Who's Who in Library and Information Services

Who's Who in Library and Information Services

Joel M. Lee, EDITOR IN CHIEF

Robert J. Beran, MANAGING EDITOR

Sandra Whiteley, ASSISTANT EDITOR

AMERICAN LIBRARY ASSOCIATION Chicago 1982

Editors

Arlan Bushman
Kevin James Carey
Beverly S. Goldberg
Judith Goldberger
Sarah Elizabeth How
Rob Kosin
Carol S. Nielsen
Marybeth Schroeder
Helen Verhoek Yarbrough

Proofreaders

Martin Brady
Bartow Culp
Mildred Farrow
Gregory Finnegan
Curtis L. Johnson
Sarah O'Brien
Anne Marie Takach
Keith R. Schlesinger
Necia Wakefield

Library of Congress Cataloging in Publication Data
Main entry under title:
Who's who in library and information services.

   1. Librarians—United States—Biography—Directories.
2. Librarians—Canada—Biography—Directories.
3. Information scientists—United States—
Biography—Directories. 4. Information
scientists—Canada—Biography—Directories. I. Lee, Joel M.
II. Beran, Robert J., 1927– . III. Whiteley, Sandra, 1943– .
IV. American Library Association.
Z720.A4W45   020′.92′2[B]   81-20480
ISBN 0-8389-0351-7   AACR2

Contents

Editor's Introduction

The editor of the previous version of this work described it as the product of "many years of experimentation and a variety of mixed parentages stemming from an unstable and makeshift ancestry." A new biographical directory of librarians and information specialists comes forth now, reflecting not only the mixed parentages of five earlier, numbered editions issued by different publishers, but also —and perhaps most significant—the ever changing patterns of employment and professional activity in the field.

The need, indeed the demand, for an accurate and up-to-date directory of leading members of the library and information services profession was evident almost immediately after the publication of *A Biographical Directory of Librarians in the United States and Canada* in 1970. That work was the fifth edition of *Who's Who in Library Service*, which had appeared at irregular intervals since 1933 under several imprints and under the sponsorship of several library organizations, but largely under the direction of the American Library Association (ALA) and the Council of National Library Associations, now the Council of National Library and Information Associations (CNLIA).

That the responsibility for issuing a new directory should again fall upon the American Library Association, the oldest and largest of the many library and information associations in North America, seems appropriate. As the earlier editions aged and the profession continued to voice its desire for a new biographical directory, the ALA sought for a number of years to issue a new edition, one which could overcome the substantial problems of scope, accuracy, and production limitation noted in previous versions and which could be produced with a minimum of financial risk. The utility and motivation for such a work needs no defense; unfortunately, the actual editorial and production demands and the economics of contemporary publishing in the library marketplace cause discouragement when the real costs are measured against sales of the finished work. These realities long impeded progress toward a new edition. This book reflects another attempt—and, we believe, a successful one—on the part of the library community to meet the need in the context of a different demographic and economic setting.

The production of this entirely new biographical directory, now entitled *Who's Who in Library and Information Services,* was finally launched in spring 1979 under the editorial direction of the American Library Association, with the participation of the Council of National Library and Information Associations. Initially, another publisher was to produce this edition under an agreement with ALA. The editors took a new and broader approach to the information services field, striving to overcome the problems of earlier works through careful editorial strategy and use of advanced technology for production of a machine-readable biographical database.

The editorial work begun in 1979 suffered a delay of many months in 1980 when the co-publisher found it necessary to withdraw from the project, but in the winter of 1980–81 production resumed as ALA took full responsibility for the work, culminating with the spring 1982 publication of this volume.

EDITORIAL AND PRODUCTION PLAN

The editorial plan for the work was developed by the project staff in concert with a committee of distinguished advisers representing varied constituencies within the field. From the beginning, the editors and advisers sought to create a directory which would be *comprehensive* in scope, reflecting the diversity of the profession and the many ways its leaders contribute to it; *selective,* including the most significant members of the library and information community according to a set of eligibility guidelines; and *accurate,* relying on multiple mailings, press releases, and galley proofs to ensure that a broad spectrum of the profession had been informed of the project and that the actual entries, once edited, were approved, corrected, or updated by the respondents themselves. To achieve these goals, the publication plan for the directory emphasized the following major phases:

Mailings and announcements. To survey the field for inclusion, a master mailing list was compiled by securing and merging the most recent available personal membership lists of some thirty-six national associations in library and information services in the U.S. and Canada. Biographical questionnaires designed by advisers and staff, with a cover letter explaining the project and presenting the eligibility guidelines, were sent to approximately 55,-000 individuals. Simultaneously, announcements of the project were made to the library press, and individuals were encouraged to request questionnaires if for some reason they failed to receive them by mail. The mailing list was developed during the summer and fall of 1979, and the first mailing sent in December 1979.

Incoming questionnaires were then checked against the mailing list, and a follow-up mailing was prepared to encourage those who had not responded to the first mailing to submit their entries. The second mailing of some 30,000 questionnaires went out on ALA's letterhead in January 1981, accompanied by press announcements of a "last call" for questionnaires.

Selection. Each questionnaire submitted was reviewed by a member of the editorial staff, according to the eligibility guidelines developed by the Advisory Committee, to determine which of the entries submitted actually warranted inclusion in the work. This long and arduous process proved a challenging aspect of the project, and the advisers themselves also reviewed entries to verify the staff work in selection. The text of these guidelines appears in the *User's Guide* to the book.

Final call. A final follow-up step was built into the planning to ensure that the most important members of the field were included. The Advisory Committee directed the formulation of a limited list of individuals whose inclusion was considered essential by virtue of their positions in the field. Those on this list who had not responded earlier received an additional personal letter from the editor, and in some cases a telephone call, so that biographical information could be obtained directly from the individual. When all attempts failed, the editorial staff compiled entries for these individuals. (Staff-written entries are identified in the text with an asterisk.)

The editorial plan and eligibility guidelines indicate the breadth of coverage sought. Relying on repeated mailings to tens of thousands of individuals, and on multiple announcements in the press, participation was ambitiously and repeatedly encouraged. Still, inclusion in *Who's Who in Library and Information Services* is essentially voluntary. Many additional librarians, archivists, and information specialists might have appeared in the work had they chosen to respond to the mailings and press announce-ments. The editors have been unable to include many who, for one reason or another, did not respond to our solicitations and are not among the limited number identified as "essential" by the advisers. Some specifically requested that they *not* be included, a request that the editors could scarcely deny. These factors serve to qualify the comprehensiveness of the work, and should be kept in mind by the user.

Accuracy. The delay in production of some months during 1980 placed an even greater emphasis on a key element in the plan—the provision for a proof of each edited entry to be sent to each of the over 12,000 individuals selected for inclusion. These "galley" proofs were actually computer printouts of the entries as keyboarded for the database and typesetting. They were sent to each biographee with the request that they be checked for accuracy and currency of data and returned promptly to the editors. Compliance was remarkable. Most of those who have been included in the work personally saw to the accuracy of their entries.

Editing. Actual editorial work was performed by a group of part-time freelance editors, most of them librarians, under the direction of the editorial staff and working under strict editorial instructions indicating the manner in which information was to be presented for typesetting, the set of abbreviations to be used in the work, and guidelines concerning the quantity of data that could be provided for each respondent.

The editorial instructions reflected principles established by the Advisory Committee and sought to balance the need for information against stringent space limitations. Proofreading was conducted by a second group of freelance readers, who relied on both the original edited questionnaires and the respondents' galleys to update the data and correct any errors of fact or interpretation. A close examination of the file was made before production of final copy to eliminate duplications and catch any obvious errors which might have been missed earlier.

The editorial plan sought to minimize error and permit as much late amendment as possible. The advisers and editors, well aware that perfection is beyond the reach of mortals, sought to achieve as much accuracy, consistency, and intelligibility as such works permit.

Further details on editorial matters are found in the *User's Guide.*

ACKNOWLEDGMENTS

The Editor in Chief acknowledges with gratitude the contributions of a number of individuals and groups whose support and work throughout the project were essential to its completion. Chief among them are Donald E. Stewart, ALA's Associate Executive Director for Publishing Services; ALA Executive Director Robert Wedgeworth; and the staff of the ALA Headquarters Library. The Advisory Committee, chaired by Robert D. Stueart, participated in every significant phase of the project. A dedicated and diligent staff of editors and proofreaders brought the work to fruition, under the daily direction of Robert Beran and Sandra Whiteley.

The editors express special appreciation for the support of K. G. Saur Publishing, Inc. Under the editorial direction of ALA and the Advisory Committee, K. G. Saur's staff conducted the first phases of the project, from its initial conception, through the development of the questionnaires and production plan, and through the first mailings. That early financial and editorial support by K. G. Saur Publishing, Inc. made this work possible.

Recognition is due in particular to Edith Meta Jaenike, who, as K. G. Saur's Editorial Director, directed the initial production and planning. With Assistant Editor Patricia Grant, Ms. Jaenike planned and executed the many tasks involved in developing the questionnaire, first mailings, and editorial and production procedures.

Joel M. Lee
ALA Headquarters Librarian
Editor in Chief

Chicago, Illinois
April 1982

User's Guide

ELIGIBILITY GUIDELINES

These guidelines were developed by the editors and advisers to govern the selection of biographees for inclusion in the work:

Fields of Activity: Librarians and information scientists; archivists; library school faculty and other educators; scholars in subject specialties associated with libraries or library education programs; publishers, editors, and journalists whose primary activity is in librarianship and information fields; trustees; others who have made notable contributions to library and information services.

Educational Requirements for Librarians: The bachelor's degree, with a bachelor's or master's in librarianship, or other professional credentials; or the bachelor's, with at least five years' work experience at the professional level; or a combination of education and experience that indicate attainment of equivalent professional qualifications.

Geographical Requirements: Persons working in the United States, Canada, their territories, and North Americans working in U.S. and Canadian military, diplomatic, professional, and other agencies abroad.

Currency of Activity: Currently active in library and information work or recently retired.

Qualifications for Inclusion (one or more of the following):

• Evidence of active participation in professional, educational, and service organizations (such as associations, networks, and consortia), including responsible positions on boards or committees; offices; program development or other activities.

• A record of activity in support of libraries and information services through philanthropy, political leadership, public service, or other means, and through such groups as boards of trustees, friends' groups, citizens' or library-related organizations.

• Substantial experience as a practitioner or educator.

• Contributions to professional literature, through monographs, significant journal articles, or other media.

• Receipt of awards or honors from professional and educational organizations and institutions, or of special fellowships or research grants.

BIOGRAPHICAL DATA AND EDITORIAL POLICIES

The following biographical information was sought in the questionnaire that biographees completed. These general editorial policies governed the manner in which editors codified and selected data for inclusion in the work.

Biographee's Name: The style of name indicated or preferred by the respondent is the form presented.

Birth Data: When the respondent provided birth data, it has been included; country of birth is provided if outside the U.S. or Canada.

Employment History: Current position is entered first, with previous positions following, most recent leading the order. Positions at the professional level and higher levels of business are included; earlier part-time, nonprofessional jobs are usually excluded. Because of space limitations, some extremely lengthy, complex employment histories have been summarized.

Education: Undergraduate and graduate study are recorded in progressive order, along with special diplomas, certificates, and other recognitions of achievement.

Library/Information-Related Organization Memberships: The extent and variety of information presented by respondents, coupled with the number and complexity of associations in the field, required the editors to exercise judgment frequently in determining the information to be recorded. Space requirements required that some long records of association activity be summarized, according to the editorial instructions; the number of organizations reported has also been limited.

Other Organizations: A pattern analogous to, but more stringent than, that for library organizations has been applied to non-library organizations.

Honors, Awards: The four most recent awards have generally been recorded, with additional information summarized. Library/information-related honors have been given preference.

Principal Publications: A limit of five publications per biographee was set as the general guideline, with preference given in order to monographs, articles or chapters, and other types of publications. The title and date are the key bibliographical elements included, with journal or book titles provided for articles or chapters; this limitation on bibliographical citations recognizes that the object here is to identify or characterize the contributions; generally available library indexes and catalogs provide the librarian and user complete citations to publications by individual biographees.

Principal Areas of Professional Activities: These have been entered as numeric codes in each sketch. The legend at the foot of the page throughout the book explains the meaning of the codes. The use of codes for these data elements is an obvious capitulation to the limitations of space, which would otherwise have been used to costly extravagance.

The selective list of activities is divided into three major categories: *Type of Institution, Functions/Activities, and Special Subjects/Services.* Respondents were limited to eight principal areas. A listing of the codes and their full interpretations is also included in this *User's Guide.*

Mailing Address: The address preferred by the respondent was recorded.

SYMBOLS AND ABBREVIATIONS

*	Staff-written entry
†	Deceased

State Library Associations: Abbreviation formed by the postal code for the state with the acronym LA, e.g., PA LA for Pennsylvania Library Association.

AAAS	American Association for the Advancement of Science
AALL	American Association of Law Libraries
AALS	Association of American Library Schools
AAP	Association of American Publishers
AASL	American Association of School Librarians
AAUP	American Association of University Professors
AAUW	American Association of University Women
AB	Alberta
Abr.	Abridge, -ed
Abs.	Abstract, -ing, -s
Abstctr.	Abstractor
Acad.	Academic, Académie (Fr.), Academy
Accred.	Accreditation
Acct.	Account, -ant, -ing
Achvmt.	Achievement
Acq.	Acquisitions
ACRL	Association of College and Research Libraries (ALA)
Actg.	Acting
Actv.	Activities
Adj.	Adjunct, Adjoint (Fr.-Assistant)
Adlsnt.	Adolescent
Admin.	Administration, -ive, -or
Admis.	Admission, -s
Adv.	Advisory, Adviser

Advert.	Advertising
Advnc.	Advance, -ed, -ment
AECT	Association for Educational Communication and Technology
Aerosp.	Aerospace
Afflt.	Affiliate
Afnty.	Affinity
Ag.	August
Agmnt.	Agreement
Agr.	Agriculture
Agt.	Agent
AJL	Association of Jewish Libraries
AK	Alaska
AL	Alabama
ALA	American Library Association
Alchl.	Alcoholism, Alcohol
Alloc.	Allocate, -tion, -s
ALSC	Association for Library Service to Children (ALA)
ALTA	American Library Trustee Association (ALA)
Alum.	Alumni, -ae, -us
Amat.	Amateur
Amer.	America, American
Anal.	Analysis, Analyst
Anl.	Annual
Anniv.	Anniversary
Anthro.	Anthropology
Antiq.	Antiquarian, Antiquaries
Ap.	April
Appld.	Applied
Apprais.	Appraisal, -s
Apprec.	Appreciation
Appt.	Appointment
Apt.	Apartment
AR	Arkansas
Arbit.	Arbitrate, -ion, -or
Arch.	Archive, -s, -al
Archdio.	Archdiocese
Archit.	Architect, -ural, -ure

Archlg.	Archaeology
Archvst.	Archivist
ARL	Association of Research Libraries
ARLIS/NA	Art Libraries Society/North America
Arrange.	Arranging, -ment, -or
Artly.	Artillery
ASCLA	Association of Specialized and Cooperative Library Agencies (ALA)
ASIS	American Society for Information Science
Asm.	Assembly
Assess.	Assessment
Assn.	Association
Assoc.	Associate, -ed
Asst.	Assistant
ASTED	Association pour l'avancement des sciences techniques de la documentation
Astr.	Astronomy, -ical
Athen.	Athenaeum
Athl.	Athletic
Athrty.	Authority
Atl.	Atlantic
ATLA	American Theological Library Association
Audit.	Audit, -ing, -or
Aut.	Autumn
Auth.	Author
Auto.	Automobile
Autom.	Automation
AV	Audiovisual
Ave.	Avenue
Awd.	Award
AZ	Arizona
Bapt.	Baptist
BC	British Columbia
Bd.	Board
Bhvl.	Behavioral
Bib.	Bibliothèque (Fr.-Library); Biblioteca (Sp.-Library)

Bibl.	Bibliography, -graphical	Cnsvty.	Conservatory	Doct.	Doctoral, -ate
Biblgphr.	Bibliographer	Cntrl.	Control	Docum.	Document, -s
Biblther.	Bibliotherapy	Cnty.	County	Documtn.	Documentation
Bibtcr.	Bibliothècaire (Fr.-Librarian); Bibliotecario, -a (Sp.-Librarian)	CO	Colorado	Dr.	Drive
		Co.	Company	Dsgn.	Design, -ed, -er, -s
		Coal.	Coalition	Dssm.	Disseminate, -ion
Bicent.	Bicentennial	Col.	Collect, -ion, -ive, -s	Dupl.	Duplicate
Biling.	Bilingual	Coll.	College	Dvnty.	Divinity
Bio.	Biology, -ical	Com.	Committee; Comité (Fr.)	E.	East
Bk.	Book	Comm.	Communication, -cator	Ecol.	Ecology
Bkmobile.	Bookmobile	Comp.	Computer, -ing	Econ.	Economics
Bldgs.	Buildings	Compar.	Compare, -ative, -ing, -ison	Ed.	Editor, -ed, -ial, -tion
Bltn.	Bulletin	Comsn.	Commission, -er	Edshp.	Editorship
Blvd.	Boulevard	Con.	Consumer	Educ.	Education, -al, -or; Educación (Sp.)
Boro.	Borough	Conf.	Conference		
Bot.	Botany	Congs.	Congress	EFLA	Educational Film Library Association
Brit.	British	Congsnl.	Congressional		
Bur.	Bureau	Cons.	Conservation	Elec.	Elected, -ing, -ion
Bus.	Business	Constn.	Constitution	Elem.	Elementary
CA	California	Construct.	Construction	Elig.	Eligible, -ility
CALS	Canadian Association of Library Schools	Consult.	Consultant, -ing	Empl.	Employee, -s, -ment, -er
		Cont.	Continuing	Encyc.	Encyclopedia
CAML	Canadian Association of Music Libraries	Contl.	Continental	Endow.	Endowment
		Contrib.	Contribute, -ing, -or	Eng.	England, English
Can.	Canada, Canadian	Conv.	Convention, Convenor	Engin.	Engineer, Engineering
Can. ALL	Canadian Association of Law Libraries	Coop.	Cooperate, -ion, -ive	Enrich.	Enriched, -ment
		Coord.	Coordinate, -ing, -or; Coordinateur (Fr.)	Ens.	Enseignement (Fr.-Education)
Can. LA	Canadian Library Association				
		Copyrt.	Copyright	Env.	Environment, -al
Cand.	Candidate	Corp.	Corporation	ERT	Exhibits Round Table (ALA)
Cap.	Capital, Capitol	Correct.	Correctional, -tive	Estab.	Establish, -ing, -ment
CARL	Canadian Association of Research Libraries	Corres.	Corresponding	Eth.	Ethnic
		COSLA	Chief Officers of State Library Agencies	Eval.	Evaluate, -ator, -ion
Cat.	Catalog, -ing			Evang.	Evangelical
Cath.	Catholic	Couns.	Counsel, -ing, -or	Excel.	Excellence, -ent
Catlgr.	Cataloger	Creat.	Creative	Except.	Exceptional
Cert.	Certificate, -ion	Cred.	Credential	Exch.	Exchange
Ch.	Chair	Crftsmn.	Craftsman	Exec.	Executive
Cham.	Chamber	Crs.	Course, -s	Exper.	Experiment, -al
Chap.	Chapter	CSLA	Church and Synagogue Library Association	Expy.	Expressway
Chem.	Chemical, Chemist, -ry			Ext.	Extension
Chin. Amer. LA	Chinese American Library Association	CT	Connecticut	F.	February
		Ct.	Court	Fac.	Faculty; Faculté (Fr.); Facultad (Sp.)
Chiro.	Chiropracter, -ic	Ctr.	Center, Centre		
CHLA	Canadian Health Libraries Association	Ctrl.	Central	Fam.	Family
		Cult.	Cultural	Fed.	Federal, -ted, -tion
Chld.	Children, -'s	CUNY	City University of New York	Fest.	Festival
Christ.	Christian	Cur.	Curator	Filmstp.	Filmstrip
Chrt.	Charter	Curric.	Curricula, -ar, -um	Fin.	Finance
Cin.	Cinéma (Fr. -Film)	Cust.	Custom, -er	FL	Florida
Cir.	Circle	Cvl.	Civil	FLC	Federal Library Committee
Circ.	Circulation	Cvlztn.	Civilization	Fld.	Field
Cit.	Citation	CZ	Canal Zone	FLRT	Federal Librarians Round Table (ALA)
Clasfd.	Classified	D.	December		
Clasfr.	Classifier	DC	District of Columbia	Flwshp.	Fellowship
Class.	Classification	DE	Delaware	Fncl.	Financial
Clear.	Clearinghouse	Decor.	Decorate, -ion, -ive	Fndn.	Foundation, -ing
CLENE	Continuing Library Education Network and Exchange	Del.	Delegate, -ion	Fndr.	Founder
		Dem.	Democratic	Fr.	French
		Demog.	Demographer, -y	Frc.	Force
Clmn.	Column	Depos.	Depository	Frdm.	Freedom
Cmdn.	Commendation	Dept.	Department, -al	Freelnc.	Freelance, -er
Cmnd.	Command	Descr.	Description, -ive	Frgn.	Foreign
Cmnl.	Communal	Det.	Detention	Fund.	Fund raising
Cmnty.	Community	Dev.	Developer, -ing, -ment	GA	Georgia
Cmplr.	Compiler	Diag.	Diagnostic, -ian	Gen.	General
Cmrce.	Commerce	Dip.	Diploma	Geneal.	Genealogy, -ical
Cmrcl.	Commercial	Dir.	Director, -ing, -tory; Directeur (Fr.)	Geo.	Geography
Cmwlth.	Commonwealth			Geol.	Geological, -y
Cncl.	Council	Disadv.	Disadvantaged	Gld.	Guild
Cnclr.	Councilor	Discuss.	Discussion	GODORT	Government Documents Round Table (ALA)
CNLIA	Council of National Library and Information Associations	Dist.	District		
		Disting.	Distinguished	Grad.	Graduate
		Div.	Division, -al	Graph.	Graphic
Cnsl.	Conseil (Fr. -Board, Council)	Dlrs.	Dealers	Grd.	Guard
Cnsrtm.	Consortium	Docmlst.	Documentaliste (Fr.)	Grk.	Greek
Cnsvtr.	Conservateur (Fr. -Curator)				

Grmn.	German	Lg.	Large	Nat.	Natural
Grntlgcl.	Gerontological	LHRT	Library History Round Table (ALA)	Natl.	National
Grntlgy.	Gerontology			Nav.	Navigator
Grp.	Group	Lib.	Library	NB	New Brunswick
Grt.	Great, -er	Libn.	Librarian	NC	North Carolina
GU	Guam	Libnshp.	Librarianship	NCLIS	National Commission on Libraries and Information Science
Guid.	Guidance	Licn.	License, -ing		
Gvr.	Governor	Ling.	Linguist, -istics		
Gvt.	Government	LIRT	Library Instruction Round Table (ALA)	ND	North Dakota
Gvtl	Governmental			NE	Nebraska
Handcpd.	Handicapped	Lit.	Literature, -ary	Negtns.	Negotiations
HI	Hawaii	LITA	Library and Information Technology Association (ALA)	Netwks.	Networks
Hisp.	Hispanic			Newsp.	Newspapers
Histn.	Historian			NF	Newfoundland
Hlth.	Health	Litcy.	Literacy	NH	New Hampshire
Hon.	Honor, -ary	Ln.	Lane	NJ	New Jersey
Hosp.	Hospital	Lrng.	Learning	NLA	National Librarians Association
Hosplty.	Hospitality	LRRT	Library Research Round Table (ALA)		
HQ	Headquarters			NM	New Mexico
HS	High School	LS	Library Science	No.	Number
Hse.	House	Luth.	Lutheran	Nom.	Nominate, -ing, -ion
HSLN	Health Science Library Network	M.	March	North.	Northern
		MA	Massachusetts	NS	Nova Scotia
Hts.	Heights	Mach.	Machinery	Nsltr.	Newsletter
Hum.	Humanities	Mag.	Magazine	NT	Northwest Territories
Hwy.	Highway	Manip.	Manipulative	Nuc.	Nuclear
IA	Iowa	Math.	Mathematics	Nutr.	Nutrition
ID	Idaho	Matric.	Matriculate, -ion	NV	Nevada
Ident.	Identification	MB	Manitoba	Nvl.	Naval
IFLA	International Federation of Library Associations and Institutions	MD	Maryland	NY	New York
		Mdrtr.	Moderator	NZ	New Zealand
		ME	Maine	O.	October
IFRT	Intellectual Freedom Round Table (ALA)	Measur.	Measure, -ing, -ment	Ofc.	Office
		Mech.	Mechanical	Ofcr.	Officer
IL	Illinois	Med.	Medical, -ine	OH	Ohio
ILL	Interlibrary Loan	Medvl.	Medieval	OK	Oklahoma
IN	Indiana	Mem.	Member, -ship; Membre (Fr.)	OLUG	Online Users Group
Indp.	Independent			ON	Ontario
Indus.	Industrial, -y	Meml.	Memorial	Oper.	Operate, -ation, -ational, -or
Indxr.	Indexer	Merit.	Meritorious	OR	Oregon
Infirm.	Infirmary	Meth.	Methodist	Orch.	Orchestra
Info.	Information	Metro.	Metropolitan	Ord.	Order
Infotste.	Informatiste (Fr.-Information Scientist)	Mex.	Mexico, -can	Org.	Organize, -er, -ation, -ational
		MFLA	Midwest Federation of Library Associations		
Insr.	Insurance			Orien.	Orientation
Inst.	Institute, -ion, -ional	Mfr.	Manufacture, -ed, -er, -ing	Orig.	Original
Instr.	Instruct, -ion, -ional, -or	Mgr.	Manager	Ornith.	Ornithology, -ist
Int.	Intellectual	Mgt.	Management	Outrch.	Outreach
Intercoll.	Intercollegiate	MI	Michigan	Outstan.	Outstanding
Intl.	International	Micro.	Microform, -graphics	PA	Pennsylvania
IRRT	International Relations Round Table (ALA)	Mid.	Middle	Pac.	Pacific
		Milit.	Military	Paleon.	Paleontology
Ja.	January	Min.	Minimum	Par.	Parish
Je.	June	Missn.	Mission, -ary	Parlmt.	Parliament, -arian
Jl.	July	Mktg.	Marketing	PE	Prince Edward Island
JMRT	Junior Members Round Table (ALA)	MN	Minnesota	Ped.	Pédagogique (Fr. -Pedagogy)
		Mncpl.	Municipal	Per.	Periodical
Jnl.	Journal	Mnstr.	Minister	Perpet.	Perpetuation
Jnlsm.	Journalism	Mnstry.	Ministry	Persnl.	Personnel
Jnlst.	Journalist	MO	Missouri	Petr.	Petroleum
Jr.	Junior	Mod.	Modern	Pharm.	Pharmaceuticals, Pharmacy
Jt.	Joint	Molec.	Molecular	Pharmgy.	Pharmacology
KS	Kansas	Mono.	Monograph, -ic, -s	Phil.	Philosophy
KY	Kentucky	MS	Mississippi	Philan.	Philanthropy, -pist, -opic
LA	Library Association; Louisiana	Msc.	Music	Photodup.	Photoduplication
		Msclgy.	Musicology	Photogram.	Photogrammetry
Lab.	Laboratory	Mss.	Manuscripts	Phys.	Physics, Physical, -ly
LAMA	Library Administration and Management Association (ALA)	Mstrs.	Masters	Physio.	Physiological
		MT	Montana	Pic.	Picture
		Mt.	Mount, -ain	Pk.	Park
		Mtg.	Meeting	Pkwy.	Parkway
Lang.	Language	Mtrls.	Materials	Pl.	Place
Lcl.	Local	Musm.	Museum	PLA	Public Library Association (ALA)
Leag.	League	My.	May		
Lect.	Lecture	Myco.	Mycology, -ical	Place.	Placement
Lectr.	Lecturer	N.	North; November	Plng.	Planning
Legis.	Legislation, -ive	NAACP	National Association for the Advancement of Colored People	Plz.	Plaza

Pol.	Political	Rm.	Room	SUNY	State University of New York
Poll.	Pollution	Rom.	Romance		
Polytech.	Polytechnic	Rpt.	Report, -er, -ing	Supt.	Superintendent
Pop.	Popular	RR	Rural Route	Supvsg.	Supervising
Popltn.	Population	Rsv.	Reserve	Supvsn.	Supervision
PQ	Quebec	RT	Round Table	Supvsr.	Supervisor
PR	Puerto Rico; Public Relations	Rte.	Route	SWLA	Southwest Library Association
		Rtl.	Retail, -ing		
Prac.	Practice, -ing, -s	RTSD	Resources and Technical Services Division (ALA)	Symp.	Symposium, -ia
Prcs.	Process, -ing, -or			Symph.	Symphony
Prep.	Prepare, -ation, -atory	Russ.	Russian	Syst.	System
Pres.	President	S.	September; South	Tchg.	Teaching
Presby.	Presbyterian	SAA	Society of American Archivists	Tchr.	Teacher
Prev.	Prevention			Tech.	Technical, -ology, -cian
Prin.	Principal	SALALM	Seminar on the Acquisition of Latin American Library Materials	Techq.	Technique
Proc.	Procedure, Proceeding			Telecom.	Telecommunications
Prod.	Production, -ion			Telefac.	Telefacsimile
Prof.	Profess, -or, -ional, -ion; Professeur (Fr.); Profesor (Sp.)	SBPR	Sociedad de Bibliotecarios de Puerto Rico	Terr.	Terrace
				Thea.	Theater
		Sbtcl.	Sabbatical	Theo.	Theology, -ical
Prog.	Program	SC	South Carolina	Therap.	Therapeutics
Progmr.	Programmer	Scan.	Scandinavian	TN	Tennessee
Proj.	Project	Sch.	School	Transl.	Translate, -or, -ion
Promo.	Promotion	Schol.	Scholar, -ship	Transp.	Transportation
Prov.	Province, -ial	Sci.	Science, -tist	Treas.	Treasurer, -y
Prsrvn.	Preservation	SD	South Dakota	Trng.	Training
Prsrvnst.	Preservationist	Sec.	Second, -ary; Secondaire (Fr.)	TV	Television
Prtg.	Printing			Twp.	Township
Psy.	Psychology, -ical			TX	Texas
Psyt.	Psychiatry, -atric	Secret.	Secretariat	UK	United Kingdom
Ptl.	Patrol	Sect.	Section	ULC	Urban Libraries Council
Pub.	Public	Secur.	Security	Un.	Union
Pubcty.	Publicity	Secy.	Secretary	Undergrad.	Undergraduate
Publshg.	Publishing	Sel.	Selected, -ion	Unfd.	Unified
Publshr.	Publisher	SELA	Southeastern Library Association	Univ.	University; Université (Fr.); Universidad (Sp.)
Pubn.	Publication				
Pvt.	Private	Sem.	Seminar	Untd.	United
Qtly.	Quarterly	Semy.	Seminary	Unvsl.	Universal
Qual.	Quality	Sen.	Senate, -or	UT	Utah
RASD	Reference and Adult Services Division (ALA)	Sept.	Separate	Util.	Utility, -ization
		SK	Saskatchewan	VA	Virginia
Ratif.	Ratify, -ication	SLA	Special Libraries Association	Venez.	Venezuela
Rcrt.	Recruit, -ing, -ment			Vetny.	Veterinary
Rd.	Road	Snd.	Sound	Vets.	Veterans
Readg.	Reading	Soc.	Social	VI	Virgin Islands
Rec.	Record, -ing	Soclgy.	Sociology	Vict.	Victorian
Recog.	Recognition	Socty.	Society	Vid.	Video
Recvy.	Recovery	SORT	Staff Organizations Round Table (ALA)	Visit.	Visiting
Red.	Rédaction (Fr. -Editing)			Vlgs.	Villages
Ref.	Reference, Referral	South.	Southern	Volun.	Volunteer
REFORMA	National Association of Spanish Speaking Librarians	Sp.	Speech	VP	Vice President
		Span.	Spanish	VT	Vermont
		Spec.	Special, -ist	W.	West
Reg.	Region, -al	Spr.	Spring	WA	Washington
Regis.	Register, -ed, -ing, -rar, -ration	Sq.	Square	West.	Western
		Sr.	Senior; Sister	WHCOLIS	White House Conference on Library and Information Services
		Src.	Source		
Rehab.	Rehabilitate, -tation, -ive	Srch.	Search, -er, -ing		
Rel.	Relationed, Relations	SRRT	Social Responsibilities Round Table (ALA)		
Relig.	Religion, -ious			WI	Wisconsin
Relshps.	Relationships	Srv.	Service	Win.	Winter
Rep.	Representative	Srvg.	Serving	Wkly.	Weekly
Repro.	Reprographics	Srvy.	Survey	Wkshp.	Workshop
Reprodct.	Reproduction	St.	Street	Wrtg.	Writing
Repub.	Republic	Stan.	Standard	WV	West Virginia
Resol.	Resolution	Stats.	Statistics	WY	Wyoming
Resp.	Responsible, -ities; Résponsable (Fr. -In charge)	Std.	Studies	YA	Young Adult
		Stdg.	Standing	YASD	Young Adult Services Division
		Storytel.	Storytelling		
Resrc.	Resource	Strg.	Steering	Yr.	Year
Resrch.	Research, -er, -ing	Sub.	Substitute, -ed, -ion	YT	Yukon Territory
Rev.	Revise, -ion, -ing, -or	Subj.	Subject	Zlgy.	Zoology
Review.	Reviewing	Subscrpn.	Subscription		
RI	Rhode Island	Sum.	Summer		

PRINCIPAL AREAS OF PROFESSIONAL ACTIVITIES

Type of Institution
1. Academic library
2. Archives
3. Association
4. Federal or governmental library
5. Institutional library
6. Manufacturer/Supplier
7. Military library
8. Museum
9. Public library
10. School library/media center
11. School of library/information science
12. Special library/information center
13. State or provincial library agency
14. (Other)

Functions/Activities
15. Acquisitions/Collection development
16. Adult services
17. Administration/Management
18. Appraisals
19. Architecture/Buildings
20. Cataloging/Classification
21. Children's services
22. Circulation
23. Conservation and preservation
24. Consulting
25. Continuing education
26. Education for librarianship/information science
27. Extension services
28. Fund raising/Grants
29. Government publications
30. Indexing/Abstracting

31. Instruction in library use
32. Media services
33. Microforms/Micrographics
34. Networks/Interlibrary cooperation
35. Personnel
36. Public relations
37. Publishing
38. Records management
39. Reference services
40. Reprographics
41. Research
42. Reviewing
43. Security
44. Serials
45. Special collections/Rare books/Manuscripts
46. Technical services
47. Trustees and boards
48. Young adult services
49. (Other)

Special Subjects/Services
50. Adult education
51. Advertising/Marketing
52. Aerospace
53. Agriculture
54. Area studies/International relations
55. Arts/Humanities
56. Automation/Computers/Systems
57. Bibliography/Printing
58. Biological sciences
59. Business/Finance
60. Chemistry
61. Copyright

62. Documentation
63. Education
64. Engineering
65. Environment
66. Ethnic groups
67. Film
68. Food/Nutrition
69. Genealogy
70. Geography/Maps
71. Geology
72. Handicapped
73. History
74. Intellectual freedom/Censorship
75. Information science
76. Insurance
77. Law
78. Legislation
79. Mathematics/Computer science
80. Medicine
81. Metals/Materials
82. Natural resources
83. Newspapers
84. Nuclear science
85. Oral history
86. Petroleum/Energy resources
87. Pharmaceuticals
88. Physics/Astronomy/Mathematics
89. Reading/Literacy
90. Religion
91. Science/Technology
92. Social sciences
93. Telecommunications/Communications
94. Transportation
95. (Other)

A

Aagaard, James S. (Jl. 20, 1930, Lake Forest, IL) Head, Info. Syst. Dev., Northwestern Univ. Lib., 1970–, Prof. Comp. Sci. and Electrical Engin., 1957–. **Educ.:** Northwestern Univ., 1948–53, BSEE (Elect. Engin.), 1953–57, MS, PhD (Elect. Engin.). **Orgs.:** ASIS. ALA. Assn. for Comp. Mach. Inst. of Electrical and Electronic Engins. Amer. Socty. for Engin. Educ. **Pubns.:** "NOTIS: an Integrated Computer System for a Large Research Library", *IL Libs.* (Ap. 1978); "An Interactive Computer-Based Circulation System", *Jnl. of Lib. Auto.* (Mar. 1972). **Activities:** 1; 17, 34; 56, 75, 93 **Addr.:** Northwestern Univ. Library, 1935 Sheridan Rd., Evanston, IL 60201.

Aaron, Shirley Louise (Ja. 2, 1941, Crowley, LA) Assoc. Prof., Sch. of LS, FL State Univ., 1975–; Asst. Prof., Univ. of FL, 1973–75; Media Spec., Northshore Jr/Sr. High, 1967–70; Media Spec., E. L. Hardee Elem. Sch., 1966–67. **Educ.:** Univ. of Southwest. LA, 1958–61, BA (Eng.); FL State Univ., 1970–73, PhD (LS). **Orgs.:** ALA: AASL, 2nd VP (1980–81). FL Assn. for Media in Educ.: Pres. (1980–81). AECT. Assn. of Supvsn. and Curric. Dev. **Honors:** Phi Delta Kappa. **Pubns.:** *A Study of the Combined School/Public Library* (1980); *Personalizing Instruction for the Middle School Learner* (1975); "The Media Supervisor and Collective Bargaining," *Drexel Lib. Qtly.* (Ap. 1977); "The Role of the School Media Program in the Curriculum," *Southeast. Libn.* (Win. 1977); "Library Cooperation: School Library Media Centers," *Encyc. of Lib. and Info. Sci.* (1980). **Activities:** 10, 11; 17, 31, 41; 63, 74, 78 **Addr.:** School of Library Science, Florida State University, Tallahassee, FL 32306.

Abajian, James de Tarr (My. 30, 1914, Sacramento, CA) Archvst., Archdiocese of San Francisco, 1978–; Cur., Kemble Cols. on West. Printing, CA Hist. Socty., 1975–77; Cur., Martin Luther King, Jr. Coll., San Francisco Pub. Lib., 1969–71; Lib. Dir., CA Hist. Socty., 1950–68. **Educ.:** Univ. of WI, 1932–36, BS (Educ.), 1937–39 (Hist.); Univ. of MI, 1939–43, (Lib. Sci.). **Orgs.:** SAA. Socty. of CA Archvsts. Org. of Amer. Hists. Amer. Hist. Assn., Pac. Cst. Brnch. Amer. Cath. Hist. Assn. **Pubns.:** *Blacks in newspapers, censuses, and other sources; an index to names and subjects* (1977); *Blacks and Their Contributions to the American West; a Bibliography and Union List of Library Holdings* (1974); Jt. Auth., *A Walking Tour of the Black Presence in San Francisco During the Nineteenth Century* (1974); Various articles and reviews. **Activities:** 1, 2; 17, 24, 41; 57, 66, 90 **Addr.:** 4801 17th St., San Francisco, CA 94117.

Abaray, Michael J. (O. 27, 1940, Pittsburgh, PA) Tech. Svcs. Libn., IN Univ. NW, 1976–; Assoc. Libn., Coll. of VI, 1972–76; Head Ref. Libn., IN Univ., South Bend, 1969–72; Docum. Libn., Brandeis Univ., 1968–69; Catlgr., Serials Libn., Univ. Notre Dame, 1966–68. **Educ.:** St. Vincent Coll., 1960–64, BA (Phil.); Univ. Pittsburgh, 1965–66, MLS. **Orgs.:** ALA. Cncl. of Plng. Libns. Inter-Amer. Bibl. and Lib. Assn. **Pubns.:** "Wilson Harris: A Bibliography", *Bltn. of Bibl.* **Activities:** 1; 15, 34, 46; 56, 66, 75 **Addr.:** 8248 E. Old Lincolnway, Hobart, IN 46342.

Abbe, Elizabeth Jane (O. 6, 1950, Hartford, CT) Libn., CT Hist. Socty., 1973–. **Educ.:** Wells Coll., 1969–72, BA (Hist., Phil. of Relig.); Simmons Coll., 1972–73, MSLS. **Orgs.:** CT Valley Chap. (Rec. Secy., 1978); Nom. Com. (1979). CT LA: Lcl. Hist. and Geneal. Sect. (Fndr., 1980). New Engl. Archvsts. Fed. of Geneal. Socty. Assn. for Std. of CT Hist. **Pubns.:** "Connecticut Genealogical Research: Sources and Suggestions", *New Eng. Historic Geneal. Socty. Rgstr.* (Ja. 1980); "The Connecticut Historical Society", *The CT Nutmegger* (S. 1976). **Activities:** 2, 12; 23, 43, 45; 55, 69, 73, 93 **Addr.:** The Connecticut Historical Society, 1 Elizabeth St., Hartford, CT 06105.

Abbott, George L. (Jl. 11, 1941, Rutland, VT) Media Libn., Syracuse Univ., 1969–, Catlgr., 1966–69; Catlgr., St. Michael's (VT) Coll., 1963–64. **Educ.:** St. Michael's Coll., 1959–63, BA (Math); Syracuse Univ., 1964–66, MSLS; Post-Grad. Crs., Instr. Tech., 1966–69. **Orgs.:** ASIS: SIG Deputy Cabinet Cnclr. (1979–); SIG/Autom. Ofc. of Future, Secy., Treas. (1979–); Mem. Com. (1977–79); Upstate NY Chap. (Ch., 1972–73). ALA: LITA/Prog. Plng. Com. (1977–); /Legis. Com. (1977–); /Gvr. Confs. Adv. Com. on Info. Tech. (Ch., 1978–79); ISAD AV Sect. (Ch., 1976–77). AECT: Info. Syst. Div., Bd. (1970–72). Socty. of Motion Pic. and TV Engins. **Pubns.:** *Videodisc, A Selected Bibliography* (1980); *Card Catalogs–Alternative Futures, A Selected Bibliography* (1979); "Information Science, What Is It?", Slide/Tape Presentation for ASIS (1979). **Activities:** 1; 49-OL srch, 32, 40; 67, 75, 93 **Addr.:** 311 Stonecrest Dr., Syracuse, NY 13214.

Abbott, John C. (Ap. 12, 1921, Auburn, ME) Dir., South. IL Univ. Lib., 1960–; Libn., Trinity Univ., TX, 1955–60; Head, Orient. Exch. Sect., Lib. of Congs., 1952–54, Asst. Ed. Subj. Heads., 1951–52, Spec. Recruit, 1950–51. **Educ.:** Bowdoin Coll., 1939–43, BA (Hist.); Syracuse Univ., 1946–49, MA (Hist.); Univ. MI, 1949–50, MA (LS), 1957, PhD (LS). **Orgs.:** ALA. IL LA. Sierra Clb. Other env. clbs. **Activities:** 1; 17 **Addr.:** 1324 Grand Ave., Edwardsville, IL 62025.

Abell, Millicent D. (F. 15, 1934, Wichita, KS) Univ. Libn., Univ. of CA, San Diego, 1977–; Assoc. Dir., Univ. Libs., SUNY, Buffalo, 1973–76; Asst. Dir., Libs., Univ. of WA, 1971–73, Asst. Libn., Bus. Admin. Lib., 1969–71. **Educ.:** CO Coll., 1956, BA (Psy.); Columbia Univ., 1958, MA (Persnl.); SUNY, Albany, 1965, MLS; Univ. of CO, 1969, MA (Pol. Sci.). **Orgs.:** ACRL: Bd. of Dirs. (1976–78, 1979–82); Pres. (1980–81). ARL: Bd. of Dirs. (1979–82); Pres. (1981–82). Ctr. for Resrch. Libs.: Bd. (1979–82). **Pubns.:** Ed., *Collective Bargaining in Higher Education: Its Implications for Governance and Faculty Status for Librarians* (1976); "The Changing Role of the Academic Librarian: Drift and Mastery," *Coll. & Resrch. Libs.* (Mr. 1979); "Undergraduate Library Programs and Problems in Educating Library Users," *Educating the Lib. User* (1974); assoc. ed., *Lib. Resrch.* (1978–); bd. of eds., *Jnl. of Acad. Libnshp.* (1974–76). **Activities:** 1; 17 **Addr.:** Central University Library C–075, University of California, San Diego, La Jolla, CA 92093.

Abella, Rosa M. (F. 13, 1920, Havana, Cuba) Prof., Otto Richter Lib., Univ. of Miami, 1962–; Head, Circ. Dept., Bib. Natl. Jose Martí, Cuba, 1959–61; Libn., Inst. de Segunda Enseñanza, Cuba, 1951–59; Libn., Lyceum, Cuba, 1948–51. **Educ.:** Inst. de Segunda Enseñanza, Cuba, 1935–39, Bachiller (Letras y Ciencias); Técnica Bib., Univ. de la Habana, 1956, Dip., 1958, PhD (Hist.). **Orgs.:** Dade Cnty. LA. Assn. de Bibs. Univ. y de Investigación del Caribe. FL LA. SALALM. Musm. of Cuban Art and Culture. Cuban Women's Club. **Honors:** US Dept of Hlth., Educ. and Welfare, Premio Lincoln Marti; Cruzada Educ. Cubana, Premio Juan J. Remos. **Pubns.:** Various articles, bibls., indxs. **Activities:** 1; 15; 55, 57 **Addr.:** 7541 S.W. 62 St., Miami, FL 33143.

Abernathy, William Fraher (N. 12, 1936, Blackstone, VA) Dir. of Lrng. Resrc., Columbia Bible Coll., 1973–. **Educ.:** VA Cmwth. Univ., 1959–63, BS (Soc. Wk.); Asbury Theo. Sem., 1968–70, MDiv (Theol.); Univ. of SC, 1973–74, ML (Libnshp). **Orgs.:** Christ. Libns. Flwshp.: Bd. (1974–76). Amer. Theo. LA: Com. on Pub. Srvs. (1979–80). SC LA: Acad. Lib. Sect. (Secy). Assn. of Evangelicals in SC: Pres. (1979–80). Evgls. for Soc. Action. **Activities:** 1; 15, 17, 31; 66, 90 **Addr.:** Columbia Bible College, PO Box 3122, Columbia, SC 29230.

Ablove, Gayle J. (N. 21, 1952, Buffalo, NY) Asst. Libn., Roswell Park Meml. Inst., 1976–. **Educ.:** SUNY, Buffalo,

1972–74, BA (Psy.), 1974–76, MLS; Med. LA, 1977, Cert.; NY State, 1977, Pub. Libns. Prof. Cert. **Orgs.:** Med. LA: Upstate NY and ON Chap. West. NY Hlth. Sci. Libns. Hlth. Sci. OCLC Users Grp.: Cat. Code: Descr. and Access Com. (1980–). SUNY Sch. of Info. and Lib. Std. Alum. Assn.: Co-Pres. (1979–81). Reg. Med. Lib.: Reg. 2, Tech. Srvs. Subcom. (1979–81). **Honors:** Phi Beta Kappa, 1974; Alpha Lambda Delta, 1971. **Activities:** 1, 5; 15, 20, 32; 80 **Addr.:** Roswell Park Memorial Institute, Medical & Scientific Library, 666 Elm St., Buffalo, NY 14263.

Aborn, Peter Keith (Mr. 5, 1938, Denver, CO) VP, Admin. Srvs. Inst. for Sci. Info., 1978–, Dir., Admin. Srvs., 1976–78, Asst. to VP, Admin., 1974–76, Dir., Latin Amer. Rel., 1972–74, Mktg. Rep., Europe, 1967–72, W. Coast Rep., 1965–67. **Educ.:** OH State Univ., Student Body Pres., 1957–61, BA (Hist.). **Orgs.:** ASIS. Fullfillment Mgt. Assn. IIA Postal Affairs Com.: Ch. Indus. Task Frc. on Alternate Delivery Syst. Admin. Mgt. Socty. Admin. Mgt. Assn. **Pubns.:** "How ISI Designed Its New Work Space," *Bltn. of ASIS* (Ag. 1979). **Activities:** 6; 17, 19, 22; 56, 57, 78 **Addr.:** Institute for Scientific Information, 3501 Market St., Philadelphia, PA 19104.

Abraham, Terry P. (O. 6, 1944, Portland, OR) Mss. and Arch. Libn., WA State Univ., 1970–. **Educ.:** Univ. WA, 1963–65, BA, (Fine Arts); WA State Univ., 1966–68, MFA, (Ceramics); Univ. OR, 1969–70, MLS; Inst. in Arch. Libnshp., Univ. OR, 1970, Cert. **Orgs.:** SAA: Find. Aids Com. (1972–79); Com. on Amer. Revolution Bicent. (1974–76). NW Archsts.: Fnd. mem. and co-ch. (1972–74). Socty. of GA Archsts. Frnds. of the Lib., WA State Univ., 1968 to date. Assn. of ID. Latah Cnty. Hist. Socty. **Pubns.:** *Selected Mss. Resrcs. in the WA State Univ. Lib.* (1974). *A Un. List of the Papers of Mems. of Congs. from the Pac. NWest.* (1976). "Mss.: a continuum of Descr.", *GA Arch.* (Win. 1974). "NUCMC and the Lcl. Repository", *Amer. Arch.* (Ja. 1977). Various articles. "Managerial Rating: A Lib. Effectiveness Model" (1980). **Activities:** 1, 2; 45; 54, 85 **Addr.:** Manuscripts, Archives and Special Collections, Washington State University Libraries, Pullman, WA 99164.

Abrahamson, Aina M. (Ap. 18, 1915, Warren, MN) Lib. Dir., CA Luth. Coll., 1971–; Pub. Srvs. Libn., 1962–71; Sch. Libn., Long Beach Unfd. Sch. Dist., 1954–58, 1959–62; Libn., Tchr., Ashira Girls' Sch., Tanzania, Afr., 1958–59; Libn., Marangu Tchr. Trng. Coll., Tanzania, Sum. 1961; Libn., Phys. Ed. Prof., Luther Jr. Coll., 1946–54; Libn., Tchr., Various MN HSchs., 1935–46. **Educ.:** Gustavus Adolphus Coll., 1931–32, 1933–35, BA (Eng.); Luther Jr. Coll., 1932–33, AA; Univ. of South. CA, 1954, MSLS; Addtl. crs. several univs. **Orgs.:** CA LA. Christ. Libns. Assn. South. CA: VP (1973–74); Pres. (1974–75). South. CA Cncl. of Lit. for Chld. and Young People. Conejo Valley Frnds. of Lib.: VP (1971–72); Other orgs. Delta Kappa Gamma: Chap. Pres. (1972–73), Area Conf. Chmn. (1971); Area Dir. (1973–75). CA Luth. Coll. Women's Leag.: Pres. (1969–70). CA Luth. Coll. Auxiliary: VP (1976–77). Conejo Valley Hist. Socty. Swedish Amer. Hist. Assn. of CA: Bd. (1977–). Other orgs. **Honors:** CA Luth. Coll., Fac. Dev. Grant, 1977; Beta Phi Mu, Beta Chap., Pres. (1976–78). **Pubns.:** "Is It Fun to Be a Librarian?" *CA Sch. Lib. Assn. Bltn.* (Fall 1955), "Enthusiasm for Library Careers" (1955), "I Lived on Kilimanjaro" (Nov. 1960); Bk. reviews for *Luth. Libs.* (1975–80); Various papers, speeches, etc. **Addr.:** 555 Laurie Ln., Apt. B–12, Thousand Oaks, CA 91360.

Abrams, Lofton W. (Je. 23, 1930, Okmulgee, OK) Proj. Coord., Ms. and Arch. Dept., Yale Univ. Lib. IV, 1981–, Head Libn., Autom. Div., Cat. Dept., 1980–81, Supvsr., Autom. Proj., 1973–75, Catlgr., Cat. Dept., 1970–73; Catlgr., Cat. Dept., IA State Univ., 1969–70; Catlgr., Morrisville Agr. and Tech. Sch., SUNY, 1968–69. **Educ.:** CT Coll., 1948–52, BA (Hist.); Syracuse

Univ., 1966–68, MSLS. **Orgs.:** ALA. NY Tech. Srvs. Libns. **Honors:** Beta Phi Mu, 1969. **Activities:** 1; 20, 45, 46; 56 **Addr.:** 1722 Whitney Ave., Hamden, CT 06517.

Abrera, Josefa B. (Je. 6, 1930, Aborlan, Palawan, Philippines) Assoc. Prof., IN Univ. Sch. of Lib. and Info. Sci., 1976–; Assoc. Prof., Univ. of HI, 1975–76, Asst. Prof., 1970–75; Coll. Libn., Ateneo de Manila Univ., 1963–65; Biblgphr., OH State Univ. Libs., 1958–60; Catlgr., Univ. of the Philippines, 1953–57. **Educ.:** Univ. of the Philippines, 1949–53, BSE (LS); IN Univ., 1957–58, MA (LS), 1965–70, PhD (LS). **Orgs.:** HI LA. ASIS. AALS. ALA: Subj. Analysis Com. (1972–74); Lib. Educ. Div., Grants Com. (1972–73); Margaret Mann Awds. Com. (1979–80). **Pubns.:** *Monographic Searching on the OCLC Terminal* (1980); *An Annotated Bibliography of the Sugar Industry in Panay and Negros* (1963); "Traditional Classification," *Drexel Lib. Qtly.* (O. 1974); "Application of Programmed Instruction to Teaching of OCLC Data Base Searching," *Jnl. of Educ. for Libnshp.* (Spr. 1980); "Southeast Asian Librarians' Dialogue," *Lib. and Info. Sci. News* (Spr. 1975). **Activities:** 11; 26; 62, 75 **Addr.:** School of Library and Information Science, Indiana University, Bloomington, IN 47401.

Acerri, Federico Urbano (Jl. 20, 1938, Detroit, MI) Info. Spec., Head, Ref., Wayne Cnty. Intermediate Sch. Dist., 1973–; Acq. Libn., Wayne State Univ., 1970–73; Info. Spec., Wayne Cnty. Intermediate Sch. Dist., 1968–70. **Educ.:** Wayne State Univ., 1959–61, BA (Pol. Sci.), 1966–68, MS (LS). **Orgs.:** ASIS. Assn. of Info. Mgrs. MI Assn. for Comp. Users. MI Assn. of Comp. Machines. **Pubns.:** *Educational Acronyms and Abbreviations* (1969); "Methadone Maintenance; A Bibliography," *Jnl. of Drug Issues* (Spr. 1974). **Activities:** 12; 17, 24, 39; 56, 63, 72 **Addr.:** 8837 Nevada, Livonia, MI 48150.

Aceto, Vincent John (F. 5, 1932, Schenectady, NY) Prof., Sch. of Lib. and Info. Sci., SUNY, Albany, 1969–; Assoc. Prof., 1963–69, Asst. Prof., 1959–63; Visit. Lectr., Univ. of Dacca, E. Pakistan, 1964–65; Dir., Ballston Pub. Lib., 1958–60; Dir., Sch. Libs., Burnt-Hills-Ballston Lake Ctrl. Schs., 1957–59. **Educ.:** SUNY, Albany, 1949–53, AB (Hist.), 1953–54, MA (Guid. Persnl.), 1957–59, MLS. **Orgs.:** ASIS. AALS. Assn. of Educ. Comm. and Tech. ALA: Coord. Com. on Lib. Srvc. to Disadv. (1969–73, Chmn. 1970–73); AASL/Ed. Com. (1969–72); Resrch. Com., Chmn. (1970–73); IRRT/S. Asia Sect., Chmn. (1971–75); YASD/Media Sel. and Eval. Com. (1976–77); Sel. Films for YA Com. (1977–80); other coms. Other orgs. Univ. Film Assn. Socty. for Cin. Stds. Amer. Film Inst.: Film/TV Arch./Libs./Subj. Access Com., Chmn. (1978–). **Honors:** Fulbright, Fulbright Schol., Univ. of Dacca, E. Pakistan, 1964; Phi Delta Kappa; NY State Cncl. on Arts, Resrch. grant, 1971–72; Natl. Endow. for Arts, Resrch. grant, 1979; Other grants. **Pubns.:** *Film Literature Index* (1973–); *A Survey of Central Processing in Public Schools of New York State* (1962); "Panacea or Pandora's Box–A Look at Central Processing in New York State", *Lib. Jnl.* (Jan. 15, 1964); "Children's Librarian–Passive Provider or Active Agent for Change?", *Ref. Qtly.* (Win. 1967); "The Purpose of a College Library," *East. Libn.* (Sept. 1966); "Opening New Doors to Film Literacy", *Film Lib. Qtly.* (Sum. 1968). **Activities:** 10, 12; 26, 30; 55, 56, 67 **Addr.:** 950 Madison Ave., Albany, NY 12208.

Ackerman, Carolyn S. (New York, NY) Acq. Libn., Hofstra Univ. Lib., 1966–; VP, Am Finn Sauna of Long Island, 1963–79; Job Anal., Brooklyn Army Base, Vets. Admin., 1944–48; Tchr., New York City Sec. Schs., 1940–43. **Educ.:** Hunter Coll., 1934–38, BA (Hist.); Columbia Univ., 1938–40, MA (Hist.); Long Island Univ., 1964–66, MLS. **Orgs.:** ALA. Nassau Cnty. LA: Coll. and Univ. Div., Stats. and Prof. Pracs. Com. (1972–). Hofstra Lib. Assocs.: Serials Com. (1972–75); Un. List Com. (1977–). Long Island Lib. Resrcs. Cncl. AAUP. **Honors:** Hafstra Univ., Disting. Srv. Libn., 1980; Beta Phi Mu; Alpha Chi Alpha; Phi Beta Kappa. **Pubns.:** "Acquisitions Hang-Ups," *Lib. Jnl.* (Mr. 1, 1971); "And Book Selection," *Lib. Jnl.* (F. 15, 1972); "Joys of Standing Orders," *Wilson Lib. Bltn.* (D. 1974); various bk. reviews, *Title Varies*; ed., *Hofstra Lib. Nsltr.* (1972–); jt. ed., *Facts and Figures* (1974, 1976, 1979). **Activities:** 1; 15, 44 **Addr.:** 195 N. Village Ave., Rockville Centre, NY 11570.

Ackerman, Page (Je. 30, 1912, Evanston, IL) Univ. Libn., Emeritus, Univ. of CA, Los Angeles, 1977–, Univ. Libn., 1973–77, Prof., Sch. of Lib. and Info. Sci., 1973–77, Assoc. Univ. Libn., 1965–73; Asst. Univ. Libn., 1954–65. **Educ.:** Agnes Scott Coll., 1931–33, AB (Eng.); Univ. of NC, 1938–40, BSLS. **Orgs.:** ALA: Cncl. (1971–75); Prof. Ethics Com. (1976–). ARL: Ofc. of Mgt. Std., Adv. Com. (1976–). Cncl. on Lib. Resrcs.: Bd. (1974–). Frdm. to Read Fndn. Natl. Enquiry into Schol. Comm.: Adv. Bd. Amer. Cvl. Liberties Un. Immaculate Heart Coll.: Bd. of Trustees (1978–79). **Honors:** Univ. of NC, Disting. Alum. Awd., 1973; AAUW, Santa Monica Branch, Status of Women Awd., 1973; Univ. of CA, Los Angeles, Alum. Assn., Awd. of Distinction, LS, 1977; Agnes Scott Coll., Alum. Assn., Disting. Alum. Awd., 1978. **Pubns.:** Jt. auth., *A Survey of the Library of the University of Arizona* (1972); "Research Needs Relating to the Library School and Requirements for Staffing Libraries," *A Study of the Needs for Research in Library and Information Science Education* (1970); "Academic Governance and Libraries," *Lib. Resrch.* (Spr. 1980). **Activities:** 1; 17, 26, 35; 63, 74 **Addr.:** 310 20th St., Santa Monica, CA 90402.

Acosta, Lydia Burguet (N. 4, 1947, New York, NY) Dir., Merl Kelce Lib., Univ. of Tampa, 1977–, Deputy Dir., 1976, Head, Pub. Srvcs. 1975–76, Ref. Libn., 1973–75. **Educ.:** Univ. S. FL, 1965–70, BA (Span.), 1970–73, MLS. **Orgs.:** Lib. Sci. Alum. Assn.: Pres. (1977–79). Assoc. Mid-FL Coll. Libs.: Pres. (1979–). FL LA: JMRT (Ch., 1978–79; Vice Ch., 1977–78). Hillsborough Cnty. Lib. Assn.: VP (1979–). ALA: ACRL/JMRT (1978–). Henry B. Plant Musm.: Bd. of Trustees (1978–). Gulf Tchrs. of Eng. to Speakers of Other Langs.: Treas. (1974). Frnds. Merl Kelce Lib.: Secy. (1979–). **Pubns.:** Oral presentations. **Activities:** 1; 17, 33, 39; 63, 74 **Addr.:** Merl Kelce Library, University of Tampa, 401 W. Kennedy Blvd., Tampa, FL 33606.

Acton, Patricia Lynn (Ap. 7, 1945, Calgary, AB) Pres., Acton Info. Resrcs. Mgt. Ltd., 1980–; Pres., Schick Info. Syst. Ltd., 1973–80; Libn., AB Dept. of the Env., 1971–73; Gen. Sci. Ref. Libn., Univ. of AB, 1969–71. **Educ.:** Univ. of SK, 1966, BA; Univ. of AB, 1969, BLS. **Orgs.:** Assn. of Recs. Mgrs. and Admins. ASIS: Can. LA. Various other orgs. **Pubns.:** *Pollution in Alberta: A Bibliography* (1974); "Kwic, But Effective - Indexing the Unindexed Speedily," Procs. *West. Can. Chap., Amer. Socty. for Info. Sci.* (1973); "The Information Company," *Procs. Can. ASIS* (1977); "Information for Sale," *Procs. West. Can. Chap., ASIS* (1975). **Activities:** 14-Info. Consult.; 24, 33, 38 **Addr.:** Acton Information Resources Management Ltd., 1923 Quadra St., Victoria, BC V8T 4C1 Canada.

Adamonis, Beverly A. (F. 6, 1953, Norwood, MA) Advert. Mgr., *The Library Scene*, Lib. Binding Inst., 1979–, PR Dir., Lib. Binding Inst., 1978–, Ed., 1978–. **Educ.:** Univ. of MA, 1971–75, BA (Communications); Boston Univ., 1977–, (PR). **Orgs.:** ALA: RTSD/Prsrvn. of Lib. Mtrls. Sect. Amer. Socty. for Assn. Execs. **Pubns.:** "Profile of a Public Library–The L.A.P.L.," *The Library Scene* (S. 1979); "Library and Aerospace Personnel Match Wits to Restore Damaged Books," *The Library Scene* (D. 1979). **Activities:** 3; 36, 37, 41; 51, 75, 93 **Addr.:** Suite 633, 50 Congress St., Boston, MA 02109.

Adamovich, Frank W. (Ja. 30, 1929, Pepperell, MA) Docum. Libn., Univ. of NH, 1968–; Assoc. Prof., Nathaniel Hawthorne Coll., 1963–68; Tchr., Eng. HS, Boston, 1961–63; various lectr. positions, wkshps. **Educ.:** Univ. of MA, 1956–60, BS (Math.); Simmons Coll., 1965–68, MS; various crs. **Orgs.:** New Eng. LA: Bibl. Com. (1975); Mem. Com. (1981). ALA: GODORT (New Eng. Rep., 1973), Machine-Readable Data Files Task Frc. (Ch., 1980–81). NH LA: CATA Com. (Ch., 1973). NELINET: Docum. Task Grp. (Ch., 1972). State Univ. of New Eng.: Docum. Libns (Ch., 1971). **Pubns.:** Ed., *NELINET Docum. Task Frc. Nsltr.* (1973); *Index to U.S. Depository Serials, Directory and Union List* (1975); "The Use of Computers in the Bibliographic Control of Government Documents" audio-cassette series (1975); *Index to Federal Documents in the UNH Library* (1976–78); *Index to Selected New Hampshire Depository Documents, 1973–1979* (1979); various bibls. **Activities:** 1; 29, 30; 56 **Addr.:** University of New Hampshire Library, Durham, NH 03824.

Adamovich, Shirley Gray (Pepperell, MA) Actg. State Libn., NH State Lib., 1979–; Instr., Lib. Sci., Univ. of NH, 1972–79, Dir., Lib. Tech. Prog., 1972–75. **Educ.:** Univ. of NH, 1954, BA (Eng.); Simmons Coll., 1954–55, MSLS. **Orgs.:** ALA. New Eng. LA. NH LA. **Honors:** Kappa Delta Pi, 1949. **Pubns.:** "A Reader in Library Technology," *Microcard Editions* (1975). **Activities:** 1, 13; 17, 20, 26; 50, 63 **Addr.:** Actg. State Librarian, New Hampshire State Library, 20 Park St., Concord, NH 03301.

Adams, Ann (My. 5, 1946, Houston, TX) Head, Cat. Dept., Houston Pub. Lib., 1973–; Pub. Libn., Consult., TX State Lib., 1972-73; Subj. Catlgr., Duke Univ. Lib., 1970–72. **Educ.:** Baylor Univ., 1964–68, BA (Hist.); Univ. of TX, 1968–70, MLS. **Orgs.:** ALA: RASD/Cat. Use Com. (1973–77). TX LA: TX Reg. Grp. of Catlgrs. and Clasfrs. (Ch., 1977–78). SWLA. **Activities:** 9; 20, 24, 46 **Addr.:** 2335 Albans, Houston, TX 77005.

Adams, Charles M. (Ag. 24, 1907, LaMoure, ND) Emeritus, Univ. of NC, 1969–; Dir., Sinclair Lib., Univ. HI, 1969–73; Libn., Univ. NC, at Greenshow, 1945–69; Ast. to Dir. and Spec. Colls. Libn., Columbus Univ., 1937–45. **Educ.:** Amherst Coll., 1926–29, AB (Lit.); Columbia Univ., 1933–34, BSLS; **Orgs.:** ALA: ACRL (Pres.); numerous bds. and coms. Sierre Clb. Audubon Society. Other orgs. **Honors:** Univ. NC, Hon. DHL, 1978. **Pubns.:** *Bibliography of Randall Jarrell* (1958); "Randall Jarrell: poet and librarian" *NC Libs.* (O., 1956); numerous articles in prof. jnls. **Activities:** 1; 17, 39, 45 **Addr.:** 214 Ridgeway Dr., Greensboro, NC 27403.

Adams, Elaine Parker (N. 12, 1940, New Orleans, LA) Supvsr., Lib. Srvs., Getty Oil Resrch. Ctr., 1980– LRC Coor., TX South. Univ., 1976–80; Media Spec., Norris Med. Lib. Univ. South. CA, 1974–75; Ast. Prof., Univ. MD, 1973; Libn., Upper St. Clair Sch. Dist., 1972–73; Cat. Libn., Grossmont Un. HS Dist., 1971–72; Libn., New Orleans Pub. Schls., 1967–68; Ref. Libn., Xavier Univ. of LA, 1966–67; Tchr., New Orleans Pub. Schls., 1961–66. **Educ.:** Xavier Univ. of LA, 1957–61, BA, (Span. Educ.); LA State Univ., 1963–66, MS, (LS); Univ. of South. CA, 1968–73, PhD, (LS). **Orgs.:** ALA: Ofc. for Lib. Svcs. to the Disadv., Adv. Com. (1977–79); YASD Resrch. Com. (1974–83); Media Sel. and Usage Com. (1972–75); Black Caucus Steer. Com. (1970–72); Other coms. CA Libns. Black Caucus: South. Area (Ch., 1975). Med. Lib. Assn.: Hlth. Sci. AV Grp. (Ch., 1976). Youth for Understand. Intl. Student Exch.: Area Rep. (1979–). **Honors:** Beta Phi Mu, 1965; Phi Kappa Phi, 1965. **Pubns.:** Co-ed., *Media and the YA, 1973-1977* (1981); Contrib, *Media and the YA* (1977); "Photograph a Good Library When You See One", *AV Instr.* (Nov. 1977); "Crisis on the UCLA Campus", *CA Libn.* (July 1970); "CLA San Francisco", *CA Libn.* (Apr. 1970); Various Reviews for *Previews* (1973–). **Activities:** 1, 10; 17, 32, 48; 63, 66, 67 **Addr.:** 10906 Holly Springs Dr., Houston, TX 77042.

Adams, Elizabeth Byrne (S. 9, 1933, Brooklyn, NY) Prof. of Mgt., George Washington Univ., 1966–; Staff Systs. Anal., I.B.M., 1955–63; Prof. Lectr., Amer. Univ., 1960–66;Ofcr., U.S. Marine Corps, 1958–60. **Educ.:** Queens Coll., NY, 1951–55, BS (Biochem.); George Washington Univ., 1955–57, MA (Adult Educ.); Amer. Univ., 1966–72, PhD (Mgt. Tech.). **Orgs.:** Amer. Socty. for Pub. Admin.: Sci. and Tech. in Gvt./Exec. Com. (1974–); Nsltr. Ed. ASIS: Pub. and Pvt. Interface Com. Assn. of Info. Mgrs. Assn. for Comp. Mach. Amer. Assn. for Advcmt. of Sci. World Future Socty. **Pubns.:** *Report of the National Forum on Scientific and Technical Communication* (1978); *Case Studies in the Management of Information Technology* (1976); "Management of the New Information Environment", *ASIS Bltn.* (Ap. 1976); "The National Forum on Scientific and Technical Communication", *ASIS Bltn.* (Mr. 1978); Various papers. **Activities:** 11; 24, 26; 75, 91, 93 **Addr.:** George Washington University, School of Government and Business Administration - Management Science, Washington, DC 20052.

Adams, Grover C. (O. 14, 1924, Bennettsville, SC) Coord. of Libs., Copiaguc Pub. Schs., 1957–; Libn., Brooklyn Pub. Lib., 1955–57; Tchr., Peabody HS, 1949–55. **Educ.:** Johnson C. Smith Univ., 1945–49, BA (Soc. Std.); Columbia Univ. Tchr. Coll., 1950–53, MA (Educ.); Columbia Univ., 1957–59, MLS. **Orgs.:** ALA. NY LA. **Activities:** 10, 11 **Addr.:** 223 Grand Blvd., Brentwood, NY 11717.

Adams, Gustav C. (D. 9, 1908, South Boston, VA) Ref. Libn., Lindsey Hopkins Tech. Educ. Ctr., 1972–; Libn., Tchrs. Prof. Lib., 1960–62; Libn., Hialeah HS, 1956–60; Libn., Palatka HS, 1948–56; Libn. Ref. Dept., NY Pub. Lib., 1947–48. **Educ.:** Presby. Coll., 1928–32, AB (Eng.); Stetson Univ., 1932–33, MA (Eng.); Columbia Univ., 1946–47, BS (LS, Pub. Lib.). **Orgs.:** ALA: AASL; RASD. FL Assn. for Media in Educ. FL LA. Dade Cnty. Media Spec. Assn. Pi Kappa Phi Soc. Fraternity: Archon (1927–28). Blue Key Hon.: Pan-Hellenic Cncl. (Pres., 1927–28). Amer. Vocational Assn. FL Vocational Assn. FL Educ. Assn./Untd. **Pubns.:** Ed., *Bookcase* (1960–65); bk. reviewer for Dade cnty. Schs. and Miami pub. lib. (1960–). **Activities:** 10, 12; 20, 39; 50 **Addr.:** 7600 N. W. 27 Ave., Miami, FL 33147.

Adams, J. Robert (F. 14, 1938, Plainview, TX) Univ. Libn., Wesleyan Univ., 1979–; Assoc. Univ. Libn., Univ. of AZ, 1973–79; Asst. Univ. Libn., Washington Univ., 1972–73, Asst. Dir. for Readrs. Srvs., 1970–72, Ast. to Dir., 1968–70; Asst. Circ. Libn., Univ. of Chicago, 1965–68. **Educ.:** Baylor Univ., 1957–60, BA (Relig., Hist.); SW Baptist Theol. Sem., 1960–63, BD (Theo.); Univ. of Chicago, 1964–68, MA (Libnshp.). **Orgs.:** ALA. **Activities:** 1; 16, 19, 35 **Addr.:** Olin Library, Wesleyan University, Middletown, CT 06457.

Adams, John M. (Je. 10, 1950, Chicago, IL) Dir., Moline Pub. Lib., 1978–; Head, Gen. Readrs. Svcs., Los Angeles Pub. Lib., 1976–78, Sr. Libn., Phil. Dept., 1975–76; Ref. Libn., Sherman Oaks Branch, 1973–75. **Educ.:** Univ. IL, 1968–72, BA (Eng. Lit.), 1972–73, MS (LS). **Orgs.:** IL LA: SRRT, Treas. (1979–80). ALA. Rotary Intl. **Activities:** 9; 17, 28, 35; 55, 92 **Addr.:** Moline Public Library, 504 17 St., Moline, IL 61265.

Adams, June (Bowen) (N. 12, 1926, Fresno, CA) Dir., Somerset Cnty. Lib., 1976–; Dir., W. New York Pub. Lib., 1973–75; Dir., Westwood Pub. Lib., 1969–73; Ref. and Docum. Libn., Hackensack Pub. Lib., 1965–69. **Educ.:** City Coll. of NY, 1955–57, BA (Psy.); Rutgers Univ., 1961–64, MLS; Univ. of Grenoble, 1964–65, Fr. Lang. and Lit. **Orgs.:** NJ LA: Pres. (1981–82); Lib. Dev. Com. (Ch., 1979–80); Exec. Bd.; other ofcs. and coms. ALA: PLA; LAD. Paramus Leag. of Women Voters: Pres.; Exec. Bd. **Activities:** 9; 17 **Addr.:** 466 Hauck Rd., Bridgewater, NJ 08807.

Adams, Katherine Jean (Jl. 20, 1945, Chicago, IL) Asst. Head Libn./Archvst., Barker TX Hist. Ctr., Univ. of TX at Austin, 1981–; Coord., TX State Pubns. Clearhse., TX State Lib., 1980–81, Asst. Coord., 1979–80; Index, 1978–79. **Educ.:** Knox Coll., 1963–67, BA (Hist.); Univ. OK, 1967–70, MA (Amer. Hist.); Univ. OK. Press, 1970–71, (Ed. Flwshp.); Natl. Arch., 1976, Arch. Admin. Trng. Cert; Univ. of TX at Austin, 1981, MLIS **Orgs.:** ASIS. Amer. Socty. of Indxrs. SAA. Socty. of Southwest Archvsts. **Pubns.:** *Texas State Documents Index: 1977, Title-Subject* (1979); *Information Available by County*

PROFESSIONAL ACTIVITIES: Institutions: 1. Acad. lib.; 2. Arch.; 3. Assn.; 4. Fed./Gvt. lib.; 5. Inst. lib.; 6. Mfr./Suppl.; 7. Milit. lib.; 8. Musm.; 9. Pub. lib.; 10. Sch. lib.; 11. Sch. of lib. sci.; 12. Spec. lib.; 13. State lib.; 14. (other). **Functions/Activities:** 15. Acq./Col. dev.; 16. Adult srvs.; 17. Admin.; 18. Apprais.; 19. Archit./Bldgs.; 20. Cat./Class.; 21. Chld. srvs.; 22. Circ.; 23. Cons./Pres.; 24. Consult.; 25. Cont. ed.; 26. Educ. lib. sci.; 27. Ext. srvs.; 28. Fund/Grants; 29. Gvt. pubs.; 30. Indx./Abs.; 31. Instr. lib. use; 32. Media srvs.; 33. Micro.; 34. Netwks./Coop.; 35. Persnl.; 36. PR; 37. Publshg.; 38. Recs. mgt.; 39. Ref. srvs.; 40. Repro.; 41. Resrch.; 42. Review.; 43. Secur.; 44. Serials; 45. Spec. col.; 46. Tech. srvs.; 47. Trustees/Bds.; 48. YA srvs.; 49. (other).

From Selected Texas State Documents (1979); *Texas State Documents: A Manual of Guidelines for Texas State Agencies* (1980). **Activities:** 13; 29, 30; 75, 92 **Addr.:** 2208 Spring Creek Dr., Austin, TX 78704.

Adams, Kathlyn C. (Ap. 7, 1921, Northampton, MA) Outrch. Consult., Monroe Cnty. Lib. Syst., 1964–; Dir., Riga Free Lib., 1952–64. **Educ.:** Smith Coll., 1942, BA (Soclgy./Econ.); SUNY, Geneseo, 1967, MLS. **Orgs.:** ALA: PLA/Conf. Plng. Com.; Nom. Com.; other coms. NY LA: Cncl. (1979–80); VP, Pres.-Elect (1978–79); Pres. (1979–80); Nom. Com. (1972–74); Ch. (1973–74); Margaret Martinoni Schol. Com.: Ch., (1972); Gvrs. Conf. Com. (1976–78); Cncl. (1979–80). Amer. Socty. of Pub. Admins.: Prog. Com. Natl. Assn. of Parents of the Deaf. Natl. Cncl. on Aging. Genesee Conf. Sr. Citizen Dir. **Honors:** Cmnty. Srv. Awds., 1974, 1978. **Pubns.:** Jt. auth., "Collections in a Capsule"; "Library Aides," *Bookmark;* "Recruitment of Minorities," *ALA Bltn.;* "A Golden Opportunity," *Cath. Lib. Jnl.;* other articles. **Activities:** 9, 11; 24, 28, 36; 50, 66, 72 **Addr.:** Monroe County Library System, 115 South Ave., Rochester, NY 14604.

Adams, Mary D. (D. 26, 1927, Minneapolis, MN) Libn., Metro. Cncl., 1970–. **Educ.:** Univ. of MN, 1944–48, BA (Phil.), 1969–70, MA (LS). **Orgs.:** SLA. MN LA: Spec. Lib. RT (Ch.-elect, 1979–80; Ch., 1980–81). AFSCME Lcl. 839. **Activities:** 13; 15, 20, 22; 65, 82, 94 **Addr.:** 300 Metro Sq. Bldg., St. Paul, MN 55101.

Adams, Maureen Dolores (Mr. 25, 1924, Toronto, ON) Tchr., Libn., Agnes Taylor Pub. Sch., 1970–; Tchr., Libn., Dufferin-Peel Sep. Sch. Bd., 1969–70; Lib. Consult., Etobicoke Sch. Bd., 1963–64; Child. Libn., Welland Pub. Lib., 1952–59; Elem. Tchr., E. York Bd. of Educ., 1942–44. **Educ.:** Univ. of Toronto, 1945–49, BA, 1949–50, BLS; Toronto Tchr. Coll., 1941–42, Elem. Tchr. Cert. **Orgs.:** ON LA. CAN LA: CAN Bk. Awd. Com. (1968–70), Ch. (1969–70). Intnl. Sch. LA. CAN Assn. for Young Chld. Assn. for Media Litcy. ON Puppetry Assn. **Activities:** 10; 22, 31, 32 **Addr.:** 27 Ladne Ave., Brampton, ON L6Y 1V4, Canada.

Adams, Mignon S. (N. 6, 1941, Chickasha, OK) Co-ord. of Info Srvs., Penfield Lib., SUNY, Oswego, 1980–; Co-ord., Lib. Instr., 1977–80; Ref. Libn., 1976–77; Instr. Designer, South. IL Univ., 1975–76; Lib. Dir., Lakeland Coll., 1967–69; Libn., Lab. Sch., East. IL Univ., 1966–67; Libn., Unity HS, 1963–66. **Educ.:** East. IL Univ., 1958–62, BS (Eng. ed.); Univ. IL, 1963–65, MSLS, 1969–72, Doct. in progress. **Orgs.:** ALA: ACRL/BIS; /Resrch. Com. (1977–80); Ch. (1979–81), /CLS (Prog. Com., 1979–80); LIRT/Pubn. Com. (Ch., 1979–81); Ed. Nsltr. NY Lib. Instr. Clearhse.: Bd. (1978–80). SUNY Fac. Sen.: Undergrad. Progs. Com. (1978–80); Ch., 1979–80). SUCO Women's Caucus: Co-ch. (1978–79; 1980-81). SUCO Fac. Asm.: Rep. (1978–82); Undergrad. Curric. Com. (1977–80; Ch., 1979–80). **Honors:** Danforth Fndn., Danforth Assoc., 1978. **Pubns.:** "Individualized Approach to Library Skills Instruction", *Lib. Trends* (Sum. 1980); "Evaluating Library Instruction", Proc. of 8th Anl. LOEX Conf. (1979). **Activities:** 1; 31; 63, 95-indust. arts, 92 **Addr.:** Co-Ordinator of Information Services, Penfield Library, SUNY/Oswego, Oswego, NY 13126.

Adams, Scott (N. 20, 1909, Agawam, MA) Consul., 1975–; Prof. Intl. Ctr. for Educ., Univ. of Louisville, 1973–75; Sr. Sci. Bio. Sci. Comm. Proj., Geo. Washington Univ., 1971–73; Spec. Asst. to Frgn. Secy., Natl. Acad. of Sci., 1970–71; Deputy Dir., Natl. Lib. of Med., 1960–70; Prog. Dir., Frgn. Sci. Info., Natl. Sci. Fndn., 1959–60; Libn., Natl. Inst. of Hlth., 1950–59; Actg. Libn., Army Med. Lib., 1946–50. **Educ.:** Yale Univ., 1926–30, AB (Eng.); Columbia Univ., 1939–40, MLS. **Orgs.:** ALA: Various coms. Med. LA: Pres. (1967–68). ASIS: Pres. (1955). Many orgs. and intl. assigns. Amer. Assn. Advnc. of Sci.: Info. Comp. Comm. Sect. (Secy). **Honors:** US Dept. HEW, Superior Svc. Awd., 1969; Med. LA, Marcia C. Noyes Awd., 1974; Med. LA, Fellow, 1978; Amer. Assn. Advnc. Sci., Fellow, 1970. **Pubns.:** *Medical Bibliography in an Age of Discontinuity* (1981); CoAuth., "Cooperation in Information Activities through International Organizations", *Anl. Review of Info. Sci. and Tech.*. ASIS (1975); "Scientific and Technical Information Services in Eight Latin American Countries: Developments, Technical Assistance; Opportunities for Development", *Natl. Tech. Info. Svc.* (1976); CoAuth., "U.S. Participation in World Information Activities," ASIS Bltn. (Mar. 1976); other pubns. **Activities:** 4, 12; 17, 24, 30; 62, 80, 91 **Addr.:** 2350 Valletta La., Louisville, KY 40205.

Adams, Sharon S. (Mr. 6, 1950, Anchorage, AK) Ref. Libn., Austin Cmnty. Coll., 1980–; Dissemination Spec., Resrch. and Dev., Exch. Info. Netwk., Sw. Educ. Dev. Lab., 1976–80, Info. Spec., Parenting Mtrls. Info. Ctr., 1974–76. **Educ.:** Univ. of CO, 1972, BA (Eng. Lit.); Univ. of TX, 1974, MLS. **Orgs.:** ALA. TX LA. **Pubns.:** Jt. auth., *Information Search Services for Educators* (1980); *Catalog of NIE Education Products: Subject and Title Index* (1977); *Parenting in 1976: A Listing from PMIC* (1976). **Activities:** 1; 15, 22, 39; 50 **Addr.:** 5908 Nasco Dr., Austin, TX 78757.

Adams, Stanley E. (Mr. 10, 1928, Greenwich Twp., PA) Info. Consult., IL State Lib., 1972–, Legis. Resrch. Libn., 1966–72; Head Libn., Punahou Sch., 1964–66; Dir., Reader Srvs. Div., NV State Lib., 1957–64; Actg. State Libn., 1962; Lectr. in State Srvs., Univ. NV, 1961–62; Ref. Libn. and LS Instr., Millersville State Coll., 1956–57; Libn., Towson Jr. HS, 1953–56. **Educ.:** Kutztown State Coll., 1949–53, BS (LS, Span.); Univ. of San Carlos, Guatemala, 1951; Univ. of Denver, 1954–57, MA (LS); Certs., IL Ofc. of State Secy., 1971, Comp. Concepts for Mgt. and Intro. to Syst. Analy. **Orgs.:** ALA: GODORT; State Docum. Task Frc. (Coord., 1974–76). IL LA. Springfield Lib. Clb.: Pres. (1979). Other orgs. Amer. Socty. for Pub. Admin. IL Fed. of State Lib. Employees: Treas. (1979–80). **Honors:** Kappa Delta Pi, 1953. **Pubns.:** *The Constitution of Illinois: A Selective Bibliography* (1970); Ed., *Nevada In Print;* Ed., *Library Information Bulletin* (1976–78); "On Being An Information Consultant," *IL Libs.* (June 1977). **Activities:** 13; 24, 29, 39; 75, 77, 78 **Addr.:** P.O. Box 2041, Springfield, IL 62705.

Adams, Velma Lee (N. 20, 1909, Columbus, MS) Libn. Emeritus, South. AR Univ., 1976–, and Libn., Belhaven Coll., 1976–; Libn., Spec. Col. and Arch., South. AR Univ., 1975–76, Head Libn., 1953–75, Asst. Libn., 1950–53, Tchr., Libn., MS HSs., 1940–50; HS Eng. Tchr., MS HSs., 1937–40. **Educ.:** MS Univ. for Women, 1927–30, BA (Eng.); LA State Univ., 1947–51, BS (LS); Univ. TX, 1962 (LS), Arch. Mgt. Cert., 1960. **Orgs.:** ALA. AR LA. SW LA: Coll. and Univ. Sect. VP (1956–58); Pres. (1958–60). MS LA.: Arch. and Hist. Com. (1981). AAUW: Pres. (Magnolia, 1957–59); AR Flwshp. Ch. (1970–71); MS Div. (Corres. Secy., 1978–80). Delta Kappa Gamma. AR Hist. Assn. MS Hist. Socty. **Honors** MS Gov. Ofc. of Volun. Svcs., Disting. Srv. Awd., 1978; Beta Phi Mu. **Activities:** 1, 10; 17, 20, 39; 50, 55, 63 **Addr.:** 155 Hayes Dr., Jackson, MS 39209.

Adamshick, Robert David (D. 29, 1948, Hazleton, PA) Dir. of Libs., NY Inst. of Tech., 1981–, Branch Libn., 1980–81; Serials Libn., St. John's Univ., 1976–79; Circ., Ref. Libn., Univ. of New Haven, 1975–76; Circ. Libn., Bethlehem Pub. Lib., 1974–75. **Educ.:** Bloomsburg State Coll., 1966–70, BA (Span.); Univ. of Pittsburgh, 1970–71, MLS; Univ. of New Haven, NY Inst. of Tech., 1975–, MBA. **Orgs.:** ALA: ACRL. DE LA. NY LA. PA LA. AAUP. **Honors:** Beta Phi Mu, 1971. **Pubns.:** Various Reviews. **Activities:** 1, 9; 15, 16, 17, 22, 31; 59 **Addr.:** 270 Burns St., Forest Hills, NY 11375.

Adamson, Martha C. (F. 20, 1947, Indianapolis, IN) Head Libn., Raytheon Co. Resrch. Div. Lib., 1981–; Libn., Phys. Sci. and Engin. Air Frc. Weapons Lab. Tech. Lib., 1976–81. **Educ.:** Kalamazoo Coll., 1965–69, BA (Grmn.); Univ. of IL, 1975–76, MS (LS); NM Highlands Univ., 1978–80, MA (Bus. Admin.). **Orgs.:** SLA: Rio Grande Chap., Secy., (1978–80), Proj. Ch. (1977–78); Boston Chap. Grt. Albuquerque LA: Wkshp. Plng. Com. (1978). **Honors:** Beta Phi Mu, 1976. **Pubns.:** Jt. ed., *Conference Literature in Science and Technology* (1981); ed., *Resource Sharing II, Proceedings of the 22nd Military Librarians Workshop* (1979); jt. auth., "Publishing in Library Science Journals: A Test of the Olsgaard Profile," *Coll. and Resrch. Libs.* (My. 1981); jt. auth., "The Experienced Microfilm User: Answering More Sophisticated Needs," *Jnl. of Micro.* (S.–O. 1979); jt. auth., "Looking Back at the Microfilm Decision: Expectations and Experiences," *Spec. Libs.* (Ap. 1979). **Activities:** 4, 12; 15, 34, 39; 64, 74, 88 **Addr.:** Raytheon Company Research Div. Library, 28 Seyon St., Waltham, MA 02254.

Adan, Adrienne Hinds (O. 17, 1942, New York, NY) Assoc. Libn., UCLA Law Sch. Lib., 1978–; Ed., 1976–78; Ref. Libn., Head of Pub. Srvs., Stanford Univ. Law Lib., 1970–76; Head, Tech. Info. Srvs., 1969–70. **Educ.:** Hebrew Univ., Jerusalem, Israel, 1960–66, BA (Romance Langs., Pol. Sci.); Univ. of TX, 1967–68, MLS; Univ. Santa Clara Law Sch., 1971–75, JD. **Orgs.:** Amer. Assn. of Law Libs.: Schol. Com. ALA. CA LA. South. CA Assn. of Law Libs.: Treas. (1978–79). CA State Bar Assn. Amer. Bar Assn. **Pubns.:** Resrch. ast. and Ed., *Federal Taxation of Trusts, Grantors, and Beneficiaries* (1978); various reviews and editing. **Activities:** 1, 12; 15, 17, 39; 56, 77, 78 **Addr.:** UCLA Law Library, 405 Hilgard Ave., Los Angeles, CA 90024.

Adcock, Donald C. (Jl. 22, 1934, Du Bois, IL) Dir. of Lib. Srvs., Glen Ellyn Pub. Schs., 1963–; Tchr., Virden Comnty. Unit Schs., 1961–63; Tchr., Libn., Tamaroa Comnty. HS, 1959–61, Tchr., Libn., 1956–57. **Educ.:** South. IL Univ., 1952–56, BS (Eng.), 1964, MS (Instr. Mtls.). **Orgs.:** ALA: Stand. Com. on Lib. Educ. (1979–81). AASL: 2nd VP (1977), By Laws Com. (1978–80), Resol., Ch. (1977), Supervisors Sect., Secy. (1978), Nom. (1979), Prog. (1976–78), Other coms. IL LA: 2nd VP (1972), Exec. Secy. Eval. Com., Ch. (1974), Libn. Citation Com., Ch. (1974), Nom./Elect. Com. (1978–80), Ch. (1978), Other coms. IL Assn. for Media Educ.: Pres. (1971), Treas. (1967); Other orgs. IL Ofc. of Educ., Title IV, ESEA Adv. Cncl.: Exec. Com. (1979), Eval. Com., Ch. (1979). **Honors:** IL Assn. of Sch. Libns., Honor Awd., 1977. **Pubns.:** "Realities in Implementation," *Objective Setting for Illinois Libraries* (1978); "Media Services for Exceptional Children", *IL Libs.* (Sept. 1977); "Setting Objectives for School Media Programs", *IL Libs.* (June 1978); "Symptoms of a Larger Problem", *IL Libs.* (Sept. 1978). **Activities:** 10; 17 **Addr.:** Glen Ellyn Public Schools, 793 N. Main St., Glen Ellyn, IL 60137.

Adelman, Jean Shaw (N. 23, 1930, Toledo, OH) Head Libn., Univ. Musm., Univ. PA, 1971–; Staff Libn., West. PA Reg. Med. Prog., 1969–71; Visit. Ast. Prof., Sch. of Lib. and Info. Sci., Univ. West. ON, 1968–69; LS Instr., Allegheny Cnty. Cmnty. Coll., 1967–68; LS Instr., Grad. Lib. Sch., Drexel Inst., 1964–65; Tchng. Fellow, Grad. Sch. of Lib. and Info. Sci., Univ. Pittsburgh, 1963–64. **Educ.:** Univ. PA, 1948–52, AB (Anthro.), 1951–54, (Anthro.); Univ. WA, Russian and Far East. Inst., 1954–55, (Anthro. and area std.); Univ. Pittsburgh, Grad. Sch. Lib. and Info. Sci., 1962–63, MLS, 1963, LS Adv. cert. **Orgs.:** SLA: Philadelphia Chap. (Pres., 1976–77); Bd. (1974–). ALA: RASD/Wilson Indexes Com. (1977–81). Philadelphia Anthro. Socty.: Bltn. Ed. (1953–54). Univ. PA, Alum. Assn.: Exec. Bd. (1973–77). Leag. of Women Voters of Pittsburgh: Exec. Bd. (1961–63). **Pubns.:** "Imaginative Mining of Resources", *Lib. Jnl.* (O. 15, 1966). **Activities:** 1, 12; 15, 16, 17; 55, 92, 95 **Addr.:** Library, University Museum, University of Pennsylvania, Philadelphia, PA 19104.

Adelsperger, Robert James (Je. 19, 1925, Hammond, IN) Spec. Coll. Libn. and Cur. of Rare Bks., Univ. of IL, Chicago Circle, 1965–, Asst. Ref. Libn., 1960–65, Asst. Serials-Acq. Libn., 1959–60; Ref. Libn. and Biblgphr., Bowling Green State Univ., 1958–59. **Educ.:** Univ. IL, AB (Eng.), MS (LS). **Orgs.:** LA: JMRT (Ch., 1963–64); Chicago Chap. (Ch., 1962–63); Ref. Svcs. Div./Pubn. Com. (1963–69); Hist. Sect. (Ch., 1971–72); Bd. (1970–72); Legis. Rep. (1968–70); ACRL/RBMS (Ch., 1969–70). IL LA: Bd. of Dir. (1974–76). SAA: Com. on Lib., Arch. Rel. (1970–71; 1980-82). Chicago Lib. Clb.: Pres. (1975–76). AAUP: Chicago Circle Chap. (Treas., 1971–75; VP, 1975–77; Pres., 1977–79); Exec. Com. (1979–81). Socty. of Midland Auths.: Bd. of Dir. (1975–80); Corres. Secy. (1977–). Frnds. of Lit.: Pres. (1974–); Bd. of Dir. (1968–74). Chicago Fndn. for Lit.: Pres. (1974–). **Honors:** Socty. of Midland Auths., Disting. Svc. Awd., 1972; Phi Beta Kappa, 1956; Phi Kappa Phi, 1956; Phi Eta Sigma, 1953. **Pubns.:** "Help your RSD Representative", *RQ* (Spr. 1971); "Special Collections", *ALA YRBK* (1976, 1978). **Activities:** 1; 18, 23, 45; 55, 57, 70 **Addr.:** University of Illinois at Chicago Circle, P.O. Box 8198, Chicago, IL 60680.

Adeniran, Dixie D. (My. 26, 1943, Los Angeles, CA) Dir., Ventura Cnty. Lib. Srvs. Agency, 1979–, Prin. Libn., 1978–79, Supvsg. Libn., 1976–77, Sr. Libn., 1975–76; Serials Libn., Coll. of Sci. and Tech., Port Harcourt, Nigeria, 1972–74; Libn., Free Lib. of Philadelphia, 1970–72. **Educ.:** Univ. of CA, Santa Barbara, 1961–65, BA (Eng. Lit.); MI State Univ., 1965–68, MA (Sec. Educ.); Univ. of MI, 1969–70, MLS. **Orgs.:** ALA. CA LA. SLA. **Activities:** 9; 17, 46 **Addr.:** Ventura County Library Services Agency, P.O. Box 771, Ventura, CA 93002.

Adler, Marianne Gresham (Dallas, TX) Head, Bibl. Prcs., Fondren Lib., Rice Univ., 1978–, Actg. Head, Acq. Dept., 1977–78, Head, Bibl. Srch. Unit, 1976–77, Orig. Catlgr., 1975–76. **Educ.:** Rice Univ., 1970–73, BA (Fr.); TX Univ., 1973–74, MLS; Rice Univ., 1974–76, MA (Fr.). **Orgs.:** ALA: Retrospective Discuss. Grp. Org. (Head, 1980); LITA/Info. Sci. and Autom. Sect., Bibl. of Lib. Autom. Task Frc. 1978–81. TX LA: 1981 Anl. Mtg., Hosplty. Com. SLA. **Honors:** Pi Delta Phi, 1973. **Activities:** 1, 4; 17, 20, 31 **Addr.:** Fondren Library/ Rice University, Box 1892, Houston, TX 77001.

Adrian, Donna J. (Ag. 28, 1940, Mordon, MB) Lib. Consult., Laurenval Sch. Bd., 1979–; Lectr., Concordia Univ., 1974–; Libn., Lib. Consult., N. Island Reg. Sch. Bd., 1974–79; Libn., Rosemere HS, 1966–74; Libn., Laurenvale Sch. Bd., 1963–66. **Educ.:** Brandon Coll., 1958–62, BA; McGill Univ., 1962–63, BLS; 1964, PQ Class I Tchrs. Cert. (LS); McGill Univ., 1967–69, MLS. **Orgs.:** Can. LA: Can. Sch. LA (Pres., 1977). PQ Assn. of Sch. Libns.: Pres. (1972–73). Intl. Assn. of Sch. Libnshp.: Conf. Co-Coord. (1977). Corp. of Prof. Libns. of PQ: Sch. Lib. Com. (1977–79). Various other orgs. Mayor of Lavan Lib. Com. **Pubns.:** "Magazines Published in Quebec," *Moccasin Telegraph.* **Activities:** 10; 21, 32, 48 **Addr.:** 194 Roi Du Nord, Ste Rose, Laval, PQ H7L 1W5 Canada.

Aeschbacher, William D. (Ja. 12, 1919, Tonganxie, KS) Prof., Hist., Univ. Archvst., Univ. of Cincinnati, 1968–; Prof., Hist., Univ. of UT, 1966–68; Dir., Eisenhower Lib., 1963–66; Dir., NE State Hist. Socty., 1956–63; Assoc. Prof., Hist., Murray State Coll., 1948–56. **Educ.:** Univ. of NE, 1935–40, BSc in Ed (Hist.), 1945–46, MA (Hist.), 1946–48, PhD (Hist.). **Orgs.:** SAA. Socty. of OH Archvsts. Amer. Assn. for State and Lcl. Hist. Org. of Amer. Histns.: Secy.-Treas. (1956–69); Treas. (1969–76). Amer. Hist. Assn.: Com. on PhD Progs. (Ch., 1973); Com. on Educ. (1974); various coms. West. Hist. Assn.: Various coms. South. Hist. Assn.: Nom. Com. (Ch., 1977). **Activities:** 2, 4; 15, 17 **Addr.:** Dept. of History, University of Cincinnati, Cincinnati, OH 45221.

Afflerbach, Betty L. (My. 22, 1927, Fabens, TX) Lib. Dir., Meml. Lib., TX Med. Assn., 1977–, Actg. Libn., 1976–77, Asst. Libn., Pub. Srvs., 1972–76, Ref. Libn., 1969–72; Lib. Mtls. Coor., Corpus Christi Indp. Sch. Syst., 1966–68); Libn., Saints Cyril and Methodius Elem. Sch., 1964–66. **Educ.:** Univ. of TX, 1944–48, BA (Eng.); Our Lady of Lake Univ., 1968–69, MSLS. **Orgs.:** Med. Lib. Assn.: Med. Socty. Libs. Grp. (Co-ch., 1974); Bylaws Com. (Ch., 1980); S. Ctrl. Reg. Grp.: Ad Hoc Com. on Goals and

Special Subjects/Services: 50. Adult educ.; 51. Advert./Mktg.; 52. Aerosp.; 53. Agric.; 54. Area std.; 55. Arts/Hum.; 56. Autom.; 57. Bibl./Prtg.; 58. Bio. sci.; 59. Bus./Fin.; 60. Chem.; 61. Copyrt.; 62. Documtn.; 63. Educ.; 64. Engin.; 65. Env.; 66. Eth. grps.; 67. Film; 68. Food/Nutr.; 69. Geneal.; 70. Geo.; 71. Geol.; 72. Handcpd.; 73. Hist.; 74. Int. frdm.; 75. Info. sci.; 76. Insr.; 77. Law; 78. Legis.; 79. Math./Comp. sci.; 80. Med.; 81. Metals; 82. Nat. resrcs.; 83. Newsp.; 84. Nuc. sci.; 85. Oral hist.; 86. Petr./Energy; 87. Pharm.; 88. Phys./Astr./Math.; 89. Readg.; 90. Relig.; 91. Sci./Tech.; 92. Soc. sci.; 93. Telecom.; 94. Transp.; 95. (other).

Objectives (Ch., 1980–); Contrib. Papers Com. (1975); Prog. Com. (1978); Treas. (1980). S. Ctrl. Reg. Med. Lib. Prog. Reg. Adv. Com.: Secy. (1978); Mem. Unit Ident. Com. (1979–). SLA. TX LA. Austin Lib. Clb. TX Med. Assn.: Com. on Aging and Nursing Homes (Secy., 1974–). **Activities:** 5, 12; 17, 34, 39; 80 **Addr.:** Memorial Library, Texas Medical Association, Austin, TX 78701.

Agard, Robert Mason (Ap. 1, 1916, Williamstown, MA) Libn., Bennington Coll., 1968–; Asst. Libn., Univ. of MA, 1961–67; Libn., Earlham Coll., 1950–61; Libn., Ripon Coll., 1946–50; Lectr., WE State Coll., 1950; Lectr., Catholic Univ., 1944–46. **Educ.:** Wesleyan Univ., 1935–39, AB (Hist.); Columbia Univ., 1939–40, BS (LS); Brown Univ., 1940–44, MA (Hist.). **Orgs.:** ALA. VT LA. Lincoln Sch.: Overseer (1966–76). **Pubns.:** "Library in the Undergraduate College", *N. Cntrl. Assn. Qtly.* (Win. 1962). **Activities:** 1; 17, 39 **Addr.:** Box 49, North Bennington, VT 05257.

Agee, Victoria L. V. (S. 21, 1947, Los Angeles, CA) Freelance Indxr., Lib. Consult., 1979–; Libn., HI Planned Parenthood, 1977–78; Pub. Srvs. Libn., Urban Inst., 1973–77; Libn., Cable TV Info. Ctr., 1972–73; Chief, Tech. Prcsg., Natl. Leag. of Cities and U.S. Conf. of Mayors, 1971–72; Catlgr., UCLA Engin. and Math. Sci. Lib., 1970–71; Lib. Resrchr., Marquardt Corp., 1969–71. **Educ.:** Univ. CA Los Angeles, 1969, BA (Eng.), 1970, MLS; Med. Lib. Assn., 1971, Grade I Cert. **Orgs.:** Amer. Socty. of Indxrs.: Secy. (1981–). Assn. for Popltn., Family Plng. Libs. and Info. Ctrs., Intl. Law Libns. Socty. of Washington, DC. SLA: DC Chap. (Audit., 1979–80), Soc. Sci. Grp. (Treas., 1976–77; 1981-82); Nom. Com. (Ch., 1975), Soc. Sci. Div., Urban Affairs Sect. (1977–78), Mem. Dir. Com. (Ch., 1976–77). Natl. Trust for Hist. Prsrvn. Parent and Child. Smithsonian Assoc. **Honors:** Beta Phi Mu, 1970. **Pubns.:** Co-Auth., *SMITHSONIAN Index-Volume X, April 1979 through March 1980* (1981); *Smithsonian Index-Volume IX, April 1978 through March 1979* (1980); Contrib., "An Evaluation with Recommendations for Action of the Government Printing Offices Services from the User's Point of View," (1978); Ed., *Urban Affairs Library Directory: A Membership and Resources Directory of the Urban Affairs Section, 1976* (1977); Contrib., *Update 76: Selected Recent Works in the Social Sciences* (1976). **Activities:** 4; 30; 55, 91 **Addr.:** 15 E. Myrtle St., Alexandria, VA 22301.

Agenbroad, James Edward (D. 9, 1934, Dayton, OH) Syst. Anal., Lib. of Congs., 1969–; Asst. Libn., Univ. of NH, 1968–69; Syst. Anal., Inforonics, Inc., 1967–68; Serials Libn., Catlgr., Univ. of NH, 1960–67. **Educ.:** Miami Univ., 1952–56, BA (Hist.); Rutgers Univ., 1959–60, MLS. **Orgs.:** ALA: Cat./Class. Sect. Policy and Res. Comm. (1973–77). ASIS. NH LA: Treas. (1965). Lib. of Congs. Prof. Assn.: Treas. (1973). **Pubns.:** "Character Sets: Current Status and East Asian Prospects," *Jnl. of Lib. Autom.* (Mr. 1980). **Activities:** 4; 20, 41; 56, 57, 95-non-Roman wrtng. systs. **Addr.:** Box 291, Garrett Park, MD 20766.

Aggarwal, Narindar Kumar (F. 15, 1934, Hoshiarpur, Punjab, India) S. and W. Asian Libn., Asst. Head, Asian Lib., Univ. IL, 1964–; S. Asian Biblgphr., Univ. PA, 1960–64; Indic Catlgr., Harvard Univ., 1959–60. **Educ.:** Panjab Univ., India, 1949–53, BA (Eng., Econ., Sanskrit); Emporia State Univ., 1958–59, MS (LS); Panjab Univ. Library, 1955, LS Cert. **Orgs.:** ALA: RTSD/CCS Com. on Cat., Asian and African Mtls. (1979–82). Assn. for Asian Stds. **Pubns.:** *A Bibliography of Studies on Hindi Language and Linguistics* (1978); *English in South Asia: A Bibliographical Survey of Resources;* "Die Sud-und Westasiatische Bibliothek der University of Illinois", *Dockumentationsdienst Asien Mitteilungen* (1974); *"Library Tools in Hindi & Punjabi", Indian Libn.* (1977). **Activities:** 1; 15, 20, 46; 50, 54, 57 **Addr.:** University of Illinois Library, Urbana, IL 61801.

Agler, Raymond Bruce (Mr. 1, 1936, Denver, CO) Coord. of Hum., Resrch. Lib., Boston Pub. Lib., 1972–, ILL Ofcr., 1968–72, Brnch. Libn., Hyde Pk. Brnch., 1966–68; Brnch. Admin. Ast., Enoch Pratt Free Lib., 1963–66. **Educ.:** Univ. of MO, 1957–60, AB (Lit.); Drexel Univ., 1961–63, MSLS. **Orgs.:** ALA: Notable Bks. Cncl. (1969–71), Ch. (1971); Ref. and Subscrpn. Bks. Review Com. (1976–79). MA LA. **Pubns.:** "Problem Books Revisited", *Lib. Jnl.* (My. 15, 1964). **Activities:** 9; 16, 34, 39 **Addr.:** Mills Hill, 300 Chestnut St., North Andover, MA 01845.

Agnew, Ellen Yale (Saville) (Ja. 15, 1921, Boston, MA) Head, Ginter Park Branch, Richmond Pub. Lib., 1977–, Head, Cat. Dept., 1971–77, Asst. Cat. Libn., 1969–71; Libn., Ctrl. Ref. Coord., Adriance Meml. Lib., 1965–68; Asst., Ref. Dept., Mid-Hudson Libs. Syst., 1965; Volun., Blodgett Meml. Lib., 1963–65; Chem., Texaco, Inc., 1942–43. **Educ.:** Smith Coll., 1938–42, AB (Chem.); SUNY, Albany, 1963–65, MLS. **Orgs.:** Dutchess Cnty. LA: VP (1967–68). VA LA: Reg. IV (Secy., 1979); Conf. 1980, Lcl. Arrange. Com. Richmond Area Libs. Club: Treas. (1971); Nom. Com. (1974). ALA. AAUW: Richmond Branch (Treas., 1969–73); Budget Com.; Nom. Com.; various other coms. **Activities:** 9; 16, 17, 39 **Addr.:** Richmond Public Library, 101 E. Franklin St., Richmond, VA 23219.

Agnew, Nancy Rutland (S. 13, 1913, Cherokee, AL) Dir., Wheeler Basin Reg. Lib., 1964–; Dir., Decatur Pub. Lib., 1960–64; Libn., Decatur Jr. HS, 1958–60; Libn., Decatur HS, 1956–58. **Educ.:** Univ. of Montevallo, 1933–35, BA (Eng.-Hist.); Emory Univ., 1935–36, Lib. Sci. **Orgs.:** AL LA: Pres. (1971–72). SE LA. ALA. Decatur Chamber of Cmrc.: Dir. DAR. **Honors:** Bus. Prof. Women's Clb., Woman of Achievement, 1972. **Activities:** 9; 17, 21, 22; 50, 72, 75 **Addr.:** 1612 Stratford Road, Decatur, AL 35601.

Agrawal, G.P. (Ja. 17, 1940, Tasing, Rajasthan, India) Dir., Lib. Svcs., Robert Morris Coll., 1979–, Ast. Dir., Lib. Svcs., 1974–79, Co-ord., Pub. Svcs. 1973–74, Pub. Svcs. Libn., 1972–73; Mktg. Resrch. Exec., Ashoka Mktg. Ltd., 1959–70. **Educ.:** Univ. of Calcutta, India, 1959–61, BCom (Cmrce.), 1962–64, MCom (Cmrce.), 1962–65, LLB, 1964–67, Dip. in Mgt.; Cath. Univ. of Amer., 1970–72, MSLS. **Orgs.:** Pittsburgh Reg. Lib. Ctr.: User's Svcs. Com. (1972–73); AV Com. (1973–79); Resrc. Dir. Com. (1975–79). ALA. SLA. PA LA. Amer. Prod. and Inventory Cntrl. Socty.: Educ. Com. (1979–). **Activities:** 1, 12; 17, 31, 39; 51, 56, 59 **Addr.:** Robert Morris College Library, Narrows Run Rd., Coraopolis, PA 15108.

Aguirre, Anthony R. (Ja. 13, 1938, Buenos Aires, Arg.) Assoc. Dir., Univ. of CT Hlth. Cntr. Lib., 1977–; Asst. Dir., Pub. Srvs., Univ. of CO Med. Cntr., 1974–77; Ref. Libn., Info. Anal., Univ. of CA, Los Angeles Biomed. Lib., 1972–74. **Educ.:** Univ. of WA, 1956–60, BA (Chem.); San Diego State Univ., 1963–66, MS (Biochem.); Univ. of WA, 1971–72, MLib. **Orgs.:** Med. LA: Cont. Ed. Com. (1976–80). New Eng. Reg. Med. Lib. Adv. Cncl.: Educ. Comm., Ch. (1979–80). Sigma Xi. **Activities:** 1; 17, 24, 35; 56, 80 **Addr.:** University of Connecticut, Health Center Library, Farmington, CT 06032.

Ahearn, Carolyn Pisha (Je. 3, 1950, Schenectady, NY) Head Libn., Shaw, Pittman, Potts and Trowbridge, 1979–; Libn., Pierson, Ball and Dowd, 1976–79; Ast. Libn., Arent, Fox, Kintner, Plotkin and Kahn, 1975–76; Resrch. Biblgphr., Econ. Dept., Univ. PA, 1973–75. **Educ.:** Union Coll., 1970–72, BA; Cath. Univ. of Amer., 1972–73, MLS. **Orgs.:** SLA; Amer. Assn. of Law Libs.; ALA; DC Law Libns. Socty. Pvt. Firm Libns. SIS.: Per. Un. List Rev. Com. **Honors:** Beta Phi Mu, 1973. **Activities:** 12; 17, 39; 77 **Addr.:** Shaw, Pittman, Potts and Trowbridge, 1800 M St., NW, Washington, DC 20036.

Ahern, Arleen Fleming (O. 15, 1922, Mt. Harris, CO) Assoc. Prof. of Libnshp. and Acq. Libn., CO Women's Coll., 1959–. **Educ.:** Univ. of UT, 1939–43, BA (Soclgy.); Univ. of Denver, 1959–62, MA (Libnshp.); Univ. of CO, Grad. Studies, 1967. **Orgs.:** ALA: Dupl. Ex. Un. Com. (1976–77). Mt. Plains Lib. Assn.: Plng. Com. (1975). CO LA: Pres. (1969–70); VP (1968–69); Bd. Mem. (1968–70); Other coms. Altrusa Intl.: VP (1969); Bd. Mem. (1970–79). Leag. of Women Voters. SAA. Adult Ed. Cncl. of Educ., Denver and Mt. Plains. **Pubns.:** State Library of CO, Library studies. **Activities:** 1; 15, 17, 18; 50, 55, 92 **Addr.:** 746 Monaco Pkwy., Denver, CO 80220.

Ahl, Ruth Elaine (O. 20, 1936, Orange, CA) Asst. Dir., Resrch. Libs. Div., Purdue Univ., 1978–, Life Sci. Libn., 1976–78; Actg. Dir., Libs., Univ. of WY, 1975–76, Head, Sci. and Tech. Lib., 1970–76; Med. Libn., Vets. Admin. Hosp., DC, 1965–70; Probation Ofcr., Juvenile Ct., Montgomery Cnty., Rockville, MD, 1961–63; Supvsr., Ref. Sect., Armed Srvs. Comsn., 1960–61, Resrch. and Stats., 1958–60. **Educ.:** Valparaiso Univ., 1954–58, BA (Soclgy.); Drexel Univ., 1963–65, MSLS (Libnshp.); Med. LA, 1972, Cert. Grade I. **Orgs.:** ALA: Ref. and Subscrpn. Bk. Review Com. (1973–75); Guest Reviewer (1978–). SLA. Med. LA: Midcontl. Reg. Med. Grp. (1974–76). Cncl. on Bot. and Horticult. Libs. **Honors:** Srvs. for the Visually Handcpd., WY State Dept. of Educ., Cheyenne, WY, Cert. of Merit, 1976. **Pubns.:** Jt. auth., "Retention Periods for Journals in a Small Academic Library," *Spec. Libs.* (S. 1979); various bk. reviews, *Booklist, Ref. and Subscrpn. Bks. Reviews* (1972–76, 1978–79). **Activities:** 1; 17, 39; 53, 80 **Addr.:** 900 Garden St., West Lafayette, IN 47906.

Ahlers, Eleanor E. (My. 16, 1911, Seattle, WA) Prof. Emeritus, Univ. of WA, 1976–, Prof., Sch. of Libnshp., 1966–76; State Sch. Lib. Supvsr., Ofc. of Pub. Instr., Olympia, WA, 1961–66; Exec. Secy., AASL, ALA, 1957–61. **Educ.:** Univ. of WA, 1928–32, AB (Fr.); Univ. of Denver, 1940–42, BLS (Libnshp.); Univ. of WA, 1955–57, MA (Curric.). **Orgs.:** WA State Assn. Sch. Libns.: 1st Pres. (1950–51); various coms. WA LA. ALA: AASL (Pres., 1965–66); Cncl. (1962–65); Lippicott Com.; Nom. Com. Pi Lambda Theta: Seattle Area Chap. (Pres., 1980–81). Women's Univ. Club, Seattle: Lib. Com., Ch.; Bk. Review Com., Ch. **Honors:** Univ. of WA Sch. of Libnshp., Estab. Eleanor Ahlers Schol. Fund, 1976; Phi Beta Kappa, 1932; Univ. of Denver Grad. Sch. of Libnshp., Disting. Alum. Awd., 1978. **Pubns.:** Various rpts. **Activities:** 10, 13; 17, 26, 48; 63 **Addr.:** 900 University St. #602, Seattle, WA 98101.

Ahlin, Nancy G. (N. 16, 1926, Oak Park, IL) Libn., Pub. Participation, E. Ctrl. FL Reg. Plng. Cncl., 1980–; Dir., Maitland Pub. Lib., 1970–74; Libn., Dept. of Defense, 1949–69. **Educ.:** Rosary Coll., 1944–48, BA (LS); Rollins Coll., 1977–78 (Readg.). **Orgs.:** CS LA: VP (1978–80). SLA: FL Chap. Sr. Churchman Task Grp., Episcopal Dio. of Orlando: Secy. (1977–79). **Honors:** SLAVA, 1979. **Pubns.:** *Thermodynamics of Mars* bibl. (1968). **Activities:** 3, 4; 17, 30, 36; 65, 86, 94 **Addr.:** Central Florida Regional Planning Council, 1011 Wymore Rd., Winter Park, FL 32789.

Ahouse, John B. (Ag. 2, 1935, New York, NY) Head, Dept. of Spec. Col. and Arch., CA State Univ., Long Beach, 1977–; Head, Spec. Col., Univ. TX, El Paso, 1974–77, ILL, 1974. **Educ.:** Columbia Univ., 1953–57, BA (Germ.); Univ. TX, El Paso, 1973–75, MA (Ling.); Univ. South. CA, 1975–76, MSLS. **Orgs.:** SAA. Socty. of CA Archvsts. **Pubns.:** Ed., *Upton Sinclair Quarterly* (1979–). **Addr.:** P.O. Box 15573, Long Beach, CA 90815.

Aichele, Jean R. (O. 16, 1926, St. Paul, MN) Instr. Dev., St. Cloud State Univ., 1977–; Admin., NW Reg. Lib. Syst., 1975–76; Consult., Lib. Dir., Pub. Lib. NJ and NY, 1963–68; Med. Libn., VA, Head, Media Ctr. Sch. Libs., 1954–63. **Educ.:** Univ. of MN, 1944–48, BS (Hist.), 1953–54, MSLS; San Jose State Univ., 1975–78, MA (Inst. Tech.); Libre Univ. de Bruxelles, 1970–71, (Fr.). **Orgs.:** ALA. AECT: Eval. Com. (1978). MN Educ. Mem. Org.: Comp. Com. (1978); Endow. Com. (1979). World Future Socty.; ULLR: Outrch. Progs. (Ch.), Nsltr. Ed.; MN AACR II Trainers, Inc. (1979–81). **Honors:** MLA, Merit Cit., 1981; ALA, Mann Cit. Nom., 1981; MEMO, AACR II Rep., 1979; NJ State Lib., NY Worlds Fair, 1965. **Pubns.:** AACR II Series Training Manuals (1980–81); *Motion Pic. and Vid. Rec. Trng. Manual of AACR 2 Examples* (1981). **Activities:** 1, 9; 17, 26, 32; 50, 67, 93 **Addr.:** 1188 McLean Ave., St. Paul, MN 55106.

Aiello, Toni L. (Je. 21, 1947, Ancon, CZ, Panama) Ast. Undergraduate Svcs. Libn., Northwestern Univ. Lib., 1977–. **Educ.:** Trinity Coll., Washington, D.C., 1965–69, AB, (Hist.); Brown Univ., 1969–70, MAT (Soc. Sci.); Simmons Coll., 1973–76, MLS. **Orgs.:** ALA: ACRL; LAMA/Mid. Mgt. Discuss. Grp. Plan. Com. Pubcty. and Mem. Com. (1979–81), Ch. (1980-81). **Honors:** Beta Phi Mu, 1976. **Activities:** 1; 15, 16, 31; 92, 95-Rsv. Svcs. **Addr.:** Undergraduate Services Department, Northwestern University Library, Evanston, IL 60201.

Aiken, Mary Peirano (N. 22, 1927, Pickens, SC) Retired, 1980–; Coord., Chld. Srvs., Greenville Cnty. Lib., 1978–80, Head, Ctrl. Chld. Rm., 1970–78; Dir., Pickens Cnty. Lib., 1961–70. **Educ.:** Salem Coll., 1945–49, AB (Eng.); Univ. of NC, 1950–53, MA (Eng.); FL State Univ., 1958–61, MLS. **Orgs.:** ALA: ALSC, Lib. Srv. to Disadv. Chld. Com. (1975–76), Newbery Com. (1980–81). SC LA: Exec. Bd. (1980); Chld. and Young People Sect. (Ch., 1980). Greenville SC Urban Leag. SC Assn. for Chld. Under Six. Oconee-Pickens SC Econ. Oppt. Fed.: Exec. Bd. (Ch., 1966–68). Natl. Assn. for the Prsrvn. and Perpet. of Storytel. **Honors:** SE LA, Disting. Srv. Proj. of the Yr., 1979; US Dept. of Hlth., Educ. and Welfare, Spec. Srv. Awd., 1979. **Activities:** 9; 15, 21, 32; 50, 55, 72 **Addr.:** 220 Ann St., Pickens, SC 29671.

Aimee, Sr. Mary S.N.D. (Je. 18, 1910, Cleveland, OH) Libn., Notre Dame Acad., 1969–; Sec. Sch. Tchr., Cardinal Mooney HS, 1963–69; Tchr., Libn., Elyria Cath. HS, 1949–63; Instr., Notre Dame Coll., 1947–49. **Educ.:** Notre Dame Coll. of OH, 1928–33, AB (Hist.); Marquette Univ., 1944–49, MA (Hist.). **Orgs.:** Cath. LA. OH Educ. Lib./Media Assn. **Activities:** 10; 17, 20, 48 **Addr.:** Notre Dame Academy Library, 13000 Auburn Rd., Chardon, OH 44024.

Ainsworth, Mary Lynn (D. 7, 1943, St. Catherines, ON) Mgr. Tech. Info. Ctr., Pitney Bowes, Inc., 1976–; Corp. Libn., Champion Intl., 1975–76; Libn., Stauffer Chem. Co., 1969–75; Jr. Libn., Rochester Pub. Lib., 1967–69. **Educ.:** Findlay Coll., 1961–65, BA (Hist., Eng.); Rutgers Univ., 1965–66, MLS. **Orgs.:** SLA: Hudson Val. Chap. (Secy., Treas., 1974–75). Lib. Grp. of SW CT: Bd. (1976). SW CT Lib. Cncl.: Secy. (1978, 1981), Dev. Com. (1979–81), Bd. (1978–). **Pubns.:** *Directory of Selected Reference Materials in Libraries and Historical Societies in Fairfield County, Connecticut* (May, 1977). **Activities:** 12; 15, 17, 39; 60, 64 **Addr.:** 27 A Nelson St., Stamford, CT 06902.

Airel, Walter F. (D. 23, 1925, Bayonne, NJ) Dir., Livingston Cnty. Lib. Syst., 1960–; Branch Head, Rochester Pub. Lib., 1953–60. **Educ.:** Assoc. Coll. of Champlain Coll., NY, 1948–51, BA (Acct.); State Tchrs. Coll., Albany, 1951–53, MSLS (Lib.). **Orgs.:** Monroe Cnty. LA: Pres. (1958). NY LA: Mem. Com. (1963–). ALA: Mem. Com. (1974–). Kiwanis Club of Geneseo: Pres. (1969). Bic Tree Skiers, Geneseo: Pres. (1963). Albany Lib. Sch. Alum. Assn.: Pres. (1968). **Activities:** 9, 11; 17, 24, 47; 51, 59, 78 **Addr.:** 756 W. Lake Rd., Geneseo, NY 14454.

Airth, Elizabeth J. (Jl. 10, 1927, Spokane, WA) Ref. Libn., Ref. Dept., Gen. Libs., Univ. of TX at Austin, 1981–, Libn., Spec. Srvs. Dept., 1977–81. Ref. Libn., Main Lib., 1972–77, Ref. Libn., Hum. Ref. Rm., 1971–72. **Educ.:** WA State Univ., 1945–49, BS (Bot.); Univ. of TX, Austin, 1969–71, MLS. **Orgs.:** SLA: TX Chap. ALA: RASD/Machine-Assisted Ref. Sect.; Coll. and Resrch. Libs. Div. TX LA: Nom. Com. (1978). TX Assn. of Coll. Tchrs. **Honors:** Phi Beta Kappa, 1949; Phi Kappa Phi, 1949. **Pubns.:** Subj. ed., anthro. and ethnology, geo. recreation, travel sects., *Texas Reference Sources: A Selective Guide* (1978); update ed., "Texas Reference Sources: A Selective Guide," anthro., ethnology, soclgy., geo., recreation, sports sects. *TX Lib. Jnl.* (Fall 1976, Fall 1977); "Selected Reference Sources," *Anthro.* (1981); *University of TX General Libraries Selected Reference*

PROFESSIONAL ACTIVITIES: Institutions: 1. Acad. lib.; 2. Arch.; 3. Assn.; 4. Fed./Gvt. lib.; 5. Inst. lib.; 6. Mfr./Suppl.; 7. Milit. lib.; 8. Musm.; 9. Pub. lib.; 10. Sch. lib.; 11. Sch. of lib. sci.; 12. Spec. lib.; 13. State lib.; 14. (other). **Functions/Activities:** 15. Acq./Col. dev.; 16. Adult srvs.; 17. Admin.; 18. Apprais.; 19. Archit./Bldgs.; 20. Cat./Class.; 21. Chld. srvs.; 22. Circ.; 23. Cons./Pres.; 24. Consult.; 25. Cont. ed.; 26. Educ. lib. sci.; 27. Ext. srvs.; 28. Fund/Grants; 29. Gvt. pubs.; 30. Indx./Abs.; 31. Instr. lib. use; 32. Media srvs.; 33. Micro.; 34. Netwks./Coop.; 35. Persnl.; 36. PR; 37. Publshg.; 38. Recs. mgt.; 39. Ref. srvs.; 40. Repro.; 41. Resrch.; 42. Review.; 43. Secur.; 44. Serials; 45. Spec. col.; 46. Tech. srvs.; 47. Trustees/Bds.; 48. YA srvs.; 49. (other).

Sources no. 1 (1981); ed., *Grants* no. 44 (1979); *Hlth. Sci.* no. 55 (1980); *Nursing* no. 35 (1980). **Activities:** 1; 31, 39; 66, 80, 92 **Addr.:** Reference Services Dept., The General Libraries, The University of Texas at Austin, Austin, TX 78712.

Ake, Mary W. (Mr. 2, 1930, E. Chicago, IN) Libn., Media Spec., Laura Ingalls Wilder Elem. Sch., 1974–; Chld. Libn., Pub. Lib., Youngstown and Mahoning Cnty., OH, 1950–55. **Educ.:** Youngstown State Univ., 1948–52, BA (Eng.); Carnegie Mellon Univ., 1952–53, MSLS; Seminar, Manila, 1979. **Orgs.:** Chld. Lit. Assn.: Panel Ch., Baylor Univ. Conf. (Mr. 1980). CO Educ. Media Assn. ALA. Dr. Watson's Neglected Patients (Sherlockian Socty.): Consult. (1974–); Amer. Assn. of Univ. Women: Littleton, Cnty, Brnch. (Fndr., First Pres., 1961–62); Frnds. of Littleton Lib./Musm.: Fndr. (1964). **Honors:** Encyc. Brit. and AASL, Sch. Lib. Media Prog. of Yr., 1976. **Pubns.:** Copyrt., INDEPENDENT LEARNING SYSTEM for lib. skills (1978). **Activities:** 9, 10; 17, 21, 32; 75, 89 **Addr.:** Wilder School, 4300 W. Ponds Circle, Littleton, CO 80123.

Akeroyd, Richard G., Jr. (Ja. 25, 1942, Queens, NY) Ast. City Libn., Dir. Pub. Svcs., Denver Pub. Lib., 1980–; Prog. and Plng. Consult., WHCOLIS, 1977–79; Dir., Plng. and Resrch., CT State Lib., 1974–77; Catlgr. and Ast. to Dir., Spec. Cols., Univ. CT Lib., 1969–74. **Educ.:** Univ. CT, 1965–68, BA (Eng.); Univ. Pittsburgh, 1968–69, MLS. **Orgs.:** ALA: ASCLA/Compar. Std. of Admin. Prcs. in State Lib. Agncy. Com. (1975–77), Interlib. Coop. Com. (1977–79), Plng., Org. and By-Laws Com. (1979–); Lib. Educ. Div./Media Resrch. Com. (1976–77); SRRT (1970–77), Action Cncl., Secy. (1970–72); ACRL (1970–74); Other coms. CT LA: Target '76 Com. (1971–75), Task Grp. on Cable Comm., Chmn. (1974–75); Com. on Cable Com., Chmn. (1973–74); Dev. Com. (1975–77); other coms. NEng. LA: Reg. Plng. Com. (1976–77). CT Educ. Media Assn. Other orgs. Colorado Mt. Club. Appalachian Mt. Club. Adirondack Mt. Club. **Honors:** Beta Phi Mu, 1970; Phi Delta Kappa, 1974. **Pubns.:** "A Directory of Ephemera Collections in a National Underground Network," *Wilson Library Bulletin* (November 1973); "Cable and Libraries: Developing Community Information Resource and Service Centers," *Connecticut Audio Visual Education Association bulletin* (March 1974); "Total Media Integration in Academic Libraries," *International Journal of Instructional Media* (1975); "Selected Readings in Systems: A Bibliography," *A Systems Approach to Learning Environments* (1975); *The ASLA Report on Interlibrary Cooperation, 1978.* 2d ed. (1978). **Addr.:** Denver Public Library, Administrative Center, 3840 York St., Denver, CO 80205.

Alain, Jean-Marc (Je. 26, 1945, Ancienne Lorette, PQ) Coord. des Cen. de Documtn., Univ. du PQ, Ecole Natl. d'Admin. Pub., 1972–. **Educ.:** Univ. Laval, 1967–70, Lich. (Hist.); Univ. De Montreal, 1970–72, Master (Bibl.). **Orgs.:** Conf. des Recteurs et des Prin. des Univ. de PQ. Inst. Can. des Aff. Int. Can. LA. Amer. Mgt. Assn. **Pubns.:** *Le Centre de Documentation* (1976); *Une Bibliothèque Pour Montréal* (1973); Cont., *Public Enterprise and the Public Interest* (1978); *L'influence du Nom d'une Maison d'Édition dans le Choix des Livres* (1972); Cont., *Documentation et Bibliothèque.* **Activities:** 1; 15, 17, 46 **Addr.:** Ecole nationale d'administration publique, Centre de documentation, 945 Ave. Wolfe, Sainte-Foy, PQ 61V 3J9 Canada.

Alamo de Torres, Daisy (Ag. 13, 1923, Caguas, PR) Catlgr., Gen. Lib., Univ. of PR, 1978–, Head, LS Lib., Grad. Sch. of Libnshp., 1976–78, Catlgr., Asst. Libn., Gen. Lib., 1966–76; Tchr., Jr. HSs., Caguas, PR, 1943–58. **Educ.:** Univ. of PR, 1951–57, BA (Educ.); 1943–45, Native Handicraft Tchr. Cert., 1946–50, Normal Dip.; Univ. of PR, 1969–70, MLS. **Orgs.:** SBPR. Assn. of Caribbean Univ. and Resrch. Libs. Assn. Ex-Alum. Esc. Gradide Bibliotecologia: Secy. **Pubns.:** "La nuena ley de derecho de autor: seccioms 107 y 108," *Bltn. Info., Univ. of PR* (1977); *Directorio de bibliotecos de Puerto Rico* (1979); *Bibliografiá de Ester Feliciano Mendoza (1935–1980)* (1980). **Activities:** 1, 11; 20, 46; 57, 63 **Addr.:** Box 21047, Rio Piedras, PR 00928.

Albano, Anne W. (Ag. 3, 1924, E. Orange, NJ) Ref. Libn., W. Caldwell Pub. Lib., 1980–; Dir., Lyndhurst Pub. Lib., 1976–79; Ref. Libn., 1975. **Educ.:** Coll. of St. Elizabeth, 1942–46, BA (Msc.); Caldwell Coll., 1972–75, LS Cert. **Orgs.:** ALA. NJ LA: Exec. Bd. (1979–82). Jr. Leag. of Oranges and Short Hills: Sustaining Mem. **Activities:** 9; 17, 36, 39; 55, 75, 78 **Addr.:** 17 Knollwood Terr., Caldwell, NJ 07006.

Alberts, Pearl Lewis (Mr. 30, 1928, Boston, MA) Sr. Ref. Libn., Sch. of Mgt. Lib., Boston Coll., 1978–, Ref. Libn., 1968–78; Vail Libn., MA Inst. of Tech., 1955–59; Ref. Libn., Boston Pub. Lib., 1951–55. **Educ.:** Univ. of NH, 1945–49, BA (Eng.); Simmons Coll., 1950–52, MSLS. **Orgs.:** SLA. ACRL. **Activities:** 1; 15, 31, 39; 51, 59 **Addr.:** School of Management Library, Boston College, Fulton Hall, Chestnut Hill, MA 02167.

Albertson, Christopher A. (D. 10, 1951, Oak Park, IL) City Libn., Tyler, TX Pub. Lib., 1981–; Dir., Orange, TX Pub. Lib., 1979–, Asst. Dir., 1974–78, Catlgr., 1974. **Educ.:** Univ. of New Orleans, 1969–70 (Hist.); Univ. of TX at Arlington, 1970–72, BA (Hist.); N. TX State Univ., 1973–73, MLS. **Orgs.:** ALA: PLA/SMLS, Nom. Com. (1980). SWLA. TX LA: Plng. Com. (1980-82); Cont. Ed.Com. (1976–78). ASIS. Amer. Socty. for Pub. Admin. **Honors:** Beta Phi Mu; Alpha Chi; Phi Alpha Theta. **Pubns.:** Various articles. **Activities:** 9; 17, 38; 95-Public adm. **Addr.:** Tyler Public Library, 201 S. College Ave., Tyler, TX 75702.

Albrecht, Alyce B. (Mr. 18, 1925, Stratford, CT) Dir., Tech. Info., Merrell Intl., 1973–; Assoc. Dir., Med. Affairs, Bristol Intl., 1968–73; Assoc. Dir., Med. Info., E. R. Squibb Intl., 1963–68; Med. Abstctr., Merck and Co., 1954–63. **Educ.:** Ursinus Coll., 1946, BS (Bio., Chem.); Long Island Coll. of Med., 1947–49 (Med.); Med. Lib. Assn. cont. ed. crs.; Natl. Lib. Med. Online training. **Orgs.:** Med. LA. Lib. Grp. of SW CT.: VP, Various coms. SW CT Lib. Cncl.: Bd. of Trustees. SW CT Lib. Cncl. Online Users Grp.: Founder, first Coord. Other orgs. Amer. Med. Writers Assn.: Natl. Bd. of Dirs.; NY Chap. Bd. of Dirs. and other offices; Ed. Com.; By-laws Com. Drug Info. Assn. **Pubns.:** Tech. Ed., *Gastroenterology Symposium* (1979); Various articles. **Activities:** 12; 17, 39, 46; 60, 68, 80, 87 **Addr.:** 29 Lakeview Drive, Brookfield, CT 06804.

Albrecht, Cheryl C. (N. 9, 1951, Beloit, WI) Dir. of Lib., Coll. of Mount St. Joseph, 1981–; Coord., Grt. Cincinnati Lib. Cnsrtm., 1976–81; Bibl. Resrchr., Univ. of WI and R. R. Bowker, 1975; Eng. Tchr., Berlitz de Mexico, Mexico City, 1973–74. **Educ.:** St. Olaf Coll., 1969–73, BA (Span., Latin Amer. Std.); Univ. of WI, 1974–75, MA (LS); La Univ. Ibero-Amer., Mexico City, 1972; Grantsmanship Training Prog., 1977, Cert.; Seminar in Public Relations for Libs., Case Western Reserve University, School of Library Science, 1977, Cert.; Exec. Dev. Prog. for Lib. Admins., Miami Univ., 1978, Cert. **Orgs.:** ALA: ASCLA/MLCS, Conf. Prog. Com. (1980 and 1982); Nom. Com. (1980-81); Rept. on Lib. Coop. Com. (1979–80); OH LA: Lib. Dev. Com. (1980-83). Acad. Lib. Assn. of OH. LAMA. OH White Hse. Conf.: Cincinnati Preconf. Com., Coord. (1978). Assn. of Women Admins., Univ. of Cincinnati. NOW. **Honors:** OH LA, Diana Vescelius Awd., 1979. **Pubns.:** Contrib., *Costing Collegiate Cooperation* (1979). **Activities:** 1, 14-Coop. Agncy.; 17, 28, 34; 95-Coop. **Addr.:** 3301 Eastside Ave., Cincinnati, OH 45208.

Albrecht, Lois K. (O. 3, 1930, Wheeling, WV) Coord., Adv. Svcs., PA State Lib., 1975–, Actg. Dir. Lib. Dev., 1980–81, Pub. Lib. Dev. Adv., 1973–75, Spec. Lib. Svcs. Adv., 1972–73; Syst. Libn., WA Cnty. MD Bd. of Educ., 1968–71; Head, Tech. Svcs., Washington Cnty. MD Lib. Syst., 1963–68; Libn., Richland Twp. HS, 1952–62. **Educ.:** Clarion State Coll., 1948–52, BS Ed, (LS, Math); Univ. Pittsburgh, 1962–63, MLS; Univ. MD, 1970–71, grad. crs. **Orgs.:** ALA: PLA Mem. Com. (1980–81); Assn. of State and Coop. Lib. Agencies. Mem. Com. (1978, 1979); Assn. of Hosp. and Inst. Libs.; Stan. Com. (Ch., 1973–77). PA LA: Schol. Com. (1979–80); Lib. Dev. Com. (1976–80); other coms. Cumberland Valley LA: Pres. (1968–69). AAUW: Hagerstown, MD Bnch., Pres. (1970–72). **Honors:** Beta Phi Mu, 1963. **Pubns.:** "A Lifetime of Learning", *Rural Libs.* (Win. 1980); Contrib. to manuals (1977). **Activities:** 9, 13; 16, 24, 47; 50, 63, 92 **Addr.:** 502 Ellen Rd., Camp Hill, PA 17011.

Albrecht, Otto E. (Jl. 8, 1899, Philadelphia, PA) Prof. Emeritus, Msc., Univ. of PA, 1970–, Cur., Albrecht Msc. Lib., 1937–, Prof., Msc., 1962–70, Lectr. in Msc., 1938–62; Instr., Asst. Prof. of Fr., 1923–62. **Educ.:** Univ. of PA, 1917–22, AB (Fr.); Univ. of Copenhagen, 1922–23 (Fr.); Univ. of PA, 1923–25, MA (Fr.), 1925–31, PhD (Fr.). **Orgs.:** Amer. Musicological Socty.: Treas. (1954–74). Msc. LA: VP (1940–45, 1951–52); Com. on Photodup. (Ch., 1939–43); Jt. Com. with Amer. Musicological Socty. for the Intl. Repertory of Musical Srcs. (Ch., 1975–). Intl. Assn. of Msc. Libs. Intl. Musicological Socty. **Honors:** Pierpont Morgan Lib., Hon. Fellow, 1972; Msc. LA, Cit., 1979; Msc. Lib., Univ. of PA, named O. E. Albrecht Msc. Lib., 1970. **Pubns.:** "America's Early Acquaintance with Beethoven," *Musik Ed. Interpretation* (1980); jt. auth., *Marian Anderson: A Catalog of the Collection at the University of Pennsylvania Library* (1981); "Opera in Philadelphia, 1800–1830," *Jnl. of the Amer. Musicological Socty.* (Fall 1979); "Beethoven Autographs in the United States," *Beiträge zur Beethoven-Bibliographie* (1978); ed., *Music Microfilm Archive* (1940); various mono., chaps. **Activities:** 1; 45; 57, 95-Msc. **Addr.:** Music Dept., University of Pennsylvania, 201 S. 34 St., Philadelphia, PA 19104.

Albrecht, Sterling J. (Je. 22, 1937, Loa, UT) Univ. Libn., Brigham Young Univ., 1980–, Assoc. Dir., Libs., 1972–80, Hum. and Arts Libn., 1970–72, Gifts and Acq. Libn., 1966–70. **Educ.:** Univ. of UT, 1962, BS (Bus. Mgt.); Brigham Young Univ., 1970, MLS; Univ. of MD, 1976, Cert. of Completion of Advnc. Std. (Lib. Admins. Dev. Prog.). **Orgs.:** ALA: Cncl. (1978–80). Mt. Plains LA: Acad. Sect. (Ch., 1979). UT LA: Ed. Bd. (Ch., 1975–78); ARL: Bd. of Dirs. (1980–). Resrch. Libs. Grp.: Bd. of Gvrs. (1979–). UT Coll. Lib. Cncl.: Ch. (1981–82). **Pubns.:** Jt. auth., "The Traditional Library Setting...Can It Meet the Profession's Needs?" *What Else You Can Do With a Library Degree* (1980). **Activities:** 1; 15, 17, 39 **Addr.:** 3080 HBLL, Brigham Young University, Provo, UT 84602.

Albright, Elaine M. (Ag. 21, 1946, Waterville, ME) Exec. Dir., Lincoln Trail Libs. Syst., 1977–; Visit. Instr., Univ. IL, Sum. 1979 and Sum. 1980, Assoc. Prof., Coord. of IL Rsrch. and Ref. Actv., 1975–77, Ast. Prof., IL Ref. and Res. Libn., 1969–75. **Educ.:** Univ. ME, 1964–68, BS (Soclgy.); Univ. IL, 1968–69, MLS. **Orgs.:** IL State Lib.: Adv. Com./LSCA (1979–81); Ref. and Resrc. Ctr. Com. on Coop. Coll. Dev. (1975–78); ALA: Cncl. (1975–79); RASD/ILL Discuss. Grp. (Co-Ch., 1977–79), /Prof. Dev. Com. (1981–). IL LA: JMRT/Exec. Com. (1974–75). Univ. IL Fac. Sen.: Ext. Com. (1974–75). **Pubns.:** "Attitudes Toward Political and Ideological Issues," *Studies in Public Library Government Organization & Support* (1968); "Handling Employee Problems", *Supervision of Employees in Libraries* (1979); "The Organization of Data Library Services at the University of Illinois at Urbana-Champaign", *Some Current Repro. Concerns Related to ILL,* ALA-RLMS Microfile Series (1977). **Activities:** 1, 13; 17, 24, 34 **Addr.:** Lincoln Trail Libraries System, 1704 West Interstate Dr., Champaign, IL 61820.

Albright, Jane A. (Ap. 7, 1926, Birmingham, AL) Ref. Libn., Bibl. Instr., Carson-Newman Coll., 1973–; various other positions, 1970–72. **Educ.:** Univ. of AL, 1943–46, BS (Home Econ., Art); Univ. of TN, 1972–73, MSLS; 1978–80, Post-grad. work (Comp. Prog., Span., Grmn., Sp.). **Orgs.:** ALA. SE LA: Bibl. Instr. Com.; Bibl. Instr. Prog. Com. (1978). TN LA. E. TN LA. **Honors:** Beta Phi Mu, 1975. **Pubns.:** *Bibliographic Instruction Directory: Academic Libraries* (1978); video tape prog., Carson-Newman Lib. (1973); slide tape prog., gvt. docum. (1975); slide tape prog., Carson-Newman Lib. (1977); slide tape prog., psy. abs. (1980). **Activities:** 1; 15, 31, 39; 55, 59, 90 **Addr.:** Rte. 1, Box 2, Jefferson City, TN 37760.

Albright, Penny E. (My. 24, 1946, Stillwater, OK) Dir., Kershaw Cnty. Lib., 1978–; Chld. Libn., Lexington Cnty. Circ. Lib., 1974–78; Catlgr., McKissick Lib., Univ. of SC, 1973–74; Sch. Libn., Dept. of Educ., St. Thomas, VI, 1972–73; Cur., VI Musm., 1970–72. **Educ.:** OK State Univ., 1964–68, BA (Hist.); Univ. of OK, 1968–69, MLS. **Orgs.:** ALA. SC LA: Chld. and YA Sect., Strg. Com. (Ch., 1978); 2nd VP (1980); Pub. Lib. Sect., Stans. Com. (1981). SE LA. Kershaw Cnty. Litcy. Assn. **Activities:** 9, 10; 17, 21, 36; 54, 55, 89 **Addr.:** Kershaw County Library, 1304 Broad St., Camden, SC 29020.

Alburger, Thomas P. (S. 10, 1937, Camden, NJ) Acq. Libn., Atomic Energy of Can., Ltd., 1976–, Ref. and Repts. Libn., 1972–76; Catlgr., Univ. of Waterloo Lib., 1969–72; Med. Libn., Mt. Auburn Hosp., 1963–69; Catlgr., Boston Pub. Lib., 1962–63. **Educ.:** Rutgers Univ., 1956–60, AB (Fr., Grmn.); West. Reserve Univ., 1960–62, MSLS. **Orgs.:** CAN LA. SLA. **Activities:** 4, 12; 15, 22, 44; 64, 84, 91 **Addr.:** Box 1553, Deep River, ON K0J 1P0, Canada.

Alderman, Alice M. (Westby, WI) Ast. Gvt. Pubns. Libn., State Hist. Socty. of WI, 1974–, Catlgr., 1966–67, Docum. Catlgr., 1967–73. **Educ.:** N. Park Coll., 1943–45, AA; Univ. WI, LaCrosse, 1963–65, BS (Eng.); Univ. WI, Madison, 1965–66, MLS, Post Grad. Std., 1967–79 (Scand. Std. and Comp. Sci.). **Orgs.:** ALA: Various GODORT Coms. (1970–). WI LA. Amer. Scand. Fndn. **Honors:** Kappa Delta Phi, 1965; Beta Phi Mu, 1966. **Pubns.:** *Organizing Wisconsin Public Documents* (1974); "Classifying State Documents", *Dttp* (May 1976); CoEd., "Wisconsin Public Documents, 1974–" (1974–). **Activities:** 13; 20, 29, 44; 56, 66, 69 **Addr.:** 1715 Laurel Crest, Madison, WI 53705.

Alderson, William T. (My. 8, 1926, Schenectady, NY) Dir., Musm. Std., Univ. of DE, 1978–; Dir., Amer. Assn. for State and Lcl. Hist., 1964–78; State Libn., Archvst., State of TN, 1961–64; Exec. Secy., TN Hist. Comsn., 1957–61; Sr. Archvst., TN State Lib. and Arch., 1952–57. **Educ.:** Colgate Univ., 1943–47, AB (Hist.); Vanderbilt Univ., 1948–52, MA, PHD (Hist.); Amer. Univ., 1952, Cert. (Arch. Admin.), 1954, Cert. (Recs. Mgt.). **Orgs.:** SAA: Cncl. (1963–67). Amer. Assn. for State and Lcl. Hist.: Cncl. (1957–64). Amer. Assn. of Musms.: Cncl. (1978–79, 1981–); Exec. Com. (1978–79); Accred. Comsn. (Ch., 1970–73). N.E. Musms. Conf.: VP (1979–80); Pres. (1981–). TN Hist. Socty.: VP (1969–71); *TN Hist. Qtly.* Ed. (1956–65); *Hist. News* Ed. (1964–78). Various other orgs. **Honors:** SAA, Fellow; Amer. Assn. for State and Lcl. Hist., Awds. of Merit, 1959, 1966; Can. Musms. Assn., Fellows Lectr., 1979. **Pubns.:** Jt. Author., *Interpretation of Historic Sites* (1976); ed., *American Issues, Understanding Who We Are* (1976); jt. ed., *Landmarks of Tennessee History* (1965); jt. auth., *Historic Sites in Tennessee* (1963); *Tennessee History in Brief* (1964); various bks., edshps., articles. **Activities:** 1; 17, 24, 45; 55, 59, 63 **Addr.:** Museum Studies Program, University of Delaware, Newark, DE 19711.

Aldous, Mary E. (Jl. 8, 1942, New York, NY) Head Libn., Nvl. Hlth. Resrch. Ctr., 1978–; Tech. Rpts./Ref. Libn., Nvl. Electronics Lab. Ctr., 1969–78; Asst. Ref. Libn., Marine Corps Dev. & Educ. Com, 1967–69; Asst. Ref. Libn., CA West. Univ., 1966–67; Readrs. Srvs. Libn., Marquette Univ. Lib., 1965–66; Msc. Cat., Nashville Pub. Lib., 1962–65. **Educ.:** St. Joseph Coll., Emmitsburg, MD, 1960–64, BA (Eng.); Peabody Lib. Sch., 1961–65, MLS. **Orgs.:** SLA: Bulletin Editor (1973–76). Med. Libns. Grp. of South. CA & AZ. Med. LA. **Honors:** Lambda Iota Tau, 1964; Beta Phi Mu, 1966. **Activities:** 4, 7, 12; 15, 17, 39; 58, 80 **Addr.:** 637 Savoy Street, San Diego, CA 92106

Aldrich, Barbara Jane (Ag. 8, 1943, Mitchell, SD) Chief, Tech. Info. Sect. Data User Srvs. Div., Bur. of the Census, 1980–; Tech. Docum. Spec., 1978–80; Data Libn., Ctr. for Demog.,

Special Subjects/Services: 50. Adult educ.; 51. Advert./Mktg.; 52. Aerosp.; 53. Agric.; 54. Area std.; 55. Arts/Hum.; 56. Autom.; 57. Bibl./Prtg.; 58. Bio. sci.; 59. Bus./Fin.; 60. Chem.; 61. Copyrt.; 62. Documtn.; 63. Educ.; 64. Engin.; 65. Env.; 66. Eth. grps.; 67. Film; 68. Food/Nutr.; 69. Geneal.; 70. Geo.; 71. Geol.; 72. Handcpd.; 73. Hist.; 74. Int. frdm.; 75. Info. sci.; 76. Insr.; 77. Law; 78. Legis.; 79. Math./Comp. sci.; 80. Med.; 81. Metals; 82. Nat. resrcs.; 83. Newsp.; 84. Nuc. sci.; 85. Oral hist.; 86. Petr./Energy; 87. Pharm.; 88. Phys./Astr./Math.; 89. Readg.; 90. Relig.; 91. Sci./Tech.; 92. Soc. sci.; 93. Telecom.; 94. Transp.; 95. (other).

Who's Who in Library and Information Services

Univ. of WI, 1971–78, Resrch. Anal., 1966–71; Mgt. Trainee, Nwest. Bell Telephone Co., 1965–66. **Educ.:** Univ. of IA, 1961–65, BA (Pol. Sci.); Univ. of WI, 1977–78, (LS). **Orgs.:** ALA. ASIS. Intl. Assn. for Soc. Sci., Info. Svc. and Tech.: Conf. Wkshp., Ch. (1980). Amer. Stat. Assn. Assn. of Pub. Data Users: Bd. Dir. (1979–80); VP (1980); Conf. Prog. Ch. (1980). **Pubns.:** Various presentations (1979). **Activities:** 4; 30, 38, 39; 56, 95-mach. read data files, 92 **Addr.:** 2715–A S. Walter Reed Dr., Arlington, VA 22206.

Aldrich, Patricia M. (Ag. 9, 1952, Findlay, OH) Asst. Law Libn., Gvt. Docum., Washington Univ., 1975–; Asst. Libn., Marathon Oil Co., 1975. **Educ.:** DePauw Univ., 1970–74, BA (Fr., Pol. Sci.); IN Univ., 1974–75, MLS. **Orgs.:** AALL: Southwest. Chap. **Pubns.:** *A Law Librarian's Introduction to Missouri State Publications* (1980). **Activities:** 1; 29, 33, 45; 77, 78 **Addr.:** Law Library, Campus Box 1120, Washington University, St. Louis, MO 63130.

Aldrich, Willie Lee (Banks), Reverend Mrs. (S. 9, 1924, Cleveland, OH) Head Libn., Hood Theo. Semy., 1960–; Libn., Dunbar HS, 1960; Tchr., Libn., Cleveland HS; Ast. Libn., Rowan Cnty. Pub. Lib. **Educ.:** Livingstone Coll., 1943–45, BA (Hist., Eng.); Hood Theo. Semy., 1974, MDIV; Atlanta Univ. Sch. of LS, MSLS. **Orgs.:** NC LA. ALA. SE LA. Amer. Theo. LA. Delta Delta Sigma Theta Sorority Inc.: Pres. (1960–63); VP (1950–56); Undergrad. Adv. (1960–72); Other coms. Church Women Untd.: Secy.; VP (1977–80). Livingstone Coll. Prayer Mtg. Choir: Advisor. Other orgs. **Honors:** Delta Sigma Theta, Svc. Awd., 1972; Livingstone Coll., Svc. Awd., 1979, 1981. **Pubns.:** Various pamphlets. **Activities:** 2, 12; 17, 31, 47; 63, 85, 90 **Addr.:** Hood Theological Seminary, W.J. Walls Center, 800 W. Thomas St., Salisbury, NC 28144.

Alessi, Dana Louise Bennett (S. 2, 1943, Colorado Springs, CO) Reg. Sales Mgr., Blackwell N. Amer., 1978–; Head of Acqs., Univ. of Houston, 1977–78, Asst. Head, Acq. and Prcs., 1975–76; Actg. Dir., Wartburg Coll., 1975, Readrs. Srvs. Libn., 1973–74; Catlgr., Stephens Coll., 1972–73; Libn., MO Sch. of Rel., 1971–73. **Educ.:** Univ. of CO, 1962–65, BA (Classics); Knox Coll., 1961–62; Univ. of MO, 1970–72, MA (LS); IN Univ., 1965–66, MA (Classics). **Orgs.:** ALA: LAMA/PAS, Exec. Com. (1978–80); ACRL/Mem. Com. (1976–80); Chap. Rel. Com. (1977–79); Com. on Econ. Status, Fringe Benefits, and Welfare (1975–79); RTSD/OCLC, Users Discuss. Grp., Org. and Ch. (1976); Acqs. of Lib. Mtls. Discuss. Grp., Vice-Ch. (1978); Ch. (1979). SW LA. TX LA. IA LA. **Honors:** Beta Phi Mu, 1972; Phi Beta Kappa, 1964. **Activities:** 1, 6; 15, 35, 46 **Addr.:** 3851 Gramercy, Houston, TX 77025.

Alexander, Carol Greene (O. 13, 1933, Washington, DC) Dir., Ofc. of Lib. Systs., U.S. Env. Protection Agency, 1980–, Deputy, 1977–80; Tech. Info. Ofcr., U.S. Energy Resrch. and Dev. Agency, 1974–77; Chief Libn., John Jay Coll., 1972–74; Deputy Dir., Lib. Srvs., U.S. Natl. Agr. Lib., 1970–72; Chief, Ref. Sect., U.S. Atomic Energy Comsn., HQ Lib., 1966–70; Tech. Info. Anal., U.S. Lib. of Congs., Legis. Ref. Srv., Sci. Policy Resrch. Div., 1965–66, Sci. Ref. Libn., Sci. and Tech. Div., 1960–65; various libn. positions, 1957–60. **Educ.:** Pembroke Coll., Brown Univ., 1951–55, AB (Geol.); Case West. Rsv. Univ., 1956–57, MS (LS). **Orgs.:** Fed. Lib. Com.: Exec. Adv. Com. of Fed. Lib. Netwk., Secy. **Activities:** 4, 12; 17, 26, 34; 65, 78, 91 **Addr.:** P.O. Box 24131, Washington, DC 20024.

Alexander, Carolyn Inez (D. 7, 1943, Shenandoah, IA) Chief Libn., Tech. Info. Ctr., U.S. Army Combat Dev. Exper. Cmnd., Fort Ord, CA, 1975–; Dir., HQ Air Frc. European Cmnd. Lib. Srv. Ctr., Germany, 1971–75; Libn., Anderson Air Frc. Base Lib., Guam, 1969–71; LS Instr., Univ. of Guam, 1969–71; Ref. Libn., Main Post Lib., Fort Riley, KS, 1968; Admin. Libn., Wheeler Air Frc. Base Lib., HI, 1966–68; Branch Libn., Funston Lib., Fort Riley, KS, 1965–66. **Educ.:** NW MO State, 1962–65, BS (Elem. Educ.); Univ. of HI, 1967–68, MLS; various crs. in pub. admin., mgt. **Orgs.:** ALA: Armed Frcs. Lib. Sect., Nom. Com. (Ch., 1979–81), Army Rep. (1981–); VP, Pres.-Elect (1970–71). GU LA: ALA Rep. (1969–71). Coop. Info. Netwk.: Exec. Bd. of Dirs. (1978–80). Cmnty. Progs. Bd. (Hlth. Educ. and Welfare): Bd. (1969–71). Civilian Trng. Com.: Bd. (1979–81). Various youth adv. bds. **Pubns.:** Various poems, TV progs. for chld. (1970–71), radio series in GU (1969–71), sps., soc. clmns. **Activities:** 4, 12; 17, 26, 34; 50, 59, 74 **Addr.:** U.S. Army Combat Developments Experimentation Command Technical Information Center, Fort Ord, CA 93941.

Alexander, Cheryl L. (Mr. 9, 1948, Buffalo, NY) Tech. Info. Spec., U.S. Dept. of Cmrce., Natl. Oceanic and Atmospheric Admin., 1980–; Marine Info. Spec., Intergvt. Exch. of Persnl., Univ. of MI, Dept. of Cmrce., 1977–79, Resrch. Assoc. II, 1976–77, Resrch. Assoc. I, 1972–76. **Educ.:** Harpur Coll., SUNY, Binghamton, 1966–70, BA (Geol.); Univ. of MI, 1970–71, MA (LS). **Orgs.:** ASIS. SLA. Oceanic Socty. World Future Socty. **Pubns.:** *ASFA Database User Guide* (1980); "A National Information Policy–Pandora's Box Revised," *Amer. Socty. for Info. Sci. Bltn.* (My. 1978); "The NOAA Regional Coastal Information Center Program," *Procs., Anl. Mtg. of ASIS* (1978). **Activities:** 4; 17, 18, 46; 56, 65, 91 **Addr.:** Environmental Science Information Center, NOAA D8 U.S. Dept. of Commerce, Rockville, MD 20852.

Alexander, David (N. 6, 1947, Berkeley, CA) Archvst., Cur., Univ. of CO at Denver, 1979–; Archvst., Cur., North. IL Univ., 1977–79;Ref. Libn., Univ. of RI, 1975–77; Law Libn., Covington and Burling, 1971–73. **Educ.:** Univ. of WI, 1966–70, BA (Hist.); Univ. of RI, 1973–76, MA (Hist.), 1975–76, MLS; Univ. of Vienna, 1974–75, Dip. (Grmn.). **Orgs.:** SAA: Mss. Com. (1979–). Midwest Arch. Conf.: Cons. Com. (1976–77). Socty. of CO Archvsts.: VP/Prog. Ch., 1980–81; Constn. and Bylaws Com. (1979–). CO LA: Coll. and Univ. Com. (1979–). Bibl. Ctr. for Resrch.: Consult., Reg. Disaster Team Com. Co State Lib. consult. for CO Cons. Study (1980–81). West. Cons. Congs. Adv. Bd. (1980–81). **Honors:** Phi Alpha Theta, 1976. **Pubns.:** "Regional Disaster Preparedness and Recovery: A Project Proposal", *CO Libs.* (S. 1981); "Education in Transition: Legacy of the Founders", Major Exhibit (1979). **Activities:** 1, 2; 23, 39, 45; 55, 85, 95-Col. Dev. **Addr.:** 735 Elm St., Denver, CO 80220.

Alexander, Malcolm Douglas (O. 17, 1939, Potlatch, ID) Assoc. Prof., Libnshp., Ctrl. WA Univ., 1965–; Tchr., Libn., Lake Stevens Sch. Dist., 1961–64. **Educ.:** Univ. of ID, 1957–61, BA (Soc. Sci.); Univ. of WA, 1964–65, MLibr; Ctrl. WA State Coll., 1966–73, MEd (Curric.); WA State Univ., 1977–79, ABD (Educ.). **Orgs.:** ALA: ACRL. WA LA: Bd. (1970–79); Pres. (1975–77). Pac. NW LA. Assn. of Acad. and Resrch. Libns. of WA LA: Pres. (1969–70). Assn. for the Std. of Higher Educ. AAUP. **Honors:** Phi Delta Kappa. **Pubns.:** "Washington Library Association," *Encyc. of Lib. and Info. Sci.* (1981); *A Measure of Library Skills of High School Graduates of Washington State As Demonstrated by Freshmen of Central Washington State College* ERIC (1972). **Activities:** 1; 31, 39; 63, 92 **Addr.:** 900 E. 1st, Ellensburg, WA 98926.

Alexander, Susanna (F. 13, 1917, St. James, MO) Assoc. State Libn., MO State Lib., 1965–; Interim State Libn., 1976–77; Dir., Daniel Boone Reg. Lib., 1959–65; Dir., Columbia Pub. Lib., 1955–59; Head, Tech. Srvs. Dept., Stephens Coll., 1952–55. **Educ.:** Stephens Coll., 1934–36, AA; Northwestern Univ., 1936–38, BS (Bus.); Univ. of Denver, 1949–52, MALS. **Orgs.:** ALA: Constn. and Bylaws Com. (Ch., 1979–80); Com. on Accred. (1973–78), Nom. Com. (Ch., 1971). MO LA: Treas. (1957–59); VP (1962); Pres. (1963); Lib. Dev. Com. (Ch., 1964). Leag. of Women Voters. Stephens Coll. Alum. Clb. AAUW. **Honors:** Stephens Coll., Alum. Achvmnt. Awd., 1959; MO Coord. Bd. of Higher Educ., Spec. Recog., 1977; Beta Phi Mu, Awd. of Merit, 1978. **Activities:** 9, 13; 17, 26; 59, 74, 78 **Addr.:** 408 Crystal View Terr., Jefferson City, MO 65101.

Alexander, William D., IV (Jl. 4, 1940, High Point, NC) Lib. Dir., S. Portland Pub. Lib., 1973–; Lib. Dir., Westerly Pub. Lib., 1968–73; Lib. Dir., Abington Lib. Socty., 1966–68. **Educ.:** Whittier Coll., 1962, BA (Psy.); Syracuse Univ., 1965–66, MS (LS). **Orgs.:** RI LA: Pres. (1971–72). New Eng. LA: Secy. (1974–75). ME LA: Treas. (1974–75). **Honors:** Beta Phi Mu, 1966. **Pubns.:** "Organizing The Library's Support," *Downeast Libs.* (F. 1980). **Activities:** 9, 16, 26 **Addr.:** South Portland Public Library, 482 Broadway, South Portland, ME 04106.

Alford, Thomas E. (Mr. 5, 1935, McKeesport, PA) Asst. City Libn., Los Angeles Pub. Lib., 1980–; Dir., Macomb Cnty. Lib., 1974–80; Dir., Benton Harbor Pub. Lib., Berrien Cnty. Lib. Leag., 1969–74; Coord., YA Srvs., Mideast. MI Lib. Coop., 1967–69; Head, YA Dept., Flint Pub. Lib., 1965–67. **Educ.:** East. MI Univ., 1958, BS; Univ. of MI, 1964, MALS. **Orgs.:** ALA: YASD (Pres., 1972–73); Cncl. (1972–73); LAMA/Circ. Srvs. Sect. (Ch., 1978–79), Org. Com. (1978–79); various other coms., ofcs. MI LA: Pub. Lib. Div. (Ch., 1974–75); Lib. Syst. RT (Ch., 1971–72); Legis. Com. (Ch., 1979–80). WHCOLIS: MI Del. (Co-Ch.). Untd. Cmnty. Srvs. of Metro. Detroit: Macomb Div. (Vice-Ch., 1979–80); Bd. of Trustees. **Pubns.:** Chap. in *Black Librarian in America* (1970); chap. in *What Black Librarians Are Saying* (1972); chap. in *Libraries in the Political Process* (1980). **Addr.:** Los Angeles Public Library, 630 W. 5th St., Los Angeles, CA 90071.

Algermissen, Virginia Lantz–Lutterbie (Je. 30, 1929, Kearney, NE) Dir. Med. Sci. Lib., TX A and M Univ., 1976–; Head, Med. Sci. Lib., Univ. MO, Kansas City, 1973–76; Asst. Prof., Univ. MO, Columbia, 1968–73. **Educ.:** Univ. of CO, 1945–49, BM; Univ. of Denver, 1961, MA (LS); Med. LA, Cert. **Orgs.:** Med. LA. TX LA. Hlth. Sci. Comm. Assn. Talon Reg. Med. Lib.: S. Ctrl. Sect. Assn. of Amer. Med. Colls. **Honors:** Phi Kappa Phi; Sigma Alpha Iota; Phi Delta Gamma. **Pubns.:** "Medical Library Awareness Seminar", *Lib. Notes* (June 1979); "A Role for the Clinical Medical Librarian in Continuing Education", *Jnl. of Med. Educ.* (June 1978); "Texas A&M Medical Sciences Library," *Lib. Notes* (December 1977); "University of Missouri-Kansas City Medical Library: New Services for a Nontraditional School," *Show-Me Libraries* (June 1976); Jt. auth., "Biomedical Slide Classification using MeSH," *Bull. of the Med. LA* (April 1976); Other articles. **Activities:** 1, 12; 17, 26, 41 **Addr.:** Medical Sciences Library, Texas A and M University, College Station, TX 77843.

Allain, Alex P. (Je. 27, 1920, Albania Plantation, LA) Attorney, 1942–. **Educ.:** Loyola Univ., New Orleans, JD. **Orgs.:** ALA: Code of Ethics Com. (1970–); Com. on Org. (1974–); Com. on Accred. (1974–78); ALTA. Frdm. to Read Fndn.: Fndr., Ch. (1970). LA LA: Lib. Trustee Assn. (Pres., 1967); Int. Frdm. Com. (Ch.). St. Mary Par. Lib.: Trustee. Amer. Bar Assn. **Honors:** LA Trustee Cit. of Merit Highest Awd., Modisette, 1965; ALTA, Trustee Cit. of Merit, 1969; Downs Awd., 1973; ALA, Hon. Mem., 1975. **Activities:** 14-Attorney; 47; 74 **Addr.:** Box 329, Jeanerette, LA 70544.*

Allan, Ann G. (Ja. 9, 1940, Youngstown, OH) Assoc. Prof. LS, Kent State Univ., 1975–; Ast. Univ. Libn., Tech. Srvs., Univ. of Akron Lib., 1968–71; Asst. Head, Acq., Kent State Univ., 1966–67; Acq. Biblgphr., Univ. MI, 1964–65. **Educ.:** Univ. MI, 1958–62, BA (Soclgy.); Simmons Coll., 1962–63, MLS; Case West. Rsv. Univ., 1971–76, PhD (LS). **Orgs.:** ALA: LAMA/LOMS. OH LA. North. OH Tech. Svc. Assn. Jr. Leag. of Akron: Bd. (1973 and 1976). Various other coms. Alpha Delta Pi. **Pubns.:** *OCLC: A National Library Network* (1979); "A Method for Determining Interdisciplinary Activities within a University", *Lib. Resrch.* (Feb. 1980). **Activities:** 1; 17, 20, 46; 56 **Addr.:** School of Library Science, Kent State University, Kent, OH 44242.

Allan, Ferne C. (Ag. 26, 1937, Upper Sandusky, OH) Supvsr., Tech. Lit. Sect., Texaco Chem. Co., 1976–, Resrch. Libn., 1975–76; Jnlst., TX State Dept. of Hwys., 1974–75; Asst. Resrch., Univ. of MI Dental Mtrls., 1963–68; Info. Anal., Battelle Meml. Inst., 1959–60. **Educ.:** OH State Univ., 1955–61, BMetE (Engin.); Univ. of TX, Austin, 1972–74, MLS (Spec. Libs.). **Orgs.:** SLA: Austin Chap., Cont. Ed. Com. (1977–79), Prog. Com. (1979–80). Austin OLUG: Pres. (1981). Amer. Socty. for Metals. Amer. Chem. Socty. **Honors:** Alpha Sigma Mu, 1961; Beta Phi Mu, 1974; Sigma Xi, 1965. **Pubns.:** Chap. in *Special Librarianship: A Reader* (1980); ed., *Index to Courses for Undergraduates* (1974); jt. auth., "Microstructure of Dental Amalgam," *Jnl. of Dental Resrch.* (S.–O. 1965); jt. auth., "Reaction of Cobalt-Chromium Casting Alloy with Investment," *Jnl. Dental Resrch.* (S.–O. 1966); jt. auth., "Microstructure and Physical Properties of Alloys for Partial Denture Castings," *Jnl. Dental Resrch.* (Mr.–Ap. 1968). **Activities:** 12; 17; 60, 64, 86 **Addr.:** P.O. Box 15730, Austin, TX 78761.

Allard, C. Gabriel (O. 18, 1922, Weedon, PQ) Chief Libn., Col. de Maisonneuve, 1952–; Prof., LS, Univ. de Montréal, 1974–76; Prof., Col. Ste-Croix, 1951–59. **Educ.:** Coll. de St-Laurent, Séminaire Ste-Croix, Univ. of Montreal, 1938–43, BA; McGill Univ., 1960–65, BLS, MLS; Univ. de Montréal, 1946–51, Bth. (Theo.), 1951–52, BPed. (Pedagogy). **Orgs.:** ASTED: Col. Lib. Sect. Assn. Can. des Bibtcrs. de Langue Fr.: VP (1962–63); Prés. (1963–64). **Pubns.:** *Programme pour la Construction d'une Bibliothèque au Cégep de Maisonneuve* (1970); *Projet d'un Index Coopératif des Périodiques de Langue Francaise pour Nos Bibliothèques d'Enseignement* (1965); "Le financement des Bibliothèques de Collège," *Argus* (Mr. 1979); "Construction d'une Bibliothèque de College," *Bltn. of Assn. Can. Bibl. Langue Fr.* (O. 1971). **Activities:** 1; 17, 31, 39; 55, 89, 90 **Addr.:** Cégep de Maisonneuve, bibliothèque, 3800 est, rue Sherbrooke, Montréal, PQ H1X 2A2 Canada.

Alldredge, Noreen S. (Ap. 8, 1939, Sacramento, CA) Dir. of Libs., MT State Univ. Libs., 1981–; Asst. Dir. for Col. Dev., TX A and M Univ. Libs., 1977–81, Asst. Dir. Tech. Srvs., 1976–77; Head, Col. Dev., Univ. of NV, 1974–76, Biblgphr., Circ. Libn., 1970–74, Desert Resrch. Inst. Libn., 1966–76, Ref. Libn., 1965–66; Film Libn., NY Pub. Lib.,1963–65. **Educ.:** Mount St. Mary's Coll., 1957–61, BA (Eng. Lit.); Columbia Univ., 1962–65, MS (LS); TX A and M Univ., 1977–80, MA (Amer. Hist.). **Orgs.:** ALA: Resrcs. Sect./Lib. Mtrls. Price Indx. Com. (Ch., 1977–79); Col. Dev. Com. (1979–); ACRL/Univ. Libs. Steer. Com. (1979–); Chap. Cncl. (1972–74). Houston Area Resrch. Libs. Cnsrtm. Tech. Srvs. Com.: Ch. (1978–79). NV LA: IFC (1970–74); Exec. Bd. (1972–73). ARL: Consult. (1979). **Pubns.:** "Symbiotic Relationship of Approval Plans and Collection Development, *Shaping Lib. Cols. for the 1980's* (1981); "Prices of U.S. and Foreign Published Materials", *Bowker Anl.* (1978 and '79); "Bibliography on Geostatistics", *Intl. Stat. Inst. Review* (1978); "Ridge Regression", *Intl. Stat. Review* (1976). **Activities:** 1; 15, 17, 41 **Addr.:** Montana State Univ. Library, Bozeman, MT 59717.

Alldredge, Shirley A. (Jl. 6, 1919, Norfolk, NE) Head, Pub. Srvs., Natl. Oceanic and Atmospheric Admin., 1967–; Ref. Libn., Denver Pub. Lib., 1952–53; Ref. Libn., Univ. of Denver, 1946–51; Clasfd. Docum. Libn., Manhattan Proj., Los Alamos, NM, 1944–46. **Educ.:** Univ. of Denver, 1938–42, BA (LS). **Orgs.:** SLA: Rocky Mt. Chap., CO ILL Com. (Chap. Rep., 1975–78); Cont. Ed. Com. (1976–80); Pres. (1979–80). **Pubns.:** "Unconventional Ways to Retrieve Literature," *Procs., SLA Wkshp. on Conf. Lit.* (1980). **Activities:** 1, 4; 17, 38, 44; 64, 88, 91 **Addr.:** 130 Pearl St., #1108, Denver, CO 80203.

Allen, Albert Harold (D. 4, 1929, Middletown, NY) Resrch. Libn., IBM Corp., 1968–, Abstctr., Transl., Indxr., 1962–68, Prod. Cntrl. Spec., 1956–62. **Educ.:** Lehigh Univ., 1949–53, AB (Lib. Arts); NY Univ., 1960–63, MPA (Pub. Ad-

PROFESSIONAL ACTIVITIES: Institutions: 1. Acad. lib.; 2. Arch.; 3. Assn.; 4. Fed./Gvt. lib.; 5. Inst. lib.; 6. Mfr./Suppl.; 7. Milit. lib.; 8. Musm.; 9. Pub. lib.; 10. Sch. lib.; 11. Sch. of lib. sci.; 12. Spec. lib.; 13. State lib.; 14. (other). **Functions/Activities:** 15. Acq./Col. dev.; 16. Adult srvs.; 17. Admin.; 18. Apprais.; 19. Archit./Bldgs.; 20. Cat./Class.; 21. Chld. srvs.; 22. Circ.; 23. Cons./Pres.; 24. Consult.; 25. Cont. ed.; 26. Educ. lib. sci.; 27. Ext. srvs.; 28. Fund/Grants; 29. Gvt. pubs.; 30. Indx./Abs.; 31. Instr. lib. use; 32. Media srvs.; 33. Micro.; 34. Netwks./Coop.; 35. Persnl.; 36. PR; 37. Publshg.; 38. Recs. mgt.; 39. Ref. srvs.; 40. Repro.; 41. Resrch.; 42. Review.; 43. Secur.; 44. Serials; 45. Spec. col.; 46. Tech. srvs.; 47. Trustees/Bds.; 48. YA srvs.; 49. (other).

min.); SUNY, Albany, 1966–68, MLS. **Orgs.:** ASIS. Amer. Socty. for Pub. Admin.: Nat. Resrcs. and Env. Admin. Sect. Env. Comsn., Saugerties, NY: Ch. Env. Comsn., Ulster Cnty., NY: Resrc. Recvry. Com. **Pubns.:** "Systems to Manage the Industrial Library," *Jnl. of Systs. Mgt.* (Je., 1972); "On-line Logging In of Periodicals by CODEN Using Interactive Query Report Processor", *ASIS Jnl.* (1976); Various papers. **Addr.:** 17 Redwood Rd., Saugerties, NY 12477.

Allen, Anita A. (Cincinnati, OH) Serials catlgr., Univ. NM, 1979–, Head of Cat., Med. Ctr. Lib., 1974–79; Serials catlgr., Univ. KY, 1973–74; Libn., Kirtland AFB, 1971–72; Serial Catlgr., Univ. NM, 1968–72; Genl. Catlgr., Baltimore Co. Pub. Lib., 1967–68; Libn., St. Maur's Priory and Semy., 1965–66; Libn., Fort Chaffee Post Lib., 1961–62. **Educ.:** West. KY Univ., 1954–59, BA (LS, Eng., Fr.); Univ. KY, 1967–68, MSLS; various courses workshops, etc. **Orgs.:** Med. LA. Grt. Albuquerque LA. Hlth. Sci. OCLC Users Grp. NM Solar Energy Assn. **Pubns.:** "Library automation at the U. of NM Health Sciences Library", *Hlth. Sci. Libs.* (1975); various panel presentations. **Activities:** 1, 12; 17, 46; 56, 80 **Addr.:** 1233 Vassar NE, Albuquerque, NM 87106.

Allen, Cameron (F. 7, 1928, Springfield, OH) Law Libn., Rutgers Univ. Law Lib., 1965–, Asst. Law Libn., 1959–65. **Educ.:** Otterbein Coll., 1944–47, BA (Hist.); Univ. of WI, 1949–51, MA (Hist.); Univ. of IL, 1954–56 MS (LS); Duke Univ., 1956–59, JD. **Orgs.:** Law LA of Grt. NY. Resrch. Libs. Grp., Inc.: Resrch. Libs. Info. Netwk., Law Lib. Adv. Cncl. (Vice-Ch., 1979–), Law Lib. Prog. Com. (Vice-Ch., 1979). Intl. Assn. of Law Libs. AALL: Secy. (1977–80); Place. Com. (Ch., 1973–74); Com. on Noms. (Ch., 1971–72); Rcrt. Com. (1969–71); Com. on the Indx. to Legal Pers. (Ch., 1974–77). Assn. of Amer. Law Schs.: Com. on Libs. (1977–80); Com. on Accred. of Law Schs. (1981–83). NJ Supreme Ct.: Com. on the Pubn. of NJ Ct. Opinions (1973–77). **Pubns.:** "Suggestions for Researching the Legislative History of Federal Legislative Enactments," *Materials and Problems on Legislation* (1967); "Law Libraries and Collections," *Encyc. of Lib. and Info. Sci.* (1975); "Legal Literature," *Encyc. of Lib. and Info. Sci.* (1975); "Citators," *How to Find the Law* (1976); "Whom We Shall Serve: Secondary Patrons of the University Law School Library," *Reader in Law Librarianship* (1976); various articles, bk. reviews, papers. **Activities:** 1; 15, 17, 31; 74, 77, 78 **Addr.:** Rutgers University School of Law, 15 Washington St., Newark, NJ 07102.

Allen, Daniel (D. 13, 1947, Brooklyn, NY) Owner, Walter C. Allen of Can., 1975–; Bus. Mgr., Coda Pubns., 1973–. **Educ.:** MA Inst. of Tech., 1965–69, BS (Geol.); Univ. of Toronto, 1971–72, MLS. **Orgs.:** Msc. LA. Assn. for Rec. Snd. Cols. Intl. Socty. for Jazz Resrch. **Pubns.:** *Bibliography of Discographies, Vol. 2: Jazz and Related Music* (1981); "78-rpm Phonorecords in the Jazz Archive," *IPLO Qtly.* (Ja. 1972); "Geomorphological Maps of Canada; a Bibliography," *SLA Bltn., Geo. and Map Div.* (D. 1972). **Activities:** 6; 37, 41; 55 **Addr.:** Box 929, Adelaide Station, Toronto, ON M5C 2K3 Canada.

Allen, Edna E. (Jl. 20, 1938, Carrollton, AL) Dir. of Prog. Dev. Gifted Chldn., E. St. Louis Pub. Sch. Dist. 189, 1971–; Couns., 1970–71, Bus. Educ. Tchr., 1963–70. **Educ.:** Lincoln Univ. (MO), 1957–60, BS (Bus. Educ.); Univ. of IL, 1969–71, MS (Couns. Educ.); Gen. Admin. Cert., 1971. **Orgs.:** Natl. Assn. for Gifted Chld.: Exec. Com. (1972–). ALA: ALTA Conf. Prog. (1975–), Eval. Com. (1975–). E. St. Louis State Comm. Coll.: Lcl. Adv. Com. (1976–). Delta Sigma Theta Sorority, Inc.: Soc. Action and Civic Projs. (Co-Ch.). **Honors:** IL Ed., "Those Who Excel", Awd. for Educ. Excellence, 1978; State Comm. Coll., Pub. Svc. Awd., 1978. **Pubns.:** "Gifted Can Push Beyond", *Gifted Gazer Newsp.* (Jan. 1979); Various presentations for ASC and Natl. Assn. for Gifted, (1976–78). **Addr.:** 664 North 33rd St., East St. Louis, IL 62205.

Allen, Eleanor Bross (N. 15, 1915, Philadelphia, PA) Head Libn., Lippincott Lib., Wharton Sch., Univ. of PA, 1952–, Assoc. Libn., 1945–51, Ref. Libn., 1942–44, Catlgr., 1941–42; Consult., Lib. of the Sch. of Cmrce. and Fin., Villanova Univ., 1959–60; U.S.A. Lib. Liaison, Inst. of Pub. and Bus. Admin., Univ. of Karachi, Wharton Sch./Intl. Coop. Admin. Jt. Proj., 1954–59. **Educ.:** Univ. of PA, 1933–37, BS, magna cum laude (Educ.), 1937–38, MS (Educ.); Drexel Univ., 1939–42, BS (LS). **Orgs.:** ALA: ACRL, Philadelphia Chap., Bd. of Dirs. (1955–57, 1975–77). SLA: Bus. Fin. Div., 1st Vice-Ch., *Bltn.* Ed. (1951–53), Div. Ch. (1953–54), Mem. Ch. (1961–63); Philadelphia Chap., (Secy., 1945–46), Bltn. Ed. (1949–51), Fin. Com. (Ch., 1963–64), Prog. Com. (Ch., 1942–43); Exec. Bd. (1946–47); various other coms., ofcs. Univ. of PA Alum.: Class of 1937 Strg. Com. (1976–). Univ. of PA Fac. Club: Chrt. Mem. (1958–). Drexel Lib. Sch. Alum. Assn.: Advnc. and Spec. Gifts Com. (1959); Exec. Com. (1959–63); Plng. Com. for Fall Wkshp. (1974) Zeta Tau Alpha Fraternity: Alpha Beta Chap. (Pres., 1936–37). **Honors:** Pi Lambda Theta, 1936; Eta Sigma Phi, 1936. **Pubns.:** Assoc. ed., *Encyclopedia of Business Information Sources* (1976); assoc. ed., *Statistics Sources* (1971); assoc. ed., *Encyclopedia of Business Information Sources* (1970); jt. ed., *Literature of Executive Management* bibl. (1963); contrib., *Special Libraries Association: Its First Fifty Years, 1909–1959* (1959). **Activities:** 1; 17; 59 **Addr.:** 527 Idlewild Cir., Media, PA 19063.

Allen, Jane D. (D. 22, 1930, Concord, NH) Sr. Libn., NY State Dept. of Hlth., 1974–; Ast. Catlgr., Union Coll., 1969–74. **Educ.:** Jackson Coll., Tufts Univ., 1948–52, BS (Bio./Chem.); SUNY, Albany, 1963–68, MLS. **Orgs.:** Med. LA: Upstate NY Ontario Reg. Grp., Educ. Com. (1980). Albany Area Hlth. Lib. Afflts.: Ch. (1979). **Activities:** 12; 20, 29, 38, 58, 80, 91 **Addr.:** Division of Labs. and Research Library, NY State Dept. of Health, Empire State Plz., Albany, NY 12201.

Allen, Joanne L. (My. 13, 1946, Regina, SK) Co-Owner, The Chld. Corner Bookstore Inc., 1980–; Asst. Dept. Head, Chld. Srvs., Regina Pub. Lib., 1977–80, Branch Head, 1974–77; Tchr., Div. II and III, Regina Bd. of Educ., 1967–71. **Educ.:** Univ. of SK, 1964–67, BEd (Eng.); Univ. of BC, 1970–71 (Sch. Libnshp.), 1971–73, MLS (Pub., Chld. Libnshp.). **Orgs.:** Can. LA. Can. Assn. of Pub. Libs. SK LA: Chld. Lib. Srvs. Sect. (Treas., 1979–81). Can. Booksellers Assn. Regina Zone II Cmnty. Assn.: Bd. (1974–78). Various cmnty. orgs. **Pubns.:** "Jobsharing," *Feliciter* (1979). **Activities:** 9; 15, 17, 21; 50, 57, 75 **Addr.:** 3142 Athol St., Regina, SK S4P 0K2 Canada.

Allen, Lawrence A. (Mr. 3, 1926, Lynn, MA) Prof., Univ. of KY, 1966–; Dean, Coll. of Cont. Ed., Northeast. Univ., 1962–66; Dir., Mgt. Educ., Amer. Hosp. Assn., 1960–62; Instr., Univ. of Chicago, 1958–60. **Educ.:** Boston Univ., 1946–50, BS (Hist.); Emmons Coll., 1950–51, MS; Univ. of Chicago, 1958–60, PhD (Adult Educ.). **Orgs.:** ALA. Adult Educ. Assn. Org. Dev. Netwk. Amer. Mgt. Assn. Organizational Behavior Tchrs. Assn. **Honors:** Ford Fndn., Flwshp., 1958. **Pubns.:** "Continuing Education: State of the Art," *Spec. Libs.* (1974); "Developing Social Interestive Skills," *Lib. Trends* (Win. 1971); "First College of Library Science," *Encyc. of Info. Sci.* (1974). **Activities:** 9, 13; 17, 24; 50 **Addr.:** College of Library Science, University of KY, Lexington, KY 40506.

Allen, Nancy H. (O. 4, 1950, Oak Park, IL) Comm. Libn., Assoc. Prof., Univ. of IL, 1978–, Asst. Undergrad. Libn., 1973–78. **Educ.:** Univ. of IL, 1968–72, MA (Eng., Educ.), 1972–73, MS (LS). **Orgs.:** ALA: ACRL/Cin. Libns. Discuss Grp. (Ch., 1977–79); LIRT. Amer. Film Inst. **Pubns.:** *Film Study Collections: a Guide to Their Development & Use* (1979); "Film Books for Students and Teachers", *Film Lib. Qtly.* (v. 9#2); "Other Books and Pamphlets on Journalistic Subjects", *Jnlsm. Qtly.* (Win. 1978 and cont.); Ed., *Cin. Libns. Nwsltr.* **Activities:** 1; 15, 31, 39; 51, 67, 93 **Addr.:** Communications Library, 122 Gregory Hall, University of Illinois, Urbana, IL 61801.

Allen, Robert Douglas (Jl. 5, 1938, Deville, LA) Asst. Prof., Head, Media Div., Northwestern State Univ. of LA, 1972–; Head, Dept. of Lib. Sci., LA Coll., 1970–71. **Educ.:** LA Coll., 1957–61, BA, (Educ.); LA State Univ., 1969–71, MLS; McNeese State Univ., 1973–75, MEd, (Educ. Tech.); Nova Univ., 1981, EdD. **Orgs.:** LA LA. Phi Delta Kappa. **Honors:** Beta Phi Mu. **Pubns.:** "Encyclopedias: Usage Techqs.", *Film News: the Intl. Rev. of AV Mtrls. and Equipment* (S./O. 1976); Various reviews. **Activities:** 1; 16, 32, 33 **Addr.:** Media Division, Watson Library, Northwestern State Univ., Natchitoches, LA 71457.

Allen, Ronald (F. 8, 1950, New York, NY) Ref. Libn., Asst. Prof., VA Cmwlth. Univ., 1978–; Ref. Libn., Wayne State Univ., 1976–78; Ref. Libn., Trenton State Lib., 1975–76. **Educ.:** Brooklyn Coll., 1967–71, BA (Soclgy.); Rutgers Univ., 1974–75, MLS. **Orgs.:** ALA. VA LA. **Pubns.:** Ed., *Urban Research Resources Directory: Detroit* (1979); *Report on Visual Display at Purdy Library (ERIC- ED167 130)* (1978). **Activities:** 1; 39; 59 **Addr.:** Cabell Library, Reference Dept., Virginia Commonwealth University, Richmond, VA 23284.

Allen, Rosanna Phillips (My. 20, 1923, Jamestown, OH) Chief, Hum., Soc. Sci. Dept., PA State Univ., 1977–, Head, Ref. Dept., 1967–77; Assoc. Libn., Engin. Lib., Cornell Univ. Lib., 1966–67; Lib. Consult., Univ. of Liberia, Cornell/USAID Proj., 1964–65; Assoc. Libn., Vetny. Lib., Cornell Univ., 1961–64; Ref. Libn., Tech. Lib., E.I. du Pont de Nemours, 1958–61; Libn., Amer. Cancer Socty., 1956–57; Libn., Rockefeller Fndn., 1950–55; various positions in cat., 1946–50. **Educ.:** Wilmington Coll., 1941–45, BA (Lit.); Columbia Univ., 1945–46, BSLS (Univ. Lib. Admin.). **Orgs.:** ALA. PA LA. **Addr.:** 511 Ridge Ave., State College, PA 16801.

Allen, Stephanie Nicely (S. 9, 1948, Indianapolis, IN) Srch. Anal. and Ref. Libn., Univ. of KY Med. Ctr., 1980–; Info. Spec., Clinical Libn., Univ. of MS Med. Ctr., 1978–, Head, Instr. and Loans, 1976–78, Medline Libn., Ast. Ref. Libn., 1975–76. **Educ.:** Univ. of KY, 1966–70, BS (Microbio.), 1973–75, MSLS; Med. LA, 1975, Cert. **Orgs.:** Med. LA KY LA. Phi Beta Mu (Treas. 1980–81). MS Humane Socty. **Honors:** Beta Phi Mu, 1975; Delta Phi Alpha, 1969. **Pubns.:** Jt. Auth., "An Evaluation of a Large-scale Self-instructional Course in Medical Information Resources", *Bltn. Med. Lib. Assn.* (Jl. 1979); Jt. Auth., "Introduction to Bibliographic Information Sources", *Rowland Med. Lib.* (1977); Jt. Prod., "Rowland Medical Library Tour", Audiotape (1977); Jt. Prod., "The Biomedical Information Network", Videotape (1977); Other progs. **Activities:** 5, 12; 31, 39; 58, 80 **Addr.:** Reference Dept., Albert B. Chandler Medical Library, University of Kentucky, Medical Center, Lexington, KY 40536.

Allen, Walter C. (N. 23, 1927, Troy, OH) Assoc. Prof., Grad. Sch. of Lib. Sci., Univ. IL, 1968–; Head, Lit. and Fine Arts Div., Dayton/Montgomery Cnty. Pub. Lib., 1962–67, Asst. Head, Ref. Dept., 1957–61, Asst. Head, Cat. Dept., 1954–57, Cat. Asst., 1953–54; Ref. Asst., Northwestern Univ., 1951–52. **Educ.:** Williams Coll., 1945–49, AB (Geol.); Columbia Univ., 1950–51, MS (LS). **Orgs.:** ALA: Adult Svcs. Div., Notable Bks. Cncl. (1969–72), Ch. (1970–71), RASD, Co-Pres. (1972–73), SORT, Chmn. (1959–60), Ref. Srvs. Div., Chapts. Com. (1964–66). OH LA: Ref. Srvs. RT, Ch. (1963–64), Dist. Mtgs. Com., Ch. (1963–65). IL LA. AALS. Other orgs. Socty. of Archit. Histn.; Socty. of Auto. Histns. **Honors:** Cncl. on Lib. Resrcs., Flwshp., 1978. **Pubns.:** Ed., *Serial Publications in Large Libraries* (1970); "Services", *Lib. Trends* (Ja. 1975); "Library Buildings", *Lib. Trends* (Jl. 1976). **Activities:** 9, 11; 16, 19, 37, 39; 74 **Addr.:** 1115 West Union St., Champaign, IL 61820.

Alley, Brian (F. 27, 1933, Waterville, ME) Ast. Dir. of Libs., Miami Univ., 1969–, Undergrad. Libn., 1968–69; Actg. Dir. of Libs., Elmira Coll., 1967–68, Ref. Libn., 1966–67; Ast. Hum. Libn., Portland State Univ., 1963–65. **Educ.:** Colby Coll., 1952–56, AB (Art Hist.); FL State Univ., 1962–63, MS (LS); Univ. MD, Lib. Admin. Dev. Prog., 1973, (cert.); IBM Customer Trng. Prog., 1965. **Orgs.:** ALA: ACRL; RTSD; LITA. OH Inter Univ. Lib. Cncl. Tech. Srvs. Grp. Tech. Srvs. Libns., OH Valley Grp. **Pubns.:** Jt. Auth., *Practical Approval Plan Management* (1979); *Technical Services Staff Directory for Academic Libraries: Indiana-Kentucky-Ohio 1978/79* (1978); Jt. Auth., "Inventory and Selection Techniques for Large Unorganized Collections", *Lib. Acq.: Pract. and Theory* (1978); "A Utility Book Truck Designed for Moving Library Collections", *Lib. Acq.: Pract. and Theory;* Jt. cmplr., *IULC Tech. Svcs. Nsltr.* (1977–80); "Use of a Commercial Acquisitions . System", *OLA Bltn.* (1980); Ed., Inter Univ. Lib. Cncl. Tech. Svcs. Nsltr. (1972–). **Activities:** 1; 17, 35, 46 **Addr.:** 410 E. Chestnut, Oxford, OH 45056.

Alligood, Elaine Catherine (Ja. 10, 1950, Washington, DC) Asst. Prof., Head Pub. Srvs., Health Sci. Lib., Univ. VA, 1980–; Chief, Lib. Srv., U.S. Vets. Admin. Med. Ctr., 1978–80; Co-ord., Ref. and Circ., Med. Lib., Johns Hopkins Univ., 1976–78; Tech. Info. Spec., U.S. Natl. Cancer Inst., 1974–76. **Educ.:** Univ. of MD, 1969–72, BA (Art Hist., Anth.), 1973–74, MLS; Med. LA, 1974–, Grade I Med. Libn. **Orgs.:** Med. LA; MD Assn. Hlth. Sci. Libns.: Pres. (1979–81), VP (1977–79); Med. LA, Mid-Atl.: Chap. VP/Pres.-elect (1980-81); Nom. Com. (1978); Bylaws Com. (1980); Prog. Speaker, Anl. Mtg. (1979); Proj. Team (1980). **Pubns.:** Co-Auth., *Union List of Biomedical Seriaes* (1977, 1978). **Activities:** 1, 12; 17, 39, 41; 75, 80, 91 **Addr.:** Chief, Library Service 142–D, Veterans Administration Medical Center, 3900 Loch Raven Blvd., Baltimore, MD 21218.

Allison, Ann Evelyn Frear (Ag. 25, 1929, New Haven, CT) Ref. Libn., Bucks Cnty. Cmnty. Coll., 1969–; Catlgr., Sci. Libn., Oakland Univ., 1967–68; Engin. Libn., PA State Univ., 1956–59; Serials Acq. Ast., Univ. WI, 1954–56; Ref. Ast., Engin. Lib., Columbia Univ., 1953–54. **Educ.:** Mt. Holyoke Coll., 1947–51, AB (Hist.); Columbia Univ. LS Sch., 1952–53, MS (Lib. Svc.). **Orgs.:** ALA. PA LA. AAUW: Treas. for 3 bnchs. (1964–66, 1967–68, 1976–78). **Activities:** 1; 31, 39 **Addr.:** Landisville Rd., R.D. 2, Doylestown, PA 18901.

Allison, Anne Marie (O. 3, 1931, Oak Park, IL) Ast. Dir. Lib. Srvs., FL Atl. Univ., 1979–; Head, Prcs. Dept., Kent State Univ., 1973–79, Asst. Head, Cat. Dept., 1971–73; Dir., Lrng. Resrce. Ctr., Coll. of Lake Cnty., 1970–71, Coll. Libn., 1969–70; Asst. Libn., Moraine Valley Cmnty. Coll., 1968–69; Asst. Libn., Triton Coll., 1967–68. **Educ.:** St. Mary of the Woods, 1949–53, BA (Fr.); Univ. of Fribourg, 1951–52; Rosary Coll., 1965–68, MLS; North. IL Univ., 1968–70. **Orgs.:** ALA: RTSD/Educ. for Tech. Srvs. Com. (1976–79); LAMA/Compar. Lib. Org. Com. (1976–79); Un. Rel. for Lib. Mgrs. Com. (1979–81). LRRT. IL LA. OH LA. Other orgs. AAUP. **Pubns.:** *OCLC: A NATIONAL LIBRARY NETWORK* (1979); *Factors Affecting Administration in Academic Libraries in the United States during the Period 1970–1975* (1979); "CHORALIST: A Computerized Index to Choral Octavo Scores", *Coll. Mgt.* (Spr. 1979); "United States Documents in an On-Line Union Catalog", *Serials Libn.* (Sum. 1977); "OCLC at Kent," "Exploring the Use of Kent's OCLC Terminals", "On-Line Cataloging", and other video tapes (1973–76). **Activities:** 1; 17, 28, 34; 50, 56 **Addr.:** University Library, Florida Atlantic University, Boca Raton, FL 33432.

Allison, Frederick E. (O. 22, 1943, Alliance, OH) Dir., Grove City (OH) Pub. Lib., 1977–; Dir., Richmond Meml. Lib., 1971–76; Head, Data Prcs. Dept., Rodman Pub. Lib., 1967–71. **Educ.:** Mt. Union Coll., 1962–67, BA (Germ.); SUNY, Geneseo, 1969–71, MLS. **Orgs.:** ALA. OH LA. **Activities:** 9; 17 **Addr.:** Grove City Public Library, Grove City, OH 43123.

Allison, Malinda B. (S. 30, 1947, Vernon, TX) Libn., Legis. Ref. Lib., 1978–; Libn., Luce, Forward, Hamilton and Scripps, 1976–77; Docum. Libn., Univ. of San Diego Law Lib., 1974–76; Libn., Legis. Ref. Lib., 1970–74. **Educ.:** Univ. of TX, Austin, 1966–69, BS (Educ.), 1969–70, MLS. **Orgs.:** AALL. Southwest. Assn. of Law Libns. Natl. Conf. of State Legis.: Legis. Libs. Sect. **Pubns.:** *Texas Legislative History; A Manual of Sources* (1980).

Special Subjects/Services: 50. Adult educ.; 51. Advert./Mktg.; 52. Aerosp.; 53. Agric.; 54. Area std.; 55. Arts/Hum.; 56. Autom.; 57. Bibl./Prtg.; 58. Bio. sci.; 59. Bus./Fin.; 60. Chem.; 61. Copyrt.; 62. Documtn.; 63. Educ.; 64. Engin.; 65. Env.; 66. Eth. grps.; 67. Film; 68. Food/Nutr.; 69. Geneal.; 70. Geo.; 71. Geol.; 72. Handcpd.; 73. Hist.; 74. Int. frdm.; 75. Info. sci.; 76. Insr.; 77. Law; 78. Legis.; 79. Math./Comp. sci.; 80. Med.; 81. Metals; 82. Nat. resrcs.; 83. Newsp.; 84. Nuc. sci.; 85. Oral hist.; 86. Petr./Energy; 87. Pharm.; 88. Phys./Astr./Math.; 89. Readg.; 90. Relig.; 91. Sci./Tech.; 92. Soc. sci.; 93. Telecom.; 94. Transp.; 95. (other).

Activities: 12, 13; 39, 49-In-Hse. Data Bases; 77, 78, 95-Pub. Affairs. **Addr.:** Legislative Reference Library, P.O. Box 12488–Capitol Station, Austin, TX 78711.

Allmand, Linda F. (Ja. 31, 1937, Port Arthur, TX) Dir., Fort Worth Pub. Lib., 1981–; Chief, Branch Srvs., Dallas Pub. Lib., 1971–81; Instr., Lib. Bldgs., N. TX State Univ., 1977–81; Pub. Lib. Bldg. Consult., 1971–; 1975–, Asst. Chief, Branch Srvs., 1971; Instr., Chld. Lit., N. TX State Univ., 1967-69; Branch Mgr., Dallas Pub. Lib., 1965–71; Coord. Chld. Srvs., Anaheim Pub. Lib., 1963–65; Asst. Libn. and Chld. Libn., Denver Pub. Lib., 1960–63. **Educ.:** N. TX State Univ., 1956–58, BA (Info. Sci., Hist.); Univ. of Denver, 1960–62, MA (Libnshp.); Univ. CA, 1966; Dallas Cnty. Comnty. Coll., 1971–79; Various wkshps. **Orgs.:** ALA: Repn. to Natl. Conf. on Soc. Welfare (1971), Task Frc. for Goals on Chld. Srvs. (1972–74), Pub. Lib. Div., Stand. Com. (1974–78), Lib. Admin. Div., Task Frc. on Lib. Bldg. Consult., Ch. (1978–). Dallas Cnty. LA: Pres. (1968–69). SW LA: Mem. Ch. (1973–75). TX LA: Pub. Lib. Assn., Vice Ch., Ch. (1979–81). Bus. and Prof. Women's Assn. N. Texas Alumni Assn. Sch. of Lib. and Info. Sci.: VP, Pres. (1978–80). NOW. Other orgs. **Honors:** Beta Phi Mu, Alpha Lambda Sigma; Phi Alpha Theta; Lib. Binding Inst. Schol., 1958. **Activities:** 9; 17, 19, 24 **Addr.:** 2409 Stanley, Fort Worth, TX 76110.

Allmen, Diane Cynthia (D. 6, 1944, Detroit, MI) Sr. Supvsr., Info. Sci., Travenol Labs., Inc., 1974–; Assoc. Ed., Wood and Wood Prod., Vance Publshng. Co., 1973; Mgr., Barbara's Bkstore., 1970–72; Rsrch. Ed., Bio., Encyc. Britannica, 1968–70; Sci. Ast., Argonne Natl. Lab., 1967–68. **Educ.:** Univ. MI, 1963–67, BS (Microbio.); Univ. of Chicago, 1978–, MBA (Mgt. Sci). **Orgs.:** COLUG: Plan. Com. (1978–80); Prog. Ch. (1979); Pubcty. Ch. (1979). SLA. ASIS: SIG Mgt. Nsltr. (Ed., 1980–). Other orgs. **Activities:** 12; 24, 30, 38; 56, 75, 91 **Addr.:** Scientific Services MG–11C, Baxter Travenol Laboratories, Inc., 6301 Lincoln, Morton Grove, IL 60053.

Almes, June C. (F. 14, 1934, PA) Assoc. Prof., Lock Haven State Coll., 1971–; Resrch. Libn., Univ. of Pittsburgh, 1970–71; Sch. Libn., Shippensburg Sch. Dist., 1964–68; Tchr., Altoona Sch. Dist., 1961–64. **Educ.:** IN Univ., 1951–55, BS Ed (Eng., Hist., Geo.); Univ. of Pittsburgh, 1968–69 (LS), 1969–70, Advnc. Cert. **Orgs.:** ALA. PA LA. PA Sch. Libns. Assn. Amer. Cvl. Liberties Un. **Honors:** Beta Phi Mu; Phi Delta Kappa. **Pubns.:** *PA Authors: Adult and Children Authors Who Were Born Or Lived In Pennsylvania* booklet, map (1976); *Lock Haven State College Student Teaching Handbook* (1977). **Activities:** 9, 11; 26, 31, 47; 63, 74, 89 **Addr.:** Lock Haven State College, Lock Haven, PA 17745.

Almony, Robert A., Jr. (O. 14, 1945, Charleston, WV) Ast. Dir. Admin. Svcs., Ellis Lib., Univ. MO., 1979–; Ast. to Dir., Ref. Libn., Oberlin Coll., 1977–79; Resrch. Ast., Univ. of CA, Berkeley, Lib. Sch., 1976–77; VP, Genl. Mgr., CA Tchrs. Fncl. Svcs., 1969–76. **Educ.:** San Diego State Univ., 1968, AB (Soc. Sci.); Univ. of CA, Berkeley, 1976–77, MLS; Natl. Assn. of Security Dlrs., 1974, Regis. Prin. **Orgs.:** ALA: ACRL; RTSD; RASD. ASIS: Rep. to OH Conf. on Libs. and Info. Svcs. Intl. Assn. of Fncl. Plan. **Pubns.:** Cmplr., *Administrative and Professional Staff Handbook* (1979); "The Concept of Systematic Duplication: A Survey of the Literature", *Coll. Mgt.* (Sum. 1978); "Library Cooperation–Networking–As a Function of Library Size," *N. Amer. Netwk. Coll. Papers* (1979); "Ohio White House Conference Report", *ASIS Bltn.* (Ap. 1979); Jt. Auth., "Library Performance Measurement Through an Automated Circulation System: Attitude and System State Variables", *The Info. Age in Perspective* (1978). **Activities:** 1; 17, 28 **Addr.:** Ellis Library, University of Missouri, Columbia, MO 65201.

Almquist, Deborah T. (O. 11, 1946, Washington, DC) Med. Libn., St. Elizabeth's Hosp., 1974–; Libn., Goethe Inst., 1968–73. **Educ.:** Clark Univ., 1964–68, BA (Grmn.); Simmons Coll., 1973, MSLS; Med. Lib. Assoc. Cert., Level I Libn.; MA Cert., Tchr. of Sec. Sch. Grmn. and Sec. Sch. Libn. **Orgs.:** Boston Biomed. Lib. Cnsrtm.: Ch. (1979–80). New Eng. LA. Med. LA. **Pubns.:** *Isadora Duncan (1878–1927): A Selected Bibliography with Annotations* (D. 1972); Several bibliographies. **Activities:** 12; 15, 17, 39; 80 **Addr.:** Medical Library, St. Elizabeth's, 736 Cambridge St., Brighton, MA 02135.

Alpers, Helmut A. (Jl. 10, 1930, Cleveland, OH) VP, Gen. Bkbinding Co., 1975–; Prod. Admin., Netwkng., IBM, 1972–75, Mktg. Prog. Mgr., 1971–72, Admin. Ast. to Chmn. of Bd., 1969–71. **Educ.:** Case Inst. of Tech., 1948–52, BS (Chem. Engin.); Harvard Bus. Sch., 1952–54, MBA. **Orgs.:** NCLIS: Comsnr. Natl. White Hse. Conf.: Ch., OH Del. OH White Hse. Conf. for Libs.: Adv. Com. **Activities:** 4, 6; 23; 56, 75, 93 **Addr.:** General Bookbinding Co., 8844 Mayfield Rd., Chesterland, OH 44026.

Alperstein, David M. (Ja. 17, 1950, Bronx, NY) Libn., Queens Boro. Pub. Lib., 1978–; Libn., Plainview-Old Bethpage Pub. Lib., 1976–77; Libn., Queens Borough Public Library, 1974–76; Libn., Henry Waldinger Meml. Lib., 1974. **Educ.:** C.W. Post Coll., 1973, BS (Elem. Educ.); Long Island Univ., 1974, MLS; Long Island Univ., 1975–80, MPA. **Orgs.:** ALA: PLA Mem. Com.; JMRT/Const. and By-Laws Com. (1980–82). NY LA: Pub. Lib. Sect./Legis. Study Com.; RASD Ref. Com.; JMRT Mem-at-Lg. Cncl. on Abandoned Milit. Posts. **Pubns.:** "Under Three Flags: Fort Wadsworth", *The Per.* (1980); "Fort Hamilton," *The Per.* (1980); "The Fort at Willets Point: Fort Totten", *The Per.* (1977); Reviews. **Activities:** 9; 39, 41, 45; 69, 83, 93 **Addr.:** 72–35 150th St., Apt. #2G, Flushing, NY 11367.

Alsmeyer, Henry Louis, Jr. (S. 13, 1926, San Benito, TX) Dir., Libs., Hendrix Coll., 1976–; Assoc. Dir., Libs., TX A&M Univ. Libs., 1973–76, Asst. Dir., Tech. Srvs., 1970–73, Hum., Soc. Sci. Div. Libn., 1968–70, Asst. Ref. Libn., 1966–68, Info. Rep., 1962–66; Dir., PR, Maryville Coll., 1961–62; Managing Ed., *Kingsville Rec.*, Kingsville, TX, 1960–61; various positions in tchg., jnlsm., 1948–60. **Educ.:** TX A&M Coll., 1943 (Liberal Arts); Univ. of TX, 1944, 1947–48, BJ (Jnlsm.); Texas A and I Univ., 1956–58, MA (Eng.); LA State Univ., 1965–66, MS (LS); TX A&M Univ., 1967–73, PhD (Eng.); various crs. **Orgs.:** TX LA: Various coms. (1974–76). AR LA: Various coms. (1977–). ALA: Lib. Admin. Div., PR Sect., Frnds. of Libs. Com. (Ch., 1976–77). Various other orgs. TX Assn. of Coll. Tchrs.: TX A&M Univ. Chap. (Pres., 1975). West. Lit. Assn.: Exec. Com. (1971–74). Beta Phi Mu: Beta Eta TX Chap. (Pres., 1976). **Honors:** Sigma Delta Chi. **Pubns.:** "J. Frank Dobie," *Literary History of the American West* (forthcoming); "Cleo Dawson," "John Houghton Allen," "Religion," *Southwestern American Literature: A Bibliography* (1980); "Academic Library–Campus Community Communications," *Cath. Lib. World* (1979); "A Librarian Looks at Local History," *AR Libs.* (1978); "Introduction," *The Land-Grant Movement and the Development of Academic Libraries* (1977); various other articles. **Activities:** 1; 15, 17, 39 **Addr.:** 1901 Creekwood Dr., Conway, AR 72032.

Alsworth, Frances W. (Ja. 19, 1927, Jackson, MS) Assoc. Prof., Chmn. of Lib. Sci. Dept., Central State Univ., 1966–; Libn., Del City HS, 1964–66; Eng. Tchr., Midwest City Schs., 1960–64; Elem. Tchr., Camp Lejeune Schs., 1958–60. **Educ.:** Millsaps Coll., 1944–47, BA, (Eng.); Univ. of OK, 1964–66, MLS; Univ. of OK, 1977–80, EdD (Educ. Tech.). **Orgs.:** ALA. SWLA. OK LA. OK Untd. Tchg. Prof. Assn. Amer. Assn. of Univ. Prof. **Activities:** 11; 26, 31; 63 **Addr.:** Library Science Dept., Central State Univ., Edmond, OK 73034.

Altan, Susan Borah (Mr. 21, 1944, Greensboro, NC) Sr. Libn., Columbus Sch. for Girls, 1975–; Libn., Instr., OH State Univ., 1974–75; Libn., Du Pont Bus. and Tech. Lib., 1967–68. **Educ.:** Univ. of CA, Berkeley, 1961–65, BA (Fr.), 1965–66, MLS. **Orgs.:** OH LA. OH Educ. Lib. Media Assn. ALA. **Honors:** Beta Phi Mu. **Pubns.:** "A Broad Program of Bibliographic Instruction For A Small School," *NAIS Tchrs. Srvs.: Lib. Connection* (Spr. 1979). **Activities:** 10; 15, 21, 31; 55, 57, 92 **Addr.:** Beaton Library, Columbus School for Girls, 56 S. Columbia Ave., Columbus, OH 43209.

Alter, Forrest Henrici, Jr. (Jl. 15, 1915, Pittsburgh, PA) Head, Art, Music, Drama Dept., Flint Pub. Lib., 1958–; US Liaison Rep. and Libn., Nat. Inst. Adult Ed., London, 1955–57; Libn., Film Cncl. of Amer., 1953–55; 1st Ast., AV Dept., Detroit Pub. Lib., 1951–53; 1st Ast., Butzel Bnch., 1951; Ref. Ast., Msc. and Drama Dept., 1949–50; Ref. Ast., Soc. Sci. Dept., 1947–49. **Educ.:** Univ. Pittsburgh, 1932–36, AB (Educ.); Columbia Univ. 1946–47, BS (Libnshp.). **Orgs.:** SLA: Adv. Cncl. (Ch. 1971–72); Rep. to Msc. LA (1972–); Pic. Div. (Vice-Ch., 1960–62; Ch., 1962–64); MI Chap. (Pres., 1966–67, 1969–70; Pres.-elect and prog. chmn., 1968–69); By-Laws Com. (Ch., 1975–80); Intl. Fed. of LAs., RT for Msc. in Libs. ALA. Msc. LA: Various positions. Flint Cmnty. Msc. Assn.: Bd. Dir. (1959–68); Pres. (1963–64); Treas. 1964–65). Intl. Inst. of Flint: Bd. Dir. (1962–68). MI Adult Ed. Assn.: Bd. Dir. (1962–66), Secy. (1964–66). MI Cncl. for Arts: Msc. Adv. Panel (1963–79). **Honors:** Beta Phi Mu, Natl. Inst. of Adult Ed., England and Wales, Hon. Life Mem., 1957; Flint Area LA, Libn. of Yr., 1971, 1981; Intl. Inst. of Flint, Hon. Life Mem., 1978; Frnds. of Flint Pub. Lib., Hon. Mem., 1981. **Activities:** 9, 12; 16, 17, 39 **Addr.:** Flint Public Library, 1026 E. Kearsley, Flint, MI 48502.

Altgilbers, Cynthia J. (Jl. 8, 1950, Quincy, IL) Asst. Libn., Quincy Coll., 1979–; Interlib. Coop. Libn., Grt. River Lib. Syst., 1975–79. **Educ.:** Quincy Coll., 1968–73, BS (Econ.); Univ. of IL, 1974–75, MS (LS). **Orgs.:** ALA: LAMA; ACRL. IL LA: Pubcty. and PR Com. IL ACRL. **Pubns.:** "Serving the Exceptional Child–A System Response," *IL Libs.* (S. 1977); "School-Public Library Cooperation," *Reg. Rag* (My.–Je. 1980). **Activities:** 1; 15, 17, 22; 56, 59 **Addr.:** 2306 Ohio, Quincy, IL 62301.

Altman, Ellen (Ja. 1, 1936, Pittsburgh, PA) Dir., Grad. Lib. Sch., Univ. of AZ, 1979–; Assoc. Prof., IN Univ., 1976–79; Ast. Prof., Univ. of Toronto, 1974–76; Ast. Prof., Univ. of KY, 1972–73. **Educ.:** Duquesne, 1953–57, AB; Rutgers, 1964, MLS, 1967–70, PhD, (LS). **Orgs.:** ALA: LRRT/Strg. Com.; Com. on Resrch. (Ch.). Amer. Natl. Standards Com. on Lib. Stat. Z 39.7. Amer. Mgt. Assn. AAUP. **Honors:** Fulbright Hays Sr. Lectureship, 1979. **Pubns.:** *Local Public Library Administration* (1980); *Performance Measures for Public Libraries 1973, A data-gathering Manual for PMPR* (1976). **Addr.:** University of Arizona, College of Education, Graduate Library School, 1515 East First St., Tucson, AZ 85721.

Aluri, Rao (Jl. 10, 1944, Moparru, India) Asst. Prof., Div. of Lib. & Info. Mgt., Emory Univ., 1981–; Ref. Libn., Univ. of NE, 1973–77; Lectr., V.S.R. Coll., India, 1966–69. **Educ.:** Andhra Univ., India, 1959–63, BSc (Phys.); Univ. of West. ON, 1969–71, MSc (Physics), 1971–72, MLS; Ph.D, 1977–81. **Orgs.:** ALA: Ref. & Subscrpn. Bks. Review Com. ASIS. **Honors:** Cncl. on Lib. Resrcs., Flwshp., 1979. **Pubns.:** Jt. auth., *U.S. Government Scientific and Technical Periodicals* (1976); Jt. auth., *Subject Heading Patterns in OCLC Monographic Records* (1979); Jt. auth., "Staffing the Reference Desk: Professionals or Nonprofessionals?", *Jnl. of Acad. Libnshp.* (July 1977); Jt. auth., "Academic Reference Librarians–Endangered Species?", *Jnl. of Acad. Libnshp.* (May 1978); Jt. auth., "Periodicals loan policies in urban commuter colleges," *Serials Librarian* (Winter 1978); Various other articles. **Activities:** 1; 29, 39, 42; 64, 75, 91 **Addr.:** 3779 Yucatan Ct., Clarkston, GA 30021.

Alvarez, Octavio (Ap. 10, 1927, Lima, Peru) Branch Libn., Soc. Secur. Admin., 1980–; Chief Libn., Natl. Inst. on Aging, 1977–80; Libn., Natl. Inst. of Mental Hlth., 1971–77; Ref. Libn., Armed Forces Rad. Bio. Resrch. Inst., 1967–71; Ref. Libn., Lib. of Congs., 1963–67. **Educ.:** Goddard Coll., 1967–71, BA (Soc. Sci.); Univ. of MD, 1974–75, MLS; Univ. of MD, 1978– (Grntlgy.). Republican Hisp. Asm. Image. **Pubns.:** Jt. auth., *A Report on Library Education in the United States*, student contrib. series, no. 7, MD Univ. (1975). **Activities:** 4, 12; 15, 17, 24; 75, 92 **Addr.:** 20801 Apollo Ln., Gaithersburg, MD 20760.

Alvey, Celine (F. 16, 1940, Washington, DC) Head, Info. Srvs. Brnch., U.S. Nvl. Med. Resrch. Inst., 1979–, Admin. Libn., 1978–79; Assoc. Libn., Natl. Acad. of Scis., 1975–78, Ast. Libn., 1972–75; Adj. Inst., Univ. of MD Coll. of Lib. Srv., 1977. **Educ.:** Mount St. Mary's Coll., 1958–62, BA (Eng.); Univ. of South. CA, Wash. Pub. Affairs Cntr., 1980–, DPA; Cath. Univ. of Amer., 1970–72, MSLS; Johns Hopkins Univ., 1965–68, MA (Eng.); Dominican Coll., 1962–63, MA (Eng.). **Orgs.:** Assoc. Info. Mgrs. ASIS. SLA. **Honors:** U.S. Naval Med. Resrch. Inst., Commanding Officer's Awd., 1979. **Pubns.:** "Guide to Dialog Databases–A Review", *ONLINE* (Jl. 1978). **Activities:** 4, 12; 17; 56, 59, 80 **Addr.:** Head, Information Services Branch, Naval Medical Research Institute, Bethesda, MD 20014.

Alvin, Glenda Marie (D. 31, 1953, Landstuhl, Germany) Fine Arts Ref. Libn., Tampa Pub. Lib., 1976–; Chld. Libn., 1976–77. **Educ.:** Kent State Univ., 1971–74, BA, (Hist.); Atlanta Univ., 1975–76, MSLS. **Orgs.:** ALA: Black Caucus (1978–). Neighborhood Dir., Sacajawea Neigh. of Sun Coast Girl Scout Cncl. NAACP: Tampa Chap., Exec. Bd. (1976–78). Tampa Chap., Natl. Cncl. of Negro Women: Exec. Com. (1978–), Urban Sect. Pres. (1979). FL Endow. for the Hum: Proj. Dir. (1981). **Honors:** Cncl. on Interracial Bks., Mss. for Chld., Recog. Awd., 1978. **Pubns.:** *A Thesaurus of Planning Terms from the Atlanta Regional Commission Library* (1978); *A Bibliography on Architecture for Public Libraries* (1978). **Activities:** 9; 21, 39; 55, 67 **Addr.:** 806 1/2 E. Ida St., Tampa, FL 33603.

Alzofon, Sammy Rebecca (O. 24, 1942, Los Angeles, CA) Ref. Libn., OH State Univ. Libs., 1980–; Owner, Alzofon Bks., 1973–80; Libn., Ctr. for Human Resrc. Resrch., OH State Univ., 1973–77, Latin Amer. Biblgphr., Lib., 1971–73; Ref. Libn., Latin Amer. Col., Univ. of FL Libs., 1969–71. **Educ.:** Merritt Coll. 1966, AA (Span.); Univ. of CA, Berkeley, 1964–68, AB (Span.), 1968–69, MLS; Arch.-Lib. Inst. on Hist. Resrch. Mtrls., 1973. **Orgs.:** SALALM: Subcom. on Lib., Bkdlr., Publshr. Rel. (Ch., 1978–); Nsltr. Ed. (1981–). ALA. OH LA. Acad. Lib. Assn. of OH. Latin Amer. Std. Assn. Conf. on Latin Amer. Hist. AAUP. **Honors:** Phi Beta Kappa. **Pubns.:** *Working Papers of SALALM: List and Index* (1971). **Activities:** 1; 15, 29, 39; 54, 92 **Addr.:** 2662 Glenmawr Ave., Columbus, OH 43202.

Aman, Mohammed M. (Ja. 3, 1940, Alexandria, Egypt) Dean, Sch. of LS, Univ. WI, Milwaukee, 1979–; Dean, Grad. Lib. Sch., Long Island Univ., C.W. Post Ctr., 1976–79; Dir., Div. of Lib. and Info. Sci., St. John's Univ., 1973–76, Ast. Assoc. and Prof. of Lib. and Info. Sci., 1969–76; Ast. Prof., Grad. Sch. of Lib. and Info. Sci., Pratt Inst., 1968–69; Ref. and Gvt. Docum. Libn., Duquesne Univ. Lib., 1966–68; Head, Info. Ctr., Arab Leag., 1964–65; Ref. Libn., Egyptian Natl. Lib., 1961–63; Various consult. **Educ.:** Cairo Univ., Egypt, 1957–61, BLS Columbia Univ., 1963–65, MSLS; Univ. Pittsburgh, Grad. Sch. of Lib. and Info. Sci., 1965–69, PhD. **Orgs.:** ALA: IRRT (Ch., 1976–77); IRC (1976–78); ACRL Pubns. in Libnshp., Ed. Bd. (1976–80); Lib. Educ. Div./Grants Com. (1976–78). ASIS: IRC (1974–76). SLA. Drug Info. Assn. Other orgs. Egyptian-Amer. Schol. Assn.: Visit. Schol. Prog. Mid. E Stds. Assn.: Fellow. **Honors:** Beta Phi Mu. **Pubns.:** *Cataloging and Classification of Non-Western Library Materials: Issues, Trends and Practices* (1980); *Arab Serials and Periodicals: A Subject Bibliography* (1979); *Librarianship and the Third World* (1976); "Library Developments in the Middle East," *Librarianship in Five Continents* (1979); "Libraries in the Arab World," *Handbook of Comparative Librarianship* (1979); Numerous other pubns. **Activities:** 1, 12; 17, 20, 24; 54, 56, 75 **Addr.:** School of Library and Info. Science, University of Wisconsin, Milwaukee, P.O. Box 413, Milwaukee, WI 53201.

Amaral, Anne (My. 24, 1980, Columbus, OH) Life and Hlth. Sci. Libn., Univ. of NV, 1978–; Asst. Ref. Libn., 1973–77,

PROFESSIONAL ACTIVITIES: Institutions: 1. Acad. lib.; 2. Arch.; 3. Assn.; 4. Fed./Gvt. lib.; 5. Inst. lib.; 6. Mfr./Suppl.; 7. Milit. lib.; 8. Musm.; 9. Pub. lib.; 10. Sch. lib.; 11. Sch. of lib. sci.; 12. Spec. lib.; 13. State lib.; 14. (other). **Functions/Activities:** 15. Acq./Col. dev.; 16. Adult srvs.; 17. Admin.; 18. Apprais.; 19. Archit./Bldgs.; 20. Cat./Class.; 21. Chld. srvs.; 22. Circ.; 23. Cons./Pres.; 24. Consult.; 25. Cont. ed.; 26. Educ. lib. sci.; 27. Ext. srvs.; 28. Fund/Grants; 29. Gvt. pubs.; 30. Indx./Abs.; 31. Instr. lib. use; 32. Media srvs.; 33. Micro.; 34. Netwks./Coop.; 35. Persnl.; 36. PR; 37. Publshg.; 38. Recs. mgt.; 39. Ref. srvs.; 40. Repro.; 41. Resrch.; 42. Review.; 43. Secur.; 44. Serials; 45. Spec. col.; 46. Tech. srvs.; 47. Trustees/Bds.; 48. YA srvs.; 49. (other).

Asst. Cat. Libn., 1972–73; Pub. Srvcs. Libn., NV State Lib., 1967–72. **Educ.:** Univ. of CA, Berkeley, 1947–52, BA, 1962–63, MLS. **Orgs.:** ALA. NV LA. SLA. **Activities:** 1; 15, 17, 39; 58, 65, 68 **Addr.:** P.O. Box 8159, Reno, NV 89507.

Ambrose, Ethel N. (Jl. 3, 1929, Moravian Falls, NC) Coord. of Chld. Srvs., Stockton-San Joaquin Cnty. Pub. Lib., 1972–; Coord. of Chld. Srvs., Sacramento Pub. Lib., 1970–72, Chld. Libn., 1968–70; Instr. in Eng. as Sec. Lang., Rpblc. of Niger, 1965–68; Dist. Sch. Libn., Harlan Cnty. Schs., 1960–65. **Educ.:** Berea Coll., 1947–48; Univ. of AZ, 1955–57; Univ. of KY, 1959–60, AB (Hist.); George Peabody Coll. for Tchrs., MLS. **Orgs.:** ALA: ALSC/Com. on Liaison With Natl. Orgs. Srvng. Child (Ch., 1976–79); ALSC/Newbery-Caldecott Com. (1978); PLA/Srvs. to Chld. Com. (1979–). CA LA: Chld. Srvs. Chap. Bd. (1981–); Chld. Srvs. Chap. Com. on Stds. Rev. (1975–79). KY LA. AAUW. Natl. Assn. for Educ. of Young Chld. Intnl. Readng. Assn. **Honors:** Phi Alpha Theta, 1960. **Pubns.:** "Working With Organizations That Serve the Child", *Show-Me Libs.* (Oct., Nov. 1979). **Activities:** 9; 17, 21, 36 **Addr.:** 8419 Burns Pl., Stockton, CA 95209.

Amdursky, Saul J. (Ag. 11, 1945, Rochester, NY) Syst. Admin., Racine Cnty. Lib. Syst., 1979–; Dir., Albion Pub. Lib., 1975–79; Interim Admin., Woodlands Lib. Coop., 1978–79; Supvsng. Libn., Centrl. Lib. of Prince Wm. Cnty. Pub. Lib. Syst., 1973–75. **Educ.:** St. John Fisher Coll., 1966–69, BA, (Hist.); Univ. of KY, 1970–71, MSLS; Mgt. Sem., VA Poly Tech Inst., 1974. **Orgs.:** ALA. WI LA. Willard Lib. Syst.: Pres. (1977–78). **Pubns.:** *Virginia Librarian* (Sum. 1972); *Illinois Libraries* (S. 1975); Reviews. **Activities:** 9, 14-Syst.; 34 **Addr.:** 1445 Park Ave., Racine, WI 53403.

Amelang, Jean Swift (Ap. 9, 1951, Louisville, KY) Readrs. Srvs. Libn., Elbert Ivey Meml. Lib., 1977–; Ast. Ref. Libn., Muncie Pub. Lib., 1975–77. **Educ.:** Univ. of KY, 1969–73, BA (Eng.); IN Univ., 1973–74, MLS. **Orgs.:** ALA. NC LA: IFC Secy. (1978–80). Altrusa Clb. of Hickory, NC. NOW. **Pubns.:** Co-Auth., Elbert Ivey Memorial Library Community Analysis (1978). **Activities:** 9; 16, 39, 48; 67, 69, 74 **Addr.:** Elbert Ivey Memorial Library, 420 Third Ave., N.W., Hickory, NC 28601.

Amend, John David (Ag. 9, 1928, Alva, OK) Lib. Consult., CA State Lib., 1965–; Dist. Libn., 11th Nvl. Dist., 1963–64; Supvsg. Libn., San Diego Pub. Lib., 1954–63; Tchr. Libn., White Pine Cnty. HS, 1950–52. **Educ.:** KS State Coll., 1946–50, BS (Fr., Eng.); Univ. of CA, Berkeley, 1952–54, BLS (Chld. Libnshp.). **Orgs.:** ALA. SLA. CA LA. **Honors:** Beta Phi Mu; Cncl. on Lib. Resrcs., Flwshp., (1974). **Pubns.:** *Library Service for the County of Madera, California* (1965). **Activities:** 9, 13; 24 **Addr.:** 74 Macondray Ln., San Francisco, CA 94133.

Ames, Gregory P. (My. 24, 1951, Warsaw, NY) Docum., Microtext Libn., Univ. of Rochester, 1979–; Asst. Ref. Libn., SUNY, Brockport, 1979; Lib. Asst., Univ. of Rochester, 1976–78. **Educ.:** SUNY, Brockport, 1969–73, BA (Fr., Grmn.); SUNY, Geneseo, 1975–76, MLS. **Orgs.:** West. NY, ON Acad. Resrch. LA: Secy. (1980–81). Litcy. Voluns. of Rochester NY. Lexington Grp. in Transp. Hist. **Pubns.:** *Pilot Library Workshop on Term Paper Writing: Proposal and Final Report* ERIC (1980); *Recreational Reuse of Abandoned Railroad Rights of Way: a Bibliography and Technical Resource Guide for Planners* Cncl. of Plng. Libns. Bibl. (N. 1981); "Federal Documents Sources for International & Foreign Lang. Studies," *DTTP* (My. 1980); "Remembering a Congressman...," *Congressional Rec.* (Ap. 16, 1980); "Special Olympics: A General Bibliography," *Being a Coach for SO* (1981). **Activities:** 1; 29, 33, 39; 78, 91, 92 **Addr.:** Rush Rhees Library, Documents Section, University of Rochester, Rochester, NY 14627.

Amestoy, Helen Hull Monnette (Ag. 26, 1920, Los Angeles, CA) Sr. Libn., Angelo M. Iacoboni Lib. Los Angeles Cnty. Pub. Lib., 1968–; Libn., Lynwood Lib., LACPL, 1967–68; Libn., Carson Lib., LACPL, 1965–67. **Educ.:** Bryn Mawr Coll., 1937–40; UCLA, 1963, BA (Art Hist.); UCLA, 1963–64, MSL. **Orgs.:** ALA. CA LA: Cncl. (1977–79); Libns. and Publshrs. Com. (1978–); IFC (1976–78); Socty. of Libns. Bd. (1977–79), Pres. (1982). South. CA Cncl. on Lit. for Chld. and Young People. Natl. Charity Leag. Lakewood Coord. Cncl.: Pres. (1970–72). Lakewood PanAmer. Assn.: Exec. Bd. (1974–). Lakewood Cham. of Cmrc., Women's Div. Other orgs. **Honors:** Beta Phi Mu; LA County, Libn. of the Year Awd., 1980. **Activities:** 9; 16, 36, 40; 55, 74, 92 **Addr.:** 3330 Club Dr., Los Angeles, CA 90064.

Amey, Lorne James (Ag. 2, 1940, Montreal, PQ) Assoc. Prof., Sch. of LS, Dalhousie Univ., 1976–; Assoc. Instr., Univ. of Toronto, 1974–75; Prof., Ahmadu Bello Univ., Nigeria, 1972–73; Prof., Univ. of Ibadan, Nigeria, 1970–72; Ref. and Cat. Libn., Amer. Musm. of Nat. Hist., 1969–70. **Educ.:** Acadia Univ., 1959–62, BSc (Biol.), BEd.; Univ. of NB, 1964–65, MEd; Columbia Univ., 1968–69, MSLS. **Orgs.:** ALA: Taskfrc. on Crisis Info. for YA (1976–79); YASD/Resrch. Com. (1979–); Best Bks. Com. (1980–). CAN LA. NS LA. NS Sch. Lib. Assn. **Pubns.:** Ed., *The Canadian School -Housed Public Library* (1979); *Visual Literacy: Implications for the Production of Children's TV Programs* (1976); "Com bination School and Public Libraries..." and "The Combination School and Public Library...", *Can. Lib. Jnl.* (June 1976). **Activities:** 11; 15, 21, 26 **Addr.:** School of Library Service, Dalhousie University, Halifax, NS B3H 4H8, Canada.

Amick, Charles W. (O. 31, 1929, LaCrosse, KS) Head, Chld. Dept., Yonkers Pub. Lib., 1977–, Circ. Dept., Branch Lib., 1976–77, Br. Libn., 1976, Head, Ref. Dept., 1968–76; Staff, Queens Boro. Pub. Lib., 1964–68. **Educ.:** Friends Jr. Coll., 1947–49; Friends Univ., 1949–51, BA (Hist.); Univ. of Wichita, 1955–61, MA (Hist.); Univ. of Denver, 1963–64, MA (Libnshp.). **Orgs.:** ALA. Yonkers Hist. Socty.: Libn. (1976–78). Natl. Educ. Assn. **Activities:** 9; 21 **Addr.:** 139–55 35th Ave., Apt. 3A, Flushing, NY 11354.

Amos, Mary Lucille (Jl. 22, 1923, Ft. Worth, TX) Assoc. Prof., Bowling Green State Univ., 1969–; Spec. in Chld. Lit. and TV Tchr., Toledo Bd. of Educ., 1961–68; Tchr., Maumee Bd. of Educ., 1957–61; Head, Chld. Dept., Lucas Cnty. Lib., 1950–57; Lect., Adrian Coll., 1966–68; Lect., Univ. of Toledo, 1959–69; Pers. Libn., Univ. of Toledo, 1946–49. **Educ.:** N. TX State Univ., 1941–45, BS (LS); Univ. of MI, 1968–69, MALS. **Orgs.:** ALA. AASL. OH Educ. Lib. and Media Assn.: Bd. of Dirs. (1979–81); Com. on Srvy. Class. and Cat. of OH Sch. Libs. and Media Ctrs., Ch. (1979–); Task Frc. on Lib. Coop. (1979–80); Nom. Com. (1975–76; Ch., 1976–77). Other coms. OH LA: Chld. Div., Exec. Bd. (1976–77); Mem. Com. (1975–76); Persnl. Functions, Educ. and Staff Dev. Div., Nom. Com. Ch. (1973–74); Action Cncl. (1973–74); Coord. (1972–73); Lib. Educ. Task Frc. (1973–74); Other coms. Pi Lambda Theta; Delta Kappa Gamma: Gamma Delta Chap., Pres. (1969–72); Kappa Delta Pi; Alpha Lambda Delta. **Honors:** Kappa Delta Pi, Compatriot in Educ., 1976; Bowling Green State Univ., Disting. Tchg. Awd., 1973. **Pubns.:** "Classification and Cataloging Practices in Ohio Schools," *OH Media Spectrum* (Mr. 1981); Co-Auth. "Ohio Children's Library Bill of Rights", *Lib. Jnl.* (Nov. 15, 1972) and *OH Assn. of Sch. Libns. Bltn.* (Jan. 1973); Various TV scripts (1968–69). **Activities:** 9, 10; 20, 21, 26; 63 **Addr.:** Dept. of Library and Educational Media, Bowling Green State University, Bowling Green, OH 43402.

Amport, Fredrick R., Jr. (Ap. 29, 1930, Detroit, MI) Dir., Info. Mgt. Consult. Srvcs., A. T. Kearney, Inc., 1976–; Mgr. Admin., Word Prcs. Consult., Advnc. Comp. Techq., 1972–76; N.E. Reg. Mgr., Clasco Syst., Inc., 1970–72; VP, Oyer Info. Sr., 1968–70; Reg. Mgr., DPF, Inc., 1967–68; Area Prod. Mgr., Control Data Corp., 1965–67; Mgr., Info. Plan. and Syst., Union Carbide Corp., 1953–65. **Educ.:** Univ. of Detroit, 1948–53, BChem.; Case West. Rsv. Univ., 1956–59, MBA, Mktg.; Sales Anal. Inst. Sem., 1965. **Orgs.:** OH Word Prcs. Socty.: Prog. VP (1977–78). Assn. of Recs. Mgrs. and Admin. Natl. Micro. Assn.: Ohio Chapter, Exec. Bd. (1977–80). Intnl. Word Prcs. Socty. Cleveland Rotary Clb.: Intnl. Srvc. Prog. Amer. Mgt. Assn. **Honors:** Beta Gamma Sigma, 1960. **Pubns.:** "Word Processing–How to Improve Productivity and Reduce Costs by Using It," *Handbook of Business Problem Solving* (1980); "Organization Change Required for Improved Effectiveness", *Can. Office* (D. 1979); "Is Word Processing for You?", *CAN Mag.* (Ag. 1977); "Is Word Processing for You?–Small Office", *Amer. Sch. and Univ. Mag.* (D. 1979); "Building an Information Machine", *Word Prcs. Rpt.* (D. 1, 1975); "Productivity and the Automated Office–Circa 80's", *Can Office Mag.* (D. 1979); Various articles. **Activities:** 5; 24, 33, 38; 56, 75 **Addr.:** A. T. Kearney, Inc., 29425 Chagrin Blvd., Pepper Pike, OH 44122.

Amrhein, John K. (S. 20, 1938, Pittsburgh, PA) Libn., Kutztown State Coll., 1971–; Circ. Libn., Kent State Univ., 1967–71; Ast. Libn., PA State Univ., 1965–66, Pers. Libn., 1963–65. **Educ.:** Duquesne Univ., 1961, BA (Classics); Univ. of Pittsburgh, 1963, MLS; PA State Univ., 1967, MA (Phil.). **Orgs.:** Cncl. of PA State Coll. and Univ. Lib. Dirs.: Secy. (1979–80). PA LA: Coll. and Resrch. Div., Treas. (1979). **Pubns.:** Philosophy Section in *Magazines for Libraries,* 2nd and 3rd eds. (1972, 1978); Various reviews. **Activities:** 1; 15, 17, 31 **Addr.:** Kutztown State College, Kutztown, PA 19530.

Amron, Irving (D. 4, 1917, New York, NY) Dir. of Info. Srvs., Thomas Natl., Inc., 1980–; Ed. of Info. Srvs., Amer. Socty. of Cvl. Engin., 1968–80; Ed., Engin. Indx., 1966–68; Engin., Harold S. Seldin, 1964–66; Engin., Blauvelt Engin., 1962–64; Techn. Transl., USSR Cham. of Cmrc., 1952–62. **Educ.:** Moscow Auto. and Hwy. Inst., 1936–41, MS, (Engin.); Amer. Arbit. Assn. Panel of Arbits., 1976. **Orgs.:** ASIS: Metro. Sect., Memb. Chmn.; Assoc. Info. Mgrs. **Honors:** Amer. Socty. of Cvl. Engin., Srv. Awd., 1978. **Pubns.:** "Data Mgt. for Info", *Comps. in Cvl. Engin.* (1981); "Use of Computers for Information Processing at ASCE", *Comp. in Cvl. Engin.* (1978); "History of ASCE Indexing and Abstracting", *Scientific Info. Transfer: The Editor's Role* (1978). **Activities:** 12; 17, 30, 37; 56, 64, 75 **Addr.:** 1035 Nicholas Ave., Union, NJ 07083.

Amster, Linda Meyerson (My. 21, 1938, New York, NY) News Resrch. Mgr., The New York Times, 1975–, Supvsr., Newsroom Resrch. Libn., 1971–75, News Resrch. Libn., 1968–71; Resrch., The Detroit News, 1965–67. **Educ.:** Univ. of MI, 1956–60, BA (Eng.); Columbia Univ., 1967–68, MLS. **Orgs.:** SLA. **Pubns.:** *The Watergate Hearings* (1973); *The White House Transcripts* (1974); *The End of a Presidency* (1974); *The Pentagon Papers* (1971); *Who Said What, 1971* (1972); Various articles. **Activities:** 12; 17, 39, 41 **Addr.:** The New York Times, 229 W. 43d St., New York, NY 10036.

Anable, Richard (Jl. 14, 1944, Monson, MA) Pres., Richard Anable and Assoc., Inc., 1980–; Assoc. Dir. of Libs., SUNY, Binghamton, 1978–80; Info. Syst. Spec., Cncl. on Lib. Resrcs., 1974–78; Syst. Libn., York Univ., 1969–74; Syst. Anal., NY State Educ. Dept., 1966–69. **Educ.:** Univ. MA, 1962–66, BA (Gvt.); SUNY, Albany, 1967–69, MLS. **Orgs.:** ALA. **Pubns.:** "CONSER: Bibliographic Considerations", *LRTS* (Fall 1975); "CONSER: An Update", *JOLA* (Mar. 1975). **Activities:** 1; 16, 24, 34; 56 **Addr.:** Richard Anable and Associates, Inc., 633 Harvard St., Vestal, NY 13850.

Anand, Mrs. Havelin (D. 14, 1948, Bombay, India) Systs. Libn., Natl. Lib. of Can., 1979–, Cat. in Pubn. Prog. Mgr. 1977–79, Systs. Libn., 1976–77. **Educ.:** Univ. of MB, 1967–70, BA (Psy.); Univ. of Ottawa, 1970–71, BLS; Univ. of West. ON, 1977–81, MLS. **Orgs.:** Can. LA. Can. Assn. of Lib. and Info. Sci. Can. Assn. Info. Sci. **Pubns.:** "Canadian Cataloguing in Publication Program," *ON Lib. Review* (Mr. 1979); "Bibliographic Sharing through the Canadian Cataloguing in Publication Program," *Procs. of the 7th Anl. Can. Conf. on Info. Sci.* (1979); "Telefacsimile Transmission Of Information In Libraries," *Procs. of the 8th Anl. Can. Conf. on Info. Sci.* (1980). **Activities:** 4, 12; 17, 36, 46; 56, 75, 93 **Addr.:** 1980 Rideau River Dr., Ottawa, ON K1S 1T9 Canada.

Anastasion, Joan D. (Mr. 24, 1929, Vancouver, BC) Coord. Lib. Tech. Prog., Vancouver Comnty. Coll., 1974–; Libn., Agr. Can., 1973–74; Rev., Univ. BC, 1971–73; Instr., Citrus Jr. Coll., 1961–62. **Educ.:** Univ. BC, 1947–52, BA, 1953–55, MA (Bot.), 1969–76, BLS, MLS. **Orgs.:** CAN LA: CACUL; SLA. Cncl. on Lib. Media Tech. Asst.: Ed. Com. BC Hlth. Libs.; Other orgs. **Pubns.:** "Swedish Library Training", *Spec. Libs.* (F. 1978); "Swedish Public Libraries Do Not Serve Isolated Areas: They Serve Isolated People", *BCLA Rep.* (Mr., Ap. 1978); "The Library Technician", *BC Lib. Qtly.* (Sum. 1974). **Activities:** 1; 26 **Addr.:** VCC Langara, 100 West 49th, Vancouver, BC V5Y 2Z6, Canada.

Anders, Roger M. (Ag. 17, 1949, Parkersburg, WV) Archvst., U.S. Dept. of Energy, 1977–; Archvst., U.S. Energy Resrch. and Dev. Admin., 1975–77; Resrch. Ast., U.S. Atomic Energy Comsn., 1972–75. **Educ.:** Univ. of GA, 1969–71, AB (Fr. Hist.); Duke Univ., 1971–72, MA (Hist.). **Orgs.:** SAA. Socty. for Hist. in Fed. Gvt.: Rec. Secy. (1979–80); Dir. Com. (Ch., 1979–81). Org. of Amer. Histns. Amer. Military Inst. **Honors:** Phi Beta Kappa, 1971. **Pubns.:** "The Rosenberg Case Revisited: The Greenglass Testimony and the Protection of Atomic Secrets", *Amer. Hist. Review* (Ap. 1978). **Activities:** 2; 17, 18, 39; 84, 86 **Addr.:** Historian's Office, Rm. 7-G-033, Forrestal Bldg., Department of Energy, Washington, DC 20585.

Andersen, Althea F. (Je. 21, 1931, Gilroy, CA) Libn. III, Youth, AV Srvs., Clearwater Pub. Lib., 1978–, Actg. Dir., 1976–78, Chld. Libn., 1971–76. **Educ.:** Simmons Coll., 1951–53, BLS; Nova Univ., 1978–80, MS (Pub. Admin.). **Orgs.:** FL LA: Chld. and Sch. Caucus (Ch., 1978–). Frnds. of Pinellas Cnty. Libs.: Strg. Com. (1979–). ALA. AAUW: Histn. (1978–). **Pubns.:** Reviews, *Clearwater Sun* (1979–). **Activities:** 9; 17, 21, 34; 67, 74 **Addr.:** Clearwater Public Library, 100 N. Osceola Ave., Clearwater, FL 33515.

Anderson, Albert G., Jr. (Jl. 19, 1929, Fargo, ND) Dir., Libs., Clark Univ. and Worcester Polytech. Inst., 1978–, Head Libn., Assoc. Prof., 1963–78; Tech. Info. Coord., Bendix Corp., 1960–63; Circ. Libn., Univ. of Pittsburgh, 1958–60. **Educ.:** ND State Univ., 1948–52, BS; Univ. of WY, 1952–53, MA; Univ. of IL, 1955–56, MSLS. **Orgs.:** ALA: Various coms. SLA: Various coms. **Honors:** Cncl. on Lib. Resrcs., Fellow, 1972. **Pubns.:** *John Woodman Higgins Armory Catalogue* (1969); *Study to Determine the Tangible and Intangible Benefits To Be Gained By Institutions In Cooperating Library Organizations* (1973). **Activities:** 1; 17, 24; 64, 91 **Addr.:** Gordon Library, Worcester Polytechnic Institute, Worcester, MA 01609.

Anderson, Barbara Elaine (S. 10, 1934, Los Angeles, CA) Mgr., Pubns., DIALOG Info. Srvs. Inc., 1978–; Instr., Sch. of Lib. and Info. Std., Univ. of CA, Berkeley, 1976–78; Head, Educ. and Psy. Lib., San Francisco State Univ., 1959–75; Lib. Adv., Univ. of Isfahan, Iran, 1971–73; Libn. II, Free Lib. of Philadelphia, 1957–59. **Educ.:** Univ. of CA, Los Angeles, 1952–56, BA (Prelibnshp.); Univ. of CA, Berkeley, 1956–57, MLS, 1975–77, Post-MLS Cert., 1977 (Lib. Autom.), work toward PhD (Libnshp.) **Orgs.:** ALA. SLA. ASIS. CA LA. **Honors:** Fulbright Lectshp., Dir. of Libs., Pahlavi Univ., Iran, 1966–67. **Pubns.:** *Urban Studies; A Study of Bibliographic Access and Control* (1977); "Ordeal at San Francisco State College," *Lib. Jnl.* (Ap. 1, 1970); jt. auth., *Observations on the Use of the Lockheed DIALOG System for Laboratory Work in a Fall 1975 Course on Computer-Based Reference Service at the UCB School of Librarianship* (1976); jt. auth., *Selected Search Subroutines for Searching the ERIC Data Base With Lockheed DIALOG Information Retrieval Service* (1977); jt. auth., *Standards for Curriculum Material Libraries in California* (1966); various mono. **Activities:**

Special Subjects/Services: 50. Adult educ.; 51. Advert./Mktg.; 52. Aerosp.; 53. Agric.; 54. Area std.; 55. Arts/Hum.; 56. Autom.; 57. Bibl./Prtg.; 58. Bio. sci.; 59. Bus./Fin.; 60. Chem.; 61. Copyrt.; 62. Documtn.; 63. Educ.; 64. Engin.; 65. Env.; 66. Eth. grps.; 67. Film; 68. Food/Nutr.; 69. Geneal.; 70. Geo.; 71. Geol.; 72. Handcpd.; 73. Hist.; 74. Int. frdm.; 75. Info. sci.; 76. Insr.; 77. Law; 78. Legis.; 79. Math./Comp. sci.; 80. Med.; 81. Metals; 82. Nat. resrcs.; 83. Newsp.; 84. Nuc. sci.; 85. Oral hist.; 86. Petr./Energy; 87. Pharm.; 88. Phys./Astr./Math.; 89. Readg.; 90. Relig.; 91. Sci./Tech.; 92. Soc. sci.; 93. Telecom.; 94. Transp.; 95. (other).

12; 26, 30, 39; 61, 62, 75 **Addr.:** 3460 Park Blvd. #2B, Palo Alto, CA 94306.

Anderson, Barbara Louise (Ja. 5, 1933, San Diego, CA) Lib. Dir., Cnty. Libn., San Bernardino Cnty. Lib., 1974–; Head, Readrs. Srvs., Riverside City and Cnty. Pub. Lib., 1972–74; Proj. Coord., Serra Reg. Lib. Syst., 1969–71; Army Libn., U.S. Army, Europe, 1964–69. **Educ.:** San Diego State Coll., 1950–55, BS (Engl., Bus., Geog.); KS State Tchrs. Coll., 1955–56, MS (LS). **Orgs.:** CA LA. CA Socty. of Libns.: Pres. (1974). ALA: Chap. Rel. Com. (Ch., 1978). Natl. Cncl. of Negro Women. AAUW: Riverside Branch, Pres. (1976). **Honors:** Riverside City Coll. Black Students, Nommo–community leadership, 1974; Univ. CA, Riverside Black Students, Comnty. Awd., 1975. **Activities:** 9; 17, 19, 27 **Addr.:** 2974 Redwood Dr., Riverside, CA 92501.

Anderson, Beryl Lapham (Ap. 15, 1925, Canso, NS) Chief, Lib. Doc. Ctr., Natl. Lib. of CAN, 1973–; Assoc. Prof., Lectr., Libn., McGill Univ., 1956–71; Lectr., Dalhousie Univ., 1950–55; Tchr., Various schs., NS and PQ, 1946–50. **Educ.:** Dalhousie Univ., 1943–46, BA, (Classics), 1948–49, MA, (Gk. Hist.); McGill Univ., 1955–56, BLS; Walden Univ., 1978–80, PhD, (Spec. Libs. Ref. Svc.). **Orgs.:** Can. LA: Cat. Sect. (Ch., 1963–64); Com. Assoc. Spec. Libs. and Info. Svcs. (Pres., 1970–71); Stats. Com. (Ch., 1977–78); other coms. SLA: Resrch. Com. (1973–78); Dir. (1978–81); Montreal Chap., Archvst. (1959–66); Consult. Ofcr. (1967–71). Atlantic Prov. LA. ASIS. Other orgs. Archlg. Inst. of Amer. **Honors:** CASLIS, Awd. for Spec. Libnshp., 1980. (CAN LA) Howard V. Phalin World Bk. Flwshp., 1971. Gvr.-Gen. Gold Medal, Dalhasie Univ., 1946. **Pubns.:** *Special Libraries in Canada; a Statistical Analysis and Commentary* (1969); Ed., *Union List of Serials in Libraries of Montreal and Vicinity* (1965); "Special Libraries in Canada, 1976–78", *CAN Lib. Handbk. 1979–80* (1979); "Special Libraries in Canada", *CAN Libs. in Changing Env.* (1977); Other books; "Special Library Statistics", *Feliciter* (S. 1977); Other articles. **Activities:** 4, 11; 17, 26, 39; 62, 75 **Addr.:** Library Documentation Centre, National Library of Canada, 395 Wellington St., Ottawa, ON K1A 0N4 Canada.

Anderson, Carol Lee (N. 21, 1951, St. Louis, MO) Access Srvs. Libn., Univ. OK, 1978–, Interim Syst. Anal., 1978, Asst. Acq. Libn., 1976–78. **Educ.:** SUNY, Geneseo, 1970–74, BA (Hist.); Univ. MO, 1974–75, MA (Lib. Sci.). **Orgs.:** ALA: JMRT Suite Com. (1977); JMRT/LITA Liaison (1979–80). OK LA: Audit. Com. (1977–78; Ch., 1979–80); Un. List of Serials Com. (1977–78); Autom. RT Nom. Com. (Ch., 1978); Coll. and Univ. Div. (Secy., Treas., 1980–81). **Activities:** 1; 17, 22, 34; 56 **Addr.:** University of Oklahoma Libraries, 41 West Brooks, Room 124, Norman, OK 73019.

Anderson, Carolyn McCown (Ja. 23, 1947, Winona, MN) Hlth. Sci. Libn., Mennonite Hosp. and Sch. of Nursing, 1979–; Spec. Srvs. Ast., Corn Belt Lib. Syst., 1977–78; Mid. Sch. Libn., New Richmond Pub. Schs., 1973–76. **Educ.:** St. Olaf Coll., 1965–69, BA (Eng.); Univ. of WI, Eau Claire, 1972–73; Univ. of MN, 1976–77, MA (LS). **Orgs.:** Med. Lib. Assn.: Midwest Reg. Grp. IL Hlth. Sci. Libns. Ctrl. IL Hlth. Sci. Libs. Cnsrtm.: Coord. (1980–). McLean Cnty. Lib. Assn.: Pres. (1981-82). Various other orgs. **Honors:** Beta Phi Mu, 1978. **Activities:** 12; 17, 24, 39; 59, 80 **Addr.:** Health Sciences Library, Mennonite Hospital and School of Nursing, 807 North Main St., Bloomington, IL 61701.

Anderson, Charles R. (Ap. 13, 1935, St. Louis, MO) Ref. Libn., N. Suburban Lib. Syst., 1975–; Info. Spec., Baltimore Cnty. Pub. Lib., 1973; Resrch., Univ. of MD, 1972–73; Ref. Libn., St. Mary's Coll. of MD, 1970–72. **Educ.:** Univ. of FL, 1955–57; FL State Univ., 1967–68, BA (Hum.), 1969, MLS; Univ. of MD, 1972–73, Post Mstrs. Study. **Orgs.:** ALA. Amer. Socty. of Indxrs. IL LA. **Honors:** Phi Kappa Phi, 1968; Beta Phi Mu, 1969; Natl. Agr. Lib., Resrch. Gnt., 1972. **Pubns.:** *Alternative Educational Patterns for Career Opportunities* (ERIC) (1973). **Addr.:** 1618 Elder Ln., Northfield, IL 60093.

Anderson, Christine Eleanor (S. 17, 1948, Watseka, IL) Asst. Dean, Swest. Univ. Sch. of Law, 1979–; Asst. Prof. of Law and Dir., Law Lib., De Paul Univ., 1977–79, Catlgr. to Actg. Law Libn., 1970–73. **Educ.:** Univ. IL, 1969, BS, 1970, MLS; De Paul Univ., 1976, JD. **Orgs.:** Amer. Assn. of Law Libs.: Com. on Exch. of Dupls. (List Cmplr., 1972–74); Law Lib. Jnl. Com. (1973–74); Com. on Rel. with Publshrs. and Dlrs. (1975–76); Indx. to Legal Pers. Com. (1978–). ASIS. Assn. of Amer. Law Schs. Chicago Assn. of Law Libs.: Educ. Com. (Co-Ch., 1974–75); CALL Inst. on Networks (Co-Ch., 1975); Admin. Code Com. (1978–79). NOW. Amer. Cvl. Liberties Un. Oral Hist. Assn. **Pubns.:** "Bicentennial History of American Law Libraries–History Through the Looking Glass; or, The Web of Our Past is the Network of our Future", *Law Lib. Jnl.* (1976); "Conference on Indexing Secondary Legal Materials", *IDEA* (1976); "Why Networks for Libraries", *Law Lib. Jnl.* (1977); Co-Auth., "Teaching Practices of Academic Law Librarians", *Law Lib. Jnl.* (1978); "The Past is a Bucket of Ashes; or, Why Archives for Law Schools", *Law Lib. Jnl.* (1978); Other articles and reviews. **Addr.:** 10447 Cumpston, North Hollywood, CA 91601.

Anderson, D. Gail (My. 2, 1938, Bayville, NJ) Libn., Media Spec., Seaside Park Elem. Sch., 1970–; Asst. Libn., Spec. Srvs., US Army, Fort Jay Lib., New York City, 1961–62, Libn., Camp Drum Lib., Watertown, NY, 1961. **Educ.:** Kutztown State Coll., 1956–60, BS (LS); Syracuse Univ., 1960–61, MLS. **Orgs.:** ALA. NJ LA. Educ. Media Assn. of NJ. Libns. Assn. of Ocean Cnty. NJ. Delta Kappa Gamma: Various chs. Ocean Cnty. Hist. Socty. Seaside Park Parent—Tchrs. Assn. Faith Luth. Church. Various orgs. **Pubns.:** *The Seventy-Five Years of Seaside Park 1898–1973* (1973). **Activities:** 10; 20, 21, 22 **Addr.:** 114 9th Ave., P.O. Box 129, Seaside Park, NJ 08752.

Anderson, David Charles (Ap. 27, 1931, Oakland, CA) Tech. Srcs. Libn., Hlth. Sci. Lib., Univ. CA, Davis, 1968–; Serials Catlgr., 1966–68, Catlgr., 1962–66; Libn., CA State Dept. of Finance, 1959–62. **Educ.:** Univ. of CA, Berkeley, 1948–52, BA (Lib. Arts), 1952–53, BLS. **Orgs.:** Med. LA: Publ. Info. Indus. Rel. Com. (1979–82), Vet. Med. Lib. Sect., Com. on Un. List of Sel. Vet. Serials. North. CA Med. Lib. Grp. **Pubns.:** "CATLINE: Use and Costs at the Health Sciences Library, University of California, Davis", *Med. LA Bltn.* (Je. 1976); Jt. auth., "Veterinary serials, a unionlist of titles not indexed by Index Medicus and held by veterinary collections in the U.S. and Canada." (1980); "Deciding the future of the catalog in small libraries," *Lib. Jnl.* (O. 1980). **Activities:** 1; 46; 80 **Addr.:** Health Sciences Library, University of California, Davis, Davis, CA 95616.

Anderson, Dorothy J. (Je. 19, 1934, Winnipeg, MB) Lib. Consult., 1976–; DC Coord., Lead. Trng. Inst., FL State Univ., 1972–75; Assoc. Dir., Assoc. Prof. Media Svcs., Fed. City Coll., 1969–71; Consult., IL State Lib., 1964–69: Prof. Ast. to Exec. Secy., ALA, 1962–64; Chld. Libn., Seattle Pub. Lib., 1958–62. **Educ.:** Seattle Pac. Coll., 1956–58, BA (Eng., Psy.); Univ. WA, 1959–61, MLS; TX Woman's Univ., 1978–81, DLS. **Orgs.:** ALA: Chld. Svc. Div. (Bd. Dir., 1966–68); Newbery-Caldecott Awds. Com. (1968). AALS. Oral Hist. Assn. **Honors:** Chicago Metro. Citizens Cncl., Outstand. New Citizen of 1965. **Pubns.:** Jt. auth., Seattle Images (1960); "A Tiger is a Tiger", *Media Manpower* (Fall 1972); "Human Values in Children's Media", *IL Libs.* (S. 1971); Ed., "Recruitment and Library Education", *IL Libs.* (My. 1967); "Land of Lincoln Recruits Librarians", *ALA Bltn.* (D. 1966); other articles. **Activities:** 1, 13; 17, 24, 25; 50, 74, 93 **Addr.:** 1317 Austin St., Denton, TX 76201

Anderson, Dorrine A. (F. 24, 1923, Ishpeming, MI) Dir., Media Srvs., Gladstone Area Schs., 1970–; Lib. Dir., Gladstone Sch. and Pub. Lib., 1961–70; Tchr., Gladstone Schs., 1960–61; HS Tchr., Nahma Twp. Sch., 1949–59; Tchr., Arlington Heights Twp. HS, 1945–49; Jr. High Eng., Eaton Rapids, MI, 1944–45. **Educ.:** North. MI Univ., 1940–44, BS (Eng., Bio., Hist.); West. MI Univ., 1967–69, MSLS. **Orgs.:** ALA: AASL. MI LA. MI Assn. for Media in Educ. AAUW: Chap. Secy. (1970–72). Reg. Educ. Media Ctr. 21. Leag. of Women Voters. Delta Kappa Gamma: Chap. VP (1980–). **Honors:** MI Educ. Assn., Reg. 17, Tchr. of the Year, 1969; Beta Phi Mu, 1967. **Activities:** 9, 10; 17 **Addr.:** 1723 Montana Ave., Gladstone, MI 49837.

Anderson, Elizabeth M. (F. 27, 1925, Los Angeles, CA) Head Libn., Hempfield Pub. Lib., 1979–; Libn., N. IL Univ., 1977; Lib. Media Spec., Fr. Hill Sch., 1970–76. **Educ.:** Washburn Univ., 1943–47, BA (Soc. Sci.); S. CT State Coll., 1970–73, MLS. **Orgs.:** ALA. PA LA. AAUW. Murrysville Lib. Bd.: Secy. **Activities:** 9, 10; 17, 21, 32; 63 **Addr.:** 118 Shangri-la Dr., Monroeville, PA 15146.

Anderson, Frank J(ohn) (Ja. 29, 1919, Chicago, IL) Dir., Wofford Coll., 1966–; Libn., KS Wesleyan, 1960–66; Dir., Submarine Lib., 1957–60; Branch Libn., E. Chicago Pub. Lib., 1956–57; Libn., KS Wesleyan, 1952–56. **Educ.:** IN Univ., 1948–50, AB (Eng.); Syracuse Univ., 1950–51, MSLS. **Orgs.:** SELA: So. Books Competition Prog. Dir. (1975–). SC LA: Coll. & Univ. Sect. Ch. (1968–69); Planning Com. (1976–). Amer. Prtg. Hist. Assn. Amalgamated Printers Assn. Gld. of Bk. Workers. S. Caroliniana Soc. **Pubns.:** *Private Presswork* (1977); *Private Presses of S.E. U.S.* (1972); Ed., SLA Geo. & Map Div. *Bulletin* (1966–75); Various articles; reviews. **Activities:** 1; 17, 37, 45; 57 **Addr.:** 229 Mohawk Dr., Spartanburg, SC 29301.

Anderson, Glenda Elaine (My. 4, 1951, Augusta, GA) Mncpl. Resrch. Libn., City of Savannah, GA, 1978–; Chatham Cnty. Ext. Coord., Savannah Pub. and Chatham-Effingham-Liberty Reg. Lib., 1977–78; Asst. Dept. Head, Gen. Ref. Dept., Atlanta Pub. Lib., Ctrl. Lib., 1974–77. **Educ.:** Armstrong State Coll., 1969–73, BA, summa cum laude (Eng.); Emory Univ., 1973–74, MLn (Libnshp.). **Orgs.:** GA LA: JMRT, Pres. (1981), VP (1979–81), Secy. (1978–79); Int. Frdm. Com. (1978–81). GA Hist. Socty.: Bd. of Curs. (1980–83). Coastal GA LA: Pres. (1979–80). Metro. Atlanta LA: Dir. Ed. (1976–77). The GA Conservancy. Amer. Assn. for State and Lcl. Hist. Socty. of GA Archvsts. **Honors:** Beta Phi Mu, 1975. **Activities:** 4, 12; 29, 39; 57, 95-Pub. Admin. **Addr.:** Municipal Research Library, Office of the City Manager, City of Savannah, GA, P.O. Box 1027, Savannah, GA 31402.

Anderson, Harold P. (O. 4, 1946, Darby, PA) Asst. VP, Corporate Archvst., Wells Fargo Bank, 1979–, Asst. Archvst., PR Ofcr., 1977–79; Arch., Lib. Spec., Hoover Inst. on War, Revolution and Peace, 1975–77; Tchg., Resrch. Fellow, Stanford Univ., 1973–75. **Educ.:** Villanova Univ., 1964–68, BA (Hist.); OH State Univ., 1969, MA (Hist.); Arch. Inst., Natl. Arch., 1976, Cert. (Arch. Admin.); OH State Univ., 1978, PhD (Hist.). **Orgs.:** SAA. Socty. of CA Archvsts.: Secy. (1978–79). Amer. Hist. Assn.: Amer. Hist. Assn./Org. of Amer. Histns./SAA Jt. Com. of Histns. and Archvsts. (1980–82). Org. of Amer. Histns. **Pubns.:** "The Corporate History Department: The Wells Fargo Model," *The Pub. Histn.* (forthcoming); "Bank History and Archives," *The MD Histn.* (Spr. 1979). **Activities:** 2; 17, 37, 41; 55, 59, 77 **Addr.:** History Dept. (921), Wells Fargo Bank, 475 Sansome St., San Francisco, CA 94111.

Anderson, Herschel Vincent (Mr. 14, 1932, Charlotte, NC) State Libn., SD State Lib., 1973–; Unit Dir., Lib. Mtrls. and Ref. Srcs., CO State Lib., 1972–73; Assoc. State Libn., TN State Lib. and Arch., 1970–72; Dir., Sandhill Reg. Lib., 1968–70; AV Consult., NC State Lib., 1964–68; Libn., NC Musm. of Art, 1964, Ast. Libn., 1963; Ast. Libn., Longview Pub. Lib., 1962–63. **Educ.:** Duke Univ., 1950–54, BA (Pol. Sci.); Columbia Univ., 1954–59, MS (LS). **Orgs.:** West. Cncl. of State Libs.: Pres. (1979–80), VP (1978–79). Bibl. Ctr. for Rsrch.: Bd. of Trustees (1973–), VP (1977). Chief Ofcrs. State Lib. Agncy.: Exec. Bd. (1974–75). ALA: PLA/AV Com. Chmn.; Other orgs. Kiwanis Clb.: Bd. of Dir. (1978–). Rotary Clb. EFLA: Juror, Amer. Film Fest. (1966–70). SD Hist. Soc. **Honors:** Mt. Plains LA, Int. Frdm. Awd., 1979; SD LA, Innovative Libn. of Yr., 1977. **Pubns.:** "Audio-visual Services in the Small Public Library", *ALA Small Libs. Proj.* (1969); "South Dakota Codified Laws," Chap. 14–1, *State Lib. Ofc.* (1975); "South Dakota Codified Laws," Chap. 14–2, *Pub. Libs.* (1976). **Activities:** 12, 13; 17, 19, 34; 67, 74 **Addr.:** Box 71, Pierre, SD 57501.

Anderson, Jack Ronald (Je. 20, 1923, Moline, IL) Coord., AV Srvs., Naperville Ctrl. HS, 1967–; Asst. AV Coord., Tchr., Bowling Green State Univ., 1966–67; AV Coord., Tchr., E. Moline Elem. Dist., 1961–66; AV Coord., Tchr., Carbon Cliff, IL, 1957–61. **Educ.:** Univ. of IL, 1947–51, BS (Cmrce.); Univ. of IA, 1958–61, MA (Sch. Super.); various grad. crs. **Orgs.:** IL AV Assn.: Prog. Ch. (1970). Chicago Suburban RT: VP (1974). Div. of AV: Eval. Com. (1968). AECT. AV Inst. of DuPage Cnty. **Honors:** Phi Delta Kappa, 1978. **Pubns.:** "More People Eat Rice Than Any Other Food," *IL Geo. Socty.* (1963); "Geography On The March," *IL Geo. Socty.* (1965); "Today We Are Going to Read a Comic Magazine," *IL Geo. Socty.* (1964). **Activities:** 10; 24, 32, 46; 50, 61, 63 **Addr.:** Naperville Central H.S., 440 W. Aurora Ave., Naperville, IL 60540.

Anderson, James Doig (N. 22, 1940, Caldwell, ID) Assoc. Prof., Grad. Sch. of Lib. and Info. Std., Rutgers Univ., 1977–; Asst. Prof., Queens Coll., CUNY, 1973–77; Asst. Prof., St. John's Univ., 1972–73; Libn., Sheldon Jackson Coll., 1964–68. **Educ.:** Harvard Coll., 1959–63, BA (Hist., Lang.); Columbia Univ., 1963–64, MSLS (Lib. Srv.), 1968–72, DLS (Lib. Srv.). **Orgs.:** Amer. Socty. of Indxrs.: Com. on Indxr. Educ. (Ch., 1975–); Dir. (1977–80). ALA: RTSD, Educ. Com. (1979–81); Ref. and Subscrpn. Bks. Review Com. (1977–81). ASIS. NJ LA. Untd. Presby. Church in the U.S.A.: Ruling Elder (1972–). Presbys. for Lesbian/Gay Concerns: Coord. for Synod of the N.E. (1977–); Comms. Secy. (1980–). **Honors:** Columbia Univ., Joseph Towne Wheeler Awd., 1964; Columbia Univ., R. Krystyna Dietrich Awd., 1964. **Pubns.:** *Education and Training in Indexing for Document and Information Retrieval* (1981); "Cataloging and Classification of Chinese Language Materials," *Cataloging and Classification of Non-Western Material* (1980); "Structure in Database Indexing," *The Indxr.* (Ap. 1980); "Contextual Indexing and Faceted Classification for Databases in the Humanities," *ASIS Procs.* (1979); "Across the Language Barrier: Translations of Scientific and Technical Journal Literature: A Test of Their Predictability on the Basis of Bibliometric Criteria," *ASIS Procs.* (1978); "Ad Hoc and Selective Translations of Scientific and Technical Journal Literature: Their Characteristics and Possible Predictability," *Jnl. of the Amer. Socty. for Info. Sci.* (My. 1978). **Activities:** 11, 12; 20, 26, 30; 62, 75 **Addr.:** Graduate School of Library & Information Studies, Rutgers University, 4 Huntington St., New Brunswick, NJ 08903.

Anderson, James F. (My. 22, 1941, Prairie, MS) Dir., First Reg. Lib., 1972–; Head Cat. Libn., AR State Univ. Lib., 1966–71. **Educ.:** MS State Univ., 1959–63, BS (Math); LA State Univ., 1965–66, MSLS AR State Univ., 1970–71, MBA. **Orgs.:** MS LA: Pres. (1977); VP (1976); Pub. Lib. Sect., (Ch., 1975), various coms. SE LA. ALA: AR LA: Coll. and Univ. Lib. Sect. (Pres., 1970); RTSD (Pres., 1971). Hernando Cham. of Comrc.: Bd. of Dir. (1975–76). AR State Univ.: Fac. Sen. (1969–71). **Honors:** MS LA, Peggy May Awd., 1979. **Pubns.:** "Break-even Point for a Proof Slip Operation", *Coll. and Resrch. Libs.* (Mr. 1972); Jt. Auth., "Cut to Fit", *Lib. Resrc. and Tech. Prcs.* (Win. 1970); Jt. Auth., "It Will Cost More Tomorrow", *Lib. Resrc. and Tech. Prcs.* (Win. 1972); "Cooperation by Discussion", *AR Libs.* (Spr. 1970); Other articles *MS Lib. News.* **Activities:** 1, 9; 17, 25; 59, 78, 89 **Addr.:** First Regional Library, 59 Commerce St., N.W., Hernando, MS 38632.

Anderson, Joan T. (Ap. 18, 1930, Wahoo, NE) Msc. Libn., Head Catlgr., CA Inst. of the Arts, 1969–; Msc. Catlgr., Univ. of AZ, 1967–69. **Educ.:** Northwest. Univ., 1950–53, BM (Msc.), 1955–56 (Msc.); Univ. of IL, 1965–67, MLS. **Orgs.:** Msc. LA: South. CA Chap. (Ch., 1980–81). **Activities:** 1; 15, 20, 46; 56

PROFESSIONAL ACTIVITIES: Institutions: 1. Acad. lib.; 2. Arch.; 3. Assn.; 4. Fed./Gvt. lib.; 5. Inst. lib.; 6. Mfr./Suppl.; 7. Milit. lib.; 8. Musm.; 9. Pub. lib.; 10. Sch. lib.; 11. Sch. of lib. sci.; 12. Spec. lib.; 13. State lib.; 14. (other). **Functions/Activities:** 15. Acq./Col. dev.; 16. Adult srvs.; 17. Admin.; 18. Apprais.; 19. Archit./Bldgs.; 20. Cat./Class.; 21. Chld. srvs.; 22. Circ.; 23. Cons./Pres.; 24. Consult.; 25. Cont. ed.; 26. Educ. lib. sci.; 27. Ext. srvs.; 28. Fund/Grants; 29. Gvt. pubs.; 30. Indx./Abs.; 31. Instr. lib. use; 32. Media srvs.; 33. Micro.; 34. Netwks./Coop.; 35. Persnl.; 36. PR; 37. Publshg.; 38. Recs. mgt.; 39. Ref. srvs.; 40. Repro.; 41. Resrch.; 42. Review.; 43. Secur.; 44. Serials; 45. Spec. col.; 46. Tech. srvs.; 47. Trustees/Bds.; 48. YA srvs.; 49. (other).

Addr.: California Institute of the Arts Library, 24700 McBean Pkwy., Valencia, CA 91355.

Anderson, John F. (O. 5, 1928, Saginaw, MI) Dir., Tucson Pub. Lib., 1962–68, 1973–); City Libn., San Francisco Pub. Lib., 1968–73; Dir., Knoxville Pub. Lib., 1958–62; Asst. Cnty. Libn., Baltimore Cnty. Pub. Lib., 1956–58, Supvsr. of Adult Work, 1955, Area Libn., 1954, Bkmobile Libn., 1952–54; Young People's Libn., Enoch Pratt Free Lib., 1950–52. **Educ.:** MI State Univ., 1946–49, BA (Hist. and Pol. Sci.); Univ. IL, 1949–50, MS (LS). **Orgs.:** ALA: Cncl. (1962–65, 1966–70), PLA/Bd. of Dir. (1961–65); Lib. Admin. Div., Bd. of Dir. (1964–65, 1967–70); Pres. (1968–69); Lib. Admin. Dev. Com., Ch. (1962–64); other coms. SWLA: Pres. (1976–78); Bd. of Dir. (1974–80). AZ LA: Pres. (1967–68); Pub. Libs. Div. (Pres., 1964–65); other ofcs. and coms. CA LA. Other orgs. Kiwanis Intnl.; St. Andrew's Housing for the Elderly, Inc.: Bd. of Dir. AZ Theatre Co., Bd. (1978–). AZ China Cncl.: Pres. (1978–80). Other orgs. **Honors:** AZ LA, Libn. of the Year, 1966; Amer. Bus. Women's Assn. Cable Car Chap., Boss of the Year, 1973; Beta Phi Mu, 1951; H.W. Wilson Periodical Award for SYNERGY, 1970, 1972. **Pubns.:** L.J. Special Report #1: Library Space Planning "Main Libraries: Time for Mutation?"; The Library Reaches Out "Trauma and Triumph in Tucson" (1965); Numerous articles in prof. jnls. **Activities:** 9; 17, 19, 24 **Addr.:** Tucson Public Library, Administrative Offices, P.O. Box 27470, Tucson, AZ 85726.

Anderson, Joseph James (Je. 28, 1932, Dubuque, IA) State Libn., NV State Lib., 1970–; Dir., Pub. Srvs. Div., 1967–70; Mgr., Tech. Prcs., Ampex Corp., 1964–67; Sr. Tech. Libn., Lockheed Missiles and Space Co., 1961–64. **Educ.:** St. Mary's Univ. of TX, 1949–53, BA (Hist.); Univ. CA, Berkeley, 1960–61, MLS. **Orgs.:** ALA. NV LA. SLA. Mt. Plains LA: Pres. (1979–80). West. Cncl. of State Libs.: Secy.-Treas. (1977–); West. Interstate Com. for Higher Educ. Lib. Coop. Org.: Chmn. (1973–75). **Pubns.:** Ed., "Dateline State Library", *State Nsltr.* (1970–). **Activities:** 12, 13; 17; 59, 78, 83 **Addr.:** Nevada State Library, Capitol Complex, Carson City, NV 89710.

Anderson, Kathie P. (N. 2, 1949, Sayre, PA) Corporate Libn., Reynolds Metals Co., 1974–, Asst. Libn., 1973–74. **Educ.:** Univ. of Rochester, 1967–71, AB (Russ. Lang., Amer. Hist.); McGill Univ., 1971–73, MLS. **Orgs.:** SLA: VA Chap. (Pres., 1977–78). SE LA. AALL. VA LA. Natl. Hist. Socty. Natl. Socty. Daughters of the Amer. Revolution. **Pubns.:** *Season in the Sun* (1975); *A Small Town in New Hampshire* (1976). **Activities:** 12; 17, 34; 59, 77, 81 **Addr.:** Reynolds Metals Co., Corporate Information Center, 6601 W. Broad St., Richmond, VA 23261.

Anderson, Le Moyne W. (Ag. 16, 1923, Wheaton, MN) Dir. of Libs., CO State Univ., 1957–; Ref. Libn., Univ. of IL, Chicago Circle, 1951–57; Serials Libn., IA State Univ., 1948–50. **Educ.:** Gustavus Adolphus Coll., 1942–43 and 1946 (Hist.); Univ. of MN, 1946–48, BA (Hist.), 1947–48, BSLS; Univ. of IL, 1950–51, MS (Lib. Sci.), 1966–69, PhD (Lib. Sci.). **Orgs.:** ALA: Cncl. (1959–63), ACRL (Pres., 1979–80). ARL: Pres. (1978–79). Unvsl. Serials and Bk. Exch.: Pres. (1979). Ctr. for Rsrch. Libs.: Bd. of Dir. (1977–79). Amer. Scndvn. Fndn. Sigma Xi. Phi Kappa Phi. Lions Intntl. **Pubns.:** Numerous Book and Articles. **Activities:** 1; 17 **Addr.:** 3606 Woodridge Rd., Fort Collins, CO 80524.

Anderson, Linda L. (D. 20, 1943, Timmins, ON) Head, Pub. Srvs. Div., Brock Univ. Lib., 1977–; Head, Docum. Dept. and Comp. Srch. Srvs., 1975–77, Head, Circ. and Docum. Depts., 1969–75, Head, Circ. Dept., 1967–69. **Educ.:** McMaster Univ., 1962–65, BA (Psych. and Soc.); Univ. Toronto, 1966–67, BLS. **Orgs.:** Can. Assn. Info. Sci. Can. LA. Can. Assn. of Coll. and Univ. Libs. **Activities:** 1; 17, 29; 92, 95-Online Searching. **Addr.:** Brock University Library, St. Catharines, ON L2S 3A1, Canada.

Anderson, Marg H.J. (S. 26, 1947, Toronto, ON) Lib. Arts Instr., South. AB Inst. of Technology, 1980–; Libn., Cntrl. Meml. Sr. HS, 1978–80; Libn., H. D. Cartwright Jr. HS, 1975–78; Libn., Sherwood Elem. and Jr. HS, 1973–75. **Educ.:** Univ. of SK, 1965–68, BA (Hist., Eng.); Univ. of AB, 1972–73, BLS; Univ. of SK, 1968–69, Prof. Tchg. Cert. **Orgs.:** Foothills LA; CAN LA; AB LA; Calgary Lrng. Resrc. Cncl. Kaliedoscope Chld. and YA Lit. Conf.: Strng. Com. (1979–). **Activities:** 10; 17, 32, 48 **Addr.:** 119 Stradwick Rise SW, Calgary, AB T3H 1G7, Canada.

Anderson, Margaret W. (Jl. 4, 1929, Columbia, TN) Acq. Libn., Lib., Mid. TN State Univ., 1980–, Asst. Acq. Libn., 1971–80; Sch. Libn., Metro Nashville, TN, 1969–71; Sch. Libn., Maury Cnty., TN, 1966–68; Bkmobile. Libn., Blue Grass Reg. Lib., 1966; Libn., Maury Cnty. Pub. Lib., 1963–65. **Educ.:** Mid. TN State Univ., 1964–66, BS (Elem. Educ.); George Peabody Coll., 1967–69, MLS. **Orgs.:** ALA. SE LA. TN LA: Coll. and Univ. Sect. (Secy.-Rec., 1972–73); Grievance Com. (1975–76); Exec. Bd. (1977–79); Tech. Srvs. Sect. (Secy.-Treas., 1978–79). Mid-State LA (TN): Exec. Cncl. (Ch., 1977–79); Adv. Bd. (1974–76); various coms. AAUW: Murfreesboro Branch, Rec. Secy. (1977–79), Corres. Secy. (1975–77); Columbia Branch (1st VP, 1968–69). **Honors:** Beta Phi Mu, 1969. **Activities:** 1; 15 **Addr.:** Acquisitions Dept., Library, Middle Tennessee State University, Murfreesboro, TN 37132.

Anderson, Marilyn C. (Lynne) Bush Sci. Libn., Asst. Prof., Rollins Coll., 1980–; Lrng. Resrcs. Ctr. Dir., Stephens Coll., 1974–76; Dir., Readrs. Srvs., Smith Coll., William Allan Neilson Lib., 1971–74; Dir., Media Srvs., Asso. Dir., Lib. Srvs. N. Country Cmnty. Coll., SUNY, 1968–71; Media Spec., Asst. Libn., Skagit Valley Coll., 1967–68. **Educ.:** Univ. of Tulsa, 1948, BA (Sp., Drama); Smith Coll., 1952, MA (Drama); Univ. of WA, 1964, MALS; various crs. **Orgs.:** FL LA. FL Assn. For Media in Educ. Ctrl. FL On-Line Searchers: Strg. Com. **Honors:** Theta Alpha Phi; Fullbright Schol., Eng., 1952–53. **Pubns.:** Jt. Auth., *Theatre Student: Makeup and Masks* (1972, 1981). **Addr.:** 1026 Kirk St., Orlando, FL 32808.

Anderson, Mary Jane (Ja. 23, 1935, Des Moines, IA) Exec. Dir., ALA, ALSC, 1973–; Exec. Secy., ALA, YASD, 1973–75; Coord., Chld. Srvs., Baltimore Cnty. Pub. Lib., 1972–73; Head, Tech. Prcs., St. Mary's Coll. of MD, 1970–72; Pub. Lib. Chld. Srvs. Consul., FL State Lib., 1967–70; Chief, Chld. Srvs., Jacksonville Pub. Lib., 1964–67, Branch Libn., 1963–64; Reg. Chld. and YA Libn., Santa Fe Reg. Lib., 1961–63; Elem. Sch. Libn., Dade Cnty. Pub. Schs., 1957-61. **Educ.:** Univ. FL, 1953–57, BAE (Educ.); FL State Univ., 1959, MS (LS). **Orgs.:** ALA: PLA/Stds. Com. (1971–73); YASD Srv. to Disadv. Youth Com. (1968–70). MD LA: Sec. VP (1973–74). FL LA: Sch. and Chld. Div., Ch. (1967–68); PR Com. (1968–70); Rcrmt. Com. (1961–64; Ch., 1963–64). Chld. Dev. Assoc. Cnsrtm.: Bd. Dir. (1975–81; Secy., 1977–81). Coal. for Chld. and Youth: Bd. of Dir. (1978–). **Honors:** Beta Phi Mu, Gamma Chap., Pres., 1968–69. **Pubns.:** "Library Service to Children in the U.S.S.R.," *Top of the News* (Winter 1981); U.S.A. Chapter in *Library Service to Children: An International Survey* (1978); "Service for the Eighties...", *IL Libs.* (Dec. 1978); Ed., *FL State Lib. Newsletter* (1967–70). **Activities:** 14-Library association; 17, 21 **Addr.:** ALSC/ALA, 50 E. Huron St., Chicago, IL 60611.

Anderson, Nancy D. (Ja. 19, 1940, Whitefish, MT) Math. Libn., Assoc. Prof. of Lib. Admin., Univ. of IL, 1972–, Serials Biblgphr., 1968–72, Asst. Geol. Libn., 1968; Geol. Libn., Columbia Univ., 1966–67. **Educ.:** Smith Coll., 1958–62, BA (Geol.); Columbia Univ., 1965–66, MS (LS). **Orgs.:** SLA: PAM. Div., Ch.; Div. Scope Com. ALA: ACRL. IL LA. Ctrl. IL Smith Clb.: Pres. (1976–78). Socty. of Sigma Xi. **Honors:** Fulbright Fellowship, 1962; Beta Phi Mu. **Pubns.:** *French Mathematical Seminars: a Union List* (1978). **Activities:** 1; 15, 17, 39; 88 **Addr.:** Mathematics Library, 216 Altgeld Hall, University of Illinois at U.C., Urbana, IL 61801.

Anderson, Olga (D. 20, 1931, Hafford, SK) Ch., Lrng. Resrc. Ctr., Grande Prairie Reg. Coll., 1980–; Supvsr., Info. Div., Edmonton Pub. Lib., 1976–80; Asst. Dir., Pub. Srvs., Concordia Univ., 1974–76; Head, Ref. Dept., Hum., Soc. Sci., Univ. of Alta, 1968–74. **Educ.:** Univ. of SK, 1947–50, BA (Bio.); Univ. of Alta, 1953–55, BED; Univ. of WA, 1955–56, MLSc. **Orgs.:** LA of AB: Cnclr. (1978–80) Un. List of Serials, Ch. ALA: ACRL; RASD. Can. LA: Can. Assn. Coll. Univ. Libs. (Secy., 1975–76); Can. Assn. Spec. Libs. and Info. Srvs. **Honors** Phi Delta Kappa. **Activities:** 1; 15, 17, 39; 56, 63 **Addr.:** 10218–111 Ave., Grande Prairie, AB T8U 1T8 Canada.

Anderson, Oriole Pamela (Je. 26, 1935, Saskatoon, SK) Chief Libn., Mfrs. Life Insr. Co., 1977–; Chief Libn., Equitable Life Assurance Socty., 1966–77; Catlgr., North York Pub. Lib., 1963–65; Head Libn., St. Vital Pub. Lib., 1960–62. **Educ.:** Untd. Coll., Univ. of MB, 1952–56, BA (Phil.); Univ. of Toronto, 1957–58, BLS. **Orgs.:** SLA: Insr. Div. (Dir., 1974–75), various ofcs., Nom. Com. (1975–76), Insr. Pers. Indx. Online Com. (1979–). **Pubns.:** Ed., *Insurance Periodicals Index* (1972–). **Activities:** 12; 17, 30, 41; 59, 76 **Addr.:** Manufacturers' Life Insurance Co., Business Library, 200 Bloor St. E., Toronto, ON M4W 1E5 Canada.

Anderson, Pauline H. (N. 27, 1918, Broadalbin, NY) Dir. of The Andrew Mellon Lib., Choate Rosemary Hall, 1950–; Dir. of Lib. Wkshps. for Natl. Assoc. of Indp. Schs., 1977–; Indp. Sch. Lib. Consult., 1963–; Libn., Abbot Acad., 1945–50. **Educ.:** Keuka Coll., 1935–39, BA (Eng.); NY State Univ., 1939–43, BLS. **Orgs.:** Amer. Assoc. of Sch. Libs.: Bd. (1979–); Non Pub. Sch. Sect. (Ch., 1979–). ALA: ACRL. New Eng. Media Assoc. Wallingford Pub. Lib.: Bd. of Mgrs. (1976–); Pres. (1979–). Eng. Speaking Union. **Honors:** Natl. Assoc. of Indp. Schs., Braitmayer Fellowship, 1966; Leader of Amer. Sec. Educ., 1972; Outstanding Sec. Educ. of Amer., 1973. **Pubns.:** Rev. ed., *The Library in the Independent School* (1980); *The Library in the Independent School* (1968); *A Selected Bibliography of Literature on the Independent School* (1961); "What's Going on In Independent School Libraries", *School Library Journal* (N. 1979); Ed., *Books for Secondary School Libraries* (1971, 1976). **Activities:** 10; 24, 45, 47; 55 **Addr.:** The Andrew Mellon Library, Choate Rosemary Hall, Wallingford, CT 06492.

Anderson, Peter Gillespie (My. 27, 1936, Norwood, MA) Head, Curric. Mtls. Dept., CA State Univ., Chico, 1974–; Curric. Lbn. and Biblgphr., Univ. IL, Chicago Circle, 1970–74; Tchr., Portsmouth, Sch. Dept., 1967–68; Tchr., Milton, Sch. Dept., 1965–67. **Educ.:** Marietta Coll., 1956–60, BA (Eng.); Boston State Coll., 1964–65, MEd; FL State Univ., 1969–70, MS (LS). **Orgs.:** ALA. CA LA. Tri-Cnts. LA. **Activities:** 1; 17, 39, 45; 63 **Addr.:** Curriculum Materials Dept., University Library, California State University, Chico, Chico, CA 95926.

Anderson, R. Joseph (N. 6, 1946, Zanesville, OH) Archvst., Mss. and Arch. Div., Yale Univ Lib., 1979–; Arch. Ast., WI State Histcl. Socty., 1978–79; Soc. Wkr., OH Yth. Comsn., 1974–78. **Educ.:** OH Univ., 1964–68, AB (Hist. and Gvt.), 1971–73, MA (Amer. Hist.); Univ. of WI, 1978, MLS. **Orgs.:** SAA: Coll. and Univ. Prof. Afnty. Grp., Theme Col. Grp. New Eng. Archvsts. Socty. of GA Archvsts. Org. of Amer. Histns. **Pubns.:** "C.-E.A. Winslow Papers," *Blth. of the Hist. of Med.* (Winter, 1980); "Public Welfare Case Records: A Study of Archival Practices," *The Amer. Archvst.* (Spring, 1980). **Activities:** 95-American history. **Addr.:** 98 Norton St. E–4, New Haven, CT 06511.

Anderson, R. Wayne (Mr. 10, 1942, Fulton, KY) Dir., Oral Hist. Ofc., Northeastern Univ., 1980–, Instr., 1974–80; Lectr., Bellarmine Coll., 1968; Instr., Univ. of Southwest. LA, 1966–68. **Educ.:** Murray State Univ., 1960–64, BA (Hist.); Tulane Univ., 1964–66, MA (Hist.); Univ. KY, 1968–74, PhD (Hist.). **Orgs.:** Oral Hist. Assn. SAA. New Eng. Assn. of Oral Hist. Org. of Amer. Hists. New Eng. Hist. Assn. Other orgs. **Pubns.:** "A Proposal for Psychologically Oriented History Courses", *New Eng. Hist. Assn. Nsltr.* (Ap. 1978); "USS KEARSARGE: Forty-six Years and Three Careers", *US Naval Inst. Proc.* (Ja. 1960); Other articles, etc. **Activities:** 1, 2; 17; 85 **Addr.:** Oral History Office, Department of History, Northeastern University, 360 Huntington Ave., Boston, MA 02115.

Anderson, Robert G. (Ja. 17, 1943, Kenosha, WI) Libn., Reuther Alternative HS, 1974–; Asst. Prof., Coll. of Racine, Dominican Coll., 1972–74, Instr., 1969–72, Asst. Libn., Tchr., LS Prog., 1968–69, Catlgr., Dir., Class. Change, Dewey to Lib. of Congs. Syst., 1967. **Educ.:** Dominican Coll., 1965, BA (Eng., Hist., Fr., Psy.); Rosary Coll., 1967, MA (LS); various crs. **Orgs.:** Kenosha Area LA: Pres. (1977–78). Tri-Cnty. Lib. Cncl.: Kenosha Unfd. Sch. Rep. (1976–77); Pubns. Com. (Ch., 1979–80). WI Cath. LA: Acad. and Spec. Libs. Sect., Ch.-Elect (1968–69, 1971–73), Ch. (1973–75); Pres.-Elect (1975–77); Pres. (1977–79). ALA. Various other orgs. Southeast. WI Comics Club: Pres. (1980–81); VP (1979–80). **Activities:** 10, 13; 31, 39, 48; 55, 63 **Addr.:** 7914-21st Ave., Kenosha, WI 53140.

Anderson, Sharon McClure (Je. 8, 1935, Emporia, KS) Head, Gvt. Docum., Maps, Micros. Dept., Univ. of CA, San Diego, 1963–, Ref. Libn., 1963–67, ILL Libn., 1963–65. **Educ.:** Univ. of KS, 1953–57, BA (Eng. and Ger.); Univ. CA, 1962–63, MLS. **Orgs.:** ALA: GODORT. CA LA: Gvt. Pubs. Chap./Gvt. Pubs. Div. (Ch., 1968). West. Assn. of Map Libs. South. CA Assn. of Law Libs. **Pubns.:** "Reference Material in Microformat–A Government Documents Librarian's View", *Microform Review* (O. 1979). **Activities:** 1; 29, 39 **Addr.:** Documents Department, Central University Library C-075-P, University of California, San Diego, La Jolla, CA 92093.

Anderson, Sherman A. (Ja. 18, 1919, Maddock, ND) Music Catlgr., SUNY, Binghamton, 1970–; Music Catlgr., Univ. of IL, 1968–69; Phonorec. Catlgr., Detroit Pub. Lib., 1955–68; Asst. Libn., Milwaukee Pub. Lib., 1951–55. **Educ.:** Univ. of MN, 1937–42, BBA; Drexel Univ., 1950–51, MSLS; Philadelphia Cnsvty. of Music, 1946–50, BM (music). **Orgs.:** Ms. LA. **Pubns.:** "Cataloging of Folk Music on Records", *Lib. Resrcs. and Tech. Srcs.* (Win. 1959); "Cataloging the Contents of Certain Recordings", *Lib. Resrs. and Tech. Svcs.* (Sum. 1965). **Activities:** 1, 12; 20, 32, 45; 55 **Addr.:** Library, State University of New York at Binghamton, Binghamton, NY 13901.

Anderson, Sherry (O. 1, 1951, Cincinnati, OH) Asst. Dir., Spec. Projs., Hlth. Sci. Lib., E. Carolina Univ., 1980–, Asst. Dir., Tech. Srvs., 1978–80, Acq. Libn., 1976–78, Ref., Cat., 1975–76. **Educ.:** Univ. of ND, 1969–73, BS (LS); Case West. Rsv. Univ., 1974–75, MSLS (Med. LS). **Orgs.:** Med. LA: Mid-Atl. Reg. Grp. NC LA. **Activities:** 1; 17, 41, 46; 58, 80 **Addr.:** GreeneWay Apts. #87, Greenville, NC 27834.

Anderson, Susan R. (Mr. 17, 1938, Painesville, OH) Lib. Dir., Coshocton Pub. Lib., 1978–, Ast. Libn., 1972–77; Catlgr., SUNY at Albany Lib., 1966–67; YA Libn., Free Lib. of Philadelphia, 1965–66. **Educ.:** Carnegie-Mellon Univ., 1956–60, BS (Gen. Stds.); Carnegie Lib. Sch., 1960–61, MLS. **Orgs.:** OH LA. Natl. Libns. Assn. Human Dev. Com.: Ch. (1970–71). Mideast. OH Lib. Org.: Exec. Com. (1979). **Activities:** 9; 17, 39 **Addr.:** 48 Sheridan Rd., Coshocton, OH 43812.

Andis, Norma B. (Washington, IN) Dir., Lrng. Resrcs., Missn. Cons. Indp. Sch. Dist., 1975–, Dir., Lib. Srvs., 1969–75, Media Coord., 1965–69. **Educ.:** Pan Amer. Univ., 1963–69, BA (Eng., Hist.); Univ. of TX, Austin, 1968–71, M (LS); 1975, Supvsrs. Cert.; various crs. **Orgs.:** ALA. TX LA: Dist. IV, Pres., VP, State Mem. Com. Chld. RT Div. (Secy.-Treas., 1977); Schol. and Resrch. Com. (Ch., 1981); Ad Hoc Com. on Netwks. (1979–80). Hidalgo Cnty. Lib. Syst.: VP (1980–81); Pres. (1975–76). Speer Meml. Lib.: Pres. (1978–). Delta Kappa Gamma: Epsilon Upsilon Chap. (Pres., 1978–80). **Honors:** TX LA, Libn. of the Yr., 1978; City of Mission, TX, First Lady of the Yr., 1960; Beta Pi Mu; Alpha Chi; other hons. **Pubns.:** Various poems,

Special Subjects/Services: 50. Adult educ.; 51. Advert./Mktg.; 52. Aerosp.; 53. Agric.; 54. Area std.; 55. Arts/Hum.; 56. Autom.; 57. Bibl./Prtg.; 58. Bio. sci.; 59. Bus./Fin.; 60. Chem.; 61. Copyrt.; 62. Documtn.; 63. Educ.; 64. Engin.; 65. Env.; 66. Eth. grps.; 67. Film; 68. Food/Nutr.; 69. Geneal.; 70. Geo.; 71. Geol.; 72. Handcpd.; 73. Hist.; 74. Int. frdm.; 75. Info. sci.; 76. Insr.; 77. Law; 78. Legis.; 79. Math./Comp. sci.; 80. Med.; 81. Metals; 82. Nat. resrcs.; 83. Newsp.; 84. Nuc. sci.; 85. Oral hist.; 86. Petr./Energy; 87. Pharm.; 88. Phys./Astr./Math.; 89. Readg.; 90. Relig.; 91. Sci./Tech.; 92. Soc. sci.; 93. Telecom.; 94. Transp.; 95. (other).

Who's Who in Library and Information Services

prose in relig. pers. **Activities:** 9, 10; 17, 21, 32; 63, 67, 89 **Addr.:** P.O. Box 953, Mission, TX 78572.

Andrews, Anne Elizabeth (F. 5, 1925, Wilmington, NC) Asst. Reg. Dir., Ext. Srvs., Ctrl. NC Reg. Lib., 1955–; Onslow Cnty. Libn., Onslow Cnty. Lib., 1953–55; Guildford Cnty. Libn., Greensboro Pub. Lib., 1951–53. **Educ.:** Univ. of NC, 1942–46, AB (Eng.), 1950–51, BS (LS). **Orgs.:** ALA. SE LA. NC LA: Pub. Lib. Sect., Adult Educ. Com. (Ch., 1965). Jr. Woman's Club, Jacksonville NC: Treas. (1952–53). Pilot Club of Burlington, NC: Rec. Secy. (1958, 1963); VP (1959, 1964, 1980); Pres. (1960, 1965, 1981). **Activities:** 9; 15, 21, 27 **Addr.:** Central North Carolina Regional Library, 342 S. Spring St., Burlington, NC 27215.

Andrews, Barbara Parker (Mr. 18, 1918, Nantucket, MA) Libn., Nantucket Athen., 1965–; Resrch. Asst., Descr. Cat. Div., Lib. of Congs., 1963–65, Admin. Asst., Descr. Cat. Div., 1950–62, Serials Catlgr., Descr. Cat. Div., 1947–50. **Educ.:** Simmons Coll., 1940–44, BS (LS). **Orgs.:** ALA. Nantucket Hist. Assn. Nantucket Maria Mitchell Assn. **Activities:** 4, 9; 17, 20 **Addr.:** 1 East York St., Nantucket, MA 02554.

Andrews, Charles R. (Jl. 5, 1930, Scranton, PA) Dean, Lib. Srvs., Hofstra Univ., 1976–; Univ. Libn., S. East. MA Univ., 1974–76; Ast. Dir., Pub. Srvs., Univ. Libs., Case West. Rsv. Univ., 1971–74, Libn., Freiberger Library, 1969–71, Chief, Ref. Dept., 1968–69; Head, Gen. Ref. Dept., Cleveland Pub. Lib., 1966–68, Ref. Libn., 1964–66. **Educ.:** State Coll., Bloomsburg, PA, 1950–54, BS (Educ.); Univ. of OK, 1956–59, MA (Eng. Lit.); Case West. Rsv. Univ., 1963–64, MSLS, 1964–67, DLS, PhD (Eng.). **Orgs.:** ALA: RASD/Pubns. Com. (Ch., 1971–72); (VP, 1973–74; Pres., 1974–75); ACRL. NY LA. Nassau Cnty. LA. Long Island Lib. Resrcs. Cncl.: Bd. of Trustees (1977–); Plng. Com. (Ch., 1978–); VP (1978–79); Pres. (1979–80). Other orgs. Case West. Rsv. Univ.: Bd. of Overseers (1978–). **Honors:** Beta Phi Mu. **Pubns.:** Ch., Rev. Com., *Reference Books for Small and Medium-Sized Libraries, 2nd ed.* (1973); Abstctr., *Abstracts of English Studies* (1961–69); Reviews. **Activities:** 1; 17, 42, 47; 57 **Addr.:** Administrative Offices, University Library, Hofstra University, Hempstead, NY 11550.

Andrews, (Rev) Dean Timothy (F. 2, 1914, Salem, MA) Dir. of Libs., Hellenic Coll., 1953–. **Educ.:** Gordon Coll., 1937, ThB; Univ. of Athens, Greece, 1939; Holy Cross Orthodox Theo. Sch., 1942; Pratt Inst., 1944–45, BLS; Columbia Univ., 1948–50, MA. **Orgs.:** ALA. Amer. Theo. LA. Boston Theo. Inst. **Pubns.:** *Eastern Orthodox Church; A Bibliography* (1943, 1947); *Classification Scheme for Eastern Orthodox Seminary Libraries; Classification Scheme for Hellenic and Byzantine Studies Libraries;* Assoc. Ed., *Orthodox (Church) Encyclopedia.* **Activities:** 1, 12; 17, 20, 31; 55, 90, 93 **Addr.:** Hellenic College Library, 50 Goddard Ave., Brookline, MA 02146.

Andrews, Elliott E. (S. 28, 1921, Springfield, MA) State Libn., State Lib., Statehse., Providence, RI, 1962–; Dir., Lib. and Info. Srvs., Providence Lib., Jnl. Co., 1951–62. **Educ.:** Brown Univ., 1940–46, AbB (Pol. Sci.), 1946–47 AM (Intl. Rel.); Univ. of RI, 1964–67, MLS; 1972, Cert. Law Libn. **Orgs.:** ALA. AALL. SLA. Amer. Assn. State Libs. New Eng. LA. Brown Univ. Alum. Assn.: Class 1947, Secy. **Activities:** 13; 17, 24, 29; 78, 83 **Addr.:** State Library, Statehouse, Providence, RI 02903.

Andrews, James Crandall (Ap. 18, 1921, Philadelphia, PA) Consult. on Lib. Bldgs., 1974–; Dir. of Libs., Rensselaer Polytech. Inst., 1972–; Univ. Libn., Univ. of TX, Dallas, 1970–72; Lib. Consult., Ctrl. Amer., Ford Fndn., 1966 and '68; Lib. Dir., Argonne Natl. Lab., 1959–70; Head of Tech. Info. Srv., E.I. duPont de Nemours & Co., Savannah River Plant, 1950–58. **Educ.:** Univ. of NC, 1938–42, BS (Phys.); Univ. of IL, 1946–47, BSLS, 1947–48, MSLS. **Orgs.:** ALA; OCLC Users: Cncl. (1978–); Netwk. Adv. Com. (Ch., 1978–). Troy Pub. Lib.: Trustee (1974–). Boy Scouts of America; Amer. Philatelic Socty. Appalachian Mtn. Clb. **Activities:** 1, 12; 17, 19, 47; 56, 91, 95-Philately. **Addr.:** Rensselaer Polytechnic Institute, Troy, NY 12181.

Andrews, Jean M. (S. 16, 1919, Kewanee, IL) Lib. Dir., Waterford Twp. Pub. Lib., 1966–; Dir., Branch Libs., Pontiac Pub. Lib., 1956–66, Ref. Libn., 1949–56; Bkmobile Libn., IL State Lib., 1947–49, Ref. Libn., 1943–45. **Educ.:** Knox Coll., 1937–41, AB (Hist.); Case West. Rsv., 1942–43, BSLS; State of MI, 1949–, Permanent Prof. Cert. **Orgs.:** MI LA: Intel. Frdm. Com. (1960). ALA. Delta Kappa Gamma: Secy. (1975–77). Zonta Intl.: Secy. (1961–63). **Activities:** 9, 13; 17, 39 **Addr.:** 766 Colonial Ct., Birmingham, MI 48009.

Andrews, Karen L. (My. 27, 1950, Attleboro, MA) Head, Engin., Math. Sci. Lib., Univ. of CA, Los Angeles, 1979–; Engin. Libn., Univ. of OK, 1976–79, Catlgr., 1973–76. **Educ.:** Univ. of MA, 1968–72, BA (Fr.); Univ. of MI, 1972–73, AMLS. **Orgs.:** ALA. Amer. Socty. for Engin. Educ.: Engin. Libs. Div. (Ch., 1980–81); Prog. Ch., Ch.-Elect (1979–80). ASIS. SLA. Various other orgs. Assn. of Acad. Women. **Honors:** Phi Beta Kappa, 1972. **Pubns.:** Jt. auth., "Communicating Information," *Procs. of the 43rd ASIS Anl. Mtg.* (1980). **Addr.:** University of California, Los Angeles Engineering & Mathematical Sciences Library, 405 Hilgard Ave., Los Angeles, CA 90024.

Andrews, Loretta Kreider (O. 22, 1931, Istanbul, Turkey) Educ. Subj. Spec., Sci., Soc. Hist. Dept., Enoch Pratt Free Lib., 1981–, Ref., Gen. Info. Dept., 1980–81; Cat. Libn., St. Mary's Semy. and Univ. Lib., 1978–80; Tchr., Bryn Mawr Sch., 1972–76; Visit. Asst. Prof., African Hist., Towson State Univ., 1966–71. **Educ.:** Carleton Coll., 1949–53, BA (Hist.); Northwest. Univ., 1955–57, MA (Hist.); MD State Dept. of Educ., 1974, Advnc. Prof. Tchr. Cert.; Univ. of MD, 1976–78, MLS. **Orgs.:** MD LA: Acad. and Resrch. Libs. Div., Prog. Com. (1978–80). ALA. SLA. African Std. Assn.: 1972 Anl. Mtg., Org., Ch. **Honors:** Phi Beta Kappa, 1953; Mortar Bd., 1953; Beta Phi Mu, 1979. **Pubns.:** *Sub-Saharan Africa: A Culture Area in Perspective* (1970); Africa Unit, *Readings in World History* (1970); jt. auth., "The Church and the Birth of a Nation," *Jnl. of Church and State* (1975). **Activities:** 1, 9; 20, 39; 54, 63, 90 **Addr.:** Social Science and History Dept., Enoch Pratt Free Library, 400 Cathedral St., Baltimore, MD 21201.

Andrews, Sara W. (F. 17, 1941, Mt. Holly, NJ) Head, Ref. Dept., Dana Med. Lib., Univ. of VT, 1976–, Ref. Libn., 1973–76, Catlgr., 1969–73; Sch. Libn., Barre City Schs., 1966–68. **Educ.:** Ursinus Coll., 1959–63, BS (Hlth., Phys. Educ.); Drexel Univ., 1964–69, MSLS. **Orgs.:** Med. LA. N. Atl. Hlth. Sci. Libs. Hlth. Sci. Libs. of NH/VT. **Pubns.:** *Cataloging and Processing Audiovisual Materials; A Manual* (1971). **Activities:** 1, 12; 31, 39; 80 **Addr.:** Dana Medical Library, University of Vermont, Burlington, VT 05405.

Andrews, Theodora Anne (O. 14, 1921, Carroll Cnty., IN) LS Prof., Pharm., Nursing, and Hlth. Sci. Libn., Purdue Univ., 1979–, Pharm. Libn., 1956–79, Ast. Ref. Libn., 1955–56, Ast. Catlgr., 1955; Visit. Lectr., Syracuse, IL, IN Univs., Summers 1958–69. **Educ.:** Purdue Univ., 1939–53, BS; Univ. IL, 1954–55, MS, (LS); Med. LA, 1958, Med. Lib. Cert. **Orgs.:** SLA: IN Chap., VP (1961–62), Pres. (1962–63), Bd. of Dir. (1963–64), Other coms.; Med. LA: Pharm. Grp. Ch. (1960–61), Midw. Reg. Grp., Bd. of Dir. (1966–69), Nom. Com. (1970–72), Bylaws Com. (1972–73); Other coms.; IN LA: Awds. Com. (1965–66), Lib. Plng. Com. (1966–67); Amer. Assn. of Colls. of Phar.: Libns. Sect., Stan. Com., Ch. (1971–), Spec. Com. to Assess Needs for Coop. Acq., Ch. (1975–76), Other coms.; Other orgs. AAUP: Purdue Chap., Com. W (1976–77), Treas. (1977–82); Purdue Women's Caucus: VP, Pres. (1976–77). **Honors:** SLA IN Chap., John H. Moriarty Awd. for Disting. Libnship., 1972. **Pubns.:** *A Bibliography of Drug Abuse, Including Alcohol and Tobacco* (1977); *A Bibliography of the Socioeconomic Aspects of Medicine* (1975); *Thesis Manual for Students in the Pharmaceutical Sciences. Rev. ed.* (1966); Co. Auth., "Subject Journal Review: Drug and Alcohol Abuse Periodicals", *Bhvl. and Soc. Sci. Libn.* (Fall, 1979); Co. Auth., "Implications of Faculty Status for University Librarians", *Jnl. of Acad. Libnshp.* (M., 1978); Numerous articles, reviews, etc. **Activities:** 1, 12; 15, 17, 39; 58, 80, 87 **Addr.:** 2209 Indian Trails Dr., P.O. Box 2362, W. Lafayette, IN 47906.

Andrist, Shirley Anne (N. 6, 1932, Estevan, SK) Tchr.-Libn., Estevan Comprehensive Sch., 1980–; Tchr.-Libn., Hillside Elem. Sch., 1970–80; Instr., Chld. Lit., Regina Univ., 1978–79. **Educ.:** Univ. of SK, 1954–55, (Arts, Sci.); Univ. of Regina, 1970–77, BEd (LS). **Orgs.:** SK Assn. of Educ. Media Specs.: Ed., *The Medium* (1980–81). Can. Sch. Libns. Assn. Assn. of Media Techs. for Educ. in Can. Beta Sigma Phi: Secy. (1979–81). Univ. Women's Club. Estevan Arts Cncl. **Pubns.:** "A Love Affair with Dennis Lee," *The Medium* (Fall 1980); Reviews. **Activities:** 10; 42; 63, 67 **Addr.:** Box 761, Estevan, SK S4A 2A6 Canada.

Andrus, Lillian S. (Jl. 4, 1919, Frost, TX) Head Libn., Port Neches–Groves HS, 1971–; Libn., Hamshire–Fannett HS, 1966–70; Libn., Orangefield HS, 1961–70; Ast. Libn. and Eng. Tchr., Nederland HS, 1950–57. **Educ.:** Howard Payne Univ., 1936–41, BA (Eng., Educ.); TX Woman's Univ., 1952–54, MLS, Library Science; Univ. TX, 1971, various courses. **Orgs.:** TX LA: Dist. VIII (Ch., 1979–80); (Vice-Ch., 1978–79); Conv. (Minutes Ch., 1979). Jefferson Cnty. LA: Pres. (1972–73), Asm. Minutes Ch. (1979); Schol. Com. (1976). Delta Kappa Gamma: Chap. Pres. (1960–62), Sec. VP (1958–60). **Activities:** 10; 17 **Addr.:** P.O. Box 805, Nederland, TX 77627.

Angel, Michael R. (Mr. 15, 1940, Edmonton, AL) Pub. Srvs. Coord., Dafoe Lib., 1980–; Head, Ref. Srvcs. Dept., Univ. MB, 1977–80; Suprvsr. of Sch. Libs., MB Dept. of Educ., 1974–77, Ast. Suprvsr. of Sch. Libs., 1973–74; Lib. Tech. Instr., Red River Comnty. Coll., 1969–73; Curric. Libn., Lib. Consult., Guyana Mnstry. of Educ., 1967–69; Bkstks., Rsv. Libn., Univ. IA, 1965–67; Ref. Libn., Catlgr., Edmonton Pub. Lib., 1963–67. **Educ.:** Univ. of AB, 1958–61, BA (Hist.); Univ. of BC, 1962–63, BLS; Univ. of IA, 1965–67, (Hist.); Adult Ed., 1970–73, (Cert.). **Orgs.:** MB LA: Cncl. (1971–73); Pres. (1973–74); numerous coms. Can. LA: Cncl. (1973–74); VP, 1980–81; CACUL (Pres., 1981–82); various committees. MB Env. Comsn.: Pubn. Com. (1974–78). Can. Univ. Svc. Overseas: Urban Com. (Ch., 1974–76); Univ. Com. (Ch., 1977–78). **Pubns.:** "Survey of library Technician Programs in Canada", *Can. Lib. Jnl.* (F. 1977); "Computer Searches at the University of Manitoba", *MB LA Jnl.* (Mr. 1978); Survey of Winnipeg School Library Services (1975); "The Reference Interview", vid. prod. (1978). **Activities:** 1, 4; 17, 39; 55, 95-Intl. libnshp. **Addr.:** 134 Niagra, Winnipeg, MB R3N 0T8, Canada.

Angelo, Alice Marie (Ja. 14, 1947, Terre Haute, IN) Lib. Dir., Pope Pius XII Lib., St. Joseph Coll., 1979–, Ref. Libn. and Biblgphr., 1970–79; Chlds. Libn., CT State Lib., Lib. for the Blind and Handicpd., 1969–70. **Educ.:** St. Mary-of-the-Woods Coll., 1964–68, BA(Eng.); IN Univ., 1968–69, MLS; St. Joseph Coll., 1974–79, MA (Educ.). **Orgs.:** Cath. LA. CT LA: Exec. Bd.; Coll. and Univ. Sec. (1977–80). Cap. Reg. Lib. Cncl.: Pubns. Com., Co-Ch. AAUP. **Honors:** Outstanding Young Woman of Amer. Awd., 1978. **Pubns.:** Ed. and Jt. Cmplr., *Directory of Connecticut Region II Libraries* (1978); Ed., *Catalog of Micrographic Hardware, Microfiche Collections and Computerized Data Bases in Libraries Within the Capitol Region* (1977). **Activities:** 1; 15, 17, 39; 63, 72 **Addr.:** Pope Pius XII Library, Saint Joseph College, 1678 Asylum Ave., West Hartford, CT 06117.

Angier, Jennifer J. (S. 27, 19–, Wellwyn Garden City, Eng.) Ref. Libn., West. Psyt. Inst. and Clinic, School of Med., Univ. of Pittsburgh, 1976–. **Educ.:** Dickinson Coll., 1972–75, BA (Eng., Fine Arts); Univ. of Pittsburgh, 1976–78, MLS (Spec. Libnshp., Resrcs.). **Orgs.:** Med. LA: Mental Hlth. Libns. Sect. (Secy., 1980–81). Pittsburgh Online Users Forum. Assn. of Univ. Libns.: Univ. of Pittsburgh, Exec. Com. (1980–81). **Honors:** Phi Beta Kappa, 1976; Beta Phi Mu, 1978. **Pubns.:** Jt. auth., "Multidatabase Searching in the Behavioral Sciences. Part I. Core Databases," *Database* (1980); jt. auth., "Multidatabase Searching in the Behavioral Sciences. Part II. Special Applications," *Database* (1980); various presentations. **Activities:** 12, 14-Med. Resrch.; 20, 39, 49-Online Srvs.; 80, 92 **Addr.:** Western Psychiatric Institute and Clinic, 3811 O'Hara St., Pittsburgh, PA 15221.

Angione, Pauline V. (S. 19, 1944, Rochester, NY) Customer Srvc. Mgr., SDC Srch. Srvc., 1979–; Ast. Prof., Rosary Coll., Grad. Sch. of LS, 1972–79. **Educ.:** Nazareth Coll. of Rochester, 1962–66, BS (Bio/Chem.); Univ. Chicago Grad. Lib. Sch., 1966–68, AMLS, 1970–71, CAS (LS), 1971–, PhD. **Orgs.:** ASIS: Spec. Interest Grp. on Educ. (Ch., 1978–79). Med. LA: Chairman, Cert. Review Com. (Ch., 1978–79); Ad Hoc Com. to Dev. Cert. Code (1973–78); other coms. SLA. CLENE. other orgs. **Pubns.:** Jt. auth., *Continuing Education for Health Science Library Personnel* (1977); Jt. auth., *Experimental Dissemination of Biomedical Information* (1970); "Education for Information Science-Evaluation in Interesting Times", *ASIS Bltn.* (1977); "On the Equivalence of Boolean and Weighted Searching . . .", *ASIS Jnl.* (1975); "On the Equivalence of Boolean and Weighted Searching Based on the Convertibility of Query Forms", *ASIS Jnl.* (Mr.–Ap. 1975); Various reviews and papers. **Addr.:** System Development Corporation, 2500 Colorado Ave., Santa Monica, CA 90406.

Angle, Joanne G. (Mr. 16, 1941, St. Helens, OR) Mgr., Proj. Dir., Natl. Hlth. Info. Clearhse., 1979–; Hosp. Libn., Mt. Vernon Hosp., 1976–79; Libn., Patton Jr. HS, 1975–76; Instr., Med. and Serials Libn., Cameron Univ., 1973–75. **Educ.:** Portland State Univ., 1960–63, BS (Hist.); Univ. of OR, 1972–73, MLS; Univ. of OK, 1973–78, MPA; Med. Libn. Cert., 1975. **Orgs.:** ALA. Med. Lib. Assn.: Com. on Econ. Status of Hlth. Sci. Libns. (1978–81). Hlth. Sci. Comm. Assn. Amer. Socty. for Pub. Admin. Amer. Socty. for Hlth. Educ. Manpower and Trng. **Honors:** Beta Phi Mu, 1973. **Pubns.:** "We Had a Book Sale", *Hosp. Libs.* (Oct. 1979); "Volunteers in a Hospital Library", *Hosp. Libs.* (Oct. 1979). **Activities:** 12; 17, 24, 39; 75, 80, 92 **Addr.:** 7923 Jansen Dr., Springfield, VA 22152.

Angoff, Allan (Jl. 30, 1910, Boston, MA) Ch., Domestic and Intl. Progs., Consult., Libs, Lit., Trustee, Parapsy. Fndn., 1951–; PR Dir., Chief, Ref. Dept., Teaneck Pub. Lib., 1965–77; Asst. Libn., Ed. Ref. Lib., *NY Times*, 1965–68; Dir., Glen Rock Pub. Lib., 1965; Lib. Consult., Clifton NJ Jewish Ctr., 1964–65; Consult., Libs. Univ. Presses, Ford Fndn., 1961–62; Asst. Lib. Dir., Fair Lawn Pub. Lib., 1960–65; Sr. Ref. Libn., Montclair Pub. Lib., 1957–60; various writing, ed. positions, 1934–57. **Educ.:** Boston Univ., 1927–32, BS (Jnlsm.); Columbia Univ., 1950–52, MSLS. **Orgs.:** NJ LA: Prog. Com. (Ch., 1968–69). Bergen and Passaic Lib. Club: VP (1961–62). Frnds. of the Clifton Pub. Lib.: Pres. (1963–64). Melvil Dui Chowder and Marching Assn. Adult Sch. of Montclair: Eval. Com. (Ch., 1958–59). **Pubns.:** Ed., *American Writing Today: Its Independence and Vigor* (1957); ed., *The Psychic Force* (1970); *Hypnotism in the United States During 19th Century* (1968); *Eileen Garrett and The World Beyond the Senses* (1974); ed., *Public Relations for Libraries: Essays in Communications Techniques* (1973); various other bks., articles, bk. reviews. **Activities:** 9, 12; 16, 24, 37, 39 **Addr.:** Parapsychology Foundation, 228 E. 71st St., New York, NY 10021.

Angoff, Florence Adelson (O. 29, 1922, Boston, MA) Educ. Media Spec., Bd. of Educ., Clifton HS, 1964–; Libn., Bd. of Educ., Montclair, NJ, 1962–64; Serials Libn., Montclair State Coll., 1957–62; Branch Libn., Montclair Pub. Lib., 1948–50; Young People's Libn., Shute Meml. Lib., 1945–48; Asst. Chld. Libn., Boston Pub. Lib., 1943–45. **Educ.:** Simmons Coll., 1939–43, BS (LS); State of NJ, Cert. (Tchr.-Libn., Media Spec., Prof. Libn.). Natl. Educ. Assn. Clifton (NJ) Coll. Women's Club. NJ Educ. Assn. Educ. Media Assn. of NJ. Passaic Cnty. Sch.

PROFESSIONAL ACTIVITIES: Institutions: 1. Acad. lib.; 2. Arch.; 3. Assn.; 4. Fed./Gvt. lib.; 5. Inst. lib.; 6. Mfr./Suppl.; 7. Milit. lib.; 8. Musm.; 9. Pub. lib.; 10. Sch. lib.; 11. Sch. of lib. sci.; 12. Spec. lib.; 13. State lib.; 14. (other). **Functions/Activities:** 15. Acq./Col. dev.; 16. Adult srvs.; 17. Admin.; 18. Apprais.; 19. Archit./Bldgs.; 20. Cat./Class.; 21. Chld. srvs.; 22. Circ.; 23. Cons./Pres.; 24. Consult.; 25. Cont. ed.; 26. Educ. lib. sci.; 27. Ext. srvs.; 28. Fund/Grants; 29. Gvt. pubs.; 30. Indx./Abs.; 31. Instr. lib. use; 32. Media srvs.; 33. Micro.; 34. Netwks./Coop.; 35. Persnl.; 36. PR; 37. Publshg.; 38. Recs. mgt.; 39. Ref. srvs.; 40. Repro.; 41. Resrch.; 42. Review.; 43. Secur.; 44. Serials; 45. Spec. col.; 46. Tech. srvs.; 47. Trustees/Bds.; 48. YA srvs.; 49. (other).

Media Assn. **Activities:** 1, 10; 20, 31, 48; 63, 89 **Addr.:** 159 McCosh Rd., Upper Montclair, NJ 07043.

Angstadt, Susan Joan (O. 22, 1954, Emmaus, PA) AV Libn., West. PA Spec. Educ. Reg. Resrc. Ctr., 1980–; Ast. Libn., S. Pk. Twp. Lib., 1980 Ref. Libn., 1978–79. **Educ.:** Millersville State Coll., 1974–76, BA (Grmn.); Univ. of Pittsburgh, 1976–77, MLS; Drexel Univ., 1980, (Vid. in Libs.). **Orgs.:** PA LA: New Libns. (1979–); Cnty. Pub. (1979–). ALA. **Honors:** Beta Phi Mu, 1977. **Activities:** 9; 15, 16, 32, 39; 50, 57, 93 **Addr.:** South Park Township Library, 2575 Brownsville Rd., Library, PA 15129.

Anker, Anita L. (F. 13, 1949, St. Paul, MN) Oper. Mgr., Univ. PA Career Place. Svc., 1980–; Coord., Serials Dept., Univ. ND Libs., 1973–76. **Educ.:** St. Olaf Coll., 1967–71, BA (Hist., Eng.); Drexel Univ., Sch. of Lib. and Info. Sci., 1977, MA, PhD (in progress). **Orgs.:** ALA: ERA Ratif. Task Frc. (1979–). ASIS. **Pubns.:** "The Dragon's Day–An Epistomological Study," *Jnl. of Infomatics* (D. 1978); Jt. auth., "Serials Evaluation–The North Dakota Project", *Serials Libn.* (1980); Jt. auth., "Utilizing Constituents' Perceived Needs for Serial Titles", *ASIS Jnl.* (N. 1979); Jt. auth., "The Aging of Scientific Literature", *Jnl. of Documtn.* (1979); Several reports. **Activities:** 1; 15, 17, 29, 38, 41, 44; 75 **Addr.:** 2221 Delancey Pl., Philadelphia, PA 19103.

Ankudowich, Mary M. (N. 7, 1917, Horthampton, MA) Libn., Werner Josten Lib. of the Performing Arts, Smith College, 1943–. **Educ.:** Smith College, 1935–39, AB (Msc.); Columbia Univ., 1941–44, BSLS. **Orgs.:** Msc. LA: New Eng. Chap. Thea. LA. **Pubns.:** Various reviews. **Activities:** 1; 17, 35, 39; 91 **Addr.:** Werner Josten Library of the Performing Arts, Smith College, Northampton, MA 01063.

Annett, Adele M. (Toronto, ON) Head, Serials Cat. Sect., Serials Dept., Univ. Toronto Lib., 1978–; Quality Cntrl. Libn., 1977–78, Head, Orig. Cat. Sect.–Mono., 1973–78, Cat. Libn., 1966–73; Cat. Libn., St. Michael's Coll. Lib., 1963–66. **Educ.:** Univ. of Toronto, 1946–50, BA, 1962–63, BLS. **Orgs.:** Can. LA. ALA. Univ. Toronto Libns. Assn. Art Gallery of ON. **Activities:** 1; 20, 44, 46 **Addr.:** Serials Dept., University of Toronto Library, 130 St. George St., Toronto, ON M5S 1A5, Canada.

Ansari, Mary B. (Ja. 15, 1939, Lincoln, IL) Actg. Head, Ref. Dept., Univ. NV, 1981–; Mines/Engin. Libn., 1976–81, Mines Libn., 1969–76, Ast. Ref. Libn., 1969; Ast. Ref. Libn., Gary Pub. Lib., 1964–66. **Educ.:** Univ. IL, 1959–61, BA (Finance), 1961–63, MLS; West. MI Univ., 1966–67, MBA. **Orgs.:** SLA. Geosci. Info. Socty. West. Assn. of Map Libs.: Nom. Com. (1974–75 and 1977–78); NV LA. Washoe Cnty. Hist. Socty.: Bd. of Dir. (1977–79). **Honors:** Phi Beta Kappa, 1961; Phi Kappa Phi, 1961; Beta Phi Mu, 1963. **Pubns.:** *Nevada Collections of Maps and Aerial Photographs* (1976); *Bibliography of Nevada Mining and Geology, 1966–1970* (1975); CoAuth., *Recent English Language Literature of Mine Ventilation, Intl. MIne Ventilation Congs.* (1979); *Gold and Silver Prospecting Bks. in Print*; "Birth and Growth of the Nevada Mining and Geology File", *CA Libn.* (O. 1977). **Activities:** 1, 14-bnch. libs.; 39; 64, 70, 71 **Addr.:** 11105 Caribou Rd., Reno, NV 89511.

Ansett, John F. (S. 26, 1921, Cornwell, PA) Pres., Book House, Inc., 1962–. **Educ.:** Valparaiso Univ., 1945–48, BA (Bus. Admin.); Northwestern Univ., 1948–51 (Bus. Admin.). **Orgs.:** ALA: Com. on Book dealer relshps. **Addr.:** The Book House, 208 West Chicago Street, Jonesville, MI 49250.

Anske, Kay L. (O. 10, 1952, San Antonio, TX) Dir./Libn., Oblate Coll. of the Southwest, 1979–; Tchr., N.E. IN Sch. Dist., 1974–79. **Educ.:** St. Mary's Univ., 1970–73, BA (Hist. Pol. Sci.); Univ. of TX, 1974–78, MLS. **Orgs.:** SLA. TX LA. Cath. LA. ATLA. Phi Kappa Phi. Phi Alpha Theta. **Honors:** Beta Phi Mu. **Activities:** 12; 17, 34, 39; 90 **Addr.:** Oblate College of the Southwest, San Antonio, TX 78216.

Ansley, Anne Cooney (Mr. 6, 1914, Birmingham, AL) Educ. Adv., GA Dept. of Educ., 1968–; Libn., Dykes HS, Atlanta, 1960–68; Ast. Libn., Sch. of Bus. Admin., Emory Univ., 1956–60. **Educ.:** Birmingham-South. Coll., 1931–36, AB (Eng., Soc. Std.); George Peabody Coll. for Tchrs., 1962–64, MLS; Emory Univ., 1956–60, Libn. Certif.; Univ. of GA, Crs. for Eds. **Orgs.:** ALA. GA LA: Sec. VP (1979–81). AASL: Sec. VP (1979–80); Reg. Dir. (1972–74); Various coms. Natl. Assn. Educ. Media Prof.: Secy. (1976–77). GA Assn. of Educrs.: 5th Dist. Libns. (Ch., 1964). GA Lib. Media Dept.: Adv. (1968–). Alpha Chi Omega. Intntl. Assn. Sch. Libns. **Pubns.:** Various articles and poetry. **Activities:** 10, 13; 21, 26, 32; 63, 67 **Addr.:** 139 Osner Dr., Atlanta, GA 30342.

Ansley, Elizabeth Glen (D. 7, 1948, Moultrie, GA) Lib. Srvs. Supvsr., GA Power Co., 1977–; Head Libn., GA Acad. for the Blind, 1976–77; Ref. Libn., Pub. Lib. Syst., Macon, GA, 1971–72. **Educ.:** Mercer Univ., 1968–70, BA (Eng.); Emory Univ., 1972–73, MLS (Libnshp.). **Orgs.:** GA LA: Gvtl. Rel. Com. ASIS. SLA: State Lib. Srvs. and Construct. Act Adv. Cncl. (Del., 1980–82); Stats. Com., Natl. Ch.; Rep. to ALA: LAMA/Stats. Sect.; S. Atl. Chap., Secy. ALA. Frnds. of the Lib., Inc. Macon, GA: VP (1973–74); Pres. (1975–77). Jr. Leag. of Atlanta, Inc.: Prof. Place. Adv. (1979–81); Proj. Coord. to Bring State Prison Lib. Syst. Up to ALA Stans. (1981–84). Women's Career Dev. Org.: Pubcty. Ch., Secy., VP (1977–79). **Honors:** Women's Career Dev. Org., Outstan. Achvmt., 1978. **Pubns.:** "Six Steps to Using the Library" pamphlet (1980); "On-Line Information–A User's Guide" pamphlet (1981); "GPC Library Answers Company's Information Needs," *Citizen* (F. 1978); "Management Training Film in Uses of On-Line Information as Planning Tool" film (1981); "Orientation to User Services of Company Library" film (1981). **Activities:** 5, 12; 17, 19, 47; 50, 78, 91 **Addr.:** Georgia Power Co., 333 Piedmont Ave., P.O. Box 4545, Atlanta, GA 30302.

Anspaugh, Judith Ford (O. 29, 1940, Akron, OH) Pub. Srvs. Libn., MS Coll. Law Lib., 1978–; Media Spec., Crestwood Mid. Sch., 1970–78. **Educ.:** Kent State Univ., 1958–62, BS (Educ.); 1974–77, MA (LS); various crs. in law. **Orgs.:** AALL. MS Coll. Law Review. **Honors:** Phi Alpha Delta; Lawyers Co-op Publshg. Co., Amer. Jur. Awd. Contracts I, 1980; Lawyers Co-op Publshg. Co., Amer. Jur. Awd. Property II, 1981. **Pubns.:** "Power of Settlor-Sole Beneficiary To Terminate An Irrevocable Trust," *MS Coll. Law Review* (Ja. 1981). **Activities:** 1; 22, 39, 41; 77 **Addr.:** Mississippi College Law Library, 151 E. Griffith St., Jackson, MS 39202.

Anspaugh, Sheryl (Je. 8, 1946, Oklahoma City, OK) Dir. of Lrng. Resrcs., Houston Cmnty. Coll. Syst., 1977–; Admin. Asst., Tulsa City-Cnty. Lib. Syst., 1975–77; Head Libn., S. OK City Jr. Coll., 1972–75; Ref., Pub. Srvs. Libn., Neast. A and M Jr. Coll., 1969–72. **Educ.:** OK Univ., 1964–67, BA (Hist.), 1969, MLS; MA (Pub. Admin.), 1981. **Orgs.:** TX LA. SW LA. ALA. OK LA: Secy. (1976–77); IFC (Rep. and State Co-Ch., 1973–74); Coll. and Univ. Div. (Ch., 1974–75); ILL Com. (1973–75); Lib. Dev. Com. (1974–75). Other orgs. OK Assn. of Cmnty. and Jr. Colls.: Lib. Div. (Secy., 1973–74; Consult., 1976). **Honors:** John Cotton Dana Spec. Awd., 1977. **Pubns.:** "Leadership in Community and Junior College Libraries," *Leadership in Libnshp.* (1981); "Public Relations in Public Libraries," *Educating the Pub. Lib. User* (1981). "Public Libraries: Teaching the User?" *Progress in Educating the Library User* (1978); "Educating the Student of a Two-Year Higher Education Institution", *Educating the Library User* (1974); "Election Day–USA. This Year Has Special Meaning For Oklahoma Libraries", *OK Libn.* (Oct. 1976); **Activities:** 1, 10; 17; 50 **Addr.:** Learning Resources Center, Houston Community College System, 2801 Travis, Houston, TX 77006.

Antczak, Janice (S. 9, 1947, Jersey City, NJ) Assoc. Prof., Brookdale Community Coll., 1974–; Head, Chld. Svcs., Middletown Twp. Lib., 1972–74; Chld. Libn., Matawan Jt. Pub. Lib., 1970–72. **Educ.:** Seton Hill Coll., 1965–69, BA, (Hist.); Simmons Coll., 1969–70, MLS; Rutgers Univ., 1971–74, MEd; Columbia Univ., 1975–79, DLS. **Orgs.:** ALA. NJ LA: Educ. for Libnshp. (1978); IFC (1975–78); Mem. (1972–74); Awds. Com. (1976); Monmouth Libns. Assn.: Exec. Bd. (1973–74, 1976–77); Pres. (1974–75). Chld. Lit. Assn. **Honors:** Monmouth LA, Past Pres. Src. Recog., 1975. **Activities:** 9, 10; 21, 26, 48; 63, 95-chld. lit. **Addr.:** Institute of Applied Humanities, Brookdale Community College, Newman Springs Road, Lincroft, NJ 07738.

Anthony, Deborah L. (S. 20, 1952, Detroit, MI) Supvsr., Media Srvs., Rochester Cmnty. Schs., 1979–; Off Campus Instr., MI State Univ., 1980; Elem. Lib. Coord., Sch. Dist., City of Berkley, 1975–79. **Educ.:** Adrian Coll., 1970–74, BA (Eng. Earth Sci., Educ.); Wayne State Univ., 1974–75, MSLS (Sch. Lib., Media); Permanent MI Tchg. Cert. (K–12). **Orgs.:** ALA: AASL; YASD; Chld. Srvs. Div. AECT. MI Assn. for Media in Educ.: Reg. 17, Ch. (1980), Prog. Ch. (1979); N. Ctrl. Accred. Com. (Ch., 1979–81); State Conf. Com. (1980–81); Legis. Com. (1979–); Legis. Day (Ch., 1981). Assn. for Supvsn. and Curric. Dev. Rochester Admin. Assns.: Negtns. Team (1981–83). **Pubns.:** "Issue: The Projected Role of the REMC in Michigan," *Media Spectrum* (1978); "White House Conference in Oakland County," *Rumbles from Mame* (Fall 1978); "Leaders in Volunteer Service," *Media Spectrum* (1980); "Leadership Is....," *Media Spectrum* (1980). **Addr.:** 1415 John R Rd., Rochester, MI 48063.

Anthony, Donald C. (Mr. 29, 1926, New York, NY) Dir. of Libs., Syracuse Univ., 1974–; Assoc. Dir. of Libs., Columbia Univ., 1969–74, Ast. Dir. of Libs., 1966–69; Assoc. Libn., Head, Mss. and Hist. Sect., NY State Lib., 1961–66; Dir., Fargo Publ Lib., 1959–61; Head Libn., Eleutherian Mills Hagley Fndn., 1955–59; Libn. I, Enoch Pratt Free Lib., 1954–55. **Educ.:** Dartmouth Coll., 1944, (Nvl., V-12); Univ. of WI, 1949–51, BA, (Hist.), 1953–54, MA, (LS); Univ. of Geneva, 1952–53, Hist. Cert. **Orgs.:** AcRL: Prsrvn. Com. (Secy., 1969–72). ALA: Com. on Appts. and Noms. (Ch., 1972–73); Rep., Amer. Cncl. on Educ. (1973–74). SAA: Prsrvn. Com. (1968–75). SLA: Tellers Com. (1968); Srch. Com. for Exec. Dir. (1970). NY Metro. Ref. and Resrch. Lib. Agncy.: Trustee (1969–74); Various coms. (1967–74). Dobbs Ferry Sch. Syst.: Trustee (1971–74); Bldg. Com. (Ch., 1972–74). **Honors:** Univ. WI, Inst. for Internatl. Educ., Schol., 1951; Cncl. on Lib. Resrcs., Flwshp., 1970. **Activities:** 1; 17 **Addr.:** 100 Bird Library, Syracuse University, Syracuse, NY 13210.

Anthony, Emily H. (Ag. 3, 1925, Camden, AL) Dir., NE GA Reg. Lib., 1972–; Media Spec., East Cobb Jr. HS, 1967–72. **Educ.:** Huntingdon Coll., 1942–46, AB (Bus. Admin.); Emory Univ., 1966–67, MLbn. **Orgs.:** GA LA: Pub. Libn. Sect. (Vice-Ch., 1979–81). GA Cncl. for Pub. Libs.: Legis. Com. (Ch., 1979–80). ALA: Adv. Com. on Libs. to Supt. of Schs., Ch. N. GA Assoc. Libs. Helen Cham. of Cmrce. GA Mt. Travel Assn. **Activities:** 9; 17, 19, 35; 69, 78, 86 **Addr.:** P.O. Box 378, Clarkesville, GA 30523.

Anthony, Susan Shelly (N. 15, 1952, Cincinnati, OH) Head of Info. Access, Univ. of Cincinnati Med. Ctr. Libs., 1978–; Circuit Libn., Cleveland Hlth. Sci. Lib., 1975–78. **Educ.:** Miami Univ., 1970–74, AB (Zlgy.); Univ. of MI, 1974–75, MLS; Med. LA, 1975, Grade I Cert. **Orgs.:** Med. LA. Cincinnati Area Hlth. Sci. Libns. Assn.: VP (1978–79). Chld. Intl. Sum. Vlgs. **Pubns.:** "One librarian for Six Hospitals", *Hosp. Libs.* (Mr. 1977); "Incremental charges for Online Srvs.: An Analysis", Proceedings of the 2nd Natl. Online Mtg., Mr. 24-26, 1981. **Activities:** 1, 12; 27, 31, 39; 58, 80, 87 **Addr.:** Univ. of Cincinnati, Medical Center Libraries, 231 Bethesda Ave., Cincinnati, OH 45267.

Antonietti, Reno M. (Ag. 29, 1937, Olean, NY) Dir., Instr. Media Srvs., Rochester Inst. of Tech., 1977–, Dir., AV Srvs., 1974–77, AV Libn., 1964–74. **Educ.:** Rochester Inst. of Tech., 1964–68, BS (Ind. Mgt.); SUNY, Geneseo, 1968–70, MLS. **Orgs.:** AECT. Rochester AV Assn. Brighton, NY Pub. Lib.: Trustee. Rochester Reg. Resrch. Lib. Cncl.: Media Com. (Ch.) **Activities:** 1; 32; 61, 67 **Addr.:** Director, Instructional Media Services, Rochester Institute of Technology, Rochester, NY 14623.

Antony, Arthur Andrew (Ja. 3, 1937, New Orleans, LA) Info. anal., Chevron Resrch. Co., 1981– Assoc. Libn., Univ. CA, Santa Barbara, 1974–80, Resrch. Assoc. in Chem., Wayne State Univ., 1972–72; Resrch. Assoc. in Chem., Univ. Coll., London, 1971–72. **Educ.:** Loyola Univ., 1955–59, BS (Chem.); Princeton Univ., 1959–63, MS, PhD (Chem.); LA State Univ., 1973–73, MLS. **Orgs.:** ALA. ASIS. SLA. Bay Area Online Users' Grp. **Honors:** Univer. CA, Santa Barbara Lib., Amy and Jens Nyholm Awd., 1978; Beta Phi Mu. **Pubns.:** *Guide to Basic Information Sources in Chemistry* (1979); "An Examination of Search Strategy and an On-Line Bibliographic System", *Spec. Libs.* (1979); "Searching the Chemistry Files for Synthetic Organic Chemistry Database", (1978); "An Online Component in an Interdisciplinary Course on Information Resources for Science and Engineering Students". *On-l-ine Review* (1978); "Networking in the Microcosm, or Reference Referrals" *RQ* (1978); various reviews. **Activities:** 1; 31, OL info, 39; 60, 91 **Addr.:** Chevron Research Co., P.O. Box 1627 Richmond, CA 94802.

Anzalone, Alfred M. (Ap. 23, 1926, Kearny, NJ) Admin. Libn., Plastics Tech. Eval. Ctr., 1960–; Lit. Resrch. Chem., Picatinny Arsenal Sci.-Tech. Lib., 1956–60, Asst. Chief Plng., Tech. Srvs. Dir., 1956, Resrch. Chem., Chem. Resrch., 1951–56; Analytical Chem., F.W. Berk and Co., 1949–51. **Educ.:** Newark Coll. of Engin., 1943–46 (Chem. Engin.); Seton Hall Univ., 1947–49, BS (Chem.); Rutgers Univ., 1958–60, MLS. **Orgs.:** SLA: Pres.; VP; Prog. Ch.; Bus. Mgr.; Nom. Ch.; Bylaws Ch. ASIS. Picatinny Arsenal Tech. Assn.: Pres. (1955–56). NJ Alum. Club: Pres. (1951–52). Kearny Area Jr. Cham. of Cmrce.: Pres. (1956–57). Mondham NJ Parent-Tchr. Assn.: Pres. (1970–71). **Honors:** Alpha Phi Delta. **Pubns.:** Various articles. **Activities:** 4; 15, 17, 30; 74 **Addr.:** Plastec–Bldg. 3401, ORRADCOM, Dover, NJ 07801.

Aoyama, Karen Marshall (F. 16, 1951, Pittsburgh, PA) Coord., Basic Srch., Trng., Pac. NW Bibl. Ctr., 1979–; Ref., ILL Libn., ID State Lib., 1978–79; Ref. Libn., Shaker Heights Pub. Lib., 1977–78; Bibl. Srch., Pac. NW Bibl. Ctr., 1976–77. **Educ.:** Brown Univ., 1969–73, AB (Amer. Cvlzn.); Univ. of Chicago, 1973–76, MA (Libnshp.). **Orgs.:** Pac. NW LA: Ref. Div., Vice-Ch. (1979–81), Ch. (1981–83). ALA: RASD; ASCLA; Int. Frdm. Com. Progressive Animal Welfare Socty. Immoral Minority of WA. **Honors:** Phi Beta Kappa, 1973. **Pubns.:** "Idaho Plus WLN – Better Library Service," *ID Libn.* (Ap. 1979). **Activities:** 3, 12; 24, 34, 39; 56, 57, 93 **Addr.:** Pacific Northwest Bibliographic Center, University of Washington Libraries FM–25, Seattle, WA 98195.

Apedaile, Marilyn E. (Ag. 22, 1944, Smiths Falls, ON) Bd. Mem., Rideau Twp. Pub. Lib., 1979–, Libn. In Charge, 1965–77. **Educ.:** Univ. of Ottawa, 1973–75, BA (Hons. Msc.); Univ. of West. ON, MLS in progress; Univ. of Toronto, 1972, ARCT. **Orgs.:** ON LA. CAN LA. ON Regis. Msc. Tchrs. Assn. **Activities:** 9; 22, 36, 47; 55, 63 **Addr.:** Box 98, North Gower, ON K0A 2T0, Canada.

Appel, Anne M. (S. 2, 1940, New York City, NY) Dir., Denville Free Pub. Lib., 1980–; Dir., North Plainfield Lib., 1978–79; Libn. II, Somerset Cnty. Lib., 1973–78. **Educ.:** Cooper Un. Sch. of Art, 1958–61, Cert. (Art); Univ. of CA, Los Angeles, 1963–65, BA (Art); Rutgers Univ., 1965–67, MA (Rom. Langs.), 1967–70, PhD (Rom. Langs.), 1976–77, MLS (Lib. Srv.). **Orgs.:** NJ LA. ALA. **Honors:** Beta Phi Mu; Phi Beta Kappa, 1965; Woodrow Wilson Flwshps., 1967–68, 1969–70; Fulbright, Std. Grant, 1969–70. **Activities:** 9; 17, 34, 38; 55, 75 **Addr.:** 18 Richter St., Randolph, NJ 07869.

Special Subjects/Services: 50. Adult educ.; 51. Advert./Mktg.; 52. Aerosp.; 53. Agric.; 54. Area std.; 55. Arts/Hum.; 56. Autom.; 57. Bibl./Prtg.; 58. Bio. sci.; 59. Bus./Fin.; 60. Chem.; 61. Copyrt.; 62. Documtn.; 63. Educ.; 64. Engin.; 65. Env.; 66. Eth. grps.; 67. Film; 68. Food/Nutr.; 69. Geneal.; 70. Geo.; 71. Geol.; 72. Handcpd.; 73. Hist.; 74. Int. frdm.; 75. Info. sci.; 76. Insr.; 77. Law; 78. Legis.; 79. Math./Comp. sci.; 80. Med.; 81. Metals; 82. Nat. resrcs.; 83. Newsp.; 84. Nuc. sci.; 85. Oral hist.; 86. Petr./Energy; 87. Pharm.; 88. Phys./Astr./Math.; 89. Readg.; 90. Relig.; 91. Sci./Tech.; 92. Soc. sci.; 93. Telecom.; 94. Transp.; 95. (other).

Appel, Marsha Ceil (D. 3, 1953, New York, NY) Staff Exec., Mem. Info. Srvc., Amer. Assn. of Advert. Agencies, 1976–. **Educ.:** SUNY, Albany, 1970–74, BA, (Soclgy., Hist.); Syracuse Univ., 1974–75, MSLS. **Orgs.:** SLA: NY Chap.; Advert./Mktg. Grp. (Secy.-Treas., 1978–79). **Honors:** Beta Phi Mu, 1975. **Pubns.:** *Illustration Index, 4th Edition* (1980); Ed., *What's New in Advertising and Marketing* (1978–80). **Activities:** 12; 17, 30, 41; 51, 56 **Addr.:** American Association of Advertising Agencies, 666 Third Ave., New York, NY 10017.

Appel, Rhoda Sara (O. 24, 1920, Brooklyn, NY) Dir., Bur. of Libs. and AV Educ., Newark Bd. of Educ., 1969–; Head Libn., Weequahic HS, 1965–69; Head Libn., Clinton Pl. Jr. HS, 1957–65; Libn., Madison Jr. HS, 1946–57; Libn., Natl. Trng. Sch. for Boys, Bur. of Prisons, US Dept. of Justice, 1944–46. **Educ.:** Douglass Coll., 1936–40, BSc (Math, LS); Rutgers Sch. of Educ., 1948–49, MEd. **Orgs.:** NJ Sch. Media Assn.: VP (1971–73). Chld. Bk. Cncl.: Dir. (1976–78). ALA. Newark Sch. Libns. Assn. Other orgs. Assn. Supvsr. and Curric. Dev. Newark Assn. Dirs. and Supvsr.: Secy. (1976–). Newark Youth Cncl.: Adv. (1958–60). **Pubns.:** "A Functional Library Serving Boys", *Lib. Jnl.* (1945); Coord. Guid. Film on Orien. of Jr. HS Students (1960). **Activities:** 10; 17, 21, 32; 63, 67, 89 **Addr.:** 203 Ivy St., Newark, NJ 07106.

Apple, Ethel Bayless (D. 1, 1927, Elgin, IL) Libn., Elgin Cmnty. Coll., 1967–; Child. Libn., Gail Borden Pub. Lib., 1951–56. **Educ.:** IL Wesleyon Univ., 1946–50, BM (Msc.); North. IL Univ., 1966–70, MA (LS); Various grad. crs. (LS). **Orgs.:** ALA: ACRL/CJCLS Nom. Com. (1977–78); Instr. and Use Com. (1975–77). IL LA. Ref. Libns. Assn. of N. Suburban Lib. Syst.: Adv. Com. IL Reg. Lib. Cncl.: Nom. Com. (1977). Sigma Alpha Iota. AAUW. **Honors:** Beta Phi Mu. **Pubns.:** "Survey of a Learning Resources Center: Facilities and Use," *Quantitative Measurement and Dynamic Library Service* (1978). **Activities:** 1; 31, 34, 39; 56 **Addr.:** 402 Miller Dr., Elgin, IL 60120.

Applebaum, Edmond Lewis (D. 19, 1924, Boston, MA) Retired, 1980–; Assoc. Libn. for Mgt., Lib. of Congs., 1978–80, Dir., Admin. Dept., 1976–78, Ast. and Assoc. Dir., Processing Dept., 1956–76, Various Other Positions, 1950–66. **Educ.:** Harvard, 1946–49, BA (Eng. Lit.); Columbia, 1949–50, MSLS Harvard, 1954–55, MPA. **Orgs.:** ALA: ACRL; LITA. Cosmos Clb. Harvard Clb. of Wash. **Honors:** ALA, Margaret Mann Cit., 1972; Lib. of Congs., Superior Srv. Awd., 1967. **Pubns.:** Ed., *Reader in Technical Services* (1973); "Wartime Preservation of Libraries", *Encyc. Amer.* (1969); Ed., "Foreign Acquisitions Programs of the Library of Congress", *Frgn. Acq.* (1972); "Centralized Cataloging for the Country–Now and in the Future", *Changing Concept of Srv. in Libs.* (1970); "The National Program for Acquisitions and Cataloging", *Lib. Res. and Tech. Servs.* (vol. 12, No. 1, 1968). **Activities:** 1, 4; 15, 17, 26 **Addr.:** 7322 Edmonston Rd., College Park, MD 20740.

Appleby, Judith Ann (Ap. 26, 1947, Montreal, PQ) Asst. Libn., Vanier Lib., Concordia Univ., 1972–; Ref./Cat. Libn., Cote St. Luc Pub. Lib., 1971–72. **Educ.:** Sir Geo. Williams Univ., 1965–68, BA (Hist.); McGill Univ., 1969–71, MLS. **Orgs.:** CAN Assn. for Info. Sci.; CAN LA. SLA: East. CAN Chap., Mem. and Rcrmt. Com. (Ch., 1979–81). Assn. for the Bibl. of Hist. Internatl. Wildlife Fed. **Activities:** 1; 15, 31, 39; 55 **Addr.:** Concordia University, Vanier Library, Reference Department, 7141 Sherbrooke St. W., Montreal, PQ H4B 1R6, Canada.

Arader, W. Graham, III (N. 16, 1950, Bryn Mawr, PA) Owner, W. Graham Arader III, Pubshlg., 1979–; Owner, W. Graham Arader III, Rare maps bks. and prints, 1973–; Owner, Charles Sessler, Inc. **Educ.:** Yale Univ., 1968–73, BA (Econ.). **Orgs.:** Antiq. Booksellers Assn. of Amer. Intl. Leag. of Antiq. Booksellers. Appraisers Assns. of Amer. **Activities:** 14-Bookstore; 18, 23, 45; 54, 57, 70 **Addr.:** W. Graham Arader III, 1000 Boxwood Ct., King of Prussia, PA 19406.

Aramayo, Susan B. (O. 31, 1942, Pittsburgh, PA) Chief, Copyrt. Cat. Div., Lib. of Congs., 1981–; Asst. Chief, Copyrt. Cat. Div., 1979–, Chief, Licn. Div., Copyrt. Ofc., 1977–79, Educ. Liaison Ofcr., 1975–77, Deputy Chief, Cat. Instr., Prcs. Dept., 1969–75, Asst. Cat. Instr., 1967–69, Descr. Catlgr., Eng. Sect., 1965–67. **Educ.:** Univ. of Pittsburgh, 1960–63, BA (Eng. Lit.), 1964–65, MLS. **Orgs.:** ALA. Lib. of Congs. Prof. Assn.: VP (1973), Pres. (1974). **Honors:** Lib. of Congs., Meritorious Srv. Awd., 1969, 1979. **Activities:** 4; 17, 20, 26; 61 **Addr.:** 6056 River Dr., Lorton, VA 22079.

Aranow, Nancy Oberdorfer (New York, NY) Emeritus, 1981–; Libn., Warburg, Paribas, Becker, 1976–80; Circ. Dept. Head, Boston Univ., 1973–75; Asst. Libn., Watson Lib. of Bus., Columbia Univ., 1971–72, Rsv. Bk. Libn., 1970–71, Ref. Libn., 1969–70. **Educ.:** Wellesley Coll., 1964–68, BA (Hist.); Columbia Univ., 1968–69, MLS. **Orgs.:** SLA: NY Chap., Bus. and Fin. Grp. (1976); Coll. Mem. Rcrt. Prog. (Head, 1977–79). **Activities:** 1, 12; 15, 22, 39; 59 **Addr.:** Warburg Paribas Becker, 55 Water St., New York, NY 10041.

Arbuckle, Jennifer C. (My. 26, 1947, Toronto, ON) Deputy Dir., Etobicoke Pub. Lib., 1981–; Head, Ctrl. Lib., North York Pub. Lib., 1980–81, Head, Don Mills Pub. Lib., 1980, Asst. Head, Ctrl. Lib., 1975–80. **Educ.:** York Univ., Glendon Coll., 1965–68, BA (Eng.); Univ. of Toronto, 1968–69, BLS. **Orgs.:** ON LA. Can. LA. Can. Assn. Info. Sci. **Activities:** 9; 16, 17, 35; 56 **Addr.:** Etobicoke Public Library, Box 501, Etobicoke, ON M9C-5G1 Canada.

Arbuckle, Marybeth M. (Je. 9, 1943, Walla Walla, WA) Acq. Libn., Ft. Vancouver Reg. Lib., 1981–; Cnty. Libn., Deschutes Cnty. Lib., 1978–81; City Libn., OR City Pub. Lib., 1972–78; Assoc. Cat. Libn., Univ. KS Libs., 1969–71; Asst. Hum. Libn., Portland State Univ. Lib., 1966–69. **Educ.:** Univ. of Puget Sound, 1961–65, BA (Music); Univ. of Denver, 1965–66, MA (Libnshp.). **Orgs.:** OR LA: Secy. (1979–80). Pacific NW LA. ALA. Bend, OR Cham. of Cmrce.: Visitors and Conv. Com. (1978–81). McLoughlin Meml. Assn.: Bd. of Dirs. (Secy., 1975–76). **Activities:** 1, 9; 17, 20, 39; 55, 69 **Addr.:** Ft. Vancouver Regional Library, 1007 E. Mill Plain Blvd., Vancouver, WA 98663.

Arcari, Ralph D. (Ja. 31, 1943, Hartford, CT) Dir., Hlth. Ctr. Lib., Univ. of CT, 1977–, Asst. Dir., Pub. Srvs., 1975–76; Asst. Libn., Trinity Coll., 1974–75, Chief, Readrs. Srvs., 1969–75. **Educ.:** Cath. Univ. of Amer., 1963–65, BA (Phil.); Drexel Univ., 1965–66, MS (LS); Trinity Coll., 1968–72, MA (Pol. Sci.). **Orgs.:** Med. LA. ALA. CT Assn. of Hlth. Sci. Libs. Cap. Reg. Lib. Cncl.: Bd. (1979–82). New Eng. Reg. Med. Lib. Srv. Adv. Cncl.: Ch. (1979). **Pubns.:** "The Librarian in Clinical Care," *Hosp. Med. Staff* (1977). **Activities:** 1; 17 **Addr.:** Health Center Library, University of Connecticut, Farmington, CT 06032.

Arce de Llorente, Maria M. (Sagua de Tanamo, Oriente, Cuba) Resrch., Univ. of PR, 1980–, Ref. Libn., 1969–80, Asst. Libn., Circ. Dept., 1965–68, Asst. Libn., Pharm. Lib., 1961–65. **Educ.:** Normal Sch. for Tchrs., Havana, Cuba, 1945–49 (Tchr., Readg.); Univ. of Havana, Cuba, 1950–56, DEd (Psy.); Pratt Inst., 1968–69, MLS (Coll., Resrch. Libs.). **Orgs.:** ALA. SBPR: Secy. (1977–78); Mem. Com. (1966–67). Coll. de Pedagogos, Havana, Cuba. **Pubns.:** "Alice Jones: A Biography," *Bib. Gen.* **Activities:** 1, 5; 31, 39, 41; 57, 63, 89 **Addr.:** Box 22687, University of Puerto Rico Station, San Juan, PR 00931.

Archer, Jean Monson (Je. 24, 1930, Lehigh, IA) Sch. Libn., Shelby Cnty. Schs., 1971–; AV Catlgr., Disciples of Christ Hist. Socty., 1979. **Educ.:** Memphis State Univ., 1967–71, BS (Educ.); Peabody Sch. of LS, 1978–79, MLS. **Orgs.:** ALA. TN LA. SELA. Natl. Educ. Assn. TN Educ. Assn. W. TN Educ. Assn.; Lib. Sect., Secy.-Treas. (1977). Shelby Cnty. Educ. Assn.: Fac. Rep. (1976). **Honors:** Beta Phi Mu, 1979; Kappa Delta Pi, 1971; ALA/Ecyc. Britannica, Outstanding Sch. Lib. Prog., 1974. **Pubns.:** "Audio-Visuals in the Historical Society", *Discipliana* (Mr. 1980); Documentary–History of 1st Christian Church, Nashville, TN, *Slide/Tape* (1979). **Activities:** 2, 10; 20, 32, 48; 63, 67 **Addr.:** 3086 Scotland Rd., Memphis, TN 38128.

Archer, John Hall (Jl. 11, 1914, Broadview, SK) Pres. Emeritus and Prof. of West. Can. Hist., Univ. of Regina, 1976–, Pres., 1974–76; Princ., Univ. SK, 1970–74; Archvst. and Prof. of Hist., Queen's Univ., 1967–69; Dir., McGill Libs., 1964–67; Prov. Archvst., SK Prov., 1957–62, Legis. Libn., 1950–64; Vice-Princ., Wawota HS, 1939. **Educ.:** Scott Coll. and Tchrs. Coll., 1933, Dip.; Univ. of SK, 1947, BA (Hist.), 1948, MA (Hist.); McGill Univ., 1949, BLS; Queen's Univ., 1969, PhD (Hist.). **Orgs.:** Can. LA. ALA. Assn. of Can. Archvsts. Natl. Apprais. Bd. (Arch.). Can. Hist. Assn. Soc. Sci. Fed. Cncl. for CAN Unity: SK Pres. (1976–). Royal Can. Artillery Assn. Other orgs. **Honors:** Coronation Medal, 1953; 25th Anniv. Com., Jubilee Medal, 1977. **Pubns.:** *Saskatchewan: A History, 1980* (1981); Ed., *The Book of Humbug* (1958); CoAuth., *Footprints in Time* (1965); Ed., *Search for Stability* (1959); "Acquisition of Canadian Provincial Government Documents", *Lib. Resrcs. and Tech. Bltn.* (Win. 1961); "The Public Records in Saskatchewan", *Socty. of Archvsts. Jnl.* (Apr. 1960); "The Saskatchewan Story", Broadcast series (1978–79); Other bks. articles, etc. **Activities:** 2; 18, 24, 38; 92 **Addr.:** President Emeritus and Professor of Western Canadian History, University of Regina, Regina, SK S4S 0A2, Canada.

Archer, Mary Ann Elizabeth (Mr. 7, 1930, Rochester, NY) Sr. Info. Anal., Resrch. Labs, Eastman Kodak Co., 1967–; Tech. Libn., Xerox Corp., 1966–67; Libn. and Biblgphr., Sybron Corp., 1962–65; Freelance Indxr. **Educ.:** SUNY, Geneseo, 1949–53, BS (Lib. Ed.), 1972–77, MSLS. **Orgs.:** ASIS: Upstate NY Ch. (1972). Assoc. Info. Mgrs. Women's Career Ctr.: Bd. of Dir. (1977–79). Socty. of Photograph. Sci. and Engins.: Educ. Com. (1977–79). **Pubns.:** *Spacecraft Sterilization, Annotated Bibliography* (1964); "The Make or Buy Decision", *ONLINE* (July 1978); "INSPEC, a Database Review", *ONLINE* (Oct. 1977). **Addr.:** Department of Information Services, Research Laboratories, Eastman Kodak Company, 1669 Lake Ave., Rochester, NY 14650.

Archibald, Jean K. (O. 31, 1917, Newton, MA) Adj. Assoc. Prof., Lib. Dir., Macalester Coll., 1978–, Assoc. Dir., 1970–78, Ref. Libn., 1967–69. **Educ.:** Simmons Coll., 1935–39, BS (Lib. Sci.). **Orgs.:** MN LA: Acad. Div. (Ch., 1971–72); Bd. of Dir. (1971–72); GODORT (Secy., 1973–74). ALA. Coll. Libs. in Cnstm.: Dir. (1969, 1978–); Pres. (1981–82). St. Paul Civic Symp. Assn.: Bd. of Dir. (1977–); Libn. (1979–). **Honors:** Phi Beta Kappa, 1975. **Activities:** 1; 29, 31, 45; 57, 75, 78 **Addr.:** 1425 Englewood Ave., St. Paul, MN 55104.

Ard, Harold J. (Ag. 26, 1940, Herrick, IL) Assoc. Dir., Univ. MS Med. Ctr. Lib., 1978–; Dir., Jackson Metro. Lib. Syst., 1972–78; Dir., Arlington Hts. Meml. Lib., 1969–72; Head Libn., Barrington Pub. Lib., 1965–69. **Educ.:** IL State Univ., 1958–62, BS (Spec. Educ.); Rosary Coll., 1964–68, MS (LS); IL State Univ. (grad. crs. in psy.) 1962–64. **Orgs.:** ALA: Archit. Com., Insr. Com., MS Rcrt. Chn. SE LA: Med. Lib. Assn. MS LA: Const. and Bylaws Com., Cont. Ed. Com., Nom. Com., IFC; Other coms. Rotary Clb. **Pubns.:** "The Arlington Heights Memorial Library: A Building for the Community", *Lib. Binder* (Dec. 1969); "The Double Referendum", *IL Libs.* (May 1970); "A Modern Library for a Mobile Public", *Personal Bk. Guide* (Feb. 1972); "Of Times Remembered: A Review of Frances Rogers' The Story of a Small Town Library: the Development of the Woodstock, N.Y. Library", *Lib. Jnl.* (Sept. 1, 1974); "A Year of Change for Jackson: From City Library to Unified Metropolitan System", *Seast. Libn.* (Spring 1974). **Activities:** 9, 12; 17, 19, 24; 56, 63, 67 **Addr.:** 804 Briarwood Dr., Jackson, MS 39211.

Arden, Caroline (O. 16, 1928, Thomasville, GA) Instr., Coord., VA Prog., Cath. Univ. of Amer., 1978–; Coord. Pub. Svcs., Arlington Cnty. (Va.) Pub. Lib., 1973–78, Bk. Sel. Libn., 1969–73; Comm. Consult., Smithsonian Inst., 1968–69; YA Svcs. Coord., Prince George's Cnty. Pub. Lib., 1966–67; Lib. Consult., Woodberry Forest Sch., 1965–66; YA Svcs. Supvsr., Arlington Cnty. Pub. Lib., 1961–65; Chld. Libn., Braswell Mem. Lib., 1959–60. **Educ.:** FL State Univ., 1947–58, BA, (LS), 1960–61, MS, (LS); Cath. Univ. of Amer., 1979–, (PhD in progress); Univ. MD, 1967–68, Post-Master Certif., (LS). **Orgs.:** ALA: VA Cncl. rep. (1980–84). VA LA: Legis. Com. (Chmn., 1976–78); Fed-State Coord. (1976–). SE LA: Gvt. Rel. Com., (1978–). DC LA: Legis. Com. (1964–67). Other orgs. Adult Ed. Assn.: Natl. Legis. Policy Com. (1976–). Adult Ed. Assn. of VA: Secy. (1979–). Press Clb. of North. VA: Treas. (1977–79). **Honors:** Beta Phi Mu, 1961. **Pubns.:** Jt. Auth., *Non-Conventional File Structure Data-Collecting Projects in the Smithsonian Institution* (1969); "Librarianship", *Encyclopedia of Education* (1970). **Activities:** 9; 16, 26, 36; 50, 78 **Addr.:** 5999 9th Street, N., Arlington, VA 22205.

Arden, Sandra E. Rose (D. 29, 1929, New York, NY) Asst. Dir., Troy Pub. Lib., 1978–, Head, Adult Srvs., Ref., 1977–, Ref. Libn., 1975–77, Chld. Libn., 1973–75; Libn., Port Washington Pub. Lib., 1969–72. **Educ.:** Hunter Coll., 1947–51, BA (Eng., Drama); Long Island Univ., 1969–71, MLS; State of MI, 1978, Permanent Prof. Cert. **Orgs.:** MI LA: Ref. Caucus (1978–80). ALA. B'Nai B'Rith Women: Ctrl. Nassau Chap., Pres.; Nassau Cncl., VP. Hadassah. **Honors:** Alpha Lambda Delta, 1949. **Activities:** 9; 16, 17, 39; 50, 59, 80 **Addr.:** Troy Public Library, 510 W. Big Beaver, Troy, MI 48084.

Ardito, Stephanie C. (My. 29, 1951, Cortland, NY) Dir., Grntlgcl. Info. Prog., Syracuse Univ. Grntlgy. Cntr., 1977–; Span. Proj. Fld. Libn., Palatine Pub. Lib. Dist., 1975–77;Aging Prog. Libn., Houston Pub. Lib., 1974–75. **Educ.:** Syracuse Univ., 1969–73, BA (Amer. Lit.), 1973–74, MLS. **Orgs.:** ALA. ASIS. Assoc. Info. Mgrs. NY LA. Grntlgl. Socty. **Pubns.:** Co-Auth., *Information in Social Gerontology* (1978); "Chicago–Suburban Libraries and the Spanish Speaking," *Wilson Lib. Bltn.* (N. 1978); Paper, 32nd Anl. Sci. Mtg. Grntlgy. Socty. (1979). **Activities:** 1, 9; 17, 24, 49-Dssm. syst. Grntlgy.; 66, 95-Grntlgy. **Addr.:** Gerontological Information Program (GRIP), Syracuse University Gerontology Center, Brockway Hall, Syracuse, NY 13210.

Arguello de Cardona, María Elena (Ja. 18, 1925, Managua, Nicaragua) Dir. of Lib., Inter Amer. Univ. of PR, 1977–; Dir., Caribbean Reg. Lib., 1970–77; Libn., Biblgphr., Univ. of PR, Inst. of Caribbean Std., 1968–70; Co-ed., Cumulative Subj. Index, *Handbook of Latin Amer. Std.*, Hisp. Fndn., Lib. of Congs., 1967–68; Sr. Libn., Latin Amer. Cat., Univ. of FL Lib., 1966–67; Libn. II, Latin Amer. Catlgr., NY Pub. Lib., 1963–65, Libn., Latin Amer. Catlgr., 1962–63; various other lib. positions. **Educ.:** Univ. of PR, 1958, BA (Hum.); Pratt Inst., 1962, MLS. **Orgs.:** Assn. de Comms. y Tech. Educ. SALALM: Caribbean Bibl. Com. (Ch., 1970–76). Assn. of Caribbean Univ. and Resrch. Insts. Libs.: Secy. (1971); Exec. Cncl. (Pres., 1976); Bibl. Com. (Ch., 1971–74); PR Com. (Ch., 1977–81). SBPR: Com. de Mejoramiento Prof. (Ch., 1975–76); Junta Directiva (1977–80). PR Cncl on Higher Educ.: Consult. Bd. (1979–1981). **Honors:** Univ. of PR, Pedreira Awd. PR Lit., 1958. **Pubns.:** Various compilations, sps. **Activities:** 1; 17, 31, 46; 57, 62, 75 **Addr.:** Box 1293, Inter American University of Puerto Rico Metropolitan Campus, Hato Rey, PR 00919.

Ariail, Julius F. (Ag. 27, 1944, Alexandria, LA) Circ. Libn., GA South. Coll., 1977–; Asst. Cat. Libn., 1976–77. **Educ.:** Emory Univ., 1964–67, BA (Eng.); FL State Univ., 1975–76, MLS; GA South. Coll., 1977–80, MA (Eng.). **Orgs.:** ALA. SELA. GA LA. Amer. Soc. of Indxrs. Amer. Prtg. Hist. Assoc. **Honors:** Woodrow Wilson Fndn., Flwshp., 1967; Phi Beta Kappa, 1967. **Pubns.:** Cumulative Index, *Philosophical Books,* Volumes 1-15

PROFESSIONAL ACTIVITIES: Institutions: 1. Acad. lib.; 2. Arch.; 3. Assn.; 4. Fed./Gvt. lib.; 5. Inst. lib.; 6. Mfr./Suppl.; 7. Milit. lib.; 8. Musm.; 9. Pub. lib.; 10. Sch. lib.; 11. Sch. of lib. sci.; 12. Spec. lib.; 13. State lib.; 14. (other). **Functions/Activities:** 15. Acq./Col. dev.; 16. Adult srvs.; 17. Admin.; 18. Apprais.; 19. Archit./Bldgs.; 20. Cat./Class.; 21. Chld. srvs.; 22. Circ.; 23. Cons./Pres.; 24. Consult.; 25. Cont. ed.; 26. Educ. lib. sci.; 27. Ext. srvs.; 28. Fund/Grants; 29. Gvt. pubs.; 30. Indx./Abs.; 31. Instr. lib. use; 32. Media srvs.; 33. Micro.; 34. Netwks./Coop.; 35. Persnl.; 36. PR; 37. Publshg.; 38. Recs. mgt.; 39. Ref. srvs.; 40. Repro.; 41. Resrch.; 42. Review.; 43. Secur.; 44. Serials; 45. Spec. col.; 46. Tech. srvs.; 47. Trustees/Bds.; 48. YA srvs.; 49. (other).

(1980). **Activities:** 1; 22, 30, 31; 51, 55, 57 **Addr.:** 109 Simmons Rd., Statesboro, GA 30458.

Armer, Paul (N. 8, 1924, Montebello, CA) Pres., Teknowledge, 1981–; Exec. Secy., Charles Babbage Inst., 1978–81; Asst. to Pres., ON-Line Bus. Syst., 1976–78; Fellow, Prog. Coord., Ctr. for Advnc. Study in Bhvl. Sci., 1972–76; Resrch. Assoc., Lect., Harvard Univ. Sch. of Bus., 1970–72; Dir., Computation Ctr., Stanford Univ., 1968–70; Head, Comp. Sci. Dept., RAND Corp., 1947–68. **Educ.:** Univ. of CA, Los Angeles, 1946, BA, 1960, Cert. (Exec. Prog.) **Orgs.:** Oral Hist. Assn. Assn. for Comp. Mach.: Natl. Cncl. (1964–68). AAAS. Hist. of Sci. Socty. Socty. for Hist. of Tech. NY Acad. of Sci. Other orgs. **Honors:** Von Karman Lect., City of Los Angeles, 1967; Natl. Lect., Assn. for Comp. Mach., 1966. **Pubns.:** Jt. auth. *Management of Information and Knowledge* (1971); Jt. auth., *Automation and Economic Progress* (1966); Jt. auth., *Computers and Thought* (1963); other books. **Addr.:** 105 Hillside Ave., Menlo Park, CA 94025.

Armistead, Henry T. (S. 16, 1940, Philadelphia, PA) Head, Col. Dev., Thomas Jefferson Univ. Lib., 1977–; Head, Tech. Srvs., 1970–77, Acqs. Libn., 1968–70. **Educ.:** Univ. of PA, 1958–63, BA (Eng. Lit.); Drexel Univ., 1965–67, MS (LS). **Orgs.:** Med. LA: Phila. Reg. Grp. (Treas., 1973–75). Amer. Ornith. Un. Brit. Ornith. Un. **Honors:** Beta Phi Mu. **Pubns.:** Various bk. reviews (1969–). **Activities:** 1; 15, 29, 44; 55, 80, 92 **Addr.:** 28 E. Springfield Ave., Philadelphia, PA 19118.

Armitage, Katherine Y. (Je. 29, 1936, Bakersville, NC) Dir., Haywood Cnty. Pub. Lib., 1978–; Consult., Cont. Ed., Univ. of SC, 1975–76; Instr. Srvs. Libn., Sangamon State Univ., 1970–75; Biblgphr., Eng. Dept., Univ. of Pittsburgh, 1967–70; Biblgphr., York Univ. Lib., 1965–67. **Educ.:** Morris Harvey Coll., 1956–59, BS (Hist.); PA State Univ., 1960–62 (Hist.); Univ. of Denver, 1964–65, MA (Libnshp.). **Orgs.:** ALA: RTSD/Acq. Sect. (Secy., 1970–73); ACRL, Plng. Com. (1974–78); PLA, Educ. of Pub. Libns. Com. (1980–). NC LA. NC Pub. Lib. Dirs. Assn. Cncl. on Appalachian Women. **Activities:** 1, 9; 15, 25, 31 **Addr.:** Haywood County Public Library, 402 S. Haywood St., Waynesville, NC 28786.

Armour, Charles Arthur (Mr. 5, 1934, Taylor Village, NB) Univ. Archvst., Dalhousie Univ., 1970–. **Educ.:** Mt. Allison Univ., Sackville, NB, 1953–56, BSc (Chem.); Dalhousie Univ., 1956–57, MSc (Chem.); Univ. Coll. London, 1950–60, PhD; Arch. Admin., Pub. Arch. of Can., 1970, Cert. Arch. Natl. Arch. Apprais. Bd., Atl. Reg.: (Ch., 1978). **Pubns.:** *Sailing Ships of the Maritimes* (1975). **Activities:** 1, 2; 15, 17 **Addr.:** Dalhousie University Archives, Killam Memorial Library, Dalhousie University, Halifax, NS B3H 4H8, Canada.

Armstrong, HelenJane (Ja. 5, 1939, Neemah, WI) Map Libn., Assoc. Libn., Univ. of FL, 1973–; Map Libn., North. IL Univ., 1965–72; Map Libn., Natl. Geo. Socty., 1963–65. **Educ.:** Carroll Coll., 1960–61, BS (Geo., Hist.); Univ. of OK, 1966, MLS (Geo.); OR State Univ., 1977, PhD (Geo.). **Orgs.:** Map OLUG: Bylaws Com. (Ch., 1980–81). SLA: Geo. and Map Div., Ch.-Elect (1977–78), Ch. (1978–79), Bd. (1979–80), Mem. Ch. (1967–72), Stans. Com., Liaison Com. with Lib. of Congs.; Div. Cabinet Com. on the Formation of New Divs., Ch.; FL Chap., Pres.-Elect (1980–81), Pres. (1981–82), Pubcty. Ch. (1979–80). FL State Univ. Lib. Sch.: Dean's Adv. Cncl. (1979–80). Assn. of Amer. Geographers: Southeast. Div., Com. on South. Map Libns. (Ch., 1977–82). **Pubns.:** "The Case of the Disappearing Keys: Historical Florida in Maps," *Florida and the Bicentennial Years...Florida Chapter, Special Libraries Association* (1976); "A Map Librarian on AACR 2," *FL Chap. Spec. Lib. Assn. Bltn.* (Ja. 1981); "Maps in Libraries," *Final Working Papers Assn. of Caribbean, Univ. Resrch. and Inst. Libs., 10th Anl. Mtg. Barbados, 1978* (forthcoming); "A Co-operative Map Cataloging Experiment" *SLA Geo. and Map Div. Bltn.* (Je. 1977); "Analysis of the Visual Resources of Mount St. Helens; Maps, Aerial Photographs and Satellite Imagery," *Southeast. Div. Assn. of Amer. Geographers Com. on South. Map Libns. Nsltr.* (Spr. 1981); various bk. reviews, *Geo. and Map Div. Bltn.* (1968–). **Activities:** 1, 12; 39, 45, 46; 70, 95-Aerial Photography. **Addr.:** Map Library, University of Florida Libraries, Gainesville, FL 32611.

Armstrong, Joanne E. (S. 16, 1946, DE) Lib. Dept. Chmn., Old Court Jr. HS, 1974–; Catlgr., State of DE, Div. of Hist. and Cult. Affairs Arch., 1974; Sch. Libn., Redding Middle Sch., 1968–74. **Educ.:** Univ. of DE, 1964–68, BA (Hist., Amer. Studies); Cath. Univ. of Amer., 1976–78, MSLS; Univ. of DE, 1969–72, Lib. Cert. **Orgs.:** ALA. AASL. Baltimore Cnty. Sch. Libns. Assn.: VP (1977–78), Secy. (1978–79). Cath. Univ. of Amer., Frnds. of the Lib. Natl. Educ. Assn. MD State Tchrs. Assn. Amer. Assn. of Univ. Women, MD Brnch.: Mem. VP (1976–79). Amer. Assn. of Univ. Women, DE Brnch.: Prog. VP (1972–73); Legis. Ch. (1970–72); Cable T.V. Action Com. (1973). **Pubns.:** "Books for Children", *A Librarian's Review* (No. 2, 1972–73). **Activities:** 10; 32, 48 **Addr.:** 11 Spinners Ct., Apt. 2A, Randallstown, MD 21133.

Armstrong, Judith G. (N. 23, 1933, Jersey City, NJ) Dir. of Lib., Drury Coll., 1969–; Docum. Libn. and Lib. Sci. Instr., SW MO State Univ., 1965–69; AV and Prog. Plng. Libn., Daniel Boone Reg. Lib., 1964–65; Jr. Libn., Univ. of MO, 1962–64. **Educ.:** N. TX State Univ., 1951–55, BBA (Bus. Admin.); TX Woman's Univ., 1961–62, MLS; SW MO State Univ., 1969–72, MA (Theatre Hist.). **Orgs.:** MO LA: VP and Pres. Elect (1977–79). Biblgphcl. Cntr. for Rsrch.: Adv. Cncl. (1979–82). ALA. SW MO Lib. Netwk.: Ch. (1974–78, 1981). AAUP. **Honors:** Cncl. on Lib. Rsrcs., Flwshp., 1975. **Activities:** 1, 15, 17, 45 **Addr.:** Director of Library, Drury College, Springfield, MO 65802.

Armstrong, Lewis A. (Ag. 18, 1941, Seiling, OK) Cur., Maps, Univ. of KS, 1970–. **Educ.:** OK State Univ., 1961–65, BA (Geo.); Univ. of KS, 1968–75, MA (Cartography); Emporia State Univ., 1975–81, MLS. **Orgs.:** SLA: Geo. and Map Div., Awds. Com. (1977–78), Stans. Com. (1979–). West. Assn. Map Libs. KS LA. Univ. of KS Clasfd. Sen.: Exec. Cncl. Rsv. Ofcrs. Assn. **Pubns.:** Jt. auth., "Preparing Acquisition Lists," *Bltn. Geo. and Map Div. Spec. Libs. Assn.* (Je. 1976); jt. auth., "Illustrating the Contour Interval of the Contour Symbol, Interval and Spacing Via 3-D Maps," *Jnl. of Geo.* (My. 1971); various maps for bks. **Activities:** 1; 15, 20, 39; 70 **Addr.:** Map Library, University of Kansas, Lawrence, KS 66045.

Armstrong, Marian (Je. 24, 1929, Bedford, IN) Ast. Prof., IN Univ. Sch. of Lib. and Info Srvc. 1969–; Instr., Sch. of Lib. and Info Srvc. and Head, Univ. Sch. Libs., 1958–68; Libn., Paris Amer. Sch., France, 1956–57; Libn., Edison Sch., 1952–56. **Educ.:** IN Univ., 1949–52, BS (Educ., Eng.), 1952–58, MLS. **Orgs.:** ALA; INULA; Assn. for IN Media Educ. AASL. Other orgs. Beta Phi Mu: Chi Chap., Secy., Treas. (1979–). IN Univ. Sch. of Lib. and Info Srvc. Alum. Assn.: Secy., Treas. (1969–). Monroe Cnty. Pub. Lib. Fndn. **Honors:** Delta Kappa Gamma; Pi Lambda Theta. **Pubns.:** Ed., *AIME News* (1979); Ed., IN Univ. Sch. of Lib. and Info. Srvc. Alum. Nsltr. (1969–); Adv., *OPEN ENTRY* Student Pubn. (1973–). **Activities:** 10, 11; 16, 39, 48; 50 **Addr.:** School of Library and Information Science, Library 015, Indiana University, Bloomington, IN 47405.

Armstrong, Mary Lou (My. 26, 1929, Edmonton, AB) Readrs. Srvs. Libn., Red Deer Coll., Univ. AB, 1981–, Sbtcl., 1980–81; Actg. Chmn., Lrng. Rsrc. Cntr., Red Deer Coll., 1978–79, Readrs. Srvcs. Libn., 1971–78. **Educ.:** Univ. AB, 1947–51, BA (Eng.), 1970–71, BLS, 1980–81, MLS. **Orgs.:** LA AB: Dir. (1972–74); Mem. Ch. (1972–73); Downey Srvy. of Libs. (Rep., 1973–74); other coms. AB Cncl. of Coll. Libns.: Nsltr. Ed. (1979–). CAN LA: CACUL; CASLIS. Fac. Assn., Red Deer Coll.: Secy. (1981–); Negtns. Com. (1972–73); Col. Agmnt. Adv. Com. (1974–75); Prof. Dev. Com. (1977–79). Univ. of AB Alum. Assn., Red Deer Brnch.: Pres. (1974–76). **Honors:** Univ. of AB Alum. Assn., G.B. Taylor Awd., 1975. **Pubns.:** "Learning Resources Centre", Videotape (1975). **Activities:** 1, 10; 17, 31, 39 **Addr.:** 4402 Springbett Dr., Red Deer, AB T4N 3N6, Canada.

Armstrong, Rodney (Mr. 5, 1923, Atlanta, GA) Dir. and Libn., Boston Athenaeum, 1973–; Libn., Phillips Exeter Acad., 1950–73. **Educ.:** Williams Coll., 1945–48, AB (Eng.); Columbia Univ., 1949–50, MS (LS). **Orgs.:** ALA: ACRL. NH LA. Ms. Socty.: Pres. (1975–77). Amer. Antiqn. Socty.: Lib. Com. (1974–76). New Eng. Hist. Geneal. Socty.: Pres. (1976–). Clb. of Odd Volumes: Pres. (1980–). Other orgs. **Honors:** Amer. Acad. of Arts and Sci., Fellow, 1976; Royal Socty. of Arts, Benjamin Franklin Fellow, 1974; Socty. of Antiq., Fellow, 1979. **Activities:** 1, 12; 18, 24, 45; 55, 57, 69 **Addr.:** 10-1/2 Beacon St., Boston, MA 02108.

Arnam, Mary Jane (N. 9, 1933, Chicago, IL) Tchr. and Libn., Roosevelt HS, 1966–; Tchr. and Libn., Pulaski Elem. Sch., 1955–59; Tchr. and Libn., Blaine Elem. Sch., 1960–66. **Educ.:** North. IL Univ., 1951–55, BA (Educ.); Chicago Tchrs. Coll., 1955–59, MS (LS). **Orgs.:** Chicago Tchr.-Libns. Clb.: Pres. and Secy. (1964–65). Chicagoland Libns. ALA. IL LA. **Pubns.:** *Children's Libraries in England* (1959). **Activities:** 10; 15, 17, 31, 32; 95-curric. plng. **Addr.:** Roosevelt High School, Library Media Center, 3436 W. Wilson Ave., Chicago, IL 60625.

Arndt, John Mark (Ja. 22, 1942, Hespeler, ON) Head, Coll. Dev. and Ref. Svcs., Wilfrid Laurier Univ., 1971–; Tchr., Libn., Waterloo Cnty. Bd. of Educ., 1967–71; Ref. Libn., Waterloo Luth. Univ., 1966–67; Tchr., Brantford Bd. of Educ., 1964–65. **Educ.:** Waterloo Luth. Univ., 1961–64, BA (Hist.); Univ. of Toronto, 1965–66, BLS, 1972, MLS; ON Coll. of Educ., 1964, Tchg. Cert.; Spec. Certif., Sch. Libnshp. and Lrng. Mtrls. **Orgs.:** Inst. of Prof. Libns. of ON: VP (1974); Pres. (1975); Mem. Com. (Ch., 1974); Contract Com. (Ch., 1976); Other coms. CAN LA. ON LA. CAN Inst. of Intl. Affairs. **Pubns.:** Ed., Institute of Professional Librarians of Ontario, Labour Relations Seminar Proceedings (1974). **Activities:** 1; 16, 40; 60, 93 **Addr.:** 54 Forestwood Dr., Kitchener, ON N2N 1B2, Canada.

Arneson, Arne Jon (Jl. 30, 1943, Eau Claire, WI) Persnl./Bus. Libn., Univ. of CO, 1981–, Msc. Libn., 1976–81; Msc. Libn., SUNY, Binghamton, 1973–76; Msc. Libn., SUNY, Coll. at Fredonia, 1970–73; Msc. Catlgr., Univ. of WI, 1968–70. **Educ.:** Univ. of WI, 1961–65, BM (Msc. Educ.), 1967–69, MM (Msclgy.), 1969–70, MA (LS). **Orgs.:** Msc. LA: AV Micro Com. (Ch., 1976–79); AV Com. (Ch., 1979); Micro. Com. (1980–). **Pubns.:** Jt. auth., *Index to Audio Equipment Reviews 1978–* (1979–); "Microformats and the Music Library: A Bibliographic–Use Survey of Recent Trends," *Micro. Review* (Ja. 1975). **Activities:** 1, 9; 15, 17, 39; 55 **Addr.:** 8523 Middlefork Rd., Boulder, CO 80302.

Arnett, Stanley K., II (Ja. 24, 1945, Fayetteville, NC) Head, Ext. Srvs., St. Clair Cnty. Lib., 1978–, Asst. to Dir., 1978–78; Head, AV Dept., 1977–78, Asst. Pub. Srvs. Libn., 1976–77; Ref. Libn., Detroit Pub. Lib., 1975–76, Adult Ref. Libn., 1974–75. **Educ.:** St. Clair Cnty. Cmnty. Coll., Port Huron, MI, 1963–70, AA (Lib. Art); MI State Univ., 1970–72, BS (Geog., Hist.); Univ. MI, 1972–74, MALS. **Orgs.:** ALA. SLA: Geog. and Map Div., Mem. Ch. (1974–76). MI LA. Amer. Radio Relay Leag. **Pubns.:** "A Classified System for the Reference Books in the Division of Maps, William L. Clements Library", *SLA Geog. and Map Div. Bltn.* (June 1973). **Activities:** 9, 12; 16, 32, 35; 70, 72, 93 **Addr.:** St. Clair County Library, 210 McMorran Blvd., Port Huron, MI 48060.

Arnhold, Katharina Pavlova (Ja. 16, 1944, Greifswald, Germany) Catlgr., Libn., Lib. of Congs., 1967–. **Educ.:** Georgetown Univ., 1963–66, BS (Russ.); Univ. of Hawaii, 1977–78, MSLS. **Orgs.:** ALA: Com. on the Status of Women (1979–). SLA: D.C. Chap. (1979–). Amer. Fed. of State, Cnty., and Mncpl. Empl.: Lib. of Congs. Univ (1977–). **Activities:** 4; 20, 24, 25; 55, 56 **Addr.:** 2105 Popkins Ln., Alexandria, VA 22307.

Arnold, Barbara Jeanne (S. 21, 1950, New York City, NY) WI Sea Grant Spec., Univ. of WI Ext., 1978–, Dir., Nat. Resrcs. Ctr., Steenbock Meml., 1975–78; LTE Libn., WI Dept. of Nat. Resrcs., 1974–75. **Educ.:** Marquette Univ., 1968–72, AB (Eng.); Univ. of WI, 1973, MA (LS); various crs., wkshps. **Orgs.:** WI LA: Ref. and Adult Srvs. Sect., Mem. Com. (1979), Nom. Com. (1980); JMRT (Secy., 1979–80). SLA: NR Div. (Nsltr. Ed., 1980); WI Div., Nom. Com. (1980–81). Grt. Lakes Env. Info. Sharing Grp.: Conf. Plng. Ch. (1977–78). Madison Area Lib. Cncl.: VP (1978); Educ. and Progs. Com. (Ch., 1974–76); Plng. and Eval. Com. (1978–80); Grant and Contracts Com. (1979–80). Madison Acad. Staff Assn.: Liaison Com. (Ch., 1977). Univ. of WI Madison Lib. Sch. Alum. Assn.: Pres.-ELect, VP (1976–77); Pres. (1977–78); Muriel Fuller Day Com. (Alum. Liaison, 1979). **Pubns.:** *A Select Bibliography of Public Information Materials on PCB's* (1980); *Periodical Publishing in Wisconsin. Proceedings of Conference, May 1978* (1980); *State of the Art of Existing Information Services* (1978); *Wisconsin's State Agency Librarians Council* (1978); *Women in Library Administration: An Institute* (1976); various mono., bibls. **Activities:** 12; 25, 27, 39; 65, 82 **Addr.:** Sea Grant Advisory Services, 1815 University Ave., Madison, WI 53706.

Arnold, Carol Post (S. 9, 1931, New Haven, CT) Adj. Lectr., Univ. of HI, 1979–, Libn., School of Pub. Hlth. 1976–; Resrc. Mtrls. Spec., East-West Ctr., 1972–76. **Educ.:** New Eng. Cnsvty. of Msc., 1949–53, BMsc; Geo. Peabody Coll. for Tchrs., 1960–61, MMsc; Univ. of HI, 1970–71, MLS. **Orgs.:** Med. LA: Mem. Com. (1979–81); Spec. Interest Grp. Liaison (Ch., 1979); Pub. Hlth. and Hlth. Admin. Grp. (Ch., 1980–81). Med. Lib. Grp. of HI: Pres. (1977–79). HI Reg. Grp. of Med. Libs.: Ch. (1977–79). HI LA. Beta Phi Mu: Xi Chap. (VP, 1978). HI Pub. Hlth. Assoc. **Honors:** UNESCO Travel/Std., Grant, 1975. **Pubns.:** Co-Auth., *A Study of Marijuana's Therapeutic Potential: Report to the 9th Legislature of Hawaii* (1977); "Clearinghouse Services of the East-West Communication Institute", *ARLIC-International* (1975); Various guides to cols. (1974–76). **Activities:** 1, 12; 17; 80, 95-Pub. Hlth. **Addr.:** School of Public Health Reference Room, University of Hawaii at Manoa, 1960 East-West Rd., D-206, Honolulu, HI 96822.

Arnold, Cynthia A. (F. 14, 1946, Berlin, NH) Libn., Lincoln Acad., 1980–; Coord., Ref. Srvs., ME State Lib., 1977–80, Coord., Spec. Srvs., 1974–77; Proofreader, Geiger Brothers, 1974; Ref. Libn., Harvard Univ., 1971–73; Acq. Libn., Radcliffe Coll., 1970–71; Photograph. Ref. Libn., Harvard Univ., 1969–70; Ed. Asst., Frgn. Lang. Dept., Ginn and Co. Publshrs., 1968–69. **Educ.:** Univ. of NH, 1964–68, BA (Eng. Lit.); Simmons Coll., 1969–71, MLS. **Orgs.:** ALA: Cnclr. (1978–82). New Eng. LA: State Lib. Sect., Nom. Com. (Ch., 1978). ME LA. New Eng. Educ. Media Assn. ME Educ. Media Assn. **Activities:** 10, 13; 34, 39, 48; 50, 63, 72 **Addr.:** Box 127, Augusta, ME 04330.

Arnold, Frederick L. (O. 26, 1923, Bedford, PA) Ref. Libn., Princeton Univ., 1954–; Ref. Libn., Lib. of Congs., 1949–54; Libn., Amer. Univ. in Cairo, 1965–66. **Educ.:** Univ. PA, 1939–48, AB (Psych.); Drexel Univ., 1949, BLS; Univ. de Grenoble, 1945, Cert. d'Etat. **Orgs.:** ALA. NJ LA. Princeton Clb. of NY. **Activities:** 1; 39; 54, 55 **Addr.:** PO Box 6003, 6 Green Ave., Lawrenceville, NJ 08648.

Arnold, Gary James (F. 27, 1947, Cleveland, OH) Archvst., OH Hist. Socty., 1971–; Mss. Libn., Rutherford B. Hayes Lib., 1973–74; Micro. Prep., MD Hist. Socty., 1972. **Educ.:** Cleveland State Univ., 1965–69, BA (Hist.), 1969–71, MA (Hist.). **Orgs.:** SAA. Socty. of OH Archvsts. Natl. Hist. Cmnl. Socty. Assn. Amer. Philatelic Socty. **Pubns.:** *The Washington Gladden Collection: An Inventory to the Microfilm Edition* (1972); *The Lloyd Family Papers: An Inventory to the Microfilm Edition* (1972); *The Papers of Thirteen Early Ohio Political Lea-*

Special Subjects/Services: 50. Adult educ.; 51. Advert./Mktg.; 52. Aerosp.; 53. Agric.; 54. Area std.; 55. Arts/Hum.; 56. Autom.; 57. Bibl./Prtg.; 58. Bio. sci.; 59. Bus./Fin.; 60. Chem.; 61. Copyrt.; 62. Documtn.; 63. Educ.; 64. Engin.; 65. Env.; 66. Eth. grps.; 67. Film; 68. Food/Nutr.; 69. Geneal.; 70. Geo.; 71. Geol.; 72. Handcpd.; 73. Hist.; 74. Int. frdm.; 75. Info. sci.; 76. Insr.; 77. Law; 78. Legis.; 79. Math./Comp. sci.; 80. Med.; 81. Metals; 82. Nat. resrcs.; 83. Newsp.; 84. Nuc. sci.; 85. Oral hist.; 86. Petr./Energy; 87. Pharm.; 88. Phys./Astr./Math.; 89. Readg.; 90. Relig.; 91. Sci./Tech.; 92. Soc. sci.; 93. Telecom.; 94. Transp.; 95. (other).

ders: An Inventory to the 1976–77 Microfilm Editions (1977); *Guide to the Microfilm Edition of Temperance and Prohibition Papers* (1977); "The Charles Emil Ruthenberg Papers", Microfilm prep. (1976). **Activities:** 1, 2; 20, 39, 45; 55, 90 **Addr.:** Archives-Library Division, Ohio Historical Society, Interstate 71 and 17th Avenue, Columbus, OH 43211.

Arnold, Mary Jo V. (D. 8, 1943, Bremen, KY) Head, Engin. and Archit. Lib., OH State Univ., 1975–; Ref. Libn., 1970–74; Ref. and Catlgr., Univ. of KY, 1969–70. **Educ.:** West. KY State Univ., 1961–65; Univ. of KY, 1967–68. **Orgs.:** Amer. Socty. for Engin. Educ.: Prog. Ch. (1975); Ch. (1976–78). SLA: Sci. Tech. Div. (Treas., 1978–80). Acad. Libs. of OH. **Activities:** 1; 15, 17, 39; 64, 81, 91 **Addr.:** OSU Engineering Library, 112 Caldwell Laboratory, 2024 Neil Ave., Columbus, OH 43210.

Arnold, Mary Lake (Ag. 1, 1921, Marshall, TX) Libn., Carlos Rivera Elem. Sch., 1975–; Instr., Lib. Srv., Educ., Univ. of TX, El Paso, 1965–72; Libn., Coronado HS, 1962–75; Libn., Maple Lawn Elem. Sch., 1960–62; Libn., Edwin J. Kiest Elem. Sch., 1955–60; Libn., San Jacinto Elem. Sch., 1953–55. **Educ.:** Univ. of TX, Austin, 1950–52, BA (Eng.), 1952–53, MEd (Educ., Lib. Srv.). **Orgs.:** ALA. TX Assn. of Sch. Libns.: Ch. (1977); Vice-Ch. (1976); Secy.; Nom. Com.; Resols. Com.; Bylaws Com. TX State Tchrs. Assn. Natl. Educ. Assn. El Paso Tchrs. Assn. Daughters of the Amer. Revolution: Lib. Com. **Activities:** 10; 21, 31; 63 **Addr.:** 1010 Galloway, El Paso, TX 79902.

Arnold, Nancy Irvin (N. 23, 1914, St. Marys, PA) Asst. Law Libn., Ref., Univ. of PA Law Lib., 1977–; Ref. Libn., 1969–77, Head Circ., Ref. Libn., 1958–69, Asst. in Acq. Dept., 1946–58. **Educ.:** MA State Tchrs. Coll., 1933–34; PA Sch. of Horticult., 1936–37. **Orgs.:** AALL. **Pubns.:** Cmplr., *Space Law Bibliography* (1970); Cmplr., *Nuremberg War Crimes Trials; Bibliography* (1969). **Addr.:** Biddle Law Library, University of Pennsylvania Law School, 3400 Chestnut St., Philadelphia, PA 19104.

Arnold, Nellye Kathryn (Mr. 25, 1925, Pikeville, TN) Dir., Libs., Chattanooga-Hamilton Cnty. Bicent. Lib., 1967–; Actg. Dir., Chattanooga Pub. Lib., 1966–67, Asst. Dir., 1965–66, Head, Ref. Info., Tech. Info. Ctr., 1965–66, Head, Hist. Dept., 1956–64. **Educ.:** Univ. of Chattanooga, 1948–52, BA (Span.); Univ. of CA, Los Angeles, 1964–65, MLS (Libnshp.). **Orgs.:** Chattanooga Area LA. TN LA: Legis. Netwk. (Reg. Coord., 1978–81); Nom. Com. (1975–76); Int. Frdm. (1974–75); Pub. Libs. Sect. (Ch., 1967–68); Anl. Conv. (Lcl. Arrange. Ch., 1970, 1978). SE LA. TN Adv. Cncl. on Libs.: PR Com., Ch. Chattanooga Area Hist. Assn.: Secy. (1972). Untd. Fund Alloc. Panel. **Honors:** Amer. Bus. Women's Assn., Dixie Land Chap., Boss of the Yr., 1977; Alpha Socty., 1977. **Activities:** 9; 17, 39, 47 **Addr.:** 2550 Avalon Cir., Chattanooga, TN 37415.

Arnold, Ruth Gertrude Liberty (Rabinoff) (Ap. 6, 1918, New York, NY) Ref. Libn., Ast. Prof., Jersey City State Coll., 1964–, Adj. Chld. Lit., 1969–70; Lib. Assoc., Dental Lib., NY Univ., 1963–64; Copyrtr., Parents' Mag., 1945–49. **Educ.:** Antioch Coll., 1934–39, AB (Soc. Sci.); NY Univ., 1940–41, MS (Rtlg.); Columbia Univ., 1960–63, MSLS; NY Univ. Grad. Sch. of Educ., 1963–64. **Orgs.:** ALA: RASD. METRO. Woodstock Gld. of Crftsmn.; Woodstock Hadassah; Woodstock Lib. **Honors:** Eta Mu Pi, 1941. **Activities:** 1; 31, 39 **Addr.:** 565 W. 169th St., New York, NY 10032.

Arnold, Wilnora Barton (N. 11, 1923, Burnet, TX) Assoc. Prof., Lib. Srvs., San Antonio Coll., 1961–; Libn., John Marshall HS, 1958–61; Libn., St. Mary's Hall, San Antonio, 1949–50; Asst. Libn., TX A&M Univ., 1947–49. **Educ.:** Univ. of TX, Austin, 1941–44, BA (Eng.); LA State Univ., 1946–47, BS (LS); TX Educ. Agency, 1968, Tech. Educ. Cert. **Orgs.:** ALA. Bexar LA: Secy. (1964–65). Cncl. on Lib. Tech. AAUP. TX Jr. Coll. Tchrs. Assn. **Activities:** 1, 10; 15, 26, 39 **Addr.:** 1001 Howard St., San Antonio, TX 78284.

Aronoff, Carol Armstrong (D. 3, 1945, Denver, CO) City Libn., Santa Monica Pub. Lib., 1974–, Head, Borrowers' Srvs., 1972–74, Ref. Libn., 1968–72. **Educ.:** Univ. of CA, Los Angeles, 1963–67, BA (Hist.), 1967–68, MLS. **Orgs.:** ALA. CA LA: VP, Pres.-Elect (1981); Pres. (1982); Gvt. Rel. Com. (1980); Forum Coord. Com. (Ch., 1976–77); Cncl. (1975–77). Congs. of CA Pub. Lib. Syst.: Ch. (1980). Metro. Coop. Lib. Syst.: Ch. (1979). Bel Air Presby. Church: Elder (1979–81). Gen. Adv. Bd. of Santa Monica Coll. Univ. of CA Los Angeles GSLIS Adv. Cncl. **Activities:** 9; 17, 32, 39 **Addr.:** 1343 6th St., Santa Monica, CA 90401.

Arora, Ved Parkash (N. 18, 1936, Mintgomery, Panjab, India) Dir., Bibl. Srcs. Div., SK Prov. Lib., 1970–; Catlgr., Wandsworth Boro. Pub. Libs., London, Eng., 1965–70; Chief Libn., Small Scale Indus., Lib., Gvt. of India, 1961–65. **Educ.:** Arya Coll., Panjab Univ., 1954–58, BA (Eng., Math, Econ.); Vikram Univ., India, 1960–61, BLS; UK LA, 1968, ALA (Cat., Class., Bibl.). **Orgs.:** SK LA: Bibl. Com. (1975–78). CAN LA. UK LA. India CAN Assn. of SK: Pres. (1980). **Pubns.:** *The Saskatchewan Bibliography, 1905–1979* (1980); *Royal Canadian Mounted Police: A Bibliography* (1973); *Indians of Americas: A Bibliography* (1973); *Saskatchewan History: A Bibliography* (1973); Various Bibls.; "Interlibrary Loan in Saskatchewan", *QLA Bltn.* (Oct.–Dec. 1978). **Activities:** 9, 13; 15, 34, 46; 57, 66 **Addr.:** 3538 Queen St., Regina, SK S4S 2G3, Canada.

Arrington, Frances T. (Ag. 10, 1931, Fyffe, AL) Head Libn., Lee Coll., 1977–, Catlgr., 1964–77; Readrs. Adv., Meramec Cmnty. Coll., 1971–73; Libn., SEast. Bible Coll., 1961–64; Catlgr., Atlanta Pub. Lib., 1957–60; Libn., Lee Coll., 1953–57; Asst. Libn., Jacksonville State Coll., 1953. **Educ.:** Lee Coll., 1949–51, AA; Jacksonville State Coll., 1951–53, BS (Math); George Peabody Coll., 1953–57, MA (LS). **Orgs.:** TN LA. SE LA. **Honors:** Kappa Delta Pi, 1953. **Activities:** 1; 15, 17, 20; 63, 90 **Addr.:** Lee College Library, Cleveland, TN 37311.

Arrivée, Sally D. (S. 26, 1949, Chicago, IL) Chld. Srvcs. Libn., Portage Pub. Lib., 1971–. **Educ.:** West. MI Univ., 1967–71, BA, (Hist.), 1971–72, MSL. **Orgs.:** ALA: YASD/Awd. Dev. Com. (1976–77); AV Producers & Distributors Liaison (1978–80). MI LA: PR Com. (1976–77); Anl. Conf. Prog. Plan. Com. (1978); Anl. YART Wkshp. Prog. Coord. (1978); Legis. Com. (1978–). **Activities:** 9; 17, 21, 48; 78 **Addr.:** Portage Public Library, 300 Library La., Portage, MI 49002.

Arrondo, Ondina J. (Ap. 12, 1936, Havana, Cuba) Head Libn., Miami-Dade Pub. Lib. Syst., Hisp. Branch, 1976–, Adult Libn., 1968–76, Chld. Libn., 1962–68; Art and Msc. Libn., Natl. Lib., Havana, Cuba, 1960–61. **Educ.:** Univ. of Havana, Cuba, 1955–59, BE (Educ.), 1959–60, MLS. **Orgs.:** Dade Cnty. LA. **Honors:** Miami-Dade Cmnty. Coll., Cert. de Apprec., 1978; Miami-Cubans Lions Club, Ano Intl. del Nino, 1979. **Activities:** 9, 10; 16, 21, 22; 50, 55, 63 **Addr.:** 1654 S.W. 19 St., Miami, FL 33145.

Arsenault, Alban (Ag. 31, 1930, Dieppe, NB) Head, Cat. Dept., Univ. of Moncton, 1982–, Catlgr., 1980–82, Head of Tech. Srv., 1974–79, Head of Cat. Dept., 1964–74. **Educ.:** Univ. St. Joseph, 1946–52, BA (Arts); Univ. de Montreal, 1963–64, BLS; Univ. de Moncton, 1970, BED (Educ.). **Orgs.:** Atl. Prov. LA. Can. LA. ASTED. Assn. des Bibl. Et Des Prof. De L'Univ. de Moncton. **Pubns.:** Jt. auth., *Directory of New Brunswick Libraries* (1976); Jt. auth., *Livres de Langue Francaise Pour Les 10E, 11E et 12E Année* (1969); *Catalogue Systématique APLA Bltn.* (D. 1969); "Service de Traduction Automatique," *Nouvelles de l'ASTED* (Jl.–O. 1981). **Activities:** 1; 20, 46; 56 **Addr.:** Bibliothèque Champlain, Univesité de Moncton, Moncton, NB E1A 3E9 Canada.

Arterbery, Vivian J. (Je. 21, 1937, Houston, TX) Lib. Dir., Rand Corp., 1979–; Supvsr., User Srvs., Aerosp. Corp., 1967–79, Ref. Libn., 1960–67; Indxr., Space Tech. Labs., 1959–60; Consult., Hlth., Educ. and Welfare, Ofc. of Educ., 1974–76. **Educ.:** Howard Univ., 1954–58, BA (Hist.); Univ. of South. CA, 1965, MS (LS); various crs. in bus. admin., data prcs. **Orgs.:** Libraria Sodalitas: Pres. (1981–82). SLA: South. CA Chap., Pres.; Corres. Secy. (1966–67); Rec. Secy. (1967–68); Place. Com. (Ch., 1968–70); various coms., ofcs. CA State Conf. on Libs. and Info. Sci.: Pre-Conf. Plng. Com. (1978). CA LA: Cnclr. (1973–75). Various other orgs. Links, Inc.: San Fernando Valley Chap., VP (1980–81); 2nd VP (1978–79); Secy. (1976–77). Univ. of South. CA Lib. Sch. Alum. Assn.: Pres. (1972–73). **Pubns.:** *Directory of Special Libraries of Southern California* (1965); "Mechanized Circulation Control System" aerosp. tech. rpt. (1967); various sps. **Activities:** 12; 17, 38, 39; 56, 91, 92 **Addr.:** Rand Corp., 1700 Main St., Santa Monica, CA 90406.

Arvin, Charles Stanford (Ap. 17, 1931, Loogootee, IN) Head, Ref., Genesee Dist. Lib., 1980–; Head, Ref., Genesee Cnty. Lib., 1962–79; Asst. Div. Libn., Univ. of MI Lib., 1960–62. **Educ.:** Wayne State Univ., 1949–53, AB (Gvt.), 1956–57, (Hist.); Univ. of MI, 1959–60, AMLS. **Orgs.:** ALA. MI LA. Flint Area Lib. Assn.: Secy.-Treas.; Various coms. Flint Geneal. Socty.: Exec. Bd. (1972–). Shiawassee Cnty. Hist. Socty.: Treas. (1976–). Owosso Y's Men's Club: Secy. (1979–). Amer. Film Inst. Other orgs. **Activities:** 9; 15, 39; 69 **Addr.:** 702 W. Oliver, Owosso, MI 48867.

Asbell, Mary M. (D. 12, 1947, Maryville, MO) Ext. Libn., Univ. of TX Med. Branch, 1974–; Secy., Rolling Hills Lib., 1972–73; Instr. of Eng., St. Joseph Sch. Dist., 1969–71. **Educ.:** NW MO State Univ., 1965–69, BS, Ed (Lit., Lang. and Comp.); MO Univ., 1973–74, MS (LS). **Orgs.:** Med. Lib. Assn. SLA. Houston OLUG. Hlth. Sci. Comm. Assn. Other orgs. PEO: Pres. (1980–); MO State Tchrs. Assn. **Pubns.:** "Creating a Union List of Serials", *User Svcs.: What's New with You* (1979); "South and East Texas Hospital Libraries", *Hosp. Libs.* (1977); "UTMB's Services to Hospital Libraries in South and East Texas", *The Bkman.* (1977); various articles, nwsltr., etc. **Activities:** 5, 12; 24, 27, 36; 50, 56, 80 **Addr.:** 3311 Ashton Pl. #16, Galveston, TX 77551.

Asencio-Toro, Doris (F. 21, 1948, Cabo Rojo, PR) Head Libn., PR Supreme Ct. Lib., 1980–; Libn., Cath. Univ. of PR Law Lib., 1977–80; Libn., San Juan Judicial Ctr., 1975–77; Libn., Superior Ct., Mayaguez, PR, 1969–74. **Educ.:** Interamer. Univ., San Germán, PR, 1965–68, BA (Soclgy.); Grad. Sch. of Libnshp., Univ. of PR, 1974–75, ML. **Orgs.:** Assn. Ex-Alum. Escuela Grad. de Bibliotecología. SBPR. Assn. de Bibs. de Derecho de PR. AALL: Southeast. Chap. **Activities:** 4; 17, 39; 77 **Addr.:** Box 161, Cabo Rojo, PR 00623.

Ash, Joan S. (Ag. 12, 1945, Fall River, MA) Assoc. Dir., Univ. OR Hlth. Sci. Ctr. Lib., 1976–; Ast. Dir. for Tech. Srvs., Univ. of CT Hlth. Ctr. Libs., 1974–76; Sr. Ref. Libn. and Ext. Libn., Yale Med. Lib., 1972–74; Sci. and Tech. Biblgphr., CA State Univ., Northridge, 1969–72. **Educ.:** Emmanual Coll., 1963–67, AB (Eng.); Columbia Univ., 1967–68, MS (Med. Libnshp.); CA State Univ., Northridge, 1970–72, MS (Hlth. Sci.); UCLA, 1968–69, Cert. Med. Libnshp. **Orgs.:** Med. LA: Bltn. Ed. Com., (1976–79; Ch., 1978–79); Bltn. Bd. of Consult. Ed. (1975–78); NLM Liaison Com. (1978–); Pac. NW Grp. (Bylaws Com., 1977–78); New Eng. Reg. Grp. Lake Oswego Pub. Lib.: Bd. of Trustees (1978–). **Pubns.:** Jt. Auth., *Health: A Multimedia Source Guide* (1976); "Journal Evaluation Study at the University of Connecticut Health Center", *Med. Lib. Assn. Bltn.* (Apr. 1977); "Library Use of Public Health Materials", *Med. Lib. Assn. Bltn.* (Apr. 1974); "A Prediction Equation Providing ...", *Lib. Resrcs. and Tech. Svcs.* (1973); "Selected Reference Works in Public Health", *Amer. Jnl. of Pub. Hlth.* (1972). **Activities:** 1, 12; 17, 35; 80 **Addr.:** University of Oregon Health Sciences Center Libraries, P.O. Box 573, Portland, OR 97207.

Ash, Lee (Michael) (S. 15, 1917, New York, NY) Lib. Consult., Rare Book Spec., 1958–; Ed., *Lib. Jnl.*, 1957–59; Libn., Carnegie Endowment for Intl. Peace, 1953–57; Biblgphr., Argosy Bk. Stores, 1946–53; Asst. Head Rare Bk Dept., Brentanos Bk. Stores, 1944–46; Head, Trade Order and Intl. Acq. Dept., other positions. **Educ.:** Columbia Univ., 1932–37, (Hist., Anthro.); Pratt Inst., 1936, Cert. (BLS); Univ. of Chicago, 1939–41, (LS). **Orgs.:** ALA: Cncl.; ACRL; various coms. Can. LA. CT LA. Bibl. Socty. of Amer. Amer. Hist. Assn. Amer. Assn. State & Local Hist. Amer. Socty. for Print. Hist. Archons of Colophon. Other orgs. **Pubns.:** Ed., *Special Collections* (1980–); *Serial Publications Containing Medical Classics* (1961; 1979); *Subject Collections* (1958–78); Ed., *American Notes & Queries* (1962–74); Ed., *Biographical Directory of Librarians in U.S. & Canada* (1955–70); other books and articles. **Activities:** 1, 12; 15, 18, 24; 55, 57, 92 **Addr.:** Bethany, CT 06525.

Ashby, Anna Lou S. (Canyon, TX) Rare Bk. Catlgr., Pierpont Morgan Lib., 1980–; Arents Coll., NY Pub. Lib., 1979–80; Catlgr., 1978; Ed. Asst., Jnl. of Lib. Hist., Univ. TX, 1976–78; Lect., Univ. of Sacred Heart, Tokyo, 1974–76; Head Libn., Amer. Intl. Sch., New Delhi, India, 1970–71; Asst. Prof., Dept. of Eng., FL A. and M. Univ., 1968–69. **Educ.:** W TX State Univ., BA (Eng.); Univ. TX, MA (Amer. Lit.), 1974, PhD (Amer. Lit. and Bibl.), 1977, MLS. **Orgs.:** ALA.: ACRL/RBMS, Nom. Com. (1980-81); Stans. Com. (1980-81); RTSD; LHRT/Nom. Com. (1978). Bibl. Socty. (London). Bibl. Socty. of Amer. NY Lib. Clb. Mod. Lang. Assn. Amer. Prntg. Hist. Assn. **Honors:** Fulbright Fndn. sem., 1970–73; Phi Kappa Phi; Beta Phi Mu. **Pubns.:** "Irwin P. Beadle", "Donnelley, Loyd & Co.", "Harper & Bros.", and "Porter and Coates," *Publishers for Mass Entertainment* (1980); "The Writer as Bookman: Christopher Morley's Library", *Lib. Chronicle of Univ. TX* (Nov. 1970); "Juliette's Door", *Lib. Chronicle of Univ. TX* (Sept. 1972); various reviews and articles. **Activities:** 1; 23, 37, 45; 55, 57, 89 **Addr.:** 300 W. 106th St., No. 61, New York, NY 10025.

Ashby, M. Adèle (S. 27, 1943, Toronto, ON) Editor, **CM: Can. Mtrls., for Schls. and Libs.** 1975–; Util. Ofcr., ON Educ. Comm. Athrty., 1974–78; Head, Chld. Srvs., Brampton Pub. Lib., 1971–74; Head, Chld. Dept., Scarborough Pub. Lib., 1969–71. **Educ.:** Univ. of Toronto, 1962–67, BA, (Langs.), 1967–68, BLS, 1968–69, MLS, 1978–80, MeD, (Adult Educ.). **Orgs.:** CAN LA: Bk. of Yr. Awd. Com. (Ch., 1972, 1978). ON LA. Assn. for Media and Tech. in Educ. in Can.; ON Film Assn. **Pubns.:** Various Reviews. **Activities:** 9, 10; 21, 24, 32; 50, 67, 93 **Addr.:** 60 Southport St., Unit 109, Toronto, ON M6S 3N4, Canada.

Asheim, Lester Eugene (Ja. 22, 1914, Spokane, WA) William Rand Kenan, Jr., Prof. of LS, Univ. NC, 1975–; Prof., Univ. Chicago Grad. Lib. Sch., 1971–74; Dir., Ofc. for Lib. Educ., ALA, 1966–71, Dir., Intl. Rel. Ofc., 1961–66; Dean and Assoc. Prof., Univ. Chicago, Grad. Lib. Sch., 1952–61; Ast. Prof., 1948–52; Reg. Libn., US Fed. Pub. Housing Athrty., 1946. **Educ.:** Univ. WA, 1936, BA (Eng. Lit.), 1937, BLS 1941, MA (Amer. Lit.); Univ. Chicago, 1949, PhD (Libnshp.). **Orgs.:** ALA: Nom. Com. IRRT (Ch., 1971–72); Lib. Educ. Div. (VP, Pres. Elect, 1975–76); Com. on Accred. (1958–61), Ch. (1958–59). AALS. Other orgs. AAUP. **Honors:** Joseph W. Lippincott Awd., Disting. Svc. in Libnshp., 1976; Beta Phi Mu, Disting. Svc. to Educ. for Libnshp., 1973; Scarecrow Press, Awd. for Lib. Lit., 1968; Univ. WA Sch. of Libnshp., Disting. Alum. Awd., 1966; Other awds. **Pubns.:** Co-Ed., *Differentiating the Media* (1975); *Librarianship in the Developing Countries* (1966); "Trends in Library Education–U.S.A.," *Advnc. in Libnshp.* (1975); "Librarianship as a Profession," *Lib. Trends* (1979); Ed., *Lib. Qtly.* (1972–74); Other articles and pubns. **Activities:** 11; 26; 63, 93, 95-Intl. Lib. Rels. **Addr.:** School of Library Science, Manning Hall 026A, University of North Carolina at Chapel Hill, Chapel Hill, NC 27514.

Asher, Helen R. (Ja. 7, 1927, Knoxville, TN) Libn., Auburn Faith Cmnty. Hosp., 1980–; Dir. Lib. Servcs., St. Joseph Hosp., Orange, CA., 1959–79. **Educ.:** UCLA, UCI, Santa Ana Coll.,

PROFESSIONAL ACTIVITIES: Institutions: 1. Acad. lib.; 2. Arch.; 3. Assn.; 4. Fed./Gvt. lib.; 5. Inst. lib.; 6. Mfr./Suppl.; 7. Milit. lib.; 8. Musm.; 9. Pub. lib.; 10. Sch. lib.; 11. Sch. of lib. sci.; 12. Spec. lib.; 13. State lib.; 14. (other). **Functions/Activities:** 15. Acq./Col. dev.; 16. Adult srvs.; 17. Admin.; 18. Apprais.; 19. Archit./Bldgs.; 20. Cat./Class.; 21. Chld. srvs.; 22. Circ.; 23. Cons./Pres.; 24. Consult.; 25. Cont. ed.; 26. Educ. lib. sci.; 27. Ext. srvs.; 28. Fund/Grants; 29. Gvt. pubs.; 30. Indx./Abs.; 31. Instr. lib. use; 32. Media srvs.; 33. Micro.; 34. Netwks./Coop.; 35. Persnl.; 36. PR; 37. Publshg.; 38. Recs. mgt.; 39. Ref. srvs.; 40. Repro.; 41. Resrch.; 42. Review.; 43. Secur.; 44. Serials; 45. Spec. col.; 46. Tech. srvs.; 47. Trustees/Bds.; 48. YA srvs.; 49. (other).

Chapman Coll. 1957–61, AA (LS); UCLA, UCI, 1957–59, MLS; Medline - UCLA, 1973–74, CBRT. (Medline). **Orgs.:** Med. LA. Sacramento Area Hlth. Sci. Libns. Grp. Assn. West. Hosp. **Honors:** Med. Tech. Lib. Grp. of Orange Cnty., Hon. Mem., 1979. **Activities:** 1, 12; 17, 20, 49; 63, 80 **Addr.:** 14145 Wolf Rd., Auburn CA 95603.

Asher, Richard E. (O. 2, 1947, Indianapolis, IN) Cat. Mgt. Unit Supvsr., IN State Lib., 1977–, Cat. Libn., 1975–77; Catlgr., Lilly Lib., IN Univ., 1974–75; Catlgr., IN Christ. Univ., 1972–74. **Educ.:** Marian Coll., 1965–70, BA (Hist.); Christ. Theo. Semy., 1970–72, MAR (Relig.); IN Univ., 1974–75, MLS. **Orgs.:** Cath. LA. ALA. IN LA: Tech. Srvs. Div., Dist. IV Rep. (1979), Vice-Ch. (1980), Ch. (1981). Amer. Acad. of Relig.: *Sem. on East. Christ. Bibl.* Ed. Com. (1977–). **Pubns.:** "AACR2 and Card Catalog Maintenance," *Cath. Lib. World* (D. 1980); "AACR2 Impact Study, Indiana State Library," *Alternative Cat. Nsltr.* (My. 1980); "The Mystical Theology of St. Maximus the Confessor," *Amer. Benedictine Review* (Mr. 1978); various bk. reviews, *Lib. Jnl., Relig. Std. Review, The Christ. Libn.* **Activities:** 13; 20, 42; 90 **Addr.:** 964 Lexington Ave., Indianapolis, IN 46203.

Ashford, Marguerite K. (F. 4, 1953, Honolulu, HI) Ref. Libn., Bernice P. Bishop Musm. Lib., 1976–. **Educ.:** Stanford Univ., 1971–74, BA, hons. (Hist.); Univ. of Otago, Dunedin, NZ, 1975, PGD (Pac. Hist.); Univ. of HI, 1974–76, MLS. **Orgs.:** SAA. HI LA. Grad. Sch. Lib. Std. Alum. Grp., Univ. of HI: Bd. (1979–); Pres.-Elect (1979–80); Pres. (1980–81); Cont. Ed. Com. (1979–); HI Musm. Assn. Adv. Bd. Ahahui 'Olelo HI. Univ. of HI Com. for the Prsrvn. and Std. of Hawaiian Lang., Art, and Culture. Punahou Alum. Assn. Otago Univ. Graduands. **Honors:** Beta Phi Mu. **Pubns.:** "Bernice P. Bishop Museum Library," *Pac. Info. and Lib. Srvs. Nsltr.* (1978). **Activities:** 12; 20, 39, 45; 54, 55, 66 **Addr.:** Bishop Museum Library, P.O. Box 19000–A, Honolulu, HI 96819.

Ashford, Richard K. (S. 22, 1950, Washington, DC) Instr., Grad. Sch. of Lib. and Info. Sci., Simmons Coll., 1980–; Chld. Libn., Boston Pub. Lib., 1977–79; Chld. Libn., Prince George's Co. Meml. Lib., 1974–77; Libn., Calverton Sch., 1972–73. **Educ.:** Carleton Coll., 1968–72, BA (Eng. Lit.); Cath. Univ. of Amer., 1973–74, MSLS; Simmons Coll., 1977–79, MA (Chld. Lit.); Columbia Univ., 1978–, PhD. **Orgs.:** ALA. New Eng. LA: RT of Chld. Libns.; MA Rep. (1979–). MA LA. Chld. Lit. Assn. Natl. Assn. for the Prsrvn. and Perpet. of Storytelling. **Pubns.:** "Tomboys and Saints; American Girls' Stories of the Latter 19th Century", *Sch. Lib. Jnl.* (Ja. 1980). **Activities:** 9, 11; 17, 21, 26 **Addr.:** Graduate School of Library and Information Science, Simmons College, 300 The Fenway, Boston, MA 02115.

Ashley, Grover C. (D. 5, 1915, Springfield, MO) Dir., Cook Lib., Univ. of South. MS., 1976–, Assoc. Univ. Libn., 1969–76. **Educ.:** AR State Coll., 1935–39, BS (Hist.); Univ. of South. MS, 1968–69, MS (Lib. Sci.). **Orgs.:** MS LA: Coll. and Univ. Sect. (Ch., 1972); Natl. Libr. Week (1972). SELA. ALA. **Activities:** 1; 17 **Addr.:** 2503 Villa Verde, Hattiesburg, MS 39401.

Ashley, Patrick (F. 23, 1946, Port Angeles, WA) Head, Acqs. Dept., Northwestern Univ. Lib., 1978–, Srch. Libn., 1973–78, Gifts and Exch. Libn., 1970–73. **Educ.:** Univ. WA., 1964–68, BA, (Anthro., Educ.); Univ. MI, 1968–70, AMLS. **Orgs.:** ALA: RTSD/RS (1972–75), /Org. Std. Com. (1974–75); SORT/Steer. Com. (1973–79), Ch. (1974–76); AACRL/ANTS, Nom. Com. (1972–74); IL LA: RTS Sect. (1974–75). Univ. MI LS Alum. Socty.: Pres. (1976–77). **Honors:** Beta Phi Mu, 1969. **Activities:** 1; 15, 44 **Addr.:** Head, Acquisitions Department, Northwestern University Library, Evanston, IL 60201.

Ashley, Roger Samuel (Ap. 16, 1940, Ishpeming, MI) Dir., Andover HS Media Ctr., 1972–; Trustee, Bloomfield Twp. Lib.; Trustee, Oakland Cnty. Lib. Trustee Assn.; Adjunct Lectr., Univ. of MI Sch. of Lib. Sci. **Educ.:** North. MI Univ., 1962, BA (Sec. Educ.); MI State Univ., 1967, MA (Educ.); Wayne State Univ., 1980, MLS. **Orgs.:** MI Assn. for Media in Educ.: State Mem. Ch. (1980–81); Ed. Staff, *Media Spectrum*. ALA: AASL. MI LA. AECT. **Honors:** Phi Delta Kappa. **Activities:** 9, 10; 26, 32, 47; 63 **Addr.:** 4200 Andover Rd., Bloomfield Hills, MI 48013.

Ashton, Rick J. (S. 18, 1945, Middletown, OH) Dir., Allen Cty. Pub. Lib., 1980–; Ast. Dir., Ft. Wayne Allen Cnty. Pub. Lib., 1977–80; Cur., Lcl. and Family Hist., Newberry Lib., 1974–77; Ast. Prof. of Hist., Northwestern Univ., 1972–74. **Educ.:** Harvard Univ., 1963–67, AB, (Hist.); Northwestern Univ., 1967–69, MA, (Hist.), 1971–73, PhD, (Hist.); Univ. Chicago, 1974–76, MA, (Libnshp.). **Orgs.:** ALA: Geneal. Com. (1977–79); IN LA: Legis. Com. (1977–80); Ft. Wayne Lib. Assn. Amer. Hist. Assn.; Org. of Amer. Histns.; Bd. for Cert. of Geneal.: Trustee (1977–79). **Honors** Beta Phi Mu, 1977. **Pubns.:** *The Life of Henry Ruiter, 1742–1819* (1974); *The Genealogy Beginner's Manual: A New Edition* (1977); "The Loyalist Congressmen of New York", *NY Hist. Socty. Qtly* (1976); "Curators, Hobbyists, and Historians: 90 Years of Genealogy at the Newberry Library", *Lib. Qtly* (1977); "Who Uses Public Libraries?", *Approaches to the Study of Public Library Services and Users* (1979). **Activities:** 9; 17, 45, 47; 55, 69 **Addr.:** Allen Cty. Pub. Lib., 900 Webster St., Box 2270, Fort Wayne, IN 46801.

Ashworth, Edith E. (Je. 9, 1920, Danville, VA) Supvsr. Lib. Srvs., Fairfax Cnty. Pub. Schs., 1975–, Asst. Supvsr. Lib. Srvs., 1973–75, Area I Media Spec., 1970–73; Title II Proj. Dir., Brookfield Elem. Sch., 1969–70; Libn., VA Hills Elem. Sch., 1958–69. **Educ.:** James Madison Univ., 1938–42, BS (LS); Univ. VA, 1948–53, MEd (Guid.); Catholic Univ., 1960–62, MLS. **Orgs.:** VA LA: Strng. Com. VA Educ. Assn.: Sch. Lib. Dept. (Secy., Pres.-elect, Pres., 1970–74). Assoc. Sch. Libns. Fairfax Cnty.: Pres. (1963–65). VA Educ. Media Assn.: Bd. Dir. (1975–78). ALA: AASL/Mtls. Sel. Com. (1976). Delta Kappa Gamma. **Pubns.:** Ed., Fairfax Cnty. Mediagram (1975–80). **Activities:** 10; 15, 17, 32; 56, 63, 74 **Addr.:** James Lee Media Center, 2855 Annandale Rd., Falls Church, VA 22042.

Asp, William G. (Jl. 4, 1943, Hutchinson, MN) Dir., MN Office of Pub. Libs. and IL Coop., 1975–; Ast. Prof., Univ. of IA, Sch. of Lib. Sci., 1970–75; Dir., East Central Reg. Lib., 1967–70. **Educ.:** Univ. of MN, 1961–66, BA (Hist.); Univ. of MN, 1966–67, MLA; Univ. of IA, Post-grad. work, 1971–75. **Orgs.:** Chief Officers of State Lib. Agencies: Ch. (1979–80); Vice-Ch. (1977–78). ALA. MN LA. MN Educ. Media Org. Other orgs. Amer. Field Srv. **Pubns.:** Ed., *Minnesota Libraries* (1975–). **Activities:** 13; 17, 34; 78 **Addr.:** Office of Public Libraries and Interlibrary Cooperation, 301 Hanover Building, 480 Cedar Street, St. Paul, MN 55101.

Aspnes, Grieg Garfield (N. 21, 1912, Montevideo, MN) Mgr., Info. Srvs., Experience, Incorporated, 1981–; Mgr., Lib. Info. Ctr., Cargill, Inc., 1956–77; Advert. Mgr., Brown and Bigelow, 1950–56, Resrch. Libn., 1943–50; Instr., Univ. of MN, Grad. Sch. of LS, 1963–70. **Educ.:** Univ. of MN, 1937–40, BA (Liberal Arts), 1940–41, BS (LS). **Orgs.:** SLA: VP, Pres.-Elect (1950–51); Pres. (1951–52); Educ. Com. (Ch., 1961–65); Nom. Com. (Ch., 1959–60); various ofcs, coms. Natl. Agr. Lib.: Adv. Com. (1964–65). MN Gvrs. Pre-WHCOLIS: Coord. (1977–78). Fed. of Soctys. for Paint Tech.: Tech. Info. Systs. Com., Ch. Univ. of MN Grad. Sch. of LS: Adv. Com. on Curric. (1972–73). **Honors:** SLA, Hall of Fame, 1977. **Pubns.:** "A Philosophy of Special Librarianship," *Special Librarianship – A New Reader* (1980); "Reference Information Service is the Essence of Librarianship," *Present Status and Future Prospects of Reference Information Service* (1967); "INFORM–An Evaluation Study," *MN Libs.* (Fall 1974); "Special Libraries in Minnesota," *MN Libs.* (Fall 1968); "Special Librarianship – What Will Change, What Must Change?" *MN Univ. Bltn.* (O. 1970); various articles, rpts., sps. **Activities:** 12; 17, 24, 26; 50, 59, 75 **Addr.:** 4324 S. Drew Ave., Minneapolis, MN 55410.

Assaf, Nancy Corbin (S. 21, 1935, San Diego, CA) Coord. of Lib. Srvs., N. Cnty. Ctr., San Diego State Univ., 1979–; Actg. Ch., Media and Curric. Ctr., 1978–79, Coord. of Lib. Instr. Srvs., 1976–80; As-. Univ. Libn., Tech. Srvs., Amer. Univ. of Beirut, 1968–75; Head, Serials Dept., Univ. of CA, San Diego, 1964–68, Serials Acq. Libn., 1962–64; Cat. Libn., Univ. of MN, 1961–62, Jr. Ref. Libn., 1959–61. **Educ.:** Occidental Coll., 1953–55; Univ. of CO, 1955–57, BA (Eng. Lit.); Univ. of WA, 1958; Univ. of Denver, 1958–59, MA (Libnshp.); San Diego State Univ., 1977–, Mass Comm. **Orgs.:** ALA. CA LA: Palomar Chap., State Univ. and Coll. Chap. Sierra Club. **Pubns.:** Co Ed., *Education: A Guide to Reference Sources* (1980); various tchg. aids, bibls. etc. (1976–79). **Activities:** 1; 15, 17, 31; 54, 92, 93 **Addr.:** 326 Mesa Way, La Jolla, CA 92037.

Astbury, Effie C. (D. 9, 1916, Montreal, PQ) Retired, 1979–; Prof. of Lib. Sci., McGill Univ. LS Grad. Sch., 1949–79, Dir., 1972–76, Head, Ref. and Circ., Med. Lib., 1939–49. **Educ.:** McGill Univ., 1934–38, BA (Classics), 1938–39, BLS; Univ. of Toronto, 1953–56, MLS; various wkshps. **Orgs.:** PQ LA: Cncl. (1957–59). CAN LA: Cncl. (1958–61). CAN Assn. of Coll. and Univ. Libs.: Cncl. (1967–69). ASIS; other orgs. McGill Univ.: Sen. (1971–74). **Honors:** Beta Phi Mu, 1958. **Pubns.:** Co. auth., "Congenital Cardiac Disease; Bibliography of the 1,000 Cases Analysed in Maude Abbott's Atlas", *Amer. Heart Jnl.* (May 1944); "Library Technicians and the Reference Service", *Can. Lib. Jnl.* (Jan./Feb. 1969); *Casey A. Wood: A Bio-Bibliography* (1981). **Activities:** 1, 11; 17, 26, 39; 55, 95-gvt. pubns., 80 **Addr.:** 3450 Drummond St., Apt. 1414, Montreal, PQ H3G 1Y2, Canada.

Astle, Deana L. (Jl. 18, 1945, Martinez, CA) Head, Serials Dept., Univ. of MO, 1978–; Serials Ord. Libn., Univ. of UT, 1968–78. **Educ.:** Brown Univ., 1963–67, AB (Eng. Lit.); Univ. of CA, Los Angeles, 1967–68, MLS; Univ. of UT, 1971–76, MA (Eng.). **Orgs.:** ALA: RTSD/Reg. Serials Wkshp. Com. (1980–83; Ch., 1981-82); RTSD/Prsrvn. Micro. Com. (1981-83). UT Coll. Lib. Cncl.: Serials Com. (1975–78). UT LA: Conv. Hosplty. Com. (Ch., 1977). **Honors:** Beta Phi Mu, 1968; Phi Beta Kappa, 1967. **Activities:** 1; 15, 23, 44 **Addr.:** Head, Serials Department, Ellis Library, University of Missouri, Columbia, MO 65201.

Atcher, Tagalie L. (Ag. 19, 1947, S. Weymouth, MA) Dir. of Med. Libs., Grp. Hlth. Coop. of Puget Snd., 1979–; Head, Pub. Srvs., Univ. of KY Med. Cntr., 1977–79, Head, Ref. Dept., 1976–77, Ref. Libn., 1976. **Educ.:** Longwood Coll., 1965–69, BS (Eng., Educ.); Univ. of KY, 1974–75, MSLS. **Orgs.:** Med. LA. Seattle Area Hosp. Lib. Cnstm.: (Ch., 1980). **Honors:** Beta Phi Mu, 1976. **Pubns.:** "Resident Selection Process: Description and Annotated Bibliography," *Med. LA Bltn.* (Oct. 1979). **Activities:** 12; 15, 17, 39; 80 **Addr.:** Group Health Cooperative, Medical Library, 200 15 Ave. E., Seattle, WA 98112.

Atherton, James J. (D. 17, 1936, Vancouver, BC) Dir. Gen., Res. Mgt. Brnch., Pub. Arch. of Can., 1978–; Prog. Plng. Ofcr., Arch. Brnch., Pub. Arch. of Can., 1976–77, Chief, Pub. Recs. Div., 1973–76. **Educ.:** Univ. of BC, 1956–61, BA (Hist.); Carleton Univ., 1961–72, MA (Hist.). **Orgs.:** Assn. of Can. Archvsts.: Recs. Mgt. Com., Ch. (1979–80), Secy. (1977–78). SAA. Assn. of Recs. Mgrs. and Admin. Can. Hist. Assn.: Cncl (1973–76). **Pubns.:** "Origins of Public Archives Records Centre", *Archivaria* (Sum. 1979); "British Columbia Origins of Federal Department of Labour", *BC Std.* (Win. 1976–77). **Addr.:** Rural Route 3, Wakefield, PQ J0X 3G0, Canada.

Atkins, Thomas Victor (D. 29, 1923, Poland) Chief, Lib. Inst. Srvs., Baruch Coll., CUNY, 1969–; Sr. Libn., Resrch. Libs., NYPL, 1965–68. **Educ.:** Columbia Univ., 1966–68, MLS; New Sch. for Soc. Resrch., 1972–76, PhD (Pol. Sci.). **Orgs.:** ALA: LIRT/Plng. Task Frc. (1978–79). CUNY LA: Pres. (1971–72). **Pubns.:** Ed., *LACUNY Journal* (1972–76); Ed., *Cross-Reference Index* (1974); Co. Auth., *Access to Information: Library Research Methods* (1979); "Library Encounter", AV tape. **Activities:** 1; 31; 54, 59, 92 **Addr.:** 120 E. 34th St., #16–A, New York, NY 10016.

Atkinson, Charles M. (Ag. 15, 1941, Crockett, TX) Assoc. Prof. of Msc., OH State Univ., 1978–; Ast. Prof., Univ. of CA, 1973–78; Clarinetist, W. Point Band, 1966–69; Msc. Tchr., Westport, CT, 1964–66. **Educ.:** Univ. of NM, 1959–63, BFA (Msc. Educ.); Univ. of MI, 1963–65, MM (Msc. Educ.); Univ. of NC, 1969–72, PhD (Msclgy.); Univ. of Erlangen, Germany, 1972–73, (Msclgy.). **Orgs.:** Msc. LA. Amer. Msclgcl. Socty.: AMS Cncl. (1977–79); Einstein Awd. Com. (1979–81). Internatl. Msclgcl. Socty. Mediaeval Acad. of Amer. Amer. Fed. of Mscns. **Honors:** Amer. Msclgcl. Socty., Alfred Einstein Awd., 1978; Mediaeval Acad. of Amer., Van Courtlandt Elliott Prize, 1979. **Pubns.:** Ed., Bk. Reviews, Msc. LA *Notes* (1975–78); "Romano Micheli", *Grove's Dictionary of Music and Musicians* (1980); "The Earliest Agnus Dei Melody and its Tropes", *Jnl. of the Amer. Msclgcl. Socty.* (1977); "Parapter", *Handwörterbuch der musikalischen Terminologie* (1979); "The *Parapteres:* a Perspective on Changes in the Concept of *Tonus* in the 9th and 10th Centuries", *Proceedings* (1980); Various reviews. **Activities:** 41 **Addr.:** 372 Fallis Rd., Columbus, OH 43214.

Atkinson, Ernest Edwin (Jl. 15, 1923, Jesup, GA) Archvst., Mexican Bapt. Conv. of TX, 1974–, Prof. and Libn., Mex. Bapt. Bible Inst., 1960–; Elem. Tchr., Lakeview Bapt. Sch., 1960–62; Missn. pastor, Home Missn. Bd., S.B.C., 1948–60. **Educ.:** Howard Payne Coll., 1949, BA (Span. Hist.); Swest. Bapt. Theo. Semy., 1950–54, MDiv. (Theo.); Austin Presby. Theo. Semy., DMin. in progress. **Orgs.:** Amer. Theo. LA. Bexar Lib. Assn. Arch. Assoc. SAA. Amer. Assn. for State and Lcl. Hist. Oral Hist. Assn. Other orgs. **Pubns.:** *Indice de materias de Publicaciones Periódicas Bautistas* (1976–); *A Selected Bibliography of Hispanic Baptist History* (1981). **Activities:** 2, 12; 17, 30; 66, 85, 90 **Addr.:** 8019 Panam Expy. S., San Antonio, TX 78224.

Atkinson, Gloria Jean Lewis (St. Joseph, MO) Dir., Arch. & Musm. Dept., MS Univ. for Women; Dir., TN-Tombigbee Waterway Dev. Athrty., 1978–; Chief, Arch. (USAF), Albert F. Simpson Hist. Resrch. Ctr., 1972–75; Resrch. Archvst., 1964–72; Catlgr./Archvst., 1960–63. **Educ.:** Auburn Univ., 1956–59, BS (Hist.); MS Univ. for Women, 1978–80, MA (Hist.); Air Univ., Maxwell AFB. **Orgs.:** SAA: Com. on Colls. & Univs. (1980–81). South. Hist. Assn. Soc. of MS Archvsts.: Prog. Ch. (1980). AAUW. Phi Alpha Theta. Pi Gamma Mu. **Honors:** State of MS, State Hist. Recs. Bd., 1980. **Pubns.:** *German Air Force Monograph Project* (1972); *Personal Files in the U. S. Air Force Historical Collection* (1975); "Meditations on Professionalism," *The Primary Source* (D. 1979). **Activities:** 2, 4, 7; 17, 23, 24; 55, 63 **Addr.:** Clio Archives Consulting Company, P. O. Box 2033, Fairlane Station, Columbus, MS 39701.

Atkinson, Hugh C. (N. 27, 1933, Chicago, IL) Univ. Libn. and Prof. of Lib. Admin., Univ. IL, 1976–; Dir. of Libs. and Prof. of Lib. Admin., OH State Univ., 1971–76, Asst. Dir. of Libs., 1967–71, Pub. Srvs. and Assoc. Prof. of Lib. Admin., 1969–74, Asst. Prof. of Lib. Admin., 1967–69; Asst. Dir. of Libs., Tech. Svcs., SUNY, 1964–67, Actg. Asst. Dir. of Libs. for Hlth. Sci., 1966–67, Head, Ref. Dept., 1961–64. **Educ.:** St. Benedict's Coll., 1951–53 (Act.); Univ. of Chicago, 1953–57 (Eng.), 1957–59, MA (LS); US Natl. Arch., 1958–, Cert. in Arch. Admin. **Orgs.:** ALA: LAMA/CSS (Ch., 1979–80); LITA/Bd. (1981–83); ACRL/Com. on Stand. and Accred. (1973–77); Cncl. (1970–73); RTSD/Lib. Mtls. Price Indx. Com. (1966–75; Ch., 1969–72; Consul., 1972–74); other coms. IL LA: OCLC Steer. Com. (1976–). ASIS. ARL: Inst. Rep. (1971–). Other orgs. AAUP: Buffalo Chap. (Treas., 1965–67). **Pubns.:** Cmplr., *The Merrill Checklist of Theodore Dreiser* (1969); CoEd., *Twenty-One Letters from Hart Crane to George Bryan* (1968); *Theodore Dreiser: a checklist* (1971); Co Auth., "The Ohio State University", *Encyc. of Lib. and Info. Sci.* (1977); "LCS, Its Future", *IL Libs.* (Apr. 1978); Other articles and reviews. **Activities:** 1; 17, 34; 56, 93 **Addr.:** 230

Special Subjects/Services: 50. Adult educ.; 51. Advert./Mktg.; 52. Aerosp.; 53. Agric.; 54. Area std.; 55. Arts/Hum.; 56. Autom.; 57. Bibl./Prtg.; 58. Bio. sci.; 59. Bus./Fin.; 60. Chem.; 61. Copyrt.; 62. Documtn.; 63. Educ.; 64. Engin.; 65. Env.; 66. Eth. grps.; 67. Film; 68. Food/Nutr.; 69. Geneal.; 70. Geo.; 71. Geol.; 72. Handcpd.; 73. Hist.; 74. Int. frdm.; 75. Info. sci.; 76. Insr.; 77. Law; 78. Legis.; 79. Math./Comp. sci.; 80. Med.; 81. Metals; 82. Nat. resrcs.; 83. Newsp.; 84. Nuc. sci.; 85. Oral hist.; 86. Petr./Energy; 87. Pharm.; 88. Phys./Astr./Math.; 89. Readg.; 90. Relig.; 91. Sci./Tech.; 92. Soc. sci.; 93. Telecom.; 94. Transp.; 95. (other).

Library, University of Illinois at Urbana-Champaign, 1408 W. Gregory, Urbana, IL 61801.

Atkinson, Joan Lyon (N. 23, 1939, Memphis, TN) Ast. Prof., Univ. of AL, 1972–; Libn. and Tchr., Erasmus Hall HS, 1965–70; Instr. of Eng., Abilene Christ. Coll., 1963–65. **Educ.:** Harding Coll., 19S7–61, BA (Eng., Hist.); Univ. of TX, 1961–63, MA (Eng. Lit.); Pratt Inst., 1969–70, MLS. **Orgs.:** ALA: YASD/ Media Sel. and Usage Com. (Ch., 1977–79); Educ. Com. (1979–). AL LA: YASRT (Mdrtr., 1976–78); Chld. and Sch. Libns. Div., Ch. (1980–81). SE LA. Natl. Cncl. of Tchrs. of Eng., Adsnt. Lit. Asm. Natl. Assn. for Pres. and Perpet. of Strytlng. **Honors:** Beta Phi Mu. **Pubns.:** "Young Adult Library Services," *ALA Yrbk.* (1979–80). **Activities:** 10, 11; 21, 39, 48; 63, 67, 89 **Addr.:** 183 Woodland Hills, Tuscaloosa, AL 35405.

Atkinson, Ross W. (D. 18, 1945, San Jose, CA) Hum. Biblgphr., Northwest. Univ. Lib., 1980–, Schol.-Libn. Prog., 1977–80. **Educ.:** Univ. of the Pac., 1963–67, BA (Grmn.); Harvard Univ., 1967–69, MA (Grmn. Lit.), 1973–76, PhD (Grmn. Lit.); Simmons Coll., 1976–77, MLS. **Orgs.:** ACRL: Bibl. Instr. Sect., Prog. Com. (Ch., 1982); West. European Spec. Sect., Bylaws Com. (Ch., 1980), Nom. Com. (Ch., 1981). Mod. Lang. Assn. **Pubns.:** "An Application of Semiotics to the Definition of Bibliography," *Studies in Bibliography* (1980); "Irony and Commitment in Heine's *Deutschland. Ein Wintermärchen*," *Germanic Review* (1975). **Activities:** 1; 15, 31, 41; 55, 57 **Addr.:** Collection Management Div., Northwestern University Library, Evanston, IL 60201.

Atwood, Ruth C. (Ag. 28, 1919, New York, NY) Dir., Lib. Ofc. of Syst. Resrch. and Dev., Univ. of Louisville, 1968–; Dir., Info. Srvs., Kornhauser Med. Lib., 1955–68; Supvsr., Milk, Water and Food Lab., KY State Bd. of Hlth., 1943–44; Resrch. chem., Seagram Distillers Lab., 1942–43. **Educ.:** Cornell Univ., 1936–40, BS (Microbiol.); IA State Univ., 1940–42, MS (Physiol.); Catharine Spalding Coll., 1950–57, MS (LS). **Orgs.:** KY LA: Spec. Lib. Sect. (Ch., 1960–); Secy., 1969–70). SLA. SE LA. ASIS. Other orgs. KY Comp. Users Grp. AAUP. **Pubns.:** Contrib., *Computerized Serials Systems Series* (1973); Ed., *Bibliography of Kentuckiana Metroversity Grant* (1972); "Technical Information Retrieval", *Louisville Engin. Sci.* (Dec. 1968); "An Annemometer for I. L. L. Winds", *Coll. and Resrch. Libs.* (1968); Ed., Technical Serials in Kentucky (1970); Various articles and videotapes. **Activities:** 1; 34; 56 **Addr.:** Library Office of System Research and Development, University Library, University of Louisville, 2301 S. Third St., Louisville, KY 40208.

Aubin, Robert (Ag. 10, 1942, Montreal, PQ) Lib. Head, Hopital Reviere-des-Pravies, 1981–; Head, of Documtn. Ctrs., Coll. de l'Assomption, 1979–81; Lib. Head, Ecole Polytech. de Thies, Senegal, 1975–79; Info. Sci., Inst. Philippe Pinel, Montreal, 1972–75. **Educ.:** Univ. de Montreal, 1967–70, DENS (Educ., 1970–72, MBibl. (LS). **Orgs.:** ASTED: Cnslr. (1974–75). Corp. des Bibtcrs. Prof. du PQ. **Activities:** 1, 10; 17, 32, 48; 63 **Addr.:** 700, chemin Seigneurial, L'Epiphanie, PQ J0K 1J0 Canada.

Aubrey, Irene Elizabeth (Ja. 7, 1928, Ottawa, ON) Chief, Chld. Lit. Srv., Natl. Lib. of Can., 1975–; Head, Chld. Sect., Westmount Pub. Lib., 1968–75; Chld. Srvs. Consult., W.-Island Reg. Lib. Srv., 1966–68; Branch Libn., Ottawa Pub. Lib., 1962–66; Stagiaire, Hachette Publshg. Co., Paris, France, 1960–61; Branch Libn., Ottawa Pub. Lib., 1956–60, Chld. Libn., 1951–56. **Educ.:** Univ. of Ottawa, 1945–49, BA (Gen.); Lafortune Bus. Coll., 1949–50, Dip.; Univ. of Toronto, 1950–51, BLS (Gen.). **Orgs.:** ASTED: Sect. Scolaire; Sect. des Bib. Pubs.; Exec. Com., Com. de Lit. de jeunesse. IFLA: RT of Libns. Representing Documtn. Ctrs. Srvg. Resrch. in Chld. Lit. PQ LA: Pub. Libs. Sect; Youth Sect. Intl. Bd. on Bks. for Young People: Can. Sect., Exec. Com., Natl. Lib. Liaison Ofcr. Various other orgs. Chld. Bk. Ctr., Toronto. Bibl. Socty. of Can. Natl. Lib. of Can.: Notable Can. Chld. Bk. Com., Ch. Bib. Natl. du Can.: Com. pour la sél. des meilleurs livres Can. pour les jeunes, Ch. Various other orgs. **Pubns.:** *Storytellers' Rendezvous: Canadian Stories to Tell to Children* (1979); *La biche miraculeuse* transl. *The Miraculous Hind* (1973); "Green Gables: Prince Edward Island National Park, Canada," *The Calendar* (N. 1979–Je. 1980); "Dialogue 1979," *Bookbird* (Ja. 1980); "The National Library's Role in the Bibliographical Access to Canadian Children's Literature," *The Bibl. Socty. of Can. Colloquium* (O. 1978); various presentations. **Activities:** 4; 15, 17, 21; 57 **Addr.:** Children's Literature Service, National Library of Canada, Ottawa, ON K1A 0N4 Canada.

Auchstetter, Rosann M. (Ja. 31, 1947, Mendota, IL) Head, Slide Dept., Art Inst. of Chicago, 1969–. **Educ.:** Marycrest Coll., 1965–69, BA (Art); Columbia Univ., Metro. Musm. Sem., 1975. **Orgs.:** ARLIS/NA: Stans. for Slide Cols. Com. (1978–); Circ. Slide Cols. Panel (1977); Visual Resrcs. Cols. N. Amer.; IL State Reg. Co-ord. (1977). Mid-Amer. Coll. Art Assn.: Rec. Secy. (1977–79). Coll. Art Assn.: Committee member, Stan. for Slide Cols. Com. (1978–). Art Libs. Socty. of N. Amer.: IN-IL Chap., Ch. (1979–81). Prof. Musm. Assn. of Art Inst. of Chicago: Secy. (1975). **Activities:** 1, 8; 15, 17, 20; 55 **Addr.:** Ryerson and Burnham Libraries, Art Institute of Chicago, Michigan Ave. at Adams St., Chicago, IL 60603.

Aucoin, Sharilynn Allison (Ja. 21, 1942, El Dorado, KS) Asst. Exec. Dir., LA LA, 1976–; Young People's Libn., Sect. for Blind and Phys. Handcpd., LA State Lib., 1974–75; various secretarial positions, 1964–67. **Educ.:** LA State Univ., 1960–64, BA (Grmn.), 1971–73, MLS; State of LA, 1979, Real Estate Salesman's Licn. **Orgs.:** ALA. Intl. Cncl. of LA Execs. LA LA: Asst. Exec. Dir. (1976–). Baton Rouge Lib. Club: Treas. (1979); Pres.-Elect (1981). Baton Rouge, LA Realtors Assn. Baton Rouge Bd. of Realtors. Natl Realtor's Assn. Beta Phi Mu: Beta Zeta Chap. (Chrt. Pres., 1973). **Honors:** Alpha Lambda Delta, 1961; Mu Sigma Rho, 1962; Phi Kappa Phi, 1963. **Activities:** 3; 17, 37, 38; 51 **Addr.:** Louisiana Library Association, P.O. Box 131, Baton Rouge, LA 70821.

Audretsch, Robert W. (N. 9, 1941, Detroit, MI) Syst. Dir., Three Rivers Reg. Lib. Srv. Syst., 1978–; Dir., Salem, OH Pub. Lib., 1973–77; Ast. Dir., Warren, OH Pub. Lib., 1972–73; Head, Cat. Dept., Wayne-Oakland Cnty. MI Lib. Fed., 1972. **Educ.:** Wayne State Univ., 1960–69, BA (Hist.), 1969–70, MSLS. **Orgs.:** ALA. CO LA. CO Educ. Media Assn. Mountain-Plains LA. **Pubns.:** Ed., *Salem, Ohio 1850 Women's Rights Convention Proceedings* (1976). **Activities:** 9, 13; 17, 36, 39; 77, 78, 95-Mult-Type Coop. **Addr.:** Three Rivers Regional Library Service System, Box 396, New Castle, CO 81647.

Auerbach, Bob Shipley (D. 14, 1919, New York, NY) Sr. Media Spec., Ref., Univ. of DC, 1972–; Dir., Catlgr., Cap. Lib. Srv., 1961–72; Libn., Urbana Coll., 1959–61; Libn., Tecumseh HS, 1958–59. **Educ.:** NY Univ., 1939–50, BA (Pol. Sci.); Columbia, CUNY, New Sch. for Soc. Resrch., 1948–51; George Peabody Coll., 1955–56, MA (LS). **Orgs.:** DC LA. Potomac Tech. Prcs. Libns. MD LA. ALA: ACRL, Com. on Coll. Lib. Coop. (1965–66). Socialist Party: WA Area Org. (1980–81). Citizens Party: Prince Georges Cnty. Org. (1980–81). Amer. Philatelic Socty. Amer. Pol. Items Collectors. **Pubns.:** "Experimental College," *Lib. Coll. Wkshp.* (1962); contrib., *Lib. Jnl.*, *RQ*. **Activities:** 1, 10; 20, 31, 39 **Addr.:** 14–X Ridge Rd., Greenbelt, MD 20770.

Auerbach, Rita (Jl. 23, 1944, New York, NY) Chld. Libn., Connetquot Pub. Lib., 1975–; Tch., Garden City Sr. HS, 1972–74. **Educ.:** Barnard Coll., 1961–66, AB (Hist.); Tchr. Coll., Columbia Univ., 1969–71, MA; Columbia Univ., 1974–75, MLS. **Orgs.:** Chld. Libn. Assn. of Suffolk Cnty., Inc.: Pres. (1978–80), Bd. of Dir. (1977–78), Lib. Pract. Com. (1976–78). Suffolk Cnty. Lib. Assn.: Cvl. Srvc. Com. (1980–). NY LA: Concerns of Women RT, Steer. Com. (1977). **Honors:** ALA/ALSC, Charles Scribner's Sons Awd., 1979; Beta Phi Mu. **Pubns.:** "On Aging—Where are the Advocates? An Annotated Bibliography", *Col. Bldg.* (1979). **Activities:** 9; 21, 39, 49-Storytel. **Addr.:** Connetquot Public Library, 760 Ocean Ave., Bohemia, NY 11716.

Aufdenkamp, Jo Ann (Mr. 22, 1926, Springfield, IL) Pvt. Consult., 1981–; Admin., Info. Srvs., Legal Dept., Lincoln Natl. Life Insr. Co., 1980–81; Libn., Fed. Rsv. Bank of Chicago, 1948–80; Asst. Libn., Cmrc. Lib., Univ. IL, 1946–48. **Educ.:** MacMurray Coll. for Women, 1942–45, BS (Bus.); Univ. of IL, 1945–46, BLS; John Marshall Law Sch., 1976, JD; Univ. of Chicago, Grad. Lib. Sch., 1964–66, (LS). **Orgs.:** SLA: IL Chap., Pres. (1954–55); Fncl. Div., Chmn. (1951–52). Amer. Assn. of Law Libs. Amer. Bar Assn. Chicago Bar Assn. IL Bar Assn. **Pubns.:** "Career Paths for Special Librarians," *Lib. Mgt.* (1981); Co-Auth., *Special Libraries: A Guide for Management* (1975); "The Free Spirit of the Special Librarian", *Spec. Libnshp., A New Reader* (1980); "Guidelines for Consultants to Libraries in Developing Countries", *Spec. Libs.* (Feb. 1965). **Activities:** 12; 17, 29, 39; 59, 77 **Addr.:** 636 Park Blvd., Glen Ellyn, IL 60137.

August, Sidney (Philadelphia, PA) Dir., Div. of Educ. Resrcs., Cmnty. Coll. of Philadelphia, 1970–; Supvsr., Sch. Libs., Sch. Dist. of Philadelphia, 1969–70; Head Libn., Pedagogical Lib., 1966–69; Libn., Sch. Dist. of Philadelphia, 1948–66; Catlgr., Univ. PA, 1942–43; Ast. Ref. Libn., Lib. of Congs., 1940–42. **Educ.:** Temple Univ., 1935–39, BA (Eng.); Drexel Univ., 1939–40, BSLS; Temple Univ., 1950–52, MEd (Educ. Admin.); Drexel Univ., 1965–66. **Orgs.:** ALA: ACRL/CJCLS, Plng. and Proc. Com. (Ch.). SLA. Film Lib. Intercoll. Coop.: Place. Policy Com. (Ch.); Pres. (1971–72). **Pubns.:** *Student Use of Libraries* (1962); *Two Plus Two: Community College Voc-Ed.* (1973). **Activities:** 1; 17 **Addr.:** Div. of Educational Resources, Community College of Philadelphia, 34 S 11th St., Philadelphia, PA 19107.

Auh, Y. John (Mr. 18, 1934, Mokpo, Chulla Namdo, Korea) Chief Libn., Wagner Coll., 1972–, Tech. Srvs. Libn., 1968–71; Head, Un. Cat., Long Island Univ., 1965–68; Asst. Libn., Branch Cnty. Lib., 1964–65; Tech. Srvs. Libn., Korean Milit. Acad., 1958–61; Asst. Catlgr., Korean Natl. Lib., 1957–58. **Educ.:** Chung-ang Univ., 1953–57, BA (Econ.); West. MI Univ., 1962–64, MA (Libnshp.); Columbia Univ., 1972–75, Cert. Advnc. Libnshp.; Univ. of MD, 1973, Cert. (Lib. Admin. Dev. Prog.); St. John's Univ., NY, 1975–79, MBA (Mgt.); Clarkson Coll., 1978, Cert. (Lib. Mgt.). **Orgs.:** ALA: APALS, Rcrt. and Mem. Com. NY LA. Libns. Club (NY Area). Songlee Corp.: Bd. of Trustees, Ch. Amer. Frnds. of Chung-ang Univ.: Bd. of Trustees. **Honors:** Cmnty. Leaders of Amer., Plaque, 1979–80. **Pubns.:** *A Survey of Wagner College Library at Bregenz, Austria* (1971); ed., *Faculty Publications of Wagner College* (1978). **Activities:** 1, 12; 15, 17; 59 **Addr.:** 126 Beverly Ave., Staten Island, NY 10301.

Aulbach, Louis Frederick (Jl. 12, 1948, Houston, TX) Tech. Info. Res. Anal., Phillips Petroleum Co., 1979–; Supvsr., Info. Sys., Ashland Exploration Co., 1976–79; Purch. Agt., Wessendorff, Nelms and Co., Inc., 1974–76; Purch. Agt., Marchem Res., Inc., 1973–74. **Educ.:** Rice Univ., 1966–70, BA (Behvl. Sci.); Univ. of Chicago, 1971–73, MBA (Info. Mgt.), 1971–73, MLS; TX State Tchrs. Cert., 1970. **Orgs.:** SLA. Natl. Micro. Assn. Assn. of Recs. Mgrs. and Admin. Houston OL Users Grp. Cvl. Air Ptl. Amat. Athl. Un., Gulf Assn. **Activities:** 12; 17, 30, 38; 56, 70, 86 **Addr.:** Phillips Petroleum Company, P.O. Box 1967, Houston, TX 77001.

Auld, Lawrence W. S. (S. 19, 1933, Joplin, MO) Ast. Dean, Grad. Sch. of Lib. Sci., Univ. IL, 1979–, Ast. Prof. and Actg. Ast. Dir., 1976–78, Tchr. and Supvsr. Lib. Sch. AV Lab., 1973–76; Assoc. Prof., Ast. Libn. and Head, Tech. Svcs., OR State Univ., 1968–73; Univ. Libn. for Syst. and Resrch., Oakland Univ., 1967–68, Ast. Univ. Libn. for Tech. Srcs., 1965–67; Dir., Prcs. Ctr., HI State Lib., 1961–65; Catlgr., Univ. TX, 1958–61. **Educ.:** Univ. of North. IA, 1952–55, BA (Eng.); Columbia Univ., 1956–58, MSLS; Univ. IL, 1973–78, DLS. **Orgs.:** ALA: ACRL (1958–); RTSD (1958–); LITA (1966–). ASIS. AALS. Other orgs. **Honors:** Phi Kappa Phi, 1977. **Pubns.:** "Automated Book Order and Circulation Control Procedures at the Oakland University Library", *Jnl. of Lib. Auto.* (Je. 1968); "ALA and Collective Bargaining", *ALA Bltn.* (Ja. 1969); "Functional Organization Plan for Technical Services", *Lib. Rsrcs. and Tech. Svcs.* (Sum. 1970); "KWOC Indexes and Vocabulary Comparisons of Summaries of LC and DC Classification Schedules", *ASIS Jnl.* (S.–O. 1971); Co Auth., "Library Group Practice", *Coll. and Resrch. Libs.* (Ja. 1973); Other articles. **Activities:** 11; 17, 41 **Addr.:** 906 E. Michigan, Urbana, IL 61801.

Aull, Sara A. (Ap. 2, 1910, China Grove, NC) Retired, 1973–; Head, Sci. and Engin. Div., Univ. of Houston Lib., 1971–73, 1951–69, Actg. Asst. Dir., Pub. Srvs., 1970; Resrch. Asst., PR Dept., Assn. of Amer. Railroads, 1946–49; Catlgr., U.S. Frgn. Econ. Admin. Lib., 1943–45; HS Libn., NY Pub. Sch. Syst., 1940–42; Head Catlgr., Lansing Pub. Sch. Lib., 1939; Serials Catlgr., NY Pub. Lib., Ref. Dept., 1934–38. **Educ.:** Lenoir Rhyne Coll., 1926–30, BA (Eng.); Columbia Univ., 1931–32, BS (LS); Univ. of Houston, 1963–65, MA (Radio, TV). **Orgs.:** SLA: Dir. (1960–63); Com. on Coms. (Ch., 1968–69); Plng. Com. (Ch., 1971–72, 1972–73); TX Chap. (Pres., 1959–60, 1966–67); NC Chap. (*Bltn.* Ed. 1975–). **Honors:** SLA, Hall of Fame Awd., 1973. **Activities:** 1, 12; 39, 44; 64, 86, 91 **Addr.:** 201 W. Rice St., Landis, NC 28088.

Auster, Ethel W. (Je. 4, 1942, Montreal, PQ) Libn., OISE, 1972–, Head, Ref., 1972–75; Libn., Toronto Bd. of Educ., 1969–71; Libn., Brookline HS, 1966–69. **Educ.:** Boston Univ., 1962–65, AB (Eng.); Simmons Coll., 1965–66, SM (LS); Univ. of Toronto, 1971–72, BEd, 1972–75, MEd, 1975–78, EdD. **Orgs.:** SLA: Educ. Div. (Ch., 1978–79). ALA: ACRL/BIS (1979–81). Can. Assn. for Info. Sci.: Anl. Conf. (Vice ch., 1980). ASIS. Can. Socty. for Std. of Educ. Amer. Educ. Rsrch. Assn. **Honors:** Soc. Sci. and Hum. Rsrch. Cncl. of Can., Rsrch. Grant, 1979–81. **Pubns.:** *Reference Sources on Canadian Education: An Annotated Bibliography* (1978); "The Educational Information System for Ontario: Summary of Selected Research Findings", *ON Lib. Review* (Sept. 1979); "Factors Affecting the Use of Educational Information: A Canadian Experience", *Educ. Libs. Bltn.* (London Institute of Education) (Sum. 1979); "The Negotiation Process in Online Bibliographic Retrieval", *Can. Jnl. of Info. Sci.* (May 1979); "ERIC in Canada: Problems and Prospects", *Can. Lib. Jnl.* (Feb. 1978); Various articles. **Activities:** 11, 12; 18, 27, 42; 64, 76, 93 **Addr.:** 39 Edgecombe Ave., Toronto, ON M5N 2X4, Canada.

Austin, David L. (F. 11, 1942, Fergus Falls, MN) Asst. Prof., Msc. Lib. and Theory, Wichita State Univ., 1966–. **Educ.:** Univ. of MI, 1960–64, BMus (Msc. Theory), 1964–67, MA (Msclgy.); Univ. of CA, 1977–78, MLS (Libnshp.). **Orgs.:** Msc. LA: Mt. Plains Chap. Amer. Musicological Socty. Lute Socty. of Amer. **Honors:** Wichita State Univ., Univ. Resrch. Grant, 1972; Beta Phi Mu, 1979. **Pubns.:** "Folilore in A Spanish Liturgical Drama," *Relig. Thea. #5* (1967); "Music Drama," *Relig. Thea. #6* (1968); *Manuscripts of the University of California, Berkeley Music Library: MSS 757–763* (Je. 1978); radio critic, KMUW pub. radio; various classical msc. articles, *Wichita Indp.* **Activities:** 1; 15, 20, 39; 55 **Addr.:** Music Library, Box 53, Wichita State University, Wichita, KS 67208.

Austin, Roxanna (Je. 5, 1919, Kenwood, GA) Dir., Athens Reg. Lib., 1976–; Assoc. Prof., Sch. of LS, FL State Univ., 1969–76; Consult., Pub. Lib. Srv., GA Dept. of Educ., 1951–68; Dir., Towns-Un. Reg. Lib., 1947–51; Asst. to Sch. Lib. Supvsr., GA Dept. of Educ., 1945–47; Asst. Libn., North Fulton HS, 1942–45; Tchr., R. L. Hope Elem. Sch., 1941–42; Tchr.-Libn., Pike Cnty. HS, 1939–41. **Educ.:** GA State Coll. for Women, 1935–39, AB (Hist., Eng.); Univ. of NC, 1943–45, BS (LS); FL State Univ., 1968–69, Advnc. Mstrs. (LS). **Orgs.:** ALA: Awds. Com. (Ch., 1963–64); *ALA Booklist* Ed. Adv. Bd. (1967–73). SE LA: Treas. (1964–66); Budget Com. (1978–80). Delta Kappa Gamma Socty.: Alpha Nu Chap. (Pres., 1963); Gamma Chap. (Pres., 1978–79). Leag. of Women Voters: Tallahassee Chap. (Dir., 1974). Pilot Club: Tallahassee Chap. (Secy., 1973–74);

PROFESSIONAL ACTIVITIES: Institutions: 1. Acad. lib.; 2. Arch.; 3. Assn.; 4. Fed./Gvt. lib.; 5. Inst. lib.; 6. Mfr./Suppl.; 7. Milit. lib.; 8. Musm.; 9. Pub. lib.; 10. Sch. lib.; 11. Sch. of lib. sci.; 12. Spec. lib.; 13. State lib.; 14. (other). **Functions/Activities:** 15. Acq./Col. dev.; 16. Adult srvs.; 17. Admin.; 18. Apprais.; 19. Archit./Bldgs.; 20. Cat./Class.; 21. Chld. srvs.; 22. Circ.; 23. Cons./Pres.; 24. Consult.; 25. Cont. ed.; 26. Educ. lib. sci.; 27. Ext. srvs.; 28. Fund/Grants; 29. Gvt. pubs.; 30. Indx./Abs.; 31. Instr. lib. use; 32. Media srvs.; 33. Micro.; 34. Netwks./Coop.; 35. Persnl.; 36. PR; 37. Publshg.; 38. Recs. mgt.; 39. Ref. srvs.; 40. Repro.; 41. Resrch.; 42. Review.; 43. Secur.; 44. Serials; 45. Spec. col.; 46. Tech. srvs.; 47. Trustees/Bds.; 48. YA srvs.; 49. (other).

Athens Chap., Corres. Secy. (1981), Dir. (1979–80). **Honors:** Beta Phi Mu, 1969; Phi Kappa Phi, 1971; Phoenix Socty., 1939. **Activities:** 9, 13; 15, 17, 26; 67, 89 **Addr.:** 13 LaFayette Sq. Apts., 680 Hill St., Athens, GA 30606.

Auston, Ione C. (S. 4, 1946, LaGrange, GA) Data Base Coord., Ref. Libn., Natl. Lib. of Med., 1978–; Tech. Info. Spec., Natl. Inst. of Neurological and Communicative Disords. and Stroke, 1977–78; Grady Libn., Emory Univ. Sch. of Med., 1973–77; Libn. I, Hlth. Sci. Lib., Univ. of MD Sch. of Med., 1972–73. **Educ.:** St. Mary's Jr. Coll. 1964–66; Univ. of GA, 1966–68, BA (Econ.); Univ. of MD, 1971–72, MLS. **Orgs.:** Med. LA. ASIS. DC LA. **Pubns.:** *Neoplasia: A Guide to Sources of Information* bibl. (1980); *Biomedical Effects of Volcanoes* bibl. (1980). **Activities:** 4; 31, 36, 39; 80, 87, 91 **Addr.:** National Library of Medicine, Rm. 153, 8600 Rockville Pike, Bethesda, MD 20209.

Autrey, Pamela Sanders (O. 13, 1945, Dallas, TX) Ed. of *EXTRACT,* SW Educ. Dev. Lab, 1978–; Info. Syst. Anal., TX Dept. of Comnty. Affairs, 1974–77; Ref. Libn., Univ. of TX, 1970–73, Libn. I, Lyndon B. Johnson Sch. of Pub. Affairs, 1970. **Educ.:** Univ. of TX, 1964–68, BA (Gvt., Fr.), 1968–70, MLS; Dip. d'Alliance Française, 1966; Univ. de las Amer., Mexico City, 1965. **Orgs.:** ASIS. Austin OLUG. Austin Readg. Is FUNdamental: Steer. Com. (Ch., 1978–79). **Honors:** Beta Phi Mu; Phi Beta Kappa, 1967; Pi Delta Phi, 1967; Phi Kappa Phi, 1969. **Pubns.:** Ed., *Change and the Public Schools: State Leadership Challenges* (1979); Ed., *Regional Needs Study: A Statistical Profile of Arkansas, Louisiana, Mississippi, New Mexico, Oklahoma and Texas* (1978); "Family and Child Statistics Available from TDCA," *TX Libs.* (Fall 1977); "My Experience in Alternative Information Careers," *SLA TX Chap. Bltn.* (Feb. 1979); Coprod., "How to Turn People on with Statistics," Videotape presentation (Apr. 1976). **Activities:** 12; 17, 24, 30; 56, 63, 92 **Addr.:** 3503 Windsor Rd., Austin, TX 78703.

Autry, Brick Dir., Rhoads Meml. Lib., 1976–; Asst. Dir., Libn., Title IV Prog., Cocopah Tribe, AZ, 1975. **Educ.:** East. NM Univ., 1969–73, BS (Drama); Univ. of AZ, 1974–75, MLS (Amer. Indian, Lib.). **Orgs.:** ALA. TX LA. Amer. Indian LA. **Honors:** TX Lib., J. Frank Dobie Awd., 1978. **Pubns.:** "Indian Library," *La Confluencia* (1978). **Activities:** 9; 24, 45; 66 **Addr.:** 121 E. Bedford, Dimmitt, TX 79027.

Avant, Julia King (O. 14, 1934, Marion, LA) Ast. Prof., Sch. of Lib. Sci., FL State Univ., 1980– Ast. Prof., Sch. of Lib. Sci., Univ. of South. CA, 1978–80; Dir., Ouachita Par. Pub. Lib., 1973–78; Dir., Trail Blazer Lib. Syst., 1973–74, Consult., 1974–78; Assoc. Prof., NWest. State Univ., 1972–73; Ast. Prof., LA State Univ., 1970–72, Catlgr., 1967; Ast. Libn., Ouachita Par. Pub. Lib., 1960–67. **Educ.:** NWest. State Coll., LA, 1953–57, BA, (Soc. Std.); LA State Univ., 1960–64, MSLS); IN Univ., 1967–72, DLS. **Orgs.:** ALA: PLA/Pub. Lib. Rpt. Com. (1979–81). LA LA: Sec. VP (1978); Conf. Ch. (1978); Secy. (1974–75). Assn. of Amer. Lib. Schls. Amer. Cntr. of Films for Chld.: Fest. Film Sel. Com. (1978), Ch. (1979–80). Delta Kappa Gamma. AAUW. Frnds. of Chld. and Lit. **Honors:** Beta Phi Mu; LA LA, Modisette Awd. for Pub. Libs., 1978. **Pubns.:** Jt. Auth., "Selecting films for Children", *Sightlines* (Win. 1980); Various reviews; "Guide to Good Reading", *Montoe News-Star World* (1973–78); "Library Bookshelf", Wkly. radio show (1973–78); "Library Viewpoint", Wkly. radio show (1976–78); Biweekly 5 minute radio broadcast, KLIC-AM, Monroe, La. (1977–78); "KNOE Open-House", Monthly TV show (1973–74); Other radio shows. **Activities:** 9, 11; 17, 26, 36; 59, 67, 92 **Addr.:** Box 112–A, Route 2, Downsville, LA 71234.

Aveney, Brian Henry (Ja. 24, 1940, Bronx, NY) Dir., Resrch. and Dev., Blackwell N. Amer., 1980–; Mgr., Comp. Systs., Info. Dsgn., 1978–80; Visit. Asst. Prof., Univ. of OR, 1977–78; Head, Tech. Srvs., Sacramento Pub. Lib., 1975–77; Mgr., Bibl. Ctr., Univ. of CA, 1974–75; Mgr., Syst. Dsgn., Richard Abel and Co., 1973–74; Head, Lib. Syst. Plng. Ofc., Univ. of PA, 1971–73; various positions in syst. analysis, tchg., consult. **Educ.:** Colgate Univ., 1957–61, BA (Fine Arts); Columbia Univ., 1965–67, MS (LS); various crs. **Orgs.:** ALA: LITA/Info. Sci. and Autom. Sect., Exec. Bd. (1978–80), Prog. Plng. Com. (1975–77); Lib. Autom. Discuss. Grp. (Ch., 1973–75); various other coms. ASIS: Conf. Com. (1976); Bay Area Chap., Ch. (1975–76), Prog. Ch. (1974–75). CA Lib. Athrty. for Systs. and Srvs.: Conf. Ch.; various coms. SLA: Various ofcs., coms. Various other orgs. Lib. of Congs. Prof. Assn.: Prog. Ch. (1969). **Pubns.:** "Special Section on Micrographics: Introduction," *Bltn. of the Amer. Socty. for Info. Sci.* (O. 1980); "Competition in New Data Bases," *Online* (Ap. 1979); jt. auth., "Reactions Measured: 600 Users Meet the COM Catalog," *Amer. Libs.* (F. 1979); jt. auth., "Indexing of Popular Periodicals: The State of the Art," *Lib. Jnl.* (O. 1, 1978); jt. auth., "Conversion of Manual Catalogs to Collection Data Bases," *Lib. Tech. Rpt.* (Mr.–Ap. 1978); ed., *Jnl. of Lib. Autom.* (1980–); various articles, rpts., bk. reviews. **Activities:** 1, 11; 17, 46; 56 **Addr.:** Blackwell North America, Beaverton, OR 97005.

Averdick, Michael Robert (N. 22, 1948, Covington, KY) Assoc. Dir., Kenton Cnty. Pub. Lib., 1978–, Head, Adult Srvs. Dept., 1973–78; Admin., Spec. Proj., KY Dept. of Libs., 1971–73; Bkmobile. Libn., Lexington Pub. Lib., 1970–71. **Educ.:** Univ. of KY, 1969–70, BA (Soclgy.); Univ. of Cincinnati, 1966–68 (Dsgn.); Univ. of KY, 1970–71, MSLS (Cmnty. Srvs.); various crs. **Orgs.:** KY LA: Exec. Nom. Com. (1981); Bd. of Dirs. (1977–78); Pub. Lib. Sect., Ch. (1977–78), Vice-Ch. (1976–77), Secy.-Treas. (1975–76), Schol. Com. (1975–78); State Conf., Lcl. Arrange. (Ch., 1977); Legis. Com. (1975); Int. Frdm. Com. (1975). ALA. Covington Rotary Club. Behringer-Crawford Musm. Bd. of Trustees: Vice-Ch. (1979–). Kenton Cnty. Hist. Socty.: Fndr. (1977); Bd. of Trustees (1979–). Retired Sr. Volun. Prog.: Adv. Cncl. (1973–76); Co-Ch. (1975–76). Various other orgs. **Honors:** Phi Beta Kappa, 1971. **Pubns.:** Ed., *Kenton Cnty. Hist. Socty. Qtly.* (1977–78, 1980); ed., *Jnl. of the KY State Lib.* (1972–73); "Tour Guide to Cincinnati," *KY Monthly* (My. 1981); "Information Boom," *KY Post* (Ap. 24, 1978); jt. auth., *Governor's Pre-White House Conference on Libraries and Information Services Blueprint for Direction Task Force Report on Delivery of Services* (1978); contrib., various cmnty. newsps. **Activities:** 9; 16, 17, 36; 69, 73, 92 **Addr.:** 213 Covington Ave., Covington, KY 41011.

Averitt, George Robert (Ag. 5, 1931, Peru, IN) Assoc. Publshr., The News-Dispatch, 1973–; Bd. Treas., MI City Pub. Lib., 1968–78; Trustee, 1965–78. **Educ.:** IN Univ., 1949–53, AB (Jnlsm.); MI State Univ. 1954; 1956–59, (Econ.). **Orgs.:** ALA. IN LA: Plng. Com. (1979–80); Pubns. Task Frc. (Ch., 1979–80); Pubns. Bd (1980–); Dist. Treas. (1980); Dist. Ch. (1981–). Amer. Econ. Assn. Socty. of Prof. Jnlsts. **Honors:** Jaycees, Distinguished Srv., 1965. **Activities:** 9; 47; 74, 75, 83 **Addr.:** 121 W. Michigan Blvd., Michigan City, IN 46360.

Aversa, Mary E. (D. 10, 1951, Pasadena, TX) Mgr., Info. Ctr., Doane Agr. Srv., Inc., 1978–; Dir., Lrng. Resrcs., WA Univ. Sch. of Soc. Work, 1976–78; Libn., Tobacco Merchants Assn., 1974–76. **Educ.:** St. Louis Univ., 1969–72, BA (Hist.); Columbia Univ., 1973–74, MSLS (Info. Sci.). **Orgs.:** SLA: Slate Ed. (1977–79); Pres.-Elect (1981–82); St. Louis Metro Area Chap., Food and Nutr. Div., Dir. St. Louis OLUG: Ch. (1980–81). ASIS. St. Louis Reg. Lib. Netwk.: Cncl. Rep. (1980–82). **Honors:** Phi Beta Kappa, 1972. **Pubns.:** "Knowledge About Knowledge Is Power," *Soc. Work Resrch. and Abs.* (Sum. 1979). **Activities:** 12; 17, 30, 49-data base prod., info. broker; 53, 59, 68 **Addr.:** Doane-Western, Inc., 8900 Manchester Rd., St. Louis, MO 63144.

Avery, May S. (My. 6, 1925, Schenectady, NY) Libn., Natl. Safety Cncl., 1974–; Chem. Libn., Argonne Natl. Lab., 1948–54. **Educ.:** OH State Univ., 1942–45, BSc (Chem); Rosary Coll., 1973–74, MALS. **Orgs.:** SLA. ASIS. **Honors:** Beta Phi Mu, 1974. **Activities:** 12; 15, 20, 30; 95-Safety, 94 **Addr.:** National Safety Council Library, 444 N. Michigan Ave., Chicago, IL 60611.

Avison, M. Elizabeth (D. 23, 1941, Montreal, PQ) AV Libn., Univ. of Toronto, 1974–; Ref. and Circ. Libn., Fac. of Lib. Sci., U of T, 1970–74; Ed., Clarke, Irwin Co. Ltd., 1966–70. **Educ.:** McGill Univ., 1966, BA; Univ of Toronto, 1969–70, BLS, 1971–78, MLS. **Orgs.:** ALA. Can. Assn. Coll. and Univ. Libs.: Non-Bk Mtls. Com. (1975–76). Can. LA: Bk. Dev. Com. (1975–76). Inst. of Prof. Libns. of ON: Assoc. ed. *Qtly.* (1974–76). Other orgs. Univ. of Toronto Lib. Syst.: Adv. Com. (1975–76). Lib. Sci. Fac.: Lect. Com. (1971–73); Lib. and Media Com. (1973–74); Resrch. and Pubns. Com. (1970–71). Univ. of Toronto Libns. Assn.: Pres. (1976–77). Univ. of Toronto Fac. Assn.: Cncl. (1976–79); Univ. Gvt. Com. (1976–77); Nom. Com. (1976–77). **Honors:** Beta Phi Mu, 1970. **Pubns.:** Various panel presentations. **Addr.:** Audio-Visual Library, 9 King's College Circle, University of Toronto, Toronto, ON M5S 1A5, Canada.

Avram, Henriette D. (O. 7, 1919, New York, NY) Dir., Pres. Systs., Netwks. and Autom. Plng., 1980–, and Dir., Network Dev. Ofc., Lib. of Congs., 1976–; Chief, MARC Dev. Ofc., 1970–76; Asst. Coord., Info. Syst., 1965–70; Sr. Syst. Anal., Oatatrol Corp., 1961–65. **Educ.:** Hunter Coll., 1936–38, (PreMed); George Washington Univ., 1953–55, (Math.). **Orgs.:** ALA: LITA, Bd. of Dirs., Pres. CLENE: Bd. of Dirs. ASIS. IFLA: Prof. Bd., Sect. on Info. Tech., Ch.; Div. of Mgt. and Tech., Ch. Other orgs. and coms. Natl. Women's Book Assn. **Honors:** ALA, RTSD, Margaret Mann Awd., 1971; ALA, ACRL, Acad./Resrch. Libn. of the Year, 1979; South. IL Univ., Edwardsville, Honorary Dr. of Sci., 1977; other awds. **Pubns.:** "Standards for Bibliographical Character Sets," *GCCA Jnl.* (1976); Jt. auth., "The Next Generation of CONSER," *Amer. Libs.* (Ja. 1977); "The Library of Congress–National and International Automation Activities," *Biblos,* (Ja. 1977); "Production, Dissemination, and Use of Bibliographic Data and Summary of the Conference" in *Prospects for Change in Bibliographic Control* (1977); "Library of Congress Networking Activities," *Unesco Bulletin for Libraries,* (Mr.–Ap. 1978); other books and articles. **Activities:** 4; 17, 34; 56, 93 **Addr.:** Processing Systems, Networks and Automation Planning, Library of Congress, Washington, DC 20540.

Awad, Amal (Mr. 27, 1933, Cairo, Egypt) Chief, Tech. Srvs., Montreal Cath. Sch. Comsn., 1970–; Asst. Libn., Montreal Univ., 1967–70; Chief Libn., Ctrl. Bank of Egypt, 1952–67. **Educ.:** Pensionnat du Sacré–Coeur, Cairo, 1938–52, Bacc. (Phil.); Montreal Univ., 1968–72, MALS; Éole des Hautes Etudes Comm., Montrèal, 1973–79, DSA (Admin.). **Orgs.:** ASTED. **Pubns.:** *Les Bibliothèques Canadiennes à l'ere de l'automatisation* (1972). **Activities:** 11, 12; 17, 20, 23; 50, 57, 63 **Addr.:** 11871 James Morrice, Montreal, PQ H3M 2G5 Canada.

Awkard, Julita Castro (N. 18, 1929, Manila, Philippines.) Head, Ref. Dept., FL A 7 M Univ., 1962–, Pharm. Libn., 1962–79; Circ. Libn., Albany State Coll., 1961–62. **Educ.:** FL A and M Univ., 1957–61, BS (LS, Fr.); 1968–70, MEd (Guid. Couns.); FL State Univ., 1970–72, MSLS. **Orgs.:** Amer. Assn. Colls. of Pharm: Libs. and Educ. Resrcs. Sect. Stand. Com. (Ch., Vice Ch.); Admin. Bd. Rep. Med. LA: Pharm. Sect. (Secy.). SLA: Pharm. and FL (News Rpt.). ALA: ACRL, FL Chap. (Ch.-elec., 1981–82). other orgs. **Honors:** Kappa Delta Pi; Phi Delta Kappa. **Pubns.:** CoAuth., "Drug Information Gathering as Part of Continuing Education in Pharmacy", *FL Pharm. Jnl.* (N. 1967); "Services that the Pharmacy Library Can Render to the Practicing Pharmacist as Part of His Continuing Education in Pharmacy", *FL Pharm. Jnl.* (O., 1973); other papers. **Activities:** 1, 11; 16, 17, 45; 75, 80, 87 **Addr.:** Coleman Library, Box 78–A, Florida A and M University, Tallahassee, FL 32307.

Axam, John Arthur (F. 12, 1930, Cincinnati, OH) Area Admin., Free Lib. of Philadelphia, 1978–, Head, Stations Dept., 1964–78, Bnch. Head, Paschalville Bnch., 1962–64, Head, Queen Meml. Bnch., 1960–62. **Educ.:** Cheyney State Coll., 1949–53, BS (Educ.); Drexel Univ., 1955–58, MSLS. **Orgs.:** ALA: LAMA/SS, Oper. Resrch. Com.; PLA/Basic Educ. and Litcy. Com. PA LA: Southeast Chap. Bd. Un. Way of Southeast PA: Trustee (1977–); Ctrl. Alloc. Com. (1975–). NAACP. **Honors:** Chapel of the Four Chaplains, Legion of Hon., 1970. **Pubns.:** "Reader Development Program", *Wilson Lib. Bltn.;* "Adult Literacy and Public Libraries", *PA Lib. Assoc. Bltn.* **Activities:** 9; 17 **Addr.:** Extension Division Office, Free Library of Philadelphia, Logan Sq., Philadelphia, PA 19103.

Axel-Lute, Paul (D. 4, 1945, New York, NY) Ast. Law Libn. for User Srvs. and Admin. Rutgers (Newark) Law Sch. Lib., 1979–, Fed. Doc. Libn., 1973–79. **Educ.:** Brandeis Univ., 1964–68, BA (Soclgy.); Rutgers Univ., 1972–73, MLS; Rutgers Law School, 1970–71; Amer. Assn. of Law Libs., 1979, Law Libn. Cert. **Orgs.:** Amer. Assn. of Law Libs. Gvt. Doc. Assn. of NJ: Pres. (1977–78). **Pubns.:** *Legislation Regulating Smoking Areas: A Selective Annotated Bibliography* (1976); "Federal Documents, 1978," *Law Lib. Jnl.* (1979); "Legislation Against Smoking Pollution," *Env. Affairs* (1978); "Recent Developments in Federal Documents," *Law Lib. Jnl.* (1978). **Activities:** 1; 17, 29, 39; 77, 78 **Addr.:** Rutgers Law Library, 15 Washington St., Newark, NJ 07102.

Axelrod, Helene Bernice (New York, NY) Media Spec., Hamden HS Lib., 1967–; Libn., South. CT State Coll., 1961–67. **Educ.:** Hunter Coll., CUNY, 1942–46, BA (Econ.); South. CT State Coll., 1966, MS (Lib. Sci.), Prof. Dip. of Adv. Std. Admin. and Supervsn., 1976. **Orgs.:** ALA. CT Educ. Media Assn. Phi Delta Kappa: South. CT State Coll. Chap., Mem. Com. (1978); Hist. (1979). Amer. Fed. of Tchrs. **Honors:** Univ. of CT, Inst. of Pub. Srv., Making Cable Work, 1976. **Pubns.:** *After Hamden High: a Career Guide for Students* (1976); "Independent Study: Report from Hamden High", *Clearing Hse.* (Oct. 1973). **Activities:** 10; 15, 17, 32; 55, 63, 92 **Addr.:** 125 Twin Brook Rd., Hamden, CT 06514.

Ayala, John L. (Ag. 28, 1943, Long Beach, CA) Libn., Asst. Prof., Long Beach City Coll., 1972–; Span. Biling. Ref. Libn., Los Angeles Cnty. Pub. Lib., 1971–72. **Educ.:** CA State Univ., Long Beach, 1961–70 (Hist.); Immaculate Heart Coll., Los Angeles, CA, 1970–71, MLS; CA State Univ., Long Beach, 1978–81, MPA (Pub. Admin.). **Orgs.:** CA LA: Cnclr. (1973–76). REFORMA: VP, Pres. (1974–76); Fndn. Mem. Assn. of Mex.-Amer. Educ. L.B.C.C. Acad. Sen.: Asst. Pres. (1979–80). **Activities:** 1, 9; 15, 17, 26; 50, 66, 92 **Addr.:** Long Beach City College, Pacific Coast Campus, 1305 E. Pacific Coast Hwy., Long Beach, CA 90806.

Ayala, Marta Stiefel (Je. 1, 1937, Pascanas, Cordoba, Argentina) Libn., Imperial Valley Coll., 1980–; Libn., San Diego State Univ.-Imperial Valley Campus, 1977–79; Ed., "La Cronica", Calexico Chronicle, 1977–77; Asst. Dir., Summer Study Tours, San Diego State Univ.-I.V. Campus, 1972–78. **Educ.:** Univ. of MN, 1956–60, BS (Occupational Therapy); Univ. of AZ, 1975–76, MLS; Univ. de Antioquia, Medellin, Colombia, 1976, Cert. (Sch. Libn.). **Orgs.:** REFORMA: Recruitment Com. Ch., (1977–79); Executive Board (1977–79). CA Media and Lib. Educators Assn. ALA. Asociacion de Bibs. Chicanas. Southwestern Missions Resrch. Ctr. Imperial Valley Coll. Musm. **Honors:** Graduate Library Institute for Spanish-Speaking Americans, Flwshp, 1975; Organization of American States, Flwshp, 1976; Phi Beta Mu, 1978. **Pubns.:** Contrib., *Spanish Language Health Materials: A Selected Bibliography* (1978); "How One Library-less Librarian Got the Word out," *Wilson Lib. Bltn.* (N. 1978); "Interviews with Spanish-Speaking Librarians,"; "Two Countries, One Workshop," *CMLEA Jnl.* (Fall 1978); "Los Centros de Medios Como Promotores de la Investigacion Creativa," *Revista Interamericana de Bibliotecologia* (Fall 1978). **Activities:** 1, 10; 15, 16, 39; 55, 66, 74 **Addr.:** 508 Second St., Calexico, CA 92231.

Ayotte, Richard G. (O. 20, 1947, Flint, MI) Pub. Srvs. Libn., Orange Cnty. Law Lib., 1979–; Circ. Dept. Head, Wayne

Special Subjects/Services: 50. Adult educ.; 51. Advert./Mktg.; 52. Aerosp.; 53. Agric.; 54. Area std.; 55. Arts/Hum.; 56. Autom.; 57. Bibl./Prtg.; 58. Bio. sci.; 59. Bus./Fin.; 60. Chem.; 61. Copyrt.; 62. Documtn.; 63. Educ.; 64. Engin.; 65. Env.; 66. Eth. grps.; 67. Film; 68. Food/Nutr.; 69. Geneal.; 70. Geo.; 71. Geol.; 72. Handcpd.; 73. Hist.; 74. Int. frdm.; 75. Info. sci.; 76. Insr.; 77. Law; 78. Legis.; 79. Math./Comp. sci.; 80. Med.; 81. Metals; 82. Nat. resrcs.; 83. Newsp.; 84. Nuc. sci.; 85. Oral hist.; 86. Petr./Energy; 87. Pharm.; 88. Phys./Astr./Math.; 89. Readg.; 90. Relig.; 91. Sci./Tech.; 92. Soc. sci.; 93. Telecom.; 94. Transp.; 95. (other).

State Univ. Law Lib., 1975–79. **Educ.:** Univ. of MI, 1965–69, BA (Hist.); Wayne State Univ. Law Sch., 1969–73, JD (Law), 1975–78, MSLS. **Orgs.:** South. CA Assn. of Law Libs.: Grants and Educ. Com. (1979–80). Amer. Assn. of Law Libs. MI Assn. of Law Libs. MI State Bar Assn.: Libs., Legal Resrch. and Pubns.; Amer. Bar Assn. **Addr.:** Orange County Law Library, 515 N. Flower St., Santa Ana, CA 92703.

Aytona, Cleotilde A. (Je. 3, 1941, Balayan, Batangas, Philippines) Sch. Libn., T.A. Neelin HS, 1971–; Tchr.-Libn., Margaret Barbour Collegiate, 1967–70; Resrch. Asst. Popltn. Inst., Univ. of Philippines, 1964–66. **Educ.:** Univ. of Philippines, 1959–63, AB (Pol. Sci.); George Peabody Coll. for Tchrs., 1970–71, MLS; Brandon Univ., 1966–67, Cert., (Educ.). **Orgs.:** Can. LA. Manitoba Sch. Lib. and AV Assn. **Activities:** 10; 15, 17, 22, 39, 48; 63 **Addr.:** 27 Balmoral Bay, Brandon, MB R7A 6E5, Canada.

Azusenis, Helen V. (My. 1, 1941, Cleveland, OH) Head, Plng. and Resrch., Cleveland Pub. Lib., 1979–, Head, Pop. Lib., 1977–79, Head, ILL, 1974–77; Dir., Henderson Meml. Pub. Lib., 1971–74. **Educ.:** Mather Coll., West. Rsv. Univ., 1959–63, BA (Eng.); Case-West. Rsv. Univ., 1969–71, MSLS. **Orgs.:** ALA. OH LA: Lib. Dev. (1977–79); Ad Hoc Com. on Ill (1980–). OHIONET: ILL Adv. Cncl. (1980–), Ch. (1980–81). OCLC ILL Adv. Com. (1979–). Case-West. Rsv. Univ.: Alum. Assn. (1978–81); Cont. Educ. Com. (1978–). **Honors:** Beta Phi Mu. **Activities:** 9; 17, 27, 34 **Addr.:** 17600 Detroit Ave. #510, Lakewood, OH 44107.

B

Baade, Harley D. (Ja 13, 1941, Guthrie, OK) Info. Systs. Coord., Shell Oil Co., 1980–, Lib. Syst. Spc., 1978–80; Supvsr., Lib. Oper., 1977–78; Info. Anal., 1974–77; Supvsr., Ofc. and Lib. Srvs., GE-Apollo Syst. Dept., 1967–73. **Educ.:** Univ. of OK, 1959–64, BA (Germn.); Univ. of TX, 1973–74, MLS. **Orgs.:** ASIS: Conf. and Mtgs. Com. (1980–81); Const. and Bylaws Com. (Ch., 1980–81). TX Chapt. Asm. Rep. (1980–81); Secy./Treas. SLA: TX Chap. (Treas., 1978–80). TX LA: Netwk. Com. (1978–79). **Honors:** Beta Phi Mu. **Pubns.:** "The Corporate Environment and the Librarian," *Special Librarianship, A New Reader* (1980); Jt. auth., "Information Systems Study", Ctr. for Highway Resrch. (1974); *Bltn. of ASIS* (Ag. 1977). **Activities:** 12; 17, 38; 52, 64, 86 **Addr.:** 1615 W. 12th, Houston, TX 77008.

Baatz, Wilmer H. (O. 23, 1915, Fort Wayne, IN) Educ. Libn., IN Univ., 1979–; Asst. Dir. for Col. Div., 1977–79, Asst. Dir. for Admin., 1973–76, Asst. Dir. for Oper. and Srvs., 1965–72; Chief Libn., Fed. Aviation Agency, 1960–65; Asst. Dir., Lib. Srvs., Vetrns. Admin., 1955–60; Chief., Tech. Srvs., Milwaukee Pub. Lib., 1950–55; Various other positions. **Educ.:** IN Univ., 1935–40, AB (Eng.), 1940–41, AM, (Eng.); Univ. of Chicago, 1945–46, BLS. **Orgs.:** ALA: RASD/Disc. Grp. Lg. Resrch. Libs., Tech. Srvs. (Ch. 1970–71), Col. Dev. (Ch., 1977–78). SLA: Transport. Div. (Ch., 1964); WI Chap. (Ch., 1953); IN Chap. (Ch., 1968). **Honors:** Cert. of Achievement, Fed. Aviation Agency, 1965; Phi Beta Kappa. **Pubns.:** Jt. Auth., *The Black Family and the Black Woman* (1978); "Recent Changes and Current Status of Collection Development in Large Research Libraries," *Emerging Trends in Library Organization* (1978); "Collection Development in 19 Libraries of the Association of Research Libraries," *Library Acquisitions: Practice and Theory* (1978); Various other articles. **Activities:** 1; 15, 46; 57, 63 **Addr.:** 3501 Park Lane, Bloomington, IN 47401.

Babcock, James M. (Jl. 4, 1926, Oklahoma City, OK) Bkseller, 1973–; Dir. of Libs., Assoc. Prof., Alma Coll., 1968–73; Chief, Burton Hist. Col., 1957–68; Actg. Archvst., Univ. of OK, 1955–56. **Educ.:** Univ. of OK, 1946–49, BA (Hist.); 1949–52, MA (Hist.); Univ. MI, 1956–57, AMLS. **Orgs.:** ALA: RASD/HS (Ch. 1977–78). Amer. Inst. of Graph. Arts. Hist. Socty. of MI: Trustee (1961–67, 1969–70); Pres. (1964). **Activities:** 14-Bk. store; 18, 24, 26; 95-Bk. Col. **Addr.:** 5055 Pte. Tremble Rd., Algonac, MI 48028.

Babian, Mary C. (D. 25, 1928, Highland Park, MI) Supvsr., Acq./Prcs., General Motors Corp. Resrch. Labs. Lib., 1969–; Libn., General Motors Corp. Electro-Motive Div. Lib., 1969. **Educ.:** East. MI Univ., 1963–65, BS (Lib. Sci.); Highland Park Jr. Coll., 1947–49. **Orgs.:** SLA: Michigan Chap. Pubcty. Ch. (1971–72); Ad Hoc Com. of the MI Partners of the Americas (1978–). ASIS. Engin. Soc. of Detroit. **Activities:** 12; 15, 17, 46; 64, 91, 94 **Addr.:** General Motors Corporation, Research Laboratories Library, General Motors Technical Center, Warren, MI 48090.

Babin, Lawrence James (Jl. 15, 1931, Hartford, CT) Libn., Media Spec., CT Pub. Sec. Sch., 1960–; Tchr., Libn., ME Pub. Sec. Sch., 1956. **Educ.:** Univ. of Hartford, Ctrl. CT State Coll., Univ. of CT, South. CT State Coll., NY Univ., Columbia Univ., Univ. of London, Untd. Kingdom; BA, MEd, Cert. (LS); PhD. **Orgs.:** ALA: AASL. CT LA. New Eng. LA. AECT. Various other orgs. Natl. Educ. Assn. Natl. Cncl. of Tchrs. of Eng. New Eng. Assn. of Tchrs. of Eng. New Eng. Educ. Media Assn. Various other orgs. **Honors:** Fiction Laureate, Natl. Competition, U-A Press, 1980. **Pubns.:** *Teacher; Twenty-Five Years Later* (1981); *Library Media Center in the Public School* (1979); *Books Are Like Flowers* (1981); *Gift for the Gifted; Cecilia of Rome* biog.; various bks. of poetry. **Activities:** 10, 11; 21, 32, 37; 55, 63, 90 **Addr.:** P.O. Box 328, Wethersfield, CT 06109.

Bacon, Agnes K. (Mr. 16, 1940, Békéscsaba, Hun) Head, Tech. Info. Dept., Nordson Corp., 1974–; Tech. Libn., Union Carbide Corp., 1967–73, Resrch. Chem., 1966–67; Comp. Progmr., 1963–65. **Educ.:** Ursuline Coll., 1958–62, BA (Chem.); Case-West. Rsv. Univ., 1968–71, MS (Info. Sci.). **Orgs.:** SLA: Cleveland Chap. (Pres., 1979–80). ASIS: North. OH Chap. (Bltn. Ed., 1976–77). **Honors:** Kappa Gamma Pi. **Activities:** 12; 15, 17, 20, 24; 59, 60, 64 **Addr.:** 28529 W. Oviatt Rd., Bay Village, OH 44140.

Badal, Jindriska (D. 4, 1944, Kolin, Czech.) Info. Spec., MA Inst. of Tech. Lab. for Comp. Sci., 1980–; Libn., Univ. of CA, Los Angeles, 1976–79. **Educ.:** Univ. of 17th N., Prague, Czech., 1965–1968; Univ. of SK, 1968–70, BA (Ger.); Univ. of South. CA, 1974–75; MS (LS); Coll. of Foreign Travel Trade, Czech., 1963–65, Dip. **Orgs.:** ASIS: Los Angeles Chap. (Exec. Bd., 1978). Assn. for Comp. Mach. **Activities:** 1, 5; 15, 20, 37; 56, 62, 75 **Addr.:** MIT - Laboratory for Computer Science, NE43-114, 545 Technology Sq., Cambridge, MA 02139.

Baechtold, Marguerite (Ap 16, 1916, Elmhurst, NY) Assoc. Prof., West. MI Univ., 1967–; Asst. Prof., Newark State Coll., 1964–66; Libn., W. Essex High Sch., 1960–64; Libn., Ridgewood, Pub. Sch., 1946–60. **Educ.:** Montclair State Coll., 1934–38, AB (Eng.); Columbia Univ., 1949–, BLS; West. MI Univ., 1968–, Ed S LS. **Orgs.:** ALA: AASL. AALS. MI LA. Assn. for Supervsn. and Curric. Dev. **Honors:** Beta Phi Mu; Delta Kappa Gamma. **Pubns.:** Jt. Auth., *Library Service to Families* (1980); *Excel: Workshop Planning Guide* (1978); "Early Childhood Library Programming", *Cath. Lib. World* (1979); Self Instructional Progs. for LS Stds. (1976). **Activities:** 10, 11; 21, 26, 32; 63 **Addr.:** 3226 Tamsin Ave., Kalamazoo, MI 49008.

Baer, Eberhard Alex (O. 8, 1929, Oelsnitz, Germany) Head, Ref./Col. Dev. Dept., VPI & SU, VA Polytechnic Inst., 1974–; Slavic Biblgphr., Univ. Lib., Regensburg, W. Germany, 1972–74; Dir., Slavic Bibl. & Documtnc Cntr., Assn. of Resrch. Libs., 1969–72; Slavic Biblgphr., Univ. Lib., Constance, W. Germany, 1968–69; Slavic Biblgphr. and Catlgr., Univ. of CA, Los Angeles, 1959–68. **Educ.:** Univ. of CA, Los Angeles, 1954–57, AB (Slavic Langs.); Harvard Univ., 1957–58, AM (Slavic Langs. & Lits); Univ. of CA, Berkeley, 1958–59, MLS. **Orgs.:** ALA: ACRL/Slavic & E. European Sect., Exec. Com. (1965–66); Ch., Nom. Com. (1979–80). Amer. Assn. for the Advnc. of Slavic Std.: Com. on Bibl. & Docum. (1970–1972). **Pubns.:** Jt. ed., *Dissertations-in-Progress in Slavic and East European Studies.* (1972). **Activities:** 1; 15, 17, 39; 54, 57, 73 **Addr.:** 209 Ardmore St., Blacksburg, VA 24060.

Baer, Eleanora A. (D. 22, 1907, Springfield, MO) Instr., LS, Fontbonne Coll., 1973–; HS Libn., Dist. Lib. Coord., Clayton Sch. Dist., 1953–73; Asst. Libn., St. Louis Univ. Libs., 1946–52; Libn., Fontbonne Coll., 1929–46. **Educ.:** Fontbonne Coll., 1926–31, AB (Eng.); St. Louis Univ., 1939–44, MEd; Univ. of WI, 1954–58, MS (LS); St. Louis Pub. Lib. Sch., 1926–27, Cert. **Orgs.:** ALA. Cath. LA: Lcl. Chap., Ch. NEA. **Honors:** Fontbonne Coll., Delta Epilson Sigma, 1942; Univ. of WI, Beta Phi Mu, 1958; Cath. LA, Fons Sapientiae Awd., 1978. **Pubns.:** *Titles in Series* (1978); *School Media Center* (1978); "Effects of Two Years of War on the Four-Year Catholic Women's Colleges," *Jnl. of Educ. Resrch.* (Mar., 1945); "Catholic Women's College and the War," *Jnl. of Higher Educ.* (Dec., 1945); "Books, Newspapers and Libraries in Pioneer St. Louis," *MO Hist. Review* (July, 1962). **Activities:** 1; 26 **Addr.:** 1359 McCutcheon Rd., St. Louis, MO 63144.

Baer, Mark H. (Je. 24, 1923, Pendleton, OR) Dir., Libs., Hewlett-Packard Corp., 1966–; Dir., Tech. Info. Srvs., Ampex Corp., 1959–66; Engin. and Tech. Div. Libn., OR State Univ., 1957–59; Chem. Branch Libn., Univ. of WA, 1956–57. **Educ.:** Univ. of WA, 1947–50, BA (Hist.), 1954–55, MLS (Libnshp.). **Orgs.:** SLA: Task Frc. on the Role of Spec. Libs. in Networking; Pres. (1976–77). Natl. Com. on Libs. and Info. Sci. Coop. Info. Netwk.: Dir. (1980–82). Inst. of Electrical and Electronics Engins. **Honors:** Univ. of WA, Sch. of Libnshp., Alum. of the Yr., 1976. **Pubns.:** *The Special Library in Industry* (1973); ed., *Union List of Periodicals: Science Technology, Economics* (1966). **Activities:** 12; 17; 59, 91 **Addr.:** Corporate Library, Hewlett-Packard Corp., 1501 Page Mill Rd., Palo Alto, CA 94304.

Baetge, Dorothy S. (F. 2, 1936, Victoria, TX) Supvsr., Elem. Libs., Pasadena (TX) Indp. Sch. Dist., 1975–, Libn., 1971–75, Tchr., 1966–71; Tchr., Edinburg Indp. Sch. Dist., 1965–66; Tchr., New Braunfels Indp. Sch. Dist., 1959–65. **Educ.:** SW TX State Univ., 1954–58, BS Ed (Msc.); Sam Houston State Univ., 1971–73, MLS, 1976–78, Supervisory Cert. **Orgs.:** ALA: AASL. TX LA: Dist. 8 (Treas., 1981–82). Lrng. Resrcs. Prog. Dirs. of TX: Pres. (1979–80). TX Assn. of Sch. Libns: Dist. 4 Lib. Sect. (Ch., 1980–81). Delta Kappa Gamma: Epsilon Rho Chap., TX Secy. (1976–78), 2nd VP (1978–80). **Activities:** 10; 21, 32; 63, 89 **Addr.:** 2013 S. Fisher Ct., Pasadena, TX 77502.

Baggett, Marjorie Dixon (My. 17, 1922, Birmingham, AL) Asst. Prof., Ref. Biblgphr., Gvt. Docums., Univ. of AL, in Birmingham, 1971. Libn., Samford Univ., 1964–71; Libn., Carraway Meth. Hosp. Sch. of Nursing, 1955–64. **Educ.:** Samford Univ., 1965–70, BA (Eng., Jnlsm., Hist.); Univ. of AL-Tuscaloosa, 1971–74, MSLS. **Orgs.:** AL LA: (Ch. PR, 1979–80); Godart (Vice Ch. 1976–78, Ch. 1978–79). SELA: Phys. Facilities Com. for 1980 Conv. Greater Birmingham Lib. Club. Order of East. Star; AL Writer's Conclave. **Honors:** Sigma Tau Delta, 1970. **Pubns.:** *AL LA GODORT: History and Procedural Manual* (1981); *Alabama Directory of Federal Depositories* (1980); "Local Documents & Public Access Workshop: A Report", *AL Libn.* (N./D. 1977). **Activities:** 1, 4; 15, 16, 29; 57, 62, 78 **Addr.:** Marjorie D. Baggett, 304 Chestnut St. (Roebuck), Birmingham, AL 35206.

Baggley, Roger (Mr. 24, 1944, Altrincham, Eng) Chief, Ofcl. Pubns. Div., Tech. Srvs. Branch, Lib. of Parmt., 1979–; Head, Ofcl. Publn. Sect. Tech. Srvs. Branch, 1976–79; Catlgr., 1970–76. **Educ.:** McMaster Univ., 1962–66, BA (Eng., Fr.); Univ. of West. ON, 1969–70, MLS. **Orgs.:** Can. LA. **Activities:** 4, 12; 17, 20, 29 **Addr.:** 2023 Deerhurst Ct., Ottawa, ON K1J 8H2 Canada.

Baginski, Doris Ann (Je. 14, 1938, Middletown, CT) Head, Ref. Libn., US Naval War Coll., 1970–; Sr. Catlgr., Yale Univ., 1969–70; Subj. Spec., Enoch Pratt Free Lib., 1966–69, Ref. Libn., 1963–66. **Educ.:** Univ. of CT, 1956–60, BA (Hist.); Syracuse Univ., 1961–63, MSLS. **Orgs.:** ALA. SLA. New Eng. LA. RI LA. **Honors:** Beta Phi Mu. **Activities:** 1, 4; 16, 17, 39; 54, 74, 92 **Addr.:** 63 Poplar St., Newport, RI 02840.

Bagnall, Norma (O. 27, 1929, St. Louis, MO) Resrch. Assoc., TX A&M Univ., 1978–. **Educ.:** TX A&M Univ., 1969–73, BS (Educ.), 1974–77, MA (Eng.), 1977–, PhD in progress (Eng.). **Orgs.:** ALA: ALSC. Adolescent Lit. Assn., Chld. Lit. Assn.: Regis. (1979–81). Mod. Langs. Assn. Natl. Cncl. of Tchrs. of Eng. **Honors** Phi Kappa Phi, TX A&M Lib. Student Book Contest, Van Domelen Awd., 1975. **Pubns.:** *A Child's Guide to the Brazos Valley* (1978); "The Formidable Sea," *Child. Lit. Qtly.*, (1978); "Books Introduce Young Readers to the Mysteries of the Sea" in *The University and the Sea* (1978); "Terabithia: Bridge to a Better World," *Lang. Arts* (Ap. 1979). "Realism: How Realistic Is It?" *Top of the News* (Win. 1980). **Activities:** 12; 21, 36, 48; 63, 65, 89 **Addr.:** Department of English, Texas A&M University, College Station, TX 77843.

Bagnell, Prisca von Dorotka (F. 16, 1928, Novi Sad, Vojvodina, Yugo.) Educ. Resrcs. Assoc., All-Univ. Grntlgy. Ctr., Syracuse Univ., 1972–; Libn., Sch. of Soc. Wk., 1970–72; Ast. Archvst., 1967–70; Asst. Slavic Biblgphr., 1963–67. **Educ.:** Syracuse Univ., 1959–63, BA (Grmn.); Syracuse Univ., 1963–77, MA PhD (Soc. Sci.); Amer. Univ., 1967, Archvst. Cert. **Orgs.:** Grntlgcl. Socty: Com. on Hist. and Arch. (Ch., 1979–80). SAA: Arch. of Sci. and Tech. Com. (1979–). Natl. Endow. for the Hum.: Div. Pub. Progs. (Review. Bd. 1979–). **Honors:** Intl. Resrch. and Exch. Bd., Resrch. grant, 1978. **Pubns.:** *Information Resources in Social Gerontology* (1979); Ed. Bd., *Jnl. of Exper. Aging Resrch.* (1975–); various papers. **Activities:** 1, 12; 15, 17, 39, 80, 95-Grntlgy. **Addr.:** All-University Gerontology Center, Syracuse University, Brockway Hall, Syracuse, NY 13210.

Bailey, George M. (F. 13, 1924, Millers, MD) Assoc. Dir. of Libs., The Claremont Colls., 1971–; Chief Libn., York Coll., CUNY, 1968–71; Exec. Secy., ACRL, ALA, 1963–68; Chief of Ref. and Spec. Srvs., Northwest. Univ., 1959–63; Head, Ref. Dept., Univ. of CA, Davis, 1958–59; Subj. Spec. in Soc. Sci. & Doc. Libn., 1955–58; Soc. Sci. Librarian, Univ. of Calif., Berkeley, 1954–55; Intern in Lib. Admin., 1953–54. **Educ.:** Franklin & Marshall Coll., 1942–46, BA (Hist.); Univ. of PA, 1946–47, MA (Hist.); Univ. of WI, 1952–53, MLS; Univ. of WI, 1948–49, 1951–52 (Hist.); Claremont Grad. Sch., 1976–78, Cert. Mgt. **Orgs.:** Beta Phi Mu (Pres., 1979–80). ALA: Cncl. (1975–79); ACRL, Chapts. Com. (1975–79); (Ch., 1978–79), *Coll. & Resrch. Libs.* Ed. Bd. (1974–80); Lib. Educ. Div.; RASD: Nom. Com. (1976–77). CA LA: CA Acad. and Resrch. Libns. (Ch., 1979). Many other ofcs. Zamarano Club. West. Assn. of Schs. & Colls.: Visit. team. **Activities:** 1; 17, 34, 39; 56 **Addr.:** 2129 Villa Maria Rd., Claremont, CA 91711.

Bailey, J. Russell (O. 19, 1905, Southampton, NY) Archit. Partner, 1946–; Sr. Partner, Bailey and Gardner, 1945–81. **Educ.:** Park Coll., BA; Univ. of MI, AB (Archit., Hist., Math.). **Orgs.:** ALA: Bldgs. Com. Orange Presby. Church: Elder. Amer. Inst. Archit.: VA Chap., VP, Treas.; N. VA Chap. **Honors:** Amer. Inst. of Archits., VA Chap., Nom. for Flwshp. **Pubns.:** "Listen Mr. Architect," *Lib. Jnl.* **Activities:** 1, 9; 19, 24; 95-Lib. Bldgs. Plg. **Addr.:** Bailey & Gardner Architects, P.O. Box 229, Orange, VA 22960.

Bailey, Martha J. (Jy. 24, 1929, Beech Grove, IN) Life Sci. Libn., Purdue Univ., 1979–, Phys. and Geo. Libn., 1976–79, Phys. Libn., 1970–76; Tech. Libn., Union Carbide Corp., 1957–70. **Educ.:** Butler Univ., 1951, AB (Eng.); Drexel Univ.,

PROFESSIONAL ACTIVITIES: Institutions: 1. Acad. lib.; 2. Arch.; 3. Assn.; 4. Fed./Gvt. lib.; 5. Inst. lib.; 6. Mfr./Suppl.; 7. Milit. lib.; 8. Musm.; 9. Pub. lib.; 10. Sch. lib.; 11. Sch. of lib. sci.; 12. Spec. lib.; 13. State lib.; 14. (other). **Functions/Activities:** 15. Acq./Col. dev.; 16. Adult srvs.; 17. Admin.; 18. Apprais.; 19. Archit./Bldgs.; 20. Cat./Class.; 21. Chld. srvs.; 22. Circ.; 23. Cons./Pres.; 24. Consult.; 25. Cont. ed.; 26. Educ. lib. sci.; 27. Ext. srvs.; 28. Fund/Grants; 29. Gvt. pubs.; 30. Indx./Abs.; 31. Instr. lib. use; 32. Media srvs.; 33. Micro.; 34. Netwks./Coop.; 35. Persnl.; 36. PR; 37. Publshg.; 38. Recs. mgt.; 39. Ref. srvs.; 40. Repro.; 41. Resrch.; 42. Review.; 43. Secur.; 44. Serials; 45. Spec. col.; 46. Tech. srvs.; 47. Trustees/Bds.; 48. YA srvs.; 49. (other).

Who's Who in Library and Information Services

1956, MS (LS). **Orgs.:** ALA: Resrch. Com. 1977–79). SLA: IN Chap., Treas. (1959–61), Rep. to LSCA Adv. Com. (1968–78). Metals–Mtrls. Div. (Treas. 1969–71). ASIS: IN Chap.: Ch. (1977–78). **Honors:** SLA, Resrch. Com. grant, 1975–76; Cncl. on Lib. Resrcs., Flwshp., 1975–76. **Pubns.:** *The Special Librarian as a Supervisor or Middle Manager* (1977); "Middle Managers who are Heads of Company Libraries/Information Services," *Spec. Libs.* (1979); "Some Effects of Faculty Status on Supervision in Academic Libraries," *Coll. and Resrch. Libs.* (1976); "Compensation Plans for Library Faculty Members," *New Horizons for Academic Libraries* (1979); "Supervision in Libraries," (ED 102 958) (1974). **Activities:** 1, 12; 17, 39; 58, 65, 82 **Addr.:** Purdue University, Life Science Library, West Lafayette, IN 47907.

Baillie, Jack (Mr. 3, 1938, Glenwood Springs, CO) Admin., Spec. Srvs., NE Dept. of Educ., 1974–. **Educ.:** Univ. of North. CO, 1958–60, BA (Sci.), 1960–63, MA (Sch. Admin.); AZ State Univ., 1964–65, MNS (Sci.); Univ. of NE, 1967–69, EdS (Sch. Admin.). **Honors:** Phi Delta Kappa. **Activities:** 14; 17; 50, 63 **Addr.:** Special Services, Nebraska Dept. of Education, P.O. Box 94987, Lincoln, NE 68509.

Baillie, Joan Louise (O. 16, 1923, Toronto, ON) Archvst., Recs. Mgr., Can. Opera Co., 1974–; Photo Archvst., OPERA Can, 1974–76; Archvst., 1969–74; Asst. Libn., Can. Bank of Cmrce., Lib. Arch., 1944–50. **Educ.:** Various courses. **Orgs.:** Assn. of Can. Archvsts. Toronto Area Archvsts. Grp. ON Hist. Socty. Can. Opera Women's Com.: Pubcty. Ch. (1964–65); Treas. (1966–70, 1972–73). Intl. Inst. of Metro. Toronto: Treas. (1973–74). **Pubns.:** "Table Talk of a History Addict: Lucia di Lammermoor," *Can. Opera Co. Souvenir Bk.* (1981–82); "The Fugitive Consul," *Can. Opera Co. Souvenir Prog.* (1976); "England, France & The Middle Ages," (1978); various lectures; "Simon Boccanegra: Oil on Troubled Waters," *Can. Opera Co. Souvenir Prog.* (1979); "Once Upon a Time in Toronto," *OVERTURES* (1979). **Activities:** 2, 12; 15, 39, 41; 51, 55 **Addr.:** Canadian Opera Company, 417 Queen's Quay West, Toronto, ON M5V 1A2 Canada.

Baillio, O. Dallas (F. 16, 1940, Shreveport, LA) Lib. Dir., Mobile Pub. Lib., 1977–; Lib. Dir., Withers Pub. Lib., 1972–77; Acct., Peat, Marwick Mitchell CPA's, 1962–63. **Educ.:** LA Tech. Univ., 1958–62, BS (Acct.); Univ. of South. CA, 1967–69, MAOM (Aerosp. Mgt.); LA State Univ., 1970–71, MS (LS). **Orgs.:** AL LA: VP, Pres.-Elect (1979–81); Lib. Srvs. and Construct. Act Adv. Com. SE LA. **Addr.:** Mobile Public Library, Mobile, AL 36602.

Baily, Diette Marie (My. 10, 1949, Mitchell, SD) Msc. Libn., Brooklyn Coll., CUNY, 1976–; Ref. Libn. II, Msc. Div., New York Pub. Lib., 1974–76; Asst. Msc. Libn., Mannes Coll. of Msc., 1972–74. **Educ.:** Univ. of MI, 1968–71, BM (Msc. Hist., Lit.), 1971–72, MALS; NY Univ., 1974–77, MA (Msclgy.). **Orgs.:** Msc. LA: NY Chap. (Ch., 1978–81; Secy.-Treas., 1977–79). Amer. Msclgy. Socty.: Amer. Msclgy. Socty.-Msc. LA Transls. Ctr. (Ch.). Intl. Assn. of Msc. Libs. LA of CUNY. **Pubns.:** *A Checklist of Music Bibliographies in Progress and Unpublished* (forthcoming); "A Report on the American Musicological Society/Music Library Association Committee on Unpublished Musicological Translations," *Msc. LA Notes* (S. 1978); Reviews. **Activities:** 1, 12; 15, 17, 22; 95-music; dance; performing arts. **Addr.:** Brooklyn College Music Library, 417 Gershwin Hall, Brooklyn, NY 11210.

Baily, Kay H. (Jl. 5, 1952, Roxboro, NC) Chief, Lib. Div., U.S. Gvt. Prtg. Ofc., 1981–, Chief, Recs. Branch, 1979–81; Ref. Libn., U.S. Gen. Acct. Ofc., 1977–79; Head Libn., Mid-Continent Pub. Lib., 1974–77. **Educ.:** Elon Coll., 1970–73, BA (Soc. Sci.); Univ. of MD, 1973–74, MLS (LS, Info. Srvs.). **Orgs.:** ALA: Fed. Docum. Task Frc., Reg. Depos. Libs. Com., Secy. SLA. **Honors** U.S. Gen. Acct. Ofc., Lib., Cert. of Apprec., 1978; U.S. Gen. Acct. Ofc., Energy and Minerals Div., Cert. of Apprec., 1979. **Pubns.:** *PRF Users' Manual* (1981); "Writing for Satisfaction and Recognition," *Gvt. Acct. Ofc. Review* (1979). **Activities:** 4; 17, 29, 30; 56, 57 **Addr.:** 12118 Harbor Dr., Woodbridge, VA 22192.

Bain, George W. (S. 14, 1942, Crozet, VA) Lcl. Recs. Spec., OH Hist. Socty., 1977–; Consult., WA Cnty. (OH) Pub. Lib., 1980; Asst. Prof., OH State Univ., Newark Branch Campus, 1975–76; Instr., Ctrl. MI Univ., 1971–72; Instr., Hamline Univ. **Educ.:** Benedictine Coll., 1961–64, BA (Hist.); Univ. of MN, 1964–66, MA (Hist.), 1966–75, PhD (Hist.); Kent State Univ., 1978–, (LS). **Orgs.:** SAA. Socty. of OH Archvsts. OH Assn. of Hist. Soctys. and Musms. Amer. Assn. for State and Lcl. Hist. Athens Cnty. Hist. Socty. OH Geneal. Socty. **Pubns.:** "Township Records: A Neglected Area of Public Records," *Echoes* (O. 1980). **Activities:** 2, 12; 17, 38, 45; 55, 69, 92 **Addr.:** Archives & Special Collections, Ohio University Library, Athens, OH 45701.

Bain, Janice W. (N. 1, 1941, Philippi, WV) Libn., Transp. Resrch. Bd., Natl. Resrch. Cncl., 1979–; Chief, Resrch & Info. Srvs., Natl. Transp. Policy Study Com., 1977–79; Libn., Manalytics, Inc., 1970–72, 74–76; Lib., Washington Cntr. for Metro. Std., 1967–70. **Educ.:** Davis & Elkins Coll., 1959–63, BA (Psych.); Univ. of MD, 1965–66, MLS. **Orgs.:** SLA: Rep. Bd. of Dirs., Documtn. Abs., Inc. (1980–); Chmn., Transp. Div. (1979–80); TRISNET Coord. Com., (1976–); Secy., Soc. Sci. Div., Wash., DC Chap. (1967–69). **Pubns.:** Comp., *The Intercity Bus Industry: A Bibliography* (1979); *Port Planning and Development: A Bibliography* 2nd ed. (1976); *Transportation of Fresh Fruits & Vegetables: A Bibliography;* "From a Safe Port", *Scitech News* (April 1978); Col. ed., "New Reference Works in Science and Technology", *Science and Technology Libraries.* **Activities:** 12; 17, 39; 64, 93, 94 **Addr.:** 5480 Wisconsin Ave., Apt. 905, Chevy Chase, MD 20015.

Baines, Grace Evelyn Ackerman (Jl. 2, 1936, Goshen, NY) Head, Cat. Dept., Buffalo and Erie Cnty. Pub. Lib., 1978–; Asst. Head, 1967–78; Catlgr., 1960–67. **Educ.:** Russell Sage Coll., 1954–58, BA (Eng.); Syracuse Univ., 1959–60, MS (LS). **Orgs.:** ALA. NY LA. Libns. Assn., Buffalo and Erie Cnty. Pub. Lib. **Activities:** 9; 20 **Addr.:** Catalog Department, Buffalo and Erie County Public Library, Lafayette Sq., Buffalo, NY 14203.

Baird, Donald Alexander (Ja. 29, 1926, Edmonton, AB, Can) Univ. Archvst., Simon Fraser Univ., 1978–, Univ. Libn., 1964–77; Asst. Libn., Univ. of AB, 1960–64, Cat. Dept. Head, 1957–60. **Educ.:** Univ. of BC, 1945–49, BA (Phil.); Columbia Univ., 1950–51, MS (LS); Pub. Arch. of Can., 1978, Cert. in Arch. **Orgs.:** ALA. Socty. of Archvsts. SAA: Task Frc. on Autom. Recs. and Techqs. (1978–). Can. Assn. of Univ. Tchrs. **Honors:** Can. Gvt., Can. Medal, 1967. **Pubns.:** Jt. auth, *The English Novel; A Checklist of 20C. Criticism* (1958). **Activities:** 1, 2; 17, 38, 41; 56, 66, 85 **Addr.:** Simon Fraser University Archives, Burnaby, BC V5A 1S6 Canada.

Baird, Lynn Norris (Ag. 17, 1950, Oakland, CA) Head, Serials Dept., Univ. of ID, 1978–, Asst. Soc. Sci. Libn., Cat. Libn., 1976–78, Cat. Libn., 1974–76. **Educ.:** Univ. of the Pac., Raymond Coll., 1968–72, BA (Liberal Arts); Univ. of OR, 1973–74, MLS; Univ. of ID, 1975–79, MPA (Pub. Admin.). **Orgs.:** ALA: JMRT, Afflts. Cncl. (1977–79). Pac. NW LA. ID LA: Treas. (1980–81). Sierra Clb. **Pubns.:** "Extending Curiosity: Children's Information Books," *ID Libn.* (O. 1974); "Communication Graphics in Library Orientation," *Cath. Lib. World* (D. 1975). **Activities:** 1; 17, 44; 92, 95-Admin. **Addr.:** P.O. Box 8787, Moscow, ID 83843.

Baird, Margaret Lucille (My. 5, 1930, Cox City, OK) Ch., Dept. of Spec. Progs., Sch. of Educ., East. NM Univ., 1980–; Asst. Prof., Educ./LS, East. NM Univ., 1976–; Asst. Prof. of Lib. Sci., Murray State Univ., 1973–74; Media Catlgr./Instr. of Media Tech., Southwest. Cmnty. Coll., 1971–73; Head Catlgr., Southwest. OK State Univ., 1969–71; Sch. Libn., Alex (OK) Pub. Sch., 1964–69. **Educ.:** OK Coll. for Women, 1948–52, BA (Bio. Sch.), 1952–53, BS (Elem. Educ.); Univ. of OK, 1966–68, MLS; IA State Univ., 1973–76, PhD (Educ.). **Orgs.:** ALA. NM LA: Lib. Dev. Com. (1976–). NM Media Assn.: Cont. Ed. Com. (1979–). Intl. Readg. Assn. NM Cncl. of Intl. Readg. Assn.: Treas. (1979–). NM Chld. Bk. Awd. Com. (Ch., 1978–79). Various other organizations. **Pubns.:** *Media Programs in Selected Public Elementary Schools in Oklahoma* (1976); "Media Programs and Teacher Education," *IA Media Message* (Spr. 1975); ERIC docum. (1978); Ed., *Teaching Learning Review* (1980–). **Activities:** 10; 25, 26, 49-Friends of the Library; 63 **Addr.:** 1720 South Avenue M, Portales, NM 88130.

Baker, Antonie L. (Mr. 16, 1944, Bryn Mawr, PA) Asst. Dir. of Lib., FL Intl. Univ., 1976–; Head, Coll. Lib., Univ. of Notre Dame, 1974; Admin. Libn., U.S. Army Lib., Munich, 1970–74; Admin. Libn., Allied Frcs. Ctrl. Europe, NATO/SHAPE, 1969–70. **Educ.:** Ohio Wesleyan Univ., 1966, BA (Hist.); Univ. of WI, 1968, MA (LS). **Orgs.:** Intl. Affairs: Soc. Sci. Sect. (Ch., 1979). Amer. Libns. in Europe: Pres. (1971–72). SLA: European Chap. (Pres., 1972–73). Conf. of Admin. Libns.: Ch. **Activities:** 1; 17 **Addr.:** Florida International University, Bay Vista Campus, North Miami, FL 33181.

Baker, Augusta (Ap. 1, 1911, Baltimore, MD) Storyteller-in-Residence, Coll. of Libnshp., Univ. of SC, 1980–; Coord., Chld. Srvs., NY Pub. Lib., 1961–74, Asst. Coord., Storytel. Spec., 1953–61, Chld. Libn., 1937–53; various positions as consult. **Educ.:** SUNY, Albany, 1929–33, AB (Educ.), 1933–34, BS (LS). **Orgs.:** ALA: Cnclr. (1965–72); Chld. Srvs. Div. (Pres., 1967–68), Bd. of Dirs. (1958–61, 1966–69); Exec. Bd. (1968–72); Newbery-Caldecott Com. (Ch., 1966); ALA/Chld. Bk. Cncl. Jt. Com.; PLA, various coms. NY LA: CYASS, Exec. Bd. (1960). SC LA. Assn. of Early Childhood Educ. Intl. Good Neighbor Civic Assn. Soc. Action Com. NY Pub. Lib. Frnds. of Chld. Srvs. Various other orgs. **Honors:** Cath. LA, Regina Medal, 1981; St. John's Univ., Jamaica, NY, Hon. Doct., 1978; Harold Jackson Meml. Awd., 1974; SUNY, Albany, Disting. Alum. Awd., 1974; other hons. **Pubns.:** Jt. auth., *Storytelling: Art and Technique* (1977); ed., *Once Upon a Time* (1964); *The Golden Lynx* (1960); ed.-in-chief, *Young Years* (1960); various bk. introductions. **Activities:** 9; 21, 25, 26 **Addr.:** 830 Armour St., Columbia, SC 29203.

Baker, Barry Boyd (S. 3, 1944, Louisville, KY) Asst. Dir. for Tech. Srvs., Univ. of GA, 1980–; Assoc. Univ. Libn., Tech. Srvs., Appalachian State Univ., 1978–80; Asst. Dir., Tech. Srvs., Univ. of SC, 1975–78; Head, Order Dept., 1972–75; Asst. Order Libn., 1970–72; Asst. Libn., Head Tech. Srvs., Instr. LS, Macon Jr. Coll., 1968–70; Sr. Libn., LA State Univ., 1967–68. **Educ.:** LA State Univ., 1962–66, BA (Hist.); 1966–67, MS (LS). **Orgs.:** ALA: RTSD/Tech. Srvs. Costs Com. (1979–); Ch. (1981–); RTSD/Cncl. of Reg. Grp. Ch. (1980–); ACRL/Univ. Lib. Sect., Strg. Com. (1980–). SELA/RTSD, Vice-Ch. 1978–80, Ch., 1980–82; Nom. Com. (1972–74). SC LA: JMRT: (Vice-Ch., 1970–72); Ch., 1972–74; Exec. Com., 1970–76); Exec. Bd. (1972–74); Nom. Com. (1972–74, 1977); other coms. NC LA: Constn. and Bylaws Com. (1980–). Other orgs. OCLC, Inc.: Adv. Com. on Acqs.: (1976–). AAUP. **Honors:** Beta Phi Mu. **Pubns.:** "Something in Our Midst," *SC Libn.* (Fall, 1971); various reviews. **Activities:** 1; 17, 46; 56, 66 **Addr.:** 325 Snapfinger Dr., Athens, GA 30605.

Baker, Bruce S. (Je. 22, 1939, Worcester, MA) Reg. Admin., West. Reg. Pub. Lib. Syst., 1972–; Dir., Leominster Pub. Lib., 1965–72; Asst. Dir., 1963–65. **Educ.:** Clark Univ., 1958–62, AB (Hist.); Simmons Coll., 1962–63, MSLS. **Orgs.:** MA. LA: Pres. (1979–81). New Eng. LA. ALA. State Adv. Cncl. on Libs. **Activities:** 9, 13; 17, 24, 34; 63 **Addr.:** Box 131, Sterling, MA 01564.

Baker, Carol J. (O. 10, 1925, Cincinnati, OH) Libn., St. Gertrude Sch., 1969–. **Educ.:** Univ. of Cincinnati, 1943–48, BBA (Acct.). **Orgs.:** Cath. LA. Grt. Cinncinati Unit Cath. LA: Elem. Sch. Sect. (Ch., 1977–79); VP, Prog. Ch., Pres.-Elect (1979–81) Pres. (1981–83). **Activities:** 10; 15, 21, 32 **Addr.:** 6534 Kenwood Rd., Cincinnati, OH 45243.

Baker, D. Philip (F. 2, 1937, Hornell, NY) Coord. of Lib. Media Progs., Stamford CT Pub. Schs., 1971–; Dir. of Libs., Darien CT Pub. Schs., 1967–71; Tchr., 1961–67; Resrch. Asst., Ofc. of U.S. Sen. Javits, 1960–61. **Educ.:** Alfred Univ., 1954–58, BA (Hist.); 1958–59, MSE (Educ.); Pratt Inst., 1967–70, MLS; Fairfield Univ., 1966–67 (Admin.). **Orgs.:** Beta Phi Mu. ALA: AASL (Pres., 1980–81). AECT. Various other orgs. and ofcs. Assoc. for Curric. Dev. and Supervision. **Honors** CT Educ. Media Assoc., Rheta Clark Awd., 1977. **Pubns.:** Jt. auth., *Library Media Programs and the Special Learner* (1981); *School and Public Library Media Programs for Children and Young Adults* (1977); "School and Public Library Programs and Information Dissemination," *Sch. Media Qtly* (Winter 1977); "A Library That's Long on Learning," *Early Years* (N. 1976); Various other articles and eds. **Activities:** 10; 17, 32; 63, 67, 93 **Addr.:** Stamford Public Schools, 195 Hillandale Ave., Stamford, CT 06902.

Baker, Dale B. (S. 19, 1920, Bucyrus, OH) Dir., Chief Operating Ofcr., Chem. Abs. Srv., 1980–, Actg. Mgr., Amer. Chem. Socty., Columbus OH Ofc., 1972; Dir., Chem. Abs. Srv., 1958–80, Assoc. Dir., 1958, Assoc. Ed., 1951–57, 1946–50; Chem.-Supvsr., E. I. du Pont de Nemours and Co., 1942–46. **Educ.:** OH State Univ., 1938–42, BChE (Chem.), 1946–48, MSc (Chem.); various crs. **Orgs.:** ASIS: Pres. (1975); Pres.-Elect (1974); Cnclr. (1970–76); Exec. Com. (1971–72, 1973–76); various other coms., ofcs. Natl. Fed. of Sci. Abs. and Index Srvs.: Past Pres. (1962–63); Treas. (1970–72); Bd. of Dirs. (1959–65, 1969–72); various coms., ofcs. Intl. Cncl. of Sci. Un. Abs. Bd.: Exec. Com. (1964–69, 1973–); Working Grp. on Copyrt. (1977–); various other coms., ofcs. Natl. Acad. of Sci./Natl. Acad. of Engin.: Com. on Intl. Sci. and Tech. Info. Prog. (1973–); various other coms. Various other orgs. Amer. Mgt. Assn. AAAS: Fellow (1955–). Amer. Inst. of Chem. Engin. Amer. Chem. Socty.: Div. Chem. Info. (1950–). Various other orgs. **Honors:** Amer. Chem. Socty., Patterson-Crane Awd., 1979; Natl. Fed. Abs. Indexing Srv., Miles G. Conrad Lectr., 1974; Sigma Xi; OH State Univ., Coll. of Engin., Disting. Alum. Awd., 1970; other hons. **Pubns.:** "History of Abstracting at Chemical Abstracts Service," *Jnl. Chem. Info. Comp. Sci.* (1980); "Recent Trends in Growth of Chemical Literature," *Chem. Engin. News* (1976); various presentations. **Activities:** 12; 60, 75, 91 **Addr.:** Chemical Abstracts Service, P. O. Box 3012, Columbus, OH 43210.

Baker, Douglas (Jl. 21, 1950, Highland, IL) Dir., NW WI Lib. Syst., 1978–; Dir., Ofc. of Interlib. Coop., State Lib. Comsn. of IA, 1975–78; Libn., Des Moines Pub. Lib., 1974–75. **Educ.:** Univ. of IA, 1968–72, BA (Eng., Anthro.), 1973, MA (LS); State of WI, 1978, Grade I Pub. Lib. Cert. **Orgs.:** WI LA. WI Cncl. on Lib. and Netwk. Dev. Syst. and Resrc. Lib. Admin. Assn. of WI. **Activities:** 9, 13; 17, 24, 35; 56 **Addr.:** Northwest Wisconsin Library System, P.O. Box 440, Ashland, WI 54806.

Baker, J. Wayne (Ag. 25, 1933, Hamilton, OH) Lib. Dir., OH North. Univ., 1967–; Assoc. Libn., Univ. of Evansville, 1965–67; Lib. Dir., Owensboro/Daviess Cnty. Pub. Lib., 1963–65. **Educ.:** Murray State Univ., 1953–57 (Soc. Std. Area); IN Univ., 1961–66, MA (LS); Lib. Admin. Mgt. Dev. Inst., 1969. **Orgs.:** OH LA: NW Reg. Mtg. (Ch., 1969–70); Coll. and Univ. RT, Vice-Ch. (1970–71), Ch. (1971–72); Hons. and Awds. Com. (Ch., 1977–78). Acad. LA of OH: OH Coll. Assn., VP (1971–72); Pres. (1972–73); Nom. Com. (Ch., 1975–76); OHIONET: Nom. Com. (1981). Boy Scouts of Amer.: Cubmstr. (1961–62); Advnc. Ch. (1969–70). Hon. Ord. of KY Colonels. **Pubns.:** "Heart of Academic Life," *OH North. Alum.* (My. 1973); *Abstracts of Popular Culture* (1976–77); reviews. **Activities:** 1, 9; 17, 22, 32; 63, 92 **Addr.:** Heterick Memorial Library, Ohio Northern University, Ada, OH 45810.

Special Subjects/Services: 50. Adult educ.; 51. Advert./Mktg.; 52. Aerosp.; 53. Agric.; 54. Area std.; 55. Arts/Hum.; 56. Autom.; 57. Bibl./Prtg.; 58. Bio. sci.; 59. Bus./Fin.; 60. Chem.; 61. Copyrt.; 62. Documtn.; 63. Educ.; 64. Engin.; 65. Env.; 66. Eth. grps.; 67. Film; 68. Food/Nutr.; 69. Geneal.; 70. Geo.; 71. Geol.; 72. Handcpd.; 73. Hist.; 74. Int. frdm.; 75. Info. sci.; 76. Insr.; 77. Law; 78. Legis.; 79. Math./Comp. sci.; 80. Med.; 81. Metals; 82. Nat. resrcs.; 83. Newsp.; 84. Nuc. sci.; 85. Oral hist.; 86. Petr./Energy; 87. Pharm.; 88. Phys./Astr./Math.; 89. Readg.; 90. Relig.; 91. Sci./Tech.; 92. Soc. sci.; 93. Telecom.; 94. Transp.; 95. (other).

Baker, John Philip (Ja. 23, 1933, Belmont, MA) Chief, Cons. Div., N.Y. Pub. Lib., 1972–; Exec. Ofcr., 1969–72; Ref. Libn., 1965–69. **Educ.:** Boston Univ., 1950–55, BA (Eng.); Columbia Univ., 1963–65, MLS. **Orgs.:** ALA: Lib. Binders Rel. Com., CH. (1980–82). Amer. Inst. for Cons. of Hist. and Artistic Works; Bibl. Socty. of Amer. New York Lib. Club: Pres. (1978–79). Various other orgs. Archons of Colophon. **Honors:** Beta Phi Mu. **Pubns.:** Jt. ed. *Library Conservation; Preservation in Perspective* (1978); "Conservation and Preservation of Library Materials," *ALA World Encyc. of Lib. and Info. Srvs.* (1980); "Restoration of Library Materials: Some Administrative Considerations", *Lib. Scene* (1974). **Activities:** 1, 9; 17, 23, 33 **Addr.:** 160 West 73rd Street, Apt. 13-F, New York, NY 10023.

Baker, Judith Marion (Mr 29, 1931, Philadelphia, PA) Assoc. Dir., Readers. Srvs., Sr. Srch. Anal., Hahnemann Med. Coll. Lib., 1979–; Head, Ref. Circ., 1977–79; Head, Ref., 1975–77; Med. Lit. Sci., Coll. of Physicians of Phila., 1974–75. **Educ.:** Univ. of PA, 1949–52, AB (Microbio.); Drexel Univ., 1969–71, MSLS; Med LA, 1971–, Med. Lib. Cert. **Orgs.:** Med. LA: Mideast. Reg. online Coord. Com. (1977–). SLA. ASIS. Tri-State Col. Lib. Coop.: Com. on Readrs. Srvcs. (1978); Consultant on ONLINE Services (1978). Univ. of PA Alum.; Drexel Univ. Alum. **Honors:** Beta Phi Mu, 1971. **Activities:** 1, 12; 31, 39, 46; 56, 80, 87 **Addr.:** Hahnemann Medical College Library, 245 N. 15th St., Philadelphia, PA 19102.

Baker, Phyllis E. (S. 19, 1947, OH) Consult., Cont. Ed., CO State Lib., 1978–; Asst. Libn., Contl. Oil Co., 1977–78; Resrch. Assoc., Denver Resrch. Inst., 1976–77; Consult., WY State Lib., 1974–76; Libn., Columbus Pub. Lib., 1970–73. **Educ.:** OH State Univ., 1969, BFA; Univ. of MI, 1970, AMLS; Univ. of CO, 1980 (Bus.). **Orgs.:** Mt. Plains LA: Cont. Ed. Com. (1976); Prof. Dev. Grants Com. (1981); State Lib. Sect. (Ch., 1980–82). ALA: SRRT, Task Frc. on Jobs and Place., Org. (1972); Coord. (1972–73, 1975); ASCLA, San Francisco Conf. Prog. Com. CO LA: Educ. Com. (1978–). Zonta Intl. **Pubns.:** Ed., *CO State Lib. Nsltr.*; ed., *Directory of Colorado Libraries and Library Statistics* (1980). **Activities:** 9, 13; 25, 35, 36; 55, 59 **Addr.:** 4698 E. Montana Pl., Denver, CO 80222.

Baker, Robert K. (N. 24, 1948, Glendale, CA) Tchnl. Srvs. Libn., Spokane Cmnty. Coll., 1981–. Pub. Srvs. Libn., Spokane Cmnty. Coll., 1977–1981; Asst. Cat. Libn., Gonzaga Univ., 1976–77. **Educ.:** CA St. Univ., Northridge, 1966–71, BA (Fr.); Univ. of CA, Los Angeles, 1974–76, MLS; 1971–74, MA (Fr.). **Orgs.:** WA LA: Exhibits (Ch. 1980, VP Ch. 1979 Cont.); Mem. Com. (1977–79). Spokane and Inland Empire Libs.: (SPIEL) Pres. (1977–78). St. Bd. for Cmnty. Coll. Educ. Cmnty. Coll. Libns. and Media Spec.: Copyrt. Rev. Act Comm. (1978). **Pubns.:** *Doing Library Research: An Introduction For Community College Students* (Westview Press) (1981); *Introduction to Library Research in French Literature.* (1978); Series ed., "Westview Guides to Library Research." (1979–); Ed. *SPIEL Resource Directory* and *Who's Who in SPIEL* (1977). **Activities:** 1; 22, 31, 39; 55 **Addr.:** Spokane Community College Library, North 1810 Greene St., Spokane, WA 99207.

Baker, Ronald (Ag. 8, 1932, Merton, Surrey, Untd. Kingdom) Cnty. Libn., Lambton Cnty. Lib., 1967–; Deputy, Middlesex Cnty. Lib., 1964–67; Branch Libn., Exmouth, Devon Cnty. Lib., 1962–67; Asst. Libn., Battersea Pub. Lib. **Educ.:** UK LA, 1963, Fellow. **Orgs.:** ON LA. ON Pub. Libns. Adv. Com. Cnty. and Reg. Municipality Libns. **Pubns.:** *Ontario Public Librarians Advisory Committee Long Range Planning Task Force* (1979–80). **Activities:** 9; 17 **Addr.:** Lambton County Library, Box 100, Wyoming, ON N0N 1T0 Canada.

Baker, Russell Pierce (S. 16, 1943, Little Rock, AR) Archvst., AR Hist. Comsn., 1970–. **Educ.:** Univ. of AR, 1964–67, BA (Hist.); 1967–69. **Orgs.:** SAA: Relig. Arch. (1973–78). AR Archvsts. and Rec. Mgrs.: VP (1979–80); Pres. (1980–81). Amer. Bapt. Assn.: Hist. and Arch. Com. (Ch., 1973–81). **Honors:** Phi Beta Kappa. **Pubns.:** Ed., *The American Baptist Association: 1924 to 1974* (1979); *Obituaries and Marriage Notices From the Tennessee Baptist: 1844–1863* (1979); "James H. Howard," *AR Hist. Qtly.* (Win. 1976); "Jacob Wolf," *AR Hist. Qtly.* (Sum. 1978). **Activities:** 2, 13; 17, 41, 45; 69, 90, 92 **Addr.:** Arkansas History Commission, One Capitol Mall, Little Rock, AR 72201.

Baker, Samuel M., Jr. (D. 28, 1929, Knoxville, TN) Univ. Libn., Univ. of New Haven, 1966–; Per. Libn., Miami-Dade Jr. Coll., 1965–66; Cat. Libn., Wake Forest Univ., 1964–65; Acq. Libn., Univ. of New Orleans, 1963–64. **Educ.:** Randolph-Macon Coll., 1948–49; Guilford Coll., 1949–52, BA (Eng., Hist.); Univ. of NC, 1952–53, BS (LS), 1955–56, 1957–60, MA. **Orgs.:** ALA. NY LA. New Eng. LA. CT LA. AAUP. Musm. of Mod. Art. SC Hist. Socty. Metro. Musm. of Art. Various other orgs. **Activities:** 1; 17, 19, 45; 55, 57, 74 **Addr.:** University of New Haven Library, P.O. Box 1306, New Haven, CT 06505.

Baker, Shirley Kistler (Mr. 16, 1943, Lehighton, PA) Access Libn., The Johns Hopkins Univ., 1978–; Undergrad. Libn., The Johns Hopkins Univ., 1976–78; Asst., Undergrad. Srvs. Libn., Northwest. Univ. Lib., 1974–76. **Educ.:** Muhlenberg Coll., 1961–65, BA (Econ.); Univ. of Chicago, 1971–74, MA (LS), U MA, (South Asian std.). **Orgs.:** ALA. MD LA: Acad. and Res. Lib. Prog. Com., (1980–81), VP.-Pres. Elect, (1981–82). Assn. for Asian Stud. **Activities:** 1; 17, 22; 54, 56 **Addr.:** The Milton S. Eisenhower Library, The Johns Hopkins University, 34th & Charles Sts., Baltimore, MD 21218.

Baker, Zachary Moshe (Je. 8, 1950, Minneapolis, MN) Asst. Libn., Yivo Inst. for Jewish Resrch., 1976–. **Educ.:** Univ. Chicago, 1968–72, AB (U.S. Hist.); Brandeis Univ., 1973–74, MA (Hist. Amer. Cvlztn.); Univ. MN, 1974–75, MA (LS). **Orgs.:** ALA. AJL. Assocs. of James Ford Bell Lib. **Honors:** Phi Beta Kappa, 1972; Beta Phi Mu, 1975. **Pubns.:** "Yiddish Books," *Jewish Bk. Anl.* (1976–81); "Landsmanshaftn and the Jewish Genealogist," *Toledot* (Sum. 1978); "Local history and the Jewish Genealogist," *Toledot* (Fall 1978); "Eastern European Jewish Geography: Some Problems and Suggestions," *Toledot* (Win. 1978–79); "More Eastern European Jewish Geography," *Toledot* (Spr. 1979). **Activities:** 12; 20, 39; 66, 69, 70 **Addr.:** c/o Yivo Institute for Jewish Research, 1048 5th Ave., New York, NY 10028.

Baker-Batsel, John David (N. 29, 1933, Greenville, KY) Lib. Dir., Graduate Theo. Union, 1977–; Lib. Dir., Garrett-Evang. Theo. Semy., 1964–77; Lib. Dir., Lambuth Col., 1963–64. **Educ.:** Lambuth Coll., 1951–55, BA (Msc.); Vanderbilt Univ., 1956–59, BD (Relig.); Peabody Coll., 1959–62, MA (Relig.); 1962–63, MALS; Cambridge Univ., Sr. Visit. Schol., 1970–71. **Orgs.:** Amer. Theo. LA: Pres. (1973–74); Bd. of Dir. (1972–75, 1977–); Bd. of Microtext (1964–70). ALA. **Honors:** Beta Phi Mu, 1963. **Pubns.:** Co-Auth., *Union List of United Methodist Serials, 1773–1973* (1974). **Activities:** 1; 17, 24, 28 **Addr.:** Graduate Theological Union Library, 2400 Ridge Rd., Berkeley, CA 94709.

Bakken, Douglas A. (Mr. 12, 1939, Breckenridge, MN) Dir., Arch., Resrch. Lib., Greenfield Vlg., Henry Ford Musm., 1977–; Admin., Arch., Lib., Recs., Anheuser-Busch, Inc., 1971–77; Assoc. Archvst., Cornell Univ., 1967–71; Archvst., NE State Hist. Socty., 1966–67. **Educ.:** ND State Univ., 1957–61, BS (Hist.); Amer. Univ., 1966 (Arch. Admin.); Univ. of NE, 1964–67, MA (Hist.). **Orgs.:** SAA: Bus. Prog. Com. (Co-Ch., 1979); Arch. Com. (Ch., 1979–80); Inst. Eval. Task Frc. (1980–81). Hist. Socty. of MI: Bd. of Trustees (1979–); Exec. Com. (1980–); Long-Range Plng. (Ch., 1979–81). Socty. of Automotive Histns.: Prof. Stans. Amer. Assn. for State and Lcl. Hist. **Honors:** SAA, Fellow, 1981. **Pubns.:** "Adjusting To Urbanity (The Roaring Twenties)," *The Herald* (Win. 1979); "Archives and American Business," *Brewers Digest* (My. 1973); "NPL in Nebraska 1917–1920," *ND Hist.* (Spr. 1972); ed.-in-chief, *The Herald* (1977–81). **Activities:** 2, 8; 17, 24, 45; 55, 59 **Addr.:** Archives & Research Library, Greenfield Village & Henry Ford Museum, Dearborn, MI 48121.

Balázs, Andrew Joseph (My. 15, 1944, Kaposvár, Hungary) Dept. Libn., AB Attorney Gen. Law Lib., 1977–; Ref. and Hist. Libn., Univ. of AB, 1974–76. **Educ.:** Univ. of Windsor, 1965–69, BA (Hist.); Wayne State Univ., 1970–71, MSLS; Univ. of Windsor, 1971–73, MA (Hist.). **Orgs.:** Edmonton Law Libns. Assn.: Exec. Com. (1978–79). Can. ALL; AALL. AB Gvt. Libs. Cncl. (1977–). Royal Astronomical Socty. of Can. **Pubns.:** "Canadian Immigration Law; A Selective Bibliography" (1979). **Activities:** 4, 12; 15, 17, 20; 57, 77, 78 **Addr.:** Alberta Attorney General Law Library, 4th Floor, North wing, 9983-109 St., Edmonton, AB T5K 2E8 Canada.

Balbach, Edith D. (Ap. 20, 1953, Urbana, IL) Exec. Asst., Univ. of IL at Chicago Circle, 1978; Resrch. Assoc., Univ. of IL at Urbana-Champaign, 1975–77. **Educ.:** Univ. of IL at Urbana-Champaign, 1970–74, BS (Jnlsm.), 1974–75, MS (LS). **Orgs.:** ALA: ACRL. **Honors:** Beta Phi Mu, 1976. **Activities:** 1; 17, 35, 36 **Addr.:** University of Illinois at Chicago Circle, P.O. Box 8198, Chicago, IL 60680.

Balcom, Karen Suzanne (F. 15, 1949, San Antonio, TX) Systems Libn., Asst. Prof., San Antonio Coll., 1975–, Catlgr., Inst., 1973–75. **Educ.:** San Antonio Coll., 1967–69, AA (Hum.); Univ. of TX at Austin, 1969–71, BA (Hist.), 1971–72, MLS. **Orgs.:** SLA. ASIS. TX LA: Registration Com. (1979). MARCIVE Users' Grp.: Pres. (1978–79). AAUP. TX Jr. Coll. Tchrs. Assn. **Activities:** 1, 12; 34, 38, 39 **Addr.:** San Antonio College Library, 1001 Howard St., San Antonio, TX 78284.

Balderas, Lynn Rose Pete Dir., Lrng. Resrc. Ctr., TX Southmost Coll. Lib., 1974–; Libn., Cameron Cnty., TX, 1976–; Asst. Libn., Lrng. Resrc. Ctr., TX Southmost Coll. Lib., 1972–74; Adult Libn., San Antonio Pub. Lib., 1971–72; Tchr., Brownsville (TX) pub. sch., 1969–70. **Educ.:** TX Women's Univ., 1969, BA (LS), 1979, MLS. **Orgs.:** ALA. TX LA: Admin. RT (Secy. 1976–77); Awds. Com. (1976–77); Dist. IV (Secy.-Treas. 1975–76). SWLA. Valley LA: Treas. (1978–80); Nom. Com. (1976–77). Bus. and Prof. Women. **Activities:** 1, 9; 17 **Addr.:** 264 Park West Dr., Brownsville, TX 78520.

Baldino, Donald James (Mr. 13, 1953, Philadelphia, PA) Info. Systs. Anal., Keystone Auto. Club, Amer. Auto. Assn., 1979–; Dir., Mktg., Ofc. of Cont. Prof. Educ., Drexel Univ., 1977–79; Data Ed., Inst. for Sci. Info., 1976–77. **Educ.:** St. Joseph's Univ., 1971–75, BA (Eng.); Drexel Univ., 1976–79, MS (Info. Sci.). **Orgs.:** ASIS: DE Valley Chap., Nsltr. Co-ed. (1978–80); Pubcty. Dir. (1978–80). **Addr.:** Keystone Automobile Club, American Automobile Assocation, 2040 Market St., Philadelphia, PA 19131.

Baldwin, Carol Ann (Mr. 25, 1949, St. Paul, MN) Libn., Engin. Lib., Univ. of MN, 1979–; Libn., Bio-Med. Lib., Univ. of MN, 1972–79. **Educ.:** Univ. of MN, 1967–71, BA (Anthro.), 1971–73, MA (LS); Med. LA Cert. **Orgs.:** MLA. ALA. ASIS. Socty. Amer. Archlg. **Honors:** Phi Beta Kappa. **Pubns.:** "Evaluation of Library Service to Rural Physician Associate Students," *Bltn. Med. LA* (O. 1976); "Use of Multiple Data Bases in Bibliographic Services," *Bltn. Med. LA* (Ja. 1976). **Activities:** 1; 39, 49-Online searching; 64, 80 **Addr.:** Engineering Library, Lind Hall 128, University of Minnesota, Minneapolis, MN 55455.

Baldwin, Charlene Marie (Ja. 12, 1946, San Francisco, CA) Chief Ref. Libn., Lockheed-CA Co., 1981–; Libn., Tetra Tech. Inc., 1976–81; Libn., Munger Africana Lib., 1974–75; CA Inst. of Tech.; Peace Corps Volun., U.S. Dept. of State, West. State, Nigeria, 1966–68. **Educ.:** CA State Univ., 1969–70, BA (Eng.); Univ. of Chicago, 1971–73, MA (LS); CA Cmnty. Coll., 1975, Lifetime Cert. (Libn. Cred.). **Orgs.:** SLA. ALA. Frnds. of the CA Tech. Libs.: Bd. of Dirs. (1979–). Grad. Lib. Sch. Alum. Assn. **Honors:** Phi Kappa Phi, 1970; Sacramento Bk. Collector's Club, Prizewinner, Anl. Contest, 1970; Cncl. of Chiefs, Lalupon Town, Nigeria, Iyalaje, 1976. **Pubns.:** Jt. auth., *The Yoruba of Southwestern Nigeria* (1976); *South African Political Ephemera* (1975). **Activities:** 12; 17, 36, 39; 64, 65, 86 **Addr.:** Lockheed-California Co., Central Library, P.O. Box 551, Burbank, CA 91520.

Baldwin, Paul E. (Ja. 7, 1938, Lincoln, NB) Dir., BC Union Cat., 1977–; Head, Cat., Simon Fraser Univ. Lib., 1971–77; Head, Cat., Univ. of CA, Santa Cruz, 1966–71; Asst. Dir., Tech. Srvs., Bibl. Ctr., Grad. Theo. Union, 1963–66. **Educ.:** Univ. of NB, 1956–60, BA (Hist.); Univ. of CA, Berkeley, 1961–62, MLS; Simon Fraser Univ., 1973–76, MBA. **Orgs.:** ALA. Can. LA. BC LA. **Honors:** Phi Beta Kappa. **Pubns.:** "The BC Union Catalogue Project and the Replication of the WLN System," *BCLA Reporter* (Ap.–My. 1979). **Pubns.:** "The BC Union Catalogue Project: Background and Progress Report", *BCLA Reporter* (Mr.–Ap. 1978); "The BC Union Catalogue Project (or Network?)", *BCLA Reporter* (O.–N. 1978); "BCUC Launched into a Replication Study," *C Lib. Jnl.* (D. 1980). **Activities:** 1, 14-Netwk.; 17, 34, 46; 56, 75, 93 **Addr.:** 2249 West 51st Ave., Vancouver, BC V6P 1E7 Canada.

Baldwin, Ruth M. (S. 29, 1918, Due West, SC) Libn., Baldwin Lib., Prof. of Eng., Univ. of FL, 1977–; Prof. of LS, LA St. Univ., 1967–77; Assoc. Prof., 1959–67; Asst. Prof., 1956–59; Asst. Prof., Sch. of LS, Univ. of South. CA, 1950–53; Resrch. Asst., Sch. of LS, Univ. of IL, 1949–50; Ref. Libn., Instr., San Jose St. Coll., 1946–49; Libn., Cambridge (Guernsey Cnty.) Pub. Lib., 1946; Various other Pub. lib. positions. **Educ.:** Muskingum Coll., 1939, BA (Sp., Eng.); Univ. of IL, 1939–40, BS (LS), 1944–45, MS 1953–55, PhD. **Orgs.:** ALA. AALS. LA LA. SLA: LA Chap., Pres. (1966). AAUP: LA St. Univ. Chap., Pres. (1968–69). **Honors:** Beta Phi Mu, 1953; LA St. Univ., Prof. Emeritus, 1977. **Pubns.:** *100 Nineteenth-Century Rhyming Alphabets in English From the Library of Ruth M. Baldwin* (1972); "The Whole Book, Please," *Wilson Lib. Bltn.* "An Index to Children's Book in English Before 1900 Catalog of the Baldwin Library of the University of Florida", 1981. **Activities:** 1, 12; 15, 41, 45 **Addr.:** Baldwin Library, University of Florida Libraries, Gainesville, FL 32611.

Balester, Vivian S. (D. 10, 1931, Pine Bluff, AR) Law Libn., Squire, Sanders and Dempsey, 1975–. **Educ.:** Vanderbilt Univ., 1955, BA (Psy.); Case West. Rsv. Univ., 1972, MSLS, 1975, JD (Law). **Orgs.:** AALL: Liaison to Amer. Bar Assn. (1977). ASIS: Law Sect. (Ch., 1978). OH Reg. Assn. of Law Libs.: Legis. Com. (Ch., 1977–78). WHCOLIS: Del. (1979). Various other orgs. Amer. Bar Assn.: Lib. Com. (1976–77). Cleveland Bar Assn. Greater Cleveland Interchurch Cncl.: Exec. Com. (1979–). Greater Cleveland Martin Luther King Celebration: Co-Ch. (1980, 81, 82). Vanderbilt Univ. Alum. Educ. Cabinet (1981–). Various other orgs. **Honors:** Federation for Cmnty. Plng., Outstanding Cmnty. Srv. Awd., 1981; NEH Fellow, Univ. of KS, 1980; Cleveland Bar Assn., Merit Srv., 1979; Beta Phi Mu, 1973. **Activities:** 14-Law Firm; 17, 24, 41; 75, 77, 78 **Addr.:** Squire, Sanders & Dempsey, 1800 Union Commerce Bldg., Cleveland, OH 44115.

Balke, Mary Noel (D. 25, 1918, Londonderry, North. Ireland) Retired, 1980–; Chief Libn., Natl. Gallery of Can., 1964–79; Asst. Head, Bus. and Tech. Dept., Ottawa Pub. Lib., 1960–64, Librn., Ref. Dept., 1958–60. **Educ.:** Sheffield Univ., 1935–39, BA (Math. and Langs.); Assoc., LA (London), 1942–. **Orgs.:** Can. LA: Art Libs. Com. (Ch., 1967–69). SLA: Musms., Arts, Hum. Div. (Ch., 1974–75). LA (London). IFLA: Art Libns. RT (Secy., 1978–79). **Honors:** Can. Women's Press Club, Meml. Awd., 1956. **Pubns.:** "Art Libraries in Canada," *ARLIS/NA Nsltr.* (F. 1979); "Acquisition of Exhibition Catalogues," *Spec. Libs.* (D. 1975); Radio Scripts for Can. Broadcasting Corp. Broadcast Talks (1950–57); Reviews broadcast. **Activities:** 4, 9; 17, 23; 55 **Addr.:** 2694 Dupont St., Ottawa, ON K1V 8N3 Canada.

PROFESSIONAL ACTIVITIES: Institutions: 1. Acad. lib.; 2. Arch.; 3. Assn.; 4. Fed./Gvt. lib.; 5. Inst. lib.; 6. Mfr./Suppl.; 7. Milit. lib.; 8. Musm.; 9. Pub. lib.; 10. Sch. lib.; 11. Sch. of lib. sci.; 12. Spec. lib.; 13. State lib.; 14. (other). **Functions/Activities:** 15. Acq./Col. dev.; 16. Adult srvs.; 17. Admin.; 18. Apprais.; 19. Archit./Bldgs.; 20. Cat./Class.; 21. Chld. srvs.; 22. Circ.; 23. Cons./Pres.; 24. Consult.; 25. Cont. ed.; 26. Educ. lib. sci.; 27. Ext. srvs.; 28. Fund/Grants; 29. Gvt. pubs.; 30. Indx./Abs.; 31. Instr. lib. use; 32. Media srvs.; 33. Micro.; 34. Netwks./Coop.; 35. Persnl.; 36. PR; 37. Publshg.; 38. Recs. mgt.; 39. Ref. srvs.; 40. Repro.; 41. Resrch.; 42. Review.; 43. Secur.; 44. Serials; 45. Spec. col.; 46. Tech. srvs.; 47. Trustees/Bds.; 48. YA srvs.; 49. (other).

Balkema, John B. (Ag. 10, 1927, Orange City, IA) Libn., Natl. Cncl. on the Aging, 1971–; Head, Pub. Srvs., Welch Med. Lib., Johns Hopkins Univ., 1964–71; Ref. Libn., Downstate Med. Ctr., 1962–64; Libn., NY State Psyt. Inst., 1959–62. **Educ.:** Morningside Coll., 1944–48, BA (Eng.); Drexel Univ., 1954–58, MS (LS). **Orgs.:** ALA: LSIES (Ch., 1978–79); Lib. Srvs. Aging Popltn. Com. (Ch., 1976–77). **Pubns.:** "The Library & Coordinated Service Delivery for Elders," *Cath. Lib. World* (F. 1980); "Interagency Cooperation for Service to Older Adults," *Drexel Lib. Qtly.* (F. 1980). **Activities:** 12; 17, 30, 37; 50, 95-Grntlgy. **Addr.:** 3325 N. 23rd Rd., Arlington, VA 22201.

Ball, Alan J. S. (My. 11, 1943, Ross-on-Wye, UK) Pres., BCD Lib. and Info. Consult., 1978–; Sci. Ref. Libn., Univ. Regina, 1977–78; Assoc. Prof., Bio. Sci., Brock Univ., 1974–77, Asst. Prof., 1971–74. **Educ.:** Univ. London, 1962–65, BSc (Microbio.); McMaster, 1965–69, PhD (Molec. Bio.); Univ. West. ON, 1976–77, MLS. **Orgs.:** SK LA: Task Frc. on Pub. Lib. Stand. (1977–78); Cncl. (1977–79). Can. LA. ASIS. Amer. Mgt. Assn. **Pubns.:** *The Automation of Saskatchewan's Public Library Systems:* (1979); *S.L.I.S. Orbit Simulator: User Manual* (1978); Co–Auth., "Computerisation of Saskatchewans Libraries," *SK Lib.* (31/4 1978); numerous (31/4 1978); numerous papers. **Activities:** 9; 24, 25, 34, 46; 56, 75, 93 **Addr.:** BCD Library and Information Consultants, 2268 Osler St., Regina, SK S4P 1W8 Canada.

Ball, Alice Dulany (Jl. 3, 1913, Washington, DC) Exec. Dir., Unvsl. Serials and Bk. Exch., Inc., 1948–; Actg. Exec. Dir., Amer. Bk. Ctr. for War Devastated Libs., 1946–48; Expediter, Hughes Aircraft Corp., 1945; Grp. Head, Lockheed Aircraft Corp., 1941–44; Accessioner, Clark Lib., Univ. of CA, Los Angeles, 1941, Secy., Eng. Dept., 1936–41, Tchg. Asst., 1934, 1936, 1939. **Educ.:** Univ. of CA, Los Angeles, 1930–34, AB (Eng.), 1934–41, MA (Eng.). **Orgs.:** ALA: Cncl. (1956–60); Acq. Sect. (Ch., 1964–65). SALAM: Bd. (1968–70); Acq. Sect. (Ch., 1964–65). SLA: DC Chap. (Pres., 1960–61). DC LA: Pres. (1968–69). Various other orgs. Mod. Lang. Assn. **Honors:** Chungang Univ., Seoul, Korea, Hon. Doctor of Humane Letters, 1971; Phi Beta Kappa; Chi Delta Phi. **Pubns.:** Various articles. **Activities:** 12; 17, 34, 44 **Addr.:** 2931 Kanawha St. N.W., Washington, DC 20015.

Ball, Darlene L. (S. 26, 1940, Washington, DC) Mgr., Lib. Info. Srvs., Burlington Indus., Inc., 1967–, Asst. Mgr., Lib. Info. Srvs., 1964–67; Libn., Dan River Mills, 1962–64. **Educ.:** Catawba Coll., 1958–62, BA (Biol.). **Orgs.:** SLA: NC Chap. (Pres., 1968–69). Textile Info. Users Cncl.: Strg. Com. (1969–). **Pubns.:** "The Textile Information Users Council," *Spec. Libs.;* "The Textile Information Users Council," *Textile Inst. and Indus.* **Activities:** 12; 17, 41, 46; 59, 64, 95-Textiles. **Addr.:** Manager, Library Information Services, Burlington Industries, PO Box 20288, Greensboro, NC 27420.

Ball, John Leslie (S. 16, 1933, Mitcham, Surrey, Eng) Coll. Libn., Scarborough Coll., Univ. of Toronto, 1964–; Ref. Libn., 1959–64. **Educ.:** Cambridge Univ., 1954–57, MA (Mod. Langs.); Univ. of Toronto, 1963–70, MLS; Univ. of London, 1958–59, Dip., Libnshp. **Orgs.:** Can. LA. ALA. LA (London). Bibl. Socty. of Can. Assn. for Can. Thea. Hist. **Pubns.:** *Bibliography of Canadian Theatre History 1583–1975* (1976); 1975–76 Supplement, (1979); Scarborough College: An Outline History, 1962–1972 (1973). **Activities:** 1; 17; 95-Theatre. **Addr.:** Chilterns R.R. 1, King City, ON L0G 1K0 Canada.

Ball, Joyce (O. 31, 1932, Paterson, NJ) Univ. Libn., CA State Univ., Sacramento, 1980–; Pub. Srvs. Libn., Univ. of NV (Reno), (1975–80); Ref. Libn., 1969–74; Gvt. Pubs. Libn., 1966–69; Foreign Docums. Libn., Stanford Univ., 1959–66. **Educ.:** Douglass Coll., Rutgers Univ., 1950–54, AB (Econ.); Indiana Univ., 1955–59, MA (Lib. Sci.); Golden Gate Univ., 1978–79, MBA. **Orgs.:** ALA: Public Docums. Comm. (1967–73). RASD Standards Comm (1974–76). ACRL *College and Research Libraries* Editorial Board, (1975–); Council, (1972–74). NV LA: Treas. (1974–75); VP (1976); President, (1977); Finance Committee, (1979–80); NV Gvr's Adv. Cncl. on Libs. (1974–78). AAUP. Natl. Soc. of Profs. UNR Executive Bd. **Pubns.:** *Foreign Statistical Documents* (1967); Ed. Adv. Bd., Congrsnl. Info. Srv.; Ed. Adv. Bd. *Gvt. Pubs. Review;* various articles and bk. reviews. **Activities:** 1; 17, 29, 39; 95-Management. **Addr.:** 8181 Folsom Blvd., #180, Sacramento, CA 95826.

Ballard, Robert Melvyn (F. 21, 1937, Atlanta, GA) Assoc. Prof., NC Ctrl. Univ., Sch. of LS, 1976–; Asst. Prof., West. MI Univ., 1972–76; Reg. Libn., U.S. Bur. of Commercial Fisheries, 1966–70. **Educ.:** Morehouse Coll., 1954–58, AB (Hist.); Atlanta Univ., 1959–61, MSLS; Atlanta Univ., 1963–64 (Hist.); East. MI Univ., 1967–69, MA (Educ.); Univ. MI, 1969–72, PhD (LS). **Orgs.:** SLA: H.H. Wilson Awds. Com. (1979–81). AALS: Resrch. Interest Grp. (Co-Conv., 1976). NC OLUG. **Honors:** Fulbright-Hays Assoc. Prof., Univ. of Zambia, 1977. **Pubns.:** Jt. auth., *Achieving Equal Pay for Equal Work: Women in Special Libraries* (1976); *The Relevance of the Core Curriculum in Preparation of Library School Students for Professional Library Duties* (1977); "Government Publications–A Course Outline," *Gvt. Pubns. Review* (1975); "Pollution in Lake Erie, 1872–1965," *Spec. Libs.* (1975); "Special Libraries and Information Centers in South Eastern Africa," *Spec. Libs.* (1979); other articles. **Activities:** 11; 29, 30; 91 **Addr.:** School of Library Science, North Carolina Central University, Durham, NC 27707.

Ballentine, Rebecca S. (Mr. 8, 1927, Raleigh, NC) Libn., Inst. of Gvt., Univ. of NC, 1965–; Dir., Pettigrew Reg. Lib., 1963–65. **Educ.:** Meredith Coll., 1944–48, AB (Hist.); Univ. of NC, 1962–63, MSLS. **Orgs.:** SLA: NC Chap.; Bd. of Dirs. (1978–80). NC LA: Red. Secy. (1969–71). ALA. SELA. AALL. Alum. Assoc., Univ. of NC, Sch. of LS: Pres. (1974–75). **Pubns.:** Co-Auth., "Public Library Services", *Cnty. Gvt. in NC (1979).;* "The New Copyright Law and the Public Schools," *Sch. Law Bltn.* (Jan. 1977). **Activities:** 12; 17, 39; 77, 78 **Addr.:** Institute of Government, University of North Carolina at Chapel Hill, Chapel Hill, NC 27514.

Ballou, Hubbard W. (Ja. 26, 1917, Peking, Hopei, China) Lectr., Photoreprodct., Sch. of Lib. Srv., Columbia Univ., 1950–, Sr. Spec., Repro., Prsrvn. Dept., Columbia Univ. Lib., 1948–; Photodup. Libn., Univ. of IL Lib., 1947–48; Mstr. of Sci., Darrow Sch., 1939–42. **Educ.:** Yenching Univ., Peiping, China, 1934–36 (Liberal Arts); Yale Univ., 1936–39, AB (Pre-Med.); Columbia Univ., 1946–47, BS (Lib.); Univ. of IL, 1947–48 (Lib.). **Orgs.:** SLA. ALA: Photodup. Ord. Forms Com. (Ch., 1960–63); Amer. Natl. Stan. Inst. Rep., 1956–70), PH5-Photograph. Reprodct. of Docum., Secy., Stan. for Micro. Com. (1960–65). Natl. Micro. Assn.: Dir. (1965–68); *Natl. Micro-News* Assoc. Ed. (1959–67). Socty. Photograph. Sci. and Engin.: Sect. Ed., Copying, *Abs. Photographic Sci. and Engin.* (1963–64). **Honors:** Natl. Micro. Assn., Fellow, 1964. **Pubns.:** Ed., *Guide to Micrographic Equipment* (1959–76); "Microcopying," *Information Processing Equipment* (1955); "Photography and the Library," *Lib. Trends* (O. 1956); "Microphotography," *Encyc. Intl.* (1964); "Microform Technology," *Anl. Review Info. Sci. and Tech.* (1973); various edshps. **Activities:** 1, 11; 23, 33, 40; 75 **Addr.:** 90 Morningside Dr., Apt. 2J, New York, NY 10027.

Ballou, Patricia K. (Jl. 2, 1924, Detroit, MI) Archvst., Tech. Srvs. Libn., Barnard Coll., 1978–, Tech. Srvs. Libn., 1969–78, Asst. Ref. Libn., 1967–69, Asst. Ref. and Circ. Libn., 1961–66; Serials Asst., City Coll., New York, 1948–50; Ref. Asst., Brown Univ., 1947–48. **Educ.:** Oberlin Coll., 1942–46, BA, summa cum laude (Hist.); Columbia Univ., 1946–47, BS; American Univ. Inst., 1977, Cert. (Introduction to Mod. Arch. Admin.). **Orgs.:** ALA. NY Tech. Srvs. Libns.: Secy.-Treas. (1977–78). SAA. Mid-Atl. Reg. Archvsts. Conf. Various other orgs. Natl. Women's Std. Assn. Columbia Sch. of Lib. Srv. Alum. Assn.: Secy. (1968–71). **Honors:** Phi Beta Kappa, 1946. **Pubns.:** *Women: A Bibliography of Bibliographies* (1980); "Bibliographies for Research on Women," *Signs* (Win. 1977); jt. auth., "Encyclopedia," *Collier's Encyc.* (1974). **Activities:** 1, 2; 23, 45, 46; 92 **Addr.:** 90 Morningside Dr., New York, NY 10027.

Balon, Brett J. S. (Ap. 26, 1953, Regina, SK) Branch Supvsr., Southeast Reg. Lib., 1978–. **Educ.:** Univ. of Regina, 1971–76, BA (Hon.) (Anthro.); Univ. of West. ON, 1976–77, MLS; Southeast (SK) Comm. Coll., 1979, Litcy. Wkshp. Leadership Cert. **Orgs.:** SK LA: Cnclr., Exec. (1979–80); Conv., SK Lib. Week Com. Can. LA. Can. Ethnological Scty. SK Writer's Gld. **Pubns.:** *Social and Demographic Change in South-Central Saskatchewan* (1976); "Scientific Laws and the Computer," SK Lib. (D. 1978); "Rusty," (Fiction) (1979). **Activities:** 9; 16, 24, 36; 55, 56, 89 **Addr.:** 104–1205 1st. Ave NE, Weyburn, SK S4H 2Y3 Canada.

Balshone, Cathy S. (Ap. 1, 1946, Columbus, OH) Head Libn., Boston Cnsvty. of Msc., 1977–; Libn., Fort Lauderdale Musm. of the Arts, 1974–77; Libn. II, Fort Lauderdale Pub. Lib., 1970–72. **Educ.:** Sarah Lawrence Coll., 1964–68, BA (Msc.); Columbia Univ., 1969–70, MS (LS). **Orgs.:** Msc. LA. Boston Area Msc. LA. Fort Lauderdale Jr. Symph. Gld.: Educ. Chmn. **Honors:** Amer. Symph. Orch. Leag., Sarah Parker Awd., 1976. **Activities:** 1, 12; 15, 39; 55 **Addr.:** Albert Alphin Music Library, Boston Conservatory of Music, 8 The Fenway, Boston, MA 02215.

Baltis, Nancy Reed (S 27, 1937, Los Angeles, CA) Mgr., Lib./Info. Srvcs., Syntex, Inc., 1975–; Infor. Spec., 1972–75. **Educ.:** San Jose State Univ., 1955–60, BA, (Soclgy.), 1971–72, MLS. **Orgs.:** SLA: Bay Reg. Chap., (Pres. 1975–76; Nom. Com., Ch., 1978–79; Prog. Com., 1979–80); Pharma. Div.: Treas. (1979–81). Pharm. Mfrs. Assn., Sci. Inf. Subsect.: Strg. Com. (1981–83). Univ. of CA Sch. of Lib. and Infor. Sci.: Adv. Com. (1980). Assoc. Info. Mgrs. **Honors** Beta Phi Mu, **Activities:** 12; 17; 58, 60, 80 **Addr.:** 109 Los Montes, Burlingame, CA 94010.

Bamberger, Mary Ann (F. 9, 1941, Chicago, IL) Univ. Arch., Univ. of IL, Chicago Circle, 1966–; Tchr., Mother McAuley Liberal Arts HS, 1962–66. **Educ.:** Loyola Univ., 1958–62, BS (Hist.); DePaul Univ., 1963–66, MA (Hist.). **Orgs.:** Midwest Arch. Conf.: Founding Mem.; Secy.-Treas. (1972–75); Pres. (1977–79). SAA: Coll. and Univ. Arch. Com. (1975–); Reg. Actv. Com. (1972–74). Amer. Assoc. of State and Lcl. Hist. Chicago Area Women's Hist. Conf. Chicago Area Cons. Grp. **Pubns.:** "The Manuscript Collection at the University of Illinois at Chicago Circle," *IL Libs.* (Mr. 1975, April 1981); "Repository Guides Report," *Book of Readings;* "Copyright and the University Archivist," *Midwestern Archivist* (1981). **Activities:** 1, 2; 38, 45; 95-Lcl. Hist. **Addr.:** 843 S. Madison, LaGrange, IL 60525.

Bamford, Harold E. (Ag. 12, 1927, San Francisco, CA) Prog. Dir., Natl Sci Fndn. Div. of Info. Sci. and Tech., 1966–; Staff Mgr., Syst. Dev. Corp., 1962–66. **Educ.:** Univ. of CA, Berkeley, 1945–49, AB (Psy), 1949–51, MA (Psy), 1951–1953, PhD (Psy); Many other courses and inst. **Orgs.:** ASIS. AAAS (fellow). Amer. Psyc. Assn. (fellow). Sigma Xi (fellow). Opers. Resrch. Socty. of Amer. **Honors:** Natl. Sci. Fndn., Cert. of Cmdn., 1970, Spec. Achvmt. Awd., 1977. **Pubns.:** "Policy implications of networks for editorial processing," *Jnl. Resrch. Comm. Std.* (N. 1979); "Assessing the effect of computer augmentation on staff productivity," *Jnl. of the Amer. Socty. for Info. Sci.* (My. 1979); "Electronic information exchange: the National Science Foundation's developing role," *Bltn. of the Amer. Soty. for Info. Sci.* (Je. 1978); Jt. Auth. "Editorial processing centers: a progress report," *The Amer. Sociologist* (Ag. 1976); "The electronic alternative to paper-based communication," *Intl. Forum Info. Documtn.* (v. 1:3 1976); Various articles. **Activities:** 4; 17, 41; 56, 75 **Addr.:** Division of Information Science & Technology, National Science Foundation, Washington, DC 20550.

Bandemer, June E. (Jl. 18, 1930, Connellsville, PA) Asst. Dir., Head of Ref., Falk Lib. of the Hlth. Sciences, Univ. of Pittsburgh, 1975–; Sr. Ref. Libn., 1974–75; Ref. Libn., 1969–74; Acq. Libn., 1966–69. **Educ.:** Westminster Coll., 1948–52, BA cum laude (Hist.); Univ. of Pittsburgh, 1965–66, MLS, Advnc. Cert., 1966–69, Addiontional credits in info. sci, 1974–78. **Orgs.:** Med. LA. **Honors:** Cncl. on Lib. Resrc./Natl. Lib. of Med., CLR-NLM Hlth. Sci. Lib. Mgt. Intershp., 1979. **Activities:** 12, 14-Health Sciences; 17, 31, 39; 75, 80, 87 **Addr.:** Assistant Director, Falk Library of the Health Sciences, University of Pittsburgh, Scaife Hall, Pittsburgh, PA 15261.

Bander, Edward Julius (Ag. 10, 1923, Boston, MA) Law Libn., Suffolk Univ., 1978–; Assoc. Law Libn., NY Univ., 1960–78; Libn., U.S. Court of Appeals, 1955–60; Asst. Ref. Libn. Harvard Law School, 1954–55. **Educ.:** Boston Univ., 1946–49, AB (Lit.); 1948–51, LLB; Simmons, 1954–56, MLS. **Orgs.:** AALL. **Pubns.:** *Mr. Dooley on the Choice of Law* (1963); "Wading Through the Congressional Morass N.Y.U.," *Jnl. of Law and Soc. Change* (Sp. 1978); "The Path of the Law, A Lawyers Tour of Boston," *Boston Bar Jnl.* (Spr. 1979). **Addr.:** 41 Temple St., Beacon Hill, Boston, MA 02114.

Bandyk, Mary Stephania (S. 18, 1949, Pittsburgh, PA) Asst. Branch Libn., Frederiksted Pub. Lib., 1979–; Sub. Tchr. and Libn., Brockway Area Schs., 1978; Libn., Brockway Glass Co., Inc., 1978; Libn., Philipsburg State Gen. Hosp. Sch. of Nursing, 1976–77. **Educ.:** Duquesne Univ., 1967–71, BS (Educ., Eng.); 1971–72, MS (Educ., LS); Univ. of Pittsburgh, 1977–78, MLS. **Orgs.:** SLA. St. Croix LA: Pres. (1980–81); Nsltr. Ed. (1979–80). St. Croix Women's Clb. Intl. Side-Saddle Org. **Activities:** 9, 12; 21, 39, 45; 54, 80, 91 **Addr.:** #17, Liberty Hall, Hosoital St., Frederiksted, St. Croix, VI 00840.

Banfill, Arnold D. (F. 16, 1914, E. Angus, PQ) Retired, 1979–; Catlgr., Fac. of Law Lib., McGill Univ., 1968–79; Chief Libn., Bishop's Univ. Lib., Lennoxville, PQ, 1951–67; Asst. to Dir., Harvard Law Lib., 1947–51. **Educ.:** Bishop's Univ., Lennoxville, PQ, 1932–35, BA hons. (Hist.); McGill Univ., 1935–40, BCL (Law), 1946–47, BLS. **Orgs.:** Can. LA. Can. ALL. Assn. of McGill Univ. Libns. **Pubns.:** Transl., "The Case for the Special Status of the University Law Library," *Law Lib. Jnl.* (F. 1973); Indxr., *Index to Canadian Legal Periodical Literature* (1972). **Activities:** 1, 12; 17, 20, 30; 77 **Addr.:** 6955 Fielding Ave., Apt. 107, Montreal, PQ H4V 1P8 Canada.

Banks, Doris H. (My. 1, 1925, Auburn, NY) Pub. Srvs. Libn., Whitworth Coll., 1979–; Dir., Prof., Div. of LS, CA St. Univ., Fullerton, CA, 1970–79, Assoc. Coll. Libn., 1967–70; Chief Libn., Hughes Aircraft Co., 1957–67; Chief Libn., Robertshaw-Fulton Controls Co., 1955–57; YA Libn., Phoenix Mncpl. Lib., 1954–55; Asst. Libn., Brookline Pub. Lib., 1949–54; Libn., Mohawk Ctrl. Sch., 1947–49. other positions. **Educ.:** St. Univ. NY, Geneseo, 1946, BA (Educ.); Univ. of South. CA, 1967, MA (Pub.Admn.); Syracuse Univ., Master of Science in Library Science, 1953, MLS. **Orgs.:** ALA: ASIS. SLA. WA LA. **Honors:** Beta Phi Mu; Kappa Delta Pi, Epsilon Tau Chap. **Pubns.:** "Planning the New Library: Hughes Aircraft Company's Ground Systems Group Technical Library," *Spec. Libs.* (Ap. 1961); "User Habits as Predictors of User Needs." *Proceedings Spec. Lib. Assn. Reg. Wkshp. Rpt. Lit.* (1965); "The Greening of the Classroom." SLA, Anl. Conf., Pittsburgh. (1972). **Activities:** 1, 12; 15, 39; 59, 63, 89 **Addr.:** 8713 N. Alcan, Spokane, WA 99218.

Banks, Joyce M. (S. 26, 1935, Stratford, ON) Rare Bks., Cons. Libn., Natl. Lib. of Can., 1974–, Sel. Libn., Antiq. Can., 1968–74. **Educ.:** Waterloo Luth. Univ., 1965–67, BA (Eng., Hist.); Univ. of Toronto, 1967–68, BLS; Univ. Coll. London, 1974–75, MA (Cons. and Print. Hist.). **Orgs.:** Cncl. of Fed. Libs., Can.: Com. on Cons./Prsrvn. of Lib. Mtrls. Assn. Can. Archvsts. **Pubns.:** *Books in Native Languages in the Collection of the Rare Books and Manuscripts Division of the National Library of Canada/Livres en Langues Autochtones Dans la Divsion des Livres Rares et des Manuscrits de la Bibliothèque Nationale du Canada*

Special Subjects/Services: 50. Adult educ.; 51. Advert./Mktg.; 52. Aerosp.; 53. Agric.; 54. Area std.; 55. Arts/Hum.; 56. Autom.; 57. Bibl./Prtg.; 58. Bio. sci.; 59. Bus./Fin.; 60. Chem.; 61. Copyrt.; 62. Documtn.; 63. Educ.; 64. Engin.; 65. Env.; 66. Eth. grps.; 67. Film; 68. Food/Nutr.; 69. Geneal.; 70. Geo.; 71. Geol.; 72. Handcpd.; 73. Hist.; 74. Int. frdm.; 75. Info. sci.; 76. Insr.; 77. Law; 78. Legis.; 79. Math./Comp. sci.; 80. Med.; 81. Metals; 82. Nat. resrcs.; 83. Newsp.; 84. Nuc. sci.; 85. Oral hist.; 86. Petr./Energy; 87. Pharm.; 88. Phys./Astr./Math.; 89. Readg.; 90. Relig.; 91. Sci./Tech.; 92. Soc. sci.; 93. Telecom.; 94. Transp.; 95. (other).

(1980); *Guidelines for Preventive Conservation and Disaster Planning* (1981); "James Constantine Pilling and the Literature of the Native Peoples," *Colloquium III* (1979); "Paper Conservation: a Basic Reading List," *Archivaria* (Sum. 1976). **Activities:** 2 **Addr.:** 512–111 Wurtemburg St., Ottawa, ON K1N 8M1 Canada.

Banks, Margaret Amelia (Jl. 3, 1928, Quebec, PQ) Law Libn., Univ. of West. ON, 1961–; Archvst., ON Dept. of Pub. Recs. and Arch., 1953–61. **Educ.:** Bishop's Univ., 1946–49, BA (Hist.); Univ. of Toronto, 1949–50, MA, 1950–53, PhD (Hist.). **Orgs.:** AALL. Can. ALL: Treas. (1964–66). Bylaws Com. (Ch., 1972–). Amer. Inst. of Parlmt.: Educ. Com. (1976–79); Resrch. Com. Natl. Assn. of Parlmt.: ON (Ch., 1979–). **Pubns.:** *Using a Law Library* (3d ed., 1980); *Edward Blake, Irish Nationalist* (1957); "An Introduction to British Government Documents," *Intl. Jnl. of Law Libs.* (Jl. 1977); "Robert's Rules of Order," *Natl. Parlmt.* (1979); many other articles and reviews. **Activities:** 1, 12; 15, 17, 39; 61, 77, 78 **Addr.:** Faculty of Law Library, The University of Western Ontario, 1151 Richmond Street, London, ON N6A 3K7 Canada.

Banks, Roderick E. (F. 26, 1933, Edmonton, AB, Can) Head, Admin. Srvs., Lib., Univ. of AB, 1968–; Mgr., Admin. Data Prcs., Univ. of AB, 1961–68. **Educ.:** Univ. of AB, 1961–65, BA (Phil.); Univ. of West. ON, 1975–77, MLS; Socty. of Mgt. Accts., 1957–61, RIA (Acct.). **Orgs.:** CA LA: Treas. (1973–75). LA of AB: Treas. (1976–77). Edmonton LA. Socty. of Mgt. Accts.: Lcl. Chap. (Ch., 1964–65). Admin. Sci. Assn. of Can. **Activities:** 1; 17, 19, 35; 56, 59, 93 **Addr.:** Cameron Library, University of Alberta, Edmonton, AB T6G 2J8 Canada.

Bannan, Victoria Lee (N. 20, 1946, Lincoln, NE) Sch. Libn., R. L. Stevenson Intermediate Sch., 1971–; Sch. Libn., Trona Intermediate Sch., 1968–70. **Educ.:** West. State Coll., Gunnison, CO, 1964–68, BA (Eng.); Univ. of HI, Manoa, 1970–71, MLS. **Orgs.:** ALA. AECT. HI Assn. of Sch. Libns.: Rec. Secy. (1975–76). Pac. Assn. of Comm. and Tech. HI State Tchrs. Assn.: Libns. Com. (Co-Ch., 1978–79). **Honors:** Beta Phi Mu. **Activities:** 10; 31, 32, 49-Gen.; 63 **Addr.:** 1983 Puowaina Dr., Honolulu, HI 96813.

Bannen, Carol A. (O. 4, 1951, St. Paul, MN) Head Libn., Reinhart, Boerner, Van Deuren, Norris and Rieselbach, s.c., 1975–; Head Libn., Peat, Marwick, Mitchell, 1973–75. **Educ.:** Coll. of St. Catherine, 1969–73, BA (LS, Hist.). **Orgs.:** AALL. SLA: WI Chap. (Pres., 1980–81; Networking Ch., 1978–80). Lib. Cncl. of Metro. Milwaukee: Bd. of Dirs. (1979–81). MN Assn. of Law Libs. Various other orgs. **Activities:** 12, 14-Law Lib.; 25, 41; 77 **Addr.:** Reinhart, Boerner, Van Deuren, Norris & Rieselbach, s.c., 1800 Marine Plz., Milwaukee, WI 53202.

Bansal, Arlene R. (Ja. 17, 1938, Chicago, IL) Deputy Dir., AZ State Dept. of Lib., Arch. and Pub. Recs., 1980–; Head Libn., AZ State Lib. for the Blind and Phys. Handcpd., 1969–80; Ref. Libn., City of Monrovia Pub. Lib., 1968–69; Lib. Consult., U.S. Agency for Intl. Dev., New Delhi, India, 1965–67. **Educ.:** Bob Jones Univ., 1958–62, BA (Hum.); Univ. of Chicago, 1962–64, Inc. (LS). **Orgs.:** AZ State LA: Pub. Libs. Div., Pres. (1977), Pres.-Elect (1976); Natl. Lib. Week Com. (Ch., 1972–75); Pub. Lib. Stans. Com. (Ch., 1976). ALA: ASCLA, Lib. Srv. to the Blind and Phys. Handcpd., Ch.-Elect (1980–81), Vice-Ch. (1979–80); Hlth. and Rehab. Lib. Srvs. Div., Lib. Srv. to the Blind and Phys. Handcpd., Secy.; Francis Joseph Campbell Awd. Com. **Honors:** AZ State LA, Libn. of the Yr., 1973. **Activities:** 13; 17, 25, 35; 56, 72 **Addr.:** Arizona State Dept. of Library, Archives & Public Records, 3rd Floor, State Capitol, 1700 W. Washington, Phoenix, AZ 85007.

Banting, Bruce W. (S. 9, 1947, Simcoe, ON, Can) Visit. Lectr., Sch. of Lib. & Info. Sci., Univ. of West. ON, 1979–, Asst. Libn., 1977–78, Col. Dev. Libn., 1974–77, Serials Libn., 1974–74. **Educ.:** Univ. of West. ON, 1967–70, BA (Psy.), 1972–73, MLS, 1978–, LLB. **Orgs.:** Can. LA. ON LA: Various coms. Can. Assn. of Info. Sci. Univ. of West. ON Libns. Assn. Can. Assn. of Lib. Schs. Univ. of West. ON Staff Assn.: Various coms. Can. Bar Assn. **Activities:** 11; 15, 17, 26; 77 **Addr.:** School of Library & Information Science, University of Western Ontario, London, ON N6A 5B9 Canada.

Baranowski, George V. (S. 8, 1951, Chicago, IL) Admin. Assoc., Opers., Dialog Info. Srvs., 1979–. **Educ.:** San Diego State Univ., 1970–74, BA (Hist.); Univ. of CA, Berkeley, 1978–79, MLS. **Orgs.:** ALA. SLA. Sierra Club. Audubon Socty. **Pubns.:** "Comparison of Psych Abstracts and NIMH Databases," *Bhvl. and Soc. Sci. Libn.* (Fall 1980); contrib., *Sierra Club History Series* (1979–). **Activities:** 12, 14-Online srch. srv.; 49-Data analysis; 56, 65, 85 **Addr.:** Dialog Information Services, Inc., 3460 Hillview Ave., Palo Alto, CA 94304.

Barbee, Norman Nathaniel (O. 2, 1936, Durham, NC) Col. Dev. Coord., U.S. Dept. of Interior Lib., 1981–; Chief, Cat. Branch, 1980–81; Admin. Libn., U.S. Gvt. Prtg. Ofc., 1973–80; Libn., GPO-Docum. Lib., 1970–72. **Educ.:** Jackson State Univ., 1972–75, BLS; University of MD, 1975–78, MLS. **Orgs.:** ALA. SLA. AALL. DC LA. NLA. **Pubns.:** *An Explanation of the Supt. of Documents Classification System* (1979). **Activities:** 4, 12; 15, 17, 29; 69, 75, 92 **Addr.:** P.O. Box 2233, Washington, DC 20013.

Barber, Constance R. (S. 26, 1923, Atlanta, GA) Lib. Media Spec., Hart Jr. HS, 1963–; Libn., Anacostia HS, 1962–63; Lib. Asst., Montreal Chld. Lib., 1959–60; Catlgr., Fed. Trade Comsn., 1956–57; Libn., Okinawa Spec. Srvs., 1955–56; Libn., Howard Univ. Lib., 1947–51. **Educ.:** Howard Univ., 1941–45, AB (Soc.); Catholic Univ., 1946–47, BS (Lib. Sci). **Orgs.:** DC Assn. Sch. Libns.: Past Pres. DC LA. ALA. South Manor Neighborhood Assn. Auxiliary to Medico - Chirurgical Soc. **Activities:** 10; 17, 31, 32 **Addr.:** Hart Jr. High School Library, 601 Mississippi Ave., S.E., Washington, DC 20032.

Barber, Cyril John (My. 18, 1934, Pretoria, S. Africa) Assoc. Prof. of Bibl., Lib. Dir., Rosemead Grad. Sch. of Prof. Psy., 1972–; Head Libn., Trinity Evang. Dvnty. Sch., 1969–72; Libn., Winnipeg Bible Coll., 1967–69. **Educ.:** Witwatersrand Tech. Coll., 1950–57, Dipl. (Bus. Admin.); Winnipeg Bible Coll., 1967–68, BREd (Hum.); Dallas Theol. Semy., 1962–67, Dipl. (Theo.), 1968, MTh (Theo.); Rosary Coll., 1970–71, MALS; Talbot Theo. Semy., 1977–79, DMin (Marriage & Fam.). **Orgs.:** ATLA. ALA. CA LA. Evang. Theo. Socty. Socty. of Biblical Lit. Royal Socty. of Lit. Royal Geo. Socty. Other orgs. **Honors** Beta Phi Mu. **Pubns.:** *The Minister's Library* (1974); *Successful Church Libraries* (1970); Contrib., *Tyndale Encyc. of Relig. Knowledge* (1979–); other devotional books and articles. **Activities:** 1; 17, 35, 41; 57, 90, 92 **Addr.:** P. O. Box 5181, Hacienda Heights, CA 91745.

Barber, Gary DeForest (F. 26, 1941, N. Tonawanda, NY) Coord., Ref. Srvs., SUNY, Fredonia, 1969–. **Educ.:** SUNY, Fredonia, 1959–64, BA; SUNY, Geneseo, 1964–67, MLS; SUNY, Buffalo, 1975–77, MS (Soc. Sci.). **Orgs.:** SUNY LA. ALA: ACRL, West. NY, ON Chap. Untd. Univ. Profs. **Pubns.:** "Current Survey of American History Reference Sources," *Ref. Srvs. Review* (Ap./Je. 1978); (Jl./S. 1979); (Ap./Je. 1980). **Activities:** 1; 15, 31, 39; 63, 85, 92 **Addr.:** Daniel A. Reed Library, State University College, Fredonia, NY 14063.

Barber, Margaret Ellen (Ag. 26, 1943, Pasadena, CA) Dir., Pub. Info. Ofc., ALA, 1974–; Dir., Ofc. for Rcrt., 1969–74; Ref. Libn., San Francisco Pub. Lib., 1968–69; Spec. Projs. Libn., Orange Cnty. Pub. Lib., 1966–68. **Educ.:** Univ. of CA, Riverside, 1961–65, BA (Eng.); Rutgers Univ., 1965–66, MLS. **Orgs.:** ALA. IL LA. Amer. Socty. of Assn. Execs. Pubcty. Club of Chicago. **Honors:** Phi Beta Kappa, 1965; Beta Phi Mu, 1966; PR Socty. of Amer., Silver Anvil, 1975; Pubcty. Club, Chicago, Golden Trumpet, 1975, 1976. **Pubns.:** "Public Relations," *ALA World Encyc. of Lib. and Info. Sci.* (1980); "Public Relations", *ALA Yearbk.* (1977); "Savoring ALA's Centennial," *Lib. Jnl.* (Je. 15, 1976). **Activities:** 3; 36; 51 **Addr.:** Public Information Office, American Library Association, 50 E. Huron, Chicago, IL 60611.

Barber, Raymond R. (Mr. 22, 1925, Duluth, MN) Lib. Supvsr., Corning Glass Works, 1964–; Lib. supvsr., Boeing Airplane Co., 1955–64; Ref. Libn., Genl. Electric Co., 1952–55; Tech. Asst., Carnegie Lib. of Pittsburgh, 1950–52. **Educ.:** MI Col. of Mining & Tech., 1948–49, BS (Chem Engr.); West. Rsrv. Univ., 1949–50, MS (Lib. Sci). **Orgs.:** SLA. **Activities:** 12; 17, 39; 60, 64, 91 **Addr.:** Corning Glass Works, Technical Information Center, Sullivan Park, Corning, NY 14830.

Barbour, Wendell Allen (Mr. 8, 1939, Chicago, IL) Assoc. Dir. for Oper., GA South. Coll., 1975–; Head of Ref., Indiana Univ. at S. Bend, 1974–75; Bkstacks Libn., Univ. of IL, 1971–74; Newsp. Libn., Asst. Archvst., 1970–71. **Educ.:** Univ. of FL, 1957–62, BA (Hist.); Univ. of IL, 1963–66, MA (Hist.), 1967–70, MS (LS); John Marshall Law Sch., 1976–80, (Law). **Orgs.:** ALA: ACRL Legis. Com.; Lama Coll. and Univ. Lib.; Bldgs. and Equipment Com. (1980–); GA LA: Handbook Com. (1981–83) Schol. Com. (1978–80); SELA; Com. on Com. (1981–) Statesboro Cmnty. Theater: Pres. (1978–79); GA South. Coll. Fac. Club: Pres. (1977–78). **Honors:** Phi Alpha Theta, 1966. **Pubns.:** *Newspaper Microfilm Holdings List: Univ. of IL.* (1970); Co-Ed. GA South. Coll. Lib. Nsltr. (1979); Co-Ed. Univ. of IL Lib. Staff Bltn. (1970–71); Ed. *Proceedings of the First Congressional District's Hearings on the Governor's Conference on Libraries and Information Services: A Pre-White House Conference.* (1979). **Activities:** 1; 17, 22, 39; 56, 61, 77 **Addr.:** Route #1, Circle Drive - Grove Lakes, Statesboro, GA 30458.

Barcellona, Edmere C. (Jl. 31, 1896, Buffalo, NY) Mem. of Mncpl. Lib. Adv. Bd., Dallas Pub. Lib., 1978; Pubcty. Mgr. & Ed., Buffalo Musm. of Sci., 1928–43; Secy. & Bd. Mem., Buffalo Plng. Assn., 1920–28; Occupational Therapist, U.S. Med. Corps, 1919–20. **Educ.:** Wm. Smith Coll., 1914–16, (Greek); Barnard Col., 1916–18, BA (Eng.). **Orgs.:** ALA. ALTA. Zonta Club of Buffalo. Buffalo Camp Fire Girls Cncl: Pres. (1936–37). Dallas Indp. Sch. Dist. Vol. Prog., Mem. of Exec. Com. (1969–75). South. Meth. Univ. Fine Arts Previewers (1975); Pres. (1978–79). Barnard Coll. Alum. of Buffalo, Bd and Pres. (1920–30's); Amer. Assoc. of Univ. Women (1920–). Various other orgs. **Honors:** Camp Fire Girls: Gulick Awd. 1937; Barcellona Awd. (named in my honor) 1979; Dallas County Council of Republican Women, „Hats Off" Award (non partisn), 1975; Dallas Indp. Sch. Dist. Vol. Prog. Ten-year Award, 1979. **Pubns.:** Ed., Hobbies Magazine (1920–). **Activities:** 9; 21, 36, 47 **Addr.:** 7507 Wellcrest Dr., Dallas, TX 75230.

Bard, Harriet E. (Springfield, MA) Dir., Morrisson-Reeves Lib., 1945–; Dir., Hagerstown-Jefferson Twp. Lib., 1937–45. **Educ.:** Boston Univ., 1926–28, BA (Eng. Lit.); Univ. of MI, 1939–41, ABLS. **Orgs.:** ALA: Cncl. (1952–53); Com. to Std. State Agencies (1953–54, 1956–57, 1959–60); Com. on Natl. Lib. Week (Ch., 1962–63). IN LA: Cert. Bd. (Ch., 1947, 1951); Legis. Com. (Ch., 1958–59); various other coms., ofcs. Lib. Srvs. and Construct. Act: Adv. Bd. (Ch., 1968). Area Lib. Srvs. Athrty.: Adv. Cncl. (Ch., 1978). Wayne Cnty. Chap. Amer. Red Cross: Secy. (1963–68). Musical Arts Socty.: Pres. (1958–59). Wayne Cnty. Cmnty. Action Comsn. OEO: Asst. Secy. (1967–68). Area TB Assn. and Respiratory Diseases: Fund Dr. (Ch., 1969); Bd. of Dirs. (1972). Various other orgs. **Honors** IN LA, ILTA Conf., Libn. of the Yr., 1966; ALA, First Recipient Allie Beth Martin Awd., 1979; Univ. of MI, Sch. of LS, Disting. Alum. Awd., 1980; Staff and Bd. of Morrisson-Reeves Lib., Cert. of Cmdn., 1980; other hons. **Pubns.:** "Student Staff at Morrisson-Reeves Library," *Focus on IN Libs.* (Je. 1967); "Reaching the Unreached," *Wilson Lib. Bltn.* (Ja.–F. 1966); "Let's Promote Librarianship," *Lib. Occurrent* (Mr. 1963); "What I See Ahead for Libraries," *Lib. Occurrent* (Je. 1957); various other articles. **Activities:** 9; 17 **Addr.:** Morrisson-Reeves Library, 80 N. 6th St., Richmond, IN 47374.

Bard, Kaye L. (Ap. 10, 1950, Trenton, NJ) Law Libn., NJ State Lib., 1976–; Libn., Mercer Cnty. Lib., 1973–76. **Educ.:** Douglass Coll., 1968–72, BA (Soclgy.); Drexel Univ., 1972–73, MS (Lib. Sci.); NJ Prof. Libns. Cert. **Orgs.:** SLA: Prog. Com. (1979–80). NJ LA: Inst. Com. (1976–77); Educ. for Libnshp. (1979–80). Greater Philadelphia Law Lib. Assn. Douglass Coll. Alumnae Assn.: Class Secy. (1972–77). **Activities:** 13; 39, 41; 77, 78 **Addr.:** NJ State Library, Law Section, 185 W. State St., Trenton, NJ 08625.

Bard, Therese Bissen (Ag. 8, 1926, Caledonia, MN) Asst. Prof., Grad. Sch. of Lib. Std., Univ. of HI, 1973–; Libn., Lrng. Resrcs. Ctr., Portland State Univ., 1972–73; Sch. Libn., Chicago Pub. Schs., 1959–63; Ref. Libn., Newberry Lib., 1957–59. **Educ.:** Coll. of St. Teresa, 1943–46 (Hist.), 1947–48, AB (Fr.); Univ. of CA, Berkeley, 1956–57, MLS (Libnshp.); Univ. of WA, 1969–77, PhD (Educ.). **Orgs.:** ALA. Chld. Lit. Assn. Pac. Assn. for Comm. and Tech.: Pres. (1979–80). HI Assn. of Sch. Libns.: Grad. Sch. of Lib. Std.; Exec. Bd. (Liaison Mem., 1974–80). **Honors:** Beta Phi Mu, 1957. **Pubns.:** "The *Katei Bunko* of Japan: A Model for An Innovative Approach to Library Service for Children," *Top of the News* (Spr. 1980); "School Libraries in the United States, 1945 to the Present," *Intl. Handbk. Contemporary Devs. in World Libnshp.* (1981). **Activities:** 10, 11; 21, 26, 32; 63, 67, 89 **Addr.:** 529–5 Pepeekeo St., Honolulu, HI 96825.

Bardwell, Sylverna V. (Ja. 29, 1950, Columbia, VA)) Branch Libn., Univ. of DC, 1978–; Ref. Libn., Washington Tech. Inst., 1974–78. **Educ.:** Univ. of MD, 1968–72, BS (Textile Sci.), 1972–74, MLS. **Orgs.:** ALA: ACRL; LAMA; RASD; JMRT; SORT. SLA. ASIS. VA LA; Various other orgs. Univ. of DC Fac. Sen. **Activities:** 1; 17, 31, 39; 51, 59 **Addr.:** University of the District of Columbia, Business Library, 1331 H St., NW #100, Washington, DC 20005.

Bareño, Laura D. (Ap. 9, 1944, South Bend, IN) Head, Outrch. Srvs., San Diego Cnty. Lib., 1972–; Chld. Libn., Venice Branch, Los Angeles Pub. Lib., 1970–72; Ref., Grp. Loan Libn., FL State Lib., 1966–68. **Educ.:** FL State Univ., 1961–65, BA (Psy.), 1965–66, MS (LS). **Orgs.:** CA LA: Palomar Chap. REFORMA. CA Eth. Srvs. Task Frc. Assn. of Mex.-Amer. Educs. **Honors:** Heartland Human Rel. Assn., Prog. of Distinction, 1974. **Pubns.:** Ed., *Guide for Developing Ethnic Library Services* (1979); ed., *CA Eth. Srvs. Task Frc. Nsltr.* (1980). **Activities:** 9; 16, 35, 36; 66, 72, 89 **Addr.:** San Diego County Library, 5555 Overland Ave., Bldg. 15, San Diego, CA 92123.

Baretski, Charles Allan (N. 21, 1918, Mt. Carmel, PA) Dir., Van Buren Branch, Newark Pub. Lib., 1954–, Sr. Libn., Art and Msc. Dept., 1944–54, Libn., various Depts., 1938–44; Dir., Ethnic Resrch Arch., Newark, NJ, 1972–. **Educ.:** NY Univ., 1935–37 (Liberal Arts); Rutgers Univ., 1939–45, BA (Hum.); Columbia Univ., 1945–46, BS (LS), 1946–51, MS (LS); Univ. of Notre Dame, 1956–57, MA (Pol. Sci.), 1957–58, PhD (Pol. Sci.); NY Univ., 1959–65, MA (Gvt.), 1965–69, PhD (Politics); American Univ., 1951, Dipl. (Arch. Adm.), 1955, Dipl. (Advnc. Arch. Admin.). **Orgs.:** ALA: SORT, Reg. Dir. (1960–63); Exec. Bd.; JMRT (Exec. Bd., 1950–53). NJ LA: Educ. for Libnshp. Com. (Ch. 1950–51). Newark Pub. Lib. Gld.: Pres. (1970). Newark Pub. Lib. Emp. Un.: Pres. (1970–77); Del. to Intl. Conv. of AFSCME (1974, 1976, 1978, 1980). Polish Amer. Hist. Assn.: Ed., *Monthly Bltn.* (1961–65). Polish Univ. Club of NJ: Pres. (1953–54); Histn. (1967–). Inst. of Polish Culture: Fndr., Exec. Dir. (1953–54). Writers' Socty. of NJ: Fndr., Exec. Dir. (1947–56). Other orgs. **Honors** Assoc. Cmnty Cncls. of Newark, Disting. Educ. of America, 1979; Newark City Cncl, 2nd Anl. Brotherhood Awd., 1962; NJ Pub. Empl. Cncl., Outstan. NJ State Labor Leader Awd., 1978; Newark Pub. Lib., 40 Yrs. Srv. Awd., 1978; NJ Polish Amer. Congs., NJ Bicentennial Amer. Heritage Awd., 1976; other awds. **Pubns.:** "History of the Polish Settlement in New Jersey and its Notables" in *The New Jersey*

PROFESSIONAL ACTIVITIES: Institutions: 1. Acad. lib.; 2. Arch.; 3. Assn.; 4. Fed./Gvt. lib.; 5. Inst. lib.; 6. Mfr./Suppl.; 7. Milit. lib.; 8. Musm.; 9. Pub. lib.; 10. Sch. lib.; 11. Sch. of lib. sci.; 12. Spec. lib.; 13. State lib.; 14. (other). **Functions/Activities:** 15. Acq./Col. dev.; 16. Adult srvs.; 17. Admin.; 18. Apprais.; 19. Archit./Bldgs.; 20. Cat./Class.; 21. Chld. srvs.; 22. Circ.; 23. Cons./Pres.; 24. Consult.; 25. Cont. ed.; 26. Educ. lib. sci.; 27. Ext. srvs.; 28. Fund/Grants; 29. Gvt. pubs.; 30. Indx./Abs.; 31. Instr. lib. use; 32. Media srvs.; 33. Micro.; 34. Netwks./Coop.; 35. Persnl.; 36. PR; 37. Publshg.; 38. Recs. mgt.; 39. Ref. srvs.; 40. Repro.; 41. Resrch.; 42. Review.; 43. Secur.; 44. Serials; 45. Spec. col.; 46. Tech. srvs.; 47. Trustees/Bds.; 48. YA srvs.; 49. (other).

Ethnic Experience (1977); "A Fateful Choice, A Polish Tale," *NY Folklore Qtly.* (Sum. 1952); "Lamplighters of Liberty, Unite," *Sch. and Socty.* (My. 1952); "America's Aesthetic Awakening," *Coll. Art Jnl.* (Win. 1951–52); "Cabbages or Artichokes," *Sch. and Socty.* (D. 1951); other books and articles. **Activities:** 2, 9; 16, 17, 38; 50, 66 **Addr.:** 229 Montclair Ave., Newark, NJ 07104.

Barhydt, Gordon C. (My. 28, 1932, Batavia, NY) Chief Libn., North York Pub. Lib., 1977–, Deputy Chief Libn., 1976–77; Actg. Chief, Ctrl. Lib. and Documtn. Branch, Intl. Labour Ofc., Geneva, 1974–75; Assoc. Dir., Metro. Toronto Lib. Bd., 1972–74; Asst. Prof., Sch. of LS, Case West. Rsv. Univ., 1961–67. **Educ.:** Case West. Rsv. Univ., 1957, BA (Eng.), 1966, MS (LS). **Orgs.:** Can. LA ALA. Cncl. of Admins. of Lg. Urban Pub. Libs.: Secy.-Treas. (1978–80). Chief Execs. of Lg. Pub. Libs. of ON: Ch. (1981–). **Pubns.:** *Information Retrieval Thesaurus of Education Terms* (1968); "The Effectiveness of Non-user Relevance Assessments," *Jnl. of Documtn.* (Je. 1967). **Activities:** 9; 17, 30, 35 **Addr.:** North York Public Library, 35 Fairview Mall Dr., Willowdale, ON M2J 4S4 Canada.

Barkalow, Patricia Walker (Mr. 14, 1939, Meadville, PA) Prin. Libn. for Support Srvs., Pasadena Pub. Lib., 1981–; Adj. Instr., Grad. Sch. of LS, Univ. of TN, 1979–80; Asst. Prof., Head, Syst. Dept., Univ. of TN, 1978–81; Head, Tech. Srvs., E. Brunswick Pub. Lib., 1975–78. **Educ.:** Rutgers, 1965–73, BA (Pol. Sci.); 1974–75, MLS. **Orgs.:** ALA: LITA (Ed. Bd. 1979–82)/VCC5, Comm. Com. (1979–82). ASIS. E. TN LA. **Pubns.:** Ed. *LITA Newsletter* (1979–82); "File Conversion," *Jnl. of Lib. Autom.* (Sept. 1979); "Library Automation," *Lib. Trustee Nsltr.* (Jul., Aug. 1979); "Generic Features of Internally Developed Systems," (audiocassette) (1977). **Activities:** 1, 9; 26, 38; 56, 75, 93 **Addr.:** University of Tennessee, Main Library, Room 105, Knoxville, TN 37916.

Barker, Aileen M. (N. 3, 1943, Ft. McMurray, AB, Can) Chief Libn., Dartmouth Reg. Lib., 1978–; Chief Libn., Halifax Cnty. Reg. Lib., 1973–78; Asst. Libn., 1971–73; Cat., Nova Scotia Prov. Lib. **Educ.:** Mount Allison Univ., 1961–64, BA (Hist.); McGill Univ., 1964–65, BLS. **Orgs.:** Atlantic Provs. Lib. Assn.: Bibl. Ctr. Com. Jt. Reg. Libr. Bds. Assn.: Secy. Can. LA. Dartmouth Cmnty. Srvs. Adv. Bd.: Secy. **Pubns.:** Ed. Bd., *Can. Lib. Jnl.* **Activities:** 9; 17, 34, 47 **Addr.:** c/o Dartmouth Regional Library, 100 Wyse Road, Dartmouth, NS B3A 1M1 Canada.

Barker, Dale L. (O. 18, 1919, Pensacola, FL) Assoc. Dir., Univ. of Miami (Coral Gables), 1969–; Lib. Syst. Anal., Univ. of GA, 1966–69; Assoc. Dir., GA Inst. of Tech., 1952–66, Asst. Libn. Tech. Prcs., 1951–52, Acq. Libn., 1950–51. **Educ.:** GA Inst. of Tech., 1946–49, BEE (Electrical Engin.); Univ. of IL, 1949–50, MS (LS); 1965, PhD (LS). **Orgs.:** ALA. GA LA. FL LA. ASIS; SELA. Member of Various Coms. of all above orgs. **Activities:** 1; 17 **Addr.:** 8320 S. W. 52 Ave., Miami, FL 33143.

Barker, Lillian Haber (Mr. 18, 1924, New York, NY) Branch Libn., Prince George's Cnty. Meml. Lib., 1975–; Adult Srvs. Consult., Ramapo Catskill Lib. Syst., 1974–75; Head, Cnty. Srvs. Branch Libn., Enoch Pratt Free Libr., 1966–74; Asst. Libn., West. MD Coll. 1961–66. **Educ.:** NY Univ., 1940–44, BA (Eng., Hist.); Columbia Univ., 1946–47, BSLS. **Orgs.:** ALA. RASD: ILL (1972–76) Notable Bks. (1981–83). MD LA: Conf. Plng. (1979–81). Toastmasters Intl. Richard III Society: Mid Atl. Reg. Chmn. (1977–). Friends of Montpelier. **Activities:** 9; 16, 17, 34; 50, 55, 67 **Addr.:** Laurel Library, PGCML, 507 7 St., Laurel, MD 20810.

Barker, M. Elizabeth (Jl. 31, 1939, Astoria, OR) Libn., Educ. Dept., Pub. Lib. of Cincinnati and Hamilton Cnty., 1966–, Libn., Art and Msc. Dept., 1962–66. **Educ.:** Lewis and Clark Coll., 1957–61, BA cum laude, (Psy., Msc.); George Peabody Coll. for Tchrs., 1961–62, MALS. **Orgs.:** ALA. OH LA. Natl. Audubon Socty. Mental Hlth. Assn. Nu Phi Epsilon. **Honors:** Beta Phi Mu. **Activities:** 9; 16, 31, 39; 63, 90, 92 **Addr.:** 3424 Brookline - Apt. 3, Cincinnati, OH 45220.

Barker, Margaret M. (N. 4, 1949, Baltimore, MD) Lib. Consult., Roger Wells, Inc., Haddonfield, NJ, 1979–; Indxr/Ed., Compset Publshrs., 1977–79; Rsrch. Assoc., Univ. of NH, 1975–77; Resrch. Assoc./Photograph Archvst., Winterthur Musm., 1974–75. **Educ.:** Dunbarton Coll., 1967–71, AB (Hist.); Drexel Univ., 1971–73, MS, LS; Natl. Arch. Cert., 1976–. **Orgs.:** ALA. Furniture Hist. Soc. (London). **Honors:** Beta Phi Mu, 1973. **Pubns.:** "A Bibliography of Publications by and about Robert Wemyss Symonds," *Furniture Hist.* (1975). **Activities:** 1, 12; 20, 30, 41; 55, 57, 61 **Addr.:** 28 Evergreen Circle, Maple Shade, NJ 08052.

Barker, Richard T. (O. 3, 1932, Mooresville, NC) Univ. Libn., Appalachian State Univ., 1972–; Ast. Libn., 1956–72. **Educ.:** Appalachian State Univ., 1951–55, BS (Eng.); 1955–56, MA (LS); addt'l. crs. **Orgs.:** ALA. SE LA. NC LA: Treas. (1971–79). Kiwanis: Pres. (1976–77). Phi Delta Kappa. **Activities:** 1; 17, 22; 56, 74, 85 **Addr.:** 306 Poplar Hill Dr., Boone, NC 28607.

Barkey, Patrick T. (F. 11, 1922, Flint, MI) Dir. of Libs., The Claremont Colls., 1974–; Dir., OCLC West. Srv. Ctr., 1976–; Dir. of Libs., Univ. of Toledo, 1967–74; Head Libn., Texas A&I Univ., 1964–67; Head, Circ. Dept., East. IL Univ., 1960–64. **Educ.:** Pomona Coll., BA (Eng.); Univ. of MI, 1951, AMLS. **Orgs.:** EDUCOM: Nom. Com. ALA. CA LA. **Pubns.:** "Flextime: The Workweek Revolution," *Lib. Jhl.* (Ap. 1, 1978); Various other articles and speeches. **Activities:** 1; 17, 28, 34; 56, 75, 93 **Addr.:** Honnold Library, The Claremont Colleges, Claremont, CA 91711.

Barkman, H. Frank (Ap. 19, 1909, Chicago, IL) Pres., Bd. of Trustees, Pueblo (CO) Lib. Dist. **Orgs.:** ALA. CO LA. Intl. Fndn. of Empl. Benefit Plans. VP, Frank I. Lamb Fndn. Fndr., Frank I. Lamb Meml. Col. for Bus. and Indust., Pueblo Lib. Dist. Rotary. **Activities:** 9; 17, 28, 47; 59, 76 **Addr.:** Suite LL-101, First National Bank Building, P. O. Box 444, Pueblo, CO 81002.

Barksdale, Milton Kendall (S. 15, 1945, Richmond, KY) Acq. Libn., East. KY Univ., 1969–. **Educ.:** East. KY Univ., 1963–67, BS (Math.); Univ. of KY, 1967–68, MSLS. **Orgs.:** Beta Phi Mu: Upsilon Chap., Pres. (1977). OH Valley Grp. of Tech. Srvc. Libns.: Ch. (1975). KY LA. Phi Kappa Phi: EKU Chap., Pres. (1976). **Honors:** Phi Delta Kappa. **Pubns.:** Reports for Ed. Rsrcs. Info. Ctr. (1978). **Activities:** 1; 15, 17, 46; 56, 63 **Addr.:** Acquisitions Section, John Grant Crabbe Library, East. KY Univ., Richmond KY 40475.

Barlow, Elizabeth A. (D. 19, 1950, Drumheller, AB) Govt. Pubns. Libn., Univ. of SK, 1978–, Hlth. Sci. Ref. Libn., 1974–77; Catlgr., Univ. of MB, 1972–74. **Educ.:** Univ. of AB, 1968–71, BSc (Math.), 1971–72, BLS. **Orgs.:** SK LA: Cnclr. (1979–81). CA LA: Dir. (1977–78). Can. Assn. of Spec. Libs. and Info. Srvs.: Pres. (1977–78). **Activities:** 1; 17, 29, 33; 78, 92, 95-Agriculture. **Addr.:** Government Publications, University of Saskatchewan Library, Saskatoon, SK S7N 0W0 Canada.

Barnard, Jean Lynn (O. 24, 1918, Tiffin, OH) Med. Ref. Libn., Univ. of MI, 1970–, Cat. Libn., 1954–70; Cat. Libn., Oxford Univ., Miami, OH, 1951–54. **Educ.:** Univ. of MI, 1936–40, AB (Econ.), 1949–51, AMLS. **Orgs.:** Med. LA. Sci. Fiction Oral Hist. Assn.: VP (1979–). Ann Arbor Sci. Fiction Assn.: Treas. (1980–). Beta Phi Mu: Mu Chap., Pres. (1979–81), VP (1977–79). **Activities:** 1; 39, 45; 80 **Addr.:** 1810 Charlton Ave., Ann Arbor, MI 48103.

Barnard, Walter Monroe (Jl. 31, 1930, Camden, NC) Biblgphr., Columbia Univ. Lib., 1965–; Docum. Catlgr., 1962–65; Circ. Libn., Bus. Lib., 1959–61; Serial Catlgr., Lib. of Congs., 1957–59. **Educ.:** Wake Forest Coll., 1948–52, AB (Soclgy.); Univ. of NC, 1955–57, MSLS. **Orgs.:** NY Tech. Libns. METRO: Resrc. Dev. Com. (1977–80); Coop. Acq. Com. (1972–80). **Honors** Beta Phi Mu, 1957. **Pubns.:** Co-Auth., "Cataloging statistics: report on an experiment," *Lib. Resrcs. and Tech. Srvs.* (Spr. 1957); "Characteristics of the Literature by American Authors of Journal Articles in Library Science" (microfilms) (1957). **Activities:** 1; 15, 20, 31 **Addr.:** 400 W 119th St., New York, NY 10027.

Barnet, Roberta Selig (D. 29, 1906, Boston, MA) Trustee, Lib. Bd., New Bedford Free Pub. Lib., 1941–; Tchr., Boston Pub. Schs., 1926–36. **Educ.:** Boston Tchrs. Coll., 1923–26, Cert.; MA Assn. for the Blind, Cert. Braille Transcriber. **Orgs.:** Frnds. of New Bedford Free Pub. Lib.: Pres. (1973–75). MA Lib. Trustee Assn.: Southeast. MA Mem. Ch. Hadassah. Garden Club of Grt. New Bedford. Women's Leag. of Untd. Synagogue of Amer. Sisterhood of Tifereth Israel Synagogue. **Honors:** MA Lib. Trustee Assn., MA Lib. Trustee of the Year, 1980; Israel Bonds, Woman of Valor, 1975. **Addr.:** 20 Morelands Terr., New Bedford, MA 02740.

Barnett, Juanita (McMillan) (My. 3, 1915, Hope, AR) Libn., Ouachita Bapt. Univ., 1956–, 1936–40. **Educ.:** Ouachita Coll., 1932–36, AB (Eng.); George Peabody Coll., 1936–37, BS (LS). **Orgs.:** ALA: State Mem. Com. (1964). AR LA: 2nd VP (1964); Coll. Sect. (Ch., 1959–60). AR Fndn. of Assoc. Colls.: Secy. (1966–67); Pres. (1970, 1977); Com. of Libns. Clark Cnty. Hist. Assn.: Asst. Exec. Secy. (1972–79). First Presby. Church, Arkadelphia: Deacon (1971–76), Elder (1977–). **Pubns.:** Ed., *Periodical Holdings in the Arkansas Foundation Associated Colleges* (1963). **Activities:** 1; 15, 17, 34 **Addr.:** Riley Library, Box 742, Ouachita Baptist University, Arkadelphia, AR 71923.

Barnett, Judith Brodkin (Ag. 13, 1939, New York, NY) Asst. Libn., Pell Marine Sci. Lib., Univ. of RI, 1971–; Sr. Catlgr., Temple Univ., 1965–69; Sr. Libn., Newark Pub. Lib., 1963–64; Libn. I, Free Lib. of Philadelphia, 1962–63. **Educ.:** Barnard Coll., 1955–59, BA (Hist.); Drexel Univ., 1961–62, MLS. **Orgs.:** ALA: ACRL. SLA. RI LA. **Honors:** Beta Phi Mu, 1962; Phi Beta Kappa, 1959. **Activities:** 1, 12; 20, 46; 91 **Addr.:** 103 Pond St., Wakefield, RI 02879.

Barnum, Joyce Lillian (F. 28, 1927, Seattle, WA) Ref. Libn., Univ. WA Libs., 1964–. **Educ.:** Univ. WA, 1943–47, BA (Msc.); 1961–64, ML (Libnshp.). **Orgs.:** ALA: Ref. and Subscrpn. Bks. Review Com. (1974–78); RASD/Coop. Ref. Srvs. Com. (1975–78, Ch., 1977–78). Pac. NW LA. WA LA. **Honors:** Beta Phi Mu. **Pubns.:** *American Library Association Reference and Subscription Books Review Committee Manual* (1979); Contrib., *Amer. Ref. Bks. Anl.* (1976–79). **Activities:** 1; 39; 54, 55, 92 **Addr.:** 16920 26th Ave. N.E., Seattle, WA 98155.

Barone, Richard Melvin (Je. 12, 1945, Buffalo, NY) Libn., US Coast Grd., 1980–; Ref. Libn., US Naval Acad., 1977–80; Libn., Admin. Conf. of the US, 1976–77; Sr. Libn., NY State Dept. of Correct. Srvs., 1973–76. **Educ.:** Canisius Coll., 1963–67, BA (Phil.); SUNY, Buffalo, 1972–73, MLS; Univ. of New Haven, 1973–74, MS (Crim. Justice). **Orgs.:** AALL. **Pubns.:** "American Prisoners of War in Vietnam," *Readers Adv. Srv.* (1979); "Administrative Conference of the United States: A Selected Bibliography 1968–1977," *Admin. Law Review* (Spr. 1978); "De-Programming Prison Libraries," *Special Libs.* (S. 1977). **Activities:** 4, 12; 17, 29, 39; 77, 74, 92 **Addr.:** 291 Berkeley Dr., Severna Park, MD 21146.

Barr, Phyllis (Ja. 10, 1943, New York, NY) Archvst., Par. Rec., Cur., Trinity Church Par., 1980–; Consult. Archvst., 1978–80; Dir., Trng. and Oper., Petry TV, 1974–75. **Educ.:** Adelphi Univ., 1960–64, BA (Eng.); MA (Amer. Hist.); NY Univ., 1975–76, MPhil. (Am. Hist.); 1976–79, Cert. (Arch. Mgt.) **Orgs.:** SAA. Archvsts. RT: Plng. Com. (1979–). Mid-Atl. Reg. Arch. Conf. Amer. Hist. Assn. Amer. Socty. for Legal Hist.: Docum. Prsvtn. Com. **Activities:** 2, 12; 17, 20, 23; 55, 85, 90 **Addr.:** Parish of Trinity Church, 74 Trinity Pl., New York, NY 10006.

Barra, Carol H. (Ap. 7, 1946, Ithaca, NY) Libn., Breed, Abbott & Morgan, 1974–; Libn., Proskauer, Rose, Goetz & Mendelsohn, 1972–74; Libn., Symmers, Fish & Warner, 1971–72); Law Libn., John Hancock Life Ins., 1969–71. **Educ.:** SUNY, Albany, 1964–68, AB (Eng.); 1968–69, MLS. **Orgs.:** AALL. SLA. Law Lib. Assn. of Greater NY. **Activities:** 12; 15, 17, 35, 39; 77 **Addr.:** Breed, Abbott & Morgan, 153 East 53rd Street, New York, NY 10022.

Barrett, Carol Ann (Everhart) (Je. 6, 1949, Center, TX) Libn., Bell Helicopter Textron, 1973–; Libn., Carter & Burgess, Inc., 1971–73. **Educ.:** TX Woman's Univ., 1967–71, BA (Lib. Sci.). **Orgs.:** SLA: TX Chap. Minorities Liasion Com. (1979–80); Mem. Com. (1981-82); Lcl. Plng. Group Ch. (1980-81). **Activities:** 12; 52, 64 **Addr.:** Bell Helicopter Textron, Technical Library, PO Box 482, Fort Worth, TX 76101.

Barrett, Darryl Dean (Mr. 3, 1942, Little Falls, MN) Libn., Art/Music/Films Dept., Minneapolis Pub. Lib., 1972–; Libn., Tech. Srvs. Div., St. Paul Campus Lib. Univ. of MN, 1969–72. **Educ.:** Univ. of MN, 1963–66, BS (Educ.); 1972, MA (Lib. Sci.). **Orgs.:** ARLIS/NA: Ch., Twin Cities Chap. (1977–78). SLA: Networking Com. (1979–80). MN State-wide Lib. Srvs. Forum: 1981 All-Assn. Conf. Com. (1979–80). **Pubns.:** Reviews. **Activities:** 1, 9; 32, 34, 39; 55, 56 **Addr.:** Art/Music/Films Department, Minneapolis Public Library and Information Center, 300 Nicollet Mall, Minneapolis, MN 55401.

Barrett, Donald J. (S. 30, 1927, St. Paul MN) Asst. Dir. for Pub. Srvs., U.S. Air Force Acad. Lib., 1970–; Chief, Pub. Srvs., 1959–69; Chief, Ref. Branch, 1955–59; Libn., Electronic Supply Ofc., 1954–55. **Educ.:** Coll. of St. Thomas, 1945–50, BS (Chem.); Univ. of MN, 1950–53, MA (LS). **Orgs.:** ALA. CO LA. Plains & Peaks Lib. Syst.: Governing Bd. (1977–). **Honors:** U.S. Air Frc., Merit. Civilian Srv. Awd., 1972. **Pubns.:** "Science and Engineering Reference Books," *Reporting Technical Information* (1972, 1975, 1979). **Activities:** 1, 4; 17, 39, 45; 52, 74, 91 **Addr.:** 2624 Flintridge Dr., Colorado Springs, CO 80907.

Barrett, G. Jaia Heymann (F. 20, 1947, Houston, TX) Head, Pub. Docum. and Maps Dept., Duke Univ., 1980–; Ref. Libn., Gvt. Docum., Drew Univ. Lib., 1972–79. **Educ.:** Washington Coll., 1965–69, BA (Intl. Stds.); Columbia Univ., 1971–72, MLS. **Orgs.:** ALA: *Docum. to People* Ed. Adv. Bd. (1979–); GODORT Liaison to Ad Hoc Copyrt. Subcom. Gvt. Docum. Assn. of NJ: Del. to NJ Conf. on Libs. and Info. Srvcs. (1979); Clearhse. Chmn. and Nsltr. Ed., (1975–76, 1978–79); Pubns. Com. (Chmn. 1977–78). U.S. Gvt. Prtg. Ofc. Depos. Lib. Cncl.: Secy. (1976–77), Com. on GPO Oper. (Ch. 1978–79); Com. on Depos. Libs. (1976–78, Ch. 1977–78). **Pubns.:** Co-ed., *Directory of Government Document Collections and Librarians* (1978). **Activities:** 1; 29, 39 **Addr.:** Public Documents and Maps Department, William Perkins Library, Duke University, Durham, NC 27706.

Barrett, Laura P. (Mr. 1, 1949, Newark, NJ) Supvsg. AV Libn., Coll. of Med. and Dentistry of NJ, 1975–, Asst. Supvsg. AV Libn., 1974–75, Ref. Libn., AV Spec., 1972–74, Dental, Med. Ref. Libn., Jersey City Med. Ctr., 1971–72. **Educ.:** Bucknell Univ., 1966–70, AB (Span.); Rutgers Univ., 1970–71, MLS, cum laude (Lib. Srv.); Med. LA, Cert. Grade I; various crs. **Orgs.:** Med. LA: ILL Resrc. Sharing Stans. and Pracs. Subcom. (1978–79); NY/NJ Reg. Med. Lib. AV Subcom. (Ch., 1978–79); NY Reg. Grp., (Secy., 1980–81), Prog. Com., Vice-Ch. (1975), Ch. (1976). Hlth. Sci. Comms. Assn.: Biomed. Libs. Sect. (Ch., 1976–77). Assn. of NJ State Coll. Media Dirs. **Honors:** Sigma Delta Pi, 1968; Beta Phi Mu, 1971. **Pubns.:** "The Multimedia Complex," *Biomed. Comms.* (S. 1977); abs. ed., *The Jnl. of Biocomm.* (1979–); various wrkshps., sems. **Addr.:** George F. Smith

Special Subjects/Services: 50. Adult educ.; 51. Advert./Mktg.; 52. Aerosp.; 53. Agric.; 54. Area std.; 55. Arts/Hum.; 56. Autom.; 57. Bibl./Prtg.; 58. Bio. sci.; 59. Bus./Fin.; 60. Chem.; 61. Copyrt.; 62. Documtn.; 63. Educ.; 64. Engin.; 65. Env.; 66. Eth. grps.; 67. Film; 68. Food/Nutr.; 69. Geneal.; 70. Geo.; 71. Geol.; 72. Handcpd.; 73. Hist.; 74. Int. frdm.; 75. Info. sci.; 76. Insr.; 77. Law; 78. Legis.; 79. Math./Comp. sci.; 80. Med.; 81. Metals; 82. Nat. resrcs.; 83. Newsp.; 84. Nuc. sci.; 85. Oral hist.; 86. Petr./Energy; 87. Pharm.; 88. Phys./Astr./Math.; 89. Readg.; 90. Relig.; 91. Sci./Tech.; 92. Soc. sci.; 93. Telecom.; 94. Transp.; 95. (other).

Library, College of Medicine and Dentistry of New Jersey, 100 Bergen St., Newark, NJ 07103.

Barrette, Pierre P. (Ja. 18, 1940, St. Louis, MO) Asst. Prof. Inf. Sci., S. IL Univ.; Assoc. Prof. (Lib. Sci.), James Madison Univ., 1974–78; Dir. of Media, Berkshire Cmnty. Coll., 1972–74; Instr., S. Hadley HS, 1966–71. **Educ.:** Univ. of MA, 1966, BS (Chem.), 1970, MEd (AV Mgt.); Univ. of MA, 1971, EdD (Educ. Media); Univ. of RI, 1974, MLS. **Orgs.:** ALA. AECT. Assn. for Educ. Data Systs. Assn. for the Dev. of Comp. Based Instr. Systs. Phi Delta Kappa. **Honors:** Phi Delta Kappan Award, Outstanding Innovations in Teaching, 1971; Intl. Congs. on the Atom, Outstanding Sci. Tchr., 1971; Rotary Club of Pittsfield Award, Service Beyond Self, 1973; VA Educ. Media Assoc., Distinq. Ser. Awd., 1976. **Pubns.:** *The Microcomputer and the School Library Media Specialist* (1981); *Equipment Operation: Principles, Practices, Competencies* (1978); "Microcomputers in Education," *Compute; the Jnl. of Progressive Comp.* (S. 1979); "Certification of School Library Media Professionals in Virginia," *VEMA Mediagram* (1976). **Activities:** 10, 11; 24, 26, 41; 56, 63, 75 **Addr.:** Dept. Curric., Instr., and Media, College of Education, Southern Illinois University, Carbondale, IL 62901.

Barron, Robert Edward (Mr. 25, 1930, Woodhaven, NY) Sch.-Lib. Liaison, NY State Educ. Dept., 1966–; Lib. Supvsr., White Plains HS, 1959–66; Dir., North Castle Free Lib., 1956–59; Asst. Ref. Libn., Trenton Pub. Lib., 1955–56; Asst. Dir., Armed Forces Info. Sch., Fort Slocum, 1953–55. **Educ.:** SUNY, 1948–52, BA (Soc. Std.); 1952–53, MSLS. **Orgs.:** ALA: Ch., Films for YA (1970–76); LAMA Pub. Rel. Sect. (John Cotton Dana Lib. Pub. Rel. Awards Com. 1976–80); (Ch. 1978–80). NY LA: State Liaison, Exec. Bd., Sch. Lib. Media Sect. (1966–). Sch. Libns. of Southeastern NY: Pres. (1964–66). Voorheesville Sch. Dist. Pub. Lib., Trustee (1970–76). **Honors:** Sch. Lib. Media Sect., Exceptional Service; NY LA, Citation, 1979. **Pubns.:** *Towards a Common Goal* (1968). **Activities:** 10, 13; 17, 24, 27; 55, 63, 67 **Addr.:** P.O. Box 612, Voorheesville, NY 12186.

Barrows, Richard Shepard (Jl. 1, 1920, Brookline, MA) Libn., Ofc. of the Navy Judge Advocate Gen., 1961–; Law Libn., U.S. Post Ofc. Dept., 1960–61; Libn., Asst. Prof., Law, Univ. of MT, 1957–60; Treasure Rm. Libn., Harvard Law Sch., 1955–57. **Educ.:** Harvard Univ., 1939–43, SB (Phil.), 1945–48, JD (Law); various crs. **Orgs.:** AALL: Nom. Com. (1965); Fed. Lib. Com. (Ch., 1965–67). The Law Libns. Socty. (DC): Pres. (1964–66). Cncl. of Navy Sci. and Tech. Libns.: Ch. (1978). **Pubns.:** "Law Libraries in Montana," *MT Law Review* (1959); "Study Aides in Law School Libraries," *Harvard Law Sch. Bltn.* (1955–56). **Activities:** 4, 5 **Addr.:** Library, Office of the Navy Judge Advocate General, 200 Stovall St., Alexandria, VA 22332.

Barry, James W. (Je. 27, 1919, Altoona, PA) Deputy Assoc. Dir., Lib. Oper., Natl. Lib. of Med., 1977–; Med. Ctr. Libn., Univ. of AZ (Tucson), 1971–76; Libn., Lib. of Sci. and Med., Rutgers Univ., 1963–71; Head, Acq., Natl. Lib. of Med., 1955–63; Natl. Agr. Lib., 1952–55; Asst. Acq. Libn., Purdue Univ., 1949–51. **Educ.:** Univ. of Pittsburgh, 1947, AB (Hist.); Carnegie Inst. of Tech., 1942–48, BSLS; Univ. of Pittsburgh, 1951–52, MED (Educ., Hist.); U.S. Civil Srv. Mid. Mgt. Inst. (1960). **Orgs.:** ALA: various coms. (1955–65). Med. LA: various coms. (1961–). **Honors:** Phi Alpha Theta, Beta Chap.; Natl. Lib. of Med., Superior Performance Awd., 1958. **Pubns.:** "U.S. Medical Periodical Price Index," *Med. LA Bltn.* (1955–); "New Medical Library Buildings," *Med. LA Bltn.* (O. 1971); "Central Science Library: A Prospectus," *Rutgers Med. Sch. Nsltr.* (My 1964); "Long Term Periodical Subscriptions," *Lib. Resrc. Tech. Srvs.* (Win. 1959); Reviews. **Activities:** 1, 4; 15, 17; 56, 57, 80 **Addr.:** 8200 Wisconsin Ave., #509, Bethesda, MD 20014.

Barsumyan, Silva E. (Aleppo, Syria) Dir., Un. City Pub. Lib., 1974–; Ref. Libn., River Vale Pub. Lib., 1973–74; Libn. Archvst., SLA, 1972–73. **Educ.:** Albertus Magnus Coll., 1967–71, AB (Psy.); Univ. of MI, 1971–72, MLS; Seton Hall Univ. **Orgs.:** NJ LA: VP (1980); Leag. of Municipalities (Ch., 1980); Gvt. Rel. Lobbyist; Admin. Sect. (Treas., 1978); various coms. NJ State Lib.: Eval. Area Coord. Cncls., Ad-Hoc Com. NJ Gvrs. Conf. on Lib. and Info. Srvs.: Del. (1979). IFLA: U.S. Del. (1977–80). Rutger's Grad. Sch. of Lib. and Info. Srvs.: Adv. Assoc. (1980–83). NJ State Cvl. Srv.: Consult. Reg. Film Ctr. Com. **Pubns.:** Ed. bds., *NJ LA Directions* nsltr. (1978). **Activities:** 9, 11; 17, 36, 39; 61, 75, 77 **Addr.:** Union City Public Library, 324–43rd St., Union City, NJ 07087.

Bartage, Ramona McInnis (D. 2, 1951, Shreveport, LA) Libn., Oil City Sch. Lib., 1978–; Asst. Par. Libn., Natchitoches Par. Lib., 1975–77. **Educ.:** LA Tech. Univ., 1969–73, BA (Educ.); LA State Univ., 1974–75, MLS; 1978, Cert. (Med. Libnshp.). **Orgs.:** LA LA. Med. LA. Shreveport Writers Club. **Honors:** Beta Phi Mu; Phi Kappa Phi. **Activities:** 10; 21, 48; 63, 68 **Addr.:** 1012 Blvd., Shreveport, LA 71104.

Bartelme, Sr. Mary O.S.F. (Jl. 19, 1914, Oconomowoc, WI) Asst. Libn. Salzmann Lib., 1979– and Libn., St. Francis Convent, Milwaukee, 1962–; Libn., Cardinal Cushing Educ. Clinic, Boston, 1951–62; Tchr.-Libn., St. John's HS, Houghton, IA, 1949–51; Asst. Libn., Cardinal Stritch Coll., Milwaukee, 1941–49. **Educ.:** Cardinal Stritch Coll., 1932–37, PhB (Eng. Lit.); Catholic Univ. of Amer., 1940–41, BSLS. **Orgs.:** Catholic LA: Coll. Libs. Sect. (Ch.). WI Cath. LA: Coll. Lib. Sect.; *ABC Bltn.* (Ed., 1962–76); Catholic Bk. Week (Ch., 1971). Sisters of St. Francis of Assisi. **Pubns.:** Reviews in various Cath. lib. pubns. **Addr.:** 3221 S. Lake Dr., Milwaukee, WI 53207.

Bartenbach, Wilhelm K. (N. 27, 1938, Heilbronn, Germany) Exec. Dir., Pub. Affairs Info. Service, 1976–; Assoc. Ed., 1971–76; Asst. Ed., 1970–71; Ref. Libn., NY Pub. Lib., Resrch. Libs., 1968–70. **Educ.:** Inter-American Univ., 1962–66, BA (Hist. and Fr.); Univ. of Denver, 1966–67, MA (Lib. Sci); City Univ. of NY, 1969–72, (Grmn. Lit.); 1973–75, (Info. Sci.). **Orgs.:** Amer. Soc. of Indxrs.: Pres.-elect, Pres. (1977–79); Treas. (1975–77); Com. on Ethics Standards and Specifications (1974–79); Bd. of Dirs. (1979–). SLA: NY Chap., Dir. of Pubn. (1979–); Secy. (1976–77). ASIS: Metro. NY Chapter; Memb. Secy. (1977–79). ALA. Various other organizations and offices. Amer. Civil Liberties Un. **Pubns.:** *Public Affairs Information Service Foreign Language Index, Vols. 1-5* (1972–76); "Public Affairs Information Service (PAIS)" *Encyclopedia of Library and Information Science* (1978). **Activities:** 3; 17, 30, 37; 59, 78, 92 **Addr.:** Public Affairs Information Service, 11 West 40th St., New York, NY 10018.

Barth, Edward W. (Mr. 7, 1930, Chicago, IL) Supvsr. Lib. Media Srvs., Prince George's Cnty. Pub. Schs., 1970–; Libn., John F. Kennedy HS, Montgomery Cnty., MD, 1965–70; Mgr., Ctrl. Prcs. Dept. Instruc. Mtrls., Montgomery Cnty., MD, 1963–65; Libn., Julius West Jr. HS, Montgomery Cnty., MD, 1961–63; Libn., Jr. HS, LeMesa-Spring Valley Pub. Schs., 1955–61; Libn., HS, Huron, SD, 1951–52. **Educ.:** Luther Coll., 1949–51, AB (Hist.); Univ. of Denver, 1954–55, MA (LS); George Washington Univ., 1967–71, EdD (Sec. Educ.). **Orgs.:** ALA: Peace Corp Com. (Ch. 1962–63). Com. on Lib. Instruc. (1979–81). Ad Hoc Copyrt. Com. (1979–81). MD Educ. Media Orgs. AECT. Natl. Educ. Assn. MD St. Tchrs. Assn. Prince George's Cnty. Educ. Assn. Phi Delta Kappa, George Washington Univ. Chap.: Mem. and Ethics Com. (1975–76); Nswltr. Ed. (1976–78); VP/Mem. Ch. (1978–79); Pres. (1979–80). **Honors:** U.S. Ofc. of Educ., Natl. Defense Educ. Act., Educ. Awd., 1965. **Pubns.:** "Looking Beyond-To Next Year," *Phi Delta Kappa Nsltr.* (Ap. 1979), "It's That Time of the Year," (Jl. 1979), "What's Basic," (Jl. 1979), "How Can Schools Make the Most of Their Shrinking Library Dollars," *Curric. Prod. Review* (N. 1979); "Closing Schools Means Moving Library Materials," *Amer. Sch. and Univ.* (My. 1978). **Activities:** 10; 17, 32; 63 **Addr.:** 13802 Loree Lane, Rockville, MD 20853.

Barth, Joseph M. (Mr. 10, 1945, Jamaica, NY) Asst. Libn., U.S. Military Acad., 1979–; Acq. Libn., 1974–79; Admin. Libn., Spec. Srvs. Lib., 1971–74; AV Libn., U.S. Military Acad., 1968–71. **Educ.:** Iona Coll., 1963–66, BA (Eng.); St. John's Univ., 1967–68, MLS. **Orgs.:** ALA. SLA. **Pubns.:** Numerous Reviews (1975–79). **Activities:** 1, 4; 15, 37, 42; 55, 57, 59 **Addr.:** 43 Spruce St., Cornwall–On–Hudson, NY 12520.

Barthell, Daniel W. (S. 8, 1938, Peoria, IL) Head, Srch. Sect., Northwestern Univ. Lib., 1979; Resrch. Assoc., Venez. Proj., 1976–79; Ref. Libn., Per. Indxr., Lib. of Intl. Rel., 1973–75. **Educ.:** Notre Dame Univ., 1956–60, BA (Hist.); Univ. of IL, 1970–72, MS (LS); 1972, PhD (Hist.). **Orgs.:** ALA. IL LA. SALALM. **Honors:** Beta Phi Mu, 1972. **Pubns.:** "Honduras," *ALA World Encyc. of Lib. and Info. Srvs.* (1980). **Activities:** 1; 15; 54 **Addr.:** Northwestern University Library, Acquisitions Dept., Evanston, IL 60201.

Bartolini, R. Paul (Jl. 21, 1920, Spring Valley, IL) Dir., Knoxville and Knox Cnty. Pub. Lib., 1979; Dir., Lake Conty. (IN) Pub. Lib., 1965–79; Asst. City Libn., Ext. srvs., Milwaukee Pub. Lib., 1956–65; Coord., Adult Srvs., Free Lib. of Philadelphia, 1953–56. **Educ.:** IL St. Univ., 1938–42, BS (Educ.); Univ. of IL, 1946–47, MS (LS); Univ. of UT, 1943–44, ASTP, (Cult., Grmn.). **Orgs.:** ALA: Cncl. (1949–54, 1968–72); LAD (Bldg. & Equipment Sect. Archit. Com., 1974–76. Econ., Status, Welfare & Fringe Benefits Com., 1966–69). PLA (Bd. of Dirs., 1968–72; Stans. for Pub. Libs. Com. 1965–69). ALTA (Legis. Com. 1970–); various other ALA coms. Lake Co. Hist. Socty.; Lake Co. Com. Dev. Comm.; Rotary Intl.; Amer. Inst. of Planners. **Honors:** Pi Gamma Mu, 1941; Kappa Phi Pappa, 1950; Beta Phi Mu, 1951. **Pubns.:** "In the Spot That's Hot. . .," *WI Lib. Bltn.*, (S./O. 1975); "Breakthrough in Cooperative Action - Reference Services Planned," *Focus on IN Libs.* (Mr. 1967); "Seven for Lake County," *Lib. Jnl.* (D. 1966); "Double Header in Milwaukee," *Lib. Jnl.* (D. 1964); "Library Service to the Blind," *WI Lib. Bltn.* (My./Je., 1962). **Activities:** 2, 9; 17, 19, 24; 56, 78, 93 **Addr.:** R. Paul Bartolini, 7140 Dan Rose Lane, Knoxville, TN 37920.

Barton, Mary Neill (Mr. 20, 1899, Winchester, VA) Retired; Head Libn., Gen. Ref. Dept., Enoch Pratt Free Lib. (Baltimore), 1938–59; Asst. Libn., 1927–37; Instr., LS, Columbia Univ., 1943, 1946; Instr., LS, Drexel Univ., 1937; Various post-retirement assignments. **Educ.:** Agnes Scott Coll., 1918–22, BA (Math.); Columbia Univ., 1926–27, BS (LS), 1938–42, MS (LS). **Orgs.:** ALA: Cncl. (1951–53; 1957–58); RASD (Pres., 1957–58). Baltimore Bibliophiles (Life Mem.). Phi Beta Kappa. **Honors:** ALA, Isadore Gilbert Mudge Awd., 1959; Enoch Pratt Free Lib., William G. Baker Awd., 1958. **Pubns.:** *Reference Books: A Brief Guide* (7 eds., 1947–70); Jt. auth., *Samuel Taylor Coleridge: A Selected Bibliography* (1935); "Administrative Problems in Reference Work," *Reference Function of the Library* (1943). **Activities:** 9; 31, 39 **Addr.:** Goodwin House, 4800 Fillmore Ave., Apt. 310, Alexandria, VA 22311.

Barton, Virginia Lee (Je. 8, 1922, Redlands, CA) Assoc. Dir., Resrch. and Plng., Timberland Reg. Lib., 1979–; Asst. Dir., West. Area, 1975–79; Asst. Dir., 1968–75; Libn., Readg. Bibltherap. Supvsr., Green Hill Sch., 1960–68. **Educ.:** Univ. CA, Santa Barbara, 1939–43, BA (Educ., Eng., Soc. Sci.); Univ. WA, 1958–60, MLS; Lib. Supvsrs. Inst., Univ. WA, 1965. **Orgs.:** ALA. WA LA. WA Lib. Media Assn.: Lib. Fld. Relshps. (Chmn.). Pac. NW LA. Other orgs. AAUW. WA State Cmnty. Educ. Assn. WA Cont. Ed. Assn. Other orgs. **Pubns.:** "Services to Children and Schools in Timberland Regional Library," *The Medium* (Fall 1979). **Activities:** 9, 10; 17, 22, 41; 50, 74, 89 **Addr.:** 579 NW Pennsylvania Av., Chehalis, WA 98532.

Barton, William H. (My. 12, 1944, Cheyenne, WY) Dir., Hist. Resrch. and Pubns., WY State Arch., Musms. and Hist. Dept., 1980–; Sr. Histn., 1978–80. **Educ.:** Univ. of AZ, 1964–69, BA (Hist.). **Orgs.:** WY State Hist. Socty. WY Oral Hist. and Folklore Assn. Cheyenne Corral of Westerners. Amer. Assn. for State and Lcl. Hist. West. Hist. Assn. Cheyenne Little Thea. Players. **Pubns.:** "David Dare and the American Dream," *Annals of Wyoming* (1979); "The Phantom of Fletcher Park," *Boomerang* (1981); "Cheyenne's Unique Heritage," *Sun-Day* (1980). **Activities:** 1, 2; 15, 23, 24; 69, 85, 95-Publshg. **Addr.:** Wyoming State Archives, Museums and Historical Dept., Barrett Bldg., Cheyenne, WY 82002.

Bartoshesky, Florence (Mr. 22, 1947, Wilmington, DE) Cur. Assoc., Baker Lib., Harvard Univ., 1979–. **Educ.:** Univ. of Toronto, 1965–70, BA (Soclgy.); Univ. of Rochester, 1971–76, MAT (Amer. Hist.); Newberry Lib., 1972, Fellow (Fam. and Quantative Hist.); Simmons Coll., 1977–81, MS (LS); Case West. Rsv. Univ., 1980, Cert. (Arch. Admin.). **Orgs.:** SAA. New Eng. Archvsts. Boston Archvst. Grp. Boston Food Coop.: Archvst. (1981–). **Pubns.:** Cmplr., "Raymond A. Bauer: A List of His Works," *Accounting, Organization and Society* (forthcoming); cmplr., "Bibliographies: Advertising; Chemicals and Pharmaceuticals; Computers; Food and Beverage; Transportation," *Careers and the MBA* (1980); jt. cmplr., "Bibliographies," *Careers and the MBA* (1979). **Activities:** 1, 2; 15, 39, 45; 55, 59, 73 **Addr.:** 44 Meacham Rd., Somerville, MA 02144.

Bartucca, Peter J. (D. 6, 1948, Bristol, CT) Libn., Burke and Burke Law Firm, 1979–; Asst. Libn., 1976–79; Arch. Asst., Yale Univ., 1975–76; Head of Circ., Med. Lib., 1974–75; Bus. and Tech. Libn., Bristol Pub. Lib., 1972–74. **Educ.:** Marist Coll., 1968–70, BA (Eng.). **Orgs.:** AALL. Law LA of Greater NY. Murray Hill Com.: Bd. of Trustees; Hist. Dist. Com. (Ch.). Natl. Trust for Hist. Prsrvn. Film Socty. of Lincoln Ctr., Inc. **Activities:** 12, 14-Law Library; 30, 39, 41; 77, 78 **Addr.:** Burke and Burke, 30 Rockefeller Plz., New York, NY 10020.

Bartz, Alice P. (Je. 19, 1915, Brunswick Cnty., VA) Sch. Lib. Spec., Sch. Dist. of Philadelphia and PA Dept. of Educ., 1968–; Libn., Abington (PA) Sch. Dist., 1960–68; Libn., Germantown Acad., Philadelphia, 1955–60; Child. Libn., Free Lib. of Philadelphia, 1940–43; Chld. Libn., New York Pub. Lib., 1938–40; Chld. Libn., Richmond (VA) Pub. Lib., 1936–38. **Educ.:** Univ. of Richmond, 1932–36, BA; Univ. of NC, Chapel Hill, 1936–38, BSLS; Univ. of IL, NDEA Inst., 1967; Drexel Univ., Temple Univ., Grad. Std. **Orgs.:** PA Sch. Libns. Assn.: Pres. (1966–68); Adv. Bd. (1978–80). ALA: ALSC (Newbery, Caldecott Com., 1978; Intl. Rel. Com., 1979–81); *Booklist* Adv. Bd. (1978–); AASL. PA LA: Various coms. Philadelphia Chld. Readg. RT: Exec. Bd., Strg. Com. (1977–). various other orgs. Lib. Publ. Rel. Assn. of Greater Philadelphia: Pres. (1973–74). Fed. Adv. Cncl. for the PA State Lib. Dev. Bur. (1972–78). Natl. Cncl. Tchrs. of Eng. Assn. of Supvsn. and Curric. Dev. various other orgs. **Honors:** PA Sch. Libns. Assn., Outstan. Contrib. Awd., 1978; Disting. Alumna Awd., Westhampton Coll., Univ. of Richmond, 1981. **Pubns.:** "Teacher Center and Staff Development," *Drexel Lib. Qtly.* (Jl. 1978); "Role of Library Media Specialist in Pennsylvania Comprehensive Reading/Communication Arts Plan," *Lrng. and Media* (Spr. 1978); "Two-Way Street to the Library," *Early Yrs.* (Ap. 1975); "Reading Motivation and the Media Specialist," *Sch. Media Qtly.* (Fall 1973). **Activities:** 14-Sch. Lib. Exam. & Evaluation Center; 19, 21, 24 **Addr.:** 646 Pine Tree Rd., Jenkintown, PA 19046.

Basart, Ann Phillips (Ag 26, 1931, Denver, CO) Ref. Libn., Msc. Lib., Univ. of CA, Berkeley, 1970–; Ed., *Cum notis variorum* UCB Msc. Lib. Nsltr., 1976–; Instr., Lone Mountain Coll., 1963–66. **Educ.:** Univ. of CA-LA, 1948–50, 1951–53, BA (msc.); UC-Berkeley, 1954–60, MA, MLS (msc.); 1976–78, Cert. in Libnshp. **Orgs.:** Msc. LA: Brd. (1978–80). North. CA, Ch. (1960–61). Intl. Assn. of Msc. Libs. **Honors:** Phi Beta Kappa, 1953; Fulbright Schol., 1956–57. **Pubns.:** Jt. auth., *Union List of Music Periodicals in Northern California Libraries* (1979); Jt. auth., *Listening to Music* (1971); *Serial Music* (1961); "Weeding books in an academic music library", *Msc Lib. Assn. Notes,* (1980); articles in *Cum notis variorum,* (1976–). **Activities:** 1, 13;

PROFESSIONAL ACTIVITIES: Institutions: 1. Acad. lib.; 2. Arch.; 3. Assn.; 4. Fed./Gvt. lib.; 5. Inst. lib.; 6. Mfr./Suppl.; 7. Milit. lib.; 8. Musm.; 9. Pub. lib.; 10. Sch. lib.; 11. Sch. of lib. sci.; 12. Spec. lib.; 13. State lib.; 14. (other). **Functions/Activities:** 15. Acq./Col. dev.; 16. Adult srvs.; 17. Admin.; 18. Apprais.; 19. Archit./Bldgs.; 20. Cat./Class.; 21. Chld. srvs.; 22. Circ.; 23. Cons./Pres.; 24. Consult.; 25. Cont. ed.; 26. Educ. lib. sci.; 27. Ext. srvs.; 28. Fund/Grants; 29. Gvt. pubs.; 30. Indx./Abs.; 31. Instr. lib. use; 32. Media srvs.; 33. Micro.; 34. Netwks./Coop.; 35. Persnl.; 36. PR; 37. Publshg.; 38. Recs. mgt.; 39. Ref. srvs.; 40. Repro.; 41. Resrch.; 42. Review.; 43. Secur.; 44. Serials; 45. Spec. col.; 46. Tech. srvs.; 47. Trustees/Bds.; 48. YA srvs.; 49. (other).

31, 37, 39; 55, 95-Msc. **Addr.:** Music Library, 240 Morrison Hall, University of California, Berkeley, CA 94720.

Basch, N. Bernard (Ap. 7, 1934, Boston, MA) Oper. VP, F.W. Faxon Co., 1970–; Fac. Mem., Neast. Univ., 1968–; Dir., Blue Hills Reg. Sch., 1978–. **Educ.:** Washington Univ., 1952–56, BSBA (Bus.); 1960–61, MS (Acct.). **Orgs.:** ASIS: Cncl. (1979–1980); Sic Mgt. (Ch., 1978–80); Conf. and Mtg. Ch. (1976–79); Ch.-Elect, New Eng. Chap. (1981). SLA: Mgt. Div. (Educ. Coord. 1979–80). Assn. for Syst. Mgt.: Bay State Chap. Pres., Div. Dir. (1977–79). New Eng. LA. Assn. for Comp. Machinery. **Pubns.:** "On Line Agency Offers Libraries Uniqus Service," *Com. World* (Ap. 24, 1978); "On Line Data Entry System Handles Subscription," *Info. Syst.* (Dec. 1977); "F.W. Faxon: Automated Subcription Agency", *ASM* (1974). **Addr.:** F. W. Faxon Co., Inc., 15 Southwest Pk., Westwood, MA 02090.

Basche, Sr. Elaine (Mr. 21, 1916, Green Bay, WI) Libn., Media, St. Lawrence Semy., 1980–; Traveling Libn., various elem. schs., 1977–80; Upper Elem., Notre Dame of De Pere, 1975–76; Libn., St. Peter, Beaver Dam, 1973–75. **Educ.:** St. Norbert Coll., 1937–59, BS (Hist.); Post Univ. of WI, 1967–71; WI Elem. and Sec. Lib. and Media, 1975, Unlimited Cert. **Orgs.:** WI Cath. LA. Cath. LA. WI LA. **Activities:** 10; 15, 20, 22 **Addr.:** St. Lawrence Seminary, Mt. Calvary, WI 53057.

Basinski, William L. (Ap. 10, 1943, Cleveland, OH) Dir., Systs., NELINET, Inc., 1979–; Chief, Litigation Systs. Div., US Railway Assn., 1977–79; Sr. Systs. Spec., Gen. Electric Co., 1976–77; Sr. Systs. Anal., Info. Dynamics Corp., 1970–76; Sr. Systs. Anal., Techlops Inc.; Systs. Consult., Info. Dynamics Corp.; Dev. Engin., Reliance Electric Co.; Info. Retrieval Anal., Amer. Socty. for Metals. **Educ.:** John Carroll Univ., 1960–64, BS (Phys.); Univ. of MD, 1966–70, MLS; Boston Univ., 1970–76, MS (Comp. Sci.). **Orgs.:** ASIS. Assn. for Comp. Mach. Amer. Inst. of Phys. **Honors:** Beta Phi Mu, 1970. **Pubns.:** *The Role of the Library of Congress in an Emerging National Network* (1976); jt. auth., *NASA Thesaurus* (1967). **Activities:** 3, 12; 34; 56, 93 **Addr.:** NELINET, Inc., 385 Elliot St., Newton, MA 02164.

Baskett, D. Adeline (Thomas) (Jl. 27, 1940, Benton, TN) Head Libn., Cleveland St. Cmnty. Coll., 1969–; Libn., Polk Cnty. HS, 1962–67; Circ. Libn., Columbia Coll., 1967–69; Ref. Libn., Cleveland St. Cmnty. Coll., 1969–72. **Educ.:** Univ. of TN, 1959–62, BA (Eng.); George Peabody Coll. for Tchrs., 1965–67, MLS. **Orgs.:** Chattanooga Area LA. TN LA: TN St. Lib. Plan Com. (1975–76); Int. Frdm. Com. (1977–81). SELA. ALA: Legis. Netwks. Com. Ladies Golf Assn. Rolling Hills Country Club. Cleveland Dupl. Bridge Club. Pilot Club of Cleveland: Secy. (1978–81). **Activities:** 1; 15, 17, 32, 39; 55, 74, 75 **Addr.:** Box 3570, Cleveland State Community College, Cleveland, TN 37311.

Basler, Beatrice Kovacs (Je. 2, 1945, Zeekirchen, Austria) Col. Dev. Libn., Med. Coll. of GA, 1978–; Cat., Asst. Acq. Libn., Augusta Reg. Lib., 1974–78; Libn., Nassau Acad. of Med., 1967–70. **Educ.:** Syracuse Univ., 1962–66, BA (Eng.); Rutgers Univ., 1966–67, MLS; Med. LA Cert., 1977. **Orgs.:** Med. LA: Med. Soctys. Libs. (Secy. 1967–69). GA LA: Spec. Libs. Sect., (VCh. 1977–79). S. East. LA. Med. LA: South. Reg. Grp. GA Hlth. Sci. LA. Augusta Archlg. Socty. **Pubns.:** *Health Sciences Librarianship: an annotated bibliography* (1977). Ed. "Secys. Minutes", *Bltn. of the Med. LA* (1967–69). **Activities:** 1, 12; 15, 20, 39; 58, 80 **Addr.:** Medical College of Georgia, Library, Augusta, GA 30912.

Basler, Thomas G. (Mr. 8, 1940, Cleveland, OH) Dir. of Libs., Prof., Med. Col. of GA, 1972–; Libn., NY Acad. of Med., 1970–72; Libn., Amer. Musm. of Natl. Hist., 1968–70; Lib., Inst. of Marine Sci., 1966–68. **Educ.:** Univ. of Miami, 1958–62, BEd (Scis.); FL State Univ., 1963–64, MLS; Laurence Univ., (CA), 1974–77, PhD, (Higher Ed.); Emory Univ. Internship in Med. Libnshp., 1964–65. **Orgs.:** Med. LA, South. Reg. Gp: Ch. (1975–76). SLA: Bio. Sci. Div., Ch. (1974–75). Augusta Area Com. for AHL. Info. Rsrcs. ACRL. various other orgs. Med. Archvsts. of NY. Amer. Assn. of State & Local Hist. Amer. Mgt. Assn. Natl. Educ. Assn. **Pubns.:** *Medical School Library Directorship* (1977); Jt. Auth., *Health Sciences Librarianship* (1977); H. Auth., "Health Sciences Librarianship in Transition" *Cath. Lib. World* (Nv 1976); Jt. Auth., "Aspects of the Modern Health Sciences Library" *The Tattler* (N/D 1975); "The American Museum of American History Library" *Bookmark* (Je 1969). **Activities:** 1, 12; 17, 19, 35; 58, 80, 91 **Addr.:** Medical College of GA, Augusta, GA 30912.

Bassett, Betty A. (My. 26, 1943, Beaver Falls, PA) Mgr., Tech. Info. Ctr., Xerox Resrch. Ctr. of Can., 1974–, Tech. Libn., 1970–74; Supvsg. Libn., Gates-Chili Sch. Dist., 1969–70; Libn., Berkshire Sch. Dist., 1966–69. **Educ.:** Grove City Coll., 1961–65, BA (Hist.); Case West. Rsv. Univ., 1965–66, MSLS. **Orgs.:** SLA: Toronto Chap., Pres. (1981–82), Pres.-Elect (1980–81), Dir. (1979–80). Can. Assn. Info. Sci. Can. LA. Sheridan Park Assn.: Lib. and Info. Sci. Com. (Ch., 1977–79), Un. List of Serials (Ed., 1976). Sheridan Coll.: Lib. Techqs. Prog. Adv. Com. (1979–82). **Pubns.:** "Sheridan Park Association: A Model in Sharing Resources," *Sharing Resrcs. - Sharing Costs: Procs. of the 7th Anl. Can. Conf. on Info. Sci.* (1979); various presentations on spec. libs. **Activities:** 12; 17; 60, 64, 88 **Addr.:** Xerox Research Centre of Canada, 2480 Dunwin Dr., Mississauga, ON L5L 1J9 Canada.

Bassett, Robert Julian (Jl. 22, 1929, Coshocton, OH) Head, Ref. and Docums., Univ. of TN, Knoxville, 1972–, Head, Undergrad. Lib., 1969–72; Asst. Acq. Libn., 1966–69; Order Libn., TN Tech. Univ., 1964–66. **Educ.:** Murray State Univ., 1947–51, BA (Hist.); Univ. of MI, 1955–56, MALS. **Orgs.:** ALA. TN LA. Southeastern LA. **Honors:** Beta Phi Mu, 1956; Kappa Delta Pi, 1950. **Pubns.:** "William Herman Jesse," *Dictionary of Amer. Lib. Biog.* (1978). **Activities:** 1; 15, 33, 39; 57 **Addr.:** 7905 Livingston Dr., Knoxville, TN 37919.

Bassett, Thomas Day Seymour (D. 21, 1913, Burlington, VT) Retired, 1981–; Ed., Com. for a New Eng. Bibl., Inc., 1978–81; Univ. Archvst., Cur., Wilbur Col., Univ. of VT, 1958–77, Assoc. Prof., Hist., 1958–65; Visit. Lectr., Univ. of CA, Riverside, 1957–58; Assoc. Prof., Hist., Earlham Coll., 1948–57; Resrch. Assoc., Prog. of Std. in Amer. Cvlztn., Princeton Univ., 1946–48. **Educ.:** Yale Univ., 1931–35, AB (Hist.); grad. std. at Univ. of CA, Berkeley, Harvard Univ.; 1952, PhD (Hist.). **Orgs.:** SAA: Coll. and Univ. Arch. Com. New Eng. Archvsts.: Exec. Com. (1972–77). VT LA: Exec. Com. (1965). Com. for a New Eng. Bibl.: Dir. (1969–78). VT Hist. Socty. Amer. Hist. Assn. Frnds. Hist. Socty. (London). Frnds. Hist. Assn.: Resrch. Com. Org. of Amer. Histns. Various other orgs. **Honors:** Phi Beta Kappa, 1935; Soc. Sci. Resrch. Cncl., Fac. Awd., 1952. **Pubns.:** Ed., *Vermont: A Bibliography of Its History* (1981); jt. ed., *New Hampshire: a Bibliography of Its History* (1979); *Outsiders Inside Vermont: Three Centuries of Visitors' Viewpoints On the Green Mountain State* (1976); *A History of the Vermont Geological Surveys and State Geologists* (1976); "Burlington in History," Sunday clmn. *Burlington Free Press* (S. 5, 1976–Jl. 8, 1979); various articles. **Activities:** 1, 2; 15, 41, 45; 55, 57, 92 **Addr.:** 11 Bilodeau Pkwy., Burlington, VT 05401.

Bassnett, Peter J. (N. 16, 1933, Sutton Coldfield, Warwickshire, England) Dir. of Libs., Scarborough Pub. Lib., 1975–; Dir. of Syst. & Mgt. Srvs., N. York Pub. Lib., 1972–75; Admin. Asst. to the Dir., Calgary Pub. Lib., 1970–72, Head, Bus., Sci. & Tech. Dept., 1966–70. **Educ.:** Lib. Assn. (UK), 1962–64, ALA, (Libnshp.), 1966–71, FLA. **Orgs.:** ON Lib. Assn. Can. LA: Resrch. & Dev. Com. (1971–75). Lib. Assn. (UK). LA of AB: Past Pres. (1969–70). Private Libs. Assn. **Pubns.:** *Spatial and Administrative Relationships in Large Public Libraries* (1970); "Library Research in Canada", *Can. Lib. Jnl.* (Jl.–Ag. 1972); "Librarian-Manager or Professional Manager", *Lib. Mgt.* (1969). **Activities:** 9; 17, 19, 47; 57, 59, 91 **Addr.:** Scarborough Public Library, Administration Centre, 1076 Ellesmere Rd., Scarborough, ON M1P 4P4 Canada.

Batchelder, Joyce E. (Ja. 24, 1929, Decatur, IL) Elem. Sch. Libn., Dist. Lib. Coord., Katonah-Lewisboro Sch. Dist., 1963–. **Educ.:** James Millikin Univ., 1946–49, AB; Columbia Univ., 1962–63, MS (LS). **Orgs.:** ALA: Filmstp. Eval. Com. (1977–79); Adv. Com. to *Abr. Readrs. Guide* (1979). NY State LA. Chld. Lit. Assn. Sch. Libns. of S.E. NY. **Honors:** Beta Phi Mu, 1963; Outstand. Elem. Tchrs. of Amer., 1972. **Activities:** 10; 17, 21, 32 **Addr.:** R.F.D. 1, 85 Allison Rd., Katonah, NY 10536.

Batchelder, Robert Nelson (Ag. 1, 1943, Boston, MA) Map and Air Photo Libn., Univ. of Calgary, 1972–; Map Libn., Dalhousie Univ., 1968–72. **Educ.:** McMaster Univ., 1963–71, BA (Hist. and Relig.). **Orgs.:** Assn. of Can. Map Libs.: Bltn. Ed., (1978–). SLA: Geo. and Map Div. West. Assn. of Map Libns. Can. Cartographic Assn. **Pubns.:** "Energy and cartography" (Exhibition Cat.), *Assn. of Can. Map* Libs. Bltn. (Jn. 1978). **Activities:** 1, 12; 15, 20, 39; 65, 70, 82 **Addr.:** Map and Air Photo Division, University of Calgary Library, Calgary, AB T2N 1N4 Canada.

Bates, Barbara S. (Ap. 28, 1919, Philadelphia, PA) Chld. Bk. Ed., The Westminster Press, 1967–; Freelnc. Writer, Lectr., 1946–67, Ed., Chld. Mags., 1941–46. **Educ.:** Wellesley Coll., 1936–40, BA (Eng. Lit.). **Orgs.:** ALA. Philadelphia Booksellers Assn.: Bd. of Dirs. (1977–81); Pres. (1979). Philadelphia Chld. Readg. RT: Strg. Com. (1972–). Chld. Bk. Cncl.: Bd. of Dirs. (1978–80). PA LA. Various other orgs. **Pubns.:** "Denominational Periodicals: The Invisible Literature," *Phaedrus* (Spr.–Sum. 1980); "Hard Questions About Easy Books," *High/Low Rpt.* (D. 1979); "Identifying High Interest/Low Reading Level Books," *Sch. Lib. Jnl.* (N. 1977); "Photography as Art in Children's Books," *Sch. Lib. Jnl.* (My. 1975); "The Young Adult Editor and Book Selection," *Cath. LA Std. in Libnshp. No. 3* (1979). **Activities:** 14-Publshr.; 21, 37, 48; 55, 89 **Addr.:** CBE 925 Chestnut St., Philadelphia, PA 19107.

Bates, Henry E. (D. 2, 1932, Quincy, MA) City Libn., Milwaukee Pub. Lib., 1975–; Deputy City Libn., DC Pub. Lib., 1973–75; Asst. Chief Libn., Chicago Pub. Lib., 1970–73; Head Libn., Newton Free Lib., 1965–70; Head Libn., Quincy Pub. Lib., 1962–65. **Educ.:** Boston Univ., 1956–60, BA (Hist.); Simmons Coll., 1960–62, MLS. **Orgs.:** WI Lib. Cnsrtm.: Ch. (1980–81). ALA: PLA, Natl. Conf. Plng. Com. (1980–83). Goals 2000-Milwaukee: Exec. Bd. (1980–). Goethe Hse. Milwaukee: Bd. (1980–). **Pubns.:** "Milwaukee Public Library, 1942–1980: A Pioneer in Data Processing," *Pub. Lib. Qtly.* (Sum. 1980); "Varied Opinion," *Wilson Lib. Bltn.* (Mr. 1981). **Activities:** 9; 17, 34 **Addr.:** 814 W. Wisconsin Ave., Milwaukee, WI 53233.

Bates, Marcia J. (Jl. 30, 1942, Terre Haute, IN) Assoc. Prof., Grad. Sch. of Lib. and Info. Sci., UCLA, 1981–; Assoc. Prof., Univ. WA, Sch. of Libnshp., 1980–81, Asst. Prof., 1976–80; Asst. Prof., Univ. of MD, Coll. of Lib. and Info. Srvs., 1972–76; Peace Corps Volun., Thailand, 1963–65. **Educ.:** Pomona Coll., 1959–63, BA (Germ.); Univ. of CA, 1966–67, MLS; 1967–72, PhD (Libnshp.) **Orgs.:** ASIS: Spec. Interest Grp. Cncl. (1973–74). Internl. Comm. Assn.; Amer. Assn. for Advnc. Sci. **Honors:** Phi Beta Kappa, 1963. **Pubns.:** Co–Ed., *Library and Information Service Needs of the Nation: Proceedings of a Conference on the Needs of Occupational, Ethnic, and Other Groups in the U.S.* (1974); "Idea Tactics," *ASIS Jnl.* (Sept. 1979); "Information Search Tactics," *ASIS Jnl.* (July 1979); "System Meets User: Problems in Matching Subject Search Terms," *Info. Prcs. and Mgt.* (vol. 13, no. 6); "Factors Affecting Subject Catalog Search Success," *ASIS Jnl.* (May 1977); "Rigorous Systematic Bibliography," *RQ* (Fall 1976). **Activities:** 11; 26, 41; 75, 91, 95-user std. **Addr.:** Graduate School of Library and Information Science, University of California at Los Angeles, Los Angeles, CA 90024.

Bates, Mary L. (Ag. 28, 1926, Ordway, CO) Dir. of Lib. Srvs., Blue Mountain Cmnty. Coll., 1965–; Visit. Prof., University of Oregon, Summers 1971–73. **Educ.:** Linfield Coll., 1944–48, BA (Msc.); Univ. of WA, 1964–68, MLS. **Orgs.:** ALA. Pac. Northwest LA: Pres. (1977–78). OR LA: Pres. (1973–74). OR Cmnty. Coll. LA: Pres. (1969–70). various other organizations and ofcs. Pendleton Woman's Club: Pres. (1971–72). OR Fed. of Women's Clubs: Bd. (1971–72). Amer. Assoc. of Univ. Women: Pendleton Branch (Pres., 1971–72). OR State Div. (various positions, 1972–75). **Honors:** Pendleton Cham. of Cmrce., First Woman Citizen, 1971; Gvr.'s Comsn. for Women, 1975–78. **Pubns.:** Locally produced AV Bibl. Inst. kits. **Activities:** 1; 17, 24, 26, 34; 74, 78 **Addr.:** Box 1091, Pendleton, OR 97801.

Bates, Peter J. (D. 22, 1940, Maindenhead, Berks, Eng) Info. Spec., Syncrude Can. Ltd., 1972–; Libn., Resrch. Cncl. of AB, 1968–72; Lib. Asst., Univ. of SK, 1967–68; Asst. Lib., Assoc. Lead MFRS, 1964–67. **Educ.:** London Univ. 1960–64, BSc. (Geol.). **Orgs.:** AB Inf. Retrieval Assn: Dir. (1975–). ASIS: W. Can. Chap. Inst. Info Sci, London. **Pubns.:** "Argon Plasma Sections: bibliography", *ICP Information Newsletter* (1976). **Activities:** 12; 15, 30, 39; 60, 86 **Addr.:** Syncrude Canada Ltd, Research Department Library, P.O. Box 5790, Edmonton, AB T6C 4G3 Canada.

Batliner, Doris J. (Mr. 24, 1929, Louisville, KY) Chief Libn., Courier-Journal & Louisville Times, 1974–; Libn., Chemetron Corp., 1958–74; Chem., DuPont & Co., 1952–58. **Educ.:** Nazareth (Now Spalding) Coll., 1947–51, BA (Chem.), 1954–58, MS (LS). **Orgs.:** SLA. KY LA. KY Opera Assn. **Honors:** Amos Tuck Sch. of Bus. Admin., Co-recipient, 1978 Media Awards Econ. Understanding; Libn. (Spec.) of Yr., KY LA, 1971. **Pubns.:** "Hydrogenation & Dehydrogenation," *Indust. & Engin. Chem.* (1962); "Hydrogenation and Dehydrogenation," *Indus. & Engin. Chem.* (1963). **Activities:** 14-Newspaper; 17, 41 **Addr.:** Courier-Journal & Louisville Times Library, 525 W. Broadway, Louisville, KY 40202.

Batson, Darrell L. (N. 24, 1951, Las Vegas, NV) Admin., Metro Jail Lib., 1980–; Outrch. Libn., Clark Cnty. Lib. Dist., 1978–80; Ref. Libn., Elko Cnty. Lib., 1977–78. **Educ.:** Dixie Jr. Coll., 1969–71, AS (Hist.); Brigham Young Univ., 1973–75, BA (Hist.), 1975–76, MLS. **Orgs.:** ALA: ASCLA/Lib. Srv. to Prisoners Sect., Nom. Com. (1981–82). Mt. Plains LA. NV LA: Sect. on Underserved Popltns. (Ch., 1981); Pub. LA of NV/NV LA of Trustees (Ch., 1980); N.E. Dist. (Pres., 1978); Persnl. Dev. Com. (1978); ILL Com. (Ch., 1978). **Addr.:** Metro Jail Library, LVMPD Detention Facility, 200 E. Carson Ave., Las Vegas, NV 89101.

Batt, Fred (My. 7, 1946, New Brunswick, NJ) Head of Ref. Srvs., Cleveland State Univ. 1980–; Soc. and Bhvl. Sci. Libn., Asst. Prof., Mansfield St. Coll., 1976–80; Educ. and Psy. Ref. Bibl., Univ. of Cincinnati, 1974–76; Asst. Educ. and Psy. Instr., East. Michigan Univ., 1972–74. **Educ.:** Rutgers Univ., 1964–68, BA (Psy.); Indiana Univ., 1968–71; 1972–72, MLS; U.S. Census Bureau, Online Training, 1979, Cert; ARL-OMS Lib. Mgt. Skills Inst., 1981. **Orgs.:** ALA: LRRT/Chap. Dev. Subcom. (1978). AAUP. ALAO. **Pubns.:** "Education is Illogical," *Improving Coll. & Univ. Tchg.* (Sum. 1977); Reviews. Short stories in lit. jnls. (1973–); "Folly of Book Reviews," ACRL, Minneapolis. **Activities:** 1; 29, 31, 39; 63, 92 **Addr.:** Head of Ref. Srvs., Main Library, Cleveland State University, Cleveland, OH 44115.

Battey, Jean D. (Mr. 7, 1926, Chicago, IL) Sch. Lib./Media Coord., VT Dept. of Educ., 1975–; Lib./Media Dir., Shelburne Vlg. Sch., 1974–75; Lib./Media Dir., E. Montpelier Elem. Sch., 1968–74. **Educ.:** Middlebury Coll., 1943–47, BA (Amer. Lit.); Dartmouth Coll., 1971–73, MALS (Hum.). **Orgs.:** VT Educ. Media Assn.: Pres. (1970–71). New Eng. Educ. Media Assn.: Exec. Bd. (1975–). ALA: AASL, Bylaws Com. (Ch., 1981–82). VT LA: Prog. Co-Ch. (1981–82). Delta Kappa Gamma; Sigma

Special Subjects/Services: 50. Adult educ.; 51. Advert./Mktg.; 52. Aerosp.; 53. Agric.; 54. Area std.; 55. Arts/Hum.; 56. Autom.; 57. Bibl./Prtg.; 58. Bio. sci.; 59. Bus./Fin.; 60. Chem.; 61. Copyrt.; 62. Documtn.; 63. Educ.; 64. Engin.; 65. Env.; 66. Eth. grps.; 67. Film; 68. Food/Nutr.; 69. Geneal.; 70. Geo.; 71. Geol.; 72. Handcpd.; 73. Hist.; 74. Int. frdm.; 75. Info. sci.; 76. Insr.; 77. Law; 78. Legis.; 79. Math./Comp. sci.; 80. Med.; 81. Metals; 82. Nat. resrcs.; 83. Newsp.; 84. Nuc. sci.; 85. Oral hist.; 86. Petr./Energy; 87. Pharm.; 88. Phys./Astr./Math.; 89. Readg.; 90. Relig.; 91. Sci./Tech.; 92. Soc. sci.; 93. Telecom.; 94. Transp.; 95. (other).

Who's Who in Library and Information Services

Kappa. **Pubns.:** "From Pooh's End," *VT Educ. Media Assn. News.* **Activities:** 10, 13; 17, 24, 46; 63, 74, 89 **Addr.:** Vermont Dept. of Education, Montpelier, VT 05602.

Battin, Patricia M. (Je. 2, 1929, Gettysburg, PA) VP, Univ. Libn., Columbia Univ., 1978–; Dir., Lib. Srvs. Grp., 1974–78; Asst. Dir., Pub. Srvs., SUNY, Binghamton, 1969–74; Asst. to Dir. of Libs., 1968–69. **Educ.:** Swarthmore Coll., 1947–51, BA (Eng.); Syracuse Univ., 1966–67, MSLS. **Orgs.:** ALA. ARL: Task Frc. on Netwk. Dev. (1979–). Resrch. Libs. Grp. Bd. of Gvrs. Grolier Clb. **Honors:** Phi Beta Kappa, 1951; Beta Phi Mu, 1967. **Pubns.:** "The Library of the Future *Has* Books," *Columbia Clmns.* (N. 1978); "The Research Library in the Network Environment," *Jnl. of Acad. Libnshp.* **Activities:** 1; 17, 34 **Addr.:** Columbia University Libraries, 535 West 114th St., New York, NY 10027.

Batton, Delma-Jane (Heck) (D. 10, 1915, Tampa, FL) Dir., Dover Pub. Lib., 1968–; Actg. State Libn., DE State Lib. Comsn., 1964–67; Fld. Consult., 1961–64. **Educ.:** Coll. of William & Mary, 1937–38; Univ. of IL, 1948–50, BLS; 1950–51, grad. crs. (LS); Syracuse Univ. **Orgs.:** DE LA: Secy.; Pres.; Pub. Lib. Div. (Pres.). **Pubns.:** Ed., *DE LA Bltn.* **Activities:** 9, 13; 17, 21, 24; 69, 72, 89 **Addr.:** Dover Public Library, 45 S. State St., Dover, DE 19901.

Batts, Nathalie C. (N. 3, 1918, Baltimore, MD) Serials Cat., Columbia Univ. Libs., 1962–; Ref. Libn., Sch. of Bus. Lib., 1955–62; Asst. Ref. Libn., 1951–55; Order Libn., Mount Holyoke Coll. Lib., 1949–51; First Asst., Cir., 1945–49; **Educ.:** Coll. of Notre Dame of MD, 1940, AB (Hist., Educ.); Columbia Univ., 1946, BS (LS); Mount Holyoke Coll., 1951, MA (Econ); Columbia Univ., 1966, MS with honors (LS). **Orgs.:** ALA. NY Tech. Srvs. Libns.: Secy./Treas. (1968–69). Amer. Natl. Stan. Inst.: Com. Z39/Subcom. Bibl. Ref. (1967–70). ASIS: NY Chap., Treas. (1971–73). Beta Phi Mu: Nu Chap., Treas. (1967–68), VP (1968–69), Pres. (1969–70); Columbia Univ., Sch. of LS, Alum. Assn.: Bd. of Dir. (1972–); Fac. House, Columbia Univ.: Corres. Secy. (1970–72); Amer. Econ. Assn.; Other orgs. **Honors:** Beta Phi Mu, 1966. **Pubns.:** Jt. Ed., *The Dewey Decimal Classification: Outlines and Papers* (1968); Cmplr., *Organization Charts* (1st, 2nd ed.) (1953, 1961); Ed., *Library Service News* (1972–). **Activities:** 1; 20, 44, 46; 57, 75, 92 **Addr.:** Mrs. Walter Batts, 21 Claremont Avenue, New York, NY 10027.

Batty, Charles David (Jl. 8, 1932, Tynemouth, Northumberland, England) VP, Alpha Omega Grp Inc., 1981–. Visit. Prof., Coll. of Lib. and Info. Srvs., Univ. of MD, 1976–81; Prof., Grad. Sch. of Lib. Sci., McGill Univ., 1971–76; Head, Dept. of Info. Retrieval Studies, Coll. of Libnshp., Wales, 1964–71; Lect., Sch. of Libnshp., Birmingham, England, 1962–64. **Educ.:** Univ. of Durham, England, 1951–54, BA (Msc., Eng., Ancient Hist.); Birmingham Sch. of Libnshp., 1954–55, ALA (Libshp); 1963, FLA (Libshp). **Orgs.:** Lib. Assn. (UK): Vice-Chm., Cat. & Indexing Grp (1964–71). PQ LA: Pres. 1973–74). ASIS: Councillor-at-Large (1974–77). **Pubns.:** *Introduction to the Dewey Decimal Classification (19th ed)* (1981); Ed., *Knowledge and Its Organization* (1975); *Introduction to Colon Classification* (1966); "The Universal Decimal Classification," *Encyc. of Lib. & Info. Sci.* (1981); "The Sheaf Catalog," ELIS (1979). "Dewey Abroad," *Lib. of Congs. Quarterly Jnl.* (1976); *"SIMULE:* An Experiment in Teaching Information Storage and Retrieval", Jnl. of Educ. for Libnshp. (1977). **Activities:** 20, 25, 30; 56, 62, 75 **Addr.:** 11608 Gilsan St., Silver Spring, MD 20902.

Bauer, Caroline Feller (My. 12, 1935, Washington, DC) Consult., Educ. Consult. Assoc., 1979–; Assoc. Prof., Univ. of OR, 1966–79; Lib., CO Rocky Mt. Sch., 1963; Chlds. Libn., NY Pub. Lib., 1960–63. **Educ.:** Sarah Lawrence Coll., 1957, BA; Columbia Univ., 1958, MLS; Univ. of OR, 1971, PhD. **Orgs.:** ALA: ALSC/Notable Chlds. Bks. Com. (Ch., 1980). Socty. of Amer. Magicians. Intl. Brotherhood of Magicians. Puppeteers of Amer. **Honors:** Univ. of OR, Ersted Awd. for Disting. Tchng., 1968. **Pubns.:** *Handbook for Storytellers* (1977); Regular contrib., *Cricket Magazine;* "Creative Storytelling" (Vid.) (1978); "Humor in Childrens Literature" (audio cassette), Children's Bk. Cncl. (1976); *This Way to Books* (1981). **Activities:** 21, 36; 63, 89, 95-Storytelling. **Addr.:** 6535 SW Chelsea, Portland, OR 97223.

Bauer, Charles K. (N. 23, 1913, Vienna, Austria) Mgr., Tech. Info. Dept., Lockheed-GA Co., 1955–; Lectr., Sch. of Lib. and Info. Srvs., Atlanta Univ., 1967–80; Asst. Chief, Tech. Srvs. Branch, U.S. Atomic Energy Comsn., 1952–55; Chief Res. Info. Engin., Guided Missle Proj., Gen. Electric Co., 1945–52. **Educ.:** Polytechnicum, Vienna, Austria, 1930–33, BS (Engin.); Cath. Univ. of Amer., 1952–55 Postgrad. in LS. **Orgs.:** ASIS: Chrt. Mem. SLA: Engin. Div. (Ch., 1952–53); Sci.-Tech. Div. (Ch., 1959–60); Fin. Com., Bd. of Dirs. (Ch., 1968–70); Chap. Pres. (1977–78). GA LA: Gvr.'s Conf. on GA Libs. and Info. Srvs., Strg. Com. (1976–79). Natl. Mgt. Assn.: Chap. VP (1972–74). Amer. Inst. of Aeronautics and Astronautics: Pubns. Com. (1978–). **Honors:** Natl. Secur. Indus. Assn., Cert. of Merit, 1968; Natl. Mgt. Assn., Medal of Valor, 1977; Natl. Mgt. Assn., Lockheed-Man-of-the-Yr., 1967. **Pubns.:** "Managing Management," *Spec. Libs.* (Ap. 1980); "Public Relations: Another Link in the Success of Information Management," *Special Librarianship–A New Reader* (1980); "What's In A Statistic," *Spec. Libs.* (O. 1966); "Computerized Information System at the Lockheed-Georgia Company," *HI Jnl.* (Je. 1967); "Automation and the Lessons We Have Learned," *Spec. Libs.* (F. 1972); various presentations, articles. **Activities:** 12; 17, 49-Tchg.; 52, 59, 64 **Addr.:** 1145 Tamworth Dr., N.E., Atlanta, GA 30328.

Bauer, Frederick E., Jr. (Jl. 12, 1922, Union City, NJ) Assoc. Libn., Amer. Antiq. Socty., 1973–, Head, Tech. Srvs., 1970–73; Libn., Mt. Hermon Sch., 1968–70, Ch., Dept. of Hist., 1960–70. **Educ.:** Princeton Univ., 1939–43, AB (Econ.); Columbia Univ., 1946–47, MA (Persnl. Admin.), 1967–68, MLS (Libnshp.). **Orgs.:** ALA. New Eng. LA. Resrch. Libs. Grp.: Prsrvn. Com. Worcester Area Coop. Libs. N.E. Docum. Cons. Ctr.: Adv. Com. Amer. Antiq. Socty. MA Hist. Socty. Holden Hist. Socty.: Pres. (1975–79). **Pubns.:** "Random Notes on the Preservation of Children's Books," *Socty. and Chld. Lit.* (1978); "The American Antiquarian Society and Children's Literature," *Phaedrus* (Spr. 1976); "American Antiquarian Society," *CT Nutmegger* (S. 1975); jt. auth., *Liberty and Power in the Making of the Constitution* (1963); jt. auth., *Democracy in the Age of Jackson* (1965). **Activities:** 2, 12; 17, 23, 45; 55, 57, 73 **Addr.:** Avery Hts. Dr., Holden, MA 01520.

Baughman, James C. (N. 13, 1941, Oil City, PA) Assoc. Prof., Grad. Sch. of Lib. and Info. Sci., Simmons Coll., 1971–; Supvsr., Lib. Dev., MA State Dept. of Educ., 1966–68; Libn., Weymouth, MA, 1965–66; Libn., Phillipsburg, NJ, 1963–65. **Educ.:** Clarion State Coll., 1959–63, BS (Eng.); Drexel Univ., 1964–67, MS (LS); Case West. Rsv., 1968–70, MA, PhD. **Orgs.:** ALA: ACRL. **Honors:** ALA, Resrch. Competition Awd., 1976; Beta Phi Mu, 1967. **Pubns.:** "A Structural Analysis of the Literature of Sociology," *Lib. Qtly.* (O. 1974); "National Survival, Information, and the Student of Society," *Lib. Jnl.* (S. 1979); "The Invisible Director: The Emerging Metropolitan Library Executive," *Lib. Jnl.* (Je. 1980). **Activities:** 1, 10; 17, 24; 63, 65, 75 **Addr.:** Graduate School of Library and Information Science, Simmons College, 300 The Fenway, Boston, MA 02115.

Baum, Willa K. (O 4, 1929, Chicago, IL) Dept. Head Reg. Oral Hist. Ofc., Bancroft Lib. Univ. of CA-Berkely, 1954–. **Educ.:** Whittier Coll., 1949, BA, (Hist.); Mills Coll., 1950, MA (Hist.); Univ. of CA-Berkely, 1954, Grad. Work. **Orgs.:** Oral Hist. Assn: Cncl (1967–69). SAA. Socty of CA Arch. West. Hist. Assn. **Pubns.:** *Transcribing and Editing Oral History.* (1977); *Oral History for the Local Historical Society.* (1969); "Therapeutic Value of Oral History", *Jrnl of Aging and Human Dev.,* (1979); "The Expanding Role of the Librarian in Oral History," LA State Univ. *Libr. Lect.* (1978); "The Library as Guardian of Oral History Materials" *Cath. Lib. World,* (1975); "A Bibliography on Oral History for the Local Historical Society", *Hist. News,* (1976); various articles, reviews. **Activities:** 1; 28, 41; 85, 92 **Addr.:** Regional Oral History Ofc., 486 The Bancroft Library, University of California, Berkeley, CA 94720.

Bauman, William A. (N. 23, 1923, New York, NY) VP, Med. Affairs, Danbury Hosp., 1979–; Sr. VP, Grp. Hlth. Incorp., 1974–79; Dir., Med. Admin. Data Prcs., Presby. Hosp., New York City, 1966–74, Chief, Pediatric Clinics, 1954–66. **Educ.:** Harvard Univ., 1942–43 (Chem.); Columbia Univ., 1944–47, MD (Med.); 1960–63, MS equivalent (Biostats.). **Orgs.:** Assn. for Comp. Mach. Socty. of Comp. Med.: Trustee (1973–); Dir. (1973–). ASIS. Amer. Acad. of Pediatrics. **Honors:** NY Acad. of Med., Fellow, 1969. **Pubns.:** *Cystic Fibrosis a study of cost and care of 265 afflicted children* (1965); Chap. in *Use of Computers* (1978); "Chest Radiography of Prematures," *Pediatrics* (1958); "Is Audit Relevent to Medical Wards at a Teachers Hospital," *Arch. Int. Med.* (1976). **Activities:** 14; 17, 47; 56, 80 **Addr.:** Danbury Hospital, 24 Hospital Ave., Danbury, CT 06810.

Baumann, Charles Henry (O. 24, 1926, Brooklyn, NY) Univ. Libn., East. WA Univ., 1969–; Acq. Lib., Asst. Dir., Univ. of WY, 1954–69; Branch Libn., Niagara Falls Pub. Lib., 1953–54; Asst. Ref. Libn., Champlain Coll., SUNY, 1952–53. **Educ.:** WA Univ., St. Louis, MO, 1947–51, BS (Educ., Math.); Pratt Inst., 1951–52, MLS; Univ. of IL, 1962–69, PhD (LS). **Orgs.:** ALA: RTSD, Reprodct. of Lib. Mtrls. (1974–77); ACRL, Pubns. in Libnshp., Ed. Bd. (1976–). Frdm. to Read Fndn.: Bd. of Dirs. (1975–78). WY LA: Pres.-Elect (1968–69). Untd. Way of Spokane Cnty.: Bd. of Dirs. (1974–80). Spokane Reg. Agency on Aging: Admin. Panel (Ch., 1975–77). Spokane Meml. Educ. Fund: Bd. of Trustees (Ch., 1979–). **Honors:** Beta Phi Mu, 1969; Phi Delta Kappa, 1971. **Pubns.:** *Influence of Angus Snead Macdonald and the Snead Book Stack on Modern Library Architecture* (1972); "Wyoming Goes Modular," *Lib. Jnl.* (D. 15, 1959); jt. auth., "Coping With the Information Explosion: Electronic Data Bases," *E. WA Univ. Bus. Jnl.* (Win. 1980); "Angus Snead Macdonald," *Dictionary of American Library Biography* (1978). **Activities:** 1; 15, 17, 19; 74, 75 **Addr.:** Eastern Washington University Library, Cheney, WA 99004.

Baumann, Roland M. (Mr 7, 1942, Sheboygan, WI) Chief, Div. of Arc. & Mss., PA Histo. and Musm. Cosm., 1977–; Arch. Consult., Co-Proj. Dir., 1975–77; Asst. Prof. of Hist., Bowling Green State Univ., 1970–73; Instr. of Hist., Monmouth (IL) Coll., 1966–67. **Educ.:** Univ. of WI-Madison, 1960–64, BSE (Hist.); North. IL Univ., 1964–66, MA (Hist.); PA State Univ., 1967–70, PhD (Hist.); Amer. Univ., 1976, Cert, Arch. Admin.; Univ. of SC, 1976, Cert, Hist. Docum. **Orgs.:** SAA. Mid-Atl. Reg. Arch. Conf. Reg. Econ. Hist. Ctr. State Lib. of PA, Harrisburg: Adv. Com. (1979–); Luth. Church: Adv. Com. on Arch. (1978–); PA Hist. Assn.: Cncl., Ed. Bd. (1977–); State Lib. of PA: Adv. Bd. (1977–80). **Honors:** Phi Alpha Theta, 1966; Phi Kappa Phi, 1969. **Pubns.:** *George Stevenson (1718–1783),* (1978); "Dr. Shenk's Missing Series of the Published Pennsylvania Archives", *PA Mag. of Hist. & Biog.* (1979); Ed., *A Manual of Archival Techniques* (1978); *PA State Arch. Rec. Guide* (1978); Various Articles. **Addr.:** Division of Archives & Manuscripts, P.O. Box 1026, Harrisburg, PA 17120.

Baumann, Susan H. (Mr. 25, 1948, Granby, PQ, Can) Exec. Asst. 1980–; Ed., *Informart,* 1978–1980; Ref. Libn., Imperial Oil Ltd., 1975–78; Ref. Libn., Bus. Div., Metro Toronto Lib. Bd., 1971–75; Halifax City Reg. Lib., 1970–71. **Educ.:** Bishop's Univ., 1965–69, BA (Phil.); Univ. of Toronto, 1969–70, BLS. **Orgs.:** Can. LA. Can. Assn. for Info. Sci. SLA. **Pubns.:** *Bus. and Gvt. News* (Index and Abs.) (1979–). **Activities:** 6, 12; 30, 37, 39; 56, 59, 83 **Addr.:** Infomart, 122 St. Patrick St., 3rd Floor, Toronto, ON M5T 2X8 Canada.

Baumruk, Robert (F 23, 1930, Chicago, IL) Chief, Soc. Sci. and Hist. Div., Chicago Pub. Lib., 1975–; Chief, Soc. Sci. and Bus. Dept., 1967–74; Head, Pub. Dept., 1964–67; Head, Newsp. Srvs., 1959–64. **Educ.:** Morton Jr. Coll., 1948–50, BEd; Univ. of Chicago, 1950–56, AM (LS). **Orgs.:** SLA: IL Chap., Pres. (1975–76); Soc. Sci. Div., Ch. (1978–79). ALA. Chicago Lib. Club: Pres. (1968–69). IL Lib. Assn. Czechoslovak Socty of America; Dobrovsky Club: VP (1980), Pres. (1981). **Activities:** 9, 12; 16, 39; 54, 63, 92 **Addr.:** Social Sciences and History Division, The Chicago Public Library, 425 N. Michigan Ave., Chicago, IL 60611.

Bauner, Ruth E. (S. 21, 1928, Quincy, IL) Educ., Psy. Libn., Assc. Prof., Curric., Instr. and Media, South. IL Univ., 1965–; Asst. Educ. Libn., 1956–64; Circ. Dept. Asst., Univ. of IL, 1954–55; Tchr., Libn., Sandwich Township HS, 1950–54. **Educ.:** West. IL Univ., 1946–50, BS (Eng.); Univ. of IL, 1954–56, MS (LS); South. IL Univ., 1974–78, PhD, (Educ.); 1970–74, SEd, (Admn.) **Honors:** Beta Phi Mu. **Pubns.:** Contrib. Auth., *The Teacher's Library* (1966), *The Teacher's Library* (rev. ed.) (1968); "The Dewey School Photographs," *I CarbS* (Spr./Sum. 1978); "The Instructional Materials Center: A Controversy Resolved," *IL Libs* (Mr. 1959). **Activities:** 1; 17, 31, 39; 63, 75, 95-Psychology. **Addr.:** 1206 West Freeman, Carbondale, IL 62901.

Baus, J. William (O. 11, 1945, Oakland, CA) Asst. Archvst., IN Univ. Arch., 1980–; Newsp. Index Libn., IN State Lib., 1979–80, Asst. Fld. Agt., 1975–79. **Educ.:** Univ. of Evansville, 1963–67, BA (Hist.); IN Univ., 1971–74, MA (Pol. Sci.), 1972, Sec. Educ. Tchg. Cert., 1973–74, MLS. **Orgs.:** SAA. Socty. of IN Archvsts.: Nsltr. Co-ed. (1980–). IN State Lib. Staff Assn.: Pres. (1978–79). SLA. IN Hist. Socty. Amer. Assn. for State and Lcl. Hist. **Activities:** 2; 15, 39, 46 **Addr.:** University Archives, Bryan Hall, 201, Indiana University, Bloomington, IN 47405.

Bayard, Mary Ivy (D. 14, 1940, Hazelton, PA) Head Libn., Tyler Sch. of Art, Temple Univ., 1970–; Asst. Dir., Montgomery Cnty. Pub. Lib., Norristown, PA, 1967–70, Head, Adult Srvs., 1965–67; Head, Ref. Dept., Norristown Pub. Lib., 1963–65. **Educ.:** Wilson Coll., 1958–62, BA (Eng.); Drexel Univ., 1962–63, MSLS. **Orgs.:** ALA: Mem. Com. (1968–72); ACRL/Art Sect. (Secy., 1973–75). PA LA: Pres.-Elect (1980–81); 2nd VP (1972–73); SE Chap. (Ch., 1970–72); Educ. and Schol. Com. (1977–79); various other coms. (1965–80). Bksellers. Assn. of Philadelphia. Lib. PR Assn. of Philadelphia. Various other orgs. Drexel Univ. Gen. Alum. Assn.: Bd. of Gvrs. (1978–80). **Honors:** Beta Phi Mu. **Pubns.:** "PLA Membership–Why and Why Not," *PLA Bltn.* (Ja. 1976). **Activities:** 1, 12; 15, 17; 55 **Addr.:** 3016 Old Arch Rd., Norristown, PA 19401.

Bayer, Bernard (Ap. 5, 1933, Chicago, IL) Head, Mechanized Info. Ctr., Univ. Libs., OH State Univ., 1970–; Head, Tech. Info. Dissemination Bur., SUNY, Buffalo, 1967–70; Ed., Cornell Aeronautical Lab., Cornell Univ., 1965–67; Writer-Ed., Electronics Lab., Gen. Electric Co., 1961–65; Sci. Writer, Resrch. Labs., Gen. Motors Corp., 1960–61; Engin., Heavy Milit. Electronics Dept., Gen. Electric Co., 1959–60; Ed. Resrchr., *Encyc. Britannica,* 1957–59; Tech. Writer, Teletype Corp., 1955–56. **Educ.:** Univ. of IL, 1950–55, BS (Engin., Phys.); Syracuse Univ., 1961–63 (Jnlsm.); Case West. Rsv. Univ., 1977–79, MSLS. **Orgs.:** ALA: LRRT; LITA Acad. LA of OH. ASIS. OH State Univ.: Pubns. Com. (Ch., 1973–74); Srch. and Screen Com. for Persnl. Libn. (1977); Srch. and Screen Com. for Undergrad. Ref. Libn. (1980). AAAS. Intl. Comm. Assn. Inst. of Electrical and Electronics Engin. Various other orgs. **Honors:** Beta Phi Mu. **Pubns.:** *Providing Computer-Based Information Services to an Academic Community* (1977); *Third Annual Report of the Mechanized Information Center* ERIC (1975); *Providing Computer-Based Information Services to an Academic Community* ERIC (1977); various presentations, sems., rpts. **Activities:** 1; 17, 31, 49-comp.-based lit. srch.; 56, 63, 75 **Addr.:** Mechanized Information Center, Ohio State University Libraries, 1858 Neil Ave. Mall, Columbus, OH 43210.

PROFESSIONAL ACTIVITIES: Institutions: 1. Acad. lib.; 2. Arch.; 3. Assn.; 4. Fed./Gvt. lib.; 5. Inst. lib.; 6. Mfr./Suppl.; 7. Milit. lib.; 8. Musm.; 9. Pub. lib.; 10. Sch. lib.; 11. Sch. of lib. sci.; 12. Spec. lib.; 13. State lib.; 14. (other). **Functions/Activities:** 15. Acq./Col. dev.; 16. Adult srvs.; 17. Admin.; 18. Apprais.; 19. Archit./Bldgs.; 20. Cat./Class.; 21. Chld. srvs.; 22. Circ.; 23. Cons./Pres.; 24. Consult.; 25. Cont. ed.; 26. Educ. lib. sci.; 27. Ext. srvs.; 28. Fund/Grants; 29. Gvt. pubs.; 30. Indx./Abs.; 31. Instr. lib. use; 32. Media srvs.; 33. Micro.; 34. Netwks./Coop.; 35. Persnl.; 36. PR; 37. Publshg.; 38. Recs. mgt.; 39. Ref. srvs.; 40. Repro.; 41. Resrch.; 42. Review.; 43. Secur.; 44. Serials; 45. Spec. col.; 46. Tech. srvs.; 47. Trustees/Bds.; 48. YA srvs.; 49. (other).

Who's Who in Library and Information Services

Bayles, Carmen L. (S. 30, 1935, Effingham, IL) Dir., Lib. Srvs., Hutchinson Cmnty. Coll., 1976–; Libn., Hutchinson Cmnty. Coll., 1967–76. **Educ.:** KS State Univ., 1953–56, BA (Eng.); Emporia State Univ., 1970–72, ML (LS). **Orgs.:** ALA. KS LA: Coll. and Univ. Libs. Sect., Nom. Com. (Ch., 1980–81). KS Lib. Netwk. Athty. Cncl. KS Lib. Netwk. Task Frc. on Ills. KS Lib. Netwk. Bd. (1981–). **Activities:** 1; 15, 17, 25 **Addr.:** Hutchinson Community College, 1300 N. Plum, Hutchinson, KS 67501.

Bayless, June Elizabeth (Je. 8, 1915, Chicago, IL) City Libn., Whittier Pub. Lib., 1972–; City Libn., Beverly Hills Pub. Lib., 1969–72; City Libn., San Marino Pub. Lib., 1952–69; Chief Circ. Dept., Pasadena Pub. Lib. 1950–52, Branch Libn., 1948–50, Libn., 1945–48; Knoxville (TN) HS Libn., 1937–38, 1938–45. **Educ.:** Univ. of TN, 1933–37, BA (Eng. Lit.); George Peabody Coll., 1938–39, BS (LS). **Orgs.:** ALA: Cnclr. (1961–65; 1969–70); Jury on Trustee Citations (1972); PLA (Bd. of Dir., 1961–65; 1968–71); (Pres., 1969–70); other coms. CA LA: Pres. (1960) Cnclr.-at-large (1955–57; 1967–69); other coms. Univ. of CA State Wide Adv. Cncl. on Educ. for Libnshp. (1963–67); Ch., (1965). Pub. Lib. Exec. Assn. of South. CA Pres. (1966–67). CA Cncl. PTA. San Gabriel Hist. Socty. Red Cross Bd. Beverly Hills, CA. Pasadena Area Girl Scout Cncl. **Pubns.:** Ed., "My Story at Molino Viejo," *CA Hist. Socty. Qtly.* (Je. 1969); "Edna Holroyd Yelland: Secretary-Treasurer, California Library Association, 1947–63," *CA Libn.* (O. 1968); "Site for CLA," *CA Libn.* (Ja. 1962); "Who's Your Bottleneck?", *News Notes CA Libn.* (Ap. 1958). **Activities:** 9; 17, 36, 47; 50, 85 **Addr.:** 11846 Floral Dr., #13, Whittier, CA 90601.

Bayley, Linda F. (Mr. 15, 1948, San Francisco, CA) Prog./Mtrls. Consul., Dimensions (Educ. Consult.), 1979–; Tchr. Trainer/Writer, Univ. of TX, 1975–80; Reg. Libn., Tulsa City Cnty. Lib., 1974–75; Lib./Adult Basic Educ. Coord., Univ. of TX, 1973–74. **Educ.:** Univ. of TX at Austin, 1966–70, MA (Soclgy., Span.); 1970–71, MLS. **Orgs.:** ALA. Natl. Assn. for Public Contin. and Adult Educ. **Pubns.:** Jt. auth., *Jail Library Services Planning and Implementation Guide* (1980); Jt. auth., *Reading to Learn: Focus on Leisure Time* (1980); Jt. auth., "A Model for Public Library Service in the Mexican-American Community," *Chicano Library Services: A Reader* (ERIC Cleaning house) (1978); Jt. auth., *The APL Series: Coping in Today's Society* (1979–80); Jt. auth., *ABE: Guide to Library Materials* (1975); Other publications. **Activities:** 16, 24, 25; 50, 63, 89 **Addr.:** Linda Bayley, "Dimensions", 2405 Dip Cove, Austin, TX 78704.

Bayne, Pauline Shaw (F. 15, 1946, Berwyn, IL) Assoc. Prof./Head, Music Lib., Univ. of TN, Knoxville, 1973; Music Tchr, various schools, suburban Chicago, 1968–69; 1971–73. **Educ.:** Morton Jr. Coll., 1964–66, AA (Msc.); Millikin Univ., 1966–68, BME (Msc. Educ.); N. West. Univ., 1969–70, MMus (Msc. Hist.); Univ. of NC, Chapel Hill, 1972–73, MSLS. **Orgs.:** Msc. LA: Open Forum (Ch., 1974–77); Subcom. on Basic Msc. Col., (mem. 1975–77, ch. 1977–); Pubs. Cncl., 1977–; Nominating Com., (ch. 1978); S.E. Chap., (Ch. 1974–76). AAUP; Univ. of TN Fac. Sen.: Secy. (1976–79); Pres.-Elect (1979–80); Pres. (1980–81); Ed. Fac. Senate *Newsletter*, (1979–80). **Honors:** Phi Kappa Phi; Beta Phi Mu; Sigma Alpha Iota, Sword of Honor, 1976; Millikin Univ., Summa cum Laude, 1968. **Pubns.:** Ed. *Library Lectures: Numbers Twenty-eight, Twenty-nine and Thirty, 1976–78* (1979); *The Gottfried Galston Music Collection and the Galston-Busoni Archive* (1978); Ed. *A Basic Music Library: Essential Scores and Books* (1978); Reviews. **Activities:** 1; 15, 17, 39; 55 **Addr.:** Music Library, University of TN, Knoxville, TN 37916.

Bayorgeon, Mary M. (O. 9, 1934, Berlin, WI) Dir. of Lib. Srvs., St. Elizabeth Hosp. Hlth. Sci. Lib., 1973–; Asst. Gvt. Docum. and Ref. Libn., Univ. of WI-Oshkosh, 1971–73. **Educ.:** Marquette Univ., 1952–57, BS summa cum laude (Hist.); Univ. of WI-Oshkosh, 1969–71, MA (LS); Med. LA courses. **Orgs.:** WI LA: Hlth. and Rehab. Lib. Srvs. (Exec. Com., 1977). Med. LA: Midwest Reg. Grp. (Exec. Com., 1977–80); Ad Hoc Com. to Study ILL (1976–77). SLA. WI Hlth. Sci. LA: Bylaws Com. (Ch., 1977–78); Exec. Com. (1978); Rep. at Large (1978). Other orgs. **Activities:** 12; 17, 24; 58, 80, 91 **Addr.:** St. Elizabeth Hospital Health Science Library, 1506 S. Oneida St., Appleton, WI 54911.

Bayrak, F. Elizabeth (Jl. 21, 1952, Summerside, PE) Ch. of Lib. Srvcs., Grande Prairie Regl. Coll., 1977–; Libn., AB Vocational Ctr., 1976–77; Micromaterials Libn., Univ. of AB, 1975–76. **Educ.:** Univ. of PE, 1970–74, BA (Eng.); Univ. of AB, 1974–75, BLS. **Orgs.:** LA of AB. Can. LA. AB Cncl. of Col. Libns.: Secy-Treas (1979–81). **Activities:** 1; 17, 31, 39; 50, 93 **Addr.:** Grande Prairie, Regional College Library, 10726 - 106th Ave., Grande Prairie, AB T8V 4C4 Canada.

Bayus, Lenore (Weatherly) (Ap. 11, 1923, New York, NY) PR Dir., Carnegie Lib. of Pittsburgh, 1973–; YA Coord., 1972–73; Ref. Libn., 1969–72; Educ. Col. Eval., Hillman Lib., Univ. of Pittsburgh, 1968–69. **Educ.:** IN Univ. of PA, 1940–44, BS (Eng., Soc. Sci.); Case-West. Rsv., 1947 (LS); Univ. of Pittsburgh, 1965–67, MLS; 1972–73 (Ed. Comm.). **Orgs.:** ALA: Conf. Wkshp. Consult. (1976). PA LA: PR Ch. (1978–79). Beta Phi Mu: Pres. (1979–80). Women in Comm., Inc.: VP (1978–79); Prog. Ch. AAUW. **Honors:** Lib. PR Cncl., Best Logo Design, 1976; ALA, John Cotton Dana Awd., 1978. **Pubns.:** "Fall Foliage," *Pittsburgh Mag.* (Oct. 1978); "Neighborhood" (TV scripts) (1978); various reviews. **Activities:** 9; 17, 31, 36 **Addr.:** Carnegie Library of Pittsburgh, 4400 Forbes Ave., Pittsburgh, PA 15213.

Bazillion, Richard J. (F. 25, 1943, Saint John, NB) Chief Libn., Univ. Archvst., Algoma Univ. Coll., 1980; Assoc. Prof. of Hist., 1974–80; Asst. Prof., 1971–74; Asst. Prof., Sir Geo. Williams Univ., 1969–71. **Educ.:** Boston Univ., 1961–65, AB (Hist.); Harvard Univ., 1965–66, MAT (Hist., Educ.); Univ. of Freiburg i.B. W. Germ., 1968–69, Certif. Proficiency in Germ.; Univ. WI, 1966–70, PhD (Mod. European Hist.); 1977–78, MLS. **Orgs.:** Can. LA. SAA. Can Assn. of Univ. Tchrs. **Honors:** Phi Alpha Theta, 1965; Germ. Acad. Exch. Srvs., Dankstipendium, 1968; Beta Phi Mu, 1979. **Pubns.:** "Access to Departmental Records, Cabinet Documents and Ministerial Papers in Canada," *Amer. Archvst.* (Apr. 1980); "Saxon Liberalism and the German Question in the Wake of the 1848 Revolution," *Can Jnl. of Hist.* (Apr. 1978); "East German Elites in Historical Perspective," *E. Ctrl. Europe* (1976); "A Scholar in Politics in Pre-March Saxony: The Biedermann Case," *Societas–A Review of Soc. Hist.* (Sum. 1975); "A German Liberal's Changing Perspective on the Social Question: Karl Biedermann in the 1840's and 1890's," *Laurentian Univ. Review* (June 1973); "Zeitungswissenschaft in the Two Germanies", *Can. Slavic Std.* (Win. 1971). **Activities:** 1, 2; 15, 17, 39; 63, 92 **Addr.:** Algoma University College Library, Sault Ste. Marie, ON Canada.

Beach, Cecil P. (Jl. 12, 1927, Knoxville, TN) Dir., Broward Cnty. Lib., 1977–; Dir., Div. of Libs., St. of FL., 1972–77; Dir., Tampa, Hillsborough Co. Pub. Lib., 1965–72; Dir., Gadsden Pub. Lib., 1960–65; Dir., Piedmont Reg. Lib., 1954–60; Ext. Libn., Decatur-DeKalb Reg. Lib., 1952–54; Bkmobile Libn., Chattanooga Pub. Lib., 1948–51. **Educ.:** Univ. of Chattanooga, 1946–50, AB (Eng.); FL St. Univ., 1951–52, MA (LS). **Orgs.:** FL LA: Pres. (1969). SELA: Pres. (1972–74). ALA: Cncl. (1974–78). AL LA: Treas. (1964–65); many other orgs. Easter Seal Socty.: Bd. of Dir. (1975–77); Parent Tchrs. Assn.: Pres. (1975); Boy Scouts of Amer.: Den Leader (1974); Rotary Club: Bd. of Dir. (1975); other orgs. **Honors:** Jaycees, Young Man of the Yr., 1965; City of Tampa, Cmdn., 1972; Tampa City Cncl., Cit. for Outstand. Srv., 1972; Jr. Womans Club, Tallahassee, Family of the Yr., 1974; other honors. **Activities:** 9, 13; 17, 19, 24; 56, 78 **Addr.:** Cecil P. Beach, Broward County Library, P.O. Box 5463, Fort Lauderdale, FL 33310.

Beach, Rose Mary Randall (D. 11, 1921, Waterloo, IA) Lib. Dir., Goldey Beacom Coll., 1970–, Fac., 1956–69; Fac., Green Mt. Jr. Coll., 1951–54; Radio News, Feature Writer, A.P. Radio, Rockefeller Ctr., 1944–47. **Educ.:** State Univ. of IA, 1940–43, BA (Jnlsm.); Univ. of IA, 1943, Cert. (Jnlsm.); Drexel Univ., 1969–71, MS (LS). **Orgs.:** ALA. DE LA: Coll. and Resrch. Lib. Div. (Pres., 1978–79). DE Cncl. of Acad. Lib. Dirs. Drexel Lib. Sch. Alum. Assn. **Honors:** Beta Phi Mu; Phi Beta Kappa; Kappa Tau Alpha; Sigma Delta Chi. **Pubns.:** Various pubns. **Activities:** 1; 15, 17, 28 **Addr.:** 5 Deville Ct., Newark, DE 19711.

Beacock, E. Stanley (Ja. 21, 1921, Tiny Twp. Simcoe Cnty., ON) Adj. Prof., Sch. of Lib. and Info. Sci., Univ. of West. ON, 1975–; Dir., Secy. Treas., London Pub. Libs. and Musms., 1974–; Dir., Midwest. Reg. Lib. Syst., Kitchener, ON, 1966–74; Asst. Dir., London Pub. Lib. and Art Musm., 1961–66; Libn., Troy-Miami OH Cnty. Pub. Lib., 1953–61; Libn., Kenton Pub. Lib., 1949–53; Libn., Lambton (ON) Cnty. Lib., 1947–49. **Educ.:** Queens Univ., 1939–42, BA (Phil.); Univ. of Toronto, 1946–47, BLS, 1964–68, MLS. **Orgs.:** ON LA. Can. LA. CALS. Rotary Club of London. **Honors:** ON Lib. Trustees' Assn. Awd., 1972. **Activities:** 9, 11; 17, 47; 50, 75 **Addr.:** London Public Libraries & Museums, 305 Queens Ave., London, ON N6B 3L7 Canada.

Beacom, Marjorie L. (Pittston, PA) Dir., Reg. Ref. Ctr., Orange Cnty. Pub. Lib., 1979–; Ref. Libn., Chapman Branch Lib., 1977–79; Ref. Libn., Garden Grove Reg. Lib., 1972–77; Cat. Libn., Orange Cnty. Pub. Lib. 1971–72; Ref. Libn., Arcadia Pub. Lib., 1970–71; Head, Dept. Lib., CA Inst. of Tech., 1968–69; Ref. Libn., Altadena Pub. Lib., 1966–67. **Educ.:** CA State Univ., Los Angeles, 1959–63, BA (Eng.); Univ. of South. CA, 1963–66, MLS. **Orgs.:** ALA:RASD/Bus. Ref. Com. (1975–77). SLA. CA LA. Orange Cnty. Philharmonic Socty. Garden Grove Women's Civic Club. **Activities:** 9, 12; 17, 29, 39; 55, 59, 78 **Addr.:** 2825 North Olive Ln., Santa Ana, CA 92706.

Beahan, Gary W. (Ap. 29, 1946, Mexico, MO) State Archvst., MO Rec. Mgt. and Arch. Srvs., 1975. **Educ.:** Wm. Jewell Coll., 1964–68, BA (Hist.); Univ. MO, 1973–74, MA (LS); KS State Univ., 1971–73, 1976, MA (Hist.); Mod. Arch. Inst., 1977, Cert. **Orgs.:** SAA. Natl. Assn. of State Archvsts. & Recs. Admins.: Stans. Com. (1978–). Midwest Arch. Conf. Beta Phi Mu: Oral Hist. Com. (1976–); Past Pres. (1976). Other orgs. Cole Cnty. Hist. Socty.: Cnty. Hist. Com. (1979–). Mid-MO Geneal. Socty: Pres. (1978); Qtly. Ed. (1977–78). Audrain Cnty. Hist. Socty. Other orgs. **Honors:** U.S. Army, Army Cmdn. Medal, Bronze Star, 1970. **Pubns.:** *Missouri State Archives: Guide to County Records on Microfilm* (1979); "The Future of Genealogy," *Pioneer Times* (O. 1977); various papers. **Activities:** 2, 12; 18, 38, 45; 62, 69, 78 **Addr.:** 723 Kevin Dr., Jefferson City, MO 65101.

Beaird, A. Michael (D. 5, 1940, Lufkin, TX) Law Libn., Asst. Prof. of Law, Law Lib., Univ. of MS, 1977–; Asst. Law Libn., Asst. Prof., Law, Univ. of Houston, 1975–77. **Educ.:** Univ. of TX, Austin, 1964–69, BA (Hist.); Univ. of OK, 1971–74, JD (Law); Univ. of WA, 1974–75, MLL (Law Libnshp.). **Orgs.:** AALL: *Law Lib Jnl.* Com. (Vice-Ch., 1979–80); SE Chap., VP, Pres.-Elect (1980–82). State Bar of TX. **Pubns.:** "Products Liability: Bibliography," *74 Law Lib. Jnl.* (1980); "Texas Agency Rule," *Houston Lawyer* (1976); various bk. reviews. **Activities:** 1, 12; 15, 17, 31; 61, 77 **Addr.:** University, MS 38677.

Beal, Sarell Wood (Ap. 3, 1945, Pittsburgh, PA) Assoc. Prof., East MI Univ., 1980–; Asst. Prof., 1974-80; Instr., 1970–74. **Educ.:** MI State Univ., 1965–67, BA (High Honor) (Pol. Sci.); Rosary Coll., 1969–70, MALS; East. MI Univ., 1975–76, MA, (Soc. Sci.). **Orgs.:** ALA. MI Assn. of Law Libs. AAUP. Phi Kappa Phi; Pi Sigma Alpha. **Pubns.:** *Legal Reference Collections for Non-Law Libraries* (1973); Reviews. **Activities:** 1; 15, 39; 59, 77, 92 **Addr.:** 312 Library, Eastern Michigan University, Ypsilanti, MI 48197.

Beal, William C. (N. 21, 1926, Mt. Pleasant, PA) Archvst., Recs. Admin., Gen. Comsn. on Arch. and Hist., The Untd. Meth. Church, 1974. Untd. Meth. Clergyman, 1950–. **Educ.:** Albright Coll., 1943–47, BS; Untd. Theo. Semy., Dayton, OH, 1947–50, M of Div; Emory State Univ., 1971, Cert. (Arch. Admin.), 1972–M. of Sacred Theo. **Orgs.:** SAA: Relig. Arch. (1974–80). Assn. of Recs. Mgrs. and Admins. Inc. **Pubns.:** "A Heap of Stuff," *Media: Lib. Srvs. Jnl.* (Ja., F., Mr., 1979). **Activities:** 2; 15, 18, 23 **Addr.:** 133 Keller St., Waynesville, NC 28786.

Beall, Barbara A. (Ag. 6, 1940, Washington, DC) Mgr., Info. Ctr., Natl. Forest Prods. Assn., 1972–; Assoc. Libn., MD Rm., McKeldin Lib., Univ. of MD, 1967–72, Assoc. Libn., Gen. Ref., 1967–67; Resrch. Assoc., Chase Manhattan Bank, 1965–67; Catlgr., Engin. Soctys. Lib., 1963–65. **Educ.:** George Washington Univ., 1960–62, BA (Eng.); Columbia Univ., 1962–63, MSLS; Amer. Univ., 1970, Cert. (Mod. Arch. Admin.). **Orgs.:** SLA: DC Chap. (Treas., 1978–81). SAA. Assn. of Recs. Mgrs. and Admins.: DC Chap. (Secy., 1975–76; Histn., 1979–). **Honors:** Phi Beta Kappa, 1963; Beta Phi Mu, 1963. **Activities:** 12; 17, 20, 39; 59, 65, 82 **Addr.:** National Forest Products Association, 1619 Massachusetts Ave., N.W., Washington, DC 20036.

Beall, C. E. Campbell (S. 22, 19–, Hedgesville WV) VP, A and S Warehouse Inc., 1968; Owner, F. L. Beall and Sons Food Brokers, 1942–. **Educ.:** WV Univ., 1941, BS (Bus.). **Orgs.:** WV Lib. Comsn.: Ch. (1975–). Martinsburg, WV Pub. Lib. Bd. of Trustees: Ch. (1956–). Natl. Conf. Lib. and Info. Srvs.: Adv. Com. (1979–80). Martinsburg WV Rotary Club: Pres. (1975). Martinsburg WV Jaycees: Pres. (1951). **Honors:** ALA, Trustee Cit., 1977; WV LA, Merit Awd., 1975. **Activities:** 4, 9; 24, 28, 36 **Addr.:** Box 528, Martinsburg, WV 25401.

Beamguard, (Mrs.) Elizabeth P. (Fayetteville, TN) Retired State Dir., AL Pub. Lib. Srv., 1960–, Fld. Rep., 1956–60; Admin., Huntsville-Madison Cnty. Reg., 1944–56; Ref. Libn., Hamilton Cnty. HS, 1940–44. **Educ.:** Univ. of TN, 1928–31, AB (LS, Eng. Lit.); Emory Univ., 1944, BS (LS); Univ. of Chattanooga, Cert.; Rutgers Univ., Cert. **Orgs.:** AL LA: Exec. Cncl. (1968–73); Plng. Com.; Stans. Com. SE LA: Pub. Lib. Div. (Ch., 1956). ALA: Pub. Lib. Div.; Cncl. of State Agencies. Com. for the Hum. in AL. AAUW: Montgomery Branch (Pres. 1978–80). Zonta, Intl.: Montgomery Club (Pres. 1975–77). **Honors:** AL LA, Awd. for Excep. and Enduring Srv., 1976; AAUW, Montgomery Branch Educ. Fndn., "Named Gift Awd.," 1980; AL LA, Schol. in Hon. of, 1975; State of AL Legis., Cit. of Hon. for Dev. and Expansion of Rural Lib. Srv., 1965; other hons. **Pubns.:** *Profiles of Public Libraries in Alabama* (1962); "Regional Library Development," *AL Leag. of Municipalities* (1967); *HQ Nsltr.; Montgomery Branch AAUW Bltn.* (1968–70). **Addr.:** 3373 Dartmouth Cir., Montgomery, AL 36111.

Beamish, Betsey S. Info. Spec., Biomed. Lib., Univ. of CA, Los Angeles, 1974–; Head, Consult. & Trng. Srvs., PSRMLS-Biomed. Lib., 1971-74; Head, Info. Srvs. Sect., PSRMLS-Biomedical Library, 1969–71; MEDLARS Srchr., Biomed. Lib., 1965–69. **Educ.:** Duke Univ., 1952–56, AB (Zlgy.); Univ. of CA, Los Angeles, 1965–68, MLS. **Orgs.:** Med. LA: Exchange Com. (Ch., 1977–80). Med. Lib. Grp. of South. CA and AZ: Schol. Com. (Ch., 1976–77). **Honors:** Beta Phi Mu; Natl. Sci. Fndn., Fellowship, 1963. **Pubns.:** *Reference Materials for a Health Science Core Library* (Revised Anly., 1971–79). **Activities:** 1; 26; 80, 91 **Addr.:** PSRMLS - Biomedical Library, Center for the Health Sciences, University of California, Los Angeles, CA 90272.

Bean, Gordon A. (Mr. 13, 1930, Toronto, ON) Prof., Lib. Arts Dept., Ryerson Polytech. Inst., 1971–; Libn., St. Augustine's Coll., Toronto, 1965–71. **Educ.:** Univ. of Toronto, 1948–51, BA (Phil.); Univ. of MI, 1964–65, AMLS. **Orgs.:** ALA. Can. LA. ON LA. Can. Assn. Info. Sci. Ryerson Fac. Assn.: Prof. Affairs Com. (Ch., 1979–81). **Honors:** Beta Phi Mu. **Activities:** 11; 20, 26, 46 **Addr.:** 1145 Logan Ave., Apt. 1102, Toronto, ON M4K 3G9 Canada.

Special Subjects/Services: 50. Adult educ.; 51. Advert./Mktg.; 52. Aerosp.; 53. Agric.; 54. Area std.; 55. Arts/Hum.; 56. Autom.; 57. Bibl./Prtg.; 58. Bio. sci.; 59. Bus./Fin.; 60. Chem.; 61. Copyrt.; 62. Documtn.; 63. Educ.; 64. Engin.; 65. Env.; 66. Eth. grps.; 67. Film; 68. Food/Nutr.; 69. Geneal.; 70. Geo.; 71. Geol.; 72. Handcpd.; 73. Hist.; 74. Int. frdm.; 75. Info. sci.; 76. Insr.; 77. Law; 78. Legis.; 79. Math./Comp. sci.; 80. Med.; 81. Metals; 82. Nat. resrcs.; 83. Newsp.; 84. Nuc. sci.; 85. Oral hist.; 86. Petr./Energy; 87. Pharm.; 88. Phys./Astr./Math.; 89. Readg.; 90. Relig.; 91. Sci./Tech.; 92. Soc. sci.; 93. Telecom.; 94. Transp.; 95. (other).

Bean, Janet R. (My. 27, 1945, Youngstown, OH) Dir., Cult. Ctr., Chicago Pub. Lib., 1978–, Chief, Gen. Info. Srvs., 1975–78, Head, Info. Cntr., 1971–74, Ref. Libn., 1968–71. **Educ.:** Youngstown Univ., 1963–67, BA (Eng.); Univ. of IL, 1967–68, MSLS. **Orgs.:** ALA: Conf. Plng. Com. (1976); Mach. Assisted Ref. Srvs. Com. (1978–81). Chicago Lib. Club: V.P., Pres. (1981); IL LA: Workshop on Workshop Com. (1976). SLA: IL Chap., Exec. Bd. (1975–76). Art Inst. of Chicago. Chicago Hist. Soc. Field Musm. of Nat. Hist. Musm. of Contemporary Art. **Honors:** Beta Phi Mu, 1968. **Pubns.:** Comp., Chicago Public Library Serials List (1977); SLA Chicago Chap. Membership Dir. (1976); "Chicago", *Funk and Wagnalls Encyclopedia.* **Activities:** 9; 17; 75 **Addr.:** The Chicago Public Library Cultural Center, 78 E. Washington St., Chicago, IL 60602.

Beard, Charles E. (Jl. 24, 1940, New Orleans, LA) Dir. of Libs., W. GA Coll., 1978–; Dir. of Libs., Coord. Educ. Lib. Media Dept., GA Coll., 1971–78; Dir. of Lib. Srvs., Judson Coll., 1970–71; Head, Acq., Univ. of AL (Tuscaloosa), 1969–70, Head, Ref. Dept., 1966–69; Admn. Ofcr., U.S. Command and Gen. Staff Coll. Lib., 1964–66. **Educ.:** Univ. of AL (Tuscaloosa), 1958–62, BA (Hist.); FL St. Univ., 1962–64, MLS. **Orgs.:** SELA: JMRT Prog. Com. (1974–76); Prog. Com. (1978–80). GA LA: JMRT, (Ch. 1973–75), VP/Pres. Elect (1979–). GA Assn. of Instr. Tech. Univ. of GA, Acad. Com. on Libs., (Ch. 1978–79). Phi Alpha Theta. Beta Sigma Phi. Central Georgia Associated Libraries, Chairman, 1974–75; Secretary/Treasurer 1979–80. **Honors:** WHCOLIS, Alternate Del., 1979; Mem. Ad Hoc Com. of 118 on White House Conf. Resol., 1980–; GA LA, JRMT Achvmt. Awd., 1975; Milledgeville Kiwanis Club, Outstan. Pres. Awd., 1975. **Pubns.:** Ed. *The GA Libn.* (1975–79). **Activities:** 1; 17, 26, 32; 50, 63, 74 **Addr.:** West Georgia College, Carrollton, GA 30118.

Beard, John R. (D. 29, 1918, Milk River, AB) Dir., Lib., Dowling Coll., 1976–; Visit. Prof., Grad. Sch. of Lib. and Info. Sci., Pratt Inst., 1973; Head Libn., Prof., Montclair State Coll., 1966–74, Assoc. Libn., Assoc. Prof., 1965–66; Actg. Chief, Div. of Libs., Untd. Nations Educ., Sci. and Cult. Org., 1964, Chief, Libs. Dev. Sect., 1962–64; Head, Acq. Div., Vancouver Pub. Lib., 1959–61; Circ. Libn., Bus. Lib., Columbia Univ., 1956–58; various tchg. and other positions, 1939–59. **Educ.:** Calgary Normal Sch., 1938–39, Elem., Intermediate Tchr.'s Cert.; Univ. of BC, 1949–52, BA (Fr., Span.); Univ. of Toronto, 1953–54, BLS; Columbia Univ., 1956–65, DLS (Lib. Admin.); various crs. **Orgs.:** ALA: ACRL/Coll. Libs. Sect. (Ch., 1972–73), Bd. of Dirs. (1971–73). NJ LA: Coll. and Univ. Sect. (Pres., 1970–71), Lib. Resrcs. Com. (Ch., 1968–72); Nom. Com. (1970–74); Lib. Dev. Com. (1971–74). Suffolk Cnty. LA: Coll. and Univ. Libs. Com. (Ch., 1976–77). NY Metro Ref. and Resrch. Lib. Agency: Lib. Use and Resrcs. Com. (1967–70). Various other orgs. AAUP: Montclair State Coll. Chap. (Secy., 1966–71). NJ Dept. of Higher Educ.: Comp.-Aided Prcs. and Terminal Access Info. Netwk., Strg. Com. (1970–71), Bd. of Dirs., Exec. Com. (1971–73); Budget Task Frc., Lib. Subcom. (1969). Cncl. of NJ State Coll. and Univ. Libns.: VP (1969–72); Coop. Proj. Com. (1969–70); Lib. Stans. Com. (1971–73). Long Island Lib. Resrcs. Cncl.: Com. on Resrc. Sharing and Coop. Acq. (1978–). **Honors:** NJ LA, Coll. and Univ. Sect., Disting. Srv. Awd., 1970. **Pubns.:** *Canadian Provincial Libraries* (1967); "Canadian Provincial Libraries," *Can. Lib.* (My., Jl., N. 1966, Ja. 1967); "A Regressive Step in New Jersey Higher Education," *NJ Libs.* (Fall 1970); contrib., *Lib. Jnl., Can. Lib., NJ Libs.* **Activities:** 1; 17 **Addr.:** 501 W. 123rd St., New York, NY 10027.

Bearden, Joseph M. (D. 5, 1948, Fort Worth, TX) Branch Mgr., Dallas Pub. Lib., 1979–; Branch Mgr., Denver Pub. Lib., 1978, Chld. Spec., 1976–78; Youth Libn., Fort Worth Pub. Lib., 1974–76, Ref. Asst., 1973–74. **Educ.:** TX Christ. Univ., 1967–71, BA (Hist. Pol. Sci.); Univ. of TX, 1971–72, MLS; Univ. of TX, Arlington, 1980–, (Bus. Adm.); Various courses and seminars. **Orgs.:** ALA: ALSC/Filmstrip Eval. Com. (1977–79). TX LA: Mem. Com. (1974–76). SWLA. Film Lib. Info. Cncl. AECT. Amer. Numismatic Assn. Alpha Phi Omega. **Honors:** Phi Alpha Theta, 1969; Pi Sigma Alpha, 1970; Beta Phi Mu, 1973; Delegate, Gvr. Conf. on TX Libs., 1974. **Pubns.:** Reviews. **Activities:** 9; 17, 21, 42; 59, 67, 92 **Addr.:** Skyline Library, Dallas Public Library, 6006 Everglade Rd., Dallas, TX 75227.

Beardsley, Barbara E. (Jl. 12, 1927, Ottawa, ON) Prin. Resrch., ONTERIS and Resrch Ofcr., Metro. Toronto Sch. Bd. 1970–; Acq. Dept., Univ. of W. Indies, Trinidad, 1969; Resrch., Metro. Toronto Sch. Bd., 1967–68; Deputy Head, Ref., Circ., Educ. Ctr. Lib., Toronto Bd. of Educ., 1962–67. **Educ.:** Univ. of Toronto, 1945–49, BA honors, (Eng.), 1961–62, BLS. **Orgs.:** Can. Assn. Info. Sci.; Can. LA; ASIS: Nsltr. Com. (1979). SIG/Info. Srvs. to Educ.; Can. Sch. Lib. Assn.: Stan. Com. (1973). EAGER (Effective Auto. Grp. for Educ. Resrch.): Fndn. mem. (1975). Can. Socty. Study Educ.; Can. Educ. Resrchs. Assn.; Assn. Educ. Resrchs. of ON: Fndn. Mem. (1972). Nom. Com. (1975, 78). Metro. Toronto Educ. Resrch. Com. Various other orgs. **Pubns.:** Jt. Ed., *ONTERIS Abstracts* v. 1 (1978); Jt. Ed., *ONTERIS Printed Index* (1978); Jt. Auth. "Hints for Survival in Open Plan Schools," *Curric. Theory Netwk.* (Sp. 1973); Jt. Auth. *Educational Specification and User Requirements for Intermediate Schools* (1969); various other speeches, papers, brochures. **Activities:** 13; 17, 30, 41; 57, 63, 75 **Addr.:** ONTERIS, Ontario Ministry of Education, Mowat Block, Queen's Park, Toronto, ON M7A 1L2 Canada.

Bearman, Toni Carbo (N. 14, 1942, Middletown, CT) Exec. Dir., NCLIS, 1981–; Spec. Projs. Consult., Inst. of Electrical Engins., 1979–81; Exec. Dir., Natl. Fed. of Abs. and Indexing Srvs., 1974–79; Bibliographic Consult., 1973–74; Proj. Coord., NSF-funded study of technically-oriented house jnls. in coop. with Antwerp (Belgium) Lib. Sch., 1972–73; Resrch. Asst., Drexel Univ. Grad. Sch. of LS, 1971–72; Supvsr., Physical Sci. Lib., Brown Univ., 1968–71; Lib. Asst., Bio. Sci. Lib., 1967–68; Subj. Spec., Engin. Lib., Univ. of WA, Seattle, 1966–67; various other lib. positions, 1962–66. **Educ.:** Brown Univ., 1969, BA (Eng., Amer. Lit.); Drexel Univ., 1973, MSLS, 1977, PhD (Info. Sci.). **Orgs.:** ASIS: Cncl. (1978–); Netwking. Com. (Ch., 1978–79); Spec. Interest Grp. on Lib. Autom. and Netwks. (Ch., 1978–79); various other coms. Cmrce. Tech. Adv. Bd.: Scientific and Tech. Info. Policy Working Grp. 1978–). Amer. Socty. of Indxrs.: Bd. of Dirs. (1978–79). *Serials Libn.*: Ed. Bd. (1976–). various other orgs. AAAS. **Honors:** ASIS, Spec. Interest Grp. of the Yr., 1979. **Pubns.:** *UNISIST/NFAIS Indexing in Perspective Education Kit* (1979); *A Study of Coverage Overlap Among Major Science and Techology Abstracting and Indexing Services* (1977); "What's New with Secondary Services," *Bltn. of ASIS* (Ag. 1979); "Indexing and Abstracting," *ALA Encyclopedia* (1980); "Secondary Information Systems and Services," *Anl. Review of Info. Sci. and Tech.* (1978); various other articles. **Activities:** 14-nonprofit inst., abs. and indexing srv.; 17, 30, 34; 56, 57, 75 **Addr.:** National Commission on Library and Information Science Washington, DC 20036.

Beary, Eugene G. (Mr. 2, 1926, Whitman, MA) Chief, Tech. Lib., US Army Natick R&D Labs, 1970–; Head, Readrs. Srvs., US Army Natick Labs., 1969–70; Ref. Libn., 1963–69; Asst. Libn., Armed Frcs. Food and Container Inst., 1962–63. **Educ.:** Boston Univ., 1947–51, AB (Geo.); Simmons Coll., 1958–66, MS (LS); MA Div. Lib. Ext., 1966, Prof. Libn Cert. **Orgs.:** SLA. **Honors:** US Army R&D Cmnd., Cmndrs. Gold Key for Excel. in Admin., 1977. **Activities:** 4, 12; 17; 64, 74, 91 **Addr.:** 16 Meeting House Ln., South Easton, MA 02375.

Beasley, Kenneth Ephraim (Ag. 27, 1925, Terre Haute, IN) Prof. of Pol. Sci., Univ. of TX, El Paso, 1967–, VP, Acad. Affairs, 1974–75, Dean, Grad. Sch., 1969–74, Ch., Dept. of Pol. Sci., 1967–69; Dir. of Resrch., KS State Legis., Prof. of Pol. Sci., Univ. of KS, 1964–67; Assoc. Prof., PA State Univ., 1961–64; Asst. Prof., Univ. of KS, 1956–69. **Educ.:** Univ. of KS, 1945–48, BA (Pol. Sci), 1948–49, MA (Pol. Sci.), 1949–55, PhD (Pol. Sci.). **Orgs.:** ALA: Com. on Accred. (1978–). TX Conf. on Libs. and Info. Srvs.: Del. (1978). Amer. Pol. Sci. Assn. Amer. Socty. of Pub. Admin. **Pubns.:** "The Changing Role of the State Library," *Advances in Libnshp.* (1971); jt. auth., *Performance Measures for Public Libraries* (1973); "Librarians Continued Efforts to Understand and Adapt to community Analysis and Libraries," *Lib. Trends* (Ja. 1976); "Evaluation of Libraries: Requirements for Continued Progress," *Lib. Trends* (Ja. 1974); "Political Parameters Affecting Library Service," *Lib. Trends* (O. 1974); other books, articles, oral presentations. **Activities:** 9; 41 **Addr.:** Education 910, Univ. of Texas at El Paso, El Paso, TX 79968.

Beattie, Judith Hudson (N. 15, 1944, Sydney, NS) Archvst., CRCCF, Ottawa Univ., 1977–; Archvst., ON Arch., 1969–73; Hist. Reschr., Hist. Sites, 1966–69. **Educ.:** Carleton Univ., 1963–67, BA Hons, (Hist.); Univ. of Toronto, 1967–68, MA (Hist.); Records Management Course (ON Govt). **Orgs.:** Assn. Can. Archvsts. Assn. des Archivistes du PQ. East. ON Archvsts. Assn.: Secy. (1978–79). **Pubns.:** *Inventaire du Fonds Union du Canada* no. 7, (1979); "The Battle of the Restigouche", *Historic Sites* (1978). **Activities:** 2; 45; 66, 95-Photographs. **Addr.:** Centre de Recherche en Civilisation, Canadienne-Francaise, Pavillon Morisset, 65 Hastey, Ottawa, ON K1N 6N5 Canada.

Beatty, Virginia Lewis (Mr. 8, 1930, Quirigua, Izabal, Guatemala) Dir., Med. Lit. Srv., 1953–. **Educ.:** Purdue Univ., 1947–51, BS (Sci.); Columbia Univ., 1951–53, MS (LS); Med. LA, 1972, Grade I Cert. **Orgs.:** Med. LA: Com. on Per. and Serial Pubns. (1954–61); Vital Notes on Med. Per. Com. (1961–74); Co-Archvst. (1979–). **Pubns.:** Jt. auth., *Vital Notes on Medical Periodicals–Five Year Cumulative Index* (1958); "Walter L. Necker (1913–1979)," *Bltn. Med. LA* (Jl. 1980); "Thoughts on Planning or Remodeling the Hospital Library," *Hosp. Libs.* (1976); "Sources of Medical Information," *Jnl. Amer. Med. Assn.* (Jl. 1976); *Rating and Raising Indoor Plants* (1975); various articles. **Activities:** 12; 24, 39, 41; 58, 75, 80 **Addr.:** 1509 Forest Ave., Evanston, IL 60201.

Beatty, William Kaye (F. 5, 1926, Toronto, ON) Prof. of Med. Bibl., Northwestern Univ. Med. Sch., 1962–; Libn., 1962–74; Assoc. Libn. & Assoc. Prof., Med. Bibliog., Univ. of MO Med. Sch., 1957–62; Assoc. Libn. & Asst. Prof., Med. Bibliog., 1956–57; College of Physicians of Philadelphia: Asst. Librn, Readers Services, 1954–56; Circ. Asst., 1952–53. **Educ.:** Harvard Univ., 1946–49, (Classics); Columbia Univ., 1950–51, BA (Classics); Columbia Univ. 1951–52, MS (LS); Med. LA, Cert. Grade I, 1955. **Orgs.:** ALA: Assn. of Hosp. and Inst. Libs. (VP, 1964–1965); (Pres., 1965–1966); ASCLA/Hlth. Care Libs. Sect., Bylaws Com. (Ch., 1979). IL LA: Pres. (1964–67). Med. LA: Archvst.; Bd. of Dirs. (1966–1969); Nom. Com., (1976–1977); Med. Hist. Grp. (Vice-Ch., 1978–79; Ch., 1979–80). SLA: Bd. of Dirs. (1964–67). Chicago Literary Club: VP, (1978–79); Pres., (1979–80). Amer. Assn. for the Hist. of Med.: Cncl. (1965–1968). Osler Medal Com. (Ch., 1965–1966). Amer. Med. Writers Assn.: Awds. Com. (1966–1970). Amer. Osler Socty: Bd. of Gvrs. (1976–1979). **Honors:** SLA, John Cotton Dana Lect., 1968; Med. LA, IDA and George Eliot Prize, 1973; D. J. Davis Lecture on Med. Hist., Univ. of IL, 1974. **Pubns.:** Jt. auth., *Epidemics* (1976); "Hippocrates - A Man, An Influence," *Med. and Health Anl.* (1977); "The Physicians of Ancient China," *Med. and Health Anl.* (1978); "William T. Bovie, Inventor and Teacher", *Transactions & Std. of the Coll. of Physicians of Philadelphia* (June 1979); "Searching the Literature and Computerized Services in Medicine," *Annals of Internal Med.* (Ag. 1979); other books, articles, and reviews. **Activities:** 1, 12; 24; 57, 80, 73 **Addr.:** Northwestern University Medical School, 303 E. Chicago Ave., Chicago, IL 60611.

Beaty, Sally K. Carroll (S. 23, 1945, San Diego, CA) AV Libn., Stephen F. Austin State Univ. Lib., 1978–; Voice Tchr., Univ. of NV, Las Vegas, 1974–75; Voice Tchr., McLennon Cmnty. Coll., Waco, TX, 1972–73; Spec. Actr. Coord., Armstrong Browning Lib., Waco, TX, 1970–73. **Educ.:** LA State Univ. 1964–67, BM (Msc.); Baylor Univ., 1967–70, MM (Msc.); Univ. of TX, 1977–78, MLS; Msc. Tchrs. Natl. Assn., 1974–79, cert. voice and piano tchr. **Orgs.:** TX Msc. LA: Natl. Regis. Com. (1980); Nsltr. Ed. (1979–); Com. on Interlib. Coop. (1980–). Msc. LA. Msc. OCLC Users Grp. Assn. Sonneck Society. Pi Kappa Lambda. **Pubns.:** *Browning Music: A Descriptive Catalog of the Music Related to Robert and Elizabeth Barrett Browning in the Armstrong Browning Library: 1972* (1973); "List of the Musical Settings in the Armstrong Browning Library Omitted in the BNP Bibliography," *The Browning Nsltr.* (Fall 1971); "Record Manufacturer's Number File," *TX Quarter-Notes Nsltr.* (My. 1979); "Music in the Armstrong Browning Library Collection" paper and recital (1974). **Activities:** 1, 12; 15, 31, 32; 55, 67, 95-AV. **Addr.:** 830 Sarah Ann, Nacogdoches, TX 75961.

Beaubien, Anne Kathleen (S. 15, 1947, Detroit, MI) Mgr. and Coord., MI Info. Transfer Servce, Univ. of MI, 1980–; Soc. Sci. Ref. Libn. & Bibl. Instr., Univ. of MI, 1971–80. **Educ.:** West. MI Univ., 1965–67; MI State Univ., 1967–69, BA (Soc. Sci.); Univ. of MI, 1970, AMLS, 1972–73 (Soc. Psych.). **Orgs.:** ALA: ACRL Bd. of Dir. (1978–80); Anthro. Sect. (Ch., 1979–80); Bibl. Instruct. Sect., Com. on Cooperation, Subcom. on Prof. Orgs. (Ch., 1977–80); RASD: Bibl. Com. (1979–81); Bibl. Instr. Sect. Com. on Cooperation (Ch., 1981–83). MI On-line Users Grp. **Pubns.:** Jt. auth., "Things We Weren't Taught in Library School: Some Thoughts to Take Home," *Putting Library Instruction in Its Place* (1978); "Library Resources for the Community Organizer," *Tactics and Techniques for Cmnty. Practice* (1977); Jt. auth., "Reaching Graduate Students: Techniques and Administration," *Fac. Involvement in Lib. Instr.* (1976). **Activities:** 1, 11; 31, 39, 49-Online Srchg.; 92 **Addr.:** Michigan Information Transfer Source, Graduate Library, University of Michigan, Ann Arbor, MI 48109.

Beauchamp, Nancy J. (D. 25, 1937, Honolulu, HI) Libn., HI-Kai County. Lib. and Kansai Gaidai HI Coll., 1980–; Libn., Japan-Amer. Inst. of Mgt. Sci., 1973–80; Sec. Tchr., Dept. of Defense, 1962–65; Sec. Tchr., Dept. of Educ., State of HI, 1959–62. **Educ.:** Univ. of HI, 1955–59, BEd (Eng. Hist.), 1972–73, MLS; 1959–60, Fifth-Yr. Dip., (Educ.). **Orgs.:** ALA; HI LA: various coms. Beta Phi Mu: Xi Chap. (Secy., 1978–79). **Honors:** Phi Kappa Phi, 1959. **Pubns.:** *Modern Japanese Novels in English: An Annotated Bibliography* (1974). **Activities:** 1, 12; 15, 20, 22; 54, 56, 59 **Addr.:** 854 Hahaione St., Honolulu, HI 96825.

Beaupré, Linda J. (Ag. 5, 1943, Oakland, CA) Assoc. Dir., Pub. Srvs., Univ. of TX, Austin, 1980–, Actg. Asst. Dir., Pub. Srvs., 1979–80, Head Libn., Ref. Srvs. Dept., 1978–80; Admin. Asst., Assoc. Univ. Libn. for Pub. Srvs., Moffitt Undergrad. Lib., Univ. of CA, Berkeley, 1977–78, Admin. Asst. to Head, E. Asiatic Lib., 1976–77, Coord., Pub. Srvs., Asst. Head, Moffitt Undergrad. Lib., Ref. Libn., Moffitt Undergrad. Lib., 1970–72; Supvsr., Micro. Col., Pers. Readg. Rm., ILL Dept., Grad. Lib., Univ. of MI, 1967–69. **Educ.:** Univ. of CA, Berkeley, 1961–65, AB (Hist.); Univ. of MI, 1966–67, AMLS. **Orgs.:** TX LA. CA LA. ALA: Instr. in the Use of Libs. Com. (1976–80); RASD, Pubns. Com. (1978–82); Lib. Admin. Div./Lib. Orgs. and Mgt. Sect., Com. on Compar. Lib. Org. (1976–78); *C&RL News* Ed. Bd. (1980–82). **Honors:** Cncl. on Lib. Resrcs., Acad. Lib. Mgt. Intern, 1975–76. **Pubns.:** *Cooperative Activities of the University of California Libraries* (1976); "CLR Academic Library Management Interns: A Symposium," *Jnl. of Acad. Libnshp.* (S. 1980); ed. bd., *Jnl. of Acad. Libnshp.* (1980–). **Activities:** 1; 17, 31, 39 **Addr.:** The General Libraries, PCL 3200, The University of Texas, Austin, TX 78712.

Beaver, Lucile E. (F. 1, 1926, Gainesville, GA) Lib. Dir., U.S. Dept. of Transp. Lib., 1976–; Chief, 10A Services Branch (Aviation Branch), Dept. of Transp. Lib., 1969–76; Chief, Ref. and Resrch., Fed. Aviation Admn. Lib., 1965–69; Ref. Libn., 1963–65; Rcrt. Rep., Spec. Srvs., Dept. of the Army, 1959–63;

PROFESSIONAL ACTIVITIES: Institutions: 1. Acad. lib.; 2. Arch.; 3. Assn.; 4. Fed./Gvt. lib.; 5. Inst. lib.; 6. Mfr./Suppl.; 7. Milit. lib.; 8. Musm.; 9. Pub. lib.; 10. Sch. lib.; 11. Sch. of lib. sci.; 12. Spec. lib.; 13. State lib.; 14. (other). **Functions/Activities:** 15. Acq./Col. dev.; 16. Adult srvs.; 17. Admin.; 18. Apprais.; 19. Archit./Bldgs.; 20. Cat./Class.; 21. Chld. srvs.; 22. Circ.; 23. Cons./Pres.; 24. Consult.; 25. Cont. ed.; 26. Educ. lib. sci.; 27. Ext. srvs.; 28. Fund/Grants; 29. Gvt. pubs.; 30. Indx./Abs.; 31. Instr. lib. use; 32. Media srvs.; 33. Micro.; 34. Netwks./Coop.; 35. Persnl.; 36. PR; 37. Publshg.; 38. Recs. mgt.; 39. Ref. srvs.; 40. Repro.; 41. Resrch.; 42. Review.; 43. Secur.; 44. Serials; 45. Spec. col.; 46. Tech. srvs.; 47. Trustees/Bds.; 48. YA srvs.; 49. (other).

Asst. Libn., North. Area Cmnd., U.S. Army, Europe, 1956–59, Army Libn., 1954–56; Libn., Riverside Milit. Acad., 1949–54. **Educ.:** Agnes Scott Coll., 1942–46, BA (Math); Univ. of GA, 1946–48, MA (Math); Columbia Univ., 1948–49, MS, (LS). **Orgs.:** ALA: Mem. Bd. Dir. FLRT (1976–79). ASIS. SLA. Sigma Xi. Pi Mu Epsilon. **Honors:** U.S. Army, Europe, Cert. of Accomplishment, 1959; Dept. of Army, Washington, Outstan. Performance, 1961; Fed. Aviation Admn., Outstan. Performance, 1968, 1969; Phi Beta Kappa. **Pubns.:** *Transportation for the Handicapped* (1969). **Activities:** 4; 17, 35, 39; 52, 94 **Addr.:** Chief, Library Services Division, M-49, U.S. Dept. of Transportation, 400 Seventh Street, S.W., Washington, DC 20590.

Bebout, Lois (My. 14, 1930, Amherst, OH) Coord., Spec. Srvs., LA State Lib., 1980–; Head, Films and Rec. Sec., 1979–80; Lib. Info. Consult., 1975–79; Assoc. Dir. for Pub. Srvcs., Univ. of TX, Austin, 1974–75; Head, Hu. Resrch. Ctr. Cat., 1973–74; Univ. of Houston Libs. Docum. Libn., 1966–68; Asst. Sci. Lib., 1970–71; Asst. Hum. Libn., 1971–72; Head, Hum. and Soc. Sci. Div., 1972-73; various other positions. **Educ.:** Mt. Union Coll., 1948–52, BA (Eng.); Univ. of WI, Madison, 1953–54, MALS. **Orgs.:** ALA: RASD Info. Retrieval (1978). SLA. ASIS. TX LA: Ref. RT (Ch., 1974–75). **Honors:** RASD Mudge Citation, 1973–74; Dartmouth Medal, 1974–75. **Pubns.:** *The Texas List* ed. (1962, 1965, 1977–78); *Texas Reference Sources*, ed. (1975–78); *Microforms in Texas Libraries: A Selective Union List.* "User Studies in the Humanities" Jt. Auth. (1975). **Activities:** 1, 13; 17, 29, 39; 67, 92 **Addr.:** 220 Delgado Drive, Baton Rouge, LA 70808.

Becham, Gerald Charles (Jl. 20, 1938, Thomaston, GA) Asst. Dir. of the Lib., Georgia Col., 1970–; Tech. Libn., ARO, Inc., 1964–70; Tech. Lib., Thiokol Chem. Corp., 1963–64; Music Tchr., Toccoa Pub. Schs., 1960–62. **Educ.:** LaGrange Col., GA, 1956–60, BA (Music); Emory Univ., Ga., 1962–63, MLn (Lib. Sc). **Orgs.:** SELA. GA LA. Flannery O'Connor Bltn.: Bd. of Eds. **Honors:** Outstan. Young Men of America, 1969. **Pubns.:** "The Flannery O'Connor Collection", *Flannery O'Connor Bltn.* (1972). **Activities:** 1; 17, 20, 45 **Addr.:** Georgia College Library, Milledgeville, GA 31061.

Bechanan, H. Gordon Dir., VA Polytech. Univ., 1980–, Asst. Dir., 1972–80; Assoc. Univ. Libn., Harvard Univ., 1972, Asst. Dir., Admin. Asst., Dir., 1957–72. **Educ.:** Transylvania Univ., 1947, AB; Univ. KY, 1947–50; Columbia Univ., 1956, MLS. **Orgs.:** VA LA. SELA. ALA.: Com. Accred. (1965–71); LAD, various com. VA St. Cncl. Higher Educ.: Lib. Adv. Com. (1974–). Assn. S.E. Resrch. Lib.: ILL Com. ARL: ILL Com. **Addr.:** Director, Virginia Polytechnic University Library, Blacksburg, VA*

Bechtel, Joan M. (My. 22, 1933, Salem, NJ) Ch., Dept. of Lib. Resrcs., Dickinson Coll., 1980–, Head, Cat. Dept., 1978–80, Catlgr., 1971–78. **Educ.:** Wilson Coll., 1951–55, BA (Hist.); Drexel Univ., 1969–70, MS (LS); Univ. of PA, 1974–78, MA (European Int. Hist.). **Orgs.:** PA LA: Legis. Com.; Tech. Srvs. Com. ALA. Cnsrtm. to Dev. an Online Cat.: Strg. Com. **Honors:** Phi Beta Kappa, 1955; Beta Phi Mu, 1971. **Pubns.:** "Cambridge, My Loving Mother and Tender Nurse," *John and Mary's Jnl.* (Sum. 1979); "A Possible Contribution of The Library College Idea to Modern Education," *Drexel Lib. Qtly.* (Sum. 1971). **Activities:** 1; 17, 20, 31 **Addr.:** Dickinson College Library, Carlisle, PA 17013.

Beck, Beatrice Mae (S. 1, 19–, Pasadena, CA) Libn., Rancho Santa Ana Botanic Garden, 1970–; Head, Cat. Dept., CA State Univ. Polytech., Pomona, 1969–70; Educ., Acq. Libn., CA State Univ. Polytech., Los Angeles, 1960–69; Chld. Libn., Los Angeles Cnty., 1959–60. **Educ.:** John Muir Coll., 1952–54, AA (Hist.); Whittier Coll., 1954–55, BA (Psy.); Univ. of South. CA, 1955–56, MS (LS). **Orgs.:** Cncl. of Horticult. and Botanical Libs. Pomona Valley Geneal. Socty. NS DAR. **Pubns.:** "The Bowman-Bauman-Fox-Fuchs Families," *Settler* (My. 1981); "Shakespeare's Knowledge of Gardening," *St. Margaret's Jnl.* (Je.–S. 1980). **Activities:** 1; 15, 20, 23; 58, 69 **Addr.:** Rancho Santa Ana Botanic Garden, 1500 N. College Ave., Claremont, CA 91711.

Beck, Lois J. (Mr. 2, 1921, Avoca, PA) Head Catlgr., St. Paul Campus Lib., Univ. of MN, 1973–, Actg. Head, Cat. Sect., 1969–73, Catlgr., 1968–69. **Educ.:** Univ. of MN, 1962–67, BA summa cum laude (Eng. Lit.), 1967–68, MALS. **Orgs.:** ALA: ACRL; RTSD. MN LA. **Honors:** Phi Beta Kappa, 1967; Beta Phi Mu, 1968. **Activities:** 1; 15, 20, 46; 63, 92 **Addr.:** 1778 Eustis St., St. Paul, MN 55113.

Beck, Mary Clare Gvt. Docum. Libn., East. MI Univ., 1970–; Ref. Libn., Fordham Univ., 1966–70. **Educ.:** Univ. of Chicago, 1960–63, BA (Hist.); Univ. of Denver, 1964–66, MA (Libnshp.); East. MI Univ., 1973–76, MA (Soc. Std.). **Orgs.:** ALA: ILL Com. (1970–73); Cmnty. Use of Acad. Libs. Com. (1970–74); GODORT Constn. Com. (1973–76). MI GODORT: Nom. Com. (1980). **Honors:** Phi Kappa Phi, 1976. **Pubns.:** *1980 Census Resources; A Directory for Washtenaw County Data Users* (1980); "State of the Art Survey of U.S. Legal Documents," *Ref. Srv. Review* (Ja.–Mr. 1978). **Activities:** 1; 29, 39; 78 **Addr.:** Library, Documents Office, Eastern Michigan University, Ypsilanti, MI 48197.

Beck, Richard J. (Jl. 1, 1928, St. Paul, MN) Prof., Assoc. Dir. of Libs., Univ. of ID, 1960–, Sci. Libn., 1957–60; Loan Libn., Univ. of Detroit, 1955–57; Acq. Libn., Univ. of MN, 1954–55; Catlgr., IA State Univ., 1953–54, Ref. Libn., 1953; Gifts and Exch. Libn. 1950–52. **Educ.:** St. Thomas Coll., 1946–49, BA (Econ.); Univ. of MN, 1949–50, BSLS, 1954–55, MALS. **Orgs.:** ID LA: Pres. (1967–68); various coms. Pac. NW LA: various coms. ALA: various coms. Catholic LA. Various other orgs. Moscow United Way Bd. ID Pub. Empl. Assn. Knights of Columbus; Moscow Dist. Campfire Com. Various other orgs. **Honors:** ID LA, Libn. of the Yr., 1973; Beta Phi Mu. **Pubns.:** *A History of the Moscow Council #1397, Knights of Columbus* (1972); "Communication Graphics in Library Orientation," *Catholic Lib. World* (D. 1975); "The Washington State Advisory Council on Libraries," *ID Libn.* (Ap. 1975); "Fifty-Nine Footnotes (A Survey of Academic Library Hours and Use)," *PNLA Qtly.* (Spr. 1974); "PNNC'N You," *ID Libn.* (AP. 1974–); various other articles and numerous articles written as ed. of the Univ. of ID's qtly., *The Bookmark.* **Activities:** 1; 17, 25, 36; 50, 69, 85 **Addr.:** 418 East C, Moscow, ID 83843.

Beck, Sara Ramser (Jl. 10, 1940, Youngstown, OH) Ref. Srvs. Coord., Educ. Lib., Univ. MO, St. Louis, 1971–; Asst. Head, Acq., St. Louis Univ., 1969–71; Asst. Acq. Libn., Kent State Univ., 1968–69; Libn., Old Trail Sch., 1966–67; Actg. Head, Bus. and Tech., Canton Pub. Lib., 1964–66; Libn., Babcock-Wilcox Co., 1962–64; Readrs. Adv., Youngstown and Mahoning Cnty. Pub. Lib., 1961–62. **Educ.:** OH Wesleyan Univ., 1957–61, BA (Econ., Eng.); Kent State Univ., 1964–68, MLS; St. Louis Univ., 1975–78, MBA (Mgt. Sci.). **Orgs.:** ALA: ACRL. AAUP: Univ. of MO, St. Louis Chap. (Treas. 1975–76). St. Louis Univ. Assn. MBA Women: Prog. Chmn. (1977–78). **Pubns.:** "Research Skills for Graduate Students," *Coll. Outlk. and Career Oppts.* (Feb. 1979); "Resources for College Students," *Coll Outlk. and Career Oppts.* (Sept. 1979); "Canton Public Library Column", *Canton Repository* (1964–1966); "Children's Books," *Youngstown Vindicator* (Dec. 1961). **Activities:** 1, 9; 17, 31, 39; 51, 59, 63 **Addr.:** 520 Edgar Ct., St. Louis, MO 63119.

Beck, William L. (Mr. 8, 1943, Indiana, PA) Dir. of Lib. Srvs., California (PA) State Coll., 1970; AV Libn., Glenville State Coll., 1969–70; Tchr., Fox Chapel Area Schs. 1965–69. **Educ.:** Indiana Univ. of PA, 1961–65, BS (Educ.); Univ. of Pittsburgh, 1967–69, MLS; Univ. of Pittsburgh, 1971–74, Advnc. Cert. (LS). **Orgs.:** ALA. PA LA: Exec. Bd. S.W. Chap. (1973–74, 1978–79). Beta Phi Mu; Pi Chap., Pres. (1972–73). Phi Delta Kappa. **Pubns.:** "Selection of Library Materials," *Encyc. of Lib. & Info. Sci.*, vol. 27 (1979); "Effective Management of Microforms," *Microform Review* (Jl. 1973). **Activities:** 1; 17, 19, 33, 34 **Addr.:** R.D. #1, Box 13-1, Fredericktown, PA 15333.

Becker, James Louis (Ja. 9, 1927, San Francisco, CA) Docum. Dept., St. Louis Pub. Lib., 1976–; Ofc. of Chief Supvsr., 1975–76; Appld. Sci. Dept., 1967–71; 1973–75, Hum. and Soc. Sci. Dept., 1973, Ref. Dept., 1972–73, Chief, ILL Srvs., 1971–72, Mncpl. Ref. Lib., Asst. Libn., 1964–67. **Educ.:** City Coll. of San Francisco, 1953–55, AA; Univ. of CA, Berkeley, 1957–58, BA (Pol. Sci); West. MI Univ., 1962–64, MA (Libnshp.) **Orgs.:** ALA. SLA: Treas., Greater St. Louis Chap. (1975). MO LA. Cath. LA: Greater St. Louis Unit, Treas. (1975–76); Various other orgs. Amer. Pol. Sci. Assn. **Honors:** Alpha Gamma Sigma. **Pubns.:** Various articles in lib. jnls. **Addr.:** St. Louis Public Library, 1301 Olive Street, St. Louis, MO 63103.

Becker, Joseph (Ap. 15, 1923, New York, NY) Pres., Becker and Hayes, Inc., 1969–; VP, EDUCOM, 1966–69; Libn., US Gvt., 1944–66. **Educ.:** Brooklyn Polytech. Inst., 1944, BS (Engin.); Catholic Univ., 1955, MLS; Comp. Resrch. Fellow, Univ. of CA, Los Angeles, 1958–60. **Orgs.:** ALA: ISAD, Past Pres. (1968). ASIS: Past Pres. (1969). Info. Indus. Assn. AAAS: Sec. T (Secy., 1973–77). Assn. for Comp. Mach. Amer. Cybernetics Socty. **Honors:** Member, NCLIS, 1971–79. **Pubns.:** Jt. auth., *Handbook of Data Processing for Libraries* (1970, 1975); *Planning for Information Technology* (1974); *First Book of Information Science* (1973); *Library Automation–Introduction to Data Processing* (1973); *Application of Computer Technology to Library Processes* (1973); other books and articles. **Activities:** 4; 19, 24, 34; 62, 75, 93 **Addr.:** Becker & Hayes Inc., 2800 Olympic Blvd., Santa Monica, CA 90404.

Becker, Ronald L. (F. 16, 1950, New York, NY) Asst. Cur. of Spec. Col., Rutgers Univ., 1974–; Catlgr. & Biblgphr., NJ Hist. Soc., 1973–74. **Educ.:** Duke Univ., 1968–71, AB (Hist.); Rutgers Univ., 1971–73, MA (Hist.); MLS; OH Hist. Soc., Arch.-Lib. Inst., 1972–72, Cert. **Orgs.:** Mid-Atl. Reg. Arch. Conf.: Prog. Com. (1973–75, Chmn., 1974); Steering Com. (1974–77 Chmn., 1975–77). SAA: Reg. Archival Actv. Com. (1975–77). Metuchen Pub. Lib. Bd. of Trustees: Treas. (1978–). **Pubns.:** *A Union List of Annual Publications in the Library Collections of the NJ Historical Society and Rutgers Univ.* (1977); "A Republican Meeting in Burlington County-1800," *New Jersey History* (Summer 1974); "Amusement Hall; An Unusual Morristown Pamphlet," *New Jersey History* (Autumn-Winter 1975). **Activities:** 1; 45; 57, 69, 73 **Addr.:** Special Collections Dept., Alexander Lib., Rutgers Univ., New Brunswick, NJ 08903.

Beckerman, Edwin P. (N. 27, 1927, New York, NY) Dir., Woodbridge Pub. Lib., 1964–; Asst. Dir., Yonkers Pub. Lib., 1961–63; Pub. Lib. Consult., NY State Lib., 1959–61; Libn., NY Pub. Lib., 1952–59. **Educ.:** Univ. of MO, 1946–49, AB (Eng. Lit.); Columbia Univ., 1951–52, MSLS. **Orgs.:** NJ LA: Pres. (1970–71). ALA: Com. on Org. (1975–76); Com. on Prog. Eval. and Support (1977–81). **Pubns.:** Chap. in *Local Public Library Administration* (1981); chap. in *Libraries in the Political Process* (1980). **Addr.:** Woodbridge Public Library, George Frederick Plz., Woodbridge, NJ 07095.

Beckman, Margaret L. (Ja. 22, 1926, Hartford, CT) Chief Libn., Univ. of Guelph, 1971–, Deputy Libn., Univ. of Guelph, 1970–71, Syst. Libn., 1966–70; Head, Tech. Srvs., Univ. of Waterloo, 1960–65. **Educ.:** Univ. of West. ON, 1943–46, BA (Hist.); Univ. of Toronto, 1948–49, BLS, 1964–69, (MLS). **Orgs.:** Can. Assn. of Coll. and Univ. Libs.: (Ch. 1972–73). ALA. Can. LA. ON LA. ASIS. Adv. Bd. for Sci. and Tech. Info., Natl. Resrch. Cncl. of Can.: (Ch. 1980–); Exec. Com. (1976–80). Waterloo Pub. Lib. Bd.: (Ch. 1966–68). **Honors:** Prov. of ON, Outstand. Woman, 1975. **Pubns.:** Jt.-auth., *New Library Design* (1971); Jt.-auth., "On-line acquisitions–circulation interfaces at the University of Guelph," Lib. Acq.: Prac. and Theory (1980); "On-line circulation: First step in a cost effective integrated total library system," *Expression* (S.–O. 1979); "Automated cataloguing systems and networks in Canada," *Can. Lib. Jnl.* (Jn. 1978); Many other papers and presentations. **Addr.:** 168 John Blvd., Waterloo, ON N2L 1C5 Canada.

Beckwith, Herbert H. (Mr. 16, 1930, Pittsburgh, PA) Head Cat. Libn., Natl. Maritime Musm., 1975–; Head, Ref. Srvs. Unit, VT Dept. of Libs., 1968–72; Soc. Sci. Libn., KS State Univ., 1967–68; Ref. Libn., AZ State Univ., 1964–67; Head Loan Libn., 1962–64; Ref./Cir. Libn., CA Inst. of Tech., 1960–62; Ref. Libn./Asst. Catlgr., Lake Forest Coll., 1958–60; Circ. Desk Libn., OH State Univ., 1957–58. **Educ.:** Lake Forest Col., 1956, BA (Fr.); Univ. of NC, 1956–58, MSLS; Univ. of Santa Clara, 1973–75, MA work (Hist.). **Orgs.:** ALA. SLA. Epis. Diocese of CA. **Pubns.:** Jt. Ed., *Index to theses at KS State Univ.*, (1967); "ILL: the view from up here", *North Country Libs.* (My.-Je. 1969); Jt. Auth., "Ref. workshops: implications.", *VT Libs.* (Jl-Ag 1971). **Activities:** 1, 4; 20, 22, 39; 55, 91 **Addr.:** 1824 Doris Dr., Menlo Park, CA 94025.

Bedard, Evelyn Margaret (O. 9, 1917, Worcester, MA) Coord. for Nursing and Allied Hlth., Houston Acad. of Med.- TX Med. Ctr. Lib., 1972–; Assoc. Dir. for Nursing, Duke Univ. Hosp., 1967–69; Asst. Prof., Comm. Med. & Research Associate, Sch. of Med., Univ. of MO, 1964–67; Command Nurse, USAF, U.S.A., 1941–62. **Educ.:** NY Univ., 1955–56, BS (Nursing Ed); Johns Hopkins Univ., 1962–63, MPH (Pub. Hlth. Admin.); Univ. of NC, 1970–72, MSLS; Mem. Hosp. Sch. of Nursing, 1935–38, Dip., (Nursing). **Orgs.:** Med LA: S. Cent. Reg. Assoc. Amer. Nurses' Assn. TX Nurse's Assn.: Pub. Inf. Com., Ch. Amer. Pub. Hlth. Assn. Sigma Theta Tau, Upsilon Chap. **Honors:** USAF, Commendation Medal, 1962; Sigma Theta Tau. **Activities:** 1, 12; 31, 36, 39; 78, 80, 92 **Addr.:** 5410 Spellman Rd., Houston, TX 77096.

Bedford, Louise C. (My. 6, 1917, Des Moines, IA) Instr. Media Coord., Montgomery Cnty., KY, 1975–; Media Libn., Mt. Sterling City Schs., 1955–75; Tchr. and Libn., 1950–55; Expediter, Gen. Electric Co., 1942–50; Tchr., Montgomery Cnty. Bd. of Educ. (KY), 1938–42. **Educ.:** Drake Univ., 1934–38, AB (Hist.); Univ. of KY, 1951–53, MSLS, 1956–59, Rank I (Sec. Sch. Admin). **Orgs.:** KY Sch. Media Assn.: Pres. (1975); Secy. (1963). KY LA: Pres. (1979–80). SELA: Exec. Bd. (1974–78). ALA-:AASL/Legislative Com. (1979–81). KY Educ. Assn.: Ctrl. KY Div. Libns. (Pres., 1958). Natl. Educ. Assn. **Honors:** KY LA, Outstan. KY Sch. Libn., 1975; Appt. to State of KY, Oral Hist. Comm., 1974–; Task Force on Educ., 1978–79; Gvr.'s Adv. Cncl. on Libs., 1979–81. **Activities:** 10; 17, 21, 48; 74, 78, 89 **Addr.:** Montgomery County Board of Education, R.5-Woodford Road, Mt. Sterling, KY 40353.

Beecher, John William (Ja. 20, 1941, Bloomington, IL) Head, Pub. Srvs., St. Paul Campus Libs., Univ. of MN, 1982–; Agr. Libn., Univ. of IL, 1973–82; Asst. Sci. Libn., NM State Univ., 1970–73; Asst. Acq. Libn., TX Christ. Univ., 1969–70. **Educ.:** Univ. of IL, 1959–64, BS (Horticulture), 1965–66, MLS. **Orgs.:** ALA: Sci. and Tech. Div., Oberly Awd. for Bibl. in Agr. Sci. (Ch., 1980–81). SLA: Bio. Sci. Div., New Projs. Ch. (1977–78), Pubcty. Ch. (1979). ASIS. Intl. Assn. of Agr. Libns. and Docmlsts. Cncl. on Bot. and Horticult. Libs. **Pubns.:** "Use of Random Alarm Mechanisms for Analyzing Professional and Support Staff Activities in Science Libraries," *Lib. Resrch.* (forthcoming); jt. auth., *An Agricultural Data Bank and Communications Center for the Mano River Union* (1978); *A 5-Year Development Program for the Library at the Institute of Agriculture and Animal Science, Rampur, Nepal* (1979); "Offering Successful Self-Instructional Services in the Library," *Procs. of the 5a Reun. Interamer. de Bibtcr. y Documentalistas Agricolas, San Jose, Costa Rica, 10–14 Ap. 1978* (1980); jt. auth., "Agricultural Librarianship and Documentation as a Profession," *Procs. of the 6th World Congs. of the Intl. Assn. of Agr. Libns. and Docmlsts. Manila, Philippines, Mr., 1980* (forthcoming). **Ac-**

Special Subjects/Services: 50. Adult educ.; 51. Advert./Mktg.; 52. Aerosp.; 53. Agric.; 54. Area std.; 55. Arts/Hum.; 56. Autom.; 57. Bibl./Prtg.; 58. Bio. sci.; 59. Bus./Fin.; 60. Chem.; 61. Copyrt.; 62. Documtn.; 63. Educ.; 64. Engin.; 65. Env.; 66. Eth. grps.; 67. Film; 68. Food/Nutr.; 69. Geneal.; 70. Geo.; 71. Geol.; 72. Handcpd.; 73. Hist.; 74. Int. frdm.; 75. Info. sci.; 76. Insr.; 77. Law; 78. Legis.; 79. Math./Comp. sci.; 80. Med.; 81. Metals; 82. Nat. resrcs.; 83. Newsp.; 84. Nuc. sci.; 85. Oral hist.; 86. Petr./Energy; 87. Pharm.; 88. Phys./Astr./Math.; 89. Readg.; 90. Relig.; 91. Sci./Tech.; 92. Soc. sci.; 93. Telecom.; 94. Transp.; 95. (other).

tivities: 1; 15, 17, 39; 58, 82, 91 **Addr.:** 1984 Buford Ave., St. Paul, MN 55108.

Beede, Benjamin R. (Ja. 12, 1939, Portland, ME) Head of Ref. Kilmer Area Lib., Rutgers Univ., 1981–; Asst. Law Libn., Rutgers Univ., 1969–80; Supvsg. Ref. Libn., Linden Pub. Lib., 1968–69. **Educ.:** Rutgers Univ., 1957–61, AB (Pol. Sci.); 1962–63, MLS; 1971–79, MA (Pol. Sci.). **Orgs.:** ALA. SLA. Greater Phil. Law LA: Pres. (1974–75). NJ LA: Ed. Adv. Board (1977–78); Secy. (1978–79). Amer. Pol. Sci. Assn. Amer. Hist. Assn. NJ Pol. Sci. Assn.: Secy-Treas. (1975–79). **Honors:** Phi Beta Kappa, 1961. **Pubns.:** Jt. Auth., *Legal Sources of Public Policy* (1977); Jt. Auth., *Independence Documents of the World* (1977); "American Librarianship", *Signs: Jnl. of Women in Culture and Soc.*, (Sum. 1976); "Library Instruction in American Law Schools", *Law Lib Jnl.*, (F. 1975). **Activities:** 1, 12; 31, 39, 41; 77, 78, 92 **Addr.:** 7 Thrush Mews, North Brunswick, NJ 08902.

Beeler, Linda Diann (Ap. 11, 1939, Peru, IA) Lib. Dept. Ch., Thornridge HS, Dolton, IL, 1961–. **Educ.:** Univ. of North. IA, 1959–61, BA (Educ.); Univ. of Chicago, 1962–67, MALS; 1972–78, CAS (Educ.). **Orgs.:** IFLA/Sect. on Sch. Libs., Plng. Grp. (1974–75), Secy. (1977–). Intl. Assn. of Sch. Libnshp.: Ed. Com. (1974–). ALA: Ad Hoc Com. on Intl. Rel. (1972–74); AASL/Intl. Rel. (1979–), Leg. Com. (1977–79). IL LA. various other orgs. World Confederation of Orgs. of the Tchg. Prof.: Del. (1970, 75, 76). Natl. Educ. Assn. IL Educ. Assn. **Pubns.:** Jt. auth., "So You're Expecting an International Visitor" brochure (1974); Jt. auth., "Welcome to the U.S.A." brochure (1975). **Activities:** 10; 17, 48, 49-International Cooperation; 54 **Addr.:** Thornridge High School Library, Sibley Blvd. and Cottage Grove, Dolton, IL 60419.

Beer, Florence Greenberg (Jl. 22, 1930, Brooklyn, NY) Lib. Dir., SUNY, Educ. Oppt. Ctr., Syracuse, 1969–; Volun. Libn., Congregation Beth Shalom, 1978–; Volun. Libn., Max Gilbert Day Sch., 1968–78; Libn., Hillel Acad., Pittsburgh, PA, 1965–68. **Educ.:** Brooklyn Coll., 1947–54, BA (Art, Educ.); Univ. of Pittsburgh, 1963–67, MLS; State of NY, 1972, Permanent Pub. Libn. Cert., Sch. Libn. Cert. (Lib. Media Spec.). **Orgs.:** Libns. Unlimited, Syracuse, NY: VP (1980–). NY LA. ALA. Amer. Jewish Com. Brooklyn Coll. Alum. Assn. Beta Phi Mu: Pi Lambda Sigma Chap. (Secy., 1979–). **Honors:** SUNY, 10 Yr. Srv. Awd., 1980. **Activities:** 10, 12; 15, 17, 31; 50, 66 **Addr.:** Paul Robeson Library, SUNY, Educational Opportunity Center, 100 New St., Syracuse, NY 13202.

Beer, Richard Lambert (S 14, 1930, Detroit, MI) Dir., Adams-Pratt Oakland Cnty. Law Li., 1960–. **Educ.:** Univ. of MI, 1957–, BA, (Pol. Sci.); Wayne State Univ., 1971–, MSLS. **Orgs.:** AALL: Pubns. Com., Ch. (1979–80). OH Reg. Assn. Law Libns.: Pres. (1978). MI Assn. Law Libns.: Educ. Com., Ch. (1979). Cncl. on Resrc. Dev.: V Ch. (1979–80). **Honors:** Oakland Cnty Bd of Comsns., Srv. Recog., 1981; Oakland Univ., Cert. of Abr., 1979. **Pubns.:** *An Annotated Guide to the Legal Literature of Michigan* (1973); Jt. Auth., *Legal Research and Writing* (1976); Jt. Auth., *Access to America* (1976); "Librarians and the Law" (1979). **Activities:** 4, 9; 17, 24, 25; 50, 72, 77 **Addr.:** Adams-Pratt, Oakland County Law Library, 1200 North Telegraph Rd., Pontiac, MI 48053.

Beers, Henry Putney (My. 7, 1907, Scranton, PA) Retired, 1968–; Finding Aids Spec., Natl. Arch., 1958–68; Asst. Ed., *Territorial Papers of the U. S.*, 1950–58; Hist., U.S. Dept. of State, 1946–50 Hist., U.S. Navy, 1944–46. **Educ.:** Lafayette Coll., 1926–30, BS (Govt., Hist.); Univ. of PA, 1930–31, MA (Hist.), 1931–35, PhD (Hist.). **Honors:** SAA, Waldo Gifford Leland Prize for Guide to Federal Archives Relating to the Civil War, 1963; Same for Guide to the Archives of the Government of the Confederate States of America, 1969; Gen. Srvs. Admin. (Natl. Arch.) for the foregoing publications, Merit. Srvc. Awd., 1963; Commendable Srvc. Awd., 1968. **Pubns.:** *Spanish and Mexican Records of the American Southwest: A Bibliographical Guide* (1979); *The French and British in the Old Northwest: A Bibliographical Guide* (1964); Many articles and bibliographies. **Activities:** 2; 18, 41; 57 **Addr.:** 2372 N. Quincy St., Arlington, VA 22207.

Beery, Carl (F. 17, 1935, Yakima, WA) Consult., Suburban Lib. Syst. and AV Ser., Burr Ridge, IL, 1977; Head Libn., Berkeley Pub. Lib., Berkeley, IL, 1974–77; Media Ctr. Supvsr. Cook Cnty. Sch. Dist. No. 87, Berkeley, IL, 1972–74. **Educ.:** Shenandoah Conservatory of Music, 1967–70, BM (Music); Rosary Coll., 1972–75, MA (LS). **Orgs.:** ALA: By-Laws Comm. Blind and Phys. Handcpd. (1979–80). ILLA (Mem. and Pubcty. Comm.). Chicago Lib. Club. WHCOLIS. **Honors:** IL LA., De Lafayette Reid Award, 1979. **Pubns.:** *Guide to Chicago for the Handicapped.* (1978); *Adapting an Existing Computer System to the Talking Books Program.* (1978); "Some Benefits to Public Libraries Providing Direct Service for Talking Book Patrons", *Dikta* (Fall 1978); Ed., *Suburban Lib. Syst. News* (1977–); Ed., IL LA., *Nsltr. of the Spec. Lib. Sers. Sect.* (1979–). **Activities:** 4, 9; 17, 24, 36, 47; 56, 72 **Addr.:** Box 838, Hillside, IL 60163.

Befu, Kei Tomita (Sacramento, CA) Assoc. Libn., East Asian Col., Hoover Inst., 1978–; Head Libn., St. Patrick's Coll., Mountain View, 1975–78; Libn., Stanford Ctr. for R. and D. in Teaching, Stanford Univ., 1973–75; Libn., Univ. of MI Lib., 1964–64. **Educ.:** Univ. of CA, Berkeley, 1954–56, AB (Soclgy.), 1962–64, MLS. **Orgs.:** ALA. **Honors:** Beta Phi Mu. **Activities:** 1, 12; 20, 39, 46; 54, 92, 95-Japanese Std. **Addr.:** East Asian Collection, Hoover Institution, Stanford, CA 94305.

Begg, Karin E. (Mr. 7, 1939, Stockholm, Sweden) Systs. Libn., Boston Univ., 1980–, OCLC Supvsr., Coord., 1980; Circ. Libn., Univ. of VA, 1977–79; Cat. Ed., Univ. of PA, 1973–76, Acq. Asst., 1972–73, Anglo-Germanic Orig. Catlgr., 1968–72, Asst. Libn., Univ. Musm. Lib., 1966–68. **Educ.:** Brown Univ., 1957–61, BA (Art); Drexel Univ., 1970–72, MLS. **Orgs.:** ALA: LITA. New Eng. Chap. ACRL: Archvst. (1981). MA Lib. Legis. Info. Netwk. New Eng. LA. Natl. Org. of Women. Common Cause. Brown Univ. Club of Boston. **Honors:** Beta Phi Mu, 1972. **Pubns.:** "Tools of the Serials Trade" clmn. *Serials Review* (O.–D. 1981); "Report of the Task Force on Catalog Use," *Resrcs. Educ.* (Ja. 1981). **Activities:** 1; 17, 20, 34; 56 **Addr.:** Mugar Library, Boston University, 771 Commonwealth Ave., Boston, MA 02215.

Begg, Robert Thomas (Ag. 14, 1947, Pittsburgh, PA) Head Law Libn., OH North. Univ., 1976–; Asst. Law Libn., Univ. of Akron, 1974–76; Law Libn., Lane Cnty. (OR) Law Lib., 1972–73. **Educ.:** Slippery Rock State Coll., 1965–69, BS (Educ.); Rutgers Univ., 1973–74, MLS; Univ. of OR, 1970–73, JD (Law). **Orgs.:** AALL. OH Reg. Assn. of Law Libs: Treas. (1979–). **Pubns.:** The Reference Librarian and the Pro Se Patron," *Law Lib. Jnl.* (1976); "Disabled Libraries: An Examination of Physical and Attitudinal Barriers to Handicapped Library Users," *Law Lib. Jnl.* (Sum. 1979). **Activities:** 1; 15, 17; 77 **Addr.:** Taggart Law Library, Ohio Northern University, ADA, OH 45810.

Beglo, Joanne K. (Ja. 15, 1948, Edgeley, ND) Ref. and Col. Dev. Libn., Univ. of Waterloo, 1975–; Lang. Instr., Montreal YWCA, 1972–74; Supply Tchr., Protestant Sch. Bd of Montreal, 1972. **Educ.:** Univ. of ND, 1966–68; Waterloo Lutheran Univ., 1968–70, BA (German Lit.); McGill Univ., 1973–74; Univ. of Toronto, 1974–75, MLS; Univ. of Waterloo, 1980, BA, honors, (Art Hist.). **Orgs.:** Can. LA. ALA. ARLIS/NA. Univ. of Waterloo Libns. Assn.: Pres (1980–81); Prog. Com., Ch. (1978–79). Univ. Art Assn. of Can. Col. Art Assn. of America. Can. Assn. of Univ. Tchrs. **Activities:** 1; 15, 31, 39; 55, 90, 95-Arch. **Addr.:** Reference and Collections, Development Department, Dana Porter Arts Library, University of Waterloo, Waterloo, ON N2L 3G1 Canada.

Behn, Roger Frederick (My. 15, 1930, Liverpool, Eng.) Alderman, Vlg. of Chase, 1981–82; Ch., Bd. of Mgt., Cariboo-Thompson Nicola Lib. Syst., 1974–81, Pres., Overlander Lib. Socty., 1974–; Pres., 1972–73; Sch. Libn., Chase Sec. Sch., 1964; Sch. Libn., John Tod Elem. Sch., 1963; Tchr., Sch. Dist. #36, Survey, 1962. **Educ.:** MacDonald Coll., McGill Univ., 1952–54, Dip. (Agr.); Univ. of BC, 1967, BEdSec (Lib., Geo.). **Orgs.:** BC Sch. Libns. Assn.: Pres. (1971); Treas. (1969–70). BC Lib. Trustees' Assn. Can. LA. Can. Sch. Libns. Assn. Various other orgs. Natl. Model Railroaders Assn. Can. Power Squadrons. Royal Can. Legion. BC Rifle Assn. **Activities:** 9, 10; 47, 48 **Addr.:** Box 353, Chase, BC V0E 1M0 Canada.

Behrens, Elizabeth Mary-Ann (Ap. 20, 1947, Oslo, Norway) Coll. Libn., Sir Wilfred Grenfell Coll., 1975–; Campus Lib. Mgr., Dawson Coll., 1971–74, Ref. Libn., 1969–71. **Educ.:** Univ. de Montreal, 1964–67, BA (Hist.); McGill Univ., 1967–69, MLS. **Orgs.:** NF LA: Pres. (1979–80). CA LA. ALA. Corp. of Prof. Libns. of Québec. Atl. Provs. LA. **Activities:** 1; 17, 31, 39 **Addr.:** College Library, Sir Wilfred Grenfell College, University Drive, Corner Brook, NF A2H 6P9 Canada.

Beilby, Mary (Heying) (Ja. 10, 1940, Alma, MI) Col. Dev. Libn., SUNY, Cortland, 1968–; Serials Acq. Libn., Princeton Univ., 1967–68; Ref. Cat. Libn., Cornell Univ., 1965–67. **Educ.:** Alma Coll., 1958–62, BA (Eng.); Univ. of CA, Los Angeles, 1964–65, MSLS; Rutgers Univ., 1974–, PhD in progress (LS). **Orgs.:** ALA. ASIS. SUNY Libns. Assn. **Pubns.:** Co-Auth., *Development of a Responsive Library Acquisitions Formula* (1978); Co-Auth., "An Information System for Collection Development in SUNY," *Col. Mgt.* (Fall 1978). **Activities:** 1; 15, 34, 41; 56, 63, 75 **Addr.:** Memorial Library, State University of New York, Cortland, NY 13045.

Beilke, Patricia Fay (O. 10, 1933, Austin, TX) Assoc. Prof., LS, Ball State Univ., 1978–; Assoc. Prof., Sch. of LS, Emporia State Univ., 1976–78; Asst. Prof., Dept. of Educ. Media, Auburn Univ., 1971–76; Instr., Coll. of ID, 1969; Sch. Libn., La Mesa-Spr. Valley Sch. Dist., 1958–70; Chld. Libn., Wayne Cnty. Lib., 1955–57. **Educ.:** West. MI Univ., 1951–55, BA (Fr.), 1957–58, MA (Eng., Educ.); CA State Bd. of Educ., 1966, Libnshp. Life Dip.; West. MI Univ., 1967–68, MSL (LS); State of CA, 1969, Stan. Supvsn. Cred. (Lib. Srvs.); West. MI Univ., 1968–74, Ed D (Educ. Leadership). **Orgs.:** IFLA: Stats. and Stans. Sect., Stdg. Com. (1979–). Intl. Assn. of Sch. Libnshp.: Resrch. and Stats. Com. (Ch., 1975–). ALA: LIRT, Natl. Progs. Std. Task Frc. (1979–); Lib. Admin. Div., Nom. Com. (1975–76), Lib. Org. and Mgt. Sect., Stats. for Sch. Lib. Media Ctrs. Com., Secy. (1970–72); Ch. (1972–74); Stats. for Ref. Srvs. Com. (1973–77); Prog. Plng. Subcom. (Ch., 1975); AASL, various coms. AECT: Accred. Com. (1976–78). IN LA: Nom. Com. (1980–); Chld. and YA Div. Bd. (1979–). Intl. Readg. Assn. Acad. for Intl. Bus. Natl. Educ. Assn.: Assn. for Supvsn. and Curric. Dev. **Honors:** Phi Delta Kappa, 1975; Beta Phi Mu, Kappa Chap., 1968; Kappa Delta Pi, 1954. **Pubns.:** Jt. auth., *Guidelines for the Planning and Organization of School Library Media Centres* (1979); "Field Experiences for Media Specialists," *Strategies for Change in Information Programs* (1974); "Librarianship: 'Becoming' as Preparation for the Future," *AECT Resrch. and Theory Div. Nsltr.* (F. 1977); "IASL Committee on Research and Statistics," *Sch. Media Qtly.* (Win. 1976); "Program for Education in Educational Media," *The Pahlavi National Library of the Future: Its Resources, Services, Programs and Building Requirements* (1976); various articles. **Activities:** 10, 11; 17, 19, 32; 63, 72 **Addr.:** Dept. of Library Science, Ball State University, Muncie, IN 47306.

Beintema, William J. (Je. 2, 1944, Bayshore, NY) Dir., Law Lib., OK City Univ., 1978–; Asst. Law Libn., Univ. of Miami, 1970–78. **Educ.:** Univ. of Miami, 1962–67, BBA (Fin.), 1967–70, JD (Law); FL State Univ., 1970–78, MSLS. **Orgs.:** AALL: *Law Lib. Jnl.* Com. (1976–77); Place. Com. (1975–77). Southwest. Assn. of Law Libs. **Honors:** Beta Phi Mu, 1978; Omicron Delta Kappa, 1976. **Activities:** 12; 17; 77 **Addr.:** Law Library, Oklahoma City University, 2501 N. Blackwelder, Oklahoma City, OK 73106.

Beland, Andre (My. 20, 1942, Beaudry, PQ) Ref. Srvs., Acq. Libn., Coll. de Rouyn, 1975–; Chief Libn., Polyvalente D'Iberville, 1972–75; Cat. and Class. Dept., Coll. de Rouyn, 1963–65. **Educ.:** Univ. de Montreal, 1963, BA, 1966, BBibl. **Orgs.:** Corp. des Bibtcrs. Prof. du PQ. ASTED. **Pubns.:** *Bibliographie de L'Abitibi-Temiscamincue* (1979). **Activities:** 1, 10; 15, 20, 39 **Addr.:** 435 Montee du Sourire, Rouyn, PQ J9X 5L2 Canada.

Belanger, Sandra Emily (Ja. 17, 1944, Sault Ste. Marie, MI) Sr. Asst. Libn., Ref., San Jose State Univ. Lib., 1975–; Asst. Ed., *The Bio. Bltn.*, Marine Bio. Lab., Syracuse Univ., 1968–74; Tchr., Wells St. Jr. High, 1966–68. **Educ.:** Univ. of WI, 1962–66, BS (Educ., Hist.); Syracuse Univ., 1969–74, MS (Libnshp.); San Jose State Univ., 1976–79, MS (Educ.). **Orgs.:** CA Media and Lib. Educs. Assn.: *CMLEA Jnl.* Managing Ed. (1979–). SLA: San Andreas Chap., Ch.; Student Rel. Com. CA LA: State Univs. and Colls. Chap. **Pubns.:** "History of the Library of the Marine Biological Laboratory 1888–1973," *Jnl. of Lib. Hist.* (Jl. 1975). **Activities:** 1, 12; 39; 51, 59, 63 **Addr.:** General Reference, San Jose State University Library, San Jose, CA 95192.

Belanger, Terry (Mr. 21, 1941, Hartford, CT) Asst. Dean, Sch. of Lib. Srv., Columbia Univ., 1980; Asst. Prof., 1972–79. **Educ.:** Haverford Coll., 1959–63, AB (Eng.); Columbia Univ., 1963–64, MA (Eng.); 1964–70, PhD (Eng.). **Orgs.:** ALA: Adv. Comm., ALA Glossary, (1978–); ACRL/Rare Bks. and Mss., (Ch. 1977–78, Bd. of Dir. 1976–8). Prtg. Hist. Soc.: Amer. Mem. Secy. 1976–80); Amer. Prtg. Hist. Assn.: Trustee (1974–79), NY Chapt., Pres. (1979–82); Ctr. Bk., Lib. of Congs.: Natl. Adv. Bd. (1978–); Exec. com. (1981–). **Pubns.:** Jt. Auth. *The Art of Persuasion* (1972); Jt. Auth. "Book Production & Distribution," *New Cambridge Bibliography of English Literature, vol. 2, 1660–1800;* Jt. Auth. "Rare Book Cataloguing & Computers", *AB BKman's Wkly.* (F. 1979); Ed., *Bibliography Newsletter,* 1973; Adv. Ed., *Publishing History.* **Activities:** 1; 23, 26, 45; 55, 57 **Addr.:** 516 Butler Library, School of Library Service, Columbia University, New York, NY 10027.

Belch, Caroline Jean (Seattle, WA) Head, Curric. Mtrls. Ctr., Univ. of WA, 1968–; Head, Tech. Srvs., Seattle Pacific Univ., 1964–68; Libn., Forest Ridge Convent, 1962–64. **Educ.:** Univ. of WA, 1934–38, BA (Eng.), 1959–60, MBL (LS). **Pubns.:** *Contemporary Games* (1974). **Activities:** 1; 15, 21; 63 **Addr.:** Curriculum Materials Center, University of Washington Libraries, Seattle, WA 98195.

Belcher, Faye (F. 29, 1932, Belcher, KY) Assoc. Dir. of Libs., Morehead State Univ., 1971–, Asst. Dir. of Libs., 1970–71, Asst. Libn., 1965–70; Libn., Pike Cnty. Schs., 1965; Libn., Lexington Schs., 1962–64; Libn., Pike Cnty. Schs., 1960–62. **Educ.:** Univ. of KY, 1956, AB (Educ., Eng.), 1961, MA (Educ., LS), 1968, MS in LS equiv.; Peabody Coll. for Tchrs., 1972 (Educ., LS). **Orgs.:** ALA. SELA: Prog. Dev. Com. (1973); Manpower Com. (1972). KY LA: Prof. Dev. Com. (1976–77); Coll. and Resrch. Nom. Com. (1977). AAUW. Ky Hist. Socty. Bus. and Prof. Women's Club: Pres. Univ. Senate: Secy. (1978–79). **Honors:** Phi Kappa Phi. **Pubns.:** "The Instructional Materials Center" *KY LA Bltn.* (O. 1967). **Activities:** 1; 17; 63, 75, 89 **Addr.:** Camden-Carroll Library, Morehead State University, Morehead, KY 40351.

Belknap, Gerda Moore (D. 2, 1941, Columbia, SC) Chief, Ext. Srvs., Richland Cnty. Pub. Lib., 1974; Chld. Srvs. Libn., 1970–74; Libn., Crayton Sch., 1967–70; Libn., Episcopal Church Exec. Cncl., 1965–67; Libn., Evans Jr. HS, 1964–65. **Educ.:** Univ. of SC, 1960–63, AB (Educ.); Univ. of NC, 1963–64, MS (LS). **Orgs.:** SE LA: Bd. Dir. (1976–80); Cont. Ed. Com. (1977–). SC LA: Cont. Ed. Com. (1977–80); Pres.-Elect (1981); Bd. Dir.

PROFESSIONAL ACTIVITIES: Institutions: 1. Acad. lib.; 2. Arch.; 3. Assn.; 4. Fed./Gvt. lib.; 5. Inst. lib.; 6. Mfr./Suppl.; 7. Milit. lib.; 8. Musm.; 9. Pub. lib.; 10. Sch. lib.; 11. Sch. of lib. sci.; 12. Spec. lib.; 13. State lib.; 14. (other). **Functions/Activities:** 15. Acq./Col. dev.; 16. Adult srvs.; 17. Admin.; 18. Apprais.; 19. Archit./Bldgs.; 20. Cat./Class.; 21. Chld. srvs.; 22. Circ.; 23. Cons./Pres.; 24. Consult.; 25. Cont. ed.; 26. Educ. lib. sci.; 27. Ext. srvs.; 28. Fund/Grants; 29. Gvt. pubs.; 30. Indx./Abs.; 31. Instr. lib. use; 32. Media srvs.; 33. Micro.; 34. Netwks./Coop.; 35. Persnl.; 36. PR; 37. Publshg.; 38. Recs. mgt.; 39. Ref. srvs.; 40. Repro.; 41. Resrch.; 42. Review.; 43. Secur.; 44. Serials; 45. Spec. col.; 46. Tech. srvs.; 47. Trustees/Bds.; 48. YA srvs.; 49. (other).

(1974–); Ch., Pub. Lib. Sect. (1974–75); 2nd VP (1978); Ch., Const. and By-Laws Com. (1977). ALA. Junior League of Columbia: VP (1976–1977); Bd. of Dir. (1975–1977). **Activities:** 9, 12; 17, 27, 35 **Addr.:** 4730 Cedar Springs Rd., Columbia, SC 29206.

Bell, C. Margaret (D. 31, 1956, Winsted, CT) Info. Spec., Gen. Foods Tech. Ctr., 1979–; Catlgr. (part-time), Gen. Electric Whitney Lib., Schenectedy, 1978–79. **Educ.:** St. Joseph Coll., 1975–78, (Home Econ.); SUNY, Albany, 1978–79, MLS. **Orgs.:** ALA. SLA: Hudson Valley Chap., OL User Grp. (Ch., 1979–); Arrangements (Ch., 1979–). **Pubns.:** "Identifying Food Dyes by Chromatography," *Sci. Tchr.* (N. 1979); "Laboratory Notebook Storage and Retrieval Systems," *Food for Thought* (S. 1979); oral presentations (1978). **Activities:** 12; 30, 39, 49-on line searching; 58, 60, 68 **Addr.:** General Foods Technical Information Center, 555 S. Broadway, Tarrytown, NY 10591.

Bell, Edith Helen (My. 7, 1926, Waldoboro, ME) Libn., Media Spec., Westbrook Jr. HS, 1960–, Tchr., 1956–60; Tchr., Windham Sch. Dept., 1947–49. **Educ.:** Gorham State Tchrs., 1943–47, BS (Eng. Lit.); Univ. of ME, Orono, 1960–65, MEd (Soc. Std.); Univ. of ME, Portland, 1969–71, MLS. **Orgs.:** New Eng. Educ. Media Assn.: Secy. (1971–73). ME Educ. Media Assn.: Bd. Mem. (1972–73). South. ME Lib. Dist. Windham Pub. Lib.: Trustee (1978–). Various other orgs. Delta Kappa Gamma Socty. Intl.: VP (1978–80). **Honors:** Girl Scouts of Amer., Thanks Badge, 1975. **Activities:** 10; 17, 32, 48; 63 **Addr.:** R.D. #2, River Rd., South Windham, ME 04082.

Bell, Elsie Lilias (Je. 12, 1922, Clydebank, Scotland) Chief, Main Lib., Metro. Lib. Syst., 1975–; Chief, Sel. and Prcs., OK Cnty. Syst., 1972–75, Head, Qual. Cntrl., Sel., 1970–72, Reg. Head, 1968–70. **Educ.:** Univ. of MI, 1946–50, BM (Msc., Voice); Univ. of OK, 1964–68, MLS. **Orgs.:** ALA: ILL Com. (1980–81). OK LA: Lib. Dev. Com. (Ch., 1975–). SW LA. OK City Cham. of Cmrce.: Booster Club Com. (Co-Ch., 1979–80). Downtown Now!: Slide/Tape Com. (Ch., 1981). **Honors:** Cncl. on Lib. Resrcs., Flwshp., 1977–78. **Activities:** 9; 17, 28, 34; 75, 78 **Addr.:** Metropolitan Library System, Main Library, 131 Dean A. McGee Ave., Oklahoma City, OK 73102.

Bell, Geraldine Watts (Ag. 29, 1936, Camden, AL) Coord., Media Resrcs., Birmingham Pub. Sch. Syst., 1973–; Asst. Prof., Sch. of Educ., Univ. of AL, Birmingham, 1976–; Asst. Supvsr., Elem. Libs., Birmingham Bd. of Educ., 1973–74; Ref. Libn., Dir. of Instr. Resrcs. Ctr., Univ. of AL, Birmingham, 1971–73; Ref. Libn., Birmingham-South. Coll., 1970–71; Sch. Libn., Hayes HS, Birmingham, 1966–69; Sch. Libn., Alden HS, Graysville, AL, 1965–66. **Educ.:** AL State Univ., 1953–57, BS (Eng., LS); IN Univ., 1962–65, MALS; Univ. of AL, University, 1975–77, EdD (Educ. Admin.); Univ. of PA, 1966, (Educ. Media). **Orgs.:** ALA: Nom. Com. (1978–79). AL LA: Natl. Lib. Week Com. (Ch., 1978–79). AL Instr. Media Assn.: Pres. (1970); Legis. Com. (1979–80). WHOCLIS: Del. (1979). Various other orgs. Natl. Cncl. of Soc. Std.: Carter G. Woodson Bk. Sel. Com. (1977–). Natl. Educ. Assn. AL Educ. Assn. Phi Delta Kappa. Various other orgs. **Honors:** AL Instr. Media Assn., President's Plaque, 1967; Birmingham Educ. Assn., Excel. in Libnshp., 1966; AL A & M Univ., Excel. in Instr., 1966. **Pubns.:** *Determining A Job Performance Basis for the Development of an Individualized Staff Development Program for School Library Media Specialists* (1977); "Certification Guidelines for School Librarians," *AL Libn.* (Sum. 1973); "Librarians Make A Difference in Birmingham Schools," *Wilson Lib. Bltn.* (O. 1976); "Birmingham Librarians Stimulate Reading Interest," *AL Libn.* (O. 1978); "Libraries: A Vast National Resource," *The Birmingham News-Post Herald* (AP. 1, 1979). **Activities:** 10; 17, 24, 25; 66 **Addr.:** Birmingham Board of Education, 2015 Park Pl., Birmingham, AL 35202.

Bell, Inglis Freeman (Mr. 27, 1917, Medicine Hat, AB) Assoc. Univ. Libn., Univ. of BC, 1961–, Head, Circ. Div., 1960–62, Asst. Head, 1954–60, Ref. Libn., 1952–54. **Educ.:** Univ. of BC, 1946–50 (Eng. Lit.); Univ. of Toronto, 1951–52, BLS. **Orgs.:** Can. Assn. of Coll. and Univ. Libs.: Pres. (1970–71). Bibl. Socty. of Can.: Pres. (1968–69, 1969–70). Can. LA: Mem. Com. **Pubns.:** Jt. auth., *The English Novel 1578–1956* (1974); jt. auth., *Reference Guide to English American and Canadian Literature* (1971); jt. auth., *On Canadian Literature 1806–1960* (1966); jt. auth., *Canadian Literature/Littereture Canadienne 1959–63* (1966). **Addr.:** University of British Columbia Library, 1956 Main Mall, Vancouver, BC V6T 1Y3 Canada.

Bell, Jo Ann G. (Ag. 12, 1933, Golden, TX) Dir., Lib. Srvs., Richardson Indp. Sch. Dist., 1962–, Tchr., 1961–62; Tchr., Spring Branch Indp. Sch. Dist., 1959–61. **Educ.:** N. TX State Univ., 1956–59, BSE (Elem. Educ., Eng.), 1962–66, MLS. **Orgs.:** AECT. ALA. TX Assn. for Educ. Tech. TX LA. TX State Tchrs. Assn. Natl. Educ. Assn. SW LA. **Honors:** TX Assn. of Sch. Libns., Disting. Lib. Srv. Awd., 1981; Alpha Delta Kappa; Delta Kappa Gamma. **Pubns.:** "Media Mix: Students Learn About Books from Tapes," *Top of the News* (Je. 1971); "Cataloging and Storing Audio Visual Materials," *Educ. Resrcs. and Techqs.* (N. 1967); "School Libraries Reach Out to Involve All Students," *TX Libs.* (Spr. 1972); "Keeping Pace with Pacesetter: A Media Center Project that Spread," *TX Lib. Jnl.* (Ja. 1977); "Science Fiction, Fantasy, and the Gifted Reader: A Pooling of Community Efforts," *Gifted Students Inst. Nsltr.* (Spr. 1981). **Activities:** 10; 17; 63 **Addr.:** 801 Carney Dr., Garland, TX 75041.

Bell, JoAnn Hardison (Mr. 25, 1941, Wilmington, NC) Dir., Hlth. Sci. Lib., E. Carolina Univ., 1969–; Ast. Prof., LS Dept., 1969; Head Libn., Pitt Tech. Inst., 1967–69; Asst. Libn. Spec. Col., E. Carolina Univ., 1966–67. **Educ.:** Duke Univ., 1959–63, BA (Hist.); Univ. of NC, 1965–66, MS (LS); 1977–80, PhD (LS); E. Carolina Univ., 1974–76, MBA. **Orgs.:** NC LA: Dir. (1969–71). SLA. ALA. Med. LA: Cont. Ed. Com. (1974–77); Cert. Exam. Review Com. (1978–80); Srch. Com. for Dir. of Educ. (1979). Other orgs. East. Area Hlth. Educ. Ctr.: Ad Hoc Com. on Lrng. Resrcs. (1979–80). Pitt Cnty. Duke Alum. Assn.: Secy. (1969–70); VP (1970–71); Pres. (1971–72); Nom. Com. (1974). Other orgs. **Honors:** Beta Phi Mu, 1967; Beta Gamma Sigma, 1975. **Pubns.:** "Comprehensive Planning for Libraries," *Long Range Plng.* (1976); "Logging Current Journals in a Library of Small or Medium Size," *NC Libs.* (1976); "Microforms: Uses and Potential," *Med. LA Bltn.* 1978; "The Role of Library Schools in Providing Continuing Education for the Profession", *Jnl. of Educ. for Libnshp.* (1979); Co Auth., "Sex, Sin, and Dirty Books," *Med. LA Bltn.* (1974); other articles, reviews. **Activities:** 12; 17, 25, 36; 59 **Addr.:** Rt. 8, Box 760, Greenville, NC 27834.

Bell, John P. (O. 8, 1946, Chicago, IL) Dir., Info. Srvs., Million Dollar RT, 1974–; Claims Anal., Combined Insr., Amer., 1973–74; Lectr., Loyola Univ., Chicago, 1971–73. **Educ.:** Loyola Univ., Chicago, 1964–69, BS (Psy.), 1969–73, MA (Psy.); Roosevelt Univ., 1979–81, BGS (Comp. Sci.). **Orgs.:** SLA: Insr. Pers. Index Online Com. (1979–81). Socty. of Insr. Resrch.: Pub. Educ. Com. (1980–81). Amer. Risk and Insr. Assn. AAAS. **Pubns.:** "I/R System: From Facts to Information," *Resrch. Review* (Jl. 1979); jt. cmplr., *Life Insurance Index* (1979). **Activities:** 12; 25, 39, 41; 59, 76, 92 **Addr.:** Information Services, Million Dollar Round Table, 2340 River Rd., Des Plaines, IL 60018.

Bell, Joy Ann (Je. 9, 1944, Cross Plains, TN) Med. Libn., St. Francis Hosp., Miami Beach, 1979–; Asst. Libn., Asst. Prof., Sch. of Marine and Atmospheric Sci., Univ. of Miami, 1976–79; Spec. Col. Cat., Instr., Trinity Univ., San Antonio, TX, 1974–75, Cat., Instr., 1974–74; Asst. Cat. Libn.; Asst. Instr. Med. Bibl. Univ. of TX Hlth. Sci. Ctr., San Antonio, TX, 1973–73; Cat. Intern, Harvard Coll. Lib., 1969–71. **Educ.:** West. KY, 1961–64, BA cum laude (Fr., Lat., Hist.); Simmons Coll., 1970–72, MS (LS); Med. LA, Cert., 1975. **Orgs.:** Med. LA. Miami Hlth. Scis. Lib. Cnsrtm.: Union List of Serials Com. (1979–80). By-Laws Com. (1979–80); Grants Com., 1980; V.CH., 1980; CH., 1981. **Honors:** Hon. Ord. of KY Colonels, KY Colonel, 1975; Amer. Socty. of Anesthesiologists, Cert. of Apprec., 1976, 1977; Intl. Anesthesia Resrch. Socty., Third Awd. 1978. **Pubns.:** "'Tight Girdle or Sömmerring's syndrome," *New England Jnl. of Med.* (S. 1973); "The Anarchist Cookbook: Banned?", *Bay St. Libn.* (O. 1972); Many other articles, Exhibits, Abstracts. **Activities:** 5, 14-Hospital Library; 20, 39, 41; 80, 91 **Addr.:** 7272 S.W. 132 St., Miami, FL 33156.

Bell, Rebecca (Becky) L. (My. 28, 1952, Estherville, IA) Tech. Srvs. Libn. SD State Lib., 1977–; Libn., West. IA Tech. Cmnty. Coll., 1975–76. **Educ.:** Univ. of SD, 1970–73, BS (Ed., LS); Univ. of Denver, 1974–75, MA (LS). **Orgs.:** ALA. Mt. Plains LA; SD LA: Lib. Issues Com. (Ch., 1978–79; 1980). SD State Empl. Org.: Chap. Ch. (1979–). **Activities:** 13; 21, 45, 47; 57, 68 **Addr.:** South Dakota State Library, State Library Building, Pierre, SD 57501.

Bell, Robert E(ugene) (O. 13, 1926, Tarrant City, AL) Head, Hum./Soc. Sci. Ref., Univ. of CA, Davis, 1976–; Lect., Sch. of Lib. & Info. Serv., Univ. of CA, Berkeley, 1974–76; Ref. Libn., City Coll. of San Francisco, 1974–76; Asst. Prof., Coll. of Libnshp., Univer. of SC, 1971–73; Head, Adult Srvs., New Orleans Pub. Lib., 1965–66; Head, Adult Srvs., Mobile (AL) Pub. Lib., 1963–65; Exec. Secy., Book Club of CA, 1960–62; Asst. Dir., Fort Worth Pub. Lib., 1955–60. **Educ.:** Birmingham-Southern Coll., 1944–50, BA (Eng.); Harvard Univ., 1950–51, AM (Eng.); LA State Univ., 1966–67, MS (Libnshp.); Univ. of CA, Berkeley, 1967–74, PhD, (Libnshp.). **Orgs.:** ALA. CA LA. Grolier Club. **Honors:** Phi Beta Kappa, 1950; Phi Kappa Phi, 1967; Beta Phi Mu, 1967. **Pubns.:** *Dictionary of Symbols, Attributes, and Associations in Classical Myth* (1981); *The Butterfly Tree, a Novel* (1959); *Bibliography of Mobile, Alabama* (1956); "S.H. Goetzel, Publisher, Mobile, Ala., 1857–1865", *Quarterly News-Letter, Book Club of CA* (Spr. 1969); "The Grabhorn Press", *Encyclopedia of Library and Information Science* (1973). **Activities:** 1, 9; 26, 34, 39; 55, 57, 92 **Addr.:** Humanities & Social Sciences, Reference Dept., Shields Library, University of California, Davis, Davis, CA 95616.

Bell, Shelah A. (Ag. 23, 1943, Selma, AL) Dir., Libs., Irving Pub. Lib. Syst., 1974–; Asst. Dir., El Paso Pub. Lib., 1968–74; Coord., Ext. Srvcs., 1967–68; Head, Gen. Ref., 1966–67. **Educ.:** MS State Coll. for Women, 1961–64, BS; TX Woman's Univ., 1965–66, MLS; Univ. of Dallas, 1978–, (Bus.). **Orgs.:** TX LA: Pres. (1977–78), Exec. Brd. (1976–79), Pub. Rel. Com. Ch., Conf. Prog. Ch., Legis. Com. Ch., Exec. Dir. NE TX Lib. Syst.: Long Range Plng. Com., Legis. Com. Ch. Border Reg. Lib. Assn.: Pres. (1971–72). ALA: Sect. Ch.; various other orgs. TX Mncpl. Leag.: Exec. Brd.; Altrusa Intl.; Amer. Bus. Womens Assn.; Natl. Assn. of Parlmt.; various other orgs. **Honors:** Border Reg. Lib. Assn., Libn. of the Yr., 1970. **Pubns.:** Jt. auth., "City-School Library Cooperation," *TX Town and Country* (1977). **Activities:** 9; 17, 47; 56 **Addr.:** Irving Public Library System, P.O. Box 766, Irving, TX 75060.

Bell, Virginia R. (F. 24, 1924, Rochester, NY) Dir., Grt. Rivers Tchr. Ctr., 1978–; IMC Dir., Dept. Ch., Black River Falls Jr. High, 1968–78; Libn., Alma Ctr., WI, 1962–68. **Educ.:** Purdue Univ., 1941–45, BS (Hist., Soc. Std.); Univ. of WI, La Crosse, 1974–76, MS (AV Media). **Orgs.:** ALA: AASL. WI LA: Exec. Bd. (1978–79). WI Sch. Lib. Media Assn.: Pres. (1979). Coulee Educ. Media Assn.: Ch. (1977). Various other orgs. Natl. Republican Party. WI Republican Party. Jackson Cnty. WI Republicans. Failsplayers. **Pubns.:** *Teacher Centers: Theory and Reality* (1980); "Teacher Centering," *WI Sch. Lib. Media Jnl.* (F. 1980). **Activities:** 10, 14-Teacher Center; 17, 24, 36; 63, 75 **Addr.:** 411 N. 9th St., Black River Falls, WI 54615.

Bell, Whitfield J. Jr. (D. 3, 1914, Newburgh, NY) Libn., Amer. Philosophical Socty., 1966–80, Assoc. Libn., 1961–65; Assoc. Ed., Papers of Benjamin Franklin, 1955–61, Asst. Ed., 1954–55; Prof. **Educ.:** Dickinson Coll., 1935, AB (Hist.); Univ. PA, 1938, AM, 1947, PhD. Amer. Hist. Assn. **Honors:** Franklin Coll., LittD, 1960; Dickinson Coll., LLD, 1964. **Pubns.:** Various pubns. in Hist. **Activities:** 2, 14-Private Lib.; 45; 55 **Addr.:** American Philosophical Society, 105 S. Fifth St., Philadelphia, PA 19106.*

Bell, Winnie E. (Jl. 7, 1925, Waxahachie, TX) Lib. Dir., Harding Univ., 1975–, Asst. Libn., 1959–75. **Educ.:** Harding Coll., 1946–49, BA (Bus. Educ.); George Peabody Coll., 1960–61, MALS. **Orgs.:** ALA. Southwestern LA. AR LA: RTSD (Ch., 1975–76); Ref. Resrcs.; Ident. Com. (1974–75); SLA Un. List of Serials Com. (1974–75). AMIGOS Bibliographic Cncl. AAUW; Kappa Delta Pi. Harding Bus. Women. **Honors:** Harding Coll., Disting. Srv. Awd., 1978. **Pubns.:** Ed., *Periodical Holdings, Arkansas Foundation of Associated Colleges* 3rd ed. (1968); "Serials: Implication of cost and copyright," *AR Libs.* (1976). **Addr.:** Box 928, Harding College, Searcy, AR 72143.

Bellardo, Lewis Joseph (Je. 15, 1943, Trenton, NJ) St. Arch. and Recs. Admin., 1980–; Arch. and Recs. Admin., 1980–; Deputy St. Arch. and Recs., KY Dept. of Lib. and Archs., 1978–80; Asst. St. Arch., KY Dept. of Lib. and Archs., 1972–78; Assoc. Ed., *The Public Papers of the Governors of Kentucky*, Vol. 1., 1970–71; Consult. in ethnic hist., KY Educ. TV Athrty., 1971. **Educ.:** Rutgers Univ., 1961–65, BA (Hist.); Univ. of KY, 1965–68, MA (Hist.), 1977–79, PhD. **Orgs.:** SAA: Autom. Com. (1977–79), Prog. Com. (1978). Assn. of Recs. Mgrs. and Admins.; Natl. Assn. of St. Archs. and Recs. Admins.; KY Cncl. on Archs.: Pres. (1977–78), Cncls. Del. to SAA (1979–). Various other orgs. KY Hist. Socty. **Honors:** Phi Beta Kappa, 1965. **Pubns.:** *The Public Papers of Governor Louie B. Nunn* (1976); "Frankfort, Kentucky, Census of Free Blacks, 1842," *Natl. Geneal. Socty. Qtly.* (1975). **Activities:** 2, 13; 17, 38, 45; 56, 75, 92 **Addr.:** Division of Archives and Records Management, Kentucky Department of Library and Archives, Box 537, Frankfort, KY 40602.

Bellardo, Trudi (Jl. 1, 1944, Camden, NJ) Asst. Prof., Coll. of LS, 1981–; Data Srvs. Libn., Univ. of KY Libs., 1975–79, Math. Libn., 1974–75. **Educ.:** Univ. of KY, 1969–71, BA (Ling.), 1974–76, MSLS. **Orgs.:** ASIS: Educ. Com. (Ch., 1978–80); Awds. and Hons. Com. (Ch., 1980–); SIG/ED (Ch., 1981–82). ALA: RASD/Machine-Assisted Ref. Sect., Educ. and Trng. Com., Ch. **Honors:** Phi Beta Kappa, 1971; Beta Phi Mu, 1976. **Pubns.:** "The Use of Co-citations to Study Science," *Lib. Resrch.* (Fall 1980); "Education and Training for On-line Searching: A Bibliography," *RQ* (Win. 1979); "User Fees in Publicly Funded Libraries," *Advncs. in Libnshp.* (1979); "On-line Bibliographic System Instruction: A Classroom Experience and Evaluation," *Jnl. of Educ. for Libnshp.* (Sum. 1978); "Marketing Products and Services in Academic Libraries," *Libri* (S. 1977). **Activities:** 11; 26, 41; 62, 75 **Addr.:** College of Library Science, University of Kentucky, Lexington, KY 40506.

Bellassai, Marcia Courtney (Mr. 5, 1919, Hartford, WI) Consult., 1972–. **Educ.:** Univ. of WI, 1936–41, BA (Pol. Sci.); Univ. of MD, 1970–72, MLS. **Orgs.:** ALA. SLA. ASIS. **Honors:** Beta Phi Mu. **Pubns.:** *Survey of Federal Libraries* (1981); "Public Library Planning and the PLA Process: What's In It for Your Library?" *Jnl. of Lib. Admin.* (1982); *Libraries and Literacy: A Theme Conference Summary* (1979); Jt. auth., *A Planning Process for Public Libraries* (1980); Jt. auth., *Study of U. S. Army Libraries* (1976); Jt. auth., *Survey of Federal Libraries, 1972* (1975); other reports. **Activities:** 14-Multi-type; 24, 41, 49-Plng. **Addr.:** 12608 Ivystone Ln., Laurel, MD 20811.

Bellefontaine, Arnold George (N. 23, 1945, Framingham, MA) Exec. Ofcr., Assoc. Libn. for Natl. Progs., Lib. of Congs., 1979–; Admin. Ofcr., Congsnl. Resrch. Srv., 1975–79; Resrch. Anal., 1973–76. **Educ.:** Geo. Washington Univ., 1964–68, BA (Intl. Rel.); Univ. of MD, 1976–79, MLS (Lib. Mgt.). **Orgs.:** ALA. Alex. Graham Bell Assn. for the Deaf: Lib. Com. ARL: OMS Consult., 1981. **Honors:** Lib. of Congs., Merit.

Special Subjects/Services: 50. Adult educ.; 51. Advert./Mktg.; 52. Aerosp.; 53. Agric.; 54. Area std.; 55. Arts/Hum.; 56. Autom.; 57. Bibl./Prtg.; 58. Bio. sci.; 59. Bus./Fin.; 60. Chem.; 61. Copyrt.; 62. Documtn.; 63. Educ.; 64. Engin.; 65. Env.; 66. Eth. grps.; 67. Film; 68. Food/Nutr.; 69. Geneal.; 70. Geo.; 71. Geol.; 72. Handcpd.; 73. Hist.; 74. Int. frdm.; 75. Info. sci.; 76. Insr.; 77. Law; 78. Legis.; 79. Math./Comp. sci.; 80. Med.; 81. Metals; 82. Nat. resrcs.; 83. Newsp.; 84. Nuc. sci.; 85. Oral hist.; 86. Petr./Energy; 87. Pharm.; 88. Phys./Astr./Math.; 89. Readg.; 90. Relig.; 91. Sci./Tech.; 92. Soc. sci.; 93. Telecom.; 94. Transp.; 95. (other).

Srv. Awd., 1975; Intern Prog., 1978. **Activities:** 1, 4; 17, 28, 37; 55, 72 **Addr.:** Library of Congress, Washington, DC 20540.

Bellomy, Fred L. (My. 10, 1934, St. Joseph, MO) Owner, The INFO-MART, 1973–; Mgr. Lib. Autom. Proj., Univ. of CA, 1970–73; Lib. Autom. Coord., Univ. of CA, Santa Barbara, 1969–70; Prog. Dir., Giannia Controls Corp., 1964–69. **Educ.:** Univ. of CA, Berkeley, 1953–57, BA (Phys.); Univ. of CA, Los Angeles, 1957–65 (Mgt.). **Orgs.:** CA LA. SLA. Inst. Electric and Electronic Engin.: Santa Barbara Chap. (Ch., 1970). **Pubns.:** "Determining Requirements for a New System," *Lib. Trends* (Jl. 1973); "Management Planning for Library Systems Development," *J. of Lib. Autom.* (D. 1969). **Activities:** 1, 6; 49-Syst.; 56 **Addr.:** The INFO-MART, P.O. Box 2400, Santa Barbara, CA 93120.

Belsky, Susan M. (N. 24, 1948, Milwaukee, WI) Resrch. Coord., Metro. Milwaukee Fair Housing Cncl., 1979–; Dir., Metro and Rural Info. Exch., 1978–79; Info. Spec., Univ. of WI-Ext., 1974–78. **Educ.:** Univ. of WI, Milwaukee, 1968–71, BA (Jnlsm.); 1974–78, MLS. **Orgs.:** ALA. Lib. Cncl. of Metro. Milwaukee. Great Lakes Women's Std. Assn.: Strg. Com. Southeastern WI Hlth. Systs. Agency: Implementation Plng. Com. **Pubns.:** "Your Move, Your Choice" (1980); *How to Start A Women's Resource Center* (1979); *Urban Sprawl: A Bibliography* (1977). **Activities:** 12; 15, 17, 24; 70, 78, 95-Housing. **Addr.:** Metropolitan Milwaukee Fair Housing Council, 1133 W. Center St., Milwaukee, WI 53206.

Belt, Sarah Jane (Ag. 5, 1928, Cumberland, MD) Med. Libn., Coord. of Cont. Ed., Hlth. Sci. Lib., Ctrl. WA Hosp., 1972–; Nursing Sch. Libn., Deaconess Hosp., 1967–71; Bkmobile Libn., N. Ctrl. WA Lib. 1958–59; Chld. Libn., Wenatchee and Chelan Cnty. Lib., 1956–58; Educ. Libn. Syracuse Univ., 1955–56; Asst. Archit. Libn., 1954–55; Chld. Branch Libn., Dayton and MAntgomery Lib., 1953–54. **Educ.:** Millersville State Tchrs. Col., 1946–50, BS (Educ.); Syracuse Univ., 1954–56, MS (LS). **Orgs.:** OH LA. WA State LA: Gvr. Lib. Conf. (Prog. Com. 1968); Netwk. Task Frc. (1973–74); Lib. Netwk. (Assem. 1977–); Secy. (1977). Med. LA: Nat. Mtg. (Sharing Grp. Lead. 1977); Hosp. Interest Grp. (Prog. Com. 1977). Pac. NW Reg. Med. LA: Reg. Conf. Chmn., Coord., Prog. Org. (1972). Other orgs. **Honors:** Beta Phi Mu, 1956. **Pubns.:** Reviews. **Activities:** 12; 25, 32; 80, 95-allied hlth. **Addr.:** Rt. #3, Box 3193, Wenatchee, WA 98801.

Beltran, Ann Bristow (Ja. 11, 1940, Chicago, IL) Head, Ref. Dept., IN Univ. Libs., 1979–; Persnl. Libn., 1977–79; Asst. Ref. Libn., 1974–77; Asst. Docums. Libn., 1965–67. **Educ.:** Univ. of MI, 1958–61, AB (Eng.); 1962–64, AM (Eng.); 1972, AMLS. **Orgs.:** ALA: ACRL/Acad. Status Com. (1977–81; Ch., 1981); LAMA/Econ. Status Fringe Benefits and Welfare Com. (1977–81); Persnl. Admin. Sect. (Ch., 1981-82). Mod. Lang. Assn. of America. **Activities:** 1; 31, 35, 39 **Addr.:** IN University Libraries, 10th & Jordan, Bloomington, IN 47405.

Belzer, Jack (Je. 15, 1910, Russia) Disting. Prof., Info. and Comp. Sci., Florida Intl. Univ., 1980–; Prof., Univ. of Pittsburgh, 1964–80; Assoc. Prof., Sch. of LS, West. Reserve Univ., 1960–64; Dir., Comp. Ctr., Battelle Meml. Inst., 1952–59; Dir., Comp. Ctr., OH St. Univ., 1947–52. **Educ.:** Cooper Union, 1927–32, BS (Engin.); Catholic Univ., 1940, (Math, Phys.); Cert. relating to Comp., 1958–60. **Orgs.:** ASIS: SIGIS (Ch. 1975–76). Assn. Comp. Mach.: SIGIR Info. Retrieval (1972–73). ACM Rep. to AAAS (1976–). Amer. Socty. Engin. Educ.: Info. Syst. Com. (Ch.); AAAS: Cncl. (1976–78); Encyc. of Lib. and Info. Sci.: Adv. Bd. **Honors:** Prof. Emeritas, Univ. of Pittsburgh, 1980; Techion, Haifa, Israel, Lady Davis Flwshp. Awd., 1978; Tau Beta Pi; Assn. Comp. Mach., Invited Sci. Lecture, 1964–65). **Pubns.:** Sr. Ed., *Encyclopedia of Computer Science and Technology* (1975–80); "Information Theory" in *Encyc. of Comp. Sci. and Tech, v. 9;* "Turing Machines" in *Encyc. of comp. Sci. and Tech., v. 13;* "Zero Memory and Markov Information Source" in *Encyc. of Comp. Sci. and Tech., v. 14;* "Paperless Office", *Info. World* (D. 1979); Various other pubns. **Activities:** 11, 12; 17, 24, 26; 56, 60, 75 **Addr.:** Department of Mathematical Sciences, Florida International University, Miami, FL 33199

Bement, James Harry (Ag. 20, 1939, Elmira, NY) Syst. Anal., Progmr., Tech. Info. Ctr., Xerox Corp., 1980–; Tech. Info. Spec. I, Xerox Corp., 1970–80; Tech. Info. Spec., Electronics Division, General Dynamics, 1968–70; Sr. Libn., Sylvania Electronic Systems, 1966–68; Lib. Intern, SUNY, Buffalo, 1962–66. **Educ.:** SUNY, Buffalo, 1957–66, BA (Msc.); State Univ. Coll., Geneseo, 1968–77, MLS. **Orgs.:** ASIS. SLA: Info. Tech. Div. (Ch., 1980–). Assoc. of Comp. Mach. **Pubns.:** "The New Prices - Some Comparisons," *Online* (Ap. 1977); "Online Systems" (Clmn.), *The Info. Mgr.* (1979–). **Activities:** 12; 17, 39, 49-Online Searching; 56, 59, 91 **Addr.:** 84 Sherwood Ave., Webster, NY 14580.

Bemko, Leila Jane (Mr. 13, 1936, Houston, TX) Libn., Addiction Resrc. Ctr., Baylor Coll. of Med., 1972–; Resrch. Libn., TX Resrch. Inst. of Mental Sci., 1972–75; Ref. Libn., TX Med. Ctr. Lib., 1970–72; Resrch. Libn., Inst. of Relig., Med. Ctr., 1968–69. **Educ.:** Dominican Coll., 1952–63, BA (Hist.); Univ. of TX, 1965–72, MLS. **Orgs.:** SLA. Substance Abuse Libns. and Info. Specs.: Fndr. and Dir. (1978–). Libns. and Info. Specs.: Intl. Rep. (1979–). Galveston Hist. Fndn. **Pubns.:** Cmplr., *Substance Abuse Book Review Index* (1980); "International Review of Women and Drug Abuse (1966–1975)," *Jnl. of Amer. Med. Womens Assn.* (Dec., 1978); Cmplr. and Ed., *Current Items of Interest in the Field of Alcohol and Drug Misuse* (1972–). **Activities:** 1, 12; 15, 17, 41; 95-Alchl./Drug Abuse, 57, 80 **Addr.:** Addiction Resource Center, Baylor College of Medicine, Texas Medical Center, Houston, TX 77030.

Benamati, Dennis C. (O. 30, 1948, Orlando, FL) Asst. Law Libn., Tech. Srvs., Univ. of ME, 1979–; Ref. Libn., Univ. of Bridgeport Sch. of Law, 1979–; Libn., Stamford Law Unit, CT State Lib., 1976–78. **Educ.:** St. Francis Coll. (PA), 1966–70, BA (Pol. Sci.); Fordham Univ., 1971–74, MA (Pol. Sci.); South. CT State Coll., 1974–75, MLS. **Orgs.:** AALL. South. New Eng. Law Libn. Assn.: Secy.-Treas. (1977–). **Activities:** 1; 46; 77 **Addr.:** Donald L. Garbrecht Law Library, Univ. of Maine School of Law, 246 Deering Ave., Portland, ME 04102.

Benchik, Barbara A. (F. 24, 1949, Chicago, IL) Chief Libn., Peoples Gas, Light and Coke Co., 1974–; Libn., 1972–74. **Educ.:** Univ. of IL, 1967–71, BA (Eng.); Simmons Coll., 1971–72, MS (LS). **Orgs.:** Amer. Gas Assn.: Lib. Srvs. Com. (Ch., 1976–77). SLA. ASIS. Chicago Jaycees: Bd. of Dir. (1977–78). Amer. Mgt. Assn. **Honors:** Various civic awds. **Activities:** 12; 15, 17, 39; 59, 86 **Addr.:** Library, Peoples Gas Light & Coke Co., 122 S. Michigan Ave., Room 727, Chicago, IL 60603.

Benck, June (Je. 4, 1917, Fresno, CA) Coord., Dist. Libs. K–12, Fresno Unfd. Sch. Dist., 1972–; Instr., Lib. Tech., Fresno City Coll., 1974; Puppeteer, Fresno Cnty. Pub. Lib., 1964–72; Libn., Wawona Jr. HS, Fresno Unfd. Sch. Dist., 1962–72, Drama, Eng. Tchr., 1957–62. **Educ.:** CA State Univ., Fresno, 1934–39, BA (Drama); 1966, Sch. Lib. Cred.; 1974, Cmnty. Coll. Tchg. Cred. **Orgs.:** ALA: AASL. CA Media LA. Ctrl. Sierra Lib. Media Assn. Storyland of Fresno: Bd. of Dirs. (1966–). CA State Univ., Fresno: Bd. of Dirs. (1955–58, 1970–75). Assn. of CA Sch. Admin. Mid. Sch. Assn. various org. **Honors:** Phi Delta Kappa; Delta Kappa Gamma; Kappa Alpha Theta. **Pubns.:** "Bound to be Read," *Mid. Sch. Jnl.* (My. 1981); "Greening of the Library," *CA Sch. Libs.* (Sum. 1975); "About the Author," *A History of Swimming and Diving in Fresno (1890–1975);* "Say It...Share It," *Top of the News* (Ap. 1969). **Activities:** 10; 17, 31, 48 **Addr.:** 739 N. Ferger, Fresno, CA 93728.

Bender, Alice C. (N. 2, 1927, Chicago, IL) Chld. Libn., Waikiki-Kapahulu Lib., 1977–; Coord., Chld. Srvs., HI State Lib. Syst., 1970–77; Head, Ctrl. Prcs., Kamehameha Schs., 1964–69; Sch. Libn., Paramus Pub. Schs., 1961–63; Chld. Libn., HI Pub. Libs., 1951–60. **Educ.:** Colby Coll., 1945–49, BA (Eng.); Simmons Coll., 1950–51, MSLS. **Orgs.:** HI LA: Dir. (1959–60, 1968–69); Chld. and Youth Sect. (Ch., 1970–71). HI Assn. of Sch. Libns.: *Golden Key Nsltr.* Ed. (1964–65). ALA. **Honors:** HI State Dept. of Educ., Supt.'s Awd. and Sustained Superior Performance Awd., 1980. **Activities:** 9; 21 **Addr.:** 1937 Kakela Dr., Honolulu, HI 96822.

Bender, Ann G. (My. 21, 1938, Peabody, MA) Chief, Srvs. to the Aging, Brooklyn Pub. Lib., 1979–, Branch Libn., 1978–79, Senior Libn., 1977; Head, Undergrad. Lib., Cornell Univ., 1976–77; Senior Libn., Brooklyn Pub. Lib., 1972–76. **Educ.:** Wellesley, 1955–59, BA (Pol. Sci.); Radcliffe, 1969–63, MA (Gvt.); Simmons Coll., 1967–68, MSLS. **Orgs.:** ALA: Jewish Libns. Caucus; SRRT/Task Force on Women. NY LA. Assn. of Jewish Libns. Congregation Beth Elohim. **Honors:** Phi Beta Kappa, 1959; Woodrow Wilson Fellow, 1959–60. **Pubns.:** "Allocation of Funds in Support of Collection Development in Public Libraries," *Lib. Resrcs.* (Win. 1979); reviews. **Activities:** 9; 16, 17, 25; 50, 66, 90 **Addr.:** 78 8th Ave., Brooklyn, NY 11215.

Bender, Betty W. (F. 26, 1925, Mt. Ayr, IA) Lib. Dir., Spokane Pub. Lib., 1973–; Circ. Libn., 1968–73; Ref. Libn., 1968; Libn., East. WA State Hist. Socty., 1960–67. **Educ.:** Drake Univ., 1942–44; N. TX Univ., 1944–46, BS (LS, Math); Univ. Denver, 1950–57, MA (LS). **Orgs.:** ALA: Circ. Srvs. Sect. (Ch., 1975–76; LAMA/Small Libs. Pubns. Com. (1977–80; Ch. 1978–79); Com. Org. (1980); Pac. NW LA: Cir. Div. (Ch., 1972–75). WA LA: Pres. (1977–79); First VP, Pres. Elect (1975–77); Treas., (1973–75); Dir., (1971–73); other ofcs. and coms. WA Lib. Netwk.: Rep. Assem. (1977–80); Exec. Cncl., 1977–79). Other orgs. AAUW: State Bd. (1967–69); Spokane Branch (Pres., 1969–71); Area Rep. for Cmnty. Affairs, Prog. Dev. Com. (1972–73); Nom. Com. (Chmn., 1980); other coms. Zonta Intl: Dist. VIII Conf. (Treas., 1972); Spokane Clb. (Pres., 1976–77); 1st-VP 1976–76; Treas., 1973–1975); several coms. **Honors:** AAUW, Betty W. Bender Fwshp., 1972. **Addr.:** Spokane Public Library, West 906 Main Ave., Spokane, WA 99201.

Bender, David R. (Je. 12, 1942, Canton, OH) Exec. Dir., SLA, 1979–; Branch Chief, Sch. Lib. Media Srvs. Branch, MD St. Dept. of Educ., 1972–79; Resrch. Assc., OH St. Univ., 1970–72; Consult., Sch. Lib. Srvs., OH Dept. of Educ., 1969–70; Libn., S. HS Willoughby, OH, 1964–68. **Educ.:** Kent St. Univ., 1960–64, BS (Educ.); Case West. Reserve Univ., 1965–69, MSLS; Ohio St. Univ., 1969–77, PhD (Educ. Tech.); Univ. of HI, Inst. on Asian Std., 1966. **Orgs.:** ALA: AASL, many coms. YASD: many coms.; AECT: various coms. MD LA.: many coms. SLA. Many other orgs. with com. srv. Amer. Socty. of Assn. Execs. NY Socty. of Assn. Execs. **Honors:** MD Educ. Media, Awd. for Outstan. Srvs., 1980; ALA., J. Morris Jones-World Bk. Encyc., AASL, 1974; MD Lib. Info. Functional Exch., Grant Natl. Inst. Educ. Grant, 1978; Beta Phi Mu. **Pubns.:** *Learning Resources and the Instructional Program in Community Colleges* 1980; *Library Media Programs and the Special Learner* 1980; "Special Libraries: Their Stake in the Future," *Educ. Media YrBk.* (1979–80); "Special Libraries," *Bowker Anl. of Lib. and Bk. Trade Info.* (1980); "Networking and School Library Media Programs," *Sch. Lib. Jnl.* (N. 1979); Many other articles, brochures, non-print pubns. **Activities:** 12, 3; 17, 25, 37; 63, 78, 93 **Addr.:** Executive Director, Special Libraries Association, 235 Park Avenue South, New York, NY 10003.

Bender, Elizabeth Harrington (Jl. 27, 1929, Manchester, NH) Dir., Comm. and Info. Srvs., Env. Resrch. and 1975–80; Inc., 1977–; Head, Resrch. Lib., Arthur D. Little, Inc., 1961–77; Libn., Genl. Instrument, Harris ASW Div., 1960–61; Sci. Libn., Boston Pub. Lib., 1959–60; Fine Arts, Msc. Libn., Manchester Pub. Lib., 1955–59. **Educ.:** Boston Univ., 1957–60, AB (Hist. of Fine Arts); Simmons Coll., 1974–76, MLS; Vesper George Sch. of Art, 1948–50, Cert. (Cmrcl. Art). **Orgs.:** SLA: Boston Chap. (Pres. 1972–73); Sci. Tech. Div. (Secy., 1976–77. NETLINET: Exec. Com., (1976–77). **Activities:** 9, 12; 15, 17, 24; 55, 65, 91 **Addr.:** Environmental Research and Technology, Inc., 696 Virginia Rd., Concord, MA 01742.

Bender, Evelyn (F. 15, 1936, Bridgeport, CT) Ref. Libn., Zahn Instr. Media Ctr., Temple Univ., 1981–; Libn., Hackett Elem. Sch., 1980–; Ref. Libn., Philadelphia Coll. of Textiles and Sci., 1974–80; Libn. I, II, III, Free Lib. of Philadelphia, 1969–72, Branch Head, 1966–67. **Educ.:** PA State Univ., 1953–57, BS (Educ., Bio., Eng.); Drexel Univ., 1967–68, MS (LS), 1975–76, Cert. (Sch. Libn.); various crs. **Orgs.:** ALA. PA LA: SE Chap. (Secy., 1970–71, 1976–77); Prog. Info. Exch. Com. (Ch., 1977–79). Assn. of Philadelphia Sch. Libns.: Mem. Com. (Co-Ch., 1980–81). Drexel Alum. Plng. Bd. Drexel Lib. Sch. Alum. Assn.: Nom. Com. (Ch., 1978). Beta Phi Mu: Sigma Chap. (Dir., 1975–77). Amer. Film Inst. **Pubns.:** AV reviewer, *Sch. Lib. Jnl.* ; *Program Information Exchange Booklet* (1978). **Activities:** 10; 21, 32 **Addr.:** 7704 Mill Rd., Elkins Park, PA 19117.

Benedetti, Joan M. (D. 28, 1937, New York, NY) Libn., Craft and Folk Art Musm., 1976–; Decor. Arts Libn., Milwaukee Pub. Lib., 1967–68; Asst. to Managing Ed., IN Univ. Press, 1963–66; Chld. Libn., Gary Pub. Lib., 1959–62. **Educ.:** IN Univ., 1954–58, BA (Thea.), 1963–66, MA (LS). **Orgs.:** ARLIS/NA: South. CA Chap. (Ch., 1979–80). SLA. ALA. **Activities:** 8, 12; 15, 17, 20 **Addr.:** Craft & Folk Art Museum, Library/Media Resource Center, 5814 Wilshire Blvd., Los Angeles, CA 90036.

Benedict, Karen M. (D. 19, 1944, Chicago, IL) Corporate Archvst., Nationwide Insr. Co., 1975–; Asst. Coord. of Juvenile Srvs., Houston Pub. Lib., 1970–; Asst. Univ. Archvst., Rice Univ., 1969–70. **Educ.:** Univ. of IL, 1962–66, BA (Sp.); Univ. of MD, 1979, MLS; Mod. Arch. Inst., Natl. Arch., 1979, cert.; Arch., Lib. Inst., OH Hist. Socty., 1975, cert. **Orgs.:** SAA: Bus Arch. Prof. Afnty. Grp. (1975–80). Spindex Users Network. ALA. **Honors:** Lib. of Congs., Intern Prog. Finalist, 1980; Beta Phi Mu. **Pubns.:** *Select Annotated Bibliography of Business Archives and Records Management* (1981); "Archives, Automation and National Networking: Is There a Future?" *GA Arch.* (N. 1980); "Archives and Information Centers," *ASIS Proceedings* (1981). **Activities:** 2; 15, 17, 18; 59, 76 **Addr.:** 2665 Howey Rd., Columbus, OH 43211.

Benedict, Marjorie Alice (Racine, WI) Sr. Asst. Libn., SUNY, Albany, Dept. of Ref. & Col. Dev. Srvs., 1977–; Libn., Tchr Educ. Dev. Service, State Univ. of NY at Albany, 1974–77; Instr., Fr., Emma Willard School, 1966–73. **Educ.:** CA State Univ., Chico, 1961, AB cum laude (Fr., Span.); Univ. of WI, Madison, 1965–66, MA (Fr.); SUNY, Albany, 1973–74, MLS. **Orgs.:** ALA: ACRL/East. NY Chap. NY LA. SLA: Secy. of Student Chap. (1973–74). State Univ. of NY Libns. Assn. Amer. Assn. of Tchrs. of Fr. AAUW: Corp. Rep. for the Univ. at Albany (1978–80). NY State Assn. of Foreign Language Tchrs.: Stdg. Com. on Pub. Rel. (1972–73); Stdg. Com. on the Less-able Student (1968–71); Reg. Conf. Plng. Com. (1968–71); Phi Delta Kappa. **Honors:** Beta Phi Mu, 1974. **Pubns.:** Jt. Auth., "New York State Governor's Conference on Libraries as Perceived by the Delegates", *Bookmark* (Fall 1979); "Le Passé Simple sans peine", *Foreign Language Annals* (1980); "Competency-based Teacher Education: A Bibliography of Bibliographies", *ERIC Document* (1976); Indexer/Abstractor for *Women's Studies Abstracts* (1974–); Various oral presentations. **Activities:** 1, 12; 15, 31, 39; 55, 75 **Addr.:** University Library, State University of New York at Albany, 1400 Washington Ave., Albany, NY 12222.

Benedict, Michael J. (S. 13, 1941, Seagraves, TX.) Coord., Mtrls. Sel., Houston Pub. Lib., 1976–; Hum. Head, 1975–76; First Asst., Lit. and Biog., 1974–75; Supvsr., ILL, 1971–74. **Educ.:** Univ. of TX, 1960–65, BA (Eng.); SW TX State Coll., 1966–68, MA (Eng.); N. TX State Univ., 1970–71, MLS. **Orgs.:** ALA. TX LA. Houston Area Resrch. Lib. Cnsrtm.: Col. Dev. Com. (Ch., 1977–79). **Activities:** 1, 9; 15, 17, 34 **Addr.:** Office of Materials

PROFESSIONAL ACTIVITIES: Institutions: 1. Acad. lib.; 2. Arch.; 3. Assn.; 4. Fed./Gvt. lib.; 5. Inst. lib.; 6. Mfr./Suppl.; 7. Milit. lib.; 8. Musm.; 9. Pub. lib.; 10. Sch. lib.; 11. Sch. of lib. sci.; 12. Spec. lib.; 13. State lib.; 14. (other). **Functions/Activities:** 15. Acq./Col. dev.; 16. Adult srvs.; 17. Admin.; 18. Apprais.; 19. Archit./Bldgs.; 20. Cat./Class.; 21. Chld. srvs.; 22. Circ.; 23. Cons./Pres.; 24. Consult.; 25. Cont. ed.; 26. Educ. lib. sci.; 27. Ext. srvs.; 28. Fund/Grants; 29. Gvt. pubs.; 30. Indx./Abs.; 31. Instr. lib. use; 32. Media srvs.; 33. Micro.; 34. Netwks./Coop.; 35. Persnl.; 36. PR; 37. Publshg.; 38. Recs. mgt.; 39. Ref. srvs.; 40. Repro.; 41. Resrch.; 42. Review.; 43. Secur.; 44. Serials; 45. Spec. col.; 46. Tech. srvs.; 47. Trustees/Bds.; 48. YA srvs.; 49. (other).

Selection, Houston Public Library, 500 McKinney Ave., Houston, TX 77002.

Beneduce, Ann K. (S. 16, 1918, Maplewood, NJ) Dr., Ed. in Chief, Philomel Bks. Div. Putnam Pub. Group, 1980–; VP, Dir., Ed. in Chief, Chld. Bk. Div., Collins Pubs. Inc., 1977–80; VP, Ed. in Chief, Chld. Bk. Div., Thomas Y. Crowell Co., 1969–77; VP, Ed. in Chief, Chld. Bks., World Publishing Co., 1963–69; Assoc. Ed., Chld. Bks., J.B. Lippincott Co., 1960–63. **Educ.:** Bryn Mawr Coll., Barnard Coll., 1946, BA (Eng., Psych.); Columbia Univ., 1947, (Psych.). **Orgs.:** Chld. Bk. Cncl.: Bd. of Dir., Various coms. U.S. Com. for UNICEF. U.S. Frnds. of Intl. Bd. on Bks. for Yng. People.: Pres., (1980–). Intl. Bd. on Bks. for Yng. People: Exec. Com. (1974–78). ALA. **Activities:** 14-Publisher; 21, 48; 74, 89, 95-Intl. Coop. **Addr.:** 52 Locust Lane, Princeton, NJ 08540.

Benemann, William E. (O 29, 1949, Riverside, CA) Tech. Srvs. Libn., Golden Gate Univ. Law Lib., 1978–; Tech. Syst. Libn., 1976–78; Asst. to the Law Libns., 1975–76. **Educ.:** Harvard Univ., 1967–71, BA (Eng.); Univ. of CA-Berkeley, 1974–75, MLS. **Orgs.:** AALL: Bay Area Law Libns. North. CA Tech. Pres. Grp. Law Libs. Ballots User Grp.: Ch. (1976–77). **Honors:** Beta Phi Mu. **Pubns.:** "Tears and Ivory Towers", *Amer. Libs.*, (1977); Reviews. **Activities:** 1, 12; 15, 20, 46; 56, 77 **Addr.:** Golden Gate University Law Library, 536 Mission Street, San Francisco, CA 94105.

Benenfeld, Alan R. (O. 3, 1939, Brooklyn, NY) Coord., Phys. Sci. and Tech. Libs., Univ. of CA, Los Angeles, 1975–; Sr. Info. Sci., NASIC, MA Inst. Tech., 1972–74, Resrch. Staff, Intrex, 1966–72, Asst. Engin. Libn., 1965–66. **Educ.:** NY Univ., 1957–61, BMetE (Metallurgy); Rutgers Univ., 1964–65, MLS; Northeast. Univ., 1972–75, MS (Mgt.). **Orgs.:** ALA: RASD, Pubns. Com. (1978–); RTSD, Piercy Awd. Jury (1980–81); LITA, Ed. Bd. (1974–79); various coms. ASIS: Nom. Com. (1980); Anl. Mtg. Tech. Prog. (Ch., 1980); New Eng. Chap., Prog. Ch. (1968), Pres. (1969), Secy. (1973); various coms., ofcs. CA Acad. and Resrch. Libns. South. CA Tech. Prcs. Grp. Rutgers Grad. Sch. of Lib. Srv. Alum. Assn.: Pres. (1965). **Honors:** Tau Beta Pi. **Pubns.:** Jt. ed., "Communicating Information," *Procs. of the 43rd ASIS Anl. Mtg.* (1980); jt. auth., "Microcomputers, Minicomputers, or Private Database Services in Reference Work: Some Decision Factors," *Procs. of ASIS Anl. Mtg.* (1980); "Information Literacy–Awareness of and Access to Information Resources," *Eight Key Issues for the White House Conference on Library and Information Services* (1978); "Catalog Information and Text as Indicators of Relevance," *Jnl. of ASIS* (Ja. 1980); jt. auth., "User Receptivity to Fee-for-Service Computer-Based Reference in a University Community," *Procs. of ASIS Anl. Mtg.* (1975); bd. of eds., *Cat. and Class. Qtly.* (1980–); bd. of eds., *Jnl. of Lib. Autom.* (1974–79); various tech. rpts., bk. reviews. **Activities:** 1; 17, 41; 64, 75, 91 **Addr.:** Physical Sciences and Technology Libraries, 8251 Boelter Hall, University of California, Los Angeles, CA 90024.

Benet, Sandra Lee (My. 5, 1946, Detroit, MI) Msc. Libn., Univ. of Victoria, 1974–. **Educ.:** Univ. of MI, 1964–68, BA (Msc.); WA State Univ., 1968–71, MA (Msc.); Univ. of AB, 1973–74, BLS. **Orgs.:** Msc. LA: Reg. Chap., VP (1978–). Can. Assn. of Msc. Libs.: VP (1979–80), Cnslr. (1975–76, 1978–79); Elec. Com., Prog. Com. Msc. OCLC Users Grp. **Activities:** 1; 15, 17, 39; 55 **Addr.:** McPherson Library, University of Victoria, P.O. Box 1800, Victoria, BC V8W 2Y3 Canada.

Bengtson, Betty G. (Je. 22, 1940, Milledgeville, GA) Head, Cat. Dept., Georgetown Univ. Lib., 1975–; Asst. Acq. Libn., 1974–75; Cat., 1972–74; Cat., Coll. of Notre Dame Lib., 1968–72; Cat., Macalester Coll. Lib., 1967–68. **Educ.:** Duke Univ., 1958–62, BA (Hist.); Catholic Univ., 1966–67, MS (LS). **Orgs.:** ALA. Potomac Tech. Proc. Libns. DC LA: Tech. Srvs. Interest Group (Ch., 1979–80); AACR Task Frc. (Ch., 1978–79). **Pubns.:** "Post-1980 Headings and the Georgetown Univ. Library Catalog," *Alternative Cat. Nsltr* (D. 1979). **Activities:** 1; 15, 20, 46 **Addr.:** 19315 Frenchton Pl., Gaithersburg, MD 20760.

Bengtson, Marjorie C. (Ja. 21, 1934, Wheaton, IL) Asst. Docum. Libn., Univ. of IL, Chicago, 1969–, Asst. Ref. Libn., 1959–69; Church Organist, various churches, 1962–; Elem. Tchr., Chicago Pub. Schs., 1956–57. **Educ.:** Chicago Tchrs. Coll., 1952–56, BEd (Educ.); Univ. of IL, 1958–59, MS (LS); various crs. **Orgs.:** Chicago Reg. Grp. of Libns. in Tech. Srvs.: Secy.-Treas. (1963–64). ALA: Mem. Com. (1963–65). Chicago Club of Women Organists: Treas. (1973–74, 1976–80); Secy. (1969–73). **Pubns.:** "Chronological Guide to Selected Indexes to Technical Reports," *From Press to People* (1979). **Activities:** 1; 29, 39, 46; 78 **Addr.:** 5134 W. Strong St., Chicago, IL 60630.

Benham, Frances (Jl. 13, 1937, Gladewater, TX) Doct. Cand., FL State Univ., 1977–; Lib. Dir., Univ. Houston, Victoria, 1973–77; Head, Educ. Div., Univ. Houston Libs. 1972–72; Soc. Sci. Ref. Libn., 1969–71; Tchr., San Antonio Sch. Dist., 1962–68; Tchr., Albuquerque Pub. Schs., 1961–62. **Educ.:** TX Tech. Univ., 1958–61, BS (Sec. Educ.); N. TX State Univ., 1968–69, MLS; FL State Univ., 1977–78, ADM (Lib.); 1978–, PhD in Progress (LS). **Orgs.:** ALA. TX LA. NEA. **Honors:** Beta Phi Mu; Phi Delta Kappa. **Pubns.:** "Foundations of Librarianship for Service to the Handicapped," *ERIC* (1978); "Administration of Library Services to the Handicapped," *ERIC* (1978); "Library Service to the Blind and Physically Handicapped: A Selected Bibliography," *ERIC* (1978). **Activities:** 1; 17, 35, 39; 63, 72, 92 **Addr.:** 300 So. Bolivar, Cleveland, MS 38732.

Benn, James R. (S. 5, 1949, New York, NY) Reg. Coord., Southeast. CT LA, 1978–; Dir., Ledyard (CT) Pub. Libs., 1975–78. **Educ.:** Univ. of CT, 1967–69, 71–73, BA (Soclgy); Univ. of Denver, South. CT State Coll., 1974–75, MLS. **Orgs.:** ALA:LAMA/PR Srvs. to State Libs. and Assns. Com. CT LA: Exec. Bd. (1979–). NELA. **Activities:** 9; 17, 34; 67 **Addr.:** Southeastern Connecticut Library Association, c/o Public Library of New London, 63 Huntington St., New London, CT 06320.

Benne, Mae M. (F. 22, 1924, Morrowville, KS) Prof. Libnshp., Univ. WA, 1965–; Actg. Dir., 1973–74; Assoc. Dir., 1971–73; Asst. Prof., 1965–70; Coord., Chld. Srvs., N. Ctrl. Reg. Lib., 1961–65; Libn., Southfield Pub. Lib., Wayne Cnty. Lib. Syst., 1959–61; Chld. Libn., Yakima Valley Reg. Lib., 1955–59. **Educ.:** Univ. NE, 1947–50, BS (Educ.); Univ. IL, 1953–55, MS (LS); Univ. Chicago, 1970–71, Cert. (Advnc. Std.). **Orgs.:** ALA-:Org. and Bylaws CSD (1971–75); ALSC (Bd. Dir. 1978–79); Cont. Ed. Com. (1977–79); Pac. NW LA: YASD (Ch., 1973–74); Young Readrs. Choice Awd. (Secy. 1965–). WA LA: Bd. Dir. (1968–70). Internl. Readg. Assn.: Chld. Bk. Awd. Com. (1978–79). Frnds. of Int. Bd. on Bks. for Youth: U.S. Chap. **Honors:** Cncl. on Lib. Resrcs., Inc., Flwshp. 1976. **Pubns.:** *Central Children's Library in Metropolitan Public Libraries* (1977); *Policies and Practices Affecting Juvenile Library Collection in County and Regional Libraries* (1970); "Educational and Recreational Services of the Public Library for Children," *Lib. Qtly.* (Oct. 1978); "Leavening for the Youth Culture," *Wilson Lib. Bltn.* (Dec. 1977). **Activities:** 9, 11; 21, 26, 27 **Addr.:** School of Librarianship FM–30, University of Washington, Seattle, WA 98195.

Bennett, Helen Haddon (Peekskill, NY) Retired, 19—; State Supvsr., Lib., Media Srvs., Dept. of Pub. Instr., 1963–71; Coord., Sch. Libs., Pub. Schs., Harrison, NY, 1961–63, Libn., Eng. Dept. Head, HS, 1953–61; Dir., U.S. Libs., U.S. Info. Srv., Tehran, Iran, 1951–53; various lib. tchg. positions, 1928–73. **Educ.:** NY State Coll. for Tchrs., Albany, 1920–24, AB (Eng.); Columbia Univ., 1935, BS (LS), 1955, MS (Lib. Srv.); various crs. **Orgs.:** ALA: Cncl. (1968–69, 1972–75, 1976–81); Cncl. Resols. Com. (1979–81); AASL, Reg. Dir. (1959); Prof. Status and Growth Com. on Coms. (1954); ALA/Natl. Educ. Assn. Jt. Com. (1970–71). State of DE Gvr.'s Lib. Coord. Com. (1965). DE LA: Pres. (1966–67). Delta Kappa Gamma Intl.: Prof. Affairs (1980–81). Harrison (NY) Tchrs. Assn.: Pres. (1941). **Honors:** DE Sch./Media Assn., Estab. Helen H. Bennett Schol., 1971. **Pubns.:** "Demonstrating Library Use to Teachers and Administrators," *ALA Bltn.* (F. 1963); "Continuing Education: A Survey of Staff Development Programs," *Sch. Libs.* (Spr. 1970); "Delaware Library Association," *Encyc. of Lib. and Info. Sci.* (1970); contrib., *DE LA Bltn.;* various articles, "Subscription Books Bulletin" sect. of *The Booklist* (1970–71), *DE Bibl., World Bk. Encyc.* (1971). **Activities:** 10, 13; 17, 20, 32 **Addr.:** Country Club Apts., 0–23, Dover, DE 19901.

Bennett, Helen L. (Burkhart) (Jl. 30, 1917, Clinton, IA) Ref. Libn., Univ. of MO, Kansas City, 1967–; Cur., Snyder Coll. of Amer., 1961–67; Head of Ref. Dept., KA City (KA) Pub. Lib., 1954–60; Ref. Libn., Pub. Lib., Denver, CO, 1953–54. **Educ.:** Phillips Univ., 1935–37; S. West. OK St. Univ., 1937–39, AB (Eng., Span.); Univ. of Denver, 1952–53, MA (LS). **Orgs.:** ALA: Ref. and Subscrpn. Bks. Com. (1961–63), Guest Reviewer (1974–77); RASD/Hist. Sec. (Secy. 1971–72). Jackson Cnty. Hist. Socty. Frnds. of the Lib., MO LA. **Activities:** 1, 9; 16, 39, 45; 55, 75 **Addr.:** General Library, University of Missouri - Kansas City, 5100 Rockhill Road, Kansas City, MO 64110.

Bennett, James F. (D. 29, 1943, Elmira, NY) Libn., Shoreham-Wading River Sr. HS, 1974–; Visit. Consult., Sbtcl., NZ Sch. Libs., 1981–82; Libn., Deer Park Sr. HS, 1972–74; Libn., East Islip Sr. HS, 1970–72; Libn., Hauppauge Sr. HS, 1968–70. **Educ.:** Elmira Coll., 1966, BS (Hist.); Long Island Univ., 1967–70, MS (LS); NY State, 1977, Admin. Cert. **Orgs.:** Suffolk Sch. Lib. Media Assn.: Pres. (1980–81). ALA: AASL, Intl. Rel. Com. (1979–81), Sch. Lib. Media Facilities Com. (1980–); LAMA, Sch. Lib. Media Facilities Com. (1980–). **Activities:** 10; 32; 63 **Addr.:** Shoreham-Wading River Sr. High School, Rte. 25A, Shoreham, NY 11786.

Bennett, Joyce Stewart (Mr. 25, 1944, Madison, WI) Assoc. Prof., Lib. Instr. srvs., Sangamon St. Univ., 1980; Asst. Prof., Lib. Instr. Srvs., Srvs., Sangamon St. Univ., 1974–80; Instr., Lib. Tech., IL Ctrl. Coll., 1971–74; Ref. Libn., 1969–71. **Educ.:** Bradley Univ., 1962–66, BA; Univ. of IL, 1969–71, MS (LS). AAUW: IL St. Div./Stan. Com. on Women (1977–78), Springfield Branch (Ch., Stan. Comm. and Bd. Mem., 1976–78). Natl. Org. for Women: Springfield Chap./Pub. Rel. (Ch. 1977–78). **Honors:** Beta Phi Mu, 1971; IL Bicent. Comsn., Cert. of Recog., 1974; Sangamon St. Univ., Extra Merit Awd., 1979; Tenure, 1980. **Pubns.:** "Sangamon State Experience," *Putting Library Instruction in Its Place: In the Library and the Library School* (1978). **Addr.:** Norris L. Brookens Library, Sangamon State University, Springfield, IL 62708.

Bennett, Rowland F. (O. 17, 1940, Rochester, NY) Dir., Maplewood Meml. Lib., 1974–; Asst. Dir., Princeton (NJ) Pub. Lib., 1971–73; Catlgr., 1968–71. **Educ.:** Wheaton (IL) Coll., 1958–62, BA (Eng.); Case West. Rsv. Univ., 1966–67, MLS; Princeton Theo. Semy., 1967–73, MA (Relig. Ed.). **Orgs.:** NJ LA: Treas. (1980–); Pres. Tech. Srvs. Sect. (1969). ALA. **Pubns.:** Film reviews, *Film News* (1979-80). **Activities:** 9; 16, 17, 46 **Addr.:** 51 Baker St., Maplewood, NJ 07040.

Bennett, Scott B. (Jl. 22, 1939, Kansas City, KS) Asst. Univ. Libn. for Col. Mgt., Northwestern Univ. Lib., 1981–; Spec. Cols. Consult., Univ. of IL Lib., 1974–81; Asst. Prof. of Eng., 1967–74. **Educ.:** Oberlin Coll., 1956–60, AB (Eng.); IN Univ., 1960–67, MA PhD (Eng.); Univ. of IL, 1974–76, MS (LS). **Orgs.:** ALA: ACRL. AAUP: various state and local ofcs. Resrch. Socty. for Vict. Pers.: Pres. (1977–); various coms. **Honors:** Amer. Cncl. of Learned Socty., Flwshp., 1978. **Pubns.:** Co-Auth., *Art and Error: Modern Textual Editing* (1970); "Bibliographic Control of Victorian Serials," *Vann, Vict. Pers.* (1978); "Prolegomenon to Serials Bibliography," *Vict. Pers. Review* (1979). **Activities:** 1; 15, 28, 36, 45; 57 **Addr.:** Northwestern University Library, Evanston, IL 60201.

Bennett, W. Ann (N. 2, 1944, Dallas, TX) Media, Resrc. Coord., Henry W. Longfellow Elem. Sch., 1975–; Media Coord., Stephen F. Austin Elem., 1971–75; Libn., Reinhardt Elem., 1966–71. **Educ.:** TX Woman's Univ., 1962–66, BS (LS), 1967–72, MEd (Educ.); N. TX State Univ., 1980–, MLS. **Orgs.:** TX Assn. of Sch. Libns.: Outstan. Admin. Awd. Com. (1980–81); AV Prod. Awd. (Ch., 1976–78); Conf. Swap Shop Booth (Co-Ch., 1979–80); various ofcs. Dallas Assn. of Sch. Libns.: Various ofcs., coms. ALA: AASL, Fiesta (1979), Awds. Luncheon Com. (1979); Hosplty. Com. (1979); Storytel. Wkshp. (1978). Classrm. Tchrs. of Dallas: Fac. Rep. (1973–76); Prof. Rights and Resp. Com. (1974–76). TX State Tchrs. Assn.: Dist. Conv. (Del., 1974); State Conv. (Del., 1974); Hosplty. Com. (Helper, 1980). Natl. Educ. Assn.: Alternate Del. (1979). **Activities:** 10; 21, 32, 36; 56, 83, 89 **Addr.:** 6011 Prospect Ave., Dallas, TX 75206.

Bennion, Bruce Carver (N. 2, 1941, Ogden, UT) Assoc. Prof., Sch. of LS, Univ. of South. CA, 1974–; Resrch. Chem., Amalgamated Sugar Co., 1972–73. **Educ.:** Brigham Young Univ., 1959–61, 1964–66, BS (Chem.); Univ. of UT, 1966–69, PhD (Chem.); Uppsala Univ., Uppsala, Sweden, 1969–72 (Postdoctoral Resrch.); Columbia Univ., 1973–74, MS (Lib. Srv.). **Orgs.:** ASIS: Los Angeles Chap. (Ch., 1979). AALS. Libraria Sodalitas. Sigma Xi. **Pubns.:** "The Epidemiology of Research on Anomalous Water," *JASIS* (Ja. 1976); "The Use of Standard Selection Sources in Undergraduate Libraries," *Coll. Mgt.* (1977); "Performance Testing of the Book and Its Index as an Information Retrieval System," *JASIS* (Ja. 1980); "Online Systems of Disciplines and Specialty Areas in Science and Technology," *JASIS* (My. 1980). **Activities:** 11; 26, 41; 56, 75, 91 **Addr.:** School of Library and Information Management, University of Southern California, University Park, Los Angeles, CA 90007.

Bennorth, Barbara (D. 15, 1936, Chicago, IL) Dir., Kent Free Pub. Lib., 1978–; Head, Chld. Srvs., Mahopac Lib., 1977–78; Head, Pers. and Microfilm, Carmel HS, 1973–76. **Educ.:** Beloit Coll., 1954–58, BA (Fr., Span.); Columbia Univ., 1975–76, MSLS; Univ. of Chicago, 1962–64, (Intl. Rel.). **Orgs.:** ALA. NY LA. Putnam Cnty. LA: Treas. (1979–). **Activities:** 9; 15, 16, 17 **Addr.:** Kent Free Public Library, 42 Smadbeck Ave., Carmel, NY 10512.

Benoit, Anthony H. (Mr. 16, 1951, Crowley, LA) Pub. Lib. Consult., LA State Lib., 1980–; Admin. Libn., Morehse. Par. Lib., 1975–80; Libn., LA State Penitentiary, 1974–75. **Educ.:** LA State Univ., 1969–73, BA (Anthro.), 1973–75, MLS. **Orgs.:** ALA: JMRT Afflt. Cncl. (2nd VP, 1977–79). SW LA. LA LA: Pub. Lib. Sect. (Ch., 1979–80); Legis. Com. (Ch., 1978–80); Legis. Netwk. (Coord., 1978–80). **Pubns.:** "1980 Legislative Wrap-up," *LA LA Bltn.* (Fall 1980); "Louisiana Libraries' Cope with Copyright'–The Public Library," *LA LA Bltn.* (Win. 1978). **Activities:** 9, 13; 17, 19, 24; 78 **Addr.:** 4265 Hyacinth Ave., Baton Rouge, LA 70808.

Benschoter, Reba Ann (Je. 14, 1930, Smithland, IA) Dir., Biomed. Comms., Univ. of NE Med. Ctr., 1957–; Writer-Producer, KTVO TV, Ottumwa, IA, 1956–57; Writer-Producer, WOI-TV, Ames, IA, 1954–55, News Film Ed., 1953–54; Instr., IA State Univ., English Dept., 1952–53. **Educ.:** Briar Cliff Coll., 1948–52, BA (Eng.); IA State Univ., 1952–56, MS (Indus. Psy.); Univ. of NE, 1978, PhD (Adult, Cont. Ed.). **Orgs.:** Med. LA. Assn. of Biomed. Comms. Dirs.: Various coms. Assn. of Med. Illustrators. Hlth. Sci. Comms. Assn.: Bd. (1966–67, 1975–79); Pres. (1976–77); various coms. **Honors:** Sch. of Allied Hlth., Univ. of NE Med. Ctr., Outstan. Srv. to Allied Hlth. Profs., 1979; Hlth. Sci. Comms. Assn., Golden Roster Awd., 1981. **Pubns.:** *Eight Millimeter Films in Medicine and Allied Health Sciences* (1977); "Using Media in Rural Clerkships," *Jnl. of Biocomms.* (Mr. 1980); "A Challenge to Medical Communications," *Jnl. of Biocomms.* (Mr. 1979); "'Communications in American Medical Centers,' Revisited," *Jnl. of Biocomms.* (Jl. 1978); "A Challenge

Special Subjects/Services: 50. Adult educ.; 51. Advert./Mktg.; 52. Aerosp.; 53. Agric.; 54. Area std.; 55. Arts/Hum.; 56. Autom.; 57. Bibl./Prtg.; 58. Bio. sci.; 59. Bus./Fin.; 60. Chem.; 61. Copyrt.; 62. Documtn.; 63. Educ.; 64. Engin.; 65. Env.; 66. Eth. grps.; 67. Film; 68. Food/Nutr.; 69. Geneal.; 70. Geo.; 71. Geol.; 72. Handcpd.; 73. Hist.; 74. Int. frdm.; 75. Info. sci.; 76. Insr.; 77. Law; 78. Legis.; 79. Math./Comp. sci.; 80. Med.; 81. Metals; 82. Nat. resrcs.; 83. Newsp.; 84. Nuc. sci.; 85. Oral hist.; 86. Petr./Energy; 87. Pharm.; 88. Phys./Astr./Math.; 89. Readg.; 90. Relig.; 91. Sci./Tech.; 92. Soc. sci.; 93. Telecom.; 94. Transp.; 95. (other).

Who's Who in Library and Information Services

to Medical Communications," *Jnl. of Biocomms.* (Mr. 1979); jt. auth., "Using Media in Rural Clerkships," *Jnl. of Biocomms.* (Mr. 1980); various articles, papers, 16mm films. **Activities:** 12; 32; 50, 93 **Addr.:** Biomedical Communications Center, University of Nebraska Medical Center, 42nd & Dewey, Omaha, NE 68105.

Benson, Harriet (My. 17, 1941, Kansas City, MO) Dir., Tech. Info. and Pub., ALZA Corp., 1969–; Tech. files, Shell Dev. Co., 1963–64. **Educ.:** Wellesley Coll., 1959–63, BA (Chem.); Univ. of KS, 1964–67, PhD (Chem.). **Orgs.:** Drug Info. Assn.: Bd. of Dirs. (1977–). Pharmaceutical Mfrs. Assn.: Sci. Info. Subsection, Steering Com. (1977–80). ASIS. Amer. Medical Writers Assn.: Exec. Com. (1978–80). Amer. Chem. Soc. **Pubns.:** Jt. Auth., "An On-line Database for Tracking Product Complaints", *Drug Information Journal* (1979); Various articles in medical journals. **Addr.:** 2825 Ramona, Palo Alto, CA 94306.

Benson, Jane A. (N. 8, 1943, Davenport, IA) Prog. Assoc., Cncl. on Lib. Resrcs. an Resrch. Spec., Ofc. of Mgt. Std., Assn. of Resrch. Libs., 1981–; Ref. Libn., Asst. Prof., Lib. Admin., Kent State Univ., 1969–81, Supvsr., ILL Srvs., 1969–75, Cat. Libn., 1968–69; Docum. Libn., IN Univ., 1966–68. **Educ.:** Drake Univ., 1961–64; IN Univ., 1964–65, BA (Hist.); 1965–66, MA (LS); Kent State Univ., 1969–77, MA (Hist.). **Orgs.:** ALA; Assn. for Bibl. of Hist. Amer. Hist. Assn. Org. of Amer. Histns. Soc. Sci. Hist. Assn. **Honors:** Cncl. on Lib. Resrcs., Flwshp. for Adv. Study, 1978. **Pubns.:** "Civil War Bibliography for 1975," *Civil War Hist.* (1976); "Civil War Bibliography for 1976," *Civil War Hist.* (1977); "Harrison Williams," *Dictionary of Amer. Biography* (1977). **Activities:** 1; 15, 29, 39; 54, 78, 92 **Addr.:** One Dupont Cir., Suite 620, Washington, DC 20036.

Benson, Joseph (O. 9, 1919, Chicago, IL) Dir., Lib. Srvs., Chicago Transit Athrty., 1974–; Libn., Jt. Ref. Lib., Pub. Admin. Srv., 1967–74; Mncpl. Ref. Libn., City of Chicago, 1956–67; Asst. Libn., Wright Jr. Coll., 1951–56. **Educ.:** Univ. of Chicago, 1948–51, AM (Libnshp.). **Orgs.:** SLA: Soc. Sci. Div. (Ch., 1961–62). IL Reg. Lib. Cncl.: VP; Bd. of Dirs. (1971–76). AALL: Treas. (1967–69). IL State Lib. Adv. Cncl. Comsn. Chicago Hist. and Archit. Landmarks: Secy. (1957–67, 1981–). **Addr.:** Chicago Transit Authority, Library, Rm. 450, P.O. Box 3555, Chicago, IL 60654.

Benson, Marjorie C. (S. 28, 1935, Yuma, CO) Spec. Libn., Access Innovations, Sandia Labs., 1979–81; Info. Spec., Natl. Energy Info. Ctr., 1978–79; Libn., Naval Arctic Resrch. Lab., 1976–78; Adams Cnty. Libs., 1974–76; NY Univ., 1972–74; Univ. CA, Davis, 1969–72; NY Pub. Lib., 1965–69. **Educ.:** Univ. CO, 1953–57, BMsc. Ed; Univ. Denver, 1963–65, MA (Libnshp.). **Orgs.:** ALA. SLA. NM LA. ALA: RTSD; ACRL; SRRT; JMRT. Univ. Denver Grad. Sch. Libnshp. Alum. Assn. **Activities:** 4, 12; 39, 46; 58, 84, 94 **Addr.:** 609 S. Ash St., Yuma, CO 80759.

Benson, Stanley H. (O. 1, 1930, Sparta, IL) Dir., Mabee Lrng. Ctr., OK Bapt. Univ., 1971–; Head Libn., Berry Coll., 1969–71; Head Libn., Gardner-Webb Coll., 1968–69; Head Libn., KY South. Coll., 1964–68. **Educ.:** South. IL Univ., 1948–52, BS (Educ.); Southwest. Bapt. Theo. Sem., 1954, MRE, 1964, ThD; Univ. of TX, 1965, MLS; Univ. of OK, 1979, PhD. **Orgs.:** OK LA: Lib. Dev. Com. (Ch., 1979–80). ALA:ACRL/AV Com. OK Dept. of Libs.: Netwk Adv. Com. (Ch., 1980–81). OK Univ. Sch. of LS: Visit. Com. **Pubns.:** *Recorded Library Use Statistics for Four-Year Liberal Arts Institutions*, ERIC Docum. # ED 119 658 (1976); "The Nature of Bibliographic/Library Instruction in Academic Libraries Today," *Learning Today* (Winter 1981). **Activities:** 1; 15, 17, 31; 90 **Addr.:** Mabee Learning Center, Oklahoma Baptist University, Shawnee, OK 74801.

Benson, Susan Shattuck (Ap. 12, 1939, Missoula, MT) Sr. Spec., Lib. and Arch. Dev. in Latin Amer. and the Caribbean, Org. of Amer. States, 1973–; Exec. Dir., Consult., Proyecto LEER, 1971–81; Sr. Assoc. Ed., *Américas*, Org. of Amer. States, 1970–73; Assoc. Proj. Dir., Bks. for the People Fund, Inc., 1969–70; Catlgr., Latin Amer. Mtrls., Hum. Resrch. Ctr., The Univ. of TX, Austin, 1966–67; Shelflister, Lib. of Congs., 1963–64; Tchr., of Emotionally Disturbed, Mumford Sch., 1962–63; Tchr., Grmn., Eng., Cypress-Fairbanks HS, 1961–62. **Educ.:** Univ. of TX, Austin, 1957–61, BA (Pol. Sci.), 1964–66, MLS; Freie Univ., Berlin, 1967–68, grad. work (Latin Amer. Std.). **Orgs.:** SALALM: Exec. Bd. (1979–81); Jt. Com. on Lib. Mtrls. for the Span.-and Portuguese-speaking in the U.S. (Ch., 1971–74); Postconf., "First Symposium on Span. Lang. Mtrls. for Chld. and YAs, "Austin, TX (Dir., 1974); Wkshp. on Dev. of Lib. Srvs., Sel. and Procurement of Mtrls. for the Span.-and Portuguese-speaking, Amherst, MA (Dir., 1972); Anl. Mtg. (Rapporteur Gen., 1969–70). Assn. Interamer. de Arch.: Sem. Interamer. Sobre Coop. Reg. para el Desarrollo de Arch., DC (Dir., 1976). Caribbean Arch. Assn. Assn. of Caribbean Univ. and Resrch. Inst. Libs. Premera Reun. Técnica Interamer. sobre "Casas de Cultura Popular," La Paz Bolivia: (Co-Dir., 1980). Univ. of AZ, Grad. Sch. of LS and Sch. of Biling. Educ.: Grad. Inst. for Sel. and Acq. of Lib. Mtrls. for the US Span.-speaking (Dir., 1976). **Honors:** Ford Fndn., Grad. Std. Grant, 1964–65; Fulbright, Post-Grad. Std., Berlin, West Germany, 1967–68. **Pubns.:** Ed., *Report on the First Symposium on Spanish-Language Materials for Children and Young Adults* (1975); "Scientific Expeditions of the Spanish Crown," *The Rediscovery of the New World* (1972); "Birds of the Americas," *Américas* (O. 1971); ed., "Fourteenth Seminar on the Acquisition of Latin American Library Materials," *Final Report and Working Papers* (1970); ed., "Fifteenth Seminar on the Acquisition of Latin American Library Materials," *Final Report and Working Pepers* (1971). **Activities:** 4, 12; 17, 24, 28; 54, 57, 89 **Addr.:** Technical Unit on Information, Communication and Cultural Diffusion, Dept. of Cultural Affairs, Organization of American States, Washington, DC 20006.

Bente, June E. (Jn. 14, 1943, Philadelphia, PA) Mgr., Lib. Srvs., Ortho Pharmaceutical Corp., 1977–, Libn., 1973–77, Asst. Libn., 1970–73. **Educ.:** Temple Univ., 1961–65, AB (Biol.); Univ. of IL, 1968–69, MLS; Med. LA, Cert., 1977. **Orgs.:** SLA: Nom. Com. (1980); Prog. Com. (1979); Princeton–Trenton Chap. (Dir., 1976–77). ASIS. Med. LA. Assn. Info. Mgrs. Med. Resrcs. Cnsrtm. of Ctrl. NJ: Secy. (1975–77). **Honors:** Beta Phi Mu. **Activities:** 12; 17, 34, 44; 80, 87, 91 **Addr.:** 203 Loetscher Pl., Princeton, NJ 08540.

Bentke, Delores A. (D 10, 1939, Hempstead, TX) Branch Libn., Hillendahl Branch, Houston Pub. Lib., 1980–; Asst. Libn., Houston Pub. Lib., 1973–; Supvsr.-Key Punch Dept., TX Marine & Indus. Sup. Co., 1958–68. **Educ.:** San Jacinto Coll., 1968–70, AA; Sam Houston State Univ., 1970–72, BA (Eng.); TX Woman's Univ., 1972–73, MLS. **Orgs.:** TX LA: Pub. Com. (1979–82); Ref. RT/Nom. Com. (1979–80). ALA. En Amie Bk Review Club (1st VP, 1980–81). YWCA. **Honors:** Beta Phi Mu, 1973; Pi Delta Phi, 1972; Alpha Chi, 1972; Kappa Delta Pi, 1972. **Pubns.:** "TWU Library Science Students Study in London", *TX Lib. Jrnl.* (1978). **Activities:** 9; 16, 36, 39; 50, 89 **Addr.:** P.O. Box 55775, Houston, TX 77055.

Bentley, James Robert (F. 14, 1942, Louisville, KY) Secy. and Cur., Mss., The Filson Club, Inc., 1968–; Resrch. Asst., Resrch. Dept., Colonial Williamsburg, 1966–67; Asst. to Cur., The Filson Club, 1964–65; various tchg. positions. **Educ.:** Ctr. Coll., 1960–64, BA (Hist.); Coll. of William and Mary, 1965–66, MA (Hist.); various crs. **Orgs.:** SAA. The Ms. Socty. KY Socty. of Mayflower Descendants. KY Socty. Sons of the Amer. Revolution. Jeffersontown Hist. Socty. City of Louisville Hist. Landmarks and Prsrvn. Dists. Comsn. various orgs. **Honors:** Sigma Chi. **Pubns.:** Ed., *The KY Genealogist* (1979–); "Jefferson B. Nones Family Bible," *The PA Genealogical Mag.* (1975); "The Family of Andrew Jackson Alexander," *The VA Genealogist* (O.–D. 1976); "A Letter From Harrodsburg, 1780," *The Filson Club Hist. Qtly.* (O. 1976); "Cousinage—Louisville's Intertwining Roots," *Louisville Mag.* (F. 1978); various articles, bk. reviews, lcl. TV progs. **Activities:** 12; 15, 20, 45; 69 **Addr.:** 3621 Brownsboro Rd., 201B, Louisville, KY 40207.

Bentley, Janice Babb (Ja. 13, 1933, Philadelphia, PA) Libn., Mayer, Brown and Platt, 1976–; Libn., CNA Fncl. Corp., 1963–76; Libn., Natl. Assn. of Realtors, 1956–76. **Educ.:** Univ. of IL, 1950–54, AB (Econ.), 1954–56, MS (LS). **Orgs.:** AALL. ASIS: Chicago Area Chap. (Secy.-Treas., 1963–64, 1971–72). Chicago Assn. Law Libs.: Pres. (1978–79). SLA: Housing Bldg. and Plng. Sect. (Ch., 1962–63); Soc. Sci. Div. (Ch., 1965–66); IL Chap. (Pres., 1967–68); Insr. Div. (Ch., 1974–75). Illiniweks: Chicago Ch. (1959). **Pubns.:** Jt. auth., *Real Estate Appraisal Bibliography* (1965); jt. auth., *Real Estate Information Sources* (1963). **Activities:** 12; 15, 29, 39; 59, 77, 78 **Addr.:** Mayer, Brown & Platt, 231 S. La Salle St., Chicago, IL 60604.

Bentley, Stella (My. 19, 1943, San Pedro, CA) Ref. Libn., Educ. Lib., IN Univ., 1978–; Resrch. Assoc., IN Univ., 1977–78; Tchr., Gary, 1966–76. **Educ.:** Univ. CA, Berkeley, 1961–65, AB (Eng.); IN State Univ., 1966–68, MS (Educ.); IN Univ., 1976–77, MLS. **Orgs.:** ALA: ACRL Stand. and Guid. for Coll. Lib. (1980). IN Univ. Libns. Assn.: Secy. (1979–80). **Honors:** Beta Phi Mu, 1978. **Pubns.:** "Collective Bargaining & Faculty Status," *Jnl. of Acad. Libnshp.* (May 1978); "Academic Library Statistics," *Lib. Resrch.* (Sum. 1979); "Factors Affecting Faculty Perceptions of Academic Libraries," *Coll. and Resrch. Libs.* (Nov. 1979). **Activities:** 1; 39; 63 **Addr.:** Education Library, Education 024, Indiana University, Bloomington, IN 47405.

Benton, Charles William (F. 13, 1931, New York, NY) Ch., Chief Exe. Ofcr., Films Inc., 1968–; Pres., Fund for Media Resrch., 1967–69; Pres., Encyclopaedia Britannica Educ. Corp, 1966–67; Encyclopaedia Britannica Films, 1953–66. **Educ.:** Yale Univ., 1953, BA; Northwestern Univ. & Natl. Col. of Educ., grad. work. **Orgs.:** NCLIS: Ch. (1978–). WHCOLIS: Ch. (1979). Natl. Citizens Com. for Broadcasting: Adv. Brd., Ch./Pres. (1972–75). Action for Child. TV Adv. Brd. Chicago Educ. TV. Assn.: Trustee (1969–1979). **Honors** Chicago Intl. Film Fest., Golden Hugo Awd., 1977. **Pubns.:** "How The Debates Came to Be", *Encyclopaedia Britannica Yearbk.* (1977); "Challenge from the White House & The National Commission:"; "The Presidential Forums", *Great Debates* (1979). **Addr.:** Films Incorporated, 1144 Wilmette Ave., Wilmette, IL 60091.

Benton, Evelyn Fleming (Ag. 10, 1921, Ponchatoula, LA) Dir., Deer Pk. Pub. Lib., 1967–; Asst. Libn., Lee Coll. Lib., 1960–67; Jr. Ref. Libn., OK State Univ., 1948–50. **Educ.:** OK State Univ., 1939–43, BFA (Msc.); Univ. TX, 1959–60, (LS); Intl. City Mgs. Assn., 1967, Cert. (Suprvsn.); Univ. of Houston, 1978, Cert. (Per. Admin.). **Orgs.:** TX LA: Dist. VIII, Vice-Ch., Ch.-Elect (1980); Treas. (1971); Ref. RT (Ch., 1973); Dist. V, Secy. (1969). Houston Area Lib. Syst.: PR Com. (1979–); Autom. Srvs. Com. (1978–). SW LA: TX Mem. Ch. (1976); Conf. Prog. Com. (1974). ALA: PLA/Ed. Com. (1974–76); RSD/Coop. Ref. Srvs. Com. (1972–74). Other orgs. Deer Pk. Bicent. Comsn.: Heritage '76 Com., Ch. **Pubns.:** Co-Auth., *An Introduction to the Houston Area Library System Computer Access Network* (1978); "Library Systems and Deer Park Public Library," *TX Libs.* (Sum., 1974). **Activities:** 9; 15, 17, 39; 55, 56, 61 **Addr.:** 5874 Doliver, Houston, TX 77057.

Benton, Rita (Je. 28, 1920, New York, NY) Msc. Libn. & Prof. of Msc., Univ. of IA, 1952–. **Educ.:** Juilliard Sch. of Msc., 1937, Diploma (Piano); Hunter Coll., 1939, BA (Msc.), 1951, MA (Msclgy.); Univ. of IA, 1961, PhD (Msclgy.). **Orgs.:** Msc. LA: Pres. 1961–62). Intl. Assoc. of Msc. Libs.: Comsn. of Resrch. Libs. (Pres., 1964–76); Ed., *Fontes Artis Musicae* (1976–). Amer. Msclgy. Socty.: Secy. (1972–77). **Honors:** Amer. Cncl. of Learned Soctys., grant-in aid & various travel grants, 1963–74; Fulbright Sr. Resrch. Scholar, Univ. of Paris, 1968; NEH, Project Grant, 1977–78; Other grants. **Pubns.:** *Directory of Music Research Libraries, vol. 4: Australia, Israel, Japan, New Zealand* (1977); *Ignace Pleyel: A Thematic Catalogue of His Compositions* (1972); "The Music Publisher Pleyel," *Jnl. of the Amer. Msclgy. Socty.* (1979); "the Nature of Music and Some Implications for the University Music Library," *Fontes Artis Musicae* (1976); many other articles, compilations, and introductions; reviews. **Activities:** 1; 15, 17, 39; 55, 57, 62 **Addr.:** School of Music, University of Iowa, Iowa City, IA 52242.†

Bentz, Dale M. (Ja. 3, 1919, York County, PA) Univ. Libn., Univ. of IA, 1970–, Assoc. Dir., 1953–70; Head, Prcs. Dept., Univ. of TN Lib., 1948–53; Asst. Libn., E. Carolina Tchrs. Coll., 1946–48; Asst., Serials Dept., Duke Univ. Lib., 1941–42; Asst., Per. Dept., Univ. of NC, 1940–41. **Educ.:** Gettysburg Coll., 1939, AB; Univ. of NC, 1940, BSLS; Univ. of IL, 1951, MS. **Orgs.:** ALA: Cncl. (1978–82); RTSD (Pres. 1975–76; Bd. of Dir. 1965–69, 1974–77); ACRL (Bd. of Dir., 1962–65); other coms. IA LA: Pres. (1959–60). Beta Phi Mu: Pres. (1966–67). AAUP. Univ. Fac. Senate. Books at Iowa: Bus. Mgr. (1964–). **Honors:** Kappa Phi Kappa. **Pubns.:** "Reclassification and Recataloging," *Lib. Trends* (1953); "An Evaluation of the ACRL Statistics Report," *Coll. and Resrch. Libs.* (1955); "College and University Library Statistics," *Coll. and Resrch. Libs.* (1956, 1957, 1958); reviews. **Activities:** 1; 17, 20, 46; 56, 74, 75 **Addr.:** 1615 East College, Iowa City, IA 52240.

Ben-Zvi, Hava (Warsaw, Poland) Head Libn., Jewish Cmnty. Lib.; Sr. Libn., Los Angeles Cnty, Lib. Syst., 1966–69. **Educ.:** CA State Univ., Los Angeles, 1960–62, BA (Soclgy.); Immaculate Heart Coll., Los Angeles, 1962–63, MALS; Libnshp. Cred., Tchg. Cred., Israel. **Orgs.:** AJL: South. CA, Liaison Com. (Ch.). **Pubns.:** Various bibl. compilations on Jewish life and thought (1970–). **Addr.:** Jewish Community Library, 6505 Wilshire Blvd., Los Angeles, CA 90048.

Berg, Ann T. (N. 14, 1923, South Bend, IN) Gvt. Ref. Lib., Tucson Pub. Lib., 1976–; Plng. Dept. Libn., City of Tucson, 1974–76; Base Libn., Sandia Base, Albuquerque, NM, 1967–72, Gen. Ref. Libn., FC, DASA, 1963–67. **Educ.:** Carleton College, 1941–45, BA (Eng.); Univ. of AZ, 1973–74, MLS. **Orgs.:** SLA: Rio Grande Chap., Pres. (1977–78); Urban Affairs Sect. Chmn. (1979–80); Soc. Sci. Div., Ch-elect (1981–), AZ Chap., Career Guidance Ch. (1978–80); AZ State LA: Spec. Libs. Div., Secy.-Treas. (1978–79). Southwest Lib. Assn. **Pubns.:** "Writing a Procedures Manual," *Newsletter* Mgt. Div. SLA (Win. 1978). **Activities:** 4, 12; 16, 17, 20; 64, 78, 95-Urban Affairs. **Addr.:** P.O. Box 27210, Governmental Reference Library, City Hall, Tucson, AZ 85726.

Berg, Edna Barrowclough (Mr. 17, 1915, Paterson, NJ) Libn., Bozeman Sr. HS, 1961–; Tchr., Libn., Hampton Pub. Sch., 1936–37. **Educ.:** Montclair State Coll., 1932–36, BA (Eng.); Columbia Univ., 1936–37 (LS); MN State Univ., 1960–61, MS (Eng.). **Orgs.:** ALA. MN LA: Cont. Educ. Com. (1976–78); Ch., Sch. Lib. Media Div. (1971–72); Pres. (1979–80). Friends of Gallatin Libs.: Bd. Delta Kappa Gamma. AAUW. **Pubns.:** Contrib., *Children's Library Service: School or Public* (1974). **Activities:** 10 **Addr.:** 1314 South Third Ave., Bozeman, MT 59715.

Bergan, Helen J. (Jl. 20, 1937, Fargo, ND) Chief, Biog. Div., DC Pub. Lib., 1972–, Readers Adv., Soclgy. Div., 1969–72; Libn. and Resrch. Ofcr., Luth. World Fed., Broadcasting Srv. Addis Ababa, Ethiopia, 1965–68; Ref. Libn., Yonkers Pub. Lib., 1964–65. **Educ.:** Augsburg College, Minneapolis, 1957–61, BA (Eng.); Univ. of MN, 1963–64, MALS. **Orgs.:** DC LA: Ref. Interest Grp. (Ch., 1979–81). **Activities:** 9; 16, 31, 39 **Addr.:** 1225 Martha Custis Dr., Alexandria, VA 22302.

Bergen, Daniel Patrick (My. 25, 1935, Albert Lea, MN) Prof., Grad. Lib. Sch., Univ. of RI, 1970–; Assoc. Prof., Dept. of Lib. Sci., Univ. of MS, 1966–70; Asst. Prof., Coll. of Lib. and Info. Srvs., Univ. of MD, 1965–66; Asst. Dean and Lectr., Sch. of LS, Syracuse Univ., 1964–65. **Educ.:** Univ. of Notre Dame, 1953–57, BA (Hist./Phil.), 1962, MA (Poli. Sci.); Univ. of Chicago, 1961, MA (LS), 1969, CAS (LS); Univ. of MN, 1968, MA (Amer.

PROFESSIONAL ACTIVITIES: Institutions: 1. Acad. lib.; 2. Arch.; 3. Assn.; 4. Fed./Gvt. lib.; 5. Inst. lib.; 6. Mfr./Suppl.; 7. Milit. lib.; 8. Musm.; 9. Pub. lib.; 10. Sch. lib.; 11. Sch. of lib. sci.; 12. Spec. lib.; 13. State lib.; 14. (other). **Functions/Activities:** 15. Acq./Col. dev.; 16. Adult srvs.; 17. Admin.; 18. Apprais.; 19. Archit./Bldgs.; 20. Cat./Class.; 21. Chld. srvs.; 22. Circ.; 23. Cons./Pres.; 24. Consult.; 25. Cont. ed.; 26. Educ. lib. sci.; 27. Ext. srvs.; 28. Fund/Grants; 29. Gvt. pubs.; 30. Indx./Abs.; 31. Instr. lib. use; 32. Media srvs.; 33. Micro.; 34. Netwks./Coop.; 35. Persnl.; 36. PR; 37. Publshg.; 38. Recs. mgt.; 39. Ref. srvs.; 40. Repro.; 41. Resrch.; 42. Review.; 43. Secur.; 44. Serials; 45. Spec. col.; 46. Tech. srvs.; 47. Trustees/Bds.; 48. YA srvs.; 49. (other).

Stud.), 1970, PhD (Amer. Stud.). **Orgs.:** ALA: Melvil Dewey Awd. Com. (1964–65). RI LA: Pres. 1976–77). AALS: Mem. Com. (1980–81); Resrch. Com. (1971–72). New England. LA. Amer. Stud. Assn. AAUP. Socty. for Gen. Syst. Resrch. Amer. Assn. for the Advnc. of Sci. **Honors:** Beta Phi Mu. **Pubns.:** Jt. ed., *Libraries and the College Climate of Learning* (1966); "The Communication System of the Social Sciences," *Coll. and Resrch. Libs.* (1967); "The Implications of General Systems Theory for Librarianship and Higher Education," *Coll. and Resrch. Libs.* (1966); Various reviews, reports, and other publications. **Activities:** 1, 11; 26, 39, 41; 54, 92, 93 **Addr.:** Graduate Library School, Rodman Hall, University of Rhode Island, Kingston, RI 02881.

Berger, Carol A. (Stamford, CT) Mgr., Lib. and Info. Srvs., Beatrice Foods Resrch. Ctr., 1979–; Lib. Dir., Natl. Livestock & Meat Bd., 1976–79; Libn., Air Transport Assn., 1970–72; Mgr., Lib. Srvs., Herner & Co., 1967–69. **Educ.:** Catholic Univ., 1960–64, BA (Eng.), 1964–68, MSLS. **Orgs.:** SLA: Dupl. Exch. (Ch., 1977–80). ASIS: Ed., Chicago Chap. Nsltr. **Activities:** 12; 17; 68, 75, 94 **Addr.:** Research Center Library, Beatrice Foods Co., 1526 S. State St., Chicago, IL 60605.

Berger, Kenneth W. (N. 1, 1949, New York, NY) Ref. Libn., Duke Univ., 1980–, Ref. Libn. and Mss. Catlgr., 1977–80. **Educ.:** Eckerd Coll., 1968–72, BA (East Asian Area Std.); FL State Univ., 1973–74, MA (East Asian Std.); 1976–77, MS (LS); Univ. of Pittsburgh, 1979, Cont. Ed. Prog. (OL Bibl. Srvs.). **Orgs.:** ALA. SELA. NC OLUG. Durham Cnty. LA: Treas. (1979–80); Ch., Bylaws Com. (1980–81). Assn. for the Bibl. of Hist. Assn. for Asian Std. AAUP. **Honors:** Beta Phi Mu. **Pubns.:** Abs. and Reviews. **Activities:** 54 **Addr.:** Reference Department, Perkins Library, Duke University, Durham, NC 27706.

Berger, Mary C. (O. 14, 1944, Cleveland, OH) Info. Spec., Cuadra Assoc., Inc., 1978–; Libn., Ferro Corp., 1972–78; Tech. Libn., Union Carbide Corp., 1969–72; Info. Retrieval Spec., Harshaw Chem. Co., 1966–68. **Educ.:** Ursuline Coll., 1962–66, BA (Chem.); Case West. Rsv. Univ., 1966–68, MLS. **Orgs.:** ASIS: Pres. (1981); Comp. Retrieval Srvs. Spec. Interest Grp. Ch., 1980). SLA: Info. Tech. Div. (Treas.). Amer. Chem. Socty. **Honors:** ASIS, Watson Davis Award, 1978; Beta Phi Mu. **Pubns.:** Jt. ed., *Directory of Online Databases* (1979); Jt. auth., *Evaluation of the Online Search Process* (1979); "Berger Bytes," *Online* (Ap. 1978). **Activities:** 12, 14-Resrch. and Dev.; 24, 25, 41; 56, 75, 91 **Addr.:** Cuadra Associates, Inc., 1523 Sixth St., Suite 12, Santa Monica, CA 90401.

Berger, Morey R. (Jl. 5, 1918, Elmira, NY) Supvsg. Libn., East. Br., Monmouth Cnty. Lib., 1975–; Film, Ref. Libn., 1970–75. **Educ.:** Cornell Univ., 1935–39, AB (Eng.); Rutgers Univ., 1969–70, MLS. **Orgs.:** NJ LA: Convention Ch. (1976–78). ALA. Congregation Beth Miriam; Masons; Friends of Steele Mem. Lib: Pres. (1965–66). **Honors:** Beta Phi Mu. **Pubns.:** Reviews. **Activities:** 9; 16, 17, 39; 54, 59 **Addr.:** 92 Friendship Ct., Red Bank, NJ 07701.

Berger, Patricia Wilson (My. 1, 1926, Washington, DC) Chief, Lib. and Info. Srvs. Div., US Natl. Bur. of Stans., 1979–; Chief, Info. Resrcs. and Srvs. Branch, US Env. Protection Agency, 1978–79; Chief, Lib. Div., US Natl. Bur. of Stans., 1976–78; Deputy Chief Libn., US Patent and Trademark Ofc., 1972–76; Chief Libn., US Comsn. on Gvt. Procurement, 1971–72; Dir., Tech. Info. and Security, Lambda Corp., 1967–71; Chief Libn., Inst. for Defense Anal., 1957–67. **Educ.:** George Washington Univ., BA; Cath. Univ., MLS. **Orgs.:** ALA: FLRT (Secy., 1978–79). ASIS. SLA: Washington Chap., (Pres., 1977–78; Corresp. Secy., 1970–71); Spec. Com. on WHCOLIS (1980). Natl. Org. of Women: Dir., North. VA Chap. (1973–74). **Honors:** Beta Phi Mu, 1974; US Dept. of Cmrc., Spec. Achieve. Awd. for Intl. Women's Yr. Actv., 1976. **Pubns.:** Jt. auth., "Standards and Guidelines for Data" in *A Sourcebook on Handling Scientific and Technical Data,* (1980); Ed., *Telecommunications Technologies, Networking and Libraries: Proceedings of a Conference, National Bureau of Standards* (1980). "Closing the Card Catalog - A Management Overview," *Procs.,* Washington, U.S. Defense Documentation Center (1980); Jt. auth., "SLA Faces the Equal Rights Amendment," *Spec. Libs.* (My.-Je. 1978); "Public Relations in the National Bureau of Standards Library," *Procs., 20th Annual Military Librarians' Workshop, Annapolis, MD* (1978); oral presentations. **Activities:** 4, 12; 17, 24, 34; 56, 62, 91 **Addr.:** US National Bureau of Standards, Washington, DC 20234.

Berger, Pearl (N. 30, 1943, New York, NY) Head Libn. Pollack Lib., Yeshiva Univ. 1981–; Head, Tech. Srvs., Yeshiva Univ., 1980–81; Asst. Libn., YIVO Inst. for Jewish Resrch., 1976–80. **Educ.:** Brooklyn Coll., 1960–65, BA (Math, Phil.); Tchrs. Inst. for Women, Yeshiva Univ., 1960–62, B Relig. Educ. (Jewish Std.); Columbia Univ., 1970–73, MLS; Yeshiva Univ., 1965–67, (Jewish Std.). **Orgs.:** ALA. ACRL. RTSD. Assn. of Jewish Libs. **Honors:** Beta Phi Mu. **Pubns.:** "Minor Repairs in a Small Research Library," *Lib. Jnl.* (Je. 1979); Assoc. Ed., *CAN (Conservation Administration News).* **Activities:** 1; 20, 23, 46 **Addr.:** Head Librarian, Pollack Library, Yeshiva University Libraries, 500 W. 185th St., New York, NY 10033.

Bergeron, Cheri Y. (D. 25, 1949, Lihue, HI) Libn., MT Ofc. of Pub. Instr., 1976–; Asst. Libn., Geol. Lib., Univ. of ND, 1973–76; Sch. Libn., Crestview Elem. Sch., 1972–73. **Educ.:** Univ. of ND, 1967–71, BS (Educ., Soc. Sci.), 1971–72, MS (Educ.); ND, 1971–76, First Grade Prof. Cert.; WI, 1972–75, Tchg. Cert. **Orgs.:** MT LA: Cont. Ed. Com. (1979–82); Spec. Libs. Dir. Com. (1979–80). SLA. **Activities:** 10, 12; 15, 17, 20; 63 **Addr.:** Office of Public Instruction, Rm. 106 State Capitol Bldg., Helena, MT 59620.

Bergeron, Louisette (Ja. 6, 1941, Saint-Jérôme, Lac St-Jean, PQ) Prof. de Lit. de jeunesse, Dept. de Francais, Univ. du PQ a Trois Rivieres, 1981–; Prof. de Lit. de Jeunesse, Ecole de bibliothéconomie, Univ. de Montréal, 1975–80; Fac. des Sci. de l'Éduc., Univ. of Laval, PQ, 1975–81; Sch. Tchr., Comsn. Scol. de Ste-Foy, 1963–70; Tchr., St-Félicien, 1958–63. **Educ.:** Univ. de Montréal, 1973–75, MA (Bibliothéconomie); Univ. Laval, 1970–73, Bac. (Hist.). **Orgs.:** Chld. Chld. Lit. Assn. *Ctr. de Recherche Intl. pour la Lit. de Jeunesse.* ALA. Assn. Can. pour l'Advnc. de la Lit. de Jeunesse (Sherbrooke). Assn. Can. de Langue Fr.: Mem., Jury du Prix Lit. de Jeunesse (1979; 1980). Other orgs. **Pubns.:** "L'image dans les Livres pour Enfants," *Docum. et Bibl.* (Mr. 1977); "L'enfant, l'image et le Récit," *Docum. et Bibl.* (1979); "Les livres que Nous avons Lus pour Vous," *Des Livres et des Jeunes* (1978–81). *Le Roman Apprevoisé* (1980); Jt. auth., *A la decouverte de la Littérature Enfantile* (1981). **Activities:** 11; 26, 41; 63 **Addr.:** 425 Learmonth, app. 6, Quebec, PQ G1S 1P7 Canada.

Bergles, Frances Daw (Ja. 15, 1943, Vancouver, BC, Can) Fine and Performing Arts Dept. Head, Saskatoon Pub. Lib., 1967–. **Educ.:** Univ. of SK, 1960–63, BA (Eng.); Univ. of Toronto, 1966–67, (BLS). **Orgs.:** Can. Assn. Msc. Libs. SK AV Assn. SK LA: AV Com. Univ. of SK Film Socty. **Honors:** SK Prov. Lib., Bursary, 1966. **Pubns.:** "Norman McLaren," *SK Lib.* (D. 1971); "Women and Film," *Cinema Can.* (Ag. 1973); "In defense of the audiovisual," *SK Lib.* (D. 1967); "Library as Total Access System: Challenge for Change," (Win. 1973–74). **Activities:** 9; 15, 17, 32; 55, 67 **Addr.:** Saskatoon Public Library, 311-23 St. E., Saskatoon, SK S7K 0J6 Canada.

Bergman, J. Peter (Ap. 29, 1946, New York, NY) Freelnc. Writer/Resrchr., 1978–; Thea., Msc. & Spoken Word Spec., Rodgers & Hammerstein Arch., NYPL at Lincoln Center, 1968–78. **Educ.:** Queens Coll., NY, 1964–69, (Eng.); Juilliard Sch. of Msc., 1969–70, (Compos.); New Sch. for Soc. Resrch., 1969-73, (Film/Theatre). **Orgs.:** Assn. for Recorded Sound Collections: Mem. Dir. Com., Chmn. (1979–). Amer. Soc. for Theatre Resrch. Thea. LA. S.W. Soho Prsrvn. Assn: Pres. (1981). The New Amsterdam Theatre Co: Bd. of Dirs. **Pubns.:** *The Films of Jeanette MacDonald & Nelson Eddy - Discography* (1975); *The Final Word,* a play (1979); "Plays for Posterity", *Playbill Mag.* (N. 1979); A series of articles on Roots of the NY Theatre, *Washington Mkt Review* (Mr.-Ag. 1979); Reviews. **Activities:** 12 10-Private Coll.; 24, 41, 42; 55, 67, 85 **Addr.:** 18 Thompson St., New York, NY 10013.

Bergman, Rita F. (S. 24, 1949, Albany, NY) Branch Mgr., Advnc. Dev. Div., Computer Corp. of Amer., 1980–; Mgr., Info. Srvs. Grp., Sigma Data Computing Corp., 1977–80; Head, Lib. and Info. Srvs., Geo. Washington Univ. Med. Cntr. Population Info. Prog., 1974–77; Libn., Phila. Gen. Hosp. Med. Lib., 1972–73. **Educ.:** SUNY, Buffalo, 1967–71, BA (Pol. Sci.); Drexel Univ., 1971–72, MS (Lib. and Info. Sci.). **Orgs.:** Assn. for Popltn./Family Plng. Libs. and Info. Cntrs.: Bd. of Dir. (1977–78); Popltn. Info. Network Com. (1976–78); Conf. Com. (1978–79). ASIS. Natl. Abortion Rights Action Leag. Natl. Org. of Women. **Honors:** Phi Beta Kappa, 1971; Beta Phi Mu, 1972. **Pubns.:** Jt. comp., *Population/Fertility Control Thesaurus* (1975). **Activities:** 12; 17, 24; 56, 65 **Addr.:** Computer Corporation of America, 1600 Wilson Blvd., Arlington, VA 22209.

Bergquist, Ann F. (Ag. 18, 1925, Flushing, NY) Tech. Info. Ofcr., Chief, Sci. Proj. Analysis and Retrieval Syst., Alchl., Drug Abuse and Mental Hlth. Admin. of DHHS, 1969–; Chief, Prog. Analysis Branch, Natl. Inst. of Allergy and Infectious Diseases, Dept. of Hlth., Educ. and Welfare, 1966–69, Staff Asst., Natl. Clearinghse. for Mental Hlth. Info., Natl. Inst. of Mental Hlth., 1962–66; Staff Asst., Prof. Spec., Pres. Cncl. on Youth Fitness, 1956–60; Confidential Asst. to Secy., Dept. of Hlth., Educ. and Welfare, 1953–56. **Educ.:** Univ. of MD, 1943–47, BS (Educ.), 1953, MA (Educ.); 1949–53, Tchr. Cert.; 1953, Real Estate Salesman Cert. **Orgs.:** Amer. Documtn. Inst.: Exec. Com. (1963–65). ASIS: Mem. Com. (1980–81); Prof. Com. (1980–81). Natl. Micro. Assn. Amer. Sch. Hlth. Assn. Amer. Assn. for Hlth., Phys. Educ. and Recreation. **Honors:** Alchl., Drug Abuse, and Mental Hlth. Admin., Qual. Increase Awd., Spec. Achvmt. Awd., 1976; Natl. Inst. of Mental Hlth., Superior Work Performance Awd., 1971. **Activities:** 12; 17, 30, 33; 80, 92 **Addr.:** Scientific Project Analysis and Retrieval System, Office of Extramural Programs, 5600 Fishers Ln., Rm. 7C26, Rockville, MD 20857.

Berk, Jack M. (Mr. 15, 1942, Philadelphia, PA) Dir., Bethlehem Pub. Lib., 1973–; Head Libn., Wolfsohn Meml. Lib., 1970–73; Libn., LA Cnty. Lib., 1969–70; Lib. Trainee, Free Lib. of Philadelphia, 1968–69. **Educ.:** Temple Univ., 1960–64, BS (Mktg.); Drexel Univ., 1967–68, MSLS. **Orgs.:** ALA. PA LA: Various offices. **Activities:** 9; 17, 25, 35 **Addr.:** 11 West Church St., Bethlehem, PA 18018.

Berk, Robert Ashby (Ja. 8, 1935, Portland, OR) Assoc. Prof., Univ. of AZ Grad. Lib. Sch., 1979–; Dir. of Educ., Med. LA, 1977–79; Curric. Spec., Natl. Lib. of Med., 1976–77; Assoc. Prof., Univ. of OR Sch. of Libnshp., 1971–77. **Educ.:** Univ. of OR, 1961–62, BA (Eng.); FL State Univ., 1963–64, MSLS; Emory Univ., 1965–66, Cert. (Med. Lib.); Univ. of IL, 1968–74, DLS. **Orgs.:** Med. LA. SLA. **Honors:** Beta Phi Mu. **Pubns.:** Ed., *Allerton Invitational Conference on Education for Health Sciences Librarianship, Proceedings* (1979); Jt. auth., "MEDLINE Training within the Library School Curriculum," *Bltn. of the Med. LA* (Jl. 1978). **Activities:** 12, 14-Medical; 17, 25, 39; 58, 80, 91 **Addr.:** Graduate Library School, University of Arizona, Tucson, AZ 85721.

Berkeley, Edmund, Jr. (Ap. 1, 1937, Charlottesville, VA) Cur. of Mss./Univ. Archvst., Univ. of VA, 1965–; Asst. Archvst., VA State Lib., 1963–65; Tchr., 1961–65. **Educ.:** Univ. of the South, 1954–58, BA (Hist.); Univ. of VA, 1958–61, MA (Hist.). **Orgs.:** SAA: Cncl. (1977–81); Arch. Secur. Prog. Adv. Com. (Ch., 1974–79); Com. to Draft a Code of Ethics (1977–); Mid-Atl. Reg. Arch. Conf. VA Oral Hist. Assoc.: VP (1978–). VA Hist. Recs. Adv. Bd. Albemarle Cnty. Hist. Soc.: Bd. (1969–72, 1977–). Various other organizations and ofcs. **Honors:** SAA, Fellow, 1976. **Pubns.:** Ed., *Autographs and Manuscripts: A Collector's Manual* (1979); Various articles in *VA Magazine of Hist. and Biog., The Amer. Archvst., Georgia Arch., VA Libn.;* Reviews. **Activities:** 1, 2; 15, 17, 45; 55, 62 **Addr.:** Manuscripts Department, University of Virginia Library, Charlottesville, VA 22901.

Berkner, Dimity S. (Jl. 2, 1941, Philadelphia, PA) VP, Taylor-Carlisle, Booksellers, 1978–; Acad. and Approval Prog., Baker & Taylor Co., 1975–78; Soc. Sci. Biblgphr., Univ. of South. CA Lib., 1971–75; YA Libn., Los Angeles Pub. Lib., 1970–71; Libn., W. European Std., Harvard Univ., 1969–70; Rotating Libn., Intl. Atomic Energy Agency, 1968; Ref. Libn., Harvard Coll. Lib., 1967–68. **Educ.:** Univ. of PA, 1960–64, AB (Int. Rel.); Simmons Coll., 1965–67, MLS; Univ. of South. CA, 1974–77, MPA (Pub. Admin.). **Orgs.:** ALA: Bookdealer-Lib. Rel. Com. (1979–81); Alternative Career Libns. Discuss. Grp. (1980). ASIS: Los Angeles Chap. Secy. (1974). **Pubns.:** "Considerations in Selecting an Approval Plan," *Shaping Library Collections for the 1980s* (1980); "Case Study: A Library Bookjobber," *What Else You Can Do with a Library Degree* (1980); "Communication between Vendors and Librarians: The Bookseller's Point of View," *Library Acquisitions: Practice and Theory* (1979); "Library Staff Development through Performance Appraisal," *Coll. and Resrch. Libs.* (Jl. 1979); "Two Library Work-Study Programs in the Boston Area," *Coll. and Resrch. Libs.* (Mr. 1967). **Activities:** 37 **Addr.:** 58 Dorann Ave., Princeton, NJ 08540.

Berkowitz, Albert M. (Je. 27, 1921, New Rochelle, NY) Chief, Ref. Srvcs. Div., Natl. Lib. of Med., 1971–; Deputy Chief, Ref. Srvcs. Div., 1969–71; Head, Loan and Stack Sec., 1966–69; Branch Libn., D.C. Pub. Lib., 1961–66. **Educ.:** NY Univ., 1938–42, BS (Bus. Admn.); Catholic Univ., 1959–61, MSLS. **Orgs.:** Med. LA: Copyrt. Com. ASIS. MD Assn. of Hlth. Scis. Libns. **Honors:** Natl. Lib. of Med., Dirs. Honor Awd., 1976. **Activities:** 4, 12; 23; 61, 80 **Addr.:** National Library of Medicine, 8600 Rockville Pike, Bethesda, MD 20209.

Berlin, Arthur E. (My. 7, 1941, Woburn, MA) Media Dir., Salem Sch. Dist., 1970–; Tchr., Salem HS, 1967–69; Tchr., Pinkerton Acad., 1963–67. **Educ.:** Gordon Coll., 1958–62, AB (Hist.); Boston Univ., 1969–70, MEd (Educ. Media). **Orgs.:** NH Educ. Media Assoc.: Pres. (1971–72). AECT: Cncl. (1972–75). New Eng. Educ. Media Assn. ALA:AASL. Auburn NH Sch. Bd.: Mem. (1969–72), Ch. (1969–70); NH Sch. Bds. Assn.: Exec. Com. (1969–72). **Activities:** 10; 24, 32; 93 **Addr.:** 23 Marsh Ave., Salem, NH 03079.

Berlin, Ira Richard (S 4, 1941, Chicago, IL) Arch./Li. Admin., Northwestern Meml. Hosp., 1974–; Archvst./Libn., Med. Trial Tech. Qtly., 1968–74; Dir., Info. & Docum., Transcopy, Inc., 1961–67; Consult. Rec. Mgr., Chrysler Corp., 1960–66. **Educ.:** Northeast. IL State Col., 1969–70, BA (Hist.); 1971–74, MA (Hist.); Rosary Col., 1973–74, MALS. **Orgs.:** SAA: Arrange. Com. (1979). Med. LA. Midwest Arc. Conf.: Arrange. Ch. (1978). Assn. of Recs. Mgrs. and Admin.: Archvst. (1978–79). **Pubns.:** "Coming Home-1978" *Bltn. of the Med. Lib. Assn.* (1978). **Activities:** 2, 12; 17, 38, 45; 59, 77, 80 **Addr.:** P.O. Box 59139, Chicago, IL 60659.

Berling, John G. (Je. 26, 1934, Melrose, MN) Dean, Lrng. Resrcs. Srvs., St. Cloud State Univ., 1977–; Dir., Media Srvs., Staples Pub. Schs., 1962–68; Dir., Media Srvs., Apollo HS, St. Cloud, MN, 1968–75; Asst. Prof., Media Educ., St. Cloud State Univ., 1975–77. **Educ.:** St. Cloud State Univ., 1952–57, BS (Bus./Eng.); Wayne State Univ., 1966–67, MSLS; Univ. of NE, 1973–75, PhD (Educ. Admin.). **Orgs.:** AECT: Prog. Consult. and Eval. Com. (Ch., 1979); AALS. MN Educ. Media Org. ALA. St. Cloud Area Cham. of Cmrce. **Pubns.:** Helped produce a vid. tape on censorship (1979). **Activities:** 1, 10; 17, 26, 34; 63, 74, 93 **Addr.:** 3011 20th St. So., St. Cloud, MN 56301.

Special Subjects/Services: 50. Adult educ.; 51. Advert./Mktg.; 52. Aerosp.; 53. Agric.; 54. Area std.; 55. Arts/Hum.; 56. Autom.; 57. Bibl./Prtg.; 58. Bio. sci.; 59. Bus./Fin.; 60. Chem.; 61. Copyrt.; 62. Documtn.; 63. Educ.; 64. Engin.; 65. Env.; 66. Eth. grps.; 67. Film; 68. Food/Nutr.; 69. Geneal.; 70. Geo.; 71. Geol.; 72. Handcpd.; 73. Hist.; 74. Int. frdm.; 75. Info. sci.; 76. Insr.; 77. Law; 78. Legis.; 79. Math./Comp. sci.; 80. Med.; 81. Metals; 82. Nat. resrcs.; 83. Newsp.; 84. Nuc. sci.; 85. Oral hist.; 86. Petr./Energy; 87. Pharm.; 88. Phys./Astr./Math.; 89. Readg.; 90. Relig.; 91. Sci./Tech.; 92. Soc. sci.; 93. Telecom.; 94. Transp.; 95. (other).

Berman, Ellen L. (My. 28, 1948, Boston, MA) Lib. Mgr., TRW Systs. and Energy, TRW Energy Systs. Lib., 1979–; Lib. Mgr. TRW Defense and Space Systs. Grp., Tech. Lib., 1975–79, Libn., 1975. **Educ.:** Univ. of WI, 1966–68; Boston Univ., 1968–70, BS (Educ.); Simmons Coll., 1973–75, MLS; various crs. **Orgs.:** Interlib. Users Assn.: Bd. of Dirs. (1979–); Ed. Com. (1977); Conf. Un. List Com. (1978–80). Com. on Info. Hang-Ups: Subcom. on Energy and Env. Info. (Ch., 1980–). SLA: Ed. Com. for Chap. Notes (1978–79). Metro. WA Lib. Cncl.: Adv. Com. for Mgt. Curric. for Spec. Libs. (1978–79). Various other orgs. **Honors:** TRW, Inc., TRW Systs. and Energy, Cost Reduction Prog. Awd. of Recog., 1979. **Pubns.:** Ed. com., *Interlibrary Users Association Journal Holdings in the Washington-Baltimore Area* (1977); ed., *Directory of Energy and Environment Libraries and Information Centers in the Metropolitan Washington, DC Area.* TRW services: "Finding Your Way Around TRW Energy Systems Library" **Activities:** 12; 17, 29, 46; 74, 86, 91 **Addr.:** TRW Energy Systems Library, 8301 Greensboro Dr., McLean, VA 22102.

Berman, Leslie M. (S. 28, 1951, Bridgeport, CT) Dir., Dept. of Plng. and Rsrch., CT State Lib., 1977–; LSCA Coord., 1976–77; Proj. Coord., Human Resrc. Info. Netwk., Bridgeport Pub. Lib., 1974–76; Resrch. Assoc., Urban Info. Interpreters, Inc., 1973–74. **Educ.:** South. CT State Coll., 1969–73, BS; Univ. of MD, Coll. Pk., 1973–74, MLS. **Orgs.:** CT LA: VP/Pres.-elect, 1981; NELA Rep. (1979–81). NELA. ALA:ASCLA/Pubn. Com. (1979–81), State Lib. Agency Sect. (Exec. Com., 1981); LAMA/Stats. Sect., Stats. for State Lib. Agencies Com. (1980–82); SRRT, Action Cncl. CT Hum. Cncl. (1978–81). **Honors:** Beta Phi Mu, 1974. **Pubns.:** *The Sourcebook: A Guide to Information on Human Resources in the Bridgeport Area* (1975); "Secrecy and Medical Experimentation on Prisoners," *Med. Experimentation on Prisoners Must Stop* (1974). **Activities:** 9, 13; 17, 34, 49-Cmnty. Info. Srvs.; 78 **Addr.:** 18 Lostbrook Road, West Hartford, CT 06117.

Berman, Margot S. (Ap. 12, 1929, Reinheim, Germany) Libn., Beth Am Sch. and Temple Lib., Miami, 1965–. **Educ.:** City Coll. of NY, 1947–50, Miami Dade Cmnty. Coll., BS; FL Intl. Univ., 1973–75, (Hist.); 1964–66, AA. **Orgs.:** AJL: Pres. (1976–78). Cncl. of Natl. Lib. and Info. Assn.: Cnclr. (1976–82). **Honors:** Jewish Bk. Cncl. of Amer., Merit Awd., 1969. **Pubns.:** "A History of the Kent Street (London) Synagogue Library," *AJL Bltn.* (1974); Various reviews, Clmns., articles in *AJL Bltn.* (1970–). **Activities:** 10, 12; 15, 21, 41; 50, 63, 90 **Addr.:** Beth Am Library, 5950 N. Kendall Dr., Miami, FL 33156.

Berman, Marsha F. (F. 23, 1935, Los Angeles, CA) Assoc. Msc. Lib., Msc. Lib., Univ. of CA, Los Angeles, 1966–; Supvsr., Msc. Lib. Internship Prog., Univ. of CA, LA, 1968–; Acq. Libn., UCLA Ed./Psyc. Lib., 1965–66; Adult Srvs. Libn., Brooklyn Pub. Lib., 1959–62, 1963–64; Libn., San Francisco Pub. Lib., Art & Msc. Dept., 1962–63. **Educ.:** Univ. of CA, Los Angeles, 1952–57, BA (Msc.); Univ. of CA, Berkeley, 1957–63, MLS. **Orgs.:** Msc. LA: Placement Com. (1969–71); Acq. Subcom. (1972–73); Nom. Com. (1978). Msc. LA: South. CA Chap., Nsltr. (1976–78); Prog. Ch. (1976–79); Chap. Ch. (1974–75). Intl. Assn. of Msc. Libs. Ed. Media Assocs.: Treas., Bd. of Dir. (1979–). **Pubns.:** "Current Bibliography...", *Journal of the Arnold Schoenberg Institute* (O. 1976); (F. 1977); (Je. 1977); Reviews. **Activities:** 1, 12; 15, 26, 39; 55 **Addr.:** UCLA Music Library, University of California, Los Angeles, Schoenberg Hall, Los Angeles, CA 90024.

Bernard, Bobbi (F. 26, 1940, Toledo, OH) Tech. Libn., AMF, Inc., 1979–; Libn., Fed. Rsv., 1975–77; Adult Srvs., Ref., Fairfield Pub. Lib., 1971–74; Circ. Staff, Miami Univ., Oxford, OH, 1959–61. **Educ.:** CA State Coll., 1969, BA (Lit.); South. CT State, 1973–75, MLS; N. TX State Univ. 1975, (Libs., Comps.). **Orgs.:** SLA: Chem. Div. (Mem. Ch., 1980–82), Engin. Stans. Com. Southwest. CT Lib. Cncl.: Bd. (1980). Southwest. CT Lib. OLUG. ALA. Various other orgs. **Pubns.:** "Education for Librarianship," *CT Libs.* (Ap. 1974). **Activities:** 9, 12; 34, 39; 91 **Addr.:** AMF Inc., 689 Hope St., Stamford, CT 06907.

Bernard, Hugh Y. (Jr.) (Jl. 17, 1919, Athens, GA) Prof. and Libn. Emeritus, 1981–; Prof., Libn. of the Law Lib., George Washington Univ., 1960–81; Sr. Cat., Descr. Cat., Lib. of Cong., 1959–60; Rev., Copyrt. Cat., 1952–59; Cat. Copyrt. Cat., 1947–52. **Educ.:** Univ. of GA, 1938–41, AB (Hist.); Columbia Univ., 1946–47, BS (LS); George Washington Univ., 1957–61, JD. **Orgs.:** Law Libns. Socty. of Washington, D.C.: VP (1964–66); Pres. (1966). AALL: Ch. Constn. and By-Laws Com. (1973–74). Copyrt. Com. (1974–78). Cat./Class. Com. (1961–64). SLA: Soc. Sci. Div. Amer. Bar Assn. Amer. Judicature Socty. D.C. Bar. **Honors:** Phi Beta Kappa, 1941; Order of the Coif, 1966; Kappa Delta Pi, 1940. **Pubns.:** *The Law of Death and Disposal of the Dead* (1979); *Public Officials, Elected and Appointed* (1968); Reviews; Ed. "Book Reviews", *George Washington Law Review* (1959–60). **Activities:** 1; 15, 17, 24; 61, 77, 92 **Addr.:** 3563 South Leisure World Blvd., Apt. 1A, Silver Spring, MD 20906.

Bernardin, Luce (Montreal, PQ) Dir., St. Bruno-de-Montarville Pub. Lib., 1963–; Dir., Outremont Pub. Lib., 1955–63. **Educ.:** Univ. of Montreal, 1955–61, BB (LS). **Orgs.:** Corp. des Bibtcrs. Prof. du PQ. Can. LA. ASTED. Assn. des bibtcrs. du PQ. **Activities:** 9; 15, 17, 18; 50, 63, 92 **Addr.:** Public Library, 1605 Montarville, St-Bruno, PQ J3V 3T8 Canada.

Berney, Bruce R. (F. 3, 1935, Walla Walla, WA) Dir., Astoria Pub. Lib., 1967–; Sch. Libn., Highline Sch. Dist., 1963–66; Eng. Conversation Tchr., Toyama, Japan, 1961–63; HS Tchr., Soap Lake, WA, 1959–60. **Educ.:** Univ. of Puget Snd., 1953–57, AB (Educ.); Lewis and Clark Coll., 1960–61, MEd (Libnshp.); Univ. of WA, 1964–66, MLS (Libnshp.). **Orgs.:** OR LA: Conf. Ch. (1968). Pac. NW LA: 2nd VP (1978–80). Pac. NW Bibl. Ctr.: Pac. NW LA Rep. (1978–80). Kiwanis Club of Astoria: Pres. (1970–71). Clatsop Cnty. Hist. Socty.: VP (1980–). **Activities:** 9; 17, 30 **Addr.:** Astoria Public Library, 450 10th St., Astoria, OR 97103.

Bernhardt, Frances Simonsen (My 4, 1932, Kennecott, AK) Acq. Libn., North. VA Com. Coll., 1978–; Tech. Srvcs. Libn., Clayton Jr. Coll., 1971–78; Libn., Fort Sill Indian Sch., 1968–70; Acq. and Cat., Univ. of MN, 1958–68. **Educ.:** St. Cloud State Coll. and Univ. of MN, 1955–, BS, (Educ.); Univ. of MN, 1957–58, MALS; Cath. Univ., 1979–, Post MLS Prog. **Orgs.:** ALA. SE LA. **Pubns.:** *Introduction to Library Technical Services* (1979); "Searching", *Library Resources & Technical Services* (Fall 1966). **Activities:** 1; 15, 20, 46 **Addr.:** 5647 Mt. Burnside Way, Burke, VA 22015.

Bernier, Gaston (Je. 19, 1938, Saint-Pascal, PQ) Dir. Adj., Bibl. de L'Asm. Natl., 1979–, Dir., Srv. de Recherche, 1977–79; Chef, Dept. du Cat., Bibl. Natl. de Côte d'Ivoire, 1975–77; Res., Srv. de Réf., Bibl. de L'Asm. Natl., 1970–75; Resp., Sect. des Sci. Soc. et Docum. Ofc., Univ. Laval, 1962–70. **Educ.:** Coll. de Victoriaville, 1954–58; Univ. Laval, 1958–62, MScSoc (Pol.); Univ. de Montréal, 1964–65, BBibl. **Orgs.:** Corp. des Bibtcrs. Prof. du PQ. ASTED. Assn. Can des Sci. de l'Info. Soc. Québécoise de Sci. Pol. **Pubns.:** "Le Droit à l'Information au Québec," *Documtn. et Bibl.* (1979); "Publications Officielles Québécoises," *Documtn. et Bibl.* (D. 1974). **Activities:** 15, 17, 47; 78, 92 **Addr.:** 315 ouest, rue des Peupliers, Québec PQ G1L 1J1 Canada.

Bernier, Roger B. (S. 28, 1942, Drummondville, PQ) Head, Sci. Lib., Univ. of Sherbrooke, 1981–, Head, Info., Prog. de Recherche Sur L'Amiante, 1977–81, Head, Gen. Lib., 1976–77, Head, Cedobus, 1973–76, Head, Sci. Lib., 1971–73; Head, Cat. Dept, Univ. Du PQ, Montreal, 1970–71; Supvsr. of Class., Cat. Dept., Univ. de Sherbrooke, 1967–70; Catlgr., Semy. de Sherbrooke, 1965–67. **Educ.:** Semy. de Sherbrooke, 1956–64, BA (Phil.); Univ. de Montreal, 1964–65, BBibl; Univ. de Sherbrooke, 1965–66, MA (Hist.). **Orgs.:** Corp. des Bibtcrs. Prof. du PQ: Bur. de Dir. (1976–79); Com. de Formation Prof. (1979); Anl. Mtg. (Pres., 1980–81). ASTED. ACSL. Caisse Pop. Ste Jeanne D'Arc: Credit Comsnr. (1974–). Cham. of Cmrce. **Pubns.:** *Etablissement D'un Catalogue Systematique* (1969); *La Classification Library of Congress: Cours et Exercices* (1973); *Abrege de la Classification Library of Congress* (1974). **Activities:** 1, 12; 17, 20, 30; 65, 80, 91 **Addr.:** Bibliotheque des Sciences, Universite de Sherbrooke, Sherbrooke, PQ J1K 2R1 Canada.

Berninghausen, David K. (F. 5, 1916, Beaman, IA) Prof. Sch. of LS, Univ. of MN, 1953, Dir., 1953–74; Visit. Prof., Natl. Taiwan Univ., 1962–63; Dir., Cooper Union Libs., 1947–53; Dir., Birmingham - Southern Coll. Lib., 1944–47; Tchr., IA HS and Jr. HS, 1936–40. **Educ.:** IA St. Tchr. Coll., 1932–36, BA (Sp.); Columbia Univ., 1938–41, BLS; Drake Univ., 1940–43, MA (Eng. Phil.); Univ. of NC, 1944, (Eng. Phil.); Harvard Educ. Fellow, 1950–51, (Educ. Admn.). **Orgs.:** ALA: Cncl., Com. on Inf. Frdm. (1948–50, 1970–71). MN LA: Pres. (1957–58). AALS: Pres. (1959–60). Amer. Cvl. Liberties Un.: St. of NY Chap., Bd. of Dir., (1951–53). St. of MN Chap., Bd. of Dir. (1954–61). AAUP: Univ. of MN Chap., Pres. (1961–62). **Honors:** Drake Univ., Alum. Disting. Srv. Awd., 1964; Univ. of IA, Alum. Achvmt. Awd., 1966. **Pubns.:** "Intellectual Freedom in Librarianship: Advances and Retreats," in *Advances in Librarianship* (1979); *The Flight from Reason, Essays on Intellectual Freedom in the Academy, the Press, and the Library* (1975); Jt. Auth., *Library Services in North Dakota* (1966); Ed., *Libraries of Seven South Dakota Institutions of Higher Learning,* (1965); *Undergraduate Library Education: Accreditation, Standards, Articulation* (1959); Many other articles. **Activities:** 1, 11; 74 **Addr.:** Library School, University of Minnesota, Minneapolis, MN 55455.

Bernstein, Judith (O. 2, 1931, New York, NY) Head, Parish Mem. Lib., Anderson Sch. of Mgt., Univ. of NM, 1980–; Ref. Libn., 1978–79; Dir., Adult Srvs., White Plains Pub. Lib., 1977–78; Head, Circ. Srvs., 1971–77. **Educ.:** Cornell Univ., 1948–52, BA (Hist.), 1952–54, MA (South East Asian Area Std. and Pol. Sci.); Columbia Univ., 1961–64, MLS. **Orgs.:** ALA: LAMA/Circ. Srvs. Eval. Com. (Ch., 1978–); Circ. Srvs. Prog. Com. (1975–78); Mem. Srvs. Rep., NM (1979–). NM LA: Native Amer. RT (1979–). Leag. of Women Voters: White Plains (VP, 1969–71). NM Cactus & Succulent Socty.: Secy. (1980–); Educ. Com. (Ch., 1967–69). **Activities:** 1, 9; 17, 22, 39; 59, 63, 92 **Addr.:** 11512 Manitoba NE, Albuquerque, NM 87111.

Berring, Robert C. (N. 20, 1949, Canton, OH) Prof. of Law and Law Libn., Univ. of WA, 1981–; Actg. Dir., Harvard Law Lib., 1979–81; Assoc. Libn., 1978; Assoc. Dir., Univ. TX Law Lib., 1976–78; Asst. Libn., Univ. IL Law Lib., 1975–76. **Educ.:** Harvard Coll., 1967–71, BA (Gvt.); Univ. of CA, Berkeley, 1971–74, JD; 1973–74, MLS. **Orgs.:** AALL: Educ. Com. New Eng. Law Libns. ALA. Amer. Bar Assn. CA Bar Assn. **Pubns.:** *Authors Guide to Journalism Law, Criminal Justice and Criminology* (1979); Ed., *Legal Ref. Qtly.* (1980–); Contrib., *Audio Resrch. in the Law* (1978); several wkshps. and panels. **Activities:** 1; 17, 24, 41; 77 **Addr.:** University of Washington Law Library, Seattle, WA 98105.

Berrisford, Paul D. (N. 3, 1925, St. Paul, MN) Dir., Ctrl. Tech. Srv., Univ. of MN, 1957–; Libn., St. Paul Pub. Schs., 1953–57. **Educ.:** Univ. of MN, 1950, BA (Hist., Pol. Sci.), 1950–52, BS (Educ.), 1950–52, BSLS. **Orgs.:** ALA: RTSD, Dir., Descr. Cat. Com. (Ch., 1969), Prsrvn. of Lib. Mtrls. Com. (Ch., 1973–74), Cat. and Class. Exec. Com. (1973–74), Margaret Mann Cit. Com. (1974–75); *Lib. Resrcs. & Tech. Srvs.* Ed. Bd. (1974–79); Twin City Catlgrs. RT (Ch., 1959). MN LA. Unvsl. Serials and Bk. Exch. AAUP. **Honors:** Phi Delta Kappa. **Pubns.:** *A Survey of the Libraries of the University of Western Ontario* (1979); "Year's Work in Cataloging and Classification: 1976," *Lib. Resrcs. & Tech. Srvs.* (Sum. 1977); "Year's Work in Cataloging and Classification: 1977," *Lib. Resrcs. & Tech. Srvs.* (Sum. 1978). **Activities:** 1; 17 **Addr.:** 2245 Princeton Ave., St. Paul, MN 55105.

Berrocal-Lopez, Ramon (F. 10, 1936, Mayaguez, Puerto Rico) Prof., Soc. Sci. Dept., Univ. of PR, Mayaguez campus, 1981–; Sub-dir., Univ. of Pr, Mayaguez, Campus Gen. Lib., 1978–80; Dir., Univ. of Puerto Rico, Arecibo, 1974–78; Head Tech. Srvs., Univ. of Puerto Rico, Mayaguez, 1971–74, Head Cat., 1970–71. **Educ.:** Univ. of Puerto Rico, Rio Piedras, 1953–57, BA (Econ.); Syracuse Univ., 1968–69, MS (LS); Univ. of Puerto Rico Rio, Piedras, 1963–65 (Cert., Pub. Admn.). **Orgs.:** Socty. de Bibter. de Puerto Rico. Phi Epsilon Chi. Phi Delta Kappa. **Activities:** 1; 17, 20, 46 **Addr.:** Box 5351 College Station, Mayaguez, PR 00708.

Berry, John N., III (Je. 12, 1933, Montclair, NJ) Ed.-in-chief, *Lib. Jnl.,* R. R. Bowker Co., 1969–, Lectr., Sch. of Lib. and Info. Sci., Univ. of Pittsburgh, 1972–73; Ed., Bk. Ed. Dept., 1966–68, Asst. Ed., 1964–66; Ed., *Bay State Libn.,* 1962–64; Asst. Dir., Lib., Simmons Coll., 1962–64, Lectr., Sch. of LS, 1961–64, Ref. Libn., 1960–62. **Educ.:** Boston Univ., 1951–58, AB (Hist.); Simmons Coll., 1959–60, SM (LS). **Orgs.:** SLA: Publshg. Div. (Ch., 1969). ALA. **Honors:** Simmons Coll., Sch. of LS, First Anl. Alum. Achvmt., 1970; ALA/H.W. Wilson, Lib. Per. Awd. for *Bay State Libn.,* 1962. **Pubns.:** Ed., *Directory of Library Consultants* (1969); various articles, *Lib. Jnl., Spec. Libs.* **Activities:** 1, 9; 16, 17, 26; 74, 78, 92 **Addr.:** Library Journal, 1180 Ave. of Americas, New York, NY 10036.

Bert, Sister Rita Ann (F. 2, 1934, Chester, IL) Chld. Libn., Oak Lawn Pub. Lib., 1974–; Libn., Aurora Ctrl. Catholic HS, 1968–74; Tchr., Various Catholic schs., 1953– 68. **Educ.:** Alverno Coll., 1953–65, BS (Educ.); Rosary Coll., 1965–70, MLS. **Orgs.:** Catholic LA: Mem. Ch. (1977–); North. IL Chap. (Vice Ch., Ch. elect., 1978–80); Chld. Sect. (Vice-Ch., Ch. elect, 1981–83); Regina Medal Com. (Ch., 1981–83). **Activities:** 9, 10; 15, 17, 21; 63 **Addr.:** Oak Lawn Public Library, 9427 S. Raymond Ave., Oak Lawn, IL 60453.

Bertels, S.J., Henry J. (Ag. 11, 1926, Jersey City, NJ) Dir., Woodstock Theo. Ctr. Lib. 1975–; Dir., Woodstock Coll. Lib., 1970–75. **Educ.:** Fordham Univ. Coll., 1954–58, BA (Eng.), 1958–59, MA (Eng.); Woodstock Coll., 1959–63, BST, (Theo.); Columbia Univ., 1964–66, MLS. **Orgs.:** ALA. ATLA. **Activities:** 12; 15, 17, 45; 90 **Addr.:** Woodstock Theological Center Library, Georgetown University, Box 37445 Washington, DC 20013.

Berthrong, Merrill Gray (Jl. 18, 1919, Cambridge, MA) Dir., Libs., Wake Forest Univ., 1964–; Libn., Admin., Univ. of PA, 1958–64, Circ. Libn., 1957–58, Rsv. Bk. Libn., 1956–57. **Educ.:** Tufts Univ., 1937–41, BA (Hist.); Fletcher Sch. of Law and Diplomacy, 1946–47, MA (Hist.); Univ. of PA, 1950–58, PhD (Hist.). **Orgs.:** ALA. SELA. NC LA. Amer. Hist. Assn. AAUP. **Activities:** 1; 17; 55, 74 **Addr.:** Z. Smith Reynolds Library, Wake Forest University, Box 7777, Winston-Salem, NC 27109.

Bertolucci, Ysabel R. (N. 13, 1949, Alameda, CA) Health Sciences Libn., Kaiser Permanente Med. Cntr., 1975–; Libn. Kaiser Fndn. Sch. of Nursing, 1973–75. **Educ.:** Univ. of CA, Berkeley, 1967–71, BA (Lang.); Univ. of South. CA, Los Angeles, 1971–72, MS (Lib. Sci.). **Orgs.:** Med. LA. SLA. CA LA. North. CA Med. Lib. Grp.: Nom. Com. (1977); Ch., Contin. Educ. Com. (1978); Pres. (1981). ALA. ASIS. West Bay Health Srvs. Agency. Friends of the San Francisco Pub. Lib. Del. CA Conf. on Lib. and Info. Srvs. (1978). **Activities:** 12; 17, 39; 80 **Addr.:** Health Sciences Library, Kaiser Permanente Medical Center, 1200 El Camino Real, South San Francisco, CA 94080.

Bertram, Lee Ann (O. 10, 1938, Harlingen, TX) Sci. Ref. Libn., Eli Lilly and Co., 1976–, Sci. Cat., 1967–76, Info. Syst. Dev. Asso., 1965–67, Sci. Cat., 1962–64. **Educ.:** Southwest. Univ., 1956–60, BS (Chem.); Carnegie-Mellon Univ., 1960–61, MLS; Emory Univ., 1961–62, Cert., Med. LS. **Orgs.:** SLA: IN

Chap.; Pres. 1975–76, Secy. 1965–66. Med. LA. **Activities:** 12; 15, 39; 60, 80, 87 **Addr.:** Scientific Library, Eli Lilly and Company, 307 E. McCarty Street, Indianapolis, IN 46285.

Bertrand-Gastaldy, Suzanne (Ja. 22, 19–, Albertville, France) Actg. Dir., Ecole de bibliothéconomie, Univ. de Montréal, 1981–, Asst. Prof., 1978–81; Libn., Univ. du Québec à Montréal, 1976–78; Asst. Libn., Comm. Scolaire Rég. du Golfe-Sept-Iles, PQ, 1973–74, Tchr. 1969–73; Tchr., Lycée de Jeunes Filles, Sfax, Tunisie, 1967–69. **Educ.:** Fac. des lettres et Sci. humaines, Lyon, France, 1962–67, Lic. ès lettres (Lett. classiques); 1967–68 Dip. d'études supérieures (Lettres classiques), 1968–69, CAPES (Lettres classiques); Univ. de Montréal, 1974–76, MLS. **Orgs.:** ASTED: Aegidius-Fauteux Conf., Org. Com. (1979–81). Can. Assn. Info. Sci.: Montreal Sect. (Ch., 1977–78). Assn. Intl. des Écoles des Sci. de l'Info.: Org. Com., Biennial Mtg., Liege, Belgium (1982). Corp. des bibtcrs. profs. du PQ: Prof. Trng. Com. (Ch., 1980–81); Com. on Sci. and Tech. Info. (1981). **Pubns.:** Ed. Com. Ch., *Argus* (1978–80); "La science de l'information à l'Ecole de Bibliothéconomie," *Can. Jnl. of Info. Sci.* (1980); "Bibliothéconomie, information documentaire, science de l'information, ou quoi?" *Argus* (1980). **Activities:** 1; 26, 30; 75 **Addr.:** Ecole de bibliothéconomie, Université de Montréal, C.P. 6128, Montréal, PQ H3C 3J7 Canada.

Berul, Lawrence Herbert (Ap. 29, 1934, Camden, NJ) Pres., Berul Assocs., Ltd., 1979–; Ch., Amicus Res. Grp. Ltd., 1981–; Pres., Applications Res. Grp., 1981– Exec. VP, Aspen Systs. Corp., 1970–79; Dir., Mktg., Auerbach Publshrs., Inc., 1968–70, Prog. Mgr., 1963–68; Dir., Washington Ofc., Info. Dynamics Corp., 1961–63; Attorney, CEIR, Inc., 1960–61; Patent Examiner and Mgt. Anal., U.S. Patent Ofc., 1957–60. **Educ.:** Drexel Univ., 1952–57, BS (Cmrc.) 1963–69, MBA; George Washington Univ., 1957–61, JD; Columbia Univ., Exec. Prog. in Bus. Admin., 1977. **Orgs.:** ASIS: Mktg. Com. (1979–80). Info. Indus. Assn.: Govt. Rel. Com. (1974–75). Amer. Bar. Assn. **Pubns.:** "Computerized Files – A Powerful Weapon," *NY Law Jnl.* (Ag. 1977); "Building a Data-Base Defense against Product Liability," *Mgt. Rev.* (N. 1977); Various other articles and tech. rpts. **Activities:** 14-Consult.; 24; 56, 75, 77 **Addr.:** 5010 Nicholson Lane, Rockville, MD 20852.

Besant, Larry X. (Mr. 13, 1935, Centralia, IL) Asst. Dir., Pub. Srvs., OH State Univ. Libs., 1972–; Asst. Dir., Tech. Srvs., Univ. of Houston Libs., 1968–71, Actg. Dir. of Libs., 1971; Tech. Info. Consult., Lunar Sci. Inst. of the Univs. Space Resrch. Assn.; Asst. Libn., Chemical Abs. Srv., 1966–68; Tech. Pres. Libn., 1962–65. **Educ.:** Centralia Twp. Jr. Coll., 1959, AA; Univ. of IL, 1961, BS (Chem.); 1962, MSLS. **Orgs.:** ALA: Plng. Com. (Ch., 1977–79). SLA: Empl. Com. (Ch., 1974–75); Dayton Chap. (Pres., 1964–65); various other coms. Acad. LA of OH: Task Force on Sharing Acad. Lib. Resrcs. Franklin Cnty. (OH) LA: Pres. (1966). Various other orgs. Amer. Chemical Socty. OH State Univ.: various coms. AAUP. Various other orgs. **Pubns.:** "The New Copyright Law–A Primer," *OSU On Campus* (Ja. 12, 1978); "Special Report: The Copyright Dilemma," *Lib. Jnl.* (Je. 15, 1977); "The Self-Destructing Constitution: 'Chousing' Up Sides at the Cincinnati Conference," *Bltn. of the OH LA* (Ja. 1973); oral presentations. **Activities:** 1; 17 **Addr.:** Public Services, The Ohio State University Libraries, 1858 Neil Ave. Mall, Columbus, OH 43210.

Bess, Elvin D. (O. 20, 1916, East St. Louis, IL) Col. Dev. Ofcr., Med. Ctr. Lib., Univ. of NM, 1977–; Chief, Tech. Srvs., 1976–77, Assoc. Libn., 1969–76, Chief, Tech. Srvs., 1968–69; Trainee in Lib. Mgt., Welch Medical Library, The Johns Hopkins Univ., 1967–68. **Educ.:** Washington Univ., 1946–49, AB (Phil.); Univ. of KY, MSLS; Med. Lib. Cert., Grade II, 1968. **Orgs.:** Med. LA. Grt. Albuquerque LA. Common Cause. Natl. Rifle Assn. **Pubns.:** "Faculty Participation in an Evaluation Review of Low-Use Journals," *Med. LA Bltn.* (O. 1978); "A Core Textbook Collection in a Health Science Library," *Med. LA Bltn.*; Jt. auth., "Cataloging," *LARC Series on Automated* - 1(4) (1976). **Activities:** 1, 12; 15; 80, 95-Pharmacy, Nursing. **Addr.:** Medical Center Library, Univ. of New Mexico, North Campus, Albuquerque, NM 87131.

Besterman, Elaine F. (S. 3, 1936, Covington, KY) Mgr., Lib. Srvs., Merrell Dow Pharm., 1972–; Supvsr., Scientific Docum., 1970–72; Indxr.-Abstctr., Scientific Docum., 1968–70. **Educ.:** Edgecliff Coll., Cincinnati, 1954–58, BA (Bio. Sci.); Univ. of Cincinnati Evening Coll., 1972–75, AS, (Info. Prcs. Syst.). **Orgs.:** ASIS: South. OH Chap., Chap. Asm. Rep. (1979–80); Ch. (1978–79); Bylaws Com. (Ch., 1974–75). SLA: Cincinnati Chap., Pres. (1976–77). **Honors:** ASIS, South. OH Chap., Outstan. Mem., 1976; Delta Mu Delta, 1975. **Activities:** 5; 15, 17, 44; 58, 80, 87 **Addr.:** Library, Merrell Dow Pharmaceuticals, Inc., 2110 E. Galbraith Rd., Cincinnati, OH 45215.

Bethel, Marilyn Joyce (Ja. 14, 1935, Detroit, MI) Consult. Libn., FL Diag. and Lrng. Resrcs. Syst., 1979–; Libn., Deerfield Beach HS, 1977–78. **Educ.:** FL Atl. Univ., 1972–74, BAE (Ed. Media); LA State Univ., 1974–75, MLS; 1975–76, MEd; Basic OL Srchg., 1979. **Orgs.:** ALA:JMRT (Liaison to FRF, 1979–80). AASL. Assn. for Educ. Comm. and Tech. FRF. Other orgs. Intl. Readg. Assn. Cncl. For Excep. Chld. **Honors:** Bd. of Cnty. Cmsnrs., Cert. Apprec., 1978. **Activities:** 12; 20, 24, 41; 63, 72, 95-Wkshp. Coord. **Addr.:** 272 N.E. 39th Ct., Pompano, FL 33064.

Bett, Carolynn E. (D. 9, 1943, Toronto, ON) Pres., CEBET Bibls., 1981–; Prin. Investigator, Feasibility Std. for Database, ON Mnstry. of Culture and Recreation, 1981–; Proj. Dir., Thesaurus, 1978–80; AV Head, St. Catharines Pub. Lib., 1977–78; Instr., Univ. of Regina, Fac. of Educ., 1977; Ed., *Can. Ed. Indx.*, Can. Educ. Assn., 1973–76. **Educ.:** Univ. of Toronto, 1962–66, BA (Eng.), 1966–67, MA (Eng.), 1968–69, Dip. HSA Type A (Educ.), 1971–73, MLS. **Orgs.:** Can. Assn. Info. Sci.: 1980 Conf., Prog. Ch.; Toronto Chap. (Fndr., 1974); Natl. Bd. of Dirs. (1975). Can. Assn. of Spec. Libs. and Info. Srvs.: Toronto Chap. (Fndn. Exec., 1975). Movement for Can. Litcy.: Tutor, Ed. of Readg. Mtrls. Can. Save the Chld.: Sponsor. **Pubns.:** "GEAC, A Brief Introduction," *ON Lib. Review* (S. 1981); *Do You Believe This: Stories for Adult New Readers* (1981); "Project to Automate the Canadian Education Index," *Open Conference on Information Science in Canada* (1975); "The Subject Access Project: A Comparison with Precis," *The Indxr.* (Ap. 1979); "Inside Information," *Educ. Can.* (Spr. 1975); various bk. reviews, *Can. Bk. Review Anl.* (1975–81). **Activities:** 4, 13; 24, 26, 30; 56, 63, 66 **Addr.:** 50 Hillsboro Ave. #202, Toronto, ON M5R 1S8 Canada.

Bettencourt, Nancy J. (Ap. 17, 1949, Fayetteville, AR) Dir., Pickens Cnty. Lib., 1978–; Coord., Baldwin Cnty. Lib. Syst., 1976–78; Libn., Irondale Pub. Lib., 1975–76; Bks.-by-Mail Libn., Friedman Meml. Lib., 1974–75. **Educ.:** Univ. of AL, 1967–69, 1973–74, BS (Sch. Libnshp.), 1974–75, MLS (Lib. Srv.). **Orgs.:** ALA: ERT (1980–); PLA (1975–); LAMA (1978–); JMRT, Orien. Com. (Ch., 1979), Liaison to ERT (1981), Booth Com. (Ch., 1978), Mem. Com. (Ch., 1979–81); Mem. Promo. Task Frc. (1979–). SC LA: Cont. Ed. Com. (1981–) AL LA: Various coms., ofcs. NLA. Various other orgs. Pickens Cnty. Foster Parents Assn.: VP (1980–). Easley Arts Cncl.: Pres. (1980–81); Secy. (1980). U.S. Ski Assn.: South. Div. (1980–). Pickens Cnty. Srvs. Org.: VP (1981–82). **Honors:** Bus. and Prof. Women's Club, Woman of the Yr. Finalist, 1980, 1981; Pickens Cnty. Career Woman of the Yr., 1981. **Activities:** 9; 17, 25, 47; 56, 74 **Addr.:** Pickens County Library, 110 W. 1st Ave., Easley, SC 29640.

Betts, Renee Allard (Ja. 29, 1946, Detroit, MI) Supvsg. Libn., PA Appellate Cts. Lib., 1981–; Consult., Betts/Allard Assocs., 1977–80; Consult., Self-Empl., 1972–77; Libn., Montgomery McCracken Walker and Rhoads, 1969–72. **Educ.:** Bryn Mawr Coll., 1963–67, AB (Hist.); Drexel Univ., 1968–70, MSLS. **Orgs.:** Grt. Philadelphia Law LA: Consult. Com. (1975–78); Educ. Com. (Ch., 1978). AALL. SLA. **Activities:** 12, 13; 24, 39; 77 **Addr.:** Pennsylvania Appellate Cts. Library, 2061 Old Federal Ct. House, 9th and Market Sts., Philadelphia, PA 19107.

Beugin, Susan A. (O. 2, 1947, Hamilton, ON) Libn., Law Info. AB, Calgary, 1980–; Libn., Calgary Courthse., 1975–80; Ref. Libn., York Univ. Lib., 1973–75, Cat. Dept., Law Lib., 1972–73. **Educ.:** Univ. of Toronto, 1965–69, BA (Hist.), 1970–72, MLS. **Orgs.:** Can. ALL: Features Ed., *CALL Nsltr.* **Pubns.:** Ed., *Law Library Guide for Alberta Practitioners* (1979); ed., *Procs. of the Can. ALL Conf., 1979* (1980). **Activities:** 12; 17, 39, 41; 56, 77 **Addr.:** Law Information Alberta, 611–4th St. S.W., Calgary, AB T2P 1T5 Canada.

Bevan, Barbara H. (Wilkes-Barre, PA) Chief Libn., York Hospital, 1969–, Asst. Libn., 1968–69; Libn., Red Lion Jr. High, 1967–68. **Educ.:** Millersville State Coll., 1968, BSLS. **Orgs.:** Ctrl. PA Hlth. Sci. Lib.: Actg. Secy. and Treas. (1975–76). Mid-East. Reg. Med. Lib. Srv.: Ext. Srv. Com. (Ch., 1979–80). **Activities:** 5; 15, 17, 39; 58, 80, 95-Nursing. **Addr.:** York Hospital Librarian, 1001 S. George St., York, PA 17405.

Bewley, Gladys P. (Mr. 19, 1923, NJ) Retired, 198–; Dir., Haddonfield Pub. Lib., 1974–81, Asst. Dir., 1967–74; Asst. Pub. Lib. Consult., Drexel Univ., 1966–67; Ref. Libn., Catlgr., Haddonfield Pub. Lib., 1961–66; various positions as wkshp. instr., 1967–80. **Educ.:** Rutgers Univ., 1940–44, BA (Span.), 1959–63, MLS. **Orgs.:** Mid. Atl. Reg. Lib. Fed.: Dir. ALA: Mem. Promo. Task Frc. (1974–78). NJ LA: Secy. (1973–74). **Honors:** Beta Phi Mu. **Activities:** 9, 13; 17, 24, 25 **Addr.:** 208 Mt. Vernon Ave., Haddonfield, NJ 08033.

Bewley, Lois M. (Ap. 3, 1926, Regina, SK) Assoc. Prof., Univ. of BC, 1969–; Lectr., Univ. of CA, Berkeley, 1968–69; Coord., N. St. Coop. Lib. Syst. (Chico, CA) 1967–68; Resrch. Assoc., Univ. of IL, 1965–67. **Educ.:** Univ. of BC, 1943–47, BA (Eng., Hist.); Univ. of Toronto, 1948–49, BLS; Univ. of IL, 1965–66, MSLS. **Orgs.:** ALA. AALS. Can. LA. BC LA. CALS. Can. Assn. of Univ. Tchr. **Honors:** BC LA Bursary, 1948; Beta Phi Mu, 1966. **Pubns.:** *Public Library Legislation in Saskatchewan: Analysis and Recommendations* (1978); "Public Libraries" in *Canadian Libraries in Their Changing Environment* (1977); "A Proposal for Legislation," *BCLA Rpt.* (F./Mr. 1979); "Future is Now for B.C. Public Libraries" *B.C.L.A. Rpt.* (Ag./S. 1978); "A Canadian Caution" *Lib. Jnl.* (S. 1977); Other pubns. **Activities:** 11; 15, 16, 19, 25; 50, 74, 78 **Addr.:** School of Librarianship, University of B.C., Vancouver, BC V6T 1W5 Canada.

Bey, Lois A. (My. 8, 1929, Chicago, IL) Mgr., Info. Ctr., Sci. Srvs., Travenol Labs., Inc., 1960–; Sales Engin., F.M. de Beers Assoc., 1956–60; Ast. Engin., Armour Resrch. Fndn., 1952–56; Asst. Engin., Underwriters Labs., Inc., 1950–52. **Educ.:** IL Inst. of Techn., 1947–50, BS (Chem. Engin.); Rosary Coll., 1964–67, MA (LS); various cont. Educ. Crs., 1967–. **Orgs.:** SLA. Med. LA. ASIS. Drug Info. Assn. Amer. Inst. of Chem. Engin. Socty. of Women Engin. AAAS. **Pubns.:** Co-Cmplr., *Bibliography of Ozone*, vol. 1 (1955). **Activities:** 12; 17; 59, 87, 91 **Addr.:** Travenol Laboratories, Inc., 6301 Lincoln Ave., Morton Grove, IL 60053.

Beyer, Ann Hatch (Jl. 14, 1929, Evanston, IL) Ref. Libn., Los Alamos Natl. Lab., 1965–; Asst. Libn., Branches, Los Alamos Sci. Lab., 1961–65; Libn., Ordnance Resrch. Lab., PA State Univ., 1957–59; Catlgr., Aircraft Gas Turbine Div., Gen. Electric Co., 1956–57; Agr. Ref. Asst., PA State Univ., 1954–55; Asst. Libn., Sci., Tech. Div., Univ. of NE, 1952–54. **Educ.:** Carroll Coll., 1947–51, BA (Bio.); Univ. of WI, 1951–52, MA (LS). **Orgs.:** SLA: Rio Grande Chap., Treas. (1967–70), Pres. (1970–71). NM LA. **Activities:** 12; 39; 91 **Addr.:** Los Alamos National Laboratory Libraries, 15D–4, MS–362, Box 1663, Los Alamos, NM 87545.

Beynen, G. Koolemans (Je. 12, 1935, Surabaya, E. Java, Indonesia) Slavic Biblgphr., OH State Univ., 1974–; Asst. Prof., Russ. Ling., Univ. of Rochester, 1969–73; Asst. Prof., Slavic Ling., Fordham Univ., 1966–69; Asst. Prof., Russ., Emporia State Univ., 1963–66. **Educ.:** Leiden Univ., Netherlands, 1954–60, Cand. (Slavic Langs.); Stanford Univ., 1960–63, PhD (Slavic Ling.); SUNY, Geneseo, 1973–74, MLS. **Orgs.:** Amer. Assn. for the Advnc. of Slavic Std. Mod. Lang. Assn. Amer. Assn. of Tchrs. of Slavic and E. European Lang. Amer. Oriental Socty. Courtly Lit. Socty. **Honors:** Midwest Univs. Cnsrtm. on Intl. Affairs, Flwshp. to Stanford Univ., 1981–82; Natl. Endow. for Hum., Transl. Grant, 1981; Intl. Resrch. and Exch. Bd., Resrch. Flwshp., 1971–72. **Pubns.:** "Semantic Differences Between *No* and *Odnako*," *Slavic and E. European Jnl.* (Sum. 1976); "The Slavic Animal Language Tales," *American Contributions to the Eighth International Congress of Slavists* (Volume 2); "The Slavic Collection," *Frnds. Line; Frnds. of the Libs. of the OH State Univ. Libs.* (O. 1978); "Reading Rooms Have Specialized Resources," *OH State Univ. Libs.* (S. 28, 1977). **Activities:** 1; 15, 39; 54, 55, 57 **Addr.:** 460 E. Norwich, #C, Columbus, OH 43201.

Bhirud, Susan McWilliams (Je. 27, 1948, Rochester, NY) Per. Libn., Met. Musm. of Art Lib., 1978–; Asst. Fine Arts Libn., Princeton Univ., 1974–78. **Educ.:** Hollins Coll., 1966–68; Keuka Coll., 1968–70, BA (Art); Rutgers Univ., 1972–74, MLS; Hunter Coll., 1980– (Art Hist.). **Orgs.:** Art Libs. Socty. of N. Amer.: Modrtr., Acad. Libns. Grp. (1977–78). Art Lib. Socty.: NY Chap. (Pub. Com., Hosp. Com., 1979–). SLA: Prog. Com. (1977). Victorian Socty. of Amer. **Pubns.:** Column, "Serials Update," *Art Lib. Socty. of N. Amer. Nwsltr.*. **Activities:** 5, 12; 31, 39, 44; 55 **Addr.:** Metropolitan Museum of Art Library, Fifth Ave. at 82nd St., New York, NY 10028.

Bianchi, Susan Bunting (D. 23, 1950, Philadelphia, PA) Mgr., Corp. Resrch., PA Blue Shield, 1981–; Sr. Resrch. Anal., 1980–81; Sr. Resrch. Anal., Hershey Med. Ctr., PA State Univ., 1977–79; Info. Spec., Lederle Labs., 1974–76. **Educ.:** Wilson Coll., 1968–72, BA (Bio.); Drexel Univ., 1972–74, MS (LS). **Orgs.:** Data Prcs. Mgt. Assn. ASIS. Issue Inc. SLA: Hudson Valley, *Bltn.* Co-Ed. (1975–76); Ctrl. PA *Bltn.* Ed., Exec. Com. (1979–80). **Pubns.:** *Minocin R (Minocycline Hydrochloride) Annotated Bibliography* (1975); *Annotated Bibliography on Cable Television for Librarians* (1973); Jt. Auth., "Subjective Characteristics of Insomniac Patients," *Procs. of the 1978 Mtg. of the Assn. for the Psychophysio. Std. of Sleep* (1978); External Reviewer, *Hlth. Srvs. Resrch.* (1980–81). **Activities:** 14-Database Resrch. Dept.; 41, 49-Data Analysis; 56, 59, 80 **Addr.:** 64 Ethel Ave., Hummelstown, PA 17036.

Bianchini, Lucian (Mr. 15, 1929, Ferrara, Italy) Univ. Libn., Mt. St. Vincent Univ., 1973–; Head, Hum. Div., Lib., Univ. of Calgary, 1970–73, Subj. Catlgr., 1967–70. **Educ.:** Istituto Scalabrini-O'Brien, Cermenate, Italy, 1945–49, BA; Rosary Coll., 1951–54, MALS; Dalhousie Univ., 1978–81, MPA (Pub. Admin.). **Orgs.:** Can. LA. Cath. LA. Atl. Assn. of Univs.: Libns. Cncl. (Secy., 1980–). Natl. Congs. of Italian Cans. **Pubns.:** Jt. Ed., Jt. Transl., *Commentarius De Rebus A Lusitanis In India...Gestis* (1973); *Italian-Can. Periodical Publications, Canadian Ethnic Studies a Preliminary Checklist* (1970, 1973). **Activities:** 1, 2; 17, 19, 35; 55 **Addr.:** 9 School Ave., Halifax, NS B3N 2E1 Canada.

Bias, Georgene I. (Ap. 1, 1926, San Antonio, TX) Dir., Learning Resrc. Ctr., St. Philip's Coll., 1961–; Inst. (Vets. Prog.), Gross HS, 1951–53. **Educ.:** Prairie View Univ., 1943–47, BS, (Voc. Ed.), 1951–53, M Ed (Educ.); Cert., LS, 1961–62, (Lib. Sci.); Our Lady of the Lake Univ., 1970–73, MSLS; Nova Univ. 1978–, (Educ.). **Orgs.:** TX LA: Nominating Com. (1977–78). Bexar LA. ALA. TX Jr. Coll. Tchrs. Assn.: Local Mem. Chmn. (1970–76). Alpha Kappa Alpha. **Activities:** 1; 17 **Addr.:** St. Philip's College, 2111 Nevada St., San Antonio, TX 78203.

Biblarz, Dora (Mr. 25, 1944, Bogotá, Colombia) Head, Col. and Acq. Srvs., AZ State Univ. Lib., 1980–; Actg. Asst. Dean, Col. Dev., Univ. of NM Gen. Lib., 1979–80; Acq. Libn., 1978;

Special Subjects/Services: 50. Adult educ.; 51. Advert./Mktg.; 52. Aerosp.; 53. Agric.; 54. Area std.; 55. Arts/Hum.; 56. Autom.; 57. Bibl./Prtg.; 58. Bio. sci.; 59. Bus./Fin.; 60. Chem.; 61. Copyrt.; 62. Documtn.; 63. Educ.; 64. Engin.; 65. Env.; 66. Eth. grps.; 67. Film; 68. Food/Nutr.; 69. Geneal.; 70. Geo.; 71. Geol.; 72. Handcpd.; 73. Hist.; 74. Int. frdm.; 75. Info. sci.; 76. Insr.; 77. Law; 78. Legis.; 79. Math./Comp. sci.; 80. Med.; 81. Metals; 82. Nat. resrcs.; 83. Newsp.; 84. Nuc. sci.; 85. Oral hist.; 86. Petr./Energy; 87. Pharm.; 88. Phys./Astr./Math.; 89. Readg.; 90. Relig.; 91. Sci./Tech.; 92. Soc. sci.; 93. Telecom.; 94. Transp.; 95. (other).

Asst. Head, Acq. Dept., Univ. of CA, Davis, 1976–78; Asst. Libn., Acq. Dept., 1972–76. **Educ.:** Univ. of CA, Los Angeles, 1970, BA (French), 1971–72, MLS; Univ. of CA, Los Angeles, Davis, 1970–77, MA (French Lit.). **Orgs.:** ALA. NM LA. CA LA. Libns. Assn. of the Univ. of CA: Davis Div. (Ch., 1977–78). **Pubns.:** "Special Emphasis Acquisitions Plans," *Proceedings of the 4th Intl. Conf. on Approval Plans-Collection Development* (1980); Jt. auth., "Professional Associations and Unions," *Coll. & Resrch Libs.* (19–). **Activities:** 1; 15, 17, 44; 95-Women in Librarianship. **Addr.:** Hayden Library, Arizona State University, Tempe, AZ 85287.

Bible, Amanda R. (O. 19, 1932, Cerro Gordo, NC) Dir., Columbus Cnty. Pub. Lib., 1973–; Coord., Pub. Srvs., Chld. Libn., El Paso Pub. Lib., 1971–73; Libn., Tchr., Gadsden Jr. HS, 1962–71; various bus. positions, 1956–61. **Educ.:** East. NM Univ., 1958–61, BA (Elem. Educ., Eng.); TX Woman's Univ., 1966–68, MLS; Univ. of NC, 1977, Cnty. Admin. Cert.; various crs. **Orgs.:** Border Reg. LA: Treas. (1972); Pubcty. Com. (1973); Natl. Lib. Week Com. (Ch., 1973). SE LA: Pub. Lib. Com. (1978–80). NC LA: Pub. Lib. Sect., YA Com. (Ch., 1973–77), Stans. Com. (1977–81); State Lib. AV Adv. Com. (1975–78); State Lib. Pres. Ctr. Adv. Com. (1978–81). Various other orgs. Natl. Educ. Assn. NM Educ. Assn. Gadsden Classrm. Tchrs. Assn.: Secy. (1968–70). NC Symph. Assocs. Various other orgs. **Honors:** Delta Kappa Gamma, 1967–80; Chadbourn NCGFWC Sorosis Club, Outstan. Woman of the Yr., 1979; Chadbourn NCGFWC Sorosis Club, Juanita Bryant Citizenship Awd., 1980; NC LA, Int. Frdm. Com., Philip J. Imroth Awd. Nominee, 1981. **Activities:** 9; 17, 21 **Addr.:** Columbus County Public Library, 117 E. Columbus St., Whiteville, NC 28472.

Biblo, Herbert (O. 17, 1924, Brooklyn, NY) Asst. Libn., Pub. Srvs., The John Crerar Lib., 1970–; Libn., Chicago Bd. of Educ., 1960–70. **Educ.:** Baruch Coll., CUNY, 1942–43, 1946–49, BBA (Econ.); Chicago State Univ., 1962, MS (LS); Univ. of Chicago, 1968–70, CAS; various crs. **Orgs.:** ALA: Cncl., Cnclr.-at-lg. (1977–80), Cnclr. (1980–84); Exec. Bd. (1980–84); Treas. (1980–84); Exec. Bd. Com. on Resrc. Dev. (1980–); various coms.; ACRL/Sci. and Tech. Sect., various coms. IL ACRL: Exec. Bd. (1977–79); IL ACRL-IL Bd. of Higher Educ. Liaison Com. (1981–). SLA: Bio. and Med. Lib. Sect. of IFLA, Rep. Chicago Acad. Lib. Cncl.: Treas. (1979). IL Inst. of Tech.: Various coms. Daley Coll. Lib. Tech. Adv. Cncl. Pvt. Acad. Libs. of IL. **Honors:** Cncl. on Lib. Resrcs., Flwshp., 1974–75. **Pubns.:** "Librarians and Trade Unionism: A Prologue," *Lib. Trends* (O. 1976); "Into a Second Decade of Service to Conscience: Special Report on SRRT," *ALA Yearbk.* (1981); ed., *IACRL Nsltr.* (1974–78); various presentations. **Activities:** 1, 12; 15, 17, 18; 54, 59, 91 **Addr.:** 5225 S. Blackstone Ave., Chicago, IL 60615.

Biblo, Mary (D. 29, 1927, E. Chicago, IN) Tchr.-Libn., Univ. of Chicago Lab. Schs., 1970–; Libn., Chicago Bd. of Educ., 1964–70; Libn., S. Chicago Cmnty. Hosp. Sch. of Nursing, 1963–64. **Educ.:** Roosevelt Univ., 1959–63, BS (Bio.); Rosary Coll., 1967–69, MS (LS). **Orgs.:** ALA: Cncl. (1978–81); Com. on Org. (1976–80); SRRT (Action Cncl. Coord., 1977–78); AASL, Int. Frdm. Com. (Lcl. Rep., 1974–76); IFRT, John Phillip Immroth Meml. Awd. Com. (1979–); IFRT, Exec. Bd. (1977–78); various coms. IL Assn. for Media in Educ.: Various com. chs. Natl. Caucus of Black Libns.: Chicago Chap., Treas., 1974–79), Pres. (1980–), Exec. Bd. (1974–80). IL WHCOLIS: Del. (1978). Various other orgs. Chld. Readg. RT: VP, Pres.-Elect (1981–82); Awds. Com. (Ch., 1980–81). **Pubns.:** "Gifted Students as Part of the Total School Environment," *The Bookmark* (Win. 1980); "Social Responsibilities Round Table," *ALA Yrbk.* (1977, 1978, 1979). **Activities:** 10; 31, 39, 48; 74, 91 **Addr.:** 5225 S. Blackstone Ave., Chicago, IL 60615.

Bichteler, Julie Hallmark (My. 27, 1938, Houston, TX) Assoc. Prof., Grad. Sch. of Lib. and Info. Sci., Univ. of TX, 1978–; Asst. Prof. and Lect., 1969–77; Ref. Libn. for the Southwest Cntr. for Advnc. Std., South. Methodist Univ., 1964–69; Chemist, Dow Chemical Co., Midland, MI, 1960–62. **Educ.:** University of TX, 1956–60, BS (Chem.), 1963–65, MLS, 1970–73, PhD (Lib. and Info. Sci.); Southern Methodist Univ., 1965–69, (Geol). **Orgs.:** SLA: Div. Cabinet Ch. (1981–82); Mem., Bd. of Dirs. (1980–82); TX Chap. Pres. (1975–76); Sci-Tech Div., Treas. (1974–76); Ch. (1977–78). AALS: Ed. Bd. *Journal of Education for Librarianship* 1977–81). ASIS: TX Chap. Ch. (1975–76); National Committees: Com. on Education for Information Science, 1973–74; Doctoral Forum Com., 1977; Co-Ch., Technical Sessions, 1978 Mid-Year Meeting; Geoscience Info. Soc.: Pres. (1978–79); Various other orgs. Amer. Geol. Inst.: Bd. of Gvrs. (1979–81). **Honors:** Phi Beta Kappa; Alpha Lambda Delta; Phi Kappa Phi; Beta Phi Mu. **Pubns.:** Ed. *Geoscience Information: Publication - Processing - Management.* (1979); "Geoscience Information Sources and Services from the User's Viewpoint," *Geoscience Information.* (1979); Jt. auth., "Comparing Two Algorithms for Document Retrieval Using Citation Links," *Jnl. of the ASIS* (1977); "Publications of the International Union of Geological Sciences: Their Influence on U.S. Geoscientists," Proceedings of the *Geoscience Information Society* (1977); "Special Libraries in the Philippines," *Special Libraries* (1977); Various other articles. **Activities:** 11, 12; 15, 29, 39; 56, 71, 75 **Addr.:** Graduate School of Library and Information Science, University of Texas, Box 7576, Univ. Station, Austin, TX 78712.

Bickel, Jane Elizabeth (O. 25, 1948, Hudson, NY) Head, Chld. Srv., Chappaqua Lib., 1979–, Proj. Dir., Gateway to Readg. Grant, 1977–79, Chld. Libn., 1971–76. **Educ.:** Mary Baldwin Coll., 1966–70, BA (Art Hist., Phil.); Columbia Univ., 1970–71, MLS (Lib.). **Orgs.:** ALA: Chld. Mtrls. and Mass Media (1976–78). Westchester LA: ALA/Chld. Bk. Cncl. Jt. Com. (1978–79). ALA: Newberry Com. (1982). Frnds. of IBBY Notable Films Com. (1980–82). **Honors:** NY State Cncl. on the Arts, Grant, 1979. **Pubns.:** Various bk. reviews, *Sch. Lib. Jnl., Westchester Lib. Syst. Bk. Examination Ctr.* **Activities:** 9; 21, 28, 32; 67, 89 **Addr.:** 17 Otsego Rd., Pleasantville, NY 10570.

Biddle, Stanton F. (S. 16, 1943, Cuba, NY) Assoc. Dir. of Libs., SUNY, Buffalo, 1979–; Assoc. Dir. of Libs., Howard Univ., 1973–76; NEH Proj. Dir., Schomburg Cntr., New York Pub. Lib., 1972–73; Archvst. Supvsg. Libn., Schomburg Center, New York Pub. Lib., 1969–72. **Educ.:** Howard Univ., 1961–65, BA (Gvt.); New York Univ., 1968–73, MPA (Urban Affairs); Atlanta Univ., 1965–66, MLS; Univ. of CA, Berkeley, 1977–, (Lib. Sci.); Univ. of MD, 1974, Cert., Lib. Admin. Dev. Prog.; American Univ., 1969, Cert., Modern Arch. Admin. **Orgs.:** ALA: ALA/SAA Joint Comm. (1973–75); LITA/Legis. Com. (1976–78); Black Caucus, Exec. Bd. Mem. 1976–78). SAA. NAACP: Hist. Proj. Steering Com. (1978–79). Afro-American Hist. Assn. of the Niagara Frontier: Exec. Bd. (1980–82). **Honors:** Cncl. on Lib. Resrcs., Acad. Lib. Mgt. Internship, 1976; Phi Alpha Theta. **Pubns.:** "The Negro in the United States; a list of significant books, A supplement to the Ninth Revised Edition", BRANCH LIBRARY BOOK NEWS (Ap. 1968); "A Partnership in Progress", *Jnl. of the Schomburg Center for Research in Black Culture.* (Spr. 1978); "The Puerto Rican New Yorkers, a guide to available materials at the Municipal Reference Library," *Municipal Reference Library Notes* (S. 1967); "The Schomburg Center for Research in Black Culture: Documenting the Black Experience." *Bull. of the New York Pub. Lib* (1972); Contrib., *No Crystal Stair; a bibliography of Black Literature,* 10th Edition (1971). **Activities:** 1; 17; 56, 66 **Addr.:** Rm. 433 Capen Hall, University Libraries, State University of New York at Buffalo, Buffalo, NY 14260.

Bidlack, Russell E. (My. 25, 1920, Manilla, IA) Dean, Sch. of LS, Univ. of MI, 1969–, Prof. of LS, 1965–, Assoc. Prof., 1960–65, Asst. Prof., 1956–60, Instr., 1953–56. **Educ.:** Simpson Coll., 1938–41, 1946–47, BA (Eng.); Univ. of MI, 1948, ABLS, 1949, AMLS, 1950, AM (Hist.), 1954, PhD (LS). **Orgs.:** ALA: Cncl. (1972–76); Nom. Com. (Ch., 1980–81); Com. on Accred. (Ch., 1974–76); LED, Bd. of Dir. (1976–78). MI LA: Tech. Srvs. Sect. (Pres., 1959–60; Dir. 1964–66). SLA. AALS: Deans and Dir. Grp. (Ch., 1979–80). **Honors:** Simpson Coll., Litt.D., 1976; Beta Phi Mu, Awd. for Disting. Srv. to Educ. for Libnshp., 1977; ALA, Melvil Dewey Medal for Recent Creative Prof. Achvmt. of a High Order, 1979. **Pubns.:** "Fifty Years of Accreditation by the American Library Association," *Procs. of the Fortieth Annual Meeting of ASIS* (1977); "Gjelsness, Rudolph H. (1894–1968)-," *Dict. of Amer. Lib. Biog.* (1978); "Some Trends and Issues in Library Education Today," *Lib. Sch. Review* (1978); "Genealogy As It Relates to Library Service," *ALA Yrbk.* (1978); "A Statistical Survey of 67 Library Schools, 1978–79," *Jnl. of Educ. for Libnshp.* (1979); other articles. **Activities:** 1, 11; 24, 26, 41; 63, 69 **Addr.:** 1709 Cherokee Rd., Ann Arbor, MI 48104.

Biebesheimer, Mary Lee (F. 9, 1927, Farmersburg, IN) Ref. Libn. and Comp. Info. Libn., Toledo-Lucas Cnty. Pub. Lib., 1975–; Instr. of General Studies, Univ. of Toledo Comnty. and Tech. Coll., 1967–68. **Educ.:** Univ. of Toledo, 1944–48, B of Ed, (Hist.), 1963–67, MA (Hist.); Univ. of OK, 1972–74, MLS. **Orgs.:** ALA: Immroth Int. Frdm. Com. (1977–79); Liaison, Int. Frdm. RT & Int. Frdm. Com. (1978–80). **Honors:** Beta Phi Mu, 1974; Phi Kappa Phi, 1967; Phi Alpha Theta, 1947; Pi Gamma Mu, 1947. **Activities:** 9, 12; 24, 39, 49-Online Searching; 59, 73, 92 **Addr.:** Business Service, Toledo-Lucas County Public Library, 325 Michigan, Toledo, OH 43624.

Bier, Robert A., Jr. (F. 9, 1942, Washington, DC) Chief Libn., Denver Lib., U.S. Geol. Srvy., 1981–, Ref. Libn., 1978–81, Map Libn., 1971–78; Sci. Anal., Smithsonian Inst., Sci. Info. Exch., 1968–69. **Educ.:** Middlebury Coll., 1960–65, BA (Geol.); Univ. of MD, 1969–71, MLS. **Orgs.:** SLA: DC Chap., Geo. and Map Div. (Treas., 1973–75). Geosci. Info. Socty.: Treas. (1977–79). **Pubns.:** Jt. auth., *Geologic Reference Sources* (1981); "On-Demand Computer Cartography and Its Effect on Map Libraries," *Spec. Libs.* (F. 1978); jt. auth., "New Maps," clmn. *Geotimes* (1975–81). **Activities:** 4, 12; 17; 70, 82, 86 **Addr.:** U.S. Geological Survey Library, Mail Stop 914, Box 25046, Federal Center, Denver, CO 80225.

Bierman, Kenneth J. (My. 27, 1944, Aberdeen, SD) Asst. Dir. for Tech. Srvs. & Auto., Tucson Pub. Lib., 1975–; Asst. Dir. for Plng. & Resrch., VA Polytechnic & State Univ., 1972–75; Data Prcs. Coord., OK Dept. of Lib., 1968–72. **Educ.:** Hanover Coll., 1962–66, BA (Eng./Math.); Univ. of OK, 1966–68, MLS; OK State Univ. Tech. Inst., Comp. Sci. Cert., 1968–70. **Orgs.:** ASIS. SWLA. AZ LA; ALA: Couns. at Large (1977–81); LITA, Bd. of Dir. (1978–81), Prog. Plng. Com. (1977–79). **Honors:** Cncl. on Lib. Resrcs., Resrch. Flwshp (1974); Disting. Libn., VA Polytechnic & State Univ. (1974/75). **Pubns.:** "Automated Alternatives to Card Catalogs: The Current State of Planning and Implementation," *Jnl. of Lib. Autom.* (D. 1975); "Library Automation," *Annual Review of Information Science and Technology* (1974); "A MARC Based SDI Service," *Jnl. of Lib. Autom.* (D. 1970). **Activities:** 1, 9; 22, 34, 46; 56, 75, 93 **Addr.:** Tucson Public Library, P.O. Box 27470, Tucson, AZ 85726.

Biggert, Elizabeth C. (S. 23, 1915, Columbus, OH) Lib. Consult., 1978–; Libn., Tech. Econ. Lib., Battelle Columbus Labs., 1956–78; Ref. Libn., Columbus Pub. Lib., 1953–56; Mss. Libn., OH Hist. Socty., 1946–54; Ref. Libn., 1940–43; Catlgr., Toledo Pub. Lib., 1939–40. **Educ.:** St. Mary of the Springs Coll., 1933–37, Summa Cum Laude (Eng.); Western Reserve Univ., 1937–38, BS in LS. **Orgs.:** SLA: Ctrl. OH Chap., (Pres., 1975–76; Secy., 1972–73); Metals/Materials Div.; Bus./Finance Div. Columbus Symph. Orch.: Bd. of Trustees (1965–67). OH Histn.: 1958–61. OH Dominican Coll. Alum. Assn.: Pres. (1951–52); Bd. (1969–72). **Pubns.:** *Guide to the Manuscripts in the Library of the Ohio State Archoeological and Historical Society* (1953); "Information for the Chemical Engineer in Federal, State and Local Sources," *Chemical Engin.* (1973). **Activities:** 12; 39, 41; 59, 81, 95-Industry. **Addr.:** 2851 Bexley Park Rd., Columbus, OH 43209.

Biggs, Debra R. (Je. 27, 1955, Cleveland, OH) Archvst., Lcl. Gvt. Recs., The OH Hist. Socty., 1979–81; Mss. Spec., OH Labor Hist. Proj., West. Rsv. Hist. Socty., 1978–79, Mss. Intern, 1978; Eng. Composition Instr., Bowling Green State Univ., 1977. **Educ.:** Bowling Green State Univ., 1973–77, BA (Amer. Std.), 1977–78, MA (Amer. Std. and Arch. Admin.); Univ. of MI, Sch. of Lib. Sci., Cncl. on Lib. Resrc. Flwshp., 1981– (LS). **Orgs.:** ALA. Socty. of OH Archvsts. Amer. Assn. for State and Lcl. Hist. Frnds. of Bowling Green State Univ. Lib./Ctr. for Arch. Cols. **Pubns.:** Jt. Auth., *Ohio Municipal Records Manual*; "Guide to Local Government Records at the Center for Archival Collections," (forthcoming). **Activities:** 1, 2; 15, 33, 38; 75 **Addr.:** Center for Archival Collections, 5th Floor, University Library, Bowling Green State University, Bowling Green, OH 43403.

Bilancio, Lewis A. (F. 16, 1915, Trenton, NJ) Ref. Libn., Glassboro State Coll., NJ, 1955–; Tchr., Libn., Solebury Sch., PA, 1954–55; Libn. II, Free Lib. of Philadelphia, 1953–54. **Educ.:** Trenton State Tchrs. Coll., 1935–39; Rutgers Univ., 1939–40, SB (Geol.); Columbia Univ., 1940–42, BLS; Univ. of IL, Army Spec. Trng. Prog., 1943; Univ. of Chicago, 1946–49, MA (LS); Univ. of Rome, Italy, 1949–51. **Orgs.:** Libs. Unlimited: Secy. (1967); VP (1968). Amer. Soc. of Travel Agts. Glassboro Cham. of Cmrce. Amer.-Ital. Hist. Assn. Various other travel, Ital., civic orgs. **Honors:** Fulbright, Schol., 1949–51. **Pubns.:** "Italian Education as of Now," *Progressive Educ.* (N 1946); Ed., *Libs. Unlimited Nsltr.* (1967–69). **Activities:** 1; 26, 39, 45; 50, 54, 66 **Addr.:** 324 N. Delsea Drive, Glassboro, NJ 08028.

Bilbie, Nancy L. (D. 6, 1946, Houston, TX) Dir. of Lib. Srvs., Farrar, Stravs & Giroux, 1980–; Instr., Chld. Lit., Univ. Houston, Victoria, 1975–80; Libn., Mitchell and Offer Elem. Schs., 1973–79; Libn., Pecan Spr. Elem. Sch., 1972–73; Tchr., Harlingen ISD, 1969–71. **Educ.:** Swest. Univ., 1964–68, BA (Eng.); Univ. TX, 1971–72, MLS. **Orgs.:** ALA: ALSC/IFC (1975–78); Newbery/Caldecott Com. (1977, 1980); Batchelder Com. (1979–80); Mem. Com. 1978–80). TX Assn. Sch. Libns. and Chld. RT Jt. Com. on TX Chld. Bk. Awd. 1977–78); TX LA: Chld. RT (Ch., 1979–80; Vice-Ch., 1978–79; Secy.-Treas., 1976–77). **Honors:** ALA Chld. Srv. Div., Charles Scribner's Sons Awd., 1975. **Pubns.:** Reviews. **Activities:** 10; 21; 95-chld. lit. **Addr.:** 215 E. 77th, New York, NY 10021. Victoria, TX 77901.

Billeter, Anne Margaret (Ap. 11, 1946, Sanford, FL) Consult., Entwood Assoc., 1979–; Children's Libn., Crescenta Valley Branch, Glendale (CA) Pub. Lib., 1976–78; Visit. Lectr., Sch. of LS, Univ. of South. CA, 1975–77 (Sum.); Resrch. Assoc., Library Research Center, Univ. of Illinois, 1972–74; Child Libn., Rockingham Cnty. (NC) Pub. Lib., 1969–71. **Educ.:** Rutgers Univ., 1964–68, BA (Eng.); Univ. of NC (Chapel Hill), 1968–69, MS (LS); Univ. of IL, 1971–79, PHD, (LS). **Orgs.:** ALA: ALSC/Resrch. and Dev. Com. (Ch., 1974–76). Josephine Cnty. Hist. Socty.: Bd. of Dir. (1979–). Phi Kappa Phi. **Honors:** Beta Phi Mu. **Pubns.:** "Research and Evaluation in the Administration of Children's Work in the Public Library," *IL Libs* (Ja. 1975); Ed. Bd., "Current Studies in Librarianship," (Univ. of RI). **Activities:** 9, 11; 21, 24, 26; 63, 89 **Addr.:** 120 Crystal Dr., Grants Pass, OR 97526.

Billings, Harold Wayne (N. 12, 1931, Cain City, TX) Dir., Gen. Libs., Univ. of TX at Austin, 1978–; Actg. Dir., Gen. Libs., 1977–78, Assoc. Dir., Gen. Libs., 1973–77, Asst. Univ. Libn., 1967–73, Chief Acq. Libn., 1965–67, Asst. Chief Cat. Libn., 1957–65, Lib. Asst., 1954–57; Tchr., Pharr-San Juan-Alamo High School, Pharr, TX, 1953–54. **Educ.:** Pan American Coll., 1949–53, BA (Phys.); Univ. of TX, 1954–57, MLS. **Orgs.:** ALA: RTSD/Tech. Srvs. Dir. of Lg. Rsch. Libs. Discuss. Grp.; Ch. (1972–73); Secy (1973–74); Chief Coll. Dev. Ofcr. of Lg. Resch. Lib. Discuss. Grp.; Secy. 1973–75). TX Cncl. of State Univ. Libns.: Book Contract Com.; Status Com. Collector's Inst.; Cncl. of Acad. Rsch. Lib. in AMIGOS: Ch. (1979–). Bd. of Trustees of the Littlefield Fund for Southern Hist.: Secy. (1977–). TX State Bd. of Lib. Examiners: Secy. (1977–). **Pubns.:** "Introduction" to Edward Dahlberg's *Bottom Dogs ... and Hitherto Unpub-*

PROFESSIONAL ACTIVITIES: Institutions: 1. Acad. lib.; 2. Arch.; 3. Assn.; 4. Fed./Gvt. lib.; 5. Inst. lib.; 6. Mfr./Suppl.; 7. Milit. lib.; 8. Musm.; 9. Pub. lib.; 10. Sch. lib.; 11. Sch. of lib. sci.; 12. Spec. lib.; 13. State lib.; 14. (other). **Functions/Activities:** 15. Acq./Col. dev.; 16. Adult srvs.; 17. Admin.; 18. Apprais.; 19. Archit./Bldgs.; 20. Cat./Class.; 21. Chld. srvs.; 22. Circ.; 23. Cons./Pres.; 24. Consult.; 25. Cont. ed.; 26. Educ. lib. sci.; 27. Ext. srvs.; 28. Fund/Grants; 29. Gvt. pubs.; 30. Indx./Abs.; 31. Instr. lib. use; 32. Media srvs.; 33. Micro.; 34. Netwks./Coop.; 35. Persnl.; 36. PR; 37. Publshg.; 38. Recs. mgt.; 39. Ref. srvs.; 40. Repro.; 41. Resrch.; 42. Review.; 43. Secur.; 44. Serials; 45. Spec. col.; 46. Tech. srvs.; 47. Trustees/Bds.; 48. YA srvs.; 49. (other).

lished and Uncollected Works (1976); *A Bibliography of Edward Dahlberg* (1971); *Edward Dahlberg: American Ishmael of Letters* (1968); Ed., Edward Dahlberg's *The Leafless American* (1967); "An Early Dahlberg Manuscript", *The Library Chronicle* (Fall 1974); Various other articles. **Activities:** 1; 15, 17, 34; 55, 56, 57 **Addr.:** General Libraries, University of Texas, Austin, TX 78712.

Billingsley, Barbara (N. 5, 1946, Cincinnati, OH) Head, Ctrl. Chld. Rm., Rochester Pub. Lib., 1977–; Chld. Libn., 1969–77. **Educ.:** Oberlin Coll., 1964–68, AB (Art Hist.); Simmons Coll., 1968–69, MS (LS). **Orgs.:** ALA. NY LA. Frdm. to Read Fndn. Chld. Lit. Assn. Natl. Assn. for the Prsrvn. and Perpet. of Storytl. **Activities:** 9; 21 **Addr.:** 205 Highland Pkwy., Rochester, NY 14620.

Billman, Betty Virginia (Ag. 15, 1948, Bloomington, IN) Instr. Media Consult., CT State Dept. of Educ., 1977–; Adj. Fac., Ctrl. CT State Coll., 1979–80; Visit. Fac., Univ. of South. ME, 1976–78; Prog. Supvsr., IN Univ., 1972–76. **Educ.:** IN Univ., 1966–70, AB (Bio. Sci.), 1970–71, MS, 1972–76, Ed. S. Instr. Syst. Tech. and LS). **Orgs.:** ALA: AASL/Eval. of Sch. Media Progs. Com. (1980–). AECT: Conf. Eval. (1979). CT Educ. Media Assn.: various ofcs. CT LA: State Dept. of Educ. Rep. (1979). CT Educ. Forum: Vice-ch. (1980). CT Instr. TV Cncl. (1979–). **Pubns.:** "The School Library Media Program of the Year Award," *Sch. Media Qtly* (Fall 1979); "Media Skills and Competencies," *CT Educ. Media Assn. Bltn.* (O. 1979). **Activities:** 14-State Dept. of Educ.; 24, 31, 32; 63, 93 **Addr.:** Connecticut State Department of Education, Box 2219, Room 364, Hartford, CT 06115.

Binder, Michael Bernard (Mr. 19, 1943, Brooklyn, NY) Dir. of Lib., Fairleigh Dickinson Univ., 1978–; Head Libn., Clinch Valley Coll., Univ. of VA, 1974–78; Dir. of Lib. Srvs., Univ. of Pittsburgh, Bradford, 1972–74; Tchg. Fellow, Univ. of Pittsburgh, 1969–70. **Educ.:** New York Univ., 1961–65, BA (Hist.); Rutgers Univ., 1965–67, MLS; Univ. of Pittsburgh, 1967–73, PhD. **Orgs.:** ALA: ACRL/NJ Chap. (Pres., 1979–). PA Area Lib. Info. Network: Finance Com. (1980–). NJ State Lib.: Statewide Plng. Grp. (1979–). State Cncl. of Higher Educ. for VA: Lib. Adv. Com. (1974–78); West. Reg. Cnsrtm. on Cont. Higher Ed. for VA: Adv. Com. on Lib. Networking (Vice-Ch., 1977–78). **Honors:** White House Conf. on Lib. & Info. Srvs., NJ delegation, 1979; U.S. Ofc. of Educ., Post Mstrs. Flwshp., 1968; Beta Phi Mu. **Pubns.:** "Going from Here to the Limitless," *Lrng. Today* (Win. 1976); Jt. auth., "A New Curriculum for New Kinds of Students," *Proc. 4th International Conference on Improving University Education* (1978); Ed., *Directions*, Admin. Sect., NJ LA, (1979–); Reviews. **Activities:** 1; 17 **Addr.:** Messler Library, Fairleigh Dickinson University, Rutherford, NJ 07070.

Binder, Richard A. (Ap. 30, 1945, Oak Park, IL) Hum., Soc. Sci. Libn., Bibl. Instr. Libn., Drexel Univ., 1973–, Gen. Ref. Libn., 1970–72; U.S. Peace Corps, Iran Libn., Instr., LS, Univ. of Tehran, 1969–70; Libn., Instr., Eng., Gondi Shapur Univ., Ahwas, Iran, 1968–69. **Educ.:** Knox Coll., 1963–67, BA (Hist.): Univ. of IL, 1967–68, MS (LS); various crs. **Orgs.:** ALA: ACRL/Bibl. Instr. Sect., Resrch. Com. (1978–80). PA LA: Bd. of Dirs. (1976–77); Coll. and Resrch. Libs. Div., Int. Frdm. Com. (Ch., 1976–77), Nom. Com. (1975, 1978); SE Chap., Bd. of Dirs. (1975–76). Intl. Std. Assn. **Honors:** Beta Phi Mu, 1968; Phi Alpa Theta, 1980. **Pubns.:** "New Towns," *Sociological Symp.* (Fall 1974); "Bibliographic Instruction Dissertations," *Jnl. of Educ. for Libnshp.* (1981). **Activities:** 1; 31, 39; 74, 92 **Addr.:** Drexel University Libraries, Philadelphia, PA 19104.

Bindman, Fred M. (Ag. 24, 1929, New York, NY) Head, Msc. Sect., Descr. Cat. Div., Lib. of Congs., 1972–; Asst. Head, Msc. Sect., Lib. of Congs., 1968–72; Sr. Msc. Cat., 1960–68. **Educ.:** Boston Univ., 1947–51, BM (Msclgy.), 1951–52, MA (Msc. composition); Simmons Coll., 1952–53, MLS. **Orgs.:** Msc. LA: Cat. Cncl. (1970–). Intl. Assn. of Msc. Libns.: Cat. Comm. (1975–). Assn. of Recorded Sound Cols. **Pubns.:** Contrib., *Msc. Cat. Bltn.* (1972–). **Activities:** 1, 4; 17, 20; 55, 95-Music, ed. **Addr.:** 832 Loxford Terrace, Silver Spring, MD 20901.

Bingham, Elizabeth E. (Je. 29, 1948, Butler, AL) Head, Adult Srvs., E. Baton Rouge Parish Lib., 1975–; Head, Mid City Branch, 1974–75; Asst. Head, Ref., 1973–74; Ref. Libn., 1970–73. **Educ.:** LA St. Univ., 1966–70, BS (Educ.), 1970–71, MS (LS). **Orgs.:** ALA: JMRT (VP, 1978–79; Pres. 1979–80). ERT (Liason for JMRT, 1976–78); Various other coms. SWLA: JMRT (Ch., 1976–80); Cont. Educ. Adv. Cncl. (1975–78); Various other coms. LA LA: Exec. Bd. (1979–80); Constn. and Bylaws Com. (1979–81); Various other Coms. Baton Rouge Lib. Club. Altrusa Intl.: Mem. Com. (1978–80). LA St. Litcy. Cncl.: Bylaws Com. (Ch. 1979–8). Career Club: Secy. (1977); VP (1978); Pres. (1979–80). **Pubns.:** "Junior Members Round Table," *Amer. Libs.* (Je. 1979); "American Library Association is for You," *LA LA Bltn.* (Spr. 1977). **Activities:** 9, 16, 22, 36, 50, 51, 67 **Addr.:** East Baton Rouge Parish Library, 7711 Goodwood Blvd., Baton Rouge, LA 70806.

Bingham, Jane Marie (S. 21, 1941, Huntington, WV) Assoc. Prof. of Chld. Lit., Oakland Univ., 1969–; NDEA Fellow, MI State Univ., 1966–69; Primary Tchr., Flint Pub. Schs., 1961–65. **Educ.:** Ctrl. MI Univ., 1960–64, BA (Educ.); MI State Univ., 1965–66, MA (Educ.); 1966–70, PhD (Educ.). **Orgs.:** ALA: Laura Ingalls Wilder Com. (1978–80); Natl. Plng. Com. for Spec. Col. for Resrch. in Chld. Lit. (1979–81). Natl. Cncl. of Tchrs. of Eng.: Chld. Lit. Asm. (Pres., 1978–79; Treas., 1976–78). Chld. Lit. Assn.: Bd. of Dirs. (1975–77); Secy. (1976–77); Awds. Com. (1977–80). **Pubns.:** Jt. auth., *Fifteen Centuries of Children's Books* (1981); Jt. auth., "Why Teach Fantasy?" *CEA Critic* (Spr. 1978); Jt. auth., "Didacticism in New Dress," *Top of the News* (Ap. 1976); "Need to Find Just the Right Book?" *MI Eng. Tchr.* (S. 1975); "The Pictorial Treatment of Afro-Americans in Books for Young Children," *Elem. Eng.* (N. 1971); Reviews. **Activities:** 14-Univ. Educ. Dept.; 21, 41, 42; 57, 63, 66 **Addr.:** Oakland University, School of Education, Rochester, MI 48063.

Bingham, Rebecca J. Taylor (Jl. 14, 1928, Indianapolis, IN) Dir., Lib. Media Srvs., Jefferson Cnty. Pub. Schs., 1975–; Dir., Lib. Media Srvs., Louisville Pub. Schs., 1970–75, Supvsr., 1966–70; Libn., Jackson Jr. High, 1963–66; Tchr., Russell Jr. High, 1962–63; Jr. HS Libn., 1960–62; Libn., Sch. Srvs. Dept., Indianapolis Pub. Lib., 1957; Actg. Libn., Jarvis Christ. Coll., Hawkins, TX, 1955–57; various libn. positions, 1950–53. **Educ.:** IN Univ., 1946–50, BS (Educ.); Univ. of Tulsa, 1958–61, MA (Educ.); IN Univ., 1966–69, MLS. **Orgs.:** ALA: Cncl. (1972–75); Exec. Bd. (1974–78); AASL, VP, Pres.-Elect (1978–79), Pres. (1979–80), Natl. Lib. Week Com. (1969–72), various coms., ofcs. KY LA: Pres. (1971); Legis. Com. (1973–74). WHCOLIS: Pres. Adv. Com. (1979). Southeast. Reg. LA: Resrcs. and Tech. Srvs. Div. (Secy.-Treas., 1973–75). Various other orgs. Phi Lambda Theta: KY Alum. Chap. (Treas., 1970–74); Pres.-Elect (1980–81). Christ. Church Fndn.: Bd. of Dirs. (1973–75). Louisville Chld. Thea. Bd. Louisville Urban Leag. Various other orgs. **Honors:** KY Lib. Trustees, Outstan. Sch. Libn., 1969; IN Univ., Grad. Lib. Sch., Louise Maxwell Awd., 1977; Kappa Delta Pi; Beta Phi Mu; other hons. **Pubns.:** "Kentucky," *Amer. Educ. Encyc.* (1974); contrib., *Compton's Encyc.* (1974); jt. auth., *Cataloging Manual For Nonbook Materials* (1974); 1975–80 adv. com., *Elementary School Library Collection;* 1975–76 adv. bd., *Britannica Jr. Encyc.;* "Components of Effective Supervision at the District Level," *Sch. Media Qtly.* (Spr. 1979). **Activities:** 10; 17, 21, 48; 56, 63 **Addr.:** Library Media Services, Jefferson County Public Schools, Brown Education Center, 675 River City Mall, Louisville, KY 40202.

Binks, Malcolm H. (My. 24, 1932, Niagara, ON, Can) Media–Lib. Resrcs. Consult., Lincoln Cnty. Bd. of Educ., 1964–, Media Consult., 1964–78; Tchr., St. Catharines, 1953–64. **Educ.:** Hamilton Tchrs. Coll., 1952–53, Cert.; Brock Univ., 1978, BA (Geo.). **Orgs.:** ON Sch. LA. Can. Sch. Lib. Assn. Assn. for Media and Tech. in Educ. in Can.: Pres. (1977–78); Awds. (Ch., 1978–79). **Honors:** Assn. for Media and Tech. in Educ. in Canada, Hon. Life Mem., 1979. **Activities:** 10; 15, 17, 24, 32; 63, 67 **Addr.:** Media Resources Centre, Lincoln County Bd. of Education, St. Catharines, ON L2P 3J9 Canada.

Birch, Grace M. (Je. 3, 1925, New York, NY) Lib. Dir., Trumbull Lib. Syst., 1969–; Ast. Town Libn., Fairfield Pub. Lib., 1966–69; Branch Libn., Bridgeport Pub. Lib., 1949–66. **Educ.:** Hunter Coll. 1942–44 (Soclgy.); Univ. of Bridgeport, 1960–63, BA (Psy.); Pratt Institute, 1966–68, MLS; Renssalear Poly. Inst., 1968, Cert. (Comps.); Fairfield Univ., 1975, Cert. (Budget). **Orgs.:** ALA. New Eng. LA. CT LA: Nom. Com. (Ch., 1981); Legis. Com. (Ch. 1970); VP (1971); Pres. (1972). SW CT Lib. Cncl.: Pres. (1977); Comp. User's Grp. (Ch., 1981); Mem. Com. (Ch., 1980). Fairfield Lib. Admin. Grp.: Pres. (1976, 1977). **Activities:** 9, 11; 17, 26, 34; 56, 75, 93 **Addr.:** The Trumbull Library, 33 Quality St., Trumbull, CT 06611.

Birchfield, James de Maris (O. 1, 1946, Mayo, FL) Cur. of Rare Books, Univ. of KY, 1980–; Asst. Libn., FL State Univ., 1977–79; Asst. Cur., Shaw Col., 1973–77; Milit. Instr., USAF, 1969–73. **Educ.:** FL State Univ., 1964–67, BA (Pol. Sci.); 1967–69, MA (Eng.); 1973–76, DPhil (Eng.); 1976–77, MS (LS). **Orgs.:** FL LA. Mss Socty. Bibl. Socty. Prtg. Hist. Socty. Amer. Prtg. Hist. Assn. Modern Lang. Assn. **Honors** Phi Beta Kappa; Beta Phi Mu. **Pubns.:** "Jim's Coat of Arms," *Mark Twain Jnl.* (Sum. 1969); "Banned in Dublin: The Parson's Horn Book," *Jnl. of Lib. Hist.* (July 1975); "Source of Housman's Classification of Poetry," *Amer. Notes and Queries* (Feb. 1973). **Activities:** 1; 15, 18, 45; 55, 57 **Addr.:** University of Kentucky Libraries, Lexington, KY 40506.

Bird, Viola A. (Je. 7, 1905, Fall River, WI) Law Libn., Preston, Thorgrimson, Ellis and Holman, 1976–; Asst. Law Libn., Univ. of WA Law Lib., 1953–73. **Educ.:** Lawrence Coll., 1924–27, BA (Pol., Sci.); Univ. of WA, 1950, JD, 1951–53, MLL (Lib. Sci.). **Orgs.:** AALL: Executive Bd. (1968–71, 1972–73), Pres. (1971–72). **Pubns.:** *"Order Procedures* (AALL Pub. 2) (1960); *Research Collections in Canadian Law Libraries* (1975); Ed. "Current Comments," (Column), *Law Library Journal* (1956–68). **Activities:** 14-Law Firm-Law Library; 39; 77 **Addr.:** 5233 Pullman Ave. N.E., Seattle, WA 98105.

Bird, Warren Phillip (D. 27, 1933, Rochester, NY) Dir., Assoc. Prof., Med. Lit., Duke Univ. Med. Ctr. Lib., 1974–, Assoc. Dir., Asst. Prof., Med. Lit., 1968–74; Visit. Lectr., Sch. of LS, Univ. of NC, 1967; Chief, Lib. Mechanization, Duke Univ. Med. Ctr. Lib., 1965–68; Lib. Syst. Anal., Columbia Univ., 1964–65, Biophysicist, 1958–64. **Educ.:** Georgetown Univ., 1953–56, BS (Phys.); Columbia Univ., 1963–64, MS (LS); Med. LA, 1965, Cert. Grade I. **Orgs.:** Med. LA: Com. on Cont. Ed. Bibl. Socty. of Amer. Amer. Assn. of Hlth. Sci. Lib. Dirs. AAUP. AAAS. **Pubns.:** Jt. auth., *Planning Academic Health Science Libraries* (1979); ed., *Library Telecommunications Directory* (1967–76); "TWX and Interlibrary Loans," *Med. LA Bltn.* (1969). **Activities:** 1, 12; 17, 19, 24; 80 **Addr.:** Duke University Medical Center Library, Durham, NC 27710.

Birdsall, Douglas George (Jy. 1, 1947, Wyandotte, MI) Hum. Libn., ID State Univ. Lib., 1975–. **Educ.:** Univ. of MI, 1965–69, AB (Eng.), 1974–75, AMLS; Ctrl. MI Univ., 1973–74, MA (Eng.); West. MI Univ., 1970–71, Sec. Tchg. Cert. **Orgs.:** ALA:ACRL. Pac. Northwest LA: Bibl. Com. (1977–). ID LA: Bibl. Com. (Ch., 1977–); Pubns. Com. (Ch., 1980–). Msc. LA.: Mt. Plains Chap. Thea. LA (1980–). **Pubns.:** Ed., *Dissertations and Theses about Idaho, 1900–1978: A Bibliography with a Checklist of Library Holdings* (1980); "Library Skills and Freshman English: A Librarian's Perspective," *Coll. Composition and Comm.* (1981); Ed., *The Idaho Librarian* (1980–); Reviews. **Activities:** 1; 15, 31, 39; 55 **Addr.:** Idaho State University, Box 8170, Pocatello, ID 83209.

Birdsall, William F. (O. 30, 1937, Farmington, MN) Assoc. Dir., Pub. Srvs., Univ. of MB Libs., 1977–, Asst. Dir., Pub. Srvs., 1973–77; Head, Pub. Srvs., Univ. of WI, La Crosse, 1965–70; Ref. Libn., IA State Univ., 1961–63. **Educ.:** Univ. of MN, 1955–59, BA (Hist.), 1960–61, MA (LS); Univ. of WI, 1971–73, PhD (LS). **Orgs.:** ALA. CA LA. MB LA: VP–Pres. elect (1980), Cont. Educ. Com. (Ch., 1979–80). **Pubns.:** "Librarians and Professionalism, Status Measured by Outmoded Models," Can. Lib. Jnl. (1980); "Librarianship, Professionalism, and Social Change," Lib. Jnl. (1981); "Social Change and Library Development," *Assistance to Libraries in Developing Nations* (1971); "Archivists, Librarians, and Issues during the Pioneering Era of the American Archival Movement," *Jnl. of Lib. Hist.* (1979); "The Two Sides of the Desk: The Archivist and the Historian, 1909–1935," *Amer. Archvst.* (1975). **Activities:** 1; 17, 39 **Addr.:** Elizabeth Dafoe Library, University of Manitoba, Winnipeg, MB R3T 2N2 Canada.

Birkel, Paul Edward (Jl 13, 1931, Louisville, KY) Univ. Libn., Univ. of San Francisco, 1976–; Assoc. Libn., 1973–75; Coord. of Lib. Srvs., 1970–73; Head, Tech. Prcs., 1969–70. **Educ.:** Bellarmine Col., 1950–54, (Eng.); Cat. Univ., 1954–55, MSLS. **Orgs.:** ALA: RTSD/Resrcs. Sect. Exec. Com. (1974–77); Lib. Mtrls. Price Index Com. (1972–75. CA LA. Bk Club of CA. Roxburghe Club. Colophon Club. **Honors:** Beta Phi Mu, 1955. **Pubns.:** Co-Ed., *Cath. Per. Index,* (1961–62). **Activities:** 1; 15, 17, 46 **Addr.:** 1899 Diamond St., San Francisco, CA 94131.

Birmingham, Dr. Frank R. (Ag. 31, 1941, Bangor, ME) Dept. Ch., Prof., Lib. Media Educ. Dept., Mankato State Univ., 1970–; Dir., AV Skills Inst. for Pub. Libns., 1979–80; Dir., Sch. Lib. Media Educ. Prog., Mankato State Univ., 1971–73, Prog. Leader, Assoc. Prof., Instr. Media and Tech., 1971–72, Assoc. Prof., LS, 1970–71; Instr., Media Educ., DC Tchrs. Coll., 1968–70; Asst. Prof., LS, Cath. Univ., 1968–70; Co-Dir., Lrng. Resrc. Ctr., McKinley High, 1967–70. **Educ.:** St. Francis Coll., 1963, BA (Hist.); Georgetown Univ., 1967, MA (Amer. Diplomatic Hist.); Cath. Univ., 1970, PhD (Educ. Tech.). **Orgs.:** ALA: Bylaws and Org. Com. (1981–83); Staff Dev. Com. (1969–73); LITA, Vid. and Cable Util. Com. (Ch., 1980–81); AASL, various coms. AALS: Cont. Lib. Educ. Com. (1972). AECT: Natl. Nom. Com. (1975, 1981). CLENE: Adv. Cncl. (1976–78). Natl. Assn. of Educ. Broadcasters. Natl. Educ. Assn. MN Educ. Media Org.: Awds. and Prof. Dev. Com. (Ch., 1976–78); Media Educ. Spec. Interest Div. (Ch., 1978–80, 1981–82); Media Educ. Licensure Com. (Ch., 1980–); Telecom. Spec. Interest Div. Exec. Bd. (1979–80); Long Range Goals and Plng. Com. (Ch., 1980–81); various coms. MN Media Educs.: Anl. Conf. Plng. Com. (Ch., Conv., 1976). Various other orgs. **Honors:** Fed. Comm. Comsn., Natl. Com. for the Full Dev. of Instr. TV Fixed Srv., Appointee, 1971–73; M.I. Smith Leadership Conf., Appointee, 1972–76. **Pubns.:** "Instructional Television Fixed Service," *EPIE Educational Product Report* (1971); jt. auth., "An Experimental Program in School Library Media Education, 1971–73," *Curriculum Alternatives: Experiments in School Library Media Education* (1974); various sps., presentations. **Activities:** 10, 11; 26, 32, 49-Chld. and TV. **Addr.:** Library Media Education, P.O. 20 Mankato State University, Mankato, MN 56001.

Birschel, Dee Baltzer (Ag. 14, 1947, Waukesha, WI) Assoc. Dir., Info. Srvs., Intl. Fndn. of Empl. Benefit Plans, 1974–; Libn., Vets. Admin., 1971–74. **Educ.:** Univ. of WI, 1965–70, BS (Con. Sci.), 1971–74, MLS. **Orgs.:** ASIS. SLA: WI Chap. (Secy., 1978–81); Insr. and Empl. Benefits Div. (Secy., 1980–81). Lib. Cncl. of Metro. Milwaukee: Nom. Com. (1978). Amer. Socty. for Trng. and Dev. **Pubns.:** "Information Please," monthly clmn. *I.F. Digest.* **Activities:** 12; 15, 17, 39; 59, 76, 77 **Addr.:** Information Center, International Foundation of Employee Benefit Plans, 18700 W. Bluemound Rd., P.O. Box 69, Brookfield, WI 53005.

Birtha, Jessie Moore (F. 5, 1920, Norfolk, VA) Retired, 1980–; Adj. Prof., Chld. Lit., Antioch Grad. Sch., Philadelphia Ctr., 1975–76; Publshrs. Consult., McGraw Hill Lang. Arts Prog.,

Special Subjects/Services: 50. Adult educ.; 51. Advert./Mktg.; 52. Aerosp.; 53. Agric.; 54. Area std.; 55. Arts/Hum.; 56. Autom.; 57. Bibl./Prtg.; 58. Bio. sci.; 59. Bus./Fin.; 60. Chem.; 61. Copyrt.; 62. Documtn.; 63. Educ.; 64. Engin.; 65. Env.; 66. Eth. grps.; 67. Film; 68. Food/Nutr.; 69. Geneal.; 70. Geo.; 71. Geol.; 72. Handcpd.; 73. Hist.; 74. Int. frdm.; 75. Info. sci.; 76. Insr.; 77. Law; 78. Legis.; 79. Math./Comp. sci.; 80. Med.; 81. Metals; 82. Nat. resrcs.; 83. Newsp.; 84. Nuc. sci.; 85. Oral hist.; 86. Petr./Energy; 87. Pharm.; 88. Phys./Astr./Math.; 89. Readg.; 90. Relig.; 91. Sci./Tech.; 92. Soc. sci.; 93. Telecom.; 94. Transp.; 95. (other).

Amer. Lang. Today, 1974; Asst. Head, Chld. Bk. Sel., Free Library of Philadelphia, 1967–69, Chld. Libn., Branch Head, 1959–80; Elem. Sch. Tchr., Pub. Schs., Norfolk, VA, 1942–46; Sec. Educ. Tchr., Penn Sch., 1940–41. **Educ.:** Hampton Inst., 1936–40, BS (Sec. Educ.); Drexel Univ., 1962, MLS. **Orgs.:** ALA: Soc. Resp. Task Frc. on Minority Rcrt.; Newbery-Caldecott Awds. Com. (1975). PA LA. Frnds. of the Free Lib., Philadelphia. Chicago Chld. Readg. RT: Assoc. Mem. **Honors:** Free Lib. of Philadelphia, Supvsr. of the Yr. Awd., 1973; Chapel of the Four Chaplains, Legion of Hon. Awd. (for outstan. work with minority chld.), 1979. **Pubns.:** "Juvenile Book Selection with Emphasis on Urban Minorities," *Bookmark* (Fall 1980); jt. auth., "What To Do When They Ask For Nancy Drew," *Cath. Lib. World* (1979); jt. auth., *Guidelines for Libraries to Serve Special Patrons* (1977); "The Black Parent, the Black Child and Books," *Sunaru* (1979); "Children's Library Service and Black American Children," *Handbook of Black Librarianship* (1977); various chaps. **Activities:** 9; 21 **Addr.:** 433 Glen Echo Rd., Philadelphia, PA 19119.

Bish, Dianne Lee (D. 19, 1946, Detroit, MI) Dir., Novi Pub. Lib., 1978–; Libn., Detroit Pub. Lib., 1973–78; Legis. Spec., MO State Lib., 1972–73; Law Libn., Clark, Klein, et. al., 1970–72. **Educ.:** MI State Univ., 1965–69, BA (Eng.); Wayne State Univ., 1970–72, MSLS; various crs. **Orgs.:** ALA. SLA: MI Chap. (Archvst., 1978–). GODORT of MI: Bylaws Com. (Ch., 1978); Secy. (1978–). SW Oakland Cnty. Libns.: Fndn. Mem. (1978); Ch. (1978–). MI Hist. Socty. MI Fed. of Bus. and Prof. Women's Clubs: Dist. Legis. Ch. (1975–76); Garden City Chap., Bicent. Ch. (1975–76), Secy. (1976–77). Novi Hist. Socty.: Archvst. (1979–). Frnds. of the Novi Lib. **Honors:** MI Fed. of Bus. and Prof. Women's Clubs, Dist. 9, Dist. "Young Career Woman," 1975; Pi Lambda Theta; Beta Phi Mu. **Pubns.:** "On Local Documents," bimonthly clmn. *Red Tape* (1978–); "History of Michigan Chapter, Special Libraries Association," *Bltn. MI Chap. SLA* (O. 1978, D. 1978). **Activities:** 9; 17, 34; 59, 77, 93 **Addr.:** Novi Public Library, 45245 W. Ten Mile Rd., Novi, MI 48050.

Bishoff, Lizbeth J. (N. 6, 1949, Chicago, IL) Admin. Libn., Ela Area Pub. Lib., 1977–; Head, Ref., Tech. Srv., Waukegan Pub. Lib., 1975–77; Media Spec., Grant Cmnty. HS, 1973–75; Head, Tech. Srv., Northbrook Pub. Lib., 1973–70. **Educ.:** West. IL Univ., 1967–70, BA (Hist.); Rosary Coll., 1971–74, MA (LS); Roosevelt Univ., 1977–81, MA (Pub. Admin.). **Orgs.:** IL LA: RTSS Bd. of Dirs. (1977–78). ALA: RTSD, Cat. Code Rev. (1974–78), Subj. Analysis Com. (1974–78), Dewey Ed. Policy Com. (ALA Rep., 1979–82), Subcom. on Subj. Analysis of AV Mtrls. (Ch., 1975–77). **Activities:** 9; 17, 20, 35 **Addr.:** 887 Hillandale Dr., Antioch, IL 60002.

Bishop, David. (S. 23, 1928, Pouch Cove, NF) Univ. Libn., Univ. of CA, San Francisco, 1977–; Lib. Dir., Univ. of NE Med. Ctr., 1973–77; Med. Libn., McGill Univ., 1971–73; Libn., AZ Med. Ctr., Univ. of AZ, 1965–71; Serials Libn., Biomed. Lib., Univ. of CA, Los Angeles, 1961–65; Ref. Libn., Los Angeles Cnty. Med. Assn., 1958–61. **Educ.:** Dalhousie Univ., 1949–52, BA (Econ.); Columbia Univ., 1957–58, MS (LS). **Orgs.:** Med. LA: Bd. Dir. (1971–74); Co.-ed., *Handbook* (1976–). ALA. ASIS. Assn. of Amer. Med. Colls. Soc. for the Hist. of Tech. **Honors** AZ State LA, Libn. of the Year, 1970; Med. LA, Janet Doe Lectureship, 1976; Assn. of Amer. Med. Colls., Grp. on PR, Disting. Srv. Awd., 1976. **Pubns.:** Co.-ed., *Handbook of Medical Library Practice,* (4th Ed., 1981–); "On the Uses of Diversity," *Bltn. Med. LA* (O. 1976); "Control & Dissemination of Information in Medicine," *Advncs. in Libnshp.* (1971); Various other articles and reviews. **Activities:** 1, 12; 17; 80, 95-Health sci. **Addr.:** The Library, S 257, University of California, San Francisco, San Francisco, CA 94143.

Bishop, David F. (N. 23, 1937, New York, NY) Dir., Univ. of GA, 1979–; Asst. Dir. Tech. Srvcs., Univ. of Chicago, 1975–79; Head Cat., 1973–75; Head, Syst. and Prog., Univ. of MD, 1970–73; Coord. of Tech. Srvcs., 1969–70; Head, Serials Dept., 1967–69; Asst. Head, Cat. Dept., 1966–67; Head, Serials Cata., 1965–66; Other positions. **Educ.:** Univ. of Rochester, 1955–59, BM (Music Educ.); Catholic Univ., 1962–64, MS (LS). **Orgs.:** ALA: ACRL: Com. on Legis. (1975–77), Ch. (1978–79). RTSD (Legis. Com. 1971–73. Cat./Class. Sec. Conf. Plng. Com. 1976). GA LA. SELA. Athens, GA. Rotary Club. **Pubns.:** "ACRL Legislative Network Backs Title 11A," *Coll. and Resrch. Libs. News* (1979). **Activities:** 1; 17, 46; 56, 78 **Addr.:** 300 Sandstone Drive, Athens, GA 30605.

Bishop, Etta May (Ja. 27, 1937, Lyndonville, VT) Asst. to Dir., Ctr. for Instr. Media and Tech., Univ. of CT, 1979–; Adj. Fac., Grad. Media Prog., Ctrl. CT State Coll., 1978–; Dir., Media, Canton Pub. Schs., CT, 1965–79; Tchr., Natchaug Sch., 1964–65; Tchr., Woodstock Jr. High, 1963–64; Tchr., Woodsville Elem. Sch., 1961–63. **Educ.:** Lyndon State Coll., 1955–59, BS (Educ.); Univ. of CT, 1968, MA (Educ.), 1972, 6th Yr. Instr. Media; various crs. **Orgs.:** CT Educ. Media Assn.: Pres. (1977–78); Secy. (1976–77); various ofcs. New Eng. Educ. Media Assn.: Bd. (1977–78); Mem. Com. (1980–81); Schol. Com. (1980–82). CT Lib. Fndn.: Bd. of Dirs. (1977–78). AECT: Various ofcs. Various other orgs. New Eng. Assn. of Schs. and Colls.: Educ. Lib./Media Com. (Ch., 1971, 1974); various coms. Natl. Cncl. for Accred. of Tchr. Educ.: Visit. Team Ch. (1977, 1978, 1981). CT Assn. for Supvsn. and Curric. Dev. Assn. for Supvsn. and Curric. Dev. **Honors:** Phi Delta Kappa; Lyndon State Coll., Disting. Alum. Awd., 1979; Canton Jaycees, Jr. Cham. of Congs., Outstan. Young Educ. Awd., 1969; WRCH Radio, WRCH Disting. Srv. Awd., 1969. **Pubns.:** Ed., *CT AV Educ. Assn. Nsltr.* (1975–76); ed., *Interface* (1981–); various presentations. **Activities:** 12, 13; 17, 24, 32; 63, 75, 93 **Addr.:** Center for Instructional Media & Technology, Box U–1, University of Connecticut, Storrs, CT 06268.

Bishop, Rev. James P. (My. 22, 1925, Chicago, IL) Dir. of Lib. Srvs., Prof., Carthage Coll., 1961–; Pastor, St. John's Lutheran Church, El Cajon, CA, 1953–61; Libn., Northwestern Lutheran Theo. Sem., Minneapolis, MN, 1950–53. **Educ.:** Wittenberg Univ., 1946–49, BSEd (Eng.); Univ. of South. CA, 1949–50, MSLS; Northwestern Lutheran Theo. Semy., 1950–53, MDiv (Theol.). **Orgs.:** Cncl. of WI Libns., Inc.: Ch. (1977–78); Secy. (1975–77). WI Assn. of Acad. Libns.: Ch. (1978). WI LA: Exec. Com. (1977–79). WI Lib. Cnsrtm.: Adv. Com. (1976–79). Various other orgs. WI-Upper MI Synod, Lutheran Church in Amer.: Archvst. (1962–). **Honors:** Phi Alpha Theta, 1948; Phi Eta Sigma, 1946; Alpha Lambda Delta, 1978. **Pubns.:** "Lamentationes ex Bibliotheca," *WI Lib. Bltn.* (Ja. 1971); "ACRL Standards, 1975," *WI Lib. Bltn.* (N. 1975); column for coll. paper (1973–78). **Activities:** 1; 17, 34, 46; 55, 58, 90 **Addr.:** 1502 22d St., Kenosha, WI 53140.

Bishop, Mary L. (N. 24, 1915, Edinburg, IN) Dir., Crawfordsville Dist. Pub. Lib., 1963–; Dir., Marion Pub. Lib., 1947–62. **Educ.:** Butler Univ., 1933–37, AB (Latin, Eng.), 1938–39 (LS); various crs. **Orgs.:** ALA. IN LA: Secy. (1958, 1963). IN Coop. Lib. Srv. Athrty.: Treas. (1976). IN LA: VP (1980); Pres. (1981). AAUW: Pres. (1967–69). Zonta: Crawfordsville Chap. (Pres., 1969–70, 1972–73). Delta Kappa Gamma: Hist. Com., Ch. **Honors:** IN LA, Libn. of the Yr., 1978; Kappa Delta Phi; Phi Kappa Phi. **Pubns.:** "Wanted! Books to Process," *Lib. Occurent* (Mr. 1964). **Activities:** 9; 17, 19, 46; 74, 78, 89 **Addr.:** Crawfordsville District Public Library, 222 S. Washington St., Crawfordsville, IN 47933.

Bishop, Olga Bernice (Je. 24, 1911, Dover, NB) Prof. Emeritus, Univ. of Toronto, 1977–, Prof., 1970–77, Assoc. Prof., 1965–70; Med. Libn., Univ. of West. ON, 1954–65, Gen. Libn., 1953–54; Asst. Libn., Actg. Libn., Mt Allison Univ., 1946–53. **Educ.:** Mt Allison Univ., 1938, BA; Carleton Univ., 1946, B Pub Adm., Mt Allison Univ., 1951, MA; Univ. of MI, 1952, AMLS, 1962, PhD. **Orgs.:** Can. Assn. of Lib. Schs.: VP (1972–73); Pres. (1973–74). Can. LA: Cnclr. (1967–68); Com. on Educ. for Lib. Manpower (Ch., 1971–72); other coms. Inst. of Prof. Libns. of ON: Pres. (1966–67) ON LA: Cnclr. (1966–67). Other orgs. and coms. Can. Assn. of Univ. Tchrs.: Com. on Status of Women (1971–75). Univ. of Toronto Fac. Assn.: Cnclr. (1967–73). ON Hist. Socty. Geosci. Info. Socty. **Honors:** Beta Phi Mu, 1962; Mt. Allison Univ., Doctor of Laws, 1971. **Pubns.:** *Canadian Association of Special Libraries and Information Services Handbook* (1970); *Publications of the Government of Ontario, 1867–1900* (1976); *Bibliography of Ontario History 1867–1976: Cultural, Economic, Political, Social* (1980); "The First Printing Press in Canada, 1751–1800" in *Books in America's Past: Essays Honoring Rudolph H. Gjelsness* (1966); "Library Collections in Science" in *Guide to Basic Reference Books for Canadian Libraries,* (1968); other books, articles. **Activities:** 1, 12; 17, 24, 25; 57, 80, 91 **Addr.:** 62 Thornton Ave., London, ON N5Y 2Y3 Canada.

Bishop, Twyla B. (N. 28, 1947, Cleveland, OH) Info. Systs. Spec., Pres. Persnl., White Hse., 1981–; Systs. Anal., MITRE Corp., 1978–81; Pres., BRAINS, Inc., 1977–78; Dir., Div. Info. Systs., JRB Assoc., Inc., 1975–77; Ref. Libn., Search Anal., Med. Coll. of GA, 1972–75; Acq. Libn., Clayton Jr. Coll., 1972. **Educ.:** Stetson Univ., 1966–69, BA (Eng.); Emory Univ., 1970–71, MLn (Libnshp.); Med. LA, Cert. **Orgs.:** SLA. Med. LA. ASIS: SIG/BC Nsltr Ed. (1978–80) Ch.-Elect (1980–81). Assoc. Info. Mgrs. Capitol Park Condominium Bd. of Dirs.: Secy. (1979–80); Bd. (1980–83). **Pubns.:** *Reference Manual, Presidential Personnel Office Placement System* (1980); *General Requirements Specification for a Self-Help Information Network Exchange* (1979); *Chemical Information Resources Directory* (1979); *Thesaurus: Chemical Information Network Directory* (1978); *Protection of Confidential Information in the German Environmental Protection Agency* (1978). **Addr.:** Presidential Personnel Office, Old Executive Office Bldg., 17th & Pennsylvania Ave. N.W., Washington, DC 20500.

Bissell, Catharine P. (O. 25, 1946, San Bernardino, CA) Asst. Libn., Spec. Col., San Jose State Univ., 1980–, Asst. Libn., Serials, 1976–80, Asst. Libn., Hum., 1974–76, Asst. Libn., Serials, 1971–74. **Educ.:** Foothill Coll., 1964–66, AA (Eng. Lit.); Univ. of CA, Riverside, 1966–68, BA (Eng. Lit.); Univ. of CA, Berkeley, 1969–71, MLS (Libnshp.); Heald Bus. Coll., 1977–78, Dip. (Career Secretarial); various crs. **Orgs.:** ARLIS/NA. SLA: Bay Reg. Chap., Un. List of Serials Com. (Co-Ch., 1973–76), Hosp. Com. (1978), Student Rel. Com. (Ch., 1979); San Andreas Chap., Student Rel. Com. (Ch., 1980). CA LA. SAA. SC LA. Assn. of CA State Univ. Profs. Assn. of Recs. Mgrs. and Admins. Smithsonian Inst. Assocs. **Pubns.:** Jt. ed., *Union List of Periodicals, San Francisco Bay Region Chapter LA* (1976); jt. auth., "Survey of Union Lists of Serials Sponsored by SLA Chapters," *Spec. Libs.* (Ag. 1974). **Activities:** 1, 2; 23, 44, 45; 55 **Addr.:** Library/Special Collections, San Jose State University, 250 S. 4th St., San Jose, CA 95192.

Bitner, Harry (Jl. 22, 1916, Kansas City, MO) Legal Biblgphr., Columbia Univ. Law Lib., 1978–; Prof. of Law, Law Libn., Cornell Univ., 1965–75; Law Libn., Yale Univ., 1957–65; Libn., U.S. Dept. of Justice, 1954–57; Assoc. Law Libn., Columbia Univ., 1946–54; Ref. Law Libn., Univ. of PA, 1954; Law Libn., Instr., Univ. of MO, Kansas City, 1939–43. **Educ.:** Univ. of MO, Kansas City, 1939–41, AB (Hist., Pol. Sci.), 1936–39, JD; Univ. of IL, 1939–42, BS (LS). **Orgs.:** AALL: Pres. (1963–64); Exec. Bd. (1953–56). Intl. Assn. of Law Libs. ALA. SLA. Various other orgs. Amer. Socty. for Legal Hist. **Honors** AALL, Joseph L. Andrews Bibligph. Awd., 1971. **Pubns.:** Jt. Auth. *Effective Legal Research* (1979); "Inexpensive Justice," *Univ. of MO (Kansas City) Law Review* (F. 1943); "The Educational Background of the University's Law Librarian," *Law Lib. Jnl.* (My. 1947); Dir., AALL Libs. Std. Proj., *Law Books Recommended For Law Libraries* (1966–). **Activities:** 1, 4; 15, 17, 31 **Addr.:** 280 Prospect Ave., Apt 4M, Hackensack, NJ 07601.

Bitting, Judith C. (Philadelphia, PA) R & D Libn., Smith Kline and French Labs., 1955–, FDA Coord., 1967–72, Sci. Ed., 1955–67. **Educ.:** Rosemont Coll., 1950–54, BS (Chem.); Drexel Univ., 1963–66, MSLS. **Orgs.:** SLA. Med. LA. ASIS. Amer. Chemical Socty. **Activities:** 12; 15, 17, 39 **Addr.:** Smith Kline & French Laboratories, 1500 Spring Garden St., Philadelphia, PA 19101.

Bivans, Margaret M. (Jl. 18, 1915, Ojus, FL) Libn., Physical Sci. and Engin. Lib., Natl. Oceanic and Atmospheric Admin., Env. Resrch. Labs, Boulder, 1973–, Admin. Asst., 1969–73, Admin. Asst., Scientific Documtn. Div., Env. Sci. Srvs. Admin., 1966–69; Qualifications Rating Examiner, Cvl. Srv. Bd. of Examiners, Natl. Bur. of Stans., Boulder, 1963– 66; various nonlib. positions, 1936–63. **Educ.:** NE Wesleyan Univ., 1932–36, BA (Bot.); Univ. of Denver, 1970–73, MALS. **Orgs.:** SLA: Math-Astronomy-Phys. Div.; Natl. Conv. Com. (1976). ALA. Univ. of Denver Grad. Sch. of Libnshp. Alum. Photographic Socty. of Amer. Rocky Mt. Climbers Clb. CO Open Space Cncl. AAUW. Various other orgs. **Honors:** Natl. Bur. of Stans., Sustained Superior Performance Awds., 1959, 1966. **Pubns.:** "Computer at NOAA: Installing Online Literature Search Services in the Library," *The Columbine* (1975); "A Comparison of Manual and Machine Literature Searches," *Spec. Libs.* (1974); "Implementation of Online Literature Searching and OASIS Program in Boulder" (wkshp. panel) (1974); various other nature articles and slide presentations. **Activities:** 4, 12; 49-Branch Libn.; 65, 88, 91 **Addr.:** 3140 Folsom St., Boulder, CO 80302.

Bivins, Hulen E. (O. 17, 1949, Lewisburg, TN) Head, Reg. Lib. for Blind and Physically Handcpd. (APLS), 1981–; Consult., AL Pub. Lib. Srv., 1979–; Media Coord., Nashville Pub. Lib., 1974–79; Asst. Ref. Libn., Marshall Univ., 1972–74. **Educ.:** David Lipscomb Coll., 1967–71, BA (Hist.); Univ. of TN, 1971–72, MSLS. **Orgs.:** AL LA. ALA. Natl. Film Market: Bd. (Ch., 1978–81); Amer. Film. Inst. Various other orgs. Civitan Intl., Nashville: Treas. (1978–79). **Honors:** Amer. Bus. & Prof. Woman's Assn., Metro Nashville Boss of Year, 1979; Civitan Intl., Nashville, Pres. Awd., 1978. **Pubns.:** Reviews. **Activities:** 9, 13; 17, 24, 32; 55, 67, 93 **Addr.:** 312 Navajo Drive, Montgomery, AL 36117.

Bivins, Kathleen T. (Jl. 29, 1940, Washington, DC) Asst. Prof., Univ. of CA, Los Angeles, 1978–; Lectr., Univ. of MD, 1976–78; Systems Anal., Lib. of Congs., 1972–75; Consult., 1975–. **Educ.:** Brown Univ., 1958–62, AB; Univ. of MD, MLS, PhD (Info. Sci.). **Orgs.:** ASIS: Intl. Rel. Com. (1978–80). AALS. IFLA: Class. Resrch. RT. Ling. Socty. of Amer. Assn. for Comp. Mach. **Honors:** Beta Phi Mu; Natl. Sci. Fndn., Travel Grants. **Pubns.:** Jt. auth., "REFLES (Ref. Libn. Enhancement Syst.): Microcomputers and Fact Retrieval," *Info. Proc. and Mgt.* (in press).; "Frame Searching and Indexing Languages," *Klassifikation und Erkenntnis II* (1979); "Aspects of Information Systems and Semantics," *Information Sciences: The Systems Design Process* (forthcoming); Various other articles. **Activities:** 11; 24, 26, 41; 56, 75, 95-Linguistics. **Addr.:** University of California, Graduate School of Library and Information Science, Los Angeles, CA 90024.

Bixler, Paul H(oward) (O. 27, 1899, Union City, MI) Libn. Emeritus, Antioch Coll., 1965–, Libn., 1935–65; Lib. Consult., Ford Fndn, 1964–71; Libn., Soc. Sci. Lib., Univ. of Rangoon, Burma, 1958–60; Eng. Instr., West. Rsv. Univ., 1928–35; Rpt., *Cleveland Press,* 1927; Rpt., *Cleveland Plain Dealer,* 1926; Eng. Instr., OH Wesleyan Univ., 1924–26. **Educ.:** Harvard Univ., 1923–24, MA (Eng.); West. Rsv. Univ., 1932–33, BSLS. **Orgs.:** ALA: Int. Frdm. Nsltr. (Fndr., Ed., 1952–56). Assn. for Asian Std. Ford Fndn.; Staff mem. (1949). **Honors:** Natl. Book Awd, Judge in Nonfiction, 1955; Univ. Ctr., Atlanta, Visit. Schol., 1963; Ford Fndn, Bibl. Resrch. Grant, 1962–63. **Pubns.:** *Southeast Asia: Bibliographic Directions* (1974); *The Mexican Library* (1969); "Are You Glad to Be Back, Jack?" *The Antioch Review* (Sum. 1979); Study of Proposed Library Standards and Growth

PROFESSIONAL ACTIVITIES: Institutions: 1. Acad. lib.; 2. Arch.; 3. Assn.; 4. Fed./Gvt. lib.; 5. Inst. lib.; 6. Mfr./Suppl.; 7. Milit. lib.; 8. Musm.; 9. Pub. lib.; 10. Sch. lib.; 11. Sch. of lib. sci.; 12. Spec. lib.; 13. State lib.; 14. (other). **Functions/Activities:** 15. Acq./Col. dev.; 16. Adult srvs.; 17. Admin.; 18. Apprais.; 19. Archit./Bldgs.; 20. Cat./Class.; 21. Chld. srvs.; 22. Circ.; 23. Cons./Pres.; 24. Consult.; 25. Cont. ed.; 26. Educ. lib. sci.; 27. Ext. srvs.; 28. Fund/Grants; 29. Gvt. pubs.; 30. Indx./Abs.; 31. Instr. lib. use; 32. Media srvs.; 33. Micro.; 34. Netwks./Coop.; 35. Persnl.; 36. PR; 37. Publshg.; 38. Recs. mgt.; 39. Ref. srvs.; 40. Repro.; 41. Resrch.; 42. Review.; 43. Secur.; 44. Serials; 45. Spec. col.; 46. Tech. srvs.; 47. Trustees/Bds.; 48. YA srvs.; 49. (other).

Patterns for MD State Council for Higher Education report (1969). **Activities:** 1; 15, 17, 24; 54, 74, 92 **Addr.:** 1345 Rice Rd., Yellow Springs, OH 45387.

Bjerke, Robert Alan (D. 23, 1939, Eau Claire, WI) Libn., Univ. of WI Ctr., Manitowoc Cnty., 1973–; Asst. Prof. of Norwegian, St. Olaf Coll., 1966–71. **Educ.:** Univ. of WI, Madison, 1959–61, BA (Hist.); 1961–62, MA (Grmn.); 1962–66, PhD (Grmn.); Univ. of MN, 1972–78, MALS. **Orgs.:** WI LA. Fox Valley LA: VP (1979–80). **Activities:** 1; 15, 17 **Addr.:** University of Wisconsin Center, 705 Viebahn St., Manitowoc, WI 54220.

Bjorncrantz, Leslie Benton (Mr. 1, 1945, Jersey City, NJ) Curr. Lib., Northwestern Univ. Lib., 1970–; Ref. Lib., 1974–78; Rsrch. Lib., Univ. of VA, 1968–70. **Educ.:** Wellesley Coll., 1963–67, BA (Eng.); Columbia Univ., 1967–68, MLS. **Orgs.:** ALA: ACRL/Ref. and Subscrptn. Bks. Review Com. Mem. (1972–75); Guest Reviewer (1975–80); Educ. and Bhvl. Sci. Sect. (1977–79); Nom. Com. (1973–74, 1979–80). Chicago On-Line Users Grp. ASIS. IL LA. various other orgs. Amer. Socty. for Trng. and Dev. Intl. Visitors' Ctr. Chicago: Bd. of Dirs. (1975–77). **Honors:** Beta Phi Mu, 1968; Phi Delta Kappa, 1981. **Pubns.:** Reviews (1972–76). **Activities:** 1; 15, 17, 39; 63, 92 **Addr.:** Curriculum Collection, Northwestern University Library, 1935 Sheridan Road, Evanston, IL 60201.

Black, Bernice Blythe (Je. 22, 1932, Cedar Bluff, AL) Chief, Lib. Branch, Tech. Info. Ctr., U.S. Army Engin. Waterways Exper. Station, 1980–; Chief Docum. Libn., Redstone Sci. Info. Ctr., U.S. Army Missile Cmnd., 1979–80, Libn., 1958–79. **Educ.:** Berry Coll., 1950–54, BS (Bus. Admin.); AL A and M Univ., 1972, MLS. **Orgs.:** AL LA. MS LA. **Activities:** 4; 17; 75 **Addr.:** P.O. Box 631, Vicksburg, MS 39180.

Black, Ferne M. (My. 16, 1920, Cleveland, OH) Coord. Libn., Cuyahoga Cmnty. Coll., (Cleveland) 1977–, Mgr., Tech. Prcs., 1975–77, Asst. Prof., Lib.-Media Tech. Prog., 1974–76, Mem. Adv. Cncl., 1975–76, Head, Acq., 1970–75; Asst. Libn., Parma Hts. (OH) Pub. Lib., 1969–70; Libn., Cleveland-Seven Cntys. Land Use/Transp. Study, 1967–69; Supvsr., Acq., Aerospace Corp., Los Angeles, 1966–67; Info. Spec., Battelle Meml. Inst., Columbus, 1965–66; Resrch. Libn., Aeronutronic Div., Ford Motor Co., Newport Beach, CA, 1961–65. **Educ.:** OH Univ., 1938–40, CA State Univ., Los Angeles, 1958–59, BA (Eng.); Univ. of South. CA, 1960–61, MSLS cum laude. **Orgs.:** SLA: Cleveland Chap. (Pres., 1972–73). South. CA Chap., various coms. (1961–65). Cleveland Area Metro. Lib. Syst., Lib. Rescrs. Com. (Vice Ch., 1980). Acad. LA of OH. Zonta Intl: Cleveland (Dir. 1974-75; Sec. 1977-78; Vice Pres. 1979-81); UNICEF: Cleveland (Bd. of Dir. 1978–). AAUP. **Honors:** Beta Phi Mu. **Activities:** 1, 12; 15, 17, 46; 50, 52, 91 **Addr.:** 12040 Lake Ave., Apt. 102, Lakewood, OH 44107.

Black, Frances P. (Jl. 27, 1949, Huntsville, AL) Head, Tech. and Ext. Srvs., Grove City Pub. Lib., 1978–; Admin. Ast., State Lib. of OH, 1977–78; Dir., Fairhope Pub. Lib., 1972–77. **Educ.:** Univ. of AL, 1969–71, BA (Eng., Soclgy.); 1971–72, MLS. **Orgs.:** ALA. OH LA: Reg. Mtg. Com. (1980). Leag. of Women Voters: Lib. Mtrls. Com. (1975–76). **Honors:** Jayceettes, Outstan. Young Women of Amer. 1975, 1977. **Activities:** 9; 15, 27, 46; 72 **Addr.:** Grove City Public Library, 3359 Park St., Grove City, OH 43123.

Black, George W., Jr. (Ap. 1, 1930, Brooklyn, NY) Sci. Libn. and Assoc. Prof., South. IL Univ. at Carbondale, 1968–; Chem. Libn., Univ. of MD, 1966–68; Asst. Prof., Div. of Nat. Scis., Southhampton Coll. of Long Island Univ., 1963–65. **Educ.:** St. Francis Coll., Brooklyn, NY, 1953–56, BS (Bio.); St. John's Univ., Jamaica, NY, 1956–58, MS (Chem.); Columbia Univ., 1964–66, MSLS. **Orgs.:** ASIS. Amer. Chem. Socty.: Sect. Secy. (1977–). Sigma Xi: Chap. Secy. (1975–). Amer. Assn. for the Advnc. of Sci. **Pubns.:** *American Science and Technology, 1776–1976: a Bibliography,* (1979); *A KWIC Index to Theses and Dissertations, 1949–1972, Southern Illinois University at Carbondale,* (1975); "Frank Bursley Taylor - Forgotten Pioneer of Continental Drift," *J of Geol. Educ.* (Mr 1979); "Justus Liebig's Contributions to Agricultural Chemistry," *J. Chem. Educ.* (J 1978); *"ASCA IV* Experience of a University Science Library," *Il Lib.,* (Ap 1977); various other articles. **Activities:** 1; 15, 17, 39; 53, 80, 91 **Addr.:** Science Division, Morris Library, Southern IL Univ.-Carbondale, Carbondale, IL 62901.

Black, John B. (Ag. 5, 1940, Guelph, ON, Can) Assoc. Libn., Univ. of Guelph, 1974–, Asst. Libn., Srvs., 1972–73, Assoc. Prof., Pol. Std., 1972, Asst. Prof., 1968–72, Lectr., Pol. Std., 1966–68. **Educ.:** Univ. of West. ON, 1958–62, BA (Jnlsm.), 1963–64, MA (Pol. Sci.); Univ. of London, Sch. of Econ. & Pol. Sci., 1964–66, 1968–69, PhD (Intl. Rel.). **Orgs.:** Intl. Com. for Soc. Sci. Documtn.: Assoc. Mem. (1978–79); Mem. titulaire (1980–). Can. Assn. for Info. Sci. ALA. ASIS. Various other orgs. Can. Inst. of Intl. Affairs. Intl. Pol. Sci. Assn. Intl. Assn. for Mass Comm. Resrch. **Pubns.:** *Organising the Propaganda Instrument: The British Experience* (1975); Communications Information (Online Data Base) (1979–). **Addr.:** McLaughlin Library, University of Guelph, Guelph, ON N1G 2W1 Canada.

Black, Larry D. (Mr. 3, 1949, Scottsboro, AL) Dir. of Main Lib., Pub. Lib. of Columbus, 1977–; Dir., Lib. Srvs., Troy State Univ., 1976–77; Dir., Baldwin Cnty. Lib. Syst., 1973–77; Asst. Dir., Mobile Coll., 1972–73. **Educ.:** Univ. of AL, 1967–71, BA (Hist.), 1971–72, MLS (Lib. Srv.); OH State Univ., 1978–81, MPA (Pub. Admin.). **Orgs.:** ALA: PLA, Pubns. Com. (Ch., 1979–80). OH LA: Ctrl. Reg. Conf. Com. (Ch., 1979). Amer. Socty. for Pub. Admin. **Activities:** 9; 17, 26, 35; 56, 59, 75 **Addr.:** Main Library, 96 S. Grant Ave., Columbus, OH 43215.

Black, Lawrence (My. 28, 1940, New York, NY) Sr. Libn., NY State Inst. for Basic Resrch. in Mental Retardation, 1968–; Lib. Assoc., Gen. Univ. Lib., NY Univ., 1967–68; Hosp. Libn., Vet. Admin. Hosp., Northport, NY, 1965–66; Tchr., New York City Bd. of Educ., 1963–64. **Educ.:** Long Island Univ., 1960–63, BA (Hist.); Pratt Inst., 1964–65, MLS; NY Univ., 1967–73, MA (Hebrew Culture); Columbia Univ., 1974–81, Cert. AL. **Orgs.:** Med. LA: NY Reg. Grp. Brooklyn, Queens, Staten Island Med. Lib. Grp. **Pubns.:** Complr., *Bibliography of the Writings of Dr. George A. Jervis* (1978); Jt. complr., *Bibliography on Idiot Savants* (1978); Complr., *A Bibliography of Bibliographies on Mental Retardation, 1963–June 1975* (1975). **Activities:** 12, 13; 17, 39, 46; 57, 58, 80 **Addr.:** New York State Institute for Basic Research in Mental Retardation, 1050 Forest Hill Rd., Staten Island, NYC, NY 10314.

Black, Sandra Mary (My. 9, 1935, Toronto, ON) Actg. Chief Libn., Mohawk Coll., 1972–; Systs. Libn., Univ. of MB, 1970–71; Systs. and Ref. Libn., McMaster Univ., 1968–70; Info. Ofcr., IBM Can., 1962–67, Instr., 1960–62. **Educ.:** Queen's Univ., 1954–57, BA (Econ., Eng., Fr.); Ryerson Polytech., 1964–65 (PR); Univ. of Toronto, 1967–68, BLS, 1977–81, MLS. **Orgs.:** Can. LA: Info. Srvs. Coord. Grp. (1972–75); Can. Assn. Coll. and Univ. Libs., Lcl. Arrange. Prog. Coord. (1980–81). Wkshp. on Lib. Instr.: Strg. Com. (1980–). Queen's Univ. Alum. Assn.: Toronto Pres., Secy. (1964–66); Hamilton Secy., Pres. (1974–79). **Pubns.:** Jt. auth., *Resources For Searching the Literature: With Examples in the Field of Business - Economics* (1969); "Personality–Librarians as Communicators," *Can. Lib. Jnl.* (Ap. 1981). **Activities:** 1; 17, 31, 39; 56, 59 **Addr.:** Mohawk College, Box 2034, Hamilton, ON L8N 3T2 Canada.

Blackaby, Sandra L. (D. 6, 1945, Redding, CA) Head Libn., Treasure Valley Cmnty. Coll., 1974–; Head Libn., New Plymouth, ID HS, 1973–74; Fr. Tchr., Wichita, KS HS, 1969–72. **Educ.:** Univ. of OR, 1964–68, BA (Fr.), 1972–73, MLS; Institut. Catholique de Paris, France, 1967–68, Degré Supérieur d' études françaises. **Orgs.:** ALA. OR LA. East. OR LA:Ch. (1976–77). various other organizations. Phi Beta Kappa. Beta Phi Mu. **Addr.:** T.V.C.C. Library, 650 College Blvd., Ontario, OR 97914.

Blackburn, Alice K. (F. 2, 1917, La Junta, CO) City Libn., Neill Pub. Lib., 1964–; Ref. Libn., Univ. of WA, 1959–64, Libn., Bur. of Bus. Resrch., 1942–47. **Educ.:** Univ. of WA, 1937–41, BA (Eng.), 1941–42, BLS (Libnshp.); Columbia Univ., 1970–71, MLS. **Orgs.:** WA State Adv. Cncl. on Libs. WA Cmnty. Lib. Cncl.: Ch., Secy. ALA. SLA: Puget Snd. Chap., Chrt. Mem. Fac. Women's Club, Univ. of WA: Constn. Com. (Ch., 1963–64). **Honors:** Phi Beta Kappa, 1941; Beta Phi Mu, 1971. **Pubns.:** Sr. auth., *NELSA Grant Report, Palouse Area Resource Sharing Service* (1978); asst. biblgphr., indxr., *Aluminum: An Industrial Marketing Appraisal,* various other pubns., *Bur. of Bus. Resrch.* (1941–44). **Activities:** 1, 9; 15, 17, 20 **Addr.:** N.W. 605 Charlotte St., Pullman, WA 99163.

Blackburn, Frank M. (My. 31, 1917, Akron, OH) Libn., W. TX State Univ., 1958–; Asst. to the Libn., Univ. of MO, 1956–58; Base Libn., Sheppard Air Force Base, 1953–56; Acq. Libn., AZ State Univ., 1951–53. **Educ.:** Kent State Univ., 1936–41, AB (Eng.); 1941–46, MA (Eng.); 1950–51, MA (LS). **Orgs.:** ALA. SWLA. TX LA: Dist. Chmn. (1960–62). TX Assn. of Coll. Tchrs. **Pubns.:** "Recruiting for Librarianship," *Coll. and Resrch. Libs.* (Nov. 1957). **Activities:** 1; 17 **Addr.:** One Windwood Pl., Canyon, TX 79015.

Blackburn, Robert H. (Fb. 3, 1919, Vegreville, AB, Can) Chief Libn., Univ. of Toronto, 1954–, Asst. Libn., 1947–54; Gen. Asst., Calgary Pub. Lib., 1945–46. **Educ.:** Univ. of AB, 1936–40, BA (Eng.), 1940–41, MA (Eng.); Univ. of Toronto, 1941–42, BLS; Columbia Univ., 1946–47, MS. **Orgs.:** Can. LA: Treas. (1953–56); Pres. (1958–59). Can. Assn. Coll. and Univ. Libs.: Pres. (1963–64). Assn. of Resrch. Libs.: Bd. of Dir. (1965–67, 1969). Can. Lib. Week: Co.-Ch. (1959). Streetsville Pub. Libn. Bd.: Ch. (1956–64). Ctr. for Resrch. Libs. Bd.: Ch. (1967). Bd. of Lib. Visitors, MA Inst. of Tech. (1970–73). Various other orgs. Adv. Com. on Sci. and Tech. Info., Natl. Resrch. Cncl., Can. (1961–73). **Honors:** Univ. of Waterloo, LL.D. (Hon.), 1965; Can. Centennial Medal, 1967; Queen's Jubilee Medal, 1977. **Pubns.:** Ed., *Joint Catalogue of Serials in Toronto Libraries* (1953); "Of Mice and Lions and Battleships and Interlibrary Things," *Qtly, Inst. of Prof. Libns. of ON* (1972); "Photocopying in a University Library," *Schol. Pub.* (1970); "Two Years with a Closed Catalogue," *Jnl. of Acad. Libnshp.* (1979); Various articles, poems, stories, briefs, and a radio play. **Activities:** 1; 17, 24; 56, 61, 78 **Addr.:** 5324 Durie Rd., Streetsville, ON L5M 2C7 Canada.

Blackmon, W. Dee (S. 18, 1921, Lancaster, SC) Dir., Abilene Pub. Lib. Syst., Big Country Lib. Syst., 1971–; Assoc. Dir., Stephen F. Austin State Univ., 1967–71; Dir., Sul Ross State Univ., 1965–67; Head, Ref. Dept., Hardin-Simmons Univ., 1963–65. **Educ.:** Univ. of AR, 1946–50, BSBA; Geo. Peabody Coll. for Tchrs., 1962–63, MALS. **Orgs.:** ALA. SWLA. TX LA. TX Mncpl. Lib. Dirs. Assn.: Pres. (1977–78). **Activities:** 9; 17, 34, 35 **Addr.:** Abilene Public Library, Abilene, TX 79601.

Blair, David C. (My. 23, 1947, Salem, OR) Asst. Prof. Comp. and Info. Systs., Univ. of MI, 1979–; Consultant, Bechtel Engin. Corp., 1977–79. **Educ.:** Whitman Coll., 1964–68, AB (Math/Phil.); Univ. of WA, 1972–73, MLS; Univ. of CA, Berkeley, 1973–79, PhD. **Orgs.:** ASIS. Assn. for Comp. Machinery. AAUP. Bay Area Artificial Intelligence Grp. **Honors:** Beta Phi Mu, 1973. **Pubns.:** "Searching Biases on Large, Interactive Document Retrieval Systems", *J. of the Amer. Socty. for Info. Sci.* (v 31 n 3); "Information Retrieval", *JASIS* (v 30 n 6). **Activities:** 14-Sch. of Bus. Adm.; 24, 26, 41; 56, 75 **Addr.:** Graduate School of Business Administration, University of Michigan, Ann Arbor, MI 48109.

Blair, Joan (My. 15, 1946, New York, NY) Dir. of Lib. Rel., C L Syst., Inc., 1974–; Reader Srvs. Libn., NY Univ., 1973–74; Staff Mem., Arthur D. Little, Inc., 1969–73; Libn., Taipei Amer. Sch., 1968–69. **Educ.:** Connecticut Coll., 1963–67, BA (Hist.); Simmons Coll., 1967–68, MLS; Neast. Univ., 1979, Mgt. Cert. **Orgs.:** ALA. ASIS. **Activities:** 17, 24; 56 **Addr.:** 81 Norwood Ave., Neutonville, MA 02160.

Blair, John C., Jr. (N. 26, 1938, Birmingham, AL) Comp. Applications Libn., TX A&M Med. Sci. Lib., 1981–, Info. Spec., 1979–81; Comp. Applications Spec., Info. Spec. in Systs. Analysis (New Orleans), 1976–79; Biling. Spec., New Orleans Pub. Schs., 1971–74. **Educ.:** Southwest. at Memphis, 1956–60, BA (Psy., Lang.); Univ. of NC, 1960–61, M Ed (Ling.); Univ. of Florence, Italy, 1965–66 (Art Hist., Italian); LA State Univ., 1976–77, MLS (Med./Data Prcs.); Med. LA, 1977, Cert. **Orgs.:** Med. LA: Entry-Level and Student Info. Netwk. (1977–78); Ad Hoc Com. to Dev. a Statement of Goals (1979–81); Med. Lib. Educ. Grp. (Secy., 1979–80). AECT. SLA. **Pubns.:** "Measurement and Evaluation of Online Services," *The Library and Information Manager's Guide to Online Services* (1980); "Online Drug Literature Searching: Excerpta Medica," *Online* (O. 1980); "Utilization of 1200 Baud for On-Line Retrieval in a Health Sciences Library," *Bltn. of the Med. LA* (Jl. 1980); "Chemical Compound Searching: Cross-Database and Cross-Vendor," *Online* (Ap. 1981); "Searching the Chemical Literature in the Health Sciences" crs. dev. with videotape (1981); various articles, bk. reviews, papers. **Activities:** 1, 12; 24, 26, 37; 56, 60, 80 **Addr.:** Texas A&M University, Medical Sciences Library, College Station, TX 77843.

Blair, Sr. Kathleen (F. 5, 1937, Erie, PA) Libn., Villa Maria Acad., Erie, PA, 1977–; Libn., Tchr., St. Peter Cathedral Ctr., Erie, PA, 1968–76; Libn., Blessed Sacrament Sch., Erie, PA, 1963–68; Tchr., St. Francis, Clearfield, PA, 1957–63. **Educ.:** Villa Maria Coll., Erie, PA, 1954–65, BS (Educ.); Edinboro State Coll., 1964–68, LS Cert.; Univ. of Pittsburgh, 1976–77, MS (LS). **Orgs.:** Cath. LA: West. PA Unit, VP (1979–81), Pres.-Designate (1981), Pres. (1981–83); Sec. Div., Geo. Rep. **Activities:** 10, 12; 31, 32, 39; 55, 75, 92 **Addr.:** Villa Maria Academy, 2403 W. Lake Rd., Erie, PA 16505.

Blair, Shirley Marlene (Ag. 27, 1938, Winnipeg, MB) Tchr., Libn., Maple Ridge Sch. Dist., 1974–; Tchr., 1959–73. **Educ.:** Univ. of BC, 1956–69, BEd; 1975–79, MEd (LS). **Orgs.:** Can Sch. LA. BC Sch. Libns. Assn.: Maple Ridge Chap. (Pres.). **Pubns.:** "Teachers and the School Resource Centre," *Can Lib. Jnl.* and *Can LS Socty. Jnl.* (Apr. 1978, 1979), reprinted in *The Library Media Specialist in Curriculum Development* (1981). **Addr.:** 12507 Grace St., Maple Ridge, BC V2X 5N3 Canada.

Blaise, Sue A. (My. 17, 1934, Tulsa, OK) Head Libn., Univ. of CA, San Diego, Med. Ctr. Lib., 1971–, Ref. Libn., Biomed. Lib., 1971, Head Catlgr., 1969–71; Lib. Consult., OK Dept. of Libs., 1968–69. **Educ.:** Univ. of OK, 1952–55, Cert. (Nursing), 1965–67, BA (Eng.), 1967–68, MLS; Med. LA, Cert. **Orgs.:** Med. LA. Med. Lib. Grp. of South. CA and AZ. **Pubns.:** "Developing Your Own Resource Library," *Infection Cntrl. and Urological Care* (1980). **Activities:** 1, 12; 15, 31, 39; 80 **Addr.:** University of California, San Diego, San Diego Medical Society, University Library, 225 W. Dickinson St., San Diego, CA 92103.

Blake, Fay M. (S. 15, 1920, New York, NY) Sr. Lectr., Sch. of Lib. & Info. Std., Univ. of CA, Berkeley, 1971–; Reader Srvs. Libn., CA Polytechnic Univ., 1976–77; Consult. NY State Educ. Dept., 1968–69; Head, Gifts & Exch., Univ. of CA, Los Angeles, 1961–68. **Educ.:** Hunter Coll., 1936–40, BA (Eng.); Univ. of So. CA, 1958–61, MS in LS; Univ. of CA, Los Angeles, 1961–70, MA (Eng.), PhD (Amer & Eng. Lit.); Univ. of Hokkaido, 1975, Cert. Cambridge Univ., 1976, Cert.; Univ. of London, 1979, Cert. **Orgs.:** CA LA: Pres. CA Soc. of Libns. (1979). ALA: Cnclr. (1978–). CA Libr. Srvs. Bd: (1978–81). Mod. Lang. Assn. Pop. Culture Assn. Amer. Std. Assn. **Honors** Phi Beta Kappa, 1939; Beta Phi Mu, 1961. **Pubns.:** *The Strike in the American Novel* (1972); "Frances Newman," *Journal of Library History* (1981);

Special Subjects/Services: 50. Adult educ.; 51. Advert./Mktg.; 52. Aerosp.; 53. Agric.; 54. Area std.; 55. Arts/Hum.; 56. Autom.; 57. Bibl./Prtg.; 58. Bio. sci.; 59. Bus./Fin.; 60. Chem.; 61. Copyrt.; 62. Documtn.; 63. Educ.; 64. Engin.; 65. Env.; 66. Eth. grps.; 67. Film; 68. Food/Nutr.; 69. Geneal.; 70. Geo.; 71. Geol.; 72. Handcpd.; 73. Hist.; 74. Int. frdm.; 75. Info. sci.; 76. Insr.; 77. Law; 78. Legis.; 79. Math./Comp. sci.; 80. Med.; 81. Metals; 82. Nat. resrcs.; 83. Newsp.; 84. Nuc. sci.; 85. Oral hist.; 86. Petr./Energy; 87. Pharm.; 88. Phys./Astr./Math.; 89. Readg.; 90. Relig.; 91. Sci./Tech.; 92. Soc. sci.; 93. Telecom.; 94. Transp.; 95. (other).

"Access to Information in a Post-Industrial Society", *The Information Society.* (1978); "Libraries in the Marketplace", *Background Readings in Building Library Collections* (1979); "Let My People Know - Access to Information in a Post-Industrial Society," *Wilson Library Bulletin* (Ja. 1978); Various articles. **Activities:** 11; 26, 41, 63; 74, 95-Info. & Ref. **Addr.:** 2398 Parker St., Berkeley, CA 94704.

Blake, John B. (O. 29, 1922, New Haven, CT) Chief, Hist. of Med. Div., Natl. Lib. of Med., 1961–; Cur., Div. of Med. Sci., Smithsonian Inst., 1959–61; Assoc. Cur., 1957–59; Asst. Hist., Rockefeller Inst. for Med. Resrch. (now Rockefeller Univ.), 1955–57. **Educ.:** Yale Univ., 1939–43, BA (Hist.); Harvard Univ., 1946–54, PhD (Hist.); Johns Hopkins Univ., Fellow, Inst. of the Hist. of Med., 1951–52; Yale Univ. Sch. of Med., Fellow, Hist. of Med., 1953–54, 1954–55. **Orgs.:** Med. LA. Amer. Assn. for the Hist. of Med: Secy.-Treas. (1956–67); Cncl. (1967–70); VP (1970–72); Pres. (1972–74). Amer. Hist. Assn. Hist. of Sci. Socty. Intl. Socty. of the Hist. of Med. **Honors:** CT State Med. Socty., Honorary M.D., 1966; Med. LA, Ida and George Eliot Awd., 1968; Amer. Assn. for the Hist. of Med., Welch Medal, 1980. **Pubns.:** Comp., *A Short Title Catalogue of Eighteenth Century Printed Books in the National Library of Medicine* (1979); Ed., *Centenary of Index Medicus, 1879–1979* (1980); "From Buchan to Fishbein; the Literature of Domestic Medicine," *Medicine without Doctors* (1977); "Early American Medical Literature," *Jnl. of the Amer. Med. Assn.* (Jl. 1976). Various other bks. and articles. **Activities:** 4; 17, 41, 45; 57, 58, 80 **Addr.:** History of Medicine Division, National Library of Medicine, 8600 Rockville Pike, Bethesda, MD 20209.

Blake, Margery S. (Ap. 14, 1928, Hartford, CT) Actg. Fac. Libn., John F. Kennedy Sch. of Gvt., Harvard Univ., 1978–; Spec. Libn., Princeton Univ. Libs., 1968–78; Asst. Ref. Libn., 1979–78. **Educ.:** Wellesley Coll., 1945–49, BA (Hist.); Columbia Univ., 1965–67, MS (LS). **Orgs.:** SLA: Soc. Sci. Div. (Mem. Ch. 1978–79). ALA. **Activities:** 1; 29, 31, 39; 95-pub. admin., 92 **Addr.:** 21 Lancaster St., Cambridge, MA 02140.

Blake, Martha A. (O. 14, 1945, San Diego, CA) Libn., U.S. Army Construct. Eng. Resrch. Lab, 1971–; Indxr., Amer. Geol. Inst., 1969–70. **Educ.:** Univ. of CA, Berkeley, 1963–66, BA (Paleon.); Univ. of IL, 1967–69, MS (Zlgy.); 1970–71, MS (LS). **Orgs.:** SLA: Milit. Libns. Div. (Ch., 1981–82). Beta Phi Mu: Alpha Chap. (Pres., 1980–81). Altrusa. **Activities:** 4, 12; 15, 29, 39; 64, 65, 74 **Addr.:** U.S. Army Construction Engineering Research Laboratory, Library, P.O. Box 4005, Champaign, IL 61820.

Blake, Virgil L. P. (D. 10, 1940, Groton, MA) Co-Adj. Instr., Rutgers Univ., G.S.L.I.S., 1978–; Dir., Media Resrc. Ctr., 1976–; Sch. Libn., Westborough Sr. HS, 1973–76; Soc. Std. Tchr., Various N.E. HS, 1965–71. **Educ.:** Clark Univ., 1958–62, AB (Hist.); Fitchburg State Coll., 1963–64, Cert. (Educ.); SUNY Albany, 1971–73, MLS; Rutgers Univ. 1976–, PhD Cand. **Orgs.:** ALA. NJ LA. **Pubns.:** Several reviews. **Activities:** 10, 11; 15, 26, 32; 63, 74 **Addr.:** Rutgers University, Grad. Sch. of Lib./Inf. Studies, 4 Huntington St., New Brunswick, NJ 08904.

Blakeley, Phyllis Ruth (Ag. 2, 1922, Halifax, NS, Can) Assoc. Archvst., Pub. Arch. of NS, 1977–, Asst. Arch., 1959–77, Sr. Resrch. Asst., 1957–59, Resrch. Asst., 1945–57; Elem. Sch. Tchr., Halifax NS, 1944–45. **Educ.:** Dalhousie Univ., 1939–42, BA, 1943–45, MA (Hist.). **Orgs.:** Assn. Can. Archvsts.: Educ. Com. (1976–78). Heritage Trust of NS: Pres. (1976–78). Zonta Intl.: Halifax Branch (Pres., 1968–69). Various other orgs. **Honors:** Order of Canada, 1979; Dalhousie Univ, LL.D. (Hon.), 1977; Can., Cert. for contrib. to Can. Hist. Heritage. **Pubns.:** Jt.-auth, *The Story of Prince Edward Island* (1963); *Nova Scotia, a brief history* (1955); *The Story of Nova Scotia* (1950); *Glimpses of Halifax, 1867–1900* (1949); various articles. **Activities:** 2; 17, 24, 41; 69, 95-Nova Scotian History. **Addr.:** Public Archives of Nova Scotia, 6016 University Avenue, Halifax, NS B3H 1W4 Canada.

Blakely, Florence Ella (S. 3, 1923, Clinton, SC) Asst. Univ. Libn., Col. Dev., Duke Univ., 1979–, Head, Ref. Dept., 1956–79, Ref. Libn., 1948–56; Branch Libn., Greenville Cnty. Lib., 1947–48; Ref. Libn., Greenville Pub. Lib., 1945–47. **Educ.:** Presby. Coll. Clinton, SC, 1940–43, BA (Eng., Hist.); George Peabody Coll., 1944–45, BS (LS), 1959–60, MALS. **Orgs.:** ALA: Cnclr. (1973–77). SE LA: Outstan. Auth. Com. (1979–81). NC LA: Exec. Bd. (1973–77). AAUP. AAUW: Durham Chap., Pres. **Honors:** ALA, RASD, Gilbert Isadore Mudge Awd., 1974; Cncl. on Lib. Resrcs., Flwshp., 1970; Phi Beta Kappa. **Pubns.:** "The North Carolina Union Catalog," *A Guide to Union Catalogs in The Southeastern States* (1965); "Perceiving Patterns of Reference Service," *RQ* (Fall 1971); "Current Newspaper Indexing in North Carolina," *NC Libs.* (Fall 1960). **Activities:** 1; 15, 17, 39; 55, 92 **Addr.:** Perkins Library, Duke University, Durham, NC 27706.

Blalock, Susan L. (Ja. 25, 1956, Ann Arbor, MI) Hist. Resrch., Suquamish Indian Tribe, 1978–. **Educ.:** Oberlin Coll., 1974–78, BA (Anthro., Psy.); CA State Univ., 1977 (Archaeological Fld. Sch.); Univ. of WA, 1979 (Oral Hist.). **Orgs.:** SAA. Amer. Assn. for State and Lcl. Hist. Oral Hist. Assn. **Pubns.:** Prod. asst., "Suquamish Elder" TV documentary (1980); asst., *1981 Suquamish Tribe Calendar* (1980). **Activities:** 2, 12; 15, 28, 41; 55, 66, 86 **Addr.:** 646 Dayton, Edmonds, WA 98020.

Blanchard, J. Richard (Mr. 3, 1912, Delphos, KS) Univ. Libn. Emeritus, Univ. of CA, Davis, 1974–; Univ. Libn., 1951–74; Div. Libn., Sci./Tech., Univ. of NE, Lincoln, 1949–51; Chief, Ref. Dept., U.S. Natl. Agr. Lib., 1947–49; Ref. Libn., Lib. of Congs., 1933–46. **Educ.:** Univ. of OK, 1929–33, AB (LS); George Washington Univ., 1934-35, AB (Eng.); Univ. of IL, 1950–53, MSLS. **Orgs.:** ALA: ACRL/Appld. Sci. Sect. (1956); Delegate, Int. Cong. of Libs. and Docmtn. Ctrs., Brussels (1955); Cncl. (1954-56, 1960–63); Univ. Libs. Sect. (Ch., 1973–74). CA LA: Pres., Coll. Univ. Resrch. Lib. Sect. (1953); Pres., Golden Empire Dist. (1954). Roxburghe Clb., San Francisco. Bk. Clb. of CA. Sacramento Bk. Collectors' Clb.: Pres. (1965). Audubon Socty.: Secy., Davis Ch. (1980–). **Honors:** ALA, Oberly Meml. Awd., 1960. **Pubns.:** Jt. auth., *Guide to Sources for Agricultural and Biological Research* (1980); Jt. Auth., *Literature of Agricultural Research* (1958); "Planning the Conversion of a College to a University Library," *Coll. and Resrch. Libs.* (Jl. 1968); "History of Agricultural Libraries in the U.S.," *Bicent. Symposium on Agr. Lit.*, Natl. Agr. Lib. (1975). **Activities:** 1; 17, 24; 58, 91, 95-Agr. **Addr.:** University Library, Special Collections Department, University of California, Davis, Davis, CA 95616.

Blanchard, Joan M. (My. 19, 1947, Auburn, NY) Dir., Ext. and Lib. Dev., NH State Lib., 1977–, Pub. Lib. Consult., 1972–77; Jr. Ref. Libn., Newark (NJ) Pub. Lib., 1970–72. **Educ.:** St. Mary's Coll., Notre Dame, IN, 1965–69, BA (Hist.); SUNY at Albany, 1969–70, MLS. **Orgs.:** NH LA: Contin. Educ. Com. (1977–). New England Lib. Assn.: Vice-Chmn., State Lib. Srvs. Sect. (1979–80). **Activities:** 9, 13; 27, 39 **Addr.:** NH State Library, 20 Park St., Concord, NH 03301.

Blanco, Mary Galligan (O. 19, 1946, Portsmouth, NH) Matrls. Ctr. Libn., Texas A & I Univ., 1980–; Biling. Ctr. Libn., 1976–80; Asst. Cat. Libn. 1973–76. **Educ.:** Univ. of TX, 1966–69, BA (Ling.); 1972–73, MLS. **Orgs.:** ALA. Natl. Libns. Assn. TX LA: Admin. RT (Secy.-Treas., 1979–80). Reforma. **Activities:** 1; 15, 20, 24; 63, 66, 95-Ling. **Addr.:** P.O. Box 2374, A&I, Kingsville, TX 78363.

Blank, Annette Chotin (Je. 1, 1925, New York, NY) Head, Ctrl. Chld. Dept., Enoch Pratt Free Lib., 1973–; Admin. Asst., Reisterstown Road Branch, 1973; Head Chld. Libn., Bkmobiles., 1964–71; Branch Libn., various branches, 1957–64. **Educ.:** Wilson Tchr.'s Coll., BS (Educ.); Univ. of South. CA, 1950–51, BS (LS). **Orgs.:** ALA: Mem. Promo. Task Force (1971–77); ALSC/Newbery-Caldecott Com. (1976). MD LA: Mem. Com. (1978–79). Jane Addams Peace Assn.: Chld. Bk. Awd. Com. (Ch., 1978–). **Pubns.:** Reviews of bks. and recs. **Activities:** 9; 21, 31, 42 **Addr.:** 5477 Cedonia Avenue, Baltimore, MD 21206.

Blank, Ruth (Jl. 26, 1917, Hartford, CT) Libn., Indian Cntr. Lib., San Jose, 1972–; Libn., Peninsula Conservation Cntr., 1971–72. **Educ.:** Columbia Univ., 1935–39, BS (Pharm.); San Jose State Univ., 1967–69, BA (Anthro.), 1969–71, MA (LS). **Orgs.:** ALA: RASD/Amer. Indian Mat. and Srvs. Com. CA LA. **Honors:** Edna B. Anthony Awd., San Jose State Univ. 1969; Beta Phi Mu, 1970. **Pubns.:** "Do Native Americans Want Libraries?", *American Indian Libraries Newsletter* (Spr. 1978); *What Shall Our Children Read? A selected Bibliography of Native American Literature for Young People* (1977). **Activities:** 12; 66 **Addr.:** Indian Center Library, 3485 East Hills Drive, San Jose, CA 95127.

Blankenburg, Judith B. (Ja. 10, 1933, Herndon, KS) Asst. Prof., Dept. Lib. Sci. and Educ. Media, James Madison Univ., 1969–; Asst. Libn., Madison Coll., 1969–71; Spec. Mtrls. Catlgr., Colby Cmnty. Coll., 1968–69; Sch. Libn., KS Pub. Sch., 1955–61, 1968–69; Sch. Libn., Dept. of Defense Schs., Europe, Japan, 1961–67; GED Instr., Bitburg Air Base, Germany, 1963–65. **Educ.:** Fort Hays State Univ., 1951–55, BA (Hist./Eng.); Emporia State Univ., 1968–69, ML (LS); Univ. of VA, 1974–. **Orgs.:** ALA. AASL. NCTE. VA Educ. Media Assn.: Intellectual Freedom Com., Ch. (1976–79). Higher Educ. Media Assn.; VA Ch. (1979–80. AECT: Int. Frdm. Com. (1976–79). Phi Delta Kappa. AAUP. **Activities:** 11; 20, 26, 48; 63, 74 **Addr.:** 551 Ott St., Harrisonburg, VA 22801.

Blanks, Eleanor Wilson (O. 13, 1927, Marlin, TX) Media Spec., Roosevelt HS, Des Moines (IA), 1979–; Media Spec., Kurtz Jr. HS, 1970–79; Libn., North HS, 1967–70; Libn., Maury Elem. Sch. (Richmond, VA), 1955–60; Libn., Marlin (TX) Elem. Sch. (1953–54). **Educ.:** TX Women's Univ., 1944–48, BA (Soclgy.); Univ. of TX, Austin, 1949–50, MA (Soclgy.), 1965–66, MLS. **Orgs.:** IA Educ. Media Assn.: Bd. of Dir. (1977–80); Pres. (1980–81). ALA. AECT. IA LA. Natl. Educ. Assn.; IA State Educ. Assn. **Activities:** 10; 31, 39, 48 **Addr.:** 635-46th St., Des Moines, IA 50312.

Blase, Nancy G. (D. 4, 1941, New Rochelle, NY) Asst. Nat. Sci. Libn., Univ. of WA, 1979–, MEDLINE Coord., Hlth. Sci. Lib., 1970–79, Ref. Libn., 1966–68; Ref. Libn., Biomed. Lib., Univ. of CA, Los Angeles, 1965–66. **Educ.:** Marietta Coll., 1960–64, BA (Bio.); Univ. of IL, 1964–65, MS (LS). **Orgs.:** ASIS. SLA. Geosci. Info. Socty. AAAS. **Honors:** Beta Phi Mu; Phi Beta Kappa. **Pubns.:** "An Experimental Cancer Information Service Using AM-TWX," *Bltn. of the Med. LA* (Ja. 1972); "An SDI-LINE Evaluation," *Bltn. of the Med. LA* (O. 1976). **Activities:** 1; 39; 58 **Addr.:** Natural Sciences Library, University of Washington, Seattle, WA 98195.

Blasingame, Ralph (O. 9, 1920, State Coll., PA) Prof., Grad. Sch. of Lib. and Info. Std., Rutgers Univ., 1964–; State Libn., PA State Lib., 1957–64; Asst. State Libn., CA State Lib., 1952–57; Asst. to the Dean, Sch. of Lib. Srv., Columbia Univ., 1950–52. **Educ.:** PA State Univ., 1938–42, BA (Eng.); Columbia Univ., 1946–73, BLS, MS (Lib. Sci), DLS. **Orgs.:** ALA: LAMA (Pres., 19–; Treas., 1964–68). **Honors:** St. Francis Coll., D. Litt. **Pubns.:** Various publications. **Activities:** 9, 13; 17, 24; 78 **Addr.:** 24 Pine Ridge Drive, East Brunswick, NJ 08816.

Blauvelt, Thomas J. (Mr. 10, 1944, New York City, NY) Dir., Ref. Srvs., N. Country Ref. and Resrch. Resrcs. Cncl., 1971–; Ref. Libn., Freeport Meml. Lib., 1969–71. **Educ.:** Cathedral Coll., Brooklyn, NY, 1962–66, BA (Phil.); Queens Coll., CUNY, 1968–69, MLS. **Orgs.:** ALA. NY LA: ILL Com. (1978–). SUNY/OCLC ILL Adv. Com. **Pubns.:** Ed., *Guide to Indexed Periodicals* (1979); *Microforms in North Country Libraries* (1979); "3 R's Bibliographic Center in Regional Reference Services," *Bookmark* (Spr. 1977). **Activities:** 3, 12; 34, 39 **Addr.:** North Country Reference and Research Resources Council, P.O. Box 568, Canton, NY 13617.

Blazek, Ronald D. (Je. 13, 1936, Chicago, IL) Prof., FL State Univ., 1981–, Assoc. Prof., 1971–81; Asst. Prof., Chicago State Univ., 1968–71, Head, Circ. Dept., 1965–68; Libn., Tchr., Chicago Pub. Schs., 1958–64. **Educ.:** Univ. of IL, 1954–56 (Hum.); Chicago Tchrs. Coll., 1956–58, BEd, 1958–61, MEd (Sch. Libnshp.); Univ. of IL, 1963–65, MS (LS), 1965–71, PhD. **Orgs.:** ALA: RASD, Adult Lib. Mtrls. Com. (Ch., 1975–77), various coms.; Lib. Educ. Div., Resrch. Com. (1974–78); ACRL Constn. and Bylaws Com. (1979–80)/Art Sect., Pubcty. Com. (Ch., 1975–77); LH RT, various coms. AALS. SE LA: Various coms. IL LA: Various coms. FL LA: Com. on Lib. and Cont. Ed. (1979–80); Acad. and Spec. Lib. Caucus, Nom. Com. (Ch., 1978–79). Various other orgs. **Honors:** FL State Univ., Cmdn. Provost's Tchg. Awd., 1977. **Pubns.:** *Influencing Students Toward Media Center Use: An Experimental Investigation in Mathematics* (1975); jt. auth., *The Black Experience: A Bibliography of Bibliographies, 1970–75* (1978); *Achieving Accountability in Media Centers* (forthcoming); various articles on lib. hist., tchg. techqs., ref. libnshp., bk. reviews. **Activities:** 1, 10; 16, 39; 55 **Addr.:** 2409 Limerick Dr., Tallahassee, FL 32308.

Bleiweis, Maxine A. (F. 4, 1951, Providence, RI) Dir., Lucy Robbins Welles Lib., 1979–; Dir., Kent Meml. Lib., 1974–79; Branch Head, Mercer Cnty. Lib., 1973–74. **Educ.:** Elmira Coll., 1969–72, BA (Soc. Sci.); Rutgers, 1972–73, MLS. **Orgs.:** Cap. Reg. Lib. Cncl.: VP (1977–). CT LA: Mem. Ch. (1977). **Honors:** Suffield Jaycees, Outstan. Young Woman, 1979. **Activities:** 9; 17 **Addr.:** Lucy Robbins Welles Library, 95 Cedar St., Newington, CT 06111.

Bloesch, Ethel (Je. 16, 1932, Manchester, MO) Asst. to the Dir./Lectr., Univ. of IA Sch. of LS, 1970–; Msc. Catlgr., Univ. of IA Libs., 1967–70. **Educ.:** Elmhurst Coll., 1949–53, BA (Msc.); Union Theo. Semy., 1953–55, MSM (Organ); Univ. of IL, 1964–67, MSLS. **Orgs.:** ALA: Beta Phi Mu Awd. Jury (1980); AALS. IA LA. Msc. LA: Insts. Com. (1972–75). State Lib. Comsn. of IA: Adv. Cncl. for Lib. Cont. Ed. (1976–). **Pubns.:** "Music Autographs and First Editions on Postage Stamps," *Fontes Artis Musicae* (Fall 1978); "Iowa. University of Iowa, School of Library Science," *Ency. of Lib. and Info. Sci.* (1975); Ed., *Univ. of IA Sch. of LS Nsltr.* (1970–); Reviews. **Activities:** 1, 11; 20, 25, 26; 55 **Addr.:** School of Library Science, 3087 Library, The University of Iowa, Iowa City, IA 52242.

Blomeley, Sherry Lynn (Ag. 23, 1948, Miami, FL) Libn., Management Science America (MSA), 1979–; Law Libn., Jones, Bird and Howell, 1978–79; Lib. Consult., St. of GA, Dept. of Offender Rehab., 1977; Law Libn., Kutak, Rock and Huie, 1976–78; Resrch. Libn., Landauer Assoc., 1973–75; Resrch. Libn., Andrew E. McColgan, MAI, 1973; Libn., Our Lady of the Assumption Sch., 1971–72. **Educ.:** Florida Presbyterian Coll., 1966–70, BA (Soclgy., Anthro.); Emory Univ., 1970–71, MLn (LS). **Orgs.:** SLA: Chap. Cabinet (1977–79). S. Atlantic Chap., Bd. of Dir. (1977–81), Pres. Elect (1977–78), Pres. (1978–79), Bltn. Ed. (1975–77); Pub. Rel. Com. (Ch., 1974–75). ASIS: Ga. Chap. Ch-Elect (1980–81). Atlanta Law Libs. Assn.: Various com. Acad. Thea., Avocational Co.: Performance Coord., Actor (1973). **Pubns.:** Reviews. **Activities:** 12; 17, 39, 41; 56, 59, 77 **Addr.:** Management Science America, Inc., Corporate Library, 3445 Peachtree Rd., N.E., Atlanta, GA 30326.

Blood, Richard W. (My 22, 1942, St. Paul, MN) Asst. Dir. Lib. for Circ. Srvs. and Autom., San Francisco State Univ., 1979–; Asst. to the Dir., for Systs. and Autom., Univ. of Houston, 1977–79; Ref. Libn., Univ. of TX, Austin, 1976–77. **Educ.:** Univ of MN, 1960–65, BS (Econ.); 1966–68, MA (Geo.); 1968–72, PhD (Geo.); Univ. of TX, Austin, 1974–75, MLS. **Orgs.:** ALA:

PROFESSIONAL ACTIVITIES: Institutions: 1. Acad. lib.; 2. Arch.; 3. Assn.; 4. Fed./Gvt. lib.; 5. Inst. lib.; 6. Mfr./Suppl.; 7. Milit. lib.; 8. Musm.; 9. Pub. lib.; 10. Sch. lib.; 11. Sch. of lib. sci.; 12. Spec. lib.; 13. State lib.; 14. (other). **Functions/Activities:** 15. Acq./Col. dev.; 16. Adult srvs.; 17. Admin.; 18. Apprais.; 19. Archit./Bldgs.; 20. Cat./Class.; 21. Chld. srvs.; 22. Circ.; 23. Cons./Pres.; 24. Consult.; 25. Cont. ed.; 26. Educ. lib. sci.; 27. Ext. srvs.; 28. Fund/Grants; 29. Gvt. pubs.; 30. Indx./Abs.; 31. Instr. lib. use; 32. Media srvs.; 33. Micro.; 34. Netwks./Coop.; 35. Persnl.; 36. PR; 37. Publshg.; 38. Recs. mgt.; 39. Ref. srvs.; 40. Repro.; 41. Resrch.; 42. Review.; 43. Secur.; 44. Serials; 45. Spec. col.; 46. Tech. srvs.; 47. Trustees/Bds.; 48. YA srvs.; 49. (other).

Com. on Eval. of Srvs.; Machine-Assisted Ref. Sec. (Ch., 1977–); Circ. Srvs. Sect.; Com. on Circ. Systs. Eval. (1979–). CA LA. **Honors:** Beta Gamma Sigma, 1965; Beta Phi Mu, 1975; Phi Kappa Phi, 1975. **Pubns.:** *Social Science Data File Directory* (1975); "Impact of OCLC on Reference Service", *Jrnl. of Acad. Libnshp.* (My. 1977); "Report on the Second Annual BATAB Users' Meeting", *Lib. Acq.* (1978). **Activities:** 1; 17, 22; 56, 70, 92 **Addr.:** San Francisco State, University Library, 1630 Holloway Ave., San Francisco, CA 94132.

Bloom, John Porter (D. 30, 1924, Albuquerque, NM) Cur. of Spec. Col. and Ed., *The Pac. Histn.*, Univ. of the Pac., 1980–; Sr. Spec., West. Hist. and Ed., *Territorial Papers of U.S.*, Natl. Arch., 1964–80; Ed., Natl. Srvy. Hist. Sites and Bldgs., Natl. Pk. Srvs., 1962–64; Asst. Prof. of Hist., Univ. TX, El Paso, 1956–60. **Educ.:** Univ. NM, 1942–47, AB (Inter-Amer. Affairs); Geo. Washington Univ., 1947–49, AM (U.S. Hist.); Emory Univ., 1949–56, PhD (U.S. Hist.); Reed Coll., 1943–44, USAF Cert., (Pre-Meteorol.). **Orgs.:** SAA: Philip Hamer Awd. Com. (Ch., 1979). Amer. Assn. for State and Lcl. Hist.: VA Ch., (1977–79), Awd. Com. West. Hist. Assn.: Pres. (1973–74); (VP, (1972–73); Secy. Treas. (1962–67). Org. of Amer. Histns.: Bicent. Com., (1974–76). Amer. Hist. Assn. Other orgs. **Pubns.:** Ed., *The American Territorial System* (1973); Ed., *Territorial Papers of the U.S.*, Vols. 27–28 (1975); "The Continental Nation–Our Trinity of Revoluntionary Testaments," *West. Hist. Qtly.* (Jan. 1975). **Activities:** 2; 37, 41; 73 **Addr.:** National Archives, Washington, DC 20408.

Bloom, Wendy B. (My. 19, 1948, Brooklyn, NY) YA-Ref. Libn., Harrison Pub. Lib., 1975–; Senior YA Libn., New York Pub. Lib., 1972–75; Libn., Morris Cnty. Free Lib., 1971–72. **Educ.:** Skidmore Coll., 1966–70, BA (Amer. Std.); Rutgers Univ., 1970–71, MLS. **Orgs.:** ALA: YASD. NY LA. Westchester LA. **Honors:** Beta Phi Mu, 1971. **Pubns.:** Annotated bibls. for G. Robert Carlsen's *Books and the Teenage Reader* (1980). **Activities:** 9; 31, 39, 48 **Addr.:** 9-6 Tudor Court, Pleasantville, NY 10570.

Bloombecker, Jay Joseph (D. 18, 1944, New York, NY) Dir., Natl. Ctr. for Comp. Crime Data, 1978–; Formerly head, Antitrust Sect., Los Angeles Cnty. Dist. Attorney's Ofc., 1978–. **Educ.:** City Coll. of NY, 1961–65, BA (Pol. Sci.); Harvard Law Sch., 1965–68, JD. **Orgs.:** ASIS. Assn. for Comp. Mach. Amer. Bar Assn.: Sect. of Sci. and Tech. Natl. Dist. Attorney's Assn.: Com. on Info. Systs. (Ch.). CA Dist. Attorney's Assn.: Law and Comp. Tech. Com. (Ch.). Various other orgs. **Pubns.:** *Investigation of Computer Crime;* "Demythologizing Computer Crime," *Proceedings,* Honeywell Info. Systs. Symps.; "(Appellate) Power to the People–A Primer of Prosecution Appeal in California," *Univ. of West Los Angeles Law Review* (Win. 1975); various other articles; reviews; Lectures. **Activities:** 12; 24, 25, 36; 77, 91, 95-comp. crime. **Addr.:** 2700 N. Cahuenga Blvd. St. 2113, Los Angeles, CA 90068.

Bloomfield, Masse (Ag. 20, 1923, Franklin, NH) Supvsr., Tech. Lib., Hughes Aircraft Co., 1962–; Admin. Asst., Gen. Dev. Div., Atomics Intl., 1957–62, Asst. Libn., 1956–57; Branch Chief, Acq. and Recs. Branch, Tech. Lib., US Nvl. Ordnance Test Station, 1953–55; Catlgr., US Dept. of Agr. Lib., 1951–53. **Educ.:** Univ. of NH, 1940–48, BS (Bacteriology); Carnegie Inst. of Tech., 1950–51, MLS. **Orgs.:** SLA: Advert. Mgr. for the S. CA Chap. Bltn. (1957); Elec. Com., Sci-Tech Div. (1965–66). ASIS. United Jewish Welfare Fund, W. Valley Div. (Ch., 1962–64). **Honors:** Disting. Flying Cross. **Pubns.:** *How to Use a Library* (1970); Jt. auth., *Man in Transition* (1973); other articles and reviews. **Activities:** 5, 12; 17; 52 **Addr.:** 20733 Stephanie Dr., Canoga Park, CA 91306.

Blooming, (Sr.) Mary Catherine (Ap. 13, 1936, Cleveland, OH) Dir., Relig. Educ., Holy Spirit Par., Uniontown, OH, 1981–; Dir., Media Srvs., Canton Ctrl. Cath. HS, 1975–81; Media Libn., Dio. of Youngstown, 1973–75; Asst. Catlgr., Youngstown State Univ., 1972–73; Libn., St. John HS, 1962–71. **Educ.:** Notre Dame Coll., Cleveland, 1953–59, BA (Educ., Eng.); Duquesne Univ., 1964–67, MEd (LS); Youngstown State Univ., 1971–73 (Educ.). **Orgs.:** ALA. Cath. LA: VP (1979–81); Pres. (1981–). PA LA. AMC Oper. Bd.: East. Reg. Film Ctr., OH. AAUW. Channel 45/49 Vid. Tape Lib. Com. **Honors:** PA LA, Cont. Ed. Grant, Kent State Univ., 1974. **Pubns.:** "The Role of Matter in Eastern Christian Spirituality," *Diakonia* (Win. 1975). **Activities:** 9, 10; 15, 48; 90 **Addr.:** 4824 W. Tuscarawas, Canton, OH 44708.

Bloss, Alexander B. (Apr. 13, 1943, Rochester, NY) Serials/Docum. Libn., Rochester Pub. Lib., 1979–; Catlgr., 1975–79; Head, Sci. and Tech. Div., 1974–75. **Educ.:** Univ. Rochester, 1960–65, BA (Eng.); Case West. Resrv. Univ., 1965–66, MSLS. **Orgs.:** ALA: Com. to Study Serials Cat. (1981–); Chld. Mtrls. Cat. Com. (Ch., 1979–81). **Activities:** 9; 20, 44; 91 **Addr.:** Rochester Public Library, 115 South Ave., Rochester, NY 14604.

Bloss, Marjorie E. (Mr. 5, 1944, Brooklyn, NY) *Un. List of Serials* Proj. Dir., Rochester Reg. Resrch. Lib. Cncl., 1979–; Asst. Prof., LS, SUNY, Geneseo, 1975–; Head, Tech. Srvs., Rochester Inst. of Tech., 1976–78, Head, Serials Div., 1974–75, Serials Catlgr., 1971–74; Army Libn., U.S. Spec. Srvs., Goeppingen, Germany, 1968–71; Army Libn., U.S. Spec. Srvs., Ft. Benning, GA, 1967; Ref. Libn., Rochester Pub. Lib., 1966–67. **Educ.:** Univ. of Rochester, 1961–65, BA (Eng.) Case West. Rsv. Univ., 1965–66, MLS (Acad. Lib.). **Orgs.:** ALA: Un. Lists of Serials Com. (Ch., 1980–); RTSD/Serials Sect., Policy and Resrch. Com. (1978–80); ASCLA, Legis. Com. (1979). **Pubns.:** *Rochester 3R's Union List of Serials* (1981); *Location Guide to Engineering Standards and Related Materials in Rochester Area Libraries* (1980). **Activities:** 1, 13; 20, 34, 46 **Addr.:** Rochester Regional Research Library Council, 339 East Ave., Rm. 300, Rochester, NY 14604.

Bloss, Meredith (D. 17, 1908, Prairieville, MI) Retired, 1978–; City Libn., New Haven Free Pub. Lib., 1959–78; Asst. City Libn., Milwaukee Pub. Lib., 1952–59; Asst. Libn., Pub. Lib. Of Youngstown and Mahoning Cnty., OH, 1948–52; Libn., Adriance Meml. Lib., 1946–48; Dir., PR, Asst. Libn., Hartford Pub. Lib., 1940–43. **Educ.:** Oberlin Coll., 1929–32, AB (Eng. Lit.); Columbia Univ., 1939–40, BS (LS). **Orgs.:** CT LA: Pres. (1966–67); *CT Libs.* Ed. (1967–74). ALA: PLA, Goals, Guidelines and Stans. Com. (Ch., 1974–76); Lib. Srv. to Functionally Illiterate Com. (1965–66); Com. on Lib. Srv. to the Disadv. (Ch., 1973–74); Com. on Econ. Oppt. Prog. (1967–68). Univ. of WI Lib. Sch.: Lib. Mtrls. Resrch. Proj., Adv. Com. (1966–67). **Pubns.:** "Conversations on Libraries," *Lib. Jnl. Spec. Rpt. #12* (1979); "Research; and Standards for Library Service," *Lib. Resrch.* (Mr. 1981); "Standards for Library Service: Quo Vadis?" *Lib. Jnl.* (Je. 1, 1976); "Branch Collections," *Lib. Trends* (Ap. 1966); "New Alignment Based in Part on Library Ideals," *Wilson Lib. Bltn.* (My. 1967); various articles. **Activities:** 9; 17 **Addr.:** Box 2356, Short Beach, CT 06405.

Blouin, Francis X., Jr. (Jl. 29, 1946, Belmont, MA) Asst. Prof., LS, Univ. of MI, 1979–; Lectr., LS, 1977–79; Lectr., Hist., 1976–; Dir., Bentley Hist. Lib., 1981–. **Educ.:** Univ. of Notre Dame, 1963–67, AB (Hist.); Univ. of MN, 1970–78, PhD (Hist.). **Orgs.:** SAA. AALS. Org. of Amer. Histns. Econ. Hist. Assn. **Pubns.:** Jt. auth., *Sources for the Study of Migration and Ethnicity* (1979); "A New Perspective on the Appraisal of Business Records," *Amer. Archvst.* (1979); "The Relevance of the Case Method to Archival Education," *Amer. Archvst.* (1978). **Activities:** 2; 26, 45 **Addr.:** Bentley Historical Library, University of Michigan, 1150 Beal Ave., Ann Arbor, MI 48109.

Blouin-Cliche, Odette (D. 26, 1937, PQ) Dir. of the Lib., Bibl. Admin., Gvt. de PQ, 1976–; Dir. of the Lib., PQ Pension Bd., 1965–76; Ref. Libn., Univ. Laval, 1964–65, Catlgr., 1958–63. **Educ.:** Coll. des Ursulines, 1953–57, BA (Hum.); Univ. de Montréal, 1963–64, BBibl (LS); École Natl. D'Admin. Pub., Univ. du PQ, 1974–77, MAdmin. Pub. **Orgs.:** ASTED: Comsn. des Bibl. de Recherche et Spéc. **Pubns.:** Cont., *Guide Pratique de Correspondance* (1976); "Politiques D'Acquisition dans les Bibliothèques Spécialisees" (1970); "Le Financement des Services Documentaires au Gouvernement Du Québec," *ARGUS* (Ap. 1980). **Activities:** 4, 12; 17, 41; 59, 63, 93 **Addr.:** Bibliothèque Administrative, Ministère des Communications, Edifice G, 1037 de la Chevrotière, Québec, PQ G1R 4Y7 Canada.

Blount, Edward F. (D. 26, 1916, Holyoke, MA) Asst. Libn., Holyoke Pub. Lib., 1977–; Asst. Libn., Ref. Libn., Bates Coll., 1967–76; Sr. Subj. Catlgr., Yale Univ., 1959–67; Sr. Serials Catlgr., 1957–59; Catlgr., Amherst Coll., 1955–57; Instr., Capital Univ., 1949–50. **Educ.:** Yale Univ., 1935–39, BA (Hist.); Harvard Univ., 1939–40, MA (Hist.); Columbia Univ., 1953–55, MS (LS); 1976–77, Cert. (Adv. Libnshp.). **Orgs.:** NY Tech. Srvcs. Libns.: Nom. Com. (Ch., 1960–61); Prog. Com. (1962–63). ME LA: Plng. and Dev. Com. (1972–73). ME Acad. and Resrch. Libns.: Strg. Com. (Ch., 1974–75). ALA. Other orgs. Holyoke Rotary Club. **Pubns.:** *Historical Notes on the Construction of the First Universalist Church, Auburn, Maine, One Hundred Years Ago* (1976). **Activities:** 1, 9; 17, 39, 46; 92 **Addr.:** 35 Lindor Hts., Holyoke, MA 01040.

Blowers, Malcolm E. (Ap. 15, 1939, Rochester, NY) Univ. Libn., Assoc. Prof. Bibl., Univ. of NC, Asheville, 1977–; Lib. Dir., Findlay Coll., 1975–77; Ref. Libn., Assoc. Prof., Univ. TN, 1972–75; Asst. Prof., Greenville Coll., 1967–69; Asst. Prof., Roberts Wesleyan Coll., 1969–71. **Educ.:** Roberts Wesleyan Coll., 1963, BA (Hist.); OH State Univ., 1964, MA (Hist.); Univ. IL, 1966–67, Doct. crs.; 1972 MSLS; Univ. of TN, 1975–, Doct. Cand. **Orgs.:** ALA: Ref. Bks. Com. (1975–79). NC LA. **Honors:** Beta Phi Mu; Phi Alpha Theta; Phi Delta Kappa. **Pubns.:** "On Futurism, Educational Folklore, and the Learning Society," *Lrng. Today* (Sum. 1975); "Library-College Mid-Seventies Style: Maverick or Mainstream of Librarianship?" *TN Libn.* (Spr. 1974); "On Futurism and Continuing Education: An Exploratory Essay," *TN Adult Educ.* (Win. 1975); other papers; reviews. **Activities:** 1; 17, 31; 63, 92 **Addr.:** D. Hiden Ramsey Library, University of North Carolina at Asheville, Asheville, NC 28804.

Bludnicki, Mary A. (O. 28, 1950, Derby, CT) AV Libn., Asst. Libn., Lrng. Resrc. Ctr., Clinton Cmnty. Coll., 1980–. **Educ.:** Sacred Heart Univ., Bridgeport, CT, 1968–72, BA (Soclgy.); Univ. of Denver, 1975–76, MSLS (Libnshp.); South. CT State Coll., 1978–80, MSEd (Educ. Media). **Orgs.:** CS LA: CT Chap. (Pres., 1980–81). ALA. AECT. **Pubns.:** "A Study of Congregational Libraries," *Church and Synagogue Libs.* (Mr.–Ap. 1978). **Activities:** 1; 32; 67, 93 **Addr.:** 6 McMartin St., Apt. 4, Plattsburgh, NY 12901.

Blue, Margaret Linn (Je. 15, 1934, Seattle, WA) Prin. Lib., Tech. Srvs., Chula Vista Pub. Lib., 1974; Dir. Srvs., San Diego Pub. Lib., 1973; Ref. Libn., U.S.I. Univ., CA West. Campus, 1969–73; Coord., Lib. Educ., OK State Univ., 1967–68; Asst. Prof., San Diego State Coll., 1966–67; Elem. Sch. Libn., Ctrl. WA State Coll., 1961–65; Asst. Libn., Univ. of Portland, (OR), 1959–61; Actg. Libn., Marylhurst Coll., (OR), 1957–58. **Educ.:** Marylhurst Col., 1952–56, AB, (Eng. Lit.); Univ. of WA, 1958–59, MLS; Columbia Univ., 1965–66, (Cert. Adv. Lib.). **Orgs.:** ALA. **Activities:** 1, 9; 26, 39, 46 **Addr.:** 4411 Santa Monica Ave., San Diego, CA 92107.

Blue, Margaret R. (Mr. 16, 1934, Le Mars, IA) Chief, Cat. Dept., The John Crerar Lib., 1973–, Serials Catlgr., 1970–72; Serials Catlgr., Univ. of NE, 1969–70, Asst. Libn., Sci. and Tech., 1967–69. **Educ.:** Cornell Coll., 1952–56, BA (Math.); OH State Univ., 1956–61 (Math.); Univ. of Pittsburgh, 1966–67, MLS. **Orgs.:** ALA. SLA. Phi Beta Kappa Assn. of Chicago. Morgan Park Presby. Church: Bd. of Trustees, Secy. **Honors:** Phi Beta Kappa, 1955; Beta Phi Mu, 1967. **Activities:** 1, 12; 20, 44; 80, 91 **Addr.:** 11643 S. Hale Ave., Chicago, IL 60643.

Blue, Richard I. (O 19, 1941, Saginaw, MI) Doct. cand., Univ. of IL, 1975–; Actg. Dir., Lib. Rsrch. Ctr., Univ. of IL, 1978–79; Branch Libn., Flint Pub. Lib., 1973–75; Libn. I Bus. & Indus. Dept., 1971–73. **Educ.:** MI State Univ., 1966–67, BA (Russ.); Univ. of MI, 1970–72, MALS. **Orgs.:** ALA. SLA. ASIS. **Pubns.:** "Directory of U.S. Full-Text System Vendors", "Questions for Selection of Information Retrieval Systems", *OL Review* (1979); Jt auth., "Optimizing Selection of Library School Student", *Jnl. of Educ. for Libnshp.* (forthcoming. 1981). **Activities:** 9, 11; 17, 26, 41; 56, 75, 93 **Addr.:** 410 David Kinley Hall, Graduate School of Library and Information Science, University of Illinois, Urbana, IL 61801.

Blum, Fred (N. 27, 1932, New York, NY) Prof., Ref. Libn., East. MI Univ., 1980; Dir., Ctr. of Educ. Resrcs., 1974–79; Head, Tech. Srvs., Cath. Univ. of Amer., 1971–74; Head, Spec. Srvcs. Dept., 1967–71; Ed., Natl. Regis. of Micro. Masters, Lib. of Congs., 1966–67; Ref. Libn., Msc. Div., 1961–66. **Educ.:** Oberlin Coll., 1950–54, BM (Msc.); OH Univ., 1954–55, MFA (MSC); Univ. IA, 1955–59, PhD (Msc.); Cath. Univ. of Amer., 1966–68, MSLS. **Orgs.:** ALA: Amer. Natl. Stand. Inst. Com. Z39 on Lib. Work, Docum., and Related Publshng. Prac. (Rep., 1972–77); ACRL/Pubns. Com. (1971–73; Ch., 1973–76)/Ed. Bd. (1974–80). Beta Phi Mu: Iota Chap. (Pres. 1973–74). MI Lib. Cnsrtm.: Trustee (1973–79); Bd. of Trustees (Vice Ch. 1977–78). Msc. LA: AV and Micro. Com. (Ch., 1966–74). Other orgs. Rotary Intnl.: Ypsilanti Clb. Schol. Com. (Ch. 1975–80); Dist. 638, Educ. Awds. Com. (1979–80). **Pubns.:** *Music Monographs in Series* (1964); *Jean Sibelius; An International Bibliography* (1965); *Guide to Selected Research Materials on Microform.* (1968); "Santayana's Music Aesthetics," *Jnl. of Amer. Msclgy. Socty.* (Spr. 1958); "Catholica on Microforms," *Cath. Lib. World* (May/June 1969); "Standards Update" and "International Standards Update," *LRTS* (Win., Fall 1974); Asst. Ed., *D.C. Libs.* (1968–70). **Activities:** 1; 17, 26, 39; 55, 92 **Addr.:** 3161 Lakehaven Dr., Ann Arbor, MI 48105.

Blum, John P. (Ap. 2, 1930, Warren, OH) Dir., NM Supreme Court Lib., 1967–; Cur., Musm of NM, 1962–67; Asst. Libn., Berkeley Pub. Lib., 1960–61; Circ. Asst., Univ. of NM Lib., 1957–59. **Educ.:** Univ. of NM, 1952–57, BA (Anthro.); Univ. of CA, Berkeley, 1960–61, MA; Univ. of CA, Boalt Hall Sch. of Law, 1968, Cert. (Law Lib. Adm.). **Orgs.:** AALL: Nom. Com.; Place. Com. Southwest Assn. of Law Libs. **Activities:** 12; 17; 77 **Addr.:** P.O. Drawer L, Santa Fe, NM 87501.

Blum, Judith Evans (Jl. 31, 1950, Lawrence, KS) Resrch. Assoc., Denver Resrch. Inst., 1977–; Libn., Bemis Pub. Lib., 1977–78; Libn., Summit Cnty. Lib., 1973–76; Rpt., *Summit Sentinel,* 1972–74. **Educ.:** Middlebury Coll., 1968–72, BA (Amer. Lit.); Univ. of Denver, 1976–77, MA (Libnshp., Info. Mgt.). **Orgs.:** ASIS. Intl. Assn. for the Advnc. of Appropriate Tech. for Dev. Countries. Socty. for Appld. Lrng. Tech. **Honors:** Beta Phi Mu, 1977. **Pubns.:** *Information Handbook: Techniques and Tools for Scientific and Technical Information Service in Developing Countries* (forthcoming); various presentations. **Activities:** 12; 24, 41; 75 **Addr.:** Denver Research Institute/SSRE, University of Denver, Denver, CO 80208.

Blumberg, Janet L. (Ag. 22, 1941, Carlisle, PA) Chief, Consult. Srvs. Div., WA State Lib., 1979–; Consult., Contin. Ed., 1976–79; Supvsr., Persnl. Admin., Timberland Reg. Lib., 1975–76; Ext. Srvs. Libn., 1973–75; Resrch. Asst., Lib. Dev. Div., WA State Lib., 1971–73; Catlgr., 1970–1971. **Educ.:** Albright Coll., 1959–63, BA (Eng. Lit.); Univ. WA, 1969–70, ML (LS). **Orgs.:** ALA: Ofc. for Lib. Persnl. Resrcs. Adv. Com. (1979–81); ASCLA/Plng. Org. and Bylaws Com. (1979–1981); ASCLA/SLAS, Plng. Com. (1978–80), Cont. Ed. Com. (1977–78), Exec. Com. (1981–84). CLENE: Exec. Bd. (1977–78); Pres.-Elect (1980–81); Pres. (1981–82). PAC. NW LA: Lib. Educ. Div. (Ch.-Elect, 1979). LA: Conf. Treas. (1979); Conf. Ch. (1977); Secy. (1976–77); other coms. Other orgs. Natl.

Special Subjects/Services: 50. Adult educ.; 51. Advert./Mktg.; 52. Aerosp.; 53. Agric.; 54. Area std.; 55. Arts/Hum.; 56. Autom.; 57. Bibl./Prtg.; 58. Bio. sci.; 59. Bus./Fin.; 60. Chem.; 61. Copyrt.; 62. Documtn.; 63. Educ.; 64. Engin.; 65. Env.; 66. Eth. grps.; 67. Film; 68. Food/Nutr.; 69. Geneal.; 70. Geo.; 71. Geol.; 72. Handcpd.; 73. Hist.; 74. Int. frdm.; 75. Info. sci.; 76. Insr.; 77. Law; 78. Legis.; 79. Math./Comp. sci.; 80. Med.; 81. Metals; 82. Nat. resrcs.; 83. Newsp.; 84. Nuc. sci.; 85. Oral hist.; 86. Petr./Energy; 87. Pharm.; 88. Phys./Astr./Math.; 89. Readg.; 90. Relig.; 91. Sci./Tech.; 92. Soc. sci.; 93. Telecom.; 94. Transp.; 95. (other).

Audubon Socty. **Activities:** 9, 13; 17, 24, 25 **Addr.:** Washington State Library AJ-11, Olympia, WA 98504.

Blume, Julie (S. 9, 1953, Washington, DC) Dir. of Educ., Med. Lib. Assn., 1980–; Coord. of User Educ./Ref. Libn., Univ. of NC Hlth. Scis. Lib., 1977–79; Asst. Dir. of Educ., Med. Lib. Assn., 1975–77; Resrch. Tech., Duke Univ. Aging Ctr., 1972–74. **Educ.:** Duke Univ., 1970–74, AB (Russ.); Univ. of Chicago, 1974–75, AM (LS); Cert. Med. LA, 1976, (LS). **Orgs.:** ALA: Lib. Educ. Div. Cont. ed. Com. (1975–77); ACRL Cont. ed. Com. (1977–79); Stdg. Com. on Lib. Educ. (1977–80); and ASCLA Prog. Comm (1980–81); various other coms. Med. LA, Recert. Com. (1978–80); CLENE Treas., Bd. of Dirs. (1978–80); AALS. **Honors:** Phi Beta Kappa, 1974; Beta Phi Mu, 1976. **Pubns.:** "Assuring Professional Competence through Education or Examination: Bibl." (1977); (ALA. Ofc. for Lib. Persnl. Resrcs.). **Activities:** 1, 12; 25, 26, 35; 50, 63, 80 **Addr.:** Div. of Educ. Medical Library Association, 919 N. Michigan Ave., Suite 3208, Chicago, IL 60611.

Boardman, Charlotte K. (N. 9, 1917, Cedar Grove, NJ) Libn., EDO Corp., 1972–; Libn., Amer. Smelting and Refining Co., Ctrl. Resrch. Labs., 1968–72; Libn., Catlgr., Ref., Gen. Precision Aerosp., 1964–68; Libn., Info. Tech. Div., Lockheed Electronics Co., 1962–64; Libn., Thomas A. Edison, Inc., 1948–57. **Educ.:** Skidmore Coll., 1936–38 (Sec. Sci.); Rutgers Univ., 1957–64, AB (Math.), 1964–67, LS. **Orgs.:** SLA: NJ Chap., Past Secy.; NY and Long Island Chaps., Nom. Com. (1974). **Activities:** 12; 17, 20, 43; 52, 64, 81 **Addr.:** EDO Corp., Government Products Div., Engineering Library, College Point, NY 11356.

Boast, Carol (O. 4, 1944, Waukegan, IL) Actg. Dir., Law Lib., Univ. of IL, 1980–, Asst. Law Libn., Head, Acq. and Ref., Docum. and Ref., Asst. Agr. Libn., Agr. Lib. **Educ.:** IA State Univ., 1962–65, BS (Math.); Univ. of IL, 1963, MS (Pol. Sci.), MLS. **Orgs.:** AALL: Com. on the Index to Pers. Mid-Amer. Assn. of Law Libs.: VP, Pres.-Elect (1980). **Honors:** Univ. of IL Law Sch., Spec. Awd. for Disting. Srv. to the Class of 1976, 1976. **Pubns.:** Jt. auth., *Subject Compilations of State Laws: Research Guide and Annotated Bibliography* (1981); jt. auth., *Illinois Legal Research Sourcebook* (1977); jt. auth., "The Monthly Catalog, July 1976–Aug. 1977," *Gvt. Pubns. Review* (1978); jt. auth., *Planning, Housing, and Environmental Looseleaf Services* (1978); jt. auth., "Current Subject Compilations of State Laws: Research Guide and Annotated Bibliography," *Law Lib. Jnl.* (Spr. 1979); various articles. **Addr.:** 104 J Law, University of Illinois, 504 E. Pennsylvannia Ave., Champaign, IL 61820.

Boaz, Martha T. (Stuart, VA) Resrch. Assoc., Annenberg Ctr., Univ. of South. CA, 1979–; Dean and Prof., Sch. of LS, Univ. of South. CA, 1955–79, Assoc. Prof., 1953–55; various positions in coll. and univ. libs., 1935–53. **Educ.:** Madison Coll., 1932–35, BS (Eng.); George Peabody Coll., 1937, BS (LS); Univ. of MI, 1950, MS, 1955, PhD (LS). **Orgs.:** ALA: Lib. Educ. Assoc. (Pres., 1968–69). AALS: Pres. (1962–63). CA LA: Pres. (1962). Many other memberships and offices. Los Angeles LA: Bd. of Dir. (1970–80); Beta Phi Mu: Pres. (1962). **Honors:** Univ. of MI, Sesquicentennial Awd., 1967; Beta Phi Mu, Nat. Awd. for Disting. Srv. to Lib. Educ., 1974. **Pubns.:** Ed., *Current Concepts in Library Management* (1980); Ed., *Towards the Improvement of Library Education* (1973); "Academic Libraries - Some Issues - No Answers," *Jnl. Acad. Libnship.* (S. 1975); "Censorship," *Ency. of Lib. and Info. Sci.* (1970); "The Living Library" *36 TV shows* (1970); many other publications. **Activities:** 1, 11; 17, 26, 39; 63, 74, 92 **Addr.:** 1849 Campus Rd., Los Angeles, CA 90041.

Boaz, Ruth Lavonne (Mr. 27, 1926, Water Valley, KY) Educ. Prog. Spec., Natl. Cntr. for Educ. Stats., 1968–; Asst. Libn. and Sr. Lib. Supvsr., NY State Educ. Dept., 1964–68; Cir. Asst., Memphis Pub. Lib., 1960–64; Catlgr., Methodist Publshg. House Lib., 1956–59; Libn. I, San Francisco State Coll., 1954–55; Asst. Libn., IL Wesleyan Univ., 1953–1954; Libn., Wynne AR HS, 1951–52. **Educ.:** Memphis State Coll., 1946–48, BS (Eng.); George Peabody Coll., 1951–53, MA (Lib. Sci.); Vanderbilt Univ. Divinity Sch., 1955–59. **Orgs.:** ALA. Natl. Cmnty. Educ. Assn. Adult Educ. Assn. of the USA. Forum for Death Educ. and Couns. AAUW. **Pubns.:** *Participation in Adult Education, Final Report 1975* (1978); *Participation in Adult Education, Final Report, 1978* (1980). **Activities:** 14-Fed. Gvt. agency; 41, 49-Surveys, statistics; 50 **Addr.:** National Center for Education Statistics, 400 MD Ave., S.W., Washington, DC 20202.

Bob, Murray L. (F. 12, 1930, New York City, NY) Dir., Chautauqua-Cattaraugus Lib. Syst., Dir., James Prendergast LA, 1963–; Asst. Dir., Richmond (CA) Pub. Lib., 1961–63; Ref. Libn., Branch Head, Bk. Selector, Free Lib. of Philadelphia, 1953–61. **Educ.:** Coll. of the City of New York, 1947–51, BS (Soc. Sci.); State Tchrs. Coll., Albany, NY, 1952–53, MS (LS). **Orgs.:** NY LA: Pres. (1976); Legis. Ch. (1973). Pub. Lib. Syst. Dirs. Org.: Ch. (1972). **Pubns.:** *A Plan of Service for the Central Minnesota Libraries Exchange* (1980); *A Library System For Wayne and Pike Counties, Pennsylvania* (1979); *Regional Intertype Library Cooperation in Windham and Tolland Counties, Connecticut* (1978); "Access to Libraries and Information Services," *BookMark* (Fall 1978); "The Commercialization of Public Libraries," *NY LA Bltn.* (O. 1980). **Activities:** 9, 13; 17, 24, 28; 55, 72, 78 **Addr.:** 66 Andrews Ave., Jamestown, NY 14701.

Bobbie, Constance H. (Ag. 20, 1935, Dryden, ON) Asst. Cat. Libn., Edinboro State Col., 1971–; Cat., OH State Univ., 1962–71; Tchr., John Marshall Sr. High Sch., 1958–60; Tchr., Roseau Pub. Sch., 1956–58. **Educ.:** Bemidji State Col., MN, 1952–56, BS (Eng.); Univ. of MN, 1960–62, MA (Lib. Sci.); Univ. of Pittsburgh. **Orgs.:** ALA. PA LA: Tech. Srvcs. RT, Ch., (1975–76). AAUP: Edinboro State Col. VP (1977–78); Pres. (1978). **Honors:** Beta Phi Mu, 1962; Alpha Phi Sigma, 1956. **Activities:** 1; 20, 39, 44 **Addr.:** Baron-Forness Library, Edinboro State Col., Edinboro, PA 16444.

Bobick, James E. (Je. 7, 1943, Indiana, PA) Head, Col. Dept., Temple Univ., 1981–, Coord., Sci. Libs., 1975–; Adj. Prof., Sch. of Lib. and Info. Sci., Drexel Univ., 1977–; Coord., Sci. Libs., Temple Univ., 1975–; Biomed. Ref. Libn., Brown Univ., 1972–75; Instr., Bio., Coll. of Mt. Saint Joseph, 1968–71; Lectr., Bio., Saint Joseph Hall Prep. Sch., 1965–68. **Educ.:** IN Univ. of PA, 1961–65, BS (Bio.); Duquesne Univ., 1966–69, MS (Bio.); Univ. of IL, 1971–72, MSLS. **Orgs.:** ALA. Med. La: Srvys. and Stats. Com. (1978–81); Philadelphia Reg. Grp., Exec. Bd. (1980–82), Nom. Com. (Ch., 1979). SLA: Bio. Sci. Div. (Dir., 1980–82), Nom. Com. (Ch., 1979), *Nsltr.* Assoc. Ed. (1973–75), Ed. (1975–77); Philadelphia Chap., Nom. Com. (Ch., 1981). Amer. Assn. for the Hist. of Med. AAUP. **Pubns.:** "Patterns of Journal Use in a Departmental Library; A Citation Analysis," *Jnl. of the Amer. Socty. for Info. Sci.* (Jl. 1981); "Citation Data for Selected Journals in Reproductive Biology," *Fertility and Sterility* (F. 1981); "New Library Buildings: Part VI. Sciences Library, Brown University," *Bltn. of the Med. LA* (Ap. 1976); "Medical Periodicals of Rhode Island: Part I. Transactions of the Rhode Island Medical Society," *RI Med. Jnl.* (D. 1973); *Monograph Selection, Acquisition, and Management* (1981). **Activities:** 1; 15, 17, 26; 58, 80, 91 **Addr.:** Temple University, Paley Library, Rm. 211, Philadelphia, PA 19122.

Bobinski, George S. (O. 24, 1929, Cleveland, OH) Dean and Prof. SUNY, Buffalo, Sch. of Info. and Lib. Std., 1970–; Assoc. Prof., Asst. Dean, Univ. KY, Sch. of LS, 1967–70; Dir. of Libs., SUNY, Cortland, 1960–67; Asst. Dir., Royal Oak Pub. Lib., 1955–59; Ref. Asst., Cleveland Pub. Lib. Bus. Info. Bur., 1954–55; Milit. Intelligence Anal., U.S. Army, 1952–54. **Educ.:** Case West. Rsv. Univ., 1947–51, BA (Hist.); 1951–52, MSLS; Univ. MI, 1957–61, MA (Hist.); 1959–66, PHD (LS). **Orgs.:** ALA: Cncl. (1974–78); ACRL (Bd. Dir. 1973–77); Amer. Lib. Hist. RT (Ch., 1974–75); Pubshng. Com. (1975–79), Ch. (1975–1977); *Choice* Pubns. Bd., 1966–73, Ch., (1970–73). West. NY Lib. Resrcs. Cncl.: Bd. Dir. (Pres., 1972; VP, Pres.-Elect, 1981–82). NY LA. AALS. **Honors:** Beta Phi Mu. Cncl. on Lib. Resrcs., Fellow, 1973–74. Fulbright Schol. and Lectr. (Poland), 1977. **Pubns.:** *Carnegie Libraries: Their History & Impact on American Public Library Development* (1969); *Dictionary of American Library Biography* (1978); Contrib., *ALA Yrbk.; Encyc. Lib. and Info. Sci.; ALA World Encyc. of Lib. Sci.;* numerous articles. **Activities:** 11; 17, 24, 26 **Addr.:** School of Information and Library Studies, State University of New York at Buffalo, Buffalo, NY 14260.

Bobinski, Mary F. (Ag. 29, 1928, Rochester, NY) Dir., Amherst Pub. Libs., 1973–; Lectr., Univ. KY, Sch. of LS, 1968–70; Dir., Royal Oak Pub. Lib., Dept. of Work with Chld., 1955–59; Supvsr., Sch. Libs., Fort Bragg, 1953–54; Dir., Royal Oak Pub. Lib., Dept. of Work with Chldn., 1952–53. **Educ.:** Univ. Rochester, 1946–51, BA (Eng.); Case West. Rsv. Univ., 1951–52, MSLS. **Orgs.:** ALA: LITA/VCCS (Secy., 1977–1979); Video Dist. and Exch. Com. (Ch., 1974–75); PLA/Actv. Com. (1975–77), Mem. Com. (1976–78). NY LA: Pub. Lib. Sect. (VP 1977–78; Pres., 1978–79): Prof. Dev. Com. (Ch., 1976–77); Legis. Com. (1979–82). NY State Educ. Dept.: Pub. Lib. Cert. Com. (1976–). **Honors:** Beta Phi Mu. **Pubns.:** "Library Limelight," weekly TV prog. (1974–). **Activities:** 9; 17, 49-cable TV; lib. prog. **Addr.:** Amherst Public Library, 770 Hopkins Rd., Williamsville, NY 14221.

Boccaccio, Mary Andrea (N. 15, 1943, San Antonio, TX) Archvst., Univ. of MD, 1972–; Archvst., Rockefeller Fndn., 1969–71. **Educ.:** Albion Coll., 1961–65, BA (Hist.); Univ. of PA, 1965–66, MA (Hist.); Wayne State Univ., 1967–68, MSLS. **Orgs.:** SAA: Bldg. & Tech. Equipment (1973–77). Mid Atl. Reg. Arch. Conf.: Treas./Secy. (1972–76); Ed. (1974–77); Ed. Bd. (1978–). **Honors:** Phi Alpha Theta, 1963. **Pubns.:** Ed., *Paper & Leather Conservation* (1978); "Ground Itch & Dew Poison," *Jnl. of the Hist. of Med.* (1972). **Activities:** 1, 2; 15, 17, 20; 73 **Addr.:** Archives & Manuscripts Department, McKeldin Library, University of Maryland, College Park, MD 20742.

Bock, D. Joleen (S. 30, 1925, Bennington, KS) Dean, Lib. Srvs., Univ. of GU, 1980–; Prof., Educ. Media, Appalachian State Univ., 1977–80; Dean, Instr. Resrcs., Coll. of the Canyons, 1969–77; Dir., Lib. Srvs., Rio Hondo Coll., 1963–69; Libn., Whittier HS, Catlgr., Whittier Un. HS Dist., 1960–63; various instr. positions. **Educ.:** Univ. of Denver, 1943–47, BA (Thea.), 1947–48, MA (Thea.); Univ. of South. CA, 1961–63, MSLS (Coll. Lib.), 1973–76, Edd (Higher Educ.). **Orgs.:** ALA: Jr. Coll. Lib. Sect. (Ch., 1970–71); LAMA, Bd. of Dirs., Lib. Bldgs. Awd. Com., Bldgs. for Coll. and Univ. Libs. Com.; Lib. Admin. Div./Bldgs. and Equip., Cmnty. and Jr. Coll. Lrng. Resrcs. Ctrs. Facilities Com. (Ch., 1976–78); Lib. Educ. Com. on Para-prof. Trng. (1970–75); Amer. Inst. Archit.-ALA Jury, Natl. Lib. Dsgn. Awds. (1978). AECT: Cmnty. Coll. Assn. for Instr. and Tech. (Bd., 1973–75). Cncl. on Lib. Tech. Assts.: Bd. (1975–76). Amer. Assn. of Jr. Colls. Adv. Com. on Micro. Various other orgs. Ofc. of the Chancellor, CA Cmnty. Colls.: Adv. Com. for Lib./Media Tech. Asst. Trng. Progs. (1970–76). CA Lrng. Resrcs. Guidelines Com. **Pubns.:** *Learning Laboratories* (1980); jt. auth., *The LRC: A Planning Primer for Libraries in Transition* (1977); "From Library to LRC," *Cmnty. Coll. Frontiers* (Fall 1979); "Two-Year College LRC Buildings," *Lib. Jnl.* (D. 1978); "Role of the Library/Media Specialist in Curriculum Development," *OH Media Spectrum* (O. 1977); various articles, rpts, sems., confs. **Activities:** 1, 11; 17, 19, 24 **Addr.:** P.O. Box 22454, Guam Main Facility, GU 96921.

Bock, Rochelle L. (Je. 16, 1947, Baltimore, MD) Head, Ref. Dept., UC Irvine Biomedical Lib., 1979–; Coord. for Physician Srvs., Houston Acad. of Med.–TX Med. Cntr., 1977–79; Resrch. Asst., Univ. of Nottingham Med. Sch., England, 1976–77; Ref./Cat. Libn., Univ. of CO Med. Cntr. Lib., 1973–76. **Educ.:** Univ. of MD, 1965–69, BA (Eng.); 1972–73, MLS. **Orgs.:** Med. LA. Med. Lib. Grp. of South. CA and AZ: Exch. Com. Ch. (1979–80); Co-ch Legis. Com. (1980–81). **Pubns.:** Jt. auth., "Cataloging costs with CATLINE," *Bull. of the Med. LA* (O. 1975). **Activities:** 1; 36, 39, 41; 58, 80, 91 **Addr.:** University of California, Irvine/Biomedical Library, P.O. Box 19556, Irvine, CA 92713.

Bockman, Eugene J. (Jl. 23, 1923, New York, NY) Comsn., N.Y.C. Dept. of Recs. and Info. Srvs., 1977–; Dir., N.Y.C. Mncpl. Arch. and Recs. Ctr., 1975–77; Dir., N.Y.C. Mncpl. Ref. and Resrch. Ctr., 1969–77; Mncpl. Ref. Libn., N.Y.C. Mncpl. Ref. Lib., 1958–69. **Educ.:** City Coll. of NY, 1942–49, BSS (Soc. Sci.); Pratt Inst., 1949–50, BLS (Lib. Sc.); City Coll. of NY, 1950–51, MA (Pol. Sci.). **Orgs.:** SAA: various Coms. ALA: various coms. SLA: various coms. N.Y. State Hist. Recs. Adv. Bd.: Gvrs. Appt. (1976–83). Boro. Histn., Manhattan, NY Cnty.: Appt. of Boro. Pres. (1976). **Honors:** Fund for the City of NY, Pub. Srv. Awd., 1974. **Pubns.:** *Community Library Information Centers MRRC Notes* (1970); *Functional Directory of New York City-Boards Departments, Commissions, etc.* (1962, 1963, 1964, 1966); "Municipal and Local Government", *Bk. of Knowledge* (1966, 1980); "Municipal Reference Libraries, Parts I and II," *Lib. Jnl.* (1961); Ed., Municipal Reference Library Notes (1958–75). **Activities:** 2, 4; 17, 29, 38; 69, 78, 92 **Addr.:** New York City Department of Records and Information Services, 31 Chambers St., New York, NY 10007.

Bockstruck, Lloyd DeWitt (My. 26, 1945, Vandalia, IL) Head, Geneal. Sec., Dallas Pub. Lib., 1979–; First Asst., Hist. & Soc. Sci. Div., 1973–79; Lib., Geneal. Div., 1973–; Continuing Education Dept., South. Meth. Univ., 1974–; Fac. Geneal. and Hist. Resrch., Samford Univ., 1974–. **Educ.:** Greenville Coll., 1963–67, AB (bio.); South. IL Univ., 1967–69, MA (hist.); Univ. of IL, 1971–73, MLS; Inst. of Geneal. and Hist. Resrch. Samford Univ., 1973–, (Cert. geneal.). **Orgs.:** ALA: RASD/Geneal. Com. 1974–77). Dallas Cnty. LA. Natl. Geneal. Soc.; VA Geneal. Soc.; VA Hist. Soc.; Dallas Geneal. Soc.: Bd. Dirs. (1979). **Honors:** Phi Alpha Theta, Schol. Key, 1967; Greenville Coll., Coll. Schol., 1964. **Activities:** 9; 15, 16, 39; 69, 92 **Addr.:** Dallas Public Library, 1954 Commerce St., Dallas, TX 75201.

Bodart, Joni (D. 16, 1947, Winchester, VA) Ph.D., MA (Psy.) Candidate, TX Woman's Univ., 1979–; YA Libn., Stanislaus Co. Free Lib., 1978–79; YA Libn., Alameda Co. Lib. Syst., 1973–78; YA Libn., Sonoma Co. Lib., 1971–73. **Educ.:** TX Woman's Univ., 1965–69, BA/BS (Eng., LS); 1970–71, MLS. **Orgs.:** ALA: YASD/ Best Bks. for YA (Ch., 1973–77); (1979–81) Nom. Com. (1979–80); Lcl. Arrange. (Ch. 1975); Outstan. Fiction for the Coll.-Bound (1979). Bay Area YA Libns.: VP (1975); Bk. review ed. (1974); Pres. (1976). **Pubns.:** *Book Talk! Booktalking and Schoolvisiting for Young Adults* (1980); "Hip Pocket Books: BAYA Reading Interest Report," *Sch. Lib. Jnl.* (N. 1973); "Booktalks: What, Why, and How-To," *Top of the News* (Spr. 1979); "The Community Library is Alive and Well in Olney, Texas," *TX Libs.* (Win. 1979); "Bibliotherapy: The Right Book for the Right Person at the Right Time–and More!" *Top of the News* (Win. 1980); "Some Libraries do Everything Well!" *Top of the News* (Sum. 1980); other articles. **Activities:** 9; 21, 39, 48 **Addr.:** 713 Woodland, Denton, TX 76201.

Bodine, Christine Marie (D. 1, 1954, Denville, NJ) State Docum. Libn., Rutgers Univ., 1979–; Gvt. Docum. Libn., Newark Pub. Lib., 1978–79; Law Libn., Allied Chemical Corp., 1976–78; Law Libn., Morris Cnty. Law Lib., 1976–76. **Educ.:** Univ. of Bridgeport, 1971–75, BA (Hist.); Columbia Univ., 1975–76, MLS; Seton Hall Univ., 1977–81, JD, (Law). **Orgs.:** AALL. Gvt. Docum. Assn. of NJ. **Pubns.:** "The March of This Government": Joel Barlow's Unwritten History of the United States," *The William and Mary Quarterly* (Ap. 1976); "Evaluating the Quality of the Corporate Law Library," *The Lawyer's Assistant: Administrator, Paraprofessional and Secretary.* (1977). **Activities:** 1; 15, 17, 29; 77, 78, 92 **Addr.:** Rutgers Law Library, State Documents Dept., 15 Washington St., Newark, NJ 07102.

Boehm, Eric H. (Jl. 15, 1918, Hof, Germany) Publshr., *Env. Per. Bibl.*, 1971–; Pres., Ch. of Bd., ABC-Clio, Inc., 1955–; Pres.,

PROFESSIONAL ACTIVITIES: Institutions: 1. Acad. lib.; 2. Arch.; 3. Assn.; 4. Fed./Gvt. lib.; 5. Inst. lib.; 6. Mfr./Suppl.; 7. Milit. lib.; 8. Musm.; 9. Pub. lib.; 10. Sch. lib.; 11. Sch. of lib. sci.; 12. Spec. lib.; 13. State lib.; 14. (other). **Functions/Activities:** 15. Acq./Col. dev.; 16. Adult srvs.; 17. Admin.; 18. Apprais.; 19. Archit./Bldgs.; 20. Cat./Class.; 21. Chld. srvs.; 22. Circ.; 23. Cons./Pres.; 24. Consult.; 25. Cont. ed.; 26. Educ. lib. sci.; 27. Ext. srvs.; 28. Fund/Grants; 29. Gvt. pubs.; 30. Indx./Abs.; 31. Instr. lib. use; 32. Media srvs.; 33. Micro.; 34. Netwks./Coop.; 35. Persnl.; 36. PR; 37. Publshg.; 38. Recs. mgt.; 39. Ref. srvs.; 40. Repro.; 41. Resrch.; 42. Review.; 43. Secur.; 44. Serials; 45. Spec. col.; 46. Tech. srvs.; 47. Trustees/Bds.; 48. YA srvs.; 49. (other).

Intl. Acad. at Santa Barbara, 1961–; Civilian with Milit. Gvt., Berlin, 1946–47. **Educ.:** Wooster Coll., 1940, BA (Hist.); Fletcher Sch. of Law and Diplomacy, 1942, MA; Yale Univ., 1951, PhD (Intl. Rel.); Wooster Coll., 1973, LittD. **Orgs.:** Jt. Com. on Bibl. Srvs. to Hist. Assn. for Bibl. in Hist.: Cncl. ASIS. ALA. Amer. Hist. Assn. West. Hist. Assn. West. Slavic Assn.: Dir. (1974). Amer. Std. Assn. Various other orgs. **Honors:** Phi Beta Kappa; Class of 1920 Prize in Hist.; Various Flwshps., Resrch. Grants. **Pubns.:** *We Survived* (1949); *Historical Periodicals* (1961); "Current Emphases in the Dissemination of Information About Manuscripts," *Publication of American Historical Manuscripts* (1976); "Twenty-five Years of History in Indexing," *The Indxr.* (Ap. 1978); "The Data Bank of the American Bibliographical Center-Clio Press," *Computers and the Humanities* (1975); various articles, chaps. **Activities:** 12; 26, 30, 37 **Addr.:** ABC-Clio, Inc., 2040 Alameda Padre Serra, Santa Barbara, CA 93105.

Boelke, Joanne H. (O. 11, 1938, Springfield, MN) Undergrad. Srvs. Libn., Northwestern Univ. Lib., 1972–; Asst. Head, Ref. Dept., 1970–72; Docum. Anal., ERIC Clearinghse. for Lib. and Info. Sci., 1968–70; Ref. and Readrs. Adv. Libn., Madison Pub. Lib., 1964–67. **Educ.:** Univ. of MN, 1957–60, BA (Eng.); 1963–64, MA (LS). **Orgs.:** ALA: LAMA/Orien. Prog. Com. (1980–81); ACRL/Undergrad. Libns. Discuss. Grp. (Ch. 1976). **Honors:** Phi Beta Kappa, 1960; Beta Phi Mu, 1964. **Pubns.:** *Library Technicians: A Survey of Current Developments* (1968); Co-Auth., *Library Service to the Disadvantaged: A Bibliography* (1968); *Library Service to the Visually and Physically Handicapped: An Annotated Bibliography* (1969). **Activities:** 1; 15, 17, 49-Undergrad. srvs. **Addr.:** Undergraduate Services Department, Northwestern University Library, Evanston, IL 60201.

Bogan, Mary Elizabeth (Ap. 6, 1940, Pottsville, PA) Spec. Col. Libn., Emporia St. Univ., 1976–; Ref. Libn., Univ. of WI–Stout, 1974; Chlds. Libn., San Diego Pub. Lib., 1963–73; Libn. (Part time), Cabrillo Natl. Monument, 1969–70, 1973. **Educ.:** Coll. of Mt. St. Vincent, 1958–62, BA Cum Laude (Hist.); Univ. of MI, 1962–63, MALS; Univ. of WI–Stout, 1973–75, MS (AV Comm.). **Orgs.:** ALA: ALSC, Com. Natl. Plng. Spec. Coll. (1979–81); Local Mem. Ch. (Palomar Dist.) (1967–73); KS Assn. of Sch. Libns. CA LA: Prof. Stan. Com. (1972). William Allen White Chlds. Bk. Awd. Prog.: Various ofcs. connected with awd. (1976–). KS St. Dept. Educ.: Bk. Adoption Com. (1978–). **Honors:** Beta Phi Mu, 1974; Phi Kappa Phi, 1974; CA PTA, Srvs. to YA Awd., 1971. **Pubns.:** "A Survey of Audiovisual Resources in Selected California Public Libraries," *CA Libn* (D. 1976); "The William Allen White Children's Book Award Program," *Top of the News* (Fall, 1979); "How Books are Selected for the William Allen White Master List," *KS Assn. Sch. Libns. Nsltr.* (D. 1977); "Twenty-sixth Winner," *KS Assn. Sch. Libns. Nsltr.* (D. 1978); "The May Masse Collection," *KS Assn. Sch. Libns. Nsltr.* (Je. 1979); Other pubns. **Activities:** 1, 2; 21, 39, 45; 55, 57, 92 **Addr.:** P.O. Box 891, Emporia, KS 66801.

Bogart, Betty Brociner (Je. 10, 1923, Bolton, MA) Presn., Bogart-Brociner Assocs., Inc., 1977–; Libn., MIT Lincoln Lab., 1959–77. **Educ.:** Univ. of MA, 1941–45, BS (Home Econ./Eng.); Simmons Coll., 1973–75, MS (LS). **Orgs.:** SLA: Rep., Natl. Transl. Cntr. (1975–78); Transl. Probs. Com. (1973–76); Gvt. Info. Srvs. Com. (1969–72); Transl. Actv. Com. (1965–69). ASIS: Natl. Conf. (Publcty Ch., 1981); Natl. Transl. Ctr. (Rep., 1979–); Lcl. Arrange. Com.; Natl. Conf. (Ch., 1975). Soc. of Fed. Ling. DC LA: Treas. (1980–82); Mem. Com. (1979–80). **Pubns.:** *A Guide to Scientific and Technical Publications,* 1st Ed. (1968), 2d Ed. (1972); *How to Obtain a Translation* (1976); "Translations - An Uncoordinated Jungle," *Transl. News* (1974). **Activities:** 6; 15, 17, 39; 56, 80, 91 **Addr.:** Bogart-Brociner Associates, Inc., 47 Williams Drive, Annapolis, MD 21401.

Bogen, Betty (Ag. 30, 1947, Poking, Germany) Chief, Lib. Srv., Dayton Vets. Admin. Med. Ctr., 1977–; Head, AV Srvs., Houston Acad. of Med.–TX Med. Ctr. Lib., 1977; Media Srvs. Libn., Univ. of UT Hlth. Sci. Lib., 1973–77; Grp. Hlth. Claims Adjuster, Occidental Life Insr. Co., 1970–71. **Educ.:** Univ. of CA, Los Angeles, 1965–70, BA (Eng.); Univ. of South. CA, 1971–73, MLS, MA (Pub. Admin.); Cert. (Med. Libnshp.) 1976. **Orgs.:** Med. LA: Bibl. and Info. Srvs. Assess. (1976–77); AV Stans. (1978–); Cont. Ed. Crs. Instr. (1974–). Hlth. Sci. Comm. Assn. OH Hlth. Info. Org.: Bylaws (1979–). Amer. Bus. Woman's Assn. **Honors:** Natl. Insts. of Hlth.–Natl. Lib. of Med., Flwshp., 1971. **Pubns.:** *Basic Media Management–Hardware and Physical Facilities* (1976); "Guidelines for Producers and Distributors of Media for the Health Sciences," *Jnl. of Biocomm.* (N. 1977); "Organization of a Pharmacy Film Festival," *Amer. Jnl. of Pharm. Educ.* (F. 1977); "A Computer-Generated Catalog of Audiovisuals," *Bltn. of the Med. LA* (Ap. 1976). **Activities:** 4, 12; 17, 32, 39; 80, 74, 92 **Addr.:** Library Service, Dayton Veterans Administration Medical Center, Dayton, OH 45428.

Bogis, Nana E. (F. 4, 1938, Philadelphia, PA) Dir., Free Pub. Lib. of Monroe Twp., 1974–; Dir., Mount Holly Pub. Lib., 1969–73; Head, Tech. Srvs., Montgomery Cnty.–Pub. Lib., 1968–69; Catlgr., Bucks Cnty. Free Pub. Lib., 1966–67. **Educ.:** Temple Univ., 1956–60, BA (Sp. and Drama); Drexel Univ., 1965–66, MSLS; NJ Prof. Libn.'s Cert., 1970–. **Orgs.:** ALA. NJ LA. Libs. Unlimited: VP (1979–80). **Activities:** 9, 11; 17, 20, 36; 67 **Addr.:** Free Public Library of Monroe Township, 306 S. Main St., Williamstown, NJ 08094.

Bohlen, Jeanne L. (Jl. 30, 1938, Kansas City, MO) Dir., Fndn. Ctr., 1977–; Ref. Supvsr., KS City Pub. Lib., 1972–77; Warrensburg Libn., Trails Reg. Lib., 1965–67; Ed., Bk. Pubns., Xerox-Univ. Micro., Inc., 1963–65; Resrch. Libn., Bendix Syst. Div., 1962–63. **Educ.:** Oberlin Coll., 1956–60, BA (Phys.); Rutgers Univ., 1960–62, MLS. **Orgs.:** SLA: PR, Nom. Com. (1979–80); Cleveland Chap. (Pres.-Elect, 1981–82). OH LA. Women and Fndns./Corp. Philan. **Pubns.:** "Foundation Grants," *OH Mus. Jnl.* (1980); "Foundation Center-Cleveland," *OH Media Spectrum* (1979); Contrib., to *Src. Bk Profiles* (1980). **Activities:** 9, 12; 28, 31, 39; 95-Philan., 91, 92 **Addr.:** Foundation Center-Cleveland, 739 National City Bank Bldg., Cleveland, OH 44114.

Bohley, Ronald (F. 17, 1942, Indianapolis, IN) Dir., Lib. and Lrng. Resrcs., Univ. of MO, Rolla, 1976–; Lib. Dir., Purdue Univ., N. Ctrl. Campus, 1967–76. **Educ.:** Purdue Univ., 1960–64, BA (Eng.); IN Univ., 1964–67, MALS; 1974–75, Phil. Cand. **Orgs.:** ALA. MO LA. **Honors:** Beta Phi Mu; MO Governor's Conf. LIS; Act. Del., WHCLIS. **Pubns.:** *Historic Photographs at the University of Missouri-Rolla* (1979); "Historical Photographs Project," *Show-Me Libs.* (Jl. 1979); "Final Report from MO's Del. to WHCLIS" (1980). **Activities:** 1; 17 **Addr.:** Curtis Laws Wilson Library, University of Missouri-Rolla, Rolla, MO 65401.

Bohling, Raymond A. (Ja. 12, 1928, Auburn, NE) Head, Engin. Lib., Univ. of MN, 1980–; Asst. Dir., Admin., 1962–80, Supvsr., Dept. Libs., 1960–62; Asst. Dir., Libs. for Sci. Tech., Univ. of NE, 1955–60. **Educ.:** Univ. of NE, 1948–51, BA (Psy.); Univ. of Denver, 1951–52, MA (LS). **Orgs.:** ASIS: MN Chap. (Pres., 1975–76). SLA: MN Chap. (Pres., 1964–65). ALA: ACRL, Bd. of Dirs. (1972–76), Budget and Finance Com. (1977–81). **Activities:** 1; 17, 19, 35; 64, 91 **Addr.:** 2142 Inca Ln., New Brighton, MN 55112.

Boissé, Joseph A. (Je. 20, 1937, Marlboro, MA) Prof., Dir. of Libs., Temple Univ., 1979–; Dir. of Lib., Univ. of Wisconsin-Parkside, 1973–79; Asst. State Libn., Vermont Dept. of Libs., 1971–73; Asst. Dir. of Lib., Lawrence Univ., 1968–71. **Educ.:** Stonehill Coll., 1960–63, AB (Fr.); Brown Univ., 1963–65, MA (Fr.); Simmons Coll., 1966–67, MLS. **Orgs.:** ALA: Com. on Instr. Lib. Use (1980); ACRL: Com. on Legis. (1976–79); Com. on White House Conf. Ch. (1977–80); Bibl. Instr. Sec.; LAMA: various offices (1977–80). Midwest Fed. LA: Pres. (1975–79). WI LA: Conf. Ch. (1974–76). Franklin Inn Club of Philadelphia. **Honors:** WI LA, Disting. Srvs. Awd., 1978. **Pubns.:** Jt. Auth., "The Academic Library as a Teaching Library", *Lib. Trends* (1979); "Dealing with the Fear of Change through the Self-Study Process," *New Horizons for Acad. Libs.* (1979); "Library Instruction and the Administration," in *Putting Lib. Inst. In Its Place* (1978); "Epilogue: Issues and Answers", Jt. Auth., *Info. Socty.* (1978). **Activities:** 1, 13; 17, 24, 34; 61, 74, 78 **Addr.:** Temple University, Philadelphia, PA 19122.

Boivin, Hélène M. L. (Jl. 29, 1949; Montreal, PQ) Slide Libn., Univ. of Ottawa, 1972–; Guide, Natl. Gallery of Can., 1970–71. **Educ.:** Univ. of Ottawa, 1967–71, BA (Visual Arts); PA State Univ., 1971–74, MEd (Art Ed.). **Orgs.:** ARLIS/NA. Mid-America Col. Art Assn. Univ. Art Assn. of Can. Col. Art Assn. **Pubns.:** "Canadian Slide Suppliers", (1977, 79, 80); Jt. Auth., *MACAA Guide to Equipment for Slide Maintenance & Viewing* (1978–79). **Activities:** 1; 15, 20, 39, 55 **Addr.:** Department of Visual Arts, University of Ottawa, 600 Cumberland, room 101–102, Ottawa, ON K1N 6N5 Canada.

Bold, Rudolph (D. 10, 1938, Brooklyn, NY) Branch Lib., Ozone Park Branch, Queens Boro Pub. Lib., 1963–; Prod. Asst., Musm. of Modern Art, 1962–63. **Educ.:** St. Johns Univ., Brooklyn NY, 1956–60, BA (Phil.); Fordham Univ., 1961–62, MS (Psych.); Pratt Inst. Lib. Sch., 1963–65, MLS. **Orgs.:** NY LA. Beta Phi Mu: Theta Chapter, Pres. (1965–66). Amer. Mgt. Assn. NY Civil Liberties Union: various committees (1978–); Mayor's Urban Task Force, NYC: Unit Chairman, Air & Noise Pollution (1971–75). Ridgewood N.Y. BiCentennial Com.: Ch. (1975–76). Kiwanis Intl.: Queens W. Div., Prog. Ch. **Pubns.:** "Rocky Horror: The Newest Cult", *Christian Century* (S. 12, 1979); "The Sensored Public Library", *Wilson Lib. Bull.* (S. 1978); "Trash in the Library", *Lib. Jnl.* (My. 15, 1980); other criticism. **Activities:** 9; 16, 24, 27; 65, 66, 67 **Addr.:** 49 Campbell Ave., Williston Park, NY 11596.

Bolden, Connie E. (D. 1, 1933, Newton, NC) State Law Libn., WA State Law Lib., 1966–; Asst. Prof., Law and Libn., Stetson Univ., 1965–66; Asst. State Law Libn., WA State Law Lib., 1963–65; Prac. Attorney, NC, 1959–63. **Educ.:** Univ. of NC, 1952–56, BS (Bus. Admin.), 1957–59, JD (Law), 1963, MLS. **Orgs.:** AALL: Pres. (1979–80); VP (1978–79); Exec. Bd. (1971–74); various coms., chs. AALL: Various coms., chs. West.-Pac. Assn. of Law Libs.: Pres. (1971). ALA. Amer. Bar Assn. NC Bar Assn. Amer. Socty. for Legal Hist. Intl. Assn. of Law Libs. **Honors:** Beta Phi Mu, 1963. **Pubns.:** *Appellate Opinion Preparation* (1978); *The American Judge* (1968); *Evaluation of the Montana State Law Library* (1979); ed., *Modern Legal Research* (1979); ed., *Law Lib. Jnl.* (1967–77); various mono., articles. **Activities:** 13; 17; 77 **Addr.:** Washington State Law Library, Temple of Justice, Olympia, WA 98504.

Boldrick, Samuel James (O. 18, 1947, Lebanon, KY) Head, FL. Col., Miami-Dade Pub. Lib., 1977–; Asst. Libn. FL. Col., 1972–77. **Educ.:** Spring Hill Coll., 1965–69, AB (Hist.); Emory Univ., 1969–70, MLN (LS); GA Dept. of Arc. and Hist., 1970, (Arch. Admn.). **Orgs.:** FL LA. ALA: Lib. Arch. Com. (1973–75), RASD (Mem. Com., 1980–) **Orgs.:** RASD Local Hist. Com. (1980–). Dade Heritage Trust: Trustee (1971–75), Pres. (1975–78). Hist. Musm. of S. FL: Trustee (1975–) FL. Hist. Socty.: Trustee (1981–). **Pubns.:** "Disinfection of Books," *Encyc. of Lib. and Info. Sci.* (1972); Various Historical Articles. **Activities:** 2, 9; 30, 39, 45; 54, 70, 83 **Addr.:** Florida Collection, Miami-Dade Public Library, One Biscayne Blvd., Miami, FL 33101.

Bolef, Doris (Mr. 26, 1922, Philadelphia, PA) Dir., Lib. of Rush Univ. Med. Ctr., 1978–; Asst. Dean for Lrng. Resrcs., E. TN State Univ. Coll. of Med., 1975–78; Proj. Dir., part-time, OH Coll. Lib. Ctr., Demonstration Proj., MO, 1974–75; Catlgr., Deputy Libn., Washington Univ., St. Louis, MO, 1963–74. **Educ.:** Temple Univ., 1939–43, BS (Educ.); Drexel Inst., 1944–45, BS (Lib. Sci.); Columbia Univ., 1947–51, MS (Lib. Sci.). **Orgs.:** SLA: Ch., Hosp. Div. (1952). Med. LA: Prof. Consult., (1962–); Ch., Pubns. Com. (1970–72); ALA: Agr. and Bio. sci. Vice-Ch., Ch.-elect./ch. (1976–78). S. East. Reg. Med. Lib. Prog.: Ch., Com. on Autom. Systs. (1975–78). **Pubns.:** *Microforms Management in Special Libraries:* A Reader (1978); Jt. author "Health Science Library Consortia in a Rural Setting," *Bltn. of the Med. Lib. Assn.* (Ap 1978); "Computer-assisted Cataloging: the First Decade," *Bltn. of the Med. Lib. Assn.* (Jl 1975); Computer Output Microfilm. *Special Libraries,* 65:169–175. (Ap 1974); Jt. author "Printed Catalogs: retrospect and prospect," *Special Libraries* (D 1968); various articles and syllabi. Reviews. **Activities:** 1; 17, 46; 80 **Addr.:** Library of Rush University, 600 S. Paulina St., Chicago, IL 60612.

Boles, Suzanne E. (Mr. 16, 1941, Grove, OK) Indp. Consult., Auth., 1980–; Cmnty. Srvs. Coord., Tulsa City-Cnty. Lib., 1970–80. **Educ.:** OK State Univ., 1959–63, BS (Dsgn.); Univ. of Tulsa, 1973–79, MA (Urban Std.). **Orgs.:** ALA: PLA, Org. Com.; LI RT, Alternative Educ. Sect. OK LA: *Un. List of Serials* Com., Inter-lib. Coop. Com.; SRRT. OK Netwk. Adv. Cncl. Task Frc. on Netwk. Srvs. Amer. Socty. for Pub. Admin. Amer. Assn. for State and Lcl. Hist. Prsrvn., Inc.: Lcl. Bd. of Dirs. Tulsa Cnty. Hist. Socty.: Bd. of Dirs.; Pres. (1980). Frnds. of the Pub. Lib. **Pubns.:** "The Learner's Advisory Service," *Lib. Trends* (Fall 1979); various presentations, wkshps. **Activities:** 9; 16, 24, 25; 50, 55, 59 **Addr.:** 4006 S. New Haven, Tulsa, OK 74135.

Bolgiano, Christina E. (D. 23, 1948, Munich, W. Germ) Ref. Libn., James Madison Univ., 1975–80, Coord. Tech. Srvs., 1975–80, Asst. Cat. Libn., 1974–75, Tech. Info. Spec., Germ. Langs., Natl. Agri. Lib., 1970–72. **Educ.:** Univ. MD, 1966–70, BA (Hist.); 1973–74, MLS. **Orgs.:** ALA. SELA. VA LA. Potomac Tech. Prcsg. Libns.: Exec. Cncl. (VA Reg. Rep. 1980–82). **Honors:** Phi Beta Kappa. **Pubns.:** "Libraries as an art form," *Jnl. of Acad. Libnshp.* (forthcoming); "Division and Revision: Modernizing the Card Catalog," *SE Libn.* (Sum. 1970); Jt. auth., "Profiling a Periodicals Collection," *Coll. and Resrch. Libs.* (Mar. 1978); "A Systems approach to label production through the OCLC system," *Jnl. of Lib. Autom.* (Dec. 1979); "Toward retrospective conversion," *Alternative Cat. Nsltr.* **Activities:** 1, 4; 20, 41, 46 **Addr.:** Rt. 2, Box 59, Broadway, VA 22815.

Bolin, Nancy Clare (Ag. 17, 1946, Columbus, OH) Dir., Resrc. Srvs., Cambridge Mental Hlth. and Developmental Ctr., 1977–; Head, Media Resrc. Ctr., St. Francis Indian Sch., 1974–76; Head, Adult Srvs., Berea Bravel, Cuyahoza Cnty. Pub. Lib., 1972–74; Asst. Branch Libn., Cleveland Pub. Lib., 1969–72. **Educ.:** Coll. of St. Mary of the Springs, 1965–68, BA (Liberal Arts); Univ. of MI, 1968–69, MALS; Univ. of WI, Madison, 1976–78, Spec. in Lib. Srvs. to Aging. **Orgs.:** OH LA: Task Force on Srv. to Older Adults (1979–). Southeastern OH Lib. Org.: Ch. (1980); Libns. Cncl. (1978–). Natl. Cncl. on Aging. **Pubns.:** "Aging as a Mass Media Experience," *Perspective: Information About Aging* (1979); "Library Service to Older People," *OH LA* (1980); "Training Volunteers to Work with the Confined Elderly," (ERIC) (1980). **Activities:** 5, 9; 16, 25, 28; 50, 72, 95-Grntlgy. **Addr.:** Director of Resource Services, Cambridge Mental Health and Developmental Center, Rte. 35 North, Cambridge, OH 43725.

Boll, John J. (Ag. 12, 1921, Berlin, Germany) Prof. LS, Univ. of WI-Madison, 1968–; Assoc. Prof., 1961–68; Asst. Prof., 1956–61; Asst. Libn., Tech. Prcs., Univ. of Tx., 1954–56; Lib. Asst., Univ. of IL, 1952–54; Descr. Cat., Lib. of Congs., 1949–51. **Educ.:** Union Coll., 1938–42, AB (LS); Columbia Univ., 1942–43, 1948–49, MS (LS); Univ. of IL, 1961, PhD. **Orgs.:** WI LA: Schol. Com. (1965–66); Coll. Univ. Sec. (Ch., 1966); Nom. Com. Tech. Srvs. (1971–72); Spec. Com. Lib. Educ. (1966–67). AALS: Curric. Com. (Ch. 1966–67). **Honors:** Beta Phi Mu. **Pubns.:** *Introduction to Cataloging, vol. 1: Descriptive Cataloging* (1970); *Introduction to Cataloging, vol. 2: Entry Headings* (1974); "A Basis for Library Education," *Lib. Qtly.* (Ap. 1972); "Tame the terror for its use; or, What are Wisconsin documents?," *WI Lib.*

Special Subjects/Services: 50. Adult educ.; 51. Advert./Mktg.; 52. Aerosp.; 53. Agric.; 54. Area std.; 55. Arts/Hum.; 56. Autom.; 57. Bibl./Prtg.; 58. Bio. sci.; 59. Bus./Fin.; 60. Chem.; 61. Copyrt.; 62. Documtn.; 63. Educ.; 64. Engin.; 65. Env.; 66. Eth. grps.; 67. Film; 68. Food/Nutr.; 69. Geneal.; 70. Geo.; 71. Geol.; 72. Handcpd.; 73. Hist.; 74. Int. frdm.; 75. Info. sci.; 76. Insr.; 77. Law; 78. Legis.; 79. Math./Comp. sci.; 80. Med.; 81. Metals; 82. Nat. resrcs.; 83. Newsp.; 84. Nuc. sci.; 85. Oral hist.; 86. Petr./Energy; 87. Pharm.; 88. Phys./Astr./Math.; 89. Readg.; 90. Relig.; 91. Sci./Tech.; 92. Soc. sci.; 93. Telecom.; 94. Transp.; 95. (other).

Bltn. (Mr./Ap. 1974); Reviews. **Activities:** 1, 11; 19, 20, 29, 30; 62, 75 **Addr.:** Library School, University of Wisconsin–Madison, 600 North Park Street, Madison, WI 53706.

Bolles, Charles A. (Ag. 10, 1940, Pine Island, MN) State Libn., ID State Lib., 1980–; Dir., Sch. of LS, Emporia State Univ., 1978–80; Dir., Lib. Dev. Div., KS State Lib., 1976–78; Assoc. Prof., Emporia State Univ., 1970–76; Serials Libn., Univ. of IA, 1965–67, Cat. Libn., 1964–65. **Educ.:** Univ. of MN, 1958–62, BA (Hist.), 1962–63, MA (LS), 1967–69, MA (Amer. Std.), 1969–75, PhD (LS). **Orgs.:** ALA: State Lib. Agency Sect. (Ch., 1980–81). ID LA: Exec. Bd. (1980–). CLENE: Adv. Com. (1977–80); Exec. Bd. (1981–). KS LA: Pres. (1977–78); Exec. Cncl. (1974–79). Bibl. Ctr. for Resrch.: Adv. Cncl. (1979–81). Pac. NW Bibl. Ctr.: Exec. Bd. (1980–); Ch. (1981–). **Pubns.:** Jt. auth., *Staff Development Bibliography* (1976); jt. auth., "Statewide Needs Assessments," *Cath. Lib. World* (Mr. 1981); "Challenges and Changes for Libraries in the 1980's," *ID Libn.* (Ja. 1981). **Activities:** 13; 17, 25, 34; 50, 56, 63 **Addr.:** Idaho State Library, 325 W. State St., Boise, ID 83702.

Bollier, John Albert (O. 12, 1927, North Tonawanda, NY) Asst. Dvnty. Lib., Yale Univ. D. Lib., 1980–; Pub. Srvs. Libn., 1973–80; Ref. Libn. and Bibl., CA State Univ. Northridge, 1971–72; Pastor, St. Stephen Presby. Church, Chatsworth, CA, 1963–70; Pastor, First Presby. Church, Stroudsburg, PA, 1954–63; Pastor, New Harmony Presby. Church, Brogue, PA, 1952–54; Tchg. Fellow, Princeton Theo. Sem., 1951–52. **Educ.:** Univ. of MI, 1944–48, BA (Hist.); Princeton Theo. Sem., 1948–51, BD (Theo.), 1951–52, ThM; Univ. of Geneva, Switzerland, 1957–58 (Ecum. Stud.); Univ. of CA, Los Angeles, 1970–71, MLS. **Orgs.:** ALA:ACRL. ATLA: Ad Hoc Com. on Cont. Ed. and Prof. Dev. (Conv., 1978–). **Honors:** Beta Phi Mu. **Pubns.:** *The Literature of Theology: A Guide for Students and Pastors* (1979); "Bibliographic Instruction in the Graduate/Professional Theological School," chap. in *New Horizons For Academic Libraries* (1979); "The Righteousness of God: A Word Study," *Interpretation* (O. 1954); "Judgment in the Apocalypse," *Interpretation* (Ja. 1953); Various other publications. **Activities:** 1, 2; 17, 31, 39; 57, 90 **Addr.:** Yale Divinity Library, 409 Prospect St., New Haven CT 06510.

Bollinger, Mary Faith (Vesper, KS) Retired, 1956–; Sch. Libn., Jefferson Jr. High, 1942–56; Tchr. KS Pub. Schs., 1934–42. **Educ.:** Baker Univ., 1934, AB (Eng., Hist., Latin); Univ. of Leicester, Eng., 1972 (Spec. Wkshp., Youth and Readg.) various crs. **Orgs.:** ID LA: Pres. (1969–70); Exec. Bd. (1965–71); ch., various coms. ALA: Natl. Com. to Elect Britannica Sch. Media Awd. (1970); AASL, ID Del. (1968, 1975). ID Sch. Libns.: Pres. (1965–67). Gvrs. Cncl. of ID Lib. Srvs. Parent-Tchrs. Assn. and Cncl. Fac. and Wives of Coll. of ID. ID Educ. Assn. Natl. Educ. Assn. various orgs. **Honors** Alpha Delta Sigma. **Pubns.:** "Observations on European Libraries," *The ID Libn.* (Ap. 1974); "Jefferson Junior Library," *The ID Libn.* (Ap. 1975); "School Days in San Francisco," *The ID Libn.* (Ja. 1976); "Survey of Library-Media Centers," *The ID Libn.* (Ja. 1977). **Activities:** 10; 31, 32; 63, 89 **Addr.:** 1805 Everett, Caldwell, ID 83605.

Bolt, Janice Ann (Ap. 27, 1941, Chicago, IL) Asst. Prof. Lib. Sci., Chicago State Univ., 1969–; Libn., Daley Cmnty. Coll., 1966–69; Libn., DuSable HS, 1963–66; Libn., Banneker Elem., 1962–63. **Educ.:** Chicago Tchrs. Coll., 1960–62, BA (Educ.); 1962–65, MS (LS); Univ. of Chicago, 1972–75, 6th-Year Certificate (LS); Florida State Univ., 1977–78, Advnc. Mstrs. **Orgs.:** IL LA: IL Assoc. Media Educ. (Nsltr. Ed., 1972–74). ALA. AECT. Cath. LA: N. IL Reg., Elem. Sch. Sect. (Ch., 1977). **Pubns.:** Guest Ed., *IL Libs.* (S. 1974–76); reviews. **Activities:** 1; 26, 42 **Addr.:** Dept. of Library Science & Media Communications, Douglas Library, Chicago State University, 95th King Dr., Chicago, IL 60628.

Bolt, Joan M. (Ja. 1, 1942, St. Thomas, ON, Can) Coord., Lrng. Mtrls., London and Middlesex Cnty. Catholic Sch. Syst., 1975–, Instr., Mnstry. of Educ., 1977–79; Tchr., Catholic Ctrl. HS, 1968–69; Tchr., F.J. Brennan HS, Windsor Sp. Schs., 1966–68. **Educ.:** Univ. of West. ON, 1960–63, BA (Eng.), 1975–76, MLS; Althouse Coll., 1979–, (Educ.); ON Coll. of Educ., 1959–63, AMus. **Orgs.:** Can. LA. ON LA. Delta Kappa Gamma: ETA Chap. (Pres., 1973–75). South Ont. Media Assn. Fanshaw Coll. Lib. Tech. Prog.: Adv. Com. **Honors** Delta Kappa Gamma, Olive Marcoux Award, 1975. **Pubns.:** Lib. media prog., 1977. **Activities:** 10; 17, 21, 32; 63, 67, 89 **Addr.:** Learning Materials Centre, 85 Charles St., London, ON N6H 1H1 Canada.

Bolt, Nancy Doyle (O. 16, 1945, St. Louis, MO) Branch Chief, Div. of Lib. Dev. and Srvs., MD Dept. of Educ., 1979–; Dir., Pub. Lib. Prog., Natl. Endow. for the Hum., 1977–79; Dir., Main Lib., Forsyth Cnty. Pub. Lib., 1977–; Dir., Adult Cont. Ed. Prog., Winston-Salem, NC, 1975–77; Head, Ref. Dept., Meadville Pub. Lib., 1972–74; Ref. Dept., Daniel Boone Reg. Lib., 1971–72; Exec. Secy., MO LA, 1970–71. **Educ.:** Southeast MO State Coll., 1963–68, BS (Ed, Hist/Soc. Sci); Univ. of MO, 1969–70, MLS; grad. credit in adult educ. Univ. of Pittsburgh, NC State Univ. **Orgs.:** ALA: Com. on Org. (1978–82). PLA: Bd. of Dir. (1979–82); Goals, Guidelines and Stans. Com., (1978–82). JMRT: Pres. 1975–76); Com. on Governance (1970–72); Ed., *Cognotes* (1970–74). RASD: Bd. of Dirs. (1976–79). Frdm. to Read Fndn.: Bd. of Dirs. (1973–75, 1978–80); Exec. Com. (1974–75). **Pubns.:** *ACE Directory of Adult Continuing Education Activities in Forsyth County* (1976); *Resource Book on CLEP* (1977); *Directory of Trade and Professional Associations in Missouri* (1970); Ed., *Public Libraries* (1974–78); Ed., *JMRT Footnotes* (1970–73). **Activities:** 9, 13; 16, 27, 47; 50 **Addr.:** Division of Library Development and Services, MD Department of Education, 200 W. Baltimore St., Baltimore, MD 21201.

Bolte, William Frank (S. 28, 1946, Yonkers, NY) Dir., Jeffersonville Twp. Pub. Lib., IN, 1981–; Dir., State Lib. Div., KY Dept. of Lib. and Arch., 1978–; Dir., Bowling Green Pub. Lib., 1972–78; Libn., Oldham Cnty. Sr. HS, 1971–72; Tchr./Libn., Christian Cnty. Sch. Syst., 1967–70. **Educ.:** Austin Peay State Univ., 1964–68, BS (Geo.); Univ. of KY, 1970–71, MSLS; West. KY Univ., 1973–, MS (Geo.). **Orgs.:** ALA: Mem. Promo. Task Force (1977–81); KY LA: Treas. (1976); Mem. Ch. (1976, 78, 79, 80); Natl. Lib. Week (Ch., 1977); Pub. Lib. Sect. (Secy./Treas., 1975; Ch., 1977). SELA: KY Mem. (Ch., 1979–80). OH Valley Grp. Tech. Srvs. Libns. Socty. for the Pres. & Encouragement of Barbershop Quartet Singing in Amer.: VP for Prog. (1980); Stage Mgr. (1980). Various other associations. **Pubns.:** "Kentucky Kaleidoscope" (Qtly. Bibl.), *KLA Bulletin* (1975–78); "Use of Government Documents in Small and Medium-Sized Public Libraries in Kentucky," *ERIC* (1979); Ed., *Keynote* (Nsltr. for KY Dept. of Lib. and Arch.), 1979–81. **Activities:** 9, 13; 16, 17, 35; 70, 92 **Addr.:** 4025 Summer Place, New Albany, IN 47150.

Bolton, Phyllis L. (Je. 5, 1928, Boston, MA) Supvsr., Tech. Info. Srvs., GAF Corp., 1966–; Tech. Ed., Associated Tech. Srvs., 1955–66; Tech. Transl., Amer. Cyanamid Co., 1951–55. **Educ.:** Bryn Mawr Coll., 1945–49, AB (Eng.); George Washington Univ., 1949–51, MA (Eng.). **Orgs.:** SLA. ASIS. Amer. Transl. Assn.: Trustee (1977–79). **Pubns.:** Transl., *Simultaneous Combustion* (1964); Comp., *German-English Science Dictionary,* 4th Ed., Supplement (1978). **Activities:** 12; 17, 49-Transl.; 60, 64, 86†

Bomar, Cora Paul (S. 8, 1913, Memphis, TN) Assoc. Prof. Emeritus of LS, Univ. of NC, Greensboro, 1979–, Assoc. Prof. of LS, 1969–79; Dir., Div. of Educ. Media, NC Dept. of Pub. Instr., 1966–69; State Sch. Lib. Supvsr., 1951–66; Dir. of Instr., Orange Cnty. (NC) Bd. of Educ., 1949–51; Elem. Sch. Libn., Chapel Hill (NC) Bd. of Educ., 1947–49; Ref. Libn., Univ. of TN, Martin, 1946–47; Tchr. and-or Sch. Libn., TN and GA Sch. Systs. 1932–42, 45–46. **Educ.:** Bethel Coll., 1930–32, Cert. (Liberal Arts); Univ. of TN, Knoxville, 1938–39, BS (Soc. Educ., Hist., Eng.); George Peabody Coll., 1945–46, BSLS; Univ. of NC, Chapel Hill, 1949–50, MA (Elem. Educ.). **Orgs.:** ALA: Cncl. (1962–67); Legis. Com. (1962–66); Lib. Educ. Div. (Pres., 1969–70), Exec. Bd. (1966–75); AASL: (Pres., 1962–63). Assn. of State Sch. Lib. Supvsrs.: Pres. (1956–57). Beta Phi Mu: Intl. Pres. (1965–66). Southeastern LA: Pres. (1966–68). Various other orgs. Delta Kappa Gamma. Natl. Catholic Educ. Assn.: Adv. Cncl. on Educ. Tech. (1968–70). US Ofc. of Educ., Adv. Com. on New Educ. Media (1966–68). State Cncl. for Soc. Legis. (NC): Pres. (1969); various other orgs. **Honors** NC Assn. of Sch. Libs., The Mary Peacock Douglas Awd., 1970; Univ. of NC, Greensboro, LS Alum. Assn., The Cora Paul Bomar Anl. Endowed Lect. Prog., 1979. **Pubns.:** *Guide to the Development of Educational Media Selection Centers* (1973); "School and Public Library Cooperation: For What?" *Southeastern Libn.* (Spr. 1970); "The Impact of Federal Legislation on School Libraries," *Federal Legislation,* Allerton Pk. Inst. (1966). **Activities:** 10, 11; 17, 26, 32; 63, 74, 78 **Addr.:** 107 W. Avondale Dr., Greensboro, NC 27403.

Bommer, Michael R. W. (Je. 30, 1940, Batavia, NY) Assoc. Prof., Clarkson Coll., 1973–; Asst. Prof., Temple Univ., 1970–73; Resrch. Assoc., Univ. of PA, 1968–70. **Educ.:** Cornell Univ., 1958–63, BS (Mech. Engin.); OH State Univ., 1963–64, MS (Indus. Engin.); Univ. of PA, 1966–70, PhD (Stats.). **Orgs.:** ASIS; Mgt. Sci.; Decision Sci. **Pubns.:** *Decision-Making For Library Management* Knowledge Industry Publications, Inc. (1981); *Library Planning and Decision-Making Systems* (1974); "Performance Assessment Model for Academic Libraries," *Jnl. of ASIS* (Mr. 1979); "Operations Research in Libraries: A Critical Assessment," *JASIS* (My. 1975); "A Systems Approach to Library Management," *Jnl. of Systs. Engin.* (Je. 1976); "A Cost-Benefit Analysis for Determining the Value of an Electronic Security System," *Coll. and Resrch. Libs.* (Jl. 1974). **Activities:** 1; 17, 24, 41; 75, 95-Mgt. **Addr.:** School of Management, Clarkson College, Potsdam, NY 13676.

Bonath, Gail Jean (S. 13, 1950, Harlan, IA) Asst. Libn. for Tech. Srvs., Grinnell Coll., 1977–; Acq. Libn., Cornell Coll., 1973–75. **Educ.:** IA State Univ., 1968–72, BS (Distributed Std.); Univ. of IA, 1972–73, MA (LS). **Orgs.:** ALA. IA LA: Resrcs. and Tech. Srvs. Sect. (Vice-Ch., 1979–80), (Ch. 1980–1981). IA OCLC Cncl.: Exec. Com. (1978–80). **Activities:** 1; 20, 23, 46 **Addr.:** Burling Library, Grinnell College, Grinnell, IA 50112.

Bond, Marvin A., Jr. (Ja. 7, 1939, Kansas City, MO) Chief, Resrcs. Dev. and Maintenance, Natl. Bur. of Stans. Lib., 1974–, ILL Srch., Lib. of Congs., 1973; Catlgr., 1972–74, Chief, Lib. Auxiliaries Sect., 1969–72. **Educ.:** Univ. of MO, 1962–64, BA (Eng.); Univ. of MD, 1968–69, MLS; Frostburg State Coll., 1975–80, MSM (Mgt. Sci.). **Orgs.:** Fed. Lib. Info. Netwk.: Tape Users Grp., VP (1975); NBS Rep. (1974–76). Interlib. Users Assn.: Ed. Com. (Ch., 1979); VP, Pres. (1978–81); Exec. Bd. (1977). Task Frc. on Dept. of Cmrce. LS Career Mgt. Prog. JOURNALINK Subscribers: Coord. (1978–79). **Pubns.:** Ed., *DC LA Nsltr.* (1969–70). **Activities:** 4, 12; 15, 17, 20; 56, 91 **Addr.:** Library, E104 Administration Bldg., National Bureau of Standards, Washington, DC 20234.

Bondarovich, Mary Frances (N. 2, 1928, Elizabeth, NJ) Mgr., Tech. Info. Ctr., Bristol-Myers Prod., 1969–; Resrch. Librn., Coca-Cola Co., 1965–69; Resrch. Libn., White Lab., 1957–65; Branch Librn., Elizabeth Pub. Lib., 1957. **Educ.:** Rutgers Univ., AB (Eng.); 1964–67, MLS. **Orgs.:** SLA: NJ Chap., Pres. (1973–74), Ch. Pharm. Div. (1976–77), NJ Chap. Nom. Com. (1976), many other offices. ASIS; Drug Info. Assn. NY Acad. of Scis. **Activities:** 9, 12; 15, 17, 39; 58, 60, 87 **Addr.:** Technical Information Center, Bristol-Myers Products, 225 Long Ave., Hillside, NJ 07207.

Bone, Larry Earl (O. 31, 1932, Memphis, TN) Dir. of Libs. and Prof., Mercy Coll., 1977–; Dir., Assoc. Prof. of Bibl., Southwestern At Memphis, 1975–77; Asst. Dir. for Pub. Srvs., Memphis Pub. Lib. and Info. Ctr., 1970–75; Asst. Dir., Asst. Prof., Sch. of LS, Univ. of IL, 1966–70; Visiting Deputy Libn., Amer. Lib., Paris, France, 1968–69; Cnty. Libn., Shelby Cnty. Libs., Memphis, TN, 1963–66; Dir., Mentor (Ohio) Pub. Lib., 1962–63; Head Libn., Avon Lake (Ohio) Pub. Lib., 1959–62; Various other library positions. **Educ.:** Southwestern At Memphis, 1950–54, BA (Fr.); Case West. Reserve Univ., 1954–55, MS (LS); Oxford Univ., Sum., 1979, Cert. (Brit. Stud.). **Orgs.:** ALA: Cncl. (1972–76); RASD (Pres., 1978–79; Bd. of Dir., 1974–77, 1979–80; Outstan. Ref. Bk. Com. (Ch., 1972–74); Pubn. Com. (1979–); Various other coms. TN LA. OH LA. Various coms. and orgs. Sch. of LS, Queens Coll.: Adv. Com. (1977–). **Honors:** Phi Beta Kappa, 1955; Beta Phi Mu, 1968; Ford Fndn., Cncl. on Lib. Resrc. Flwshp., 1974. **Pubns.:** *Library Education: An International Survey.* (1968); *Library School Teaching Methods: Courses in the Selection.* (1969); *The Goals and Objectives Experience.* (1975); *Reference Books for Small and Medium-sized Libraries.* (1979); Ed. *Lib. Trends* (Ap. 1972, Ja. 1976); many other articles in lib. pubn. **Activities:** 95-Literature, 89-Emily Dickinson. **Addr.:** Director of Libraries and Professor, Mercy College, 555 Broadway, Dobbs Ferry, NY 10522.

Boner, Marian O. (Je. 25, 1909, Cleburne, TX) Retired, 1981–; Dir., State Law Lib., 1972–81; Assoc. Libn., Assoc. Prof., Law, Univ. of TX Sch. of Law, 1969–72, 1965–69, Ref. Libn., 1960–65. **Educ.:** Univ. of TX, 1926–30, BA (Phys.), 1930–31, MA (Phys.), 1950–55, LLB. **Orgs.:** AALL: Secy. (1970–73); Pres. (1974–75). Southwest. Assn. of Law Libs.: Pres. (1969–70). State Bar of TX: Com. on Legal Pubns. (Ch., 1975–77); Com. on Hist. and Traditions of the Bar (1978–81). **Pubns.:** *Reference Guide to Texas Law and Legal History* (1976); "Erie v. Tompkins, a Study in Judicial Precedent," *TX Law Review* (Ap.–My. 1962); "Index to Chambers Opinions," *Law Lib. Jnl.* (My. 1972). **Activities:** 77 **Addr.:** 1508 Hardouin Ave., Austin, TX 78703.

Bonfield, Lynn (Ap. 6, 1939) Arch. Consult, Self-empl., 1978–; Mss. Libn., CA Hist. Socty., 1971–78, Actg. Lib. Dir., 1974; Archvst., Urban Arch., Temple Univ., 1969–70; Coll. Arch., Cur. of Mss. Schlesinger Lib., Radcliffe Coll., 1966–68; Asst. Archvst., Harvard Univ., 1965–66. **Educ.:** Oberlin Coll., 1961, AB (Hist.); Simmons Coll., 1967, MLS (LS); Oral Hist. Cert., Univ. of CA, Los Angeles, 1968. **Orgs.:** SAA: Cncl. (1979–), various coms. Socty. of CA Arch.: Co-fndr., Cncl. (1973–75). CA Heritage Prsrvn. Comsn. W. Coast Assn. Women Hist. Frnds. San Francisco Pub. Lib.: Bd. of Dir., VP. Frnds. Bancroft Lib. Frnds. Schlesinger Lib. **Pubns.:** "Day-by-Day Records: Diaries from the California Historical Society Library," *CA Hist.* (Win. 1975, Spr. 1977); "Women's History: A Listing of West Coast Archival and Manuscript Sources," *CA Hist.* (Spr., Sum. 1976); slide/tape progs, reviews. **Activities:** 2, 9; 24, 45; 85 **Addr.:** 4171 23rd St., San Francisco, CA 94114.

Bonfili, Barbara Davis (D. 20, 1923, Morgantown, WV) Head Libn., Morgantown Sr. HS, 1965–; Catlgr., WV Univ., 1960–64. **Educ.:** WV Univ., 1957–60, BS (Elem. Educ.); Univ. of Pittsburgh, 1963–65, MLS; Advnc. Cert., Educ., WV Univ., 1974–. **Orgs.:** WV LA: Conf. Ch. (1974); VP (1975); Pres. (1976–77). SELA: Non-bk Media Com. (1975–). ALA: AASL/Video Comm. Com. (1976–81). Morgantown Pub. Lib: Trustee VP (1979–). **Pubns.:** Ed., *West Virginia Libraries* (1978–). **Activities:** 1, 10; 15, 17, 20; 63, 75, 92 **Addr.:** 746 Amherst Road, Morgantown, WV 26505.

Bonis, Eva M. (D. 12, 1930, Budapest, Hungary) Corp. Libn., Dennison Mfr. Co., 1972–; Ast. Sci. Libn., MA Inst. Tech., 1968–70; Sci. Libn., Univ. MA, 1967–68. **Educ.:** Tech. Univ. of Budapest, 1951–56, Eng. (Chem. Eng.); Simmons Coll., 1962–67, MS (LS). **Orgs.:** SLA: Boston Chap., Sci. and Tech. Div. (Ch., 1978–79); Hosplty. (Ch., 1975–77); Prog. Com. (1974–75). Assoc. Info. Mgrs. Assn. Amer. Chem. Socty. Amer. Mktg. Assn. **Activities:** 12; 15, 20, 39; 59 **Addr.:** Dennison Manufacturing Company, 300 Howard St., Building 26, Framingham, MA 01701.

PROFESSIONAL ACTIVITIES: Institutions: 1. Acad. lib.; 2. Arch.; 3. Assn.; 4. Fed./Gvt. lib.; 5. Inst. lib.; 6. Mfr./Suppl.; 7. Milit. lib.; 8. Musm.; 9. Pub. lib.; 10. Sch. lib.; 11. Sch. of lib. sci.; 12. Spec. lib.; 13. State lib.; 14. (other). **Functions/Activities:** 15. Acq./Col. dev.; 16. Adult srvs.; 17. Admin.; 18. Apprais.; 19. Archit./Bldgs.; 20. Cat./Class.; 21. Chld. srvs.; 22. Circ.; 23. Cons./Pres.; 24. Consult.; 25. Cont. ed.; 26. Educ. lib. sci.; 27. Ext. srvs.; 28. Fund/Grants; 29. Gvt. pubs.; 30. Indx./Abs.; 31. Instr. lib. use; 32. Media srvs.; 33. Micro.; 34. Netwks./Coop.; 35. Persnl.; 36. PR; 37. Publshg.; 38. Recs. mgt.; 39. Ref. srvs.; 40. Repro.; 41. Resrch.; 42. Review.; 43. Secur.; 44. Serials; 45. Spec. col.; 46. Tech. srvs.; 47. Trustees/Bds.; 48. YA srvs.; 49. (other).

Bonn, Jane H. (S. 13, 1937, Denver, CO) Ref. Libn., U.S. Geol. Srvy. Lib., 1981–; Ref. Libn., U.S. Bur. of Reclamation, 1977–81; Libn., U.S. Bur. of Mines, 1976–77; Libn., Arapahoe Reg. Lib., 1974–76. **Educ.:** Purdue Univ., 1957–59, BS (Soc. Sci.); Univ. of Denver, 1974, MAL (Lib.). **Orgs.:** SLA: Nsltr. Co-Ed.; Hosplty. Ch. Rocky Mt. OLUG. Denver Univ. Lib. Sch. Alum. Assn. **Honors:** Beta Phi Mu, 1974. **Pubns.:** "Terminal Equipment for Online Interactive Information Retrieval Using Telecommunications," *Spec. Libs.* (Ja. 1976). **Activities:** 4; 39; 64, 65, 81 **Addr.:** 2372 S. Locust St., Denver, CO 80222.

Bonnaffon, Anna C. (O. 14, 1925, Philadelphia, PA) Med. Libn., U S Walson Army Hosp., 1959–; Med. Libn., Valley Forge Army Hosp., 1957–59; Asst. Libn., Patients' Lib., US Philadelphia Naval Hosp., 1951–59; Asst. Libn., Med. Lib., Womens' Med. Col., PA, 1949–51. **Educ.:** Univ. of PA, 1944–48, AB (Eng/Jnlsm); Drexel Univ., 1948–49, BS (Lib. Sci). **Orgs.:** Med. LA. NJ Hosp. LA. **Activities:** 4, 12; 17, 39; 58, 80, 74 **Addr.:** Medical Library, US Walson Army Hospital, Ft. Dix, NJ 08640.

Bonnell, Pamela G. (F. 2, 1948, Monterey, CA) Dir. of Audience Div., Dallas Symph. Orch., 1980–; Libn., Mgmt. Srvs. Resrch. Lib., 1977–80. Lib. Consult., US Fed. Energy Admin., 1977; Ref. and YA Libn., OK Cnty. Libs., 1974–75. **Educ.:** Cameron Univ., 1969–72, BA (Lang. Arts); Univ. of OK, 1972–73, MLS. **Orgs.:** ALA: IFRT (Secy. 1978–80). JMRT (Liaison to Freedom to Read Fndn., 1977–78. Ch., Local Arrange. Conf. 1978–79. Liaison to the Lib. Admin. and Mgt. Assn. 1979–80). TX LA (Int. Frdm. Com. 1979–83; Spec. Mncpl. Docums. Adv. 1978–79). OK LA (Int. Frdm. Com., Secy. 1974–75). **Honors:** ALA, Shirley Olofson Mem. Awd., 1974. **Pubns.:** "Intellectual Freedom," *OK Libn.* (1974); "A Taste of Texas," *Lib. Jrnl.* (1979). **Activities:** 9, 12; 59, 62 **Addr.:** 1317 Regal Apt. 521, Richardson, TX 75080.

Bonnelly, Claude (Fb. 4, 1946, Quebec City, PQ, Can) Asst. Chief Libn., Laval Univ., Lib., 1978–, Head Ref. Dept., 1975–78, Ref. Libn., 1968–75. **Educ.:** Laval Univ., 1965–68, LPh (Phil.); Univ. de Montreal, 1971–73, MLS. **Orgs.:** Assn. Pour L'Avancement des Sci. et des Techq. de la Documtn.: Com. des Bibs. de Recharche et Spec. (1978–). Can. Assn. Info. Sci.: Fr. Ed., *Can. Jnl. of Info. Sci.* (1977–78). Corp. des Bibtcr. Prof. du Quebec. **Pubns.:** Jt.-auth., "Searching the Social Sciences Literature Online: Social Sci. Search," *Database* (1978); Jt.-auth., "DSI/LAVAL. Organisation et gestion d'un service automatisé de recherches bibliographiques dans une bibliothèque universitaire," *Documtn. et bibs.* (1976); "Banques de données et diffusion sélective de l'information en sciences humaines," *Stage pratique en informatique documentaire. Comptes rendus* (1975); "La référence automatisée dans les bibliothèques d'université et de recherche," *Documtn. et bibs.* (1973); Various other articles. **Activities:** 1; 17, 31, 39; 55, 56, 92 **Addr.:** Bibliotheque Pavillon Bonenfant, Universite Laval, Ste-Foy, PQ G1K 7P4 Canada.

Bonner, Robert J. (Jl. 3, 1941, Hazleton, PA) Dir., Libs., IN Purdue Univ., 1974–; Coord., Cmwlth. Campus Libs., PA State Univ., 1970–74, 1968–70; Pottsville Free Pub. Lib., 1966–68. **Educ.:** King's Coll., AB (Econ.); Rutgers Univ., 1965–66, MLS. **Orgs.:** ALA: RTSD/Reprodct. of Lib. Mtrls. Sect., Telefac. Com. (1973–76); ACRL/Natl. Univ. Ext. Assn. Jt. Liaison Com. on Ext. Lib. Srvs. IN LA: Plng. Com., Ch. PA LA: Conf. Tech. Arrange. Com. (1969); Juniata-Conemaugh Chap., Secy.-Treas., Nom. Com., Ch., Mem. Com., Vice-Ch.; various coms. SLA: IN Chap., Dir.-at-Lg. PA Assn. for Adult Educ.: Lib. Com. (1974). Natl. Univ. Ext. Assn. Indianapolis Lit. Club. **Pubns.:** *A Survey on Telefacsimile Use in Libraries in the United States by Hans Engelke.* **Activities:** 1, 2; 17, 26, 28; 59, 63, 72 **Addr.:** University Library, 815 W. Michigan St., Indianapolis, IN 46202.

Bonner, Sandra J. (Ja. 6, 1948, Brooklyn, NY) Dir. of Lib. Srvs., Rec. for the Blind, 1981–; Head, Ref., Thomas J. Shanahan Lib., Marymount Manhattan Coll., 1977–81, Lectr., Div. of Hum., 1979–80; Libn., Hist. and Soc. Sci. Dept., Mid-Manhattan Lib. of New York Pub. Lib., 1973–77; Tchr., Correct. Readg., Bd. of Educ., New York City, 1971–73; Tchr. of Early Childhood Classes, 1969–71. **Educ.:** Brooklyn Coll. of CUNY, 1964–68, BA (Educ., Eng.); Univ. of MI, 1968–69, MA (Psy. of Readg.); Columbia Univ., 1972–73, MLS. **Orgs.:** ALA. SLA: Cont. Educ. Com. (1979–80). NY Metro. Ref. and Resrch. Lib. Agency: Educ. and Psy. Libns. Discuss. Grp. (Ch., 1976–77); Pub. Srvs. Com./Task Force on Closing the Cat. (1979). **Activities:** 1, 9; 15, 31, 39; 59, 63, 92 **Addr.:** 528 W. 111 St., New York, NY 10025.

Bonta, Bruce D. (Jl. 10, 1941, East Orange, NJ) Head, Gen. Ref., PA St. Univ., 1977–, Asst. Head, Ref. Dept., 1971–77; Readers Srvs. Libn., Colby Coll., 1966–71; Ref. Libn., Lib. of Cong., 1963–66. **Educ.:** Bucknell Univ., 1959–63, AB (Hist.); Univ. of ME, 1966–69, MLS. **Orgs.:** ALA: RASD/Mach. Assisted Ref. Sect., Costs and Financing Com. (Ch., 1978–80), Ref. Srvs. Lg. Resrch. Libs. Discuss. Grp. (Ch., 1978–79). **Honors:** Phi Kappa Phi, 1969. **Activities:** 1; 31, 39 **Addr.:** E110 Pattee Library, Pennsylvania State University, University Park, PA 16802.

Bonynge, Jeanne Redfield (F. 10, 1925, Bronxville, NY) Libn., US Tax Ct., 1978–; Ast. Libn., IRS, 1974–78; Asst. Libn., Schiff, Hardin and Waite, 1971–73. **Educ.:** Denison Univ., 1942–46, BA (Soc. Sci.); Rosary Coll., 1970, MALS. **Orgs.:** AALL. Law Libns. Socty. of Washington, D.C. Chicago Assn. of Law Libs.: Hosplty. Com. (1971–73). Wilmette Leag. of Women Voters: Pres. (1965–67). Grt. Chicago Area Com. for UNICEF: Pres. (1969–73). Lake MI Inter-Leag. Grp.: Ch. (1967–69). **Honors:** Vlg. of Wilmette, IL - Cent. - Outstan. Citizen Awd., 1972. **Activities:** 4; 15, 17, 39; 59, 77, 78 **Addr.:** Library, United States Tax Court, 400 Second St., N.W., Washington, DC 20217.

Boody, Patricia W. (Ja. 24, 1954, Raleigh, NC) Info. Sci., FL Inst. of Phosphate Resrch., 1980–; Libn., Tampa Subdist. Ofc., US Geol. Srvy., 1979–80; Lit. Srchr., ILL, Univ. of NC, US Env. Protection Agency, 1978–79. **Educ.:** Pfeiffer Coll., 1972–75, AB (Eng.); Univ. of NC, 1977–78, MS (LS). **Orgs.:** SLA: FL Chap. (Secy., 1981–82), Lcl. Arrange. Com. (State Coord., 1980–81). FL LA: Site Sel. Com. (1981). Polk Cnty. Acad. Pub., and Spec. Libns. Assn.: Un. List of Serials Com. (Ch., 1980–81). Tampa Bay Libs. Cnsrtm. **Pubns.:** Jt. ed., *Phosphogypsum: An International Symposium on Phosphogypsum* (1981). **Activities:** 12, 13; 15, 17, 39; 65, 91 **Addr.:** Florida Institute of Phosphate Research, P. O. Box 877, Bartow, FL 33830.

Booher, Harold Hasting (Jl. 14, 1929, Fort Worth, TX) Libn., Assoc. Prof., New Testament, Episcopal Theo. Semy. of the SW, 1974–; Asst. Prof., Relig., Salem Coll., 1966–67; Actg. Libn., Episcopal Theo. Semy. of the SW, 1965–66, Instr., New Testament, 1964–65; Instr., Relig., Miami Univ., OH, 1963–64. **Educ.:** TX Wesleyan Coll., 1947–51, BS (Chem.); South. Meth. Univ., 1955–57, MA (Bible); Columbia Univ., 1957–63, MPhil (Bible); Univ. of TX, Austin, 1968–72, MLS. **Orgs.:** ATLA: Com. on Anl. Confs. (1977–80). **Activities:** 1; 15, 17, 20; 90 **Addr.:** Episcopal Theological Seminary of the Southwest, P.O. Box 2247, Austin, TX 78768.

Booker, Barbara Ann (Ja. 10, 1932, Powhatan Cnty., VA) Supvsr., Media and Lib. Srvs., Charlottesville City Schs., 1974–; Asst. Supvsr., Sch. Libs., VA Dept. of Educ., 1970–74; Supvsr., Libs., Chesterfield Cnty. Pub. Schs., 1966–70; Libn., Huguenot HS, 1960–66. **Educ.:** Longwood Coll., 1949–53, BS (LS, Elem. Educ.); Univ. of VA, 1964–66, MED (AV Educ.). **Orgs.:** Gvr.'s Conf. Lib. and Info. Srvs.: Del. (1979). ALA. VA LA: Bd. of Dirs. (1970). VA Educ. Media Assn.: Bd. of Dirs. (1978); Pres.-Elect (1980); Pres. (1981). Chesterfield Cnty. Lib. Bd. Cmnty. Srvs. Bd.: Ch. (1981). Gvr.'s Conf. on Lib. and Info. Srvs.: Del. (1979). **Honors:** VA Assn. for Educ. Comm. and Tech., Media Educ. of Yr., 1974; **Activities:** 10, 13; 26, 32, 36 **Addr.:** Charlottesville City Schools, 4th St. N.W., Charlottesville, VA 22901.

Bookstein, Abraham (Mr. 22, 1940, New York, NY) Assoc. Prof., Univ. of Chicago Lib. Sch., 1971–. **Educ.:** City Coll. of NY, 1957–61, BS (Phys.); Univ. of CA, Berkeley, 1961–66, MS (Phys.); Yeshiva Univ., 1966–69, PhD (Phys.); Univ. of Chicago, 1969–70, MA (LS). **Orgs.:** Assn. for Comp. Mach. ASIS. **Pubns.:** Co-Auth., *Prospects for Change in Bibliographic Control* (1977); Jt. auth., *Operative Research: Prospects for Libraries* (1972); "Operations Research in Libraries," *Advncs. in Libnshp.* (1979); "Explanations of the Bibliomatric Laws," *Col. Mgt.* (1980). **Activities:** 11; 26, 41; 56, 75 **Addr.:** Graduate Library School, 1100 E. 57 St., Chicago, IL 60637.

Boone, Edward James, Jr. (N. 22, 1926, Reading, PA) Archvst., MacArthur Meml., 1973–; Tchr., Bayside HS, Virginia Beach, 1971–73; Naval Ofcr., U.S. Navy, 1952–70, Petty Ofcr., 1951–52, 1944–46. **Educ.:** Fordham Coll., 1950–51, AB (Eng.); Old Dominion Univ., 1970–73, (Hist.); U.S. Navy Lang. Sch., Washington, DC, 1954–55, Cert. in Russ. **Orgs.:** Middle Atl. Reg. Arch. Conf. SAA. Amer. Assn. for Advnc. of Slavic Std. **Addr.:** MacArthur Memorial, MacArthur Square, Norfolk, VA 23510.

Boone, Jon A. (Ja. 4, 1937, Orange City, IA) Coord., Col. Dev. and Acq., Univ. of ND, 1981–. Head, Col. Dev., North. IL Univ., 1977–81; Head, Acq., Univ. of NE-Omaha, 1970–76; Lib. Dir., Midwest. Col., 1966–70; Sci. Ref. Libn., MT State Univ., 1962–65. **Educ.:** IA State Univ., 1955–56; Univ. of IA, 1956–59, BA (Geol.); 1959–60, BA (Eng.); Univ. of Denver, 1960–61, MA (LS); Univ. of IA, 1965–66, (Amer. Std.); Univ. of NE-Lincoln, 1976–77, MA, (Eng.). **Orgs.:** ALA. AAUP: Univ. of NE-Omaha Chap. Pres. (1974–76); NE State Exec. Bd. (1974–75). **Pubns.:** "When Are Two Better Than One", *NE Assn. Qtly.* (Sum. 1972). **Activities:** 1; 15, 17 **Addr.:** 30 Conklin Ave , Grand Forks, ND 58202.

Boone, Mary L. (D. 29, 1944, Durham, NC) Lib. Dir., Chapel Hill Pub. Lib., 1978–; Asst. to Dir., U.S. Army Lib. Prog., Europe, 1977–78, Admin. Libn., 1974–77; Resrc. Libn., ACTION Lib., 1973–74. **Educ.:** Univ. of NC, 1962–67, BA (Eng.), 1972–73, MSLS. **Orgs.:** ALA: PLA/Small and Medium Sized Libs. Sect., Pubns. Com. (1980–82); LAMA/various sects. NC LA: Pub. Lib. Sect., Exec. Bd. (Dir., 1980–82). NC Pub. Lib. Dirs. Assn.: Exec. Bd. (Mncpl. Lib. Rep., 1980–81). Zonta Intl. Univ. of NC Sch. of LS Alum. Assn.: Exec. Bd. (*Nsltr.* Ed., 1980–); Pubcty. Com. **Pubns.:** *Our Library and the Community, a community analysis* (1979). **Activities:** 9; 17 **Addr.:** Chapel Hill Public Library, 523 E. Franklin St., Chapel Hill, NC 27514.

Boone, Morell D. (D. 15, 1942, Londonderry, Derry, N. Ire) Dean, Lrng. Resrcs., Univ. of Bridgeport, 1977–; Visit. Asst. Prof., Syracuse Univ., 1976–77; Libn., Univ. of Bridgeport, 1973–76; Lectr., Syracuse Univ., 1970–72; Asst. Ref. Libn., Hobart and Wm. Smith Colls., 1968–70. **Educ.:** Kutztown State Coll., 1960–64, BS (Educ.); Syracuse Univ., 1966–68, MS (LS); Syracuse Univ., 1970–80, PhD Cand. (Instr. Tech.). **Orgs.:** ALA: AV Com. (1978–); Stdg. Com. on Stans. (1973–77). CT State Lib.: Com. to Estab. Coop. Units (1975–77). CT Gvrs. Conf. on Lib. and Info. Srvs.: Del. (Dec., 1978). **Pubns.:** Ed., *Approaches to Measuring Library Effectiveness* (1972); Contrib., *Use, Misuse, and Nonuse of Academic Libraries* (1970); "Iran's Learning Resource Centers," *Jnl. of World Educ.* (Spr./Sum. 1978); "Camelot...A Quest or a Kingdom?" *Coll. and Resrch. Libs.* (Jan. 1973); "Survey of User Education in N.Y. State Academic Libraries," (ERIC microfiche) (1971). **Activities:** 1, 10; 17, 19, 32; 56, 63, 93 **Addr.:** University of Bridgeport, 126 Park Ave., Bridgeport, CT 06602.

Boone, Samuel Moyle (Ap. 9, 1919, Gates, NC) Newsp. & Micros. Libn., Perkins Lib., Duke Univ., 1980–; Head, Interlib. Srvs., Ctr., Univ. NC, 1952–80; Signal Corps Radio Oper., US Army, 1942–45. **Educ.:** Univ. of NC, 1946–49, AB (Jnlsm.); 1958–64, MS (LS). **Orgs.:** ALA: Reprodct. of Lib. Mtrls. Sect. (Ch. 1969–70); Prsvtn. Com. (1975–78); Telefac. Com. (1977–79); Copyrt. Update (1978–80). Natl. Micro. Assn.: Newsp. Stan. Com. (1969–74); Tar Heel Chap., (Dir., 1977–80). **Honors:** Natl. Micro. Assn., Cert. of Appreciation, 1974. **Pubns.:** *Current Practices in the Administration of Library Photographic Services* (1964); Co-Auth., "An Ordering Procedure Utilizing the Xerox Process," *Lib. Resrcs. and Tech. Srvcs.* (Win. 1966); "A Regional Approach to Catalog Card Reproduction Using Electrostatic and Micrographic Techniques," *Micro and Lib. Cats.* (1977). **Activities:** 1; 23, 33, 34; 61 **Addr.:** 57 Oakwood Dr., Chapel Hill, NC 27514.

Boorkman, Jo Anne (Jl. 21, 1947, San Jose, CA) Asst. Dir., Pub. Srvs., Hlth. Sci. Lib., Univ. of NC, 1977–; Asst. Head Ref., Biomed. Lib., Univ. of CA, Los Angeles, 1973–77, Bibl. Srch. Anal., Pac. S.W. RML, 1971–73. **Educ.:** Scripps Coll., 1965–69, BA (Bio.); Univ. of IL, 1969–71, MSLS; Med. LA, 1972, Cert. **Orgs.:** Med. LA: Schol. Com. (1978–). SLA. Med. Lib. Grp. of South. CA: Career Guid. Com. (Ch., 1973–74). NC SLA: Career Guid. Com. (1977–;) *NCSLA Bltn.* (Rpt., 1978–); Univ. of NC Libns. Assn. Univ. of NC Fac. Clb. **Honors:** Beta Phi Mu, 1971. **Pubns.:** *Introduction to Reference Sources in the Health Sciences* (1980). **Activities:** 1; 17, 39, 49-Online bibl. srvs.; 58, 68, 80 **Addr.:** Health Sciences Library 223 H, University of North Carolina, Chapel Hill, NC 27514.

Boorstin, Daniel J. (O. 1, 1914, Atlanta, Ga) Libn. of Cong., Lib. of Cong., 1975–; Sr. Histn., Smithsonian Inst., 1973–75; Dir., Natl. Musm. of Hist. & Tech., Smithsonian Institution, 1969–73; Preston and Sterling Morton Disting. Service Prof. of Amer. Hist., Univ. of Chicago, 1965–69; Assoc. Prof., 1949–56; Asst. Prof., 1944–49; Ofc. of Land-Lease Admn., 1942–43; various other tchg. positions. **Educ.:** Harvard Coll., 1930–34, AB summa cum laude; Rhodes Scholar, Balliol Coll., Oxford Univ., 1934–37, BA Jurisprudence, 1st class honors, Bachelor, Civil Law, 1st class honors; Yale Univ., 1940, JSD. **Orgs.:** ALA. **Honors:** Friends of Lit., Award, 1959; Columbia Univ., Bancroft Prize, 1959; Parkman Prize, 1966; Pulitzer Prize for History, 1974; Drexel Univ. Lib. Sch. Alumni Assn., Disting. Scr. Award, 1976; numerous other honors and awards. **Pubns.:** *Democracy and Its Discontents* (1974); *The Americans: The Democratic Experience* (1973); *The Americans: The Colonial Experience* (1958); *The Decline of Radicalism* (1969); *The Americans: The National Experience* (1965); many other books. **Activities:** 4; 41 **Addr.:** Library of Congress, Washington, DC 20540.

Booth, Robert Edmond (My. 21, 1917, Bridgeport, CT) Prof. & Dir., Div. of Lib. Sci., Wayne State Univ., 1960–; Rsrch. Assoc. & Instr., Western Reserve Univ. Sch. of Lib. Sci., 1956–60; Assoc. Libn., MIT, 1947–56; Ref. Libn., Peabody Inst. Lib., 1946–47; Ed. and Bib., 1944–46; Jr. Asst., Detroit Pub. Lib., 1943–44. **Educ.:** Wayne State Univ., 1936–41; AB (Hist.); Columbia Univ., 1941–42, ABLS; Univ. of MI, 1942–43, AMLS; Case/Western Resv. Univ., 1956–60, PhD (Lib. Sci). **Orgs.:** ALA: IRRT, Secy, Treas. (1976–79). MI Lib. Assoc: Pres. (1970–71); Cncl. of Deans, Secy, Treas. (1978–80). AALS. SLA. Beta Phi Mu; Phi Delta Kappa; World Future Soc. **Honors:** Univ. of MI, Disting. Alum. Awd. 1977; Case-Western Rsv. Univ., Disting. Alum. Awd., 1979; MI Lib. Assoc., Libn. of the Year, 1979. **Pubns.:** jt. Auth. *Personnel Utilization in Libraries* (1974); *Culturally Disadvantaged* (1967); *Index to Poverty, Human Resources and Manpower Information* (1967); *Personnel Utilization in Libraries* (1974); "Dard Hunter & His Life with Paper" *Among Friends* (1979). **Activities:** 1, 11; 17, 26 **Addr.:** Wayne State Univ., Division of Library Science, Detroit, MI 48202.

Borchin, Anna P. (My. 31, 1909, Klcove Dluhe, Czechoslovakia) Retired, 1975–; Visit. Prof., Univ. of Cincinnati, 1966–70; Head Libn., Woodward HS, 1953–75; Libn., Lloyd HS, Erlanger, KY, 1949–53, Tchr., 1945–49; Tchr., Lynch, KY Schs., 1928–1943. **Educ.:** Univ. of KY, 1928–38, BA (Sec. Educ.), 1950–54, MA (LS and Sec. Educ.). **Orgs.:** OH Assn. of Sch.

Special Subjects/Services: 50. Adult educ.; 51. Advert./Mktg.; 52. Aerosp.; 53. Agric.; 54. Area std.; 55. Arts/Hum.; 56. Autom.; 57. Bibl./Prtg.; 58. Bio. sci.; 59. Bus./Fin.; 60. Chem.; 61. Copyrt.; 62. Documtn.; 63. Educ.; 64. Engin.; 65. Env.; 66. Eth. grps.; 67. Film; 68. Food/Nutr.; 69. Geneal.; 70. Geo.; 71. Geol.; 72. Handcpd.; 73. Hist.; 74. Int. frdm.; 75. Info. sci.; 76. Insr.; 77. Law; 78. Legis.; 79. Math./Comp. sci.; 80. Med.; 81. Metals; 82. Nat. resrcs.; 83. Newsp.; 84. Nuc. sci.; 85. Oral hist.; 86. Petr./Energy; 87. Pharm.; 88. Phys./Astr./Math.; 89. Readg.; 90. Relig.; 91. Sci./Tech.; 92. Soc. sci.; 93. Telecom.; 94. Transp.; 95. (other).

Libns.: Secy. (1960), Pres. (1963); Catholic Lib. Assn.: Pres. (1969–70, 1977–79); Cincinnati Sec. Sch. Libns. Assn.: Pres. and founder (1970), Prog. Com. (1975–78). Natl. Lib. Week: Dir. for OH (1966); Delta Kappa Gamma: Xi Chap. (VP, Mem. Ch., Pubcty. Ch.). **Honors:** OH Educ. Lib./Media Assoc., Awd. of Merit, 1979. **Pubns.:** "History of Cincinnati," *Catholic Lib. World* (1970); "Tips for Exhibit," *OH Assoc. of Sch. Libns. Bltn.* (Ja. 1965); Ed., *OH Assn. of Sch. Libns. Bltn.* (1965–67); Various other articles and columns. **Activities:** 10; 15, 17, 20; 57, 63, 75 **Addr.:** 3175 Hulbert Ave., Erlanger, KY 41018.

Borchuck, Fred P. (F 6, 1934, Newark, NJ) Dir., Univ. Lib., East Tennessee State Univ., 1981–; Dir. of Lib. & Media Srvs., Shippensburg State Coll., 1978–81; Dir. of Lib. Srvs., Coe Coll., 1974–78; Circ. Libn., A. R. Mann Lib., Cornell Univ., 1965–71. **Educ.:** Rutgers Univ., 1959–62, BA (Eng.); Rutgers Univ., 1963–65, MLS; 1971–78, PhD (Lib. Srvs.). **Orgs.:** ALA. Oral Hist. Assn. **Activities:** 1, 11; 17, 31, 39; 55, 65, 91 **Addr.:** ETSU, Box 24, 450A, Johnson City, TN 37614.

Borders, Florence M. (Edwards) (F. 24, 1924, New Iberia, LA) Sr. Archvst., Amistad Resrch. Cntr., 1970–; Head of Tech. Srvs., Grambling State Univ., 1959–70; Cat. Libn., TN State Univ., 1958–59; Asst. Librn. in charge of Cat., Bethune-Cookman Coll., 1947–58. **Educ.:** Southern Univ., 1941–45, BA (Eng.); Rosary Coll., 1946–47, BA, (LS); 1964, MA (LS); LA State Univ., 1966–67, Post-master's fellow. **Orgs.:** SAA. Frnds. of Arch. Greater New Orleans Lib Club. Zeta Phi Beta Sorority, Inc. Ladies Auxiliary, Knights of Peter Claver. St. Theresa Little Flower Ct. #52. **Honors:** Phi Alpha Theta, 1979; Phi Beta Sigma Fraternity, Citation, 1969. **Pubns.:** "The Amistad Research Center," *LA Lib. Assn.* (Sum. 1974); *Guide to the Microfilm Edition of the Countee Cullen Papers,* Bulletin, (1975). **Activities:** 2; 20, 39, 41; 66, 69, 85 **Addr.:** Amistad Research Center, 2601 Gentilly Blvd., New Orleans, LA 70122.

Boren, Michael E. (Ja. 11, 1952, Ft. Sill, OK) Libn., Cohen and Uretz, 1981–; Libn., Jt. Com. on Taxation, U.S. Congs., 1979–81; Libn., Dechert, Price and Rhoads, 1978–79; Libn., Miller and Chevalier, 1977–78; Libn., Cohen and Uretz, 1975–77. **Educ.:** Oberlin Coll., 1970–73, BMus (Msc.); Guildhall Sch. of Msc. and Drama, London, Eng., 1973 (Msc.); Cath. Univ. of Amer., 1977–, MSLS. **Orgs.:** SLA. AALL: Legis. and Legal Dev. Com. (1977–); Pvt. Law Libs. Spec. Interest Sect. (Secy.-Treas., 1980–81). Law Libns.' Socty. of DC. Treas. (1979–80). **Pubns.:** Ed., *Pvt. Law Libs. Nsltr.* (1977–79). **Activities:** 12; 15, 39, 41; 77 **Addr.:** Cohen & Uretz, 1775 K St., N.W., Washington, DC 20006.

Borgeson, Earl C. (D. 2, 1922, Boyd, MN) Law Lib., Southern Methodist University, 1978; Assoc. Libn., LA Cnty. Law Lib., 1975; Assoc. Dir., Stanford Univ. Lib., 1970–; Libn. Harvard Law Sch. Lib., 1952–70. **Educ.:** Univ. Minnesota, BSL, 1947; LLB, 1949; Univ. Washington, 1949–50, BA (Law Libnshp.). **Orgs.:** AALL: Exec. Bd. (1967–69); Pres. (1968). **Activities:** 1, 12; 17, 24, 39; 77 **Addr.:** 10724-B Park Village Pl., Dallas, TX 75230.

Borglund, Shirley Alice (Ap. 24, 1935, Salina, KS) Lib. Dir., Hlth. Sci. Lib., Stormont-Vail Reg. Med. Ctr., 1979–; Acq., Cat. Libn., 1977–79, Lib. Asst., 1975–77; Cat. Libn., KS State Hist. Socty. Lib., 1972–73, 1969–70. **Educ.:** Ottawa Univ., 1953–61, BA (Home Econ.); Emporia KS State Univ., 1974–76, MLS; Med. LA, 1978, Cert. (Hlth. Sci. Libnshp.). **Orgs.:** Med. LA: Hosp. Lib. Sect.; Midcontl. Chap., Educ. Com. (1980–). Topeka Area Med. Lib. Grp. KS Online Grp. AAUW. **Honors:** Beta Phi Mu, 1976. **Activities:** 5, 12; 15, 17, 41; 58, 59, 80 **Addr.:** Health Sciences Library, Stormont-Vail Regional Medical Center, 1500 W. 10th St., Topeka, KS 66606.

Borko, Harold (F. 4, 1922, New York, NY) Prof., Univ. of CA, Los Angeles, 1967–; Assoc. Staff Head, Lang. Prcs. and Retrieval Staff, Syst. Dev. Corp., 1957–67; Syst. Trng. Spec., RAND Corp., 1956–57. **Educ.:** Univ. of CA, Los Angeles, 1946–48, AB (Psych.); Univ. of South. CA, 1948–49, MA, 1949–52, PhD (Psych.). **Orgs.:** ASIS: Pres. (1966). AALS. Assn. for Comp. Mach. Amer. Psychological Assn.: Fellow. Amer. Federation of Info. Prcs. Soctys.: Bd. of Dir. **Honors:** Phi Beta Kappa, Sigma Xi, Phi Gamma Mu. **Pubns.:** Jt. auth., *Indexing Concepts and Methods* (1978); Jt. auth., *Information Systems and Networks* (1977).; Jt. auth., *Abstracting Concepts and Methods* (1975); Ed., *Targets for Research in Library Education* (1973); Jt. auth., *Computers and the Problems of Society* (1972); Various other monographs and articles. **Addr.:** Graduate School of Library and Information Science, Univ. of California, Los Angeles, 405 Hilgard Ave., Los Angeles, CA 90024.

Born, Gerald M. (My. 16, 1936, Hammond, IN) Pres., Celadon Press, 1976–; Exec. Secy., PLA & ASLA, ALA, 1970–76; Resrcs. Coord., North Suburban Lib. Syst., 1968–70; Bldg. Consult., IL State Lib., 1966–68. **Educ.:** Butler Univ., 1955–59, BA (Hist.); IN Univ., 1960–61, MA (Lib. Sci.). Soc. of Golden Section: Pres. (1970–74). **Activities:** 9, 13; 17, 20, 24 **Addr.:** 5039 N. Winthrop, Chicago, IL 60640.

Bornt, Phyllis (S. 14, 1929, Schenectady, NY) Coord. of Branches, Schenectady Cnty. Pub. Lib., 1975–; Head, Ref. Dept., 1971–75; Branch Libn., 1960–71; Asst. Libn., Brooklyn Pub. Lib., 1955–60. **Educ.:** Central Coll., 1947–51, BA (Eng. Lit.); Columbia Univ., 1951–52, MLS. **Orgs.:** ALA. NY LA. Hudson-Mohawk LA. **Activities:** 9; 16, 17, 39 **Addr.:** Schenectady County Public Library, Clinton & Liberty St., Schenectady, NY 12305.

Borock, Freddie (Ms.) (Ja. 2, 1931, Brooklyn, NY) Med. Libn., Brookhaven Meml. Hosp., 1975. **Educ.:** Brooklyn Coll., 1948–52, BA (Eng. Lit.); C.W. Post Coll., 1974–76, MLS. **Orgs.:** Med. and Sci. Libs. of Long Island: Pres. (1978–79); Prog. Ch., (1977–78); CE Ch. (1979–80). Med. LA: NY Reg. Grp.; Small Hlth. Sci. Libs. Com. (1979–80). Med. LA. Reg. Med. Lib.: Adv. and Plng. Com. (1979–); ILL Com. (1979–81); Ad Hoc Com. (1979–80). **Activities:** 12; 15, 17, 20, 39; 80 **Addr.:** 2 Milleridge Ln., Smithtown, NY 11787.

Borovansky, Vladimir Theodore (My. 25, 1931, Prague, Czechoslovakia) Head, D.E. Noble Sci. & Engin. Lib., AZ State Univ., 1968–; Head, Ref. Dept., Univ. of Petr. & Minerals Lib., Dhahran, Saudi Arabia, 1978–79; Asst. Head, Info. Ctr., Resrch. Inst. for Ferrous Metallurgy, Prague, Czechoslovakia, 1959–67, Mgr., Heat treatment lab., 1955–59. **Educ.:** Charles University, Prague, Czechoslovakia, 1960–65, Grad.Libr. (LS/Tech.); Cmrcl. Acad., Prague, Czechoslovakia, 1946–49; 1956–57, Cert., (Bus.). **Orgs.:** Amer. Inst. of Aeronautics & Astronautics. Czechoslovak Soc. for Arts & Scis. in Amer. **Pubns.:** "Academic Reference Librarians," *J. Acad. Libnshp.* (Mr. 1979); "Solar Energy Collection at ASU", *ASHRAE J.* (N. 1977); H. Auth., *Collection Analysis Project.* Final report (1978); "Solar Energy Information System" (A Proposal) *Sharing the Sun, Solar Technology in the Seventies* (1976); "Use of Faculty Profile Cards for Disseminating Information", *Network* (1975); Various other articles. **Activities:** 1; 17, 31, 39; 52, 64, 91 **Addr.:** 7026 N. 14th Street, Phoenix, AZ 85020.

Bortnick, Jane (Ap. 7, 1947, St. Louis, MO) Anal. in Info. Scis., Lib. of Congs./Congsnl. Resrch. Srvs., 1976–, Spec. Asst., 1974–76; Staff Asst., U.S. Senate, 1973–74; Instr., Cnty. Coll. of Morris, NJ, 1970–73. **Educ.:** Univ. of WI, Madison, 1965–69, BA (Hist.); Rutgers Univ., 1969–71, MA (Hist.); American Univ., 1975–76, (Tech. Mgt.). **Orgs.:** ASIS. Amer. Assn. for the Advnc. of Sci. **Honors:** Phi Kappa Phi; Phi Alpha Theta. **Pubns.:** Jt. auth., *State Legislature Use of Information Technology* (1978); Jt. auth., "An Overview of Computerized Legal Information Systems", *Law & Computer Technology* (1st Quarter 1977); "Revista de Informacao Legislativa," *Brazilian Senate Jnl.* (1979); "State Legislatures and Information Technology", *Law & Computer Technology* (2nd Quarter, 1978); Jt. author: "Scientific and Technical Information (STI) Activities: Issues and Opportunities", Com. Print, Com. on Sci. & Tech., U.S. House of Representatives (1979). **Activities:** 4; 24, 41; 75, 78, 91 **Addr.:** Science Policy Research Division, Congressional Research Service, Library of Congress, Washington, DC 20540.

Bosca, David Thomas (D. 20, 1947, Jackson, MI) Chief, Lit. and Phil. Div., Chicago Pub. Lib., 1977–; Dir., Vicksburg-Warren Cnty. Pub. Lib., 1975–77; Coord., Ref. and Info. Div., Jackson Metro. Lib. Syst., 1974–75; Ref. Libn., 1973–74. **Educ.:** Univ. of Notre Dame, 1966–71, BA; Univ. of MI, 1972–73, MALS; MS Coll., 1974–77, MA (Eng.). **Orgs.:** ALA:RASD/Outstan. Ref. Srcs. Com. (1978–). IL LA. Chicago Lib. Clb. **Pubns.:** "Library of the Mississippi School for the Blind," *MS Library News* (June 1974). **Activities:** 9; 15, 17, 39; 55, 75, 90 **Addr.:** 3168 North Pine Grove Ave. #2, Chicago, IL 60657.

Bose, Anindya (Ja. 1, 1928, Mymensing, Bengal, India) Dir., Comp. Access Lab., Univ. of Denver, 1979–; Assoc. Prof., Pratt Inst., 1973–78; Asst. Prof., Stockton State Coll., 1972–73. **Educ.:** Univ. of Calcutta, 1958, BA (Econ.); Univ. of Pittsburgh, 1964–70, PhD (Info. Sci.). **Orgs.:** ALA: Country Resrcs. Panel: India (Ch.); LITA. ASIS. **Honors:** Beta Phi Mu. **Pubns.:** "Consumer Protection for the Information User" (1981); *Information System Design Methodology* (1970); "Program Evaluation and Review Technique (PERT) and Critical Path Method (CPM)" in *Encycl. of Lib. and Info. Sci.* (1978); "Automation and the Penrose Library" (videotape) (1979). **Activities:** 11; 26; 56, 75, 93 **Addr.:** University of Denver, Graduate School of Librarianship and Information Management, Denver, CO 80208.

Boshears, Onva K., Jr. (Ag. 31, 1939, Bloomington, IN) Dean, Prof., Sch. of Lib. Srv., Univ. of South. MS, 1976–; Asst. Prof., Lib. Srv., Univ. of KY, 1971–75; Dir. of Lib. Srvs., Asbury Theo. Semy., 1967–70; Residence Halls Libn., Univ. of MI, 1965–67; Asst. Libn., Asbury Theo. Semy., 1962–65; various positions as consult. **Educ.:** Greenville Coll., 1957–61, AB, cum laude (Hist.); Univ. of IL, 1961–62, MS (LS); Asbury Theo. Semy., 1962–65, MAR (Relig.); Univ. of MI, 1965–67, PhD (LS); various crs. **Orgs.:** KY LA: Various sects. MS LA: White Hse. Conf. Com. (Ch., 1977–78); Educ. Com. (Co-Ch., 1980–81); various coms. AALS: Cncl. of Deans and Dirs. (1976–). ALA: ACRL; AASL; RASD; RTSD, Educ. for Resrcs. and Tech. Srvs. Com. (1977–78), Resrch. Com. (1981–); various other coms. Various other orgs. Univ. of MI LS Alum. Socty. Episcopal Church. **Honors:** Beta Phi Mu, 1967; Phi Alpha Theta, 1961. **Pubns.:** Jt. auth., *A Directory of Special Subject Resources in Mississippi Libraries* (1977); "The Public Library and the Senior Citizen; An Annotated Bibliography," *A Demonstration Pilot Program of Comprehensive Library Services for the Aged in Selected Communities in Kentucky* (1974); various confs., sps. **Activities:** 1, 11; 26, 39, 45; 57, 78, 90 **Addr.:** School of Library Service, Southern Station, Box 5146, University of Southern Mississippi, Hattiesburg, MS 39401.

Boss, Richard W. (O. 31, 1937, Arnhem, Netherlands) Info. Systs. Consult., Inc.; Univ. Libn., Princeton Univ., 1975–78; Dir. of Libs., Univ. of TN-Knoxville, 1970–75; Assoc. Dir., Actg. Dir., Univ. of UT, 1966–70; Asst. Dir., 1963–64; Ord. Libn., 1962–63. **Educ.:** Univ. of UT, 1960, BA (Pol. Sci.); Univ. of WA, 1962, MA (LS); Univ. of UT, additional coursework, (Pol. Sci.). **Orgs.:** ALA: Com. on Org. (1970–77); Cncl. (1976–); LAD Tech. Srvs. Stats. Com. (1970–73); ACRL Legis. Com. (1973–74). SELA. TN LA. ARL: Bd. (1975–77). Phi Beta Kappa: Ad hoc Com. to Dev. Criteria for Eval. of Libs. (1974); TN Chap., Pres. (1974–75). **Pubns.:** "Putting the Horse Before the Cart, Planning Microforms Facilities and Services," MICROFORMS REVIEW (Mr.-Ap. 1978); "Circulation Systems: The Options," *Lib. Tech. Reports* (Ja.-F. 1979); "The Library as an Information Broker," *Coll. and Resrch. Libs.* (Mr. 1979); *The Library Manager's Guide to Automation* (1979); *Grant Money and How to Get It* (1980); other bks. and articles. **Addr.:** Information Systems Consultants, Inc., Box 34504, Bethesda, MD 20817.

Bosseau, Don L. (N. 28, 1936, Pittsburg, KS) Univ. Libn., Univ. of HI, 1977–; Dir. of Libs., Emory Univ., 1973–77; Dir. of Libs., Univ. of TX at El Paso, 1972–73; Asst. Univ. Libn., Univ. of CA, San Diego, 1970–72; Head Lib. Syst. Dept., 1966–70; Ref. Libn., General Dynamics Corp. Tech. Info. Cntr. 1964–65; Engineering positions, 1957–64. **Educ.:** KS State Univ., 1956–58, BS (Engin.); Univ. of HI, 1965–66, MLS; Univ. of KS, 1960–61, MS (Engin.). **Orgs.:** Lib. Autom. Resrch. & Consult. Assn.: Pres. (1975). ALA: Ch., Com. on Lib. Autom. Discus. Grp. (1970–73); Ed., Technical Communications, Jnl. of Lib. Autom. (1972–77); Lib. Tech. Prog., Adv. Bd. (1973–74); Nom. Com., Chmn. (1976). HI LA. SOLINET: Bd. of Dir. (1977). Infill-Phot, Inc. Publications: VP, BD. of Dir. (1974–76). Bosso-Nova, Inc.: VP (1979–). Marina Towers, Honolulu: Bd. of Dir. (1979–). **Honors:** Kappa Mu Epsilon, 1956; Mellon/ACRL: Host Director for Minority Administrative Intern Program 1976–77. **Pubns.:** "The Computer in Serials Processing and Control," *Advances in Librarianship Vol 2* (1971); "The University of California at San Diego Serials System - Revisited," *PROGRAM* (Jan. 1970); "COM - Administrative Decisions," *Pcs. of the Natl. Conf. on New Dirs. in Law Libs.* (April 15, 1977); "University of California, San Diego Serials System," *Computerized Systems - Serials,* (1973); "COM Catalogs: An Analysis of the Administrative Decision Points," Sec. Anl. Lib. Micro Law Conf. (1976); Various other articles, papers & films. **Activities:** 1; 17, 24, 32; 56, 91, 93 **Addr.:** University Librarian, University of Hawaii at Manoa, Honolulu, HI 96822.

Bostian, Irma R. (Mr. 27, 1929, DeKalb, IL) Ed. IL. Libs. and Head, Pubns. Unit, IL State Lib., 1965–; Head, Art Srvs., IL State Lib., 1959–65. **Educ.:** North. IL Univ., 1946–50, (Sp/Eng.); Univ. of IL, 1960–62, (LS). **Orgs.:** IL LA: Numerous Comms. Ch. ALA: Ed.: *COSLA Nsltr.* (1974–79). Lawyers Wives Assn.; Delta Zeta; Pi Kappa Delta. **Honors:** H. W. Wilson, Per. Awd., 1972; Springfield Advert. Cncl., 1st place in "Pub. Srvc. and PR, 1979. **Pubns.:** Ed., St. Lib. Rpt. Series (1979); Ed., IL Nodes 1979; Ed., ASLA Pres. Nsltr. 1979. **Activities:** 13; 36, 37; 50, 57, 75 **Addr.:** 15 Timber Hill, Springfield, IL 62704.

Bostley, Sr. Jean R., SSJ, (S. 26, 1940, Greenfield, MA) Libn., St. Joseph Ctrl. HS, Pittsfield, MA, 1969–; Tchr., Libn., St. Thomas the Apostle Sch., West Springfield, MA, 1963–69; Tchr., Sacred Heart Acad., Worcester, MA, 1961–63. **Educ.:** Coll. of Our Lady of the Elms, 1958–69, BA (Soclgy.); SUNY, Albany, 1970–74, MLS; various crs. **Orgs.:** New Eng. LA. ALA. Cath. LA: HS Libs. Sect., Vice-Ch. (1979–81), Ch. (1981–83); New England Chap. (Secy., 1977–81). Srs. of St. Joseph of Springfield: Com. on Wrtg. the Hist. of... (1980–83). **Pubns.:** Contrib., "Salvation History Since Pius IX: A Review of Literature," *Cath. Lib. World* (My.–Je. 1980); invited respondent, "Comment on...Student Library Assistants," *Cath. Lib. World* (Ap. 1978). **Activities:** 10; 17, 20, 32; 63, 90, 93 **Addr.:** St. Joseph Central High School Library, 22 Maplewood Ave., Pittsfield, MA 01201.

Bostwick, Joan E. (Ag. 24, 1948, Kingston, NY) Inst. Lib. Consult., MA Bd. of Lib. Comsns., 1975–80; Inst. Lib. Spec., IL State Lib., 1972–74. **Educ.:** Ursinus Coll., 1966–70, BS (Psy.); FL State Univ., 1971–72, MS (LS). **Orgs.:** ALA: Hlth. and Rehab. Lib. Srvcs. Div./Bd. Dir. (Secy. 1976); Biblther. Com. (1974–76); RASD/Bd. Dir. (1975–77); YASD/Bd. Dir. (Ref. and Adult Srvs. Liason 1975). New Engl. LA: Inst. Libns. Sect. (Ch., 1976–78). est: Logistics Team (Spr. 1978); Bus. and Finance Asst. (Spr. 1979). Amer. Psyt. Assn.: Biblther. RT. Correct. Educ. Assn. **Pubns.:** "Regional Library System-Based Library Service to Residents of State Correctional Institutions," *IL Libs.* (Sept. 1974); *Assessment of Library Services Provided in Bergen County (NJ) Institutions* (1975). **Activities:** 5, 13; 17, 24, 27; 72, 80 **Addr.:** 281 Walden St., Cambridge, MA 02138.

Botkin, Karen R. (O. 16, 1956, New York City, NY) Resrch. Libn., Natl. Broadcasting Co., 1980–. **Educ.:** William Paterson Coll., 1974–77, BA (Performing Arts); Columbia Univ.,

PROFESSIONAL ACTIVITIES: **Institutions:** 1. Acad. lib.; 2. Arch.; 3. Assn.; 4. Fed./Gvt. lib.; 5. Inst. lib.; 6. Mfr./Suppl.; 7. Milit. lib.; 8. Musm.; 9. Pub. lib.; 10. Sch. lib.; 11. Sch. of lib. sci.; 12. Spec. lib.; 13. State lib.; 14. (other). **Functions/Activities:** 15. Acq./Col. dev.; 16. Adult srvs.; 17. Admin.; 18. Apprais.; 19. Archit./Bldgs.; 20. Cat./Class.; 21. Chld. srvs.; 22. Circ.; 23. Cons./Pres.; 24. Consult.; 25. Cont. ed.; 26. Educ. lib. sci.; 27. Ext. srvs.; 28. Fund/Grants; 29. Gvt. pubs.; 30. Indx./Abs.; 31. Instr. lib. use; 32. Media srvs.; 33. Micro.; 34. Netwks./Coop.; 35. Persnl.; 36. PR; 37. Publshg.; 38. Recs. mgt.; 39. Ref. srvs.; 40. Repro.; 41. Resrch.; 42. Review.; 43. Secur.; 44. Serials; 45. Spec. col.; 46. Tech. srvs.; 47. Trustees/Bds.; 48. YA srvs.; 49. (other).

1977–78, MS (LS). **Orgs.:** Assn. of Rec. Snd. Cols. Msc. LA. Thea. LA. **Activities:** 12; 30, 39, 41 **Addr.:** NBC, 30 Rockefeller Plz., Rm. 1426, New York City, NY 10020.

Bouchard-Hall, Robert W. (Ag. 5, 1941, Santa Cruz, CA) Head, Cat. Dept., Stonehill Coll., 1978–; Cat. Spec., Brown Univ., 1976–78; Ref. Libn., Riverside Pub. Lib., 1972–76. **Educ.:** Univ. of Redlands, 1959–63, BA (Hist., Gvt.); CA State Univ., San Jose, 1970–72, MA (LS); various courses. **Orgs.:** New Eng. Lib. Info. Netwk.: Qual. Cntrl. and Cat. Com. (1979–). ALA. **Honors:** Beta Phi Mu, 1971. **Activities:** 1, 9; 20, 39, 44; 54, 70, 83 **Addr.:** 18 Eisenhower Dr., Norton, MA 02766.

Boucher, Virginia (My. 26, 1929, Bloomington, IL) Head, Interlibrary Coop., Univ. of CO, Boulder, 1979–, Head, ILL Srv., 1967–79, Actg. Resrch. and Plng. Libn., 1978; Netwk. Coord., CO State Lib., 1976–77; Ref. Libn., Mncpl. Gvt. Ref. Ctr., Boulder Pub. Lib., 1965–67; various positions as catlgr. or spec. libn., 1953–65. **Educ.:** CO Coll., 1948–51, BA cum laude, (Eng.); Univ. of MI, 1951–52, MALS. **Orgs.:** ALA: Cncl. (1976–); Div. Interests Spec. Com. (1976–79); ACRL; RASD (Pres., 1977–78), Natl. ILL Code Rev. Subcom. (1978–), various coms. Bibl. Ctr. for Resrch.: Adv. Cncl. (1977–). Ctrl. CO Lib. Syst.: Bd. (1979–). Unvsl. Serials and Bk. Exch.: Bd. of Dirs. (1980–). Various other orgs. CO Mt. Clb. Denver Art Musm. Leag. of Women Voters. **Pubns.:** *Colorado Library Network Plan* (1977); Ed., *just b'TWX us; an interlibrary loan information bulletin* (My. 1970–); "Reference and Adult Services Division," *ALA Yrbk, 1977* (1978); "Interlibrary Loan Basics: A Workshop Package" (mimeo.) (1976); "Nonverbal Communication and the Library Reference Interview," *RQ* (Fall 1976). **Activities:** 1; 34, 49-ILL; 61 **Addr.:** Interlibrary Cooperation, University Libraries, Campus Box 184, University of Colorado at Boulder, Boulder, CO 80309.

Boudreau, A. Allan (Ag. 1, 1936, Albany, NY) Cur., Dir., Grand Lodge Lib. and Musm., 1972–; Asst. Dir., Univ. Libs., NY Univ., 1962–72; Admin. Ofcr., NY State Lib., 1958–62. **Educ.:** Russell Sage Coll., 1955–58, BS (Acct.); NY Univ., 1958–62, MBA (Pub. Admin.); Columbia Univ., 1970–72, MS (LS); NY Univ., 1970–73, PhD (Hist.). **Orgs.:** Lib. Trustees Fndn. of NY State: Secy. (1972–). ALA: ALTA, various coms. Various Hist., Lib. Assns. Amer. Mgt. Assn. **Pubns.:** *Role of the Library in Scientific and Scholarly Research* (1965); *Urban University Library Resources* (1973). **Activities:** 14-Pvt.; 24, 47; 50, 75, 92 **Addr.:** One Washington Sq. Vlg., New York, NY 10012.

Boudreau, Berthe (Jl. 21, 1937, Petit Rocher, NB) Prof., Libn., Univ. de Moncton, 1973–; Prof., Libn., Ecole normale, Moncton, 1968–73; Libn., College N. D. d'Acadie, Moncton, 1966–68, Tchr., 1960–65. **Educ.:** Univ. de Moncton, 1956–60, BA; Univ. de Montréal, 1965–66, BLS; Univ. of MI, 1970–72, AMLS; IN Univ., 1975–78, Cert. (Phil., LS). **Orgs.:** ALA. Can. LA. Atl. Prov. LA. ASTED. **Pubns.:** Collaborator, *Guide de la bibliothèque scolaire pour les écoles du Nouveau-Brunswick* (1972); *Selected Curriculum Materials Centers: Organisation and Services* ERIC; "La bibliothèque de l'école élémentaire" 80 slides, cassette, text (1973). **Activities:** 1, 12; 15, 17, 20; 63 **Addr.:** Centre de ressources pédagogiques, Faculté de l'éducation, Université de Moncton, Moncton, NB E1A 3E9 Canada.

Bougas, Stanley J. (D. 7, 1921, Norfolk, VA) Lib. Dir., Dept. of Cmrce. Lib., 1969–; Libn., Assoc. Prof., Washington Coll. Law, Amer. Univ., 1966–69; Law Libn., HEW Lib. 1965–66; Libn., Assoc. Prof. Cath. Univ. Sch. Law, Ponce, PR, 1962–65; Libn., Admin. Asst. to Dean, Emory Univ., Sch. Law, 1961–62; Libn., 1954–61; Asst. Ref. Libn., NY Univ. Sch. Law, 1953–54. **Educ.:** NY Univ., 1946–50, AB (Hist.); Columbia Univ., 1952, MS (LS); Emory Univ. Sch. Law, 1955–62, JD. **Orgs.:** ALA: FLRT (Pres. 1973). FLC: Pres. (1974). SLA: GA Chap., (Treas. 1959). AALL. **Activities:** 1, 4; 17, 25; 77, 78 **Addr.:** 2801 Park Center Dr. (A-612), Alexandria, VA 22302.

Boulet, Paul-Emile (Jn. 19, 1920, Cap St-Ignace, PQ, Can) Univ. Libn., Univ. of PQ, Chicoutimi, 1975–, Libn., 1973–75, Asst. to the Chancellor, 1969–71, Dean, Sci. and Engin., 1969–70; Dean, Engin., Montreal Univ., 1966–69, Prof. Engin., 1958–66. **Educ.:** Montreal Univ., 1938–42, BA (Lit.); Catholic Univ., 1955–58, BEng (Engin.), 1958–59, MS (Phys.); Univ. of Pittsburg, 1971–73, MLS. **Orgs.:** Can. LA. Assn. des Tech. et Sci. de L'Info. Assn. des Bibtcr. Prof. du Québec. Bd. of Chancellors and Rectors of Quebec Univs. **Pubns.:** *Ultrasonic Relaxation Effects in Mixtures of Monochloroethane and Ethyl Alcohol* (1958). **Activities:** 1, 5; 17, 39; 64, 75, 88 **Addr.:** 930 est, rue Jacques Cartier, University of Quebec at Chicoutimi, Chicoutimi, PQ G7H 2B1 Canada.

Boulton, Earl M. (S. 21, 1924, Milwaukee, WI) Head, Ref. and Medline Srvs., Hlth. Sci. Lib., Creighton Univ., 1978–; Coord., Ref. and Autom., Lib. of Rush Univ., 1975–78; Libn. of Prof. Lib., IL State Psyt. Inst., 1972–75; Sci. Libn., IL Wesleyan Univ. Lib., 1969–72; Resrch. Asst., Neurochem. and Pharmgy., Univ. of IA Coll. of Med., 1962–68; Resrch. Asst. in Psychopharmgy., Univ. of IL Coll. of Med., Chicago, 1959–62; Rehab. Shop Supvsr., Jewish Vocational Srv., Milwaukee, 1957–59; Interviewer, WI State Empl. Srv., Milwaukee, 1955–57. **Educ.:** Univ. of WI, Roosevelt Univ., 1951–55, BS (Psy.); North. IL Univ., 1968–69, MALS; Emory Univ., 1971, (Med. Lib.); Cert. (Med. Libn. I), 1972. **Orgs.:** Med. LA. Metro. Omaha Hlth. Sci. Lib. Grp. **Pubns.:** Jt. auth., "Chemical Constitution and Biochemical Correlates of Aryloxyalkylpiperazines," *Arch. Intl. Pharmacodynamics* (1961). **Activities:** 15, 39, 41; 80, 87, 91 **Addr.:** Creighton University Health Sciences Library, 2500 California, Omaha, NE 68178.

Bourne, Charles P. (S. 2, 1931, San Francisco, CA) Head, Prod. Dev., DIALOG Info. Srvs., Inc., 1977–; Dir., Inst. of Lib. Resrch., Prof.-in-Residence, Univ. of CA, Berkeley, Sch. of LS, 1971–77; Pres., Charles Bourne & Assoc., 1968–71; VP, Info. Gen. Corp., 1966–68; Resrch. Engin., Stanford Resrch. Inst., 1957–66. **Educ.:** Univ. of CA, Berkeley, 1957, BS (Electrical Engin.); Stanford Univ., 1963, MS (Indus. Engin.). **Orgs.:** ASIS: Pres. (1970). ALA: ISAD (Dir. 1966–67). Ency. of Lib. and Info. Sci.: Adv. Bd. (1967–). **Honors:** Amer. Documen. Inst., Anl. Awd. of Merit, 1965; Sarada Ranganathan Endowment, Lectr. for 1978. **Pubns.:** *Methods of Information Handling* (1963); "Frequency and Impact of Spelling Errors in Bibliographic Data Bases," *Info. Prcs. and Mgt.* (1977); "Computer-Based Reference Services as an Alternative Means to Improve Resource-Poor Local Libraries in Developing Countries," *Intl. Lib. Review* (1977); jt. auth., "An Improved Title Word Search Key for Large Catalog Files," *Jnl. of Lib. Autom.* (D. 1976); "Improvements in the Coupling of SDI System Output with Document Delivery Systems," *Jnl. of Chem. Info. and Comp. Sci.* (F. 1976); other reports and articles. **Activities:** 6; 41, 49-Online Search Service; 56 **Addr.:** 1619 Santa Cruz Ave., Menlo Park, CA 94025.

Bouton, Marla K. (N. 27, 1946, Denver, CO) Coord., Ctrl. Lib. Netwk., NE Lib. Comsn., 1977–; Dir., User Srvs., Lib. Lrng. Prog., Kearney State Coll., 1975–77. **Educ.:** Hastings Coll., 1964–68, BA (Soclgy.); KS State Univ., 1968–74, MA (Soclgy.); George Peabody Coll., 1974–75, MLS. **Orgs.:** ALA. Mt. Plains LA. NE LA: Int. Frdm. Com. (Ch., 1976–78); PR Com. (Ch., 1979–). NE JMRT: Ch. (1979). Nebraskans for Pub. TV. NE Educ. Media Assn. Nebraskans for Pub. Radio. Frdm. to Read Fndn. **Honors:** Beta Phi Mu. **Pubns.:** "'Bookmarker'-a Cataloging Road Show," *NE LA Qtly.* (Spr. 1979). **Activities:** 13; 24, 25, 34; 74, 92 **Addr.:** P.O. Box 1068, Kearney, NE 68847.

Boutros, Gail A. (Mr. 29, 1938, Painesville, OH) Proj. Libn., Docum. Syst., Ebon Resrch. Syst., Env. Protection Agency, 1980–; Assoc. State Srvs. Libn., Clendening Lib., Univ. of KS Med. Ctr., 1979–80; Med. Libn., Lakeside Hosp., 1975–79; Clinical Med. Libn., Truman Med. Ctr., 1976–77; Ref. Asst., Kansas City Pub. Lib., 1972–75. **Educ.:** OH State Univ., 1957–60, BA (Econ.); Univ. of MO, 1971–72, MA (Lib., Info. Sci.); various crs; wkshps., confs. **Orgs.:** Hlth. Sci. Lib. Grp. of Grt. Kansas City: Cont. Educ. Ch. (1980). Med. LA: Midcontl. Chap. Kansas City MO Pub. Lib. Staff Assn.: Pres. (1974). Clendening Lib. Fac.: Secy. (1979–80). **Honors:** Beta Phi Mu, 1972. **Activities:** 12; 24, 27, 39; 56 **Addr.:** 5708 The Paseo, Kansas City, MO 64110.

Bowden, Ann (F. 7, 1924, East Orange, NJ) Assoc. Dir., Austin Pub. Lib., 1977–; Assoc. Ed., *Papers*, Bibl. Socty. of Amer., 1967–; Lectr., Grad. Sch. of Lib., Info. Sci., Univ. of TX, Austin, 1964–; Libn., Acad. Ctr., 1963, Libn., Hum. Resrch. Ctr., 1960–63, Rare Bk. Libn., 1959–60, Ms. Catlgr., Rare Bk. Lib., 1958–59; various positions in lib., Henry L. Stimson Coll., Yale Univ., 1948–53. **Educ.:** Radcliffe Coll., 1942–44, 1946–48, BA (Scan. Lang., Lit.); Columbia Univ., 1950–51, MS (Lib. Srv.); Univ. of TX, Austin, 1972–75, PhD (Comm.). **Orgs.:** ALA: Cncl. (1975–79); various coms., ofcs.; ACRL/Rare Bk. and Ms. Sect., Vice-ch. (1974–75), Ch. (1975–76), Nom. Com. (Ch., 1979–80), Exec. Bd. (1974–76). SW LA: NEH Southwest. Libs. Proj. (State Ch., 1974–75). TX LA: Pubns. Com. (Ch., 1965–71); various coms. TX Conf. on Lib. and Info. Srvs.: Adv. Com. (1977–79). AMIGOS Bibl. Cncl., Inc.: Bd. of Trustees, Ch. (1980–81), Vice-Ch. (1979–80). TX Info. Exch.: Bd. of Dirs. (1977–78). **Honors:** Kappa Tau Alpha, 1975; Phi Kappa Phi, 1975. **Pubns.:** Ed., *Maps and Atlases* (1978); *Report of a Planning Conference for Solar Technology Transfer, Austin, Texas, 12–13 June 1979* (1979). **Activities:** 2, 9; 41, 45; 57 **Addr.:** 2109 B Exposition Blvd., Austin, TX 78703.

Bowden, Virginia Massey (Jl. 22, 1939, Houston, TX) Assoc. Lib. Dir., Univ. of TX Health Sci. Cntr., 1978–; Asst. to Dir., 1974–78; Syst. Anal., 1970–74; Sr. Progmr., Anal., Bamberger's Dept. Store, 1967–68; Sr. Progmr., Anal., C.E.J.R. Inc., 1965–66; Sr. Progmr., Amer. Medical Assn., 1964–65; Sr. Progmr., Texaco Inc., 1960–64. **Educ.:** Univ. of TX at Austin, 1957–60, BA (Math); Univ. of KY, 1968–70, MS (LS). **Orgs.:** Med. LA: Survey and Stats. Com. (1975–77); MLA News Ed. Com. (1978–80); S. Ctrl. Reg. Grp.; Liason to the MLA. Legis. Com.; Pres. (1980-81). ALA. TX LA. ASIS. **Honors:** Phi Beta Kappa; Bet Phi Mu, Cncl. on Lib. Resrcs. Flwshp., 1978–79; Del., TX Conf. on Libs. and Info. Sci., 1978. **Pubns.:** Jt. auth., "A union catalog of monographs, another approach" *Bltn. of the Med. LA* (1978); "Comparative analysis of health science libraries' monograph collections by computer" *Proc. of the ASIS Annual Mtg.* (1978); Jt. auth., "Management data for collection analysis and development" *Bltn. of the Med. LA* (1978); Jt. auth., "Comparison of holdings of NLM (CATLINE) with those of resource libraries" *Bltn. of the Med. LA* (1979); "Serial transactions in an online circulation system" *Bltn. of the Med. LA* (O. 1979); various other articles. **Activities:** 12; 17, 41, 44; 56, 80 **Addr.:** Library, The University of Texas Health Science Center, 7703 Floyd Curl Dr., San Antonio, TX 78284.

Bowen, Christopher E. (Jl. 24, 1947, New York, NY) Libn., NY Post, 1977–; Head Libn., L. I. Press Pub. Co., 1975–77; Libn., 1972–75. **Educ.:** St. John's Univ. (NY), 1965–70, BA, (Eng.); Queens Coll. (NY), 1972–75, MLS; St. Johns Univ. (NY), 1975–79, BS (Pharm.). **Orgs.:** SLA: Comm. Div. Chmn. (1978–79). **Activities:** 12; 20, 39, 41; 83 **Addr.:** New York Post, 210 South St., New York, NY 10002.

Bowen, Madge Durden (D. 14, 1914, Swainsboro, GA) Lib. Media Spec., Swainsboro HS, 1957–; Tchr., Swainsboro HS, 1954–57; Tchr., Emanuel Cnty. Inst., 1952–53; Lib. Consult. 1969–72. **Educ.:** Univ. of GA, 1932–35, ABJ (Jnlsn.), 1965–69, Med, Eds (LS). **Orgs.:** ALA. GA LA: Sch. Stand. (1968–71), Gvt. Affairs (1978, 79). GA Lib. Trustees Assn.; GA Bd. of Cert. Libns.: Mem. (1971–). St. Adv. Cncl. Elem. Sec. Act. Natl. Educ. Assn. GA Assn. of Educ. Phi Kappa Phi. Various other orgs. **Honors:** GA Cncl. of Pub. Libs., Cert. of Apprec., 1976; Jr. Woman's Club, Citizen of the Yr., 1958; Swainsboro HS, Tchr. of the Yr., 1958. **Pubns.:** "Multi Media–Do or Die", *GA Libn.* (Spr. 1975). **Activities:** 10; 17, 32 **Addr.:** Post Office Box 388, Swainsboro, GA 30401.

Bowers, Elizabeth A. (N. 7, 1917, Riverton, WY) Dir., Weld Cnty. Lib., 1954–; Ref. and Cat. Asst., Univ. of North. CO, 1946–53; Libn., Greeley HS, 1942–43; Circ. Libn. and Asst. Cat., DePauw Univ., 1938–40. **Educ.:** Univ. of North. CO, 1933–37, BA (Eng.); Univ. of Denver, 1937–38, BS (LS). **Orgs.:** ALA: Cncl. (1972–74). CO LA: Pres. (1961–62). CO Cncl. for Lib. Dev.: Ch. (1966–67). P.E.O. **Honors:** CO LA, Cert. of Merit, 1966; Altrusa Club of Greeley, Bus. Woman of the Year, 1966; Altrusa Club of Denver, Beautiful Activist, 1972; CO LA, Libn. of the Year, 1977. **Pubns.:** Jt. auth., *Colorado Plan for Library Development* (1967); Jt. auth., *Standards for Bookmobile Service* (1965); "Centralized Technical Processes in a County Library," Lib. Resrcs. & Tech. Srvs. (Summer 1958). **Activities:** 9; 15, 17, 20 **Addr.:** 2227 23rd Ave., Greeley, CO 80631.

Bowler, Richard L. (Mr. 3, 1943, Lockport, NY) Assoc. Libn./Ref. Srvs., Univ. of NM Sch. of Law Lib., 1981–; Col. Dev. Libn., Univ. of Chicago Law Lib., 1980–81, Law Libn., 1974–80, Head, Pub. Srvs., 1972–73, Ref. Libn., 1970–72, Docum. Libn., 1968–70. **Educ.:** Hobart Coll., 1960–64, BA (Soc.); Univ. of Chicago, 1964–67, JD (Law). **Orgs.:** AALL: Com. on Indexing of Per. Lit. (Ch., 1978–79). Chicago Assn. of Law Libs.: Pres. (1975–76). **Pubns.:** "A Uniform System of Citation," *Univ. of Chicago Law Review* (Spr. 1977). **Activities:** 1; 15; 77 **Addr.:** University of New Mexico School of Law Library, 1117 Stanford Dr. N.E., Albuquerque, NM 87131.

Bowles, Carol A. (Ja. 8, 1948, Lancaster, PA) Asst. Tech. Srvs. Libn., San Mateo Cnty. Lib., 1981–, Ref. Libn., Chld. Libn., 1979–80; Ref. Libn., Oakland Pub. Lib., 1978–79; Gen. Srvs. Libn., N. Babylon Pub. Lib., 1973–78, Chld. Libn., 1971–72; Asst. Bkmobile. Libn., Madison Pub. Lib., 1970–71. **Educ.:** Millersville State Coll., 1965–69, BA (Russ. Lang., Lit.); Univ. of WI, 1969–71, MA (LS); Univ. of IL, 1970, Slavic Libnshp. Inst. **Orgs.:** ALA: Mildred L. Batchelder Awd. Com. (1971–72); Liason with Natl. Org. Srvg. the Child Com. (1971–72). CA LA. CLENE. Sierra Club. Nat. Conservancy. Telephone Action Netwk. Natl. Parks and Cons. Assn. **Honors:** Beta Phi Mu. **Activities:** 9; 15, 16, 20; 55, 56, 67 **Addr.:** San Mateo County Library, 25 Tower Rd., Belmont, CA 94002.

Bowles, Garrett H. (F. 3, 1938, San Francisco, CA) Msc. Libn., Univ. of CA, San Diego, 1979–; Head Msc. Catlgr., Stanford Univ., 1968–79; Msc. Catlgr., 1965–68. **Educ.:** Univ. of CA, Davis, 1955–60, AB (Msc.); San Jose State Univ., 1961–62, MA (Msc.); Univ. of CA, Berkeley, 1963–65, MLS; Stanford Univ., 1970–78, PhD (Msclgy.). **Orgs.:** Msc. LA: Autom. Com. (Ch. 1970–); Mem. at Large (1980–82). Assn. for Rec. Snd. Col.: Pres. (1978–80). Intl. Assn. for Msc. Libs.: Cat. Comsn. (1976–). **Honors:** Beta Phi Mu, 1965. **Pubns.:** *Directory of Music Library Automation Projects*, 2d ed. (1979); "The AAA Project: a Report," *ARSC Jnl.* (vol. 9, 1977); "A Computer-Produced Thematic Catalog: the *Pièces de violes* of Marin Marais," *Fontes Artis Musicae* (vol. 26, 1979); reviews. **Activities:** 1; 15, 39, 45; 56, 75, 95-Rec. Snd. **Addr.:** Music Collections, Central University Library, University of California, San Diego, La Jolla, CA 92093.

Bowling, Mary Boone (Ap. 20, 1950, Pottstown, PA) Ref. Libn., Mss., Columbia Univ., 1974–; Asst. Libn., Amer. Heart Assn., 1972–74; Mss. Prcs., West. Rsv. Hist. Socty., 1968–71; **Educ.:** Case West. Rsv. Univ., 1967–71, BA (Eng.); Columbia Univ., 1971–72, MLS. **Orgs.:** SAA: Status of Women Com. (1976–); Ref. and Access Policies Com. (1974–1976). Mid-Atl. Reg. Arch. Conf. Archvsts. RT of Metro. NY: Secy./Treas. (1980–). **Pubns.:** "Such Interesting People: Singers, Musicians and Constance Hope," *Columbia Lib. Clmns.* (Nov. 1976); oral presentations. **Activities:** 1, 12; 39, 45; 55, 63, 85 **Addr.:** Rare Book and Manuscript Library, 800 Butler Library, Columbia University, New York, NY 10027.

Bowman, Carlos Morales (Mr. 4, 1935, Mexico, DF, Mexico) Lab. Dir., Dow Chemical Co., 1968–, Asst. Lab. Dir.,

Special Subjects/Services: 50. Adult educ.; 51. Advert./Mktg.; 52. Aerosp.; 53. Agric.; 54. Area std.; 55. Arts/Hum.; 56. Autom.; 57. Bibl./Prtg.; 58. Bio. sci.; 59. Bus./Fin.; 60. Chem.; 61. Copyrt.; 62. Documtn.; 63. Educ.; 64. Engin.; 65. Env.; 66. Eth. grps.; 67. Film; 68. Food/Nutr.; 69. Geneal.; 70. Geo.; 71. Geol.; 72. Handcpd.; 73. Hist.; 74. Int. frdm.; 75. Info. sci.; 76. Insr.; 77. Law; 78. Legis.; 79. Math./Comp. sci.; 80. Med.; 81. Metals; 82. Nat. resrcs.; 83. Newsp.; 84. Nuc. sci.; 85. Oral hist.; 86. Petr./Energy; 87. Pharm.; 88. Phys./Astr./Math.; 89. Readg.; 90. Relig.; 91. Sci./Tech.; 92. Soc. sci.; 93. Telecom.; 94. Transp.; 95. (other).

1967–68, Grp. Leader, 1965–67, Info. Retrieval Anal., 1961–65. **Educ.:** Univ. of UT, 1951–54, BA (Chem.); 1954–57, PhD (Chem.). **Orgs.:** ASIS. Assn. for Comp. Mach. Amer. Chemical Socty: Div. of Chemical Info. (Ch., 1968; Cncl., 1970–). Socty. of the Sigma XI: Ch., (1967). AAAS. **Pubns.:** Contrib., *Chemical Information Systems* (1975); "On-Line Storage and Retrieval of Chemical Information. I Structure Entry," *Jnl. of Chemical Info. and Comp. Sci.* (1979); "On-Line Storage and Retrieval of Chemical Information. II Substructure Search and Biological Activity Searching," *Jnl. of Chemical Info. and Comp. Sci.* (1979). **Activities:** 12; 17, 41; 56, 60, 75 **Addr.:** 1414 Timber Dr., Midland, MI 48640.

Bowman, Martha A. (Je. 8, 1945, Washington, DC) Assoc. Univ. Libn., George Washington Univ., 1978–, Asst. Univ. Libn., 1975–78; Head, Acq. Dept., Univ. of MD, 1974–75, Asst. Head, 1973–74, Serials Libn., Serials Dept., 1969–73. **Educ.:** Univ. of MD, 1963–67, BA (Eng.); Cath. Univ. of Amer., 1968–69, MSLS. **Orgs.:** ALA: LITA. DC LA: Pres. (1981–82), VP, Pres.-Elect (1980–81); Tech. Srvs. Interest Grp. (Ch., 1978–79). Univ. of MD: Lib. Asm. (Ch., 1974–75); Mgt. Review and Analysis Prog., Policy Task Frc. (1974). **Honors:** Beta Phi Mu. **Activities:** 1; 15, 17, 44 **Addr.:** Gelman Library, George Washington University, Washington, DC 20052.

Bowron, Albert Wilson (O. 13, 1919, Hamilton, ON) Lib. Consult., pvt. inst., 1969–; Dir., Scarboro. Pub. Lib., 1964–69; Head, Tech. Srv. Div., Toronto Pub. Lib., 1958–64; Chief Libn., Galt Pub. Lib., 1954–58. **Educ.:** Univ. of Toronto, 1945–48, BA (Gen.), 1948–49, BLS. **Orgs.:** ON LA: Pres. (1966–67); various coms., divs. Can. LA: Various sects., coms. Writers Dev. Trust: Bd. ON Prov. Lib. Cncl. **Pubns.:** *The Ontario Public Library: Review and Reorganization* (1969–81); various articles. **Activities:** 9, 13; 17, 19, 24; 74 **Addr.:** 55 Westmount Ave., Toronto, ON M6H 3K2 Canada.

Bowser, Eugene O. (Je. 18, 1933, Fall River, KS) Serials Libn., Univ. of North. CO, 1977–; Asst. Ed., *CO Libs.*, 1981–; Ref. Libn., 1973–77, Instr., Hist., 1969–73. **Educ.:** KS State Univ., 1951–55, BS (Geol.); Univ. of KS, 1955–58 (Paleon.); Ctrl. Bapt. Theo. Semy., 1961–65, BD (Biblical Interpretation); Brandeis Univ., 1965–68, MA (Mediterranean Std.); Univ. of Denver, 1974–75, MA (Libnshp.). **Orgs.:** ALA: RTSD; LITA. CO LA: Tech. Srvs. RT (Ch., 1980); Tech. Srvs. Div./Serials Sect. (Ch., 1981). Genescope Assocs. **Honors:** Sigma Gamma Epsilon, 1953; Beta Phi Mu, 1975. **Pubns.:** "Automated Serials Control is Here," *CO Libs.* (D. 1980); "Citation Analysis – Practical Tool or Esoteric Plaything?" *CO Libs.* (S. 1979); "Colleague Relations," *CO Libs.* (Je. 1979); "A New Serials Evaluation Process at the University of Northern Colorado," *CO Libs.* (Mr. 1979). **Activities:** 1; 15, 20, 44 **Addr.:** 2531 – 15th Ave., Greeley, CO 80631.

Boyce, Bert R. (Ja. 10, 1938, Sharon, PA) Assoc. Prof., Dept. of Info. Sci., Univ. of MO, 1978–, Ch., 1976–, Actg. Dean, Sch. of Lib. and Info. Sci., 1980–81; Asst. Prof., Info. Sci., 1972–76; Lectr., Case West. Rsv. Univ., 1972; Info. Systs. Resrch. Anal., Lib. of Congs., 1968–69; Asst. Dir., Redev. Athrty., City of Sharon, PA, 1966–67. **Educ.:** Marietta Coll., 1955–59, BA (Hist.); Case West. Rsv. Univ., 1967–68, MSLS, 1969–72, PhD (Info. Sci.); various crs. **Orgs.:** ALA. ASIS. AALS. Univ. of MO: Fac. Cncl., Exec. Com. (1979–80); Spec. Projs. Com.; Campus Com. on Resrch. Policies and Procs. (1981–); Sch. of Lib. and Info. Sci., Persnl. Com. (1976–), Educ. Policy Com. (1977–), Campus Flwshps., Traineeships and Assistanceships Com. (1978–); various coms. **Honors:** Sr. Fulbright-Hayes Fellow, 1974. **Pubns.:** "Instruction in Online Library Tool.....," *Jnl. of Educ. for Libnshp.* (Fall 1979); jt. auth., "Bradford's Law and the Selection of High Quality Papers," *Lib. Resrcs. & Tech. Srvs.* (Fall 1978); jt. auth., "Data Accuracy in Citation Studies," *RQ* (Sum. 1979); "Instruction in Online Library Tools at the University of Missouri," in "Visible College," *Jnl. of Educ. for Libnshp.* (Fall 1979); "In Support of Technology in Libraries," *Show-Me Libs.* (My. 1979); jt. auth., "The Brillouin Measure of an Author's Contribution to a Literature in Psychology," *Jnl. of the Amer. Socty. for Info. Sci.* (Ja. 1981); various articles. **Activities:** 4, 11; 20, 26, 30; 56, 75 **Addr.:** Dept. of Information Science, University of Missouri, 110 Stewart Hall, Columbia, MO 65211.

Boyce, Emily Stewart (Ag. 18, 1933, Raleigh, NC) Prof., E. Carolina Univ., 1959–; Prof. of LS, 1964; Cat. Libn. III, 1962–63; Educ. Supvsr. II, Educ. Media Div. NC State Dept. Pub. Instr., 1961–62; Ast. Libn., E. Carolina Univ., 1959–61; Chld. Libn., Wilmington Pub. Lib., 1957–58; Libn., Tileston Jr. HS, 1955–57. **Educ.:** E. Carolina Univ., 1951–55, BS (Hist., LS); 1960–61, MA (Guid.); Univ. of NC, 1968, MLS; Cath. Univ. of Amer., 1977. **Orgs.:** ALA:AASL/Legis. Com. (1970–72); RTSD/Plng. Com. (1977–81). SE LA: Sch. and Chld. Sect. (Ch., 1969); NC LA: NC Assn. of Sch. Libns. Pubn. Com. (Ch., 1968–71); Discuss. Ldr., 1971; Coll. and Univ. Sect., Serials Wkshp., Coord. (1972); IFC (1964–66; 1974–76; Secy., 1977–79); Bd. of Dir. (1979–81); other coms. AALS. Other orgs. NOW: Secy. (1974–76). Leag. of Women Voters. AAUP. **Honors:** Beta Phi Mu. **Pubns.:** "The United States Supreme Court and North Carolina Obscenity Laws," *NC Libs.* (Win., 1974); "Special Programs in North Carolina and Implications for the Media Staff," *NC Libs.* (Sum., 1976). **Activities:** 10, 11; 24, 26, 32; 63, 72, 74 **Addr.:** 1406 Rondo Dr., Greenville, NC 27834.

Boyce, Harold Walter (My. 13, 1927, Mishawaka, IN) Dir. of Lib. Srvs., Marion Coll., 1966–. **Educ.:** Marion Coll., 1952, AB (Relig.); Ball State Univ., 1966, MA (Educ.); IN Univ., 1974, Ed.D., (Higher Educ., LS). **Orgs.:** IN LA: Coll. and Univ. Div. (Ch., 1979–80). ALA. Amer. Assn. of Higher Educ. Midwest Coop. Educ. Assn. **Activities:** 1; 17, 24; 56, 63, 90 **Addr.:** Marion College Library, 4201 S. Washington St., Marion, IN 46952.

Boyce, Joseph A. (Ap. 12, 1938, Trinidad, W. Indies) Lib. Dir., Parlett L. Moore Lib., Coppin State Coll., 1977–; Actg. Dir., Lib., Lrng. Resrcs. Srvs., 1976–77, Assoc. Dir., Lib., 1973–76; Evening Ref. Dept., Univ. of Baltimore, 1972–76; Dir., Tech. Srvs., Coppin State Coll., 1970–73; Asst. Libn., Catlgr., Univ. of MD East. Shore, 1965–70; Asst. Libn., Catlgr., Atlanta Univ. Ctr., 1962–65; various tchg., adv. positions. **Educ.:** Shorter Jr. Coll., 1959, AA; Morris Brown Coll., 1961, BA (Phil., Psy.); Atlanta Univ., 1964, MS (LS); various crs., wkshps. **Orgs.:** ALA. MD LA. State Coll. Lib. Dirs. Cncl. on Acad. Dirs. Cont. Lib. Educ. of MD. NAACP. Amer. Fed. of Tchrs. various orgs. **Activities:** 1, 13; 17 **Addr.:** Parlett Moore Library, Coppin State College, 2500 W. North Ave., Baltimore, MD 21216.

Boyd, Catherine A. (My. 29, 1951, South Bend, IN) Mgt. Info. Anal. Argonne Natl. Lab., 1979–; Info. Spec., Old West Reg. Comsn., 1975–79. **Educ.:** Carroll Coll., 1969–73, BA (Eng. and Psy.); Univ. of Denver, 1974–75, MALS. **Orgs.:** Assoc. Inf. Mgrs. ASIS. SLA. West. Info. Netwk. on Energy: North. Rockies Dep. (1978–79). Bus. and Prof. Women. **Pubns.:** *Energy Research Information System: Projects Reports* (1975–79); "Energy Research Information System." Jt. Auth. (Spec. Libs. Assn., 67th Conf.) (1976); *Environmental Research Series: Land Reclamation Research* (Brochure) (1979); "A Selective Bibliography of Surface Coal Mining and Reclamation Literature: Western Coal Provinces" (Ja. 1981). **Activities:** 14-Fed. Lab. Prog.; 36, 38, 49-Tech. Transfer; 57, 65, 91 **Addr.:** Building 8, Argonne National Laboratory, Argonne, IL 60439.

Boyd, Daphne Gwendolyn (Jl. 5, 1927, Calgary, AB) Catlgr., Calgary Pub. Lib., 1969–; Head, Hum., 1968, Head, Circ., 1964–67, Branch Libn., 1960–64, various other positions. **Educ.:** Mount Royal Coll., 1946–47; Univ. AB, 1948–49, BA (Eng.); McGill Univ., 1949–50, BS. **Orgs.:** Calgary LA: Soc. Conv. LA of AB. Can. LA. **Activities:** 9, 12; 20, 22, 39 **Addr.:** 304-105-26th Ave., SW, Calgary, AB T2S 0M3 Canada.

Boyd, Elizabeth Ann (Je. 17, 1950, Chattanooga, TN) Media Spec., Acworth Elem. Sch., Cobb Cnty. Pub. Sch. Syst., 1972–. **Educ.:** David Lipscomb Coll., 1968–71, BS (Elem. Educ.); George Peabody Coll., 1971–72, MLS; State of GA, T–5 Cert. **Orgs.:** Cobb Cnty. Assn. of Sch. Media Specs. ALA: AASL. GA LA. GA Assn. of Educs.: GA Lib. Media Dept., 7th Dist. Ch. (1976–77), Handbk. Ed. (1978–79); Legis. Com. (1980–81). Cobb Cnty. Assn. of Educs., Tchr. Educ. and Prof. Stans. Com. (1974–75), Nsltr. Ed. (1975–76), Corres. Secy. (1977–78), Rpt. Secy. (1978–79), PR Com. (1979–81). **Honors:** GA Assn. of Educs., Sch. Bell Nsltr. Excel. Awd., 1976. **Activities:** 10; 20, 21, 32; 63 **Addr.:** 4514 Dallas St. N.W., Acworth, GA 30101.

Boyd, Kenneth W. (O. 2, 1938, Jacksonville, FL) Pres., Larlin Corp., 1976–; S. East. Rep., Congsnl. Info. Srv., 1974–76; Gen. Mgr., Coord. of Sales, Josten's Lib. Supplies, 1967–74; Asst. Serials Dept., Atlanta Pub. Lib., 1965–66. **Educ.:** The Citadel, 1956–60, AB (Hist.); Drexel Univ. 1962–63, MS (LS). **Orgs.:** Metro Atlanta LA: Pres. (1969). S. East. LA: Mem. Com. (1979–80). GA LA: Mem. Com. (1979–80). **Activities:** 10, 6; 31, 37, 46 **Addr.:** Larlin Corporation, P.O. Box 1523, Marietta, GA 30061.

Boyd, R. Virginia (O. 1, 1938, Pelham, GA) Assoc. Libn., Brunswick Jr. Coll., 1969–; Asst. Libn., GA Southwest. Coll., 1966–69; Secy. to Libn., GA Coll., 1962–65. **Educ.:** Young Harris Coll., 1956–58, AA; GA Coll., 1962–65, AB (Hist., LS); George Peabody Coll., 1965–66, MLS. **Orgs.:** ALA. SE LA. GA LA: Mem. Com. (1977–79); Gvtl. Rel. Com. (1979–81). Glynn Cnty. LA: Secy. (1972–73); Pres. (1974–75). Phi Delta Kappa: Secy. (1978–79); Del. (1979–80); Pres. (1980–82). AAUW: VP (1980–82); various coms. (1975–79). Coastal GA LA. Frnds. of the Brunswick Reg. Lib.: Secy. (1978–). **Honors:** Beta Phi Mu. **Activities:** 1; 29, 38, 39 **Addr.:** Brunswick Junior College Library, Brunswick, GA 31523.

Boyd, Sandra Hughes (D. 29, 1938, Council Bluffs, IA) Ref. Libn., Episcopal Dvnty. Sch.-Weston Sch. of Theology Libs., 1978–; Cat. Libn., OH State Univ., 1972–73; Jnlsm. Libn., 1967–68; Cat. Libn., 1966–67; Libn., Luth. Brotherhood Insr. Co., 1964–66. **Educ.:** CO Coll., 1957–61, BA (Econ.); Univ. of MN, 1962–64, MALS; Episcopal Dvnty. Sch. 1976–78, MDvnty. **Orgs.:** SLA. ATLA. **Pubns.:** *Women in American Religious History: A Bibliography* (1982); Jt. auth., "Women in Religion," *Women's Anl.* (D. 1981). **Activities:** 1, 12; 20, 37, 39; 90, 92, 95-Hist. **Addr.:** 263 Payson Rd., Belmont, MA 02178.

Boyd, William Douglas, Jr. (D. 15, 1929, Pulaski, TN) Assoc. Prof., Sch. of Lib. Srv., Univ. of South. MS, 1973–; Asst. Law Libn., IN Univ., 1972–73; Asst. Pastor, Indp. Presby. Church, Birmingham, AL, 1963–67; Pastor, First Presby. Church, Mt. Pleasant, IN, 1956–63. **Educ.:** Southwest. At Memphis, 1948–52, BA (Phil.); Un. Theo. Semy., NY, 1952–55, BD (Old Testament); Univ. of Muenster, W. Germany, 1955–56, (Bible, Ecumenics); Princeton Theo. Semy., 1957–58, ThM (Church Hist.); IN Univ., 1957–72, MLS, 1967–75, PhD (Adult Educ., LS). **Orgs.:** ALA. MS LA. AALS. AAUP. Adult Educ. Assn. of the U.S.A. Presbytery of Birmingham. MS Inst. of Arts and Letters. **Honors:** Southwest. at Memphis, NY South. Socty., Algernon Sydney Sullivan Awd., 1952; Omicron Delta Kappa; Eta Sigma Phi; Alpha Tau Omega; other hons. **Pubns.:** "Alexander MacWhorter: The Blackcoat from Newark," *Daughters of the Amer. Revolution Mag.* (F. 1981); "The Prison and Educational Possibility," *Adult Leadership* (O. 1973). **Activities:** 11; 26; 50, 55, 90 **Addr.:** 104 Lee Cir., Hattiesburg, MS 39401.

Boyer, Alta E. (O. 18, 1914, Lodi, NY) Consult., Prsrvnst., Lib. Mtrls., 1978–; Chief of Lib. Srvs., Willard Psyt. Ctr., 1970–78; Head Libn., 1962–70; Asst. Libn., 1957–62. **Educ.:** William Smith Coll., 1932–36, BA; Syracuse Univ., SUNY Geneseo, 1960–63, MLS; New Eng. Ctr. Doc. Pres., 1972; RCHA 1979. **Orgs.:** NY LA: Finger Lakes Library System: Trustee. Med. LA: Exec. Com., NYS & Can. S. Ctrl. Resrch. Lib. Cncl.: Consult. (1969). Wm. Smith Coll. Alumnae Assn: Exec. Cncl. (1969–71). Amer. Red Cross: Exec. Com. (1973–79). Lodi Hist. Society: Pres., Prog. Ch. (1976–78). Prsrvn. Leag. of NY (1975–). **Pubns.:** *Guide to Historic Houses of Lodi* (1975–79). **Activities:** 2, 9, 14; 23, 24, 47; 69 **Addr.:** 8678 Watkins Glen Rd., Lodi, NY 14860.

Boyer, Calvin James (Mr. 4, 1939, Charleston, IL) Univ. Libn., Univ. of CA, Irvine, 1980–; Dir. of Libs., Univ. of MS, 1975–80; Assoc. Prof., IN Univ., 1972–75; Libn., Midwestern Univ., 1967–69. **Educ.:** East. IL Univ., 1958–62, BSEd (Foreign Lang.); Univ. of TX, Austin, 1963–64, MLS; 1969–72, PhD, (Lib. Sci.). **Orgs.:** ALA. **Pubns.:** *Descriptive Cataloging Sampler* (1970); *Book Selection Policies in American Libraries* (1971); *The Doctoral Dissertation as an Information Source* (1973); "State-wide Contracts for Library Materials," *College and Research Libraries* (Mr. 1974); "Nonconventional Information Sources and Services", *RQ* (Fall, 1975). **Activities:** 1; 15, 17, 37 **Addr.:** University of California Library, Irvine, Irvine, CA 92713.

Boyer, Denis P. (Jl. 10, 1945, St-Edouard, PQ) Dir., Bibl. Mncpl. de Hull, 1969–; Catlgr., Cegep de Hull, 1968–69; Catlgr., Bibl. Ctrl. de Pret de L'Outaouais, 1966–68. **Educ.:** Univ. de Montreal, 1965, BA, 1966, BLS, 1976–79, MAP. **Orgs.:** ASTED. Can. LA. Salon du Livre de l'Outaouais. **Activities:** 9; 17; 61 **Addr.:** 8 Helmer, Hull, PQ J8Y 1H2 Canada.

Boyer, Laura M. (Madison, IN) Head, Ref. Dept., Univ. of the Pac. Lib., 1965–, Asst. Ref. Libn., 1963–65; Asst. Circ. Libn., Univ. of KS, 1961–63; Pub. Sch. Tchr., 1957–58. **Educ.:** Univ. of MS, 1952–54; George Washington Univ., 1954–56, AB (Relig.); Univ. of Denver, 1958–59, AM (Sec. Educ.); George Peabody Coll., 1960–61, AM (LS). **Orgs.:** ALA. CA Assn. of Resrch. Libs. CA LA. ASIS. AAUP. **Honors:** Phi Beta Kappa; Beta Phi Mu; Kappa Delta Pi. **Pubns.:** Cmplr., *Play Anthologies Union List* 1976; jt. auth., "The Use and Training of Nonprofessional Personnel at Reference Desks in Selected College and University Libraries," *Coll. & Resrch. Libs.* (My. 1975). **Activities:** 1; 31, 39, 41; 63 **Addr.:** 5650 Stratford Cir., Apt. 29, Stockton, CA 95207.

Boyer, Robert Earl (N. 1, 1947, Dallas, TX) Assoc. Dir., Arlington (TX) Pub. Lib., 1975–, Asst. Dir., 1971–75. **Educ.:** Univ. of Dallas, 1966–70, BA (Eng., Grmn.); Univ. of KY, 1970–71, MSLS; various crs. **Orgs.:** TX LA: Pub. Lib. Div., (Treas., 1981); Nom. Com. (Ch., 1977), Cont. Educ. Com. (1978), Lib. Week Com. (1981), JMRT (Treas., 1974). Tarrant Reg. LA: Treas. (1974); VP (1979); Pres. (1980). ALA: RTSD, Cat. of Chld. Mtrls. Com. (1980–82); PLA, Swap and Shop (1979); JMRT; various coms. N. TX Co-Op for Adult Basic Educ.: Adv. Bd. (1978–). **Pubns.:** "Do We Use Standards? Yes, but...," *Cath. Lib. World* (F. 1977); cmplr., *Union List of Local Newspaper Backfiles in Public Libraries of the Greater Fort Worth Region* (1980). **Activities:** 9; 15, 17, 20; 56, 72 **Addr.:** Arlington Public Library, 101 E. Abram St., Arlington, TX 76010.

Boykin, Joseph F., Jr. (N. 7, 1940, Pensacola, FL) Dir. of Lib., Clemson Univ., 1981–; Dir. of Lib., Univ. of NC, Charlotte, 1970–81, Actg. Head Libn., 1968–70; Asst. to Libn., 1965–68. **Educ.:** FL State Univ., 1960–62, BS (Hist.); 1964–65, MS (LS). **Orgs.:** ALA. SE LA. NC LA: Gvt. Rel. Com. (1977–79); SC LA. SE Lib. Netwk., Inc.: Bd. Dir. (1975–78), Ch., 1977–78); Adv., Consult. (1978–79). OCLC, Inc. Users Cncl.: Del. (1978–82), Pres. (1978–80). **Pubns.:** Jt. auth., "The Academic Library Development Program," *Coll. and Resrch. Libs.* (Jan. 1977). **Activities:** 1; 17, 34 **Addr.:** Library, Clemson University, Clemson, SC 29631.

Boyko, Maksym (F. 22, 1912, Pochaiv, Volhynia, Ukraine) Slavic Catlgr., IN Univ. Lib., 1966–; Econ. & Pol. Sci. Catlgr., West. ON Univ., 1962–64; Secy., Fndr., Resrch. Inst. of Volhynia, 1953–60. **Educ.:** Grand Sch. of Econ., Munich, West Germany, 1945–48, BA & MA (Econ.); Univ. of Ottawa, 1961–62, BLS; Ukrainian Free Univ., Munich, West Germany, 1967–68, PhD (Law & Econ.). Volhynian Bibl. Ctr.: Fndr., Dir., Ed., (1967–). Shevchenko Sci. Socty. Research Inst. of Volhynia: Secy. **Pubns.:** Various books and articles in Ukrainian, English,

PROFESSIONAL ACTIVITIES: Institutions: 1. Acad. lib.; 2. Arch.; 3. Assn.; 4. Fed./Gvt. lib.; 5. Inst. lib.; 6. Mfr./Suppl.; 7. Milit. lib.; 8. Musm.; 9. Pub. lib.; 10. Sch. lib.; 11. Sch. of lib. sci.; 12. Spec. lib.; 13. State lib.; 14. (other). **Functions/Activities:** 15. Acq./Col. dev.; 16. Adult srvs.; 17. Admin.; 18. Apprais.; 19. Archit./Bldgs.; 20. Cat./Class.; 21. Chld. srvs.; 22. Circ.; 23. Cons./Pres.; 24. Consult.; 25. Cont. ed.; 26. Educ. lib. sci.; 27. Ext. srvs.; 28. Fund/Grants; 29. Gvt. pubs.; 30. Indx./Abs.; 31. Instr. lib. use; 32. Media srvs.; 33. Micro.; 34. Netwks./Coop.; 35. Persnl.; 36. PR; 37. Publshg.; 38. Recs. mgt.; 39. Ref. srvs.; 40. Repro.; 41. Resrch.; 42. Review.; 43. Secur.; 44. Serials; 45. Spec. col.; 46. Tech. srvs.; 47. Trustees/Bds.; 48. YA srvs.; 49. (other).

Who's Who in Library and Information Services

and Polish. **Activities:** 1; 20, 33; 57, 66 **Addr.:** 307 N. Overhill Dr., Bloomington, IN 47401.

Boylan, Merle Nelson (F. 24, 1925, Youngstown, OH) Dir. of Libs., Univ. of WA, 1977–; Dir. of Gen. Libs., Univ. of TX, 1973–77; Dir. of Libs., Univ. of MA (Amherst), 1970–72, Assoc. Dir. Tech. Srvs., 1969–70; Chief Libn., NASA-Ames Resrch. Ctr., 1967–69; Lib. Mgr., Univ. of CA, Lawrence Livermore Lab., 1964–67; Assoc. Dir., Tech. Srvs., 1962–64; Engin. Libn., General Dynamics/Astronautics, 1961–62; Other lib. positions. **Educ.:** Youngstown Coll., 1946–50, BA (Bio. Sci.); Carnegie-Mellon Univ., 1955–56, MLS; Univ. of AZ, 1950–52 (Bio. Sci.); Indiana Univ., 1952 (Bio. Sci.). **Orgs.:** ALA: ACRL (Legis. Com., 1977–79). SLA. ASIS. WA LA. Pacific N.W. LA. Pacific N.W. Bibl. Ctr.: Exec. Bd., Secy. (1977–). AMIGOS Bibl. Cncl.: Exec. Bd. (1974–77). WA Lib. Netwk.: Fncl. Com. (1977–79). Various other orgs. and com. **Honors:** Beta Phi Mu. **Activities:** 1, 12; 17, 34, 46; 56, 58, 75 **Addr.:** 1354 Bellefield Park Lane, Bellevue, WA 98004.

Boylan, Ray P. (Ja. 7, 1938, Gary, IN) Ast. Dir., Ctr. for Resrch. Libs., 1971–; Circ. Libn., 1969–71; Catlgr., 1967–69; Assoc. Mnstr., Good Shepherd Untd. Church of Christ, 1964–66. **Educ.:** Kalamazoo Coll., 1957–61, BA (Phil.); Colgate Rochester Dvnty. Sch., 1961–64, BD; Grad. Lib. Sch., Univ. of Chicago, 1966–67. **Orgs.:** ALA. IL Reg. Lib. Cncl.: Plng. Com. (1977–). Assn. for Asian Std. **Pubns.:** "Serial Publications In The Center for Research Libraries," *Serials Review* (Jan./Mar., 1979); "Scholarly Citadel in Chicago: The Center for Research Libraries," *Wilson Lib. Bltn.* (Mar., 1979). **Activities:** 12; 17, 33, 34; 54 **Addr.:** 5721 S. Cottage Grove Ave., Chicago, IL 60637.

Boyle, Deirdre (Jl. 12, 1949, New York, NY) Fac., Fordham Univ. Coll. at Lincoln Ctr., 1979–81; Fac., Rutgers Univ. GSLIS (1979–80); Fac. New Sch. for Social Resrch., 1978–81; Lib. media consult., educ., writer, 1979–; Asst. ed., Wilson Lib. Bltn., 1978–79; Asst. ed., R. R. Bowker Co., 1973–74; AV Coord. and Tchr., Cathedral HS, 1971–72. **Educ.:** Coll. of Mt. St. Vincent, 1966–70, BA (Eng.); Antioch Coll., 1973–76, MA (Media Study). **Orgs.:** ALA: LITA/Video and Cable Comm. Sect., Comm. Com. (Ch., 1980); AV Sect. Corres., LITA News (1980); NY Film Cncl. Assn. of Indep. Video and Filmmakers. **Pubns.:** Jt. ed., *Mediamobiles: Views from the Road* (1979); Jt. ed., *Children's Media Market Place* (1978); Ed., *Expanding Media* (1977); "In the beginning was the word...Libraries and Media," *Lib. Jnl.* (Ja. 1, 1976); "The Library, Television, and the Unconscious Mind," *Wilson Lib. Bltn.* (My. 1978); reprinted in *Lib. Lit: Best of 1978* (1979); other articles. **Activities:** 11, 14-Media consult.; 26, 32, 37; 67, 93, 95-Media Arts. **Addr.:** 3 West 29th St. (11th floor), New York, NY 10001.

Boyle, Jeanne E. (Ja. 30, 1945, Englewood, NJ) Head, Gvt. Docum. Dept., Lib. of Sci. & Med., Rutgers Univ., 1978–; Prin. Libn., U.S. Docum., Newark Pub. Lib., 1976–78; Prin. Libn. & Coord. of Interlib. Srvs., 1973–76; Sr. Libn., Interlib. Srvs., 1970–73; Sr. Libn., 1969–70; Libn. III, NJ State Lib., 1968–69. **Educ.:** Douglass Coll., 1963–67, AB (Eng.); Rutgers Univ., 1967–68, MLS. **Orgs.:** Gvt. Docum. Assn. of NJ: various offices and coms. NJ LA: various offices and coms. ALA: ACRL; GODORT; various comms. SLA. Grad. Sch. of Lib. and Info. Stud., Rutgers Univ.: Adv. Assoc. (1979). **Pubns.:** Various articles on gvt. docum. **Addr.:** Government Documents Department, Library of Science and Medicine, Rutgers University, P.O. Box 1029, Piscataway, NJ 08854.

Boyles, Linda K. (Je. 18, 1949, Gainesville, FL) Supvsr. of Chlds. Srvcs., Santa Fe Reg. Pub. Lib., 1977–; Chlds. Libn., 1974–77. **Educ.:** Univ. of FL, 1967–71, BA (LS, Eng.); FL St. Univ., 1973–74, MLS. **Orgs.:** FL LA: Ch., Chlds. Caucus (1977–78). ALA. Chlds. Lit. Assn. **Honors:** ALA, Charles Scribner Award, 1978. **Pubns.:** "Storytelling", *FL Libs.* (N., D. 1978). **Activities:** 9; 17, 21, 27; 95-Parent Education Early Childhood Education. **Addr.:** Gainesville Public Library, 222 East University Avenue, Gainesville, FL 32601.

Boyvey, Mary R. (S. 10, 1920, Ft. Worth, TX) Lib. Prog. Dir., Instr. Media Div., TX Educ. Agency, 1965–, Lib. Consult., State Dept. Educ. (TX), 1963–65; Libn., Jr HS Lib., Corpus Christi, 1951–63; Libn., Jr HS Beaumont, 1948–51; Libn., Orange HS (TX), 1947–48; Libn., Big Spring (TX) HS, 1945–47; Libn., Lockhart (TX) HS, 1943–45. **Educ.:** TX Women's Univ., 1938–40, BA (LS, Eng.); Univ. TX, 1945, MA (Eng.); Univ. Chicago, 1956, MALS. **Orgs.:** TX LA. ALA. Delta Kappa Gamma. TX AECT. Natl. Educ. Assn. **Activities:** 10, 13; 63 **Addr.:** Library Program Director, Instructional Media Division, Texas Education Agency, 11th and Brazos, Austin, TX 78701.*

Bozone, Billie Rae (O. 7, 1935, Norphlet, AR) Coll. Libn., Smith Coll., 1971; Asst. Libn., 1969–71; Head, Circ. Dept., 1968; Sr. Ref. Libn., Univ. MA, 1967–68; Asst. Libn., New Eng. Mutual Life Ins. Co., 1965–67; Asst. Ref. Libn., Univ. IL 1963–65; Serials Libn., MS State Univ., 1961–63, Asst. Ref. Libn., 1958–63. **Educ.:** MS State Coll. for Women, 1953–57, BS (LS); Geo. Peabody Coll. for Tchrs., 1957–58, MA (LS). **Orgs.:** ALA: ACRL, New Eng. Chap. New Eng. Lib. Info. Network: Bd. of Dir. (1977–79). **Activities:** 1; 17, 19, 35 **Addr.:** Smith College Library, Northampton, MA 01063.

Brabham, Robert Franklin, Jr. (Jl. 25, 1946, Sumter, SC) Spec. Cols. Libn., Univ. Archvst., Univ. NC, Charlotte, 1973–; Order Libn., 1969–73. **Educ.:** Furman Univ., 1964–68, BA (Fr., Hist.); Emory Univ., 1968–69, MLn (Libnshp.); Univ. of NC at Chapel Hill, 1976–77, MA (Hist.); Cert., Arch. Inst., GA Dept. of Arch. & Hist., 1975. **Orgs.:** SAA. Socty. of GA Archvsts. Mss. Socty. NC Lit. and Hist. Assn. Hist. of Educ. Socty. **Honors:** Beta Phi Mu. **Pubns.:** "Defining the American University: The University of North Carolina, 1865–1875," *NC Hist. Review* (Aut. 1980). **Activities:** 1, 2; 15, 45; 57, 73, 93 **Addr.:** Box 211, Newell, NC 28126.

Brace, Phyllis Mayer (D. 18, 1931, Jersey City, NJ) Head Libn., Cicero Pub. Lib., 1979–; Asst., Readers Srv. Dept. and Branch Libn., Oak Park Pub. Lib., 1961–78; Asst. Libn., Amundsent Branch, Chicago City Jr. Coll., 1960; Libn., Southeast Branch, 1958–60. **Educ.:** Simmons Coll., 1949–53, BS (Eng.); Univ. of Chicago, 1953–55, MA (LS); Rosary Coll., 1978– (Bus. Admin.). **Orgs.:** ALA: NLA: IL LA: Pub. Libs. Sect. (Ch., 1962). Chicago On-Line Users Grp. Chicago Lib. Club. AAUW. Women in Mgt., West Suburban Exec. Breakfast Club. **Activities:** 9, 12; 16, 17, 22 **Addr.:** P. O. Box 655, Oak Park, IL 60303.

Bracewell, R. Grant (My. 20, 1928, Penticton, BC) Lib. Coord., Toronto Sch. of Theo., 1969–; Emmanuel Coll. Libn., Victoria Univ. Libs. 1968–; Ref. Libn., BC Inst. of Tech., 1967–68; Pastor, Royal Hts. Untd. Church, N. Delta, BC, 1963–66; Pastor, Trinity Untd. Church, Merritt, BC, 1958–63; Pastor, Bella Coola Untd. Church, Bella Coola, BC, 1955–58. **Educ.:** Univ. of BC, 1948–50, BA (Zlgy.); Univ. of WA, 1966–67, MLibr (Libnshp.); Un. Coll. of BC, 1952–55, (Testamur Theo.), 1967, BD (Theo.). **Orgs.:** Can. LA: Can. Assn. of Coll. and Univ. Libs.; Can. Assn. of Spec. Libs. and Info. Srvs. Libns. Assn. of the Univ. of Toronto. ALA: ACRL; LITA. ATLA: Index Bd., Secy. (1970–79), Ch. (1979–); Jt. Task Frc. on Strategy for Semy. Libs. and Lrng. Ctrs. for the '70s (1972–73); Ad Hoc Com. for Implementation of the ATS/ATLA Task Frc. Rpt. (Ch., 1974–75); Com. on Amer. Theo. Lib. Needs (Ch., 1976–78). Bd. of Dirs. of Bella Coola Gen. Hosp.: Bd. of Dirs. (Ch., 1955–58). Boy Scouts of Can.: Various lcl. grp. coms., ofcs. (1955–68). Can. Red Cross Socty.: Various lcl. chaps., ofcs. (1955–63). Can. Cancer Socty.: Various lcl. chaps., ofcs. (1955–63). Various other orgs. **Activities:** 1, 14-Netwk.; 15, 34, 39; 90 **Addr.:** Rm. 36, Emmanuel College, 75 Queen's Park Crescent E., Toronto, ON M5S 1K7 Canada.

Bracey, Ann Elizabeth (N. 5, 1942, Oklahoma City, OK) Br. Mgr. Ft. Worth Pub. Lib., 1977–; Br. Libn., 1972–76; Lib. Asst., 1971–72. **Educ.:** TX Christ. Univ., 1964–66, BA (Eng.); N. TX St. Univ., 1970–72, MLS. **Orgs.:** ALA: TX Mem. Com. (1973). TX Lib. Assn: Schol. & Resrch. Com. (1975). Ft. Worth Lib. Assn.: Treas. (1975); Trustee (1976). N. TX St. Univ. Lib. Sch. Alum. Socty. (Secy-Treas., 1980–81). AAUW: Legis. Ch. (1977); VP (1979); Nsltr. ed., 1980–81. Jr. Womans Clb: Various positions. **Honors:** Beta Phi Mu; Omniana, JWC, Nominee, for Most Outstanding Mem., 1979, 1980. **Activities:** 9; 16, 17, 39 **Addr.:** 3955 Shannon Dr., Ft. Worth, TX 76116.

Brackney, William Henry (Ja. 30, 1948, Washington, DC) Exec. Dir., Archvst., Amer. Bapt. Hist. Socty., 1979–; Mnstr., United Meth. Church, 1974–79; Asst. Prof. Houghton Coll., 1976–79. **Educ.:** Univ. MD, 1966–70, BA (Hist.); East. Bapt. Semy., 1970–72, MA (Rel.); Temple Univ., 1972–76, MA, PhD (Hist.); SUNY, Geneseo, 1980–, MLS in progress. **Orgs.:** Amer. Theo. LA. SAA. ALA. Amer. Assn. of State and Lcl. Hist. Lake ON Arch. Grp. **Honors:** Houghton Coll., Outstan. Fac. Mem., 1978. **Pubns.:** "Expedience versus Conviction: Baptist Responses to Antimasonry," *Fndtns.* (Apr. 1978); "The Fruits of a Crusade: Wesleyan Opposition to The Antimasonic Crusade," *Meth. Hist.* (July 1979); "Yankee Benevolence in Yorker Lands: The Origins of The Baptist Home Missions Movement," *Andover Newton Qtly.* (Spr. 1980). **Addr.:** 1106 S. Goodman St., Rochester, NY 14620.

Bradbury, Daniel J. (D. 7, 1945, Kansas City, KS) Dir., Janesville (WI) Pub. Lib., 1977–; Dir., Rolling Hills Consolidated Lib., MO, 1974–77; Assoc. Dir., for Ext. Srvs., Waco-McLennan Cnty. Lib., TX, 1972–74; Asst. Pub. Srvs. Libn., Coll. of Emporia, 1971–72. **Educ.:** Univ. of MO, Kansas City, 1968–71, BA (Eng.); Emporia KS State Coll., 1971–72, MLS. **Orgs.:** ALA: ALA Mem. Ch. for WI (1979–81); LAMA, Compar. Lib. Org. Com. (1979–8); PLA, Mem. Com. Task Force (1979–81). WI LA: Lib. Dev. and Legis. Com. (Ch., 1979–); Admin. RT (Vice Ch., 1980). WI Gvr.'s Conf. on Lib. and Info. Srvs. (Del., 1978). Janesville Lions Clb. Janesville Serra Clb. Janesville Chamber of Cmrce. **Honors:** Beta Phi Mu. **Pubns.:** "Overview of New State and Federal Legislation," *WI Lib. Bltn.* (Sum. 1979); *Missouri State Network Plan,* Com. Ch. for MO LA (S. 1977). **Addr.:** Janesville Public Library, 316 S. Main St., Janesville, WI 53545.

Bradbury, Frances J. (Detroit, MI) Exec. Libn., Northbrook Pub. Lib., 1976–; Head, Adult Srvcs., 1973–76. **Educ.:** Smith Col., BA (Eng.); Rosary Col., 1968–70, MLS. **Orgs.:** ALA. IL LA. State Adv. Com. for Srvc. to Blind & Physically Handicapped: ch. (1977–80). Reg. Lib. Adv. Cncl.: Exec. Com. (1977–79); ch. of Exec. Com. (1979); NSLS Coop. Computerized Circ. Systs. (Ch. 1981–82). **Activities:** 9; 17 **Addr.:** Northbrook Public Library, 1201 Cedar Ln., Northbrook, IL 60062.

Bradbury, Kathleen G. (Je. 19, 1949, Cleburne, TX) Branch Mgr., Fort Worth Pub. Lib., 1980–; Asst. Branch Mgr., 1975–80, Ref. Libn., 1972–75. **Educ.:** TX Woman's Univ., 1967–71, BA (LS), 1971–72, MLS. **Orgs.:** ALA. TX LA: VP (1979–80); Dist. 7 (Pres., 1981). Fort Worth Pub. Libns. Assn.: Secy.-Treas. (1980–81). AAUW: Cmnty. Ch. (1978–80); Intl. Std. (Co-Ch., 1980–81). **Activities:** 9; 16, 35, 39; 50, 55, 72 **Addr.:** 5812 Wessex Ave., Fort Worth, TX 76133.

Bradbury, Phillip John (Ja. 14, 1946, Newark, NJ) Pres., Lib. Educ. Inst., 1977–; Pres., Parrot Graph., Inc., 1974–; Head, Graph. Arts Dept., Bloomfield (NJ) Pub. Lib., 1972–77. **Educ.:** Montclair State Coll., 1968–72, BA (Eng.). **Orgs.:** Lib. PR Cncl.: Awds. Com. (1976), Exec. Bd. (1976–). ALA: LAMA/PR Srvs. to Libs. Com. (1977–); Nom. Com. (1978–). NJ LA: *NJ Libs.* Com. (Ch., 1974–76); PR Com. (Ch., 1975–76). **Honors:** Lib. PR Cncl., Ed./Designer, Best Lib. Nsltr., 1976. **Pubns.:** *Library Border Book* (1978); Ed., *Library of Clip Art* (1978); Ed. *Lib. PR News* (1978–); Ed. *Lib. Trustee Nsltr.* (1978–79); Ed. *Evil John's Almanac* (1974–77); Ed. *NJ Libs.* (1974–76). **Activities:** 9, 10; 24, 36, 37 **Addr.:** L.E.I., Inc., RD 1, Box 219, New Albany, PA 18833.

Bradford, Daniel L. (D. 26, 1926, Washington, DC) Head, Subscrpn. & Micro. Sect., Lib of Congs., 1973–; Supvsr., Continuations Unit, 1971–73; Asst. Supvsr., 1968–71; other positions at Lib. Congs. since 1945. **Educ.:** Amer. Univ. and Fed. City Coll., 1971, BA (Urban Std.); Fed. City Coll., 1971–72, MS (Media Sci.). US Dept. of Agr. Grad. Sch., Cert., Admin. Procs., 1964, Lib. Techqs., 1965. **Orgs.:** ALA. DC LA. U.S. Dept. of Agr. Grad. Sch. Soc. of Lib. and Info. Technicians: Instr.; Com. of Lib. Techqs. **Activities:** 4; 15, 44; 50, 75 **Addr.:** Library of Congress, Order Division, Washington, DC 20540.

Bradley, Carol June (Ag. 12, 1934, Huntingdon, PA) Assoc. Dir., Msc. Lib., St. Univ. of NY at Buffalo, 1967–; Msc. Cat., Vassar Coll., 1960–67; Msc. Libn., US Milit. Acad., W. Point, 1959–60; Libn., Drinker Lib. of Choral Msc., Free Lib. of Philadelphia, 1957–59. **Educ.:** Lebanon Valley Coll., 1952–56, BS (Msc.); West. Rsv. Univ., 1956–57, MLS; FL St. Univ., 1970–78, PhD (LS). **Orgs.:** Msc. LA: Info. and Org. Com. (Ch. 1959–67); Autom. Com. (Ch. 1969–71); Rep. to various other assns. (1965–71). Assn. Intl. des Bibs. Musicales. ALA. Oral Hist. Assn. Assn. for Rec. Snd. Cols. **Honors:** St. Univ. of NY, Chancellor's Awd for Excel. in Libnshp., 1977. **Pubns.:** *Music Collections in American Libraries: A Chronology* (1981); *The Genesis of American Music Librarianship, 1902–1942* (1978); *Reader in Music Librarianship* (1973); *The Dickinson Classification; A Cataloguing & Classification Manual for Music* (1968); Ed., *Manual of Music Librarianship* (1966); Various other articles. **Activities:** 1, 20, 26, 41, 85, 95-Music libraries. **Addr.:** 818 Delaware Road, Kenmore, NY 14223.

Bradley, Jared William (Ag. 2, 1931, New Orleans, LA) Ref. Libn. and Gvt. Docum. Spec., LA State Lib., 1981–; Head, Spec. Col. and Ref. Libn., Centroplex Lib., Baton Rouge, 1978–81; Ref. Libn., Main Lib., E. Baton Rouge Parish Lib., 1978; Ref. Libn., Docum. Dept., LA State Univ., 1977; Dir., LA Hist. Prsrvn. and Cult. Comsn., 1972; Lib. Asst., US Geol. Srvy. Lib., Dept. of Interior, 1960. **Educ.:** LA State Univ., 1951–55, BA (Hist.); 1959–60, MA (Amer. Hist.); 1976–77, MLS. **Orgs.:** ALA. SLA. LA LA: Subj. Spec. Sect., Nom. Com. (Ch., 1979). Baton Rouge Lib. Clb.: Pres. (1980). Fndn. for Hist. LA: Bd. Mem. (1978–79); various coms. Amer. Hist. Assn. Org. of Amer. Histus. Natl. Trust for Hist. Prsrvn.; various other orgs. **Honors:** Phi Alpha Theta. **Pubns.:** "Personnel/Manpower," *History of Air Force Systems Command, 1 July 1973–30 June 1974, Fiscal Year 1974,* (1974); "W. C. C. Claiborne, the Old Southwest and the Development of American Indian Policy," *TN Hist. Qtly.* (Fall 1974); "Walker Percy and the Search for Wisdom," *LA Std.* (Win. 1973); "W.C.C. Claiborne and Spain: Foreign Affairs under Jefferson and Madison, 1801-1811," *La. Hist.* (Fall 1971); "Louisiana: An Historic Preservation Plan," *Toward Preservation...-Problems and Projects in Louisiana* (1972); various other articles. **Activities:** 9, 12; 29, 39, 41; 62, 69, 92 **Addr.:** Jared W. Bradley, 5920 Forsythia Ave., Baton Rouge, LA 70808.

Bradshaw, Lillian Moore (Ja. 10, 1915, Hagerstown, MD) Dir., Dallas Pub. Lib., 1962–, Actg. Dir., 1961–62, Asst. Dir., 1958–61, Adult Srvs. Coord., 1955–58, Circ. Dept. Head, 1952–55, Dir., Readers Adv. Srv., 1946–52; Asst. YA Coord., Enoch Pratt Free Lib., 1944–46, Adult Lib., 1943–44; various libn. positions, 1938–43. **Educ.:** West. MD Coll., 1933–37, BA (Hum.); Drexel Univ., 1937–38, BS (LS). **Orgs.:** ALA: Pres. (1970–71); 1st VP, Pres.-Elect (1969–70); Frdm. to Read Fndn. Bd. of Trustees (1969–71); Cncl. (1968–69); Adult Srvs. Div., Pres. (1967–68), VP (1966–67). TX LA: Awds. Com. (Ch., 1973–74, 1979–80); Legis. Task Frc. (Ch., 1967–69); Pres. (1964–65); VP (1963–64). WHCOLIS: Del. (1979). Pub. Admins. of N. TX: Pres. (1969). Various other orgs. Ctrl. Bus. Dist. Assn.: Qual. of Life Com. (1977–). Hoblitzelle Fndn.: Dir. (1971–). Goals for Dallas: Exec. Com. (1977–); Bd. of Trustees (1977–); Secy. (1977–78); Treas. (1979–); Goals Achvmt. Com. for Cont. Educ., Vice-Ch. (1971), Ch. (1972); Conf. and Asst.

Special Subjects/Services: 50. Adult educ.; 51. Advert./Mktg.; 52. Aerosp.; 53. Agric.; 54. Area std.; 55. Arts/Hum.; 56. Autom.; 57. Bibl./Prtg.; 58. Bio. sci.; 59. Bus./Fin.; 60. Chem.; 61. Copyrt.; 62. Documtn.; 63. Educ.; 64. Engin.; 65. Env.; 66. Eth. grps.; 67. Film; 68. Food/Nutr.; 69. Geneal.; 70. Geo.; 71. Geol.; 72. Handcpd.; 73. Hist.; 74. Int. frdm.; 75. Info. sci.; 76. Insr.; 77. Law; 78. Legis.; 79. Math./Comp. sci.; 80. Med.; 81. Metals; 82. Nat. resrcs.; 83. Newsp.; 84. Nuc. sci.; 85. Oral hist.; 86. Petr./Energy; 87. Pharm.; 88. Phys./Astr./Math.; 89. Readg.; 90. Relig.; 91. Sci./Tech.; 92. Soc. sci.; 93. Telecom.; 94. Transp.; 95. (other).

Task Frc. Leader (1966–69); Citizen Info. and Participation Com. (Ch., 1976–77). Zonta Club of Dallas I: Pres. (1976–77). Various other orgs. **Honors:** Zonta Club of Dallas I, 48th Anl. Srv. Awd., 1981; TX LA, Disting. Srv. Awd., 1975; Dallas Hist. Socty., Execel. in Cmnty. Srvs. Awd., 1981; Drexel Univ., Hon. Doctor of Letters, 1981; other hons. **Pubns.:** "Public Library Funding Through a Local Government Unit," *PLA Nsltr.* (Fall 1977); "Opportunities for Growth," *Personnel Utilization in Libraries* (1970); "Goals for Library Progress–Inaugural Address by Lillian M. Bradshaw," *AB Bookman's Wkly.* (Jl. 20–27, 1970); "Service Is Our Product–How Do We Measure Productivity?" *TX Lib. Jnl.* (Sum. 1969); "Cultural Programs–The Dallas Public Library," *Lib. Trends* (Jl. 1968); various articles. **Addr.:** Dallas Public Library, 1954 Commerce St., Dallas, TX 75201.

Brady, J. Ben (S. 7, 1941, Simmesport, LA) Assoc. State Libn., LA State Lib., 1979; Lib. Prog. Coord., 1977–79; Inst. Lib. Consult., 1971–77; Libn., Cntrl. LA State Hosp., 1970–71; Libn., N. Caddo HS, 1963–69. **Educ.:** Nwest. State Univ., 1959–63, BA (Soc. Sci.); LA State Univ., 1968–69, MSLS. **Orgs.:** ALA: Legis. Com./Ad Hoc Copyrt. Subcom. (Liason). SW LA: Prog. Coord. and Mdrtr. for Inst. SELA/SWLA, (1972). LA LA: Secy. (1976–77); VP, Pres.-Elect (1980–81); Pres. (1981–82); Fed. Rel. Com. (Ch. 1978–). Baton Rouge Lib. Club: Pres. (1979–80). **Honors:** Beta Phi Mu, 1969. **Pubns.:** *Jails Need Libraries, Too!* (1973); "Brighter Tomorrows Through Public and Institutional Cooperation," *LA LA Bltn.* (Spr., Sum. 1979). **Activities:** 13; 27; 50, 74, 78 **Addr.:** Louisiana State Library, P.O. Box 131, Baton Rouge, LA 70821.

Bragg, Mary Jane (N. 2, 1918, Missoula, MT) Ref. Lib., CA State Univ., Fullerton, 1966–; Ed., Pubs. Dept., Huntington Lib., 1959–65; Hungarian Refugee relief worker, Quäkerhilfe, Vienna, Austria, 1958; various positions in Amer. Friends Srvc. Com., 1950–57; Lib. Asst. Ref.; Huntington Lib., 1949–50; 1942–45; Engl. Tchr., Carlsbad Union High Sch., 1948–49; Relief Worker, Germany, Amer. Friends Srvc. Com., 1947–48. **Educ.:** Occidental Col., 1935–39, BA (Eng.); Columbia Univ., 1939–41, MA (Eng. lit.); Univ. of CA, LA, 1965–66, MLS. **Orgs.:** ALA. CA LA **Honors:** Beta Phi Mu. **Pubns.:** "Some Southwest Imprints.", *Southwest Review* (1967). **Activities:** 1; 31, 39; 55, 57 **Addr.:** Lib., CA State Univ., Fullerton, P.O. Box 4150, Fullerton, CA 92634.

Brahm, Walter T. (O. 19, 1910, Massillon, OH) Dir. Dev., OH Lib. Fndn., 1977–; St. Libn., CT St. Lib., 1964–75; St. Libn., OH St. Lib., 1942–63; Asst. Libn., Toledo Pub. Lib., 1939–41, Head, Sci. and Tech., 1937–38. **Educ.:** Case Western Reserve Univ., 1928–32, AB; 1933, MSLS. **Orgs.:** ALA: Finance Com. OH LA: Various coms. CT LA: Various coms. New England Lib. Bd.: Ch. **Honors:** OH LA., First Outstan. Libn. of the Yr. Awd., 1959; OH LA Hall of Fame, Mem., 1978; OH LA., Ohioana Cit. for Disting. Srv., 1962; Sch. of LS, Case Western Reserve Univ. Cert. of Hon., 1979. **Pubns.:** *Index to Publications of Western Reserve University* (1937); "Regional Approaches to Conservation," *Amer. Archvst.* (Oct. 1977). **Activities:** 9, 13; 17, 23, 24; 75, 78, 91 **Addr.:** 3168 Lilly Mar Ct., Dublin, OH 43017.

Branch, Olive H. (F. 5, 1913, Clinton, SC) Col. Dev. Libn., Univ. of TN, 1974–; Acq. Libn., 1963–73; Head, Order Dept., 1948–62; Asst. Circ. Libn., 1947. **Educ.:** Converse Coll., 1929–33, BA; Emory Univ., 1933–34, BS (LS). **Orgs.:** ALA. SELA. TN LA. AAUP. **Activities:** 1; 15, 45; 55, 72, 89 **Addr.:** Library, University of Tennessee, Knoxville, TN 37916.

Brand, Mary Guilbert (Mr. 26, 1936, Oak Park, IL) Libn. Jr.-Sr. Lib., Hebrew Acad. of Grt. Miami, Miami Beach, FL, 1970–; Ref. Libn. and Head of Centralized Cat., US Virgin Islands Lib., 1966–68. **Educ.:** FL St. Univ., 1953–60, BALS, 1961–62, (LS). **Orgs.:** Assoc. of Jewish Libs.: Treas. (1979–). S. FL Chap., Assn. of Jewish Lib.: Pres. (1976–). S. FL Jewish Hist. Socty.: Corres. Secy. (1978–). **Pubns.:** Ed., *The Jewish Biblio-File, Newsletter.*, Ed. "Convention Proceedings", AJL, (1976–79). **Activities:** 10, 13; 15, 21, 23; 66, 85 **Addr.:** 2842 Pine Tree Drive #6, Miami Beach, FL 33140.

Brandak, George M. (Ag. 10, 1943, Regina, SK) Mss. Cur., Univ. of BC, 1973–; Arch. Ast., Univ. of SK, 1971–73; Archvst., Prov. Arch. of AB, 1966–69. **Educ.:** Univ. of SK, Regina, 1963–66, BA (Hist.); Wilfrid Laurier Univ., 1970–71, MA (1973), History thesis; Carleton Univ., 1968, Cert. in Arch. Admin. **Orgs.:** Assn. Can. Archvsts. Assn. of BC Archvsts.: Pres. (1975–76); Secy.-Treas. (1977–78). Can. Hist. Assn.: Arch. Sect. (Treas., 1968). Can. Hist. Assn. Steveston Hist. Socty.: VP (1979–80). Richmond Cent. Socty.: Hist. Com. (1979). **Pubns.:** "Labour Sources in the UBC Library's Special Collections Division," *Archivaria* (Sum 1977); various reviews. **Activities:** 1, 2; 18, 39, 45; 66, 95-Labor Rel., Lit. Mss. **Addr.:** University of B.C., Library - Special Collections, 1956 Main Mall, University Campus, Vancouver, BC V6T 1Y3 Canada.

Brandeau, John Harrison (My. 30, 1945, Troy, NY) Head, AV Dept., Mercy Coll. Lib., 1979–; Media Resrcs. Adv./Fac. Assoc. in Film, Hampshire Coll., 1975–76; Non-Print Media Libn., 1973–75; Archvst., Adirondack Musm., 1972–73. **Educ.:** Assumption Coll., 1962–66, BA (Frgn. Affairs); SUNY, Albany, 1971, MA (Eng.), 1972, MLS; Univ. of MI, 1978–, DLS. **Orgs.:** ALA. METRO Film Coop. Five Coll. Lib. Lecture Com.: Ch. (1974–75). Univ. of MI Sch. of LS Doct. Students Org.: Pres. (1977–78). **Honors:** Beta Phi Mu, 1972. **Activities:** 1; 15, 32, 39; 67, 72 **Addr.:** Mercy College Library, 555 Broadway, Dobbs Ferry, NY 10522.

Branden, Shirley (Crane Creek, MO) Head Ref. Libn., Univ. of TN, 1977–; Med. Libn., TX Tech. Univ., 1975–77; Ref. Libn., Creighton Univ., 1972–75. **Educ.:** Univ. of MO, 1957, BS (Educ.), 1962, MA (Span.), 1972, MA (LS); Med. LA, 1972, Cert. **Orgs.:** Med. LA: South. Reg. Grp. **Pubns.:** Ed. com., *Bltn. of the Med. LA* (1978–); "Monitoring MEDLINE Activity at the University of Tennessee Center for the Health Sciences Library," *Proceedings of the Second Joint Conference of the Southern and South Central Regional Groups of the Medical Library Association, New Orleans, LA, O. 16, 1980* (1981); "Bibliographic Instruction," *TN Libn.* (1980). **Activities:** 1, 12; 39 **Addr.:** 6035 Bangalore Ct., Memphis, TN 38119.

Brandhorst, Wesley T. (Ted) (My. 9, 1933, Portland, OR) Dir., ERIC Prcs. and Ref. Facility, Operations Resrch., Inc., 1970–, Prin. Info. Sci., 1969, Asst. Dir., NASA Facility, 1962–68, Libn., Info. Sci., 1960–61; Intern, Lib. of Congs., 1957–59. **Educ.:** Univ. of CA, Berkeley, 1951–55, BA (Eng.), 1955–57, MLS; American Univ., 1960–64. **Orgs.:** ASIS: Cnclr. (1977–79); Standards Com. (Ch., 1978–). ALA. SLA. Info. Indus. Assn. AAAS. Amer. Anthro. Assn. **Pubns.:** "A Table of Set Theory Notations," *Jnl. of the Amer. Socty. for Info. Sci.* (N.-D. 1970); "Document Retrieval and Dissemination Systems" in *Anl. Review of Info. Sci. and Tech.* (1972); "Managing the ERIC Data Base" in *Computers in Information Data Centers* (1973); "ANSI Z39 Romanization Standards and Reversibility: A Dialog to Arrive at a Policy," *Jnl. of the Amer. Socty. for Info. Sci.* (Ja. 1979); jt. cmplr., *A Bibliography of Publications About the Educational Resources Information Center* (1978); other articles. **Activities:** 12; 20, 30, 46; 62, 63, 75 **Addr.:** ERIC Processing & Reference Facility, 4833 Rugby Ave., Suite 303, Bethesda, MD 20014.

Brandon, Alfred N. (S. 10, 1922, Ogden, UT) Med. Lib. Consult., 1979–; Head Libn., NY Acad. of Med., 1973–78; Ch. & Prof., Dept. LS, Mt. Sinai Sch. of Med., 1969–73; Dir., Welch Med. Lib., Johns Hopkins Univ. Sch. of Med., 1963–69; Head Libn., Univ. of KY Med. Ctr., 1957–63; Head Libn., Loma Linda Univ., 1953–57; Head Libn., Transp. Lib., Univ. of MI, 1952–53; Head Libn., Atl. Union Coll., 1948–52. **Educ.:** Atl. Union Coll., 1940–45, ThB (Theo.); Syracuse Univ., 1947–48, BS (LS); Univ. of IL, 1950–51, MS (LS); Univ. of MI, 1952–56, MA (Hist.). **Orgs.:** Med. LA: Pres. (1965–66); Ed., *Bltn. MLA* (1961–69). SLA. ALA. **Honors:** Med. LA, Marcia C. Noyes Awd., 1977; Med. LA, Ida & George Eliot Prize Essay Awd., 1972; Med. LA, Janet Doe Lecture, 1969; Beta Phi Mu. **Pubns.:** Jt. auth., "Selected List of Nursing Books and Journals," *Nursing Outlook* (O. 1979); "Selected List of Books and Journals for the Small Medical Library," *Bltn. Med. LA* (Ap. 1981); "The emergence of the modern medical library" in *Handbook of Med. Lib. Practice.* (1970); "Academic status for medical school librarians," *Bltn. Med. LA* (Ja. 1970); "The controversy over change," *Bltn. Med. LA* (Ja. 1978); other articles, reviews. **Activities:** 1, 14-Medical Library; 17, 24, 34; 57, 63, 80 **Addr.:** 805 E. South St., Orlando, FL 32801.

Brandt, Ingeborg Kiessel (O. 16, 1922, Manor Radenhausen, Hesse, W. Germany) Head, Serials Dept., Hlth. Sci. Ctr. Lib., TX Tech Univ., 1977–81, Asst. Catlgr., 1975–77. **Educ.:** Philipps Univ., (Germany), 1943–44 (Chem.); NM State Univ., 1955–74 BA (Langs., Scis.); TX Woman's Univ., 1974–75, MLS. **Orgs.:** Med. LA. SLA. TX LA. AAAS. **Activities:** 1, 12; 44, 45, 46; 58, 80, 86 **Addr.:** Sanborn Rd., Hampton Falls, NH 03844.

Brandwein, Larry (Ag. 20, 1931, New York City, NY) Deputy Dir., Brooklyn Pub. Lib., 1970–, Branch Libn., 1967–70, Dist. Libn., 1965–67, Branch Libn., 1960–65. **Educ.:** Brooklyn Coll., 1951–54, BA (Hist., Gvt.); Columbia Univ., 1956–57, MLS. **Orgs.:** ALA: LAMA/Lib. Org. and Mgt. Sect. (1979–). NY LA: Legis. Com. (1975–77). NY State LSCA Adv. Cncl. (1977–). Natl. Pub. Empl. Labor Rel. Assn. (1978). **Pubns.:** "Developing a Service Rating Program," *Lib. Jnl.* (F. 1, 1975); "Library Service to Labor," *RQ* (Win. 1977); "Management and Labor, from Confrontation to Coexistence," *Lib. Jnl.* (Mr. 15, 1979). **Activities:** 9; 17, 35 **Addr.:** Brooklyn Public Library, Brooklyn, NY 11238.

Branham, Gloria Kay (O. 9, 1953, Perryton, TX) Libn., Southwest. Pub. Srv. Co., 1980–; Libn., First Presby. Church, 1979–; Asst. Ref. Libn., W. TX State Univ., 1977–80, Jr. Libn., Ref., Cat., 1976–77. **Educ.:** Amarillo Coll., 1972–74, AS (Gen.); W. TX State Univ., 1974–75, BA (Soc. Std., Educ.); TX Educ. Agency Cert., 1975 (Sec. Schs., Soc. Std.); TX Woman's Univ., 1975–77, MLS. **Orgs.:** TX LA: Dist. 2, Lcl. Arrange. Com. (1978), Legis. Com. (1978–79); Cont. Educ. Com. (Secy., 1980–81); Ref. RT, Pubcty. Com. (Ch., 1979–80). Lib. Cont. Educ. in TX Task Frc. SW LA. SLA. W. TX State Univ. Stdg. Com. Orien. Com. (1979–80). TX Woman's Univ. Alum. Assn.: Panhandle Chap. (Co-Ch., 1978–79). Amer. Bus. Women's Assn.: Tascosa Chap. (1981–). Frnds. of the W. TX State Univ. Cornette Lib. **Honors:** Kappa Delta Pi; Phi Alpha Theta; Pi Gamma Mu; Pi Delta Phi. **Pubns.:** Educ. chap., *Texas Reference Sources: A Selective Guide* (1978). **Activities:** 12; 17, 39, 46; 59, 64, 91 **Addr.:** 3004 Brentwood, Amarillo, TX 79106.

Branin, Joseph J. (Mr. 26, 1947, Philadelphia, PA) Hum. Libn., Univ. GA Libs., 1977–; Libn., Kent State Univ., Salem, 1975–77. **Educ.:** La Salle Coll., 1965–69, BA (Eng.); Univ. Pittsburgh, 1971–74, MA (Eng.); 1974–75, MLS. **Orgs.:** ALA. GA LA. OH Acad. LA. **Honors:** Beta Phi Mu, 1975. **Pubns.:** "Elizabeth Hardwick" in *American Novelists Since World War II* (1980); numerous reviews (1976–77). **Activities:** 1, 13; 15, 17, 39; 55, 75, 93 **Addr.:** University of Georgia Libraries, Athens, GA 30602.

Branscomb, Lewis Capers, Jr. (Ag. 5, 1911, Birmingham, AL) Prof. of Thurber Std., OH State Univ., 1971–; Dir. of Libs., Prof. of Lib. Admin, 1952–71; Assoc. Dir. of Libs., Prof. of Lib. Admin., 1948–52; Asst. Dir., Pub. Service Depts., Assoc. Prof. of LS, Univ. of IL, 1944–48; Libn., Prof. of LS, Univ. of SC, 1942–44; Libn., Mercer Univ., 1941–42; Order Libn., Univ. of GA, 1939–41. **Educ.:** Birmingham-South. Coll., 1929–30 (Pre-Med.); Duke Univ., 1930–33, AB (Pre-Med., Eng.); Univ. of MI, 1938–39, BLS; 1939–41, MALS; Univ. of Chicago, 1945–54, DLS. **Orgs.:** ALA: Nom. Com. (Ch., 1954–55); ACRL (Dir., 1953–55; Pres., 1958–59). Ctr. for Resrch. Libs.: Bd. of Dirs. (1953–64); Ch. (1961–62). Beta Phi Mu: Exec. Cncl. (1955–58). OCLC: Bd. of Trustees (1967–72); Ch. (1968–70). various other lib. orgs. AAUP: OH State Univ. Chap. (Pres., 1953–54); Natl. Cncl. (1952–55). Amer. Cvl. Liberties Un. Torch Clb. Crichton Clb. various other orgs. **Honors:** OH LA, Awd. of Merit, 1971. **Pubns.:** Ed., *The Case for Faculty Status for Academic Libraries* (1971); Jt. auth., *History of The Ohio Conference, American Association of University Professors, 1949–1974* (1974); "James Thurber and Oral History at Ohio State University," *Lost Generation Jnl.* (Win. 1975); "Thurber at Ohio State," *OH LA Bltn.* (Ap. 1973); "Tenure for Professional Librarians on Appointment at Colleges and Universities," *Coll. and Resrch. Libs.* (Jl. 1965); various articles. **Activities:** 1; 24, 41, 45; 55, 57, 95-James Thurber. **Addr.:** Main Library, Ohio State University, Columbus, OH 43210.

Branscombe, Frederic Ray (Je. 4, 1914, Moncton, NB) Consult., 1976–; Coord. of Educ. Media Servs., N York Bd. of Educ., 1965–76; Sup. of Teaching Aids, Weston Bd. of Educ., 1963–64; Head of Dept. of Teaching Aids, Weston Collegiate & Vocational Sch., 1954–62. **Educ.:** Univ. of Toronto, 1933–37, BA (Eng. & Hist.); New York Univ., 1960–61, MA 1961–69, PhD (Educ. Communications); ON Coll. of Educ., 1937–38, (Spec. in Eng. & Hist.). **Orgs.:** AECT: Consult. Ed. *Instructional Innovator* (1978–); International Div.: Bd. of Dir. (1977–); Pres. 1981–82). Assn. for Media & Tech. in Educ. in Canada: Bd. of Dir. (1974–77); Pres. (1975–76). Can. LA. Can. Sch. Lib. Assn. Can. Coll. of Tchrs.: Exec., Central ON Chap. (1974–77). Phi Delta Kappa. ON Educ. Assn.: Senate (1961–71). ON Tchrs. Fed.: AV Com. (1959–70). **Honors:** Assn. for Media & Tech. in Educ. in Can., Natl. Leadership Medalion and Honorary Life Membership, 1979; Can. Coll. of Tchrs., Fellow of the College, 1972; New York Univ., Founders Day Award, 1970. **Pubns.:** Jt. ed., *Resource Services for Canadian Schools* (1977); "Challenges and Changes: Resource Guidelines for Canadian Schools", *Can. Lib. Jnl.* (Ag. 1978); "It's Time to Break the Impasse Between Library and Audio-Visual", *School Progress in Canada* (Mr. 1971); "Educational Media and Teacher Training", *School Progress in Canada* (D. 1970); "Computer Based Resource Units", *Audiovisual Instruction* (Je.–Jl. 1970); Other articles. **Activities:** 9, 10; 17, 24, 26; 50, 56, 63 **Addr.:** 11 St. Leonards Ave., Toronto, ON M4N 1K1 Canada.

Brant, Marjorie H. (Jl. 27, 1947, Pittsburgh, PA) Resrch. Libn., Columbia Gas Syst. Srv. Corp., 1973–. **Educ.:** IN Univ. of PA, 1965–69, BA (Eng.); Purdue Univ., 1969–71, MA (Eng.); Univ. of Pittsburgh, 1972–73, MLS. **Orgs.:** SLA: Pub. Utils. Div. (Ch., 1980–81). Ctrl. OH Chap. (Pres., 1977–78). Columbus Area Lib. and Info. Cncl. of OH: Bd. of Trustees (1977–80). OH LA: OLDP Draft Com. (1976). Ctrl. OH Fed. of Info. Soctys.: Strg. Com. (1975–76). Amer. Gas Assn.: Lib. Srvs. Com. (Ch., 1981). **Pubns.:** "Selling Microforms to Management," *Spec. Libs.* (Ag. 1978); "Help Is at Hand–the A.G.A. Network," *Oper. Sect. Proceedings*, Amer. Gas Assn. (1980); oral presentations. **Activities:** 12; 15, 17, 39; 64, 86, 91 **Addr.:** Columbia Gas System Service Corp., 1600 Dublin Rd., Columbus, OH 43216.

Brant, Virginia A. (Ja. 16, 1933, Akron, OH) Lib. Supvsr., AV Coord., Title IV, Crestline HS, 1978–; Libn., Mayer Jr. High, 1972–78; Elem. Sch. Libn., Coffinberry Sch., 1969–72. **Educ.:** Kent State Univ., 1950–54, BA (Eng.); Case West. Rsv. Univ., 1966–69, MS (LS). **Orgs.:** ALA: AASL. OH Educ. Lib./Media Assn. N. Ctrl. OH Educ. Lib./Media Assn.: Prog. Ch. (1980–81); VP, Pres.-Elect. NE OH Educ. Lib./Media Assn.: NEOTA Day (Jr. High Ch., 1979). **Pubns.:** Various presentations. **Activities:** 10; 15, 17, 20 **Addr.:** 340 Emmet St., Crestline, OH 44827.

Brantz, Malcolm H. (Je. 1, 1945, Hartford, CT) Dir., Lrng. Resrcs. Ctr., Univ. of CT Health Ctr., 1973–. **Educ.:** Univ. of Hawaii, 1964–68, BA (Psy.); 1972–73, MLS; University of CT, 1976–80, MBA. **Orgs.:** Med. LA: AV Stans. Com. (1979–80). ALA. **Pubns.:** Ed., *Health Sciences Audiovisual Resource List* (1977–78); "Hospital Audiovisual Equipment Policy," *Hospitals*

PROFESSIONAL ACTIVITIES: Institutions: 1. Acad. lib.; 2. Arch.; 3. Assn.; 4. Fed./Gvt. lib.; 5. Inst. lib.; 6. Mfr./Suppl.; 7. Milit. lib.; 8. Musm.; 9. Pub. lib.; 10. Sch. lib.; 11. Sch. of lib. sci.; 12. Spec. lib.; 13. State lib.; 14. (other). **Functions/Activities:** 15. Acq./Col. dev.; 16. Adult srvs.; 17. Admin.; 18. Apprais.; 19. Archit./Bldgs.; 20. Cat./Class.; 21. Chld. srvs.; 22. Circ.; 23. Cons./Pres.; 24. Consult.; 25. Cont. ed.; 26. Educ. lib. sci.; 27. Ext. srvs.; 28. Fund/Grants; 29. Gvt. pubs.; 30. Indx./Abs.; 31. Instr. lib. use; 32. Media srvs.; 33. Micro.; 34. Netwks./Coop.; 35. Persnl.; 36. PR; 37. Publshg.; 38. Recs. mgt.; 39. Ref. srvs.; 40. Repro.; 41. Resrch.; 42. Review.; 43. Secur.; 44. Serials; 45. Spec. col.; 46. Tech. srvs.; 47. Trustees/Bds.; 48. YA srvs.; 49. (other).

(S. 1978); Jt. auth., "Classification and Audiovisuals," *Bltn. Med. LA* (Ap. 1977); Patent No. 3,694,645 (1970); Various other publications in AV. **Addr.:** 28 Francis Street, Avon, CT 06001.

Branyan, Brenda May (Jl. 16, 1932, Coloma, MI) Assoc. Prof., UT State Univ., 1976–; Asst. Prof., Dept. Info. Sci., IL State Univ., 1975–76; Asst. Prof., Dept. Lrng. Resrc., West. IL Univ., 1969–74; Lib. Media Spec., Lakeview Pub. Schs., 1954–69; Visit. Asst. Prof., Univ. of NC, 1974–76; Asst. Prof., E. TN State Univ., 1971–72; Visit. Instr., West. MI Univ., 1968–69. **Educ.:** Lake MI Coll., 1950–52, A Arts (Elem. Educ.); West. MI Univ., 1952–54, BA (Elem. Educ., LS); 1966–67, MSL; South. IL Univ., 1973–77, PhD (Curric. Instr. and Instr. Media). **Orgs.:** ALA: AASL. AALS. UT LA: IFC (1979–80). Other orgs. **Honors:** Beta Phi Mu, 1967. **Pubns.:** *Outstanding Women Who Pioneered the School Library Media Concept* (1980); "Report on the Follow-up Committee: Utah Gov Conf on Libr & Infor Sys," *UEMA Jnl.* (Mr. 1980); "Critical Issues Facing School Lib/Media Personnel in Utah," *UEMA Jnl.* (N. 1978); "Materials Selection: The Possible, The Practical & the Potentially Pleasing," *UEMA JNL.* (S. 1977); various wkshps. and progs. **Activities:** 10, 11; 17, 26, 32; 56, 63, 74 **Addr.:** Nibley Mobile Pk., Lot 11, Rte. 1, Logan, UT 84321.

Brassil, Ellen Christina (Jl. 28, 1952, Schenectady, NY) Ref. Libn., Coord. of User Educ., Hlth. Sci. Lib., Univ. of NC, 1979–; Ref. Libn., St. Francis Hosp. and Med. Ctr., 1976–79. **Educ.:** Drew Univ., 1970–74, BA (Eng.); Simmons Coll., 1974–75, MS (LS). **Orgs.:** Med. LA. CT Assn. of Hlth. Sci. Libs.: Ed. CAHSL Nsltr. (1978–79); Exec. Bd. (1978–79); Pubcty. Com. (Ch. 1978–79). **Activities:** 1, 12; 16, 25, 29; 54, 58, 59 **Addr.:** Chateau Apts. #309, Hwy. 54 ByPass, Carrboro, NC 27510.

Bratton, John T. (O. 17, 1933, Camden, AR) Head, Tech. Srvs., East. MT Coll. Lib., 1979–; Acq. Libn., Ball State Univ., 1978–79; Asst. Acq. Libn., 1977–78; Acq. Libn., Univ. of Denver, 1969–75; Head, Acq.-Serials Dept., 1969–69; Serials Libn., 1968–69; Acq. Libn., ID State Univ., 1967–68; Catlgr., Univ. of Rochester, 1966–67; various other lib. positions. **Educ.:** Hendrix Coll., 1951–55, BA (Lit. Phil.); LA State Univ., 1955–57, MSLS; Univ. of CO, Boulder, 1975, MA (Hist.). **Orgs.:** ALA: ACRL; RTSD. MT LA. AAUP; Natl. Educ. Assn. **Activities:** 1; 15, 20, 46 **Addr.:** Eastern Montana College Library, Billings, MT 59101.

Bratton, Phyllis (My. 8, 1947, New York, NY) Head Ref. Srvs., Coral Gables Pub. Lib., 1980–, YA Libn., 1978–80; Branch Libn., Northfield Cmnty. Lib., 1974–78; Proj. Libn., Akrow-Summit Cnty. Pub. Lib., 1973–74; Ref. Libn., San Francisco Pub. Lib., 1972–73. **Educ.:** Kent State Univ., 1964–68, BA (Psych.); 1970–71, MLS. **Orgs.:** OH LA. FL LA. **Pubns.:** Draft "Guidelines for Establishing I & R Services in Public Libraries", *Public Libraries* (Fall 1979); "Community Services Staff Development Project: An Overview" summarized in *New Media in Public Libraries* (1978). **Activities:** 9; 16, 39, 48; 50, 59, 95-Staff Development & Training. **Addr.:** 5325 SW77 Ct. F-204, Miami, FL 33155.

Braude, Robert M. (S. 27, 1939, Los Angeles, CA) Dir., McGoogan Lib. of Med., Univ. of NE Med. Ctr., 1978–; Dir., Denison Meml. Lib., Univ. of CO Med. Ctr., 1975–77; Assoc. Dir., 1968–75; Head, MEDLARS Search Station, Biomed. Lib., Univ. of CA, Los Angeles, 1965–68; Ref. Libn., 1964–65. **Educ.:** Univ. of CA, Los Angeles, 1957–62, BA (Psy.); 1961–64, MA (Psy.); 1963–64, MLS. **Orgs.:** Med. LA: Bd. of Dirs. (Secy., 1972–75); Prog. and Conv. Com., (1976–1980; Ch., 1979–80); Chairman, Ad Hoc Com. to Study ILL Practices and Problems (Ch., 1976–78); Nom. Com. (1978–79). NE LA; ALA. Other orgs. and coms. **Pubns.:** "Automated circulation systems," *The CO Acad. Lib.* (5:1–6, 1969); Jt. auth., "Cost-performance analysis of TWX-mediated interlibrary loans in a medium-sized medical center library," *Bltn. Med. LA* (59:65–70, 1971); Jt. Auth., "Cost-performance analysis of cataloging and card production in a medical center library," *Bltn. Med. LA* (63:29–34, 1975); Jt. Auth., "Cataloging costs with CATLINE: A follow-up study," *Bltn. Med. LA* (63:414–5, 1975); Jt. Auth., "Determination of overlap in coverage of Excerpta Medica and Index Medicus through SERLINE," *Bltn. Med. LA.* (64:324–5, 1976). **Activities:** 1, 14-Medical Center; 17, 80 **Addr.:** McGoogan Library of Medicine, University of Nebraska Medical Center, 42nd Street & Dewey Ave., Omaha, NE 68105.

Brauer, Regina (New York, NY) Libn., Hunter Coll. Elem. Sch., 1977–; Slide Libn., Guggenheim Musm., 1975–77; Libn., Cncl. of Jewish Feds. and Welfare Funds, 1971–74. **Educ.:** Adelphi Univ., 1939–42, BA (Bus. Admin.); Columbia Univ., 1968–70, MLS. **Orgs.:** ALA. ARLIS. NY LA. **Activities:** 10; 15, 17, 21 **Addr.:** 525 E. 86 St., New York, NY 10028.

Brault, Jean-Rémi (S. 16, 1926, Montreal, PQ) Dir., PQ Natl. Lib., 1974–; Chief Libn., Coll. Montmorency, 1970–72; Chief Libn., Coll. Lionel-Groulx, 1951–70. **Educ.:** Univ. of Montreal, 1939–47, BA; Univ. of Ottawa, 1959–61, MA (Hist.), 1961–62, PhD (Hist.). **Pubns.:** "Dans la Maison du Père," *Assn. Can. des. Bibtcrs. de Lang. Fr. Bltn.* (D. 1975). "Commission de Revision des Objectifs et des Structures," *Assn. Can. des Bibtcrs. de Lang. Fr. Bltn.* (N. 1972); "La Commission de Revision des Objectifs et des Structures," *Assn. Can. des Bibtcrs. de Lang. Fr. Nouvelles* (Jl. 1972); "Commission de Revision des Objectifs et des Structures," *Assn. Can. des Bibtcrs. de Lang. Fr. Rpts. Anl.* (1972); "Conférence Nationale sur les Statistiques des Bibliothèques," *Assn. pour l'Advnc. des Sci. et des Tech. de la Documtn.* (1974); various articles. **Activities:** 9, 13; 17, 46; 57 **Addr.:** 55 Cote Ste-Catherine, Apt. 1506, Outremont, PQ H3V 2A5 Canada.

Braun, Beverly J. (Ap. 12, 1941, Sanger, CA) Dist. Libn., Monterey Peninsula Unfd. Sch. Dist., 1976–; Consult., Lib., Media, Fresno Cnty. Dept. of Educ., 1973–76; Asst. Prof., Libnshp., Univ. of OR, 1969–76; Libn., Santa Barbara City Schs., 1970–73. **Educ.:** Univ. of OR, 1964–67, BS (Hist.), 1967–68, MLS (Libnshp.); CA State Univ., 1973–75 (Admin.). **Orgs.:** CA State Lib. Bd.: VP (1978–80). ALA: Notable Chld. Bks. (1980–82); ALSC, Film Com. (1978–80). CA Media and Lib. Educs.: Treas. (1976–78); Conf. Coord. (1979–80). Coop. Info. Netwks.: Exec. Bd. (1977–79). CA Young Reader Medal: Bd. (1975–80). Assn. CA Sch. Admins. **Honors:** Delta Kappa Gamma. **Pubns.:** *Cultural Understanding through Picture Books* (1973); *Reference Books for Elementary Schools* (1974); "California Children Elect Their Favorite Author," *CA Sch. Libs.* (Fall 1976); "Student TV Newscast Feature New Materials," *News and Views* (F. 1975). **Activities:** 10, 11; 17, 21, 48; 63, 67, 89 **Addr.:** P.O. 22604, Carmel, CA 93723.

Braunstein, Yale M. (Ja. 12, 1945, Philadelphia, PA) Asst. Prof. of Econ., Brandeis Univ., 1977–; Asst. Prof. of Econ., NY Univ., 1974–77. **Educ.:** Rensselaer Polytechnic Inst., 1962–66, BS (Econ.); Stanford Univ., 1967–74, PhD (Econ.). **Orgs.:** ASIS. Amer. Econ. Assn. **Pubns.:** *Manual of Pricing and Cost Determination for Information Organizations* (1977); *Economics of Property Rights as Applied to Computer Software and Data Bases* (1977); "Empirical Study of Scale Economics and Production Complementarity," *Jour. Pol. Econ.* (O. 1977); "Economic Rationale for Page and Submission Charges," *Jour. Am. Soc. for Int. Sci.* (N. 1978); "Costs and Benefits of Library Information," *Lib. Trends,* (Sum. 1979). **Activities:** 14-Univ. Dept.; 24, 41, 49-Teaching; 61, 93, 95-Economics. **Addr.:** Department of Economics, Brandeis University, Waltham, MA 02254.

Bravard, Robert Staton (N. 2, 1935, Dayton, OH) Dir. of Lib. Srvs., Lock Haven State Coll., 1970–, Tech. Srvs. Libn., 1963–70; Head Libn., Findlay Coll., 1960–63, Asst. Libn., 1959–60. **Educ.:** Wilmington Coll., 1953–57, BA (Eng., Hist.); Syracuse Univ., 1957–59, MSLS. **Orgs.:** Cncl. of PA State Coll. and Univ. Lib. Dirs.: Ch. (1976–78); Secy. (1973–76). Susquehanna Lib. Coop.: Ch. (1974–76). Interlib. Delivery Srv. of PA: Bd. of Dirs. (1979–). Ctrl. PA Hlth. Systs. Agency: Bd. of Dirs. (1978–). Lock Haven Hosp. Con. Adv. Com.: Ch. (1973–81). **Honors:** Beta Phi Mu. **Pubns.:** Jt. auth., *Samuel R. Delany: A Primary and Secondary Bibliography* (1980); "American Erotica at the Close of the Sixties," *Choice* (N. 1970). **Activities:** 1; 15, 17, 20; 57, 74 **Addr.:** Stevenson Library, Lock Haven State College, Lock Haven, PA 17745.

Braver, Norma B. (Jl. 30, 1927, Brooklyn, NY) Ref. Libn., Asst. Prof., Univ. of Louisville, 1977; Vetny. Med. Libn., TX A&M Univ., 1975–77; Resrch. Asst. to Dr. Daniel Mazia, 1957–58; Radioactive Tracer Work, Radiation Lab., Donner Lab., Univ. of CA, Berkeley, 1955–57; Resrch. Asst. to Dr. Lloyd Thomas, Univ. of MO Med. Sch., 1954; Gen. Med. Tech., Ellis Fischel State Cancer Hosp., 1953–54; Gen. Med. Tech., The NY Hosp., 1952–53. **Educ.:** Brooklyn Coll., 1948, AB (Zlgy., Clinical Pathology); Univ. of MO, 1949–52, MA (Zlgy.); Univ. of OK, 1973–75, MLS; various crs. **Orgs.:** ALA: ACRL/Coll. and Resrch. Libs. Sect./Bio. Sci. Sect., Com. on Goals and Structure (1977–); RASD/Machine-Assisted Ref. Sect. (1979–). KY LA: Hlth. Sci. RT (Secy., 1978–79); Spec. Libs. Sect. (Secy., 1980–81). SLA: KY Chap., Bd. (Del., 1979–80), Ad Hoc Com. Dir. of Spec. Libs. of KY (1979–), Networking Ch. (1980–81); TX Chap. (1975–77); OK Chap. (1974–75). TX LA: Cont. Educ. Com. (1977). Various other orgs. AAUP. NY Acad. of Sci. AAAS. **Honors:** Beta Phi Mu; Sigma Xi. **Pubns.:** *The Mutants of Drosophila melanogaster Classified According to Body Parts Affected* (1956); *The Literature of Zoology: an Annotated Bibliography* (1975); various bk. reviews, *Amer. Ref. Bks. Anl.* **Activities:** 31, 39, 41; 58, 80 **Addr.:** 190 Breckinridge Sq., Louisville, KY 40220.

Brawley, Paul Holm (S. 27, 1942, Granite City, IL) Ed.-in-chief, *Booklist,* ALA, 1973–, Ed., Nonprint Mtrls., 1969–73; AV Libn., Boston Pub. Lib., 1967–69, Recs. Libn., 1965–67; various wkshps. **Educ.:** South. IL Univ., 1960–65, BA (Eng.); Simmons Coll., 1965–68, MS (LS); various crs. World Hunger Proj. Breakthrough Fndn. Erhard Sems. Trng. **Activities:** 3; 37, 42 **Addr.:** 916 W. Willow St., Chicago, IL 60614.

Brawner, Lee B. (My. 1, 1935, Seguin, TX) Exec. Dir., Metro. Lib. Syst., Oklahoma City, OK, 1971–; Asst. State Libn., TX State Lib., 1967–71; Chief, Branch Srvs., Dallas Pub. Lib., 1964–67; Dir., Waco Pub. Lib., 1962–64. **Educ.:** N. TX State Univ., 1955–57, BA (LS); George Peabody Coll., 1960–61, MA (LS). **Orgs.:** AMIGOS Bibl. Cncl.: Bd. of Trustees (Vice-Ch., 1979–81). ALA: Cncl. (Cnclr.-At-Lg., 1979–82); Int. Frdm. Com. (1979–81). NEH Oral Hist. Plng. Proj.: Adv. Bd. (1978–79). OK Hum. Com.: Ch. (1977–78). Frnds. of Libs. in OK: Bd. of Dirs. (1979–). **Honors:** OK Chap., Amer. Inst. of Archits., Merit Awds. for Branch Lib. Bldgs. Planned, 1974, 1979. **Pubns.:** Jt. auth., *Building Program Study with Recommendations for the Central Library; Broward County Library* (1979); *Facilities Planning Study; Irving Public Library System* (1979); "The Fine Art of Associating," *ALA Yrbk.* (1979); jt. auth., "A Regional Association Launches Cooperative Endeavors," *Lib. Trends* (O. 1975). **Activities:** 9; 17, 24, 34; 50, 55, 74 **Addr.:** Metropolitan Library System, 131 Dean A. McGee, Oklahoma City, OK 73102.

Brazile, Orella R. (My. 28, 1945, Leesville, LA) Dir., Lib., Media Srvs., South. Univ., 1978–, Circ. Libn., 1968–78; Libn., Pine Valley Elem. Sch., 1968. **Educ.:** Grambling State Univ., 1964–67, BS (Soc. Sci.); E. TX State Univ., 1971–73, MSLS; South. Univ., 1975–76, MEd (Media). **Orgs.:** ALA. LA LA. AECT. Grambling State Alum. Assn.: Corres. Secy. **Honors:** H. W. Wilson, Staff Dev. Grant, 1980; Assn. of Women Students (Campus), Cert. of Apprec., 1978. **Pubns.:** "Staff Development Workshop" one hour vid. cassette (1980); "Seminar on the History of the Cooper Road" 3 half-hour vid. cassettes (1981). **Addr.:** 4396 Worth Cir., Shreveport, LA 71109.

Bream, Elizabeth M. (My. 19, 1936, Guelph, ON) Assoc. Chmn. of Comm. (Library), L'Amoreaux Collegiate Inst., 1973–; Head Libn., Agincourt Collegiate Inst., 1971–73; Tchr.–Libn., Victoria Park Sec. Sch., 1969–70; Tchr.–Libn., Milneford Jr. HS, 1968–69. **Educ.:** Univ. of Toronto, 1955–58, BA (Eng.); Fac. of Educ., 1958–59, ON Teacher's Cert.; ON Ministry of Educ., Specialist's Cert. in Sch. Libnshp., 1971. **Orgs.:** ON Sch. Lib. Assn.: Exec. Cncl.; Ed., *The Revolting Librarian* (1978–); Wkshp. Leader (1978, 1979, 1980, 1981). Can. LA: ON Ed., *Moccasin Telegraph* (1973). Scarborough Sec. Sch.: Secy. (1972–73). Libns. Assn.: Chmn. (1974–75). **Pubns.:** Ed., *L'Amoreaux Life* (1977–78); "Satellite Libraries; A Case Study", *Moccasin Telegraph* (My. 1972); Book reviews. **Activities:** 10; 31, 49-Editing; 63 **Addr.:** L'Amoreaux Collegiate Institute, 2501 Bridletowne Circle, Agincourt, ON M1W 2K1 Canada.

Brearley, Neil (Ap. 22, 1928, Rochdale, Lancashire, Eng) Assoc. Libn., Reader Srvs., Carleton Univ. Lib., 1976–, Head, Sci. and Engin. Div., 1972–75; Info. Ofcr., TRIUMF Proj., Univ. of BC, 1969–72; Head, Sci. Div., Simon Fraser Univ. Lib., 1968–69; Resrch. Ofcr., BC Resrch. Cncl., 1956–67; Resrch. Sci., Tootal Ltd., 1952–56; Military Service, British Army, 1949–52. **Educ.:** Univ. of London, 1945–49, BSc (Phy.); Univ. of BC, 1967–68, BLS. **Orgs.:** Can. LA. Can. Assn. for Info. Sci.: Ottawa Chap. (Treas., 1978–). Alcuin Socty.: Pres. (1970–71). **Honors:** Univ. of BC, Neal Harlow Prize, 1978. **Pubns.:** Ed., *The journal and narrative of R.H. Alexander* (1973); *A selection of old Canadian bookplates* (1967); "Resource sharing at the information interface," Proceedings, Can. Assn. for Info. Sci. (1979); Various other articles; Reviews. **Activities:** 1, 12; 15, 17, 39; 88, 91 **Addr.:** Carleton University Library, Colonel By Drive, Ottawa, ON K1S 6J7 Canada.

Breaux, Cheryl S. (Je. 4, 1944, Jennings, LA) Med. Libn., Lafayette Charity Hosp., 1973–. **Educ.:** Univ. of Southwestern LA, 1962–66, BA (Eng.); LA State Univ., 1974–76, MLS; Med. Lib. I, 1977. **Orgs.:** Med. LA: Cont. Ed. Hlth. Scis. LA of LA: VP (1976–78); Pres. (1978–present). **Pubns.:** Reviews; "The Effect of Local Resource - Sharing on Interlibrary Loan in Two Hospital Libraries" (1978). **Activities:** 5, 12; 15, 34, 39; 80 **Addr.:** Lafayette Charity Hospital, Health Science Library, Lafayette, LA 70502.

Brechon, Melissa Jane (Je. 17, 1942, Dixon, IL) Libn., Resrch., Guthrie Thea. Fndn., 1979–; Chld. Paperback Bookseller, Bookmen, Inc., 1977–79. **Educ.:** Coll. of St. Catherine, St. Paul, MN, 1975–77 BA (LS). **Orgs.:** SLA. MN LA: Pubns. Com. (1981–82); Exhibits Com. (1981–82). Cath. LA ARLIS/NA: Twin City Chap., Spec. Libns. Caucus to Metronet Exhibits Com. for All-Assn. Conf. 1 (Ch., 1981). **Activities:** 12 **Addr.:** Guthrie Theater Staff Reference Library, 725 Vineland Pl., Minneapolis, MN 55403.

Brecht, Albert O. (N. 19, 1946, Dallas, TX) Prof. and Dir. of the Law Lib., Univ. South. CA Law Sch., 1979–; Assoc. Prof. and Lib. Dir., 1977–79; Asst. Prof. and Dir., 1975–77; Asst. Dir., Law Lib, 1973–75. **Educ.:** North TX State Univ., 1965–69, BA (Govt. and Soclgy.); Univ. Houston, 1969–72, JD; Univ. WA, 1972–73, MLL (Law Libnshp.). **Orgs.:** South. CA Assn. of Law Libs.: Pres. (1975–76). AALL: Placement Ch. (1978–80). SLA. **Pubns.:** "Minorities Employed in Law Libraries," *Law Lib. Jnl.* (1978); "Turning Off the Volume," *Law Lib. Jnl.* (1978). **Activities:** 12; 35; 77 **Addr.:** USC Law Library, University of Southern California, Los Angeles, CA 90007.

Breed, Patricia Ann (D. 23, 1941, Berwyn, IL) Prog. Dir., LS, Instr. Media, Foster G. McGaw Grad. Sch., Natl. Coll. of Educ., 1980–; Resrch. Ctr. Coord., Wilmette Jr. High, 1979–80; Resrch. Ctr. Coord., Howard Jr. High, 1966–79. **Educ.:** North. IL Univ., 1963–66, BSE (Eng., LS), 1968–71, MSE (LS, Instr. Media), 1971–77, EDD (Instr. Tech.). **Orgs.:** IL LA: Legis. Dev. Com.; Reg. I IL Assn. for Media Educ., Ch., Coord. (1980); Legis. Day in Springfield (Coord., My. 24, 1978, My. 1979). AECT:

Special Subjects/Services: 50. Adult educ.; 51. Advert./Mktg.; 52. Aerosp.; 53. Agric.; 54. Area std.; 55. Arts/Hum.; 56. Autom.; 57. Bibl./Prtg.; 58. Bio. sci.; 59. Bus./Fin.; 60. Chem.; 61. Copyrt.; 62. Documtn.; 63. Educ.; 64. Engin.; 65. Env.; 66. Eth. grps.; 67. Film; 68. Food/Nutr.; 69. Geneal.; 70. Geo.; 71. Geol.; 72. Handcpd.; 73. Hist.; 74. Int. frdm.; 75. Info. sci.; 76. Insr.; 77. Law; 78. Legis.; 79. Math./Comp. sci.; 80. Med.; 81. Metals; 82. Nat. resrcs.; 83. Newsp.; 84. Nuc. sci.; 85. Oral hist.; 86. Petr./Energy; 87. Pharm.; 88. Phys./Astr./Math.; 89. Readg.; 90. Relig.; 91. Sci./Tech.; 92. Soc. sci.; 93. Telecom.; 94. Transp.; 95. (other).

Who's Who in Library and Information Services

Gvtl. Rel. Com.; Cert. Com. North. IL Media Assn.: Mem. Ch. (1974–77); Pres.-Elect (1978–79); Pres. (1979–80). IL AECT: Secy. (1980–82); Legis. Ch.; IL LA Legis. Dev. Com., IL AV Assn. Rep. Alpha Delta Kappa: Corres. Secy. (1976–78); Altruistic Ch. (1978–80); Ways and Means (1980–). Phi Delta Kappa: Bd. Natl. Educ. Assn. IL Educ. Assn. Various other orgs. **Honors:** IL AECT, Pres. Awd. for Current Contrib. to the Assn., 1980; Pi Lamda Theta, 1975. **Pubns.:** "The Squeaky Wheel," *IL Libs.* (O. 1978); various legis. com. rpts., *IL AV Assn. Jnl.*, various confs. **Addr.:** National College of Education Library, 2840 Sheridon Rd., Evanston, IL 60201.

Breeden, Barbara K. (F. 13, 1947, Philadephia, PA) Libn., Anne Arundel Genl. Hosp., 1979–; Libn., Higgs, Fletcher & Mack, 1976–77; Head Libn., Trident Tech. Coll., 1974–76; Libn., C. S. Draper Lab. Lib., 1973. **Educ.:** Beaver Coll., 1965–69, BS (Elem. Educ.); Simmons Coll., 1972–73, MLS; Univ. of SC, 1973–74, (higher ed.). **Orgs.:** ALA. Med. LA. MD LA. Med. Assn. of Hlth Sci. Libns. AAUW. Beaver Col. Alum. Assn: Bd. of Dir. (1979–81). **Activities:** 5, 12; 17, 22, 39; 63, 80 **Addr.:** 1090 Sun Valley Dr., Annapolis, MD 21401.

Breedlove, Elizabeth Ann (My. 30, 1943, New York, NY) Head, Bur. Tech. Lib. Srvs., NJ State Lib., 1976–; Lib. Consult., NY State Lib., 1975–76; Head, L.C. Cat. Sect., Univ. PA, 1970–74; Serials Catlgr., 1968–70; Ref. Libn., WA Univ. Lib., 1967–68. **Educ.:** Manhattanville Coll., 1961–65, BA (Eng.); IN Univ., 1966–67, MLS. **Orgs.:** ASIS. NJ LA. ALA: ASCLA/ Interlib. Coop. Discuss. Grp. (Ch., 1979–); MLCS (Exec. Com., 1980–); LAMA/LOMS Budget Acct. and Costs Com., (1979–); Stats. for Tech. Srvs. Com. (1976–80); PLA/Interlib. Coop. Com. (1975–79); RTSD/Cat.: Descr. and Access Com. (1979–). PALINET: Bd. of Trustees (1980–). **Honors:** Beta Phi Mu, 1968. **Pubns.:** "Experimental Use of Computerized Literature Searches in Public and Academic Libraries," *Bookmark* (v. 35 no 2 1976). **Activities:** 1, 13; 17, 34, 46; 56, 75 **Addr.:** New Jersey State Library, Bureau of Technical Library Services, 185 W. State St., Trenton, NJ 08625.

Breedlove, William O., II (Ja. 15, 1941, Indianapolis, IN) Dir., Louis Bay 2nd Lib., Hawthorne, NJ, 1979–; Branch Libn., The Free Lib. of Philadelphia, 1978–79; Asst. Head, Stations Dept., 1976–78; Cmnty. Srvs. Libn., 1971–76. **Educ.:** Butler Univ., 1959–63, BA (Relig., Grk.); Univ. of Chicago, 1963–66, BD (Theol.); Univ. of IL, 1967–68, MS (LS). **Orgs.:** ALA: PLA/ Alternative Educ. Programs Sect., Task Frc. on Litcy. (Co-Ch., 1978–79); Pubn. Com. (1979–81). PA LA (Co-Ch., Adult Srvs. Com.); NJ LA. Natl. Affiliation for Litcy. Adv.: (Treas., New Eng. Reg., 1975–77; Chmn., Natl. Nom. Com., 1977–78). **Honors:** Phi Beta Mu. **Pubns.:** Asst. Ed. and regular contrib. to *PIVOT* (1971–76); "Illiteracy in the United States: Definitions and Statistics," *Notes on Adult Educ.* (1976). **Activities:** 9; 16, 17, 27; 50, 89, 90 **Addr.:** 10 Winthrop Road, Somerset, NJ 08873.

Bregaint-Joling, Geertje (Carole) (S. 27, 1944, Assen, Drente, Netherlands) Asst. Dir., Field Lib. Srvs., Agr. Can., 1979–; Chief Libn., Secy. of State Dept., Can., 1974–79, Ref. Libn., 1971–74; Govt. Docum. Libn., Univ. of BC, 1969–71. **Educ.:** Univ. of BC, 1963–67, BA (Compar. Lit.), 1968–69, BLS. **Orgs.:** Can. Assn. Info. Sci.: VP (1979–80). Can. LA: Can. LA–ASTED Liason, 1981–84. Cncl. of Fed. Libns.: Working Grp. on Access to Gvt. Info. ASIS. **Pubns.:** Ed., Bltn., Can. Ethnic Std. Assn. (1974–79); "Federal Government Libraries and Access to Government Documents; a Report" (1980). **Activities:** 4; 17, 24, 29; 66, 75 **Addr.:** 1360 Maxime St., Gloucester, ON K1B 3L1 Canada.

Breinich, John A. (O. 20, 1943, Davenport, IA) Dir., HI Med. Lib., 1975–; Spec. Asst. to the Dir., Houston Acad. of Med., Med. Ctr. Lib., 1974–75; Assoc. Dir., Univ. of CT Hlth. Ctr. Lib., 1966–71. **Educ.:** Univ. of IA, 1963–65, BA (Psy); Univ. of IL, 1965–66, MS (LS). **Orgs.:** Med. LA: Ad Hoc Com. on Grp. Structure (1975–76). Co-Ch. Anl. Mtg. (1979). HI LA. **Honors:** Beta Phi Mu, 1966. **Activities:** 1, 12; 17, 19; 80 **Addr.:** Hawaii Medical Library, 1221 Punchbowl St., Honolulu, HI 96813.

Breivik, Patricia Senn (Ag. 17, 1939, Pittsburgh, PA) Dir., Auraria Lib. and Media Center. 1979–; Dean of Lib. Srvs., Sangamon State Univ., 1976–79; Asst. Dean, Pratt Inst. Grad. Sch. of Lib. and Info. Sci., 1972–76. **Educ.:** Brooklyn Coll., 1968, BA (Eng.); Pratt Inst., 1969, MLS; Columbia Univ., 1974, DLS. **Orgs.:** ALA: LIRT (Ch., 1978–79); Plng. Com. **Pubns.:** Jt. auth., *Funding Alternatives for Libraries* (1979); *Open Admissions and the Academic Library* (1977); "The Neglected Horizon, or An Expanded Educational Role for Academic Libraries," *New Horizons for Acad. Libs.* (1979); "A Model for Library Management," *Lib. Jnl.* (Spec. Rept. #10, 1979); Ed., Cont. Ed. Clmn., *Jnl. of Educ. for Libnshp.* (1974–76); Various other publications. **Activities:** 1; 17, 26, 31; 50 **Addr.:** Director, Auraria Library and Media Center, 11th & Lawrence, Denver, CO 80204.

Brennan, Exir B. (Jl. 29, 1937, West Point, MS) Asst. Prof./Coord. Lib. Instr., Univ. of AL, 1972–; Coord. Lib. Instr., 1977–80; Ref. Libn., Hum., 1974–77; Ref. Libn., Educ., 1972–74. **Educ.:** Univ. of AL, 1963–67, BA (Eng.), 1971–72, MLS. **Orgs.:** AL LA: Treas. (1977–79); Jr. Mem. RT (Mdrtr., 1978–79). ALA. Southeast. LA. Beta Phi Mu: VP (1975). **Pubns.:** "Bibliographic Instruction: a Review of Research and Applications", *Progress in Educating the Library User* (1979). "Something New Under the Sun–Library Instruction Clearinghouses" *AL Libn.* (1978). **Activities:** 1; 17, 31, 36; 50, 63, 75 **Addr.:** P.O. Box S, University, AL 35486.

Brennan, Sister Mary E. (Ja. 1, 1923, Worchester, MA) Media Libn., Coll. of Our Lady of Elms, 1972–; Ast. Libn., Catlgr., 1967–72; Tchr., St. Mary HS, 1955–66; Tchr., Holy Name Jr. HS, 1952–55. **Educ.:** Coll. of Our Lady of Elms, 1947–58, AB (Eng.); Cath. Univ. of Amer., 1966–67, MSLS; Simmons Coll., 1979, Cont. Ed. Cert. **Orgs.:** Cath. LA: New Eng. Chap. Pioneer Valley Assn. of Acad. Libns. Natl. Assem. of Women Rel. **Honors:** Beta Phi Mu, 1969; Delta Epsilon Sigma, 1977. **Activities:** 1; 17, 20, 32; 63 **Addr.:** College of Our Lady of the Elms, 291 Springfield St., Chicopee, MA 01013.

Brennan, Robert Gilbert (Mr. 26, 1927, Mount Vernon, NY) Asst. Dir. for Pub. Srvs., CA State Univ., Chico, 1962–; Lib. Dir., Howard Whittemore Mem. Lib., 1954–62; Ref. Libn., Dayton Pub. Lib., 1952–54. **Educ.:** Mt. Union Coll., 1945–51, BA (Soclgy.); Pratt Inst., 1951–52, MLS. **Orgs.:** ALA. CA LA. Pratt Inst. Grad. Lib. Sch. Alum. Assn. CA Tchr's Assn. **Pubns.:** Communication Studies, Report, Task Force for the Center for Information (1974); Report, Task Force on Instructional Media (1972). **Activities:** 1; 15, 17; 61 **Addr.:** Meriam Library, CA State University, Chico, Chico, CA 95929.

Brennen, Patrick Wayne (Ja. 24, 1940, Regina, SK) Dir., Univ. of SD, Sch. of Med., Lommen Health Sci. Lib., 1974–; Agr. Libn., Univ. of DE, 1971–73; Bio. Tchr., John Carroll HS, Bel Air, MD, 1967–70; Chem. Tchr., St. Patrick's HS, Hull, PQ, 1966–67; Chem. Tchr., Gonzaga HS, St. John's, NE, 1962–66. **Educ.:** Coll. of Great Falls, 1958–61, BA (Bio., Chem.); Univ. of IL, 1970–71, MS (Lib. Sci.); Univ. of TN, 1961–62, Microbio.; Johns Hopkins Univ., 1968, Educ. **Orgs.:** Med. LA: Bib. and Info. Srvs. Com. (1979–81). SLA. SDLA. Midcontinental Reg. Med. Lib. Grp. (Pres.-Elect): Legis. Liason Com. (Ch., 1979–80); Union List of Serials Com. (1979); Ed. Srvs. Subcom. (1979); other orgs. **Pubns.:** "Informational Flow in American Agricultural Literature", *Qtly. Bltn. of the Intl. Assn. of Agri. Libns. & Docmlsts.* (v. 20, no. 2, 1975); *A Select Bibliography of Reference Books for Medical Students* (1975); Jt. auth., "Reclassification in a Small Decentralized Medical Library". *Bltn. of the Med. LA* (July 1977); Jt. auth., "Citation Analysis in the Literature of Tropical Medicine," *Bltn. of the Med. LA* (January 1978); Jt. auth., "Medical Library Service in a Community-Based Medical School: A Case Study in South Dakota," *Bltn. of the Med. LA* (Ja. 1981); other articles. **Activities:** 1, 14-Med. Lib.; 17, 24, 35; 80 **Addr.:** Lommen Health Sciences Library, School of Medicine, University of South Dakota, Vermillion, SD 57069.

Brenner, Everett H. (F. 3, 1926, Lynn, MA) Mgr., Ctrl. Abs. and Indexing Srv., Amer. Petr. Inst., 1959–; Mgr., Lib. Opers., Dow Chem., 1958–59; Tech. Abstctr., Texaco Inc., 1952–58. **Educ.:** Bates Coll., 1943–48, BS (Chem.); Univ. of MI, 1948–50, MA (Grmn.). **Orgs.:** ASIS: 1978 Anl. Mtg., Tech. Ch. Natl. Fed. of Abs. and Indexing Srvs.: Pres. (1972). Engin. Index: Bd. of Trustees (1969–82). **Pubns.:** Ed. bd., *Sci. and Tech. Libs.* (1980–); ed. bd., *Jnl. of Amer. Socty. of Info. Sci.* (1979–82); jt. auth., "Petroleum Information Services: API's CAIS," *Bltn. of the ASIS* (D. 1979); "Euronet and its Effects on the U.S. Information Market," *JASIS* (Ja. 1979); "Petroleum Literature and Patent Retrieval. Centralized Information Processing," *Spec. Libs.* (Mr. 1969); various articles. **Activities:** 3; 30 **Addr.:** American Petroleum Institute, 156 William St., New York, NY 10038.

Brenner, Joseph S. (Mr. 17, 1950, Baltimore, MD) Acq. Libn., General Motors Resrch. Labs., 1978–; Asst. Netwk. Coord., MI Lib. Cnsrtm., 1976–78; Asst. Head, Acq. Dept., Drexel Univ. Lib., 1973–76. **Educ.:** Drexel Univ., 1968–73, BS (Hum. & Soc. Sci.), 1973–75, MLS. **Orgs.:** MI LA: Cont. Ed. Com. (1977–78); Mem. Com. (1978–). SLA. **Activities:** 12; 46 **Addr.:** Research Laboratories Library, General Motors Corp., General Motors Tech. Ctr., Warren, MI 48090.

Brenner, Lawrence (S. 19, 1939, Lynn, MA) Sr. Med. Libn., Boston City Hosp., 1962–, Asst. Med. Libn., 1962–64. **Educ.:** Northeast. Univ., 1957–62, BS (Educ.); various crs., 1963–65 (LS); 1973–76, PRA Cert.; Northeastern Univ., 1979–81, MPA. **Orgs.:** ALA: ACRL; SRRT. Med. LA. New Eng. LA. Mens Lib. Club. Amer. Med. Rec. Assn. MA Med. Rec. Assn.: Ed. Com. (1977–). **Pubns.:** "A history of the Boston City Hospital Medical Library", in *A History of Boston City Hospital 1905–1964;* "A report on LATCH," *Med. Rec. News* (Aug. 1976); "A Design for the Display and Storage of Current Periodicals," *Med. LA Bltn.* (July 1969). **Activities:** 5; 17; 68, 80, 87 **Addr.:** 44 Elwin St., Swampscott, MA 01907.

Brenner, M. Diane (S. 25, 1946, Walla Walla, WA) Musm. Archvst., Anchorage Hist. and Fine Arts Musm., 1975–; Sci.-Tech. Libn., OR State Univ. Lib., 1972–74; ILL Libn., OR State Lib., 1969–71. **Educ.:** Univ. of OR, 1968, BS (Soc. Sci.), 1971–72, MLS; Inst. of Arch. Admin., Univ. of WA, 1976. **Orgs.:** AK LA: Lcl. Chap., various coms., ofcs.; State Mem. Ch. (1976–80). SAA. SLA. AK State Hist. Recs. Adv. Bd. **Honors:** AK LA, Schol. Awd., 1980. **Activities:** 2, 12; 20, 23, 39; 55, 66 **Addr.:** Anchorage Historical and Fine Arts Museum, 121 W. 7th Ave., Anchorage, AK 99501.

Brenni, Vito Joseph (Mr. 15, 1923, Highland, NY) Lib. Dir., Siena Hts. Coll., 1971–74; Visit. Prof., Coll. of Libnshp., Aberystwyth, Wales, 1968–69; Biblgphr., SUNY, Plattsburgh, 1966–68; Asst. Prof., Head Lib. Educ., Duquesne Univ. 1962–65; Chief Ref. Libn., Villanova Univ., 1960–62; Jr., Sr., Chief Ref. Libn., W. VA Univ., 1951–57; Tchr., Fonda HS, 1949–50. **Educ.:** SUNY, Albany, 1940–47, BA (Eng.); Columbia Univ., 1950–51, MSLS; 1957–58, Cert. (Adv. Libnshp.); MI State Univ., 1978, PhD (Eng.). **Orgs.:** ALA. W. VA LA: Bibl. Com. (1953–56); W. VA Libs. (Bus. Mgr.). Cath. LA: Lib. Educ. Sect.; (Secy., 1965–67); MI Unit, Coll. Lib. (1972–73). **Honors:** W. VA LA, Tribute, 1957. **Pubns.:** *William Dean Howells: A Bibliography* (1973); *Water Resources of West Virginia: a bibliography* (1954); "Children's Literature: a selected bibliography," *Cath. Lib. World* (Oct. 1964); "The Bibliographer in the College Library", *Cath. Lib. World* (Apr. 1969); Cmplr., Ed., *Essays on Bibliography* (1975); other pubns. **Activities:** 1, 11; 15, 26, 29; 55, 57, 92 **Addr.:** 1991 Lake Lansing Rd., Haslett, MI 48840.

Bresie, Mayellen (Ag. 25, 1928, Lafayette, LA) Dir., Harold R. Yeary Lib., Laredo Jr. Coll., Laredo State Univ., 1976–; Head, Tech. Srvs., Assoc. Prof., Inter Amer. Univ., San Juan, PR, 1974–76; Libn., Mendel Coll., Lilly Lib., IN Univ., 1967–74; Libn. I, Latin Amer. Col., Univ. of TX, 1964–67. **Educ.:** Univ. of TX, 1945–49, BA (Latin Amer. Std.); 1963–64, MLS; IN Univ., 1970–73, MA (Latin Amer. Hist.); Natl. Arch., 1973, Cert., (Arch. Mgt.). **Orgs.:** TX LA: Lib. Netwks. Com. (1978–). SWLA: Coop. with Mex. Com. (1976–); SALALM: Adv. Com. to the Secret. (Ch., 1970–74); Rpt. Gen. (1974); Ed. Bd. (Ch., 1976–78). TX Assn. of Coll. Tchrs. TX Jr. Coll. Tchrs. Assn. AAUP. **Honors:** Beta Phi Mu. **Pubns.:** "Eighteenth Century News Sheets. . .," *Bltn.* NYPL (Fall 1974); "Mendel Collection of the Lilly Library," *Latin Amer. Std. Resrcs. Bk.* (1972); "Exotic Printing and the Expansion of Europe, 1492–1840" (exhibit) (1972); "Brazil from Discovery to Independence" (exhibit) (1972). **Activities:** 1; 17, 20, 45; 54, 57; **Addr.:** Harold R. Yeary Library, Laredo Junior College/Laredo State University, West End Washington St., Laredo, TX 78040.

Breslauer, Lester M. (N. 23, 1923, New Philadelphia, OH) Chief Libn., Bell Aerospace Textron, 1974–; Chief Libn., Buffalo Musm. of Sci., 1973–74; Tech. Libn., Calspan Corp., 1971–73. **Educ.:** NY Univ., 1941–46, BAE; SUNY, Buffalo, 1970–72, MLS. **Orgs.:** SLA: Upstate NY Chap. (Treas., 1978–). West. NY Lib. Resrcs. Cncl.: ILL Com. (1977–78); Coop. Acq. Com. (1977–). ACRL: West. NY-ON Chap. **Activities:** 12; 17, 33, 34; 52, 75, 91 **Addr.:** Bell Aerospace Textron, Technical Library, P.O. Box 1, Buffalo, NY 14240.

Brett, William H. (Mr. 2, 1914, New York, NY) Trustee, Mechanics Inst. and Mercantile Lib., 1977–; Dir., Oakland Pub. Lib., 1959–65, various other positions, 1949–65. **Educ.:** Stanford Univ., 1931–38, AB (Jnlsm.); Univ. of CA, Berkeley, 1940–41, Cert. (Sch. Libnshp.), 1948–49, M (LS). **Orgs.:** ALA. CA LA: Pres. (1967). Trustee Fort Point and Army Musm. Assn.: San Francisco Presidio. **Addr.:** 7 Embarcadero W., Apt. 114, Oakland, CA 94607.

Brewer, Annie M. (Mr. 31, 1925, Rahway, NJ) Sr. Ed., Gale Resrch. Co., 1969–. **Educ.:** Univ. of MI, 1966, BA (Eng.); 1968, MALS; Henry Ford Cmnty. Coll., 1960–63, Cert. **Orgs.:** SLA: MI Chap. (Audit. of the Treas., 1980). Book Clb. of Detroit. Book and Auth. Socty. of Metro-Detroit. **Pubns.:** *Biography Almanac* (1981); *Abbreviations, Acronyms, Ciphers, and Signs* (1981); *Dictionaries, Encyclopedias and Other Word Related Books,* 2nd. ed. (1979); *Book Publishers Directory,* 2nd ed. (1979); *Youth Serving Organizations Directory* (1978). **Activities:** 12; 17, 37, 41; 57, 69 **Addr.:** Gale Research Company, 700 Book Tower, Detroit, MI 48226.

Brewer, Joan Scherer (Je. 21, 1930, New York, NY) Info. Srvs. Ofcr., Inst. for Sex Resrch., Inc., 1975–; Asst. Libn., Inst. for Sex Resrch., Inc., 1973–75; Serials Catlgr., IN Univ., 1971–73; Women's Ed., Garden Grove Daily News, 1958–60. **Educ.:** Syracuse Univ., 1949–51, BA (Eng.); IN Univ., 1968–71, MS (LS). **Orgs.:** IN Univ. Lib. Fac. Cncl.: Elec. Ch. Beta Phi Mu: Chi Chap.; VP. **Pubns.:** *Sex Research: Bibliographies from the Institute for Sex Research* (1979); "A Guide to Sex Education Books," *Interracial Bks. for Chld. Bltn.* (no. 3, 1975); "The Library of the Institute for Sex Research," *InULA Bltn.* (no. 3, 1979). **Addr.:** Institute for Sex Research, Inc., Indiana University, Morrison 416, Bloomington, IN 47405.

Brewer, Karen L. (Ap. 29, 1943, Janesville, WI) Dir. and Chief Libn., Northeastern OH Univs. Coll. of Med., 1976–; Head of Serials, Cleveland Hlth. Sci. Lib., 1971–76; Ref. and Actg. Libn., Sch. of Med. Lib., Case West. Rsv. Univ., 1970–71; Ref. and ILL Libn., Mooney Med. Lib., Univ. of TN, 1968–69; Ref. Libn., Memphis Pub. Lib., 1967–68; Head, Rsv. Col., W. S. Middleton Med. Lib., Univ. of WI, 1966–67. **Educ.:** Univ. of WI, 1961–65, BA (Asian Std.); 1965–66, MALS; Case West. Rsv. Univ., 1975–, PhD cand., (Hist.). **Orgs.:** Med. LA: Ad-Hoc Com. to Study Intl. Exch. and Redistribution of Lib. Mtrls. (1979); Exhibits Com. (Ch., 1975). OH Hlth. Info. Org.: Com. on Struc-

PROFESSIONAL ACTIVITIES: Institutions: 1. Acad. lib.; 2. Arch.; 3. Assn.; 4. Fed./Gvt. lib.; 5. Inst. lib.; 6. Mfr./Suppl.; 7. Milit. lib.; 8. Musm.; 9. Pub. lib.; 10. Sch. lib.; 11. Sch. of lib. sci.; 12. Spec. lib.; 13. State lib.; 14. (other). **Functions/Activities:** 15. Acq./Col. dev.; 16. Adult srvs.; 17. Admin.; 18. Apprais.; 19. Archit./Bldgs.; 20. Cat./Class.; 21. Chld. srvs.; 22. Circ.; 23. Cons./Pres.; 24. Consult.; 25. Cont. ed.; 26. Educ. lib. sci.; 27. Ext. srvs.; 28. Fund/Grants; 29. Gvt. pubs.; 30. Indx./Abs.; 31. Instr. lib. use; 32. Media srvs.; 33. Micro.; 34. Netwks./Coop.; 35. Persnl.; 36. PR; 37. Publshg.; 38. Recs. mgt.; 39. Ref. srvs.; 40. Repro.; 41. Resrch.; 42. Review.; 43. Secur.; 44. Serials; 45. Spec. col.; 46. Tech. srvs.; 47. Trustees/Bds.; 48. YA srvs.; 49. (other).

ture (1978–79). OH Area Hlth. Educ. Ctr.: various coms. Northeastern OH Univs. Coll. of Med.: various coms. **Pubns.:** "Method for Cooperative Serials Selection and Cancellation through Consortium Activities," Jnl. of Acad. Libnshp. (Fall 1978). **Activities:** 1, 12; 15, 17, 34; 58, 80 **Addr.:** Basic Medical Sciences Library, Northeastern Ohio Universities College of Medicine, Rootstown, OH 44272.

Brewer, Stanley E. (F 24, 1944, Glendale, CA) Lib. Dir., Gulf Refining & Mktg. Co., 1974–; Hist. & Pol. Sci. Libn. Univ. of Houston, 1972–74; Asst. Soc. Sci. Libn., 1970–72. **Educ.:** OK State Univ., 1962–66, BA, (Hist.); Univ. of OK, 1966–67, MLS; Univ. of Houston, 1970–71, Law studies. **Orgs.:** SLA: TX Chap., Treas. (1975–77); Nom. Com., Ch. (1977–78); Pub. Rel., Ch. (1978–79); Petroleum and Energy Resrcs. Div.: Treas. (1978–80); Prog. Com. (1978–79); Ch.-Elect (1980–81); Ch. (1981-82). Assoc. Info. Mgrs.; Univ. of Houston Fac. Sen. (1972–74). **Honors:** Beta Phi Mu; Phi Kappa Phi; Phi Alpha Theta (Hist.). **Pubns.:** "Gulf Refining & Marketing Co (Library Profile)", SLA Petroleum & Energy Resrcs. Div. *Bltn.* (1978). **Activities:** 12; 15, 17, 39; 59, 86 **Addr.:** 814 Kipling, Houston, TX 77006.

Brewitt, Laura E. (O. 31, 1935, Sherman, TX) Lib. Dir., N. Richland Hills Pub. Lib., 1972–; Libn., Dir., Forbes Air Frc. Base Lib., KS, 1960–61; Readers Adv., Youth Libn., Topeka Pub. Lib., 1955–56. **Educ.:** TX Woman's Univ., 1951–55, BA (LS), 1974–77, MLS. **Orgs.:** ALA. TX LA: Dist. VII (Treas., 1981–82). Tarrant Reg. LA: Secy. (1973); VP (1974); Pres. (1975). N. TX Lib. Syst.: Media Com. (1976–77, 1981); Plng. Com. (1978–79). Cncl. for Educ. TV in Tarrant Cnty. N. Ctrl. TX Film Assn.: Pres. (1977). **Honors:** Beta Phi Mu. **Activities:** 9; 16, 17 **Addr.:** 7301 N.E. Loop 820, P.O. Box 18609, N. Richland Hills, TX 76118.

Brewster, Evelyn S. (F. 1, 1916, Volin, SD) Lib. Consult., Self-empl., 1981–; Pub. Lib. Consult., CO State Lib., 1957–81; Libn., Deadwood Pub. Lib., 1949–57; Libn., Grad. Sch. of Libnshp., Univ. of Denver, 1947–49. **Educ.:** Univ. of Denver, 1947–48, BA (Educ.), 1948–49, MA (LS). **Orgs.:** ALA: Mem. Com. (1973–74); Cnclr. (1980–84). Mt. Plains LA: Pres. (1968–69). CO LA: Pres. (1964). SD LA: Pres. (1954–56). Delta Kappa Gamma Socty. Intl.: Lcl. Chap. Pres. (1976–78). P.E.O. Sisterhood: Lcl. Chap. Pres. (1970–71). Luth. Church LA: CO Mile-High Chap. (Pres., 1981–82). **Honors:** Mt. Plains LA, Recog. of Srv., 1967, Disting. Srv. Awd., 1978; CO LA, Libn. of the Yr., 1976; Delta Kappa Gamma Socty. Intl., Omega State Awd., 1981; Univ. of Denver Grad. Sch. of Libnshp. and Info. Mgt., Disting. Alum. Awd., 1981. **Pubns.:** *Public Library Trustees of Colorado* (1980); *Trustees Handbook for Colorado Public Libraries* (1963); jt. auth., "Colorado Library Association," *Encyc. of Lib. and Info. Sci.* (1971); "Keys to Cooperation," *SD Lib. Bltn.* (O.–D. 1964); "Denver: Rapport and Round Robin," *Wilson Lib. Bltn.* (N. 1963); various pub. lib. srvys. **Activities:** 9, 13; 24, 27, 47; 50, 63 **Addr.:** 1125 Jersey St., Denver, CO 80220.

Breyfogle, Donna Helen (Mr. 21, 1953, Morris, MB) Ref. Libn., Elizabeth Dafoe Lib., Univ. of MB, 1978–; Ref. Libn., Faculty of Ed. Lib. Univ. of MB, 1978–79. **Educ.:** Univ. of Winnipeg, 1971–75, BA (Hons.) (French & Hist.); Univ. of Toronto, 1976–78, MLS. **Orgs.:** MB LA: Corres. Secy. (1979–). Can. LA. **Pubns.:** Jt. comp., *Blacks in Ontario: A Selective Bibliography* (1977); "A Selective Bibliography on Censorship," *MB LA Bltn.* (Mr. 1979); "LIBFIND: A Short Title Search System," MB LA Bltn. (1980); "A Selective Bibliography on Censorship," MB LA Bltn. (1979); Various book reviews in *Can. Lib. Jnl.* (1980–81). **Activities:** 1, 10; 31, 39; 55, 63, 90 **Addr.:** Ref. Srvs. & Dafoe Cols. Dept., Elizabeth Dafoe Library, University of Manitoba, Winnipeg, MB Canada.

Brian, Ray (My. 22, 1924, Stockton, CA) Libn., CA Acad. of Sci., 1963–; Lectr., Univ. of CA, Berkeley, Sch. of Libnshp., 1969; Libn., Hyman Labs., Inc., 1961–63; Adult Probation Ofcr., Contra Costa Cnty., 1957–61; Persnl. Anal., CA State Persnl. Bd., 1956–57; Libn. I, Univ. of CA, Los Angeles, Ref. Dept., 1953–55; Libn., Lear, Inc., 1954–55. **Educ.:** Univ. of CA, Berkeley, 1942–43, 1946–49, BA (Psy.), 1949–52, MA (Psy.), 1952–53, BLS (Libnshp.). **Orgs.:** SLA: San Francisco Bay Reg. Chap. (Pres., 1971–72). ALA. CA LA: Mem. Com. (1969–71). Bay Area Ref. Libns. Cncl. Amer. Psy. Assn. Univ. of CA Lib. Sch. Alum. Assn. **Activities:** 12; 15, 17, 18; 58, 82, 95-Musm. **Addr.:** 3330 21st St., San Francisco, CA 94110.

Brice, Heather W. (Jl. 9, 1941, Hobart, Tasmania, Australia) Dir., Laurel Highlands Hlth. Sci. Lib. Cnsrtm., 1978–; Med. Libn. (part-time), Windber Hosp. and Wheeling Clinic, 1976–; Night Supvsr., Olin Lib., Cornell Univ., 1969–71; Libn., Hobart Matric. Coll., 1964–65; Lib. Asst., Univ. of Tasmania, 1959–64. **Educ.:** Univ. of Tasmania, 1959–65, BA (Asian Cvlztn.); Univ. of Pittsburgh, 1975, MLS, 1981, MS (Info. Sci.); Med. LA, 1976, Cert. (Med. Libnshp.). **Orgs.:** ALA. ASIS. Med. LA. Mid-East. Reg. Med. Lib. Srv.: Bd. Resrc. Sharing Com. (1978–). AAUW. **Honors:** Beta Phi Mu, 1976. **Activities:** 1, 12; 24, 28, 34; 75, 80, 93 **Addr.:** 531 Highland Ave., Johnstown, PA 15902.

Brich, George Michael (Mr. 31, 1935, Palmerton, PA) Dir., Elkhart Pub. Lib., 1976–; Coord., Area Lib. Srvs. Athrty. 2, 1976; Asst. Dir., Bur Oak Lib. Syst., 1972–75; Asst. to Dir., Ofc. for Int. Frdm., ALA, 1971–72; Asst. Dir., Norwich Univ., 1967–71. **Educ.:** E. Stroudsburg State Coll., 1959–61, BS (Eng., Sec. Educ.); Drexel Univ., 1963–67, MLS. **Orgs.:** ALA. IN LA: Int. Frdm. Com. (Ch., 1979). **Activities:** 9; 17 **Addr.:** P.O. Box 471, Elkhart, IN 46515.

Brichford, Maynard J. (Ag. 6, 1926, Madison, OH) Univ. Archvst., Univ. of IL, 1963–; Admin. Ofcr., WI Dept. of Admin., 1959–63; Methods & Proc. Anal., IL State Arch., 1956–59; Asst. Arch., WI State Hist. Soc., 1952–56. **Educ.:** Hiram Col., 1944–51, BA (Soc. Std.); Univ. of WI, 1951–53, MS (Hist.); Amer. Univ., 1954, Cert. Recs. Mgt. **Orgs.:** SAA: Cncl. (1965–69; Pres., 1979–80). Midwest Arch. Conf. **Honors:** SAA, Fellow, 1970. **Pubns.:** *Appraisal Manual* (1977); *Scientific and Technological Documentation* (1969); "University Archives", *Amer. Archvst.* (Ap. 1971); "Historians and Mirrors", *AA* (Jl. 1973); "Guide to ALA Archives" (1979). **Activities:** 1, 2; 26, 41, 45; 56, 62, 91 **Addr.:** 409 Eliot Dr., Urbana, IL 61801.

Brickman, Sally F. (F. 15, 1936, Cleveland, OH) Lib. Ed., Publicist, Case West. Rsv. Univ. Lib., 1975–; Freelnc. Writer, *Properties Mag.*, 1973–; Ed. Staff Writer, Sun Newsp., 1972–74; Chld. Libn., Cleveland Bd. of Educ., 1966–71; Sub. Libn., Shaker Hts., Cleveland Hts., Univ. Hts. Schs., 1966–71; various positions as PR consult. **Educ.:** Brown Univ. 1954–56; Case West. Rsv. Univ., 1956–58, BA (Eng.), 1960–64, MLS. **Orgs.:** ALA: Exec. Com. (1980–82); LAMA/PR Sect., John Cotton Dana PR Awd. (1978–79). OH LA: PR Srvs. to Libs. (1978–). Women in Comms. PR Socty. of Amer. **Pubns.:** Various PR presentations. **Activities:** 1; 36 **Addr.:** Freiberger Library, 11161 E. Blvd., Cleveland, OH 44106.

Bridegam, Willis E., Jr. (O. 15, 1935, Pettstown, PA) Coll. Libn., Amherst Coll., 1975–; Dir. of Libs., SUNY, Binghamton, 1972–75; Assoc. Dir. of Libs., Univ. Rochester, 1969–72; Med. Libn., 1966–69. **Educ.:** Univ. Rochester, 1953–57, BM (Msc.); Syracuse Univ., 1958–63, MS (LS). **Orgs.:** ALA: Ed. Bd. *Coll. and Resrch. Libs.* (1980–81); ACRL Acad. Status Com. (1976–80); Conv. Budget and Finance Com. (1978). Grolier Club. **Pubns.:** "Perspectives on Cooperation: The Evaluation of a Consortium," in *New Horizons for Academic Libraries* (1979); "A Research Requirement for Librarians?" *Jnl. of Acad. Libnshp.* (July 1978); "Library Participation in a Biomedical Communication Network," (Ap. 1970). **Activities:** 1; 15, 17; 55, 57 **Addr.:** 52 High Point Dr., Amherst, MA 01002.

Bridewell, Juanita (Mr. 27, 1915, Coushatta, LA) Asst. Prof. LA State Univ., Alexandria; Gen. Libn. and Instr., 1966–79; Ref. Libn., Rapides Par. Lib., 1959–66; Sch. Libn., Poland HS (Alexandria, LA), 1956–59. **Educ.:** LA State Univ., 1930–35, BA (Eng.); 1936–39, MA (Eng.); 19—, (LS); Northwest. State Univ. of LA, Sch. Libn. Cert., 1959. **Orgs.:** LA LA: LA State Lit. Awd. (Ch., 1970–73). ALA: ACRL. SWLA. Phi Kappa Phi. Kappa Delta Pi. Reading Is Fun-damental Cmnty. Bd. **Pubns.:** "Storytelling" (Cont. Educ. course) (Spr. 1980); Story hours. **Activities:** 1; 31, 32, 39 **Addr.:** 135 Hudson St., Pineville, LA 71360.

Bridge, Stephen W. (N. 3, 1948, Logansport, IN) Branch Admin. Asst., Indianapolis-Marion Cnty. Pub. Lib., 1978–, Chld. Libn., 1974–. **Educ.:** DePauw Univ., 1966–70, BA (Sp., Thea.); IN Univ., 1973–74, MLS. **Orgs.:** ALA: ALSC (1974–); Int. Frdm. Com. (1977–). IN LA: Chld. and Young People Div., Exec. Bd. (1977–79); IL LA Anl. Conf., Lcl. Arrange. (Co-Ch., 1980). Amer. Cvl. Liberties Un. IN Univ. Grad. Lib. Sch. Alum. Assn.: Alum. Bd. (1976–78). Inst. for Advnc. Bio. Std., Inc.: Pres. (1976–79); Treas. (1979–). Readers and Collectors. **Pubns.:** *Cryonics: Threshold to Immortality* (1979). **Activities:** 9; 17, 21; 55 **Addr.:** Indianapolis-Marion County Public Library, 40 E. St. Clair, Indianapolis, IN 46204.

Bridges, Barbara S. (O. 7, 1942, New Orleans, LA) Gvt. Docum. Libn., Tarlton Law Lib., Univ. of TX, Austin, 1973–, Libn., Criminal Justice Ref. Lib., 1971–73, Ref. Libn., Docum. Col., 1970–71, Ref. Libn., Undergrad. Lib., 1968–70. **Educ.:** Sophie Newcomb Coll., 1960–64, BA (Msc. Hist.); Inst. Tech. de Monterrey, Mex., 1962 (Span.); Tulane Univ., 1964–66 (Msclgy.); Univ. of TX, Austin, 1966–69, MLS, 6th yr. prog. **Orgs.:** ALA: ACRL, Acad. Status Com. (1971–73); RTSD, ILL Com. (1970–72); JMRT, Carhart Task Frc. on Lib. Resrch. (1971–72). TX LA: Int. Frdm. Com. (Secy., 1971–72); JMRT, Educ. Com. (Ch., 1971–73); Docum. RT. SW LA. Beta Phi Mu: Beta Eta Chap. (Pres., 1975–76). Grad. Sch. LS Alum. Assn.: Nsltr. Ed. (1970–72). **Pubns.:** Jt. auth., *The Adjudication and Disposition Phases in Court Handling of Juveniles: An Annotated Bibliography* (1972); ed., *CRJL Nsltr.* (1971–73); "A Miscellany of Multi-Media Materials on Environmental Control," *Educ. Resrcs. and Techq.* (Spr. 1971); "Junior College Training of Library Technical Assistants: A Negative Viewpoint," *TX Lib. Jnl.* (Fall 1968). **Activities:** 1, 12; 29, 31, 39; 65, 77, 78 **Addr.:** Tarlton Law Library, 727 E. 26th St., Austin, TX 78705.

Bridgman, David L. (Mr. 26, 1949, Los Angeles, CA) Pub. Srvs. Libn., Santa Clara Cnty. Law Lib., 1977–, Ref. Libn., 1974–77. **Educ.:** San Jose State Univ., 1973–75, BS (Admin. of Justice), 1975–77, MS (Justice Mgt.), 1977–78, MLS. **Orgs.:** AALL: Spec. Interest Sect. on Law Lib. Srv. to Inst. Residents Nsltr. Ed., Nom. Com. (1980–81); North. CA Chap., Nsltr. Com. Ch., Nsltr. Ed. **Activities:** 12; 22, 24, 39; 57, 77, 78 **Addr.:** Santa Clara County Law Library, Superior Ct. Bldg., 191 N. 1st St., San Jose, CA 95113.

Brière, Jean-Marie (S. 15, 1951, Lac-Saint-Paul, PQ) Bibtcr., Bibl. Resrch., Bib. Natl. Du Can., 1981–; Bibtcr. De Réf., Ministère De L'Energie et des Resrcs. Du PQ, 1979–80; Bibtcr. De Réf., Pubns. Officielles, Bib. Natl. Du Can., 1977–79, Bibtcr., Bibl. Resrch., 1976–77. **Educ.:** Univ. de Sherbrooke, 1971–74, BA (Lit.); Univ. De Montréal, 1974–76, MABibl (Bibliothéconomie). **Orgs.:** ASTED. Assn. Des Bibs. D'Ottawa, Hull. Societé. Bib. Du Can. **Pubns.:** *L'information Gouvernementale Au Québec: Bibliographie Analytique* (1977); *L'information Gouvernementale Au Québec et au Canada: Bibliographie Signalétique* (1975). **Activities:** 4, 5; 39, 41; 55 **Addr.:** Bibliotheque Nationale Du Canada, 395, Rue Wellington, Ottawa, ON K1A 0N4 Canada.

Brigandi, Carmen Elisabeth (O. 10, 1948, Ft. Worth, TX) Law Libn., State of NY, Supreme Ct. Lib., 1978–; Law Libn., Mackenzie Law Firm, 1975–78. **Educ.:** TX Woman's Univ., 1966–70, BA (Hist.); Syracuse Univ., 1972–74, MLS. **Orgs.:** AALL: 1978 AALL Anl. Mtg., Lcl. Arrange. Ch.; Autom. and Sci. Dsgn. Com. (1977–80); Rel. with Publshrs. Com. (1980–81); Assn. of Law Libs. of Upstate NY: Treas. (1978–80). Onondaga Free Lib.: Bd. of Trustees (1979–82); Bd. Pres. (1980–81). **Activities:** 13; 15, 20, 41; 77, 78 **Addr.:** Supreme Ct. Library, 500 Ct. House, Syracuse, NY 13202.

Briggs, Cherylyn J. (O. 26, 1951, Arlington, VA) Libn., West. Electric Co., Inc., 1979–; Head, Tech. Srvs., Benjamin N. Cardozo Sch. of Law, 1977–79, Head Catlgr., 1976–77, Catlgr., 1976–77. **Educ.:** William Smith Coll., 1969–73, BA (Hist.); C.W. Post Coll., 1974–75, MALS. **Orgs.:** AALL: OCLC-Spec. Interest Sect. (Ch., 1978–79). Law Lib. Assn. of Greater NY. **Activities:** 12; 15, 17, 39; 77 **Addr.:** Western Electric Co., Inc.-Legal Library, 222 Broadway, New York, NY 10038.

Briggs, Geoffrey Hugh (Ap. 14, 1926, Leeds, Yorkshire, Eng) Univ. Libn., Carleton Univ., 1969–; Deputy Libn., Univ. of Calgary, 1967–69; Deputy Libn., Victoria Univ., Wellington, NZ, 1954–67. **Educ.:** St. John's Coll., Cambridge, 1943–47, MA (Classics); Univ. London, 1947–49, Dip. (Arch. Admin. and Libnshp.). **Orgs.:** CARL: Pres. (1979–80). ON Cncl Univ. Libns.: Chmn. (1971–72). **Activities:** 1; 17, 19, 34; 55, 57, 93 **Addr.:** Carleton University Library, Colonel By Drive, Ottawa, ON K1S 5J7 Canada.

Briggs, Nathalie E. (Ja. 22, 1912, Woonsocket, RI) Retired; Spec. Catlgr., Kelvin Grove Coll. of Advnc. Educ., Brisbane, 1972–73; Head Catlgr., Univ. of RI, Kingston, 1960–72; various lib. positions, Univ. of RI, Kingston, 1934–59. **Educ.:** RI State Coll., 1929–33, BS (Bio.); Syracuse Univ., 1933–34, BSLS. **Orgs.:** RI LA: various coms. ALA. New Eng. LA. Kingston Free Lib.: Trustee. Univ. of RI Fndn. Pettaquamscutt Hist. Socty. Various other orgs. **Honors:** Univ. of RI, Alum. Srv. Awd., 1977; Chi Omega RI Chap., Nathalie E. Briggs Anl. Schol., 1978–. **Activities:** 1, 12; 20, 39, 46; 58, 80 **Addr.:** P.O. Box 3, Kingston, RI 02881.

Bright, Franklyn F. (Mr. 24, 1919, Rochester, NY) Asst. Dir. for Tech. Srvcs., Univ. of WI-Madison Lib., 1965–; Chief of Acq., 1948–65; Head, Acq. Dept., Brown Univ. Lib., 1946–48. **Educ.:** Oberlin Col., 1937–41, BA (Pre Lib.); Univ. of MI, 1941–42, BLS. **Orgs.:** ALA: RTSD/Bylaws Com., Organ. Com. WI LA: Elec. Com. **Honors:** Phi Beta Kappa, 1941. **Addr.:** University of Wisconsin-Madison, Library, 728 State St., Madison, WI 53706.

Brightwell, Juanita Sumner (Ja. 4, 1918, Sylvester, GA) Dir., Lake Blackshear Reg. Lib., 1962–80; Eng. Tchr., Libn., Americus HS, 1956–62; Elem. Tchr., New Era Elem. Sch., 1955–56; Asst. Libn., Americus Carnegie Lib., 1952–55; Oper., Brightwell's Nursery, 1946–52; Tchr., Libn., Americus HS, 1942–43; Tchr., Libn., Smithville HS, 1941–42; Tchr., Weston HS, 1937–38. **Educ.:** GA Coll. at Milledgeville, 1938, BS (Educ.); Emory Univ., 1965, MLS. **Orgs.:** ALA. S. East. LA: Ch. Pub. Lib. Sec. (1969–71). GA LA. Editorial Resrch. Bd, ABI. Delta Kappa Gamma, 1969–. Alpha Chi Omega, 1972–. Americus-Sumter Cnty. Bus. and Prof. Women's Club: Pres. (1968–69). Daughters of Amer. Revolution. **Honors:** Natl. Tchr. Scho., 1962–65; Woman of the Yr., 1968; Americus Civitan Club, Outstan. Pub. Servant Awd. 1973. **Pubns.:** *The Organization of the Americus Library Association* (1965); Various articles. **Activities:** 9; 17; 63, 69, 78 **Addr.:** 1307 Hancock Dr., Americus, GA 31709.

Bril, Patricia L. (My 6, 1948, Santa Monica, CA) Coord., Ref. Sect., CA State Univ., Fullerton, 1977–; Ref. Libn., 1971–77. **Educ.:** Univ. of CA, Irvine, 1966–70, BA (Soc. Sci.); Univ. of South. CA, 1970–71, MSLS; CA State Univ., Fullerton, 1973–76, MPA (Pub. Adm.). **Orgs.:** ALA: ACRL/Bibl. Instr. Sect. Pre-conf. Plan. Com. (1979–81); S. CA. Ch., Exec. Bd. (1980). CA LA: Acad. and Resrch. Libns., Secy. (1980–81); Clearinghouse on Lib. Instr., Coord. (1978). **Honors:** Beta Phi Mu, 1972. **Activities:** 1; 17, 31, 39; 55, 92 **Addr.:** Library-Reference, California State University, P.O. Box 4150, Fullerton, CA 92634.

Special Subjects/Services: 50. Adult educ.; 51. Advert./Mktg.; 52. Aerosp.; 53. Agric.; 54. Area std.; 55. Arts/Hum.; 56. Autom.; 57. Bibl./Prtg.; 58. Bio. sci.; 59. Bus./Fin.; 60. Chem.; 61. Copyrt.; 62. Documtn.; 63. Educ.; 64. Engin.; 65. Env.; 66. Eth. grps.; 67. Film; 68. Food/Nutr.; 69. Geneal.; 70. Geo.; 71. Geol.; 72. Handcpd.; 73. Hist.; 74. Int. frdm.; 75. Info. sci.; 76. Insr.; 77. Law; 78. Legis.; 79. Math./Comp. sci.; 80. Med.; 81. Metals; 82. Nat. resrcs.; 83. Newsp.; 84. Nuc. sci.; 85. Oral hist.; 86. Petr./Energy; 87. Pharm.; 88. Phys./Astr./Math.; 89. Readg.; 90. Relig.; 91. Sci./Tech.; 92. Soc. sci.; 93. Telecom.; 94. Transp.; 95. (other).

Brinkler, Bartol (O. 2, 1915, Portland, ME) Class. Spec., Widener Lib., Harvard Univ., 1965–, Chief Subj. Catlgr., 1950–65, Catlgr., Clasfr., 1947–50; Asst. Instr., Eng., LA State Univ., 1940–41. **Educ.:** Princeton Univ., 1933–37, BA (Eng.), 1937–40, MA (Eng.); Columbia Univ., 1946–47, BS (Lib. Srv.). **Orgs.:** ALA: Com. on Subj. Headings (Ch., 1958–60). New Eng. Tech. Srv. Libns.: Secy.-Treas. (1949–50); Vice-Ch. (1954–55); Ch. (1955–56). Cambridge Hist. Socty. Harvard Lib. Club: Treas. (1953–54); Nom. Com. (Ch., 1968, 1972–73). Socty. for the Prsrvn. of New Eng. Antiquities. **Pubns.:** "The Geographical Approach to Materials in the Library of Congress Subject Headings," *Lib. Resrcs. & Tech. Srvs.* (Win. 1962). **Activities:** 1; 20, 24; 55 **Addr.:** 5 Craigie Cir., Apt. 38, Cambridge, MA 02138.

Brinton, Edgar Harry (Jl. 5, 1916, Kansas City, MO) Dir. of Libs., Jacksonville Pub. Lib., 1959–; Chief of Order Dept., Chief of Ext. Dept., Actg. Libn., Admn. Asst., Kansas City, MO. Pub. Lib., 1941–59; Catlgr. and Mgr., Traveling Libs., MO St. Lib., 1940–41; Libn., Topeka HS, Topeka, KS, 1939–40; Gvt. Docums. Libn., OK St. Univ., 1938–39. **Educ.:** Univ. of Denver, 1938, AB (LS); Columbia Univ., 1957, MS (LS). **Orgs.:** ALA. FL LA: Pres. (1964–65). SELA; Lib. Bldgs. Consult., St. of FL. Civitan Clb. of Jacksonville; Jacksonville Area Chamber of Commerce; Mem. of Bd. of Trustees for Jacksonville Episcopal HS; Univ. Clb. of Jacksonville. **Activities:** 9; 17, 19, 35; 56, 74, 75 **Addr.:** Jacksonville Public Library System, 122 North Ocean Street, Jacksonville, FL 32202.

Briscoe, Peter M. (Ag. 10, 1942, Glendale, CA) Chief Col. Dev. Ofcr., Univ. of CA, Riverside, 1978–; Lib. Biblgphr., CA State Coll., San Bernardino, 1973–78; Ref. & Micro. Libn., CA State Coll., Sonoma, 1970–73. **Educ.:** San Bernardino Valley Coll., 1960–62; Univ. of CA, Riverside, 1962–64, BA (Phil.); Univ. of HI at Manoa, 1969–70, MLS; Univ. of CA, Riverside, 1977–81, M Admin. **Orgs.:** ALA. CA LA: Ch., State Univ. and Coll. Chap. (1978). SALALM; West. Assn. of Map Libs. Les Amis du Vin. **Honors:** Beta Phi Mu, 1970. **Pubns.:** "Paris", *Books at UCR* (Fall 1979). **Activities:** 1; 15, 17, 45 **Addr.:** Collection Development Department, The Library, University of California, Riverside, CA 92517.

Brislin, Jane F. (F. 23, 1920, PA) Dir. of Info. Srvs., Indus. Hlth. Fndn., 1973–; Libn., Graphic Arts Tech. Fndn., 1966–73; Jr. Flw., Mellon Inst., Carnegie-Mellon Univ., 1965–66; Resrch. Assoc., Sch. of Dentistry, Univ. Pittsburgh, 1959–64. **Educ.:** Mt. Mercy Coll., 1938–42, BA (Bio.); Carnegie Inst. of Tech., 1954–58, MLS; Univ. of Pittsburgh, 1944–48, (Bio.). **Orgs.:** SLA: Mem. Com. (Ch., 1972–73). Pittsburgh Reg. Lib. Ctr.: Bd. of Trustees (1968–79). **Honors:** Beta Phi Mu, 1958. **Pubns.:** Jt. Auth., *Survey of the Literature of Dental Caries, 1948–1960.* (1964); Ed., *Industrial Hygiene Digest* (1973–). **Activities:** 12; 17, 30; 80, 91 **Addr.:** 340 S. Highland Ave., Pittsburgh, PA 15206.

Britton, Helen H. (N 20, 1922, Tuskegee Inst., AL) Asst. Dir. for Ref. and Instr. Srvs., CA State Univ., Long Beach, 1981–; Head, Cat. and Prcs. Dept., Univ. of Houston, 1974–81; Head, Docum. Div., TX A&M Univ., 1972–74; Sr. Catlgr., 1971–72; Sr. Cat. and Asst. Catl. Reviser, OH State Univ., 1968–71; Cat., 1966–68; Circ. Desk and Bkstk. Libn., 1963–66; Catlgr., 1962–63; Lib. Field Consult. and Spec. Srvs. Dept. Libn., LA State Lib., 1956–62. **Educ.:** Leland Col., 1939–43, BA (Educ.); Univ. of IA, 1944–45, MA (Eng.); Univ. of MI, 1952–53, MALS. **Orgs.:** ALA: ACRL; RTSD: Cat. Class. Sect., Nom. Com. (1978–79). RASD. TX LA. Southwest LA. AAUW: Coll. Stat., TX, Secy. (1973–74). AAUP: TX Conf., Reg. VP (1978–80); other ofcs. **Honors** Pi Lambda Theta. **Pubns.:** "Cataloging and Classifying Documents", TX Libs. (Sum. 1976); Jt. auth., "Government Documents in the Public Catalog", Govt. Pub. Review (1978); Jt. auth., "Utilization of Personnel and Bibliographic Resources in OCLC Participating Libraries", *Lib. Resrcs. and Tech. Srvs.* (1979). **Activities:** 1; 17, 20, 46 **Addr.:** H. H. Britton, 2032 Bermuda St., Apt. 307, Long Beach, CA 90814.

Brizendine, Margaret (Kingsley) S. (S. 19, 1926, Richmond, VA) Lib. Media Spec., Knox Meml. Sch. Lib., Dir., Russell Pub. Lib., 1972–; Asst. Libn., Canton HS, 1968–70. **Educ.:** Univ. of Richmond, 1944–48, BA (Hist., Gvt.); Cath. Univ. of Amer., 1972–76, MLS; NY State, 1975, Permanent Cert. (Lib. Media Spec.), Permanent Tchg. Cert. (Soc. Std., 7–12). **Orgs.:** ALA. NY LA: Sch. Lib. Media Sect. N. Country Assn. Sch. Media Specs.: Pres. (1978–80). Pub. Lib. Cnty. Funds Com.: Ch. (1977–79). Knox Meml. Tchrs. Assn. Girl Scouts of Amer. Frnds. of Canton Free Lib. **Activities:** 9, 10; 15, 17, 39 **Addr.:** 4 Judson St., Canton, NY 13617.

Broadbent, H. E., III (My 28, 1947, Abington, PA) Lib. Dir., Ursinus Coll., 1975–; Head, Ref. & Ill., Philadelphia Coll., 1972–75; Adult/YA Lib., Free Lib. of Philadelphia, 1970–72. **Educ.:** Ursinus Coll., 1965–69, BA (Eng.); Drexel Univ., 1969–70, MSLS; Villanova Univ., 1970–72, MA, (Thea.). **Orgs.:** ALA. PA LA: Col. & Resrch. Div., Ch. (1979). Tri-State Col. Lib. Coop.: Pres. (1978). Beta Phi Mu: Sigma Chap. Pres. (1977–78). **Activities:** 1; 17; 93 **Addr.:** Ursinus College, Myrin Library, Collegeville, PA 19926.

Broaddus, Gloria H. (F. 25, 1949, Pine Bluff, AR) Libn., Babcock and Wilcox, 1979–; Resrch. Libn., Monsanto Co., 1973–77. **Educ.:** Univ. of AR, 1968–72, BS (Bio.). **Orgs.:** SLA: Corres. Secy. (1976–77); Positive Action Com. (1977). ASIS. Amer. Socty. for Metals. Alpha Kappa Alpha; NAACP. **Activities:** 12; 15, 17, 20; 64, 84, 86 **Addr.:** Babcock and Wilcox Co., 20th S. Van Buren Ave., Barberton, OH 44203.

Broadus, Robert N. (D. 3, 1922, Stanford, KY) Prof. of LS, Univ. NC at Chapel Hill, 1976–; Prof. of LS, North. IL Univ., 1965–76; Assoc. Prof., 1961–65; Lib. Spec., Sperry Rand Corp., 1956–61; Assoc. Prof., North. IL State Coll., 1955–56; Libn., David Lipscomb Coll., 1953–55; Libn., Pepperdine Coll., 1947–53. **Educ.:** David Lipscomb Coll., 1941–43, Pepperdine Coll., 1943–45, BA (Relig.); Univ. Chicago, 1946–47, BLS (LS); Univ. South. CA, 1948–52, PhD, (Sp. Comm.). **Orgs.:** ALA: various coms. AALS. SE LA. NC LA. AAUP. **Pubns.:** *Selecting Materials for Libraries* (1973), 2nd ed. (1981); Co-ed., *The Short Story* (1967); Ed., *The Role of the Humanities in the Public Library* (1980); "Applications of Citation Analyses to Library Collection Building," *Advncs. in Libnshp.* (1977); "The Literature of the Social Sciences," *Intl. Soc. Sci. Jnl.* (1971); other articles. **Activities:** 1; 15, 19, 26; 55, 57, 92 **Addr.:** School of Library Science, University of North Carolina at Chapel Hill, Manning Hall 026A, Chapel Hill, NC 27514.

Brockman, Norbert C. (Mr. 2, 1934, Cincinnati, OH) Dir., Marianist Trng. Netwk., 1973–; Prog. Dir., Bergamo Ctr., 1973–80; Visit. Schol., St. Louis Univ., 1971–73; Assoc. Prof., Univ. of Dayton, 1962–70. **Educ.:** Univ. of Dayton, 1951–55, BA (Pol. Sci.); Catholic Univ. of Amer., 1957–63, MA, PhD (Politics); Untd. Theo. Sem., 1970–72, STM (Theology). **Orgs.:** SAA: Consult. on Cont. Ed. Socty. of CA Archvsts. LCWR Arch. Proj.: Adv. Bd. Assn. for Creative Change: Bd. (1971–73, 75). **Pubns.:** Four books, numerous articles, none germane to arch. work; developed trng. mtrls. for arch. educ. **Activities:** 2; 24, 25; 50, 90, 95-Access. **Addr.:** P.O. Box 1283, Dayton, OH 45401.

Brockway, Duncan (Jl. 23, 1932, Manchester, NH) Dir., Lib. Srvs., Schs. of Theo., Dubuque, 1977–; Libn., Hartford Semy. Fndn., 1965–76; Ord. Libn., Princeton Theo. Semy., 1958–62. **Educ.:** St. John's Coll., 1949–53, BA (Liberal Arts); Harvard Dvnty. Sch., 1953–55; Princeton Theo. Semy., 1955–56, BD; Rutgers Univ., 1958–60, MLS. **Orgs.:** ALA. ATLA. **Pubns.:** Jt. auth., *The Health Sciences Audiovisual Resource List 1977* (1977); "The Reading and Library Habits of Connecticut Pastors," *ATLA Procs.* (1974). **Activities:** 1; 15, 17, 46; 90 **Addr.:** 2245 Bennett, Dubuque, IA 52001.

Broderick, Donald C. (Mr. 21, 1922, Lynn, MA) Dir., Lrng. Resrcs., Univ. of ME, Augusta, 1971–; **Educ.:** Univ. of MA, 1940–42, 1946–48, BS (Econ.); Univ. of ME, 1970–71, MLS. **Orgs.:** ALA: ACRL. ME LA. New Eng. LA. New Eng. Coll. Libn. **Activities:** 1; 17 **Addr.:** RFD #1, Vassalboro, ME 04989.

Broderick, John C. (S. 6, 1926, Memphis, TN) Asst. Libn. for Rsrch. Srvs., Lib. of Congs., 1979–; Chief, Mss. Div., 1975–79, Asst. Chief, Mss. Div., 1965–75, Spec. in Amer. Cult. Hist., 1964–65; Adj. Prof. of Eng., Geo. Washington Univ., 1964–; Prof. of Eng., Wake Forest Univ., 1957–64; Instr. in Eng., Univ. TX, 1952–57. **Educ.:** Southwestern at Memphis, 1943–48, AB (Eng.); Univ. of NC, 1948–53, MA, PhD (Eng.); Yale Univ. (U.S. Army Lang. Prog.), 1945–46, Cert. (Japanese). **Orgs.:** Mod. Lang. Assn.: Com. on Bibl., Amer. Lit. Sect. 1964–). SAA: Archival Secur. Bd. (1975–). Bibl. Soc. of Amer. Natl. Hist. Pubns. & Recs. Comsn. Amer. Antiq. Soc. **Honors:** Danforth Fndn. Grant, 1960; Amer. Cncl. of Learned Socs., Grant, 1962; Cncl. on Lib. Resrcs., Flwshp., 1970. **Pubns.:** Cont., *American Studies: Topics and Sources* (1976); Cont., *The Librarians of Congress, 1802–1975* (1977); "John Russell Young: The Internationalist as Librarian", *Qtly. Jnl. of the Lib. of Congs.* (Ap. 1976); "The Greatest Whitman Collector and the Greatest Whitman Collection", (Ap. 1970); Cont. *American Literary Scholarship* (1970–73); Various other articles. **Activities:** 4; 15, 17 **Addr.:** Library of Congress, Washington, DC 20540.

Brodhead, Thomasene (Honolulu, HI) Dir., Ewa Beach Sch. Lib., 1977–; Chlds. Libn., Kaimuk, Reg. Lib., 1974–77; YA Libn., HI Pub. Lib., 1970–74. **Educ.:** Shimer Coll., 1966–68, AB (Soc. Sci); Emory Univ., 1969–70, MLN, (LS). **Orgs.:** HI LA: VP (1978), Pres. (1979). **Activities:** 9; 16, 17, 32 **Addr.:** Ewa Beach C S Library, 91-950 North Rd., Ewa Beach, HI 96706.

Brodie, Linda Grace (N. 10, 1944, St. Louis, MO) Media Spec., Roosevelt Jr. High, 1973–; Media Spec., Lincoln and Laurel Hill Elem., 1970–73. **Educ.:** CA State Univ., Fullerton, 1964–68, BA (Phil.); Univ. of OR, 1969–70, MA (Libnshp.); 1970, Stan. OR Tchg Cert. K-12. **Orgs.:** OR Educ. Media Assn.: Prog. Com. (1979–80). ALA: Best Bks. (1976–78); Selected Fndns. (1978–82); *Booklist* Adv. (1979–81). AECT. Eugene Educ. Assn. OR Women in Educ. Admin. **Activities:** 10; 31, 39, 48; 89, 93, 95-Couns. **Addr.:** 3590 Donald St., Eugene, OR 97405.

Brodie, Nancy E. (Mr. 1, 1947, Montreal, PQ) Chief, Jn. Cat. of Bks. Div., Natl. Lib. of Can., 1981–; Chief, Un. Cat. of Serials Div., 1976–81; Sr. MARC Libn., Can. MARC Ofc., 1975–76; Engin. Libn., Concordia Univ., 1972–74; Syst. Libn., Univ. of Victoria, 1969–72. **Educ.:** Bishop's Univ., 1963–68, BSc (Math); Univ. BC, 1968–69, BLS. **Orgs.:** Can. Assn. Info. Sci.: Ottawa Chap., (Pres., 1977–78); Pubn. Com. (Ch., 1978–). Can. LA: Per. Indx. Review Com. (Ch., 1975–77); Lcl. Arrange. Com. 1978–79). SLA: East. Can. Chap., Nom. Com. (1979). Inst. of Victoria Libns.: Exec. Cncl. (1971–72). **Pubns.:** "DOBIS: The Canadian Government Version," *Can. Lib. Jnl.* (Ag. 1979); "Evaluation of a KWIC Index for Library Literature," *ASIS Jnl.* (Ja.-F. 1970). **Activities:** 1, 4; 35, 45; 57 **Addr.:** Public Services Branch, National Library of Canada, 395 Wellington St., Ottawa, ON K1R 7T7 Canada.

Brodman, Estelle (Je. 1, 1914, New York, NY) Retired. Libn., Prof. of Med. Hist., Washington Univ. Sch. of Med., 1961–81; Asst. Libn. for Ref. Srv., Natl. Lib. of Med., 1949–61; Columbia Univ. Med. Lib., 1937–49. **Educ.:** Cornell Univ., 1931–35, AB (Histology & Embryology); Columbia Univ., 1936, BS 1943, MS, 1953, PhD (Libnshp., Hist. Med.). **Honors:** Noyes Awd., Med. LA, Honorary DSc, Univ. of IL, Murray Gottlieb Awd., Med. LA, President's Natl. Adv. Cmsn. on Libs. **Pubns.:** *Development of medical bibliography* (1956); *Bibliographical lists for medical libraries* (1946); "Medical Libraries," *ALA Yrbk.* (1975–78); "Pediatrics in an 18th-century home remedy book," *Bull. Med. Lib. A,* (1978); "Reactions to failures in library automation," *Clinic on Lib. Applications of Data Processing* (1978); other articles. **Activities:** 1; 17; 56, 80, 85 **Addr.:** 19-09 Meadow Lakes, Highstown, NJ 08520.

Brodsky, Caren S. (My. 13, 1956, Abington, PA) Info. Anal., InfoSrc., 1980–; Catlgr., Hlth. Systs. Agency, 1980; Ref. Libn., Point Park Coll., 1979–80; Freelnc. Lexicographer, Random Hse., 1978–79. **Educ.:** Temple Univ., 1974–78, BA, magna cum laude (Eng.); Columbia Univ., 1978–79, MSLS (Lib. Srv.); various crs. **Orgs.:** OLUG: Ch. (1981–) SLA. ALA. ASIS. **Honors:** Phi Beta Kappa, 1978; Beta Phi Mu, 1979. **Activities:** 12; 24, 41; 59, 81, 91 **Addr.:** 1850 Edumnd Rd., Abington, PA 19001.

Brody, Catherine Tyler (S. 7, –, Chicago, IL) Actg. Chief Libn. & Dept. Chmn., NYC Tech. Coll., CUNY, 1978–; Ch., Lib. Ref. Srvs., 1976-78, Exhibits Coord., Archvst., 1968–79, Ref. Libn., 1966–78; Branch Libn., 1966–76. **Educ.:** Rosary Coll., BA, (Eng.); St. Louis Univ., (Eng. & Comp. Lit.); Pratt Inst., 1964–66, MLS; Hunter Coll., 1974–76, MA (Eng. Lit.). **Orgs.:** Beta Phi Mu: Pres., Theta Chap. (1972–76). Cncl. of Chief Libs., CUNY: Secy. (1978–81). ALA. LA of the City Univ. of NY: Secy. (1969–71). Amer. Prntg. Hist. Assn.: Pres. (1978–82); VP (1974–78). Typophiles: Secy.-Treas. (1972–). South Street Seaport Musm.: Advisory Com., Prntg. Shop Restoration (1973–). Grolier Club: Lib. Com. (1977–); Admis. Com. (1977–). **Honors:** Typophiles, Inc. "Catherine Brody Day" Recognition, 1975; Richter Award for Graduate Scholarship, 1976. **Pubns.:** Asst. ed., *Long Island Printing, 1791–1830; A Checklist of Imprints* (1979); Asst. ed., *Hellmut Lehmann-Haupt, A Bibliography* (1975); Contrib. Ed., *Printing News,* (1974–); Ed., *APHA Letter,* (1974–); Co-Ed., *The Independent Shavian* (1969–73); Other articles, book reviews. **Activities:** 1; 17, 39, 45; 57, 61 **Addr.:** New York City Technical College, City University of NY, 300 Jay Street, Brooklyn, NY 11201.

Brody, Lynne M. (Ap. 9, 1942, Los Angeles, CA) Head Libn., Undergrad. Lib., Univ. of TX at Austin, 1979–, Col. Dev. Libn., Undergrad. Lib., 1974–79; Reserve Room and Asst. Ref. Libn., Barnard Coll., Columbia Univ., 1968–74; Ref. Lib., M.I.T., Rotch Lib. of Archit. & City Plng., 1967–68. **Educ.:** Douglass Coll., Rutgers Univ., 1958–62, BA (Soc.); Simmons Coll., 1965–66, MLS. **Orgs.:** ALA: Undergrad. Lib. Discuss. Grp. (1979–). Soc. of Univ. of TX Libns.: Pres. (1978–79). TX Assn. of Coll. Tchrs. **Activities:** 1; 15, 17; 55, 92 **Addr.:** Undergraduate Library, ACA 101, University of Texas, Austin, TX 78712.

Broering, Naomi C. (N. 24, 1929, New York, NY) Med. Ctr. Libn., Georgetown Univ. Med. Ctr., 1978–, Assoc. Med. Ctr. Libn., 1975–78; Prog. Ofcr., Manpower Grants, Vet. Admin., 1974–75, Chief, Readers Srvs., 1972–74; Asst. Libn., Walter Reed Gen. Hosp., 1971–72; Chief Libn., Chld. Hosp. of Los Angeles, 1968–71; Ref., Acq. Libn., Univ. of South. CA, 1962–68. **Educ.:** CA State Univ., Long Beach, 1957–60, BA (Hist., Soc. Sci.); 1961–63, MA (Hist.); Univ. of CA, Los Angeles, 1963–66, MLS, 1966–67; Postgrad. Internship-Cert. (Biomed. Lib.). **Orgs.:** Med. LA: Bd. of Dirs. (1979–82); Legis Com. (Ch., 1970–72). ALA. SLA. ASIS. Various other orgs. AAAS; Amer. Hist. Assn. **Honors:** Vet. Admin., Performance Awd., 1973. **Pubns.:** *Laws and Legislation in Medical Librarianship* (1980); "Renewal of the Medical Library Assistance Act," *Bltn. of the Med. LA* (Ap. 1978). **Activities:** 1, 12; 17, 28, 34; 58, 78, 80 **Addr.:** Dahlgren Memorial Library, Georgetown University Medical Center, 3900 Reservoir Rd., N.W., Washington, DC 20007.

Brogden, Stephen R. (S. 26, 1948, Des Moines, IA) Head, Fine Arts Dept., Pub. Lib. of Des Moines, 1980–; Film Srvs. Libn., 1979–80; Visit. Lectr., Grad. Lib. Sch., Univ. of AZ, 1975–76; Dir., Harwood Fndn., Univ. of NM, 1972–75. **Educ.:** Univ. of IA, 1966–70, BA (Eng.), 1970–72, MA (LS). **Orgs.:** ALA. IA LA. Metro. Des Moines LA: VP, Pres.-Elect (1980–81). **Pubns.:** Reviews. **Activities:** 1, 9; 16, 26, 32; 55, 67 **Addr.:** Public Library of Des Moines, 100 Locust St., Des Moines, IA 50311.

PROFESSIONAL ACTIVITIES: Institutions: 1. Acad. lib.; 2. Arch.; 3. Assn.; 4. Fed./Gvt. lib.; 5. Inst. lib.; 6. Mfr./Suppl.; 7. Milit. lib.; 8. Musm.; 9. Pub. lib.; 10. Sch. lib.; 11. Sch. of lib. sci.; 12. Spec. lib.; 13. State lib.; 14. (other). **Functions/Activities:** 15. Acq./Col. dev.; 16. Adult srvs.; 17. Admin.; 18. Apprais.; 19. Archit./Bldgs.; 20. Cat./Class.; 21. Chld. srvs.; 22. Circ.; 23. Cons./Pres.; 24. Consult.; 25. Cont. ed.; 26. Educ. lib. sci.; 27. Ext. srvs.; 28. Fund/Grants; 29. Gvt. pubs.; 30. Indx./Abs.; 31. Instr. lib. use; 32. Media srvs.; 33. Micro.; 34. Netwks./Coop.; 35. Persnl.; 36. PR; 37. Publshg.; 38. Recs. mgt.; 39. Ref. srvs.; 40. Repro.; 41. Resrch.; 42. Review.; 43. Secur.; 44. Serials; 45. Spec. col.; 46. Tech. srvs.; 47. Trustees/Bds.; 48. YA srvs.; 49. (other).

Brokalakis, Melissa Chait (Je. 15, 1950, Brockton, MA) Mgr., Info. and Lib. Srvs., Honeywell Inf. Systs. 1980–. Documtn. Spec., Honeywell Info. Systs., 1978–80; Asst. Dir., Wayland Pub. Lib., 1975–80; Visit. Lectr. in Lib. Sci., Framingham State Coll., 1978–79. **Educ.:** Smith Coll. 1967–72, BA (Anthro.); Simmons Coll. 1974–75, MLS. **Orgs.:** MA LA: Pub. Rel. Com. (1978–79); Int. Frdm. Com. (Secy, 1979–80). SLA: Boston Chap. Greater Boston Pub. Lib. Asst. Dir. Grp. **Pubns.:** "Quantification of Reference Services at the Wayland Public Library", *Quantitative measurement and Dynamic Library Services* (1978). **Activities:** 9, 12; 16, 17, 39; 50, 62, 67 **Addr.:** Honeywell Information Systems, 200 Smith St., MS423, Waltham, MA 02154.

Brome, Eleanor C. (D. 23, 1929, Washington, DC) Dir., Cranford Pub. Libs., 1974–; Dir., LS Prog., Caldwell Coll., 1972–74, Catlgr., Instr., 1969–72; Jr. Libn., Cat., Ref., Verona Pub. Lib., 1967–69. **Educ.:** West. State Coll., 1950–51, BA (Soclgy., Lit.); Rutger Univ., 1965–68, MLS. **Orgs.:** ALA: Stats. for Pub. Lib. Com. (1978). NJ LA: Tech. Srv. Sect., VP (1972–73), Pres. (1973–74); Admin. Sect., VP (1977–78), Pres. (1978–79); Exec. Bd. (1980–); Awds. Com. (1980–); Gvt. Rel. Com. (1980–). NJ Cncl. on Lib. Educ. (1973–74). Coord. Cncl. of Elizabeth Area Libs.: Pres. (1977–79). Various other orgs. Summit Monthly Mtg.: Lib. Com. **Honors** Beta Phi Mu, 1968. **Activities:** 1, 9; 15, 17, 47 **Addr.:** Cranford Public Library, 224 Walnut Ave., Cranford, NJ 07016.

Bromert, Jane Doyle (S. 26, 1947, Beatrice, NE) Assoc. Dean of the Coll., Huron Coll., 1979–, Coord. of Title III & Fac. Dev., Adj. Instr. of LS, 1978–79, Asst. Libn., Instr. of LS, 1977–78; Libn., Toldeo Lucas Cnty. Pub. Lib., 1976–77; Intern Arch., Univ. of SD, 1975, Head and Asst. Head of Circ., 1972–74. **Educ.:** St. Mary's Univ., 1971–72, BA (Eng.); Wayne State Univ., 1974–75, MSLS; Univ. of SD, 1981–, PhD (Adult and Higher Educ. Admin.). **Orgs.:** ALA:ACRL. SD LA: Exec. Cncl. (1978–79); Acad. Sect. (Pres., 1978–79; Secy.-Treas., 1977–78). Amer. Assn. of Higher Educ. Prof. and Organizational Net. of Higher Educ. **Honors:** Danforth Fndn., Danforth Assoc., 1979. **Pubns.:** Jt. auth., "Huron College: An Intergenerational Experience," chapter in *New Directions in Higher Education: Teaching Adults of All Ages* (1980). **Activities:** 1, 2; 17, 25, 28 **Addr.:** 1320 Campbell Drive, Huron, SD 57350.

Brong, Gerald R. (Jl. 20, 1939, Tacoma, WA) Dir., Fac. Srvs., Instr. Media Srvs., WA State Univ., 1965–; Dir., Lib. Futures Plng. Task Force, WA State Lib., 1973–74; Elem. Tchr., Tacoma (WA) Pub. Sch., 1961–65. **Educ.:** Ctrl. WA State Coll., 1957–61, BA Educ. (Psy.), 1963–65, MEduc (Psy.); WA State Univ., 1969–71, EdD (Higher Educ). **Orgs.:** AECT: Bd of Dir (1972–74); Info. Syst. Div., (Pres. 1971–72); other coms. ALA: LITA (Pres. 1972–73); ISAD (Bd. of Dirs. 1975–76); AV Sect. (Ch., 1975–76). WHCOLIS: Ad Hoc Adv. Com. (1976–80). Phi Delta Kappa. NW Coll. & Univ. Cncl. for Mgrs. of Educ. Tech. in H Educ.: Pres. (1979). Rotary Intl. Ctrl. WA State Univ. Alum. Assn: Bd. of Dir. (1977–). **Honors:** WA AECT: Disting. Srv. Awd., 1975. **Pubns.:** "Non-print Media–1971, The Year of Minimal Change," *Bowker Lib. Anl.* (1971); "Library Networks and Non-print Resources," *Lib. News Bltn.* (Jl.-S. 1970). **Activities:** 17, 24, 32, 61, 63, 67 **Addr.:** Instructional Media Services, Washington State University, Pullman, WA 99164.

Brongers, Reinder Jan (Ap. 14, 1926, Rotterdam, Netherlands) Head, Sci. Div., Univ. of BC Lib., 1967–; Asst., Chief Engin., AMFAB Prods. Ltd., (Burnaby, B.C.), 1959–66; Design Engin., John Laing Ltd., 1957–59; Asst. Engin., New Zealand Mnstry. of Works, 1952–57. **Educ.:** Tech. Univ. of Delft, 1945–51, Ir., (Engin.); Univ. of BC, 1966–67, BLS; Regis. Prof. Engin., BC, 1957. **Orgs.:** ASIS: West. Can. Chap., Chap. Rep. (1974–75), Treas. (1975–77). Assn. of Prof. Engins. of BC: PR Com. (1967/68). **Honors:** Beta Phi Mu. **Activities:** 1; 39; 64, 91 **Addr.:** Science Division/The Library, University of British Columbia, 1956 Main Mall, Vancouver, BC V6T 1Y3 Canada.

Brooke, Lee (Jl. 5, 1930, Rochester, NY) Lib. Consult., 1966–; Dir. of Libs., Chicago Coll. of Osteopathic Med., 1970–80; Michael Reese Hosp., Head Libn., 1969–70; Various consult. and lib. design appts. **Educ.:** Elmhurst Coll., 1950–56, AB (Eng.); Rosary Coll., 1962–65, MALS. **Orgs.:** Various mems. Friends of Oak Park Pub. Lib.: Bd. of Dir. **Pubns.:** Ed. and Publshr., *Hosp. Libs.* (1976–80). **Activities:** 1, 12; 19, 24, 28; 51 **Addr.:** 1029 Belleforte, Oak Park, IL 60302.

Brooks, Benedict (Ap. 18, 1935, Pearl Creek, NY) Self-Empl. Indxr-Ed., 1975–; Ed., Prod. Mgr., Paul de Haen, 1976–78; Ed., Bio. and Agr. Indx., H.W. Wilson Co., 1970–76; Instr., Brooklyn Coll. Lib., 1968–70. **Educ.:** Univ. of Rochester, 1952–56, AB (Fr.); Columbia Univ., 1956–57, MS (LS); PA State Univ., 1958–61; Yale Univ. Sch. of Med., 1961–65. **Orgs.:** NY Lib. Clb. Ed. Freelnc. Assn. Amer. Socty. of Indxrs. **Honors:** Beta Phi Mu, 1957. **Pubns.:** Co-Auth., "Catalog Subject Searches in the Yale Medical Library, Coll. and Resrch. Libs.," (N. 1964); Co-Auth., *Bltn. of the Med. LA* "A Comparison of Library of Congress Subject Headings and Medical Subject Headings," *Bltn. of the Med. LA* (Apr. 1964). **Activities:** 1, 12; 20, 30, 37; 58, 80, 87 **Addr.:** Box 56, Apartment 1421, 155 W. 68th St., New York, NY 10023.

Brooks, Burton Howard (My 30, 1935, Chicago, IL) Dir. Instr. Media Srvcs., Grand Haven Pub. Sch., 1968–; Media Spec., Grand Haven HS, 1967–68; Libn., Tchr, Climax-Scotts HS, 1961–67; Tchr., Bellevue HS, 1957–61. **Educ.:** MI State Univ., 1953–56, BA (Jnlsm.); MI State Univ., 1957–60, MA (Educ.); West. MI Univ., 1965–68, MSL. **Orgs.:** MI Assn. of Sch. Libns.: Pres. (1973). MI Assn. for Media in Educ.: Pres. (1974); Policy Com., Ch. (1975–81); Newsletter Ed. (1977–81). ALA. MI LA. AECT. MI AV Assn. MI Assn. for Supervsn. and Curric. Dev. **Honors:** Sigma Delta Chi, 1955; Be Phi Mu, 1968. **Pubns.:** "A Task Analysis of the District Media Director", *Media Spectrum* (1976); "Career Education Media", *Previews* 1978); "Selling Your Organization: Survival Strategies for the 80s", *Media Spectrum* (1981); Reviews. **Activities:** 10; 17, 32, 40; 57, 63 **Addr.:** P.O. Box 211, Grand Haven, MI 49417.

Brooks, Clifford J. (N. 27, 1951, Jersey City, NJ) Dir., of Educ., Opera Co. of Boston, 1979–; Asst. Coord. of Jr. Srvcs., E. Orange Pub. Lib., 1978–79; Head, Adult Srvs., Hoboken Pub. Lib., 1977–78; Pub. Rel. Libn., La Joie par les livres (France), 1975–77. **Educ.:** Georgetown Univ., 1969–73, BSL (Fr.); Rutgers Univ., 1974–75, MLS. **Orgs.:** ALA. NJ LA. Les Amis de la Joie parles livres. **Honors:** Phi Beta Kappa, 1972–; Beta Phi Mu, 1976–. **Pubns.:** Trans., *Let Them Read!* (1980); "International Trends in French Childrens' Literature," *Book Bird* (D. 1976); "Pour une Méthode D'Analyses", *La Revue de livres pour Enfants* (O. 1976). **Activities:** 14-Opera Co.; 21, 25; 55 **Addr.:** 594 Forest St., Kearny, NJ 07032.

Brooks, D. Dee (Ja. 18, 1951, Kingman, KS) Tech. Dir., Syst. Anal., North. IL Lrng. Resrc. Coop., 1978–; Progmr., Anal., Mgt. Syst. Tech., Inc., 1977–78; Asst. Libn., Info. Syst. Dev. Ofc., Northwest. Univ., 1974–77; Progmr., KS Bur. of Educ. Measur., 1973–74. **Educ.:** Hutchinson Cmnty. Jr. Coll., 1969–71, AA (Math); KS State Univ., Manhattan, 1971–73, BA (Comp. Sci.); KS State Univ., Emporia, 1973–74, ML; Northwest. Univ., 1976 (Comp. Sci.). **Orgs.:** ALA. ASIS: Chap. Asm. Rep. (Chicago, 1980); Nat. Chap. Awd. Jury (1980); SIG/LAN (Chap. Coordn. Ch., 1980); Chicago Chap. (Ch., 1978–79); other coms. Assn. of Comp. Mach.: KSU Student Chap. Secy., 1972–1973. **Pubns.:** *CALS Management Overview* (1979); "Introduction to CALS: Design and Development," (slide show) (1979). **Activities:** 1, 10; 24, 34; 56, 62, 75 **Addr.:** Renner Learning Resource Center, Elgin Community College, 1700 Spartan Dr., Elgin, IL 60120.

Brooks, Janet (Strattan) (Peters) (D. 27, 1918, Detroit, MI) Chief Libn., Defense Comm. Agency, U.S. Dept. of Defense, 1973–; Proj. Ofcr., Tech. Info. Support Actv. Proj., Army Resrch. Ofc., 1971–73; Dir., Lib. Srvs., U.S. Natl. Comsn. on Prod. Safety, 1968–70; Actg. Chief, Sci. and Tech. Info. Ofc., U.S. Army Engin. Geodesy, Intelligence, and Mapping Agency, 1966–67; Info. Spec., U.S. Navy, Nvl. Autom. Resrch. and Dev. Info. Syst., 1965–66; Asst. Libn., U.S. Nvl. Observatory, 1960–65. **Educ.:** OH State Univ., 1940–41, BSEd (Fr., Eng.); Univ. of MD, 1967–68, MLS. **Orgs.:** ALA. SLA: DC Chap., Milit. Libns. (Ch., 1968–69); Soc. Sci. Div., Housing and Urban Affairs Sect. (Ch., 1969–71). ASIS. Fed. Libns. Assn. Various other orgs. Armed Frcs. Comm./Electronics Assn. Toastmstrs. **Activities:** 4, 12; 17, 34; 75, 74, 93 **Addr.:** Box 39096, Friendship Station, 4620 Windom Pl., N.W., Washington, DC 20016.

Brooks, Jean S. (S. 19, 1914, Torrance, CA) Retired, 1979–; Proj. Mgr., Prin., Dallas Pub. Lib., 1978–79, Libn. for Indp. Lrng., 1977–78, Proj. Dir., 3D Lrng. Ctrs., 1973–76, Proj. Dir., Indp. Std. Proj., 1972–73, Inst. Srvs. Libn., 1969–72, Libn., St. Louis Cnty. Lib., 1965–68; Asst. Branch Head, Torrance Pub. Lib., 1939–41; Libn., Glendale Pub. Lib., 1938–39. **Educ.:** Univ. of CA, Los Angeles, 1935, BA (Eng.); Univ. of MO, 1969, MLS. **Orgs.:** ALA: PLA, Alternative Educ. Prog. Strg. Com. (1976–77); HRLSD, Stans. Review Com. (1975–77), Ad Hoc Com. on Lib. Srvs. to Shut-ins (1974–75); RASD, Com. on Lib. Srvs. to an Aging Popltn. (Ch., 1972–76). Dallas Cnty. Mental Hlth. Assn.: Com. on Aging (1979–80). Adv. Cncl. Retired Sr. Volun. Prog.: Ch. (1973–77). Park Manor Pub. Housing for Sr. Citizens: Citizens Adv. Grp. (1971–74). **Pubns.:** "Special Information Services" ERIC (1979); "Independent Study: How Nontraditional Is It?" *Jnl. of Acad. Libnshp.* (S. 1976); "Cracking the Structure" ERIC (1974); jt. auth., *The Public Library in Non-Traditional Education* (1974); "Older Persons and the College Level Exam Program," *Assn. of Hosp. and Inst. Libs. Qtly.* (Spr.–Sum. 1972). **Activities:** 9; 16, 17, 41; 50, 75, 89 **Addr.:** 2011 Cap Rock Cir., Richardson, TX 75080.

Brooks, Judith A. (F. 25, 1942, Pontiac, MI) Dir., Lib. Srvs., Oakland Schs., 1980–, Resrch. Libn., 1970–80; Nurse, St. Joseph Hosp., 1968–70; Tchr., Waterford Kettering HS, 1963–68. **Educ.:** Oakland Univ., 1959–63, BA (Sec. Educ., Eng.); Wayne State Univ., 1966–70, MSLS; Oakland Cmnty. Coll., 1970–72, Assoc. Degree (Nursing, R.N.). **Orgs.:** ALA: ASCLA, Bibliother./Lib. Srv. to the Blind and Phys. Handcpd., Pres.'s Ad Hoc Com. on Empl. of the Handcpd. (1977–78). Natl. Educ. Assn. MI Educ. Assn. Amer. Nurses' Assn. **Honors:** MI State Univ., Outstan. Srv. in Sec. Educ., 1965. **Pubns.:** Jt. auth., *Employment-Related Materials for Disabled People* (1977–78). **Activities:** 1, 12; 15, 17, 41; 63, 72, 80 **Addr.:** Oakland Schools Library, 2100 Pontiac Lake Rd., Pontiac, MI 48054.

Brooks, Kristina M. (Ag. 29, 1949, Ft. Leavenworth, KS) Coord., Lib. Info. Retrieval Srv., OR State Univ., 1975. **Educ.:** Univ. of WA, 1967–70, BA (Pol. Sci.); NM State Univ., 1970–72, MAT (Educ.); Univ. of OR, 1974–75, MLS. **Orgs.:** SLA: OR Chap. (Pres., 1979–80). ASIS: Pac. NW Chap. (Treas., 1978–79). OR OLUG: Coord. (1976–78); Cncl. of Plng. Libns. **Pubns.:** "A Comparison of the Coverage of Agricultural and Forestry Literature on AGRICOLA, BIOSIS, CAB and SCISEARCH," *Data-Base* (Mr. 1980); "Requirements for a Statewide Geographic Information System," (1980). **Activities:** 1; 24, 39; 70, 82, 91 **Addr.:** LIRS, Kerr Library, Oregon State University, Corvallis, OR 97331.

Broome, Frances M. (Ja. 29, 1947, Ottawa, ON) Pres., Kinetic Film Enterprises Limited, 1976–; Mgr., City Films, 1972–75; Statistical Resrch. Ofcr., OECA Channel 19 Educ. TV, 1973–74; Film Fest. Planner, Can. Film Inst. **Educ.:** Carleton Univ., BA (Eng.); Dips. in Photography, Animation. **Orgs.:** EFLA. AECT. ASTED. Various Can. lib. assns. **Pubns.:** Various articles. **Activities:** 9, 10; 25, 32, 49; 50, 63, 67 **Addr.:** Kinetic Film Enterprises, Ltd., 781 Gerrard St., E., Toronto, ON M4M 1Y5 Canada.

Brophy, Charles A., Jr. (Jl. 9, 1913, Columbus, OH) Self-empl. Info. Consult., 1974–; Dir. of Libs., Battelle Meml. Inst., 1951–74; Head Libn., White Cross Hosp., 1950–51; Head of Circ., Univ. of NM, 1949–50. **Educ.:** OH State Univ., 1931–32, 1938–40, BS (Educ.); Univ. of IL, 1941–42, BS (LS). **Orgs.:** SLA. Univ. Clb. of Columbus. **Pubns.:** *Titanium Bibliography* (1952). **Activities:** 1, 12; 17, 24, 34; 64, 80, 91 **Addr.:** 303 South Ardmore Rd., Bexley, OH 43209.

Brophy, Edward G. (Ap. 3, 1939, New York, NY) Head Libn., Msgr. McClancy Meml. HS, 1966–; Ast. Libn., St. John's Prep., 1962–66. **Educ.:** St. John's Univ., 1957–60, BA (Eng.); 1961–65 (LS). **Orgs.:** ALA. Cath. LA: B'klny-Long Island Unit (VP, Pres.-Elect, 1979). Cath. Forensic Leag.: Treas. (1966–76). **Activities:** 10; 31, 32, 48; 57, 89 **Addr.:** Msgr. McClancy Memorial H.S., 71-06 31st Ave., East Elmhurst, NY 11370.

Brophy, Mary Jill (Ag. 6, 1949, Cleveland, OH) Head, Cat. Dept., Law Lib., Univ. of CA, Los Angeles, 1976–; Head, Cat. Dept., DePaul Univ. Law Lib., 1975–76; Cat., 1974–75; Libn., Isham, Lincoln & Beale Law Firm, 1973–74. **Educ.:** Univ. of IL, AB (Hist.), MSLS. **Orgs.:** AALL: Govern. Docum. Spec. Interest Sect. (1979–); On-Line Bibl. Srvs. Spec. Interest Sect. (1979–); Tech. Srvs. Spec. Interest Sect. (1978–). South. CA Assn. of Law Libs.: Treas. (1978–79); Mem. Com. (1977–78). South. CA Tech. Proc. Grp. Various other mems. **Pubns.:** Contrib. Ed., *The Law Cat.* (1975–79); Contrib. Ed., *The Tech. Srvs. Law Libn.* (1979–). **Activities:** 1; 17, 20; 77 **Addr.:** UCLA Law Library, 405 Hilgard Ave., Los Angeles, CA 90049.

Brose, Friedrich K. (F. 29, 1936, Potsdam, Brandenburg, Germany) Assoc. Prof., Lib. Srvs., Riverside City Coll., 1970–; Libn. II, San Diego State Univ., 1969–70; Acq. Libn., U.S. Intl. Univ., 1968–69; Libn. II, Univ. of CA, Santa Barbara, 1967–68. **Educ.:** Australian Natl. Univ., Canberra, 1960–63, BA (Asian Cvlztn.); Univ. of New S. Wales, Sydney, 1964–65, Dip. (Lib.); McGill Univ., 1966–67, MLS; San Diego State Univ., 1969–70, MA (Grmn. Lit.). **Orgs.:** CA LA: Chap. of Acad. and Resrch. Libns., Acad. Status Com. (1974–75); Lib. Dev. and Stans. Com. (1973–76); Cmnty. Coll. Libns. Chap., Legis. Com. (Ch., 1973–75), Secy.-Treas. (1974–75). ALA. South. CA Tech. Prcs. Grp.: Prog. Com. (Ch., 1971–72). COLT. Various other orgs. CA Cmnty. and Jr. Coll. Assn.: Com. on Values in Higher Educ. (1974–76); Reg. 7 (RCC Fac. Rep., 1973–75, 1981–). **Pubns.:** Ed., *Intercom; the Nsltr. for CA Cmnty. Coll. Libns.* (1972–74); "Accepting Employment: the Problem of Insufficient Data for the Applicant," *CA Libn.* (XXXIII, Ap.–Jl.); "RCC's 'Library 59' Work Experience Class," *COLT Nsltr.* (O. 1974); "Collective Bargaining: Can We Adjust to It?" *CA Libn.* (Ap. 1975); "Summary of Our New Collective Bargaining Law," *Intercom: the Nsltr. of CA Cmnty. Coll. Libns.* (N. 1975); various articles. **Activities:** 1; 15, 20, 39 **Addr.:** Riverside City College Library, 4800 Magnolia Ave., Riverside, CA 92506.

Brosky, Catherine M. (Ap. 2, 1926, Pittsburgh, PA) Head, Sci. and Tech. Dept., Carnegie Lib. of Pittsburgh, 1979–; Dir., Grad. Sch. of Pub. Hlth. Lib., Univ. Pittsburgh, 1955–79; Ast., Libn., US Bur. Mines, Region V, 1952–55; Libn., Sci. and Tech. Dept., Carnegie Lib., 1947–52. **Educ.:** Carnegie Inst. of Tech., 1942–46, BS (Chem.); 1946–47, BS (LS). **Orgs.:** SLA: numerous lcl. coms.; Chap. Pres. ALA. Amer. Socty. of Indxrs. **Addr.:** Science and Technology Department, Carnegie Library of Pittsburgh, 4400 Forbes Ave., Pittsburgh, PA 15213.

Brosnan, Donald P. (Mr. 6, 1925, Oakland, CA) Arch., Hist., and Recs. Mgt., Pima Cnty., AZ, 1979–; Recs. Mgr., Tucson, AZ, 1974–78; Admin. Srvs. Mgr., U.S. Dept. of the Army, 1950–74. **Educ.:** Pima Coll., 1974–77, AA (Educ.); Univ. of AZ, 1977–80, BA (Gen. Stud., Hist.); Atlantic Coll., Dublin, Ireland, 1949–50, DP (Radio Engin.); Inst. of Cert. Recs. Mgt., 1976, Cert. Recs. Mgr. (CRM). **Orgs.:** SAA. Bus. Forms Mgt. Assn.: Tuscon Chap. (Cht. Mem.). Natl. Micro. Assn.; Association of Records Managers and Administrators: Tuscon Chapter; Cofounder (1979); Board of Directors (1979–81); Membership

Special Subjects/Services: 50. Adult educ.; 51. Advert./Mktg.; 52. Aerosp.; 53. Agric.; 54. Area std.; 55. Arts/Hum.; 56. Autom.; 57. Bibl./Prtg.; 58. Bio. sci.; 59. Bus./Fin.; 60. Chem.; 61. Copyrt.; 62. Documtn.; 63. Educ.; 64. Engin.; 65. Env.; 66. Eth. grps.; 67. Film; 68. Food/Nutr.; 69. Geneal.; 70. Geo.; 71. Geol.; 72. Handcpd.; 73. Hist.; 74. Int. frdm.; 75. Info. sci.; 76. Insr.; 77. Law; 78. Legis.; 79. Math./Comp. sci.; 80. Med.; 81. Metals; 82. Nat. resrcs.; 83. Newsp.; 84. Nuc. sci.; 85. Oral hist.; 86. Petr./Energy; 87. Pharm.; 88. Phys./Astr./Math.; 89. Readg.; 90. Relig.; 91. Sci./Tech.; 92. Soc. sci.; 93. Telecom.; 94. Transp.; 95. (other).

Committee (Ch., 1979–80); various offices and committees. Various other orgs. AZ Hist. Socty. Amer. Assn. for State and Lcl. Hist. Amer. Legion; Various Vets. Assns. **Honors:** Various military honors. **Activities:** 2, 4; 17, 33, 38 **Addr.:** 9031 E. Kenyon Dr., Tucson, AZ 85710.

Brothers, Cassie C. (O. 20, 1928, Wabash, AR) Lib. Supvsr., Helena-W. Helena Sch. Dist., 1965–; Libn., Helena Jr. HS, 1958–65, Tchr., 1952–58. **Educ.:** Univ. of AR, 1946–50, BSE (Msc.); Univ. of MS, 1959–62, MLS; various crs. **Orgs.:** AR LA: Pres. (1978); VP, Conf. Ch. (1977). SW LA: Exec. Bd. (1978); Cncl. (1977). ALA: AASL (Del., 1977). AR AV Assn.: Exec. Bd. (1980). Delta Kappa Gamma: Lcl. Chap. Pres. (1975). AR Assn. of Educ. Admins. Assn. of Prof. Educs. AR Educ. TV Netwk.: Sec. Curric. Com. (1978–). **Honors:** Sigma Alpha Iota, 1950. **Pubns.:** *Bibliography of Arkansas and Arkansas Author Materials* (1962). **Activities:** 10, 14-Dist. supv.; 17, 32, 36; 63, 89, 93 **Addr.:** Helena-West Helena School District, 123 Summit Dr., Helena, AR 72342.

Brou, Marguerite–Marie (My. 3, 1922, Wallace, LA) Archvst., Roman Cath. Archdio., New Orleans, 1971–; Prof. of Fr., Hum. Div. Chmn., St. Mary's Dominican Coll., 1965–69; Ast. Prof. of French, 1955–61; Instr. of French, 1945–55; Regis., 1947–58; Ast. Regis., 1945–47. **Educ.:** St. Mary's Dominican Coll., 1938–42, AB (Fr.); Laval Univ., 1961–65, PhD (Fr.); LA State Univ., 1949–55, MA (Fr.); 1969–71, MS (LS). **Orgs.:** Socty. of SW Archvsts.: Charter mem. SAA. LA Assn. of Coll. Regis. and Admis. Ofcrs.: Chrt., lifetime mem. **Honors:** Phi Kappa Phi, 1955; Delta Epsilon Sigma, 1957; Beta Phi Mu, 1971. **Activities:** 2; 20, 39, 41; 90 **Addr.:** 7214 St. Charles Ave., New Orleans, LA 70118.

Broussard, Harry C. (New Orleans, LA) Ast. to Dean, Syst. and Dev., Univ. NM Genl. Lib., 1975–; Head, Serials Dept., North. IL Univ. Lib., 1972–75; Head, Serials Sect., Tulane Univ. Lib., 1967–70; Acq. Libn., TX State Lib., 1965–66. **Educ.:** Tulane Univ., 1958–63, BA (Fr.); LA State Univ., 1963–65, MS (LS); Univ. TX, 1965–67, Crs. (Ling.). **Orgs.:** ALA: LAMA/SS, Dev. and Plng. Com. (1979–); ACRL; LITA/ISAS. SW LA. NM LA. AAUP. **Honors:** Beta Phi Mu, 1965. **Pubns.:** Ed., Rio Grande Chap., *SLA Bltn.* (1978–79); Contrib. ed., *Magazines for Libraries* (1972); Jt. auth., "Postcripts to a Preconference," *LA Chap. Bltn. SLA* (v. 18, #2). **Activities:** 1; 17, 24, 34, 41; 44, 56 **Addr.:** Univ. of New Mexico General Library, Albuquerque, NM 87131.

Brow, Ellen H. (D. 23, 1936, Williams, CA) Actg. Dir., Ctr. of Latin Amer. Std., Univ. of KS, 1980–, Biblgphr. for Spain, Portugal, Latin Amer., 1975–; Ibero-Amer. Ref., Cat. Libn., Univ. of NM, 1974, Latin Amer. Biblgphr., 1969–73; Proj. Asst., Meml. Lib., Univ. of WI, 1968–69, Catlgr., 1965–66. **Educ.:** Univ. of CA, Davis, 1954–58, BA (Pol. Sci.); San Jose State Univ., 1963–65, MALS (Libnshp.); Univ. of WI, 1966–69, MA (Ibero-Amer. Area Std.), various crs. in Iberian hist. **Orgs.:** SALALM. KS LA. ALA: RASD (Dir.-at-Lg., 1975–77); Org. Com. (Ch., 1976–77)/Hist. Sect., Ch.; GODORT; RTSD; ACRL; LITA; LIRT; SRRT. Latin Amer. Std. Assn. Socty. for Span. and Portuguese Hist. Std. Intl. Working Grp. on Mod. Portugal. Conf. on Latin Amer. Hist. **Activities:** 1, 12; 15, 17, 46; 54, 73 **Addr.:** P.O. Box 684, Lawrence, KS 66044.

Browar, Lisa M. (Ja. 22, 1951, Jamaica, NY) Archvst., Latin Amer. Pamphlet Col., Yale Univ., 1981–, Asst. to Cur., Yale Col. Of Amer. Lit., Beinecke Rare Bk. and Ms. Lib., 1979–80; Ref. Libn., Johnson Cnty. Pub. Lib., 1979. **Educ.:** IN Univ., 1969–73, BA (Eng. Lit.); Univ. of KS, 1975–76, MA (Eng., Amer. Lit.); IN Univ., 1976–77, MLS; Mod. Arch. Inst., Natl. Arch. and Recs. Srv., 1980, Cert. (Arch. Admin.). **Orgs.:** ALA: ACRL/Rare Bk. and Ms. Sect. SAA: Acq. and Univ. Arch. Afnty. Grps.; Ms. Repositories Afnty. Grp. Mod. Lang. Assn. **Pubns.:** "The Discovery of a Ghost in Edgar Fawcett's Canon," *Papers of the Bibl. Socty. Of Amer.* (3rd Quarter 1978); reviewer, consult., *Choice Mag.* (1981–). **Activities:** 1, 2; 20, 23, 45; 55, 57 **Addr.:** 925 Mix Ave. #2–0, Hamden, CT 06514.

Browder, Martha Cline Holsoinger (D. 31, 1913, Harrisonburg, VA) HS Libn., Chesterfield Cnty., VA, 1970–78; HS Libn., Waynesboro HS, 1955–70; HS Libn., Meadowbrook HS, 1970–78; Tchr., McGaheysville HS, McIntire HS, 1936–50; HS Libn., Scottsvill HS, 1950–1951. **Educ.:** Madison Univ., 1930–34, BS (Hist., Eng.); William and Mary Coll., 1947, (Lib. Sci.); Univ. of Chicago, Sum. 1948, (Lib. Sci.); Univ. of VA, 1959–63, MEd, (AV). **Orgs.:** VA LA: Ch., Sch. Lib. Sect. (1968–69); Mem. Com. for ALA (1966–68). ALA: Del. (1968–69). Sch. Lib. Assn. of VA Ed Assn.: ALA Mem. Ch. (1967–69). VA Educ. Assn.: Del. (1946–48, 1966). Albemarle Educ. Assn.: Secy. (1949). Natl. Educ. Assn.: Del. (1968). **Activities:** 10; 21, 48 **Addr.:** 1915 Park Road, Waynesboro, VA 22980.

Brower, June B. (Jl. 12, 1937, East Orange, NJ) Dir., Dev. Srvs., Syracuse Univ., 1978; Dir., Educ. Resrc. Ctr., Syracuse, 1974–78. **Educ.:** Amer. Univ., 1959, MA (Comm.); Syracuse Univ., 1963, MA (Educ.); 1969, MLS. **Orgs.:** ASIS. Assn. Info. Mgrs. ALA. **Activities:** 12; 17, 28, 38; 59, 63, 93 **Addr.:** Development Services, 820 Comstock Ave., Syracuse, NY 13210.

Brown, Alberta L. (Ja 9, 1894, Chicago, IL) Retired; Catlgr., Council Bluffs, IA. Pub. Lib., 1920–24; Head Libn., Upjohn Co., 1941–59; Libn., H.A. Brassert Co., 1939–40; Head Libn., St. Mary's Col. 1933–38; Head Catlgr., Univ. of ND-Grand Forks, 1929–33; Head Libn., Creighton Univ., 1925–29; Assoc. Prof., West. MI Univ. Lib. Sc., 1963–70. **Educ.:** Tabor Coll., AB (Hist.); Univ. of WI, 1924–25, lib. cert.; Univ. of IA, 1921, lib. cert. **Orgs.:** ALA. SLA: Pres. (1957–58). Cncl. of Natl. LA, (1958–59); various positions since 1951. Altrusa Club: Pres. (1949–51). **Honors:** Upjohn Co., Upjohn Awd., 1954; SLA, Hall of Fame Awd., 1961; Beta Phi Mu, 1977. **Pubns.:** Jt. Auth., *Scientific and Technical Libraries* 1964; 2d ed. (1972); "Planning the New Library", *SL* (1958); "Special Librarianship in the United States", *Review of Docum.* (1959); "Survey of Translation Activity in the United States and Canada", *Special Libraries*, 53: 34-36 (1962); "Special Libraries", *MI Challenge* (1965). **Activities:** 11, 12; 20, 24, 26; 64, 80, 87 **Addr.:** 1400 N. Drake Rd., Apt. 247, Kalamazoo, MI 49007.

Brown, Atlanta Thomas (O. 30, 1931, Bennettsville, SC) Head Libn., Newark HS, 1981–; Head Libn., Pierre S. duPont HS, 1963–; Libn., Richmond City Schs., 1958–63; Libn., Columbia City Schs., 1953–58. **Educ.:** SC State Coll., 1949–53, BS (LS); Univ. of WI, 1963, MS (LS). **Orgs.:** ALA. DE Sch. Lib. Media Assn.: Pres. (1977–78). DE State Adv. Cncl. on Libs.: Secy. (1971–75). Delta Kappa Gamma Socty. Intl. AAUW. **Honors:** NAACP Mem. Dr. Awd., 1979. **Pubns.:** "Activity During Story Hour," *Wilson Lib. Bltn.* (Apr. 1958). **Activities:** 10; 17, 31, 32 **Addr.:** 4502 Pickwick Dr., Limestone Gardens, Wilmington, DE 19808.

Brown, Barbara Elizabeth (My. 27, 1933, Montreal, PQ) Head, Cat. Sect., Lib. of Parliament, 1976–, Cat., 1958–76. **Educ.:** McGill Univ., 1949–53, BA (Lang.), 1957–58, BLS; Univ. of Toronto, 1966–68, MLS. **Orgs.:** Can. LA. ALA. Can. Assn. Info. Sci. Assn. Adv. Sci. Tech. Doc. **Pubns.:** *Canadian Business and Economics: A Guide to Sources of Information* (1976); and 2d. ed. (1981); "Update to Canadian Business and Economics," *Can. Lib. Jnl.* (D. 1976, and F. 1978). **Addr.:** Technical Services Branch, Library of Parliament, Ottawa, ON K1A 0A9 Canada.

Brown, Barbara Jeanne (O. 9, 1941, Charles City, IA) Assoc. Dir., Prog. Resrch. Libs. Grp., Inc., 1980–; Asst. Univ. Libn., Gen. Reader Srvs., Princeton Univ., 1976–80; Head, Ref. and Pub. Srvs., WA and Lee Univ., 1971–76; Assoc. Libn., Ref. Dept., Cornell Univ., 1968–71. **Educ.:** IA State Univ., 1959–63, BS (Eng.); Columbia Univ., 1963–64, MS (LS); Cncl. on Lib. Resrcs., 1974–75 (Mgt. Intern Prog.). **Orgs.:** ALA: ACRL, *C & RL* Ed. Bd. (1980–), Pubns. Com. (1974–78); RASD, Bd. of Dirs. (Secy., 1976–78), Dartmouth Medal Com. (1980–81). **Honors:** WA and Lee Univ., Ring-Tum-Phi Awd., 1976. **Activities:** 1; 17, 34, 39 **Addr.:** Research Libraries Group, Inc., Jordan Quadrangle, Stanford, CA 94305.

Brown, Bruce B. (Je. 26, 1938, Flint, MI) Spec. Srvs. Libn., Corn Belt Lib. Syst., Lincoln Trail Libs. Syst., Lib. Srvs., for the Blind and Phys. Handcpd., 1979–. **Educ.:** Flint Cmnty. Jr. Coll., 1957–59, AA (Soc. Sci.); Univ. of MI, 1959–62, AB (Soc. Sci.); Wayne State Univ., 1978–79, MSLS; Inst. of Grntlgy., Wayne State Univ., 1978–79, Spec. Cert. **Orgs.:** CSLA: Treas. (1979–81). ALA. SLA. IL LA. **Honors:** Beta Phi Mu. **Activities:** 13; 24, 27, 34; 95-Grntlgy., 72 **Addr.:** CBLS/LTLS Library Services for the Blind and Physically Handicapped, 1809 West Hovey Ave., Normal, IL 61761.

Brown, Bruce McClave (Je. 11, 1917, New York, NY) Col. Libn., Colgate Univ., 1980–; Univ. Libn., 1959–80; Ref. Libn., 1948–59; Ref. Libn., Englewood (NJ) Free Pub. Lib., 1947–48; various positions in advert. and prtg., 1941–45. **Educ.:** Middlebury Coll., 1934–38, BA (Hist.); NY Univ., 1945–46, MA (Soc. Std.); Columbia Univ., 1946–47, BSLS. **Orgs.:** ALA. NY LA: Pres. (1970–71); various coms. Ctrl. NY Lib. Resrcs. Cncl.: Pres. (1972); Bd. (1967–73). Mid-York Lib. Syst.: Pres. (1978–79); Bd. (1974–83). Various nature and railroad orgs. **Activities:** 1, 9; 15, 39, 45; 74, 94 **Addr.:** Rd. 2, Earlville Rd. Box 167, Hamilton, NY 13346.

Brown, Carolyn P. Chief, User Srvs., Natl. Oceanic and Atmospheric Admn., 1977–; Chief, Information Services, Nat'l Bureau of Standards, 1975–77; Librarian, Naval Medical Research Inst., 1972–75; Librarian, Div. Computer Research and Technology, Nat'l Institutes of Health, 1968–72. **Educ.:** Univ. of MS, 1941–45, BA MA; Univ. of MD, 1967–68, MLS; Lib. Admn. Dev. Course, Univ. of MD., 1976; Various other courses and On-line training. **Orgs.:** ALA: Chair, Mars Measur. of Srv. Com. (Ch. 1978–80). SLA: Chair, Info. Tech. Div. (Ch. 1979–80). ASIS. Various other coms., orgs. AAAS. **Honors:** U.S. Dept. of Cmrce., Outstan. Performance, (1979); Cncl. on Lib. Resrc., Flwshp., (1977); Beta Phi Mu. **Pubns.:** "What is an Online Search?" *ONLINE* (J. 1980); "On-Line bibliographic retrieval systems", *Spec. Libs.* (Ap. 1977); "Use of Online bibliographic retrieval systems in science and technology libraries", Cncl. of Lib. *Resrc.* Rpt. (1978). **Activities:** 4; 17, 34, 39; 82 **Addr.:** Carolyn P. Brown, 3517 Chevy Chase Lake Dr., Chevy Chase, MD 20015.

Brown, Charles M. (O. 4, 1948, St. Louis, MO) Asst. Exec. Dir., Columbus Pub. Lib., 1980–; Asst. Dir. Head of Ctrl. Lib., Prince Wm. Pub. Lib., 1978–79; Branch Libn., D.C. Pub. Lib., 1974–78; Cmnty. Coord., Orange Pub. Lib., 1973; Branch Asst., Newark Pub. Lib., 1971–73; Branch Head, St. Louis Pub. Lib., 1969–71. **Educ.:** Rutgers Univ., 1971–73, BA (Eng.); Columbia Univ., 1973–74, MLS. **Orgs.:** ALA: JMRT/Mem. and Rel. Com. (1975–76); PLA/Litcy. and Lrng. Com. (1975–76); Mem. Com. (1979–80) Prog. Com. Natl. Conf. (1981–83). DC LA: JMRT afflt., Ch. (1975–79). OH LA. Urban League. Assn. for the Std. of Afro-Amer. Life and Hist. YMCA. **Activities:** 9; 17 **Addr.:** Public Library of Columbus and Franklin County, 28 S. Hamilton Rd., Columbus, OH 43213.

Brown, Christine (Je. 20, 1923, Springfield, TN) Dir., School Lib. Resrcs., State Dept. Educ. (TN), 1966–; Matls. Supvsr., Robertson City Sch. (TN), 1948–66; Tchr. **Educ.:** Mid. TN State Univ., 1945; Univ. TN, 1966. **Orgs.:** ALA. SELA. TN LA. TN Educ. Assn. Bus. and Prof. Women's Club. Natl. Educ. Assn. Springfield Fed. Women's Clubs. **Activities:** 13 **Addr.:** School Library Resources, State Dept. of Education, 111 Cordell Hull Bldg., Nashville, TN 37219.*

Brown, Clara D. (Ap. 13, 1905, Portland, OR) Retired, Serials Libn., LA State Univ. Lib., 1947–70; Circ. and Ref. Libn., WA State Univ. Lib., 1937–47. **Educ.:** Univ. WA, 1935, BA (Art); 1936–37, BA (Libnshp.); WA State Univ., 1943, MFA. **Orgs.:** ALA. LA LA. Baton Rouge LA. **Pubns.:** *Serials: Acquisition & Maintenance* (1976); *Serials: Past, Present and Future* (1980); "57 Ways of Keeping a Serials Librarian Happy," *Stechert Hafner News.* (1969); reprint of above, *Serials Libn.* (1967–77); "Computers the Monsters," *Stechert Hafner News* (1969). **Addr.:** 1180 Stanford Ave., Baton Rouge, LA 70808.

Brown, Curtis Leslie (My. 31, 1921, Vienna, Austria) Ed., *Abstract Bltn.*, Inst. of Paper Chem., Lawrence Univ. Afflt., 1956–; Biblgphr., & Assoc. Prof. and Actg. Libn., 1955–75; Ed., *Prev. Deter. Abstracts*, Natl. Resrch. Cncl., Natl. Acad. Sci., 1948–55. **Educ.:** Bolyai Univ., Cluj; Univ. of Vienna, 1945–47 (Phil., Math); Geo. Washington Univ., 1948–53, MS (Phys., Chem.); Lawrence Univ., Grad. Crs. (Symb. Logic and Ling.). **Orgs.:** ASIS: *Mgt. of Info. Actv.*, Nsltr. Ed. (1976–78). Amer. Socty. of Indxrs. Tech. Assn. of the Pulp and Paper Indus.: Com. on Info. Mgt. (1964–). **Honors:** Info. Sci. Abstracts, Cert. of Apprec., 1972. **Pubns.:** "Using the Computer to Store Type on Tape," *Reprodct. Review and Methods* (F. 1972); "Mechanized Information Retrieval for the Paper Industry," *Indian Pulp and Paper* (Jl. 1968); "Experiments in Centralized Literature Processing," *Tappi* (S. 1966); "Two Approaches to the Retrieval of Information from a Special Library," *Advncs. in Docum. and LS* (1957); "The Scientific Literature of Israel," *Jnl. of Chem. Educ.* (Je. 1957); other articles, numerous reviews. **Activities:** 12; 25, 30, 37; 57, 62, 75 **Addr.:** P.O. Box 1039, Appleton, WI 54912.

Brown, Dale W. (Jl. 21, 1932, Benton, KY) Lib. and Media Srvs. Supvsr., Alexandria City Pub. Schs., 1969–; Asst. Prof., Univ. MD, 1961–69; Instr., Wayne State Univ., 1958–61; Tchr., Libn., Livonia, MI, 1956–58; Instr., David Lipscomb Coll., 1954–56. **Educ.:** David Lipscomb Coll., 1949–53, BA (Sp.); Geo. Peabody Coll., 1954–55, MA (Educ. Admin.); Univ. MI, 1965, AMLS; Wayne State Univ., 1957–60, addtl. crs. **Orgs.:** ALA: Cncl. (1975–77); Budget Asm. (1975–76). Assn. for Lib. Srvcs. to Chld. AASL: Afflt. Asm. (VA Rep. 1976–79); Vice Ch., 1979–80; Bd. Dirs., 1980–82; Nom. Com. (1979–80); SS/Prog. Com. (1978–79); ByLaws Com. (Chmn., 1978–79). AECT: Cncl. (1976–77); Nom. Com. (1976–77). VA LA. Other orgs. Alexandria Sch. Admin. Alexandria Hist. Socty. Cable TV Adv. Cmsn.; Other orgs. **Honors:** Phi Delta Kappa. **Pubns.:** Jt. auth., *Elementary and Secondary Teachers Use ERIC* (1978); various articles. **Activities:** 10; 17, 24, 32; 63, 67, 75 **Addr.:** Educational Media Center, Alexandria City Public Schools, 3801 W. Braddock Rd., Alexandria, VA 22302.

Brown, David Carl (S. 30, 1929, Milwaukee, WI) Admin. Libn., Marine Corps Educ. Ctr. Lib., 1979–; Asst. Libn., 1965–79; LS Instr. Univ. WI, Whitewater, 1961–63; Libn., Milwaukee Pub. Lib., 1956–60. **Educ.:** Univ. WI, 1947–56, BS (Hist.); Rutgers Univ., 1957–58, MLS. **Orgs.:** ALA. Sierra Club. Toastmasters Intl. **Activities:** 1, 4; 17, 20, 29; 57, 74, 92 **Addr.:** J. C. Breckinridge Library, Education Center, MCDEC, Quantico, VA 22134.

Brown, Donald Raymond (N 19, 1930, Lebanon, PA) Coord., Matrls. Sel. Prog., State Lib. of PA, 1974–; Coord., Ref. and Inf. Srvs., 1970–74; Chief Ref. Libn., West. MI Univ., 1961–68; Ref. Libn., Detroit Pub. Lib., 1957–61. **Educ.:** Ursinus Col., 1948–52, AB (Hist.); Univ. of IL, Urbana, 1953–54, MA (Hist.); Univ. of WI, Madison, 1956–1957, MSLS. **Orgs.:** ALA: RASD, Secy., Ch. (1979–81); Hist. Sect., Ch. (1976); Ref. Sect. MI LA: Ch. (1965). Amer. Assn. for State and Local Hist. Socty. of Archit. Histns. **Honors:** Beta Phi Mu, 1957. **Pubns.:** "Michigan Bibliography: 1958", *MI Hist.* (1959); "Michigan Bibliography: 1959", *MH* (1960); "Jonathan B. Turner and the Land Grant Idea", *Jrl. of the IL State Hist. Socty.* (1962). **Activities:** 12, 13; 15, 39; 55, 57, 85 **Addr.:** State Library of PA, Library Services Division, Box 1601, Harrisburg, PA 17105.

PROFESSIONAL ACTIVITIES: Institutions: 1. Acad. lib.; 2. Arch.; 3. Assn.; 4. Fed./Gvt. lib.; 5. Inst. lib.; 6. Mfr./Suppl.; 7. Milit. lib.; 8. Musm.; 9. Pub. lib.; 10. Sch. lib.; 11. Sch. of lib. sci.; 12. Spec. lib.; 13. State lib.; 14. (other). **Functions/Activities:** 15. Acq./Col. dev.; 16. Adult srvs.; 17. Admin.; 18. Apprais.; 19. Archit./Bldgs.; 20. Cat./Class.; 21. Chld. srvs.; 22. Circ.; 23. Cons./Pres.; 24. Consult.; 25. Cont. ed.; 26. Educ. lib. sci.; 27. Ext. srvs.; 28. Fund/Grants; 29. Gvt. pubs.; 30. Indx./Abs.; 31. Instr. lib. use; 32. Media srvs.; 33. Micro.; 34. Netwks./Coop.; 35. Persnl.; 36. PR; 37. Publshg.; 38. Recs. mgt.; 39. Ref. srvs.; 40. Repro.; 41. Resrch.; 42. Review.; 43. Secur.; 44. Serials; 45. Spec. col.; 46. Tech. srvs.; 47. Trustees/Bds.; 48. YA srvs.; 49. (other).

Brown, Donna M. (Ja. 5, 1943, Lewisburg, KY) Asst. Dir., Lib. Srvs., Stockton-San Joaquin Cty. Pub. Lib., 1981–; Branch Coord., 1979–81; Branch Libn., 1978–79; Pub. Lib. Consult., VA State Lib., 1973–78; Head Libn., Amherst Cnty. (VA) Pub. Lib., 1970–73. **Educ.:** West. KY State Coll. 1961–65, BS (Hist.); Univ. of KY, 1969–70, MLS. **Orgs.:** ALA. CA LA: Standards & Lib. Dev. Com. (1980, 1981). VA LA: Nom. Com. (1976); Pub. Lib. Sect., Ch. (1973); Secy. (1972). SELA. AAUW. Pilot Intl. **Activities:** 9; 17, 27 **Addr.:** 1249 Stratford Circle #13, Stockton, CA 95207.

Brown, Doris Rahe (D. 26, 1943, Dyersville, IA) Assoc. Dir., Tech. Srvs., DePaul Univ. Lib., Chicago, 1976–; Biblgphr., Acq. Dept., Univ. of CT, 1971–76. **Educ.:** Rosary Coll., 1961–65, BA (Span./Por.); Univ. of WI, Madison, 1968–69, MA (Latin Amer. Area Studies), 1970–71, MA (Lib. Sci.). **Orgs.:** ALA; LAMA: Stats. for Tech. Srvs. Com. (1978–82), Ch. (1980-82); RTSD: Tech. Srvs. Admin. of Smaller Resrch. Libs. Discuss. Grp., Ch. (1978–79). IL ACRL: Exec. Bd., Dir.-at Large (1979–81); Contin. Educ. Com. (1977–79); Ch. (1978–79). IL OCLC Users Group; Exec. Bd., Mem.-at large (1977–79); Contin. Educ. Com. (1977–80), Ch. (1979–80). SALALM: Exec. Bd. (1975–76); Com. on Bibl., Vice-ch. (1974–75); Com. on Reporting Bibl. Activities (1973–75). **Pubns.:** Jt. auth., "From Purchase Order to Processing Slip on OCLC", *Lib. Jnl.* (O. 15, 1979); "Putting the 'LC' on OCLC: Illinois Reclassification on OCLC", *Wilson Lib. Bull.* (Ap. 1979); "Retention of Dewey Decimal Classification at DePaul University Library," *ERIC Reports* (ED 160 057). **Activities:** 1; 17, 25, 46; 54 **Addr.:** 2741 Simpson, Evanston, IL 60201.

Brown, Dorothy Eady (My. 5, 1925, Crystal Springs, MS) Head, Bus. Lib., Univ. of AL, 1969–; Readers Srv. Libn., New Eng. Coll., 1967–69; Readers Srv. Libn., Florida South. Coll., 1965–67; Head, Chem. Lib., Univ. of NC, 1964–65. **Educ.:** Millsaps Coll., 1943–46, BA (Hist.); Florida State Univ., 1960–61, MSLS. **Orgs.:** ALA: ACRL, Mem. Com. (1978–80); RASD, Isadore Mudge Cit. Com. (1979–80). SLA: AL Chap. (Pres., 1976–77). AL LA: Coll., Univ., and Spec. Lib. Div. (Ch., 1975–76). AAUW: Tuscaloosa Branch, Intl. Rel. Com. (Ch.); Altrusa: Treas. **Activities:** 1; 17, 31, 39; 54, 59, 94 **Addr.:** 3-C River Road Apts., Tuscaloosa, AL 35401.

Brown, Edna Earle (D. 31, 1923, Nashville, TN) Assoc. Dir. of Libs., Assoc. Prof., Georgia South. Coll., 1969–; Head, Acq. Dept., Univ. of FL, 1964–69; Serials Libn., Auburn Univ., 1952–64; Actg. Head, Serials Sect., Duke Univ., 1946–48. **Educ.:** George Peabody Coll. of Vanderbilt Univ., 1942–45, BA (Hist.); Univ. of IL, 1945–46, BSLS. **Orgs.:** ALA: ACRL; LAMA; RTSD. Southeastern LA: Exec. Bd. (1960–62). GA LA: RTSD (Secy., 1977–79); Exhibit Com. (1971–73). AAUP. AAUW. Pi Gamma Mu. **Honors:** Beta Phi Mu. **Activities:** 1; 15, 46 **Addr.:** Georgia Southern College Library, Statesboro, GA 30460.

Brown, Elinor D. (Ap. 18, 1924, Millsboro, DE) Lib. Media Spec., Linden Elem. Sch., 1970–; Head, Readrs. Srvs., Oak Ridge Pub. Lib., 1950–55; Catalgr., Drew Univ. Lib., 1949–50; Catalgr., Dickinson Coll. Lib., 1947–49. **Educ.:** Mary Washington Coll., 1942–46, AB (Eng.); Drexel Inst. of Tech., 1946–47, BS (LS); Univ. of TN, crs. in LS, 1968–77. **Orgs.:** ALA. TN LA: Nom. Com. (1979–80). E. TN LA. NEA. TN Educ. Assn. E. TN Educ. Assn. **Pubns.:** "Media Education Leads the Fight for Truth and Justice," *AV Instr.* (O. 1979). **Activities:** 10; 15, 21, 31 **Addr.:** Linden Elementary School, Robertsville Rd., Oak Ridge, TN 37830.

Brown, Elizabeth E. (Ag. 29, 1921, Charlotte, MI) Info. Retrieval Spec., IBM, 1969–; Resrch. Libn., 1953–69; Rpt. Indxr., Bakelite Co., 1950–52; Info. Spec., Enjay Co., 1943–50. **Educ.:** Albion Coll., 1939–43, BA (Chem., Med. Lang.); Pratt Inst., 1952–53, MLS. **Orgs.:** SLA: Eng. Div. (Secy./Tres. 1968–70). NY Chap., Tech. Sci. Grp. (Ch. 1970–71). Hudson Valley Chap. (Pres. 1974–75). ALA. ASIS. Westchester LA. Amer. Chem. Socty. AAAS. Natl. Micro. Assn. **Activities:** 12; 15, 17, 39; 56, 93 **Addr.:** IBM Corp - DPH706 Info Center, 1133 Westchester Ave., White Plains, NY 10604.

Brown, Eva R. (D. 31, 1927, Magdeburg, Germany) Coord., IL Coop., Chicago Lib. Syst., 1975; Cncl. Libn., IL Reg. Lib. Cncl., 1972–75. **Educ.:** Roosevelt Univ., 1970, BA (Grmn.); Rosary Coll., 1970–72, MLS. **Orgs.:** ALA: ASCLA/MLCS, Pub. Com. (Ch., 1978), Legis. Com. SLA. ASIS. IL LA. **Pubns.:** "Chicago Library System," *IL Libs.* (S. 1979); "Special Librarians, the Original Cooperators," *IL Libs.* (Spr. 1980); Nsltr. Ed., *Chicago Lib. Syst. Comm.* (1976–); Co-Ed., *Union List of Serials Holdings in Illinois Special Libraries* (1977). **Activities:** 14-Multi. Lib. Coop.; 24, 25, 34 **Addr.:** Chicago Library System, Interlibrary Cooperation Office, 425 N. Michigan Ave., 13th Floor, Chicago, IL 60611.

Brown, Forrest E. (Ag. 2, 1928, Princeton, MN) Lib. Dir., St. Olaf Coll., 1961–; Lib. Dir., Cornell Coll., 1956–61; Cat. Libn., Lawrence Univ., 1954–56. **Educ.:** Hamline Univ., 1946–50, BA (Hist., Phil.); Univ. of MN, 1950–54, MA (Hist.), MSLS. **Orgs.:** ALA: ACRL. MN LA: Acad. and Resrch. Lib. Div. (Pres., 1978–79). **Activities:** 1; 15, 17, 45; 55, 57, 66 **Addr.:** Rolvaag Memorial Library, St. Olaf College, Northfield, MN 55057.

Brown, Freddiemae E. (O. 16, 1928, Racine, WI) Asst. Prof., Wayne State Univ., 1974–; Asst. Dir., Branch Srvs., Detroit Pub. Lib., 1970–74, Chief, Dept., 1968–70, Chief, Div., 1966–68. **Educ.:** Fisk Univ., 1947–51, BA (Soclgy.); Univ. of MI, 1956–59, AMLS, 1977–, Doct. Cand. **Orgs.:** AALS. AALL. ALA: Ref. and Subscrpn. Bks. (1966–70); PLA, Educ. for Pub. Libns. Com. (1978–79). MI LA: Dist. III (Secy., 1966–68). Women's Natl. Bk. Assn.: Secy. (1968–70). Univ. of MI, Sch. of LS, Alum. Assn. Wayne State Univ., Div. of LS Alum. Assn. Fisk Univ., Alum. Assn. Wayne State Univ. Phylon Socty. **Honors:** Higher Educ. Act, Title II B, Flwshp., 1973; Wayne State Univ., Pres. Awd. for Excel. in Tchg., 1977. **Activities:** 9, 11; 16, 17, 21; 50 **Addr.:** 315 Kresge Library, Wayne State University, Detroit, MI 48202.

Brown, Gerald Robert (My. 21, 1937, Rossburn, MB, Can) Chief Libn., Winnipeg Sch. Div. #1, 1977–, Conslt., Ref., 1967–76, Catlgr., 1965–67; Tchr., 1956–65. **Educ.:** Brandon Coll., 1955–56, Cert., (Tch.); Univ. of MB, 1958–65, BA B. Educ.; West. MI. Univ., 1965–68, MS (LS); Univ. of MB, 1966–72, M. Educ. **Orgs.:** ALA: AASL. AECT. Assn. for Media and Tech. in Can. Can. LA: Can. Sch. Libn. Assn. Various other orgs. **Honors:** Beta Phi Mu. **Pubns.:** "B.E.W.A.R.E.," *Moccasin Telegraph* (Win. 1979); "AMTEC Special Interest Group: Media Utilization Personnel," *Media Message* (Sum. 1979); "Bibliotherapy: A New Way for Home Economics Teachers and Librarians to Help Kids," *Jnl of MB Home Econ. Tchrs. Assn.* (Ap. 1979); Comp., *AMTEC Communications Directory 1978*, (My. 1978); Various other rpts. and articles. **Activities:** 10; 17, 24, 35; 63, 69, 89 **Addr.:** 3003-55 Nassau St. N, Winnipeg, MB R3L 2G8 Canada.

Brown, Gloria Primm (O., 1941, Williamson, WV) Prog. Assoc., Carnegie Corp., 1968–, Prog. Asst., 1977–78, Admin. Asst., Libn., 1969–77, Supvsr., Files, Libn., 1968–69; Chld. Libn., DC Pub. Lib., 1963–68. **Educ.:** Howard Univ., 1959–63, BA (Eng.); Columbia Univ., 1971–72, MLS (Chld. Srvs.). **Orgs.:** ALA: Cnclr. (1978–82); Plng. and Budget Asm. (1979–80); Constn. and Bylaws Com. (1980–82); U.S. Missn. (ALA Rep., 1978–82). NY Black Libns. Caucus. Cnsrtm. of Fndn. Libs. Assn. of Black Women in Higher Educ.: Pres. (1981–82); Bd. (1979–). Frnds. of the New York City Comsn. on the Status of Women. Assn. of Black Fndn. Execs. Natl. Black Child Dev. Inst. **Honors:** NY Black Libns. Caucus, Achvmt., 1979. **Pubns.:** Contrib., *ALA World Encyclopedia of Library and Information Services* (1980). **Activities:** 3; 28; 63 **Addr.:** Carnegie Corporation of New York, 437 Madison Ave., New York, NY 10022.

Brown, Grace T. (F. 1, 1926, New York, NY) Head, Circ., Head Rsv. Libn., Hofstra Univ., 1972–; Head, Circ., Wantagh Pub. Lib., 1966–72. **Educ.:** Fordham Univ., 1972–75, BA, magna cum laude (Hum.); Long Island Univ., 1975–76, MLS, 1976–80, MPA (Pub. Admin.). **Orgs.:** ALA. NY LA: Coll. and Univ. Lib. Sect., Prog. Com. (1979). Nassau Cnty. LA: Pres., VP (1974–75); Com. on Exec. Bd. Procs. (1976–); Coll. and Univ. Div., Constn. and Bylaws Com. (Ch., 1974), Nom. Com. (Ch., 1977), Legis. Com. (Ch., 1974); Persnl. Policy Com. (Ch., 1973); various coms. **Honors:** Alpha Sigma Lambda, 1975. **Pubns.:** *To Find A Book: How to Use the Hofstra University Library* (1973, 1977, 1980); *Training Guide for Student Aides* (1973); *How to Find Articles in Periodicals and Newspapers* (1974); "Brief Encounters" trng. film (1971); *Newsletter* monthly (1975–76). **Activities:** 1; 22 **Addr.:** Hofstra University Library, Hempstead, NY 11550.

Brown, Harold L. (S. 6, 1952, Taber, AB) Dir., Deptl. Support Branch, Admin. Srvs. Div., AB Gvt. Srvs., 1981–; Dir., Recs. Mgt., AB Prov. Gvt., 1976–81; Recs. and Micro. Anal., Can. Dept. of Indian and North. Affairs, 1974–76, Admin. Srvs. Branch, 1971–74. **Educ.:** Inst. of Cert. Recs. Mgrs., 1979–; other courses in recs. mgt. **Orgs.:** ASIS: West. Can. Chap. (Secy., 1979–). Natl. Micro. Assn. Assn. of Recs. Mgrs. and Admin. Can. Micro. Assn. Can. Inst. of Mgt. **Pubns.:** "Total Information Systems Design," *ARMA Recs. Mgt. Qtly.* (Ap. 1981). **Activities:** 14-Prov. Recs. & Info. Srv.; 17, 33, 38; 56 **Addr.:** Alberta Government Services, Park Sq., 10001 Bellamy Hill, Edmonton, AB T5J 3C1 Canada.

Brown, Harriet Baltimore (S. 13, 1911, Gendale, MD) Retired. Libn., Ethical Cult., 1973–76; Supvsr., Bd. of Educ., New York, 1948–73; Chlds. Libn., New York Pub. Lib., 1937–48. **Educ.:** Hunter Coll., 1930–34, AB (Educ.); Columbia Univ., 1935–37, BLS. **Orgs.:** Cncl. on Interracial Bks.: Bd. of Trustees (1979–). New York Black Libns. Caucus: Pres. (1979–81). Schomburg Lib.: Bd. of Trustees (1979). New York Lib. Assn.: VP (1976). NAACP: Afro-Amer. Com. (1978–). Coretta Scott Awd: Exec. Com. (1970–). St. Philips Church: Anl. Luncheon (Ch. 1974–). **Addr.:** 328 Central Park West, New York, NY 10025.

Brown, Jack E. (Mr. 1, 1914, Edmonton, AB) Assoc. Prof., McGill Univ. Grad. Sch. of LS, 1978–; Dir., Can. Inst. for Sci. and Tech. Info., Nat. Res. Cncl., 1974–77; Dir., Natl. Sci. Lib., 1963–74; Chief Libn., Nat. Res. Cncl. of Can., 1957–63; 1st Asst., Sci. and Tech. Div., NY Pub. Lib., 1947–57; Asst. Libn., Brown Univ., 1946–47; Lib. Asst., Sci. and Tech. Div., NY Pub. Lib., 1942–45; Ref. Libn., Edmonton Pub. Lib., 1940–42. **Educ.:** Univ. of AB, 1934–38, BA; McGill Univ., 1938–39, BLS; Univ. of Chicago, 1939–40, MA (LS). **Orgs.:** Nat. Res. Cncl.: Assoc. Com. on Sci. Info. (Secy., 1958–70). Can. Nat. Com. for FID: Secy. (1962–70). Intl. Fed. for Documtn.: VP (1964–68). ALA: Cnclr. (1961–64); ACRL (Dir.-at-Lg., 1961–65); ALA/Can. LA Liaison Com. (Ch., 1963–64). UNESCO Intl. Gvtl. Conf. for UNISIST. UNESCO Adv. Com. for Gen. Info. Prog. OECD Grp. on STI Policy. **Honors:** Waterloo Univ., LLD, 1965; McMaster Univ., LLD, 1978; Can. Assn. Spec. Libs. and Info. Srvs., Awd. for Spec. Libnshp. in Can., 1979; Can. LA, Outstan. Srv. to Libnshp. Awd., 1979. **Pubns.:** "L'IST au Canada," *La Revue de l'AUPELF* (Je. 1978); "Information Users versus Information Systems," *Can. Lib. Jnl.* (D. 1978); "Developing SDI Services: Canadian Contribution to UNISIST," *Can. Lib. Jnl.* (D. 1975); "L'organisation de la documentation scientific et technique au Canada," *Réseaux et Systèmes de Documentation* (1975); "National Science Library of Canada," *Encyc. of Lib. and Info. Sci.* (1976); various articles. **Activities:** 4, 11; 17, 19, 24; 75, 91 **Addr.:** 417 Meadow Dr., Ottawa, ON K1K 0M3 Canada.

Brown, James Wilson (S. 18, 1913, Hanford, WA) Ed., *Educ. Media Yearbook*, Libs. Unlimited, Inc., 1973–; Dean and Prof., Instr. Tech., San Jose State Univ., 1953–79; Dir., Film Ctr., Univ. of WA, 1948–53; Info. Spec., Marshall Plan in Europe, Paris, 1951–52; Asst. Prof., Instr. Tech., Syracuse Univ., 1947–48; Dir., Bur. of Tchg. Mtrls., Richmond (VA), 1941–42, 1945–46. **Educ.:** Univ. of WA, 1931–33; Ctrl. WA Univ., 1933–35, BA; Univ. of Chicago, 1939–41, MA, 1945–47, PhD. **Orgs.:** ALA: AASL. AECT: Pres. (1951–53); Found. Bd. CA Media/Lib. Educators Assn. **Honors:** Disting. Alum., Ctrl. WA Univ., 1973; AECT, Disting. Srv. Awd., 1977; AECT, Spec. Srv. Awd., 1975. **Pubns.:** Jt. auth., *Administering Educational Media* (1965, 1971); Jt. auth., *AV Instruction: Technology, Media, and Methods* (5 eds., 1959–1980); Jt. auth., *AV Instructional Technology Manual for Independent Study* (6 eds., 1957–77); Various other reports, studies, articles. **Activities:** 1; 26, 32, 37; 57, 67, 93 **Addr.:** 8413 Chenin Blanc Drive, San Jose, CA 95135.

Brown, Jean Isobel (Ag. 27, 1927, Montreal, PQ) Volun. Consult., Potton Pub. Lib., 1975–; Libn., Protestant Sch. Bd. of Grt. Montreal, 1960–74; Asst. Libn., Shawinigan Water & Power Co., 1958–60; Ref. Libn., Toronto Pub. Lib., 1957–58. **Educ.:** Sir George Williams Univ., 1945–55, BA (Soc. Sci.); McGill Univ., 1956–57, BLS; 1970–72, MLS. **Orgs.:** Can. LA. PQ LA: 1968–69, Pres. Young Peoples; 1969–70, VP; 1970–71, Pres.; 1971–72 Past Pres. PQ Assn. of Sch. Libns.: VP. Corp. of Prof. Libns. of PQ. Montreal Musm. of Fine Arts. Can. Amateur Msc. Makers; Can. Wildlife Assn. **Pubns.:** "Support Systems for School Libraries in England," *Argus* (S.-O. 1979). **Activities:** 9, 10; 17, 20, 24 **Addr.:** #33, 4865 Queen Mary Rd., Montreal, PQ H3W 1X1 Canada.

Brown, Jovana J. (D. 8, 1937, Los Angeles, CA) Dean, Lib. Srvs., Evergreen State Coll., 1974–; Head, Ref., Univ. CA, Santa Cruz, 1970–74; Ast. Ref. and Docum. Libn., Univ. San Francisco, 1965–66. **Educ.:** Univ., CA, Riverside, 1958–59, BA (Pol. Sci.); Univ. CA, Berkeley, 1959–61, MA (Pol. Sci.); 1964–65, MLS, 1966–70, PhD. **Orgs.:** ALA: Nom. Com. (1976–77); ACRL/Legis. Com., (1979–81). WA LA: Exec. Bd. Dir., (1977–79). Career Dev. for Women Libns.: Adv. Cncl., (1977–). Amer. Cncl. on Educ.: Natl. Ident. Prog., (1979). **Activities:** 1, 11; 17, 26, 39; 54, 66, 92 **Addr.:** Library 2300, The Evergreen State College, Olympia, WA 98505.

Brown, June Evelyn (Je. 29, 1925, Ipswich, Suffolk, Eng) Univ. Libn., Alfred Univ., 1977; Acq. Libn., 1970–77. **Educ.:** Alfred Univ., 1967–69, BA (Frgn. Lang.); SUNY, Geneseo, 1969–70, MLS; Leicester Coll. of Arts and Sci., Eng., 1943–45, Nat. Dsgn. Dip. (Indus. Dsgn.). **Orgs.:** ALA. Natl. LA. NY LA. AAUP. **Honors:** Beta Phi Mu, 1970. **Pubns.:** "Bindery Records for the Academic Library," *Lib. Scene* (Mr. 1976). **Activities:** 1; 15, 17, 45; 55, 65, 67 **Addr.:** Herrick Memorial Library, Alfred University, Alfred, NY 14802.

Brown, Lucille Gregor (My 15, 1927, Ottumwa, IA) Prog. Admin. II, Lib. Srvs., Mt. Diablo Unfd. Sch. Dist., 1969–; Dist. Libn., Burlingame City Sch. Dist., 1968–69; HS Libn., Dos Pueblos HS, 1965–68. **Educ.:** Coe Coll., 1945–50, BA (Lib. Arts); Univ. of South. CA, 1962–67, MALS; Univ. of CA, Santa Barbara, 1968, (Admin.). **Orgs.:** CA Media and Lib. Educ. Assn.: Pres. ALA: AASL. Educ. Congs. of CA. Educ. Innovation and Plng. Comm.: CA Commsn. (1975–79). **Pubns.:** *Core Media Collection for Secondary Schools*, (1975); *Core Media Collection for Elementary Schools, 1978*, (1979). **Activities:** 10; 17, 26, 42; 63, 67, 78 **Addr.:** Mt. Diablo Unified School District, 1936 Carlotta Dr., Concord, CA 94519.

Brown, Lucille W. (S. 10, 1924, New York, NY) Libn., Albany Coll. of Pharm., 1980–; Circ. Libn., Hudson Valley Cmnty. Coll., 1979–80; Catlgr., Asst. Prof., Union Coll., 1973–79; Head, Circ. and ILL, Instr., Siena Coll., 1972–73. **Educ.:** Hunter Coll., 1942–46, BA (Labor Eco., Pol. Sci.); SUNY, Albany, 1969–71, MLS (LS). **Orgs.:** NY LA. Cap. Dist. Lib. Cncl. Socty. of Bibliophiles. Oral Hist. Assn. Other orgs. **Honors:** Beta Phi Mu, 1971; Union Coll., Hum. Fac. Dev. Com. Awds, 1975, 1979. **Pubns.:** "Fathers and Sons....A View from Eastern Europe," *Oral Hist. Review* (1977); "Municipal Mediation Plans," *Univ. IL Bltn.* (1946). **Activities:** 1; 20, 22, 41; 66, 85, 92 **Addr.:** 1157 Highland Pk. Rd., Schenectady, NY 12309.

Special Subjects/Services: 50. Adult educ.; 51. Advert./Mktg.; 52. Aerosp.; 53. Agric.; 54. Area std.; 55. Arts/Hum.; 56. Autom.; 57. Bibl./Prtg.; 58. Bio. sci.; 59. Bus./Fin.; 60. Chem.; 61. Copyrt.; 62. Documtn.; 63. Educ.; 64. Engin.; 65. Env.; 66. Eth. grps.; 67. Film; 68. Food/Nutr.; 69. Geneal.; 70. Geo.; 71. Geol.; 72. Handcpd.; 73. Hist.; 74. Int. frdm.; 75. Info. sci.; 76. Insr.; 77. Law; 78. Legis.; 79. Math./Comp. sci.; 80. Med.; 81. Metals; 82. Nat. resrcs.; 83. Newsp.; 84. Nuc. sci.; 85. Oral hist.; 86. Petr./Energy; 87. Pharm.; 88. Phys./Astr./Math.; 89. Readg.; 90. Relig.; 91. Sci./Tech.; 92. Soc. sci.; 93. Telecom.; 94. Transp.; 95. (other).

Brown, Luther (Mr. 9, 1912, Swain Cnty., NC) Emeritus Prof. and Dean, of Lrng. Resrcs. Srvs., and Ch., Dept. Lib. & AV Educ., St. Cloud State Univ., 1958–, Prof., Dir., AV Educ. and Curric. Mtrls., 1956–58; Pres., Northwestern State Univ., 1955–56; Dir., Tchr. Educ. and Placement Srv., Northeastern State Univ., 1946–55; Tchr., Dewey, OK, 1935–42. **Educ.:** Northeastern State Univ. (OK), 1935, BS; OK State Univ., 1938, MS; Vanderbilt Univ., George Peabody Coll., 1953, PhD. **Orgs.:** AECT: Nom. Com. (1974). ALA. MN LA. MN Assn. Sch. Libns. Natl. Educ. Assn. MN Educ. Media Assn. Assn. for Supvsn. and Curric. Dev. Natl. Socty. for the Study of Educ. **Honors:** MN LA, Libn. of Yr. **Activities:** 1, 11; 17, 26, 32 **Addr.:** Nisswa, MN 56468.

Brown, Mabel C. (N. 13, 1932, Ottawa, ON) Dir., Lib. Srvs., Ottawa Civic Hosp., 1970–, Nursing Libn., 1966–70; Nursing Libn., Toronto West. Hosp., 1960–66; Nursing Instr., Toronto E. Gen. Hosp., 1957–59. **Educ.:** Toronto Univ., 1956–60, BSc (Nursing); Ottawa Civic Hosp., 1950–53, Dip. (Nursing); Toronto Univ., 1956–57, Cert. (Nursing Educ.), 1965–66, BLS. **Orgs.:** Med. LA: Nursing Lib. Grp. (Ch., 1964–65). CHLA: Ottawa/Hull Chap. (Ch., 1976–77). ON Hosp. Assn.: Reg. 9, Lib. Sect. (Ch., 1978–79). Toronto Bus. and Prof. Women's Club: Bursary (1959). **Pubns.:** *The Library Service Needs of the Eighteen Educational Programs in the Ottawa Civic Hospital* (N. 1979); "Giving Seniors a Choice of Services and Facilities," *ON Med. Review* (Ja. 1981); "The Multiple Services of a Hospital Library," *Dimensions In Hlth. Srv.* (Jl. 1976); "The Library and Nursing Education," *The Can. Nurse* (Ap. 1964). **Activities:** 12; 17, 20, 39; 80, 92 **Addr.:** Library Services, Dr. G.S. Williamson Health Sciences Library, Ottawa Civic Hospital, 1053 Carling Ave., Ottawa, ON K1Y 4E9 Canada.

Brown, Sr. Margaret Rose (My. 5, 1911, Germantown, PA) Biblther., Libn., Mt. St. Joseph Convent, 1973–; Libn., St. Thomas More Paroch. Sch., 1967–69; Cat., 1941–43; Asst. Libn, Cecilian AS Acad., 1938–40. **Educ.:** Chestnut Hill Coll., 1928–32, AB (Eng.); Villanova Univ.; Catholic Univ., 1950–58, MA (Rel. Educ.); Chestnut Hill Coll, 1978–, Cert., (C. Educ.). **Orgs.:** Catholic LA: HS Sect., Arch. Sect., Neumann Chap. (1968–). Church and Synagogue LA. Chestnut Hill Coll. Alum. Assn.; Wyck Guide Com.; Irish–Amer. Intercult. Inst.; Germn. Hist. Socty. **Honors:** Kappa Gamma Pi, 1932. **Pubns.:** Contrib., *Sisters Book of St. Joseph of Philadelphia,* 1950; "God's Image in the Media," *Catholic Lib. World* (1975); "The Golden Griffin," *Chestnut Hill Coll. Alum. Assn.* (1964); "Teaching Baptism through Scripture", *Orate Fratres* (1951). **Activities:** 2, 12; 23, 37, 41; 55, 57, 90 **Addr.:** Mt. St. Joseph Convent, Chestnut Hill, Philadelphia, PA 19118.

Brown, Mary Ann (Ag. 10, 1936, Lyles-Wrigley, TN) Chief, Readrs. Srvcs., Duke Univ. Med. Cntr. Lib., 1969–; Ext. Lib. Admin., 1968–72; Ref. Libn., 1965–68; Pub. Srvcs. Libn., A W Calhoun Med. Lib., Emory Univ., 1962–65. **Educ.:** Geo. Peabody Coll., 1954–58, BS (Bio.); 1958–59, MA (LS); US Pub. Hlth. Srvcs. Prog., Emory Univ. 1961–62, Med. Lib. Intern. **Orgs.:** Med. LA: Rcrt. Com. (1968–72); Mid-Atl. Reg. Grp. (Prog. Ch., 1976). Reg. Med. Lib. Prog.: Reg. IV, Duke Rep. to Reg. Adv. Cncl. (1975–); ILL Com. (1976–78); Exec. Bd. (Resrce. Lib. Rep., 1977); Vice Ch., 1978–79; Ch. (1979–80). SLA: NC SLA Bltn. (Co-ed., 1973–74); NC Chap. (VP, 1976–77). **Activities:** 1, 12; 17, 34, 39; 58, 80 **Addr.:** Medical Center Library, Box 3702, Duke University Medical Center, Durham, NC 27710.

Brown, Mary Grace Hawkins (O. 22, 1915, Petersburg, VA) Media Srvcs. Dir., Med. Lib., Petersburg Gen. Hosp., 1956–; Libn., Bolling Jr. HS, 1943–63. **Educ.:** Mary Washington Coll., 1934–38, BS; Univ. of VA, 1940–41 (LS); William and Mary, 1947 (LS); Columbia Univ., Summer 1958 (LS). **Orgs.:** VA LA: Jr. Mem. RT (Pres., 1946); Dist. D (Pres., 1955). Petersburg Tchrs. Assoc.: Pres. (1955); VP (1960–66). Quota Club Intl.: VP (1977–78); Secy. 1975–77). **Honors:** Various civic awards. **Pubns.:** "Epidemics and Therapy," *VA Med. Monthly* (D. 1959); "Dr. John Herbert Claiborne," *VA Med. Monthly* (O. 1961). **Activities:** 12; 15, 16, 20 **Addr.:** Medical Library, Petersburg General Hospital, 801 S. Adams St., Petersburg, VA 23803.

Brown, Maryann Kevin (Je. 9, 1949, Sacramento, CA) Sr. Staff Assoc., Natl. Cntr. for Higher Educ. Mgt. Systs., 1978–; Sr. Staff Assoc., West. Interstate Lib. Coord. Org., 1975–78; Lib. and Info. Spec., Westat, Inc., 1974–75. **Educ.:** Univ. of CA, Davis, 1967–71, BA (Hist.); Univ. of CA, Berkeley, 1972–74, MLS. **Orgs.:** ALA: Com. Mem., Machine-Assisted Ref. Srvs. Measur. of Service; Com. Mem., Assn. of Spec. and Coop. Lib. Agencies Ad Hoc Com. on Study of Compar. Procs. of State Lib. Agencies (1976–80). CO LA: Treas., Jr. Members RT. ASIS. Resrch. in Higher Educ. Admin.: Ed. Bd. **Pubns.:** Handbook of Standard Terminology for Reporting and Recording Information about Libraries (1979); Library Statistical Data Base Commentary and Formats and Definitions (1977); Cost and Funding Studies Regarding a Western Interstate Bibliographic Network (1976). **Activities:** 3; 24, 28, 41; 63, 75 **Addr.:** NCHEMS, P.O. Drawer P, Boulder, CO 80302.

Brown, Mirneal C. (Ja. 14, 1935, Grundy, VA) Head, Acq. Dept., Univ. of TN, Chattanooga, 1969–; Sr. Nonprof. Asst., Univ. of MS, 1967–68; Circ. Libn., Univ. of Chattanooga, 1966–67; Tchr., Ringgold HS (GA), 1965–66. **Educ.:** Radford Coll., 1952–53; Berea Coll., 1953–56, BS (Bus. Admin.); Univ. of Chattanooga, 1963–66, M.Ed. (Educ. Admin.). **Orgs.:** TN LA: Mem. Com. (1968). Chattanooga Area LA. SELA. ALA. AAUP. **Activities:** 1; 15, 17, 44; 59, 74 **Addr.:** 1001 Arden Way, Signal Mountain, TN 37377.

Brown, Muriel Windham (N. 19, 1926, Dallas, TX) Chld. Lit. Spec., Dallas Pub. Lib., 1977–; Chld. Lib., 1969–72; 1965-77, in various capacities; Head, Ctr. Chld. Rm., 1967–69; Lib. Lit. and Hist. Div., 1964–65. **Educ.:** South. Meth. Univ., 1947–49, BA (Eng.); 1949–50, MA (Eng.); North TX State Univ., 1971–74, MLS; 1974–, PhD, work in prog. **Orgs.:** ALA. TX LA. Dallas Cnty. LA. **Honors:** Alpha Lambda Sigma; Beta Phi Mu. **Activities:** 9; 15, 21, 48; 95-Resrch in Chld. Lit. **Addr.:** Dallas Public Library, 1954 Commerce, Dallas, TX 75201.

Brown, Nancy Ann (London, ON) Univ. Libn. and Dir. of Libs., Univ. of SK, 1979–; Head, Sci. Div., Univ. of Guelph, 1971–79; Math., Phys. Libn., Queen's Univ., 1969–71; Phys. Libn., Univ. of Toronto, 1966–69. **Educ.:** Carleton Univ., 1953–57, BSc (Geol.); McGill Univ., 1963–64, BLS; Univ. of Toronto, 1964–68, MLS, 1979, MBA (Bus.). **Orgs.:** Can. LA. **Pubns.:** Jt. auth., "The Role of the Librarian in Management," *Spec. Libs.* (Ja. 1975); jt. auth., "Libraries as Consumers of Micrographics," *Jnl. of Appld. Photographic Engin.* (Win. 1977); jt. auth., "Microforms: User Requirements and Response," *The Can. Micro. Socty.* (1977); jt. auth., "COM Catalogues at the University of Guelph Library," *Micro. Review* (Jl.–Ag. 1978); "Management by Objectives," *Expression* (Spr. 1980). **Activities:** 1; 17 **Addr.:** University of Saskatchewan, Saskatoon, SK S7N 0W0 Canada.

Brown, Norman B. (F. 25, 1926, Rochester, NY) Head, Co. Dev. Div., Univ. of IL Li., 1978–, Serials Acq. Libn., 1958–78; Docum. Biblgrphr., 1957–58; Asst. Ref. Libn., 1953–57. **Educ.:** Univ. of Rochester, 1945–48, AB (Eng.); Case-Western Rsv. Univ., 1948–49, MS (LS). **Orgs.:** ALA: ACRL; RTSD Lib Mtrls. Pr. Indx Com. (1972). **Honors:** Phi Beta Kappa; Beta Phi Mu. **Pubns.:** "Price indexes for 1979", *Lib. Jnl.* (1979); Reviews. **Activities:** 1; 15, 44, 46; 55, 57 **Addr.:** 111 University of IL Library, Urbana, IL 61801.

Brown, Pat L. (Ap. 15, 1933, Van Nuys, CA) Coord., Hlth. Info., East. OR State Coll., 1979–; Sch. Libn., Roosevelt Sch. Dist., 1971–76. **Educ.:** AZ State Univ., 1966, BA (Eng.), 1970, MA (Eng.); Univ. of AZ, 1978, MLS. **Orgs.:** OR Hlth. Sci. Libs. Assn.: Consult. Com. (Ch., 1980); Pres.-Elect (1981–). Med. LA. **Pubns.:** "Curriculum Guide for Teaching Library Skills, Roosevelt School District" (1975). **Activities:** 1, 12; 20, 24, 39; 56, 75, 80 **Addr.:** Eastern Oregon State College Library, La Grande, OR 97850.

Brown, Patricia B. (O. 20, 1943, Chicago, IL) Lrng. Resrc. Ctr. Dir., Natl. Coll. of Chiro., 1976; Consult., Reg. Srv. Agncy., 1975; Catlgr., Sch. Dist. 034, 1973–75. **Educ.:** Mundelein Coll., 1971, BA (Psy.); Rosary Coll., 1972–74, MA (LS). **Orgs.:** Chiro. Lib. Cnsrtm.: Vice-Ch. (1979–); Ch. (1980). ALA. **Pubns.:** "Online Searching: An Intro," *Jnl. Manip. & Physiol. Therap.* (Mr. 1980); reviews. **Activities:** 1; 17; 80 **Addr.:** National College of Chiropractic, Learning Resource Center, 200 E. Roosevelt Rd., Lombard, IL 60148.

Brown, Patricia L. (Ap. 23, 1954, Torrance, CA) Assoc. Libn., *Los Angeles Times* Lib., 1981–; Consult., Savage Info. Srvs., 1981–; Info. Spec., NASA Indus. Application Center/USC, 1978–; Asst. Resrch. Libn., Metro-Goldwyn-Mayer Resrch. Lib., 1978–78; Ref. Libn., *Los Angeles Times* Lib., 1977–77. **Educ.:** Univ. of CA, Irvine, 1972–76, BA (Eng.); Univ. of CA, Los Angeles, 1976–78, MLS. **Orgs.:** ALA. SLA. ASIS: Conv. Spec. Events Com. (1979–80). Natl. Women's Pol. Caucus: Mem.-at-Large (1981); Mem. Ch. (1980); Comm. Com. (1979–80). **Honors:** Participant, CA Conf. for WHCLIS, Mr. 1979. **Activities:** 4, 12; 39, 41, 49-Online Srch.; 56, 62, 75 **Addr.:** 11391 Larkin Drive, Garden Grove, CA 92641.

Brown, Patricia L. (O. 1, 1928, Lafayette, LA) Assoc. Dir., Travenol Labs., Inc., 1976–; Sr. Resrch., Info. and Comms., Battelle Columbus Labs., 1966–76; Info. Srvs., TX Instruments, 1957–66; Tech. Writing-Ed., Westinghse. Atomic Power Div., 1955–57; Info. Srvs. Staff, Ethyl Corp., 1951–55; Resrch. Assoc. Indus. Toxicology, Albany Med. Coll., 1950–51; Chem., R and M Labs., 1950; Instr., Anal. Chem., Smith Coll., 1949–50. **Educ.:** Univ. of Southwest. LA, 1944–47, BS (Chem. Engin.); Univ. of TX, 1947–49, MA (Chem.). **Orgs.:** SLA. ASIS. Assoc. Info. Mgrs. Engin. Soctys. Lib.: Bd. of Dirs. (1961–63, 1966–71). Socty. of Women Engins.: Pres. (1961–63). Amer. Chem. Socty. Socty. for Tech. Comm. **Pubns.:** Jt. auth., "Document Retrieval and Dissemination in Libraries and Information Centers," *Annual Review of Information Science* (1967) "Redesigning Information Systems," *Jnl. of Systs. Mgt.* (1972); jt. auth., "A Network for Army Technical Library Information Services," *Contemporary Problems in Technical Library and Information Center Management: A State of the Art* (1974); jt. auth., "Automated Retrieval and Remote Viewing of COSATI Microfiche–Problems and Prospects," *Procs. of the Amer. Socty. for Info. Sci.* (1970); jt. auth., "The Information Analysis Center–Key to Better Use of the Information Resource," *Jnl. of Chem. Documtn.* (My. 1968). **Activities:** 12; 17; 56, 75, 91 **Addr.:** Travenol Labs., Inc., 6301 Lincoln Ave., Morton Grove, IL 60053.

Brown, Peter Bennett (D. 10, 1946, Los Angeles, CA) Accts. Libn. (Catlgr.), Theodore Front Mscl. Lit., 1975–; Sub. Catlgr., UCLA Univ. Resrch. Lib., 1975–75. **Educ.:** CA State Univ., Long Beach, 1966–69, BA (Msc., Math); 1969–72, MA (Msc.); Univ. of CA, Los Angeles, 1972–75, MLS; CA State Univ., Long Beach, CA Life Tchg. Cred. **Orgs.:** Msc. LA: South. CA Chap. (Vice-Ch., Ch., 1978–80). **Pubns.:** "Ordering and Claiming Music Materials" (1981); reviews. **Activities:** 1, 98; 15, 20, 39; 95 **Addr.:** Theodore Front Musical Literature, 155 N. San Vicente Blvd., Beverly Hills, CA 90211.

Brown, Philip L. (D. 22, 1942, Hillsboro, OH) Pub. Srvs. Libn., SD State Univ. Lib., 1979–; Ref. Dept. Head, SD State Univ. Lib., 1974–79; Ref. Libn., Univ. of MO–Kansas City Lib., 1971–74. **Educ.:** OH State Univ., 1961–65, BA (Hist.), BS (Educ.), 1965–67, MA (Hist.), 1967–70 (Hist.); Univ. of MI, 1970–71, AMLS. **Orgs.:** ALA:ACRL. Mt. Plns. LA. SD LA: Docum. Com. (Ch., 1975–77); PR Com. (Ch., 1980–). Rotary. **Honors:** Mt. Plns. LA, One to One Awd., 1978; Phi Beta Kappa. **Pubns.:** "Multi-type Library Cooperation: Colorado and MINITEX," *MPLA Nsltr.* (F. 1979); "South Dakota Voters Reject 'Parrish Law,'" *Nsltr on Int. Frdm.* (Ja. 1979); "South Dakota," *The ALA Yearbook* (1979–80); Ed., *Book Marks,* SD LA nsltr. (1977–). **Activities:** 1; 17, 31, 39 **Addr.:** Philip L. Brown, Hilton M. Briggs Library, Box 2115, South Dakota State University, Brookings, SD 57007.

Brown, Phyllis E. M. (Saint John, NB) Head, Cat. Copy and Data Entry, Hamilton Pub. Lib., 1976–; Catlgr., Hamilton Pub. Lib., 1971–76; Catlgr., White Plains Pub. Lib., 1968–71; Catlgr., Montreal Star Lib., 1964–68. **Educ.:** Mt. Allison Univ., Sackville, NB, 1940–44, BA (Eng.); McGill Univ., 1945–46, BLS; 1966–67, MLS. **Orgs.:** Can. LA. ON LA. Can. Auths. Assn. **Pubns.:** Poems "Yacht Race," "Scottish Tattoo" *Alberta Poetry Yearbook* (1979). **Activities:** 9; 20, 33, 34; 56 **Addr.:** Technical Services Hamilton Public Library, Hamilton, ON Canada.

Brown, Stanley Wright (My. 10, 1945, Cambridge, MA) Chief, Spec. Col. and Cur. Rare Bks., Dartmouth Coll. Lib., 1980–; Chief, Pub. Srvs., 1975–80; Chief, Circ. Srvs., 1972–75; Asst. to the Libn., 1970–72. **Educ.:** Dartmouth Coll., 1963–67, AB (Eng.); Oxford Univ., 1967–69, MA (Eng.); Simmons Coll., 1969–70, MS (LS). **Orgs.:** New Eng. LA: Secy. (1977–78); Dir. (1978–80); various coms. and chs. ALA. NS LA. NELA Cncl. (1973–75); VP (1980–81); Pres. (1981–82). New Eng. Lib. Bd.: Couns. (1972–75). Other orgs. Lebanon, NH: City Cncl. (Elect. 1979). **Honors:** New Eng. LA., Cert. of Apprec., 1975. **Activities:** 1; 17, 33, 45 **Addr.:** Dartmouth College Library, Hanover, NH 03755.

Brown, Thomas Elton (S. 19, 1946, Lubbock, TX) Arch., Natl. Arch., 1976–; Asst. Prof., Grand Valley State Colls., 1975–76. **Educ.:** St. Meinrad Coll., 1968, BA (Hist.); OK State Univ., 1974, MA, PhD (Hist.). **Orgs.:** SAA: Task Force on Autom. Recs. and Techs. Amer. Hist. Assn. Amer. Catholic Hist. Assn. **Pubns.:** *Bible-Belt Catholicism: A History of the Roman Catholic Church in Oklahoma, 1905–1945* (1977); "Appraisal of Machine-Readable Records," (sem.), SAA Anl. Mtg., 1978, 1979. **Activities:** 2; 15, 38; 56, 62 **Addr.:** 33 Q Street, NE, Washington, DC 20002.

Brown, Thomas Markwell (My 19, 1930, Los Angeles, CA) Head Libn., New Trier High Sch., 1966–; Lib. Consult., Meth. Sch. of Malaya, 1961–65; Libn., Univ. of Chicago Lab. Sch., 1960–61; Tchr., Libn., Anglo-Chinese Sch., Malaya, 1954–59. **Educ.:** Univ. of CA-Berkeley, 1948–52, BA (Eng.); Univ. of Chicago, 1959–60, MALS; Los Angeles State Col., Tch. Cred., 1953. **Orgs.:** IL LA: IL Lib. Task Anal. Proj. Ch., Treas. (1979); Nom. (1978). IL Assn. Sch. Libn.: Treas., (1970). ALA: Cncl. 1981–84). IL Reg. Lib. Cncl.: Bd. (1979). IL State Lib. Adv. Com.: Sub Com. on Interlib. Coop., Ch. **Honors:** Beta Phi Mu. **Activities:** 10; 17, 35, 48; 89, 91, 92 **Addr.:** 604 Drexel Ave., Glencoe, IL 60022.

Brown, Timothy A. (S. 30, 1940, Galesburg, IL) Univ. Libn., Boise State Univ., 1977–; Asst. Dir., Admin. Srvs., IA State Univ. Lib., 1970–77; Dir., Pub. Srvs., Univ. of MT Lib., 1969–70, Ref. Libn., 1968–69; Adv., Univ. Libs., U.S. Peace Corps, Brazil, 1966–67; Head, Docum. Dept., Univ. of UT Libs., 1965–66, Instr., LS, 1964–65. **Educ.:** St. Paul Semy., 1960–62, BA (Phil.); Univ. of IL, 1963–64, MS (LS). **Orgs.:** ALA. Pac. NW LA: Ref. Div., Pubns. Com. (1969–70). ID LA: Coll. Univ. and Spec. Libs. Sect. (Ch., 1980–81). **Honors:** Beta Phi Mu, 1964. **Pubns.:** "The Choice of MRAP as a Vehicle of Change," *Jnl. of Acad. Libnshp.* (Ja. 1976). **Activities:** 1; 17, 39 **Addr.:** Boise State University Library, Boise, ID 83725.

Brown, William A. (Ap. 16, 1943, Portsmouth, VA) Asst. City Lib. Dir., Portsmouth Pub. Lib., 1974–, Branch Libn., 1973–74, Ref. Staff, 1970–72. **Educ.:** Randolph-Macon Coll., 1961–65, BA (Hist.); Univ. of VA, 1965–69, MA (Hist.); Univ. of NC, 1972–73, MS (LS); Univ. of MD, 1977, Lib. Admin. Dev. Prog. **Orgs.:** VA LA: Reg. III (Ch., 1979); Lib. Coop. Com.

PROFESSIONAL ACTIVITIES: Institutions: 1. Acad. lib.; 2. Arch.; 3. Assn.; 4. Fed./Gvt. lib.; 5. Inst. lib.; 6. Mfr./Suppl.; 7. Milit. lib.; 8. Musm.; 9. Pub. lib.; 10. Sch. lib.; 11. Sch. of lib. sci.; 12. Spec. lib.; 13. State lib.; 14. (other). **Functions/Activities:** 15. Acq./Col. dev.; 16. Adult srvs.; 17. Admin.; 18. Apprais.; 19. Archit./Bldgs.; 20. Cat./Class.; 21. Chld. srvs.; 22. Circ.; 23. Cons./Pres.; 24. Consult.; 25. Cont. ed.; 26. Educ. lib. sci.; 27. Ext. srvs.; 28. Fund/Grants; 29. Gvt. pubs.; 30. Indx./Abs.; 31. Instr. lib. use; 32. Media srvs.; 33. Micro.; 34. Netwks./Coop.; 35. Persnl.; 36. PR; 37. Publshg.; 38. Recs. mgt.; 39. Ref. srvs.; 40. Repro.; 41. Resrch.; 42. Review.; 43. Secur.; 44. Serials; 45. Spec. col.; 46. Tech. srvs.; 47. Trustees/Bds.; 48. YA srvs.; 49. (other).

(1981). ALA: JMRT, Handbk. Com. (1976–77). Tidewater Area Dirs.: Secy. (1974–). WA Lafayette Lodge: Chaplain (1981). Kiwanis Club of Portsmouth. Cncl. of Agencies, Tidewater Asm. on Fam. Life: Fam. Fair Ch. (1976). Tidewater Litcy. Cncl.: Bd. (1975–76). Various other orgs. **Honors:** Phi Beta Kappa, 1965; Beta Phi Mu, 1972; Pi Gamma Mu, 1965. **Activities:** 9; 15, 16, 27 **Addr.:** Portsmouth Public Library, 601 Court St., Portsmouth, VA 23704.

Brown, William Joseph (N. 9, 1930, Buffalo, NY) Asst. Supt., Curric. (LS), Metro. Sp. Sch. Bd., 1977–, Coord. Lib. Srvs., 1974–77, Consult. for Sch. Libs., 1968–74; Libn., St. Michael's Coll. Sch., 1964–68. **Educ.:** Univ. of Windsor, 1955, BA (Hist.); Univ. of St. Michael's Coll., 1960, STB (Theo.); West. Rsv. Univ., 1965, MS, (LS); MI: Tchr. Cert.; ON: Elem. Sch. Tchr. Cert.; HS Asst. Cert., Spec. Cert. in Sch. Libnshp. **Orgs.:** ALA. AECT. Can. LA. Beta Phi Mu. Various other orgs. **Activities:** 10; 15, 17, 24 **Addr.:** Metropolitan Separate School Board, 146 Laird Drive, Toronto, ON M4G 3V8 Canada.

Browne, C.S.C., Joseph P. (Je. 12, 1929, Detroit, MI) Dir., Univ. of Portland Lib., 1976–; Dir., Grad. Sch. of LS, Our Lady of the Lake Coll., 1973–75; Dean, Coll. of Arts & Scis., Univ. of Portland, 1970–73, Dir. Lib., 1966–70, Dir. of the Sum. Session, Univ. of Portland, 1964–66, Head, Dept. of LS, Univ. of Portland, 1964–70; Libn., Holy Cross Coll., 1959–64. **Educ.:** Univ. of Notre Dame, 1946–51, AB (Phil.); Holy Cross Coll., 1951–55, (Theo.); Pontificium Athenaeum (Angelicum), Rome, Italy, 1956–58, STL, STD, (Theo.); Catholic Univ. of Amer., 1959–64, MSLS. **Orgs.:** OR LA: Natl. Lib. Wk., (Exec. Dir., 1965–), VP (1966–67), Pres. (1967–68). Catholic LA: Lib. Educ. Sect. (Actg. Ch., 1968–69), VP (1969–71), Pres. (1971–73). ALA: ACRL; Pacific N.W. LA; Catholic Theo. Socty. of Amer. Univ. of Portland, Bd. of Regents (1969–70, 1977–81), Acad. Sen. (Ch. 1968–70, Mem. 1968–73). Archdio. of Portland, Sen. of Priests (1967–69). Columbia Interstate Lib. Bd.: VCh. (1977–79). Prov. Chap., IN Prov., Congregation of Holy Cross: Mdrtr. (1976–79). **Honors:** Beta Phi Mu, 1965; Knights of Columbus, OR Knight of the Yr., 1973; Univ. of Portland, Culligan Fac. Awd., 1979. **Pubns.:** *Some Moral Implications of the Privilege Against Self-Incrimination in the Fifth Amendment to the Constitution of the United States.* (1960); contributions to the New Catholic Encyclopedia and to library periodicals. **Activities:** 1; 17, 34, 35; 61, 75, 90 **Addr.:** Wilson W. Clark Memorial Library, PO Box 03017, Portland, OR 97203.

Brown-Slusher, Shirley (My. 28, 1923, Covington, KY) Law Libn., Mulcahy & Wherry, S. C., 1980–80; Info. Sci. Spec., Rexnord, Inc. Tech. Lib., 1975–79; Acct., 1973–75. **Educ.:** Univ. of Evansville, 1950–53, BS (Bus. Admin.) Magna Cum Laude; Univ. of WI, Milwaukee, 1970–73, MLS. **Orgs.:** ALA. SLA: WI Chap., Pres.-Elect (1978–79); Pres. (1979–80). Waukesha Pub. Lib.: Trustee (1977–80). **Activities:** 12; 39, 41, 49-Comp. assisted Resrch. Syst.; 77 **Addr.:** 913 E. Juneau Ave., Apt. 42, Milwaukee, WI 53202.

Bruce, Dennis Luther (Ja. 3, 1944, Elizabeth City, NC) Dir., Spartanburg Cnty. Pub. Lib., 1975; Ast. Dir., Admin. Srvs., Wake Cnty. Pub. Libs., 1971–75; Ref. Libn., 1970–71. **Educ.:** Methodist Coll., 1966–68, AB (Eng.); Univ. NC, 1969–70, MS (LS). **Orgs.:** ALA: PLA/AV Com. (1979–80). SE LA. SC LA: Pub. Lib. Sect. (Ch., 1978); NC LA: Pub. Lib. Sect./Lib. Dev. Com. (1974); Persnl. Com. (Ch., 1975). Other orgs. Soc. Srvcs. Assn.: Pres. (1979). **Honors:** Spartanburg (SC) Jaycees, Disting. Srvc. Awd., 1978. **Activities:** 9; 17, 35, 39 **Addr.:** Spartanburg County Public Library, 333 S. Pine St., P.O. Box 2409, Spartanburg, SC 29304.

Bruch, Virginia I. (My. 26, 1921, Hickman, KY) Chief, Spec. Srvs. Branch, Army Lib., Dept. of the Army, 1955–; Chief, Cat. Sect., 1965–71; Catlgr., 1955–65; Catlgr., Fed. Trade Comsn. Lib., 1949–55. **Educ.:** B.S. Murray Univ., 1939–43, BS (LS, Eng.). **Orgs.:** ALA: Milit. Libns. SLA: Milit. Libns. Daughters of the Amer. Revolution. **Honors:** Fed. Poet, 1956; Army Lib., Outstan. Awd., 1979. **Pubns.:** "Forever Young," *Fam. Heritage,* (Oct. 1978); poems in various mags. **Activities:** 2, 12; 20, 21, 37; 55, 69, 85 **Addr.:** 15 West Howell Ave., Alexandria, VA 22301.

Brudvig, Glenn L. (O. 14, 1931, Kenosha, WI) Dir., Bio-Med. Lib., Univ. of MN, 1964–, Asst. Dir. for Resrch. and Dev., 1968–79, Supvsr. of Dept. Libs., 1963–64; Asst. Libn., Univ. of ND, 1962–63, Acq. Libn., Archvst., 1958–62. **Educ.:** Univ. of ND, 1954, BS Ed (Hist.); 1956, MA (Hist.); Univ. of MN, 1962, MALS. **Orgs.:** ALA. ASIS: MN Chap. (Ch., 1972). Med. LA: Natl. Issues Adv. Com. (1979–); Ed. Consult. (1979–82). Assn. of Acad. Hlth. Sci. Lib. Dirs.: Bd. of Dirs. (1976–79). Various other orgs. **Pubns.:** "The Development of a Minicomputer System for the University of Minnesota Bio-Medical Library," *Clinics on Library Applications of Data Processing, Proceedings* (1974); "The Development of Public Library Services in North Dakota," *ND Qtly.* (1963); "The Catalog of the Orin G. Libby Historical Manuscripts Collection, University of North Dakota," *ND Hist.* (1963). **Activities:** 1, 12; 17, 34; 56, 80 **Addr.:** Bio-Medical Library, University of Minnesota, 505 Essex St., S.E., Minneapolis, MN 55455.

Bruer, John Michael (Jl. 23, 1940, Knoxville, TN) Assoc. Dir., CA Lib. Athrty., 1978–; Assoc. Univ. Libn., NYU., 1975–78; Assoc. Dir., Libs., Univ. of Houston, 1972–75; Dir., Acq. Dept., Univ. of KY, 1969–72; Admin. Asst., 1966–69; Head, Circ. Dept., Univ. of Notre Dame, 1965–66; Asst. Circ. Supvsr., Vanderbilt Univ., 1963–65; Genl. Ref. Asst., TN State Lib., 1958–62. **Educ.:** Vanderbilt Univ., 1958–62, BA (Greek); 1962–65, MA (Latin); G. Peabody Coll., 1963–65, MALS. **Orgs.:** ALA: ACRL (Nom. Com., 1977–78, Strg. Com., 1975–78). RTSD (Resrcs. Sect., 1973–74, Bkdealer. 1970–74. Plng. 1976–78, Nom. 1978–79. RASD (Eval. of Srvcs., 1979–, Exec., 1977–). **Honors:** ALA, Resrcs. Sect. Publ. Awd., 1978; Cncl. on Lib. Resrcs, Flwship, 1972; Lib. of Congs., Internship, 1965. **Pubns.:** *Toward A California Document Conservation Program,* (1978); *Guidelines for Publishers, Agents, and Librarians in Handling Library Orders for Serials and Periodicals,* (1973); "Implementations of Automated Circulation Systems: Public Relations", *Jrnl. of Lib. Autom.* (D. 1979); "Management Information Aspects of Automated Acquisitions Systems" *ALA* (1979); "Resources in 1976" *Lib. Resrcs. and Tech. Srvcs.* (1977); "Bereitstellung und Einsatz von Mitteln für amerikanische Bibliotheken", *Bibl. Forschung und Praxis* (1977). **Activities:** 1, 4; 15, 23, 34; 56, 75, 93 **Addr.:** California Library Authority, 1415 Koll Circle, Suite 101, San Jose, CA 95112.

Brugh, Anne Elizabeth (Je. 4, 1924, Logan, WV) Ref. Libn., Rutgers Univ., Douglass Coll. Lib., 1969–, Head, Circ. Dept., 1959–69; Sr. Circ. Libn., 1955–59; Asst. Ref. Libn., Univ. of IL Lib., 1953–55; Sr. Circ. Asst., Univ. of VA Lib., 1951–53. **Educ.:** Roanoke Coll., 1943–47, BS (Econ.); Univ. of MI, 1950–51, AMLS; Rutgers Univ. 1973–76, MA (Hist.). **Orgs.:** NJ LA: Exec. Bd. (1976–79); Secy., Coll. and Univ. Sect. (1967–68, 1971–72). AAUP: Rutgers Chap, Cncl. (1977–80); Com. W (1976–80), Ch. (1977–78). **Honors:** Beta Phi Mu, 1954. **Pubns.:** "American Librarianship", *Signs: Journal of Women in Culture and Society* (Sum. 1976); Reprinted in *Best of Library Literature 1977; The Role of Women in Librarianship 1876–1976* (1979). **Activities:** 1; 22, 39, 44; 59, 92 **Addr.:** 7 Thrush Mews, North Brunswick, NJ 08902.

Bruguera, Eva A. (D 23, 1927, Viipuri, Finland) Libn., Bio. & Med. Sci., Vets. Admin. Med. Ctr., Palo Alto, CA, 1963–; Order Libn., SRI Intl., 1962–63. **Educ.:** Univ. of Helsinki, 1946–48; Univ. of Paris, La Sorbonne, 1948–49, 1950–51, Cert. Fr.; Univ. of Pittsburgh, 1956, MA, (Fr.); Carnegie Inst. Tech., 1961, MLS. **Orgs.:** Med. LA. North. CA Med. Lib. Grp.: Secy (1978–79). **Activities:** 4, 5; 34, 39, 49-On-Line Search.; 80, 92 **Addr.:** 3537 Murdoch Dr., Palo Alto, CA 94306.

Brumback, Elsie Lawson (O. 1, 1934, Lumberton, NC) Dir. of Educ. Media, NC Dept, Pub. Instr., 1974–; Supvsr. of Libs., Fairfax (VA) Cnty. Pub. Sch., 1968–74; Asst. Supvsr. of Libs., 1965–68; Educ. Media Spec., Curric. Lab Supvsr., 1965–68; Head Libn., Fairfax HS, 1963–65; Organized Lib., Cooper Intermediate Sch. (Fairfax, VA), 1962–63; Head Libn., Osburn HS (Manassas, VA), 1955–61. **Educ.:** E. Carolina Univ., 1952–55, BS (Eng., LS); Univ. of VA, 1967–68, MA (Educ. Media); Univ. of NC at Chapel Hill, G.W. Univ., 1968–69. **Orgs.:** NC Assn. Sch. Libns.: Exec. Bd. (1974–79). NC Lib. Srvs. Construction Act Adv. Bd.: (1974–79). AECT: Natl. Nom. Com. (1974, 1979). ALA: AASL/Natl. Stan. Com. (1969). SELA: Nom. Com. (1979). Many other orgs. and coms. Delta Kappa Gamma Socty. Phi Delta Kappa: Cap. Area Chap./Mem. Com. (1979–80). Many other prof. orgs. and coms. **Honors:** NC Gvr. Conf. on Libs., Exec. Com. and Del., 1978; WHCOLIS, Del. from NC, 1979. **Pubns.:** "Eight Exemplary School Media Programs", *NC Libs* (4: 1978); "Accessibility is the Key", *HS Jnl.,* (My. 1976); "The Open Classroom and Its Effect on the School Library Program", *VA Libn.* (3, 4: 1972); "Classrooms Need Their Own Equipment", *The Instr.* (Je./Jl. 1968); "The Right Film At The Right Moment", *The Scholastic Tchr.* (Ja. 1968); Many other articles, multi-media presentations, and speeches. **Activities:** 10; 17, 32; 63, 93 **Addr.:** Division of Educational Media, Department Public Instruction, Raleigh, NC 27611.

Brumberg, G. David (Je. 7, 1939, Ironton, OH) Dir., NY Hist. Resrcs. Ctr., Olin Lib., Cornell Univ., 1977–; Dir., Geneva Hist. Socty., 1973–76; Archvst., Papers of the Contl. Congs. Proj., Natl. Arch., 1971–73. **Educ.:** Univ. of PA, 1957–61, BS (Econ., Mktg.); Miami Univ., 1966–71, MA, PhD (Hist.); 1971, Cert. (Arch. Admin.). **Orgs.:** SAA. Mid-Atl. Reg. Arch. Conf. Lake ON Arch. Conf. Hist. Ithaca.: Bd. Amer. Assn. for State and Lcl. Hist. Org. of Amer. Histns. NY State Hist. Assn. **Pubns.:** *The Making of an Upstate Community: Geneva, New York 1789–1920* (1976); "Sources and Uses of Local History Materials," *Bookmark* (1981). **Activities:** 1, 2; 17, 28, 45; 54, 55, 56 **Addr.:** New York Historical Resources Center, Olin Library, Cornell University, Ithaca, NY 14853.

Brun, Christian M. F. (O. 3, 1920, Trondheim, Nor) Head, Dept. of Spec. Col., Univ. of CA, Santa Barbara, 1963–; Cur. of Maps, Clements Lib., Univ. of MI, 1958–63; Ast. Cur. of Maps, 1952–58; Asst. Cur. of Rare Bks., Univ. of PA, 1950–51. **Educ.:** Univ. of WA, 1939–41, BA (Econ., Bus.); Univ. of NC, 1949–50, BS (LS); Univ. of MI, 1951–52, AM (LS); Univ. of MI, Adv. Grad. crs., 1952–56. **Orgs.:** Bibl. Socty. of Amer. Socty. of CA Archvsts. Map Socty. of CA. ALA. Amer. Scan. Fndn. **Pubns.:** *Guide to the Manuscript Maps in the William L. Clements Library* (1959); Co-Auth., *Bibliography of Maps and Charts published in America before 1800* (1969), 2nd ed., 1978; "Dobbs and the Passage," *The Beaver* (Aut. 1958); "Maps of the 16th and 17th Centuries," *Dimension* (Fall 1960); other articles. **Activities:** 1, 2; 15, 17, 45; 57, 70, 93 **Addr.:** Department of Special Collections, Library, University of California, Santa Barbara, Santa Barbara, CA 93106.

Brundin, Robert E. (D. 10, 1929, Los Angeles, CA) Prof., LS, Univ. of AB, 1980–, Assoc. Prof., 1975–80, Vist. Assoc. Prof., 1972–73; Dir. of Lib. Srvs., San Jose City Coll., 1963–75, Libn., 1959–63; Reporter and copy ed., Calexico Chronicle, 1953–54. **Educ.:** Univ. of CA, 1948–52, AB (Jnlsm.), 1952–53, MJ, (Jnlsm.); CA Jr. Coll. Tchng. Cred., Univ. of CA, 1959; Natl. Univ. of Mexico, 1956–57, (Span.); Univ. of CA, 1958–59, MLS; Stanford Univ., 1963–70, PhD (Educ.). **Orgs.:** ALA. AALS. CALS. Can. LA. Various other orgs. Can. Assn. of Univ. Tchrs. Gen. Faculties Cncl., Univ. of AB: Rep., LS (1979–). **Pubns.:** *Price Guide to Books on Canada and the Canadian Arctic* (1979); "Winsor, Justin (1831–1897)," *ALA World Ency. of Lib. and Info. Srvs.* (1980); "Justin Winsor and the Liberalizing of the College Library," *Jnl. of Lib. Hist.* (Ja. 1975). **Activities:** 1, 11; 19, 39, 41 **Addr.:** Faculty of Library Science, University of Alberta, Edmonton, AB T6G 2J4 Canada.

Brunelle, Eugene A. (O. 31, 1925, Providence, RI) Dir., LS, E. Carolina Univ., 1976–; Dir., LS, St. Mary's Coll., 1972–76; Head, Reader's Srvcs., SUNY, Buffalo, 1968–72; Ed., *Jnl. of Creat. Behv.* 1960–68; Asst. Prof., CA State Univ., 1963–66; Inst., Mills Coll., 1960–63. **Educ.:** Harvard Univ., 1946–50, AB (Eng.); Simmons Coll., 1950–51, MLS; Univ. of CA, Berkeley, 1954–57, MA (Eng.); SUNY, Buffalo, 1966–71, EdD (Psy.). **Orgs.:** ALA: ACRL. NC LA. SE LA. AAUP; Amer. Assn. Univ. Admin. **Honors** Danforth Fndn., Assoc., (1963); Educ. Prcs. Assn., Jnlsm., (1967). **Pubns.:** "A Semantic Rhetoric," *Educ. in Innovative Socty.* (1965); "An Experiment in Exposition," *CA Eng. Jnl.* (Win., 1967); "New Learning, New Libraries, New Librarians," *Jnl. of Acad. Libnshp.* (Nov. 1975); other papers, reviews. **Activities:** 1; 17, 19, 34; 55, 63 **Addr.:** Joyner Library, East Carolina University, Greenville, NC 27834.

Brunswick, Sheldon Roy (O. 5, 1938, Somerville, NJ) Judaica Libn., Univ. of CA, Berkeley, 1968–; Libn., SUNY, Binghamton, 1966–68; Semitics Libn., Brandeis Univ., 1963–66. **Educ.:** Yeshiva Univ., 1956–60, BA (Soclgy.); Jewish Theol. Semy. of America, 1961–62, MHL, (Judaica); Columbia Univ., 1962–63, MLS. **Orgs.:** AJL; Resrch. and Spec. Libs. Div.: Pres. (1978–80). **Pubns.:** Contrib., *Nemoy Festschrift* (1980); Reviews and articles. **Activities:** 1, 5; 15, 17, 20; 54, 90 **Addr.:** University of California Library, Berkeley, CA 94720.

Bruntjen, Scott (S. 10, 1943, Pittsburgh, PA) Exec. Dir., Pittsburgh Reg. Lib. Ctr., 1979–; Head, Pub. Srvs., Shippensburg State Coll. Lib., 1969–79. **Educ.:** Univ. of IA, 1961–65, BA (Hist.); 1967–69, MA (LS); Shippensburg State Coll., 1971–74, MA (Pol. Sci.); Simmons Col., 1974–75, DA, (Lib. Admin.). **Orgs.:** PA LA: 2nd VP (1978); VP (1979); Pres. (1980). ALA: ACRL. **Honors:** PA LA, Cert. of Merit, 1978; PA Dept. of Educ., Excep. Acad. Srv. Cert., 1976. **Pubns.:** *The Checklist of American Imprints, 1831* (1975); *The Checklist of American Imprints, 1832* (1977); *The Checklist of American Imprints, 1833* (1979); *Douglas C. McMurtrie: Bibliographer and Historian of Printing* (1979); *The Checklist of American Imprints, 1834* (1981); **Activities:** 1; 24, 26, 34; 56, 59, 93 **Addr.:** Pittsburgh Regional Library Center, Chatham College, Pittsburgh, PA 15232.

Brunton, David W. (N. 9, 1929, Oak Park, IL) Free-lance ed., writer, consult.; Asst. to the Dir., Englewood Pub. Lib., 1974–1980; Dir., Douglas Cnty. (CO) Lib., 1973–74; Asst. Dir., Longmont CO Pub. Lib., 1970–73; Staff Dev. Ofcr., Univ. of CA, Irvine, 1969–70; Exec. Dir., CA LA, 1964–69. **Educ.:** Ripon Coll., 1950–54, BA (Hist.); Univ. of IL, 1955–56, MS (LS). **Orgs.:** ALA: IFRT (Ch., 1975–76); Secy., Persnl. Admin. Sect. (1973–75). CO LA. Various positions in state lib. assns. Conf. of Intermt. Arch. Georgetown Socty., Inc. **Honors:** CA LA, Cit., 1969. **Pubns.:** *Index to the Contemporary Scene,* vol. 1 (1973), vol. 2 (1975); *Douglas County Library, Perspectives on Development* (1975); "Non-Profit Association Law and Taxes," *Drexel Lib. Qtly.* (Jl. 1967); Regular column, "025.5," *Nexus* (1974–); Ed., *Nexus* (1981–); Reviews. **Activities:** 2, 9; 17, 39, 45; 56, 59; 95-Local hist. **Addr.:** P.O. Box 184, Englewood, CO 80151.

Bruwelheide, Janis H. (Ag. 9, 1948, Lakeland, FL) Asst. Prof., LS, MT State Univ., 1974–; Asst. to Dean, Coll. of Educ., UT State Univ., 1979–80; Tchr., Godby HS, 1970–72. **Educ.:** FL State Univ., 1968–70, BS (Eng. Educ.), 1972–73, MS (LS); UT State Univ., 1979–, EdD (Curric. Dev., Supvsn.). **Orgs.:** ALA: JMRT, Prof. Dev. Com. (Ch., 1978–80); Lib. Admin. Div., Sch. Media Facilities Plng. Com.; AASL, Prof. Dev. Com. (1978–). AECT: Int. Frdm. Com. (1979–); Tchr. Educ. Com. (1979–). MT LA: Cont. Educ. Com. (1978–79). MT Sch. Lib. Media Assn.: Ch. (1979). **Honors:** ALA, JMRT, Prof. Dev. Awd., 1976. **Activities:** 11; 26; 63, 74 **Addr.:** Library Science, Renne Library, Montana State University, Bozeman, MT 59717.

Special Subjects/Services: 50. Adult educ.; 51. Advert./Mktg.; 52. Aerosp.; 53. Agric.; 54. Area std.; 55. Arts/Hum.; 56. Autom.; 57. Bibl./Prtg.; 58. Bio. sci.; 59. Bus./Fin.; 60. Chem.; 61. Copyrt.; 62. Documtn.; 63. Educ.; 64. Engin.; 65. Env.; 66. Eth. grps.; 67. Film; 68. Food/Nutr.; 69. Geneal.; 70. Geo.; 71. Geol.; 72. Handcpd.; 73. Hist.; 74. Int. frdm.; 75. Info. sci.; 76. Insr.; 77. Law; 78. Legis.; 79. Math./Comp. sci.; 80. Med.; 81. Metals; 82. Nat. resrcs.; 83. Newsp.; 84. Nuc. sci.; 85. Oral hist.; 86. Petr./Energy; 87. Pharm.; 88. Phys./Astr./Math.; 89. Readg.; 90. Relig.; 91. Sci./Tech.; 92. Soc. sci.; 93. Telecom.; 94. Transp.; 95. (other).

Bryan, Arthur L. (Je. 4, 1945, Summit, NJ) Dir., Jacob Edwards Lib., 1977–; Head, Msc., Art, Film Dept., Nashua Pub. Lib., 1976–77; Dir., Instr. Media, North. Essex Cmnty. Coll., 1971–76. **Educ.:** Middlebury Coll., 1963–65, 1967–69, BA (Geo.); SUNY, Albany, 1970–71, MLS. **Orgs.:** ALA. New Eng. LA. MA LA. Ctrl. MA Reg. Lib. Syst. Adv. Cncl.: Exec. Bd. Rotary Club. Tri-Cmnty. Cham. of Cmrce.: Bd. Dir. **Pubns.:** Proj. Dir. and Ed., *Cmnty. Srvy. and Anal. of Lib. Needs* (1979); several rec. albums (1973–79). **Activities:** 9; 17, 28, 34; 55 **Addr.:** Jacob Edwards Library, 236 Main St., Southbridge, MA 01550.

Bryan, Barbara D. (My. 20, 1927, Livermore Falls, ME) Univ. Libn., Fairfield Univ., 1974–; Asst. Dir., Fairfield Univ. Lib., 1965–74; Asst. Libn., Fairfield Pub. Lib., 1957–65; Ref. Libn., 1954–57. **Educ.:** Univ. of ME, Orono, 1944–48, BA (Psych.); South. CT State Coll., 1960–64, MLS. **Orgs.:** CT State Lib. Bd., 1978–. Southwest. CT Lib. Cncl., Trustees, (1978–). ALA: Chap. Rel. Com. (1978–82); ERA Task Force (1979–); CT Chap., Cncl. (1977–80); Various other organizations and offices. Leag. of Women Voters. CT Audubon Socty. **Honors:** Phi Beta Kappa; South. CT State Coll, Div. of LS, Disting. Alum. Awd., 1979. **Pubns.:** "Connecticut Report," *ALA Yearbook* (1978, 1979, 1980, 1981). **Activities:** 1; 15, 17, 46 **Addr.:** Nyselius Library, Fairfield University, Fairfield, CT 06430.

Bryan, Carol L. (Ap. 11, 1942, Charleston, WV) Ed., Graph. Dsgn., Carol Bryan Imagines, *The Lib. Imagination Paper!* (pubn.), 1978–; Head, PR, Dsgn., Prtg. Div., WV Lib. Comsn., 1974–78; Art Dir., Rose City Press, 1973–74; Dsgn., Wrtr., Hallmark Cards, Inc., 1965–66. **Educ.:** Univ. Cincinnati, 1960–65, BS (Dsgn.) **Orgs.:** ALA: PR Com. (1979–80); John Cotton Dana PR Com. (Judge 1980–81). Lib. PR Cncl. WV LA. WV Comm. WV Press Women. **Honors:** John Cotton Dana Com., HW Wilson Co., Lib. PR Awd., First, 1974; Merit, 1975; Special, 1976; First, 1977; other awds. **Pubns.:** Publshr., graph. dsgn., *The Library Imagination Paper* (1979–80); "Graphic Design For Libraries," *Prepare, ALA PR Recipe Bk.* (1978); "The Pet Bookmark," *UNABASHED Libn.* (#20, 1976); "The John Cotton Dana Awards: "Pack Your PR Into A Scrapbook and WIN"... The Library Imagination Paper (Win. 1979); other articles. **Activities:** 36, 37, 49-graph. dsgn; 98, 6 **Addr.:** The Library Imagination Paper, 1000 Byus Dr., Charleston, WV 25311.†

Bryan, James E. (Jl. 11, 1909, Easton, PA) Lib. Consult., 1972–; Dir., Newark Pub. Lib., 1958–72, Asst. Dir., 1943–58; Head, Adult Lending Dept., Carnegie Lib. of Pittsburgh, 1938–43; Libn., Easton (PA) Pub. Lib., 1936–38. **Educ.:** Lafayette Coll., 1927–31, BS (Econ.); Drexel Univ., 1931–32, BLS; Amer. Univ., 1935–37, MA (Econ.). **Orgs.:** ALA: Pres. (1962–63); PLA: (Pres., 1959–60). NJ LA: Pres. (1952–54). Mid. Atl. States Reg. Lib. Conf.: Ch. (1949). Rutgers Univ. Grad. Lib. Sch.: Adv. Bd. (Ch.). **Honors:** Drexel Univ., 70th Anniv. Alum. Cit., 1961; Lafayette Coll., George Washington Kidd Awd., 1974; Rutgers Univ., Litt. D., 1964. **Pubns.:** Contrib. to prof. pers.; Auth. of numerous bldg. progs. and std. **Activities:** 9; 19, 24 **Addr.:** Ellis Rd., East Sullivan, NH 03445; and 217 W. Comstock Ave., Winter Park, FL 32789.

Bryan, Vivian (Je. 24, 1921, Elizabeth, NJ) Div. Dir., VT Dept. of Libs. **Educ.:** Northwestern Univ., 1938–42, BA; 1944–46, MS; SUNY - Albany, 1969–70, MLS. **Orgs.:** VT LA. Law Libn. of New Engl. AALL. Geneal. Soc. of VT. Vt Hist. Soc. VT Audubon Soc. New England Archvst. **Pubns.:** "The Law Library 1825–1977", *The Vermont Bar* (D. 1977); VT State Pubn. Checklist (1971–). **Activities:** 12, 13; 15, 16, 17 **Addr.:** Vermont Department of Libraries, Law and Documents Unit, Montpelier, VT 05602.

Bryant, Douglas Wallace (Je. 20, 1913, Visalia, CA) Trustee, Exec. Dir., Amer. Trust for the British Lib., 1979–; Prof., Bibl. and Libn. Emeritus, Harvard Univ. 1979–; Dir., Harvard Univ. Lib., 1971–79, Univ. Libn., 1964–71, Assoc. Dir., 1956–64, Admin. Asst., 1952–56; Dir. of Libs., US Info. Srv., London, 1949–52; Asst. Libn., Univ. of CA, Berkeley, 1946–49; Asst. Chief, Burton Hist. Col. Detroit Pub. Lib., 1941–42. **Educ.:** Stanford Univ., 1931–35, AB (Eng.); Univ. of Munich, 1932–33, Univ. of MI, 1935–38, AMLS. **Orgs.:** IFLA: VP (1952–58). ALA: Intl. Rel. Com. (1952–58, Ch., 1952–55). ARL: Pres. (1969). Ctr. for Resrch. Libs.: Bd. of Dir. (1968–71, 1973–79; Ch., 1970). Other orgs. Flw., Amer. Acad. Arts and Sci. MA Hist. Socty. Amer. Antiq. Socty. Grolier Club. Club of Odd Volumes. **Pubns.:** "The American Scholar and Barriers to Knowledge" in *Iron Curtains and Scholarship, the Exchange of Knowledge in a Divided World* (1958); "Centralization and Decentralization at Harvard (The Organization of the Harvard University Library)," *Coll. and Resrch. Libs.* (S. 1961); "An American View of University Libraries," *Jahrbuch für Amerikastudien* (1965); "The Changing Research Library," *Harvard Lib. Bltn.* (O. 1974); "Strengthening the Strong: The Cooperative Future of Research Libraries," *Harvard Lib. Bltn.* (Ja. 1976); other articles. **Activities:** 1, 4; 17, 19, 45; 55, 57 **Addr.:** 35 Woodland Rd., Lexington, MA 02173.

Bryant, Frederick David (Jl. 18, 1924, El Paso, TX) Dir., Med. Ctr. Lib., Univ. of S. FL, 1971–; Dir., Med. Ctr. Lib., PA St. Univ. 1965–71; Dir., Hlth., Ctr. Lib., Univ. of FL., 1954–64; Sci. Cat., 1952–53; Cat., Natl. Lib. of Med., 1949–51. **Educ.:** Univ. of FL, 1942–46, BA (Pol. Sci.); Emory Univ., 1946–47, ABLS; Cert. Med. Lib. Assoc., 26 lib. crs. and wkshps. (1954–80). **Orgs.:** Med. LA: Bus. Mgr., *Med. LA Bltn.* (1958–62). Med. LA: South. Grp.; Numerous ofcs. and coms., (1948–80). FL Med. Libns. Consult. Med. Libs. (1955–80). **Pubns.:** "The J. Hillis Miller Health Center Library", *Med. LA Bltn.* (Spr. 1955); "New Medical Library Buildings," *Med. LA Bltn.* (Fall 1969); "Costs to Establish the University of Florida Medical Center Library," *Med. LA Bltn.* (Win. 1979); Ed. *FL Libs.* (1954–64). **Addr.:** Medical Center Library, University of South Florida, 12901 N. 30th St., Box 31, Tampa, FL 33612.

Brynteson, Susan (F. 18, 1936) Dir. of Libs., Univ. of DE, 1980–; Asst. Dir. for Tech. Srvs., IN Univ., 1977–80; Assoc. Dir. for Tech. Srvs., Univ. of TN, 1974–77; Head, Ser. Dept., Univ. of MA, 1969–74; Cat. Libn., Skidmore Coll., 1964–69; Acq. Libn., San Diego State Univ., 1963–64; Ser. Libn., Univ. of WI, 1963. **Educ.:** Univ. of WI, Madison, BA (Phil.), 1958, MALS, 1963. **Orgs.:** ALA: Legis. Com. (1979–83); Legis. Asm. (1974–78); Melvil Dewey Medal Jury (1978–79); ACRL/Com. on Legis. (Ch., 1974–78); RTSD/Nom. Com. (Ch., 1978–79), Tech. Srvs. Dirs. of Lg. Resrch. Libs. Disc. Grp. (Ch., 1978–79); ARL: Task Force on Bibl. Cntrl.; Various other orgs. and ofcs. **Honors:** Beta Phi Mu. **Addr.:** University of Delaware Library, Newark, DE 19711.

Bryson, Shauna (O. 26, 1947, Oakland, CA) Head, Cat., ICI Americas, Inc., 1978–; Head, Acq. Dept., ICI Americas, Inc., 1973–78. **Educ.:** Univ. of CA, Santa Cruz, 1965–69, BA (Hist.); Drexel Univ., 1970–72, MS (Info. Sci.). **Orgs.:** DE LA: Treas. (1979–). SLA. ASIS. **Honors:** ALA, J. Morris Jones Awd., 1971. **Activities:** 12; 15, 20, 44; 82, 87, 91 **Addr.:** 3102 Swarthmore Rd., Wilmington, DE 19807.

Bryson, Verena L. (F. 22, 1927, Brevard, NC) Ast. Dir., Cmnty. Srvs., Greenville Cnty. Lib., 1963–; Head Libn., Donaldson Air Frc. Base, 1960–62; Head Libn., Woman's Coll., Furman Univ., 1953–55; Head Ref. Libn., Greenville Cnty. Lib., 1952–53. **Educ.:** Univ. of NC, 1944–46; Univ. SC, 1946–48, BA (Hist., Pol. Sci.); Univ. of NC, 1949, BS (LS). **Orgs.:** SC LA: Pub. Lib. Sect. (Ch., 1975–76); Exec. Bd. 1975–79); Nom. Com. (1976) 2nd VP (1977–79); other coms. SELA: Lib. Admin. Sect. and Pub. Lib. Sect. (1979–); PR Com. 1975–77). ALA: Mem. Com. (1977–79); LAD/PR Sect.; Pubns. Com. (1977–79). Greenville Arts Festival (Bd., 1979–80). **Honors:** U.S. Air Frce., Milit. Air Transp., Outstan. Libn. Awd.; ALA, John Cotton Awd., 1961, 71, 72, 74, 75. **Pubns.:** "Banned Books," *SC Libn.* (1970); feature articles on Greenville Cnty. Lib. in *SE Libn., Lib. Jnl., Amer. Libs.* **Activities:** 9; 17, 36, 37; 51 **Addr.:** 127 Howell Cir., Greenville, SC 29615.

Brzezinski, Sister Mary Carmelle (D. 19, 1934, Milwaukee, WI) HS Libn., St. Joseph HS, Chicago, 1981– Libn., St. Turibius Media Center, Chicago, 1974–81; Tchr./Libn., St. Mary School, Downers Grove, 1965–74; Tchr., Sacred Heart Sch., Two Rivers, WI, 1964–65; Tchr., Good Shepherd, Chicago, 1961–64; Tchr., St. John of God, Chicago, 1959–61; Tchr., Sacred Heart, Chicago, 1956–59. **Educ.:** De Paul Univ., 1956–63, BA (Educ.); Chicago State Univ., 1972–75, MA. **Orgs.:** Cath. LA: Ed. of Chlds. Sect. Nsltr. (1979–81). North. IL Unit of Cath. LA: Vice-Chmn. of Chlds. Sect. (1972–74); Chmn. of Chlds. Sect.; Chmn. of Elect. Com. WI Unit of Cath. LA; MN/ND Unit of Cath. LA; Felician Lib. Srv.; Ed. Nsltr. (1971–). Cath. Assn. of Student Cncls. **Pubns.:** "The School Media Center a Teacher's and Student's Paradise! Is it Really?" *IL Libs.* (S 1976); "An Inside Look," *IL Libs.* (S 1973). **Activities:** 10; 17, 20, 21; 89, 91, 92 **Addr.:** St. Joseph High School Library, 4831 South Hermitage Ave., Chicago, IL 60609.

Buchanan, Holly Shipp (O. 10, 1949, Louisville, KY) Dir., Med. Lib., NKC, Inc., Instr., Bibl., Spalding Coll., 1975–; Ast. Asst. Med. Libn., Norton Meml. Infirm., 1971–72. **Educ.:** Georgetown Coll., 1967–71, BA (Bio.); Emory Univ., 1972–73, MLn; Med. LA Cert., 1975. **Orgs.:** Med. LA: Hosp. Lib. Sect; Mem. Com. (Ch., 1978–); Cont. Ed. Com. (1979–); Sect. Cncl. (1981–84). OH Valley Area Hlth. Sci. LA. Ch. (1974–76). KY LA. KY Metroversity Lib. Cncl.: Secy. (1976–77). **Pubns.:** Several papers. **Activities:** 12; 17, 39; 59, 80 **Addr.:** NKC, Inc., Medical Library, P.O. Box 35070, Louisville, KY 40232.

Buchanan, Joel R. (N. 19, 1928, Darwin, VA) Mgr., Nuc. Safety Info. Ctr., 1963–; Dev. Engin., Oak Ridge Natl. Lab, 1951–63; various other positions in engineering. **Educ.:** Vanderbilt Univ., 1948–51, BE (Chem. Engin.); Oak Ridge Sch. of Reactor Tech., 1962–63, Cert. in Nuc. Engin. **Orgs.:** ASIS. AAAS. Amer. Nuc. Socty. Natl. Socty. of Prof. Engin. **Honors:** NSIC Pubns., Tech. Com. Awd., 1978, 1979. **Pubns.:** many pubns. in nuc. engin., lab rpts. **Activities:** 4, 12; 17, 29, 46; 56, 84, 91 **Addr.:** Nuclear Safety Information Center, Oak Ridge National Laboratory, P.O. Box Y, Oak Ridge, TN 37830.

Buchanan, Robert J. C., Jr. (Jim) (O. 9, 1949, Toronto, ON) Libn., The Housing Advocates, Inc., 1979–. **Educ.:** Kent State Univ., 1967–71, BS (Educ.); 1971–74, MA (Geo.); 1977–79, MLS. **Orgs.:** ALA: RASD/Amer. Indian Mtrls. Com. (1978). **Honors:** Beta Phi Mu. **Pubns.:** "Consumerism and Consumer Resources for the Public Library," *Lib. Jnl.* (1981); Five bibls., Pub. Admin. Series, Vance Bibls. (1979–80); "American Indian Periodical Literature," *RQ* (Spr., 1977); numerous pubs. **Activities:** 12; 17, 28, 41; 95-Con. Affairs, 77, 78 **Addr.:** 7435 Pearl Rd., Middleburg Hts., OH 44130.

Buchanan, William Charles (Je. 25, 1940, Cuba Landing, TN) Asst. Prof., LS, East Carolina Univ., 1978–; Ast. Prof., Educ. Media, Univ. of Cntrl. AR, 1977–78; Asst. Libn., LSU Lab. Sch., 1976–77; Dir. of Lrng. Resrcs., Geo. C. Wallace St. Comm. Coll., 1971–76. **Educ.:** Mid. TN State Univ., 1960–62; Belmont Coll., 1962–64, BA (Eng.); Mid. TN State Univ., 1965–67, MEd; LA State Univ., 1968–71, MSLS; 1975–78, EdD. **Orgs.:** AALS. ALA. NC LA. AECT. Phi Delta Kappa. **Honors:** Beta Phi Mu. **Pubns.:** "Classification & Cataloging of Multi-Media Resources," *AR News & Views* (Ap. 1978); "Learning Center at UCA," *AR News & Views* (De. 1977). **Activities:** 1, 11; 17, 20, 32; 56, 63, 67 **Addr.:** Department of Library Science, East Carolina University, Greenville, NC 27834.

Bucher, Katherine T. (Jl. 30, 1947, Shickshinny, PA) Asst. Prof., Old Dominion Univ., 1975–; Adj. Asst. Prof., Univ. of NC, 1979–; Lectr., Catholic Univ., 1979–; Dir., Macon Cnty.-Tuskegee Pub. Lib., 1971–74; Libn., Radford Coll., 1970–71; Libn., Appleman Elem. Sch., 1968–69. **Educ.:** Millersville State Coll., 1965–69, BS (LS); Rutgers Univ., 1969–70, MLS; Auburn Univ., 1973–75, Ed.D. **Orgs.:** ALA: AASL. VA LA: Sch. Lib. Sect. (Pres. elect, 1979–). AECT: Natl. Conf. Eval. Com. (1979). VA Educ. Media Assoc: Ways and Means Com. (1978–). Assn. for Supervision and Curric. Dev. AAUW. Various other orgs. **Honors:** Beta Phi Mu; VA Educ. Media Assoc., Media Award, 1978; AAUW, Outstanding Young Women of America, 1974, 1976. **Pubns.:** "Visual Literacy," *Virginia Resolves* (Winter 1978); Reviews. **Activities:** 10, 11; 26, 32; 63, 89 **Addr.:** 1229 Benefit Rd., Chesapeake, VA 23322.

Buchholz, Janis D. (Ag. 4, 1947, Medford, WI) Serials Libn., Wayne State Univ., 1976–; Tech. Info. Spec., Lawrence Berkeley Lab., 1975–76. **Educ.:** Univ. of WI-Eau Claire, 1965–69, BA (Fr.); Univ. of WI-Madison, 1971–72, MALS. **Orgs.:** SLA. MI LA. MI Data Base Users' Grp.: Coord. Com. (1979–) **Activities:** 1; 39, 44; 60, 88 **Addr.:** Wayne State University, Science Library, Detroit, MI 48202.

Buck, Jeremy R. (O. 29, 1943, Boston, MA) Asst. Dir., Dayton and Montgomery Cnty. Pub. Lib., 1978–; Asst. Dir., Erie (PA) City and Cnty. Lib., 1976–78; Dir., Erie (PA) Cnty. Pub. Lib., 1976; Asst. Dir., 1975–76. **Educ.:** OH State Univ., 1967–70, BA (German); Case West. Rsv. Univ., 1970–71, MSLS. **Orgs.:** ALA. OH LA. **Activities:** 9; 17, 35 **Addr.:** Dayton and Montgomery County Public Library, 215 E. 3rd St., Dayton, OH 45402.

Buck, Michael Dennis (N. 27, 1949, Sidney, NY) Lib. Dir., TX State Tech. Inst., 1979–; Libn., 1978–79; Asst. Libn., 1976–78. **Educ.:** Univ. of TX, Arlington, 1970–74, BA (Hist.); N. TX State Univ., 1975–76, MLS; SUNY, Alfred, 1968–70, AAS (Mech. Tech.). **Orgs.:** ALA. TX LA. Harlingen Civitan Intl.: VP (1979–80). **Honors:** Beta Phi Mu, 1976. **Pubns.:** "Data Analysis of the use of Materials in a Metropolitan Public Library," *ERIC* (1977). **Activities:** 1; 17, 31, 36 **Addr.:** 307 E. Flynn, Harlingen, TX 78550.

Buck, Richard MacDonald (Je. 16, 1930, Albion, NY) Asst. to Chief Performing Arts Resrch. Ctr., NY Pub. Lib., 1967–, Adult Bk. Review Spec., 1965–67, Asst. Branch Libn., 1962–65. **Educ.:** SUNY, Albany, 1948–52, BA, cum laude (Educ.), 1952–53, MA (Educ.); Columbia Univ., 1959–60, MS cum laude (LS). **Orgs.:** ALA: Int. Frdm. Com. (1978–79, 1981–); Cncl. (1975–79, 1980–84), IFRT, Exec. Com. (1979–80) Thea. LA: Secy.-Treas. (1970–); Prog. Com. (1970–). Cncl. of Natl. Lib. and Info. Assns.: Ch. (1980–81); Thea. LA Cnclr. (1972–). EFLA. Various other orgs. **Pubns.:** Contrib., *Funding Alternatives for Libraries* (1979); "Theatre Library Association," *ALA Yrbk.* (1976–). **Activities:** 2, 12; 17, 28, 42; 55, 67 **Addr.:** Performing Arts Research Center, New York Public Library at Lincoln Center, 111 Amsterdam Ave., New York, NY 10023.

Buckingham, Barbara L. (D. 18, 1938, Detroit, MI) AV Div., Head, Macomb Cnty. Lib., 1968–; Branch Libn., Warren Pub. Lib., 1965–68. **Educ.:** Wayne State Univ., 1957–61, BS (Ed.); 1965–70, MSLS; Waldorf Tchr. Training Inst., Mercy Coll., 1968–69, Dipl., (El. Ed.). **Orgs.:** Film Lib. Info. Cncl.: Co-ch. (1979–80). EFLA: Amer. Film Fest. Juror (1970–80). AECT. MI LA: AV Div. Ch. (1975). Detroit Area Film Tchrs.: Newsletter Ed. (1970); Bd. Mem. (1973–76). **Pubns.:** "From Globe to Video Cassettes," *Michigan Librarian* (Win. 75); Reviews. **Activities:** 9; 15, 17, 32; 67, 85, 93 **Addr.:** Macomb County Library, 16480 Hall Rd., Mt. Clemens, MI 48044.

Buckingham, Betty Jo (Ag. 6, 1927, Prairie City, IA) Consult. Lib. Media, IA State Dept. of Pub. Instr., 1964–; Lectr., Univ. of MN Lib. Sch., Sum., 1970; Libn., Kurtz Jr. HS, Des Moines, 1960–64; Libn., Fort Madison (IA) HS, 1954–60; Tchr.-Libn., Harlan (IA) Cmnty. Schs., 1950–54; Tchr., Earlham (IA) Cmnty. Schs., 1948–50. **Educ.:** IA State Tchrs. Coll., 1945–48, BA (Eng.); Univ. of IL, Sums. 1949–53, MSLS; Univ. of MN, 1969–78, PhD (LS). **Orgs.:** ALA: Cncl. (1980–83); AASL (Pres.-Elect/Pres. 1980–82; Secy., 1980), Unit Head, Unit Grp. V-Pub. Info. (1978–79), various other coms. (1976–79); YASD. IA Educ.

PROFESSIONAL ACTIVITIES: Institutions: 1. Acad. lib.; 2. Arch.; 3. Assn.; 4. Fed./Gvt. lib.; 5. Inst. lib.; 6. Mfr./Suppl.; 7. Milit. lib.; 8. Musm.; 9. Pub. lib.; 10. Sch. lib.; 11. Sch. of lib. sci.; 12. Spec. lib.; 13. State lib.; 14. (other). **Functions/Activities:** 15. Acq./Col. dev.; 16. Adult srvs.; 17. Admin.; 18. Apprais.; 19. Archit./Bldgs.; 20. Cat./Class.; 21. Chld. srvs.; 22. Circ.; 23. Cons./Pres.; 24. Consult.; 25. Cont. ed.; 26. Educ. lib. sci.; 27. Ext. srvs.; 28. Fund/Grants; 29. Gvt. pubs.; 30. Indx./Abs.; 31. Instr. lib. use; 32. Media srvs.; 33. Micro.; 34. Netwks./Coop.; 35. Persnl.; 36. PR; 37. Publshg.; 38. Recs. mgt.; 39. Ref. srvs.; 40. Repro.; 41. Resrch.; 42. Review.; 43. Secur.; 44. Serials; 45. Spec. col.; 46. Tech. srvs.; 47. Trustees/Bds.; 48. YA srvs.; 49. (other).

Media Assn.: Consult., Ex Officio (1972–); Cert. and Stans. Com. (1977–); Srvy. Com. (1975–). IA LA. Natl. Educ. Assn. **Honors:** Beta Phi Mu; Kappa Delta Pi. **Pubns.:** Ed., *Plan for Progress in the Media Center, 7–12,* Rev. ed. (1980); Ed., *Plan for Progress in the Media Center, K–6,* Rev. ed. (1979); Ed., *Selection Bibliography,* 4th ed. (1979); Ed., *Iowa and Some Iowans, Supplement to Second Edition* (1978); Jt. auth. *Survey of the Status of Media Service in Iowa Public Schools* (1978). **Addr.:** Alternative Programs Section, Instruction and Curriculum Division, Iowa State Department of Public Instruction, Grimes State Office Building, Des Moines, IA 50319.

Buckland, Lawrence Fogler (Ag. 5, 1929, Schenectady, NY) Pres., Inforonics, Inc., 1962–; Mgr., Info. Sci. Dept., Itek Corp., 1958–62; Lieutenant, USAF, 1954–58. **Educ.:** MA Inst. of Tech., 1948–52, BS (Mech. Engin.). **Orgs.:** ALA. SLA. Soc. for Scholarly Publshg. Bd. of Dirs. **Pubns.:** Various conf. papers and reports. **Activities:** 6; 24, 30, 34; 57, 75, 93 **Addr.:** 18 Ridge Rd., Hudson, MA 01749.

Buckland, Michael K. (N. 23, 1941, Wantage, Oxfordshire, Eng) Dean, Sch. of Lib. and Info. Std., Univ. of CA, Berkeley, 1976–; Asst. Dir., Purdue Univ. Libs., 1972–75; Asst. Libn., Univ. of Lancaster Lib., 1965–72. **Educ.:** Oxford Univ., 1960–63, BA (Hist.); Sheffield Univ., 1964–65, Postgrad. Dip. (Libnshp.), 1968–72, PhD (LS). **Orgs.:** ALA. ASIS. CA LA. LA (London). IN Coop. Lib. Srvs. Athrty.: VP (1974–75). **Honors:** Univ. of West. MI, Visit. Schol., 1979. **Pubns.:** Co.-ed., *Reader in Operations Research for Libraries* (1976); *Book Availability and the Library* (1975); Co-auth., *The Use of Gaming in Education for Library Management* (1976); "Library Education–Meeting the Needs of the Future," Cath. Lib. World (My/Je 1979); "On Types of Search and the Allocation of Library Resources," Jhl. Amer. Socty. for Info. Sci. (My. 1979); Various other publications. **Activities:** 11; 17, 26, 41 **Addr.:** School of Library and Information Studies, University of California, Berkeley, CA 94720.

Buckley, Cozetta W. (O. 21, 1926, Rio, MS) Head Dept. & Assoc. Prof. of Lib. Sci., Jackson State Univ., 1967–; Libn., Brinkley HS, 1959–67; Tchr., Smith Elem. Sch., 1955–59; Tchr., Leflore Cnty. Schs., 1948–55. **Educ.:** Jackson State Univ., 1944–48, BS (Educ.); Atlanta Univ., 1960, MSLS; Univ. of IL, 1971–72, CAS (Lib. Sci); Univ. of MI, 1976–78, PhD, (Lib. Sci.). **Orgs.:** ALA: Nominations, (Techrs. Section, Lib Ed. Div.) (1969). AALS: Nominations (1980). MS LA: Education (1975–76, 1980); Long Range Plan (1974); Standards and Planning (1979–1980). SELA. MS Assn. of Educators. MS Assn. of Higher Educ. **Honors:** Beta Phi Mu; Pi Lambda Theta; Sigma Tau Delta. **Activities:** 10, 11; 21, 25, 26; 57, 63, 72 **Addr.:** 6340 Whitestone Rd., Jackson, MS 39206.

Buckley, Francis J., Jr. (Ag 7, 1942, Lynn, MA) Coord., Col. Dev., Detroit Pub. Lib., 1980–. Docum. Spec., 1972–80; Ref. Libn., 1966–72. **Educ.:** Univ. of MI, 1962–65, BA (Hist.); 1965–, MLS. **Orgs.:** ALA: GODORT/V. Ch. (1977–78), Ch. (1978–80). Depos. Lib. Cncl. to the Pub. Printer: Ch. (1977–79). Prof. Org. of Libns., Detroit Pub. Lib.: Pres. (1972–73, 1974–75). SLA. various other orgs. **Pubns.:** "Library Publishing & Information", *Amer. Libs.* (S. 1979). **Activities:** 9; 15, 29, 34; 78, 95-Labor Rel. **Addr.:** Detroit Public Library, 5201 Woodward Avenue, Detroit, MI 48202.

Buckley, Hope Tillman (S. 8, 1941, Baltimore, MD) Ref. Libn., Rider Coll., 1970–; Branch Libn., Trenton Pub. Lib., 1968–69; Lib. Trainee, Free Lib. of Philadelphia, 1965. **Educ.:** Goucher Coll., 1959–60, Middlebury Coll., 1960–62; Univ. of PA, 1962–64, AB (Eng.); Rutgers Univ., 1965–66, MLS; Rider Coll., 1976–79, MBA (Indus. Rel.). **Orgs.:** ALA; SLA: Princeton-Trenton Chap. **Honors:** Sigma Iota Epsilon, 1979; Beta Phi Mu, 1966. **Activities:** 1; 29, 31, 39; 51, 59, 77 **Addr.:** 33 Bruce Dr., Holland, PA 18966.

Buckley, James Whitney (Ag. 16, 1933, Los Angeles, CA) City Libn., Torrance Pub. Lib., 1979–; Cnty. Libn., Marin Cnty. Pub. Lib., 1979; Cnty. Libn., San Mateo Cnty. Pub. Lib., 1974–78; Dir. of Pub. Srvs., Orange Cnty. Pub. Lib., 1969–74; Reg. Libn., Orange Cnty. Pub. Lib., 1968–69; Branch Libn., Los Angeles Cnty. Pub. Lib., 1961–68. **Educ.:** Los Angeles Harbor Coll., 1951–53, AA (Liberal Arts); CA State Univ., Long Beach, 1958–60, BA (Eng.); Univ. of South. CA, 1960–61, MLS, 1972–74, MPA (Pub. Admin.); CA Sec. Tchg. Cred., 1975. **Orgs.:** ALA. CA LA: Com. on Coms. (1964); Rcrt. Com. (1967); Gvt. Rel. Com. (1977); Nom. Com. (Ch., 1970, 1973). Cnty. Supvsrs. Assoc. CA: Cnty Libns. (Pres., 1974). Leag. of California Cities: Cmnty Srvs. Com. (1980–81). Amer. Socty. for Pub. Admin. Rotary: various ofcs. **Activities:** 9; 17, 35, 36; 63, 75, 78 **Addr.:** 3301 Torrance Boulevard, Torrance, CA 90503.

Buckley, Jeanne (N. 8, 1950, Melrose, MA) Coord. of Instr. Media, St. Joseph's Univ., 1979–; Circ. Libn., Coll. of Wm. and Mary, 1977–79; Circ. Libn., Simmons Coll., 1976–77; Asst. Circ. and Rsrvs. Libn., 1975–76. **Educ.:** Univ. of ME, 1969–73, BA (Eng.); Simmons Coll., 1975–77, MLS. **Orgs.:** ALA: ACRL. AECT. VA Photographer's Assn. **Pubns.:** Bibl., *Women's Studies Materials,* Coll. of Wm. and Mary (1979); Photographs *Wm. and Mary Review,* (1978–79). **Activities:** 10; 28, 32; 50, 67 **Addr.:** St. Joseph's University, 54th and City Line Ave., Philadelphia, PA 19131.

Buckley, Steven F. (Jl. 14, 1938, Marietta, OH) Head, Tech. Srvs., SUNY, Brockport, 1970–; Head, Prcs. Dept., Rutgers Univ. Lib., 1969–70; Head, Prcs. Sect., Cat. Dept., 1966–69; Serials Libn., Lib. of Sci. and Med., 1965–66. **Educ.:** Rutgers, 1956–60, BA (Geo.); 1963–65, MA (Geo.); 1966–69, MLS. **Orgs.:** ALA. SUNY Libns. Assn. **Activities:** 1; 17, 46 **Addr.:** 41 Chappell St., Apt 8, Brockport, NY 14420.

Buckman, Thomas R. (May 3, 1923, Reno, NV) Pres., The Fndn. Ctr., 1971–; Libn., Northwestern Univ., 1968–71; Dir. of Libs., Univ. of KS, 1961–68. **Educ.:** Univ. of the Pac., 1943–47, BA; Univ. of MN, 1951–52, MA (Scan. Std.); 1952–53, BLS; Univ. of Stockholm, 1948–51, Cert. Lit. **Orgs.:** ALA. ASIS. ARL: Pres. (1971–72). Assn. for the Study of Grants Econ. Telecomm. Coop. Netwk.: Chmn. (1979–). **Honors:** John Simon Guggenheim Meml. Fndn., Guggenheim Fellow, 1964–65. **Pubns.:** *University and Research Libraries in Japan and the United States* (1972); Publshr. and Intro. Auth., *The Foundation Directory,* Ed. 5, 6, 7 (1975, 1977, 1979); Ed., "The Impact of Economic Change on Libraries," *Josey;* "The Information Society: Issues and Answers," *Phoenix* (1979). **Activities:** 12; 17, 37, 47; 93, 95-Grant/Fndns., **Addr.:** The Foundation Center, 888 Seventh Ave., New York, NY 10019.

Bucknall, Carolyn Foreman (D. 14, 1931, Port Arthur, TX) Asst. Dir. for Col. Dev., Univ. TX, 1974–; Head, Mono. Unit, 1973–74; Head, Acq. Dept., 1967–73; Head, Acq. Dept., SUNY, Binghamton, 1965–67; Head, Serials Acq. and Cat., Univ. MA, 1963–65; Serials Catlgr., Univ. WA, 1961–63; Serials Catlgr., Univ. TX, 1959–61. **Honors:** Phi Beta Kappa; Beta Phi Mu. **Pubns.:** "Texas University of Texas Libraries," *Encyc. of Lib. and Info. Sci.;* "An Analysis of Publications Issued by the American Library Association, 1907–57," *ACRL Microcard Series, no. 118* (1960). **Activities:** 1; 15, 28, 45; 54, 55, 57 **Addr.:** General Libraries, University of Texas at Austin, Austin, TX 78712.

Buckwald, Joel (Je. 29, 1917, New York, NY) Chief, Arch. Branch, Fed. Arch. and Recs. Ctr., Natl. Arch. and Recs. Srv., Gen. Srvs. Admin., 1970–, Consult., Arch. and Recs., Mgt. to Mnstry. of Frgn. Affairs, Peru, Org. of Amer. States, 1963; Archvst., Fed. Rec. Ctr., 1950–70; Archvst., Natl. Arch., 1947–50, 1942, Arch. Asst., 1941–42. **Educ.:** Coll. of the City of New York, 1934–38, BSS (Hist.); Columbia Univ., 1969, MA (Hist.). **Orgs.:** SAA: NY Area, Mem. Com. (Ch., 1954–56); Cncl., Alternate Rep. SAA Amer. Stans. Assn.: Sect. Com. 239 on Lib. Work and Documtn. (1963–67). **Pubns.:** "Aims in Teaching World History," *The Social Studies* (1968); contrib., *Handbook of Federal World War Agencies and Their Records, 1917–21* (1943). **Activities:** 2; 18, 41; 69 **Addr.:** 3835 Sedgwick Ave., Bronx, NY 10463.

Buckwalter, Robert L. (N. 29, 1941, Baltimore, MD) Head, Resrcs. and Tech. Srvs., Columbia Univ. Law Lib., 1976–, Acq. Libn., 1973–76. **Educ.:** Johns Hopkins Univ., 1959–63, BA (Eng.); Columbia Univ. Sch. of Lib. Srv., 1972–73, MS. **Orgs.:** AALL: Rel. with Publshrs. and Dlrs. (1976–77). Law LA of Grt. NY. NY Tech. Srvs. Libns. Assn. **Honors:** Beta Phi Mu, 1973; Phi Beta Kappa, 1963. **Pubns.:** Ed., cmplr., *Law Books Published* (1979–); ed., cmplr., *Law Books in Print* (1982). **Activities:** 1, 12; 15, 23, 46; 77 **Addr.:** Columbia University Law Library, 435 W. 116th St., New York, NY 10027.

Buder, Christine L. (S. 12, 1924, St. Louis, MO) Spec. Cols. Libn., NM State Univ. Lib., 1977–, Ref. Libn., Dept. Head, 1974–77, Soc. Sci., Bus. Admin. Div. Libn., 1966–74, Ref. Libn., 1965–66, Circ. Libn., 1962–65; Libn., Christ. Bd. of Publ., 1955–62; Asst. Cur., Disciples of Christ Hist. Socty., 1952–55; Asst. Libn., Culver-Stockton Coll., 1949–52. **Educ.:** Culver-Stockton Coll., 1944–48, BS (Bus. Admin., Econ.); Univ. of IL, 1948–49, MS (LS); various crs. **Orgs.:** ALA: RASD/Hist. Sect., Bibl. Com. (1970–73); Amer. Indian Mtrls. and Srvs. Com. (1974–76). NM LA: Pres. (1975–76); various ofcs., coms. SW LA: Exec. Bd. (1975–76). **Honors:** Beta Phi Mu, 1949. **Pubns.:** *The Newspaper Collection of the New Mexico State University Library: A Holdings List* (1981); *How To Build A Church Library* (1955); ed., *NM Libs.* (1968–72). **Activities:** 1, 12; 39, 45; 70, 73, 83 **Addr.:** 1120 N. Mesilla St., Las Cruces, NM 88005.

Budington, William S. (Jl. 3, 1919, Oberlin, OH) Exec. Dir., Libn., The John Crerar Lib., 1969; Libn., 1965–69; Assoc. Libn., 1952–65; Libn., Engin. and Phys. Sci., Columbia Univ., 1947–52. **Educ.:** Williams Coll., 1936–40, BA (Amer. Lit.); Columbia Univ., 1940–41, BS (LS); Virginia Polytech. Inst., 1946–, BS (Elec. Engin.). **Orgs.:** ALA: Cncl. (1960–63, 1967–71, 1979–82); various bds. and coms. SLA: Pres. (1964–65); Bd. of Dir. (1961–66). ARL: Pres. (1973); Bd. of Dir., (1969–74). Med. LA: various coms.; ASIS. AAAS. Amer. Socty. for Engin. Educ. **Honors:** Williams Coll., Hon. L.H.D. Degree, 1975; Phi Beta Kappa, 1940. **Pubns.:** Contrib., *Special Libraries: A Guide for Management,* 1st and 2nd ed. (1966, 1975); numerous articles. **Activities:** 12; 17; 64, 80, 91 **Addr.:** The John Crerar Library, 35 W. 33rd St., Chicago IL 60616.

Buechler, John L. (Mr. 26, 1926, Milwaukee, WI) Head, Spec. Col., Bailey/Howe Lib., Univ. of VT, 1962–; Head, Spec. Col., Univ. of FL, 1959–62; Librn., Eng. and Sp. Grad. Lib., Ohio State Univ., 1956–59; Asst. Hum. Libn., Univ. of Notre Dame, 1955–56. **Educ.:** Marquette Univ., 1946–50, BA (Eng.); 1950–51, MA (Eng.); Univ. of WI, 1954–55, MS (LS). **Orgs.:** Bibl. Socty. of Amer. Amer. Prtg. Hist. Assn. Royal Untd. Srv. Inst. for Defence Std. VT Hist. Socty. VT Acad. of Arts and Sci.: Interuniv. Ctr. for European Std. **Honors:** Univ. of VT Fac. Resrch. Awds., 1969, 1975; Natl. Hist. Pubns. and Recs. Comsn., 1977–78. **Pubns.:** *Henry Stevens - His Autobiography & the Noviomagus Club* (1978); Ed., *Correspondence of Francis Parkman and Henry Stevens* (1967); "Brace, Bran & St Albans," *New Eng. Galaxy* (Fall 1978); "Ethan's Youngest Brother," *Manuscripts* (Win. 1977); other articles. **Activities:** 1; 15, 41, 45; 55, 57, 74 **Addr.:** Special Collections, Bailey/Howe Library, University of Vermont, Burlington, VT 05405.

Buehler, Dale A. (F 28, 1932, Hazleton, PA) Chief Libn., Wilkes Col., 1971–; Acq. Libn., 1962–71. **Educ.:** Franklin & Marshall Col., 1950–54, AB (Soclgy.); Drexel Univ., 1958–60, MSLS. **Orgs.:** ALA. PA LA: Northeast Chap., Ch. (1977–78). **Activities:** 1; 17 **Addr.:** Eugene Shedden Farley Library, Wilkes College, Wilkes-Barre, PA 18766.

Buhr, Lorne Richard Mr. 25, 1942, Borden SK) Head of Ref. and Info. Srvs., AB Legis. Lib., 1981–, Docum. Ref. Libn., 1977–81; Gvt. Pubns. Libn., Univ. SK, 1971–77. **Educ.:** Can. Mennonite Bible Coll., 1960–64, BChrEd (Theo.); Univ. SK, 1965–69, BA (Hist.); Univ. Toronto, 1969–70, BLS. **Orgs.:** Can. LA. AB LA: Gvt. Docum. Com. CALL. Edmonton Law Libns. Assn. **Pubns.:** "Selective Dissimination of MARC: a User Evaluation," *Jnl. of Lib. Autom.* (1972); Jt. auth., *"Using MARC to Catalogue Monographs in Series" 6th Annual WES CAN ASIS Conference, Saskatoon, Sept. 25–27, 1974.* **Activities:** 15, 29, 39; 75, 78, 92 **Addr.:** Alberta Legislature Library, 216 Legislature Building, Edmonton, AB T5K 2B6 Canada.

Buist, Eleanor (Jl. 9, 1916, Brooklyn, NY) Indxr.-Transl. (Lib. Lit.), The H. W. Wilson Co., 1971–; Slavic Bibl., Columbia Univ., 1964–66, Sr. Ref. Libn., 1954–64, Resrch. Asst., Russ. Inst., 1946–54; Assoc. Dir., Slavic Lib. Inst. and Visit. Lect., Sch. of LS, Univ. of IL, Sum. 1970. **Educ.:** Vassar Coll., 1933–37, BA (Grmn.); Middlebury Coll., Sums. 1946–49, MA, (Russ.); Columbia Univ., 1951–54, MSLS. **Orgs.:** ALA: Ref. and Subscrpn. Bks. Review Com. (1971–75; Guest Reviewer, 1975–79); ACRL/Slavic Subsect. (Ch., 1965–66)/Subj. Spec. Sect. (Ch., 1970–71). Coord. Com. for Slavic and E. European Lib. Resrcs.: Exec. Secy. (1962–66). NY LA. Amer. Assn. for the Advnc. of Slavic Std. **Pubns.:** Jt. auth., *Guide to Reference Books,* 7th ed., *3rd Supplement* (1960); *4th Supplement* (1963); "Steps toward Cataloging at Source in the U.S.S.R.," *Wilson Lib. Bltn.* (Je. 1970); "Soviet Centralized Cataloging: a View from Abroad," *Lib. Trends* (Jl. 1967); "Advanced Study: Trends in the USSR" in *Library Education: An International Survey* (1968). "Area Programs for the Soviet Union and East Europe: Some Current Concerns of the Libraries," *Lib. Qtly.* (O. 1965); Reviews. **Activities:** 1; 20, 30, 39, 54 **Addr.:** 90 LaSalle St., New York, NY 10027.

Bulaong, Grace F. (N. 22, 1939, Manila, Philippines) Head, Cat. Dept., Metro. Toronto Lib., 1971–, Asst. Head of Lib., 1980–; Sr. Catlgr., Queen's Univ., 1968–70; Catlgr., Asst. Prof., North. IL Univ., 1967; Instr., Secy. of Inst., Inst. of Lib. Sci., Univ. of the Phil. 1963–67. **Educ.:** Univ. of the Philippines, 1955–59, BSLS, 1959–62, 67, MA (Asian Studies); Univ. of MI, 1962–63, AMLS; Cert. on Supervision, 1975. **Orgs.:** ALA. Can. LA. ON LA. Dirs. of ON Reg. Lib. Systs.: Ch., Tech. Srvs. Com. (1979–81); Ch., Multilingual Srvs. Com. (1976–79); Admins. of Borough and City Libs.: Ch., Subcom. on Stats. & Authority Files (1978–79). Union Cat. Proj.: Subcom. on Authority Files. Shared Authority Files: Bd. of Dirs. (1979–). **Honors:** Pi Gamma Mu, 1959; Phi Kappa Phi, 1959; Philippine Bd. of Schols. for SE Asia, grantee. **Pubns.:** *Satire in the Philippines* (1969); "Dewey 19", *DORLS Information Exchange* (D. 1979); "Authorities and Standards in a Changing World", DORLS Tech. Srv. Com., Information Exchange (1980). **Activities:** 1, 9; 20, 46; 54, 56, 66 **Addr.:** Cataloguing Dept., Metropolitan Toronto Library, 789 Yonge St., Toronto, ON M4W 2G8, Canada.

Bullen, Robert Whitefield (Ag. 12, 1927, Vicksburg, MS) Admin. Srvs. Libn., N Suburban Lib. Syst., 1968–; Dir., Cobb Cty. Pub. Lib., 1962–68; Dir., Peidmont Regl. Lib., 1961–62; Consult., W VA Lib. Comsn., 1957–60; Lib., MS State Col., 1953–57; Lib., Univ. of GA, 1950–53. **Educ.:** Millsaps Col., 1944–47, BA (Eng.); Emory Univ., 1950–51, MA (Lib. Sci.); **Orgs.:** GA LA: Mem. Com. Ch. (1963–65); Pub. Lib. Com. Ch. (1965–67); Exec. Board (1965–67). IL LA: Ch (1971). MFLA: Conf. Com. Ch. (1972). Kiwanis Intl.: Ed. Exec. Bd. Boy Scouts: Exec. Com. (1968–78). PTA. Pi Kappa Alpha: Alum. Com. (1968–). **Honors:** Natl. Lib. Weeks, Cert., 1960. **Pubns.:** *McDowell Cnty., W. VA.* and *Marshall Cty., W. VA.* (1957); *Survey for Raleigh and Fayette Counties, W. VA.* (1959); *Conference for Library Trustees Proceedings,* (1961); Ed., *Non Easter* (1968–73). **Activities:** 4, 9; 17, 26 **Addr.:** North Suburban Lib. System, 200 W. Dundee Road, Wheeling, IL 60090.

Special Subjects/Services: 50. Adult educ.; 51. Advert./Mktg.; 52. Aerosp.; 53. Agric.; 54. Area std.; 55. Arts/Hum.; 56. Autom.; 57. Bibl./Prtg.; 58. Bio. sci.; 59. Bus./Fin.; 60. Chem.; 61. Copyrt.; 62. Documtn.; 63. Educ.; 64. Engin.; 65. Env.; 66. Eth. grps.; 67. Film; 68. Food/Nutr.; 69. Geneal.; 70. Geo.; 71. Geol.; 72. Handcpd.; 73. Hist.; 74. Int. frdm.; 75. Info. sci.; 76. Insr.; 77. Law; 78. Legis.; 79. Math./Comp. sci.; 80. Med.; 81. Metals; 82. Nat. resrcs.; 83. Newsp.; 84. Nuc. sci.; 85. Oral hist.; 86. Petr./Energy; 87. Pharm.; 88. Phys./Astr./Math.; 89. Readg.; 90. Relig.; 91. Sci./Tech.; 92. Soc. sci.; 93. Telecom.; 94. Transp.; 95. (other).

Buller, Nora Grace (Jl. 20, 1926, Porthope, ON) Actg. Dir., Libs. and Cmnty. Info. Branch, ON Mnstry. of Culture and Recreation, 1980–; Coord. of Pub. Lib. Srvs., ON Prov. Service Lib., 1970–80; Head, Young People's Srvs., Toronto Pub. Lib., 1967–69; Branch Head, 1959–67. **Educ.:** Univ. of Toronto, 1944–47, BA (Gen. Arts), 1949–50, BLS. **Orgs.:** ON LA. Can. LA: Chmn. of Int. Frdm. Com. (1972–75). ALA. **Pubns.:** Ed., *ON Lib. Review* (1975–); Various articles. **Activities:** 9, 13; 16, 17, 24; 50, 72, 74 **Addr.:** Ontario Ministry of Culture and Recreation, W. Toronto, ON M7A 2R9 Canada.

Bulman, Learned Thomas (F. 23, 1923, Norwich, CT) Supvsr., Tech. Srvs., Cnty. Coll. of Morris Randolph (NJ), 1976–; Dir., E. Orange Pub. Lib., 1970–76; Asst. Dir., 1966–70; Supvsr., Youth Srvs., 1951–66; Youth Libn., Detroit Pub. Lib., 1949–51. **Educ.:** Washington and Jefferson Coll., 1946–48, AB (Hist.); Columbia Univ., 1948–49, MLS. **Orgs.:** NJ LA: Chld. Sect., Pres. (1966–67); Pres. (1974–75); Cnclr. (1978–81); Schol. Trustees Fund, Ch. (1978–); Lib. Dev. Com. (1973–). ALA; NJ Area Libs.; Archons of Colophon. Little Theatre, E. Orange: Pres. (1958–59); Masons: Pres., E. Orange Hi-12 Clb. (1959); E. Orange Sr. Citizen's Cncl.; Mayor's Youth Cncl. **Pubns.:** Reviews, Articles. **Activities:** 1, 9; 15, 17, 20 **Addr.:** 30-3B Mt. Pleasant Village, Morris Plains, NJ 07950.

Bulow, Jack F. (Je. 7, 1942, Elmira, NY) Assoc. Dir., Birmingham Pub. Lib., 1977–, Cmnty. Srvs. Libn., 1973–77. **Educ.:** Univ. of AL, Birmingham, 1968–71, BA (Hist., Pol. Sci.); Univ. of AL, Tuscaloosa, 1972–73, MLS; Corning (NY) Cmnty. Cdl., 1966–68, AAS (Sci.). **Orgs.:** AL LA: Pub. Rel. Com. (Ch., 1977); Constn. and Bylaws Com. (1976); Lib. Manpower Srvy. Com. (Ch., 1976); various other coms. ALA. Southeastern LA. Cystic Fibrosis Fndn.: Reg. VIII (Pres., 1978–). Downtown Action Com. Greater Birmingham Arts Alliance: Bd. of Dirs. (1976–). Various other orgs. **Activities:** 9; 17, 27 **Addr.:** 2020 Park Pl., Birmingham, AL 35203.

Bulson, Christine E. (Mr. 11, 1942, Cooperstown, NY) Assoc. Libn., SUNY, Oneonta, 1968–; Libn., Pleasantville HS, 1967–68; Ctrl. Sch. Libn., Margaretville, 1964–66. **Educ.:** Hartwick Coll., 1960–64, BA (Eng.); SUNY, Albany, 1966–67, MLS; 6th-Yr. Cert. in progress. **Orgs.:** SUNY LA. NY LA. ALA: ACRL, East. NY (Prog. Com. 1977–78). Worcester Free Lib.: Bd. of Trustees (1975–). **Pubns.:** Numerous bk. reviews *Lib. Jnl.* (1974–); other reviews. **Activities:** 1; 17, 31, 39; 68, 77, 92 **Addr.:** Milne Library, SUNY, Oneonta, Oneonta, NY 13820.

Bulthuis, G. Thomas (Je. 21, 1935, Grand Haven, MI) VP, Microfilming Corp. of Amer., 1976–; Dir., Lib. Srvs., Ramapo Coll. of NJ, 1970–74; Asst. Dir., Lib., Grand Valley State Coll., 1964–69. **Educ.:** Calvin Coll., 1961–63, BA (Hist.); Univ. of MI, 1963–64, MALS. **Orgs.:** ALA: Micropublshg. Com.; Natl. Micro. Assn. Archons of Colophon. **Activities:** 1, 14-Publshr.; 15, 33, 37; 83, 85 **Addr.:** Microfilming Corporation of America, 1620 Hawkins Ave., Sanford, NC 27330.

Bumgardner, Georgia Brady (D. 8, 1944, Mt. Kisco, NY) Andrew W. Mellon Cur. of Graph. Arts, Amer. Antiq. Socty., 1969–. **Educ.:** Wellesley Coll., 1962–66, BA (Art Hist.). **Orgs.:** New Eng. Adv. Com. of Arch. of Amer. Art. Print Cncl. of Amer. New Eng. Mus. Assn. Amer. Hist. Print Col. Socty. Other orgs. **Pubns.:** Co-Auth., *Massachusetts Broadsides of the American Revolution* (1976); *American Broadsides* (1971); "American Almanac Illustrations in the Eighteenth Century" in *Eighteenth-Century Prints in Colonial America* (1979); Cmplr., "Graphic Arts: Seventeenth-Nineteenth Century" in *Arts in America: A Bibliography* (1979): "Aspects of American Book Illustration," *Imprint* (Aut. 1980). **Activities:** 12; 15, 20, 45; 55, 70 **Addr.:** American Antiquarian Society, 185 Salisbury St., Worcester, MA 01609.

Bundy, Annalee M. (F. 11, 1938, Chicago, IL) Dir., Providence Pub. Lib., 1978–; Dir., Pub. Lib. of the City of Somerville, MA, 1973–78; Asst. Dir., Medford (MA) Pub. Lib., 1967–73; Docum. and Per. Libn., Grad. Sch. of Pub. Affairs, SUNY, Albany, 1966–67; Head Libn., Children's Room, Schnectady, NY Cnty Pub. Lib., 1965–66; Tech. Libn., E.I. DuPont de Nemours, Londonderry, N. Ireland, 1963–65; Head and Assoc. Head Libn., Coll. of Guam, 1961–63; Asst. Libn., Pine Manor Jr. Coll., 1960–61. **Educ.:** Univ. of NH, 1960, BA; Simmons Coll., 1961, MLS. **Orgs.:** New England LA: Secy. (1978–79). ALA: Mem. Ch., New England Region (1974–78); PLA/VP/Pres. Elect of the Metropolitan Sec. (1980–). RI LA: Ch., Standards Com. (1979–80). RI Governor's Conf.: Del. Massachusetts Cable TV Comsn.: Commissioner (1975–79). Massachusetts Consumer's Cncl: Pub. Mem. Providence Chamber of Cmrce.; RI Sch. of Design: Lib. Adv. Com. **Pubns.:** Comp., Alternatives in Print, II (1972); "Defense of a Library Budget", *Cath. Lib. World* (S. 1978). **Activities:** 9, 13; 17, 24, 47; 50, 56, 93 **Addr.:** Providence Public Library, 150 Empire St., Providence, RI 02903.

Bunge, Charles A. (Mr. 18, 1936, Kimball, NE) Prof., Lib. Sch., Univ. of WI, Madison, 1977–; Prof. and Dir., Lib. Sch., 1971–81, Asst. and Assoc. Prof., 1967–71; Resrch. Assoc., Lib. Resrch. Ctr., Univ. of IL, 1964–67; Ref. Libn., Ball State Tchrs. Coll., 1962–64; Ref. Libn., Daniel Boone Reg. Lib., 1960–62. **Educ.:** Univ. of MO, 1954–59, BA (Phil.); Univ. of IL, 1959–60, MSLS, 1964–67, PhD (LS). **Orgs.:** ALA: Cncl. (1975–79); RASD (Bd., 1979–82). AALS: Pres. (1980–81); Bd. (1969–72). WI LA: Pres. (1972–73). **Honors:** Beta Phi Mu, 1960; Phi Beta Kappa, 1959. **Pubns.:** *Professional Education and Reference Efficiency* (1967); "Current Reference Books," *Wilson Lib. Bltn.* (1972–81); "Approaches to the Evaluation of Library Reference Service" in *Evaluation and Scientific Management of Libraries and Information Centers* (1977); "Reference Service in the Information Network" in *Interlibrary Communications and Information Networks* (1971). **Activities:** 1, 9; 26, 34, 39; 55, 92 **Addr.:** Library School, University of Wisconsin, Helen White Hall, 600 N. Park St., Madison, WI 53706.

Bunn, Dumont C. (Ja. 15, 1936, Vero Beach, FL) Asst. Lib. Dir., Mercer Univ., 1971–; Head, Pub. Srvs., 1965–71, Head Catlgr., 1964–65; Asst. to Head of Acq., GA State Univ., 1962–64; Asst. Libn., Emory Univ. Dental Sch. Lib., 1961–62. **Educ.:** Univ. of GA, 1955–59, BA (Eng.); Emory Univ., 1959–61, MLn (Libnshp.); various crs. **Orgs.:** SELA. GA LA. Mercer Univ. Cncl. of Libns. Ingleside Neighborhood Assn. Macon-Bibb Cnty. Beautification-Clean Cmnty. Comsn. Various cmnty. orgs. **Activities:** 1; 17, 34, 37 **Addr.:** Stetson Memorial Library, Mercer University, Macon, GA 31207.

Bunnell, Chester S. (Ap. 3, 1946, Auburn, NY) Ref. Libn., Univ. of MS Law Lib., 1980–, Circ. Libn., 1978–80; Ref. Libn., SUNY, Plattsburgh, 1973–78. **Educ.:** Auburn Cmnty. Coll., 1964–66, AA (Eng. Lit.); Bowling Green State Univ., 1970–72, BA (Eng. Lit.); SUNY, Albany, 1973, MLS. **Orgs.:** MS LA: Interlib. Com. (1979–). AALL: Copyrt. Com. (1979–); Pubns. Com. (1979). SLA. **Pubns.:** "Mississippi Legislative Information," *Southeast. Law Libs.* (F. 1981); various bk. reviews, *Lib. Jnl.* (1980–). **Activities:** 1, 12; 22, 31, 39; 55, 57, 92 **Addr.:** Law Library, University of Mississippi, University, MS 38677.

Bunnell, William I. (O. 25, 1940, Fairfield, IA) Exec. Secy., RTSD, ALA, 1978–; Dir. of Lib. Srvs., Cnty. Coll. of Morris, 1968–78; Dir. of Lib. Srvs., Bloomfield Coll., 1965–68; Asst. Cat./Ref. Libn., Cornell Univ., 1963–65. **Educ.:** Trinity Coll., Hartford, CT., 1958–62, AB (Amer. Hist.); Columbia Univ., 1962–63, MLS. **Orgs.:** NJ LA: Pres. (1976–77); Coll. and Univ. Sec: Pres. (1972–73). ALA: RTSD; Logis. ASM. Rep. (1976–78); AAP: RTSD Jt. Com., Mem. (1975–78). **Activities:** 1; 15, 17, 46; 55, 78 **Addr.:** 5813 N. Bernard St., Chicago, IL 60659.

Bunting, Anne Carroll (D. 8, 1936, Memphis, TN) Asst. Prof., Head of Tech. Srvs., Univ. of TN Hlth. Sci. Lib., 1972–; Head, Tech. and Pub. Srvs., 1969–72; Actg. Head Libn., 1971; Asst. Libn., Rotating Srvs., 1966–69. **Educ.:** MI St. Coll. for Women, 1954–58, BA (Eng., LS); Univ. of NC, Chapel Hill, 1965–66, MS (LS); Med. LA, Grade I Cert., 1967–; Med. LA, Hlth. Sci. Libnshp. Cert., 1983–1987. **Orgs.:** Med. LA. Memphis Lib. Cncl.: Secy. (1976–79); Ch. (1979–80). TN LA: Ad-Hoc Com. Hon. and Awds. Ch. (1975–76); Com. Hon. and Awds. Ch. (1976–77). Hlth. Sci. OCLC Users Grp. Univ. of TN, Hlth. Sci. Fac. Club: Bd. of Dir. (1975–78). **Activities:** 12; 15, 17, 20, 46; 80 **Addr.:** University of Tennessee Center for the Health Sciences, Library, 800 Madison Ave., Memphis, TN 38163.

Buntrock, Robert E. (N. 19, 1940, Minneapolis, MN) Snr. Resrch. Info. Sci., Standard Oil Co. (IN), 1981–; Staff Resrch. Info. Sci., Standard Oil Co. (IN), 1979–81; Resrch. Info. Sci., Standard Oil Co. (IN), 1971–79; Proj. Chem., Amoco Oil Co., 1970–71; Resrch Chem., Air Prod. and Chemicals, 1967–70. **Educ.:** Univ. of MN, 1958–62, B (Chem.); Princeton Univ., 1962–67, MA, PhD (Chem.). **Orgs.:** ASIS: Computerized Retrieval Srvs. Spec. Interest Grp. (Secy., 1975–76); Chicago Chap. Rep. (1977–78); Bio./Chem. Spec. Interest Grp.; User OL Interaction Spec. Interest Grp. Amer. Chem. Socty.: Div. Chem. Info. (Ch. Elec., 1980; Ch., 1981); Prog. Com. (1975); Chicago Sect., Lit. Topical Grp. (Ch., 1974–75); Amer. Assn. for the Advnc. of Sci: Sect. T. Sigma Xi: Amoco Resrch. Clb. Prog. Com. (1979–80). Naperville Area Transcribing for the Blind (Pres., Tape Ch., 1973–80). Various other orgs. **Pubns.:** "The Effect of the Searching Environment on Search Performance," *ONLINE* (O. 1979); "Searching Chemical Abstracts vs. CA Condensates," *Jnl. Chem. Info. Comp. Sci.* (1975); Other columns in *Online Datebase*. **Activities:** 12; 25, 49-Lit./patent searching, 49A-Selective Dissemination of Information; 60, 86, 91 **Addr.:** Standard Oil Co. (Indiana), Amoco Research Center, P.O. Box 400, Naperville, IL 60566.

Burch, James R. (My 16, 1926, Portland, OR) Asst. Head, Env. Design Lib., Univ. of CA, Berkeley, 1953–; Ref. Lib., Sacramento City Lib., 1952–53. **Educ.:** Sacramento City Coll., 1944–48, AA; Univ. of CA, Berkeley, 1948–50, BA; Columbia Univ. 1951–52, MSLS. **Orgs.:** ALA: Art Sect., Secy. (1977–79). ARLIS/NA. Socty. of Arch. Hist. **Activities:** 1; 15, 39, 46; 55, 65 **Addr.:** 1531 Edith St., Berkeley, CA 94703.

Burch, Mary S. (O. 16, 1925, Worcester, MA) Law Libn., NY State Supreme Court Lib., 1969–. **Educ.:** SUNY, Albany, 1976, BS (Admin.); Pratt Inst., 1979, MSLS; Univ. of MN Sch. of Law, 1974, Cert. (Cat. and Class.); Univ. of WA Sch. of Law, 1973, Cert. (Book Sel. and Acq.); Univ. of IL Coll. of Law, 1972, Cert. (Legal Bibl.). **Orgs.:** AALL: Cat. and Class. Com. (1972); Educ. Com. (1977–). State, Court and Cnty. Law Libs.: Exec. Bd. Assn. of Law Libs. of Upstate NY: Pres. (1971); Nsltr. Ed. (1971–78); Mem. Com. (Ch., 1978–). **Pubns.:** Reviews (1973–75); "The Problems in Setting Up a Microform Library" lecture (1978). **Activities:** 4; 15, 17, 41; 77 **Addr.:** 946 Hoosick Rd., Troy, NY 12180.

Burchinal, Lee G. (O. 23, 1927, Altoona, PA) Sr. Prog. Assoc., Natl. Sci. Fndn., 1972–, Dir., Div. of Sci. Info., 1972–78; Asst. Comsn., Natl. Ctr. for Educ. Comm., U.S. Ofc. of Educ., 1970–72, Dir., Div. of Info. Dssm., 1969–70. **Educ.:** Otterbein Coll., 1948–51, BA (Soc. Sci.); OH State Univ., 1952–56, PhD (Soc.). **Orgs.:** ASIS. Natl. Micro. Assn.: Bd. of Dirs. (1971–73); Pres. (1973–74); Fellow (1975). **Pubns.:** Various articles on info. sci., info. srvs., soclgy. (1958–). **Activities:** 12; 30, 33, 41; 56, 75, 91 **Addr.:** K-300, National Science Foundation, 1800 G St., N.W., Washington, DC 20550.

Burckel, Nicholas C. (Ag. 15, 1943, Evansville, IN) Exec. Asst. to Chancellor, Univ. WI, Parkside, 1975; Dir., Arch. and Area Resrch. Ctr., 1972; Ast. Archvst., Univ. WI, Madison, 1971–72. **Educ.:** Georgetown Univ., 1961–65, BA (Hist.); Univ. WI, 1965–67, MA (Hist.); 1967–71, PhD (Hist.). **Orgs.:** SAA: Coll. and Univ. Arch. Com. (1972–79); Ch., 1977–79); Com. on Awds. (1974–76); Com. on Coms. (1976–79); Ch., 1977–79); Com. on Reg. Arch. Actvs. (1979–81). Midwest Arch. Conf.: Prog. Com. (Ch., 1972–73); Bks. Review Ed., (1973–79); VP, (1976–78); Pres., (1979–81). Tri-Cnty. Lib. Cncl.: Secy., (1975–76). Org. of Amer. Histns. Amer. Hist. Assn. **Honors:** Cncl. for WI Writers, Schol. Bk Awd., First, 1977; WI Hist. Socty., Awd. of Merit, 1978; Amer. Assn. for State Lcl. Hist., Cert. of Cmdn., 1978. **Pubns.:** Co-Ed., *Progressive Reform* (1980); Ed., *Racine: Growth and Change in a Wisconsin County* (1977); Co-Ed., *Immigration and Ethnicity* (1977); "Establishing a College Archives: Possibilities and Priorities," *Coll. and Resrch. Libs.* (Sept., 1975); "The Expanding Role of a College or University Archives," *Midest. Archvst.* (Apr. 1976); other articles, bks. **Activities:** 1, 2; 38; 66, 85, 92 **Addr.:** University Archives and Area Research Center, University of Wisconsin-Parkside, Kenosha, WI 53141.

Burcsu, James E. (Mr. 11, 1940, Columbus, OH) Head, Sci. Documtn. Dept., Burroughs Wellcome Co., 1977–; Mgr., Data Cntrl., 1977; Plng. and Mfr. Data Coord., 1975–77; Sr. Resrch. Organic Chem., 1968–75. **Educ.:** OH State Univ., 1958–62, BSc (Chem.); Univ. of MN, 1963–68, PhD (Organic Chem.); Duke Univ., 1976–78, MM (Mgt.). **Orgs.:** Drug Info. Assn. ASIS. Amer. Chem. Socty. Proj. Mgt. Inst. **Activities:** 12; 17, 30, 38; 58, 60, 87 **Addr.:** Burroughs Wellcome Co., 3030 Cornwallis Rd., Research Triangle Park, NC 27709.

Burdash, David H. (Mr. 23, 1941, Johnson City, NY) Dir., The Wilmington Inst., 1975–, Asst. Dir., 1972–75; Tchr., W. Jefferson Hills Sch. Dist., 1967–72; Tchr., Butler Sch. Dist., 1964–67. **Educ.:** Lehigh Univ., 1958–62, BA (Classical Lang.); Duquesne Univ., 1967–71, MA (Classical Lang.); Univ. of Pittsburgh, 1971–72, MLS (Lib. Admin.). **Orgs.:** ALA. DE LA: Pub. Lib. Div., Pres. MD LA: Ed. Com. PA LA. Amer. Classical Leag. Classical Assn. of Atl. States. Rotary Intl. of Wilmington: Prog. Ch. Youth Comms., Inc.: Treas. Various other orgs. **Honors:** Beta Phi Mu. **Activities:** 9; 17, 35, 36 **Addr.:** The Wilmington Institute, 10th and Market Sts., Wilmington, DE 19801.

Burdenuk, Eugene L. (O. 27, 1942, Sudbury, ON, Can) Asst. Prof., Univ. West. ON, 1975–; Head Libn., Timmins HS., 1967–75; Visit. Prof., Kent State Univ., Sum. 1978. **Educ.:** Laurentian Univ., 1961–64, BA (Hist.); Univ. of West. ON, 1966–67, MLS; Univ. of West. ON, 1974–75, Dip.Educ. **Orgs.:** Can. Sch. LA: Secy.-Treas. (1979–80); Exemplary Resrc. Ctr. Com. (Ch., 1977–). ON LA: Educ. Action Grp. (Ch., 1975–76). ON Educ. Comm. Athrty.: Reg. Cnclr. (1972–74); Fanshawe Coll. Lib. Tech. Adv. Com. **Pubns.:** *Canadian School Library Programmes of Interest to Visitors* (1975); *An Annotated Guide to Selection Sources for Secondary School Resource Centres* (1977); "Adolescents and Recreational Reading," *In Review* (Sum. 1978); "The Teacher Librarian as an Integral Member of the School Staff," *Expression* (Aut. 1977). **Activities:** 10, 11; 25, 26, 48; 63 **Addr.:** Faculty of Education, The University of Western Ontario, 1137 Western Rd., London, ON N6G 1G7 Canada.

Burdick, Elizabeth Birdsall (Ap. 15, 1920, Haddonfield, NJ) Dir., Org., Intl. Theat. Col., Intl. Theat. Inst. of U.S., 1968–; Dir., Natl. Theat. Srv. Dept., Amer. Natl. Theat. and Acad., 1951–58; Staff, Natl. and Int. Srv. Depts., 1948–57; Prod. Ast., NY Theat. Prod., 1946–48. **Educ.:** Wellesley Coll., 1938–43, BA (Eng. Lit., Drama); Yale Univ., 1943–46, MFA (Theatre). **Orgs.:** Theat. LA. Amer. Socty. Theat. Resrch. **Pubns.:** Co-Ed., *Contemporary Stage Design - USA* (1974); Co-Auth., *International Directory of Theatre, Dance and Folklore Festivals* (1979); Cmplr., "Annotated Bibliographies of Theatre Books" in *Theatre 5: The American Theatre 1971–72* (1972); *Theatre 4: The American Theatre 1970–71* (1971); *Theatre 3: The American Theatre 1969–70* (1970); Theatre 1970–71 (1971); Theatre 3: The American Theatre 1969–70 (1970); *Theatre 2: The American Theatre 1968–69* (1969). **Activities:** 2, 5; 15, 17, 39, 41; 95-intl. thea. **Addr.:** International Theatre Institute of the United States, Inc., 1860 Broadway-Suite 1510, New York, NY 10023.

PROFESSIONAL ACTIVITIES: Institutions: 1. Acad. lib.; 2. Arch.; 3. Assn.; 4. Fed./Gvt. lib.; 5. Inst. lib.; 6. Mfr./Suppl.; 7. Milit. lib.; 8. Musm.; 9. Pub. lib.; 10. Sch. lib.; 11. Sch. of lib. sci.; 12. Spec. lib.; 13. State lib.; 14. (other). **Functions/Activities:** 15. Acq./Col. dev.; 16. Adult srvs.; 17. Admin.; 18. Apprais.; 19. Archit./Bldgs.; 20. Cat./Class.; 21. Chld. srvs.; 22. Circ.; 23. Cons./Pres.; 24. Consult.; 25. Cont. ed.; 26. Educ. lib. sci.; 27. Ext. srvs.; 28. Fund/Grants; 29. Gvt. pubs.; 30. Indx./Abs.; 31. Instr. lib. use; 32. Media srvs.; 33. Micro.; 34. Netwks./Coop.; 35. Persnl.; 36. PR; 37. Publshg.; 38. Recs. mgt.; 39. Ref. srvs.; 40. Repro.; 41. Resrch.; 42. Review.; 43. Secur.; 44. Serials; 45. Spec. col.; 46. Tech. srvs.; 47. Trustees/Bds.; 48. YA srvs.; 49. (other).

Burdick, Oscar Charles (Ja. 2, 1929, Milton, WI) Assoc. Libn., Col. Dev., Grad. Theo. Un., 1966–; Organist, Arlington Cmnty. Church, Kensington, CA, 1958–; Libn., Pac. Sch. of Relig., 1969–80, Assoc. Libn., 1962–69, Asst. Libn., 1956–62; Pastor, 7th Day Bapt. Church, Daytona Beach, FL, 1954–56. **Educ.:** Milton Coll., 1946–50, BA, Cert. (Pipe Organ); Alfred Univ., 1950–53, BD; various crs. **Orgs.:** ATLA: Pres. (1974–75); various ofcs. Amer. Gld. of Organists: San Francisco Chap., various ofcs. **Pubns.:** Various articles in 7th Day Bapt. pubns. **Activities:** 1; 15, 44; 90 **Addr.:** 2400 Ridge Rd., Berkeley, CA 94709.

Burgan, Anne Shaw, (F. 14, 1935, New York, NY) Adj. Prof., Gvt. Info. Systs., Univ. of MD., 1981–; Chief, MD State Netwk. Srvs., Enoch Pratt Free Lib., 1979–; Deputy Dir., RI Dept. of State Lib. Srvs., 1978–; Gvt. Docum. Lib., Asst. Prof., Univ. of RI, 1972–77, Prof., Grad. Lib. Sch., 1976–77. **Educ.:** Hunter Coll., 1957, BA (Pol. Sci.); Univ. of RI, 1975, MLS. **Orgs.:** MD Gvr.'s Task Frc. on Docum.: Ch. (1980–). MD LA. SLA. State Agency LA of MD. ALA: GODORT, Micro. Task Grp. (Coord., 1977–). Various other orgs. **Pubns.:** "Microform Survey," *Micro. Review* (Ja. 1978); "Government Inspection of U.S. Depository," *Biblio* (N. 1976); "Rhode Island State Documents," *Biblio* (Mr. 1976); "State Documents," *Biblio* (Mr. 1975); "Documents for Rhode Islanders," *RI LA Bltn.* (1975–76). **Activities:** 1, 9; 17, 29, 34; 77, 78 **Addr.:** Enoch Pratt Free Library, 400 Cathedral St., Baltimore, MD 21201.

Burgarella, Mary M. (Je. 27, 1923, Gloucester, MA) Head of Lib. Dev., MA Bd. of Lib. Commissioners, 1965–; Pub. Lib. Consult., CT State Dept. Ed., 1960–65; Head Tech. Srvs., Robbins Lib, 1959–60; Chief Librn., USAF, Hawaii, 1956–59; Base Libn., USAF, Philippines, 1956; Spec. Srvs. Lib., US Army, Japan, 1953–55; Head Catlgr., Greenwich (CT) Lib. 1951–53; Asst. Cat. Libn., PA State Univ., 1946–51. **Educ.:** Salem State Coll., 1941–45, BS (Ed.); Simmons Coll., 1945–46, BS, LS. **Orgs.:** ALA. New England LA; Treas. (1974–77, 1978–79). MA LA. **Pubns.:** Ed., *LSCA Special Project Reports* (1971–). **Activities:** 13; 17, 19, 47; 63, 89, 93 **Addr.:** 44 Beach Rd., Gloucester, MA 01930.

Burger, Henry G. (Je. 27, 1923, New York, NY) Prof. of Anthro. & Educ., Univ. of MO-Kansas City, 1969–; Anthro., Southwest. Coop. Educ. Lab., 1967–69; Soc. Sci. Consult., 1956–67; Lectr., City Univ. of NY, 1957–65; Design Tester, various orgs., 1947–55. **Educ.:** Columbia Univ., 1940–47, BA with honors (Soc. Sci.), 1962–67, MA, PhD (Anthro.). **Orgs.:** ASIS. The Class. Socty. Dictionary Socty. of N. America. AAUP. Socty. for Med. Anthro. Socty. of Prof. Anthro.: Pres. (1963–64); Dir. (1964–68). Amer. Anthro. Assn. Other orgs. **Honors:** Natl. Sci. Fndn., Inst. Fac. Resrch. Grant, 1970; Phi Beta Kappa. **Pubns.:** *The Wordtree: A Transitive Taxonomy...* (1981); "Cultural Materialism: Efficiencies, Not Descriptions," *Gen. Syst.* (1975); "Piaget's Maturational Phases as Merely Consecutive Definitions," *Comm. & Cognition* (1977); "Panculture: A Hominization-Derived Processual Taxonomy" in *The Concept and Dynamics of Culture* (1977); "A Transitive Taxonomy as a Dictionary of Cause and Effect," *Socty. for Gen. Syst. Resrch., Procs.* (1979); other books and articles. **Activities:** 5, 6; 37, 39, 49-Editing; 56, 75, 92 **Addr.:** 7306 Brittany, Shawnee Mission, KS 66203.

Burger, Robert Harold (S. 2, 1947, Bronxville, NY) Slavic Catlgr, Assoc. Prof. of Lib. Admin., Univ. of IL-Urbana, 1981–. Asst. Prof. of Lib. Admin., Univ. of IL-Urbana, 1976-81. **Educ.:** Tufts Univ., 1965–69, BA (Russian); Univ. of NC-Chapel Hill, 1973–75, MA (Slavic); 1975–76, MSLS; Univ. of IL, 1976–78, Cert. of Adnc. Std. in Libnshp. **Orgs.:** ALA: ACRL. Amer. Soc. of Indxrs. Assn. for the Bibl. of His. Amer. Assn. for the Adv. of Slavic Std. **Honors** Beta Phi Mu, 1978; Phi Kappa Phi, 1978. **Pubns.:** "The Kanawha County Textbook Controversy", *Lib. Qtly.* (1978); "General Retrospective Indexes to Pre-revolutionary Russian Periodicals" *Libri* (1979); "Circulation Automation", "Teaching Library Automation" *Bltn. of the Amer. Socty. for Info. Sci* (1978); "Caveat lector, caveat descriptor *JAL* (1980); Jt. auth, "Serial Control in a Developed Machine System", *Ser. Libn.* (1980); Various articles in history journals. **Addr.:** 225 Library, University of Illinois, Urbana, IL 61801.

Burgess, Dean (Mr. 27, 1937, Buffalo, NY) Lib. Dir., Portsmouth Pub. Lib., 1974–, Asst. Dir., 1966–74, Head, Ref. and Main Lib. Mgr., 1965–66. **Educ.:** Kenyon Coll., 1954–58, AB (Eng.); Univ. of NC, 1965–66, MS (LS); Univ. of MD, 1976, Lib. Admin. Dev. Wkshp. **Orgs.:** VA LA: Pres. (1983); VP (1982); *VA Libn.* Ed. (1966–71); AV RT (Ch., 1966); Subcom. to Write Pub. Lib. Stans. (Ch., 1979); Legis. Drafting Com. (Ch., 1980). WHCOLIS: Alternate Del. (1979). ALA: LAMA. Lib. Srvs. and Construct. Act VA Adv. Com. Plng. Com. (Ch., 1981). Various other orgs. Portsmouth Cham. of Cmrce. Mncpl. Execs. Club. Tidewater Litcy. Cncl. Kiwanis. **Honors:** Beta Phi Mu, 1966. **Pubns.:** *Minimum Standards for Virginia Libraries* (1976); *Sources of Income of All Virginia Libraries* (1978); "The Access Exception," *Sch. Lib. Jnl.* (O. 1980); "School Library Public Library Combination," *VA Libn.* (1975); "Subject Use of Public Library Collections," *Torch Mag.* (1968); various articles, films. **Activities:** 9; 17 **Addr.:** Portsmouth Public Library, 601 Court St., Portsmouth, VA 23704.

Burgess, Robert S. (N. 22, 1917, Pulaski, TN) Prof., Sch. of LS, St. Univ. of NY, Albany, 1948–; Actg. Dean, 1977–78; Visit. Prof., Univ. of Puerto Rico, 1968–69; Visit. Prof., Yonsei Univ., Seoul, Korea, 1959–61; Libn., Talladega Coll., 1943–48; Libn., Shimer Coll., 1942–43; Assoc. Libn., N. West. Univ., 1941-42; Sci. Libn., Stephens Coll., 1939–41. **Educ.:** Vanderbilt Univ., 1934–38, BA (Math.); George Peabody Coll., 1938–39, BS (LS); Univ. of Chicago, 1941–42, MA (LA); 1946–47, Doctoral Study. **Orgs.:** ALA: various coms. in all orgs. NY LA. AALS. **Honors:** Phi Beta Kappa, 1938; Fulbright, Hayes Lectureship in Iceland, 1980; Kappa Delta Pi, 1939; Sigma Delta Kappa, 1938. **Pubns.:** *The Classified Catalog* (1960); Ed. *Library Literature 5-The Best of 1974.* (1975); "Education for Librarianship us Assistance," *Lib. Trends* (Ja. 1972); Jt. Auth., "How Library Schools Respond to Inquiries," *Jnl. of Educ. for Libnshp.* (Fall 1969); "Korea: A Case Study in American Assistance," *Jnl. of Educ.* for *Libnshp.* (Spr. 1961); Many other pubns., speeches, consult. Reviews. **Activities:** 11; 25, 26; 56, 59 **Addr.:** School of Library & Information Sciences, St. University of NY, Albany, NY 12222.

Burgis, Grover C. (Ap. 20, 1933, Toronto, ON) Chief Libn., Thunder Bay Pub. Lib., 1976–; Exec. Dir., CAPTAIN Lib. Srvs., 1975–76; Dir., Resrch. and Plng., Natl. Lib. of Can., 1970–73; Head, Tech. Srvs., Univ. of SK, 1967–70. **Educ.:** Wheaton Coll., 1953–56, B Sc (Hr. Chem.); Univ. of Pittsburgh, 1957–58 (Mktg. Resrch.), 1966–67, MLIS; MA Inst. of Tech., 1968 (Info. Mgt. Tech.); Univ. of Pittsburgh, 1973–75, Ph D Student. **Orgs.:** Can. LA. ON LA. Can. Assn. Info. Sci. ALA. Chief Exec. Ofcrs. of Lg. Pub. Libs. of ON: Secy.-Treas. (1979–80). Adv. Bd. of Netwk. Dev. Ofc. Task Frc. on the N. for the Prog. Review of the Mnstry. Task Grp. on Comp. Dev. **Honors:** Beta Phi Mu. **Pubns.:** "Ontario Universities Library Cooperative System," *Encyc. of Info. and Lib. Sci.* (1977); jt. auth., *Canadian MARC: A Report of the Activities of the MARC Task Group Resulting in a Recommended Canadian MARC Format for Monographs and a Canadian MARC Format for Serials* (1972); jt. auth., *Cataloguing Standards: Report of the Canadian Task Group on Cataloguing Standards* (1972); *Research Collections in Canadian Libraries* (1972); "What's the National Library Doing," *LA of AB Bltn.* (Ag. 1971); various articles. **Activities:** 1, 4; 17, 19, 35; 56, 60 **Addr.:** Thunder Bay Public Library, 285 Red River Rd., Thunder Bay, ON P7B 1A9 Canada.

Burhans, Barbara Carroll (N. 9, 1927, Morristown, TN) Ref. Libn., Natl. Lib. of Med., 1973–, Cat. Libn., 1955–73; Ref. libn., Gen. Ref. Div., Cleveland Pub. Lib., 1954–55; Jr. Ref. libn., Univ. of WV, 1951–54. **Educ.:** George Washington Univ., 1945–48, BA (Eng. lit); Catholic Univ., 1949–51, MS in LS; Univ. of MD, 1948–49 (lit.); Columbia Univ., 1963 (LS). **Orgs.:** ALA: JMRT (Ch.). Natl. Women's Std. Assn. **Activities:** 4, 12; 39, 49-Online Services; 80, 92 **Addr.:** 1806 Orchard St., Alexandria, VA 22302.

Burich, Nancy J. (Ag. 12, 1943, Orange Cnty., CA) Dir., Univ. of KS Regents, Center Lib., 1976–; Ref. Libn., Columbia Univ. Med. Lib., 1970–71; Head, Bus. Lib., MI State Univ. Lib., 1969–70; Ref. Libn., 1967–69. **Educ.:** Kent State Univ., 1961–65, BA (Hist.); 1965–68, MLS. **Orgs.:** SLA. KS LA. ALA. AAUP: Univ. of KS Chap. (Treas., 1979–80). **Pubns.:** "Coping with Changing Tradition: The University of Kansas Regents Center Library," *Wilson Lib. Bltn.* (Je. 1980); *Alexander the Great: a bibliography* (1970). **Activities:** 1, 10; 16, 17, 39; 59, 80, 92 **Addr.:** K.U. Regents Center Library, 9900 Mission Rd., Shawnee Mission, KS 66206.

Burk, Cornelius F., Jr. (Ja. 8, 1933, Sarnia, ON) Dir., Can. Centre for Geoscience Data, Dept of Energy, Mines, and Resrcs., 1970–; Natl. Coord., Secretariat for Geoscience Data, 1968–70; Resrch. Sci., Geological Srvy. of Can., 1960–68; Petr. Geologist, Texaco, Inc., 1959–60. **Educ.:** Univ. of West. ON, 1952–56, BSc (Geol.); Northwestern Univ., 1956–59, PhD (Geol.). **Orgs.:** Geoscience Inf. Soc.: Pres. (1971). Assoc. Info. Mgrs. Can. Assn. for Info. Sci.: Info. Policy Com. (1977–). ASIS. Various other orgs. and offices. **Honors:** AB Soc. of Pet. Geologists, Outstanding Service Awd, 1968. **Pubns.:** "The national data referral system for Canadian geoscience," *Geoscience Info. Soc.* (1978); "Canada: Current activities and issues in geological documentation," *Geoscience Info., an international state-of-the-art review.* (1979); "The link between "data" and "documentation"," *Geoscience Info., an international state-of-the-art review* (1979); "Proposal to establish international federation of geological documentation services," *Geoscience Info. Society Proc.* (1979); "International review of geoscience databases", *Australian Mineral Foundation,* (1981); Various other books and articles. **Activities:** 12; 18, 31, 40; 63, 71, 83 **Addr.:** Canada Centre for Geoscience Data, Department of Energy, Mines and Resources, Ottawa, ON K1A 0E4 Canada.

Burk, William Robert (Je. 25, 1945, Norwalk, CT) Bot. Libn., Univ. of NC, 1979–; Sci. Catlgr., Univ. of CA, Santa Barbara, 1977–79; Acq. Libn., Univ. of GU, 1977; Sci. Catlgr., Univ. of UT, 1973–76. **Educ.:** Central CT State Coll., 1963–67, BA (Bio.); MI State Univ., 1969–71, MS (Bot.); Univ. of MI, 1972, AMLS. **Orgs.:** ALA. Myco. Socty. of Amer. **Pubns.:** *"Pseudocolus javanicus* in Connecticut and its Distribution in the United States," *Mycotaxon,* (vol. 3, 1976); *"Pseudocolus fusiformis,* Synonymy and Distributional Records," *Mycologia* (vol. 70, 1978); Co-Auth., *"Dictyophoora multicolor,* New to Guam," *Mycologia* (vol. 70, 1978); *"Clathrus ruber* in California and worldwide distributional records," *Mycotaxon* (vol. 8, 1979); Co-Ed., *Terrarium Topics* (1974–77); numerous reviews. **Activities:** 1; 15, 22, 39; 58 **Addr.:** John N. Couch Library, University of North Carolina, 301 Coker Hall 010-A, Chapel Hill, NC 27514.

Burke, Frank G. (Ap. 22, 1927, New York, NY) Exec. Dir., Natl. Hist. Pubns. and Recs. Cmnsn., 1975–; Asst. to the Archvst. of the U.S., U.S. Natl. Arch., 1974–75, Asst. Archvst. for Educ. Prog., 1968–74, Info. Retrieval Spec., 1967–68; Head, Prep. Sect., Mss. Div., Lib. of Congs., 1964–67; Asst. Cur., Arch. and Mss., Univ. of Chicago, 1962–64. **Educ.:** Univ. of AK, Fairbanks, 1952–55, (Hist); Univ. of Chicago, 1955–69, MA, PhD (Hist). **Orgs.:** SAA: Autom. Com. (Ch., 1967–70); Finding Aids Com. (Ch., 1971–73); Cncl. (1977–81). Mss. Socty. Assn. for the Bibl. of Hist.: Cncl., (1979–81). Amer. Hist. Assn. Assn. for Documentary Editing. **Honors:** SAA, Fellow, 1970. **Pubns.:** Contrib., *Archive Library Relations* (1976); "The Rheinsberg Stage," *Eighteenth-Century Life* (D. 1974); "Impact of the Specialist on Archives," *Coll. & Resrch. Libs.* (Jl. 1972); "Automation and Historical Research," *Libri* (1969); "SPINDEX II, an Aspect of Archival Information Retrieval," *Recs. Mgt. Jnl.* (Sum. 1970); other articles, film, tape cassette. **Activities:** 2; 17, 28; 56, 92 **Addr.:** N.H.P.R.C., National Archives Building, Washington, DC 20408.

Burke, Sr. Grace (O. 3, 1922, New York, NY) Media Libn., Molloy Coll. Rockville Centre, NY, 1978–, Ref. Libn., 1976–78; Lib. Dir., St. Michael's HS, Brooklyn, 1974–76, AV, Ref. Libn., 1972–74, Eng. Tchr., 1970–72; Prin., Christ the King Elem. Sch., 1967–70; Eng. Tchr., Dominican Commercial HS, 1953–67; various other tchg. positions. **Educ.:** St. John's Univ., 1952, BA (Eng.); Coll. of St. Rose, Albany, 1968, MA (Eng.); St. John's Univ., 1972–74, MLS. **Orgs.:** Nassau Cnty. LA: Coll. and Univ. Lib. Div., Prog. Com. (1978–). Catholic LA. AECT. Molloy Coll: Fac.-Student Affairs Com. (1979–); Sbtcl. Com. (1979–); Experiential Life Com. (1979–). **Honors:** Lambda Iota Tau Hon. Socty., 1977. **Activities:** 1; 31, 32, 34; 55, 63, 92 **Addr.:** Molloy College, 1000 Hempstead Ave., Rockville Centre, NY 11570.

Burke, Margaret Elsie (Ag. 4, 1921, Winnipeg, MB, Can) Admis. Coord., Sch. of Libnshp., Univ. of BC, 1968–; Rev., 1965–68. **Educ.:** Univ. of BC, 1961–64, BA (Grmn.), 1964–65, BLS; Royal Schs. of Msc., London, 1950–52, LRSM (Piano). **Orgs.:** BC LA: Pres. (1973–74), VP (1972–73), Cnclr. (1973–74). Can. LA. AALS. CALS. **Pubns.:** Ed., *B.C. L.A. Reporter* (1970–73). **Activities:** 11; 17, 25, 26 **Addr.:** School of Librarianship, The University of British Columbia, 2075 Wesbrook Mall, Vancouver, BC V6T 1W5 Canada.

Burkett, Nancy Hall (Je. 22, 1943) Head, Readrs. Srvcs., Amer. Antiq. Socty., 1978–; Ast. Cur. of Mss., 1973–78. **Educ.:** Amer. Univ., 1961–65, AB (Intl. Rel.); Boston Univ., 1968–69, MA (Hist.); Univ. of CA, Los Angeles, 1972–73, MLS. **Orgs.:** MA Gvr. Conf. on Libs. and Info. Srvcs.: Del. (1978). MA Bd. Lib. Comsn.: Com. on Min. Stan. State Aid Elig., (1979–82). Worcester Pub. Lib. Bd. Dir. (1976–82). Worcester Opera: Bd. Dir. (1975–78). **Activities:** 14-Indp. Resrch. Lib.; 39, 47; 55 **Addr.:** American Antiquarian Society, 185 Salisbury St., Worcester, MA 01609.

Burkett, Phyllis G. (F. 10, 1952, Searcy, AR) Dir. Crowley Ridge Reg. and Craighead Cnty. Jonesboro Pub. Lib., 1980–; Dir., White Cnty. Pub. Lib., 1975–80. **Educ.:** State Coll. of AR, 1970–74, BA (Hist.); Univ. of Denver, 1974–75, Mstr. (Libnshp.). **Orgs.:** AR LA: VP (1980); Pres. (1981). SWLA: Exec. Bd. (1981). ALA. AAUW: Various ofcs. **Honors:** Searcy Bus. and Prof. Women, Young Careerist, 1977. **Activities:** 9; 17, 35; 50 **Addr.:** 1208 S. Madison #5, Jonesboro, AR 72401.

Burkhardt, Frederick H. (S. 13, 1912, New York City, NY) Retired, 1974–; Ch. Emeritus, Natl. Comsn. on Libs. and Info. Sci., 1978–, Ch., 1971–78; Pres. Emeritus, Amer. Cncl. of Learned Soctys., 1974–, Pres., 1957–74. **Educ.:** Columbia Univ., 1929–33, BA (Phil.); Oriel Coll., Oxford, 1933–35, BLitt (Phil.); Columbia Univ., 1940, PhD (Phil.). **Orgs.:** NY Pub. Lib.: Ch. (1974); Bd. of Trustees (1970–71). **Addr.:** Box 1067, Bennington, VT 05201.

Burkhart, Velda Betts (Jl. 15, 1918, Grantsville, WV) Head, Cat. Dept., VA Polytech. Inst. & State Univ., 1975–; Asst. Head, Cat. Dept., 1974–75; Supvsr., Hum. Cat., 1971–73; Cat., 1969–70; Cat., OH State Univ., 1965–68; Cat., Kenyon Coll, 1963–65; Cat., OH Wesleyan Univ., 1949–52; Cat. OH State Univ., 1946–49. **Educ.:** Glenville State Coll., 1935–37, 1941–43, AB (Eng.); Univ. of MI, 1945–48, ABLS. **Orgs.:** ALA: RTSD. VA LA. Potomac Tech. Proc. Libns. Southeast. LA. Blacksburg Baptist Church: Music Com. Ch., 1973–74, 1978–79). Order of East. Star. **Activities:** 1; 17, 20, 46 **Addr.:** 802 Dickerson Ln., NE, Blacksburg, VA 24060.

Burlingame, Dwight F. (Jl. 28, 1945, Park Rapids, MN) Dean of Libs., and Lrng. Resrcs., Bowling Green State Univ., 1978–; Dean of Libs. and Lrng. Resrcs., Univ. of Evansville, 1974–78; Head., Tech. Srvs; Head Acq., Head of Ref., St. Cloud State Univ., 1969–73; Ref. Libn. and Bus. Libn., Univ. of IA,

Special Subjects/Services: 50. Adult educ.; 51. Advert./Mktg.; 52. Aerosp.; 53. Agric.; 54. Area std.; 55. Arts/Hum.; 56. Autom.; 57. Bibl./Prtg.; 58. Bio. sci.; 59. Bus./Fin.; 60. Chem.; 61. Copyrt.; 62. Documtn.; 63. Educ.; 64. Engin.; 65. Env.; 66. Eth. grps.; 67. Film; 68. Food/Nutr.; 69. Geneal.; 70. Geo.; 71. Geol.; 72. Handcpd.; 73. Hist.; 74. Int. frdm.; 75. Info. sci.; 76. Insr.; 77. Law; 78. Legis.; 79. Math./Comp. sci.; 80. Med.; 81. Metals; 82. Nat. resrcs.; 83. Newsp.; 84. Nuc. sci.; 85. Oral hist.; 86. Petr./Energy; 87. Pharm.; 88. Phys./Astr./Math.; 89. Readg.; 90. Relig.; 91. Sci./Tech.; 92. Soc. sci.; 93. Telecom.; 94. Transp.; 95. (other).

1967–68. **Educ.:** Moorhead State Univ., 1962–65, BS (Pol. Sci. and Bus); Univ. of IL, 1966–67, MS (LS); Univ. of MN, 1970–72 (Higher Educ.); FL State Univ., 1973–74, PhD (LS). **Orgs.:** ALA: ACRL/AV Com. (1970–74); Ed. Bd., *Choice* (1981–); Coll. Libs. Sect., Nom. Com. (1977–78); Legis. Network (1977–). AECT: Accred. Com. (1977–78). OH LA. Acad. LA of OH: Pres. (1979–80). Amer. Assn. for Higher Educ. Toledo Opera: Bd. of Dirs. (1979–). **Honors:** Beta Phi Mu; Phi Delta Kappa. **Pubns.:** Jt. auth., "Staff Development and Continuing Education in the University Library Setting," *Jnl. of Lib. Admin.* (Win. 1980); Jt. auth., *The College Learning Resource Center* (1978); Jt. auth., "Utilizing Technological Developments for the Improvement of Teaching in Higher Education," *Intl. Jnl. of Instructional Media* (1977–78); "Film," *Nonprint Media in Acad. Libs.* (1975); "Adulthood in the Underground Press: What the Future Holds." *Southeastern Libn.* (Sum., 1974); reviews. **Activities:** 1; 17, 26; 55 **Addr.:** 1209 Lyn Rd., Bowling Green, OH 43402.

Burlingham, Esther H. (Ap. 11, 1920, Meriden, CT) Libn., Oxford Pub. Lib., 1978–; Libn., Escola Graduada de Sao Paulo, Brazil, 1974–76; Libn., Sanford Sch., Hockessin, DE, 1966–74; Libn., George Gray Sch., Wilmington, DE, 1950–55; Libn., Bigelow Jr. High, Newton, MA, 1947–50. **Educ.:** State Tchrs. Coll., Framingham, MA, 1938–42, BS (Elem. Educ.); Columbia Univ., 1947–52, MSLS. **Orgs.:** ALA. PA LA. **Addr.:** Box 365, R.D.1, West Grove, PA 19390.

Burnett, Betty W. (Ap. 16, 1932, Itasca, TX) Libn., Los Alamos Natl. Lab., 1964. **Educ.:** Univ. of TX, Austin, 1950–53, BA; various crs. **Orgs.:** SLA: Rio Grande Chap., President-Elect (1975–76) Pres. (1976–77); Nuc. Sci. Div., Ch.-Elect (1978–79), Ch. (1979–80). **Activities:** 12; 15, 20, 22 **Addr.:** 203 Venado, Los Alamos, NM 87544.

Burnett, Ruth Pitkin (My. 23, 1919, Coventry, CT) Head, Acq. SUNY, Oneonta, 1962–; Libn., N.E. Electric Syst. Lib., 1945–46; Asst. Libn., Providence Pub. Lib., 1943–45; Libn., Sch. of LS, Simmons Coll., 1942–43. **Educ.:** Simmons Coll., 1937–41, BS (LS). **Orgs.:** ALA: ACRL, E. NY Chap. SUNY Libns. Assn. **Activities:** 1; 15, 39 **Addr.:** R.D. 2, Oneonta, NY 13820.

Burney, Thomas D. (N. 12, 1938, Middletown, OH) Asst. Chief, Rare Bk. & Spec. Cols. Div., Lib of Congress, 1972–; Asst. Prof., Classics, Miami Univ., 1968–69; Asst. Prof., Classics, Univ. of CA, Riverside, 1964–67. **Educ.:** Fordham Univ., 1958–60, BA (Classics), 1960–63, MA; Univ. of CA, Los Angeles, 1970–71, MLS. **Orgs.:** ALA: ACRL/Rare Bk. and Mss. Sect., Recommendations for Marking Rare Mtrls. (1977–79); Secur. (1979–). Amer. Philological Assn. Amer. Classical Leag. Prtg. Hist. Assn. **Honors:** U.S. Dept. of St., Fulbright Flw., Italy, 1963; Lib. of Congs., Spec. Rcrt., 1971. **Activities:** 4; 17, 45; 55, 57 **Addr.:** Rare Book and Special Collections Division, Library of Congress, Washington, DC 20540.

Burnison, Judith Coate (Ap. 4, 1943, Atlanta, GA) Exec. Dir., IL LA, 1981–; various positions as prog. coord., Northwest. Univ., 1977–; Spec. Projs. Coord., Dept. of Human Resrcs., City of Bloomington, IN 1975–76; Asst. Advert. Mgr., The Mart, Inc., 1972–73; various positions as artist, jnlst., acct. exec. **Educ.:** IN Univ., 1969, BS, 1976, MS (Adult Cont. Educ.), Doct. Cand. (Adult and Cont. Educ.). **Orgs.:** Women in Comms.: Mem. Vice-ch.; Progs. VP. Chicago Pub. Lib. Volun. Srvs. Adv. Com. Comprehensive Cmnty. Srvs. of Metro. Chicago, Inc. **Pubns.:** Various presentations. **Addr.:** Illinois Library Association, 425 N. Michigan Ave. Suite 1304, Chicago, IL 60611.

Burns, Barrie A. F. (Ja. 3, 1939, Winnepeg, MB, Can) Actg. Dir., Cat. Branch, Natl. Lib. of Can., 1979–, Asst. Dir. (Systs.), Cat. Branch, 1976–79; Asst. to Univ. Libn. Syst. and Plng., Univ. of SK, 1973–76; Syst. Libn., 1971–73; Serials Libn., Env. Can., 1967–71. **Educ.:** Univ. of MB, 1957–61, (Archit.), 1962–66, BA (Hist., Phil.); Univ. of BC, 1966–67, BLS. **Orgs.:** Can. Assn. Info. Sci.: Bd. of Dir. (1977–79). ASIS. West. Can. Chap. (Ch., 1975–76). ALA. Can. LA. **Pubns.:** "Alternatives For Library Catalogues: Tools for Catalogue Planning", *Cataloguing and Classification Quarterly* Vol. 1 (1) (Fall 1980); "The Authority Subsystem of the National Library of Canada," *Whats in a Name? Cntrl. of Cat. Recs. through Auto. Athrty. Files* Univ. of Toronto (1978); "The CONSER Minimum Element Data Set," *Automation in Libraries,* Can. Assn. of Coll. and Univ. Libs. (1975); Jt.-auth., "TESA-1 Cataloguing: A Second Look," *Lib. Autom. in the Nation* Can. Assn. of Coll. and Univ. Libs. (1973). **Activities:** 1, 4; 17, 20, 46; 56, 75 **Addr.:** 235 Somerset St., W, Apt. 1106, Ottawa, ON K2P 0J3 Canada.

Burns, Helen Marie (Ag. 15, 1922, Baltimore, MD) Consult., 1980–; Chief Law Libn., Fed. Rsv. Bank of NY, 1966–79; Head Law Libn., 1957–66; Asst. Law Libn., 1953–57; Libn., MD State Plng. Comsn., 1949–53. **Educ.:** Coll. of Notre Dame of MD, 1940–44, BA (Eng.); Drexel Univ., BS (LS); NY Univ., 1959–66, MA, PhD (Hist.). **Orgs.:** ALA. SLA. AALL: Educ. Com. (1977–78). Private Law Libs. (1975–76). Law Library Assn. of Grt. New York: Secy. (1969–72); Bd. of Dir. (1962–63). Amer. Socty. of Indxrs. (1974–81). Amer. Hist. Assn. Org. of Amer. Histns. MD Hist. Socty. **Honors:** New York Univ. Founders Day Honors, 1966. **Pubns.:** *American Banking Community and New Deal Banking Reforms, 1933–35* (1974); Reviews and abstracts. **Activities:** 12; 17, 30, 41; 59, 77, 92 **Addr.:** 5903 Aylesshire Rd., Baltimore, MD 21239.

Burns, John Andrew (S. 25, 1928, Baltimore, MD) Dir., Wayne (NJ) Pub. Lib., 1972–; Assoc. Dir., Anne Arundel Cnty. (MD) Pub. Lib., 1967–72; Branch Libn., Prince George's Cnty. (MD) Pub. Lib., 1965–67; Asst. Dir., Onondaga Cnty. (NY) Pub. Lib., 1962–65; Director, Ossining (NY) Pub. Lib., 1959–62; Jr. and Sr. Libn., Enoch Pratt Free Lib., 1955–59. **Educ.:** The Johns Hopkins Univ., 1946–50, BA (Eng.); Columbia Univ., 1951–55, MS (LS). **Orgs.:** ALA: Jt. Com. on Lib. Srv. to Labor (Ch. 1968). MD LA: Pres. (1969–70). NJ LA: Pres. (1979–80). Lib. PR Cncl.: Pres. (1978–79). **Activities:** 9; 17, 18, 24 **Addr.:** Wayne Public Library, 475 Valley Rd., Wayne, NJ 07470.

Burns, John F. (S. 13, 1945, Joliet, IL) Chief of Arch., CA State Arch., 1981–; Admin., WA State Hist. Recs. and Arch. Proj., 1977–81; Admin. Intern, West. WA Univ., WA State Arch., 1976–77; Instr., Chapman Coll. PACE Prog., 1975–76; Instr., Dept. Ch., Skagit Valley Coll., 1972–75; Cmsn. Ofcr., US Navy, 1967–70. **Educ.:** Lewis Coll., 1963–67, BA (Hist.); WA State Univ., 1970–72, MA (Hist.); West. WA Univ., 1976–77, Cert. (Arch. Admin.). **Orgs.:** Spindex Users' Netwk: Exec. Com. (Ch. 1979–81). SAA. NW Archvsts. Amer. Assn. for State and Lcl. Hist. **Pubns.:** Co-cmplr., *Washington State Archives Guide to the Governor's Papers, 1853–1976* (1977); "Statewide Surveying: Some Lessons Learned," *Amer. Archvst.* (July 1979); "The NHPRC and the State of Washington's Historical Records," *Prologue* (Spr. 1979); Supvsg. Ed., *Historical Record of Washington State,* 4 vols. (1981). **Activities:** 2; 17, 28, 39; 56, 57 **Addr.:** California State Archives, 1020 "O" St., Rm. 130, Sacramento, CA 95814.

Burns, Mary Ada (S 20, 1928, Sarasota, FL) Sr. Asst. Libn., Media & Curric. Ctr., San Diego State Univ. Lib., 1975–; Col. Head Libn., Barat Coll., 1972–74; Asst. Libn., Maryville Coll., 1972; Elem. Libn., Convent of the Sacred Heart, 1968–70. **Educ.:** San Francisco Coll. for Women, 1950–59, BA (Educ.); Cath. Univ., 1971–72, MSLS; San Diego State Univ., 1975–77, MA (Educ.). **Orgs.:** ALA. CA LA. CCLI. AAUP. **Activities:** 1; 31, 32, 39; 63, 95-Bibl. Computer Srch. **Addr.:** 1638 Corsica St., San Diego, CA 92111.

Burns, Mary Mehlman (Gloucester, MA) Coord., Curric. Lib., Framingham State Coll., 1969–, Instr., Hist. Dept., 1962–69; Chld. Libn., Boston Pub. Lib., 1952–58; Tchr., Mt. St. Mary Semy., Nashua, NH, 1950–52. **Educ.:** Mt. St. Mary Coll., Hooksett, NH, 1945–49, AB (Eng., Hist.); Boston Coll., 1949–50, AM (Eng.); Simmons Coll., Grad. Sch. of LS, 1966, MS; various crs. **Orgs.:** ALA: Mildred L. Batchelder Awd. Com. (Ch., 1975); Newbery-Caldecott Com. (1980); Hans Christian Andersen Awd. Com. (1981). New Eng. LA: RT of Chld. Libns. (Adv. to Ch., 1972–76). CLENE. Framingham State Coll. Prof. Assn.: Nom. and Elecs. (Ch., 1978–81). Nobscot Readg. Assn. Intl. Readg. Assn.: Chld. Choices Com. (1979–81). **Honors:** Framingham State Coll., Disting. Srv. Awd., 1979; Alum. Assn. of Framingham State Coll., Disting. Srv. Awd., 1980; New Eng. LA, RT of Chld. Libns., Hewins-Melcher Lectr., 1971; Delta Kappa Gamma; other hons. **Pubns.:** Introduction, *The Hurdy Gurdy Man* (1980); introduction, *Robbut: A Tale of Tails* (1981); "There Is Enough for All: Robert Lawson's America," *The Horn Bk. Mag.* (F.–Ap.–Je. 1972); "In the Spotlight: The 1975 Mildred Batchelder Award," *Top of the News* (Ja. 1976); reviewing staff, *The Horn Book Mag.* (1970–). **Activities:** 1, 9; 15, 25, 42; 55, 63 **Addr.:** Curriculum Library, Framingham State College, Framingham, MA 01701.

Burns, Richard K. (Ja. 9, 1935, Blackmountain, KY) Ed., Legacy Bks., COME-ALL-YE (A Review Jnl.), 1971–; Dir., Falls Church, Pub. Lib., 1960–71; Writer/Resrchr.; White House Natl. Comsn. on Libs., 1967–; Circ. Supvsr., U. of IL, 1959–60; Ref. Libn., Louisville, Free Pub. Lib., 1957–59. **Educ.:** Morehead Univ., 1953–57, BS; 1958–60, MSLS; Inst. for Trng. in Muncpl. Admin., 1965, Cert. **Orgs.:** ALA. DC LA: Pres. (1970). VA LA: *VA Libn.*, ed. Amer. Folklore Society. Natl. Bk. Cncl. **Honors:** BOMC Lib. Awrd., 1965. **Pubns.:** Ed., *The Broadside Ballad;* Rpts., Msc. LA, Assn. Anl. Conf., *Lib. Jnl.*, (1976–80); "History & Development of the White House Nat'l Commission on Libraries" *Lib. Jnl.*, (1968); Reviews. **Activities:** 9, 6; 17, 39, 41; 57, 66, 85 **Addr.:** P.O. Box 494, Hatboro, PA 19040.

Burns, Robert W., Jr. (Jl. 5, 1928, St. Louis, MO) Asst. Dir. of Libs., CO State Univ., 1968–; Head, Sci. Lib., Univ. of ID, 1957–68; Head, Ref. Libn., Omaha Pub. Lib., 1955–59. **Educ.:** Univ. of CO, 1949–51, BA (Hist.); Univ. of Denver, 1954–55, MSLS. **Orgs.:** ASIS: Const. and Bylaws Com. (1976–80). ALA: ACRL Plng. Com. (1978–81); LRRT Strg. Com. (1975–79); Planned Resrch. Forum (1976). CO LA: Spr. Panel (1974, 1976–78). Fort Collins Pub. Lib.: Trustee (1974–78). NCLIS: Comsn. (1978–81). CO Mt. Club: Various Ofcs. **Honors:** Beta Phi Mu; Cncl. on Lib. Resrscs., Fellow, 1975; LRRT, Best Paper of the Year, 1977. **Pubns.:** "Library Use as a Performance Measure," *Jnl. of Acad. Libnshp* (Mr. 1978); "An Empirical Rationale for the Accumulation of Statistical Information," *Lib. Resrcs. and Tech. Srvs* (Sum. 1974); "A Generalized Methodology for Library Systems Analysis," *Coll. & Resrch. Libs.* (Jl. 1971); Various other articles; Mem. various ed. bds. **Activities:** 1; 24, 28, 41; 56, 75 **Addr.:** 1504 Emigh, Fort Collins, CO 80521.

Burns, Teresa A. (Ja. 19, 1938, Grand Rapids, MI) Libn., Info. and Ref. Dept., Cuyahoga Cnty. Pub. Lib., 1978–, Adult Srvs. Libn., 1969–81. **Educ.:** Aquinas Coll., 1956–60, BS (Bio.); John Carroll Univ., 1965–67, (Eng. Lit., Educ.); Case West. Rsv. Univ., 1969–72, MSLS. **Orgs.:** ALA: PLA/Cmnty. Info. Sect. OH LA: Div. IV Action Cncl. (1980–81); Cmnty. Info. Task Frc. (Ch., 1979–81); Cmnty. Info. State Wkshp. (Ch., 1981). OH Cncl. of Info. and Ref. Providers: Lib. Com. (Ch., 1980–81). Alliance of Info. and Ref. Srvs.: Lib. Com. (1979–81). Con.'s Leag. of OH. Womenspace: Lib. Com. for Wkshp. on Women and Personal Fin. (Ch., 1979). **Activities:** 9; 16, 39; 93 **Addr.:** Cuyahoga County Public Library, Parma Regional Branch, 5850 Ridge Rd., Parma, OH 44129.

Burns, (Rev. Msgr.) Vincent L. (Ag. 30, 1926, Philadelphia, PA) Pres., St. Charles Semy., 1974–, VP, 1966–74; Prin., Bishop Kenrick HS, 1966. **Educ.:** St. Charles Semy., 1948–52, BA (Phil.); Villanova Univ., 1962–64, MA (Educ.); Cath. Univ. of Amer., 1964–66, PhD (Educ. Admin.). **Orgs.:** Free Lib. of Philadelphia: Trustee (1969–); Exec. Com. Secy. Fed. Adv. Cncl. of PA. Gvr.'s Adv. Cncl. on Libs. of PA. **Activities:** 4 **Addr.:** Saint Charles Seminary, Overbrook, Philadelphia, PA 19151.

Burr, Catherine Murray (O. 9, 1939, Minneapolis, MN) Libn., Clayton Woods Sch., Parkway Sch. Dist., 1979–; Instr., Lindenwood Coll., 1973–80; Dir., Lib. Srvs., Parkway Sch. Dist., 1970–74; Head Libn., Paul, Weiss, Goldberg, et al Law Firm, 1969–70; Asst. Law Libn., Univ. of IA, 1966–68; Elem. Sch. Libn., Marine Corps Sch., 1963–64; Chld. Libn., Arlington Pub. Lib., VA, 1962. **Educ.:** IA State Univ., 1957–61, BS; Columbia Univ., 1961–62, MS hons. (LS); St. Louis Univ., 1976–81, PhD (Educ.). **Orgs.:** MO Assn. of Sch. Libns.: Pres. (1980–81). ALA: AASL. MO LA: Bd. (1980–81). Univ. of MO Sch. of Lib. and Info. Sci.: Adv. Cncl. (1979–82). **Activities:** 10; 21, 31; 63 **Addr.:** 5 Summersweet Ln., Ballwin, MO 63011.

Burr, Elizabeth (My. 27, 1908, Waco, TX) Retired, 1973–; Pub. Lib. Consult., Chld. and YA Srv., WI Div. for Lib. Srvs., Dept of Pub. Instr., 1946–73; Head, Chld. Dept., Lincoln Lib., Springfield, IL, 1943–46, Chld. Libn., 1931–43. **Educ.:** Oxford Coll. for Women, 1925–27; Univ. of IL, 1942–43, BS; West Rsv. Univ., 1930–31, Cert. (Lib.). **Orgs.:** ALA: Cncl. (1960–61); Chld. Srvs. Div. (Pres., 1960–61), Newbery-Caldecott Com. (Ch., 1959–60). WI LA. AAUW. WI Hist. Socty. Nature Conservaney. Friends of the CCBC, Inc. Various other orgs. **Honors:** WI LA, Libn. of the Yr., 1956. **Pubns.:** Numerous articles in *Lib. Jnl., ALA Bltn.,* and other lib. jnls. **Activities:** 9, 13; 21, 25, 48 **Addr.:** 302 S. Owen Dr., Madison, WI 53705.

Burrier, Donald H. Jr. (S. 30, 1945, Avignon, France) Dir., Elyria Pub. Lib., 1978–; Persnl. Ofcr., Toledo-Lucas Cnty. Pub. Lib., 1976–78; Persnl. and Budget Ofcr., Univ. Lib., Kent St. Univ., 1973–75. **Educ.:** Kent St. Univ., 1963–68, BA 1973–75, MLS; Univ. D'Aix-Marseille, 1972; Univ. of Toledo, Pub. Srv. Mgt. Sem., 1976; Miami Univ. (Ohio), Exec. Dev. Prog. Lib. Admn., 1976. **Orgs.:** ALA: PLA; OH LA. Info. Multi. Cnty. Coop.: Pres. (1981–). Lorain Cnty. Fed. for Human. Srvs.: Pres. Bd. of Trustees (1980–81), Elyria Concert Assn.: Bd. of Trustees (1979–); Untd. Way of Greater Lorain Cnty.: Bd. of Trustees (1981) N.W. OH. Cnsrtm. for Pub. Sec. Labor Rel.: Exec. Com. (1977–78). **Honors:** OH. Rehab. Conf., N.W. OH. Nom. Empl. of the Yr., 1977; U.S. Army, Bronze Star, 1971. **Activities:** 9; 17 **Addr.:** 320 Washington Ave., Elyria, OH 44035.

Burrows, Suzetta Cecile (N. 22, 1944, New York, NY) Head, Cat., Prcs. Dept., Univ. of MS Med. Ctr., 1979–; Bibl. Resrch. Srvs. Libn., Univ. of MS Med. Ctr., 1977–79; Library Consultant, Eliot Hlth. Scis. Bks., Inc., 1974–76; Libn., Memorial Sloan-Kettering Cancer Ctr., 1968–74. **Educ.:** Brooklyn Coll., 1961–65, BS (Bio.); Columbia Univ., 1965–68, MLS; Med. LA Cert., 1980. **Orgs.:** Med. LA: Pubcty. Com. (1969–70), Secy. (1971–73). Med. LA: NY Reg. Grp., Pubcty. Com. (1969–71). Med. LA: South. Reg. Grp., Nom. Com. (1979). **Pubns.:** "Searching the MEDLARS file on NLM and BRS; a comparative study," *Bltn. of the Med. LA.* (Ja. 1979). **Activities:** 1, 12; 17, 20, 39; 56, 75, 80 **Addr.:** Univ. of Mississippi Med. Ctr. Library, 2500 North State St., Jackson, MS 39209.

Burson, (Mrs.) Phyllis S. (Mr. 31, 1914, Seattle, WA) Dir. of Libs., City of Corpus Christi, 1956–74 and 1980–; Dir. of Ofc. of Cmnty. Enrich., City of Corpus Christi, 1974–79; Asst. Libn., Del Mar Coll., 1951–53; Law Libn., Univ. of ID, 1940–45. **Educ.:** Univ. of WA, 1938, BA; 1939, MLS; Univ. of ID Coll. of Law, 1940–46. **Orgs.:** ALA: Cncl. (1972–74). TX LA: Pres. (1970–71). SWLA: Pub. Lib. Sect. (Ch., 1974–76); SLICE: Exec. Com. of Cncl. (1971–72). Other orgs. Numerous city bds. **Honors:** TX LA, TX Libn. of the Yr., 1966; Corpus Christi Woman of the Yr., 1963. **Pubns.:** "A Place in City Government," *What Else You Can Do With a Library Degree* (1980). **Activities:** 9; 17, 24 **Addr.:** Corpus Christi Public Libraries, 505 North Mesquite St., Corpus Christi, TX 78401.

Burstein, Lee (Ag. 15, 1952, Chicago, IL) Chief Acq. Libn., Cook Cnty. Law Lib., 1979–, Adm. Asst., 1978–79, Asst. Ref.

PROFESSIONAL ACTIVITIES: Institutions: 1. Acad. lib.; 2. Arch.; 3. Assn.; 4. Fed./Gvt. lib.; 5. Inst. lib.; 6. Mfr./Suppl.; 7. Milit. lib.; 8. Musm.; 9. Pub. lib.; 10. Sch. lib.; 11. Sch. of lib. sci.; 12. Spec. lib.; 13. State lib.; 14. (other). **Functions/Activities:** 15. Acq./Col. dev.; 16. Adult srvs.; 17. Admin.; 18. Apprais.; 19. Archit./Bldgs.; 20. Cat./Class.; 21. Chld. srvs.; 22. Circ.; 23. Cons./Pres.; 24. Consult.; 25. Cont. ed.; 26. Educ. lib. sci.; 27. Ext. srvs.; 28. Fund/Grants; 29. Gvt. pubs.; 30. Indx./Abs.; 31. Instr. lib. use; 32. Media srvs.; 33. Micro.; 34. Netwks./Coop.; 35. Persnl.; 36. PR; 37. Publshg.; 38. Recs. mgt.; 39. Ref. srvs.; 40. Repro.; 41. Resrch.; 42. Review.; 43. Secur.; 44. Serials; 45. Spec. col.; 46. Tech. srvs.; 47. Trustees/Bds.; 48. YA srvs.; 49. (other).

Libn., 1976–78. **Educ.:** Univ. of IL, Chicago Circle, 1970–74, BA (Pol. Sci.); Rosary Coll., 1974–76, MLS. **Orgs.:** AALL: Rel. with Publshrs. and Dirs. Com. (1981-82); Educ. Com. (1979–80); Chicago Assn. of Law Libs.: Pres. (1980–81); Secy. (1978). **Pubns.:** *Entertainment Law and the Arts: a Bibliography* (1978); *Cable Television: a Selective Bibliography.* **Activities:** 4, 12; 15, 38, 46; 77, 78 **Addr.:** Cook County Law Library, Chicago, IL 60602.

Burt, Lesta Jeanne (Norris) (Ja. 24, 1928, Harmon, OK) Dir., Prof., Sam Houston State Univ., 1972–, Inst., 1966–69; Libn., Fort Worth I.S.D., 1965–66; Tchr./Libn., Arlington I.S.D., 1963–65. **Educ.:** TX Woman's Univ., 1945–48, BA (Sp./Eng.), 1963–66, MLS; University of WI, Madison, 1969–72, PhD (Lib. Sci.); A & M, College Teaching courses, 1967–68. **Orgs.:** Texas Cncl. of Lib. Educ.: Pres. (1967–69; 1976–79). SWLA: CELS Adv. Bd. (1972–). ALA: HRLS Awds. Com. (1977); ASCLA Improving Jail Lib. Srvs. Consult. (1979–); ASCLA Rep. to ALA CLENE Network (1980–82). TX LA: TLA Plng. Com., (1980–82). TX Assn. of Coll. Tchr.: Secy., Local Chap. (1967–68). Univ. Women. Book Discussion League. **Pubns.:** *Bibliotherapy: The Effect of Group Book Discussion on the Attitudes of Inmates in Two Correctional Institutions* (1972); "Information Needs of Inmates", *Lib. Trends* (1977); "Keepers of Men Need Keepers of Books", *Jnl. of Crime and Delinquency* (1972). **Activities:** 10, 11; 17, 36, 41; 89, 95-Children's and YA Lit. **Addr.:** Library Science Department, Sam Houston State University, P.O. Box 2236, Huntsville, TX 77341.

Burtis, Alyce Rodgers (My. 10, 1921, Charleston, SC) Dir., Instr. Mtrls. Ctr., Hunterdon Ctrl. HS, 1971–; Libn., Zuegner Meml. Lib., 1969–71; Libn., Hunterdon Ctrl. HS, 1956–69; Libn., Flemington HS, 1951–56; Libn., Upper Freehold Twp. HS, 1945–50. **Educ.:** Syracuse Univ., 1939–43, AB (Zlgy.); Columbia Univ., 1947–52, MLS. **Orgs.:** ALA. NJ LA: Mem.-at-Lg. (1969–71); Educ. Media Assn. NJ: Pres. (1976–77). AAUW, Flemington Branch: Pres. (1965–67). NJ Sch. Women's Club: Pres. (1972–74). **Pubns.:** "Precis", *NJ Libs.* (S. 1977); "Precis", Dalhousie Univ. Nsltr., (D. 1977). **Activities:** 10; 17; 58, 83, 92 **Addr.:** Route 6, Hickory Trail, Flemington, NJ 08822.

Burtner, Susan Burns (N. 30, 1942, Chicago, IL) Dir., Ofc. of Info. Systs. and Srvs., U.S. Gen. Acct. Ofc., 1980–, Dir., Ofc. of Libn., 1976–80, Chief, Readers Srvs., 1973–76; Chief, Ref. Srvs., U.S. Dept. of Cmrce., 1970–73; Base Libn., Dept. of Air Frc., Fuchu, Japan, 1968–70; Catlgr., Dept. of HEW, 1967–68. **Educ.:** Purdue Univ., 1960–64, BA (Soc. Std.); Univ. of IL, 1965–67, MSLS; George Washington Univ., 1968–70, MS (Human Resrcs. Dev.). **Orgs.:** SLA: DC Chap., Soc. Sci. Div. (Treas., 1973–74). ALA: Fed. Libns. RT (Exec. Secy., 1973–74). DC LA. **Honors:** Gen. Acct. Ofc. Mgt. Srvs. Org., Dirs. Awd., 1977. **Activities:** 4; 17, 30, 38; 77 **Addr.:** 4013 N. Tazewell St., Arlington, VA 22207.

Burtniak, John (F. 12, 1941, Ethelbert, MB, CAN) Head, Tech. Srvs. Div., Brock Univ. Lib., 1970–, Acq. and Serials Libn., 1968–70, Admin. Asst. to Chief Libn., 1967–68, Acq. Libn., 1966–67, Catlgr., 1965–66. **Educ.:** Univ. of Ottawa, 1961–64, BA (Arts); Univ. of Toronto, 1964–65, BLS, 1965–69, MLS. **Orgs.:** Can. LA. ON. LA. Bibl. Socty. of Can. ON Hist. Socty. ON Geneal. Socty: Pres (1981-1983), VP (1979–81). Grt. Lakes Hist. Socty. Alcuin Socty. Various other socty. **Pubns.:** Jt. Auth. *Railways in the Niagara Peninsula* (1978); Jt. Ed., *The Welland Canals* (1979); Jt. Ed., *Villages in the Niagara Peninsula* (1980); Jt. Ed., *Immigration and Settlement in the Niagara Peninsula* (1981); "Local Sources for Searchers in the Niagara Peninsula," *Families* (Fall 1973). **Activities:** 1, 2; 15, 45, 46; 55, 69, 73-History. **Addr.:** R.R. #2 Barron Road, Niagara Falls, ON L2E 6S5, Canada.

Burton, Arlynn R. (O. 15, Cleveland, OH) Maple Hts. Reg. Libn., Cuyahoga Cnty. Pub. Lib., 1969–; Parma Hts. Branch Libn., 1966–69; Brooklyn Branch Libn., 1957–66; Parma Reg. Chldn. Libn., 1952–57; Tchr., Parma City Schs., 1941–42. **Educ.:** Kent State Univ., 1938–41, BS (Educ.); Case West. Resrv. Univ., 1951–52, MLS. **Orgs.:** ALA. OH LA. Zonta Clb: Bedford Area (Secy., 1978–79, VP 1979–80; Pres., 1980–82). **Activities:** 9 **Addr.:** 9230 Independence Blvd., Parma Heights, OH 44130.

Burton, Hilary D. (Je. 26, 1943, Pittsburgh, PA) Tech. Info. Spec., Sci. and Educ. Admin., U.S. Dept. of Agr., 1977–; Consult., Brazilian Dept. of Agr., 1976–; Tech. Info. Spec., Agr. Resrch. Srvs., U.S. Dept. of Agr., 1975–77; Comp. Syst. Anal., 1971–75; Visit. Prof., Emory Univ., 1973; Comp. Srvs. Libn., U.S. Forest Srv., 1966–70. **Educ.:** Univ. of CA, Berkeley, 1961–65, AB (Pol. Sci., Russ.), 1966–72, MLS, PhD (Info. Sci.). **Orgs.:** Amer. Assn. for the Advnc. of Sci.: Sect. T. ASIS: Chapt. Ofcr. (1966–70, 1975). Assn. of Info. Dissm. Ctrs. **Honors:** U.S. Dept. of Agr. Superior Srv. Awd., 1973. **Pubns.:** "FAMULUS Revisited: Ten Years of Personal Information Systems," *J. ASIS* (1981); "Multi-Data Base Searching in Agriculture," *Spec. Libs.* (Jl. 1978); "Computerized Bibliographic Services for USDA Research," *J. Forrestry* (F. 1978); "Techniques for Educating SDI Users," *Spec. Libs.* (My/Je 1975); "A User Dependent SDI System," *Spec. Libs.* (D. 1973); Reviews; Various other articles. **Activities:** 4, 12; 24, 49-Tech. Transfer Online Srvs.; 75, 91, 93 **Addr.:** USDA, SEA, TIS, 1333 Broadway, Suite #400, Oakland, CA 94612.

Burton, Melvin K. (Jl. 21, 1952, St. Louis, MO) Chld. Libn., St. Louis Pub. Lib., 1981–; Chld. Libn., Phoenix Pub. Lib., 1979–81; Chld. Libn., Nationa Cnty. Lib., 1976–79. **Educ.:** Ctrl. Meth. Coll., 1969–73, BA (Pol. Sci.); Univ. of MO, 1973–74, MA (LS). **Orgs.:** AZ State LA. ALA: ALSC, Caldecott Com. Natl. Assn. for the Prsrvn. and Perpet. of Storytel. **Honors:** JRMT, 3M/JMRT Prof. Dev. Grant, 1978. **Pubns.:** Storyteller, "Story Kaleidoscope Cassettes" (1979). **Activities:** 9; 21 **Addr.:** Divoll Branch Library, 4234 N. Grand, St. Louis, MO 63107.

Burton, Riley Paul (Ja. 6, 1921, Franklin, NE) Prof. of Law and Cur. of Law Lib., Univ. of South. CA, 1972–; Prof. and Law Libn., 1959–72, Assoc. Prof. and Law Libn., 1956–59, Asst. Prof. and Law Libn., 1953–56; Asst. Prof. and Law Libn., Univ. of UT, 1952–53. **Educ.:** Univ. of WA, 1938–41, 1946–48, BA (Law/Hist.), 1948–50, JD (Law), 1950–51, BA (Law Libr.). **Orgs.:** AALL: Chap. (1954–55); Ch., Const. & By-Laws (1955–56); Co-op. with Assn. of Am. Law Schools (1957–60); Recruitment (1961–62). South. CA Assn. of Law Libs.: Pres. (1954–55). Amer. Judicature Soc. Law and Soc. Assn. WA State Bar Assn. **Pubns.:** "General Reference Materials", *How to Find the Law*, 7 ed. 1976; "Non-Legal Materials", *How to Find the Law, 6th ed.* (1965); "Consciousness in Connecticut" *Jnl. of Beverly Hills Bar Assn.,* (Ja. 1971); "Readings in Legal Literature" *American Bar Association Jnl.,* (Oct. 1955; S., N., 1957). **Activities:** 1, 12; 15, 39, 41; 55, 77, 92 **Addr.:** Law Center Library, University of Southern California, University Park, Los Angeles, CA 90007.

Burton, Robert Edward (F. 16, 1927, Detroit, MI) Dir. of Libs., SUNY, Plattsburgh, 1976–; Ast. Pub. Srvs. Dir., SUNY, Buffalo, 1975–76; Head, Div. Libs., Univ. of MI, 1962–75; Libn., Union Carbide Corp., 1956–62. **Educ.:** Univ. of MI, 1945–48, BS (Math); 1954–56, AMLS. **Orgs.:** ALA. Bibl. Socty. of Amer. Bibl. Socty. of the Univ. of VA. **Pubns.:** Co-Auth., *Roses: A Bibliography* (1972); *Travel in Oceania* (1980); numerous articles. **Activities:** 1; 15, 17 **Addr.:** Benjamin F. Feinberg Library, Plattsburgh State University College, Plattsburgh, NY 12901.

Bury, Peter Paul (N 29, 1927, Hartford, CT) Dir., Glenview Pub. Lib., 1958–; Consult., CT State Lib., 1960–62; Libn., Detroit Pub. Lib., 1955–58. **Educ.:** Boston Univ., 1944–48, BA (Hist.); 1948–49, MA (Hist.); Simmons Col., 1954–55, MSLS. **Orgs.:** IL LA: Treas. (1967); Pres. (1972–73); Stan. Com., Ch. (1970–72); IL Natl. Lib. Wk.: Ch. (1965). ALA: Stan. Com. (1971–74); Frnds. of Lib. Ch. (1972–73). N Shore Lib. Club: Pres. (1962–63). Glenview Rotary Club: various offices since 1960. Glenview Area Hist. Socty.: VP (1977–79). Glenview Volun. Bur.: VP (1977–81). **Honors:** U.S. Army, Bronze Star, 1953. **Pubns.:** "Publicity for small libraries", *IL Libs.* (F. 1961). Reports. **Activities:** 9; 17, 19, 24 **Addr.:** 1537 Brandon Rd., Glenview, IL 60025.

Busbin, O. Mell (Winterville, GA) Assoc. Prof., Appalachian State Univ., 1980–; Asst. Prof., E. TN State Univ., 1974–79; Assoc. Prof., Ch., Media Educ. Dept., Univ. of ND, 1973–74; Asst. Prof., Med. Educ. Dept., Appalachian State Univ., 1968–72; Libn., Ctr. for Sch. Experimentation, OH State Univ., 1961–66. **Educ.:** High Point Coll., 1955–59, AB (Eng.); Appalachian State Univ., 1961–63, MA (LS); West. MI Univ., 1972–73, SPA (LS); FL State Univ., 1980, Advnc. MLS. **Orgs.:** TN LA. NC LA. ALA. SELA. Natl. Cncl. of Tchrs. of Eng. **Honors:** Beta Phi Mu, 1974; Phi Delta Kappa, 1966. **Pubns.:** Ed., *NC Libraries* (1969–72); "Reading Guidance–What It IS," *Readg. Improvement* (1966). **Activities:** 1; 21, 26, 32 **Addr.:** P.O. Box 411, Boone, NC 28607.

Busch, B. J. (N. 12, 1943, Ypsilanti, MI) Head, Educ. Lib., and Lectr., LS, Univ. of AB, 1975–, Supvsr., Soc. Sci. Cat., 1974–75, Catlgr., 1971–74; Cat. Libn., Marburg (Grmn.) Univ., 1970–71; Libn., St. Joseph Acad. (Adrian, MI), 1968–70; Subj. Cat., Univ. of MI Lib., 1967–70. **Educ.:** Univ. of MI, 1961–65, BA (Russ.), 1966–67, MA (LS); Univ. of AB, 1973–79, MA (Compar. Lit.). **Orgs.:** Can. Assn. of Spec. Libs. and Info. Srvs.: Edmonton Chap., Vice-ch. (1975–76). ALA. Edmonton LA: Nom. Com. (Ch., 1976–77). Assn. of Prof. Libns., Univ. of AB: Pres. (1973–74), Treas. (1973). ABLA: Vice–Pres. (1980–81), Pres. (1981–82). Various other orgs. Can. Assn. of Univ. Tchrs. Assn. of Acad. Staff, Univ. of AB. **Pubns.:** Reviews and abstracts. **Activities:** 1, 12; 17, 20, 42; 54, 63, 92 **Addr.:** Education Library, Education Building South, University of Alberta, Edmonton, AB T6G 2G5 Canada.

Busch, Joseph A. (My. 23, 1952, New York, NY) Dir., Bradford M. Field. Meml. Lib., 1980–, and Asst. Dir., Tech. Srvs., Hampshire Coll., 1979–; Chief, Tech. Srvs., Paul, Weiss, Rifkind, Wharton and Garrison Law Lib., 1977–79. **Educ.:** Portland State Univ., OR, 1974, BA (Lit.); SUNY, Albany, 1977, MLS. **Orgs.:** ASIS. AALL. **Honors:** Beta Phi Mu, 1977. **Pubns.:** "OCLC Quality Control Practices in NELINET," *Procs. of the ASIS Anl. Mtg.* (1981); "The Supt. of Docs.' *Publications Reference File (PRF)*", 5 *Gvt. Pubns. Review* (No. 4, 1978); "A Method for Evaluating the Multiple Relations Between Subject Descriptors–Related Terms," *Procs. of the ASIS Anl. Mtg.* (1978). **Activities:** 1, 12; 24, 41, 46; 55, 56, 75 **Addr.:** 200 Long Plain Rd., RFD 3, Amherst, MA 01002.

Buser-Molatore, Marcia (N. 29, 1952, Ft. Meade, MD) Info. Mgr., Precision Castparts Corp., 1979–; Law Libn., Spears, Lubersky et al., 1977–79; Ref. Libn., Univ. of OR Hlth. Sci. Ctr., 1976–77. **Educ.:** OH State Univ., 1971–74, BA (Hist. Art); Univ. of OR, 1975–76, MLS. **Orgs.:** SLA: OR Chap., Pres.; OR Guide to Metallurgical Lit. Rev. Com. **Pubns.:** *Managing Special Library Collections; A Bibliography and Oregon Union List* (1981). **Activities:** 12; 15, 17, 30; 81 **Addr.:** Precision Castparts Corp., 4600 S.E. Harney Dr., Portland, OR 97206.

Bush, Donna Dianne (D. 15, 1948, Columbus, WI) Libn., Fac., WI Luth. Coll., 1978–; Bk. Selector, Blackwell's, Eng., 1977–78; Acq. Tech., Univ. of WI, 1976–77, Rsv., Pers. Asst. Supvsr., 1974–76. **Educ.:** WI Luth. Coll., 1967–69, AA (Educ.); Univ. of WI, 1970–72, BS (Elem. Educ.), 1974–77, MA (LS). **Orgs.:** ALA: ACRL. WI LA. Natl. Cncl. of Tchrs. of Eng. **Honors:** Beta Phi Mu, 1978. **Pubns.:** "Discards 'Worth Fort Knox'," *Amer. Libs.* (O. 1979); "Women Library Workers" slide-tape presentation (1976). **Activities:** 1; 15, 17, 22; 63, 90, 92 **Addr.:** N78W12648 Fond du lac Ave., Menomonee Falls, WI 53051.

Bush, Douglas P. (O. 14, 1930, Monterey Park, CA) Asst. Dir. of Libs., Brigham Young Univ., 1972–; Asst. Dir. of Libs., San Diego State Univ., 1968–72; Head, Ref. Srvs., Univ. of WA, 1967–68; Head of Acq., Univ. of UT, 1965–67; Head, Undergrad. Lib., Brigham Young Univ., 1963–65; Bk. Sel. Libn., Univ. of CA, La Jolla, 1962; Ref. Libn., San Diego Pub. Lib., 1961. **Educ.:** Brigham Young Univ. 1959, BS (Hist.); Univ. of WA, 1959–61, MLS; Brigham Young Univ., 1979, M.Ed. (Hist. of Ed.). **Orgs.:** ALA. UT LA. **Activities:** 1; 16, 17, 19 **Addr.:** Harold B Lee Library, Brigham Young University, Provo, UT 84602.

Bush, Gail (My. 2, 1952, Chicago, IL) Lib. Resrch. Mgr., Heidrick and Struggles, Inc., 1979–; Head Libn., Natl. Coll. of Educ.-Chicago Campus, 1977–79. **Educ.:** Univ. of IL, 1970–73, AB (Anthro.), 1975–77, MSLS. **Orgs.:** IL Reg. Lib. Cncl.: Cont. Ed. Com. (1977–79). ASIS. SLA. ALA. **Honors:** Phi Beta Mu. **Activities:** 12; 15, 41, 49-Develop on-line library data base; 59, 95-Biographical Data. **Addr.:** Heidrick & Struggles, Inc., 125 S. Wacker Dr., #2800, Chicago, IL 60606.

Bush, Margaret (Jody) (Pitsenberger) (Je. 25, 1936, Klamath Falls, OR) Chief, Branches, Cmnty. Srvs., Providence Pub. Lib., 1979–; Branch Libn., DC Pub. Lib., 1965–79. **Educ.:** Stanford Univ., 1954–58, BA (European Lit.); Univ. of WA, 1961–62, MLS. **Orgs.:** New Eng. LA. RI LA: Exec. Bd., Persnl. Com. (1980–81). ALA: Cnclr. (1980–84); LAMA; SRRT, Feminist Task Frc. Reg. Lib. for the Blind and Phys. Handcpd. Educ. Info. Ctrs. of RI. Adult Basic Skills Acad. **Honors:** Mayor, DC Gvt., Outstan. Performance Awd., 1978. **Pubns.:** "ALA Column," *RI LA Bltn.* (monthly). **Activities:** 9; 16, 17, 27; 50, 66, 89 **Addr.:** Providence Public Library, 150 Empire St., Providence, RI 02903.

Bush, Margaret A. (Ag. 14, 1937, Webster, SD) Assoc. Ref. Libn., Founders Library, Howard Univ, 1981–; Netwk. Consult., Natl. Lib. Ser. for the Blind and Phys. Handcpd., 1979–81; Ref. Libn., Biblgphr., Lib. of Cong., 1978; Asst. Prof., Simmons Coll., 1976–78; Circ. Libn., Chlds. Lit. Specialist, Natl. Coll. of Educ., 1974–76; Head of Chlds. Dept., Oak Park Pub. Lib., Oak Park, IL, 1967–74; Chlds. Libn., NY Pub. Lib., 1960–67. **Educ.:** Univ. of CA at Berkeley, 1955–59, BA (Eng.); 1959–60, MLS; Ctrl. MI Univ., 1978–79, Mgt., Econ., Comms. **Orgs.:** ALA: ALA Cncl./ALSC Cnclr., 1981–84 ALSC/Bd. of Directors (1976–79); Priority Grp. Ch. (1979–81). Chlds. Film Eval. Comm. (1976–78). Newbery Caldecott Awds. Comm. (1972–73). Comm. on Natl. Plng. for Spec. Collections (1978–80). Comm. Liason with Bk. stores (1970–72). DC LA; Freedom to Read Fndn.; Chlds. Readg. RT of Chicago. Indp. Voters of IL: Bd. of Dir. (1972–74); Amer. for Dem. Action: Bd. of Dir. (1974, 1975); Oak Park (IL) Women's Exch.: Bd. of Dir. (1974, 1975). **Honors:** Beta Phi Mu, 1960; IL LA., Davis Awd. for Leadership in Lib. Srv. to Chld., 1974. **Pubns.:** Ed. *Storytelling: Readings, Bibliographies, Resources* (1978); "In Search of the Perfect Shark," *Sch. Lib. Jnl.* (Mr. 1979); "Space: Factors in Planning and Use," *IL Libs.* (D. 1978); "Serving the Interests of Children,-' *Appraisal* (Spr. 1977); "Library Facilities for Children. . .", *Children's Services in Public Libraries* (1978); Many other articles, reviews. **Activities:** 9, 11; 21, 24, 26; 63, 67, 72 **Addr.:** 319 10th St. SE, Washington, DC 20003.

Bush, Nancy Wagoner (Ag. 6, 1934, Malvern, PA) Assoc. Prof., Head of Dept. of Educ. Media, Auburn Univ., 1976–; Asst. to Vice Chancellor, Acad. Affairs, Appalachian State Univ., 1975–76, Dir., Resrcs. Ctrs. Prog., Assoc. Prof., 1972–75; Asst. Dir., Mtrls. Ctr., Sch. of LS, Asst. Prof., Nonprint Media, FL State Univ., 1971–72; Visit. Assoc. Prof., Sch. of LS, Univ. of NC, Chapel Hill, Sum. 1973; Visit. Lectr., Sch. of LS, FL State Univ., Sum. 1969; Chief, Circ. and Col., Branch Libn., Jacksonville Pub. Lib., 1966–68; Branch Libn., Miami Pub. Lib., 1960–66; various tchg. and other positions, 1947–56. **Educ.:** W. Chester State Coll., 1949–53, BS (Eng., Soc. Sci.); FL State Univ., 1962–63, MSLS, 1968–71, PhD (Mgt., Psy. Stats.), 1972, Post-doct. Std. (Finance, Law); Univ. of South. CA, 1979, Cmnty. Analysis Resrch. Inst.

Special Subjects/Services: 50. Adult educ.; 51. Advert./Mktg.; 52. Aerosp.; 53. Agric.; 54. Area std.; 55. Arts/Hum.; 56. Autom.; 57. Bibl./Prtg.; 58. Bio. sci.; 59. Bus./Fin.; 60. Chem.; 61. Copyrt.; 62. Documtn.; 63. Educ.; 64. Engin.; 65. Env.; 66. Eth. grps.; 67. Film; 68. Food/Nutr.; 69. Geneal.; 70. Geo.; 71. Geol.; 72. Handcpd.; 73. Hist.; 74. Int. frdm.; 75. Info. sci.; 76. Insr.; 77. Law; 78. Legis.; 79. Math./Comp. sci.; 80. Med.; 81. Metals; 82. Nat. resrcs.; 83. Newsp.; 84. Nuc. sci.; 85. Oral hist.; 86. Petr./Energy; 87. Pharm.; 88. Phys./Astr./Math.; 89. Readg.; 90. Relig.; 91. Sci./Tech.; 92. Soc. sci.; 93. Telecom.; 94. Transp.; 95. (other).

Orgs.: SLA: AL Chap. (Pres., 1980–81), Mem. Com. (Ch., 1977–79). AL Gvr.'s Task Force on Libs. (1979–). ALA: LAMA, Ref. Stats. Com. (1976–81); RTSD, Plng. Com. (Ch., 1975–78); various coms. AL LA: Educ. Com. (Ch., 1978–79); Stans. and Cert. Com. (Ch., 1978–). Various other orgs. AAUP. AAUW. Natl. Educ. Assn. East. Educ. Resrch. Assn. Various other orgs. **Honors:** Beta Phi Mu. **Pubns.:** "Justification of the Media Center Budget," *ALAC Open Circuit* (Fall 1978); "Getting Acquainted," and "In Conclusion," *Who Runs Your Library? 1978* (in press); "Academic Library Service: Can It Be High Quality with Limited Resources and Tomorrow's Future Scarcity," *Alabama Governor's Conference on Library and Information Services Proceedings* (in press); various other articles; Ed., *ALMA Nsltr.* (1978–). **Addr.:** P.O. Box 970, Auburn, AL 36830.

Busha, Charles H. (D. 14, 1931, Liberty, SC) Indp. Lib. Consult., Auth., 1976–; Assoc. Prof., Univ. S. FL., 1973–76; Asst. Prof., Lectr., IN Univ., 1970–73; Ref. Consult., SC State Lib., 1963–67; Ref. Libn., Greenville Cnty. Lib., 1961–63; Fld. Artly. Ofcr., U.S. Army, 1951–54. **Educ.:** Furman Univ., 1954–58, BA (Pol. Sci.); Rutgers Univ., 1959–60, MLS; IN Univ., 1967–71, PhD (LS and Mass Comm.); U.S. Army Fld. Artly. Ofcr. Cand. Sch., 1952, 2nd Lt. **Orgs.:** Beta Phi Mu: IN Univ. Chap. (Pres. 1972–73). SC LA: Pubns. Com. (Ch. 1962–63). FL LA. SE LA. Frnds. of Tampa Pub. Lib.: Pres. (1974–76). Frnds. of Sarlin Cmnty. Lib.; Liberty Arts Cncl.: Pres. (1978–80). **Pubns.:** Ed., *A Library Science Research Reader and Bibliographic Guide* (1981); Ed., *An Intellectual Freedom Primer* (1977); Co-auth. *Research Methods in Librarianship: Techniques and Interpretation* (1980); "Research Methods," *Encyc. of Lib. and Info. Sci.;* Co-Auth., "Libraries and Privacy Legislation," *Lib. Jnl.* Feb. 1, 1976); other articles. **Activities:** 9, 11; 26, 39, 41; 74, 92, 93 **Addr.:** Summit Dr., Rt. 2 - Box 301, Liberty, SC 29657.

Bushnell, Peter S. (S. 9, 1948, Bogotá, Cundinamarca, Colombia) Assoc. Univ. Libn., Cat. Dept., Univ. of FL, 1975–, Asst. Univ. Libn. Latin Amer. Col., 1972–75. **Educ.:** Univ. of Rochester, 1966–70, BA (Hist.); FL State Univ., 1971–72, MS (LS); Univ. of FL, 1973–80, MFA (Msc.). **Orgs.:** Msc. LA. Msc. OCLC Users Grp. Natl. Flute Assn. Amer. Recorder Socty.: Gainesville Chap., Pres. (1977–79), VP (1973–74, 1981). Univ. of FL Lib. Staff Assn.: VP (1973–74); Bd. (1974–77, 1980–); Treas. (1979–80). **Activities:** 1; 20, 39; 54, 55 **Addr.:** 636 N.W. 26th Ave. #112, Gainesville, FL 32601.

Busquets, Carmen Liliana (Ap. 14, 1954, Fajardo, PR) Libn., Sellés Lib., Coll. of Educ., Univ. of PR, 1971. **Educ.:** Coll. of the Sacred Heart, 1968–71, BA (Art and Psy.); Univ. of PR, 1972–77, MLS. **Orgs.:** Socty. de Bibtcr. de PR: Com. of Admns. (1979–82). Fundación Puertorriqueña de Zarzuela y Opereta. Amigos de Ballet de San Juan. Actividades Culturales y Programa de la Univ. de PR. **Honors:** Highest academic average medal, Sociedad de Bibtcrs. de PR, 1977. **Activities:** 1; 20, 30, 39; 63 **Addr.:** Abolición 569 St., Baldrich, Hato Rey, PR 00918.

Butcher, Dina S. (S. 10, 1940, Gordon, NE) Coord., Minot Tchr. Lrng. Ctr. and Cmnty. Exch., 1978–; Coord., ND Gvr.'s Conf. on Libs., ND LA and State Lib., 1977–78; Consult. and Exec. Sec. Gvr. Adv. Cncl. on Libs., ND State Lib., 1975–77; Tchr., Minot Pub. Schs., 1970–74. **Educ.:** Skidmore Coll., 1959–63, BA (Grmn.); Freiburg Univ., Germany, 1963–64; Minot State Coll., 1967–69, BS (Sec. Educ.). **Orgs.:** ND Lib. Assn.: Pres. (1976); Trustee Pres. (1973–76). ALA: Legis Com. (1979–81). ALTA: Speaker's Bur. (1978–80); Prog. Com. (1977–79); Legis. Com. (1976–78). various other orgs. and ofcs. ND Citizens for the Arts: Secy. (1978–80). YMCA Bd. of Dir.: VIP Ch. (1978–80). Cham. of Cmrce.: Bus. and Con. Affairs Com. (Ch., 1979–80). various other orgs. and ofcs. **Honors:** ND Lib. Trustees, Trustee of the Year Awd., 1978. **Activities:** 12; 16, 17, 24; 50, 63 **Addr.:** 610 S. Main, Minot, ND 58701.

Buterbaugh, James G. (Mr. 20, 1936, Kearney, NE) Dir., Media/Telecom., Auraria Lib. and Media Ctr., Denver, CO., 1981–; Prof., Ch., Univ. of UT, 1977–81; Dir., Assoc. Prof., Instr. Media Ctr., Univ. of NE, 1966–77; Campus Dev. Dir., NE West. Coll. (Scottsbluff), 1960–66; Prin., Dalton (NE) Consolidated Sch., 1956–60. **Educ.:** NE St. Coll. (Kearney), 1953–56, BA (Educ., Sp., and Thea.); Univ. of North. CO, 1958–60, MA (Educ. Admn.); Univ. of NE, 1966–70, PhD, (Instr. Dev.). **Orgs.:** EFLA: Pres. and Bd. of Dir. (1976–77). Cnsrtm. of Univ. Film Ctrs.: Pres., Bd. of Dir. (1976–77). AECT. Phi Delta Kappa: Fac. Adv.; Assn. for Supvsn. and Curric. Dev. **Honors:** AECT/EBE, Fac. Insrv. Awd., 1976; Phi Delta Kappa, Tchr. Technologist, 1980. **Pubns.:** "Countdown-to-Dawn," *Videodisc News* (Mr. 1981); "New Video Technologies," *Sightlines* (Spr. 1980); Alternative Media Delivery Technologies: A Forecast for the Future, (1980); "Future Film Delivery Options," *Sightlines* (Spr. 1980); "Holography: Art in an Ephemeral Medium," *AV Instr.* (O. 1979); "Threading Ladders with Personal Visions," *AV Instr.* (My. 1979); Other articles and media. **Addr.:** Media/Telecommunications, Auraria Library and Media Center, Lawrence at 11th St., Denver, CO 80204.

Buthod, J. Craig (Je. 13, 1954, Tulsa, OK) Head, Bus. and Tech. Dept., Tulsa City-Cnty. Lib., 1979–; Tech. Libn., Williams Brothers Engin. Co., 1977–79. **Educ.:** Univ. of Tulsa, 1972–75, BS (Eng.); Univ. of Denver, 1976–77, MA (Libnshp.). **Orgs.:** SLA: OK Chap., VP, Pres.-Elect (1981–82); Bus. and Fin. Div., Pub. and Gvt. Libs. RT (Ch., 1980–). Tulsa Cnty. Hist. Socty.: Bd. of Dirs. (1981–). **Honors:** Beta Phi Mu, 1977. **Pubns.:** Ed., *INFO* (1979–); "Triage," *Ref. Libn.* (Sum. 1982). **Activities:** 9; 39; 59, 86, 91 **Addr.:** Business & Technology Dept., Tulsa City-County Library, 400 Civic Center, Tulsa, OK 74103.

Butler, Anne H. (Jl. 3, 1947, Charleston, WV) Libn., Alston, Miller, Gaines, 1971–; **Educ.:** Univ. of NC at Greensboro, 1965–69, BA (Eng.); Emory Univ., 1970–71, MLn (LS). **Orgs.:** AALL: Conf. of Newer Law Libns., Vice Ch., 1977), Ch. (1978). AALL: S. East. Chap., Pres. (1978–80), VP (1976–78). Atlanta Law Libs. Assn.: Pres. (1974). **Pubns.:** "Guide for Developing a Law Library for the Practitioner," (1977). **Activities:** 12, 14-Law Firm; 15, 17, 41; 77, 78 **Addr.:** Alston, Miller & Gaines, 1200 C & S National Bank Bldg., Atlanta, GA 30335.

Butler, Brett (Ja 13, 1941, San Francisco, CA) Pres., Information Access Corp., 1977–; Dir., Butler Assoc., 1969–71; 1973–78; Assoc., R & D Consult., 1974–76; Dir./VP, Mktg., Info. Design, 1971–73; VP, Stacey Div., Brodart Indus., 1968–69; Asst. VP/Head; J.W. Stacey, Inc., 1964–68. **Educ.:** Stanford Univ., 1958–62, BA (Soclgy.); 1964, MBA (Mktg.); San Jose State Univ., 1975, MA (Libnshp). **Orgs.:** ALA: Inf. Sci. and Autom.; Inst. Com. Ch. (1973–75); Las Vegas Preconf. Co-Ch. (1973); Libr. Auto. Discus. Grp. Ch. (1976–); RTSD; Reprodct. of Lib. Matrls./ Sect. Stan. Com. (1973–75). ASIS/various coms. since 1965). Infor. Indus. Assn. Natl. Micro. Assn. (1972–78), various coms. since 1972. **Pubns.:** "Beyond the Library-U.S. Online Trends" , *Online Info.* (1979); "The Energy Validation Information Management System". *N Amer. Netwk.*, (1979); Jt. Auth., "Feasibility Study, Final Report". Los Altos, CA: Info. Access Corp. (1979); "Collection and Resource Data Bases in Bibliographic Management.", *Requiem for the Card Cat.* (1979); Jt. Auth. "Lib. and Patron Response to the Com Catalog". Infor. Access Corp. (1979); various articles on lib. tech. **Activities:** 6; 24, 30, 37; 56, 62, 75 **Addr.:** Information Access Corporation, 404 Sixth Ave., Menlo Park CA 94025.

Butler, Cynthia (F. 19, 1936, Los Angeles, CA) Head, Pub. Srvs., Biomedical Lib., Univ. of CA, Irvine, 1969–; Readers Srvs. Libn., Anaheim Pub. Lib., 1964–68; Asst. Libn., Gen. Atomic, 1963–64; Tech. Docum. Libn., Hughes Aircraft Co., 1960–63. **Educ.:** Scripps Coll., 1954–58, BA (Span.); Univ. of CA, Berkeley, 1958–59, MLS; Med. LA Cert., 1975. **Orgs.:** Med. LA: Memb. Com. (1969–72); Bibl. and Info. Srvs. Assess. Com. (1978–). Med. Lib. Grp. of South. CA and AZ: Secy. (1974–75); Treas. (1976–77); Cont. ed. Com. (1977–); Pres.-elect (1981–82). Orange Cnty. LA: Nom. Com. (1976). Various other ofcs. **Pubns.:** "Medico-legal Research: Don't Overlook the Medical Textbooks," *Trauma* (D. 1978); Jt. auth., "Journal Titles Held by Forty Health Institutions in Southern California," *Bltn. Med. LA* (O. 1975). **Activities:** 1; 22, 39; 80 **Addr.:** Biomedical Library, University of CA, Irvine, P.O. Box 19556, Irvine, CA 92713.

Butler, Evelyn (Ag. 23, 1915, Saginaw, MI) Soc. Work Libn., Univ. of PA, 1946–; Head, Bus. and Tech. Dept., Lib. of the New Britain Inst., 1942–46; Head, Soc. Admin., Univ. of MI, Detroit, 1938–42. **Educ.:** Univ. of MI, 1933–37, AB (Span.); 1937–38, ABLS; 1946, AMLS. **Orgs.:** ALA: Urban Univ. Libn. Ad Hoc Com. (1977–79); Mid-Atlantic Recruit. Com. (1961–62); ACRL: Delaware Valley Chap.; SLA: CT Valley Chap. (Pres., 1945–46; VP, 1944–45); Philadelphia Chap, (Secy., 1947–48, Dir., 1958–60; Mem. Ch. 1960–61); Soc. Sci. Div. (ch. 1951–53); Soc. Welfare Sect. (Ch. 1960–66); Spec. Proj. Com. (Ch., 1975–). PA LA. AAUW; Natl. Assn. of Soc. Workers; Philadelphia Flwshp Comsn; Socty. for Crippled Chld. and Adults. **Honors:** Univ. of MI: Alum. Schol., 1933–37. **Pubns.:** Jt. ed., *Building A Social Work Library* (1962); "The Rule of Thumb," SLA Jrnl, (1960); "Social Welfare Libraries and Collections," Encyc. of Lib. and IS (1980). **Activities:** 1, 12; 15, 17, 39; 92 **Addr.:** Smalley Library of Social Work, 3701 Locust Walk, Castor Building C3, Philadelphia, PA 19104.

Butler, Karen A. (F. 11, 1948, Terre Haute, IN) Head, Pub. Srvs. Hlth. Sci. Lib., Univ. UT, 1978–; Ext. Libn., 1976–78; Ext. Ref. Libn., 1974–76; Ref. Libn., St. Lukes Hosp., 1972–74. **Educ.:** Univ. CA, Berkeley, 1968–70, AB (Soclgy.); Emporia State Univ., 1971–72, MLS. **Orgs.:** Med. LA: Mem. Com. (1978–). Midcont. Chap., Med. Lib. Grp.: Ch. (1978–79); Secy. (1975–76); Rep. (1981–84). UT LA, (1974–). Leag. of Women Voters. **Pubns.:** Ed., UT Hlth. Sci. Lib. Netwk. Nsltr. (1975–77). **Activities:** 12; 27, 34; 80 **Addr.:** Spences S. Eccles Health Sciences Library, Salt Lake City, UT 84112.

Butler, Kenneth W. (D. 10, 1922, Leeds, UK) Asst. Dir., Portland State Univ., 1977–; Dir., AV Srvs., 1953–77; Branch Libn., Multnomah Cnty. Lib., 1951–52; Branch Libn., Leeds Pub. Lib., UK, 1948–51. **Educ.:** Univ. of Portland, 1952–53, BA (Eng. Lit.); 1953–58, MA (Eng. Lit.); Lib. Assn., UK, 1947–48, ALA (Libnshp.). **Orgs.:** Pac. NW LA. ASIS. **Pubns.:** "A Modest Proposal for a School Library," *Educ.* (Mr. 1966). **Activities:** 1; 17, 32; 55, 67, 74 **Addr.:** Portland State University Library, P.O. Box 1151, Portland, OR 97207.

Butler, Matilda L. (F. 5, 1942, Oklahoma City, OK) Ch., Educ. Comm. Dept., Far West Lab., 1980–; Component Leader, Women's Concerns, 1979–; Dir., Comm. Netwk., 1977–; VP, Applied Comm. Resrch. Inc., 1974–77; Resrch. Assoc. & Lectr., Stanford Univ., 1970–77. **Educ.:** Univ. of OK, 1960–62; Boston Univ., 1962–64, BS (Comm. Arts); Stanford Univ., 1964–66, MA (Comm. Res.); Northwestern Univ., 1968–70, PhD (Soc. Psy.). **Orgs.:** ALA. ASIS. Intl. Comm. Assn.: Com. on Status of Women, Co-Ch. (1975). Amer. Educ. Resrch. Assn. AAAS. Amer. Assn. for Pub. Opinion Resrch.: Pacific Chap., Prog. Ch. (1972). **Pubns.:** Jt. Auth., *Women and the Mass Media* (1980); Jt. Auth., *Conceptualization of Information Equity Issues in Education* (1979); Chapter in *Coordinated-Career Couples:* (1980); Chapter in *The Potential of Mass Communication & Interpersonal Communication for Cancer Control* (1976); "Trends in Research Concerning Women's Educational Equity", *Educ. Libs.* (1978); Various articles. **Activities:** 12, 14-non-profit educ. inst.; 17, 28, 41; 63, 92, 93 **Addr.:** Far West Laboratory for Educational Research and Development 1855 Folsom St., San Francisco, CA 94103.

Butler, Naomi W. (Ag. 25, 1934, Boonsboro, MD) Spec., Field Srvs., Div. of Lib. Dev., MD, St. Dept. of Educ., 1970–; Asst. Prof., LS, Shepherd Coll., 1968–70; Asst. Prof., LS, Shippensburg St. Coll., 1966–67; Lib. Media Spec., Frederick Cnty. (MD) Sch., 1957–66, 1967–68. **Educ.:** Shepherd Coll., 1954–57, AB (Eng.); Univ. NC, 1959–66, MS (LS); Univ. MD, 1969–78, Advnc. Grad. Spec., 1969, PhD in prog. **Orgs.:** ALA. AECT. Md. Educ. Media Org. Cumberland Valley LA. Boonsboro Free Lib., Bd. of Trustees (Pres.). **Honors:** Hagerstown Jr. Coll., Outstan. Alumnus, 1967. **Pubns.:** "The Planning and Modification of Library Media Center Facilities," *Drexel Lib. Qtly.* (Ap. 1977); *Planning and Designing a Library Media Center* (1978). **Activities:** 13; 21, 24, 32; 63, 78 **Addr.:** 26 S. Main St., Boonsboro, MD 21713.

Butler, Patricia Smith (N. 14, 1942, Joplin, MO) Mgr. of Lib. Dev., DataPhase Systems, Kansas City, MO., 1980–; Head of Ref., Wichita State Univ. Lib., 1979–80; Biomed. Ref. Libn., 1978–79; Health Sciences Libn., Reg. Mem. Hosp., Brunswick, ME, 1977–78; Dir. of Media Prod. and AV Libn., Univ. of OK Health Sci. Ctr., 1972–76, Acq. and Ser. Libn., 1971–72; Coord., Lib. and Info. Srvs. Proj., OK Reg. Med. Prog., 1967–70; Circ. and ILL Libn., Univ. of OK Health Sci. Ctr., 1966–67. **Educ.:** Univ. of OK, 1959–63, BA (Eng.), 1965–66, MLS, 1973–77, PhD (Educ.); Med. LA, Grade 1, 1968. **Orgs.:** ALA: ACRL. Med. LA: Publshg. and Info. Industries Rel. Com. (1979–81); Educ. Sect. (Sec.-Treas., 1980–81; Ch.–Elect, 1981–82); Midcontinental Chap., Legis. Com. KS LA: Coll. and Univ. Libs. Sect. KS Online Grp. Coord., (1979–80). Various other associations. **Pubns.:** Jt. auth., "Books as Clinical Tools: Your Working Library," *Jnl. of OK State Med. Assn.* (F. 1969); *Hospital Library Resources in Oklahoma,* Univ. of OK Med. Ctr., Lib. Resrch. Rpt. 2 (1968). **Activities:** 1, 12; 17, 31, 39; 56, 63, 80 **Addr.:** 6018 Sunrise, Fairway, KS 66205.

Butler, Ruth G. (O. 6, 1921, Buffalo, NY) Ref. Libn., W. Seneca Pub. Lib., 1972–; Libn., Houghton Coll., 1970–; Libn., Buffalo Bible Inst., 1956–69; Fld. Socty., Campfire, 1944–45; Tchr.-Libn., Ten Broeck Acad., 1943–45. **Educ.:** SUNY, 1943, BEd, 1964, MLS. **Orgs.:** Assn. of Christ. Libns.: Bd. of Trustees (1960–78); Pres. (1977). NY LA. Trocaire Coll.: Lib. Adv. Bd. **Pubns.:** Ed., *Christ. Per. Index* (1958–75). **Activities:** 1; 17, 20, 25; 75, 89, 90 **Addr.:** Ada M. Kidder Library, Houghton College/ Buffalo Suburban Campus, 910 Union Rd., W. Seneca, NY 14224.

Butler, Tyrone G. (Ja. 15, 1948, Morehead, KY) Coll. Archvst. and Rec. Mgr., Medgar Evers Coll., 1981–; Asst. Archvst., Salvation Army Arch. and Resrch. Ctr., 1979–81; Archvst. TN State Lib. & Arch., 1977–79. **Educ.:** Xavier Univ., 1966–70, BA (Hist.); Boston Coll., 1971–72, MA (Hist.); Vanderbilt Univ., 1973–79 (Hist.); Nat. Arch. Inst., 1978, Cert., Mod. Arch. Admin.; 1978, Cert., Spindex III Users Crs.; 1978, Cert., Case Recs. **Orgs.:** SAA: Lcl. Arrange. Com. (1978). NY City Archvst. RT: Prog. Com. (1980). Metro. Area Rel. Arch. Long Island Archvsts. Amer. Assn. for State and Lcl. Hist. Natl. Trust for Hist. Prsrvn. TN Hist. Socty. **Activities:** 2; 23, 39, 43; 69, 90 **Addr.:** Medgar Evers College, 1150 Carroll St., Brooklyn, NY 11225.

Butorac, Frank George (F. 12, 1927, Crosby, MN) Dir. of Lib. Srvs., and Ch., Lib.–Media Cntr. Tech. Asst. Curric., Mercer Cnty. Cmnty. Coll., 1974–; Dir., Spec. Progs., 1971–74; Registrar, 1966–68; Asst. Dir., cnty. & Ext. Srvs., 1968–70; Dir., Evening & Ext. Oper., 1970–71; Order Libn., Holy Cross Coll., 1962–66; Circ. Libn., Univ. of MI, 1958–59. **Educ.:** Univ. of MI, 1948–50, Cornell Law School, 1950–51; Harvard Univ., 1953, (Educ.); AB (Pol. Sci.), 1953–56, AM (Educ. Admin.), 1956–58, Univ. of Notre Dame, 1959, AMLS; NY Univ., 1979–, (Higher Ed. Admin.). **Orgs.:** ALA: ACRL. NJ LA: Exec. Bd. (1978); SLA: Princeton–Trenton Chap. (Secy. 1977). Cncl. on Lib. Tech.: East Coast Conf., 1978, Speaker. Trenton Lions Club: Pres. (1972). Trenton Torch Club: Pres. (1972). Cornell Club of Cntrl. NJ: Pres. (1977). **Honors:** Tall Cedars of Lebanon, Comnty. Srvs. Awd., 1974. **Pubns.:** "Defining the Role of the Library Technical Assistant," *Bltn. Princeton/Trenton Chap., SLA* (March 1976). **Activities:** 1; 17, 24, 26; 63, 75 **Addr.:** 44 East Union St., Bordentown, NJ 08505.

PROFESSIONAL ACTIVITIES: Institutions: 1. Acad. lib.; 2. Arch.; 3. Assn.; 4. Fed./Gvt. lib.; 5. Inst. lib.; 6. Mfr./Suppl.; 7. Milit. lib.; 8. Musm.; 9. Pub. lib.; 10. Sch. lib.; 11. Sch. of lib. sci.; 12. Spec. lib.; 13. State lib.; 14. (other). **Functions/Activities:** 15. Acq./Col. dev.; 16. Adult srvs.; 17. Admin.; 18. Apprais.; 19. Archit./Bldgs.; 20. Cat./Class.; 21. Chld. srvs.; 22. Circ.; 23. Cons./Pres.; 24. Consult.; 25. Cont. ed.; 26. Educ. lib. sci.; 27. Ext. srvs.; 28. Fund/Grants; 29. Gvt. pubs.; 30. Indx./Abs.; 31. Instr. lib. use; 32. Media srvs.; 33. Micro.; 34. Netwks./Coop.; 35. Persnl.; 36. PR; 37. Publshg.; 38. Recs. mgt.; 39. Ref. srvs.; 40. Repro.; 41. Resrch.; 42. Review.; 43. Secur.; 44. Serials; 45. Spec. col.; 46. Tech. srvs.; 47. Trustees/Bds.; 48. YA srvs.; 49. (other).

Butt, Jean Frances (N. 3, 1927; Portland, ME) Head of Ref. and Spec. Cols. and Srvs., Tufts Univ., 1971–; Docum. Libn., 1965–70; Admin. Asst., Cambridge YWCA, 1960–64; Recreation Worker, Amer. Natl. Red Cross, 1958–60. **Educ.:** Chicago Musical College, 1947–50, (Music.); Univ. of Chicago, 1953–58, MA (Human.); Simmons Col., 1964–65, MLS, Univ. of Denver, On-Line Inst. work, 1974. **Orgs.:** New Eng. OLUG: Secy. (1979–80); Ch. Mgt. Com. (1978–79). **Pubns.:** Jt. Auth. *Library Materials in Psychology* (1976); *Jean Mayer: A bibliography, 1948–1976* (1976). **Activities:** 1; 39, 45; 55, 92 **Addr.:** Tufts University Library, Medford, MA 02155.

Buttler, Erwin (Mr. 27, 1925, Hungary) Sr. Libn., Span. Spec., NY Pub. Lib., Donnell Lib. Ctr., Frgn. Lang. Lib., 1980–; Libn., Lang. and Lit. Dept., Queensboro Pub. Lib., 1970–80; Libn., Escuela Graduada de Planificacion, Univ. of PR, 1968–69; Sr. Clerk, Libn., Donnell Frgn. Lang. Lib., NY Pub. Lib., 1961–67. **Educ.:** Dartmouth Coll., 1957–59, BA (Fr.); Columbia Univ., 1966–67, MLS. **Orgs.:** ALA: Pub. Libs. (1979). **Pubns.:** "Hungarian Books Bibliographies," *Booklist* (1970–); "Spanish Books Bibliographies," *Booklist* (1979–). **Activities:** 9, 12; 15, 39; 63, 66, 92 **Addr.:** The New York Public Library, Donnell Library Center, Foreign Language Library, 20 W. 53rd St., New York, NY 10019.

Butz, Helen S. (O 12, 1925, Newark, NJ) Head, Rare Bk. Cat. Div., Univ. of MI, 1968–. Coord. of Tech. Srvcs., Syracuse Univ., 1966–68; Catlgr., Univ. of MI, 1961–66; Catlgr., Princeton Theo. Semy., 1948–61. **Educ.:** Wellesley Coll., 1943–47, BA (Biblical Hist.); Drexel Univ., 1954–55, MSLS. **Orgs.:** ALA: ACRL/Rare Bks. and Mss. Sect., Nom. Com. (1971–72); Arrange. Com (1975–76); Stans. Com (1979–); RTSD/Prsvn. of Lib. Mtrls. Sect.: Nom. Com. (1979–80). Bibl. Socty. of America. Prtg. Hist. Socty. (London). AAUP. **Honors:** Beta Phi Mu; Phi Kappa Phi. **Activities:** 1; 20, 23, 45; 57 **Addr.:** 1221 Island Dr. #103, Ann Arbor, MI 48105.

Buvinger, Jan (O. 4, 1943, Lampasas, TX) Dir., Charleston Cnty. Lib., 1981–, Deputy Dir., 1978–81; Ref. Libn., Dept. Head, 1974–78, Prof. Asst., Ref. and Adult Srvs., 1971–74, Prof. Asst., Chld. Dept., 1970–71; Secy., Cornish and Horlbeck, Attorneys, 1965–69. **Educ.:** Coll. of Charleston, 1961–65, BS (Hist.); Emory Univ., 1969–70, MLS (Lib.). **Orgs.:** ALA: SC Fed. Rel. Coord. (1979). SC LA: Secy.; Exec. Bd.; Legis. Com.; Pub. Lib. Sect. (Pres.-Elect, 1981). SC Gvr.'s Conf. on Libs. (1977–78): Pub. Lib. Resrc. Com.; Berkeley-Charleston-Dorchester Reg. Mtg. Plng. Com.; Display Ch. SE LA: Gvtl. Rel. Com. (1979–80); Nom. Com. (SC LA Rep., 1980). Coll. of Charleston Alum. Assn.: Exec. Bd. (1977–); VP (1981–82); various coms., ofcs. Sum. Wkshp. Thea.: Exec. Bd. (1981–). Charleston Higher Educ. Cnsrtm.: Lib. Com. (Pub. Lib. Rep., 1980–). Tri-Cnty. Arts Cncl.: Pub. Lib., Lib. Rep. Various other orgs. **Activities:** 9; 15, 17, 39; 77, 78 **Addr.:** 404 King St., Charleston, SC 29403.

Buyansky, Fr. Timothy D. (N. 16, 1942, Cleveland, OH) Head Libn. Benedictine HS, 1970–. **Educ.:** St. John's Univ.-Borromeo Semy., 1960–65, BA (Phir.); Rosary Coll. 1969–70, MALS; St. Mary's Semy., 1966–69, M Div. **Orgs.:** Catholic LA: HS Sect. (Ch., 1980–81); North. OH Unit (HS Rep., 1977–). **Pubns.:** AV reviews, 1978. **Activities:** 10; 31, 42, 48; 55 **Addr.:** Benedictine High School, 2900 E. Blvd., Cleveland, OH 44104.

Buzzard, Marion L. (D. 26, 1922, Rio de Janeiro, Brazil) Col. Dev. Ofcr. and Head, Acq., and Art biblgphr., Univ. of CA, Irvine, 1974–, Frgn. lang. and Latin American biblgphr., 1972–74; Latin American catlgr. and biblgphr., Univ. of CA, Riverside, 1970–72. **Educ.:** Oberlin Coll., 1940–44, AB (Span./Art Hist.); Univ. of MI, 1967–69, MLS; Univ. of CA, Riverside, 1976–79, MA (Art Hist.). **Orgs.:** CA LA. ALA. ARLIS/NA: Ch., Art Publshg. Awd. Com. (1979). Coll. Art Assn. **Honors:** Phi Beta Kappa, 1944; Beta Phi Mu, 1969; Phi Kappa Phi, 1969. **Pubns.:** Contrib., Kathe Kollwitz (exhibition catalogue) (1977); Anni Albers; Prints and Drawings (exhibition catalogue) (F. 1980); "Writing a Collection Development Policy for an Academic Library", *Collection Management* (Win. 1978). **Activities:** 1; 15, 17; 55 **Addr.:** 815 Bellis St., Newport Beach, CA 92660.

Byam, Milton S. (Mr. 15, 1922, New York, NY) Pres., Byam et al Consult., Inc., 1979–; Dir., Queens Borough Pub. Lib., 1974–79; Dir., DC Pub. Lib., 1972–74; Chmn., Dept. of Lib. Sci., St. Johns Univ., 1968–72; Teaching, Pratt Inst., (1956–67); Teaching, St. John's Univ., (1956–68). **Educ.:** City Coll. of NY, 1940–47, BSS (Eng.); Columbia Univ., 1947–49, MSLS. **Orgs.:** ALA: Cncl. (1973–77); Copes (1974–78); Com. on Coms. (1974–75); PLA Nom. Com. (1975–76); Comm. on Org. (1970–74). NYLA: Legis. Com. (1975–79). ASIS. Cath. LA. Rotary Club of Jamaica: Pres. (1978–79). Queensboro Cncl. for Soc. Welfare: Pres. (1979–). Queens Council on the Arts. AAUP. **Honors:** Brotherhood Award, National Conference of Christians and Jews, 1977; Brotherhood Award, St. Albans Civic Improvement Association, 1977; Award, Queens Interfaith Clergy Council, 1977; February 20, 1977 - declared Milton S. Byam Day in Queens by the Borough President; Bronze Star Medal. **Pubns.:** "Consulting in Staff Development," *Library Trends* (Win. 80); "An Approach to Public Library Signage", *SIGN/SYSTEMS for Libraries* (1979); "Remodeling and expanding for new services". Martin Luther King Memorial Library," *An Architectural Strategy for Change* (1976); "Public Library site selection," A Public Library site symposium. *Library Journal Special Report #1. Library Space Planning* (1976); "Kiosks and porta-branches, an LJ mini-symposium," *Lib. Jnl.* (Ja. 15, 1977); Various other articles. **Activities:** 9, 13; 17, 19, 24; 50, 78, 89 **Addr.:** 162-04 75 Rd., Flushing, NY 11366.

Bye, John Edward (Ag. 20, 1948, Northwood, ND) Cur. of Mss., Assoc. Univ. Arch., ND Inst. for Reg. Std., ND State Univ., 1976–; Assoc. Cur., ND Inst. for Reg. Std., 1975–76; Serials Libn., ND State Univ. Lib., 1973–75. **Educ.:** ND State Univ., 1966–70, BS (Hist.); Univ. of WI, 1972–73, MA (Lib. Sci./Arch. Admin.). **Orgs.:** SAA. Midwest Arch. Conf. ND LA. Heritage Educ. Comsn.: Treas. (1978–). **Pubns.:** *Guide to the Small Collection Manuscripts of the North Dakota Institute for Regional Studies* (1977); Reviews. **Activities:** 1, 2; 45; 66, 95-ND Hist., Photographs. **Addr.:** North Dakota Institute for Regional Studies, North Dakota State University, Fargo, ND 58105.

Byerly, Greg W. (S. 13, 1949, Lima, OH) Ref. Libn., Kent State Univ., 1975–; HS Libn., Wapakoneta (Ohio) Pub. Schs., 1973–74, HS Eng. Tchr., 1971–73. **Educ.:** Wittenberg Univ., 1967–71, BA (Eng.); Kent State Univ., 1974–75, MLS, 1975–76, MA (Eng.), 1977–79, PhD (Higher Educ. Admin.). **Orgs.:** ALA: Machine-Assisted Ref. Sect., Educ. and Trng. of Srch. Anals. Com. (Ch., 1979–80). OH LA. ASIS. AAUP. **Honors:** Kent State Univ. Sch. of LS, Crawford Bindery Awd., 1975. **Pubns.:** Jt. auth., *Pornography: An Annotated Bibliography of the Conflict over Sexually Explicit Materials in the United States* (1980). **Activities:** 1; 26, 31, 39; 56, 63, 75 **Addr.:** Reference Department, Kent State University Libraries, Kent, OH 44242.

Byers, Cora Mae (Ag. 10, 1929, Arkansas City, KS) Circ. Dept., Head, LA Tech. Univ., 1966–; Asst. Circ. Libn., 1964–66; Asst. Ref. Libn., Univ. of Houston, 1960–63. **Educ.:** LA Tech. Univ., 1974, BA (LS); LA State Univ., 1979, MLS. **Orgs.:** LA LA: Int. Frdm. Com. (Ch. 1981). SWLA. Med. LA. Arts Clb. of Ruston: Pres. (1978–79). Alpha Beta Alpha. **Pubns.:** "Wooten Richardson: The Man Who Sold Ruston," *N. LA Hist. Assoc. Jnl.* (Sum. 1972). **Activities:** 1; 17, 22, 39; 61, 75, 85 **Addr.:** Prescott Memorial Library, Louisiana Tech University, Ruston, LA 71272.

Byers, Edward W. (Ja. 2, 1948, Pittsburgh, PA) Dir., Laramie Cnty. Lib. Syst., 1977–; Head of Main Lib., Warder Pub. Lib., Springfield, OH, 1974–77; Head of Ref., 1973; Sci. Ref. Libn., Pub. Lib. of Cincinnati and Hamilton Cnty., 1972–73. **Educ.:** Lawrence Univ., 1967–71, BA (Hist.); Univ. of Denver, 1971–72, MALS. **Orgs.:** WY LA: Exec. Bd. (1980–); Legis. Com. (Ch., 1978–). ALA: Cncl. (1980–); RASD, Geneal. Com. (1978–80); PLA, Pub. Lib. Actv. Com. (1973–76); LAMA, various coms. (1977–80). Mt. Plains LA. Miami Valley List of Un. Serials: Bd. of Eds. (1973–77). Amer. Mgt. Assn. **Activities:** 9; 17, 34, 39; 56, 78 **Addr.:** Laramie County Library System, 2800 Central Ave., Cheyenne, WY 82001.

Byers, James B. (Ap. 11, 1943, Massillon, OH) Chief, Resrch Rooms Branch, Natl. Arch. and Recs. Service, 1978–; Chief, Arch. Branch, Fed. Arch. and Recs. Cntr., 1976–78, Archvst., Office of Presidential Lib., 1972–76. **Educ.:** Ohio Univ., 1961–65, AB (Hist.); Miami Univ., 1965–67, MA (Amer. Hist.). **Orgs.:** SAA. Amer. Assn. for State and Local Hist. Mid Atl. Reg. Arch. Conf. Amer. Hist. Assn. Org. of Amer. Histns. **Activities:** 2; 24, 39 **Addr.:** 7813 Evening Ln., Alexandria, VA 22306.

Bynagle, Hans Edward (F. 24, 1946, Ruurlo, Netherlands) Dir., Lrng. Resrcs. Ctr., Frnds. Univ., 1976–; Asst. Prof., Phil., Coll. of Wooster, 1974–75; Asst. Prof., Phil., Un. Coll., 1972–73. **Educ.:** Calvin Coll., 1964–68, BA (Phil.); Columbia Univ., 1968–72, PhD (Phil.); Kent State Univ., 1975–76, MLS. **Orgs.:** ALA. KS LA: Lcl. Arrange. Com., Jt. Conf. of KS LA, KS ASL, KS AECT (1981). KS Chap. ACRL: Ch. (1980–81); Vice-Ch. (1979–80); Secy.-Treas. (1978–79). Amer. Phil. Assn. **Pubns.:** Various reviews, *Lib. Jnl., Amer. Ref. Bks. Anl.* (1977–). **Activities:** 1; 15, 17, 39; 55, 90 **Addr.:** Edmund Stanley Library, Friends University, Wichita, KS 67213.

Bynum, Mollie Beth (O. 8, 1943, Carlsbad, NM) Resrc. Libn., Media Spec., Mt. View Elem. Sch., 1976–; Resrc. Libn., Fort Richardson, AK On-Base Sch. Syst., 1974–76; Tchr., Ursa Minor Elem., 1973–74; Elem. Msc. Tchr., Fort Richardson, AK, 1968–72; Elem. Msc. Tchr., Ben F. Dowell Elem., 1965–68. **Educ.:** McMurry Coll., 1961–65, BS (Msc. Educ.); N. TX State Univ., 1972–73, MLS. **Orgs.:** AK LA: Anchorage Area Chap. (Pres., 1976); State Pres. (1981). ALA: AASL/EBE Sch. Media Prog. of the Yr. Awd. Sel. (State Ch., 1976–80); ALSC. Pac. NW LA: Young Readers Choice Awd. (State Contact Person, 1979–81). Natl. Educ. Assn. Anchorage Educ. Assn.: Legis./Pol. Action Ch., (1976–77). Alpha Delta Kappa: Corres. Secy. (1980–81). AK Readg. Assn. AK Sci. Tchrs. Assn. **Honors:** Kappa Delta Pi; Beta Phi Mu. **Activities:** 10; 21, 31, 32; 63, 78, 89 **Addr.:** P.O. Box 8722, Anchorage, AK 99508.

Byrd, Gary D. (My. 30, 1945, Columbus, OH) Chief Med. Libn., Univ. of MO, Kansas City, 1976–; Asst. Dir., Hlth. Sci. Lib., Univ. of SD, 1974–76; Tech. Info. Spec., Natl. Lib. of Med., 1973–74, Lib. Assoc., 1972–73. **Educ.:** Rutgers Univ., 1963–67, BA (Eng.); Univ. of VA, 1968–71, MA (Eng.); Univ. of MN, 1971–72, MA (LS); Med. LA, Cert. **Orgs.:** Hlth. Scis. Libs. Grp. of Grt. Kansas City: Pres. (1978–79). Med. LA: Bibl. and Info. Srvs. Assess. Com. (1976–79, Ch., 1978–79); Cont. Ed. Com. (1980–84). Assn. of Acad. Hlth. Scis. Lib. Dirs.: Kansas City Lib. Network: Pres. (1980). Other orgs. Univ. of MO, Kansas City Univ. Senate: Exec. Com. (1978–79). **Honors:** Phi Beta Kappa; Beta Phi Mu. **Pubns.:** Jt. auth., "A Role for Clinical Medical Librarians in Continuing Medical Education," *Jnl. of Med. Educ.* (Je. 1978); jt. auth., "Systematic Serial Selection Analysis in a Small Academic Health Sciences Library," *Bltn. of the Med. LA* (O. 1978); jt. auth., "The Urban University Library: Effectiveness Models for 1989" in *New Horizons for Academic Libraries* (1979); Jt. auth., "The Kansas City Libraries Metropolitan Online Bibliographic Information Network (MINET)," *Lib. Jnl.* (O. 1979); jt. auth., "Medical School Graduates' Retrospective Evaluation of a Clinical Medical Librarian Program," *Bltn. of the Med. LA* (Jl. 1979); other articles. **Activities:** 1, 12; 15, 17, 34; 58, 80, 95-Nursing. **Addr.:** University of Missouri-Kansas City, Health Sciences Library, 2411 Holmes St., Kansas City, MO 64108.

Byrd, Robert L. (Ag. 26, 1950, Mobile, AL) Mss. Libn., Duke Univ., 1980–, Ast. Cur., Mss. for Read. Srvs., 1978–80. **Educ.:** Duke Univ., 1970–72, AB (Hist.); Yale Univ., 1976–77, MPhil (Hist.); Univ. of NC, 1977–78, MSLS. **Orgs.:** SAA. NC LA. South. Hist. Assn. **Pubns.:** Assoc. Ed., *North Carolina Libraries* (Jan. 1979–). **Activities:** 1; 39, 45; 73, 93 **Addr.:** Manuscript Department, William R. Perkins Library, Duke University, Durham, NC 27706.

Byrn, James H. (Ja. 10, 1935, Lawton, OK) Dir. Lib. Syst. and Tralinet, US Army Trng. and Doctrine Cmnd., 1978–; Lib. Dir., US Army Fld. Artly. Sch., 1974–78; Lib. Dir., Cameron State Univ., 1969–74; Ofcr., US Army, 1958–68. **Educ.:** Cameron State Univ., 1953–55, AA (Engin.); Univ. OK, 1955–58, BA (Hist.); 1968–69, MLS; 1969–74, (Admin. Higher Ed.); US Army Cmnd. and Gnl. Staff Coll., 1970–72, Dip., (Milit. Sci.); Indus. Coll. of Armed Frcs., 1976–78, Dip. (Milit. Sci.). **Orgs.:** US Army Lib. Cncl. US Army Rsrv.: Col. Optimist Intl. **Pubns.:** "Field Artilleryman's Library," *Fld. Artly. Jnl.* (Mar/Apr. 1976); "Automation in University Libraries," *Lib. Resrcs. and Tech. Srvs.* (Fall 1969). **Activities:** 1, 4; 17, 34, 35; 56, 75, 74 **Addr.:** HQ TRADOC, Attn: ATPL-AOL, Fort Monroe, VA 23651.

Byrne, Sr. Anne Lucille, S.C. (My. 2, 1913, Orange, NJ) Supvsr., Elem. Sch. Libs., Srs. of Charity of St. Elizabeth, 1960–; Mod., Seton Lib. Gld., 1960–79; Libn., Bayley-Ellard Reg. HS (NJ), 1949–69; Tchr., Libn., Our Lady of Victories Sch. (NJ), 1935–49. **Educ.:** Coll. of St. Elizabeth, 1934–43, BS (Educ.); Catholic Univ., 1953–57, MS (LS). **Orgs.:** Paterson Diocesan Lib. Cncl.: Ch. (1960–62). Hudson Cnty. Pub. LA. Catholic LA: Bk. Rev. Com. (1966); /NJ Chap. (Ch., 1966–68). ALA. **Honors:** Ency. Britannica and ALA, AASL: Sch. Lib. Med. Prog. Awd., 1968. Grolier Interstate, Educ. Srvs. Awd., 1974. Srs. of Charity of St. Elizabeth, Disting. Educ. Awd., 1977. **Pubns.:** *Centralization of Professional Library Services for Elementary Schools* (1958); *Handbook of Policies and Procedures for Library Volunteers* (1967); *Library Science Series–Graded Lessons 1-8* (1972); Various articles on pre-prcs. bks. for sch. libs. Various AV prods. **Activities:** 9, 10; 26; 50, 56, 89 **Addr.:** Sisters of Charity of Saint Elizabeth, League House–Park Avenue, Convent Station, NJ 07961.

Byrne, Dorothy Johnson (D. 22, 1916, Camden, NJ) Dir., Seguin-Guadalupe Cnty. Pub. Lib., 1967–; Libn., Bandera Cnty. Pub. Lib., 1962–67; Libn., Bandera HS, 1965–67; Lib. Asst., Chardon Pub. Lib., Story Teller, Chardon Pub. Sch. Syst., 1953–56. **Educ.:** Univ. of Akron, 1933–36 (Educ.); Cnty. Libn. Cert., Anl.; various crs. **Orgs.:** ALA. TX LA: Lcl. Arrange. (Ch., 1972); Pubcty. Com. (1980–81), Dist. 10 Ch. (1981–82). SW LA. Natl. Assn. for the Prsrvn. and Perpet. of Storytel. Zonta Intl. TX Press Women. Natl. Fed. of Press Women. Seguin Std. Club: VP (1980–81). **Pubns.:** 5 minute wkly. lib. radio prog., KWED, (1969–); various articles, Seguin newsp. (1967–). **Activities:** 9; 15, 17, 36 **Addr.:** Seguin-Guadalupe County Public Library, Seguin, TX 78155.

Byrne, Elizabeth Douthitt (D. 16, 1946, Louisville, KY) Head, Dsgn., Archit. and Art Lib., Univ. of Cincinnati, 1978–; Ref. Libn., San Diego Pub. Lib., 1977–78; Asst. Head, Fine Arts Dept., Detroit Pub. Lib., 1972–76; Art Libn., Univ. of Louisville, 1969–71. **Educ.:** Univ. of Louisville, 1964–68, BA (Art); IN Univ., 1968–69, MLS. **Orgs.:** ARLIS/NA. Art Libs. Socty. of KY/TN. Art Libs. Socty. of OH. Assn. of Archit. Libns. **Pubns.:** Jt. auth., *Great Cooks of the Western World* (1977); ed., *D.A.A. Jnl.* (1980–81). **Activities:** 1; 15, 17; 55, 64 **Addr.:** 405 Lafayette Ave., Cincinnati, OH 45220.

Byrne, Janice Durack (My. 14, 1949, Chicago, IL) Head, Garfield Ridge Branch, Chicago Pub. Lib., 1978–; st Asst., Scottsdale Branch, 1976–78, Ref. Libn., 1973–76; Prof. Asst., Summit-Argo Pub. Lib., 1972–73. **Educ.:** Univ. of IL, Chicago Circle, 1967–71, AB cum laude (Hist.); Rosary Coll., 1971–73, MALS; Certs., City of Chicago, Management, 1977–79. **Orgs.:** ALA. IL LA. Lib. Admins. Conf. of North. IL. **Activities:** 9; 16, 17, 39; 50

Special Subjects/Services: 50. Adult educ.; 51. Advert./Mktg.; 52. Aerosp.; 53. Agric.; 54. Area std.; 55. Arts/Hum.; 56. Autom.; 57. Bibl./Prtg.; 58. Bio. sci.; 59. Bus./Fin.; 60. Chem.; 61. Copyrt.; 62. Documtn.; 63. Educ.; 64. Engin.; 65. Env.; 66. Eth. grps.; 67. Film; 68. Food/Nutr.; 69. Geneal.; 70. Geo.; 71. Geol.; 72. Handcpd.; 73. Hist.; 74. Int. frdm.; 75. Info. sci.; 76. Insr.; 77. Law; 78. Legis.; 79. Math./Comp. sci.; 80. Med.; 81. Metals; 82. Nat. resrcs.; 83. Newsp.; 84. Nuc. sci.; 85. Oral hist.; 86. Petr./Energy; 87. Pharm.; 88. Phys./Astr./Math.; 89. Readg.; 90. Relig.; 91. Sci./Tech.; 92. Soc. sci.; 93. Telecom.; 94. Transp.; 95. (other).

Addr.: Garfield Ridge Branch, Chicago Public Library, 6322 Archer Ave., Chicago, IL 60638.

Byrne, Jerry R. (Ag 30, 1934, Toledo, OH) Staff Asst. for Lib. Syst., Lawrence Livermore Lab., 1979–; Head of Ref., 1974–79; Info. Spec., 1968–74; Tec. Biblgphr., Inst. of Paper Chem., 1959–68. **Educ.:** Univ. of WI, 1952–56, BS (Chem.). **Orgs.:** ASIS: Chap. Ch. (1980). SLA. **Pubns.:** "Relative Effectiveness of Titles, Abstracts, and Subject Headings for Machine Retrieval from the COMPENDEX Services.", *Jrnl. of ASIS*, (Jl.-Ag. 1975). **Activities:** 4; 15; 84 **Addr.:** Lawrence Livermore Laboratory, P.O. Box 5500, Livermore, CA 94550.

Byrum, John D., Jr. (Je. 10, 1940, Wenatchee, WA) Chief, Descr. Cat. Div., Lib. of Congs., 1976–; Head Catlgr., Princeton Univ., 1968–76, Actg. Head Catlgr., 1968, Descr. Catlgr., 1966–68. **Educ.:** Harvard Coll., 1958–62, AB, magna cum laude (Hist); Rutgers Univ., 1965–66, MLS; various grad. crs. **Orgs.:** ALA: RTSD/Cat. and Class. Sect., Margaret Mann Cit. Com. (1968–69), DCC Subcom. on Rules for Cat. Machine-Readable Data Files (Ch., 1970–74)/RSD/ISAD, Interdiv. Com. on Bibl. Rep. in Machine-Readable Form (1971–74), Cat. Code Rev. Com. (Ch., 1974–78), Spec. Com. on Intl. Cat. Consult. (Ch., 1976–80); GODORT, Docum. Cat. Manual Com. (Lib. of Congs. Rep., 1977–). NY Tech. Srvs. Libns. DC LA. Various adv. grps. Beta Phi Mu: Mss. Srch. Com. (1970–72). **Honors:** Cncl. on Lib. Resrcs., Fellow, 1974–75; ALA, RTSD, Esther J. Piercy Awd., 1975. **Pubns.:** Jt. auth., "AACR 2: Background and Summary," *Lib. of Congs. Info. Bltn.* (O. 1978); jt. auth., "AACR 1 as Applied by Research Libraries to Determine Entry and Headings," *Lib. Resrcs & Tech. Srvs.* (Win. 1980); jt. auth., "AACR as Applied by Research Libraries for Serials Cataloging," *Lib. Resrcs. & Tech. Srvs.* (Spr. 1979); jt. auth., "The Newest Anglo-American Cataloging Rules," *The Nature and Future of the Catalog: Proceedings of the ALA's Information Science and Automation Division's 1975 and 1977 Institutes on the Catalog* (1979); jt. auth., "AACR Chapter 6 as Adopted, Applied, and Assessed by Research Libraries," *Lib. Resrcs. & Tech. Srvs.* (Win. 1977); various other articles, sps. **Activities:** 4; 17, 20 **Addr.:** 400 Madison St. #1504, Alexandria, VA 22314.

Bysiewicz, Shirley Raissi (Middletown, CT) Law Libn., Prof. of Law, Univ. of CT Sch. of Law, 1956–; Asst. Prosecutor, Town of Enfield, 1956–57; Partner, Raissi and Raissi, 1954–56. **Educ.:** Univ. of CT, 1951, BA; 1954, JD (Law); South. CT State Coll., 1967, MSLS. **Orgs.:** New Eng. Law Libns. Assn.: Pres. (1967–68); VP (1964–66). AALL: Sec. (1980–83); Exec. Com. (1973–74); Legis. Com. (1979). CT Law Lib. Adv. Com. Amer. Assn. of Law Schs.: Sect. on Legal Resrch. Amer. Bar Assn. Natl. Assn. of Women Lawyers: CT State Del. CT Bar Assn.: Civil Rights Com., Status of Women Com. (Ch., 1973–75); Juvenile Justice Com. (Ch., 1980–82); Treas. (1975–78); Exec. Com. and Family Law Sect. (1980–82); other coms. **Honors:** South. CT State Coll., Disting. Alum. Awd., 1977. **Pubns.:** "Women Lawyers in Connecticut: A Survey," *49 Conn B J 123* (1975); "The Legal Status of the Dakota Indian Woman," *Amer. Indian Law Review* (1975); *Conn. - ERA, 41 Conn B J 113* (1977); Contrib., *Issues in Feminism* (1979); jt. auth., *Effective Legal Research.* (1979); other articles, reviews. **Activities:** 14-Law Library; 15, 20; 77 **Addr.:** The University of Connecticut, School of Law Library, Greater Hartford Campus, West Hartford, CT 06117.

C

Caballero, Cesar (My. 26, 1949, Puebla, Mexico) Head, Spec. Coll., Univ. of TX, El Paso Lib., 1978–, Asst. Head of Circ. and Ref., 1974–78, Chicano Studies Libn., 1971–73. **Educ.:** Univ. of TX at El Paso, 1967–71, BBA (Acct.); Univ. of TX at Austin, 1973–74, MLS. **Orgs.:** ALA. REFORMA: Pres. (1980–82); Bd. of Dir. (1978); El Paso Chap., Pres. (1977). El Paso Pub. LA: Bd. of Dir. (1978–84). Border Reg. LA. Chicano Fac. Assn., U.T. El Paso, Pres. (1979–80). **Pubns.:** "Non-Print Materials and the Mexican-American," *Library's*, Resources on Latin America, New Perspectives for the *1980's*, SALALM (1981); contributor, *Chicano Periodicals Index* (1981); "Public Library Boards, the Chicano and the Political Process," *Library Services to Mexican Americans: Policies, Practices, Prospects* (1978); "El Paso: The Movement Is Forward", *Wilson Library Journal* (N. 1978). **Addr.:** 204 Alvarez, El Paso, TX 79932.

Caballero, Isabel Seijo (My. 7, 1926, Havana, Cuba) Hist. of Med. Libn., Univ. of Miami, Sch. of Med. Lib., 1980–, Head Catlgr., 1975–80, Interlib. Loan Libn., 1967–75; First Asst. Libn., Per. Dept., NY Acad. of Med. Lib., 1965–66; Catlgr., Cornell Univ. Med. Coll. Lib., 1964–65; Asst. Libn., NY Pub. Lib., 1961–65; Dir., Nat. Hosp. Lib., Havana, 1960–61; Head Libn., Cuban Engineers Assn., 1955–61. **Educ.:** Havana Univ., 1946–50, BA (Arts), 1950–51, PhD (Arts), 1952, MSLS, 1952–60, PhD (Educ.). **Orgs.:** Med. LA: South. Reg. Grp. (Secy./Treas., 1971). Dada Cnty. LA: (VP, 1972–73. Pres., 1973–74). Univ. of Miami Intl. Med. Educ. Prog. S. FL Hosp. Libns. **Pubns.:** "Biblioteca del Instituto Nacional de Cultura," *Boletin de la Asociacion Cubana de Bibliotecarios* (1956); "La Biblioteca de la F.A.C.E.P.," *Cuba Bibliotecologica* (1953). **Activities:** 1, 2; 20, 45, 46; 58, 62, 80 **Addr.:** 160 N.E. 95th St., Miami Shores, FL 33138.

Cabeceiras, James (Mr. 7, 193-, Fall River, MA) Prof., San Jose State Univ., 1968–; Curric. Supvsr., Syracuse City Sch. Dist., 1967–68; Instr., Syracuse Univ., 1966–67; Resrchr., Ford Fndn., 1963–65. **Educ.:** Bridgewater State Coll., 1959–63, BS (Educ.); Syracuse Univ., 1963–67, PhD (Instr. Comm.). **Orgs.:** CA Assn. of Media Libns. AECT. **Honors:** Kappa Delta Pi, 1961. **Pubns.:** "A Cure for Multiple Video-itis," *A V Instr.* (S. 1976); "Categorizing and Organizing Curriculum Components," *Educ. Tech.* (Jl. 1974); "The Application Of Media in Various Forms to Assist Teachers in Specific Learning Objectives," *Cath. Lib. World.* (Ap. 1979); "Exercise on Tape and Disc Recordings" in *A V Instructional Materials Manual* (1969; 1973; 1976); *The Multimedia Library: Materials Selection and Use* (1978); other articles, videotapes. **Activities:** 14-Univ.; 26, 32; 63, 93, 95-TV. **Addr.:** Division of Library Science, San Jose State Univ., San Jose, CA 95192.

Cabeen, Samuel Kirkland (Ja. 22, 1931, Easton, PA) Dir., Engin. Societies Lib., 1964–; Libn., Ford Instrument Co., 1958–64; Asst. Libn., American Metal Co., 1956–58. **Educ.:** Lafayette Coll., 1948–52, BA (Chem.); Syracuse Univ., 1952–54, MS (LS). **Orgs.:** SLA: NY Chap., Pres. (1966–67), Sci-Tech Div., Ch. (1970–71). ALA. ASIS. NY Lib. Club. Amer. Chem. Soc. Electrochemical Soc. **Activities:** 12; 17; 64, 91 **Addr.:** Engineering Societies Library, 345 East 47th St., New York, NY 10017.

Cabello-Argandoña, Roberto O. (N. 12, 1939, Antotagasta, Chile) Exec. Dir., CA Span. Lang. Data Base, 1980–; Head Libn., Haskett Lib., Anaheim Pub. Lib., 1977–80; Coord., Bibl. Unit, CSC, Univ. of CA, Los Angeles, 1975–77, Head Libn., Lib., 1972–75. **Educ.:** Univ. of CA, Los Angeles, 1969–70, BA (Pol. Sci.), 1971–75, MLS, 1973–75, MPA (Pub. Admin.). **Orgs.:** CA LA. ALA. REFORMA: Pres. **Pubns.:** *The Chicana: A Comprehensive Bibliographic Study* (1976); *List of Ethnic Studies Serials* (1976); "Recruiting Spanish-speaking Library Students," *Lib. Jnl.* (Jl. 1975); *System Analysis of Library and Information Services to the Spanish Speaking* (1977). **Activities:** 9; 20, 41 **Addr.:** 21212 Lull St., Canoga Park, CA 91304.

Cable, Carole L. (Ja. 21, 1944, New Orleans, LA) Archit., Fine Arts Libn., Univ. of TX, Austin, 1979–, Archit. Libn., 1976–79, Rare Bks. Catlgr., 1973–76; Slide Cur., Univ. of IL, 1971–72. **Educ.:** Tulane Univ., 1962–65, BA (Hist.); Univ. of TX, Austin, 1965–68, MLS; Univ. of IL, 1969–72, MA (Art Hist.). **Orgs.:** ARLIS/NA: TX Chap. (Ch., 1976–77). **Pubns.:** Various articles, *The Bk. Collector, Lib. Chronicle of the Univ. of TX, The Lib. Qtly., The Serif, Vance Archit. Bibl. Series.* **Activities:** 1; 15, 31, 32; 55 **Addr.:** Fine Arts Library, University of Texas, Austin, TX 78712.

Cable, Leslie Gibbs (S. 1, 1943, Cincinnati, OH) Ref. Libn., OR Hlth. Sci. Univ. Lib., 1967–; Reclass. Libn., Wellesley Coll. Lib., 1966–67. **Educ.:** Stanford Univ., 1961–65, BA (Psy.); Simmons Coll., 1965–66, MLS. **Orgs.:** Med. LA: Pac. NW Reg. Grp. OR Hlth. Sci. LA. Portland Area Hlth. Sci. Libns. OR OLUG. **Pubns.:** "Cost Analysis of Reference Service to Outside Users," *Bltn. of the Med. LA* (Ap. 1980). **Activities:** 1; 27, 31, 34; 56, 63, 80 **Addr.:** Oregon Health Science University Library, P.O. Box 573, Portland, OR 97207.

Cackowski, Irene Kathleen (S. 9, 1946, Englewood, NJ) Dir., S. River Pub. Lib., 1972–; Libn., S. River HS, 1970–72; Chld. Libn., Hackensack Pub. Lib., 1969–70; Chld. Libn., New Rochelle Pub. Lib., 1968–69. **Educ.:** Coll. of New Rochelle, 1964–68, BA (Eng.); Long Island Univ., 1968–69, MLS (Lib.); various crs. in advnc. lib. srv. **Orgs.:** ALA. NJ LA: Leag. of Municipalities (1980); Admin. Sect. (Hosplty. Ch., 1979–80); Nom. Com. (1980); Dir. (1978–80). E. Brunswick Area Coord. Cncl.: Pres. (1980). S. River Civic Assn. E. Brunswick Woman's Club. **Activities:** 9; 15, 16, 17 **Addr.:** South River Public Library, 55 Appleby Ave., South River, NJ 08882.

Cadle, David Dean (Ja. 16, 1920, Middlesboro, KY) Assoc. Libn., Tech. Srvs., Univ. of NC, Asheville, 1966–; Libn., Southeast Cmnty. Coll. (KY), 1960–66; Catlgr., Univ. of KY, 1959–60; Ext. Libn., KY State Dept. of Libs., 1957–59. **Educ.:** Berea Coll., 1938–41, 1946–47, BA (Lit.); State Univ. of IA, 1949–50, MA (Lit.); Univ. of KY, 1956–57, MS (LS); Stanford Univ. Fellow in Creative Wrtg., 1947–48. Prof. Photographers of Amer. **Honors:** Var. awds. for creative wrtg. **Pubns.:** Various articles and short stories. **Activities:** 1; 15, 20, 31; 55 **Addr.:** D. Hiden Ramsey Library, University of North Carolina at Asheville, Asheville, NC 28804.

Cagle, R. Brantley, Jr. (Jl. 18, 1941, New Orleans, LA) Docum. Libn., Assoc. Prof. of LS, McNeese State Univ., 1967–. **Educ.:** McNeese State Univ., 1961–65, BA cum laude (Hist.); LA State Univ., 1965–67, MA (Hist.); Cath. Univ., 1974, MSLS. **Orgs.:** ALA: Com. on Lib. srvs. to Dev. Disabled Persons (Ch., 1979–80). SWLA. LA LA: Docum. Com. (1976–80). SAA. SW LA Hlth. Counseling Srv.: Prog. Dev. Com. (Ch., 1977–78); Bd. of Dirs. (1979). LA Statewide Hlth. Coord. Cncl. LA State Plng. and Adv. Cncl. on Dev. Disabilities: Plng. and Exec. Com. (Ch., 1978). LA Comsn. on Residential Alternatives for the Dev. Disabled: Vice Ch. (1978–79). Other orgs. **Honors:** Beta Phi Mu, 1975; Phi Kappa Phi, 1967; Phi Alpha Theta, 1967. **Pubns.:** "Politics and Government 1890–1967: A Study in Progressive Change" in *Lake Charles Centennial Celebration* (1967); jt. auth., "The Library Profession," *Rehab. Gazette* (O. 1974); *Government Documents on the Physically Handicapped: A Selected Bibliography* (1975); "Federal Documents: A Vital Advocacy Resource," *Amer. Rehab.* (S.-O. 1977); "Advocacy, A Novel Approach for Delivering Documents to the People," *Cath. Lib. World*, (N. 1977); other articles. **Activities:** 1; 29, 41; 70, 72, 77 **Addr.:** Fraser Memorial Libr., McNeese State U., Lake Charles, LA 70601.

Cahoon, Andrea Ruth (My. 6, 1949, Brooklyn, NY) Dir., Ringwood Pub. Lib., 1975–. **Educ.:** Univ. of RI, 1967–71, BA (Eng.), 1973–75, MLS. **Orgs.:** NJ LA: Pub. Rel. Com., Ch. (1978–). ALA. Bergen Passaic Lib. Assn.: Treas. (1978–79), Mem. at Large (1979–80). Lib. Pub. Rel. Cncl. League of Women Voters: Treas. (1977–). Ringwood Manor Assn. of Arts. **Honors:** Ringwood (NJ) Jaycees, Outstan. Pub. Servant, 1979; Beta Phi Mu, 1975. **Activities:** 9; 17, 28, 36; 51 **Addr.:** 34 Lake Riconda Dr., Ringwood, NJ 07456.

Cahoon, Herbert (Thomas Fuller) (D. 29, 1918, West Chatham, MA) Cur. of Autograph Mss., Pierpont Morgan Lib., 1954–; First Asst., Rare Book Div., NY Pub. Lib., 1948–54; Ref. Asst., 1941–48. **Educ.:** Harvard Coll., 1936–40, AB (Hist.); Columbia Univ., 1942–43, SBLS. **Orgs.:** ALA. Bibli. Socty. (London). Bibli. Socty. of America. Bibli. Socty. (Univ. of VA). Mss. Socty. Melville Socty. Poetry Socty. of America. Grolier Club. **Pubns.:** Jt. comp., *A Bibliography of James Joyce* (1953); Contrib., *Oxford Companion to the Theatre* (1951); *The Clifton Waller Barrett Library* (1960); *The Overbrook Press Bibliography* (1963); *American Literary Manuscripts* (1977); Numerous exhibition cats. for The Pierpont Morgan Lib. **Activities:** 1, 5; 41, 45; 55 **Addr.:** 29 East 36th St., New York, NY 10016.

Cain, Carolyn Louise (Mr. 27, 1935, Berwyn, IL) Dir., Instr. Mtrls. Ctr., LaFollette HS, 1969–; Dist. Consult., Madison Metro. Sch. Dist., 1976–78; Libn., Nakoma Elem. Sch., 1968–69; Head Libn., West Sr. HS, 1964–66; Libn., Elkhorn Jr. HS, 1962–64. **Educ.:** Univ. of WI, 1952–56, BA (Eng.); 1967–68, MA (LS); State Cert. as Sch. Lib. Supvsr. and AV Coord.; 1971–78; Univ. of WI, grad. work, 1979–80 (Cont. Educ.). **Orgs.:** WI Sch. Lib. Media Assn.: Secy. (1975, 1976); Ed., *Communique* (1978, 79, 80); Co-Ch., Pub. Rel. Conf. (1979). Madison Area Lib. Cncl.: Pres. (1979); Policy and Plng Bd. (1978–79). AASL: Eval. Com. (1979–80). ALA. WI Educ. Assn. Natl. Educ. Assn. **Honors:** WI Sch. Lib. Media Assn., Sch. Libn. of Year, 1979. **Pubns.:** "To Meet the Needs of a Certain Subject; Planning and administering resource materials centers," *WI Lib. Bltn.* (Mr/Ap. 1972); "Overdues; a new look at an old problem," *WI Ideas in Media* (F. 1971). **Activities:** 10, 14-District IMC Services; 25, 32 **Addr.:** 5406 Whitcomb Drive, Madison, WI 53711.

Cain, Jack (D. 16, 1940, Newmarket, ON) Mgr., Prod. Dev., Univ. of Toronto Lib. Autom. Syst., 1979–, Sr. Consult., 1977–79; Head, Cat. Dept., Univ. of Toronto Lib., 1972–77, Asst. Head, Cat. Dept., 1969–72. **Educ.:** Univ. of Toronto, 1958–62, BA (Gen. Arts); Univ. of BC, 1965–66, BLS. **Pubns.:** "Aperçus sur un grand réseau automatisé," *Documentaliste* (N./D. 1978). **Activities:** 1; 17, 20, 34 **Addr.:** UTLAS, 130 St. George St., Toronto, ON M5S 1A5 Canada.

Cain, Rita Ranson (Mr. 14, 1946, Cherokee, OK) Dir., Elem. Libs., Enid Pub. Schs., 1977–81; Elem. Fld. Libn., 1974–77, HS Libn., 1972–74; Elem. Fld. Libn., Oklahoma City Pub. Schs., 1968–72. **Educ.:** OK State Univ., 1964–68, BS (Educ.); Univ. of OK, 1970–72, MLS. **Orgs.:** ALA. OK LA: Sequoyah Chld. Bk. Awd. Com. (Ch., 1972–73); Chld. Srvs. Div. (Ch., 1974–75); Right to Read Com. (1979–80). OK Assn. of Sch. Lib. Media Specs.: Task Frc. on Re-Org. (1980). Natl. Educ. Assn. OK Educ. Assn. Delta Kappa Gamma Socty.: Kappa Chap. (VP, 1980–82). **Activities:** 10; 17, 24, 32; 63 **Addr.:** 7109 Wind Chime, Ft. Worth, TX 76133.

Cain, Robert Evans (Jl. 21, 1938, Marble City, OK) Asst. Chief Libn., Fitchburg Pub. Lib., 1974–; Ref. Supvsr., Cary Meml. Lib., Lexington, MA, 1966–74, Ref. Libn., 1964–66; Ref. Libn., Reading (MA) Pub. Lib., 1963–64. **Educ.:** Lawrence Coll., 1957–61, AB cum laude (Eng.); Simmons Coll., 1962–64, MS (LS). **Orgs.:** MA LA: Ed., Bay State Libn. (1970–74); Co-Ch., Int. Frdm. Com. (1978–79); Ch., Personnel Issues Com. (1980–); Handbook Com. (1973–74). New Eng. LA: Ch., PR Com. (1966–68). **Pubns.:** "The Original Print," *Lib. Jnl.* (N. 1, 1966); "Due Process? It's Due", *Bay State Libn.* (Win., 1979); Other articles. **Activities:** 9; 16, 35, 39; 74 **Addr.:** 508 West St., Leominster, MA 01453.

Cairns, Eleanor C. (Jl. 23, 1909, Boston, MA) Chief Libn., ME Med. Ctr. Lib., 1966–; Libn., Chld. Hosp., Sch. of Nursing, Boston, 1963–66; Libn., Burbank Hosp., Fitchburg, MA, 1945–63; Libn., Harvard Coll. Lib., 1943–45; Libn., Dalton Sch., 1939–42. **Educ.:** Columbia Univ., 1939–40, (LS). **Orgs.:** Med. LA: New Eng. Mem. Com. (Ch., 1974–77). New Eng. LA: Hosp. Lib. Sect. Hlth. Sci. Lib. and Info. Coop. of ME: Exec. Com. (1974–79). ME LA: Educ. Com. (1976–78). Other orgs. Amer.

PROFESSIONAL ACTIVITIES: Institutions: 1. Acad. lib.; 2. Arch.; 3. Assn.; 4. Fed./Gvt. lib.; 5. Inst. lib.; 6. Mfr./Suppl.; 7. Milit. lib.; 8. Musm.; 9. Pub. lib.; 10. Sch. lib.; 11. Sch. of lib. sci.; 12. Spec. lib.; 13. State lib.; 14. (other). **Functions/Activities:** 15. Acq./Col. dev.; 16. Adult srvs.; 17. Admin.; 18. Apprais.; 19. Archit./Bldgs.; 20. Cat./Class.; 21. Chld. srvs.; 22. Circ.; 23. Cons./Pres.; 24. Consult.; 25. Cont. ed.; 26. Educ. lib. sci.; 27. Ext. srvs.; 28. Fund/Grants; 29. Gvt. pubs.; 30. Indx./Abs.; 31. Instr. lib. use; 32. Media srvs.; 33. Micro.; 34. Netwks./Coop.; 35. Persnl.; 36. PR; 37. Publshg.; 38. Recs. mgt.; 39. Ref. srvs.; 40. Repro.; 41. Resrch.; 42. Review.; 43. Secur.; 44. Serials; 45. Spec. col.; 46. Tech. srvs.; 47. Trustees/Bds.; 48. YA srvs.; 49. (other).

Lung Assn. of MA: Exec. Com. Amer. Cancer Socty. **Pubns.:** "An Adequate Budget for the School of Nursing Library," *Hosp. Progress* (Je. 1960); "The Extra-curricular Library," *Trained Nurse and Hosp. Review* (N. 1947). **Activities:** 12; 15, 17, 20; 58, 63, 80 **Addr.:** Maine Medical Center Library, 22 Bramhall St., Portland, ME 04102.

Cairns, Sr. Marie Laurine (N. 2, 1914, Midway, OK) Asst. Dean, Assoc. Prof., Sch. of Lib. and Info. Sci., LA State Univ., 1972–; Tchg. Asst., FL State Univ., 1969–72; Dir., Media Ctr., Tampa Cath. High, 1966–69; Tchr.-Libn., St. Patrick High, 1964–66; Tchr., Parochial Schs., 1935–64. **Educ.:** Siena Hts. Coll., 1944, BA (Educ., Msc.); MI State Univ., 1953, M Mus (Msc.); FL State Univ., 1969, MS (LS); 1971, AMD (LS); 1972 PhD (LS). **Orgs.:** ALA: AASL. Cath. LA. AALS. AECT. Various other orgs. AAUP: Treas. (1975–76). **Honors:** Beta Phi Mu, 1970; Phi Kappa Phi, 1971. **Pubns.:** *Factors Affecting Selective Admission and Retention of Students in Graduate Library Programs* (1972); *Staff Survey Development by Type of Function: Children and Young People's Services* (1975); "SLIS Student Profile–Spring 1981," *LA LA Bltn.* (Spr. 1981); "LSU Summer School Library Science Student Profile," *LA LA Bltn.* (Sum. 1975); "GSLS Student Profile," *LA LA Bltn.* (Win. 1975). **Activities:** 10, 11; 17, 21, 26 **Addr.:** School of Library and Information Science, Louisiana State University, Baton Rouge, LA 70803.

Cairns, Roberta A. E. (F. 1, 1945, Waltham, MA) Dir. Lib. Srvs., E. Providence Pub. Lib., RI, 1979–; Lib. Dir., Barrington Pub. Lib., RI, 1971–79; Libn., Fiske Pub. Lib., 1966–71. **Educ.:** Stonehill Coll., 1962–66, AB (Eng.); Univ. of RI, 1967–69, MLS. **Orgs.:** ALA: Pub. Rel. Srvcs. to Libs. Com. (1979). Lib. Admin. and Mgt. Assn. Rep. (1979). New England LA: Mem. Com. (1975–76); Bibl. Com. (1976–77); Pub. Rel. Com. (1978–80); Conf. Com. (1980–). RI LA: Admin. Com. Ch. (1972–74); Conf. Com. Ch. (1973–75); Com. for Pub. Lib. Stan. (1971–73), (1978–79); Exec. Brd. (1972–75); Govt. Rel. Com. (1971–72); Long Range Plng. Com. (1973–75). Gov. Conf. on Lib. and Info. Srvs.: Plng. Com. Ch. (1976–78); Steering Com. (1978–79); Lib. Assn. Rep. (1978–79); Pub. Rel. Com. Co-Ch. (1978–79); Task Force on Non-Users, Ch. (1978–79). RI League of Women Voters: ERA Ch. (1976–77). RI Women's Political Caucus. **Pubns.:** *A History of St. Mary's Church–Wrentham, Ma.* (1978). **Activities:** 9; 17, 36, 43; 50, 51, 89 **Addr.:** 1355 Wampanoag Trail, East Providence, RI 02915.

Calabrese, Alice M. (O. 24, 1944, Chicago, IL) Lib. Admin., Geneva Pub. Lib., 1979–; Head, Chld. Srvs., Schaumburg Twp. Pub. Lib., 1976–79; Chld. Libn., Elmwood Park Pub. Lib., 1972–76; Chld. Libn., Skokie Pub. Lib., 1971–72. **Educ.:** Rosary Coll., 1967–70, BA (Hist.), 1970–71, MALS. **Orgs.:** IL LA: Pub. Lib. Sect. (Secy., 1981); Chld. Libns. Sect. (Pres., 1977). ALA. **Pubns.:** "An Image-Status Study," *IL Libs.* (D. 1976); "Skills in Sharing: Storytelling for Preschoolers" vid.-cassette (1978). **Activities:** 9; 17, 21, 24 **Addr.:** 2 Hatherley Ct., Prestbury-Aurora, IL 60504.

Calcagno, Philip Marino (N. 29, 1946, St. Louis, MO) Head, Serials Dept., Lovejoy Lib., South. IL Univ., 1971–; Lect., Univ. of IL, Grad Sch. of Lib. Sci., Fall 1976; Catlgr., S. IL Univ., 1969–70. **Educ.:** South. IL Univ., 1964–68, BA (Eng. Lit.); Univ. of IL, 1968–69, MSLS. **Orgs.:** ALA. IL LA. Msc. LA. **Honors:** Beta Phi Mu, 1969. **Pubns.:** Jt. ed., *Catalog of Cards for Printed Music, 1953–1972* (1974). **Activities:** 1; 17, 26, 44; Music. **Addr.:** Serials Dept., Lovejoy Library, Southern Illinois University, Edwardsville, IL 62026.

Calcaterra, Loretta M. (Ja. 27, 1943, St. Louis, MO) Head, Sci.-Engin. Srvs., Washington Univ. Libs., 1981–; Ref. Libn., 1976–80, Resrch. Libn., Washington Univ., Comp. Labs., 1972–76; Tchr., St. Louis Pub. Schs., 1965–70. **Educ.:** St. Louis Univ., 1961–65, BA (Math); Univ. of MO, 1971–72, MALS. **Orgs.:** SLA: St. Louis Metro Area Chap., Secy. (1973–74), Pres.-Elect (1981–82); Bltn. Ed. (1974–78). **Activities:** 1; 39, 41; 56, 64, 91 **Addr.:** 4966 a Sutherland Ave., St. Louis, MO 63109.

Calderisi, Maria Vincenza (Mr. 17, 1935, Montreal, PQ) Head, Printed Coll., Msc. Div., Natl. Lib. of Canada, 1973–; **Educ.:** McGill Univ., 1967–72, BMus (Msc. Hist.); Univ. of MI, 1972–73, AMLS; McGill Univ., 1975–76, MMA (Musicology). **Orgs.:** Can. Assn. of Msc. Libs.: VP (1975–76), Pres. (1976–78). Intl. Assn. of Msc. Libs.: Secy., Bibl. Resrch. Comsn. (1976–). Msc. Lib. Assn.: Bd. (1977–79). IFLA: Secy., RT for Msc. in Libs. (1977–), VP (1980). Amer. Musicological Socty. Intl. Musicological Socty. **Pubns.:** *Music publishing in the Canadas: 1800–1867* (1980); "Sheet Music Publishing in the Canadas," *Papers of the Bibl. Socty. of Can.* (XVIII, 1979). **Activities:** 4; 15, 39, 45; 54, 55, 57 **Addr.:** Music Division, National Library of Canada, Ottawa, ON K1A 0N4, Canada.

Caldiero, Wendy A. (Mr. 30, 1944, Goshen, NY) Bronx Chld. Spec., NY Pub. Lib., 1978–, Sr. Chld. Libn., Fordham Lib. Ctr., 1973–77, Sr. Chld. Libn., Bronx Bkmobiles., 1970–73, Chld. Libn., Bronx Bkmobiles., 1968–70. **Educ.:** Wilson Coll., 1962–66, BA (Eng.); Univ. of IL, 1966–67, MLS; Manhattan Coll., 1975–80, MA (Eng.). **Orgs.:** NY LA: Bkmobile. Com. (Ch., 1972–73); CYASS Bd. (Secy., 1981–82); Int. Frdm. and Due Prcs. Com. (1980–82). ALA. Bronx LA. Amer. Prtg. Hist. Assn. **Honors:** Beta Phi Mu, 1968. **Activities:** 9; 21 **Addr.:** New York Public Library, Bronx Borough Office, 2556 Bainbridge Ave., Bronx, NY 10458.

Caldwell, Alva R. (D. 28, 1941, Little Sioux, IA) Libn., Garrett-Evang. Theo. Semy., 1978–; Asst. Libn., 1972–78, Ref. Libn., 1969–72. **Educ.:** Buena Vista Coll., 1960–64, BA, (Reli. Phil.); Garrett-Evang. Theo. Semy., 1966–69, MDiv, (Theo.); Rosary Coll., 1971–72, MLS. **Orgs.:** Chicago Area Theo. Lib. Assn.: Secy. (1970–73), Vice-Ch. (1973–74), Ch. (1974–75). Meth. Libns. Flwshp.: Vice-Ch. (1973–75), Ch. (1975–77). ATLA: Nom. Com. (1973–76), Persnl. Exch. Com. (1974–75). Iowa Conf. Untd. Meth. Church: Ordained Mnstr. (1971). **Honors:** Beta Phi Mu, 1971. **Activities:** 1; 17, 35, 39; 90 **Addr.:** Garrett-Evangelical Theological Seminary, 2121 Sheridan Rd., Evanston, IL 60201.

Caldwell, George Howard (S. 29, 1926, Holton, KS) Sr. Spec., U.S. Gvt. Docum., Lib. of Congs., 1978–, Head, Pub. Ref. Sect., 1966–78; Instr., U.S. Dept. of Agr. Grad. Sch., 1967–69; Head, Ref. Dept., Univ. of KS Lib., 1961–66, Head, Docum. Sect., 1957–61; Asst. Head, European Exch. Sect., Lib. of Congs., 1956–57, Biblgphr., Legis. Ref. Srv., 1956; Tech. Writer, Trng. Dept., Boeing Aircraft Corp., 1951–54. **Educ.:** Univ. of KS, 1944–48, BA (Pol. Sci.); Harvard Univ., 1948–50, MA (Gvt.); Columbia Univ., 1954–55, MLS (Lib. Srv.). **Orgs.:** ALA: Sci. Ref. Com. (1967–69); Coop. Ref. Srv. Com. (1977–79); Cat. in Pubn. for Gvt. Pubns. Com. (1979–80); Supt. of Docum. Nos. Std. Grp. (1979–); Eval. Com. on Fed. Gvt. Info. Progs. (1979–). Lib. of Congs. Prof. Assn. (Pres., 1975). KS Adv. Cncl. on Cvl. Rights: 2nd VP (1965–66). **Honors:** Phi Beta Kappa, 1947; Harvard Univ. Grad. Sch. of Bus. Admin., Std. Grant, 1962. **Pubns.:** "Concept of Provenance in SuDocs Numbers," *Docum. to the People* (S. 1979); "A View from the Top (on natl. tel. ref. srv.)," *RQ* (Sum. 1979); "Joint Pubns. Research Serv. Pubns." *Coll. & Resrch. Libs.* (Mr. 1964); "University Libraries and Government Publications," *C&RL* (Ja. 1961). **Activities:** 1, 4; 15, 29, 39 **Addr.:** 10010 Frederick Ave., Kensington, MD 20895.

Caldwell, Jane L. (My. 30, 1949, Minneapolis, MN) Educ. and Mktg. Srvs. Rep., BRS, 1980–; Coord. of Ref. & Datapage Srvs., Univ. of MN, 1979–80; Ref. Libn., Univ. of MN, 1975–79. **Educ.:** Univ. of MN, Minneapolis, 1967–71, BA (Eng.), 1971–74, MALS. **Orgs.:** ASIS: MN Chap. (Mem. Ch. 1978–79; Treas., 1979–80; Nat. Mtg., 1979). **Pubns.:** "A Comparison of Overlap: Eric and Psychological Abstracts," *Database* (Je. 1979). **Activities:** 1; 15, 31, 39; 63, 75, 92 **Addr.:** 5337 Colfax Ave. So., Minneapolis, MN 55419.

Caldwell, John (Charles) (Ag. 28, 1926, Latrobe, PA) Lib. Dir., Augustana Coll., Rock Island, Ill., 1975–; Head, Tech. Srvs., CA State Coll., Stanislous, 1970–74; Libn., CA Lutheran Coll., 1961–70; Asst. Libn., Tech. Srvs., Drew Univ., 1956–61, Catlgr., 1954–56; Inst., Grad. Lib. Sch., Univ. of IL, Summers 1976, 1978. **Educ.:** St. Vincent Coll., 1946–50, BS (Hist.); Univ. of PA, 1950–52, MA (Am. Studies); Drexel Inst., 1953–54, MSLS (LS). **Orgs.:** ALA. IL LA. Pvt. Acad. Libs. of IL: Secy./Treas. (1977); Pres. (1981). CA LA: State Coll. Libns. Chap., Pres. (1973). West. Lit. Assn. Assn. for Can. Studies. **Honors** Beta Phi Mu. **Pubns.:** *George R. Stewart* (1981); *Histories of American Colleges and Universities: A Bibliography* (1977); "The International Dramatic Critiques' Anti-Playwriting Association," *Menckeniona* (Win. 1970); "Degrees Held by Head Librarians of Colleges and Universities," *College & Research Libraries* (My. 1962); "Conventional Titles," *Library Resources and Technical Services* (Sum. 1960). **Activities:** 1; 17, 34, 46; 57, 66 **Addr.:** Denkmann Memorial Library, Augustana College, Rock Island, IL 61201.

Caldwell, Rossie Brower (N. 4, –, Columbia, SC) Assoc. Prof., SC State Coll., 1957–; Various other positions. **Educ.:** Claflin Coll., 1933–37, AB (Eng.); SC State Coll., 1950–52, MS (Educ.); Univ. of IL, 1954–59, MS (LS). **Orgs.:** ALA: Lib. Resrch. RT (1972). SC LA. SELA. AECT: Conf. Eval. (1975, 1978). AAUP: Secy. (1975–79). Histn. (1979–). Natl. Educ. Assn. AAUW. Phi Delta Kappa: Pubn. Com. (1978–). Various other orgs. and ofcs. **Honors:** Beta Phi Mu. **Pubns.:** "History of South Carolina Black Library Organization," in *Handbk. of Black Libnshp.* (1977); "Needed: Definitions in Action!" *SC Libn.* (Fall 1979); "Appraisal of Instructional Procedures," *Explorations* (Spr. 1968); "The Media Concept," *Explorations* (Spr. 1973). **Activities:** 10, 11; 26 **Addr.:** P.O. Box 686, Orangeburg, SC 29115.

Calhoun, Clayne M. (Jl. 22, 1950, Orange, NJ) Libn., Roanoke Law Lib., 1977–; Asst. Libn., Caplin & Drysdale, 1975–77. **Educ.:** Stratford Coll., 1970–72, BA (Pol. Sci.); Cath. Univ., 1973–76, MSLS. **Orgs.:** AALL: Law Lib. Srv. to Institutional Residents (1976–); S. East. Chap./Ch., State, Cnty. & Court Lib. Com. **Activities:** 9, 12; 17, 39; 77, 78, 95-Service to prisoners. **Addr.:** Roanoke Law Library, 210 Campbell Avenue, S.W., Roanoke, VA 24011.

Calhoun, Ernestine A. (Ja. 14, 1923, Crystal Springs, MS) Ed., Chld. Resrcs., Abingdon Press, Utd. Meth. Publishg. House, 1973–; Ed., KINDERGARTNER magazine, Untd. Meth. Church, 1970–73; Tchr., Meridian Pub. Schs., 1958–70. **Educ.:** Jackson State Univ., 1954–58, BS (Elem. Educ.); Scarritt Coll., 1970–73, MA (Christ. Educ.). **Orgs.:** Woman's Natl. Bk. Assn.: Bd. Mem. (1973–75). Assn. of Childhood Educ. Intl. ALA. Natl. Cncl. of Tchrs. of Eng. Altrusa Club of Nashville: Ch., Vocational Srvs. (1976–77). Intl. Readg. Assn. **Activities:** 6; 18; 90 **Addr.:** Abingdon Press, 201 Eighth Ave., South, Nashville, TN 37202.

Calhoun, Wanda J. (Ja. 23, 1932, Mayfield, KY) Dir., Augusta Reg. Lib., 1975–; Visit. Spec., Lib. Srvs., Untd. Bd. for Christ. Higher Educ. in Asia, 1971, 1965–66; Head Libn., Eckerd Coll., 1963–75; Head Libn., Heidelberg Coll., 1958–63; Div. Libn., Univ. of MI, 1955–58. **Educ.:** Murray State Univ., 1950–53, BS (Math., LS); Univ. of MI, 1953–55, AMLS; various crs. **Orgs.:** ALA. SE LA: Ed. Bd. GA LA. Quota Club of Augusta: Bd. of Dirs. **Pubns.:** Ed., *The GA Libn.* **Activities:** 1, 9; 17, 36, 47; 63, 74 **Addr.:** 2905 Arrowhead Dr., #C–1, Augusta, GA 30909.

Cali, Joseph J. (O. 17, 1928, Amsterdam, NY) Assoc. Libn., Antioch Coll., 1969–, Libn. for Pub. Srvs., 1965–69, Serials Libn., 1954–65. **Educ.:** Union Coll., 1947–51, BA; Western Reserve Univ., 1951–52, MSLS; Univ. of MI, 1957–65, grad. work (LS, Hist.). **Orgs.:** Dayton-Miami Valley Cnsrtm.: Resrcs. & Spec. Col. Com. (1969–); Ed. Bd., Un. List of Serials (1969/70, 1978–). **Activities:** 1; 22, 39, 44; 55, 57, 92 **Addr.:** Olive Kettering Library, Antioch College, Yellow Springs, OH 45387.

Callaham, Betty Elgin (O. 8, 1929, Honea Path, SC) State Libn., SC State Lib., 1979–, Deputy Libn., 1974–79, Dir., Field Srvs., 1965–74, Field Srvs. Libn., 1961–65. **Educ.:** Duke Univ., 1946–50, BA (Hist.); Emory Univ., 1953–54, MA (Hist.), 1960–61, MLS. **Orgs.:** ALA: Chap. Cnclr. (1976–80). SC LA: Pub. Lib. Sect. (Ch., 1965). Southeast. States Coop. Lib. Survey Com. (Ch., 1973–74); Plng. Com. (Ch. 1974–76); Fed. Rel. (Coord., 1976–78). SELA: Cont. Educ. Com. (1975–76). Hist. Columbia Fndn. Amer. Socty. for Pub. Admin. Caroliniana Socty. Natl. Trust. for Hist. Pres. **Honors:** Coord., SC Governor's Conf. on Pub. Libs., 1965; Coord., SC Governor's Conf. on Lib. and Info. Srvs., 1978–79; Alternate delegate, WHCLIS, 1979. **Pubns.:** "The Carnegie Library School of Atlanta (1905–1925)," *Lib. Qtly.* (Ap., 1967). **Activities:** 13 **Addr.:** South Carolina State Library, 1500 Senate Street, Post Office Box 11469, Columbia, SC 29211.

Callan, Frances (N. 23, 1936, Youngstown, OH) Chld. Lit. Catlgr., Lib. of Congs., 1972–, Asst. Head, State Docum. Sect., 1971–72; Elem. Sch. Tchr., OH, Eng., Colombia, DC, MD, 1958–68. **Educ.:** Kent State Univ., 1954–58, BS (Educ.); Univ. of the Amer., Mex., 1957; Univ. of MD, 1969–70, MLS. **Orgs.:** ALA. DC LA. Frnds. of IBBY. **Activities:** 4; 20, 21, 48; 55, 63, 89 **Addr.:** 1900 S. Eads, Arlington, VA 22202.

Callard, Carole Crawford (Ag. 8, 1941, Charleston, WV) Branch Libn., Ann Arbor Pub. Lib., 1974–; Libn. I, WV Lib. Comsn., 1973; Head, Docum. Dept., Haile Sellassie I Univ., 1970–71; Adult Srvs. Libn., Tompkins Cnty. Pub. Lib., 1966–69. **Educ.:** Morris Harvey Coll., 1959–63, BA (Hist. & Educ.); Univ. of Pittsburgh, 1965–66, MLS; East. MI Univ., 1976–78, MA (Soc. Fndns.). **Orgs.:** ALA: GODORT (1966–69, 1976–). MI LA. Washtenaw Lib. Club. Other orgs. AAUW: Secy. (1976–77, 1978–79); Geneal. Socty. of Washtenaw Cnty.: Pres. (1978–79); MI Geneal. Cncl.: Del. (1978–80); Fed. of Geneal. Societies: Del. (1980–); Other orgs. **Honors:** Beta Phi Mu. **Pubns.:** *Index of the Ithaca Journal 150 Anniv. Ed.* (1967); "Dry Branch Cemetery," *Journal of the Kanawha Valley Genealogical Society* (Jl., Ag., S. 1979); Ed., *Ann Arbor AAUW* (1975–77); Ed., *Giles, West Virginia Cemetary Inscription,* (1980). **Activities:** 1, 9; 20, 29, 39; 63, 69, 92 **Addr.:** 1033 Pomona, Ann Arbor, MI 48103.

Callard, Joanne C. (S. 7, 1925, Eads, CO) Adjunct Inst., Coll. of Pharmacy, 1977–; Interlib. Loan Libn., Univ. of OK Hlth. Scis. Ctr., 1979–; Assistant Professor, Medical Library Science. OUHSC 1978. Asst. Coord., Ext. Lib. Srvs., 1977–79; Interlib. Loan Libn., Ext. Lib. Srvcs., 1976–77; Pharmacy Libn., 1976–76. **Educ.:** Univ. of CO, 1943–48, BA (Pre-Law); Univ. of OK, 1975–76, MLS; West. State Coll., Gunnison, CO, 1974, CO Tchg. Cert. **Orgs.:** Med. LA: S. Cent. Reg. Grp. ALA. OK LA: Ch., Interlib. Coop. Com. (1978); Ch., Prog. Mtg. (1978). Network Adv. Cncl. for OK Libs. **Honors:** Beta Phi Mu, 1976. **Pubns.:** Cont., *Manual for Hospital Librarians* (D. 1979); jt. Ed., *Union List of Serials in Oklahoma Medical Libraries,* (D. 1977); "The Medical Librarian's Role as Adjunct Faculty Member of a College Within A Health Sciences Center," *Btln. of the Med. LA* (O. 1979); "Guide to Interlibrary Loan Practices in Oklahoma," *OK Libn.* (Ap. 1979). **Activities:** 1; 31, 34; 80, 87 **Addr.:** Library, University of Oklahoma Health Sciences Center, P.O. Box 26901, Oklahoma City, OK 73190.

Callinan, Mary L. Mgr., Inf. Ctr., Union Dime Savings Bank, 1976–; Catlgr., St. John's Univ., Jamaica, NY, 1966–76; Libn., Red Bank Pub. Lib., 1958–59; Libn., Philip Morris Inc., 1957–58. **Educ.:** Marywood Coll., AB (LS); St. John's Univ., 1976–80, MLS. **Orgs.:** SLA. ASIS. NY Lib. Club. **Pubns.:** *E.F.T.: 1976–1978; A Selected Bibliography* (1978); *Sources of Management/Finance Information for Today's Savings Banker; A Select-*

Special Subjects/Services: 50. Adult educ.; 51. Advert./Mktg.; 52. Aerosp.; 53. Agric.; 54. Area std.; 55. Arts/Hum.; 56. Autom.; 57. Bibl./Prtg.; 58. Bio. sci.; 59. Bus./Fin.; 60. Chem.; 61. Copyrt.; 62. Documtn.; 63. Educ.; 64. Engin.; 65. Env.; 66. Eth. grps.; 67. Film; 68. Food/Nutr.; 69. Geneal.; 70. Geo.; 71. Geol.; 72. Handcpd.; 73. Hist.; 74. Int. frdm.; 75. Info. sci.; 76. Insr.; 77. Law; 78. Legis.; 79. Math./Comp. sci.; 80. Med.; 81. Metals; 82. Nat. resrcs.; 83. Newsp.; 84. Nuc. sci.; 85. Oral hist.; 86. Petr./Energy; 87. Pharm.; 88. Phys./Astr./Math.; 89. Readg.; 90. Relig.; 91. Sci./Tech.; 92. Soc. sci.; 93. Telecom.; 94. Transp.; 95. (other).

Who's Who in Library and Information Services

ed List, 1976-1980. (1980). **Activities:** 1, 5; 20, 45; 57, 59 **Addr.:** Information Center, Union Dime Savings Bank, 1065 Ave. of the Americas, New York, NY 10018.

Caltabiano, Marilyn (Ap. 19, 1933, Trenton, NJ) Lib. Dir., Meml. Lib. of Radnor Twp., 1971–, Ref. Libn., 1965–67; Serials Libn., Chance Vought Aircraft, 1956–57. **Educ.:** Wellesley Coll., 1951–55, BA (Eng.); Drexel Univ. 1963–67, MLS. **Orgs.:** Frnds. of the Radnor Lib.: Bd. (1971). PA LA: Adult Srvs. Com. (Dir., 1973–74). DE Cnty. Libns. Assn.: Ch. (1974–76). Philadelphia Dist. Adv. Com. Radnor Hist. Socty.: Dir. (1978–). Wellesley Class of 1955: Pres. (1966–70). Wellesley Coll. Club in Philadelphia. Beta Phi Mu: Sigma Chap. (Treas., 1974–76). **Honors:** Beta Phi Mu, 1967; Phi Kappa Phi, 1967. **Activities:** 9; 15, 17, 19; 75, 86 **Addr.:** Memorial Library of Radnor Township, 114 W. Wayne Ave., Wayne, PA 19087.

Calvert, Lois M. (My. 19, 1940; Rockford, IL) Assoc. Law Libn., Univ. of CO, 1978–; Asst. Law Libn., 1966–78; Asst. Serials Libn., 1963–66. **Educ.:** Beloit Coll., 1958–60; Univ. of WI, 1960–62, BS (Eng/Hist.); Univ. of Denver, 1962–63, MA (LS). **Orgs.:** AALL: various com. (1966–). Southwestern Chap.: Various com. (1966–). CO Cnsrtm. of Law Libs.: Pres. (1978); Prog. Com. (1979). **Activities:** 1, 12; 17, 39 **Addr.:** University of Colorado Law Library, Boulder, CO 80309.

Calvert, Stephen Jared (Mr. 7, 1940, Benton, WI) Sponsoring Ed., Market Places and Directories, R. R. Bowker Co., 1979–; Free-lance auth., ed., indxr., 1976–79; Asst. Ed., *Weekly Record* and *American Book Publishing Record,* R. R. Bowker Co., 1975–76, Asst. Editor, *Books in Print,* 1974–75, Asst. Ed., *International Bibliography, Information, Documentation,* 1972–74; Head, FAO & GATT Publns. Sales, Unipub, 1970–72; Ref. Libn.; Asst. Circ. Libn., Engin. Societies Lib., 1966–69; Head, Circ. Dept.; Ref. Libn., Amer. Inst. of Aeronautics and Astronautics, 1962–65. **Educ.:** Oberlin Coll. & Univ. of WI, 1958–62, 1970, BS (Psy.); Pratt Inst., 1976–78, MLS. **Orgs.:** ALA. OR Historical Soc. **Pubns.:** Jt. ed., *Literary and Library Prizes,* 10th ed. (1980); Collab., *Subject Collections,* 5th ed. (1978); Jt. ed., *Children's Media Market Place* (1978); "A Select Bibliography of Science Fiction Bibliographies, Indexes, and Checklists," *The Great Science Fiction Pictures* (1977); "Resources Untapped: Publications of the U.N. Agencies," *Directions* (O. 1975). **Activities:** 6, 12; 22, 37, 39; 52, 64, 75 **Addr.:** R. R. Bowker Co., 1180 Ave. of the Americas, New York, NY 10036.

Camacho, Nancy Sue (N. 7, 1946, Houston, TX) Libn., Proctor Cmnty. Hosp., 1972–; Asst. Libn., Univ. of NE Med. Ctr. Lib., 1970–72. **Educ.:** Kent State Univ., 1965–69, BA (Fr.); Univ. of MI, 1969–70, MALS. **Orgs.:** Med. LA: Hosp. Lib. Sect.; Midwest Reg. Grp. Hlth. Sci. Libns. of IL. IL Valley Lib. Syst.: Interlibrary Coop. Cncl. (1973–75); Adv. Cncl. (1977–80). Heart of IL Lib. Consortium: Coord. (1979–). Other orgs. **Activities:** 12; 17, 34, 39; 80 **Addr.:** Proctor Community Hospital Medical Library, 5409 N. Knoxville Ave., Peoria, IL 61614.

Cameron, Dee Birch (Je. 25, 1943, Somerset, PA) Ref. Libn., Univ. of TX at El Paso, 1972–; Consult. to Tech. Info. Ctr., El Paso Co., 1977–79; Tchr., Ysleta HS, 1969–69. **Educ.:** Oberlin Coll., 1961–63; Univ. of Pittsburgh, 1963–64, AB (Eng. & Grmn.); George Washington Univ., 1965–68, MA (Eng. & Amer. Lit.); Univ. of Pittsburgh, 1974–75, MLS. **Orgs.:** Border Reg. LA: Constitution Com. (Ch., 1971); Second VP (1973); Schol. Com. (Ch., 1974); Southwest Book Awds. Com. (1979). ALA: RASD. Pi Lambda Theta. **Honors:** Beta Phi Mu. **Pubns.:** "The Unitarian Woman and the One-Eyed Man: Updike's *Marry Me* and 'Sunday Teasing,'" *Ball State Univ. Forum* (Spr. 1980); "The Credentials Question: Why We Care," *Jnl. of Acad. Libnshp.* (My. 1979); "Maya Angelou Bibliography," *Bltn. of Bibl. and Magazine Notes* (Ja. 1979); "On My Mind: Professor Smith and Pandora's Box," *Jnl. of Acad. Libnshp.* (Ja. 1977); "Public and Academic Library Reference Questions," *RQ* (Win. 1976). **Activities:** 1; 31, 39; 55 **Addr.:** Reference Department, The Library, The University of Texas at El Paso, El Paso, TX 79968.

Cameron, Lynn E. (Ag. 7, 1951, Pontiac, MI) Cur. of Slides, Slide Libn., Oakland Univ., 1976–. **Educ.:** MI State Univ., 1969–73, BA (Art Hist.); Wayne State Univ., 1973–77, MA (Art Hist.); Workshop for Art Slide Cur., Univ. of MO, 1977; Oakland Univ., 1980, MBA; Columbia Univ., PhD (in progress). **Orgs.:** ARLIS/NA: Visual Resrcs. Com. (1976–); Coll. Art Assn. Founders Socty. of the Detroit Inst. of Arts. **Pubns.:** Ed., *Focalpoint Gallery Guide* (1976–); MI rep., *National Arts Guide* (1979–). **Activities:** 1, 12; 15, 17, 32; 54, 55, 67 **Addr.:** 1742 Bedford Square #203, Rochester, MI 48063.

Cameron, M. Francesca (Jl. 31, 1924, Fairfax Cnty., VA) Dir., Media Ctr., St. Catharine Coll., 1975–; Prof. of Educ., Bishop Coll., 1971–75; Acad. Dean, St. Catharine Coll., 1966–71, Prof. of Educ., 1961–66. **Educ.:** FL State Coll. for Women, 1941–45, AB (Sec. Educ.); FL State Univ., 1947–48, MLS; Columbia Univ. Tchrs. Coll., 1950–63, EdD (Curric. & Tchg.). **Orgs.:** AECT. KY LA. Pi Lambda Theta. Kappa Delta Pi. **Honors:** Beta Phi Mu. **Pubns.:** *Education as Ministry* (1974); "Putting Pamphlets in Circulation," *Wilson Lib. Bltn.* (F. 1960); "Recreating with the Evangelists," *DEA Bltn.* (Spr. 1960); "The Alabaster Jar," *Review for Religions* (Jl. 1977). **Activities:** 1, 10; 17, 32, 39; 63, 67, 90 **Addr.:** St. Catharine P.O., KY 40061.

Cameron, Sam Archie (My. 25, 1943, Chattanooga, TN) Archvst., Fisk Univ., 1972–. **Educ.:** TN State Univ., 1966–70, BS (Soclgy.), 1970–72, MS (Hist.); SAA Wkshp., 1978. **Orgs.:** SAA. Assn. for the Std. of Afro-Amer. Life and Hist. TN State Univ.: Curric. Com. (1969). **Activities:** 1, 2; 38; 66 **Addr.:** 1906 S. St. #303, Nashville, TN 37212.

Cameron, William James (O. 29, 1926, Paekakariki, NZ) Dean and Prof., Sch. of Lib. and Info. Sci., Univ. of West. ON, 1970–, Assoc. Dean and Prof., 1968–70; Prof., Dept. of Eng., McMaster Univ., 1964–68; Sr. Lectr., Dept. of Eng., Univ. of Auckland, 1960–64, Lectr., 1958–60; Asst. Lectr., Dept. of Eng., Reading Univ., 1953–56; Jr. Lectr., Dept. of Eng., Victoria Univ. of Wellington, 1950–53. **Educ.:** Victoria Univ. of Wellington, 1949, BA (Eng.), 1950–51, MA (Eng.); Reading Univ., Eng., 1952–58, PhD (Eng.). **Orgs.:** ALA. Can. LA: Resrch. and Dev. Com. AALS: Liaison Com. with Latin Amer. Lib. Schs. (1980–82). Assn. of Caribbean Univ., Resrch. and Inst. Libs.: Lib. Educ. Com. (1978–82). Amer. Socty. for 18th Century Std. Can. Socty. for 18th Century Std. Various bibl. soctys. **Honors:** Cmwlth. Visit. Flwshp., 1966; Can. Cncl. Resrch. Flwshp., 1976–77. **Pubns.:** *Bibliographical Control of Early Books* (1978); "The *Lexicon Technicum* of John Harris," *Papers on Lexicography in Honor of Warren N. Cordell* (1979); *The HPB Project: Phase IV. The French Canadian Contribution to the Development of A Western Hemisphere Short Title Catalog (WHSTC) of Spanish, French and Portuguese Language Books Printed Before 1801* (1980); "Lodes of French-Canadian Gold in U.S. Libraries," *Can. Jnl. of Info. Sci.* (1980); "La School of Library and Information Science de l'Université Western Ontario," *Argus* (1980); various articles, bks. **Activities:** 1, 11; 26, 37, 45; 55, 57, 75 **Addr.:** School of Library and Information Science, University of Western Ontario, London, ON N6A 5B9 Canada.

Camp, Thomas Edward (Jl. 12, 1929, Haynesville, LA) Libn. of the Sch. of Theo., 1957– and Assoc. Univ. Libn., Univ. of the South, 1976–; Circ. Libn., Bridwell Lib., Perkins Sch. of Theo., S.M.U., 1955–57. **Educ.:** Centenary Coll. of LA, 1946–50, BA (Eng.); LA State Univ., 1951–53, MSLS; Vanderbilt Dvnty. Sch., 1950–51, 1965. **Orgs.:** ATLA: Exec. Secy. (1965–67); Ad Hoc Com. on Persnl. Exch. (1974–76). ALA. TN LA: Legis. Com. (1979–). SELA. AAUP. **Honors:** Omicron Delta Kappa, 1950; Phi Kappa Phi, 1953; Beta Phi Mu, 1954. **Pubns.:** Jt. auth., *Using Theol. Bks. and Libs.* (1963); "The Librarian on the Teaching Team," *Theol. Educ.* (Sum. 1965); "Evaluation of 'Religion' and 'Philosophy' sections of Choice," *MO Lib. Assn. Qtly.* (Mar. 1968); "The American Theological Library Association" in *The Encyc. of Lib. and Info. Sci.* (1968). **Activities:** 1, 14-Theol. Lit.; 15, 17, 44; 57, 90, 92 **Addr.:** Carruthers Road, Sewanee, TN 37375.

Campanelli, Richard Lee (Ag. 16, 1925, Bell, CA) Dir., Instr. Mtrls. and Lib. Srvs., Walla Walla Sch. Dist. # 140, 1958–, Tchr., 1953–58. **Educ.:** East. WA Univ., 1945–49, BA (Eng. Soc. Std., Educ.); Columbia Univ., 1962, MA (Curric., Instr.); various crs. **Orgs.:** ALA. WA Lib. Media Assn.: State Mem. Ch.; Dir. SE Lib. Srv. Area: Ch. AECT. Phi Delta Kappa: Blue Mt. Chap., Secy., Nsltr. Ed. Intl. Readg. Assn.: Ch.; Secy. Assn. for Childhood Educ.: Past Lcl. Ch.; various coms. WA Assn. of Sch. Admins.: Job Alike Com. Various other orgs. **Honors:** Parent Tchr. Assn., Golden Acorn Awd., 1957. **Pubns.:** "The Use of Instructional Materials with Severely Retarded Youngsters," *Resrcs. for Tchg. and Lrng.* (Sum. 1969). **Activities:** 10; 17, 24, 32; 61, 63, 67 **Addr.:** P.O. Box 752, 49 Jade St., Walla Walla, WA 99362.

Campbell, Alma B. (Jl. 1, 1928, Keene, NH) Mgr., Info. Ctr., Sperry Univac, 1966–; Docum. Libn., Bell Labs., 1958; Catlgr., Mt. Holyoke Coll., 1954–57; Resrch. Libn., Raytheon Co., 1951–54. **Educ.:** Boston Univ., 1946–50, BA (Chem.); Simmons Coll., 1950–51, MLS. **Orgs.:** SLA. Assn. of Info. Mgrs. **Activities:** 12; 17; 59, 64, 91 **Addr.:** Sperry Univac, Information Center E2–112, Blue Bell, PA 19424.

Campbell, Ann Morgan (My. 15, 1937, Beckely, WV) Exec. Dir., SAA, 1974–; Chief, Arch. Branch, Natl. Arch., San Francisco, 1972–74; Admin. Ofcr., Natl. Arch., Reg. 9, 1971–72; Admin. Ofcr., John F. Kennedy Lib., 1969–71. **Educ.:** Univ. of FL, 1954–57, AA (Educ.); Old Dominion Univ., 1964–67, BA (Hist.); Coll. of William & Mary, 1967–68 (Hist.); FL Atl. Univ., 1978–81, MBA; Seminar for Hist. Admin., Cert., 1968; Mod. Arch. Admin., Cert., 1970. **Orgs.:** SAA: Cncl. (1973–74), Exec. Dir. (1974–). U.S. Natl. Com. for the UNESCO Gen. Info. Prog.: Bureau Mem. (1977–). Natl. Study Comsn. on the Records & Docum. of Fed. Officials: Comsn. (1975–77). Intl. Cncl. on Arch.: Sect. of Prof. Archival Assn., Secy. (1976-80). Amer. Socty. of Assn. Exec.: Individual Memb. Org. Cncl. (1978–). **Honors:** SAA, Fellow, 1976; Certified Assn. Exec., 1977. **Pubns.:** "Archives," *ALA YEARBOOK* (1977, 1978, 1979, 1980); "Reports from Weedpatch, California: The Records of the Farm Security Administration," *Agr. Hist.* (Jl. 1974); "In Nineteenth Century Nevada: Federal Records as Sources for Local History," (NV Hist. Qtly.) (S. 1974); "Reaping the Records: Sources for Archival Research," *Agr. Hist.* (Ja. 1975); "Trappings of the Trade: Oral History Equipment," in *A Guide for Oral History Programs* (1973). **Addr.:** 1510 W. Jackson Blvd., Chicago, IL 60607.

Campbell, Archibald D. (Ag. 23, 1946, Chatham, ON) Chief, Lib. Srvs. Div., Pub. Srv. Comsn. of Can., 1977–; Head, Circ. Sect., Natl. Lib. of Can., 1975–77, Trainer, Location Sect., 1973–75, Srch., Location Sect., 1971–73. **Educ.:** Univ. of West. ON, 1965–69, BA, hons. (Hist.), 1969–71, MLS. **Orgs.:** Cncl. of Fed. Libs.: Strg. Com. (1980–); Integrated Lib. Systs. Com. (Conv., 1980–); Com. on Cont. Educ. (Conv., 1980–). **Activities:** 4, 12; 17, 25, 34; 50, 59, 63 **Addr.:** Library Services Division, Rm. 935, 300 Laurier St., L'Esplanade Laurier, Ottawa, ON K1A 0M7 Canada.

Campbell, Cathrin M. (S. 20, 1947, Ottawa, ON) Assoc. Prof., 1981–, Asst. Coord., Lib. Std. Prog., Concordia Univ., 1976–, Actg Coord., Lib. Std. Prog., 1980–81; Head, Sci. & Engin. Lib., 1973–76; Sr. Ref. Libn., Sir George Williams Univ., 1971–73; Libn., Dominion Bridge Co., 1971. **Educ.:** Univ. of Ottawa, 1965–69, BSc (Physio.), 1969, BLS; McGill Univ., 1973–75, MLS. **Orgs.:** SLA: Exec. Secy. (1973–74), VP & Pres. Elect (1977–78), Pres. (1978–79). Can. LA. **Activities:** 1, 11; 17, 26, 35; 50, 75, 91 **Addr.:** Concordia University, Library Studies Program, 7141 Sherbrooke St. W., Montreal, PQ H4B 1R6, Canada.

Campbell, Corinne A. (My. 10, 1940, Tacoma, WA) Mgr., Tech. Libs., Boeing Co., 1979–, Supvsr., Kent Tech. Lib. (Boeing), 1979–79, Supvsr., Renton Tech. Lib. (Boeing), 1974–79, Head, Resrch. and Ref. Srvs., 1970–74, Resrch. Libn. (Boeing), 1966–70; Various Tchg. positions. **Educ.:** WA State Univ., 1958–62, BA (Eng.); Univ. of WA, 1964–66, M. Libnshp. **Orgs.:** SLA: Pac. Northwest Chap. (Pres., 1976–77). WA Lib. Netwk. Exec. Cncl. (Ch., 1978–79). ASIS; WA State Adv. Cncl. on Libs., Resrc. Ctrs.: Task Frc. (1974–76). New Beginnings (Shelter for Battered Women) Bd. of Dir. (1977; Pres., 1978–80). United Way of King Cnty.: Loaned Exec. (1979). **Honors:** Phi Kappa Phi, 1962; Pi Lambda Theta, 1961; Beta Phi Mu, 1966. **Pubns.:** Jt.-auth., *Specialized Resource Centers in Washington State: Potential for Network Involvement,* (1975). **Activities:** 12; 17, 41; 52, 59, 94 **Addr.:** 2525 - 175th N.E., Redmond, WA 98052.

Campbell, Deas P. (Ap. 18, 1946, Monroe, LA) Head, Pub. Srvs., Austin Cmnty. Coll., 1976–; Educ. Coord., Yavapai-Prescott Tribe, 1975–76; Consult., Srv. to Indians, AZ Lib. Ext., 1974–75; Bkmobile Libn., Papago Tribe of AZ, 1971–73; Instr. (part-time), Univ. of AZ (Indian Program), 1973–74. **Educ.:** Northeast LA, 1966–68, BA (Eng.); Univ. of AZ, 1970–71, MLS; Univ. of TX, 1977–80, (LS); LA State Univ., 1969, (LS). **Orgs.:** ALA: American Indian People (1971–78). TX Jr. Coll. Lrng. Resrcs.: Secy. (1979–80). TX LA. Amer. Civil Liberties Un.: Ctrl. TX Bd. of Dir. (1979–). **Pubns.:** "Where is the Library?", *Accolade* (Ja. 1980); Photography–Teaching Indian Dances, *Young Horizons* (1973). **Activities:** 1, 12; 17, 27, 32; 50, 66, 89 **Addr.:** 1713 Enfield Rd., Apt. F, Austin, TX 78703.

Campbell, Evelyn M. (O. 29, 1907, Arichat, NS) Libn., Retired, 1971; Libn., Info. Srvs., NS Resrch. Fndn., 1948–71; Libn., Prov. Sci. Lib., 1936–48. **Educ.:** Mt. St. Vincent Univ., 1925–29, BA, BEd; McGill Univ., 1930–31, MLS; various crs. **Orgs.:** Halifax LA: Pres., Secy. (1950–55). Atl. Prov. LA: Secy. (1945–56). SLA. ALA. **Honors:** Atl. Prov. LA, Merit, 1977. **Pubns.:** Ed., *Selected Bibliography on Algae* (1952–71); "History Halifax Library Association," *Dalhousie Lib. Sch. of LS* (1976); various articles, *Can. LA Bltn.* **Activities:** 4, 12; 30, 39 **Addr.:** 1101 Wellington St., Halifax, NS B3H 3A1 Canada.

Campbell, Frances D. (Je. 11, 1937, Cape Girardeau, MO) Supreme Ct. Libn., CO Supreme Ct., 1964–; Libn., Denver Pub. Lib., 1962–64. **Educ.:** CO Univ., 1955–60, BA (Eng.); Denver Univ., 1961–62, MS (LS), 1963–69, JD (Law). **Orgs.:** AALL. CO Cnsrtm. of Law Libns. SLA. CO Bar Assn. CO Women's Bar Assn. **Pubns.:** *District and County Court Law Libraries* (1971). **Addr.:** Colorado Supreme Ct. Library, B112 State Judicial Bldg., 2 E. 14th Ave., Denver, CO 80203.

Campbell, Francis D. (My. 26, 1942, New York, NY) Head Libn., Amer. Numismatic Socty., 1975–, Asst. Libn., 1966–75. **Educ.:** Fordham Univ., 1959–63, BS (Comm. Arts); Queens Coll., 1969–73, MLS. **Orgs.:** SLA. ASIS. Esperanza Ctr.: Pres., Bd. Ch. (1974–). Spuyten Duyvil Assn.: VP (1980–). **Honors:** ALA, J. Morris Jones–World Bk. Encyc. Awd., 1970; Beta Phi Mu, 1973; NEH, grant support for proj., 1978–. **Pubns.:** "Numismatic Bibliography and Libraries," *Encyc. of Lib. and Info. Sci.* (forthcoming); various bk. reviews, *Lib. Jnl.* (1963–68). **Activities:** 12; 15, 17, 39; 55, 95-Numismatics. **Addr.:** American Numismatic Society, Broadway at 155 St., New York, NY 10032.

Campbell, Frank Carter (S. 26, 1916, Winston-Salem, NC) Chief, Msc. Div., NY Pub. Lib., 1966–, Asst. Chief, 1959–66; Libn., Msc. Div., Lib. of Congs., 1943–59; Catlgr., Sibley Lib., Eastman Sch. of Msc., 1943. **Educ.:** Salem Coll., 1933–38, BMsc (Piano); Eastman Sch. of Msc., 1940–43, MMsc (Msclgy.). **Orgs.:** Msc. LA: Ed., *Notes* (1971–74); Secy. (1948–50); Pres. (1967–69). Intl. Assn. of Msc. Libs. Amer. Msclgl. Socty. Clarion Msc. Socty. Aston Magna Fndn. Cantata

Singers. **Pubns.:** "Schubert Song Autographs in the Library of Congress," Lib. of Congs. *Qtly Jnl. of Current Acq.;* "The Musical Scores of George Gershwin," Lib. of Congs. *Qtly Jnl. of Current Acq.;* "Some Manuscripts of George Gershwin," *Mss.;* "The Music Library Association," *Msc. Pubshrs. Jnl.* (My.-Je. 1946); "The Music Division of The New York Public Library," *Fontes Artis Musicae* (1969/3). **Addr.:** Nevada Towers, 1 Nevada Pl., Apt. 16A, New York, NY 10023.

Campbell, Helen Woerner (O. 17, 1918, Indianapolis, IN) Chief Libn., IN Univ. Sch. of Den., 1966–80, Retired Je. 30, 1980; Asst. Libn., 1965–66, Libn., 1942–46, Asst. Order Libn., 1937–42. **Educ.:** IN Univ. 1935–41; Butler Univ., 1963–67, BS (Bus. Admin.). **Orgs.:** SLA: IN Chap., (Treas. 1963–64, Pub. Rel. Ch., 1967–69, Secy., 1969–70, Pres.-elect, 1971–72, Pres., 1972–73). SLA: Adv. Cncl. (1971–73). Med. LA: Ch. Annual Mtg. (1975). Midwest Reg. Grp. Exec. Com. (1966–69). Nom. Com. (1970). Amer. Assn. of Dental Schls. Amer. Acad. of the Hist. of Dent. **Honors:** Omicron Kappa Upsilon, 1977. **Pubns.:** "The School of Dentistry Library," Alum. Bltn., IN Univ. Sch. of Dent. (1979); "A Look Behind the Scenes at the School of Dentistry Library," (1973). **Activities:** 1, 12; 17, 31, 39; 58, 63, 80 **Addr.:** 1865 N. Norfolk St., Indianapolis, IN 46224.

Campbell, Henry Cummings (Ap. 22, 1919, Vancouver, BC) Dir., Urban Lib. Study Proj., Toronto Pub. Lib., 1978–; Chief Libn., 1956–78; Head, Clearing House for Libs., UNESCO, Paris, 1949–56; Producer, Natl. Film Bd. of Can., 1942–46. **Educ.:** Univ. of BC, 1936–40, BA (Hist.); Columbia Univ., 1946–48, MA (Adult Educ.); Univ. of Toronto, 1940–41, BLS. **Orgs.:** Can. LA: Pres. (1974–75). IFLA: 1st VP (1974–78). **Honors:** IFLA, Honorary Fellow, 1979. **Pubns.:** *Early Days on the Great Lakes* (1972); *Metropolitan Public Library Planning throughout the World* (1973); *UNESCO Manual on Developing Public Library Systems and Services* (1981). **Activities:** 9, 12; 17; 50, 75, 78 **Addr.:** P.O.B. 624 Station K, Toronto, ON M4P 2H1, Canada.

Campbell, Jerry D. (S. 25, 1945, Matador, TX) Dir. of the Lib., Iliff Sch. of Theo., 1976–, Act. Libn., 1975–76, Assoc. Libn., 1974–75, Asst. Libn., 1972–74. **Educ.:** McMurry Coll., 1964–68, BA (Relig.); Divinity Sch., Duke Univ., 1968–71, MDiv.; Univ. of NC, Chapel Hill, 1971–72, MSLS: Certificate in Archive Management, Case Western Reserve, 1976. **Orgs.:** CO LA. ATLA: Ch., Per. Exch. Com. (1974–77); Prog. Com. (1974, 1980); Bd. of Dir. (1977–80). Meth. Libn.: Secy./Treas. (1977–79). AAUP. Denver Unit. Meth. Min. Assn. **Honors:** United Meth. Church, Cokesbury Grad. Awd., 1978; Assn. of Theo. Sch., Faculty Dev. Grant, 1976; U.S. Jaycees, Outstanding Young Man of America, 1976. **Pubns.:** "Fastcat Considered," *Proceedings Amer. Theo. Lib. Assn.* (1973); Jt. Auth., "Video Usage in the Seminary Setting," (1975); "How Does Your Soul Prosper: A Play in Two Acts," *Comsn. on Arch. and Hist.,* Meth. Ch. (1975). **Activities:** 2, 12; 15, 17, 45; 90 **Addr.:** 2233 South University Blvd., Denver, CO 80210.

Campbell, John D. (Ja. 5, 1946, Philadelphia, PA) Dir., Pathfinder Lib. Syst., CO, 1980–; Head, Cir.-Ext., Great Falls Pub. Lib., MT, 1977–80; Libn. at Large, Occidental Coll. Lib., 1974–77. **Educ.:** Univ. of AZ, Tucson, 1963–73, BA (Classics), 1973–74, MLS. **Orgs.:** Co LA. ALA. MT LA: Ch., Pub. Libs. Div. (1979–80). **Pubns.:** "Publish or Perish, Library Style," *Wilson Lib. Bltn.* (N. 1977); Reviews. **Activities:** 9; 17, 31; 57, 62 **Addr.:** South First and Uncompahgre, Montrose, CO 81401.

Campbell, John Lewis (Ja. 1, 1943, Akron, OH) Online Srvs. Coord., Ref. Libn. Ref. Dept., Univ. of GA Libs., 1981–, Ref. Libn., 1978–80; Asst. Gvt. Docum. Libn., West. IL Univ. Lib., 1974–78, Asst. Ref. Libn., 1971–74. **Educ.:** N. Ctrl. Coll., 1961–65, BA (Classical Langs., Phil.); Evang. Theo. Semy., 1966–69, MDiv; Univ. of IL, 1969–71, MLS. **Orgs.:** IL LA: GODORT (Treas., 1975–77). ALA. GA LA. Amer. Cvl. Liberties Un. **Honors:** Beta Phi Mu, 1971. **Activities:** 1; 39, 49-Online bibl. retrieval. **Addr.:** Reference Dept., University of Georgia Libraries, Athens, GA 30602.

Campbell, Kenneth A. (Jl. 30, 1922, Detroit, MI) Mgr., Info. Ctrs. Pro., Gen. Elec. Co., 1971–; Mgr., Appollo and Ground Syst., 1962–71; Mgt., Convair Corp., 1951–62; Fac./Staff, MI State Univ. and South. Meth. Univ., 1947–54. **Educ.:** Wayne State Univ., 1940–47, BS (Civ. Eng.); MI State Univ., 1948–51, MS (Civ. Eng.). **Orgs.:** ASIS. **Pubns.:** Extensive Info. Syst. and Srvs. **Activities:** 12; 17, 26, 46; 75 **Addr.:** General Electric Company, 9119 Gaither Rd., Gaithersburg, MD 20760.

Campbell, Lucy Barnes (O. 30, –, Windsor, NC) Asst. Prof., Head Per. Dept., Hampton Inst., 1966–, Asst. Ref. Libn., 1964–65, Actg. Dir., Coord., Student Actv., 1964, Circ. Libn., 1963; Asst. Libn., AL State Univ., 1945–63; Libn., Darden HS, 1942–45. **Educ.:** NC Ctrl. Univ., 1937–41, AB (Eng.), 1941–42, BLS, 1958–60, MLS; Cert., Inst. on Sel. Org. and Use of Mat. by and about Blacks-Fisk Univ., 1970. **Orgs.:** ALA: ACRL; Black Caucus. SELA. VA LA. Assn. Study Afro American Life and Hist. NAACP. Women's Service Leag. YWCA. **Honors:** AL State Univ., Cit. for Srv. and Leadership, 1962; Women's Sen., Hampton Inst., Cert. of Merit; Mother of the Year, 1965; Men's Cncl., Hampton Inst., Mother of the Men of Hampton, 1968. **Pubns.:** "The Hampton Institute Library School, 1925–1939," *Handbook of Black Librarianship,* (1977); "Black Librarians in Virginia", *Black Librarian in the South,* (1976). **Activities:** 1, 12; 17, 41, 44; 66, 75, 91 **Addr.:** 819 Lincoln St., Portsmouth, VA 23704.

Campbell, Mary Elizabeth (Jl. 23, 1939, London, ON) Autom. Srvs. Libn., ON Inst. for Studies in Educ., 1979–; Procs. Libn., 1971–79; Catlgr. 1966–71; Gen. Libn., 1966; Home Ofc. Underwriter, Mfrs. Life Ins. Co., 1961–65. **Educ.:** Univ. of Toronto, 1957–61, BA (Household Sci.); 1965–66, BLS; 1968–71, MLS; 1976–79, M Ed. **Orgs.:** SLA: Toronto Chap., Secretary, 1973/74); Pres. (1975–76); Ch., Nom. com. 1977–78); Ch., Ret. Com., 1977–78); Budget Com. (1978–79, 1979–80). Can. LA: Mem. Com. (1977). Can. Assn. for Info. Sci.: Conf. Secy. (1980). Inst. of Prof. Libn. of ON: VP (1975–76). Toronto Pub. Libs. Citizen's Adv. Com.: North-end Com. (1976). Deer Park South Residents' Assn.: Bd. of Dirs. (1976). English-Speaking Un. of Can. Bootmakers of Toronto. **Honors:** Bootmakers of Toronto, True Davidson Meml. Awd. for Excellence, 1977; Beta Phi Mu, 1966. **Activities:** 1, 5; 20, 34, 46; 56, 63, 92 **Addr.:** Library, Ontario Institute for Studies in Education, 252 Bloor St. W., Toronto, ON M5S 1V6, Canada.

Campbell, Mary Joan (Ag. 18, 1920, Winnipeg, MB) Emeritus, Univ. of IL, 1980; Asst. Dir. for Tech. Srvs., Univ. of IL Med. Ctr. Lib., 1971–80; Acq. Libn., 1955–71, Catlgr./Ref. Libn., 1950–71; Libn., St. Luke's Hosp. Sch. of Nursing, 1948–50; Cat./Ref. Libn., Univ. of MB. Lib., 1946–48. **Educ.:** Univ. of MB, 1937–41, BA (Eng., Fr.); McGill Univ., 1945–46, BLS; Univ. of Chicago, 1960–62, MA (LS). **Orgs.:** Med. LA: Intl. Ed. (1973–); Nom. Com. (1973); Midwest Reg. Grp.: Exec. Com. (1962–64); Nom. Com. (Ch. 1965). SLA, IL Chap.: Memb. Com. (1960–62). Chicago Lib. Club, Pres. (1971–72). Univ. of IL, Med. Ctr. Senate: Honorary Degrees Com. (Ch. 1973–76); Com. on Com. (Ch. 1977–78); Educ. Policy Com. (1978–); Acad. Frdm. & Tenure Com. (1978–). **Honors:** Med. LA: Murray Gottlieb Hist. of Med. Essay Awd., 1976. **Pubns.:** "Health Library Science," *Comparative and International Library Science* (1977); "Development of Criteria and Procedures for Appointment, Promotion and Tenure of Library Faculty in an Academic Health Sciences Library," *Bltn. Med. LA* (Ja. 1977); column "International Notes," *Med. LA News* (1973–). **Activities:** 1; 15, 17, 20; 58, 80, 87 **Addr.:** 401 W. Fullerton, # 1602, Chicago, IL 60614.

Campbell, Mary Katherine (Ag. 13, 1943, Mineral Wells, TX) Educ. Libn., Hardin-Simmons Univ., 1971–; Dir. of Lib., Philippine Baptist Theo. Semy., Baguio City, Philippines, 1968–70; Tchr., Allison Elem. Sch., 1965–68. **Educ.:** Hardin-Simmons Univ., 1961–65, BS (Elem. Ed/Special Ed.); Univ. of TX, 1968, 1970–71, MLS. **Orgs.:** ALA. TX LA. XXI Club: Pres. (1978–80). AAUW. Kappa Delta Pi. First Baptist Church, Abilene, TX: Church Libn. (1975–77). **Activities:** 1, 14-Church Library; 15, 20, 21, 39; 63 **Addr.:** 1010 Mulberry, Abilene, TX 79601.

Campbell, Nina S. (Anselmo, NE) Assoc. Dir., IN Univ. Sch. of Med. Lib., 1978–, Asst. Libn. and Dir. of Info. Srvs.; Ref. Libn.; Catlgr., 1951–78; Chld. Libn., Shreve Meml. Pub. Lib., 1948–49; Catlgr., CO State Coll. of Educ., 1943–46; Catlgr., TX Coll. of Arts and Industries, 1942–43; Asst. Libn., NM State Tchrs. Coll., 1941–42. **Educ.:** Univ. of NE, 1933–37, BS with Distinction (Educ.); Univ. of Denver, 1940–41, BSLS with Honors; CO State Coll. of Educ., 1943–46, MA (Educ.). **Orgs.:** Med. LA: Exch. Com. (1973–76). Midwest Chap., Med. LA. PEO. **Pubns.:** Jt. auth., "The Indiana Biomedical Information Program," *Bull. Med. Libr. Ass.* (Ja. 1970); Jt. ed., *InU-M Library Newsletter.* **Activities:** 12; 17, 39; 80 **Addr.:** Indiana University, School of Medicine Library, 1100 West Michigan St., Indianapolis, IN 46223.

Campbell, Sally S. (F. 12, 1934, Santa Ana, CA) Info. Mgr., Bank of HI, 1977–; Catlgr., HI Loa Coll., 1977; Libn., Milton Roy Co., 1973–75. **Educ.:** Whittier Coll., 1951–55, BA (Soc. Psy.); Univ. of FL, 1969–70, Cert. (LS, AV); Univ. of HI, 1976–77, MLS. **Orgs.:** SLA: Hawaiian Pac. Treas. (1979–80); Secy. (1980–81). HI LA. HI Econ. Assn.: Treas. (1978–81). Univ. of HI Grad. Sch. of LS Alum. Assn.: Pres.-Elect (1980–81); Pres. (1981–82). **Activities:** 12; 17, 20, 44; 59 **Addr.:** Bank of Hawaii Information Center, P.O. Box 2900, Honolulu, HI 96846.

Campbell, Stuart W. (Jl. 30, 1944, Dayton, KY) Asst. Archvst., Clark Univ., 1978–; Asst. Prof., Archvst., Mercyhurst Coll., 1973–78; Visit. Instr., Hist., Sweet Briar Coll., 1972–73. **Educ.:** Kenyon Coll., 1962–66, BA (Hist.); Univ. of DE, 1968, MA (U.S. Hist.), 1978, PhD, (U.S. Hist.); Natl. Arch., 1978, Cert. (Introduction to Mod. Arch. Admin.); Case West. Rsv. Univ., 1979, Cert. (Advnc. Wkshp. in Higher Educ. Arch.). **Orgs.:** SAA. New Eng. Archvsts. Mid. Atl. Reg. Archvsts. Conf. PA Hist. Assn.: Bd. (1975–78). Natl. Hist. Pubns. and Recs. Comsn.: PA Adv. Bd. (1976–78). Org. of Amer. Histns. **Pubns.:** Jt. auth., "H.B. Gantt and the Bancrofts," *Bus. Hist. Review* (Spr. 1972); ed., *Jnl. of Erie Std.* (1973–78). **Activities:** 2; 17, 38, 45; 55, 67, 92 **Addr.:** Clark University Archives, 950 Main St., Worcester, MA 01610.

Campbell, Winifred (Jl. 15, 1918, Cleveland, OH) Catlgr., Andover-Harvard Theo. Lib., Harvard Dvnty. Sch., 1974–; Catlgr., Widener Lib., Harvard Univ., 1966–74; Catlgr., Haverford Coll. Lib., 1964–66; Sub. Catlgr., Swarthmore, 1964. **Educ.:** Radcliffe Coll., 1935–39, AB (Gvt.); Columbia Univ., 1939–41, BS (LS). **Orgs.:** ATLA: Bibl. Systs. Com. (1979–81). **Addr.:** Andover-Harvard Theological Library, Divinity School, 45 Francis Ave., Cambridge, MA 02138.

Camper-Titsingh, Mary Elisabeth (O. 11, 1924, Monheim, Rhineland, Germany) Mgr., Investment Resrch. Lib., The Ford Fndn., 1971–; Prog. Staff member, The Choate Fndn., 1964–65. **Educ.:** Lake Forest Coll., 1966–69, BA (Pol. Sci.); Columbia Univ., 1970–71, MS (LS); Sems., Pratt Inst. & CUNY Grad. School, 1973, 1976. **Orgs.:** SLA: Coord., Intl. Rel. Com. (1973); NY Chap. Nom. Com. (1976); Soc. Sci. Plng. Grp. (1979), Treas., 1980. Amer. for Dem. Action: Exec. Com., Natl. Bd. of Dirs. (1970), Natl. Bd. of Dirs. (1966–76). Chicago Child Care Soc.: Bd. of Mgrs. (1966–68). **Pubns.:** Contrib., *Business Roles in Economic Development,* (1979). **Activities:** 3, 12; 17, 39, 41; 59, 95-corp. soc. responsibility. **Addr.:** 35 East 35th St., New York, NY 10016.

Campese, Michael Angelo A. (Ja. 24, 1953, Chicago, IL) Lib. Dir., St. Elizabeth's Hosp., Belleville, IL, 1977–; Libn., Deaconess Hosp., 1977. **Educ.:** Univ. of Evansville, 1971–75, BA (Hist., Pol. Sci.); IN Univ., 1975–76, MLS. **Orgs.:** Areawide Hosp. Lib. Cnsrtm. of Southwest. IL: Past Coord. (1978–79); Past Proj. Ch. (1979–80). Midwest Hlth. Sci. Lib. Netwk.: Governing Bd., IL Rep. Med. LA. IL Pub. Lib. Syst./Illinet. **Pubns.:** "Adopt-a-journal," *Bltn. of the Med. LA* (Ap. 1979). **Activities:** 5, 12; 17, 24, 41; 80, 87 **Addr.:** Health Science Library, St. Elizabeth's Hospital, 211 S. 3rd St., Belleville, IL 62221.

Campion, Carol-Mae Sack (Ap. 8, 1950, Atlantic City, NJ) Head Libn., Lackawanna Jr. Coll., 1977–; Proj. Libn., White Haven Ctr., 1976–77; Libn., Mid-Valley Jr. High, 1974–75; Libn., Bishop O'Hara HS, 1973–74. **Educ.:** Georgetown Univ., 1968–72, BA (Hist.); Rutgers Univ., 1972–73, MLS; Univ. of Scranton, 1979–81, MA (Hist.). **Orgs.:** ALA. PA LA. EFLA. Altrusa Intl. Young Women's Christ. Assn. **Activities:** 1; 15, 17, 39; 59, 66, 77 **Addr.:** 1041 N. Webster Ave., Scranton, PA 18510.

Campion, Serge G. (Ap. 25, 1942, Mont-Louis, Gaspe, PQ, Can) Chief Libn., Transport Can. Lib. and Info. Ctr., 1976–; Info. Sci., Transport Can., 1975–76; Search Ed., Can. Inst. for Sci. and Tech. Info., 1971–75; Officer-Inst., Can. Forces Fleet Sch., 1967–70. **Educ.:** Univ. de Sherbrooke, 1960–65, BEd (Physics, Math); Univ. of West. ON, 1970–71, MLS. **Orgs.:** Cncl. of Fed. Libs.: Strg. Com. (1977–79). Can. Trans. Resrch. and Info. Srvs.: Ch. (1976–78). **Pubns.:** "Demonstration of Multi-File Interactive Searching for Transportation Information," *Spec. Libs.* (1977); "Examination of the principles of selection", *Intl. Road Resrch. Docu. Working Rules* (1977); "Banques de données et diffusion sélective de l'information en sciences pures et appliquées," *Stage prat. en inf. doc.* (1974). **Activities:** 4, 12; 17; 75, 94 **Addr.:** Chief Librarian, Transport Canada Library and Information Centre, 2A Transport Canada Building, Place de Ville, Ottawa, ON K1A 0N5 Canada.

Candelmo, Emily T. (Jl. 31, 1948, Brooklyn, NY) Lib., Consult., TAMS Engin. & Archit., 1973–; Libn., NY Christ. Acad., 1972–73; Catlgr., Consult., Bd. of Coop. Educ. Srvs., Nassau Educ. Resrc. Ctr., 1972. **Educ.:** Suffolk Cmnty. Coll., 1966–68, AA, (Hist.); Hofstra Univ., 1968–70, BA (Hist.); St. John's Univ. (NY), 1970–72, MLS. **Orgs.:** SLA. LS Socty. of St. John's Univ.: Past Pres. St. John's Univ. LS Alum. **Pubns.:** Ed., *Catalog of the Documentation Center-Inter-African Committee for Hydraulics Studies* (1977); Jt. ed., *Thesaurus des Termes des Ressources en Eau et des Terres/Thesaurus of Water & Land Resources Terms.* (1979); Cmplr., "Bibliography Savannah Regional Water Resources & Land Use," NTIS (1979). **Activities:** 12; 20, 24, 39; 54, 62, 64 **Addr.:** TAMS Engineers & Architects, 655 Third Avenue, New York, NY 10017.

Canelas, Dale Brunelle (Ja. 13, 1938, Chicago, IL) Assoc. Dir. of Pub. Srvs., Stanford Univ., 1975–; Asst. Univ. Libn. for Admin. Srvs., Northwestern Univ., 1971–75; Budget and Plng. Ofcr., 1969–71; Asst. Dir./Act. Dir., Palatine Pub. Lib., 1967–69. **Educ.:** Loyola Univ., Chicago, 1956–60, BS (Span., Hist. & Eng.); Rosary Coll., 1965–66, MA (LS); Cert.: Lib. Admin. Dev. Prog., 1971; Universidad Nacional Autónoma de México, 1958–59. **Orgs.:** ALA: Com. on Org., Ch. (1973–74); Com. on Accred.; Visiting Teams (1973–79); ACRL: *Col. and Resrch. Libs.* Ed. Bd. (1975, 1976, 1977–80); LAMA/Lib. Admin. Div.: Pres./Pres.-Elect (1978–80); Persnl. Admin. Sect.; Bd., ch. (1974–76); Frdm. to Read Fndn.: VP (1977–78); Resrch. Libs. Grp.: Pub. Srvs. Com. (1979–p.). Northwestern Univ.: Fac. Club Bd. of Trustees; VP (1975). Stanford Univ.: Acad. Cncl. Com. on Libs., Secy. (1979–p.). Univ. Lib. Cncl. (1975–p). **Pubns.:** "Task Analysis of Library Jobs in the State of Illinois: A Working Paper on the Relevance of the Study to Academic Libraries," *ERIC/CLIS* (1971); Jt. auth., "Guidelines for Staff Development," *Lib. Trends* (July 1971); reviews. **Activities:** 1; 17, 25, 35; 74, 75 **Addr.:** Green Library - Director's Office, Stanford University, Stanford, CA 94305.

Special Subjects/Services: 50. Adult educ.; 51. Advert./Mktg.; 52. Aerosp.; 53. Agric.; 54. Area std.; 55. Arts/Hum.; 56. Autom.; 57. Bibl./Prtg.; 58. Bio. sci.; 59. Bus./Fin.; 60. Chem.; 61. Copyrt.; 62. Documtn.; 63. Educ.; 64. Engin.; 65. Env.; 66. Eth. grps.; 67. Film; 68. Food/Nutr.; 69. Geneal.; 70. Geo.; 71. Geol.; 72. Handcpd.; 73. Hist.; 74. Int. frdm.; 75. Info. sci.; 76. Insr.; 77. Law; 78. Legis.; 79. Math./Comp. sci.; 80. Med.; 81. Metals; 82. Nat. resrcs.; 83. Newsp.; 84. Nuc. sci.; 85. Oral hist.; 86. Petr./Energy; 87. Pharm.; 88. Phys./Astr./Math.; 89. Readg.; 90. Relig.; 91. Sci./Tech.; 92. Soc. sci.; 93. Telecom.; 94. Transp.; 95. (other).

Canevari, Donna Adeline (Jl. 6, 1951, Bridgeport, CT) Libn. II, Univ. of SK, 1974. **Educ.:** Skidmore Coll., 1969–73, BA (Hist.); Columbia Univ., 1973–74, MS (LS). **Orgs.:** ALA. Bibl. Socty. of Can. Can. LA: Int. Frdm. Com. (Monitor, 1980–82). SK LA: Cnclr. (1978–80); SK Lib. Week (Conv., 1978–79); Int. Frdm. Com. (Conv., 1979–). Amer. Assn. for the Advnc. of Slavic Std.: Com. on Bibl. and Documtn. (1979–). Can. Assn. Slavists: Slavic Libns. Com. (1979–). Univ. of SK Fac. Assn.: Exec. (1980–82); Com. on the Status of Women Acads. (Conv., 1977–). **Pubns.:** "The Left Book Club," *Notable Works and Cols.* (Je. 1978); ed., *Notable Works and Cols.* (1975–77); contrib. ed., *Notable Works and Cols.* (1977–); "Russian Futurism, 1910–1916: Poetry and Manifestoes," *Notable Works and CoL.* (Je. 1981). **Activities:** 1; 15; 54, 66, 74 **Addr.:** Main Library–Collection Development, University of Saskatchewan, Saskatoon, SK S7N 0W0 Canada.

Cann, Sharon Lee (Ag. 14, 1935, Ft. Riley, KS) Hlth. Sci. Libn., Woodruff Hlth. Sci. Lib., 1977–. **Educ.:** Sacramento State Univ., 1957–59, BA (Soc. Sci.); Atlanta Univ., 1976–77, MSLS; Med. LA, 1978, Cert. **Orgs.:** GA Hlth. Sci. LA: Ch. (1981–82). GA LA: Spec. Lib. Sec. (Secy.–Treas., 1978–79). Atlanta Hlth. Sci. Lib. Cnsrtm.: Ch. (1979). ALA. Med. LA. Various other orgs. Sacramento State Univ. Alumni Assn.: Bd. (1959–60). **Activities:** 12; 20, 32, 39; 58, 80, 87 **Addr.:** Woodruff Health Science Library, Northside Hospital, 1000 Johnson Ferry Rd., N.E., Atlanta, GA 30042.

Cannici, Peter (D. 2, 1908, Schenectady, NY) Retired, 1971–; Supt. of Schs., Passaic Pub. Schs., 1964–71; Prin., Passaic Sr. HS, 1959–64, Tchr., 1931–63. **Educ.:** Tusculum Coll., 1927–31, BA, hons.; Rutgers Univ., 1941, MEd (Admin., Supvsn.), DED (Equivalency). **Orgs.:** Passaic Pub. Lib. Bd. of Trustees: Pres. (1974–). NJ Lib. Trustee Assn.: Pres. (1975–78). **Orgs.:** ALA: Staff Com. on Arbit., Mediation and Inquiry; ALTA, Task Frc. Persnl. Policies and Pracs. (Ch., 1980–81); Speakers' Bur. (1976–). Various other confs. NJ Legis. Task Frc.: Lib. Legis. (1980–). **Honors:** NJ LA, NJ Trustee of the Yr., 1978; Cham. of Cmrce., Man of the Yr., 1964; *Clifton Leader* (newsp.), Man of the Yr., 1979. **Pubns.:** "A Trustee Dreams: Let There Be Libraries," *The Pub. Lib. Trustee* (S.–D. 1980); ed., *NJ Lib. Trustee Assn. Nsltr.* (1974–78). **Activities:** 9, 10; 24, 35, 47; 74, 78, 89 **Addr.:** 212 Howard Ave., Passaic, NJ 07055.

Canning, Bonnie (O. 4, 1948, Pensacola, FL) VP, Micronet, Inc., 1978–; Info. Coord., Nat. Micrographics Assn., 1976–78; Asst. to Dir., Microform Div., Greenwood Pr., 1975–76; Nat. Educ. Prog. Assoc., 1970–72. **Educ.:** George Washington Univ., 1967–70, BA (Chinese); Univ. of MD, 1973–75, MLS. **Orgs.:** Nat. Micrographics Assn.: Secy., Natl. Capitol Chap. (1979–80). Annual Conf. Prog. Com. (1979–80). SLA: Cont. Educ. Sem. Instr., (1978–79). Info. Industries Assn. **Honors:** Beta Phi Mu, 1976; Phi Kappa Phi, 1976. **Pubns.:** *Micrographics: Its Relation to Other Information Handling Technologies,* (1979); Ed., *Micrographics Index,* (1976–79); *A Report on Library & Information Science Education in the United States,* (1975); "Micrographics Speeds Information Handling," *The Office* (S. 1977). **Activities:** 5, 12; 17, 30, 33; 56 **Addr.:** Micronet, Inc., 2551 Virginia Avenue, N.W., Washington, DC 20037.

Cannon, Carl F., Jr. (Ag. 21, 1928, Newport News, VA) Asst. Libn., U.S. Army Transp. Tech. Info. and Resrch. Ctr., 1979–; Circ. Libn., U.S. Armed Forces Staff Coll., 1974–79; Mgr., Info. Srvs. Dept., Newport News Shipbuilding, 1963–74; Dir., Greensboro Hist. Musm., 1961–63. **Educ.:** Mars Hill Coll., 1951–52, AA (Hist.); Duke Univ., 1952–54, AB (US Hist.), 1954–57, MA (Hist.). **Orgs.:** SLA: Gvt. Rel. Com. (1963–73); VA Chap. (Pres., 1974–75); Consult. Com. (Ch., 1969–74). Amer. Recs. Mgt. Assn. SELA. Amer. Mgt. Assn. **Activities:** 12; 17, 22, 46 **Addr.:** U.S. Army Transportation Technical Information and Research Center, DAC-ET-L, U.S. Army Transportation School, Fort Eustis, VA 23604.

Cannon, Ruth M. Eggleston (Ag. 8, 1923, Brookneal, VA) Libn., Fed. Resrv. Bank of Richmond, 1962–; Libn., U.S. Army, Quartermaster Corp., 1958–62; Chld. Libn., Richmond Pub. Lib., 1952–58. **Educ.:** Longwood Coll., 1946–49, BA (Hist.); Univ. of NC, 1950–52, BSLS **Orgs.:** SLA: VA Chap. (Pres., 1966–67); Dir. (1978–79); Bus. & Finance Div. (Ch., 1975–76). VA LA: Secy. (1962–65). **Activities:** 4, 9; 17, 21; 59 **Addr.:** Research Library, Federal Reserve Bank of Richmond, P.O. Box 27622, Richmond, VA 23261.

Cantone, Sister Paschal Marie, O.S.F. (Jl. 4, 1912, Johnston, RI) Med. Libn., St. Francis Hospital, Inc., 1974–; Med. Libn., St. Francis Hosp. Med. Ctr., Trenton, NJ, 1964–74; Nurses Lib., St. Joseph Hosp. Sch. of Nursing, Philadelphia, PA, 1949–54. **Educ.:** Sch. of Nursing, St. Joseph Hospital, Providence, RI, 1930–33, Dipl. (Nursing); Villanova Univ., Catholic Univ., Rutgers Univ.; attended Lib. Wkshps. given by Amer. Hosp. Assn., Col. of Physicians in Philadelphia, and Med. LA. (General Educ., Nursing, Mgt., LS.). **Orgs.:** DE LA. Med. LA. Cath. LA: Ch., Philadelphia Cath. LA Hosp. Sect. Trenton Med. LA: Secy. (1970). **Activities:** 12; 17, 20, 39; 63, 80 **Addr.:** St. Francis Hospital Library, 7th & Clayton Sts., Wilmington, DE 19805.

Canuti, Teresa D. (Jl. 8, 1950, Westfield, NY) Dir., Dansville Pub. Lib., 1976–; Dir., Mt. Morris Pub. Lib., 1973–76. **Educ.:** State Univ. Coll., Geneseo, 1968–72, BA (Eng.); Sch. of Lib. & Info. Sci., Geneseo, 1975, MLS. **Orgs.:** NY LA. ALA. **Activities:** 9; 15, 17 **Addr.:** Dansville Public Library, 200 Main St., Dansville, NY 14437.

Cao, Jerry (Madisonville, KY) Asst. Prof., Sch. of Lib. and Info. Mgt., Univ. of South. CA, 1975–; Sr. Libn., TRW Syst. Grp., 1972–75; Head, Govt. Docus. Dept., Univ. of IA, 1966–68; Cat. Libn., Univ. of IA, 1965–66; Univ. of South. CA, 1965–65. **Educ.:** Loma Linda Univ., La Sierra Campus, 1960–64, BA (Hist.); Univ. of South, CA, 1964–65, MSLS, 1968–78, PhD (LibSci). **Orgs.:** ALA. SLA. Various other orgs. AAUP. **Honors:** U.S. Office of Educ., Flwshp., 1968–71; San Bernardino Cnty. Lib., Schol., 1965. **Pubns.:** "Managing the Technical Library," *Current Concepts in Lib. Mgt.* (1979). **Activities:** 12, 14-Lib. Educ.; 20, 29, 30; 52, 64, 91 **Addr.:** 2211 Wanderer Dr., San Pedro, CA 90732.

Caparros, Ilona Siren (F. 2, 1937, Newport, NH) Head, Micro. Dept., Alexander Lib., Rutgers Univ., 1980–; Asst. Head, Tech. Srvs., Rutgers Univ., 1973–80; Reclassification Proj. Libn., Newark State Coll., 1972–73; Tech. Srvs. Libn., Plymouth State Coll., 1966–72; Catlgr., Harvard Univ., 1960–66. **Educ.:** Univ. of NH, 1955–59, BA (Eng. Lit.); Simmons Coll., 1961–63, MSLS; Univ. of MI, 1959–60 (Msc. Ed.). **Orgs.:** NY Tech. Srvs. Libns.: Mem. Com. Ch. (1979–80); Secy.-Treas. (1978–79). ALA: ACRL; RSTD; RASD; GODORT. Citizens Leag. of Elizabeth, NJ: Treas. (1979–80), Nsltr. Ed. (1979–80). **Activities:** 1; 17, 39, 46 **Addr.:** 825 N. Broad St., Elizabeth, NJ 07208.

Capitani, Cheryl A. (My. 29, 1946, Pittsburgh, PA) Dir., Lib., Media Srvs., Harrisburg Hosp., 1980–; Asst. Libn., Ref., PA State Univ., Coll. of Med., The Milton S. Hershey Med. Ctr., 1978–80; Info. Retrieval Spec., Soc. Sci. Info. Util. Lab. GSPIA Lib., Univ. of Pittsburgh, 1978; Lib. Evening and Weekend Supvsr., West. Psyt. Inst. and Clinic Lib., 1977–78; Elem. Sch., Remedial Readg. Tchr., Bd. of Educ., Columbus, Pickerton, OH, 1968–75. **Educ.:** OH Univ., 1968, BS; OH Dominican Coll., 1975, Cert. (Educ. Media); Univ. of Pittsburgh, 1978, MLS; various crs., wkshps. **Orgs.:** ALA: RASD/Machine-Assisted Ref. Sect. (1977–78). Ctrl. PA Hlth. Sci. LA: Nom. Com. (1979–80). Med. LA. SLA: Cntrl. PA Prov. Chap., Nom. Com. (1979–80), OLUG (Ch., 1979–). PA State Univ. Lib. Fac. Org.: Assoc. Mem. (1979–80). **Pubns.:** Jt. auth., "A Medical Library's Response to Three Mile Island," *Bltn. Med. LA* (Ap. 1980). **Activities:** 14-Hosp.; 17, 32, 39; 80 **Addr.:** Library/Media Services, Hospital Library, Harrisburg Hospital, S. Front St., Harrisburg, PA 17101.

Caponio, Joseph F. (Mr. 25, 1926, Canton, MA) Deputy Dir., Dept. of Commerce Natl. Techn. Info. Srv., 1979–; Actg. Deputy Dir., Environmental Data & Info. Srv., 1978–79; Dir., Environmental Sci. Info. Ctr., 1974–78; Actg. Dir., Natl. Agric. Lib., 1973–74. **Educ.:** St. Anselm's Coll., 1947–51, BA (Chem.); Georgetown Univ., 1951–59, PhD (Chem.). **Orgs.:** Natl. Sci. Fndn.: Sci. Info. Cncl. (1972); Info. Anal. Ctrs. (Ch.). ASIS: Pub. Affairs Com. (Ch., 1977–); Potomac Valley Chap. (Pres., 1974–75); Washington Update, ASIS Bltn (Ed., 1977–). Fed. Lib. Com.: Exec. Adv. Com. (1974–79). FAO/IOC/UN–Aquatic Sci. & Fisheries Info. Syst.: Panel of Experts (Ch., 1974–). **Pubns.:** "ASFIS–International Info. Sys.," *Jnl. Sea Tech.* (1978); "AGRIS–Intl. System in Agr. Science", *Science* (1975); Cain: The Natl. Agri. Library Data Base for the Agricultural Sciences, (1974); Various articles. **Activities:** 4; 17; 58, 75 **Addr.:** 8417 Ft. Hunt Rd., Alexandria, VA 22308.

Capoor, Asha (Jl. 24, 1941, Ajmer, Raj, India) Dir., Tech. Srvs., Baker and Taylor Co., 1976–, Mgr., Bibl. Cntrl., 1976–81; Supvsr., Wkly. Rec., R. R. Bowker, 1973–76. **Educ.:** Rajasthan Univ., India, 1958–60, BA (Hist.), 1960–62, MA (Hist.); Pratt Inst., 1970–72, MLS. **Orgs.:** ASIS: Mem. Com. (Ch., 1980–). SLA: SLA/ASIS Liasion (1980–). NJ Tech. Libn. Assn.: Pres.-Elect (1980–). ALA. **Honors:** Rajasthan Univ., Flwshp., 1964. **Activities:** 1, 9; 15, 17, 20; 56, 75 **Addr.:** The Baker & Taylor Co., 6 Kirby Ave., Somerville, NJ 08876.

Caputo, Anne Spencer (Ja. 14, 1947, Eugene, OR) Visit. Asst. Prof., Cath. Univ. Grad. Dept. of Lib. and Info. Sci., 1978–; Online Consult., Self Employed, 1977–; Info. Syst. Anal., Lockheed Info. Syst., 1976–; Micro. Libn., San Jose State Univ., 1971–76. **Educ.:** Lewis and Clark Coll., 1965–69, BA (Hist.); San Jose State Univ., 1973–76, MALS; Univ. of OR, 1969–70, (Archit. Hist.). **Orgs.:** ALA. ASIS. SLA. AALS. Phi Alpha Theta. Phi Kappa Delta. **Honors:** Beta Phi Mu, Outstan. Grad., 1976. **Pubns.:** Jt. auth., *Brief Guide to DIALOG Searching* (1976); *Microform Collections in the Libraries of the California State University and Colleges* (1976). **Addr.:** 5314 26th Road North, Arlington, VA 22207.

Caputo, Janette S. (N. 16, 1946, Detroit, MI) Dir., Saginaw Hlth. Sci. Lib., 1981–; Sci. Libn., Wayne State Univ., 1977–81; Dir. of Libs., St. Joseph Mercy Hosp., Pontiac, Mich., 1973–77, Chief Med. Libn., 1971–73; Med. Libn., Metro. Hosp., Detroit, 1970–71; Serials Libn., Univ. Detroit Dental Lib., 1969–70. **Educ.:** Wayne State Univ., 1964–68, BA (Psy., Eng.), 1968–69, MSLS, 1973–76, PhD (Instr. Tech.); Med. LA, Cert., 1971. **Orgs.:** SLA: MI Chap., Contin. Educ. Com. (1979–). Med. LA: Exec. Com. (1971–), Contin. Educ. Com. of Hosp. Libs. Grp. (1976–), Hlth. Sci. AV Grp., pres.-elect (1976–77); Consult. Ed. *MLA Bulletin* (1977–). MI LA. Amer. Socty. for Engin. Educ. Elephant Interest Grp. AAAS. **Pubns.:** Jt. auth., "P.A.I.R.: A Cooperative Effort to Meet Information Needs," *Bltn. of the Med. LA* (1973); Jt. auth., "The Concept of the Three-Way Marriage: Librarians, Media Specialists, and Educators," *Bltn. of the MI Chap. of the SLA* (1973); "Teaching Library Skills," *Hosp. Progress* (1974); "Behavior Modification and the Nursing Process," *Perspectives in Psyt. Care* (1975); *A Program Guide to the Use of Index Medicus* (1977); other articles, various oral presentations. **Activities:** 1, 12; 17, 24, 25; 59, 80, 91 **Addr.:** Saginaw Sciences Library, 1000 Houghton, Saginaw, MI 48602.

Carbery, Mance G. (Ag. 3, 1933, Toronto, ON) Admin. Mgr., Pubns. Serv., ON Mnstry. of Govt. Servs., 1979–; Sr. Cat. Libn., Bibl. Servs., 1977–79; Chief Libn., ON Mnstry. of Revenue, 1973–77; Asst. Head Libn., ON Mnstry. of the Environment, 1971–73. **Educ.:** Univ. of Toronto, 1951–55, BA (Eng.); Ryerson Polytechnical Inst. 1970–72 (LS). **Orgs.:** Can. LA. ON LA: Govt. Docum. Com. Index. and Abs. Socty. of Can. ON Govt. Libns. Cncl.: Secy. to the Exec. (1973–75); Ch. (1979–80). Alpha Gamma Delta. Jr. Leag. of Toronto. **Pubns.:** Ed., *Ontario Government Publications* (1976, 1977, 1978); Ed., *Catalogue Des Publications En Francais Du Gouvernement De L'Ontario* (1979–80). **Activities:** 13; 20, 29, 37; 57, 62, 78 **Addr.:** Publications Service, Ontario Ministry of Government Services, 880 Bay Street, 5th Floor, Toronto, ON M7A 1N8 Canada.

Cardinal, Robert (My. 20, 1936, Dunham, PQ) Biblgphr., Ctrl. Des Bibs., 1972–; Ref. Libn., Coll. Edouard-Montpetit, 1969–71; Catlgr., Bib. Natl. Du PQ, 1966–69. **Educ.:** Univ. De Sherbrooke, 1956–59, B Ped; Univ. De Montréal, 1971–74, MLS. **Orgs.:** Corp. of Prof. Libns. of PQ. ASTED. **Pubns.:** *Les Bibliothèques Canadiennes À L'Ère De L'Automatisation* (1972); *Le Syndicalisme À La B.N.Q.* (1968); "Le Professionnalisme Et Les Bibliothécaires," *Argus* (1973). **Activities:** 4; 15, 30, 42; 57 **Addr.:** 454 Brixton, St-Lambert, PQ J4P 3A7 Canada.

Carducci, Frances A. (D. 24, 1938, Syracuse, NY) Systs. Anal., Rochester Pub. Lib., 1979–; Head, Circ., Syracuse Univ., 1975–79, Systs. Anal., 1973–75, Acq. Libn., 1970–73. **Educ.:** Syracuse Univ. 1957–61, BS (Bus. Admin.), 1969–70, MSLS; MPA in progress. **Orgs.:** NY LA. ALA: LITA/Info. Sci. and Autom. Sect., Prog. Plng. Com.; LRRT, Cont. Educ. Com. **Activities:** 1, 9; 15, 17, 22; 56, 75, 91 **Addr.:** 12 Blackwatch Trail Apt. #9, Fairport, NY 14450.

Cargill, Jennifer Sue (Jl. 15, 1944, Ruston, LA) Acq. Libn., Miami Univ. Libs., 1974–, Sci. Libn., 1972–74; Hlth. Sci. Libn., Univ. of Houston Libs., 1969–72, Asst. Acq. Libn., 1967–68. **Educ.:** LA Tech Univ., 1962–65, BA (Hist.); LA State Univ., 1965–67, MS (LS); Exec. Dev. Prog. for Lib. Admin., 1975, Cert. Miami Univ. Sch. of Bus. Admin.; Miami Univ., 1972–75, MEd (Higher Educ. Admin.); Miami Admin. Fellow Prog. Intern, 1977–78. **Orgs.:** ALA: Ref. and Subscription Books Review Com. (1977–81); ACRL; RTSD; LITA. SLA: Treas., TX Chap. (1970). OHIONET Acq. Cncl. Phi Kappa Phi. LA Hist. Assn. Univ. of Houston Fac. Sen. (1971–72). Miami Univ., Ch., Affirmative Action Adv. Com. (1978–79). **Pubns.:** Jt. auth., *Keeping Track of What You Spend* (1981); Jt. Auth., *Practical Approval Plan Management* (1979); Jt. Complr. *Technical Services Staff Director for Academic Libraries: Indiana-Kentucky-Ohio, 1978/79* (1978); Jt. Auth., "Inventory and Selection Techniques for Large Unorganized Collections", *Lib. Acq.: Practice and Theory,* (1978); "Bridging the Gap Between Acquisitions and Public Services: One Approach", *Lib. Acq.: Practice and Theory,* (1979). Other articles. **Activities:** 1; 15, 17, 38; 56 **Addr.:** 209 South Main, Oxford, OH 45056.

Carlen, IHM, Claudia (Jl. 24, 1906, Detroit, MI) Admin. Asst. to the Rector, St. John's Prov. Semy., 1979–, Libn., 1972–79; Lib. Consult., North American Coll. Grad. Div. (Rome), 1971–72; Assoc. Libn., Marygrove Coll., 1970–71; Managing Ed., Corpus Dictionary Prog., 1969–70; Index Ed., Theo. Resrcs., 1968–70; Index Ed., *New Cath. Encyc.,* 1963–67; Libn., Marygrove Coll., 1944–69. **Educ.:** Marygrove Coll., 1924–26, (Rom. Lang.); Univ. of MI, 1926–28, ABLS, 1936–38, AMLS; Univ. of Chicago, 1953; Natl. Arch., 1971; Case Western Reserve Univ., 1976; Univ. of MT, Inst. on Scholarly Pubshg., 1977. **Orgs.:** ALA: Cncl. (1958–61; 1968–71); Cath. LA: Pres. (1965–67). SAA. Amer. Socty. of Indxrs. Other orgs. The Pope Speaks: Adv. Bd. (1963–). Wayne State Univ. Press: Hilberry Publication Jury (1963–64). Marygrove Coll. Bd. of Trustees: VP (1977–79). Other orgs. **Honors:** Phi Beta Kappa, 1928; Beta Phi Mu, 1955; Univ. of MI, Sch. of LS, Disting. Alum. Awd., 1974; Cath. LA, honorary Life Membership, 1978. **Pubns.:** *Guide to the Encyclicals* (1939); *Guide to the Documents of Pius XII* (1951); *Dictionary of Papal Pronouncements* (1958); "Catholic Bibliographical Sources," *Catholic Bookman's Manual* (1961); "State of the Art Survey: Reference Sources in Religion and Philosophy." *Reference Services Review* (Ap./Je. 1978); Other articles. **Activities:** 1, 2; 17, 30, 41; 57, 63, 90 **Addr.:** Marygrove College Library, Detroit, MI 48221.

Carlson, Denise Eileen (Ap. 1, 1949, St. Paul, MN) Ref. Libn., James J. Hill Ref. Lib., 1975–. **Educ.:** Univ. of MN,

PROFESSIONAL ACTIVITIES: Institutions: 1. Acad. lib.; 2. Arch.; 3. Assn.; 4. Fed./Gvt. lib.; 5. Inst. lib.; 6. Mfr./Suppl.; 7. Milit. lib.; 8. Musm.; 9. Pub. lib.; 10. Sch. lib.; 11. Sch. of lib. sci.; 12. Spec. lib.; 13. State lib.; 14. (other). **Functions/Activities:** 15. Acq./Col. dev.; 16. Adult srvs.; 17. Admin.; 18. Apprais.; 19. Archit./Bldgs.; 20. Cat./Class.; 21. Chld. srvs.; 22. Circ.; 23. Cons./Pres.; 24. Consult.; 25. Cont. ed.; 26. Educ. lib. sci.; 27. Ext. srvs.; 28. Fund/Grants; 29. Gvt. pubs.; 30. Indx./Abs.; 31. Instr. lib. use; 32. Media srvs.; 33. Micro.; 34. Netwks./Coop.; 35. Persnl.; 36. PR; 37. Publshg.; 38. Recs. mgt.; 39. Ref. srvs.; 40. Repro.; 41. Resrch.; 42. Review.; 43. Secur.; 44. Serials; 45. Spec. col.; 46. Tech. srvs.; 47. Trustees/Bds.; 48. YA srvs.; 49. (other).

1967–71, BA (Soclgy.), 1973–76, MA (LS). **Orgs.:** MN LA. MN OLUG. SLA. Parent-Tchr.-Student Assn. **Pubns.:** Various bus. bk. reviews, *St. Paul Pioneer Press* (1981). **Activities:** 12; 20, 39, 42; 59, 92, 94 **Addr.:** James J. Hill Reference Library, 80 W. 4th St., St. Paul, MN 55102.

Carlson, Karen R. (O. 5, 1950, Springfield, MA) Asst. Ed., Wilson Lib. Bltn., 1979–; Catlgr., H.W. Wilson Co., 1973–79. **Educ.:** Wheaton Coll., Norton MA 1968–72, BA (Fr.); Columbia Univ., 1972–73, MLS. **Orgs.:** ALA: YASD/TV Com. (1978–80); JMRT/Affiliates Cncl. (1976–79), Exec. Bd. NY LA: Exhibits Com. (1978–); JMRT. New York Lib. Club. Women's Natl. Book Assn. Wheaton Club of New York. **Pubns.:** Jt. ed., *Senior High School Library Catalog* (1977). **Activities:** 6, 9; 20, 37, 48; 63 **Addr.:** Wilson Library Bulletin, 950 University Ave., Bronx, NY 10452.

Carlson, Patricia T. (N. 4, 1932, Oakland, CA) Head Libn., South. CA Coll. of Optometry, 1975–. **Educ.:** Stanford Univ., 1951–55, AB (Econ.); CA State Univ., Fullerton, 1972–74, MSLS. **Orgs.:** Assn. of Visual Sci. Libns.: Pres.-Elect (1981); Treas. (1979–80). Med. Lib. Grp. of South. CA and AZ: Treas. (1980–82); Nom. Com. (Ch., 1978). Med.-Tech. Libns. of Orange Cnty.: Pres. (1978). **Honors:** Phi Kappa Phi, 1973. **Activities:** 1, 12; 17; 80 **Addr.:** Southern California College of Optometry, 2001 Associated Rd., Fullerton, CA 92631.

Carlson, Rena M. (N. 4, 1898, Simpson, PA) Libn. Emeritus, Clarion State Coll., 1963–, Head Libn., 1929–63; Libn., Wagner Jr. HS, 1928–29; Libn., Reading HS, 1927–28; Libn., HS for Girls, Reading, PA 1925–27; HS Tchr., 1921–24. **Educ.:** Greenville Coll., 1917–21, AB (Eng.); Carnegie Mellon, 1924–25, BSLS; Univ. of MI, 1935–36, AMLS; various crs. **Orgs.:** ALA: Cncl. (1954–56). PA LA: Coll. Sect., Ch. Frnds. of the Lib., Clarion, PA: Pres. (1971–73). Fort Myers FL Frnds. of the Lib. AAUW: Clarion PA Pres. (1969–71). Leag. of Women Voters of Clarion Cnty. PA: Chavrinall-Clarion Cnty. Std. (1968–70). **Honors:** Clarion State Coll., Lib. named Rena M. Carlson Lib., 1964; Delta Kappa Gamma. **Activities:** 1; 17, 21, 31; 63 **Addr.:** 521 Periwinkle Ct., Shell Point Vlg., Fort Myers, FL 33908.

Carlson, Sandra Louise (My. 6, 1947, Bremerton, WA) Coord., Chld. Srvs., Kitsap Reg. Lib., 1976–, Coord., Chld. Prog., 1974–76; Weekend Libn., Olympic Coll., 1972–75; Chld. Libn., Baker Cnty. Lib., 1971–71. **Educ.:** Olympic Coll., 1965–67, AA; West. WA State Coll., 1967–69, BA (Hist.); Univ. of OR, 1969–70, MLS. **Orgs.:** WA LA: Chld. and YA Srvs. (Ch., 1979–80). ALA. Pac. Northwest LA. Puget Sound Cncl. for the Review. of Chld. Media. **Activities:** 9; 21, 31, 48 **Addr.:** Kitsap Regional Library, 1301 Sylvan Way, Bremerton, WA 98310.

Carlsson, Vera R. (S. 9, 1921, Minneapolis, MN) Head, Acq., Univ. of MN Law Lib., 1951–; Libn., Cat. Dept., 1950–51; Libn., Serials Div., Univ. of MN Walter Lib., 1948–49; Jr. Libn., Acq. Dept., 1946–48. **Educ.:** Univ. of MN, 1939–43, BS (Soc. Stud. Educ.), 1945–46, BSLS. **Orgs.:** AALL: Com. on New Mem., Ch. (1956–57); Com. on Rel. with Publ. and Dealers; Ed., Pub. Bltn. (1978–79); Ch., Sub-Com. on Complaints (1977–78); MN Assn. of Law Libs.: Pres., (1967–68). **Honors:** Pi Lambda Theta, 1943; Delta Phi Lambda, 1942. **Activities:** 1; 15 **Addr.:** Law Library, Law Center, 229 19th Ave. South, Minneapolis, MN 55455.

Carmack, Bob (Mr. 15, 1937, Quail, TX) Dean, Lib. Srvs., Univ. of SD, 1979–; Dir. of Libs., 1971–79; Asst. Dir. for Pub. Srvs., Univ. of NE/Lincoln, 1970–71; Undergrad. Libn., 1967–70; Asst. Hum. Libn., 1966–67. **Educ.:** CO State Univ., 1959–65, BA (Hist.); Univ. of Denver, 1965–66, MA (Lib. Sci.); Postmstrs work, Univ. of SD, 1977–. **Orgs.:** ALA: Cncl. (1972–76); ACRL: Legis. Com. (1974–78, 1979–); LAMA AIA/ALA: Ch., Bldgs. Awd. Com. (1979–); LAMA: Ch. Bldgs. & Equipment Sect., 1974–75; Ofc. for Lib. Srv. to the Disadv., Mem., Subcom. on Lib. Srv. for Amer. Indian People (1977–79); various other coms. Mountain Plains LA: Ch., Coll. and Univ. Sect. (1976–77). SD LA: Pres. (1979–80). West. Amer. Lit.; Bibliographic Ctr. for Resrch.: Bd. of Trustees (1972–77); various other orgs. **Pubns.:** Jt. auth., "Population Characteristics of Academic Librarians", *Coll. & Resrch. Libs. News* (My. 1981); "Staff Development Model for I. D. Weeks Library, University of South Dakota,", *Staff Development Model Book: Program Designs for Library Personnel* (1976); "South Dakota Public Documents: Report of a Study," *Gvt. Pubns. Review* (1974); "Library Reserve System - Another Look," *Coll. and Rerch. Libs.* (March, 1970); SD. Interim Public Documents Study Commission. *Report to the 48th Session of the South Dakota Legislative Assembly* (1972). **Activities:** 1; 17 **Addr.:** I. D. Weeks Library, University of South Dakota, Vermillion, SD 57069.

Carmack, Mona (My. 10, 1940, Deadwood, SD) Dir., Ames Pub. Lib., 1975–; Head Libn., Brookings Pub. Lib., 1969–75. **Educ.:** North. State Coll., Aberdeen, SD, 1958–62, BS (Educ.); West. MI Univ., Kalamazoo, 1968–69, MSL. **Orgs.:** ALA: Arch. for Pub. Libs. Com., Lib. Admin. Div., (1974–77); Leg. Com., Pub. Lib. Assn. (1974–77); Ins. for Libs. Com., Lib. Admin. and Mgt. Assn. (1978–); Cncl. (1980). IA LA: Exec. Brd. (1977–). State Lib. Com. of IA: Gov. Conf. (1979); Adv. Cncl. for Lib. Cont. Educ. (1976–77); Ch., Pub. Libs. Auto. Tech. Srvs. Adv. Grp. (1977–78); Interlib. Loan Adv. Cncl. (1978–). Bibl. Ctr. for Rsrch.: VP, Bd. of Dir. (1980); Ch., Adv. Cncl. (1980); Interlib. Loan Com. (1973–74); Various other orgs. **Activities:** 9; 17, 19, 36 **Addr.:** Ames Public Library, 210 Sixth St., Ames, IA 50010.

Carmack, Norma J. (Jl. 29, 1930, Morgantown, WV) Soc. Sci. Libn., Trinity Univ., 1976–, Serials Libn., 1970–71, Catlgr., 1970. **Educ.:** WV Univ., 1948–52, BA (Hist.); Our Lady of the Lake Univ., 1967–69, MSLS. **Orgs.:** SLA. TX LA: Acq. RT (Secy., 1971); Coop. Com. (1979). Bexar LA: Exec. Bd. (1980–81). San Antonio OLUG: Mem. Ch. (1981). Phi Beta Kappa: Trinity Univ. Chap. (Histn., 1979–81). **Honors:** Phi Beta Kappa, 1952; Phi Alpha Theta, 1952; Kappa Delta Pi, 1951. **Pubns.:** *Information Sources for Research in Urbanology: A Basic Bibliography* (1979). **Activities:** 1; 15, 39; 92 **Addr.:** 219 Pike Rd., San Antonio, TX 78209.

Carmichael, Eleanor Johnson (Mrs. Charles W.) (Ag. 31, 1916, Mooresville, IN) Tech. Srvs. Libn., Assoc. Prof., Depauw Univ., 1960–; Libn., Indianapolis Musm. of Art, 1956–60; Libn., Dept. of Physics Lib., Purdue Univ., 1946–49; Libn., Coll. of Archit. & Art, Cornell Univ., 1942–46. **Educ.:** Earlham Coll., 1934–38, AB (Eng. Lit.); Columbia Univ., 1940–41, BS in LS; IN Univ., 1968–70, MLS. **Orgs.:** ALA. IN LA. OH Valley Grp. Tech. Srv. Libns.: Secy. (1962–63). Task Force Coop, Bibli. Ctr. for IN Libs. Alpha Phi. Tri Kappa. Daughters of the Amer. Revolution. **Honors:** Beta Phi Mu. **Pubns.:** Jt. Auth., *A chronology of Scientific Development, 1848–1948* (1948); "The Birthday Book of Hattie Carter Johnson, Mooresville, Indiana, 1864–1883," *IN Hist. Bltn.* (Ag. 1978). **Activities:** 1; 20; 55, 91 **Addr.:** 702 Highwood Ave., Greencastle, IN 46135.

Carnovsky, Ruth French (WI) Prof. Emeritus, Univ. of Chicago, 1971–; Prof., 1954–71; Visit. prof., Keio University, Tokyo, 1953–54; Assoc. prof., Univ. of Denver, 1949–53; Art Libn., Minneapolis Pub. Lib., 1945–48. **Educ.:** Carroll Coll., 1928, BA (Classics); Yale Univ., (Classics); Univ. of IL, 1935, PhD (Classics); Univ. of MN, 1945, BS (LS). **Orgs.:** ALA: Ch., Cat. Policy & Resrch. Com.; Ch., Margaret Mann Awd. Com.; Ch., Ester J. Piercy Awd. Com. **Pubns.:** *Development of Subject Access to Literature* (1969); *Toward a Better Cataloging Code* (1957; *Library Catalogs: Changing Dimensions* (1964); various articles. **Activities:** 11; 20, 26, 46; 55 **Addr.:** 1200 Lakeshore Avenue, Oakland, CA 94606.

Caron, Gilles (D. 27, 1945, St. Martin, PQ) Head, Pub. Srvs., Univ. Du PQ A Chicoutimi, 1977–; Subj. Spec., Soc. Sci., Laval Univ., 1970–77. **Educ.:** Laval Univ., 1967–70, BA (Pol. Sci.); McGill Univ., 1974–75, MLS. **Orgs.:** Corp. of Prof. Libns. of PQ: *ARGUS* (1976–77). **Pubns.:** "Librarians and Change," *ARGUS* (1980); "Librarian or Administrator: A Choice to Make," *ARGUS* (1977). **Activities:** 1; 17, 31, 39; 92 **Addr.:** Bibliotheque - Universite Du Quebec A Chicoutimi, 930 est. Rue Jacques–Cartier, Chicoutimi, PQ G7H 2B1 Canada.

Carothers, Diane F. (D. 30, 1927, Philadelphia, PA) Head, Mono. Order, Claiming & Receipt Unit, Univ. of IL, 1980–, Head, Bibl. Srch. & Cat. Maintenance Unit, 1979–80, Catlgr., 1977–79; Catlgr., Parkland Coll., 1975–77. **Educ.:** Parkland Coll., 1970, AA (Gen. Studies); Univ. of IL, 1973, BA (Hist.), 1975, MS (LS). **Orgs.:** ALA: RTSD; RASD/Hist. Sect. IL LA: Resources and Tech. Srvs. Sect.; IL ACRL. Beta Phi Mu: Treas., Alpha Chapter (1978–80). Natl. Geneal. Socty. IL State Geneal. Socty. Champaign Cnty. Geneal. Socty. Champaign Cnty. Hist. Socty. **Pubns.:** *Complete surname index to the Commemorative Biographical Encyclopedia of the Juniata Valley, comprising the counties of Huntingdon, Mifflin, Juniata, and Perry, Pennsylvania* (1979); "A brief history of English parish registers," *Geneal. Jnl.* (Mr. 1980); *Self-Instruction Manual for the Filing of Catalog Cards* (1981); **Activities:** 1; 15, 46; 56, 69 **Addr.:** 220a Library, University of Illinois, 1408 W. Gregory Dr., Urbana, IL 61801.

Carparelli, Felicia A. (N. 9, 1952, Chicago, IL) Libn., Msc. Sect., Chicago Pub. Lib., 1977–; Ref. Libn., Du Page Lib. Syst., 1975–77. **Educ.:** Univ. of IL, 1970–73, BS (Msc., Psy.), 1974–75, MSLS. **Orgs.:** ALA: RASD, Adult Lib. Mtrls. (1980–82). IL LA. Msc. LA. **Activities:** 9; 15, 32, 39; 50, 55, 61 **Addr.:** Music Section, Chicago Public Library, 78 E. Washington, Chicago, IL 60602.

Carpenter, Barbara E. (Odgers) (Ja. 24, 1930, Detroit, MI) Asst. Libn., Pers., Harrisburg Area Cmnty. Coll., 1970–; Ref. Libn., W. Shore Pub. Lib., 1967–70; Catlgr., IN State Univ., 1965–67; Catlgr., Univ. of MI, 1956–57; Asst. Libn., Henry Ford Hosp. Med. Lib., 1955–56; Circ. Libn., various branches, NY Pub. Lib., 1954–55. **Educ.:** Albion Coll., 1948–51, BA (Eng., Msc.); Columbia Univ., 1952–54, MSLS (Lib. Srv.). **Orgs.:** Assoc. Coll. Libs. of Ctrl. PA: Pers. Com. (Ch., 1976–78). PA LA: Bd. of Dirs. (1972–73, 1979–80); Cmnty. and Jr. Coll. Sect. (Ch., 1979–80); Tech. Srvs. RT (Ch., 1972–73). Amer. Gld. of Organists. **Honors:** Delta Zelta; Sigma Alpha Iota. **Activities:** 1; 33, 39, 44; 55, 63 **Addr.:** 4108 Linglestown Rd., Harrisburg, PA 17112.

Carpenter, Eric James (My. 14, 1944, Fond du Lac, WI) Biblgphr. for Eng. & Amer. Lit., SUNY at Buffalo, 1972–; Actg. Cur., Poetry & Rare Book Col., 1978–79; Head, Lockwood Col. Dev., 1977–78; Info. Libn., Univ. of WI-Madison, 1972; Inst. of Eng., Dominican College, Racine, WI, 1970–71. **Educ.:** Univ. of WI, 1962–66, BS (Eng.), 1966–70, MA (Eng.), 1971–72, MS (LS). **Orgs.:** ALA: ACRL/West. European Spec. Sect.: Ch. (1974–77); ACRL Constn. and Bylaws Com.: (1974–78); RTSD/Reprtg. Com.: (1975–76). Mod. Lang. Assn.: Organizer and Presider, "Literary Research Scholar, Libraries, & Librarians," MLA Anl. Conv. (1976). **Honors:** Beta Phi Mu, 1972. **Pubns.:** Contrib., *MLA Handbook for Writers of Research Papers, Theses and Dissertations* (1977); "The Literary Research Scholar, the Librarian, and the Future of Literary Research," *Lit. Resrch. Nwsltr.* (O. 1977); Jt. auth., "A Zero-Base Budget Approach to Staff Justification for a combined Reference and Collection Development Department" in *New Horizons for Academic Libraries* (1979). **Activities:** 1; 15, 39, 45; 55, 57, 67 **Addr.:** Reference Department, Lockwood Library, SUNY at Buffalo, NY 14260.

Carpenter, Michael Anthony (Jl. 30, 1940, Los Angeles, CA) Lib. Consult., 1973–; Lect., Univ. of CA, Los Angeles, 1976–77; Ser. Catlgr., Lib. of Congs., 1968–69; Spec. Recruit, 1967–68. **Educ.:** Occidental Coll., 1958–63, AB (Phil.); Univ. of CA, Los Angeles, 1966–67, MLS; Univ. of CA, Berkeley, 1969–79, PhD (Libnshp.). **Orgs.:** ALA; ASIS. ASLIB. Assoc. Gen. Cont. of CA: Tax and Industry Fin. Com. (1978–). **Honors:** Beta Phi Mu, 1967. **Pubns.:** *Corporate Authorship; Its Role in Library Cataloging* (1981); "No Special Rules for Entry of Serials," *Lib. Resrcs. and Tech. Srvs.* (1975); Reviews. **Activities:** 1; 19, 20, 24; 62, 75 **Addr.:** 6424 Orion Ave., Van Nuys, CA 91406.

Carpenter, Patricia A. (Jl. 28, 1938, Atlanta, GA) Assoc. Dir., Univ. Place. Srvs., Univ. of NC, 1976–; Catlgr. of pvt. book col., 1973–; Resrch. Asst., Univ. of NC, 1970–72. **Educ.:** Agnes Scott Coll., 1956–60, AB (Psych.); Univ. of NC, 1961–64, MS (LS). **Orgs.:** ALA: David Clift Schol. Awd. Com. (1979–80; Ch. 1980–81). AALS. SELA. NC LA. NC Place. Assn.; **Honors:** Beta Phi Mu, 1962; Eta Sigma Phi, 1958. **Pubns.:** Ed., *Directory of NC Employers and Educational Insts.;* Jt. auth., "The Doctorate in Library Science and An Assessment of Graduate Library Education", *Jnl. of Educ. for Librarianship* (Sum. 1970); "The Adequacy of Selected Book Reviewing Media in the History of Medicine", *ACRL Microcards Series* (1965). **Activities:** 12; 15, 17, 39 **Addr.:** 107 Stateside Dr., Chapel Hill, NC 27514.

Carpenter, Ray Leonard (D. 1, 1926, Watertown, NY) Prof., Sch. of Lib. Sci., Univ. of NC, 1981–; Assoc. Prof., Sch. of Lib. Sci., 1960-81; Biblgphr., Duke Univ., 1959; Head, Srch. Sect., Univ. of NC, 1957–58, Gen. Lib. Asst., 1956–57, Asst. Mgr., Bull's Head Bookshop, 1952–55. **Educ.:** St. Lawrence Univ., 1946–49, AB (Soclgy.); Univ. of NC, 1949–51, MA (Soclgy.), 1956–59, MS (LS), 1966–69, PhD (Soclgy.). **Orgs.:** ALA: Coll. Lib. Standards (1979–), Ref. and Subscrpn. Books Review Com. (1968–73). LED: Resrch. Com., Ch. (1971–73). LAMA: Statistics Com. for Lib. Educ. (1978–79). Lippincott Awd. Jury (1978–). AALS: Com. on Resrch. by Corres., Ch. (1971–73). ASIS. Amer. Sociological Assn. AAUP. Alpha Kappa Delta. **Honors:** Fulbright-Hays Comsn., Sr. Resrch. Fellow, Italy, 1974; Beta Phi Mu, 1959. **Pubns.:** *Statistical Methods for Librarians* (1978); *Public Library Patrons in N.C.* (1975); *Public Library Executive* (1969); "College Libraries: A Comparative Analysis," *Coll. & Resrch. Libs.* (Ja. 1981); Jt. auth., "Public Library Support and Salaries and the Seventies," *Lib. Jnl.* (Mr. 15, 1976); Other articles, reviews. **Activities:** 11; 24, 26, 41; 92 **Addr.:** School of Library Science, University of North Carolina, Chapel Hill, NC 27514.

Carpino, Linda M. (N. 3, 1946, Clarksburg, WV) Coord., Chld. Srvs., Toledo-Lucas Cnty. Lib., 1979–, Branch Head, 1978–79, Chld. Libn., 1977–78. **Educ.:** Miami Univ., 1967–70, BA (Eng.); West. MI Univ., 1976–77, MSLS (Lib.). **Orgs.:** ALA: Newbery/Caldecott Com. (1979). OH LA. **Activities:** 9, 11; 15, 17, 21; 69, 74, 89 **Addr.:** Toledo-Lucas County Library, 324 Michigan, Toledo, OH 43624.

Carr, Charles Edward (Mr. 13, 1939, Wildwood, NJ) Prin. Libn., HQ Readers Adv., Burlington Cnty. (NJ) Lib., 1973–, Prin. Libn., Ext. Srvs., Cinnaminson Branch, 1965–73, Sr. Libn., Ext. Srvs., Bkmobiles, 1962–65. **Educ.:** Wagner Coll., 1957–61, BA (Hist.); Drexel Univ., 1961–62, MSLS. **Orgs.:** NJ LA: Adult and YA Srvs. Sect. ALA: YASD. Phi Mu Alpha Sinfonia. Cont. Educ. Cncl. of Burlington Cnty.: Exec. Com. (1979); Corres. Sey. (1980). **Pubns.:** Jt. Ed., *Burlington Cnty. Area Lib. Nsltr.* (1973–). **Activities:** 9; 16, 36, 48; 50, 72 **Addr.:** 2000 Atlantic Ave., North Wildwood, NJ 08260.

Carr, Jo Ann Daly (Jn. 15, 1952, Lafayette, IN) Pub. Srvs. Libn., Instr. Mtrls. Ctr., Univ. of WI, 1976–, Actg. Dir., 1975–76, Catlgr., 1974–75. **Educ.:** IN Univ., 1970–73, BA (Hist.), 1973–74, (MLS). **Orgs.:** ALA. WI LA: Literary Awds. Com. (1975–77). WI Assn. of Acad. Libns.: Conf. Plng. Com. (1979). WI Sch. Lib. Media Assn.: Cont. Plng. Com. (1976), Pubn. Com. (1977). Spec. Campus Libs. Grp.: Various coms. **Activities:** 1; 22, 39 **Addr.:**

Special Subjects/Services: 50. Adult educ.; 51. Advert./Mktg.; 52. Aerosp.; 53. Agric.; 54. Area std.; 55. Arts/Hum.; 56. Autom.; 57. Bibl./Prtg.; 58. Bio. sci.; 59. Bus./Fin.; 60. Chem.; 61. Copyrt.; 62. Documtn.; 63. Educ.; 64. Engin.; 65. Env.; 66. Eth. grps.; 67. Film; 68. Food/Nutr.; 69. Geneal.; 70. Geo.; 71. Geol.; 72. Handcpd.; 73. Hist.; 74. Int. frdm.; 75. Info. sci.; 76. Insr.; 77. Law; 78. Legis.; 79. Math./Comp. sci.; 80. Med.; 81. Metals; 82. Nat. resrcs.; 83. Newsp.; 84. Nuc. sci.; 85. Oral hist.; 86. Petr./Energy; 87. Pharm.; 88. Phys./Astr./Math.; 89. Readg.; 90. Relig.; 91. Sci./Tech.; 92. Soc. sci.; 93. Telecom.; 94. Transp.; 95. (other).

Who's Who in Library and Information Services

University of Wisconsin-Madison, School of Education IMC, 225 N. Mills, Madison, WI 53706.

Carr, Mary M. (Ja. 4, 1950, Everett, WA) Head of Technical Sus., Gonzaga Univ., 1974–; Latin Tchr. and Head Libn., Gonzaga Prep. Sch., 1973–74. **Educ.:** Univ. of WA, 1968–72, BA (Latin), 1972–73, M. Libnshp.; Teaching Cert., 1972; WA Libn. Cert., 1973. **Orgs.:** ALA: RTSD. NLA. Pac. Northwest LA. WA LA: Tech. Srvs. Interest Grp. (Ch., 1980–81) /Strg. Com. (1978–79). WA Lib. Netwk.: Asm. (Rep., 1977–80), Exec. Cncl. (mem. 1980–82). Northeast Lib. Srvc. Area: Secy. (1977–78), Ch. (1978–80). Amer. Classical Leag. Classical Assn. of the Pac. Northwest. **Honors:** Phi Beta Kappa; Beta Phi Mu. **Pubns.:** Reviews. **Activities:** 1; 17, 20, 29; 55, 59 **Addr.:** E. 502 Boone Ave., Crosby Library, Gonzaga University, Spokane, WA 99258.

Carr, Mildred Lee (F. 10, 1915, Norfolk, VA) Retired, 1980; Head Circ. Libn., Univ. of NC, Greensboro Lib., 1970-80; Rsv. Libn., 1958–70; Ref. Libn., Towson State Tchrs. Coll., 1951–52; First Asst., Lit. Dept., Enoch Pratt Free Lib., 1939–43. **Educ.:** Coll. of William and Mary, 1931–34, BA (Eng.); Columbia Univ., 1938–39, BS (LS); E.P.F.L. Training Class, Cert., 1935–36. **Orgs.:** ALA: LITA. NC LA. SELA. Moses Cone Hosp. Auxiliary, Greensboro: Org. Patients Lib. (1954–55). **Pubns.:** Ed. "The St. John's List of Great Books," *Enoch Pratt Free Library* (1943); Comp. "Catching Up With the Twentieth Century," (1961). **Activities:** 1, 9; 16, 22, 36; 50, 56, 75 **Addr.:** 202 Meadowbrook Terr., Greensboro, NC 27408.

Carrasco, Alys Godsil (S. 8, 1937, Fairbanks, AK) Media Spec., Lake Shore Elem. Sch., 1977–; Libn., Klickitat Sch. Dist., 1974–77; Lib. Asst., Chapman Elem. Sch., 1973–74. **Educ.:** Portland State Univ., 1969–71, BA (Elem. Ed.); Univ. of WA, 1971–72, MLS; Univ. of Mexico & Univ. of the Americas, 1958–59 (Span.). **Orgs.:** ALA: ALSC; AASL. WA State Lib. Media Assn.: Int. Frdm. Rep for Region 9 (1978), Jr. HS Levels Ch. (1978), Legis. Rep for Region 9 (1979–). AAUW: Vancouver Branch 2nd V.P. (1980–). Natl. Educ. Assn. WA Educ. Assn. Vancouver Educ. Assn.: Fac. Rep (1978–79). **Honors:** ALSC/Scribner, to attend ALA conf., 1976; Eleanor Ahlers Scholarship, to attend ALSC conference, 1979; Beta Phi Mu. **Pubns.:** "Puppetry and the International Year of the Child," *The Medium* (Spr. 1980). **Activities:** 10; 21, 31, 32; 63 **Addr.:** 1901 N. W. 100th St., Vancouver, WA 98665.

Carreau, Janice E. (Ja. 9, 1934, Haverhill, MA) Libn., Westerly HS, 1977–; Libn., Stonington HS, 1974–75. **Educ.:** Mt. Holyoke Coll., 1951–55, AB (Relig.); Univ. of RI, 1971–74, MLS. **Orgs.:** ALA: AASL. RI Educ. Media Assn. Republican Party: Town Com. (1980–). Meth. Church: Lcl. Church Trustees (Pres., 1980–); Educ. Comsn. (1963–75). **Honors:** Phi Beta Kappa, 1955; Beta Phi Mu. **Activities:** 10; 31, 32, 48 **Addr.:** RFD 1, Box 486, Mystic, CT 06355.

Carrick, Bruce R. (F. 5, 1937, New York, NY) VP, H.W. Wilson Co., 1975–; Sr. Ed., Macmillan Co., 1971–75; Dir., Trade and Ref. Depts., T.Y. Crowell and Co., 1970–71; Sr. Ed., Charles Scribner's Sons, 1968–70. **Educ.:** Princeton Univ., 1954–61, AB (Hist.). **Orgs.:** ALA. NY LA. **Addr.:** Chestnut Ridge Rd., Mt. Kisco, NY 10549.

Carrick, Kathleen Michele (Je. 11, 1950, Cleveland, OH) Asst. Prof., Law, Dir., Law Lib., SUNY, Buffalo, 1980–, Assoc. Dir., 1978–80, Head Ref. Libn., 1977–78; Resrch. Asst., *Plain Dealer*, 1973–75. **Educ.:** Duquesne Univ., 1968–72, BA (Jnlsm.); Univ. of Pittsburgh, 1972–73, MLS; Cleveland State Univ., 1974–77, JD; OH Bar, Mem. **Orgs.:** AALL. AALS. Amer. Bar Assn. **Pubns.:** "A Case Study Approach to Legal Research: The Kent State Case," *Law Lib. Jnl.* (1980); "Status of Librarians at SUNY/Buffalo," *Law Lib. Jnl.* (1980); "Regulating Rehabilitation–A Selective Bibliography on the Federal Regulations Promulgated through 1980 as a Result of Section 504, the Rehabilitation Act of 1973, with Emphasis on Federal Rehabilitation Legislation," *Law Lib. Jnl.* (Sum. 1981). **Activities:** 1; 41; 77 **Addr.:** SUNY at Buffalo, O'Brian Hall, Buffalo, NY 14260.

Carrier, Esther Jane (Je. 22, 1925, Punxsutawney, PA) Ref. Libn., Lock Haven State Coll., 1978–; Libn., Houghton Coll., 1950–77. **Educ.:** Bob Jones Coll., 1942–44; Geneva Coll., 1944–46, AB, (Eng.); Carnegie Lib. Sch., 1946–47, BSLS; PA State Univ., 1947–50, MA (Eng.); Univ. of MI, 1957–60, AMLS, DLS. **Orgs.:** ALA. **Honors:** Beta Phi Mu. **Pubns.:** *Fiction in public libraries, 1876–1900* (1965). **Activities:** 1; 17, 39 **Addr.:** 225 1/2 W. Clinton St., Lock Haven, PA 17745.

Carrigan, John L. (S. 9, 1948, Leadville, CO) Dir., Lib. Srvs., City of Hope Natl. Med. Ctr., 1976–, Asst. Libn., 1974–76, Resrch. Tech., 1974. **Educ.:** TX A&M Univ., 1966–70, BS (Phys.); CA Inst. of Tech., 1970–73, MS (Bio.); CA State Univ., Fullerton, 1975–78, MLS. **Orgs.:** SLA. ASIS. Med. LA. Assoc. Info. Mgrs. NY Acad. of Sci. **Honors:** Sigma Xi; Phi Kappa Phi; Sigma Pi Sigma. **Activities:** 5, 12; 17, 24, 39; 58, 80, 91 **Addr.:** 4811 Orchard, Montclair, CA 91763.

Carrington, David K. (Ap. 10, 1938, Washington, DC) Head, Tech. Srvs. Sect., Geo. and Map Div., Lib. of Congs., 1968–; Chief, Source Mat. Sect., Ofc. of Geo., U.S. Dept. of the Interior, 1966–68. **Educ.:** Univ. of MD, 1956–61, BS (Geo.); FL State Univ., 1964–65, MS (LS). **Orgs.:** SLA: Geo. and Map Div. (Secy./Treas., 1977–); ALA. **Honors:** Lib. of Congs., Merit. Srv. Awd., 1971. **Pubns.:** *Map Collections in the United States and Canada; a directory* (1977). **Activities:** 4; 17, 45, 46; 56, 70 **Addr.:** Technical Services Section, Geography and Map Division, Library of Congress, Washington, DC 20540.

Carrington, Samuel M., Jr. (Je. 22, 1939, Durham, NC.) Prof. of Fr. and Univ. Libn., Rice Univ., 1979–; Assoc. Prof. of Fr., Rice Univ., 1971–79, Asst. Prof. of Fr., 1967–71; Asst. Prof. of Fr., Univ. of CO, 1965–67. **Educ.:** Univ. of NC, 1957–60, AB (Fr.), 1960–65, MA, PhD (Romance Lang.). **Orgs.:** ALA. Mod. Lang. Assn. Amer. Assn. of Tchrs. of Fr. Other Orgs. **Pubns.:** *Les Oeuvres poétiques d'Amadis Jamyn*, t. I & II, Édition Critique, (1973–78); "Deux pièces comiques in édites du ms. B.N. fr. 904," *Romania, XCI*, (1970); "Amadis Jamyn's Theory of Translation," *KY Romance Quarterly* (1975); Other articles. **Activities:** 1; 17; 95-Fr. **Addr.:** Fondren Library, Rice University, Houston, TX 77001.

Carrison, Dale K. (Ap. 29, 1936, Macomb, IL) Dean of Libs., Mankato State Univ., 1968–; LS Instr., Asst. to the Dean, Univ. of Denver Grad. Sch. of Libnshp., 1964–68; Asst. Prof., Dept. of LS, West. IL Univ., 1962–64; HS Libn., Adult Bus. Educ. Instr., Untd. Twp. HS, 1958–61. **Educ.:** West. IL Univ., 1957, BS (Bus. Educ.), 1959, MS (Bus. Admin.); Univ. of Denver, 1962, MALS, PhD in progress (Higher Educ.). **Orgs.:** ALA: ACRL/Coll. Libs. Sect. (Ch., 1978–79; Bd. of Dirs., 1977–79); Oberly Awd. Com. (1978–79). AALS: Nom. Com. (1977–78). MN LA: VP, Pres. (1974–77); Long-Range Plng. Com. (1976–78, Ch., 1976–77). Multi-Church Educ. Comsn.: Ch. (1975–78). **Honors:** Beta Phi Mu; MN LA: 1981 Libn. of Year. **Pubns.:** Ed., *Literature for the Young Adult, A Compilation of Papers and Bibliographies from an NDEA Institute for School Librarians* (1968); Ed., *A Media Resources and Services Budgetary Analysis and Allocation System for the Minnesota State University System* ERIC (1975); jt. auth., "An Experimental Program in School Library Media Education, 1971–73" in *Curriculum Alternatives: Experiments in School Library Media Education* (1974). **Activities:** 1, 11; 17, 26, 34; 50, 56, 72 **Addr.:** Mankato State University Library, Mankato, MN 56001.

Carro, Jorge L. (N. 27, 1924, Havana, Cuba) Assoc. Prof., Prof. of Law and Head Law Libn., Univ. of Cincinnati Law School, 1976–, Actg. Dean, 1978–79; Head Law Libn., Assoc. Prof., OH North. Univ. Coll. of Law, 1972–76; Asst. Libn., Catlgr., Univ. of WI, Whitewater, 1969–72; Asst. Libn., Catlgr., Univ. of WI, Milwaukee, 1969. **Educ.:** Havana Inst., 1940–45, BA; Univ. of Havana, 1945–50, JD (Law); Emporia State Univ., 1968–69, MLS; Marquette Univ. Law Sch.-Univ. of WI, Milwaukee, 1969, Law Lib. Inst., Cert.; AALL, 1972, Law Lib. Cert. **Orgs.:** OH Reg. Assn. of Law Libs.: Nom. Com. (Ch., 1972–75); Treas. (1975–77); Exec. Bd. (1975–77). AALL: Com. on Autom. (1973–76); Com. on Ethics (1976–78); Com. on Foreign, Comparative and Intl. Law (1978–). Assn. of Amer. Law Schs.: House of Del. (1974, 1975). Morgan Inst. on Intl. Human Rights: Adv. Bd. (1978–). **Pubns.:** "The Use of Spanish and Latin American Legal Encyclopedias as an Alternative in Building a Minimum Collection of Those Jurisdictions." *Intl. Jnl. of Law Libs.* (N. 1978); Intl. Assn. of Law Libs. Jnl., Bk. review ed. (1977–). **Activities:** 1, 12; 17, 19, 24; 54, 56, 77 **Addr.:** 1015 Paxton, Cincinnati, OH 45208.

Carroad, Eva G. (F. 26, 1950, Oakland, CA) Head Libn., Bio. Lib., Univ. of CA, Berkeley, 1979–; Hlth. Scis. Libn., 1974–79; Inst., Sch. of Lib. & Info. Studies, 1976–80. **Educ.:** Univ. of CA, Berkeley, 1972, BA (Biochem. and Grmn.), 1973, MLS; Cert. Biomed. libnshp., 1973–74. **Orgs.:** Med. LA. N. CA Med. Lib. Grp.: Pres. (1978–79); Prog. Ch. (1977–78). **Honors:** Phi Beta Kappa, 1971; Beta Phi Mu, 1973. **Activities:** 1, 12; 15, 17, 39; 58, 80 **Addr.:** Biology Library, University of California, Berkeley, CA 94720.

Carroll, C. Edward (O. 8, 1923, Grahn, KY) Prof. of Lib. and IS, Univ. of MO, Columbia, 1970–, Dir. of Libs., 1970–73; Dir. of Libs., Wichita State Univ., 1967–70; Head Libn., South. OR Coll., 1965–67. **Educ.:** Univ. of Toledo, 1947, PhB (Eng.); Univ. of Toledo, 1951, BEd (Educ.); Univ. of Toledo, 1950, MA (Eng.); Univ. of CA, Los Angeles, 1961, MLS; Univ. of CA, Berkeley, 1969, PhD (Higher Educ.). **Orgs.:** AALS. ALA. MO LA. Natl. Micro. Assn. AAUP: MO State Pres. (1981–82); Rotary Intl. NY Acad. of Sci. KY Colonels. **Honors:** Beta Phi Mu; Phi Delta Kappa. **Pubns.:** *The Professionalization of Education for Librarianship* (1970); "Microfilmed Catalogs," *Microform Review* (1972); "Some Problems of Microform Utilization in Large Academic Libraries," *Micro. in Libs.: A Reader* (1975); "Bibliographic Control of Microforms," *Micro. Review* (1978); *Administrative Aspects of Educ. for Librarianship*, chap., (1975). **Activities:** 1; 17, 25, 26; 63, 72, 90 **Addr.:** 2001 Country Club Dr., Columbia, MO 65201.

Carroll, Dewey Eugene (Ag. 30, 1926, Monterey, TN) Dean, Prof., Sch. of Lib. and Info. Sci., N. TX State Univ., 1973–; Dir., Libs., Prof., Univ. of TN, 1969–73; Asst. Prof., Resrch. Assoc., Grad. Sch. of LS, Univ. of IL, 1965–69; Asst. Prof., Sch. of Info. Sci., GA Inst. of Tech., 1963–65; Instr., Asst. Prof., Div. of Libnshp., Emory Univ., 1960–63, Sci. Libn., 1957–58; Head, Sci. and Indus. Div., Atlanta Pub. Lib., 1955–57. **Educ.:** Univ. of S., 1944–45 (Engin.); Univ. of Chattanooga, 1946–49, BA (Hist., Psy.); Emory Univ., 1954–55, MLN (Libnshp.); Univ. of IL, 1959–65, PhD (LS). **Orgs.:** ALA. ASIS. AALS. TX LA. TN LA. **Honors:** Pi Gamma Mu; Phi Kappa Phi; Beta Phi Mu. **Pubns.:** Ed., *Library Applications of Data Processing: Proceedings of the 5th Annual Clinic 1967* (1968); ed., *Library Applications of Data Processing: Proceedings of the 6th Annual Clinic 1968* (1969); ed., *Library Applications of Data Processing: Proceedings of the 7th Annual Clinic 1969* (1970); jt. auth., *Statement of Program: Library Building—Chattanooga Campus, University of Tennessee* (1969); ed., *School of Library and Information Sciences, North Texas State University: Self Study Report Submitted to the Committee on Accreditation, American Library Association* (1975); various bks., articles, papers, presentations. **Activities:** 1, 9; 15, 17, 39; 75, 91, 92 **Addr.:** 2121 Pembrooke Pl., Denton, TX 76201.

Carroll, Frances Laverne (D. 6, 1923, Scammon, KS) Prof., Sch. of Lib. Sci., Univ. of OK, 1962–; Sr. Lectur., West. Australian Tchrs. Coll., 1977–79; Libn. and Supvsr. of Sch. Libs., Coffeyville Jr. Coll., 1953–62; Libn., Field Kindley Mem. HS, 1949–53. **Educ.:** KS State Tchrs. Coll., 1944–48, BS (Eng.); Univ. of Denver, 1954–56, MALS; Univ. of OK, 1968–70, PhD (Educ.). **Orgs.:** IFLA: Ch., Sch. Libs. (1973–77). ALA: Intl. Lib. Educ. Com. (1973–77). AALS: Co-Ch., Fac. Exc. Subcom., (1972–77). LA of Australia: Ed., *Biblia* (News.) (1979). Chld. Book Cncl.: Exec. Com. (1978). AAUP: VP, O.U. Br. (1973–74). AAUW. Intl. Assn. of Sch. Libns. **Pubns.:** Jt. auth., *The Library at Mount Vernon* (1977); *Recent Advances in School Librarianship* (1981); "An Internationalized Children's Literature," *UNESCO Jnl.* of Info. Sci. (Ja. 1979); "School Library Studies, Proposed Guidelines for School Libraries," *Intl. Lib. Review* (1978); "World Librarianship," *Encyclopedia of Library and Information Science* (1981); various articles and reviews. **Activities:** 10, 11; 21, 48; 54 **Addr.:** School of Library Science, University of Oklahoma, 401 W. Brooks Street, Norman, OK 73019.

Carroll, Hardy (F. 24, 1930, Kernersville, NC) Assoc. Prof., West. MI Univ., 1970–; Persnl. Libn., PA State Univ., 1966–67, Asst. Cat. Libn., 1965–66; Catlgr., Univ. of PA, 1963–65, 1957–59. **Educ.:** Guilford Coll., 1947–51, BA (Phil.); Hartford Theo. Semy., 1951–54, BD (Phil. of Rel.); Univ. of Edinburgh, 1954–56 (Hist.); Drexel Univ., 1963–65, MS in LS; Case Western Reserve Univ., 1967–70, PhD (Lib. and Info. Sci.). **Orgs.:** ALA: Copyright Com. 1975–77). ASIS: AALS: Org. and Bylaws Com. Assn. for Computing Mach. Other orgs. AAUP. **Pubns.:** Ed., *Environmental Information Programs for Public Libraries* (1973); "Primary Sources for Understanding the New Copyright Law," *Coll. and Resrch. Libs. News* (Ja. 1977). **Activities:** 1, 12; 26, 30, 41; 56, 61, 75 **Addr.:** 618 Axtell St., Kalamazoo, MI 49008.

Carroll, John Millar (D. 6, 1925, Philadelphia, PA) Prof., Univ. of West. ON, 1968–; Assoc. Prof., Lehigh Univ., 1964–68; Managing Ed., *Electronics Mag.*, 1952–64. **Educ.:** Lehigh Univ., 1944–50, BSIE (Indus. Engin.); Hofstra Univ., 1952–55, MA (Phys.); NY Univ., 1959–68, DR (Engin. Sci., Indus. Engin.). **Orgs.:** Can. Assn. Info. Sci. ASIS. Can. Info. Prcs. Socty. Inst. of Electrical and Electronics Engin.: Info. Retrival Com. (1960–64). *Engin. Index:* Trustee (1962–65). **Pubns.:** *Confidential Information Sources* (1974); *Computer Security* (1977); "Computer Selection of Key Words (Using Word-Frequency Analysis)," *Amer. Doc.* (Jl. 1969); "Explorations into Informatic Geometry," *Can. Jnl. of Info. Sci.* (My. 1980). **Activities:** 11; 26, 30, 43; 64, 75, 93 **Addr.:** Dept. of Computer Science, University of Western Ontario, London, ON N6A 5B9 Canada.

Carroon, Robert Girard (My. 24, 1937, Kansas City, MO) Dir., Litchfield Hist. Socty, Litchfield, CT (1968–81); Episcopal Clergyman, Diocese of Milwaukee, 1962. **Educ.:** IN State Univ., 1955–60, BA (Hist.); Univ. of WI, 1966–70, MA (Hist.); Nashotah House, 1959–60, MDiv; Marquette Univ., 1975–, PhD cand. **Orgs.:** SAA: Immigration/Ethnic & Church Coms.; Lib. Cncl. of Milwaukee: Arch. & Coord. Col. Com. Socty. of Antiq. of Scotland: Fellow; Socty. of Colonial Wars in WI: Gvr.; Sons of Amer. Revolution: Geneal. Gen. (1977–79); WI Pres. (1979–80); Huguenot Socty. of WI: Pres. (1977–79); Other orgs. **Honors:** Sussex Coll., Hon. D. Litt., 1977. **Pubns.:** *Milwaukee and the American Revolution* (1973); "Scotsmen in Old Milwaukee," *Hist. Messenger* (Mr. 1969); "Arms and the Clans", *Hist. Messenger* (S./D. 1969); "Chief Blackbird," *The Badger State* (1979); "The Judge & the General," *The MacArthurs of Milwaukee* (1979). **Activities:** 2, 12; 15, 23, 39; 54, 66, 69 **Addr.:** Litchfield Historical Society, On-The-Green, Litchfield, CT 06759.

Carruthers, Ralph H. (S. 2, 1903, Thornhill, MB) Retired, 19–; Chief, Photograph. Srvs., NY Pub. Lib., 1945–65; Overseas Rep., Interdept. Com. for Acq. of Frgn. Pubns., ETO OSS, 1942–45; Head, Photograph. Srv., NY Pub. Lib., 1938–42, Asst., Main Info. Desk, 1932–38, Head, Photograph. Srv., 1928–32, Asst., Sci. and Tech., 1927–28. **Educ.:** Queen's Univ., 1924–26, BA, hons. (Sci. for Tchg.); Columbia Univ., 1926–27, BS (Lib.), 1937–38 (Documentary Photography). **Orgs.:** ALA. Natl. Micro.

PROFESSIONAL ACTIVITIES: Institutions: 1. Acad. lib.; 2. Arch.; 3. Assn.; 4. Fed./Gvt. lib.; 5. Inst. lib.; 6. Mfr./Suppl.; 7. Milit. lib.; 8. Musm.; 9. Pub. lib.; 10. Sch. lib.; 11. Sch. of lib. sci.; 12. Spec. lib.; 13. State lib.; 14. (other). **Functions/Activities:** 15. Acq./Col. dev.; 16. Adult srvs.; 17. Admin.; 18. Apprais.; 19. Archit./Bldgs.; 20. Cat./Class.; 21. Chld. srvs.; 22. Circ.; 23. Cons./Pres.; 24. Consult.; 25. Cont. ed.; 26. Educ. lib. sci.; 27. Ext. srvs.; 28. Fund/Grants; 29. Gvt. pubs.; 30. Indx./Abs.; 31. Instr. lib. use; 32. Media srvs.; 33. Micro.; 34. Netwks./Coop.; 35. Persnl.; 36. PR; 37. Publshg.; 38. Recs. mgt.; 39. Ref. srvs.; 40. Repro.; 41. Resrch.; 42. Review.; 43. Secur.; 44. Serials; 45. Spec. col.; 46. Tech. srvs.; 47. Trustees/Bds.; 48. YA srvs.; 49. (other).

Assn. NY Lib. Club. **Honors:** Natl. Micro. Assn., Fellow, 1965. **Pubns.:** Various articles on photographic reprodct.; assoc. ed., bibl., *Jnl. of Documentary Reprodct.* (1939–42). **Activities:** 9; 33, 40; 62, 75 **Addr.:** 233–A Heritage Vlg., Southbury, CT 06488.

Carsch, Ruth Elizabeth (R.E.) (My. 3, 1945, London, Eng.) Consult. Info. Spec., 1973–; Mgr., Info. Srvs. Sect., AK Pipeline, Bechtel Inc., 1973–74; Dir., Info. Ctr./Arts Resrcs. Dept., NY State Cncl. on Arts, 1970–73; Libn., NY Pub. Lib., 1968–70. **Educ.:** Hunter Coll., CUNY, 1963–67, BA (Comp. Lit., Hum.) Columbia Univ., 1967–68, Mstrs.; NY State Libns. Cert.; AMA Supervisory Mgt. Cert.; various crs. **Orgs.:** Media Alliance. SLA. **Pubns.:** Consult., *Lit. Market Pl.* (1981); consult., *Info. Indus. Market Pl.* (1980). **Activities:** 5, 9; 17, 19, 24; 51, 55, 56 **Addr.:** 1453 Rhode Island St., San Francisco, CA 94107.

Carson, Donald E. (Ja. 3, 1922, Douglas, AZ) Chief Libn., The Coll. of Insurance Lib., 1980–; Assoc. Libn., 1965–79; Assoc. Libn., Wagner Coll., 1957–65; Asst. Libn., Univ. Club Lib., 1953–57; Catlgr., Coll., of the City of New York, 1950–53. **Educ.:** Univ. of CO, 1939–43, BA (Eng. Lit.); Univ. of MI, 1948–49, AMLS. **Orgs.:** SLA: Insurance Div. ALA. **Activities:** 1, 12; 20; 76 **Addr.:** The College of Insurance Library, 123 William Street, New York, NY 10038.

Carstater, Sister Mary Esther (Jl. 30, 1931, Jamestown, NY) Libn., Media Spec., Our Lady of Mercy HS, 1962–; Asst. Libn. & Tchr., Notre Dame HS, 1959–62; Tchr., Mercy HS, 1957–59; Tchr., St. Charles Sch., 1954–57. **Educ.:** Nazareth Coll. of Rochester, 1949–55, BA (Eng.); SUNY, Geneseo, 1957–59, MLS; Pub. Libn. Cert., 1963; Lib. Media Spec. Cert., 1972. **Orgs.:** ALA. Cath. LA. AECT. NY LA. Other orgs. Greater Rochester Area Sch. Media Specs. **Honors:** National Poetry Prize, 1960. **Pubns.:** "Making Education Live," *Cath. Sch. Jnl.* (My. 1967); "Challenge of Change," *Cath. Lib. World* (My.-Je. 1966); "Teaching English", *Cath. Educator* (Je. 1966); "Character Formation Through Books", *Cath. Educator* (My. 1960); Poetry. **Activities:** 10; 17, 31, 48 **Addr.:** Our Lady of Mercy High School, 1437 Blossom Road, Rochester, NY 14610.

Carter, Bobby R. (N. 26, 1941, Baytown, TX) Dir. of Lib. Srvs., Assoc. Prof. of Med. Educ., TX Coll. of Osteopathic Med., 1978–; Med. Ctr. Libn., Georgetown Univ., 1973–78; Assoc. Dir. & Actg. Dir., Univ. of TX Med. Branch, Galveston, 1969–73; Pharm. Libn., Univ. of Houston Coll. of Pharm., 1967–69. **Educ.:** Univ. of Houston, 1963–65, BS (Comm.); LA State Univ., 1965–68, MSLS. **Orgs.:** Med. LA: Pub. Com. (1976). DC Hlth. Sci. Info. Network: Founder, Pres. (1973–77). ALA. AAUP. **Pubns.:** "The University of Texas Medical Branch at Galveston: An Expanding Medical Campus and Library," *South. Med.* (D. 1973); "The Moody Medical Library and Its Historical Relevance," *Bltn. of the Med. LA* (Ja. 1974). **Activities:** 1, 14-Medical School Library; 17, 24, 36; 58, 80, 87 **Addr.:** 4320 Westdale Dr., Fort Worth, TX 76109.

Carter, C. Ross (Mr. 18, 1929, Vancouver, BC) Dir., Coll. Resrcs., Vancouver Cmnty. Coll., 1969–; Asst. Dir., Yakima Reg. Lib., 1965–69; Film Libn., Portland State Univ. Lib., 1963–65; Asst. Dir., Plainfield (NJ) Pub. Lib., 1959–63. **Educ.:** Univ. of BC, 1948–51, BA (Hist.), 1951–52, Dipl. (Educ.); Univ. of WA, 1956–57, MLS. **Orgs.:** BC LA: Treas. (1978–79). Can. LA: CACUL/Local Arrange. Com. (1980 AGM). Langara Fac. Assn., VCC: Pres. (1974–75). **Pubns.:** Jt. auth., *Development of Academic Libraries in British Columbia* (1976); "Newsnotes, British Columbia", *PNLA Qtly.* (1975–); "Community College Libraries in BC", *BCLA Qtly.* (#3, 1973). **Activities:** 1; 17, 34 **Addr.:** Vancouver Community College, Regional Offices, 675 W. Hastings Street, Vancouver, BC Canada.

Carter, Catherine Ann (My. 26, 1925, Council Bluffs, IA) Head, Orig. Cat. Sect., PA State Univ., 1955–; Catlgr., 1951–53; Catlgr., Univ. of IA, 1949–51. **Educ.:** Univ. of KS, 1944–47, AB (Span.); Univ. of MI, 1947–49, MALS; Columbia Univ., 1953–55, MA (Ling.). **Orgs.:** ALA. PA LA. ASIS. Intl. Ling. Assn. **Pubns.:** "Cataloging and classification of State documents," *PLA Bltn.* (Mr. 1970). **Addr.:** 447 Hillcrest, State College, PA 16801.

Carter, Darline L. (D. 7, 1933, Pinola, MS) Pub. Lib. Dir., W. Islip Pub. Lib., 1969–, Asst. Dir., 1966–69, Chld. Libn., 1962–66; Circ. Libn., Tougaloo Coll., 1960–62; Asst. Libn., Syracuse Univ., 1959–60; Libn., Cleveland (MS) HS, 1955–59. **Educ.:** Tougaloo Coll., 1951–55, BS (Elem. Educ.); Syracuse Univ., 1959–60, MLS. **Orgs.:** Suffolk Cnty. LA: Past Pres. Suffolk Cnty. Dir.'s Assn.: CEU Com., Past Ch. NY LA: Exhibits Com.; Mem. Com. ALA: Natl. Lib. Week Com. Adv. Com. for C. W. Post Lib. Schs. Accred. NY State's Gvr.'s Conf. on Libs. **Honors:** Parent-Tchr. Assn., Hon. Life Mem.; Univ. of MD, Flwshp., 6th Anl. Lib. Admin. Dev. Prog. **Addr.:** Public Library, 3 Higbie Ln., W. Islip, NY 11795.

Carter, Gesina C. (D. 15, 1939, Nootdorp, Netherlands) Exec. Secy., Numerical Data Adv. Bd., U.S. Natl. Com. for CODATA, Natl. Acad. of Sci., 1978–; Dir., Alloy Data Ctr., Natl. Bur. of Stans., 1966–78; Resrch. Assoc., Cath. Univ. of Amer., 1965–66. **Educ.:** Univ. of MI, 1957–60, BS (Phys.); Carnegie Mellon Univ., 1961–65, MS, PhD (Phys.). **Orgs.:** ASIS. Amer. Chem. Socty.: Div. of Chem. Info. Amer. Phys. Socty. Amer. Socty. for Metals. Intl. Assn. for Hydrogen. NY Acad. of Sci. **Honors:** U.S. Dept. of Cmrce., Silver Medal. **Pubns.:** *The NBS Alloy Data Center: Function, Bibliographic System, Related Data Centers, and Reference Books* (1968); *National Bureau Standards Technical Note* (1968); "Numerical Data Retrieval in the U.S. and Abroad," *Jnl. Chem. Info. Comp. Sci.* (1980); various tech. articles on metal phys.; "The NBS Alloy Data Center: Permuted Materials Index," *Natl. Bur. Stans. Spec. Pubn.* (1971); "Metallic Shifts in NMR," *Prog. Mtrls. Sci.* (1977). **Activities:** 3; 42, 47; 91 **Addr.:** Numerical Data Advisory Board, National Academy of Sciences, 2101 Constitution Ave. N.W., Washington, DC 20418.

Carter, Helen S. (Je. 20, 1926, Hobart, OK) Prof. (Legal Resrch., Wrtg.), Univ. of Albuquerque, 1979–; Lectr. III (Law Libnshp.), Univ. NM, 1966–80; Attorney, 1951–; Attorney, for U.S. Sen. Clinton P. Anderson, 1950–51. **Educ.:** Stephens Coll., 1943–44; Univ. of OK, 1944; Kiowa Cnty. Jr. Coll. 1945; Univ. of NM, 1945–47, BA (Eng., Drama); George Washington Univ. 1948; Univ. of UT, 1948–51, LLB; AALL, 1970, Cert. **Orgs.:** AALL. NM LA. **Activities:** 1, 5; 31, 36, 39; 56, 77, 78 **Addr.:** 2913 Cutler Ave., N.E., Albuquerque, NM 87106.

Carter, Nancy Carol (N. 12, 1942, Tacoma, WA) Prof. (Law), Dir., Law Lib. Srvs., Golden Gate Univ., 1975–; Govt. Docum. Libn., OK Cnty. Lib. Syst., 1974–75; Asst. Acq. Libn., Univ. of OK Libs., 1967–71. **Educ.:** TX A & I Univ., 1960–63, BS (Hist.), 1967–69, MS (Hist.); Univ. of OK, 1965–67, MLS, 1972–75, JD. **Orgs.:** AALL. North. CA Assn. Law Libs. West.-Pac. Assn. Law Libs. Amer. Bar Assn. State Bar of OK. **Pubns.:** *Meeting the Legal Information Needs of Michigan, A Study of the Michigan State Law Library* (Rprt.) (1980); "Race and Power Politics as Aspects of Federal Guardianship Over American Indians," *Amer. Indian Law Rev.* (1976). **Activities:** 1, 12; 17; 66, 77 **Addr.:** Golden Gate Univ., 536 Mission St., San Francisco, CA 94105.

Carter, Robert R. (F. 29, 1932, Riverside, CA) Consult., Asst. Prof., CA State Univ., Los Angeles, 1979–; Dir., Lrng. Assistance Ctr., Pasadena City Coll., 1976–79, Libn., 1967–76; Tchr., Pasadena Unified Sch. Dist., 1960–67. **Educ.:** Orange Coast Coll., 1956–57, AA; CA State Univ., Los Angeles, 1957–60, BA (Eng.); Immaculate Heart Coll., 1963–66, MALS. **Orgs.:** West. Coll. Readg. Assn. Cmnty. Coll. Assn. for Instr. and Tech. CA Tchrs. Assn.: Pres., Pasadena City Coll. Chap. (1976–77). **Honors:** Disting. Srv. Awd., Omicron Mu Delta, 1975. **Pubns.:** *Ready Reference: a Workbook on Reference Materials* (1977); *Social Science: a Workbook on Reference Materials* (1971); "New Multimedia Center", *Journal of Media and Technology* (Fall 1972); "Just for Fun–a Bookish Kind of Quiz", *California School Libraries* (Spr. 1971). **Activities:** 1, 10; 24, 26, 32; 50, 63, 75 **Addr.:** 5451 Reef Way, Channel Islands Harbor, Oxnard, CA 93030.

Carter, Ruth C. (D. 13, 1937, Cincinnati, OH) Head, Cat. Dept., Head, Ser. Unit, Univ. of Pittsburgh, 1981–; 1973–81; Syst. Libn., 1972–73; Head, Tech. Srvs., Parkland Coll., 1970–72; Comp. Syst. Anal., U.S. Army, 1964–66. **Educ.:** Univ. of Cincinnati, 1955–59, BSEd (Hist.), 1960–61, MA (Eur. Hist.); Univ. of IL, 1969–70, MSLS. **Orgs.:** ALA: RTSD (Pol. and Resrch. Com., 1980–81; Resrch. Libs. Disc. Grp., Ch., 1978). PA LA. Pittsburgh Reg. Lib. Ctr.: Ch., Ad Hoc Com. on Union List of Per. (1975–); Peer Cncl., (1975–78). **Pubns.:** Jt. Auth., *Bibliography and index of North American Carboniferous brachiopods,* (1970); "Steps toward an on-line union list," *Jnl. of Lib. Auto.* (Mr. 1978); "Systems analysis as a prelude to library automation," *Lib. Trends* (Ap. 1973). **Activities:** 1, 10; 34, 44, 46; 56, 75 **Addr.:** 121 Pikemont Dr., Wexford, PA 15090.

Carter, Selina Jewell (Alexander) (Ja. 3, 1928, Birmingham, AL) Lib. Dir., Ida V. Moffett Sch. of Nursing, Samford Univ., 1978–; Reader Srvs. Libn., Golden Gate Theo. Semy., 1971–78; Circ., Ref. Libn., Univ. of AL, Birmingham, 1968–71; Reader Srvs. Libn., Asst. Libn., Samford Univ. Lib., 1963–68. **Educ.:** Samford Univ., 1957–62, BS (Human Rel.); Univ. of Denver, 1962–63, MA (Libnshp.). **Orgs.:** AL LA: PR Com. (1979–). Med. LA. SELA. ALA. Other orgs. Natl. Leag. for Nursing; Hlth. Educ. Media Assn. Huffman Bapt. Church. **Activities:** 1, 14-Sch. of Nursing; 17, 24 **Addr.:** Ida V. Moffett School of Nursing of Samford University, 820 Montclair Rd., Birmingham, AL 35213.

Carter, Thomas George (N. 11, 1949, Joliet, IL) Dir., Wilmington (IL) Pub. Lib., 1976–; Head of Bkmobile and Chld. Srvs., Joliet Pub. Lib., 1975–76; Head of Div. Data Ctr. Computer Lib., US Army, 1972–75. **Educ.:** IL State Univ., 1969–72, BA (LS); Governor's State Univ., 1976–78, MA (Comm.). **Orgs.:** ALA: JMRT Memb. Mtg., Ch., (1978–79), Chicago Conf. Arrange. Comm. (1978), Midwinter Actv. Com. Ch. (1977–78). IL LA: JMRT Pres. (1979), Treas. (1977–78), Chicago Conf. Arrange. Com. (1978–79). Chicago Lib. Club. AECT. Other orgs. Wilmington Rotary Club. Wilmington Hist. Socty. **Pubns.:** "Librarians and Trustees: What we expect from each other?" *Sum and Substance* (May 1978). **Activities:** 9, 14-Computer Library; 17, 32; 56, 67, 69, 93 **Addr.:** 412 So. Main St., Wilmington, IL 60481.

Carter, Yvonne Breaux (Ag. 3, 1922, Crowley, LA) Educ. Prog. Spec., U.S. Office of Ed., 1967–; Asst. Prof., Lib. Sci., Univ. of Southwest. LA, 1966–67; Sch. Libn., Gueydan HS, LA, 1965–66; Asst. Prof., Lib. Sci., Northwest. State Univ., LA, 1964–65; Principal, Sardis High Sch., TN, 1943–45. **Educ.:** Univ. of Southeast LA, 1939–43, BSE (Math); George Peabody Coll., 1949–50, BSLS, 1959–60, MA (LS), 1963–66, EdS. **Orgs.:** ALA: AASL: (Guidance Com; Counsel. Liaison Com.). Southwest. LA. LA LA. LA Assn. of Sch. Libns.: VP (1965–66); Pres. (1966–67). Delta Kappa Gamma: Pres. (1977–79); VP (1975–77); Chap. Pres. Alpha Epsilon. Pres., DC Chap. Assn. for Educ. Com. and Tech. **Honors:** Kappa Delta Phi; Beta Phi Mu. **Pubns.:** Jt. Auth., *Aids to Media Selection for Children and Teachers* (1979); "Towards Common Goals," LA Schs. (O. 1960); "Leadership Role and Future," OH Media Assn. (O. 1977). **Activities:** 4, 10; 17; 63 **Addr.:** 301 G St. S.W., Apt. 213, Washington, DC 20024.

Cartier, Céline (My. 10, 1930, Lacolle, PQ) Dir. Gén. des Bib., Univ. Laval, 1978–, Chef de la Bib. Gén., 1977–78; Dir. des Bib. de Sect., Univ. du PQ, 1976–77, Dir. des Col. Spéc., 1973–76; Dir. de la Bib. Ctrl., Comsn. des Écoles Cath. de Montreal, 1964–73. **Educ.:** Ecole Natl. d'Admin. Pub., 1973–76, MAP (Pub. Admin.); Univ. de Montreal, 1946–48, Dipl. Sup. (Ped.), 1950–52, Cert. (Lit., Lang); École de Bibtcrs., 1961–62, Dipl. (Bibl.); Univ. de Montreal, 1976–, (Bibl.) **Orgs.:** ASTED. ALA. Can LA. **Pubns.:** "L'Auto-évaluation et les Instruments de Mesure dans les Bibliothèques de Recherche," *ASTED* (1978); "L'influence de la France sur la Bibliothéconomie Québecoise," *ASTED* (1977); "La Promotion des Bibliothèques dans une Société de Consommation," *Lecture et Bibl. de France* (1973); *Rencontre sur la Bibliothéconomie Québécoise* (1975). **Activities:** 1; 17, 34; 67, 70 **Addr.:** Bibliothèque, Université Laval, Cité universitaire, Québec, PQ G1K 7P4 Canada.

Cartledge, Ellen Giordano (Ja. 21, 1947, NY, NY) Libn., CT Mutual Life Insurance Co., 1977–; Docmst., Resrchr., Intl. Cncl. for Educ. Dev., 1971–77. **Educ.:** Bard Coll., 1965–69, BA (Drama); South. CT State Coll., 1971–74, MS (LS). **Orgs.:** SLA: CT Chap. (Pres., 1977–78), Prog. Ch. (1976–77), Bltn. Ed. (1975–76). **Pubns.:** Jt. Auth., "The Construction of Delphi Event Statements," *Tech. Forecasting and Soc. Change* (1971). **Activities:** 12; 17, 39, 41; 59, 76 **Addr.:** Connecticut Mutual Life Insurance Co., 140 Garden St., Hartford, CT 06115.

Cartmell, Vivien M. (D. 16, 1945, Kabwe, Zambia) Documtn. Ofcr., Cat. Ed., Pub. Arch. of Can., Natl. Map Coll., 1973–; Catlgr., Natl. Lib. of Can., 1972–73; Resrch. Asst., Geo. Dept., Univ. of Zambia, 1970–71. **Educ.:** Univ. of Otago, New Zealand, 1965–67, BA (Geo.); 1968–69, MA (Geo.); (Graduate) Univ. of West. ON, 1971–72, MLS. **Orgs.:** Assn. of Can. Map Libs.: Natl. Un. Cat. Com. Anglo-Amer. Cat. Com. for Cartographic Mat.: Secretariat, Ed. Com. (1979–81). Can. Cat. Com.: Observer for Assn. of Can. Map Libs. **Activities:** 20, 24; 70 **Addr.:** Public Archives of Canada, National Map Collection, 395 Wellington Street, Ottawa, ON K1A 0N3 Canada.

Cartwright, Moira Catherine (Je. 16, 1921, Macleod, AB) Chief Libn., Kingston Pub. Lib., 1978–; Head of Adult Srvs., 1969–77; Libn., Alcan Resrch. & Dev., 1947–66. **Educ.:** Univ. of AB, 1939–42, BA (Hons. Mods.); Univ. of Toronto, 1966–67, BLS; Lib. Admin. Dev. Course, Univ. of MD, 1975. **Orgs.:** Can. LA. ON LA: Ch., Litcy. Gld. (1979–80). SLA: Ch., Metals Div. (1959–60); Ch., Resol. Com. (1966–67); John Cotton Dana Lect. (1967). Can. Fed. of Univ. Women: Pres., Kingston Branch (1955–56). Kingston Symphony Assn.: Pres. (1973–75). **Pubns.:** "Selected bibliography of metals library literature," *Spec. Libs.* (Mr. 1965); "Survey of the history of academic libraries in Canada," *Can. Libs.* (S.-O. 1968). **Activities:** 9, 12; 16, 17, 39; 81, 89, 91 **Addr.:** Kingston Public Library, 130 Johnson St., Kingston, ON K7L 1X8 Canada.

Cartwright, Phyllis B. (My. 29, 1925, Middletown, OH) Syst. Libn., Tech. Srvs., Broward (FL) Cnty. Libs., 1978–; Corp. Libn., FL Power and Light Co., 1975–78; Asst. Dir., FL Intl. Univ., 1971–75; Asst. Dir., FL Atl. Univ., 1967–71; Dir., Converse Coll. Lib., 1964–67; Cat. Libn., Armstrong Jr. Coll., 1961–64. **Educ.:** Univ. of Miami, 1951–55, BM (Msc. Educ.); FL State Univ., 1961–63, MS (LS). **Orgs.:** FL LA: Coll. and Spec. Lib. Div. (Ch., 1973). SLA: Pub. Utilities Div.; Nuclear Energy Div. ALA: Internship Com. (1969–74); RTSD/Serials Sect., Policy and Resrch. Com. (Secy., 1973, Ch., 1975), Tech. Srvs. Admin. of Med.-Sized Resrch. Libs. Discuss. Grp. (1971–75); other coms. Zonta Intl. **Activities:** 9; 17, 34, 46; 56, 75, 93 **Addr.:** 1301 River Reach Dr., Apt. 117, Fort Lauderdale, FL 33315.

Caruso, Elaine (Je. 2, 1926, Ronco, PA) Pres., Caruso Assocs., Inc. 1980–; Consult., Lib., Univ. of Pittsburgh, 1979–81, Assoc. Prof. (LS), 1976–79, Asst. Prof. (LS), 1970–76. **Educ.:** CA State Tchrs. Coll., 1943–47, BS ED (Biol.); Carnegie Inst. of Tech., 1957–58, MLS; Univ. of Pittsburgh, 1963–69, PHD (Info. Sci.). **Orgs.:** ASIS. AAAS. **Pubns.:** "Trainer," *ONLINE Mag.* (Ja. 1981); "Online Scholars, Save Time & Dollars," *Intl. Std. Assn. Nsltr.* (Spr. 1981); "CAI for Online Retrieval," *Anl. Rev. of Info. Sci. and Tech.* (1981). **Activities:** 1, 4; 24, 25, 31 **Addr.:** CARUSO Associates, Inc., 440 Second St., California, PA 15419.

Special Subjects/Services: 50. Adult educ.; 51. Advert./Mktg.; 52. Aerosp.; 53. Agric.; 54. Area std.; 55. Arts/Hum.; 56. Autom.; 57. Bibl./Prtg.; 58. Bio. sci.; 59. Bus./Fin.; 60. Chem.; 61. Copyrt.; 62. Documtn.; 63. Educ.; 64. Engin.; 65. Env.; 66. Eth. grps.; 67. Film; 68. Food/Nutr.; 69. Geneal.; 70. Geo.; 71. Geol.; 72. Handcpd.; 73. Hist.; 74. Int. frdm.; 75. Info. sci.; 76. Insr.; 77. Law; 78. Legis.; 79. Math./Comp. sci.; 80. Med.; 81. Metals; 82. Nat. resrcs.; 83. Newsp.; 84. Nuc. sci.; 85. Oral hist.; 86. Petr./Energy; 87. Pharm.; 88. Phys./Astr./Math.; 89. Readg.; 90. Relig.; 91. Sci./Tech.; 92. Soc. sci.; 93. Telecom.; 94. Transp.; 95. (other).

Caruso, Rose Marie (N. 21, 1944, Madison, WI) Asst. Dir., Coll. Lib., Univ. of WI, Madison, 1972–; Ref. Libn., Univ. of WI Mem. Lib., 1970–72. **Educ.:** Univ. of WI, Madison, 1963–69, BS (Eng.), 1969–70, MLS, 1978–, (Acad. Lib.). **Orgs.:** ALA: ACRL/JMRT (Chap. Cnsl., 1980–83; Ch., Olofson Awd. Com., 1974–75; Ch., Mem. Com., 1975–76; Secy./Treas., 1976–77; Ch., Nom. Com., 1977–78); RASD (Ch., Dartmouth Medal Awd. Com., 1979–80); (Mem. Dartmouth Medal Awd. Com., 1981–82). WI LA: JMRT (Mem. Coord., 1974–75; Ch., Lib. Careers Com. 1972–73; Res. Com., 1975–76; Natl. Lib. Week Com., 1976–77; Ref. and AS Sect. Nom. Com., 1974–75). Madison Area Lib. Cncl. (Ch., Educ. and Prog. Com., 1972–74). Univ. of WI, Madison Lib. Sch. Alum. Assn. (VP, 1973–74; Pres. 1974–75). **Pubns.:** Added Entries (editorial responsibilities) U.W. Memorial Library. **Activities:** 1; 17, 31, 39; 67, 93 **Addr.:** 5459 W. Netherwood, Oregon, WI 53575.

Caruthers, Robert Lee (My. 3, 1945, Jacksonville, FL) Ref., Docum. Libn., Univ. of Louisville, 1973–; Intern Libn. (Circ., Ref.) IN Univ. 1971–73; Instr. (Fr.), Manchester Coll., 1970–71; Instr. (Eng.), École Superieure des Sci. Econ. et Commerciales, Paris, 1969–70. **Educ.:** Univ. of NC, 1963–67, BA (Fr.) IN Univ., 1967–69, MA (Fr.), 1971–73, MLS. **Orgs.:** KY LA: Gvt. Docum. RT (Treas., 1978–80); Acad. Libs. Sect. (Treas., 1974–75). SELA. AAUP. **Honors:** Phi Beta Kappa. **Pubns.:** "Affirmative Action and the Hiring of Professional Librarians," *KY LA Bltn.* (Win. 1976). **Activities:** 1; 29, 31, 39 **Addr.:** Library, University of Louisville, Belknap Campus, Louisville, KY 40292.

Casas de Faunce, Maria (Madrid, Spain) Assoc. Prof., Univ. of PR, 1968–; Asst. Prof., Ling., Assoc. Libn., Inter-Amer. Univ., 1966–67; Acq. Libn., Undergrad. Lib., Univ. of MI, 1964–66, Asst. Head, Slavic Cat., 1961–64. **Educ.:** Univ. of MN, 1957–60, BA (Ling.); Univ. of MI, 1960–66, MLS, MA (Rom. Langs.); Univ. of PR, 1968–75, PhD (Latin Amer. Lit.); Consejo Superior de Investigaciones Cientificas, 1977, Dipl. Phil. **Orgs.:** Sem. on Acq. Latin Amer. Lib. Mtrls.: Oral Hist. Com. (1967–77); Persnl. Com. (1968–). Socty. de Bibtcr. de PR: Prof. Trng. (Ch., 1973–75). AALS. Various other orgs. Lambda Alpha Psi. Asociación de Lingüistas y Filólogos de America Latina. Latin Amer. Std. Assn. **Pubns.:** *Aplicación descriptiva de las normas catalográficas angloamericanas 2* (1980); *La Novela Picaresca Latinoamericana* (1977); Jt.-auth., *MARCAL: Manual de Catalogación Mecanizada para America Latina* (1976, 1978); "Bibliotecología en el Banquilio," *Revista Colegio Abogados PR* (N. 1979); Various other articles. **Activities:** 1, 12; 15, 20, 29; 55, 57, 83 **Addr.:** Escuela Graduada de Bibliotecologia, Universidad de Puerto Rico, P.O. Box 21 906, San Juan, PR 00931.

Casciero, Albert J. (D. 27, 1941, Junin, Buenos Aires, Argentina) Dir., Learning Resrcs., Univ. of the DC, 1978–; Dir., Media Facilities, Assoc. Dir., Inst. Dsgn. Ctr. for Adult Educ., City Coll. of NY, 1967–77. **Educ.:** City Coll. of NY, 1973, BA (Fine Arts); Columbia Univ., 1975, MA (Educ. Tech.). **Orgs.:** ALA; AECT. Socty. of Motion Pics. and TV Engin.; Amer. Film Inst. **Honors:** Phi Beta Kappa, 1973; Golden Awd., Mod. Lang. Film Fest., 1979; Golden Image Cert., Long Island Film Fest., 1978. **Pubns.:** *Introduction to A-V for Technical Assistants* (1981); "AV Materials: A Need for Dialogue," *Educ./Instr. Broadcasting* (1970); "Building a Darkroom," *AV Instr.* (1977); Several films, videotapes, slide shows. **Activities:** 1, 14-Lrng. Resrcs.; 17, 26, 32; 55, 67 **Addr.:** Learning Resources Division, Building 41, Room 106, Van Ness Campus, 4200 Connecticut Ave. N.W., Washington, DC 20008.

Case, Ann Massie (F. 9, 1944, Scottsbluff, NE) Asst. Dir. of Indxg. Srvs. for Ed. Resrch. H. W. Wilson Co., 1981–, Ed., *Bibliographic Index,* 1973–81, Asst. Ed., 1971–73, Indxr., 1968–71. **Educ.:** Univ. of WY, 1962–66, BA (Eng.), 1966–67, MA (Eng.); Rutgers Univ., 1967–68, MLS. **Orgs.:** ALA. SLA. NY Lib. Club. NY Tech. Srvs. Libns. **Honors:** Phi Beta Kappa. Beta Phi Mu. **Activities:** 6; 20, 30, 37 **Addr.:** The H. W. Wilson Co., 950 University Ave., Bronx, NY 10452.

Case, Barbara Sharon (N. 21, 1946, San Pedro, CA) Head, Cat. Sect., CA State Univ., Los Angeles, 1975–, Admin. Asst., 1973–75; Catlgr., Univ. of CA, Santa Barbara, 1970–71. **Educ.:** Univ. of CA, Santa Barbara, 1965–66; Georg-August Univ., W. Germany, 1967–68; Univ. of CA, Berkeley, 1966–69, BA (Grmn.), 1969–70, MLS; Harvard Grad. Sch. of Bus. Admin., 1972–1973; CA State Univ., Los Angeles, 1975–81, (Bus. Admin.). **Orgs.:** ALA: Promotion Task Frc. (Los Angeles Area Rep.); RTSD; LITA. CA LA. CA State Univ. and Colls.: various coms. **Activities:** 1; 17, 20, 46; 56, 59, 75 **Addr.:** 612 S. Gertruda Ave., Redondo Beach, CA 90277.

Case, Patricia J. (Jl. 24, 1952, Hartford, CT) Spec. Cols. Asst., Univ. of CT Lib., 1976–. **Educ.:** Univ. of CT, 1970–75, BA (Phil.); South. CT State Coll., 1977–81, MLS. **Orgs.:** ALA: ACRL; SRRT, *Alternatives in Print* (Managing Ed., 1981–82). **Pubns.:** Jt. ed., *Alternative Papers* (1981); "Collections of Contemporary Alternative Materials in Libraries: A Directory," *Alternative Materials in Libraries: A Handbook* (1981). **Activities:** 1; 15, 37, 45 **Addr.:** University of Connecticut Library, Storrs, CT 06268.

Case, Robert N. (Mr. 22, 1931, Lorain, OH) Dir., Lancaster Cnty. Lib., 1974–; Dir., Sch. Lib. Manpower Proj., ALA, 1968–74; Sch. Lib. Consul., OH Dept. of Educ., 1965–68; Head Libn., Rocky River, (OH) HS, 1958–65; Eng. Tchr., Napoleon, (OH) HS, 1955–58. **Educ.:** Miami Univ., 1949–53, BS (Educ.); Case-Western Reserve Univ., 1955–60, MSLS. **Orgs.:** OH LA: Dev. Com. (1965–68). OH Assn. of Sch. Libns.: Pres. (1967–68). ALA: PLA Lib. Srvs. & Chld. Com., Ch. (1977–80); Open Meeting Policy Statement, Ch. (1977–80); PA LA: Cnty.-Pub. Div., Ch. (1976–77); Cont. Educ. Com., Ch. (1977–80). Other orgs. Amer. Cancer Socty.: Campaign Ch. (1959–64). Grosse Pointe Lighthouse Nature Ctr.: Bd. of Dir. (1969–74); Pres. (1972–74). Ladd Arboretum Ecology Ctr.: Bd. of Dir. (1973–75). Lancaster Rotary Club: Newsletter Ed. (1981-82). **Honors:** Beta Phi Mu; Proposal Evaluator Higher Education Act, USOE, 1971. **Pubns.:** Jt. auth., *Evaluation of Alternative Curriculum* (1975); *Curriculum Alternatives* (1974); "The Knapp Foundation," *Encyclopedia of Library and Information Sciences* (1972); "Measuring Program Effectiveness," *Drexel Lib. Qtly.* (July 1978); Other bks. and articles. **Activities:** 9, 10; 16, 17, 21; 55, 85 **Addr.:** Lancaster County Library, 125 N. Duke St., Lancaster, PA 17602.

Case, Suzanne Espenett (N. 29, 1928, Jefferson City, MO) Actg. Prin., Hanahauoli Sch., 1980–, Libn., 1969–79. **Educ.:** Wellesley Coll., 1946–49; Univ. of HI, 1949–58, BA (Sp.); Univ. of HI, 1966–69, MLS. **Orgs.:** HI Assn. of Sch. Libns.: Pres. (1978–79); VP (1977–78); Dir. (1975–77). HI LA. ALA. **Honors:** Beta Phi Mu. **Activities:** 10; 21 **Addr.:** 3757 Round Top Drive, Honolulu, HI 96822.

Casebier, Janet Jenks (O. 11, 1946, Hollywood, CA) Hum. and Soc. Sci. Libn., CA Inst. of Tech., 1975–; Docum. and Hum. Per. Libn., 1974–75; Docum. Libn., Univ. of South. CA Law Sch. Lib., 1970–73. **Educ.:** Los Angeles Valley Comnty. Coll., 1964–67, AA (Pol. Sci.); Univ. of CA, Los Angeles, 1967–69, BA (Soclgy.); Univ. of South. CA, 1969–70, MLS. **Orgs.:** NLA: Mem. Dir. (1979–81). CA LA: Gvt. Docum. Chapt., Nsltr. Ed. (1978–79); Chap. of Acad. & Resrch. Libs. SLA: South. CA Chap. Amer. Soc. for Aesthetics, Pacific Div.: Treas. (1979–80). Natl. Org. for Women. Natl. Alliance for Optional Parenthood. **Pubns.:** Jt. ed., *Social Responsibilities of the Mass Media,* (1978); "Bibliography on Dreams and Films," *Dreamworks* (1980). **Activities:** 1; 17, 29, 33; 55, 92 **Addr.:** Caltech Pasadena, CA 91125.

Casellas, Elizabeth Reed Brannon (Ja. 7, 1925, New Orleans, LA) Art Resrch. and Writer, 1977–; Assoc. Prof., Tulane Univ., Grad. Sch. of Bus., 1969–77; Head, Bus., Sci. and Tech. Dept., Orlando Pub. Lib., 1965–69; Asst. Prof. and Bus. Biblgphr., Univ. of HI, 1964–65; Dir., Lib., Stewart, Dougall & Associates, New York, 1960–64; Dir., Lib., Cresap, McCormick & Paget, New York, 1959–60; Dir., Lib., Comm. Couns., Inc., New York, 1957–59. **Educ.:** Chicago Musical Coll., 1942–48, BM; Columbia Univ., 1959–64, MS (Lib. Sci.); 1948–49, MA (Educ.); 1949–52, (Spec. in Educ.); New York Univ., 1950–51, (Grmn.); Univ. of Paris, 1953–54, (Fr.); Tulane Univ., 1970, (Span.). **Orgs.:** SLA: (Founder, FL Chap., 1968–69; NY Chap. Advert. Grp: Lectr., 1958; Pres., LA Chap. 1974–75). ALA. **Honors:** Beta Gamma Sigma, Tulane Univ. Chap., 1973; Kappa Delta Pi, 1951, Phi Mu Gamma, Composition Award, 1948. **Pubns.:** *Academic Business Librarians in the United States: Their Faculty Status and Its Relationship to the Development of Their Professional Activities and Published Writings* (1979); *Guide to Basic Information Sources in Business Administration,* (1974); "Library of Congress Proof Slips: The Overlooked Selection Medium for Business Libraries," *Spec. Libs.,* (March 1972); "Relative Effectiveness of the Harvard Business, Library of Congress and the Dewey Decimal Classifications for a Marketing Collection," *Lib. Resrcs. & Tech. Srvs.* (Fall 1965); "Business, Science and Technology Services in Florida Public Libraries," *FL Libs.* (March 1968); other articles. **Activities:** 1, 12; 17, 26, 39; 51, 57, 59 **Addr.:** 2442 Dauphine St., New Orleans, LA 70117.

Caselli, Jaclyn R. (Mr. 28, 1921, Boston, MA) Lib. Oper., Resrch. Libs. Grp., Resrch. Libs. Info. Ntwk., 1978–; Lib. Coord., BALLOTS, 1976–78; Dir., Acq., ERIC Clearinghouse on Info., 1973–76; Dir., Acq., ERIC Clearinghouse on Educ. Media, 1969–73. **Educ.:** San Jose State Univ., 1971–76, BA (Eng.), 1976–79, MLS. **Orgs.:** ALA. SLA. CA LA. **Honors:** Phi Kappa Phi. **Pubns.:** "John Steinbeck and the American Patchwork Quilt," *San Jose Std.* (N. 1975). **Activities:** 1, 12; 34, 46; 56 **Addr.:** 1528 Carmel Dr., San Jose, CA 95125.

Casey, Daniel W. (Ja. 13, 1921, Malone, NY) Trustee, Solnay Pub. Lib., 1954–; Trustee, Onondaga Cnty. Pub. Lib., 1974–. **Educ.:** Niagara Univ., 1938–42, BS (Jnlsm.). **Orgs.:** ALA: Cncl. (1977–81); ALTA, Endowment Com. (Ch.); Pres. (1973–74); Bd. of Dirs.; PLA, Bd. of Dirs. NY LA: Dev. Com. (1968–71, Ch.). NCLIS. NY State Bd. of Regents: Adv. Cncl. on Libs. (Vice-Ch. 1975–80). Woman's Natl. Book Assn. Syracuse Rotary Club. Literacy Volum. of Amer.: Natl. Bd. Onondaga Citizens Leag. **Honors:** ALA: ALTA, Trustee Cit., 1977; NY State Assn. of Lib. Bds., Velma K. Moore Meml. Awd., 1974; Onondaga Lib. Syst., Cit., 1969. **Activities:** 9, 10; 24, 36, 47; 51, 74, 78 **Addr.:** 202 Scarboro Dr., Syracuse, NY 13209.

Casey, Genevieve M. (Jl. 13, 1916, Minneapolis, MN) Prof. (LS), Wayne State Univ., 1967–; State Libn., MI State Lib., 1961–67; Chief, Ext. Div., Detroit Pub. Lib., 1948–60; US Army Libn., Europe, 1947–48. **Educ.:** Coll. of St. Catherine, 1933–37, BS (LS); Univ. of MI, 1956, MLS. **Orgs.:** ALA: PLA (Pres., 1973–75), Lib. Educ. Div. (Pres. 1970); AHIL (Pres., 1960–61). AALS: Pres. (1978), Legis Com. (Ch., 1979–). MI LA. **Honors:** MI LA, Libn. of the Yr., 1978; Univ. of MI, Disting. Alum., 1975; ASCLA, Excep. Srv. Awd., 1979. **Pubns.:** *Public Library in the Network Mode: A Preliminary Investigation* (1974); "Public Library Collections and Materials," *ALA World Ency. of Lib. and Info. Srvs.* (1980); "The Management of Retrenchment," *Pub. Libs.* (Sum. 1979); "Administration of State and Federal Funds for Library Development," Lib. Trends (Fall 1978); many other articles. **Activities:** 5, 9; 16, 17, 24; 50, 78, 90 **Addr.:** 373 Rivard, Grosse Pointe, MI 48230.

Casey, Marion T. (N. 7, 1930, Chicago, IL) Asst. Prof., Univ. of CA, Berkeley, 1979–; Asst. Prof., Univ. of Richmond, 1976–78; Fulbright Prof., Univ. of Saigon & Univ. of Seoul, Korea, 1974–76. **Educ.:** Rosary Coll., 1957, BA (Hist.); Univ. of IL, 1964, MA (Hist.); Univ. of WI, 1971, PhD (Hist.). **Orgs.:** ALA. Amer. Hist. Assn. Org. of Amer. Histns. **Honors:** Natl. Endowment for the Hum., 1974, 1978; Smithsonian Awd., 1973. **Pubns.:** "Efficiency, Taylorism & Libraries in Progressive America," *Jnl. of Lib. Hist.* (Ja. 1980); "Charles McCarthy's 'Idea': A Library to Change Government," *Lib. Qtly.,* (Ja. 1974). **Activities:** 1, 4; 41, 42; 73, 78, 85, 92 **Addr.:** School of Library & Information Studies, U. of California, Berkeley, Berkeley, CA 94720.

Cash, Pamela J. (O. 26, 1948, Cleburne, TX) Libn., Johnson Pub. Co., 1973–; Libn., Univ. of TX, Arlington, 1972–73. **Educ.:** Univ. of OK, 1966–70, BA (Soclgy.); Univ. of IL, 1970–72, MLS. **Orgs.:** SLA: Pub. Div. (Treas. 1976–77). ALA. ASIS. YWCA. Assn. for the Study of Afro-Amer. Life and Hist. **Activities:** 12; 17, 39, 41 **Addr.:** Library, Johnson Publishing Co., 820 S. Michigan Ave., Chicago, IL 60605.

Casini, Barbara Palmer (Mr. 1, 1940, Philadelphia, PA) Head Libn., Easttown Twp. Lib. (Berwyn, PA), 1981–; Managing Ed., Drexel Lib. Qtly., Drexel Univ., 1974–81. **Educ.:** Swarthmore Coll., 1959–62, BA (Latin); Drexel Univ., 1972–74, MS (LS). **Orgs.:** PA LA: Ed., *PLA Bulletin* (1980–). ALA. Ridley Township Pub. Lib.: Trustee (1978–); Bd. Pres. (1979–). PA Citizens for Better Libraries. **Honors:** Beta Phi Mu, 1974. **Pubns.:** "Private Foundations," *ALA Yrbk.* (1980); Jt. ed., "Library and Information Services for Older Adults," *Drexel Library Quarterly* (1979); Jt. Auth., *Curriculum and Instruction: A Guide to Alternatives* (1976); column "From the States" *New Library World* (London) (1979–). **Activities:** 9, 11; 24, 37, 47; 63, 95-Lib. Srvs. for Older Adults. **Addr.:** Easttown Township Library, Berwyn, PA 19312.

Caskey, Jefferson Dixon (Jl. 31, 1922, Lancaster, SC) Prof. of Lib. Sci. and Instr. Media, West. KY Univ., 1974–; Asso. Prof., Dir. of Lib. Sci. Prog., TX A & I Univ., 1970–74; Head Libn., Houston Baptist Univ., 1963–70; Head Libn. and Asst. Prof. of Lib. Sci., Little Rock Univ., 1960–63; Head Libn. and Assoc. Prof. of Lib. Sci., Pfeiffer Coll., 1956–60; Assoc. Libn. and Asst. Prof., Shepherd Coll., 1954–56; Cat. Libn., Asst. Ref. Libn., Auburn Univ., 1953–54; Eng. Tchr., SC Pub. Sch., 1948–52. **Educ.:** Erskine Coll., 1945–48, AB (Eng.); Syracuse Univ., 1952–53, MS (LS); Univ. of Houston, 1964–66, MA (Eng.); 1967–72, EdD (Eng. Educ.); Inst. of Chld. Lit., 1975–76, Dipl. (Writing for Children). **Orgs.:** KY LA. KY Sch. Media Assn. Natl. Concl. of Tchrs. of Eng. Church and Synagogue LA. Other orgs. Odd Fellows. Phi Delta Kappa. **Pubns.:** *Samuel Taylor Coleridge: A Selective Bibliography of Criticism* (1979); "No time to be lonely: A biographical sketch of Beatrix Potter," *Rainbow Mag.* (1977); "Reference books on religions reviewed," *Church & Synagogue Libs.* (1978); "Miss Barbara's dividends," *Face to Face Mag.* (1978); "We have Many Sources for Creative Storytelling," *Church Tchrs.* (1979); other articles, reviews. **Activities:** 10, 11; 16, 26, 39; 50, 57, 72 **Addr.:** 1016 Meadowwood, Bowling Green, KY 42101.

Caskey, Mary Lou (D. 6, 1951, Herkimer, NY) Cmnty. Srvs. Consult., Mid-York Lib. Syst., 1981–, Outrch. Consult., 1978–81; Branch Libn., Utica Pub. Lib., 1978; Rare Book Prcs., George Arents Resrch. Lib., 1976–77. **Educ.:** SUNY Oswego, 1969–73, BA (Russ.); Syracuse Univ., 1975–78; MLS; NY State Pub. Libns. Cert. **Orgs.:** NY LA: Pub. Lib. Sect., Outreach Com. (1979–); Ref. and Adult Srvs. Sect., Lcl. Jails Com. (1979–). Ctrl. NY LA: Pres. (1981). Poland Cmnty. Civic Club. **Activities:** 1, 9; 27, 36, 45; 54, 55, 72 **Addr.:** Box 127, Poland, NY 13431.

Casno, Pierre-Peteris (Je. 2, 1922, Aizkalne, Latvia) Sr. Ref. Libn., Bib. E.P.C., Univ. of Montreal, 1960–, Fac. of Educ., 1967–. **Educ.:** Classical Gymnasium Aglona (Latvia), 1939–43, BA (Latin, Greek); Baltic Univ., Hamburg, 1947–49, MA (Phil.); Univ. de Louvain (Belgium), 1950–57, MA (Ped.), 1960–69, PhD (Educ.). **Orgs.:** Corp. des Bibtcrs. Prof. du PQ. CAIS. Amer. Assn. for Higher Educ. Intl. Assn. for Appld. Psy. Assn. Intl. de la Recherche en Educ. de la Lang. Fr. **Pubns.:** Jt. auth., *Bibliographie Sur l'Education du Canada Francais* (1975); Autre Aspects (1976; 1977; 1978). **Activities:** 1, 12; 39, 41, 45; 63, 92 **Addr.:** 200, Ave. Lagace, Dorval, PQ H9S 2M1 Canada.

PROFESSIONAL ACTIVITIES: Institutions: 1. Acad. lib.; 2. Arch.; 3. Assn.; 4. Fed./Gvt. lib.; 5. Inst. lib.; 6. Mfr./Suppl.; 7. Milit. lib.; 8. Musm.; 9. Pub. lib.; 10. Sch. lib.; 11. Sch. of lib. sci.; 12. Spec. lib.; 13. State lib.; 14. (other). **Functions/Activities:** 15. Acq./Col. dev.; 16. Adult srvs.; 17. Admin.; 18. Apprais.; 19. Archit./Bldgs.; 20. Cat./Class.; 21. Chld. srvs.; 22. Circ.; 23. Cons./Pres.; 24. Consult.; 25. Cont. ed.; 26. Educ. lib. sci.; 27. Ext. srvs.; 28. Fund/Grants; 29. Gvt. pubs.; 30. Indx./Abs.; 31. Instr. lib. use; 32. Media srvs.; 33. Micro.; 34. Netwks./Coop.; 35. Persnl.; 36. PR; 37. Publshg.; 38. Recs. mgt.; 39. Ref. srvs.; 40. Repro.; 41. Resrch.; 42. Review.; 43. Secur.; 44. Serials; 45. Spec. col.; 46. Tech. srvs.; 47. Trustees/Bds.; 48. YA srvs.; 49. (other).

Cason, Cleo (Stargel) (Je. 24, 1910, Dahlonega, GA) Chief Libn., Madison Cnty. Pub. Law Lib., 1973–; Chief Tech. Libn., U. S. Army, Redstone Arsenal, AL, 1949–73. **Educ.:** N. GA Coll., 1926–28; Univ. of AL, 1951–53; Univ. Sch. of Law, 1946–49, LLB (Law). **Orgs.:** SLA: Pres., AL Chap. (1955–56). AL LA: Ch., Univ. & Spec. Libs. Div. (1959–60). Bus. and Prof. Women's Club: Chap. Pres. (1950–51). Aladdin Club of Huntsville: Pres. (1958, 1967, 1976). **Honors:** Dept. of the Army, Meritorious Civilian Service Awd., 1970; Madison Cnty., AL, Citation of Merit for Outstanding Srvc., 1971. **Pubns.:** *Huntsville Hist. Review,* Member Editorial Board (1971–75); military librarians wkshps., contrib. (1949–73). **Activities:** 12; 17; 64, 77, 74 **Addr.:** 700 Watts Drive, SE, Huntsville, AL 35801.

Casper, Dale Edward (F. 24, 1947, Mt. Clemens, MI) User Srvs. Coord., St. Clair Cnty. Cmnty. Coll., 1976–; Libn., Dakota Cnty. (MN), 1975–76; Libn., Tchr., Maternity of Mary Sch., 1972–75; Libn., MN Pub. Lib., 1974–76. **Educ.:** MI State Univ., 1965–69, BA (Hist.); Univ. of MN, 1969–72, MA (Hist.), 1972–75, MA (LS), 1975–81, PhD (Hist.). **Orgs.:** MI LA. Southeast. MI Leag. of Libs. Thumb Area Med. Info. Cnsrtm. Amer. Hist. Assn. MI Assn. for Higher Educ. **Honors:** Phi Kappa Phi. Phi Beta Kappa. **Activities:** 1; 20, 31, 39; 55, 63, 92 **Addr.:** St Clair County Community College, 323 Erie St., Port Huron, MI 48060.

Cassell, Kay Ann (S. 24, 1941, Van Wert, OH) Dir., Huntington Pub. Lib., 1981–; Dir., Bethlehem (NY) Pub. Lib., 1975–81; Adult Srvs. Consult., Westchester Lib. Syst., 1973–75; Peace Corps Volun., Rabat, Morocco, 1971–73; Adult Srvs. Consult., NJ State Lib., 1968–71; Ref. Libn., Brooklyn Coll. Lib., 1965–68. **Educ.:** Carnegie-Mellon Univ., 1959–63, BS (Mod. Lang.); Rutgers Univ., 1963–65, MLS; Brooklyn Coll., 1965–69, MA (Comp. Lit.); **Orgs.:** ALA: Ch., Awd. Com. (1977–79); Co-Ch., ERA Task Force (1979–). NY LA: Pres., RASD (1975–78). NJ LA: Pres., Adult Srvs. Sect.. (1970–71). **Honors:** Beta Phi Mu. **Pubns.:** "Libraries to serve the people of New Jersey," *Sch. Bd. Notes* (Mr.-Ap. 1970); "An International Woman - Assignment: Morocco," *Wilson Lib. Bltn.* (June 1973); "Women in Print: An Update" *Lib. Jnl.* (Je. 15, 1977). **Activities:** 9; 16, 17, 36; 50, 55, 95-Women's studies. **Addr.:** Huntington Public Library, 338 Main St., Huntington, NY 11743.

Cassels, Sheila E. (Mr. 30, 1938, Granville, NY) Resrch. Libn., Inst. of Nat. Resrcs., 1977–; Serials Catlgr., Arlington Cnty. Dept. of Libs., 1974–76. **Educ.:** Oberlin Coll., 1956–60, BA (Eng. Lit.); Univ. of WI, Madison, 1973–74, MALS. **Orgs.:** IL LA: SLSS Sect., Secy.-Treas. (1981–82). SLA. ALA. Leag. of Women Voters of Morgan Cnty.: Bd. Mem. (1977–). **Honors:** Beta Phi Mu. **Activities:** 4, 12; 15, 17, 19; 65, 82, 86 **Addr.:** 335 N. Webster Ave., Jacksonville, IL 62650.

Cassidy, Lelia B (S. 3, 1921, Kansas City, MO) Dir., Lib. Srvs., Mendocino Coll., 1973–; Lib., Media Spec., Pasco-Hernando Cmnty. Coll., 1972–73; Asst. Libn., Santa Fe Jr. Coll., 1971–72; Pub. Srvs. Libn., Coll. of the Redwoods, 1967–70. **Educ.:** Univ. of CA, Los Angeles, 1940–42, BA (Psy.); Univ. of South. CA, 1962–63, MSLS. **Orgs.:** ALA. CA LA. Lrng. Resrcs. Assn., CA Cmnty. Colls. **Pubns.:** *Archaeology; Selections for the Small College Library* (1979); "I Can't Hear the Flutes," *Amer. Libs.* (O. 1970); presented papers. **Activities:** 1; 17, 31, 39; 55, 91 **Addr.:** P.O. Box 3000, Ukiah, CA 95482.

Castagna, Edwin (My. 1, 1909, Petaluma, CA) Resrch., Reading on Behavior, 1977–; City Libn., San Francisco Pub. Lib., 1976–77; Dir., Enoch Pratt Free Lib., MD, 1960–75; City Libn., Long Beach Pub. Lib., CA, 1950–60; City Libn., Glendale Pub. Lib., CA, 1949; Dir., Washoe Cnty. Lib., NV, 1940–49; City Libn., Ukiah Pub. Lib., CA, 1937–40. **Educ.:** Univ. of CA, Berkeley, 1932–35, AB (Eng.), 1935–36, Cert. in Lib. **Orgs.:** NV LA: Pres. (1946–47). CA LA: Pres. (1954–55). ALA: Pres. (1964–65): Intl. Assn. of Metro. Libs.: VP (1967–70). Baltimore Bibl.: Pres. (1975). Union de Bibl. Taurinos (Spain). MD Com. for the Human. and Pub. Pol., (1973–75). Fourteen W. Hamilton St. Club, Baltimore. **Pubns.:** *History of the 771st Tank Battalion,* (1946); Co.Ed., *The Library Reaches Out,* (1965); Various other articles. **Activities:** 9; 15, 17, 24; 50, 67, 74 **Addr.:** 3601 Greenway, Apt. 305, Baltimore, MD 21218.

Castle, Geoffrey (Uxbridge, Middlesex, Eng.) Head, Map Div., Prov. Arch. of BC, 1975–; Tech. Planner, BC Mnstry. of Lands, Parks and Housing, 1965–75; Supvsg. Draughtsman, BC Forest Srv., 1955–65; Asst. Land Surveyor, BC Lands Srv., 1952–55. **Educ.:** Univ. of Victoria, BA (Geo., Hist.), MPA (Pub. Admin.) **Orgs.:** Assn. of Can. Map Libs.: 2nd VP, (1979–80). BC Hist. Assn.: Victoria Branch (VP 1980–81). Royal Geographical Socty.: BC Grp. (Secy., 1979–81). **Pubns.:** "Victoria Landmarks," weekly column, *Victoria Press* (1981). **Activities:** 2; 15, 20; 70 **Addr.:** Map Division, BC Provincial Archives, 655 Belleville St., Victoria, BC V8V 1X4 Canada.

Castro, Augustine Camacho (My. 26, 1935, Saipan, Mariana Islands) Retired, 1981–; Cmwlth. Libn., Dept. of Educ., 1978–81, Supvsr., Lib. Srvs. 1966–78, Tchr., Jr. HS, 1962–66, Asst. Tchr. Trainer, 1957–62. **Educ.:** Univ. Tchrs. Coll. at Geneseo, 1962 (LS); E.-W. Ctr., 1970 (Refresher Crs. in Lib. Techqs.); various crs. in LS. **Orgs.:** NCLIS: Ad Hoc Com. (1980). ALA. Pre-White Hse. Conf. on NCLIS: Coord., Planner (1978). LSCA Adv. Cncl.: Org. Com., Trust Territory Pre-White Hse. Conf.: Resrc. Person (1978). Various other orgs., confs. Parents, Tchrs. Assn. **Activities:** 9, 10 **Addr.:** Saipan, Commonwealth of Northern Mariana Islands 96950.

Caswell, Lucy Shelton (O. 22, 1944, Brownwood, TX) Cur., Libn. for Comm. and Graphic Arts, OH State Univ. Libs., 1977–, Head, Jnlsm. Lib., 1970–75; Tchr., MI Pub. Schs., 1967–68. **Educ.:** Austin Coll., 1962–66, AB (Hist.); Univ. of MI, 1969–70, AMLS. **Orgs.:** ALA: RASD/Hist. Sect., Comm. Com. (1970–72); ACRL. Acad. LA of OH. **Honors:** OH LA Florence Head Meml. Awd. (for *Billy Ireland*), 1981; Beta Phi Mu. **Pubns.:** Jt. auth., *Billy Ireland* (1980); "Milton Caniff - Art for Everybody," exhibit cat. (1979); "Jon Whitcomb Retrospective," exhibit cat. (1980); reviews. **Activities:** 1; 15, 23, 45; 55, 95-comic strips and cartoons. **Addr.:** Library for Communication and Graphic Arts, 242 West 18th Ave., Ohio State University, Columbus, OH 43210.

Caton, Doyle L. (Mr. 21, 1934, Ada, OK) Dir., Info. Srvs., Natl. Info. Ctr. Apflt., Univ. of NM, 1978–; Mgr., Energy Info. Prog., Tech. Appl. Ctr. (NASA), Univ. of NM, 1974–78; Asst. Dir., OK Env. Info. Ctr., 1970–74; Tech. Transfer. Spec., Tech. Use Std. Ctr. (NASA), 1966–70; Tech. Info. Spec., Melpar Corp., Goddard Space Ctr., 1965–66; Strategic Intelligence Spec., U.S. Army Secur. Agency, 1959–65; Ballistics Data Spec., White Sands Missile Range, 1955–59. **Educ.:** East Ctr. State Univ. (OK), 1952–55; Southeast. State Univ. (OK), 1967–69, BS (Indus. Tech.); East Ctr. State Univ. (OK), 1970–72, MT (Indus. Educ.); Cert., Cryptography, Photo Interpretation. **Orgs.:** ASIS: Energy Spec. Int. Grp. (Ch., 1979–80). West. Info. Netwk. on Energy: Co-founder; ch.-elect (1980). Tech. Transfer Socty.: Chrt. Mem. NM Solar Energy Assn.: Chrt. Mem. MENSA Intl. **Activities:** 12; 34, 39, 46; 65, 91 **Addr.:** National Energy Information Center Affiliate (NEICHA), Univ. of New Mexico, Albuquerque, NM 87131.

Causley, Monroe Sweeney, Jr. (D. 28, 1929, Bay City, MI) 1975–; Asst. Dir., Support Srvs., 1980–; Morris Cnty. Free Lib., Head of Ref., 1976-80; Ch., Dept. of LS, FL Atl. Univ., 1969–75; Head of Tech. Srvs., Fort Lauderdale Pub. Lib., 1967–68; Head of Bus. & Tech. Dept., Saginaw Pub. Lib., 1963–66. **Educ.:** Central MI Univ., 1960–62, BA (Hist.); Univ. of MI, 1962–63, AMLS. **Orgs.:** ALA. Lib. Consult. NJ Dept. of Civil Srv. (1978–). Amer. Prtg. Hist. Assn. Univ. of MI Sch. of LS Alumni. **Pubns.:** *Bibliography of Holdings of the FL Atl. Univ. Library dealing with Black America* (1969); "The Theodore Pratt Collection," *FL Libn.* (Sum. 1970); *Innokentii, Metropolitan of Moscow, 1797–1879: A Bibliography* (1979). **Activities:** 9; 39, 45; 57 **Addr.:** 2 Green Tree Ln., Dover, NJ 07801.

Cavaleri, Tish A. (O. 19, 1947, Poughkeepsie, NY) Grad. Asst., Exceptional Child Cntr., Utah St. 1981; Lib.-Media Spec., Ramah Navajo Pine Hill Sch., 1977–81; Dir., ITC Lib., Essex Comm. Coll., 1976–77; Head, Tech. Srvs., Dundalk Comm. Coll., 1974–76; Child. Libn., Wissahickon Valley Pub. Lib., 1973–74; Catlgr., Engin. Socty. Lib., NY, 1971–73; Libn., NY State Med. Lib., 1970–71. **Educ.:** Elmira Coll., 1965–69, BA (Lit.); SUNY, Albany, 1969–70, MLS; Various Libn. Certs., PA, NM, NY. **Orgs.:** SLA: Ch. Network Com. (1979–80); Ch., Nom. Com. (1978); Leg. Liaison (1979–80). NM LA: Leg. and Intell. Freedom Com. (1978–80). NMMA: Mem. Ch. (1979–80); Legis. Ch. (1979–80). AECT: Cncl. (1979–81); Gov. Rel. Com. (1979–81); Ed. Ad. Brd., (1979); Okoboji Leadership Conf. Del. (1979); Conv. Plng. Com. (1979). Phi Delta Kappa. Socty. for Creative Anachronism. **Pubns.:** *Dií Shaghandi Hóló,* (1978); "Prickly Pear Cactus," *Tsá'ászi'* (1979). **Activities:** 9, 10; 34, 39, 46; 50, 63 **Addr.:** 715 E Center St., Logan, UT 84321.

Cavallari, Elfrieda L. (S. 9, 1929, Talsi, Latvia) Chief, Cat. Sect., AFGL Resrch. Lib., 1972–, Libn.-Catlgr., 1964–72; Docum. Engin., ITEK Corp., 1963–64; Libn., TX Eastern Transmission Corp., 1957–59. **Educ.:** Ukrainian Politech, Inst., Munich, Germany, 1945–49, (Chem.); Clark Univ., 1951–53, AB (Grmn./Russ.); Simmons Coll., 1961–63, MS (LS); Simmons Coll., Middle Mgt. Prog., 1978. **Orgs.:** SLA: Boston Chap., Recruitment, (Ch. 1967–69); Prog. Com. (1977–78); PR (Ch. 1978–80). ACRL New Eng. Chap. MA Gen. Pub. Awareness Endeavor. ASIS. AAUW. Federally Employed Women: Patriot Chap., VP (1977–78); Pres. (1978–79). **Pubns.:** *Bibliography on Natural Disasters.* (1979). **Activities:** 4, 12; 20, 36, 46; 56, 74, 91 **Addr.:** 18 Lantern Ln., Chelmsford, MA 0 824.

Cavanagh, G. S. Terence (S. 16, 1923, Winnipeg, MB) Cur., Trent Col. in Hist. of Med., Prof., (Med. Lit.), Duke Univ., 1975–, Dir. Med. Ctr. Lib., 1962–75; Libn., Med. Ctr. Lib., Univ. of KS Med. Ctr., 1953–62. **Educ.:** Univ. of MB, 1946–50, BA; McGill Univ., 1950–51, BLS. **Activities:** 1; 18, 45; 57, 80 **Addr.:** Medical Center Library, Duke University, Durham, NC 27710.

Cavanagh, Gladys Louise (O. 26, 1901, Minden City, MI) Ed., *Subject Index to Children's Magazines,* 1967–; Asst. Prof., Lib. Sch., Univ. of WI, 1952–67; Instr., 1948–52; Sch. Lib. Supvsr., 1941–48. **Educ.:** Univ. of WI, 1920–24, BA (Fr.), 1951, MS (Elem. Educ.); Columbia Univ., 1937, BLS. **Orgs.:** WI LA: Ch., State Lib. Com. WI Plng. Prog. (1947–50). ALA. Delta Kappa Gamma. Pi Lambda Theta. **Honors:** WI LA, Cit. of Merit, 1967; Delta Kappa Gamma; Pi Lambda Theta. **Pubns.:** Ed., *Subject Index to Chld. Mags.* (1967–81). **Activities:** 10, 11; 21, 39 **Addr.:** 12049 Pastoral Rd., San Diego, CA 92128.

Cavender, Carol J. (Je. 17, 1947, San Fernando, CA) Mgr., Search and Info. Analysis, Patent Dept., The Dow Chem. Co., 1977–; Patent Searcher, 1974–77; Libn., 1973–74. **Educ.:** Univ. of Houston, 1965–69, BS (Chem.); IN Univ., 1971–73, MLS, 1969–73, PhD (Chem.); Registered Patent Agent, 1975. **Orgs.:** Indus. Tech. Info. Mgr. Grp.: Ch./Coord., Patent Info. Com. (1979–). Derwent On-Line Options Subscriber Com. Info. for Indus. Quality Control Com.: Ch. (1978–). Div. of Chem. Info. of Amer. Chem. Socty. ASIS. Amer. Chem. Socty. Sigma Xi: Chap. Secy. (1976–77). **Pubns.:** "Patent Information," *Midland Chem.* (Ja. 1980); "Trifluoromethanesulfonyl Azide. Its Reaction with Alkyl Amines to Form Alkyl Azides," *Jnl. Org. Chem.,* 37 (1972); "Facile Thermal Cyclization of 6-vinylfulvene to Dihydropentalene" *Tetrahedron Letters,* 1057-60 (1971). **Activities:** 12, 14-Patent Dept.; 17, 39; 60, 91, 95-Patents. **Addr.:** Search and Information Analysis, Patent Department, 1776 Building, The Dow Chemical Company, Midland, MI 48640.

Cavill, Patricia Mary (S. 10, 1947, Gillingham, Kent, Eng) Dir., Marigold Lib. Syst. (Strathmore, AB), 1981–; Asst. Prov. Libn., SK Prov. Lib., 1979–, PR Consult., 1977–79; Reg. Libn., Lakeland Lib. Region, 1973–77; Lib. Consult., SK Prov. Lib., 1970–73. **Educ.:** Univ. of AB, 1965–68, BA (Hist.), 1969–70, BLS; Prof. Mgr. Cert., Can. Inst. of Mgt., 1977. **Orgs.:** Can. LA. LA of AB. Can. LA: VP (1979), Pres. (1980), Can. Assn. of Pub. Libs; Com. on Future of Pub. Lib. Bds. (1979). SK LA: Ch., Elec. Com.; Pres. (1977–78); VP (1976–77); Cnclr. (1973–77). Regina LA. Can. Inst. of Mgt. **Pubns.:** "Bridging the publisher-librarian gulf," *Quill & Quire* (Jl. 1978); "Howie Meeker, where were you when we needed you?," *SK Lib.* (My. 1974); "Setting up a regional library," *Quill & Quire* (My. 1973); Co-ed., "Focus on SK Libs." (1977–); SK corres., "Feliciter", (1977–79). **Activities:** 4, 9; 17, 24, 36; 51, Public Relations. **Addr.:** Marigold Library System, Box 1830, Strathmore, AB T0T 3H0, Canada.

Caya, Marcel (F. 25, 1947, Montréal, PQ) Univ. Archvst., McGill Univ., 1977–; Head, Human Resrc. Recs. Sect., Pub. Arch. of Can., 1976–77, Archvst., 1974–76. **Educ.:** Univ. de Montréal, 1967, BA; Univ. de Sherbrooke, 1967–69, LèsL (Hist.); Carleton Univ., 1969–70, MA (Hist.); Cert. Arch. Mgt., 1970; York Univ., 1971-81, Phd (Hist.). **Orgs.:** Assn. des archivistes du Québec: Ed., *Archives* (1978–80). Assn. of Can. Archvsts.: Prog. Ch. (1980). Can. Micrographics Soc. Assn. Recs. Mgrs. and Admin. Other orgs. Institut d'histoire de l'Amérique française: Secy. (1979). Can. Hist. Assn.: Frdm. of Info. Com. (1978). **Pubns.:** *Treasury Board Records, Inventory, Ottawa, Public Archives of Canada* (1977); "Aperçu sur les élections provinciales au Québec de 1867 à 1887," *Revue d'histoire de l'Amérique française* (S. 1975); Jt. auth., *Archives in Canada Communiqué* (Spr. 1980). **Activities:** 2; 17, 26, 38; 56 **Addr.:** 3459 McTavish Street, Montréal, PQ H3A 1Y1, Canada.

Caynon, William A. (F. 25, 1940, Miami, FL) Asst. Prof., Kent State Univ., 1976–; Head, Circ., IN Univ., 1974–75; Prog. Coord., AL Cntr. for Higher Educ., 1971–73; Asst. Head, Fine Arts Dept., Atlanta Pub. Lib., 1969–71. **Educ.:** Talladega Coll., 1958–64, BA (Msc.); Atlanta Univ., 1968–69, MSLS; IN Univ., 1973-80 Ph.D. **Orgs.:** OH LA. ALA. AAUP. **Activities:** 1, 9; 17, 20, 39 **Addr.:** School of Library Science, Kent State University, Kent, OH 44242.

Cayton, Colleen U. (Jl. 2, 1942, Mound City, KS) Dir., Dev. and PR, Denver Pub. Lib., 1978–; Asst. Dir., Dev. and PR, Presby. Med. Ctr., 1978; Dir., Dev. and Cmnty. Rel., Littleton Hosp. Assn., 1976–78; Dir. of Mktg., Bristol Mt. Ski Resort (NY), 1972–75; Legis. Asst., U.S., Congressman William L. Clay, 1968–70. **Educ.:** KS State Univ., 1959–63, BA (Eng., Sp.). **Orgs.:** CO LA: PR Com. (Ch., 1981). WHCOLIS, Facilitator (1979). Rocky Mountain Inventor's Congs.: Pres. (1980–81). **Pubns.:** "An Uncommon Cooperative Venture," *Lib. Jnl.* (Ja. 1, 1981); presented papers. **Activities:** 9; 36 **Addr.:** 13795 Berry Rd., Golden, CO 80401.

Caywood, Carolyn (N. 29, 1947, Mansfield, OH) Chld. Coord., VA Beach Pub. Lib., 1979–; Chld. Libn., Cleveland Pub. Lib., 1972–79. **Educ.:** Kent State Univ., 1965–68, BS Ed (Eng., Hist.); Wayne State Univ., 1971–72, MSLS. **Orgs.:** VA LA: Chld., YA RT (Bd., 1979–81). ALA: ALSC, Com. on the Disadvantaged Chld. (1978–79). Chld. Lit. Assn. **Pubns.:** Reviews. **Activities:** 9; 21 **Addr.:** Virginia Beach Public Library, 3612 S. Plaza Trail, Virginia Beach, VA 23452.

Caywood, Gladys R. (N. 26, 1930, Hancock Cnty., TN) Supvsr., Lib. Srvs., Newport News Pub. Sch., 1966–; Libn., Denbigh HS, 1965–66; Elem. Sch. Libn., Sanford & South Morrison, 1964–65; Libn., John Battle HS, 1960–64; Elem. Libn., Abingdon Elem. Sch., 1959–60; Elem. Libn., Clintwood Elem. Sch., 1952–59; Tchr., 1948–52; Instr. LS, Coll. of William & Mary, 1978–. **Educ.:** Lincoln Meml. Univ., 1949–51; E. TN State Univ., 1959–61, BS LS (Elem. Educ.); Coll. of William & Mary, 1969–73, MEd (Supvsn.); Coll. of William & Mary, Adv. Cert. of Study, 1973–78, (Educ. Admin.). **Orgs.:** ALA: Legis. Com.

Special Subjects/Services: 50. Adult educ.; 51. Advert./Mktg.; 52. Aerosp.; 53. Agric.; 54. Area std.; 55. Arts/Hum.; 56. Autom.; 57. Bibl./Prtg.; 58. Bio. sci.; 59. Bus./Fin.; 60. Chem.; 61. Copyrt.; 62. Documtn.; 63. Educ.; 64. Engin.; 65. Env.; 66. Eth. grps.; 67. Film; 68. Food/Nutr.; 69. Geneal.; 70. Geo.; 71. Geol.; 72. Handcpd.; 73. Hist.; 74. Int. frdm.; 75. Info. sci.; 76. Insr.; 77. Law; 78. Legis.; 79. Math./Comp. sci.; 80. Med.; 81. Metals; 82. Nat. resrcs.; 83. Newsp.; 84. Nuc. sci.; 85. Oral hist.; 86. Petr./Energy; 87. Pharm.; 88. Phys./Astr./Math.; 89. Readg.; 90. Relig.; 91. Sci./Tech.; 92. Soc. sci.; 93. Telecom.; 94. Transp.; 95. (other).

(1973–74). VA LA: Secy. (1974–76); Nom. Com. (1976); Ch., Sch. Libs. Sect. (1979–80). SELA: Co-Ch., Mem. Com. for VA (1974–76); Nom. Com. (1976–77). VA Educ. Media Assn.: Exec. Bd. (1975–76; 1978–80); Treas. (1978). Other orgs. and coms. VA Assn. Sch. Exec.: Coord. Cncl. (1974–76); Ch., Instr. Leaders Sect.; Nom. Com. (1976–); Resolutions Com. (1976); Mem. Ch. (1976–77). Delta Kappa Pi. VA Readg. Assn. **Honors:** VA Educ. Media Assn., Media Educ. of the Year, 1979; Encyclopedia Britannica & AASL, Third Place Winner, 1969. **Pubns.:** *Manual for Cataloging Non-Book Materials, Newport New Public Schools* (1970); *Library Media Center Skills Continuum & Guide, K-7* (1978). **Activities:** 9, 10; 17, 26, 32, 47; 50, 63 **Addr.:** 382 B Deputy Ln., Newport News, VA 23602.

Cazden, Robert E. (Ag. 29, 1930, New York, NY) Prof. (LS), Univ. of KY, 1966–; Bibl. Coord., OR State Univ., 1959–65; Actg. Gifts Libn., Univ. of CA, Berkeley, 1955–57. **Educ.:** Univ. of CA, Los Angeles, 1951–52, BA (Eng.); Univ. of South. CA, 1953–54, MA (Msclgy.); Univ. of CA, Berkeley, 1954–55, MLS; Univ. of Chicago, 1965, PhD (LS). **Orgs.:** Gutenberg Gesellschaft. Prtg. Hist. Socty. Wolfenbütteler Arbeitskreise für Geschichte des Buchwesens. Socty. for Grmn.-Amer. Std. Immigration Hist. Socty. **Honors:** Socty. for Grmn.-Amer. Std., Cit., 1973. **Pubns.:** *German Exile Literature in America 1933–1950* (1970); "The German Book Trade in Ohio Before 1848," *OH Hist.* (Win. 1975); "Some Developments in Nineteenth Century Bibliography: Germany," *LIBRI* (1977); "Libraries in the German-American Community and the Rise of the Public Library Movement," *Milestones to the Present* (1978); and others. **Activities:** 1; 15, 26, 45; 55, 57, 66 **Addr.:** College of Library Science, University of Kentucky, Lexington, KY 40506.

Cazeaux, Isabelle (F. 24, 1926, New York, NY) Alice Carter Dickerman Prof. and Ch., Msc. Dept., Bryn Mawr Coll., 1963–; Fac. of Msclgy. and Msc. Hist., Manhattan Sch. of Msc., 1969–; Visit. Prof. of Msc., Douglass Coll., 1978; Sr. Msc. Catlgr., Head, Msc. and Phonorecord Cat., NY Pub. Lib., 1957–63. **Educ.:** Hunter Coll., 1941–45, BA magna cum laude (Msc.); Smith Coll., 1945–46, MA (Msc.); Ecole Normale de Musique, Paris, 1948–50, Lic.; Columbia Univ., 1957–59, MSLS, 1961, PhD (Msclgy.). **Orgs.:** Msc. LA: Cat. Com.; Bibl. Com.; NY Chap., Asst. Ch. Intl. Assn. of Msc. Libs. ALA. Amer. Musicological Socty.: Cncl. (1968–70); Com. on the Status of Women (1976–78). Société française de musicologie. AAUP. Coll. Msc. Socty. **Honors:** Phi Beta Kappa, 1944, Martha Baird Rockefeller Fund, Grant, 1971–72. **Pubns.:** *French Music in the Fifteenth and Sixteenth Centuries* (1975); Transl., *Memoirs of Philippe de Commynes* (1969–73); "Musicology and other friendly musical disciplines," *Current Msclgy.* (1972); "Alfred Einstein," *Revue de Musicologie* (1952); several entries, *Grove's Dictionary of Music and Musicians* (1981); other articles. **Activities:** 14-Univ.; 49-Tchg.; 55 **Addr.:** 415 E. 72nd St., New York, NY 10021.

Ceceri, Mildred B. Petolina (N. 16, 1934, Newark, NJ) Bd. of Trustees, Newark Pub. Libs., 1978–, Pres., 1978–80, Secy., 1980–81, Treas., 1981–; Elem. Tchr., 1973–. **Educ.:** Kean Coll., 1969–73, BA (Educ.), 1976–77, MA (Spec. Educ.). **Orgs.:** ALA. ALTA. NJ LA. NJ Lib. Trustee Assn. Other orgs. Girl Scouts of Amer. Our Lady of Good Counsel Parish. Amer. Legion. Residents for Cmnty. Action. Other orgs. **Honors:** Newark Pub. Lib. Bd. of Trustees, Resol. of Apprec., 1980. **Activities:** 9; 47 **Addr.:** 665 Clifton Ave., Newark, NJ 07104.

Cederholm, Theresa Dickason (Jl. 31, 1945, Washington, DC) Actg. Cur. of Fine Arts, Resrch. Div., Boston Pub. Lib., 1981–, Fine Arts Libn., 1968–81; Prod. 1968–; Prod. Supvsr., Art Dept., Little Brown & Co., 1967–68. **Educ.:** Cornell Univ., 1963–67, AB (Art Hist. & Comp. Lit.); Simmons Coll., 1968–70, MLS; Cornell Univ., Grad. work (Art Hist.). **Orgs.:** ARLIS/NA: Treas. (1980–); Standards Com. (1978–). ARLIS/NA: New Eng. Chap. MA LA. Plng. Com. for the First Intl. Conf. of Art Libns. (1976). City Cons. Leag.: Dir. 1976–). MA Com. for the Prsrvn. of Archit. Recs.: VP (1978–); Strg. Com. (1979–). Socty. of Archit. Histns. Coll. Art Assn. Other orgs. **Pubns.:** *Afro-American Artists: A Bio-Bibliographical Directory,* (1973); Ed., Royal Institute of British Architects. *Architectural Index Thesaurus of Terms* (1976). **Activities:** 9, 12; 15, 30, 39, 41; 55 **Addr.:** Fine Arts Department, Research Division, Boston Public Library, Boston, MA 02117.

Celigoj, Carmen Z. (Ja. 11, 1947, Painesville, OH) Dir., Kent Free Lib., 1973–; Asst. Prof. (LS), Kent State Univ. 1972, 1977; Libn., Cleveland Musm. of Art, 1971–73. **Educ.:** Lake Erie Coll., 1965–69 BA magna cum laude (Langs.); Kent State Univ., 1969–71, MLS; Miami Univ., Exec. Dev. Prog., 1975. **Orgs.:** OH LA. ALA. Beta Phi Mu: Rho Chap. (Pres. 1979). Bus. and Prof. Women. AAUW. **Honors:** OH LA, Diane Vescelius Awd., 1979. **Pubns.:** "Faulkner's Use of Dante in 'The Sound and The Fury'," *Nota Bene* (1969). **Activities:** 9; 15, 17, 36; 55 **Addr.:** Kent Free Library, 312 W. Main St., Kent, OH 44240.

Cella, Sr. Marian Auxilia (Jl. 11, 1934, Philadelphia, PA) Libn., Wildwood Cath. HS, 1976–; Libn., Cecilian Acad., 1970–76; Tchr., Libn. Star of the Sea Grade Sch., 1963–70; Tchr. St. Ann's, 1957–63. **Educ.:** Chestnut Hill Coll., 1953–65, BS (Educ.); Villanova Univ., 1966–70, MLS. **Orgs.:** Cath. LA: Treas. (1968–70). **Activities:** 10; 17, 20, 22 **Addr.:** St. Ann's Convent, 119 E. Glenwood Ave., wildwood, NJ 08260.

Cellini, Nicholas J. (Ag. 2, 1947, Lake Placid, NY) Fine Arts Libn., Beverly Hills Pub. Lib., 1974–; Art Libn., CA Inst. of the Arts, 1970–72; Instr. (Art), Pepperdine Univ., 1972–74. **Educ.:** Hunter Coll., 1967–68, AB (Art); Univ. of CA, Los Angeles, 1968–69, MA (Art Hist.); Univ. of South. CA, 1969–70, MLS. **Orgs.:** ARLIS/NA. Coll. Art. Assn. **Activities:** 9; 15, 36, 41; 55, 67 **Addr.:** Beverly Hills Public Library, 444 N. Rexford Dr., Beverly Hills, CA 90210.

Centing, Richard Ronald (S. 16, 1936, Detroit, MI) Head, Eng., Thea., Comm. Lib., OH State Univ., 1969–; Ref. Libn., Oakland Univ., 1967–68; Ref. Supvsr., Campbell-Ewald Co., 1964–67; Ref. Libn., Detroit Pub. Lib., 1961–63. **Educ.:** Wayne State Univ., 1954–58, BA (Eng.); Univ. of MI, 1960–61, 1963–64, MLS. **Orgs.:** ALA: Ref. and Adlt. Srvs. Bibl. Com. (1974–76). Modern Lang. Assn. Ohio. Lib. Assn.: Jury on Ed. Excell. (1979). Acad. Lib. Assn. of Ohio. Society of OH Archvsts.: Ref./Arch. Com., Ch. (1973–74). **Pubns.:** Reviews; Ed., *Under the Sign of Pisces;* Ed., *Serials Review* (1975–77). **Activities:** 1; 39, 42, 44; 54, 55, 93 **Addr.:** Ohio State University Libraries, 1858 Neil Avenue Mall, Columbus, OH 43210.

Cenzer, Pamela S. (S. 22, 1949, Akron, OH) Asst. Ch., Acq., Univ. of FL, 1979–, Mono. Order Libn., 1977–79, Gift and Exch. Libn., 1976–77, Soc. Sci. Catlgr., 1975–76. **Educ.:** Univ. of MI, 1967–75. **Orgs.:** ALA. FL LA. **Pubns.:** Contrib., *Shaping Library Collections for the Eighties* (1981). **Activities:** 1; 15, 35, 37; 55 **Addr.:** 149 Library West, University of Florida, Gainesville, FL 32611.

Ceresa, Mario A. (Mr. 3, 1932, Puerto Padre, Cuba) Lib. Dir., Asst. Prof., Detroit Coll. of Law, 1970–; Lib. Asst., Univ. of MI Law Lib., 1968–70; Pub. Defender, Cuba Mnstry. of Justice, 1957–67. **Educ.:** Belen Coll. (Havana), 1945–51; Univ. of Havana Law Sch., 1951–56; Univ. of MI Sch. of LS, 1967–69, MALS. **Orgs.:** AALL. ALA. **Activities:** 1; 77 **Addr.:** 3600 Eli, Ann Arbor, MI 48104.

Cerutti, Elsie (Mr. 3, 1931, Seminole, PA) Chief, Info. Srvs., Natl. Bur. of Stans. Lib., 1980–, Ref. Libn., 1974–80; Libn., Asst. Prof., Clarion State Coll., 1972–74; Progmr., Head, Users Srvs., Brown Univ. Comp. Lab., 1965–69. **Educ.:** Univ. of Pittsburgh, 1949–53, BS (Math); Purdue Univ., 1954–56, MS (Math); Univ. of Pittsburgh, 1969–72, MLS. **Orgs.:** ALA: RASD Mach. Asst. Ref. Com. (1980–). ASIS. Potomac Appalachian Trail Club. **Pubns.:** "Management of Online Reference Search Services in Federal Libraries," *Sci. and Tech. Libs.* (1981); "FORMAC Meets Pappus," *Amer. Math. Monthly* (O. 1969). **Activities:** 4; 39; 60, 64, 91 **Addr.:** National Bureau of Standards Library, Adm E106, Washington, DC 20234.

Cetina, Judith Gladys (My. 30, 1949, Cleveland, OH) Cur., Cnty. Mss., Cuyahoga Cnty. Arch., 1977–. **Educ.:** Case West. Rsv. Univ., 1967–71, BA (Hist.), 1971–77, MA, PhD (Hist.); Natl. Arch., Mod. Arch. Inst., 1980. **Orgs.:** SAA. Socty. of OH Archvsts. Arch. Assocs. OH WHCOLIS, Del. (1978). Women Histns. of Greater Cleveland; Org. of Amer. Histns. Amer. Hist. Assn. **Honors:** Phi Beta Kappa. **Pubns.:** "History of Cuyahoga County Archives," Socty. of OH Archvsts. Nsltr. (Spr. 1981); reviews. **Activities:** 2; 17, 39, 41; 69, 85, 73 **Addr.:** 3391 Tullamore Rd., Cleveland Heights, OH 44118.

Chabot, Juliette (Ja. 24, 1902, Montrèal, PQ) Asst. Chief-Libn., Montrèal Pub. Lib., 1970–, various positions, 1930–1965. **Educ.:** Univ. de Montrèal, 1930–40; Coll. Marguerite Bourgeoys, 1940–65; McGill Univ., 1938–40, MALS; L'Inst. Cath. (Paris), 1940, Dip; Ecole Natl. des Chartes *Paris,* 1940, Cert. **Orgs.:** Can LA. ACBLF. Ctr. d'oecumemisme: Bibtcr. (1965–). **Pubns.:** Jt. auth., *Vocabulaire Technique de la Bibliothècànomie de la Bibliographie* (1969); *Montreal et le Rayonnement des Bibliothèques Publiques* (1963); *Classification des Livres* (1952); *Bio-bibliographies d'Écrivains Canadiens-Français* (1948). **Addr.:** 4245 rue de Lanaudiere, Montreal, PQ Canada.

Chadbourn, Erika S. (Ja. 21, 1915, Nuremberg, Bavaria, W. Germany) Cur. of Mss. and Arch., Harvard Law Sch. Lib., 1966–; Catlgr., Temple Univ., 1939–40; Asst. to Libn., Hunterdon Cnty. Lib., 1938–39; Circ./Ref. Asst., Middlebury Coll., 1937–38. **Educ.:** Univ. of DE, 1934–36, BA (Fr.); Drexel Univ., 1936–37, BS in LS; Inst. in Arch. Admin., U. of Denver, 1968, Cert. **Orgs.:** SAA: Exhibits Wkshp. demonstration, Ann. Conf. 1978. AALL. New Eng. Archvsts.: Ch., Nom. Com. (1978/79); Local Arrange. Ch., (1976). Law Libns. of New Eng. Other orgs. Museum of Fine Arts (Boston). Friends of the Schlesinger Library, Radcliffe Coll. **Pubns.:** "Charles C. Burlingham: Twentieth Century Crusader. A Retrospective Exhibit at the Harvard Law School Library" (1980); "A Passionate Intensity: The Felix Frankfurter Exhibit at the Harvard L.S. Library" (1977); "Library Administration of Historical Materials: Exhibits". *Law Library Journal,* (Ag. 1976); Other exhibition catalogs and reviews. **Activities:** 1, 2; 20, 39, 45; 77 **Addr.:** Manuscript Division, Harvard Law School Library, Langdell Hall, Cambridge, MA 02138.

Chadwick, Regina E. (My. 6, 1918, Atascadero, CA) Head Libn., CA Med. Assn., 1959–; Docum. Libn., Univ. of AZ, 1955–59; Asst. Libn., Standard Oil of CA, 1941–43; Asst. Ref. Libn., Univ. of CA, Davis, 1940–41. **Educ.:** San Francisco Coll. for Women, 1935–39, BA (Eng.); Univ. of CA, Berkeley, 1939–40, MS (LS). **Orgs.:** SLA: Nom. Com. (1966). Med. LA. **Activities:** 3; 17, 20, 39; 76, 78, 80 **Addr.:** 731 Market St., San Francisco, CA 94103.

Chafe, H. David (F. 4, 1932, St. John's, NF) Dir., Metals Socty. (London, Eng.) 1981–, Dir., Metals Info., Amer. Socty. for Metals, 1964–81; Metallurgical Engin., Reynolds Metals Co., 1963–64. **Educ.:** Nova Scotia Tech. Univ., 1961–63, BE (Metals. Engin.); Meml. Univ. of NF, 1957–60 Dipl. (Engin.). **Orgs.:** Natl. Fed. of Abs. and Indxg. Srvs.: Secy. (1975–76), Treas. (1977–78), Bd. (1974–77). ASIS. Assn. of Info. Dssm. Ctrs. AAAS. **Pubns.:** *METADEX: A User Guide to the Database* (1980); Ed., *Metals Abs.* (1972–); Ed., *World Aluminum Abs.* (1968–). **Activities:** 12; 30; 81 **Addr.:** American Society for Metals, Metals Park, OH 44073.

Chait, William (D. 5, 1915, NY, NY) Dir. Emeritus, Dayton & Montgomery Cnty. Pub. Lib., 1979–, Dir., 1956–78; Dir., Kalamazoo Pub. Lib., 1948–56; Chief, Trng. and Persnl., Ctrl. Milwaukee Pub. Lib., 1946–48; various visit. faculty positions. **Educ.:** Brooklyn Coll., 1931–34, BA (Hist.); Pratt Inst., 1934–35, BSLS; Columbia Univ., 1936–38, MSLS. **Orgs.:** ALA: Treas. (1976–80); COPES (1970–74); Chap. Cnclr. (OH); PLA (Pres., 1964–65). OH LA: Pres. (1964–65). Mich. LA: Pres. (1955–56). OCLC: Trustee (1974–); Treas. (1976–79). SC LA. Various other orgs. **Honors:** OH LA, Hall of Fame, 1980; Libn. of the Year, 1975. **Pubns.:** Jt.-auth., *Survey of the public libraries of Norwalk, Conn.* (1966); Jt.-auth., *Survey of the public libraries of Ashville and Buncombe Co., NC* (1965); Various other articles. **Activities:** 9, 14-Netwk.; 17, 19, 24; 54, 56, 74 **Addr.:** 38 Deer Run Ln., Hilton Head Island, SC 29928.

Chall, Leo P. (Jl. 21, 1921, Daugavpils, Latvia) Pres., Sociological Abs., Inc., 1953–; Instr., Brooklyn Coll., 1961–64; Lectr., 1953–61. **Educ.:** OH State Univ., 1946–48, BA (Hist., Soclgy.); 1949 (Soclgy.); Columbia Univ., 1950–53, (Soclgy.). **Orgs.:** Natl. Fed. of Sci. Abs. Srvs.: Com. on Ethics, (1979–). **Honors:** Amer. Sociological Assn., Commendation for Contrib. to Resrch., 1957. **Pubns.:** Contrib., *The Reception of the Kinsey Report in the Periodical Press of the US: 1947–49* (1955); Contrib., *The Sociology of Knowledge* (1958); Introd., *The First 10 Years of Sociological Abstracts* (1969); *The Quinquennial Years: 1963–67* (1977); "A Comparison of Psychological & Sociologicals: 1845–1953," *Procs. Southwestern Sociological Assn.* (1966). **Activities:** 6; 30, 33, 37, 44; 62, 92 **Addr.:** P. O. Box 22206, San Diego, CA 92122.

Chamberlain, Merle J. (Ag. 19, 1919, Chicago, IL) Asst. Libn., Archvst., Philadelphia Musm. of Art, 1975–, Catlgr. (Volun.), 1970–75; Circ. Libn., Philadelphia Coll. of Art, 1966–69. **Educ.:** Wellesley Coll., 1938–41, BS (Eng.); Drexel Univ., 1963–66, MSLS; Amer. Univ., 1975, Cert. (Arch). **Orgs.:** ARLIS/NA. SAA. Amer. Socty. of State and Lcl. Hist. **Activities:** 2, 12; 20, 39; 55, 73 **Addr.:** Philadelphia Museum of Art, P.O. Box 7646, Philadelphia, PA 19101.

Chamberlain, Ruth Brown (Mr. 16, 1948, Amherst, MA) Dir., Plymouth Pub. Lib., 1976–, Asst. Dir., 1975–76; Libn., Nauset Reg. HS, 1974–75; Ref., Adult Srvs. Libn., Falmouth Pub. Lib., 1971–74. **Educ.:** Syracuse Univ., 1966–70, BA (Anthro.); Simmons Coll., 1970–71, MLS. **Orgs.:** East. MA Reg. Lib. Syst.: PR Com. (1978–). ALA. **Activities:** 9; 17, 35, 36; 56 **Addr.:** Plymouth Public Library, Plymouth, MA 02360.

Chamberlin, Charles E. (Ap. 9, 1947, Uniontown, PA) Head, Prsnl. and Admin. Srvs., Univ. of WA, 1981–; Prsnl. and Budget Ofcr., Univ. of NE, 1976–80, Circ. Libn., 1975–76, Asst. Undergrad. Libn., 1974–75. **Educ.:** Marshall Univ., 1965–70, BA (Hist.); Univ. of WI, 1973–74, MALS. **Orgs.:** ALA. WA LA. **Activities:** 1; 17, 35 **Addr.:** 6013 N.E. 204th St., Seattle, WA 98155.

Chamberlin, Edgar Wilbur (Ag. 1, 1923, Mishawaka, IN) Exec. Dir., Kaskaskia Library Syst., 1967–; Asst. Dir., IN State Lib., 1960–67; Head, Bus. and Tech. Dept., South Bend Pub. Lib., 1955–60; Asst., Bus. and Tech. Dept., KS City Pub. Lib., 1952–55. **Educ.:** IN Univ., 1942–49, BS (Educ.); Univ. of IL, 1950–52, MSLS. **Orgs.:** ALA. IL LA: Autom. Com. (1979–80). **Activities:** 9, 14-Reg.; 17, 24, 34; 70, 74, 91 **Addr.:** Kaskaskia Library System, 306 N. Main St., Smithton, IL 62285.

Chamberlin, Lawrence C. (Ap. 17, 1921, St. Louis, MO) Rare Bks. Catlgr., Georgetown Univ. Lib., 1962–; Gvt. Docum. Libn., St. Louis Univ., 1948–56. **Educ.:** St. Louis Univ., 1939–43, AB, 1949, AM; Cath. Univ., 1962, MSLS. **Orgs.:** DC LA. Cath. LA: DC Chap. Archlg. Inst. of Amer. **Honors:** Georgetown Univ., Vicennial Medal, 1976. **Activities:** 1; 20, 41, 45; 55, 57 **Addr.:** 2700 Que St. N.W. Apt. 319, Washington, DC 20007.

Chamberlin, Leslie Burk (D 4, 1946, Passaic, NJ) Head, Child. Srvcs., Napa City Cnty. Lib., 1978–; Coord. of Child. Srvcs, Phillipsburg Pub. Lib., 1976–78; Cable TV Coord., Ocean

Cnty. Lib., 1971–76; Bibl. Asst., Columbia Univ., 1967–68. **Educ.:** San Francisco State Univ., 1968–71, BA, (Eng. & Am. Lit.); Rutgers Univ., 1973–74; MLS. **Orgs.:** ALA: LITA/various coms. since 1976; SRRT: JMRT/various coms. since 1975. Beta Phi Mu: Omicron Chap., Treas. (1977–78). Intl. Readg. Assn. NJ LA. Various other orgs. NOW. **Honors:** Beta Phi Mu, ALA/JMRT, Novia Awrd., 1975; **Pubns.:** *Video and Cable Guidelines* (1980); Reviews. **Activities:** 9; 21, 24, 36 **Addr.:** Box 71, Napa, CA 94558.

Chamberlin, Leslie Burk (D. 4, 1946, Passaic, NJ) Head, Chld. Srvs., Napa City-Cnty. Lib., 1978–; Chld. Coord., Philipsburg Free Pub. Lib., 1976–78; CATV Coord., Ocean Cnty. Lib., 1971–76. **Educ.:** San Francisco State Univ., 1968–71, BA (Eng., Amer. Lit.); Rutgers Univ., 1973–74, MLS (Educ. Tech.). **Orgs.:** ALA: LITA, Nom. Com. (1978–79), Vid. and Cable Comm. Sect., Dist. and Exch. Com. (1975–77), Prog. Plng. Com. (Ch., 1978–79, 1980–81), other ofcs.; SRRT; JMRT, various coms.; LAMA/PR Sect., PR Srvs. to Libs. Com. (1981–83). NJ LA: PR Com. (1976–78). Lib. Pub. Rel. Coord.: (Lcl. Arrange. Coord. 1980). Bay Area Soc. Resp. RT. Other orgs. and coms. Intl. Reading Assn. Natl. Org. for Women. **Honors:** ALA, Novia Awd., 1975; 3M/JMRT Prof. Dev. Grant, 1976. **Pubns.:** *Video & Cable Guidelines* (1980); reviews. **Activities:** 9; 21, 36; 93 **Addr.:** Box 71, Napa, CA 94559-0071.

Chamberlin, Richard Ralph (Ag. 9, 1935, Great Barrington, MA) Ref. Libn., Indiana Univ. of PA, 1967–; Head, Readers Servs., Univ. of Guyana, 1977–78; Docum. Libn., Wellesley Coll., 1964–67; Circ./Ref., Springfield Coll., 1963–64. **Educ.:** Northeastern Univ., 1953–58, BA (Hist.); MI State Univ., 1961–62, MA (Hist.); Univ. of Denver, 1962–63, MA, (LS). **Orgs.:** ALA. PA LA: Southwest Chap.-Treas. (1972); Pres. (1973); State Mem. Com. (1973–1974); State Awds. (1974–75). Tri-State Assn. of Col. and Resrch. Libs. **Activities:** 1, 2; 30; 55, 70, 77 **Addr.:** University Library, Indiana University of Pennsylvania, Indiana, PA 15705.

Chambers, Elizabeth (Jl. 24, 1916, New Cumberland, WV) Asst. Prof., North. IL Univ., 1973–; Dir. of Libs., Central Philippine Univ., 1954–72; Head, Acq., WA State Univ., 1951–52; Head Catlgr., Univ. of Louisville, 1945–51; Catlgr., MI State Univ., 1943–44; Gen. Catlgr., Univ. of Cincinnati, 1941–43. **Educ.:** Univ. of Cincinnati, 1935–38, BA (Eng.); Univ. of IL, 1940–41, BSLS; 1959–61, MSLS; Berkeley Baptist Dvnty. Sch., 1952–54, MA (Relig. Educ.); George Peabody Coll., 1971–74 (Educ. Spec., LS). **Orgs.:** ALA: Ch., JMRT (1945); Ch., OH Valley Reg. Gp. of Catlgrs. (1950). Philippine LA. IL LA. ATLA. **Honors:** Philippine LA, Disting. Srvs. to Philippine Libnshp., 1970. **Pubns.:** "New Trends in Classification and Cataloging," in *Librarianship as a Profession in the Philippines* (1969); "Central Philippine University; Filipiniana Collection," *ASLP* (Assn. of Spec. Libs. of the Philippines) *Bulletin* (D. 1964); "Index to Volumes VIII-IX, 1949–50," *Jnl. of the Socty. of Archit. Histns.* (D. 1950); "The Saint with Heart Aflame," *The Tchrs. Jnl.* (October 1964). **Activities:** 1, 11; 17, 20, 26; 90 **Addr.:** 807 W. Taylor, Apt. 507, DeKalb, IL 60115.

Chambers, Joan Louise (Mr. 22, 1937, Denver, CO) Univ. Libn., Univ. of CA, Riverside, 1981 Asst. Univ. Libn. for Pub. Srvs., Univ. of CA, San Diego, 1979–81; Gov. Pub. Libn., Univ. of NV, Reno, 1972–78; Ref. and Interlib. Loan Libn., 1970–72; Secondary Sch. Tchr. and Libn., CA Pub. Sch., 1958–70. **Educ.:** Univ. of North. CO, 1955–58, BA (Eng.); Univ. of CA, Berkeley, 1969–70, MLA; Univ. of Edinburgh, Scotland, 1957, (Eng. Lit.). **Orgs.:** ALA: Chap. Cncl. (1977–78); ACRL (Law and Pol. Sci. Sect., Secy. 1973–78); Ad Hoc Com., Deposit. Lib. Syst. (1974–77). CA LA. NV LA: Conf. Pub. Com. (1970); Leg. Com. (1972); Nat. Lib. Week Dir. (1972); ALA Mem. Ch. (1973–). SLA. AAUP. Sierra Club. **Honors:** Beta Phi Mu, 1970. **Pubns.:** "Government Publications," *Energy and NV* (1977); Reviews; "Federal Documents in Microform", *Microform Review* (1978); Ed., *Selected List of Publications Received, Gov. Pub. Dept.* (1972–78); Various papers. **Activities:** 1, 12; 17, 31, 39; 57, 77, 78 **Addr.:** University Librarian, University of California, Riverside, CA 92521.

Chambers, Paula Haver (Ja. 21, 1947, Atlanta, GA) Chld. Libn., S.W. GA Reg. Lib., 1978–81. **Educ.:** Univ. GA, Oglethorpe Coll., 1965–69, BA (Elem. Educ.); Duke Univ., 1969–70, MEduc. (Elem.); GA State Univ., 1970, 1976–77 (Educ., Hist.); FL State Univ., 1978– (LS). **Orgs.:** GA LA: Chld. Sect. (Treas., 1980–), PR Com. (1980–). ALA. AAUW. Soltas. **Pubns.:** "Word Attack: 'R' Blends," *Early Years* (Ap. 1977); "Children's Poetry Workshops," *The GA Libn.* (My. 1979); "Library Day at the Mall," *GA Libn.*, (Ag. 1980); "UNICEF and Children's Art," *GA Libn.*, (Ag. 1979). **Activities:** 9; 15, 21, 48; 63, 72, 89 **Addr.:** 1405 Pineland Dr., Bainbridge, GA 31717.

Chamis, Alice Yanosko (Ap. 25, 1939, Kenogami, PQ) Asst. to Dir., Cuyahoga Cnty. Pub. Lib., 1970–; Mgr. of Lib., B.F. Goodrich Co., 1962–69; Lit. Chem., ALCAN Aluminum Labs., 1959–61. **Educ.:** McGill Univ., 1955–59, BSc (Chem.); Case Western Reserve Univ., 1961–62, MLS. **Orgs.:** SLA: Cleveland Chap. (Pres., 1969–70); Placement Ch. (1970–76). ASIS: Northeast OH Chap., Pres.-Elect (1981–82), Placement Ch. (1975–). OH LA: Div. III (Coord., 1980–81; Asst. Coord., 1979–80); Div. II (Bd., 1974–75). ALA: LITA. **Pubns.:** "The Literature of Synthetic Rubber" in *Literature of Chemical Technology*, (1969); "Managing Tech Records," *Info. and Recs. Mgt.* (Ap./My. 1970); "The Design of Information Systems," *Spec. Libs.* (Ja. 1969); "The Application of Computers at the B.F. Goodrich Research Center Library," *Spec. Libs.* (Ja. 1968); "The B.F. Goodrich Information Retrieval System and Automatic Information Distribution," *Jnl. of Chem. Documtn.* (1967). **Activities:** 9, 12; 16, 17, 24; 56, 60, 75 **Addr.:** 24534 Framingham Dr., Westlake, OH 44145.

Champlin, Constance J. (Mr. 2, 1942, Perth Amboy, NJ) Lib. Resrc. Spec., OM Pub. Sch., 1976–; Libn., Mercer Crest Sch., Mercer Is, WA, 1975–76; Libn., Belmont St. Comm. Sch., Worcester, MA, 1973–74; Lib. Consul. Peace Corps., Korea Dev. Inst., Seoul, 1971–72. **Educ.:** Syracuse Univ., 1961–63, BS (Educ.); George Peabody Coll. for Tchrs., 1967–69, MLS; Univ. of WA, 1974–76, MA (Drama). **Orgs.:** ALA. NE LA: Conf. Wkshp., (1977). NE Educ. Media Assn.: Conf. Com. (1978); Wkshp. (1978). Puppeteers of America. Nat. Fest. Wksp. Ldr. (1978–80). Pub. Rel. Com. (1979). **Pubns.:** *Overhead Projector Shadow Puppets*, (1978); "Puppetry and Creative Dramatics in Storytelling," (1980); "Books, Puppets and the Mentally Retarded Student," (1981). **Activities:** 10; 21, 24, 32; 75, 95-Puppetry/Storytelling. **Addr.:** 2051 N 54th St., Omaha, NE 68104.

Champlin, Peggy (Margaret D.) (O. 13, 1925, Bryn Mawr, PA) Sr. Asst. Libn., Sci. & Tech., Kennedy Meml. Lib., CA State Univ., Los Angeles, 1972–. **Educ.:** Wesleyan Coll., 1943–47, BA (Chem.); Immaculate Heart Coll., 1970–71, MLS; CA State Univ., Los Angeles, 1977–, (Hist. of Sci.). **Orgs.:** SLA. Hist. of Sci. Socty. **Pubns.:** Reviews. **Activities:** 1; 39, 49-Computerized Lit. Searching; 91, 95-Hist. of Sci. **Addr.:** Kennedy Memorial Library, California State University, Los Angeles, 5151 State University Dr., Los Angeles, CA 90032.

Chan, Florence May Harn. (S. 29, 1929, Victoria, BC) Head Libn., Cañada Coll., 1968–; Cat., Ref. Libn., Coll. of San Mateo, 1957–60; Catlgr., Golden Gate Coll., 1956–57. **Educ.:** Victoria Coll., 1950–52; Univ. of BC, 1952–53, BA (Hist.); Univ. of CA, Berkeley, 1955–56, MLS; San Jose State Univ., 1973–76, MA (Educ.). **Orgs.:** CA LA. ALA. Cmnty. Coll. Media Assn.: Pres. (1979–80). Suicide Prevention Ctr., San Mateo Cnty.: Lib. Adv. Com. (1976). San Jose State Univ., Dept. of Instr. Tech.: Adv. Com. (1977–). **Honors:** Phi Kappa Phi, 1977. **Pubns.:** *Using Library Resources, a worktext* (1976). **Activities:** 1; 15, 17, 20 **Addr.:** Cañada College Library, 4200 Farm Hill Blvd., Redwood City, CA 94061.

Chan, Lois Mai (Jl. 30, 1934, Nanking, China) Prof., Prof., Coll. of Lib. Sci., Univ. of KY, 1970–; Ser. Catlgr., Univ. of KY, 1966–67; Asst. Libn., Lake Forest Coll., 1964–66; Serials Acq. Libn., Northwestern Univ., 1963–64; Asst. Catlgr., Purdue Univ., 1961–63; Asst. Acq. Libn., Purdue Univ., 1960–61. **Educ.:** Nat. Taiwan Univ., 1952–56, AB (For. Langs.); FL State Univ., 1956–58, MA (Eng.), 1958–60, MS (Lib. Sci.); Univ. of KY, 1967–70, PhD (Comp. Lit.). **Orgs.:** ALA: Cat. & Class. Sect., Pol. and Resrch. Com. (1976–80); Ch. (1977–78); Exec. Com. (1977–78). Dec. Class. Ed. Pol. Com. (1975–); Vice Ch. (1980). AALS: (1970–). **Honors:** Cncl. on Lib. Resrcs. Flwshp., 1977. **Pubns.:** *Library of Congress Subject Headings: Principles and Application* (1978); *Marlowe Criticism: A Bibliography* (1978); *Immroth's Guide to Library of Congress Classification* (3rd Edition) (1980); *Cataloging and Classifications: An Introduction* (1981); jt. Auth., "When Do You Use a Jobber," *Coll. and Resrch. Libs.* (1962); "The Form Distinction in the 800 Class of the Dewey Decimal Scheme," *Lib. Resrcs. and Tech. Srvs. XV* (1971); "Technical Processing in the School Libraries in Kentucky; Some Random Observations," *KY Lib. Assn. Bltn.* (1972); Various other articles and reviews. **Activities:** 1; 20, 44, 46 **Addr.:** College of Library Science, University of Kentucky, Lexington, KY 40506.

Chan, Mary Lu (Jl. 19, 1946, Hardisty, AB) Area Chld. Libn., Fraser Valley Reg. Lib., 1974–; Branch Asst. Supvsr., Edmonton Pub. Lib., 1972–74, Ref., Chld. Libn., 1969–72. **Educ.:** Univ. of AB, 1965–68, BA (Eng.); 1968–69, BLS. **Orgs.:** Can. LA. BC LA. **Activities:** 9 **Addr.:** 11232 Sussex Pl., Delta, BC V4E 2J9 Canada.

Chan, Wing K. (Je. 4, 19–, Canton, China) Ref. Libn., Kilmer Area Lib., Rutgers Univ., 1971–; Tchr., (Sci., Math), St. Joan of Arc HS 1962–69; Tech. Salesman, Dow Chem. Co., 1961–62. **Educ.:** Cheng Kung Univ. (Taiwan), 1956–60, BSE (Chem. Engin.); Wayne State Univ., 1969–70, MSLS; Hong Kong Univ., 1965–67, Cert. (Educ.). **Orgs.:** NJ LA: Lib. Dev. Com., Subcom. on Lib. Autom. (1978–79). Chinese Amer. Libns. Assn.: Bd. of Dir. (1980–81), Northeast Chap. (VP, 1979–81). AAUP. **Activities:** 1; 39; 58, 91, 92 **Addr.:** 5 Continental Rd., Somerset, NJ 08873.

Chanaud, Josephine P. (Je. 26, 1927, Denver, CO) Asst. Dir., CO Technical Ref. Cntr., Univ. of CO Libn., 1980–; Ser. Catlgr., 1978–80; Info. Spec., Eng. Dynamics, 1974–77; Libn., Ball Brothers Resrch. Corp., 1969–70; Asst. Chief Libn., Nat. Ctr. for Atmospheric Resrch., 1962–69. **Educ.:** Reed Coll., 1944–49, BA (Lit. & lang.); Univ. of Denver, 1973–74, MALA. **Orgs.:** ASIS: Ch., CO Centennial Chap. 1980–81. ALA. CO LA. Colorado Mntn. Club: Brd. of Dir., Boulder Chap. (1963–64). Boulder Tennis Assn.: Nsltr. Ed. (1969–70). **Honors:** ASIS, Career Profile Contest Winner, 1976. **Pubns.:** Jt. Auth., "The Independent Information Specialist and the Research Library," Jrnl. of the Socty. of Resrch. Admin. (1975); Newsletter, WICHE Cont. Educ. (1974–). **Activities:** 1, 12; 17, 39, 44 **Addr.:** 1708 Hillside Rd., Boulder, CO 80302.

Chandler, Devon (Jl. 1, 1934, Yreka, CA) Dir., Instr. Mtrls. Srv., Prof., Univ. of MT, 1967–. **Educ.:** OR State Coll., 1952–56, BS (Sci.); Univ. of OR, 1967, MS (Educ.), 1973, EdD. **Orgs.:** AECT, MT LA. Cnsrtm. of Univ. Film Ctrs. Mt. Plains Leadership Symp. **Pubns.:** "Transparency Microfiche: A New Dimension," *AV Instr.* (D. 1975); "Non-Print Media and Mediaware Availability to Students of College and University," *Intl. Jnl. of Instr. Media* (1974). **Activities:** 1, 14-Instr. Media Ctr.; 15, 32; 67 **Addr.:** Instructional Materials Service, University of Montana, Missoula, MT 59801.

Chandler, James Greenough (My. 8, 1917, Dedham, MA) Indp. Dev. and Instr. of Voice Indexing; Ch. Lib. Com., Amer. Cncl. of the Blind, 1976–; Asst. Dir. of Libs., Univ. of MD, 1967–72. **Educ.:** Univ. of HI, 1938–1940; Pomona Coll., 1940–42, AB (Eng.); Cath. Univ., 1946–50, BS (LS). **Orgs.:** Beta Phi Mu: Iota Chap. (Pres., 1967–69). Amer. Assn. of Workers for the Blind: Spec. Interest Grp. on Libs. (1977–), MD–DC Chap., Bd. of Dir. (1980–). Intl. Innovations for the Blind: Treas. (1977–). Volunteers for the Visually Hndcpd.: Pres. (1972–1974). **Honors:** Lions, Schnebly Meml. Awd., 1978; Amer. Cncl. of the Blind, Ned Freeman Awd., 1978; Phi Beta Kappa. **Pubns.:** "Library Service to the Blind," Braille Forum (N. 1979); "Voice Indexing of Tape Recordings," *Jnl. of Visual Impairment and Blindness* (My. 1979); "A Dictionary on Tape," *Braille Forum* (S.-O. 1975); designed and coordinated the voice indexed rec. ed. of *Coping with Sight Loss: The VISION Resource Book* (1980), and *Amana Microwave Oven Cookbook* (1980); ed. and voice indexed other vols. **Activities:** 10; 30, 34, 39; 50, 63, 72 **Addr.:** 9116 St. Andrews Pl., College Park, MD 20740.

Chandler, Joan Barbara Barbee (Ja. 18, 1941, Minneapolis, MN) Retrospective Conversion Projs. Supvsr. AMIGOS Bibl. Cncl., 1980–81, Serials Proj., 1980; Asst. Head, Order Dept. South. Meth. Univ. Lib., 1970–74; Head Catlgr., Nicholson Meml. Lib., 1966–67; Catlgr., TX State Lib. Prcs. Ctr., 1964–66; Libn., Prof. Col., TX State Lib. Field Srvs. Div., 1963–64. **Educ.:** N. TX State Univ., 1959–63, BS (LS), 1977–78, MLS. **Orgs.:** TX LA. ALA. **Pubns.:** "Professional Collection Texas State Library," *TX Libs.* (Spr. 1973). **Activities:** 1, 14-Ntwk.; 20, 44, 46; 56 **Addr.:** 3617 Granada, Dallas, TX 75205.

Chang, Chien-heh Y. (N. 21, 1936, Taichung, Taiwan) Assoc. Libn., SUNY, State Coll. of Optometry, 1977–, Asst. Libn., 1971–77. **Educ.:** Tunghai Univ., Taiwan, 1955–59, BA (Lit.); St. John's Univ. (NY), 1969–71, MLS. **Orgs.:** Med. LA. SUNY LA. Amer. Socty. of Indxrs. **Pubns.:** Indxr. of several jnls. **Activities:** 1, 12; 30, 39, 46; 72, 75, 80 **Addr.:** Library, State College of Optometry, 100 E. 24th St., New York, NY 10010.

Chang, Frances M. (F. 20, 1936, Hankow, Hu-Pei, China) Libn. (Physical Scis. and Engin.), Naval Sea Systems Cmnd., Dept. of the Navy, 1981–; Libn., U.S. Office of Naval Resrch., 1979–81; Libn., Intl. Food Pol. Resrch. Inst., 1975–78; Head, Tech. Srvs., Amer. Bankers Assn., 1970–75. **Educ.:** Nat. Taiwan Normal Univ., 1956–60, BA (Chinese Lit.); East. MI Univ., 1964–66, MA (Educ.); Univ. of MI, 1968, MSLS; Montgomery Coll., 1978, (Comp. Sci.). **Orgs.:** SLA. ASIS. AALL. Potomac Chinese Sch.: Ch. Brd., Prin. of Sch. (1976–77). **Activities:** 4, 11, 12; 17, 20, 46; 59, 77, 91 **Addr.:** 12320 Rivers Edge Dr., Potomac, MD 20854.

Chang, Helen S. (Ap. 20, 1953, Navasota, TX) Ref. Libn., Thomas Nelson Cmnty. Coll., 1978–; Branch Libn., Chesapeake Pub. Lib. Syst., 1976–78, Ref. Libn., 1976–76. **Educ.:** PA State Univ., 1971–75, BA (Eng.); Univ. of MI, 1975–76, AMLS. **Orgs.:** ALA. VA LA: Prog. Com. (Ch., 1980–81). **Activities:** 1, 9; 16, 31, 39; 55, 92 **Addr.:** Thomas Nelson Community College Library, P.O. Box 9407, Hampton, VA 23670.

Chang, Henry C. (S. 15, 1941, Canton, China) Dir. & Territorial Libn., Gvt. of U.S. VI, 1975–; Dir., Inst. for Trng. in Libnshp., Coll. of the VI, 1975–79, Chief Libn. & Lect. in Soc. Sci., 1974–75; Asst. Head, Gvt. Pubn. Div., Univ. of MN Libs., 1972–74. **Educ.:** Natl. Chengchi Univ., Taipei, 1958–62, BLL; Univ. of MO, 1964–65, MA (Demog.); Univ. of MN, 1967–68, MA (LS), 1970–74, PhD (Soclgy.); Lib. Admin. Dev. Prog., Univ. of MD, 1972–72, Cert. (Lib. Admin.). **Orgs.:** ALA: ASCLA, Legis. Com. (1979–81); Cnclr. at Lg. (1980–84); PLA; ACRL, GODORT; various RTS. ACURIAL: Exec. Cncl.; various functions. Asian Amer. LA. VILA. Amer. Assn. of Musm. Amer. Soclgl. Assn. Popltn. Assn. of Amer. Caribbean Arch. Assn. **Honors:** Fort Frederik Comsn., VI, Cert. of Apprec., 1978; Amer. Revolution Bicentennial Comsn. of the VI, Cert. of Apprec., 1977; Coll. of the VI, Fac. and Staff of the Year, 1974–75. **Pubns.:** *Final Report: V.I. Governor's Conference on Library and Information Services*, (1979); *Institute for Training in Library Management and Communications Skills: A Project Report,*

Special Subjects/Services: 50. Adult educ.; 51. Advert./Mktg.; 52. Aerosp.; 53. Agric.; 54. Area std.; 55. Arts/Hum.; 56. Autom.; 57. Bibl./Prtg.; 58. Bio. sci.; 59. Bus./Fin.; 60. Chem.; 61. Copyrt.; 62. Documtn.; 63. Educ.; 64. Engin.; 65. Env.; 66. Eth. grps.; 67. Film; 68. Food/Nutr.; 69. Geneal.; 70. Geo.; 71. Geol.; 72. Handcpd.; 73. Hist.; 74. Int. frdm.; 75. Info. sci.; 76. Insr.; 77. Law; 78. Legis.; 79. Math./Comp. sci.; 80. Med.; 81. Metals; 82. Nat. resrcs.; 83. Newsp.; 84. Nuc. sci.; 85. Oral hist.; 86. Petr./Energy; 87. Pharm.; 88. Phys./Astr./Math.; 89. Readg.; 90. Relig.; 91. Sci./Tech.; 92. Soc. sci.; 93. Telecom.; 94. Transp.; 95. (other).

Who's Who in Library and Information Services

(1979); "Use of Microforms in Libraries," *Caribbean Arch. Bltn.* (1978); "Library Networks in Remote, Disadvantaged Areas: A Survey Report," *Serials Libn.* (Fall 1978); "A Selected Annotated Bibliography of Caribbean Bibliographies in English", *Research in the Humanties and Social Sciences* (1975–76); Other reports and articles. **Activities:** 9, 13; 17, 26; 62 **Addr.:** Bureau of Libraries, Museums, and Archaeological Services, P. O. Box 390, Charlotte Amalie, St. Thomas, VI 00801.

Chang, Min-min (O. 18, 1940, China) Head, Cat. Dept. McGill Univ. Lib., 1981–, Tech. Prcs. Libn., 1978–81; Head, Cat. Dept., Concordia Univ. Libs., 1976–78; Head, Syst. Cat., SUNY Buffalo, 1969–76; Orig. Catlgr., Northwestern Univ. Libs., 1966–68. **Educ.:** Natl. Taiwan Univ., 1958–62, BA (Pol. Sci.); Univ. of CA, Berkeley, 1964–65, MLS. **Orgs.:** ALA: ACRL; LITA; RTSD. Can. LA. UTLAS-UNICAT/TELECAT: Oper. Com. (1976–79); Cat., Coding Com. (1976–79, Ch. 1977–79). **Activities:** 1; 20, 46; 56 **Addr.:** 4 Chesterfield Ave., Westmount, PQ H3Y 2M2 Canada.

Chang, Robert Huei (F. 20, 1932, Taiwan, Shangtung, China) Lib. Dir., Univ. of Houston, Downtown Coll., 1977–; Asst. Prof. & Dir. of IMC, Univ. of MO, 1975–77; Asst. Prof., Upper IA Univ., 1970–71; Head of Acq., Univ. of TN, Chattanooga, 1969–70; Acq. Libn., E. TN State Univ., 1968–69; Docum. Libn., KS State Coll. of Pittsburg, 1967–68. **Educ.:** Natl. Cheng Chi Univ., 1956–60, LLB (Jnlsm.); Univ. of MO, 1963–65, MA (Jnlsm.); West. MI Univ., 1966–67, MLS; Univ. of IA, 1971–75, PhD (Educ. Media). **Orgs.:** ALA. Chinese-Amer. Libns. Assn., Southwest Chap.: Secy., Pres. elect (1979–81). AECT. Phi Delta Kappa. **Honors:** Beta Phi Mu. **Pubns.:** "Systematic Approach to Your P.R. Program," *A V Instruc.* (F. 1977). **Activities:** 1; 17, 32 **Addr.:** 5531 Bolivia Blvd., Houston, TX 77091.

Chang, Roy Tingkwo (S. 27, 1935, Taitung, Taiwan) Cat. libn., West. IL Univ., 1974–; Asst. Circ. Libn., 1970–74, Rsv. Libn., 1964–69. **Educ.:** Natl. Taiwan Normal Univ., 1958–62, BA (Eng. Lit.); George Peabody Tchrs. Coll., 1963–64, MLS; IN Univ., 1969–72 (Anthro.). **Orgs.:** Asian Amer. Libns. Caucus: Mem. Com., Ch. (1977–78). ALA: RTSD/Com. on Cat.: Description and Access. Rep. (1979–); ACRL; LITA. Chinese Amer. Libns. Assn.: Bd. (1978–81); VP (1977–78); Midwest Chap. (Ch., 1979–80). **Activities:** 1; 20, 46 **Addr.:** 152 Penny Ln., Macomb, IL 61455.

Chang, Sookang Han (D. 28, 1941, Seoul, Korea) Head, Serials Dept., Chicago State Univ., 1971–. **Educ.:** Ewha Woman's Univ., 1961–65, BA (Eng.) North. IL Univ., 1966–69, MA (LS); Rosary Coll., 1977–80, Cert. **Orgs.:** ALA. IL LA: Exhibit Com. (1978–). Phi Delta Kappa (1979–). Chicago Acad. Libs. Cncl. **Pubns.:** "What Does Research Say About Mainstreaming," *Jnl. for Spec. Educ.* (Fall 1981); "Introduction to Waldorf Education: Curriclum and Methods," *Educ. Stds.* (Sum. 1980). **Activities:** 1; 15, 17, 44; 66, 72 **Addr.:** Chicago State University Library 95th St. at King Dr., Chicago, IL 60628.

Chang, Tohsook P. (O. 15, 1936, Seoul, Rep. of Korea) Catlgr., Asst. Prof. in Lib. Sci., Univ. of Alaska, 1972–; Catlgr., AK Methodist Univ. Lib., 1970–71; Catlgr., Univ. of Louisville Med. Sch. Lib., 1968; Catlgr., WA State Univ. Lib., Pullman, 1964–65; Catlgr., Boston Univ. Lib., 1963–64. **Educ.:** Ewha Womans Univ., Seoul, Korea, 1955–59, BA (Eng.); NY State Univ., Albany, 1962–63, MLS. **Orgs.:** ALA. Pacific Northwest LA. AK LA. Asian Amr. Assembly for Pol. Resrch.: AK Reg. Chap., Adv. Com. (1978–). **Honors:** AAUW, Flwshp., 1962. **Pubns.:** Jt. Ed., Anchorage Times Obituaries Index (1979). **Activities:** 1; 20, 46; 89 **Addr.:** Technical Services Dept., University of Alaska Anchorage Library, 3211 Providence Dr., Anchorage, AK 99504.

Channing, Rhoda K. (O. 7, 1941, New York, NY) Chief Libn., Sch. of Mgt., Boston Coll., 1979–; Bus. and Econ. Libn., Univ. of KY, 1974–79; Actg. Undergrad. Libn., Univ. of NC, 1966–68; Asst. Branch Libn., Queensborough Pub. Lib., 1963–65. **Educ.:** Brooklyn Coll., 1958–62, BA (Eng.); Columbia Univ., 1962–63, MSLS. **Orgs.:** SLA: KY Chap., PR Com. (1977–78); Student Chap. Sponsor (1978–79). KY LA: Acad. Sect. (Mem. Ch., 1978–79). ALA. **Pubns.:** "Epilogue", *Richard Whittington and His Cat* (1974); "Independent unions" *Library Trends* (O. 1976); "Chapbooks: a neglected resource" *KLA Bltn.* (Spring 1976); "Conference Report-67th Annual SLA Conference" *Kentucky Chapter (SLA) Bulletin* (Jl., 1976); "Research in Accounting," Slide-Tape (1979). **Activities:** 1, 12; 15, 17, 31; 51, 59, 92 **Addr.:** SOM Library, Boston College, Chestnut Hill, MA 02167.

Chao, Jennifer J. (Ap. 2, 1949, New York, NY) Libn., Boston Globe Newsp. Co., 1980–, Asst. Libn., 1974–79; Tech. Srvs. Libn., Houston Pub. Lib., 1973–74; Libn., TX East. Transmission Corp., 1973. **Educ.:** Boston Univ., 1967–71, BA (Russ.); Columbia Univ., 1971–72, MLS. **Orgs.:** SLA. **Activities:** 12; 32, 39, 41 **Addr.:** Boston Globe Library, Boston Globe Newspaper, Boston, MA 02107.

Chaparro, Luis F. (Ap. 1, 1944, Ciudad Juarez, Chihuahua, Mexico) Pub. Srvs. Libn., El Paso Cmnty. Coll., 1977–; Asst. Ref. Libn., Univ. of the Americas, 1970–72. **Educ.:** Univ. of Texas at El Paso, 1963–67, BA (Inter-American St.); Univ. Nacional Autonoma de Mexico, 1969–71, (Latin Amer. St.); Univ. of BC, 1972–75, MLS, 1976–77, MA (Latin Amer. Lit.). **Orgs.:** SALALM: Com. on Bibl. (1977–78). REFORMA: El Paso Chap. (Pres. 1977–78). Amer. Assn. of Tchrs. of Span. and Portuguese. Latin Amer. Studies Assn. **Pubns.:** Ed., *Amoxcalli Newsletter.* **Activities:** 1; 15, 31, 39; 55, 66 **Addr.:** 3025 Memphis, El Paso, TX 79930.

Chapel, Nancy A. (D. 11, 1936, Ft. Smith, AR) Former Media Coord., Dallas Indp. Sch. Dist., 1971–81; Tchr., Garland Indp. Sch. Dist., 1967–69. **Educ.:** E. TX State Univ., 1955–67, BS (Elem. Educ./Eng.), 1970–71, Cert. (LS). **Orgs.:** ALA. Dallas Assn. of Sch. Libns. Dallas Cnty. Lib. Assn. TX LA. Other orgs. Puppeteers of Amer. Lone Star Puppet Gld. Dallas Musm. of Fine Arts. Dallas Musm. of Nat. Hist. **Activities:** 10; 21, 32; 63, 95-AV, free-lance writer. **Addr.:** 1618 South Highway 121, #1005, Lewisville, TX 75067.

Chapin, Richard E. (Ap. 29, 1925, Danville, IL) Dir. of Libs., MI State Univ., 1959–, Assoc. Dir. of Libs., 1955–59; Asst. Dir., Sch. of LS, Univ. of OK, 1953–55; Circ. Asst., Univ. of IL, 1950–53; Ref. Asst., FL State Univ., 1949–50. **Educ.:** Wabash Coll., 1944–48, AB (Econ.); Univ. of IL, 1948–49, MS (LS), 1949–54, PhD, (Comm.). **Orgs.:** ALA: ACRL/Univ. Libs. Sect. (Ch., 1960); Nom. Com. (Ch., 1967–68); Cncl. Assn. of Resrch. Libs.: ILL Com. (1973–78). Ctr. for Resrch. Libs.: Bd. of Dir. (1977–82). MI LA: Pres. (1966–67). MI Lib. Consortium Exec. Com. (1975–). OCLC Users Cncl: Pres. (1981). E. Lansing Human Rel. Cmsn.: Ch. (1968). E. Lansing Bd. of Educ.: (1970–75); Pres. (1973–74). **Pubns.:** *Mass Communications, A Statistical Analysis,* (1957); Contrib. to encyclopedias, jnls. and conf. proc. **Activities:** 1; 17, 34; 61, 93 **Addr.:** Director of Libraries, Michigan State University, East Lansing, MI 48824.

Chaplock, Sharon Katherine Kayne (Ap. 27, 1948, Milwaukee, WI) Dir., Audiovisual Ctr., Milwaukee Pub. Musm., 1975–; Media Technician–Film, Learning Resrc. Ctr. Goodwill Rehab. Ctr., 1971–74; Advert. Asst., Roa's Films, 1970–71. **Educ.:** Marquette Univ., 1965–69, BA (Jrnlsm.); Univ. of WI, Stout, 1974–75, MS (Media Tech.). **Orgs.:** Nat. Film Market: Bd. of Dirs. (1979–82). AECT. Educ. Film Lib. Assn.: Juror, 1979–80–81. Amer. Film Fest. WI Audiovisual Assn. Women in Comm.: Pub. Ch. (1973). Amer. Assn. of Musms.: Com. on nonprint media (1979–82). Altrusa Int.: Ed. *Altrusagram* (1978–79). Milwaukee Cncl. for Adlt. Lrng. **Pubns.:** Film Ed. *Lore* Mag. (1977–); Ed., *Altrusagram* (1978–79); Ed., "This is Milwaukee," (Film) (1974). **Activities:** 10, 12; 15, 17, 32; 55, 56, 67 **Addr.:** Director, Audiovisual Center, Milwaukee Public Museum, 800 W. Wells St., Milwaukee, WI 53233.

Chapman, Geoffrey Leigh (S. 6, 1937, Sydney, Australia) Sr. Lectr., Dept. of Sch. Libnshp., Kelvin Grove Coll. of Advnc. Educ., Brisbane, Australia, 1981–; Asst. Prof., Sch. of Libnshp., Univ. of BC, 1973–81; Asst. Prof., Fac. of Educ., Univ. of MB, 1968–73; Libn., Loyalist Collegiate and Vocational Inst., 1966–68; Tchr., Nakusp Secondary Sch., Nakusp, BC, 1963–65; Tchr., Narrabai High School, Narrabai, Australia, 1958–62. **Educ.:** Univ. of Sydney, 1958, BA (Latin); Univ. of BC, 1965–66, BLS; Assoc. of the LA of Australia. **Orgs.:** Can. Lib. Assn. Can. Sch. LA. LA of Australia. BC LA; Other orgs. BC Tchrs. Fed. Can. Civil Liberties Assn. **Honors:** Sch. of Libnshp., Univ. of BC, Ruth Cameron Medal for Librarianship, 1966; Univ. of BC, Alma Mater Socty. Awd., 1966. **Pubns.:** "School-Housed Public Libraries in British Columbia," *The Canadian School-Housed Public Library* (1979); *Prospective Manitoba Teachers and the Library; A Study of University of Manitoba Faculty of Education Students Basic Library Knowledge and Attitudes Concerning the Use of Libraries* (1975); "Canadian Reference and Information Materials for Children," *Canadian Children's Literature* (Spr., Sum., 1975); "Continuous Progress Education Curriculum and Resources–A Linear Probe," *MB Jnl. of Educ.* (1970). **Activities:** 10, 11; 20, 21, 26; 63, 89 **Addr.:** Dept. of School Librarianship, Kelvin Grove College of Advanced Education, Victoria Park Rd., Kelvin Grove, Brisbane, Queensland 4059 Australia.

Chapman, Mary R. (O. 20, 1944, Cortland, NY) Head, Cat. and Tech. Srvs., NY Univ. Sch. of Law Lib., 1980–, Assoc. Head, Cat. and Tech. Srvs., 1978–80, Assoc. Head, Cat., 1972–78, Catlgr., 1967–72. **Educ.:** Syracuse Univ., 1962–66, AB (Hist.), 1966–67, MSLS; AALL, 1975, Cert. (Law Lib Admin.); New Sch. for Soc. Resrch., 1971–74, MA (Pol. Sci.), 1979– (Pol. Sci.). **Orgs.:** ALA. AALL. Intl. Assn. of Law Libs. Natl. Org. for Women. Natl. Abortion Rights Action Leag. **Pubns.:** Reviews, indxs. **Activities:** 1, 12; 20, 46; 77 **Addr.:** New York University, Library of the School of Law, 40 Washington Sq. S., New York, NY 10012.

Chapman, Renee Diamond (Jl. 13, 1949, Detroit, MI) Tech. Srvs. Libn., Assoc. Prof., Drake Univ. Law Lib., 1975–. **Educ.:** Univ. of MI, 1968–71, AB (Pol. Sci.); Wayne State Univ., 1974–75, MSLS. **Orgs.:** AALL: Cat. and Class. Com. (1975–77), Online Srvs. Spec. Interest Sect. (1977–). **Activities:** 12; 15, 20, 39; 77 **Addr.:** Law Library, Drake University, 27th & Carpenter Sts., Des Moines, IA 50311.

Chappell, Barbara A. (S. 20, 1938, Brownwood, TX) Chief of Ref. and Circ., U.S. Geol. Survey Lib., 1974–; Geol. Libn., Univ. of TX, 1972–73, Undergrad. Libn., 1970–72. **Educ.:** Univ. of TX, 1966–69, BS (Educ.), 1969–70, MLS. **Orgs.:** SLA. Geoscience Info. Socty.: Guidebook Com. **Activities:** 1, 4; 16, 17, 22 **Addr.:** 3720 Camelot Dr., Annandale, VA 22003.

Chappell, Dick LaMont (Ag. 3, 1936, Lyman, UT) Dean, Instr. Srvs., Univ. of TX, Permian Basin, 1980–, Dir., Lrng. Resrcs. Center, Actg. Dean, Coll. of Arts and Educ., 1977–80, Dir., Lrng. Resrcs. Ctr., 1971–76; Assoc. Dir., Lrng. Resrcs., UT State Univ., 1969–71, Dir., Comp. Ctr., 1966–69, Assoc. Univ. Libn., 1962–66. **Educ.:** UT State Univ., 1961, BS (Bus. Educ.); Univ. of WA, 1961–62, MSLS; Univ. of TX, Permian Basin, 1979–81, MBA. **Orgs.:** ALA: Ad Hoc Com. on Upper Level Univs. (Ch., 1977–79). TX LA: Coll. and Univ. Div. (Secy. 1978–79); Dist. Ch. (1976). TX Cncl. of Univ. Libn.: Formula Com. (1973–75). Univ. of TX Data Prcs. Cncl. **Pubns.:** "The Role of the Computer in Integrating and Utilizing Multi-media in the Library," *UT Acad. of Arts, Scis., and Letters, Proc.* (Fall 1970); "Automation and the Library," *UT Acad. of Arts, Scis. and Letters, Proc.* (Fall 1968); "Operation Move," *UT Libs.* (Fall 1964); "The Conception of a Research Center," *Permian Hist.* Anl. (D. 1972). **Activities:** 1, 14-Acad. Admin.; 17, 19; 56, 75 **Addr.:** 4607 Somerset Ln., Odessa, TX 79761.

Charbonneau, Bernard (F. 15, 1939, Laval-Des-Rapides, PQ) Tchr., Head of Dept., Tech. de la Documtn., Coll. de Jonquière, 1973–; Tchr., C.S.R. Alma, PQ, 1963–73. **Educ.:** B.A., (B. Pédagogie); B. Bib. **Orgs.:** Socty. Can. pour l'Analyse de Docum. **Pubns.:** *Recueil des Sentences de L'Éducation* (1979); *Index Cumulatif du Saguenay Médical* (1975); *Index de la Revue Saguenayensia* (1979). **Activities:** 30; 63 **Addr.:** 218 St-Georges, Arvida, PQ G7S 1W5 Canada.

Charbonneau, Monique (Ap. 7, 1948, Ottawa, ON) Dir., Bib. Admin., Dept. of Comms., PQ, 1980–; Chef, Srv. de la Documtn. Term. et des Bib., Ofc. de la Lang. Fr., 1979–80; Dir., Reg. Lib. Srvs., Dept. of the Env., 1977–79; Chief, Lib., Can. Labour Rel. Bd., 1976–77; Chief, Reg. Lib., Dept. of Manpower and Immigration, 1969–75. **Educ.:** Ottawa Univ., 1967–69, BLS; Univ. de Montréal, 1972–76, MLS. **Orgs.:** ASTED: Comsn. des Bibl. de Recherche et Spéc. (Près., 1978–79). Corp. des Bibtcrs. Prof. du PQ. Assn. Can. des Bibtcrs. de Lang. Fr.: Com. du Bltn. (Secy., 1970–75). IFLA: Pubns. Com. (1980–). **Pubns.:** Jt. auth., *Service d'information bibliographiques* (1978); *Le programme de dépôt des publications governementales du Québec dans les bibliothéques* (1981). **Activities:** 4; 17, 29, 39; 65 **Addr.:** Bibliothéque Administrative, Ministére des Communications, 1037 de la Chevrotière, Québec, PQ G1R 4Y7 Canada.

Charette, Christiane (N. 16, 1950, Verdun, PQ) Bibtcr., Bib. Municipale de St-Eustache, 1980–; Responsable De Succursale, Bib. Municipale de Montréal 1975–80. **Educ.:** Univ. de Montréal, 1970–73, BS (Educ.), 1973–75 M (LS). **Orgs.:** Corp. Des Bibltcrs. Prof. du PQ. ASTED. Com. Bib. Et Lectures Pour Jeunes. LURELU: Com. de Redaction (1980–81). **Pubns.:** Jt. auth., *Enfin, Je Lis! Bibliographie Selective Pour Enfants 7à 10 Ans* (1978); Jt. auth., *Ten Dances Actuelles De La Littérature De Jeunesse Langue Française* (1980); "Contes Et Legendes Du Québec," *LURELU* (Spr. 1981). **Activities:** 9; 15, 39, 49-Animation. **Addr.:** Bibliothèque Municipale De St-Eustache, St-Eustache, PQ J7R 2H7 Canada.

Charette, Réjean (N. 12, 1940, St-Léon-le-Grand de Maskinongé, PQ) Bibl. Prof., Ecole polyvalente Calixa-Lavallée, 1974–; Bibl. Prof., Ecole polyvalente Edouard-Montpetit, 1972–74; Serv.-tech., Bib. centrale des professeurs de la C.E.C.M., 1970–72; Professeur-Titulaire, Ecole Adélard-Langevin, 1963–67. **Educ.:** Univ. de Montréal, 1959–63, BA (Ens.), 1959–63, BPéd (Ens.), 1963–67, Dipl. (Théol. past.), 1968–70, B.Bibl. (Bibl.). **Orgs.:** Corp. des bibl. prof. du Québec: Com. des bibl. scolaires (1974–77); Sous-com. de Statut et Traitement: Bibl. scholaires (1977–78). Ass. pour l'avancement des sc. et des tech. de la doc.: Cons. de la sect. scolaire (1975–78); Com. de recrutement (1979–). **Pubns.:** *Mémoire relatif au Livre vert sur l'enseignement primaire et secondaire au Québec* (1978). **Activities:** 10; 17, 48; 63 **Addr.:** 7225, rue Marie-Victorin, Montréal, PQ H1G 2J7, Canada.

Chariton, May (Ja. 18, 1926, New York, NY) Med. Libn., Southside Hosp., 1980–; Med. Libn., St. John's Episcopal Hosp., 1977–80; Ref. Libn., Valley Stream Pub. Lib., 1967–74. **Educ.:** Hunter Coll., 1943–47, (Psy.); Long Island Univ., 1962–67, (LS); Columbia Univ. (1975). **Orgs.:** Med. LA: NY Grp., ILL Com. 1981. Med. and Sci. Libs. of Long Island: Pres. (1979–80). **Activities:** 12; 17, 34, 39; 80 **Addr.:** Medical Library, Southside Hospital, Bay Shore, NY 11706.

Charles, Sharon Ashenbrenner (Ap. 21, 1947, Shawano, WI) Coord., Indianhead Fed. Lib. Syst., 1979–; Adult Srvs. Libn., Cook Meml. Pub. Lib. Dist., 1977–79, Asst. Adult Srvs. Libn., 1976–77; Asst. to the Nursing Supvsr., Sauk Cnty. Hlth. Care Ctr., 1971–75. **Educ.:** St. Norbert Coll., 1965–68; Univ. of WI, 1969–71, BA (Comp. Lit.), 1975–76, MA (LS), 1972–74 (Comp. Lit.). **Orgs.:** ALA. WI LA. Lib. Admin. Cncl. of North. IL: Prog. Plng. Com. (1978–79). **Pubns.:** *Drugs:A Mul-*

PROFESSIONAL ACTIVITIES: Institutions: 1. Acad. lib.; 2. Arch.; 3. Assn.; 4. Fed./Gvt. lib.; 5. Inst. lib.; 6. Mfr./Suppl.; 7. Milit. lib.; 8. Musm.; 9. Pub. lib.; 10. Sch. lib.; 11. Sch. of lib. sci.; 12. Spec. lib.; 13. State lib.; 14. (other). **Functions/Activities:** 15. Acq./Col. dev.; 16. Adult srvs.; 17. Admin.; 18. Apprais.; 19. Archit./Bldgs.; 20. Cat./Class.; 21. Chld. srvs.; 22. Circ.; 23. Cons./Pres.; 24. Consult.; 25. Cont. ed.; 26. Educ. lib. sci.; 27. Ext. srvs.; 28. Fund/Grants; 29. Gvt. pubs.; 30. Indx./Abs.; 31. Instr. lib. use; 32. Media srvs.; 33. Micro.; 34. Netwks./Coop.; 35. Persnl.; 36. PR; 37. Publshg.; 38. Recs. mgt.; 39. Ref. srvs.; 40. Repro.; 41. Resrch.; 42. Review.; 43. Secur.; 44. Serials; 45. Spec. col.; 46. Tech. srvs.; 47. Trustees/Bds.; 48. YA srvs.; 49. (other).

Who's Who in Library and Information Services

timedia Sourcebook for Young Adults. (1980). **Activities:** 9; 16, 24, 25 **Addr.:** 2515 Diane Ln., Eau Claire, WI 54701.

Charpentier, Arthur A. (Ag. 13, 1919, Waterbury, CT) Retired 1981; Assoc. Dean for Lib. Mgt., Yale Univ. Law Sch., 1967–; Libn., The Assn. of the Bar of the City of New York, 1957–67; Asst. Libn., 1950–57; Libn., Boston Univ. Sch. of Law, 1948–50. **Educ.:** Springfield Coll., 1937–41, BS (Grp. Work); Boston Univ., 1946–48, LLB (Law); Admitted, MA Bar, 1948. **Orgs.:** AALL: Pres. (1965–66); Intl. Assn. of Law Libs.: VP (1968–71). Amer. Arbitration Assn: Ch., Library Com. (1978–); CT Law Lib. Adv. Com.: Secy. (1976–). **Addr.:** Box 22, Mount Desert, ME 04660.

Chartrand, Margaret (Ag. 4, 1943, Saint John, NB) Head, PR, Metro. Toronto Lib. Bd., 1976–; PR Ofcr., Govt. of ON 1973–75; Info. Ofcr., ON Coll. of Art 1972–73; Info. Ofcr., Bell Can. 1971–72; Info. Ofcr., Univ. of West. ON, 1967–71. **Educ.:** Carleton Univ., 1963–66 B. of Jnlsm., various insts. **Orgs.:** Can. LA. ON LA. ALA. Various PR Coms. Toronto Press Club. **Honors:** ALA, John Cotton Dana Awd., 1978. Intl. Assn. of Bus. Comm. Awd. of Merit, 1978, 71, 70. **Pubns.:** Many newsp., mag. and jnl. articles, directories, and media presentations. **Activities:** 9; 28, 36, 37; 51 **Addr.:** Metropolitan Toronto Library Board, 789 Yonge St., Toronto, ON M4W 2G8 Canada.

Chartrand, Robert Lee (Mr. 6, 1928, Kansas City, MO) Sr. Spec. in Info. Policy and Tech., Lib. of Congs., 1966–; Mgr., Applications Dev., Plng. Resrch. Corp., 1964–66; Tech. and Mgt., IBM Fed. Syst. Div., 1961–64; Tech. Staff, TRW, Inc., 1959–61. **Educ.:** Univ. of MO, Kansas City, 1945–48, BA (Eng. and Hist.), 1948–49, MA (Hist., Govt.); LA State Univ., 1949–50, (Hist.); Univ. of MD, 1956, (Govt.). **Orgs.:** ASIS: Consult. Ed., *Bulletin* (1975). Ch., Bicentennial Conf. on "America in the Information Age," (1976). Amer. Assn. for the Adv. of Sci.: Fellow (1977–). Fulbright Alumni Assn. **Honors:** Dept. of State, Fulbright-Hays lect., 1968; Pres. of the Italian Republic, Cavaliere Ufficiale (Order of Merit), 1968. Interagency Com. on Automatic Data Processing, Cert. of Appre., 1976. Test of Time Awd., 1979. **Pubns.:** *Systems Technology Applied To Social and Community Problems,* 1971; Ed., *Hope for the Cities,* 1971; Ed., Jt. Auth., *Computers In the Service of Society,* 1972; *Computers and Political Campaigning,* 1972; Jt. Ed., *Information Support, Program Budgeting, And The Congress,* 1972; Jt. Auth., *State Legislature Use of Information Technology,* 1978; Jt. Ed., *Information Technology Serving Society,* 1979; Various other publications. **Activities:** 4; 17, 24, 29; 56, 75, 78 **Addr.:** 5406 Dorset Ave., Chevy Chase, MD 20015.

Chase, Frank R. (Je. 9, 1915, Chicago, IL) Retired, 1980–; Law Libn., Coord. of Spec. Srvs., East. KY Univ., 1965–80; Asst. Sci. Libn., South. IL Univ., 1959–65; Asst. Ref. Libn., Peoria Pub. Lib., 1952–59; Ref. Libn., Bradley Univ., 1947–52. **Educ.:** Univ. of IL, 1938–42, BA (Hist.); Columbia Univ., 1946–47, BSLS. **Orgs.:** IL LA. KY LA. ALA. **Activities:** 1; 39; 77 **Addr.:** Route 2, Lancaster Woods, Richmond, KY 40475.

Chase, Peter Frank (D. 13, 1949, New Bedford, MA) Lib. Dir., Plainville Pub. Lib., 1981–; Dir., Phoebe Griffin Noyes Lib., 1977–81; YA Libn., Enoch Pratt Lib., 1973–77. **Educ.:** Univ. of RI, 1967–71, BA (Educ.); Univ. of Pittsburgh, 1972–73, MLS; Emergency Med. Tech., CT, 1978. **Orgs.:** ALA: YASD, Logo Com. (1976). CT LA: Small Pub. Libs. Com. (1979). Southeast. CT LA: Bd. of Dir. (1979). **Pubns.:** "What's In It For You At the Library," *Top of the News* (Je. 1976). **Activities:** 9; 17, 48; 63, 92 **Addr.:** Plainville Public Library, 56 E. Main St., Plainville, CT 06026.

Chasen, Larry I. (S. 20, 1924, Philadelphia, PA) Mgr., GE Space/RSD Librs., General Electric Co., 1956–; Chief Libn., Boeing Co. Vertol Div., 1949–56; Admin. Ofcr., U.S. Naval Ship Services, 1947–49; Tech. Librn., US Army Signal Corps, 1942–47. **Educ.:** Gratz Coll., 1942–44, AB (Lang.); Dept. of Defense, Tech. Info. Ctr. Training Prog., 1978. **Orgs.:** SLA. Amer. Inst. of Aeronautics and Astronautics: Techn. Info. Consult. (1965–68). **Honors:** GE Co., One in a Thousand Awd. for Outstan. Achvmt. in Lib. Syst., 1968. **Pubns.:** "Information and Retrieval Systems and Technology in Library Systems," *SLA Journal* (D. 1966); "An On-Line System with the Department of Defense," *SLA Journal* (Ja. 1980); various speeches. **Activities:** 5; 15, 17, 20; 88, 91, 93 **Addr.:** P.O. Box 8555, Philadelphia, PA 19101.

Chatfield, Michele R. (Mr. 4, 1947, Brooklyn, NY) Tech. Info. Spec., Food & Drug Admin., 1974–; Ref. Libn., Lib. of the Hlth. Scis., U. IL Med. Ctr., 1971–73; Tech. Libn., Julius Schmid, Inc., 1969–70; Tech. Info. Spec., Intl. Nickel Co., Inc., 1968–69. **Educ.:** Beaver Coll., 1963–67, BA (Chem.); Pratt Inst., 1969–71, MLS. **Orgs.:** Med. LA: Mid Atlantic Reg. Grp. (Educ. Com. 1976–79; Nom. Com. 1979; On-Line Srvs. Com. 1981); Bibl. and Assess. Com. 1977–80; Anl. Mtg. Com. 1979–. **Honors:** Beta Phi Mu, 1971. **Activities:** 4, 12; 17, 38, 39; 60, 68, 80 **Addr.:** 3701 Mass. Ave. N.W., Washington, DC 20016.

Chatfield, Robert Warner (D. 5, 1932, Newton, MA) Dir., Lib. Resrcs. Ctr., Franklin Pierce Coll., 1970–; Chief, Acq. Div., Boston Univ., 1969–70, Head, Order Dept., 1964–69; Circ., Ref. Libn., Lamont Lib., Harvard Coll., 1961–64. **Educ.:** Columbia Univ., 1955–59, AB (Eng.), 1959–61, MSLS. **Activities:** 1; 15, 17 **Addr.:** Pratt Rd., Alstead Center, NH 03602.

Chaturvedi, Malya Momaya (Jl. 20, 1947, Bombay, India) Media Spec., High Hills Middle Sch., 1975–; Libn., Mayesville Elem. Sch., 1972–75; Libn., Queensborough Pub. Lib., 1970–71. **Educ.:** Univ. of Bombay, 1964–68, BA (Pol. Sci.); Atlanta Univ., 1969–70, MS (LS); Univ. of SC, 1972–74, MEd. **Orgs.:** SC Assn. of Sch. Libns.: Com. of Creative Handouts (Ch., 1978–79); *Media Messenger* (Ed., 1979). **Activities:** 9, 10; 17, 21, 32; 63 **Addr.:** Malya Chaturvedi, 817 Rockwood Rd., Columbia, SC 29209.

Chauhan, Ram P.S. (Ja. 12, 1932, U. P., India) Asst. Dir., E. St. Louis Pub. Lib., 1972–; Dir., Pub. Lib., Fremont, MI, 1971–72; Lect. in LS, Univ. of Rajasthan, Jaipur, India, 1968–70; Libn., Brooklyn Pub. Lib., 1966–68; Head Libn., Coll. of Educ., G.V.M. Sardarshahr, India, 1956–66, Lect. in LS, 1961–66; Catlgr., Univ. Lib., Rajasthan Univ. Jaipur, India, 1955–56. **Educ.:** Agra Univ., India, 1950–52, BA (Pol. Sci.); Rajasthan Univ., India, 1956–58, MA (Pol. Sci.); Banaras Hindu Univ., India, 1954–55, Dipl. (LS); Long Island Univ., 1967–68, MSLS; South. IL Univ., Edwardsville, 1974–76, MS, (Educ.); South. IL Univ., Carbondale, 1978–, Doctoral Cand. (Educ. Media). **Orgs.:** ALA. IL LA. **Pubns.:** "History of Delhi Public Library from 1951 to 1969," *LIBRA*. **Activities:** 1, 9; 15, 17, 46 **Addr.:** 16 Northland Dr., Belleville, IL 62221.

Cheatham, Bertha M. (S. 1, 1932, Ossining, NY) Assoc. Ed., Sch. Lib. Jnl., R. R. Bowker Co., 1973–; Sch. Libn., Greenburgh Ctrl. Sch. Dist., 1961–73; Chld. Libn., Brooklyn Pub. Lib., 1957–61. **Educ.:** Hunter Coll., 1951–55, BA (Eng./Ed.); Pratt Inst., 1958–60, MLS; Univ. of HI, 1973–74, MA (Educ.). **Orgs.:** ALA: ALA/Chld. Book Cncl. Jt. Com. NY LA; Women's Natl. Book Assn. **Honors:** Pi Lamda Theta. **Pubns.:** "News Events of the Year," *Sch. Lib. Jnl.,* annually. **Activities:** 6; 21, 32, 37, 42 **Addr.:** 81 Bischoff Ave., Chappaqua, NY 10514.

Cheeseman, E. Margaret (Muncie, IN) Doctoral Student, Univ. of WI, 1979–; Lib. Adv., State Lib. of PA, 1968–79; Consult., MI State Lib., 1966–68; Head Libn., Lakeview HS, 1960–66; Bkmobile Libn., Grace A. Dow Meml. Lib., 1958–60; Asst. Libn., Lab. Sch., Univ. of Chicago, 1957–58; Tchr., Libn., Mt. Morris HS, 1953–55. **Educ.:** Northwestern Univ., 1949–53, BS (Eng., Math); Univ. of Chicago, 1956–58, MLS; Miscellaneous workshops, seminars, inst. **Orgs.:** CLENE. MI LA: Newcomers Com. (Ch., 1965). ALA: LAD/Buildings and Equipment Sect., Exec. Com. (1972–74); AHIL. (VP, Pres. Elect, Exec. Bd., 1973–74); HRLSD (Co-Pres., 1974–75); Exec. Bd. (1975–76); Bylaws Com. (1976–77). AECT. Other orgs. and coms. Amer. Correctional Assn. Correctional Educ. Assn. **Honors:** ALA, Cert. of recog. as Dir. of MI Lib. Week, 1963; ALA, ASCLA, Excep. Srv. Awd., 1980. **Pubns.:** *Guidelines to Help Libraries Serve Special Patrons* (1977); "Prison (Correctional) Libraries," *Encyclopedia of Library and Information Science* (1978); "Special Patron At the Library," *PLA News* (Spr. 1976); "Give Us Your Poor," *Cath. Lib. World* (My. 1976); "Library Services to Young People and Children in Correctional Facilities," *Lib. Trends* (Summer 1977); Other articles. **Activities:** 5, 10; 17, 24, 25; 56, 72 **Addr.:** R #5, Box 283, Portland, IN 47371.

Chelton, Mary K. (F. 9, 1942, Baltimore, MD) Co-Ed., *Voice of Youth Advocates,* 1981–; Asst. Prof., Rutgers Univ. Grad. LS, 1978–; YA Consult., Westchester (NY) Lib. Syst., 1974–78; Prin. YA Libn., Prince George's Co. (MD) Library Syst., 1970–73; YA Libn., Sacramento (CA) City-Cnty. Lib. Syst., 1969–70. **Educ.:** Mt. St. Agnes College, Baltimore, MD, 1959–63, BA (Eng.); Rutgers Univ., 1964–65, MLS. **Orgs.:** ALA: YASD, Pres., (1976–77); Cncl. (1977–81); Com. on Org. (1977–81); YASD IFC (1979–80). NJLA: IFC (1979–). Frd. to Read Fndn: Bd (1980–81). Soc. for Adlsnt. Med. Natl. Cncl. of Tchrs. of Eng. **Pubns.:** "Educational and Recreational Information for Young Adults," *Lib. Qtly.* (O. 1978); "Booktalking: You Can Do It!", *Sch. Lib. Jnl* (Ap. 1976). **Activities:** 9; 26, 48 **Addr.:** P.O. Box 6569, University, AL 35486.

Chen, Catherine W. (S. 19, 1938, Chengtu, Szechuan, China) Head Libn., Northwood Inst., 1974–, Catlgr., 1971–74; Lectr., Univ. of MI, 1970–71; Instr., Univ. of MN, 1966–69. **Educ.:** Natl. Taiwan Univ., 1956–60, BA (Frgn. Langs.); Univ. of MN, 1963–66, MA (LS), 1967–75, PhD (E. Asian Lit.). **Orgs.:** ALA. SLA. MI LA. Assn. of Asian Stds. **Activities:** 1; 17 **Addr.:** Strosacker Library, Northwood Institute, Midland, MI 48640.

Chen, Ching-chih (S. 3, 1937, Foochow, Fukien, China) Assoc. Dean & Prof., Grad. Sch. of Lib. & Info. Sci., Simmons Coll., 1979–, Asst. Dean for Acad. Affairs, 1976–79, Assoc. Prof., 1975–79, Asst. Prof., 1971–75; Assoc. Sci. Libn., M.I.T., 1968–71; Head, Engin., Math. & Sci. Lib., Univ. of Waterloo, 1965–68, Sr. Sci. Libn., 1964–65; Head, Sci. Lib., McMaster Univ., 1963–64. **Educ.:** Natl. Taiwan Univ., 1956–59, BA (Lang. & Lit.); Univ. of MI, 1959–61, AMLS; Case Western Reserve Univ., 1972–74, PhD (Info. Sci.). **Orgs.:** SLA. ASIS: New Eng. Chap., Vice-Ch., Ch.-Elect (1976–77); Ch., (1977–78); SIG/ED, Ch. (1979–80). Med. LA: Ch., Surveys and Statistics Com., (1979–80); Cert. Examination Review Com. (1977–79); Ad Hoc Com. to Study MLA's Role in Lib. Resrch. (1979–). ALA: Cncl. (1981–85); Cncl. Legislative Com. (1981–83); Resource member on Taiwan, Intl. Lib. Educ. Com. (1978–). Other orgs. and coms. **Honors:** Univ. of MI, Disting. Alumnus Awd., 1980; ASIS, First runner-up, 1976 ASIS Best Info. Sci. Book Awd., 1978; Beta Phi Mu, 1972. **Pubns.:** *Health Sciences Information Sources* (1981); *Library Management Without Bias* (1981); *Zero-Base Budgeting in Library Management: A Manual for Librarians* (1980); *Scientific & Technical Information Sources* (1978); *Application of Operations Research Models to Libraries: A Case Study of the Use of Monographs in the Francis A. Countway Library of Medicine.* (1976); *Biomedical Scientific and Technical Book Reviewing.* (1976); other books and articles. **Addr.:** Graduate School of Library & Information Science, Simmons College, 300 The Fenway, Boston, MA 02115.

Chen, David W. R. (Jl. 9, 1939, Lo-tung, Taiwan, Rep. of China) Asst. Libn., Pitts Theo. Lib., Emory Univ., 1978–; Catlgr., 1971–78; Catlgr., Hartford Sem. Fndn., 1969–71. **Educ.:** Taiwan Theo. Coll., 1959–65, BTh (Theo.); Yale Univ. Dvnty. Sch., 1965–68, BD (Theo.); Univ. of Pittsburgh, 1968–69, MLS. **Orgs.:** ATLA: Com. on Cat. and Class. (1975–78). Meth. Libn. Flwshp. **Pubns.:** Trans., *The Study of Nestorian Church in China* (1965); "The Chinese-Japanese Collection at the Pitts Theology Library," *Ex Libris* (O. 1979). **Activities:** 1; 20, 45; 90 **Addr.:** Pitts Theology Library, Emory University, Atlanta, GA 30322.

Chen, Donna H. (S. 24, 1935, Shanghai, China) Head, ILL, OH Univ., 1978–, Tchg. Assoc., 1973–78; Head, Serial Cat., Syracuse Univ., 1963–66, Soc. Sci. Cat., 1961–63. **Educ.:** Natl. Taiwan Univ., 1954–58, BA (Eng.); Univ. of WA, 1959–61, MLS; OH Univ., 1973–75, MA (Ling.), 1975–, (Eng.). **Orgs.:** ALA. OH LA. Chinese Amer. Libns. Assn. Mod. Langs. Assoc. Phi Kappa Phi. **Activities:** 1; 17, 34, 41; 95-Ling. **Addr.:** Main Campus Library, Ohio University, Athens, OH 45701.

Chen, Effie Y. H. (Mr. 22, 1935, Taipei, Taiwan, China) Actg. Cur., Gest Oriental Lib., Princeton Univ., 1979–, Assoc. Cur. & Head, Chinese Sect., 1975–79, Chinese Head Catlgr., 1968–75; Ref. Libn., Catlgr., Citizens Lib., Washington, PA, 1965–68; Chinese Catlgr., Gest Oriental Lib., 1963–65. **Educ.:** Taiwan Normal Univ., 1953–57, BEd; Drexel Univ., 1959–61, MS (Nutr.), 1961–63, MLS. **Orgs.:** ALA: RTSD/Descr. Cat. Com., Ad Hoc Subcom. on the Descr. Cat. of Asian & African Mat. (1976–78). Assn. for Asian Stds.: Subcom. on Tech. Proc./Com. on East Asian Libs. (1974–). **Pubns.:** "A Summary of Problem areas in Descriptive Cataloging and Subject Analysis of East Asian Materials," *Com. on East Asian Libs. Bltn.,* (N. 1977). **Addr.:** Gest Library & East Asian Collections, 317 Palmer Hall, Princeton University, Princeton, NJ 08540.

Chen, John H. M. (Je. 24, 1931, China) Exec. Dir., Nat. Lib./Info. Syst. and Netwks., 1972–; Dean Libs. & Lrng. Resrcs., AL State Univ., 1975–77; Prof., Ch. of Lib. Sci., Univ. of So. MI, 1970–72; Dir. of Libs., WI State Univ., 1970–72. **Educ.:** VA Polytech. Inst., 1957, MS; Columbia Univ., 1963, MSLS; NY Univ., 1964, MA; PA State Univ., 1968, EdD; v. of Pittsburgh, 1972, Adv. Study in Info. Sci. **Orgs.:** ALA. ASIS. **Honors:** White House Conf. on Lib. and Info. Srvcs. Adv. Com. Mem., 1972–79; UNEXCO, Spec. Awd. for Lit. Comp. and Effects; Int. Book Yr., 1972; NATO Merit. Cit. for Info. Sci., 1973. **Pubns.:** *Vietnam: A Comprehensive Bibliography* (1973); Cont., *Information Science:* (1974); Cont., *Sufi Studies: East and West,* (1975). *Historical Development of Land-Grant Universities,* (NALINETS) (1980). **Activities:** 1; 34; 54, 56, 75 **Addr.:** NALINETS, P.O. Box 602, Beltsville, MD 20705.

Chen, Simon P. J. (S. 25, 1931, Peking, China) Head of Cat., Cleveland State Univ. Lib., 1979–; Coord. of Orig. Cat., San Jose State Univ. Lib., 1973–79; Head Cat. Libn., West. KY Univ. Lib., 1967–73; Cat. Libn., North. IL Univ. Lib., 1963–67; Asst. Cat. Libn., Univ. of NV Lib., Reno, 1961–63; Cat., Univ. of Chicago, 1959–61. **Educ.:** Natl. Taiwan Univ., 1950–54, BA (Hist.); Cath. Univ. of Amer., 1956–59, MSLS; San Jose State Univ., 1976–79, MA (Hist.); Additional coursework, 1959–66. **Orgs.:** KY LA. North. OH Tech. Srvs. Libns. ALA. Chinese Libns. Assn.: Reg. Dir. (1974–75); Ch., Affirmative Action Com. (1976); Act. Dir. (1977); Memb. Dir. (1978); Exec. Dir. (1979). Chinese for Affirmative Action. Chinese Assn. in Grt. Cleveland. AAUP. **Honors:** Phi Alpha Theta, 1976. **Pubns.:** *East Asian Language Works in the San Jose State University Library* (1975); *On-line Cataloging and Circulation at Western Kentucky University; an Approach to Automated Instructional Resources Management* (1973); "Automated Cataloging and Reclassification by ATS," *Special Libs.* (Ap. 1973); "Swen Parson Library, Northern Illinois University," *IL Libs.* (Je. 1965). **Activities:** 1; 20, 46; 54, 56, 92 **Addr.:** 3281 Berkeley Rd., Cleveland Heights, OH 44118.

Chenevert, Edward V. (Ja. 24, 1933, Waterville, ME) Exec. Dir., Portland Pub. Lib., (ME), 1970–. **Educ.:** Boston Univ., 1946–48, AB (Hist.); Columbia Univ., 1949–50, MLS. **Orgs.:** New Eng. Lib. Bd.: Panel of Couns., Ch. (1973–76). New Eng. LA: VP (1978–79); Pres. (1979–80). **Honors:** Columbia Univ., Joseph Towne Wheeler Awd., 1950. **Addr.:** Five Monument Sq., Portland, ME 04101.

Special Subjects/Services: 50. Adult educ.; 51. Advert./Mktg.; 52. Aerosp.; 53. Agric.; 54. Area std.; 55. Arts/Hum.; 56. Autom.; 57. Bibl./Prtg.; 58. Bio. sci.; 59. Bus./Fin.; 60. Chem.; 61. Copyrt.; 62. Documtn.; 63. Educ.; 64. Engin.; 65. Env.; 66. Eth. grps.; 67. Film; 68. Food/Nutr.; 69. Geneal.; 70. Geo.; 71. Geol.; 72. Handcpd.; 73. Hist.; 74. Int. frdm.; 75. Info. sci.; 76. Insr.; 77. Law; 78. Legis.; 79. Math./Comp. sci.; 80. Med.; 81. Metals; 82. Nat. resrcs.; 83. Newsp.; 84. Nuc. sci.; 85. Oral hist.; 86. Petr./Energy; 87. Pharm.; 88. Phys./Astr./Math.; 89. Readg.; 90. Relig.; 91. Sci./Tech.; 92. Soc. sci.; 93. Telecom.; 94. Transp.; 95. (other).

Who's Who in Library and Information Services

Cheney, Frances Neel (Ag. 9, 1906, Washington, DC) Prof. Emeritus, Peabody Sch. of LS, 1975–, Prof., Assoc. Dir., 1967–75, Assoc. Prof., 1949–67, Asst. Prof., 1946–49. **Educ.:** Vanderbilt Univ., 1924–28, BA (Soclgy.); Columbia Univ., 1938–40, MLS. **Orgs.:** ALA: Cncl. (1954–68); Exec. Bd. (1956–61); Ref. Srvs. Div. (Pres., 1960–61); Lib. Educ. Div. (Pres., 1964–65). AALS: Pres. (1956–57). Beta Phi Mu: Pres. (1961). SELA: Pres. (1960–62). Other orgs. and ofcs. TN Hist. Socty. TN Folklore Socty. TN Cmsn. for the Hums. **Honors:** SELA Mary U. Rothrock Awd., 1980; TN LA, various Hons., 1976, 1980; Women's Natl. Bk. Assn., Skinner Awd., 1976; Peabody Coll., Awd. for Excel. in Tchg., 1971; other hons. **Pubns.:** *Fundamental Reference Sources* (1971, 1980); *Annotated List of Selected Japanese Reference Materials* (1952); *Sixty American Poets, 1886–1944* (1944); "Current Reference Books," monthly column *Wilson Lib. Bltn* (1942–72); reviews; many articles. **Activities:** 1, 11; 17, 26, 39 **Addr.:** 112 Oak St., Box 223, Smyrna, TN 37167.

Cheng, Chao-Sheng (Ag. 10, 1939, Tainai, Taiwan, Repub. of China) Acq. Lib., Hlth. Sci. Lib., E. Carolina Univ., 1980–; Head Catlgr., 1976–80; Catlgr., 1974–76; Catlgr., Univ. of WI, La Crosse, 1969–72. **Educ.:** Taiwan Normal Univ., 1959–63, BEd (Adult Educ.); Univ. of Pittsburgh, 1967–68, MLS, 1968–69, Advanced Cert. (LS); E. Carolina Univ., 1975–77, MAED (Adult Educ.). **Orgs.:** ALA. Med. LA. **Honors:** Kappa Delta Pi. **Pubns.:** "The 501 Years of the Oxford University Press," *Jnl. of Lib. & Info. Sci.* (O. 1979); "The Beginning of the Western Encyclopedia," *Jnl. of Lib. & Info. Sci.* (Ap. 1978); "U.S. Saturday Evening Post," *Central Daily News* (Mr. 30, 31, Ap. 1, 1972); "The Shortcut from Milwaukee to Washington D.C.–the library," *Overseas Intellectual* (Ap. 15, 1972); Other articles. **Activities:** 1, 12; 17, 20, 39; 80 **Addr.:** Health Sciences Library, East Carolina University, Greenville, NC 27834.

Cheng, Hsueh-Chen (Jeannette) W. (My. 15, 1936, Yüng-Chun, Fu-Kien, China) Sr. Cat/gr., Tech. Prcs. Div., Madison Pub. Lib., 1980–; Asst. Supvsr., 1979–1980 Suprvsr, Reader's Srvs. Div., Natl. Tsing-Hua Univ. Lib., 1977–78; Catlgr., Madison Pub. Lib., 1978–79, 1973–77; Bibl., Acq., Ctrl. WA State Coll. Lib., 1970–72. **Educ.:** Natl. Taiwan Univ., 1954–58, BA (Chinese Lit.); Univ. of WI, 1967–69, MA (Asian Std.), MLS; WI Pub. Libn. Cert., 1974. **Orgs.:** ALA. Org. of Chinese Amers. **Pubns.:** Textual Std. of Han-shih Wai-chüan, (1962); Study of Li-Po's poetry illustrated with maps, (1964); Translations. **Activities:** 1, 9; 15, 20, 39; 57, 75, 91 **Addr.:** 1022 Friar Ln., Madison, WI 53711.

Cheng, James K. M. (F. 12, 1947, Canton, Kwangtung, China) Actg. Cur., Far Eastern Lib., Univ. of Chicago, 1981–, Actg. Cur., 1980-81; Asst. cur, 1979-80, Bibligphr. for Spec. Proj., 1977–79; Bibligphr., Ctr. for Chinese Resrch. Mat., Assn. of Resrch. Libr., 1973-75; Chinese Catlgr., Far Eastern Lib., Univ. of Chicago, 1972–73. **Educ.:** Chinese Univ. of Hong Kong, 1966–70, BA (Lit.); Univ. of KY, 1970–71, MSLS; Univ. of Chicago, 1977–; Cert. of Advnc. Studies, 1972–77 (LS). **Orgs.:** Assn. for Asian Studies: com. on E. Asian Libs. **Pubns.:** Jt. auth., *Research Materials on Twentieth-Century China, A List of CCRM Publications* (1975); Jt. auth., *China: A Bibliography of Bibliographies* (1978); "Rarities and specialties of East Asian materials in American libraries," *Com. on East Asian Libs. Nsltr.* (N. 1976). **Activities:** 1; 15, 17, 23, 39; 54, 57 **Addr.:** Far Eastern Library, The University of Chicago Library, 1100 E. 57th St., Chicago, IL 60637.

Chenier, André (Jl. 20, 1930, Maniwaki, PQ) Dir. des Bibs., Univ. du PQ a Hull, 1974–; Chef, Sect. du Pret, Bib. Natl. du Can., 1972–74; Dir., Bib., Gén., Univ. de Sherbrooke, 1964–72; Bibtcr.-en-chef, Coll. des Jésuites de PQ, 1957–64. **Educ.:** Univ. d'Ottawa, 1949–53, BA, BPh (Phil.), 1954–55, BLS. **Orgs.:** ASTED. Corp. des Bibtcrs. Prof. du PQ. Can LA. ALA. Conf. des Recteurs et des Principaux des Univ. du PQ. **Activities:** 1; 17, 34 **Addr.:** 805 Hamlet, Ottawa, ON K1G 1R1 Canada.

Chepesiuk, Ronald Joseph (Je. 14, 1944, Thunderbay, ON, Can) Head, Spec. Col., Winthrop Coll., 1973–. **Educ.:** Moorhead State Univ., MN, 1964–68, BA (Hist.); AT Univ., 1971–72, MLS; Inst. on Arch. Admin., 1973, Cert. **Orgs.:** SAA: Arch. Lib. Rel. Com. (1974–77). Socty. of GA Archvsts.: Ed. Brd. (1979–). SC LA. S. Atlantic Arch. and Records Conf. **Honors:** Beta Phi Mu; Phi Alpha Theta. **Pubns.:** *Winthrop College Archives and Special Collections* (1978); "Ida Jones Dacus," *SC Libn.* (1977). **Activities:** 1; 45; 55, 85 **Addr.:** 5 Dacus Library, Winthrop College, Rock Hill, SC 29733.

Chernik, Barbara E. (F. 18, 1938, Washington, DC) Head Libn., Warren-Newport Pub. Lib., 1980–; Instr. (Lib. Media Tech. Asst. Prog.), Gateway Tech. Inst., 1970–80, Tech. Srvs. Libn., 1967–69; Army Libn., Europe, 1962–64; Chld. Libn., Arlington Cnty. Libs., 1960–62. **Educ.:** Dickinson Coll., 1955–59, BA (Hist.); Univ. of IL, 1959–60, MS (LS). **Orgs.:** ALA. WI LA. IL LA. AAUW. Bd. of Trustees, Kenosha Pub. Lib. (1972–79). **Activities:** 1, 9; 17, 26, 47 **Addr.:** 120 68th Pl., Kenosha, WI 53140.

Chernofsky, Jacob L. (Ap. 11, 1928, Brooklyn, NY) Ed., Publshr., *AB Bookman's Wkly.*, 1972–; various ed. and publshg. positions, 1954–72. **Educ.:** NY Univ., 1949–53, BA (Jnlsm.), 1953–54 (Hist.). **Orgs.:** ALA: ACRL. Frdm. to Read Fndn. Bibl. Socty. of Amer. Ms. Socty. Amer. Prtg. Hist. Assn. **Activities:** 14; 37, 41, 45; 57 **Addr.:** Antiquarian Bookman, Box AB, Clifton, NJ 07015.

Cherry, Joan M. (Mr. 9, 1947, Saint John, NB) Ph.D. student, Info. Sci., Univ. of Pittsburgh, 1979–; Head of Pub. Srvs., St. Mary's Univ. Lib., Halifax, 1978–79; Head of Info. Srvs., Macdonald Sci. Lib., Dalhousie Univ., 1976–79, Ref. Libn., 1972–76. **Educ.:** St. Francis Xavier Univ., 1965–69, BSc (Chem.); Univ. of West. ON, 1971–72, MLS. **Orgs.:** Halifax LA: Prog. Conv. (1977–78). Atl. Prov. LA: Treas. (1978–79). Can. LA. ASIS. Other orgs. **Pubns.:** Oral presentations. **Activities:** 11; 26, 41; 56, 75, 93 **Addr.:** Interdisciplinary Department of Information Science, School of Library and Information Science, University of Pittsburgh, Pittsburgh, PA 15206.

Cheshier, Robert Grant (S. 28, 1930, Goldendale, WA) Dir., Cleveland Hlth. Sci. Lib., Case-West. Reserve Univ. and Cleveland Med. Lib. Assn., 1966–, Asst. Prof. of LS, 1966–, Dir., Med. Lib. Trng. Prog., Sch. of LS, 1974–, Asst. Prof., Dept. of Resrch. in Med. Educ., 1979–81. **Educ.:** Univ. of WA, 1956–60, BA (Gen. Std.), 1963, MA (Libnshp.); Univ. of Chicago, 1964–66, (LS); Case West. Reserve Univ., (LS). **Orgs.:** AALS: Resol. Com. (1978) Cleveland Area Metro. Lib. Syst.: Bd. of Trustees (Ch., 1979–). Lib. Cncl. of Grt. Cleveland: Secy. (1974); V-Ch. (1975); Ch. (1976). Med. LA: Exec. Com., Ch., 1975 Anl. Mtg. Other orgs. Amer. Assn. for Hist. of Med. Rowfant Club: Libn. Metro. Hlth. Plng. Corp. Univ. Circle: Bd. of Trustees. **Pubns.:** Ed., *Information in the Health Sciences: Working to the Future* (1972); Ed., *The Environment Affecting Health Science Libraries* (1977); "Providing Library Services in a Time of Fiscal Crisis," *Bltn. of Med. Lib. Assn.* (O. 1977); "The Medical Center and the Community: Communications and Fees," *Rocky Mt. Med. Jnl.* (Jl. 1978); "The Work and Impact of Jesse Hauk Shera," *Herald of Lib. Sci.* (Ap.-Jl. 1978); other articles. **Addr.:** Cleveland Health Sciences Library, 2119 Abington Rd., Cleveland, OH 44106.

Cheski, Richard M. (S. 29, 1935, Canton, OH) State Libn., State Lib. of OH, 1978–; Dir., Oceanside Free Lib., 1976–78; Asst. Comsn., Libs., CO State Lib., 1974–76; Asst. State Libn., State Lib. of OH, 1969–74. **Educ.:** Kent State Univ., 1957, BA (Sp., Math.), 1958, BS (Educ.), 1963, MA (LS). **Orgs.:** ALA: ASCLA/State Lib. Agency Sect. (Vice-Ch./Ch.-Elect, 1981–83). COSLA. OH LA. OH Educ. Lib. Media Assn. OH Pub. Prog. for Hum.: Ch. (1981–83). Amer. Socty. for Trng. and Dev. **Honors:** Kent State Univ., Outstan. Alum., 1978. **Activities:** 4, 13; 17, 24, 26; 50, 55, 93 **Addr.:** State Library of Ohio, 65 S. Front St., Columbus, OH 43215.

Cheslock, Rosalind Pleet (Ag. 6, 1946, Baltimore, MD) Mgr., Tech. Info. Srvs., Martin Marietta Labs., 1979–, Sci., Tech. Libn., 1976–79, Info. Spec., 1975–76, Asst. Libn., 1974–75; Asst. Dir., Bkmobiles., Enoch Pratt Free Lib., 1971–73, YA Spec., 1968–71. **Educ.:** Goucher Coll., 1963–67, BA, magna cum laude (Latin, Grk.); Univ. of MD, 1973–74, MLS; Johns Hopkins Univ., 1967–68, MA (Latin, Grk.); various crs., insts. **Orgs.:** Interlib. Users Assn.: Bd. of Dirs. (1981–84). Defense Remote Online Syst. Users Cncl. (1981–83). ASIS. SLA: Metals and Mtrls. Div., various coms. Assoc. Info. Mgrs. Aluminum Assn.: Subcom. on *World Aluminium Abstracts* (ch., 1981). Tech. Info. Com. (1979–). *Modern Plastics* Mgt. Adv. Panel (1981). Neighborhood Bus. Adv. Com. **Honors:** Phi Beta Kappa; Beta Phi Mu. **Pubns.:** Jt. ed., *Guide to Metallurgical Information.* **Activities:** 12; 15, 17; 64, 81, 91 **Addr.:** Martin Marietta Laboratories, 1450 S. Rolling Rd., Baltimore, MD 21227.

Chestnut, Paul I. (Je. 7, 1939, Charleston, SC) Asst. State Archvst. for Arch., VA State Lib., 1978–; Asst. Cur. of Mss. for Reader Srvs., Duke Univ., 1971–78. **Educ.:** Duke Univ., 1957–61, AB (Hist.), 1964–74, PhD (Hist.); Yale Univ., 1961–64, BD (Church Hist.); Natl. Arch. Inst. in Modern Arch. Admin., 1976, Cert. **Orgs.:** SAA: Ref., Access, and Outreach Com. (1976–); Steering Com. (1979–). Mid-Atl. Reg. Arch. Conf.: Prog. Com. (1980). S. Atl. Arch. and Recs. Conf. VA Hist. Socty. South. Hist. Assn. **Pubns.:** "The Moravians," *Encyc. of Southern History* (1979); Essays in *Dictionary of North Carolina Biography* (1979); Reviews. **Activities:** 2, 13; 17, 39, 46; 55, 69 **Addr.:** Archives Branch, Virginia State Library, Richmond, VA 23219.

Chiarmonte, Paula L. (O. 14, 1952, Buffalo, NY) Archit. Libn., SUNY, Buffalo, 1981–; Slide Cur., Art Histn., Univ. of NV, Las Vegas, 1980–81; Slide Cur., Cornell Univ., 1979–80. **Educ.:** SUNY Buffalo, 1970–74, BA (Art); 1978–79, MLS; Univ. of Siena, Italy, 1973–74 (Art Hist.). **Orgs.:** ARLIS/NA: various coms. Natl. Micro. Assn. Women's Caucus For Art. **Pubns.:** "Microform Collection Development Policy for Art Librarians and Visual Resources Curator," *Intl. Bltn. for Photographic Documtn. of Visual Art* (D. 1980). **Activities:** 1, 12; 24, 33; 55 **Addr.:** College of Architecture, Hayes Hall, SUNY, Buffalo, 3435 Main St., Buffalo, NY 14221.

Chiasson, Gilles (O. 4, 1937, Paquetville, NB, Can) Mgr., Sport Info. Resrce. Ctr., 1973–; Chief, Tec. Srvs., Dept. of I.T. and C. Lib., 1972–73; Chief Catlgr., Dept. of Finance Lib., 1971–72; Catlgr., Univ. of Ottawa, 1969–71. **Educ.:** Univ. of Moncton, 1958–62, BA (Gen.); Univ. of Ottawa, 1967–68, MTh (Theo.), 1968–69, BLS. **Orgs.:** Can. Assn. Info. Sci. CLA. ASIS. **Activities:** 12; 17, 30; 95-Recreation. **Addr.:** Sport Information Resource Centre, 333 River Rd., Ottawa, ON K1L 8B9 Canada.

Chiasson, Gilles (D. 21, 1942, Shippegan, NB, Can) Reg. Libn., Haut-Saint-Jean Reg. Lib., 1975–; Chief Libn., Bathurst Col., Can., 1966–75. **Educ.:** Le Collège de Bathurst, NB, 1957–65, BA; Univ. of Ottawa, 1965–66, BLS; Univ. of West. ON, 1971–72, MLS. **Orgs.:** Atlantic Provinces LA: VP NB Chap. (1978–79). Cncl. of Head Libns. of NB: Ch. (1970–73). Secy./Treas. (1977–80). Can. LA; Assn. pour l'avancement des Sci. et des tech. de la Docu. Lions Club. **Activities:** 1, 9; 15, 17, 35; 56, 75 **Addr.:** 50 Queen St., Edmundston, NB E3V 1A6 Canada.

Chicco, Meg (Je. 9, 1949, Queens, NY) Head Libn., Trubin Sillcocks Edelman & Knapp, 1975–; Head Libn., The Legal Aid Soc., 1972–75; Asst. Libn., Cravath, Swaine & Moore, 1970–71. **Educ.:** York College, New York Univ., 1974–. **Orgs.:** AALL: Pvt. Law Lib. Grp. SLA. Law Lib. Assn. of Greater NY: Dir., (1979–). **Activities:** 12; 15, 17, 41; 77 **Addr.:** Trubin Sillcocks Edelman & Knapp, 375 Park Ave., New York, NY 10022.

Chickanzeff, Sharon (O. 12, 1950, Los Angeles, CA) Head Libn., San Francisco Art Inst. Lib., 1978–, Cat. Libn., 1977–78; Asst. to Ed., ARLIS/NA Nsltr., 1976–77. **Educ.:** Univ. of CO, 1973, BA (Art Hist.); Univ. of South. CA, 1975–76, MLS. **Orgs.:** ARLIS/NA. Coll. Art Assn. **Activities:** 2, 10; 15, 17, 39; 55, 67 **Addr.:** San Francisco Art Institute, 800 Chestnut St., San Francisco, CA 94133.

Chicorel, Marietta (My. 22, –, Vienna, Austria) Pres., Amer. Lib. Pubshg. Co., Inc., 1979–; Pres., Chicorel Lib. Pubshg. Corp., 1969–79; Prof. of LS, Queens Coll., 1971–72; Proj. Mgr., Info. Sci., Inc., MacMillan Pubshg. Co., 1968–69; Chief Ed., R.R. Bowker Co., 1966–68. **Educ.:** Wayne State Univ., 1949–52, BA; Univ. of MI, 1957–60, MA (LS). **Orgs.:** ALA: Cncl. (1969–73); Ch., Lib. Mtrls. Price Index Com. (1965–68); Tech. Srvs. Div. (Exec. Bd. 1965–68). ASIS. NY Lib. Club. NY Tech. Srvs. Libns. Gvr. Cmsn. on the Status of Women: Educ. Com. (1963–65). Booksellers Leag. of NY: Bd. of Gvrs. (1968–). **Honors:** ALA, Outstan. Ref. Books Awds. **Pubns.:** *Chicorel Index Series* (1969–80); various articles. **Activities:** 1, 9; 15, 26, 37; 51, 55, 57 **Addr.:** American Library Publishing Co., Inc., 275 Central Park West, New York, NY 10024.

Childers, Thomas A. (Jl. 2, 1940, Chillicothe, OH) Prof., Sch. of Lib. and Info. Sci., Drexel Univ., 1970–; Visit. Fac., Sch. of LS, Syracuse Univ., 1970; Adj. Instr., Rutgers Univ., 1970; Sr. Prof. Asst., Baltimore Cnty. Pub. Lib., 1965–67; Libn., U.S. Army, Fort Lewis (WA), 1963–65. **Educ.:** Univ. of MD, 1958–62, BA magna cum laude (Eng.); Rutgers Univ., 1962–63, MLS, 1967–70, PhD. **Orgs.:** ALA: Adv. Com. to the Office for Rcrt. (1968–73); Cncl. (1972–74); RASD (Dir., 1978–81); Strg. Com., Resrch. RT (Dir., 1972–75); Com. on Prog. Eval. and Support (1973–77; Ch. 1976–77). Ctr. for Litcy., Philadelphia: Trustee (1976–79). AAUP. Amer. Civil Liberties Un. **Honors:** Fellow, British Lib. Resrch. and Dev. Dept., 1978. **Pubns.:** *The Information-Poor in America* (1975); Jt. auth., *Information Service in Public Libraries: Two Studies* (1971); "Trends in Public Library I&R Services," *Lib. Jnl.* (O. 1979); "The Future of Reference and Information Service in the Public Library" in *The Public Library: Circumstances and Prospects,* (1978); "Community Referral Centers: Impact Measures" in *Information for the Community* (1976); other articles. **Activities:** 11; 26, 41 **Addr.:** School of Library and Information Science, Drexel University, Philadelphia, PA 19104.

Childs, Margaretta P. (S. 29, 1912, Charleston, SC) Archvst., City of Charleston, 1977–; Rare Bks, Arch., Coll. of Charleston, 1972–76; Bibl., Rare Bks. Catlgr., PA State Univ., 1968–72; Rare Bks. Catlgr., The Johns Hopkins Univ., 1966–68. **Educ.:** Wellesley Coll., 1928–32, BA (Hist.); The Johns Hopkins Univ., 1938–40, PhD (Hist.); Emory Univ., 1967–68, MLn (LS). **Orgs.:** SAA. Assn. for the Std. of Negro Life and Hist. Avery Inst. of Afro-Amer. Hist. and Culture: Exec. Com. (1978, 1979, 1981). **Pubns.:** Reviews. **Activities:** 2, 4; 15, 19, 41; 66, 69 **Addr.:** Division of Archives & Records, City of Charleston, City Hall, Charleston, SC 29402.

Childs, Martha C. (S. 30, 1947, Knoxville, TN) Lib. Dir., Univ. of TN Ctr. for the Hlth. Sci., Knoxville, 1978–; Libn., Clatsop Cmnty. Coll., 1972–73. **Educ.:** Univ. of TN, 1965–69, BS (Bio.); Emory Univ., 1969–70, MSLS; Med. LA Cert. **Orgs.:** Knoxville Area Hlth. Sci. Lib. Cnsrtm.: Pres. (1978–79); Ch. Union List Com. (1978–80). Med. LA.; Southern Chap., By-Laws Com. (1980). E. TN LA. TN AB Area Coord., Lib. Legis. Network (1978–80). Other orgs. **Activities:** 12; 31, 34, 39; 58, 80 **Addr.:** Preston Medical Library, University of Tennessee Center for the Health Sciences/Knoxville, Knoxville, TN 37920.

Chin, Cecilia Hui-hsin (F. 25, 1938, Tientsin, China). Assoc. Libn., Head of the Ref. Dept., Ryerson & Burnham Libraries, Art Inst. of Chicago, 1975–; Actg. Dir. of Libraries, 1976–77; Head of Ref. Dept. & Indxr., 1970–75; Ref. Libn. & Indxr., 1963–70; Cat./Ref. Libn., Roosevelt Univ. Lib., 1963.

PROFESSIONAL ACTIVITIES: Institutions: 1. Acad. lib.; 2. Arch.; 3. Assn.; 4. Fed./Gvt. lib.; 5. Inst. lib.; 6. Mfr./Suppl.; 7. Milit. lib.; 8. Musm.; 9. Pub. lib.; 10. Sch. lib.; 11. Sch. of lib. sci.; 12. Spec. lib.; 13. State lib.; 14. (other). **Functions/Activities:** 15. Acq./Col. dev.; 16. Adult srvs.; 17. Admin.; 18. Apprais.; 19. Archit./Bldgs.; 20. Cat./Class.; 21. Chld. srvs.; 22. Circ.; 23. Cons./Pres.; 24. Consult.; 25. Cont. ed.; 26. Educ. lib. sci.; 27. Ext. srvs.; 28. Fund/Grants; 29. Gvt. pubs.; 30. Indx./Abs.; 31. Instr. lib. use; 32. Media srvs.; 33. Micro.; 34. Netwks./Coop.; 35. Persnl.; 36. PR; 37. Publshg.; 38. Recs. mgt.; 39. Ref. srvs.; 40. Repro.; 41. Resrch.; 42. Review.; 43. Secur.; 44. Serials; 45. Spec. col.; 46. Tech. srvs.; 47. Trustees/Bds.; 48. YA srvs.; 49. (other).

Educ.: Natl. Taiwan Univ., 1957–61, BA (Lit.); Univ. of IL, 1961–63. **Orgs.:** ALA. SLA. ARLIS/NA. Chicago Area Cons. Grp. Other orgs. Soc. of Architectural Histns. Coll. Art Assn. **Pubns.:** Comp. *The Art Institute of Chicago. Index to Art Periodicals, First Supplement* (1975). **Activities:** 1, 12; 23, 39, 45; 55, 57 **Addr.:** Ryerson & Burnham Libraries, Art Institute of Chicago, Michigan & Adams, Chicago, IL 60603.

Ching, Lillian Y. (Ap. 5, 1924, Honolulu, HI) Head Libn., Cooke Lib., Punahou Sch., 1969–, Libn., Bishop Lib., 1961–69; Pers., Ref. Libn., Lib. of HI, 1946–51, 1960–61. **Educ.:** Mills Coll., 1941–45, BA (Langs., Lit.); Columbia Univ., 1945–46, MLS. **Orgs.:** ALA. HI LA. HI Assn. of Sch. Libns. **Honors:** Phi Beta Kappa. **Activities:** 2, 10; 15, 17, 48 **Addr.:** Cooke Library, Punahou School, 1601 Punahou St., Honolulu, HI 96822.

Chinik, Mildred Katella (My. 20, 1910, Pittsburgh, PA) Retired, 1975–; Branch Libn. Carnegie Lib., 1963–75, previously chld. libn., various branches. **Educ.:** Univ. of Pittsburgh, 1929–32, AB; Carnegie Mellon Univ., 1935–37, BS (LS). **Orgs.:** ALA. PA LA. **Activities:** 9; 21, 48 **Addr.:** 4649 Cook Ave., Pittsburgh, PA 15236.

Chipman, Mary L. (Ap. 2, 1942, Calgary, Alta) Trustee, Vice-Ch. of Bd., Toronto Pub. Lib., 1978–, Ch., Bldg. Com., Wychwood Branch, 1977–78. **Educ.:** Univ. of Toronto, 1960–64, BSc (Math., Phys.), 1964–65, MA (Math., Stats.). **Orgs.:** Can. LA. ON LA. **Activities:** 9; 17, 19, 47; 72, 74, 89 **Addr.:** Toronto Public Library, 40 Orchard View Blvd., Toronto, ON M4R 1B9 Canada.

Chisholm, Margaret E. (Jl. 25, 1921, Grey Eagle, MN) Actg. Dir., Sch. of LS, Univ. of WA, 1981–, VP, Univ. Rel. and Dev., 1975–81; Prof., Dean (LS), Univ. of MD, 1969–75. **Educ.:** Univ. of WA, 1957, BA (Educ.), 1958, ML, 1966, PhD (Higher Educ. Admin.). **Orgs.:** ALA: Cncl. (1980–), Resols. Com. (1977–). AECT: Prof. Ethics Com. (1977–). **Honors:** Univ. of WA, Sch. of LS, Ruth Worden Awd., 1957, Disting. Alum., 1979; St. Cloud State Univ., Disting. Alum., 1977; Beta Phi Mu. **Pubns.:** *Instructional Design and the Library Media Specialist* (1979); jt. Auth., *Media Personnel in Education; A Competency Approach* (1979); *Reader in Media, Technology and Libraries* (1976). **Activities:** 11; 17, 26, 32 **Addr.:** 4915 N.E. 85th St., Seattle, WA 98115.

Chisum, Emmett D. (Mr. 19, 1922, Monroe, LA) Prof., Resrch. Hist., Arch., Univ. of WY, 1977–; Soc. Sci. Libn., 1954–77; Tchr., Eng., Welsh HS, 1946–47; Tchr., Sci., Cameron Parish Sch. Syst., LA, 1947–51. **Educ.:** Northwest. State Univ., 1938–42, BA (Soc. Sci.); LA State Univ., 1945–46, MA (Soc. Sci.); Univ. of WY, 1951–52, MA, (Hist.), 1960–61, MA, (Pol. Sci.-Anthr.). **Orgs.:** ALA. WY LA. Univ. of WY, Senate, Lib. Rep. (1973–76). Amer. Archaeological Socty. West. Pol. Sci. Assn. AAUP. **Honors:** Phi Delta Kappa. **Pubns.:** *Guide to Library Research* (1969); *Guide to Research in Political Science* (1970); *Guide to Research in Education* (1974); "Boom Towns on The Union Pacific" *Annals of Wy. Vol. 53 No. I* (Spring 1981); "Crossing Wyoming By Car In 1908", "The New York To Paris Automobile Race" *Annals of Wy. Vol. 52 No. I* (Spring 1980). **Activities:** 1, 2; 15, 39, 41; 54, 63, 92 **Addr.:** 2032 Holliday Dr., Laramie, WY 82070.

Chitwood, Julius R. (Jack) (Je. 1, 1921, Magazine, AR) Consul., Lib. & Info. Srvs., 1979–; Exec. Dir., Rockford (IL) Pub. Lib., 1961–79; Exec. Dir., North. IL Lib. Syst., 1966–76; Coord., Adult Srvs., Indianapolis Pub. Lib., 1957–61. **Educ.:** Ouachita Baptist Coll., 1938–42, BA cum laude (Msc.); IN Univ., 1947–48, M (Mus.); Univ. of Chicago, 1948–54, MA (LS). **Orgs.:** ALA: Cncl. (1969–70); LAMA: Pres. (1969–70); Persnl. Admin. Sect.; Staff Dev. Com., Ch. (1967–71); Adult Srvs. Div.: Bd. (1963–67). IL LA: Pres. (1965–66). IL State Lib. Adv. Com.: Sub-committee for System Development, Ch. (1975–79). Rotary Club: Bd. (1965–67). Rockford Reg. Acad. Ctr., Bd. (1972–); Pres. (1974–76). Rockford Area Cham. of Cmrce.: Bd. (1966–68). Univ. Club. **Honors:** IL LA, Libn. of the Year, 1974. **Activities:** 9; 16, 17, 24; 50, 55, 56 **Addr.:** 4036 East State St., Rockford, IL 61108.

Chiu, Kai-Yun (Kweilin, Kwangsi, China) Dir., Lib. Co. of the Baltimore Bar, 1976–; Head, Docu. Ctr., Eisenhower Lib., Johns Hopkins Univ., 1968–76; Docu. Libn., Enoch Pratt Free Lib., 1965–68, Ref. Libn., 1962–65. **Educ.:** Coll. of the Holy Names, Oakland, CA, 1959–61, BA (pol. Sci.); Univ. of CA, Berkeley, 1961–62, MLS; Johns Hopkins Univ., 1974–78, MAS (Adm. Sci.). **Orgs.:** ALA. AALL. SLA: Baltimore Chap., Nwsltr. Ed.; Pres., Employ. Com. MD LA: Acad. and Resrch. Lib. Div.; Employ. Com.; Prog. Com.; Nom. Com. **Pubns.:** "Membership/Subscription Law Libraries–A Round Table in the Making," *AALL, St., Ct., and Cnty. Law Lib. Section Newsletter,* (Vol. 8, No. 2), (M. 1981). **Activities:** 12; 17; 77, 92 **Addr.:** 10615 Lancewood Rd., Cockeysville, MD 21030.

Chmura, Catherine Welsh (Ag. 12, 1949, Utica, NY) Asst. Libn., Serials, Siena Coll., 1974–. **Educ.:** SUNY Oswego, 1967–71, BA (Eng.); SUNY Albany, 1973–74, MLS, 1976–81, MA (Econ.). **Orgs.:** ALA: ACRL/East. NY Chap. (Pres., 1979–80, VP, 1978–79). Capital Dist. Lib. Cncl.: Bd. of Trustees (Secy. 1980–). AAUP Siena Coll., Fac. Com. **Activities:** 1; 44; 51, 59, 92 **Addr.:** 866 Lishakill Rd., Schenectady, NY 12309.

Cho, Keiko (Ap. 12, 1943, Winnipeg, MB) Asst. Head, Cat. and Prcs., Head, Autom. Cat., Univ. of Houston 1980–; Head, LC Mono. Cat. Sect., Rice Univ., 1968–80; Catlgr., Univ. of WI, Milwaukee, 1967–68; Head, Educ. Lib., Univ. of MB, 1966–67. **Educ.:** Univ. of MB, 1960–64, BA (Fr., Latin); Univ. of Toronto, 1964–65, BLS; Royal Cnsvty. of Toronto, 1952–66 ARCT (Piano). **Orgs.:** TX LA. Msc. LA. Msc. OCLC Users Grp. ALA. **Activities:** 1; 20, 46; 56 **Addr.:** 3818 Linklea Dr., Houston, TX 77025.

Cho, Sung Yoon (S. 10, 1928, Shinuiju, Pyongbuk, Korea) Asst. to the Chief, Far East. Law Div., Lib. of Congs., 1976–; Sr. Legal Spec., Lib. of Congs., 1968–76, Legal Spec., 1963–68, Resrch. Asst., 1959–63; Korean Attorney, United Nations Civil Asst. Command, 1953–55. **Educ.:** Seoul Natl. Univ., 1946–53, LLB; Tulane Univ., 1955–57, MA, 1958–63, PhD (Intl. Law); George Washington Univ., 1964–66, MCL, (Comp. Law). **Orgs.:** AALL: Foreign Law Indx. Com. (1974–80). WA DC Law Libn. Socty. Intl. Assn. of Law Libs. Amer. Socty. of Intl. Law. Assoc. for Asian Std. Japanese Amer. Socty. for Legal Std. **Pubns.:** *Japanese Writings on Communist Chinese Law 1946–1974* (1977); "The Judicial System of North Korea," *Asian Srvy.* (1971); "Law and Justice in North Korea," *Jnl. of Korean Affairs* (1973). **Activities:** 4; 30, 39, 41; 77, 78 **Addr.:** Far Eastern Law Division, Library of Congress, 10 First St. SE, Washington, DC 20540.

Chobot, Mary Casella (Mr. 24, 1945, Oneida, NY) Instr. (LS), Cath. Univ. of Amer., 1976–, Resrch. Assoc, Proj. Mgr., Home Study Proj., 1975–76; Lectr., Coord., Field Stds. (LS), Syracuse Univ., 1974–75; Dist. Lib. Media Srvs. Dept. Head, Baldwinsville Sch. Dist., 1973–75; Elem. Libn., McNamara Sch., 1970–73; Libn., Indxr., Amer. Mgt. Assn., 1969–70; Base Libn., U.S. Air Force, Syracuse NY, 1968–69. **Educ.:** Le Moyne Coll., 1963–67, BA (Eng.); Syracuse Univ., 1967–68, MSLS; 1972–74 (Educ. Admin.); Cath. Univ., 1982– (Educ. Psy., Eval.) **Orgs.:** ALA: Poster Session Strg. Com. (1981); AASL; LITA; Resrch. RT. AALS. CLENE. **Honors:** Beta Phi Mu. NY State Regents Schol. Oneida Zonta Club Schol. **Pubns.:** Jt. Auth., *Motivation: A Vital Force in the Organization; A Home Study Course* (1978). **Activities:** 11; 25, 26, 41 **Addr.:** 4950 Andrea Ave., Annandale, VA 22003.

Choi, Susan E. (N. 23, 1948, Duluth, MN) Supvsr., Lib. Srvs., Santa Clara Cnty. Superintendent of Sch., 1971–. **Educ.:** Sacramento State Univ., 1966–70, BA (Pol. Sci.); San Jose State Univ., 1972–73, MA (LS). **Orgs.:** CA Media & Lib. Educ. Assn.: Mem. Ch. (1978–79). Bay Area Educ. Libns.: Secy./Treas. (1973–75, 1979–80). Peninsula Media Admin. Women Leaders in Educ.: Pres. (1981–82), Comm. Ch. (1978–80). **Pubns.:** *A Comparison of the Recommendations of the RISE, NASSP, and Kettering Reports on Secondary Education* ERIC (1976); *The Cooperative Information Network* ERIC (1973); "Data Acquisition Advisory Committee," *CMLEA Jnl.* (Fall 1978); Jt. auth., *Selected References in Educational Planning: Bibliography and Selection Criteria* ERIC (1975); Jt. auth., *Selected References in Educational Planning: Part 2 - A Supplement* ERIC (1975). **Activities:** 10; 15, 17, 20; 63 **Addr.:** Instructional Resources and Information Center, 100 Skyport Dr., San Jose, CA 95110.

Choldin, Marianna Tax (F. 26, 1942, Chicago, IL) Slavic Ref. Libn., Assoc. Prof., Univ. of IL, 1969–; Slavic Biblgphr., MI State Univ., 1967–69. **Educ.:** Univ. of Chicago, 1959–62, BA (Russ.), 1963–67, MA (Slavic), 1976–79, PhD (Libnshp.). **Orgs.:** ALA: ACRL/Slavic and E. European Sect.: Mem. at large (1977–78); RASD: Coop. Ref. Srvs. Com. (1979–); Ref. and Subscrpn. Bks. Review Com. (1980–). Amer. Assn. for the Advnc. of Slavic Studies: Bibl. and Documtn. Com. (1974–), Ch. (1978–). **Honors:** Phi Beta Kappa, 1962. **Pubns.:** "A Nineteenth Century Russian View of Bibliography," *Jnl. of Lib. Hist.,* 10 (1975); "The Russian Bibliographical Society; 1889–1930," *Lib. Qtly.* 46 (1976); "Some Developments in Nineteenth Century Bibliography: Russia," *Libri,* 27 (1977); "'The Russian Connection': The Bureau of International Bibliography and the *International Catalogue of Scientific Literature,"* *Jnl. of Lib. Hist.,* 13 (1978); Jt. auth. "Slavica," *Non Solus,* no. 6 (1979); other articles, reviews, transl., and oral presentations. **Activities:** 1; 15, 26, 39; 54, 57, 95-Slavic & East European. **Addr.:** Slavic and East European Department, 225 Library, 1408 W. Gregory Dr., University of Illinois, Urbana, IL 61801.

Choncoff, Mary (Jl. 28, 1923, Gary, IN) Coord. ESEA IV-B AZ Dept. of Educ., 1975–, State Sch. Lib. Consult., Dir., ESEA Title II, 1970–75; Instr., Chld. Lit., Purdue Univ., Sum. 1970; Libn., Tchr., Gary (IN) Pub. Schs., 1956–69; Asst. to Dean of Women, OH State Univ., 1954–56; Instr., AZ State Coll., Tempe, 1952–54. **Educ.:** West. KY State Coll., 1942–46, AB (Hist., Eng.); AZ State Coll., 1948–50, MA (Guid.); Lib. courses at Univs. of West. MI, Purdue, IN. **Orgs.:** ALA. Maricopa Sch. Lib. Assn. Natl. Assn. of State Media Profs. AZ LA: Sch. Libs. Div. (Exec. Bd., 1970–); Exec. Bd. (1970–); Pres. (1975–76); other orgs. Bus. and Prof. Women's Club. **Honors:** AZ LA, Libn. of the Yr., 1975. **Pubns.:** "Federal Funding," *AV Jnl. of AZ* (Spr., 1972); "ESEA IV-B Moves Into Third Year," *AZ Media Jnl.* (Fall, 1977). **Activities:** 10, 13; 21, 24 **Addr.:** 5101 S. Birch, Tempe, AZ 85282.

Chou, Michaelyn Pi-hsia (O. 12, 1928, Porterville, CA) Resrc. Libn. & Head of Pub. Srvs. for Spec. Col., Univ. of HI at Manoa, 1976–; Catlgr., 1971–76; Head of Proc. Branch, 1967–71; Asst. Order Libn. & Acting Chief of Serials, 1964–65; Head of Circ., 1960–61; Head of Fine Arts & Hum., Univ. of CA, Sacramento, 1959; Ref. Libn., 1955–59. **Educ.:** Univ. of CA, Berkeley, 1949–54, BA (Gen. Curric.); 1954–55, MLS; Univ. of HI, 1972–75, MA (Amer. Std.); PhD cand. 1975–. **Orgs.:** ALA. HI LA: various coms. SLA. Beta Phi Mu: XI Chap., Pres. (1974–75); VP (1973–74). Oral Hist. Assn. Amer. Std. Assn. AAUP: HI Chap., Secy. and Dir. (1973–74). HI Hist. Soc. Other orgs. **Pubns.:** *Memories of Hiram L. Fong, U.S. Senator from Hawaii, 1959–1977* (1979); *Memories of Elizabeth Farrington, Delegate to the U.S. Congress from Hawaii* (1978); *Memories of Thomas P. Gill, Member of the U.S. House of Representatives from Hawaii* (1978); "Library Friends at Manoa," *HI Lib. Assn. Jnl.* (1976); "Musical Chairs," *HI Lib. Assn. Jnl.* (May 1961). **Activities:** 1; 15, 39, 45; 66, 85 **Addr.:** Hamilton Library 519, The University of Hawaii at Manoa, Honolulu, HI 96822.

Chou, Nelson Ling-sun (Jl. 2, 1935, Nanking, China) Libn., East Asian Lib., Rutgers Univ., 1970–; Assoc., Grad. Sch. of Lib. and Info. Std., 1973–; Asst. Libn., Far East. Lib., Univ. of Chicago, 1968–70, Head Chinese Catlgr., 1965–68, Chinese Catlgr., 1963–65, Asst. Chinese Catlgr., 1962–63. **Educ.:** Natl. Taiwan Univ., 1953–57, BA (Eng.); Rosary Coll., 1961–63, MLS; Univ. of Chicago, 1964–70, DLS. **Orgs.:** ALA. ASIS. LA of China. Chinese Amer. Libns. Assn.: Org. Com.; Exec. Cncl. (1975/76); Org. Com. for N./E. Chap. (1979). Assn. for Asian Std.: Com. on E. Asian Libs. (1970–); Coord., Subcom. for Tech. Srv. (1972–73); Co-ed., CEAL Nsltr., (1973–74); Subcom. on Autom. (1978–). Chinese Lang. Comp. Socty. **Pubns.:** Trans., *Chung-kuo ku tai shu shih* (1975); "A New Alphameric Code for Chinese Ideographs", *Proc. of the First Intl. Symp. on Comp. and Chinese Input/Output Systems,* (1974); "On Designing and Evaluating a Chinese Input/Output System," *Jnl. of Lib. and Info. Sci.,* (1975); Other articles. **Activities:** 1; 15, 17, 26; 54, 75, 95-E. Asian Std. **Addr.:** East Asian Library, Alexander Library, Rutgers University, New Brunswick, NJ 08903.

Chou, Pei Hua (Ja. 14, 1936, China) Coll. Libn., Cuyamaca Coll., 1978–; Head, Govt. Pub. Dept., Univ. of CA, Irvine, 1967–78; Asst. Supvsr. of Cat. Dept., Xerox-Prof. Lib. Servs., 1965–67; Gvt. Pubs. Libn.; Ref. Libn., Univ. of KS, 1961–65. **Educ.:** Tunghai Univ., Taiwan, 1955–59, BA (Hist.); Colorado Coll., 1959–60, Cert. (Hist.); Univ. of Denver, 1960–61, MA, (LS); Univ. of South. CA., 1980–, PhD Prog. (Higher Educ.). **Orgs.:** ALA. CA LA. Assn. of CA Comnty Coll. Admin. **Activities:** 1; 15, 17, 29 **Addr.:** Cuyamaca College, 2950 Jamacha Rd., El Cajon, CA 92020.

Chouinard, Germain (Ag. 30, 1943, Woburn, PQ) Dir., Hlth. Sci. Lib., 1974–; Resrch. Asst. in Gastroenterology, Univ. de Sherbrooke, 1971–72. **Educ.:** Univ. de Sherbrooke, 1966, BA; 1967–71, BSCS (Microb.); Univ. of West. ON, 1973–73, MLS. **Orgs.:** ASTED: Hlth Sect. (1978). Assoc. Des Bibliothèques De La Sante Du Can.; Bd. of Dir. (1979); Rcrt. Com. (1979). Assn. Des Facultes De Med. Du Can.: Spec. Resrc. Com. on Med. Sch. Libs. (1974). Med. LA. Other orgs. **Activities:** 1, 12; 25, 32, 35; 68, 80, 95-Nursing. **Addr.:** Chus - Bibliothèque Des Sciences De La Santé, Université De Sherbrooke, Sherbrooke, PQ J1H 5N4 Canada.

Chouinard, Joseph Jerod (My. 7, 1926, Middletown, CT) Msc. Libn., State Univ. Coll. at Fredonia, 1977–; Asst. Libn. in Msc., SUNY, Buffalo, 1973–77; Msc. & Art Libn., CA State Coll. at San Bernardino, 1970–73. **Educ.:** Univ. of CT., 1946–50, BA (Msc.); 1950–51, MA (Msc.); State Univ. Coll. at Geneseo, 1969–70, MLS. **Orgs.:** SUNY: Libns. Assn. Msc. LA: West. NY/ON Chap. Untd. Univ. Prof. Amer. Musicological Socty. Natl. Assn. of Tchrs. of Singing. Natl. Retired Tchrs. Assn. **Activities:** 1; 15, 39, 42; 55 **Addr.:** 71 Central Ave., Fredonia, NY 14063.

Chowdhury, Manny D. (Ag. 1, 1926, Calcutta, India) Libn., Harlem Hosp. Med. Ctr., Columbia Univ., 1968–; Asst. Libn., NY State Depts. of Educ. and Mental Hygiene, 1964–68; Intern, Fordham Univ. Lib., 1963–64; Trainee, Brooklyn Pub. Lib., 1960–63. **Educ.:** Calcutta Univ., 1944–48, BCom (Bus. Adm.); Pratt Inst., 1960–63, MLS; Grad. work, Columbia Univ., 1967–68, Rutgers Univ., 1979– (LS). **Orgs.:** ALA. SLA. Med. LA. ASIS. NY Lib. Club. AAUP. AAAS. **Activities:** 1, 12; 17; 56, 63 **Addr.:** Harlem Hospital Medical Center, 506 Lenox Ave., KP 6108, New York, NY 10037.

Chretien, Muriette N. (D. 23, 1938, Amqui, PQ) Ref. Libn., Univ. of Ottawa Law Lib., 1981–, Actg. Dir., 1979-81; Ref. Libn., Civil Law Sect., 1975–79; Dir., Law Lib., 1968–73. **Educ.:** Univ. of Ottawa, 1959–61, BA (Pol.Sci.); 1963–67, LLL (Civil Law); 1968–73, BLS. **Orgs.:** Assn. des Professeurs de Droit due Québec: Comité des bibliothécaires de Droit. Assn. des bibliothèques de Droit du Can. **Pubns.:** *Répertoire des thèses de doctorat et de maîtrise soutenues dans les facultés de Droit des Universités de Québec et de l'Université d'Ottawa, Section Droit civil* (1978). **Activities:** 1; 17, 31, 39; 77 **Addr.:** University of Ottawa Law Library, Fauteux Hall, 57 Copernicus Street, Ottawa, ON K1N 6N5 Canada.

Special Subjects/Services: 50. Adult educ.; 51. Advert./Mktg.; 52. Aerosp.; 53. Agric.; 54. Area std.; 55. Arts/Hum.; 56. Autom.; 57. Bibl./Prtg.; 58. Bio. sci.; 59. Bus./Fin.; 60. Chem.; 61. Copyrt.; 62. Documtn.; 63. Educ.; 64. Engin.; 65. Env.; 66. Eth. grps.; 67. Film; 68. Food/Nutr.; 69. Geneal.; 70. Geo.; 71. Geol.; 72. Handcpd.; 73. Hist.; 74. Int. frdm.; 75. Info. sci.; 76. Insr.; 77. Law; 78. Legis.; 79. Math./Comp. sci.; 80. Med.; 81. Metals; 82. Nat. resrcs.; 83. Newsp.; 84. Nuc. sci.; 85. Oral hist.; 86. Petr./Energy; 87. Pharm.; 88. Phys./Astr./Math.; 89. Readg.; 90. Relig.; 91. Sci./Tech.; 92. Soc. sci.; 93. Telecom.; 94. Transp.; 95. (other).

Chrisant, Rosemarie Kathryn (O. 9, 1946, Chicago, IL) Lib. Dir., Akron Law Lib. Assn., 1976–; Asst. Libn., Akron Law Lib., 1973–76, Catlgr., 1971–73; HS Tchr. (Eng.), Chicago Pub. Schs., 1967–70. **Educ.:** North. IL Univ., 1964–67, BS (Educ.); Rosary Coll., 1970–71, MSLS; various insts. in law libnshp.; AALL Cert. 1978. **Orgs.:** Assoc. Info. Mgrs. OH Reg. Assn. of Libs.: Actv. Com. (1980–81). AALL. **Activities:** 4, 12; 17, 35, 47; 77, 78 **Addr.:** Akron Law Library Assn., Summit County Courthouse, 209 S. High St., Akron, OH 44308.

Chrisman, Larry George (N. 27, 1940, Glendale, CA) Asst. Prof., Univ. of S. FL, 1978–; Asst. Prof., Univ. of MS, 1972–78; Catlgr. I and II, Univ. of South. CA Lib., 1966–69. **Educ.:** WA State Univ., 1960–62, BA (Pol. Sci.); Univ. of South. CA, 1964–66, MSLS; IN Univ., 1969–75, PhD (LS). **Orgs.:** ALA: RTSD. **Honors:** Beta Phi Mu. **Pubns.:** "Job Satisfaction and the Academic Library Cataloger," *The Southeastern Libn.* (Sum. 1976); Reviews. **Activities:** 1, 11; 20, 44, 46; 92 **Addr.:** Library, Media, and Information Studies Department, University of South Florida, Tampa, FL 33620.

Christensen, Beth E. (My. 10, 1954, Mendota, IL) Msc. and Ref. Libn., Saint Olaf Coll., 1977–. **Educ.:** IL State Univ., 1972–76, BM (Msc.); Univ. of IL, 1976–77, MS (LS); Univ. of MN, 1979–, (Msc.). **Orgs.:** ALA. Msc. LA: Midwest. Chap./Bibl. Instr. Com. (1978–). Msc. OCLC User's Grp. Intl. Assn. of Msc. Libs. MN LA. **Pubns.:** Reviews. **Activities:** 1; 15, 20, 39; 55 **Addr.:** Music Library, Saint Olaf College, Northfield, MN 55057.

Christensen, Fern (Breakenridge) (Mr. 26, 1923, Winterset, IA) Assoc. Prof., Dept. of Sec. Educ., Northwestern State Univ., 1966–; Lib. Media Ctr. Dir., DuQuoin HS, 1963–66. **Educ.:** Drake Univ., 1959, BSEd (Hist. Eng.); South. IL Univ., Carbondale, 1965, MSEd (Instr. Mat.); Univ. of CO, 1969, Cert. (Media Spec.). **Orgs.:** SW LA: Pub. Com. (1977–78). Alpha Beta Alpha: Nat. Adv. Bd. (1979–80). Delta Kappa Gamma: Finance Com. (1979–80). Phi Delta Kappa: Ed., Kappanette (1977–79), VP (1979–80), Chap. Pres. (1980-81); Assn. for Genealogical Educ. **Pubns.:** "Relative Seeking," *The Natchitoches Genealogist* (1977–); "Relative Seeking," *Natchitoches Times* (1975–77); Jt. auth., *Natchitoches Cemeteries* (1977). **Activities:** 11, 14-Church Library Media Center; 17, 26; 63, 69, 90 **Addr.:** 1017 Oma St., Natchitoches, LA 71457.

Christenson, John D. (S. 2, 1936, Amherst, WI) Exec. Dir., Traverse des Sioux Lib. Syst., 1975–; Dir., Brevard Cnty. Lib. Syst., FL, 1971–75; Cmnty. Rel. Libn., Ferguson Lib., Stamford, CT, 1969–71; Adult Srvs. Coord., Lake Cnty. Pub. Lib., IN, 1967–69. **Educ.:** WI State Univ., Oshkosh, 1954–62, BS (Eng.); Univ. of WI, Madison, 1962–63, MSLS. **Orgs.:** ALA: Notable Books Cncl., Pub. Lib. Assn. MN LA: Pub. Lib. Div., Ch., (1976–78). Southcen. MN Inter-lib. Exch.: Pres. (1978). City of Good Thunder: Mayor (1977–). Good Thunder Chamber of Commerce: Brd. Mem. (1979–). **Activities:** 9; 17, 34, 36; 50, 67, 78 **Addr.:** Traverse des Sioux Library System, 100 East Main St., Mankato, MN 56001.

Christian, Dorothy A. (Ja. 9, 1944, NJ) Assoc. Dir., Regulatory Affairs, Amer. Cyanamid Co., 1980–, Mgr., Plng. and Admin., Regulatory Affairs, 1976–80; Resrch. Lit. Syst. Coord., Schering-Plough Corp., 1972–76; Info. Sci., Hoffmann-LaRoche, Inc., 1967–70. **Educ.:** William Paterson Coll., 1962–66, BA (Bio.); Rutgers Univ., 1966–77, MS (Genetics); Pratt Inst., 1976, MLS; NY Univ., 1974, Cert. (Data Prcs. and Systs. Anal.). **Orgs.:** ASIS. Drug Info. Assn. Assn. of Systs. Mgt. Pharmaceutical Spec. Interest Grp. **Honors:** Beta Phi Mu. **Activities:** 12; 17, 30, 38; 56, 58, 87 **Addr.:** American Cyanamid, Middletown Rd., Pearl River, NY 10965.

Christian, Roger W. (Mr. 27, 1928, Neenah, WI) Pres., Creative Consult. Srv., 1969–; Managing Ed., McGraw-Hill Publshg. Co., 1960–69; Dir., Adv. & PR, Babcock & Wilcox Co., 1957–59; Field Tech. Rep., IBM, 1956–57. **Educ.:** Lawrence Univ., 1950–54, BA with high honors (Lib. Arts); Univ. of CA, Berkeley, 1954–55. (Eng. Lit.); NY Univ., 1960–63. (Finance). **Orgs.:** Socty. for Scholarly Publshg.: Anl. Conf. Prog. Com. Authors Gld. **Honors:** Indus. Mktg. mag., Cert. of Merit for Outstan. Orig. Resrch., 1961, 1963; Commu. Arts mag., Awd. of Excel., 1971. **Pubns.:** *The Electronic Library: Bibliographic Data Bases 1978–79* (1978); Jt. auth., *Librarians & Online Services* (1977); *The Electronic Library: Bibliographic Data Bases 1975–76* (1975). **Activities:** 6; 24, 37; 56, 75 **Addr.:** Creative Consulting Service, Goldens Bridge Rd., Katonah, NY 10536.

Christianson, Elin J. Ballantyne (N. 11, 1936, Gary, IN) Lib. Consult., 1968–; Libn., J. Walter Thompson Co., 1959–68; Ed. Asst., *Journal of Business* (Grad. Sch. of Bus., Univ. of Chicago), 1956–59. **Educ.:** Univ. of Chicago, 1954–58, BA (Lib. arts); Univ. of Chicago, 1958–61, MALS, 1968–74, (Cert. of Adv. Study). **Orgs.:** ALA: Ref. Srvcs. Div. (Ch., Spec. Com. to Study Index. of Variant Ed. of Per., 1966–68). Consult., (Spec. ALA Cncl. Com., Freedom of Access to Libs., 1968). SLA: IL Chap. (Asst. Ed., *Informant* 1960–61. Ed. 1961–63, Mem. Ch. 1963–64. Treas., 1965–66. Ad. and Mktg. Ch., 1967–68. Chap. Manual Comm., 1966–67. Ch., Comm. on New Special Lib., 1979–80. various other offices. Hobart Hist. Socty.: Exec. Brd., Curator, Pleak Lib. (1971–). Hobart Amer. Rev. Bicen. Comsn.: Ch. (1974–76). **Honors:** IN Awd. of Achvmt., 1975; Laura Bracken Awd., of Hobart, IN, 1976. **Pubns.:** *New Special Libraries,* (1980); *Non-Professional and Paraprofessional Staff in Special Libraries,* (1973); Jt. Auth., *Subject Headings in Advertising, Marketing and Communications Media,* (1964); *Directory of Library Resources in Northwest Indiana,* (1976); *Special Libraries: A Guide for Management* (1981); *Daniel NASH Handy and the Special Library Movement* (1980); various articles. **Activities:** 12; 24, 39, 41; 51, 59 **Addr.:** 141 Beverly Blvd., Hobart, IN 46342.

Christolon, Blair Birkholz (O. 1, 1947, Oak Park, IL) Lib. Consult., Dept. of Educ., 1979–; Dir. of Lib., Overseas Private Investment Corp., 1978; Asst. Dir. of Chld. Srvs., Weber Cnty. Pub. Lib., 1976–77; Asst. Branch Libn., 1975–76; Asst. Circ. Lib., Johns Hopkins USIS Lib., Bologna, Italy, 1972–73. **Educ.:** Univ. of Denver, 1965–69, BA (Educ.); Brigham Young Univ., 1974–76, MLS; Univ. of Bologna, Italy, 1972–73 (Lit.). **Orgs.:** ALA. H.E.W.: Grant Application Reviewer (1979–). Washington Area, Cncl. of Gvts.: Loan Task Force (1978). UT LA: Pub. Lib. Div., VP/Pres.-Elect (1977). Parent-Infant Educ. **Pubns.:** "The Social Support Factors that Encourage a Preschooler to Participate in a Summer Read-to-Me Program," *Encyclia* (Spr. 1977); Reviews. **Activities:** 4, 9; 21, 24, 42; 54, 63, 72 **Addr.:** 8396 Briarmont Ln., Manassas, VA 22110.

Christopher, Irene (N. 17, 1922, Greece) Chief Libn., Boston Univ. Med. Ctr., 1970–; Libn., Harvard Univ. Gordon McKay Lib., 1968–70; Libn., G. K. Hall, 1968; Dir., Emerson Coll. Lib., 1962–68; Chief Ref. Libn., Boston Univ., Chenery Lib., 1948–62, Head, Circ. Dept., 1946–48; Gen. Asst., Arlington (MA) Pub. Lib., 1945–46. **Educ.:** Boston Univ., 1940–44, AB (Eng); Simmons Coll., 1944–45, BS in LS. **Orgs.:** ALA: Cncl. (1970–74); RASD, Cat. Use Com. (Ch., 1968–69); RASD/Com. on Rel. with State and Reg. Lib. Assns. (Ch., 1974–79); Com. on Dartmouth Medal Awd. (1980–81). SLA: Boston Chap., Dir. (1968–70). New Eng. Tech. Srvs. Libns.: Ch., Nom. Com. (1966/67). Boston Univ. Lib. Club: Pres. (1955–56). AAUP: Emerson Coll. Chap., Secy.-Treas. (1965–66); Secy. (1966/67; 1967/68). **Pubns.:** "Developing Reference Services in a College Library," *Choice* (Je., 1965); "Translating Services," *Boston Univ. Grad. Jnl.* (My., 1955). **Activities:** 1, 12; 15, 17, 39; 58, 60, 80 **Addr.:** 790 Boylston St., Boston, MA 02199.

Christopher, James R. (Ag. 10, 1943, Oak Park, IL) Head Libn., Simpson Coll., 1971–; Actg. Serials Libn., Univ. of WI, Whitewater, 1970–71, Asst. Circ. Libn., 1969–70; Pub. Srvs. Libn., Simpson Coll., 1967–69. **Educ.:** Ripon Coll., 1962–65, BA (Hist., Art Hist.); Univ. of IL, 1965–67, MSLS. **Orgs.:** IA LA: Exec. Com. (1976–78). IA Pvt. Acad. Lib. Cnsrtm.: Pres. (1979–80); Strg. Com. (1977–78). Southeast IA Lib. Cnsrtm.: Pres. (1978–79). IA OCLC Cncl.: Secy. (1977–); Strg. Com. (1979–). **Activities:** 1; 17 **Addr.:** Dunn Library, Simpson College, Indianola, IA 50125.

Christopher, Paul (Ja. 20, 1931, New York, NY) Ref. Libn., Archvst., Univ. of South. CA, 1975–; Ref. Libn., Los Angeles and Long Beach Pub. Libs., 1974–76; Asst. Prof., Dept. of Hist., CA St. Univ., Long Beach, 1964–68. **Educ.:** Pratt Inst., 1949–52, Cert. (Archit.); Pomona Coll., 1955–58, BA (Hist.); Univ. of MI, 1958–59, AM (Hist.); Univ. of CA, Berkeley, 1959–64, (Hist.); Univ. of South. CA, 1973–74, MSLS. **Orgs.:** SAA. CA Socty. of Archvsts. Renaissance Socty. of Amer. Amer. Hist. Assn. **Pubns.:** "Placer County in 1874; the Letters of Duncan Mackenzie," *The Pacific Historian* (Spr. 1975); "Louis Fabian Bachrach", *Dictionary of American Biography, 1961–1965*; Medieval and Renaissance authors in *Magill's Bibliography of Literary Criticism* (1979); Reviews. **Activities:** 1, 2; 15, 23, 39; 55, 92, 95-Exhibits. **Addr.:** 15 Cinnamon Lane, Portuguese Bend, CA 90274.

Christy, Ann K. (N. 13, 1939, Montgomery, AL) Systs. Anal., Lib. of Congs., 1979–; Tech. Srvs. Libn., Natl. Transp. Policy Std. Cmsn., 1978–79; Info. Spec., Natl. Acad. of Scis., 1976–77; Libn., Barton-Aschman Assoc., 1974–76. **Educ.:** Univ. of AL, 1958–61, BS (Chem.); Case West. Rsv. Univ., 1967–68, MSLS. **Orgs.:** ALA. ASIS. **Honors:** Beta Phi Mu. **Activities:** 4; 41, 46; 56 **Addr.:** Library of Congress, Washington, DC 20540.

Chu, Ellen Moy (Ap. 7, 1938, New York, NY) Libn., Natl. Inst. of Hlth., 1974–. **Educ.:** Wellesley Coll., 1955–59, BA (Geo.); Catholic Univ., 1972–74, MSLS. **Orgs.:** DC LA: Dir. (1981–). DC OLUG. SLA: DC Chap., Nom. Com. (1979–80); Info. Tech. Grp. (Vice-Ch., 1977–78). Metro. Washington Lib. Cncl.: Libns. Tech. Com. (Fed. Rep., 1978–79). OCLC Users Cncl., Secy. (1981–82). **Honors:** Beta Phi Mu, 1974. **Pubns.:** Ed., *Interlibrary Users Association Directory and Subject Index* (1978). **Activities:** 4, 12; 17, 34; 56 **Addr.:** National Institutes of Health, Division of Computer Research and Technology Library, Bg 12A Rm 3018, Bethesda, MD 20205.

Chu, Sally Chen (My. 19, 1939, Tainan, Taiwan) Clinical Med. Libn., Hlth. Scis. Lib., Univ. of MO, Kansas City, 1980–; Chief Libn., Natl. Yang-Ming Med. Coll., (Taiwan), 1976–79; Chld. Libn., San Bruno Pub. Lib., 1966–70; Chld. Libn., San Diego Pub. Lib., 1965–66. **Educ.:** Natl. Taiwan Univ., 1958–62, BA (Chinese Lit.) TX Woman's Univ., 1963–65, MLS. **Orgs.:** Med. LA. Hlth. Sci. Lib. Grp. of Grt. Kansas City. Chinese Club of Grt. Kansas City. Emmanuel Bapt. Church. **Activities:** 1, 12; 39; 80 **Addr.:** Health Sciences Library, University of Missouri Kansas City, 2411 Holmes, Kansas City, KS 64108.

Chubb, William O. (N. 2, 1916, Quebec, PQ) Ch., Bd. of Trustees, South-Central Reg. Lib., MB, 1978–, Citizen Trustee, 1969–80. **Educ.:** Laval Univ., 1933–37, BScA (Chem.), 1938–41, DScA (Plant Biochem.). **Orgs.:** MB Lib. Trustees Assn.: Publicity Ch. (1979–80); Pres. (1975–76). MB LA. **Addr.:** Box 699, Morden, MB R0G 1J0 Canada.

Chudacoff, Nancy Fisher (My. 21, 1945, Muskegon, MI) Lib. consult., 1979–; Lib. Dir., RI Hist. Socty., 1976–79; Asst. Libn., 1975–76; Ed., *RI Hist.,* 1976–79. **Educ.:** Northwestern Univ., IL, 1963–67, BA (Hist.); Univ. of RI, 1971–73, MLS; Arch.-Lib. Inst., OH Hist. Socty., 1973; Univ. of RI, 1974–76, MA (Hist.); Boston Univ. Sch. of Law, 1979–82, (J.D. expected). **Orgs.:** New England Arcvsts.: treas., (1973–75); Rep. at large (1975–77). Consortium of RI Acad. & Resrch. Libs.: vice-ch., (1978–79). SAA. RI LA: Ch., Nom. Com. (1978); Schol. Com. (1973). Various other orgs. Amer. Civil Lib. Union. Appalachian Mtn. Club. **Pubns.:** *Providence Newspapers on Microfilm 1762 to the Present: A Bibliography,* (1974); "Archivists and Librarians,": *Amer. Archvst.* (O. 1979); "Copyright, Don't Copy Wrong," *RI Roots,* (1978); "The Revolution and the Town: Providence 1775–1783," *RI Hist.* (Ag. 1976); "Woman in the News 1762–1770–Sarah Updike Goddard," (N. 1973). **Activities:** 14-Consultant; 15, 24, 45; 61, 74, 77 **Addr.:** 84 Cole Ave., Providence, RI 02906.

Chumbler, Sara Darnall (Je. 1, 1940, Dawson Springs, KY) Elem. Libn., D.T. Cooper Sch., Paducah Pub. Sch., 1972–; Libn., Clark Elem. Sch., 1969–72; Tchr., 1964–69; Tchr., Clay Elem. Sch., 1961–64. **Educ.:** Murray State Univ., 1958–61, BS (Elem. Ed.), 1965–70, MA (Elem. Ed.), 1969–72, (Lib. Sci.); Univ. of KY, (Grad. work in Lib. Sci.). **Orgs.:** First Dist. LA: Secy./Treas. (1979–80). KY LA: Ch., Schol. Com. (1979–80); Outstan. Libn. Com. (1979); Pub. Rel. Ch. (1975). ALA: Renovations and Con. of Media Fac. (1978–81). Paducah Educ. Assn.: Bldg. Rep. (1970–72; 1979–80). KY Educ. Assn. Nat. Educ. Assn. KY Sch.: Media Assn. **Honors:** KY Colonel, 1978; KY Ambassador, 1978. **Activities:** 10, 12; 21, 36, 48; 50, 72, 85 **Addr.:** 3814 Phillips Ave., Paducah, KY 42001.

Chung, Wen G. (D. 5, 1940, Ping-tung, Taiwan) Head, Acq./Bib. Search, Univ. of Guelph Lib., 1975–; Sr. Acq. Libn., 1973–75; Coll. Libn., Univ. of West. ON, 1972-73, Acq. Libn., 1970–72. **Educ.:** Natl. Chengchi Univ., 1960–64, BA (Russ.); Univ. of Waterloo, 1966–68, MA (Russ.); Univ. of West. ON, 1969–70, MLS. **Orgs.:** ALA. Can. LA. ACRL West. NY/ON Chap. **Pubns.:** *Acquisitions Bibliography: A Guide to Articles in English* (1974). **Activities:** 1; 15 **Addr.:** 217 Gordon St., Guelph, ON N1G 1X4 Canada.

Church, John G. (Mr. 11, 1929, Globe, AZ) Admin., Resrcs. Ctr., CA State Dept. of Educ., 1962–; Consult., Educ. Comms., NY Educ. Dept., 1960–62; Dir., Instr. Mtrls. Ctr., East. WA State Coll., 1958–60; Dir., Curric. Lab., Univ. of UT, 1957–58; Dir., Lib. and Media Srvs., Westminster Coll., 1953–57. **Educ.:** Univ. of UT, 1945–48, BA (Soc. Sci.), 1949–50, MA (Sec. Educ.); Univ. of UT, Univ. of WA, 1954–57, PhD (Educ. Admin., LS); State of CA, 1962, Elem., Sec., Admin., Libnshp. Creds. **Orgs.:** ALA. CA Media Educs. and Libns. Assn.: Conf. Prog. Co-Ch. (1980). UT LA: Pres. (1954–55). Phi Delta Kappa: Area 2 (Coord., 1976–). Natl. Educ. Assn. CA Assn. for Compensatory Educ.: Reg. II, Prog. Com., Co-Ch. **Honors:** Phi Delta Kappa, Outstan. Srv. as Coord., 1976; CA Assn. for Compensatory Educ., Contribs. to Educ., 1978; CA Assn. for Compensatory Educ., Yrs. of Outstan. Srv. in Providing Insrv. Educ., 1981. **Pubns.:** "Ways to Help Your Child to Develop Thinking Skills," *Children's World* (1981); *Administration of Instructional Materials Organizations, Analysis and Evaluative Criteria for Materials Centers* (1970); Jt. auth., *Beginning Global Geography* (1967); "Information Centers Now Located Coast to Coast," *The Lib.-Coll. Omnibus* (S. 1972); "Making a Wide Variety of Educational Resources Available," *AV Instr.* (Ap. 1973); various articles, mono. **Activities:** 10, 12; 17, 34; 63, 75 **Addr.:** 440 Bret Harte Rd., Sacramento, CA 95825.

Churchman, Alice M. Guignard (Jy. 11, 1931, Ottawa, ON Can.) Coord. of Resrc. Ctr. Srvs., Etobicoke Bd. of Educ., 1975–, Resrc. Ctr. Consult., 1967–75; Tchr., Ottawa Bd. of Educ., 1959–66. **Educ.:** Univ. of Toronto, 1949–52, BA (Gen.); Columbia Univ., 1964–67, MS (LS); Ottawa Tchrs. Coll., 1958–59, Cert. **Orgs.:** Can. LA. Ont. LA. Chlds. Bk. Ctr. (Toronto). Frnds. of the Osborne and Lillian H. Smith Cols. **Activities:** 10, 12; 17, 24; 63, 92, 95-Chlds. Mtrls. **Addr.:** 300 Mill Rd., Apt. B21, Etobicoke, ON Canada.

Churchville, Lida Holland (My. 5, 1933, Dallas, TX) Libn., Natl. Arch. & Recs. Srvc., 1979–; Law Libn., Army Lib., Pentagon, 1976–79; Legis. Lib. Chief, NY State Senate, 1967–75. **Educ.:** Russell Sage Coll., 1950–52, 1963–65, BA (Hist.); SUNY, Albany, 1965–67, MLS; NY Pub. Libn. Prof. Cert., 1978–. **Orgs.:** DC LA. DC Law Lib. Assn. SUNY Lib. Sch. Alumni Task Force (1972–75). Geneal. & Local Hist. Interest Grp.: Co-Ch.

PROFESSIONAL ACTIVITIES: Institutions: 1. Acad. lib.; 2. Arch.; 3. Assn.; 4. Fed./Gvt. lib.; 5. Inst. lib.; 6. Mfr./Suppl.; 7. Milit. lib.; 8. Musm.; 9. Pub. lib.; 10. Sch. lib.; 11. Sch. of lib. sci.; 12. Spec. lib.; 13. State lib.; 14. (other). **Functions/Activities:** 15. Acq./Col. dev.; 16. Adult srvs.; 17. Admin.; 18. Apprais.; 19. Archit./Bldgs.; 20. Cat./Class.; 21. Chld. srvs.; 22. Circ.; 23. Cons./Pres.; 24. Consult.; 25. Cont. ed.; 26. Educ. lib. sci.; 27. Ext. srvs.; 28. Fund/Grants; 29. Gvt. pubs.; 30. Indx./Abs.; 31. Instr. lib. use; 32. Media srvs.; 33. Micro.; 34. Netwks./Coop.; 35. Persnl.; 36. PR; 37. Publshg.; 38. Recs. mgt.; 39. Ref. srvs.; 40. Repro.; 41. Resrch.; 42. Review.; 43. Secur.; 44. Serials; 45. Spec. col.; 46. Tech. srvs.; 47. Trustees/Bds.; 48. YA srvs.; 49. (other).

(1980–81). Arena Stage Repertory Theater: Volunteer (1976–). Waterside Residents Assn.: Secy. (1980–81). Natl. Geneal. Soc. **Honors:** Army Lib., Letter of Comdn., 1976. **Pubns.:** Jt. cmplr., "Writings on Archives, Historical Manuscripts, and Current Records: 1978," *The American Archivist* (Sum. 1980). **Activities:** 2, 4; 15, 17, 42; 56, 69, 77 **Addr.:** Apt. 512B, 905 6th St. S.W., Washington, DC 20024.

Churchwell, Charles D. (N. 7, 1926, Dunnellon, FL) Dean, Lib. Srvs., WA Univ., 1978–; Univ. Libn., Brown Univ., 1974–78; Assoc. Provost, Miami Univ., 1972–74; Prof., Dir. Libs., Miami Univ., 1969–72; Asst. Dir., Univ. of Houston, 1967–69. **Educ.:** Morehouse Coll., 1948–52, BS (Math.); Atlanta Univ., 1952–53, MLS; Univ. of IL, 1961–66, PhD (LS); Amer. Cncl. on Educ., 1971–72, Acad. Admin. Fellow. **Orgs.:** ALA: Com. of Accred. (1976–80). MO LA. **Pubns.:** *History of Education for Librarianship* (1974); "The Library in Academia: An Associate Provost's View," *New Dimensions for Academic Library Service* (1975). **Activities:** 1; 26 **Addr.:** Library Services, Olin Library, Box 1061, Washington University, St. Louis, MO 63130.

Chvatal, Donald P. (My. 14, 1940, Waverly, IA) VP, Acad. Book Ctr., 1975–; Dir., Mktg., Richard Abel & Co., 1973–74, Mgr., of Tech. Srvs., 1967–72; Dir. of Pub. Srvs., Univ. of MT, 1964–67. **Educ.:** St. John's Univ. (MN), 1958–63, BA (Phil.); Univ. of IL, 1963–64, MSLS. **Orgs.:** ALA. Pac. NW LA. **Pubns.:** "A Computer-Based Acquisitions System for Libraries," ASIS Proc. (1971). **Activities:** 1, 6; 15, 20, 37 **Addr.:** 13770 S.W. Parkway, Beaverton, OR 97005.

Chwalek, Adele R. (Je. 3, 1939, Ludlow, MA) Interim Head of Circ., Catholic Univ., 1980–; Head, Educ./Psy. Srvs. & Col., 1976–80; Cat. Libn., Trinity Coll., Washington, DC, 1972–76, Dominican Coll., Washington, DC, 1971–72; Libn., Dept. of Educ., U.S. Catholic Conf., 1970–72; Libn., Longview Coll., 1967–70. **Educ.:** Coll. of St. Catherine, 1965–67, BA (Lib. Sci.); Catholic Univ., 1970–72, MSLS; Tchr. Cert., NY, MA, 1967. **Orgs.:** ALA. ACRL: Com. on Stan. for Educ. Libs. (1978–). Cath. LA: Cont. Educ. Com. (1979–). Coll. Univ./Sem. Lib. Sect., Secy./Treas., (1979–). **Honors:** Beta Phi Mu. **Pubns.:** *Materials about poverty and human development: a bibliography* (1971). **Activities:** 1, 10; 31, 32, 39; 63, 72, 92 **Addr.:** Mullen Library, The Catholic University of America, Washington, DC 20064.

Chweh, Steven Seokho (Ja. 15, 1944, Naju, Chonnam, Korea) Asst. Prof., Sch. of Lib. Sci., Univ. of South. CA, 1976–; Head, Acq. Libn., Henderson State Univ., AR, 1971–74; Korean Lang. Instr., U.S. Peace Corps, 1968–69. **Educ.:** Kyung Hee Univ., Seoul, Korea, 1962–66, BA (Eng.); LA State Univ., Baton Rouge, 1969–71, MSLS; Univ. of Pittsburgh, 1974–76, PhD (Lib. & Info. Sci.). **Orgs.:** ALA; ASIS: Los Angeles Chap., Ch., Elec. Com. (1979–80); AALS; Friends of the Korea Town Lib. (Los Angeles): Pres. (1977–). Assn. for Korean Stud.: Secy. Gen., VP Brd. of Dir.; Univ. of South CA Univ. CA Los Angeles Jt. E. Asian Stud. Ctr. **Honors:** Outstanding Young Men of America, Awd., 1979; Beta Phi Mu. **Pubns.:** "A Study of Data Elements for the COM Catalog", *Jrnl. of Lib. Auto.* (Mr. 1979); "A Comparative Study of Job Satisfaction," *Jrnl. of Acad. Libnshp.* (1978); "A Model Instrument for User-rating of Library Service," *CA Libn.* (Ap. 1978); "Early Korean Printing," *Papers of Bibl. Socty. of Amer.* (Je. 1979); "Recommended Books to Read," *The Korea Times, Amer. News* (Je. 1978); "Evaluation Criteria For Library Service," *Jnl. of Lib. Administration* (Je. 1981); Reviews. **Activities:** 11; 20, 26, 35, 41; 56, 75 **Addr.:** School of Library and Information Management, University of Southern California, University Park, Los Angeles, CA 90007.

Ciallella, Carol Ann (F. 28, 1939, Milford, MA) Adult Srv. Coord., Barrington Pub. Lib., 1977–80; Reg. Coord., Island Interrelated Lib. Syst., 1969–77; Bkmobile Libn., Worcester Pub. Lib., 1965–69, Lib. Asst., 1964–65. **Educ.:** Anna Maria Coll., 1957–61, BA (Hist.); Simmons Coll., 1962–64, MSLS. **Orgs.:** ALA: RI Chap. Cnclr. (1972–76). RI LA: Chap. Cnclr. (1972–76). New England LA. MA LA. **Activities:** 9; 16, 39 **Addr.:** 78 Arnold St., East Providence, RI

Ciallella, Emil A., Jr. (Jl. 1, 1943, Fall River, MA) Dir., Ctrl. Falls Free Pub. Lib., 1974–; Asst. Ref. Libn., Barrington Pub. Lib., 1971–74. **Educ.:** Providence Coll., 1961–65, BA (Educ., Langs.); Assumption Coll., 1965–66, MA (Fr.); Univ. of RI, 1970–1971, MLS. **Orgs.:** RI LA: Conf. Com. (1975–76); Gvt. Rel. Com. (1975–77, 1979–); Ad Hoc Com. on the Statewide Lib. Card (1976–77). New Eng. LA. ALA. RI Hist. Socty. **Pubns.:** "Rhode Island," *ALA Yearbook* (1976–81). **Activities:** 9; 17, 24, 28; 66, 85 **Addr.:** 78 Arnold St., East Providence, RI 02915.

Ciccariello, Priscilla C. (O. 27, 1925, Ann Arbor, MI) Ref. Libn., Port Washington Pub. Lib., 1975– Libn. (Stipendiate) Intl. Youth Lib., Munich, W. Germany, 1974. **Educ.:** Queens Coll., 1970–73, BA, 1973–74, MLS; Columbia Univ., 1975–80, Sixth Year Cert. (LS). **Orgs.:** ALA. NY LA. Nassau Cnty. LA. **Activities:** 9; 23, 29, 39 **Addr.:** 54 Ima Ave., Port Washington, NY 11050.

Cinquemani, Frank L. (N. 16, 1922, Jamaica, NY) Retired, 1978–; Chief, Ref. Div., Baruch Coll., CUNY, 1951–78; Asst. Ref. Libn., Bus. Lib., Columbia Univ., 1949–50. **Educ.:** Queens Coll., 1946–49, BS (Econ.); Columbia Univ., 1949–51, MS (LS); NY Univ., 1958–64, MA (Educ.). **Orgs.:** ALA. NY Lib. Club. **Pubns.:** "Robert's Revisited; Parliamentary Practice in Perspective," *RQ* (1976, no. 1); "The Bibliographic Essay," *RQ* (1972, no. 3); "The Story of a Scroll," *The City Coll. Alum.* (1963, no. 2); reviews. **Activities:** 1; 15, 17, 39; 59 **Addr.:** 535 Upper Mountain Ave., Montclair, NJ 07043.

Ciolli, Antoinette (Ag. 20, 1915, New York, NY) Chief, Spec. Col., Brooklyn Coll. Lib., 1970–81, Chief Sci. Libn., 1959–70, Ref. Libn., 1947–59, Lectr. (Hist.), 1944–50, Lectr. (Lib. User), 1947–56. **Educ.:** Brooklyn Coll., 1933–37, AB (Hist.), 1937–40, AM (Amer. Hist.); Columbia Univ., 1940–43, BS (LS), additional grad. work. **Orgs.:** ALA: Sci. and Tech. Ref. Srvs. Com. (1964–67). Amer. Hist. Assn. NY Lib. Club. SLA. Other orgs. AAUP. **Honors:** Beta Phi Mu. NY City Univ. Chancellor's Fund, Grant for Gideonse Bibl., 1968. **Pubns.:** Jt. Comp., *Urban Educator: Harry D. Gideonse...* (1970); "Research Use of Student Archives: A Brooklyn College Experience," Mid-Atl. *Archvst.* (Ap. 1980); "Brooklyn College Library...," *Brooklyn Coll. Alum. Assn. Bltn.* (Fall 1977); "The Subject Division Organization in a Liberal Arts College Library," *Coll. and Resrch. Libs.* (Jl. 1961). **Activities:** 1, 2; 15, 17, 31; 57, 62, 85 **Addr.:** 1129 Bay Ridge Pkwy., Brooklyn, NY 11228.

Cipolla, Wilma Reid (O. 18, 1930, Moberly, MO) Head, Serials Dept., SUNY, Buffalo, 1978–, Head, Serial Recs., 1974–77. **Educ.:** Pomona Coll., 1949–51, BA (Msc.); Eastman Sch. of Msc., 1951–52, MM (Msc. Lit.); SUNY, Buffalo, 1972–74, MLS. **Orgs.:** ALA: RTSD/Serials Sect.: Ad Hoc Com. on Union Lists of Serials (1980–). Five Assoc. Univ. Libs.: Rep. to OCLC Adv. Com. on Serials (1978–). Msc. LA: Rep. to Jt. Com. on the Union List of Serials (1978–). West. NY Lib. Resrcs. Cncl.: Tech. Srvs./Union List of Serials Com. (1978–80). **Honors:** Beta Phi Mu, 1974. **Pubns.:** *A Catalog of the Works of Arthur Foote, 1853–1937* (1980); "Introduction and Notes", *Arthur Foote, 1853–1937: An Autobiography* (1979); *Keyboard Realizations of Giuseppe Torelli, "Sinfonia for Four Trumpets."* (1974); *Keyboard Realizations of Giuseppe Jacchini, "Sonate con trombe, 1695."* (1977); "Music Subject Headings: A Comparison," *Lib. Resrcs. and Tech. Srvs.* (Fall 1974). **Activities:** 1; 17, 44, 46; 55 **Addr.:** 79 Roycroft Blvd., Buffalo, NY 14226.

Citron, Caryl Graham (Ap. 21, 1953, Syracuse, NY) Head Libn., C.S. Draper Lab., Inc., 1978–. **Educ.:** Vassar Coll., 1970–74, AB (Ital.); Simmons Coll., 1976–78 MS (LS). **Orgs.:** SLA: Sci. Tech. Com. (Ch., 1979–80); Educ. Com. (1980–81); Legis. Liaison (1980–81); New Eng. OLUG. NELINET. Amer. Fld. Srv. Scottish Country Dance Socty. **Activities:** 12; 15, 17, 49-Autom.; 52, 64, 91 **Addr.:** C. S. Draper Lab, Inc., Tech. Info. Center, 555 Tech. Sq., Cambridge, MA 02139.

Ciucki, Marcella A. (Ja. 30, 1931, Hammond, IN) Chief, Tech. Srvs., Lake Cnty. Pub. Lib., 1978–; Chief, Ref. Srvs., 1966–78; Info./Syst. Spec., U.S. Naval Ord. Lab., 1963–66; Elem. Tchr., E. Chicago Pub. Schls., 1960–61; Analyst, Lever Bros. Co., 1952–59. **Educ.:** Indiana Univ., 1948–52, BA (Math.), 1962, MS (Educ.), 1962–63, MALS. **Orgs.:** ALA: Com. on Stat. for Ref. Srvs. SLA. **Pubns.:** "Recording of Reference/Information Service Activities," *RQ* (1977). **Activities:** 9; 22, 39, 46; 56, 91 **Addr.:** 8723 Oakwood Ave., Munster, IN 46321.

Claassen, Lynda Corey (Mr. 29, 1943, Troy, NY) Consultant, Smithsonian Inst., 1981–; Resrch. Spec./Ed., Smithsonian Inst., 1979–81; Head, Rare Books & Spe. Coll., Mills Coll., 1974–79; Cur., Slides & Photo., Cornell Univ., Coll. of Arch., 1965–72. **Educ.:** Smith Coll., 1961–65, BA (Art hist.); Univ. of CA, Berkeley, 1973–74, MLS; Cornell Univ., 1966–69, (Art Hist.). **Orgs.:** ALA: ACRL, Ch., Cont. Educ. Com., Rare Books & Manu. Sect. (1979–81). College Art Assn. Dist. of Columbia LA: Fed. Rel. Coord. (1979–80). Book Club of CA: Ed. Brd. (1978–79). Amer. Printing Hist. Assn. **Pubns.:** *Finders' Guide to Drawings & Prints in the Smithsonian Institution* (1981); *Franklin D. Walker: A Checklist of His Writings* (1978); "The Eucalyptus Press at Mills College," (1978). **Activities:** 1; 28, 40, 41, 45; 55, 57 **Addr.:** 505 G St., S.E., Washington, DC 20003.

Clancy, Ron (My. 1, 1947, Windsor, ON) Asst. Dir., Vancouver Island Reg. Lib., 1980–; Head, Sci. Lib., Univ. of AB, 1974–80; Sci. Ref. Libn., Univ. of BC, 1972–74. **Educ.:** Univ. of Windsor, 1965–70, BSc (Chem.); Trent Univ., 1970–71, MSc (Chem.); Univ. of West. ON, 1971–72, MLS. **Orgs.:** LA AB: Councillor & Mem. Ch. (1977–79). AB Info. Retrieval Assn.: Bd. of Dir. (1975–); Secy. (1979–). Polish Can. Libns. Assn.: Pres. (1977–78). Can. Assn. for Info. Sci. Amer. Chem. Soc. **Pubns.:** Jt. auth., *Foodmonton: An Edmonton Bibliogastronomy* (1978); *Library Association of Alberta Membership Directory* (1978). **Activities:** 1, 12; 15, 17, 39; 60, 88, 91 **Addr.:** Vancouver Island Regional Library, Strickland St., Nanaimo, BC V9R 5J7 Canada. Edmonton, AB T6G 2J8 Canada.

Clarie, Thomas C. (D. 21, 1943, Providence, RI) Head Ref. Libn., South. CT State Coll., 1973–; Ref. Libn., Univ. of CT, 1973–; Libn., Avon Old Farms School, 1969–71; Libn., Miller Memorial Lib., Hamden, CT, 1967–69. **Educ.:** Holy Cross Coll., 1961–65, BS (Hist.); South. CT State Coll., 1970–72, MS (LS); Univ. of CT, 1972–73, MA (Hist.). **Orgs.:** CT LA: Memb. Ch. (1979–80); Coll./Univ. Div., Exec. Bd. (1977–80). **Honors:** Carrollton Press Prize, Best New Ref. Book Concept, 1978. **Pubns.:** *Occult Bibliography.* (1978); Reviewer, *American Reference Books Annual.* (1977–). **Activities:** 1; 16, 31, 39; 57, 59, 83 **Addr.:** Reference Dept., Buley Library, Southern Connecticut State College, New Haven, CT 06515.

Clark, Alice Sandell (N. 24, 1922, Oneonta, NY) Asst. Dean for Readers' Srvs., Univ. of NM Gen. Lib., 1974–; Head, Undergrad. Libs., OH State Univ., 1970–74; Ref. Libn., 1969–70; Asst. Head, Persnl., 1968–69; Lect., SUNY Sch. of Lib. and Info. Sci., 1968. **Educ.:** State Univ. Coll., Oneonta, 1964–67, BA (Soc. Sci. Ed.); SUNY, Albany, 1967–68, MLS; State Univ. Coll., Oneonta, 1971–78, MA (Hist.) **Orgs.:** ALA: Cncl. (1977–); Plng. and Budget Asm. (1979–); RASD: Nom. Com., Hist. Sect. (1979); NM LA: Bd. of Dir. (1977–). Franklin Cnty. Lib. Assn.: Pres. (1974). Grt. Albuquerque Lib. Assn.: Constn. & Bylaws Com. (1979–80). AAUP. **Pubns.:** Jt. Auth., *Quantitative Methods in Librarianship: Standards, Research, Management* (1972); "Computer Assisted Instruction in the Use of the Library: One Solution for the Large University" in *A Challenge for Academic Libraries* (1973); "Computer-Assisted Library Instruction" in *Educating the Library User,* (1974); "Microforms as a Substitute for the Original in the Collection Development Process" in *Collection Development in Libraries* (1980); "Reserve Processing, An Automated System," *Southwest Acad. Lib. Cnsrtm. Nsltr.* (March 1976); other articles. **Activities:** 1, 10; 17, 33, 40; 61, 72, 92 **Addr.:** Zimmerman Library, University of New Mexico, Albuquerque, NM 87131.

Clark, Barbara Campbell (My. 10, 1933, Elizabethtown, NC) Asst. Dean of Instr. for Learning Resrc., Pitt Cmnty. Coll., 1979–; Asst. Dean of Instr. for Library Resrc., Pitt Tech. Inst., 1977–79, Dir. of Lib. Resrc., 1972–77, Lib. Dir., 1970–72, Head Libn., 1969–70; Tchg. Fellow, E. Carolina Univ. Lib. Sci. Dept., 1968–69; Asst. Mgr., Duke Univ. Dining Halls, 1960–61; Asst. Home Demonstration Agent, NC Agricultural Extension Service, 1955–58. **Educ.:** Univ. of NC at Greensboro, 1951–55, BS (Home Econ. Educ.); E. Carolina Univ., 1967–69, MAEd (LS), 1971–73, MLS; NC State Univ., 1974–, EdD in progress. **Orgs.:** ALA. SELA. NC LA: Com. on Lib. Resrcs., Ch. (1979–81). NC Comnty. Coll. Learning Resources Assn.: Distr. Dir. (1977–78), Priorities Com. (1978–79), Mem. Ch. (1979–80), Exec. Bd. (1977–78, 1979–80); Other orgs. Adult Educ. Assn. of the U.S.A. NC Adult Educ. Assn. NC Comnty. Coll. Adult Educ. Assn.: Fall Conf. Plng. Com. (1977), Fall Conf. Recorder (1979). Greenville Area Cham. of Cmrc.: Com. on Recreation and Culture (1978–79), Com. on Plng. (1980–). **Activities:** 1; 17; 50 **Addr.:** Pitt Community College, P.O. Drawer 7007, Greenville, NC 27834.

Clark, Barbara Lee (Jl. 17, 1939, Columbus, OH) Branch Mgr., Pub. Lib. of Columbus and Franklin Cnty., 1975–, Bkmobile. Dept. Head, 1966–74; Intl. Exch. Prog. Libn., Gloucestershire (Eng.) Cnty. Lib. Syst., 1979–80. **Educ.:** Capital Univ. 1957–61, BS in Ed; Kent State Univ., 1974–75, MLS; Miami Univ., Lib. Exec. Dev. Prog., 1978. **Orgs.:** ALA. OH LA: Lcl. Arrange Com. (1976), Org. Com. (1976–79, Ch., 1978–79) Franklin Cnty. LA. NLA. Natl. Assn. for the Pres. and Protection of Storytel. Southwest Hlth. Ctrs., Inc. **Honors** OH LA, Best Article of the Year, 1980. **Pubns.:** "The England Experience/The Gloucestershire Connection," *OH LA Bltn.* (Jl. 1980). **Activities:** 9; 16, 17, 27 **Addr.:** Hilltop Branch, Public Library of Columbus and Franklin Co., 2955 W Broad St., Columbus, OH 43204.

Clark, Barton M. (N. 11, 1939, Omaha, NE) Asst. Dir., of Pub. Srvs., Soc. Scis. Libs., Univ. of IL, 1981–, Educ., Soc. Scis. Libn., 1977–81; Head, Soc. Stds. and Hum. Div., Univ. of NE, 1972–73, Undergrad. Libn., 1971–72, Asst. Soc. Stds. Libn., 1970–71. **Educ.:** Univ. of CO, 1957–68, BA (Anthro.) Univ. of IL, 1968–70, MS (LS), 1970, MA (Anthro.); Univ. of AZ, 1973–76 (Anthro.). **Orgs.:** ALA: ACRL/ANSS (Exec. Com., 1972–73, 1977–79), Comm. Com. (Ch., 1977–79);/EBSS, Psy. Psyt. Com. (1978–); RASD, Amer. Ind. Mtrls. and Srvs. Com. (1972–73); Mem. Com. (1971–72). NE LA: Exec. Com. (1971–72). Other orgs. and ofcs. Intl. Un. of Anthro. and Ethnological Scis.: Cmsn. on Documtn. (1979–), Subcom. on Comp.-Based Systs. for Anthro. Documtn. (Ch., 1980–). Socty. for Applied Anthro. Amer. Anthro. Assn. **Honors:** Smithsonian Inst., Travel Grant (India), 1978; Wenner-Gren Fndn., Info. Resrcs. Flwshp., 1977; Beta Phi Mu. **Pubns.:** "Social Science Data Libraries: A View to the Future," *Lib. Trends* (in press); jt. auth, "Documentation and Data Management in Applied Anthropology," *Jnl. of Cult. and Educ. Futures* (1981); jt. auth., "Professional and Nonprofessional Staffing Patterns in Departmental Libraries," *Lib. Resrch.* (1979); jt. auth., "Socialization of Library School Students," *Jnl. of Educ. for Libnshp.* (1979). **Activities:** 1; 15, 17, 39; 62, 92, 93 **Addr.:** Library, University of Illinois at Urbana-Champaign 1408 W. Gregory Dr., Urbana, IL 61801.

Clark, Elaine M. (S. 27, 1948, Lancaster, PA) Head Libn., Springfield (PA) Township Lib., 1974–; Head Libn., Glenside Free Lib., 1971–74. **Educ.:** Ursinus Coll., 1966–70, BA (Pol. Sci.); Rutgers Univ., 1970–71, MLS. **Orgs.:** ALA. PA LA: Southeast

Special Subjects/Services: 50. Adult educ.; 51. Advert./Mktg.; 52. Aerosp.; 53. Agric.; 54. Area std.; 55. Arts/Hum.; 56. Autom.; 57. Bibl./Prtg.; 58. Bio. sci.; 59. Bus./Fin.; 60. Chem.; 61. Copyrt.; 62. Documtn.; 63. Educ.; 64. Engin.; 65. Env.; 66. Eth. grps.; 67. Film; 68. Food/Nutr.; 69. Geneal.; 70. Geo.; 71. Geol.; 72. Handcpd.; 73. Hist.; 74. Int. frdm.; 75. Info. sci.; 76. Insr.; 77. Law; 78. Legis.; 79. Math./Comp. sci.; 80. Med.; 81. Metals; 82. Nat. resrcs.; 83. Newsp.; 84. Nuc. sci.; 85. Oral hist.; 86. Petr./Energy; 87. Pharm.; 88. Phys./Astr./Math.; 89. Readg.; 90. Relig.; 91. Sci./Tech.; 92. Soc. sci.; 93. Telecom.; 94. Transp.; 95. (other).

Chap. (Ch., 1979–80). Delaware Cnty. LA: Ch. (1977–78). Pi Nu Epsilon. Pi Gamma Mu. **Honors:** Beta Phi Mu. **Activities:** 9; 16, 17, 39; 92 **Addr.:** Springfield Township Library, 70 Powell Rd., Springfield, PA 19064.

Clark, George C. (Ap. 7, 1937, Port Chester, NY) Head Libn., Minot State Coll., 1972–, Ref. Libn., 1969–72. **Educ.:** CO State Coll., 1955–59, BA (Msc. Educ.), 1962–64, MA (Msc. Educ.); Denver Univ., 1968–69 MA (LS). **Orgs.:** ALA. Mt. Plains LA. ND LA. Kiwanis. Antique Auto. Club of Amer. Amer. Fed. of Musicians. Minot Symph. Orch. Libn. **Activities:** 1; 15, 17, 34; 55 **Addr.:** 204 7th St S.E., Minot, ND 58701.

Clark, Georgia Ann M. (S. 19, 1942, Duluth, MN) Law Libn., Wayne State Univ., 1975–, Asst. Dir., Law Lib., 1973–75; Serials Libn., Law Lib., Univ. of MI, 1967–73, Circ. Libn., 1965–67. **Educ.:** Coll. of St. Scholastica, 1960–64, BS (Hist.); Univ. of MI, 1964–65, AMLS. **Orgs.:** MI Assn. Law Libs.: Strg. Com. (Pres., 1977). AALL. Law Lib. Micro. Cnsrtm.: Bd. of Dir. (1976–). **Pubns.:** "The Problem Patron," *Law Lib. Jnl.* (Win. 1979). **Activities:** 1; 17; 77 **Addr.:** Law Library, Wayne State University, 468 W. Ferry Mall, Detroit, MI 48202.

Clark, Gertrude M. (Mr. 14, 1915, Vienna, Austria) Freelance Libn., 1970–; Serials Libn., Portland State Univ. Lib., 1968–70; Ref., Circ. Libn., Med. Scis. Lib., Univ. of UT, 1968–69; Chief Libn., Stuart Co. Div., Atlas Chem. Indus., 1959–68; Libn., Los Angeles City Pub. Lib., 1957–59; Asst., then Chief Libn., Los Angeles Cnty. Med. Assn., 1951–57; Tech. Libn., Harrower Labs., 1946–49. **Educ.:** Occidental Coll., 1939–40, AB (Mod. Langs.); Univ. of South. CA, 1940–41 BS (LS). Med. LA Cert.; SLA Cert. (Tech. Transl.). **Orgs.:** SLA: South. CA Chap. Spec. Libns. in Pasadena. Med. LA. Med. Lib. Grp. of South. CA. Various ofcs. **Pubns.:** Jt. auth., *I. Kant, Lectures on Philosophical Theology* (1978); articles in *Spec. Libs.* and *Bltn. Med. Lib. Assn.* **Activities:** 1, 12; 39, 41; 58, 80, 87 **Addr.:** 1950 SW Camelot Ct., #505, Portland, OR 97225.

Clark, Harry (D. 16, 1917, San Diego, CA) Assoc. Prof., Sch. of Lib. Sci., Univ. of OK, 1969–; Circ. Libn., CA State Univ., Chico, 1962–63, Catlgr., 1958–62; Libn. I (pub. srvs.), LA, Portland, OR, 1956–58. **Educ.:** Univ. of CA, Berkeley, 1936–40, BA (Hist.), 1955–56, MLS, 1963–69, PhD (Libnshp.). **Orgs.:** ALA. Freedom to Read Fndn. OK LA: (Cont. Educ. Com., 1975–77; Pr. Arts Rd Tbl. Ch., 1978). AAUP. Amer. Pr. Hist. Assn. **Pubns.:** *A Venture in History,* (1973); "Four Pieces in a Press; Gutenberg's Activities in Strasbourg," *Lib. Qtrly.* (Jl. 1979); "The Huckster in the Parlor," *Jrnl. of Lib. Hist.* (Jl. 1973). **Activities:** 11; 26, 31; 57, 74 **Addr.:** School of Library Science, University of Oklahoma, Norman, OK 73019.

Clark, Margery Marston (O. 30, 1926, Manhattan, KS) Assoc. Libn., Natl. Housing Cntr. Lib., 1962–; ILL Libn., Johns Hopkins Univ., Appld. Phys. Lab., 1958–62. **Educ.:** Univ. of DE, 1944–48, BA (Hist.); Cath. Univ., 1958–62, MSLS. **Orgs.:** SLA: Urban Affairs Sect./Soc. Sci. Div. (Ch., 1974). **Honors:** Phi Kappa Phi, 1948; Beta Phi Mu, 1962. **Activities:** 12; 39, 41; 64, 65, 86 **Addr.:** National Housing Center Library, 15th & M Streets N.W., Washington, DC 20005.

Clark, Marilyn S. (My. 1, 1938, Silver Creek, NY) Coord., Grants and Funding, Head, Ref. Dept., Univ. of KS Libs., 1972–, Ch. Col. Dev. Cncl., 1975–79, Ref., ILL Libn., 1970–72, Msc. Catlgr., 1969–70. **Educ.:** Univ. of MI, 1956–59, BMus (Msc.); Univ. of Chicago, 1959–63, MA (LS); Univ. of KS, 1980, MA (Hist.). **Orgs.:** ALA. Coll. Msc. Socty. Medieval Acad. of Amer. **Pubns.:** Co-Ed., Bibliographies of American Music Series (1978–). **Activities:** 1; 28, 39 **Addr.:** University of Kansas Libraries, Lawrence, KS 66045.

Clark, Marjorie J. (Ja. 19, 1929, Tallulah Falls, GA) Head Libn., North Georgia Coll., 1973–; Head Libn., Gainesville Jr. Coll., 1966–73; Tchr., Atlanta Pub. Schs., 1948–64. **Educ.:** Piedmont Coll., 1945–48, AB (Engl.); Emory Univ., 1965–66, M.Libn. **Orgs.:** GA LA: Secy. (1979–81). Northeast GA Assoc. Libs.: Ch. (1979–80). Southeast. LA. AAUP: Lcl. Chap. (Pres., 1978–79). Untd. Meth. Women: Bk. Review. (1979–). **Activities:** 1; 15, 17, 34; 63 **Addr.:** Stewart Library, North Georgia College, Dahlonega, GA 30533.

Clark, Robert L., Jr. (S. 12, 1945, McAlester, OK) Dir., OK Dept. of Lib., 1976–; Dir., Mid MI Reg. Lib. Syst., 1974–76; Asst. Dir. for Pub. Srvs., Jackson Met. Lib. Syst., 1973–74; Data Processing Coord., OK Dept. of Libs., 1972–73; Dir. of Div. of Arch. and Rec., 1968–72. **Educ.:** Univ. of OK, 1966–68, BA (Hist. and Pol. Sci.); Univ. of Denver, Univ. of OK, 1969, MLS. **Orgs.:** ALA: Stan. Com. Chief Officers of State Lib. Agencies: Ch., Leg. Com. (1979). Southwest. LA: Pres. (1980–). OK LA. OK Arts Cncl.: Secy. **Pubns.:** *Archive-Library Relations,* (1976); "New Dimensions in Archive-Library Relations," Southwest. LA Conf. Proc. (1972); "The Centennial Celebration of OK. Pr. and Pub." *Chron. of OK* (1970); "Local History," *OK Libn.* (1970). **Activities:** 2, 13; 17, 28; 55, 78 **Addr.:** Oklahoma Department of Libraries, 200 N.E. 18th, Oklahoma City, OK 73105.

Clark, Thomas A. (Mr. 12, 1936, Iuka, MS) Head, User Srvs., Valdosta State Coll. Lib., 1966–; Libn., Belmont (MS) HS, 1958–66. **Educ.:** Univ. of South. MS, 1956–58, BS (Hist.) Univ. of MS, 1964–66 MLS. **Orgs.:** Valdosta Lowndes Cnty. LA. GA LA. SELA. ALA. AAUP. **Activities:** 1, 10; 17, 22, 39; 68, 80, 95-Nursing. **Addr.:** 1909 Jerry Jones Dr., Valdosta, GA 31601.

Clark, Virginia (O. 4, 1929, Alliance, OH) Asst. Ed., *Choice* 1974–, Ed., *Books for Coll. Libs.* 2d ed., 1972–74; Catlgr., State Lib. of OH, 1968–72; Catlgr., City of Westminster Coll., (Eng.), 1967–68; Ref., Docum. Libn., Kenyon Coll., 1965–67, 1961–63; Asst. Ed., *Choice* 1963–64; Ref. Libn., Wright Branch, Chicago City Colls., 1955–61. **Educ.:** Mt. Un. Coll., 1947–51, BA; Univ. of Chicago, 1953–55, MA (LS). **Orgs.:** ALA: ACRL/Jr. Colls. Sect. (Secy. 1960, Vice-Ch., 1961, Ch., 1962). **Pubns.:** Jt. auth., "Suggested Classification for the Literature of Documentation," *Amer. Docum.* (Ja. 1961); "Teaching Students to Use the Library: Whose Responsibility?" *Coll. and Resrch. Libs.* (S. 1960); "Student Use of a Junior College Library," *IL Libs.* (My. 1960); "Punch Cards in Reference Work," *IL Libs.* (Je. 1958); Reviews. **Activities:** 1, 3; 20, 37, 39 **Addr.:** *Choice* 100 Riverview Ctr., Middletown, CT 06457.

Clarke, D. Sherman (Je. 19, 1946, Westerly, RI) Head, Hum. Cat. Team, Cornell Univ. Libs., 1979–; Catlgr. and Per. Libn., Frick Fine Arts Lib., Univ. of Pittsburgh, 1973–78. **Educ.:** SUNY Coll. at New Paltz, 1965–68, BA (Art Hist.); Case Western Reserve Univ., 1968–72, MA (Art Hist.), 1972–73, MS (LS). **Orgs.:** ARLIS/NA: Treas. (1977–79), Co-coord., Cat. Problems Discuss. Grp. (1975–). ALA. Coll. Art Assn. of America. Intl. Ctr. of Medieval Art. Soc. of Archit. Histns. Natl. Trust for Hist. Prsrvn. **Activities:** 1; 20; 55 **Addr.:** P.O. Box 91, Ithaca, NY 14850.

Clarke, Jack Alden (F. 20, 1924, Bay City, MI) Prof. of Lib. Sci., Univ. of WI-Madison, 1965–; Dir. of Libs., Prof., Univ of WI-Eau Claire, 1962–65; Asst. Libn., Univ. of WI-Madison; Dir. of Libs., Doane Coll. **Educ.:** MI State Univ., 1949–, BA Univ. of WI, MA (LS); PhD (Hist.); Diplome d études francaises, 1950. **Orgs.:** WI Assn. of Acad. Libns.: various com. WI LA. ALA. WI Acad. of Sci. and Arts: Libn. AAUP. **Pubns.:** Complr., *Modern French Literature and Language: A Bibliography of Homage Studies* (1976); *Gabriel Naude* (1970); *Huguenot Warrior: The Life and Times of Henri de Rahan* (1967); various articles. **Activities:** 1, 2; 29, 34, 39; 57, 69, 92 **Addr.:** 600 N. Park St., Madison, WI 53706.

Clarke, James P. (O. 9, 1926, Wilkes-Barre, PA) Lib. Dir., Marywood Coll., 1968–. **Educ.:** King's Coll., 1946–50, AB (Eng.); Drexel Univ., 1950–51, MLS. **Orgs.:** PA LA: Pres. (1969/70). Cath. LA. PA Citizens For Better Libs. **Activities:** 1; 17 **Addr.:** 10 E. South St., Apt. 750, Wilkes-Barre, PA 18701.

Clarke, Norman F. (My. 7, 1928, St. Paul, MN) Lcl. and MN Info. Spec., St. Cloud State Univ., 1974–; Dir., Sch. of LS, KS State Tchrs. Coll., 1971–73; Ch., Dept. of LS, IN State Univ., 1965–71; Asst. Prof., LS, Univ. of KY, 1963–65; Dir., Jamestown Coll. Lib., 1956–62. **Educ.:** IN Univ., 1946–50, AB (Jnlsm.), MA (Pol. Sci.); Univ. of MN, 1950–55, MS (LS); Univ. of MI, 1959–65, (LS). **Orgs.:** Mtn. Plains LA: Bd. of Dir. (1959–61). various other assns. and ofcs. ND Cncl. of Presby. Men: Pres. (1958–61). Rotary: Terre Haute, IN (Secy., 1968–70). MN Indp. Republican Party: Ctr. MN Reg. (Ch.) **Pubns.:** *Media Documentation of Local History* (1976); *Logsleds to Snowmobiles: a history of Pine River, Minnesota* (1979); "Cataloging, Classification, and Storage of Government Documents," *Lib. Trends* (Jl. 1966); "A Team for Learning: Teacher-Student-Librarian," *Contemporary Educ.* (N. 1969); "Kensington Rune Stone and Olof Ohman" (Oral Hist. Tapes) (1977). **Activities:** 1, 11; 30, 39, 45; 69, 83, 85 **Addr.:** Local and Minnesota Information, Learning Resources Services, St. Cloud State University, St. Cloud, MN 56301.

Clarke, Robert Flanders (Je. 20, 1932, Newport News, VA) Lib. Dir. & Prog. Chief, US Mental Hlth. Study Ctr., Natl. Inst. of Mental Hlth., 1977–; Spec. Asst. to Dir. for Biomed. Comm., US Food & Drug Admin., 1972–77; Spec. Asst. to Chief, Ref. & Bib. Natl. Inst. of Hlth., 1968–72; Chief, LS, Natl. Clearinghouse for Smoking & Hlth., 1965–68; Deputy Chief, Tech. Srvs., Natl. Lib. of Med., 1964–65, Syst. Anal., 1963–64. **Educ.:** US Coast Guard Acad., 1949–50 (Engin.); US Nvl. Acad., 1950–54, BS (Engin.); Rutgers Univ., 1960–61, MLS, 1961–63, PhD (LS). **Orgs.:** DC LA. ALA. SLA. Med. Lib. Assn. Comm. Ofcr. Assn. of the US Pub. Hlth. Srv. **Honors:** Beta Phi Mu, 1961; US Pub. Hlth. Serv. Cmdn. Medal, 1969. **Pubns.:** *Sports Car Events* (1959); *Drug Interactions, an Annotated Bibliography, vol. 3* (1976); "Impact of photocopying on scholarly publishing," *Lib. Jnl.* (1963); "Repeat photocopying of journal articles," *Coll. & Resrch. Libs.* (1966). **Activities:** 4; 17, 33, 41; 61 **Addr.:** 2710 Elsmore St., Fairfax, VA 22031.

Clarke, Virginia (N. 8, 1907, Albany, TX) Retired, 1973–; Adj. Prof. (LS), TX Woman's Univ., 1974–, Consult., 1974–; Asst. Dir., Autom. Srvs., Tarrant Cnty. Jr. Coll. Dist., 1969–73; Libn., Instr. (LS), N. TX State Univ., 1943–55, 1958–69; Consult., 1956–58; Sch. Libn., 1936–43. **Educ.:** N. TX State Univ., 1932–39, BA (Span., LS), 1940–44, MA (LS, Educ.); TX Lib. Cert., 1940; various Certs., 1956; various courses in LS, 1947–79. **Orgs.:** ALA. TX LA. TX Assn. for Educ. Tech. SWLA. Media Tech. Adv. Com. for Tarrant Cnty. Jr. Coll. **Honors:** Tarrant Cnty. Jr. Coll. Dist., Prof. Emeritus, 1978. **Pubns.:** *Organization of Nonbook Materials in the Laboratory School* (1965, 1969); "Gear Organization to Elementary School Needs," *Jr. Libs.* (Ap. 1960). **Activities:** 10, 11; 17, 26, 46 **Addr.:** 1112 Bell Ave., #7, Denton, TX 76201.

Clarkson, Sara H. (O. 23, 1951, Fort Dix, NJ) Head, A-V, Microforms Cat., SUNY, Buffalo, 1980–, Orig. Catlgr., 1977–80. **Educ.:** SUNY, Stony Brook, 1969–73, BA (Eng.); SUNY, Buffalo, 1975–76, MLS. **Orgs.:** ALA: LAMA/Stats. Sect., Stats. for Non-Print Media Com. (1979–81); RTSD, AV Com. (1980–82); JMRT, Com. to the Liaison to LITA (1980). NYLA: Resrcs. and Tech. Srvs. Sect. SUNY Libns. Assn. Beta Phi Mu: Beta Delta Chap., Bd. of Dirs. (1977–79). **Activities:** 1; 20 **Addr.:** 90 Radcliffe Rd., Buffalo, NY 14214.

Clarkson, Teresa N. (N. 30, 1951, Chester, PA) Law Libn., Duane, Morris & Heckscher, 1976–; **Educ.:** George Washington Univ., 1969–71; Villanova Univ., 1971–73, BA (Psy.); Drexel Univ., 1975–76, MS (LS). **Orgs.:** AALL: Place. Com. (1977–79); Pvt. Law Lib.-Retirem. Plan (1979). SLA; Greater Phila. Law Lib. Assn.: Place. Dir. (1977–80); Treas. (1978); Consultation Ch. (1979–80); Pres. (1981-82). PA Citizens for Better Libs. **Activities:** 12; 17, 39, 41; 77, 78 **Addr.:** Duane, Morris & Heckscher, Library, 1500 One Franklin Plz., Philadelphia, PA 19102.

Clary, Ann Roane (Ap. 5, 1931, Washington, DC) Chief Libn., Resrch. Lib., Fed. Res. Syst., 1960–; Chief Libn., Amer. Nat. Red Cross, 1955–60; Tchr., Montgomery Cnty. MD Sch. Syst., 1952–54. **Educ.:** Wilson Tchr. Coll. 1949–1950; Mary Washington Coll., 1950–52, BA (Eng.); Catholic Univ., 1954–56, MSLS. **Orgs.:** SLA. DCLA. ASIS. Fed. Lib. Com.: Rep. (1976–78). Chancel Guild: All Souls Episcopal Church. **Activities:** 4; 17, 39; 59, 92 **Addr.:** Research Library, Board of Governors of the Federal Reserve System, Washington, DC 20551.

Clary, Lydia Sharon. (N. 22, 1947, New York, NY) Coord., Resrc. Ctr. for Hlth. Servs. Admin. Educ.-ACEHSA/AUPHA, 1977–; Resrch. Asst., Assn. of Univ. Prog. in Hlth. Admn., 1975–78; Asst. Libn., McKinsey & Company, Inc., 1972–75. **Educ.:** Syracuse Univ., 1966–70, BA (Hist. & Pol. Sci.); Catholic Univ., Sch. of Lib. and Info.; Alliance francaise de Washington, 1979–80, (Fr.). **Orgs.:** SLA. Bus. Interest Grp. Libns. ASIS. Am. Film Inst. member. **Pubns.:** *The Utility of Student Selection Criteria for Predicting Academic Outcomes in the Health Administration Field: Literature Review & Recommendations,* (1976); "Oversupply of health administrators: true or false?," *Hosp. Progress,* (Ap. 1977). **Activities:** 2, 12; 15, 17, 39; 63, 92, Hlth. Srvs. Admin. **Addr.:** Resource Center for Health Services Administration Education, One Dupont Circle, Suite 420, Washington, DC 20036.

Clasper, James W. (N. 30, 1948, Niagara Falls, NY) Asst. Corp. Libn., Cincinnati Milacron Inc., 1979–; Mss. Cur., Amer. Jewish Arch., 1975–79; Bibligphr., Univ. of WI-Madison, 1974–75. **Educ.:** SUNY Coll. at Geneseo, 1966–70, BScED (Educ.), 1972–73, MA (Hist.); Univ. of WI-Madison, 1974–75, MA (LS). **Orgs.:** SAA: Anl. Conv. Local Arrange. (1980). ALA. ASIS. Assn. of Records Mgrs. and Admin. Other orgs. **Pubns.:** *Guide to the Holdings of the American Jewish Archives* (1979). **Activities:** 2, 12; 17, 38, 39; 56, 75, 91 **Addr.:** 3301 Eastside Ave., Cincinnati, OH 45208.

Clasquin, Frank F. (N. 2, 1915, Jacksonville, FL) Retired, 1980; VP, Resrch. & Dev., F. W. Faxon Co., 1961–; VP & Mgr., Cook Paint & Varnish Co., 1938–61. **Educ.:** Washington Univ., 1934–38, BS (Chem. Educ.). **Orgs.:** ALA: Price Index Com.; ANSI Std. Claim Form; Core List of Per. **Pubns.:** "The Subscription Agency and Lower Serials Budgets." *Serials Librarian,* (1976); Jt. auth., "Prices of Physics and Chemistry Journals." *Science,* (1977); "Financial Management of Serials and Journals through Subject 'Core' Lists." *Serials Librarian,* (1978); "Periodical Prices: 1977–79 Update." *Lib. Jnl.* (1978); "Physics & Chemistry Journal Prices in 1977–78", *Serials Librarian* (Sum. 1979); Other articles. **Activities:** 1, 4, 6; 38, 44, 46; 56 **Addr.:** 100 Lowder St., Dedham, MA 02026.

Clausen, Elizabeth P. (Je. 24, 1931, Lawrenceville, VA) Med. Libn., Augustana Hosp., 1981–; Med. Libn., Holy Cross Hosp., 1975–81; Ed., *Login New Title Abs.* Login Brothers Book Co., 1974. **Educ.:** Mary Washington Coll., 1948–52, BA (Art); Rosary Coll., 1972–73, MA (LS); Med. LA Cert., 1974. **Orgs.:** Med. LA. Hlth. Sci. Libns. of IL: Mem. Com. (1979), Bylaws Com. (1980). Frank Lloyd Wright Hist. Dist.: Interpreter. **Pubns.:** Contrib., *From Radical Right to Extreme Left* (1974). **Activities:** 1, 5; 15, 17; 72, 80, 87 **Addr.:** 500 Washington Blvd., Oak Park, IL 60302.

Clausen, Nancy M. (O. 7, 1942, Independence, MO) Mgr. Info. Srvs., Tracy-Locke Advert. Inc., 1979–; Mgr., Persnl. Admin., Borg-Warner Corp., 1978–79, Mgr., Info. Srvs., 1971–78; Info. Spec., UARCO Inc., 1969–71. **Educ.:** Univ. of North. IA, 1960–64, BA (LS); Rosary Coll., 1966–68, MLS; Univ. of Chicago, 1975–81, MBA (Mktg.). **Orgs.:** SLA. **Pubns.:** Jt. auth., *R&D on a Minimum Budget* (1979); "Automation in Special Li-

PROFESSIONAL ACTIVITIES: Institutions: 1. Acad. lib.; 2. Arch.; 3. Assn.; 4. Fed./Gvt. lib.; 5. Inst. lib.; 6. Mfr./Suppl.; 7. Milit. lib.; 8. Musm.; 9. Pub. lib.; 10. Sch. lib.; 11. Sch. of lib. sci.; 12. Spec. lib.; 13. State lib.; 14. (other). **Functions/Activities:** 15. Acq./Col. dev.; 16. Adult srvs.; 17. Admin.; 18. Apprais.; 19. Archit./Bldgs.; 20. Cat./Class.; 21. Chld. srvs.; 22. Circ.; 23. Cons./Pres.; 24. Consult.; 25. Cont. ed.; 26. Educ. lib. sci.; 27. Ext. srvs.; 28. Fund/Grants; 29. Gvt. pubs.; 30. Indx./Abs.; 31. Instr. lib. use; 32. Media srvs.; 33. Micro.; 34. Netwks./Coop.; 35. Persnl.; 36. PR; 37. Publshg.; 38. Recs. mgt.; 39. Ref. srvs.; 40. Repro.; 41. Resrch.; 42. Review.; 43. Secur.; 44. Serials; 45. Spec. col.; 46. Tech. srvs.; 47. Trustees/Bds.; 48. YA srvs.; 49. (other).

braries," *IL Libs.* (Spr. 1979); "You Can Use Your R&D Library More Than You Think," *Indus. Resrch. & Dev.* (S. 1979). **Activities:** 12; 17; 51 **Addr.:** Tracy-Locke Co. Inc., Plaza of the Americas, Texas Commerce Bank Tower, Dallas, TX 75201.

Clausman, Gilbert Joseph (N. 8, 1921, Los Angeles, CA) Libn., New York Univ. Med. Ctr., 1955–; Ref. Asst., New York Acad. of Med., 1948–55. **Educ.:** Willamette Univ., 1947, AB; Columbia University, 1948, BS; 1952, MS. **Orgs.:** Med. Lib. Assn.: various com. and offices (1948–79); Bd. of Dir. (1959–63); Exchange Mgr. (1960–62); Pres. (1977–78). Assoc. Med. Sch. of NY and NJ: Lib. Com., Ch., Task Force (1972–73). NY and North. NJ Reg. Med. Lib.: Adv. Com. (1969–73); Subcom. on Direction and Guid. (1972). NY State Lib.: Adv. Com. on Med. Lib. Srv. (1969–72). Amer. Rock Garden Soc. Metropolitan Opera Gld. Amer. Horticultural Soc. New York City Opera Gld. **Honors:** New York Univ. Sch. of Med., Honorary Mem., Alumni Assn., 1969. **Pubns.:** Articles and reviews. **Activities:** 1; 15, 17, 24; 80 **Addr.:** New York University Medical Center Library, 550 First Avenue, New York, NY 10016.

Clay, Debra Jones (O. 18, 1951, Baton Rouge, LA) Tech. Srch. Libn., Getty Oil Co., 1981–; Coord., Hosp. Lib. Dev., Houston Acad. of Med.-TX Med. Ctr. Lib., 1978–81; Libn., St. Dominic-Jackson Meml. Hosp., 1974–78; Coord., Tech. Srvs., Shreve Meml. Lib., 1974. **Educ.:** LA Tech Univ., 1969–72, BS (LS); LA State Univ., 1973–74 MLS. **Orgs.:** Med. LA: South Ctrl. Reg. Grp., Com. to Dev. Core Wkshps. (1980). SLA. ASIS. Houston OLUG. **Activities:** 12; 24, 27, 39; 80, 86, 91 **Addr.:** 15758 Boulder Oaks, Houston, TX 77084.

Clay, Lawrence Edward (O. 8, 1934, Broken Bow, NE) Trustee, Beatrice, NE Pub. Lib., 1971–. **Educ.:** Univ. of NE, 1952–57, BS (Chem. Engin.). **Orgs.:** ALA: Legis. Com. (1979–81). NE LA: Legis. Com. (1978–80). Beatrice Pub. Lib. Fndn.: Trustee (1979–). NE Lib. Trustee Assn.: Pres. (1977–78). Other lib. orgs. and ofcs. Three Rivers Dist. Cornhusker Cncl., Boy Scouts of Amer. Sertoma. Trinity Lutheran Church. Southeast NE Geneal. Socty. **Honors:** NE LA, Trustee Citn., 1980; Cornhusker Council, Boy Scouts of Amer., Silver Beaver, 1975; Three Rivers Dist., Boy Souths of Amer., Dist. Awd. of Merit, 1979; Phillips Petroleum Co., Disting. Cmnty. Srv. Awd., 1975. **Activities:** 9; 47 **Addr.:** 1712 Hoyt, Beatrice, NE 68310.

Clay, Mattie Elrichard (Ja. 12, 1931, Richmond, KY) Lib. Media Spec., Dann C. Byck Elem. Sch., 1972–; Tchr., 1964–72; Tchr., Paul Lawrence Dunbar Elem. Sch., 1961–64. **Educ.:** Fayetteville State Tchrs. Coll., 1952–55, BS (Elem. Educ.); Univ. of KY, 1972–75, MSLS. **Orgs.:** ALA: AASL; Mem.-at-Large/West & Treas. KY AV Assn. KY LA: Bd. of Dirs. & Schol. Ch. KY Sch. Media Assn. Natl. Educ. Assn. KY Educ. Assn.: Sch. Rep. Louisville Educ. Assn. Jefferson Cnty. Tchrs. Assn. **Honors:** KY AV Assn., Class AAA Runner-Up Elem. Media Awd. Cert., 1974; Outstanding Elem. Tchrs. of America, Outstanding T. of Amer. Awd., 1974; Natl. Educ. Assn., Cert. of Prof. Acceptance (1972). **Activities:** 10; 21, 31, 32; 63, 72, 89 **Addr.:** 923 South Western Parkway, Louisville, KY 40211.

Clayborne, Jon L. (Ja. 29, 1948, New York, NY) Asst. Ref. Libn., Jersey City State Coll., 1977–; Ref. Libn., Woodbridge Pub. Lib., 1975–76; Libn., Trenton State Prison Lib., 1973–74; Ref. Libn., Rutgers Univ. Lib., 1972–73. **Educ.:** Bowdoin Coll., 1965–69, BA (Eng.); Rutgers Univ., 1971–72, MLS. **Orgs.:** ALA. Screen Actors Guild. Actors' Equity Assn. **Pubns.:** "Modern Black Drama and the Gay Image," *Coll. Eng.* (N. 1974); "Gay Liberation and Blacks," *Lavender Culture* (19–). **Activities:** 1, 12; 31, 34, 39; 51, 59, 95-Gay Stds. **Addr.:** 315 Tenth Ave., #8, New York, NY 10001.

Claypool, Richard D. (Mr. 11, 1936, Camden, NJ) Musicologist-Resrchr., Moravian Msc. Fndn., 1973–; Lectr. (Fine Arts), Loyola Univ. of Chicago, 1970–72; Libn., Programmer (Classical Msc.), Radio Station WEFM, Chicago, 1969–70. **Educ.:** Univ. of Chicago, 1961–64, BA Msc., Northwest. Univ., 1970–75, PhD (Msc. Hist.). **Orgs.:** Intl. Assn. of Msc. Libs. Msc. LA: PA Chap. (Ch. elect, 1981). Hist. Socty. of PA. Amer. Musicological Socty. Neue Bach-Gesellschaft. **Honors:** Msc. LA, Best article prize, 1978. **Pubns.:** Ed., *Catalog of the Philharmonic Society of Bethlehem Collection* (in press); "Archival Collections of The Moravian Music Foundation and Some Notes on The Philharmonic Society of Bethlehem," *Fontes Artis Musicae* (O.-D. 1976); Several articles in *Moravian Msc. Fndn. Bltn.* **Activities:** 2; 20, 23, 41; 55 **Addr.:** 116 Beth Dr., Lansdale, PA 19446.

Clayton, John Middleton, Jr. (My. 4, 1941, West Grove, PA) Univ. Archvst., Dir., of Recs. Mgt., Univ. of DE, 1969–, Reader Srvs. Libn., 1967–69; HS Tchr., West Grove, PA, 1966–67. **Educ.:** W. Chester State Coll., 1959–63, BS (Msc.); Drexel Univ., 1963–66, MSLS; Univ. of WI, 1969 (Arch. Admin). **Orgs.:** SAA: Coll. and Univ. Arch. (1970–), Subcom. on Theses and Dissertations (1975), Subcom. on Stans. (1978). Mid.-Atl. Reg. Arch. Conf.: Strg. Com. (1978). Assn. of Rec. Mgrs. and Admins.: DE Valley Chap. (Pres., 1978). Jt. Com. on Arch. of Sci. and Tech. (1981–). Presby. Hist. Socty.: Bd. of Dir. (1980). Organ Hist. Socty. **Activities:** 1, 2; 16, 17, 22, 26, 38; 69 **Addr.:** University of Delaware Archives, 78 E. Delaware Ave., Newark, DE 19711.

Clayton, Margaret Diane (My. 4, 1950, Denver, CO) Info. Spec., Soc. Scis., Hamline Univ., 1978–. **Educ.:** Macalester Coll., 1968–73, BA (Hist.); Univ. of WI, 1974–76, MA (S. Asian Stds.), 1977–78, MA (LS); New Delhi, India, 1976–77, Dipl. (Hindi). **Orgs.:** ALA: ACRL. Assn. of Asian Schol. AAUP. **Activities:** 1; 39; 54, 92 **Addr.:** Bush Library, Hamline University, St. Paul, MN 55104.

Clayton, Sheryl A. Howard (My. 17, 1929, Kansas City, MO) Dir., Pub. Lib., E. St. Louis Pub. Lib., 1975–; Ref. Libn., State Cmnty. Coll., 1970–75; Ref. Libn., Washington Univ. Biomed. Lab, 1970; Sch. Libn., Clark Jr. HS, 1963–69. **Educ.:** Prairie View A N & M Coll., 1945–48, BA (Soclgy.); Univ. of IL, 1952–58, MSLS; South. IL Univ., Edwardsville, 1972–76, MS (Couns.); South. IL Univ., Carbondale, 1977–, (Adult Educ.). **Orgs.:** ALA. IL LA. Alpha Kappa Alpha Sorority: Parlmt. (1979–80). Toastmasters Intl. Chld. and Fam. Srvs. of IL: Adv. Com. (1978–). **Honors:** Child Care Assn. of IL, Friend of Chld. Awd., 1976; IL Assn. of Club Women, Cult. Enrichment Awd., 1977. **Pubns.:** Ed., *Who's Who in Central Region of Alpha Kappa Alpha Sorority* (1979); *Guide to Black Churches in Illinois* (1973); "Reassurance, A Key to Adult Education," *Reg. V Adult Educ. Srv. Ctr. Spotlight* (Vol. 4 No. 2). **Activities:** 9; 17, 36; 50, 89 **Addr.:** 405 N. 9th St., East St. Louis, IL 62201.

Cleaver, Betty P. (Camden, NJ) Dir., Edgar Dale Educ. Media Ctr., Coll. of Educ., 1978–; Dir., Instructional Mts. Ctr., Sch. of Educ., Univ. of NC, Chapel Hill, 1969–78. **Educ.:** Hood Coll., 1940–44, AB (Eng.); Univ. of NC, 1967–69, MSLS; Duke Univ., 1972–76, EdD (Cur. Instr.). **Orgs.:** ALA: ACRL (Educ. and Bhvl. Scis. Sect. Com.). AASL. AECT (Div. of Educ. Media Mgt.). **Honors:** Phi Delta Kappa; Beta Phi Mu; Kappa Delta Pi. **Pubns.:** "A Media Faculty Make-over" *Instructional Innovator* (Mr. 1981); Chap., "Listening," in *Questions English Teachers Ask* (1977); Chap., "Media and the English Curriculum," in *English in the 80's* (1980); "Sight and Sound," *Clearinghouse* (1979); "Survey of Values Education," *ERIC* (1974). **Activities:** 5, 10; 17, 26, 32; 63 **Addr.:** Edgar Dale Educational Media Center, The Ohio State University, 260 Ramseyer Hall, 29 W. Woodruff, Columbus, OH 43210.

Cleland, Margaret I. (N. 20, 1920, Passaic, NJ) Proj. Dir.: Info. on Tech./Org. of Amer. States Transfer, 1979–; Exec. Ofcr., CT State Comsn. on Educ. and Info. Uses of Cable Telecom., 1975–76; Dir., Pub. Info. Prog., CT State Lib., 1974–76; Various other positions. **Educ.:** Mount Holyoke, Barnard Coll., 1938–42, BA (Span.); American Univ., 1957–59, (Intl. Rel.). **Orgs.:** ALA: LITA/Leg. and Regulation Com. (1975–77); Cable Telecom. Com. (1975–77). CT LA. Partners for Progress (Conn.–Brazil). Mount Holyoke Club of Hartford, CT. **Honors:** John Cotton Dana Awd., 1975. **Pubns.:** *Public Use of Public Channels: Opportunities in Cable Telecommunications* (1976); *Cable in Connecticut: A Citizens's Manual* (1976); Ed., *Cable Libraries* (1973–77); *Connecticut Cable Clips* (a weekly statewide review) Published by Conn. State Library (1976–77). **Activities:** 13; 17, 36, 41; 54, 78, 93 **Addr.:** 32 Bolton Center Rd., Manchester, CT 06040.

Cleland, Mary Valerie (Ag. 15, 1942, Budapest, Hungary) Adult Srvs. Libn., Ref., Mayfield Reg. Lib., Cuyahoga Cnty. Lib., 1976–; Slide Libn., Seattle Art Musm., 1970–72. **Educ.:** Ohio State Univ., 1961–63; Univ. of WA, 1969–70, BA (Art Hist.), 1972–73, MLS; other courses. **Orgs.:** ALA. ARLIS/OH: *College* Nsltr. Ed. (1980–). **Activities:** 9; 16, 31, 39; 50, 55, 75 **Addr.:** 21203 Hillgrove Ave., Cleveland, OH 44137.

Clem, Harriet M. (N. 8, 1940, Akron, OH) Dir., Rodman Pub. Lib., 1969–, Head of Ext. Dept., 1965–68; Bkmobile Libn., Wasdworth Pub. Lib., 1963–64. **Educ.:** Kent State Univ., 1959–63, BA cum laude, 1964–65, MLS. **Orgs.:** Beta Phi Mu: Natl. Bd. of Dir. (1978–81). OH LA: Legis. Com. (1975–81); Coord. of Div. V (1979–80). Alliance Cham. of Cmrce.: Bd. of Dir. (1977–80). Alliance Red Cross Chap.: Pres. (1975–77). Alliance Y.M.C.A.: Bd. of Dir. (1974–77, 1979–81). Alliance Woman's Club: Pres. (1977–78). **Activities:** 9; 17, 35, 42 **Addr.:** 13484 Louisville St., N.E., Paris, OH 44669.

Clemens, Lindell S. (Ag. 29, 1944, Toledo, OH) Ref. Libn., Toledo-Lucas Cnty. Pub. Lib., 1971–; Tchr., Marcellus Cntrl. Schs., 1968–71; Tchr., Washington Local Schs., 1966–68. **Educ.:** Univ. of Toledo, 1962–66, B of ED (Eng.); Univ. of MI, 1973–74, AMLS. **Orgs.:** ALA: PLA/Info. & Referral Com. (1978–). OH LA: Info. & Referral Task Force (1979–). OH Cncl. of Info. and Referral Providers. Info. and Referral of United Way: Operating Bd. (1976–). AAUW. Leag. of Women Voters of Toledo-Lucas Cnty. Women Involved in Toledo, Inc. **Activities:** 9; 28, 36, 49-I&R; 92 **Addr.:** 6135 South Chanticleer Dr., Maumee, OH 43537.

Clement, Evelyn G. (S. 1, 1926, Springfield, MA) Prof., Ch., Lib. Sci. Dept., Memphis State Univ., 1972–; Lrng. Resrcs. Libn., Oral Roberts Univ., 1966–68; Spec. Instr., Univ. of OK, 1966–70; Bkmobile; Ref., Readers Adv., Tulsa City/Cnty. Lib. Syst., 1960–66. **Educ.:** Univ. of Tulsa, 1961–65, BA (Hist.); Univ. of OK, 1965–66, MLS; IN Univ., 1968–75, PhD (LS). **Orgs.:** ALA: AV Com. Ch. (1974–76); AV Rep., Cat. Code Rev. Com. (1974–76); ISAD, AV Sect., Ch. (1978–79). AALS: Deans and Dir. Cncl.; Nom. Com. (1976–77). SELA: Manpower Com. (1978–). TN LA: Treas. (1975-76); Finance Com., Ch. (1976–77). Other orgs. and coms. AAUP: Pres., MSU Chap. (1976–78); Ch., Com. A, TN Conf. (1978–79). **Honors:** Beta Phi Mu, 1966; Phi Alpha Theta, 1964; Pi Gamma Mu, 1964. **Pubns.:** Jt. ed., *Bibliographic Control of Nonprint Media* (1972); "Standards" in *Nonprint Media in Acad. Librs.* (1975); Guest ed., "Students Look at Library Schools" *Focus on Indiana Libs.* (S. 1970). **Activities:** 1, 11; 17, 26, 39; 57 **Addr.:** 280 Patterson, Memphis, TN 38111.

Clement, Hope E. A. (D. 29, 1930, North Sydney, NS) Assoc. Natl. Libn., Natl. Lib. of Can., 1977–, Dir., Resrch. & Plng. Branch, 1973–77, Asst. Dir., Resrch. & Plng. Br., 1970–73, Chief, Natl. Bibli. Div., 1966–70; Ed., *Canadiana* (1966–69). **Educ.:** Dalhousie Univ., 1948–51, BA (Eng.), 1951–53, MA (Fr.); Univ. of Toronto, 1954–55, BLS. **Orgs.:** Can. LA; Can. Assn. of Info. Sci. **Pubns.:** "Developments toward a National Bibliographic Data Base," *Automation in Libraries* (1974); "The Canadian Union Catalogues: Plans & Developments," *Library Automation in the Nation* (1973); "The Automated Authority File at the National Library of Canada," *IFLA and Institutions Cataloguing* (1980). **Activities:** 4; 17, 34, 46; 56, 57 **Addr.:** National Library of Canada, 395 Wellington Street, Ottawa, ON K1A 0N4, Canada.

Clements, Cynthia Lea (My. 23, 1950, Dallas, TX) Libn., Richland Coll., Dallas, 1974–. **Educ.:** Univ. of Dallas, 1968–72, BA (Hist.); TX Woman's Univ., 1973–74, MLS; Univ. of TX at Dallas, 1976–80, MA (Hum.); Other courses. **Orgs.:** ALA. TX LA: Ed., *TX Lib. Jnl.* (1978–79); Pubn. Com. (1977–79). Phi Alpha Theta. **Activities:** 1; 17, 35, 39 **Addr.:** Richland College, Learning Resource Center, 12800 Abrams Rd., Dallas, TX 75243.

Clemmer, Joel G. (S. 13, 1948, Philadelphia, PA) Chief of Pub. Srvs., Bertrand Lib., Bucknell Univ., 1980–, Head, Ref. Dept., 1979–80, Ref. Libn., 1975–79; Ref. Libn., Susquehanna Univ., 1973–75. **Educ.:** Lehigh Univ., 1966–70, BA (Hist.); Northwestern Univ., 1970–72, MA (Hist.); Univ. of Pittsburgh, 1972–73, MLS. **Orgs.:** APA. PA LA: Int. Frdm. Com. (1975–77); Coll. and Resrch. Lib. Div. (Secy., 1981–); W. Branch Chap. (Vice-Ch./Ch. elect, 1978–79; Ch., 1979–80). Assoc. Coll. Libs. of Ctrl. PA: Treas. (1975–77); Budget Com. (Ch., 1977–). **Activities:** 1; 17, 34, 39 **Addr.:** Ellen Clarke, Bertrand Library, Bucknell Univ., Lewisburg, PA 17837.

Clemons, John E. (Ag. 1, 1928, Sumner, FL) Assoc. Prof. and Asst. Dir., Div. of Libnshp., Emory Univ., 1966–; Univ. Biblgphr., FL State Univ. Lib., 1955–66, Gen. Asst., 1954–55; Educ. and Personal Affairs Office, U.S. Marine Corps, 1952–54; Asst. in Per., FL State Univ. Lib., 1949–52. **Educ.:** FL State Univ. 1947–48, BA (LS), 1948–49, MA (LS). **Orgs.:** AALS: Dir. (1978–81); Jnl. of Educ. for Libnshp. Ed. Srch. Com., Ch. (1979); ALA: Cncl. (1974–78); Plng. and Budget Asm. (1976–78). SELA: Exec. Bd. (1964–66). GA LA: Exec. Bd. (1974–78). Other orgs. and coms. **Honors:** Beta Phi Mu. **Pubns.:** Jt. auth., *Graduate Thesis and Dissertation Handbook* (1965); "Teaching Bibliographic Sources and Styles," *Coll. & Resrch. Libs.* (S. 1956); "Research Activity at the ... Library School," *Southeast. Libn.* (Sum. 1965); "Paradox of Shortages," *FL Libs.* (1971); "Georgia," *ALA Yearbook* (1976–78); Other articles. **Activities:** 11; 17, 24, 26 **Addr.:** Division of Librarianship, Emory University, Atlanta, GA 30322.

Cleveland, Mary Louise Jones (D. 4, 1922, Clarksdale, MS) Assoc. Prof. of Lib. Media, AL A & M Univ., 1977–; Head Libn., Wiley Coll., 1971–77; Asst. Prof. of Lib. Sci., E. TX State Univ., 1972; Asst. Prof. of Lib. Svc., Atlanta Univ., 1966–71; Head Libn., Asst. Prof. of Educ., Talladega Coll., 1965–66; Acqu. Libn., Asst Prof. of Lib. Educ., AL State Univ., 1963–65; Per. Libn., 1957–63. **Educ.:** AL State Univ., 1945–47, BS (Eng.); Case-Western Reserve Univ., 1955–57, MSLS; courses at Indiana Univ., Syracuse Univ., Atlanta Univ., 1968–71, (LS, Educ.); E. TX State Univ., 1972–, (Admin., Higher Educ.). **Orgs.:** ALA: RTSD. AALS: Resrch. (1979–81); Liaison (1977–). AL Instructional Media Assn. AL Educ. Assn. 1979–80). Friends of the Lib., Marshall, TX: Ch., Com. on Community Srvs., (1975–76). TX Assn. of Developing Coll.: Secy. (1975–77). Alpha Kappa Alpha. Natl. Educ. Assn. **Pubns.:** *"The American Indian: a selected bibliography of distinguished titles in the East Texas State University Library," ERIC* (1972); "Using PSI (Personalized System of Instruction) in Teaching the Use of the College Library," *TX Libraries* (1973). **Activities:** 1, 11; 17, 20, 26; 56, 63, 75 **Addr.:** School of Library Media, Alabama A & M University, Normal, AL 35762.

Cleveland, Phyllis L. (D. 12, 1927, Bedford, IN) Libn., Natl. Agr. Lib., 1978–; Media Spec., DC Pub. Sch., 1975–77; Libn., Holy Trinity HS, 1973–75; Libn., DC Public Sch., 1973–73. **Educ.:** IN State Univ., 1945–49, BS (Eng.; Soc. Studies); Cath. Univ. of Amer., 1970–72, MSLS; Courses at Univ. of MO; IN Univ.; Univ. of MD. **Orgs.:** ALA. DC LA. DC Assn. of Sch. Libns.: Exec. bd. (1975–77); ed. of nwsltr., (1976–77); Hospity. Ch. (1975–76). AECT. Other orgs. Woodside Park Civic Assn.: Secy. (1978–). IN Sesquicentennial Com.: Local organiz-

Special Subjects/Services: 50. Adult educ.; 51. Advert./Mktg.; 52. Aerosp.; 53. Agric.; 54. Area std.; 55. Arts/Hum.; 56. Autom.; 57. Bibl./Prtg.; 58. Bio. sci.; 59. Bus./Fin.; 60. Chem.; 61. Copyrt.; 62. Documtn.; 63. Educ.; 64. Engin.; 65. Env.; 66. Eth. grps.; 67. Film; 68. Food/Nutr.; 69. Geneal.; 70. Geo.; 71. Geol.; 72. Handcpd.; 73. Hist.; 74. Int. frdm.; 75. Info. sci.; 76. Insr.; 77. Law; 78. Legis.; 79. Math./Comp. sci.; 80. Med.; 81. Metals; 82. Nat. resrcs.; 83. Newsp.; 84. Nuc. sci.; 85. Oral hist.; 86. Petr./Energy; 87. Pharm.; 88. Phys./Astr./Math.; 89. Readg.; 90. Relig.; 91. Sci./Tech.; 92. Soc. sci.; 93. Telecom.; 94. Transp.; 95. (other).

ing com. (1966). Vincennes Hist. and Antiq. Socty. **Honors:** Beta Phi Mu, 1972; Phi Gamma Mu, 1943. **Activities:** 4, 10; 21, 32, 34; 63, 82, 91 **Addr.:** 1220 Burton St., Silver Spring, MD 20910.

Cleveland, Susan E. (Mr. 14, 1946, Plainfield, NJ) Hosp. Lib. Dir., Univ. of PA, 1974–; Cat. Libn., Univ. of AZ Hlth. Sci. Ctr., 1973–74; Med. Libn., VA Hosp., Hines, IL, 1972; Acq. Libn., Thomas Jefferson Univ., 1970–71. **Educ.:** Douglass Coll., 1964–68, BA (Amer. Std.); Rutgers Univ., 1968–69, MLS; Med. LA Cert., 1971, 1981. **Orgs.:** Med. LA. **Honors:** Chapel of the Four Chaplains, Legion of Honor, 1979. **Activities:** 5; 15, 17, 39; 80 **Addr.:** University of Pennsylvania Hospital, 3400 Spruce St., Philadelphia, PA 19104.

Clevenger, Judy Beth (O. 15, 1950, Maryville, MO) Lib. Dir., Scott-Sebastian Reg. Lib., 1977–; Asst. Dir., Rolling Hills Consolidated Lib., 1975–77, Admin. Asst., 1973–75. **Educ.:** NW MO State Univ., 1968–72, BS (Educ., LS); Univ. of OK, 1972–73, MLS. **Orgs.:** ALA. AR LA: Mem. Ch. (1980). MO LA: PR Ch. (1976). Gvr.'s WHCOLIS: Del. (1979). Bus. and Prof. Women. Daughters of Amer. Revolution. **Activities:** 9; 17, 28, 36; 57, 89 **Addr.:** Scott-Sebastian Regional Library, 18 N. Adair, Box 400, Greenwood, AR 72936.

Cline, Gloria Stark (S. 22, 1936, Eunice, LA) Asst. Dir. for Pub. Srvs., Univ. of Southwest. LA, 1973–; Ref. Libn., 1970–73; Libn., Lafayette Parish Sch. Bd., 1969–70; Ref. Libn., Univ. of TX, 1967–68. **Educ.:** Univ. of Southwest. LA, 1956–60, BA (Educ.); Univ. of TX, 1966–67, MLS; Univ. of South. CA, 1976–79, DLS. **Orgs.:** ALA: ACRL. LA LA. AAUW: Prog. Ch., Intl. Rel. Grp. (1972–74). **Honors:** Kappa Delta Pi, 1958; Phi Kappa Phi, 1959; Beta Phi Mu, 1967; ALA, RASD Com., Outstanding Reference Book, 1974. **Pubns.:** *Index to Criticisms of British and American Poetry* (1973). **Activities:** 1; 17, 22, 39 **Addr.:** Dupre Library, University of Southwestern Louisiana, St. Mary Blvd., Lafayette, LA 70504.

Cline, Helen R. (F. 14, 1932, Hennessey, OK) Managing Ed., Pubshg. Srvs., ALA, 1973–, other editorial positions, 1968–73; Ed. Asst., Colonial Williamsburg, 1965–68; Tchr., OK City Pub. Schs., 1961–63; Tchr., Normandy (MO) Pub. Schs., 1955–61. **Educ.:** OK State Univ., 1950–53, BA (Eng.); Univ. of OK, 1963–65, MLS. **Orgs.:** Amer. Socty. of Indxrs. **Honors:** Univ. of OK Press fellow. **Activities:** 37 **Addr.:** American Library Association, 50 East Huron, Chicago, IL 60611.

Cline, Nancy M. (S. 21, 1946, Chambersburg, PA) Assoc. Libn. & Chief, Bibl. Resrcs. Dept., PA State Univ. Libs., 1970–. **Educ.:** Univ. of CA, Berkeley, 1967, AB (Eng.), 1970, MLS. **Orgs.:** ALA: Ch., Govt. Docum. RT (1976–77, 1977–78). PA LA. Depository Lib. Cncl. to the Pub. Printer: Ch., Micrographics Com. (1976–79). Pub. Printers Micropublishing Cncl.: Ch. (1979–); Vice-Ch. (1978–79). **Pubns.:** Co-ed., *Directory of Government Document Collections & Librarians* (1978); "Librarian's perspective of the GPO & Micropublishing," *Microform Review* (Win. 1979); "Government Documents Roundtable," *ALA Yrbk.* (1979). **Activities:** 1; 29, 33; 56, 75 **Addr.:** Pennsylvania State University Libraries, E506 Pattee Library, University Park, PA 16802.

Clintworth, William A. (Ja. 30, 1949, Seattle, WA) Drug Lit. Spec., Univ. of South. CA, 1977–, Ref. Libn., 1974–77. **Educ.:** Ctrl. WA State Coll., 1967–72, BA (Psy.); Univ. of WA, 1972–74, M.Libr. **Orgs.:** Med. LA. Med. Lib. Grp. of South. CA & AZ: Pub. Rel. Com., Ch.; Schol. Com.; Nsltr. Ed.; Jt. Mtg., Co-Ch. **Pubns.:** "Continuing Education and Library Services for Physicians in Office Practice", *Bltn. of the Med. LA* (O. 1979); "Health Science Libraries Focus on Physicians' Needs", *Los Angeles Cnty. Med. Assn. Bltn.* (N. 1977). **Activities:** 1; 25, 27, 41; 80, 87 **Addr.:** Norris Medical Library, University of Southern California, 2025 Zonal Ave., Los Angeles, CA 90027.

Cloherty, Patrick John, Jr. (My. 7, 1942, Boston, MA) Dir., Salem Pub. Lib., 1971–; Head Libn., N. Reading Pub. Lib., 1967–71. **Educ.:** Boston Coll., 1960–64, AB (Hist.); Simmons Coll., 1968–71, MSLS; Northeastern Univ., 1972–79, MPA (Pub. Admin.); MA Prof. Libn. Cert., 1968; Wayne State Univ., Harvard Univ., Inst. **Orgs.:** MA Bd. of Lib. Comsn.: Com. on Standards (Secy., 1977–79); Adv. Com. on Reg. Srv. Prog. (1970). East. MA Reg. Lib. Syst. Adv. Cncl.: Budget Com. (Ch., 1973–75). Simmons Coll.: Sch. of Lib. Sci. Natl. Fund Drive (Ch., 1972–73). Greater Boston Pub. Lib. Admin.: Pres. (1970–71); Secy. (1969–70). Other coms. Rotary Club of Salem: Dir. (1976–78); VP (1978–80); Pres. (1980–81). Amer. Socty. for Pub. Admin. Intl. City Mgt. Assn. Friends of the Boston Pub. Garden. Other coms. **Activities:** 5, 9; 15, 19, 24 **Addr.:** Salem Public Library, 370 Essex Street, Salem, MA 01970.

Closson, Elizabeth Aldrich (Mr. 14, 1942, Springfield, MA) Asst. in Info. Srvs., Educ. Progs. & Std. Info. Srvs., NY State Lib., 1980–; Sr. Libn., Ref., 1978–80; Asst. Libn., Law Lib., 1976–78, Asst. Libn., Educ. Lib., 1976, Asst. Libn., Gen. Ref. Lib., 1972–75, Asst. Libn., Lib. for the Blind and Visually Handcpd., 1969–72. **Educ.:** Coll. of Our Lady of the Elms, 1960–64, BA (Eng.); SUNY, Albany, 1967–69, MLS. **Orgs.:** Assn. of Law Libs. of Upstate NY: Bd. of Dir. (1977–80), Ch., Nom. Com. (1980-81). AALL: Mem. Com. (1978–80), Local Arrange. Strg. Com. (1978), Autom. and Scientific Dev. Com. (1977–78). Law Lib. Assn. of Greater NY. Capitol Dist. Lib. Cncl.: Comp. Based Ref. Srvs. Com. (1975–). Other orgs. **Activities:** 13; 39, 41; 63, 77, 78 **Addr.:** New York State Library, EP515, Rm. 330 EB, Sciences, Cultural Education Center, Empire State Plaza, Albany, NY Education Department, Albany, NY 12234.

Clotfelter, Cecil F. (Ap. 3, 1929, Anthony, KS) Asst. Dir., Golden Lib., Eastern NM Univ., 1969–; Asst. Dir., Tech. Prep., TX A&M Univ., 1967–69; Asst. Libn. Pub. Srvs., NM Highlands Univ., 1959–67. **Educ.:** OK Baptist Univ., 1947–51, BA (Spa.); OK State Univ., 1953–54, MA (Span.); Univ. of OK, 1958–59, MLS. **Orgs.:** ALA. Southwest. LA. NM LA: Treas., (1979–81). Nat. Rifle Assn. **Pubns.:** *Hunting & Fishing* (1974); Jt. Auth., *Camping & Backpacking* (1979). **Activities:** 1; 15, 17, 46 **Addr.:** Rte. 3, Box 792 A, Portales, NM 88130.

Clotfelter, Elizabeth R. (O. 22, 1917, Bardstown, KY) Head of Mono. Catlgrs., Univ. of KY Libs., 1975–, Mono. Catlgr., 1957–75, State Docum. Libn., 1954–57. **Educ.:** Centre Coll., 1935–39, BA (Hist.); Univ. of KY, 1953, MA (Hist.), 1957, MSLS, other courses. **Orgs.:** ALA. KY LA. OH Valley Reg. Grp. of Tech. Srv. Libns. **Activities:** 1; 20, 25 **Addr.:** University of Kentucky Libraries, Lexington, KY 40506.

Clotfelter, Mary Long (Noble, OK) Asst. Libn., Portales Pub. Lib., 1979–; Instr., Lib. Sci., East. NM Univ., 1969–; Lib. Prcs. Ctr., Bryan Pub. Schs., 1968–69; Dir., Carnegie Pub. Lib., 1962–67; Asst. Libn., Instr., LS, OK Bapt. Univ., 1947–59. **Educ.:** Univ. of OK, 1946, BA, 1947, BALS; various crs. **Orgs.:** SWLA: Exec. Secy. (1973). NM LA. Alpha Beta Alpha: Sponsor (1976–). Portales Gem and Mineral Socty. East. NM Univ. Fac. Dames. La Escalera Art Gld. **Honors:** Phi Delta Kappa. **Pubns.:** Jt. Auth., *Camping and Backpacking* (1979). **Activities:** 9; 20, 39 **Addr.:** Rte. 3, Box 792, Portales, NM 88130.

Clough, Elaine B. (Jl. 2, 1921, Green Bay, WI) Bus. Resrch. Libn., Ventura Cnty. Lib. Srvs. Agency, 1970–; Bus. Libn., MBA Prog., CA Lutheran Coll., 1978–; Branch Libn., Conejo Library, Ventura Cnty., 1967–70; Resrch. Libn., Turck, Hill & Co., NYC, 1944–48. **Educ.:** Univ. of WI, Madison, 1939–43, BA (Comp. Lit.); Simmons Coll., 1943–44, BLS. **Orgs.:** SLA: NY Chap., Secty. (1946–48). ALA. CA LA. SCORE/ACE Couns. Prog., SBA (1974–). Total Interlibrary Exch.: Adv. Bd. (1974–75; 1979–81). Conejo Future Fndn.: Task Force on Educ. (1976–77). AAUW. Conejo Symphony Guild. WI Alumni Assn. Other orgs. **Honors:** U.S. Small Bus. Admin., "Special ACE Award" 1976; U.S. SBA and SCORE, "Cert. of Appreciation," 1977; Ventura Reg. Criminal Justice Plng. Bd., "Commendation for Pursuit of Excellence in Resrch.," 1977. **Activities:** 1, 9; 16, 39, 41; 59 **Addr.:** 1324 Buckingham Drive Thousand Oaks, CA 91360.

Clough, M. Evalyn (Jl. 10, 1930, Kansas City, MO) Asst. to the Dean, Sch. of Lib. and Info. Sci., Univ. of Pittsburgh, 1977–; Visit. Lectr., 1975–77; Actg. Exec. Dir., Pittsburgh Reg. Lib. Ctr., 1975–75; Chief Libn., PPG Industries, Inc., 1964–75; Sr. Tech. Libn., Republic Aviation Corp., 1958–64; 1st Asst., Cat. Dept., New York Acad. of Med., 1956–58; Catlgr., Med. Library, Columbia Univ., 1954–56. **Educ.:** Univ. of KS, 1947–50; Univ. of CA at Los Angeles, 1950–52, BA (Msc.); Columbia Univ., 1954–56, MS (LS); Univ. of Pittsburgh, Grad. Sch. of Lib. & Info. Sci., 1965–67, Cert. of Adv. Studies. **Orgs.:** ALA. SLA. AALS. ASIS. Phi Delta Gamma. Sigma Alpha Iota. Pittsburgh Savoyards. **Honors:** Beta Phi Mu. **Activities:** 11, 12; 17, 26, 44; 64, 81, 91 **Addr.:** School of Library and Information Science, University of Pittsburgh, 510 L15 Building, 135 No. Bellefield Ave., Pittsburgh, PA 15230.

Clouse, R. Wilburn (My. 13, 1937, Manchester, TN) Assoc. Prof. of Educ. and LS & Info. Sci., John F. Kennedy Ctr. for Rsch., Asst. Dir. for Admin., George Peabody Coll., 1969–; Actg. Dir., Comp. Ctr., Actg. Ch., Dept. of Comp. Sci., Columbia State Cmnty. Coll., 1967–69; Chem., E. I. DuPont Co., 1963–67; Resrch. Asst., Vanderbilt Univ. Sch. of Med., 1959–63. **Educ.:** David Lipscomb Coll., 1959, BA (Chem.); Univ. of TN, 1960–63, (Econ.); Middle TN State Univ., 1968, MA (Econ.); George Peabody Coll., 1977, PhD (Educ. Admin.). **Orgs.:** ALA. ASIS. TN LA: Bd. of Dirs. (1978–79). SELA. Other orgs. Alpha Kappa Psi. Socty. of Resrch. Admins. Assn. of Small Comp. Users in Educ. Amer. Assn. on Mental Deficiency. **Pubns.:** *The Expected Role of Beginning Librarians: A Comparative Analysis from Administrators, Educators, and Young Professionals* (1979); "Legal ramifications of computerized library networks and their implications for the library director," *Southeast. Libn.* (Fall 1979); Ed., *Administrators as Educators: Procs. of a National Conference for Administrators of University Affiliated Facilities,* (1976); Jt. ed., *Education of health service administrators in an interdisciplinary model* (1975); "A comparison of a manual library reclassification project with a computer automated library reclassification project," *ERIC* (1975); other articles. **Activities:** 11; 24, 26, 41; 56, 63, 75 **Addr.:** George Peabody College, Vanderbilt University, Nashville, TN 37203.

Cloutier, Guy (O. 2, 1944, Plessisville, PQ) Dir., Libs., Univ. of Sherbrooke, 1976–, Head, Main Lib., 1972–76, Ref. Libn., 1970–72, Asst. Libn., 1967–68. **Educ.:** Univ. of Sherbrooke, 1960–64, BA, 1964–67, Licn. es lettres (Lit.); Univ. of West. ON, 1968–69, MLS. **Orgs.:** CARL: Secy./Treas. (1978–79). ASTED: Pres. (1979–). PQ Ord. of Nurses: Bd. (1979–81), Exec. Com. (1979–81). **Addr.:** 422 rue Québec, Sherbrooke, PQ J1H 3L8 Canada.

Clow, Faye E. (N. 29, 1943, Berlin, WI) Dir., Bettendort Pub. Lib. and Info. Ctr., 1978–; Asst. Dir., Moline Pub. Lib., 1976–78, Fine Arts Libn., 1967–76; Catlgr./Ref. Libn., Fed. Rsv. Bank of Chicago, 1966–67. **Educ.:** Univ. of WI, Oshkosh, 1961–65, BA (Eng.) Univ. of WI, 1965–66, MLS. **Orgs.:** ALA. IA LA. ILLOWA LA. Quad City-Scott Cnty. Film Coop. Various ofcs. Playcrafters Barn Thea. Quad City Arts Cncl. Bettendorf Cham. of Cmrce. **Pubns.:** "Art Reproductions to Go," *Reg. RAG* (F.–Mr. 1981). **Activities:** 9; 17, 36; 55 **Addr.:** Bettendorf Public Library and Information Center, 2950-18th St., Bettendorf, IA 52722.

Cluff, E. Dale (Ap. 15, 1937, El Segundo, CA) Dir. of Lib. Srvs., South. IL Univ. at Carbondale, 1980–; Asst. Dir. for IIS, Univ. of UT, 1979–80, Head Info. & Instr. Srv., 1977–79, Head Media Srv. Dept., 1974–77, Head Mono. Order Dept., 1971–74. **Educ.:** Univ. of UT, 1961–67, BA (Eng.); Univ. of WA, 1967–68, MLib; Univ. of UT, 1971–76, PhD (Educ. Admin.). **Orgs.:** ALA: Ch., Reproduction of Lib. Mat. Sect. (1978/79); Micropublishing Com. (1976/80). UT LA: Pres. (1977/78). **Honors:** Phi Delta Kappa, 1977; Beta Phi Mu, 1969; UT LA, Disting. Srv. Awd. for Libnshp. in Higher Educ., 1979. **Pubns.:** "Developments in Copyright, Micrographics, and Graphic Communications, 1978", *Lib. Resrc. & Tech. Srvs.* (Sum. 1979); "Developments in Copyright, Micrographics, & Graphic Comm. 1977", *Lib. Resrc. & Tech. Srvs.* (Sum. 1978). **Activities:** 1; 17 **Addr.:** Director of Library Services, Southern Illinois University at Carbondale, Carbondale, IL 62901.

Clum, Audna T. (F. 14, 1913, Troy, NY) Libn., St. Mary's Hosp., 1963–; Libn., Averill Park HS, 1938–. **Educ.:** NY State Coll., Albany, 1934, BS in LS, 1940, MS (Educ.). **Orgs.:** ALA. NY LA. Albany Area Hlth. Libns. Hudson-Mohawk Lib. Assn. NY Tchrs.; Rensselaer Cnty. Hist. Assn. **Honors:** Delta Kappa Gamma, 1965. **Activities:** 10, 12; 22 **Addr.:** 554 Third Av., Troy, NY 12182.

Clune, John Richard (N. 22, 1933, Bronxville, NY) Chief Libn., Assoc. Prof., Kingsborough Comnty. Coll., 1979–, Actg. Chief Libn., 1977–79, Deputy Chief Libn., 1972–77, Actg. Chief Libn., 1971–72, Reader Srvs. Libn., 1966–71. **Educ.:** St. Joseph's Semy., Cathedral Coll., 1952–56, BA (Phil.); Pratt Inst., 1964–66, MLS; Long Island Univ., 1967–71, (Eng.). **Orgs.:** LA of City Univ. of NY: Pres. (1973/74); VP (1971/72); Pratt Grad. Lib. Sch. Alum. Assn. **Honors:** Beta Phi Mu. **Pubns.:** "Print and Non-Print Media; a Trial Separation," *LACUNY Jnl.* (Spr. 1975); "Local Round Tables for Fast Action," *Wilson Lib. Bltn.* (My. 1969). **Activities:** 1, 9; 16, 17, 39; 55, 90 **Addr.:** Kingsborough Community College, 2001 Oriental Blvd. (Manhattan Beach), Brooklyn, NY 11235.

Clyde, Walter Eric (Penicuik, Midlothian, Scotland) Proj. Ofcr., Can. Inst. Sci. and Tech. Info., 1980–, Head, Tech. Srvs., 1971–80, Head, Cat. Dept., 1964–71, Head, Appld. Phys. Branch, Natl. Sci. Lib., 1961–64; various positions, Natl. Resrch. Cncl. Lib., 1958–61. **Educ.:** Univ. of Edinburgh, 1948–52, BSc (Math.); Univ. of Toronto, 1957–58, BLS. **Orgs.:** Can. Assn. Info. Sci.: Pres. (1978–79), various Ofcs. Intl. Org. for Stans.: ISO/TC46/SC6 (Secy., 1977–). **Pubns.:** "Dobis: The Canadian Government Version," *Can. Lib. Jnl.* (Ag. 1979). **Activities:** 4; 17, 24; 75, 91, 93 **Addr.:** Canada Institute for Scientific & Technical Information, Montreal Rd., Ottawa, ON K1A 0S2 Canada.

Cnota, Mitchell M. (Ja. 1, 1932, Chicago, IL) Sr. Libn., CA Dept. of Justice, 1968–; Libn., CA State Lib., 1966–68. **Educ.:** Univ. of CA, Santa Barbara, 1956–58, AB (Hist.); Univ. of South. CA, 1966, MS (LS); AALL, 1974, Cert. **Orgs.:** AALL. CA LA. Intl. Assn. of Law Libs. **Activities:** 13; 77 **Addr.:** California Dept. of Justice, Office of the Attorney General Law Library, 555 Capitol Mall, Rm. 482, Sacramento, CA 95814.

Coan, La Verne Z. (Ap. 30, 1954, New Castle, PA) Computer Docum. Spec., Tetra Tech Services, Inc., 1980–; Docum. Control Spec., REMAC Info. Corp., 1978–80; Info. Anal., Franklin Inst. Resrch. Labs., 1977–78; Resrch. Asst., Univ. of MD, 1976–77. **Educ.:** Univ. of DE, 1971–75, BA (Bio.Sci.); Univ. of MD, 1976–77, MLS; Cert. of Med. Libnshp., 1977. **Orgs.:** ALA: Ref. Srcs. Com. (1979–81). Med. LA. Polish Falcons of America; Polish Nat. Alliance. **Honors:** Outstanding Young Woman of America, 1979. Beta Phi Mu, 1978. Phi Kappa Phi, 1978. **Pubns.:** *Dun & Bradstreet Exporters' Encyclopaedia,* (1980); *Federal Scientific and Technical Communication Activities–1976,* (1977). **Activities:** 12; 30, 37, 39; 56, 57, 58 **Addr.:** Tetra Tech Services, Inc., c/o Navy Tactical Support Activity, P.O. Box 1042, Silver Springs, MD 20910.

Coates, Ann S. (My. 4, 1937, Louisville, KY) Cur. of Slides, Art Histn., Univ. of Louisville, 1964–; Art Histn., Louisville Sch. of Art, 1969; KY South. Coll., 1966. **Educ.:** U of Louisville, 1963, BA (Eng.), 1969, MA (Art Hist.). **Orgs.:** Art Libs. Socty.: N. Amer. Chap., Visual Resrcs. Com.; KY/TN Chap. Coll. Art

PROFESSIONAL ACTIVITIES: Institutions: 1. Acad. lib.; 2. Arch.; 3. Assn.; 4. Fed./Gvt. lib.; 5. Inst. lib.; 6. Mfr./Suppl.; 7. Milit. lib.; 8. Musm.; 9. Pub. lib.; 10. Sch. lib.; 11. Sch. of lib. sci.; 12. Spec. lib.; 13. State lib.; 14. (other). **Functions/Activities:** 15. Acq./Col. dev.; 16. Adult srvs.; 17. Admin.; 18. Apprais.; 19. Archit./Bldgs.; 20. Cat./Class.; 21. Chld. srvs.; 22. Circ.; 23. Cons./Pres.; 24. Consult.; 25. Cont. ed.; 26. Educ. lib. sci.; 27. Ext. srvs.; 28. Fund/Grants; 29. Gvt. pubs.; 30. Indx./Abs.; 31. Instr. lib. use; 32. Media srvs.; 33. Micro.; 34. Netwks./Coop.; 35. Persnl.; 36. PR; 37. Publshg.; 38. Recs. mgt.; 39. Ref. srvs.; 40. Repro.; 41. Resrch.; 42. Review.; 43. Secur.; 44. Serials; 45. Spec. col.; 46. Tech. srvs.; 47. Trustees/Bds.; 48. YA srvs.; 49. (other).

Assn.: Visual Resrcs. Com.: Co-Ch. (1973). Socty. of Archit. Hist. **Pubns.:** Slide Catalog, Univ. of Louisville. **Activities:** 15, 17, 20; 55 **Addr.:** 1819 Woodbourne, Louisville, KY 40205.

Coates, Paul F. (Je. 17, 1934, Louisville, KY) Gvt. Archvst., Jefferson Cnty. Gvt. Fiscal Ct., 1972–; Fed. Prog. Data Spec., 1971–72; Partner, Syst. Anal., 1969–71; Admin. Anal., KY State Gvt. Dept. of Corrections, 1967–68. **Educ.:** Univ. of Louisville, 1952–56, AB (Human.), 1962–65, (Psych.), 1968–69, (Cmnty. Dev.). **Orgs.:** KY Cncl. on Arch.: Dir., Ch. Com. on Arch. Lib. Theft (1979–80). SAA: Micro. (1978). Assn. of Records Mgrs. & Admin., Inc. National & KY Micro. Assn. Filson Club. Speed Musm. **Honors:** Gov. Pre-White House Conf. on Lib. & Info. Srvs., Disting. Srvc., 1979. **Pubns.:** *Task Force Report on Archives & Records* (1978). **Activities:** 2; 23, 38, 45; 56, 69, 75, 92 **Addr.:** Archives and Records Service, Jefferson County Government, Louisville, KY 40202.

Coatsworth, Patricia A. (Ap. 19, 1940, Coleman, MI) Head Libn., Charles E. Merriam Ctr. for Pub. Admin., 1975–; Dir. Info. Ctr., Natl. Cncl. of Sci. and Tech., Mex., 1974–75; Consult., Natl. Inst. of Anthro. and Hist., Mex., 1974; Docum. Libn., Univ. of Chicago, 1970–73. **Educ.:** Univ. of WI, 1964–66, BA (Hist.), 1967–69, MA (LS). **Orgs.:** Cncl. of Plng. Libns.: Pres. (1980–81). ALA: Intl. Docum. Task Frc. (Secy., 1972–73). **Pubns.:** Ed., *Women and Urban Planning: A Bibliography* (1981) "Lista de Encabezamientos de materia e información general sobre la Biblioteca," *Cuadernos de la Biblioteca "Manuel Orozco y Berra"* (Jl. 1974); "El papel del Bibliotecario en los Estados Unidos: Su Posición Professional y sus intereses," *Archivos y Bibliotecas* (1974); "Selected Reference Resources in Urban Research," *Proceedings of the Council of Planning Librarians* (1976); jt. auth., "Urban Affairs," *Update 76: Selected Recent Works in the Social Sciences* (1976); "Sources of Information for Public Works and Utilities," in *Municipal Year Books: 1978, 1979, 1980, 1981, 1982.* **Activities:** 1, 12; 17, 24, 29; 92 **Addr.:** 5307 S. University Ave., Chicago, IL 60615.

Cobb, David A. (S. 25, 1945, Rutland, VT) Map & Geo. Libn., Univ. of IL, 1973–; Geo. & Map Libn., IN Univ., 1970–73; Map Libn., Univ. of VT, 1967–70. **Educ.:** Univ. of VT, 1968, BA (Hist.), 1968–70, MA (Geo.); IN Univ., 1971–73, MLS. **Orgs.:** ALA: Ch., Map & Geo. RT. SLA: Archvst., Geo. & Map Div. West. Assn. of Map Libs. **Pubns.:** "The Politics and economics of map librarianship," S.L.A. Geog. & Map Div., *Bltn.* (S. 1979); "Maps and Scholars," *Lib. Trends* (Spr. 1977). **Activities:** 1, 12; 15, 20, 45; 70, 92 **Addr.:** Map and Geography Library, University of Illinois, Urbana, IL 61801.

Cobb, E. Lafaye (Mr. 10, 1944, Columbus, GA) Head, Bartlett Branch, Memphis/Shelby Cnty. Pub. Lib., 1979–; Libn. II, Shelby State Cmnty. Coll., 1977–79; Head, Micro. Dept., Memphis State Univ., 1976–77; Asst. Serials Libn., W. GA Coll., 1968–76; Hum./Cat. Libn., Univ. of GA, 1966–68. **Educ.:** FL State Univ., 1963–65, BA (Eng.), 1965–66, MA (LS), W. GA Lib., 1972–76 (Eng.). **Orgs.:** ALA: RASD, Ad Hoc Com. on Goals (1978–); GODORT, Fed. Docum. Task Frc. (1976–77); JMRT, *Cognotes* Com. (1976–77). SELA. TN LA: JMRT (Ch., 1978–). **Honors:** ALA, 3M/JMRT Prof. Dev. Grant, 1976. **Activities:** 9; 16, 17, 44; 61, 85 **Addr.:** Bartlett Branch Library, 6382 Stage Rd., Memphis, TN 38134.

Cobb, Mary Louise (Mr. 16, 1937, Rose Hill, NC) Coord., Pub. Srvs., ME State Lib., 1980–; Deputy Law Libn., ME State Law and Legis., Ref. Lib., 1978–80; Head, Cat. Dept., Coll. of William and Mary, 1968–77; Ref. Libn., Grinnell Coll. Lib., 1966–67. **Educ.:** Wake Forest Univ., 1955–59, BA (Latin, Eng.); George Peabody Coll., 1964–65, MLS. **Orgs.:** ALA: Cncl. (1972–74); Assn. of Amer. Publshrs. Jt. Com. on Readg. Dev. (1972–73); SAA Jt. Com. (1970–72); ACRL, Exec. Bd. (1976–78)/Coll. Libs. Sect. (Ch., 1977–78), various ofcs.; RTSD, Lib. Admin. Div.; JMRT, various ofcs. Potomac Tech. Prcs. Libns. ME LA. Various other orgs., ofcs. Twentieth Cent. Gallery, Williamsburg, VA: Bd. of Dirs. **Honors:** Beta Phi Mu; Eta Sigma Phi; Mortar Bd. **Activities:** 1, 13; 17, 20, 29 **Addr.:** Maine State Library, LMA Bldg., Station #64, Augusta, ME 04333.

Cobb, Parris Gerald (Ap. 18, 1942, Gilmer, TX) Multi-Image Prod., Arlington Pub. Lib., 1974–; Ref. Libn., Shreve Mem. Lib., 1971–72; Prod. of Educ. Mat., UT State Lib., 1965–70; Asst. Fine Arts Libn., Salt Lake Pub. Lib., 1964–65. **Educ.:** Univ. of TX, Arlington, 1974–76, BA (Phil.); N. TX State Univ., 1976–77, MLS. **Orgs.:** TX LA: Local Arrange.-A/V Ch. (1979–80). Southwest LA. ALA. Assn. for Multi-Image: Dallas-Fort Worth Chap. (VP, 1980). **Pubns.:** Various multi-image prod. **Activities:** 9; 32, 36; 51, 55, 93 **Addr.:** 2707 Augusta Ln., Arlington, TX 76012.

Coberly, Jean A. (Je. 25, 1942, Elkins, WV) Head, Hist. Dept., Seattle Pub. Lib., 1976–, Natl. Endow. for Hum., Proj. Dir., 1978–81; Head, Ref. Dept., Univ. of Houston, 1973–76; Head, Hum. Dept., Ft. Lauderdale Pub. Lib., 1970–73. **Educ.:** Stetson Univ., 1965, BA (Eng.); Univ. of Houston, 1974, MA (Hist.); Emory Univ., 1968, MLA; Univ. of WA, 1981– (Hist.). **Orgs.:** ALA: RASD/Machine-Assisted Ref. Sect., Nom. Com. (Ch., 1979);/Hist. Sect., Lcl. Hist. Com. (1976–78). Assn. Amer. Histns. Assn. of State and Lcl. Hist. **Honors:** Univ. of Houston Resrch. Grant, 1976; Natl. Endow. for the Hum. Grant, 1979, U.S. Dept. of Educ., 1980. **Pubns.:** "Management Concern," *Online Bibl. Srvs.* (1977); "Guidelines for the Allocation of Library Materials Budgets," *Col. Dev. Guidelines* (1979). **Activities:** 1, 9; 16, 28, 41; 55, 66, 86 **Addr.:** Seattle Public Library, 1000 4th Ave., Seattle, WA 98104.

Coble, Gerald M. (S. 11, 1926, Prior, MO) Head, Naval Gen. Lib. Srvcs., U.S. Navy & Marine Corps, 1966–; Machine Applications Libn., Vets. Admin., 1963–66; Dir., Sch. of Lib. Sci., Univ. of OK, 1959–63; Asst. Dir. (Public Services), Univ. of OK Libs., 1958–59; Lib. Adv., Univ. of Peshawar, Pakistan, 1955–57. **Educ.:** Univ. of CO, 1947–51, BA (Eng.); Univ. of Denver, 1951–52, MSLS; Univ. of Chicago, 1957–58, (Lib. Sci.). **Orgs.:** ALA. SLA. FL LA. Southeast. LA. Freedom to Read Fndn. **Activities:** 4; 15, 17; 50, 56, 74 **Addr.:** 311 S. Sunset, Gulf Breeze, FL 32561.

Coburn, Louis (Ag. 13, 1915, New York, NY) Assoc. Prof., Sch. of Lib. and Info. Studies, Queens Coll., 1974–79; Asst. Prof., 1963–73; Libn. in charge, Jamaica HS, 1956–63; Libn.-in-Charge, Gompers HS, 1938–56. **Educ.:** City College, New York, 1932–36, BA (Eng.); Columbia Univ., 1936–37, MLS; Coll. of the City of New York, 1937–41, MS (Educ.); New York Univ., 1951–61, EdD (Admin.). **Orgs.:** ALA. NY City Sch. Libn. Assn. NY LA. NY Lib. Club. AAUP. New York Univ. Alumni Assn. **Honors:** City College, Library Fellow, 1937. **Pubns.:** *Classroom and Field: Internships in American Library Education* (1980); *Library Media Center Problems: Case Studies* (1973); *Case Studies in School Library Administration* (1968). **Activities:** 10, 11; 17, 26, 48; 63, 74 **Addr.:** 137-01 63rd Avenue, Flushing, NY 11367.

Cochrane, MaryJane S. (Mr. 14, 1950, Rochester, NY) Head, Comp. Assisted Resrch. Srv., Univ. of MD, 1979–; Info. Srvs. Libn., Nat. Acad. of Sci., 1977–79; Libn./Tech. Info. Spec., Capitol Syst. Grp. Inc., 1975–77. **Educ.:** Syracuse Univ., 1968–72, BA (Hist.); Univ. of MD, 1974–75, MLS; Cert. of Med. Libnshp., 1976–80. **Orgs.:** ALA. SLA. ASIS. **Honors:** Beta Phi Mu; Phi Alpha Theta **Pubns.:** "The Environment of Creativity," *Knowledge and Its Organization.*; "The Use of OnLine Databases at the Reference Desk," *National OnLine Meeting* (Mr. 1981). **Activities:** 1, 12; 17, 39; 56, 75, 93 **Addr.:** McKeldin Library–Reference, University of Maryland, College Park, MD 20742.

Cochrane, Pauline A. (D. 2, 1929, Berwyn, IL) Prof., Syracuse Univ., 1966–; Assoc. Dir., Amer. Inst. of Phys., 1961–66; Assoc. Prof., Chicago Tchrs. Coll., 1957–61; Cross Ref. Ed., World Bk. Encyc., 1957–59. **Educ.:** Illinois Coll., 1949–51, BA, (Soc. Sci.); Rosary Coll., 1951–54, MA, (LS); Univ. of Chicago, 1957–61. **Orgs.:** ASIS: Pres. (1970), Treas. (1965); ALA: Cncl.; ACRL/Bd. **Honors:** Phi Beta Kappa, 1951; Sarada Ranganathan Endowment Lect. Series, 1970; SLA, John Cotton Dana Lect., 1972. **Pubns.:** *Basics of Online Searching* (1981); *Librarians and Online Services* (1977); *Handbook of Information Systems and Services* (1975); *Putting Knowledge to Work* (1972); Numerous articles; "Books are For Use", Videotape (1978). **Activities:** 11; 24, 26, 30, 41; 56, 92 **Addr.:** Syracuse University, School of Info. Studies, 113 Euclid Ave., Syracuse, NY 13210.

Cockburn, Marjorie M. T. (Ap. 10, 1931, Fredericton, NB) VP, N.B. Lib. Trustees Assn., 1980–. **Educ.:** Univ. of NB, 1948–52, BA (Entomology). **Orgs.:** St. John Reg. Lib. Bd.: Fin. Ch. (1980); Plng. and Dev. Com. (1974–79). Can. Lib. Trustees Assn.: NB Rep. (1980). Univ. of NB Bd. of Gvrs.: Vice-Ch. (1980–); Exec. Com. (1977); various ofcs. Assoc. Alum. Univ. NB: Pres. (1980). **Honors:** St. Croix Pub. Lib., Commemorative Plaque, 1976. **Activities:** 9; 47 **Addr.:** 40 Hawthorne St., St. Stephen, NB E3L 1W6 Canada.

Cockhill, Brian Edward (Ag. 13, 1942, Devils Lake, ND) Asst. Dir., MT Hist. Socty., 1981–; State Archvst., 1977–81; Archvst., 1973–77; Asst. Archvst., 1971–73; Univ. Archvst., Univ. of MT, 1970–71. **Educ.:** MT Sch. of Mines, Univ. of MT, 1963–64, BA (Hist.), 1966–70, MA (Amer. Hist.). **Orgs.:** SAA. Northwest Archvsts. Cncl. to Preserve MT Hist. **Pubns.:** Jt. Ed. *F. Jay Haynes, Photographer* (1981); jt. Ed., *Not in Precious Metals Alone:* (1976); jt. Ed., *Guide to Manuscripts in Montana Repositories,* (1973); "The Quest of Warren Gillette," *MT, the Mag. of West. Hist.* (1972). **Activities:** 2; 17, 36, 45; 55 **Addr.:** 232 Greenwood Dr., Helena, MT 59601.

Cockrum, Frances E. (Ja. 1, 1945, Boise, ID) Libn., Med. Sch., Univ. of ND, 1975–. **Educ.:** Univ. of OR, and Portland State Univ., 1963–68, BS (Anthro.); Univ. of OR, 1973–74, MLS; Med. LA., Cert., 1978. **Orgs.:** Med. LA. Midwest Hlth. Sci. Lib. Ntwk: Medline Users Grp. Com. (1979); Rep., Cncl. of Hlth. Sci. Libs (1977–). ND LA: Hlth. Sci. Info. Sect. (Exec. Bd., 1976–78); Cont. Ed. Com. (Ch. 1978–79). Girl Scouts: Camp Com. (1979). Natl. Ski Patrol Syst. **Activities:** 12; 17, 27, 39; 80 **Addr.:** Angus L. Cameron Medical Library, Trinity Professional Building, Minot, ND 58701.

Cocks, Anna R. (Jl. 18, 1918, Moscow, MI) Sr. Libn. Tech. Srvs., Miles Lab., Inc., 1957–, Sr. Libn. and Actg. Mgr., 1979; Librarian Lincoln School Library Pub. Lib., Kalmazoo, MI, 1942–43; Asst. Libn., Agr. Lib., Penn State Univ., 1941–42. **Educ.:** Western MI Univ., 1935–40, BA (Chem.); George Peabody Coll. for Tchrs., 1940–41, BLS. **Orgs.:** Med. LA: Midwest Reg. Grp. SLA: IL and IN Chaps. ALA. ASIS. Amer. Assn. for the Adv. of Sci. AAUW; Zonta International. **Honors:** Phi Sigma Alpha. **Pubns.:** Cont. Ed., COPNIP List, *SLA* (1958–71). **Activities:** 12; 15, 20, 46; 59, 87, 91 **Addr.:** 1622 Victoria Dr., Elkhart, IN 46514.

Cocks, J. Fraser, III (Jl. 15, 1941, Detroit, MI) Cur., Spec. Co. & Asst. Prof., Hist., Colby Coll., 1975–; Asst. Dir., MI Hist. Col., 1971–74. **Educ.:** Occidental Coll., 1959–63, BA (Hist.); Univ. of MI, 1963–75, PhD (Amer. Stud.). **Orgs.:** New England Archvsts.: Treas. (1979–80). New England Doc. Cons. Ctr.: Bd. of Adv. (1979–81). SAA: Brd. of Security Adv. (1977–). New England Com. for Ir. Std. New England Amer. Std. Assn. **Honors:** Phi Beta Kappa, 1962; Woodrow Wilson Flshp., 1963. **Pubns.:** Ed., *Pictorial History of Ann Arbor* (1974); Jt. Comp., *James Augustine Healy Collection of 19th & 20th Century Irish Literature* (1978). **Activities:** 1; 15, 18, 45; 54, 66, 74 **Addr.:** Curator, Special Collections, Colby College, Waterville, ME 04901.

Coco, Alfred Joseph (F. 28, 1933, Moreauville, LA) Prof. of Law, Libnshp. & Law Libn., Univ. of Denver Coll. of Law, 1972–; Prof. of Law & Law Libn., Univ. of Houston, 1971–72, Assoc. Prof. of Law & Law Libn., 1970–71; Asst. Prof. of Law & Law Lib. Admin., St. Mary's Univ. Sch. of Law, 1962–66. **Educ.:** Univ. of TX, 1957, BA (Psy.); St. Mary's Univ. Sch. of Law, 1960, JD; Univ. of WA, 1962, MLL (LS). **Orgs.:** AALL: Southwest. Chap. (Pres. 1965); Exhibits Com., Pubcty. Com. (Ch., 1969–70); Placement Com. (Ch., 1974–75); VP, Pres-Elect (1976–77); Pres. (1977–78); Exec. Bd. (1978–79). Amer. Bar Assn. CO Bar Assn. Denver Bar Assn. Assn. of Amer. Law Schs. **Pubns.:** Jt. auth., *The Impact of the Environmental Sciences and the New Biology on Law Libraries* (1973); "Books for the Texas Lawyer," *12 Barrister's News 2* (1963); "The Proper Care of Law Books," *11 Barrister's News 3* (1963); TV scripts. **Activities:** 11, 14-Law Library; 17, 24; 77 **Addr.:** University of Denver College of Law Library, 200 West 14th Ave., Denver, CO 80204.

Cocozzoli, Gary R. (O. 27, 1951, Detroit, MI) Acting Dir., Lawrence Inst. of Tech., 1975–. **Educ.:** Wayne State Univ., 1969–73, BA (Geo.), 1973–74, MSLS. **Orgs.:** MI LA: JMRT (Secy.-Treas., 1978–79); Bd. (1977–78, 1979–80). Wayne State Univ. LS Alum. Assn.: Bd. (1978–79), VP (1979–81), Pres. (1981–83). **Pubns.:** Jt. auth., *German-American History and Life: A Guide to Information Sources* (1980). **Activities:** 1; 34, 39, 44 **Addr.:** Library, Lawrence Institute of Technology, 21000 W. Ten Mile Rd., Southfield, MI 48075.

Coe, D. Whitney (Mr. 23, 1937, Oswego, NY) Team Leader, Hum. Team, Princeton Univ. Lib. 1979–, Prin. Catlgr., 1977–79, Head, Descr. Cat. Sect. 1968–77, Russ. Catlgr., 1967–68. **Educ.:** Syracuse Univ., 1955–59, BA (Intl. Rel., Russ.); Univ. of CA, Berkeley, 1959–61, MA (Russ. Hist.); Syracuse Univ., 1966–67, MLS. **Orgs.:** ALA: ACRL; RTSD/Cat. and Class. Sect., Margaret Mann Cit. Com. (1972–73); Policy and Resrch. Com. (1980–); LITA. NY Tech. Srvs. Libns.: Pres. (1979–80), Nom. Com. (Ch., 1980–), Awds. Com. (Ch., 1974–75), various ofcs. Amer. Hist. Assn. **Pubns.:** Jt. auth., "AACR As Applied By Research Libraries for Serials Cataloging," *Lib. Resrcs. & Tech. Srvs.* (Spr. 1979); "AACR Chapter 6 as Adopted, Applied, and Addressed by Research Libraries," *Lib. Resrcs. & Tech. Srvs.* (Win. 1977); "A Cataloger's Guide to AACR Chapter 6, Separately Published Monographs, 1974," *Lib. Resrcs. & Tech. Srvs.* (Spr. 1975). **Activities:** 1; 20, 46; 54, 55 **Addr.:** 34 Franklin Corner Rd., P.O. Box 6292, Lawrenceville, NJ 08648.

Coe, Marilyn Rae (Je. 10, 1942, Kansas City, MO) Dir., Lib., Unity Sch. of Christianity, 1981–, Assoc. Libn., 1979–80; ILL Libn., Linda Hall Lib., 1976–78, Head, Copying Srvs., 1972–76. **Educ.:** Natl. Coll., 1961–64, BA (Psy.); Univ. of MO, 1968–69, MSLS; Unity Inst. of Cont. Educ., 1977–79, Cert. **Orgs.:** KS City Theo. LA. **Activities:** 5, 12; 15, 17, 39; 90, 91, 92 **Addr.:** Unity School of Christianity Library, Unity Village, MO 64065.

Coffee, E. Guy (F. 7, 1934, Kansas City, MO) Vetny. Med. Libn., KS State Univ., 1970–. **Educ.:** Univ. of MO, 1958, AB (Bio.), KS State Tchrs. Coll., 1969–70, MLS; Med. LA, 1978, Cert. **Orgs.:** Mid-Contl. Med. Lib. Grp.: Archvst. (1975–). Med. LA. **Honors:** Phi Zeta. **Pubns.:** "New Books Available to Kansas Vets," *KS Veterinarian* (1972); "Introduction to the Use of Online Information Retrieval for Conducting the Literature Search," *Procs. Anl. Conf., KS State Agr. Exper. Station, 53d* (1978). **Activities:** 1; 17, 24, 39; 58, 80 **Addr.:** Veterinary Medical Library, Kansas State University, Manhattan, KS 66506.

Coffindaffer, Clarence L. (O. 8, 1941, Clarksburg, WV) State Libn., SD State Lib., 1981–; Coord., Persnl., Labor Rel., Keister Coal Co., Inc., 1979–81; Dir., Raleigh Cnty. Pub. Lib., 1978–79; Dir., Asst. Prof., Media Educ., Media Ctr., Alderson Broaddus Coll., 1976–78; Libn., Asst. Prof., Media Educ., Glenville State Coll., 1975–76; Dir., Stonewall Jackson Reg. Lib., 1972–75; Ext. Libn., Clarksburg Pub. Lib., 1970–71; HS Tchr., 1966–70. **Educ.:** Salem Coll., 1966, BA (WV Tchr. Cert.); Univ.

Special Subjects/Services: 50. Adult educ.; 51. Advert./Mktg.; 52. Aerosp.; 53. Agric.; 54. Area std.; 55. Arts/Hum.; 56. Autom.; 57. Bibl./Prtg.; 58. Bio. sci.; 59. Bus./Fin.; 60. Chem.; 61. Copyrt.; 62. Documtn.; 63. Educ.; 64. Engin.; 65. Env.; 66. Eth. grps.; 67. Film; 68. Food/Nutr.; 69. Geneal.; 70. Geo.; 71. Geol.; 72. Handcpd.; 73. Hist.; 74. Int. frdm.; 75. Info. sci.; 76. Insr.; 77. Law; 78. Legis.; 79. Math./Comp. sci.; 80. Med.; 81. Metals; 82. Nat. resrcs.; 83. Newsp.; 84. Nuc. sci.; 85. Oral hist.; 86. Petr./Energy; 87. Pharm.; 88. Phys./Astr./Math.; 89. Readg.; 90. Relig.; 91. Sci./Tech.; 92. Soc. sci.; 93. Telecom.; 94. Transp.; 95. (other).

of Pittsburgh, 1972, MLS (Lib. Admin.); Univ. of WI, 1973, Adult Inst. on Disadv.; various crs. **Orgs.:** ALA: PLA; SRRT; IFRT; JMRT, Afflt. Cncl. (1975). WV LA: Pub. Lib. Sect. (Ch., 1973–75); JMRT (Ch., 1975); Ad Hoc Com. for Dir. for WV LA (1976); Legis. Com. (1974–78); Constn. and Bylaws Com. (1973–75). Gvrs. Conf. on Libs.: State Del. Coord. SELA. Oral Hist. Assn. Arts 7 of Lewsi Cnty., Inc. Kiwanis Club of Philippi. **Honors:** Beta Phi Mu, 1972; Alpha Si Omega, 1966. **Activities:** 9, 10; 17, 25, 34; 63, 72, 74 **Addr.:** 800 N. Illinois, State Library Bldg., Pierre, SD 57501.

Coffman, M. Hope (N. 3, 1942, Hartford, CT) Mgr., Tech. Info. Ctr., Charles Stark Draper Lab., Inc., 1972–; Intern, Serials Catlgr., Harvard Coll. Lib., 1969–72. **Educ.:** Boston Univ., 1965–69, BA (Eng.); Simmons Coll., 1969–72, MS. **Orgs.:** ALA. ASIS. SLA: Boston Chap., Educ. Com. (Ch., 1979–81), Prog. Ch., Pres.-Elect (1981–82), Prog. Com. (1979–81), Schol. Com. (1979). Assoc. Info. Mgrs. Un. Way: Adv. Trng. Com. (1978–80); Corp. Keyperson (1977). **Honors:** Beta Phi Mu; Cogswell Awd., 1976; Un. Way Grt. Boston Chap., Outstan. Achvmt. Awd., 1977, 1979. **Pubns.:** "Communication Dynamics, A Seminar Report," *SLA, Boston Chap. News Bltn.* (My. 1980); "Workshop on the Effectiveness of Small Groups," *Sem. Rpt. from 72nd Anl. Conf. SLA Boston Chap. Bltn.* (Jl.–Ag. 1981). **Activities:** 12; 17, 36, 43; 64, 91, 93 **Addr.:** Technical Information Center, 555 Technology Sq., Cambridge, MA 02139.

Coffman, Ralph J. (Jl. 16, 1940, Boston, MA) Corp. Lib. Mgr., Digital Equipment Corp., 1978–; Dir. of Lib., Northeastern Univ., 1972–78; Teaching Fellow, Harvard Univ., 1969–72; Mgr., Data Proc. Prog., Cambell & Hall, Inc., 1969–72; Rare Book and Arch. Catlgr., Andover-Harvard Lib., 1966–69; Head Libn., Franklin Inst. of Boston, 1964–66. **Educ.:** Trinity Coll., 1959–63, BA; Boston Univ., 1964–67, ED (Comp. Ed.); Simmons Coll., 1966–69, MS (LS); Harvard Univ., 1969–76, PHD (Phil.). **Orgs.:** Socty. for Mgt. of Info. Sci.: Ethics Com. (1978–79). ASIS: Com. on the Study of Info. Sci. (1979). ALA: ACRL. N. Atl. Treaty Org.: Systems Science Com. Prog. (1979). Lowell Area Cncl. on Interlibrary Networks: Pres. (1974–76). Natl. Micro. Assn. **Pubns.:** *Solomon Stoddard: Religion and Society in Colonial Northampton* (1978); "Microform Serials: A Systems Analysis," *The Serials Libn.* (1977). **Activities:** 12; 75 **Addr.:** Digital Equipment Corporation, ML4-3/A20, 146 Main St., Maynard, MA 01754.

Coggin, Mary (Vancouver, BC) Supvsr., Lib./Media Instr., Sch. Dist., 1961–; Lectr., LS, Univ. of BC, 1966–76; Lectr., LS, Univ. of Victoria, 1973; Elem. and HS Tchr. **Educ.:** Univ. of BC, 1961, BEduc., 1967, MLS. **Orgs.:** BC Sch. LA: Pres. (1966). Can. Sch. Libns. Assn.: Pres. (1968). ALA: AASL. AECT. Natl. AV Assn. **Honors:** Can. Sch. Libn. Assn., Encyc. Britannica Awd., 1975; AECT, Encyc. Britannica Educ. Awd., 1978; Can. Sch. Libns. Assn., Margaret Scott Awd. of Merit, 1981. **Activities:** 10; 17, 24 **Addr.:** 805 Cumberland St., New Westminster, BC V3L 3H2 Canada.

Coggins, Timothy L. (D. 7, 1948, Roanoke Rapids, NC) Head of Ref. Dept., NC Ctrl. Univ., 1977–; Asst. Libn., Chowan College, 1974–76; Tchr., Gumberry HS, 1972–73. **Educ.:** NC Wesleyan Coll., 1968–72, BA (Eng. Fr.); Simmons Coll., 1973–74, MS (LS). **Orgs.:** ALA. NC LA: Ed. Bd. of *NC Libraries*, Ch.-Elect of NC Jr. Mem. Durham Cnty. Lib. Assn.: Ed. *Newsletter*. Friends of Filipino People. Women's Intl. Leag. of Peace & Frdm. **Honors:** ALA, Student Awd. to ALA Conf., 1974. **Activities:** 1, 2; 29, 39, 45; 55, 66, 77 **Addr.:** 2410 West Club Blvd., Durham, NC 27705.

Cogswell, Howard L. (D. 4, 1934, Fort Fairfield, ME) Branch Supvsr., St. John Reg. Lib., 1974–; City Libn., Chaleur Reg. Lib., 1973–74; Tchr./Libn., Bethany Bible Coll., 1963–73. **Educ.:** East. Nazarene Coll., 1953–58, BA (Eng.); Tufts Univ., 1962–63, MA (Eng.); Simmons Coll., 1972–73, MS (LS). **Orgs.:** ALA. Atl. Prov. LA: V.P. (1974–75), Councilor for Aims & Objectives (1976–78). Can. LA. Church & Synagogue LA. Assn. Christian Libns. Natl. Affiliation For Litcy. Advnc.: V.P. (1980–1982). Inter-Varsity Christian Flwshp. (Can.): Bd. (1978–81). **Pubns.:** "Libraries and those who cannot read," *APLA Bltn.* (Jl. 1979); Reviews. **Activities:** 9; 17, 35, 36; 74, 90, 92 **Addr.:** Saint John Regional Library, 20 Hazen Ave., Saint John, NB E2L 3G8, Canada.

Cogswell, James A. (S. 4, 1946, Malden, MA) Circ. Libn., Princeton Univ., 1978–; Ref. & Online Srvs. Libn., Univ. of PA, 1974–78; Ref./Circ. Libn., Bennington Coll., 1972–74; Bkmobile Libn., New Brunswick (NJ) Pub. Lib., 1970–72. **Educ.:** Bowdoin Coll., 1964–68, BA (Hist.); Rutgers Univ., 1971–72, MLS; Wharton Sch. of Bus., Univ. of PA, 1976–78, Cert. Mgt. **Orgs.:** LA: ACRL; LAMA: Circ. Srvs. Sect., Prog. Plng. Com. (1978–); RASD: Machine-Assisted Ref. Sect., Exec. Com. (1977–78). **Honors:** Beta Phi Mu, 1972. **Pubns.:** "Online Search Services: Implications for Libraries and Library Users," *Coll. and Resrch. Libs.* (Jl. 1978); Videotape: "Online Search Services: An Introduction" (1977). **Activities:** 1; 17, 22, 34; 56 **Addr.:** Circulation Department, Firestone Library, Princeton University, Princeton, NJ 08544.

Cogswell, Robert Elzy (Ag. 9, 1939, Houston, TX) Catlgr. & Ref. Libn., Episcopal Theo. Semy. of the Southwest, 1979–; Spec. Proj. Libn., Tarlton Law Lib., Univ. of TX, 1964–79. **Educ.:** Univ. of TX, 1964–72, BA (Govt.), 1975–78, MLS. **Orgs.:** ATLA. ALA: RTSD; Library Hist. RT. ACRL. TX LA. CSLA. Other orgs. Amnesty Intl. Abba Books & Broadsides (a private press): Ed. and publshr. **Honors:** Beta Phi Mu, 1978. **Pubns.:** Ed. and publshr., *Abba, a Journal of Prayer;* "Hours of Opening and After-Hours Access in University Law Libraries" *Law Library Journal* (F. 1973); "Easter in October" *Spirit and Life* (O. 1979); "Three Stories of Religious Persecution" *Baseball, Popcorn, Apple Pie, & Liberty* (1979); *The Return of the King: An Exhibit of Arthurian Literature,* Humanities Research Center, Univ. of TX (July-August, 1979). **Activities:** 1; 20, 31, 39; 57, 90 **Addr.:** 3913 Wilbert Rd., Austin, TX 78751.

Cohan, Leonard (Jl. 20, 1930, New York, NY) Dir. of Libs., Polytech. Inst. of NY, 1964–; Head Libn., NY Cmnty. Coll., 1956–64; Asst. Bus. Ref., Sr. Libn., Brooklyn Pub. Lib., 1955–56; Lib. Asst., City Coll. of NY, 1954–55; Asst. Post Libn., Army Engin. Ctr., Ft. Belvoir, VA, 1953–54; Head Libn., Asst. Dir., Resrch., Parsons Sch. of Dsgn., 1952. **Educ.:** City Coll. of NY, 1948–51, BS (Soc. Sci.); Columbia Univ., 1951–52, MS (LS). **Orgs.:** Metro. Ref. and Resrch. Lib. Agency. Acad. Libs. of Brooklyn. Metro. Coll. Interlib. Assn. Amer. Socty. for Engin. Educ. NY Archlg. Socty. NY Socty. for Paint Tech. **Honors:** Various fed. grants. **Pubns.:** Ed., *Directory of Computerized Information in Science and Technology* (1968–73); *Science Information Personnel* (1961); *Improvement of College Instruction* (1959); ed., *Info. Hotline* (1971–). **Activities:** 1; 17, 41; 64, 75, 91 **Addr.:** 330 E. 33 St., Apt. 10-P, New York, NY 10016.

Cohen, Aaron (Jl. 10, 1935, New York, NY) Prin., Aaron Cohen and Assoc., 1972–; Campus Plnr., Bronx Cmnty. Coll., 1966–72; Chief Designer, Edward Durrell Stone Architect, 1960–66. **Educ.:** Georgia Inst. of Tech., 1958, BArch (Arch.); Pratt Univ., 1961, MArch. **Orgs.:** ALA. SLA. NY LA. Amer. Inst. of Arch. NY State Assn. of Arch. Natl. Cncl. Arch. Reg. Brd. Amer. Arbitration Assn. **Honors:** Fulbright Flwshp. **Pubns.:** *Designing and Space Planning for Libraries,* (1979); "101 Ways to Keep Warm," *NY Mag.* (1973); "Do Our Library Buildings have to be Discarded Every Fifteen Years?", *LJ Spec. Report* (1976); "Architectural Considerations," *LJ Spec. Report;* "Architectural Techniques for Wayfinding," *Sign Syst. for Libs.* (1979). **Addr.:** Aaron Cohen and Associates, Teatown Rd., RFD # 1, Box 636, Croton-on-Hudson, NY 10520.

Cohen, Allen (N. 7, 1935, Brooklyn, NY) Head, Cat. Dept., Univ. of CA., Santa Barbara, 1980–; Head, Cat. Dept., Free Lib. of Philadelphia, 1978–80; Head, Pres. Sect., PA State Univ., 1975–78; Cat. Dept. Trainer, 1971–75; Catlgr., United Nations Lib., 1970–71; Head Catlgr., John Jay Coll. of Criminal Justice, 1967–70; Catlgr. & Acq. Libn., NY City Cmnty. Col., 1966–67; Serials Catlgr., NY Pub. Lib., 1962–66. **Educ.:** City Coll. of New York, 1953–57, BA (Eng.); Pratt Inst., 1961–62, MLS. **Orgs.:** ALA: Sub. Analysis Com. (1973–76); Subcom. on Sub. Headings for Correctional Mat. (Ch. 1973–75); Subcom. on Sub. Headings for Individual Works of Art (1979–80); Descr. Cat. Com. (1977–79); Com. on Cat.: Descr. and Access (1980–81; Ch. 1980); Cat. & Class. Sect. Nom. Com. (Ch. 1976). PA LA: Memb. Com. (1975–77). Ctrl. PA Fest. of the Arts: Film Com. (1972–77). PA State Univ. Jazz Club: Fac. Adv. (1975–77). **Honors:** Beta Phi Mu, 1962. **Pubns.:** "Classification of four track tapes," *Lib. Resrc. & Tech. Srvs.* (Fall 1962); "Suggestions for further reading," *Pennsylvania 1776* (1975); *Jazz Music: A basic guide to the records, books, periodicals.* (1976). **Activities:** 1, 9; 15, 20, 24; 55, 57, 67 **Addr.:** 2809 Serena Rd. # B, Santa Barbara, CA 93105.

Cohen, Bill (Ag. 23, –, New York, NY) Ed., Haworth Press, Inc., 1972–; Mktg. Mgr., Human Sciences Press, Inc., 1968–71. **Educ.:** Columbia Univ., 1968–71, BA (Psy.). **Orgs.:** ALA. ASIS. Med. LA. SLA. Other orgs. **Activities:** 6; 75, 92, 93 **Addr.:** The Haworth Press, Inc., 149 Fifth Ave., New York, NY 10010.

Cohen, Bunny (Ja. 25, 1947, Seattle, WA) VP, Bd. of Trustees, Seattle Pub. Lib., 1981–. Trustee, Seattle Pub. Lib., 1978–81. **Orgs.:** ALA: ALTA/Prog. and Eval. Com. (1979–81); Persnl. Task Frc. (1979–81). Pac. Northwest LA: Trustee Div. (Ch., 1979–81). WA LA: Strg. Com. (1980). Historic Seattle Pres. and Dev. Assn.: Volun. Assn. (Pres.). **Honors:** City of Hope, Million Dollarclub, Outstan. Mem., 1978. **Activities:** 9; 47 **Addr.:** 311 W. Halladay, Seattle, WA 98119.

Cohen, David (My. 24, 1909, New York, NY) Adj. Prof., Dir., Ethnicity Libnshp. Inst. and Flwshp. Prog., Queens Coll. Sch. of Lib. and Info. Std., 1972–; Libn., Plainview - Old Bethpage HS, 1960–75; Reg. Dir., Field Enterprises–World Book, 1955–59; Elem. Tchr., NY City Bd. of Educ. 1947–54; Ref. Libn., City Coll. of NY, 1930–42. **Educ.:** City Coll. of NY, 1926–30, BSS, 1930–34, MSE (Hist. and Educ.); Columbia Univ., 1937–39, MSLS, 1967–68, Cert. in Advnc. Libnshp. **Orgs.:** ALA: SRRT; Ethnic Mtrls. Info. Exch. Task Force (Coord., 1973–). NY LA: Ethnic Srvs. Task Force (Ch., 1978–). Long Island Media Assn.: Frdm. to Read Com. (Ch., 1975–). Long Island Frdm. to Read Coal.: Coord. (1977–). Amer. Cvl. Liberties Un.: Acad. Frdm. Com. (Exec. Ofcr., 1975–). Amer. Fed. of Tchrs. Natl. Educ. Assn. **Pubns.:** *Multiethnic Media: Bibliographies Currently Available* (1975); *Recommended Paperback Books for Elementary Schools* (1976); "Plainview Welcomes Paperbacks: A High School Library Experience," *Sch. Lib. Jnl.* (Ja. 1965); "Multiethnic Media: Bibliograpies Currently Available," *Sch. Lib. Jnl.* (Je. 1974); Reviews. **Activities:** 11; 26, 28, 48; 66, 74 **Addr.:** 67-81 Bell Blvd., Bayside, NY 11364.

Cohen, Diana Barbara (S. 13, 1927, Montreal, PQ) Ref. libn., Natl. Coll. of Educ., 1978–; Ref. libn., Lib. of Intl. Rel., Chicago, 1977–78; Lib. Assoc., Lib. Ahmadu Bello Univ., Nigeria, 1972–74. **Educ.:** Univ. of Toronto, 1948–51, BA (Art Hist.); Natl. Froebel Fndn., London, 1951–52, Grad. Cert. (Educ.); Rosary Coll., 1975–76, MLS. E. Evanston Cmnty. Conf.: Pres. (1970–72). **Pubns.:** "Unesco's bibliographic services," *Intl. Lib. Review* (Ap. 1977); "Access to publications of the International Labour Office," *Intl. Lib. Review* (Jl. 1978); "Userguide to the publications & documentation of the International Labour Office, ILO," "Userguide to Unesco publications & documentation," *Gvt. Pubns. Review* (1978). **Activities:** 1, 2; 24, 31, 39; 63, 69, 75 **Addr.:** 1040 Michigan Ave., Evanston, IL 60202.

Cohen, Elaine M. (N. 13, 1938, Brooklyn, NY) Prin., Elaine Cohen Assoc., 1973–. **Educ.:** Skidmore Coll., 1960, BA (Chem.); City Coll. of NY, 1973, MA (Psy.). **Pubns.:** *Designing and Space Planning for Libraries.* (1979); LJ Spec. Report # 1: "Do Our Library Buildings Have to Be Discarded Every Fifteen Years?" (1976); LJ Spec. Report # 7: "Architectural Considerations"; "Architectural Techniques for Wayfinding," *Sign Systems for Libraries* (1979); Other articles. **Addr.:** Elaine Cohen Associates, Teatown Road, RFD # 1, Box 636, Croton-on-Hudson, NY 10520.

Cohen, Elinor Margot (Ja. 2, 1936, Long Island City, NY) Admin., Tech. Info. Srvs., General Foods Corp., 1977–; Supvsr., Info. Srvs., 1972–76; Libn., 1966–72; Chem., 1961–66. **Educ.:** New York Univ., 1956, BA (Chem.); Columbia Univ., 1968, MLS. **Orgs.:** SLA: Hudson Valley Chap., Pres. (1974–75), Food Division, Ch. (1973–74). Hlth. Info. Libns. of Westchester: Pres. (1978–79). ASIS. **Pubns.:** Jt. auth., "Food Science and Technology Abstracts," *Database* (D. 1979). **Activities:** 12; 17, 39, 41; 58, 68, 91 **Addr.:** Technical Center Library, General Foods Corp., White Plains, NY 10625.

Cohen, Gilbert (Ja. 2, 1929, New York, NY) Head of Ref., Dana Lib., Rutgers Univ., 1967–; Head of Circ., 1961–67; Ref. Libn., Newark Pub. Lib., 1959–61. **Educ.:** Queens Coll., Flushing, NY, 1947–51, BA (Eng.); Rutgers Univ., 1957–59. **Orgs.:** ALA. NJ LA: Trustee Relshps. Com. Springfield (NJ) Pub. Lib.: Trustee. AAUP. **Honors:** Beta Phi Mu. **Pubns.:** "Library Service to Labor," *ALA Lib. Srvs. to Labor Nsltr.* (Summer 1959); reprinted in: *Library Service to Labor* (1963). **Activities:** 1, 9; 31, 39; 55 **Addr.:** Dana Library, Rutgers University, Newark, NJ 07102.

Cohen, Jackson B. (Jl. 13, 1929, Detroit, MI) Head, Sci. Lib., Queens Coll., 1976–; Sci. Biblgphr., Hunter Coll. Lib., 1972–76; Head, Sci. and Tech. Dept., Pratt Inst. Lib., 1969–72; Libn., Sci. and Indus. Dept., Pub. Lib. of Cincinnati and Hamilton Cnty., 1957–69. **Educ.:** Univ. of Pittsburgh, 1948–52, AB (Eng.), 1953–56, MLitt (Eng.); Carnegie-Mellon Univ., 1956–57, MLS; Univ. of Cincinnati, 1964–68, (Sci., Hist.); SLA Contin. Educ. Sem., 1977. **Orgs.:** LA, City Univ. of NY: Prog. Com. (1972–73); Anl. Inst. Com. (1978/79). NY Lib. Club. SLA: Adv. Cncl. (1963–64); Cincinnati Chap. (Pres., 1963–64); Prog. Ch., NY Chapt., SLA and ASIS Jt. Conf. Com. (1973); NY Chap. Bylaws Com. (Ch., 1975–76); Other orgs. and coms. METRO: Sci-Tech Discuss. Grp. (Ch., 1974–76). **Honors:** Beta Phi Mu, 1957; Phi Kappa Phi, 1957. **Pubns.:** Ed., *METRO Census of Scientific and Technical Periodicals,* (1976); Ed., *CUNY Checklist of Scientific, Technical, and Medical Periodicals,* (1975); Jt. Auth., "Physics and Chemistry Journal Prices in 1977–78," *Serials Libn.* (Sum. 1979); "Management of Scientific and Technical Information in Nigeria," *Technological Development in Nigeria,* (1979); *Machine Tool Referral Guide,* (1966); Jt. Auth., "Prices of Physics and Chemistry Journals," *Science* (Jl. 29, 1977); Other articles. **Activities:** 1; 15, 17, 39; 58, 91 **Addr.:** Paul Klapper Library, Queens College, 65-30 Kissena Boulevard, Flushing, NY 11367.

Cohen, Lorraine Sterling (D. 17, 1917, Warsaw, Poland) Sch. Libn., Main St. Sch., Port Washington, NY, 1959–. **Educ.:** Chicago Tchrs. Coll., 1936–40, BE (Educ.); Queens Coll., 1958–63, MLS. **Orgs.:** LS Alum. Assn. of Queens Coll. Long Island Sch. Lib. Media Assn. ALA. Amer. Jewish Congs.: Justice Chap., Corres. Secy. (1977–79); NY State Untd. Tchrs. Women's Amer. ORT. Hadassah. **Pubns.:** "Children's Library Services in Israel," *Top of the News* (Ja. 1975); "Begin Critical Reading In Elementary School," *Elem. Eng.* (Ap. 1967); "Student Helpers in the Elementary School Library," *Sch. Lib. Jnl.* (D. 1962). **Activities:** 10; 15, 20, 21; 63, 75, 89 **Addr.:** 184-15 69th Ave., Flushing, NY 11365.

Cohen, Madeline E. (My. 28, 1948, New York, NY) Mgr. of Lib. Srvs., ABC News, 1980–; Admin. of Info. Srvs., The Resrch. Inst. of Amer., 1978–81; Ref. Ref. Libn., McGraw-Hill, Inc., 1974–78; Ref. and Cat. Libn., Amer. Bankers Assn., 1973–74. **Educ.:** Hunter Coll., 1969–72, BA (Hist.); Univ. of MD, 1972–73, MLS. **Orgs.:** SLA.: Ch.-Elect, Publshg. Div. (1979–80);

PROFESSIONAL ACTIVITIES: Institutions: 1. Acad. lib.; 2. Arch.; 3. Assn.; 4. Fed./Gvt. lib.; 5. Inst. lib.; 6. Mfr./Suppl.; 7. Milit. lib.; 8. Musm.; 9. Pub. lib.; 10. Sch. lib.; 11. Sch. of lib. sci.; 12. Spec. lib.; 13. State lib.; 14. (other). **Functions/Activities:** 15. Acq./Col. dev.; 16. Adult srvs.; 17. Admin.; 18. Apprais.; 19. Archit./Bldgs.; 20. Cat./Class.; 21. Chld. srvs.; 22. Circ.; 23. Cons./Pres.; 24. Consult.; 25. Cont. ed.; 26. Educ. lib. sci.; 27. Ext. srvs.; 28. Fund/Grants; 29. Gvt. pubs.; 30. Indx./Abs.; 31. Instr. lib. use; 32. Media srvs.; 33. Micro.; 34. Netwks./Coop.; 35. Persnl.; 36. PR; 37. Publshg.; 38. Recs. mgt.; 39. Ref. srvs.; 40. Repro.; 41. Resrch.; 42. Review.; 43. Secur.; 44. Serials; 45. Spec. col.; 46. Tech. srvs.; 47. Trustees/Bds.; 48. YA srvs.; 49. (other).

NY Chap., Cont. Educ. Com. (1979–80); *Bulletin* Ed. (1977–78); Mem. Ch. (1976–77); Arrange. Ch. (1975–76). ALA. ASIS. Admin. Mgt. Soc. **Honors:** Beta Phi Mu, 1973. **Activities:** 12; 17, 39, 41; 51, 59, 92 **Addr.:** 26 E. 60th St., New York, NY 10022.

Cohen, Morris L. (N. 2, 1927, New York, NY) Libn. & Prof. of Law, Yale Law Sch., 1981–; Libn. & Prof. of Law, Harvard Law Sch., 1971–81; Libn. & Prof. of Law, Univ. of PA Law Sch., 1963–71; Libn. & Assoc. Prof. of Law, SUNY Buffalo Law Sch., 1961–63; Asst. Libn., Columbia Univ. Sch. of Law, 1959–61; Asst. Libn., Rutgers Univ. Law Sch., 1958–59; Lect., Columbia Univ. Lib. Sch., 1963–70; Lect., Drexel Univ. Lib. Sch., 1964–71; Adj. Prof., Simmons Coll. Lib. Sch., 1976–. **Educ.:** Univ. of Chicago, 1945–48, BA (Pol. Sci.); Columbia Univ. Sch. of Law, 1948–51, JD; Pratt Inst., 1957–59, MLS. **Orgs.:** ALA: Ch., Law & Pol. Sci. Subsect. (1969–70). AALL: Pres. (1970–71); Ch., Network Com. (1975–78). Bibli. Socty. of Amer. Intl. Assn. of Law Libs. Assn. of Amer. Law Schs.: Jurimetrics Com.; Accred. Com. Amer. Bar Assn.: Ch., Jt. Task Force on Automated Legal Resrch. (1971–75). AAUP: Pres., Univ. of PA Chap. (1967–68). Amer. Civil Liberties Un.: Exec. Bd., Philadelphia Chap. (1968–71). Other orgs. **Pubns.:** *Law and Science: A Selected Bibliography* (1978); *Legal Research in a Nutshell,* 3rd ed. (1978); *How to Find the Law,* 7th ed. (1976). **Activities:** 1, 14-Law Library; 17, 26, 41; 57, 77, 95-Legal Research. **Addr.:** Yale Law School, 127 Wall St., New Haven, CT 06520.

Cohn, Alan M. (Ag. 21, 1926, St. Louis, MO) Hum. Libn. & Prof. of Eng., South. IL Univ. at Carbondale, 1955–. **Educ.:** Washington Univ., St. Louis, 1946–49, AB (Eng.), 1949–50, MA (Eng.); Univ. of IL, 1954–55, MS (LS). **Orgs.:** Bibl. Soc. of Amer. Msc. LA. Caxton Club. Mod. Lang. Assn. of America. Mod. Hum. Resrch. Assn. James Joyce Fndn.; Dickens Soc. **Honors:** Phi Beta Kappa, 1949; Beta Phi Mu, 1955; Southern IL Univ., Amoco Outstan. Tchr. Awd., 1977; Pi Delta Kappa, 1974. **Pubns.:** Jt. auth., *D.H. Lawrence: An Exhibit* (1979); Jt. auth., "Mysterious Coppinger (in *Finnegans Wake),*" *James Joyce Qtly.* (Sum. 1979); "A Vonnegut Rarissima," *Papers of Bibli. Soc. of Amer.* (3d quar. 1979); *"Ulysses,* the Son of a Beach," *Studs. in Contemporary Satire* (1978); "Additions to Dace's *LeRoi Jones,*" *Papers Bib. Soc. Amer.* (4th quar. 1976); Other articles. **Activities:** 1; 15, 39, 41; 55, 57 **Addr.:** Humanities Librarian, Southern Illinois University, Carbondale, IL 62901.

Cohn, Emma (Mr. 23, 1922, New York, NY) Freelnc. Lib./Media Consult., 1979–; Asst. Coord., YA Srvs., Bronx Pub. Lib., 1954–78. **Educ.:** NY Univ., 1940–43, BA (Eng.); Columbia Univ., 1952–54. **Orgs.:** ALA: ALSC, *Top of The News* Ed. (1957), Video-Cable Task Frc. (1973), YA Film Com. (1981). NY LA: Film-Video RT (Ch., 1982). **Pubns.:** Jt. ed., *Library Service to Young Adults* (1968), various articles, *Top of the News, Lib. Trends, Voice of Youth Advocates* on YA srvs. and non-print media; managing ed., *Film Lib. Qtly.* (1970–80). **Activities:** 9; 48; 67 **Addr.:** 2827 Valentine Ave., Bronx, NY 10458.

Cohn, John M. (N. 23, 1943, New York, NY) Dir. of Lib. Srvs., Cnty. Coll. of Morris, 1978–; Asst. Prof., Dept. of the Lib., Brooklyn Coll., 1973–78; Adj. Lect., GSLIS, Pratt Inst., 1972–; Gen. Asst. Libn., Queens Borough Pub. Lib., 1971–72. **Educ.:** Pratt Inst., 1972, MLS; NY Univ., 1974, PhD (Pol. Sci.). **Orgs.:** ALA: RTSD, Educ. Com. (1979); CJCLS, Nom. Com. (1979). NJ LA: Coop. & Networking Com., Coll. & Univ. Sect. (Ch., 1979). **Pubns.:** "Federal Aid & Local Spending: Stimulation vs. Substitution," *Lib. Jnl.* (F. 15, 1979); "The Applicability of Interest Group Theory to the Concerns of Librarianship," *Jnl. of Lib. Hist.* (Fall, 1977). **Activities:** 1, 11; 17, 26; 56, 92 **Addr.:** County College of Morris, Learning Resource Center, Route 10 & Center Grove Road, Randolph, NJ 07869.

Cohn, William L. (D. 9, 1934, Joliet, IL) Dir., Nichols Coll., 1979–; Asst. Prof., Univ. of WI-Milwaukee, 1972–79; Assoc. Dir., E. Carolina Univ., 1968–70; Dir., Drury Coll. Lib., 1966–68; Head, Hum. and Fine Arts, South. IL Univ. Lib., Edwardsville, 1964–66; Asst. Ref. Libn., Univ. of NH, 1963–64; Libn. I, Soc. Sci. Dept., Chicago Pub. Lib., 1962–63. **Educ.:** Vanderbilt Univ., 1958–60, BA MA (Eng.); George Peabody Coll., 1961–62, MALS; FL State Univ., 1970–72, AMD, DLS. **Orgs.:** AALS: Adult Srvs. (Conv., 1976–77, 1979). WI LA: Lib. Educ. Sect. (Ch., 1977). WI Lib. Trustees Assn.: Bd. of Dir. (1978–79). ALA: ACRL; RASD, Amer. Indian Mtrls. and Srvs. Com. (1976/79); Conf. Srvs. Com. (1977); Adult Lib. Mtrls. Com. (1978/80, Ch. 1978/79). Ozaukee Cnty. Cncl. of Southeast. WI Hlth. Syst. Agency: Consumer mem. (1976/78). Girl Scouts of Greater Milwaukee Area: Sustaining Mem. Drive Ch. (1975–76, 1978), Mequon area Ch. (1977). **Pubns.:** Jt. auth., "CLEP and Libraries in Wisconsin," *WI Lib. Bltn.* (Jl/Ag 1973); "Report on Adult Services Interest Group," *Jnl. of Educ. for Libnshp.* (Win. 1976), (Spr. 1977); "An Overview of ARL Directors, 1933–1973," *Coll. & Resrch. Libs.* (Mr. 1976); "The Need for Intermediaries," *ASIS Proceedings* (1976); Other articles, reviews, oral presentations. **Activities:** 1, 11; 16, 17, 26; 50, 55, 57 **Addr.:** Box 112, Nichols College, Dudley, MA 01570.

Cohrs, Joyce S. (My. 29, Pekin, IL) Dir. of Tech. Prcs., DeKalb Lib. Syst., 1977–; Recs. Admin., J. Ray McDermott Co., 1975–77; Ref. Libn., DeKalb Lib. Syst., 1972–75; Catlgr., GA State Univ. Lib., 1970–72. **Educ.:** Univ. of IL, 1946–50, BA (Psy.), 1950–51, MA (Psy.); Emory Univ., 1969–70, MLn (LS); Emory Univ., DASL, 1981. **Orgs.:** ALA. GA LA: Exec. Bd. (1973–75, 1979–81). Metro Atlanta Lib. Assn.: Pres. (1974). **Honors:** Phi Beta Kappa; Beta Phi Mu; **Activities:** 9; 17, 20, 46 **Addr.:** 307 Adair St., #B-5, Decatur, GA 30030.

Coil, Suzanne M. (F. 19, 1935, Elizabeth, NJ) Dir., Educ. Dept., Avon Books, 1977–; Educ. Dir., Bantam Books, 1976–77; Educ. Promo. Mgr., Dell Publishing Co., 1970–76. **Educ.:** Univ. of Chicago, 1952–55, AB (Lib. Arts). **Orgs.:** ALA. Intl. Reading Assn.: Adlsnt. Lit. Com. (1975–). Natl. Cncl. of Tchrs. of Eng. Natl. Cncl. for the Soc. Studies. Assn. of Amer. Publshrs.: Educ. Paperback Mktg. Com. Other orgs. **Pubns.:** "Paperbacks and Progress Against Illiteracy," *School Library Journal* (Ap. 1978). **Activities:** 6; 37; 51, 63, 89 **Addr.:** Education Department, Avon Books, 959 Eighth Ave., New York, NY 10019.

Colaianni, Lois Ann (Ag. 18, 1932, Utica, NY) Deputy, Assoc. Dir., Natl. Lib. of Med., 1980–; Dir. of Libs., Cedars-Sinai Med. Ctr., 1972–80; Head, Med. Info. Comm. Srv., Univ. of CA, Los Angeles, 1968–72, MEDLARS Srchr., 1965–68. **Educ.:** Univ. of Rochester, 1949–53, BA (Bio.); Univ. of CA, Los Angeles, 1963–64, MLS; Internship, Med. LA, 1965, Cert. **Orgs.:** Med. LA: Pres. (1979–80), South CA and AZ chaps. SLA. Assn. of West. Hosp., Libns. Sect. **Honors:** Beta Phi Mu. **Pubns.:** *Manual for Librarians in small hospitals,* (1969). **Activities:** 12; 17; 80 **Addr.:** National Library of Medicine, 8600 Rockville Pike, Bethesda, MD 20209.

Colby, Edward Eugene (Jl. 5, 1912, Oakland, CA) Retired (Emeritus), Stanford Univ., 1949–; Music Libn., 1949–78; Lec. in Music, 1951–79; Archvst., Arch. of Recorded Sound, 1958–78; Acting Chief, Music Div., Oakland Pub. Lib., 1946–49. **Educ.:** Univ. of CA, Berkeley, 1930–35, BA (Music); Stanford Univ., 1951–56, MA (Music); Univ. of CA, Berkeley, 1939–41, Cert. of Libnshp.; Pomona Coll., 1943–44, Cert., Far Eastern Area & Lang. **Orgs.:** Music LA: Pres. (1950–52). Intl. Assn. of Music Libs. Assn. for Recorded Sound Coll. Intl. Assn. of Sound Arch. Amer. Music. Socty. Visiting Intl. Schol. and Tchrs. Assn., Stanford Univ.: Pres. (1963–64). **Honors:** Music LA, Disting. Music Libn., 1978. **Pubns.:** "Sound Scholarship: Scope, Purpose, Function and Potential of Phonorecord Archives," *Lib. Trends* (Jl. 1972); "Sound Recordings in the Music Library: With Special Reference to Record Archives," (Ap. 1960); Tape recordings. **Activities:** 1, 2; 15, 17, 39; 57, 95-Music. **Addr.:** 1749 Duvall Dr., San Jose, CA 95130.

Colby, Robert Alan (Ap. 15, 1920, Chicago, IL) Prof. of Lib. Sci., Queens Coll., NY, 1966–; Assoc. Prof., Lib. Sci., South. CT State Coll., 1964–66; Lang., Lit., and Arts Libn., Queens College, NY, 1953–64; Lecturer in Eng., Hunter Coll., 1951–53; Asst. Prof. of Eng., Lake Forest Coll., 1949–51; Inst. in Eng., Speech, IL Inst. of Tech., 1947–49; Instr. in Eng., De Paul Univ., 1946. **Educ.:** Univ. of Chicago, 1937–41, BA (Eng.), 1941–42, MA (Eng.), 1947–49, PhD (Eng.); Columbia Univ., 1951–53, MSLS. **Orgs.:** ALA. AALS. NY Lib. Club. Amer. Printing Hist. Assn.: Trustee (1979–). Resrch. Socty. for Victorian Per.: Brd. of Dir. (1969–). AAUP. Mod. Lang. Assn. **Honors:** Guggenheim Fndn., Flwshp., 1978. **Pubns.:** *Thackeray's Canvass of Humanity,* (1979); *Fiction with a Purpose,* (1967); "Literary Scholars, Librarians, and Bibliographical Systems," *Lit. Resrch. Nsltr.* (1977); Jt. Auth., "Thackeray's Manuscripts," *Costerus* (1974); Jt. Ed., *Access to the Literature of the Social Sciences and the Humanities,* (1974). **Activities:** 1, 12; 26, 41, 45; 55, 57, 62 **Addr.:** 33-24 86th St., Jackson Heights, NY 11372.

Cole, Fred Carrington (Ap. 12, 1912, Franklin, TX) Retired, 1977–; Pres., Cncl. on Lib. Resrcs., 1967–77; Pres., Washington and Lee Univ., 1959–67; Academic VP, Tulane Univ., 1954–59, Dean, Coll. of Arts and Sci., 1947–54, Assoc. Prof., 1946–47; Prof., 1947–59; various ed. positions, 1938–42. **Educ.:** LA State Univ., 1934, AB, 1936, AM, 1941, PhD (Hist.). Amer. Hist. Assn. South. Hist. Assn. MS Valley Hist. Assn. Phi Beta Kappa: Cncl. Nom. Com. (Ch., 1964–67). **Honors:** ALA, Hon. Mem., 1978; ALA, Spec. Centennial Cit., 1976; Union Coll., LLD, 1961; Washington and Lee Univ., LLD, 1968; other hons. **Activities:** 14-Fndn.; 28 **Addr.:** 107 Hunters Ridge Rd., Chapel Hill, NC 27514.*

Cole, (Linda) Gayle (Jl. 14, 1941, Houston, TX) Branch Lib. Mgr., Dallas Pub. Lib., 1976–, Chld. Libn., 1970–76; Elem. Sch. Tchr., Dallas, 1969–70. **Educ.:** Univ. of TX, Austin, 1960–65, BS (Elem. Educ.); TX Woman's Univ., 1971–74, MLS. **Orgs.:** ALA: Grolier Awd. Jury (1980–81); ALSC, Newbery Caldecott Com. (1978). TX LA: Chld. RT (1978). Dallas Cnty. LA. Various other ofcs. AAUW. **Honors:** Beta Phi Mu. **Pubns.:** "Public Library/Public School Cooperation," *PLA Nsltr.* (Sum. 1977). **Activities:** 9; 17, 21, 27 **Addr.:** 8512 Charing Cross, Dallas, TX 75238.

Cole, Jim E. (My. 14, 1948, Fort Dodge, IA) Serials Catlgr., Roland R. Renne Lib., MT State Univ., 1981–; Serials Catlgr., Univ. of IA Libs., 1971–81. **Educ.:** Univ. of IA, 1966–70, BA (Math.), 1970–71, MA (LS). **Orgs.:** ALA. Pac. NW LA. Verein Deutscher Bibliothekare (W. Germany). Frnds. of the Univ. of IA Libs. State Hist. Socty. of IA. **Honors:** Phi Beta Kappa, 1970; Eta Sigma Phi, 1968. **Pubns.:** "Conference Publications: Serials or Monographs?" *Lib. Resrcs. & Tech. Srvs.* (Spr. 1978); "AACR6: Time for a Review," *Lib. Resrcs. & Tech. Srvs.* (Fall 1975); jt. auth., "Alternative III," *Title Varies* (S.–N. 1975). **Activities:** 1; 20, 44 **Addr.:** Roland R. Renne Library, Bozeman, MT 59715.

Cole, John Y. (Jl. 30, 1940, Ellensburg, WA) Exec. Dir., The Ctr. for the Book, Lib. of Congs., 1977–, Ch., The Libn. Task Force on Goals, Org., and Plng., 1976–77, Newsp. Microfilming Coord., 1975–76, Coord., Foreign Newsp. Microfilming, 1972–75. **Educ.:** Univ. of WA, 1958–62, BA (Hist.), 1962–63, MLS; Johns Hopkins Univ., 1964–66, MLA (Liberal Arts); George Washington Univ., 1968–71, PhD (Amer. Cvltzn.). **Orgs.:** ALA: Intl. Rel. Com. (1974–76); Publshg. Com. (1979–81). SAA. DC LA: Bd. of Dir. (1975–77). Amer. Studies Assn. Org. of Amer. Histns. Amer. Assn. for State and Local Hist. **Pubns.:** *For Congress and the Nation: A Chronological History of the Library of Congress* (1979); ed., *The Library of Congress in Perspective* (1978); ed., *Television, the Book, and the Classroom* (1978); ed., *Ainsworth Rand Spofford: Bookman and Librarian* (1975); "Developing a National Foreign Newspaper Microfilming Program," *Lib. Resrcs. and Tech. Srvs.* (Win. 1974); Other articles. **Activities:** 1, 4; 15, 37, 45; 55, 57, 89 **Addr.:** The Center for the Book, Library of Congress, Washington, DC 20540.

Cole, Mary Elizabeth (Ag. 4, 1921, Winchester, TN) Pub. Lib. Consult., GA State Lib. Agency, 1970–; Dir., Div. of Pub. Lib. Srvs., TN State Lib., 1967–70; Consult., FL State Lib., 1960–67; Dir., Blue Grass Reg. Lib., 1954–60; Libn., Upper Cumberland Reg. Lib., 1952–54. **Educ.:** TN Tech, 1940–45, BS (Eng.); George Peabody Coll. for Tchrs., 1949–53, MLS. **Orgs.:** ALA: Nom. Com. (1975). SELA: Pub. Lib. Sec., Ch. (1974); Mem. Com., Ch. (1972). GA LA: Ch., Lib. Dev., Ch. (1974); Site Sel. Com., Ch. (1976); Coord. of the GA Del. to the WHCOLIS (1979). IFLA. **Honors:** GA LA: Cert. of Apprec., 1977. **Pubns.:** *A Survey of Library Services in Pinellas County, Florida* (1966); *A Survey of Library Services in Charlotte Co., Fla.* (1971); *A Survey of Library Services in Polk Co., Florida* (1965); *A Survey of the Southeastern States for the National Book Committee* (1966). **Activities:** 4, 9; 27, 36 **Addr.:** 620 Peachtree St. N.E., Atlanta, GA 30308.

Cole, Maud D. (Fremont, OH) Retired, 1977–; Keeper of Rare Bks., NY Pub. Lib., 1973–, First Asst., Rare Bk. Div., 1954–73, Asst., Amer. Hist. Div., 1952–54, Ref. Libn./Atlas Catlgr., Geo. and Map Div., Lib. of Congs., 1945–52. Exch. and Gift Libn., Lib. of Congs., 1943–45; Ref. Libn., Fort Hays State Coll., 1938–40, First Asst., Rochester Pub. Lib., 1937–38; Asst., Transp. Lib., Univ. of MI, 1934–37. **Educ.:** Univ. of Toledo, 1929–33, AB (Hist.); Univ. of MI, 1933–34, ABLS. **Orgs.:** SLA: Geo. and Map Div. NY Lib. Club. Typophiles. ALA: ACRL/Rare Bk. and Mss. Div. Bibl. Socty. of Amer. Amer. Prtg. Hist. Assn.: Educ. Com. (1978–). Socty. for the Hist. of Discoveries: Anl. Conf. 1979, Gen. Session Ch. **Honors:** SLA, Geo. and Map Div., Hons. Awd., 1980. **Pubns.:** "The American Alpine Club and the Montagnier Memorial Library," *SLA Geo. and Map Div. Bltn.* (F. 1954); "Some Early Map Treasures in the New York Public Library," *SLA Geo. and Map Div. Bltn.* (F. 1955); "Children's Rare Book Treasures," *AB Bookman's Yrbk.* (1956); various exhibition cats. **Activities:** 4, 10; 39, 45; 70 **Addr.:** 21-45 28th St., Astoria, NY 11105.

Coleman, 23 Alice Rae (Jl. 3, 1935, Peoria, IL) VP, Bd. of Dir., Evanston (IL) Pub. Lib. **Orgs.:** VP, N. Suburban Lib. Syst. Mem., IL State Lib. Adv. Com. Secy., IL Lib. Trustee Assn. (1977–1979). **Honors:** Co-Winner, Outstanding Trustee of the Year (IL), 1979. **Addr.:** 2646 Bennett Ave., Evanston, IL 60201.

Coleman, Crenola Sneed (D. 16, 1916, Lafayette Springs, MS) Asst. Prof. and Libn., Grad. Sch. of Lib. and Info. Sci., Univ. of MS, 1968–; Lib. Suprv., Kosciusko Sch. Libs., 1966–68; Libn., Kosciusko Jr. HS, 1960–66; Head, Children's Department, Jackson Pub. Lib., 1949–51; Various other positions. **Educ.:** Univ. of MS, 1934–37, BA (Soc. Sci.); George Peabody Coll. for Tchrs., 1939–47, BS (LS); Univ. of MS, 1975–78, Educ. Spec. (Media). **Orgs.:** ALA. MS LA. MS Assn. for Media Educs.: Treas. (1978–79). Delta Kappa Gamma: Lcl. Treas. (1972–). **Activities:** 10, 11; 15, 17, 20 **Addr.:** 1152 South 14th St., Oxford, MS 38655.

Coleman, Jean Ellen (Brooklyn, NY) Dir., Ofc. for Lib. Srv. to the Disadvantaged, ALA, 1973–; Libn./Dir., Central Brooklyn Model Cities/Bkmobile Srv. Trust, 1968–73; Asst. Dir., Central Chld. Room, Brooklyn Pub. Lib., 1966–68; Chld. Libn., 1965–66; Asst. Libn., Lexington Sch. for the Deaf, 1964–65; Tchr., Jewish Gld. for the Blind, 1958–63; Libn. Trainee, Brooklyn Pub. Lib., 1957–58; Tchr., San Carlos Indian Sch., 1956–57. **Educ.:** Hunter Coll., 1951–56, AB (Hist.), 1957–61, MSED (Educ.); Pratt Inst., 1963–64, MLS; Rutgers Univ., 1971– (LS). **Orgs.:** ALA. NY LA. **Honors:** Beta Phi Mu, Theta Chap., Outstanding Student, 1964. **Activities:** 9; 16, 21, 27; 50, 66, 89 **Addr.:** c/o ALA-OLSD, 50 East Huron St., Chicago, IL 60611.

Coleman, Jean MacMicken. (D. 2, 1907, Rochester, NY) Pres., Bd. of Trustees, Dayton & Montgomery Cnty. Pub. Lib., 1979–, VP, Bd. of Trustees, 1976–79, Pres., 1973–76, VP, 1971–73, Pres., 1968–71. **Educ.:** Univ. of Rochester, 1925–29,

Special Subjects/Services: 50. Adult educ.; 51. Advert./Mktg.; 52. Aerosp.; 53. Agric.; 54. Area std.; 55. Arts/Hum.; 56. Autom.; 57. Bibl./Prtg.; 58. Bio. sci.; 59. Bus./Fin.; 60. Chem.; 61. Copyrt.; 62. Documtn.; 63. Educ.; 64. Engin.; 65. Env.; 66. Eth. grps.; 67. Film; 68. Food/Nutr.; 69. Geneal.; 70. Geo.; 71. Geol.; 72. Handcpd.; 73. Hist.; 74. Int. frdm.; 75. Info. sci.; 76. Insr.; 77. Law; 78. Legis.; 79. Math./Comp. sci.; 80. Med.; 81. Metals; 82. Nat. resrcs.; 83. Newsp.; 84. Nuc. sci.; 85. Oral hist.; 86. Petr./Energy; 87. Pharm.; 88. Phys./Astr./Math.; 89. Readg.; 90. Relig.; 91. Sci./Tech.; 92. Soc. sci.; 93. Telecom.; 94. Transp.; 95. (other).

BA; Cornell Univ. Law Sch., 1929–32. **Orgs.:** ALA: Cncl. (1980–); Int. Frdm. Com. (1981); Legis. Com. (1975–77); ALTA/Pres. (1974–75); Prog. Com. (Ch., 1969–70). OH Lib. Trustee Assn.: Pres. (1968–70). Amer. Bar Assn. OH Bar Assn. Dayton Bar Assn. **Honors:** ALTA, Trustee Cit., 1979; OH LA, Hall of Fame, 1976; United Hlth. Fndn. of Dayton, Honorary Life Trustee, 1976; OH LA, Trustee of the Year, 1971. **Pubns.:** "Trustees", *ALA Yearbook* (1978); "User Fees–Con", *Lib. Trustee Nsltr.* (My. 1978). **Activities:** 9; 47 **Addr.:** 191 Folsom Dr., Dayton, OH 45405.

Coleman, Karen S. (O. 25, 1948, Chattanooga, TN) Kings Park Lib. Branch Mgr., Fairfax Cnty. Pub. Lib, 1979–, Thomas Jefferson Branch Mgr., 1978–79, Asst. Libn., Reston Reg. Lib., 1977–78, Asst. Branch Mgr., Woodrow Wilson Lib., 1976–77. **Educ.:** George Mason Univ., 1966–70, BA (Hist.); Univ. of MD, 1973–74, MLS. **Orgs.:** ALA. VA LA: Chld. and YA RT (1974–76); Oral Hist. Forum (1973–79); Legis. Com.; Mem. Com. **Activities:** 9; 16, 17, 22 **Addr.:** 10622 Springmann Dr., Fairfax, VA 22030.

Coleman, Sandra S. (Mr. 20, 1943, Summit, NJ) Head, Ref. Dept. and Asst. Prof., Univ. of NM Gen. Lib., 1976–; Acad. Lib. Mgt. Intern, Stanford Univ., 1978–79; Asst. Libn. for Pub. Srvs., Acting Law Libn., Tech. Srvc. Libn., Catlgr., Univ. of NM Sch. of Law Lib., 1971–76; Asst. Docum. Libn., IN Univ. Lib., 1968–70. **Educ.:** Eckerd Coll., 1966, BA, (Pol. Sci.); IN Univ., 1970, MLS; Univ. of NM, (Mgt.); Cert. in Law Libnshp., Amer. Assn. Law Libs., 1976. **Orgs.:** ALA: LAMA/Lib. Org. and Mgt. Sect., Budgeting Acctg. and Costs Com. (1979/81). NM LA: Lib. Educ. Com. (1978–80); Treas. (1977–78). SLA: Bylaws and Proc. Com. (1975/76); Rio Grande Chap., Pres. (1974–75), Exec. Bd., Ch., Contin. Educ. Com. (1975–76). SWLA: Exec. Bd. (1978–80). **Honors:** Council on Lib. Resrc., Acad. Lib. Mgt. Internship, 1979. **Pubns.:** "Continuing Education-VIII," *Coll. and Resrch. Libs. News* (D. 1978); "Being a Library Management Intern at Stanford," *Stanford Lib. Bull.* (May 1979). **Activities:** 1; 15, 17, 39; 77, 78, 92 **Addr.:** Reference Dept., University of New Mexico General Library, Albuquerque, NM 87131.

Coleman, Theodore Hamilton, Jr. (Fb. 17, 1944, Jacksonville, FL) Asst. Prof. (LS), Chief, Lib. Proc. Srvs., Med. Coll. of GA, 1975–. **Educ.:** Duke Univ., 1962–66, AB (Gk.); Southeast. Bapt. Theo. Sem., 1966–69, MDV (Theo.); Emory Univ., 1974–75, MLn (LS); Duke Univ., 1969–77, PhD (Relig.); Med. LA, Cert. **Orgs.:** Med. LA. Socty. of Bible Lit. **Pubns.:** "Rank and promotion of library faculty in a health sciences university," Bltn of the Med. LA (Jy. 1977). **Activities:** 1, 12; 15, 20, 44; 80, 90 **Addr.:** 824-D33 Hickmon Rd., Augusta, GA 30904.

Coley, Betty (Ag. 4, 1933, Corrigan, TX) Libn., Armstrong Browning Lib., Baylor Univ., 1972–; Law Libn., Fulbright & Jaworski, 1969–72; Libn., Aldine Sch. Dist., 1967–69; Libn., Mesquite Sch. Dist., 1965–67. **Educ.:** Sam Houston State Univ., 1950–53, BS, (Soclgy.); E. TX State Univ., 1959–61, MEd (Elem. Supvsn. & LS); Teaching Cert., 1953; Libn. Cert., 1964; T.W.U., 1978–80, MLS. **Orgs.:** TX LA: District Ch. (1979–80). ALA. SWLA. SLA. AAUW: Branch pres. (1975–77); Division Histn. & District Coord. (1979–81). Arthritis Fndn. Bd.: Patient Educ. (Ch., 1979–80); Delta Kappa Gamma. **Honors:** AAUW, Outstan. Member–Waco Branch, 1980. **Pubns.:** Ed., *My Browning Family Album* (1979); "Painting by Pen Browning Acquired", *Studies in Browning & His Circle* (Spr. 1976). **Activities:** 1, 12; 17, 23, 45; 55 **Addr.:** P. O. Box 6336, Waco, TX 76706.

Colhocker, Brother Lawrence J., FSC. (Je. 7, 1936, Pittsburgh, PA) Dir. of Instr. Mat. Ctr., LaSalle Coll., 1979–; Dir. of Curric., St. Gabriel's Hall, 1974–79; Dir. of Media Srvs., W. Cath. HS, 1973–74; Principal, Bishop Walsh HS, 1966–72. **Educ.:** LaSalle Coll., 1955–58, BA (Eng.-Ed.), 1958-59, MA (Theo.); Cath. Univ., 1960–70, MA (Eng.); Drexel Univ., 1972–73, MS (LS); Univ. of PA, 1974–, EdD, in progress. **Orgs.:** ALA; AASL. AECT. PA Lrng. Resrc. Assn. Assn. for Supvsn. and Curric. Dev. PA Assn. for Supvsn. & Curric. Dev. Assn. of Tchr. Educ. Natl. Cath. Educ. Assn. Other orgs. **Honors:** Beta Phi Mu, 1973. **Activities:** 1; 17, 32; 63 **Addr.:** La Salle College, 20th St. and Olney Ave., Philadelphia, PA 19141.

Coll, John Daniel (F. 17, 1934, San Francisco, CA) Prin. Libn., San Francisco Pub. Lib., 1968–, Sr. Libn., 1957–68, Libn., 1956–57. **Educ.:** Univ. of CA, Berkeley, 1952–55, BA (Hist.), 1955–56, MLS; various crs. **Orgs.:** SLA: Prog. Com. (1964). Bay Area Ref. Libns. Assn. CA LA: Bay Area Chap. Electric Railroaders Assn. Bay Area Electric Railroad Assn. **Pubns.:** Reviews. **Activities:** 9; 15, 16, 39 **Addr.:** 241 Amber Dr., San Francisco, CA 94131.

Collard, R. Michael (S. 7, 1942, Aurora, IL) Student, Grad. Sch. of LS, Univ. of IL, 1979–; Coord., Boulder Cnty. Hist. Proj., Boulder Pub. Lib., 1977–78; Asst. Libn., 1977; Hist. Resrch., Boulder Cnty. Govt., 1976; Documentarian/Resrch. Assoc., Natl. Assessment of Educ. Progress, Denver, CO, 1975–76; Libn., Dept. of Energy and Resources, Univ. of CA, Berkeley, 1974. **Educ.:** San Francisco State Univ., 1971–74, BA (Phil. & Comp. Lit.); Univ. of CA, Berkeley, 1974 (LS); Univ. of IL, 1978–79, MS (LS); Cert. of Advnc. Study, LS, Univ. of IL, 1979–80. **Orgs.:** ASIS: Student Chap. Ch. (1979–80). IL LA. SLA: Stud. Chap. Treas. (1978–79). ALA: JMRT Handbook Com. (1979–80); Lib. Instruction RT Natl. Prog. Study Taskforce (1980–); YASD/Org. and Bylaws (1980–82). Other orgs. Oral Hist. Assn. Amer. Assn. for State and Local Hist. CO Hum. Prog., Proj. Dir. (1977–78). Boulder Cnty. Hist. Soc., Founder (1978). Other orgs. **Honors:** IL LA, JMRT/Baker & Taylor Grassroots Grant, 1979; Phi Kappa Phi, 1979; Beta Phi Mu, 1979; Boulder Cnty. Hist. Soc., Lifetime Mem., 1979. **Pubns.:** Complr., *Brief Descriptions of the Databases in the Major (Publicly Available) Online Reference Systems: BRS, INFORMATION BANK, MEDLARS, ORBIT IV, DIALOG: 1980* (1979–80); Jt. auth., "Conference Report (The Role of the Library in Electronic Society)," *Bltn. of the ASIS* (D. 1979); oral histories, Boulder Cnty. CO (1977–78). **Activities:** 1, 9; 15, 16, 17; 55, 63, 65 **Addr.:** 510 So. First St., #6, Champaign, IL 61820.

Collet, Lois Wuerdeman (Wauwatosa, WI) Mgr., Lib. Info. Srv., D'Arcy, MacManus Masius, 1966–; Libn., A.O. Smith Harvestore Div., 1961–65, Asst. Libn., 1956–61; Libn., Allis-Chalmers Mfg. Co., 1954–56, Asst. Libn., 1951–54. **Educ.:** Univ. of WI, 1938–42, BS (Amer. Inst.); Univ. of WI, Milwaukee, 1951–52 (LS). **Orgs.:** SLA: Advert. and Mktg. Div., Ch. (1978–79), Secy. (1972–73); MI Chap. (Treas., 1981–). Cncl. for Resrc. Dev.: Ch. (1979–80). Oakland Cnty. Un. List of Serials: Adv. Cncl. (1972–). Gvt. Docum. Libns. of MI. Women Overseas Srv. Leag.: Detroit Unit (Pres., 1980). **Activities:** 12; 17, 39; 51, 59 **Addr.:** Library Information Service, D'Arcy-MacManus & Masius, Inc., P.O. Box 811, Bloomfield Hills, MI 48013.

Collett, Joan (S. 13, 1926, St. Louis, MO) Dir., St. Louis Pub. Lib., 1978–; Country & Reg. Libn., U.S. Intl. Comm. Agency, 1966–78; Libn., Grailville Coll., 1964–66; Head, Ext. Dept., Gary Pub. Lib., 1957–64; Instr., Rosary Coll., 1956–57; Reg. Consult., WV Lib. Comsn., 1954–56; Asst. Dir., Clayton Pub. Lib., 1950–53. **Educ.:** Maryville Coll., St. Louis, 1943–47, BA (Lit.); Washington Univ., St. Louis, 1950, MA (Lit.); Univ. of IL, 1954, MS, (LS). **Orgs.:** ALA. MO LA: Dev. Com. (1978–). Frdm. to Read Fndn.: Trustee (1980). Altrusa Intl., St. Louis: Exec. Bd. (1979–). **Pubns.:** "American Libraries Abroad: USIA Activities," *Lib. Trends* (Ja. 1972). **Activities:** 4, 9; 15, 17 **Addr.:** 1301 Olive St., St. Louis, MO 63111.

Colley, Charles C. (Ja. 5, 1938, Indio, CA) Dir., Spec. Col., Lib., Univ. of TX at Arlington, 1981–; Head, AZ Col./Archvst., Hayden Lib., AZ State Univ., 1972–80; Instr., 1977–80; Instr., Phoenix Coll., 1976–80; Archvst., AZ Hist. Soc., 1966–72. **Educ.:** Univ. of CA, Los Angeles, 1957–60, BA (Hist.); San Diego State Univ., 1962–65, MA (Hist.); AZ State Univ., 1972–75, PhD (Hist.); Arch. Cert., Univ. of Denver, 1967. **Orgs.:** SAA: AZ Hist. Rec. Adv. Comsn. (1976–). West. Hist. Assn. AZ Hist. Soc.: Bd. of Dirs. (1976–). **Honors:** Phi Alpha Theta, 1970. **Pubns.:** *The Century of Robert H. Forbes* (1977); *Documents of Southwestern History* (1972); various articles. **Activities:** 1, 2 **Addr.:** The Library, P.O. Box 19497, The University of Texas at Arlington, Arlington, TX 76019.

Collier, Bonnie B. (D. 4, 1944, Dumont, NJ) Sr. Ref. Libn., Yale Univ., 1972–, Arch. Asst., 1970–72; Ref. Libn., Amer. Hist. Div., NY Pub. Lib., 1969–70; Assoc. Ed., Funk & Wagnalls, Inc., 1967–69. **Educ.:** Univ. of Bridgeport, 1962–66, BA (Hist.); Univ. of CT, 1966–69, MA (Hist.); Columbia Univ., 1969–71, MLS. **Orgs.:** ALA. Assn. for the Study of CT Hist. **Pubns.:** "The Ohio Western Reserve," *CT Review* (N. 1975); "The Library Journals: Putting Things in Order," *Change Magazine* (My. 1974); "Abraham Lincoln and the Trumbull Fortress," *Yale Lib. Gazette* (Ja. 1974); "Noah Webster's Notes," *Bltn. of the NY Pub. Lib.* (My. 1970). **Activities:** 1; 31, 39; 55, 57 **Addr.:** Reference Department, Sterling Memorial Library, Yale University, New Haven, CT 06520.

Collier, Monica H. (N. 7, 1953, Detroit, MI) Ref./Micro. Libn., Purdy Lib., Wayne State Univ., 1979–; Chld. Libn., Redford Pub. Lib., 1978–79. **Educ.:** MI State Univ., 1971–75, BA (Educ.); Univ. of MI, 1977–78, AMLS. **Orgs.:** Natl. Micro. Assn.: MI Chap., Eager Schol. Com. (1979–80). **Pubns.:** "Acceptance of Microfiche in Academic Libraries," *ASIS Bltn.* (O. 1980); "The John P. Eager Scholarship," *MI Micro. News* (D. 1979). **Activities:** 1, 5; 33, 39; 92 **Addr.:** Purdy Library, Wayne State University, 5244 Gullen Mall, Detroit, MI 48202.

Collier, Susan D. (Ja. 29, 1930, Oklahoma City, OK) Educ. Media Spec., Levin B. Hanigan Lib., Deerfield Sch., 1964–. **Educ.:** Carleton Coll., 1947–51, BA (Soclgy.); Rutgers Univ., 1966, MLS. **Orgs.:** ALA: ALSC, Bd. of Dirs. (1979–), Notable Chld. Bks. Com. (Ch., 1971–75); Chld. Bk. Cncl. Jt. Com. (Ch., 1975–76). New Providence Pub. Lib.: Trustee (1960–65). Leag. of Women Voters. Mountainside Tchrs. Assn. Educ. Media Assn. of NJ: Rec. Secy. (1976–77). Educ. Media Assn. of Un. Cnty. (NJ). **Activities:** 10; 21 **Addr.:** 76 Whitman Dr., New Providence, NJ 07974.

Collier, Mrs. Virginia Spore (F. 14, 1919, Dallas, TX) Libn., U.S. Gvt. Docum. Reg. Depos., OK Dept. of Libs., 1978–, Construct. Consult., 1968–77; Chief, Bkmobile Srvs., Tulsa City-Cnty. Lib. Syst., 1960–68; Dir., Okmulgee Pub. Lib., 1953–60. **Educ.:** Univ. of TX, 1936–40, BA (Eng.); Emory Univ., 1940–41, BS in LS. **Orgs.:** ALA: LAMA/Bldg. & Equipment Sect. (Secy., 1979–81); Archit. for Pub. Libs. Com. (1976–80); ALA State of OK Mem. Ch. (1964–66); Com. on Interlib. Coop. (1964–67). OK LA: Secy. (1958–59); Pub. Lib. Div. (Ch., 1956–57). SWLA: Pub. Lib. Div. (Secy., 1960–62). AAUW. **Pubns.:** "The Patients' Library," *News Notes, Bltn. of TX LA* (F. 1944); "Emergency-Damaged Books," *OK Libn.*, (Ja. 1974). **Activities:** 9, 13; 19, 24, 29 **Addr.:** U.S. Govt. Doc. Reg. Dep., Oklahoma Department of Libraries, 200 N.E. 18, Oklahoma City, OK 73105.

Collins, Christiane C. (F. 14, 1926, Hamburg, Germany) Head Libn., Parsons Sch. of Dsgn., 1973–; Catlgr., Musm. of Mod. Art, 1971–72; Readers Srvs., Donnell Art Lib., NY Pub. Lib., 1968–71. **Educ.:** Carleton Coll., 1949, BA (Art Hist.); Columbia Univ., 1954, MA (Art Hist.), 1968, MLS. **Orgs.:** ARLIS/NA. Socty. of Archit. Histns. Coll. Art Assn. **Pubns.:** Jt. transl., *The Architecture of Fantasy* (1962); Jt. transl., Camillo Sitte: *City Planning According to Artistic Principles,* (1965); Jt. transl., *Camillo Sitte and the Birth of Modern City Planning* (1965); Jt. auth., "The Humanistic City of Camillo Sitte" in *Architects' Yrbk.* (1965). **Activities:** 1; 15, 17; 55 **Addr.:** 448 Riverside Dr., New York, NY 10027.

Collins, Donald Edward (D. 6, 1934, Miami, FL) Assoc. Prof., Dept. of Lib. Sci., E. Carolina Univ., 1972–; Asst. Soc. Sci. Libn., Univ. of GA, 1963–70. **Educ.:** FL State Univ., 1959–62, BA (LS/Hist.), 1962–63, MS (LS); Univ. of GA, 1966–70, MS (Hist.), 1970–75, PhD, (Hist.). **Orgs.:** ALA: Adult Lib. Mat. Com. (1977–81). NC LA: Educ. for Libnshp. Com. (1975–78). **Pubns.:** "Reference Works, 1978," *Cath. Lib. World* (O. 1978); "A Georgian's View of Alabama in 1836," *The AL Review* (Jl. 1972). **Activities:** 1; 26, 31, 39; 57, 69, 92 **Addr.:** Dept. of Library Science, East Carolina University, Greenville, NC 27834.

Collins, John W., III (Je. 1, 1948, North Adams, MA) Coord. of Lib. Instr., Boston Univ., 1979–; Asst. Libn., Glenville State Coll., 1975–79, CLR Proj. Dir., 1977–78. **Educ.:** Univ. of MA, 1970–73, BA (Eng.); Univ. of KY, 1974, MLS. **Orgs.:** ALA. WV LA: Exec. Com.; JMRT (Ch., 1978). WV Educ. Media Assn. SELA: Lib. Instr. Com. Glenville W.V.: City Cncl. (1976–78). Gvrs. Conf. on Libs.: Gilmer Cnty. Coord. (1978). **Honors:** Beta Phi Mu, 1975. **Pubns.:** "Library Use, A Matter of Encouragement," *WV Libs.* (Fall 1978); "Bibliographic Instruction in College Libraries," (ERIC 144582); "Use of Periodical Indexes," Slide/Tape (1976). **Activities:** 1; 17, 31 **Addr.:** Mugar Memorial Library, 771 Commonwealth Ave., Boston, MA 02215.

Collins, Marcia Reed (Je. 5, 1945, Passaic, NJ) Art, Archlg., Msc. Libn., Univ. of MO, 1971–. **Educ.:** Univ. of NH, 1963–68, BA (Phil.); Univ. of MO, 1968–71, MALS, 1973–81, MA (Art Hist.). **Orgs.:** ARLIS/NA. Msc. LA. **Pubns.:** *Libraries for Small Museums* (1977); *Early Books on Art* (1977); *The Dance of Death in Book Illustration* (1978); "Archaeology in the Fine Arts Library," *ARLIS/NA Nsltr.* (O. 1979); reviews. **Activities:** 1; 15, 23, 39; 55, 57 **Addr.:** Ellis Library, University of Missouri, Columbia, MO 65201.

Collins, Mary Frances (My. 18, 1935, Albany, NY) Dir., Pub. Srvs., Univ. of IL, Urbana, 1978–; Assoc. Dir., Tech. Srvs., Rice Univ., 1977–78; Asst. Dir., Bibl. Opers., SUNY, Albany, 1975–77, Asst. Dir., Tech. Srvs., 1972–75, Head Catlgr., 1968–72; Ref. Libn., Jr. Coll. of Albany, 1967–68; Catlgr., Nvl. Post Grad. Sch., 1966–67; Catlgr., SUNY, Albany, 1964–66. **Educ.:** Simmons Coll., 1953–57, BA (LS); SUNY, Albany, 1964–66, MLS. **Orgs.:** ALA: ACRL, Pubn. Com. (Ch., 1978–80). **Pubns.:** Ed., *Coll. & Resrch. Lib. News* (1975–77). **Activities:** 1; 17, 39, 46 **Addr.:** Library, University of Illinois, 1408 W. Gregory, Urbana, IL 61801.

Collins, Richard H. (Jl. 19, 1924, Seattle, WA) Libn., Los Angeles Pub. Lib. Art & Msc. Dept., 1973–; Prin. Libn., CA Inst. of Tech., 1971–72; Adult Srvs. Libn., Downey Pub. Lib., 1969–70; Admin. Libn., CA Inst. of the Arts, 1967–68. **Educ.:** Mills College Ext., Paris, France, 1947–48, (Msc.); San Francisco State Univ., 1950–53, BA (Msc.); Univ. of South. CA, 1970–73, MSLS **Orgs.:** SLA. CA LA. South. CA Tech. Prcs. Grp. **Activities:** 1, 9; 17, 39, 46; 55, 91 **Addr.:** 1028 S. Westmoreland Ave. Apt. #1, Los Angeles, CA 90006.

Collins, Sara Jean (N. 13, 1929, Detroit, MI) Virginiana Libn., Arlington Cnty. Dept. of Libs. 1980–; Virginiana Libn., Fairfax Cnty. Pub. Lib., 1979–80; Virginiana Libn., Arlington Cnty. Dept. of Libs., 1974–79, Ref. Libn., 1965–74; Libn., Ctrl. Intelligence Agency, 1951–57. **Educ.:** Albion Coll., 1947–51, BA (Eng.); Cath. Univ. of Amer., 1952–66, MS in LS. **Orgs.:** Oral Hist. in the Mid-Atl. Reg.: Pres. (1977–78). Oral Hist. Assn.: Nom. Com. (1976–78); Reg. Org. (1978–80). VA LA: Ch., Oral History Forum (1977–78); Oral Hist. Wkshp. Com. (1975–77). DC LA. Arlington Hist. Socty.: VP (1978–79); Newsletter Ed., Secy. (1976–78); Ch., Indexing Com. (1975–81). Hist. Socty. of Fairfax Cnty. North. VA Histns. **Honors:** Arlington Cnty., VA, Merit Awd., 1975. **Pubns.:** *Arlington County in Maps, 1608–1975* (1976); "A Librarian looks at books in Arlington", *North. VA Heritage* (F. 1979); "Program in Action", *The Zontian* (Mr. 1978); Ed., *OHMAR* (1977–78). **Activities:** 2, 9; 15, 23, 45; 69, 78, 85 **Addr.:** Virginia Collection, Arlington County Dept. of Libraries, 1015 North Quincy St., Arlington, VA 22201.

PROFESSIONAL ACTIVITIES: Institutions: 1. Acad. lib.; 2. Arch.; 3. Assn.; 4. Fed./Gvt. lib.; 5. Inst. lib.; 6. Mfr./Suppl.; 7. Milit. lib.; 8. Musm.; 9. Pub. lib.; 10. Sch. lib.; 11. Sch. of lib. sci.; 12. Spec. lib.; 13. State lib.; 14. (other). **Functions/Activities:** 15. Acq./Col. dev.; 16. Adult srvs.; 17. Admin.; 18. Apprais.; 19. Archit./Bldgs.; 20. Cat./Class.; 21. Chld. srvs.; 22. Circ.; 23. Cons./Pres.; 24. Consult.; 25. Cont. ed.; 26. Educ. lib. sci.; 27. Ext. srvs.; 28. Fund/Grants; 29. Gvt. pubs.; 30. Indx./Abs.; 31. Instr. lib. use; 32. Media srvs.; 33. Micro.; 34. Netwks./Coop.; 35. Persnl.; 36. PR; 37. Publshg.; 38. Recs. mgt.; 39. Ref. srvs.; 40. Repro.; 41. Resrch.; 42. Review.; 43. Secur.; 44. Serials; 45. Spec. col.; 46. Tech. srvs.; 47. Trustees/Bds.; 48. YA srvs.; 49. (other).

Collinsworth, Barbara L. Howle (Jl. 16, 1934, Detroit, MI) Assoc. Dean, Learning Resrc., Macomb Cnty. Cmnty. Coll., 1975–; Coord. of Lib. Servs., 1968–75; Jr. HS Libn., Walled Lake Consolidated Sch., 1959–68; HS Libn., Lake Orion Cmnty. Sch., 1957–59; Elem. Libn., Pontiac Pub. Sch., 1957; HS Libn., Clawson Pub. Sch., 1955–56. **Educ.:** Ctrl. MI Univ., 1951–55, AB (LS); Univ. of MI, 1959–67, AMLS; MI State Univ., 1969–70. **Orgs.:** ALA: ACRL/Vice Ch./Ch. Elect-Cmnty. & Jr. Coll. Libs. Sect. (1979–81); Mem. Com. (1977–81); Choice Ed. Bd. (1976–78). MI Lib. Cnsrtm.: Exe. Com. (1977–79). MI LA: Cmnty. Coll. RT, Ch. (1972). Friends of Sterling Heights Pub. Lib.: Pres. (1977–78). **Honors:** Beta Phi Mu, 1967; Phi Delta Kappa, 1955. **Pubns.:** Article, *Forward* (Win. 1970). **Activities:** 1; 17, 26; 63 **Addr.:** Macomb County Community College, 14500 E. Twelve Mile Rd., Warren, MI 48093.

Colman, Gould P. (Ap. 30, 1926, Medina, NY) Univ. Archvst., Cornell Univ., 1973–; Dir., Prog. Oral Hist., 1965–72, Coll. Histn., Coll. of Agr., 1962–65. **Educ.:** Cornell Univ., 1947–51, AB, 1954–56, PhD (Amer. Hist.); 1959–61. **Orgs.:** SAA. Org. of Amer. Histns. Rural Soclgy. Socty. Agr. Hist. Socty. **Pubns.:** "Oral History, An Appeal for More Systematic Procedures," *Amer. Archvst.* (1965); "Making Library History," *Jnl. of Lib. Hist.* (Ap. 1972); "Oral History As Agricultural Literature," *Agr. Lit: Proud Heritage - Future Promise* (1977); "Women's Rights and Centralization of Libraries," *Jnl. of Lib. Hist.* (Win. 1979). **Activities:** 1, 2; 41, 45; 62, 86 **Addr.:** 101 Olin Library, Cornell University, Ithaca, NY 14853.

Colquhoun, Joan Eileen (Je. 1, 1951, Toronto, ON) Head, Msc. Sect., Cat. Branch, Natl. Lib. of Can., 1981–, Msc. Catlgr., 1978–80; Supply Libn., Etobicoke Pub. Lib., 1976–78. **Educ.:** Univ. of West. ON, 1969–73, BA (Msc.); Univ. of Toronto, 1976–78, MLS; Royal Cnsvty. of Toronto, 1974, ARCT (Cello). **Orgs.:** Can. Assn. of Msc. Libs.: Exec. Bd., mem.–at–Lg. (1980–81), Secy (1981–). Can. LA. Intl. Assn. of Msc. Libs.: Mem. of the Working Grp. on Comp. Cat. (1980–). Msc. LA: Cat. Com. on AACR2. Assn. of Rec. Snd. Cols. Ottawa Symph. Orch. **Pubns.:** "The Impact of AACR–2 on Cataloguing of Music and Sound Recording," *Can. Assn. of Msc. Libs. Nsltr.* (No. 1981). **Activities:** 4; 20; 55 **Addr.:** Music Section, Cataloguing Branch, National Library of Canada, Ottawa, ON K1A 0N4 Canada.

Colson, John Calvin (D. 9, 1926, Kingman, IN) Consult., 1979–; Asst. Prof., North. IL Univ., 1975–79; Asst. Prof., Univ. of MD, 1966–74; Lect., Coll. of Libnshp., Wales, 1971–72; Acq. Libn., State Hist. Socty. of WI, 1961–65, Pub. Srvs. Libn., 1953–60; Libn. I, Milwaukee Pub. Lib., 1951–53. **Educ.:** OH Univ., 1944–50, BA (Hist.); West. Reserve Univ., 1950–51, MS in LS; Univ. of Chicago, 1960–73, PhD (LS). **Orgs.:** AALS: Lib. Hist. Interest Grp. NLA: Prof. Educ. Com. (Ch., 1979–). SAA: Com. on Arch./Lib. Relshps. (1971/72; 1977/78); Com. on Educ. and Prof. Dev. (1970/71; 1972–76). SLA: Cncl. (1957–60); WI Chap. (Pres., 1959–60). Other orgs. and coms. **Honors:** Beta Phi Mu Prize, 1961. **Pubns.:** "The press, civic and public library development in 19th century Wisconsin: speculations on relationships," *Jnl. of Lib. Hist.* (Winter 1978); "The United States: a historical critique." *Library services to the disadvantaged* (1975); "The rise of the public library in Wisconsin, 1850–1920," *Milestones to the Present,* (1978); "Lutie Eugenia Stearns", "Henry Eduard Legler," *Dictionary of American Library Biography* (1978); "Horse-nettles in the hollyhocks: some personal views on education for librarianship," *Natl. Libn.* (Ag. 1979); Other articles, reviews, oral presentations. **Activities:** 2, 9; 16, 27, 39; 62, 73, 75 **Addr.:** Management Technology Consultants, 813 Somonauk, Sycamore, IL 60178.

Colson, Judith K. (S. 1, 1936, Syracuse, NY) Head, Docu. Dept., Univ. of NB, 1967–; Asst. Head Serials Section, Acq. Dept., Univ. of MI, 1963–67; Docu. Libn., 1961–63; Readers' Adv., Syracuse Pub. Lib., 1960–61. **Educ.:** Roberts Wesleyan Coll., 1954–58, BA (Eng.); Syracuse Univ., 1959–60, MSLS. **Orgs.:** Can. LA: Info. Can. Com. (1976). Govt. Pub. Com. (1977). Can. Assn. of Coll. and Univ. Libs.: Nom. Com. (1977). Atlantic Provinces LA. ALA. **Honors:** Beta Phi Mu, 1960. **Activities:** 1; 29, 44; 70 **Addr.:** 230 Winslow St., Fredericton, NB E3B 2A1 Canada.

Colston, Stephen A. (N. 5, 1945, La Jolla, CA) Dir., San Diego Hist. Resrch. Ctr., San Diego State Univ., 1978–, Archvst., 1977; Lectr., Dept. of Soc. and Culture, Lect., Dept. of Anthr., UCLA, 1974–76. **Educ.:** Univ. of San Diego, 1964–67, BA (Hist.); UCLA, 1970–73, PhD (Hist.), 1975–76, MLS; Cert. of Postdoctoral Study in Anthr., UCLA, 1973–74. **Orgs.:** Socty. of CA Archvsts.: Cncl. (1979–81). SAA. Société des Américanistes de Paris. West. Hist. Assn. **Pubns.:** *A Guide to the Collections of the San Diego History Research Center* (1978); "The 'Historia Mexicana' and Durán's *Historia," Journal de la Société des Américanistes* (1973). **Activities:** 1, 2; 17, 24, 49-Educ. for Arch. Mgt.; 55, 85, 95-Reg. Studies. **Addr.:** San Diego History Research Center, University Library, San Diego State University, San Diego, CA 92182.

Colter, Carole Anne (Je. 3, 1940, Detroit, MI) Hlth. Sci. Libn., Midland (MI) Hosp. Ctr., 1978–; Libn., E. Ctrl. MI Hlth. Syst. Agency, 1976–77; Libn., St. Joseph Mercy Hosp. Med. Lib. & Sch. of Nursing Lib., 1974–75; Libn. Asst., Burroughs Corp. Lib., 1973–74; Ref. Libn., The Detroit News Lib., 1970–73. **Educ.:** Wayne State Univ., 1963, BA (Pol. Sci.), 1975, MSLS; MI Permanent Teaching Cert., 1966; Grad. Studies, Wayne State Univ., 1964–65 (Pol. Sci.). **Orgs.:** MI Hlth. Sci. Libs. Assn.: Pres.-Elect (1979), Pres. (1980). Valley Reg. Hlth. Sci. Libns.: Secy.-Treas. (1976–78), VP (1979–). MI LA: Rep. Cncl. (1979–). Med. LA. **Activities:** 12, 14-Hlth. Sci. Lib.; 15, 17, 34; 80, 95-Nursing. **Addr.:** Midland Hospital Center, Health Sciences Library, 4005 Orchard Dr., Midland, MI 48640.

Comaromi, John P. (Ap. 4, 1937, Flint, MI) Ed., Dewey Decimal Class., Chief, Decimal Class. Div., Lib. of Congs., 1980–; Assoc. Prof., Grad. Sch. of Lib. & Info. Sci., Univ. of CA, Los Angeles, 1977–79; Assoc. Prof., Sch. of Libnshp., West. MI Univ., 1970–77; Asst. Prof., Sch. of Libnshp., Univ. of OR, 1968–70; Tchr., Flushing HS, 1961–64. **Educ.:** Flint Coll., Univ. of MI, 1959–61, BA (Eng.); Univ. of MI, 1961–64, AMLS, 1964–65, MA (Eng.), 1966–69, PhD (LS). **Orgs.:** ALA: Decimal Class. Ed. Policy Com. (1973–79). **Honors:** Phi Beta Kappa, 1961. **Pubns.:** *The Eighteen Editions of the Dewey Decimal Classification* (1976); "Knowledge Organized is Knowledge Kept," *Qtly. Jnl. of the Lib. of Congs.* (O. 1976); *Survey of the Use of the DDC in the U.S. and Canada* (1975). **Activities:** 1, 11; 20, 26, 30 **Addr.:** Decimal Classification Division, Processing Services, Library of Congress, Washington, DC 20540.

Combe, David A. (D. 10, 1942, New Orleans, LA) Law Libn., Tulane Univ., 1972–; Assoc., Adams and Reese, New Orleans, 1971–72. **Educ.:** Tulane Univ., 1964, BA (Anth.), 1971, JD; LA State Univ., 1975, MLS. **Orgs.:** AALL: Com. on Foreign, Intl. and Comparative Law (1977–). Intl. Assn. of Law Libs.: Ch., Com. on Rare Books and Spec. Col., (1980–). Law Lib. Microform Consortium Natl. Adv. Bd. (1979–). LA State Bar Assn. **Pubns.:** Trans., *A Historical Summary of the French Codes* (1979); "French Legal Bibliographies," *Intl. Jnl. of Law Libs.* (Mr. 1979). **Activities:** 1, 12; 24, 33, 45; 69, 77, 78 **Addr.:** Tulane University Law Library, New Orleans, LA 70118.

Combs, Adele W. (Ja. 10, 1933, Mendota, IL) Asst. Univ. Libn. for Pub. Srvs., Northwest. Univ., 1975–, Actg. Asst. Univ. Libn. for Pub. Srvs., 1973–75, Deputy Asst. Univ. Libn., 1969–73, Ref. Libn., 1968–69; Libn., Vernon Ct. Jr. Coll., 1965–68; Libn., Newport Sch. for Girls, 1965–68; Ref. Libn., Columbia Univ., 1963–65, Asst. Docum. Libn., IN Univ., 1957–63. **Educ.:** IN Univ., 1951–56, AB (Soclgy.), 1956–57, MA (LS). **Orgs.:** ALA: ACRL; LAMA, Com. on Org. (1979–). IL LA. IL Reg. Lib. Cncl.: Bd. of Dirs. (1975–81). **Honors:** Beta Phi Mu. **Activities:** 1; 17 **Addr.:** Northwestern University Library, 1935 Sheridan Rd., Evanston, IL 60201.

Comeau, Reginald A. (N. 22, 1934, St. Leonard, NB) Consult., Educ. Media Srvs., NH State Dept. of Educ., 1973–; Media Spec., E. Lyme Jr. HS, 1970–73; Consult., YA Srvs., East. MA Pub. Lib. Syst., 1969–70; Reg. Coord., S. Cnty. Interrel. Lib. Syst., 1968–69; Gen. Lib. Asst., Calgary Lib. Srv. Ctr., 1967; Sch. Libn., Housatonic Valley Reg. HS, 1965–67; Acq. Libn., Univ. of CT Sch. of Law, 1962–65. **Educ.:** Univ. of Hartford, 1957–61, BA (Hum.); South. CT State Coll., 1962–67, MSLS; Boston Univ., 1979, EdD (Educ. Media, Tech.). **Orgs.:** Natl. Assn. of State Educ. Media Profs.: Dirs. Com. (1980). New Eng. Educ. Media Assn.: Plng. Com. (1979–80); Exec. Bd. (State Rep., 1973–). NH Educ. Media Assn.: Exec. Bd. (State Rep., 1973–). **Pubns.:** *The Plain Rapper; Selection Processes* (1979); "Nothing to Fear but...," *Bay State Libn.* (O. 1970); ed., *Mediums of Comm.* nsltr. (1975–). **Activities:** 10, 14-State Dept. of Educ.; 17, 24, 32; 63, 95-Netwks. **Addr.:** New Hampshire State Dept. of Education, 64 N. Main St., Concord, NH 03301.

Compton, Anne W. (Je. 28, 1948, Stillwater, OK) Coord., Resrc. Ctr., Pop. Info. Prog., Johns Hopkins Univ., 1978–; Dir., Lib. Srvcs., Union Mem. Hosp., 1975–78; Head, Biomedical Sect., Edgewood Arsenal, 1973–75; Libn., Picctinny Arsenal, 1972–73. **Educ.:** East Carolina Univ., 1966–71, MSLS; Univ. of MD, 1971–72, MLS. **Orgs.:** SLA. **Pubns.:** "Reclassification of a small hospital library," *Bltn. of the Med. LA* (1977). **Activities:** 4, 12; 17, 39, 46; 58, 80, 91 **Addr.:** Population Information Center, Johns Hopkins University, Baltimore MD 21214.

Compton, Olga M. (Mr. 7, 1950, Milano, Italy) Mgr., Tech. Info. Ctr., Ctrl. VT Pub. Srv. Corp., 1977–; Resrch. Asst., Ofc. of Lib. Srvs., SUNY, OCLC, 1976–77; Asst. to Chief, Benefits, State of VT Dept. of Empl. Secur., 1972–73. **Educ.:** Univ. of VT, 1969–72, BA (Hist., Asian Std.); SUNY, Albany, 1974–76, MLS; Mgt. Inst., Dept. of Libs., 1979, Cert. **Orgs.:** ALA. SLA: Pub. Utils. Div. (Treas., 1979–81). VT LA: Coll. and Spec. Libs., VP (1981), Pres. (1982). Amer. Mgt. Assn. Edison Electric Inst. **Pubns.:** Jt. auth., "The Florence Floods," *Nat. Hist.* (1973). **Activities:** 12; 15, 17, 41; 59, 64, 86 **Addr.:** Central Vermont Public Service Corporation, 77 Grove St., Rutland, VT 05701.

Conable, Gordon M. (Ja. 5, 1947, Buffalo, NY) Assoc. Dir., Ft. Vancouver Reg. Lib., 1979–, Head, Comnty. Srvs., 1978–79, Vancouver Cmnty. Libn., 1975–78. **Educ.:** Antioch Coll., 1964–69, BA (Art); Columbia Univ., 1974–75, MS (LS). **Orgs.:** ALA. SLA. Interstate Lib. Plng. Cncl.: Secy. (1979–). WA LA: Int. Frdm. Com. (1976–79). Outrch. Progs. for Essential Needs (Ch., 1978–79). Various other orgs. Kiwanis. Amer. Civil Liberties Union. Natl. Org. for Women. **Honors:** Beta Phi Mu. **Activities:** 9; 16, 17, 36; 50, 74 **Addr.:** Fort Vancouver Regional Library, 1007 E. Mill Plain Blvd., Vancouver, WA 98663.

Conaway, Charles Wm. (Jl. 11, 1943, Anniston, AL) Asst. Prof., Sch. of LS, FL State Univ., 1977–; Asst. Prof., Sch. of Info. and Lib. Studies, SUNY at Buffalo, 1971–77; Fulbright Sr. Lect., Univ. of Iceland, 1974–75; Visit. Lect., Coll. of Libnshp., Univ. of SC, 1973; Resrch. Fellow, Grad. Sch. of Lib. Srv., Rutgers Univ., 1968–71; Head Ref. Libn., FL Atl. Univ., 1966–68. **Educ.:** Jacksonville (AL) State Univ., 1961–64, AB (Eng./Admin.); FL State Univ., 1964–65, MLS; Rutgers Univ., 1974, PhD (Info. Sci.); GA Dept. of Arch. and Hist., 1968, Cert.; Cornell Univ. Engin. Contin. Educ., 1973, Cert.; Univ. of WA Sch. of Libnshp., 1978, Cert. **Orgs.:** ALA. ASIS. SELA. SLA. Other orgs. Amer. Assn. for Computational Ling. **Honors:** Beta Phi Mu. **Pubns.:** *A User's Guide to Rice's KWAC* (Keyword-Alongside-Context) *Indexing Program* (1973); "Normative Values of Coefficients of Index Usability of "Off-the-Shelf" Indexes," *Lib. Resrch. RT Resrch. Forums. Proc.* (1979); "Bibliography and Indexes," *ALA Yrbk.;* "Lyman Copeland Draper," *Dictionary of Amer. Lib. Biog.* (1977); "Retrieval-Oriented Storage of Medical Data: Operational Aspects," *Jnl. of Clinical Comp.* (1973); other articles. **Activities:** 1, 11; 26, 39, 41; 56, 57, 75 **Addr.:** School of Library Science, Florida State University, Tallahassee, FL 32306.

Concepción, Luis (F. 11, 1950, Aguadilla, PR) AV Libn., Univ. of PR, Aguadilla, 1980–; Syst. Libn., Univ. of PR, Río Piedras, 1979–80, Asst. Libn., Acq., 1976–77, Admin. Asst., Acq., 1972–76. **Educ.:** Univ. of PR, Río Piedras, 1968–71, BA (Econ.); 1973–75, MLS; Univ. of TX, 1977–79, Sixth Year Cert. **Orgs.:** ALA. Assn. of Caribbean Univ. and Resrch. Libs.: Pubn. Com. (1976–80). Socty. de Bibtcr. de PR: Treas. (1976–77). Reforma. Assn. Para las Comm. y Tech. Educ. Assn. **Activities:** 1; 15, 46; 56, 75 **Addr.:** 15 D St. Urb. Jard. de Maribel, Aguadilla, PR 00603.

Condit, Martha Olson (S. 8, 1913, East Orange, NJ) Retired, 19–; Consult., Media Srvs., Montclair Pub. Schs., 1973, Coord., Lib. and AV Srvs., 1965–72, Sch. Libn., 1956–65; Chld. Libn., East Orange Pub. Schs., 1945–56; Chld. Libn., Passaic Pub. Lib., 1943–45; Chld. Libn., Nutley Pub. Lib., 1936–43. **Educ.:** Pratt Inst., 1933–34, Cert. (LS); Rutgers Univ., 1953, BA (Hist., Psy.), 1954–58, MLS. **Orgs.:** ALA: AASL; ALSC. Montclair (NJ) Operetta Club. Cable Car Playhse. Calvary Presby. Church. **Pubns.:** "If Only the Teacher Had Stayed with the Class," *Elem. Eng.* (My. 1975); "Trade Books for Beginning Readers," *Wilson Lib. Bltn.* (D. 1959); *Something to Make Something to Think About* (1975); *Easy to Make Good to Eat* (1976); *KOALA!* (1981). **Activities:** 6; 24 **Addr.:** 17 Lincoln Ave., Florham Park, NJ 07932.

Conduitte, Gretchen Garrison (F. 10, 1909, Sewickley, PA) Ref. Libn., Orlando Pub. Lib., 1975–80, Retired; Ref., 1967–75; Libn., Monroe Cnty. Pub. Lib., 1964–67; Community Rel., Jacksonville Pub. Lib., 1954–64; Libn., Jackson Lib., FL, Jackson, Tenn., 1952–54; Dir., First Reg. Lib., Hernando, MI, 1950–52; NY Pub. Lib., 1935–41; Asst. Libn., Bennington Coll., 1932–35. **Educ.:** Univ. of CA, Los Angeles, 1927–31, BA (Phil.); Columbia Univ., 1931–32, BSLS. **Orgs.:** ALA. FL LA. Southeast. LA. Lib. Pub. Rel. Cncl. League of Women Voters. AAUW. **Honors:** Peace Essay Winner, 1981, Orlando Religious Society of Friends (Quakers); Adult Literacy League at Valencia Comm. Coll. **Pubns.:** Ed., "Talents Inside," *AAUW* (1978). **Activities:** 1, 9; 16, 36, 39; 89 **Addr.:** 3508 N. Westmoreland Dr., Orlando, FL 32804.

Congdon, Nell Archer (My. 15, 1938, Augusta, GA) Head, Info. & Ref. Div., New Orleans Pub. Lib., 1969–; Head of Circ., Jefferson Parish Lib., 1968–69, Asst. Supvsr. of Branches, 1967–68; Libn. I, Atlanta Pub. Lib., 1963–64. **Educ.:** Agnes Scott Coll., 1956–60, BA (Hist. & Pol. Sci.); Emory Univ., 1961–63, MLn (LS). **Orgs.:** ALA. Freedom To Read Foundation. LA LA: Int. Frdm. Com. (1974–76), Conf. Regis. Com. (1977). SWLA. World Sci. Fiction Conv.: Supporting Mem. (1980 & 1981). **Pubns.:** "Hezekiah Alexander House," *Our North Carolina Heritage* (1960). **Activities:** 9; 16, 39, 48; 74, 89 **Addr.:** Information & Reference Division, New Orleans Public Library, 219 Loyola Ave., New Orleans, LA 70140.

Conger, Lucinda Dickinson (Je. 11, 1941, Ft. Bragg, NC) Sr. Ref. Libn., U.S. Dept. of State, 1976–; Prin. Ref. Data Arch. Libn., Yale Univ., 1973–75; Asst. Prof., Albion Coll. 1970–73, Serials/Docum. Libn., 1971–73; Dir., Reclass., 1970–71, Annex Libn., Princeton Univ, 1966–70; Catlgr., then Ref. Libn., Lib. of Congs., 1965–66; Ref. Libn., Univ. of CA, Davis, 1964–65. **Educ.:** Radcliffe Coll., 1959–63, BA (Anthro.); Rutgers Univ., 1963–64, MLS. **Orgs.:** ASIS: Numeric Data Bases Spec. Interest Grp. (Secy.-Treas., 1979–80). Intl. Assn. for Soc. Sci. Info. Srvs. and Tech. Bibl. Retrieval Srvs.: Fed. Lib. Com. (Rep., 1977–80). Radcliffe Club of DC. Washington Cathedral. **Pubns.:** "Multiple System Searching," *Online* (My. 1980); "Data Reference with MRDF," *Jnl. of Acad. Libnshp.* (My. 1976); "Annex Library of Princeton University," *Coll. & Resrch. Libs.* (My. 1970); "Online Command Chart" *Online Spec. Pubn.*

Special Subjects/Services: 50. Adult educ.; 51. Advert./Mktg.; 52. Aerosp.; 53. Agric.; 54. Area std.; 55. Arts/Hum.; 56. Autom.; 57. Bibl./Prtg.; 58. Bio. sci.; 59. Bus./Fin.; 60. Chem.; 61. Copyrt.; 62. Documtn.; 63. Educ.; 64. Engin.; 65. Env.; 66. Eth. grps.; 67. Film; 68. Food/Nutr.; 69. Geneal.; 70. Geo.; 71. Geol.; 72. Handcpd.; 73. Hist.; 74. Int. frdm.; 75. Info. sci.; 76. Insr.; 77. Law; 78. Legis.; 79. Math./Comp. sci.; 80. Med.; 81. Metals; 82. Nat. resrcs.; 83. Newsp.; 84. Nuc. sci.; 85. Oral hist.; 86. Petr./Energy; 87. Pharm.; 88. Phys./Astr./Math.; 89. Readg.; 90. Relig.; 91. Sci./Tech.; 92. Soc. sci.; 93. Telecom.; 94. Transp.; 95. (other).

(1980). **Activities:** 1, 4; 20, 31, 39; 54, 56, 92 **Addr.:** 4906 Jamestown Rd., Bethesda, MD 20016.

Conklin, Curt E. (Ap. 8, 1947, Huntington Park, CA) Cat. Libn., Law Lib., Brigham Young Univ., 1972–; Cat. Libn., UT Tech. Coll., 1979–. **Educ.:** Brigham Young Univ., 1965–72, BA (Hist.), 1972–77, MLS; AALL, 1978, Cert. **Orgs.:** AALL. UT LA: Various coms. UT Coll. Lib. Cncl. **Pubns.:** *Library of Congress KF Cross-Reference* (1979); *Library of Congress Entries For State and Local Bar Associations* (1978); jt. auth., *Foreign Law Classification Schedule, Class K* (1975). **Activities:** 1, 12; 20; 77, 78 **Addr.:** Brigham Young University, 358-B JRCB, Provo, UT 84602.

Conklin, Harriet W. (O. 1, 1926, Kewanee, IL) Dir., Kewanee Pub. Lib., 1969–; Sch. Libn., Intl. Sch. of The Hague, Holland, 1963–67; Sch. Libn., Ctrl. Jr. HS, Kewanee, IL, 1962–63. **Educ.:** Mount Holyoke Coll., 1944–48, BA (Amer. Culture); Columbia Univ., 1950–51, MLS. **Orgs.:** ALA. IL LA. Kewanee Pub. Hosp.: Bd. of Dir. (1977–). Kewanee United Fund: Bd. of Dir. (1970–76). Leag. of Women Voters. **Activities:** 9, 10; 15, 17, 19; 89 **Addr.:** Kewanee Public Library, 102 S. Tremont St., Kewanee, IL 61443.

Conley, Binford Harrison (F. 13, 1933, Madison Cnty., AL) Dir. Libs., Howard Univ. 1975–; Libn., NC A&T State Univ., 1973–75; Libn., AL A and M, 1962–76; Libn., Scar State Coll., 1960–62; Asst. Libn., Reader Srv., Atlanta Univ., 1957–60. **Educ.:** Morehouse Coll., 1950–53, AB; Atlanta Univ., 1958–60, MLS; Rutgers Univ., 1981, PhD. **Orgs.:** ALA. DC LA. **Pubns.:** Ed., *Proceedings of The Conference of Black Writers* (1965). **Activities:** 1; 66 **Addr.:** Howard University Libraries, Washington, DC 20059.*

Connan, Shere A. (N. 29, 1945, Evansville, IN) Chief Libn., Serials Dept., Stanford Univ. Lib., 1977–; Serials Libn., Univ. of CA, San Diego, 1974–77; Asst. Serials Libn., IN Univ., 1971–74. **Educ.:** IN Univ., 1966–69, AB (Eng.), 1969–70, MLS; Purdue Univ., 1963–66 (Mech. Engin.). **Orgs.:** ALA: RTSD/Serials Sect., Exec. Com. (Secy., 1976–79), Ad Hoc Com. on Lib. Sch. Educ. (1975–79). Assn. for Lib. Autom. Resrch. Comms.: Pres. Adv. Com. (1974), Constn. and Bylaws Com. (1973–74). Libns. Assn. of Univ. of CA: Com. on Coms. Rules, and Jurisdictions (1975–77). **Honors:** Beta Phi Mu. **Activities:** 1; 15, 17 **Addr.:** Stanford University Libraries, Stanford, CA 94305.

Connaughton, Theresa Gonzales (Mr. 7, 1949, Santa Fe, NM) Asst. Tech. Prcs. Libn., Los Alamos Natl. Lab., 1978–, Ref. Libn., 1975–78; Libn., U.S. Army Construct. Engin. Resrch. Lab., 1974. **Educ.:** NM State Univ., 1970–71, BA (Hist.); Coll. of Santa Fe, 1967–70; Univ. of IL, 1973–74, MS (LS). **Orgs.:** SLA: Rio Grande Chap. (Pres., Pres. Elect., 1978–80), *Bltn.* Ed. (1976–77), Proj. Com. (1979–80), Pubcty. Com. (1975–76). NM LA: Coll., Univ., and Spec. Lib. Div., ACRL Chap. Std. Com. (1981). NM State Lib. Cont. Lib. Educ. Adv. Cncl. (1980–82). NM WHCOLIS: Del. (1978). **Activities:** 12; 15, 39, 46; 84, 91 **Addr.:** Rte. 7 Box 111 D, Santa Fe, NM 87501.

Connell, Robert E. (F. 12, 1936, Winthrop, MA) Coll. Librn., Washington and Jefferson Coll., 1968–; Sr. Ref. Libn. and Instr., Lib. Sci., WV Univ., 1966–68; Head Libn. and Housemaster, HI Prep. Acad., 1964–66; Sr. Opers. Supvsr., Western Union Telegraph Co., 1960–63; Latin Inst. and Housemaster, Middlesex Sch., 1957–60. **Educ.:** Brown Univ., 1953–57, AB (Hist.); Rutgers Univ., 1963–64, MLS. **Orgs.:** Citizens Lib. of Washington, PA: Bd. of Trustees (1977–), Treas. and Ch., Finance Com. (1978–). Pittsburgh Reg. Lib. Ctr.: Bd. of Trustees (1977–). **Honors:** Beta Phi Mu, 1964. **Activities:** 1, 9; 15, 17, 47; 55, 74 **Addr.:** Library, Washington and Jefferson College, Washington, PA 15301.

Connell, Wessie G. (N. 21, 1915, Cairo, GA) Dir., Roddenbery Meml. Lib., 1939–. **Educ.:** Peabody Coll., Emory Univ., Spec. Std. **Orgs.:** ALA. GA LA. SELA. S. GA Assn. of Libs.: Pres. (1981). Various other orgs., ofcs. First Un. Meth. Church. GA Ornith. Socty. GA Hist. Socty. GA Geneal. Socty. Various other orgs. **Honors:** ALA, *Wilson Lib. Bltn.*, John Cotton Dana Awd., 1958; Lib. PR Cncl., Awd., 1949–50, Cairo Kiwanis, First Citizen of the Yr., 1948; Garden Club of GA, Merit Awd., 1948. **Pubns.:** *Gardening Handbook for Armchair Aficionados* (1975); "Public Relations in a Small Public Library," *PR for Libs.* (1974); "So You're Going to Have a Drive," *Wonderful World of Books* (1952); "One Library's Role in Adult Education," *Adult Leadership* (1972). **Addr.:** Roddenbery Memorial Library, North Broad, Cairo, GA 31728.

Conners, Margaret S. (D. 7, 1914, Cincinnati, OH) Dir., Med. Lib., Good Samaritan Hosp., 1974–; Serials Libn., Gen. Hosp., Univ. of Cincinnati, 1967–74. **Educ.:** Univ. of Cincinnati, 1972, BS (Eng.). **Orgs.:** Med. LA. SLA: Budget Com. (1979–80); Educ. Com. (Ch., 1978–79); ASIS: South. OH Chap. (Secy., 1978–79). **Activities:** 1, 12; 15, 17; 58, 63, 80 **Addr.:** Medical Library, 2d fl, Good Samaritan Hospital, Cincinnati, OH 45220.

Connick, Kathleen D. (S. 30, 1952, Cincinnati, OH) Lib. Dir., Med. Lib., Good Samaritan Hosp., Cincinnati, 1981–; Network Prof. Coord., Tampa Bay Med. Lib. Network, 1979–80; Lib. Dir., Christ Hosp. Inst. of Med. Resrch., 1976–79. **Educ.:** OH Univ., 1970–74, BA (Psy.); Univ. of KY, 1974–75, MSLS; Med. LA, Grade I Cert., 1977–81. **Orgs.:** Med. LA: Ed. Com., *MLA News* (1980–82). SLA: FL Chap. Network Com., Ch. (1979–80). Cincinnati Chap. Educ. Com. (1978–79). FL Med. Libns.: Interconsortia Coop. Com., Ch. (1980–81). Cincinnati Area Hlth. Sci. Lib. Assn.: VP (1977–78), Secy. (1978–79). **Pubns.:** Jt. auth., "Standards for Small Hospital Libraries," *Ohio Hospital Association Bulletin* (D. 1977). **Activities:** 12; 17, 34, 39; 58, 80, 87 **Addr.:** Medical Library, Good Samaritan Hospital, 3217 Clifton Ave., Cincinnati, OH 45220.

Connor, Billie M. (O. 4, 1934, Brighton, MO) Head, Sci. and Tech. Depart., Los Angeles Pub. Lib., 1979–, Head, Bus. and Econ. Dept., 1977–79, Sr. Libn., 1970–77; Bus. and Econ. Subj. Spec., South. CA Answering Network, 1969–70; Ref. Libn., Bus. and Tech. Srv., Wichita Pub. Lib., 1962–68; Ext. Libn., Southwest Reg. Lib., Bolivar, MO, 1959–62. **Educ.:** Southwest MO State Univ., 1951–55, BS in ED (Span.); Rutgers Univ., 1958–59, MLS; Univ. de Guanajuato, 1956, (Span. lang. and lit.); Miscellaneous univ. courses, 1959–; SUNY, Albany, 1975, Inst. on Lib. Srv. to the Bus. Cmnty. **Orgs.:** CA LA: Cnclr.-at-Large (1972–74; 1979–81). SLA: Bus. and Finance Div. (Ch., 1977–78); Heart of Amer. Chap. (Pres., 1967–68; Pres.-Elec., 1966–67; Treas., 1965–66). ALA: Cncl. (1980–). Libns. Guild: VP (1973–76); Treas. (1979). Other orgs. AAUW. Amer. for Democratic Action. Sierra Club. **Pubns.:** Jt. cmplr., *Ottemiller's Index to Plays in Collections* (1971, 1976); Various articles; Ed., *COMMUNICATOR* (1973–76). **Activities:** 9; 15, 17, 39; 59, 91 **Addr.:** 1707 Micheltorena, #312, Los Angeles, CA 90026.

Connors, Jean M. (My. 8, 1925, Staten Island, NY) Adult Srvs. Libn., S. Huntington Pub. Lib., 1978–; Ref. & Tech. Proc., E. Pub. Lib., 1975–78; School Libn., various NY schs., 1964–74. **Educ.:** Elmira Coll., 1943–47, AB (Eng.); Long Island Univ., 1964–66, MSLS; Southampton, Dowling & Hefsha Colls., 1965–67, (Educ. & Supvsn.). **Orgs.:** Suffolk LA: Inst. Com., Regis. (1979–80). Suffolk Sch. LA: Pres. (1968–69). **Activities:** 9; 15, 16, 39 **Addr.:** Box 757 Huntington, NY 11743.

Connors, William E. (S. 20, 1935, St. Joseph, MI) Dir., Sojourner Truth Lib., SUNY, New Paltz, 1977–; Coord. of Tech. Srvs., 1966–77; Coord. of Reclass. Ofc., Univ. of MD, 1963–66; Cat. Libn., NY State Sch. of Labor and Indust. Rel. at Cornell Univ., 1960–63. **Educ.:** Kalamazoo Coll., 1953–57, BA (Eng.); Ohio Wesleyan Univ., 1957–59, MA (Eng.); Univ. of MI, 1959–60, AMLS. **Orgs.:** ALA. NY LA: RTSS, Resrc. Com. (Ch., 1978–79; VP, 1980-81). S. East. NY Lib. Resrc. Cncl.: Pres. (1977–78), Bd. of Trustees (1975–). New Paltz Coll. Fed. Credit Un.: Treas., VP. **Pubns.:** "Reclassification at the University of Maryland," *Lib. Resrc. and Tech. Srvs.* (Spr. 1967); "The Academic Role of Librarians," *Fac. Senate Bltn.* (Ja. 1968). **Activities:** 1; 17, 35, 46; 56 **Addr.:** Sojourner Truth Library, State University of New York, College at New Paltz, New Paltz, NY 12561.

Conover, Craig Robert (O. 19, 1946, Plainfield, NJ) Lib. Dir., Sussex Cnty. Lib. Syst., 1978–; Asst. Lib. Dir., Fair Lawn Pub. Lib., 1977–78; Instr., Elem. Educ., William Paterson Coll., 1973–77; Media Spec., Brookdale Cmnty. Coll., 1971–73; Libn., Red Bank Reg. HS, 1969–71. **Educ.:** Trenton State Coll., 1964–68, BA (Pol. Sci.); Univ. of Pittsburgh, 1968–69, MLS; Rutgers Univ., 1972–78, Cert. Adv. Std. (Admin.). **Orgs.:** ALA. NJ LA: Educ. for Libnshp. Com. (1976–78); Admin. Sect. Nsltr. (Ch., 1977–78). Cnty. Libns. Assn. of NJ: Secy. (1980–82). Area Lib. Dirs. of NJ. NJ State Lib., LSCA Adv. Cncl. **Honors:** Beta Phi Mu; Bed Bank Reg. Bd. of Educ., Cert. of Apprec., Bldg. Consult., 1972. **Pubns.:** Reviews. **Activities:** 9, 11; 17, 19, 26; 63, 92, 95-Instr. tech. **Addr.:** Sussex County Library System, R.D. 3, Box 76, Newton, NJ 07860.

Conrad, Agnes Catherine (S. 7, 1917, Pasadena, CA) State Archvst., HI State Arch., 1955–; Dept. Head, Univ. of HI Lib., 1950–55; Catlgr., Univ. of CA, Los Angeles, 1946–50; Base Libn., USAAF, Victorville, CA, 1942–45; Rare Bk. Catlgr., Henry E. Huntington Lib., 1941–42. **Educ.:** Holy Names Coll., Oakland, CA, 1935–39, BA (Hist.); Univ. of CA, Berkeley, 1939–40, Cert. (LS.). **Orgs.:** SAA: Cncl. Mem. 1968–69). HI LA: Pres. (1962); Ch., By-laws (1975–79). Intl. Cncl. of Arch. HI Msms. Assn.: Pres. (1970). HI Hist. Soc.: Pres. (1967–69). Hist. HI Fndn.: Trustee (1977–1980). Amer. Assn. for State & Local Hist.: Awds. Ch., HI (1970–1978). Other orgs. **Honors:** HI Lib. Assn., Disting. Libn. Awd., 1979; Hist. HI Fndn., Presrvn. Awd., 1976; SAA, Fellow, 1964. **Pubns.:** Ed., *Don Francisco de Paula Marin, Letters and Journal* (1973); Ed., *Proc. of the 1950 Constitutional Convention, State of HI* (1960); "Hawaiian Registered Vessels," *HI Jnl. of Hist.* (1967); "Genealogical Sources in Hawaii," *HI Lib. Assn. Jnl.* (1974); Ed., *Hawaiian Journal of History* (1972, 1974–1975). **Activities:** 2; 17, 38 **Addr.:** Hawaii State Archives, Iolani Palace Grounds, Honolulu, HI 96813.

Conrad, James Henry (Jl. 13, 1940, Cleveland, OH) Head, Univ. Arch., E. TX State Univ., 1976–, Inst. of Hist., 1967–70, 1972–74. **Educ.:** Wittenberg Univ., 1958–62, AB (Hist.); OH State Univ., 1964–66, MA (Hist.); Case Western Reserve Univ., 1976–76, Cert. (Arch.); OH State Univ., 1967–74, PhD, (Hist.); TX Woman Univ., 1974–75, MLS. **Orgs.:** SAA. Socty. of Southwest Archvsts. TX State Hist. Assn.; E. TX Hist. Assn. **Pubns.:** *An Annotated Bibliography of Old Age in America* (1978); *Texas Educational History: A Bibliography* (1979). **Activities:** 1, 2; 23, 33, 45; 57, 85, 92 **Addr.:** James G. Gee Library, ET Sta, Commerce, TX 75428.

Conrow, Jane Henning (N. 30, 1944, Connersville, IN) Head, ILL Srv., AZ State Univ. Lib., 1981–, Head, Access Srv., 1976–80; Head, Howe Archit. Lib., 1968–75; Head, Ellettsville Branch, Monroe Co. (IN) Pub. Lib., 1968; Head, Circ., 1966–67. **Educ.:** IN Univ., 1962–66, BA (anthro.), 1966–68, MLS. **Orgs.:** ALA. ARLIS/NA: Ch., Archit. Spec. Interest Grp. (1977). Art Libs. Socty./AZ: Ch. (1978). Amer. Inst. of Architects Assn. for Archit. Libns. **Honors:** Cncl. on Lib. Resrcs., Fellow, 1975; AZ State Univ., Faculty Grant-in-aid, 1973. **Pubns.:** Jt. ed., *Index to the Paolo Soleri Archive,* (1973–); "Accreditation Standards and Architecture Libraries–a Status Report," *Spec. Libs.* (N. 1975); Jt. auth., "Paolo Soleri Archive, Arizona State University", *Man-Environment Systems* (V.5 #5. 1975); "The Literature of Adobe; a Biblio Brief," *CA Libn.* (Jl. 1972). **Activities:** 1; 17, 34; 55 **Addr.:** 1124 East Laguna, Tempe, AZ 85282.

Conroy, Barbara (My. 16, 1934, Sioux Falls, SD) Consult., 1973–; Dir., Outreach Leadership Network, New England Ctr. for Cont. Educ., 1971–72; Dir., Washington Seminar, Catholic Univ. Lib. Sch., 1970–71; Dept. Head, Soc. and Bus., Denver Pub. Lib., 1964–68; Head, Bus. Div., 1961–64. **Educ.:** SD State Univ., 1952–56, BS (Eng.); Univ. of Denver, 1956–57, MLS; Boston Univ., 1969–70, CAGS (Ad. Educ.). **Orgs.:** ALA: Cncl. (1974–77); Staff Dev. Com. (1970–74, 1979–81); LAMA PAS Ch. (1981). Cont. Educ. Network and Exch.: Adv. Com. (1976–80). AALS. Mountain Plains LA. Adult Educ. Assn.: Task Force on Libs. and Lifelong Lrng. (1979–80). Mountain Plains Adult Educ. Assn. Amer. Socty. for Trng. and Dev. (Rocky Mntn. Chap.). **Pubns.:** *Library Staff Development and Continuing Education* (1978); *Library Staff Development Profile Pages* (1979); "Continuing Education: Carrot or Stick?," *Cath. Lib. World* (Mr. 1978); "A Consumer's Guide to Staff Development Resources," *Jrnl. of Lib. Admin.* (My. 1980). **Activities:** 24, 25, 28; 50, 92 **Addr.:** 30 Lynx Rd., Box 520, Tabernash, CO 80478.

Considine, Joseph D. (S. 18, 1938, Lowell, MA) Head, Reader Srvs./Acq. Libn., New Eng. Coll., 1976–, Ref. Libn., 1976. **Educ.:** Univ. of NH, 1973, BA (Soclgy.); Univ. of RI, 1975, MLS. **Orgs.:** ALA: ACRL. New Eng. LA. New Eng. Tech. Srvs. Libns.: Nom. Com. (1977). NH LA: Nom. Com. (1976), Bylaws Com. (1978–80), Treas. (1978–). Amer. Cvl. Liberties Un. Dem. Soc. Org. Com. **Activities:** 1; 15, 16, 39; 74, 75, 92 **Addr.:** Box 651, Henniken, NH 03242.

Conway, Jeanne W. (Ja. 21, 1918, Chicago, IL) Pub. Srvs. Libn., Gallaudet Coll. Lib., 1973–, Circ. Libn., 1970–73; Head Ref. Libn., Georgetown Univ. Lib., 1966–70; Ref. Libn., Fairfax Cnty. Pub. Lib., 1966. **Educ.:** Rosary Coll., 1935–39, BA (Soclgy., Fr.); Cath. Univ. of America, 1964–66, MS in LS. **Orgs.:** ALA: ASCLA/LSDS Prog. and Actv. Com. (1980–81). ASIS. DC LA: Asst. Treas. (1975–77). Conv. of Amer. Instr. of the Deaf. AAUP: Pres., Gallaudet Branch (1972). **Honors:** Beta Phi Mu; Kappa Gamma Pi. **Activities:** 1; 15, 36, 39; 61, 72, 75 **Addr.:** Gallaudet College Library, 7th and Florida Ave. N.E., Washington, DC 20002.

Coogan, Helen M. (Mr. 12, 1920, Sioux Falls, SD) Lib. Supvsr., Sci. Ctr., Rockwell Intl., 1975–, Lib. Resrch. Anal., 1962–75, Cat./Acq. Libn., 1959–60; Lab Tech., 1945–56. **Educ.:** Mt. St. Mary's Coll., 1937–41, BS (Chem.); Immaculate Coll., 1958–61, MA (LS). **Orgs.:** SLA: Various coms. Cath LA. **Pubns.:** Jt. auth., *The Mossbauer Effect Data Index 1966–1968* (1975); *The Mossbauer Effect Data Index 1958–1965* (1966); "Computer Information Techniques Applied to the Mossbauer Effect," *Bltn. of the Amer. Phys. Socty.* (1967). **Activities:** 12; 15, 17, 39; 52, 60, 88 **Addr.:** Rockwell International, Science Center Library, 1049 Camino Dos Rios, Thousand Oaks, CA 91360.

Cook, C(harles) Donald (Jl. 6, 1923, Scottsbluff, NE) Assoc. Prof., Fac. of Lib. Sci., Univ. of Toronto, 1972–; Dir., Ofc. of Lib. Coord., Cncl. of ON Univs., 1969–72; Coord. of Cat., Columbia Univ. Libs., 1960–69; Asst. to the Dir., Persnl., 1957–59; Assoc. in Lib. Srv., 1952–57; Docum. Libn., United Nations Lib., 1947–52; Catlgr., Columbia Univ. Libs., 1946–47. **Educ.:** Univ. of AZ, 1945, BA (Eng.Lit.); Columbia Univ., 1946, BS (LS); 1956, MS (LS); 1977, DLS. **Orgs.:** Can. Assn. of Lib. Sch. Can. LA: ALA/CLA Jt. Com. (1971–73); Tech. Srus. Coord. Grp. (1975–77). Can. Assn. Coll. and Univ. Libs. ALA: Cncl. (1967–71); ACRL: Bd. of Dir. (1973–77); RTSD: Pres. (1970–71); Bd. of Dir. (1965–72). Other orgs. Can. Assn. of Univ. Tchrs. AAUP. **Honors:** Beta Phi Mu; Phi Beta Kappa; NY Tech. Srvs. Libns., Citation, 1977. **Pubns.:** *SIMCOE II User Manual* (1979); Jt. ed., *Use of the Library of Congress Classification* (1968); "The Practical Possibilities for PRECIS in North America," *The PRECIS Index Syst.* (1977); "Means of Achieving Standardization" in *Natl. Conf. on Cat. Standards, Ottawa, 1970,* Papers (1970); "The Year's Work in Cataloging, 1967," *Lib. Resrcs. & Tech. Srvs.* (Spring 1968); other articles. **Activities:** 11; 20, 26, 46 **Addr.:** Faculty of Library Science, University of Toronto, 140 St. George Street, Toronto, ON M5S 1A1 Canada.

PROFESSIONAL ACTIVITIES: Institutions: 1. Acad. lib.; 2. Arch.; 3. Assn.; 4. Fed./Gvt. lib.; 5. Inst. lib.; 6. Mfr./Suppl.; 7. Milit. lib.; 8. Musm.; 9. Pub. lib.; 10. Sch. lib.; 11. Sch. of lib. sci.; 12. Spec. lib.; 13. State lib.; 14. (other). **Functions/Activities:** 15. Acq./Col. dev.; 16. Adult srvs.; 17. Admin.; 18. Apprais.; 19. Archit./Bldgs.; 20. Cat./Class.; 21. Chld. srvs.; 22. Circ.; 23. Cons./Pres.; 24. Consult.; 25. Cont. ed.; 26. Educ. lib. sci.; 27. Ext. srvs.; 28. Fund/Grants; 29. Gvt. pubs.; 30. Indx./Abs.; 31. Instr. lib. use; 32. Media srvs.; 33. Micro.; 34. Netwks./Coop.; 35. Persnl.; 36. PR; 37. Publshg.; 38. Recs. mgt.; 39. Ref. srvs.; 40. Repro.; 41. Resrch.; 42. Review.; 43. Secur.; 44. Serials; 45. Spec. col.; 46. Tech. srvs.; 47. Trustees/Bds.; 48. YA srvs.; 49. (other).

Cook, Gail Fleming (Mr. 8, 1939, Salt Lake City, UT) Assoc. Dean, Lib., CA State Univ., Dominguez Hills, 1976–; Asst. Dir., Ref./Persnl., 1970–76, Head Pers. Libn., 1966–70, Asst. Educ. Libn., 1963–66. **Educ.:** OR State Univ., 1958–61, BS (Educ.); Univ. of CA, Los Angeles, 1962–63, MLS; CA State Univ., Long Beach, 1974–77, MPA; Univ. of South. CA, 1978– (Pub Admin.). **Orgs.:** CA Acad. and Resrch. Libns.: Secy. (1979), Nsltr. Ed. (1980). CA LA. ALA: ACRL. Amer. Socty. for Pub. Admin. **Activities:** 1; 17, 34, 35; 95-Pub. admin. **Addr.:** Library, California State University, Dominguez Hills, Carson, CA 90747.

Cook, J. Frank (D. 5, 1939, Lynchburg, VA) Dir. of Arch., Univ. of WI-Madison, 1971–; Archvst., 1965–71. **Educ.:** E. TN State Univ., 1958–61, BS (Hist.); Univ. of WI-Madison, 1962–70, MS, PhD (Am. Hist.). **Orgs.:** SAA: Cncl. (1974–78); Exec. Com. (1977–78); Ch., Com. on Reg. Arch. Act. (1973–74, 1979–80). *Amer. Archvst.* Ed. Bd. (1978–81); other coms. Midwest Arch. Conf.: VP (1973–76); *Midwestern Archivist* Ed. Bd. (1976–80). Org. of Amer. Histns. **Honors:** SAA, Fellow, 1978. **Pubns.:** "'Private Papers' of Public Officials," *Amer. Archvst.* (July, 1975); "The Archivist: Link Between Scientist and Historian," *Amer. Archvst.* (Oct., 1971). **Activities:** 1, 2; 17, 38, 45; 57, 63, 85 **Addr.:** University Archives, B 134 Memorial Library, University of Wisconsin-Madison, Madison, WI 53706.

Cook, Jeannine S. (Ap. 11, 1929, New York, NY) Lib. Dir., Emma S. Clark Meml. Lib., 1967–; Assoc. Libn., SUNY, Stony Brook, 1962–63; Sr. Prof. Admin., Engin. & Physical Sci. Lib., Columbia Univ., 1960–62; Ctrl. Med. Libn., Amer. Cyanamide Co., 1958–60. **Educ.:** Hunter Coll., 1947–51, AB; Columbia Univ., 1956–58, MLS; Adv. Degree in LS, 1973. **Orgs.:** SLA. Med. LA. Admin. Assn. of Brookhaven & Riverhead Libs.: Pres. Pub. Lib. Dir. of Suffolk Coop. Lib. Syst.: Exec. Bd. Amer. Chem. Socty. Three Village Comnty. Youth Srvs.: Bd. of Dirs., Persnl. Com. (1980–). **Honors:** PR Awd. of Merit, Best Budget Brochure, 1978. **Activities:** 9; 17, 36, 39; 50, 68, 73 **Addr.:** Emma S. Clark Memorial Library, 120 Main Street, Setauket, NY 11733.

Cook, Margaret Kathleen (N. 18, 1941, St. Louis, MO) Asst. Educ. Psy. Libn., South. IL Univ., Carbondale, 1977–; Visit. Instr., 1976–77. **Educ.:** OK State Univ., 1967–69, BS (Educ.); Univ. of OK, 1970–71, MLSc; South. IL Univ.-Carbondale, 1974–77, PhD (Educ.). **Orgs.:** ALA. IL LA: Comm. Com. IACRL Section (1979–80). Phi Delta Kappa. Kappa Delta Pi. Phi Kappa Phi. **Honors:** Beta Phi Mu. **Pubns.:** Jt. auth., "Research Development of Academic Librarians," *Jnl. of Acad. Libnshp.* (May 1981); "Rank, Status, and Contributions of Academic Librarians . . .," *Coll. and Resrch. Libs.* (May 1981); "Career Education: A Guide to Basic Sources," *RSR* (7:4 1980); "Reduction in Forces and Its Implication for Media Professionals," *IAVA Jnl.* (F. 1978); "The Effects of Copyright Dynamics on Educational Media," *IL AV Assn. Jnl.* (N. 1975); Various speeches. **Activities:** 1; 31, 39; 56, 63, 92 **Addr.:** Education/Psychology Division, Morris Library, Southern Illinois University, Carbondale, IL 62901.

Cook, Marilyn (My. 12, 1936, Pittsburgh, PA) Dir., Med. Lib., WA Hosp. Ctr., 1980–; NC Area Hlth. Educ. Ctr. Liaison Libn., Univ. of NC, 1978–79; Libn., St. Margaret Meml. Hosp., 1968–78. **Educ.:** Chatham Coll., 1954–58, BS (Educ.); Univ. of Pittsburgh, 1967–68, MLS. **Orgs.:** Med. LA: Mid-Atl. Reg. Grp., Ch-Elect., Educ. Com., Ad Hoc Com. on Hosp. Lib. Consults. (1979–81). Med. LA–Natl. Lib. of Med. Liaison Com. (1978–80). SLA. DC Hlth. Scis. Info. Netwk. ALA. **Activities:** 12; 17, 24, 39; 80 **Addr.:** Medical Library, Washington Hospital Center, 110 Irving St N.W., Washington, DC 20010.

Cook, Marion E. (Mr. 30, 1912, Farmington, CT) Lib. Dir., Meriden Pub. Lib., 1955–, Asst. Libn., 1950–55, Head, Cat. Dept., 1946–55; Ref. Libn./Catlgr., W. Hartford Pub. Lib., 1941–46. **Educ.:** Univ. of CT, 1931–35, AB (Eng.); Columbia Univ., 1940–41, MLS. **Orgs.:** ALA: Cncl. (1958–61). New Eng. LA. CT LA: Secy. (1945–46), Procs. Ch. (1947–54). AAUW. Soroptimist Intl. Bus. and Prof. Women. **Activities:** 9; 17, 39, 46 **Addr.:** 518 Fern St., West Hartford, CT 06107.

Cook, Sybilla Avery (Ag. 20, 1930, Buffalo, NY) Lib. Media Spec., Dist. #12, Glide, OR, 1978–; Libn., Dist. #116, Dillard, OR, 1976–78; Media Spec., Dist. #62, Des Plaines, IL, 1969–76; Libn., Dist. #103, Deerfield, IL, 1968–69; Tchr., 1951–66. **Educ.:** Smith Coll., 1948–50; Northwestern Univ., 1950–51, BS (Educ.); Rosary Coll., 1966–68, MA (LS); Univ. of OR, 1977–81, MA in progress (Curric.). **Orgs.:** ALA: AASL; ALSC, Book Discuss. Grp. (1980). OR LA: OR Auth. Com. (1978–80). Pac. NW LA. IL Assn. of Sch. Libns.: Exec. Bd. (1974–76). **Honors:** Beta Phi Mu, 1968. **Pubns.:** "The Delphi Connection," *Wilson Lib. Bltn.* (My. 1978); "Minicatalog for Second/Third Graders," *Sch. Media Qtly.* (Fall 1974); *The Library Flipper* (1974); *Library Flipper Puzzles* (1978); reviews. **Activities:** 10; 31, 32, 42; 63, 74, 75 **Addr.:** 19 North River Dr., Roseburg, OR 97470.

Cook, Terry G. (Je. 6, 1947, Vancouver, BC) Archvst., Pub. Arch. of Can., 1975–. **Educ.:** Univ. of AB, 1965–69, BA (Hist.); Carleton Univ., 1969–70, MA (Hist.); Queen's Univ., 1970–77, PhD (Hist.). **Orgs.:** Assn. of Can. Archvsts.: Assoc. Ed., *Archivaria* (1977–78). Can. Hist. Assn.: Ed., *Historical Papers* (1978–). **Pubns.:** "The Canadian Conservative Tradition: An Historical Perspective", *Jnl. of Can. Studies* (N. 1973); "George R. Parkin and the Concept of Britannic Idealism", *Jnl. of Can. Studies* (Ag. 1975); "Archives Yesterday: A Glimpse at the Enthusiasms and Tribulations of Sir Arthur Doughty", *Archivaria* (Win. 1975–76); "Clio: The Archivist's Muse", *Archivaria* (1977–78); "The Tyranny of the Medium: A Comment on Total Archives", *Archivaria* (1979–80); Other articles. **Activities:** 2; 15, 37, 39; 55, 82 **Addr.:** Public Archives of Canada, 395 Wellington Street, Ottawa, ON K1A 0N3 Canada.

Cooke, Anna L. (Fe. 14, 1923, Jackson, TN) Head Libn., Lane Coll., 1967–; Cat. Libn., 1963–67; Libn., Merry HS, Jackson, TN, 1951–63; Tchr., Jackson City Sch. Syst., 1947–51; Prin., Haywood Cnty. Sch. Syst., 1944–46. **Educ.:** Lane Coll., 1940–44, BA (Soc. Sci); Atlanta Univ., 1951–55, MSLS; TN State Univ., 1944–45, Cert. (Admin.); Univ. of Louisville, 1967, Cert. (Persnl. Admin.). **Orgs.:** ALA: ACRL/Stan. & Accred. Com. (1972–74). Southeastern LA. W. TN LA: Secy. (1981). TN LA: Coll. Sect., Secy. (1978). Delta Sigma Theta: Natl. Proj. Com. (1967–69). Links, Inc.: Area Nsltr. Ed. (1975–80); Pres. (1979–). Jackson Madison Cnty. Sesquicentennial: Secy. (1970–72). Jackson Arts Cncl.: Secy. (1974–76). Other orgs. **Honors:** Lane Coll., Plaque, 1976; American Cancer Socty., Plaque, 1973; City of Jackson, Plaque, 1972; Delta Sigma Theta Sorority, Inc. Cert., 1969–72. **Pubns.:** Ed., *Lane Coll. Reporter* (1965–69). **Activities:** 1; 17, 31, 35; 63, 78 **Addr.:** 120 Hale St., Jackson, TN 38301.

Cooke, Bette L. (O. 26, 1929, Emporia, KS) Head, Dept. of LS and Inst. Tech., Ctrl. MO State Univ., 1972–, Asso. Prof., 1972–; Asst. Prof., Lib. Sci., West. IL Univ., 1966–72; Inst. in Lib. Sci., Catlgr., Northeast MO State Univ., 1964–66. **Educ.:** Univ. of MO, 1949–51, BS (Educ.); George Peabody Coll. for Tchrs., 1963–64, MSLS; IN Univ., Bloomington, 1968–70, EdD. **Orgs.:** ALA; AALS: Liaison Rep. (1973–75). MO LA: Lib. Sci. Educ. Com. (1973–). MO Assn. of Sch. Libns. (1972–). **Honors:** Phi Lambda Theta. **Pubns.:** *Manual and Exercises for Library Usage,* (c 1978); *Interpreting Language Arts Research for the Teacher,* (c 1971). **Activities:** 11; 26; 63 **Addr.:** 1413 Grandview Dr., Warrensburg, MO 64093.

Cooke, Constance Blandy (Mr. 7, 1935, Woodbury, NJ) Dir., Queens Borough Pub. Lib., 1980–, Deputy Dir., 1975–79; Asst. Dir., Mt. Vernon Pub. Lib., 1966–75; Adult Consult., Onondaga Lib. Syst., 1965–66. **Educ.:** Univ. of PA, 1953–56, BA (Soclgy.); Univ. of Denver, 1956–57, MLS; AMA Mgt. Course, 1977–78. **Orgs.:** NYLA: Cnclr. at Large (1979–81); RASD (Pres., 1977–78). ALA: LAMA/Circ. Srvs. Sect. (Pres., 1975–76). Litcy. Volun. of NY State: Bd. (1976–77). Litcy. Volun. of Mt. Vernon: Pres. (1973–75). **Activities:** 9; 16, 17, 25, 36, 48 **Addr.:** Queens Borough Public Library, 89-11 Merrick Blvd., Jamaica, NY 11432.

Cooke, Eileen D. (D. 7, 1928, Minneapolis, MN) Assoc. Exec. Dir. and Dir., ALA, Washington, 1972–; Deputy Dir., 1969–72; Assoc. Dir., 1968–69; Asst. Dir., 1964–68; Pub. Rel. Spec., Minneapolis Pub. Lib., 1962–64. **Educ.:** Coll. of St. Catherine, 1948–52, BS (Lib. Sci.). **Orgs.:** ALA. MN LA. DC LA. Jt. Cncl. on Educ. Telecomm.: Pres. (1977–79). Womens Nat. Book Assn.: Washington/Baltimore Chap., Treas. (1978–80). **Pubns.:** "Role of ALA . . . in . . . Library Legisation," *Library Trends* (Jl. 1975); Jt. auth., "Legislation Affecting Libraries," *Bowker Annual* (1965–); "Washington Office," *ALA Yearbook* (1976–). **Activities:** 9; 17; 61, 78, 93 **Addr.:** 110 Maryland Ave. N.E., Box 54, Washington, DC 20002.

Cookston, James Sanders (Je. 7, 1926, Winnfield, LA) State Supvsr. of Sch. Libs., State Dept. of Educ., 1965–; Asst. Libn., Soc. Sci., LA State Univ. Lib., 1963–65; Admin. Asst., LA State Lib., 1959–63; Instr., Grad. Sch. of LS, LSU, 1958–59; Supvsr., Univ. HS, 1957–58; Tchr. and Libn., E. Baton Rouge Parish Schs., 1950–58; Adj. Fac. Mem., Lib. Sch. and Coll. of Ed., 1972, 1974, 1976, 1978, 1979, 1980; Visit. Prof., Sch. of Lib. Srv., Columbia Univ., 1973. **Educ.:** LA Polytechnic Inst., 1949, BA (Lang.); LA State Univ., 1951, MEd (Educ.), 1955, MSLS, 1971, PhD (Educ.); Cert., McGill Univ. Ecole d'été; Cert., Univ. of Montpelier, France, 1974; Dip., Teacher's College, Debrecen, Hungary, 1980. **Orgs.:** LA LA: Pres. (1967-68). SWLA: Treas. (1974). ALA: Natl. Lib. Week Com. (1968-71). Cath. LA. Natl. Educ. Assn. **Pubns.:** *Standards for School Libraries* (1968); *Building a Home Library* (1969); International Book Year (1972); *Selected Resources for Career Education* (1973); *Resources for Arts and Environmental Studies* (1974); Various articles. **Activities:** 14-State Dept. of Educ.; 17; 63, 92 **Addr.:** 1956 Tamarix Street, Baton Rouge, LA 70808.

Coolidge, Arlan R. (Ap. 10, 1902, Orange, MA) Prof. Emeritus (Msc.), Brown Univ., 1930–, Violinist, Cincinnati Symph. Orch., 1925–27; Various other positions. **Educ.:** Brown Univ., 1920–24, PhB (Eng.); Juilliard Grad. Sch. of Msc., 1927–29, (Violin, Viola); State Acad. of Msc., Vienna, 1929–30, Cert. **Orgs.:** Msc. LA: New Eng. Chap. Frnds. of the Lib., Brown Univ. Assoc. of John Carter Brown Lib. Amer. Msc. Socty.: Cncl. Coll. Msc. Socty.: Pres. (1948–50); Cncl. Frnds. of Providence Pub. Lib. RI Msc. Tchrs. Assoc.: Various ofcs. Various other orgs. and ofcs. **Honors:** Phi Beta Kappa; Providence Coll., Doc. of Msc. (Hon.), 1973; Brown Univ., Doc. of Msc. (Hon.), 1974; RI Coll., Doc. of Msc. (Hon.), 1976. **Pubns.:** *A Guide for Listening* (1938); "Francis H. Brown, 1819–1893, American Composer and Teacher," *Jnl. of Resrch in Msc. Educ.* (1955); "Place of the Arts in College Curricula," *Jnl. of Coll. Msc.* (1972); "Serving the General Student in the Music Curriculum," *Msc. Educs. Jnl.* (1969). **Activities:** 1; 15, 41, 45; 55 **Addr.:** 88 Meeting St., Providence, RI 02906.

Coombs, C'Ceal P. (Ag. 8, 19–, Portland, OR) Self-empl. Bus. Admin., Coombs Projs., 1945–. **Educ.:** Univ. of ID, BS (Eng. Educ.). **Orgs.:** ALA: Cncl. (1969–71); ALTA (Pres., 1968). WA State Lib. Comsn.: Ch. (1960–76). WA State Frnds. Fndn.: Pres. (1977–79). **Honors:** ALA, ALTA, Trustee Cit., 1966; WA LA, Cit., 1967, Life Mem., 1976; Yakima Valley Reg. Lib., Life Mem., 1959; other hons. **Activities:** 9; 25, 28, 47; 69, 78 **Addr.:** Coombs-Mieras Rds., Rte. 1 Box 1055, Yakima, WA 98901.

Coombs, Elisabeth G. (N. 1, 1921, Boston, MA) Head, Tech. Srvs., Nyselius Lib., Fairfield Univ., 1974–; Pub. Srvs. and Ser. Libn., 1973–74; Pub. Srvs. Libn., 1971–73; Adult Srvs. Libn., Weed Mem. Br., Ferguson Lib., Stamford, CT, 1971. **Educ.:** Smith Coll., 1938–42, AB (Premed); Pratt Sch., 1968–71, MLS. **Orgs.:** CT LA: Resrcs. and Tech. Srvs. Sect. (Secy. 1976–77); Vice-Ch. (1977–78); Ch. (1978–79); Nom. Ch. (1979–80); Exec. Bd. (1978–); Co-Ch. Ways and Means (1979–80). New England LA: Membership Com. (1981); New England Tech. Srvs. Sect. (Rec. Secy. 1976–78). New England Lib. Brd.: Serials Task Force (1976–78). Southwestern CT Lib. Cncl.: Union List of Serials Com. (1978–). Various other orgs. Smith Coll. Alum. Assn.: Class Pres. (1967); Class Reunion Ch. (1962–). Darien-New Canaan Smith Club: Pres. (1967), Ch., Used Book Sale (1966–). New Canaan Audubon Socty.: Secy. (1978–). **Honors:** Beta Phi Mu, elected, 1971. **Activities:** 1; 33, 44, 46; 56 **Addr.:** 343 South Ave., New Canaan, CT 06840.

Coombs, Ronald Lawrence (S. 17, 1944, Montpelier, VT) Asst. Libn., SUNY, Brooklyn, 1972–; Asst. Libn., Episcopal Church Ctr., 1967–70; Adlt. Srvcs., Brooklyn Pub. Lib., 1966–67; Lecturer, Pratt Inst., 1976–78. **Educ.:** Atlantic Union Coll., 1962–66, BA (Eng.); Pratt Inst., 1971–72, MLS. **Orgs.:** Med. LA: NY Reg. Grp. (Reg. Com. Ch., 1979; Hosp. Com. Ch., 1978; Pub. Com., 1975; Prog. Com., 1980). Thea. Lib. Assn. **Pubns.:** Reviews. **Activities:** 1; 20; 80 **Addr.:** 111 Eighth Ave., Brooklyn, NY 11215.

Cooney, Jane (Mr. 18, 1943, Montreal, PQ) Lib. Mgr., Can. Imperial Bank of Cmrc., 1972–; Libn., Econ. Div., 1969–72; Ref. Libn., Metro Toronto Bus. Lib., 1966–69; Circ. Libn., McGill Univ., Redpath Lib., 1965–66; Ref. Libn., Calgary Pub. Lib., 1964–65; Assoc. Instr., Univ. of Toronto Fac. of Lib. Sci., 1975–79. **Educ.:** Marianopolis Coll., 1959–63, BA; Univ. of Toronto, 1963–64, BLS, 1974, MLS. **Orgs.:** SLA: Bus. & Finance Div. (Ch., 1979–80; Dir., 1977–78); Pres., Toronto Chap. (1976–77). Can. LA: Com. on Publications (1976–79), Review Com. on *Can. Per. Index* (1974–75). Seneca Coll., Toronto: Lib. Tech. Adv. Com. (1977–81). Rathnally Area Residents Assn.: Treas. (1979–81). Micromedia Ltd - Can. Bus. Index: Ed. Bd. (1975–). **Pubns.:** "Prospects for Women in the Paid Labor Market: Response," *In Changing Times Changing Libraries* (1978); Jt. comp., "United States and Canadian Business and Banking Information Sources," *Law Lib. Jnl.* (N. 1977). **Activities:** 11, 12; 17, 26, 39; 59, 92 **Addr.:** Information Centre, Canadian Imperial Bank of Commerce, Head Office–Commerce Court, Toronto, ON M5L 1A2, Canada.

Cooney, Jane Bentley (Ag. 6, 1928, Huntsville, AL) Admin. Libn., Redstone Scientific Info. Ctr. Redstone Arsenal, 1951–. **Educ.:** Samford Univ., 1946–50, BA (Eng.); Alabama A&M Univ., 1971–75, MLS. **Orgs.:** AL LA: Pres. (1961–62); VP (1960–61); Treas. (1958–59, 1963–64). SLA: AL Chap., Pres. (1969–70); Secy./Treas. (1955–56). Natl. Micro. Assn.: Southeast. Chap., VP (1977–78); Secy. (1976–77). **Honors:** U S Army, Outstan./Sustained Superior Performance, 1960; 63; 67; 70; 71. **Pubns.:** "Automation at the Redstone Scientific Information Center - An Integrated System," *Lib. Resrcs. and Tech. Srvs.* (Sum. 1974). **Activities:** 4, 12; 17, 33, 46; 52, 56, 91 **Addr.:** Redstone Scientific Information Center, Redstone Arsenal, AL 35898.

Cooper, Arthur Gerald (Ja. 2, 1939, Far Rockaway, NY) Elem. Libn., Mineola Pub. Schs., 1964–; Ref. Libn., Bethpage Pub. Lib., 1979–; Ref. Libn., Syosset Pub. Lib., 1975–79; Ref. Libn., Plainview-Old Bethpage Pub. Lib., 1964–75; Jr. HS libn., Massapequa Pub. Schs., 1960–64. **Educ.:** Queens Coll., 1956–60, BA 1960–61, MS (Educ.), Dipl. Lib. Educ.; C. W. Post Coll., 1978–80, MLS. **Orgs.:** Nassau-Suffolk Sch. LA: Second VP (1974–75). Long Island Educ. Comm. Cncl.: Directory Ch. (1975–76). NY LA: Second VP, Sch. Lib. Media Sect. (1976–77); Ed., SLMS Nsltr. (1977–78). Long Island Sch. Media Assn.: Directory Ed. (1978–79). Mineola Tchrs. Assn.: Building Rep. (1971); Asst. Ed., Nsltr. (1979–). **Honors:** Beta Phi Mu, 1980; N.Y.S. Congs. of Parents & Tchrs., Honorary Life Memb., 1976. **Activities:** 10; 21, 39, 48 **Addr.:** 8 Woodland Drive, Old Bethpage, NY 11804.

Cooper, B. Jane (O. 5, 1929, Detroit, MI) Head Libn., Jt. Ctr. for Grad. Std., 1971–; Tech. Ref. Spec., Battelle Northwest,

Special Subjects/Services: 50. Adult educ.; 51. Advert./Mktg.; 52. Aerosp.; 53. Agric.; 54. Area std.; 55. Arts/Hum.; 56. Autom.; 57. Bibl./Prtg.; 58. Bio. sci.; 59. Bus./Fin.; 60. Chem.; 61. Copyrt.; 62. Documtn.; 63. Educ.; 64. Engin.; 65. Env.; 66. Eth. grps.; 67. Film; 68. Food/Nutr.; 69. Geneal.; 70. Geo.; 71. Geol.; 72. Handcpd.; 73. Hist.; 74. Int. frdm.; 75. Info. sci.; 76. Insr.; 77. Law; 78. Legis.; 79. Math./Comp. sci.; 80. Med.; 81. Metals; 82. Nat. resrcs.; 83. Newsp.; 84. Nuc. sci.; 85. Oral hist.; 86. Petr./Energy; 87. Pharm.; 88. Phys./Astr./Math.; 89. Readg.; 90. Relig.; 91. Sci./Tech.; 92. Soc. sci.; 93. Telecom.; 94. Transp.; 95. (other).

1967–71. **Educ.:** Univ. of MI, 1947–52, BA (Educ.); Univ. of WA, 1962–66, MA (LS). **Orgs.:** ALA. SLA. WA LA: Assn. of Acad. and Resrch. Libns. (Secy.–Treas., 1979–80). **Activities:** 1; 17, 26 **Addr.:** Joint Center for Graduate Study, 100 Sprout Rd., Richland, WA 99352.

Cooper, Barbara Duncan (Jl. 5, 1925, Los Angeles, CA) Secy., Cncl. for FL Libs., Inc., VP, Reg. IV, ALTA, 1978–; Del., White House Conf. on Lib. and Info. Srvs., 1979; Ch., Plng. Com., FL Gov. Conf. on Lib. and Info. Srvcs., 1976–78; Ch., Friends and Trustees Caucus, FL LA, 1975–77; Pres., Broward Cnty. Lib. Assn., 1972–74. **Educ.:** San Jose State Univ., 1943–44. **Orgs.:** ALTA: VP, Reg. IV (1978–79). Cits. and Awds. Com. (1978–80). FL LA: Cit. and Awds. Com., Ch. (1979–80). Cncl. for FL Libs., Inc., Secy. (1979–80). Southeast LA. Various other orgs. Jr. League, Fort Lauderdale, Inc. Women's Aux. to Broward Cnty. Med. Assn.: Pres. (1962–63). League of Women Voters, Broward Cnty. Charter Rev. Bd., City of Fort Lauderdale. **Honors:** FL LA: Friends and Trustees Awd., 1977. ALA: Trustee Cit., 1978. **Pubns.:** Various articles, *FL Libs.* (1975–). **Activities:** 9; 47; 54, 78 **Addr.:** 936 Intracoastal Dr., Apt. 60, Fort Lauderdale, FL 33304.

Cooper, Ellen R. (Ag. 9, 1950, Muskegon, MI) Dir., Lrng. Resrc. Ctr., Presby. Hosp., Charlotte, NC, 1981–; Med. Libn., St. Luke's Hosp., 1976–81; Asst. Branch Libn., Cleveland Pub. Lib., 1974–76, Lib. Srv. Rep., Unvsl. Pers., 1973–74. **Educ.:** Oakland Univ., 1970–72, BA (Hist.); Univ. of MI, 1972–73, MALS; Med. LA, 1978, Cert. **Orgs.:** Tri-Cnty. Lib. Cncl.: Bd. (1981). WI Hlth. Sci. LA: Exec. Bd. (1978–81); Cont. Educ. Com. (Ch., 1978–81). Southeast. WI Hlth. Sci. Lib. Cnsrtm.: Secy. (1978–79), Cont. Educ. Com. (Ch., 1978–81). Various other orgs. Childbirth Educ. Srvs.: Bd. (1981). **Pubns.:** "A One Year Promotion Campaign at St. Luke's Hospital," *Hosp. Libs.* (S. 1977). **Activities:** 5; 15, 17, 39; 80, 95-Nursing. **Addr.:** 3416 Champaign St., Charlotte, NC 28210.

Cooper, Hilma F. (My. 21, 1942, Elmira, NY) Dir., Cheltenham Township Libs., 1978–; Head Libn., Glenside Free Lib., 1974–78. **Educ.:** Dickinson Coll., 1960–64, AB (Eng.); Drexel Univ., 1966–67, MSLS. **Orgs.:** PA LA. ALA. **Pubns.:** Reviews. **Activities:** 9; 17, 39 **Addr.:** Cheltenham Township Libraries, Keswick Ave. and Waverly Road, Glenside, PA 19038.

Cooper, Joanne S. (N. 7, 1926, New York, NY) Libn., Dir. of Lrng. Resrc. Ctr., Mercyhurst Coll., 1972–, Ref. Libn., 1971–72; Ref. Libn., Alliance Coll., 1970–71; Asst. Ref. Libn., Merrick (N.Y.) Pub. Lib., 1967–70. **Educ.:** Cornell Univ., 1944–45; New York Univ., 1945–48, BA (Phil.); Long Island Univ., 1964–69, MLS. **Orgs.:** Northwest Interlibrary Coop. of PA: Ch. (1974–78). PA LA. ALA. Natl. Org. for Women. Amer. Civil Liberties Un. **Honors:** Beta Phi Mu, 1978. **Activities:** 1, 2; 15, 17, 34; 80, 92, Criminal Justice. **Addr.:** Learning Resource Center, Mercyhurst College, 501 E. 38 St., Erie, PA 16546.

Cooper, M. Jane (D. 17, 1934, Hamilton, ON) Head, Circ. Dept., Univ. of Toronto Lib., 1978–; Asst. Head, Circ. Dept., 1971–78; Libn.-in-Charge, Laidlaw Lib., 1968–71; Libn., Circ. Dept., 1958–60. **Educ.:** McMaster Univ., 1953–57, BA (Fr. & Germ.); Univ. of Toronto, 1957–58, BLS; 1968–71, MLS. **Orgs.:** Can. LA: ILL Com. (1979–). ON LA: Conf., Lcl. Arrange. Com. (1979); Nom. Com. (1981). Libns. Assn. of the Univ. of Toronto: Pres. (1973–74). Bibli. Socty. of Can. **Activities:** 1; 17, 22, 35 **Addr.:** University of Toronto Library, 130 St. George St., Toronto, ON M58 1A5 Canada.

Cooper, Marianne Abonyi (Ap. 14, 1938, Budapest, Hungary) Asst. Prof., Grad. Sch. of Lib. & Info. Studies, Queens Coll., CUNY, 1980–; Instr., 1975–80; Head, Studies Sect., Info. Div., Amer. Inst. of Phys., 1967–70; Chem. Libn., Columbia Univ., 1961–66. **Educ.:** Syracuse Univ., 1957–60, BA (Fine Arts); Columbia Univ., 1960–61, MS (LS), 1967–80, DLS. **Orgs.:** ALA. ASIS: Metro. New York Chap. (Ch., 1981–82; Prog. Ch., 1980–81). AALS. SLA. **Honors:** Phi Beta Kappa, 1960; Columbia Univ., George Virgil Fuller Awd., 1972. **Activities:** 11, 12; 17, 26, 41; 75, 88, 91 **Addr.:** 17 St. Lawrence Pl., Jericho, NY 11753.

Cooper, Michael D. (O. 30, 1941, Los Angeles, CA) Assoc. Prof., LS, Univ. of CA, Berkeley, 1972–; Comp. Performance Eval. Spec., Natl. Lib. of Med., 1979; Admin. Anal. V, Univ. of CA, Berkeley, 1969; Systs. Engin., IBM, Sweden, 1966–67, Systs. Progmr., IBM, Los Angeles, 1965–66. **Educ.:** Univ. of CA, Los Angeles, 1959–63, BA (Econ.); Univ. of South. CA, 1963–65, MS (Quantitative Bus. Analysis); Univ. of CA, Berkeley, 1968–71, PhD (LS). **Orgs.:** ASIS. Assn. Comp. Mach.: Various coms. Amer. Econ. Assn. Inst. of Mgt. Sci. Opers. Resrch. Socty. of Amer. **Honors:** Beta Gamma Sigma. **Pubns.:** *California's Demand for Librarians: Projecting Future Requirements* (1978); "The Economics of Library Size," *Lib. Trends* (Sum. 1979); "Charging Users for Library Service," *Info. Prcs. and Mgt.* (1978); "Input-Output Relationships in On-Line Bibliographic Searching," *Jnl. ASIS* (My. 1977); jt. auth., "Misplacement of Books on Library Shelves: A Mathematical Model," *Lib. Qtly.* (Ja. 1977); various articles. **Activities:** 11; 26, 41; 56, 75, 95-Econ. of info. **Addr.:** School of Library and Information Studies, University of California, Berkeley, CA 94720.

Cooper, Richard S. (Ag. 23, 1935, Elmira, NY) Act. Head, E. Asiatic Lib., Univ. of CA, Berkeley, 1979–; Head, Spec. Lang. Sect., Cat. Dept., 1977–79, Islamica Libn., Coll. Dev. Ofc., 1970–79. **Educ.:** Princeton Univ., 1953–57, BA (Econ. & Pub. Affairs); Univ. of CA, Berkeley, 1961–70, MA, PhD (Near East Std.); MLS; Cert. of the Woodrow Wilson School of Pub. & Intl. Affairs, Princeton Univ., 1955–57. **Orgs.:** ALA: ACRL. Mid. E. Libns. Assn.: Pub. Bd. (1972–79); Com. on Coop. Arrangements (1975–Ch.); VP (1973–75); Prog. Ch. (1973–75); Com. on Resrc. & Coop. (1976–79); Com. on Machine Readable Arabic Data; Ch. (1979). Intl. Assn. of Orientalist Libns. Amer. Oriental Soc. Mid. E. Std. Assn. **Pubns.:** "The Assessment and collection of *kharaj* tax in medieval Egypt," *Jnl. of the Amer. Oriental Socty.* (1976); "The Case for a consortium," *MELA Notes* 4, (1975); "A Survey of Turkish Acquisitions," *MELA Notes* 8 (1976); "Forward to the 1976 MELA/MESA panel discussion," *MELA Notes* 10 (1977); Co-Ed., *LAUC Seminar on Career Development for Academic Librarians* (1977); other articles. **Activities:** 1; 15, 17, 20; 54, 90 **Addr.:** East Asiatic Library, University of California, Berkeley, CA 94611.

Cooper, Sandra M. (Ag. 22, 1946, San Francisco, CA) Exec. Dir., ASCLA, ALA, 1977–; Pub. Lib. Consult., LA State Lib., 1975–77; Parish Libn., De Soto Parish Lib., 1971–75. **Educ.:** LA State Univ., 1964–68, BA (Eng.), 1968–71, MLS. **Orgs.:** ALA: Various Com. SWLA: Various Com. LA LA. Free Univ. Netwk.: Adv. Com. (1977). **Pubns.:** "Association of Specialized & Cooperative Library Agencies," *ALA Yearbook* (1979); "Association of State Library Agencies," *ALA Yearbook* (1978). **Activities:** 5, 9, 13; 24, 25, 34; 72 **Addr.:** Association of Specialized & Cooperative Library Agencies, American Library Association, 50 East Huron St., Chicago, IL 60611.

Cooper, Sylvia Jane (Je. 10, 1936, Columbia, MO) Head Med. Libn., OK Osteopathic Hosp., 1976–; Libn., Dept. of Interior, Fish-Pest. Resrch. Lab, 1970–71; Libn., Reader Srvcs. Dept., St. Louis Cnty. Lib., 1969. **Educ.:** Univ. of MO, Columbia, 1954–58, BS (Educ.), 1962, M (Educ.), 1967–72, MALS. **Orgs.:** OK Hlth. Sci. Lib. Assn.: Nom. Com. (1979). Med. LA: S. Cent. Reg. Grp. (Mem. Com. Ch. 1981; Mem. Com. 1979). SLA. ALA. Beta Sigma Phi: Pres. (1981); Srv. Ch. (1979); VP (1978); Secy. (1977). **Pubns.:** "Upgrading the Medical Library in the Community Teaching Hospital," *AHME Jrnl.* (1978). **Activities:** 5, 12; 17, 20, 39; 80 **Addr.:** L. C. Baxter Medical Library, Oklahoma Osteopathic Hospital, 9th St. & Jackson Ave., Tulsa, OK 74127.

Cooper, William Copeland (Ag. 3, 1946, Laurens, SC) Dir., Laurens Cnty. Lib., 1975–; Head, Gen. Ref. Dept., Greenville Cnty. Lib., 1972–75; Asst. Ref. Libn., Univ. of NC, Charlotte, 1971–72. **Educ.:** Presby. Coll., 1964–68, BA (Hist.); Wake Forest Univ., 1968–69, MA (Hist.); Univ. of NC, 1970–71, MSLS. **Orgs.:** ALA: PLA; JMRT, various ofcs.; Bylaws Com. (1981–83). SC LA: JMRT (Ch., 1978), Nom. Com. (1978), Cont. Educ. Com. (1979–80)/PLA Sect., Exec. Bd. (1978–80). SC LA. Assn. of Pub. Lib. Admins. of SC: VP (1981). SC Lung Assn.: Bd. (1976–79). Laurens Cnty. Cham. of Cmrce.: Mem. Com. (1980). Laurens Cnty. Cmnty. Concert Assn.: Pres. (1979–80). Laurens Cnty. Arts Comsn.: Ch. (1978–81). **Pubns.:** "Bibliography of Translation Sources for Humanities Literature," *RQ* (Fall 1972). **Activities:** 9; 17, 36, 39; 55, 77, 92 **Addr.:** P.O. Box 42, Laurens, SC 29360.

Cooper, William L. (S. 11, 1944, Highland Park, MI) Supervsry. Attorney, Resrch. Srvs., Dykema, Gossett, Spencer, Goodnow & Trigg, 1977–; Libn., Hogan & Hartson, 1975–77; Gvt. Docum. Libn., Univ. of PA Law Sch., 1974–75. **Educ.:** Dartmouth Coll., 1962–66, AB (Eng.); Univ. of MI, 1970–72, JD, 1973–74, AMLS. **Orgs.:** MI Assn. of Law Libs.: Constitution Com. (1979–). Detroit Bar Assn.: Lib. Com. (Ch. 1979–). Detroit Bar Assn. Fndn.: Trustee (1979–). MI State Bar Assn.: Com. on Legal Resrch. (Ch., 1977–78). **Pubns.:** "Survey of Prof. Attitudes toward Research Retrieval Systems", *Law Lib. Jnl.* (F. 1979). **Activities:** 12; 41, 42; 77, 78 **Addr.:** Dykema, Gossett, Spencer, Goodnow & Trigg, 35th Floor, 400 Renaissance Center, Detroit, MI 48243.

Cooper, William S. (N. 7, 1935, Winnipeg, MB) Prof., LS, Univ. of CA, Berkeley, 1970–; Asst. Prof., LS, Univ. of Chicago, 1966–70; Alexander Van Humboldt Fellow, Univ. of Erlanger, W. Germany, 1964–66. **Educ.:** Principia Coll., 1952–56, BA (Math); MA Inst. of Tech., 1956–59, MSc (Math); Univ. of CA, Berkeley, 1959–64, PhD (Logic). **Orgs.:** ASIS. Assn. Comp. Mach. AAAS. **Honors:** Best *Jnl. ASIS* Paper of Yr., 1973, 1978. **Pubns.:** *Foundations of Logico-Linguistics* (1978); *Set Theory and Syndoctic Description* (1964); "Indexing Documents by Gedanken Experimentation," *Jnl. ASIS* (1978). **Activities:** 11; 26, 41; 56, 75 **Addr.:** School of Library and Information Studies, University of California, Berkeley, CA 94720.

Coover, James B. (Je. 3, 1925, Jacksonville, IL) Prof., Dir., Msc. Lib., SUNY at Buffalo, 1967–; Head, George Sherman Dickinson Msc. Lib., Vassar Coll., 1953–67; Bibligphr. & Asst. Dir., Bibli. Ctr. for Resrch., Rocky Mt. Reg., 1950–53. **Educ.:** Univ. of North. CO, 1946–49, AB (Msc.), 1949–51, MA (Msc.); Univ. of Denver, 1950–53, MA (LS). **Orgs.:** Msc. LA: Pres. (1959–60), other ofcs. and coms. Intl. Assn. of Msc. Libs. Assn. of Recorded Sound Col. Dictionary Socty. of N. Amer.; AAUP. **Pubns.:** *Medieval and Renaissance Music on Long-Playing Records,* Supp. (1973); *Music Lexicography* (1971); "Dictionaries and Encyclopedias," *The New Grove's Dictionary* (1981); "Selection Policies for a University Music Library" in *Reader in Music Librarianship* (1974); "American Music Libraries; the Formative Years and the First Generation," *Fontes Artis Musicae* 3 (1970); other articles, reviews. **Activities:** 1; 15, 17, 26, 41; 55, 57 **Addr.:** Dept. of Music, Baird Hall, State Univ. of NY, Buffalo, NY 14214.

Coover, Robert Wingert (D. 15, 1922, Waynesboro, PA) Admin. Coord., San Jose State Univ., 1970; Chief Catlgr., PA State Univ., 1967–70; Adjunct Inst., Lib. Sci., Drexel Univ., 1966–67; Supvsr., Tech. Info. Ctr., Chrysler Corp., Space Div., 1965–66; Supvsr., Lib. & Info. Srvs., Genl. Dynamics-Convair, 1958–65; Tech. Info. Spec., G.E. Small Aircraft Eng. Dept., 1956–58. **Educ.:** Univ. of MD, 1946–49, BA (Hist.); Catholic Univ., 1951–56, MS/LS; Drexel Univ., 1966–74, MALS; CA Western Univ., 1963–64, (Data Proc.); San Jose State Univ., 1976–81, MA (Educ.). **Orgs.:** ALA. **Honors:** Phi Alpha Theta, 1949; Beta Phi Mu, 1974. **Pubns.:** *A History of the Maryland State Library, 1827–1939* (1957); "User Needs and Their Effects on Information Center Administration," *SLA Jrnl.* (S. 1969); "Worthy of Note," *CA Media and Lib. Educ. Jrnl.* (1979). **Activities:** 1; 17, 32, 46; 63, 75, 92 **Addr.:** 8105 Cabernet Ct., San Jose, CA 95135.

Cope, Johnnye Louise (D. 15, 1923, Eden, TX) Hum. Libn., N. TX State Univ. Lib., 1966–; Ref. Libn., Trinity Univ. (TX), 1956–66; Asst. Ref. Libn., El Paso Pub. Lib., 1954–56; Inst., Lab. Sch., N. TX State Univ., 1946–52. **Educ.:** N. TX State Univ., 1942–45, BA (Eng.); OH State Univ., 1948–49, MA (Eng.); Univ. of MI, 1952–54, AMLS; Cert. in Arch. Mgt., Univ. of TX, 1961. **Orgs.:** TX LA: Ref. RT, TX Pers. Indx. Subcom. (1979/80–). SW LA. ARLIS/NA. Assn. for Higher Educ. of the N. TX Area Libs.: Ref. Subcom. (Ch., 1971–73). **Activities:** 1; 25, 31, 39; 55, 57 **Addr.:** Box 5503 NTSU, Denton, TX 76203.

Cope, Mary McCarthy (O. 11, 1928, Washington, DC) Chief, Ref., City Coll. of NY, 1968–. **Educ.:** City Coll., 1958–62, BA (Art Hist.); Columbia Univ., 1962–66, MA (Art Hist.), 1966–68, MLS; MD Inst. of Fine Arts; Art Students League of NY. **Orgs.:** ALA. ARLIS/NA. CNLIA: Bd. mem. Beta Phi Mu, Nu Chap.: Secy./Treas. (1977–80). Coll. Art Assn. **Honors:** Phi Beta Kappa, 1961. **Pubns.:** Co-ed., *Circumspice,* (1975–77). **Activities:** 1; 25; 55 **Addr.:** 370 Riverside Dr., #15C, New York, NY 10025.

Copeland, Elizabeth H. (Mr. 12, 1917, Tarboro, NC) Dir., Sheppard Meml. Lib., 1954–; Libn., BHM Reg. Lib., Washington, NC, 1949–54; Libn., Bureau of Mncpl. Resrch. of Philadelphia, 1947–49; Libn., Resrch. Div., Curtis Publishing Co., 1945–47. **Educ.:** E. Carolina Univ., 1934–38, AB (Eng., Hist.); Peabody Coll., 1940–42, BLS; Graduate work, 1938–39, (Eng., Hist.). **Orgs.:** NC LA: Pub. Lib. Sect., Ch. (1967–69), VP & Pres-elect (1969–71), Pres. (1971–73), Exec. Bd. (1965–75). SELA: Various Coms. ALA. E. Carolina Art Soc.: Exec. Bd. Pitt Cnty. Hist. Soc., Pres. NC Lit. and Hist. Soc. **Pubns.:** "History of North Carolina Library Assn.," *Encyclopedia of Library and Information Science* (1977); Biographical sketches for the *Dictionary of North Carolina Biography* (1979–); Various articles for *North Carolina Libraries.* **Activities:** 9, 11; 17, 39, 41; 55, 74, 75 **Addr.:** 1302 Sonata St., Greenville, NC 27834.

Copeland, Julia Wallace (Je. 13, 1939, Minneapolis, MN) Env. Cons. Libn., Minneapolis Pub. Lib., 1970–, Cat. Libn., 1969–70, Asst. to Assoc. Dir. for Spec. Projs., 1968–69; Cat. Libn., Pikes Peak Reg. Lib. Dist., 1966–68; Ref. Libn., Minneapolis Pub. Lib., 1961–64. **Educ.:** Carleton Coll., 1956–60, BA (Eng.); Univ. of MN, 1960–61, MA (LS). **Orgs.:** SLA. MN LA. Metro. Multi-Cnty. Multi-Type Lib. Syst. Adv. Com. (1979–81). MN Env. Educ. Bd.: Vice-Ch. (1973–74). Citizens Leag. MN Acad. of Sci. **Honors:** U.S. Env. Protection Agency, Env. Qual. Awd., 1975. **Pubns.:** "EIC Provides Environmental Data to Minnesota Library," *Info. Mgr.* (Sum. 1980). **Activities:** 9, 13; 15, 17, 39; 65, 82, 86 **Addr.:** Environmental Conservation Library, Minneapolis Public Library and Information Center, 300 Nicollet Mall, Minneapolis, MN 55401.

Copenhaver, Ida L. (O. 19, 1945, Johnson City, TN) Mgr., Prod. Specifications and Srvs., Chem. Abs. Srv., 1969–, Sr. Assoc. Ed., 1975–77, Assoc. Ed., 1972–75, Asst. Ed., 1969–72. **Educ.:** Agnes Scott Coll., 1963–67, BA (Chem.); Emory Univ., 1967–69, MS (Chem.). **Orgs.:** Amer. Chem. Socty. ASIS. Amer. Women in Sci. Jr. Leag.: Columbus: Bd. Columbus Area Leadership Lab.: Bd. Cmnty. Info. Ref. Srv.: Bd. Columbus Cmnty. Conf.: Bd. (1978–79). Various coms. **Honors:** Columbus Jaycees, Ten Outstan. Young Citizens, 1977. **Activities:** 6; 17, 37, 46; 60, 75 **Addr.:** Chemical Abstracts Service, Dept. 67, P.O. Box 3012, Columbus, OH 43210.

Coplen, Ron (Ag. 2, 1936, Des Moines, IA) Libn., Harcourt Brace Jovanovich, Inc., 1970–; Libn., Fred B. Rothman, 1967–70; Libn., Oceanic Publns., 1965–67; Head, Serials Acq., Columbia Univ., 1963–65. **Educ.:** Drake Univ., 1955–59, BFA (Eng. Lit. Thea.); Columbia Univ., 1981–, (LS); Various Cont. Educ. courses, SLA, 1978–79. **Orgs.:** SLA: Conf. Ch., New York (1977),

PROFESSIONAL ACTIVITIES: Institutions/ 1. Acad. lib.; 2. Arch.; 3. Assn.; 4. Fed./Gvt. lib.; 5. Inst. lib.; 6. Mfr./Suppl.; 7. Milit. lib.; 8. Musm.; 9. Pub. lib.; 10. Sch. lib.; 11. Sch. of lib. sci.; 12. Spec. lib.; 13. State lib.; 14. (other). **Functions/Activities:** 15. Acq./Col. dev.; 16. Adult srvs.; 17. Admin.; 18. Apprais.; 19. Archit./Bldgs.; 20. Cat./Class.; 21. Chld. srvs.; 22. Circ.; 23. Cons./Pres.; 24. Consult.; 25. Cont. ed.; 26. Educ. lib. sci.; 27. Ext. srvs.; 28. Fund/Grants; 29. Gvt. pubs.; 30. Indx./Abs.; 31. Instr. lib. use; 32. Media srvs.; 33. Micro.; 34. Netwks./Coop.; 35. Persnl.; 36. PR; 37. Publshg.; 38. Recs. mgt.; 39. Ref. srvs.; 40. Repro.; 41. Resrch.; 42. Review.; 43. Secur.; 44. Serials; 45. Spec. col.; 46. Tech. srvs.; 47. Trustees/Bds.; 48. YA srvs.; 49. (other).

Schol. Com. (1979/80–1981/82); Ch., Publshg. Div. (1975/76), Nom. Com., Ch. (1975/76); NY Chap., Pres. (1978/79), Finance Com. (1977–). NY Lib. Club: Nsltr./Bltn. Ed.; Other Coms. New Dem. Asm.: Pres. (1972). Campaign Coord. for Bella Abzug (1970), Al Blumenthal (1972), John Lindsay (1966). **Honors:** The Fanny Simon Awd. for Excellence in Publshg. Co. Libs., 1980. **Pubns.:** "Publishing Industry Libraries in the New York Metropolitan Area," *Special Libraries* (O./N. 1974); "Subscription Agents–When to use," *Special Libraries* (D. 1979); Ed., *Special Libraries Index: 1971-80* and ... *1910-1970* (forthcoming); Ed., *Publishing Div. Bltn.* (1973/74); Other articles. **Activities:** 12; 15, 17, 39; 57, 75, 95-Publishing. **Addr.:** Harcourt Brace Jovanovich, Inc., 757 Third Ave., New York, NY 10017.

Coppin, Ann S. (Mr. 2, 1944, Pasadena, CA) Supvsr., Tech. Info. Srvs., Chevron Oil Field Research Co., 1974–. **Educ.:** Univ. of Redlands, 1962–66, BS (Geol.); NM Inst. of Mining & Tech., 1966–68, MS (Geol.); Univ. of AZ, 1972–74, MLS. **Orgs.:** Geoscience Info. Socty. SLA: Petroleum Grp. of South. CA Chap. (Ch., 1979–80). ASIS. Other orgs. AIM. Assn. of Women Geoscientists. **Honors:** Beta Phi Mu. **Pubns.:** "The Subject Specialist on the academic library staff", *Libri* (1974); "Lunar Science Institute", *Sci-Tech News* (1975); "From Research Laboratory to the Operating Company: How Information Travels", *Spec. Libs.* (1980). **Activities:** 12; 17, 38, 39; 71, 82, 86 **Addr.:** Chevron Oil Field Research Company, P.O. Box 446, La Habra, CA 90631.

Coral, Lenore (Ja. 30, 1939, Detroit, MI) Msc. Libn./Asst. Prof., Univ. of WI, 1972–; Fine Arts Libn., Univ. of CA, Irvine, 1967–72. **Educ.:** Univ. of Chicago, 1957–61, BA (Msc., Gen. Std.), 1963–65, MA (LS); Univ. of London, Eng., 1965–66, MMus (Msc. Hist.), 1966–74, PhD (Msc. Hist.). **Orgs.:** Msc. LA: Bd. of Dirs. (1973–75); Tech. Rpts. (Ed., 1977–), Pubns. Com. (1977–). Intl. Assn. of Msc. Libs.: Bibl. Resrch. Comsn. (1975–), Cat. Comsn. and ISBD (NBM) Working Grp.; U.S. Bd. of Dirs. (1976–78). Amer. Msclgy. Socty.: Cncl. (1975–77). Bibl. Socty. Royal Msc. Assn. **Honors:** Fulbright/Hays Resrch. Grant, 1965–67; NEH Grants, 1976–77, 1979–80. **Pubns.:** Jt. auth., *British Book Sale Catalogues, 1676-1800* (1977); *Concordance of the Thematic Indexes to the Instrumental Works of Antonio Vivaldi* (1972); "The History of Thematic Catalogues," *Reader in Msc. Libnshp.* (1973); "Sotheby's Auctioneers, Publishers and Booksellers in the Eighteenth Century," *Art at Auction* (1970); various articles. **Activities:** 1; 15; 55 **Addr.:** Mills Music Library, University of Wisconsin, 728 State St., Madison, WI 53706.

Corbett, Elizabeth M. (Mr. 23, 1926, Paterson, NJ) Libn., Barnard Coll., 1981–; Actg. Libn., 1980–81, 1976–77, Circ. Libn., 1969–80; Lib. Consult., Silliman Univ., Philippines, 1977, Treas. Dept., Amer. Telephone and Telegraph Co., 1947–68. **Educ.:** Wellesley Coll., 1943–47, BA (Econ.); Simmons Coll. 1967–69, MLS. **Orgs.:** ALA. NY LA: Acad. and Spec. Libs. Sect. (Pres., 1979–80). NY Lib. Club. Un. Bd. for Christ. Higher Educ. in Asia: Univ. Progs. Com. (1978–), China Concerns Subcom. on Lib. and Transl. Progs. (1980–). **Pubns.:** "A Civil War General Surveys the Library Field in 1876, Creates a Corps of Librarians from Scattered Troops," *Amer. Libs.* (Ja. 1976); "Conference Reviews," *ASLS/NYLA Bltn. for Prog. Reviews* (O. 1981). **Activities:** 1; 17, 24, 35; 55, 92 **Addr.:** 116 Pinehurst Ave., Apt. B-11, New York, NY 10033.

Corbin, Brenda G. (N. 29, 1942, Chickamauga, GA) Head Libn., U.S. Nvl. Observatory, 1973–; ILL Libn., Hist. of Med. Div., Natl. Lib. of Med., 1971–72; Readg. Rm. Supvsr./Libn., Folger Shakespeare Lib., 1965–69. **Educ.:** Woman's Coll. of GA, 1960–64, AB (Eng. Lit.); Univ. of MD, 1971–72, MLS. **Orgs.:** SLA: *Phys.-Astronomy-Math. Bltn.* (1980–82). DC LA. Amer. Astronomical Socty.: Hist. Astr. Div. **Pubns.:** "Preservation of Astronomical Materials," *Phys.-Astr.-Math. Bltn.* (N. 1979). **Activities:** 4; 15, 23, 39; 88, 91 **Addr.:** Library, U.S. Naval Observatory, 34th & Massachusetts Ave., N.W., Washington, DC 20390.

Corbin, John B. (Ap. 7, 1935, Moody, TX) Asst. Dir. Admin. and Systs., Univ. of Houston Libs., 1981–; Assoc. Dir. for Tech. Srvs., Stephen F. Austin State Univ., 1977–81; Asst. Prof., N. TX State Univ., 1973–77; Plng. Ofcr., CO State Lib., 1972–73; Spec. Proj. Libn., OK Dept. of Libs., 1970–72; Dir. of Autom. Srvs., Tarrant Cnty. Jr. Coll., 1967–70; Dir. of Tech. Srvs., TX State Lib., 1963–67; Acq. Libn., Univ. of TX at Arlington, 1960–63. **Educ.:** N. TX State Univ., 1955–57, BA (LS); Univ. of TX at Austin, 1959–61, MLS; Univ. of OK, 1970–73, PhD, (Lib. Syst. Mgt.). **Orgs.:** ALA: Com. for Rev. of the ALA Glossary of Lib.-Related Terms; ISAD/Com. on Lib.-Indus. Rel. (1976–77); RTSD/Piercy Awd. Jury (1974–75). CHOICE Ed. Bd. (1971–73). SWLA: Tech. Srvs. Interest Grp. (Ch. 1976–78; Secy. 1971–72). Bibli. Ctr. for Resrch., Rocky Mt. Reg.: Finance Com. (1972–73). TX LA: Ad-Hoc Com. on Networks (Ch., 1978–80); Other coms. **Honors:** ALA, Esther J. Piercy Awd., 1970. **Pubns.:** *Introduction to Computer-Based Data Processing for Libraries* (1975); *Computer-Based Acquisitions Procedures at Tarrant County Junior College District* (1974); "Library Automation: A State of the Art," *Cath. Lib. World* (My./Je. 1979); "Networks," *Lib. Jnl.* (Ja. 1, 1976); *A Technical Services Manual for Small Libraries* (1971); Other bks. and articles. **Activities:** 1, 11; 17, 34, 46; 56, 75 **Addr.:** University of Houston Libraries, 4800 Calhoun Rd., Houston, TX 77004.

Corcoran, Dennis Richard (D. 2, 1950, Cambridge, MA) Dir., Ventress Meml. Lib., Marshfield, MA, 1975–; Branch Libn., Cambridge Pub. Lib., 1973–75. **Educ.:** Boston State Coll., 1968–72, BA (Hist.); Simmons Coll., 1972–73, MLS. **Orgs.:** ALA. MA LA: Legis. Com. (1980). Grt. Boston Pub. Lib. Admins.: VP (1980). **Activities:** 9; 17 **Addr.:** 33 Trask Ave., W. Quincy, MA 02169.

Corcoran, Frances Evelyn (Je. 28, 1938, Chicago, IL) IMC Coord., Cmnty. Consolidated Sch. Dist. 62, 1973–; Instr., Natl. Coll. of Educ., 1977–; Media Spec., Orchard Place Sch., 1968–73, Tchr., 1964–68; Tchr., Barrington Pub. Sch., 1962–64; Tchr., Waukegan Pub. Sch., 1960–62. **Educ.:** N. Park Coll., 1956; Roosevelt Univ., 1956–60, BA (Elem. Educ.); Rosary Coll., 1968–70, MLS. **Orgs.:** ALA. IL LA: Citation Com. (1978), Job Place. (1976–77). IL Assn. of Media Educ. Assn. for Supvsn. and Curric. Dev. Phi Delta Kappa; Delta Kappa Gamma: Prof. Dev. Com. (1977–78). **Pubns.:** Jt. auth., *Sports: A Multimedia Guide for Children and Young Adults* (1980). **Activities:** 10; 17, 21, 26; 50, 63, 89 **Addr.:** Community Consolidated School District 62, 777 Algonquin Rd., Des Plaines, IL 60018.

Cordell, Howard William (Je. 13, 1921, Industry, IL) Docum Lib, FL Intl. Univ., Bay Vista Campus, 1981–; Dir., Lib. and Media Srvs., FL Intl. Univ., 1970–80; Dir., Lib. Srvs., Cornell Coll., 1967–70; Head, Ref. Dept., Univ. of IL, Chicago Circle, 1966–67; Assoc. Dir., Libs., FL Atl. Univ., 1963–66. **Educ.:** West. IL Univ., 1939–43, BS (Bus. Educ.), 1947–49, MS (Bus. Educ.); Univ. of IL, 1956–57, MSLS. **Orgs.:** FL LA: Ch., IFRT (1964). ALA: Ch., Reprodct. of Lib. Mats. Sect. (1972). **Pubns.:** "Library Public Services in the Age of Data Processing," *Florida Libraries* (June 1964). **Addr.:** 7158 Laurel Ln., Miami Lakes, FL 33014.

Córdova, Martha Heffernan (S. 9, 1948, Springfield, MA) Asst. Bus. & Engin. Libn., Dartmouth Coll., 1981–; Head Ref. Libn., Colgate Univ., 1977–80; Sr. Asst. Libn./Asst. Dept. Head, Grad. Sch. of Bus. & Pub. Admin. Lib., Cornell Univ., 1972–76. **Educ.:** Coll. of New Rochelle, 1966–70, AB (Eng./Educ.); Univ. of HI, 1971–72, MLS. **Orgs.:** ALA. ACRL: East. NY Chap. Ctrl. NY Lib. Resrcs. Cncl.: Secy., Prof. Dev. Com. Frnds. of the Colgate Lib. **Honors:** Beta Phi Mu, 1972. **Activities:** 1, 12; 17, 31, 39; 55, 59 **Addr.:** Feldberg Library, Dartmouth College, Hanover, NH 03755.

Core, Ofra D. Chief, Recs. Mgt. Service, United Nations, 1952–. **Educ.:** 1947, MA (Hum.); Admin. of Arch., American Univ., Natl. Arch., 1950–51, cert.; Cert. Recs. Mgr., 1976. **Orgs.:** SAA. Assn. of Recs. Exec. and Admin. Oral Hist. Assoc. Inst. of Cert. Recs. Mgrs. **Pubns.:** "Comments on Records Management", *Info. and Recs. Mgt* (Ap. 1980); "The United Nations - The Written Record," *Amer. Archvst.* (Jl. 1976); "The United Nations Correspondence Classification Manual," *Amer. Archvst.* (Jl. 1961). **Activities:** 14-Intl. Org.; 24, 38; 62 **Addr.:** Box 20, United Nations, New York, NY 10017.

Corey, James F. (N. 9, 1937, Council Grove, KS) Lib. Sys. Spec., Univ. of MO, 1979–; Mgt. Sys. Anal., Univ. of CA, Davis, 1978–79; Syst. Libn., Univ. of IL, Urbana, 1973–78; Syst. Anal., Univ. of CA Sys.-wide 1971–73. **Educ.:** Univ. of KS, 1955–59, BA (Phil.); Univ. of IL, 1973–75, MSLS. **Orgs.:** ALA. MO LA. **Pubns.:** "The Ups, Downs and Demise of a Library Circulation System"; Clinic on Lib. App. of Data Prcs., (1979); "Negotiating Computer Services within an Organization", (1978). **Activities:** 1; 17, 34; 56 **Addr.:** 410 Clark Hall, University of Missouri, Columbia, MO 65201.

Corkle, Violet Schwartz (F. 5, 1931, Chester, PA) Libn., Caesar Rodney Jr. High Media Ctr., 1967–; Elem. Libn., Caesar Rodney Sch. Dist., 1963–67; Engl Tchr., Shippensburg Area Sch. Dist., 1955–63. **Educ.:** State Teachers Coll., Shippensburg, PA, 1955, BS (Educ.); Drexel Univ., 1969, MSLS. **Orgs.:** ALA. DE Sch. Lib. Media Assn.: Pres. (1970–71). Shippensburg Pub. Lib.: Bd. of Dir. (1960–63). AAUW; DE State Educ. Assn. Nat. Educ. Assn. **Honors** Delta Kappa Gamma. **Activities:** 10; 17, 31, 32 **Addr.:** 2017 Highland Ave., Dover, DE 19901.

Corley, Nora Teresa (Montreal PQ) Freelnc. Libn., Ed. work, Wrtg., 1976–; Agency Libn., Can. Intl. Dev. Agency, 1975; Libn., in Charge, Arctic Inst. of N. Amer., 1954–72; Asst. Libn., Law Lib., McGill Univ., 1952–54. **Educ.:** McGill Univ., 1951, BA Honors (Geo.), 1952, BLS, 1961, MA (Geo.). **Orgs.:** PQ LA: Eng. Secy. (1958–59); Bltn. Ed. (1963–64). Can. LA: Vice-Ch., Resrch. Sect. (1964–65). Assn. of Can. Map Libs. SLA: Montreal Chap., Bltn. Ed. (1961–62); Pres., (1964–65); Geo. & Map Div., Ch., (1969/70). Can. Bibl. Socty. Other orgs. Univ. Womens Club of Montreal. Univ. Womens Club of Ottawa. Can. Womens Club.Club of Ottawa. Arctic Inst. of N. Amer. **Honors:** Arctic Inst. of N. Amer., Fellow, 1972. **Pubns.:** *Polar and Cold Regions Library Resources: A Directory* (1975); "The Yukon and Northwest Territories," *Can. Anl. Review of Pol. and Pub. Affairs* (1971–1978); "Geographical Literature," *Encyc. of Lib. and Info. Sci.* (1973); "The St. Lawrence Ship Channel," *Cahiers de Géographie de Quebec* (1967); Ed., *The Artic Circular* (1976–); other articles, reviews. **Activities:** 1, 12; 17, 30; 57, 70, 95-Writing, ed. **Addr.:** 185 Kamloops Ave., Ottawa, ON K1V 7E1 Canada.

Corliss, Jack Arthur (My. 6, 1933, Brookings, SD) Dir. of Libs., Arlington Pub. Lib., 1965–; YA Libn., Waco Pub. Lib., 1961–65. **Educ.:** Baylor Univ., 1961, MA. **Orgs.:** TX LA: Cncl. (1970); Grievance Com., Ch., V Ch., Secy./Treas. ALA. Tarrant Reg. LA: (Pres., Sec/Treas.). Southwest LA. Great Southwest Rotary Club: Bd. of Dir. Chamber of Commerce: Educ. Com.; Arlington Civitan Club: Pres. (1969). Arlington Rotary Club. **Activities:** 9; 17, 28, 32; 56, 93 **Addr.:** P.O. Box 1165, Arlington, TX 76010.

Corman, Linda Wilson (N. 25, 1944, Washington, DC) Coll. Libn., Trinity Coll., Univ. of Toronto, 1980–; Libn., ON Inst. for Std. in Educ., 1974–80; Instr., Eng., Univ. of IL, Chicago, 1969–70; Tchr., Eng., Ctrl. YMCA HS, 1968–69. **Educ.:** Vassar Coll., 1962–66, AB (Eng.); Univ. of Chicago, 1966–69, MA (Eng.); Univ. of Toronto, 1972–74, MLS. **Orgs.:** Can. LA. ALA. Bibl. Socty. of Can. ATLA. **Honors:** Beta Phi Mu; Phi Beta Kappa. **Pubns.:** *Declining Enrollments: Issues and Responses* (1978); *Community Education in Canada, an Annotated Bibliography* (1975); "A Library 'Alternative' at the Ontario Institute for Studies in Education," *Can. LA Jnl.* (Ap. 1977); "James Campbell and the Ontario Education Department, 1858–1884," *Papers of the Bibl. Socty. of Can.* (1975). **Addr.:** Trinity College Library, 6 Hoskin Ave., Toronto, ON M5S 1H8 Canada.

Corman, Paula Fay (Ag. 23, 1937, Boston, MA) Dir. for Admin. Srvs., NELINET, 1976–; Dir., Lrng. Resrc. Ctr., N. Shore Cmnty. Coll., 1973–76; Info. Spec., New Eng. Resrc. Ctr. for Occupational Educ., 1971–72; Coord., Lib. Tech. Prog., Quincy (MA) Vocational-Tech. Sch., 1970–71; Acq. Spec., Natl. Aeronautical and Space Admin., 1969–70; Lib. Mgr., Camp, Dresser and McKee, 1968–69. **Educ.:** Boston Univ., 1955–59, BA (Am. Lit.); Simmons Coll., 1964–68, MSLS; Suffolk Univ., 1977–79, MBA. **Orgs.:** ASIS: New Eng. Chap. (Treas. 1980–81). ACRL: New Eng. Chap., Nom. Com. (Ch., 1980). ALA: LAMA/Network Discuss. Grp. (Ch., 1980). MA LA: Fed. Rel. Coord. (1977). Other orgs. N. Amer. Socty. for Corp. Plng., New Eng. Chap.: Pub. Info. Com. (1980). Simmons Lib. Sch. Annual Alumni Day: Ch. (1980). Small Bus. Inst. Dir. Suffolk Univ. Exec. MBA Socty. **Activities:** 14-Reg. Networks. **Addr.:** NELINET, 385 Elliot St., Newton Upper Falls, MA 02164.

Cormier, John A. (Ja. 14, 1943, Worcester, MA) Dir., Lib. Srvs., Meml. Hosp., Worcester, 1969–. **Educ.:** Worcester State Coll., 1962–66, BS, 1966–69, MS (Educ.); Univ. Rhode Island, 1976–78, MS (LS). **Orgs.:** Med. LA. **Pubns.:** "Communication Consortium," *Hosp. Libs.* (Jn. 1977); "Two Projects for Patients Libraries," *Hosp. Libs.* (My. 1978); "Medical Texts for Public Libraries," *Lib. Jnl.* (O. 15, 1978); AV. **Activities:** 5†

Corning, Mary Elizabeth (O. 19, 1925, Norwich, CT) Asst. Dir., Intl. Progs., Natl. Lib. of Med., 1972–, Spec. Asst. to Dir., 1966–72, Chief, Pubns. and Transl. Div., Natl. Lib. of Med., 1964–66; Assoc. Prog. Dir., Ofc. of Intl. Sci. Actv., Natl. Sci. Fndn., 1962–64, Spec. Asst. to Head., 1961–62, Proj. Dir., Plng. Grp., Ofc. of the Assoc. Dir., 1960–61; Spec. Asst. to Sci. Adv., Ofc. of U.S. Secy. of State, 1958–60, Phys. Chem., Natl. Bur. of Stans., 1949–58. **Educ.:** CT Coll., 1943–47, BA (Chem., Fr.); Mt. Holyoke Coll., 1947–49, MA (Chem.). **Orgs.:** Med. LA. U.S. Natl. Com. for UNESCO Gen. Info. Prog. Various other ofcs. AAAS. Pan Amer. Hlth. Org. Amer. Chem. Socty. Optical Socty. of Amer.: *Jnl.* Asst. Ed. (1950–60); Volume 40 Index Ed. Various other orgs., ofcs. **Pubns.:** *A Review of the United States' Role in International Biomedical Research and Communications* (1980); "The United States National Library of Medicine's International Relationships," *Med. Informatics* (1980); jt. auth, "Biomedical Communications," *Advances in American Medicine Essays at the Bicentennial* (1976); various articles. **Activities:** 4, 12; 24, 34, 49-Intl. rel.; 54, 75, 91 **Addr.:** National Institutes of Health, National Library of Medicine, 8600 Rockville Pike, Bethesda, MD 20209.

Cornog, Martha (Ag. 21, 1944, Wayne, PA) Consult., CALCULON Corp., 1972–; Catlgr., Libn., Haddonfield Pub. Lib., 1970–72; Bibl. Asst., Temple Univ., 1968–69; Comp. Prog., Penn Mutual Life Ins. Co., 1967–68. **Educ.:** Brown Univ., 1962–66, BA (Ling.), 1966–68, MA (Ling.); Drexel Univ., 1970–71, MLS. **Orgs.:** ASIS: DE Valley Chap. (Treas., 1979–81). Assn. of Recs. Mgrs. & Admin. **Honors:** Beta Phi Mu, 1971; Phi Beta Kappa, 1966. **Pubns.:** Reports, oral presentations, reviews. **Activities:** 14-Consulting firm; 24, 42; 75 **Addr.:** CALCULON Corporation, 121 N. Broad St., Philadelphia, PA 19107.

Cornwell, Bertha Emily (O. 9, 1898, Marshall, TX) Adv. Mem. of Lib. Bd., Alma M. Carpenter Pub. Lib., 1968–; Typographer, Cornwell Printing Co., 1973–; Assoc. Ed., Oil City Visitor, 1961–73; Libn., Sour Lake HS, 1934–61; Libn. Coord., French HS, 1944–45. **Educ.:** Baylor Univ. and N. TX State Univ., 1939–42, BS (LS); N. TX State Univ., 1942–46, MS (LS); Univ. of Houston, 1950–54, (Educ.). **Orgs.:** TX LA: Pres., Co-Founder (1962–63). ALA: Ch. for TX (1964–67); Reg. dir. (1965–66). TX Federation Women's Club. **Honors:** Kappa Delta Pi, 1940; Trustee of the year for TX, 1963; Citizen of Sour Lake, 1973. **Activities:** 1 **Addr.:** P.O. Box 114, Sour Lake, TX 77659.

Corrigan, CFX, John Thomas (F. 28, 1936, Brooklyn, NY) Asst. to Exec. Dir., Cath. LA, 1973–; Dir., Media Cntr.,

Special Subjects/Services: 50. Adult educ.; 51. Advert./Mktg.; 52. Aerosp.; 53. Agric.; 54. Area std.; 55. Arts/Hum.; 56. Autom.; 57. Bibl./Prtg.; 58. Bio. sci.; 59. Bus./Fin.; 60. Chem.; 61. Copyrt.; 62. Documtn.; 63. Educ.; 64. Engin.; 65. Env.; 66. Eth. grps.; 67. Film; 68. Food/Nutr.; 69. Geneal.; 70. Geo.; 71. Geol.; 72. Handcpd.; 73. Hist.; 74. Int. frdm.; 75. Info. sci.; 76. Insr.; 77. Law; 78. Legis.; 79. Math./Comp. sci.; 80. Med.; 81. Metals; 82. Nat. resrcs.; 83. Newsp.; 84. Nuc. sci.; 85. Oral hist.; 86. Petr./Energy; 87. Pharm.; 88. Phys./Astr./Math.; 89. Readg.; 90. Relig.; 91. Sci./Tech.; 92. Soc. sci.; 93. Telecom.; 94. Transp.; 95. (other).

Spalding Coll., 1971–73; Dir., Media Cntr., Nazareth H.S., Brooklyn, NY, 1963–71; Coord. of New Proj., Brooklyn Cath. Schs., 1967–71. **Educ.:** Cath. Univ., 1956–60, BA (Hist.); St. John's Univ. (NY), 1963–67, MSLS. **Orgs.:** ALA. Cath. LA: Exec. Bd. (1971–73). PR Assn. of Philadelphia: Pres. (1977). Natl. Cath. Educ. Assn. **Honors:** Catholic LA, Brooklyn, NY: Outstan. Libn., 1971. **Pubns.:** *Relationship of the Library to Instructional Systems* (1977); *Periodicals for Religious Education Centers/Parish Libraries* (1976); *Librarian/Educator Interdependence* (1977); *Guide for the Organization and Operation of A Religious Resource Center* (1978); *Today's Youth, Today's Librarian* (1980). **Activities:** 3; 17, 36; 51, 95-Ed. **Addr.:** 22-5 Valley Rd., Drexel Hill, PA 19026.

Corry, Ann Marie (D. 31, 1943, Minneapolis, MN) Libn. III, Sch. of Dentistry, Univ. of MO, Kansas City, 1970–; Ref. Libn., Univ. of IA, 1968–69, Catlgr., 1966–68. **Educ.:** Washburn Univ., 1961–65, BA (Eng.); Univ. of Denver, 1965–66, MA (LS). **Orgs.:** Med. LA: Prog. and Conv. Com. (1980–), Mem. Com. (1975–78), Rcrt. Com. (1974–75), Dental Grp. Mtg. (Ch., 1972–73), Anl. Mtg., Lcl. Arrange. Com. (Ch., 1972–73), Midcont. Reg. Med. Lib. Com. (1980–), Coord. Com. (1982). Hlth. Scis. Lib. Grp. of Grt. Kansas City. Kansas City Lib. Netwk. Exec. Com. Various other orgs. Amer. Assn. of Dental Schs. **Activities:** 1; 15, 36, 39; 80 **Addr.:** School of Dentistry Library, University of Missouri, 650 E. 25th St., Kansas City, MO 64108.

Corry, (Brother) Emmett (D. 28, 1934, New York, NY) Assoc. Prof., Div. of Lib. & Info. Sci., St. John's Univ., 1977–; Dir., Lib. Media Ctr., St. Anthony's HS, Smithtown, NY, 1974–77; Asst. Prof., St. John's Univ., 1972–74. **Educ.:** St. Francis Coll., Brooklyn, NY, 1960, AB (Eng.); Columbia Univ., 1960–62, MS (LS); New York Univ., 1973–77, PhD (Media); Univ. of WA, 1965; Univ. of Denver, 1969. **Orgs.:** ALA: Cncl. (1977–81). Cath. LA.: Exec. Bd. (1977–83). CNLIA: CLA Rep. (1979–83). Intl. Soc. for Gen. Semantics. **Pubns.:** "The English Teacher and the Library Media Program," *Cath. LA.* (1978); "Enlightenment Intensives: A New Form of Communication," *Media Ecology Review* (Ap./My. 1974). **Addr.:** Division of Library & Information Science, St. John's University, Jamaica, NY 11439.

Cors, Paul B. (Ag. 13, 1930, Janesville, WI Col.) Dev. Libn., Univ. of WY Lib., 1978–; Acq. Libn., 1969–78; Cat. Libn., WY State Lib., 1964–69; Cat. Libn., NM State Univ. Lib., 1959–64. **Educ.:** Ripon Coll., 1950–53, BA (Classics); Rutgers Univ., 1958–59, MLS. **Orgs.:** ALA: Cncl. (1977–79). Intell. Freedom Com. (1970–74). Mountain-Plains LA: Ch., Acad. Sect. (1972–73). WY LA: Secy. (1976–79). Amer. Ornithologists' Union; Cooper Ornithological Socty. Wilson Ornithological Socty. **Honors:** Phi Beta Kappa, 1953; Beta Phi Mu, 1959. **Pubns.:** *Railroads* (1975). **Activities:** 1; 15, 42 **Addr.:** University of Wyoming Library, Box 3334, University Station, Laramie, WY 82071.

Corson, David W. (Ap. 30, 1943, Washington, DC) Head, Col. Dev., Olin Lib., Cornell Univ., 1980–; Head, Hist. of Sci. Col., Cornell University Libs., 1979–; Asst. Prof., Dept. of Hist., Univ. of AZ, 1973–78, Instr., 1970–73. **Educ.:** Cornell Univ., 1961–65, BA (Hist./Phys.), 1965–70, PhD (Hist. of Sci.); Univ. of AZ, 1978–79, MLS. **Orgs.:** ALA: ACRL. Hist. of Sci. Soc. **Honors:** Fulbright-Hays Flwshp., 1967. **Pubns.:** Ed., *Man's Place in the Universe: Changing Concepts* (1977); "Masson"/"Polinière," *Dictionary of Scientific Biography* (1974/1975); "Pierre Polinière, Francis Hauksbee, and Electroluminescence," *Isis* (1968). **Activities:** 1; 15, 17, 45; 55, 91, 92 **Addr.:** History of Science Collections, Cornell University Libraries, Ithaca, NY 14853.

Corson, Janet E. (Ja. 25, 1949, Toledo, OH) Mgr., Scientific Lib., Frederick Cancer Resrch. Ctr., 1976–; Asst. Dir., Head, Pub. Srvs., Frederick (MD) Cmnty. Coll., 1974–76; Dir., Hlth. Srvs. Lib., Johnson Cnty. (IN) Meml. Hosp., 1973–74. **Educ.:** Brown Univ., 1967–71, AB (Grmn.), 1972, AM (Grmn.); Univ. of RI, 1972–73, MLS. **Orgs.:** SLA. **Honors:** Phi Beta Kappa, 1971. **Pubns.:** "Breaking The Language Barrier: A Sociolinquistic Perspective of Online Search Strategy," *3rd International Online Information Meeting* (1979); Reviews. **Activities:** 12; 17, 24, 34; 58, 60, 91 **Addr.:** Frederick Cancer Research Center, P.O. Box B, Frederick, MD 21701.

Corson, Richard H. (N. 1, 1938, Rahway, NJ) Chief Libn., SUNY Maritime Coll., 1970–, Assoc. Libn., 1965–70, Asst. Libn., 1962–65. **Educ.:** Wesleyan Univ., 1957–61, BA (Eng.); Columbia Univ., 1961–62, MSLS. **Orgs.:** ALA. SUNY LA. Bronx LA. Archons of Colophon. **Activities:** 1, 2; 17, 32; 55, 64, 94 **Addr.:** Stephen B. Luce Library, State University of New York Maritime College, Fort Schuyler, Bronx, NY 10465.

Corth, Annette (O. 14, 1927, Newark, NJ) Head, Serials/Tech. Srvs., Lib. of Sci. & Med., Rutgers Univ., 1980–, Bio. Sci. Resrc. Libn., 1973–80; Supvsr., Ctrl. Info. Srv., Crompton & Knowles Corp., 1967–73; Ref. Libn., Bell Telephone Labs., 1963–67; Ref. Libn., Engin. Societies Lib., 1962–63. **Educ.:** Douglass Coll., 1945–49, BA (Grmn./Educ.); Columbia Univ., 1961–62, MLS; 6th-Year Spec. Prog., Rutgers Univ. Grad. Schl. Lib. and Info. Studies, 1974–80. **Orgs.:** ALA. SLA: Pres., NJ Chap. (1978–79); VP (1977–78); Prog. Ch. (1976–77); Treas. (1969–71). NJ Gvt. Docum. Assn. NJ LA. ASIS. **Pubns.:** "Coverage of Marine Biology Citations", *Spec. Libs.* (D. 1977); "Corth's Commandments", *Spec. Libs.* (O./N. 1974). **Activities:** 1, 12; 15, 39, 44, 46; 58, 91 **Addr.:** Library of Science & Medicine, Rutgers University, P.O. Box 1029, Piscataway, NJ 08854.

Cosgriff, John C., Jr. (S. 13, 1939, Oakland, CA) Copy Editing Supvsr., VA Polytechnic Inst. & State Univ., 1979–, Sci. and Tech. Cat. Supvsr., 1974–79; Sr. Catlgr., CA Inst. of Tech., 1972–74, Bio. & Chem. Libn., 1970–72. **Educ.:** Univ. of CA, Berkeley, 1957–62, AB (Zlgy.); Brigham Young Univ., 1968–70, MLS. **Orgs.:** ALA. Potomac Tech. Prcs. Libns. Natl. Cncl. on Family Relations. AAUP. **Honors:** Beta Phi Mu, Honorary Membership, 1971. **Pubns.:** "Reducing Library Costs", *Sci-Tech News* (Ja. 1976). **Activities:** 1; 20, 39; 58, 60, 91 **Addr.:** 102 Orchard View Ln., Blacksburg, VA 24060.

Costa, Robert N. (F. 3, 1938, Windber, PA) Dir., Cambria Cnty. Lib. Syst., 1976–, Assoc. Dir., 1974–76, Head, Adult Srvs., 1971–74. **Educ.:** Univ. of Pittsburgh, 1966–69, BA (Eng.), 1969–71, MLS; U.S. Naval Meteorology Schools, 1957–64. **Orgs.:** ALA. PA LA. YMCA Judo Club: Pres. (1973–75). Windber Lib. Bd.: Secy. (1972–74). **Honors:** Military honors. **Pubns.:** "Science Learning Games," *Sci. Activities* (Mr. 1971); "Project Tips," *P.L.A. Bltn.* (S. 1977). **Activities:** 9; 17, 19, 28; 63, 91 **Addr.:** Cambria County Library System, David A. Glosser Memorial Library Building, 248 Main St., Johnstown, PA 15901.

Costabile, Salvatore Louis (D. 24, 1934, Hazleton, PA) Pres., Costabile Assoc. Inc., 1974–; Asst. Dir., Amer. Assn. of Musms., 1972–74; Dep. Dir. Tech. Srvcs., Nat. Lib. of Med., 1966–72; Head of Acq., Georgetown Univ. Lib., 1956–66. **Educ.:** Georgetown Univ., 1956, BS (Hist.); Catholic Univ., 1963, MSLS; Georgetown Univ., 1956–58, (Pol. Sci.). **Orgs.:** ALA. **Pubns.:** "Proof of the Pudding," Coll. & Resrch. Libs. (Mr. 1967). **Activities:** 4, 11, 12; 17, 24, 46; 55, 75, 86 **Addr.:** Costabile Associates, Inc., 4720 Montgomery La., Bethesda, MD 20014.

Costales, Justina L. (S. 15, 1917, Naguilian, La Union, Philippines) Staff Libn., West. State Hosp., WA, 1967–80. **Educ.:** Philippine Normal Sch., 1933–36, (Teaching Cert.); Univ. of Santo Tomas, Manila, 1946–48, BS (Educ.); Univ. of CA, Los Angeles, 1948–49; Univ. of CA, Berkeley, 1950–51; Univ. of WA, 1966–67, MLS. **Orgs.:** Med. LA: Pacific Northw. Grp. ALA. WA LA. WA Med. Libns. Assn. **Pubns.:** Jt. auth., "Western State Hospital", *Illinois Libraries* (S. 1975); *Western State Hospital, Its History and Its Programs, a Bibliography* (1971); *Group Psychotherapy for Geriatric Patients; a Bibliography* (1970). **Addr.:** 8016 70th Ave. Ct. SW, Tacoma, WA 98499.

Costello, Joan M. (S. 14, 1930, Wilkes-Barre, PA) Head Libn., Osterhout Free Lib., 1973–; Asst. Dir., Scranton Pub. Lib., 1968–72; Adult Srvs. Staff, Osterhout Free Lib., 1964–68. **Educ.:** Coll. Misericordia, 1950–54, BA (Eng.); Drexel Univ., 1963–64, MLS. **Orgs.:** ALA: RASD/Adult Lib. Mat. Com. (1971–74). PA LA: Northeast Chap. Ch. (1971–72), PLA Nom. Com. (1975–76). Northeast. PA Bibl. Ctr.: VP (1974–76, 1978–79); Pres. (1980-81). Soroptimist Intl. of Wilkes-Barre: Pres. (1979–81). Greater Wilkes-Barre Cham. of Cmrce.: Community Issues (1979–81), Mem. Participation/Programming (1979–80); Flood Cntrl. (1977–80). College Misericordia Trustees (1978-81). **Pubns.:** Jt. auth., "Hannah Packard James," *Dictionary of American Library Biography* (1978); Oral presentations. **Activities:** 9; 17 **Addr.:** 71 S. Franklin Street, Wilkes-Barre, PA 18701.

Costello, Joseph Gerard (F. 17, 1943, Philadelphia, PA) Mgr., Spec. Proj., D&N (USA) Lib. Srvs. Inc.; Phd Student, Drexel Univ., 1979–81; Consult., Lib. & Info. Sci., Auerbach Assoc. Inc., 1977–79; Head, Branch Library, Free Lib. of Philadelphia, 1971–75; Resrch. Sci., Franklin Inst. Rsrch. Labs., 1967–69. **Educ.:** Villanova Univ., 1960–64, BS (Phys.), 1972–74, MS (LS); Drexel Univ., 1979–81. **Orgs.:** ASIS. ALA. PA LA. SLA. Amer. Inst. of Phy. **Pubns.:** Oral presentations, research reports, reviews. **Activities:** 4, 9, 11; 24; 88, 91 **Addr.:** 55 E. Mermaid Lane, Philadelphia, PA 19118.

Côté, Ernest Adolphe (Je. 12, 1913, Edmonton, AB) Retired, 1975–; Can. Ambassador to Finland, Gvt. of Can., 1972–75, Deputy Solicitor-Gen., 1969–72, Deputy Mnstr., Vets. Affairs, 1968–69, Deputy Mnstr., Indian Affairs and North. Dev., 1963–65. **Educ.:** Coll. des Jésuites, Edmonton, 1923–31, BSc; Univ. of AB, 1935–38, LlB; Imperial Defence Coll., London, 1949, IDC. **Orgs.:** Can. Lib. Trustees' Assn. Ottawa Pub. Lib.: Bd. of Trustees (Ch., 1981–). Royal Can. Geo. Socty.: Dir. (1964–72, 1977–). Hopital de Montfort: Trustee (1978–). **Honors:** H.M. George VI, Mem., Ord. of Brit. Empire, 1943. **Activities:** 9; 47 **Addr.:** 2 Pl. Allan, Ottawa, ON K1S 3T1 Canada.

Cottam, Keith M. (F. 13, 1941, St. George, UT) Assoc. Dir., Vanderbilt Univ. Lib., 1980–, Asst. Dir. for Pub. Srvs. & Empl. Rel., 1977–80; Asst. Dir. of Libs. for the Undergrad. Lib., Univ. of TN, Knoxville, 1972–77; Soc. Sci. Libn., Brigham Young Univ., 1967–72; Asst. Soc. Sci. Libn., South. IL Univ., Edwardsville, 1965–67; Adult Srvs. Libn., Brooklyn Pub. Lib., 1965. **Educ.:** UT State Univ., 1959–63, BS (Soclgy.); Pratt Inst., 1963–65, MSLS; ARL/OMS Consult. Trng. Prog., 1979–80. **Orgs.:** TN LA: VP/Pres. Elect (1978–79); Pres. (1979–80). ALA: Minimum Qualifications For Libns. Task Force (Ch., 1978–). UT LA. Church of Jesus Christ of Latter-day Saints. **Honors:** Phi Kappa Phi, 1972; Council on Lib. Resrcs., Flshp., 1975–76; TN Conf. on Lib. & Info. Srvs., Del., 1978. **Pubns.:** Jt. auth., *Writer's Research Handbook; a Guide to Sources* (1977); *Health, Physical Education, and Recreation: a Guide to Research in the Brigham Young University Library* (1971); "The State of Graduate Education," *The Grad.* (1974, 1975); "Library Use Instruction in Tennessee's Academic Libraries," *TN Libn.* (1974); "New Horizons for Library Service," *Reader in Library Technology* (1975); Other books, articles. **Activities:** 1; 17, 26, 35; 63, 92, 93 **Addr.:** Vanderbilt University Library, Nashville, TN 37203.

Cotter, Michael G. (O. 12, 1937, Prescott, WI) Head, Docum. & NC Unit, Lib. E. Carolina Univ., 1978–; Ref. Libn. for Docum., Harvard Coll. Library, 1975–76, Chief Docum. Libn., 1969–74, Book Sel. Spec., 1966–69. **Educ.:** WI State Coll., River Falls, 1955–60, BA (Hist.); Univ. of WI, 1963–66, MA (Hist.), MA (LS); Cert. in Vietnamese Lang., U.S. Army Lang. Sch., 1961. **Orgs.:** NC LA. ALA: Gvt. Docum. RT (1976-79). **Pubns.:** "Vietnam," *Southeast Asian Research Tools* (1979); *Vietnam, A Guide to Reference Sources* (1977); "Documents," *North Carolina Libraries* (Spr., Sum., Win. 1979); "Towards a Social History of the Vietnamese Southward Movement," *Jnl. of Southeast Asian Hist.* (1968). **Activities:** 1; 29, 39; 78 **Addr.:** J. Y. Joyner Library, East Carolina University, Greenville, NC 27834.

Cotton, Kenneth Wayne (Ag. 27, 1926, Groveton, NH) Lib. Dir., Westfield State Coll., 1966–; Chief of Acq., SUNY at Cortland, 1961–66. **Educ.:** Univ. of NH, 1944–48, AB (Eng.); OH Univ., 1956–57, MA (Hist.); Simmons Coll., 1960–61, MSLS. **Orgs.:** MA Conf. of Chief Libns. of Pub. Higher Educ. Coop. Coll. Libs. of Grt. Springfield. Natl. Educ. Assn. **Activities:** 1; 15, 17 **Addr.:** 2 Pine Wood Dr., Southampton, MA 01073.

Cottrell, Linda Diane. (Ag. 26, 1946, Santa Ana, CA) Map Libn., Univ. of AZ Lib., 1971–. **Educ.:** Coalinga Coll., 1964–66; Fresno State Coll., 1966–69, BA (Geo.); Univ. of IL, 1969–71, MSLS. **Orgs.:** SLA: AZ Chap. Pres.-elect (1978–79); Pres. (1979–80); Geo. and Map Div., Educ. Com. (1979–). AZ State LA: Spec. Libs. Div. (Secy./Treas., 1975–76). West. Assn. of Map Libs.: Car. Com. (1980–). ALA. AAUP. Phi Kappa Phi. Gamma Theta Upsilon. Pi Gamma Mu. **Honors:** Beta Phi Mu. **Activities:** 1, 12; 20, 39; 70 **Addr.:** Map Collection, University Library, University of Arizona, Tucson, AZ 85721.

Coty, Patricia Ann (Jl. 8, 1950, Niagara Falls, NY) Assoc. Dir., Pub. Srvs., Assoc. Libn., Sci. and Engin. Lib., SUNY, Buffalo, 1981–; Head, Media Ctr., Welch Med. Lib., Johns Hopkins Univ., 1978–81; Coord., Media Srvs./Assoc. Prof., Niagara Cnty. Cmnty. Coll., 1977–78, Media Libn., 1973–77; Lectr., LS, SUNY, Buffalo, 1978. **Educ.:** SUNY, Buffalo, 1972, BA (Bio.), 1973, MLS, 1979, EdM. **Orgs.:** Med. LA: Mid.-Atl. Reg. Grp., AV Com. (1978–81). SLA. AECT. **Pubns.:** "Organization of Non-Print Materials in the Library," *Cath. Lib. World* (Spr. 1980); jt. auth., "Integrated Shelving at Niagara County Community College," *Bookmark* (Sum. 1977). **Activities:** 1; 17, 32, 39; 58, 80, 91 **Addr.:** 921 Sun Valley, North Tonawanda, NY 14120.

Coughlin, Caroline M. (D. 6, 1944, New York, NY) Assoc. Dir., Rose Meml. Lib., Drew Univ., 1978–; Asst. Prof., Sch. of LS, Simmons Coll., 1974–78; Ref., Chld. Libn., Phillipsburg Pub. Lib., 1973–74; Instr., Rutgers Univ., Univ. of AL, 1971–73; Instr., Div. of Libnshp., Emory Univ., 1968–71; Ref., Cat. Libn., First Natl. City Bank, 1967–68. **Educ.:** Mercy Coll., 1962–66, AB (Eng.); Emory Univ., 1966–67, MLn (LS); Rutgers Univ., 1971–76, PhD (LS). **Orgs.:** ALA: Cncl. (1976–80); Awds. Com., J. Morris Jones, G. K. Bailey Howard ALA Goals Awd. Com. (Ch., 1980); D. Clift Schol. (Ch., 1978); Future Structure of ALA (1977–78). NJ LA: Lib. Dev. Com. (1978–80). AALS. **Honors:** Beta Phi Mu, 1967; Emory Univ., Fed. Grant, 1968–71. **Pubns.:** Ed., *Recurring Library Issues* (1979); "Childrens Librarians: Managing in the Midst of Myths," *Sch. Lib. Jnl.* (Ja. 1978) jt. auth., "Principal Library Associations," *A Century of Service* (1976); jt. ed., *Top of the News* (1974–77). **Activities:** 1, 11; 17, 26, 35 **Addr.:** Drew University, Rose Memorial Library, Madison, NJ 07940.

Coughlin, Violet L. Emeritus Prof., Univ. of Toronto Fac. of LS, McGill Univ. Lib. Sch., 1975–, Dir., 1971–73, Actg. Dir., 1970–71, various positions on fac., 1951–69; Libn., Royal Victoria Coll., 1941–51; Catlgr., Redpath Lib., 1941; Tchr., Montreal HS, 1929–34; Tech., Med. Lab., Royal Victoria Hosp., 1928–29. **Educ.:** McGill Univ., 1928, BS, magna cum laude (Arts), 1928, 1st Class HS Tchrs. Dip., 1938, BLS; Columbia Univ., 1958, MA (Adult Educ.), 1966, DLS. **Orgs.:** Can. LA: Various coms. ALA: Lib. Educ. Div., Bd. Secy., Nom. Com. AALS: Secty.-Treas. (1970–73); various coms. PQ LA: Pres. (1954–55); Legis. Com.; various coms. Beta Phi Mu: Bd. (1965–68). **Pubns.:** *Larger Units of Public Library Service in Canada* (1968); "Graduate School of Library Science, McGill University," *Encyc. of Lib. and Info. Sci.* (1968). **Addr.:** 666 Spadina Ave., Apt. 1810, Toronto, ON M5S 2H8 Canada.

PROFESSIONAL ACTIVITIES: Institutions: 1. Acad. lib.; 2. Arch.; 3. Assn.; 4. Fed./Gvt. lib.; 5. Inst. lib.; 6. Mfr./Suppl.; 7. Milit. lib.; 8. Musm.; 9. Pub. lib.; 10. Sch. lib.; 11. Sch. of lib. sci.; 12. Spec. lib.; 13. State lib.; 14. (other). **Functions/Activities:** 15. Acq./Col. dev.; 16. Adult srvs.; 17. Admin.; 18. Apprais.; 19. Archit./Bldgs.; 20. Cat./Class.; 21. Chld. srvs.; 22. Circ.; 23. Cons./Pres.; 24. Consult.; 25. Cont. ed.; 26. Educ. lib. sci.; 27. Ext. srvs.; 28. Fund/Grants; 29. Gvt. pubs.; 30. Indx./Abs.; 31. Instr. lib. use; 32. Media srvs.; 33. Micro.; 34. Netwks./Coop.; 35. Persnl.; 36. PR; 37. Publshg.; 38. Recs. mgt.; 39. Ref. srvs.; 40. Repro.; 41. Resrch.; 42. Review.; 43. Secur.; 44. Serials; 45. Spec. col.; 46. Tech. srvs.; 47. Trustees/Bds.; 48. YA srvs.; 49. (other).

Coumbe, Robert E. (Je. 20, 1933, Mount Holly, NJ) Dir., Gloucester Cnty. Lib., 1977–; Dir., N. Tonawanda, NY Pub. Lib., 1973–77; Consult., CT State Lib., 1969–73. **Educ.:** Villanova Univ., 1957–61, BA (Phil.), 1961–65, MSLS; Augustinian Coll., 1961–65, MAed (Theo.). **Pubns.:** *Guidepost: A Guide to the Religious Orders of Men in North America* (1964). **Activities:** 9; 17, 19, 47; 59, 69, 90 **Addr.:** 7 Arlington Drive, Sewell, NJ 08080.

Couper, Richard Watrous (D. 16, 1922, Binghamton, NY) Pres., Woodrow Wilson Natl. Flwshp. Fndn., 1981; Pres. Emeritus, NY Pub. Lib., 1981; Pres., Chief Exec. Ofcr., 1971–81; Deputy Comsn. for Higher Educ., NY State Educ. Dept., 1969–71; VP and Provost, Hamilton Coll., 1968–69, Actg. Pres., 1966–68, VP, 1965–66, Admin. VP, 1962–65; Treas., Dir., Couper-Ackerman-Sampson, 1948–62. **Educ.:** Hamilton Coll., 1947, BA; Harvard Univ., 1948, MA (Amer. Hist.). **Orgs.:** Univ. of Rochester Lib. Trustees: Visit. Com.; Resrch. Libs. Grp.: Ch. of Bd.; Grolier Club. Org. of Amer. Histns.; NY State Hist. Assn.: Trustee; Wesleyan Univ.: Trustee; Hamilton Coll.: Trustee; Other orgs. **Honors:** Phi Beta Kappa; Hamilton Coll., LLD, 1969; NY Univ., LHD, 1974. **Addr.:** The Woodrow Wilson Fellowship Foundation, Box 642, Princeton, NJ 08540.

Courtot, Marilyn E. (Mr. 17, 1943, Plainfield, NJ) Asst. Secy. of the U.S. Senate, 1981–, Admin. Dir., 1973–81; Sr. Systs. Anal., Lib. of Congs., 1971–73; Systs. Anal., IBM, 1968–71; Progmr., Dept. of Army, 1966–68; Progmr., Prudential Insr. Co., 1965–66. **Educ.:** Univ. of MD, 1961–65, BA (Eng.); Cath. Univ., 1972, MSLS. **Orgs.:** Natl. Micro. Assn.: Various ofcs. WHCOLIS: Adv. Com. (1979). NCLIS: Pub. Sector/Pvt. Sector Task Frc. CLENE. **Honors:** Beta Phi Mu; Assn. of Recs. Execs. and Admins., Cert. of Apprec., 1975; Natl. Micro. Assn., Certs. of Apprec., 1973, 1974, 1977; other hons. **Pubns.:** *Microform Indexing and Retrieval Systems* (1980); ed., *Glossary of Micrographics* (1980); ed., *Survey of Microforms Systems* (1976); *Microforms Systems Characteristics and Potential Senate Applications* (1975); various articles, reviews. **Activities:** 33 **Addr.:** U.S. Senate, Room S221, U.S. Capitol, Washington, DC 20510.

Coutant, Patricia C. (Ap. 13, 1949, Jacksonville, FL) Asst. Prof., Asst. Catlgr., Southeast. LA Univ., 1977–. **Educ.:** Univ. of FL, 1967–71, BEd; LA State Univ., 1976–77, MLS. **Orgs.:** LA LA: *LA LA Bltn.* Co. ed. (1980–). ALA. **Activities:** 1; 20, 39 **Addr.:** Sims Memorial Library, Southeastern Louisiana University, P.O. Drawer 896, Hammond, LA 70402.

Coutin, Rafael (Ap. 16, 1925, Baracoa, Cuba) Latin Amer. Catlgr., Univ. of NC, 1971–; Latin Amer. Catlgr., Tulane Univ., 1968–71. **Educ.:** Inst. of Sec. Tchg., Havana, 1940–45, BA; Univ. of Havana, 1945–50, Doctor of Law; Emporia State Univ., 1967–68, MA (LS). **Orgs.:** SALALM: Subcom. on Cuban Bibl. (1974–); Com. on Bibl. (1975–77); Ad Hoc Com. on Coop. Cat. of Latin Amer. Mtrls. (1976–); Com. on Lib. Oper. and Srvs. (1980–); Subcom. on Cat. and Bibl. Tech. (Ch., 1980). Libns. Assn. of Univ. of NC. **Pubns.:** Jt. cmplr., *Bibliography of Sources of Information Relative to Latin America* (1967); "Cuba: A Selected Bibliography," *Nineteenth SALALM Final Rpt. and Working Papers* (1976); contrib. indxr., *Hisp. Amer. Pers. Index* (1975–78). **Activities:** 1; 20, 30, 44; 54 **Addr.:** 112 Hamilton Rd., Chapel Hill, NC 27514.

Coven, Jane Davies (F. 12, 1922, Elyria, OH) Coord., Lib. Srvs., Elyria City Schs., 1964–; Libn., Lakewood Pub. Sch. 1960–64; Chld. Libn., Cleveland Pub. Lib., 1957–60; Libn., Elyria Lib., 1956–57. **Educ.:** West. Rsv. Univ., 1944–48, AB, magna cum laude (Geol., Geo.); Case West. Rsv. Univ., 1955–56, MS (LS), Univ. of NM, 1948–49 (Geol.). **Orgs.:** ALA. OH Educ. Lib Media Assn.: Stans. Com. (1977–79). **Honors:** Beta Phi Mu. **Activities:** 10; 17 **Addr.:** 425 East Ave., Elyria, OH 44035.

Covert, Nadine (Mr. 25, 1938, IL) Exec. Dir., EFLA, 1972–; Film Libn., YA Libn., NY Pub. Lib., 1969–72; Tchr., Scarsdale HS, 1965–68. **Educ.:** Univ. of IL, 1959–61, BA (Fr.), 1962–63, MA (Fr.); Columbia Univ., 1968–69, MLS. **Orgs.:** NY LA: Film/Video RT. Intl. Film Sems.: Treas./Trustee (1975–80). Media Ctr. for Chld.: Trustee (1976–79). Amer. Ctr. of Films for Chld.: Adv. Bd. (1977–). NY Film Cncl.: Bd. of Dir. (1972–75). Other orgs. **Honors:** Phi Beta Kappa, 1961; Phi Kappa Phi, 1961. **Pubns.:** Co-Ed., *16mm Distribution* (1977); Ed., *Films on War and Peace* (1971); "Freedom to View . . .", *Educ. Media Yearbook 1979* (1980); "EFLA: Influential Force in Media," *Educ. Media Yearbook 1977* (1978); "Voice Over", *Sightlines* (1973–); Other articles. **Activities:** 12; 17, 32, 37; 67 **Addr.:** c/o Educational Film Library Association, 43 W. 61 St., New York, NY 10023.

Covey, Elwin H. (Je. 29, 1922, Napa, CA) Anal./Data Prog. Base Mgr., Nvl. Ocean Syst. Ctr., San Diego, 1970–; Sci. Staff Asst., Nvl. Radiological Defense Lab., (S.F.), 1949–69; Chem./Jr. Exec., U.C. Radiation Lab., Berkeley, 1947–48; Resrch. Asst./Jr. Chem., Clinton Lab., Oak Ridge, TN, 1944–46; Asst. Chem., Metall. Lab., Chicago, 1942–44. **Educ.:** Univ. of CA, Berkeley, 1939–42, 1947–49, BS (Bus. Admin.); 1963–67, MLS; various ASIS/SLA workshops/tutorials, 1968–80. **Orgs.:** SLA: Pres., San Diego Chap. (1975–76). ASIS. Amer. Soc. for Recorded Sound. Sierra Club: Pres., Loma Prieta Chap. (1950–51). **Honors:** Beta Phi Mu, 1967; Naval Undersea Ctr., Sustained Superior Performance, 1970. **Activities:** 12; 17, 39, 46; 56, 74, 91 **Addr.:** 770 Loma Valley Road, San Diego, CA 92106.

Covington, Paula Anne (S. 30, 1947, Long Beach, CA) Latin Amer. Biblgphr./Ref. Libn., Vanderbilt Univ. Lib., 1978–; Proj. Coord., Cncl. on Lib. Resrc. LSEP Grant, 1977–78, Latin Amer. Biblgphr., 1976–77, Ref. Libn., 1973–75; Catlgr., Public Lib. of Nashville, 1971–72. **Educ.:** Syracuse Univ., 1965–69, BA (Latin Amer. Studies); George Peabody Coll., 1970–71, MLS; Univ. de los Andes, Bogotá, Colombia, 1968. **Orgs.:** ALA: Coop. Ref. Srvs. Com. (1976–78); ACRL: Bibli. Instr. Resrch. Com. (1979–). SALALM: Com. on Bibl. (1977–); *Hispanic American Periodical Index* Com. (1977–). SELA. TN LA. Other orgs. **Honors:** Beta Phi Mu, 1971. **Pubns.:** "Indexed Journals: A Selection of Latin American Serials," *SALALM Working Paper* (26:101, 1981) Contrib., *Hispanic American Periodical Index* (1977–); Contrib., *Bibliography of Latin American Bibliographies* (1977–); Reviews. **Activities:** 1; 15, 31, 39; 54 **Addr.:** Vanderbilt University Library, Nashville, TN 37203.

Cowan, Barbara M. (O. 6, 1946, ON) Adult Srvs. Libn., St. John Reg. Lib., 1972–. **Educ.:** Univ. of West. ON, 1966–70, BA (Eng.); Dalhousie Univ., 1970–72, MLS. **Orgs.:** Atl. Prov. LA. Can. LA: Councilor, C.A.P.L. (1979–81). John Howard Soc.: Bd. of Dir. (1977–). St. John Arts Cncl.: Secy. (1975–). St. John Heritage Trust: Secy. (1977–78). Univ. Women's Club: Prog. (1977–79), Treas. (1979–). **Pubns.:** Jt. auth., "When you are old and grey," *Can. Lib. Jnl.* (O. 1974); "Woman Is Woman's Natural Ally," *APLA Bltn.*. **Activities:** 9; 16, 48 **Addr.:** Saint John Regional Library, 20 Hazen Ave., Saint John, NB E2L 3G8, Canada.

Cowan, David G. (N. 12, 1953, Mountain Home, AR) Asst. Law Libn., Univ. of AR, 1978–. **Educ.:** Crowder Coll., 1971–73, AA; Univ. of AR, Fayetteville, 1973–75, BA (Pol. Sci.), 1975–78, JD. **Orgs.:** AALL. Southwest. Assn. Law Libs.: Cont. Educ. Com. (1980–), ILL Com. (1980–). Amer. Bar Assn. **Pubns.:** "Networking Within Swall," *Southwest. Assn. Law Libs. Bltn.* (My. 1980). **Activities:** 1; 22, 35, 39; 56, 77, 78 **Addr.:** 216 Waterman Hall, University of Arkansas Law School, Fayetteville, AR 72701.

Cowan, Georges (O. 13, 1942, Lachute, PQ) Mktg. Dir., La Société d'informatique Raymond Chabot, Inc. 1980–; Mgt. Consult. Raymond, Chabot, Martin, Paré and Cie, 1979–80; Data Base Mgr., Univ. of PQ, Montreal, 1975–79, Bus. Systs. Mgr., 1972–75; Programming and Inventory Cntrl. Syst. Mgr., North. Electric Co., 1967–71. **Educ.:** Univ. of Montreal, 1963–67, BSC (Math.), 1967–73, DSA (Admin.). **Orgs.:** Can. Assn. Info. Sci.: Prog. Ch. (1978); Montreal Chap. (VP, 1979). ASTED: Prog. Ch. (1979). Data Prcs. Mgt. Assn. Assn. for Systs. Mgt. **Pubns.:** *BADADUQ-Interrogation* (1975); "Les professionnels des sciences de l'information," *ARGUS* (Mr.–Ap. 1980); "Un réseau de documentation axé sur l'usager BADADUQ," *Docmlst.* (Mr. 1978); various presentations on the *BADADUQ* Syst. **Activities:** 6, 12; 24, 30; 56, 61, 75 **Addr.:** 111 Callieres St., Longueuil, PQ J4L 1K4 Canada.

Cowan, Lenore Elizabeth (Ja. 28, 1928, Bozeman, MT) Cur. of Pic. Col., NY Pub. Lib., 1968–; Asst. Cur., Pic. Col., 1966–68; Sr. Lib., Pic. Col., 1962–66. **Educ.:** Univ. of WI, 1942–51, BA (Eng. Lit.); Columbia Univ., 1959–62, MLS. **Orgs.:** SLA: Ch., Pic. Div. (1971–72). **Activities:** 9; 17; 95-Pictures. **Addr.:** Picture Collection, The New York Public Library, 5th Ave. & 42nd St., New York, NY 10018.

Coward, Robert Yeoman (Jl. 20, 1920, Port Huron, MI) Head Libn., Franklin Coll., 1952–; Sr. Libn., Univ. of MI, 1947–52; Asst. Circ. Dept., 1941–42. **Educ.:** Port Huron Jr. Coll., 1938–40, AA (Math.); Univ. of MI, 1940–42, AB (Germ.), 1946–50, ABLS, AMLS; Univ. of IL, 1953–55, (Lib. Sci.); IN Univ., 1963, (Audio-Visual). **Orgs.:** ALA. IN LA: Legis. Com. (1972–80). Exec. Brd. (1975–77). Nom. Com. (1978). Can. and Bylaws Com., (1978–81). AAUP: IN Conf., (VP, 1975–76). **Pubns.:** *Catalog of the David Demaree Banta Indiana Collection*, and 2d ed. (1960) (1965); "The Individual Study Carrell," *Pioneer* (1965). **Activities:** 1; 15, 17, 20; 56, 75 **Addr.:** 54 N. Dawn Dr., Franklin, IN 46131.

Cox, Beverly Anne (Jl. 7, 1945, Yakima, WA) Dir. of Lib. Srvs., Brookhaven Coll., 1978–; Instr. of LS, Baylor Univ., 1975–78; Youth Spec., Northe. TX Lib. Syst., 1974–75; Libn., OK City Pub. Sch., 1968–74. **Educ.:** OK State Univ., 1963–67, BS (Eng./Educ.); Univ. of OK, 1967–72, MLS; OK Tchr. Cert., 1967–74. **Orgs.:** ALA. OK Assn. of Sch. Libns.: Pres. (1972–73). TX LA. TX Jr. Col. Tchrs. Assn. Chld. Lit. Assn. AAUP. Bus. & Prof. Women's Club: Farmers Branch. (Prog. Ch., 1979–80). **Honors:** Beta Phi Mu. **Pubns.:** Ed. Bd., *Baylor Educator*, (1975–77). **Activities:** 1, 10, 11; 15, 26, 31; 63, 66, 75 **Addr.:** 12834 Midway Rd. #1103, Dallas, TX 75234.

Cox, Doris Walker (D. 11, 1919, Montbrook, FL) Prof. and Chair. Dept. of Lib. Sci., Ball State Univ., 1976–; Prof., Ch., Educ. Media and Lib. Sci., Appalachian State Univ., 1968–76; Assoc. Prof., Lib. Educ., Univ. of GA, 1965–68; Instruc., FL State Univ., 1964–65. **Educ.:** FL State Coll. for Women, 1936–39, AB (Eng.); FL State Univ., 1953–56, MALS, 1964–68, PhD (Educ.). **Orgs.:** ALA: AASL: (Early Chld. Educ. Com., 1975–; Chair. Stud. Involvement in Media Progs. Com., 1981–82. Com. on Lib. Educ. (1979–). Assn. of IN Media Educ.: Mat. Com. (1976–79). NC LA: Lib. Educ. Com. (1972–74). Stans. Com. (1973–76). FL Assn. of Sch. Libns.: Brd. of Dirs. (1954–65). **Honors:** Phi Delta Kappa; Beta Phi Mu. **Activities:** 10, 11; 17, 26, 41; 55, 63, 72 **Addr.:** 808 Riverside, Apt. 314, Muncie, IN 47303.

Cox, Dorothy J. (My. 2, 1923, Marion, IL) Dept. of Curric., Instr. and Media, Southern IL Univ., 1966–; Libn., Granite City (IL) Sch., 1956–66; Libn., Zeigler (IL) HS, 1954–56; Tchr., Coquille (OR) HS, 1952–54. **Educ.:** Southern IL Univ., Carbondale, 1940–44, BS (Hist./Eng.), 1945–51, MA (Hist.); Univ. of IL, 1958–61, MS (LS); Southern IL Univ., 1967–76, PhD (Educ.). **Orgs.:** Amer. Assn. of Sch. Libns. AECT: Cert. Com. (1978–). IL Assn. for Media in Educ.: Exec. Bd. (1962–68); Pres. (1966–67); Int. Frdm. Com., Ch. (1978). IL LA: Nom. Com. (1973–75, Ch. 1974–75); Int. Frdm. Com. (1978–); Future for Every Child Conf. (1979). Other orgs. and coms. Delta Kappa Gamma: Prof. Growth and Srvs., Ch. (1978–). Phi Delta Kappa. **Honors:** IL Assn. for Media in Educ., Sch. Libn. Honor Awd., 1979; Beta Phi Mu. **Pubns.:** Jt. auth., "Reference Books," *Bibliography of Books for Children* (1971); "The Role of the Librarian in the Library Without Walls," *IL Libs.* (Ap. 1966); "Education of the School Media Specialist," *IL Libs.* (S. 1970). **Activities:** 10, 14-Univ.; 24, 26, 32; 63, 74, 75 **Addr.:** Department of Curriculum, Instruction and Media, Southern Illinois University, Carbondale, IL 62901.

Cox, James C. (Jl. 8, 1927, Chicago, IL) Chief Libn., Loyola Univ. of Chicago Med. Ctr. Lib., 1974–; Asst. Libn., Lewis Towers Lib., Loyola Univ., 1972–74; Dir. of Libs., Loyola Univ., 1959–71; Assoc. Libn., 1958–59; Asst. Libn., Cudahy Lib., Loyola Univ., 1956–58; Libn., Sch. of Dentistry, Loyola Univ., 1955–56; Asst. Libn., Lewis Towers Lib., Loyola Univ., 1953–55. **Educ.:** Loyola Univ. of Chicago, 1946–50, PhB (Eng.); Rosary Coll., 1954–56, MALS; Loyola Univ., 1952–54 (Eng.); Cert. of Advnc. Study, Univ. of Chicago, 1971–72 (LS). **Orgs.:** ALA: LAMA/Publ. Com., Pub. Rel. Sect. (1965–67). Cath. LA: Cat. & Class. Sect. (Ch., 1966–67); Exec. Bd. (1967–73); VP (1973–75); Pres. (1975–77); Nom. Com. (Ch., 1980–81). Bibli. Soc. (London). Bibli. Soc. of Amer. Other orgs. **Pubns.:** Jt. auth., "Elizabeth M. Cudahy Library, Loyola University," *IL Libs.* (N. 1965); "Cataloging and Classification of Slides, Filmstrips, and Films," *Cath. LA Conf. Proc.* (1960). **Activities:** 1, 12; 17; 80 **Addr.:** 5926 North Bernard, Chicago, IL 60659.

Cox, Mary Frances (Knoxville, TN) Law Libn., TN Valley Athrty. Law Lib., 1958–. **Educ.:** South. Jr. Coll.; Columbia Jr. Coll.; South. Missionary Coll.; Columbia Univ.; Law Libn. Cert. **Orgs.:** AALL. Natl. Assn. of Legal Secys. Fort Sanders Hosp. Auxiliary. TN Bd. of Realtors. Knoxville Choral Socty. **Activities:** 4; 15, 30, 39; 77 **Addr.:** TVA Law Library, 400 Commerce Avenue E10C65, Knoxville, TN 37902.

Cox, Richard J. (F. 9, 1950, Baltimore, MD) City Arch. & Recs. Mgt. Ofcr., City of Baltimore, 1978–; Cur. of Mass., MD Hist. Socty., 1973–78. **Educ.:** Towson State Univ., 1968–72, BA (Hist. Eng.); Univ. of MD, 1975–78, MA (U.S. Hist.); Arch. Lib. Inst., OH Hist. Socty., 1974, Cert.; Mod. Arch. Admin. Natl. Arch., 1977, Cert.; Inst. in Advnc. Arch. Admin., 1979, Cert. **Orgs.:** SAA: News Notes Rept., *American Archivist* (1978–). Mid-Atl. Reg. Arch. Conf.: Strg. Com. (1976–78); Pubn. Com. (1977–); Nom. Com. (1979). Mss. Socty.: Book Review Ed., *Manuscripts* (1977–). Midwest Arch. Conf. Amer. Assn. for State and Local Hist.: MD Mem. Ch. (1976–). Org. of Amer. Histns. Amer. Hist. Assn. **Honors:** Mid-Atl. Reg. Arch. Conf., Arlene Custer Meml. Awd., 1979. **Pubns.:** *A Guide to the Microfilm Edition of the Mordecai Gist Papers* (1975); *A Guide to the Microfilm Edition of the Calvert Papers* (1973); co-ed., *A Guide to the Research Collections of the Maryland Historical Society* (1981); "The Plight of American Municipal Archives: Baltimore, 1789–1979," *Amer. Archvst.* (Jl. 1979); "Professionalism and Civil Other articles. **Activities:** 2; 38, 39, 45; 55, 69, 95-Local Government. **Addr.:** Baltimore City Archives, 211 E. Pleasant St., Baltimore, MD 21202.

Coy, Howard Louis, Jr. (Jl. 16, 1945, W. Monroe, LA) Libn., Leesville State Sch., 1970–. **Educ.:** Northeast LA State Univ., 1963–69, BA (Advert. Dsgn.). **Orgs.:** ALA. SWLA: Com. to Std. Modisette Awd. Guidelines (1979–). LA LA: LA State Lib. Adv. Com. (1976–). Amer. Assn. of Mental Deficiency. Assn. of Retarded Citizens. Vernon Bapt. Assn.: Media Dir. **Honors:** LA LA, Modisette Awd., 1979; LA Civil Srv. Leag., Charles E. Dunbar Jr. Career Srv., 1979. **Pubns.:** "PR and the Library," *LA Lib. Assn. Bltn.* (Spr. 1980); Reviews. **Activities:** 5, 10; 15, 17, 32; 67, 72 **Addr.:** 724 Sarah St., Leesville, LA 71446.

Coyle, Richard D. (Ja. 2, 1947, Lockport, NY) Head of Chld. Srvs., Brantford Pub. Lib., 1975–; Libn. I, Halifax City Reg. Lib., 1974–75. **Educ.:** Harpur Coll., 1965–69, BA (Eng.); Univ. of West. ON, 1972–74, MLS. **Orgs.:** Can. LA. ON LA. **Pubns.:** "Another Library Myth," *Emergency Libn.* (F. 1975). **Activities:** 9; 21, 36 **Addr.:** 67 Brant Ave., Apt. 201, Brantford, ON N3T 3H2 Canada.

Coyne, John R. (Jl. 30, 1930, Oak Park, IL) Head, Ref., Schaumburg Twp. Pub. Lib., 1978–; Exec. Secy., IL LA, 1976–78; IL Hlth. Sci. Libs. Coord., Midwest HSLN, 1973–76.

Special Subjects/Services: 50. Adult educ.; 51. Advert./Mktg.; 52. Aerosp.; 53. Agric.; 54. Area std.; 55. Arts/Hum.; 56. Autom.; 57. Bibl./Prtg.; 58. Bio. sci.; 59. Bus./Fin.; 60. Chem.; 61. Copyrt.; 62. Documtn.; 63. Educ.; 64. Engin.; 65. Env.; 66. Eth. grps.; 67. Film; 68. Food/Nutr.; 69. Geneal.; 70. Geo.; 71. Geol.; 72. Handcpd.; 73. Hist.; 74. Int. frdm.; 75. Info. sci.; 76. Insr.; 77. Law; 78. Legis.; 79. Math./Comp. sci.; 80. Med.; 81. Metals; 82. Nat. resrcs.; 83. Newsp.; 84. Nuc. sci.; 85. Oral hist.; 86. Petr./Energy; 87. Pharm.; 88. Phys./Astr./Math.; 89. Readg.; 90. Relig.; 91. Sci./Tech.; 92. Soc. sci.; 93. Telecom.; 94. Transp.; 95. (other).

Who's Who in Library and Information Services

Educ.: Loyola Univ., 1948–59, BS (Eng.); Univ. of Chicago, 1971–73, MA (LS). **Orgs.:** ALA. SLA. IL LA: Libn. Cit. Com. (1979–80); Conf. Com. (1980). **Activities:** 9; 16, 17, 39 **Addr.:** 728 Colfax, Evanston, IL 60201.

Crabb, Elizabeth A. (S. 1, 1925, Denton, TX) Coord., N.E. TX Lib. Syst., 1976–; Asst. Libn., Amarillo Pub. Lib., 1972–75; Asst. Chief of Branches, Austin Pub. Lib., 1971–72; Asst. Libn., Ext. Coord., Amarillo Pub. Lib., 1968–71, Head, Ref. Dept., 1966–68; Sch. Libn., Dependents' Sch., Rota, Spain, 1960–62; Asst. Head, Ref., Oakland Pub. Lib., 1958–59; various other prof. positions, 1945–58. **Educ.:** TX Woman's Univ., 1942–45, BA (LS); Univ. of TX, 1971–72, MLS. **Orgs.:** Dallas Cnty. LA: Pres. (1978–79). TX LA: Legis. Com. (1979–); Exec. Bd. (Pres.–Elect, 1981–82). SWLA: Pub. Lib. Dev. Interest Grp. (Ch., 1978–83). ALA: ASCLA/Multitype Lib. Syst. Div., Legis. Com. (1979–); Mem. Com. (TX Ch., 1972–75). **Honors:** TX LA, Libn. of the Yr., 1980; Beta Phi Mu. **Activities:** 9; 17, 25, 47 **Addr.:** Northeast Texas Library System, 1954 Commerce, Dallas, TX 75201.

Crabbe, Nancy S. (Ag. 31, 1945, Anderson, SC) Asst. City Libn., Redwood City Pub. Lib., 1979–; Prog. Mgr., Peninsula Lib. Syst. Comnty. Info. Proj., 1978–79; File Coord., 1976–78; Dept. Libn., San Mateo Cnty. Dept. of Pub. Hlth. & Welfare, 1973–76; Branch Libn., San Mateo Cnty. Lib., 1971–72; Ref. Libn., 1969–71. **Educ.:** Cornell Coll., 1963–67, BA, cum laude (Eng.); Simmons Coll., 1968–69, MS (LS). **Orgs.:** CA LA: Cncl. (1979–81). ALA. CA Women in Govt.: San Mateo Area Coord. (1979–). **Pubns.:** "The Community Information Project, San Mateo County;" LJ Special Report #5, *Community Information Services in Libraries* (1978); "Love conquers all: a cooperative program in I&R," *AIRS Newsletter* (July 1977). **Activities:** 9; 17, 35; 56, 92 **Addr.:** Redwood City Public Library 881 Jefferson Ave., Redwood City, CA 94063.

Crahan, Elizabeth Schmidt (O. 6, 1913, Cleveland, OH) Dir. of Lib. Srvs., Los Angeles Cnty. Med. Assn., 1960–; Asst., Sumner Spaulding, Architect, 1937–43. **Educ.:** Wellesley Coll., 1931–32; Univ. of South. CA, 1932–37, Bach. (Archit.), 1959–60, MSLS. **Orgs.:** Med. LA: Schol. Com. (1969–). SLA: Biological Sci. Div., South. CA Chap. (Ch., 1963–64); Corres. Secy. (1964–65); PR Dir. (1965–66). Med. Lib. Schol. Fndn.: Co-Founder (1969); Secy.-Treas. (1969–78); Pres. (1978–). USC Sch. of LS Alum. Assn.: Pres. (1965). Gen. Alum. Assn.: Bd. of Gvrs. (1971–74). Friends of the UCLA Lib.: Cncl. (1969–); VP (1976); Pres. (1977–79). Friends of the Los Angeles Cnty. Med. Assn. Lib.: Secy. (1978–). **Pubns.:** Various articles, *LACMA Physician*. **Activities:** 12; 15, 16, 26; 75, 80, 95-History of Medicine. **Addr.:** Los Angeles County Medical Association Library, 634 South Westlake Avenue, Los Angeles, CA 90057.

Craig, Sr. Agnes Gregory, SC (O. 5, 1926, Irvington, NJ) AV Libn., Coll. of St. Elizabeth Convent, 1970–, Prog. Dir. (LS), 1967–75; Libn., Marylawn HS (South Orange), 1960–70; Lib. Coord., Archdio. of Newark, 1965–70. **Educ.:** Caldwell Coll., 1944–48, BA (Eng.); St. John's Univ., 1956–60, MLS. **Orgs.:** ALA. Catholic LA: /North NJ Chap. (Various ofcs.). NJ LA: Rec. Secy. (1974–76). **Activities:** 1; 17, 25, 32; 50, 63, 92 **Addr.:** College of Saint Elizabeth, Convent Station, NJ 07961.

Craig, Marilyn Joanne (O. 29, 1932, Alameda, CA) Msc. Cat. Libn., Univ. of Houston Ctrl. Campus, 1979–; AV Cat. Libn., Univ. of AZ, 1973–79; Sch. Libn., Vail Sch. Dist. (Tuscon, AZ), 1972–73. **Educ.:** Univ. of the Pac., 1950–54, BA (Msc.); Univ. of AZ, 1969–72, MLS. **Orgs.:** ALA: RTSD, AV Com. (1975–76)/ Cat. and Class. Sect., Cat. of Chld. Mtrls. Com. (1979–83); LITA. Msc. LA. Msc. OLUG. Online AV Catlgrs. **Activities:** 1; 20, 46; 55, 56 **Addr.:** 131 Burwell Rd., Highlands, TX 77562.

Craig, Susan V. (N. 10, 1948, Newton, KS) Art Libn., Univ. of KS, 1981–; Art Hist./Classics Libn., Univ. of CA, Berkeley, 1975–81; Indxr., *Art Index*, H. W. Wilson Co., 1971–74. **Educ.:** Univ. of KS, 1970, BA (Hist. of Art); Emporia State Univ., 1971, MLS. **Orgs.:** ARLIS/NA: Secy. (1975–77); Prog. Ch. (1981). ARLIS/North. CA: Vice-Ch. (1979–80). **Activities:** 1; 15, 31, 39; 55 **Addr.:** Art Library, Spencer Museum of Art, University of Kansas, Lawrence, KS 66044.

Craighead, Gracie Mae (Ap. 24, 1920, Defeated, TN) Elem. Media Spec., Morny Elem. Sch., 1965–, Union Hill Elem. Sch., 1968–; Libn., Jere Mills School, 1965–68; Tchr., Jere Baytten Sch., 1963–65; Elem. Libn., Ft. Benning Chld. Sch., 1954–63. **Educ.:** TN Tech. Univ., 1941–45, BS (Eng.); George Peabody Coll. for Tchrs., 1952–53, MALS. **Orgs.:** ALA. SELA. TN LA. Middle TN Lib. Assn. Intl. Reading Assn. Natl. Untd. Tchrs. Org. Natl. Socty. of Published Poets. **Honors:** Freedoms Fndn., Schoolmen Medal Awd., 1975. **Pubns.:** "We Stand Responsible for our Fundamental Freedoms," *TN Libn.* (Spr. 1975); "Neither Dull Nor Dreary–Our School Library," *TN Tchr.* (D. 1972); Poetry. **Activities:** 10 **Addr.:** Morny Elementary School, 5880 Eaton's Creek Rd., Joelton, TN 37080.

Cramer, Anne O. (S. 20, 1929, Norman, OK) Dir., East. VA Med. Sch. Lib., 1972–; Ext. Libn., Univ. of UT, 1970–72; Lib. Dir., Southwest. OK State Univ., 1961–69; HQ Libn., Johnson Cnty. (KS) Lib., 1959–61; Asst. Libn., Kansas City Pub. Lib., 1951–58. **Educ.:** Stephens Coll., 1947–48; Univ. of OK, 1948–51, BA (LS), 1967–68, MLS; FL State Univ., 1969–70, Advnc. MLS (Lib. Admin.); Med. LA, Cert., 1969. **Orgs.:** Med. LA: Mid-Atl. Reg. Grp.; Com. on Grp. Structure (1975–76). SLA. VA LA. ALA. Other orgs. Weatherford (OK) Lib. Adv. Bd. (1964–69). VA Lung Assn.: Dir.-At-Large (1976–77). Soroptimist Intl. of Norfolk-VA Beach: Secy.; Exec. Bd. (1976–77). State Cncl. of Higher Educ. for VA: Lib. Adv. Com. (1978–80). Other orgs. **Honors:** Beta Phi Mu. **Pubns.:** *"First Aid" for Hospital Librarians* (1971); Hospital Library Handbook Series, No. 1–*Hospital Library Administration* (1971); No. 2–*Hospital Library Development* (1971); No. 3–*Printed Materials: Selection and Acquisition* (1972). **Activities:** 1, 12; 17, 27, 34; 55, 63, 80 **Addr.:** Eastern Virginia Medical School, Moorman Memorial Library, Post Office Box 1980, Norfolk, VA 23501.

Crampon, Jean E. (N. 9, 1947, Richmond, CA) Asst. Prof., Head Ref. Libn., South. IL Univ. Sch. of Med., 1981–, Asst. Med. Libn., Head of Ref., 1980, Ref. Libn., 1976–80, Circ. Libn., 1974–76; Chld. Libn., San Diego Pub. Lib., 1971–73. **Educ.:** San Diego State Coll., 1966–69, AB (Liberal Arts); Univ. of NC, 1969–72, MSLS; Med. LA 1975, Cert. **Orgs.:** MEDLINE Users Grp. of the Midwest: Strg. Com. (1978–81). Med. LA: Pubns. Com. (1978). SLA. IL LA: Hosplty. Com. (1974); Spec. Events Com. (1977). Various other orgs. Leag. of Women Voters. **Honors:** Midwest HSLN, Cert. of Apprec., 1980. **Pubns.:** "Introducing the Laboratory Animal Data Bank," *Database* (S. 1981); "Training Backup Searchers," *Online* (O. 1980); "Comment on Scope of Clinical Medical Library Service," *Online* (O. 1979). **Addr.:** Southern Illinois University, School of Medicine Library, P.O. Box 3926, Springfield, IL 62708.

Crane, Lilly E. (S. 12, 1937, Hackensack, NJ) Asst. Cat. Libn., South. IL Univ., 1974–, Serials Catlgr., 1969–74, Asst. Educ. Libn., 1967–69. **Educ.:** IN Univ., 1955–59, BA (Hist.); Univ. of MI, 1965–67, MALS. **Orgs.:** ALA. IL LA: Revisions Com. (1977–79). IL ACRL: Exec. Bd. (1976–78). IL OCLC Users Grp. **Activities:** 1; 20, 34 **Addr.:** Route 1, Box 92A, Makanda, IL 62958.

Crane, Maurice Aaron (Je. 6, 1926, Atlantic City, NJ) Head, Voice Lib., MI State Univ., 1974–, Prof., Hum., 1953–. **Educ.:** Princeton Univ., Villanova Univ., 1944–48; Univ. of Chicago, Univ. of IL, 1948–53, MA, PhD (Eng.). **Orgs.:** Assn. of Rec. Snd. Collectors. Oral Hist. Assn. Pop. Culture Assn. **Honors:** MI State Univ., Disting. Fac. Awd., 1979; MI State Univ., Disting. Prof. Awd., 1968. **Pubns.:** *Academic Overture* (1968); various articles, reviews, radio talks, films. **Activities:** 1; 55, 93 **Addr.:** Michigan State University Libraries, East Lansing, MI 48824.

Cranford, Theodore N. (My. 9, 1930, Portland, OR) Lib. Resrch. Anal., Rockwell Intl. Corp., 1962–; Libn. II, Univ. of CA, Lawrence Livermore Lab., 1957–62; Libn. GS-7, NACA, Ames Aeronautical Lab., 1954–57. **Educ.:** Univ. of WA, 1948–52, AB (Hist.), 1952–53, MALS. **Orgs.:** SLA. Sierra Club. Natl. Jogging Assn. **Honors** Rockwell Intl., Employee Cons. Com. Awd., 1975, Sustained Superior Performance Awd., 1972, Apollo Achvmt. Awd., 1972. **Pubns.:** *ERIC Guidelines for Abstracting and Indexing.* (1966); "Training of Indexers for Consistency", *SLA So. CA Bltn.* (Spr. 1965). **Activities:** 4, 12; 15, 39, 49-Online Lit. Search; 52, 64, 91 **Addr.:** P. O. Box 1307, Downey, CA 90240.

Craven, Timothy C. (S. 4, 1947, Vancouver, BC) Asst. Prof., Sch. of Lib. and Info. Sci., Univ. of West. ON, 1977–, Lect., 1974-77. **Educ.:** Carleton Univ., 1965–69, BA (Classics); McMaster Univ., 1969–70, MA (Classics); 1970–73, PhD (Roman Studies); Univ. of West. ON, 1973–74, MLS. **Orgs.:** ASIS. Can. Assn. for Info. Sci. Can. Class. Resrch. Grp.: Coord. (1979–). Can. LA; Other orgs. **Pubns.:** "Salient Node Notation," *The Can. Jnl. of Info. Sci.*, 4 (1979); "Linked phrase indexing," *Info. Processing and Mgt.*, 14 (1978); "A NEPHIS thesaurus for computer generation of permuted cross-references" in: ASIS, Anl. Mtg., 41st, NY (1978); "NEPHIS: a nested phrase indexing system," *Jnl. of the ASIS*, (Mr. 1977); various other articles. **Activities:** 11; 26, 41; 56, 75 **Addr.:** School of Library and Information Science, The University of Western Ontario, London, ON N6A 5B9 Canada.

Cravey, Pamela J. (Washington, DC) Head, Circ. Dept., GA State Univ., 1979–; Ref. Libn. & Bibli. Instr. Coord., 1975–79; Head Circ. Dept., FL Tech. Univ., 1972–75; Asst. Head, Circ. Dept., Univ. of GA, 1969–72. **Educ.:** Baldwin-Wallace Coll., 1967, BA (Soclgy.); FL State Univ., 1967–68, MS (LS). **Orgs.:** ALA: Various Coms. SELA: Ch. Lib. Orien. & Bibl. Instr. Com. (1978–80). GA LA. GA Sociological Assn. **Honors:** Cncl. on Lib. Resrc., Lib. Srvc. Enhancement Prog., 1977–78; GA State Univ., Urban Life Ctr., Pub. Srvc. Awd., 1977–78. **Pubns.:** "User & Bibliographic Instruction," *GA Libn.* (F. 1979); "Bibliographic Instruction & Murphy's Law," *Proceedings* (1978); Other pubs. **Activities:** 1; 22, 31; 92 **Addr.:** 2413 Harrington Dr., Decatur, GA 30033.

Crawford, Anthony R. (My. 2, 1944, Oklahoma City, OK) Asst. Dir. for Lib. & Arch., MO Hist. Socty., 1980–; Archvst., George C. Marshall Resrch. Lib., 1973–79; Resrch. Asst., Univ. of OK Lib., West. Hist. Coll., 1972–73; Hist. Tchr., Miami (OK) Pub. Sch., 1967–72. **Educ.:** OK State Univ., 1964–67, BS (Educ.); Univ. of OK, 1972–73, MLS. **Orgs.:** SAA: Finding Aids (1974–); Mss. Socty.; Oral Hist. Assn. Midatl. Reg. Arch. Conf.: Steering Com. (1979–81). **Pubns.:** Ed., *Posters of World War I and World War II in the George C. Marshall Research Foundation*, (1979). **Activities:** 12, 14-Hist. Socty.; 15, 23 **Addr.:** Missouri Historical Society, Forest Park, St. Louis, MO 63112.

Crawford, David S. (S. 16, 1943, Stowe-on-the-Wold, England) Asst. Life Sci. Area Libn., McGill Univ., 1972–; Head of Pub. Srvs., Hlth. Sci. Lib., Dalhousie Univ., 1971–72; Asst. Libn., Med. Lib., Queen's Univ., Belfast, N. Ireland, 1967–71. **Educ.:** Queen's Univ. Belfast, 1961–66, BA (Hons) (Psy.), 1966–67, Dip. (Lib. Std.); London, 1966–70, ALA. **Orgs.:** Med. LA: Ed. Com., *Bltn.* (1973–76); Ch. (1975/76). Can. Hlth. Libs. Assn.: Pres. (1976–77); Exec. Mem. (1976–78). Assn. of Can. Med. Colls.: Secy., Med. Libs. Com. (1974–76). **Activities:** 1; 17, 44; 80 **Addr.:** Medical Library, McGill University, 3655 Drummond St., Montréal, PQ H3G 1Y6 Canada.

Crawford, John Carlisle (My. 26, 1931, Ridley Park, PA) Field Dir., Lib. of Congs. Office, Jakarta, 1978–; Asst. Chief, Overseas Oper. Div., Lib. of Congs., 1976–78; Field Dir., Lib. of Congs. Office, Nairobi, 1974–76; Jakarta, 1969–74; New Delhi, 1964–69; various other positions in Lib. of Congs. **Educ.:** Univ. of PA, 1949–53, AB (Hist.); Drexel Univ., 1956–57, MSLS. **Orgs.:** ALA. Intl. Assn. of Orientalist Libns. Indian LA. **Activities:** 1, 4; 15, 17, 20; 54, 92 **Addr.:** American Embassy Box 1, APO, San Francisco, CA 96356.

Crawford, Miriam I. (Jl. 3, 1916, Brooklyn, NY) Cur., Conwellana-Templana Col., Temple Univ. Libs., 1965–; Ref. Libn., 1964–65, Asst. Head, Cat. Dept., 1962–64, Catlgr., 1958–61; Adult Educ. Dir., New Rochelle Pub. Lib., 1946–49; Soc. Sci. Libn., Brooklyn Pub. Lib., 1941–43, Branch Work Asst., 1939–41. **Educ.:** Brooklyn Coll., 1933–37, BA (Soc. Sci.); Columbia Univ., 1937–40, BS (LS); Teachers Coll., Columbia Univ., 1941–47, MA (Adult Educ.); American Univ., Cert. in Arch. Admin., 1966. **Orgs.:** ALA: Cnclr. (1972–74, 1978–82). SAA: Com. on Com. (1977–78), Arch.-Lib. Rel. Com. (1971/72, 1973–75). PA LA: Int. Frdm. Com. (Ch., 1977–78). Temple Univ. Acad. Asm. of Libn.: Ch. (1978–79). Other orgs. AAUP: Ch., Temple Chap. Libns. Caucus (1980). Natl. Women's Political Caucus. **Honors:** SAA, Fellow, 1978. **Pubns.:** Contrib., *Affirmative Action in Libraries* (1981); "Common Issues," *Archive-Library Relations* (1976); "Women in Archives: A Program for Action," *Amer. Archvst.* (Ap. 1973); "Interpreting the University Archives to the Librarian," *PLA Bltn.* (N. 1968); Comp., "Russell Herman Conwell ... an Exhibition ..." (1977). **Activities:** 1, 2; 15, 39; 63, 85 **Addr.:** Samuel Paley Library, Temple University, Philadelphia, PA 19122.

Crawford, Paul Russell (Je. 16, 1919, St. Ignatius, MT) Dir. of Cnty. Sch. Lib. Srvs., Ventura Cnty., 1961–; Asst. Libn., Ventura Coll., 1954–61; Ref. Libn., San Jose State Coll., 1952–54. **Educ.:** Univ. of WA, 1938–42, BA (Hist.); 1947–49, MA (Hist.); Univ. of CA, Berkeley, 1951–52, BLS; CA Libnshp. Lifetime Cred. **Orgs.:** CA Media and Lib. Educ. Assn.: State Ch., Cnty. Sch. Sect. (1962–66; 1976–77). ALA. CA LA. Natl. Educ. Assn. CA Tchrs. Assn. Assn. of CA Sch. Admin. Assn. for Supvsn. and Curric. Dev. **Honors** Phi Alpha Theta, 1952. **Activities:** 1, 10; 17, 21, 39; 55, 63, 74 **Addr.:** 145 Stadium Avenue, Ventura, CA 93003.

Crawford, Richard A. (My. 15, 1930, Wagner, SD) Pres., The Amer. Co., Inc., 1968–; VP, Josten's, Inc., 1962–68; Mgr. Fncl. Plng., Westinghse. Elec. Corp., 1955–62. **Educ.:** Mankato State Univ., 1949–52, BS (Bus. Admin.); IN Univ., 1953–54, MBA. **Orgs.:** KS LA: Exec. Cncl., Exhibits Mgr. (1968–79). Topeka Pub. Schs.: Sch. Bd. (1978–80). Topeka Savings Assn.: Dir. Brewster Pl.: Dir. Rosco Concrete Pipe Co.: Dir. **Honors:** KS LA, Pres. Awd., 1981. **Addr.:** The American Companies, Inc., 914 Jefferson St., Topeka, KS 66607.

Crawford, Robert G. (Jl. 29, 1945, Pittsburgh, PA) Assoc. Prof., Queen's Univ., 1972–. **Educ.:** PA State Univ., 1963–67, BSc (Engin.); Cornell Univ., 1967–71, PhD (Comp. Sci.). **Orgs.:** ASIS. Can. Assn. Info. Sci. Assn. Comp. Mach.: Info. Retrieval Spec. Interest Grp. **Pubns.:** "The Relational Model in Information Retrieval," *Jnl. ASIS* (1981); "Automatic Thesaurus Construction Based on Teum Centroids," *Can. Jnl. of Info. Sci.* (1979); "Dynamic Dictionary Updating," *Info. Prcs. and Mgt.* (1977); "The Computation of Discrimination Values," *Info. Prcs. and Mgt* (1975). **Activities:** 11; 26, 30, 41 **Addr.:** Dept. of Computer & Information Science, Queen's University, Kingston, ON K7L 3N6 Canada.

Crawford, Susan Y. (Vancouver, BC) Dir., Div. of Lib. & Arch. Srvs., Amer. Med. Assn., 1974–; Dir., Arch.-Lib. Dept., 1960–74; Assoc. Prof., Sch. of Lib. Srv., Columbia Univ., 1972–75; Resrch. Assoc., Amer. Med. Assn., 1956–59. **Educ.:** Univ. of BC, BA (Lib. Arts); Univ. of Toronto, BLS; Univ. of Chicago, MA (Biol., Soc. Sci), PhD (Lib. & Info. Sci.). **Orgs.:** Amer. Assn. for the Advnc. of Sci. ALA. ASIS. Med. Lib. Assn. **Honors:** Pi Lamda Theta, hon. educ., 1967–69; Bd. of Regents, Natl. Lib. of Med. 1971–75; U.S. Public Health Service, Cert. of

PROFESSIONAL ACTIVITIES: Institutions: 1. Acad. lib.; 2. Arch.; 3. Assn.; 4. Fed./Gvt. lib.; 5. Inst. lib.; 6. Mfr./Suppl.; 7. Milit. lib.; 8. Musm.; 9. Pub. lib.; 10. Sch. lib.; 11. Sch. of lib. sci.; 12. Spec. lib.; 13. State lib.; 14. (other). **Functions/Activities:** 15. Acq./Col. dev.; 16. Adult srvs.; 17. Admin.; 18. Apprais.; 19. Archit./Bldgs.; 20. Cat./Class.; 21. Chld. srvs.; 22. Circ.; 23. Cons./Pres.; 24. Consult.; 25. Cont. ed.; 26. Educ. lib. sci.; 27. Ext. srvs.; 28. Fund/Grants; 29. Gvt. pubs.; 30. Indx./Abs.; 31. Instr. lib. use; 32. Media srvs.; 33. Micro.; 34. Netwks./Coop.; 35. Persnl.; 36. PR; 37. Publshg.; 38. Recs. mgt.; 39. Ref. srvs.; 40. Repro.; 41. Resrch.; 42. Review.; 43. Secur.; 44. Serials; 45. Spec. col.; 46. Tech. srvs.; 47. Trustees/Bds.; 48. YA srvs.; 49. (other).

Achvmt., 1975; Med. Lib. Assn., Eliot Awd., 1976; Sigma Xi, 1978. **Pubns.:** "From hard copy to electronic publishing: problems in accessing the literature," *Jnl. Amer. Med. Assn.* (Ja. 31, 1979); "The evaluation of manuscripts in health sciences librarianship," *Bull. Med. Lib. Assn.* (O. 1979); Jt. ed., *Directory of Health Sciences Libraries in the United States* (1979); "Identification of problem domains in psychiatry," *Procs. of ASIS* (1979); Jt. auth., "Research in psychiatry: a co-citation analysis," *Amer. Jnl. Psyt.* (Ja. 1980); various other monographs and articles. **Addr.:** American Medical Association, 535 N. Dearborn St., Chicago, IL 60610.

Crawley, William D. (Jl. 31, 1938, Buenos Aires, Argentina) Exec. VP, Pergamon Press Can., 1977–; Dir., Intl. Mktg., Educ. Dev. Corp., 1975–77; Gen. Mgr., McGraw-Hill Ryerson, 1962–75. **Educ.:** Dalhousie Univ., 1958–62, BSc (Geol.). **Orgs.:** Can. LA. Can. Bk. Publshrs. Cncl. **Activities:** 6 **Addr.:** Pergamon Press Canada Ltd., Suite 104, 150 Consumers Rd., Willowdale, ON M2J 1P9 Canada.

Crayton, James Edward (D. 18, 1943, Thomasville, AL) Head of Acq., Pasadena City Coll., 1972–; Sr. A. V. Libn., Los Angeles Cnty. Pub. Lib. Syst., 1970–72; Ref. AV and Head of Acq., Anaheim Pub. Lib., 1969–70; Libn., Atlanta Trade Tech., 1967; Staff Asst., Atlanta Bd. of Educ., 1967–68; Elem. Sch. Libn., Cobb Cnty. Bd. of Educ., Marietta, GA, 1965–67. **Educ.:** AL State Univ., 1961–64, BS (Hist.); Atlanta Univ., 1965–68, MLS; CA State Univ., Long Beach, 1974–75, MA (Educ.); Claremont Grad. Sch., 1975–80, PhD, (Educ.); other courses. **Orgs.:** CA LA: Cncl. (1974–76); Gvt. Rel. Com. (1979–80). CA Libn. Black Caucus: South. Area Coord. (1979–80); ALA: LITA/AVS Mem. Com. (1979–81). NAACP. Los Angeles Urban Leag. **Pubns.:** "A Case for Afro-American Collections," *CA Libn.* (1976); "As a Black Librarian, I Am Asking–What Next?", *What Black Librarians are Saying* (1972); "The L. A. Black Caucus: Fending and Defending," *Wilson Lib. Bltn.* (Ja. 1974); "A Core Afro-American Film Collection," *Film Lib. Qtly.* (N. 2, 1974); "A Case for Afro-American Collections," *CA Libn.* (Ja. 1976). **Activities:** 1; 15, 32; 50, 66, 67 **Addr.:** Pasadena City College Library, 1570 E. Colorado Blvd., Pasadena, CA 91106.

Creaghe, Norma S. (Jl. 30, 1925, Colorado Springs, CO) Lib. Dir., St. Anselm Coll., 1971–; Asst. Dir., St. Anselm's Coll., 1969–71. **Educ.:** Univ. of CO, 1943–47, (Pol. Sci. and Econ.); Texas Woman's Univ., 1968–69, MLS. **Orgs.:** Acad. Libns. of NH: Ch. (1973). NH LA. NH Lib. Cncl.: Ch. (1976). NELINET: Bd. of Dir. (1973, 1979–). NELA: Secy. (1977); VP (1980); Pres. (1981). Educ. Assistance Com. (Ch., 1978–80). Hopkinton Woman's Club. **Honors:** Beta Phi Mu. **Activities:** 1; 17, 25, 31 **Addr.:** Geisel Library, St. Anselm's College, Manchester, NH 03102.

Creech, Chloe R. (O. 28, 1937, Tina, KY) Media Spec., Canton S. HS, 1971–; Libn., Dilce Combs HS, 1965–71; Tchr., Vest Elem. Sch., 1963–65; Tchr., Lower Ball Elem. Sch., 1958–63. **Educ.:** Univ. of KY, 1957–65, BA (Educ, Eng.); Univ. of KY, 1968–71, MLS. **Orgs.:** ALA: AASL. OH Educ. Media Assn.: Pubcty. Com. (1973–76); Schol. Com. (1977–79). **Honors:** Beta Phi Mu. **Pubns.:** "Precious Moments," *OASL Bltn.* (J. 1976); "The Creation," (sound/slide) (1974); "His Love . . . Reaching," (sound/slide) (1979). **Activities:** 10; 15, 32, 48 **Addr.:** 1125 Lakeview NW, Canton, OH 44708.

Creek, Leon Joseph (D. 18, 1936, Rochester, NY) Phil. Biblgphr., Univ. of Rochester Lib., 1970–, Serials Catlgr., 1978–, Sci. and Engin. Libn., 1967–78. **Educ.:** St. John Fisher Coll., 1956–60, BS (Educ.); Syracuse Univ., 1967, MS (LS). **Orgs.:** ALA. Phil. of Sci. Assn. Amer. Cath. Phil. Assn. **Pubns.:** Reviews. **Activities:** 1; 15, 20, 42; 55, 88 **Addr.:** 304 Mulberry St., Rochester, NY 14620.

Creighton, Alice S. (Annapolis, MD) Asst. Libn. for Spec. Co., US Naval Acad., 1974–; Catlgr., Pittsburgh Theo. Sem., 1971–74; Hist. of Med. Libn., Univ. of Rochester Sch. of Med. & Dent., 1965–71. **Educ.:** Univ. of ME, Orono, 1954–56, BS Univ. of Pittsburgh, 1962–64, MLS; Biomed. Lib. Intern., Univ. of CA, Los Angeles, 1964–65, MLA. **Orgs.:** SLA. ALA. Amer. Inst. for Cons. of Art. & Hist. Works. Amer. Assn. for State & Local Hist. NY State Hist. Assn. **Honors:** Phi Kappa Phi, 1956; Omicron Nu, 1956; Beta Phi Mu, 1964. **Pubns.:** "The Edward J. Steichen Collection," *Aerospace Hist.* (Mr. 1977); "Creatures so very Diminutive," *Univ. of Rochester Lib. Bltn.* (Winter 1967–68). **Activities:** 1; 17, 23, 45; 74, 91 **Addr.:** Special Collections Department, Nimitz Library, U.S. Naval Academy, Annapolis, MD 21402.

Crenshaw, Tena Lula (D. 15, 1930, Coleman, FL) Head, Educ. Lib., Univ. of FL, 1980–; Deputy Dir., Louis Calder Mem. Lib., Univ. of Miami, 1979–80; Head, Srv. to the Pub., A.W. Calhoun Med. Lib., Emory Univ., 1969–79; Resrch. Info. Spec., Tech. Info. Ctr., Lockheed Missiles & Space Co., 1966–68; Reader Srvs. Libn., John F. Kennedy Space Ctr., NASA, 1964–66; Acq. Libn., Martin Marietta Corp., 1961–64; Tech. Libn., Army Rocket and Guided Missile Agency, 1960–61. **Educ.:** FL South. Coll., 1948–51, BS (Educ.); Univ. of OK, 1959–60, MLS; Univ. of FL, 1952–55; Emory Univ., 1969; Med. LA, Cert., 1969. **Orgs.:** SLA: Arch. Com. (1977–78); S. Atl. Chap., Pres. (1974–75); Ch., Mem. Com. Treas. (1970–72); Bio. Sci. Div. (Ch., 1977–78). Med. LA: Southeast. Rep. (1977–79). SELA. FL LA. Kappa Delta Pi. Alpha Delta Pi. **Pubns.:** Various articles. **Activities:** 1, 12; 17, 35, 36; 63, 64, 80 **Addr.:** University of Florida, Education Library, 1500 Norman Hall, Gainesville, FL 32611.

Creps, John E. Jr. (Mr. 22, 1926, Newark, NJ) Exec. Dir., Engin. Index, Inc., 1973–; Dir. of Mktg., 1968–72; Dir. of Mktg., Biol. Abs., 1965–68. **Educ.:** Franklin and Marshall Coll., 1948–52, BS (Chem.); Univ. of Dubuque, 1952–55, BD (Theol.). **Orgs.:** Amer. Soc. of Info.: Treas. (1978–80). Natl. Fed. of Abs. & Indx. Srvs.: Pres. (1974), Treas. (1978–79). Amer. Soc. of Info. Dssmn. Ctr.: Plng. Com. (1979). SLA. World Fed. of Engin. Orgs.: Com. on Info., Plng. & Strg. Com. (1978–80). Intl. Cncl. of Sci. Un.: Abs. Bd., Ch., Mem. Com. (1977–80), Plng. & Strg. Com. (1979–80). Other orgs. **Pubns.:** *Computerization of Engineering Index* (1975); "Engineering Information," *Anl. Review of Info. Sci.* (1978). **Activities:** 6; 30, 37, 47; 64 **Addr.:** Engineering Index, Inc., 345 East 47th St., New York, NY 10017.

Cressaty, Margaret Doumar (D. 16, 1905, Pasadena, CA) Assoc. Libn., Univ. of CA, Irvine, 1968–73; Archvst., CA Coll. of Med., 1966–68; Act. Libn., 1962–66; Libn., Coll. of Osteopathic Physicians, 1947–62; Sr. Asst., Pasadena Pub. Lib., 1930–37; Sr. Asst., Lib. of World Affairs, Univ. of South. CA, 1937–39; Libn., 1939–43; Libn., John Randolph Haynes and Dora Haynes Fndn., 1943–47. **Educ.:** Pasadena Jr. Coll., 1925–27, Cert. (Eng.); Occidental Coll., 1927–29, AB (Eng. & Educ.); Lib. Sch. of the Los Angeles Pub. Lib., 1929–30, Dipl.; University of South. CA Sch. of Lib. Sci., 1966. **Orgs.:** Med. LA: Publicity & Prntg. Com. (1956). Med. Lib. Grp. of So. CA: Pres. (1961–62). Osteopathic Libs. Assn.: Pres. (1961), VP (1956), Secy.-Treas. (1955). SLA: So. CA. Chap., Pres. (1955–56). Friends of CalTech Libs.: Secy. (1979–80). **Pubns.:** "The Librarian Looks at the Inter-American Program," *Spec. Libs.* (D. 1941); "Integration of Chinese Publications," *Coll. & Resrch. Libs.* (Ja. 1952); various other articles. **Activities:** 1; 17, 39; 54, 58, 80 **Addr.:** 1401 North Holliston Ave., Pasadena, CA 91104.

Cresswell, Donald H. (My. 20, 1941, Washington, DC) Ed., W. Graham Arader III, Rare Maps, Books, and Prints, 1977–; Rare Book Libn., Univ. of NC at Charlotte, 1976–77; Dir. of Lib., Belmont Abbey Coll., 1973–76; Biblgphr., Lib. of Congs., 1973–74. **Educ.:** Belmont Abbey Coll., 1961–69, BA (Eng.); Univ. of Cincinnati, 1969–71, MA (Eng.); George Washington Univ., 1971–77, PhD (Amer. Std.). **Orgs.:** ALA: ACRL. SLA. Philobiblon Club. Socty. for the Hist. of Discoveries. Amer. Std. Assn. **Pubns.:** *The American Revolution in Drawings and Prints, 1765–1790 A Checklist of Graphics in the Library of Congress* (1975). **Activities:** 1; 18, 23, 37; 55, 70 **Addr.:** 605 Ardmore Ave., Ardmore, PA 19003.

Creth, Sheila Donovan (O. 30, 1939, Shreveport, LA) Asst. Dir., Univ. of CT Lib., 1975–; Staff Dev. Coord., Columbia Univ. Libs., 1973–75; Asst. to Dir., Columbia Univ. Comp. Ctr., 1967–73; Admin. Asst., Columbia Univ. Career Plng. and Place. Ofc., 1965–67. **Educ.:** Columbia Univ., 1973, BA (Anthro.); Univ. of CT, 1980, MA (Comms.). **Orgs.:** ALA: ACRL, Discuss. Grp. of Persnl. Admin. in Acad. Resrch. Libs. (1974–); Staff Dev. Discuss. Grp. (Ch., 1975–78); LAMA/Persnl. Admin. Sect., Staff Dev. Com. (1975–78). **Honors:** Cncl. on Lib. Resrcs., Flwshp., 1979–80. **Pubns.:** Jt. ed., *Personnel Administration in Libraries* (1981); "Cost Considerations in Personnel Management," *Strategies for Survival: Library Financial Management Today* (1979); jt. auth., "Requirements for the Entry Level Librarian in Selected Academic Research Libraries," *Lib. Jnl.* (1980); "The Impact of Changing Lifestyles on Library Administration," *Southeast. Libn.* (1980); "Conducting An Effective Employment Interview," *Jnl. of Acad. Libnshp.* (1978). **Activities:** 1; 17, 24, 35; 93 **Addr.:** University of Connecticut Library, Box 5A, Storrs, CT 06268.

Cretsos, James M. (O. 23, 1929, Athens, Greece) Dept. Head, Sci. Info. Syst., Merrell-Natl. Labs., 1969–; Dir., Info. Syst. Lab., Litton Indus., 1967–69; Mgr., Info. Srvs. Lab., Melpar, Inc., 1965–67, Head, Tech. Info. Ctr., 1964–65, Info. Sci., 1963–64, Resrch. Chem., 1961–63. **Educ.:** American Univ., 1960, BS (Chem.), 1960–62, (Chem.). **Orgs.:** ASIS: Pres. (1978–79); Nom. Com. (1980); Exec. Com. (1979); Ch., Mid-Yr. Mtg. (1976); South. OH Chap. (Ch., 1973–74). SLA: Cincinnati Chap. (Pres., 1974–75). Med. LA. Drug Info. Assn. Other orgs. Amer. Chem. Socty. AAAS. Amer. Mgt. Assn. Assn. Comp. Mach. Other orgs. **Honors:** ASIS, Watson Davis Awd., 1976. **Pubns.:** Ed., *Hlth. Aspects of Pesticides Bltn.* (1967–69). **Activities:** 12; 24; 60 **Addr.:** Merrell-National Laboratories, 110 E. Amity Rd., Cincinnati, OH 45215.*

Cribben, Sr. Mary Margaret RSM. (Ambler, PA) Assoc. Prof., Dept. of LS, Villanova Univ., 1956–, Lect., 1956–69; Adj. Prof., Drexel Univ., 1967; Visit. Lect., Gwynedd Mercy Coll., 1958–63; Libn., Merion Mercy Acad., 1952–69; Tchr./Libn., Phila. Parochial Schs., 1938–52. **Educ.:** Villanova Univ., 1935–40, BS (Educ.); Drexel Univ., 1946–50, MSLS; Case Western Reserve, 1966; Villanova Univ., 1969–72, MA (Admin.), 1973–76, MA (Rel Studies). **Orgs.:** Cath. LA: Natl. PR (Ch., 1979–83); Adv. Cncl. (1959–62, 1979–83); various orgs. Philadelphia Booksellers Assn.: Pres., (1976–77). other orgs. ALA: YASD; AASL; RASD; other orgs. PA LA. Middle States Com. on Educ.: Evaluation Com. **Honors:** Chapel of the Four Chaplains, Temple Univ., Legion of Honor Awd., 1979. **Pubns.:** *Progress Report for Program for School Librarianship* (1971); *Program for Professional Education of Librarians* (1970); *Standard Catalog for High School Libraries, Catholic Supplement,* (1961–66); Ed. "Resources Column," *Catholic Library World* (1975); Various articles and reviews. **Activities:** 10, 11; 17, 26, 31; 50, 63, 74 **Addr.:** Dept. of Library Science, Villanova University, Villanova, PA 19085.

Crickman, Robin Dee (My. 23, 1947, Mineola, NY) Asst. Prof., Univ. of MN, 1979–; Asst. Prof., Univ. of OK, 1977–79; Visiting Asst. Prof., Drexel Univ., 1976–77; Resrch. Assoc., Mental Hlth. Resrch. Inst., Univ. of MI, 1975–76. **Educ.:** SUNY, Binghamton, 1965–68, BA (Ling.); Univ. of MI, 1970–76, PhD (Plng.); Univ. of IL, 1969, MSLS. **Orgs.:** ASIS: Placement Officer (1977–). AAAS. **Pubns.:** "Community Communications Patterns," *Info. for the Community* (1976); "The Value of Computer Conferencing in Values Discussions Held Among Citizens," *Proceedings* of the Socty. for Genl. Syst. Resrch. (1977); "The Form and Implications of Bibliographic Citations to Computer Conference Comments," ASIS *Proceedings* (1978); "Citizen Participation Through Computer Conferencing," *Tech. Forecasting and Soc. Change* (1979); "The Emerging Information Professional," *Lib. Trends* (1979). **Activities:** 11; 24, 26, 41; 56, 75 **Addr.:** University of Minnesota, Library School/433 Walter Library, 117 Pleasant St. S.E., Minneapolis, MN 55455.

Crimmins, Mary E. (S. 16, 1938, Worcester, MA) Coord., Sch. Curric. and Textbook Ctr. Lib., CA State Univ., Fullerton, 1981–; Ref. Libn., Educ. Lib., WA State Univ., 1979–81; Refer. Libn., North. IL Univ., 1974–79; Libn., Laconia Jr. HS, 1974; Pub. Srvs., Educ. Libn., Plymouth State Coll., 1971–73; Chld. Libn., Roslindale Branch, Boston Pub. Lib., 1970–71; Media Spec., Quonset Elem. Sch., 1968–70; French Spec., N. Kingstown Sch. Dept., 1962–68. **Educ.:** Pembroke Coll., Brown Univ., 1956–57, (Art); RI Coll., 1959–62, EdB (Elem. Ed.); Univ. of RI, 1967–70, MLS; North. IL Univ., 1975–78, MS, (Educ. Instr. Tech.); Other insts. **Orgs.:** WA LA. ALA. IL LA: IACRL Spring Conf. Com. (1978). AECT: IL Spring Conf. Com. (1979). Other orgs. Assn. for Acad. Women, WA State Univ. Assn. for Acad. Women's Equality, Northern IL Univ.: Corres. Secy. (1978–79). Lib. Cncl., North. IL Univ. Kappa Delta Pi. **Pubns.:** "Crisis: The school Library Media Program," *Northern Illinois Media Association Newsletter* (Mr. 1976); Reviews, Videotapes and slide tapes. **Activities:** 1, 9, 10; 21, 31, 32, 39; 63, 95-Children's Literature. **Addr.:** 5700 Carbon Canyon Rd., #132, Brea, CA 92621.

Crismond, Linda F. (Mr. 1, 1943, Burbank, CA) Asst. Univ. Libn., Univ. of South. CA, 1974–; Head of Acq., San Francisco Pub. Lib., 1972–74, Head of Per., 1971–72, EDP Coord., 1968–71. **Educ.:** Univ. of CA, Santa Barbara, 1960–64, BA (Hist.); Univ. of CA, Berkeley, 1964–65, MLS. **Orgs.:** ALA: Esther Piercy Jury (Ch., 1976–78); ISAD/Prog. Plng. Com. (1975–77); RTSD/Resources Sect., Exec. Bd. (1980–82). ASIS. CA LA: Com. on Libns. and Publishers (1976–79); Cncl. (1980–82). Amer. Natl. Standards Inst.: Com. Z39, Subcom. 36 (1978–80). **Honors:** San Francisco Pub. Lib., Outstan. Staff Member of the Year, 1968. **Pubns.:** *Directory of San Francisco Bay Area Publishers* (1968); "IROS at the University of Southern California", *Jnl. of Acad. Libnshp.* (S. 1977); "Planning Strategies for Austere Times," *Proc., Conf. on Managing Under Austerity* (Je. 1976); "A Computer System for Periodicals", *Lib. Jnl.* (O. 1969); "Automated Serials Check-in and Binding Procedures at the San Francisco Public Library", *ASIS Proc.* (1969). **Activities:** 1; 17, 46; 56 **Addr.:** University of Southern California, Doheny Library, University Park, Los Angeles, CA 90007.

Crissinger, John D. (Jl. 13, 1948, Galion, OH) Geol. Libn., VA Polytech. Inst. and State Univ., 1977–. **Educ.:** OH Univ., 1966–69 (Geo.); East. IL Univ., 1969–70, BS (Geo.); Univ. of IL, 1976–77, MS (LS). **Orgs.:** SLA: Geo. and Map Div. (1976–). Geosci. Info. Socty.: Mem. Com. (1980); Ad Hoc Com. on Alternative Pubns. (Ch., 1981). Map OLUG. Roanoke Sp. Club. Assn. Amer. Geos. **Pubns.:** Jt. auth., *Environmental Implications of Karst and other Geomorphic Features of the New River Valley* (1980); "The Use of Journal Citations in Theses as a Collection Development Methodology," *Geosci. Info. Socty. Procs.* (forthcoming). **Activities:** 1; 15, 39; 91 **Addr.:** Geology Library, 3040 Derring Hall, Virginia Polytechnic and State University, Blacksburg, VA 24061.

Crist, Dorothy J. (Ja. 3, 1918, Ft. Wayne, IN) Med. Libn., Muskegon Gen. Hosp., 1969–; Med. Libn., Hackley Hosp., 1956–61. **Orgs.:** MI Hlth. Sci. LA: Exec. Com. (1978–80); Educ. Com. (1981). W. MI Hlth. Sci. LA: Pres. (1971–73, 1978–80). Med. LA. Midwest LA: KY-OH-MI Exec. Com. (1971–73). Various other orgs. Jr. Woman's Club. Ctrl. Un. Meth. Church Admin. Bd. Amer. Bus. and Prof. Women's Assn. **Pubns.:** "Doctors! Have You an Expressway to References?" *MI Osteopathic Jnl.* (Mr. 1974). **Addr.:** Muskegon General Hospital Medical Library, 1700 Oak Ave., Muskegon, MI 49442.

Special Subjects/Services: 50. Adult educ.; 51. Advert./Mktg.; 52. Aerosp.; 53. Agric.; 54. Area std.; 55. Arts/Hum.; 56. Autom.; 57. Bibl./Prtg.; 58. Bio. sci.; 59. Bus./Fin.; 60. Chem.; 61. Copyrt.; 62. Documtn.; 63. Educ.; 64. Engin.; 65. Env.; 66. Eth. grps.; 67. Film; 68. Food/Nutr.; 69. Geneal.; 70. Geo.; 71. Geol.; 72. Handcpd.; 73. Hist.; 74. Int. frdm.; 75. Info. sci.; 76. Insr.; 77. Law; 78. Legis.; 79. Math./Comp. sci.; 80. Med.; 81. Metals; 82. Nat. resrcs.; 83. Newsp.; 84. Nuc. sci.; 85. Oral hist.; 86. Petr./Energy; 87. Pharm.; 88. Phys./Astr./Math.; 89. Readg.; 90. Relig.; 91. Sci./Tech.; 92. Soc. sci.; 93. Telecom.; 94. Transp.; 95. (other).

Critchlow, Therese E. (Mr. 29, 1921, Princeton, NJ) Head, AV Srvs., Princeton Pub. Lib., 1964–. **Educ.:** Trinity Coll., 1939–43, BA (Fr.), Columbia Univ., 1955, MA (Fr.); Rutgers Univ., 1963, MLS. **Orgs.:** ALA. NJ LA: AV Sect. (Pres., 1972); various other coms. NJ Vid. Circuit. NJ Lib. Film Circuit. Princeton Med Ctr. Auxiliary. Princeton Area Cncl. of Cmnty. Srvs. Com. on Aging. St. Paul's Cath. Church Par. Cncl. (1974). Princeton Boro./Twp. Jt. Cable TV Adv. Com. (1973). **Activities:** 9; 16, 39; 67, 86 **Addr.:** 11 Westcott Rd., Princeton, NJ 08540.

Crittenden, Sara N. (O. 3, 1917, Nova, OH) Dir., Lrng. Resrcs., St. Petersburg Jr. Coll., 1955–80, Retired; Acq. Libn., FL State Univ., 1951–55; Asst. and Head Libn., Willard (OH) Mem. Lib., 1937–49. **Educ.:** Blackburn Coll., 1935–37, AAB (Educ.); FL State Univ., 1948–50, BA (LS), 1950–51, MA. Delta Kappa Gamma. **Honors:** Beta Phi Mu. **Pubns.:** "Essay and General Literature Index, an Evaluation, with Analysis of the Books for 1936 Indexed Therein," (ACRL Microcard Series, No. 24) (1954). **Activities:** 1; 17 **Addr.:** 4542 Fourth Ave. North, St. Petersburg, FL 33713.

Crocker, C. Anne (My. 27, 1944, Montreal, PQ) Law Libn., Univ. of NB, 1976–; Ext. Libn., York Reg. Lib., 1970–76. **Educ.:** Univ. of NB, 1962–66, BA (Eng., Hon.); Univ. of Toronto, 1969–70, BLS. **Orgs.:** Can. Assn. of Law Libs.: Subcom. on Micropubshg. (1979–80). Can. LA: Cnclr. (1976–79). Atl. Prov. LA: Secy. (1974–75); Ad Hoc Com. on the Status of Women (Ch., 1973–74). Women in Transition: Pres. (1977–80). NB Adv. Cncl. on the Status of Women: Vice-Ch. (1977–80). **Activities:** 1, 12; 15, 17, 39; 77, 78 **Addr.:** Faculty of Law Library, University of New Brunswick, Bay Service #44999, Fredericton, NB 6C9 Canada.

Crocker, Jane Lopes (S. 19, 1946, Wareham, MA) Dir., Lib. Media Ctr., Gloucester Cnty. Coll., 1976–; Head Libn., Sch. of Nursing, Boston City Hosp., 1973–76; Pub. Srvs. Libn., Simmons Coll., 1971–73; Pub. Rel. Libn., New Bedford (MA), Pub. Lib., 1968–71. **Educ.:** Bridgewater State Coll., 1964–68, BA (Eng.); Simmons Coll., 1969–71, MSLS; Cert., MA Bd. of Lib. Comsns., 1973. **Orgs.:** S. Jersey Coll. Lib. Coop.: Pres. (1979–). NJ LA: Pub. Rel. Com. (1976–78). Gloucester Lib. Org.: Ch., PR Com. Camden/Gloucester Area Strg. Com.: Mem.-at-large (1977). Other orgs. **Pubns.:** Contrib., *Ref. & Info. Srvs.: A Reader* (1978); Ed., *Bay State Libn.* (1973–76). **Activities:** 1; 15, 17, 39; 50, 63 **Addr.:** Gloucester County College, Sewell P.O., NJ 08080.

Crockett, C. Merritt (Jl. 22, 1932, Summerside, PE) Univ. Libn., Univ. of PE, 1969–; Chief Libn., St. Dunstans Univ., 1968–69. **Educ.:** St. Dunstans Univ., 1965–67, BA (Hist.); Univ. of Toronto, 1967–68, BLS. **Orgs.:** Can. Assn. of Coll. and Univ. Libs.: Pres. (1977–78). Can. LA. ALA. Atl. Prov. LA. Can. Table Tennis Assn.: VP (1979–). **Activities:** 1; 15, 17, 19 **Addr.:** 104 Brighton Rd., Charlottetown, PE C1A 4P3 Canada.

Crockett, Edith S. (D. 30, 1944, New York, NY) Chief, User Comms., *BIOSIS*, 1980–; Mgr., European Opers., Mgr., N.E. (U.S.) Opers., SDC Srch. Srv., 1977–80; Geol. and Psy. Libn., Columbia Univ., 1973–76; Head Libn., Ed., Horticult. Socty. of NY, 1966–72. **Educ.:** City Coll. of NY, 1961–66, BA (Bio.); Columbia Univ., 1968–72, MSLS. **Orgs.:** SLA. Cncl. on Bot. Horticult. Libs.: Bd. Pres. (1970). **Pubns.:** Jt. auth., "Sci/Tech Books: 700 Outstanding Titles," *Lib. Jnl.* (Mr. 1, 1973–81). **Activities:** 6; 26, 36; 51, 58 **Addr.:** User Communications, BIOSIS, 2100 Arch St., Philadelphia, PA 19119.

Crockett, Ethel S. (Ja. 19, 1915, Mt. Vernon, NY) Retired, 19–; CA State Libn., 1972–80; Dir., Lib. Srvs., City Coll. of San Francisco, 1968–72; Libn., San Jose City Coll., 1962–68. **Educ.:** Vassar Coll., 1932–36, BA (Eng., Econ.); San Jose State Univ., 1961–62, MA (LS). **Orgs.:** ALA. COSLA: Ch. (1974–76), Bd. of Dirs. (1974–78). SLA: Bay Area Chap. (Dir., 1970–72). CA LA: CA Inst. of Libs. (Pres., 1973–74). Various other orgs., ofcs. Bk. Club of CA. CA Sir Francis Drake Comsn.: VP (1973–80). Pvt. Press Assn. Various other orgs. **Honors:** CA State Sen., Asm., Secy. of State, Resols. of Cmdn., 1980. **Pubns.:** Preface, *Who's Who in California* 12th ed. (1979); "New Directions," *News Notes of CA Libs.* (Sum. 1975); *From the State Librarian's Desk Nsltr.* (1973–80); Ed., *Intercom, The Cmnty. Coll. Lib. Nsltr.* (1967–68). **Activities:** 1, 13; 17, 23, 34; 56, 78 **Addr.:** P.O. Box 457, Stinson Beach, CA 94970.

Croft, Vicki F. (Ja. 13, 1948, St. Louis, MO) Head, Vetny. Med. Lib., WA State Univ., 1976–; Asst. Sci. Libn., Univ. of NB, 1971–76. **Educ.:** Dana Coll., 1966–70, BS (Bio.); Univ. of IL, 1970–71, MSLS; Med. LA, 1971, Cert. **Orgs.:** Med. LA: Pac. Northwest Reg. Chapter; Vetny. Med. Libs. Section. **Honors:** Beta Phi Mu. **Activities:** 1; 15, 17, 39; 80, 95-Vetny. Med. **Addr.:** Veterinary Medical Library, 170 Wegner Hall, Washington State University, Pullman, WA 99164.

Cronshaw, Patricia (Grassington, Yorkshire, Eng) Head, Serials Dept., Univ. of CA, Santa Barbara, 1976–, Asst. Dept. Head, Serials, Gvt. Pubs/Serial Dept., 1974–76, Ref. Libn., 1971–74, Serials Catlgr., 1968–71. **Educ.:** Leeds Sch. of Libnshp., 1952–56; ALA, 1955; FLA, 1960. **Orgs.:** Library Assn. (London); ALA: RTSD; ACRL; South. CA Tech. Prcs. Grp.; Coll. and Resrch. Libs., South. CA. **Honors:** Leeds Sch. of Libnshp., Annual prize for best student, 1956; Jens and Amy Nyholm Awd., 1980. **Addr.:** Serials Department, Library, University of California, Santa Barbara, Santa Barbara, CA 93106.

Crooks, James Edward (Mr. 16, 1946, Brookville, PA) Head, Ref. and Info. Srvs., Taubman Med. Lib., Univ. of MI, 1979–; Extramural Coord., KY-OH-MI Reg. Med. Lib. Network, 1975–79; Ref. Libn., Med. Ctr. Lib., Univ. of MI, 1972–79; Libn., Baltimore Cnty. Pub. Sch., 1969–71. **Educ.:** Clarion State Coll., 1964–68, BA (Hist.); The Univ. of MI, 1968–72, AMLS; Med. LA Cert., 1972; Johns Hopkins Univ., 1970, (Hist.). **Orgs.:** Med. LA: Midwest Reg. Grp. ALA. MI Hlth. Sci. Libs. Assn.: Org. Com. (1976–77). S. Ctrl. MI Hlth. Sci. LA. Beta Phi Mu: Dir. (1973–76). Phi Gamma Mu. Alpha Mu Gamma. Kappa Delta Pi. **Activities:** 1, 10; 24, 39, 48; 58, 80 **Addr.:** Taubman Medical Library, The University of Michigan, Ann Arbor, MI 48109.

Crooks, Susan Harrah (Jl. 1, 1945, Ajrib, OH) Sr. Consult., Info. Systs., Arthur D. Little, Inc., 1976–; Inst. Libn., Ranier State Sch. for Mentally Retarded, 1971–74; Ref. Libn., Seattle Pub. Lib., 1969–71. **Educ.:** Bryn Mawr Coll., 1963–67, AB (Eng.); Univ. of Chicago, 1966–68, MA (LS); Univ. of PA, 1974–76, MBA. **Orgs.:** ASIS: New Eng. Chap. (Ch., 1980), Com. on Intl. Rel. (1980). **Honors:** Univ. of PA, Wharton Pub. Policy Fellow, 1975. **Pubns.:** *Strengthening The Law Library Of Congress* (1980); jt. auth., *Comparative Evaluation of Alternative Systems for Provision of Effectiveness Access to Periodical Literature* (1979); jt. auth., *Into the Information Age* (1978); jt. auth., *A New Governance Structure for OCLC* (1977). **Activities:** 4, 12; 17, 24, 34; 56, 93, 95-Info. policy. **Addr.:** Arthur D. Little, Inc., Acorn Park, Cambridge, MA 02140.

Crosby, Ramona C. T. (My. 18, 19–, Brooklyn, NY) Supvsr., Info. Srvs. Stauffer Chem. Co., 1973–; Sr. Lit. Chem., Warner Lambert Resrch. Inst., 1969–73; Instr., CUNY, Cmnty. Coll., 1969. **Educ.:** Brooklyn Coll., 1951–55, BS (Chem.); Howard Univ., 1955–57, MS (Chem.). **Orgs.:** ASIS. Amer. Chem. Socty.: Chem. Lit. Div. Assoc. Info. Mgrs. Amer. Mgt. Assn. Intl. Platform Assn. **Activities:** 12; 17, 38, 40; 56, 60, 75 **Addr.:** Stauffer Chemical Co., Information Service, Livingston Ave., Dobbs Ferry, NY 10522.

Crosman, Alexander C., Jr. (Mr. 9, 1940, Philadelphia, PA) Dir., Peoria Pub. Lib., 1975, Asst. Dir., 1972–75; Circ. Libn., Univ. of VA, 1967–72. **Educ.:** Univ. of VA, 1958–62, (Hist.); Univ. of KY, 1966–67 (LS); WV Univ., 1966 (Educ.). **Orgs.:** ALA: PLA, Org. Com. (1979–). Intl. Assn. of Bus. Comm. Rotary. Peoria Advert. and Selling Club. **Honors:** Beta Phi Mu. **Activities:** 9; 17, 35, 36 **Addr.:** Peoria Public Library, 107 N.E. Monroe, Peoria, IL 61602.

Cross, Geraldine P. (S. 29, 1944, Atlanta, GA) Head Libn., Mercer Univ. (Atlanta), 1976–, Head, Ref. and Reader Srvs., 1973–76, Head, Tech. Srvs., 1972–73. **Educ.:** Univ. of GA, 1962–66, BA (Psy.); Emory Univ., 1971–72, MLn; GA State Univ., 1974–78 (Educ. Admin.). **Orgs.:** ALA: ACRL. SELA. GA LA: Asst. to Exec. Secy. (1976–79); Coll. and Univ. Div., Vice Ch./Ch. Elect (1979–81), Ch. (1981–83); ACRL Sect. **Honors:** Beta Phi Mu. **Activities:** 1; 17, 19, 39; 50, 63, 92 **Addr.:** Mercer University in Atlanta Library, 3000 Flowers Rd. S., Atlanta, GA 30341.

Cross, Jennie B. (Ja. 12, 1935, Wichita Falls, TX) Dir. of Lib. Srvs., Oakland Schs., Pontiac, MI, 1980–; Lib. Consult., 1979; Docum. Libn./Asst. Prof., Oakland Univ., 1967–79; Asst. Libn., Michigan Christ. Coll., 1962–67. **Educ.:** Harding Coll., 1952–55, BA (Jnlsm.); Univ. of MI, 1966–68, AMLS, **Orgs.:** ALA: Gvt. Docum. RT, Treas. 1978–79). SLA: Gvt. Info. Srvs. Com. (1979–82). GODORT MI: Pres. (1978–79). MSU Empl. Credit Un.: Bd. of Dir. (1973–76). Hist. Socty. of MI: Trustee (1974–76). **Honors:** MSU Empl. Credit Un., Mem. of the Year, 1975. **Pubns.:** "State Documents to the People," *MI in Books* (Win. 1975). **Activities:** 12; 17, 29; 63, 95-Gov. Documents. **Addr.:** 3942 Embarcadero, Drayton Plains, MI 48020.

Cross, Joseph Russell Jr. (Jl. 29, 1945, Bennettsville, SC) Head, Reader Srvs., Law Lib., Univ. of SC, 1978–; Adj. Instr., Furman Univ., 1975–; Asst. Ref. Libn., Univ. of SC, 1972–75. **Educ.:** Wofford Coll., 1963–67, BA (Eng.); Emory Univ., 1971–72, MLn; Univ. of SC, 1975–78, JD. **Orgs.:** SC LA. ALA: AASL. Southeast. Assn. of Law Libs. SC Bar Assn. Amer. Bar Assn. **Honors:** Beta Phi Mu. **Addr.:** Law Library, University of South Carolina, Columbia, SC 29205.

Crotts, Joe L. (N. 26, 1947, Winston-Salem, NC) Map & Geography Libn., CA State Univ., Chico, 1974–; Libn., LA State Penitentiary, 1974. **Educ.:** Vanderbilt Univ., 1968–70, BS (Geography); LA State Univ., 1970–72, MA (Geography), 1973, MLS. **Orgs.:** West. Assn. of Map Libs. **Pubns.:** Ed., Geologic Index; "Index to the Defense Mapping Agency–Army Map Service Depository Cat.," Info. Bltn., Western Assn. of Map Libs. (Mr. 1977). "Geologic Index to the 7.5' and 15' Quadrangles of California," Info. Bltn., Western Assn. of Map Libs. (Je., N. 1981; Mr. 1982). **Activities:** 1; 20, 29, 30; 65, 70, 82 **Addr.:** Library–Maps, California State University, Chico, Chico, CA 95929.

Crouch, Judith Ann (F. 27, 1945, Frederick, OK) Asst. Prof., of Lib. Sci. and Cat. Libn., Northwest. OK State Univ., Alva, 1975–; Inst. of Lib. Sci., Cat. Libn., Southeast. OK State Univ., Durant, 1973–75; Lib. Dir., Derby Sr. HS, KS, 1969–72; K-12 Libn., Sch. Dist. #360 Caldwell, KS, 1967–69. **Educ.:** OK State Univ., Stillwater, 1963–67, BS (Lib. Sci. and Elem. Ed.); Univ. of OK, Norman, 1972–73, MLS. **Orgs.:** ALA. Higher Educ. Alum. Cncl. of OK. Nat. Educ. Assn. OK Educ. Assn. AAUP: Alva Br., Pres. (1978–80); Second VP, Mem., 1976–78); Nom. Com., Ch. (1977); Plng. Com. Ch. (1979). Delta Kappa Gamma Socty. Intl.: Chi Chap., Prof. Affairs Com., (1978–80); Ch. Personal Growth and Srvcs. Com. (1976–78). OK State Univ. Alum. Assn. **Honors:** Beta Phi Mu, 1974. Delta Kappa Gamma, 1976. Kappa Delta Pi, 1965. **Pubns.:** "Promoting the Sequoyah Award," *OK Libn.* (O. 1977); "Banks at Work in the Community," *OK Banker* (Ag. 1962); Slide Pres., Sequoyah Chld. Book Awd. Com. (1978). **Activities:** 1, 10; 20, 26, 46; 63, 75, 89 **Addr.:** 636 Linden, Apt. 16, Alva, OK 73717.

Crouch, Lora E. (Ja. 18, 1907, Dallas Cnty., IA) Volun., UT State Hist. Lib., 1973–; Head, Acq., Salt Lake Cnty. Lib. Syst., 1963–72; Head, Adult Srvs., Rochester Pub. Lib., 1963; Head Libn., Sioux Falls Pub. Lib., 1944–60; Libn., Forest Lib., Lake Placid Club, 1960–63. **Educ.:** Dakota Wesleyan Univ., 1929–33, BA (Eng.); Univ. of IL, 1934–39, BS (LS); Univ. of UT, 1964–70 (Hist.). **Orgs.:** ALA: Cncl. (1938–41), Cont. Mem. (1977–). Mt. Plains LA: VP, Pres. (1956–58). UT LA. UT Hist. Socty. Salt Lake Valley Hist. Socty. Natl. Fed. of Bus. and Prof. Women's Clubs. **Honors:** UT Hist. Socty., Srv. Awd., 1973, 1977; Mt. Plains LA, Cert. of Recog., 1958; UT Fed. of Bus. and Prof. Womens Clubs, Woman of the Yr., 1972. **Pubns.:** Cmplr., *Index to Utah Historical Quarterly* (1979); cmplr., "Name Index," *Tales of a Triumphant People* (1977); *Hamlin Garland, Dakota Homesteader* (1961); pres. messages, *Mt. Plains Lib. Qtly.* (1957–58). **Activities:** 9, 13; 30, 39, 41 **Addr.:** 1320 E., 5th S., Apt. 1016, Salt Lake City, UT 84102.

Crouch, Milton H. (O. 25, 1934, Martinsville, VA) Asst. Dir., Reader Srvs., Univ. of VT, 1973–, Pub. Srvs. Libn., 1969–73, Undergrad. Libn., PA State Univ., 1963–69; Asst. Soc. Scis. Libn., Univ. of FL, 1961–63. **Educ.:** Birmingham-South. Coll., 1956–60, BA (Hist., Zlgy.); LA State Univ., 1960–61; PA State Univ., 1965–68, MA (Hist.). **Orgs.:** ALA: Cncl. (1981–84); RASD, Exec. Com. (1974–79). VT LA: Various coms. **Pubns.:** *Directory of State and Local History Periodicals* (1977); "Dormitory Libraries," *Encyc. of Lib. and Info. Sci.* (1972); "Book Review Sources for Canadian and United States History," *Serials Review* (1978). **Addr.:** Bailey/Howe Library, University of Vermont, Burlington, VT 05405.

Crow, Rebecca N. (O. 5, 1949, St. Louis, MO) Div. Head of Current Col., Ctrl. Lib., Dallas Pub. Lib.; Branch Mgr., Dallas Pub. Lib., 1976–80; Head Libn., Wheeler AFB, HI, 1973–75; Media Dir., Libn., Mills Elem. Sch., 1972–73; Tchr., Holmes Jr. HS, 1971–72. **Educ.:** Univ. of TX, 1969–71, BA w/Honors (Eng./Hist.); N. TX State Univ., 1972–73, MLS; All-Level Sch. Libn., Cert., 1972–73; Sec. Tchg. Cert., 1969–71. **Orgs.:** ALA. TX LA: Conf. Local Arrange. (Pubcty. Ch.). Dallas Cnty. LA. Chi Omega Fraternity. **Honors:** ALA, John Cotton Dana Pub. Rel. Awd., 1975. **Activities:** 9, 10; 16, 17, 21; 50, 74 **Addr.:** 4309 Grassmere Ln., Dallas, TX 75205.

Crow, Richard V. (Je. 17, 1924, Threesands, OK) Acq. and Ref. Libn., Stroman HS, 1968–; Libn., Hopkins Elem. School, 1957–68; Libn., Patti Welder HS, 1956–57; Libn., Patti Welder Jr. HS, 1954–56; Asst. Ref. Libn., Texas A.&M. Lib., 1952–53. **Educ.:** OK A.&M., 1947–49; TX Christ. Univ., 1949–51, BA (Eng. & Educ.); N. TX State Univ., 1952–54, MLS. **Orgs.:** ALA: AASL. TX LA. TX Assn. of Sch. Libns.: Teenage Lib. Assn., State Com. Ch. (1975–76). Other orgs. Exec. Dinner Club. Natl. Assn. for the Deaf. First Christian Church: Church Libn. Natl. Educ. Assn. **Pubns.:** "Libraries Suffer Growing Pains," *Texas Outlook* (D. 1955). **Activities:** 10, 11; 31, 39, 48; 63, 89, 92 **Addr.:** 2001 East Power St., Victoria, TX 77901.

Crow, Rochelle (Ap. 22, 1936, Johnson City, TN) Head of Acq. and Cat., Univ. of AL in Birmingham, 1978–; Cat. Libn., 1968–78; Cat. Libn., Birmingham-Southern Coll., 1964–68; Ref. and Docum. Libn., 1962–64. **Educ.:** Birmingham-Southern Coll., 1955–59, BA (Fr.); Univ. of Denver, 1959–62, MALS. **Orgs.:** AL LA: Tech. Srvs. RT (1980); Stans. and Cert. Com. (1981). SELA. ALA. Univ. Senate: 2nd VP (1976); 1st VP (1977); Fac. Senate: Sec. (1980). **Pubns.:** "Where will your Catalog be in 1980", *Al Libn.* (Oct 1977). **Activities:** 1; 15, 20, 45 **Addr.:** Sterne Library, University of Alabama in Birmingham, University Station, Birmingham, AL 35294.

Crowe, Edith L. (N. 12, 1947, Buffalo, NY) Assoc. Libn., San José State Univ. Lib., 1980–, Sr. Asst. Libn., 1977–80; Asst. Libn., CA State Univ., Hayward, 1976–77; San José State Univ., 1971–75. **Educ.:** SUNY, Buffalo, 1968–70, BA (Art Hist.); SUNY, Geneseo, 1970–71, MLS; CA State Univ., Dominguez Hills, 1977–80, MA (Human.). **Orgs.:** Art Libs. Socty./N. Amer.: Secy./Treas. North. CA Chap. (Secy./Treas., 1979–81; Vice-Ch./Ch.-Elec., 1980–82). CA LA. CA Clearinghouse on Lib. Inst.: North. CA Steer. Com. (1977–). Mythopoeic Socty.: Bay Area Br. (Mod., 1976–77; Secy., 1978–79. **Honors:** Phi Beta

PROFESSIONAL ACTIVITIES: Institutions: 1. Acad. lib.; 2. Arch.; 3. Assn.; 4. Fed./Gvt. lib.; 5. Inst. lib.; 6. Mfr./Suppl.; 7. Milit. lib.; 8. Musm.; 9. Pub. lib.; 10. Sch. lib.; 11. Sch. of lib. sci.; 12. Spec. lib.; 13. State lib.; 14. (other). **Functions/Activities:** 15. Acq./Col. dev.; 16. Adult srvs.; 17. Admin.; 18. Apprais.; 19. Archit./Bldgs.; 20. Cat./Class.; 21. Chld. srvs.; 22. Circ.; 23. Cons./Pres.; 24. Consult.; 25. Cont. ed.; 26. Educ. lib. sci.; 27. Ext. srvs.; 28. Fund/Grants; 29. Gvt. pubs.; 30. Indx./Abs.; 31. Instr. lib. use; 32. Media srvs.; 33. Micro.; 34. Netwks./Coop.; 35. Persnl.; 36. PR; 37. Publshg.; 38. Recs. mgt.; 39. Ref. srvs.; 40. Repro.; 41. Resrch.; 42. Review.; 43. Secur.; 44. Serials; 45. Spec. col.; 46. Tech. srvs.; 47. Trustees/Bds.; 48. YA srvs.; 49. (other).

Kappa, 1969. **Pubns.:** *Fine Arts Reference Sources.* Hayward, (1978); "The Federal Government As Art Publisher", *RQ* (1978). **Activities:** 1; 15, 31, 39; 55 **Addr.:** San José State University Library, 250 South Fourth Street, San José, CA 95192.

Crowe, Linda D. (S. 1, 1937, Cleveland, OH) Syst. Dev. Ofcr., N. Suburban Lib. Syst., 1976–; Asst. Prof., Rosary College Grad. Sch. Lib Sci., 1971–76; Inst., Univ. of IL, 1969–71; Chld. Consult., Lincoln Trail Lib. Syst., 1968–70; Sch. Libn., S. Euclid Bd. of Educ., OH, 1966–68. **Educ.:** Western Reserve Univ., 1956–59, BS (Phys. Educ./Eng.), MLS; Univ. of IL, 1968–70, CAS (LS). **Orgs.:** CLENE: Adv. Com. IL LA: Ch., Contin. Educ. Com.; Ch., Int. Frdm. Com. (1974–75). ALA: Ch., YASD, Int. Frdm. Com. (1979); ALA Cncl. (1978–); Ch., ALSC, Melcher Com. (1978–1979); Mem., Standing Com. on Lib. Educ. (1979–), other coms. and ofcs. **Honors:** Beta Phi Mu, 1970. **Pubns.:** Regular reviewer of books for *Sch. Lib. Jnl.* since January 1968; Jt. auth, "Sexism in Picture Books," *IL Libs.* (O. 1971); Jt. auth., "Staffing Neighborhood Information Centers," *Ref. Qtly.* (Jl. 1973); Jt. auth., "On Beyond Children - A Look at Adult Involvement in Children's Services," *IL Libs.* (D. 1976); Jt. auth., "Examining the "IN" Groups: Intellectual Freedom and Information," *Cath. Lib. World* (Ap. 1978); Jt. Auth., "Libraries Resources are more than Materials," *Col. Bldg.* (1979); other books and articles; Jt. Auth., *Libraries and Neighborhood Information Centers.* (1972); Ed., *ALA Centennial Calendar* (1976). **Activities:** 4; 24, 25, 34; 50, 74 **Addr.:** 1356 Scott Ave., Winnetka, IL 60093.

Crowe, Susan Brennan (Jl. 30, 1934, Kansas City, MO) Supvsr., Tech. Srvs., Aerospace Corp., 1969–; Lect., Univ. of CA, Los Angeles, Grad Sch. of Lib. & Info. Sci., 1976–77; Supvsr., Acq., 1967–69; Libn., Northrop Corp. Space Labs., 1963–67; Catlgr., Hughes Aircraft Co., 1961–63. **Educ.:** Mt. St. Mary's Coll., 1953–57, BA (Eng.); Univ. of So. CA, Los Angeles, 1957–58, MSLS. **Orgs.:** ALA. SLA: South. CA Chap., Pres. (1969–70). CA LA: Various positions. ASIS. **Pubns.:** Ed., Sci-Tech News, (1976–80). **Activities:** 12; 15, 46; 52, 91 **Addr.:** Aerospace Corporation, P.O. Box 92957, Los Angeles, CA 90009.

Crowe, Virginia M. (Mr. 8, 1933, Meadville, PA) Assoc. Prof., Div. of Educ. Srvs., VA Commonwealth Univ., 1980-81; Ch., Lib. Sci. Dept., Edinboro State Coll., 1968–; Sec. Sch. Libn., General McLane Sch. Syst., 1967–68; Elem. Sch. Libn., 1965–67; Elem. Sch. Libn., Saegertown Area Schs., 1965–65. **Educ.:** Edinboro State Coll., 1961–65, BS (Elem. Educ.); Univ. of Pittsburgh, 1965–67, MLS; 1967–73, PhD (Educ. Comm.); Advnc. Cert., 1967–70 (Lib. Sci.). **Orgs.: Orgs.:** ALA. PA LA. PA Sch. Libns. Assn.: Bd. of Dir. (1977–78); Tech. Comm. (1978–80). AECT. PA Learning/Resrcs. Assn.: Memb. Ch. (1975); Bd. Mem. (1978–80). **Honors:** Beta Phi Mu, 1967. **Activities:** 10, 11; 21, 26, 32; 63, 72, 85 **Addr.:** Library Science Dept., Edinboro State College, Edinboro, PA 16444.

Crowe, William Joseph (F. 27, 1947, Boston, MA) Asst. to Dir., OH State Univ. Libs., 1979–; Admin. Asst. to Dean, IN Univ. Libs., 1977–79; Coord., Prcs., IN Univ. Reg. Campus Libs., 1971–76; Asst. to Acq. Libn., Boston Pub. Lib., 1970–71. **Educ.:** Boston State Coll., 1964–68, BA (Hist.); Rutgers Univ., 1968–69, MLS; IN Univ., 1979– (Phil.). **Orgs.:** ALA: LAMA/Persnl. Admin. Sect., Staff Dev. Com. (1980–). OH LA. **Honors:** Cncl. on Lib. Resrcs., Acad. Lib. Mgt. Intern, 1976. **Pubns.:** "Cataloging Contributed to OCLC: A Look One Year Later," *Lib. Resrcs. & Tech. Srvs.* (Ja. 1981). **Activities:** 1; 17, 35, 46 **Addr.:** Ohio State University Libraries, 1858 Neil Ave. Mall, Columbus, OH 43210.

Crowley, Bill (Jl. 4, 1949, New York) Cont. Educ. Consult., AL Pub. Lib. Srv., 1978–; Cont. Educ. & Pub. Info. Coord., 1977–78, Pub. Info. Srvs. Coord., 1976–77; PR Asst., NY Pub. Lib., 1975–76, Libn., 1974–75, PR Rep., 1972–74. **Educ.:** Hunter Coll., 1967–70, BA (Hist.); Columbia Univ., 1971–74, MS (LS). **Orgs.:** ALA: Circ. Srvs. Sect. (Secy., 1978); AL LA: PLA (Vice-ch., Ch.-elect, 1981–82). PR Com. (1976–77); Natl. Lib. Week Com. (1977–78); Educ. Com. (1979); Ch., Nom. Com. for ALA Cncl. (1979). **Pubns.:** "Readers Response: Demand on Public Libraries," *Lifelone Learning: The Adult Years* (Je. 1979); "I Have Changed My Mind (On Systems)," *AL Libn.* (My./Je., 1979). **Activities:** 9, 13; 24, 25, 47; 50, 89 **Addr.:** Alabama Public Library Service, 6030 Monticello Dr., Montgomery, AL 36130.

Crowley, Terence (My. 29, 1935, Chicago, IL) Assoc. Prof., San Jose State Univ., 1978–; Visit. Ref. Spec., CA State Univ., Chico, 1977–78; Assoc. Prof., Univ. of Toledo, 1972–77; Asst. Prof., Univ. of IL, 1969–72. **Educ.:** Univ. of Notre Dame, 1953–57, AB (Hum.); Rutgers Univ., 1960–62, MLS, 1965–68, DLS. **Orgs.:** ALA. SLA. Alliance of Info. and Referral Srvs. OH Cncl. of Info. and Referral Providers: Treas. (1976–77). **Pubns.:** Jt. Auth., *Information Service in Public Libraries: Two Studies* (1971); Jt. Auth., *Library Response to Urban Change* (1969); "Library Services for the Urban Community," *Cath. Lib. World* (Mr. 1977); "The Statewide Plan in Ohio," *Information and Referral in Public Libraries* (Cassette) (1978). **Activities:** 11; 26, 39, 41; 57, 92, 93 **Addr.:** Division of Library Science, San José State University, San José, CA 95192.

Croxton, Fred(erick) E(mory) Jr. (O. 14, 1923, Columbus, OH) 1978–; Dir., Automated Syst. Of., Lib. of Congs., 1978–; Dir., Reader Srvs. Dept., 1976–78, Dir., Admin. Dept., 1970–76; Exec. VP, Informatics/Tisco Inc., 1968–70; Dir., Redstone Scientific Info. Ctr., U.S. Army Missile Cmd., 1962–68; Supt., Info. & Recs., Goodyear Atomic Corp., 1953–62; Chief, Cat. Br., Tch. Info. Srv., U.S. Atomic Energy Comsn., 1949–53; Tech. Eng., Union Carbide Nuclear Corp., 1946–49. **Educ.:** Oberlin Coll., 1941–44, BA (Chem.); Columbia Univ., 1950–60, MLS. **Orgs.:** SLA. Amer. Chem. Socty.: Adv. Bd. Amer. Assn. for the Adv. of Sci. Assn. of the U.S. Army. Pike Cnty. Free Pub. Lib. Assn.: Ch. (1955–62); Pike Cnty. Red Cross Chap.: Ch. (1959–61). Amer. Natl. Students Inst.: Ch., Sub. Com. 20 (1966–68). **Activities:** 4; 17, 24, 34; 56, 91 **Addr.:** 12806 Kendale Le., Bowie, MD 20715.

Crum, Norman James (S. 5, 1926, Waverly, IL) Info. Resrch. Spec., Lockheed CA, 1976–; Tech. Info. Spec., Gen. Electric TEMPO, 1962–75; Head, Bus. and Indus. Dept., Omaha Pub. Lib., 1956–62; First Asst., Sci. and Indus., Pub. Lib. of Youngstown and Mahoning Cnty., 1953–55. **Educ.:** Univ. of IL, 1946–50, BS (Econ.); Univ. of IL, 1951–53, MS (LS); Columbia Univ, 1955 (LS). **Orgs.:** SLA: South. CA Chap., Pres. (1979–80), Pres-Elect, Prog. Ch. (1978–79), Treas. (1977–78), various ofcs. ASIS. **Honors:** Beta Phi Mu. **Pubns.:** "The Librarian-Customer Relationship: Dynamics of Filling Requests for Information," *Spec. Libs.* (My.–Je. 1969); "Head Librarian and Manager: Dynamics of a Creative Relationship," *Spec. Libs.* (N. 1970). **Activities:** 12; 39; 52, 59, 91 **Addr.:** 20226 Delight St., Canyon Country, CA 91351.

Crumb, Lawrence Nelson (My. 19, 1937, Palo Alto, CA) Ref. Libn., Univ. of OR, 1978–; Lib. Staff, Univ. of WI, Parkside, 1970–78; Asst. Libn., Nashotah Hs. Sem., 1965–70. **Educ.:** Pomona Coll., 1954–58, BA (Engl. lit.); Univ. of WI, Madison, 1966–67, MALS; Nashotah House, 1958–61, MDiv (Theo.); Gen. Theo. Sem., 1961–62, (church hist.). **Orgs.:** ALA. ACRL: OR Chap. (Brd. mem. 1979–). **Honors:** Phi Beta Kappa, 1958; Beta Phi Mu, 1967. **Pubns.:** *Historic Preservation in the Pacific Northwest,* (1979); Contr., *Racine: Growth and Change in a Wisconsin County,* (1977); "Presbyteral Ordination and the See of Rome," Church Qtly. Review (1963); "The Anglican Church in Colonial Maine," Hist. Mag. of the Prot. Epis. Ch. (1964); "James Albert Pike," Bltn. Bibl. (1970). **Activities:** 1, 2; 39, 41, 45; 55, 69, 90 **Addr.:** 1674 Washington St., Eugene, OR 97401.

Cruse, Larry S. (Jl. 29, 1944, Upland, CA) Head, Map Sect., Univ. CA, San Diego, 1971–. **Educ.:** Univ. of CA, San Diego, 1970–71, BA (Hist.). **Orgs.:** West. Assn. of Map Libs.: Pres.; Prog. Ch. Map Soc. of CA. **Pubns.:** "Collecting Microcartography: Sources and Prospects," *SLA Geog. and Map Div. Bltn.* (Je. 1980); "Microcartography and Cartographic Data Bases," *Lib. Trends* (Win, 1981); "Microcartography" column, *West. Assn. of Map Libs. Bltn.* (Mr. 1979–); Complr., *Microcartography in Libraries and Archives* (1981). **Activities:** 1; 29, 33; 70 **Addr.:** Map Section C-075P, University Library, University of California, San Diego, La Jolla, CA 92093.

Crutchfield, Mary Jane (O. 5, 1925, Sutton, WV) Chief, Lib. Srv., V. A. Hosp., Mountain Home, TN, 1973–; Med. Libn., V. A. Hosp., Richmond, VA, 1969–73; Branch Libn., Duke Univ. Med. Ctr. Lib., 1967–69; Bio-med. & Document-Film Libn., Armed Forces Radiobiology Resrch. Inst., 1964–66; Ref. Libn., Silver Spring (MD) Pub. Lib., 1962–64; Asst. Libn., Fairchild-Stratos Corp., 1961–62; Libn. II, Miami Pub. Lib., 1959–61; Ref. Libn., Chula Vista Pub. Lib., 1957–59. **Educ.:** WV Univ., 1943–47, BS (Ed./L.S. Soc. Sci.); Univ. of NC, 1953–55, BS in LS; Emory Univ., 1964, Med. Lib. Cert. **Orgs.:** Med. LA. SLA. Tri-Cities Hlth. Sci. Libs. Cnsrtm.: Ch. (1975). **Activities:** 4, 12; 15, 17, 39; 72, 80, 74 **Addr.:** Veterans Administration Medical Center, Mountain Home, TN 37684.

Cruzat, Gwendolyn Stiggins (Chicago, IL) Prof., Univ. of MI, 1979–, Assoc. Prof., 1976–79, Asst. Prof., 1971–76; Visit. Assoc. Prof., Univ. of HI, 1977; Med. Ref. Libn. III, Wayne State Univ., 1964–70. **Educ.:** Fisk Univ., 1953, BA (Math.); Atlanta Univ., 1954, MS (LS); Wayne State Univ., 1976, PhD (Higher Educ.). **Orgs.:** AALS: Resrch. Com. (1981–); Prog. Com. (1980–81). ALA: Com. on Col. Bargaining (1976–80); ACRL, Pubs. Libnshp. Ed. Bd. (1975–80); ASCLA, Hlth. Care Libs. Sect. Strg. Com. (1978–80). Med. LA: Goals Com. (1978–); Med. Lib. Ed. Grp. (1977–78). Various other orgs., Ofcs. **Honors:** Natl. Lib. of Med., Regent, 1980–; Med. LA, Janet Doe Lectr., 1979; Univ. MI, Disting. Srv. Awd., 1977. **Pubns.:** "Medical Librarianship: A Systems Perspective," *Bltn. Med. LA* (1980); "Issues and Strategies for Academic Librarians," *Col. Bargaining in Higher Educ.* (1976); various articles. **Activities:** 11; 17, 26, 29; 58, 75, 80 **Addr.:** School of Library Science, The University of Michigan, Ann Arbor, MI 48109.

Cruz de Escalera, Digna Rosa (S. 22, 1936, Santurce, PR) Head, Acq. Dept., Univ. of PR Lib., 1976–; Catlgr., 1971–72. **Educ.:** Univ. of PR, 1954–58, BA (Educ.), 1970–71, MLS. **Orgs.:** SBPR: Treas. (1973–75, 1978–80). Asociacion De Bibs. Univ. Y D Investigacion Del Caribe. SALALM. Asociacion de Maestros de PR. Natl. Educ. Assn. Org. de Prof. Univ. **Activities:** 1, 4; 15, 16, 20, 34; 56 **Addr.:** Felipe Roey 872, Country Club, Rio Piedras, PR 00924.

Crystal, Bernard Robert (Je. 18, 1937, Minneapolis, MN) Asst. Libn. for Mss., Columbia Univ. Libs., 1976–; Asst. Libn. for Rare Bks. and Mss., 1975–76; Ref. Libn., Spec. Col., 1970–74; Catlgr. (Rare Bks.), 1966–68; Ref. Libn., Spec. Col., 1961–66; Ref. Libn., IN Univ. Libs., 1961. **Educ.:** Univ. of MN, 1955–59, AB (Fr.), 1959–61, AM (LS); Columbia Univ., 1966–74, Cert. in Advnc. Libnshp.; Amer. Univ., 1976, Cert. (Arch.). **Orgs.:** Bibli. Soc. of Amer. SAA. Amer. Prntg. Hist. Assn.; Archvsts. RT of Metro. NY. **Pubns.:** "If the Good Lord and My Creditors Spare Me," *Columbia Lib. Columns* (My. 1973); Jt. auth. "Collections of Hebraica & Judaica at Columbia University," *Jewish Bk. Anl.* (1979); "Gonzalez Lodge, Apostle of the Classical Tradition," *Columbia Lib. Columns* (F. 1980). **Activities:** 1, 2; 17, 39, 45 **Addr.:** 531 West 217th St., New York, NY 10034.

Csaky, Susan Dischka (Ag. 25, 1926, Budapest, Hungary) Assoc. Prof. of Law, and Law Libn., Univ. of MO-Columbia, 1979–; Head, Gov. Pub. Dept., Adj. Instr., Univ. of KY, 1975–79, Law Libn., 1963–75; Lecturer and Libn., Univ. of NC, 1960–62. **Educ.:** Univ. of Budapest, 1945–47, (Law); Univ. of GA, 1947–48, AB (Econ.); Johns Hopkins Univ., 1948–53, MA (Pol. Sci.); Univ. of NC, 1959–60, MSLS; Univ. of KY, 1970–77, JD. **Orgs.:** AALL: Educ. Com. (1974–75). Gov. Doc. Com. (1975–76). Southeast Chap., Ch., Schol. Com. (1972–76). Mid Amer. Chap. (1979–). Intl. Assn. of Law Libs. Federation of Info. Users. **Honors:** Beta Phi Mu; Cncl. on Lib. Rsrcs, Fellow, 1977; Intl. Resrch. and Exch. Board, Fellow, 1977; AALL, Awd., 1976–77. **Pubns.:** *How to Use Government Documents for Legal Research* (1979). **Activities:** 1, 12; 15, 17, 31; 77 **Addr.:** University of Missouri-Columbia, Law Library, Tate Hall, Columbia, MO 65201.

Cuadra, Carlos Albert (D. 21, 1925, San Francisco, CA) Pres., Cuadra Assoc., Inc., 1978–; Gen. Mgr., SDC Search Service, System Dev. Corp., 1974–78, Mgr., Educ. & Lib. Syst. Dept., 1971–73, Mgr., Lib. and Docum. Syst. Dept., 1968–70. **Educ.:** Univ. of CA, Berkeley, 1947–49, AB (Psy.), 1949–53, PhD (Psy.). **Orgs.:** ASIS. Info. Indus. Assn.: Bd. of Dir. SLA. NCLIS: Commissioner (1971–). Univ. of South. CA: Annenberg Sch. of Comm. (Bd. of Visitors, 1979–80). *On-line Review:* Ed. Bd. (1977–). **Honors:** Info. Indus. Asn., Hall of Fame Awd., 1980; Natl. Fed. of Abs. & Indx. Srvs., Miles Conrad Award, 1980; Info. Indus. Assn., Info. Prod. of the Year, 1975; ASIS, Awd. of Merit, 1968; ASIS, Best Info. Sci. Bk., 1969; Other awds. **Pubns.:** Ed., *Annual Review of Information Science and Technology* (1966–75); "The Role of the Private Sector in the Development and Improvement of Library and Information Services," *Lib. Qtly.* (Ja. 1980); "U.S.-European Cooperation and Competition in the On-line Retrieval Services Marketplace," *Info. Scientist* (Je. 1978); "Commercially Funded On-line Retrieval Services—Past, Present, and Future," *Aslib Proc.* (Ja. 1978); Other articles and oral presentations. **Activities:** 4, 11; 24, 26, 41; 75, 95-Computer Technology. **Addr.:** Cuadra Associates, Inc., 1523 Sixth Street, Suite 12, Santa Monica, CA 90401.

Cuebas, Ana E. (Ap. 29, 19–; Mayaguez, PR) Head of Pers. Coll., Gen. Lib., Univ. of PR, Mayaguez, 1981– Dir., PR Coll.; 1980–81; Dir., Ctr. de Documentación y Promoción Cult., 1978–79; Head, Readers Srvs., Univ. of PR, 1975–78; Head, Ref., Univ. of PR, Mayaguez, 1968–74. **Educ.:** Coll. of Agr. & Mech. Arts, 1961–65, BA (Soc. Sci.); Pratt Inst., 1966–67, MLS (LS); Univ. of PR, Río Piedras, 1968–72, MPA (Pub. Admin.). **Orgs.:** Reforma. Socty. de Bibtcr. de PR: Bd. of Dir. Assn. of Carribean Univ. and Resrch. Libs.: various Coms. Oral Hist. Assn. ALA. Altrusa Intl.: Acts Secy. Bus. and Prof. Women. Carnaval Mayaguezano, Inc. Centro Cultural Eugenio María de Hostos. **Pubns.:** *Diccionario de siglas en uso en Puerto Rico* (1979); *Bibliografía del Arroz* (Rice Bibl.) (1979); *Caso de Puerto Rico ante la O.N.U.* (1978); Producer, "Bibliotecas, Libros y Autores" (TV Prog.) (1980); Simbolos que identifican nuestras instituciones. **Activities:** 1, 2; 15, 17, 23; 62, 77, 85 **Addr.:** E-36 Yaurel St., Urb. Alturas de Mayaguez, Mayaguez, PR 00708.

Cuenca, Pilar A. de (Jl. 1, 1931, Camagüey, Cuba) Sch. Lib. Media Spec., Bronx, NY Schs., 1980–; Supvsg. Libn., Reg. Biling. Trng. Resrc. Ctr., Bd. of Educ., Brooklyn, NY, 1974–80; Tchr. of Lib., Biling. Sch., 1969–74; Biling. Tchr., Bronx, NY, Brooklyn, NY Schs., 1968–69; Spec. in Vocational Orient. and Educ. Psy., Dept. of Educ. Psy., Camagüey, Cuba, 1962–66; Prof. Early Chldhd. Educ., Escuela Normal de Kindergarten, Cuba, 1961–62; Kindergarten Tchr., Pub. Sch., Cuba, 1956–61. **Educ.:** Sch. of Educ. for Kindergarten Tchrs., Cuba, 1946–49; Univ. of Havana, 1950–55, Dr. in Educ.; Queens Coll., 1969–71, MLS, Post-Grad. Cert., 1975, (Libnshp.); Additional credits. **Orgs.:** ALA. Natl. Assn. for Biling. Educ. Utd. Fed. of Tchrs. NY State Utd. Tchrs. **Pubns.:** "School Library Media Centers and Puerto Ricans", *Opportunities for Minorities in Librarianship* (1977); Other articles and bibls. **Activities:** 10, 14-Tchr. Ctr.; 15, 17, 20; 63, 66, 95-Biling. Educ. **Addr.:** P.S. 25, District 7, Bronx Public Schools, Bronx, NY

Cuesta, Yolanda J. (Ap. 24, 1947, Laredo, TX) Lib. Consult., CA State Lib., 1974–; Head Srvs. to Mex.-Amers., El Paso

Special Subjects/Services: 50. Adult educ.; 51. Advert./Mktg.; 52. Aerosp.; 53. Agric.; 54. Area std.; 55. Arts/Hum.; 56. Autom.; 57. Bibl./Prtg.; 58. Bio. sci.; 59. Bus./Fin.; 60. Chem.; 61. Copyrt.; 62. Documtn.; 63. Educ.; 64. Engin.; 65. Env.; 66. Eth. grps.; 67. Film; 68. Food/Nutr.; 69. Geneal.; 70. Geo.; 71. Geol.; 72. Handcpd.; 73. Hist.; 74. Int. frdm.; 75. Info. sci.; 76. Insr.; 77. Law; 78. Legis.; 79. Math./Comp. sci.; 80. Med.; 81. Metals; 82. Nat. resrcs.; 83. Newsp.; 84. Nuc. sci.; 85. Oral hist.; 86. Petr./Energy; 87. Pharm.; 88. Phys./Astr./Math.; 89. Readg.; 90. Relig.; 91. Sci./Tech.; 92. Soc. sci.; 93. Telecom.; 94. Transp.; 95. (other).

Pub. Lib., 1970–74. **Educ.:** Univ. of TX, Austin, 1966–68, BS (Educ.), 1968–70, MLS. **Orgs.:** ALA: PLA, Conf. Coord. Com. (1980–82) Multiling. Srvs. Com. (1978–80); Louise Giles Schol. Jury (1981); Ofc. for Lib. Persnl. Com., Equal Empl. Oppt. Subcom. (1978–80). CA LA: Cncl. (1978–80); Lib. Dev. and Stans. Com. (1980). **Pubns.:** "Guidelines for Library Services to Spanish Speaking," *Lib. Jnl.* (Jl. 1978); "Library Services to Hispanic Americans," *ALA Yrbk.* (1978); "Personnel and Employment, Affirmative Action," *ALA Yrbk.* (1979). **Activities:** 9, 13; 24, 27; 66 **Addr.:** California State Library, P.O. Box 2037, Sacramento, CA 95809.

Culbertson, Diana L. (D. 6, 1947, Toledo, IA) Libn., Natl. Dairy Cncl., 1972–; Resrch. Libn., Assn. of Sch. Bus. Officials, 1970–72. **Educ.:** Wartburg Coll., 1965–69, BA (Hist.); Rosary Coll., 1969–70, MALS; Med. LA, Cert., 1978. **Orgs.:** SLA: Ch., Food & Nutrition Div. (1980–81). Med. LA. ASIS. Assoc. Info. Mgrs. **Pubns.:** Contrib., *Food Science & Technology* (1978); monthly column, *School Business Affairs* (1970–72). **Activities:** 12; 17; 68 **Addr.:** National Dairy Council Library, 6300 N. River Rd., Rosemont, IL 60018.

Culbertson, Katheryn C. (Ag. 14, 1920, Coeburn, VA) State Libn./Archvst., TN State Lib., 1972–; Dir., Ext. Srvs., Metro Nashville Lib., 1961–72; Reg. Libn., Watauga Reg., Johnson City, TN, 1953–61; Libn., Kingsport Pub. Schs., 1949–51; Ref. Libn. Catlgr., U.S. Bur. of Ships, 1945–53. **Educ.:** E. TN State Univ., 1937–40, BS (Eng., Latin); George Peabody Coll., 1940–42, BS (LS); YMCA Night Law Sch. (Nashville, TN), 1962–68, LLB, 1971, JD. **Orgs.:** TN LA: Various ofcs. SELA. ALA. Pres. Com. on Empl. of Handcpd.: Lib. Com. (1966–). Amer. Bar Assn. TN Bar Assn. TN Fed. Bus. and Prof. Women's Clubs: Pres. (1974–75). Zonta. **Pubns.:** "Rural Library Service," *Encyc. of Educ.* (1971). **Activities:** 2, 13; 17, 36; 72, 77, 78 **Addr.:** 800 Glen Leven Dr., Nashville, TN 37204.

Culbertson, Lillian D. (N. 10, 1929, Springfield, MO) Supvsr., Tech. Srvs., Chicago Transit Athrty., 1975–; Catlgr., Spec. Proj., Oak Park Pub. Lib., 1974; Serials Catlgr./Head, Tech. Srvs., Skokie Pub. Lib., 1968–72, 1960–64; Catlgr., Wichita City Lib., 1958–60; Branch Libn., Flint Pub. Lib., 1956–57; HS Libn., MO Pub. Schs., 1951–56. **Educ.:** SW MO State Univ., 1947–51, BS (Span.); Univ. of Denver, 1956–58, MALS. **Orgs.:** SLA: Transp. Div. (Ch., 1980–81); IL LA: Schol. Com. (Ch, 1963). ALA. Chicago Lib. Club: Pres. (1979–80). Various other orgs. Pistakee Yacht Club. Art Inst. of Chicago. **Activities:** 9, 12; 15, 20, 46; 56, 92, 94 **Addr.:** 1132 Curtiss St. Apt. 1-A, Downers Grove, IL 60515.

Cullen, Linda B. (Mr. 9, 1950, LaFayette, IN) Coord., Texas-Trans-Pecos Lib. Syst., 1981–; Chief of Ext. Srvs., Augusta Reg. Lib., 1979–81; Ext. Srvs. Libn., 1978–79, Info./YA Libn., 1974–78; Asst. to the Consult., GA Lib. Srvy., Div. of Pub. Lib. Srvs., 1973–74. **Educ.:** IN Univ., 1968–72, BA (Hist.); Emory Univ., 1972–73, MLn; Med. Libn. Cert., Grade I, 1973; Augusta Coll., 1978–80, (Bus.). **Orgs.:** ALA: YASD/Media Sel. & Usage Com. (1978–); JMRT *Cognotes* Com. (1978); Pubcty. & Travel Network Com. (1980–). GA LA: JMRT, Pres. (1979–81); Pub. Lib. Div./Lib. Srvs. to YA Com., Ch., (1979–81). Ctrl. Savannah River Area Lib. Assn.: Sec.-Treas. (1975-77), VP (1977–80). **Pubns.:** "A History of Libraries in Georgia," (1973); Jt. auth., "Georgia Librarians' Concerns in the 70's," *Georgia Librarian* (N. 1974); Jt. auth., "Animation: A-Z," *Top of the News* (Win. 1980); Jt. auth., "Portrait of an Adolescent," *Top of the News* (Spr. 1980). **Activities:** 9, 12; 17, 27, 35; 59, 78, 80 **Addr.:** Texas Trans-Pecos Library System, 501 N. Oregon, El Paso, TX 79901.

Cullinan, Bernice E. (O. 12, 1926, Hamilton, OH) Prof., NY Univ., 1967–; Asst. Prof., OH State Univ., 1964–67, Instr., 1961–64; Elem. Tchr., OH Pub. Schs., 1958–61, 1946–52. **Educ.:** OH State Univ., 1943–48, BA (Educ.); 1948–51, MA (Educ.); 1961–64, PhD (Educ.). **Orgs.:** Intl. Readg. Assn.: Bd. of Dirs. (1979–82). Natl. Cncl. of Tchrs. of Eng.: Comsn. on Lit. (1979–83); Ed. Bd. (1973–76). ALA: ALSC, Multimedia Approach to Chld. Lit. Com. (1980–82), Caldecott Com. (1982). Natl. Conf. on Resrch. in Eng.: Ed. Bd. (1972–75); Secy. (1980–83). Alvina Treut Burrows Inst.: Dir. **Honors** Pi Lambda Theta. **Pubns.:** *Literature and the Child* (1981); jt. ed., *Literature and Young Children* (1977); *Literature for Children: Its Discipline and Content* (1971); jt. ed., *Books I Read When I Was Young* (1980); "Teaching Reading and Literature" 30 segment videotape series (1981). **Activities:** 14-Univ.; 41; 55, 89 **Addr.:** Dept. of Education, New York University, 200 East Bldg., New York, NY 10003.

Culnan, Mary J. (D. 9, 1944, New York, NY) Asst. Prof. (LS), Univ. of CA, Berkeley, 1980–; Asst. Prof., McIntire Sch. of Cmrc., Univ. of VA, 1979–80; Libn., Burroughs Corp., 1974–75, Syst. Anal., Burroughs Corp., 1968–74. **Educ.:** Coll. of Wooster, 1962–66, BA (Pol. Sci.); FL State Univ., 1966–68, MS (LS); Univ. of CA, Los Angeles, 1975–79, PhD (Mgt.). **Orgs.:** ASIS. Acad. of Mgt. Socty. for Mgt. Info. Syst. ACM. **Honors:** IBM Corp., Flwshp., 1978–79. **Pubns.:** Jt. auth., "Document-based Information Systems for Management Planning and Control," *MIS Qtly.* (D. 1978); "An Analysis of the Information Usage Patterns of Academics and Practitioners in the Computer Field," *Info. Prcs. Mgt.* (1978). **Activities:** 11; 26, 41; 56 **Addr.:** School of Library & Information Studies, University of California, Berkeley, CA 94720.

Culotta, Wendy Anne (My. 14, 1943, Coronado, CA) Head, Sci. and Tech. Ref. Dept., CA State Univ., Long Beach, 1973–. **Educ.:** San Diego State Univ., 1965–67, BA (Eng.); Univ. of CA, Los Angeles, 1971–73, MLS. **Orgs.:** CA Acad. and Resrch. Libs.: Mem. Com., Ch. (1980–); Pres. (1982). South. CA OLUG: Strg. Com. (1978–79). CA LA: South. CA Sect. (Coord., 1980); Coll. Dev. Ch. ACRL: Chap. Cncl. (Ch., 1982). **Pubns.:** Jt. auth., "Pelamis, Pelamis platurus," *Cat. of Amer. Amphibians and Reptiles* (1980). **Activities:** 1; 17, 31, 39; 58, 80, 91 **Addr.:** Library, California State University, Long Beach, 1250 Bellflower Blvd., Long Beach, CA 90840.

Culp, Marion E. (New York, NY) Lib. Dir., Roosevelt Pub. Lib., 1975–; Ref. Libn., Shelter Rock Pub. Lib., 1970–75. **Educ.:** Queens Coll., 1946–50, BA (Soclgy.); Long Island Univ., 1967–70, MLS; St. John's Univ., 1978–, (Adv. Cert. in prog.). **Orgs.:** ASIS. Amer. Socty. of Indkrs. ALA. NYLA. Other orgs. Archlgl. Inst. of Amer.: N. Shore Chap. **Activities:** 9; 17, 30, 39; 57, 66 **Addr.:** Roosevelt Public Library, Rose & Mansfield Avenues, Roosevelt, NY 11575.

Culpepper, Betty M. (Ja. 15, 1941, Lynchburg, VA) Biblgphr./Head of Ref., Moorland-Springarn Resrch. Ctr., Howard Univ., 1977–; Chief, Washingtoniana Div., DC Pub. Lib., 1972–77; Branch Libn., Prince George's Cnty. Meml. Lib., 1967–72; Reader's Adv., DC Pub. Lib., 1964–67. **Educ.:** Howard Univ., 1959–63, BA (Hist.); Kent State Univ., 1963–64, MA (Hist.); Cath. Univ., 1965–67, MSLS; Howard Univ., 1979–81, MA (Pub. Admin.). **Orgs.:** ALA: ACRL. Columbia Hist. Socty.: Bd. of Gvrs. (1979–82). DC Jt. Com. on Landmarks. **Pubns.:** "Genealogical Resources in Moorland-Springarn Research Center," *Jnl. of the Afro-Amer. Geneal. and Hist. Socty.* (Jl. 1981). **Activities:** 1, 12; 17, 41, 45; 66, 75 86. **Addr.:** 9770 Basket Ring Rd., Columbia, MD 21045.

Cummings, Charles F. (Je. 27, 1937, San Juan, PR) Supvsg. Libn., NJ Ref. Div., Newark Pub. Lib., 1969–, Prin. Libn., 1967–69, Sr. Libn., 1965–67, Lib. Trainee, 1963–65. **Educ.:** Univ. of AL, 1955–59, AB (Hist.); Vanderbilt Univ., MA (Hist.); Rutgers Univ., MLS. **Orgs.:** NJ LA: Pres. Hist. and Bibl. (1971–72). ALA: Hist. Sect. Prog. Com. for NYC Conf. (1980). NJ Hist. Cmsn.: Scholarly Prog. Com. NJ Hist. Soc.: Lib. Com., Pubn. Com. Newark Prsrvn. and Landmarks Com.: Vice-Ch. NJ Hist. Recs. Adv. Bd. Other orgs. **Honors:** NJ Hist. Comsn., Awd. of Recog., 1978; Newark Prsrvn. and Landmarks Com., Awd., 1978. **Pubns.:** Jt. auth., *Newark: An American City* (1979); *Records of the Township of Newark, 1666–1836* (1966); Complr., *Newark Star-Ledger Index* (1972–); Co-ed., "New Jersey Libraries," *NJ Libs.*; "A New Jersey Book List," *This is NJ* 3rd ed. **Activities:** 9; 30, 39; 83 **Addr.:** New Jersey Reference Division, Newark Public Library, 5 Washington St., Newark, NJ 07102.

Cummings, John P. (D. 29, 1941, Scranton, PA) Assoc. Dir., U.S. Nvl. Acad. Lib., 1978–; Head, Reader Srvs., 1972–78; Resrc. Coord., Navy Gen. Lib. Syst., 1971–72; Head, Acq., Nvl. Acad. Lib., 1969–71; Ref. Libn., Booz Allen Applied Resrch., 1968–69; Head, Reader Srvs., Applied Physics Laboratory, Johns Hopkins Univ., 1968; Head, Tech. Srvs., 1966–68. **Educ.:** Univ. of Scranton, 1962–64, BA (Hist.); Cath. Univ., 1964–68, MSLS. **Orgs.:** ALA. FLRT: Secy. (1979–80). **Activities:** 1, 4; 15, 17; 74 **Addr.:** Nimitz Library, U. S. Naval Academy, Annapolis, MD 21402.

Cummings, Martin Marc (S. 7, 1920, Camden, NJ) Dir., Natl. Lib. of Med., 1964–; Assoc. Dir. for Resrch. Grants, Natl. Inst. of Hlth., 1963–64, Chief, Ofc. of Intl. Resrch., 1961–63; Prof., Ch., Dept. of Microbio., Univ. of OK Sch. of Med., 1959–61; Dir., Resrch. Srvs., Vets. Admin., 1953–59; Chief, Tuberculosis Resrch. Lab., Vets. Admin. Hosp. of Atlanta, 1949–53; Instr. through Assoc. Prof. of Med., Emory Univ., 1948–53; Dir., Tuberculosis Eval. Lab., US Pub. Hlth. Srv., 1947–49. **Educ.:** Bucknell Univ., 1941, BS; Duke Univ., 1944, MD. **Orgs.:** ARL. Med. LA. Socty. of Sigma Xi. AAAS: Bd. of Dirs. Inst. of Med., Natl. Acad. of Sci. Amer. Acad. of Microbio. Other orgs. **Honors:** Disting. Alum. Awd., Duke Univ., 1969; Hon. Doct., Bucknell Univ., Univ. of NE, Emory Univ., Georgetown Univ., Acad. of Med., Poland, others. **Pubns.:** Jt. auth., "International Aspects of U.S. Biomedical Communications," in *Health Handbook* (1979); "Control of Federal Publications," *Sci.* (Jl. 1979); "NLM/MLA (Editorial)," *Bltn. Med LA* (Ja. 1972); "Preface: Information services of the National Library of Medicine," "The National Library of Medicine: Its Scope and Goals," *Hosp Form Mgt.* (Ap. 1973); Jt. auth., "Biomedical Communications" in *Advances in American Medicine: Essays at the Bicentennial* (1976); other books and articles. **Addr.:** National Library of Medicine, 8600 Rockville Pike, Bethesda, MD 20209.

Cummings, Nancy R. (Jn. 9, 1938, Reno, NV) Dir., Yuma-City Cnty. Lib., 1981–, Admin., HQ Lib., 1978–81, Young Peoples Srvs. Coord., 1972–81, Young People's Libn., 1971–72; Dir., Readg. Enrich. Prog., Armona Elem. Sch., 1966–69. **Educ.:** Univ. of NV, Las Vegas, 1972 (Psy.); San Jose State Coll., 1976, MLS. **Orgs.:** NV LA: Chld.-YA Sect. (Ch., 1973–75, 1977–78); Gvt. Rel. Sect. (1978–79); Int. Frdm. Com. (1979–). ALA: Newbery-Caldecott Com. (1977–); U.S. Natl. Parks Jt. Com. (Co.-Ch., 1977–80). **Honors:** NV, Outstan. Citizen Awd., 1963; NV LA, Libn. of the Yr., 1973; Clark Cnty. Lib. Dist., Spec. Awd. for Srv. to Chld., 1974. **Pubns.:** "The Effects of Pre-school Programming upon the Circulation of Children's Books in the Public Library," ERIC (1978); "Reflections in a Cracked Mirror; or Whoever Heard of a Blond Snow White?" *CHOICES* (Je. 1977). **Activities:** 9; 16, 17, 21; 63, 74, 89 **Addr.:** Yuma City-County Library, 350 3rd Ave., Yuma, AZ 85364.

Cummings, Peggy J. (S. 9, 1948, Portland, OR) Spec. Srvs. Libn., AK State Lib., 1975–, Blind & Phys. Handcpd. Libn., 1974–75, Interlib. Loan Libn., 1972–74; Docu. Libn., 1970–72. **Educ.:** OR State Univ., 1966–70, BS (Elem. Ed.); Univ. of HI, 1975–76, MLS. **Orgs.:** AK LA: Pres. (1977–78); Secy. (1972–73); Local Chap. Pres. 1973–74). AECT. ALA. Govr. Adv. Cncl. on Libs., AK. Educ. Telecom. Cnstm., AK. Nat. Audubon Socty. Sierra Club. **Activities:** 13; 29, 32, 39; 67, 72 **Addr.:** Alaska State Library, Pouch G, Juneau, AK 99811.

Cummings, Roberta Spikes (My. 1, 1944, Angie, LA) Asst. Law Libn., Head of Acq., South. Univ. Law School, 1973–; Ref. Libn., E. Baton Rouge Parish Pub. Lib., 1973; Libn., Lafayette Parish Sch. Bd., 1966–73. **Educ.:** Grambling State Univ., 1962–66, BS (LS); LA State Univ., 1967–72, MSLS, 1973–78, (Media & Broadcasting); AALL Cert.; LA State Dept. of Educ. Cert. **Orgs.:** AALL; Southeast. Chapt. SLA. LA LA. Lafayette Parish School Libns. Assn.: Secy.-Treas. (1973). Alpha Kappa Alpha Sorority: Secy. (1966). **Honors** Alpha Theta Pi, 1973. **Pubns.:** *Books & Nonprinted on Blacks* (1972). **Activities:** 12; 15, 32, 44 **Addr.:** Southern University Law Library, Southern Br. PO, Baton Rouge, LA 70813.

Cummins, A. Blair (F. 6, 1938, Indiana, PA) Dir., Wood Lib., Canandaigua, NY, 1968–. **Educ.:** Mt. Union Coll., 1956–60, BA (Hist.); SUNY, Geneseo, 1967–68, MLS. **Orgs.:** ALA: Mem. Com. (1970–74). NY LA; Rochester and Environs Soc. for Org. Unified Resrcs. for Comms. and Educ. Srvs.: Pres. (1976–77). City of Canandaigua, Cons. Comsn.: Secy. (1978–). **Pubns.:** "Surveys", *OC/WC News* (Ap. 1976). **Activities:** 9; 16, 17, 38 **Addr.:** Wood Library, 134 N. Main St., Canandaigua, NY 14424.

Cummins, Julie A. (N. 15, 1939, Mansfield, OH) Chld. Srvs. Consul., Monroe Cnty. Lib. Syst., 1976–; Head, Ctrl. Chld. Room, Rochester Pub. Lib., 1969–76; Chld. Libn., 1963–69. **Educ.:** Mt. Union Coll., 1957–61, BA (Eng./Drama); Syracuse Univ., 1962–63, MSLS. **Orgs.:** ALA/ALSC: Lib. Srv. to Disadvantaged Child Com. (1977–79), Laura Ingalls Wilder Awd. Com. (1980–83). NY LA, Chld. and YA Srvs. Sect.: VP (1978), Pres. (1979). **Honors:** Beta Phi Mu. **Pubns.:** "Table Legs and Chair Arms: The Anatomy of Children's Furniture in Libraries," *IL Libs.* (D. 1978); "Children's Films: Secondhand, Second-rate or Second Wind?" *Lib. Trends* (Sum. 1978). **Activities:** 9, 11; 21; 67, 95-Storytel. **Addr.:** Monroe County Library System, 115 South Ave., Rochester, NY 14604.

Cunha, George Martin (D. 25, 1911, Providence, RI) Pres., George Martin Cunha, Inc., Cons. Consult., 1978–; Dir., New Eng. Docum. Cons. Ctr., 1973–78; Chief Conservator, Lib. of the Boston Athenaeum, 1963–73; Weapons Ofcr., Carrier Pilot, US Navy, 1937–63; Chem., Vultex Chem. Co., 1934–37. **Educ.:** MA Inst. of Tech., 1930–32; Lowell Inst., 1933–34, (Chem.); U.S. Navy General Line School, 1946–47, (Engin.); U.S. Naval War Coll., 1958–59, (Intl. Rel.). **Orgs.:** SAA: Prsrvn. Methods Com. (Ch., 1976–78). New Eng. Archvsts. Amer. Inst. for Cons. Intl. Inst. for Cons. Other orgs. Fellow Royal Socty. of Arts. Fellow of the Pilgrim Socty.: Lib. Adv. Com. The Colonial Socty. of MA. Associates of the John Carter Brown Lib. **Pubns.:** Jt. Auth., *Conservation of Library Materials* (1972); Jt. ed., *Conservation Administration* (1975); Jt. ed., *Library and Archives Conservation* (1972); "Conserving Local Archival Materials", *Hist. News* (1975); "Preservation and Conservation of Legal Materials" *Law Lib. Jnl.* 69(3), (1976); Other articles. **Activities:** 14-Cons. Ctr.; 19, 23, 24; 65 **Addr.:** 4 Tanglewood Dr., Lexington, KY 40505.

Cunningham, Sally Louise (Jn. 9, 1944, Birtle, MB, Can) Archvst., Rural Arch., Brandon Univ., 1976–. **Educ.:** Brandon Univ., 1978–80, Arts, (Hist.); MB Tchg. Cert., 1965. **Orgs.:** Assoc. of Can. Archvsts. MB Geneal. Socty. Assn. of MB Archvsts. Can. Oral Hist. Assn. Assn. of MB Musms. Brandon Geneal. Socty. Assiniboine Hist. Socty. **Pubns.:** Ed., *Proceedings of the Local Histories Workshops* (1978). **Activities:** 2, 12; 23, 38, 41; 69, 85 **Addr.:** Rural Archives, Brandon University, Brandon, MB R7A 6A9 Canada.

Cunningham, Sharon K. (O. 23, 1943, Wiseman, AR) Media Libn., Georgetown Univ. Law Ctr. Lib., 1979–. **Educ.:** Ottawa (KS) Univ., 1961–65, BA (Fr.); Univ. of MD, 1976–79 MLS. **Orgs.:** AALL: Micro. and AV Spec. Interest Sect., Secy.-Treas. (1980–81) Vice-Ch., Ch.-Elect (1981–82); Conf. of Newer Law Libns. (Secy.-Treas., 1980–81). ALA. Law Libns. Socty. of DC. **Honors:** Beta Phi Mu. **Activities:** 1, 12; 32, 33, 39; 56, 77, 78 **Addr.:** 1616 15th St. N.W., Washington, DC 20009.

Cunningham, William D. (Ag. 9, 1937, Kansas City, MO) Asst. Prof., Coll. of Lib. and Info. Srvs., Univ. of MD,

PROFESSIONAL ACTIVITIES: Institutions: 1. Acad. lib.; 2. Arch.; 3. Assn.; 4. Fed./Gvt. lib.; 5. Inst. lib.; 6. Mfr./Suppl.; 7. Milit. lib.; 8. Musm.; 9. Pub. lib.; 10. Sch. lib.; 11. Sch. of lib. sci.; 12. Spec. lib.; 13. State lib.; 14. (other). **Functions/Activities:** 15. Acq./Col. dev.; 16. Adult srvs.; 17. Admin.; 18. Apprais.; 19. Archit./Bldgs.; 20. Cat./Class.; 21. Chld. srvs.; 22. Circ.; 23. Cons./Pres.; 24. Consult.; 25. Cont. ed.; 26. Educ. lib. sci.; 27. Ext. srvs.; 28. Fund/Grants; 29. Gvt. pubs.; 30. Indx./Abs.; 31. Instr. lib. use; 32. Media srvs.; 33. Micro.; 34. Netwks./Coop.; 35. Persnl.; 36. PR; 37. Publshg.; 38. Recs. mgt.; 39. Ref. srvs.; 40. Repro.; 41. Resrch.; 42. Review.; 43. Secur.; 44. Serials; 45. Spec. col.; 46. Tech. srvs.; 47. Trustees/Bds.; 48. YA srvs.; 49. (other).

1973–; Dir., Univ. Libs., Howard Univ., 1971–73; Prog. Officer, US Office of Educ., 1968–71; Chief, Lib. Srvcs., Fed. Aviation Agcy., 1965–68; Head, Adult Srvs., Topeka Pub. Lib., 1962–65. **Educ.:** Univ. of KS, 1956–59, BA (Psych.); Univ. of TX, 1961–63, MLS, 1970, PhD. **Orgs.:** ALA: ASCLA (Com. on Grantmanship, 1976–80). LAMA (Ad Hoc Com. on Sexism and Racism, 1977–79); Cnclr. at Large (1974–77); Office of Lib. Srv. to the Disadv., Adv. Com. (1979–81). Freedom to Read Fndn. (Exec. Brd., 1970–72). Assn. for the Study of Afro-Amer. Life and Hist.: Black Hist. Com. (1974–); Treas. (1976–77); Ch. (1978–80). **Honors:** Assn. for the Study of Afro-Amer. Life and Hist., Carter G. Woodson Medal, 1975. **Pubns.:** Jt. Auth., *Blacks in the Performing Arts,* (1980); *Bibliographic Guide to Washington DC,* (1980); Jt. Auth., *Black Guide to Washington,* (1976); "Anto Wicharti," *Lib. Jnl.* (1971); "The Changing Institution," *Lib. Trends* (1971); "From the Agony," *IA Lib. Qtrly.* (1970). **Activities:** 4, 11; 17, 26, 28; 66, 78, 89 **Addr.:** 3806 V St. S.E., Washington, DC 20020.

Cupoli, Patricia Dymkar (My. 25, 1948, Rochester, NY) Supvsr. and Info. Spec., GM Corp., 1978–; Circ. Libn., Univ. of Detroit Law Lib., 1977–78; Libn., Burroughs Corp., 1976–77. **Educ.:** Wayne State Univ., 1966–70, BA (Russ.); Fordham Univ., 1970–71, MA (Russ. Area Std.); Wayne State Univ., 1973–75, MSLS; Univ. of Detroit, 1977–79, MBA (Mgt.). **Orgs.:** SLA: MI Chap., Hosplty. Com. (Co-Ch., 1977–78); Bltn. Com. (1979–80); Empl. Com. (1979–80). MI Assn. of Law Libs.: Treas. (1977–80). ASIS. AIM. **Pubns.:** "Reference Tools for Data Processing, Office Automation, and Data Communications: An Introductory Guide", *Spec. Libs.* (Jl. 1981). **Activities:** 12; 17, 39, 49-On-line Searching; 75, 93 **Addr.:** 13341 Irvine, Oak Park, MI 48237.

Curley, Arthur (Ja. 22, 1938, Boston, MA) Deputy Dir., Detroit Pub. Lib., 1978–; Instr., Univ. of MI Grad. Sch. of LS, 1978–; Assoc. Dir. Pub. Srv., Detroit Pub. Lib., 1977–; Dir., Cuyahoga Cnty. Pub. Lib., 1975–76; Dir., Montclair (NJ) Pub. Lib., 1968–75; Dir., Palatine (IL) Pub. Lib., 1964–68; Dir., Avon (MA) Pub. Lib., 1961–64; Adult Srvs. Libn., Boston Pub. Lib., 1959–61. **Educ.:** Harvard Univ., 1955–59, AB (Gvt./Lit.); Simmons Coll., 1960–62, MS (LS). **Orgs.:** ALA: Com. on Org. (Ch. 1977–); Edit. Adv. Com. (Ch. 1976–77); Cncl. (1970–74); Pres. Comsn. (1976–77); Legis. Asm. (1971–74). PLA: Legis. Com. (Ch. 1971–74). SLA. ASIS. CLENE. **Honors:** ALA/BOMC, Dorothy Canfield Fisher Award, 1964; Work included in: *Best of Library Literature* 1974, 1979. **Pubns.:** Ed., *Collection Building: Studies in the Development and Effective Use of Library Resources* (1978); Jt. auth. *Simple Library Cataloging* (1977); Jt. auth. *Modern Romance Literatures: A Library of Literary Criticism* (1968); "Information from the People to the People," *Amer. Libs.* (Je. 1979); "Social Responsibility and Libraries," *Advncs. in Libnshp.* v. 4 (1974); Other articles. **Activities:** 9; 15, 17, 26; 55, 92 **Addr.:** Detroit Public Library, 5201 Woodward Avenue, Detroit, MI 48202.

Curley, Elmer F. (Ja. 13, 1929, PA) Asst. Dir., Pub. Srvs., Univ. of NV, Las Vegas, 1967–; Head, Ref., SUNY, Stony Brook, 1964–67; Ref. and ILL, Univ. of Pittsburgh., 1962–64. **Educ.:** Univ. of Pittsburgh, 1961, BA (Msc.); Carnegie Inst., 1961–62, (LS); Univ. of Pittsburgh, 1962–64, Cert. (LS). **Orgs.:** ALA: RASD/Nom. Com. (Ch., 1975–76; Secy., 1976); Bibl. Inst. Com. (1978–80); Ref. and Sub. Books Rev. Com. (1980–82). Bibl. Socty. of Amer. Bibl. Socty., Univ. of VA. **Activities:** 1; 17, 26, 39; 55, 57, 92 **Addr.:** 1170 Maryland Cl., Apt. 4, Las Vegas, NV 89109.

Curley, Thomas E. (Je. 9, 1937, Brooklyn, NY) Trustee, Asst. Treas., Queens Borough Lib., 1977–; Assoc. Prof., Queensborough Cmnty. Coll., 1973–79; Asst. Prof., 1971–73; Instr., 1969–71. **Educ.:** St. Francis Coll., Brooklyn, 1957–61, BA (Eng.); Hofstra Univ., 1965–68, BS (Readg.); NY Univ., 1969–74, PhD (Educ.). **Orgs.:** NY LA. Frnds. of Queens Borough Cmnty. Coll. ALA: ALTA. . Prof. Staff Conf. Intl. Readg. Assn. Amer. Irish Hist. Assn. NY State Assn. of Cont. Educ. Other orgs. **Honors:** NY Univ., The Founders Day Awd., 1974. **Activities:** 1, 9; 17, 36, 47 **Addr.:** 133–18 Crouston Ave., Belle Harbor, NY 11694.

Curran, Charles C. (Je. 21, 1934, Pittsburgh, PA) Assoc. Prof., LS, Univ. of SC, 1974–; Ref. Libn., E. Stroudsburgh State Coll., 1965–73; Sch. Libn., Hanover Pk. HS, 1963–65; Sch. Libn./Basketball Coach, S. Park HS, 1961–63. **Educ.:** Duquesne Univ., 1952–56, BEd (Pol. Sci.), 1958–62, MEd (LS); Rutgers Univ., 1964–67, MLS, 1970–77, PhD (LS). **Orgs.:** ALA: LRRT, Strg. Com. (Ch., 1981–82). SC LA: Lib. Educ. RT (Ch., 1979). **Pubns.:** Jt. auth., "Assessing the Information Needs of Rural People," *Lib. Trends* (Spr. 1980); "Developing Patterns of Governance in Public Organizations," *Lib. Trends* (Fall 1977). **Activities:** 11; 25, 26; 92 **Addr.:** College of Librarianship, University of South Carolina, Columbia, SC 29208.

Curran, Francis J. (Mr. 30, 1940, Boston, MA) Media Dir., Hanover Sch. Dept., 1979–, AV Dir., 1967–79, Soc. Studies Ch., 1966–67, Soc. Studies Tchr., 1961–67. **Educ.:** State Coll. at Bridgewater, 1957–61, BSEd (Hist.), 1962–65, MEd (Sch. Admin.); Boston Univ., Media Training, 1965–69, CAGS-Cand. **Orgs.:** MA Assn. for Educ. Media: Pres. (1977–78). AASL. AECT. Natl. Educ. Assn. MA Tchr. Assn. **Honors:** Plymouth Cnty. Educ. Assn., Disting. Srv. Cit., 1976. **Pubns.:** "Accountability: How Effective is Non-Print Instruction," MAECT *Focus* (S., 1975); "Camp Squanto: An Experience in Outdoor Education, 1977" MA State Winner Video Tape (1977). **Activities:** 10; 32 **Addr.:** 288 Forest St., Pembroke, MA 02359.

Curran, George Lally, III (D. 17, 1949, New York, NY) Libn./Supvsr., Bochringer Mannheim Corp., 1980–; Libn., Ctrl. IN Hlth. Syst. Agency, 1977–80; Dir., Hlth. Sci. Lib. and Med. Recs. Dept., Dunn Mem. Hosp., 1976–77; Evening Ref. Libn., Lib. of the Hlth. Sci., Univ. of IL, 1975–76. **Educ.:** Earlham Coll., 1968–72, AB (Psy./Rel.); IN Univ., 1974–75, MLS; Cert. of Med. Libnshp., 1976/77. **Orgs.:** ALA: ACRL; LAMA; LITA. Assn. of Midwest Hlth. Plng. Libs.: Pres. (1979–81); Ctrl. IN Area Lib. Srvs. Athrty.: Bd. of Dir. (1977–); ILL/Ref. Referral Com. (1979–). IN LA: Exec. Com., Ref. Div. (1978–). **Honors:** Beta Phi Mu, 1977. **Pubns.:** Jt. complr., "Selected sources of information in consumer health education", *IL Libs.,* (1976). **Activities:** 12; 17, 24, 34; 56, 80, Hlth. Plng./Pub. Hlth. Admin. **Addr.:** BMC Information Center, Boehringer Mannheim Corporation, 8021 Knue Rd., Indianapolis, IN 46250.

Curry, David S. (Je. 23, 1940, Morristown, NV) Hlth. Sci. Libn., Univ. of IA, 1976–; Engin. & Math. Libn., 1972–75. **Educ.:** Brown Univ., 1957–61, BS (Engin.); Long Island Univ., 1971–72, MLS. **Orgs.:** Med. LA: Midwest Reg. Grp., Exec. Com. (1979–). Midwest Hlth. Sci. Lib. Network: Assembly of Resrc. Libs., Ch. (1978–79); Educ. Com. (1977–). IA LA. Assn. of Acad. Hlth. Sci. Lib. Dir., (1978–). Inst. of Elec. and Electronics Engin.: Cedar Rapids Sect., Stud. Act. Ch., (1973–74); Long Island Sect., Facil. Ch., (1965–66). Unitarian/Universalist Socty., IA City: Brd. of Trustees (1977–); Mem. Com. Mem. (1977–). **Pubns.:** Jt. Auth., "Evaluation of an Approval Plan," *Coll. and Resrch. Libs.* (N. 1978). **Activities:** 1, 12; 17; 80 **Addr.:** 648 S. Lucas St., Iowa City, IA 52240.

Curry, Juanita V. (Ap. 20, 1919, Topeka, KS) Dir., Inst. Srv., Mid-Continent Pub. Lib., 1971–, Subj. Request Spec., 1968–71. **Educ.:** Univ. of MO, Kansas City, 1965–67, BA (Eng.); George Peabody Coll., 1967–68, MLS. **Orgs.:** MO LA: Outrch. RT. MO LA: Pub. Lib. Div. (Secy., 1977–78). Women's Archit. Leag.: Dir. **Activities:** 9; 16, 17, 27 **Addr.:** 5901 Rockhill Rd., Kansas City, MO 64110.

Curtis, Betty J. L. (Ap. 30, 1931, Harrisburg, PA) Libn., Vets. Admin. Med. Ctr., 1972–; Libn., St. Joseph Hosp., Reading, PA, 1971–72; Asst. Lib. Consult., PA State Lib., 1970–71; Libn., Philadelphia Free Lib., 1967–70; Asst. Ref. Libn., Univ. of PA, 1966–67; Bkmobile. Libn., Spec. Srvs., Korea, 1963–64; Libn., St. Joseph Hosp., 1960–63. **Educ.:** Los Angeles City Coll., 1954–56; Millersville State Coll., 1958–61, BS (LS); Drexel Inst., 1964–66, MS (LS); various cont. educ. crs. **Orgs.:** Ctrl. PA Hlth. Scis. LA: Treas. (1977–78). SLA: Nom. Com. (1981). West. Writers of Amer. AAUW. **Honors:** Save the Chld. Fed., Humanitarian Flwshp. Awd., 1969. **Pubns.:** "Mary Harper, R.N.," *Black Hist. Musm. Nsltr.* (Spr. 1976); "Dr. Joanne Spurlock," *Black Hist. Musm. Nsltr.* (Spr. 1976); various articles, reviews. **Activities:** 4, 5; 16, 30, 39; 72, 80, 92 **Addr.:** Library, Veterans Administration Medical Center, Lebanon, PA 17042.

Curtis, George A. (Ja. 16, 1917, Indianapolis, IN) Dir., River Bend Lib. Syst., 1966–; Head of Persnl. & Comnty. Rel., Wayne Cnty. (MI) Lib., 1963–66; Dir., Washtenaw Cnty. (MI) Lib., 1962–63; Dir., LaPorte (IN) Pub. & Cnty. Libs., 1952–62. **Educ.:** Butler Univ., 1935–40, AB (Eng. Sp., Relig.); Univ. of Chicago, 1947–51, BLS, MA (LS). **Orgs.:** ALA. IL LA. **Activities:** 9, 14-Lib. Syst.; 17, 19, 26; 50, 63 **Addr.:** 2503 29th Ave., Rock Island, IL 61201.

Curtis, George H. (D. 2, 1935, Portland, OR) Asst. Dir., Harry S. Truman Lib., 1977–; Sup. Archvst., Eisenhower Lib., 1972–77; Archvst., Center for Polar Archs., 1971–72; Archvst., Office of Pres. Libs., 1969–71. **Educ.:** Portland State Col. (OR), 1954–61, BS (Hist.); American Univ., 1961–64, MA (Hist.); Georgetown Univ., 1964–72, PhD (Hist.). **Orgs.:** SAA. Amer. Hist. Assn.; Org. of Amer. Hist. **Pubns.:** "Americus Vespucius Symmes and the North Greenland Expeditions of Robert E. Peary, 1891–1895," *The American Neptune* (1978); Jt. Auth, "Abilene, Kansas, and the History of World War II," *Military Affairs* (1977). **Activities:** 2, 12; 15, 17, 45; 55, 85 **Addr.:** Harry S. Truman Library, Highway 24 and Delaware, Independence, MO 64050.

Curtis, Ruth V. (O. 20, 1943, Syracuse, NY) Lib./Media Spec.,Dr. Edwin E. Weeks Elem. Sch., 1977–; Lib./Media Spec., Cleveland Sch., 1974–77; Elem. Tchr., Pub. Sch., Syracuse, NY, Stamford, CT, New Rochelle, NY, 1965–68. **Educ.:** Syracuse Univ., 1960–64, BS (Elem. Ed.); Hunter Coll., 1965–67, MS (Elem. Ed.); Syracuse Univ., 1974–77, MLS. **Orgs.:** Beta Phi Mu: VP, Pres.-Elect. Ctrl. NY Media Spec. NY LA. ALA. People Advocating Gifted Educ. Syracuse Tchrs. Assn. Assn. for Supvsn. and Curric. Dev. AECT. **Pubns.:** "Organizing a Nursing Home Library; A How-to Manual," *ERIC* (1980); "What Did You Do in School Today?", Slide/Tape (1978–79). **Activities:** 10; 21, 32 **Addr.:** 119 Woodmancy Ln., Fayetteville, NY 13066.

Cuseo, Allan A. (N. 9, 1940, Rochester, NY) Coord., Media Ctr., Greece Arcadia HS, 1970–; Head Libn., Gates Chili HS, 1965–69; Arts Libn., Rochester Pub. Lib., 1963–65; Visit. Fac., SUNY, Grad. Coll. of Lib. & Info. Srvs., 1970–; Part time Fac., Nazareth Coll. of Rochester, 1975–. **Educ.:** Geneseo State (SUNY), 1959–63, BSLS, 1963–69, MLS; Univ. Coll., Galway, Ireland, 1971. **Orgs.:** ALA. NY LA. Adolescent Lit. Assm. Blackfriars Inc.: Pres. (1975–). Amer. Civil Liberties Un. Natl. Cncl. of Tchrs. of Eng. Natl. Educ. Assn. **Activities:** 10, 11; 32, 48; 55, 74 **Addr.:** 15 Stonewall Ct., Rochester, NY 14615.

Cushing, Helen Grant (Jl. 22, 1896, Houlton, ME) Private Geneal. Work, 1965–; NY Genealogical Soc. Lib., 1964–66; Sub. Ctlgr., Research Libs., The NY Pub. Lib., 1945–60; Catlgr., Ed., The H. W. Wilson Co., 1930–45; Head Cat. Dept., Amer. Lib. in Paris, 1928–29; Cat. Libn., Univ. of NH Lib., 1919–28. **Educ.:** Acadia Univ., Nova Scotia, 1913–17, BA (Mod. Langs.); NY State Lib. Sch., 1917–20, BLS; Univ. of NH, 1923–27. **Orgs.:** ALA: ACRL; Ch., Sub. Headings Com. (1945–46); Pres. NY Reg. Cat. Grp. (1945–46). NH LA: Pres. (1928). **Pubns.:** Ed, *Children's Song Index* (1936); Ed., *Nineteenth Century Readers' Guide* (1945); reviews. **Activities:** 1; 20 **Addr.:** 339 East 58th St., New York, NY 10022.

Cushing, John D. (Ag. 26, 1922, Candia, NH) Libn., MA Hist. Socty., 1960–; Resrch. Asst., Old Sturbridge Vlg., 1958–60; Asst. Prof., Hist., Norwich Univ., 1950–54. **Educ.:** Univ. of NH, 1949, BA (Hist.); Clark Univ., 1960, PhD (Hist.). **Orgs.:** Arch. Adv. Comsn.: Secy. of the Cmwlth. of MA. Supreme Judicial Ct. of MA: Recs. Adv. Bd. Amer. Socty. for Legal Hist.: Pubns. Com., Ch. 10 yrs. **Pubns.:** *The Laws and Liberties of Massachusetts, 1641-1691* (1976); *The First Printed Laws of the North American Colonies* (1980); various articles. **Activities:** 3, 12; 17, 28, 45; 56, 57, 77 **Addr.:** 1154 Boylston St., Boston, MA 02215.

Cushmore, Carole L. (S. 21, 1940, Steubenville, OH) VP./Publshr., BK. Div., R. R. Bowker, 1980–; VP, Mktg., Baker & Taylor, 1975–80; Mgr., Mkt. Dev., R. R. Bowker, 1971–75; Info. Offcr., Free Lib. of Philadelphia, 1969–70; Writer/Prod., WCAU-TV, 1965–69. **Educ.:** Ohio Univ., 1958–62, BFA (Radio-TV); Penn State Univ., 1962–64, MA (Sp.). **Orgs.:** ALA. SLA. Ossining Pub. Lib.: Bd. of Trustees; Ch., Nat'l. Lib. Week (1981–82); Adv. Bd., Ctr. for the BK. (1981–83). **Honors:** YWCA, Women's Achvmt. Awd., 1978. **Pubns.:** "Alternative Careers for Librarians," *Wilson Lib. Bltn.* (F. 1980); "R. R. Bowker: 1872–1972, A Century of Service," *Indian Libn.* (Je. 1972). **Activities:** 6 **Addr.:** P.O. Box 314, Scarborough, NY 10510.

Cuyler, Margery S. (D. 31, 1948, Princeton, NJ) VP, Holiday Hse. Inc., 1974–, Ed.-in-Chief, 1974–80; Ed., Walker and Co., 1972–74; Asst. Ed., Atl. Monthly Press, 1970–72. **Educ.:** Sarah Lawrence Coll., 1966–70, BA. **Orgs.:** Women's Natl. Bk. Assn. Chld. Bk. Cncl.: Bd. (1980–82). Sarah Lawrence Coll.: Lib. Trustee. **Pubns.:** *The All-Around Pumpkin Book* (19–); *Jewish Holidays* (19–); *The Trouble With Soap* (1982); *The All-Around Christmas Book* (1982). **Activities:** 6; 37; 95-Chld. bks. **Addr.:** Holiday House, Inc., 18 E. 53rd St., New York, NY 10022.

Cveljo, Katherine (Je. 30, 1921, Farrell, PA) Assoc. Prof., LS, N. TX State Univ., 1977–; Asst. Prof., LS, Univ. of KY, 1974–77; Assoc. Prof., LS, Univ. of SC, 1970–74; Asst. Prof., LS, Dalhousie Univ., 1969–70; Ref. Libn., Cleveland Pub. Lib., 1965–67; Sci. Dept. Libn., OH State Univ., 1961–65; Sci. and Tech. Ref. Libn., Detroit Pub. Lib., 1959–61. **Educ.:** Univ. of Zagreb, 1947–51, Dip. (Econ.); West. Rsv., Univ., 1958–59, MSLS; Case West. Rsv. Univ., 1965–67, MS (Slavic Lang. Lit.), 1970–75, PhD (LS). **Orgs.:** ALA: ACRL/Slavic and E. European Sect. (Ch., 1974–75), various ofcs.; Lib. Educ. Div., Intl. Lib. Educ. Com. (1975–77). AALS. SLA. ASIS. Various other orgs. World Future Socty. Amer. Assn. Advnc. Slavic Std. Musm. of Mod. Art (NY). Smithsonian Assocs. **Honors:** Beta Phi Mu; Dobro Slovo; N TX State Univ., Fac. Resrch. Grant, 1980–81. Beta Phi Mu, Grant, 1978; other hons. **Pubns.:** "Business Librarianship," *Spec. Libs.* (Ag. 1979); "Special Librarianship in Yugoslavia," *Spec. Libs.* (My.–Je. 1979); "Education for Librarianship in Yugoslavia," *LEADS* (Mr. 1977); "Post-Graduate Education for at Yugoslavia's University of Zagreb," *Spec. Libs.* (F. 1977); various articles. **Activities:** 11, 12; 17, 34, 39; 54, 59, 75 **Addr.:** North Texas State School of Library and Information Sciences, Denton, TX 76201.

Cylke, Frank Kurt (F. 13, 1932, New Haven, CT) Dir., Natl. Lib. Srv. for the Blind and Physically Handcpd., Lib. of Congs., 1973–, Exec. Dir., Fed. Lib. Com., 1970–73; Chief, Lib. and Info. Sci. Resrch., U.S. Ofc. of Educ., 1968–69; Asst. Chief Libn., Providence (RI) Pub. Lib., 1965–68; Head, Ref. Dept., Bus. & Indus. Dept., New Haven Free Pub. Lib., 1962–65; Ref. Asst., Bridgeport Pub. Lib., 1958–62; Libn. and Resident Master, Graham-Eckes Sch., 1957–58. **Educ.:** Univ. of CT, 1949–54, BA (Amer. Lit.); Pratt Inst., 1955–57, MLS; Courses at Georgetown Univ., South. CT State Coll., Fairfield Univ., IBM, American Univ. **Orgs.:** ALA: Intl. Rel. Com. (1972–); FLRT (founder, 1971–). ASIS: Secy. (1974–76); Ch., CISCO, (1974–76). IFLA: RT of Libs. for the Blind, Founder/Ch. (1977–79); Exec. Secy. (1979–81). SLA: Pres., DC Chap. (1975–76). Other orgs. and coms. Amer. Assn. of Workers for the Blind: Prog. Com. (1975); Pubns. Com. (1975–). Civil Srv. Comsn.: Adv. Com., ADP Mgt. Training Ctr. (1969–73). Com. on Scientific and Tech. Info.: Exec. Secy., Panel on Educ. and Training (1968–72); Panel on Lib. Prog. (1968–72). Natl. Rehab. Info. Ctr.: Adv. Bd. (1978–).

Special Subjects/Services: 50. Adult educ.; 51. Advert./Mktg.; 52. Aerosp.; 53. Agric.; 54. Area std.; 55. Arts/Hum.; 56. Autom.; 57. Bibl./Prtg.; 58. Bio. sci.; 59. Bus./Fin.; 60. Chem.; 61. Copyrt.; 62. Documtn.; 63. Educ.; 64. Engin.; 65. Env.; 66. Eth. grps.; 67. Film; 68. Food/Nutr.; 69. Geneal.; 70. Geo.; 71. Geol.; 72. Handcpd.; 73. Hist.; 74. Int. frdm.; 75. Info. sci.; 76. Insr.; 77. Law; 78. Legis.; 79. Math./Comp. sci.; 80. Med.; 81. Metals; 82. Nat. resrcs.; 83. Newsp.; 84. Nuc. sci.; 85. Oral hist.; 86. Petr./Energy; 87. Pharm.; 88. Phys./Astr./Math.; 89. Readg.; 90. Relig.; 91. Sci./Tech.; 92. Soc. sci.; 93. Telecom.; 94. Transp.; 95. (other).

Other orgs. and coms. **Pubns.:** *Library Services for the Blind and Physically Handicapped: An International Approach* (1979); *African Braille Production* (1979); "Library Services to the Blind and Physically Handicapped," *American Library Association Yearbook,* (1976, 1977, 1978, and 1979); "Proposal for International Coordination of Library Service for Blind and Physically Handicapped Individuals", *Leads,* (Je. 1977); Jt. auth., "Information and Communication Devices for Blind and Physically Handicapped Readers," *Bulletin of ASIS* (Ap. 1979); Other articles. **Activities:** 4; 32, 34, 41; 72, 75, 89 **Addr.:** 1032 Harriman St., Great Falls, VA 22066.

Cyr, Helen W. (N. 18, 1926, Oakland, CA) Head, AV Dept., Enoch Pratt Free Lib., 1972–; Dir. of Instr. Media, Oakland Pub. Schs., 1963–71; Libn., Oakland HS, 1960–63; Libn., McChesney Jr. HS, 1954–60. **Educ.:** Univ. of CA, Berkeley, 1945–47, AB (Msc.), 1953–54, BLS 1947–49, Gen. Sec. Cred., 1963–64, Supvs. Cred. **Orgs.:** MD LA: AV Div. (Pres., 1979–80). ALA: ASCLA/Lib. Srv. to the Impaired Elderly Div. (Secy., 1979–80); LITA/AV Util. Com. (Ch., 1979–81). Baltimore Film Forum: VP (1978–81). **Honors:** Encyclopaedia Britannica Educational Corp., 3rd Prize–School Media Award (for Oakland Public Schools), 1971. **Pubns.:** *A Filmography of the Third World* (1976); Contrib., *How to Start an Audiovisual Collection,* (1978); "Why Not the Instant Media Center?", *School Libraries,* (Spring 1971); "Case Studies of Remodeling in California Schools," *Library Buildings for Changing Needs* (1972); "Newberry and Caldecott Awards", *Top of the News,* (Ap. 1973); Other articles, film strips. **Activities:** 9; 27, 32, 46; 67 **Addr.:** Audio-Visual Dept., Enoch Pratt Free Library, 400 Cathedral St., Baltimore, MD 21201.

D

Daane, Jeanette K. (Je. 7, 1929, Fond du Lac, WI) Educ. Srvs. Libn., Mesa Cmnty. Coll., 1975–; Lib. Dir., Scottsdale Cmnty. Coll., 1973–75; Pub. Srvs. Libn., Mesa Cmnty. Coll., 1969–73; Sch. Libn., Tempe Pub. Sch., 1963–68. **Educ.:** Rockford Coll., 1952, BA (Msc.); Indiana Univ. 1955, MS; Univ. of HI, 1968–69, MLS; AZ St. Univ., 1973–79, MA (Hum.). **Orgs.:** ALA. AZ LA: Coll. and Univ. Div., Secy./Treas. (1979–80). SWLA. Delta Kappa Gamma: Secy. (1977). **Activities:** 1; 26, 31, 39 **Addr.:** 2743 S. El Marino, Mesa, AZ 85202.

Dagenais, Michel P. (O. 8, 1949, Ste-Agathe-des-Monts, PQ) Bibtcr. de Réf., Bib. Sci., Univ. Laval, 1974–; Orienteur du Lect., Bib. de la Ville de Montréal, 1973–74. **Educ.:** Loyola Coll., Montreal, 1968–71, BA (Hist.); Univ. of West ON, 1972–73, MLS. **Orgs.:** Can. Assn. for Info. Sci. **Pubns.:** Transl., *Repertoire de Vedèttes-Mitière* (1976). **Activities:** 1, 9; 16, 40; 92 **Addr.:** Bibliothèque Scientifique, Universitè Laval, Quèbec, PQ G1K 7P4 Canada.

Dagnese, Joseph M. (O. 10, 1927, Worcester, MA) Dir. of Lib., AV Ctr., Purdue Univ., 1972–; Asst. Dir. for Tech. Srvs., MA Inst. of Tech., 1966–71; Sci. Libn., 1962–66; Head Acq. Dept., 1960–62; Libn., Nuc. Metals, Inc., 1957–60; Cat., Catholic Univ. of Amer., 1955–57; Lib. Consult., Birla Inst. of Tech., India, 1967. **Educ.:** Boston Coll., 1947–49, BA (Eng.); Catholic Univ. of Amer., 1949–51, MA (Eng.); 1951–52, MLS; Heidelberg Univ., Germany, 1954–55, (Grmn.). **Orgs.:** SLA: Rep. to ARL (1975–78); Bd. of Dir. (1974–77); Secy. to Bd. of Dir. (1975–77); Pres.-Elect (1978–79); Pres. (1979–80); many other com. ARL: Comsn. on Orgs. of Resrc., (1975–77); other Com. **Pubns.:** "SLA, or Specialized Librarians in Academe," *Special Delivery: A Collection of Papers 1974–1977.* (1978); "The Employment of Professionals in Support Positions," *Jnl. of Acad. Libnshp.* (Ja. 1978); "Managing Organizational Change: MRAP as a Vehicle," *Emerging Trends in Library Organization: What Influences Change* (1978); "The Hoosier Way to Synergism," *Spec. Libs.* (Ag. 1976); "MRAP and the Library Director," *Jnl. of Acad. Libnshp.* (Ja. 1976); Many other articles. **Activities:** 1, 12; 17 **Addr.:** Purdue University Libraries, West Lafayette, IN 47907.

Dahl, Edward H. (S. 27, 1945, Chilliwack, BC) Chief, Early Can. Cartography Sect., Natl. Map Coll., Pub. Arch. of Can., 1976–; Head, Can. Sect., 1974–76; Head, Refer. Unit, 1970–74. **Educ.:** Univ. of BC, 1963–68, BA (Hist. and Eng.); Carleton Univ., 1968–69, MA (Hist.). **Orgs.:** Assn. of Can. Archvsts.: Co-ed.; Gen. Ed., *Archivaria,* (1976–1978); Assn. of Can. Map Libs., Proceedings ed., 1973, 1974, 1976; Can. Cartographic Assn.: Ch., Hist. of Cartography Interest Grp. (1979–81). Intl. Socty. for the Hist. of Cartography. **Honors:** Man. Hist. Socty, Margaret McWilliams Medal, 1975. **Pubns.:** Jt.-auth., *La Ville de Quebec, 1800–1850: un inventaire de cartes et plans* (1975); Jt. auth., *Winnipeg in Maps, 1816–1972* (1975); "The Two States of Champlain's Carte Geographique," *Can. Cartographer,* (Jn. 1979); Jt.-auth., "Quebec: Evolution de la ville depuis 1600" (AV) (1976); various other articles and carto-bibliographies. **Activities:** 2; 15, 41, 45; 70 **Addr.:** National Map Collection, Public Archives of Canada, Ottawa, Canada K1A 0N3.

Dahlin, Therrin Carl (Mr. 10, 1947, Bremerton, WA) Head, Circ., Brigham Young Univ. Lib., 1980–, Assoc. Head, Circ., 1979–80, Rsv., Libn., 1978–79, Latin Amer. Catlgr., 1974–78. **Educ.:** Brigham Young Univ., 1970–73, BA (Hist.), 1974, MLS, 1978–79 (Pub. Admin.), 1979– (Higher Educ. Admin.). **Orgs.:** CLSI Natl. Users Grp.: Natl. VP, Pres.-Elect. ALA. SALALM. **Honors:** Phi Kappa Phi; Beta Phi Mu. **Pubns.:** *The Catholic Left in Latin America: A Comprehensive Bibliography* (1981); *Caribbean Religion: A Survey and Bibliography* (1980); "Public Library Services to Chicanos in Utah," *UT Libs.* (Spr. 1977). **Activities:** 1; 17, 22, 32; 54, 56, 75 **Addr.:** 1028 W. 1100 N., Provo, UT 84601.

Dailey, Kazuko M. (D. 12, 1927, Tokyo, Japan) Asst. Univ. Libn. for Tech. Srvs. and Autom., Univ. of CA, Davis, 1976–; Asst. Chief Libn. for Tech. Srvs., City Col. of CUNY, 1972–75; Head, Tech. Prcs. Div., Cleveland State Univ., 1970–72. **Educ.:** Univ. of MO, 1951–53, BA (Pol. Sci.), 1954–55, MA (Hist.); Columbia Univ., 1963–64, MLS. **Orgs.:** ALA. CA LA. **Honors:** Phi Beta Kappa, 1953; Beta Phi Mu, 1964. **Pubns.:** "Cost Implications of Closing the Catalog," *Alternative Cat. Nsltr.* (S. 1978). "RLIN and OCLC–Side by Side: Two Comparisons Studies," *Advances in Lib. Admin. and Org.* (1982). **Activities:** 1; 17, 46 **Addr.:** University of California-Davis, General Library, Davis, CA 95616.

Daily, Jay E. (Jn. 17, 1923, Pikeview, CO) Prof., Univ. of Pittsburgh, 1965–; Lib. Consult., Franklin Bks. Prog., 1962–65; Adv. Libn., Univ. of Mandalas, 1959–62; Consult. Libn., Ofc. of Prime Mnstr. (Rangoon, Burma), 1957–59; Head Libn., Wasner Coll., 1954–55; Admin. Ofc., Amer. Educ. Missn., Korea, 1952–53. **Educ.:** South. CO State Coll., 1942–43; New York Univ., 1949–51, BA (Span.); Columbia Univ., 1951–52, MS, 1955–57, DLS. **Orgs.:** ALA: Policy Resrch. Com. (Ch.); Ethics Com. (Ch., 1975–76); Cat. and Class. Sect. (Exec. Bd., 1967–70). SLA. AALS. AAUP. **Honors:** Repub. of Korea, Hon. Tchr., 1948. **Pubns.:** *Cataloging Phonorecordings for Library Technical Assistants* (1975); *Anatomy of Censorship* (1973); *Organizing Non-Print Collections, A Guide for Librarians* (1972); Jt.-Auth., *Library Cataloging: A Guide to a Basic Course* (1971); Various other bks. and many articles. **Activities:** 11; 15, 20, 30, 44, 46; 74 **Addr.:** School of Library and Information Science, University of Pittsburgh, Pittsburgh, PA 15260.

Dain, Phyllis (N. 29, 1929, NY, NY) Prof. of LS, Columbia Univ., 1977–, Assoc. Prof., 1971–77, Asst. Prof., 1966–71, Lectr., 1961–66, Chief, Med. Cat. Sect., 1958–60, Sr. Catlgr., 1955–58, Catlgr., 1953–55. **Educ.:** Brooklyn Coll., 1946–50, BA (Hist.); Columbia Univ., 1952–53, MS (LS), 1953–57, MA (Hist.), 1957–66, DLS. **Orgs.:** Beta Phi Mu: Nu Chap. (Pres., 1978–79); ALA: LHRT (Pres. 1980–81); Resrch. Forum Series Com. (1979–80); various other ofcs. Jnl. of Lib. Hist.: Adv. Bd. (1976–). Leonia (NJ) Pub. Lib.: Trustees (1976–; Pres., 1979–80). Amer. Hist. Assn. Columbia Univ., Sem. in Amer. Hist. (1978–). Mental Hlth. Mtrls. Ctr., NY: Bd. of Dir. (1972–). **Honors:** Phi Beta Kappa; Cncl. of Lib. Resrcs., Fellow, 1973–74. **Pubns.:** Jt.-Ed., "Libraries and Society: Research and Thought," *Lib. Trends* (Win. 1979); *The New York Public Library: A History of Its Founding and Early Years* (1972); "Outreach in Public Libraries–How New?" *Milestones to the Present,* (1978); "Harry Miller Lydenberg and American Library Resources," *Lib. Qtly.* (O. 1977); Various other articles. **Activities:** 1, 11; 26, 41; 57, 73, 92 **Addr.:** School of Library Service, Columbia University, New York, NY 10027.

Dakan, Norman E. (Tony) (S. 16, 1926, Beaver City, NB) Air Force Libn., U.S. Air Force, 1977–, Asst. Air Force Libn., 1976–77, Base Libn., Hickam AFB, HI, 1975, Base Wing Supervisory Libn., Yokota AFB, Japan, 1971–75, Chief Libn., 1970–71, Base Libn., Hickam AFB, HI, 1968–70, Chief Libn., Kadena AFB, Okinawa, 1966–68; various positions, 1954–66. **Educ.:** Univ. of CA, Berkeley, 1953, BA (Eng.), 1954, BLS. **Orgs.:** ALA: PLA/Armed Forces Libns. Sect., Achvmt. Cit. Awd. (Ch.). SLA. Bexar Cnty LA. **Pubns.:** *PACAF Basic Bibliography: Intelligence* (1958); *PACAF Basic Bibliography: Black Literature* (1971). **Activities:** 4, 12; 34, 35, 36; 52, 56, 74 **Addr.:** HQ AFMPC/MPCSOA, Air Force Library Program, Randolph AFB, TX 78150.

Dalbotten, Mary S. (Ap. 28, 1944, Waseca, MN) Spec., Educ. Media, MN Dept. of Educ., 1972–; Peace Corps Volun., St. Vincent, West Indies, 1970–72; Media Spec., Fern Hill Elem. Sch., 1967–70. **Educ.:** Hamline Univ., 1962–66, BA (Educ., Sp.); Columbia Univ., 1966–67, MS (LS); 1972, Cert. Media Generalist; 1974, Media Supvsr. **Orgs.:** ALA: AASL, Stans. Implementation (1978–80), Cert. of Sch. Media Specs. (1976–78)/Supvsrs. Sect., Pubn. Com. (1973–75); YASD. AASL. AECT. MN Educ. Media Assn. Amer. Cvl. Liberties Un. MN Assn. for Supvsn. and Curric. Dev. Natl. Assn. of State Educ. Media Profs. **Pubns.:** Ed., *Some Essential Learner Outcomes in Educational Media* (1980); "Sexism/Racism Checklist for School Librarians," *UPDATE* (D. 1974); "Capitol Comments," *MN Media* (Sum. 1977); various subj. bibls. **Activities:** 13; 24, 25, 37; 57, 63, 74 **Addr.:** Educational Media Unit, Dept. of Education, 607 Capitol Square Bldg., St. Paul, MN 55101.

Dale, Doris Cruger (Jl. 22, 1927, Madison, WI) Prof. and Mstrs. Prog. Coord., Dept. of Curric., Instr. and Media, South. IL Univ., 1969–; Tchg. Asst., Sch. LS, Columbia Univ., 1966–67; Bus. Libn., North. IL Univ., 1964–66; Ref. Libn., Univ. of WI, Milwaukee, 1962–64; Bus. and Sci. Libn., Rockford (IL) Pub. Lib., 1959–62; Circ. Libn., Appleton (WI) Pub. Lib., 1958–59; Ref. and Branch Libn., Madison (WI) Pub. Lib., 1954–58. **Educ.:** Univ. of WI, 1945–50, BA (Span.), 1952–54, MALS; Columbia Univ., 1966–68, DLS. **Orgs.:** AALS. IL LA. AECT. ALA: ACRL/Cmnty. Jr. Coll. Sect., Bibl. Com. (1977–81); Cat. Chlds. Mtrls. Com. (1977–79); LED/Tchrs. Sect. (Ch., Nom. Com., 1974–75); Amer. Lib. Hist. RT (Nom. Com., 1973–74; Ch., 1978–79); Subscrpn. Bks. Com. (1965–69). Phi Delta Kappa. AAUW. **Honors:** *Jnl. of Lib. Hist.,* Sixth Anl. Awd. Outstan. Mss. of Yr., 1972; Beta Phi Mu. **Pubns.:** *The United Nations Library: Its Origin and Development* (1970); Ed., *Carl H. Milam and the United Nations Library* (1976); *Illinois Library History: A Bibliography* (1976); "A Nineteenth-Century Cameo: Melvil Dewey in 1890," *Jnl. Lib. Hist.* (Win. 1978); "Mastering Library Research Techniques Through Self-Instruction," *Tech. Horizons in Educ.* (N.-D. 1977); many other pubns., reviews. **Activities:** 11; 26; 57, 63, 75 **Addr.:** Department of Curriculum, Instruction and Media, Southern Illinois University, Carbondale, IL 62901.

Dallas, Larayne Joyce (My. 2, 1955, Tuscola, IL) Head Ref. Libn., AR State Univ., 1980–, Ref./Pers. Libn., 1978–80; Asst. Libn., Educ. and Soc. Sci. Lib., 1978. **Educ.:** Univ. of IL, 1973–76, AB (Anthro.); 1976–77, MS (LS). **Orgs.:** N.E. AR LA: Pres. (1980–81). ALA. AR LA: Ref. Div. (Secy., 1979–80), Mem. Com. (1979–80), Schol. Com. (1979–80). AAUW. **Honors:** ALA, JMRT, Olofson Meml. Awd., 1980. **Activities:** 1; 26, 31, 39; 63, 92 **Addr.:** University Library, Box 2040, State University, AR 72467.

Dallett, Anne W. B. (Jl. 7, 1937, Birmingham, AL) Catlgr., Libn. II, Ottawa Pub. Lib., 1977–; Libn. II, Can. Cons. Inst., 1976–77; Libn., Carleton Univ., 1974–75; Asst. Art Libn., Smith Coll., 1965–66. **Educ.:** Mills Coll., 1955–59, BA (Europ. Civ. and Fine Arts); Harvard Univ., 1959–60 (Fine Arts); Univ. of CA, Berkeley, 1965, MLS; Various sems. **Orgs.:** ARLIS/NA. ARLIS/UK. Can LA. Coll. Art Assn. Intl. Cncl. of Mus. **Honors:** Beta Phi Mu. **Pubns.:** Various articles in *ARLIS/NA Nsltr* (1975–76) and *ARLIS/UK Jnl.* (1976). **Activities:** 1, 9; 15, 20; 55 **Addr.:** 45 Pentry Ln., Ottawa, ON K1S 0X1 Canada.

Dalligan, Alice Cook (Ap. 28, 1923, Detroit, MI) Chief, Burton Hist. Col., Detroit Pub. Lib., 1973–, First Asst., 1971–73, Cur. of Mss., 1964–71, Ref. Asst., 1949–64. **Educ.:** Wayne State Univ., 1941–45, BA (Educ.); Univ. of MI, 1946–48, MA (Hist.), 1949–50, MALS; Wayne State Univ., 1964 (Arch. Admin). **Orgs.:** ALA. MI LA. SAA. MI Arch. Assn. Detroit Hist. Socty. Hist. Socty. of MI. Hist. Meml. Socty. of Detroit: Pres. Oakland Cnty. Hist. Socty. **Pubns.:** Contrib., *Dictionary of American Library Biography* (1978); "Detroit's Master Archivist, Clarence M. Burton," *Detroit in Perspective* (1978); "Emily Virginia Mason," *Detroit Hist. Socty. Bltn* (1970). **Activities:** 2, 9; 15, 39, 45; 62, 69, 92 **Addr.:** Burton Historical Collection, Detroit Public Library, 5201 Woodward, Detroit, MI 48202.

Dallman, Glenn R. (Jl. 31, 1927, Oconomowoc, WI) Dir. of Lrng. Resrcs., St. Petersburg Jr. Coll. (Clearwater), 1966–; Dir. of Lib. Srvs., Indian River Cmnty. Coll., 1962–66; Libn., First Asst., Cleveland Heights Pub. Lib., 1961–62. **Educ.:** Northland Coll., 1947–50, BA (Eng.); Univ. of WI, 1953–54, ME (Educ.); Case-Western Reserve Univ., 1960–62, MSLS. **Orgs.:** FL LA: Awds. Com. (1980); Nom. Com. (1979). SELA. ALA: Bldg. and Equipment Com. (1976–79); Stans. Com. (1974–79); Bibl. Com. (1970–75); Nom. Com. (1976); Natl. Educ. Assn., Com. (1971–74). FL Assn. of Cmnty. Colls. **Activities:** 1; 17, 32 **Addr.:** St. Petersburg Junior College, 2465 Drew St., Clearwater, FL 33515.

Dalton, Jack (Mr. 21, 1908, Holland, VA) Lib. Consult., 1978–; Dir., Lib. Dev. Ctr., Columbia Univ., 1970–78, Dean, Sch. of Lib. Srv., 1959–70; Dir., Intl. Rel. Off., ALA, 1956–59; Libn., Univ. of VA, 1950–56. **Educ.:** Univ. of VA, 1927–30, BS (Eng. Lit.), MS (Eng. Lit.); Univ. of MI, 1935–36, (LS); VA Polytech. Isnt., 1924–27 (Chem.Engin.). **Orgs.:** VA LA. SELA. ALA. NY LA. AALS. **Activities:** 1, 11; 15, 17, 31; 55, 63, 75 **Addr.:** 445 Riverside Dr., New York, NY 10027.

Dalton, Phyllis I. (S. 25, 1909, Marietta, KA) Lib. Consult., Self-empl., 1972–; Asst. St. Libn., CA St. Lib., 1957–72, Chief Reader Srvs., 1953–57, Legis. Ref. Libn., 1949–53, Ref. Libn., 1948–49; Div. Libn. Hum., Univ. of NE, 1945–48, Ref. Libn., 1942–45, Circ. Libn., Lincoln (NE) Pub. Lib., 1940–41. **Educ.:** Univ. of NE (Lincoln), 1928–31, BSc (Educ.), 1938–41, MA (Eng. Lit.); Univ. of Denver, 1941–42, BS (LS); Washburn Univ., 1932 (Tchg. Cert.), Sacramento Cmnty. Coll., CA St. Gvt. Cert., 1958. **Orgs.:** ALA: Cncl. (1961–65); AHIL (Pres., 1971–72); ASCLA (Co-Pres., 1978–79); ASLA (Pres., 1961–62); many other coms. CA LA: Pres. (1968–69). Univ. of CA: Adv. Com. Libnshp. (1960–65). Amer. Correct. Assn.: Inst. Lib. Com. (1973–). Natl. Legis. Conf.: Legis. Ref. Com. (Ch., 1963–64). AAUW: many coms. West. Interstate Comsn. Higher Educ.: Adv. Com. Internships (1974–). Many other orgs. **Honors:** Beta Phi Mu, 1958; Exceptional Srv. Awd., ASCLA, 1981; NV LA, Hon. Mem., 1963; Univ. of South. CA, Libraria Sodalitas, 1972. **Pubns.:** "The Library and the Political Process" in *Local Pub. Lib. Admin.* (1980); *Coos County Library Service, Coos County, Oregon* (1979); *Village Library Project (Nome, Alaska): An*

PROFESSIONAL ACTIVITIES: Institutions: 1. Acad. lib.; 2. Arch.; 3. Assn.; 4. Fed./Gvt. lib.; 5. Inst. lib.; 6. Mfr./Suppl.; 7. Milit. lib.; 8. Musm.; 9. Pub. lib.; 10. Sch. lib.; 11. Sch. of lib. sci.; 12. Spec. lib.; 13. State lib.; 14. (other). **Functions/Activities:** 15. Acq./Col. dev.; 16. Adult srvs.; 17. Admin.; 18. Apprais.; 19. Archit./Bldgs.; 20. Cat./Class.; 21. Chld. srvs.; 22. Circ.; 23. Cons./Pres.; 24. Consult.; 25. Cont. ed.; 26. Educ. lib. sci.; 27. Ext. srvs.; 28. Fund/Grants; 29. Gvt. pubs.; 30. Indx./Abs.; 31. Instr. lib. use; 32. Media srvs.; 33. Micro.; 34. Netwks./Coop.; 35. Persnl.; 36. PR; 37. Publshg.; 38. Recs. mgt.; 39. Ref. srvs.; 40. Repro.; 41. Resrch.; 42. Review.; 43. Secur.; 44. Serials; 45. Spec. col.; 46. Tech. srvs.; 47. Trustees/Bds.; 48. YA srvs.; 49. (other).

Evaluation (1979); "Health and Rehabilitative Library Services," *ALA Yrbk.* (1980); "Health and Rehabilitative Library Services Division," *ALA Yrbk* (1979); many other pubns. **Activities:** 9, 13; 17, 24, 34; 72, 74, 78 **Addr.:** 850 East Desert Inn Rd. #1101, Las Vegas, NV 89109.

Daly, Jay (O. 5, 1946, Boston, MA) Libn., Lincoln (MA) Pub. Lib., 1979–; Branch Dir., Cambridge Pub. Lib., 1975–79; Adult & YA Srvs. Libn., Roslindale Branch, Boston Pub. Lib., 1971–75. **Educ.:** Coll. of the Holy Cross, 1964–68, AB (Eng.); Simmons Coll., 1971–74, MSLS. **Orgs.:** ALA: Com. on Instr. in the Use of Libs. (1981). MA LA. **Pubns.:** *WALLS* (1980); "Dracula Meats the Card Catalog," (Videotape) (1975); Reviews. **Activities:** 9; 17, 31, 48 **Addr.:** Lincoln Public Library, Lincoln, MA 01773.

Daly, Rev. Simeon P., O.S.B. (My. 9, 1922, Detroit, MI) Libn., St. Meinrad Sch. of Theo., St. Meinrad Col., 1951–. **Educ.:** St. Meinrad Coll., 1941–45, BA (Phil.); Catholic Univ. of Amer., 1948–49, STL (Theo.); 1950–51, MSLS. **Orgs.:** ATLA: Pres. (1979–81). Four Rivers Area Lib. Srvs. Athrty.: Pres. (1974–75). Cath. LA: Coll. and Univ. Sec./Board mem. (1974–76). **Activities:** 1, School of Theology; 15, 17, 34; 90 **Addr.:** Archabbey Library, St. Meinrad, IN 47577.

Damico, James A. (My. 22, 1932, Syracuse, NY) Dir., Cook Meml. Lib., Univ. of South. MS, 1981–; Assoc. Univ. Libn., Rice Univ., 1977–81; Head, Ref./Info. Srvs., Brown Univ., 1975–77, Sci. Libn., 1972–75; Head of Ref./Syst. Spec., Univ. of Dayton, 1968–72. **Educ.:** Post Coll., 1955–59, BS (Bus. Admin.); Rutgers Univ., 1959–61, MLS. **Orgs.:** ALA. SLA: Gvt. Info. Srvs. Com. (Ch., 1969–71). TX LA. **Activities:** 1; 17; 50, 91 **Addr.:** Cook Memorial Library, University of Southern Mississippi, Southern Station Box 5053, Hattiesburg, MS 39406-5053.

Damkoehler, Esther (Ag. 22, 1911, Milwaukee, WI) Libn., Hope Luth. Church, 1962–. **Educ.:** Univ. of UT, 1980–81 (Church Libnshp.). **Orgs.:** Natl. Luth. Church LA: VP (1980–81); Pres. (1981); Milwaukee Chap., Bd. (1981), VP, Pres. **Addr.:** Hope Lutheran Church Library, 1115 N. 35 St., Milwaukee, WI 53308-2899.

Dance, James C. (My. 30, 1929, Knoxville, TN) Coord., PR, Detroit Pub. Lib., 1955–, Asst. Coord., Bk. Sel., 1963–68, Asst. Coord., Cmnty. and Grp. Srv., 1956–63, Press Rel. Ofcr., 1955–56; Psy. Dept. Libn., Columbia Univ., 1953–55. **Educ.:** Maryville Coll., 1947–51, BA (Eng.); Columbia Univ., 1951–53, MS (LS). **Orgs.:** ALA. MI LA. Adult Educ. Assn. of MI. **Honors:** D.P.L. Staff Meml. & Flwshp. Awd., 1966. **Pubns.:** *Public Relations for the Smaller Library* (1979); "Culture in Detroit Takes No Back Seat," *Lib. Jnl.* (My. 15, 1977). **Activities:** 9; 36, 37 **Addr.:** Detroit Public Library, 5201 Woodward Ave., Detroit, MI 48202.

Dane, William J. (My. 8, 1926, Concord, NH) Supvsg. Libn., Art and Msc. Dept., Newark Pub. Lib., 1967–. **Educ.:** Univ. of NH, 1947, BA; Drexel Inst., 1951, MLS; Sorbonne, Diploma, 1950; Attingham Pk. Sch., 1967. **Orgs.:** ARLIS/NA. Vict. Socty. in Amer.: Bd. Mem. (1974–). Grolier Club: Exhibits Com. (1976–). **Pubns.:** *Picture Collection Subject Headings.* (1968); *150 Years of Graphic Art in New Jersey* (1970); *Contemporary Trends in Art: 1948–1968. A Bibliography* (1971); "Organizational Patterns in Public Libraries," *Lib. Trends.* (Ja. 1975). **Activities:** 9, 12; 32, 34, 45; 55, 95-Picutres, Film Print Collection. **Addr.:** Art & Music Department, Newark Public Library, 5 Washington St., Newark, NJ 07101.

Danford, Ardath A. (F. 11, 1930, Lima OH) Dir., Toledo-Lucas Cnty. Pub. Lib., 1977–; Asst. Dir., Toledo-Lucas Cnty. Pub. Lib., 1971–77; Dir., Way Pub. Lib., 1960–70; Head, Tech. Srvs., Lima Pub. Lib., 1956–60. **Educ.:** FL State Univ., 1947–51, BA (LS); 1951–52, MA (LS). **Orgs.:** ALA. OH LA: Pres. (1973–74). OH Lib. Foundation: Dir. (1979–83). OHIONET: Dir. (1978–80). Leag. of Women Voters. Zonta Club of Toledo: Pres. (1975–76). **Honors:** Women in Comm., Headliner Awd., 1978; Amer. Bus. Women's Assn., Boss of the Year Awd., 1978. **Pubns.:** *The Perrysburg Story* (1966). **Activities:** 9; 16, 17 **Addr.:** Toledo-Lucas County Public Library, 325 Michigan St., Toledo, OH 43624.

Danford, Helen C. (D. 4, 1914, Cleveland, OH) Univ. Libn., Head of Mono. Cat., FL State Univ., 1972–; Libn., Sch. of Lib. Sci., 1958–72; Tchr., Miss Daugherty's Prep. Sch., 1936–37. **Educ.:** Univ. of Cincinnati, 1932–36, BS (Hlth./Ph.Ed); FL State Univ., 1956–58, MSLS. **Orgs.:** ALA. SE LA. FL LA. **Honors:** Beta Phi Mu, 1958; Kappa Delta Pi. **Activities:** 1; 20, 26 **Addr.:** 925 East Magnolia Dr., Apt. M-8, Tallahassee, FL 32301.

Dang, Charlotte L. (F. 16, 1923, Honolulu, HI) Coord., Lib. Tech. Prog., Leeward Cmnty. Coll., 1970–, Pub. Srv. Libn., 1968–70; Lectr., Lib. Col., Grad. Sch. of Lib. Stud., Univ. of HI, 1968–69; YA Libn., Branch Libn., Adult Srvs. Coord., HI State Lib. Syst., 1959–65; Chld. Libn., Kauai Pub. Lib., 1957–59; YA Asst., Branch Libn., Cleveland Pub. Lib. Syst., 1952–57; Tchr., Soc. Stds., Waimea HS, Kauai, 1949–51. **Educ.:** Univ. of HI, 1940–47, EdB, 1947–48, Cert. (Tchg.); West. Rsrv. Univ., 1951–52, MSLS. **Orgs.:** ALA. HI LA: Dir. (1976–78). HI Assn. of Sch. Libns. Cncl. on Lib./Media Tech. Assts. Pac. Assn. for Comm. and Tech.: Mem. Ch. (1979–80). Delta Kappa Gamma: Lambda Chap. (Secy./Treas., 1979–). **Honors:** HI LA, Tech. and Gen. Srvs. Sect., Most outstanding member, 1979. **Pubns.:** "Palm Trees, Hula Girls...and Libraries," *Colt Nsltr.* (Ap. 1976); "Hey, Look Us Over...," *HI Lib. Jnl.* (D. 1974); "How to Answer Would-be Censors," *HI Lib. Jnl.* (Fall 1963); "Library Development Problems," *HI Lib. Jnl.* (Ap. 1960). **Activities:** 1, 9; 16, 26 **Addr.:** Leeward Community College, 96-045 Ala Ike, Pearl City, HI 96782.

Daniel, Donna Mary (O. 19, 1932, Galion, OH) Libn., Shelby Jr. HS, 1967–; Asst. Libn., OH State Univ., Mansfield Branch, 1966–67; Libn., Madison HS, 1959–66; Tchr., Northridge HS, Dayton, 1957–59; Libn. Galion Jr. and Sr. HS, Galion, 1956–57. **Educ.:** OH Univ., 1952–56, BS (Educ.); West. Rsv. Univ., 1959–64, MSLS. **Orgs.:** OH Assn. Sch. Libns.: N. Ctrl. (Reg. Dir., 1965–67, 1974–76; Mem. Ch., 1968–72). St. Joseph Church Galion. **Activities:** 10; 20, 31; 89 **Addr.:** 406 Fairview Ave., Galion, OH 44833.

Daniel, Evelyn H. (N. 23, 1933, Whitefield, ME) Dean, Sch. of Info. Std., Syracuse Univ., 1981–, Assoc. Prof., 1976–81; Asst. Prof., Univ. of RI, 1974–76; Asst. Prof., Univ. of KY, 1972–74. **Educ.:** Univ. of NC, 1968, AB (Hist.); Univ. of MD, 1969–74, MLS, PhD. **Orgs.:** ALA: Stdg. Com. on Lib. Educ. (Ch., 1979–). ASIS. SLA. Amer. Acad. of Mgt. Amer. Mgt. Assn. **Pubns.:** Jt. auth., *Assessing the Competencies of Media Professionals: A Model for Determining Costs and Effectiveness* (1979); *Media in the Library: A Selected, Annotated Bibliography* (1978); "Evaluation of School Library Media Centers," *The Bookmark* (Spr. 1980); "Measurement and Evaluation," *The ALA Encyc.* (1980). **Activities:** 10, 11; 17, 24, 26 **Addr.:** School of Information Studies, Syracuse University, 113 Euclid Ave., Syracuse, NY 13210.

Daniel, Lynn C. (Jn. 2, 1944, Seattle, WA) Libn., Educ. Dept., Seattle Pub. Lib., 1974–, Libn., 1973–74; Sch. Libn., St. Edward's Semy., 1972–73; Libn., New Orleans Pub. Lib., 1971–72. **Educ.:** WA State Univ., 1962–66, BA (Eng.); Univ. of IL, 1968–69, MLS. **Orgs.:** WA State LA. SLA: Pac. N.W. Chap. **Honors:** Beta Phi Mu. **Pubns.:** *Greater Seattle Area Clubs & Organizations* (Directory) (1979). **Activities:** 9; 16, 25, 29; 50, 63, 92 **Addr.:** Seattle Public Library, Seattle, WA 98104.

Daniells, Edith Laurenda (Je. 28, 1923, Winnipeg, MB) Univ. Archvst., Univ. of BC, 1970–. **Educ.:** Univ. of MB, 1941–44, BA (Psy./Soclgy.), 1944–45, Dip. (Soc. Work); Univ. of BC, 1969–70, BLS, 1973–1976, MLS; Carleton Univ., 1970, Cert. (Arch.). **Orgs.:** Assn. of BC Archvsts.: VP (1975–7; 1980–81); Pres. (1981–82). Assn. of Can. Archvsts.: Copyrt. Com. (Ch., 1972–4); Educ. Com. (1975–). SAA. NW Archvst. Assn. Inc. Fac. Assn. Conf. Univ. Fac. Assn.: BC Pres. (1978–79); VP (1977–78). **Pubns.:** Jt. auth., *More Recreation for the Contemplative Man* (1971); *Further Recreation For the Contemplative Man* (1972); "Archivio Segreto Vaticano," *ABCA Nsltr.* (Mr. 1976); "In Search of Papyrus and Incunabula in Italy," *Amphora* (Sum. 1976); Contrib. *Dictionary of Canadian Biography* (1980); various articles. **Activities:** 1, 2; 45 **Addr.:** Library-Special Collections, 1956 Main Mall, University of British Columbia, Vancouver, BC V6T 1Y3 Canada.

Daniells, Lorna M. (Jy. 13, 1918, Toledo, OH) Biblgphr., Baker Lib., Harvard Univ., 1979–; Head, Ref. Dept., 1969–79; Ref. Libn., 1949–69; Catlgr., 1946–49; Catlgr., Vassar Lib., 1941–46. **Educ.:** Miami Univ., 1936–40, BA (Hist.); Columbia Univ., 1940–41, BS (LS). **Orgs.:** SLA: Adv. Com. (Ch.; 1964–65); Nom. Com. (Ch., 1973–74); Boston Chap., Bylaws Com. (Ch., 1978–), various other ofcs; Bus. and Finance Div., various ofcs. N. Amer. Socty. for Corp. Plng.: Boston Chap., Comm. Com. (1979–). **Honors:** SLA, Prof. Awd., 1978; SLA, Boston Chap.; 1st Chap. Awd. 1977. **Pubns.:** *Business Information Sources* (1976); "A Study of a Business School Library," *Spec. Libs.* (Ap. 1951); Various bibls. for *Harvard Bus. Rev.* **Activities:** 1; 39, 49-Bibl.; 59 **Addr.:** Baker Library, Harvard Business School, Soldiers Field, Boston, MA 02163.

Daniels, Bruce (N. 21, 1947, Nottawa, MI) Deputy Dir., RI Dept. of State Lib. Srvs., 1979–; Asst. Coord., District Srvs., Free Lib. of Philadelphia, 1977–79; Branch Libn., 1973–77; YA Libn., 1971–73. **Educ.:** West. MI Univ., 1966–70, BA (Hist.); Univ. of MI, 1970–71, AMLS. **Orgs.:** RI LA. New Eng. LA. ALA: Cncl. (1980–); Com. on Org. (1980–); Future ALA Structure Com. (1977–1978); YASD: Pres. (1978–1979); VP/Pres.-Elect (1977–1978); Bd. of Dir. (1974–); other Coms. PA LA: Exec. Com. (1977). **Pubns.:** *Look, Listen, Explain: Developing Community Library Services for Young Adults* (1975); "Education for Young Adult Librarians", *Sch. Lib. Jnl.* (S. 1976); "Library Referral Services for Young Adults," *Cath. Lib. World* (N. 1977). **Activities:** 13; 17; 50, 78, 89 **Addr.:** Rhode Island Department of State Library Services, 95 Davis St., Providence, RI 02908.

Daniels, Jerome P. (Mr. 3, 1934, Greensburg, PA) Lib. Dir., Univ. of WI, Platteville, 1970–, Asst. Dir., 1968–69, Acq. Libn., 1965–67; Libn., WI State Hist. Socty., 1960–65. **Educ.:** Univ. of WI, Madison, 1952–57, BS (Sp.), 1959–65, MLS. **Orgs.:** WI LA: (Treas., 1971–73). WI Assn. of Acad. Libns.: (Ch., 1977). ALA. Cncl. of WI Libns.: Ch. (1974–75). **Honors:** Beta Phi Mu; Phi Delta Kappa. **Pubns.:** "View of the NCLIS Nation Program," *WI Lib. Bltn.* (1975); "You can Influence Legislation," (1976); "Politics on the Campus," (1979). **Activities:** 1; 17, 35; 56, 78, 93 **Addr.:** 1125 Hollman St., Platteville, WI 53818.

Daniels, John Edward (Ag. 17, 1932, Buffalo, NY) Dir., Natl. Energy Info. Ctr., US Dept. of Energy, 1978–; Dir., Ofc. of Proj. Accountability and Ctrl., 1977–78; Exec. Ofcr., Fed. Energy Admin., 1977; Prog. Anal., Lib. of Congs., 1975–77; Exec. Ofcr./Assoc. Asst. Admin., Fed. Energy Admin., 1973–75; Spec. Asst. and Spec. Proj. Ofcr., Dept. of Transp., 1970–73; Mgr., Spec. Proj. Staff, Comp. Usage Corp., 1969–70. **Educ.:** Univ. of Notre Dame, 1951–54, AB (Pol. Sci.); George Washington Univ., 1959–63, MBA. Amer. Socty. of Pub. Admin. **Activities:** 4, 12; 29, 32, 34; 75 **Addr.:** National Energy Information Center, Forrestral Building, Dept. of Energy, Washington, DC 20585.

Daniels, Linda Torfin (Ja. 7, 1944, Tacoma, WA) Actg. Dir., Midw. Reg. Lib. Netwk., 1976–. **Educ.:** West WA State Univ., 1962–69, BA (Eng. Educ.); Univ. of WI, 1975, MLS. **Orgs.:** Bibl. Ret. Srvs. User Adv. Bd.: Secy. (1979–80). ALA: RASD/Machine Assisted Ref. Sect. ASIS: Spec. Interest Grps. Lib. Autom., Netwks., Educ. Leag. of Women Voters of Grt. Green Bay. **Pubns.:** "A Matter of Form," *ONLINE Mag.* (O. 1978); "AACRonymania," *Booklegger/Emergency Libn.* (Win. 1976). **Activities:** 1; 25, 34; 56, 93 **Addr.:** MIDLNET, c/o UWGB, Green Bay, WI 54302.

Daniels, Mina H. (Ap. 23, 1927, Trenton, NJ) Asst. Dir., Tech. Srvs., SUNY Albany Lib., 1978–; Head, Cat. Dept., South. IL Univ. Lib., 1974–78; Head, Circ. and Ref., Ctrl. Resrch. Lib., Oak Ridge Natl. Lab., 1972–74; Asst. Prof., Univ. of TN, 1968–72; Catlgr., 1968–72; Head, Serials Cat. Sect., Duke Univ. Lib., 1965–67. **Educ.:** Coll. of Wooster, 1945–49, BA (Eng.); Univ. of NC, 1964–65, MSLS. **Orgs.:** ALA: RTSD, Cat. Norms Disc. Grp. (Ch., 1977–78); Heads of Tech. Srvs. in Medium-sized Resrch. Libs. Disc. Grp. (1978–); LAMA: Middle Mgt. Disc. Grp., Com. on Pubs. (1979–); LITA; ACRL. SUNY LA. Various other orgs. Phi Beta Kappa: Upper Hudson Assn. **Honors:** Beta Phi Mu; Phi Alpha Theta; Delta Phi Alpha; Phi Beta Kappa. **Pubns.:** "Future of the Card Catalog; a Selected Bibliography." *Alternative Cat. Nsltr.* (Jn. 1978). **Activities:** 1; 17, 20, 46; 56, 75 **Addr.:** 65 Point of Woods Dr., Albany, NY 12203.

Daniels, Ronald Backus (Jl. 25, 1935, Jamaica, NY) Head Libn., Henry Pfeiffer Meml. Lib., MacMurray Coll., 1980–; Chief of Pub. Srvs., Bucknell Univ., 1974–80; Asst. Hum. Libn., VA Polytech. Inst., 1972–74, Asst. Acq. Libn. 1968–72; Dist. Ref. Libn., Ealing Pub. Libs. (Eng), 1966–68; Asst. Circ. Libn., Cornell Univ. Libs., 1962–65, Asst. Cat. Libn., 1960–62. **Educ.:** Harvard College, 1953–58, BA (Eng. Lit.); Columbia Univ., 1959–60, MLS; Univ. of Sussex (England), 1965–66, MA. **Orgs.:** ALA. PA LA: W. Branch Chap., Nom. Com. (Ch., 1978), By-Laws Rev. Com. (Ch., 1976–77; Legis. Com. (1979–80). Susquehanna Lib. Coop.: Readers Srvs. Com. (Ch., 1980). C. C. Morris Cricket LA. Rotary. **Activities:** 1; 15, 17, 35; 61, 90 **Addr.:** Henry Pfeiffer Memorial Library, MacMurray College, Jacksonville, IL 62650.

Daniels, Westwell R. (N. 1, 1946, Webster, MA) Sr. Ref. Libn., Harvard Law Sch., 1978–79, 1981–, Ref. Libn., 1979–81, Sr. Acq. Libn., 1977–78; Head of Tech. Srvs., Univ. of Lowell Lib., 1976–77, Ser. Libn., 1974–76. **Educ.:** Fordham Univ., 1964–68, BA (Eng.); Simmons Coll., 1972–74, MLS; Harvard Law Sch., 1969–71, 1979–81 JD; Univ. De Paris, 1966–67, Cert. (Pol. Sci). **Orgs.:** AALL. Law Libns. of New England. **Pubns.:** *Strengthening the Library Profession* (1979); "An Alternative to Library School" *Lib. Jrnl.* (S. 1978); "How To Hire A Library Director" *Jrnl. of Acad. Libnshp.* (S. 1977); "Law On-Line," in *Essays from the New England Academic Libraries Writing Seminar* (1980). **Activities:** 1; 39; 77 **Addr.:** Harvard Law School Library, Langdell Hall, Cambridge, MA 02138.

Dankert, Elizabeth Jane (Je. 28, 1955, Springfield, IL) Circ. Libn., Stetson Meml. Lib., Mercer Univ., 1978–. **Educ.:** Univ. of IL, 1973–77, BA (Art Hist.), 1977–78, MLS. **Orgs.:** GA LA: Ed., "Georgia Chapter Notes". Assn. for the Dev. of Computer-Assisted Instr. Syst. **Activities:** 1; 15, 31, 39; 56, 63 **Addr.:** Stetson Memorial Library, Mercer University, Macon, GA 31207.

Dankert, Philip R. (O. 29, 1935, Hanover, NH) Col. Dev. Libn., Martin P. Catherwood Lib., Cornell Univ., 1980–, Biblgphr., 1970–80, Ref. Libn., 1968–70; Assoc. Acq. Libn., Olin Lib., Cornell Univ., 1967–68. **Educ.:** Colby Coll., 1954–58, BA (Econ.); Simmons Coll., 1961–63, MS (LS). **Orgs.:** SLA: Ed., *Upstate;* NY Chap. Bltn. (1978–); Treas. (1980–). NY LA: Cont. Ed. Com. (1981–). **Activities:** 12; 15, 17, 39; 59, 92 **Addr.:** 32 Dart Dr., Ithaca, NY 14850.

Danko, Diana M. (S. 17, 1925, Barberton, OH) Supvsr. Info. Srvs., PPG Indus., 1975–; Info. Spec., 1972–75; Indxr., 1968–72; Ed., Univ. of Akron, 1966–67; Indxr., Goodyear Tire and Rubber Co., 1965–66; Asst. Libn., Firestone Resrch., 1952–56, Chem., 1948–52. **Educ.:** Heidelberg Coll., 1943–47, BS (Chem., Biol.). **Orgs.:** ASIS.: NORASIS OLUG, (Coord., 1976–77). SLA. Akron Area Biosci. Libs. Amer. Chem. Socty.:

Special Subjects/Services: 50. Adult educ.; 51. Advert./Mktg.; 52. Aerosp.; 53. Agric.; 54. Area std.; 55. Arts/Hum.; 56. Autom.; 57. Bibl./Prtg.; 58. Bio. sci.; 59. Bus./Fin.; 60. Chem.; 61. Copyrt.; 62. Documtn.; 63. Educ.; 64. Engin.; 65. Env.; 66. Eth. grps.; 67. Film; 68. Food/Nutr.; 69. Geneal.; 70. Geo.; 71. Geol.; 72. Handcpd.; 73. Hist.; 74. Int. frdm.; 75. Info. sci.; 76. Insr.; 77. Law; 78. Legis.; 79. Math./Comp. sci.; 80. Med.; 81. Metals; 82. Nat. resrcs.; 83. Newsp.; 84. Nuc. sci.; 85. Oral hist.; 86. Petr./Energy; 87. Pharm.; 88. Phys./Astr./Math.; 89. Readg.; 90. Relig.; 91. Sci./Tech.; 92. Soc. sci.; 93. Telecom.; 94. Transp.; 95. (other).

Akron Sect., Speakers Bur. (Ch. 1980–81). **Pubns.:** Various Internal Pubs. **Activities:** 12; 17, 30, 46; 58, 60, 91 **Addr.:** P.O. Box 31, PPG Industries, Barberton, OH 44203.

Danky, James Philip (O. 3, 1947, Los Angeles, CA) Per. Libn., State Hist. Socty. of WI, 1976–, Order Libn., 1973–76. **Educ.:** Ripon Coll., 1966–70, AB (Hist.); Univ. of WI, 1972–73, MALS. **Orgs.:** ALA. Amer. Hist. Assn. State Hist. Socty of WI. **Honors:** Beta Phi Mu. **Pubns.:** Jt. ed., *Alternative Literature in Libraries: A Handbook* (1979); *Undergrounds* (1974); Jt. cmplr., *Hispanic Americans in the United States* (1979); *Women's History* (1975); Various other monographs. **Activities:** 1; 15, 17, 24; 57, 66, 83 **Addr.:** State Historical Society of Wisconsin Library, 816 State St., Madison, WI 53706.

Danowski, James A. (Ag. 2, 1949, Detroit, MI) Asst. Prof., Univ. of South. CA, Annenberg Sch. of Comms., 1974–, Dir. of Comm. Mgt. Resrch., 1978–; Resrch. Assoc., Soc. Policy Lab., Andrus Grntlgy. Ctr., Univ. of South. CA, 1974–77. **Educ.:** MI State Univ., 1971, BA (Pol. Sci.), 1974, MA (Comm.), 1974, PhD (Comm.). **Orgs.:** ASIS. Intl. Comm. Assn. Assn. for Educ. in Jnlsm. Intl. Network for Soc. Network Anal. **Honors:** Intl. Comm. Assn., Org. Comm. Div., First Place Awd., 1973; Intl. Comm. Assn., Info. Syst. Div., Top Three Paper, 1976. **Pubns.:** "Communication Network Analysis and Social Change: Group Structure and Family Planning in Two Korean Villages," *Communication and Group Transformations for Development,* (1976); "Analyzing Human Communication Networks in Organizations: Applications to Management Problems," *Readings in Managerial Communication,* (1980); "Group Attitude-Belief Uniformity and Connectivity of Organizational Communication Networks for Production, Innovation, and Maintenance Content." *Human Comm. Resrch.* (1980); "Aging and Preference for Interactive Cable Services." *Jnl. of Broadcasting* (1980); Danowski, J., and Sacks, W., "Computer Communications and the Elderly," *Exper. Aging Resrch.* (1980); Other articles. **Activities:** 14-Sch. of Comm.; 41; 75, 92, 93 **Addr.:** Annenberg School of Communications, University of Southern California, Los Angeles, CA 90007.

Dansker, Shirley E. (Ag. 1, 1922, Brooklyn, NY) Dir., Lenox Hill Hosp. Hlth. Sci. Lib., 1968–. **Educ.:** Beaver Coll., 1938–42, BA (Msc.); Columbia Univ., 1967–68, MLS. **Orgs.:** Med. LA. Med. Lib. Ctr. of NY: Libns. Adv. Bd. (1979–). Manhattan/Bronx Hlth. Sci. Libs. Grp. and Cnsrtm.: Ch. (1978–79). **Activities:** 5, 12; 15, 17, 20; 75, 80, 91 **Addr.:** Health Sciences Library, Lenox Hill Hospital, 100 East 77th St., New York, NY 10021.

Danton, J. Periam (Jl. 5, 1908, Palo Alto, CA) Prof., Sch. of Lib. & Info. Stds., Univ. of CA, Berkeley, 1946–; Dean, 1946–61; Visit. Prof., Sch. of Lib. Srv., Columbia Univ., 1946; Libn., Assoc. Prof. of Bibl., Temple Univ., 1936–41; Libn., Assoc. Prof., Colby Coll., 1935–36; Gen. Asst., ALA, 1930–1933. **Educ.:** Oberlin Coll., 1924–28, BA (Grmn.) Univ. of Leipzig, 1925–26; Columbia Univ., 1928–29, BLS; Williams Coll., 1929–30, MA (Grmn.); Univ. of Chicago, 1933–35, PhD (LS). **Orgs.:** ALA: ACRL (Treas., 1938–40); other coms. and ofcs. AALS: Pres. (1949–50). CA LA. **Honors:** Fulbright Resrch. Scholar, 1960–61, 1964–65; Guggenheim Fellow, 1971–72; Berkeley Cit., 1976. **Pubns.:** *Between M.L.S. and Ph.D.: A Study of Sixth-year Specialist Programs in Accredited Library Schools.* (1970); *Book Selection and Collections: A Comparison of German and American University Libraries.* (1963); *The Dimensions of Comparative Librarianship.* (1973); *Index to Festschriften in Librarianship.* (1970); *Jamaica: Library Development.* (1968); Other books, articles, reviews. **Activities:** 1; 15, 26, 41; 54, 63 **Addr.:** School of Library & Information Studies, University of California, Berkeley, CA 94720.

Darby, Jim L. (Jl. 10, 1946, Rome, GA) Dir., Brunswick-Glynn Reg. Lib., 1979–; Assoc. Dir., Tri-County Reg. Lib., 1973–79. **Educ.:** Shorter Coll., 1964–68, BA (Hist.); Atlanta Univ., 1973–74, MS (LS); Univ. of GA, 1969–71, MEd (Soc. Std. Educ.). **Orgs.:** ALA: Pub. Lib. Syst. Conf. Com. (1979); Video Distribution and Exch. Com. (1977–79). GA LA: Exhibits (Ch. 1979–81). SELA. GA Lib. Video Assn. S. GALA. GA Adult Educ. Assn.: Prog. Com. (1976). GA Governor's Conf. On Lib.: Strg. Com., Secy. (1977–79). **Activities:** 9; 17; 93 **Addr.:** Brunswick-Glynn Regional Library, 208 St., Brunswick, GA 31523.

Darden, Sue Eagles (Ag. 13, 1943, Miami, FL) Asst. Lib. Dir., Norfolk Pub. Lib., 1980–; Dir., Stanly Cnty. Pub. Lib., 1976–80, Asst. Lib. Dir., 1973–76; Branch Libn., LA of Portland, OR, 1971–72. **Educ.:** Atl. Christ. Coll., 1963–65, BA (Eng.); Univ. of TX, Austin, 1969–70, MLS; NC Pub. Lib. Cert. **Orgs.:** NC LA: Pub. Lib. Sect., Plng. Cncl. (1975–79), Info. Resrcs. Com. (Ch., 1978–79; Vice-Ch., 1976–77); Lib. Resrcs. Com. (1978–79). ALA. VA LA. SELA. **Pubns.:** Jt. auth., *Key to Progress* (1977). **Activities:** 10; 16, 17; 36 **Addr.:** Norfolk Public Library, 301 E. City Hall Ave., Norfolk, VA 23510.

Darken, Margaret F. (O. 21, 1914, Boston, MA) Trustee, Schlow Lib. (State Coll., PA), 1977–. **Educ.:** Hunter Coll., 1929–33, AB (Chem.); Yale Univ., 1933–36, PhD (Chem.). **Orgs.:** ALA: Trustee Awds. Com. (Ch., 1976–77). ALTA: Action Dev. Com. (1978–80). PA LA: Trustee Div. (Ch., 1973–75); Trustee Manual Com. (1975–77). PA Citizens for Better Libs.: Bd. (1979–). PA Ctl. Dist. Lib. Bd. (1979–). **Honors:** PA LA, Awd. of Merit, 1976. **Pubns.:** Various pubns. in chem. **Activities:** 9; 47 **Addr.:** Box 387-B, R.D. 1, Boalsburg, PA 16827.

Darling, John Blake (Jl. 7, 1930, San Francisco, CA) Libn., Zlgy. Lib., Univ. of NC, 1978–; Instr., Bio., Roanoke Coll., 1963–65. **Educ.:** Univ. of NV, Reno, 1950–54, BS (Bio.); Duke Univ., 1956–59, MA (Bot.); Univ. of NC, 1972–75, MSLS. **Orgs.:** ALA. SLA: Dir., NC Chap., (1979–81). ASIS. SELA. Other orgs. AAAS. Amer. Inst. of Bio. Sci. AAUP. **Honors:** Sigma Xi, 1959. **Activities:** 1; 15, 17, 39; 58, 91 **Addr.:** Zoology Library, University of North Carolina at Chapel Hill, 213 Wilson Hall 046-A, Chapel Hill, NC 27514.

Darling, Louise M. (Ag. 3, 1911, Los Angeles, CA) Libn. Emerita, Biomed. Lib., Univ. of CA, Los Angeles, 1979–; Adj. Prof., Sch. of LS, 1979–, Assoc. Univ. Libn., 1947–79, Lectr., 1961–79; Army Libn., Area Lib. Supvsr., U.S. Army Spec. Srvs., HI, 1944–47; Sci. Ref. Asst., Univ. of CA Lib., Los Angeles, 1941–44. **Educ.:** Univ. of CA, Los Angeles, 1929–33, BA (Bio.); Univ. of CA, Berkeley, 1933–35, MA (Bot.), 1935–36, Cert. (Libnshp.), 1940, Spec. Cert. (Libnshp.). **Orgs.:** Med LA: Bd. of Dir. (1961–62; 1964–65); VP (1962); Pres. (1963–64). ALA: ACRL/Agr. and Br. Scis. Subsect. (Vice Ch., 1967–68; Ch., 1968–69; Exec. Com., 1969–70), Com. on Accred. Visit. Team (1975–78). ASIS. Amer. Assn. for the Hist. of Med.: Cncl. (1961–63; 1969–71). AAAS. **Honors:** Med. LA, Janet Doe Lectr. in Hist. or Phil. of Med. Libnshp., 1973, Marcia C. Noyes Awd., 1974, Fellow 1978. **Pubns.:** Jt. auth., "Evolution of a Processing System in a Large Biomedical Library," *Bltn. of the Med. LA* (Ja. 1976); "Changes in Information Delivery Since 1960 in Health Science Libraries," *Lib. Trends* (Jl. 1974); various med. LS articles. **Activities:** 1, 12; 17, 24, 26; 58, 80 **Addr.:** Biomedical Library, Center for the Health Sciences, University of California, Los Angeles, CA 90024.

Darling, Pamela W. (Ag. 31, 1943, Lake Forest, IL) Prsrvn. Spec., Assn. of Resrch. Libs., 1981–; Head, Prsrvn. Dept., Columbia Univ. Libs., 1974–80; Head, Presrvn. Prog. Offc., NY Pub. Lib., 1973–74; Exec. Asst., Prcs. Dept., Lib. of Congs., 1972; Spec. Rcrt., 1971. **Educ.:** Northwestern Univ., 1965, BA (Eng.); Columbia Univ., 1970–71, MS (LS). **Orgs.:** ALA: Presrvn. of Lib. Mtrls. Com. (Ch., 1975–77; 1981–82); Presrvn. Discuss. Grp. (Ch., 1977–1980); other coms. ATLA: Bd. of Microtext, (1974–). Amer. Inst. for Cons. of Historic & Artistic Works: Assoc. (1978–). **Honors:** ALA; RTSD; Esther J. Piercy Awd., 1979; Beta Phi Mu. **Pubns.:** Ed., "LJ Series on Preservation" *Lib. Jnl.* (My.-S. 1979); "Our Fragile Inheritance: The Challenge of Preserving Library Materials" *ALA Yrbk.* (1978); Other articles. **Activities:** 17, 23, 33 **Addr.:** 560 Riverside Drive, Apt 3E, New York, NY 10027.

Darling, Richard L. (Ja. 19, 1925, Gt. Falls, MT) Dean, Sch. of LS, Columbia Univ., 1970–; Dir., Dept. of Educ. Media, Montgomery Cnty. Pub. Sch. (MD), 1966–70; Asst. Dir., 1965–66; Supvsr. of Libs., 1964–65; Sch. Lib. Spec., US Ofc. of Educ., 1962–64; Coord. of Libs., Livonia (MI) Pub. Schs., 1959–62; Asst. Prof., (Educ.), Univ. of MT, 1956–59. **Educ.:** Univ. of MT, 1943–48, BA (Eng.); 1948–50, MA (Eng.); Univ. of MI, 1951–54, AMLS; 1954–60, PhD (LS). **Orgs.:** ALA: VP (1970–71); Inf. Frdm. Com. (1971–75; Ch., 1971–73); Com. on Accred. (1978–); Cncl. (1963–67; 1971–80); AASL, Pres. (1966–67); Freedom to Read Fndn., Pres. (1974–77). AALS. NY LA. RTSD. Various other coms. **Honors:** Beta Phi Mu; ALA, Dutton-McRae Awd., 1939; Montgomery Cnty. Educ. Assn., Broome Awd., 1969; Univ. of MI, Sch. of LS, Disting. Alum. Awd., 1973. **Pubns.:** *The Rise of Children's Book Reviewing in America* (1968); *Survey of School Library Standards* (1964); *Public School Library Statistics, 1962–63* (1964); various articles. **Activities:** 10, 11; 17, 26; 74 **Addr.:** 560 Riverside Dr., New York, NY 10027.

Dasgupta, Krishna (D. 24, 1939, Calcutta, W. Bengal, India) Asst. Prof., Media Dept., Coord., Tech. Srv. LRC, Worcester State Coll., 1969–; Tech. Srv., Goldfarb Lib., Brandeis Univ., 1963–65. **Educ.:** Calcutta Univ. (India), 1960, MA (Lit.); Simmons Coll., 1968–69, MSLS. **Orgs.:** ALA. New Eng. LA MA LA: Tech. Srv. Sect. (Exec. Bd., 1978–79), Nom. Com. (Ch., 1978–79), Prog. Com. (1978–). Worcester Cnty Media LA. MA Tchrs. Assn. **Pubns.:** "The Impact of Technology on the Role of the Technical Services Librarians of Academia in the USA," *Intl. Lib. Review* (1981); "OCLC–The Last Word in the Present Library Services in the USA," *Annals of Lib. Sci.* (1979); "Indian Libraries: Automation and Documentation in Library Services," *Intl. Lib. Review* (1979). **Activities:** 1, 4; 17, 20, 37; 56, 62 **Addr.:** Worcester State College, Learning Resources Center, 486 Chandler St., Worcester, MA 01602.

Dash, Harriman Harvey (My. 26, 1910, New York, NY) Consult., Info. Sci., Amer. Hosp., Miami, FL, 1976–; Chief Biochem., Miami Heart Inst., 1968–76; Assoc. Biochem., N. Shore Hosp., Manhasset, NY, 1958–67; Consult., Chem. & Engin. Sci., Private Practice, 1947–57. **Educ.:** Coll. of the City of NY, 1928–33, BS (Chem. & Phys.); Brooklyn Polytech. Inst., 1947–53, MS (Macromol. Chem.); Chicago Univ. Med. Sch., 1942–43, Cert. (Lab. Sci.). **Orgs.:** Med. LA. FL Med. Libns. Miami Hlth. Sci. Libs. Cnsrtm. AAAS. Amer. Assn. of Clinical Chem. Amer. Chem. Socty.: Chem. Abs., Abstctr. (1947–77). NY Acad. of Sci. **Honors:** Amer. Chem. Socty., Chem. Abs., Cert. of Merit, 1976. **Pubns.:** "Chromium Depletion in the Pathogenesis of Diabetes and Atherosclerosis," *South. Med. Jnl., 70,* 1449 (1977); "Source Resources-New Developments in Information Retrieval," *Jnl. of Inter-American Med.,* (1979); Other articles and oral presentations. **Activities:** 5; 24, 26, 41; 60, 75, 80 **Addr.:** Box 248267, University of Miami, Coral Gables, FL 33124.

Daub, Albert Walter (Jl. 2, 1931, Hackensack, NJ) Exec. VP, Scarecrow Press, Inc., 1965–; Sales Rep, I.B.M., 1955–65. **Educ.:** Washington and Lee Univ., 1949–53, BA (Hist.); Rutgers Univ., 1968–70, MLS. **Orgs.:** ALA. **Honors:** Beta Phi Mu. **Activities:** 25, 37 **Addr.:** Scarecrow Press, Inc, 52 Liberty St., Metuchen, NJ 08846.

Daugherty, Robert Allen (D. 26, 1945, Tulsa, OK) Circ. Libn., Univ. of IL, Chicago Circle, 1977–; Asst. Head, Circ. Dept., OH State Univ. Libs., 1970–77; Ref. Libn., Battelle Meml. Inst., 1970. **Educ.:** St. Louis Univ., 1963–68, BS (Bio.); Univ. of IL, 1968–70, MS (LS); Exec. Dev. Prog. for Lib. Admin., Miami Univ., 1971. **Orgs.:** ALA: LAMA/Circ. Srvs. Sect., Nom. Com. (1980); Exec. Bd. (1980–82); LITA; ACRL. IL LA. IL ACRL, Bibl. Instr. Com. (1981, 1982). **Pubns.:** "System Statistics from the Library Computer System (LCS) at the University of Illinois", *Lib. Acq.: Practice and Theory,* (Spring 1980); Jt. auth., "Book Losses in Libraries; a pilot opinion survey", ERIC (1979); "Books in Print 1969: An Analysis of Errors," *Amer. Libs.* (O. 1970). **Activities:** 1; 22; 56 **Addr.:** University of Illinois at Chicago Circle, P.O. Box 8198, Chicago, IL 60680.

Daume, Mary Rossiter (Jl. 10, 1913, Detroit, MI) Ed., Monroe Cnty Hist. Socty., 1975–; Ch., Monroe Cnty. Cmnty. Fndn., 1975–79; Dir., Raisin Valley Lib. Syst., 1973–76; Dir., Monroe Cnty Lib., 1963–76, Libn., 1946–63; Prof., Univ. of MI, 1967–68; Prof., Wayne State Univ., Sch. of LS, 1966–68. **Educ.:** Coll. of Wooster, 1930–34, AB (Eng.); Western Rsv., 1934–35, BS (LS). **Orgs.:** ALTA: Fndn. Com. (1979–). MI LA: Pres. (1971–75); HQ and Fin. Com. (1980–); Educ. Fndn. Bd. (1980–); Task Force on the State Lib. (1981–); various coms. ALA: PLA, By Laws Com. (Ch., 1974–76), /Circ. Sect. (Secy., 1972–73); various coms. Monroe Cnty. Cham. of Cmrc. **Pubns.:** *Monroe County Centennial Farms Directory* (1978); Ed., *Exhibit Procedures Manual* (1977); *Cooperation in Library Service, St. Clair County & Port Huron* (1964); *Trinity Episcopal Church, 1831–1956* (1956); various articles. **Activities:** 9, 11; 17, 24, 47; 55, 67, 85 **Addr.:** Monroe County Community Foundation, P.O. Box 862, Monroe, MI 48161.

Daval, Nicola M. (D. 24, 1946, San Francisco, CA) Info. Ofcr., Assn. of Resrch. Libs., 1979–; Actg. Msc. Libn., Univ. of CA, San Diego, 1979; Catlgr., 1973–79. **Educ.:** Univ. of CA, Berkeley, 1964–68, AB (Hum.); 1970–71, AB (Anthr.); 1972–73, MLS. **Orgs.:** ALA. CA LA. DC LA. **Pubns.:** "IFLA/Brussels, an informal independent view" *LEADS* (S. 1977); Ed., *ARL Newsletter* 1979–. **Activities:** 1, 14-Lib. Association; 17, 34, 46 **Addr.:** Association of Research Libraries, 1527 New Hampshire Ave. N.W., Washington, DC 20009.

Davey, Nancy A. (D. 28, 1951, Gary, IN) OCLC/SOLINET Coord., Asst. Head, Cat. Dept., East Carolina Univ., 1978–; Catlgr., Purdue Univ., 1975–78. **Educ.:** IN Univ., 1970–74, BA (Eng.), 1974–75, MLS. **Orgs.:** ALA. NC LA. SELA. IN LA: Mem. Drive (Ch., 1976–78); various other orgs. AAUW: Bd.; Women Com. (Ch., 1976–79). AAUP. Purdue Womens Caucus: VP; Bd. (1976–78). Friends of the East Carolina Lib. **Pubns.:** "Implications of Faculty Status for University Librarians with Special Attention to Tenure," Jnl. of Acad. Libnshp. (My. 1978). **Activities:** 1; 20, 34, 46; 56, 75 **Addr.:** J. Y. Joyner Library, East Carolina University, Greenville, NC 27834.

David, Indra M. (Jn. 4, 1937, Palamcottah, Madras, India) Asst. Dean, Oakland Univ. Lib., 1978–, Asst. to the Dean, 1976–78; Actg. Asst. Dir., Tech. Srvs., Syracuse Univ., 1973–75, Head, Acq. Dept., Syracuse Univ., 1970–73. **Educ.:** Univ. of Madras, 1955–60, BA (Eng., Hon.); Syracuse Univ., 1965–66, MSLS. **Orgs.:** ALA. MI LA. NLA: MI Chap. (VP). **Honors:** Beta Phi Mu. **Pubns.:** Various oral presentations. **Activities:** 1; 15, 17, 35; 54, 56, 75 **Addr.:** University Library, Oakland University, Rochester, MI 48063.

David, Kay Ollerenshaw (F. 22, 1947, St. Louis, MO) Asst. Law Libn., Univ. of OR Law Lib., 1972–81. **Educ.:** Univ. of OR, 1967–69, BA (Eng.), 1971–72, MLS, 1976–79, JD (Law). **Orgs.:** AALL: Com. on Directories (1974); Com. on Indexing of Per. Lit. (1979). **Pubns.:** "How to Perform a Patent Search - A Step-by-Step Guide for the Inventor," *Law Lib. Jnl.* (Win. 1980). **Activities:** 1; 15, 36, 39; 77 **Addr.:** Library, Schwabe, Williamson, Wyatt, Moore, & Roberts, 1200 Standard Plz., Portland, OR 97204.

David, Shirley Hart (O. 21, 1949, Camp LeJeune, NC) Asst. State Law Libn., MN State Law Lib., 1977–, Docum. Libn., 1971–77. **Educ.:** Coll. of St. Catherine, St. Paul, MN, 1967–71, BA (Pol. Sci., LS). **Orgs.:** AALS: Exch. of Dupl. Com. (1978–81);

PROFESSIONAL ACTIVITIES: Institutions: 1. Acad. lib.; 2. Arch.; 3. Assn.; 4. Fed./Gvt. lib.; 5. Inst. lib.; 6. Mfr./Suppl.; 7. Milit. lib.; 8. Musm.; 9. Pub. lib.; 10. Sch. lib.; 11. Sch. of lib. sci.; 12. Spec. lib.; 13. State lib.; 14. (other). **Functions/Activities:** 15. Acq./Col. dev.; 16. Adult srvs.; 17. Admin.; 18. Apprais.; 19. Archit./Bldgs.; 20. Cat./Class.; 21. Chld. srvs.; 22. Circ.; 23. Cons./Pres.; 24. Consult.; 25. Cont. ed.; 26. Educ. lib. sci.; 27. Ext. srvs.; 28. Fund/Grants; 29. Gvt. pubs.; 30. Indx./Abs.; 31. Instr. lib. use; 32. Media srvs.; 33. Micro.; 34. Netwks./Coop.; 35. Persnl.; 36. PR; 37. Publshg.; 38. Recs. mgt.; 39. Ref. srvs.; 40. Repro.; 41. Resrch.; 42. Review.; 43. Secur.; 44. Serials; 45. Spec. col.; 46. Tech. srvs.; 47. Trustees/Bds.; 48. YA srvs.; 49. (other).

State, Cnty., Court Libs. Spec. Interest Grp. (1978–80). MN Assn. Law Libs.: Prog. Com. (1974–75); Secy./Treas. (1975–77); Stats. Com. (1977–79); Cont. Educ. Com. (1979–); Pub. Srvs. Liason Com. (1978–). SLA. MN LA. **Activities:** 13, 14-Law Library; 17, 39; 77 **Addr.:** Minnesota State Law Library, 117 University Ave., St. Paul, MN 55155.

David, Susan Thea (Ap. 3, 1951, New York, NY) Libn., Spec. in Autom. Info. Resrcs., Lib. of Congs., 1980–, Ref. Libn., 1979; Libn., Scarborough Pub. Lib., 1974–78. **Educ.:** NY Univ., 1970–73, BA, cum laude (Eng.); Univ. of MI, 1973–74, AMLS; Cath. Univ., 1979. **Orgs.:** ALA: RASD/Machine-Assisted Ref. Sect. ASIS. DC LA. **Pubns.:** "The Afternoon Library Club," *ON Lib. Review* (1978). **Activities:** 4, 9; 16, 31, 39; 55, 56, 78 **Addr.:** Library of Congress, CRS-AIS LM-218, Washington, DC 20540.

Davidoff, Marcia (N. 21, 1932, NY) Mgr., Tech. Info. Ctr., Naval Trng. Equipment Ctr., 1980–; Dir., Biomed. Lib., Univ. of S. AL, 1976–80; Assoc. Libn., NY St. Lib., and Dir. of the Med. Lib., 1969–76; Med. Libn., S.S. HOPE, 1973; Sr. Libn., NY St. Med. Lib., 1968–69; Med. Libn., Ellis Hosp., 1968–; Asst. Libn. for Extramural Progs., and Asst. Prof. LS, Univ. of NE Coll. of Med., 1967–68; Circ. and Ref. Libn., Upstate Med. Ctr. (Syracuse, NY), 1963–67; Ref. and Circ. Libn., Coll. of Physicians of Philadelphia, 1961–63. Various other positions. **Educ.:** Keuka Coll., 1954, BA, (Soclgy.); St. Univ. of NY, Albany, 1957, MS(LS); Drexel Inst., 1962 (Med. Lib.); Case-Western Reserve Univ., Sch. of Applied Soc. Sci., 1954–55; Med. Lib. Cert., Grade I, 1962; NY St. Permanent Prof. Libn. Cert., 1959. **Orgs.:** Med. LA: South. Chap., Pres. (1980–81); Cert. Com. (1963–68; Ch., 1967–68); Intl. Coop. Com. (1977–); various other coms. Assn. Acad. Hlth. Sci. Dir.: Bd. Mem. (1979–). Biomed. Comm. Netwk.: Bd. (1977–). SLA: By-laws Rev. Pharm. Div. Com. (1963); Hosplty. Com., Mid-Win. Conf. (1969). Various orgs. AAAS. Amer. Pub. Hlth. Assn. Reg. Med. Lib. Prog.: Adv. Bd. (1968–). **Honors:** Univ. of IL Med. Ctr., Inst. Dev. Med. Lib. Admn., 1962. **Activities:** 1, 14-Medical; 17, 24; 80, 95-International Librarianship. **Addr.:** TIC, Bldg. 2068, Naval Training Equipment Center, Orlando, FL 32813.

Davidson, Gail Sonnemann (S. 17, 1952, Watertown, WI) Lib. Prog. Ofcr., Reg. Lib. Consult., U.S. Intl. Comm. Agency, 1980–; Lib. Adv., Amer. Lib., USICA, Bucharest, Romania, 1979–80; Hum. and Msc. Libn., Miami Univ., 1976–78; Msc. and Art Libn., Woonsocket (RI) Harris Pub. Lib., 1975–76. **Educ.:** Lawrence Univ., 1970–74, BA (Msc. Hist.); Univ. of MI, 1974–75, AMLS. **Orgs.:** ALA. Msc. LA. Intl. Assn. of Msc. Libs. Amer. Msc. Ctr. **Activities:** 4; 15, 24, 39; 54, 55 **Addr.:** U.S. International Communication Agency, Foreign Service Center, Rm. 718, 1776 Pennsylvania Ave. NW, Washington, DC 20547.

Davidson, Mary Wallace (Je. 9, 1935, Louisville, KY) Msc. Libn., Wellesley Coll., 1967–; Msc. Libn., Radcliffe Coll., 1964–67; Msc. Spec., Brookline Pub. Lib., 1962–64. **Educ.:** Wellesley Coll., 1953–57, AB (Msc.); Simmons Coll., 1959–62, MS (LS). **Orgs.:** CNLIA: Com. on Prison Libs. (1972–74). Msc. LA: Ch., Lib. Bldgs. & Equipment Com. (1967–70); Mem.-at-large, Bd. of Dir. (1970–72); Ch., Pubn. Com. (1972–75). Msc. LA, New Eng. Chap.: VP (1968–69); Pres. (1969–71). New Eng. Lib. Info. Network: Msc. Users Grp.: Ch. (1979–). Sonneck Socty. **Pubns.:** Jt. auth., *Eighteenth-Century American Secular Music Manuscripts: An Inventory* (1980); "Libraries–U.S.A. (and) Canada," *The New Grove Dictionary of Music and Musicians* (1980); "Time-Space and the Music Library," Msc. LA *Notes* (S. 1970). **Activities:** 1; 15, 17, 18, 20, 24, 41; 55 **Addr.:** Music Library, Wellesley College, Wellesley, MA 02181.

Davidson-Arnott, Frances E. (D. 31, 1946, Winnipeg, MB) Dir., Resrce. Ctr., Centennial Coll. of Appld., 1974–; Tech. Srvs. Libn., 1973–74; Libn., Can. Assn. in Support of the Native People, 1973; Head, Order Dept., on Inst. for Stds. in Educ., 1972–73. **Educ.:** Univ. of Toronto, 1968–69, BA (Eng.); 1969–70, BLS; 1970–74, MLS. **Orgs.:** ON Colls. of Appld. Arts and Tech.: Com. of Libns. (Ch., 1978–80). Can. LA: Non-Prt. Media Com. (Ch., 1974–75). Univ. of Toronto, LS Alum.: Pres. (1980–81). New Dem. Party. **Activities:** 1, 11; 17, 26, 34; 56, 61, 63 **Addr.:** Resource Centre, Centennial College of Applied Arts & Technology, P.O. Box 631 Station A, Scarborough, ON M1K 5E9 Canada.

Davie, Judith Fields (D. 31, 1942, St. Louis, MO) Asst. Prof. of Lib. Sci./Educ. Tech., Univ. of NC/Greensboro, 1981–; Assoc. Prof., Dept. of Educ. Media, Appalachian State Univ., 1979–81; Libn., Jinks Jr. HS (Panama City, FL), 1972–76, Eng. Tchr., 1969–71; Assoc. Libn., Atlanta Pub. Lib., 1966–68. **Educ.:** Birmingham South. Coll., 1960–64, AB (Eng., cum laude); Florida State Univ., 1971–72, MS, 1976–78, PhD (LS). **Orgs.:** AECT. ALA: AASL; Prog. and Implementation Com. (1980–82); ALSC, Toys, Games, Realia Eval. Com. (1979–81). SELA. Various other orgs. Phi Beta Kappa; Phi Kappa Phi; AAUP; Delta Kappa Gamma. **Honors:** Beta Phi Mu. **Pubns.:** "A Survey of School Library Media Resources for Exceptional Children," *FL Media Qtly* (Fall 1981); Jt.-auth., "Back on the Job . . ." and "Monday Morning Bedlam in the Science Library" *In-Basket Simulation Techniques: A Sourcebook* (1978); various other papers. **Activities:** 10, 11; 26, 31, 32; 63, 72, 89 **Addr.:** Department of Library Science/Educational Technology, University of North Carolina/Greensboro, Greensboro, NC 27412.

Davies, Jeanne Brooks (Ap. 15, 1931, Denver, CO) Trustee, Arapahoe Reg. Lib. Dist., 1965–, Pres., 1978–81, VP, 1977–78. **Educ.:** CO State Univ., 1949–52. **Orgs.:** CO LA: Trustee Div. (Pres., 1969). Mt. Plains LA: Pubcty. Com. (1979). ALA: PLA, Bd. (1981–82); ALTA, 2nd VP (1978), 1st VP (1979), Pres. (1980–81). CO State Grange. Master Farm Homemakers. **Addr.:** c/o Arapahoe Regional Library District, 2305 E. Arapahoe Rd., Littleton, CO 80122.

Davies, Nicholas E. (Ja. 25, 1926, Philadelphia, PA) Physician, Piedmont Hosp., Atlanta, 1957–. **Educ.:** Univ. of VA, 1942–49, BA (Med.), 1948–52, MD. **Orgs.:** Natl. Lib. Med.: Bd. of Regents (Ch., 1980–81). Frnds. of the Atlanta Pub. Lib.: Pres. (1975–79); Ch. (1979–80). **Activities:** 4, 9; 17, 28, 47; 80 **Addr.:** Suite 650, 35 Collier Rd., Atlanta, GA 30309.

Davis, Albert H., Jr. (Je. 28, 1916, Boston, MA) Ch. of the Bd., F. W. Faxon Co., 1937–. **Educ.:** Burdett Coll., 1938–39. **Orgs.:** ALA. SLA. New Eng. LA. Library Bldg. Com., Westwood, MA: Ch. **Pubns.:** Publisher, *Bulletin of Bibliography*, Useful Reference Series. **Activities:** 6 **Addr.:** 15 Southwest Pk., Westwood, MA 02090.

Davis, Anne Crosby (Ag. 10, –), Hanover, NH) Mental Hlth. Resrch. Inst. Libn., Univ. of MI, 1979–; Pub. Hlth. Libn., 1968–70; Progmr., Inst. for Soc. Resrch., 1967–68; Libn., Progmr., Natl. Lib. of Med., 1959–67. **Educ.:** Mt. Holyoke Coll., 1948–52, BA (Zlgy.); Columbia Med. Sch., 1952–54, (Med.); Temple Univ., 1955–56, MA (Psy.); Univ. of MI, 1957–58, AMLS; Cert. of Med. Libnshp., 1979. **Orgs.:** SLA: Ed., Telecomm./Comm. Nsltr. (1979–). MI Interorganizational Com. for Cont. Lib. Educ.: Screening Com. (1979–). ASIS. Fac. Women's Club: (Fnd. Plng. Ch. 1978–79). Mt. Holyoke Coll. Alum.: Pres. (1973–77). Model Cities' Park Dev. **Honors:** Beta Phi Mu, 1958; Psy Chi, 1956. **Pubns.:** "Psychiatry for the Nonpsychiatric Physician," *Psychosomatics* (Sum. 1961); Medical Literature and Analysis Retrieval System - Demand Search Module (1966); Oral presentations. **Activities:** 1, 12; 15, 25, 46; 75, 92, 93 **Addr.:** Mental Health Research Institute Library, The University of Michigan, Ann Arbor, MI 48109.

Davis, Barbara M. (D. 23, 1926, Cranston, RI) Mgr., Tech. Info. Ctr., Resrch. and Engin. Div., Cabot Corp., 1981–; Head, Tech. Info. Srvs., Resrch. and Engin. Div., 1968–81, Resrch. Libn., Billerica Tech. Ctr., 1961–68, Res. Libn., Resrch. and Dev. Dept., 1957–61, Asst. Resrch. Libn., Resrch. and Dev. Div., 1948–57. **Educ.:** Brown Univ., 1944–48, BS (Chem.); Simmons Coll., 1954–56, MS (LS); Miami Univ., Exec. Dev. Prog. for Lib. Admins., 1979, Cert. **Orgs.:** Amer. Chem. Socty.: Div. of Chem. Info. (Secy., 1961–65; Cnclr., 1966–68). SLA: Boston Chap. (various ofcs.); Chem. Div. (various ofcs.); Sci.-Tech. Div. (various coms.)/Boston Chap. (various ofcs.). Simmons Coll., LS Alum.: VP (1965–66). **Pubns.:** "Technical Information Service in the Cabot research laboratories," *Am. Documentation* (1958); "Literature of carbon black," *Adv. in Chem.*, Series 78, (1967); "Bookbinding for special libraries is indeed 'special'," *Lib. Scene*, (1978). **Activities:** 12; 15, 20, 39 **Addr.:** Cabot Corp., Technical Information Center, Concord Rd., Billerica, MA 01821.

Davis, Betty A. (O. 10, 1943, Kannapolis, NC) Dialog Mktg. Dir., Lockheed Info. Syst., 1977–; Math-Physics Lib. Dir., Univ. of NC, 1972–77, Hum. Ref. Libn., 1970–71; Pub. Srvs. Libn., New York Pub. Lib., 1966–70. **Educ.:** St. Andrews Coll., 1961–65, BA (Eng.) Univ. of NC (Chapel Hill), 1965–66, MLS, 1974–77, MA (Art Hist.). **Orgs.:** SLA. ASIS. **Pubns.:** "Computed Based Online Access to Scientific & Technical Information," *Socty. of Mech. Engin. CASA Tech. Pap.* (1979); "Use of Computerized Bibliographic Search Services in North Carolina Libraries," *NC Libs.* (Spr. 1977). **Activities:** 1, 6; 17, 26, 39; 55, 75, 91 **Addr.:** DIALOG Marketing, 3460 Hillview Ave., Palo Alto, CA 94304.

Davis, Bonnie Dian (Ja. 16, 1943, Conway, SC) Admin. Libn., Nvl. Explosive Ord. Disposal Tech. Ctr., 1974–; Libn., Braddock, Dunn and McDonald, 1973–74; Tetra Tech, Inc., 1971–73; Insr. Inst. for Hiway Safety, 1971; Asst. Libn., MITRE Corp., 1966–71; Chld. Libn., DC Pub. Lib., 1966; Libn., Marion Jr. HS, 1965–66. **Educ.:** Withrop Coll., 1961–65, BS (LS); Ctrl. MI Univ., 1979–81, MA (Mgt.). **Orgs.:** SLA. ALA. SELA. Cncl. of Navy Sci. and Tech. Libs.: Secy. (1980–82); Trng. Com. (Ch., 1977–). **Pubns.:** Various speeches (1979). **Addr.:** Naval Explosive Ordnance Disposal Technology Center, Indian Head, MD 20640.

Davis, Bonnie Maxwell (N. 2, 1943, Lafayette, IN) Assoc., James E. Rush Assocs., 1981–; Interlib. Coop. Consult., Lincoln Trail Libs. System, 1979–81; Head, Acq. Div., Univ. of AB, 1976–79; Mgr., Col. Dev. and Bibl. Srvs., Univ. Microfilms Intl., 1971–76; Ref. Libn., Univ. of PA, 1969–71. **Educ.:** IN Univ., 1962–66, AB (Comp. Lit.), 1966–67, MALS. **Orgs.:** ASIS: Jnl. (Consult. Ed., 1975–77). ALA. IL LA. **Honors:** Phi Beta Kappa, 1962; Beta Phi Mu, 1967. **Pubns.:** *Guide to Information Sources for Reading* (1971); Jt. auth., "A Computer-Based Procedure for Keyword Indexing of Newspapers," *Jnl. of ASIS* (S./O. 1971); Ed., *ASIS, W. Can. Chap. Proc.* (1977). **Activities:** 1, 13; 15, 17, 24; 56 **Addr.:** 603 W. Church St., Savoy, IL 61874.

Davis, Charles E. (S. 28, 1927, Manhattan, KS) Dir. of Libs., Archvst., S. Missn. Coll., 1968–; Pub. Srv. Libn., Loma Linda Univ., 1966–68; Tchr., Libn., San Pasqual Acad., 1963–66; Tchr., Libn., Bass Meml. Acad., 1961–63; Tchr., Libn., Mt. Pisgah Acad., 1956–1961; Dean of Men, Tchr., Campion Acad., 1955–56; Dean of Men, Tchr., Highland Acad., 1951–55. **Educ.:** Union Coll., 1947–51, BA (Bio.); KS State Univ. 1961, MA (Hist.); Univ. of South. CA, 1967, MSLS. **Orgs.:** ALA. SELA. TN LA. SAA. Amer. Assoc. for State and Lcl. Hist. **Activities:** 1; 15, 17, 45; 73 **Addr.:** McKee Library, Southern Missionary College, Collegedale, TN 37315.

Davis, Charles H. (S. 23, 1938, Tell City, IN) Dean and Prof., Grad. Sch. of Lib. & Info. Sci., Univ. of IL, 1979–; Dean and Prof., Univ. of AB, 1976–79; Assoc. Prof., Univ. of MI, 1971–76; Ass. Prof., Drexel Univ., 1969–71. **Educ.:** IN Univ., 1956–61, BS (Chem.), AM (LS), 1965–79, PhD (LS, Info. Sci.). **Orgs.:** ASIS: IN Chap., Ch. (1968–69); Prog. Content and Papers Sel., 33rd Annual Meeting (1970); Pubns. Com. (1972–76; Cnclr., 1978–81). ALA: LRRT (Strg. Com., 1971–74; Ch., 1978–79); LED (Resrch. Com., Ch., 1973–77). AALS: Resrch. Com. (Ch., 1976–). Can. LA.; Can. Cncl. Lib. Sch. Many other com. and orgs. Assn. Comp. Mach.: AB Chap. (Ch., elect, 1978–). **Honors:** Phi Lambda Upsilon (1959); Beta Phi Mu (1972). **Pubns.:** Jt. auth., *Information Retrieval and Documentation in Chemistry* (1974); *Illustrative Computer Programming for Libraries: Selected Examples for Information Specialists* (1974); Jt. auth., *Guide to Information Science* (1979); "Problems, Real and Imaginary, in Integrating Library and Information Science Curricula," *Info. Rpts. and Bibl.* (1978); "Programming Aptitude as a Function of Undergraduate Major," *Spec. Lib.* (D. 1978). **Addr.:** 410 David Kinley Hall, Graduate School of Library and Information Science, University of Illinois, Urbana, IL 61801.

Davis, Charles Roger (Ag. 9, 1943, Peoria, IL) Biblrgphr., Smith Coll. Lib., 1975–; N. Amer. Biblgphr., Asst. Prof., Univ. of VA Lib., 1972–75. **Educ.:** Yale Univ., 1961–65, BA (Eng., Hon.); Princeton Univ., 1966–71, MA, PhD (Eng.); Columbia Univ., 1971–72, MS (LS). **Orgs.:** ALA: Ralph J. Shaw Awd. for Lib. Lit. (Jury, 1978–79); ACRL, Plng. Com. (1978–); LAMA; RTSD/Resrcs. Sect., Col. Dev. Com. (1979–). Amer. Prtg. Hist. Assn. Bibl. Socty. of Amer. Various other orgs. Assn. of Princeton Grad. Alum.: Governing Bd. (1978–). Fac. Club of Smith Coll.: Secy. (1979–). Mod. Lang. Assn. Assn. of the U.S. Army. Various other orgs. **Pubns.:** *Petrarch's RIME 323 and its Tradition Through Spenser* (1973); "The Compleat Collection Developer," *New Horizons for Acad. Libs.* (1979); "C.D. or not C.D.?," *LJ Spec. Rpt. 11: Coll. Mgt.* (1979); "Towards Comprehensive Love in Spenser's *Shepheardes Calender*," *Spenser and the Middle Ages* (1976); "Tending the Growth of the Collection," *Smith Alum. Qtly.* (Ap. 1976). **Activities:** 1; 15, 24, 37; 55, 57 **Addr.:** Smith College Library, Northampton, MA 01063.

Davis, Debra K. (S. 2, 1952, Lubbock, TX) Mktg. Rep., Source Telecomputing Corp., 1981–; Head, Info. Retr. Srvs. Dept., Bibl. Ctr. for Resrch., 1980–81, Ref. Syst. Spec., 1978–80. **Educ.:** Univ. of TX, Austin, 1971–75, BA (Fr.), 1975–77, MLS. **Orgs.:** ASIS: CO Chap. (Secy./Treas., 1979), Mem. (Ch., 1979–80). Rocky Mtn. OLUG: Secy. (1980); Ch. (1981). ALA: MARS/RASD, Mem.-at-Large, Exec. Com. BRS Tech. Com. **Pubns.:** Ed., *Jnl. of Lib. Hist., Phil. and Comp. Libnshp.: Index to vols. I–XI* (1977). **Activities:** 17, 24, 49-Online Trng. 51. **Addr.:** Source Telecomputing Corporation, 585 So. Xenon Ct., Lakewood, CO 80228.

Davis, Donald Gordon, Jr. (Ag. 15, 1939, San Marcos, TX) Assoc. Prof. (LS), Univ. of TX, 1977–; Asst. Prof. (LS), 1971–77; Head, Spec. Cols. Fresno State Coll., 1966–68; Sr. Ref. Libn., 1964–68. **Educ.:** Univ. of CA, Los Angeles, 1957–61, BA (Hist.); Univ. of CA, Berkeley, 1961–63, MA (Hist.); 1963–64, MLS; Univ. of IL, 1968–72, PhD (LS). **Orgs.:** ALA: LHRT (Ch., 1978–79), Mem. Prom. Task Frc. (1972–75); Ofc. Lib. Ed., Adv. Com. (1971–76); ACRL; RASD, Isadore Gilbert Mudge Citn. Com. (1978–80; Ch., 1979–80), Ref. and Subsc. Bks. Rev. Com. (1974–76). Beta Phi Mu: Beta Eta Chap. (Pres., 1973–75). Christian Libns. Flwshp. AALS: various coms. Various other orgs. Amer. Hist. Assn. Amer. Prtg. Hist. Assn. Amer. Sci. Affil. Assn. for the Bib. of Hist. Various other orgs. **Pubns.:** Ed., *Jnl. of Lib. Hist., Phil. and Comp. Libnshp.* (1976–); Jt. auth., *American Library History: A Bibliography* (1978); Jt. auth., *Reference Books in the Social Sciences and Humanities*, 4th ed. (1977); *The Association of American Library Schools, 1915-1968: An Analytical History* (1974); various other pubns. **Activities:** 1, 11; 26, 39, 45; 55, 57, 73-Hist. **Addr.:** Graduate School of Library Science, The University of Texas at Austin, P.O. Box 7576, University Station, Austin, TX 78712.

Davis, Elisabeth B. (Mr. 13, 1932, Effingham, IL) Bio. Libn., Univ. of IL, 1971–; Asst. Bio. Libn., Univ. of IL, 1969–71; Bacteriologist, MI Dept. of Health, 1956–59. **Educ.:** Univ. of IL, 1950–54, BS (Bacteriology), 1969–70, MLS; Med. LA, Cert., 1976–. **Orgs.:** SLA. ALA. Med. LA. Amer. Inst. of Bio. Sci. **Pubns.:** *Using the Biological Literature* (1980); "Evaluation of PLATO Library Instructional Lessons," Jnl. of Acad. Libnshp.

Special Subjects/Services: 50. Adult educ.; 51. Advert./Mktg.; 52. Aerosp.; 53. Agric.; 54. Area std.; 55. Arts/Hum.; 56. Autom.; 57. Bibl./Prtg.; 58. Bio. sci.; 59. Bus./Fin.; 60. Chem.; 61. Copyrt.; 62. Documtn.; 63. Educ.; 64. Engin.; 65. Env.; 66. Eth. grps.; 67. Film; 68. Food/Nutr.; 69. Geneal.; 70. Geo.; 71. Geol.; 72. Handcpd.; 73. Hist.; 74. Int. frdm.; 75. Info. sci.; 76. Insr.; 77. Law; 78. Legis.; 79. Math./Comp. sci.; 80. Med.; 81. Metals; 82. Nat. resrcs.; 83. Newsp.; 84. Nuc. sci.; 85. Oral hist.; 86. Petr./Energy; 87. Pharm.; 88. Phys./Astr./Math.; 89. Readg.; 90. Relig.; 91. Sci./Tech.; 92. Soc. sci.; 93. Telecom.; 94. Transp.; 95. (other).

(1979); "Current Survey of Reference Sources in Botany," Ref. Srvs. Rev. (1979). **Activities:** 1; 15, 17, 39; 58 **Addr.:** Biology Library, 101 Burrill Hall, University of Illinois, Urbana, IL 61801.

Davis, Emmett A. (My. 31, 1948, Poughkeepsie, NY) Libn., Hennepin Cnty. Lib., 1975–. **Educ.:** SUNY, Albany, 1966–70, BA (Hist.); Univ. of MN, 1970–72, MA (Hist.); 1973–75, MA (LS); Univ. of the Punjab, Lahore, 1974, Cert. (Urdu). **Orgs.:** MN LA. ALA. **Pubns.:** Jt. auth., *Mainstreaming Library Service for Disabled People* (1980); Jt. ed., *Minnesota Library Scene: A Handbook for Library Workers* (1980); Cmplr., *Mediagraphy on Mainstreaming Library Service to Disabled People* (1979). **Activities:** 9; 20, 30, 49-editing; 66, 72, 89 **Addr.:** 1370 Wellesley Ave., St. Paul, MN 55105.

Davis, Francis Raymond (F. 10, 1920, Washington, DC) Pastor, St. Patrick's Church (Corning, NY), 1980–; Pastor, St. Mary's Church (Dansville, NY), 1978–80; Pastor, Our Lady of Lourdes Church (Elmira, NY), 1969–78; Libn. and Fac. Mem., St. Bernard's Semy., 1950–69; Asst. Pastor, St. Ambrose Church (Rochester, NY), 1945–50. **Educ.:** St. Bernard's Semy. and Coll., 1937–41, BA (Phil.); 1941–45 (Theo.); Catholic Univ., 1952–53, MS (LS). **Orgs.:** Catholic LA: Sem. Sect. (Ch., 1959–60). Church and Synagogue LA: Nom. Com. (1978). ALA. NYLA. Many other orgs. Chemung Co. Ofc. for the Aging: Adv. Bd. (1973–78). Elmira and Vicinity Mnstl. Assn.: Secy./Treas. (1970–75). **Honors:** Beta Phi Mu. **Pubns.:** "Post-War Reading List for New Testament Study," *Catholic Lib. World* (D. 1958); Reviews; Various other articles. **Activities:** 1, 12; 90 **Addr.:** St. Patrick's Church, 274 Denison Pkwy. E., Corning, NY 14830.

Davis, Hiram L. (Ap. 10, 1943, St. Joseph, MO) Dir. of Univ. Libs., Univ. of the Pac., 1979–; Head, Coll. Lib., Univ. of CA, Los Angeles, 1976–79; Assoc. Dir. of Libs., Univ. of OK, 1973–76; Dir. of the Com. on Inst. Coop., 1972–73; LS Doct. Prog., Dir. of Lib. Srvs., Kalamazoo Valley Cmnty. Coll., 1969–1970; Head Ref. Libn., Muskingum Coll., 1968–1969; Libn. of Spec. Educ. Instr. Mtrls. Ctr., Univ. of KS, 1967–1968. **Educ.:** MO Valley Coll., 1962–66, BS (Econ./Eng.); KS State Tchrs. Coll., 1966–67, MLS; PhD work, Univ. of MI, 1970–72. **Orgs.:** ALA; ACRL Plng. Com. (1975–1979); RASD, Ad Hoc Com. on Goals (1977–78); LAD, Acad. Task Force (1976). OK LA: Pres.-Elect, Coll. & Univ. Lib. Div. (1975). SWLA: Bibl. Adv. Grp. and Task Force (1975). Beta Phi Mu: Pres.-Elect, Lambda Chap. (1975). **Honors:** Sigma Tau Delta, 1966. **Activities:** 1; 17, 35, 39; 55, 59 **Addr.:** University of the Pacific, Stockton, CA 95207.

Davis, Jacqueline Baas (O. 23, 1934, Kalamazoo, MI) Info. Mgr., Motorola Info. Ctr., 1980–; Asst. Libn., Tracor, Inc., 1978–80; HS Libn., Coll. Cmnty. Sch. Dist., 1964–65; Tchr. and Libn., Pub. Schs., IA and NY, 1955–64. **Educ.:** West. MI Univ., 1955, BS (Eng.); Univ. of IA, 1956–61 (Eng., LS); Univ. of TX, 1978, MLS. **Orgs.:** ALA; SLA. ASIS: Com. on Future of Info. Sci. (1979). TX LA: Com. on Legis. Action (1979). AAAS; AAUW: Schol. Ch. (1979). Assn. of Women in Comp. Austin Pub. Lib. Bd. (1976–). Other orgs. **Activities:** 12 **Addr.:** Motorola Information Center, 3501 Ed. Bluestein Blvd., Austin, TX 78721.

Davis, Jinnie Y. (D. 1, 1945, Sian, China) Asst. Head, Serials Dept., NC State Univ., 1980–; Order Libn., Auburn Univ., 1974–75; Span. Catlgr., Instr. (LS), Ohio State Univ., 1969–73; Asst. Libn., Freer Gallery of Art, 1968–69. **Educ.:** Univ. of MI, 1963–67, AB (Hist.), 1967–68, AMLS; Auburn Univ., 1973–74, MHS (Hisp. Stds.); Inst. Mexicano-Norteamer. de Rel. Cult., 1973, Cert., (Span.); IN Univ., 1976–80, PhD. **Orgs.:** ALA. SELA. NC LA. **Honors:** Beta Phi Mu. **Pubns.:** *Monograph Searching on the OCLC Terminal* (1981); "Factors Affecting Faculty Perceptions of Academic Libraries," *Coll. & Resrch. Libs.* (N. 1979); "Micropublishing in Color: An Answer to the Art Publisher's Dilemma?" *Micro. Rev.* (Sum., 1979). **Activities:** 1; 17, 34, 46 **Addr.:** 914 Tyrell Rd., Raleigh, NC 27609.

Davis, Joyce N. (O. 10, 1941, Marshall, MO) Mgr., Lib. Syst. Support Srvs., Cincinnati Electronics, 1977–; Assoc. Head, Tech. Srvs., Ferguson Lib., 1974–77; Asst. Head, Cat., Univ. of Notre Dame, 1973–74; Head, Cat., CT State Lib., 1970–72; Catlgr., Duke Univ., 1967–70. **Educ.:** William Jewell Coll., 1959–63, BA (Relig.); Univ. of NC, 1965–67, MLS; Duke Univ., 1967–70, MDiv. **Orgs.:** ALA: LAMA; LITA; RTSD/Cat. and Class. Sect., Nom. Com. (1980–81), Subj. Anal. Com. **Activities:** 6; 22, 34, 46; 56, 93 **Addr.:** Cincinnati Electronics, 2630 Glendale-Milford Rd., Cincinnati, OH 45241.

Davis, Linda Morgan (My. 14, 1953, Binghamton, NY) Info. Sci., Norwich-Eaton Pharm., 1978–; Tech. Libn., INA, Corp., 1977–78; Supvsr., Bibl. Srvs., ISI, 1977; Lit. Srchr., 1976–77. **Educ.:** Broome Cmnty. Coll., 1971–73, AA (Lib. Arts); Marywood Coll., 1973–75, BS (Elem. Ed. Libnshp.); Villanova Univ., 1975–76, MLS. **Orgs.:** SLA: Asst. Ed. *Bulletin* Phila. Chap. (1978); Advert. Mgr. *Bulletin* Upstate NY Chap. (1978–80). ASIS. S. Cntrl. Resrch. Lib. Cncl.: Cont. Educ. Rep. **Pubns.:** "Spotlight on–Information Services, Norwich-Eaton Pharmaceuticals," *Upstate NY Chapter SLA Bulletin* (D. 1980); Contrib., *Insurance Lit.* (1978); Reviews. **Activities:** 12; 29, 41; 76, 87, 91 **Addr.:** Norwich-Eaton Pharmaceuticals, P.O. 191, Norwich, NY 13815.

Davis, Lynda Chambers (My. 16, 1945, San Francisco, CA) Actg. Chief Libn., MD Legis. Ref. 1980–; Assoc. Libn., Ref. Supvsr., MD Legis. Ref., 1975–; Asst. Libn., Ref. Dept., East Baton Rouge Parish, 1970–73; Libn., Dyersburg St. Cmnty. Coll., 1969–74. **Educ.:** Univ. of TN (Martin), 1963–67, BS (Hist., Eng.); FL St. Univ., 1968–69 MLS. **Orgs.:** ALA: Gvt. Docs. RT. AALL. MD LA: Int. Frdm. Com. (1979–). St. Agency LA of MD: VP (1979), Pres. (1980). Frdm. to Read Fndn. YWCA. **Activities:** 9, 13; 20, 29, 39; 77, 78, 92 **Addr.:** Department of Legislative Reference, 90 State Cir., Annapolis, MD 21401.

Davis, Marie A. (Je. 29, 1918, Pittsburgh, PA) Deputy Dir., Free Lib. of Philadelphia, 1979–, Assoc. Dir., 1970–79, Coord., Adult and YA Srvs., 1963–70, Coord., Adult Srvs., 1956–63; Dir., PR, Carnegie Lib. of Pittsburgh, 1947–56. **Educ.:** Carnegie Mellon Univ., 1937–41, BS (Soc. Sci.), 1944–45, BS (LS). **Orgs.:** Mstr. Plan Com. for Total Lib. Srv. in PA (1971–73). PA State Lib.: Adv. Com. to Std. Mgt. Info. (1978–79). PA LA: Pres. (1962–63). ALA: Adult Srvs. Div. (Pres., 1968–69); Cncl. (PA Rep., 1968–72); PLA/Metro. Libs. Sect. (Pres., 1978–79); ASCLA/Lib. Srvs. to the Deaf Sect. (1980–81). Various other orgs. Ctr. for Litcy. (Philadelphia). Musm. Cncl. of Philadelphia. Amer. Cvl. Liberties Un. PA Acad. of Fine Arts: Peale Club. **Honors:** PA LA, Disting. Srv. Awd., 1971; Carnegie–Mellon Univ. Alum. Assn., Merit Awd., 1971; PA LA, Cert. of Merit, 1965. **Pubns.:** "Serving the Disadvantaged from the Administrative Viewpoint," *Lib. Trends* (O. 1971); various articles. **Activities:** 9; 16, 17, 48; 50, 72, 74 **Addr.:** The Free Library of Philadelphia, Logan Sq., Philadelphia, PA 19103.

Davis, Martha Harris (F. 14, 1920, Macon, NC) Dir., Rockingham Cnty. Pub. Lib., 1968–; Libn., Reidsville Jr. HS, 1962–68; Instr., Chld. Lit., Meredith Coll., 1952–53; Libn., Hugh Morson HS, 1951–52; Libn., Mary Bayley Pratt Chld. Lib.; Dir., Portsmouth Pub. Lib.; Libn., Wake Cnty. Pub. Lib. **Educ.:** Greensboro Coll., 1936–40, AB (Eng.); Univ. of NC, 1940–41, BS (LS). **Orgs.:** ALA. SELA. NC LA: Pub. Lib. Sect., Ch.; Exec. Bd. NC Cert. Comsn. Various other orgs. NC Piedmont Cncl. of Girl Scouts: Dist. Dir. (1959–60). Greensboro Coll. Alum. Assn.: Pres. (1959–61). Little Gardens Garden Club. Tuesday Afternoon Readg. Club. Various other orgs. **Activities:** 9, 10; 17, 19, 24; 56, 59, 89 **Addr.:** 1610 Country Club Rd., Reidsville, NC 27320.

Davis, Mary Byrd (S. 30, 1936, Cardiff, Wales, UK) Art Libn., Univ. of KY, 1978–; Actg. Head, Acq., 1978; Asst. Libn., Georgetown Coll., 1975–78; Acq. Libn., North. MI Univ., 1974–75. **Educ.:** Agnes Scott Coll., 1954–58, BA (Eng.); Univ. of WI, 1965–72, MA PhD (Eng.); Simmons Coll., 1973–74, MS (LS). **Orgs.:** ALA: ACRL/Coll. Sect., Cont. Educ. Com. (1977–80). Univ. of KY Lib. Assocs.: Managing Ed., *The Kentucky Review* (1979–). KY LA. ARLIS/NA. Mod. Lang. Assn. **Honors:** Phi Beta Kappa; Beta Phi Mu. **Pubns.:** *James Elroy Flecker: A Critical Study,* (1977); "George Sand and the Poetry of Matthew Arnold," *TX Studies in Lit. and Lang.* (Sum. 1977); "Model for a Vendor Study in a Manual or Semi-Automated Acquisitions System," *Lib. Acq.: Practice and Theory* (1979). **Activities:** 1; 15, 17, 39; 55 **Addr.:** Art Library, University of Kentucky Libraries, Lexington, KY 40506.

Davis, Natalia G. (S. 10, 1935, Panama, Rep. of Panama) Dir., El Centro Hispano De Info., Brooklyn Pub. Lib., 1978–; Cmnty. Coord., Bedford-Styuvesant, 1971–78; Libn., 1969–71. **Educ.:** Brooklyn Coll., 1961–69, BA (Lang.); Rutgers Univ., 1969–71, MLS. **Orgs.:** ALA: RASD/Com. on Srvs. to the Spanish-Speaking (1972–76). Reforma. NY LA: Outrch. Com. (1979–); Chld. and YA Sect. (1977–). McNaughton YA Plan: Adv. Bd. (1973–79). Brooklyn Hlth. Educ. Cncl. **Activities:** 9, 12; 17, 39, 49-Span. Lib. Ctr.; 50, 66, 95-Job Info. **Addr.:** El Centro Hispano De Informacion, C/O Williamsburgh Regional Library, Brooklyn Public Library, 240 Division Ave., Brooklyn, NY 11211.

Davis, Ollye Golden (O. 28, 1949, Mobile, AL) Resrch. Libn., South. Ctr. for Std. in Pub. Policy, Clark Coll., 1977–; Asst. Cur., Spec. Cols., Atlanta Pub. Lib., 1977, Libn., Gvt. Docum. Col., 1974–77, Libn., Bus. and Sci. Dept., 1972–74; Adult Srvs./Acad. Libn., Jordon Thomas Lib., Morris Brown Coll., 1972; Info. Spec., Cmnty. Cncl. of the Atlanta Area, Inc., 1971–72. **Educ.:** Clark Coll., 1967–71, BA (Eng.); Atlanta Univ., 1971–73, MLS. **Orgs.:** SLA: Fac. Adv., Student Chap. S. Atl. (1978–). GA LA: Site Sel. Com. (1979). ALA: ACRL/Bibl. Instr. Sect. (1979). Metro. Atlanta LA: Mem. Com. (Ch., 1972–73). Atlanta Urban Bus. and Prof. Women's Club: Legis. Ch. (1979–80). Atlanta Urban Leag. Atlanta YWCA. **Pubns.:** *Public Policy Studies in the South: A Research Guide* (1981); "A History of South Georgia" slide (1977); *Urban Development Strategies: Transportation* (1978); *Interracial Adoption in America* bibl. (1973). **Activities:** 5, 12; 30, 41; 92 **Addr.:** 1891 Idlewood Dr., East Point, GA 30344.

Davis, Richard A. (Ap. 26, 1923, Pasadena, CA) Prof. (LS), Rosary Coll., 1971–; Dir., Midwest Reg. Med. Lib., 1968–72; Adj. Prof. (LS), Univ. of Chicago, 1966–72; Prof. (LS), Drexel Univ., 1960–68; Consult., US Ofc. of Educ., 1966–67; Libn., Labs. for Appld. Sci., Univ. of Chicago, 1959–60; Ref. Libn., John Coerar Lib., 1956–59. **Educ.:** Pasadena Coll., 1939–42, 1946, AA; Univ. of CA, Berkeley, 1946–47; Northwest. Univ., 1947–48; Univ. of Chicago, 1954–58, MA. **Orgs.:** Catholic LA: North. IL Unit (Pres., 1978–80). Med. LA: Treas., (1970–72). ASIS. ALA. Various other orgs. U.S. Naval Inst. **Honors:** Phi Beta Kappa. **Pubns.:** *Thesaurus of Library and Information Science* (1977); *Marysville Public Library: A Case Study* (1976); "A Curriculum in Indexing and Abstracting," *The Indexer* (O., 1976); "Goals," *IL Libs.* (Ja., 1975); Various other articles. **Activities:** 11, 12; 17, 30, 39; 58, 64, 91 **Addr.:** 142 Park Ave., River Forest, IL 60305.

Davis, Russell Leonard (O. 25, 1924, Blackfoot, ID) Dir., State Lib. of UT, 1957–; Prof. of LS, UT State Univ., 1954–57, Circ. Libn., 1954–57, Engin. Libn., 1953–54. **Educ.:** Weber Jr. Coll., 1948–50; UT State Univ., 1950–52, BS (Pol. Sci.); Univ. of MI, 1952–53, AMLS. **Orgs.:** UT LA: Pres. (1963–65). Mt. Plains LA: Pres. (1960–61). **Activities:** 13; 17 **Addr.:** Utah State Library, 2150 South 300 West, Suite 16, Salt Lake City, UT 84115.*

Davis, Sally A. (F. 28, 1929, Chicago, IL) Libn., Lib. Sch., Univ. of WI, 1978–; Dir. of Sch. Libs., Oconomowoc (WI) Pub. Schs., 1958–78; Libn., Skokie Jr. HS, 1954–58; Tchr., Edgar (WI) HS, 1951–53. **Educ.:** Carroll Coll., 1947–51, BA (Hist.); Univ. of WI, Madison, 1953–54, MA (LS); 1973–75, PhD (Educ. Admin.). **Orgs.:** ALA: Chap. Cnclr. (1971–75). WI LA: Pres.-elect, Pres., Past Pres. (1969–71); Secy. (1965); Dir. (1966–69). State Adv. Com., Elem & Secondary Educ. Act, Title IV. **Honors:** WI Assn. of Sch. Libns., WI Sch. Libn. of the Yr., 1974. **Pubns.:** "Balanced School Library Service: Planning at the School System Level," *WI Lib. Bltn.* (S., 1968); "The Role of the School Library Media Director" *News for You* (Sum., 1976); "The Wisconsin Library Association" *Encyc. of Lib. and Info. Sci.*. **Activities:** 10, 11; 26, 34, 41; 74, 75, 93 **Addr.:** Library School, University of Wisconsin, 600 N. Park St., Madison, WI 53706.

Davis, Willard G. (N. 25, 1945, Mt. Pleasant, MI) Head, Circ. Srvs., Univ. of MI Lib., 1973–; Asst. Head, Circ., 1972–73, Head, Cat. Info., 1971–72; Head, Cat. Dept., Univ. of MI, Dearborn, 1970–71; Ref. Libn., Congsnl. Resrch. Div., Lib. of Congs., 1969–70. **Educ.:** Univ. of MI, 1963–64; Ohio State Univ., 1965–67, BA (Ling.); Univ. of MI, 1968–69, AMLS. **Orgs.:** ALA: Lib. Admin. Div., Bldgs. and Equipment Com. (1971–75); RTSD, Subj. Analysis Com. (1973–75). **Activities:** 1, 4; 17, 22, 46; 56 **Addr.:** 535 6th St., Ann Arbor, MI 48103.

Davish, William Martin (F. 1, 1913, Philadelphia, PA) Prof. of Theo., Assoc. Dean, Loyola Coll. (Baltimore) 1976–, Prof. of Theo., Secy. Dept., 1964–76, Assoc. Prof., Ch. Dept., 1957–64, Asst. Prof., Libn., 1949–64. **Educ.:** Georgetown Univ., 1933–39, AB (Educ.); Woodstock Coll., 1938–47, MA (Educ.), PHL (Phil.), STL (Theo.); Cath. Univ., 1946–48 MLS. Inst. Catholique, Paris, 1961–62; Oxford Univ., 1977, (Ethics Sem.). **Orgs.:** ALA: Intl. Rel. RT (1951–53). Catholic LA: various coms. Assn. Cont. Higher Educ.: Bd. of Dir. (1955–57); Prog. Ch. (1954–56). Amer. Cath. Theo. Socty. Coll. Theo. Socty. Amer. Conf. of Acad. Deans. East. Assn. of Coll. Deans and Advs. of Students. **Honors:** Loyola Coll., Bene Merenti Awd., 1978; Natl. Forum of Relig. Educ., Outstan. Tchr., 1976; Loyola Coll., Evening Div. Medal, 1974; Loyola Coll., Pres. Medal, 1972. **Pubns.:** *Woodstock College 1869–1944* (1944); *St. Thomas on Contrition and Sin* (1946); "Jansenism," *Corpus Dict. of West. Churches;* "Jesus Christ, Example of," *New Cath. Encyc.;* "Lateran Councils," *Collier's Encycl.;* other pubns. in relig. **Activities:** 1; 15, 17, 39; 50, 90, 95-Ethics. **Addr.:** Loyola College, Baltimore, MD 21210.

Davy, Edgar W. (Jy. 19, 1927, Newton, MA) Head, Dewey Lib., MA Inst. of Tech., 1972–; Biblgphr. for Econ. Dev., Princeton Univ., 1969–72; Intl. Credit and Mktg. Ofcr., Chase Manhattan Bank, 1958–68; Intelligence Ofcr., U.S. Air Frc., Europe, 1952–55. **Educ.:** Univ. of South CA, 1947–51, BA (Intl. Rel.); Rutgers Univ., 1968–69, MLS; Amer. Grad. Sch. for Intl. Mgt. (AZ), 1956–57, BFT, (Intl. Mgt.), **Orgs.:** ALA: ACRL. SLA. **Activities:** 1; 17, 24, 39; 59, 78, 92 **Addr.:** Dewey Library, E53–100, Massachusetts Institute of Technology, Cambridge, MA 02139.

Dawkins, Diantha Dee (O. 6, 1942, McCamey, TX) Libn., Media Coord., Lee Freshman HS, 1973–; Asst. Libn./Media Coord., Midland HS, 1970–73; Asst. Libn., R. E. Lee HS, 1966–70. **Educ.:** Univ. of TX, 1961–66, BA (Hist.), 1969–71, MLS. **Orgs.:** TX Assn. of Sch. Libns.: Dist. 18, Vice–Ch. (1973), Ch. (1974); Vice–Ch., Wkshp. Ch. (1978–79), State Ch. (1979–80); State Bd. (1978–81); various coms. TX LA: Constn. Com. (Interim Mem., 1971); Rcrt. Com. (Ch., 1975); JMRT; Dist. 9; various coms. ALA: JMRT; AASL; LIRT. CSLA. Various other orgs. TX State Tchrs. Assn.: State Exec. Com. (1979–80). TX Classrm. Tchrs. Assn.: Midland Treas. (1976–77), Vice–Ch. (1977–78), Ch.-Elect (1978–79), Ch. (1979–80), Bd. (1980–84); various coms. Meml. Christ. Church. Natl. Educ. Assn. **Pubns.:** *Media Matters* (Win. 1980); *Media Matters* (Fall 1979). **Activities:** 10; 15, 17, 20 **Addr.:** 501 W. Louisiana #203, Midland, TX 79701.

Dawson, Debra Ann (Mr. 3, 1949, Montgomery, WV) Mgr., Online Srvs., Congsnl. Info. Srv., 1979–; Mgr., Training, SDC Srch. Srv., 1977–79; Info. Spec., West. Resrch. Application Ctr., 1975–77. **Educ.:** WV Univ., 1967–71, AB (Eng.); Univ. of

PROFESSIONAL ACTIVITIES: Institutions: 1. Acad. lib.; 2. Arch.; 3. Assn.; 4. Fed./Gvt. lib.; 5. Inst. lib.; 6. Mfr./Suppl.; 7. Milit. lib.; 8. Musm.; 9. Pub. lib.; 10. Sch. lib.; 11. Sch. of lib. sci.; 12. Spec. lib.; 13. State lib.; 14. (other). **Functions/Activities:** 15. Acq./Col. dev.; 16. Adult srvs.; 17. Admin.; 18. Apprais.; 19. Archit./Bldgs.; 20. Cat./Class.; 21. Chld. srvs.; 22. Circ.; 23. Cons./Pres.; 24. Consult.; 25. Cont. ed.; 26. Educ. lib. sci.; 27. Ext. srvs.; 28. Fund/Grants; 29. Gvt. pubs.; 30. Indx./Abs.; 31. Instr. lib. use; 32. Media srvs.; 33. Micro.; 34. Netwks./Coop.; 35. Persnl.; 36. PR; 37. Publshg.; 38. Recs. mgt.; 39. Ref. srvs.; 40. Repro.; 41. Resrch.; 42. Review.; 43. Secur.; 44. Serials; 45. Spec. col.; 46. Tech. srvs.; 47. Trustees/Bds.; 48. YA srvs.; 49. (other).

South. CA, 1974–75, MSLS. **Orgs.:** SLA. ASIS: Ch., South. CA Chap. (1980); Pubcty. Com. Co-Ch., 1980 ASIS Conf. South. CA OLUG. **Activities:** 6; 25, 29, 39; 51, 59, 78 **Addr.:** 7638 Westlake Terr., Bethesda, MD 20817.

Dawson, Lawrence (Mr. 30, 1941, New York, NY) Consult., 1980–; Syst. Plng. Consult., AMMS, Div. of RTI 1980–; Spec. Asst. to Dir., Rockford (IL) Pub. Lib. 1975–80, Supvsr. Tech. Pres., 1971–75, First Asst., Bus., Sci., Tech. Div., 1969–71; Asst. Libn., Highland Cmnty. Coll., 1968–69; Asst. Libn., Auburn (NY) Cmnty. Coll., 1966–68. **Educ.:** Shimer Coll., 1963, AB (Hum.); Syracuse Univ., 1966, MLS. **Orgs.:** ALA. IL LA: Auto. Com. (1972–73); Intl. Frdm. Com. (1974). LARC Assn. ILLINET Data Base Interconnect Proj.: (1975–77). Others orgs. IL. St. Lib.: Circ. Syst. Com. (1974–75); Auto Adv. Cncl. (1974–75). **Activities:** 9; 22, 32, 49-Comp. Systs.; 56 **Addr.:** Rt #1, S. Heitter Rd., Pearl City, IL 61062.

Day, (Elizabeth) Bettie B. (O. 4, 1933, San Francisco, CA) Coord. of Lib. and Resrc. Ctr. Srvs., Santa Barbara Cnty. Schs., 1972–; Instr., Ext. Crs., Univ. of CA, Santa Barbara, 1973–74; Head Libn., Burlingame Intermediate Sch., 1969–72; Sch. Libn., Livermore Unfd. Sch. Dist., 1963–69; Tchr., Washington Sch., Alameda Unfd. Sch. Dist., 1962–63; Tchr., Livermore Unfd. Sch. Dist., 1960–62; Sch. Libn., Shoreline Sch. Dist., 1959–60; Libn., Seattle Pub. Lib., 1959; various positions, 1955–58. **Educ.:** San Jose State Univ., 1953–55, BA (Educ.); Univ. of WA, 1958–59, MLS; various crs. (1962–78). **Orgs.:** ALA: Com. on Legis. (1979–82); AASL/Supvsr.'s Sect. Ch. (1981–82), Ch.-Elect (1980–81); Secy. (1977–78), Nom. Com. (1978–79), Prog. Com. (1976–78); AASL, Conf., Prog. Ch. (1981–83); various other coms.; ALSC, Newbery–Caldecott Awd. Com. (1977). CA Media and Lib. Educs. Assn.: Pres. (1978–79); various ofcs. (1977–78). CA Assn. of Sch. Libns.: Various coms., ofcs. (1970–77). Delta Kappa Gamma: Delta Chap. (Sec. VP, 1980–82). Pi Lambda Theta: Santa Barbara Chap. Assn. of CA Sch. Admins.: South. Coast Chap. (Secy., 1974–75, 1978–80), VP (1975–76). Altrusa Club of Santa Barbara. **Pubns.:** "Forum: How Can Schools Make the Most of Their Shrinking Library Dollars," *Curric. Prod. Review* (N. 1979); "SMQ: AASL Notes: California Media Specialists Respond to Proposition 13," *Sch. Media Qtly.* (Win. 1979); "Author-Go-Round," *Lang. Arts* (Ja. 1977). **Activities:** 10, 14-Reg. ctr.; 21, 24, 32; 63 **Addr.:** Santa Barbara County Schools, 4400 Cathedral Oaks Rd., P.O. Box 6307, Santa Barbara, CA 93111.

Day, Billee M. (Ap. 5, 1925, Duncan, OK) Dir., Chickasaw Lib. Syst., 1964–, Ext. Libn., 1962–64, Bkmobile. Libn., 1960–62; Ref. Libn., OK State Univ., 1948–49; Libn., OK State Univ. Tech. Sch., 1946–47; Asst. to the Libn., OK State Univ., 1946–47; Instr., LS, Southeast. OK State Univ., 1968–69. **Educ.:** TX Woman's Univ., 1943–46, BA (LS). **Orgs.:** OK LA: *OK Libn.* Ed. (1969–71); Pub. Libs. (Ch., 1962–63, 1969–70); Pubns.; Chld. Div., Nom. Com.; Chld. Bk. Review Wkshp.; Lcl. Arranges; various other coms. ALA. SWLA. Pub. Lib. Dirs. of OK: Pres. Altrusa. AAUW. Ardmore Band Boosters. Ardmore Cncl. of Orgs. Various other orgs. **Activities:** 1, 14-Pub. lib. syst.; 15, 17, 27 **Addr.:** 1615 W. Broadway Pl., Ardmore, OK 73401.

Day, Duane R. (O. 29, 1923, Albert Lea, MN) Mgr. of Lib. Srvs., General Mills, Inc., 1965–; Libn., Campbell-Mithun, 1952–65; Asst. Libn., Brown & Bigelow, 1951–52; Asst. Libn., Veteran's Admin., Fargo, 1950–51. **Educ.:** Hamline Univ., Univ. of MN, 1946–49, BA (Eng.); Univ. of MN, 1949–50, BS in LS. **Orgs.:** SLA: MN Chap. (Pres.); Adv. & Mktg. Div. (Ch.). **Activities:** 12; 17, 41; 51, 59, 68 **Addr.:** 2233 Merrill St., St. Paul, MN 55113.

Day, Heather Ewbank (Ja. 28, 1951, Newcastle-On-Tyne, England) Resrch. Asst., Ctrl. Resrch. Systems, 1980–; Libn., Lilly Endow., 1974–80. **Educ.:** Taylor Univ., 1966–71, BA (Fr.); IN Univ., 1973–74, MLS. **Orgs.:** IN LA: Conf. Local Arrange. (Ch., 1979). Spec. LA: IN Chap./Bltn. Ed. (1976–80). Ctl. IN Area Lib. Srvs. Athrty.: Secy. (1976–78). **Honors:** Beta Phi Mu, 1974. **Pubns.:** Contrib., *Foundation Guide for Religious Grant Seekers* (1979); Jt. Auth. "The Role of the Speial Library in Networking", *Conference on Networking for Networkers: Proceedings* (1980); "Grant Seeking", *CIALSA* (O. 1978); *Nsltr.;*"Computerized Information Services in Indiana", *SLANT* (My. 1977). **Activities:** 12; 20, 39, 41; 63, 90, 92 **Addr.:** 217-8 Nimitz Dr., W., Lafayette, IN 47906.

Day, Mary H. (My. 24, 1939, Raleigh, NC) Leg. Div. Libn., Delta Air Lines, 1979–; Libn., Sutherland, Asbill and Brennan, 1978–79; Circ. Libn., Law Sch., Wake Forest Univ., 1975–76; Asst. Acq. Libn., Wake Forest Univ., 1970–75; Circ. Libn., 1964–70; Pub. Srvs. Libn., Sweet Bnar Coll., 1962–64. **Educ.:** Wake Forest Coll., 1956–60, BA (Fr.); Univ. of NC, 1960–62, MS (LS). **Orgs.:** AALL. Atlanta Law Libs. Assn.: VP (1980); Pres. (1981); Union List of Pers. Com. (1979). Epsilon Sigma Alpha: various lcl. Ofcs. **Honors** Phi Beta Kappa. **Activities:** 12; 15, 39, 46; 77 **Addr.:** 2807 Bentwood Dr., Marietta, GA 30062.

Day, Melvin S. (J. 22, 1923, Lewiston, ME) Dir., Natl. Tech. Info. Srv., 1978–; Deputy Dir., Natl. Lib. of Med., 1972–78; Ofc. of Sci. Info. Sev., Natl. Sci. Fndn., 1971–72; Deputy Asst. Admin. for Tech. Util., NASA, 1966–71; Dir., Sci. and Tech. Info. Div., NASA, 1962–66; Deputy Dir., Ofc. of Tech. Info, NASA, 1960–62; Dir., Div. of Tech. Info., Atomic Energy Comsn., 1958–60. Various other positions. **Educ.:** Bates Coll., 1943, BS; Univ. of TN, 1956–58 (Indus. Mst.). **Orgs.:** ASIS: Pres. (1975). Intl. Cncl. of Sci. Uns. Abs. Bd.: Pres. (1977–). ALA. SLA. Med. LA. Many other orgs. and ofcs. Smithsonian Sci. Info. Exchange: Bd. (1972). AAAS. Amer. Chem. Socty. **Honors:** Pub. Hlth. Srv. Superior Srv. Awd., 1976. Natl. Lib. of Med. Dir. Awd., 1975. NASA Excep. Srv. Medal, 1971. AEC Sustained Superior Srv. Awd. **Pubns.:** Many articles. **Addr.:** 7805 Beech Tree Rd., Bethesda, MD 20034.

Dayton, Donald Wilber (Jl. 25, 1942, Chicago, IL) Libn., Asst. Prof., N. Bapt. Theo. Semy., 1979–; Dir., Assoc. Prof., Mellander Lib., N. Pk. Theo. Semy., 1972–79; Acq. Libn., Asst. Prof., Asbury Theo. Semy., 1969–72. **Educ.:** Houghton Coll., 1960–63, BA (Math. and Phil.); Yale Div. Sch., 1964–69, BD (Theo.); Univ. of KY, 1968–69, MS (LS); Univ. of Chicago, 1972–; various other courses. **Orgs.:** ATLA: Mem. at Lg.; Bd. of Dir. (1976–79). Chicago Area Theo. LA: Pres. (1975–76). Karl Barth Socty. of N. Amer.: Bd. of Dir., Mem. Secy. (1972–). Wesleyan Theo. Socty.: Promo. Secy. (1974–). **Pubns.:** *Discovering an Evangelical Heritage* (1976); Ed., *Contemporary Perspectives on Pietism* (1976); *Five Sermons and a Tract by Luther Lee* (1975); "The Wesleyan Church," *Ecumenical Rev.* (1976); Various other articles, etc. **Activities:** 1; 15, 17, 37; 90 **Addr.:** N. Baptist Theological Seminary, 660 E. Butterfield Rd., Lombard, IL 60148.

Deahl, Thomas F. (F. 17, 1930, Lakewood, OH) Dir., Cmnty. Resrc. Info. Srv., Cmnty. Srvs. Plng. Cncl. of Southeast. PA, 1977–81; Proprietor, Consult., MICRODOC, 1969–; Adj. Assoc. Prof., Temple Univ., 1975–; Dir., Model Cities Cmnty. Info. Ctr., 1972–73; Managing Ed., AUERBACH Info. Inc., 1968–69. **Educ.:** OH State Univ., 1955–57, BA (Soclgy.); OH State Univ., Univ. of MN, 1957–60, (Soclgy.). **Orgs.:** ASIS: DE Valley Chap. (Ch., 1974). Assn. for Computational Ling. Alliance of Info. and Ref. Srvs. Natl. Micro. Assn. Assn. of Recs. Mgrs. and Admins. **Pubns.:** "The CRIS Project: Marrying Word Processing and Computer Output Microfilm to Publish a Directory of Human Services," *Info. and Referral* (Sum. 1979). **Activities:** 6, 12; 24, 33, 37; 72 **Addr.:** MICRODOC, 815 Carpenter Ln., Philadelphia, PA 19119.

Dealy, Ross (S. 13, 1933, Atlantic, IA) Dir. of the Lib., Univ. of WI Ctr., Marinette, 1979–, Instr., Dept. of Hist., Willamette Univ., 1977; Lectr. and Adv., External Degree Prog., St. Mary of the Woods, 1976; Assoc. Instr., Dept. of Hist., IN Univ., 1972; Asst. Prof., Dept. of Hist., Queens Coll., 1964–66; Asst. Prof., Univ. of NC, 1965. **Educ.:** South. Meth. Univ., 1952–56, BA (Soc. Sci., Lit.); Univ. of WA, 1960–62, MA (Hist. of Sci.); IN Univ., 1966–75, PhD (Hist.); Univ. of OR, 1977–78, MLS. **Orgs.:** ALA. N.E. WI ILL Assn.: Bd. of Dirs. (1979–81); Plng. Com. (1979–80). WI LA. Univ. of WI Ctr. Syst. Lib. Cncl. Amer. Hist. Assn. Conf. on Latin Amer. Hist. **Pubns.:** *The Politics of an Erasmian Lawyer, Vasco de Quiroga* (1976); "Vasco de Quiroga's 'Regula Ubi Commodum: The *Utopian* Roots," *Materiali per Una Storia della Cultura Giuridica* (1978). **Activities:** 1; 15, 17, 41; 54, 75, 92 **Addr.:** Library, University of Wisconsin Center–Marinette, Bay Shore, Marinette, WI 54143.

Dean, Carole Jackson (Jy. 28, 1940, Camilla, GA) Asst. Lib. Dir., Ctr. for Disease Control, 1975–; Ref. Libn., 1970–75; Acq. Libn., GA Inst. of Tech., 1967–70; Ref. Libn., Decatur-DeKalb Lib. Syst., 1964–65. **Educ.:** Agnes Scott Coll., 1958–62, BA (Eng.); Emory Univ., 1962–63, MLS; Med. Lib. Internshp., A.W. Calhoun Med. Lib., 1963–64, Cert. **Orgs.:** Med. LA. GA LA. GA Hlth. Sci. Lib. Assn. **Activities:** 4; 15, 17, 46; 57, 80, 91 **Addr.:** Library, 1–4104, Center for Disease Control, Atlanta, GA 30333.

Dean, Frances Childers (Ap. 20, 1930, Lipan, TX) Dir., Dept. of Instr. Resrcs., Montgomery Cnty. Pub. Sch. (Rockville, MD), 1976–, Coord., Eval. and Sel., 1969–76, Sec. Libn., Fairfax Pub. Sch., (VA), 1963–69; Elem. Libn., Dallas Pub. Sch., 1959–62. **Educ.:** TX Woman's Univ., 1957–59, BS (LS), 1959–62, MLS; Univ. of MD, 1963–69. **Orgs.:** ALA: AASL (Bd. of Dir. (1972–74), Pres. 1977–78). Intl. Frdm. Com. (Ch., 1978–). Frdm. to Read Frdn.: Bd. (1974–76, 1978–). EFLA: Bd. (1979–). NAACP. Natl. Educ. Assn. MD St. Tchrs. Assn. Intl. Reading Assn. **Honors:** D.C. Sch. Libn., Outstan. Srvs. Beta Phi Mu, 1962 Sch. Libs., 1976. **Pubns.:** "Design of Initial Media Collections," *Sch. Media Qtly.* (Spr. 1974); "Reaction to Donelson's "What to Do Before the Censor Arrives," *Today's Educ.* (Ja. 1975). **Activities:** 10, 11; 21, 42, 48; 63, 66, 74 **Addr.:** Dept. of Instructional Resources, Montgomery County Public Schools, Rockville, MD 20850.

Dean, Kathryn F. (O. 13, 1917, Calgary, AB, CAN.) Arch. & Spec. Col. Libn., Univ. of MB, 1980–, Cont. Educ. Lib., Coord., 1976–80, Head, Ref. Srvs. Dept. 1974–76; Asst. Head, Hum. Dept., Enoch Pratt Free Lib., 1970–74, Admn. Asst., Cnty. Srvs., 1967–69, Ref. Libn., 1961–67. **Educ.:** Univ. of Toronto, 1948–51, ARCT (Msc.), 1951–53, LRCT (Msc.); Catholic Univ., 1959–61, MLS Med. Lib. Cert., 1967; Licentiate, Royal Sch. Msc., London, Eng. **Orgs.:** ALA: Task Force on Gvt. Docs. (1975–76). Can LA. MB LA: Cont. Educ. Lib. Com. (1978–79). Cncl. Acad. Libs. MB: Cont. Educ. Com. (1978–79). Various other orgs. Can. Assn. of Univ. Tchrs. MB Assn. Cont. Educ. MB Liberal Assn. Can. Assn. for Univ. Cont. Educ. **Honors:** Can. Cncl., Travel Grants, 1960, 1977–78; Brit. Cncl., Travel Grant, 1977–78. **Pubns.:** Articles, reviews. **Activities:** 1, 9; 25, 41, 42; 78, 90, 92 **Addr.:** 305-333 Wellington Crescent, Winnipeg, MB R3M 0A1 Canada.

Dean, Sharon L. (N. 4, 1943, Ithaca, NY) Info. Broker, Info. Unltd., 1979–; Head Libn., J.F. Kennedy HS (Seattle), 1977–81; Soc. Stds. Libn., Mercer Island HS, 1975–77. **Educ.:** Keuka Coll., 1961–64, BA (Hist.); Syracuse Univ., 1964–65, MA (Educ.); Univ. of WA, 1976–1978, MLS. **Orgs.:** ALA: AASL, Univ. Press Com. (1978–79). WA LA. WA Lib. Media Assn. SLA; WA YA Review Grp. **Honors:** Beta Phi Mu. **Pubns.:** Reviews. **Activities:** 10, 6; 15, 24, 48; 54, 63; 92 **Addr.:** Box 385, Mercer Island, WA 98040.

Dean, Winifred Fay (Spooner) (Jl. 24, 1930, Cleveland, OH) Ref./Biblgphr. Soc. Sci., Cleveland State Univ. Libs., 1974–; Actg. Head, Col. Dev., Case Western Reserve Univ. Libs., 1973–74; Soc. Sci. Sel. Libn., 1968–73; Econ. Biblgphr., Legis. Ref. Srv., Lib. of Congs., 1966–67; Head, Bus. & Sci. Dept., Atlanta Pub. Lib., 1965–1966; 1st Asst. Libn., Bus. & Sci., 1963–1965; Adult Srvs. Libn., Cuyahoga Cnty. Pub. Lib., 1961–1963. **Educ.:** Hiram Coll., 1947–51, BA (Span.); Western Reserve Univ., 1960–61, MSLS. **Orgs.:** ALA: RTSD/Acq. Sect., Policy & Resrch. Com. (1971–74); Ch. (1972–73); Ref. & Subscrpn. Books Review Com., (1974–78); Guest reviewer, (1978–). OH LA. Acad. Lib. Assn. of OH. Women's Natl. Book Assn.: Cleveland Chap., (Pres., 1977–79). AAUP. **Activities:** 1, 9; 15, 31, 39; 59, 74, 92 **Addr.:** 4015 West 213 St., Fairview Park, OH 44126.

Deane, Shirley Park (Jl. 8, 1936, Richmond, KY) Asst. Prof., East. KY Univ., 1970–; Serials Libn., Med. Ctr. Lib., Univ. of KY, 1959–62. **Educ.:** Univ. of KY, 1954–58, BA (Eng.); 1958–59, MS (LS). **Orgs.:** ALA. KY LA. KY Sch. Media Assn. Phi Kappa Phi. **Honors:** Phi Beta Kappa. **Pubns.:** *Cataloging Manual for Non-Book Materials* (1976); *An Illustrated Guide to Typing Catalog Cards for the School Library* (1979). **Activities:** 11; 20, 21, 26 **Addr.:** Department of Curriculum and Instruction, Eastern Kentucky University, Richmond, KY 40475.

DeAngelo, Rachael Wingfield (D. 24, 1908, Franklin Cnty., VA) Prof. Emeritus, Univ. of HI, 1973–; Prof., Grad. Sch. of Lib. Studies, 1967–73; Prof., Grad. Sch. of Lib. & Info. Sci., Drexel Univ., 1961–67; Prof. & Coord., Lib. Educ. Prog., Queens Coll., 1954–61; Exec. Secy. ALA/AASL, 1952–54; Supvsr. of Sch. Libs., Yonkers, NY, 1949–52; HS Libn., Oneonta, NY, 1943–49; Libn., Hartwick Coll., 1930–43. **Educ.:** Mary Washington Coll., 1925–28, BS (Eng. & Fr.); Columbia Univ, 1928–33, BS (LS), 1947–50, MS (LS); Pratt Inst., advanced study, 1961–62, (LS);Univ. of PA, 1962 (Educ.). **Orgs.:** ALA: LED/Bd. of Dir. (1958–60); Grolier Fndn. Awd. Jury (1969–71). AASL/Bd. of Dir. (1958–60, 1969–71); Prof. Status and Growth Com. (Ch., 1960–64, 1969–72); Disting. Lib. Srv. Awd. for Sch. Admin. (Ch., 1965–68; 1969–72); other coms. AALS. Assn. of Sch. Libns., Philadelphia and Vicinity: VP (1964–65). HI LA. Other orgs. Delta Kappa Gamma Socty. Intl.: Resrch. Com. (Ch. 1973–76; 78–79). Beta Beta State: Prof. Affairs Com. (Ch. 1972–76); Prog. Com. (1970–75); YBook Com. (1977–78). Assn. Childhood Educ. Intl.: Ref. Books Eval. (1958–60). Arts Cncl. of HI. **Honors:** Beta Phi Mu, Honorary Mem., 1976; ALA, AASL, Cert. of Recog., 1974; Mary Washington Coll., Disting. Alum. Awd., 1974; Drexel Univ., Christian R. and Mary K. Lindback Fndn. Awd. for Disting. Teaching, 1964; other awds. **Pubns.:** Issue Ed. *"Book Selection for Children", Drexel Lib. Qtly* (Ja. 1966); Ed., *Bibliography of Books for Children:* 1958–60, (1962); "Children's Book Publishing," *Lib. Trends,* (Jl. 1958); "Media for Disseminating Critiques", *Evaluating Books for Children and Young People.* (1968); *"Suggested Guidelines for Planning Continuing Education Programs...for School Library Media Personnel," Sch. Lib. Media Qtly.* (Fall, 1974); Other articles, reviews. **Addr.:** Bellevue Tower, Apt. 1101, 1309 Wilder Ave., Honolulu, HI 96822.

DeBakey, Lois (Lake Charles, LA) Prof. of Sci. Comm., Baylor Coll. of Med., 1968–; Prof. of Sci. Comm., Tulane Univ., Sch. of Med., 1966–, Assoc. Prof. of Sci. Comm., 1965–66, Asst. Prof. of Sci. Comm., 1963–65, Instr. of Eng., 1960–63. **Educ.:** Tulane Univ., 1949, BA, 1959, MA, 1963, PhD. **Orgs.:** *Amer. Heritage Dict.:* Usage Panel (1980–). Natl. Lib. of Med.: Biomed. Lib. Review Com. (1973–77). South. Assn. Coll. and Sch.: Exec. Cncl. Cncl. Basic Educ.: Spec. Comsn. on Wrtg. (1977–79). Ed. Bd.: various publications. Many other orgs. Intl. Socty. for Gen. Semantics. NIH Alumni Assn. **Honors:** Amer. Med. Writers Assn., Disting. Srv. Awd., 1970; Bausch and Lomb Awd., Sci. Schol. Awd.; Phi Beta Kappa, Schol. Fraternity. **Pubns.:** *The Scientific Journal: Editorial Policies and Practices* (1976); "English Today: Are We Speaking in Tongues?" *Brit. Bk. Eng. Usage* (1980); "Relighting the Lamp of Excellence," *Forum on Med.* (Aug. 1979); "Literacy: Mirror of Society," *Jnl. of Tech. Writing and Comm.* (1978); "Art of Persuasion: Logic & Language in Proposal Writing," *Grants Mag.* (Mr. 1978); various other pubns. **Activities:** 14-Med School; 24, 25, 42, 49; 63, 80, 91, 95-Sci Comm. **Addr.:** Baylor College of Medicine, 1200 Moursund Ave., Houston, TX 77030.

Special Subjects/Services: 50. Adult educ.; 51. Advert./Mktg.; 52. Aerosp.; 53. Agric.; 54. Area std.; 55. Arts/Hum.; 56. Autom.; 57. Bibl./Prtg.; 58. Bio. sci.; 59. Bus./Fin.; 60. Chem.; 61. Copyrt.; 62. Documtn.; 63. Educ.; 64. Engin.; 65. Env.; 66. Eth. grps.; 67. Film; 68. Food/Nutr.; 69. Geneal.; 70. Geo.; 71. Geol.; 72. Handcpd.; 73. Hist.; 74. Int. frdm.; 75. Info. sci.; 76. Insr.; 77. Law; 78. Legis.; 79. Math./Comp. sci.; 80. Med.; 81. Metals; 82. Nat. resrcs.; 83. Newsp.; 84. Nuc. sci.; 85. Oral hist.; 86. Petr./Energy; 87. Pharm.; 88. Phys./Astr./Math.; 89. Readg.; 90. Relig.; 91. Sci./Tech.; 92. Soc. sci.; 93. Telecom.; 94. Transp.; 95. (other).

Who's Who in Library and Information Services

DeBardeleben, Marian Zalis (S. 30, 1946, New Brunswick, NJ) Resrch. Libn., Philip Morris U.S.A., 1978–, Info. Sci., 1974–77, Assoc. Libn., 1973–74, Asst. Libn., 1969–73. **Educ.:** Univ. of NH, 1964–68, BA (Eng. Lit.); SUNY, Albany, 1968–69, MS (LS); Univ. of the Americas, Mexico, 1967–67, (Span.). **Orgs.:** SLA. Amer. Chem. Socty.: Div. of Chem. Lit. **Pubns.:** *Dictionary of Tobacco Terminology* (1980); Oral presentations. **Activities:** 12; 17, 39, 41; 60, 91, 95-Tobacco. **Addr.:** Philip Morris U.S.A., Research Center Library, P.O. Box 26583, Richmond, VA 23261.

Debenham, W. Stuart (Ag. 30, 1937, Danville, IL) Dir., Colby Coll., 1977–81; Asst. Exec. Dir., OCLC, 1974–76; Head, Acq., Bibl. Dept., Yale Univ., 1966–74; Ref. Libn., Gift Exch. Libn., Serials Libn., Harvard Univ. Lib., 1963–66. **Educ.:** Univ. of Pittsburgh, 1957–60, BA (Phil.), 1962–63, MLS. **Orgs.:** ALA: Various coms. Bibl. Socty. of London. Prtg. Hist. Socty. Grolier Club. Nelinet: Bd. of Dir. (1978, Ch., 1979–). **Pubns.:** Tech. Rpt., Pub. Use Terminals, OCLC (1975). Reviews. **Activities:** 1; 15, 17, 34; 55, 57, 75 **Addr.:** PO Box 673, Waterville, ME 04901.

DeBolt, W. Dean (D. 2, 1950, Springfield, IL) Assoc. Univ. Libn. for Spec. Cols., Univ. of W. FL, Pensacola, 1981–; Univ. Archvst., Sangamon State Univ., 1973–81; Asst. Archvst., 1972–73. **Educ.:** Sangamon State Univ., 1970–72, BA (Hist.), 1972–74, MA (Hist.); Univ. of IL, 1976–79, MLS; Arch. Cert., OH Hist. Socty., 1973. **Orgs.:** Midwest Arch. Conf.: Nsltr. Ed., (1976–). SAA. Socty. of GA Archvsts. Sangamon Cnty. Hist. Socty.: Secy./Treas. (1976–1977). Amer. Philatelic Socty.: Paper Prsrvn. Com. (1977–). Org. of Amer. Histns. Natl. Trust for Hist. Prsrvn. **Pubns.:** *Guide to Collections: Materials on Springfield and Sangamon County.* (1978); *Cumulative Index to Illinois History Magazine, Vol. 1–25* (1972); "A Woman's Place is in the Archives" *XX Chromosone Chronicle* (N.-D. 1978); Ed., *Nsltr. of the Midwest Arch. Conf., Vol. 5 - 7.* **Activities:** 1, 2; 17, 23, 45; 55, 69, 85 **Addr.:** 4049 Alconbury Cir., Pensacola, FL 32504.

Debons, Anthony (Ap. 6, 1916, Mesida, Malta) Prof., Vice-Ch. (Info. Sci.), Univ. of Pittsburgh, 1969–; Prof., Ch. (Psy., Info. Sci.), Univ. of Dayton, 1964–69; Colonel (Resrch. and Dev.), U.S. Air Force, 1942–64. **Educ.:** Brooklyn Coll., 1936–48, BA (Psy.); Colombia Univ., 1951–54, MS, PhD (Psy.). **Orgs.:** ASIS. Fed. of Info. Users: Pres. **Honors:** Fellow, Amer. Psy. Assn. **Pubns.:** Jt.-Auth., *The Information Profession* (1981); Ed., *Information Science: Search for Identity* (1974); Jt.-ed., *Perspective in Information Science* (1975); Jt.-Auth., *Information Sciences: Basics and Challenges* (in press); Jt.-Auth., "Towards a Meta Science of Information," *Jnl. of ASIS* (Ja./F., 1970). **Activities:** 1; 24, 26, 41; 63, 75, 92 **Addr.:** 115 Edgecliff Rd., Carnegie, PA 15106.

de Brigard, Emilie (D. 11, 1943, New York, NY) Dir., FilmResearch, 1970–, Consult., on Film, 1970–; Prin. Prog., Margaret Mead Film Fest., Amer. Musm. of Nat. Hist., 1977–78. **Educ.:** Radcliffe Coll., 1960–63, AB (Soc. Anthro.); Univ. of CA at Los Angeles, 1967–68, MA (Theat. Arts); Inst. in Arts Admin. (Harvard), 1975, Cert. (Arts Admin.). **Orgs.:** Anthropological Film Resrch. Inst.: Secy. (1978–80); Bd. of Dirs. (1979–). EFLA: Pre-screening Com. (Ch., 1973–). Ctr. for the.Std. South. Cult.: Natl. Adv. Bd. (1979–). **Pubns.:** "The History of Ethnographic Film" in *Principles of Visual Anthropology* (1975); Prod., *Margaret Mead: A Portrait by a Friend* (film) (1978). **Activities:** 14-Private Consulting Firm; 20, 24, 32; 54, 66, 92 **Addr.:** Film-Research, RFD 2, Box 436, Higganum, CT 06441.

Debusman, Paul Marshall (D. 6, 1932, Wichita, KS) Ref. and Serials Libn., South. Bapt. Theo. Semy., 1974–; Order Libn., 1963–74. **Educ.:** Baylor Univ., 1950–54, BA (Rel., Eng.); South. Bapt. Theo. Semy., 1954–57, MDiv (Theo.); 1957–62, PhD (Christ. ethics); Spalding Coll., 1964–1970, MSLS. **Orgs.:** ATLA: Per. Exch. Comm. (1972–75); Ch. (1975); Stan. of Accred. Com. (1978–). Crescent Hill Bapt. Church. Crescent Hill Cmnty. Cncl. KY Bapt. Hist. Socty. **Activities:** 1, 12; 15, 39, 44; 90 **Addr.:** Southern Baptist, Theological Seminary Library, 2825 Lexington Rd., Louisville, KY 40280.

DeCandido, GraceAnne A. (Je. 6, 1947, Bronx, NY) Coord., Retrospective Conversion Proj., NY Univ., 1981–; Libn.-in-charge, Gimbel Lib., Parsons Sch. of Dsgn., 1980–81, Ref./Tech. Srvs. Libn., 1979–80; Art Catlgr., NY Pub. Lib., 1976–79, Art Ref. Libn., 1973–75. **Educ.:** Thomas More Coll., Fordham Univ., 1965–69, BA (Eng. Lit., Art Hist.); Columbia Univ., 1971–72, MLS. **Orgs.:** ARLIS/NA. Art Libs. Socty./NY: Exec. Bd. (1980–). ALA: ACRL/Art Sect. (Secy., 1981–). **Pubns.:** Various bk. reviews (1973–). **Activities:** 1; 17, 20, 46; 55 **Addr.:** 716 E. 235th St., Bronx, NY 10466.

DeCaprio, Albert A. (Ap. 3, 1926, Newton, MA) Asst. Cnty. Libn., San Bernardino Cnty. Lib., 1975–; Dir. of Lib., City of Fort Lauderdale, 1973–74; Admn., Cambria Cnty. Lib. Syst., 1969–73; Head Admn. Srvs., Miami Pub. Lib. Syst., 1964–69. **Educ.:** Kenyon Coll., 1952, BA (Eng. Lit.); Simmons Coll., 1956, MS (LS). **Orgs.:** ALA: Ad Hoc Com. on Netwks. (1977–78). Natl. Libn. Assn.: CA Chap., Secy. (1979–80). CA LA: Intl. Frdm. Com. (1978; Ch., 1979). Amer. Socty. of Pub. Admin. Kiwanis. **Activities:** 9; 17, 19, 35; 56, 74 **Addr.:** 6925 Rogers Ln., San Bernardino, CA 92404.

de Chantal, Jean (Mr.) (My. 4, 1921, Hawkesbury, ON) Chief Libn., Intl. Dev. Resrch. Ctr., 1976–; Assoc. Dir. for Lib. Dev., IDRC Reg. Ofc., Dakar, Sénégal, 1974–75; Lib. Adv., Univ. of Mauritius, 1970–74; Prog. Admin., Educ. Div., Can. Intl. Dev. Agency, 1969–70; Lib. Adv. (UNESCO), Nat. Polytech. Inst., Mexico City, 1968–69; Prog. Ofcr. (Educ. Div.), External Aid Ofc., Ottawa, 1966–68; Lib. Adv. (United Nations), Inst. of Pub. Admin., Ghana, 1962–65; Branch Libn., Natl. Resrch. Cncl. of Can., 1946–62. **Educ.:** Univ. of Ottawa, 1958–60, BA, 1960–61, BLS. **Orgs.:** Assn. Can. des Bibtcrs. de Lang. Fr.: Cnclr. on Natl. Exec. (1961). Can. LA: Elec. Com. (Ch., 1962). LA of Ottawa: Secy.-Treas. (1960–61); Ch. (1962). ASTED: Cnclr. (1979–). **Honors:** Grolier Socty. Prize, 1958. **Pubns.:** Ed., Conf. of African Univ. Libs.-East. Area *Proceedings* (1974); "Des Lecteurs Africains sans Bibliothèques," *Le CRDI Explore* (1977); "Development Needs Libraries," *IDRC Rpts.* (1977). **Activities:** 4, 12; 30, 34, 41; 68, 75, 92 **Addr.:** 18 chemin Castelbeau, Aylmer, PQ J9J 1E1 Canada.

Dechert, Dorothy (Fulkerson Bower) (Ag. 28, 1906, Chillicothe, OH) Retired, Volun. Cat. Spec. Col. Winter Park Pub. Lib., 1979–, Head of Tech. Srvs., 1962–76; Head of Acq. & Ext., Orlando Pub. Lib., 1961–62; Libn., Maitland Pub. Lib., 1960–61; Ref. Asst., Spec. Cat., Avery Arch. Lib., Columbia Univ., 1935–42; Asst. Cat., Peoria Pub. Lib., 1928–35. **Educ.:** Oberlin Coll., 1923–27, AB (Eng. Lit.); Univ. of IL, 1927–28, BSLS; Columbia Univ., 1935–42, MSLS. **Orgs.:** ALA: ALSC. The Frnd. of the Osborne & Lillian H. Smith Coll., Toronto Pub. Lib. Intl. Inst. for Chlds. Lit. and Readg. Resrch. (Vienna). Loch Haven Art Ctr., Orlando, FL. Ross Cnty. Genealogical Socty., Chillicothe, OH. **Pubns.:** Reviews. **Activities:** 9, 12; 15, 20, 39; 55, 57, 75 **Addr.:** 350 East Kings Way, Winter Park, FL 32789.

Decker, Jean S. (Franklin, NY) Head, Serials Cat., SUNY, Buffalo, 1972–; Tchr., Morris Ctrl. Sch. (NY), 1946–51; various other positions. **Educ.:** Hartwick Coll., 1942–46, BA (Fr./Span.); Syracuse Univ., 1948–49 (Fr./Voice); Univ. of NH, 1962–66 (Educ.); SUNY Buffalo, 1970–71, MLS. **Orgs.:** ALA: RTSD, Tech. Srvs. Costs Com. (1978–80). Fac. Senate, SUNY: Lib. Resrcs. Com. (Ch., 1977). Beta Phi Mu: Delta Chap. (Pres., 1978). **Pubns.:** "Serials and Catalog Closings," *Jnl. of Acad. Libnshp.* (N. 1979). **Activities:** 1; 20, 44, 46; 63, 75, 89 **Addr.:** 136 Capen Blvd., Amherst, NY 14226.

de Cordova, Diane J. (F. 15, 1934, New York City, NY) Educ. Media Spec., River Edge Elem. Sch., 1958–; Instr. (part-time), Alphonsus Coll., 1969–72. **Educ.:** Trenton St., 1952–56, BS (Educ.); Rutgers Univ., 1968–69, MLS; Seton Hall, 1971–74, MA (Educ.); 1974–76, (Supvsr. Cert.). **Orgs.:** ALA: AASL (Com. on Instruc. Media, 1971–76). AECT: Liaison Com. (Co-Ch., 1980–82). Educ. Media Assn. of NJ: Co-Pres. (1977–78). **Activities:** 10; 17, 21, 32; 55 **Addr.:** 8 Patton Pl., Dumont, NJ 07628.

Deering, Ronald F. (O. 6, 1929, Paxton, IL) Lib. Dir., South. Bapt. Theo. Semy., 1971–; Assoc. Libn., 1967–71; Resrch. Libn., 1961–67; Instr. in Greek, 1958–61. **Educ.:** Georgetown Coll., 1947–51, BA (Hist.); South. Bapt. Theo. Semy., 1951–55, MDiv (Theo.); 1955–62, PhD (New Testament); Columbia Univ., 1966–67, MS (LS). **Orgs.:** ATLA. KY LA. ALA. Sigma Tau Delta. Phi Alpha Theta. **Honors:** Beta Phi Mu. **Activities:** 1; 15, 17, 33; 63, 85, 90 **Addr.:** Southern Baptist Theological Seminary, 2825 Lexington Rd., Louisville, KY 40206.

Dees, Anthony Roane (S. 19, 1937, Pikeville, NC) Dir., GA Hist. Socty., 1977–; Cur. Mss., Dir. of GA Room, Univ. of GA, 1975–77, First Asst., Head of Cat. Dept., 1967–75; Cat. Libn., Washington & Lee Univ., 1962–67. **Educ.:** Univ. of NC (Chapel Hill), 1955–59, AB (Eng.), 1964, MSLS. **Orgs.:** SELA. GA LA: GA Reprint Com. (1976–). SAA: Personal Mss. Com. (1979). Socty. of GA Archvst.: Dir. (1977–79). Rotary Club of Savannah: Cult. Affairs Com. (1978–). **Pubns.:** "The Georgia Historical Society in Historic Preservation," *GA Hist. Qtly.* (Spr. 1979). **Activities:** 1, 2; 20, 45; 55, 69 **Addr.:** Georgia Historical Society, 501 Whitaker St., Savannah, GA 31401.

Dees, Margaret N. (Mr. 5, 1917, Dupree, SD) Prin., Yankee Ridge Sch. (Urbana, IL), 1975–; Dir. of Libs., Sch. Dist. 116 (Urbana), 1958–75; Libn., Champaign (IL) Sr. HS, 1957–58; Elem. and Sec. Tchr. (IL, CA, FL); 1939–54. **Educ.:** Univ. of IL, 1939, BS (Eng. and Hist.); 1949, MS (Educ.); 1957, MA (LS). **Orgs.:** ALA: Various coms. IL LA: Pres. (1973–74). IL Assn. of Sch. Libns.: Pres. (1967–68). Lincoln Trail Libs. Syst.: Pres. (1977–79). Urbana (IL) Free Lib.: Trustee. Delta Kappa Gamma: Beta Mu Chap. (Pres., 1970–72). **Honors:** IL Sch. Libns. Awd., 1974; Kappa Delta Pi, Compatriot Awd., 1976. **Pubns.:** Jt. auth., "How Elementary School Teachers & Librarians Cooperate in Instruction," *IL Libs.* (1966); "Peeling the Potato" *Water ReUse Conf.* Proc., Amer. Inst. of Chem. Engin. (1975); "Catch the Brass Ring," *IL Libs.* (Jn. 1975); "Who Decides?," *IL Libs.* (S. 1978). **Addr.:** 2016 Boudreau Dr., Urbana, IL 61801, and 1215 6th Ave. W., Seattle, WA 98119.

De Gennaro, Richard (Mr. 2, 1926, New Haven, CT) Dir. of Libs., Univ. of PA, 1970–; Sr. Assoc. Univ. Libn., Harvard Univ. Lib., 1969–70, Assoc. Univ. Libn., Syst. Dev., 1966–69, Asst. Dir., 1958–66; Ref. Libn., NY Pub. Lib., 1956–58; Visit. Prof. (LS), Univ. South. CA, 1968–69. **Educ.:** Wesleyan Univ. (CT), 1947–51, BA (Gvt.), 1959–60, MA (Hist.); Columbia Univ., 1955–56, MS (LS); Harvard Bus. Sch., 1956, AMP; Univs. of Paris, Poitiers, Barcelona, Madrid, and Perugia, 1951–55, (Lang. and Cult. Progs.). **Orgs.:** ARL: Pres. (1975). ALA: Info. Sci. and Autom. Div. (Pres., 1970–71). Resrch. Libs. Grp., Inc.: Bd. of Gvrs., (1979–). Univ. of PA Press: Bd. of Dir. (1978–). ASIS: Spec. Int. Grp. on Lib. Autom. and Netwks. (Ch., 1965). PA Area Lib. and Info. Netwk. (PALINET): Bd. (1974–78). Franklin Inn Club, Philadelphia. **Honors:** R.R. Bowker Meml. Lectr., 1979; ALA, 1st place, *Amer. Libs.* Prize Article Competition, 1977. **Pubns.:** "Research Libraries Enter the Information Age," *Lib. Jnl.* (N. 15, 1979); "From Monopoly to Competition: The Changing Network Scene." *Lib. Jnl.* (Jn. 1, 1979); "Library Administration and New Management Systems," *Lib. Jnl.* (D. 15, 1978); "Copyright, Resource Sharing and Hard Times," *Amer. Libs.* (S. 1977); Many other articles. **Activities:** 1, 11; 17, 24, 34; 56, 75, 93 **Addr.:** Van Pelt Library/CH, University of Pennsylvania, Philadelphia, PA 19104.

de Grasse, Charles I. (Ap. 23, 1923, Boston, MA) Dir., Inst. Mktg., Harper & Row, 1980–; Natl. Sales Mgr., J. B. Lippincott Co., 1979; Lib. Prom. Mgr., 1977–79; Reg. Sales Mgr., Doubleday & Co., 1965–77; Dist. Sales Mgr., 1956–65; Reg. Libn., MA Div. of Lib. Ext., 1953–56; Libn., Greenwich Pub. Lib., 1951–53. **Educ.:** Boston Univ., 1946–50, BA (Soc. Std.); Simmons Coll., 1950–51, MS (LS); Drexel Univ., 1978, Cert. (Chld. Lit.). **Orgs.:** Lib. PR Assn.: Pres. (1966). Philadelphia Chlds. RT: Bd. (1978). New Eng. LA. ALA. Pub. Lib. Promo. Grp. **Activities:** 9, 10; 16, 21, 37; 51, 63, 92 **Addr.:** Director, Institutional Marketing, Harper & Row, 10 East 53rd St., New York, NY 10022.

deGruyter, M. Lisa (N. 15, 1951, Spencer, WV) Lectr., Dept. of LS, North. IL Univ., 1980; Admin. Secy., PLA, 1980; Ext. Libn., Alpha Reg. Lib., 1977–78. **Educ.:** Marshall Univ., 1973, BA (Eng.); LA State Univ., 1976–77, MLS; Univ. of Chicago, 1978– (LS). **Orgs.:** ALA: PLA, Org. Com. (1980–). WV LA. **Pubns.:** "History and Development of Rural Public Libraries," *Lib. Trends* (Spr. 1980); jt. auth., "William Torrey Harris," *Dictionary of American Library Biography* (1978). **Activities:** 9; 17, 27, 41; 95-Rural lib. srv. **Addr.:** 1755 E. 55th St. #206, Chicago, IL 60615.

Deitzer, Margaret Ann (O. 26, 1943, Pittsburgh, PA) Libn., PA State Univ. (Allentown), 1977–, Radnor Grad. Ctr., 1973–76; Hunt Lib., Carnegie-Mellon Univ., 1967–73. **Educ.:** PA State Univ., 1962–65, BA (Pol. Sci.); Univ. of Pittsburgh, 1965–67, MLS; various cont. educ. crs., 1977–80. **Orgs.:** PA LA: Bd. of Dirs. (1979–80); Coll. and Resrch. Libs. Div. (Ch., 1979–80), Bd. (1978–81); Nom. Com. (1980–81); Mem. Com. (Ch., 1980–81). Philadelphia Area Ref. Libns. Info. Exch. PA Citizens for Better Libs. ALA: LIRT, PR and Mem. Com. (1981–83); ACRL, SE Chap. PA, various coms. Various other orgs. Lehigh Valley Assn. for Acad. Women. Lehigh–Northampton Area Cont. Educ. Cncl.; Exec. Com. **Honors:** Beta Phi Mu. **Activities:** 1, 10; 15, 31, 39; 50, 63, 75 **Addr.:** 1537 Pennsylvania St., Allentown, PA 18102.

DeJarnatt, James R. (My. 16, 1940, Ft. Smith, AR) Dir., GA Reg. Lib. for the Blind and Phys. Handcpd., 1976–, various positions, 1973–76; Catlgr., GA Tech., 1968–73; Asst. Libn., New Coll., 1966–68; Spec. Col., Univ. of S. FL, 1964–66. **Educ.:** Hendrix Coll., 1958–62, BA (Eng.); Emory Univ., 1962–63, MLS. **Orgs.:** GA LA: Schol. Com. (1981–82). SELA. ALA: ASCLA/Lib. Srv. to Blind and Phys. Handcpd. Sect., Bylaws Com. (Ch., 1979–80, 1980–81). GA Radio Readg. Srvs., Inc.: Bd. of Dirs. (Ch., 1980–81). Atlanta Area Srvs. for the Blind: Bd. of Dirs. (1978–). **Activities:** 9, 13; 17, 27, 34 **Addr.:** Georgia Library for the Blind & Physically Handicapped, 1050 Murphy Ave., S.W., Atlanta, GA 30310.

Deken, Jean Marie (Ap. 5, 1953, St. Louis, MO) Chief, Accession and Disposal, Natl. Arch. and Recs. Srv., Natl. Prsnl. Recs. Ctr., 1981–, Mgt. Anal., 1978–81; Archvst., MO Bot. Garden Lib., 1976–78; Cat. Asst., 1974–76. **Educ.:** Washington Univ. 1971–74, BA summa cum laude, (Eng.); 1975–76, MA (Eng.). **Orgs.:** Assn. of St. Louis Area Archvsts.: Secy. (1978–). Midwest Arch. Conf. SAA: Com. on the Arch. of Sci. MO Musms. Assoc.: Secy.-Treas. (1978–); Newsltr. Ed. (1975–78). **Pubns.:** *Henry Shaw, His Life and Legacy.* **Activities:** 2, 12; 23, 38, 45; 55 **Addr.:** Management and Technical Staff, National Personnel Records Center, 111 Winnebago St., St. Louis, MO 63118.

de Klerk, Ann M. (Eng) Univ. Libn., Bucknell Univ., 1981–; Assoc. Dir., Univ. Libs., Carnegie Mellon Univ., 1978–81, Head, Engin. and Sci. Lib., 1975–78, Assoc. Engin. and Sci. Libn., 1971–75, Asst. Ref. Libn., 1965–71. **Educ.:** Univ. of London, 1950–53, BA (Hon.), (Germ.), 1953–54, Postgrad. Cert., (Educ.); Univ. of Pittsburgh, 1963–65, MLS. **Orgs.:** ASIS: Pittsburgh Chap., Prog. Ch. (1977–78), Ch. (1978–79), Nom. Com. (1979–80). SLA: Pittsburgh Chap. (Secy., 1975–76), Docum. Div. (Secy., 1977–79). ALA: ACRL; LITA. Beta Phi Mu. Pittsburgh Reg. Lib. Ctr.: User Srvs. Com. (Ch., 1970–74); Dir. Com. (Ch., 1974–76); Bd. of Trustees (Alternate, 1973–). **Pubns.:** Ed., *Western Pennsylvania Resources* (1975, 1976). **Activities:** 1; 17,

PROFESSIONAL ACTIVITIES: Institutions: 1. Acad. lib.; 2. Arch.; 3. Assn.; 4. Fed./Gvt. lib.; 5. Inst. lib.; 6. Mfr./Suppl.; 7. Milit. lib.; 8. Musm.; 9. Pub. lib.; 10. Sch. lib.; 11. Sch. of lib. sci.; 12. Spec. lib.; 13. State lib.; 14. (other). **Functions/Activities:** 15. Acq./Col. dev.; 16. Adult srvs.; 17. Admin.; 18. Apprais.; 19. Archit./Bldgs.; 20. Cat./Class.; 21. Chld. srvs.; 22. Circ.; 23. Cons./Pres.; 24. Consult.; 25. Cont. ed.; 26. Educ. lib. sci.; 27. Ext. srvs.; 28. Fund/Grants; 29. Gvt. pubs.; 30. Indx./Abs.; 31. Instr. lib. use; 32. Media srvs.; 33. Micro.; 34. Netwks./Coop.; 35. Persnl.; 36. PR; 37. Publshg.; 38. Recs. mgt.; 39. Ref. srvs.; 40. Repro.; 41. Resrch.; 42. Review.; 43. Secur.; 44. Serials; 45. Spec. col.; 46. Tech. srvs.; 47. Trustees/Bds.; 48. YA srvs.; 49. (other).

35; 56, 91 **Addr.:** University Library, Bucknell University, Lewisburg, PA 17837.

De Klerk, Peter (Ap. 15, 1927, Amsterdam, The Netherlands) Theo. Libn., Calvin Theo. Semy., 1969–; Catlgr., Candler Sch. of Theo., 1968–69. **Educ.:** Calvin Coll., 1952–56, BA (Lit.); Westminster Theo. Semy., 1962–63, MDiv; Emory Univ., 1965–68, MLn (LS). **Orgs.:** ATLA: Pubn. Com. (1977–81). Chicago Area Theo. LA. Dutch-Amer. Hist. Comsn.: Pres. (1975–). Calvin Std. Socty.: Secy./Treas. (1978–). Amer. Socty. for Reformation Resrch. **Pubns.:** *A Bibliography of the Writings of the Professors of Calvin Theological Seminary* (1980); jt. ed., *Essays on Theological Librarianship* (1980); ed., *Renaissance, Reformation, Resurgence* (1976); "Calvin Bibliography," anl. *Calvin Theo. Jnl.* (1972–); "A Bibliography on A.C. Van Raalte," *Reformed Review* (1976–77); various bibls. (1976). **Activities:** 1; 15, 39, 45; 90 **Addr.:** Calvin Theological Seminary, 3233 Burton St., S.E., Grand Rapids, MI 49506.

de la Garza, Peter J. (My. 12, 1926, San Antonio, TX) Coord., Hisp. Acq. Proj., Lib. of Congs., 1978–, Tech. Ofcr., Prcs. Srvs., 1976–78, Asst. Chief, Overseas Opers. Div., 1971–76, Asst. Opers. Ofcr., Ord. Div., 1968–71; Head of Acq., Columbus Meml. Lib., Org. of Amer. States, 1960–68. **Educ.:** Univ. of WA, 1947–50, BA (Hist.), 1958–59, MLS. **Orgs.:** ALA: Exhibit Staff, Century 21 Expo. Seattle (1962); Mem. Com. (DC Ch., 1961–63); RTSD, Hammond Map Awd. Com. (1965)/Acq. Sect. Policy and Resrch. Com. (Ch., 1970–71); IRRT (Vice-Ch., 1972–73). Assn. of Caribbean Univ. and Resrch. Libs.: Com. on Acq. (1980–). SALALM: Subcom. on Latin Amer. Acq. in U.S. Libs. (1980–); various coms., ofcs. **Honors:** Beta Phi Mu. **Pubns.:** Ed., *International Subscription Agents* (1974); contrib., *International Guide to Educational Documentation 1955-1960* (1963); various articles, reviews and working papers in lib. pubns. **Activities:** 4; 15 **Addr.:** 902 A St. S.E., Washington, DC 20003.

Delaney, Oliver J. (Je. 30, 1941, Dublin, Ireland) Head, Legis. Ref. Div., OK Dept. of Lib., 1979–, Law Libn., 1977–79; Head, Bus., Sci. Dept., OK Cnty. Libs., 1972–77; Head, Tech. Srvs., Coppin St. Coll., 1970–72. **Educ.:** St. Mary's Coll., 1960–63, AB (Phil.); Univ. of OK, 1966–68, BA (Classics), 1968–69, MLS. **Orgs.:** OK LA: Exec. Bd. (1979); Ref. Div. (Nom. Com. Ch., 1978); SRRT, Intl. Frdm. Com. (Ch., 1973, 1974). ALA: RASD/Bus. Ref. Srvs. Com. (1973–77). NLA: Nom. Com. (Ch., 1979). Various other orgs. **Honors:** Med. LA, Natl. Schol., 1968. **Pubns.:** "Selling to the Government," *OK Libn.* (Ja. 1978); "Libraries and Obscenity," *OK Libn.* (Ap. 1976); "The Occult: Diabolica to Alchemists, A Bibliography and Reference Shelf," *Ref. Qtly.* (Fall 1971); various other pubns. **Activities:** 4, 13; 24, 36, 39; 59, 77, 78 **Addr.:** 3120 Harvey Pkwy., Oklahoma City, OK 73118.

DeLaurier, Nancy G. (Ja. 11, 1924, Kansas City, MO) Cur. of Slides and Photographs, Univ. of MO, Kansas City, Art Hist. Dept. 1962–; Jr. Musm. Staff, Metro. Musm. of Art, 1945–46. **Educ.:** Northwest. Univ., 1940–45, BS (Hist.); Inst. of Fine Arts, New York Univ., 1945–46, (Art Hist.). **Orgs.:** Art Lib. Socty.: Visual Resrcs. Slide Stan. Com. (1977–79). Coll. Art Assn. Amer.: Visual Resrcs. (Ch., 1971); Nsltr. Ed. (1971–72). Mid-Amer. Coll. Art Assn.: Secy./Treas. (1972–); Nsltr. Ed. (1974–); *GUIDE* Pubns. (Ch., 1975–77). Intl. Art Hist. Cong.: Visual Resrcs. (Ch., 1979–81); various other coms. **Pubns.:** Ed., *International Bulletin for Photographic Documentation of the Visual Arts* (1980–81); *Slide Buyers Guide* (1972, 1974, 1976, 1980); "Slide Quality," *ARLIS Nsltr.* (1978); various articles in *MACAA Slides and Photographs Nsltr.* (1974–). **Activities:** 14-Academic Department; 15, 20, 23, 49-Visual Resources & Teaching Professional Visual Resources Courses; 55 **Addr.:** Department of Art & Art History, University of Missouri-Kansas City, Kansas City, MO 64110.

Delbaum, Judith E. (S. 28, 1945, New York, NY) Libn., Blue Cross of Grt. Philadelphia, 1973–; Libn., Resrch. for Better Schs., 1970–73. **Educ.:** Queens Coll., 1964–68, BA (Educ.); Drexel Univ., 1968–69, MSLS. **Orgs.:** SLA: Insr. Div. (Dir., 1980–81). Med. LA: Philadelphia Chap. (Treas., 1978–80). **Activities:** 12; 15, 20, 39; 59, 76, 80 **Addr.:** Blue Cross of Greater Philadelphia, 1333 Chestnut St., Philadelphia, PA 19107.

de Lerma, Dominique-René (D. 8, 1928, Miami, FL) Prof. of Msc. and Grad. Msc. Coord., Morgan St. Univ., 1976–; Msc. Libn., Assoc. Prof. Msc., IN Univ., 1963–76; Assoc. Prof. Msc., Univ. of OK, 1962–63; Assoc. Prof. Msc., Univ. of Miami, 1951–62. **Educ.:** Univ. of Miami, 1946–52 BM (Comp.); Indiana Univ., 1956–58 PhD (Msclgy.); Univ. of OK and IN Univ., LS std., post doc. **Orgs.:** Msc. LA: Bd. of Dir. (1969–71). Intl. Assn. of Msc. Libs. Inst. for Resrch. in Black Amer. Msc.: Bd. (Ch., 1979–). Columbia Records, Black Composers Series: Ch., Consult. (1973–). Sonorities in Black Msc.: Artistic Dir. (1978–). **Pubns.:** *The Legacy of Black Music* (1980); *Reflections of Afro-American Music* (1973); "The Chevalier de Saint-Georges," *Revista/Review Interamer.* (Win. 1978/79); "Humanistic Perspectives from Black Music," *Msc. and Man* (1974); ed. various wks. Chevalier de Saint-Georges and José Mauricio Nunes-Garcia recorded. **Activities:** 1, 12; 24, 30, 41; 95-Black music. **Addr.:** Music Department, Morgan State University, Baltimore, MD 21239.

Delgado, Jorge Garcia (F. 28, 1953, Silver City, NM) Libn., El Paso Cmnty Col., 1978–; Substitute Tchr., El Paso Pub. Schs., 1974–76. **Educ.:** Univ. of TX, El Paso, 1971–76, BS (Educ.); Univ. of AZ, 1977–78, MLS; TX Tchng. Cert., 1976; Univ. of TX, El Paso, 1979–81, MBA. **Orgs.:** REFORMA: El Paso Chap., Resrcs. Com. (Ch., 1979–). Border Reg. LA. ALA. El Paso Cmnty. Coll. Fac. Assn.: Stud. Affairs Com. (1979–). *AMOXCALLI Nsltr.*: Advert./Circ. Ed. **Pubns.:** Articles and Reviews, *AMOXCALLI Nsltr.*; "Library Service to the Spanish-speaking" (slide-tape) (1978). **Activities:** 1, 12; 15, 17, 31; 50, 59, 66 **Addr.:** 9244 Morelia, El Paso, TX 79907.

Delgado Cintrón, Carmelo (S. 7, 1940, Guayama, PR) Prof. of Law, Law Libn., Univ. of PR, 1980–; Dir., Univ. of PR Press, 1978–80; Exec. Secy., Univ. Bd., Univ. of PR, 1974–78. **Educ.:** Univ. of PR, 1959–63, BA (Hist.); 1963–66, LLB; SUNY, 1976, MA; Univ. of Madrid, 1973–74, Dr. en Derecho (Legal Hist.). Colegio de Abogados de PR: Ed. PR Bar Assn. Legal Review. Acad. Puertorriqueña de la Hist. **Pubns.:** *Cuestiones Ideológicas del Poder Judicial de Puerto Rico* (1979); *Derecho y Colonialismo. La Trayectoria histórica del Derecho puertorriqueño* (1979); *La Transculturación del Pensamiento Juridico en Puerto Rico* (1978); *El Tribunal Federal como Factor de Transculturación en Puerto Rico* (1973); *Historia Politica de Puerto Rico* (1976); Other books and articles. **Addr.:** Box L, University of Puerto Rico Station, Río Piedras, PR 00931.

Delivuk, John Allen (S. 25, 1947, Beaver Falls, PA) Head Libn., Trinity Episcopal Sch. for Mnstry., 1978–80; Asst. Libn., Covenant Theo. Semy., 1975–78; Ref. Libn. Cmnty. Coll. of Beaver Cnty., 1974–75. **Educ.:** Geneva Coll., 1965–69, BS (Phys.); Reformed Presby. Theo. Semy., 1964–73, Dip. (Theo.); Clarion State Coll., 1973–74, MSLS; Concordia Semy., 1975–. **Orgs.:** ATLA. ALA. **Pubns.:** "An Introduction to the History, Scope and Doctrine of the Reformed Presbyterian Church of North America," *Psalm-Singing of the Covenanters* (19–). **Activities:** 1; 15, 17, 20; 88, 90 **Addr.:** 747 Penn Ave., Apt. 9, Pittsburgh PA 15221.

Delks, Patricia J. Dir., Libs., Assoc. Prof., Rollins Coll., 1979–; Lib. Dir., Asst. Prof., Educ. Lindenwood Coll., 1974–79; Head, Ref., Smith Coll., 1963–74; Head, Serials/Docum. Div., Syracuse Univ., 1956–63; Dir., Geol. Branch Lib., Univ. of CA, Los Angeles, 1954–56. **Educ.:** IN Univ., 1944–47, BA (Anthro., Geol.); Univ. of KY, 1947–48 (Anthro.); Case West. Rsv. Univ., 1953–54, MLS; various insts. **Orgs.:** MO Gvrs. Conf. on Libs. **Honors:** Beta Phi Mu. **Pubns.:** Cmplr., *Environmental Pollution; A Select Bibliography,* (1960–71); *A Guide to Chemical Abstracts* (1977). **Addr.:** Rollins College, Holt Ave., Winter Park, FL 32789.

Della Cava, Olha T. (Mr., 1937, Posnan, Poland) Archvst., Columbia Univ., 1980–; Dir. of Arch. and Lib., Ctr. for Migration Std., 1973–80. **Educ.:** Manhattanville Coll., 1955–59, MA (Russ.); Harvard Univ. and Columbia Univ., 1960–72, PhD (Slavic Lang. and Lit.); Columbia Univ., 1976–79, MS (LS). **Orgs.:** SAA: Theme Cols. Ch. ALA. SLA. **Honors:** Free Univ. of Bruxelles, Fulbright Flwshp., 1959; Harvard Univ., Woodrow Wilson Flwshp., 1960. **Pubns.:** "Human Migration: A Survey of Information Sources," *Spec. Libs.* (Ag. 1979); "Italian-American Studies: A Progress Report," *Perspectives in Italian Immigration and Ethnicity* (1977). **Activities:** 1, 12; 24, 38, 45; 62, 66, 92 **Addr.:** 131 Sylvan Ave., Leonia, NJ 07605.

Della Porta, Armand (D. 20, 1921, Philadelphia, PA) Dir., Trustee, The Free Lib. of Philadelphia, 1968–; Judge, Court of Common Pleas, 1971–. **Educ.:** Temple Univ., 1941–43, 1946–47, BA (Soclgy.), 1947–50, LLB. **Orgs.:** ALA. **Honors:** St. Joseph's Prep. Sch., Ignatian Awd., 1977. **Pubns.:** "A Survey of the Laws of Marriage and Divorce in Pennsylvania," *Temple Law Qtly.* (Win., Spr., 1950); Contrib. to *Commentaries to PA Rules of Civil Procedure,* (1950–52); Articles for *Shingle* (Philadelphia Bar Assn.). **Activities:** 47; 77 **Addr.:** Rm. 1000 One East Penn Square Building, Philadelphia, PA 19107.

Deller, A. Michael (Jl. 8, 1941, Highland Park, MI) City Libn., Madison Heights Pub. Lib., 1979–; Coord., Prog. Srvs., Detroit Pub. Lib., 1978–79; Deputy Dir., Bloomfield Township Pub. Lib., 1976–78; Coord. of Cmnty. Rel., 1973–76. **Educ.:** Oakland Univ., 1959–63, BA (Educ.); Univ. of MI, 1966–68, MALS; Northwestern Univ., NDEA Russ. Lang. Inst., 1963; IN Univ., NDEA II Russ. Lang. Inst., 1964. **Orgs.:** ALA. MI LA. MI Lib. Film Circuit. Detroit Puppeteers Guld. **Activities:** 9, 13; 17, 36, 39; 55, 66, 95-Puppetry. **Addr.:** 2165 Burns Ave., Detroit, MI 48214.

DeLoach, Marva LaVerne (O. 24, 1946, Ludowici, GA) Head Cat. Libn., Asst. Prof., Hampton Inst., 1970–; Head Cat. Libn., Instr., 1971–79; Asst. Cat. and Ref. Libn. and Instr., 1970–71; Cat. Libn. and Asst. Pub. Srvs. Libn., Voorhees Coll., 1968–70. **Educ.:** Savannah State Coll., 1963–67, BS (Math.); Atlanta Univ., 1967–68, MSLS; Univ. of Pittsburgh, 1977–80, PhD (LS). Various wkshps. **Orgs.:** ALA: OLPR Minority Rcrt. Subcom. (Ch., 1979–); Black Caucus Awds. Com., (Ch., 1979); African and Caribbean Libns. Exch. Task Frc. (Rec., 1976–). SELA. VA LA. ASIS. AAUP: various Ofcs. AAUW: various Ofcs. NAACP: various coms. Hampton Inst. Womens Bd.: Pres. (1976); various other ofcs. Various other orgs. **Honors:** Alpha Kappa Mu; Beta Kappa Chi; Various Civic Awds. **Pubns.:** "Report of the Study Committee of the King Street Community Center," (1977); "Recruitment of Afro-Americans," Opportunities for Minorities in Libnshp. (1977); "Some Notes on Groups," *The Newtonian* (1967). **Activities:** 1, 12; 17, 20, 41; 66, 75, 91 **Addr.:** P.O. Box 6599, Hampton Institute, Hampton, VA 23668.

DeLong, Douglas A. (Ag. 11, 1939, Urbana, IL) Serials Libn., IL State Univ., 1968–, Per. Libn., 1967–68; Army Libn., U.S. Army, Europe, 1964–67. **Educ.:** Knox Coll., 1957–61, BA (Hist.); Univ. of IL, 1961–62, MS (LS); Univ. of Denver, 1972–73, Cert. of Adv. Std., Libnshp. **Orgs.:** ALA. IL LA. McLean Cnty. LA (IL): Pres. (1977–78). AAUP: IL State Univ. Chap. (VP, 1977–78). **Pubns.:** Contrib. Ed., *Magazines for libraries* (1978, 1982). **Activities:** 1; 44 **Addr.:** 35 Payne Pl., Normal, IL 61761.

De Lucia, Al (Jl. 2, 1923, Rochester, NY) Freelnc. Consult., 1980–; Comp. Sci., Dept. of the Air Frc., Rome Air Dev. Ctr., 1979–80; Opers. Resrch. Anal., Shape Tech. Ctr., The Hague, Netherlands, 1974–79; Comp. Sci., Dept. of Air Frc., Rome Air Dev. Ctr., 1951–74. **Educ.:** Hamilton Coll., 1948, BA (Phys., Chem.); Syracuse Univ., 1955, MA (Educ. Admin.). **Orgs.:** ASIS: Cncl. (1960–67). Socty. for Info. Display. **Pubns.:** Various papers at confs. (1959–75). **Activities:** 12; 30, 33, 41; 56, 75, 91 **Addr.:** 105 Harrogate Rd., New Hartford, NY 13413.

Del Valle, Mayoral, Miriam L. (N. 2, 1941, Bayamón, PR) Head Libn. Judicial Ctr., PR Ofc. of Court Admn., 1975–, Libn., Law Lib. of the Admn. for Compensation, 1973–75; Libn., Blanco Lugo, Lavatida, Moran; Libn., Univ. of PR, Docum., Maps, Order Dept., 1969–74. **Educ.:** Univ. of PR, 1960–64, BA (Pol. Sci.) 1975–77, MS (LS). **Orgs.:** Socty. de Bibter. de PR. ALA. AALL. Assn. Bib. de Derecho de PR: Secy. (1979). Catholic Daughters of Amer. Girl Scouts of Amer. Liga de Mujeres Votantes de PR. Assn. Exalumnos de la Univ. PR. **Pubns.:** *Las Bibliotecas Especializadas en Puerto Rico* (1975); *El Bibliotecario Especialista* (1975); *Las Bibliotecas Especializadas en América Latina* (1976); *La Organización y Administración de las Bibliotecas en Puerto Rico* (1977). **Activities:** 4, 12; 17, 20, 24; 77, 78 **Addr.:** Teniente Cesar Gonzalez #381, Urb. Roosevelt, Hato Rey, PR 00918.

Delzell, Robert F. (S. 4, 1918, Independence, KS) Dir. of Prsnl., Prof. of Lib. Admin. *Emeritus,* Univ. of IL, 1978–; Dir. of Prsnl., Prof. Lib. Admin., 1968–78; Prsnl. Libn., Assoc. Prof., 1967–68; Admin. Asst., Asst., Assoc. Prof., 1955–67; Chief, Acq. Branch, Asst. Prof. of Libnshp., USAF Air Univ. Lib., 1953–55; Chief, Acq. Dept., Washington Univ. Libs., 1951–53. **Educ.:** Drury Coll., 1936–40, AB (Fr.); Northwestern Univ., 1940–41 (Fr.); Washington Univ., 1948–50, BS (Educ.); Univ. of IL, 1950–51, MSLS. **Orgs.:** ALA: Awds. Com. (Ch., 1971–73); Scarecrow Press Awd. Jury, (Ch., 1967–68); Grolier Awd. Jury, (Ch., 1968–69). IL LA: Secy., Coll. and Resrch. Libs. Sect. (1961–62); Freedom to Read Foundation, ALA, 1970–. Beta Phi Mu: Exec. Cncl. (1962–65); Pres. (1969–70). SLA. Other orgs. AAUP. Amer. Civil Liberties Un. Univ. of IL, Campus RT: Bd. of Dirs. (1967–68). Univ. of IL Film Socty.: Pres. (1957–58); Fac. Adv. (1961–62). **Pubns.:** "Biography of Robert B. Downs," *Research Librarianship,* (1971); "On A Clear Day. . .," *Reminiscences; Seventy-Five Years of A Library School,* (1969); Ed., *The Book of Beta Phi Mu* (1957); Jt. auth., "Professional Duties in University Libraries", *The Case for Faculty Status for Academic Librarians,* (1970); Jt. auth., "ALA Awards, Citations, Scholarships & Grants," *American Libraries,* (N. 1971); Other articles, reviews. **Activities:** 1, 4; 15, 17, 35 **Addr.:** 1655 South Marion, Apt. 103-B, Springfield, MO 65807.

Demaree, Pauline F. (My. 10, 1928, Fairmont, NB) Dir., Lorain (OH) Pub. Lib., 1978–; Asst. Dir., 1972–77; Branch Libn., Cleveland Hts./Univ. Hts. (OH) Pub. Lib., 1968–72. **Educ.:** NB Wesleyan Univ., 1944–47, BA (Soc. Sci.); West. Resrv. Univ., 1965–67, MLS; Miami Univ., 1970, Cert. (Lib. Admin.). **Orgs.:** ALA. OH LA: Resrch. and Plng. Div. (Coord., 1973); Reg. Mtgs. Com. (1974; Ch., 1975; 1979); Stan. for Pub. Lib. (1977–78); Lib. Dev. Com. (Ch., 1980). Quota Club of Lorain: Pres. (1977–78); various coms. Lorain City Cmnty Educ. Adv. Com. Lorain City Schs. Reading Improvement Proj. Adv. Com. **Honors** Beta Phi Mu **Activities:** 9; 17 **Addr.:** Lorain Public Library, 351 Sixth St., Lorain, OH 44052.

Demers, Madeleine (Ag. 4, 1926, Béthanie, PQ) Dir. de la Bib., Coll. du Sacré-Coeur, Sherbrooke, 1947–; Enseignante, 1944–47. **Educ.:** Univ. de Montréal, 1952, Dip. (LS); Univ. de Sherbrooke, 1965, Cert. (Spir.); Inst. Cath. de Paris, 1966–67, Dip. (LS). **Orgs.:** ASTED: Sect. Scolaire (Exec. and Secy.-Treas., 1972–75); Cncl. (1975–77). CADRE: Com. Ad Hoc Sur le Persnl. de Bib. Cncl. d'Admin. du Coll. du Sacré-Coeur. Assn. des Bibtcrs. Français. Various other orgs. Assn. des Rel. enseignantes du PQ. **Pubns.:** Jt. auth., *Classification décimale Dewey, Traduction, lère éd. fr. intégrale* (1974). **Activities:** 10; 17, 20, 39; 62, 89 **Addr.:** 979, Sideleau, Sherbrooke, PQ J1E 1H6 Canada.

Dempsey, Frank J. (N. 8, 1925, San Francisco, CA) Exec. Libn., Arlington Heights Meml. Lib., 1973–; Dir., Berkeley Pub. Lib., 1962–73; Asst. Dir., 1958–62; Supvsry. Libn. & Trng. Ofcr.,

Special Subjects/Services: 50. Adult educ.; 51. Advert./Mktg.; 52. Aerosp.; 53. Agric.; 54. Area std.; 55. Arts/Hum.; 56. Autom.; 57. Bibl./Prtg.; 58. Bio. sci.; 59. Bus./Fin.; 60. Chem.; 61. Copyrt.; 62. Documtn.; 63. Educ.; 64. Engin.; 65. Env.; 66. Eth. grps.; 67. Film; 68. Food/Nutr.; 69. Geneal.; 70. Geo.; 71. Geol.; 72. Handcpd.; 73. Hist.; 74. Int. frdm.; 75. Info. sci.; 76. Insr.; 77. Law; 78. Legis.; 79. Math./Comp. sci.; 80. Med.; 81. Metals; 82. Nat. resrcs.; 83. Newsp.; 84. Nuc. sci.; 85. Oral hist.; 86. Petr./Energy; 87. Pharm.; 88. Phys./Astr./Math.; 89. Readg.; 90. Relig.; 91. Sci./Tech.; 92. Soc. sci.; 93. Telecom.; 94. Transp.; 95. (other).

Indus. Rel. Dept., US Nvl. Supply Ctr., 1955–58. **Educ.:** Univ. of CA, Berkeley, 1946–50, BA (Hist.); 1952–53, BLS. **Orgs.:** IL LA: Pres. (1977–78). ALA: PR Sect. (Ch., 1977–78). Reg. Lib. Adv. Cncl. (IL): Pres. (1975–76). Arlington Heights Rotary Club: Intl. Rel. (Ch., 1975–76). Amer. Red Cross, Berkeley Chap.: VP (1971–72). **Honors:** U.S. Naval Supply Center (Oakland CA) Superior Accomplishment Award, 1956. **Pubns.:** "Public Relations" *ALA Yearbook* (1979); *A Review of Library Administration* (1961); "Berkeley, California" *Encyc. Americana* (1976); "Berkeley's Award Winning Branch Library" *CA Libn.* (Ap. 1967). **Activities:** 4, 9; 17, 19, 36 **Addr.:** Arlington Heights Memorial Library, 500 N. Dunton, Arlington Hts., IL 60004.

Dempster, Dorothea (Dora) M. (Ag. 14, 1945, Edinburgh, Scotland) Dir., Lib. Resrcs. Ctr., Seneca Coll., Finch Campus, 1978–; Coord., Lib. Srvs., Ryerson Polytech. Inst., 1974–78; Ref. Libn., Can. Broadcasting Corp. Lib., 1972–74; Ref. & Orient. Libn., Carleton Univ., 1967–72. **Educ.:** Univ. of SK, 1963–66, BA (Econ.); Univ. of BC, 1966–67, BLS. **Orgs.:** Can. LA: Conv. Info. Srvs. Coord. Grp. (1976–1978). ON LA: Conf. Plng. Com. (1978). ON Cncl. of Univ. Libs.: Ch. Interuniv. Borrowing Proj. (1976–1977). **Pubns.:** Audio Cassette: "Closing the Card Catalogue." (1977). **Activities:** 1; 18, 21, 32; 51, 57 **Addr.:** Finch Campus Library, Seneca College of Applied Arts and Technology, 1750 Finch Ave., East, Willowdale, ON M2J 2X5 Canada.

Dendy, Adele Sharp (N. 14, 1936, Philadelphia, PA) Head, Media Srvs. and Media Libn., IN Univ., 1977–; Sch. Libn./AV Coord., Monroe Cnty. Cmnty. Schs. Corp., 1972–74; Media Libn., IN Univ. Libs., 1974–75. **Educ.:** Temple Univ., 1954–63, BS (Educ.); Univ. of Pittsburgh, 1969–70, MLS; IN Univ., 1978–80, MS (Educ.); 1979– (Higher Educ. Admin.). **Orgs.:** ALA: ACRL/Educ. and Bhvl. Scis. Sect. (1980–82); LITA; Black Caucus. Assn. of IN Media Educs.: Prog. Com. (1980); Mem. Com. Dist. 10 (1978, 1979). IN Univ. Libns. Assn. Various other orgs. IN LA. Phi Delta Kappa: Resrch. Com. (1980–82). Delta Kappa Gamma: Alpha Chap., Resrch. Com. (Ch., 1980–82). Alpha Kappa Alpha: Kappa Tau Omega Chap. IN Univ. Women's Fac. Club. **Pubns.:** "Media Centers: From the School to the University," *IN Univ. Lib. Qtly.* (Spr. 1978). **Activities:** 1, 10; 15, 17, 32; 63, 93 **Addr.:** 3200 Longview Dr., D61, Kingston Manor Apts., Bloomington, IN 47401.

Denis, Laurent-G. (F. 21, 1932, Montreal, PQ, Can) Prof. of LS, Univ. of Toronto, 1970–; Dir., Univ. of Montreal-Ecole Bibter., 1961–70; Asst. Chief Libn., Coll. Milit. royal de St-Jean, 1956–61; Cat., Natl. Lib. of Can., 1955–56. **Educ.:** Loyola Coll., Montreal, 1951–54, BA (Pre-med); McGill Univ., 1954–55, BLS; 1956–59, MLS; Rutgers Univ., 1965–69, PhD (LS). **Orgs.:** Can. LA: various coms. and ofcs. ALA. Ontario LA. Assn. des Scie. et Tech. de la Documtn. **Pubns.:** *Rapport de l'Etude des bibliothèques publiques de la région de Montréal* (1975); "Full-time Faculty: Survey Describes Educators", *Can. Lib. Jnl.* (Je. 1979); Ed. "Library Education Issue", *Can. Lib. Jnl.* (Je. 1979). **Activities:** 9; 17, 24, 26 **Addr.:** Faculty of Library Science, University of Toronto, 140 St. George St., Toronto, ON M5S 1A1 Canada.

Deniston, Patricia Swan (S. 29, 1935, New York, NY) Dir. of Lrng. Resrcs., Polk Cmnty. Coll., 1972–, Prof. and Media Spec., 1971–72; Media Spec., Tampa Catholic HS, 1969–70; Media Spec. and Tchr., Hillsborough Cnty. Sch., 1963–69. **Educ.:** Univ. of Tampa, 1963, BS (Elem. Educ.); Univ. of S. FL, 1968, MA, (LS); Univ. of FL, 1978, EdD. **Orgs.:** FL Assn. for Media in Educ.: Secy. (1974–76), Pres. (1979–80). ALA. FL LA. AECT. Pi Lambda Theta. Kappa Delta Pi. Phi Kappa Phi. **Honors:** Beta Phi Mu. **Activities:** 1; 15, 17, 20; 61, 67, 72 **Addr.:** Polk Community College, 999 Ave H N.E., Winter Haven, FL 33880.

Denman, Margaret Woods (S. 11, 1926, Oklahoma City, OK) Coord., Grad. Media/LS Prog., West. MD Coll., 1977–; Fac., Dept. of LS, Ctrl. MO State Univ., 1970–77; Libn., Raytown S. HS, 1967–70; Pub. Libn., St. Louis Cnty. Lib., 1963–66. **Educ.:** Univ. of OK, 1948, BA (Eng.); Ctrl. MO State Univ., 1969, MSE (LS); TX Woman's Univ., 1979, PhD (LS). **Orgs.:** ALA: AASL; YASD, ALSC. AECT. MD Educ. Media Assn.: Treas. (1979–81); Pres.-Elect (1981–82). AALS: Mem. Com. (1980–83). Adlscnt. Lit. Asn. MD Assn. of Tchrs. of Educ. AAUP. Various other orgs. **Honors:** Beta Phi Mu; Phi Kappa Phi; Phi Delta Kappa. **Activities:** 11; 26; 63 **Addr.:** P.O. Box 056, Westminster, MD 21157.

Denman, Ruby Othella (D. 16, 1908, Iola, TX) Retired, 1972–; Head Libn., Waco HS, 1942–72; Instr., LS, Baylor Univ., 1965–67; Instr., LS, TX Women's Univ., 1958–60; Instr., E. TX State Univ., 1953; Tchr., Libn., La Vega HS, 1938–42; Tchr., Libn., Elkhart HS, 1936–38; Tchr., Garden City HS, 1931–36. **Educ.:** Baylor Univ., 1926–31, AB (Educ., Eng.); Univ. of TX, 1936–39, MA (Educ., Eng.); TX Women's Univ., 1940, 1941, 1946, BS (LS), 1954, MS (LS). **Orgs.:** ALA: AASL, Student Lib. Assts. (Ch., 1958–62), Rcrt. Com. (1958–61). SWLA: TX Rep. (1957–58). TX LA: State Pres. (1957–58); VP (1956–57); Mem. Ch. (1954–55); Natl. Lib. Week Com. (1956–60); Sch. Lib. Div., State Secy. (1945), State Treas. (1968). Delta Kappa Gamma: Various ofcs., coms. Natl. Educ. Assn.: Natl. Conv. (Waco Rep., 1964). AAUW. TX State Tchrs. Assn. Various other orgs. **Honors:** ALA, John Cotton Dana Pubcty. for HSs, 1956; Delta Kappa Gamma, State Achvmt. Awd., 1953. **Pubns.:** Various articles, *Sch. Libs.* (1955–62), *TX Lib. Jnl.* (1950–70); reviews. **Activities:** 10, 11; 26, 32, 48; 63 **Addr.:** 2912 Fort Ave., Waco, TX 76707.

Dennin, Marjorie Catherine Wilkins (O. 5, 1918, Barnesville, OH) Dir. of Lrng. Resrcs., North. VA Cmnty. Coll., Annandale Campus, 1965–; Cat. Libn., VA Theo. Semy., 1964–65; Chief Libn., Amer. Auto. Assn., 1960–64; Chief Libn., Edison Electric Inst., 1946–56. **Educ.:** Mt. Un. Coll., 1936–40, BA (Eng.); Cath. Univ. of Amer., 1960–64, MSLS. **Orgs.:** ALA: ACRL, Legis. Com. (1976–78); Stans. and Accred. Com. (1978–82),/Cmnty. and Jr. Coll. Sect. (Ch., 1974)/Coll. and Univ. Sect. (Ch., 1976), Task Frc. on Lib. Resrcs. (Ch., 1976), Maintenance Formula Com. (1975–76), various other coms. VA LA: Lib. Adv. Com. to VA State Cncl. of Educ. (1966–). Smithsonian Resident Assn. Natl. Trust for Hist. Prsrvn. **Pubns.:** Ed., *Directory of Virginia Library Resources* (1976). **Activities:** 1, 12; 17, 32, 34; 50, 75, 95-Vocational/tech. Info. **Addr.:** 4320 Old Dominion Dr., Arlington, VA 22207.

Denning, Julie Wolfson (D. 5, 1950, Chicago, IL) Libn., San Pedro Branch, Albuquerque Pub. Lib., 1978–; Info. Srvs. Libn., 1974–78; Chld. Libn., Erna Fergusson Branch, 1974. **Educ.:** Univ. of CO, 1968–72, BA (Soclgy.); Univ. of Denver, 1972–74, MA (LS). **Orgs.:** ALA. SWLA: Lcl. Arrange. Sub-Com. (1976). NM LA: Gen. Pubcty. & Natl. Lib. Week Com. (1978–81). **Honors:** Phi Beta Kappa, 1972; Beta Phi Mu, 1974. **Activities:** 9; 16, 17, 39 **Addr.:** San Pedro Branch Library, 5600 Trumbull Ave. S.E., Albuquerque, NM 87108.

Dennis, Deborah Ellis (Ja. 3, 1950, Brainerd MN) Admin. Staff Libn., Univ. of MD, 1979–; Libn., Resrch. Assoc., George Washington Univ. Social Resrch. Grp., 1978–79; Libn., Natl. Sch. Bds. Assn., 1976–77; Asst. to the Dir., Ed., Northwest. Univ. Ctr. for Urban Affairs, 1972–76. **Educ.:** Northwest. Univ., 1968–71, BSJ (Jnlsm.); Univ. of Chicago, 1974–76, AM (LS); Univ. of MD, 1979– (Gen. Mgt.). **Orgs.:** ALA: RASD Rep. to Frdm. to Rcad Fndn. (1981–82); ACRL/Bibl. Instr. Com. Prog. Com. (1981); LAMA; LRRT. SLA. Socty. of Prof. Jnlsts. (Sigma Delta Chi). **Pubns.:** Jt. auth., *Suburbia: A Guide to Information Sources* (1979); Jt. auth., *Youth in America: A Social Indicators Chartbook on the 4H Eligible Population* (1979); Jt. auth., *Child Development Within the Family–Evolving New Research Approaches.* (1978); Jt. auth., *Youth Development and Families* (1978); Jt. auth., *Suburbs, Suburbia and Suburbanization: A Bibliography,* 2nd ed. (1974). **Activities:** 1, 12; 17, 39, 41; 63, 92 **Addr.:** Office of the Director, University of Maryland Libraries, College Park, MD 20742.

Dennis, Donald D. (D. 21, 1928, Paris, France) Univ. Libn., Amer. Univ., 1971–; Chief, Ref. Srvs. Div., Natl. Lib. of Med., 1969–71; Hlth. Scis. Libn., Univ. of MI, 1967–69; Libn. and Assoc. Prof., Cedar Crest Coll., 1962–66. **Educ.:** Bowdoin Coll., 1947–51, AB (Eng.); Univ. of CA, Berkeley, 1956–57, MLS. **Orgs.:** ALA. SLA. **Honors:** Amer. Univ., Fac.–Admin. Awd. for Outstan. Srv., 1979. **Pubns.:** *Simplifying Work in Small Public Libraries* (1965). **Activities:** 1, 4; 17, 19, 24; 56, 75 **Addr.:** 9204 Seven Locks Rd., Bethesda, MD 20034.

Dennis, Willye F. (Mr. 14, 1926, Jacksonville, FL) Dept. Libn., Chld. Srvs., Outreach, Jacksonville Pub. Lib., 1953–. **Educ.:** Clark Coll., 1950–53, BA (Bus. Admn.), Atlanta Univ., 1954–56, MSLS; Nora Univ., 1976–78, DPA (Pub. Admn.). **Orgs.:** ALA: Notable Bk. Com.; Newbery/Caldecott Com. (1978–79). FL LA. (1977–78). Delta Sigma Theta: Pres. (1977–80). Jack and Jill of Amer., Inc.: Teen Adv. (1976–78). **Honors:** NAACP, Educ., 1976; Chi Eta Phi, Outstan. Citizen, 1974; YMCA, Outstan. Citizen, 1973. **Pubns.:** "Jacksonville Public Library Outreach Program," *FL Libs.* **Activities:** 9; 21, 49-Outreach; 66, 89 **Addr.:** Jacksonville Public Library, 122 N. Ocean St., Jacksonville, FL 32209.

Dennison, Lynn C. (Je. 11, 1947, Boston, MA) Student, Grad. Sch. of Mgt., Univ. of CA, Los Angeles, 1979–; Staff Asst., Lib., Univ. of IL at Chicago Circle, 1979; Prog. Ofcr., Prof. Asst., ALA, ACRL, 1972–78. **Educ.:** Grinnell Coll., 1964–66; Hiram Coll., 1967–69, BA (Span. & Msc.); Univ. of WI, Madison, 1971–72, MA (LS); Univ. of CA, Los Angeles, 1979–, MBA, in progress. **Orgs.:** ALA: ACRL. IL LA: Libn. Cit. Com. (1976–77). IL ACRL. Pub. Interest Mgt. Assn.; Assn. of MBA Execs. **Honors:** Cncl. on Lib. Resrcs., Flwshp., 1975–76. **Pubns.:** "The Organization of Library and Media Services in Community Colleges," *Coll. and Resrch. Libs.* (Mr. 1978). **Activities:** 1, 3; 17, 37; 56 **Addr.:** 1133 Elizabeth, Naperville, IL 60540.

Dennison, Sam M. (S. 26, 1926, Geary, OK) Cur., Edwin A. Fleisher Col. of Orch. Msc., 1975–; Msc. Libn., Free Lib. of Philadelphia, 1964–75; Msc. Libn., Prof., Inter Amer. Univ., 1960–64. **Educ.:** Univ. of OK, 1946–50, BM (Composition); Univ. of South. CA, 1950–53, MM (Composition); Drexel Univ., 1964–66, MSLS. **Orgs.:** Msc. LA: PA Chap. Sonneck Socty. Msc. Fund Socty.: Mus. Com. **Pubns.:** *The Edwin A. Fleisher Collection of Orchestral Music in The Free Library of Philadelphia: A Cumulative Catalog 1929–1977.* (1979). **Activities:** 9, 12; 16, 22; 55 **Addr.:** Fleisher Collection, Free Library of Philadelphia, Logan Sq., Philadelphia, PA 19103.

Densmore, Christopher (O. 8, 1949, Painesville, OH) Assoc. Archvst., SUNY, Buffalo 1974–. **Educ.:** Oberlin Coll., 1971, BA (Hist.); Univ. of WI, 1973, MA (Amer. Hist.). **Orgs.:** SAA: Task Force on a Model Finding Aid Syst. for Coll. and Univ. Arch., (Ch., 1977–79); Strg. Com., Prof. Afnty. Grp. on the Descr. of Mss. and Arch. (1979–). Lake Ontario Archival Conf.: Co-Ch., Prog. Com. (1974–1q75); Steering Com. (1975–76). Midwest Arch. Conf. Mid Atl. Arch. Conf. Other orgs. Amer. Assn. for State and Local Hist. Org. of Amer. Histns. Buffalo Cmnty. Stds. Grp.: Strg. Com. (1979–80). **Pubns.:** "Multi-Institutional Finding Aids," *The Bookmark* (Win. 1981); "Understanding and Using Early Nineteenth Century Account Books," *Midwestern Archvst.* (1980). **Activities:** 1, 2; 38, 45, 46 **Addr.:** University Archives, 420 Capen Hall, State University of New York at Buffalo, Buffalo, NY 14260.

Denson, Janeen J. (Mr. 26, 1949, Albany, GA) Circ. Libn., Duke Univ., 1975–; Sch. Libn., Fishkill Elem. Sch. (NY), 1973–74; Asst. Libn., Middle GA Coll., 1971–73. **Educ.:** Clark Coll., 1966–70, AB (Eng.); Atlanta Univ., 1970–71, MSLS. **Orgs.:** AALL. Beta Phi Mu; Alpha Kappa Alpha. **Activities:** 1, 12; 15, 22, 39; 77 **Addr.:** 602 Red Carriage Ave., Durham, NC 27704.

Denton, William Richard (Jl. 17, 1929, Seattle, WA) Serials Libn., Theo. Lib., South. CA Sch. of Theo., 1959–; Mnstr. of Educ., First Presby. Church, Oakland, CA, 1957–59; Mnstr. of Educ., St. John's Presby. Church, Reno, NV, 1954–57. **Educ.:** Whitworth Coll., 1947–51, BA (Christ. Educ.); San Francisco Theo. Semy., 1951–55, BD, MA (Christ. Educ.); Univ. of South. CA, 1959–63, MS, in LS. **Orgs.:** ATLA: Per. exchange com. West. Theo. LA: Pres. (1966–67). Christ. LA: Pres. (1964–66). Amer. Gld. of Eng. Handbell Ringers. Modified Motorcycle Assn. Amer. Bell Assn.: Dir. Ch. Amer. Motorcycle Assn. **Pubns.:** *Bells and their use as a means of Christian Education* (1961; 2d ed. 1975); Ed. *Union List of Continuations* (1961); "The Robert Dollar Memorial Chimes" *The San Francisco Theological Seminary Chimes* (S. 1953). **Activities:** 1; 15, 44, 46; 90 **Addr.:** 352 S. Annapolis Dr., Claremont, CA 91711.

DePew, John N. (N. 18, 1934, Akron, OH) Assoc. Prof., Sch. LS, FL St. Univ., 1972–; Coord. of Tech. Srvs., Univ. of Pittsburgh, 1969–72, Coord. of Acq., 1967–69; Head of Acq., Duquesne Univ., 1965–67; Asst. Librn., Bethany College (WV), 1964–65; Librn., New York Pub. Lib., 1958. **Educ.:** Bethany Coll. (WV), 1952–56, BA, (Hist.); West. Reserve Univ., 1956–58, MS (LS); Univ. of Pittsburgh, 1964–65, Advnc. Cert. (LS), 1966–71, PHD (LS). **Orgs.:** ALA: ACRL, Acad. Status Com. (1978–81); LAMA/Lib. Org. and Mgt. Sect., Compar. Lib. Org. Com. (1978–80, Ch. 1979–80); Persnl. Admn. Sect., Staff Dev. Com. (1974–78, Ch. 1976–78); various other coms. FL LA: Budget Com. (Ch., 1978–79); VP (1977–78); Pres. (1978–79); Exec. Bd. (1979–80); various other coms. AALS; SELA; St. Lib. Cncl. FL; various coms. in all orgs. U.S. Naval Reserve: Capt., Naval Reserve Assn. **Honors:** Beta Phi Mu, 1971. **Pubns.:** "An Acquisitions Decision Model for Academic Libraries," *Jnl. ASIS* (Jl./Ag. 1975). **Activities:** 1, 11; 17, 44, 46; 50, 70, 92 **Addr.:** School of Library Science, Florida State University, Tallahassee, FL 32306.

DeProspo, Ernest R. (Ja. 10, 1937, Worcester, MA) Prof. and PhD Dir., Grad. Sch. of Lib. and Info. Sci., Rutgers Univ., 1967–; Resrch. Assoc., Inst. of Pub. Admin., PA State, 1965–67; Resrch. Assoc., IPA/NY, Lima, Peru, 1964–65; Instr., Dept. of Pol. Sci., PA State, 1963–64. **Educ.:** Clark Univ., 1955–59, AB (Gvt.); Northeast. Univ., 1959–61, MA (Pol. Sci.); PA State Univ., 1961–67, PhD (Pol. Sci.). **Orgs.:** ALA: PLA, Goals, Guidelines, and Stans. Com. (1975–78). NJ LA: Lib. Dev. Com. (Co–Dir., 1969–73). ASIS. **Pubns.:** *Performance Measures for Public Libraries* (1973); *A Data Gathering and Instructional Manual for Performance Measures in Public Libraries* (1976); "Potential Limits and Abuses of Evaluation," *Sch. Media Qtly.* (Sum. 1975); "Federal Funds in Governance of Local Library Instutions," *Lib. Trends* (Fall 1975). **Addr.:** 16 Westwood Rd., East Brunswick, NJ 08816.

Dequin, Henry C. (Jn. 20, 1925, Detroit, MI) Assoc. Prof., LS, North. IL Univ., 1974–; Lib. Media Dir., Luth. HS (Detroit), 1958–74. **Educ.:** Concordia Sem., 1945–46, BA 1946–49, MDiv, 1953–55, STM (Theo.); Univ. of MI, 1958–61, AMLS; Wayne State Univ., 1968–72, PhD (Instr. Tech.). **Orgs.:** ALA: AASL, Video Comm. Com. (1978–81); YASD, Media Sel. and Usage Com. (1976–80). AECT: Cont. Educ. Com. (1978–80). IL Assn. for Educ. Comm. and Tech.: Gen. Co-Ch. Spr. 1979 Conf. (1977–79); Jt. Std. Com. (1977–79). IL LA: AV Com. (Ch., 1977–78). Various other orgs. and coms. **Honors:** Beta Phi Mu. **Pubns.:** *A Guide to Selecting Learning Resource Materials and Equipment* (1978); "Sources of Information about the Handicapped," *Sch. Lib. Jnl.* (N. 1979); "Selecting Materials for the Handicapped: A Guide to Sources," *Top of the News* (Fall 1978). **Activities:** 11; 26 **Addr.:** Dept. of Library Science, Northern Illinois University, DeKalb, IL 60115.

Dermyer, Angela L. (D. 18, 1940, Tecumseh, NE) Head Libn., Union Pacific Railroad, 1978–, Libn., 1976–78; Libn., Burke HS (Omaha, NE), 1970–71; Libn., Puohala Elem. Sch. (Kaheohe, HI), 1968–69, Libn., Moss Point, MS HS, 1967–68. **Educ.:** Univ. of NE (Lincoln), 1958–62, BA (Eng.); Univ. of NC

PROFESSIONAL ACTIVITIES: Institutions: 1. Acad. lib.; 2. Arch.; 3. Assn.; 4. Fed./Gvt. lib.; 5. Inst. lib.; 6. Mfr./Suppl.; 7. Milit. lib.; 8. Musm.; 9. Pub. lib.; 10. Sch. lib.; 11. Sch. of lib. sci.; 12. Spec. lib.; 13. State lib.; 14. (other). **Functions/Activities:** 15. Acq./Col. dev.; 16. Adult srvs.; 17. Admin.; 18. Apprais.; 19. Archit./Bldgs.; 20. Cat./Class.; 21. Chld. srvs.; 22. Circ.; 23. Cons./Pres.; 24. Consult.; 25. Cont. ed.; 26. Educ. lib. sci.; 27. Ext. srvs.; 28. Fund/Grants; 29. Gvt. pubs.; 30. Indx./Abs.; 31. Instr. lib. use; 32. Media srvs.; 33. Micro.; 34. Netwks./Coop.; 35. Persnl.; 36. PR; 37. Publshg.; 38. Recs. mgt.; 39. Ref. srvs.; 40. Repro.; 41. Resrch.; 42. Review.; 43. Secur.; 44. Serials; 45. Spec. col.; 46. Tech. srvs.; 47. Trustees/Bds.; 48. YA srvs.; 49. (other).

(Chapel Hill), 1965–67, MS (LS). **Orgs.:** SLA: Bus. Circle Coord. (1978). Assn. for Info. Mgrs. NE LA. Metro. Lib. Netwk.: Secy. (1979–80). St. Lib. Adv. Cncl. **Pubns.:** "Try on a Company Library," *Indus. Wk.* (Ag. 1977); "Libraries in Business Firms Tailor-Made to Companies' Goals," *Midlands Bus. Jnl.* (D. 1976); syndicated column, "Inside Information" (D. 1979–). **Activities:** 12; 17, 39; 51, 59, 94 **Addr.:** Union Pacific Railroad, 1416 Dodge St., Omaha, NE 68179.

De Ronde, Paula Doreen (Mr. 21, 1944, St. Andrew, Jamaica, W. Indies) YA Libn. III, Head Libn., Palmerston Lib., Toronto Pub. Lib., 1981–, Libn. II; YA Libn. I, 1976–79. **Educ.:** Univ. of Toronto, 1971–74, BA (Eng.); 1974–76, MSL. **Orgs.:** Can. LA: Intl. Frdm. Com. (1977–79). ON LA. ON Puppetry Assn. **Activities:** 9; 15, 21, 48; 66, 74, 89 **Addr.:** Palmerston Library, 560 Palmerston Ave., Toronto, ON M6G 2P7, Canada.

Dertien, James L. (D. 14, 1942, Kearney, NE) Dir. of Cmnty. Srvs. and City Libn., City of Bellevue, Bellevue Pub. Lib., 1975; Chief Libn., Bismarck Pub. Lib., 1970–75; Actg. Dir. of Libs., Univ. of SD, 1969–70; Head Libn., Sioux Falls Coll., 1967–69. **Educ.:** Univ. of SD, 1962–65, AB (Eng.); Univ. of Pittsburgh, 1965–66, MLS. **Orgs.:** Mt. Plains LA: Pres. (1979–80). ALA: PLA, Pubns. Com. (Ch., 1978–79). ND LA: Nsltr. (Ed., 1970–75). Rotary Intl. of Bellevue. Bellevue Cham. of Cmrce. **Honors:** Bellevue Cham. of Cmrce., Outstan. Dir., 1979 and 1980; Bellevue Jaycees, Outstan. Young Man, 1980. **Activities:** 9; 17, 25, 35 **Addr.:** Bellevue Public Library, 1003 Lincoln Rd., Bellevue, NE 68005.

Desch, Carol Ann (O. 11, 1952, Albany, NY) Head, Ref. and Info. Srvs., Bethlehem Pub. Lib., 1979–; Ref. Libn., Bethlehem Pub. Lib., 1977–79. **Educ.:** NY State Univ. Coll., Oneonta, 1974, BA (Educ.); SUNY Albany, 1977, MLS. **Orgs.:** ALA: Job Info. Srvs. Com. (Ch., 1980–82); NY LA: Adult Learner and Job Info. Srvs. Com. (1978–). **Honors:** Beta Phi Mu. **Pubns.:** Jt. auth., "Job Information Centers in the Public Library," *Col. Bldg.* (forthcoming). **Activities:** 9; 16, 39; 50 **Addr.:** 125 S. Main Ave., Albany, NY 12208.

Deschatelets, Gilles H. (My. 26, 1945, Montreal, PQ) Head, Sci. Lib., Univ. Laval, 1979–, Ref. Libn., 1971–79, Coord., Comp. Ref. Srvs., 1973–79. **Educ.:** Univ. de Montreal, 1958–65, BA (Econ.), 1966, BA (Educ.); McGill Univ., 1970–71, MLS; Univ. of West. ON, 1975– (LS). **Orgs.:** Can. Assn. Info. Sci.: Conf. (Ch., 1981). Can. LA. ASTED. Corp. des Bibtcrs. Prof. du PQ. Various other orgs. **Pubns.:** Jt. auth., *Recueil des instructions d'opération des systèmes documentaires en mode conversationnel offerts par DSI/LAVAL* (1975); "Problèmes et promesses de la téléréférence (Telereference: Promises and Pitfalls)," *Revue Can. Des Sci. De L'Info.* (1976); "L'intermédiaire humain: une espèce en voie de disparition? (The Human Intermediary: An Endangered Species?)," *Revue Can. des Sci. de l'Info.* (1978); *Enquête sur les services de téléréférence au Canada* (Mr. 1980); *A Survey of Online Search Service Centers in Canada* (Mr. 1980); various articles (1973–75). **Activities:** 1; 17; 75, 80, 91 **Addr.:** 1190 Colbert, Apt. 514, Ste-Foy, PQ G1V 3Y4 Canada.

Des Chene, Dorice (Warren, MN) Head, Chem.-Bio. Lib., Univ. of Cincinnati, 1973–; MEDLINE Coord., Univ. of WA, 1972–73, Head, MEDLARS/MEDLINE Ctr., 1968–72. **Educ.:** Univ. of MN, 1939–43, BS (Med. Tech.); Univ. of WA, 1967–68, ML (LS), 1972–78, MA (Biomed. Hist.); MEDLARS Trng., Natl. Lib. of Med., 1968–69. **Orgs.:** ASIS: South. OH Chap. (Ch., 1979–80). Med. LA: Nom. Com. (1971–73). SLA. AAUP. Cincinnati OLUG. **Honors:** ASIS, South. OH Chap., Kahles Awd., 1977, Outstan. Mem. Awd., 1978. **Activities:** 1; 17, 26; 58, 60, 75 **Addr.:** Chemistry-Biology Library, University of Cincinnati, Cincinnati, OH 45221.

de Sciora, Edward A. (Mr. 17, 1928, Chicago, IL) Dir., Port Washington Pub. Lib., 1959–; Adj. Assoc. Prof., Grad. Lib. Sch., Queens Coll., CUNY, 1976–79; Adj. Assoc. Prof., Grad. Lib. Sch., Long Island Univ., 1968–78; Admin. Asst. to Chief Libn., Brooklyn Pub. Lib., 1955–58. **Educ.:** Bethany Coll., 1946–51, BA (Econ.); Columbia Univ., 1951–54, MSLS. **Orgs.:** Lib. PR Cncl.: Pres. (1976–77); Secy. (1963–64). ALA: Lib. Admin. Div., Small Libs. Pubn. Com. (1973–76). NY State Assn. of Lib. Bds.: Bd. (1971–77). NY LA: Sec. VP (1975–76); Pub. Libs. Sect. (Pres., 1973–74). Various other orgs., ofcs., coms. Natl. Fed. Lcl. Cable Progs. Adelphi Univ., Univ. Coll.: Adv. Bd. (1978–). Port Washington Chld. Ctr.: Adv. Bd. (1978–). Telicmnty., Inc.: Pres., Bd. Ch., (1980–). Various other orgs., coms. **Activities:** 9, 11; 17, 19, 24; 93 **Addr.:** Port Washington Public Library, 245 Main St., Port Washington, NY 11050.

Deshaies, Louise T. (Ap. 13, 1920, Raleigh, NC) Asst. Cat. Libn., University of NC, Greensboro, 1972–; Head, Descr.-Adaptive Cat. Sect., Univ. of NC, Chapel Hill, 1967–72. **Educ.:** Meredith Coll., 1938–40, AB (Eng., Fr.); Peace Coll., 1936–1938; Univ. of NC, 1963–67, MSLS. **Orgs.:** ALA. SELA. NCLA: Resrcs. & Tech. Srv. Div. (Secy. 1968–70; Dir. 1972–74; Nom. Com., 1972, 1975). Univ. of NC Sch. of LS Alum. Assn.: Pres. (1970–71). Other orgs. NC Poetry Socty. NC Registry of Interpreters for the Deaf. Pilot Club of Greensboro. **Honors:** Beta Phi Mu. **Pubns.:** Solinet *Memoranda* Indexes, (1975–1979); *Solinews*, (1973–1979); "Capitalization of Catalog Cards: Brief Guidelines," *NC Libs.* (1972). **Activities:** 1; 20, 45, 46; 55, 92 **Addr.:** 2619 Springwood Dr., Greensboro, NC 27403.

Deshpande, Gangadhar R. (Mr. 29, 1933, WAI, Maharashtra, India) Ref. Spec., City of Brampton Pub. Lib., 1969–; Ref. Libn., Sudbury Pub. Lib., 1967–69; Asst. Libn., The British Cncl. Lib., India, 1963–67; Intern Libn., Croydon Pub. Lib., England, 1965–66; Tech. Libn., Tech. Lib., Air India Intl., 1957–63. **Educ.:** Bombay Coll., Bombay, India, BA; Univ. of Bombay, BLSc. **Orgs.:** ALA. SLA. Can. LA. Can. ALL. Ctrl. Ontario Reg. Lib. Syst.: Inf. Srvs. Com. (Mem., 1969–72; Ch., 1972). **Honors:** Township of Chinguacousy, Civic Recog. Awd., 1973. **Pubns.:** "An Airline Library: Its Organization and Functions", *IASLIC Bltn.* (S. 1958). **Activities:** 9, 12; 39, 45; 59, 69, 77 **Addr.:** 53 Briar Path, Bramalea, ON L6T 2A3 Canada.

De Simone, Mary G. (Mr. 31, 1950, Pensacola, FL) Hlth. Sci. Libn., Lynn Hosp., 1978–. **Educ.:** Salem State Coll., 1974–76, BA (Eng.); Simmons Coll., 1976–77, MS (LS). **Orgs.:** New Eng. LA: Hosp. Sect. (Secy., 1980–81). Northeast. Cnsrtm. for Hlth. Info.: Ch. (1981–82); Vice-Ch. (1980–81). Essex Cnty. Coop. Libs.: Exec. Bd. (1979–81). Med. LA. N. Atl. Hlth. Sci. Libns. MA Hlth. Sci. Libns. **Activities:** 12; 17, 32, 39; 80 **Addr.:** Health Sciences Library, Lynn Hospital, 212 Boston St., Lynn, MA 01904.

Desjardins, Alvina A. (Cheyenne, WY) Asst. Cat. Libn., CO State Univ. Libs., 1957–; Tchr., Torrington HS, 1953–56; Tchr., Kimball Co., 1944–53; Tchr., CO, WY, 1940–44. **Educ.:** CO State Univ., 1935–39, BS (Soclgy.); Univ. of CO, 1947, 1948, 1954; Univ. of Denver, 1956–1957, MA (Libnshp.); Cert., HS Libn., 1952–55. **Orgs.:** ALA. CO LA. Mt. Plains LA: Coll. & Univ. Sect. (Secy., 1973–1976. Phi Kappa Phi: Pres., CO Chap. (1978–79); Treas. (1976–77); Histn. (1975–76). Natl. Fed. of Bus. and Prof. Women: Pres., Fort Collins Club (1964–65; 1979–80). **Pubns.:** Jt. auth., "A Study of Discrepancies between CIP and Proof Slip Information" *CO Libs.* (D. 1977). **Activities:** 1; 20, 46 **Addr.:** 700 West Oak St., Fort Collins, CO 80521.

Desmarais, J. H. Raymond (Ag. 25, 1922, Montreal, PQ) Head Libn., Coll. Laval, 1969–; Tchr. of Latin and Fr. Lit., Coll. Mgr. Prince, 1965–67; Tchr. of Latin and Hist., Externat classique, St-Hyacinthe, 1963–65; Tchr., various subjs. and pls., 1939–63. **Educ.:** Univ. of Montreal, 1952–56, BA; Univ. of Ottawa, 1967–69, BLS. **Orgs.:** Comm. Jeunesse Inc.: Treas. (1975–); VP (1974). Pvt. Schs. Libns. Comsn.: Bd. of Dirs. (1972–74). Corp. des Bibtcrs. Profs. du PQ. ASTED. Laval Choral Socty. Les Insulaires de Laval, Midget Hockey Club: Bd. of Dirs. **Activities:** 10; 15, 17, 39; 55, 90, 92 **Addr.:** 275 Laval Duvernay, Ville de Laval, PQ H7C 1W8 Canada.

Desmarais, Norman Paul (D. 15, 1946, Lowell, MA) Lib. Dir., St. Mary's Semy. and Univ. (Baltimore) 1977–; Dir. of Relig. Educ./Libn., Ctrl. Falls Relig. Educ. Prog. 1974–77. **Educ.:** Pontifical Gregorian Univ., Rome, Italy, 1967–69, B.Phil. (Phil.), 1969–72, STB (Theo.); Simmons Coll., 1977, MSLS; St. John's Coll., Bar Harbor, ME, 1964–66, AA (Hum.); Inst. for Theo. Libnshp. 1979. **Orgs.:** Amer. Theo. LA.: Readrs. Srvs. Com. (1980–). Cong. of Acad. Lib. Dir. MD LA MD Indp. Coll. and Univ.: Prog. Com. (1978–79). **Pubns.:** *Basic Resources for Studying Theology* (1979); Jt. auth., *Confirmation* (1975); Transl., *The Complete Papal Encyclicals* (1980–81); reviews. **Activities:** 1; 15, 17, 45; 55, 57, 90 **Addr.:** 3104 Harview Ave., Baltimore, MD 21234.

Desnoyers, Megan Floyd (O. 31, 1945, New York, NY) Supervisory Archvst., John F. Kennedy Lib., 1970–; Lectr. Grad. Crs. in Arch., Univ. of MA, 1978–; Archvst., Franklin D. Roosevelt Lib., 1969; Libn., John Jay HS, 1968–69. **Educ.:** Vassar Coll., 1963–67, AB (Eng.); Rutgers Univ., 1967–68, MLS. **Orgs.:** SAA: Basic Level Wkshps. Lectr. (1978–). New Eng. Archvsts.: Secy. (1976–78). MA Lib. Trustees Assn. Cmwlth. of MA: Arch. Adv. Comsn. Various other orgs. Voluntary Action Ctr. of Boston: Adv. Bd. (1974–80). **Honors:** Beta Phi Mu, 1968. **Pubns.:** "The National Security Function: The Kennedy Records," *Proceedings of the Citadel Conference on War And Diplomacy* (1979); various reviews. **Activities:** 2; 26, 39, 49-Prcs. (arrange. and descr.); 85, 95-Pol. frgn. rel. **Addr.:** John F. Kennedy Library, Columbia Point, Boston, MA 02125.

Desoer, Jacqueline Johnson (Mr. 13, 1931, Barranquilla, Colombia) Resrch. Libn., Chevron Resrch. Co., 1974–; Libn., Manalytics, Inc., 1972–74; Ref. Libn., Stan. Oil Co. of CA, 1965–72; Asst. Engin. Libn., Engin. Lib., Columbia Univ., 1964–65; Ref. Libn., 1962–64; Ref. Libn., Imperial Oil Ltd., 1955–61; Bacteriologist, Sunnybrook Vets. Hosp., 1952–54. **Educ.:** McGill Univ., 1949–52, BS (Bacteriology); Case West. Rsv. Univ., 1961–62, MSLS. **Orgs.:** SLA: Dir. (1980–83); San Francisco Chap., Pres. (1977–78), Pres.-Elect (1976–77), Bylaws and Procs. Com. (Ch., 1978–79), Mem. Com. (1976–77), Empl. Com. (1973–75), various other coms., ofcs. (1969–73). ASIS. **Activities:** 12; 17, 39; 60, 86, 91 **Addr.:** 2589 Hilgard Ave., Berkeley, CA 94709.

DeSomogyi, Aileen Ada (N. 26, 1921, London, Eng) Libn., Sperry Univac Toronto Ctrl. Lib., 1980–; Student, Career Learning Centre, 1979–80; Lib. Mgr., ON Minstry. of Gvt. Srvs., 1975–78; Libn., East York Pub. Lib., 1971–74; Catlgr., Co-Op Bk. Ctr. of Can., 1971; Reg. Hist. Libn., Univ. of West. ON, 1966–71. **Educ.:** Univ. of London, 1939–41, BA (Hist.); 1941–43, MA (Hist.); Univ. of West. ON, 1967–70, MLS; LA (UK), 1946, A.L.A. Cert.; Carleton Univ., 1969, Cert. (Arch. Mgt.). **Orgs.:** ALA. Can. Info. Pres. Socty. ON Humane Socty. Pet Pride. Can. Wildlife Fed. **Pubns.:** "In Memoriam: Joseph DeSomogyi," *Stds. in Islam*, (Jy. 1978); "Library skills: now or never," *Sch. Lib. Jnl.* (N. 1975); "Communication," *Can. Lib. Jnl.* (F. 1975); "The Librarian and the Reading Habit," *Can. Lib. Jnl.* (D. 1974). **Activities:** 1, 9; 20, 39, 45; 56, 75 **Addr.:** 9 Bonnie Brae Blvd., Toronto, ON M4J 4N3 Canada.

Dessy, Blane Kent (Ag. 7, 1951, Pittsburgh, PA) Dir., Mifflin Cnty. Lib., 1979–; Dir. of Lib. Srvs., Juniata Cnty. Lib., 1976–79. **Educ.:** IN Univ. of PA, 1969–73, BA (Eng.); Univ. of PA, 1975–76, MLS. **Orgs.:** ALA. PA LA: Juniata/Conemaugh Chap. (Ch., 1979–80); Exec. Com. (1979–80). **Activities:** 9; 15, 17, 35 **Addr.:** 17 Reservoir Ln., Lewistown, PA 17044.

de Streel, Quentin (Ap. 16, 1934, Paris, Fr) Dir., Easton Area Pub. Lib., 1977–; Admin., S. Ctrl. Lib. Syst. (Madison, WI), 1975–77; Dir., Jones Lib. (Amherst, MA), 1971–75. **Educ.:** Harvard Univ., 1953–57, AB (Eng.); Simmons Coll., 1970–71, SM (LS). **Orgs.:** ALA; Easton Lib. Dist.: Dist. Admin.; Adv. Cncl. Family Couns. Srv. of Northampton Cnty.: Mem., Bd. of Dir; PR Com., Ch. Rotary: Prog. Com. Easton Area Chamber of Cmrce.: Tourist and Area Beautification Com. Downtown Improvement Grp.: Mem. Drive (Ch., VP, and Mem., Bd. of Dir.). **Activities:** 9; 17 **Addr.:** Easton Area Public Library, 6th & Church Sts., Easton, PA 18042.

Detlefsen, Ellen Gay (My. 31, 1946, Baton Rouge, LA) Assoc. Prof., LS, Univ. of Pittsburgh, 1978–; Coord. and Core Fac., Women's Std. Prog., 1979–; Asst. Prof., LS, 1975–78; Chief Libn., West. Psy. Inst. and Clinic, 1974–75; Catlgr., Ref. Libn., Musm. of Mod. Art, 1969–71. **Educ.:** Smith Coll., 1964–68, BA magna cum laude, (Amer. Std.); Columbia Univ., 1968–69, MS (LS), 1973, MA (Hist.), 1978, M Phil (Hist.), 1975, DLS. **Orgs.:** ALA: Com. on the Status of Women in Lbnshp. (Ch., 1977–1980); Cncl. (1979–1982). AALS: Conv., Women's Int. Grp. (1977–1979); Resol. Com., (1980–1982). Org. of Amer. Histns. Pittsburgh Bibliophiles: Confederate Meml. Literary Socty. **Pubns.:** *National Directory of Mental Health* (1980); "Telefacsimile in Libraries and Information Centers," *North Carolina Libraries*, (Sum. 1979); "Library Education–History," *ALA Encyc.* (1980); "United Nations Publications," *Encyc. of Lib. and Info. Sci.* (1980); "Stone, Abraham," *Dictionary of Amer. Biog.: Supplement, 1956–1960.* (1980); Other articles. **Activities:** 11; 24, 26, 29; 92, 95-Women's Std. **Addr.:** 644 LIS Building, 135 N. Bellefield Ave., School of Library and Information Science, University of Pittsburgh, Pittsburgh, PA 15260.

de Tonnancour, Paul Roger Godefroy (My. 22, 1926, Fall River, MA) Dir., Tech. Info. Progs., Gen. Dynamics, 1964–, Dir., Resrch. Lib., 1956–; Chief Libn. and Tech. Anal., Armco Steel Corp., 1954–56; Asst. Libn., Enoch Pratt Lib., 1953–54. **Educ.:** Providence Coll., 1952, AB, cum laude; Simmons Coll., 1952–53, MLS. **Orgs.:** ALA. SLA. ASIS. Assoc. Info. Mgrs. Ft. Worth Opera Assn. Chorus. Untd. Fund and Cmnty. Cncl. Big Brothers Tarrant Cnty. AAAS. Various other orgs. **Honors:** Amer. Bus. Women's Assn., Boss of Yr., 1965. **Pubns.:** Jt. auth., *Science Information Personnel* (1963); *The Exploitation of Technical Information* (1966); various articles. **Activities:** 12; 17, 24, 29; 52, 64, 88 **Addr.:** General Dynamics Corp., P.O. Box 748, Mail Zone 2246, Fort Worth, TX 76101.

deTreville, Virginia E. (Dublin, GA) Asst. Libn., Asst. Prof., Ref., Augusta Coll., 1976–, Asst. Libn, Asst. Prof., Circ., 1969–76; Info. Libn., Augusta Reg. Lib., 1966–69; Chief of Adult Srvs., 1961–66. **Educ.:** Univ. of South. CA, 1934–38, AB Magna Cum Laude (Fr.); Emory Univ., 1958–59, MLn (LS); Natl. Arch. Inst. on Genealogical Resrch., 1976 (Cert.); Arch. Inst., GA Dept. of Arch., 1978 (Cert.); various other institutes. **Orgs.:** ALA. SELA. GA LA. Ctrl. Savannah River Areas LA: VP (1977–79); Prog. Ch. (1977–79); Pres. (1979–80). Frnds. Augusta Lib.: Adv. Cncl. (1969–71, 1975–79); Secy. (1971–75). Richmond Cnty. Hist. Socty.: Asst. Cur. (1969–); Ed. (1976–). GA Hist. Socty. GA Geneal. Socty. GA Trust for Hist. Prsrvn. **Honors:** Phi Beta Kappa, 1938; Phi Kappa Phi, 1938. **Pubns.:** "George Washington Visits Augusta," *Richmond Cnty. Hist.* (Sum. 1972); "Salem Dutcher, Journalist, Lawyer, Author," *Richmond Cnty Hist.* (Win. 1970). **Activities:** 1, 2; 22, 31, 39; 69, 85 **Addr.:** Reese Library, Augusta College, 2500 Walton Way, Augusta, GA 30904.

Detty, Elizabeth Weller (Jl. 22, 1924, Biltmore, NC) Dir. of Instr. and Libs., Salisbury City Schs., 1979–, Prin., Isenberg Elem. Sch., 1977–79; Dir. of Media, Rowan Cnty. Schs., 1974–75; Visit. Instr., LS, E. Carolina Univ., 1971–73; Libn., Overton Sch., Salisbury City Schs., 1962–74. **Educ.:** Amer. Univ., 1941–45, BA (Hist.); Univ. of NC, Greensboro, 1970, MEd (Lib. Educ.), 1981, EdD (Educ. Admin.). **Orgs.:** NC LA: Int. Frdm. Com. (1980–81). NC Assn. of Sch. Libns.: Ch. (1977–79); Vice Ch. (1975–77); Prog. Ch. (1973–75); Stans. Com. (1970–73). SELA: Co–Mem. Ch. for NC (1973). ALA. Leag. of Women Voters. AAUW. **Honors:** Delta Kappa Gamma; Salisbury Civitan

Special Subjects/Services: 50. Adult educ.; 51. Advert./Mktg.; 52. Aerosp.; 53. Agric.; 54. Area std.; 55. Arts/Hum.; 56. Autom.; 57. Bibl./Prtg.; 58. Bio. sci.; 59. Bus./Fin.; 60. Chem.; 61. Copyrt.; 62. Documtn.; 63. Educ.; 64. Engin.; 65. Env.; 66. Eth. grps.; 67. Film; 68. Food/Nutr.; 69. Geneal.; 70. Geo.; 71. Geol.; 72. Handcpd.; 73. Hist.; 74. Int. frdm.; 75. Info. sci.; 76. Insr.; 77. Law; 78. Legis.; 79. Math./Comp. sci.; 80. Med.; 81. Metals; 82. Nat. resrcs.; 83. Newsp.; 84. Nuc. sci.; 85. Oral hist.; 86. Petr./Energy; 87. Pharm.; 88. Phys./Astr./Math.; 89. Readg.; 90. Relig.; 91. Sci./Tech.; 92. Soc. sci.; 93. Telecom.; 94. Transp.; 95. (other).

Club, Disting. Tchr. of Yr., 1969; Salisbury City Schs., Tchr. of the Yr., 1973; Terry Sanford Awd. for Innovative Tchg., Dist. Winner, 1974. **Activities:** 10; 21, 32; 63, 74 **Addr.:** 905 Confederate Ave., Salisbury, NC 28144.

de Usabel, Frances Esmonde (Je. 22, 1943, Brooklyn, NY) Lib. Consult., Spec. Srvs., WI Div., Lib. Srvs., 1981–; Inst. Srv. Libn., WI Ref. and Loan Lib., 1972–81; Libn., Berkeley Pub. Lib., 1969–72; Chld. Libn., NY Pub. Lib., 1966–68. **Educ.:** Queens Coll., 1961–65, BA (Anthro., Soclgy.); Columbia Univ., 1965–66, MLS; Univ. of VA, 1968–69, MA (Eng. Lit.). **Orgs.:** ALA: ASCLA/Lib. Srvs. to Prisoners Sect. (Secy., 1980–81), Prog. Com. (Ch., 1980); RASD, Notable Bks. Cncl. (1980–82). WI LA: Hlth. and Rehab. Lib. Srvs. Sect. (Ch., 1978–79); Lib. Awds. Com. (1978–79). Madison Area Lib. Cncl.: Exec. Bd. (1977–79); Cmnty. Rel. Com. (1978); Educ. and Prog. Com. (1980–). **Honors:** Phi Beta Kappa, 1965; Beta Phi Mu, 1966; Queens Coll., Emory Halloway Prize in Lit. Criticism, 1965. **Pubns.:** "Institutional Services at the Wisconsin Reference and Loan Library," *Inside/Outside* (O. 1976); "Expanding Horizons: Institutional Services, R & L Library," *WI Lib. Bltn.* (My.–Je. 1980); *Evaluation of the Federal Correctional Institution Library* (1979). **Activities:** 9, 13; 16, 21, 39; 55, 66, 92 **Addr.:** 125 S. Webster St., Madison, WI 53707.

Deuss, Jean (D. 6, 1922, Chicago, IL) Chief Libn., Resrch. Lib., Federal Rsv. Bank of NY, 1970–; Asst. Chief Libn., 1969–70; Head Catlgr., 1961–69; Catlgr., Cncl. on Foreign Rel., 1959–61. **Educ.:** Univ. of WI, 1940–44, BA (Hist.); Columbia Univ., 1957–59, MS (LS). **Orgs.:** SLA: NY Chap. (Pres., 1971–72; Treas., 1969–70), Cabinet (Ch., 1974–76), Liaison Ofcr. (1972–74). NY Tech. Libns. Assn. NY Lib. Club. **Activities:** 12; 17, 20, 46; 59, 92 **Addr.:** Research Library, Federal Reserve Bank of New York, Federal Reserve P.O. Station, New York, NY 10045.

Deutsch, James I. (Je. 9, 1948, New York, NY) Head, Ext. Srvs. and ILL, Parmly Billings Lib., 1979–; Cmnty. Info. Spec., Fairbanks North Star Borough Lib., 1973–74. **Educ.:** Williams Coll., 1966–70, BA (Amer. Civ.); Emory Univ., 1978–79, M.Ln. (Libnshp.); Univ. of MN, 1974–76, MA (Amer. Std.). **Orgs.:** ALA: Pub. Lib. Syst. Sect., Com. on Com. (1980); Com. on By-Laws (1980–). Pac. Northw. LA. MT LA. Amer. Std. Assn. Pop. Cult. Assn. **Honors:** ALA, Student Staff to Conf., 1979. **Pubns.:** Cmplr., *A Trans-Alaska Pipeline Bibliography* (1974); "Jesse James in Dime Novels" *The Dime Novel Roundup* (F. 1976). **Activities:** 9; 27, 34 **Addr.:** c/o Parmly Billings Library, 510 North Broadway, Billings, MT 59101.

Devan, Christopher B. (N. 15, 1926, Plainfield, NJ) Dir. Jefferson Madison Reg. Lib., 1975–81; Dir., Cuyahoga Cnty. (OH) Pub. Lib., 1970–75; Dir. of Libs., Wilmington Inst. Free Libs, New Castle Cnty. Free Lib., 1963–70; Coord., of Pub. Srvs., Chester Cnty. (PA) Pub. Lib., 1961–63. **Educ.:** George Washington Univ., 1946–50, AB (Soclgy.); Univ. of IL, 1955–54, MLS. **Orgs.:** ALA: Cncl. (1966–70). VA LA. Amer. Red Cross: Ctrl. VA Chap. (Ch., 1979–80). **Activities:** 9; 17 **Addr.:** 2817 Northfield Rd., Charlottesville, VA 22901.

de Vaux, Paula T. (Ap. 28, 1943, Bridgeport, CT) Freelnc. Indxr. and Ed., 1980–; Ed., Current Bk. Review Cits., H. W. Wilson Co., 1975–80; Ref. Libn., Kansas City Pub. Lib., 1974–75; Ed., Lib. Lit., H. W. Wilson Co., 1973–74, Indxr., Lib. Lit., 1971–73; Asst. Pers. Libn., Providence Pub. Lib., 1970–71; Rsvs. Libn., Undergrad. Lib., Univ. of MI, 1969–70, Pers. Libn., 1968–69; Post Libn., Fort Clayton, CZ Post Lib., 1967–68. **Educ.:** Hiram Coll., 1961–65, BA (Eng.); Univ. of MI, 1965–67, AMLS. **Orgs.:** ALA. NY Lib. Club. **Activities:** 9, 14-Publshg. co.; 37, 39, 44; 55, 56, 57 **Addr.:** 201 E. 77th St. 9F, New York, NY 10021.

DeVelbiss, Elizabeth M. (Ag. 10, 1919, Lynden, WA) Libn., II, Richmond Pub. Lib. (CA), 1956–; Catlgr., Univ. of CA, Berkeley, Lib., 1948–57; Bibgphr., Resrv. Bk. Dept., 1947–48; Catlgr., Desc. Cat. Div., Lib. of Congs., 1943–47. **Educ.:** Cornell Univ., 1936–40, BA; Simmons Coll., 1940–41, BS (LS); Univ. of CA, Berkeley, 1947–48, MLS. **Orgs.:** ALA. CA LA. Girl Scouts of U.S.A.: Berkeley-Albany Srv. Team. Bergen Swamp Prsrvn. Socty. **Honors** San Francisco Bay Girl Scout Cncl., Thanks Badge, 1979. **Activities:** 9; 21 **Addr.:** 1780 San Lorenzo Ave., Berkeley, CA 94707.

Devers, Charlotte M. (Ag. 10, 1923, NY, NY) Lib. Dir., N. Castle Pub. Lib. (NY), 1968–; Mgr., Inf. Srvs., Curtiss-Wright Corp., 1965–68; Supvsr., Tech. Lib., General Dynamics Corp., 1963–65; Head Libn., Compton Advert., Inc., 1958–63; Libn., TV Bur. of Advert., 1956–58; Resrch. Libn., Hearst Pubns., 1954–56. **Educ.:** Cornell Univ., 1941–44, BA (Zool.); Columbia Univ., 1956–58, MS (LS); Ballard Sch. (NY), 1955–56, Certs. (LS). **Orgs.:** Friends of the N. Castle Libr. (1968–). NY LA. Westchester LA: Publicity (Ch., 1978–79). SLA: various ofcs. Pub. Lib. Dirs. Assn.: Pres. (1971). Amer. Socty. of Indexers. Archlg. Inst. of Amer.: Meso Amer. Std. Grp. Green Acres Garden Club: PR Dir. (1975–79). N. Castle Hist. Socty. Leag. of Women Voters. Various other orgs. **Honors:** Delegate, Gvrs. Conf. on Libs. and Info. Sci., 1978. **Pubns.:** Jt.-Ed., *Guide to Special Issues and Indexes of Periodicals* (1963, 1975); Various panels. **Activities:** 9; 17, 26, 30; 50, 51, 59 **Addr.:** North Castle Public Library, 19 Whippoorwill Rd. E., Armonk, NY 10504.

Devine, Marie E. (O. 6, 1940, Phoenixville, PA) Instr. Srvs. Libn., Univ. of NC, Asheville, 1978–; Ref. Libn., Coll. of Physicians (Philadelphia), 1976–78; Head, Tech. Srvs., Ursinus Coll., 1967–72; Catlgr., Bryn Mawr Coll., 1965–67. **Educ.:** Ursinus Coll., 1961–64, BA (Eng.); Drexel Univ., 1964–65, MSLS; Bryn Mawr Coll., 1972–77, MA, PhD (Eng.). **Orgs.:** SELA. NC LA. Amer. Socty. for Eighteenth Century Stds. E.-Ctrl. Amer. Socty. for Eighteenth Century Stds. S. E. Amer. Socty. for Eighteenth Century Stds. **Pubns.:** Reviews. **Activities:** 1; 31, 39, 42; 55, 80 **Addr.:** Ramsey Library, University of North Carolina at Asheville, Asheville, NC 28814.

Devlin, Mary Kathleen (Ag. 17, 1946, Portland, OR) Libn., Portland Gen. Electric, 1980–; Tech. Srv. Libn., Univ. of Portland, 1978–80, Spec. Srvs. Libn., 1977–78; Approval Prog. Mgr., Richard Abel, Ltd. (London), 1971–75. **Educ.:** Lewis and Clark Coll., 1964–68, BS (Lit.), 1968–71, MAT (Educ.), Univ. of OR, 1975–76, MLS. **Orgs.:** OR LA: Lib. Dev. Com. (1977–78); Legis. Com. (1979–). SLA: OR Chap., Dir. (1977–78); Nom. Com. (1979). ALA: ACRL/OR Chap., Ch. (1977–78); Adv. Bd. (1978–); Nsltr. Ed. (1980–). Frnds. of Multnomah Cnty. Lib.: Bd. of Dir. (1979); VP (1981); Bksale Ch. (1979, 1980). Other orgs. The Wolfe Pack. **Pubns.:** Cmplr., *Directory of Special Libraries in Oregon & Southwest Washington* (1978). **Activities:** 1; 20, 31, 49-Online Searching; 55, 63, 92 **Addr.:** Portland General Electric, Technical Library, 121 SW Salmon St., Portland, OR 97204.

De Vos, Lawrence J. (Ja. 5, 1925, Detroit, MI) Head, Div. of Continuations, and Assoc. Prof. of Lib. Srv., Ball State Univ., 1971–; Admin. Asst., 1967–71; Asst. Catlgr., FL Atl. Univ., 1965–67; Asst. Dir. Admin. Srvs., MI State Lib., 1964–65; Head, Prtg. Srvs., 1963–64; Head, Burton Branch Lib., Grand Rapids Pub. Lib., 1962–63; Ref. Libn., 1961–62; Libn., Pettisville (OH) HS, 1960–61. **Educ.:** Calvin Coll., 1943–48, AB (Gen.); Univ. of MI, 1961–64, MALS; Calvin Semy. 1948–52, Cert. (Theo.); Other courses. **Orgs.:** ALA. Assn. for Comp. Mach. ASIS. Assn. of Recs. Mgrs. and Admin.: PR Com. (1970–72); Indianapolis Chap., Nsltr. Ed. (1968–72); PR Com. (Ch., 1968–74). Other orgs. Delaware (Cnty.) Lions, Intl.: Bd. (1971). NEMOS Motorcycle Club: Secy. (1977–80). **Pubns.:** "PR Politics," *Focus on IN Libs.* (S. 1970); "Wanna Sell Your Old Carnegie? Yes, You Wanna Buy It?, *Focus on IN Libs.* (F. 1972); "Indiana ILA Conference, 1971," *Amer. Libs.* (F. 1972). **Activities:** 1; 17, 33, 38, 44; 56, 59 **Addr.:** Bracken Library, Ball State University, Muncie, IN 47306.

De Waal, Ronald Burt (O. 23, 1932, Salt Lake City, UT) Hum. Libn., Exhibits Coord., CO State Univ., 1966–; Head Libn., Westminster Coll., 1964–66; Head Libn., Sperry UT Co., 1961–64; Head Libn., NM Military Inst., 1959–60; Spec. Col. Libn., Univ. of NM, 1959–60. **Educ.:** Univ. of UT, 1951–55, BS (Psy./Phil.); Univ. of Denver, 1957–58, MA (Libnshp.); Mexico City Coll., 1955; 1958. **Orgs.:** ALA. CO LA. Msc. LA. Baker Str. Irregulars. Coll. Art Assn. of Amer. Natl. Sculpture Socty. Sherlock Holmes Socty. of London. **Honors:** Union College, John H. Jenkins Awd. for best work of bibl. published in U.S. during 1974, 1976. **Pubns.:** *The International Sherlock Holmes* (1980); *The World Bibliography of Sherlock Holmes and Dr. Watson.* (1974); "Adventures of a Sherlock Holmes Bibliographer," *Baker St. Miscellanea* (Fall 1980); "I Hear of Sherlock Holmeses and Dr. Watsons Everywhere," *The Sherlock Holmes Jnl.* (Win. 1976); "Sherlock Holmes and U.S. Presidents," *Sherlock Holmes* (Jl. 1976); Other articles. **Activities:** 1; 32, 37, 41, 45; 55, 57, 67 **Addr.:** 5020 Hogan Dr., Ft. Collins, CO 80525.

Dewar, Mildred (Jo) E. (N. 9, 1925, Wilkesboro, NC) Dir., Lib. Srvs., Miami-Dade Cmnty. Coll., 1970–; Ch., Readers' Srvs., (1963–70); Libn., Lauderdale Manors Sch., (1956–63); Libn., Olsen Jr. HS, (1955–56); Chief, Post Lib. Syst., Fort Stewart, GA, (1952–54); Libn., U.S. Army Spec. Srvs., Fort Jackson, SC, (1951–52); Dept. Head, Univ. of TX Lib., (1951); Chief Libn., TN Wesleyan Coll., (1948–50). **Educ.:** Brevard Jr. Coll., 1942–44, Dipl.; Berea Coll., 1944–46, BA (Eng.); Univ. of NC, 1947–48, BS (LS); additional educ.; Barry Coll., Univ. of FL., Univ. of Miami, FL State Univ. **Orgs.:** Natl. Lib. Week in FL: Co-Exec. Dir. (1963–64). FL Assn. of Sch. Libns.: Pres. (1961–62). Broward Cnty. Assn. Sch. Libns.: Pres. (1959–61). ALA: various coms. Delta Kappa Gamma: Publcty. Ch., Nsltr. ed. (1962–64). AAUW: VP, Ft. Lauderdale Chap. (1958–61). FL Assn. of Cmnty. Colls. SE FL Educ. Cnsrtm.: Lib. Task Force (1977–). **Honors:** Alum. Cit., Brevard Coll., Disting. Srv. in Field of Educ., 1951. **Pubns.:** Contrib., *Problems in Planning Library Facilities* (1964); "Individualized Reading Program In An Elementary School Library", *ALA Bltn.* (F. 1962); "Spotlight on School Libraries", *FL Educ. Mag.* (Ap. 1962); column in *FASL Bookcase* (1961–62). **Activities:** 1; 17, 31, 34; 63 **Addr.:** 3520 Crystal View Ct., Coconut Grove, FL 33133.

Dewdney, Patricia H. (My. 8, 1942, Tonbridge, Kent, Eng.) Tchg. Asst., Sch. of Lib. and Info. Sci., Univ. of West. ON, 1979–, Visit. Lectr., 1978–79; Cmnty. Rel. Consult., London Pub. Libs., 1975–78, Head Libn., Crouch Branch, 1972–75, Cont. Educ. Ofcr., 1968–72; Ref. Libn., Ann Arbor Pub. Lib., 1967–68. **Educ.:** Univ. of West. ON, 1960–64, BA, hons. (Eng.); Univ. of MI, 1966–67, AMLS; Univ. of West. ON, 1979– (LS). **Orgs.:** Can. LA. ON LA. **Pubns.:** *Citizen Participation in Library Planning* (1975); "The Crouch Experience: An Interagency Approach to Neighbourhood Services," *Can. Lib. Jnl.* (F. 1979); jt. auth., "How to Assess the Community for Adult Education Needs," *ON Lib. Review* (S. 1978); "Citizen Participation: An Experiment in London, Ontario," *Can. Lib. Jnl.* (Je. 1977); jt. auth., "Canadian Public Libraries and the Physically Handicapped," *Can. Lib. Jnl.* (My.–Je. 1972). **Activities:** 9, 11; 26, 39; 50, 75, 95-Cmnty. info. **Addr.:** School of Library and Information Science, University of Western Ontario, London, ON N6A 5B9 Canada.

Deweese, Don B. (Jl. 2, 1940, Berryville, AR) Admn. Asst. for Info. Srvs., Fayetteville Pub. Sch., 1979–, Dir., Dist. Media Prog., 1975–79; Head Libn., Fayetteville HS, 1970–75; Head Libn., Ramay Jr. HS, 1966–69. **Educ.:** Univ. of AR, 1958–62, BA (Hist.); Univ. of TN, 1969–70, MS (LS). **Orgs.:** ALA: Ed. Bd., Index Ed., *Sch. Media Qtly.* (1971–79). AR LA: Natl. Lib. Wk. (State Ch., 1973); Pubns. Com. (Ch., 1975–76); Ed., *AR Libs.* (1979–). Natl. Educ. Assn. AR Educ. Assn. Fayetteville Educ. Assn. Phi Delta Kappa. **Honors:** WHCOLIS, Pre-Conf. Del., AR, 1978. **Activities:** 10; 17, 32, 35 **Addr.:** 742 North Sang Ave., Fayetteville, AR 72701.

DeWeese, Eldonna R. (N. 7, 1940, Seneca MO) Admn. Libn., S.W. Baptist Coll., 1972–, Ref. and Acq. Libn., 1969–72; Speech and Eng. Instr., Libn., Pierce City HS (MO), 1962–68. **Educ.:** S.W. Baptist Coll., 1958–60, AA, S.W. Mo St. Univ., 1960–62, BS (Eng.); Emporia St. Univ., 1968–69, MLS. **Orgs.:** ALA. MO LA: Int. Frdm. Com. (1970–71). Springfield Area Libns. Assn.: Union List of Serials Com. (1970–72); Secy., (1976–77); Pres. (1977–78). Adv. Cncl. to the S.W. MO Lib. Netwk.: Secy. (1976–77); Elect. Mem. (1972–80) Long-Range Plng. Com. (1980–81); Budget Com. (1980–81). Bolivar Cmnty. Thea.: V Ch. (1977–78). **Activities:** 1; 17, 32, 34 **Addr.:** Estep Library, Southwest Baptist College, Bolivar, MO 65613.

DeWeese, June LaFollette (Ag. 25, 1951, Trenton, MO) Soc. Sci. Libn., Adj. Asst. Prof., Univ. of MO (Columbia), 1975–, Geol. Libn., 1975–75, Info. Libn., 1974–75. **Educ.:** Univ. of MO (Columbia), 1969–72, AB (LS, Pol. Sci.), 1972–73, MA (LS). **Orgs.:** SLA. MO LA. Natl. Womens Std. Assn. Bus. and Prof. Women's Club. Assn. of Amer. Coll.: Proj. Status and Educ. of Women. **Honors:** Beta Phi Mu. **Pubns.:** "Title XX: One Social Service Program That Helps Children," *Show-Me Libs.* (O.-N. 1979); "Current Resources in Women's Studies," *Show-Me Libs.* (Jan. 1978); "Library Search Guides," *Show-Me Libs.* (Ja. 1977); "Centralization of Current Periodicals in Elmer Ellis Library at the University of Missouri-Columbia" ERIC Docum.; "Meramec Dam Project, Missouri: Selected Bibliography," Cncl. on Plng. Libns. *Exchange Bibliography* (Ap., 1976); "Lock and Dam 26 on the Mississippi River at Alton, Illinois: A Selected Bibliography," *Vance Biblis.* Pub. Admn. Series (Ap. 1979). **Activities:** 1; 15, 31, 39; 59, 92 **Addr.:** Social Science Library/Ellis Library, University of Missouri, Columbia, MO 65201.

Dewey, Gene L. (Jl. 19, 1938, Malone, NY) Chief, Acq. Dept., Univ. of WI (Madison), 1969–; Acq. Libn., SUNY, Buffalo, 1964–69, Asst. Circ. Libn. and Head, Rsv. Rm., 1962–64; Jr. Libn., Buffalo and Erie Cnty. Pub. Lib., 1960–62. **Educ.:** State Univ. Coll., Geneseo, NY, 1955–59, BS (LS); Univ. of IL, 1959–60, MS (LS). **Orgs.:** ALA. **Pubns.:** "The Wisconsin Experience," *Shaping Library Collections for the 1980s* (1980); jt. auth., "Evaluation of a University Library Collection: Some Guidelines," *Lib. Resrcs. & Tech. Srvs.* (Fall 1969). **Activities:** 1; 15, 46 **Addr.:** 2125 Fox Ave., Madison, WI 53711.

Dewey, Harry (F. 29, 1920, Cebu, Cebu, Philippines) Current Awareness Lit. Srv. Liaison, Agency for Intl. Dev., 1979–; Consult. on Corp. Entry, Food & Agriculture Org., United Nations, 1977–78; Consult., Agency for Intl. Dev., 1975–76; sometime lectr., Univ. of MD Lib. Sch. 1966–72. **Educ.:** Univ. of NC, Chapel Hill 1936–41, AB (Am. Hist.); Columbia Univ., 1950, MS (Lib. Srv.); Univ. Flw. Univ. of Chicago, 1949. **Orgs.:** ALA: various coms. Amer. Rock Garden Socty.: Asst. Ed. bltn. **Pubns.:** *Introduction to Library Cataloging and Classification,* 4th ed. (1956); *Specialized Cataloging and Classification,* 3d ed. (1956). **Activities:** 1, 4; 20, 26, 46; 56, 75, 91 **Addr.:** 4605 Brandon Ln., Beltsville, MD 20705.

DeWhitt, Bennie L. (Mr. 20, 1941, Oklahoma City, OK) Supvsry. Archvst., Natl. Arch., 1979–; Archvst., 1973–79; Asst. Ed., Will Rogers Papers, 1970–73; Teaching Assoc., Emory Univ., 1968–70. **Educ.:** OK State Univ., 1959–64, BA (Hist.), 1964–66, MA (Hist.); Emory Univ., 1966–77, PhD (Hist.). **Orgs.:** SAA: Task Frc. on Autom. (1979–). Assn. of Pub. Data Users: Com. on Data Access (1976–79). Washington Calligraphers Gld. **Pubns.:** "Archival Uses of Computers in the U.S. and Canada," *Amer. Archvst.* (Ap. 1979); "Can New Storage Technology Really Improve Access?", *Proceedings of the Conference on Data Bases in the Humanities and the Social Sciences.* (1980). **Activities:** 2; 15, 18, 38; 56, 75, 92 **Addr.:** NARS (NNR), Washington, DC 20408.

deWit, Dorothy Knowles (My. 24, 1916, Youngstown, OH) Head, Chlds., Srvs., Maple Heights Reg., Cuyahoga Cnty.

PROFESSIONAL ACTIVITIES: Institutions: 1. Acad. lib.; 2. Arch.; 3. Assn.; 4. Fed./Gvt. lib.; 5. Inst. lib.; 6. Mfr./Suppl.; 7. Milit. lib.; 8. Musm.; 9. Pub. lib.; 10. Sch. lib.; 11. Sch. of lib. sci.; 12. Spec. lib.; 13. State lib.; 14. (other). **Functions/Activities:** 15. Acq./Col. dev.; 16. Adult srvs.; 17. Admin.; 18. Apprais.; 19. Archit./Bldgs.; 20. Cat./Class.; 21. Chld. srvs.; 22. Circ.; 23. Cons./Pres.; 24. Consult.; 25. Cont. ed.; 26. Educ. lib. sci.; 27. Ext. srvs.; 28. Fund/Grants; 29. Gvt. pubs.; 30. Indx./Abs.; 31. Instr. lib. use; 32. Media srvs.; 33. Micro.; 34. Netwks./Coop.; 35. Persnl.; 36. PR; 37. Publshg.; 38. Recs. mgt.; 39. Ref. srvs.; 40. Repro.; 41. Resrch.; 42. Review.; 43. Secur.; 44. Serials; 45. Spec. col.; 46. Tech. srvs.; 47. Trustees/Bds.; 48. YA srvs.; 49. (other).

Pub. Lib., 1966–; Chlds. Libn., 1965–66; Asst. Chlds. Libn., 1960–65; Dir., Relig. Educ., Union Church (Balboa Canal Zone), 1947–51. **Educ.:** Schauffler Coll., 1937–40, BS (Soc. Work); Cleveland State Univ., 1940–41, BA (Soclgy.); West. Resrv. Univ., 1963–65, MSLS. **Orgs.:** OH LA: Sect. VIII, Chlds. work (1976–77). ALA: ALSC, Notable Chlds. Bks. (1978–80); Newbery Com. (1981). Netherlands Amer. Club: Northeast. OH (Nom. Com., 1976–78). S. Haven United Church, Organist, Choir Dir. **Pubns.:** *Children's Faces Looking Up* (1979); *The Talking Stone; Native American Tales and Legends* (1979). **Activities:** 9; 21; 95-Storytel. **Addr.:** 13305 Maple Leaf Dr., Garfield Hghts, OH 44125.†

Dewton, Johannes Leopold (S. 27, 1905, Vienna, Austria) Retired, 1981; Assoc. Ed., Natl. Union Cat. Pubn. Proj., Lib. of Congs., 1975–81, Head, Natl. Union Cat. Pubn. Proj., 1966–75, Chief, Shared Cat. Div., 1965–66, Asst. Chief, Union Cat. Div., 1957–65, Ed., Cat. Pubns., 1950–57, Catlgr., Descrip. Cat. Div., 1945–50, Catlgr., Univ. of IL Lib., 1941–45. **Educ.:** Univ. of Vienna, Austria, 1923–27, JurD (Law, Econ., Pol. Sci.); Univ. of IL, 1940–41, BS in LS with honors, 1941–44, MS (LS). **Orgs.:** ALA. Cncl. on Resrch. in Bibl.: Bd. of Dir. (1960–74). **Honors:** Lib. of Congs., Disting. Srv. Awd., 1975; Superior Accomplishment Awd., 1957; Beta Phi Mu. **Pubns.:** Various articles. **Activities:** 1, 4; 20; 55, 57, 77 **Addr.:** 4201 Seventh Rd. South, Arlington, VA 22204.

Deyá, Lourdes Lendián (Habana, Cuba) LS Educ. Instr., LA. St. Univ. Coll. of Educ., 1972–, Instr., Sch. of LS, 1967–72; Asst. Catlgr., LA St. Lib., 1964–66. **Educ.:** LA St. Univ., 1961–62, BA (Span.), 1962–63, MS (LS), 1966–67 post MLS, 1966– (Lang.), 1976–77 (Fr. Cert.). **Orgs.:** ALA: YASD, Srvs. to Span. Speaking YA Com. (1979–80); Sem. Acq. Latin Amer. Mtrls.: LS Educ. Amer. Com. (1979–80). LA LA: Trust. Schol. Com. REFORMA. SWLA. AAUP. Phi Sigma Iota. Phi Lambda Phi. Delta Sigma Pi. **Pubns.:** "Outline of Introductory Courses in International and Comparative Librarianship," *Intl. Lib. Review* (Ap. 1970); "How, What and Why Select Books for Children and Young Adults in Spanish," SALAM Papers XIX (Ap. 1974); "A Bilingual Libn. Looks at Book Selection," *SCOLT-Dimension Langs.* (Spr. 1976). **Activities:** 11; 20, 26; 54, 63, 66 **Addr.:** 5785 Glenwood Dr., Baton Rouge, LA 70806.

Dial, Carolyn E. (Mr. 27, 1949, Jacksonville, FL) Adult Srvs., Lib. Syst., Holdrege, NE, 1979–; AV Coord., Stetson Univ., 1976–78. **Educ.:** Stetson Univ., 1967–71, BA (Eng.); Emporia State Univ., 1978–79, MLS. **Orgs.:** NE LA: Int. Frdm. Com. (1979–80); JMRT, Pubcty. Ch. (1979–80). KS LA: JMRT (1978–79). AAUW: Topic Resrc. Person: Energy (1980–81). **Honors:** Baker & Taylor Co., Grassroots Grant, 1979; Beta Phi Mu, 1979. **Pubns.:** "JMRT: Early Career Development Opportunity" -*NE LA Qtly.* (Spring 1980). **Activities:** 9; 16, 32, 39; 67 **Addr.:** The Library System, 604 East Ave., Holdrege, NE 68949.

Diamond, Harold J. (F. 16, 1934, New York, NY) Assoc. Prof., Fine Arts Libn., Herbert H. Lehman Coll., 1959–; Msc. Libn., NY Pub. Lib., 1956–59. **Educ.:** Hunter Coll., 1952–56, BA (Msc.); Columbia Univ., 1956–58, MS (LS); NY Univ., 1963–65, MA (Msclgy.). **Orgs.:** Msc. LA: Advert. Ed., *Notes* (1975–81); Treas., (1981–); Pubn. Com. Assn. for Recorded Sound Col. (1977–). Delius Socty. Grainger Socty. **Pubns.:** *Music Criticism: An Annotated Guide to the Literature* (1979); Contrib., *Magazines for Libraries* (1972); Reviews. **Activities:** 1; 15, 39, 42; 51, 55, 95-Msc. **Addr.:** The Herbert H. Lehman College, Fine Arts Library, Bedford Park Blvd. West, Bronx, NY 10468.

Diaz, Albert James (O. 17, 1930, Philadelphia, PA) Pres., AJ Sems., 1979–; VP and Publshr., Brookhaven Press, 1974–79; VP, Info. Handling Srvs., 1973–74; Publshr., Microcard Ed., 1960–73; Visit. Lectr., Sch. LS, Univ. MD, 1966–67. **Educ.:** Swarthmore Coll., 1948–52, BA (Hist.); Univ. of NC (Chapel Hill), 1954–56, MS (LS). **Orgs.:** ALA: Copying Methods Sect. (1965–68); Reprodct. of Lib. Matls. Sect. (1971–74). Sem. Acq. Latin Amer. Lib. Mtrls. Treas. (1960–69). Natl. Micro. Assn. **Pubns.:** *Microforms and Library Catalogs* (1977); *Microforms in Libraries* (1975); "Microform Information Sources," *Micro. Review* (O. 1975). **Activities:** 1, 6; 17, 33, 40; 54, 57, 92 **Addr.:** 11205 Farmland Dr., Rockville, MD 20852.

Dible, Joan Brain (Mr. 22, 1937, Upland, PA) Sci. and Tech. Catlgr., Green Lib., Stanford Univ., 1966–; Docum. Custodian, Stanford Resrch. Inst. Lib., 1965–66; Catlgr., Univ. of CA Med. Ctr., 1963; Catlgr. of Tech. Rpts., Lockheed, 1962–63; Ref. Libn., Harvard Med. Lib., 1960–62. **Educ.:** Univ. of DE, 1954–58, BA (Bio.); Simmons Coll., 1959–60, MS (LS). **Orgs.:** ALA. SLA. **Pubns.:** *Index to the Library of Congress Cataloging Service Bulletins 108–125* (1979); "Unionization: Costs and Benefits to the Individual and the Library," *Lib. Trends* (O. 1976); *Index to the Cataloging Service Bulletin* (1979–). **Activities:** 1; 20, 30; 70, 91 **Addr.:** 3278 Fareham Ct., Fremont, CA 94536.

DiCarlo, Celeste (Jl. 30, 1944, Hibbs, PA) Libn./AV Coord., Peters Twp. Mid. Sch., 1968–; Visit. Instr. (Sums.), West. MI Univ., 1978–79; Elem. Libn., S. Fayette Twp. Sch. Dist., 1966–67. **Educ.:** Slippery Rock State Coll., 1962–66, BS (Elem. Educ., LS); West. MI Univ., 1967–68, MLS. **Orgs.:** Gvr.'s Adv. Cncl. on Lib. Dev. (1980–). ALA. PA Sch. Libns. Assn.: Treas. (1974–76); Pres. (1976–80); Past Pres. (1980–). PA LA. Cncl. of Sch. Libns. Natl. Educ. Assn. PA State Educ. Assn. PA Leag. of Mid. Schs.: Natl. Conf. Com. (1978). **Honors:** Beta Phi Mu; Slippery Rock State Coll., Dept. of LS, Outstan. Contrib., 1980. **Activities:** 10; 32 **Addr.:** 327 Ridge Point Cir., A-23, Bridgeville, PA 15017.

Dick, Esme June (Je. 14, 1933, Derby, England) Lib. AV Dir., Brunswick Sch., Greenwich, CT, 1977–; Dir. of Spec. Srvs., Eccentric Circle Cin. Wkshp., 1974–77; Admin. Dir., EFLA, 1969–74; Dir., Amer. Film Fest., 1969–72; Coord. Film Srvs., Greenwich (CT) Lib., 1965–69; Fiction Spec., YA Srvs., 1962–65; Libn., St. Mary's in the Mountains, 1957–60; Branch Libn., Tibshelf, Derbyshire England (1952–54); other lib. positions in Eng. **Educ.:** Eng. Lib. Cert., Mansfield Tech.; Coll., Chesterfield Tech. Coll., 1950–53. **Orgs.:** EFLA: Ch., Prescreening Com. Amer. Film Fest. (1973–). Wilson Publications; Member of John Cotton Dana Award Committee 1972–75. Intl. Film Sem.: Adv. (1970–1978); Trustee (1979–1985); NY Film Cncl.: Bd. (1969–74, 1977–80); Treas. (1974–76); Community Centers Inc.: Bd. (1978–); Rep. Greenwich Town Mtg., (1976–1982); Other orgs. **Honors:** Blue Ribbon Awd., EFLA, 1973. **Pubns.:** *Energy & The Way we Live* (1980); *Crime, Justice & Punishment* (1978); Jt. auth., *Alternatives* (1974); *16mm Distrbution Handbook* (1977); Managing Ed., *Film Library Quarterly* (1967–1972); Reviews. **Activities:** 10; 24, 31, 32; 63, 67, 75 **Addr.:** 77 Valley Dr., Greenwich, CT 06830.

Dickens, Janis L. (Je. 4, 1949, Des Moines, IA) Coord. of Lib. Pub. Srvs., DeAnza Cmnty. Coll., 1979–; Branch Mgr., San Jose Pub. Lib., 1977–79; I & R Coord., Los Angeles Pub. Lib., 1975–77; YA Libn., Contra Costa Cnty. Pub. Lib., 1974–75. **Educ.:** IA State Univ., 1967–71, BS (Eng.); Univ. of MI, 1971–72, AMLS. **Orgs.:** ALA: PLA/I & R Com.; JMRT/Students to ALA Com.; Prof. Dev. Grant Com. CA LA: Cncl.; Int. Frdm. Com. Union City, City of: Housing and Cmnty. Dev. Com. **Honors:** ALA, JMRT/3M Prof. Dev. Grant to attend conf., 1976. **Pubns.:** Guest Ed. *CA Libn.* (Jl. 1976). **Activities:** 1, 9; 16, 17, 48 **Addr.:** DeAnza Community College, 21250 Stevens Creek Blvd., Cupertino, CA 95014.

Dicker, Joan F. (Jl. 11, 1932, Brooklyn, NY) Head of Ref., Film Libn., Wayne Pub. Lib., 1977–; AV Dept., 1973–77. **Educ.:** Univ. of WI, 1953, BA (Pol. Sci., Law); Rutgers Univ., 1971, MLS. **Orgs.:** ALA. SLA. Educ. Film Lib. Assn. Juror, Amer. Film Fest. (1977–79). NJ LA: Exec. Bd. (1976–77); Pres., AV Sect. (1978–79); Ch., Inst. Com. (1978–79); Trustee Rel. Com. (1979–); PR Com. (1980–). **Pubns.:** "Report on Institute for Service to the Business Community," *NJ Libs.* (S. 1975). **Activities:** 9; 16, 32, 39; 59, 67 **Addr.:** 11 Mohawk Ave., Rockaway, NJ 07866.

Dickerson, L. Jane (D. 8, 1941, Shelter Island, NY) Sr. Libn., Legis./Gvtl. Srvs., NY State Lib., 1977–; Curric. Libn., 1971–77; Asst. Libn., Educ., 1968–71; Libn., Queens Borough Pub. Lib., 1963–68. **Educ.:** SUNY, Geneseo, 1959–63, BS (Educ. & Lib Sci.); Queens Coll., NY, 1964–67, MLS. **Orgs.:** ALA. NY LA. East. NY Sch. Lib. Media Assn. Capital Reg. Educ. Comm. Assn. Natl. Socty. Daughters of the Amer. Revolution. Natl. Assn. of Watch and Clock Collectors. **Pubns.:** Ed., *Legislative Trends* (1971–). **Activities:** 4, 12, 13; 16, 17, 24, 41; 78, 92 **Addr.:** Legislative and Governmental Services, New York State Library, Cultural Education Center, Empire State Plz., Albany, NY 12230.

Dickerson, Lon R. (D. 16, 1941, Ypsilanti, MI) Dir., Lake Agassiz Reg. Lib., 1972–; Actg. Libn., Head of Tech. Srvs., Univ. of Liberia Libs., 1968–72; Peace Corps Volun. Libn., Sierra Leone Lib. Bd., 1964–67. **Educ.:** Albion Coll., 1960–64, AB (Pol. Sci.); Univ. of Pittsburgh, 1967–68, MLS. **Orgs.:** ALA: Intl. Rel. Com. (1974–75). MN LA: Task Force on Lib. Futures (1975–76); Blue Ribbon Com. (1974–74). Adv. Cncl. to OPLIC: Pres. (1977–78); Task Force on Multitype Lib. Coop. (1978–78). MN Lib. Film Circuit: Bd. of Dir. (1975–78). **Pubns.:** "Where the Toys Are," *Show-Me Libraries* (O./N. 1979). **Activities:** 9; 17; 54, 78 **Addr.:** 607 South 6th St., Moorhead, MN 56560.

Dickerson, M. Maurine (Bethany, OK) Head Libn., Mid-America Nazarene Coll., 1967–; Eng. Tchr., Bethany Nazarene Coll., 1951–58, Catlgr., San Fernando Valley Coll., 1958–59; Eng. Tchr., Mutual Jr. and Sr. HS, 1948–50. **Educ.:** Bethany Nazarene Coll., 1944–48, AB (Eng.); OK St. Univ., 1950–51, MA (Eng.); Univ. of OK, 1954–58, MLS. **Orgs.:** ALA. Christ. Libns. Flwshp.: Bd. Mem. **Honors:** Beta Phi Mu, 1958; Bethany Nazarene Coll., Recipient of "B" Awd., 1976; Mid-America Nazarene Coll., Ltd, 1978; Bethany Nazarene Coll., Phi Delta Lambda, 1948; OK St. Univ., Phi Kappa Phi, 1951. **Addr.:** Mid-America Nazarene College, Box 1776, Olathe, KS 66061.

Dickey, Julia Edwards (Mr. 6, 1940, Sioux Falls, SD) Pres., Jedco Enterprises, 1981–; Dir., S. East. IN Area Lib. Srvs. Athrty., 1978–81; Coord., 1974–78; Head, Tech. Srvs., Bartholomew County Library, 1967–74; Asst. Acq. Libn., IN Univ. Reg. Campus Libs., 1965–67. **Educ.:** IN Univ., 1960–62, AB (Eng. and Hist.); 1964–67, MLS. **Orgs.:** ALA. Assn. for IN Media Educ. IN LA: Lib. Educ. Div. (Vice Ch., 1979–; Ch., 1980–81); ILTA Lib. Plng. Com. (1969–72); Ch., Tech. Srvs. RT. (1972); ILTA Leg. Com. (1978–); Lib. Asst. and Tech. RT (1969); various other com. AAUW: Columbus Chap. Pres. (1973–75); Psi Iota Xi. **Activities:** Multi-Type Regional; 17, 24, 34 **Addr.:** 021.7 Division, Jedco Enterprises, 511 Terr. Lake Rd., Columbus, IN 47201.

Dickinson, Candace S. (F. 15, 1946, Sarnia, ON) Coord. Reg. Srvs., Lake Erie Reg. Lib. Sys., 1979–; Libn., London Pub. Lib., 1971–79. **Educ.:** Univ. of West. ON, 1965–69, Honours BA (Hist.); Sch. of Lib. & Info. Sci., 1969–70, MLS. **Orgs.:** Can. LA. ON LA: Visitg. Lib. Srv. (Ch., 1979–). World Wildlife Fund. ON Nature Fed. Amnesty Intl. **Honors:** ALA, For Booklist on Underground Mag. (1972). **Activities:** 9; 16, 21, 27; 67, 72, 92 **Addr.:** 426 Pall Mall St., London, ON N5Y 2Z2 Canada.

Dickinson, Donald C. (Je. 9, 1927, Schenectady, NY) Prof. LS, Univ. of AZ, 1969–; Dir., Sch. of LS, 1969–78; Asst. Libn., Univ. of MO (Columbus), 1966–69; Libn., Bemidji St. Coll., 1958–66; Acq. Libn., Univ. of KS, 1956–58; Ref. Libn., MI St. Normal Sch., 1954–56; Ref. Libn., Ctr. MO St., 1951–54. **Educ.:** St. Univ. of NY (Albany), 1945–49, AB (Eng.); Univ. of IL, 1949–51, MLS; Univ. of MI, 1954–65, PhD (LS). **Orgs.:** ALA: Cncl. (1972–73). AZ LA: Pres. (1979–80). S. West. LA: Exec. Cncl. (1977–). AALS. Bibl. Socty. of Amer. **Honors:** ALA/ACRL, Travel Grant, 1959; Amer. Phil. Socty., Travel Grant, 1969. **Pubns.:** *Bio-bibliography of Langston Hughes, 1902–1967* (1972); *Hellmut Lehmann-Haupt, a bibliography* (1975); Ed. "Aware" in *Amer. Libs.* (1971–72); Ed. *Voices from the Southwest* (1976); Ed. *F. L. Schmied, Artist, Engraver, Printer* (1976); Other articles. **Activities:** 1; 26, 39; 55, 57 **Addr.:** 1515 E. First St., Tucson, AZ 85719.

Dickinson, Elizabeth M. (Mr. 26, 1948, Minneapolis, NM) Tech. Srvs. Coord., Stockton-San Joaquin Cnty. Pub. Lib. Stockton, CA, 1978–; Syst. Libn. for Tech. Srvs., Broward Cnty. Lib., 1977–78; Head, Ed. Sect., Tech. Srvs., Hennepin Cnty. Lib., 1975–77, Cat. Ed., Catlgr., 1971–75. **Educ.:** Lawrence Univ., 1966–70, BA cum laude, (Hist.); Coll. of St. Thomas, 1975–79, MBA; Univ. of MN, 1970–72, MA (LS). **Orgs.:** ALA: Cncl. (1978–81); Budget Asm. (1980); Ad Hoc Com. Status of Women (Ch. 1977–78); SRRT Action Cncl. (1975–76); Equal Empl. Oppt. Subcom. (1975–78); various other coms. CA LA: Tech. Srvs. Chap., VP/Pres. Elect (1979–80); various other coms. ASIS. Amer. Socty. for Pub. Admn. Stockton Chorale and Solo Chorale. Sigma Alpha Iota. **Honors:** Beta Phi Mu. **Pubns.:** Jt. auth., "Affirmative Action and American Librarianship," *Advncs. in Libnshp.* (1978); Jt. auth., *Affirmative Action and Librarianship* (forthcoming). "Library Personnel: Affirmative Action in Librarianship," *ALA Yrbk.* (1976, 1977); "Of Computers, Catalogs and Communication," *Wilson Lib. Bltn.* (F. 1976); "A Word Game," *Can. Lib. Jnl.* (Ag. 1974). **Activities:** 9; 46; 56 **Addr.:** 1358 Pelem Ct., Stockton, CA 95203.

Dickson, Katherine Murphy (Jl. 13, 1932, Boston, MA) Libn., Bus. and Prof. Women's Fndn., 1981–; Catlgr., Amer. Fed. of State, Cnty. and Mncpl. Empl., 1979–81; Libn. and Asst. Ed., Cat. Pubn., Lib. of Congs., 1978–79, Catlgr., Natl. Lib. Srv. to Blind, 1977–78, Bibl. and Sci. Ref. Libn., 1966–68; Rotch Arch. and Plng. Libn., MA Inst. of Tech., 1963–65, Assn. Ref. Libn., 1958–65; Libn., NY Pub. Lib., 1954–58. **Educ.:** Simmons Coll., 1950–54, BS (LS); Columbia Univ., 1956–58, MA, cum laude (Eng. Lit.); Univ. of MD, 1979– (Amer. Std.). **Orgs.:** ALA. SLA: Boston Chap., Prog. Com. (1965). Cncl. of Plng. Libns.: VP (1964–66). Frnds. Conf. on Rel. and Psy. **Honors:** Assoc. Electrical Indus. Ltd., Exch. Libn., 1961–62. **Pubns.:** *History of Aeronautics and Astronautics: A Preliminary Bibliography* (1968); "Reentry Professional Librarians," *Research Issues on Women in Librarianship* (1982); "Scientific and Technical Literature in England," *SLA Boston Chap. News Bltn.* (1962); "Growth," *Inward Light* (1977); "Boston Fantasy," *Wingspread: A Feminist Lit. Jnl.* (1980). **Activities:** 12; 17, 39, 41; 92 **Addr.:** 42 Castleton Dr., Upper Marlboro, MD 20870.

Dickson, Lance E. (Jl. 11, 1939, Cape Town, S. Africa) Law Libn. and Prof. of Law, LA St. Univ. Law Ctr., 1978–, Law Libn. and Assoc. Prof., 1975–78; Assoc. Libn., Univ. of TX Sch. of Law, 1973–75; Co. Secy. and Legal Couns., Mobil Oil South. Africa, 1970. **Educ.:** Univ. of Cape Town, 1960, BA (Law), 1962, LLB (Law), 1969, BCom (Bus.); Univ. of TX, Austin, 1971 MLS. **Orgs.:** Amer. Assn. of Law Libs. British & Irish Assn. of Law Libns. Can. Assn. of Law Libs. LA St. Adv. Cncl. on Libs. **Pubns.:** *LSU Law Library Dictionary Card Catalog on Microfiche* (1981); *Marine Resources: Catalog of a Special Collection* (1980); *Legal Bibliography Index* (1979). **Activities:** 1, 12; 17, 24, 26; 56, 57, 77 **Addr.:** Law Library, Louisiana State University, Baton Rouge, LA 70803.

Didier, Elaine K. (Mr. 20, 1948, Detroit, MI) Asst. Dir., Instr. Strategy Svs., Univ. of MI Sch. of Educ., 1981–; Asst. Dir., Instr. Strategy Srvs. and Lib. Consult., Univ. of MI Sch. of Educ., 1979–81; Exec. Secy., MI Assn. for Media in Educ., 1977–79; Mtlrs. Utilization Spec., Wayne Cnty. Inter. Sch. Dist., 1976–77; Lib. Media Spec., Plymouth, Ann Arbor, PR, 1971–76. **Educ.:** Univ. of MI, 1966–70, AB (Eng.); 1970–71, AM (LS); PhD in prog. (LS). **Orgs.:** ALA: AASL. AECT: Eval. of Instr. Mtls. Com. (Ch., 1977–); Div. of Educ. Mgt. (Pres.-elect, 1981). MI LA. MI

Special Subjects/Services: 50. Adult educ.; 51. Advert./Mktg.; 52. Aerosp.; 53. Agric.; 54. Area std.; 55. Arts/Hum.; 56. Autom.; 57. Bibl./Prtg.; 58. Bio. sci.; 59. Bus./Fin.; 60. Chem.; 61. Copyrt.; 62. Documtn.; 63. Educ.; 64. Engin.; 65. Env.; 66. Eth. grps.; 67. Film; 68. Food/Nutr.; 69. Geneal.; 70. Geo.; 71. Geol.; 72. Handcpd.; 73. Hist.; 74. Int. frdm.; 75. Info. sci.; 76. Insr.; 77. Law; 78. Legis.; 79. Math./Comp. sci.; 80. Med.; 81. Metals; 82. Nat. resrcs.; 83. Newsp.; 84. Nuc. sci.; 85. Oral hist.; 86. Petr./Energy; 87. Pharm.; 88. Phys./Astr./Math.; 89. Readg.; 90. Relig.; 91. Soc. sci./Tech.; 92. Soc. sci.; 93. Telecom.; 94. Transp.; 95. (other).

Assn. for Media in Educ.: Exec. Sec. (1977–79); Bd. of Dir. (1976–77). Other orgs. **Honors:** Phi Kappa Phi, 1970; Beta Phi Mu, 1971. **Pubns.:** "The Status of Building Level Media Programs in Michigan," *Media Spectrum* (1981); "Library Media Programs in Michigan," *Letter to Schools* (Mr. 1981); "Expanding the Role of the Lib. Media Spec. in Curric. Development," *Innovator* (Jl. 4, 1978); "The Coming of Age...of the Sch. Lib. Media Spec.," *MI Libn.* (Win. 1979). **Activities:** 1; 17, 24, 32; 63 **Addr.:** Instructional Strategy Services, 3001 School of Education, University of Michigan, Ann Arbor, MI 48109.

Diehl, Carol L. (Ag. 10, 1929, Milwaukee, WI) Lib. Media Dir., Sch. Dist. of New London, 1977–; Lib. Media Coord., Sch. Dist. of Manawa, WI, 1973–77; Coll. Libn., Instr., Vernon Cnty. Tchrs. Coll., 1965–67; Sch. Libn., WI Schs., 1951–65. **Educ.:** Univ. of WI, Madison, 1947–51, BS (Eng.); Univ. of WI, Oshkosh, 1970–71, MA (LS); Univ. of WI, Stout & Oshkosh, 1977–81, Lib. Supvsi. and AV Dir. Cert. **Orgs.:** ALA: AASL/ Prof. Dev. Com. (1979–81, Ch., 1980–81); Affilt. Assm. (Secy., 1979–80). AECT. WI Sch. Lib. Media Assn.: Pres. (1980); VP (1979). WI LA: Exec. Bd. (1979–80); Lib. Dev. and Legis. Com. District Coord., (1979–80). Other orgs. and coms. Natl. Educ. Assn. WI Educ. Assn.: Cncl. (1973–). Fox Valley Symph. Leag.: Bd. of Dir. (1970–81). Manawa Women's Club: Pres. (1976–77). Other orgs. **Honors:** WI Dept. of Pub. Instr., Exemplary Sch. Media Prog., 1976; WI Republican Party, William J. Campbell Awd., 1979. **Pubns.:** "Task Analysis of Elementary School Librarians", *WI Lib. Bltn.* (Mr.-Ap., 1973); "Turn the Key, Public Relations for School Media Programs," *WI Ideas in Media,* (F. 1979); Newspaper articles. **Activities:** 10, 14; 32, 36, 39; 63, 75, 93 **Addr.:** School District of New London, Library Media Services, 901 W. Washington St., New London, WI 54961.

Diehl, Katharine Smith (My. 16, 1906, Manheim, PA) Freelance Writer, 19–; Sr. Resrch. Flw., Amer. Inst. of India Studies, 1967–70; Asst. Prof. LS, Rutgers Univ., 1963–66; Bibl., Carey Lib., Serampore, W. Bengal, India, 1961–62; Sr. Fulbright Prof. LS, Dacca Univ., 1959–61; Head, Dept. LS, Univ. of TN (Knoxville), 1958–59; Libn., TX Lutheran Coll., 1938–53. **Educ.:** Boston Univ., 1926–28, BA (Relig. Educ.); Emory Univ., 1937–38, AB (LS); Univ. of MI, 1953–54, MA (LS). **Orgs.:** ALA. Amer. The. LA. Assn. Asian Studies, Inc. AAUW. Hymn Socty. Amer. **Honors:** U.S. Gvt., Sr. Fulbright Prof., 1959. **Pubns.:** *Hymns and Tunes: An Index* (1966); *Early Indian Imprints* (1964); *Religions, Mythologies, Folklores* (1962, 1956); *One Librarian* (1956); many other pubns. on Asia. **Activities:** 1, 11; 17, 26, 39; 54, 90 **Addr.:** 812 Baker Ave., Seguin, TX 78155.

Diener, Ronald Ernst (Ag. 13, 1937, Sheboygan, WI) Exec. Dir., OHIONET, 1978–; Head, Ofc. of Systs. Plng. and Resrch., Harvard Univ. Lib., 1974–78; Libn., Exec. of Coop. Lib. Prog., Boston Theo. Inst., 1969–74; Exec. Dir., Fndn. for Reformation Resrch., 1964–69. **Educ.:** Northwest. Coll., 1955–59, BA (Pre-Theo.); Univ. of MO, 1960–62, MA (Classics); Concordia Semy., 1961–64, BD (Theo.); Univ. of IL, 1964–65, MSLS; Harvard Univ., 1968–79, ThD (Hist.). **Orgs.:** OH LA: Dev. Com. (1980–). NELINET: Bd. and Coms. (1971–73, 1977–78). **Pubns.:** "Biography of Johann Wigand," *Shapers of Tradition* (1981); ed., *OHIONETWORK* (1979–); ed., *Religions and Theological Resources* (1971–74). **Activities:** 1, 14-Netwk.; 34, 49-Systs.; 56, 73, 90 **Addr.:** OHIONET, 1500 W. Lane Ave., Columbus, OH 43221.

Diffendal, Anne Polk (Ja. 3, 1943, Charlotte, NC) Mss. Cur., NE State Hist. Socty., 1974–; Instr., Asst. Prof. of Hist., Univ. of NE, Lincoln, 1972–73; Asst. Prof. of Hist., St. Dominic Coll., 1966–70; Archvst., GA Dept. of Arch. and Hist., 1965–66. **Educ.:** Barry Coll., 1960–64, BA (Hist.); Emory Univ., 1964–65, MA (Hist.); Univ. of NE, 1970–1974, PhD (Hist.); Cert. in Mod. Arch. Admin., Natl. Arch. and Recs. Srv., Amer. Univ., 1975. **Orgs.:** SAA: Arch.-Lib. Rela. Com., (1974–79), Ch., (1978–79); ALA/SAA Jt. Com. Midwest Arch. Conf.: Cncl. (1978–1980). **Honors:** NE State Hist. Socty., James E. Sellers Awd., 1979. **Pubns.:** *Centennial History of the Nebraska State Historical Society* (1978); *Guide to the Newspaper Collection of the State Archives, Nebraska State Historical Society* (1977); "Nebraska in the Centennial Exhibition at Philadelphia, 1876," *NE Hist.* (Spring 1976); "Fort Augusta," *GA Mag.* (June 1966); "Argyle, Colonial Outpost," *GA Mag.* (March 1966). **Activities:** 2, 14; 39, 41, 45; 55, 69, 83 **Addr.:** Nebraska State Historical Society, 1500 R St., Lincoln, NE 68508.

Dillard, Georgia M. (D. 5, 1938, Spring Grove, MN) Lib. Dept. Ch., Phoenix Coll. Lib., 1973–; Dept. Ch., IMC, Glendale Cmnty. Coll., 1971–73, Pers. and Circ. Libn., 1967–71; Libn., Art and Phil. Sect., Phoenix Pub. Lib., 1966–67; Libn., Loan Dept., Univ. of CA, Berkeley, 1964–66; Libn., Padelford Branch Lib., Univ. of WA, 1961–63. **Educ.:** Macalester Coll., 1957–59, BA (Intl. Rel.); Univ. of WA, 1960–61, ML (LS); U.S. Intl. Univ., 1979–80, MA (Psy.). **Orgs.:** AZ LA: Coll. and Univ. Div. (Pres., 1975–76); *AZ Highways* 50 Yr. Index Com. (Indxr., 1976–77). Phoenix Coll. Fac. Assn. Maricopa Colls. Educ. Assn. **Activities:** 1; 15, 17, 39 **Addr.:** Phoenix College, 1202 W. Thomas Rd., Phoenix, AZ 85013.

Dilley, Richard Allen (Je. 29, 1936, Richland Center, WI) Head, Serials Sect., IL St. Lib., 1975–; Ref. Libn., West. IL Univ. Lib., 1971–75; Acq. Libn., Grad. Sch. of Bus. Stanford Univ., 1968–71; Serials Libn., Univ. of IA Libs., 1964–67. **Educ.:** Univ. of WI (Madison), 1957–59, BA (Fr.), 1960–61, MALS. **Orgs.:** ALA. IL LA. **Activities:** 1, 13; 15, 39, 44 **Addr.:** Serials Section, Illinois State Library, Centennial Bldg., Springfield, IL 62756.

Dillon, Howard W. (N. 5, 1937, Green Valley, IL) Assoc. Dir., Pub. Srvs., Univ. of Chicago, 1975–; Univ. Libn., Sangamon State Univ., 1970–75; Libn., Grad. Sch. of Educ., Harvard Univ., 1965–70; Auto. and Info. Sci. Libn., Ohio State Univ., 1961–65; Ref. Libn., IN Univ., 1960–61. **Educ.:** Knox Coll., 1955–59, AB (Msc.); IN Univ., 1959–61, AM (LS). **Orgs.:** ALA: Info. Sci. and Autom. Div. (Secy., 1966–67); ACRL, Acad. Status Com. (1975–77), Budget and Finance Com. (1975–77), /Univ. Libs. Sect., Strg. Com. (1975–77). ASIS. IL LA. IL Reg. Lib. Cncl. (Pres., 1978–). Various other coms. and ofcs. Caxton Club (Chicago). Quadrangle Club (Chicago): Bd. (1978–81). **Pubns.:** Jt. ed., *Library Technology and Architecture,* (1968); "Organizing the Academic Library for Instruction," *Jnl. of Acad. Libnshp.* (S. 1975). **Activities:** 1; 17, 24, 34 **Addr.:** University of Chicago Library, 1100 East 57th St., Chicago, IL 60637.

Dillon, William A. (O. 2, 1922, Pittsburgh, PA) Dir. Jervis Pub. Lib. (Rome, NY), 1958–; Branch Libn., Brooklyn Pub. Lib., 1956–58; Stacks Cur., 1955; Genl. Asst., 1953–54. **Educ.:** Univ. of Pittsburgh, 1946–48, BA (Eng.); Columbia Univ., 1952–53, MSLS. **Orgs.:** Indp. Ctrl. LA: Pres. (1977). NYLA. ALA. **Activities:** 9; 17 **Addr.:** Jervis Public Library, 613 N. Washington St., Rome, NY 13440.

DiLoreto, Ann Marie (Jl. 4, 1953, Detroit, MI) Law Libn., Widett, Slater & Goldman, 1977–; Asst. Libn., New Eng. Hist. Geneal. Socty., 1976–77; Libn., New Eng. Aquarium, 1975–76. **Educ.:** Univ. of MI, 1971–75, BGS (Gen. Studies); Simmons Coll., 1975–76, MLS. **Orgs.:** Assn. of Boston Law Libns.: Prof. Standards Com. (Ch., 1979–); Consult. Com. Law Libns. of New Eng. SLA. AALL. **Activities:** 12, 14; 24, 41, 46; 77 **Addr.:** 1683 Cambridge St., Cambridge, MA 02138.

DiMattia, Susan S. (Jl. 28, 1942, Neptune, NJ) Lib. Consult., Freelance Ed. and Writer; Bus. Ref. Spec., Suffolk Coop. Lib. Syst., 1971–74; Head Libn., New England Merchants Bank (Boston), 1965–71. **Educ.:** Wilson Coll., 1960–64, BA (Eng., Econ.); Simmons Coll., 1964–65, MS (LS); Univ. of CT, 1981, MBA. **Orgs.:** ALA: Bus. Ref. Srvs. Comm. (Ch., 1981). SLA: Long Island Chap. (Bltn. Ed., 1972–76); Boston Chap. (Treas., 1970–71). **Pubns.:** "Business Books, 1976–80", *Lib. Jnl.* (Mr. 1977–80); "Library School Alumni Publications," *Jnl. of Educ. Libnshp.;* Ed., *Spotlight on M.B.A. Stamford* (Univ. of CT.), (1978–); Ed., *The Simmons Librarian* (1971–76); Ed. *Soundings* (1972–1976). **Activities:** 9, 12; 17, 39; 59 **Addr.:** 44 Chatham Rd., Stamford, CT 06903.

Dimmick, Mary Laverne (Jl. 13, 1930, Charleroi, PA) Sr. Info. Libn., Univ. of Pittsburgh, 1968–, Supvsr., of Lending Srvs., 1966–68, Docum. Libn., 1965–66; Per. Libn., Amer. Univ., 1963–65; Asst. Ref. Libn., Grt. Neck Lib., 1959–63; Jr. Libn., Buffalo and Erie Cnty. Lib., 1958–59. **Educ.:** CA State Coll., 1948–52, BS (Eng.); Carnegie Inst. of Tech., 1957–58, MLS; Univ. of Pittsburgh, 1969–72, Adv. Cert. (LS). **Orgs.:** ALA. ASIS. Beta Phi Mu. **Pubns.:** *The Rolling Stones: An Annotated Bibliography* (1979). **Activities:** 1; 31, 39, 49-Online Srch.; 75, 92 **Addr.:** 7013 Reynolds St., Pittsburgh, PA 15208.

Dimone, Vincent P. (My. 21, 1950, Brooklyn, NY) Info. Spec., Cravath, Swaine & Moore (NYC), 1981–; Info. Spec., FIND/SVP, 1979–81; LSCA, Title I, Proj. Dir., Suffolk Coop. Lib. Syst., 1977–78; Libn., Comm. Ctr. Mgr., Cath. Charities, Dio. of Brooklyn, 1974–76. **Educ.:** SUNY, Stony Brook, 1967–72, BS (Applied Math. & Psy.); Queens Coll., 1973–74, MLS. **Orgs.:** NY LA: RASD/Litcy. Com. (1978). ALA. Suffolk LA. **Honors:** Intl. Lib. Sci. Socty., 1974. **Activities:** 9, 12; 17, 39, 41; 59, 88, 92 **Addr.:** 1010 Bloomfield St., Hoboken, NJ 07030.

Di Muccio, Mary-Jo (Je. 16, 1930, Hanford, CA) Admin. Libn., City of Sunnyvale, 1972–; Head Libn., Immaculate Heart Coll., 1962–72; Tchr., CA and BC Schs., 1948–62. **Educ.:** Immaculate Heart Coll., 1953, BA (Eng.); 1960, MLS; CA Libn. Cred.; Lifetime Cmnty. Teaching Cred.; United States Univ., 1968–70, PhD (Psy.). **Orgs.:** Cath. LA: Pres. (1973–75). SLA: Rep. to Cath. LA (1972–). ALA. CA LA: Schol. Com. (1976). Soroptimist Intl. of Sunnyvale: Pres. (1976–78). Bus. and Prof. Women: Pres. (1978–79). Sunnyvale Cmnty. Srvs.: Pres. (1978–). Untd. Way Allocation Bd. Other orgs. **Honors:** Amer. Bicentennial Resrch. Inst. Service, 1976. **Pubns.:** *Freedom and Responsibility of the Individual in Democratic Society* (1970); *Library Informational Handbook for Elementary Schools* (1961); *Children's Choices & Parent's Choices in Selecting Children's Literature* (1960). **Activities:** 9; 16, 17, 21; 75, 92 **Addr.:** 720 C Blair Ct., Sunnyvale, CA 94087.

Dingle-Cliff, Susan M. (Ag. 31, 1950, Kankakee, IL) Libn., AB Alcoholism and Drug Abuse Cmsn., 1977–; Actg. Pub. Srvs. Libn., Grant MacEwan Cmnty. Coll., 1976–77; Sessional Libn., Educ. Ref., Univ. of AB., 1975–76. **Educ.:** Univ. of IL, 1968–72, AB (Amer. Civ.); 1973–75, MS (LS). **Orgs.:** LA AB: Secy. (1977–78). AB Gvt. Libs. Cncl.: Cnclr. (1979–80); Staff Dev. Com. (Ch., 1979–80). ASIS: West. Can. Chap. (Secy., 1978; Mem., 1979 Can. Micro. Assn.: Edmonton Chap., Pubcty. Com. (1979–80). Various other orgs. **Pubns.:** Jt. auth., "Comparison of Recent Acquisitions and OCLC Find Rates for Three Canadian Special Libraries," *Jnl. of Amer. Soc. Info. Sci.* (1981); Jt.-auth., "Collection Overlap in Canadian Addictions Libraries," *Spec. Libs.* (1979); various delivered papers and speeches. **Activities:** 4, 12; 17, 27, 39; 95-Addictions. **Addr.:** Alberta Alcoholism & Drug Abuse Commission Library, Pacific Plaza, 10909 Jasper Ave., Edmonton, AB T5J 3M9 Canada.

Diodati, C. Michael (My. 19, 1938, Brooklyn, NY) Supvsg. Head, Wakefield Lib., NY Pub. Lib., 1976–, Supvsg. Asst. Libn., Bkmobiles, 1974–76; Sr. Libn. Head, Morrisania Lib., 1972–74; Sr. Libn., Manhattan Borough Ofc., 1970–72; Libn., NY Pub. Lib., 1968–70; Ch., Eng. Dept. and Libs., Collegio San Jose (PR), 1965–68; Tchr., Libn., Marianist HS, 1959–65. **Educ.:** Univ. of Dayton, 1956–59, BS (Educ.); Pratt Inst., 1967–68, MLS; St. John's Univ., 1969–71, MS (Educ.); Catholic Univ. of PR, 1965–66, Cert. (ling.). **Orgs.:** ALA: SRRT, Info Exch. Task Frc. (1976–80); Ofc. for Lib. Outrch. Srvs., Minority concerns (1978–80). Italian Amer. LA. NY LA: Outrch. com. (1976–80). Sons of Italy, Mid-Manhattan Lodge: Vice-Ch. (1974–75). Assn. of Prof. Italian Amers.: Ch. (1973–74); Actv. Com. (1972–73); Treas. (1979). **Honors:** NY Dept. of State, Disting. Merit for Ethnic Info. Srv., 1978; Delegate, NY Gvrs. Conf. on Libs., 1979. **Pubns.:** *Writings on Italian Americans* (1976); *Finding Your Way* (1980); "Italian Americans and Libraries," *ALA Yrbk.* (1977, 1978, 1979); "Ethnic Communities and Their Needs," *Catholic Lib. World* (Mr. 1980); Various speeches. **Activities:** 9; 27, 36, 41; 50, 57, 66 **Addr.:** 6 Peter Cooper Rd. #11G, New York, NY 10010.

Dionne, Richard J. (Mr. 10, 1941, Lebanon, NH) Libn. for the Scis., Yale Univ., 1975–; Head, Sci. and Tech. Libs., Syracuse Univ., 1971–75; Ref. Libn., Engin. Trans. Lib., Univ. of MI, 1970–71; Lectr., Sch. of Lib. Sci., 1968–70. **Educ.:** Boston Coll., 1958–62, AB (Hist.); Univ. of MI, 1963–65, AMLS, 1968–69, MA (Ling.). **Orgs.:** SLA: Upstate NY Chap. (Treas., 1972–75); CT Valley Chap. (Dir., 1977–78; Pres.-elect, 1978–79; Pres. 1979–80). CT Coop. Lib. Srvs. Unit Review Bd., Ch. (1981–82). **Pubns.:** Contrib. ed., *Guide to Reference Books,* suppl. (1980); "Managing the serials budget in a large academic library," *SLA Lib. Mgt. Div. Bltn.* (1979). **Activities:** 1; 17; 91 **Addr.:** 64 Sidehill Rd., Hamden, CT 06517.

Divilbiss, J. L. (Ja. 17, 1930, Parsons, KS) Assoc. Prof., Univ. of IL, 1971–; Resrch. Engin., 1965–80; Tech. Staff, Bell Resrch. Labs., 1962–65. **Educ.:** KS State Univ., 1949–52, BS (Engin.); Univ. of IL, 1954–61, PhD (Engin.). **Orgs.:** ASIS. **Pubns.:** Ed., *Proceedings of the 1976 Clinic on Library Applications of Data Processing* (1977); Ed., *Proceedings of the 1977 Clinic on Library Applications of Data Processing* (1978). **Activities:** 11; 24, 26; 56, 93 **Addr.:** 410 DKH, University of Illinois, Urbana, IL 61801.

Djonovich, Dusan J. (My. 17, 1920, Belgrade, Yugoslavia) Prof. of Law & Libn., Cardozo Law Sch., 1979–; Law Libn., Brooklyn Law Sch., 1974–79; Assoc. Curator, Foreign Law & Libn., NY Univ., 1964–74. **Educ.:** Univ. of Belgrade Law Sch., 1938–43, Dipl.; Columbia Univ., 1963–1964, MLS; Cert. of Adv. Libnshp. **Orgs.:** Intl. Law Lib. Assn. AALL. **Honors:** Phi Beta Mu. **Pubns.:** Legal Education: A Selective Bibliography. (1970); U.N. Resolutions. Ser. 1; General Assembly, 14 Vol. (1972–78); Jt. Auth., Law of Notary Public, 2d ed. (1967). **Activities:** 1, 12; 15, 17, 24; 54, 77 **Addr.:** 70 East 10th St., New York, NY 10003.

Doak, Mary M. (Ap. 17, 1921, Belton, MO) Prof. and Ch., Hum. and Soc. Sci. Div., Univ. of NE Lib. (Lincoln), 1979–, Hum. Libn., 1974–79, Pub. Srvs. Libn., 1962–74, Soc. Std. Libn., 1949–61, Actg. Soc. Sci. Libn., 1948–49, Asst. Libn. Soc. Sci. Div., 1946–48, Asst. Lib. Soc. Sci. and Hum. Div., 1945–46. **Educ.:** Ctrl. MO Univ., 1938–41, BS (Soc. Sci., Educ.); Univ. of Chicago, 1944–45, BLS; Univ. of NE, 1956, MA (Amer. Hist.). **Orgs.:** ALA. Mt. Plains LA. NE LA: Cits. Com. (1981); Coll. and Univ. Sect. (Secy./Treas., 1976); Conv. (Ch., 1964); State Legis. Com. (1967–68); Resol. Com. (Ch., 1969–73). Lincoln LA: Nom. Com. (1979, 1980). AAUP. NE State Hist. Soct. **Activities:** 1; 15, 17, 39; 55, 92 **Addr.:** 217N Love Library, University of Nebraska Libraries, Lincoln, NE 68588.

Doak, Wesley Allen (Ja. 19, 1939, Oberlin, OH) Chief of Lib. Dev., CA State Lib., 1980–, Asst. Chief of Lib. Dev., 1975–80, Prin. Consult., 1973–80; Grad. Lib. Sch. Instr., Univ. of CA, Los Angeles, 1972–73. **Educ.:** Yankton Coll., 1957–60, BM (Msc.); CA State Univ., 1978– (Pub. Admin.); Univ. of MA, 1960–63 (LS); Univ. CA, Davis, 1974–76, CPM (Prog. Mgt.). **Orgs.:** ALA: MBSP (1971); Collective Bargaining (1973); Cable and Vid. (1976–); ISAD Bd. of Dirs.; Nom. Com. Conf. Plng. (1980); Chap. Fndr. (1979). AECT. Intl. TV Assn. Film Lib. Info. Cncl.: Bd. of Dirs. (1979–). Fremont Presby. Church. **Honors:** CA LA, Boyle Hutchenson Awd., 1978; People to People Intl., European Del. Leader, 1979. **Pubns.:** Contrib. ed., auth., *Educational Technology: The Alternative Futures* (1979); contrib. ed., auth., *New Media in (Public) Libraries* (1978); "Administrative Problems and Their Solutions," *Lib. Qtly.* (Ja. 1975); "World's First Do-it-Yourself Media Futures Game," *Pyramid Film and*

PROFESSIONAL ACTIVITIES: Institutions: 1. Acad. lib.; 2. Arch.; 3. Assn.; 4. Fed./Gvt. lib.; 5. Inst. lib.; 6. Mfr./Suppl.; 7. Milit. lib.; 8. Musm.; 9. Pub. lib.; 10. Sch. lib.; 11. Sch. of lib. sci.; 12. Spec. lib.; 13. State lib.; 14. (other). **Functions/Activities:** 15. Acq./Col. dev.; 16. Adult srvs.; 17. Admin.; 18. Apprais.; 19. Archit./Bldgs.; 20. Cat./Class.; 21. Chld. srvs.; 22. Circ.; 23. Cons./Pres.; 24. Consult.; 25. Cont. ed.; 26. Educ. lib. sci.; 27. Ext. srvs.; 28. Fund/Grants; 29. Gvt. pubs.; 30. Indx./Abs.; 31. Instr. lib. use; 32. Media srvs.; 33. Micro.; 34. Netwks./Coop.; 35. Persnl.; 36. PR; 37. Publshg.; 38. Recs. mgt.; 39. Ref. srvs.; 40. Repro.; 41. Resrch.; 42. Review.; 43. Secur.; 44. Serials; 45. Spec. col.; 46. Tech. srvs.; 47. Trustees/Bds.; 48. YA srvs.; 49. (other).

Who's Who in Library and Information Services

Vid. News (Ja. 1980); producer, TV spots, CA LA (1972); various edshps. (1968–). **Activities:** 9, 13; 17, 24, 32 **Addr.:** 4111 Winding Creek Rd., Sacramento, CA 95825.

Dobb, L. Bartley (Seattle WA) State Docum. Libn., Univ. of WA, 1981–, Asst. Libn., Pol. Sci. Lib., 1973–81; Instr., Soc. Sci., Seattle Cmnty. Coll., 1970–72; Libn., Phys./Astr./Math. Lib., Univ. of WA, 1953–70. **Educ.:** Univ. of WA, 1942–46, BA (Pol. Sci.), 1971, BA (Hist.), 1954–59, MLS, 1964–67, MA (Pol. Sci.); WA St. Tchg. Cert. 1951–53. **Orgs.:** ALA: ACRL/Law and Pol. Sci. Sect., Com. Goals Objectives (1974–76). SLA: Pacific NW Chap., Com. Educ. Spec. Libns. (1970); Prog. Com. (1979–80). WA LA: Com. to Cert. Plenary Sessions (1978); Steering Cncl., Lib. Admin. Interest Grp. (1979–). Pacific NW LA. Amer. Pol. Sci. Assn. **Honors:** Phi Beta Kappa, 1945; Phi Delta Kappa, 1953; Pi Sigma Alpha, 1946. **Pubns.:** *A Study of the King County (WA) Rural Library District* (1967). **Activities:** 1, 12; 17, 22, 39; 54, 78, 92 **Addr.:** Suzzalo Library, University of Washington FM-25, Seattle, WA 98195.

Dobbin, Geraldine F. (Je. 1, 1929, Nakuru, Kenya) Systs. Libn., Univ. of BC, 1967–, Head, Cat. Div., 1963–66, Serials Catlgr., 1956–63. **Educ.:** Univ. of BC, 1949–51, BA (Eng., Math.); Univ. of Toronto, 1955–56, BLS. **Orgs.:** BC LA: Secy. (1959–60); Treas. (1970–71). Can. LA. ALA: Cat. Code Rev. Com., Subcom. on Rules for Cat. Machine-Readable Data Files (1973–76). **Pubns.:** "Sharing Social Science Research Data," *ASIS West. Can. Chap., Procs. of Fourth Anl. Mtg.* (1972). **Activities:** 1; 29, 44, 46; 56 **Addr.:** Library Processing Centre, University of British Columbia, Vancouver, BC V6T 1Z8 Canada.

Dobbs, David L. (Jn. 28, 1923, Minneapolis, MN) Mgr., Info. Storage and Retrieval, Merrell Resrch. Ctr., 1979–; Coord., Info. Retrieval, Merrell-Natl. Labs., 1977–79, Resrch. Info. Asst., 1957–77; Chief Chem., Resrch. Labs., Inc., 1954–57. **Educ.:** Univ. of MN, 1941–48, BChem, 1948–50 (Agr. Biochem.). **Orgs.:** ASIS: South. OH Chap. (Treas., 1978–79; Ch., (1980–81). Chem. Notation Assn. Amer. Chem. Socty. **Honors:** Phi Lambda Upsilon. **Pubns.:** "Silver Plating Bath" (U.S. Patent 2,883,288) (April 21, 1959); "Irreversible Temperature Change Indicator" (U.S. Patent 2,892,798) (June 30, 1959). **Activities:** 12; 33; 56, 60 **Addr.:** Scientific Information Systems Department, Merrell Research Center, 2210 East Galbraith Rd., Cincinnati, OH 45215.

Dobbs, Sr. M. Kathryn (N. 6, 1940, Camden, NJ) Dir., Lib. Srvs., Holy Family Coll., 1973–, Actg. Dir., Lib. Srvs., 1971–73, Readers Srvs. Libn., 1969–71. **Educ.:** Holy Family Coll., 1958–66, BA (Psy.); Drexel Univ., 1967–69, MS (LS). **Orgs.:** ALA. Catholic LA: Neumann Chap./Coll. and Univ. Sect. (Ch., 1976–79). PA LA. Tri-State Coll. Lib. Coop.: Bd. of Dir. Archlg. Inst. of Amer. Camden Cnty. (NJ) Hist. Socty. Haddonfield (NJ) Hist. Socty. Hist. Socty. of PA. **Activities:** 1; 17, 25, 34; 50, 55, 66 **Addr.:** Holy Family College, Grant & Frankford Aves., Philadelphia, PA 19114.

Dockins, Glenn (D. 29, 1925, Scopus, MO) Exec. Dir., Cumberland Trail Lib. Syst., 1967–; Admn. Libn., Mexico-Audrain Cnty. Lib., 1965–67; Libn., Flat River Jr. HS, 1961–65. **Educ.:** S. E. MO St. Coll., 1946–51, BS (Educ.); George Peabody Coll., 1960–64, MLS; Univ. of NE, Sum. 1965 (AV). **Orgs.:** ALA IL LA. MO St. Tchrs. Assn. Masonic Lodge. Elks Club. Methodist Church. **Honors:** Alpha Beta Alpha. **Pubns.:** "Serving the Unserved-Along the Cumberland Trail," *IL Libs.* (Mr. 1978); "District Libraries in Rural Areas," *IL Libs.* (My. 1975); "The Non User. . .The Libraries' Untapped Resource," *IL Libs.* (Mr 1974); "Wanted–For the Small Public Library An Improved Image," *IL Libs.* (Ap. 1973). **Activities:** 9; 17, 19, 24; 56, 76, 92 **Addr.:** Cumberland Trail Library System, Twelfth & McCawley, Flora, IL 62839.

Dodd, James Arthur (F. 17, 1925, NY, NY) Lib. Dir., Adrian Coll., 1964–; Branch Libn., Grosse Pointe Pub. Lib., 1959–64; Libn., Detroit Pub. Lib., 1951–59. **Educ.:** Northland Coll., 1946–50, AB (Chem.); Univ. of WI, 1950–51, MS (LS). **Orgs.:** MI LA: PR Com. (1978–). ALA. MI Arch. Assn.; Assn. of Indp. Colls. and Univ. in MI. Kiwanis Club, Adrian MI: various coms. Goodwill-LARC: Bd. of Dir. (Pres.). Various other orgs. **Honors:** United Fund Disting. Srv. as Pres., 1973; Outstan. Kiwanis Srv., Grosse Pointe Kiwanis Club, 1964. **Pubns.:** "Building a Library Collection, the Case of the Small College," *Coll. Mgt.* (O. 1967); "Highlights in the History of Adrian College," *MI Christian Advocate* (Ap. 1971); "Automation at Adrian College Library," *MI Libn.,* (Win., 1977); "The Dawson Years: Love & Commitment," *Contact,* Adrian Coll. Bltn. (Spr., 1978). **Activities:** 1, 2; 17, 31, 34 **Addr.:** Shipman Library, Adrian College, Adrian, MI 49221.

Dodd, James Beaupré (S. 21, 1926, Eldorado, IL) Prof. and Head, Users Srvs. Div., Price Gilbert Meml. Lib., GA Inst. of Tech., 1979–, Assoc. Prof. and Coord. of Srv. to Bus. and Indus., 1971–79, Assoc. Prof. and Head, Tech. Info. Srv., 1968–71, Assoc. Prof. and Grad. Libn., 1967–68; Visit. Lectr., LS, Emory Univ., 1972, 1977, 1979; Asst. Prof. and Sci. Libn., North. IL Univ., 1962–67; Head., Info. Srvs. Sect., Babcock and Wilcox Co., Atomic Energy Div., 1955–62; Instr., LS, Univ. of VA, Div. of Ext. and Gen. Std., 1961–62; various prof. positions and consults. (1948–). **Educ.:** South. IL Univ., 1943–48, BS (Educ. Eng.), 1948–50, MS (Educ. Eng.); Univ. of IL, 1951–52, MS (LS). **Orgs.:** GA LA: Autom. Com. (1977–81). ALA. ASIS. SLA: Pres. (1980–81); Pres.-Elect (1979–80); Awds. Com. (1970–80); WHCOLIS Official Observer (1979); Assn. Ofc. Oper. Com. (1979–82); various coms., ofcs. (1962–). Various other orgs., coms., ofcs. Amer. Assn. for Engin. Educ. Phi Kappa Sigma: Fac. Adv. and Alum. Chap. Visit. Interfaith, Inc.: Bd. of Trustees (1974–79). Trinity Presby. Church (Atlanta). **Honors:** Cncl. on Lib. Resrcs., Flwshp., 1973. **Pubns.:** Ed., *A Pictorial Directory of Special Libraries Board of Directors, Association Committee Members, and SLA Representatives* (1980); "In Medias Res," *Sci. and Tech. Libs.* (F. 1981); "Strategy for Change," *Spec. Libs.* (S. 1980); "At Age 70, Is SLA Ready for the 1980's?" *Spec. Libs.* (Mr. 1980); "Information Brokers," *Spec. Libs.* (1976); various articles, edshps. (1961–76). **Activities:** 1, 12; 17, 24, 34; 59, 86, 91 **Addr.:** 2898 Rockingham Dr., N.W., Atlanta, GA 30327.

Dodd, Sue A. (Je. 18, 1937, Lexington, KY) Assoc. Resrch. Libn., Inst. for Resrch. in Soc. Sci., Soc. Sci. Data Lib., Univ. of NC, 1970–, Asst. Dir., Louis Harris Pol. Data Ctr., 1967–70, Plng. Asst., Srvy. Resrch. Sect., Div. of Hlth. Affairs, 1966–67. **Educ.:** Univ. of KY, 1955–60, AB (Pol. Sci.), 1963–65, MA (Diplomacy); Univ. of NC, 1974–77, MSLS. **Orgs.:** Intl. Assn. for Soc. Sci. Info. Srvs. and Tech.: Exec. Admin. Com. (1978–); Class. Action Grp. (Ch., 1974–). ASIS: Spec. Interest Grp. on Numeric Data Bases. SAA: Task Frc. on Autom. Recs. and Techqs. ALA: RTSD/Cat. and Class. Sect., Com. on Descr. and Access (1979–). Various other orgs. **Honors:** Cncl. on Lib. Resrcs., Grant, 1979–. **Pubns.:** *Cataloging Machine-Readable Data Files: An Interpretive Manual* (forthcoming); "Building an On-Line Bibliographic/MARC Resource Database for Machine-Readable Data Files," *Jr. Lib. Autom.* (Mr. 1979); "Bibliographic References for Numeric Social Sciences Data Files . . . Suggested Guidelines," *JASIS* (Mr. 1979); "Machine-Readable Data Files," *Intl. Cat.* (Ap.–Je. 1978); "Titles," *IASSIST Nsltr.* (Fall 1977); "Cataloging Machine-Readable Data Files–A First Step?" *Drexel Lib. Qtly.* (Ja. 1977); various articles, papers (1978–80). **Activities:** 1, 12; 15, 20, 24; 56, 75, 92 **Addr.:** Institute for Research in Social Science, Rm. 25 Manning Hall 026A, University of North Carolina, Chapel Hill, NC 27514.

Dodson, Ann T. (Jl. 2, 1930, Zanesville, OH) Mgr., OCLC Lib., 1977–; Libn., Tech. Ed., Inst. for Aerobics Resrch. (Dallas), 1974–76; Asst. Info. Syst. Sci., Univ. of Dayton Resrch. Inst., 1970–72; Asst. to the Dir., 1968–69; Resrch. Anal., 1965–67; Info. Spec.; Battelle Meml. Inst., 1957–64. **Educ.:** Muskingum Coll., 1948–52, BA (Eng. and Span.); N. TX State Univ., 1974–76, MLS; Wright State Univ., 1970–72, Cert. (Sch. Media). **Orgs.:** Beta Phi Mu, 1977. SLA: Ctrl. OH Chap., Nsltr. Ed. (1978–80). ASIS: Ctrl. OH Chap., Steering Com. For '82 Annual Conf.; Awds. and Nom. Com. (1978–79), Hosplty. Com. (Ch., 1977–78); Spec. Inf. Grp. on Lib. Autom. and Ntwks. (1979–80). **Pubns.:** Jt. auth., "Special Libraries and Data Bases: A State of the Art Report," *Spec. Libs.* (April 1981); Jt. ed., *Dallas Health Science Consortium: Union List of Periodicals* (1976); Jt.-auth., "The Physiological Consequences of Wearing Industrial Respirators: A Review," *Amer. Indus. Hygiene Assn. Jnl.,* (Jn. 1979); "Stresses Involved in Wearing PVC Supplied-Air Suits: A Review," *Amer. Indus. Hygiene Assn. Jnl.* (Jl. 1979); Various other tech. rpts. **Activities:** 12; 17, 34, 41; 64, 75, 91 **Addr.:** 1120 Firth Ave., Worthington, OH 43085.

Dodson, James T. (Je. 4, 1932, Cambridge, OH) Dir. of Libs., Univ. of TX, Dallas, 1972–; Dir. of the Lib., Wright State Univ., 1964–72; Assoc. Libn., Educ. Lib., OH State Univ., 1963–64; Ref. Libn., 1962–63. **Educ.:** Denison Univ., 1950–54, BA (Hist.); OH State Univ., 1960–61, MA (Hist.); Case Western Reserve Univ., 1961–62, MSLS. **Orgs.:** AMIGOS Bibl. Cncl.: Ch. of Bd. (1973–77, 79–80). TX LA: Ch.-Elect, Coll. & Univ. Div., (1979–80). Interuniv. Cncl. of the N. TX Area: Ch., Lib. Com. (1973–75). ALA: ACRL/Acad./Resrch. Libn. of the Yr. Awd. Com. (Ch. 1979–80); Univ. Libs. Sect. (Ch., 1978–1979); LITA/Ind./Lib. Rel. Com. (Ch., 1975–77). **Addr.:** 10506 Creekmere Dr., Dallas, TX 75218.

Dodson, Suzanne Cates (F. 3, 1933, North Vancouver, BC) Head, Gvt. Pubn. and Micro., Univ. of BC Lib., 1965–, Libn., Circ. Div., 1963–65. **Educ.:** Univ. of BC, 1950–54, BA (Zlgy.), 1962–63, BLS. **Orgs.:** Can. LA. Can. Micro. Socty.: Vancouver Chap., Pres. (1972–73); Natl. Dir. (1975–77). Natl. Micro. Assn. ALA: Guidelines for Oper. a Lib. Micro. Facility Com. (1980–). Univ. of BC LA: Pres. (1981–82). **Honors:** Univ. of BC, Marian Harlow Prize in Libnshp., 1963; Can. Micro. Socty., Fellow, 1978. **Pubns.:** *Microform Research Collections: A Guide* (1978); "Library Applications with Microforms," *MicroNotes* (1973); "Microforms for the Library," *Brit. Bk. News* (O. 1973); "The Use of Microforms in the Library," *IMC Jnl.* (1973); "Toward Bibliographic Control: The Development of a Guide to Microform Research Collections," *Microform Review* (Jl.–Ag. 1978); various articles, reviews. **Activities:** 1; 26, 29, 33 **Addr.:** Government Publications and Microforms Divisions, University of British Columbia Library, 1956 Main Mall, Vancouver, BC V6T 1Y3 Canada.

Doellman, Michael Anthony (F. 11, 1945, Quincy, IL) Ref. Libn., Burton Pub. Lib., 1971–. **Educ.:** Quincy Coll., 1964–70, BA (Eng.); North. IL Univ., 1971 (LS); Case Western Reserve Univ., 1977, MS (LS); North. OH LA, 1976, Cert.; Univ. of Akron, 1978– (Eng.); various workshops. **Orgs.:** OH LA: Div. VII, Secy., Action Cncl. (1978–79). Cath. LA: Pub. Lib. Sect. (Ch., 1976–77; Secy., 1977–78). **Activities:** 1, 9; 20, 34, 39; 55, 56, 90 **Addr.:** Burton Public Library, 14588 W. Park, Burton, OH 44021.

Doerrer, David H. (Ap. 16, 1937, Rochester, NY) Asst. Dir., Tech. Prcs., Univ. of W. FL, 1976–; Head, Cat. Dept., IA State Univ., 1973–76; Cat. Libn., NYSSILR, Cornell Univ., 1969–73, Asst. Circ. Libn., 1966–69. **Educ.:** Syracuse Univ., 1963–65, AB (Hist.), 1965–66, MSLS. **Orgs.:** ALA. FL LA. W. FL LA: Pres. (1978–79). Com. of Univ. Indus. Rel. Libns.: Subcom. on Subj. Headings (Ch., 1971–73). **Honors:** Woodrow Wilson Flwshp., Hon. Mention, 1965. **Activities:** 1; 17, 46 **Addr.:** John C. Pace Library, The University of West Florida, Pensacola, FL 32504.

Doggett, Rachel H. (O. 7, 1943, Bellefonte, PA) Accessions Libn., Folger Shakespeare Lib., 1967–; Msc. Admin., WA Natl. Symph., 1966–67; Mgt. Trainee, Maritime Admin., 1965–66. **Educ.:** Univ. of MI, 1961–65, BA (Eng.); Catholic Univ., 1973–76, MSLS. **Orgs.:** Bibl. Socty. of Amer. Bibl. Socty., London. Amer. Prtg. Hist. Assn. Smithsonian Inst.: Friends of Msc., Strg. Com. **Honors** Folger Shakespeare Lib., Virginia LaMar Bk. Prize, 1978. **Activities:** 1, 12; 15, 18, 45; 55, 57 **Addr.:** Folger Shakespeare Library, 201 East Capitol St., Washington, DC 20003.

Doherty, Edmond J. (D. 9, 1933, New York, NY) Dir., Reading Pub. Lib., 1966–; Branch Libn., Free Lib. of Philadelphia, 1961–66. **Educ.:** St. Martin's Coll., 1951–55, BA (Phil.); Rutgers Univ., 1958–60, MLS. **Orgs.:** Mid. Atl. Reg. LA: Pres. (1977–80). PA LA: Treas. (1973–75). Untd. Way of Berks. Cnty. **Honors:** Untd. Way of Berks Cnty., Doran Awd., 1979. **Activities:** 9; 17 **Addr.:** 1208 Hampden Blvd., Reading, PA 19604.

Doherty, Joseph H. (D. 19, 1923, Boston, MA) Dir., Phillips Meml. Lib., Providence Coll., 1967–; Branch Libn., Hudson Park Branch, NY Pub. Lib., 1964–67, Asst. Libn., Grand Concourse Lib., 1961–63, Asst. Cur., Schomburg Ctr. for Resrch. in Black Culture, 1957–60. **Educ.:** Fordham Coll., 1946–48, AB (Eng.); Columbia Univ., 1948–51, MA (Eng.), 1954–55, MLS. **Orgs.:** ALA: ACRL, New Eng. Chap., Bylaws Com. (Ch., 1977). RI LA. RI Adv. Bd. of Lib. Comsns.: Ch. (1975–). Cnsrtm. of RI Acad. and Resrch. Libs.: Vice–Ch. (1980–81); Ch. (1981–82). **Activities:** 1; 17, 31, 45 **Addr.:** Phillips Memorial Library, Providence College, Providence, RI 02918.

Doi, Makiko (F. 25, 1931, Okayama, Japan) Serials Libn., Assoc. Prof. of LS, Ctrl. WA Univ., 1974–; Asst. Libn., Ellensburg Pub. Lib., 1970–74; Ref. Libn., South. OR Coll., 1962–65; Catlgr., E. Asian Lib., Columbia Univ., 1957–59; Catlgr., Hoover Inst., Stanford Univ., 1955–57. **Educ.:** Univ. of the Pacific, 1951–54, BA (Eng.); Univ. of WA, 1968–71, MS; San Jose St. Coll., 1954–55 (LS). **Orgs.:** WA LA: Assn. Acad. Libns. (Vice-Ch., Ch.-Elect, 1979–80); Serials RT. Pacific N. W. LA. ALA. Japan Lib. Assn. Japanese Amer. Citizens Leag. **Pubns.:** "Patterns of Current Periodical Usage," *Pacific NW LA Qtly.* (Fall 1976); "Establishing the Subject Authority File," *Unabashed Libn.* (Win. 1973); various speeches. **Activities:** 1; 15, 44, 46 **Addr.:** Central Washington University, Library, Serials Department, Ellensburg, WA 98926.

Doig, Zelma M. (Ja. 29, 1912, Coos Bay, OR) Libn., Volun., Chapel by the Lake Lib., 1976–; Libn., Hist. Lib., AK State Lib., 1975–78; Libn., Bk./Boat Proj., 1972–75, Head Libn., Sheldon Jackson Coll., 1968–72; Libn., Sheldon Jackson HS, 1962–67; Tchr.–Libn., Cathlamet HS, 1935–36; Tchr.–Libn., Ewan HS, 1934–35. **Educ.:** Whitworth Coll., 1929–33, BA (Hist.); WA State Univ., 1934, Cert. (Tchg.); Univ. of WA, 1935–36, Cert. (Tchg., Libn.), 1964–68, AK Tchg. Cert., 1969, MA (LS). **Orgs.:** ALA. Pac. NW LA. CSLA. AK LA: Juneau Pubcty. Com. (1977–78); Com. to Develop Stans. for Sch. Libs. (1978). Various other orgs. AK Hist. Socty. Pioneers of AK Auxiliary. Amer. Assn. of Ref. Persons. Older Persons Action Grp., Inc. Various other orgs. **Pubns.:** Various exhibits (1980). **Activities:** 1, 13; 17, 20, 39; 55, 66, 73 **Addr.:** 9449 Berners Ave., Juneau, AK 99801.

Dolan, Frank T. (Jl. 1, 1935, Nelson-Miramichi, NB, Can.) Assoc. Prof., Sch. of LS, Univ. of West. ON, 1972–; Mgr., Comp. Ctr., Univ. of Calgary, 1969–72; Mgr., Tech. Info. Srv., Imperial Oil Ltd, 1966–69, Info. Spec., 1962–64; Geol., Imperial Oil Ltd., 1957–62. **Educ.:** St. Francis Xavier Univ., 1953–57, BSC (Phys. Sci.); GA Inst. of Tech., 1964–66, MSC (Info. Sci.); Stanford Univ., 1973–74 (Comm.). **Orgs.:** Can. Assn. Info. Sci. ASIS. **Pubns.:** *Textual Information Storage and Retrieval* (1980); "Teletext: Its Development and Social Implications" in *Procs. of the Seventh Anl. Can. Conf. on Info. Sci.* (1979); "A Universal Index Generator" in *Procs. of the Fifth Can. Conf. on Info. Sci.* (1977); "An Algorithm for Differentiating Natural Language Words From Nonsense Words" in *Procs of the Fourth Can. Conf. on Info. Sci.* (1976); Ed., *Can. Jnl. Info. Sci.* (1976–); many other pubns. **Activities:** 9, 11; 17, 24, 32, 41; 56, 75, 93 **Addr.:** School of Library & Information Science, The University of Western Ontario, London, ON N6A 5B9 Canada.

Special Subjects/Services: 50. Adult educ.; 51. Advert./Mktg.; 52. Aerosp.; 53. Agric.; 54. Area std.; 55. Arts/Hum.; 56. Autom.; 57. Bibl./Prtg.; 58. Bio. sci.; 59. Bus./Fin.; 60. Chem.; 61. Copyrt.; 62. Documtn.; 63. Educ.; 64. Engin.; 65. Env.; 66. Eth. grps.; 67. Film; 68. Food/Nutr.; 69. Geneal.; 70. Geo.; 71. Geol.; 72. Handcpd.; 73. Hist.; 74. Int. frdm.; 75. Info. sci.; 76. Insr.; 77. Law; 78. Legis.; 79. Math./Comp. sci.; 80. Med.; 81. Metals; 82. Nat. resrcs.; 83. Newsp.; 84. Nuc. sci.; 85. Oral hist.; 86. Petr./Energy; 87. Pharm.; 88. Phys./Astr./Math.; 89. Readg.; 90. Relig.; 91. Sci./Tech.; 92. Soc. sci.; 93. Telecom.; 94. Transp.; 95. (other).

Dolan, Pat A. (N. 13, 1945, Sioux City, IA) Asst. Libn. In Charge of Pub. Srvs., William Mitchell Coll. of Law, 1976–, Acq. Libn., 1971–76. **Educ.:** Univ. of SD, 1963–67, BA (Hist., Eng.), BS (Educ.); various LS crs. **Orgs.:** AALL: *Law Lib. Jnl.* Com. (1977–78). MN Assn. Law Libs.: Cont. Educ. (Ch., 1977–79); Pres. (1979–81). MN State Task Frc. For Cont. Educ. **Activities:** 1, 12; 16, 22, 25; 77, 78 **Addr.:** William Mitchell College of Law, 871 Summit Ave., St. Paul, MN 55105.

Dole, Grace F. (Cambridge, MA) Lib. Spec., Univ. of CT (Stamford), 1975–, Libn., 1964–75; Ref. Libn., The Ferguson Lib., Stamford, CT, 1962; Libn., Benton and Bowles, Inc., NY, 1956–62 Ref. Dept., N.Y. Pub. Lib., 1954–56. **Educ.:** Bryn Mawr Coll., 1940–44, BA (Hist.); Columbia Univ., 1950–54, MLS; Middlebury Coll., grad. wk. Frn., 1948; Columbia Univ., grad. wk. Hist., 1949. **Orgs.:** SLA: Lib. Dev. Com. (Head, 1962–63); Publicity (Ch., 1971) ALA. AAUP. Hudson Valley Art Assn.: Rec. Secy. (1973–74). Margaret F. Dole Contempory Art Club: VP (1973–74), Pres. (1974–). Other orgs. **Honors:** Amer. Artists Prof. League, Hon. Mem.; Zeta Tau Alpha, Awd. of Merit, 1979. **Pubns.:** Reviews. **Activities:** 1, 9, 12; 15, 17, 20, 31, 39 **Addr.:** 503 West Lyon Farm Dr., Greenwich, CT 06830.

Dole, Wanda V. (S. 10, 1942, Melrose Park, IL) Bibl. Hum., Univ. of IL (Chicago Circle), 1978–; Archit. Libn., Univ. of KY, 1976–78; Asst. Cur., World Heritage Musm., Univ. of IL, 1974–76; Tchg. Asst., Classics Dept., Univ. of IL, 1968–75, Asst. Ed., Scott, Foresman and Co., 1967–68; Tchr., Cambridge Sch. of Weston, 1965–66. **Educ.:** Lawrence Univ., BA (Classics); Tufts Univ., 1964–65, MA (Classics); Univ. of IL, 1974–75, MS (LS), 1968–74 (Classics). **Orgs.:** ALA: SORT (Steering Com., 1979–). Art Lib. Socty. of N. Amer.: Midwest. Reg. Rep. (1979–81); Chicago Lib. Club. Constitution Com. (1979); KY/TN Chap. SAA. (Ch., 1977). Socty. of Archit. Hist. Archlg. Inst. of Amer.: KY Chap. (Exec. Bd., 1976–78). **Pubns.:** *Historical Architecture of Lexington, Kentucky and the Blue Grass Region* (1979). **Activities:** 1; 15; 55, 57 **Addr.:** 4970 N. Marine Dr. #621, Chicago, IL 60640.

Dolgin, Jeanne Rydell (Je. 3, 1921, New York, NY) Head of Lib. and Info. Srvs., Katherine Gibbs School (NYC), 1981–; Asst. Prof., Head Instr. Libn., Mercy Coll., 1979–81; Head Pub. Srvs. Libn., 1977–79; Reader Srvs. Libn., 1969–77; Ref. Libn., Scarsdale Pub. Lib., 1964–69; Fellow, Dept. of Phil., Brooklyn Coll., 1944–1946. **Educ.:** Brooklyn Coll., 1939–44, BA (Phil.); Columbia Univ.-Grad. Sch. of Phil., 1944–48; Columbia Univ., 1960–64, MS in LS. **Orgs.:** ALA: ILL Com. (1979–1980). Westchester LA: Ch., Coll. Lib. Sect. (1973–74); Co-Ch., Com. on Coop. (1976–78). Westchester Lib. Syst.: Trustee (1976–); Ch., Com. to Review the Code of Srv. (1978); Secy. (1979–80). Ardsley Pub. Lib.: Trustee (1971–); Pres., Bd. of Trustees, (1977–). **Honors:** Beta Phi Mu, 1964. **Activities:** 1; 31, 39, 47; 55, 92 **Addr.:** 32 Mt. View Ave., Ardsley, NY 10502.

Dollard, Peter A. (Ag. 22, 1938, Ashland, KY) Lib. Dir., Alma Coll., 1974–; Head Libn., Clinch Valley Coll., Univ. of VA, 1970–74; Chief Ref. Libn., Brown Univ., 1969–70, Ref. Libn., 1969–69; Instr., Univ. of ME, 1965–67. **Educ.:** Univ. of MI, 1959–62, BA (Eng.); Univ. of WY, 1963–65, MA (Eng.); Univ. of MI, 1968, AMLS. **Orgs.:** ALA. NLA: Pres. (1977–79). MI Lib. Cnsrtm.: Bd. of Trustees (Ch., 1979–80). **Activities:** 1 **Addr.:** 227 Philadelphia, Alma, MI 48801.

Dollen, Charles Joseph (Ap. 14, 1926, Rochester, NY) Pastor, St. Gabriel's, 1973–; Lib. Dir., Univ. of San Diego, 1955–73. **Educ.:** St. Bernard's, Rochester, NY, 1947–51, BA (Phil.); Immaculate Heart Semy., 1952–54, Ordination (Theo.); Univ. of South. CA, 1956–57, MS (LS). **Orgs.:** CA LA: Int. Frdm. (Ch., 1971–72). Cath. LA: Various coms. (1957–). Poway (CA) Unfd. Sch. Dist.: Bd. of Trustees (1977–81). **Honors:** Natl. Assn. of Christs. and Jews, San Diego, Hon. Roll, 1974. **Pubns.:** *Civil Rights: A Source Book* (1964); *Messengers to the Americas* (1975); bk. review ed., *The Priest* (1965–); jt. ed., *The Catholic Tradition* (1980); ed., *Alternate Index*. **Activities:** 1, 10; 15, 21, 35; 57, 74, 90 **Addr.:** P.O. Box 887, Poway, CA 92064.

Dollerschell, Allen L. (Jl. 17, 1938, Litchfield, MN) Lib. Coord., Rochester Cmnty. Coll., 1964–; Asst. Libn., St. Louis Park HS, 1962–64; Asst. Libn., Edina Jr. HS, 1959–62. **Educ.:** St. Cloud State Univ., 1955–59, BS (Hist.); Univ. of MN., 1960–62, MA (LS). **Orgs.:** ALA: ACRL, Chap. Com. (1977–80); *Choice* Ed. Bd. (1978–80); MN LA: Acad. Div., (Ch., 1977–78); Exec. Bd. (1977–78), Task Force on Legis. Effectiveness (1978–79). Long Range Plng. and Dev. Com. Rochester Area Libn. Assn. MN Educ. Comp. Cnsrtm. MN Interlib. Telecom. Exch. Various coms., other orgs. Natl. Educ. Assn. MN Educ. Assn. MN Cmnty. Coll. Fac. Assn. Rochester Cmnty. Coll. Fac. Assn.: Secy./Treas. (1979–80); Curric. Com. (1968–79). **Pubns.:** Ed., *Directory of Minnesota Academic Librarians* (1977–78, 1980–81). **Activities:** 1; 15, 31, 37; 63, 78, 93 **Addr.:** Goddard Library, Rochester Community College, Rochester, MN 55901.

Dolnick, Sandy F. (N. 26, 1936, Milwaukee, WI) Pres., Friends of Libraries USA, 1979–; Co-pres., Friends of Milwaukee Pub. Lib., 1975–79; Dir., Friends of WI Libs., 1977–83. **Educ.:** Univ. of WI, 1954–58, BS (Eng.). **Orgs.:** WI LA. ALA: LAMA/PR Sect., Friends of Libs. Com. (Ch., 1976–80). **Pubns.:** Ed. *Friends of Libraries Source Book* (1980); Ed., *Friends of the Library National Notebook* (1978–); "Present State of Library Friends" *Organizing the Library Support* (1980). **Activities:** 1, 9; 17, 36, 49-Friends; 95-Volun. **Addr.:** 4909 N. Ardmore Ave., Milwaukee, WI 53217.

Domenech, Helen J. (My. 14, 1909, Cardiff, MD) Archvst., Widener Univ., 1978–; Asst. Libn., 1961–78; Asst. Prof., 1973–78; Libn., Eddystone HS, 1931–43. **Educ.:** Temple Univ., 1927–30, BS (Eng., Fr.); Drexel Univ., 1930–31, BS, in LS; Grad. courses at Penn, Columbia. **Orgs.:** ALA: ACRL. PA LA. Zonta Club of Philo: Secy. (1971). Messiah Proj.: Volun. Tchr. (1967–1980). Haverford Twp. Girl Scouts: Leader, Ch. (1950–1959). **Activities:** 1, 2; 23, 35, 39 **Addr.:** 151 Rockland Rd., Havertown, PA 19083.

Domescik, Carol Jo (Ag. 14, 1939, Alton, IL) Media Spec., Belle Valley Elem. Sch., 1967–; Eng. Tchr., Bement Sch. Dist., 1966–67. **Educ.:** South. IL Univ., Edwardsville, 1966, BA (Eng., LS); 1976, Spec. Cert. **Orgs.:** ALA. IL LA. IL Assn. for Media in Educ. Gateway Media RT: Secy. (1978–83). Various other orgs. Ord. of the East. Star of IL: Worthy Matron (1973). AAUW. Belle Valley Educ. Assn.: Comms. Com. (1979). **Pubns.:** "Noontime Madness at Belle Valley," *IAME News for You* (Win. 1980). **Activities:** 10; 20, 21, 22 **Addr.:** 112 Castle Dr., Belleville, IL 62221.

Domineske, Alice M. (Je. 17, 1931, Pittsburgh, PA) Lib./Media Coord., Shawnee HS, 1970–; Instr. in LS, Trenton State Coll., 1974–75; Sch. Libn., Corpus Christi Sch., 1967–70. **Educ.:** Chatham Coll., 1949–53, BA (Psy.); Drexel Univ., 1968–70, MS (LS); Monmouth Coll., 1973–76, MBA. **Orgs.:** Burlington Cnty. Sch. Media Assn.: Prog. Com.; Nom. Com. Educ. Media Assn. of NJ: Corres. Secy.; Pubcty. Ch. ALA: YASD, Media Sel. and Usage Com. Brodart: Sch. Lib. Adv. Bd. **Honors** Beta Phi Mu, 1970. **Pubns.:** Various sps., slide presentations (1973–76). **Activities:** 10; 15, 17, 31 **Addr.:** 14 Hinsdale Ln., Willingboro, NJ 08046.

Doms, Keith (Ap. 24, 1920, Endeavor, WI) Dir., The Free Lib. of Philadelphia, 1969–; Dir., Carnegie Lib. of Pittsburgh, 1964–69, Assoc. Dir., 1963–64, Asst. Dir., 1956–63; City Libn., Grace A. Dow Meml. Lib. (Midland, MI), 1951–56; City Libn., Concord (NH) Pub. Lib., 1946–51. **Educ.:** Univ. of WI, 1938–42, BA (Langs.), 1947, BLS; Harvard Univ., 1943–44, (Far East. Stds.). **Orgs.:** ALA: Pres. (1971–72); Exec. Bd. (1963–67; 1970–73). SLA. PA LA: Pres. (1960–61). Franklin Inn Club: Pres. (1978–80). PA State Bd. of Educ.: (1975–). PA Educ. Info. Ctrs.: Adv. Com. (Ch., 1979–). PA Citizens for Better Libs.: Bd. Dirs. (1980–). Various other orgs. and ofcs. **Honors:** PA LA, Awd. of Merit, 1961; PA LA, Disting. Srv. Awd., 1976; Cmwlth. of PA, Outstan. Srv. Cit., 1972. **Pubns.:** Various articles on Lib. Plng. Chaps. in *Local Public Library Administration* (1964); *A Practical Guidebook for Library Trustees* (1964, 1969). **Activities:** 9; 17, 19, 24; 50 **Addr.:** The Free Library of Philadelphia, Logan Sq., Philadelphia, PA 19103.

Doms, Margaret Taylor (Ag. 5, 1920, Bluffton, IN) Law Libn., Berger & Montague, 1977–; Law Libn., Duane, Morris & Heckscher, 1972–77; Librarian, Info. and Volun. Srvs. of Allegheny Cnty., 1968–69; Cmnty. Srv. Libn., WI State Traveling Lib., 1946–47; Genl. Libn., Pub. Lib. (Petaluma, CA), 1945–46; Libn., Natl. Defense Com., Natl. Socty. Daughters of the Amer. Revolution, 1944–45; various other positions. **Educ.:** Univ. of WI, 1937–41, BA (Amer. Insts.), 1941–42, BLS; various wkshps. **Orgs.:** AALL: Stans. Com. (1979–80); Private Law Firm Spec. Interest Sect., Prog. Com. (1978–79). Grt. Philadelphia Law Lib. Assn.: various coms. Cosmopolitan Club of Philadelphia. **Pubns.:** "A Law Library Consulting Service in the Philadelphia Area," Law Lib. Jnl. (Win. 1979). **Activities:** 12; 17, 24, 39; 77 **Addr.:** 3101 West Coulter St., Philadelphia, PA 19129.

Donahue, Kathryn (Kay) A. (Morristown, SD) Bus. and Docum. Spec., Sunnyvale Pub. Lib., 1969–; Freelnc. Jnlst., 1950–; Dir. of Pub. Info., Honolulu Army Port Cmnd., 1948–49; News Bur. Mgr., Los Angeles and Honolulu, Pan Amer. World Airways, 1943–48. **Educ.:** Univ. of South. CA, AB (Jnlsm.); San Jose State Univ., 1969, MA (LS), Golden Gate Univ., MA (Pub. Admin.). **Orgs.:** ASIS: Conv. Prog. (Ed., 1969). CA Frdm. of Info. Com.: Spec. Projs. (1969). Women in Comms. **Honors:** U.S. Small Bus. Admin., Awd. for Srv. to Bus. Cmnty., 1973; Sunnyvale Cham. of Cmrce., Cert. of Apprec. for Outstan. Srv. **Pubns.:** "Public Patent Libraries in California," *News Notes of CA Libs.* (1974); "Be an Information Specialist," *Matrix Mag.* (Je. 1967); *Technical and Materials Information Protocol* (1981); copy ed., *CA Publshr.;* columnist, *Los Angeles Cmrcl. News.* **Activities:** 9; 59, 64, 75 **Addr.:** 7545 Rainbow Dr., Cupertino, CA 95014.

Donahue, Martha (Ja. 5, 1936, Danville, KY) Head, Pub. Srvs., Assoc. Prof., Mansfield State Coll., 1971–: Ref. Libn., Univ. of WI, Whitewater, 1967–70; Ref. Libn., Ctr. Coll. (KY), 1966–67; Post Libn., U.S. Army, W. Germ., 1961–65. **Educ.:** Ctr. Coll., 1954–58, BA (Lit.); IN Univ., 1959–61, MA (LS); Univ. of WI, 1970–71, 6th Year Spec. Cert., (Lib. Admin.). **Orgs.:** ALA. PA LA: Bd. of Dir. (1978–79); West Branch Chap. (Ch., 1978–79). AAUP. **Activities:** 1; 17, 39; 59 **Addr.:** Library, Mansfield State College, Mansfield, PA 16933.

Donahue, Mary Katherine (Ja. 14, 1942, Dallas, TX) Coord., Hidalgo Cnty. Lib. Syst., 1976–80; Admin. Asst., Corpus Christi (TX) Pub. Libs., 1972–76; Corp. Libn., Univ. Computing Co., 1970–72; Libn., Univ. of TX, Arlington, 1969; Asst. Div., Lubbock (TX) Pub. Libs, 1966–69; Asst. Dept. Head, Dallas Pub. Libs., 1965–66. **Educ.:** Our Lady of the Lake Univ., 1959–63, BA (LS); Univ. of CA, Berkeley, 1964–65, MLS; Grad. Work, Texas A&M Univ. (1981–). **Orgs.:** SWLA. ALA: PLA, Cat. Needs of Pub. Libs. Com. (1977–81; Ch., 1979–81); LAMA, Stats. for Non-Prt. Media Com., 1979–81. TX LA: Plng. Com. (1976–77); Leg. Com. (1980–81). Various other coms. Hidalgo Cnty. Hist. Cmsn. Rio Grande Valley Cncl. for the Arts: Secy (1977–). **Honors:** TX Hist. Cmsn., Disting. Srv. Awd., 1975. **Pubns.:** Jt.-ed., *Texas Reference Sources: A Selective Guide* (1976); Ed., *1-2-3 Handbook* (1976). **Activities:** 9; 17, 24, 34; 56, 66, 89 **Addr.:** 504 South Dexter, College Station, TX 77840.

Donahugh, Robert Hayden (My. 20, 1930, St. Paul, MN) Dir., Pub. Lib. of Youngstown and Mahoning Cnty., 1979–; Asst. Lib. Dir., Youngstown Pub. Lib., 1962–79; Libn., Canton Pub. Lib., 1957–62; Eng. and Sp. Instr., Robert Coll., Istanbul, 1956–57; various other positions. **Educ.:** Coll. of St. Thomas, 1948–52, BA (Eng. and Educ.); Univ. of MN, 1952–53, MA (LS); Univ. of MD Overseas Prog., 1956 (Germ.); various wkshps. **Orgs.:** OH LA: Pres., (1975). MFLA: Pres. (1979–83). ALA. Various coms. and ofcs. Rotary; B.P.O.E. Lodge. **Pubns.:** *An Evaluation of Reference Resources in Eight Public Libraries in Four Ohio Counties* (1970); *Report of Kent State University's School of Library Science and Commission on Continuing Education* (1971); Reviews; Various articles. **Activities:** 9 **Addr.:** Public Library of Youngstown and Mahoning County, 305 Wick Ave., Youngstown, OH 44503.

Donaldson, Mary Anne Tay (Je. 13, 1946, Englewood, NJ) Libn., Mitchell, Silberberg & Knupp, 1972–; Ref. Libn., Amer. Bankers Assn., 1970–71, Asst. Libn., 1968–71. **Educ.:** Trinity Coll., Washington, D.C., 1964–68, BA (Hist.); Catholic Univ., 1968–70, MSLS; Amer. Assn. of Law Libs., 1975, Cert. Law Libn. **Orgs.:** South. CA Assn. of Law Libs.: Secy. (1975–76); VP (1977–78); Pres. (1978–79); Consult and Place. Com. (Ch., 1974–75). SLA. **Addr.:** Mitchell, Silberberg & Knupp, 1800 Century Park East, Los Angeles, CA 90067.

Donham, Jean O. (Ag. 9, 1946, IA City, IA) Dist. Media Coord., IA City Cmnty. Schs., 1974–. **Educ.:** Univ. of IA, 1964–67, BA (Eng. Educ.), Univ. of MD, 1972, MLS. **Orgs.:** ALA. IA Educ. Media Assn.: Bd. of Dirs. (1978–81). Intl. Readg. Assn. **Honors:** Beta Phi Mu, 1972. **Pubns.:** "Reading to Write: An Approach to Composition Using Children's Books," *Lang. Arts* (My. 1977); "Listening to Literature: An All-School Program," *Readg. Tchr.* (Ap. 1981). **Activities:** 10; 16, 21, 32; 63 **Addr.:** Iowa City Community Schools Administrative Bldg., 1040 Williams St., Iowa City, IA 52240.

Donley, Albert Murray, Jr. (O. 16, 1919, Melrose, MA) Assoc. Dir. Libs., Assoc. Prof. (LS), Univ. Archvst., 1953–; Lib. Dir., Dedham (MA) Pub. Lib., 1951–53. **Educ.:** Amer. Intl. Coll., 1946–49, AB (Hist. and Eng.); Syracuse Univ., 1950–51, MS (LS). **Orgs.:** ALA: ACRL; RTSD; LAMA. Amer. Docum. Inst. MA LA: Leg. Com. (Ch., 1955–56). New Eng. LA: Various Coms. SAA. Adult Educ. Assn. of the US. Natl. Educ. Assn. Adult Educ. Assn. of MA. **Pubns.:** *Use of Data Processing* (1967); *A Machine System for US Government Publications* (1966); "Library Ecology and Electronics," *Amer. Docum.* (O., 1957); "Using AV Materials for Orientation Lecture," *Lib. Jnl.* (My. 1956); Various bibls. and other pubns. **Addr.:** 84 Millwood St., Framingham, MA 01701.

Donley, Mary R. (Ja. 18, 1928, Minneapolis, MN) Coord. of Tech. Srvs., Univ. of WI, Stout, 1971–, Cat. Libn., 1959–69; Cat./Ref. Libn., North. State Tchrs. Coll., 1956–59. **Educ.:** Univ. of MN, 1952–55, BA (Pol. Sci.), 1955–56, MA (LS). **Orgs.:** ALA. WI LA. WI AV Assn. Metro. Opera in Upper Midwest: Reg. Ch. **Honors:** Beta Phi Mu, 1956. **Pubns.:** "Placements and Salaries," *North American Library Directory* (1972); "Placements and Salaries, 1970," *Lib. Jnl.* (Je. 1, 1971). **Activities:** 1; 20, 32, 46; 56, 75 **Addr.:** 1219 N. Shore Dr., Menomonie, WI 54751.

Donnelly, F. Dolores, (Sister Francis Dolores) (Mr. 31, 1914, St. John's, NF, Can.) Prof., Fac. LS, Univ. of Toronto, 1971–; Univ. Libn., Mt. St. Vincent Univ., 1957–68, Prof. LS, 1950–57; Consult., Dir. Reg. Lib. Proj., Cape Breton, NS, 1940–50. **Educ.:** Meml.-Univ. of NF and Mt. St. Vincent Univ., 1935–39, BA cum laude, Md. Lang. Univ. of Toronto, 1952–54, MLS; Univ. of IL, 1968–71, PhD. **Orgs.:** ALA. AALS: Policy Com. (1971–). Can. LA: Bd. Dir. (1968–69). Can. Assn. Coll. Univ. Libs.: Bd. Dir. (1963–65). CALS. Many other orgs. Inst. Prof. Libns. ON: Bd. Dir. 1972–74. Adv. Bd., *Jnl. Lib. Hist.* **Honors:** Beta Phi Mu. Phi Kappa Phi. **Pubns.:** *The National Library of Canada* (1973); "Canada's National Library Services" (1977); numerous journal articles. **Activities:** 1, 4; 26, 34, 41; 55, 56, 74 **Addr.:** Faculty of Library Science, University of Toronto, 140 St. George St., Toronto, ON M5R 2M6 Canada.

PROFESSIONAL ACTIVITIES: Institutions: 1. Acad. lib.; 2. Arch.; 3. Assn.; 4. Fed./Gvt. lib.; 5. Inst. lib.; 6. Mfr./Suppl.; 7. Milit. lib.; 8. Musm.; 9. Pub. lib.; 10. Sch. lib.; 11. Sch. of lib. sci.; 12. Spec. lib.; 13. State lib.; 14. (other). **Functions/Activities:** 15. Acq./Col. dev.; 16. Adult srvs.; 17. Admin.; 18. Apprais.; 19. Archit./Bldgs.; 20. Cat./Class.; 21. Chld. srvs.; 22. Circ.; 23. Cons./Pres.; 24. Consult.; 25. Cont. ed.; 26. Educ. lib. sci.; 27. Ext. srvs.; 28. Fund/Grants; 29. Gvt. pubs.; 30. Indx./Abs.; 31. Instr. lib. use; 32. Media srvs.; 33. Micro.; 34. Netwks./Coop.; 35. Persnl.; 36. PR; 37. Publshg.; 38. Recs. mgt.; 39. Ref. srvs.; 40. Repro.; 41. Resrch.; 42. Review.; 43. Secur.; 44. Serials; 45. Spec. col.; 46. Tech. srvs.; 47. Trustees/Bds.; 48. YA srvs.; 49. (other).

Donofrio, John S. (S. 25, 1941, San Francisco, CA) Assoc. Archvst., Bank of America, 1970–. **Educ.:** San Francisco State Univ., 1959–66, BA (Hist.); 1966–68; Cert. in Arch. Admin., Univ. of Denver, 1971. **Orgs.:** SAA: Bus. Arch. Com. (1972–). Socty. of CA Archvsts.: Secy.-Treas. (1974–1976). **Pubns.:** "The Bank of America Archives: Its Origin and Development, 1948–1977", *Bankhistorisches Archiv* (2/1977). **Activities:** 2, 12; 15, 17, 39; 56, 59, 85 **Addr.:** Bank of America Archives #3218, P.O. Box 37000, San Francisco, CA 94044.

Donohue, Gail Marie (Jl. 15, 1947, Cambridge, MA) Tchg. Flw., Dept. of Eng., Univ. of Houston, 1981–; Proj. Dir., CARE-A-VAN, Pub. Lib. of Annapolis and Anne Arundel Cnty., 1977–; Adult Srvs. Libn., Champaign Pub. Lib. and Info. Ctr., 1974–77. **Educ.:** Rosary Coll., 1965–69, AB (Eng.); Univ. of IL, 1972–73, MS (LS). **Orgs.:** ALA: ASCLA/Lib. Srv. Impaired Elderly Sect., Clear. House Info. Com. (1978–80), Manual on Srvc. to Shut-ins Com. (1979–81). Anne Arundel Cnty. Ofc. on Aging: Adv. Bd., Tech. Adv. **Honors:** Beta Phi Mu, 1973. **Pubns.:** *First Poems of Gail Donohue* (1974); "The Community Writers' Library," *IL Writers' Nsltr.* (1976); "Ocean," "Dreams, Rising" (poems), *MS Valley Review* (1979); "Timepiece," "Plain Poem," "Flight," "Dear Alice," *Matrix II: The Red Herring Poets* (1977). **Activities:** 9; 16, 27, 39; 55, 72 **Addr.:** Dept. of English, University of Houston, Houston, TX 77004.

Donohue, Joseph Chaminade (N. 26, 1930, Baltimore, MD) Deputy Dir., Div. of Appld. Tech. Ofc. of Systs., Soc. Secur. Admin., 1980; Info. Sci., Food and Drug Admin., 1972–80. Admin. Libn., Natl. Agr. Lib., 1970–72; Asst. Prof., Univ. of MD, 1969–70; Info. Syst. Spec., Informatics, Inc., 1966–69; Asst. Mgr., RAND Corp. Lib., 1964–65; Libn., Gen. Electric Co., TEMPO, 1961–64; Libn., NY Pub. Lib., 1960–61. **Educ.:** Oakland Coll., 1955-56; Univ. of CA, 1956–58, BA (Hum., Soc. Sci.); Simmons Coll., 1959–60, MS (LS); West. Resrv. Univ., 1967–70, PhD, (Info. Sci.); Grad. of non-degree progs. in mgt., including persnl., supvsn., couns., labor and indus. rel., systs. engin., law, finance, and contract negtns.; commn., intelligence, langs.; archs., recs. mgt. **Orgs.:** ASIS: Inf. Rel. Com (1980); Pub. Affairs Com. (1980); Spec. Int. Grp. of Cmnty. Info. Srvs. (Ch., 1977); SLA: South. CA Chap.: Educ. Com. (1966); Fed. Lib. Com. Pre-White House Conf.: Del., Facilitator (1979). **Pubns.:** Jt.-auth., *Information for the Community* (1976); auth., *Understanding Scientific Literatures* (1973); "The Library of Congress: A Proposed Role in a National Information and Referral Network," *Jnl. ASIS* (1979); "Some Experiments Fail," *Lib. Jnl.* (Jn. 15, 1975); Reviews, Rpts., various other articles. **Activities:** 4, 12; 17, 24; 56, 75, 91 **Addr.:** 6106 Maylane Dr., Baltimore, MD 21212.

Donohue, Mildred D. (S. 6, 1915, Baltimore, MD) Consult. and Indexr., self-empl. and retired; Head, Tech. and Sci. Div., Univ. of MD Lib., 1959–76; Med. Libn., OH St. Univ., 1956–59; Med. Libn., Amer. Cancer Socty., 1949–56. **Educ.:** Univ. of MD, 1934–38, BS (Bio.); Columbia Univ., 1943–44, BS (LS); Univ. of IL, 1957–59, MS (LS); Univ. of MD, grad. wk. in Bot. **Orgs.:** SLA.: various local coms. Med LA: various local coms. MD LA. Intl. Agr. Libns. and Docmlst. **Honors:** Beta Phi Mu; Enoch Pratt Lib., Staff Assn. Prize. **Pubns.:** Jt. auth., *Fossil Finds in Maryland* (1967); "Evaluative Checklist of the Literature of Neoplastic Diseases," *Med. LA Bltn.* (Jl. 1960). **Activities:** 1, 13; 17, 39, 41; 58 **Addr.:** 3411 Rutgers St., University Hills, MD 20783.

Donovan, Jerry J. (F. 2, 1928, Houston, TX) Bus. Ref. Libn., Coord., Online Comp. Srch., Emory Univ., 1977–; Head Libn., The Lawrenceville Sch. 1972–77; Bibl. Consult. to Population Index, Popltn. Resrch. Libn., Princeton Univ., 1971–72; Mgr. Intl. Census Docum. Proj., Univ. of CA, Berkeley, 1968–71. **Educ.:** Washington & Lee Univ., 1946–50, BA (Hum.); Univ. of CA, Berkeley, 1966–68, MLS; Merrill Lynch, Pierce, Fenner & Smith: Account Exec. Training Sch., 1956, (Finance). **Orgs.:** ALA. SLA. ASIS. Atlanta Online Srch. Grp. DeKalb Families in Action: Ch., Drug Info. Ctr. Com., Bd. **Pubns.:** *Western European Censuses, 1960: An English Language Guide* (1971); *Selected Bibliography of Planning-Programming-Budgeting Systems in Education* (1970); "Libraries in Selected NAIS Secondary Schools: Summary of a Survey," (Spr. 1977); "Making Foreign Census Documents Accessible & Available," *Spec. Libs.* (S. 1973). **Addr.:** 1270 West Peachtree St. N.W., Apt. 5-A, Atlanta, GA 30309.

Donovan, Kathryn M. (N. 24, 1935, Philadelphia, PA) Mgr., Info. Srvs., Pennwalt Corp., 1976–, Libn., 1967–76, Ref. Libn., 1959–67; Libn. I, Free Lib. of Philadelphia, 1958–59. **Educ.:** East. Coll., 1953–57, BA (Chem.); Drexel Univ., 1957–58, MSLS. **Orgs.:** Amer. Chem. Socty. SLA. Indus. Tech. Info. Mgrs. Grp. **Pubns.:** "A User's Experience with Searching the IFI Comprehensive Database," *Jnl. Chem. Info. Comp. Sci.* (1977); "Problems in the Nomenclature of Inorganic Polymers," Jnl. Chem. Documtn. (1969). **Activities:** 12; 17, 38, 39; 60 **Addr.:** Pennwalt Corporation, 900 First Ave., P.O. Box C, King of Prussia, PA 19406.

Donovan, Ruth H. (D. 1, 1927, Lincoln, NE) Asst. Dir. of Lib., Univ. of NV, Reno, 1969–, Bibl., 1967–69, Asst. Dir. of Lib., 1962–63, Ref. Lib., 1954–61; Asst. Soc. Sci. Libn., Univ. of NE, 1950–54. **Educ.:** Univ. of WI, 1945–49, BA (Eng.), 1949–50, BLS. **Orgs.:** ALA: Women Admins. Discuss. Grp. (1976–); ACRL. Mt. Plains LA: Prof. Dev. Grants Com. (1979–). NV LA: Persnl. Dev. Com. (1976–79); NV Indxr. Interest Grp. (1974–). CLENE. NV Corral, West. Intl.: Ed., *Inkslinger* (1978–79). NV Hist. Socty. Univ. Club, Univ. of NV. Common Cause. **Pubns.:** "Continuing Education: Training Resources," *Highroller* (Jl./Ag. 1976); "Personnel Development," *Highroller* (S./O. 1976, D. 1976); "Staff Development Plan for the University of Nevada, Reno Library," *Staff Dev. Model Bk.* (1976). **Activities:** 1; 17, 25, 35; 50, 61, 91 **Addr.:** P.O. Box 8352, University Station, Reno, NV 89507.

Donovan, William A. (Ja. 29, 1937, Rochester, NY) Head, Biol. Sect., Chicago Pub. Lib., 1975–, Head, Newspaper Srv. Dept., 1965–75, Asst., Natl. Sci. Dept., 1965, Pub. Srv. Libn., 1964–65. **Educ.:** St. John Fisher Coll., 1954–58, BA (Bio.); Univ. of Chicago, 1961–63; Univ. of S. FL., 1980–81. **Orgs.:** Chicago Lib. Club. SLA. **Pubns.:** "Reference Librarian and the Whole Truth," *RQ* (Spr., 1969); "Seemingly Unjustified Complaints," *RQ* (Sum., 1969); Reviews. **Activities:** 1, 9; 15, 16, 39; 58, 68, 83 **Addr.:** Chicago Public Library, 425 N. Michigan Ave., Chicago, IL 60611.

Donze, Sara Lee (N. 12, 1925, East Liberty, OH) Dir., N. Canton Pub. Lib., 1978–; Coord., Chlds. Srvs., Stark Cnty. Dist. Lib., 1964–68; Chlds. Libn., N. Canton Pub. Lib., 1955–64; Actg. Head, Adult Srvs., Canton Pub. Lib., 1947–55. **Educ.:** Mt. Union Coll., 1943–47, BA (Sp./Drama); West. Resrv., 1957–60, MLS. **Orgs.:** ALA. OH LA: Chlds. RT (Ch., 1965). Delta Kappa Gamma. Soroptimists Intl.: Pres., 1968. **Pubns.:** *Robin and the Thorn* (1965). **Activities:** 5, 9; 17, 21, 36; 55, 63, 89 **Addr.:** 290 James St. S.W., North Canton, OH 44720.

Dooling, Marie (My. 8, 1952, Brooklyn, NY) Mgr., Info. Srvs., SLA, 1977–. **Educ.:** Univ. of PA., 1970–74, BA (Hist.); Catholic Univ., 1976–77, MLS. **Orgs.:** SLA: Exec. Div. Srch. Com. (1979). Natl. Micrographics Assn. **Pubns.:** "PUBS," (Monthly Column) *Spec. Libs.* (Nov. 1978–). **Activities:** 2, 12; 17, 39; 75 **Addr.:** Special Libraries Assn., 235 Park Ave. S., New York, NY 10003.

Dorman, David C. (My. 24, 1943, Racine, WI) Head Tech. Srvs. Libn., Mercy Coll. Libs., 1979–; Head, Card Prod. Dept., Columbia Univ. Libs., 1976–79; Mgr., Bookmasters Bookstore, 1975–76. **Educ.:** Marlboro Coll., 1965–67, BA (Pol. Sci.); Columbia Univ., 1976–78, MLS. **Orgs.:** ALA: LITA Legis. Com. (1979–). Natl. LA: Cert. Standards Com. (1978–). NY Tech. Srvs. Libns.: Tech. Com., (1979–). **Honors:** Beta Phi Mu, 1978. **Activities:** 1; 17, 46; 56 **Addr.:** Mercy College Libraries, 555 Broadway, Dobbs Ferry, NY 10522.

Dorr, Ralze W. (O. 27, 1929, Kansas City, KS) Lib. Plng. Ofcr., Assoc. Prof. of LS, Univer. of Louisville, 1971–; Asst. to the Pres., Catherine Spalding Coll., 1965–70; Coord. of Tech. Srvs., Coord. of Bldg. Plng., 1962–65; Head, Circ. Dept., Univ. of Cincinnati Lib., 1961–62. **Educ.:** Univ. of Louisville, 1948–51, AB (Eng.); IN Univ., 1956–61, MA (LS). **Orgs.:** ALA: LAMA Com. on Bldg. & Equipment; Com. on Equipment. Socty. for Coll. & Univ. Plng. Environmental Action. **Pubns.:** Various Case Studies In: *The Management of Libraries and Information Centers,* (1968). **Activities:** 1; 17, 19 **Addr.:** Central University Library, University of Louisville, Belknap Campus, Louisville, KY 40208.

Dorrity, Sister Ann M. (Je. 28, 1934, Orange, NJ) Lib. Consult., Grolier Educ. Srvs., White Plains, N.Y., 1977–; Dir. of Educ., Sisters of Charity, Western Province, 1975–77; Lib. Consult., Diocese of Paterson, NJ, 1973–75; Lib. Consult., Sisters of Charity, Western Province, 1971–73. **Educ.:** Coll. of St. Elizabeth, Convent Station, NJ, 1953–61, AB (Msc, Educ.); Villanova Univ., 1969–74, MLS. **Orgs.:** ALA. Cath. Lib. Volun. of Amer.: (Exec. Secy. 1977–). Cath. LA: Chld. Lib. Sect. (Bd. 1978–). South. Passaic Cnty. Area Coord. LA: (Past Ch. 1975–76); Intl. Readg. Assn. Natl. Cath. Educ. Assn. **Pubns.:** "Library Volunteers", *Cath. Lib. World; Catholic Library Volunteers of America Manual,* (1979). **Activities:** 10; 21, 24, 26, 31; 50 **Addr.:** St. Nicholas Convent, 121 Jefferson St., Passaic, NJ 07055.

Dorsett, Cora Elliott Matheny (Jl. 15, 1921, Camden, AR) Dir., Pine Bluff and Jefferson Cnty. Lib. Syst., 1965–; Tchr., Caddo Parish (LA) Sch., 1963–64. **Educ.:** Centenary Coll. of LA, 1963, BS (Educ.) Summa Cum Laude; Univ. of MS, 1965, MS (LS); 1972, PhD (Higher Educ. Student Persnl.). **Orgs.:** ALA. S. West. LA: Cont. Educ. for Lib. Staffs (Adv. Com.). AR LA: Pub. Lib. Div. (Ch.); Natl. Lib. Week Com.; Cont. Educ. Com. **Honors:** Centenary Coll., Alpha Chi, 1962; Centenary Coll., Chi Omega Soc. Sci. Awd., 1963; Univ. of MI, Kappa Delta Pi, 1971. **Pubns.:** "Public Library of Pine Bluff & Jefferson Co.", *AR Libs.* (Fall 1968); "Library Technician - Problem or Promise," *AR Libs.* (Fall 1973); "Continuing Education Materials Fair - A Report", *S. East. Libn.* (Spr. 1978); "Whither the Technician?," *Jnl. of Educ. for Libnshp.* (Spr. 1974). **Activities:** 9; 17 **Addr.:** 200 East 8th Ave., Pine Bluff, AR 71601.

Dorsey, Bertha S. (Je. 5, 1916, Joplin, MO) Sr. Ref. Libn., Southwest. Univ. Sch. of Law, 1970; Law Libn., Nossaman, Waters, Scott, Krueger & Riordan, 1967–70; Circ. Libn., Loyola Univ. Sch. of Law, 1964–67; Law Libn., Gibson, Dunn & Crutcher, 1961–64. **Educ.:** Univ. of CA, Los Angeles, 1935–37, BA cum laude (Span.). **Orgs.:** South. CA Assn. of Law Libs.: Pres. (1972–73). AALL. Phi Beta Kappa. Sigma Delta Pi. **Activities:** 1, 12; 39; 77 **Addr.:** Southwestern University School of Law, 675 South Westmoreland Ave., Los Angeles, CA 90005.

Dosa, Marta Leszlei (Szekszard, Hungary) Prof., Sch. of Info. Std., Syracuse Univ., 1964–, Assoc. and Asst. Prof., 1964–76, Math. Libn., 1960–64, Gvt. Docum. Libn., 1957–60; Freelnc. Writer and Interpreter, Hungary, Germany, U.S. **Educ.:** Univ. of Budapest, 1942–43, BA (Compar. Lit. and Ling.); Syracuse Univ., 1956–57, MSLS; Univ. of MI, 1967–71, PhD (LS). **Orgs.:** ASIS: Intl. Rel. Com. (1980–). AALL. NY LA: Exec. Bd., Lib. Educ. Sect. (1974–77). SLA: Spec. Com. on Env. Info. (Ch., 1973–76). Various other orgs. Grntlgcl. Socty. of Amer. State Assn. of Grntlgcl. Educs. **Pubns.:** *Libraries in the Political Scene* (1974); jt. auth., *Gerontological Information Systems and Services* (1980); "Education of Environmental Information Specialists," *Spec. Libnshp.* (1980); "Information Counseling," *Info.* (1978); "Information for Environmental Policy Making," *Converging Trends* (1980); various articles, papers (1974–80). **Activities:** 11; 24, 26, 41; 65, 75, 95-Info. policy. **Addr.:** School of Information Studies, Syracuse University, 113 Euclid Ave., Syracuse, NY 13210.

Doszkocs, Tamas Endre (Mr. 26, 1942, Bánhida, Hungary) Chief, Biomedical File Implementation Branch, Natl. Lib. Med., 1980–, Chief, Tech. Srvs. Div., 1979–80; Comp. Expert, Natl. Cancer Inst., 1976–79; Comp. Spec., Natl. Lib. of Med., 1974–76; Lectr., Sch. of LS, Univ. of MD, 1970–77. **Educ.:** Kossuth Univ., Debrecen, Hungary, 1959–64, BA (Ling.); Univ. of MD, 1967–68, MLS, 1970–72, MS (Comp. Sci.), 1973–79, PhD (Info. Sci.). **Orgs.:** ALA: Tech. Srvs. Dir. Lg. Resrch. Lib. Discuss. Grp. ASIS. Assn. Comp. Mach. **Honors:** Natl. Lib. Med., Regents Awd. Tech. Excel. 1979; ASIS, Doc. Forum, 1979. **Pubns.:** "Automated Information Retrieval in Science and Technology," *Sci.* (1980); "AID, on Associative Interactive Dictionary for OnLine Searching," *Online Review* (1978); "Searching MEDLINE in English," *ASIS Proc.* (1979); *A Computerized Scheme for Duplicate Checking* (Tech. Rpt. ORNL/CSD-5, 1976). **Activities:** 4, 11; 17, 26, 46; 56, 75, 80 **Addr.:** Chief, Biomedical File Implementation Branch, National Library of Medicine, 8600 Rockville Pike, Bethesda, MD 20901.

Dotts, Maryann J. (N. 11, 1933, Pittsburgh, PA) Freelnc. Trainer & Writer, 1979–; Dir., Chld. and Adult Ministries, Belle Mead Untd. Meth. Church, 1976–79; Libn., Untd. Meth. Church Bd. of Discipleshp. Lib., 1975; Tchr., Riverside Church, NY, 1965–67; Dir., Christ. Educ., 1st Meth. Church, Arlington Heights, IL, 1958–61; Dir., Christ. Educ., 1st Meth. Church, Erie, PA, 1956–58. **Educ.:** Natl. Coll. for Christ. Workers, 1956, BA (Relig. Educ.); Scarritt Coll., 1974, MA (Christ. Educ.); George Peabody Coll. for Tchrs., 1975, MLS. **Orgs.:** CSLA: Pres. (1978–79); Awd. Ch. (1977); VP (1978); PR Ch. (1981). TN Assn. of Young Chld. Christ. Educ. Flwshp., Untd. Meth. Church. Dir. of Untd. Meth. Preschools. **Pubns.:** *The Church Resource Library* (1975); Christ. Educ. books for chld. **Activities:** 12, 14-Church Resource Center; 17, 20, 21; 90 **Addr.:** 2514 Blair Blvd., Nashville, TN 37212.

Doty, Rosamond Clark (F. 22, 1917, Foy, MN) Dist. Media Coord., Ind. Sch. Dist. 728, 1977–; HS Media Dir., 1969–77; Elem. Media Dir., 1962–69; Tchr., 1957–62. **Educ.:** Bemidji State Univ., 1935–39, (Lang. Arts & Msc.); St. Cloud State Univ., 1956–57, BS (Grmn.); Univ. of MN, 1964–67, Masters (Info. Media); St. Cloud Univ., 1972–74, Media Supvsr.; 1974–77, Spec. in Media. **Orgs.:** ALA. AECT. MN LA. Assn. for Supvsn. and Curric. Dev. MN Educ. Media Assn.: Reg. Ch. (1965–67); Intl. Frdm. Com. (1977–); Treas. (1980–81). **Pubns.:** *A Study of Professional Media Persons in the State of Minnesota as to their Membership in and Attendance of Professional Media Organizations* (1978). **Activities:** 17, 32; 74 **Addr.:** 225 East River St., Monticello, MN 55362.

Doucet, Claude W. (N. 6, 1951, Ottawa, ON, Can) Corp. Archvst., ON Hydro Arch., 1980–; Mgr., Arch., The Bank of Nova Scotia, 1975–80. **Educ.:** York Univ. (Toronto), 1970–74, BA (Hist.). **Orgs.:** Toronto Area Archvsts. Grp.: Exec. Comm. (1977–78); Ontario's Reg. Heritage Proj. (Reg. Com., 1979–80). Assn. of Can. Archvsts.: Bus. Arch. Com. (1977–80), Cons. Com. (1978–79). SAA. **Honors:** York Univ., Gvrs. Awd., 1970. **Pubns.:** "La Rentabilité Des Archives Dans L'entreprise Privée: Le Cas De La Banque De Nouvelle-Écosse," *Arch.* (1979). **Activities:** 2; 15, 17, 20, 39; 59 **Addr.:** Ontario Hydro Archives, 800 Kipling Ave., Toronto, ON M8Z 5S4, Canada.

Doudnikoff, Basil (Ap. 19, 1933, New York, NY) Pres., Dataflow Systems Inc., 1967; Asst. Mgr. Oper., Docum. Inc., 1965–67; Dir., Info. Syst. Dir., Jonker Corp., 1962–65; Syst. Anal., Westinghouse Elect., 1959–62. **Educ.:** Univ. of FL, 1955–59, BA (Indus. Engin.); George Washington Univ., 1962–64, MA (Engin. Admin.). **Orgs.:** SLA. ALA. Natl. Micro Assn. **Pubns.:** *Information Retrieval* (1973); "How to Index and Abstract," *The Ofc.* (O. 1972). **Activities:** 4, 12; 24, 30, 33 **Addr.:** Dataflow Systems Inc., 7758 Wisconsin Ave., Bethesda, MD 20014.

Special Subjects/Services: 50. Adult educ.; 51. Advert./Mktg.; 52. Aerosp.; 53. Agric.; 54. Area std.; 55. Arts/Hum.; 56. Autom.; 57. Bibl./Prtg.; 58. Bio. sci.; 59. Bus./Fin.; 60. Chem.; 61. Copyrt.; 62. Documtn.; 63. Educ.; 64. Engin.; 65. Env.; 66. Eth. grps.; 67. Film; 68. Food/Nutr.; 69. Geneal.; 70. Geo.; 71. Geol.; 72. Handcpd.; 73. Hist.; 74. Int. frdm.; 75. Info. sci.; 76. Insr.; 77. Law; 78. Legis.; 79. Math./Comp. sci.; 80. Med.; 81. Metals; 82. Nat. resrcs.; 83. Newsp.; 84. Nuc. sci.; 85. Oral hist.; 86. Petr./Energy; 87. Pharm.; 88. Phys./Astr./Math.; 89. Readg.; 90. Relig.; 91. Sci./Tech.; 92. Soc. sci.; 93. Telecom.; 94. Transp.; 95. (other).

Dougherty, Linda Anne (Ap. 16, 1947, Gary, IN) Unit Head, Clearing Branch, Chicago Pub. Lib., 1977–; Ref. Libn., Scottsdale Branch, 1976–77. **Educ.:** IN Univ., 1972, AB (Hist.); 1974, MLS (Hist.). **Orgs.:** ALA: LIRT, Prod. Mgr. (1979–80); Nsltr. Ed. (1978–79). Southwest Area Cult. Arts Cncl.: Mem. Ch. (1980). Clearing Bus. Assn. Clearing Women's Club. **Activities:** 9; 31, 36, 39; 46, 85, 95-Women's Studies. **Addr.:** 5643 W. 63rd St., Chicago, IL 60638.

Dougherty, Richard M. (Ja. 17, 1935, E. Chicago, IN) Dir., Univ. Lib. and Prof. of LS, Univ. of MI, 1978–; Univ. Libn., Univ. of CA, Berkeley, 1972–78; Prof., Grad. Sch. of Info. Std., Syracuse Univ., 1970–72; Assoc. Dir. of Libs., Univ. of CO, 1966–70; Head, Acq. Dept., Univ. of NC, 1963–66. **Educ.:** Purdue Univ., 1953–59, BS (Forestry); Rutgers Univ., 1959–63, MLS, PhD (LS). **Orgs.:** MI Lib. Cnsrtm.: Exec. Cncl. (1978–). ARL: Bd. of Dirs. (1977–80); Task Frc. on Natl. Lib. Netwk. Dev. (Ch., 1976–80); Rep. to Lib. of Congs. Netwk. Adv. Com. (1977–80). ALA: Exec. Bd. (1972–76); Cncl. (1969–76). IFLA: RT of Eds. (Secy., 1978–). Fndn. Lib. Com. RLG: Bd. of Gvrs. **Honors:** Rutgers Univ., Grad. Sch. of Lib. and Info. Sci., Disting. Alum. Awd., 1980; Cncl. on Lib. Resrcs., Inc., Flwshp., 1970; ALA, RTSD, Esther J. Piercy Awd., 1968. **Pubns.:** *Scientific Management of Library Operations* (1981); *Improving Access to Library Resources* (1974); various articles in prof. jnls.; ed. and publshr., *Jnl. of Acad. Libnshp.* (1975–); *Lib. Issues: Briefing for Acad. Ofcrs.* (1980–); ed., *Coll. & Resrch. Libs.* (1969–74). **Activities:** 1; 17, 24, 34; 56, 93, 95-Prtg./publshg. **Addr.:** 818 Hatcher Graduate Library, The University of Michigan, Ann Arbor, MI 48109.

Doughty, Barbara Parr (S. 15, 1935, New Albany, MS) Med. Ref. Libn., Univ. of AL, 1975–; Fr. Tchr., Druid HS, 1970–71; Fr.–Eng. Tchr., Knoxville City Sch. Syst., 1964–66. **Educ.:** MS State Coll. for Women, 1953–56, BA (Fr.); Univ. of AL, 1973–74, MLS. **Orgs.:** Med. LA.: South. Chap. AL Hlth. Libs. Assn. AL LA: Hlth. Scis. Libns. RT, Bylaws Com. (1977–); JMRT. **Activities:** 1, 12; 31, 39; 80 **Addr.:** Health Sciences Library, P.O. Box 6331, University of Alabama, University, AL 35486.

Douglas, Althea Cleveland (D. 25, 1926, Moncton, NB) Cur., Penfield Col., Montreal Neurological Inst., 1978–; Asst. Ed., Burney Papers, McGill Univ., 1958–80. **Educ.:** McGill Univ., 1944–47, BSc (Math, Phys.), 1958, MA (Eng.). **Orgs.:** Assn. of Can. Archvsts. **Pubns.:** Jt. auth., *A Catalogue of the Burney Family Correspondence 1748–1878* (1971); jt. ed., *The Journals and Letters of Fanny Burney (Madame d'Arblay)* (1970–); "An Eighteenth Century Journal, a Twentieth Century Restoration," *Lib. Scene* (D. 1980). **Activities:** 2; 20, 23, 45; 55, 80 **Addr.:** Penfield Collection, c/o Montreal Neurological Institute, 3081 University St., Montreal, PQ H3A 2B4 Canada.

Douglas, George Lees (O. 12, 1904, Lucknow, ON) Consult. in Lib. Srv., Knox Coll., Univ. of Toronto, 1973–; Chief Libn., 1961–73; Pastor, Knox Presby. Church (Woodstock, ON), 1946–61; Chaplain, Royal Can. Navy, 1944–45; Pastor, Drummond Hill Presby. Church (Niagara Falls, ON), 1938–44. **Educ.:** Univ. of Toronto, 1927–29; Univ. of MB, 1933–35, BA (Lib. Arts); Knox Coll., 1935–38, Dip. (Theo.); Union Theo. Semy., 1939–40, STM, Magna Cum Laude; Columbia Univ., 1964–65, MS (LS). **Orgs.:** ATLA. Toronto Sch. of Theo.: Lib. Com. (1969–73). Presby. Church in Canada Archvst. (1966–72); Gen. Asm., Articles of Faith Com. (1948–71; Conv., 1949–57); Bd. of Educ. (1959–65); various other coms. and ofcs. **Honors:** Beta Phi Mu; Presbyterian Coll. (Montreal), DD (Hon.), 1967. **Pubns.:** "Co-humanity and the covenant," *Putting Woman in Her Place.* (1964); "Election and predestination," The Presby. Church in Can., Gen. Asm., *Acts and Procs.* (1970); Various other pubns. **Activities:** 1, 2; 17, 24; 90 **Addr.:** 24 Leith Hill Rd., Apt. 1101, Willowdale, ON M2J 1Z3 Canada.

Douglas, John R. (Jack) (Ja. 1, 1933, Waukegan, IL) Libn., John Steinbeck Resrch. Ctr., San Jose State Univ., 1980–, Assoc. Libn., 1959–, Media Coord., Inst., New Coll., 1968–79, Publn. Libn., 1967–68, Circ. Libn., 1965–67. **Educ.:** Earlham Coll., 1951–53; Univ. of Denver, 1956–58, BA (Soclgy.); Univ. of Denver, 1958–59, MA (LS); San Jose State Univ., coursework. **Orgs.:** ALA. CA LA: Cncl. (1973–76); Budget Com. (1973–76). Msc. LA. Assn. for Recorded Sound Cols. CA Socty. of Libns. Untd. Prof. of CA. **Pubns.:** *San Jose State University Faculty and Staff Bibliography* (1966); "Musician and Composer Societies: a World Directory," *Notes* (Je. 1974, S. 1977); "Beecham, Bufano and the 50 cent Symphony," *San Jose Studies.* (F. 1978); "Free-Schooling: alternative education and its documentation", *Wilson Lib. Bltn.,* (S. 1972); "Publications devoted to individual musicians: a checklist", *Bltn. of Bibl.* (Ap. 1976); Other articles. **Activities:** 1, 12; 31, 32, 36; 55, 58, 63 **Addr.:** San Jose State University, San Jose, CA 95192.

Douville, Judith Ann (Piliero) (N. 3, 1937, New York, NY) Tech. Libn., T.R.C., 125 Silas Deane Hwy, Wethersfield, CT 1978–, Circ. Mgr., *Info. Sci. Abs.,* 1978–; Abstctr., *Chem. Abs.,* 1961–78; Mgr., Metals Info. Ctr., Olin Corp., 1975–78; Asst. Ed., *Info. Sci. Abs.,* 1972–75; Serials Libn., Ctrl. CT St. Coll., 1970–72, Asst. Serials Libn., 1970; Instr. Phys. Sci., East. CT St. Coll., 1967–70; various other positions in chem. and libs. **Educ.:** Univ. of CT, 1959, BA (Chem.), 1965, MS (Chem.); Univ. of RI, 1971, MLS; additional wk. in chem. **Orgs.:** SLA: CT Valley Chap., Corres. Secy. (1976–77); Rec. Secy. (1977–78). New England Lib. Bd.: Panel of Couns. (1976–80); Serials Task Force (1976–78). Amer. Chem. Socty.: CT Valley Sect., Archvst. (1970–76); Ch. (1977); many other coms. ASIS. Amer. Socty. Indxr. AAAS. Assn. Comp. Ling. **Pubns.:** "Indexing and Abstracting Services in the Air Pollution Field," *Jnl. of Air Pollution Control Assn.* (Ap. 1981); "Development of Aluminum indexing and abstracting services," *Serials Libn.* (Spr. 1980); "Literature of corrosion technology," *Mtrls. Performance* (1980); "Technical Information Centers: Specialized Services to Science and Technology," *Jnl. ASIS* (My., Je. 1972); various other pubns. **Activities:** 12; 26, 30, 44; 60, 65, 75 **Addr.:** 23 Virginia Dr., Middletown, CT 06457.

Dow, Gail M. (Ag. 9, 1945, Roseau, MN) Acq. Dept., Mgr., Denver Pub. Lib., 1973–; Coord., Reg. Libs. Courier Srv., 1972–73; Head, Ref. Srvs., Univ. of Denver, 1970–72, Ref. Libn., 1968–70. **Educ.:** Augsburg Coll., 1963–67, BA (Eng.); Univ. of Denver, 1967–68, MALS; Metro. State Coll., 1978–, BSBA Cand. (Comp. Mgt. Sci.). **Orgs.:** ALA. CO LA: Acq. RT, Ch. Mt. Plains LA: Ad Hoc Com. on CO ILLs (Ch., 1970–72). **Honors:** Lambda Iota Tau. **Activities:** 9; 15, 17, 46; 56, 75 **Addr.:** 4048 S. Wisteria Way, Denver, CO 80237.

Dow, Ronald F. (Ja. 26, 1949, Deadwood, SD) Asst. Bus. and Engin. Lib., Dartmouth Coll., 1976–; Asst. Ref. Libn., Hamilton Coll., 1972–76. **Educ.:** Augustana Coll., 1967–71, BA (Hist., Eng.); Syracuse Univ., 1971–72, MSLS. **Orgs.:** ALA: RASD, Data Base Prod. and Srch. Srvs. Vendors Com. (1977–). NH LA New England Lib. Bd.: Cnclr. (1978–). **Pubns.:** "Academic Librarians: A Survey or Benefits...," *Coll. and Resrch. Libs.* (My. 1977); "INSPEC on BRS," *Database* (Sum. 1978). **Activities:** 1; 17, 31, 39; 59, 64 **Addr.:** Fedlberg Library, Hanover, NH 03755.

Dow, Sally C. (S. 27, 1926, Hillsdale, MI) Chld. Libn., Helen Kate Furness Free Lib., Wallingford, PA, 1974–; Libn., Upchurch Jr. HS, Raeford, NC, 1969–71; Head Libn., Sumter HS, 1967–68. **Educ.:** Univ. of MI, 1946–49, BA (Soc. studies); Drexel Univ., 1972–74, MS (LS). **Orgs.:** DE Cnty. Libs. Assn.: Chld. Srvs. Div. (Ch., 1979–80; Vice Ch., 1978–79). **Activities:** 9, 10; 15, 21, 39 **Addr.:** 132 Park Ave., Swarthmore, PA 19081.

Dowd, Mary-Jane M. (F. 4, 19–, Baltimore, MD) Asst. Branch Chief, Projs., Indus. and Soc. Branch, Natl. Arch., 1978–; Arch., Spec. Projs., 1978–78; Arch., Indus. and Soc. Branch, 1974–78; Assoc. Ed., Territorial Papers of the U.S., 1973–74; Assoc. Ed., *Amer. Archvst.,* 1964–72; Various other positions. **Educ.:** Goucher Coll., 1952–56, BA (Hist.); The Johns Hopkins Univ., 1956–59, MA (Hist.); Amer. Univ., 1960–61, Cert. (Arch.); Univ. of VA, 1972, Cert. (Hist. Ed.). **Orgs.:** Intl. Cncl. on Arch. Amer. Hist. Assn. Mid-Atl. Reg. Arch. Conf. SAA: Status of Women Com. (Ch., 1980–81); Awds. Com. (1977–80); Intl. Arch. Affairs Com. (1975–); Com. on the Bicentennial. (1974–75). Socty. Ed. Bd. (1972–75). Natl. Trust. for Hist. Pres. Org. of Amer. Histns. Amer. Socty. for Eighteenth Cent. Stds. Various other orgs. **Honors:** SAA, Fellow, 1969. **Pubns.:** Jt.-ed., *Territorial Papers of the United States: Volume 28, The Territory of Wisconsin, 1839–1848* (1975); Comp., *Index to the "American Archivist, 1958-67* (1974); Jt. auth., "Among the Evils Consequent on a Depreciation of Money," *Amer. Archvst.* (Ja. 1972); "The State in the Maryland Economy, 1776–1807," *MD Hist. Mag.* (Jn., S., 1962); Reviews. **Activities:** 2, Prsrvn. **Addr.:** Industrial and Social Branch (NNFS), National Archives, Washington, DC 20408.

Dowd, Philip Michael (Ag. 17, 1915, NY, NY) Dir. of Libs., Manhattan Coll., 1969–; Libn., De La Salle Coll., 1957–69; Tchr., De La Salle Acad. (NY), 1954–57; Tchr., La Salle Acad., 1948–51; Tchr., St. Joseph's Jr., 1953–54, 1936–48. **Educ.:** Catholic Univ., 1936–39, BA (Arts), 1957–60, MSLS, 1960–63, MMsc, 1963–69, PhD. **Orgs.:** ALA. Catholic LA. **Pubns.:** Ed., *Hymns and Psalms of Lucien Deiss* (1965). **Activities:** 1; 17 **Addr.:** Manhattan College, Riverdale, NY 10471.

Dowd, Susan Correnty (N. 13, 1950, Philadelphia, PA) Mgr. of Resrch. Srvs., Calhoun's Collectors Socty., Inc., 1980–; Freelance Resrch. Consult., Self-employed, 1978–80; Libn., Resrchr., The Franklin Mint, 1977–78; Staff Artist, PR Asst., Atlanta Pub. Lib., 1973–76. **Educ.:** Agnes Scott Coll., 1968–72, BA (Art); Emory Univ., 1975–76, MLn. **Orgs.:** SLA: Bltn. Ed. (1977–78), Asst. Ed. (1976–77). PA Citizens for Better Libs. **Activities:** 12, 14-Freelance resrch. consult.; 24, 41; 51, 55 **Addr.:** 5717 Harriet Ave., Minneapolis, MN 55419.

Dowden, Keith (My. 26, 1920, Bristol, England) Asst. Dir. for Spec. Col., Purdue Univ. Libs., 1978–, Asst. Dir. for Resrc. and Ref., 1963–78, Head, Ref. Srvs., 1953–63, Asst. Ref. Libn., 1951–53; Asst. Ref. Libn. Columbia Univ. Libs., 1950–51. Visit. Lectr., various schs. LS, Sum. 1959, 1961, 1963, 1965. **Educ.:** Bowdoin Coll., 1946–49, BA (Hist.); Columbia Univ., 1949–50, MS (LS). **Orgs.:** ALA: Subscrpn. Bks. Com. (1963–69). SLA. SAA. AAUP. **Honors:** Phi Beta Kappa, 1948. **Pubns.:** "John H. Moriarty," in *Dict. of Amer. Lib. Biog.* (1978); reviews. **Activities:** 1; 45, 49-Archives. **Addr.:** Special Collections and Archives, Purdue University Libraries, West Lafayette, IN 47907.

Dowell, Arlene Taylor (D. 22, 1941, Iola, KS) Asst. Prof., Grad. Lib. Sch., Univ. of Chicago, 1981–; Asst. Prof. (LS), NC Ctrl. Uni., 1976–77, 1979; Visit. Lectr. (LS), Univ. of NC, 1976–76; Asst. Prof., Asst. Head, Cat. Dept., Iowa State Univ. Lib., 1972–75; Instr., (LS), Univ. of IL, 1971–72, 1974; Assoc. Libn., Christopher Newport Coll., 1967–70; Catlgr., Lib. of Congs., 1966–67. **Educ.:** OK Bapt. Univ., 1959–63, BA (Eng., Educ.); Univ. of IL, 1965–66, MSLS; Univ. of NC, 1977–81, PhD (LS). **Orgs.:** ALA: RTSD, Cmrcl. Prcs. Srvs. Com. (1975–79), /Cat. and Class. Sect., Com. on Cat. Desc. and Access (1977–81), Exec. Com. (1978–81), Margaret Mann Cit. Com. (1981); LITA; Lib. Resrch. RT. NC LA. AALS. SELA. Beta Phi Mu: Beta XI Chap. AAUP. **Pubns.:** Jt.-auth., *Introduction to Cataloging and Classification* (1980); *Cataloging with Copy: a Decision-Maker's Handbook* (1976); "Discrepancies in CIP: How Serious is the Problem?" *Lib. Jnl.* (N. 1, 1979); "Staying Open in 1981," *HCL Cat. Bltn.* (Mr./Ap., 1979); *AACR II* (Sound Rec.) (IA State Univ.) (1978); Various other articles. **Activities:** 1, 11; 20, 26, 46; 56 **Addr.:** 1418 Rochdale Pl., Chicago, IL 60615.

Dowell, David Ray (N. 14, 1942, Trenton, MO) Dir. of Info. and Lib. Resrcs., IL Inst. of Tech., 1981–; Asst. Univ. Libn., Admin. Srvs., Duke Univ., 1979–81, Asst. Univ. Libn., Persnl. and Staff Dev., Duke Univ., 1975–79; Head, Admin. Srvs., IA State Univ. Lib., 1972–75. **Educ.:** OK Bapt. Univ., 1960–64, BA (Hist.); Univ. of IL, 1965–66, AM (Hist.), 1971–72, MSLS; Univ. of NC, 1978–. **Orgs.:** ALA: LAMA/Persnl. Admin. Sect. (Vice-Ch./Ch.-elect, 1981–82); OLPR Adv. Com. (Ch., 1979–80); LAMA/Lib. Org. and Mgt. Assn., Exec. Com. (1979–81), /Stats. Sect., Stats. for Persnl. Com. (1979–81); ACRL/Univ. Libs. Sect., Nom. Com. (1979–80); Cncl. on Lib. Resrcs.: Adv. Com. on Auditing Resrch. Libs. (1976–77). Various other orgs. and coms. **Honors:** Beta Phi Mu. **Pubns.:** "The Role of the Supervisor in Training and Developing Staff," *Supvs. of Empl. in Libs.* (1979); "Crisis Management for the Eighties: People and Productivity," *CO Libs.* (D., 1979); "Minimum Qualifications for Librarians," *NC Libs.* (Mr., 1980); "Certification: More Study Needed," *Lib. Jnl.* (S. 1, 1977); "How Would you Rate Joe Benson?" *Southeast. Libn.* (Sum., 1977); various other articles. **Activities:** 1; 17, 35; 56, 59, 92 **Addr.:** 1418 Rochdale Pl., Chicago, IL 60615.

Dowell, Mary Evelyn Minter (Ap. 28, 1944, New Orleans, LA) Med. Libn., Singing River Hosp., 1978–; Spec. Projs. Libn., Univ. of KY Med. Ctr. Lib., 1977–78, Tobacco and Hlth. Info. Srv. Libn., 1971–77, Acq. Libn., 1970–71. **Educ.:** Transylvania Univ., 1962–66, AB (Bio.); Univ. of KY, 1966–68, MS (LS). **Orgs.:** Med. LA. SLA: KY Chap. (Pres., 1978). Gulf Coast Biomed. Lib. Cnsrtm.: Ch. (1981). Southeast. Conf. of Hosp. Libns.: Ch.-Elect (1981). **Honors:** Univ. of KY, H.W. Wilson Flwshp., 1966; Beta Phi Mu. **Pubns.:** "T.H.I.S. Is Where It's At," *Bltn. of Med. LA* (1973). **Activities:** 1, 12; 17, 39, 46; 58, 80, 87 **Addr.:** Singing River Hospital, Medical Library, 2809 Denny Ave., Pascagoula, MS 39567.

Dowlin, Charles Edwin (Je. 3, 1933, Laird, CO) Dir., Sch. of LS, Sam Houston State Univ., 1980–; Sr. Resrch. Sci., Appld. Mgt. Scis., Inc., 1978–80; Consult., Allegheny Cnty., 1977–78; Consult., Metro. Lib. Syst. of OK City–Cnty., 1976–77; State Libn., NM State Lib., 1970–77; Head, Lib. Dev., State Lib. of OH, 1968–70; City Libn., Provo City Corp., 1963–67; Qual. Cntrl. Statistician, Sundstrand Aviation, 1960–62. **Educ.:** Univ. of CO, 1951–55, BS (Bus.), 1955–56, MPS (Persnl.); Univ. of Denver, 1963, MA (LS); Univ. of Pittsburgh, 1980, PhD (LS). **Orgs.:** ALA. SWLA. TX LA. **Honors:** NM LA, Libn. of the Yr., 1977; Beta Phi Mu. **Pubns.:** Jt. auth., "The Governance of Library Networks: Purposes and Expectations," *The Structure and Governance of Library Networks* (1979); "Public Relations and the State Library," *Public Relations for Libraries: Essays in Communication Techniques* (1973); jt. auth., "Ohio's BOOKS/JOBS Program," *Lib. Jnl.* (O. 1, 1970); contrib., "Needs Assessment in New Mexico," "TV and the Library," "Opportunity Handbook for Local Library Communications," and "The Librarian's Guide to Great Speechmaking," *NM State Lib. Occ. Paper Series.* **Activities:** 4, 11; 17, 24, 26 **Addr.:** School of Library Science, Sam Houston State University, P.O. Box 2236, Huntsville, TX 77341.

Dowlin, Kenneth E. (Mr. 11, 1941, Wray, CO) Dir., Pikes Peak Lib. Dist., 1975–; Dir., Natrona Cnty. Pub. Lib., 1970–75; Admin. Asst. to Dir., Jefferson Cnty. Pub. Lib., 1969–70; City Libn., Arvada Pub. Lib., 1964–69. **Educ.:** Univ. of CO, 1960–64, BA (Hist.); Univ. of Denver, 1964–66, MA (LS); University of CO, Colorado Spr., 1981, MA (Pub. Admn.). **Orgs.:** CO LA: Pub. Lib. Div. (Ch., 1967); Mem. Com. (1967); Pres. (1968); Legis. Com. (1976, 1977). ALA. Natl. Micro. Assn. Mt. Plains LA: Mach. Readable Data Base Com. (Ch., 1973); Various other coms. Satellite Lib. Info. Netwk.: Bd. Dir. CO St. Lib: Netwk. Com. (Ch., 1976). Bibl. Ctr. Resrch.: Rocky Mt. Reg., Bd. Dirs. (1970–75), Ch. (1974, 1975). Plains Peaks Reg. Lib. Syst.: Bd. (1975–), Secy. (1977). Many other lib. coms. and orgs. **Honors:** WHCOLIS, Delegate, 1979; Mt. Plains LA, Cert. Recog., 1973; WY LA, Outstan. Lib. Wk., 1973; Denver Reg. Cncl. Gvts., Cert. of Merit for Outstand. Srv., 1969; other awds. and honors. **Pubns.:** "The Technological Setting of the Public Library," *Lib. Qtly.* (O. 1978); "CATV - NCPL - VRS: Broadcasting Reference Service Over a Community TV System," *Lib. Jnl.* (S. 1970); many other pubns. and speeches. **Activities:** 9; 17, 24; 56 **Addr.:**

PROFESSIONAL ACTIVITIES: Institutions: 1. Acad. lib.; 2. Arch.; 3. Assn.; 4. Fed./Gvt. lib.; 5. Inst. lib.; 6. Mfr./Suppl.; 7. Milit. lib.; 8. Musm.; 9. Pub. lib.; 10. Sch. lib.; 11. Sch. of lib. sci.; 12. Spec. lib.; 13. State lib.; 14. (other). **Functions/Activities:** 15. Acq./Col. dev.; 16. Adult srvs.; 17. Admin.; 18. Apprais.; 19. Archit./Bldgs.; 20. Cat./Class.; 21. Chld. srvs.; 22. Circ.; 23. Cons./Pres.; 24. Consult.; 25. Cont. ed.; 26. Educ. lib. sci.; 27. Ext. srvs.; 28. Fund/Grants; 29. Gvt. pubs.; 30. Indx./Abs.; 31. Instr. lib. use; 32. Media srvs.; 33. Micro.; 34. Netwks./Coop.; 35. Persnl.; 36. PR; 37. Publshg.; 38. Recs. mgt.; 39. Ref. srvs.; 40. Repro.; 41. Resrch.; 42. Review.; 43. Secur.; 44. Serials; 45. Spec. col.; 46. Tech. srvs.; 47. Trustees/Bds.; 48. YA srvs.; 49. (other).

Pikes Peak Library District, 20 N. Cascade Ave., P.O. Box 1579, Colorado Springs, CO 80901.

Downes, Robin N. (Ap. 23, 1932, Torrington, CT) Dir. of Libs., Univ. of Houston, 1980–; Assoc. Dir., Tech. Srvs., Univ. of MI Lib., 1978–80, Assoc. Dir., 1972–78, Asst. to the Dir., 1971–72. **Educ.:** FL State Univ., 1950–54, BA (Hist.), 1957–58, MA (LS). **Orgs.:** MI LA: Acad. Lib. Sect., Bd. of Dirs. (1971–73); Tech. Srvs. Sect. Ch.-Elect (1974–75), Ch. (1975–76); Nom. Com. (Ch., 1973–74). RLG/RLIN: Com. on Tech. Srvs. and Bibl. Cntrl. (Ch., 1979–80). ALA: RTSD Bd. of Dirs. (1980–); Tech. Srvs. Dirs. of Lg. Resrch. Libs. Discuss. Grp. (Ch., 1975–76); ACRL, Task Frc. on Cont. Educ. (1976–77). TX LA. Various other orgs., ofcs. **Pubns.:** "The Challenge of Steady-State Budgeting: A Perspective," *Library Budgeting: Critical Challenges for the Future* (1977). **Activities:** 1; 17, 39, 46; 55, 56 **Addr.:** University of Houston Central Campus Library, 4800 Calhoun Blvd., Houston, TX 77004.

Downes, Valerie Jean (Ap. 7, 1938, IL.) Dir. of Lib., Media Srvs., J.S. Morton HS, 1974–; Dir. of Title II ESEA, IL Ofc. of Educ., 1971–74; Dir. of Lib. Media Prog., Sch. Dist. 110, Deerfield, 1966–71; "Project Discovery" Media Spec., Daly City, CA, 1965–66; Adj. Prof., Loyola Univ., 1978. **Educ.:** Univ. of IL, 1956–60, BA (Eng./Educ.); San Jose State Coll., 1960–66, MA (LS); Loyola Univ., 1970–75, EdD (Curric. & Instr.). **Orgs.:** ALA: AASL/Supvsrs. Sect., (Ch. 1976); AASL/EB Sch. Lib. Media Prog. of the Yr. Awd. Com. (Ch., 1977); Member Right to Read Comm. (1972–1974); Cncl. (1977–1981). IL LA: Exec. Bd. (1971–1973). IL Assn. of Sch. Libns.: Exec. Bd. (1971–1973). IL AV Assn.: Exec. Bd. (1971–1973. **Pubns.:** "Programs of Media Services in Elementary Schools and Their Relation to Guidance Services", *IL Jnl. of Educ.* (S./O., 1972); "Complimenting and Cooperating! Total Library Service to Children Through Maximum Use of the Children's Room and Media Center", *IL Libs.* (Ja. 1975); "Blueprint for a Media Center", *Curric. Review* (F. 1977); "Media Programs Can Be Alive and Well", *Cath. Lib. World* (My.-Je., 1978); "Who's Who in Problem Solving", *IL Libs.* (S. 1978); Other articles. **Activities:** 10, 11; 17, 26 **Addr.:** J.S. Morton High School District, 2423 S. Austin Blvd., Cicero, IL 60650.

Downey, Bernard F. (Ag. 17, 1921, Boston, MA) Dir., Lib.–Info. Srvs., Inst. of Mgt. and Labor Rel., Rutgers Univ., 1957–; Head, Bus.–Tech. Dept., Trenton Pub. Lib., 1951–57; Jr. Libn., Bus. Lib., Newark Pub. Lib., 1949–51; Ref. Libn., Pub. Admin. Sch., Harvard Univ., 1947–49. **Educ.:** Boston Coll., 1939–43, BA (Lit.); Simmons Coll., 1946–47, BS (LS). **Orgs.:** SLA: Princeton–Trenton Chap. (Dir., 1980–81); NJ Chap., Consult. Com. (Ch., 1969–71). AAUP: New Brunswick Chap. **Pubns.:** Jt. cmplr., *Industrial and Labor Relations Thesaurus* (1977); jt. auth., *Library Service to Labor* (1963); "Library and Information Service Needs of Labor," *Library and Information Service Needs of the Nation* (1974). **Activities:** 1, 12; 17, 25; 50, 95-Indus. and labor Rel. **Addr.:** 3 Goodale Cir., New Brunswick, NJ 08901.

Downey, Howard R. (S. 22, 1938, Spokane, WA) Prop., Valley Books, 1980–; Dir., Bellingham (WA) Pub. Lib., 1967–, Asst. Dir., 1966–67; Ref. Libn., West. WA St. Coll., 1962–64. **Educ.:** Univ. of WA, Seattle Pacific Coll. 1956–58; 1958–60, BA (Geo.); 1960–62, MLS; Univ. of CA, Berkeley, 1964–66, LS. **Orgs.:** ALA: Various coms. WA LA: various coms. Pacific N.W. LA. Lions Club: various coms. United Way: various coms. **Honors:** Beta Phi Mu, 1963. **Pubns.:** Reviews. **Activities:** 9; 17 **Addr.:** Valley Books, 315 Main St., Mount Vernon, WA 98273.

Downey, Lawrence J. (S. 1, 1931, Indianapolis, IN) Assoc. Dir., Indianapolis-Marion Cnty. Pub. Lib., 1973–; Coord. of Persnl. Srvs., 1965–73; Coord. of Tech. Srvs., 1963–65; Branch Lib. Admn., 1961–63. **Educ.:** Butler Univ., 1949–54, BA (Span.); IN Univ., 1956–58, MLS. **Orgs.:** ALA: Cncl. (1971–72); Staff Dev. Com. (1972–74). IN LA: Treas. (1970–71); Exec. Bd (1970–71). Ctrl. IN Area Lib. Srvs. Athrty.: Exec. Com. (1974–77). **Activities:** 9; 17, 22, 35 **Addr.:** Indianapolis-Marion County, Public Library, P.O. Box 211, Indianapolis, IN 46206.

Downey, Linda K. (Ag. 26, 1941, Grinnell, IA) Instr., ESLR Dept., Univ. of UT, 1976–; Asst. Ref. Libn., Old Dominion Univ., 1973–75; YA Libn., Annapolis and Anne Arundel Pub. Lib., 1972–73; Catlgr., Shared Cat., Lib. of Congs., 1969–71; YA Libn., Enoch Pratt Free Lib., 1971–72. **Educ.:** Univ. of IA, 1959–63, BA (Eng.); Catholic Univ., 1968–69, MS (LS); Univ. of UT, 1975–78, MEd. **Orgs.:** ALA. UT LA. UT Educ. Media Assn. Wilderness Assn. **Honors:** Univ. of UT, Ralph Thompson Awd., 1978; Beta Phi Mu. **Activities:** 11; 20, 39, 48; 63 **Addr.:** 209 Marriott Library, University of Utah, Salt Lake City, UT 84112.

Downey, Margaret Abigail (Detroit, MI) Ref. Libn., Educ. Dept., Cincinnati Pub. Lib., 1972–; Libn., Merrill–Palmer Inst., 1963–71; Head, Ref./ILL, Wayne Cnty. Pub. Lib., 1951–63; Fld. Libn., U.S. Army, Germany, 1948–51. **Educ.:** Wayne State Univ., 1936–40, BA; McGill Univ., 1940–41, MLS. **Orgs.:** SLA: MI Chap., Treas., Prog. Ch., Nat. Conv. Banquet Com., Ch. ALA. MI LA: Grp. III (Secy.–Treas., 1960). Wayne State Dearborn Chap.: Schol. Com. **Activities:** 9, 12; 39; 92 **Addr.:** Education Dept., Public Library of Cincinnati & Hamilton County, 800 Vine St., Cincinnati, OH 45202.

Downing, Mildred Harlow (Ap. 30, 1929, Washington, DC) Asst. Prof., LS, Univ. of NC, 1978–; Asst. Prof., LS, Villanova Univ., 1975–78; Instr., LS, Drexel Univ., 1968–71; Resrch. Asst., Psychopharmacology, Univ. of PA, 1961–65. **Educ.:** Univ. of PA, 1948–52, BA (Psy.); Drexel Univ., 1957–58, MSLS; Univ. of PA, 1970–74, PhD (Comm.). **Orgs.:** ALA. AALS. SELA. SLA. Action for Chlds. TV. **Honors:** Delta Phi Alpha, 1951. **Pubns.:** "Three approaches to the teaching of online cataloging in an academic setting," *Jnl. Educ. for Libnshp.* (in press); *Introduction to Cataloging and Classification* (1981); "Heroine of the daytime serial," *Jnl. Comm.* (Spr. 1974); "Men, Women, Love, and Sex in Prime Time TV Drama," *Prog. in Comm. Sci.* (in press); various other articles. **Activities:** 11, 12; 20, 26, 41; 63, 72, 93 **Addr.:** School of Library Science, University of NC, Chapel Hill, NC 27514.

Downing, Thomas Allison (O. 20, 1947, Kalamazoo, MI) Libn./Info. Anal., U.S. Dept. of Defense, 1980–; Libn., U.S. Gvt. Prtg. Ofc., 1978–80; Intelligence Ofcr., Strategic Intelligence Analyst, US Army, 1970–72. **Educ.:** West. MI Univ., 1966–69, BA (Pol. Sci); Simmons Coll., 1977–78, MS (LS); Hebrew Union Coll.-Jewish Inst. of Relig., 1973–75, MA (Hebrew Lit.) **Orgs.:** ALA: GODORT Ch., Com. on CIP for Gvt. Pub. (1978–); Com. on Review Copies of Gvt. Pubn. (1979–). Working Grp. on Updating COSATI (1978–). **Honors:** Meml. Fndn. for Jewish Culture, Grant, 1976. **Pubns.:** "Federal Documents Task Force Committee Report on CIP for Government Publications," *Documents to the People* (N. 1979). **Activities:** 4; 20, 29, 30; 77, 91, 92 **Addr.:** 11303 Gilsan St., Silver Spring, MD 20902.

Downs, Robert Bingham (My. 25, 1903, Lenoir, NC) Dean, Lib. Admn., Emeritus, Univ. of IL, 1971–, Dean Lib. Admn., 1943–71; Dir. of Libs., New York Univ., 1938–43; Libn., Univ. of NC (Chapel Hill), 1932–38. **Educ.:** Univ. of NC, 1922–26, AB; Columbia Univ., 1926–27, BS, 1927–29, MS. **Orgs.:** Assn. of Coll. and Resrch. Libs., Pres., 1940–41. ALA: Pres. (1952–53); ACRL (Pres., 1940–41). IL LA: Pres. (1955–56). **Honors:** ALA, Clarence Day Awd., 1963; ALA, Lippincott Awd., 1964; ALA Melvil Dewey Awd., 1974; Univ. of NC, LLD, 1949; Guggenheim Flw., 1971–72; numerous other honors. **Pubns.:** *Books That Changed the World,* 2d ed. (1978); *In Search of New Horizons* (1978); numerous books, articles, other pubns. **Activities:** 1; 15, 24, 35, 37 **Addr.:** 708 W. Pennsylvania Ave., Urbana, IL 61801.

Downs, Rubye P. (Ap. 2, 1921, Malden, MO) Dir. of Media Srvs., USD No. 305, Instr. Media Ctr., 1966–; Tchr. and Supvsn. (Mtrls. Spec.), Oscoda Area Schs., 1962–66; Classrm. Tchr., Salina Pub. Schs., 1958–62; Classrm. Tchr., Hermiston, OR, 1954–56; Classrm. Tchr., New Madrid Cnty., MO, 1940–43; Persnl. Mgr. and Asst. Instr., U.S. Army Air Frc., 1943–45; various tchg. and wkshps. (1965–). **Educ.:** SE MO S. T. Coll. Marymount Coll., 1939–59, BA (Educ., Bus./Art); Ctrl. MI Univ., 1963–65, MA (Supvsn. and Curric.); various crs. **Orgs.:** KS LA: Rep. KASL, Exec. Bd. (1970–72); ILL for Non–Print Media (Ch., 1975–76). KS Assn. of Sch. Libns.: Exec. Bd.; Pres. (1970–72); various coms., ofcs. KS Sch. Lib. Media Dirs.: Ch. (1968–69). KS Assn. for Comm. and Tech.: Bd. of Dirs. (1970–80). Various other orgs., ofcs. KS Assn. for Supvsn. and Curric. Dev.: Secy.–Treas. (1974–75). Assn. for Supvsn. and Curric. Dev. Untd. Sch. Admins.: Mem. Com.; William White Chld. Bk. Awd. Com. First Christ. Church, Salina, KS. Various other orgs., ofcs. **Pubns.:** *Cataloging Manual for Non-Print Media* (1968). **Activities:** 10, 11; 17, 21, 24; 61, 63, 67 **Addr.:** USD No. 305, Instructional Media Center, 119 E. Mulberry, Salina, KS 67401.

Downum, Evelyn R. (Chicago, IL) Dir. Lib., and Instr., North. AZ Univ. Elem. Sch. and Univ., 1956–; Instr. Hist., AZ St. Coll., 1948. **Educ.:** Univ. of IL, 1936, BA (Hist.) with honors; Univ. of TX, 1941, MA (Hist.); Univ. of Denver, 1965. **Orgs.:** AZ LA: Sch. Lib. Div. (Exec. Bd.). Chlds. Lit. Assn. ALA. Cncl. on Interracial Bks. Many other orgs. Phi Kappa Phi. Pi Lamba Theta. Beta Sigma Phi. Delta Kappa Gamma. Other orgs. **Pubns.:** Reviews. **Activities:** 1, 10; 17, 21, 26; 63, 95 **Addr.:** 1609 N. Aztec St., Flagstaff, AZ 86001.

Doyle, Francis Robert (Je. 2, 1938, Cambridge, MA) Law Libn. and Asst. Prof. of Law, Loyola Univ., Chicago, 1978–; Ref. and Pub. Srvs. Libn., Univ. of CA, Berkeley, 1972–78; Ref. Libn., Harvard Law Sch. Lib., 1970–71; Law Libn., Middlesex Law LA, 1967–72. **Educ.:** Boston Univ., 1959–63, BA (Pol. Sci.); New Eng. Sch. of Law, 1969–72, JD; Univ. of CA, Berkeley, 1974–77, MLS. **Orgs.:** AALL: Elec. Com. (1980–81). Chicago Assn. of Law Libs.: Admin. Law (1978–80). ALA. Cath. LA. Various other orgs. Knights of Columbus. Benevolent and Protective Ord. of Elks. Loyola Univ. Empl. Credit Un. St. Athanasius Bd. of Educ. **Pubns.:** Asst. ed., *Index to Multilateral Treaties* (1965); bibl. ed., *Computer and the Law* (1966); *End of the (Red)line. Exchange Bibliography No. 1486* (1978); "A Nickle for Your...: The Copyright Problem," *Law Lib. Jnl.* (My. 1976); jt. auth., "A Bibliography: The Published Works of Albert A. Ehrenzweig," *CA Law Review* (1974); various bibls. (1975). **Activities:** 1; 17, 39; 77 **Addr.:** Loyola University School of Law, Law Library, 1 E. Pearson St., Chicago, IL 60611.

Doyle, Pamela Barefoot (D. 1, 1948, Dunn, NC) Dir., Div. of Media Prcs. Srvs., NC Dept. of Com. Colls., 1981–, Asst. Dir., 1976–81; Libn., 1971–76. **Educ.:** East Carolina Univ., 1967–71, BS (LS). **Orgs.:** NC LA: Resrcs. and Tech. Sect. (Dir., 1977–79; Secy., 1979–81); Jr. Colls. Sect. (Secy., 1977–79); JMRT, By-Laws Com. (Ch., 1975). NC Com. Colls. Lrng. Resrcs. Assn.: Autom. Com. (Ch., 1979–80). ALA. SELA. Various other orgs. **Activities:** 1; 17, 20, 46 **Addr.:** Division of Media Processing Services, North Carolina Dept. of Community Colleges, 100 S. Harrington St., Raleigh, NC 27603.

Doyle, T. Sharon (Jl. 8, 1948, Chatham, ON) Head Libn., Resrc. Ctr., Havergal Coll., 1979–; Tchr.-Libn., Lrng. Mtrls. Unit, Oxford Cnty. Bd. of Educ., 1975–79; Tchr.-Libn., Chatham Collegiate Inst., Kent Cnty. Bd. of Educ., 1971–74. **Educ.:** Univ. of Windsor, 1967–70, BA (Pol. Sci.); Univ. of West. ON, 1970–71, BEd (LS), 1974–75, MA (LS). **Orgs.:** ON LA: ON Sch. LA; Prog. Co–Ch., ON LA Anl. Conf. (1978): E. York Sch. Libns. Assn.: Rec. Secy. (1980–81). Sch. Libns. Assn., Oxford Cnty. Bd. of Educ.: Pres. (1978–79); VP (1977–78). Kent Cnty. Bd. of Educ. Libns. Assn.: Prog. Co–Ch. (1973–74). Fed. of Women Tchrs. Assn. of ON: Oxford Exec. ON Sec. Sch. Tchrs. Fed. **Pubns.:** "A Celebration...National Book Festival at Havergal College," *Revolting Libn.* (Sum. 1980); various reviews. **Activities:** 9, 10; 31, 42, 48; 55, 63, 67 **Addr.:** Resource Centre, Havergal College, 1451 Avenue Rd., Toronto, ON M5N 2H9 Canada.

Drach, Marian (Capozzi) (My. 11, 1927, Baltimore, MD) Supvsr., Lib. Srvs., Baltimore Cnty. Pub. Schs., 1966–; Libn., Westchester Cnty. Schs., 1962–65; Libn., Baltimore Cnty. Schs., 1957–61; Libn./Tchr.–Adv., U.S. Dependent Schs., 1955–57; Tchr., Baltimore Cnty. Schs., 1950–55. **Educ.:** Univ. of MD, 1945–49, BS (Home Econ.); Cath. Univ. of Amer., 1965–67, MSLS; various crs. **Orgs.:** ALA: *Booklist* Ed. Adv. Bd. (1973–74); *Pers. for Sch. Libs.* (2nd ed.) Adv. (1976–77); ALSC Sec. VP (1975–76), CSD Bd. (1975–76), Newbery–Caldecott Com. (1975–76), Mildred Batchelder Awd. Com. (1969–71), various coms; AASL, various coms. MD LA. MD Educ. Media Org. AECT. **Honors:** Beta Phi Mu, 1967. **Pubns.:** *The Elementary School Media Program: An Approach to Individualizing Instruction* (1970). **Activities:** 10; 17, 32 **Addr.:** 205 E. Joppa Rd., #602, Towson, MD 21204.

Dragon, Andrea Claire (N. 28, 1945, OR City, OR) Asst. Prof., Rutgers Univ., 1977–; Libn., Minneapolis Inst. of Arts, 1971–73; Ref. Libn., St. Olaf Coll., 1967–70. **Educ.:** Portland State Univ., 1963–66, BA (Geo.); Univ. of MN, 1966–68, MA (LS), 1973–76, PhD (LS). **Orgs.:** AALS. Acad. of Mgt. **Pubns.:** "Leader Behavior in Changing Libraries," *Lib. Resrch.* (Spr. 1979); "Marketing the Library," *Wilson Lib. Bltn.* (Mr. 1979). **Activities:** 9; 17, 24, 26; 51 **Addr.:** Graduate School of Library and Information Studies, Rutgers University, 4 Huntington St., New Brunswick, NJ 08903.

Drake, Eleanor Anne (Ja. 29, 1931, Jackson, TN) Libn., Peeples Jr. HS, Jackson, MS, 1955–; Libn., DeSoto Cnty. HS, Arcadia, FL, 1954–55; Libn., Jackson (MS) Mncpl. Lib., Sum. 1953–58, 60; Libn., U.S. Army Engin. Waterways Exper. Station, Sum. 1962; Field Libn., MI Lib. Commsn., 1964–68. **Educ.:** MS Univ. for Women, 1950–54, BS (LS); MS State Univ., 1977–78, MEd (LS). **Orgs.:** ALA. MI LA: VP (1972), Pres. (1973); Exec. Dir. MI Natl. Lib. Wk. (1965). MI Assn. of Media Educ. Jackson (MS) Assn. of Educ. MS Assn. of Educ. Delta Kappa Gamma. **Activities:** 10 **Addr.:** 276 Rosslyn Ave., Jackson, MS 39209.

Drake, Mayo (Je. 9, 1934, Tallahassee, FL) Libn. and Prof. of Med., LA St. Univ., 1968–; Asst. Libn., Hlth. Ctr. Lib. Univ. of FL, 1957–67; Asst. Acq. Libn., FL St. Univ., 1955–57. **Educ.:** FL St. Univ., 1950–54, BS (Pub. Admn.), 1954–56, MS (LS); Cert. Med. Libn. I, 1965–. **Orgs.:** Med. LA: Schol. Com. (1968–71), Mem. Com. (1971–73); South. Reg. (Ch., 1963). LA LA. **Pubns.:** *Checklist of Periodical Titles Held By Medical Libraries in Southern Region,* 3rd ed. (1967); "Priorities In Preparation for Opening Day," *Bltn. Med. LA* (1971); "The LSU Medical School Library," *LA LA Bltn.* (Spr. 1970). **Activities:** 1; 15, 17; 58, 80 **Addr.:** Louisiana State University Medical Center, P.O. Box 33932, Shreveport, LA 71130.

Drake, Miriam A. (D. 20, 1936, Boston, MA) Asst. Dir. Lib. Support Srvs., Purdue Univ. Libs., 1981–, Asst. Dir., Admn. Srvs., 1976–81, Head, Resrch. and Dev. Unit, 1974–76, Resrch. Libn., 1972–74. **Educ.:** Simmons Coll., 1954–58, BS (Econ.), Simmons Coll., 1969–71, MS (LS); Radcliffe Coll., 1959–1960, (Econ.). **Orgs.:** ALA. ASIS. SLA. OCLC Inc.: Bd. of Trustees (1978–84; Ch., 1981–); Vice-Ch. (1978–80). **Honors:** Beta Phi Mu, 1971. **Pubns.:** "Managing Innovation in Academic Libraries," *Coll. and Resrch. Libs.* (N. 1979); Jt. auth., "The Economics of Library Innovation," *Lib. Trends* (Sum. 1979); "Management Control in Academic Libraries," *New Horizons for Acad. Libs.* (1979); Jt. auth., "An Information Service for Practicing Veterinarians," *Bltn. of Med. LA* (O. 1978); "Impact of On-line Systems or Library Functions" in *The Online Revolu-*

Special Subjects/Services: 50. Adult educ.; 51. Advert./Mktg.; 52. Aerosp.; 53. Agric.; 54. Area std.; 55. Arts/Hum.; 56. Autom.; 57. Bibl./Prtg.; 58. Bio. sci.; 59. Bus./Fin.; 60. Chem.; 61. Copyrt.; 62. Documtn.; 63. Educ.; 64. Engin.; 65. Env.; 66. Eth. grps.; 67. Film; 68. Food/Nutr.; 69. Geneal.; 70. Geo.; 71. Geol.; 72. Handcpd.; 73. Hist.; 74. Int. frdm.; 75. Info. sci.; 76. Insr.; 77. Law; 78. Legis.; 79. Math./Comp. sci.; 80. Med.; 81. Metals; 82. Nat. resrcs.; 83. Newsp.; 84. Nuc. sci.; 85. Oral hist.; 86. Petr./Energy; 87. Pharm.; 88. Phys./Astr./Math.; 89. Readg.; 90. Relig.; 91. Sci./Tech.; 92. Soc. sci.; 93. Telecom.; 94. Transp.; 95. (other).

tion in Libraries (1978); various other pubns. **Activities:** 1; 17 **Addr.:** 1815 Woodland Ave., West Lafayette, IN 47906.

Draper, James Donald (F. 29, 1944, Corbin, KY) Head Libn., Doraville City Lib., 1976–; Head of Tech. Srvs., Metro. Life Insr. Co., 1973–75; Catlgr., Pace Univ. Lib., 1972–73; Head of Tech. Srvs., Coopers and Lybrand, 1969–73; Head of Tech. Srvs., Ingram Bk. Co., 1968–69. **Educ.:** Peabody Coll., 1963–67, BA (Liberal Arts); Peabody Lib. Sch., 1968–69, MLS; NY Sch. of Interior Dsgn., 1974–75, Cert. (Interior Dsgn.). **Orgs.:** ALA. SELA. GA LA: Libnshp. Com. (1980–81). Metro. Atlanta LA: Secy. (1978). **Pubns.:** Jt. auth., *Interior Design for Libraries* (1979). **Activities:** 1, 9; 15, 17, 46 **Addr.:** Doraville City Library, 3748 Central Ave., Doraville, GA 30340.

Drazan, Joseph Gerald (Je. 1, 1943, Spokane, WA) Acq. Libn., Whitman Coll. Lib., 1972–; Ref. Libn., Univ. of Alaska Lib., Fairbanks, 1970–72. **Educ.:** East. WA St. Univ., 1967–69, BA (Soclgy.); Univ. of HI, 1969–70, MLS. **Orgs.:** ALA. WA LA. **Pubns.:** *The Unknown ERIC: A Selection of Documents for the General Library* (1981); *The Pacific Northwest; an Index to People and Places in Books* (1979); *The Nightmare; a Checklist of the World Literature to 1976* (1979); *Picture Alaska; an Index to Illustrations* (1973); "Research Studies Index, 1929–1975", *Research Studies* (1976); other articles, editorships; reviews. **Activities:** 1; 15, 18, 30; 57, 95-Photography. **Addr.:** 1203 Bonsella, Walla Walla, WA 99362.

Drazic, Milimir (Ap. 22, 1926, Kikinda, Yugoslavia) Dir., Lrng. Resrc. Ctr., McCook Cmnty. Coll., 1978–; Dir. of Libs., Asso. Prof., Univ. of Houston, Victoria, 1977–78; Dir. of Lib, Asso. Prof., Castleton State Coll., 1974–77; Dir. of Lib., Coord. of LTA, Head Libn., Manchester Cmnty. Coll., 1966–74; Head Libn., Glencoe (IL) Pub. Lib., 1961–1966. **Educ.:** Univ. of Belgrade, Yugoslavia, 1945–50, M.Dipl. (Grmn.); Univ. of KY, 1956–58, MSLS; Univ. of Copenhagen, Denmark, 1953–54, Cert. (Scan.). **Orgs.:** ALA. Lib. Admin. Cncl. of N. IL: Ch. (1964–1966). Mari Sandoz (NE) Reg. Lib: Dir. (1978). NE Pre-WACOLIS: Dele. (1979). **Pubns.:** Articles and reviews. **Activities:** 1; 17; 54, 55, 56 **Addr.:** Director of Learning Resource Center, McCook Community College, 1205 East Third St., McCook, NE 69001.

Drazniowsky, Roman (Ag. 12, 1922, Chortkiv, Ukraine) Cur., Ed. of Current Geographical Pubns., Amer. Geographical Socty. Col., Univ. of WI, Milwaukee Lib., 1978–; Libn., Map Cur., Amer. Geographical Socty. (NY), 1976–78; Map Cur., 1962–75; Map Libn., Columbia Univ., 1957–62; Lect., Columbia Univ. Sch. of Lib. Serv., 1968–79. **Educ.:** Innsbruck Univ., Austria, 1953–57, PhD (Geo., Cartography). **Orgs.:** SLA: Archvst. (1974–1977); Geo. and Map Div., NY Chap. (Ch., 1974–1975). Ukrainian LA: Pres. (1976–1978). Assn. of Amer. Geographers. **Honors:** Amer. Geographical Socty., Charles P. Daly Medal, 1978; SLA, Geo. and Map Div., Spec. Cit., 1979. **Pubns.:** *Map Librarianship: Readings.* (1975); Index to Maps in Books and Periodicals. American Geographical Society. (1968); "Conference on the History of Cartography," *The Cartographer* (1967); "Cartography. Bibliography: Current State and Future Trends," *Lib. Trends* (1967); "The Need for Map Cataloging," *Spec. Libs.* (My.-Je. 1970); Other books, articles, reviews. **Activities:** 1; 15, 17, 26; 57, 63, 70 **Addr.:** AGS Collection of the UWM Library, P.O. Box 399, Milwaukee, WI 53201.

Drennan, Henry Thomas (D. 24, 1913, Portland, OR) Actg. Chief, U.S. Ofc. of Educ., Ofc. of Lib. Resrch. Demonstration Proj., 1980, Sr. Prog. Ofcr. for Resrch., 1975–80, Chief Plng. Branch, 1970–74, Coord. Pub. Lib. Srvs., 1962–69; ID State Libn., 1959–62. **Educ.:** Univ. of WA, 1948–50, BA magna cum laude (Pol. Sci.), 1950–51, BLS; Amer. Univ., 1962–64, MA (Urban Stud.). **Orgs.:** ALA: Com. on Stan. and Ref. Srvs. (1965–67); Com. on Srvs. to Aging Popltn. (1963–65); Com. on Srvs. to Functionally Illiterate (1967); various other coms. Many other orgs. and coms. U.S. Ofc. of Educ.: Comsn. Task Force on Rural Educ., 1979–. **Honors:** Phi Beta Kappa, 1949. ALA, Joseph Lippincott Awd., 1978–79; WHCOLIS, Mem. Plng. Grp. and Resrc. Rep., 1979. **Pubns.:** "Library Legislation Discovered," *Lib. Trends* (Jl. 1975); Jt. auth., "The 1971 White House Conference on Aging: Implications for Library Services," *Lib. Trends* (Ja. 1973); "Discrimination in Libraries," *Encyc. of Lib. and Info. Sci.* (1972); "New Directions in Public Library Legislation," *Lib. Trends* (O. 1970); "The Urban Public Library: Strategies for Survival," in *Changing Role of Library Consultants* (1968); many other pubns., speeches. **Activities:** 4, 13; 24, 41; 50, 66, 89 **Addr.:** 138 E. St. S.E., Washington, DC 20003.

Dresang, Eliza Timberlake (O. 21, 1941, Atlanta, GA) Mgr. of Media Srvs., Madison Metro Sch. Dist., 1980–; Lect., Univ. of WI, Madison Lib. Sch., 1978–80; Dir., Inst. Mtrls. Ctr., Lapham Elem. Sch., 1974–78; Resrch. Asst., African Educ., Univ. of WI, 1974; Resrch. Proj., Haddoof Chld. Dept., Ida Williams Branch, Atlanta Pub. Lib., 1967–68; Head of Chld. Dept., Adult Ref. Libn., Encino-Tarzana Branch, Los Angeles Pub. Lib., 1966–67; Tchr., WI and CA Sch., 1963–65. **Educ.:** Emory Univ., 1959–63, BA (Fr./Span.); Univ. of CA, Los Angeles, 1965–66, MLS; Univ. of WI, 1978–81, PhD (LS). **Orgs.:** ALA; AASL; ALSC: Lib. Srv. to Chld. With Special Needs Com. (Ch., 1979–82). AECT. WI LA (Wisconsin School Library Media Association; Audiovisual/Multi-Image Section): Legis. Com., (1980). WI AV Assn. Other orgs. Socty. for Chld. Book Writers. **Honors:** Phi Beta Kappa, 1962; Beta Phi Mu, 1966; Phi Eta Sigma, 1962; WI Sch. Lib. Media Assn., Sch. Libn. of the Yr., 1978. **Pubns.:** *The Land and People of Zambia* (1975); "An Application of Decision-Making Theory to Curriculum Change in Library Education", *Jnl. of Educ. for Libnshp.* (Win. 1980); "There Are No Other Children: Special Children in Library Media Centers," *Sch. Lib. Jnl.* (S. 1977); reprinted in *Reader in Children's Librarianship* (1978); and *Meeting Needs of the Handicapped* (1980); "Mainstreaming All Children: Exceptional Children Use School and Public Libraries," *Wisconsin Library Bulletin* (Ap./My. 1978). **Activities:** 10, 11; 21, 26, 32; 63, 72, 93 **Addr.:** 440 Virginia Terr., Madison, WI 53705.

Drescher, Judith A. (Greensburg, PA) Lib. Dir., Champaign Pub. Lib. and Info. Ctr. (IL), 1979–; Lib. Dir., Rolling Meadows Pub. Lib. (IL), 1974–79; Branch Libn., Pub. Lib. Cincinnati and Hamilton Cnty. (OH) 1972–74; Chld. Libn., 1971–72. **Educ.:** Grove City Coll., 1964–68, AB (Eng.); Univ. of Pittsburgh, 1970–71, MLIS. **Orgs.:** IL LA: PR com. (1975–79, Ch., 1978); Mem. Com. (1975–78, Ch., 1977); Intl. Frdm. Com. (1979–); other coms. ALA: Mem. Com. (1977–78); PLA Mem. Com. (1977–78); other coms. N. Suburban Lib. Syst.: Reg. Lib. Adv. Cncl. (Bd., 1978–79); various coms. Lib. Admn. Conf. North. IL. IL Reg. Lib. Cncl. Other orgs. Altrusa Club of North. Cook Cnty.: Pres. (1977–78); Cmnty. Srvs. Com. (Ch. 1978–79). Chamber of Commerce. League of Women Voters. **Honors:** Beta Phi Mu, 1971. **Pubns.:** "What's the Picture?" *IL Libs.* (D. 1976). **Activities:** 9; 17, 27, 36; 50, 78 **Addr.:** Champaign Public Library and Information Center, 505 S. Randolph, Champaign, IL 61820.

Dresp, Donald F. (F. 17, 1936, Omaha, NE) Lib. Dir., Thomas Branigan Meml. Lib., 1971–; Asst. Dir., Scottsdale Pub. Lib., 1967–71; Asst. Educ. Libn., AZ State Univ., 1965–67; Libn., Loveland HS, 1962–65; Libn., Valley HS, NE, 1960–62. **Educ.:** Immaculate Conception Coll., MO, 1955–58, BA (Phil.); Univ. of Denver, MA (LS); Creighton Univ., 1958–60, (Hist. & Educ.); AZ State Univ., Grad. work, 1968–70. **Orgs.:** NM LA: VP (1972–73); Pres. (1973–74). NM Mncpl. Libns.: VP (1975–76); Pres. (1976–77). Border Reg. LA; Salt River Valley LA: VP (1968–69); Pres. (1969–70). Other orgs. and coms. Rotary Club. Amer. Red Cross: Bd. (1977–). Dóna Ana Cnty. Hist. Socty. Las Cruces Arts & Crafts Assn. **Honors:** Border Reg. LA, Libn. of the Yr., 1975. **Activities:** 9, 10; 17, 19, 36; 55, 63 **Addr.:** 1829 Salinas Dr., Las Cruces, NM 88001.

Drew, Frances K. (D. 4, 1928, Jacksonville, FL) Archit. Libn., GA Inst. of Tech., 1977–, Cat. Libn., 1966–77; Acq. Libn., 1965–66; Sr. Cat. Libn., LA State Univ., 1963–65; Asst. Cat. Libn., Univ. of GA Libs., 1959–63; Jr. Libn., Savannah Pub. Lib., 1957–59; Tchr., Chatham Jr. HS, 1955–57. **Educ.:** Wesleyan Coll., 1948–52, AB (Eng.); Emory Univ., 1952–54, MEd (Educ.), 1957–59, MLn (LS). **Orgs.:** SLA: Geo. and Map Div. (1968–77); Musm. and Art Libs. Div. (1977–). SELA: Arch. Com. (1976–). GA LA: Libnshp. as a Career Com. (1975–). ARLIS/NA: Archit. Grp. (1980–). Various other orgs., coms. AAUP: GA Tech. Chap. Poetry Socty. of GA. GA Hist. Socty. GA Trust for Hist. Prsrvn. Various other orgs. **Pubns.:** "The Georgia Tech Map Collection," *SLA Geo. and Map Div. Bltn.* (D. 1975); "Bicentennial Roadmaps of the Thirteen Original States," *SLA Geo. and Map Div. Bltn.* (S. 1977); "Map Cataloging," *Handling Special Materials in Libraries* (1974). **Activities:** 1, 12; 15, 17, 19; 55 **Addr.:** 710 Peachtree St., N.E., Apt. 1224, Atlanta, GA 30308.

Drew, Howard P. (Ja. 5, 1925, Hartford, CT) Supvsry. Libn., Natl. Lib. of Med., 1948–. **Educ.:** Howard Univ., 1946–49, (Gvt.). **Orgs.:** Med. Lib. Assn. Disabled Amer. Vets. Airborne Assn. **Activities:** 4; 39; 80 **Addr.:** National Library of Medicine, Reference Section, Reference Service Div., 8600 Rockville Pike, Bethesda, MD 20209.

Drew, Sally J. (F. 19, 1945, Burbank, CA) Dir., Bur. of Pub. and Coop. Lib. Srvs., Div. for Lib. Srvs., 1978–, Consult., Cont. Educ., 1976–78; Coord., Task Frc. on Interlib. Coop. and Resrc. Sharing, 1975–76; Head, Ref. Dept., Redwood City Pub. Lib., 1973–75; Asst. Dir., Monroe Cnty. Pub. Lib., 1973, Chld. Libn., 1970–73. **Educ.:** Univ. of MD, 1967–68, BA; IN Univ., 1969–70, MLS. **Orgs.:** ALA. WI LA. ASIS. **Pubns.:** *Interlibrary Cooperation: A Wisconsin Plan, A Report of the Task Force on Interlibrary Cooperation and Resource Sharing* (1976); "Library Service by Computer–Wisconsin Studies New Possibilities," *WI Lib. Bltn.* (Jl.–Ag. 1980); "Grants for Libraries, Sources of Funds to Supplement the Budget," *WI Lib. Bltn.* (Mr.–Ap. 1980); "From User to Ultimate Source of Information," *WI Lib. Bltn.* (N.–D. 1976); "Ask a Data Base! Public Libraries Experiment with Computerized Searches," *WI Lib. Bltn.* (My.–Je. 1977); various papers (1975). **Activities:** 9, 13; 16, 17, 21; 56, 75, 77 **Addr.:** Bureau of Public & Cooperative Library Services, Division for Library Services, 125 S. Webster St., P.O. Box 7841, Madison, WI 53707.

Drewes, Arlene Torgerson (F. 12, 1928, Denver, CO) Catlgr., Natl. Geo. Socty., 1968–; Resrch. Assoc., Syracuse Univ., 1955–57. **Educ.:** Univ. of CO, 1946–51, BA (Geo.); Syracuse Univ., 1951–55, (Geo.); Univ. of MD, 1965–68, MLS. **Orgs.:** SLA: Geo. and Map Div., Mem. (Ch., 1978). DC LA. **Pubns.:** *Climate and related phenomena of the eastern Andean slopes of Central Peru* (1957); "Structure of the subject of Geography," and "Population Data on the La Plata River Drainage Basin," *The Study of Subject Bibliography* (1970); Sources of information on the natural resources of Latin America (Pan American Union) (1969); *Sem. on the Acq. of Latin Amer. Lib. Mtls.* 14th, San Juán (1969). **Activities:** 12; 20; 54, 70, 82 **Addr.:** Library, National Geographic Society, Washington, DC 20036.

Drewett, William O. (III) (Ag. 22, 1950, Lake Charles, LA) Prog. Ofcr. II, ALA/RTSD, 1979–; Dir., Green Gold Lib. Syst., 1974–79. **Educ.:** Rice Univ., 1968–72, BA cum laude (Eng.); LA State Univ., 1973–74, MLS; HEA Title IIB Inst. Fellow, "Cont. Educ. for Lib. Staffs in the Southwest," 1975. **Orgs.:** ALA. **Honors:** Phi Kappa Phi, 1974; Beta Phi Mu, 1975. **Pubns.:** Jt. auth., "A Continuing Education Plan for Louisiana," *LLA Bltn.* (Spr. 1978). **Activities:** 3, 14, 25; 46 **Addr.:** ALA/RTSD, 50 East Huron St., Chicago, IL 60611.

Driessen, Karen C. (Ja. 24, 1941, Missoula, MT) Media Libn./Assoc. Prof., Univ. of MT, 1976–, Lectr./Media Catlgr., 1973–76; Dir. of Lib. Purchasing and Prcs., Missoula Cnty. HS Dist., 1969–70; Dir. of Lib. Prcs., Sch. Dist. #50, Adams Cnty. (CO), 1967–69. **Educ.:** Univ. of MT, 1963–65, BA, hons. (LS); Univ. of Denver, 1966–67, MA (LS). **Orgs.:** AECT. Cnsrtm. of Univ. Film Ctrs.: Sel. and Eval. Com., New Tech. Com.; Transp. Com. MT LA: Sch. Lib. Media Div. (Secy., 1979–80), Nom. Com. (1979); Baker and Taylor JMRT Schol. (Ch., 1979); Conf. Ch. (1981); Lib. Dev. Com. (1981). Univ. Tchrs. Un. **Honors:** MT Plains Media Leadership Symp., Del., 1976–80. **Pubns.:** *Instructional Materials Service Film Catalog* (1976–77, 1977–78, 1980–81) **Activities:** 1, 10; 15, 20, 32; 55, 56, 67 **Addr.:** Instructional Materials Service, University of Montana, Missoula, MT 59812.

Drinan, Helen Gannon (My. 14, 1947, Weymonth, MA) Mgr., Systems Plng. and Coord., Human Resrcs. Div., First Natl. Bank of Boston, 1981–; Dir. of Resrch., Bartholdi and Co., 1979–81; Mgr. of Info. Srvs., Charles Rivev Assoc., 1975–79. **Educ.:** Mt. Holyoke Coll., 1965–69, AB (Fr.); Simmons Coll., 1973–75, SM (LS); 1976–78, AM (Mgt.). **Orgs.:** ASIS. Assoc. Info. Mgrs. New Eng. OLUG: Strg. Com. (1977–78). MA Bd. of Lib. Comsn.: Adv. Com. on Autom. **Pubns.:** Ed. *Management Analysis of Marketing Plans for the Northeast Academic Science Information Center* (1978); "Financial Management of On-Line Information Services," *Online* (O., 1979). **Activities:** 12; 17, 24, 41; 51, 56, 59 **Addr.:** P.O. Box 165, Babson Park, MA 02157.

Driscoll, Sr. Loretto Marie (N. 11, 1916, Ludlow, KY) Dir., Bradford Coll., 1977–81; Ch., Eng. Dept., Thomas More Coll., 1972–77; Prof. (Eng.), Thomas More Coll., 1959–77. **Educ.:** Villa Madonna Coll. (now Thomas More Coll.), 1935–39, BA (Eng.); Catholic Univ., 1945–46, MLS; 1950, MA (Eng.); Fordham Univ., 1955–59, PhD (Eng.). Postdoctoral stds. at Oxford Univ.; Univ. Coll., Dublin; Univ. of Bristol (UK); and Yeats Intl. Sum. Sch. **Orgs.:** Haverhill Area Lib. Resrscs. Cnsvtm.: Pres. (1979–81). ALA. Lawrence Area CETA Manpower Adv. Plng. Bd.: Rev. Com. **Pubns.:** "Hans Kung: His Way and His Work," *Echoes* (Sum. 1980); "Bethlehem at Christmas, *Echoes* (Win., 1971); "A Shoreline Montserrat" (poem), *Sea Bk., Gloucester* (Sum., 1980); "Bradford" (poem), *Bradford Rev.* (Fall 1977). **Activities:** 1; 17, 31, 34; 55 **Addr.:** Madeleine Cooney Hemingway Library, Haverhill, MA 01830.

Drolet, Gaëtan (Mr. 20, 1947, Québec, PQ) Cnclr. a la Documtn., Univ. Laval, 1977–; SDI Libn., Bib. Natl. du Can., 1976–77. **Educ.:** Univ. Laval, 1968–72, BS (Soc. Sci.); Univ. de Montréal, 1974–76, MALS; Univ. Laval, 1978–80, Cert. (Geo.). **Orgs.:** ASTED: Com. de Coord. des Coms. (1978–). Can. Assn. of Info. Sci. **Pubns.:** *Les Bibliothèques Universitaires du Quèbec* (1979); "Searching the Social Sciences Literature Online," *Database* (1978); "Le Bibliothécaire à l'Université, *Argus* (1981). **Activities:** 1; 15, 31, 39; 92 **Addr.:** Bibliotheque Générale, Université Laval, Ste-Foy, PQ G1K 7P4 Canada.

Drolet, Leon L., Jr. (Ja. 25, 1942, Chicago, IL) Dir., Suburban AV Srv., 1972–; Coord., Ctrl. Serials Srv., N. Suburban Lib. Syst., 1970–72; Elem. Sch. Tchr., Skokie, IL, 1966–70. **Educ.:** John Carroll Univ., 1960–64, AB (Classics); Loyola Univ. (Chicago), 1968–71, MEd; Rosary Coll., 1970–71, MLS. **Orgs.:** ALA: PLA, AV Com. (Ch., 1976–80); ASCLA, AV Com. (Ch., 1974–76). IL LA: AV Com. (Ch., 1974–76). Educ. Film LA: Nom. Com. (1974). Film Lib. Info. Cncl.: Bd. (1974–77). **Pubns.:** "Software: The Key to a Successful Video Program," *Amer. Libs.* (D. 1979); "Metropolitan Library Service via 'the Cable' in the United States of America: A Thing of the Future," *UNESCO Bltn. for Lib.* (Mr., 1975); "Give Them the Real Thing," *Tchr. Outdoors* (Win., 1976); "Audiovisual Hardware," *How to Start an Audiovisual Collection* (1978); various other articles. **Activities:** 9; 17, 32; 67, 72 **Addr.:** Suburban Audio Visual Service, 920 Barnsdale Rd., LaGrange Park, IL 60525.

Drone, Jeanette Marie (N. 18, 1940, Evansville, IN) Msc. Libn., Memphis St. Univ., 1969–. **Educ.:** George Peabody Coll., 1958–62, BS (MSc.); Univ. of MI, 1964–65, MM (Msc.); George Peabody Coll., 1968–69, MLS. **Orgs.:** Msc. LA. Msc. LA: S. East. Chap. TN LA. Sigma Alpha Iota. Phi Kappa Lambda.

PROFESSIONAL ACTIVITIES: Institutions: 1. Acad. lib.; 2. Arch.; 3. Assn.; 4. Fed./Gvt. lib.; 5. Inst. lib.; 6. Mfr./Suppl.; 7. Milit. lib.; 8. Musm.; 9. Pub. lib.; 10. Sch. lib.; 11. Sch. of lib. sci.; 12. Spec. lib.; 13. State lib.; 14. (other). **Functions/Activities:** 15. Acq./Col. dev.; 16. Adult srvs.; 17. Admin.; 18. Apprais.; 19. Archit./Bldgs.; 20. Cat./Class.; 21. Chld. srvs.; 22. Circ.; 23. Cons./Pres.; 24. Consult.; 25. Cont. ed.; 26. Educ. lib. sci.; 27. Ext. srvs.; 28. Fund/Grants; 29. Gvt. pubs.; 30. Indx./Abs.; 31. Instr. lib. use; 32. Media srvs.; 33. Micro.; 34. Netwks./Coop.; 35. Persnl.; 36. PR; 37. Publshg.; 38. Recs. mgt.; 39. Ref. srvs.; 40. Repro.; 41. Resrch.; 42. Review.; 43. Secur.; 44. Serials; 45. Spec. col.; 46. Tech. srvs.; 47. Trustees/Bds.; 48. YA srvs.; 49. (other).

Honors: Beta Phi Mu. **Pubns.:** *Index to Opera, Operetta, and Musical Comedy Synopses in Collections and Periodicals* (1978); Ed., Bk. Review Column, *Pan Pipes* (Sigma Alpha Iota) (1979–); Ed. *Directory of Music Collections in the Southeast* (1978). **Activities:** 1; 15, 39; 95-Music. **Addr.:** 572 Patterson, Apt. D, Memphis, TN 38111.

Drowne, Lawrence A. (Brother) (Ja. 21, 1916, Malone, NY) Head Libn., St. Francis Coll., 1955–; Libn. and Tchr. of Fr., Eng., St. Anthony's HS, 1950–54; Tchr. of Fr., Rel., St. Francis Prep., 1947–54. **Educ.:** St. Francis Coll., 1943–47, BA (Fr.); St. John's Univ., Jamaica, NY, 1955–56, MLS. **Orgs.:** Cath. LA: Coll. and Univ. Sect. (Ch., 1974). NY LA. Acad. Libs. of Brooklyn: Pres. (1980–81). **Activities:** 1; 17 **Addr.:** 180 Remsen St., Brooklyn, NY 11201.

Drucker, Elsalyn Palmisano (Mr. 20, 1943, Corvallis, OR) Lib. Dir., Ann May Sch. of Nursing, Jersey Shore Med. Ctr., 1980–; Media Spec., Brookdale Cmnty. Coll., 1979–81; Resrch. Asst., NJ Hist. Comsn., 1980; Libn./Archvst., Monmouth Cnty. Hist. Assn., 1974–78; Resrc. Libn., Women's Ctr., Brookdale Cmnty. Coll., 1974–80; Per. Asst., Monmouth Coll., 1968–69; Asst. Libn. and Engin. Libn., Univ. of PA, 1965–67. **Educ.:** Univ. of DE, 1961–65, BA (Amer. Std.); Drexel Univ., 1965–67, MS (LS). **Orgs.:** ALA. Mid-Atl. Reg. Archvst. Org. NJ LA: Hist. and Bibl. Sect., Pres. (1980–81), VP (1979–80), Secy. (1977–78); *Chronicle* (Ed.). Monmouth Area Ref. Cncl.: Exec. Bd. (1979–81); Secy. (1979–80); Autom. Com. (1979–81). Various other orgs. Med. Hist. Socty. of NJ. NJ Hist. Socty. Amer. Std. Assn. Vict. Socty. in Amer.: Ctrl. NJ Chap., Treas., Mem. Ch. Various other orgs., ofcs. **Honors:** Beta Phi Mu, 1968. **Pubns.:** Various pamphlets (1975–78). **Activities:** 2, 12; 17, 31, 45; 55, 69, 80 **Addr.:** 446 Monmouth Rd., West Long Branch, NJ 07764.

Druesedow, John Edward, Jr. (My. 1, 1939, Cambridge, OH) Dir., Cnsvty. Lib., Oberlin Coll., 1974–; Msc. Libn., Miami Univ., 1969–74; Instr. (Msc.), Miami Univ., 1966–69. **Educ.:** Miami Univ., 1957–61, BM (Msc.); IN Univ., 1961–66, MM (Msclgy.); MA (LS); PhD (Msclgy.). **Orgs.:** Msc. LA.; Intl. Assn. of Msc. Libs.; ALA. Amer. Msclgy. Socty. **Honors:** Phi Beta Kappa. **Pubns.:** *Library Research Guide to Music* (1981); "Orrego-Salas, Juan" *Dictionary of Contemporary Music* (1974); "Aspectos teóricos modales de un libro español," *Rev. Msc. Chilena* (O./Dec., 1975); "Cuatro Piezas de Mario Davidovsky," *Rev. Msc. Chilena* (Ja./Mr., 1966); Reviews. **Activities:** 1, 12; 15, 17, 41; 55, 57 **Addr.:** 142 S. Cedar St., Oberlin, OH 44074.

Drum, Carol A. (F. 11, 1943, Catawba, NC) Chem. Libn., Univ. FL, 1972–; Lit. Chem., Lorillard Corp., 1970–71; Lit. Chem., Celanese Corp., 1969–70, Lab. Tech., Celanese Corp., 1967–69; Chemist Collins & Aikman Inc. 1965–67. **Educ.:** Lees-McRae Jr. Coll., 1961–63, AA (Lab. Tech.); TX Christ. Univ., 1963–65, BA (Chem.) N. TX St. Univ., 1971–72, MLS. **Orgs.:** SLA: FL Chap., Treas. (1977–79); Ed., *Bltn.* (1980–81); Chem. Div. (Ch.-Elect, 1979–80; Ch., 1980–81). FL LA. SELA. Amer. Chem. Socty.: Gainesville Subsect., Secy., Treas. (1979–80). Untd. Fac. of FL: Secy. (1978–79), Mem. Ch. (1979–80). **Pubns.:** *Guide to Academic Libraries in the United States* (1981). "On-Line Data Bases in Chemistry Literature Education," *Jnl. Chem. Educ.,* (S. 1979); "From Alchemy to Apollo: A Chemistry Odessey" in *Florida and the Bicentennial Years* (1976). **Activities:** 1; 15, 17, 39; 60 **Addr.:** Chemistry Library, 216 Leigh Hall, University of Florida, Gainesville, FL 32611.

Drum, Eunice Paige (N. 19, 1928, Godwin, NC) Chief, Tech. Srvs., NC State Lib., 1976–, Consult. to State Agency Libs., 1973–76, Prcs. Ctr. Libn., 1970–73; Head, Tech. Srvs., Durham (NC) Pub. Lib., 1966–70; Circ. Libn., Catawba Cnty. Lib. (NC), 1964–65. **Educ.:** Emmanuel Coll., 1946–48, AA; Lenoir Rhyne Coll., 1949–50, BA (Eng.); Univ. of NC, 1965–66, MS (LS); Various wkshps. **Orgs.:** ALA: RTSD (Ch., 1971–73), Plng. Com. (1977–81); Comrcl. Prcs. Srvs. Com. (1973–80), Tech. Srvs. Divs. of Association of Special Library Agencies, Comparative Study of the Administrative Processin State Agencies Committee (1977–80); Prcs. Ctrs. (Ch., 1975–76). SELA: *SOLINET* Qual. Cntrl. Com.; ALSC. NC LA Jr. Mem. RT (Ch., 1969–71). AAUW: Pubcty. (Ch., 1968–69). **Honors:** Beta Phi Mu. **Pubns.:** "Automation and Networking in N.C. Public Libraries" (1981); "Technical Services in the 1980's" (1980). **Activities:** 9, 13; 17, 24, 46; 92 **Addr.:** 3001 Sherry Dr., Raleigh, NC 27604.

Drummond, Donald R. (Ag. 26, 1933, Midland, TX) AV Coord., Deputy Dir., San Antonio Coll., 1967–; Ref. Libn., Bridgeport (CT) Pub. Lib., 1964–67. **Educ.:** Univ. of TX, 1951–56, BFA; 1961–64, MLS. **Orgs.:** ALA. TX LA: Arts RT (Ch., 1974–75); LCL Arrange Com. (Co-Ch., 1979). BEXAR LA: Pres. (1978–79). TX Assn. for Educ. Tech. AECT. Presby. Church: Deacon (1973–77); Elder (1977–). **Activities:** 1; 17, 32; 55, 67, 75 **Addr.:** San Antonio College, San Antonio, TX 78284.

Drummond, Herbert William, Jr. (Ja. 2, 1924, Big Lake, WA) Asst. Dir. for Pub. Srvs., CA State Univ., Sacramento, 1978–, Asst. Univ. Libn. for Pub. Srvs., 1963–78, Soc. Sci. and Bus. Admin. Ref. Libn., 1959–65, Gen. Ref. Libn., 1958–59, Asst. Ord. and Cat. Libn., 1955–58, Circ. Libn., 1954–56. **Educ.:** Univ. of WA, 1943–45, BA (Hist.); Univ. of CA, Berkeley, 1950–52, MA (Hist.), 1953–54, BLS. **Orgs.:** CA LA. ALA. MT Valley Lib. Syst.: Exec. Cncl. (1974–). Sacramento Bk. Col. Club. Congs. of Fac. Assns. **Honors:** Sigma Alpha Epsilon. **Pubns.:** Ed. com., *California Local History, a Bibliography and Union List of Library Holdings* (1970, 1976); "The Union List of Newspapers in California Libraries," *CA Libn.* (Jl. 1958). **Activities:** 1; 15, 39; 73 **Addr.:** P.O. Box 443, Sacramento, CA 95802.

Drury, Joyce Mildred (O. 13, 1918, Cherokee Cnty., IA) Coord., Jefferson Cnty. Sch. Dist. Lib., 1974, Jr. HS Libn., 1969–73; Sec. Eng. Tchr., IA Pub. Schs., 1940–44. **Educ.:** Buena Vista Coll., Elmhurst Coll., 1936–40, BA (Eng.); Univ. of OR, 1974, MLS various crs. **Orgs.:** ALA. OR Educ. Media Assn.: Educ. Com. (1979–80). AECT. AAUW. Confed. of OR Sch. Admins. **Honors:** Phi Delta Kappa. **Activities:** 10; 20, 24, 32; 63 **Addr.:** Jefferson County School District 509J, 1355 Buff St., Madras, OR 97741.

Druschel, Joselyn A. (Jl. 12, 1933, New Castle, PA) Asst. Dir. for Autom. and Tech. Support, WA State Univ. Libs., 1976–, Libn., 1967–; Catlgr., Cleveland Pub. Lib., 1966–67; Instr., Comms., Youngstown Univ., 1964–65; Tchr., Lang. Arts, New Castle Area Sch. Dist., 1963, 1959–61; Tchr., Lang. Arts, Fox Chapel Area Sch. Dist., 1962–63. **Educ.:** Westminster Coll., 1956–59, BA (Eng.); Case West. Rsv. Univ., 1965–66, MSLS. **Orgs.:** ALA. ASIS. Pac. NWLA. WALA. AAUP. AAUW. **Pubns.:** "Cost Analysis of an Automated and Manual Cataloging and Book Processing System," *Jnl. of Lib. Autom.* (Mr. 1981). **Activities:** 1; 17, 46; 56 **Addr.:** P.O. Box 2565 C. S., Pullman, WA 99163.

Dryden, Jean E. (Je. 11, 1949, Fergus, ON) Sr. Archvst., AV, Prov. Arch. of AB, 1976–; Staff Archvst., Mss, Pub. Arch. of Can., 1972–76. **Educ.:** Queen's Univ., 1966–71, BA (Hist., Eng.); Carleton Univ., 1971–72, MA (Can. Std.), various cont. educ. crs. **Orgs.:** Assn. Can. Archvsts.: Treas. (1977–79); Copyrt. Com. (1975–) Can. Hist. Assn. Can. Com. on Women's Hist.: Reg. Coord. for ON (1975–76); Co-Ch. (1979–81). **Pubns.:** *Some Sources for Women's History at the Provincial Archives of Alberta* (1980); "The Mackenzie King Papers: An Archival Odyssey," *Archivaria* (Sum. 1978); "Physical Care of Photographs," *AB Musms. Review* (D. 1977); "Revision of the Main Entry Cards at the Provincial Archives of Alberta," *Archivaria* (Win. 1977–78); "Proposed Revision of the Copyright Act," *ON Musm. Assn. Nsltr.* (Sum. 1977); various articles, sps., reviews (1975–). **Activities:** 2; 33, 39, 45; 61 **Addr.:** Provincial Archives of Alberta, 12845–102 Ave., Edmonton, AB T5N 0M6 Canada.

Duane, James E. (My. 17, 1943, Hartford, CT) Assoc. Prof., Univ. of UT, 1970–; Pres., Media Systs., Inc., 1975–; Asst. Prof., Univ. of UT, 1970–74, Instr., IN Univ., 1968–70. **Educ.:** Hartford State Tech. Coll., 1961–63, AS (Tech.); Univ. of CT, 1963–67, BS (Bus. Admin.); IN Univ., 1967–70, EdD (Instr. Tech.). **Orgs.:** UT Educ. Media Assn.: Pres. (1974–75); VP (1973–74); Secy. (1972–73); Jnl. Ed. (1974–79). AECT: AUI Ed. Bd. (1974–75). Intl. Individualized Inst. Congs.: Bd. of Dirs. (1974–76). Olympus Kiwanis. Various other orgs. **Honors:** Phi Delta Kappa; Outstan. Educ. Amer. Awd., 1975. **Pubns.:** *Media About Media* (1981); ed., *Instructional Media Library* (1981); "Parent Participation Television Workshops," *UEMA Jnl.* (Spr. 1980); "What Media Should be Used to Individualize Instruction," *Jnl. of Personalized Instr.* (Fall 1978); "Bibliographies and Books on Individualized Instruction," *One to One: Jnl. of the Intl. Congs. for Individualized Instr.* (My. 1978); various articles, edshps., slide-tapes (1969–). **Activities:** 14-Media dept.; 26, 31, 32 **Addr.:** Dept. of Educational Studies–307MBH, University of Utah, Salt Lake City, UT 84112.

Duarte, Ana G. (My. 27, 1921, Havana, Cuba) Exch. Libn., Univ. of CA, Los Angeles, 1964–; Biblgrphr., Inter-Amer. Bank, 1963; Libn., Woodward Sch. for Boys, 1962–63; Libn., Lyceum and Lawn Tennis Club, Habana, 1959–62. **Educ.:** Escuela Cubana de Bibtcrs., 1953–54, BS (LS); various crs. **Orgs.:** Univ. of CA (Los Angeles) Libns. Assn. SALALM: Com. on Cuban Bibl.; Com. on Gifts and Exchs. Assn. of Acad. Women, UCLA. Club Cubano de Culver City. **Pubns.:** "Acquisitions of Caribbean Material on Exchange" working Paper C-8, SALALM (Je. 1979); "Exchanges at UCLA," *UCLA Libn.* (Mr. 1979), various articles (1965–75). **Activities:** 1; 44 **Addr.:** University of California (LA) Library, 405 Hilgard Ave., Los Angeles, CA 90024.

Dubberly, Ronald A. (O. 25, 1942, Jacksonville, FL) City Libn., Seattle Pub. Lib., 1975–; Dir., Sioux City Pub. Lib., 1969–75; Admin. Asst. to Dir., Baltimore Cnty. Pub. Lib., 1967–69, Ref. Libn., Branch Libn., 1965–67. **Educ.:** Jacksonville Univ., 1960–64, BA (Hist.); FL State Univ., 1964–65, MA (LS). **Orgs.:** ALA: PLA, Past Pres. (1980–81), Pres. (1978–80), Pub. Lib. Prins. Task Frc. (Ch., 1980); ALTA, Bd. of Dirs. (1980–81). Urban Libs. Cncl.: Exec. Bd. (1981–83). Adv. Cncl. on Libs. Various other orgs. Seattle Cham. of Cmrce. Seattle Rotary Club. **Honors:** IA LA, Spec. Srv. Awd., 1975. **Pubns.:** "Options to Improve Delivery," *Lib. Jnl.* (Ja. 15, 1977); "Public Libraries Today! and Tomorrow?," *FL State Rpts.* (N.–D. 1978); ed. bd., *Jnl. of Lib. Admin.* (1979–82); "Public Library Association," *ALA Yrbk.* (1978); "From the PLA President," *Pub. Libs.* (Fall 1979); various articles. **Activities:** 9; 17, 28, 47; 63 **Addr.:** Seattle Public Library, 1000 4th Ave., Seattle, WA 98104.

Dubin, Eileen (N. 2, 1932, New York, NY) Assoc. Prof., Assoc. Head of Circ., North. IL Univ., 1981–, Actg. Asst. to Dir., 1979–, Head, ILL, 1977–81, Ref. and Docum. Libn., 1973–77, Acq. Libn., 1968–73; Ref. Libn., Soc. Sci. and Bus. Dept., Chicago Pub. Lib., 1959–65; Educ. Lib., Univ. of Chicago, 1956–57. **Educ.:** Hunter Coll., 1950–53, BA (Soclgy.); North. IL Univ., 1966–68, MLS. **Orgs.:** ALA: LIRT (Treas., 1980–81); Natl. Progs. Std. Task Frc. (Ch., 1979–82). IL LA: Exec. Dir.-at-lg. (1977–80); Liaison to ALA Copyrt. Subcom. (1978–); IL Assn. of Coll. and Resrch. Libs., Com. on Bibl. Instr. (1978–80); Awds. Com. (Ch., 1977–); various other coms. DeKalb Cnty. Hist. Socty.: Pres. (1976–78); Corres. Secy. (1972–74). AAUW. DeKalb Landmarks Comsn. **Honors:** North. IL Univ., Improvement for Undergrad. Educ., 1978, 1979; IL Hum. Cncl. Grant, 1980–81. **Pubns.:** *Basic Library Skills Workbook* (1979); "The New Copyright Law–A View from Academic Libraries in Illinois," *IL Libs.* (O. 1981); jt. auth., *Library Skills Test* (1980); jt. auth., "An In Depth Analysis of a Term Paper Clinic," *IL Libs.* (Mr. 1978); "The Library Skills Test–Helping to Set Benchworks," *11th Anl. Procs. of LOEX Conf. 1981* (1982). **Activities:** 1; 22, 31, 34; 61, 86 **Addr.:** Northern Illinois University Libraries, DeKalb, IL 60115.

Dubreuil, Lorraine (Jn. 4, 1946, Montreal, PQ) Map Cur., McGill Univ., 1973–; Asst. Map Cur., 1970–73. **Educ.:** McGill Univ., 1965–70, BSc (Geo.); Univ. of MD, 1977–78, MLS. **Orgs.:** Assn. of Can. Map Libs.: Pres. (1980–82); VP (1979–80); Treas. (1974–76); Conf. Ch. (1977). Natl. Union Cat. Com. (1977–). **Honors:** Beta Phi Mu. **Pubns.:** *Directory of Canadian Map Collections*, 4th ed. (1980); African Topographic Maps (1976). **Activities:** 1, 12; 15, 17, 39; 70 **Addr.:** Map & Air Photo Library, McGill University, 805 Sherbrooke St. W., Montreal, PQ H3A 2K6 Canada.

Dubrule, Sylvia A. (Ag. 2, 1936, London, Eng) Head Libn., Ext. Lib., Univ. of AB, 1975–; Asst. Libn., M.E.LA Zerte HS, 1974–75; Head Libn., Ross Shepherd HS, 1971–74; Tchr., Laurier Hts. Jr HS, 1965–70. **Educ.:** Univ. of AB, 1961–64, BEd; 1970–71, BLS; Brighton Trng. Coll. (UK), 1954–56, Tchr. Cert. **Orgs.:** Can. LA. LA AB: Treas. (1976–80); Conf. Treas. (1976–77, 1979–80). Univ. of AB Acad. Womens Assn.: Treas. (1979–80). Delta Kappa Gamma: Chap. Pres. (1976–77). Beta Phi Mu. AB Status of Women Action Com. **Pubns.:** "A Visit to Saskatchewan," *Letter of the LA AB* (Mr., 1978). **Activities:** 12, 14-Ext. Lib.; 17, 27, 36 **Addr.:** Extension Library, Rutherford South, University of Alberta, Edmonton, AB T6G 2J4 Canada.

Dubuc, Pierrette B. (O. 27, 1927, Lévis, PQ) Head, Info. Srvs., Hôsp. Ste.-Justine, 1975–; Asst. Dir., Ctr. d'Info. sur l'Enfants, 1968–74; Docmlst., Dept. of Child Psyt., Hôsp. Ste.-Justine, 1966–68. **Educ.:** Univ. Laval, 1947–48, Cert. (LS); Univ. of Montreal, Addl. Courses. **Orgs.:** Can. Socty. for Info. Sci. Can. Hlth. LA. ASTED: Hlth. Sect. (Ch., 1970–71); various ofcs. SLA: Montreal Chap., Consult. Com. (Ch., 1973–74). Les Amis du Ctr. Monchanin Inc.: Ch. (1978). Amitié Canada-Orient. **Pubns.:** "La Matériathèque de l'Hôpital Sainte-Justine," *ARGUS* (1980); *De l'Information sur les Inadaptés? Une réponse: C.I.E.A.I.* slide-tape (1973); *Conférence Publique sur les Sciences de l'Information au Canada* (1974); "Un Reseau de Materiathèques pour le Quebec," *Revue Can. des Sci. de l'Info.* (1977); various articles. **Activities:** 17, 24, 34; 63, 72, 80 **Addr.:** Centre d'information sur la Santé de l'Enfant/CISE, Hôpital Sainte-Justine, 3175 Chemin Sainte-Catherine, Montréal, PQ H3T 1C5 Canada.

Ducat, Sr. Peter-Claver (O. 21, 1919, Milwaukee, WI) Libn., St. Joseph Cath. Sch., 1973–; Assoc. Dir. of Dev., Rosary Coll., 1971–73; Dir. of Docum., Ctr. For Appld. Resrch, 1969–1971; Dir. Dominican Educ. Ctr., 1967–1969; Dir., Grad. Dept. LS, Rosary Coll., 1957; Ref. Libn., 1953–1955; Libn., Heelan HS, 1949–1953; Tchr., Visitation HS, 1947–1949. **Educ.:** Ursinus Coll., 1938–42, BA (Eng.); Rosary Coll., 1944–45, BLS; 1950–53, MALS; Cath. Univ. 1954, (Hist.); Columbia Univ., 1955–1957, DLS. **Orgs.:** ALA: Com. on Accred. (1967–73); Pres. Lib. Educ. Div. (1965–67); Ch., PR Com. (1967–70). Cath. LA: Adv. Bd. (1959–1969); Ch., Scholar. Com., (1967–70); Pres., IL Unit-1968–70). IL LA: Com. on Reg. Dev. (1969–71). WI LA: Ch., Lib. Educ. Com. (1968–1970). AAUW: Ch., Educ. Com., Tuskegee Branch. Church Women United. NAACP. **Activities:** 10, 11; 21, 25, 26; 63, 66, 89 **Addr.:** 1105 Montgomery Rd., Tuskegee Institute, AL 36088.

Duchac, Kenneth Farnham (Ja. 8, 1923, Antigo, WI) Dir., Brooklyn Pub. Lib., 1970–; Deputy Dir., 1969–70; Pub. Lib. Supvsr., MD Dept. of Educ., 1961–68; Pub. Lib. Consult., WI Lib Comsn., 1957–60. **Educ.:** Carroll Coll., 1940–43, AB (Eng.); Univ. of Chicago, 1947–49, BLS. **Orgs.:** ALA. NY LA. INTAMEL: Secy./Treas. (1974–77). **Activities:** 9, 13; 16, 17, 46 **Addr.:** Brooklyn Public Library, Grand Army Plz., Brooklyn, NY 11238.

Duchesne, Roderick Martin (S. 23, 1937, Ash Vale, Surrey, Eng.) Sr. Netwk. Ofcr., Natl. Lib. of Can., 1974–; Head, Gen. Systs. Ofc., Brit. Lib., 1972–74; Sr. Resrch. Fellow, Univ. of Bath, 1970–71. **Educ.:** Univ. of Cambridge, 1957–60, BA (Econ.); Brit. LA, 1966–67, Assoc. (LS). **Orgs.:** Can. Assn. Info. Sci.: Ottawa Chap., Pres. **Pubns.:** *Towards More Effective Nationwide Library and Information Networking in Canada* (1980);

Special Subjects/Services: 50. Adult educ.; 51. Advert./Mktg.; 52. Aerosp.; 53. Agric.; 54. Area std.; 55. Arts/Hum.; 56. Autom.; 57. Bibl./Prtg.; 58. Bio. sci.; 59. Bus./Fin.; 60. Chem.; 61. Copyrt.; 62. Documtn.; 63. Educ.; 64. Engin.; 65. Env.; 66. Eth. grps.; 67. Film; 68. Food/Nutr.; 69. Geneal.; 70. Geo.; 71. Geol.; 72. Handcpd.; 73. Hist.; 74. Int. frdm.; 75. Info. sci.; 76. Insr.; 77. Law; 78. Legis.; 79. Math./Comp. sci.; 80. Med.; 81. Metals; 82. Nat. resrcs.; 83. Newsp.; 84. Nuc. sci.; 85. Oral hist.; 86. Petr./Energy; 87. Pharm.; 88. Phys./Astr./Math.; 89. Readg.; 90. Relig.; 91. Sci./Tech.; 92. Soc. sci.; 93. Telecom.; 94. Transp.; 95. (other).

Who's Who in Library and Information Services

Overview of Computerized Library Networking in Canada (1979); "The Role of National Libraries in National and International Information Systems," *UNESCO Bltn. for Libs.* (Ja.–F. 1977). **Activities:** 4; 17, 34; 56 **Addr.:** National Library of Canada, 395 Wellington St., Ottawa, ON K1A 0N4 Canada.

Duckett, Kenneth W. (Je. 26, 1924, Colorado Springs, CO) Cur., Spec. Cols., Univ. of OR Lib., 1979–; Univ. Archvst., Cur., Spec. Col., South. IL Univ., 1965–79; Cur., Mss., OH Hist. Socty., 1959–65; Head Libn., OR Hist. Socty., 1956–59. **Educ.:** Univ. of Denver, 1946–50, BA (Soc. Sci.); Univ. of WI, 1950–56, MA (Hist.). **Orgs.:** Ms. Socty.: Bd. of Dirs. (1962–71); Exec. Secy. (1963–71). SAA: Com. on Mss. (Ch., 1969); Prog. Com. (Ch., 1980); Nom. Com. (Ch., 1981). **Honors:** SAA, Leland Awd., 1976; SAA, Fellow, 1977. **Pubns.:** *Modern Manuscripts: A Practical Manual for Their Management, Care and Use* (1976). **Activities:** 1; 23, 45; 55, 92 **Addr.:** Special Collections, University of Oregon Library, Eugene, OR 97403.

Duckworth, Paul Marten (F. 5, 1948, Long Beach CA) Ref. Dept. Mgr., Springfield-Greene Cnty. Lib., 1979–, Supvsr. of Branches, 1978–79, Asst. Ref. Libn., 1975–78; Asst. Ref. Libn., Drury Coll., 1971–75. **Educ.:** S.W. MO St. Univ., 1967–70, BA (Eng.); Univ. of South. CA, 1970–71, MSLS. **Orgs.:** ALA. MO LA: Lib. Educ. and Manpower Com. (1977–). Sierra Club. Ozark Socty.: Outings Ch. (1976–1977); Schoolcraft Chap. (Ch. (1978–79); Nsltr. Ed. (1980–). **Activities:** 1, 9; 15, 31, 39; 65 **Addr.:** Springfield-Greene County Library, MPO Box 737, Springfield, MO 65801.

Duda, Frederick (S. 26, 1939, Linden, NJ) Asst. Univ. Libn. for Persnl., Columbia Univ. Libs., 1973–; Asst. Dir. of Libs. for Admin. Srvs., 1969–73; Asst. to the Dir., Exec. Dev. Prog., Grad. Sch. of Pub. Admin., NY, Univ., 1964–66. **Educ.:** NY Univ., 1960–63, BS (Eng. Educ.), 1963–66, MA (Amer. Lit.). **Orgs.:** Archons of Colophon. NY Lib. Club. NY Tech. Srvs. Libns. ALA: Ad hoc Com. to Revise ALA Policy on Tenure in Libs. (1973–74); LAD/Staff Dev. Com. (1969–74); Nom. Com. (1971); Persnl. Ofcrs. of Large Resrch. and Acad. Libs., (Ch., 1971–72). **Pubns.:** Co-ed. and contrib., *Library Personnel Administration* (1981); Jt. ed., *Personnel Administration in Libraries,* (1980); "Columbia's Two-Track System" *Coll. and Resrch. Lib.* (My. 1980); Crossword puzzle books. **Activities:** 1; 17, 25, 26, 35, 37; 63, 78 **Addr.:** Box 35, Butler Library, Columbia University, 535 W. 114th St., New York, NY 10027.

Dudley, Durand Stowell (F. 28, 1926, Cleveland, OH) Sr. Law Libn., Marathon Oil Co., 1975–, Head, Corporate Lib., 1960–75; Ref. Staff Libn., Akron Pub. Lib., 1955–58; Adult Srvs. Libn., Marietta Coll. Lib., 1953–55. **Educ.:** Oberlin Coll., 1944–48, AB (Econ.); Case West. Rsv. Univ., 1949–50, MS (LS). **Orgs.:** SLA: Cleveland Chap., Treas. (1962–63), Pres. (1974–75); Petr. Div., Ch. (1969–70), Secy. (1966–67). AALL. OH Reg. Assn. of Law Libs.: Various coms. **Activities:** 12; 15, 17, 39; 77, 86 **Addr.:** Marathon Oil Company, Law Library, Rm. 854-M, 539 S. Main St., Findlay, OH 45840.

Dudley, Miriam Sue (D. 25, 1924, Minot, ND) Ref. Libn., Univ. of CA, Los Angeles, 1967–, Bibl. Checker, 1949–54. **Educ.:** Univ. of CA, Los Angeles, 1942–45, BA (Eng.); Univ. of South. CA, 1947–49, MSLS. **Orgs.:** CA Clearinghouse on Lib. Instr.: Strg. Com. (1973–). CA LA: Ref. and Info. Srvs. Chap., Ch. (1975). ALA: ACRL/Bibli. Instr. Sect. (Ch., 1978). Natl. Endowment for the Hum.: Bd. of Consult. (1978–). **Pubns.:** *Chicano Library Program* (1970); *Library Instruction Workbook* (1979); "The Self-Paced Library Skills Program at UCLA's Coll. Lib." *Educating the Library User* (1974); "Teaching Library Skills to College Students," *Advances in Librarianship* (Vol. 3, 1972). **Activities:** 1; 31, 39 **Addr.:** 425 Kelton Avenue, Los Angeles, CA 90024.

Dudley, Norman Houston (Je. 24, 1923, Los Angeles, CA) Asst. Univ. Libn. for Coll. Dev., Univ. of CA, Los Angeles, 1970–, Head, Acq. Dept., 1965–70, Ref. Libn., 1964–65. **Educ.:** Harvard Univ., 1945–48, AB (Eng.); Univ. of CA, Los Angeles, 1963–64, MLS. **Orgs.:** ALA: RTSD (Pres. 1977–78); Ch., Org. Com. (1978–80); Liaison to ALA Legis. Asm. (1975–77). CA LA: Cncl. (1976–78). **Pubns.:** "Organizational Models for Collection Development" *Collection Development in Libraries* (1980); Jt. ed., *Victorian England in its Novels (1840–1870)* (1969); "Collection Development: A Summary of Workshop Discussions," *Lib. Resrcs. and Tech. Srvs.* (Win. 1979); "Resources and Technical Services Division," *The ALA Yrbk.* (1978); "The Blanket Order," *Lib. Trends* (Ja. 1970). **Addr.:** 425 Kelton Ave., Los Angeles, CA 90024.

Due, Kay Mills (Ja. 12, 1947, Batesville, AR) Assoc. Dir., NY & NJ Reg. Med. Lib., 1981–, Asst. Libn., 1980-81; Head Libn., St. Jude Chld. Resrch. Hosp., 1972–80; Lib. Asst., Univ. of TN Med. Lib., 1971–72; HS Tchr., W. Memphis, AR, Sr. HS, 1969–71. **Educ.:** AR St. Univ., 1965–69, BSE (Eng.); George Peabody Coll. for Tchr., 1977–79, MLS; Med. LA Cert., 1979. **Orgs.:** Assn. of Memphis Area Hlth. Sci. Libs.: Pres. (1974–75); VP (1976); Treas. (1977, 1979); Memphis Lib. Cncl.: Mem. Com. (1980). TN Hlth. Sci. LA. Med. LA: S.E. Reg. Grp.; Hosp. Lib. Sect. **Pubns.:** Jt. auth., "Hospital library consortia: a vital component of hospital-wide education," *Jnl. of Cont. Educ. in Nursing* (1978); Jt. ed., *Association of Memphis Area Health Science Libraries Directory and Periodicals Holdings List,* 2d ed. (1978). **Activities:** 5; 15, 17, 39, 41; 58, 80, 91 **Addr.:** New York and New Jersey Regional Medical Library, The New York Academy of Medicine, 2 E. 103rd St., New York, NY 10029.

Dueltgen, Ronald Rex (S. 21, 1940, Salem, OR) Dir., Info. and Admin. Srvs., Henkel Corp., 1977–; Dir., Sci. Info., G. D. Searle & Co., 1972–76, Resrch. Chem., G. D. Searle & Co., 1967–72. **Educ.:** OR St. Univ., 1958–62, BA (Chem.); Univ. of MI, 1962–67, PhD (Organic Chem.). **Orgs.:** ASIS: SIG/BC (Ch., 1978); SIG-of the-Year Jury (1979–81); Ch., MN Chap. (1981–82). SLA. Assoc. Info. Mgrs. Amer. Chem. Socty. AAAS. Sigma Xi. **Pubns.:** Cmplr., *Proceedings of the ASIS Annual Meeting* (1979); many articles, speeches in chem. and sci. info. **Activities:** 12; 17, 39, 49-Information Management; 60, 91 **Addr.:** Henkel Corporation, 2010 East Hennepin Ave., Minneapolis, MN 55413.

Duffett, Gorman Louis (D. 10, 1938, Cleveland, OH) Asst. Dir., Pub. Srvs., Cleveland State Univ. Libs., 1978–; Coord. Libn., Cuyahoga Cmnty. Coll., 1976–78; Ref. Libn., 1968–76; Catlgr., 1966–68. **Educ.:** Marietta Coll., 1956–60, AB (Hist.); Stanford Univ., 1960–61, MA (Hist.); West. Resrv. Univ., 1965–66, MSLS; Univ. of Pittsburgh, 1972–76, PhD (LS). **Orgs.:** ALA: Comm. Com. (Ch., 1976–78); ACRL/Cmnty. and Jr. Coll. Sect. (Exec. Com., 1976–68). Acad. Lib. Assn. of OH: Pres. (1980–81). Sch. of LS, Univ. of Pittsburgh: Pres. (1979–80). Cuyahosa Cmnty. Coll., Fac. Sen.: VP (1969–70). Afro. Amer. Hist. and Cult. Org.: Lib. Adv. Catholic Interacial Cncl. Intercity Protestant Parrish: Adv. Com. **Activities:** 1, 11; 17, 31, 39; 66, 92 **Addr.:** Asst. Director for Public Services, Cleveland State University Libraries, Cleveland, OH 44115.

Duffy, Mary Anne Burns (S. 17, 1945, Philadelphia, PA) Docum. and Map Libn., W. Chester State Coll., 1975–, Ref. Libn., 1969–75; Corporate Libn., Atl.–Richfield Co., 1968–69. **Educ.:** Immaculata Coll., 1963–67, BA (Hist.); Drexel Univ., 1967–68, MLS. **Orgs.:** PA LA: GODORT (Ch., 1977–78), Plng. Com. (1978–81). ALA: GODORT; Map and Geo. RT. **Pubns.:** "Faculty Status for Librarians at West Chester State College," *Coll. & Resrch. Libs.* (Mr. 1975). **Activities:** 1; 29, 31; 70, 85 **Addr.:** Library, West Chester State College, West Chester, PA 19380.

Duffy, Michelle (D. 12, 1946, Ft. Monmouth, NJ) Lib. Liaison Ofcr., Amigos Bibl. Cncl., Inc., 1978–; Catlgr., Colby Coll., 1974–78; Head, Mono. Cat., FL State Univ., 1973–74, various positions, 1969–73. **Educ.:** Mt. Holyoke Coll., 1964–68, BA (Msc.); FL State Univ., 1968–69, MS (LS). **Orgs.:** ALA. **Honors:** Beta Phi Mu, 1969. **Pubns.:** *Self-Instructional Introduction to Searching the OCLC On-Line Union Catalog* (1980). **Activities:** 1, 14-Netwk.; 20, 25; 55, 62 **Addr.:** Suite 321, Amigos Bibliographic Council, Dallas, TX 75243.

Duggan, Carol Cook (My. 25, 1946, Conway, SC) Chief, Adult Srvs., Richland Cnty. Pub. Lib., 1971–; Asst. to the Dir., 1970–70. **Educ.:** Columbia Coll., 1964–68, AB (Eng./Sp.); Univ. of KY, 1969–70, MS (LS). **Orgs.:** ALA: SC State Mem. Ch. (1979–); Chap. Cnclr. (1981). SELA: Pubcty. Com. (1976–78). SC LA: Secy. (1976); Vice Ch.-Ch. Elect, Pub. Lib. Sect. (1980); Conv. Com., (1979); Ed. Com. (1977–78); other coms. **Honors:** Beta Phi Mu. **Activities:** 9; 16, 17, 36 **Addr.:** 2101 Woodmere Dr., Columbia, SC 29204.

Dugger, Linda Jane (D. 26, 1945, Batesville, AK) Serials Libn., Lamar Univ., 1972–; Catlgr., 1970–72. **Educ.:** Odessa Jr. Coll., 1963–65, AA; N. TX State Univ., 1965–67, BA (LS); 1969–70, MLS. **Orgs.:** TX LA: Serials Forum (Secy., 1975–76); Acq. RT (Secy., 1978–79). Jefferson Cnty. LA. ALA. Big Thicket Assn. **Honors:** Beta Phi Mu. **Activities:** 1; 44 **Addr.:** Lamar University Library, LU Station, Box 10021, Beaumont, TX 77710.

Dujsik, Gerald (D. 17, 1946, Chicago, IL) Lib. Mgr., Christ Hosp., 1976–; Hosp. Libn., S. Chicago Cmnty. Hosp., 1975–76; Asst. Libn., Instr. Mat. Ctr. Coord., St. Xavier Coll., 1970–75. **Educ.:** Univ. of IL, Chicago Circle, 1964–68, BA (Hist.); Rosary Coll., 1968–70, MALS; Med. LA Cert., 1977. **Orgs.:** Hlth. Sci. Libns. of IL: Pres. (1980–81). Chicago and South Cnsrtm.: Coord. (1976–). Cath. LA: North. IL Unit, Secy. (1974–76). Cath. Alumni Club of Chicago: Treas. (1975); Men's VP (1976). Southwest Archdiocesan Singles: Treas. (1979–80). **Honors:** Beta Phi Mu. **Activities:** 12; 17, 34, 39; 80 **Addr.:** Christ Hospital, Library, 4440 West 95th St., Oak Lawn, IL 60453.

Duke, Lucy L. (N. 21, 1921, Eatonton, GA) Head Libn., Sheppard W. Foster Lib., Sch. of Dentistry, Emory Univ., 1966–, Libn., Lib., Sch. of Bus. Admin., 1957–66; Catlgr. and Asst. Ref. Libn., Pub. Lib. Srv., GA Dept. of Educ., 1949–57; Head, Srvs. to the Pub., Calhoun Med. Lib., Emory Univ., 1945–48. **Educ.:** GA State Coll. for Women, 1938–41, BA (Eng., Fr.); Emory Univ., 1944–45, BA (LS), 1964–66, MLibn (LS), 1976–78, Dip. Adv. Std. (LS). **Orgs.:** SLA: S. Atl. Chap. (Treas., 1958–62). Med. LA. GA LA: Lib. Dev. Com. (1979–81); Spec. Libs. Sect., Ch. 1971–73), Secy.–Treas. (1969–71); Proj. Adv. Com. for Battelle Std. (1975). **Honors:** Beta Phi Mu, 1966. **Pubns.:** "Sheppard W. Foster," *Dictionary of Georgia Biography* (forthcoming); "Thomas P. Hinman," *Dictionary of GA Biography* (forthcoming). **Activities:** 1, 12; 15, 17, 45; 58, 80, 95-Dentistry. **Addr.:** Sheppard W. Foster Library, Emory University School of Dentistry, 1462 Clifton Rd., N.E., Atlanta, GA 30322.

Dumas, Paul (N. 24, 1915, Ste Aurélie, Beauce, PQ) Univ. Archvst., Univ. of Ottawa, 1967–; Asst. Chief, Maps Div., Pub. Arch. of Can., 1959–67, Asst. Chief, Info. Srv., 1939–59. **Educ.:** Coll. de Lévis, 1928–36, BA; Univ. Laval, 1936, BA; American Univ., 1952. **Orgs.:** SAA. Assn. of Can. Archvsts. Assn. des Archvsts. du PQ. Can. Hist. Assn. Assn. des Archvsts. de France. **Pubns.:** *Catalogue de Cartes des XVIle et XVIIle Siècles Relatives au Canada.* **Activities:** 2; 15, 17, 18; 63 **Addr.:** Archives, Université d'Ottawa, 57 Copernicus, pièce 415, Ottawa, ON K1N 6N5 Canada.

Dumbauld, Betty E. (Brooklyn, IA) Head Libn., J. Walter Thompson Co., 1968–; Libn., Needham Harper and Steers, 1955–68; Libn., Meredith Publshg. Co., 1946–55; Asst. and Circ. Libn., Denison Univ. **Educ.:** Simmons Coll. **Orgs.:** ALA. SLA: Publshg. Div., Ch.; Adv. and Mktg. Div., Ch.; IL Chap., Pres. **Honors:** Alpha Omicron Pi. **Activities:** 1, 12; 17, 22, 39; 51 **Addr.:** 1255 N. Sandburg Terr., Chicago, IL 60610.

Dumond, Jean E. (Ap. 13, 1920, Albion, MI) Dir., Curric. Resrcs. Ctr., Coll. of Educ., Univ. of GU, 1975–, Libn., 1972–75; Libn., Andersen Elem. Sch., Dept. of Educ., Gvt. of GU, 1971–72; Ref. Libn., RFK Lib., Univ. of GU, 1970–71. **Educ.:** Univ. of MI, 1941–43, AB (Span.); Univ. of HI, 1976–78, MLS. **Orgs.:** ALA. GU LA. **Honors:** Phi Delta Kappa. **Activities:** 12; 15, 17; 63 **Addr.:** P.O. Box 10242, Sinajana, GU 96910.

Dumont, Monique (Jl. 22, 1952, Montreal, PQ) Info. Broker, Infoges, 1980–; Docmlst./Libn., Gerard Parizeau Ltee/Gestas Inc., 1976–80. **Educ.:** Univ. de Montreal, 1971–74, BACC (Hist.), 1974–76, MBibl. **Orgs.:** ASTED: Spec. Libs. Com. (1980). Assn. Can. des Scis. de l'Info.: Montreal Chap., Exec. Com. (1979–80). SLA: East. Can. Chap., Exec. Com. (1979–80), Dir. Com. Ch. **Pubns.:** *Répertoire des outils documentaires dans les centres de documentation* (1980); "L'assurance responsabilité professionnelle: un Pressant besoin de repérage," *Revue can. des scis. de l'info.* (1979); bibls., *Assurances and Regards/Foresight* (1976–). **Activities:** 12; 24, 30, 39; 51, 59, 76 **Addr.:** Infoges, 417 St–Pierre, Suite 403, Montreal, PQ H2Y–2M4 Canada.

Dumont, Normand E. (F. 9, 1924, Haverhill, MA) Asst. Dir., Port Washington Pub. Lib. (NY), 1969–; Asst. Dir., Clinton, Essex, Franklin Lib. Syst. (NY), 1968–69; Admin. Ofcr., Assoc. Prof. (LS), Univ. of Hawaii, 1965–68; Admin. Asst., Branch Head, Brooklyn Pub. Lib., 1955–65; Asst. Libn., Albany Med. Sch., 1954–55. **Educ.:** Univ. of NH, 1944–48, BA (Econ.); SUNY Albany, 1954–55, MS (LS). **Orgs.:** ALA: various coms. NY Lib. Club. **Activities:** 9; 17 **Addr.:** 6 Belleview Ave., Port Washington, NY 11050.

Dumont, Paul E. (Ag. 21, 1943, Sanford, ME) Dir. of Tech. Srvs., Dallas Cnty. Cmnty. Coll., 1976–; Chief of Mtrl. Prcs., Dallas Pub. Lib., 1974–76; Systs. Libn./Ref. Libn., San Antonio Coll. Lib., 1969–74; Ref. Libn., St. Francis Coll. Lib., 1968–69. **Educ.:** St. Francis Coll., 1961–66, BA (Econ.); Cath. Univ. of Amer., 1966–68, MS (LS). **Orgs.:** ASIS: TX Chap. (Ch., 1977–78). ALA. TX LA. Amer. Recs. Mgt. Assn.: Hosplty. Ch. (1980–81). Natl. Micro. Assn. **Pubns.:** "The Cars System at San Antonio College Library," *LARC Nsltr.* (O. 1972); "A Library Management Information System," *ASIS Procs.* (1973). **Activities:** 1; 17, 33, 46; 56, 63, 75 **Addr.:** 5940 Meletio Ln., Dallas, TX 75230.

Du Mont, Rosemary Ruhig (Jl. 1, 1947, Chicago, IL) Asst. Prof., Sch. of LS, Univ. of KY, 1976–; Instr., Sch. Gen. Std., 1975–76; Asst. to the Dean, Ofc. of Resrch. Admn., Univ. of HI, 1969–72; Asst. to Asst. Dir. and Coord. of Pub. Srv., Syracuse Univ. Libs., 1967–68. **Educ.:** N. West. Univ., 1964–67, BS (Comm.); Syracuse Univ., 1967–69, MSLS; Univ. of Pittsburgh, 1972–75, PhD (LS). **Orgs.:** AALS. ALA: Subcom. on Lib. Srv. Rural Poor Appalachian Peoples. **Honors:** Beta Phi Mu. **Pubns.:** *Reform and Reaction: The Big City Public Library in American Life* (1977); "Issues for Teachers of Library Science," *Jnl. of Educ. for Libnshp.* (Sum. 1979); Jt. auth., "Organizational Effectiveness in Libraries: A Review and a Reassessment," *Advncs. in Libnshp.* (1979); "The New Librarian," *Jnl. of Acad. Libnshp.* (Jl. 1978); "The Management of Public Libraries: The Tension Between Problem Solving and Purpose," *S. East. Libn.* (Spr. 1978); various other pubns. **Activities:** 9; 26; 55, 95-Management User Needs. **Addr.:** College of Library Science, University of Kentucky, Lexington, KY 40506.

Dumouchel, Bernard J. J. (Ja. 14, 1949, Ottawa, ON) Head, Tech. Srvs., Algonquin Coll. Resrce. Ctr., 1973; Libn., CEGEP of Hull (Quebec), 1970–73. **Educ.:** Ottawa Univ., 1969–70, BLS; Univ. of West. ON, 1977–80, MLS. **Orgs.:** Can. LA. ASTED: Com. du droit d'auth. (1977–). **Pubns.:** *Choix et Acquisition des Documents au Québec; vol. II: Procédures* (1978). **Activities:** 1; 17, 46; 61 **Addr.:** Algonquin College Resource Centre, 1385 Woodroffe Ave., Nepean, ON K2G 1V8 Canada.

PROFESSIONAL ACTIVITIES: Institutions: 1. Acad. lib.; 2. Arch.; 3. Assn.; 4. Fed./Gvt. lib.; 5. Inst. lib.; 6. Mfr./Suppl.; 7. Milit. lib.; 8. Musm.; 9. Pub. lib.; 10. Sch. lib.; 11. Sch. of lib. sci.; 12. Spec. lib.; 13. State lib.; 14. (other). **Functions/Activities:** 15. Acq./Col. dev.; 16. Adult srvs.; 17. Admin.; 18. Apprais.; 19. Archit./Bldgs.; 20. Cat./Class.; 21. Chld. srvs.; 22. Circ.; 23. Cons./Pres.; 24. Consult.; 25. Cont. ed.; 26. Educ. lib. sci.; 27. Ext. srvs.; 28. Fund/Grants; 29. Gvt. pubs.; 30. Indx./Abs.; 31. Instr. lib. use; 32. Media srvs.; 33. Micro.; 34. Netwks./Coop.; 35. Persnl.; 36. PR; 37. Publshg.; 38. Recs. mgt.; 39. Ref. srvs.; 40. Repro.; 41. Resrch.; 42. Review.; 43. Secur.; 44. Serials; 45. Spec. col.; 46. Tech. srvs.; 47. Trustees/Bds.; 48. YA srvs.; 49. (other).

Duncan, Cynthia B. (Ap. 26, 1932, Madison, PA) Dean, Lib. Srvs., Old Dominion Univ., 1977–; Dir. of the Lib., Prof. of LS, Northeast LA Univ., 1973–76; Adj. Prof. of LS, IN State Univ., 1972; Assoc. Prof. of LS, Winthrop Coll., 1967–70; Head of Ref., Assoc. Prof. of LS, Mansfield State Coll., 1966–67; Libn., Instr., FL State Univ. Lib. Sch., (Summer, 1966–Fall, 1965); Tchr., Gateway Union Schs., 1953–64. **Educ.:** CA State Coll., PA, 1950–53, BS (Pub. Speaking & Eng.); Univ. of Pittsburgh, 1954–58, MLitt (Drama & Lit.); FL State Univ., 1964–65, MS (LS); IN Univ., 1970–73, PhD (LS). **Orgs.:** ALA: ACRL; RASD; ISAD; LAD. LA LA: Fed. Rel. Com. (1974–77). OCLC Users Cncl. (1979–81). VA LA: Coll. and Univ. Sect. (Ch., 1980). Other orgs. Governors Conf. on Libs. and Info. Srv.: Prog. Plng. Com. (1978–79). Tidewater Cnsrtm. for Cont. Higher Educ.: Dirs. Com. (Ch., 1977–). **Pubns.:** "Reference Statistics–A Plea for Originality," *The Purposes of Reference Measurement,* (1976). **Activities:** 1, 12; 17, 34, 39; 55, 63, 75 **Addr.:** Old Dominion University, Norfolk, VA 23508.

Duncan, Donna Noreen (S. 19, 1940, Montreal, PQ) Asst. Area Libn. Hum. and Soc. Sci., McGill Univ., 1979–, Head, Cat. Dept., 1973–79, Cat. Athrty. Libn., 1971–73, Asst. Head, Cat. Dept., 1969–71, Supvsr., Cat. Sect., 1967–69, Soc. Sci. and Hum. Cat., 1962–66. **Educ.:** Marianpolis Coll. 1957–61, BA (Eng.); McGill Univ., 1961–62, BLS, 1967–68, MLS. **Orgs.:** Can. LA: Stat. Com. (Ch., 1979–83); Can. Assn. Coll. and Univ. (Secy., 1976–77); Tech. Srvs. Sect. (Vice-Ch., 1971–72). PQ LA: VP (1981–82); Cnclr. (1977–78); Coll. Resrch. Libs. Sect. (Pres., 1976–77; VP, 1975–76; Secy. 1974–75). ALA. Can. Assn. Info. Sci. Many other orgs. and coms. **Activities:** 1; 20, 34, 46; 56, 75 **Addr.:** 6550 Sherbrooke St. W., Apt. 1214, Montreal, PQ H4B 1N6 Canada.

Duncan, Winifred E. (Ap. 12, 1932, Elmhurst, IL) Dir., Bur. of Libs., Chicago Pub. Schs., 1974–; Supvsr., Cat., 1969–74, Tchr.–Libn., 1965–69, HS Libn., 1961–65, Elem. Libn., 1954–61; Instr., LS, Natl. Coll. of Educ., 1976–77. **Educ.:** Chicago Tchrs. Coll., 1950–54, BE (Educ., LS), 1956–58, ME (Educ., LS); Rosary Coll., 1973–75, MALS. **Orgs.:** IL Assn. for Media in Educ.: Stans. Com. (1979–80). AECT. IL LA. ALA: AASL, Stans. and Prog. Implementation Com. (1980–82), Task Frc., Stans. Com. (1972–74), Lib. of Congs./Cat.–in–Pubns. Adv. Com. (Rep., 1978–), Cat. of Chld. Mtrls. Com. (Rep., 1978–), Pubns. Adv. Com. (1970); RTSD, various coms; ALSC. Various other orgs., ofcs. Assn. for Supvsn. and Curric. Dev. IL Assn. for Supvsn. and Curric. Dev. **Honors:** Delta Kappa Gamma Socty. Phi Delta Kappa. **Pubns.:** "School Library Collections," *ALA World Encyclopedia of Libraries and Information Services* (1980); "AACR II: Implications for School Libraries," *IN Media Jnl.* (Spr. 1979); "LC's National Standard for Cataloging Children's Materials," *Sch. Lib. Jnl.* (Ja. 1976). **Activities:** 10, 14-Pub. sch. syst.; 17; 63, 89 **Addr.:** Bureau of Libraries, Chicago Public Schools, 228 N. LaSalle St., Chicago, IL 60601.

Dunham, Linda Baxter (My. 12, 1948, Hartshorne, OK) Dir., Curric. Media Ctr., Oral Roberts Univ., 1971–, Lrng. Resrcs. Libn., Ref. Libn. **Educ.:** Oral Roberts Univ., 1966–70, BA (Educ.); Univ. of MI, 1970–71, MA (LS). **Orgs.:** OK LA: Mem. Com. (1979–81). OK Assn. Educs. in Comms. and Tech. ALA. Civitan Intl.: Tulsa Div. **Activities:** 1, 10; 15, 17, 20; 63 **Addr.:** Oral Roberts University, 7777 S. Lewis, Tulsa, OK 74171.

Duniway, David C. (Jl. 9, 1912, Missoula, MT) Histn., Secy., Frnds. of Deepwood Missn. Mill Musm., Salem Art Assn., 1976–, Exec. Dir., Missn. Mill Musm. (Salem, OR), 1972–76; State Archvst., OR State Lib., 1946–72; various positions, Natl. Arch., 1937–45; Adjunct Prof., West. WA. State, 1973; Adjunct Prof., Univ. of OR, 1969–70. **Educ.:** Carleton Coll., 1933, AB (Hist.); Univ. of CA, Berkely, 1933–34, MA (Hist.), 1936–37, Lib. Cert. **Orgs.:** SAA: Cncl. (1955–59); Ed. Bd. (1959–66); Com. St. Arch. (1950–54); Adv. Com. Study St. Arch. (1962–63); Com. Intergvt. Rel. (Ch., 1967–72). Amer. Assn. St. Local Hist.: Secy./ Treas. (1941–45); VP (1945–48). Marion Cnty. Hist. Socty.: Pres. (1950, 1962–64). Victorian Socty.: OR Chap., Pres. (1978–80). OR Hist. Socty.: Hon. Bd. (1979). OR State Hist. Properties Comsn. (1979–). **Honors:** SAA, Flw., 1959. **Pubns.:** "Dr. Luke A. Port, builder of Deepwood," *Marion Cnty. Hist.* (1969–71); "How Does One Collect Archives?", *Indian Arch.* (1967–68); "Where do Public Records Belong?" *Amer. Archvst.* (Ja. 1968); "On The Use of Archives by Historians," *Pacific Hist. Review* (v. 28); many other pubns. **Activities:** 2, 8; 41, 49-Govt. records; 95-Local History Oregon. **Addr.:** 1365 John St. S., Salem, OR 97302.

Dunkly, James Warren (Ag. 1, 1942, Alexandria, LA) Libn., Nashotah House, 1975–; Managing Ed., New Testament Abs., 1972–75; Asst. Ed., 1971–72; Tutor, Episcopal Dvnty. Sch., 1970–71. **Educ.:** TX Christ. Univ., 1959–63, BA (Eng.); Vanderbilt Univ., 1966–69, MA (Rel.); Oxford Univ., 1963–64, Dip. (Theo.); Brite Dvnty. Sch., 1964–1966, (Theo.). **Orgs.:** ATLA: Pubn. Com. (1977–). Chicago Area Theo. Lib. Assn. Lib. Cncl. of Metro. Milwaukee. Socty. of Biblical Lit. Cath. Biblical Assn. Chicago Socty. for Biblical Resrch. **Pubns.:** Asst. Ed., *Anglican Theol. Review* (1979–). **Activities:** 1; 15, 17, 39; 90 **Addr.:** Nashotah House, Nashotah, WI 53058.

Dunlap, Alice E. (My. 10, 1915, New Plymouth, ID) Head Libn., Caldwell Pub. Lib., 1961–; Catlgr., Strahorn Lib., Coll. of ID, 1956–60; Chld. Libn., LA of Portland, OR, 1938–41. **Educ.:** Coll. of ID, 1932–37, BA (Eng.); Univ. of WA, 1937–38, BS (LS). **Orgs.:** ID LA: Pres. (1964–65). ALA. Frnds. of Caldwell Pub. Lib., Inc. Presby. Church. Daughters of the Amer. Revolution. Zonta Intl. of Caldwell. PEO. Various other orgs. **Activities:** 1, 9; 17, 20, 21 **Addr.:** Caldwell Public Library, 1010 Dearborn, Caldwell, ID 83605.

Dunlap, Barbara Jane (D. 23, 1939, Brooklyn, NY) Chief, Arch. and Spec. Col., Col. Dev. Coord., City Coll. of NY, 1978–; Ref. Libn., 1971–76; Biblgphr. in Acq., Hum. Ref. Libn., 1964–71. **Educ.:** Queens Coll., 1957–60, BA (Eng.); Hunter Coll., 1961–63, MA (Eng.); Columbia Univ., 1963–64, MS in LS; City Univ. Grad. Ctr., 1973–76 (Eng.). **Orgs.:** SAA. Amer. Inst. for Cons.: Prsrvn. Com. Pvt. Libs. Assn. William Morris Socty. Victorian Socty. in Amer. Mod. Lang. Assn. **Honors:** Phi Beta Kappa, 1959. **Activities:** 1, 2; 15, 23 **Addr.:** 420 Riverside Dr. (12G), New York, NY 10025.

Dunlap, Connie (S. 9, 1924, Lansing, MI) Univ. Libn., Duke Univ., 1975–80; Deputy Assoc. Dir., Univ. of MI, 1972–75, Head, Grad. Lib., 1967–75, Head, Acq. Dept., 1964–67, Head, Order Dept., 1961–64, Assoc. Circ. Libn., 1954–61, Sr. Circ. Libn., 1952–54. **Educ.:** Univ. of MI, 1942–46, AB (Geol. and Geog.), 1948–52, AMLS; Univ. of Paris, Sum. 1967, (Fr.). **Orgs.:** ARL: Pres. (1979–80). ALA: Exec. Bd. (1978–); Cncl. (1974–); ACRL, Pres. (1976–79), Bd. of Dir. (1975–78); RTSD, Pres. (1972–73), Organ. Com. (1973–74). Many other orgs. and ofcs. Natl. Hum. Ctr.: Tech. Adv. (1976–). NC Gvrs. Pre White Hse. Conf.: Citizens Adv. Com. (1977–80). Various other Ofcs., and Visit. Coms. **Honors:** Univ. of MI, School of LS, Disting. Alum. Awd., 1977. **Pubns.:** "Challenge of the Future," *Southeast. Libn.* (Spr., 1979); "Resource Sharing," *Library Resource Sharing* (1979); "Organizational Patterns in Academic Libraries, 1876–1976," *Coll. & Resrch. Libs.* (S., 1976); "Library Services to the graduate community," *Coll. & Resrch Libs* (My. 1976); various other pubns. **Activities:** 1; 17 **Addr.:** 1570 Westfield, Ann Arbor, MI 48103.

Dunlap, Leslie W. (Ag. 3, 1911, Portland, OR) Dean of Lib. Admn., Univ. of IA, 1958–; Assoc. Dir., Prof., Univ. of IL, 1951–58; Libn., Univ. of British Columbia, 1949–51; Asst. Chief, Mss. Div., Lib. of Cong., 1945–49. **Educ.:** Univ. of OR, 1929–33, BA (Eng.); Columbia Univ., 1935–41, AM (Eng.); BS (LS); PhD (Hist.). **Orgs.:** ALA: Bibl. Com. (1947–49). IA LA: Pres. (1969). NCLIS: Mem. (1971–75). N. Ctrl. Assn.: Consult. and examiner (1965–). U.S. Capitol Hist. Socty.: Trustee (1968–). Mss. Socty.: Dir. (1976–80). **Honors:** Phi Beta Kappa, 1933; N. West. Coll., Disting. Srv. Cit. 1964. **Pubns.:** Ed., *"Your Affectionate Husband, J. F. Culver"* (1978); Ed., *The Publication of American Historical Manuscripts* (1976); *American Historical Societies, 1790–1860* (1944). **Activities:** 1; 15, 17, 45; 55, 57, 85 **Addr.:** University of Iowa Libraries, Iowa City, IA 52242.

Dunn, Charlene Quinn (Ap. 28, 1948, Pensacola, FL) Mgr., N.E. Reg. Coastal Info. Ctr., Univ. of RI, 1977–; Resrc. Dev. Spec., Career Couns. Srv./State Dept. of Educ., RI, 1976–77; Biblgphr., Law of the Sea Inst., Univ. of RI, 1974–75. **Educ.:** Univ. of RI, 1972, BA (Phil.); 1973–74, MLS: 1974–75, MMA (Marine Affairs). **Orgs.:** New Eng. Lib. Bd.: Panel of Couns. (1979–1982). SLA. Intl. Assn. of Marine sci.; Libs. and Info. Ctrs. Assn. of Info. Mgrs. Marine Tech. Socty. Coastal Socty. RI Aquaculture Assn. **Pubns.:** Jt. auth., *Marine Policy, Law and Economics* (1975); Jt. auth. *Law of the Sea: A Bibliography of the Periodical Literature of the 70's* (1975); Jt. auth., *RI Marine Bibliography* (1978); "Regional Coastal Information Centers in New England", *Sea Grant '70's,* (1978). **Activities:** 12, 14; 17, 28, 34; 65, 82, 86 **Addr.:** Coastal Information, URI-MAS, Bay Campus, Narragansett, RI 02882.

Dunn, Christina Jordan (Mr. 30, 1946, Richmond, VA) Asst. Supvsr., Sch. Libs., VA Dept. of Educ., 1974–; Branch Head, Cnty. of Henrico Pub. Libs., 1972–73, Head of Ref. Srvs., 1971–72, Ref. Libn., 1970–71; Sch. Libn., Stafford Cnty. Pub. Schs., 1969–70. **Educ.:** Westhampton Coll., Univ. of Richmond, 1964–68, BA (Eng.); Univ. of NC, 1968–70, MLS; Cath. Univ., 1980–81, Cert. (LS). **Orgs.:** ALA: AASL, Early Childhood Educ. Com. (1976–79). VA Educ. Media Assn.: Secy. (1979–81). SELA: PR Com. (1978–80). VA LA: PR Com. (1978–79); Lib. Dev. Com. (1978–80); Coop. Progs. Com. (1980–82). Natl. Assn. of State Educ. Media Profs. AECT. **Pubns.:** "Passages: Library Instruction for Lifelong Enrichment," *School Library Response* (1979); state ed. and contrib., *The Southeast: Readings for Young People* (1980). **Activities:** 9, 10; 17, 21, 39 **Addr.:** 155 Pemberton Rd., Richmond, VA 23233.

Dunn, Donald J. (N. 9, 1945, Tyler, TX) Law Libn., Prof., West. New Eng. Coll. Sch. of Law Lib., 1973–; Libn., Criminal Justice Ref. Lib., Univ. of TX, 1972–73, Asst. to the Law Libn., 1969–72. **Educ.:** Univ. of TX, 1966–69, BA (Hist.), 1971–72, MLS. **Orgs.:** ACRL: Law and Pol. Sci. Sect., Ch. (1981–82). AALL: Vice-Ch. (1976–77); Law Lib. Srv. to Prisoners (1973–77). Law Libns. of New Eng.: Exec. Cncl. (1976–). MA State Adv. Cncl. on Libs. SLA. Various other orgs. Amer. Red Cross: Pioneer Valley Chap. (Bd. of Dir., 1979–). **Pubns.:** Jt. auth., *Five Year Index to Periodical Articles Related to Law 1969–73* (1974); Jt. auth., *Impact of the Environmental Sciences and the New Biology on Law Libraries* (1973); Jt. auth., , "The Law Library's Institutional Response to the *Pro Se* Patron: a Post-Faretta Review," *West. New Eng. Law Rev.* (Ap. 1979); "The Criminal Justice Reference Library: a Collection of Informally Published Materials Related to Criminal Law," *Amer. Jnl. of Criminal Law* (O. 1972). **Activities:** 1, 12; 15, 17, 35; 65, 77, 78 **Addr.:** Western New England College, School of Law Library, 1215 Wilbraham Rd., Springfield, MA 01119.

Dunn, Doris (R.F.) (Jl. 9, 1927, New York, NY) Asst. Prof., (LS), Univ. of South. CA, 1978–, Resrch. Assoc., 1977–78; Info. Anal., Brain Info. Srv., Univ. of Los Angeles, 1970–77; Resrch. Assoc., Univ. South. CA, 1963–66, Resrch. Flw., Sloan Kettering Inst. for Cancer Resrch., 1956–57; Resrch. Assoc., Michael Reese Hosp. Resrch. Inst., 1955–56. **Educ.:** Brooklyn Coll., 1944–47, BS (Chem.); Univ. Rochester, 1950–52, MS (Biochem.); Temple Univ., 1952–56, PhD (Biochem.); Univ. CA, Los Angeles, 1969–70, MLS. **Orgs.:** Med. LA. Med. Lib. Grp., S. CA and AZ. ASIS. SLA. AASL. AAAS. **Pubns.:** Various articles in bio. and chem. jnls. **Activities:** 11, 12; 26, 30, 49-Specialized Information Services, Computer Data Base Searching; 58, 75, 80 **Addr.:** School of Library Science, University of Southern California, Los Angeles, CA 90007.

Dunn, Willie Mae (Mr. 10, 1925, Holden, LA) Dir., Natchez Campus Lib., Copiah Lincoln Jr. Coll., 1973–; Libn., Adams Cnty. Christ. Sch., 1971–73; Libn., Morgantown Jr. HS, 1965–71; Libn., Braden Elem. Sch., 1962–65. **Educ.:** Southeastern LA Univ., 1941–44, BA (Hist.); LA State Univ., 1946–47, BSLS. **Orgs.:** MS LA. ALA. **Addr.:** 125 Hensley Dr., Natchez, MS 39120.

Dunnigan, Mary C. (My. 7, 1922, Shauvers Mill, VA) Libn., Fiske Kimball Fine Arts Lib., Univ. of VA, 1973–; Libn., Coll. of Archit., VA Polytech. Inst., 1967–73; Libn., Inst. of Textile Tech., 1965–67; Dir., Lib. & Info. Srvs., US Brewers Assn., 1948–65; Libn., Rubber Mfrs. Assn., 1947–48. **Educ.:** Mary Washington Coll., 1939–42, BA (Soc. Std.); Columbia Univ., 1945–47, BLS. **Orgs.:** SLA: NY Chap. (Pres., 1953–54); VA Chap. (Pres., 1971–72); Ch., Musm., Arts, & Hum. Div., (1973–74). ARLIS/NA. NY Hist. Socty. Socty. of Archit. Histns. Socty. of Archit. Libns.: Ch., Com. on Org. & Structure (1979). **Pubns.:** Consult., *Webster's 3rd New International Dictionary* (1966). **Activities:** 1; 17, 23; 55, 67, 95-Planning. **Addr.:** Fiske Kimball Fine Arts Library, University of Virginia, Bayly Dr., Charlottesville, VA 22901.

Dupont, A. Jerome (F. 19, 1939, Marquette, MI) Assoc. Prof. and Libn., Univ. of HI Sch. of Law Lib., 1973–; Pres., Law Lib. Micro. Cnsrtm., 1977–; Asst. Dir., Univ. of MI Law Lib., 1967–73. **Educ.:** Capuchin Semy. of St. Mary, 1957–61, BA (Phil.); Univ. of MI, 1964–67, JD, 1969–70, MALS; Univ. of HI, 1978–80, MBA. **Orgs.:** AALL: Stats. Com. (1968–70). Ethics Com. (Ch., 1974–76, 1979–81). **Activities:** 1, 6; 17, 37; 77 **Addr.:** Law Library Microform Consortium, P.O. Box 11033, 1400 Lower Campus Rd., Honolulu, HI 96828.

Dupuis, Marcel (D. 23, 1934, PQ) Head, Educ. Lib., Univ. du PQ, Montréal, 1976–, Head, Law Lib., 1975–76, Ref. Libn., Soc. Sci., 1971–74, Catlgr., Libn., 1970–71. **Educ.:** Univ. de Montréal, 1952–56, BA (Arts, Econ.), 1959–61, BA (Phil.), 1964–68, MA (Rel. Stds.), 1969–70, BA (libnshp.). **Orgs.:** ASTED: Pubns. Com. (Secy., 1972–). Corp. des Bibtcrs. Prof. du PQ: Terminology Com. (1979–); By-Laws Com. (1978–79). Couple and Famille: Bks. Review (Ed., 1974–). Amateurs du Chauffage au bois: Exec. Com. (Secy., 1979–). **Pubns.:** Contrib., *Current Words in Library Science* (1979); *Bibliographie Annotée sur l'Éducation Sexuelle des Enfants* (1973); reviews. **Activities:** 1; 17, 35, 39; 50, 63 **Addr.:** 158 Jacques Lamoureux, Boucherville, PQ J4B 4R6 Canada.

Dupuis, Noël A. (D. 25, 1947, Moncton, NB) Archvst., McGill Univ., 1978–; Archvst., Prov. Arch. of NB, 1975–78. **Educ.:** Univ. de Moncton, 1967–71, BA (Hist.), 1972–74, MA (Hist.); Case West. Rsrv. Univ., 1979, Cert. (Arch.). **Orgs.:** Assn. des Archvsts. du PQ: Bk. Review Com. (1979). Assn. of Can. Archvsts. **Pubns.:** *Archives Nationales de France, Index des Noms Propres avec un Choix de Thèmes* (1975); "Les Sources d'Archives en Histoire Acadienne aux Archives Prouinciales du Nouveau-Brunswick," *Les Cahiers* (1979); various articles. **Activities:** 2; 15, 38, 39 **Addr.:** McGill University Archives, 3459, McTavish, Montréal, PQ H3A 1Y1 Canada.

Dupuis, Onil (Ja. 2, 1950, Arthabaska, PQ) Resrch. Ofcr., Conf. of Rectors and Prins. of PQ Univs., 1975–; Dir. of Info., Socty. Cogito Ltée, 1973–75. **Educ.:** Univ. de Montréal, 1969–71, BLS, 1971–72, MLS. **Orgs.:** IFLA: Gen. Conf. Org. Com. (Ch., 1979). ASTED: Com. de Promo. (Pres., 1973–74); Com. des PR (Pres., 1974–75). Assn. Can. des Scis. de l'Info.: *Revue Can. des Scis. de l'Info.* Dir. (1980); Pres. (1977–78); Com. d'Org. de la Conf. Anl. (1977–78); Com. des Statuts et Reglements (1976–77); various coms., ofcs. SLA: Various coms., ofcs. Various other orgs. and ofcs. Bib. Natl. du Can.: Com. sur les Réseaux des Bibls. et de Docum. (1981–). **Pubns.:** "3lième Conference Annuelle de la Canadian Library Association," *Nouvelles de l'AST-*

Special Subjects/Services: 50. Adult educ.; 51. Advert./Mktg.; 52. Aerosp.; 53. Agric.; 54. Area std.; 55. Arts/Hum.; 56. Autom.; 57. Bibl./Prtg.; 58. Bio. sci.; 59. Bus./Fin.; 60. Chem.; 61. Copyrt.; 62. Documtn.; 63. Educ.; 64. Engin.; 65. Env.; 66. Eth. grps.; 67. Film; 68. Food/Nutr.; 69. Geneal.; 70. Geo.; 71. Geol.; 72. Handcpd.; 73. Hist.; 74. Int. frdm.; 75. Info. sci.; 76. Insr.; 77. Law; 78. Legis.; 79. Math./Comp. sci.; 80. Med.; 81. Metals; 82. Nat. resrcs.; 83. Newsp.; 84. Nuc. sci.; 85. Oral hist.; 86. Petr./Energy; 87. Pharm.; 88. Phys./Astr./Math.; 89. Readg.; 90. Relig.; 91. Sci./Tech.; 92. Soc. sci.; 93. Telecom.; 94. Transp.; 95. (other).

ED (Ag. 1976); jt. auth., "Le prêt entre bibliothèques," *Docmtn. et Bibs.* (Mr. 1979); "Du désir à la realité, *Argus* (Mr.–Ap. 1977); "Dix ans de coopération entre les bibliothèques universitaires du Québec," *Docmtn. et Bibs.* (S. 1977); "La dissolution du consortium télécat/Unicat," *Nouvelles de l'Asted* (Mr.–Je. 1980); various articles, conf. papers (1973–). **Activities:** 1, 13; 34, 36, 49-Coord.; 56, 93 **Addr.:** CREPUQ, 2 Complexe Desjardins, Suite 1817, Case postale 124, Succursale Place Desjardins, Montréal, PQ H5B 1B3 Canada.

Durance, Cynthia J. (O. 3, 1940, Sarnia, ON) Dir., Natl. Lib. Network Proj., Natl. Lib. of Can., 1979–; Dir., Cat. Branch, 1975–79; Asst. Libn., Plng., Univ. of Waterloo Lib., 1973–74; Head, Serials Dept., 1972–73; Head, Serials Dept., Carleton Univ. Lib., 1970–1972; Serials Catlgr., 1969–1970; Ref. Libn., Sir George Williams Univ. Lib., 1967–1969. **Educ.:** Univ. of Toronto, 1959–1962, BA (Eng.); McGill Univ., 1965–67, MLS. **Orgs.:** IF LA: Working Grp. on the Intl. Stan. Bibl. Descr. for Component Parts, (1979–); Stdg. Com. of the Sect. on Serial Pubns. (1976–). Intl. Serials Data Syst.: Rapporteur-Gén., Governing Bd. (1978–1980); Can. del., Gen. Assm. (1978–). ALA: Ch., Cat. Class. Sect. Nom. Com. (1978). Assn. of Bib. Agencies of Britain, Australia, Canada and the US: Natl. Lib. of Can. rep., (1976–). Other orgs. and coms. **Pubns.:** "Recommendations of the Canadian Task Group on Cataloguing Standards: final report on implementation," *Can. Lib. Jnl.,* (Ap. 1980); "International Serials Cataloguing," *Serials Libn.* (Spr. 1979); "Subject Authority Control in the Canadian Context," *Can. Lib. Jnl.* (O. 1976); Other articles. **Activities:** 4; 20, 34, 44; 57, 75, 93 **Addr.:** National Library Network Project, National Library of Canada, 395 Wellington St., Ottawa, ON K1A 0N4 Canada.

Durand, Gilles (Ja. 20, 1943, L'Ascension, PQ) Archvst. Rég., Arch. Natl. du PQ, Ctr. Reg. de L'Estrie, 1978–; Archvst, Arch. Natl. du PQ, Ctr. Reg. de Montreal, 1973–78. **Educ.:** Univ. de Montréal, 1965–68, Licn. Es Lettres (Hist.), 1968–69, MA (Hist.); various cont. educ. crs., 1974–77. **Orgs.:** Assn. des Archvsts. du PQ. Assn. Can. Archvsts. **Pubns.:** "L'Histoire Économique du Bas-Canada," *Revue d'Hist. de L'Amér. Française* (D. 1970); "Sources Manuscrites pour l'Histoire de la Vallée du Haut-Saguenay et du Lac Saint-Jean," *Protée* (Ap. 1972); "Histoire Urbaine: Sources," *Arch.* (1973); "Le VIII Congrès du Conseil International des Archives (Washington, D.C. - du 27 septembre au Ier octobre 1976)," *Arch.* (Je. 1977); jt. auth., "Bibliographie d'histoire Archivistique," (1975); various articles, sps., reviews (1969–80). **Activities:** 2, 4; 49-Archvst. reg. **Addr.:** Archives Nationales du Québec, Centre Regional de L'Estrie, 740 Rue Galt Ovest, Rez-de-Chaussée, Sherbrooke, PQ J1H 1Z3 Canada.

Durand, Marielle (Ap. 19, 1933, Montréal, PQ) Dir. de la Bib. EPC, Univ. de Montréal, 1977–, Dir., Adj. Bib. EPC, 1971–77, Chef de Bib. Educ., 1968–71, Bibtcr. 1966–68; Bibtcr., Ville de Montréal, 1957–66; Prof., CECM, 1952–53. **Educ.:** Univ. de Montréal, 1968–75, PhD (Educ.), 1960–65, BA, MA (Fr.), 1953–54, Dipl. (Bibl.); Inst. Péd. de Montréal, 1950–52, Dipl. Sup. Ens. (Ens.). **Orgs.:** Corp. des Bibtcrs. Prof. du PQ. ASTED: Prés. (1974–75). Comm. Jeunesse. Assn. des Cadres de l'Univ. de Montréal. Fndn. de la Maison Trestler: Amie (1979–). Com. Consult. du Livre. **Pubns.:** *L'Enfant Personnage et L'Autorité dans La Littérature Enfantine* (1966); Contrib., *Livre, Bibliothèque et Culture Quebecoise* (1976); Contrib., *Le Livre dans la Vie de L'Enfant* (1978); various articles. **Activities:** 1, 12; 17, 35, 38; 63, 93 **Addr.:** Bibliothèque EPC - Local G 305, Pavillon Marie-Victorin-Univ. de MTL, 90 Rue Vincent d'Indy, Montréal, PQ, Canada.

Durant, Anita Marshall Bims (My. 30, 1938, Newark, NJ) Lib. Media Ctr. Dir., John Hope Mid. Sch., 1973–; Dir., Federally Funded Lib. Trng. Proj., Chicago State Univ., 1978, Lectr., 1977–79, Grad. Asst. to Coord., Media Srvs., 1976–77; Tchr.-Libn., Chicago Pub. Schs., 1966–, Tchr., 1964–; Peace Corps Volun., Philippines, 1962–63; Tchr., Newark Pub. Schs., 1959–62. **Educ.:** Newark State Coll., 1955–59, BS (Kindergarten, Primary Educ.); Chicago State Univ., 1973–74, MS (LS); Grad. Crs., Univ. of Chicago. **Orgs.:** ALA: AASL, Lib. Srvs. to Disadv. (1976). IL LA. Chld. Readg. RT: Sec. Chld. Lit. Conf. (Exhibit Ch., 1976). IL Assn. of Sch. Libns.: Int. Frdm. Com. (1974–75). Chicago Tchr. Libns. Assn.: Reservation Secy.; Treas. (1974–76). Alpha Kappa Alpha: Theta Omega Chap., Histn. (1980–); Secy. (1971–75); Pubcty. Ch. (1976–80). Clifford Shaw Com. UP Beatrice Caffery Youth Org. Intl. Readg. Assn. Chicago Area Readg. Assn. various orgs. **Honors:** Cosmopolitan Cmnty. Church, Srv. Awd., Women's Day, 1977. **Activities:** 10, 11; 21, 26, 31; 63, 72 **Addr.:** 9544 S. Calhoun Ave., Chicago, IL 60617.

Durbin, Ramona J. (Jn. 10, 1928, St. Paul, MN) Head Cat., U.S. Naval Acad., 1978–; Head, Acq. and Serials, 1977–78; Head, Serials, 1969–77; Head, Lib. Srv. Ctr., U.S. Army (Vietnam), 1968–68. **Educ.:** Mankato State Coll., 1946–50, BS (Eng.); Univ. of MN, 1951–52, BSLS. **Orgs.:** ALA. SLA. **Activities:** 1, 4; 15, 17, 20; 74 **Addr.:** Nimitz Library, U.S. Naval Academy, Annapolis, MD 21402.

Duree, Barbara Joyce (Mr. 9, 1922, Las Vegas, NM) Ed., Bks. for YAs, *Booklist,* 1954–; Reader's Adv., Ext. Libn., Topeka Pub. Lib., 1951–54; Eng. Instr., Univ. of KS, 1946–48; Eng. Tchr., Council Grove (KS) HS, 1944–46. **Educ.:** Univ. of KS, 1940–44, AB (Eng.), 1946–49, MA (Eng.); Case West. Rsv. Univ., 1952–53, MS (LS). **Orgs.:** ALA. IL LA. **Honors:** Phi Beta Kappa. **Activities:** 9, 10; 42, 48 **Addr.:** 8053 S. Throop St., Chicago, IL 60620.

Durham, Mary Joines (N. 2, 1921, Sale City, GA) Head, Tech. Srvs., Valdosta State Coll., 1972–; Acq. Libn., 1968–72; Head Libn., Norman Coll., 1956–68; Head Libn., Norman Park HS, 1952–56. **Educ.:** Tift Coll., 1938–42, BA (Eng.); FL State Univ., 1957–59, MA (LS). **Orgs.:** SELA. GA LA: Stud. Assts. Com. (1979–81). Beta Phi Mu. Delta Kappa Gamma: Sigma Chap. (Pres., 1978–80; 1st VP, 1976–78; Resrch. Com. Ch., 1974–76; Ch., Finance Com., 1981–). **Addr.:** 2207 Park Ln., Valdosta, GA 31601.

Duris, Richard Martin (Ja. 28, 1931, North Braddock, PA) Ref. Libn., Msc. Biblgphr., Temple Univ., 1969–; Asst. Head, Msc. Lib., OH State Univ., 1968–69; Head Libn., Cmnty. Lib. of Castle Shannon, 1967–68; Catlgr., Hunt Lib., Carnegie-Mellon Univ., 1966–67; Libn., Art & Msc. Dept., Cincinnati and Hamilton Cnty. Pub. Lib., 1961–66; Libn., Art Div., Carnegie Lib., Pittsburgh, 1959–61. **Educ.:** Indiana Univ. of PA, 1949–53, BS (Msc. Educ.); Carnegie Lib. Sch., 1958–59, MS (LS); Carnegie Mellon Univ., 1966–68, MFA (Fine Arts); Temple Univ., 1977, (Grmn.). **Orgs.:** PA LA: Org. & Bylaws (Ch., 1972–73); Exec. Com., (1972–73). Msc. LA: Lib. Admin. Com., (1971–73, 1976–). PA Chap. Msc. LA: Fndr., Ch. (1975–76). AAUP. Amer. Gld. of Organists: Exec. Bd. (1976–77); Ch. for Busing, Intl. Congs. of Organists, (1977). **Honors:** PA LA, Cont. Educ. Grant, 1978. **Pubns.:** "Music materials in the libraries of Pennsylvania," *PA LA Bltn.* (Ja. 1975). **Activities:** 1, 9; 15, 39, 41; 55, 56, 75 **Addr.:** Samuel Paley Library, Temple University, Philadelphia, PA 19122.

Durkan, Michael J. (Louisburgh, Ireland) Coll. Libn., Swarthmore Coll., 1976–; Asst. Libn., Wesleyan Univ., 1963–76; Head, Cat. Dept., 1958–1963; Asst. Libn., Longford/Westmeath Cnty. Lib., 1956–1957; Libn., US Info. Ctr., Dublin, 1950–1956. **Educ.:** St. Patrick's Coll., Ireland, 1944–47, BA (Lat/Mod. Irish); Univ. Coll., Dublin, Ireland, 1949–50, Dipl. (LS). **Orgs.:** CT LA: Rep.-at-Large (1969–71); Resrcs. and Tech. Srvs. Sect. (Prog. Ch., 1960–61, Ch., 1961–62); Coll. and Univ. Sect. Vice Ch., 1962–63, Ch., 1963–64). New Eng. LA: Reg. Plng. Com. (1971–73). Philadelphia Area Libs. Coop. DE Cnty. Lib. Adv. Com. Philobiblon Club (Philadelphia). Bibl. Socty. of Amer. Amer. Com. for Irish Studies. Intl. Assn. for the Study of Anglo-Irish Lit. Other orgs. **Pubns.:** Jt. auth., *Sean O'Casey: A Bibliography* (1978); *W. B. Yeats 1865–1939, A Catalogue of His Works and Associated Items in Olin Library, Wesleyan University.* (1965); "A Checklist of Works by Charles Robert Marturin", *Eire 19* (1977); "A Reading List on Northern Ireland" in *Conflict in Ireland.* (1976); "The First American Production of *The Plough and the Stars", The Sean O'Casey Review* (Fall 1976); Other articles. **Activities:** 1, 2; 17, 24, 45; 54, 55, 57 **Addr.:** Swarthmore College Library, Swarthmore, PA 19081.

Durnell, Jane B. (Jl. 26, 1916, Kokomo, IN) Coord. of Lib. Instr., Univ. of OR Lib., 1978–; Ref. Libn., 1968–78; Libn., Bureau of Mncpl. Resrch. & Srv., 1962–66. **Educ.:** State Univ. of IA, 1934–38, BA (Eng.); Univ. of OR, 1964–68, MLS. **Orgs.:** Pac. North. LA. OR LA. **Honors:** Beta Phi Mu, 1968. **Pubns.:** Jt. ed., *The Librarian, Selections from the Column of That Name...* (1976); "The Cardelius Syndrome," *Imprint: Oregon* (Spr. 1976); "An Irrepressible Deceiver," *PNLA Qtly.* (Fall 1971). **Activities:** 1; 31, 39; 57 **Addr.:** 1047 W. 18th Pl., Eugene, OR 97402.

Durrance, Joan Coachman (Ap. 20, 1937, Miami, FL) Coord., Cont. educ., Sch. of LS, Univ. of MI, 1979–, Lectr., 1978–; Instr., Cmnty. Info. Spec., Univ. of Toledo, 1976; Cmnty. Srvs. Libn., Ctrl. WI Colony Lib. and Info. Ctr., 1972–73; Ref. Libn., Univ. of NC, 1963–65; Branch Libn., Miami Pub. Lib., 1960–62. **Educ.:** Palm Beach Jr. Coll., 1955–57; Univ. of FL, 1957–59, BA (Hon.) (Eng. and Psy.); Univ. of NC, 1959–60, MSLS; Univ. of WI, 1974–75, Cert.; Univ. of MI, 1980, PhD. **Orgs.:** ALA: Cncl. (1978–); PLA, Goals, Guidelines, and Standards Com. (1978). MI LA: Cont. Ed. Com. (1975–79; Ch., 1977–79). CLENE: Adv. Com. (1978–), Bd. (1981); Cont. Prog. Com. (1977); Nom. Com. (1978). MFLA: Cont. Educ. Com. (1976–). Various other orgs. Leag. of Women Voters. **Honors:** Beta Phi Mu. **Pubns.:** Jt. ed., *Public Libraries: New Directions for Adult Services,* 1981; "Emerging Patterns of Service for Citizen Groups," *Lib. Trends* (Fall, 1979); "Initiating a Statewide Continuing Education Program," *Proc of the Second CLENE Asm.* (Jn., 1976). **Activities:** 9, 11; 24, 25, 29; 50 **Addr.:** School of Library Science, Univ. of Michigan, Ann Arbor, MI 48109.

Durrance, Raymond E. (D. 7, 1936, West Palm Beach, FL) Pres., Associated Information Consultants; Asst. Prof., LS, Univ. of MI, 1975–; Asst. Prof., LS, Univ. of South. CA, 1973–74; Plng. Ofcr., Univ. of WA Lib., 1969–70; Dir., Fisheries-Oceanography Lib., Univ. of WA, 1965–69. **Educ.:** Univ. of FL, 1957–59, BS (Zlgy.); Univ. of NC, 1963–65, MSLS; Univ. of WI, 1970–75, PhD (LS). **Orgs.:** SLA: Student Rel. Ofcr. (1978–80); MI Chap. (Bltn. Ed., 1978–79; Treas., 1979–80). ASIS. AALS. **Activities:** 1, 12; 15, 17, 41; 65, 75, 91 **Addr.:** School of Library Science, University of Michigan, Ann Arbor, MI 48109.

Dutton, Brenda K. (Ja. 19, 1948, Petersburg, VA) Chld. Libn., Dayton and Montgomery Cnty. Pub. Lib., various branches, 1971–. **Educ.:** Univ. of KY, 1966–70, BA (Eng.), 1970–71, MLS; various wkshps. **Orgs.:** OH LA: Srv. to Chld. and Young Teens (Coord., 1979–80; Asst. Coord., 1978–79); Mem. Com. (Ch., 1978). ALA: Com. on Involvement (1979). **Activities:** 9; 21 **Addr.:** 2019 Harvard Blvd., Dayton, OH 45406.

Dutton, Pauline M. (Jl. 15, –, Detroit, MI) Fine Arts Libn., Pasadena Pub. Lib., 1971–; Tchr., Anaheim and Corona, 1967–69. **Educ.:** CA State Univ., Fullerton, 1964–67, BA (Art); Univ. of South. CA, 1970–71, MS (LS); CA Teaching Cred., 1969. **Orgs.:** CA LA. ARLIS/NA. Pasadena Libns. Assn.: Treas. (1979); Secy. (1978). Gilbert & Sullivan Socty. of LA. Toastmistress Intl.: Pasadena Chap., Pres. (1974); VP (1973). **Activities:** 9; 15, 20, 39; 55, 67 **Addr.:** Fine Arts Division, Pasadena Public Library, 285 East Walnut St., Pasadena, CA 91101.

Duval, Marjorie A. (Ag. 31, 1922, Leominster, MA) Univ. Archvst., Univ. of South. ME, 1972–, Assoc. Prof. of Lib. Srv., 1968–; Head Libn., Univ. of ME, Portland, 1962–72; Recreation Supvsr., U.S. Civil Srv., 1951–61. **Educ.:** New Eng. Cnsvty. of Msc., 1939–45, BMsc (Voice); Simmons Coll., 1961–62, MSLS; Amer. Univ./Natl. Arch. Inst., 1973, Cert. **Orgs.:** SAA: Com. on Reg. Arch. Act. (1979–80). New Eng. Archvsts: Pres. (1979–80); VP (1978–79); ME LA: Secty. (1971–74). Altrusa Intl., Inc.: Pres., Portland, ME (1973–74); First Dist. Com. Ch. (1974–76); Dist. Secty. (1980–82). **Activities:** 1, 2; 17, 18, 23; 85 **Addr.:** University of Southern Maine, 96 Falmouth St., Portland, ME 04110.

Dvorák, Anna M. (Mr. 7, 1930, Trebíc, Czechoslovakia) Art Libn., NC Musm. of Art, 1977–; Frgn. Lang. Catlgr., NC State Lib., 1977; Dsgn., Graph. Artist, Illustrator, Lectr. (Czechoslovakia), 1951–64. **Educ.:** Art Coll., Brno, Czechoslovakia, 1949–51, BA (Studio); Univ. of NC, 1970–72, MS (LS), 1978, PhD (Art Hist.). **Orgs.:** ARLIS/NA. **Pubns.:** Jt. auth., *Alphonse Mucha: The Complete Graphic Works* (1980); *Alphonse Mucha: Figures Décoratives* (1981); illustrator, various chld. bks., articles (1953–72). **Activities:** 41; 55 **Addr.:** North Carolina Museum of Art, Raleigh, NC 27611.

Dvorzak, Marie A. (My. 16, 1945, Sewickley, PA) Ref. Biblgrphr. and Head, Geol. Lib., Univ. of MN, 1976–, Sci. Biblgrphr., 1969–76. **Educ.:** Carnegie-Mellon Univ., 1963–67, BA (Math.); Univ. of Pittsburgh, 1967–69, MLS. **Orgs.:** Geosci. Info. Socty.: Treas. (1980–81); Com. on the Un. List of Fld. Trip Guidebks. (1977–). ALA. **Pubns.:** "Collection Development in the Geosciences: Monographs," *Geosci. Info. Socty. Procs.* (1980). **Activities:** 1; 15, 17, 39; 70, 91 **Addr.:** Winchell Library of Geology, 204 Pillsbury Hall, 310 Pillsbury Dr. S.E., University of Minnesota, Minneapolis, MN 55455.

Dworak, Marcia L. (Mr. 31, 1939, Los Angeles, CA) Lib. Dir., Coll. of the Atlantic, 1978–; Asst. Prof. of Lib. Instr. Srvs., Sangamon State Univ., 1974–78; Libn. II, CA State Univ., Fullerton, 1973–74; Librarian I, 1972–73. **Educ.:** CA State Univ., Fullerton, 1970–72, BA (Hist.), 1972–73, MSLS; Sangamon State Univ., 1976–79, MA (Pub. Admin.). **Orgs.:** ALA. ME LA: Stand. Adv. Com. on Cont. Educ. (1979–82); Cnclr. to ME Lib. Bd. (1980–82); ME Lib. Comsn. (1981–85). **Honors:** Phi Kappa Phi, 1972; Phi Alpha Theta, 1971. **Pubns.:** *Illinois Public Library Administrators: A Training Needs Assessment,* (1979); "Women in Public Library Management," *Pub. Lib. Qtly.* (1979); "If Not MBO, Then What?," *IL Lib.* (Je. 1978); "Women at Work" (Slide-tape prog.) (1975); "Ethics in the Public Service" (Videotape training package) (1974). **Activities:** 1; 17, 25, 39; 50, 65, 92 **Addr.:** Mount Desert Island, ME 04660.

Dwyer, James R. (Jl. 21, 1949, Seattle, WA) Asst. Prof., Catlgr., Univ. of OR, 1976–; Visit. Asst. Prof., Univ. of WA Sch. of Libnshp., 1978; Asst. Prof., Catlgr., SUNY, Albany, 1973–76; Indxr., Film Lit. Index, 1974–76. **Educ.:** Univ. of WA, 1967–71, BA (Eng.); 1971–73, MLibr. **Orgs.:** ALA: SRRT/Action Cncl. (1979–81), Clearhse. (1975–77); IFRT; Rep. to Cat. Code Rev. Com. (1975–78); Prog. Com. (1974–76). LITA. Clergy and Laity Concerned: Peace Conversion Task Force (Ch., 1976–78). Bus. and Prof. People for Sane Energy. **Honors:** ALA, JMRT, Shirley Olofson Novia Awd., 1974. **Pubns.:** "Public Response to an Academic Library Microcatalog," *Jnl. of Acad. Libn.* (Jl., 1979); Other articles, oral presentations. **Activities:** 1; 20, 31, 46 **Addr.:** Catalog Dept., Library, University of Oregon, Eugene, OR 97403.

Dyer, Charles Richard (Ag. 20, 1947, Richmond Height, MO) Law Libn. and Assoc. Prof. of Law, Univ. of MO, 1977–; Assoc. Law Libn. and Asst. Prof. of Law, St. Louis Univ., 1975–77; Readers' Srvs. Asst., Univ. of TX Law Lib., 1974–75. **Educ.:** Univ. of TX, 1965–69, BA (Phil.); Northwest. Univ., 1969–71, MA (Phil.); Univ. of TX, 1971–74, JD, 1974–75, MLS. **Orgs.:** AALL: Autom. Com. (Asst. Ch., 1976–78); Law Sch. Lexis Users Grp. (1977–); Rel. with Vendors (Ch., 1978–). Mid-Amer. Assn. of Law Libs.: Prog. Ch. (1975–77); Secy. (1976–78). Southwest. Assn. of Law Libs.: VP/Pres.-Elect (1981–82); Prog. Com. (1978–); Lcl. Arrange. (Co-Ch., 1978). Natl. Conf. of Law Sch. Lib. Dirs. Amer. Bar Assn.: Legal Educ. and Admis. to Bar; Pub. Util. Law; Sci. and Tech. Assn. of Amer.

PROFESSIONAL ACTIVITIES: Institutions: 1. Acad. lib.; 2. Arch.; 3. Assn.; 4. Fed./Gvt. lib.; 5. Inst. lib.; 6. Mfr./Suppl.; 7. Milit. lib.; 8. Musm.; 9. Pub. lib.; 10. Sch. lib.; 11. Sch. of lib. sci.; 12. Spec. lib.; 13. State lib.; 14. (other). **Functions/Activities:** 15. Acq./Col. dev.; 16. Adult srvs.; 17. Admin.; 18. Apprais.; 19. Archit./Bldgs.; 20. Cat./Class.; 21. Chld. srvs.; 22. Circ.; 23. Cons./Pres.; 24. Consult.; 25. Cont. ed.; 26. Educ. lib. sci.; 27. Ext. srvs.; 28. Fund/Grants; 29. Gvt. pubs.; 30. Indx./Abs.; 31. Instr. lib. use; 32. Media srvs.; 33. Micro.; 34. Netwks./Coop.; 35. Persnl.; 36. PR; 37. Publshg.; 38. Recs. mgt.; 39. Ref. srvs.; 40. Repro.; 41. Resrch.; 42. Review.; 43. Secur.; 44. Serials; 45. Spec. col.; 46. Tech. srvs.; 47. Trustees/Bds.; 48. YA srvs.; 49. (other).

Law Schs.: Econ. and the Law; Legal Resrch. and Wrtg., Exec. Bd. (1977–78). TX State Bar: Pub. Util. Law. **Honors:** Southwest. Assn. of Law Libs., Cert. of Srv., 1979. **Pubns.:** Jt./asst. ed., *Index to Periodical Articles Related to Law* (1974); ed., *Law Lib. Jnl.* (1981–82); various sps. **Activities:** 1, 12; 15, 17, 35; 77, 93 **Addr.:** University of Missouri-Kansas City Law Library, Kansas City, MO 64110.

Dyer, Esther R. (Ag. 30, 1950, Albany, NY) Asst. Prof., Grad. Sch. of Lib. & Info. Studies, Rutgers Univ., 1977–; Asst. Prof., St. John's Univ., 1976–77; Tchr./Libn., Riccardi Elem. Sch., 1973–74; Head, Chld. Dept., Troy Pub. Lib., 1972–73. **Educ.:** State Univ. Coll. at New Paltz, 1968–72, BA cum laude (Sec. Ed); SUNY, Albany, 1972–73, MLS; Columbia Univ., 1974–76, DLS; Univ. de Salamanca, Spain, 1974, Cert. (Span.). **Orgs.:** IFLA: Stdg. Com. on Theory & Resrch. (1979–81). ALA: ALA/Chld. Book Cncl. (1977–81); AASL/Intl. Rel. Com. (Co-Ch., 1979–82); LRRT/Info. Exch. Prog. (Ch., 1978); other coms. NY Lib. Club, Resrch. and Schol. Com. (Ch., 1977–80). Intl. Assn. of Sch. Libns: Resrch. Com. (1979–). NY City Jr. Cham. of Cmrce.: VP, Bd. of Dir. (1977–80). Natl. Socty. for Autistic Chld. Assn. of Chld. Lit. in Span. Natl. Arts Club: Admis. Com. (1979–). **Honors:** Beta Phi Mu, 1976. **Pubns.:** *Public, School and Academic Media Centers* (1981); *Cultural Pluralism and Children's Media* (1978); *Cooperation in Library Service to Children* (1978); "Including School Libraries in National Bibliographic Systems", *Int. Lib. Rev.* (Fall 1979); "The Delphi Technique in Library Research", *Library Research* (Spr. 1979); other books and articles. **Addr.:** 15 Gramercy Park So., New York, NY 10003.

Dyer, Susan K. (Coos Bay, OR) Info. and Gen. Srvs. Mgr., Morrison & Foerster, 1978–, Libn., Morrison & Foerster, 1968–78. **Educ.:** Univ. of OR, 1963–67, BA (Eng.), 1967–68, MLS. **Orgs.:** AALL: CONELL (Co–Ch., 1973); Rcrt. Com. (Ch., 1974–76); Nsltr. Ed. (1976–79); Exec. Bd. (1979–); SLA West. Pacific Chap. (Pres., 1977–79). **Pubns.:** "Recruiting Law Librarians," *Law Lib. Jnl.* (F. 1976). **Activities:** 12; 17, 38; 77 **Addr.:** Morrison & Foerster, One Market Plz., Spear St. Tower, San Francisco, CA 94105.

Dyess, Dessie Mae (O. 3, 1923, Smithville, TX) Cat. Libn. & Asst. OCLC Supvsr., TX Tech Univ., 1971–; Head, Cat. Dept., W. TX State Univ., 1968–71; Serials Catlgr., Dallas Pub. Lib., 1964–68; Catlgr. & Asst. Ref. Libn., TX State Lib., 1954–1963; Head Libn., Austin Presby. Theo. Semy., 1945–54. **Educ.:** Univ. of TX, 1941–44 (Eng., Ed.); N. TX State Univ., 1944–45, BS (LS); E. TX State Univ., 1965–66, MS in LS. **Orgs.:** ALA: TX Reg. Grp. of Catlgrs. and Clasfrs. TX LA: Ch., Ad Hoc Com. on Plng., (1975–76); Secy./Treas., (1977–78); Mem. Com. (1980–82). SWLA. **Pubns.:** "Catalogers and Classifiers Round Table Survey," *TX Lib. Jnl.* (N., 1976). **Activities:** 1, 9; 20, 34, 46; 63, 90 **Addr.:** 2110 56th St., Lubbock, TX 79412.

Dyess, Stewart W. (D. 25, 1933, Holland, TX) Asst. Dir., Lib. Srvs., TX Tech. Univ., 1971–; Assoc. Libn., W. TX State Univ., 1968–71; Dir., N. Branch Lib., Fort Worth Pub. Lib., 1966–68; Trng. Libn., Soc. Case Worker, TX Dept. of Pub. Welfare, 1962–66. **Educ.:** Univ. of TX, 1954–61 (Gov., Econ.); E. TX State Univ., 1965, BS (Gov., LS); 1965–1966, MS (LS); TX Tech Univ., 1971–77, EdD. **Orgs.:** ALA. TX LA: Admin. RT (Pres., 1979–80), Nom. Com. (Ch., 1976); Coll. and Univ. Div. (Ch., 1973); Cncl. (1972–73; 1980–82); various other coms. S.W. Acad. Lib. Cnsrt.: *SWAC Nsltr.* (Ed., 1977–). TX Cncl. of State Univ. Libns.: Leg. Com. (Ch., 1970–); Nom. Com. (1976). Various other orgs. TX Tech. Univ.: Various coms. Rotary. Scottish Rite Masons. Phi Delta Kappa. **Pubns.:** "Academic Status of Librarians in Texas: A Survey," *TX Lib. Jnl.* (1972); "A History and Analysis of Library Formula Funding in Texas Public Higher Education," (1977); Various delivered papers. **Activities:** 1; 17, 19, 24; 56, 63, 78 **Addr.:** 2110 56th St., Lubbock, TX 79412.

Dygert, Michael H. (N. 15, 1938, Burlington, VT) Reg. Srvs. Libn., East. MA Reg. Lib. Syst., 1975–; Dir., Winthrop (MA) Pub. Lib., 1967–75; Ref. Libn., Catlgr., Saugus (MA) Pub. Lib., 1965–67; Ref. Asst., Branch Libn., Malden (MA) Pub. Lib., 1963–65. **Educ.:** Worcester Jr. Coll., 1957–59, AA (Arts); Northeast. Univ., 1959–62, AB (Hist., Educ.); Univ. of RI, 1965–66, MLS (LS). **Orgs.:** ALA: PLA; LAMA. New Eng. LA: Bylaws Com. (Ch., 1977–78). MA LA: many Coms. Grt. Boston Pub. Lib. Admins.: VP (1969–70, 1973–74), Pres. (1974–75). **Activities:** 9; 17, 24, 35; 95 **Addr.:** 15 Belmont Pl., Melrose, MA 02176.

Dykstra, Gail S. (O. 12, 1943, NY, NY) Ed. *Legal Mtrls. Letter,* Can. Law Info. Cncl., 1977–; Consult. Can. Law Info. Cncl., 1975–77; Ref. Libn., Metro. Toronto Ctrl. Lib., 1972–73; Ref. Libn., WA State Univ., 1969–71. **Educ.:** Alma Coll., 1961–65, BA (Hist.); Univ. of WA, 1967–69, MLS. **Orgs.:** Can. Assn. Law Libs.: Mem. at Lg. (1979–81); Dev. of Law Libs. Com. (Ch., 1979–81); Access to the Law Spec. Inf. Sect. (Ch., 1978–80); Preconf. Wkshp. Subcom. (Ch., 1978–79). AALL: Co-Ch., Lcl. Arrange. (1977). Toronto Area Law Libs. Cmnty. Legal Educ. ON: Exec. Bd. (1979–). Can. Law Info. Cncl.: Law for the Layman Com. (1977–). **Pubns.:** *A Bibliography of Canadian Legal Materials* (1977); *A Bibliography of Legal Materials for Non-Law Libraries* (1975); "Public Legal Education and Information," *Can. Cmnty. Law Jnl.* (1980); "Bringing Law to the People," *Law Lib. Jnl.* (Fall 1979); "Law for the Non Specialist" (Audio Cassett) (1979); Various other articles. **Activities:** 14-Publshr.; 24, 37, 42; 77 **Addr.:** Clic's Legal Materials Letter, 31 Belvale Ave., Toronto, ON M8X 2A8, Canada.

Dykstra, Mary E. (My. 21, 1939, Philadelphia, PA) Assoc. Prof., Sch. LS, Dalhousie Univ., 1980–, Asst. Prof., 1974–79, Orientation Libn., Lect., 1973–74, Cat. Libn., Lect., 1971–73, Syst. Libn., Tech. Srvs., 1970–71. **Educ.:** Calvin Coll., 1956–60, BA (Eng.); Dalhousie Univ., 1969–70, MLS; Univ. of Sheffield, England, 1978–, PhD. **Orgs.:** Can. LA: Tech. Srv. Coord. Grp. (1977–78). Indx. and Abs. Socty. of Can.: Mem. of Exec. (1977–78; 1980–). Atlantic Provinces LA: Secy. (1973); Subcom. for Permanent Secy. (Ch., 1975); Pubn. Com. (Ch., 1976–78). Halifax LA CALS. Other Orgs. Can. Diabetic Assn.: Halifax Chap. Parents' Grp. (1973–). Com. on Tchg. and Lrng., Dalhousie Univ.: Rep. of Fac. of Admn. Std. (1975–78). Dalhousie Fac. Club: Bd. of Dir. (1977–78), Sen. Com. on Acad. Admin. (1980–81). **Honors:** Beta Phi Mu. **Pubns.:** *PRECIS: A Primer* (1981); *Access to Film Information: An Indexing and Retrieval System for the National Film Board of Canada* (Occasional Papers, 15) (1977); "The National Film Board of Canada Project" in *The PRECIS Index System: Principles, Applications, and Prospects* (1977); "A Complete Delivery Service for Canadian Non-Print Media," *Can. Jnl. of Info. Sci.* (My. 1978); "The Lion That Squeaked," *Lib. Jnl.* (S. 1978); Ed. Bd., *Cataloging and Classification Quarterly;* other pubns. **Activities:** 11; 20, 30, 38; 56, 67, 75 **Addr.:** School of Library Service, Dalhousie University, Halifax, NS B3H 4H8 Canada.

Dym, Eleanor D. (D. 5, 1930, Pittsburgh, PA) Assoc. Dir., Lectr., LS, Univ. of Pittsburgh, Knowledge Availability Syst. Ctr., 1974–; 1976–; Asst. Dir., 1967–74; Resrch. Asst., 1965–67; Asst. Instr., LS, 1970–76. **Educ.:** PA Coll. for Women, 1949–53, BA, (Econ. Info.); Univ. of Pittsburgh, 1963–65, MLS. **Orgs.:** ASIS. SLA. Phi Delta Gamma. **Pubns.:** *Information Analysis and Retrieval: Course Materials Manual* (1980); Jt.-comp., *Political Science Thesaurus* (1975); "A Statistical Decision Model for Periodical Selection for a Specialized Information Center," Jnl. of ASIS, (Mr./Ap., 1973); "Relevance Predictability in Information Retrieval Systems," *Methods of Info. in Med.* (Ap. 1967); Various other bks. **Activities:** 11, 14-Resrch. Ctr.; 17, 26, 41; 56, 62 **Addr.:** Knowledge Availability Systems Center, University of Pittsburgh, LIS Building, Room 828, Pittsburgh, PA 15260.

Dymek, Mary J. (Ja. 29, 1949, North Adams, MA) Supvsr. of Chld. Srvs., Prosser Pub. Lib., 1973–; Coord. of Chld. Srvs., Meriden Pub. Lib., 1972–73; Supvsr. of Chld. Srvs., Meml. Hall Lib., Andover, MA, 1971–72. **Educ.:** Coll. of New Rochelle, 1966–70, AB (Eng. Lit.); Simmons Coll., 1970–71, MS (LS); Mgt. Sem. for Chld. Libn., Simmons Coll., 1978, Cert; Coursework, St. Joseph Coll., 1974–80. **Orgs.:** ALA: ALSC. New Eng. LA: RT of Chld. Libns. CT LA: Chld. Srvs. Sect. (Ch. 1978–80); Rep.-at -Large (1978); Exec. Bd. (1978–80); Nom. Com. (1979, 80); New Eng. Educ. Media Assn.: Pubcty. Com. (1977). Other orgs. CT Cnl. of Tchrs. of Eng. Early Childhood Educ. Cncl. of CT. Bloomfield, CT Non-Unionized Emp.: Persnl. Com. (1975–76). Bloomfield, CT Arts Fest. Com. **Activities:** 9; 17, 21, 48; 63, 89 **Addr.:** Prosser Public Library, 1 Tunxis Ave., Bloomfield, CT 06002.

Dyment, Alan R. (Ja. 21, 1942, London, Eng.) Dir., Lrng. Resrcs. Ctr., Mt. Royal Coll., 1974–, Head of Resrc. Islands, 1973–74; AV Libn. and Campus Libn., Cent. Coll., 1967–73; Catlgr., Co–op Bk. Ctr. of Can., 1966–67. **Educ.:** LA UK, Assoc., Fellow. **Orgs.:** AB Cncl. of Coll. Libns.: Past Ch./Dir.–at–Lg. (1979–); Com. on Networking (Ch., 1980–). Can. LA: Stdg. Com. on ILL (1980–); Can. Assn. of Coll. and Univ. Libs./Cmnty. and Tech. Coll. Libs. Sect., Secy. (1980–), Vice-Ch./Ch.-Elect (1981). AB LA: Travel Exch. Com. (Ch., 1980–). **Pubns.:** *Literature of the Film* (1975). **Activities:** 1; 17, 31, 32; 56, 67, 75 **Addr.:** Mount Royal College, Learning Resources Centre, 4825 Richard Rd. S.W., Calgary, AB T3E 6K6 Canada.

Dysart, Jane I. (N. 21, 1950, Belleville, ON) Chief Libn., Info. Resrcs., Royal Bank of Can., 1975–; Asst. Libn., Can. Stans. Assn., 1974–75. **Educ.:** Univ. of Toronto, 1969–72, BSc (Psy.), 1972–74, MLS. **Orgs.:** SLA: Chap. Cabinet, Ch. (1981–82), Ch.-Elect (1980–81); Bus. and Fin. Div., Mem. Com. (Ch., 1979–81); Jt. Chap./Div. Cabinets Arch. Std. Com. (1978–79); Toronto Chap., Nom. Com. (Ch., 1980–81), Past–Pres. (1979–80), Pres., (1978–79), various ofcs. Can. LA. Univ. of Toronto Fac. of LS Fac. Cncl.: Can. LA Rep. (1979–81). Seneca Coll. of Appld. Arts and Tech. Cont. Educ. Fac. **Activities:** 12; 15, 17, 39; 59 **Addr.:** Information Resources, Royal Bank of Canada, Royal Bank Plz., Toronto, ON M5J 2J5 Canada.

Dyson, Allan J. (Mr. 28, 1942, Lawrence, MA) Univ. Libn., Univ. of CA, Santa Cruz, 1979–; Head, Moffitt Undergrad. Lib., Univ. of CA, Berkeley, 1971–79; Asst. to the Dir., Columbia Univ. Libs., 1968–71. **Educ.:** Harvard Coll., 1960–64, AB (Gvt.); Simmons Coll., 1966–68, MS (LS). **Orgs.:** ALA: Publshg. Com. (1981–); Exec. Bd. Com. *Choice* (1976); ACRL: Ch. Ed. Bd., *Choice* (1978–80); Pubn. Com. (1978–80). Libns. Assn. of the Univ. of CA: Pres. (1976). CA LA. Sierra Club. ACLU. **Honors:** Cncl. on Lib. Resrcs., Fellow, 1973–74. **Pubns.:** "Library Instruction in University Undergraduate Libraries," *Progress in Educating the Library User* (1978); "Organizing Undergraduate library instruction: the English and American Experience," *Jnl. of Acad. Libnshp.* (Mr. 1975); "Textbooks, Propaganda, and Librarians," *Wilson Lib. Bltn.* (N. 1971); Ed., *College and Research Libraries News* (1973–74). **Activities:** 1; 17 **Addr.:** University Librarian, University of California, Santa Cruz, CA 95064.

Dyson, Sam A. (S. 3, 1928, Shreveport, LA) Dir. of Lib., LA Tech. Univ., 1966–, Assoc. Libn., 1960–66; Head Libn., LA Coll., 1953–60. **Educ.:** N. West. St. Univ., 1947–50, BS (Bio.); LA St. Univ., 1952–53, MS (LS); LA Coll., 1957, (Fren.); LA Tech. Univ., 1967–70, (Comp. Sci.). **Orgs.:** ALA: ACRL (Legis. Netwk., 1976–). SWLA: Bd. Dir. (1973–75); SLICE Adv. Cncl. (1972–74); Proj. Cncl. (1978–80); Pres. (1978–80). LA LA: Pres; many other orgs. Dist. 8-L Lions Intl. Cabinet Secy./Treas. (1979–80) Boy Scouts of Amer.: Past Dist. Ch. Other orgs. **Honors:** Baptist Christ. Coll., Doctor of Laws Degree 1974; Phi Beta, Natl. Patron, 1963. **Pubns.:** *Sheppard Collection of Band Music* (1977); *Library Automation* (1971); "New Book Browse," *LA LA Bltn.* (Spr./Sum. 1977); "Electronic Learning," *LA Schs.* (My. 1975); "Regional Interlibrary Loan,..." *RQ* (Sum. 1974); "Southwestern Library Association," *ALA Yrbk.* (1979); many other pubns. **Activities:** 1; 17, 26, 32; 56, 75, 85 **Addr.:** Prescott Library, Louisiana Tech University, Ruston, LA 71272.

Dziedzic, Donna (Ag. 30, 1947, Haverhill, MA) Dir., IL Reg. Lib. for the Blind and Phys. Handcpd., 1977–; Asst. to the Comsn. for Plng. and Eval., Chicago Pub. Lib., 1976–77, Spec. Assignment to the Dir. of Lib. Systs. Engin., 1975–76, Adult Srvs. Libn., Hild Reg. Lib., 1974–75; Subj. and Lang. Spec., Bibl. Dept., Sterling Meml. Lib., Yale Univ., 1969–71. **Educ.:** Salve Regina Coll., 1965–69, AB (Hist.); Univ. of IL, 1972–73, MS (LS). **Orgs.:** IL LA: Exec. Bd. (Dir.-at-Lg., 1981–82); 1980 Anl. Conf. Ch.; 1978 Conf. Eval. Com. (1979); various coms. ALA: ASCLA/Lib. Srvs. to the Blind and Phys. Handcpd. Sect. (Vice-Ch./Ch.-Elect, 1980–81), Radio Readg. Srvs. Com. (Ch., 1979–81); Autom. for Srvs. to the Blind and Phys. Handcpd. Discuss. Grp. (Conv., 1980–81); various coms. Chicago Pub. Lib.–Chicago Lib. Syst.: Various coms., ofcs. (1975–79). Lib. of Congs.: Natl. Lib. Srv. for the Blind and Phys. Handcpd., various coms. (1979–82). Various other orgs. Mid–N. (Cmnty.) Assn. Lincoln Park Cons. Assn. Near W. Side (Cmnty.) Assn. Balzekas Musm. of Lithuanian Culture. **Activities:** 9, 12; 16, 17, 34; 72 **Addr.:** 2124 N. Sedgwick, Chicago, IL 60614.

E

Eadie, Tom (Ap. 21, 1941, Halifax, NS) Head, Arts Ref. and Col. Dev., Univ. of Waterloo, 1974–; Info. and Orien. Libn., Univ. of BC, 1972–74. **Educ.:** Queen's Univ., 1960–68, HonBA (Phil.); 1968–71, MA (Phil.); Univ. of West. ON, 1971–72, MLS. **Orgs.:** Can. LA. Can. Assn. of Coll. and Univ. Libs.: CAUT/Cacul Jt. Tsk. Frc. on Acad. Status for Libns. (1975); Acad. Status Com. (Ch., 1978–79). Can. Assn. of Univ. Tchrs.: Col. Bargaining Com. (1977–). **Pubns.:** *The Beast With Three Backs* (1965); "Librarians and Collective Bargaining," *CAUT Bltn.* (F. 1978). **Activities:** 1; 15, 17, 39; 55 **Addr.:** University of Waterloo Library, Waterloo, ON N2L 3G1 Canada.

Eager, Virginia W. (F. 14, 1919, Cleveland, OH) Head, Lib. Systs., GTE Labs., 1974–; Libn., New Eng. Instr. Mtrls. Ctr., Boston Univ., 1972–74; Chem., Stahl Finish Co., 1967–71. **Educ.:** West. Rsv. Univ., 1936–40, BA (Chem.); Radcliffe Coll., 1941–43, MA (Chem.); Simmons Sch. of LS, 1970–72, MA (LS). **Orgs.:** SLA: Boston Chap., Bd. (1980–); Treas. (1978–79). New Eng. OLUG: Bd. (1978). 128 Libns. Grp. Sigma Xi. **Honors:** Phi Beta Kappa, 1939. **Pubns.:** *Guide to Resources for Continuing Education in Online User Groups* (1980); jt. auth., *Children with Special Needs, a Brief Bibliography for Public Librarians* (1974); various sps. **Activities:** 12; 16, 17; 51 **Addr.:** GTE Laboratories, 40 Sylvan Rd., Waltham, MA 02254.

Eaglen, Audrey B. (O. 22, 1930, Cleveland, OH) Head, Order Dept., Cuyahoga Cnty. Pub. Lib., 1970–; Consult., WVIZ (Educ. TV, Cleveland), 1975–; Resrch. Assoc., Educ. Resrch. Cncl. of Amer., 1965–69; Consult., Lang. Arts, Reardon-Baer Pub. Co., 1962–65. **Educ.:** John Carroll Univ., BS MS; Univ. of Chicago, MA (LS). **Orgs.:** ALA: YASD, Pres. (1980–81); ALSC/YASD, Ed., *Top of the News.* Natl. Cncl. of Tchrs. of Eng. AAUW. **Pubns.:** *Purchasing Books for Libraries: A Practical Guide* (1980); "Book Distribution: Present Conditions," *Sch. Lib. Jnl.* (D. 1979); "The Warning Bookmark: Censorship or Selection Aid?" *Library Acq.: Practice and Theory* (Spr. 1980). **Activities:** 9; 15, 42, 48; 74 **Addr.:** 1600 Rydalmount Rd., Cleveland Hts., OH 44118.

Eagleton, Kathleen M. (Ja. 16, 1934, Preston, Eng.) Dir. of Lib. Srvs., Brandon Gen. Hosp., 1976–, Libn., Sch. of Nursing, 1972–76; Head, Verifications Dept., Univ. of MB Lib., 1968–70; Libn., Sch. Dist. of Mystery Lake, 1967–68; Catlgr., Univ. of MB Lib., 1965–67. **Educ.:** Univ. of MB, Brandon Univ., 1972, BA (Geo., Anthro.); LA UK, 1965, Assoc. **Orgs.:** CH LA. MB Hlth. LA: Pres. (1979–81). Med. LA. LA UK. **Activities:** 10, 12; 17, 39, 46; 80 **Addr.:** P.O. Box 12, Brandon, MB R7A 5Y6 Canada.

Special Subjects/Services: 50. Adult educ.; 51. Advert./Mktg.; 52. Aerosp.; 53. Agric.; 54. Area std.; 55. Arts/Hum.; 56. Autom.; 57. Bibl./Prtg.; 58. Bio. sci.; 59. Bus./Fin.; 60. Chem.; 61. Copyrt.; 62. Documtn.; 63. Educ.; 64. Engin.; 65. Env.; 66. Eth. grps.; 67. Film; 68. Food/Nutr.; 69. Geneal.; 70. Geo.; 71. Geol.; 72. Handcpd.; 73. Hist.; 74. Int. frdm.; 75. Info. sci.; 76. Insr.; 77. Law; 78. Legis.; 79. Math./Comp. sci.; 80. Med.; 81. Metals; 82. Nat. resrcs.; 83. Newsp.; 84. Nuc. sci.; 85. Oral hist.; 86. Petr./Energy; 87. Pharm.; 88. Phys./Astr./Math.; 89. Readg.; 90. Relig.; 91. Sci./Tech.; 92. Soc. sci.; 93. Telecom.; 94. Transp.; 95. (other).

Eagon, Carrie W. (Ag. 19, 1920, Chattanooga, TN) Head Libn., Esso Eastern Inc., 1971–; Head Libn., Esso Math. & Syst., 1970–71; Head Libn., Esso Prod. Resrch., 1965–70; Head Libn., Jersey Prod. Resrch., 1955–65. **Educ.:** Univ. of Tulsa, 1938–42, BA (Hum.); LA State Univ., 1950, MLS. **Orgs.:** SLA: OK Chap. (Dir. 1963–65; Pres. 1962–63); TX Chap. (Recruit. and Educ. Com., 1965–70; Natl. Consult. Com. 1958–70; Ch., Petroleum Div., 1963). **Pubns.:** John Cotton Dana, SLA, lectur. (1969). **Activities:** 5, 12; 15, 17, 39; 59, 77, 86 **Addr.:** Esso Eastern Inc., Library, P.O. Box 1415, Houston, TX 77001.

Eakin, Laurabelle (New Castle, PA) Dir., Falk Lib. of the Hlth. Scis., Univ. of Pittsburgh, 1958–, Visit. Lectr., Sch. of Lib. and Info. Scis., 1968–; Chief Libn., Vets. Admin. Hosp., 1950–57, Med. Libn., 1949–50; Libn., East Deer Twp. HS, 1944–49; Libn., Verona HS, 1941–44. **Educ.:** Grove City Coll., 1934–38, AB; West. Rsv. Univ., 1943–46, BS (LS). **Orgs.:** Med. LA: Pittsburgh Reg. Grp. SLA. Amer. Assn. of Med. Lib. Dirs. ACRL/Tri-State Chap. Hlth. Scis. Comm. Assn. **Pubns.:** Jt. auth., "A Bibliography of the History of Rheumatic Diseases, 1940–1962," *Arthritis and Rheumatism* (1964). **Activities:** 1, 12; 17, 26; 50, 80 **Addr.:** Falk Library of the Health Sciences, University of Pittsburgh, 2nd Floor-Scaife Hall, DeSoto & Terrace Sts., Pittsburgh, PA 15261.

Eames, Robert Wallace (My. 21, 1928, Canastota, NY) Head, Info. Srvs. Div., Rochester Pub. Lib., NY, 1961–; Acting Head, Gen. Ref. Div., 1959–60, Asst., Art Div., 1956–58, Asst., Lit. & Bio. Div., 1954–56. **Educ.:** Hartwick Coll., 1948–53, BA (Eng.); Columbia Univ., 1953–54, MSLS. **Orgs.:** ALA: Staff, Lib./USA, NY World's Fair (1964). NY LA. **Activities:** 9; 16, 39; 75 **Addr.:** 5 Castle Park, Rochester, NY 14620.

Earle, Elinor Southgate (Mr. 24, 1921, Union City, IN) Retired, 1981–; Br. Libn., Kenmore Br. Akron Summit Cnty. Pub. Lib., 1961–, First Asst., Gen. Ref., 1959–61; Base Libn., Phalsbourg AFB (France), 1957–59; Head, Gen. Ref. Div., Akron Summit Cnty. Pub. Lib., 1951–57; Asst. Head, Ref., 1948–51; Asst. Head, Ref., Springfield Pub. Lib., (IL), 1947–48. **Educ.:** Univ. of KY, 1938–42, AB (Eng.); OH State Univ., 1946–46, MA (Eng.); Univ. of IL, 1946–47, BS LS. **Orgs.:** ALA. OH LA. AAUW. Huguenot Society of OH: Consult. Geneal. (1972–76; 1979–). OH Soc. Daughters of Amer. Colonists: Nat. Defense Ch., (1972–75); Colonial & Geneal. Recs. Ch. (1975–78). **Activities:** 9; 16, 39, 48 **Addr.:** 77 Fir Hill #6A1, Akron, OH 44304.

Earnest, Patricia H. (Ag. 19, 1944, Hammond, IN) West. Reg. Mgr., Lib. Auto. Div., Brodart, Inc., 1977–; Mgr., Prof. Srvs., Xerox Univ. Microfilms, 1973–77; Asst. Ref. Libn., Purdue Univ. Libs., 1970–71; Sr. Catlgr., Norfolk Pub. Lib., 1969–70; Head, Tech. Prcs., Willingboro (NJ) Pub. Lib., 1967–69. **Educ.:** Purdue Univ., 1962–66, BA (Eng.); Univ. of KY, 1966–67, MSLS. **Orgs.:** CA LA. ASIS: Conf. and Meetings Com. (1978–80); Products and Srvcs. Task Force (1979–80); Treas., MI Chap. LITA (Nom. Com., 1978–79; Secy., Lib. and Info. Discuss. Grp., 1980). **Pubns.:** "What Can the Library/Information Manager Gain Through the Services of a Book Vendor," *Lib. Mgt. Bltn.*, (1980). **Activities:** 1, 9; 24, 33, 46; 56, 75, 91 **Addr.:** 2775 Mesa Verde Dr. East, Apartment U 216, Costa Mesa, CA 92626.

East, Catherine R. (D. 29, 1935, St. Louis, MO) Head, Ref. Srvs., U.S. Postal Srvs. Lib., 1980–; Asst. Dir., Head, Ref. Srvs., Cherry Hill Free Pub. Lib., 1970–80; Catlgr., Glassboro State Coll., 1968–70; Serials Libn., Philadelphia Coll. of Textiles and Sci., 1966–68. **Educ.:** Rutgers Univ., 1966, AB (Eng. Lit.); Drexel Univ., 1968, MSLS; NJ State Mncpl. Trng. Consortium, 1975, Cert. **Orgs.:** SLA. NJ LA: Ref. Sect., Secy. (1971–72); Nom. Com. (1975); VP (1977–78); Pres. (1978–79); Lib. Dev. Com. Coll. Dev. Sub. Com. (1978–). DC LA. DC Law Lib. Assn. Thomas A. Edison Coll. Acad. Cncl. NJ Higher Educ. Dept. Adv. Com. on Educ. Info. Ctrs. **Honors:** Beta Phi Mu. **Pubns.:** Column in local newspaper. **Activities:** 1, 9; 17, 25, 39; 54, 55, 59 **Addr.:** U.S. Postal Service Library, 475 L'Enfant Plaza, S.W., Washington, DC 20260.

East, Kay Ann (Kathy) (S. 18, 1942, Chicago, IL) Coord., Chlds. and YA Srvs., Pub. Lib. of Columbus and Franklin Cnty., 1979–; Coord., Presch. Experience Proj., 1978–79; Chlds. Libn., Asst. Branch Head, 1977–78. **Educ.:** Univ. of WI, 1964–65, BS (Elem. Educ.); Wayne State Univ., 1969–72, MSLS. **Orgs.:** ALA: ALSC, Presch. Srvs. and Parent Educ. Com. (1979–81). OH LA. **Activities:** 9; 21, 48 **Addr.:** Public Library of Columbus & Franklin County, 28 S. Hamilton Rd., Columbus, OH 43213.

East, Mona (Ap. 22, 1920, Worthington, IN) Asst. Dir. for Col. Dev., Univ. of MI, 1980–, Sel. Ofcr., 1955–80, Sr. Biblgrphr., 1949–55. **Educ.:** Univ. of MI, 1946–49, AB (Hist.), 1949–52, AMLS. **Orgs.:** ALA: RTSD/Resrcs. Sect. (Secy., 1978–80), Chief Col. Dev. Ofcrs. of Lg. Resrch. Libs. Discuss. Grp. (Ch., 1976–77); ACRL. **Honors:** Resrcs. Sect. Schol. Awd., 1978. **Pubns.:** Jt. auth. "Collection Development in Large University Libraries," *Advncs. in Libnshp.* (Volume 8). **Activities:** 1; 15, 23 **Addr.:** P.O. Box 1688, Ann Arbor, MI 48106.

East, Sherrod E. (N. 1, 1910, Lowndes Cnty., MS) Arch. Consult., 1967–; Actg. Asst. Archvst., Natl. Arch., 1966, Asst. Archvst. for Milit. Arch., 1963–66, Dir., World War II Recs. Div., 1958–63; Chief, Dept. Recs. Branch, Adj. Gen. Ofc., Army, 1943–58. **Educ.:** George Washington Univ., Univ. of Denver, 1929–37, BA (Pol. Sci.); Amer. Univ., 1938–40 (Pub. Admin.). **Orgs.:** SAA. **Honors:** SAA, Fellow, 1958; U.S. Army, Legion of Merit, 1969. **Pubns.:** *Records of the Constitutional Convention of Maryland, 1967-1968, A Descriptive Inventory* (1968); *Inventory of the Archives of St. Albans School* (1970); "Describable Item Cataloging," *Amer. Archvst.* (1953); "The Banishment of Captain Meigs," *Recs. of the Columbia Hist. Socty.* (1940). **Activities:** 2; 17, 20, 39; 69, 85 **Addr.:** 5830 Riggs Rd., Laytonsville, MD 20879.

Easterbrook, David L. (Ja. 25, 1947, New York, NY) African Std. Area Spec., IN Univ. Lib., 1980–; Africana Biblgphr., Syracuse Univ. Libs., 1975–79. **Educ.:** Kalamazoo Coll., 1965–69, BA (African Hist.); SUNY, Albany, 1971–72, MLS; Syracuse Univ., 1973– (African Hist.). **Orgs.:** ALA: ACRL. African Stds. Assn.: Ch., Arch.-Lib. Com. (1978–79). SAA. Coop. Africana Microform: Exec. Com.; Proj. of the Ctr. for Resrch. Libs.: (1977–). **Pubns.:** "Recent Bibliographic and Development Trends in Archives in Africa South of the Sahara and Their Impact on the Expatriate Researcher," *Africana Jnl.* (1980); *Africana Book Reviews 1885–1945* (1979); *Africana microfilms in the E.S. Bird Library, Syracuse University* (1975); "Bibliography of Africana Bibliographies, 1976–77," *Africana Jnl.* (1978); "Africana at the E.S. Bird Library, Syracuse University," *African Resrch. and Docu.* (1977). **Activities:** 1; 15, 39; 54 **Addr.:** E 660 Main Library, Indiana University, Bloomington, IN 47405.

Easterly, Ambrose (Ja. 4, 1920, Oak Grove, TN) Dir., Lib. Srvs., Harper Coll., 1967–; Univ. Libn., Murray State Univ., 1965–67; Assoc. Libn. for Reader Srvs., Univ. of MO, 1956–65; Asst. Libn. and Catlgr., Mid. TN State Univ., 1949–56. **Educ.:** Berea Coll., 1938–42, BA (Fr.), 1949, MA; Peabody Coll., 1948–54, MS (LS). **Orgs.:** ALA. SELA. IL LA. State Hist. Socty. of MO. **Honors:** Phi Kappa Phi. **Pubns.:** Article, *IL Libs.* (O. 1979); article, *KY LA Bltn.* (Jl. 1966); various radio and TV prods. (1962–73). **Activities:** 1; 15, 17; 65, 73, 82, **Addr.:** 269 Eggleston, Elmhurst, IL 60126.

Eastlick, John Taylor (Ap. 28, 1912, Norris, MT) Prof. Emeritus, Univ. of Denver, 1979–, Assoc. Dean and Prof., GSLIM, 1969–79; Libn., Denver Pub. Lib., 1951–69. **Educ.:** AZ State Tchrs. Coll., 1931–34, AB (Educ.); CO State Coll., 1939, MA (Educ.); Univ. of Denver, 1939–40, BLS. **Orgs.:** ALA: PLA (Pres., 1956–57); ACRL, Acrred. (COA) (1971–76). CO LA: Sec. VP (1964–65). Mt. Plains LA: Conf. Ch. Bibl. Ctr. for Resrch.: Exec. Bd. (1951–69). Denver Cncl. for Educ. TV: Pres. (1954–56). **Honors:** CO State Coll., Outstan. Alum., 1962; CO LA, Awd. of Merit, 1967; City of Denver, Mayor's Awd. of Merit, 1969. **Pubns.:** *Library Management* (1981); *Changing Environment of Libraries* (1971); "Impact of Serving the Unserved on Public Library Budgets," *Lib. Trends* (Ap. 1975); "Financial Problems Affecting Metropolitan Libraries," *Lib. Trends* (O. 1974). **Activities:** 9, 11; 17, 24, 26; 63, 95-Lib. archit. **Addr.:** 3914 E. Evans Ave., Denver, CO 80210.

Eastman, Ann Heidbreder (Ag. 31, 1933, Minneapolis, MN) Dir., Pub. Affairs Progs., VA Polytechnic Inst. and State Univ., 1978–; Dir. of Educ. and Lib. Srvs., Harcourt Brace Jovanovich, 1972–73; Sr. Assoc., Assn. of Amer. Publ., 1964–72; Dir., Educ. and Lib. Srvs., Random House/Knopf, Pantheon, 1962–64; Sch. and Lib. Consult., David McKay and Co., 1959–63, Ed., 1955–59. **Educ.:** Univ. of MI, Ann Arbor, 1951–55, BA (Eng.); NY Univ., Columbia Univ., 1956–60 (Eng./Publ.). **Orgs.:** Women's Nat. Book Assn.: Pres. (1976–80). ALA: RTSD; LAMA; PR Div., Publshg. Sect., VP and Pres.-Elect (1981). White House Conf. on Lib. and Info. Srvcs.: Adv. Com.; Del. Ctr. for the Book, Lib. of Cong.: Exec. Com., Brd. of Adv. (1978–). Pub. Lib. Mktg.: Founder, VP. **Honors:** Phi Beta Kappa, 1955; Phi Kappa Phi, 1955; ALA, RTSD, Cert., 1972. **Pubns.:** *Educational Media Selection Center* (1970); *A Guide to the Development of Educational Media Selection Centers* (1970); "Research Needed in the Fields of Reading and Communication," *Lib. Trends* (1973). **Activities:** 9; 28, 36, 37; 51, 55, 78 **Addr.:** 716 Burruss Dr. N.W., Blacksburg, VA 24060.

Eastmond, J. Nicholls, Jr. (F. 20, 1946, Salt Lake City, UT) Assoc. Dir., Instr. Srvs., Merrill Lib., Lrng. Resrcs. Prog. for Instr. Dev., Dir., North. Rockies Cnsrtm. for Higher Educ., Asst. Prof., Dept. of Instr. Media, UT State Univ., 1977–; Eval. Spec., 1974–77; Eval. Spec., Hlth. Care Mgt., Tooele, UT, 1975; Eval. and Needs Assess., Worldwide Educ. and Resrch. Inst., 1971–74. **Educ.:** Univ. of UT, 1965–67, BS (Econ.); OH Univ., 1967–69, MEd (Elem. Educ.); Univ. of UT, 1972–76, PhD (Educ. Psy.). **Orgs.:** Amer. Educ. Resrch. Assn. AECT: Div. of Instr. Dev., Prof. and Org. Dev. Netwk., Eval. Netwk. North. Rockies Cnsrtm. for Higher Educ. **Honors:** FIPSE, Proj. Dir., Grant Awd., 1978–81. **Pubns.:** *ID Under the Microscope: Perceptions of Faculty Members* (1975); Jt. Auth., *So What's Different? Student Achievement and Attitude Results from Instructional Development Projects* (1976); Jt. Auth., "Gaining Support for A Women's Studies Program in a Conservative Institution," *Liberal Educ.* (O. 1978); "The New Revelation: A Personal View," *Dialogue: A Jnl. of Mormon Thought* (Sum. 1979); *An Assessment of Educational Needs for the Department of Range Science* (1977); various rpts., articles, reviews. **Activities:** 1; 16, 18, 19; 63, 75, 95-Eval. **Addr.:** Instructional Services, MLLRP, UMC 30, Utah State University, Logan, UT 84322.

Eastwood, Terence M. (O. 7, 1943, Edmonton, AB) Asst. Prof., Mstrs. of Arch. Std. Prog., Sch. of Libnshp. and Dept. of Hist., Univ. of BC, 1981–; Archvst., Mss and Pub. Recs., Prov. Arch. of BC, 1973–81. **Educ.:** Univ. of AB, 1961–65, BA (Hist.); Pub. Arch. of Can., 1975, Dip. (Arch.); Univ. of AB, 1977, MA (Hist.). **Orgs.:** Assn. of BC Archvsts.: Secy. and Ed. (1973–75); Pres. (1975–76). Assn. Can. Archvsts.: *Arch. Bltn.* Ed. (1975–77); VP (1977–78); Pres. (1978–79); *Archivaria* Ed. (1981–83). **Pubns.:** "The Disposition of Ministerial Papers," *Archivaria* (1977). **Activities:** 2; 49-Mss.; 95-Pub. recs. **Addr.:** University of British Columbia, School of Librarianship, 831–1956 Main Mall, Vancouver, BC V6T 1W5 Canada.

Eatenson, Ervin Theodore (Ap. 18, 1924, Dallas, TX) Spec. Projs. Ofcr., Dallas Pub. Lib., 1980–; Head, Current Coll. Div., 1978–80, Coll. Enrichment Libn., 1976–78; Coll. Dev. Ofcr., 1973–75; Coord. of Adult Srvs., 1968–72; Head, Cmnty. Living Div., 1962–68; Head, Sci-Tech. Div., San Jose State Coll. Lib., 1956–68; Asst. Grad. Psy. Lib, Columbia Univ., 1949–51; Optometry Libn., 1951–56. **Educ.:** South. Meth. Univ., 1942–46, BS (Jnlsm.); Columbia Univ., 1955–62, MS (LS). **Orgs.:** ALA: ACRL (Bd. of Div., 1961–62); RASD, Notable Bk. Cncl. (Ch., 1969). TX LA: Com. on Grievance Procs. (Ch., 1973–74); Inf. Frdm. and Prof. Resp. Com. (1975–79). Various other orgs. and coms. Sigma Delta Chi. Cmnty. Cncl. of Grtr. Dallas Panel on Aging, 1964–66. Various other orgs. **Pubns.:** Ed., *Destiny is a Set of Plans* (1978); "Notable Books, 1944–69," Amer. Libs (J. 1971); "The Making of a History for the Dallas Public Library," *TX Libs.* (Fall, 1977); Producer and host, "Bookline Dallas" (WRR (AM)) (1974–75); Reviews. **Activities:** 9; 16, 37, 42; 67, 74, 83 **Addr.:** P.O. Box 19627, Dallas, TX 75219.

Eaton, Andrew Jackson (Jy. 5, 1914, Holley, NY) Visit. Prof., Grad. Sch. of Lib. Std., Univ. of Hawaii at Manoa, 1980–; Dir. of Libs., Emeritus, Spec. Consult., Washington Univ., 1978–, Dir. of Libs., 1953–78; Assoc. Dir., LA State Univ. Lib., 1946–53, Chief Ref. Libn., 1945–46; Ref. Libn., Lawrence Coll., 1944–45; Instructor at various lib. schs., 1947–. **Educ.:** Coll. of Wooster, 1931–35, AB (Hist.); Univ. of MI, 1935–36, AB (LS); Univ. of Chicago, 1940–44, PhD, (LS). **Orgs.:** ALA: Cncl. (1967–71); ACRL, Bd. of Dir. (1952–53; 1963–66; 1967–71) /Univ. Lib. Sect. (Ch., 1964–65). ARL: Pres. (1968). MO LA: Pres. IFLA: Univ. Libs. Sect. (Ch., 1973–77). Various other orgs. and ofcs. **Honors:** Phi Beta Kappa; Council on Library Resources, Fellowship, 1969; Fulbright Program, Lectureship at Tehran University Library School, 1972–74; Deutsche Bibliothekskon Perenz, Travel grant to visit German research libraries, 1977. **Pubns.:** "Fund Raising for University Libraries," *Coll. and Resrch. Libs.* (S., 1971); "Research in Librarianship in the U.S.A.," *Fed. Lib. Com. Nsltr.* (N. 1970); "Building Competition Prooves Successful," *Lib. Jnl.* (Ap. 1, 1958); "The American Movement for International Copyright, 1837–1860," *Lib. Qtly.* (Ap. 1945). **Activities:** 1; 17, 26 **Addr.:** Graduate School of Library Studies, University of Hawaii at Manoa, 2550 The Mall, Honolulu, HI 96822.

Eaton, Jeannine Todd (F. 18, 1931, Ellisville, MS) Libn., Provine HS, 1965–; Libn., Whitten Jr. HS, 1961–65; Tchr., Sea Isle Elem. Sch., 1958–60; Asst. Libn., Lee Cnty. Lib., 1953–55; Libn., Leland HS, 1952–53. **Educ.:** MS Univ. for Women, 1948–52, BS (LS, Soc. Sci.); Univ. of South. MS, 1969–72, MS (LS), 1972–75, Cert. (AAA Tchg.). **Orgs.:** MS Assn. of Sch. Libns.: Pres. (1972–73). MS LA: Secy. (1973); Hist. Com. (1970–76). MS Assn. of Media Educs.: VP (1978–79). Delta Kappa Gamma: Treas. (1980–). MS Educ. Assn.: Sect. Ch. (1972–73). **Honors:** MS Assn. of Media Educs., Outstan. Media Educ. of the Yr., 1980; Paul Truitt Meml. Bapt. Church, Cert. of Apprec. for LS, 1980. **Pubns.:** "As the Twig Is Bent," *A History of Mississippi Libraries* (1976). **Activities:** 10 **Addr.:** 219 Van Dorn, Jackson, MS 39208.

Eaton, M. Katherine G. (Mr. 9, 1924, St. Paul, MN) Asst. Prof., Head, Bur. of Govt. Resrch. Lib., Univ. of OR, 1970–; Consult., OR State Lib., 1968–70. **Educ.:** Univ. of MN, 1941–44, BA (Jnlsm.); Univ. of OR, 1951–52, MS (Jnlsm.); 1966–68, MLS; St. Paul Coll. of Law, 1948–51. **Orgs.:** Cncl. of Plng. Libns.: Pres. (1978–79). OR LA: Pres. (1973–74). ALA: ACRL, Bib. Resrch. Com. (1978–80), Leg. Com. (1974–78). SLA. NLA. Camp Fire Girls: various coms. AAUP: OR Chap. (various ofcs.). Leag. of Women Voters: OR (various bds. and ofcs.). AAUP: Natl. Bd. (1976–); various other ofcs. Various other orgs. **Honors:** Camp Fire Girls, various awds., 1960, 1967, 1971. Lane Cncl. of Orgs., Woman of the Year, 1974. Beta Phi Mu. **Pubns.:** "Oregon Libraries," *ALA Yrbk.* (1978, 1979, 1980); "Oregon Library Association," *Ency. of Lib. and Info Sci.* (1977); "Citizen Participation," *Grad. Woman* (F. 1978). **Activities:** 1, 12; 15, 17, 20; 78, 95-Public Planning, Public Finance. **Addr.:** Bureau of Governmental Research Library, Box 3177, University of Oregon, Eugene, OR 97403.

Eaton, Nancy L. (My. 2, 1943, Berkeley, CA) Head, of Tech. Srvs., Atlanta Pub. Lib., 1976–; Autom. Libn., SUNY Stony Brook, 1974–76; Asst. to the Univ. Libn., Univ. of TX, 1972–74; Head, of MARC Unit, 1971–72; Catlgr., Univ. of TX,

PROFESSIONAL ACTIVITIES: Institutions: 1. Acad. lib.; 2. Arch.; 3. Assn.; 4. Fed./Gvt. lib.; 5. Inst. lib.; 6. Mfr./Suppl.; 7. Milit. lib.; 8. Musm.; 9. Pub. lib.; 10. Sch. lib.; 11. Sch. of lib. sci.; 12. Spec. lib.; 13. State lib.; 14. (other). **Functions/Activities:** 15. Acq./Col. dev.; 16. Adult srvs.; 17. Admin.; 18. Apprais.; 19. Archit./Bldgs.; 20. Cat./Class.; 21. Chld. srvs.; 22. Circ.; 23. Cons./Pres.; 24. Consult.; 25. Cont. ed.; 26. Educ. lib. sci.; 27. Ext. srvs.; 28. Fund/Grants; 29. Gvt. pubs.; 30. Indx./Abs.; 31. Instr. lib. use; 32. Media srvs.; 33. Micro.; 34. Netwks./Coop.; 35. Persnl.; 36. PR; 37. Publshg.; 38. Recs. mgt.; 39. Ref. srvs.; 40. Repro.; 41. Resrch.; 42. Review.; 43. Secur.; 44. Serials; 45. Spec. col.; 46. Tech. srvs.; 47. Trustees/Bds.; 48. YA srvs.; 49. (other).

Who's Who in Library and Information Services

1968–71. **Educ.:** Stanford Univ., 1961–65, AB (Eng.); Univ. of TX, 1966–68, MLS. **Orgs.:** ALA. GA LA. **Pubns.:** Jt. ed., *Book Selection Policies in American Libraries* (1970). **Activities:** 1, 9; 17, 46; 56 **Addr.:** 200 26th St. NW, Apt H102, Atlanta, GA 30309.

Ebeling, Elinor H. (Ag. 23, 1932, Detroit, MI) Dean, Lrng. Resrcs., Brookdale Cmnty. Coll., 1977–; Ch., Tech. Srvs., 1969–76; Asst. Prof. (LS), IL State Univ., 1968–69; Catlgr., Supvsr., Tech. Srvs., Henry Ford Cmnty. Coll., 1961–67; Circ., Ref. Libn., Fordson HS, 1954–61. **Educ.:** Wayne State Univ., 1950–54, BA (Eng.) Hist.); Univ. of MI, 1954–57, MALS; West. MI Univ., 1967–68. **Orgs.:** NJ LA. Two Year Cmnty. Coll. Dirs. Org.: Pres. (1979–80). Monmouth Cnty. Area Lib. Cncl.: Exec. Bd. (1979–80). AECT. Delta Zeta: Detroit Alum. Grp. (Treas., 1957). **Honors** Beta Phi Mu; Pi Lambda Theta. **Activities:** 1, 10; 17, 32, 34; 56, 61, 92 **Addr.:** P.O. Box 148, Lincroft, NJ 07738.

Eber, Beryl E. (F. 1, 1948, New York, NY) Supvsg. Libn., Nathan Straus YA Lib., NY Pub. Lib., 1978–; Sr. YA Libn., Jefferson Market Br., NY Pub. Lib., 1972–78; YA Libn., Nathan Straus YA Lib., 1970–72; Libn., Yorkville Br., NY Pub. Lib., 1969–70. **Educ.:** City Coll. of NY, 1964–68, BA (Psych.); Columbia Univ., 1968–70, MLS. **Orgs.:** ALA. NY LA. **Activities:** 9; 17, 48 **Addr.:** Nathan Straus Young Adult Library, 20 West 53rd St., New York, NY 10019.

Eberhart, George M. (Je. 6, 1950, Hanover, PA) Ed., *Coll. & Resrch. Libs. News,* ACRL, ALA, 1980–; Serials/Reader Srvs. Libn., Univ. of KS Law Lib., 1977–80. **Educ.:** OH State Univ., 1968–73, BA (Jnlsm.); Univ. of Chicago, 1975–76, MLS. **Orgs.:** AALL. ALA: ACRL. Ctr. for UFO Std.: Staff Libn. (1980–). Mutual UFO Netwk.: Staff Libn. (1978–). **Pubns.:** *A Geo-Bibliography of Anomalies: Primary Access to Observations of UFOs, Ghosts, and Other Mysterious Phenomena* (1980); *A Survey of Ufologists and Their Use of the Library* (1978); "UFO Literature for the Serious Ufologist," *RQ* (Win. 1980); "Climatic Variation and the Exploration of Greenland," *Pursuit* (Fall 1978); "Witchcraft and Weather Modification," *Pursuit* (Spr. 1978); various articles (1977–78). **Activities:** 1, 3; 37, 44; 57, 70, 95-Parapsy. **Addr.:** Association of College & Research Libraries, 50 E. Huron St., Chicago, IL 60611.

Eberhart, Wilbur Lyle (My. 30, 1922, Topeka, KS) Asst. Supt., Admin., Div. of Lib. Srvs., WI Dept. of Pub. Instr., 1965–; Pub. Lib. Consult., WI Lib. 1962–65; Chief, Lib. Div., Detroit (MI) Pub. Lib., 1959–62; Asst. to Home Reading Srvs. Div., 1957–58. **Educ.:** Washburn Mncpl. Univ., 1941–45, AB (Hist.); University of WI, 1950–51, MSLS. **Orgs.:** ALA: Cncl. (1977–81); COSLA: Pres. (1980–81); Midwest Reg. Lib. Ntwk.: Pres. (1966–67); WI LA: Assn. of State Lib. Agencies: Pres. (1973–74). **Pubns.:** "State Libraries in the U.S.," *World Ency. of Lib and Info. Srvs.* (1980); "A Closer Look: Survey of American Adults Assesses the Role of Libraries in America," *Amer. Libs.* 1976); "Standards for State Library Agencies," *Lib. Trends,* (Fall 1978). **Activities:** 13; 17, 27, 34; 63, 78 **Addr.:** Division for Library Services, Wisconsin Department Public Instruction, 125 S. Webster St., P.O. Box 7841, Madison, WI 53707.

Ebershoff-Coles, Susan Vaughan (Lafayette, IN) Supvsr., Tech. Srvs., Indianapolis–Marion Cnty. Pub. Lib., 1976–, Asst. Supvsr., Tech. Srvs., 1969–75, Ref. Libn., 1967–69; Ref. Libn., Milwaukee Pub. Lib., 1965–67. **Educ.:** Purdue Univ., 1959–63, BS (Educ.); IN Univ., 1963–65, MLS. **Orgs.:** ALA. IN LA: Tech. Srvs. Div., Exec. Bd. (Ch., 1977). Hendricks Cnty. Humane Socty. U.S. Auto Club: Timing and Scoring Official. Sports Car Club of Amer.: Natl. Competition Licn. **Pubns.:** Jt. auth., *Motorsports: An Information Guide* (1979); various reviews, *Lib. Jnl., Amer. Ref. Bks. Anl.;* various articles in motorsports, env., animal welfare. **Activities:** 9; 15, 20, 22; 65 **Addr.:** Indianapolis–Marion County Public Library, P.O. Box 211, Indianapolis, IN 46206.

Eble, Mary Martha Coates (D. 6, 1917, Akron, OH) Lib.-Media Coord., Fairview Park Brd. of Educ., 1963–; Adjunct Prof., Case Western Resrv. Univ., Sch. of Lib. Sci., 1970–; Bkmobile Libn., Cuyahoga Cnty. Pub. Lib., 1963. **Educ.:** Notre Dame Coll., 1935–39, AB (Eng.); Case Western Resrv. Univ., 1963–67, MSLS, 1967–77 (Cert. in Supvsn.). **Orgs.:** ALA. ASIS: Pub. Com. (1970). OH Educ. Lib.-Media Assn.: Intell. Freedom Com. (1979–). Nat. Educ. Assn. OH Educ. Assn. Fairview Park Educ. Assn. Christ Child Socty. **Honors:** ALA, E.P. Dutton-John Macrae Award, 1972. **Pubns.:** "Literary Launchings," *Sch. Lib. Jnl.* (1969); "School Library Standards," *Cath. Lib. Wrld.* (1977); "Books Unlimited," *Jnl. of Readg.* (N. 1978). **Addr.:** Fairview High School, 4507 West 213 St., Fairview Park, OH 44126.

Ebner, William E. (O. 16, 1922, Canton, OH) Chief, Tech. Info. Srvs., Teledyne Ryan Aeronautical, 1967–; Resrch. and Dev. Ofcr., U.S. Air Frcs., 1942–67. **Educ.:** OH State Univ., 1947–51, BSc (Geol.); Univ. of CT, 1960–61, MBA. **Orgs.:** SLA: Aerosp. Div., Treas. (1971–73), Secy. (1979–80); San Diego Chap., Advert. Mgr. (1972–81). Natl. Class. Mgt. Socty. Natl. Mgt. Assn. Knights of Columbus. Aircraft Owner's and Pilots Assn. **Activities:** 12; 17, 24, 46; 52, 64, 91 **Addr.:** 4462 Algeciras St., San Diego, CA 92107.

Ebro, Diana Carole (Piccio) (D. 20, 1938, Bacolod City, Philippines) Asst. Dir. for Hlth. Sci., Univ. of MN-Duluth Lib., 1981–; Libn./Dept. Head, Circ./ILL, Univ. NE Med. Ctr. Lib., 1979–81; Med. Libn., Boehringer Ingelheim Ltd. Dr. Thomae Sci. Lib., Germany, 1971–78; Fachreferentin, Universitat Ulm Medizin-Naturwiss Hochschul-Bibl., Germany, 1967–71; Sr. Catlgr., Yale Univ. Sch. of Med. Lib., 1965–67; Libn. I, Univ. of the Philippines Lib., Coll. of Med. Lib., 1962–64; Grad. Sch. Pub. Admin. Lib., 1961–62; Libn., Pacifica Inc. Manila, 1959. **Educ.:** Univ. of the Philippines, 1954–58, BA (LS), 1961–63, Pub. Admin.; Simmons Coll., 1964–65, MSLS; 1964, Cert. as Jr. Mgt. Anal., 1967, Cert. in Med. Libnshp. **Orgs.:** MN LA. MN Cncl. Hlth. Sci. Libs. Med. LA: Intl. Coop. Com. (1978–79, 1980–81). Omaha Met. Area Libns. Club: Pres. (1980–81). NE LA. **Honors:** US Dept. of State, Fulbright, 1964; Sigma Delta Phi. **Pubns.:** Cmpir., *Thesaurus of Scientific Terms. Thesaurus Wissenschaftlicher Fachausdruecke;* Founded by Horst Schneider. (1978, 1979, 1980). **Activities:** 1, 12; 17, 22, 34; 58, 80, 87 **Addr.:** University of Minnesota-Duluth, Health Sciences Library, 2400 Oakland Ave., Duluth, MN 55811.

Eccles, Ann E. (N. 19, 1944, Manchester, CT) Sr. Libn., Hennepin Cnty. Lib., 1972–, Libn., 1969–72. **Educ.:** Salve Regina Coll., 1962–66, AB (Eng.); Rutgers Univ., 1967–70, GS (LS). **Orgs.:** ALA. MN LA: Mem. Com. (1977–79). Twin Cities Cath. Alum. Club. Cath. Alum. Clubs Intl.: Bd. of Dirs., Futures Com. (1978). **Activities:** 9; 16, 17, 39 **Addr.:** 6323 St. John Dr., Eden Prairie, MN 55344.

Echelman, Shirley T. (O. 7, 1934, Omaha, NE) Exec. Dir., Assn. of Resrch. Libs., 1981–; Exec. Dir., Med. LA, 1979–81; Asst. VP/Chief Libn., Chemical Bank, NY, 1966–79. **Educ.:** Univ. of NE, Omaha, 1952–56, BSc (Econ.); Rutgers Univ., 1964–66, MLS. **Orgs.:** SLA: Pres. (1977–78); Ch., Spec. Com. on Copyright Law Prac., (1977–78); Ch., Div. Cabinet (1975–76); Div. Liaison Off. (1972–75); John Cotton Dana Lectur. (1973–74); Ch., Bus. and Finance Div. (1971–72). Pub. Affairs Info. Srv., Bd. of Trustees (1972–). Natl. Lib. of Med., Bd. of Regents (1981–). ALA. Archons of Colophon. **Pubns.:** "Libraries are Businesses, Too," *SLA* (1974); "Networks and Cooperation", Lib. Jnl. (1974); "Toward the New Special Library," (1976); "Special Libraries in the Banking Industry," "The White House Conference on Library and Information Services," *ALA Yr. Bk.* (1980); *Spec. Delivery* (1978). **Activities:** 12; 17; 59, 61 **Addr.:** Association of Research Libraries, 1527 New Hampshire Ave. NW, Washington, DC 20036.

Echt, Sandy (My. 25, 1950, Pueblo, CO) Database Srvs. Libn., TX Christ. Univ., 1978–; Srch. Anal., Univ. of TX Hlth. Sci. Ctr., 1977–78; Srch. Anal./Ref. Libn., TX Coll. of Osteopathic Med., 1974–77. **Educ.:** Univ. of TX, 1969–72, BA (Eng.); N. TX State Univ., 1972–74, MLS; Med. Lib. Cert., 1974. **Orgs.:** ASIS. Med. LA. N.E. TX OLUG: Secy.–Treas. (1979–80); Fndr. (1979). **Pubns.:** Jt. auth., "Substitution of Scisearch and Social Scisearch for Their Print Versions in an Academic Library," *DATABASE* (Mr. 1980); "Save Time, Simplify Procedures, Get Better Statistics," *Online* (Ap. 1981). **Activities:** 1, 12; 41, 49-Info. retrieval; 56, 80, 91 **Addr.:** 665 Quail Ridge Rd., Aledo, TX 76008.

Eckard, Helen Marie (Mr. 17, 1930, Washington, DC) Admin. Libn., Nat. Ctr. for Educ. Stat., 1974–; Super. Libn., Defense Intelligence Agency, 1973–74; Admin. Libn., 1971–73; Bibl. Libn., 1969–71. **Educ.:** American Univ., 1948–52, BA (Eng. Lit.); Univ. of MD, College Park, 1966–68, MLS. **Orgs.:** SLA: Secy./Treas., Military Div. (1971–72); Prog./V. Ch., Washington Chap. (1972–73); Ch., (1973–74). ALA: Ex-Officio, Stat. Coord. & Ref. Com. **Honors** Phi Delta Gamma, 1966. **Pubns.:** *Statistics of Public Libraries–1974* (1978). **Activities:** 4; 17; 63 **Addr.:** National Center for Education Statistics, DMES/Learning Resources Branch, 400 Maryland Ave., S.W., Attn: 620 Presidential Building, Washington, DC 20202.

Eckel, Virginia E. (D. 20, 1924, Anderson, IN) Dir., Acad. Lib., Air Force Inst. of Tech., 1981–; Actg. Dir., 1979–81, Libn., Branch Lib., 1964–79, Libn., Catlgr., 1962–64; Libn., Ref., Tech. Lib. Wright-Patterson Air Force Base, 1952–62. **Educ.:** Ball State Univ., 1942–46, BS (Bus., LS); George Peabody Coll., 1949–53, MA (LS). **Orgs.:** SLA: Milit. Div. (Ch., 1972–73); Ctrl. OH Chap. (Treas., 1970–71). **Activities:** 1, 4 **Addr.:** 2993 Westcott Dr., Kettering, OH 45420.

Edberg, J. Fyle (Jl. 19, 1911, SD) Assoc. Prof. and Dir. of Lib. Srvs., Norwalk Cmnty. Coll., 1961–, Coord., Lib. Tech. Asst. Prog., 1970–; Supvsr., Norwalk Pub. Sch. Libs., 1956–61; Libn., Vets. Admin., 1951–56. **Educ.:** Lake Forest Coll., 1946–50, BA (U.S. Hist.); Univ. of IL, 1950–51, MLS; NY Univ., 1960–65 (Asian Std.). **Orgs.:** ALA. New Eng. LA. Fairfield Cnty. Lib. Admin. Grp., Cncl. of CT Cmnty. Coll. Libns. Asia Socty. Natl. Educ. Assn. Amer. Educ. Assn. CT Educ. Assn. Various other orgs. **Activities:** 1, 4, 13 **Addr.:** Deer Park Rd., New Canaan, CT 06840.

Eddison, Elizabeth Bole (Je. 3, 1928, Bronxville, NY) Pres., Warner-Eddison Assoc., Inc., 1980–, Ch., Treas., 1973–80; Secy., Bd. of Dirs., Colegio Nueva Granada, Colombia, 1969–71; VP, Assn. Amer. For. Srvs. Women, 1965–69; Coord., Soc. Srvs., Urban Srvs. Corps, 1965–69. **Educ.:** Vassar Coll., 1945–48, AB (Pol. Sci.); Simmons Coll., 1971–73, MS(LS). **Orgs.:** ALA. SLA: Cont. Educ. Com., Boston Chap. (1979). ASIS: Pres.-elect, Boston Chap. (1979–80). Comsn. on Engineer. Info. Adv. Com., Intl. Investment, Tech., & Dev. Dept. of State. **Honors:** Beta Phi Mu, 1973. **Pubns.:** Articles. **Activities:** 11; 17; 64, 86, 91 **Addr.:** Warner-Eddison Associates, Inc., 186 Alewife Brook Pkwy., Cambridge, MA 02138.

Eddy, Barbara J. (Ap. 28, 1941, Halifax, NS) Educ. Libn., Meml. Univ. of NF, 1966–, Lectr., Dept. of Curric. and Instr., 1970–73, Head Catlgr., 1964–66, Catlgr., 1962–64; Tchr., Brinton Meml. Sch., 1959–60. **Educ.:** Meml. Univ. of NF, 1962–67, BA, BA (Ed) (Eng., Fr., Psy.); McGill Univ., 1962–63, BLS. **Orgs.:** Atl. Provs. LA: Pres. (1981–82). Can. Sch. LA: Pres. (1975–76); Awds. Jury (1976–77). IFLA: Sch. Libs. Grp. (Secy., 1973–77). Can. LA: Bd. of Dirs. (1975–76); Cnclr. (1970–73, 1975–76); Ed. Bd. of Can. Mtrls. (1979–82); various other coms. (1966–76). Various other orgs. Meml. Univ. Fac. Assn. **Pubns.:** "Biography of Mother M. Xavier," *Dictionary of Canadian Biography* (1976); various reviews, *Can. Mtrls.* **Activities:** 1; 15, 17, 39; 56, 63, 95-Sch. libs. **Addr.:** Education Library, Memorial University of Newfoundland, St. John's, NF A1B 3Y1 Canada.

Eddy, Leonard M. (Ap. 26, 1932, Stamps, AR) Dir., Kornhauser Hlth. Sci. Lib., Univ. of Louisville, 1979–; Dir., Hlth. Sci. Ctr. Lib., Univ. of OK, 1962–79; Sci. Libn., 1961–62; Tech. Libn., ACF Industries, Inc., 1957–59. **Educ.:** South. State Coll., 1950–54, BSE (Educ.); Univ. of OK, 1959–61, MLS. **Orgs.:** Med. LA: Com. on Cert. (1970–74); Ch. (1973–74). OK LA: Treas. (1971–73); VP (1973–74); Pres. (1974–75). White House Conf. on Lib. and Info. Srvs.: Del. (1979). **Honors:** Phi Theta Kappa, 1951–52; Beta Phi Mu. **Activities:** 1; 17; 58, 80 **Addr.:** 1865 Princeton Dr., Louisville, KY 40205.

Edelen, Joseph R., Jr. (S. 5, 1944, Belleville, IL) Head, Tech. Srvs., Univ. of SD, 1969–; Catlgr., 1968–69. **Educ.:** St. Mary's Coll., 1962–66, BA (Phil., Hist.); St. Mary's Univ., 1966–67, BA (Hist., Eng.); Catholic Univ., 1967–68, MSLS. **Orgs.:** SD LA: Finance Com. (1974–77, 1977–). Mt. Plains LA: Exec. Secy. (1976–). ALA: ACRL; LITA; RTSD; JMRT, Const. and Bylaws Com. (Ch., 1976–77). Various other coms. Rotary; Pres., 1980–81. Clay Cnty. Hist. Socty. Phi Alpha Theta. **Honors:** Beta Phi Mu. **Pubns.:** "A Different Approach to Catalog Card Acquisitions," *MPLA Qtly.* (Fall, 1970); "The Faculty Library Committee: A State of the Arts Survey," *Catholic Lib. Wld.* (My., 1971). **Activities:** 1; 20, 46 **Addr.:** I. D. Weeks Library, University of South Dakota, Vermillion, SD 57069.

Edelman, Gayle Smith (F. 18, 1945, Chicago, IL) Head of Tech. Srvs., Univ. of Chicago Law Lib., 1980–; Head of Tech. Srvs., DePaul Univ. Law Lib., 1975–80, Head of Cat., 1972–75. **Educ.:** Univ. of IL, Chicago, 1963–67, BA (Soclgy., Anthro.); Univ. of IL, 1971–72, MLS; DePaul Univ., 1976–80, MA (Pub. Admin.). **Orgs.:** AALL: Tech. Srvs. Spec. Interest Sect. (Ch., 1982); Educ. Com., Liasion with Tech Srvs. Spec. Interest Sect. (1980–81); Dupls. Exch. Com. (Ch., 1978–79); OCLC Spec. Interest Sect. (Vice-Ch., 1978–79). Chicago Assn. of Law Libs.: Ch.-Elect (1981–82); Educ. Com. (Co-Ch., 1980–81); Place. Com. (Ch., 1977–79); Exec. Bd. (1974–75). IL OCLC Users' Grp.: Various ofcs. (1976–79). **Pubns.:** Jt. auth., "Teaching Practices of Academic Law Libraries," *Law Lib. Jnl.* (1978); index, *The Globe* (1976); various reviews, *Law Lib. Jnl.* (1977–78). **Activities:** 1; 17, 35, 46; 77, 78 **Addr.:** University of Chicago Law Library, 1121 E. 60th St., Chicago, IL 60637.

Edelman, Hendrik (N. 27, 1937, Wageningen, The Netherlands) Univ. Libn., Rutgers Univ., 1979–; Asst. Dir., Cornell Univ. Libs., 1970–78; Univ. Biblgphr., Jt. Univ. Libs., Vanderbilt Univ., 1967–70; D. Reidel Pub. Co. (The Netherlands), 1965–67; Martinus Nijhoff, Pub. & Bk-Sellers (the Netherlands), 1958–65. **Educ.:** George Peabody Coll., 1969, MLS. **Orgs.:** ALA. Bibl. Socty. of Amer. Socty. for Schol. Pub. NJ LA. **Honors:** ALA, Resrcs. Sect. Awd., 1976. **Pubns.:** *Dutch-American Bibliography 1693–1794,* (1974); *Short Title Check List of Dutch-American Imprints, 1848–1946* (In press); "Selection Methodology in Academic Libraries," *Lib. Resrcs. and Tech. Srvcs.* (1979); "Per. Lit. in a Changing Lib. Environment," *IEEE Transactions on Prof. Comm.* (S. 1977); "Development of the Collections in American University Libraries," *Coll. & Resrch. Libs.* (My. 1976). **Activities:** 1, 11; 15, 17, 24 **Addr.:** Rutgers University Library, New Brunswick, NJ 08903.

Edelson, Dr. Alan M. (Mr. 17, 1937, New York, NY) Pres. and Publshr., Raven Press, 1965–; Resrch. Assoc., Coll. of Physicians & Surgeons, Columbia Univ., 1972–73; Info. Sci., Columbia Med. Lib., 1964–65. **Educ.:** Univ. of Rochester, 1955–59, BS (Chem.); Columbia Univ., 1963–64, MSLS; Coll. of Physicians & Surgeons, 1966–72, PhD, (Physiology). **Orgs.:** Med. LA. NY Acad. of Sci. Amer. Chemical Socty. Socty. for Neurosci. Intl. Socty. for Neurochem. **Honors:** Phi Beta Kappa, 1959; Sigma Xi, 1971. **Pubns.:** Jt. auth., *Pre- and Post-junctional Effects of 1-Fluoro-2,4-Dinitrobenzene at the Frog Neuromuscular Junction,* (1973); Jt. auth., "Unit Responses in Anterolateral Hypothalamus to Local Stimulation," *The Physiologist* (1972); Jt. auth., "Intrinsic Connections of Caudate Neurons," *Brain Resrch.* (1973); Jt. auth., "Intrinsic Connections of Caudate Neu-

Special Subjects/Services: 50. Adult educ.; 51. Advert./Mktg.; 52. Aerosp.; 53. Agric.; 54. Area std.; 55. Arts/Hum.; 56. Autom.; 57. Bibl./Prtg.; 58. Bio. sci.; 59. Bus./Fin.; 60. Chem.; 61. Copyrt.; 62. Documtn.; 63. Educ.; 64. Engin.; 65. Env.; 66. Eth. grps.; 67. Film; 68. Food/Nutr.; 69. Geneal.; 70. Geo.; 71. Geol.; 72. Handcpd.; 73. Hist.; 74. Int. frdm.; 75. Info. sci.; 76. Insr.; 77. Law; 78. Legis.; 79. Math./Comp. sci.; 80. Med.; 81. Metals; 82. Nat. resrcs.; 83. Newsp.; 84. Nuc. sci.; 85. Oral hist.; 86. Petr./Energy; 87. Pharm.; 88. Phys./Astr./Math.; 89. Readg.; 90. Relig.; 91. Sci./Tech.; 92. Soc. sci.; 93. Telecom.; 94. Transp.; 95. (other).

rons," *Exper. Neurol.* (1973). **Activities:** 14-Publisher; 37; 58, 80, 91 **Addr.:** c/o Raven Press, 1140 Ave. of the Americas, New York, NY 10036.

Edelstein, Jerome Melvin (Jl. 31, 1924, Baltimore, MD) Chief Libn., Natl. Gallery of Art, 1972–; Hum. Biblgrphr. and Lectr. in Bibl., Univ. of CA, 1966–72; Libn. for Spec. Cols., NY Univ., 1964–66; Biblgrphr. for Medvl. and Renaissance Std., Univ. of CA, Los Angeles, 1962–64. **Educ.:** Johns Hopkins Univ., 1942–47, AB (Hist.); Univ. of MI, 1952–53, MLS. **Orgs.:** ALA: ACRL/Rare Bks. and Mss. Sect., Past Ch. Amer. Antiq. Socty. Bibl. Socty. of Amer.: BSA Papers. Bibl. Socty. (London), Notes Ed. ARLIS/NA. Various other orgs. Grolier. COSMOS. Century Assn. Rounce and Coffin. **Honors:** Phi Beta Kappa, Fulbright Comsn. Travel Grant, 1949–50. **Pubns.:** *A Bibliographical Checklist of Thornton Wilder* (1959); *A Garland for Jake Zeitlin* (1967); *The Library of Don Cameron Allen* (1968); *Wallace Stevens: A Descriptive Bibliography* (1974); various articles, reviews. **Activities:** 1, 8; 15, 17, 45; 55, 57, 74 **Addr.:** 3421 34th Pl. N.W., Washington, DC 20016.

Edgar, Neal Lowndes (Jn. 21, 1927, NY, NY) Assoc. Cur., Spcl. Cols., Kent State Univ. Lib., 1979–; Resrch. Libn., 1977–79, Acq. Libn., Serials Libn., 1967–77; Serials Catlgr., Lib. of Congs., 1965–66; Residence Halls Libn., Univ. of MI, 1961–65. **Educ.:** Trinity Coll., 1946–50, AB (Econ. Hist.); MA (Eng.); SUNY, Albany, 1956–58, MSLS; Univ. of MI, 1961–65, AMLS PhD (LS). **Orgs.:** ALA: Cat. Code Revision Com.; Jt. Com. on the Union List of Serials. OH LA. North OH Tech. Srvs. Libns.: various coms. Acad. LA of OH. AAUP. **Pubns.:** *History and Bibliography of American Magazines, 1810-1820* (1972). Contrib. to *Anglo-American Cataloguing Rules,* 2d Ed. (1978); Indexes; articles on Cat. and Pers.; Reviews. **Addr.:** Kent State University Library, Kent, OH 44242.

Edgar, Shirley A. (Jn. 30, 1935, Welland, ON) Coord., Lib. Tech. Prog., Fanshawe Coll. of Appld. Arts and Tech., 1977–; Coord., Info. Srvs., Lake Erie Reg. Lib. Syst., 1975–77; Reg. Ref. Libn., London Pub. Lib., 1972–75; Catlgr., 1969–72; Tutor (LS), Univ. of West. ON, 1967–69; Asst. Libn., Med. Lib., 1963–64; Catlgr., McMaster Univ., 1957–60. **Educ.:** McMaster Univ., 1953–57, BA (Gen.); Univ. of MI, 1957–60, AMLS. **Orgs.:** Can. LA. ON LA: Secy. (1979–81); Copyrt. Com. (1977–). Heritage Can. Hist. Mus. Adv. Com., London Public Lib. **Activities:** 9, 13; 26, 34, 39; 61, 67 **Addr.:** 270 Huron St., London, ON N6A 2J9 Canada.

Edgcombe, Frank Berkeley (My. 18, 1935, Plymouth, Devon, Eng.) Asst. Dir., Captain John Smith Lib., Christopher Newport Coll., 1978–; Dept. Head, Non Print Srvs., Montclair State Coll., 1973–78; Asst. Dir., Media, William Paterson Coll., 1970–73. **Educ.:** Bloomfield Coll., 1962–66, BA (Hist.); NY Univ., 1966–69, MA (Hist.), 1969, Dip. (TV Prod.); Rutgers Univ., 1970–72, MLS. **Orgs.:** ALA: RTSD/Reprodct. of Lib. Mtrls. Sect., Exec. Com. (1978–80); RASD, ILL Com. **Pubns.:** Photographs, *Amer. Libs.* (Mr. 1978). **Activities:** 1; 32, 33, 46; 56, 93 **Addr.:** Captain John Smith Library, Christopher Newport College, 50 Shoe Ln., Newport News, VA 23606.

Edge, Sharon M. (Ap. 10, 1945, Evansville, IN) Assoc. Prof. & Head, Circ. Dept., Univ. of Louisville Lib., 1976–; Asst. Head, Acq. Dept., 1973–75; Head, Docu. Div. & Ref. Libn., OH State Univ. Libs., 1971–73; Ref., Interlib. Loan Libn., Univ. of KY, 1968–71. **Educ.:** KY Wesleyan Coll., 1963–67, BA (Eng.); Univ. of KY, 1967–68, MSLS; IN Univ., 1976–78 (LS); Library of Congress Braille Transcription Cert., 1970–71. **Orgs.:** ALA: LITA (1968–); Lib. Resrcs. and Tech. Srvcs. (1968–69); ACRL (1968–); Gov. Docums. Roundtable (1972–79). ASIS: Costs, Budgeting, and Economics (1975–); Comput. Retrieval Srvs. (1975–77); Educ. for Info. Sci. (1975–77); Info. Srvs. to Educ. (1975–77). KY LA: Prof. Dev. Com. (1979–); Const. Rev. Com. (1971). Univ. of Louisville Lib. Assn.: Ch., Soc. Com. (1974–75). **Honors:** Beta Phi Mu; Lib. Binding Inst., Schol., 1967; Univ. of KY, Haggin Grad. Flwshp., 1967; KY Wesleyan Coll., Outstanding Schol. Ach. Gr., 1963–67. **Pubns.:** "Retrieval of Cataloged United States Government Publications From Integrated Library Collections," *KY LA Bltn.,* (1975); "Conference Report: Kentucky Libraries Association 65th Annual Conference, Toronto, Canada, June 9-13, 1974," *SLA, KY Prov. Chap. Bltn.;* "Conference Report: Kentucky Library Association, Special Libraries Section and Kentucky Provisional Chapter of SLA, Spring Meeting, Pleasant Hill, Kentucky, April 25-26, 1974" (1974); Ed., *Lib. Acq.: Practice and Theory,* (1980); Ed., *Spec. Libs. Assn., KY Chap. Bltn.* (1973–76). **Activities:** 1; 17, 22, 46; 56, 70, 72, 75 **Addr.:** Central University Library, University of Louisville, Louisville, KY 40292.

Edgerly, Linda (Ja. 9, 1950, Newton, NJ) Consult. Archvst., 1979–; Archvst., Chase Manhattan Bank, 1976–79; Archvst., Weyerhaeuser Co., 1975–76; Asst. Archvst., Rockefeller Fam. Arch., 1972–75; Asst. to Dir. and Archvst., N.E. Arch. of Folklore and Oral Hist., Univ. of ME, 1972. **Educ.:** Hood Coll., 1967–71, BA (Hist.); NY Univ., 1974–76, MA (Hist.). **Orgs.:** SAA: Bus. Arch. Com. (1975–79); Bus. Arch. Afnty. Grp., Vice-Ch. (1979–80), Ch. (1980–); Com. on Prof. Ethics (1977–79). Mid-Atl. Reg. Arch. Conf. Pac. NW Archvsts. NY Archvsts. RT: Strg. Com. (1978). Amer. Assn. for State and Lcl. Hist. Natl. Trust for Hist. Prsrvn. **Pubns.:** Ed., *The Church Pistols* (1977); various reviews (1979). **Activities:** 2; 15, 17, 24; 59, 62, 85 **Addr.:** 103 W. 75th St., New York, NY 10023.

Edlin, Katherine Chadwick (Ap. 1, 1926, Honolulu, HI) Asst. Dir., Greenwich Lib., 1969–; Libn. III, 1962–69; Photo Libn., Assoc. Press, NY, 1953–61. **Educ.:** Bryn Mawr Coll., Cornell Univ., 1946–50, BA (Fine Arts); Columbia Univ., 1961–62, MLS (Lib. Sci.). **Orgs.:** ALA. New England LA. CT LA. Target (1976). Cornell Club of Fairfield Co. **Activities:** 9; 17; 59, 65, 76 **Addr.:** Greenwich Library, 101 West Putnam Ave., Greenwich, CT 06830.

Edlund, Paul Erik (My. 11, 1922, Cortland, NY) Exec. Ofcr., Prcs. Srvs., Lib. of Congs., 1976–, Chief, Card Div., 1972–76, Exec. Ofcr., Prcs. Dept., 1968–72, Asst. Chief, Exch. and Gift Div., 1965–68, Col. Maintenance and Prsrvn. Ofcr., Admin. Dept., 1963–65, Head, Prep. Sect., Mss Div., Ref. Dept., 1961–63, Head, E. European Accessions Index Proj., Exch. and Gift Div., 1961, Head, Gift Sect., 1960–61; various prof. positions, 1955–60. **Educ.:** Yale Univ., 1945–48, BA (Hist.); Univ. of VA, 1949–54, MA (Hist.); Univ. of MI, 1954–55, MS (LS). **Orgs.:** Lib. of Congs.: Various coms. (1963–). ALA. **Pubns.:** "The Continuing Quest: Care of LCS Collections," *Lib. Jnl.* (S. 1, 1965); "A Monster and of Miracle: The Cataloging Distribution Service of the Library of Congress, 1901–76," *Qtly. Jnl. of the Lib. of Congs.* (O. 1976); various reviews, *Lib. Jnl.* (1966–70). **Activities:** 1, 4; 17, 41, 42; 55, 72, 73 **Addr.:** 11210 Kenilworth Ave., Garrett Park, MD 20896.

Edmonds, Anne Carey (D. 19, 1924, Penang, Malaysia) Libn., Mt. Holyoke Coll., 1964–; Libn., Douglass Coll./Rutgers Univ., 1961–64; Asst. Libn., Goucher Coll., 1951–60; Ref. Libn., City Coll. of NY, 1950–51; Chld. Asst., Enoch Pratt Free Lib., 1948–49. **Educ.:** Univ. of Reading, England, 1942–44, Dipl. (Com.); Barnard Coll., 1946–48, BA (Hist.); Columbia Univ., 1949–50, MLS; Johns Hopkins Univ., 1954–59, MA (Geo.); West. Resrv. Univ., 1960–61 (Lib. Sci.). **Orgs.:** MD LA. NJ LA. ALA: ACRL (Pres., 1970–71), Adv. Cncl., Acad. Lib. Dev. Proj., Univ. of NC at Charlotte (1975) and Drew. Univ. (1977–78). New Eng. Lib. Info. Network: Exec. Com. AAUP: Com. of MA State Conf. AAUW. Universal Ser. and Bk. Exch. Inc. (Bd. of Dirs.). Hist. Deerfield, Inc. (Adv. Comsn.). **Activities:** 1; 17, 24, 34 **Addr.:** Mount Holyoke College Library, South Hadley, MA 01075.

Edmonds, Edmund Patrick (Mr. 3, 1951, Omaha, NE) Assoc. Law Libn., Marshall-Wythe Sch. of Law Lib., Coll. of William and Mary, 1978–; Head, Circ. Dept., Univ. of Toledo Coll. of Law Lib., 1974–78. **Educ.:** Univ. of Notre Dame, 1969–73, BA (Hist.); Univ. of MD, 1973–74, MLS; Univ. of Toledo, 1974–78, JD, Law. **Orgs.:** AALL: Southeast. Chap. Amer. Bar Assn. **Honors:** Beta Phi Mu, 1974. **Pubns.:** "Postsecondary Athletics and the Law" *Jnl. of Coll. and Educ. Law,* (1977). **Activities:** 1; 31, 33, 39; 77 **Addr.:** Marshall-Wythe School of Law, College of William and Mary, Williamsburg, VA 23185.

Edsall, Shirley A. (Ja. 16, 1933, Bath, NY) Dir., Lrng. Resrcs., Wilson Meml. Hosp. (Johnson City, NY), 1978–; Asst. Prof., Sch. of Inf. and Lib. Stds., 1974–78; Asst. Prof. (LS), Univ. of MI, 1973–74; Head Libn., Corning Cmnty. Coll., 1961–70; Sch. Libn., Campbell Ctrl. Sch., 1955–61. **Educ.:** SUNY, Albany, 1950–54, AB (Math., Bio.); 1954–55, MSLS; Indiana Univ., 1970–73, PhD (LS); Med. LA, 1967, Cert.; NY State, 1955, Pub. Lib. Prof. Cert. **Orgs.:** Med. LA: Recert. Com. (1979–). Hlth. Resrcs. Cncl. of Ctrl. NY Strg. Com. (1978–; Secy., 1979–80). NY LA: Pers. Admin. Com. (1975–78); Coll. and Univ. Sect. (Bd. of Dir., 1967–69). ALA: various coms. CLENE. Various other orgs. AAUW. **Honors:** ALA, ACRL, Cmnty. and Jr. Coll. Libs. Sect., Cmdn. Awd., Beta Phi Mu. **Pubns.:** "AV Center for Individualized Learning," *Natl. Lib. of Med. News* (Ja. 1980); "Community College Librarian: A Profile," *Cmnty. and Jr. Coll. Jnl.* (D.-Ja. 1976); "Education of Community College Librarians," *Jnl. of Educ. for Libnshp.* (Fall 1975); A Study of the Administration... of Community College Libraries," ERIC Docum. IR 005 434 (1977). **Activities:** 1, 12; 17, 32, 39; 63, 75, 80 **Addr.:** C.S. Wilson Memorial Hospital, Department of Learning Resources, 33–55 Harrison St., Johnson City, NY 13790.

Edwards, Fern L. (N. 5, 1932, Topeka, KS) Coll. Libn., Gallaudet Coll. Lib., 1975–; User Srvs. Libn., 1973–75; Ref. Libn., 1969–73; Circ. Libn., 1967–69; Sr. Libn.; Brooklyn Pub. Lib., 1965–67; Basic Adult Educ. Spec., Bengal Soc. Srvs. Leag., Calcutta, 1960–65; Asst. Libn., Anderson Coll., 1957–59. **Educ.:** Anderson Coll., 1950–54, BS (Eng.); IN Univ., 1956–57, MA (LS). **Orgs.:** ALA. ASIS. DC LA. Metro. Washington Lib. Cncl.: Rep., Four-Year Colls., 1979–81. Conv. of Amer. Instrs. of the Deaf. **Pubns.:** "Individual Access to Nonprint Information for Deaf Students," *Catholic* Lib. *World* (S. 1974). **Activities:** 1, 9; 17, 32; 72 **Addr.:** Gallaudet College Library, 7th and Florida Ave., N.E., Washington, DC 20002.

Edwards, Ralph M. (Ap. 17, 1933, Shelley, ID) Chief of the Cen. Resrch. Lib., Dallas Pub. Lib., 1975–; Asst. Prof., Sch. of Libnshp., West. MI Univ., 1970–74; Libn., Portland (OR) Pub. Lib., 1964–67; Catlg. Libn., Univ. of IL Lib., 1961–62. **Educ.:** Univ. of WA, Seattle, 1955–59, BA (Eng.), 1959–60, MLS; Univ. of CA, Berkeley, 1967–70, DLS. **Orgs.:** Pub. LA: Com. on Interlib. Coop. (1976–78). ALA: ACRL; Lib. Admin. Div., Com. on Pub. (1977–79). **Honors:** Cncl. on Lib. Rsrcs., Univ. Lib. Mgt. Intern., 1974. **Pubns.:** *Role of the Beginning Librarian in University Libraries,* (1975); "The Management of Libraries and the Professional Functions of Librarians," *Lib. Qtly.* (Ap. 1975). **Activities:** 1, 9; 15, 17, 19 **Addr.:** Dallas Public Library, 1954 Commerce St., Dallas, TX 75201.

Edwards, Rita L. (Ap. 5, 1928, Toronto, ON) Dir., Lib. & AV Srvs., George Brown Coll. of Appld. Arts and Tech., 1980–, Dir., Lib. Srvs., 1968–80; Lectr., Lib. Arts Dept., Ryerson Polytech. Inst., 1969; Head Libn., Bathurst Heights Sec. Sch. (ON), 1963–68; Tchr., Libn., Laurentian HS (Ottawa, ON), 1961–63; various other teaching positions, 1951–61. **Educ.:** Univ. of Toronto, 1951, BA (Gen.); Univ. of Ottawa, 1962, BScB (LS; Magna cum Laude); Univ. of Toronto, 1964, BEd, 1969, MEd (Adult Educ.), 1971, MLS; Med. LA, 1975, Cert. (Nursing). **Orgs.:** Can. LA. Med. LA. ON Assn. of Coll. and Univ. Libs.: Ch. (1973–75). ON LA. Com. of Libns. Colls. of Appld. Arts and Tech. of ON: COM-O-LIB (Ed., 1979–). Various other orgs. Users Adv. Com., Coll. Bibliocentre. ON Assn. for Cont. Educ.: Cmnty. Coll. Com. (1969–70). Can. Wildlife Fed. Upper Can. Railway Socty. **Pubns.:** "Communicating With the Deaf," *COM-O-LIB* (N. 1979); "Introduction to Archives: A Seminar," *COM-O-LIB* (J. 1979); "George Brown Archives: Notes," *COM-O-LIB* (F. 1978); "The George Brown College Archives," *COM-O-LIB* (F. 1977); Various other articles. **Activities:** 1; 17, 19, 35; 50, 72, 80 **Addr.:** Apt. 1811, 33 Harbour Square, Toronto, ON M5J 2G2 Canada.

Edwards, Willie M. (Mr. 28, 1927, Winston Salem, NC) Libn., Inst. of Grntlgy., 1974–; Dir., Lrng. Resrc. Ctr., Univ. of MI, Inst. of Grntlgy., 1974; Libn., Tyler Sch., 1966–74; Head Subj. Biblgphr., MI State Univ., Agricultural Econ. Dept. Lib., 1962–64; Catlgr., Univ. of Nigeria, W. Africa, 1961–62; Asst. Div. Libn., Soc. Sci. Div., Univ. Lib., MI State Univ., 1957–60; Ref. Libn. and Book Sel. of Aged and Shut-ins, Iowa City Pub. Lib., 1955–57; Instr. in Lib. Sci., Dept. of Educ., South. Univ., Baton Rouge, 1952–55. **Educ.:** Livingstone Coll., 1945–48, BA (Soc./Econ.); Atlanta Univ., 1950–51, MSLS; Univ. of MI, 1978, Spec. in Aging Cert.; Univ. of MD, 1969 (Educ. Tech.). **Orgs.:** ALA: HRLSD (1975–76). SLA: Ref. Update, Age and Aging Sect. (1976–77, 1979–80). Grntlgy. Socty.: Hist. and Arch. Com. (1979–80). MI Socty. of Grntlgy.: Educ. Com. (1979–80). MI Acad. of Sci. **Pubns.:** *Gerontology: A Cross-National Core List of Significant Works, Revised and Expanded* (1981); Jt. auth., *Gerontology: A Core List of Significant Works,* (1978). **Activities:** 1, 2; 15, 17, 25; 58 **Addr.:** Institute of Gerontology, 520 E. Liberty St., University of Michigan, Ann Arbor, MI 48109.

Efird, Frank Kimball, Jr. (Jl. 11, 1949, Roanoke, VA) Archvst., IL State Arch., 1972–. **Educ.:** Carthage Coll., 1967–71, BA (Hist. & Span.); Univ. of WI, Madison, 1971–72, MSLS. **Orgs.:** SAA: Com. on Finding Aids (1974–79); Des. Grp. (1979–); Pub. Rec. Grp. (1979–). Midwest Arch. Conf.: Const. Com. (ad hoc) (1973). ALA. Springfield Lib. Club: Secy/Treas. (1979). Amer. Assn. for State and Local Hist. Sangamon Cnty. Hist. Socty. **Pubns.:** Contrib., IL Secy. of State Des. Inventory of the Archs. of the State of IL (1978); "A History of the Blacks of Madison, WI In Madison Black Book" (1970); "Report on the User Analysis Survey to the Committee on Finding Aids of the Society of American Archivists," *Midwestern Archvst* (1981); **Activities:** 2; 37, 41; 62 **Addr.:** Illinois State Archives, Office of the Secretary of State, Springfield, IL 62756.

Efron, Muriel C. (N. 15, 1925, Philadelphia, PA) Asst. Dir., Head, Pub. Srvs., FL Intl. Univ., 1976–; Head, Ref., 1974–76; Docum. Libn., 1971–74; Sch. Libn., Hebrew Acad. of Grtr. Miami, 1970–71. **Educ.:** San Antonio Coll., 1965–66; Univ. of TX, 1966–67; Univ. of PA, 1967–69, BA (Pol. Sci.); Drexel Univ., 1969–70, MS (LS); FL Intl. Univ., 1972–77, MS (Pub. Admin.); Univ. of Miami, 1977–81, JD (Law). **Orgs.:** ALA: GODORT (Asst. Coord., 1973–74). Dade Cnty LA. Assn. of Jewish Libs. AALL. Other orgs. United Fac. of FL: FIU Chap. (Secy., 1977–78). Leag. of Women Voters: Various Ofcs. **Activities:** 1; 17, 29, 39; 77, 78 **Addr.:** Florida International Univ. Library, Tamiami Trail, Miami, FL 33199.

Egan, Catherine M. (Mr. 3, 1943, Saskatoon, SK) Asst. Dir., AV Srvs., PA State Univ., 1977–, AV Mtrls. Spec., 1969–77. **Educ.:** Slade Sch. of Fine Art, Univ. of London, 1961–65, Dip. (Fine Art); Univ. of SK, 1966–68, BA (Fine Arts); Sir George Williams Univ., 1968–73, MA (Art Educ.). **Orgs.:** EFLA: Bd. of Dirs. (1973–76, 1981–84); Secy.; VP. AECT. PA Lrng. Resrcs. Assn. Cnsrtm. of Univ. Film Ctrs.: Eval.–Sel. Com.; Data Bank Com. **Pubns.:** Ed., *Perspectives on Film* (S. 1978, Ag. 1979, O. 1980); "Films about Artists and Their Audiences," *Sightlines* (Spr. 1981); "The Great Film Bazaar: Best Selling Educational Films of the Seventies," *Sightlines* (Fall–Win. 1980); "A-V Software" clmn. *Media and Methods* (1980–81); contrib. ed., *Sightlines, Media and Methods.* **Activities:** 1; 15, 17, 32; 55, 67, 93 **Addr.:** Audio Visual Services, The Pennsylvania State University, 208 Special Services Bldg., University Park, PA 16802.

PROFESSIONAL ACTIVITIES: Institutions: 1. Acad. lib.; 2. Arch.; 3. Assn.; 4. Fed./Gvt. lib.; 5. Inst. lib.; 6. Mfr./Suppl.; 7. Milit. lib.; 8. Musm.; 9. Pub. lib.; 10. Sch. lib.; 11. Sch. of lib. sci.; 12. Spec. lib.; 13. State lib.; 14. (other). **Functions/Activities:** 15. Acq./Col. dev.; 16. Adult srvs.; 17. Admin.; 18. Apprais.; 19. Archit./Bldgs.; 20. Cat./Class.; 21. Chld. srvs.; 22. Circ.; 23. Cons./Pres.; 24. Consult.; 25. Cont. ed.; 26. Educ. lib. sci.; 27. Ext. srvs.; 28. Fund/Grants; 29. Gvt. pubs.; 30. Indx./Abs.; 31. Instr. lib. use; 32. Media srvs.; 33. Micro.; 34. Netwks./Coop.; 35. Persnl.; 36. PR; 37. Publshg.; 38. Recs. mgt.; 39. Ref. srvs.; 40. Repro.; 41. Resrch.; 42. Review.; 43. Secur.; 44. Serials; 45. Spec. col.; 46. Tech. srvs.; 47. Trustees/Bds.; 48. YA srvs.; 49. (other).

Egan, Elizabeth M. (Ag. 19, 1930, Chicago, IL) Info. Coord., Lisle-Woodridge Pub. Lib., 1979–; Head of Adult Srvs., Lombard Pub. Lib., 1966–78. **Educ.:** Roosevelt Univ., 1975–77, BA (Eng.); Rosary Coll., 1977–79, MALS. **Orgs.:** Lib. Admins. Conf. of North. IL: Ch. (1975). ALA: Notable Bks. Com. (Ch., 1978–79); RASD. **Activities:** 9; 16, 24, 39 **Addr.:** Woodridge Public Library, 2525 Center Dr., Woodridge, IL 60517.

Egan, Sr. Kathleen, OSB (Mr. 13, 1915, Wales, Grt. Britain) Assoc. Libn., Benedictine Coll., 1972–, Ch., Drama Dept., 1948–71. **Educ.:** Mt. St. Scholastica Coll., 1946, BA (Eng.); Cath. Univ., 1947–48, MA (Drama); St. John's Univ., Jamaica, NY, 1971–72, MLS. **Orgs.:** Cath. LA: *Cath. Lib. World* Ed. Bd. (1978–). Midwest Cath. LA: Secy. (1974–76); Main Speaker (1975, 1979). KS Gvr.'s Task Frc. on Libs. Amer. Benedictine Acad. Pax Christi, U.S. CoWorkers of Mother Teresa of Calcutta: Reg. Vice-Ch. (1975–). **Pubns.:** Various reviews, sps. **Activities:** 1; 17, 32, 39 **Addr.:** Benedictine College, South Campus, 801 S. 8th St., Atchison, KS 66002.

Egan, Mary Joan (Jn. 22, 1929, Albany, NY) Dir. of Libs., Burnt Hills-Ballston Lake Schs., 1968–; Instr. (LS), SUNY Albany, 1964–; Elem. Libn., Burnt Hills Schs., 1958–61. **Educ.:** SUNY Albany, BS (LS); 1960, MS (LS); 1970, MS, (Educ. Admin.). **Orgs.:** ALA: AASL, Lib. Instr. Com. (Ch., 1970–74), Pubn. Com. (1971–75); John Cotton Dana PR Awd. Com. (1970–72; Ch., 1974–76). NY LA: Resrch. and Tech. Srvs. Div. (VP, 1970–71). Various other orgs. **Honors:** NY LA, Outstand. Sch. Lib. Media Awd., 1969; Delegate, NY Gov. Conf. on Libs., 1978–79. **Pubns.:** "Using TV to Teach Library Skills," *Instr.* (N. 1965); "Library Media Center," *AV Instr.* (O. 1972). **Activities:** 10; 20, 21, 24 **Addr.:** 2 Midline Rd., Ballston Lake, NY 12019.

Eggers, Sara H. (N. 17, 1930, Lincoln, NB) Dir., Old Bridge Pub. Lib., 1975–; Ref. Libn., Somerset Cnty. Lib., 1971–75. **Educ.:** Bryn Mawr Coll., 1948–52, BA (Phil.), Rutgers Univ., 1969–71, MLS. Various wkshps. **Orgs.:** NJ LA: Gvt. Rel. Com. (1977–80); Rec. Secy. (1980–82). Libs. of S. Middlesex: Secy.-Treas. (1978–79); Pres. of Dirs. (1980). Area Coord. Cncl.: VP (1978); Exec. Bd. (1977–80). ALA. Leag. of Women Voters. **Pubns.:** "Obscenity Law in NJ," *NJ Libs.* (O. 1977); "There Is No Free Lunch," *NJ Libs.* (Ap./My. 1978). **Activities:** 9; 17 **Addr.:** Old Bridge Public Library, 1 Old Bridge Plz., Old Bridge, NJ 08857.

Eggleton, Richard B. (F. 23, 1948, Waterbury, CT) Asst. Dir., Lib., Univ. NC, Charlotte, 1978–; Asst. Prof., Univ. NC, Greensboro, 1977–78; Dir., Thomas More Coll. Lib., 1974–76; Serials Libn., Keene State Coll., 1972–74. **Educ.:** Ctrl. CT State Coll., 1966–70, BS (Soc. Sci.); Drexel Univ., 1975–78, PhD (LS). **Orgs.:** ALA. LA (UK). **Pubns.:** "Conflict in Libraries Revisited," *Libri* (Mr. 1979); "Academic Libraries, Participative Management and Risky Shift," *Jnl. Acad. Libs.* (N. 1978); "The Tough-minded and the Tender-minded in Librarianship," *Wilson Lib. Bltn.* (O. 1978); various other articles. **Activities:** 1; 17, 26, 41; 56, 75, 92 **Addr.:** Atkins Library, Univ. of North Carolina, Charlotte, NC 28223.

Egoff, Sheila A. (Ja. 20, 1918, Auburn, ME) Prof., Sch. of Libnshp., Univ. of BC, 1961–; Ed., Can. LA, 1957–61; Ref. Libn., Toronto Pub. Lib., 1952–57, Chld. Libn., 1942–52; Chld. Libn., Galt Pub. Lib., 1938–42. **Educ.:** Univ. of Toronto, 1938, Dip. (LS), 1948, BA; Univ. of London, 1949, Dip. (LS). **Orgs.:** Can. LA. Brit. LA. ALA. BC LA. **Honors:** Univ. of Toronto, Fac. of LS Alum. Assn., Jubilee Awd., 1980; May Hill Arbuthnot Hon. Lectr., 1979. **Pubns.:** Jt. ed., *Only Connect* (1980); ed., *One Ocean Touching* (1979); *Thursday's Child: Trends and Patterns in Contemporary Children's Literature* (1981); *The Republic of Childhood: A Critical Guide to Canadian Children's Literature* (1975); "Beyond the Garden Wall," *Top of the News* (Spr. 1979). **Activities:** 9; 21, 48; 55 **Addr.:** School of Librarianship, University of British Columbia, Wesbrook Mall, Vancouver, BC V6T 1W5 Canada.

Ehlert, Arnold Douglas (Ap. 22, 1909, Mondovi, WI) Dir. of the Lib., The Institute for Creation Resrch., 1981–; Dir. of Libs., Christian Heritage Coll. and The Inst. for Creation Resrch., 1974–80; Grad. Stds. Libn., Talbot Theo. Semy., 1969–74; Libn., Prof. (LS), Biola Coll., 1955–69; Libn., Fuller Theo. Semy., 1948–55; Libn., Dallas Theo. Semy., 1942–48. **Educ.:** John Fletcher Coll., 1928–32, AB (Gk.); Dallas Theo. Semy., 1942–45, ThM ThD; Univ. of South. CA, 1949–53, MSLS. **Orgs.:** ATLA. Christ. LA; Natl. Assn. of Evangelicals. Intl. Socty. of Bible Collectors: Pres. (1964–). **Honors:** Beta Phi Mu. **Pubns.:** *The Biblical Novel, a Checklist* (1960); *Bibliographic History of Dispensationlism* (1965); *Brethren Writers,* (Checklist Intro. Essay) (1969). **Activities:** 1; 35, 39; 57, 69, 90 **Addr.:** 1262 Camillo Way, El Cajon, CA 92021.

Ehlinger, Clifford J. (Ja. 24, 1945, Chicago, IL) Dir., Div. of Media, Grant Wood Area Educ. Agency, 1973–; Instr., North. IL Univ., 1971–73; Sch. Dist. #48, Villa Park, 1966–71. **Educ.:** Elmhurst Coll., 1962–66, BA (Educ.); North. IL Univ., 1966–69, MA (Instr. Tech.), 1969–73, EdD (Instr. Tech.). **Orgs.:** ALA: AASL. AECT: Definitions Com. Natl. Assn. of Reg. Media Ctrs.: State Rep. (1978–81); Treas. (1981–83); Pubn. Ch. (1980–81). EFLA: Bd. (1980–83). IA Educ. Media Assn.: Conf. Ch. (1981). Amer. Assn. of Sch. Admins. Amer. Socty. for Trng. and Dev. **Pubns.:** "Reel Communications: Objective Film Use," *Sightlines* (Win. 1978–79); "Media Specialist and Special Educator–A Partnership That Makes Sense," *AV Instr.* (D. 1976); "Instructor's Reel Winners," *Instr.* (D. 1980). **Activities:** 14-Reg. lib. **Addr.:** Division of Media, Grant Wood Area Education Agency, 4401 Sixth St. S.W., Cedar Rapids, IA 52404.

Ehrenberg, Ralph E. (O. 14, 1937, Minneapolis, MN) Asst. Chief, Geo. and Map Div., Lib. of Congs., 1979–; Dir., Cartograph. Arch. Div., Natl. Arch. and Recs. Srv., 1966–79. **Educ.:** Univ. of MN 1963, 1968. **Orgs.:** SLA. SAA. Amer. Congs. on Surveying and Mapping. Assn. of Amer. Geographers. **Pubns.:** Jt. auth., *The Mapping of America* (1980); *Maps and Architectural Drawings* (1981); "Mapping the Nation's Capital," *Lib. of Congs. Qtly.* (1979); "Taking the Measure of the Land," *Prologue* (1977). **Activities:** 2, 4; 33, 45; 70 **Addr.:** 9219 Bells Mill Rd., Potomac, MD 20854.

Ehresmann, Julia M. (Ap. 12, 1939, New Orleans, LA) Staff reviewer, ALA, 1979–; Instr., Hum., William Rainey Harper Coll., 1972–79; Spec. Srvs. libn., Geneva Pub. Lib., 1973–79; Ref. libn., SUNY, Brockport, 1969–71. **Educ.:** Pomona Coll., 1957–61, BA (Art Hist.); Inst. of Fine Arts, NY Univ., 1961–67, MA (Art Hist.); Rutgers Univ., 1965–66, MLS. **Orgs.:** Art Libns. Socty. of N. Amer. Coll. Art Assn. IL LA. **Honors:** Beta Phi Mu. **Pubns.:** *Pocket Dictionary of Art Terms* (1979); *Geneva, IL: A History of Its Times and Places* (1977). **Activities:** 1, 9; 36, 39, 42; 55, 85 **Addr.:** 217 North St., Geneva, IL 60134.

Ehrhardt, Allyn (Ap. 13, 1940, Columbus, OH) Dir., Franklin Univ. Lib., 1966–; Asst. Libn., Ref. Dept., Columbus Pub. Lib., 1965–66; Asst. Libn., Sci. Lib., Univ. of IL, 1964–65; Asst. Libn., Ref. Dept., Columbus Pub. Lib., 1960–64. **Educ.:** OH State Univ., 1958–61, BA (Eng.); Univ. of IL, 1964–65, MS (LS). **Orgs.:** ALA. SLA. OH LA: Lib. Dev. (1969–71); Nom. Com. (1975–78). Amer. Casting Assn.: Pres. (1978–80). **Activities:** 1; 15, 17, 39; 59, 92 **Addr.:** Franklin University Library, 303 S. Grant Ave., Columbus, OH 43215.

Ehrhardt, Margaret W. (S. 17, 1918, Orangeburg, SC) Lib. & Media Consult., SC Dept. of Educ., 1965–; Order Libn., Wofford Coll., 1964–65; Asst. Order Libn., Univ. of SC, 1960–64; Chld. Libn., Richland Cnty. Pub. Lib., 1952–58. **Educ.:** Duke Univ., 1935–39, BA (Hist.); Emory Univ., 1945–49, BALS; Furman Univ., 1970; Univ. of Pittsburgh, 1978 (Media). **Orgs.:** ALA. SC LA: Pres. (1977); Secy. (1971–72). Southeast. LA: Manpower Com. (1977). Nat. Assn. of State Educ. Media Profs. Delta Kappa Gamma: Schol. Ch. (1978). **Pubns.:** "Evaluating the Performance of the School Media Specialist," *SC Libn.* (1979); "Facts & Figures; you & your SC School Library Media Centers," *Media Ctr. Messenger* (1979). **Activities:** 10, 13; 21, 24, 48; 63, 74, 89 **Addr.:** 227 Lawand Dr., Columbia, SC 29210.

Eiberson, Harold (S. 5, 1913, New York, NY) Chief Libn., Baruch Coll. Lib., 1963–; Ref., Tech. Srvs., 1933–63. **Educ.:** City Coll., NY, 1929–33, BSS (Hist.); Columbia Univ., 1934–36, MA (Hist.), 1934–37, BLS. **Orgs.:** ALA. LA, City Univ. of NY: Pres. (1943–46). NY Lib. Club: Secy. (1951–54). **Pubns.:** *Sources for the Study of the New York Area* (1960). **Activities:** 1; 17 **Addr.:** 227-08 57th Rd., Oakland Gardens, NY 11364.

Eichman, Thomas Lee (D. 17, 1940, Sibley IA) Private Resrch. and Wrtg., Asst. Prof., Hum. Div., IN State Univ., 1970–75. **Educ.:** Univ. of SD, 1958–62, BA (Math.); Univ. of IA, 1962–65, MA (Grmn.); Univ. of IL, 1967–71, PhD (Ling.); Univ. of MD, 1975–76, MLS. **Orgs.:** ASIS. Ling. Socty. of Amer. Mod. Lang. Assn. of Amer. AAUP. **Pubns.:** "Speech Action in the Library," *Lings. in the Profs.* (1980); "The Complex Nature of Opening Reference Questions," *RQ* (1978); "Applied Linguistics in Librarianship," *DE Symp. on Lang. Stds.,* I (1979); "Subject Heading Syntax and 'Natural Language' Nominal Compound Syntax," *The Info. Age in Perspective, ASIS Proceedings, 15.* (1978); Jt. auth., "Copyright Clearinghouse: In-Depth Study," *Copyright and Photocopying.* (1977). **Activities:** 14-Self-employed; 41; 55, 75 **Addr.:** 3401 Stanford St., University Hills, MD 20783.

Eidelman, Diane L. (N. 4, 1950, Youngstown, OH) Docum. Libn., Suffolk Coop. Lib. Syst., 1978–; Ref./Docum. Libn., Youngstown State Univ., 1973–78. **Educ.:** Youngstown State Univ., 1970–72, BA (Eng.); Kent State Univ., 1972–73, MLS; Youngstown State Univ., 1975–80, MA (Hist.). **Orgs.:** Suffolk Cnty. LA: Exec. Bd. (1980–). NY LA: GODORT (Prog. Ch., 1980–81). ALA: Eval. Com. on Fed. Gvt. Info. Progs. and Srvs. (1979–). **Pubns.:** Various reviews, (1981). **Activities:** 1, 9; 29, 39; 78, 92 **Addr.:** Suffolk Cooperative Library System Documents Dept., P.O. Box 187, Bellport, NY 11713.

Eidelson, Elizabeth Shaps (Ja. 16, 1936, Boston, MA) Asst. Dir., Lower Merion Lib. Assn., 1978–; Head Libn., Ludington Lib., 1978–; Head Libn., Penn Wynne Lib., 1976–78. **Educ.:** Barnard Coll., 1955–56, AB (Eng.); Simmons Coll., 1964–70, MSLS. **Orgs.:** Montgomery Cnty. Dist. Lib.: Pub. Rel. Ch. (1977–78). PA LA: S.E. Chap., Board and Arrange. Ch. (1978–79). **Activities:** 9; 16, 17, 36 **Addr.:** Lower Merion Library Assn., Bryn Mawr & Lancaster Aves., Bryn Mawr, PA 19010.

Einhorn, Nathan R. (Ja. 15, 1923, York, PA) Chief, Exch. and Gift Div., Lib. of Congs., 1968–; Asst. Chief, Order Div., 1964–68; Asst. Chief, Exch. and Gift Div., 1958–64. **Educ.:** PA State Univ., 1941–43, 1945–47, BA (Educ.); Harvard Univ., 1947–49, MA (Hist.); Columbia Univ., 1949–50, MS (LS). **Orgs.:** DC LA. ALA. COSLA: Lib. of Congs. Liaison (1968–). **Activities:** 4; 15; 62, 78 **Addr.:** 3507 DePauw Pl., College Park, MD 20740.

Eiselstein, June Ellen (D. 28, 1949, Huntington, WV) Branch Head, Enoch Pratt Free Lib., 1976–, Chlds. Libn., 1974–76; Bkmobile. Libn., Newport News Pub. Lib. Syst., 1972–74. **Educ.:** Marshall Univ., 1967–71, BA (Educ.); Univ. of Pittsburgh, 1971–72, MLS. **Orgs.:** ALA: PLA/Small and Medium Sized Libs. Sect., Starter List for New Branch Libs. Com. (1978–80); ALSC, Lib. Srv. to Chld. with Spec. Needs Com. (1976–78). **Activities:** 9, 10; 17, 21, 27; 72, 89 **Addr.:** 7723 Greenview Terr., Apt. 170, Towson, MD 21204.

Eisen, David John (D. 11, 1949, Zeeland, MI) Dir., Mishawaka-Penn Pub. Lib., 1980–; Asst. Dir., 1977–80; Head, Adlt. Srvs., 1975–77; Adjunct Prof., IN Univ., S. Bend, 1977. **Educ.:** Calvin Coll., 1968–72, BA (Hist.); Univ. of MI, 1974, MLS; Univ. of VA, 1972–73, MA (Hist.). **Orgs.:** IN LA. ALA. Friends of Libs. IN Oral Hist. Roundtable. IN Film Cncl. **Pubns.:** *Biographical Index to St. Joseph County Indiana Histories* (1978). **Honors:** Beta Phi Mu. **Activities:** 9; 17, 30, 35; 69, 75 **Addr.:** Director, Mishawaka-Penn Public Library, 209 Lincoln Way East, Mishawaka, IN 46544.

Eisen, Marc (Ap. 12, 1940, New York, NY) Asst. Dir., East Orange (NJ) Pub. Lib., 1976–; Head, Ref., 1966–76; Head, Adult Srvs., Ref., Piscataway (NJ) Pub. Lib., 1965–66. **Educ.:** Syracuse Univ., 1956–60, AB (Eng.); Rutgers Univ., 1963–65, MLS; Brooklyn Coll., 1960–61 (Eng.). **Orgs.:** Beta Phi Mu: Rutgers Chap. (Pres., 1971–72). ALA. NJLA: Ref. Sect. (Pres., 1972–73); Parlmt.; various coms. NJ Educ. Assn. **Activities:** 9; 17, 39 **Addr.:** 786 Warren St., Westfield, NJ 07090.

Eisen, Sylvia A. (Ap. 30, 1924, New York, NY) Consult., Libn., Oceanside Jewish Ctr., 1979–; Dir. (Retired 4/79), Long Beach Pub. Lib., 1975–79; Chld. Srvs., Elmont Pub. Lib., 1965–75; Consult., Adelphi Bus. Sch., 1972–73. **Educ.:** Brooklyn Coll., 1940–44, BA (Fr./Educ.); Queens Coll., 1965–68, MLS. **Orgs.:** ALA. NY LA. Nassau Cnty. LA: Stat. Ch. (1972–73); Const. and By-laws Ch. (1975–). Jewish Libns. Caucus: Treas. (1975–). **Activities:** 9, 10; 17, 21, 24 **Addr.:** 690 Anderson Avenue, Franklin Sq., NY 11010.

Eisenbach, Elizabeth R. (Terre Haute, IN) Assoc. Dean (LS), Univ. of CA, Los Angeles, 1979–; Lectr., 1966–; Libn., 1962–66. **Educ.:** Stanford Univ., BA (Econ.); Univ. of CA, Los Angeles, 1960–62, MLS. **Orgs.:** ALA. CA LA: Cont. Educ. Com. (1978–). **Pubns.:** Jt.-auth., *The Effective Reference Librarian* (1981); "Bibliographic Instruction from the Other Side of the Desk," *RQ* (Sum. 1978); "No Case Histories, No Papers, No Texts-Only the Reference Desk," *RQ* (Sum. 1978). **Activities:** 1, 11; 25, 26, 31; 57, 63, 74 **Addr.:** Graduate School of Library & Information Science, Univ. of California, Los Angeles, CA 90024.

Eisenberg, Michael B. (O. 4, 1949, Brooklyn, NY) Coord., Fld. Work/Sch. Media, Sch. of Info. Std., Syracuse Univ., 1979–, Adj. Fac., 1977–; Head, Lib. Media Spec., Manlius HS, 1974–81; Soc. Std. Tchr., Valencia HS, 1972–73. **Educ.:** SUNY, Albany, 1967–71, BA (Hist., Educ.), 1973, MLS. **Orgs.:** NY LA. Ctrl. NY Media Specs. NY State Untd. Tchrs. NY State Assn. for Hum. Educ.: Ctrl. NY Admin. (1980–81). **Pubns.:** "The View from the Other Side," *Sch. Lib. Jnl.* (D. 1980); "The High School Library Media Center and the Humanities," *Bookmark* (Win. 1980); "Book-talk Fever," *Media and Methods* (Mr. 1979). **Activities:** 10, 11; 26, 32, 48; 63 **Addr.:** School of Information Studies, Syracuse University, 113 Euclid Ave., Syracuse, NY 13210.

Eisenhart, Ruth (Cecilia) (S. 28, 1909, Binghamton, NY) Retired, 1979–; Assoc. Cat. Ed., Pre-1956 Natl. Union Cat. Pubn. Proj., Lib. of Congs., 1969–1979; London Ed., Pre-1956 Natl. Union Cat. Pubn. Proj., ALA, 1967–69; Head Catlgr., Union Theo. Semy., 1940–67; Catlgr., Yale Univ. Lib., 1932–40. **Educ.:** Mount Holyoke Coll., 1928–32, BA (Eng.); Columbia Univ., 1935–38, BS (LS). **Orgs.:** ALA: RTSD, Cat. Policy and Resrch. Com. (1962–67). ATLA: various coms.; Consult. to ALA Cat. Code Rev. Com. (1961–62). **Honors:** Phi Beta Kappa. **Pubns.:** Ed., *Classification of the Library of Union Theological Seminary* (Rev., 1967); Working paper on Liturgical and Rel. entries prepared for Intl. Conf. on Cat. Prins., Paris, 1961. Conducted wkshps. on Theo. Cat. and Class. in S.E. Asia, 1966. **Activities:** 1; 20; 90 **Addr.:** 2500 Wisconsin Ave., N.W., Washington, DC 20007.

Eiser, Mary Jo (Ag. 24, 1951, Punxsutawney, PA) Tech. Inf. Ctr. Mgr., Sybron/Taylor Instrument, 1977–; Libn., Sybron/Pfaudler, 1975–77; Sr. Lib. Clerk, Rochester Pub. Lib., 1974–75. **Educ.:** PA State Univ., 1969–73, BS (Educ.); SUNY, Geneseo, 1974–75, MLS. **Orgs.:** SLA: Employment Com. (1978–). Monroe Cnty. Lib. Club: Mem. Ch. (1977–). Rochester Online

Special Subjects/Services: 50. Adult educ.; 51. Advert./Mktg.; 52. Aerosp.; 53. Agric.; 54. Area std.; 55. Arts/Hum.; 56. Autom.; 57. Bibl./Prtg.; 58. Bio. sci.; 59. Bus./Fin.; 60. Chem.; 61. Copyrt.; 62. Documtn.; 63. Educ.; 64. Engin.; 65. Env.; 66. Eth. grps.; 67. Film; 68. Food/Nutr.; 69. Geneal.; 70. Geo.; 71. Geol.; 72. Handcpd.; 73. Hist.; 74. Int. frdm.; 75. Info. sci.; 76. Insr.; 77. Law; 78. Legis.; 79. Math./Comp. sci.; 80. Med.; 81. Metals; 82. Nat. resrcs.; 83. Newsp.; 84. Nuc. sci.; 85. Oral hist.; 86. Petr./Energy; 87. Pharm.; 88. Phys./Astr./Math.; 89. Readg.; 90. Relig.; 91. Sci./Tech.; 92. Soc. sci.; 93. Telecom.; 94. Transp.; 95. (other).

Users Group. **Pubns.:** Ed., *SLA Jobs Bltn.* **Addr.:** Taylor Instrument Company, 95 Ames St., Rochester, NY 14601.

Eiss, Merle I. (O. 10, 1935, Chicago, IL) Supvsr., Tech. Info. Ctr., McCormick and Co., 1980–; Info. Sci., 1972–79; Chem., Sinai Hosp., 1967–71; Chem., Amer. Cyanamid Co., 1957–60. **Educ.:** Purdue Univ., 1953–57, BS (Chem.). **Orgs.:** SLA: Food and Nutr. Div. (Ed., *Bltn.*, 1976–78). Amer. Chem. Socty.: Cnslr. (1978–); Bus. Ed., *Bltn.* (1978–); Middle Atl. Reg. Mtg. (Ch., 1978–). ASIS. **Pubns.:** "Irradiation Treatment of Onion Powder," *Jnl. Food* Sci. (1979); "Effect of Irradiation on ... Onion Powder," *5th Intl Congs. of Food Sci and Tech.*, Japan, 1978; "Spices, Herbs, Flavor Materials," *Food Sci. and Tech., A Bibl.*, U.S. Dept. of Agr. (F. 1978); Other articles, and presented papers. **Activities:** 12; 17, 46; 60, 68 **Addr.:** Merle I. Eiss, McCormack & Co., 204 Wight Ave., Hunt Valley, MD 21031.

Ekechukwu, Myriette Revenna Guinyard (Jn. 19, 1935, Orangeburg, SC) Columbus Branch Mgr., Tucson Pub. Lib., 1977–; Chlds. Libn., Tucson Pub. Lib., 1975–77; Head, Lib., Inst. of Mgt. and Tech. (Enugu, Nigeria), 1974–75; Head, Trng. and Resrch. Sect., State Lib. (Enugu, Nigeria), 1973–74; Branch Libn., Minneapolis Pub. Lib., 1969; Sch. Libn., Denmark, SC, 1968–69; various other positions. **Educ.:** SC State Coll., 1952–56, BS (Educ.); Univ. of SC, 1966–67, MS (LS); Univ. of WA, 1969–72, PhD (Educ.); Inst. of Libnshp., Univ. of Ibadan (Nigeria), 1961–62, (LS). **Orgs.:** ALA. SWLA. AZ LA. Beta Phi Mu, Tucson Chap. (1978–79). **Honors:** Various grants. **Pubns.:** "Library Services to Young Adults in Eastern Nigeria," *Lib. Srvs. to YAs* (1968); "Public Library Services for Children," *The Renaissance Wkly.* (N. 11, 1973); "The School Library - A Force for Educational Excellence," *The Renaissance Wkly.* (N. 9, 1974); Various other pubns. and presented papers. **Activities:** 9, 10; 17, 21, 27; 63, 66, 85 **Addr.:** 2402 East Eastland, Tucson, AZ 85719.

Elchesen, Dennis Raymond (Jl. 19, 1945, Cleveland, OH) Head, Resrch. Info. Grp., Lawrence Livermore Natl. Lab., 1979–; Head, Info. Proc. Grp., 1978–79; Head, Br. Libs., 1977–78; Tech. Info. Spec., 1969–77. **Educ.:** Cleveland State Univ., 1963–68, BS (Chem.); Case-Western Resrv. Univ., 1968–69, MSLS; Univ. of CA, Berkeley, 1974–81, PhD (expected) (Info. Sci.). **Orgs.:** ASIS: (Pres., Std. Chap., Case-Western Resrv. Univ., 1969). Assn. of Info. and Dissem. Ctrs. **Pubns.:** "Cost Effectiveness Comparison of Manual and On-Line Retrospective Bibliographic Searching," *Jnl. of the Amer. Socty. for Info. Sci.* (Mr. 1978); "Dedicated Versus Resource-Shared Library Computer Systems," *Spec. Libs.* (Jl. 1976); "A Correlation of Bibliographic Data Elements for Use in a Generalized File Management System," *Jnl. of the Amer. Socty. for Info. Sci.* (1973); "Effectiveness of Combining Title Words and Index Terms in Machine Retrieval Searches," *Nature* (1972); "Monitoring and Retrieving Literature Searches Using a Generalized File Management System," *ASIS* (1971). **Activities:** 4, 12; 17, 39, 41; 56, 75, 91 **Addr.:** Lawrence Livermore Laboratory, Technical Information Department, Library L-53, P. O. Box 5500, Livermore, CA 94550.

Elder, Eleanor Shafer (S. 18, 1935, Lake Charles, LA) Sci. Libn., Univ. of New Orleans, 1970–. **Educ.:** Univ. of Southwest. LA, 1952–55, BS (Chem.); Univ. of Houston, 1956–58, MS (Chem.); Univ. of New Orleans, 1966–69, PhD (Chem.); LA State Univ., 1977–79, MLS. **Orgs.:** LA LA: Acad. Sect., Nsltr. Co–ed.; LA Online Interest Grp. Amer. Chem. Assn.: LA Sect., Arch. Com., Ch. AAUP. **Honors:** Beta Phi Mu. **Pubns.:** "Sir William Crookes, Victorium, and the Library of Congress," *Jnl. of Chem. Educ.* (1980); jt. auth., "The Deadly Outcome of Chance–Vera Estaf'evna Bogdanovskaia," *Jnl. of Chem. Educ.* (1979); jt. auth., "Research versus Teaching: A Selected Review," *Improving Coll. and Univ. Tchg.* (1976); "Agnes Pockels–Indeed a Lady," *Chem.* (1974); jt. auth., "Final Field Results of Traditional Logic and the Venn Diagram: A Programmed Introduction," *Jnl. of Exper. Educ.* (1973); various articles in chem. (1960–67). **Activities:** 1; 39, 49-Online srvs.; 60, 91 **Addr.:** Earl K. Long Library, University of New Orleans, Lakefront, New Orleans, LA 70148.

Elder-Green, Jenelle (Je. 6, 1936, Knoxville, TN) Mass Media Spec., Milwaukee Pub. Sch., 1966–; Tchr., Libn., 1971–77; Sch. Lib. Supvsr., 1969–71; Tchr., Libn., 1966–69; Pub. Libn., Milwaukee Pub. Lib., 1962–66. **Educ.:** Knoxville Coll., 1954–58, BA (Eng.); Univ. of KY, Lexington, 1960–62, MSLS; Univ. of WI, Milwaukee, 1978 (Urban Std./Admin.). **Orgs.:** Southeast. WI LA: Pres. (1977), VP (1976), Treas. (1975). WI Sch. Lib. Media Assn.: Pres (1978), VP (1977), Secy. (1973). Amer. Sch. Lib. Assn.: Afflt. Asm., VP (1978). WI AV Assn. Alpha Kappa Alpha: VP (1973); Secy. (1972). **Honors:** WI Sch. Lib. Media Assn., Srvc. Awd., 1979; WI LA, Gov. and White House Conf. Del., 1979. **Pubns.:** "Spanish in the library media Center," *WI Lib. Bltn.* (1978); "The reluctant readers among us," *WI Lib. Bltn.* (1969). **Activities:** 10; 32, 36 **Addr.:** Division of Relationships, Milwaukee Public Schools, P.O. Drawer 10 K, Milwaukee, WI 53201.

Eldred, Heather Ann (S. 4, 1942, Racine, WI) Syst. Admin., WI Valley Lib. Srvc., 1972–; Catlgr., Holy Redeemer Coll., 1970–72; Actg. Head, Catlgr., Marquette Univ. Law Sch. Lib., 1966–70; Chld. and YA Libn., Cudahy Pub. Lib., 1965–66. **Educ.:** Univ. of WI, 1960–64, BA (Eng. Lit.), 1964–65, MALS; N. Central Tech. Inst., 1975, 1981 (Sign Lang.); Miami Univ., 1976 (Lib. Std.). **Orgs.:** WI LA. ALA. **Pubns.:** "Cooperation with potential: Wisconsin Valley school & system libraries," *WI Lib. Bltn.*, (Ja. 1974). **Activities:** 4, 9; 17, 24, 28; 50, 75, 78 **Addr.:** 914 Stewart Ave., Wausau, WI 54401.

Eldredge, Jonathan (Mr. 10, 1954, Boston, MA) Chief of Outreach Progs., Med. Ctr. Lib., Univ. of NM, 1981–; Asst. Libn., Lake Forest Coll. Lib., IL, 1979–81. **Educ.:** Beloit Coll., 1972–76, BA (Comp. Rel.); Univ. of MI, 1977–78, AMLS. **Orgs.:** ALA: ACRL; LIRT ASIS. Univ. of MI Alum. Assn. AAUP. Friends of the Earth. **Pubns.:** "ACRL's Bibliographic Instruction Preconference in Dallas," *Coll. and Resrch. Libs. News* (F. 1980); Ed., *Newsletter*, Univ. of MI (1977–78). **Activities:** 1; 29, 31, 39; 90, 92, 93 **Addr.:** 1305 Tijeras Ave., Albuquerque, NM 87106.

El-Fityani, Susan (Jn. 21, 1947, Newcastle-on-Tyne, Northumberland, UK) Libn., Brockville Psy. Hosp., 1974–; Libn., Ove Arup and Partners, Consult. Engin. (UK), 1971–72; Info. Asst. and Prod. Ed., Biodeterioration Info. Ctr., Univ. Aston, (UK), 1969–71. **Educ.:** Loughborough Sch. of Libnshp., 1967–69, ALA (Spec. Libs.). **Orgs.:** LA (UK). ASLIB. Med. LA. Can. Hlth. Libs. Assn. ON Psy. Hosp. Staff Libs. Grp.: Stans. Com. (Co-Ch., 1977–). **Pubns.:** "The work of the Biodeterioration Information Centre," *New Lib. World* (O. 1971). **Activities:** 4, 12; 15, 17, 39; 58, 64, 80 **Addr.:** Library Resources & Information Centre, Brockville Psychiatric Hospital, Box 1050, Brockville, ON K6V 5W7 Canada.

Elias, Arthur W. (F. 21, 1927, NY) Dir., Prof. Srvs., BioSci. Info. Srv., 1974–; Dir., Info. Srvs. Plng., Informatics, 1972–74; Pres., 3 I (Info. Intersci. Inc.) Co., 1971–72; Pres., ICA Info. Co. of Amer., 1968–71. **Educ.:** Univ. of AB, 1946–50, BS (Bio.); Rutgers Univ., 1955–56, MS (Med. Sci.). **Orgs.:** ASIS: Ed., Cncl., Pubn. Com. (1962–78). **Honors:** ASIS, Watson Davis Awd., 1977. **Pubns.:** Ed., *U.S. Information Services and Use* (1981); Ed., *Ency. of Comp. Sci. and Tech.* (1979); Ed., *Technical Information Center Administration* (I, 1964; II, 1965; III, 1966). "Marketing of On-Line Bibliographic Data Bases," *Online Rev.* (1979); "A General Review of Chemical and Other Information Systems," *Pure and Appld. Chem.* (1977). **Activities:** 6; 17, 25, 30; 58 **Addr.:** BIOSIS, 2100 Arch St., Philadelphia, PA 19103.

Elkins, Hilda Arnold (Jy. 26, 1935, Ennis, KY) Prof. (LS), Edinboro State Coll., 1969–; Assoc. Prof. (LS), Kutztown State Coll., 1967–69; Asst. Libn., Mary Hardin-Baylor Coll., 1963–64; Interim Libn., Little Rock Univ., 1962–63; Carver Sch. of Missions, 1959–61. **Educ.:** West. KY Univ., 1953–56, AB (LS); Univ. of KY, 1957–59, MSLS; N. TX State Univ., 1964–67, EDD. **Orgs.:** ALA: AASL, Std. Involvement in the Media Prog. Com. (Ch.). PA LA. Assn. of PA State Coll. Fac. AAUP. **Activities:** 10, 11; 20, 21, 26; 63, 65, 66 **Addr.:** R. D. 1, 13061 State Hwy. 99, Edinboro, PA 16412.

Elkouri, Jim R. (Ag. 7, 1938, Chickasha, OK) Head, Tech. Srvs., Altadena (CA) Lib. Dist., 1974–; Head, Cat. Dept., Univ. of Tulsa, 1973–74; Circ. Libn., Los Angeles City Coll., 1972–73; Sr. Catlgr., CA Inst. of the Arts, 1970–72; Cat. Libn., OK City Univ., 1963–70; Docu. Catlgr., OK State Univ., 1962–63. **Educ.:** Univ. of OK, 1956–60, BA 1960–62, MLS; Univ. of OK, OK City Univ., 1965–70 (Educ./LS). **Orgs.:** ALA. South. CA Tech. Processing Grp. **Honors:** Phi Beta Kappa, 1960; Beta Phi Mu, 1962; Phi Alpha Theta, ca. 1960. **Activities:** 1, 9; 20, 39, 46; 55, 63, 92 **Addr.:** 927 Kings Rd., #315, Los Angeles, CA 90069.

Elleman, Barbara Koplein (O. 20, 1934, Coloma, WI) Chlds. Bk. Reviewer, *Booklist*, ALA, 1975–; Sch. Lib., Media Spec., Whitefish Bay Schs., (WI), 1971–75; Chlds. Libn., Denver Pub. Lib., 1964–65; Sch. Lib., Media Spec., Cherry Creek Schs., (CO), 1965–70; Sch. Lib., Media Spec., Homestead HS (WI), 1959–64. **Educ.:** Univ. of WI, Oshkosh, 1952–56, BS (Educ.); Univ. of Denver, 1964, MA (LS). **Orgs.:** ALA: Intl. Bd. of Bks, for Young People. Intl. Assn. of Sch. Libns. Chlds. Reading RT of Chicago. Socty. of Chlds. Bk. Writers. Natl. Cncl. of Tchrs. of Eng. **Pubns.:** Essays; Reviews; freelance writer, frequent speaker. **Activities:** 3, 10; 21, 32, 42 **Addr.:** P.O. Box 1284, Milwaukee, WI 53201.

Ellenberger, Jack S. (S. 5, 1930, Lamar, CO) Libn., Shearman and Sterling, 1978–; Instr., Law Libnshp., U.S. Dept. of Agr. Grad. Sch., 1963–78; Libn., Covington and Burling, 1963–78; Libn., Bar Assn. of DC, 1961–63; Libn., Jones, Day, Cockley and Reavis, 1960–61; Libn., Carter, Ledyard and Milburn, 1957–60; Law Libn., U.S. Dept. of Hlth., Educ. and Welfare, 1957. **Educ.:** Georgetown Univ., 1955–57, BSFS; Columbia Univ., 1957–59, MSLS. **Orgs.:** AALL: Pres. (1976–77). SLA: DC Chap. (Pres., 1968–69); various coms. ALA. DC LA. **Pubns.:** *Legislative History of the U.S. Securities and Securities and Exchange Acts of 1933 and 1934* (1973); various articles, *Law Lib. Jnl.*, *Spec. Libs.* **Activities:** 12; 15, 17, 29; 77 **Addr.:** Rm. 718, 53 Wall St., New York, NY 10005.

Ellingson, Celia Sparrow (Mr. 3, 1950, Ortonville, MN) Head, Educ., Psy., LS Lib., Univ. of MN, 1979–, Coord., Ref. and Database Srvs. Educ. Lib., 1977–79, Ref. Libn., Wilson Lib., 1976–77, Srch. Anal., Educ. Lib., 1974–76. **Educ.:** Univ. of MN, 1968–72, BA, magna cum laude (Hist., Child Psy.), 1972–73, MA (LS). **Orgs.:** ASIS: Empl. Ch. (1978–79); Lcl. Arrange. Com., 1979 Conf. **Honors:** Beta Phi Mu, 1974. **Pubns.:** "A Comparison of Overlap: ERIC and Psychological Abstracts," *Database* (Je. 1979). **Activities:** 1; 15, 17, 39; 63, 92 **Addr.:** University of Minnesota Libraries Twin Cities, Walter Library, 2nd Floor, 117 Pleasant St. S.E., Minneapolis, MN 55455.

Elliott, Clark A. (Ja. 22, 1941, Ware, MA) Assoc. Cur. of Univ. Arch., Harvard Univ., 1971–; Asst. Prof. of LS, Simmons Coll., 1969–71. **Educ.:** Marietta Coll., 1959–63, AB (Hist.); Case West. Rsv. Univ., 1965, MSLS, 1968, MA (Hist.), 1970, PhD (LS). **Orgs.:** SAA: Com. on Arch. of Sci. and Tech. (Ch., 1978–80). New Eng. Archvsts. Hist. of Sci. Socty. **Pubns.:** *A Descriptive Guide to the Harvard University Archives* (1974); *Biographical Dictionary of American Science: The Seventeenth through the Nineteenth Centuries* (1979); "The American Scientist in Antebellum Society: A Quantitative View," *Soc. Std. of Sci.* (Ja. 1975); "Citation Patterns and Documentation for History of Science: Some Methodological Considerations," *Amer. Archvst.* (Spr. 1981); "Models of the American Scientist: A Look at Collective Biography," *ISIS* (Mr. 1982); ed., *Hist. of Sci. in Amer.: News and Views* (1980–). **Activities:** 1, 2; 45; 73 **Addr.:** University Archives, Pusey Library, Harvard University, Cambridge, MA 02138.

Elliott, Donald Allison (Je. 9, 1935, Lubbock, TX) VP, Dir., Div. of Sci. Affairs, Smithsonian Sci. Info. Exch., 1976–; Dir., Current Cancer Resrch. Proj. Anal. Ctr., Natl. Cancer Inst., 1976–; Asst. Prof., Rockefeller Univ., 1971–76, Grad. Fellow, 1966–71; Resident in Pediatrics, Resrch. Fellow, Johns Hopkins Univ., 1962–66. **Educ.:** TX Tech. Coll., 1953–57, BA (Chem.); Baylor Univ., 1957–61, MD; Rockefeller Univ., 1966–71, PhD (Cellular Pharm.). **Orgs.:** ASIS. Amer. Coll. of Nutr.: VP (1978–79). NY Acad. of Sci. Acad. of Med. **Pubns.:** Cmplr., ed., *Research in Progress Information Service, A Worldwide Inventory, UNESCO* (1981); prin. investigator, *Directory of Biosaline Research Projects* (1980). **Activities:** 12, 14-Resrch. in progress info. ctr.; 17, 26, 34; 75, 80, 91 **Addr.:** Smithsonian Science Information Exchange, 1730 M St. N.W., Rm. 300, Washington, DC 20036.

Elliott, Kay M. (F. 9, 1947, Minneapolis, MN) Libn., Dept. of Soc. Srvs. (Des Moines, IA), 1980–; Libn., Dept. of Pub. Instr. (Des Moines, IA), 1979–80; Head, Tech. Srvs., Drake Univ., 1977–78; Dir., St. Ambrose Coll. Lib., 1974–77; Asst. Libn., 1971–74; Asst. Libn., Pub. Lib. (Stevens Point, WI), 1968–70. **Educ.:** Coll. of St. Catherine, 1964–68, BA (Hist.); Kent State Univ., 1970–71, MLS. **Orgs.:** IA LA: Pres., 1979; Coll. and Univ. Libns. Sect. (Ch., 1977). ALA. Pilot Club Intl.: Davenport (Exec. Bd., 1977); Des Moines, (Corres. Secy., 1979). **Honors:** Pi Gamma Mu; Beta Phi Mu. **Activities:** 1, 10, 13; 17, 39, 46; 63, 92 **Addr.:** Library, Iowa State Department of Social Services, Hoover State Office Building, Des Moines, IA 50319.

Elliott, L. Gene (Jn. 16, 1940, Charleston, W VA) Lib. Dir., Bob Jones Univ., 1976–; Ref. Libn., 1974–76, Msc. Libn., 1970–72; Ref. Libn., Bibl., Asst. Prof. (LS), Univ. of MN, 1966–69. **Educ.:** Univ. of MN, 1960–63, AB (Zool.); West. Resrv. Univ., 1965–66, MS (LS); FL State Univ., 1972–73, AdvM (LS); 1973–77, PhD. **Orgs.:** SC LA. Piedmont LA: Pres. (1980–81). **Activities:** 1; 17, 26 **Addr.:** Mack Library, Bob Jones University, Greenville, SC 29614.

Elliott, Shirley B. (Jn. 4, 1916, Wolfville, NS) Legis. Libn., Legis. Lib. of NS, 1954–; Chief Libn., Colchester-East Hants Reg. Lib. (Truro, NS), 1950–54; Asst. Ed., *Canadian Index* Can. LA, 1949–50; Asst. Libn., Univ. of RI, 1946–49; Ref. Asst., Brookline Pub. Lib. (MA), 1940–46. **Educ.:** Acadia Univ., 1933–37, BA (Eng.); 1938–39, MA (Eng.); Simmons Coll., 1939–40, BS (LS). **Orgs.:** Can. LA: Cncl. (1964–67). Atlantic Provs. LA. Bibl. Socty. of Can.: Cncl. (1970–71). Can. Fed. of Univ. Women. Heritage Trust of NS. Can. Club of Halifax. Royal Commonwealth Socty.: NS Branch, Cncl. (1978–80). **Pubns.:** *Province House* (1967); *The Nova Scotia Book of Days* (1980); Ed., *Atlantic Provinces Checklist* (1957–65); "Heritage in Printing (Nova Scotia)," *Can. Antiques* (Ja/F. 1972); various other articles. **Activities:** 13; 17, 29, 39; 57, 69, 78 **Addr.:** Legislative Library of Nova Scotia, Province House, Halifax, NS B3J 2P8 Canada.

Ellis, Claudia B. (My. 28, 1950, Huntington, NY) Pres., Info. Ctr., 1980–; Lib. Consult., Adv. Marine Enterprises, Inc., 1979; Recs. Mgt. Consult., Amer. Mensa Ltd., 1979–81; Tech. Info. Spec., Nat. Oceanic and Atmospheric Admin., 1978–79; Med. Ref. Libn., Univ. of MD Hlth. Sci. Lib., 1977–78; Head of Circ., 1973–77. **Educ.:** Barnard Coll., 1968–72, BA (Bio.); Simmons Coll., 1972–73, MLS; Johns Hopkins Univ., 1974–77, MAS (Admin. Sci); Med. LA, 1977 (Cert.). **Orgs.:** Med. LA. ASIS. Mensa. **Activities:** 17, 24, 38; 75, 80, 91 **Addr.:** 3512 Gunston Rd., Alexandria, VA 22302.

Ellis, Dorothy Ann (Indianapolis, IN) Sch. Lib. Media Consult., OH Dept. of Educ., 1978–; Coord., Lib. Media, Rocky River (OH) Sch. Dist., 1960–78; Adj. Prof., Care West. Resrv. Univ., 1973–. **Educ.:** Brown Univ., 1940, BA (Latin) Case West. Resrv. Univ., 1970, MLS. **Orgs.:** OH Educ. Lib. Media Assn.:

PROFESSIONAL ACTIVITIES: Institutions: 1. Acad. lib.; 2. Arch.; 3. Assn.; 4. Fed./Gvt. lib.; 5. Inst. lib.; 6. Mfr./Suppl.; 7. Milit. lib.; 8. Musm.; 9. Pub. lib.; 10. Sch. lib.; 11. Sch. of lib. sci.; 12. Spec. lib.; 13. State lib.; 14. (other). **Functions/Activities:** 15. Acq./Col. dev.; 16. Adult srvs.; 17. Admin.; 18. Apprais.; 19. Archit./Bldgs.; 20. Cat./Class.; 21. Chld. srvs.; 22. Circ.; 23. Cons./Pres.; 24. Consult.; 25. Cont. ed.; 26. Educ. lib. sci.; 27. Ext. srvs.; 28. Fund/Grants; 29. Gvt. pubs.; 30. Indx./Abs.; 31. Instr. lib. use; 32. Media srvs.; 33. Micro.; 34. Netwks./Coop.; 35. Persnl.; 36. PR; 37. Publshg.; 38. Recs. mgt.; 39. Ref. srvs.; 40. Repro.; 41. Resrch.; 42. Review.; 43. Secur.; 44. Serials; 45. Spec. col.; 46. Tech. srvs.; 47. Trustees/Bds.; 48. YA srvs.; 49. (other).

Pres. (1978–79). ALA: YASD, Sel. Films for YA (1975–80). AECT: Delegate (1978–79). Assn. of Pilots of Amer. OH Educ. Assn. Kent State Sch. of LS: Adv. Bd. Cuyahoga Cmnty. Coll. Lib. Media: Adv. Bd. **Honors:** ALA, John Cotton Dana PR Awd., 1977; Martha Halden Jennings Awd., 1974, 1979; Case West. Resrv., Disting. Alum., 1979. **Pubns.:** *Library/Media Handbook* (1980); "Grantsmanship," *The Spectrum* (1979); "Audio Visual Instruction," (1977); Various slide tape productions. **Activities:** 13; 24, 29; 63 **Addr.:** 1060 Richmar Dr., Westlake, OH 44145.

Ellis, Edward F. (Ag. 24, 1906, Buffalo, NY) Retired; Cat., Acq., Ref. and Circ. Depts., SUNY, Buffalo, 1948–76; Ref. Dept., Buffalo Pub. Lib., 1933–48. **Educ.:** Lafayette Coll., 1925–29, BS; Columbia Univ., 1932–33, BS (LS). **Orgs.:** ALA. NY LA. Bibl. Socty. of Amer. **Pubns.:** *British Museum in Fiction* (1981); jt. auth., *Alphabet of Buffalo* (1947); transl., *Librarian Van Der Boecken of Rotterdam* (1945); jt. auth., *Alphabet of New York Bookshops* (1940); various bibls., *Bltn. of Bibl.* (1951–61). **Activities:** 1, 9; 15, 20, 39; 57 **Addr.:** 757 Bird Ave., Buffalo, NY 14209.

Ellis, Elizabeth G. (Raleigh, NC) Lib. Stds., Head, Instr., PA State Univ., 1976–, Undergrad. Libn., 1969–76; Govt. Pubns. Libn., State Lib. of PA, 1958–67; Hlth. and Med. Libn., PA Dept. of Hlth., 1956–58; Libn., Serials Dept., Lib. of Congs., 1954; Tchr., Libn., NC Pub. Schs., 1947–52. **Educ.:** NC Ctrl. Univ., 1947, AB (Eng.), 1949, BSNLS, 1962, MLS; various wkshps. **Orgs.:** ALA: ACRL; RTSD; GODORT; various Coms. PA LA: Awds. and Resols. Com. (Ch., 1977–78); Nom. Com. (1976–77); various other coms. and ofcs. AAUW: Com. on Leg. (Ch., 1972–73). Leag. of Women Voters; Various other civic, etc., orgs. **Pubns.:** "Point of Use Instruction," *Jnl. of Acad. Libnship* (N. 1978); "The Black Academic Librarian," *The Black Libn. in the Southeast* (1977); "Of Sex and Administration," *The Protean* (D. 1971); "Reference use of Legislative Publications," *PA LA Bltn.* (Mr. 1970); Other papers and presentations. **Activities:** 1, 13; 17, 24 **Addr.:** Pattee Library - E 311, Pennsylvania State University, University Park, PA 16802.

Ellis, Joan M. (N. 11, 1930, Boston, MA) Coord., of Ref. Srvs., Univ. of Lowell, 1978–; Head Libn., Purdue Frederick Pharmaceutical Co., 1976–78; Ref. Libn., Dir., Serials, Philadelphia Coll. of Pharm. and Sci., 1974–76; Dir., Tech. Srvs., 1973–74; Serials Libn., 1973. **Educ.:** Boston Univ., 1948–50, AA (Gen.); 1950–52, BS (PR); Villanova Univ., 1970–72, MSLS. **Orgs.:** New Eng. OLUG: Com. on Mgt. (1979–). Med. LA. New Eng. Lib. Ntwk.: Govt. Docum. Sect., Spr. Wkshp. Com. (1974–78). Acad. of Pharm. Sci.: Indus. Pharm. Tech. Sect. (East. Reg. Bd., 1978–). **Pubns.:** "Useful Sources of Foreign Drug Information," *Drug Info. Assn. Jnl.* (My./S. 1975); Various papers. **Activities:** 1, 12; 29, 31, 39; 87, 91 **Addr.:** Alumni/Lydon Library, University of Lowell, Lowell, MA 01854.

Ellis, Katheleen Mae (Ap. 6, 1946, Toronto, ON) Asst. Libn., Disabled Living Resrc. Ctr., Kinsmen Rehab. Fndn., 1979–; Libn., Riverview Hosp., (BC), 1970–79; Acq. Libn., Univ. of West. Ont., 1968–70; Asst. Libn., Fisheries Resrch. Inst., Cape Town, S. Africa, 1968. **Educ.:** Univ. of Cape Town, S. Africa, 1964–66, BA (Eng./Hist.), 1967–70, Final Dipl., Libnshp.; Univ. of BC, 1977–78, MLS. **Orgs.:** Govt. LA of BC: Secy. (1979); Automated Cat. Proj., (1978–79). Hlth. Libs. Assn. BC LA. **Pubns.:** *Immigration into South Africa, 1940–1967*, (1970); Ed. Govt. LA Nwsltr. (1979). **Activities:** 5, 12; 15, 20, 39; 72, 80, 92 **Addr.:** Disabled Living Resource Centre, Kinsmen Rehabilitation Foundation of B.C., 2256 West 12th Ave., Vancouver, BC V6K 2N5 Canada.

Ellison, John William (D. 6, 1941, Darke Cnty., OH) Assoc. Prof., SUNY, Buffalo, 1971–; Asst. Dir., Univ. Libs., Wright State Univ., 1969–71; Dir., Curric. Mat. Ctr., 1966–68; School Media Spec., Middletown, OH, 1964–66. **Educ.:** Morehead State Univ., 1960–63, BA (Educ.); Xavier Univ., 1964–65, MEd (Admin.); South. IL Univ., 1968–70, SEd (LS); OH State Univ., 1970–72, PhD (Educ.). **Orgs.:** Assn. of Educ. Comm. and Tech.: Pres., Div. of Info. Syst. (1975–76). NY LA: Intell. Freedom Com. (1977–). **Pubns.:** *Graduate Degree Programs In Instructional Technology 1977–78* (1978); various articles on media and libnshp. **Activities:** 1, 11; 17, 32, 36; 63, 74, 93 **Addr.:** Eggertsville, NY 14226.

Ellison, Sandra Marie (Ap. 5, 1945, Detroit, MI) Pub. Lib. Consult., OK Dept. of Libs., 1971–; Asst. Exten. Libn., Tampa (FL) Pub. Lib., 1970–71; Br. Libn., 1969–70; Bkmobile Libn., 1967–68. **Educ.:** Univ. of S. FL, 1964–67, BS (Pol. Sci); Univ. of IL, 1967–68, MSLS. **Orgs.:** ALA: ASCLA/SLA Plng. Org. and Bylaws Com. (1980–82); Gen. Consult. Disc. Grp., Ch. (1976); Statewide Borrowers Card Com. (1978–79). Southwestern LA: Const. and Bylaws Com., Ch. (1972); Cont. Educ. for Lib. Staffs in the Southwest (CELS) Adv. Com., Ch. (1976–77). OK LA: Secy., 1980–81; Cont. Educ. Com., Ch. (1977); Intell. Freedom Com.; Interlib. Coop. Com. Capitol City Camera Club. Sierra Club. **Pubns.:** "Library Continuing Education in YOUR Future," *OK Libn.* (O. 1978). **Addr.:** Oklahoma Dept. of Libraries, 200 N.E. 18th St., Oklahoma City, OK 73105.

Ellisor, F. L. Page (O. 7, 1924, Beaumont, TX) Libn., Media Spec., Kate Bell Elem. Sch. (TX), 1960–; Tchr., Houston Ind. Sch. Dist., 1955–60. **Educ.:** Univ. of Houston, 1944–46, BS (Educ.), 1946–47, MS (Psych.); Lib. Sci. study at various univs. **Orgs.:** ALA. TX LA. Houston Assn. of Sch. Libns.: VP, Treas. (1965). Cong. of Houston Tchrs.: VP (1975). Methodist Ch. Amer. Guild of Piano Tech. and Tuners. **Pubns.:** "Understanding one's Self and Others," *Study of Lit. in Grade Six* (1975); "Good Library Manners," Slide Show. **Activities:** 10; 21, 32; 67 **Addr.:** 10915 Ella Lee Ln., Houston, TX 77042.

Elliston, Margaret (Ap. 27, 1926, Peru, IL) Dir. of Libs., Biscayne Coll., 1975–; Pub. Srvs. Libn., Broward Cmnty. Coll., 1972–74; Asst. Libn., Marymount Coll., 1969–72. **Educ.:** Northwest. Univ., 1944–48, BM (Msc.); Cath. Univ. of Amer., 1967–69, MLS. **Orgs.:** SELA. FL LA. Cath. LA. Dade Cnty. LA: Pres. (1980–81). **Honors:** Beta Phi Mu, 1969. **Activities:** 1 **Addr.:** 16400 N.W. 32nd Ave., Miami, FL 33054.

Ellsworth, Dianne J. (Ap. 7, 1942, New York, NY) Prog. Mgr., CA Union List of Per., 1978–; Head, Circ. Srvcs., Mountain View Pub. Lib., 1975–78; Asst. Head Ser. Dept., Univ. of CT, 1967–74; Circ. Dept., Univ. of CA, Berkeley, 1966–67. **Educ.:** UCLA, 1958–61; Univ. of CA, Berkeley, 1961–62, BA (Art Hist.), 1964–65, MLS; Comm. Coll. Tchg. Cert. (CA), 1974. **Orgs.:** ALA: Resrcs. Tech. Srvcs. By-laws Com. (1969–70); Com. Prcs. Srvs. (1971–73); Ser. Nom. Com. (1974–75). **Pubns.:** Jt. auth., *"The Role of Women in Librarianship* (1978); Jt. auth., *Landmarks of Library Literature* (1976); "The Magazine Index," *Serials Review,* (1978); "The Academic Library looks at Union Lists," *Coll. and Resrch. Libs.* (N. 1971). **Activities:** 1; 17, 34, 46 **Addr.:** 185 Waverley St., Palo Alto, CA 94301.

Ellsworth, Ralph E. (S. 22, 1907, Forest City, IA) Dir. of Libs., Emeritus, Univ. of CO, 1958–; Dir. of Libs., Univ. of IA, 1943–58; Dir. of Libs., Univ. of CO, 1937–43; Libn., Adams State Coll., 1931–34. **Educ.:** Oberlin Coll., 1925–29, AB, (Pol. Sci.); West. Resrv. Univ., 1930–31, BS (LS); Univ. of Chicago, 1934–37, PhD (LS). **Orgs.:** CO LA: Pres. (1937, 1938, 1959). ALA: Exec. Bd. (1946–50); many other coms.; ACRL, Pres. (1944, 1955). CO Assoc. Univ. Press: Bd. of Div. (Ch., 1962–72). **Honors:** West. Resrv. Univ., LLD. (Hon.) 1956.; Denver Pub. Lib., Nell Scott Awd., 1972; Mt. Plains LA, Cert. of Recog., 1972; Case West. Resrv. Univ., Alumni, Recog. Awd., 1979; other honors. **Pubns.:** *Academic Library Buildings* (1973); Jt.-auth., Planning the Academic Library, (1971); The Economics of Book Storage, (1969); The School Library, (1965); four other bks.; over fifty articles. **Activities:** 1; 18, 19, 24 **Addr.:** 860 Willowbrook Rd., Boulder, CO 80302.

Elman, Stanley A. (Ap. 24, 1928, Buffalo, NY) Mgr., Info. Srvs. Dept., Lockheed-CA Co., 1972–; Supvsr., Lib., Jet Propulsion Lab., 1967–72; Supvsr., Lib., Thiokol Chem. Corp., Reaction Motors Div., 1963–67; Chief Tech. Abstctr./Transl., *Intl. Aerospace Abstracts,* 1962–63. **Educ.:** Univ. of Notre Dame, 1949–53, BS (Bio. Chem.); Univ. of Buffalo, 1953–58, EDM (Sci. Ed.); SUNY, Geneseo, 1960–62, MLS. **Orgs.:** SLA. ASIS. ALA. CA LA. Air Force Assn. Reserve Officers Assn. of the US. **Honors:** U. S. Air Force, Air Force Com. Medal, 1976. **Pubns.:** *A Cost-Effective Machine-Readable Technical Data Base for Aerospace Libraries,* (1976); "Politics, the Public Library and the NCLIS," *CA Libn.* (Ja. 1977); "The Humanization of Information Science," *Spec. Libs.,* (S. 1976); "Cost Comparison of Manual and On-Line Computerized Literature Searching," *Spec. Libs.* (Ja. 1975); "What's Good for General Motors is Just as Good for Our Libraries!" *CA Libn.* (Ja. 1975). **Activities:** 12; 17; 52 **Addr.:** 945 Hastings Ranch Dr., Pasadena, CA 91107.

Elrod, J. McRee (Mr. 23, 1932, Gainesville, GA) Dir., Spec. Libs. Cat., Inc., 1979–; Head, Cat. Divs., Univ. of BC Lib., 1967–78; Head, Cat., Ohio Wesleyan Univ., 1963–67; Libn., Ctrl. Coll., 1960–63; Assoc. Libn., Yonsei Univ. (Korea), 1955–60. **Educ.:** Univ. of GA, 1949–52, AB (Hist.); Scarritt Coll., 1953–54, MA (CLT)(Theo.); Peabody Coll., 1952–53, 1960, MA (LS); Yale Univ., 1954–55 (Korean). **Orgs.:** IFLA: Com. on Cat. (1978–). BC LA. ALA. Can. LA. **Honors:** Phi Beta Kappa. **Pubns.:** *Modern Library Practices* (1978); *An Index to English Language Periodical Literature Published in Korea 1890–1940* (1965); "A practical compromise between the card catalogue and the interactive on-line computerized catalogue for local and union catalogue purposes," *IFLA Pubs. 14* (1979); indexes; various other articles. **Addr.:** 2012 Dollarton Highway, North Vancouver, BC V7H 1A4 Canada.

Elsasser, Katharine K. (Jn. 19, 1942, Jacksonville, FL) Sr. Subj. Cat. Spec., Lib. of Congs., 1974–; Descr. Cat., 1972–74. **Educ.:** Newcomb Coll., 1960–64, BA (Span., Portuguese); Tulane Univ., 1964–69; LA State Univ., 1970–71, MLS, Library Science; 1971–72, (Span. Portuguese). **Orgs.:** ALA. African Stds. Assn.: Arch.-Libs. Com., Sub-Com. on Cat. and Class (Ch., 1978–). **Activities:** 4; 20, 41; 54, 55, 66 **Addr.:** 319 C St., N.E., Washington, DC 20002.

Else, Carolyn J. (Ja. 3, 1934, Minneapolis, MN) Dir., Pierce Cnty. Lib. Dist., 1965–, Branch Libn., Tenzler Branch, 1963–65; Info. Libn., Lincoln Pub. Lib., 1962–63; Spec. Srvs. Libn., France, Germany, 1959–62; Libn. I, Queensboro. Pub. Lib., 1957–59. **Educ.:** Stanford Univ., 1952–56, BS (Psy.); Univ. of WA, 1956–57, MLS. **Orgs.:** Pac. NW LA: Secy. (1969–71). ALA: PLA, Arch. for Pub. Libs., Ch.; various other coms. WA LA: Sec. VP (1969–70); Legis. Com. (Ch., 1971); New Directions Com. (Ch., 1970); Conf. Prog. (Ch., 1968, 1974). Soroptomist Intl. **Activities:** 9; 17 **Addr.:** 1414 N. Alder, Tacoma, WA 98406.

Elstein, Herman (N. 6, 1938, New York, NY) Lib. Dir., Ocean Cnty. Lib., 1980–, Head, Ref. Srvs., 1976–80, Head, Acq., 1975–76; AV Libn., Atl. Cnty. Lib., 1974; Asst. Dir. for Reader Srvs., Stockton State Coll., 1971–72; Asst. Coll. Libn., Williams Coll., 1969–71; Acq. Libn., Rider Coll., 1966–69. **Educ.:** Brooklyn Coll., 1956–60, BA (Eng.); Rutgers Univ., 1965–66, MLS; Glassboro State Coll., 1972–74, MA (Eng.). **Orgs.:** ALA. NJ LA: Int. Frdm. Com. (Ch., 1978–79). **Pubns.:** "Escaping the Gradgrinds," *Wilson Lib. Bltn.* (Ap. 1979); "Gaylord Circulation Control System: A Second View," *NJ Libs.* (F. 1976). **Activities:** 1, 9; 19, 35; 56, 74 **Addr.:** Ocean County Library, 101 Washington St., Toms River, NJ 08753.

Elston, Charles B. (Mr. 19, 1942, Schenectady, NY) Head, Spec. Colls. and Archs., Marquette Univ., 1977–; Asst. Univ. Archvst. and Newsp. Libn., Univ. of IL, 1971–77. **Educ.:** Cornell Univ., 1960–63 (Archit); Union Coll., 1963–65, BA (Soc. Stds.); Univ. of WI, 1965–71, MA (Hist.). **Orgs.:** SAA: Coll. and Univ. Arch. Com. (1975–79); Prog. Com. (1979); various other coms. Midwest Arch. Conf.: Ed. Bd. (1979–81); Exec. Cncl. (1978–80). Lib. Cncl. of Metro. Milwaukee: Arch. Com. (Ch., 1978–80). Various other coms. **Pubns.:** Jt.-auth., *College and University Archives: Selected Readings* (1979); "University Student Records: Research Use, Privacy Rights, and the Buckley Law," *Midwestern Archvst.* (Ap. 1976). **Activities:** 1, 2; 38, 45; 62, 78, 92 **Addr.:** Special Collections/Archives, Marquette University Library, 1415 W. Wisconsin Ave., Milwaukee, WI 53233.

Ely, Donald P. (S. 3, 1930, Buffalo, NY) Dir., ERIC Clearinghouse on Info. Resrcs., Syracuse Univ., 1977–, Prof. of Educ., 1956–; Senior Fulbright Prof., Univ. of Chile, 1963–64; Asst. Prof. of Educ., SUNY, New Paltz, 1952–55. **Educ.:** SUNY, Albany, 1947–51, BA (Eng.); Syracuse Univ., 1951–53, MA (AV Ed.), 1956–61, PhD (Comm.). **Orgs.:** ALA. AASL. ASIS: Ch., Nonprint SIG (1974–75). AECT: Pres. (1965–66). Dewitt Com. LA: Trustee (1969–); Pres. (1972–75). Intl. Fed. of LA: Com. on Statistics and Stan. (1973–75); Part., White House Conf. on Libs. and Info. Srvcs. (1979). **Honors:** SUNY, Albany, Disting. Alum., 1975. **Pubns.:** *Media Personnel in Education: A Competency Approach,* (1976); *Instructional Design and the Library Media Specialist,* (1979); "The Future of the Library," *NC Libs.* (1977); "The Current Status of Audiovisual Definitions," Intl. Cat. (1976); "The Changing Role of Audiovisual Media", *Comp. and Intl. Lib. Sci.* (1977). **Activities:** 12; 17, 26, 32; 50, 63, 93 **Addr.:** ERIC Clearinghouse on Information Resources, Syracuse University, School of Education, Syracuse, NY 13210.

Ember, George (N. 21, 1917, Budapest, Hungary) Asst. to Dir., Can. Inst. for Sci. and Tech. Info., Natl. Resrch. Cncl. of Can., 1980–, Chief of Opers., 1974–80; Assoc. Natl. Sci. Libn., Natl. Sci. Lib. of Can., 1971–74, Chief, Hlth. Scis. Resrc. Ctr., 1968–71; Lectr., Lib. Sch., Univ. of Ottawa, 1969–72; Lectr./Instr., Sch. of LS, Case West. Rsv. Univ., 1965–68; Mgr., Resrch. Resrcs., Ctr. for Documtn. and Comm. Resrch., 1965–68; Dir., Med. Documtn. Srv., Inst. of Exper. Med. and Surgery, Univ. de Montréal, 1962–65. **Educ.:** Sir George William Univ., 1959–64, BA (Phil., Psy.); West. Rsv. Univ., 1964–67, MSLS. **Orgs.:** Can. Assn. Info. Sci. NRC Can. Natl. Com. for Fed. Intl. de Docum.: Adv. Bd. on Sci. and Tech. Info. (Secy., 1980–). **Pubns.:** Jt. auth., *Symbolic Shorthand System for Physiology and Medicine* (1964); "Communication for Research in Biomedicine in Canada," *Hlth. Comms. and Informatics* (1980); "Dissemination of Scientific and Technical Information in Canada," *Jnl. of Chem. Documtn.* (1973); "The Health Sciences Resource Centre: A New Information Service of the National Science Library of Canada," *Procs. 3rd Intl. Congs. of Med. Libnshp.* (1970); "Training in Information Science for Scientific and Technological Information (STI) Services in Canada," *Procs. F.I.D. Intl. Sem. on Educ. in Info. Sci.* (1974); various articles, (1963–). **Activities:** 4; 17, 24, 26; 75, 80, 91 **Addr.:** 595 LaVerendrye Dr., Ottawa, ON K1J 7C1 Canada.

Embry, Jonathan D. (D. 8, 1949, NM) Dev. Mgr., Netwk. Rep. and Cntrl., Satellite Bus. Systs., 1980–; Gen. Mgr., Info. and Pub. Systs., Inc., 1977–80; Comp. Systs. Dept. Mgr., Info. Systs. Div., ORI, 1974–77; Data Prcs. Instr., Howard Cmnty. Coll., 1975–75; Dir., Comp. Srvs., Southwest Resrch. Assocs., 1972–74. **Educ.:** Univ. of NM, 1968–72, BUS (Comp. Sci.); Inst. for the Cert. of Comp. Processionals, Cert. **Orgs.:** ASIS: SIG/ISE Nsltr. Ed. Assn. for Comp. Mach. Assn. for Educ. Data Systs. **Pubns.:** Jt.-auth., "A Computer-Assisted Study of the Vocabulary of Young Navajo Children" *Comps. and the Hums.* (Mr. 1973); Various presented papers. **Activities:** 14-Private Company; 17, 24, 49; 56, 57, 75 **Addr.:** 8603 Leonard Dr., Silver Spring, MD 20910.

Embs, Ardith B. (Mr. 26, 1922, Kalamazoo, MI) Asst. Prof., Sch. of Libnshp., West. MI Univ., 1961–. **Educ.:** Kalamazoo Coll., 1939–43, BA (Bio.); West. MI Univ., 1963–66, MSL. **Orgs.:** ALA. MI LA: Nat. Lib. Week Com. (1973–74); Ed. Brd., *MI Libn.* (1974–78); Pub. Rels. Com. (1978–80). MI Assn. for Media in Educ. (Bd.). Freedom to Read Fndn. **Honors:** Beta Phi Mu.

Special Subjects/Services: 50. Adult educ.; 51. Advert./Mktg.; 52. Aerosp.; 53. Agric.; 54. Area std.; 55. Arts/Hum.; 56. Autom.; 57. Bibl./Prtg.; 58. Bio. sci.; 59. Bus./Fin.; 60. Chem.; 61. Copyrt.; 62. Documtn.; 63. Educ.; 64. Engin.; 65. Env.; 66. Eth. grps.; 67. Film; 68. Food/Nutr.; 69. Geneal.; 70. Geo.; 71. Geol.; 72. Handcpd.; 73. Hist.; 74. Int. frdm.; 75. Info. sci.; 76. Insr.; 77. Law; 78. Legis.; 79. Math./Comp. sci.; 80. Med.; 81. Metals; 82. Nat. resrcs.; 83. Newsp.; 84. Nuc. sci.; 85. Oral hist.; 86. Petr./Energy; 87. Pharm.; 88. Phys./Astr./Math.; 89. Readg.; 90. Relig.; 91. Sci./Tech.; 92. Soc. sci.; 93. Telecom.; 94. Transp.; 95. (other).

Pubns.: "Position paper on Public Relations for Libraries," MI White House Conf. on Libs. and Info. Srvs. (1979). **Activities:** 10, 11; 26, 36; 63 **Addr.:** School of Librarianship, Western Michigan University, Kalamazoo, MI 49008.

Emch, Lucille B. (Ap. 30, 1909, Toledo, OH) Rare Bks. Consult., 1979–; Rare Bks. Libn. and Prof. of Lib. Admin., Univ. of Toledo Libs., 1975–79, Assoc. Dir. for Rare Bks., Spec. Cols. and Arch., 1970–75, Assoc. Libn. and Prof. of LS, 1940–70. **Educ.:** Univ. of Toledo, 1926–30, BA (Eng. Lit.), 1939, MA (Eng. Lit.); Univ. of MI, 1935–41, BA (LS). **Orgs.:** ALA: ACRL/Rare Bks. and Mss. Sect. Mss. Socty. Bibl. Socty. (London). Bibl. Socty. of Amer. Various other orgs. Hon. Socty. of Phi Kappa Phi: Univ. of Toledo Chap. Beta Phi Mu: Mu Chap. (Pres., 1969–71). Delta Kappa Gamma: Beta Omicron Chap., various ofcs. **Honors:** Phi Kappa Phi, Disting. Mem. Awd., 1979. **Pubns.:** "Ohio in Short Stories, 1824–1839," *OH State Archaeological* (Jl.–S. 1944); "An Indian Tale by Joseph Snelling," *MN Hist.* (S. 1945); "University of Toledo's Carlson Library Offers Multi-media Resources to Researches," *OH Archvst.* (Fall 1974); "Two Anniversaries in Toledo, Ohio in the American Bicentennial Year: The Hundredth for Woodlawn Cemetery and the Seventy-fifth for the Lucas County Civil War Memorial," *NW OH Qtly.* (Spr. 1977). **Activities:** 18, 23, 45 **Addr.:** 752 Alvison Rd., Toledo, OH 43612.

Emerick, John Lee (Ap. 26, 1937, Fleetwood, PA) Supvsr., Lib. Media Srvs., Boyertown Area Sch. Dist., 1975–; Lib. Media Coord., Muhlenberg Sch. Dist., 1966–75; Tchr. (Eng.), Fleetwood Area Sch. Dist., 1962–66; Tchr. (Eng.), Libn., Daniel Boone Sch. Dist., 1959–62. **Educ.:** Kutztown State Coll., 1955–59, BS (Eng., LS); Villanova Univ., 1961–65, MS (LS); Temple Univ., PA State Univ., 1966–70, Cert. (Supvsr.). **Orgs.:** ALA. PA Sch. Libns. Assn.: Supvsrs. Com. (Ch., 1978); Leg. Com. (1979). Berks Cnty. Sch. Libns.: Treas. (1969); Nom. Com. (1971). Natl. Educ. Assn.; PA State Educ. Assn.: Delegate (1971). Fleetwood Area Educ. Assn.: Pres. (1965); various coms. (1962–66). Boyertown Area Educ. Assn. **Honors:** PA Jaycees, Disting. Srv. Awd., 1964. **Activities:** 10; 17, 20, 32; 61, 74, 78 **Addr.:** Boyertown Area School District, 911 Montgomery Ave., Boyertown, PA 19522.

Emerick, Tyron D. (Je. 30, 1937, Modesto, CA) Dir., Lrng. Resrcs., Columbia (MO) College, 1980–; Lib. Dir., Roswell (NM) Pub. Lib., 1975–79; Lib. Dir., S. Prairie Lib. Syst 1974; Dir. of Libs., Kansas City Cmnty. Coll., 1970–73; Head, Loan Div., Lincoln City Lib., 1969–70; Dir., N. Platte Pub. Lib., 1967–69; Head Libn., Newton (IA) HS, 1965–67; Dist. Libn., Milford Comnty. Sch., 1963–65. **Educ.:** Northwest MO State Univ., 1959–60, BS (Hist.); Emporia State Univ., 1963–66, MSLS. **Orgs.:** ALA; Intellectual Freedom Com. (1977–79); SRRT (Act. Cncl., 1971–73). NM LA: Schol. Com. (1976–78); Educ. Com. (1978–79); Ch., Pub. Lib. Div. (1978–79); Exec. Bd. (1978–79); Mtn. Plains LA: Exec. Bd. (1970–71). NE LA: Exec. Bd. (1968–69). Optimist International: Roswell Chap. (VP, 1976–77); Youth Work Ch., (1977–78). **Pubns.:** "SRRTI-Fied Action," *Lib. Jnl.* (F. 1972). **Activities:** 1, 19; 24, 32, 36; 74, 75 **Addr.:** 3512 Sierra Madre, Columbia, MO 65201.

Emerson, John Alfred (My. 17, 1926, Chippewa Falls, WI) Asst. Head, Msc. Lib., Univ. of CA, Berkeley, 1962–. **Educ.:** Northwest. Univ., 1948–50, BM (Msc. Composition); Mills Coll., 1950–51, (Msc. Composition); Univ. of CA, Berkeley, 1960, MA (Msclgy.), 1962, MLS. **Orgs.:** Msc. LA. Amer. Musicological Socty. Medvl. Acad. of Amer. Intl. Musicological Socty. **Honors:** Fulbright Schol., 1961–62. **Pubns.:** "The Recovery of the Wolffheim Antiphonale," *Annales musicologiques* (1963); "Über Entstehung und Inhalt von Mü D (München, Staatsbibl., Cgm. 716)," *Kirchenmusikalisches Jahrbuch* (1964); "Two Newly Identified Office for Sts. Valeria and Austriclinianus by Ademar de Chabannes," *Speculum* (Ja. 1965); amer. com., *Fontes Artis Musicae* (1964–69); eleven articles, *New Grove's Dictionary of Music and Musicians* (1980); various articles, reviews in msclgy., (1963–69). **Activities:** 1; 15, 39, 45; 55 **Addr.:** 619–30th St., Richmond, CA 94804.

Emerson, Katherine T. (Ap. 2, 1927, Jacksonville, FL) Univ. Archvst., Univ. of MA, Amherst, 1972–; Resrch. Assoc., grad. Sch. of Lib. and Info. Std., Univ. of CA, Berkeley, 1979–80; Asst. to Dir., Univ. of MA, 1967–72, Deputy Dir. for Pub. Srvs., 1969–70, Asst. Head, Mono. Cat., 1965–67; Catlgr., St. Petersburg (FL) Pub. Lib., 1963–65; Head Catlgr., Asst. Libn., Lehigh Univ., 1957–60; Catlgr., 1956–57; Catlgr., Moravian Coll., 1955–56. **Educ.:** Duke Univ., 1944–48, BA (Hist.), 1948–49, MA (Hist.); LA State Univ., 1952–53, MSLS; Univ. of Denver-Lib. Syst. Anal. Inst., 1970, Cert.; Amer. Univ.-Nat. Arch. Inst., 1973, Cert. **Orgs.:** ALA: ACRL (Ed. Brd., 1976–82); Admin. and Mat. Assn., Stat. Sect., Exec. Com. (1979–80); LAMA (Bd. of Dirs., 1978–80; Lib. Org., 1978–79; Ch., 1979–80). SAA: Coll. and Univ. Arch. Com. (1972–77); Panel of Arch. Security Consult. (1976–); Com. on Term. and Uniform Stat. (1976–77). Amer. Nat. Stan. Inst.: Lib. Com. (Ch. 1977–). Phi Beta Kappa: Secy. (1967–69); VP (1974–75); Pres. (1975–76). AAUP: Exec. Com. (1976–79); Treas. (1978–79). League of Women Voters: Bd. of Dirs. (1961–65); VP (1963–65); Amherst Chap., Bd. (1966–69); VP (1968–69). **Honors:** Phi Beta Kappa, 1947; Sigma Delta Pi, 1946; Tau Psi Omega, 1947; Cncl. on Lib. Resrcs., flwshp., 1972. **Pubns.:** Ed., *Proceedings of the Symposium on Measurement of Reference* (1974); "National Reporting on Reference Transactions, 1976–1978," *RQ* (1977); "Background and Recent Developments in ... Measurement," *Pub. Lib. Qtly.* (1979). **Activities:** 1, 2; 17, 39, 45; 75 **Addr.:** 47 Arnold Rd., Amherst, MA 01002.

Emerson, Susan Vince (Ja. 12, 1942, Budapest, Hungary) Head, Agr. Lib., OH State Univ., 1978–; Visit. Asst. Prof., Sch. of Libnshp. and Univ. Lib., Univ. of OR, 1976–78; Info. Spec., INFO, 1973–76; Tech. Asst., Ctr. for Documtn. and Comms. Resrch., Case West. Rsv. Univ., 1968–69; Ref. Libn., Food and Agr. Org. of the Untd. Nations., 1967–68; Resrch. Libn., Univ. of MI, 1966–67; Sci. Libn., Queens Coll., 1964–66. **Educ.:** City Coll. of NY, 1959–61, BS (Bio.); Pratt Inst., 1962–64, MLS; Case West. Rsv. Univ., 1971–75, PhD (Info. Sci.). **Orgs.:** ASIS. **Honors:** Beta Phi Mu, 1964. **Pubns.:** "Types of Agricultural Serials," *Serials Review* (O.–N. 1981). **Activities:** 1, 12; 17, 24, 41; 56, 75, 91 **Addr.:** 3707 Blanche Rd., Cleveland Heights, OH 44118.

Emerson, Virginia Beabes (N. 8, 1927, Somerset, PA) Chief Libn., The New School of Msc., 1969–; Chief Libn., Philadelphia Msc. Acad., 1962–65. **Educ.:** Univ. of MI, 1945–49, BA (Eng.); Univ. of CA, 1953–54 (Slavic Std.); Drexel Univ., 1959–61, MSLS. **Orgs.:** Msc. LA: PA Chap., Nom. Com. (1978). **Activities:** 1; 15, 17, 46; 55 **Addr.:** 16 Oberlin Ave., Swarthmore, PA 19081.

Emery, Sarah Snell (Jl. 29, 1918, Leadville, CO) Assoc. Libn., Ref. Dept., SUNY, Buffalo, 1970–; Libn., Cornell Aeronautics Labs, 1968–70. **Educ.:** Univ. of Denver, 1935–39, BA (Chem.); SUNY, Buffalo, 1966–70, MLS 1972–74, MA, (Latin Amer.). **Orgs.:** Sem. on Acq. of Latin Amer. Lib. Mat. (1971–). State Univ. Latin Americanists (1974–). **Pubns.:** *Mexican Agricultural Development and Education: A Select Bibliography* (1978); "Carter and the Mexican Press" *Buffalo Evening News* (Ap. 1, 1979). **Activities:** 1; 39, 41; 54 **Addr.:** E. H. Butler Library, State University College at Buffalo, 1300 Elmwood Ave., Buffalo, NY 14222.

Emmons, Paul Raymond (S. 25, 1948, Rhinelander, WI) Msc. Libn., Ctrl. WA Univ., 1979–; Msc. Libn., Millikin Univ., 1974–77. **Educ.:** Lawrence Univ., 1966–70, BMus, cum laude (Organ); Univ. of IL, 1970–72, MM, 1972–73, MS (LS). **Orgs.:** Msc. LA. Royal Sch. of Church Msc. Amer. Gld. of Organists: Yakima Valley Chap. (Secy., 1979–). **Activities:** 1; 15, 20, 39; 55, 56, 75 **Addr.:** Central Washington University Library, 8th St., Ellensburg, WA 98926.

Endelman, Judith E. (Ap. 4, 1947, Rochester, NY) Hist., Acq. Consult., Jewish Fed. of Indianapolis, IN Hist. Socty., 1979–; Archvst., Jewish Theo. Semy., 1977–79; Assoc. Libn., Amer. Jewish Hist. Socty., 1972–75; Synagogue Libn., Temple Beth Am, 1972–73. **Educ.:** Univ. of CA, Berkeley, Los Angeles, 1965–69, AB (Anthro.); Simmons Coll., 1971–72, MS (LS); Boston Coll., 1975–77, MA (Amer. Stds.). **Orgs.:** ALA. SLA. **Pubns.:** *Paintings, Daguerreotypes and Artifacts of the American Jewish Historical Society* (1974); "Genealogical Resources at the Jewish Theological Seminary," *Toledot* (Spr., 1979); "Jewish Genealogy without 'Jewish' Sources," *Toledot* (Sum., 1978); "Judaica Americana," *Amer. Jewish Hist. Qtly.* (1973, 1974, 1975). **Activities:** 1, 2; 15, 20, 41; 66, 69, 95-Jewish Hist. **Addr.:** 1200 Collinswood Dr., Bloomington, IN 47401.

Engberg, Linda L. (Ja. 14, 1943, Minot, ND) Dir., Tech. Srvs. Div., Hennepin Cnty. Lib., (MN), 1978–; Actg. Asst. Dir., Tech. Srvs., 1976–78; Area Libn., Pub. Srvs. Div., 1974–76; Bookmobile and Reading Ctr. Supvsr., 1971–74; Bookmobile Libn., 1969–71; Catlgr., 1968–69; Head Libn., James Mem. Lib., (ND), 1966–68. **Educ.:** Jamestown Coll., 1961–65, BA (Hist.); Univ. of Denver, 1965–66, MALS. **Orgs.:** ALA. MN LA. **Activities:** 9; 17, 46 **Addr.:** Technical Services Division, Hennepin County Library, York Ave. South at 70th, Edina, MN 55435.

Engeldinger, Eugene A. (O. 30, 1940, Menomonie, WI) Ref. Libn., Univ. of WI, Eau Claire, 1969–; Asst. Ref. Libn., IN Univ., 1969. **Educ.:** Univ. of WI, Eau Claire, 1961–65, BS (Hist.); Univ. of KS, 1965–68, MA (Hist.); Univ. of WI, Madison, 1968–69, MSLS. **Orgs.:** ALA. Assn. of Univ. of WI Fac. **Pubns.:** Jt. ed., *Black American Fiction: a Bibliography* (1978); "Cumulative Author and Subject Indexes, v1-6 (1970–75)," *Std. in Black Lit.* (1977); "Cumulative Author and Subject Indexes, v9-13 (1972–76)," *WI Soc.* (1977). **Activities:** 1; 30, 39, 42; 57, 92 **Addr.:** University of Wisconsin, Eau Claire, WI 54701.

Engelhardt, D. LeRoy (S. 27, 1921, Philadelphia, PA) Head Libn., New Brunswick Theo. Semy., NJ, 1967–; Gvt. Docum. Libn., Univ. of TX, Arlington, 1966–67; Pastor, First Presby. Church, Euless, TX, 1962–66; Pastor, Un. Church of Lima, Peru; Prof., San Marcos Univ. **Educ.:** Penn State, 1939–42, BA (Hum.); Princeton Theo. Semy., 1942–45, MDiv (Theo.); N. TX State Univ., 1964–67, MLS. **Orgs.:** ATLA. NY Area Theo. LA: Exec. Cncl. Secretary. PA Theo. LA. NB Presbytery, Untd. Presby. Church. **Pubns.:** Various articles and reviews, *Reformed Church in America Seminary Pubn.* **Activities:** 12; 17; 90 **Addr.:** 85 College Ave., New Brunswick, NJ 08901.

Engelke, Hans (D. 11, 1927, St. Louis, MO) Assoc. Dir. of Libs., West. MI Univ., 1975–; Asst. Dir. of Libs., 1971–75; Acting Dir. of Libs., 1970–71; Asst. Dir., Resrcs. and Tech. Srvs., 1967–70. **Educ.:** Chicago Mscl. Coll., 1948–51, BM (Comp.), 1951–52, MM (Comp.); Univ. of South. CA, 1953–59, PhD (Msc.); Univ. of Chicago, 1960–61, MALS. **Orgs.:** MI LA: Tech. Srvcs. Div. (Ch. 1968–69); Acad. Libs. Div. (Ch., Nom. Com. 1969; Ch. Sub.-Com. of the Com. of Coop. Proc. among State Coll. and Univ. in MI, 1972–73). ALA: RTSD (Ch., Tech. Srvs. Admin. of Medium-Sized Resrch. Libs. Dis. Grp. 1969–70; Telefac. Com. 1972–74; Reprod. of Lib. Mat. Sect., Nom. Com. 1976–77; Pol. and Resrch. Com. 1976–78); Info. Sci. and Auto. Div. (Sub-Com. on In-Srvc. Trng. for Comp., 1969–71). Msc. LA: Midwest Chap. (Const. Com. 1962–63; Ch., Prog. Com. 1963–64). **Pubns.:** *A Survey on Telefacsimile Use in Libraries in the United States,* (1976); "The Use of the IBM MT/ST Machine in the Labeling and Catalog Production Processes in the Western Michigan University Libraries," *Current State of Cat. Card Prod. ALA,* (1973); "Telefacsimile Use in U.S. Libraries," *Interlending Review* (1978). **Activities:** 1; 15, 17, 46; 55 **Addr.:** 640 Weaver Ave., Kalamazoo, MI 49007.

Engen, Richard B. (N. 23, 1927, Aberdeen, WA) Dir., AK State Lib., 1967–; Head, Fld. Srvs., OR State Lib., 1963–67; Cnty. Libn., Inyo-Mono, CA, 1961–63; various positions, Seattle Pub. Lib., 1952–60. **Educ.:** Northwest. Univ., 1948–52, BS (Hist.); Univ. of WA, 1952–53, MLS. **Orgs.:** ALA: Cnclr. (1970–74). AK LA. Pac. NW LA: Secy. (1967–68). AECT. Cham. of Cmrce. **Addr.:** Pouch G, Juneau, AK 99811.

England, Claire (N. 21, 1935, Toronto, ON) Assoc. Prof., Univ. of Toronto, 1975–; Lectr., College of Libnshp. (Wales), 1974–75. **Educ.:** Univ. of Toronto, BA BEd BLS; MLS, 1974, PhD. **Orgs.:** ALA. Can. LA. ON LA. **Pubns.:** Jt.-auth., *Children Using Media: Reading and Viewing Preferences Among the Users and Non-Users of the Regina Public Library* (1977); "Violence in the Literature of Children and Young Adults," ON Royal Cmsn. on Violence in the Comm. Media. (1976). **Activities:** 9, 10; 15, 21, 39; 74 **Addr.:** Faculty of Library Science, University of Toronto, 140 St. George St., Toronto, ON M5S 1A1 Canada.

Engle, Constance Black (S. 27, 1936, New York, NY) Cat. Libn., Wayne State Univ., 1978–; Catlgr., Ref. Libn., Finkelstein Mem. Lib., 1972–78; Chld. Libn., White Plains Pub. Lib., 1964–65; Catlgr., Indianapolis Pub. Lib., 1962–63. **Educ.:** Brown Univ., 1954–58, AB (Msc., Grmm.); Indiana Univ., Bloomington, 1961–62, MLS; Wayne State Univ., 1978; 1979 (Autom.). **Orgs.:** ALA. SLA. LA of Rockland Cnty.: Secy., Mem. Com. (1970–75). Rockland Cnty. Pub. Libns. Assn.: Exec. Com.; Recording Secy. (1969–78); Info. and Ref. Com. (1975–78). Tappan Lib. Brd. of Trustees: Secy., Treas., Nsltr. Ed. (1969–75). Christ Epis. Church: Sr. Warden, Jr. Warden, Asst. Treas. (1971–78). Brown Univ. Natl. Alum. Schls. Prog. 1976–78). Friends Sem.: Ed., Alum. Bltn. (1963–68). **Pubns.:** *Rockland Co. Union List of Serials* (1972). **Activities:** 1, 9; 34, 39, 46; 55, 92 **Addr.:** Longmeadow Dr., Bloomfield Township, MI 48013.

Engle, June Lester (Ag. 25, 1942, Sandersville, GA) Assoc. Prof. (LS), Libn., Emory Univ., 1981–, Asst. Prof. (LS), Libn., 1975–81; Libn., Lectr., Emory Univ., 1973–75; Asst. Prof., Catlgr., Univ. of TN, 1971–73. **Educ.:** Emory Univ., 1960–63, BA (Hist.); 1970–71, MLn. **Orgs.:** ALA: ERA Task Frc. (1979–); LAMA, Orient. Prog. Com. (1979–83), Pers. Admin. Sect., Nom. Com. (Ch., 1978–79). AALS: Nom. Com. (Ch., 1980). SELA: Inf. Frdm. Com. (1978–80). GA LA: Inf. Frdm. Com. (Co-Ch., 1977–79). Various other coms. and orgs. **Honors:** Phi Beta Kappa; Beta Phi Mu. **Pubns.:** "Bibliotherapy: An Introduction," *Exploring Mental Hlth. Parameters* (1976); "The Library of the Division of Librarianship, Emory University," *Lib. Sci. Libns. Natl. Nsltr.* (D 1976); "Library Bill of Rights Revision," *GA Libn.* (Ag. 1979); Jt.-auth., "Library Science Libraries," *Ency. of Lib. and Info. Sci.* (1975). **Activities:** 1, 11; 15, 17, 26; 74, 95-Library Administration. **Addr.:** Division of Library and Information Management, Candler Library Building, Emory University, Atlanta, GA 30322.

Engley, Donald B. (Jl. 19, 1917, Stafford Springs, CT) Assoc. Univ. Libn., Yale Univ., 1972–; Libn., Trin. Coll., CT, 1951–72; Assoc. Libn., 1949–51; Libn., Norwich Univ., 1947–49. **Educ.:** Amherst Coll., 1935–39, BA (Hist.); Columbia Univ., 1940–41, BLS; Univ. of Chicago, 1946–47, MALS. **Orgs.:** ALA: ACRL. Assn. of Coll. & Ref. Libs; Bibl. Socty. of Amer. CT Lib. Assn. **Pubns.:** "James Hammond Trumbull, Papers of the Bibliographical Bibliographer of Connecticut," *Soc. of Amer.* (1954). **Activities:** 1; 17, 34 **Addr.:** 30 Glenwood Rd., West Hartford, CT 06107.

Ennis, Mary Jane (My. 11, 1920, Cincinnati, OH) Resrch. Libn., Drackett Co. (Bristol-Myers), 1951–. **Educ.:** Univ. of Cincinnati, 1958–68, BLS. **Orgs.:** SLA: Cincinnati Chap., Long Range Plng. Com. (1979–), Hosplty. Com. (1977–78), Educ. Com. (1977–78), Treas. (1970–73), Secy. (1967–69). ASIS, OH Chap. **Activities:** 12; 16, 34, 41; 59, 60, 91 **Addr.:** The Drackett Company, Research & Development Library, 5020 Spring Grove Ave., Cincinnati, OH 45232.

Ensley, Robert Francis (O. 30, 1940, Portola, CA) Sr. Consult., Inst. Lib. Srvs., IL State Lib., 1971–; Coord., Pub. Lib. Prog., ID State Lib., 1969–71, Field Libn., 1964–69. **Educ.:** Univ.

PROFESSIONAL ACTIVITIES: Institutions: 1. Acad. lib.; 2. Arch.; 3. Assn.; 4. Fed./Gvt. lib.; 5. Inst. lib.; 6. Mfr./Suppl.; 7. Milit. lib.; 8. Musm.; 9. Pub. lib.; 10. Sch. lib.; 11. Sch. of lib. sci.; 12. Spec. lib.; 13. State lib.; 14. (other). **Functions/Activities:** 15. Acq./Col. dev.; 16. Adult srvs.; 17. Admin.; 18. Apprais.; 19. Archit./Bldgs.; 20. Cat./Class.; 21. Chld. srvs.; 22. Circ.; 23. Cons./Pres.; 24. Consult.; 25. Cont. ed.; 26. Educ. lib. sci.; 27. Ext. srvs.; 28. Fund/Grants; 29. Gvt. pubs.; 30. Indx./Abs.; 31. Instr. lib. use; 32. Media srvs.; 33. Micro.; 34. Netwks./Coop.; 35. Persnl.; 36. PR; 37. Publshg.; 38. Recs. mgt.; 39. Ref. srvs.; 40. Repro.; 41. Resrch.; 42. Review.; 43. Secur.; 44. Serials; 45. Spec. col.; 46. Tech. srvs.; 47. Trustees/Bds.; 48. YA srvs.; 49. (other).

of MO, 1960–62, AB (Lib. Sci.); Univ. of Denver, 1963–64, MALS; Graceland Coll., 1958–60, AA. **Orgs.:** ALA: Amer. Correctional Assn. Jt. Com. on Inst. Libs., Ch. (1979–80); Leg. Assembly (1976–77); H. W. Wilson Recruit. Awd. Com., Ch. (1973); Mem. Com., ID State Ch. (1971); Reg. Conf. on Educ. and Manpower (1969). Assn. of Spec. and Coop. Lib. Agnc.: Nom. Com. (1980); Rep. to the Lib. Adm. and Mgt. Assn. Bldgs. and Equip. Sect. (1979–80); State/White House Conf. (ad hoc) (1979); Lib. Srvs. to the Blind & Phys. Handcpd. Sect. Campbell Awd. Com. (1979–80); Lib. Srvs. to Prisoners Sect.; State Lib. Agncy. Sect. IL LA: Nom. Com., Ch. (1980); Spec. Lib. Srvs. Sec. (1979–); Hlth. and Rehab. Lib. Srvs. Com., Ch. (1972); Pub. Libs. Sect. (1971–78). Univ. of Denver Alum. Assn. (1967–); Secy. (1980). Various other orgs. Amer. Assn. of Workers for the Blind: (Bd. of Dir. 1979–80). IL Assn., Workers for the Blind: Bd. of Dir. (1974); VP (1978); IL Com. on Comprehensive Srvs. for the Blind (1974–80). Amer. Correct. Assn.: Inst. Libs. Com., Ch. (1979–80); Prog. Com. (1978–80). IL Correct. Assn., (1979–). Various other orgs. **Pubns.:** Jt. auth., "The Springfield Connection," *IL Libs.* (Je. 1977); "Library Service for the Blind and Physically Handicapped," *IL Libs.* (S. 1975); "Library Service in State Correctional Facilities," *IL Libs.* (S. 1974); "Interlibrary Cooperation," *ID Libn.* (Ja. 1968). **Activities:** 12, 13; 24, 25, 34; 72, 90 **Addr.:** 2650 Cooper Ave. 212, Springfield, IL 62704.

Enyingi, Peter (O. 6, 1926, Budapest, Hungary) Head Cat. Libn., Los Angeles Cnty. Law Lib., 1970–; Asst. Law Libn. for Tech. Srvs., Cornell Law Lib., 1960–68. **Educ.:** Kiralyi Katolikus Egyetemi Gimnazium, 1940–44, (Erettsegi); Columbia Univ. 1959–60, MSLS; Pázmány Péter Tudományegyetem, 1944–48, Dr.iur (Law). **Orgs.:** AALL. **Pubns.:** Articles in *Law Lib. Jnl.* **Activities:** 1, 12; 20, 24, 46; 56, 77 **Addr.:** Los Angeles County Law Library, 301 West First St., Los Angeles, CA 90012.

Enz, Philip I(rwin) (S. 25, 1937, Oklahoma City, OK) Lib. Dir., Larue D. Carter Meml. Hosp. (Indianapolis); 1968–; Info. Spec., P.R. Mallory and Co., 1963–67; Electrochem. Engin., 1959–63; Analytical Chem., New Era Milling Co., 1959. **Educ.:** Phillips Univ., 1955–58, BA (Chem.); IN Univ., 1963–68, MA (LS); Libn. I, IN State Lib., 1972–, Cert. **Orgs.:** SLA. IN State Libs. Adv. Cncl. Med. LA: Mental Hlth. Grp. (Ch., 1969–71). Alternate, Gvr.'s Conf. on IN Libs. and Info. Srvs., Ag., 1978. **Pubns.:** "The Library: An Aid to the Resourceful," *Lib. Occurrent* (1970); Jt.-holder, U.S. Patent 4,089,125 (My. 16, 1978). **Activities:** 5, 12; 17, 24, 39; 80 **Addr.:** Medical Library, Larue D. Carter Memorial Hospital, 1315 W. 10th St., Indianapolis, IN 46202.

Epps, Helen Reese (O. 1, 1928, Pickens Cnty., SC) Dir. of Media Srvs., Bibb Cnty. Pub. Schs., 1980–; Media Spec., N.E. HS, 1969–80; Media Spec., Appling HS, 1962–69; Tchr., Elem. Grades, Hamilton Elem. Sch., 1961–62; Bio. Tchr.–Libn., Elm St. HS, 1959–61; Bio. Tchr.–Libn., Dickerson Trng. Sch., 1956–58; Sci. Tchr.–Libn., Lumber City HS, 1952–56; Sci. Tchr.–Libn., Twin City HS, 1949–52. **Educ.:** Johnson C. Smith Univ., 1945–49, BS (Gen. Sci., Bio.); Atlanta Univ., 1950–55, MLS; Univ. of GA, 1980, Dir. of Libs. Cert. **Orgs.:** ALA: AASL, Nom. Com. (1978–79), Conv. Del. (1977, 1978), GA Mem. Netwk. (Ch., 1979–80). GA LA: Awds. and Bylaws Com. (1977–79). GA Assn. of Educs.: Lib. Media Dept., Pres. (1977–78), VP and PR Ch. (1973–74), Sixth Dist. (Ch., 1971–72, 1975–76); various other coms., ofcs. Bibb Assn. of Media Specs.: Pres. (1979–80). Various other orgs. Bibb Assn. of Educs.: Corres. Secy. (1975–76); Bldg. Rep. (1972–75); Necrology Com. (Ch., 1972–73, 1974–75); Legis. Lobbyist (1975–78). Natl. Educ. Assn.: Conv. Del. (1973, 1976–81). GA Assn. of Educs.: Conv. Del. (1971–80). AAUW. Various other orgs. **Honors:** Lib. Dept. of GA Assn. of Educs., Plaque for Dedicated Srvs., 1978, Plaque for Pres., 1978. **Activities:** 10; 17, 24, 32; 63 **Addr.:** 389 Astor St., Macon, GA 31201.

Epstein, Barbara A. (Ap. 21, 1951, Cleveland, OH) Libn., West. Psyt. Inst. and Clinic, 1974–; Instr., Sch. of LS, Univ. of Pittsburgh, 1979–; Libn., Carrick HS, 1973–74. **Educ.:** Univ. of Pittsburgh, 1969–72, BA (Pol. Sci., Fr.), Case West. Rsv. Univ., 1972–73, MSLS; Med. LA, 1976, Cert. **Orgs.:** Med. LA: Com. on Hosp. Lib. Stans. and Pracs. (1979–81); Chap. Cncl. (1981–); Mental Hlth. Libns. Sect. (Ch., 1978–79); Dev. and Instr., CE464-81: Online Srch. in Psyt. Natl. Lib. of Med.: Stdg. Com. for Online Retrieval Educ., Subcom. to Dev. a Crs. in Psyt. (1979–80). **Honors:** Beta Phi Mu, 1973. **Pubns.:** Jt. auth., "Multidatabase Searching in the Behavioral Sciences, Part II," *Database* (D. 1980); jt. auth., "Multidatabase Searching in the Behavioral Sciences: Part I," *Database* (S. 1980); jt. auth., "JCAH Accreditation and the Hospital Library: A Guide for Librarians," *Bltn. of the Med. LA* (1980). **Activities:** 1, 5; 26, 31, 39; 80 **Addr.:** Western Psychiatric Institute & Clinic Library, 3811 O'Hara St., Pittsburgh, PA 15261.

Epstein, Dena Julia (N. 30, 1916, Milwaukee, WI) Asst. Msc. Libn., Univ. of Chicago, 1964–; Msc. Catlgr. and Rev., Copyrt. Cat. Div., Lib. of Congs., 1946–48; Sr. Msc. Libn., Newark Pub. Lib., 1943–45; Catlgr. in Art and Msc., Univ. of IL, 1939–43. **Educ.:** Univ. of Chicago, 1934–37, BA (Msc.); Univ. of IL, 1938–43, BLS, MA (LS). **Orgs.:** Msc. LA: Bd. of Dirs. (1970–73); Pres. (1977–79). ALA. Intl. Assn. of Msc. Libs. Amer. Musicological Socty. Intl. Folk Msc. Cncl. **Honors:** Univ. of Chicago, Chicago Folklore Prize, 1978; South. Hist. Assn., Francis Butler Simkins Awd., 1979; Univ. of TN, 30th Anl. Lib. Lectr., 1978. **Pubns.:** *Music Publishing in Chicago before 1871: The Firm of Root and Cady, 1858–1871* (1969); *Sinful Tunes and Spirituals: Black Folk Music to the Civil War* (1977); "African Music in British and French America," *Musical Qtly.* (Ja. 1973); "The Folk Banjo: A Documentary History," *Ethnomsclgy.* (S. 1975). **Activities:** 1, 9; 20, 39, 41; 55, 57 **Addr.:** 5039 S. Ellis Ave., Chicago, IL 60615.

Epstein, Hank (Ja. 13, 1934, New York, NY) Pres., Info. Transform, 1977–; Dir., Ballots Ctr., Stanford Univ., 1969–77; Mgr., Advnc. Tech., Apollo, N. Amer. Aviation, 1962–69. **Educ.:** CUNY, 1951–55, BS (Engin.). **Orgs.:** ALA. ASIS: Lib. Autom. and Netwks. Spec. Interest Grp. (Ch., 1979); COM Spec. Interest Grp. (Ch., 1975, 1980). **Pubns.:** "Network Technology Today," *Networks for Networkers* (1980); "The Technology of Library and Information Networks," *Jnl. of ASIS* (N. 1980); "The Networking of Networks," *Bltn. of ASIS* (Je. 1979). **Activities:** 9, 13; 24, 33, 34; 56, 83 **Addr.:** Information Transform, 502 Leonard St., Madison, WI 53711.

Epstein, Rheda (My. 26, 1945, Birmingham, AL) Head, Tech. Srvs. Div., VA Beach Pub. Lib., 1976–; Catlgr., Libn. II, Trenton State Coll., 1971–76; Catlgr., Asst. Libn., Univ. of S. FL, 1968–71. **Educ.:** Univ. of FL, 1963–67, BAE; Drexel Univ., 1967–68, MLS; Rutgers Univ., 1972–77, EdM. **Orgs.:** Southeast. LA. VA LA: JMRT. ALA: JMRT (Prof. Dev. Grant Com. 1975–76; Travel Ntwk. Com., Ch., 1975–76; Handbk. Com., Ch. 1977–78); RTSD (Cat. and Class. Div., Nom. Com. 1977–78; Subj. Anal. Com. 1978–80). NJ LA: JMRT, Pres. (1974–76); Legis. Com. (1973–76). **Honors:** ALA, JMRT Prof. Dev. Grant, 1975. **Addr.:** Technical Services Division, Virginia Beach Public Library, 1251 Bayne Dr., Virginia Beach, VA 23454.

Erbes, Raymond Gustave (N. 18, 1922, Mendota, IL) Dir. of Lib. Srvs., Reavis HS, 1950–; Libn., Evanston Township HS, 1948–50. **Educ.:** Univ. of IL, 1936–40, BS (Educ.), 1948–50, MLS. **Orgs.:** IL Assn. of Sch. Libn.: Pres. (1958); Exec. Bd. (1955–59). ALA: AASL (Treas. Exec. (Bd.). Nat. Assn. of Educ. **Pubns.:** "Try a Display," *IL Sch. Brd. Jnl.,* (Mr. 1979). **Activities:** 10, 11; 15, 17, 31; 50, 63 **Addr.:** 915 South LaGrange Rd., LaGrange, IL 60525.

Eres, Beth Krevitt (D. 11, 1950, NY, NY) Costi and Weizmann Inst., Israel, 1977–79; Grp. Mgr. Info. Tech., Franklin Inst. Resrch. Labs., 1974–77; Proj. Mgr., Aspen Syst. Corp., 1973–74; Spec. Recruit, Lib. of Congs., 1972. **Educ.:** SUNY, Stony Brook, 1967–70, BA (Grmn.); Drexel Univ., 1970–72, MS (Info. Sci.); 1979–, PhD, cand. **Orgs.:** ASIS: Comsn., Long Range Plng. Comsn. (1973–75); Secy., Potomac Valley Chapter (1974); Pres., Drexel Student Chap. (1971); Beta Phi Mu. Sigma Xi. **Pubns.:** Ed., *Legal and Legislative Information Processing* (1980); Jt. auth., "The Impact of Editorial Processing Centers on Developing Nations," *Proceedings, Conf. on Info. Tech.,* Jerusalem, (1974); Jt.-auth., "Evaluation of Information Systems," *Info., pt. II* (1973); Jt.-auth., "A Comparison of Several Zipt-type Distributions," *Jnl.* of ASIS (My./Jn. 1972); Various other articles and presented papers. **Activities:** 11, 12; 24, 26, 41; 91, 93 **Addr.:** School of Library and Information Science, Drexel University, Philadelphia, PA 19104.

Erickson, Donald Robert (O. 2, 1932, Chicago, IL) Head, Tech. Lib., Naval Sea Systems Command, Washington, DC, 1978–; Libn., 1972–78; Asst. Naval Reg. Libn., Naval Educ. & Trng. Support Ctr., San Diego, CA, 1971–72; Dir. of Libs., U.S. Fleet Activities, Yokosuka, Japan, 1967–71; Asst. Sci. and Tech. Ref. Libn., CA State Univ., Long Beach, 1961–66. **Educ.:** West. MI Univ., Kalamazoo, 1959–60, BA (Eng.), 1960–61, MALS. **Orgs.:** SLA: Docu. and Info. Retrvl. **Activities:** 4, 12; 17; 64, 91 **Addr.:** Naval Sea Systems Command, Technical Library, SEA 99612, Department of the Navy, Washington, DC 20362.

Erickson, Harold H. J. (O. 22, 1931, Point Mills, MI) Dir. of Libs., Univ. of NV, 1965–; Head, Acq., Syracuse Univ., 1963–65, Head, Gift and Exch., 1961–62; Biblgrphr., Univ. of Cincinnati, 1959–61. **Educ.:** MI State Univ., 1950–54, BA (Eng.); Univ. of MI, 1958–59, MALS. **Orgs.:** ALA: ACRL, Legis. Com. Mt. Plains LA. NV LA: Lib. Plng. Com. NV Cncl. on Libs.: Ch. Various other orgs. **Activities:** 1; 15, 28; 78 **Addr.:** 217 Redstone, Las Vegas, NV 89128.

Erickson, Ture Rexford (O. 26, 1936, New Westminster, BC) Head, Sedgewick Lib., Univ. of BC, 1965–; Ref. Libn., 1964–65. **Educ.:** Univ. of BC, 1954–62, BA (Hist.); 1963–64, BLS. **Orgs.:** Can. LA: Lcl. Arrange. Com. (1979–80). BC LA. Univ. of BC Libns. Assn.: Pres. (1979–80). Can. Assn. of Univ. Tchrs. **Activities:** 1; 17, 19, 34 **Addr.:** Sedgewick Library, 1958 Main Mall, Univ. of BC, Vancouver, BC V6T 1W5 Canada.

Ericson, Richard James (Jl. 7, 1951, Milwaukee, WI) Chief, Lawbk. Sect., Admin. Ofc. of the U.S. Cts., 1981–; Acq. Libn., Georgetown Univ., Law Ctr. Lib., 1980–81; Catlgr., Serials Recs. Div., Lib. of Congs., 1980–81; Acq. Libn., Econ. Growth Ctr. Col., Yale Univ., 1978–80; Serials Catlgr., Latin Amer. Mtrls., Univ. of TX, 1976–78; Serials Catlgr., Univ. of WI, 1976. **Educ.:** Univ. of WI, 1970–73, BA (Span.), 1974–75, MLS. **Orgs.:** SALALM: Acq. Com. (1978–79); Nsltr. Com. (1976–78). **Honors:** Beta Phi Mu, 1976; Sigma Delta Pi, 1973. **Pubns.:** Contrib., *Hispanic American Periodicals Index* (1976–). **Activities:** 1, 4; 15, 44, 46; 54, 92 **Addr.:** 1414 17th St. N.W., Washington, DC 20036.

Erlandsson, Alf M. E. (Je. 5, 1931, Lidköping, Sweden) Chief, U.N. Arch., 1971–; Deputy Chief, Landsarkivet Lund, Sweden, 1967–71, Archvst., 1962–67, Asst. Archvst., 1958–62. **Educ.:** Univ. of Lund, Sweden, 1951–56, MA, 1967, PhD (Hist.). **Orgs.:** Svenska Arkivsamfundet. SAA. Intl. Cncl. on Arch.: Sect. for Archvsts. of Intl. Orgs., Ch. **Pubns.:** *Skanska Generalguvernementet och dess arkiv, 1658–1693* (1967); various articles in Swedish pers. **Activities:** 2 **Addr.:** United Nations Archives, Rm. PK1214, United Nations, New York, NY 10017.

Erlen, Jonathon (O. 11, 1946, Louisville, KY) Hist. of Med. Libn., Univ. of TX Hlth. Sci. Ctr., Dallas, 1974–; Lib. Dir., Paducah Com. Coll., 1974. **Educ.:** IN Univ., 1964–68, BA (Hist.); Univ. of KY, 1968–70, MA (Hist.), 1970–73, PhD (Hist.), 1972–73, MSLS; Med. LA, 1975, Cert. **Orgs.:** Assn. of Libns. for the Hist. of the Hlth. Sci.: Secy/Treas. Med. LA: Oral Hist. Com. (1979–81); Hist. of Med. Com.; Steering Com. (1977–81). Socty. for Hlth. and Human Values. Hastings Ctr. Amer. Assn. of the Hist. of Med. **Honors:** Phi Alpha Theta, 1969. **Pubns.:** "The New Medical Humanities Program at Texas A & M" *The Watermark* (Jnl. of the Amer. Assn. for Hist. of Biol. Sci. Libns.) (1977); "Old Medical Journals, Clipping Files Aid Researchers," *TX Times,* 5:5, (Mr., 1977). "Librarians as Academicians," *Frontiers in Hlth. Sci. Libnshp.* (Je., 1976); "Revolutionary War Medicine in America," *Dallas Med. Jnl.* (Mr., 1976); "Revolutionary Medicine," *Dallas Med. Jnl.* (1976); Reviews. **Activities:** 1, 5; 39; 55, 80 **Addr.:** Medical Library, UTHSCD, 5323 Harry Hines Blvd., Dallas, TX 75235.

Erlich, Martin (Jn. 20, 1924, Philadelphia, PA) Dir., Orange Pub. Lib. (CA), 1966–; Cnty. Libn., Stanislaus Cnty. Free Lib., (CA), 1965–66; Dir., Mineola Meml. Lib. (NY), 1956–65. **Educ.:** Temple Univ., 1942–47, BA (Hist.); Drexel Inst., 1948–48, BSLS; Wayne State Univ., 1949–54, MA, (Hist.). **Orgs.:** ALA. CA LA. NLA. Los Compadres. **Pubns.:** Articles in *Lib. Jnl., Wilson Lib. Bltn. and Cath. Lib. World.* **Activities:** 9; 17, 36 **Addr.:** Orange Public Library, 101 N. Center St., Orange, CA 92666.

Ernest, Judith Ellen (N. 6, 1938, Hammond, IN) Lib. Trustee, Lake Cnty. Pub. Lib., 1979–. **Educ.:** Valparaiso Univ., 1956–60, BA (Bio., Hist.); Northwest. Univ., 1962–66, MA (U.S. Hist.). **Orgs.:** North. IN Lib. Bds. Assn.: VP (1979–80); Pres. (1980–81). ALA: ALTA: Int. Frdm. Com. (1980–83). Natl. Cncl. for the Soc. Std. Natl. Educ. Assn. **Activities:** 9; 47; 74, 95-Org. lcl. trustees. **Addr.:** 9100 W. 129th Pl., Cedar Lake, IN 46303.

Erwin, Joan Rhoads (S. 30, 1943, Columbus, GA) Cmnty. Rel. Coord., Orlando Pub. Lib. Syst., 1973–; Promo. Dir., WMFE-TV (Pub. TV, Orlando, FL), 1972–73; Prog. Asst., KY Educ. TV Ntwk., 1968–71. **Educ.:** Univ. of KY, 1961–65, BA (Intl. Rel.); 1967–68, MA (Comm.). **Orgs.:** ALA: LAMA, Pub. Rel. Sect. (Ch., 1980–81). FL LA PR Caucus: Chair, 1974. **Honors:** ALA, John Cotton Dana PR Awd., 1973, 1975. **Addr.:** Orlando Public Library, 10 North Rosalind, Orlando, FL 32801.

Esala, Lillian H. (F. 16, 1923, Toledo, OH) Dir., Esala Assocs., 1974–; Dir., VA (MN) Pub. Lib., 1961–74; Dir., Hoyt Lakes, (MN) Pub. Lib., 1959–60; Cnty. Libn., VA Pub. Lib., 1945–46. **Educ.:** Univ. of Toledo, 1941–44, BA (Hist.); Columbia Univ., 1944–45, BSLS. **Orgs.:** ALA. MN LA: various coms. Arrowhead LA: Past Pres., coms. MN Hist. Socty. Various other orgs. VA Study Club: Pres. (1978–80). MN Fed. of Women's Clubs: various ofcs. **Honors:** MN LA, Cert. of Merit, 1966. **Pubns.:** *Genealogical Helper* "How to Use Your Public Library," *Geneal. Helper* (1978). **Activities:** 9; 23, 34, 41; 66, 69, 85 **Addr.:** Box 180, R. 1, Embarrass, MN 55732.

Escoffier, Alfred H. (Jl. 18, 1948, Portland, OR) Chief, Ref. Dept., Burlingame Pub. Lib., 1975–; Lib. Consult., 1981–; Spec. Srvs. Libn., 1971–75. **Educ.:** Stanford Univ., 1970, AB (Art Hist.); Univ. of Denver, 1971, MLS; CA State Univ., Hayward, 1978, MPA. **Orgs.:** ALA. CA LA: Bay Area Chap. (Pres., 1980); Cont. Educ. Com. (1981). Peninsula Lib. Syst.: Ref. Com. (Ch., 1976); Coop. Sel. Com. (Ch., 1977); Cmnty. Awareness Prod. Com., Ch. **Pubns.:** *PLS Cooperative Selection Directory* (1978); *Five Year Staff Development Plan for Medium Sized Public Library* (1978); *Reference Services Development Plan, South San Francisco Public Library* (1982); various reviews (1973–78). **Activities:** 9; 16, 17, 36 **Addr.:** Burlingame Public Library, 480 Primrose Rd., Burlingame, CA 94010.

Esdon, Robert E. (Ag. 16, 1931, Greensboro, VT) Elem. Lib. Coord., IMC Dir., Fall Mt. Reg. Sch. Dist., 1970–; Tchr., Bristol Elem. Sch. (VT), 1969–70; Libn., Williston Ctrl. Sch., (VT), 1967–69; Tchr. Bridgewater Vlg. Sch. (VT), 1963–67. **Educ.:** Johnson Tchrs. Coll., 1949–53, BS (Educ.); Univ. of RI, 1971–74, MLS; NH Bd. of Educ., 1974, Prof. Cert. (Sch. Lib.); Univ. of VT, Sums., 1965–70, (LS). **Orgs.:** ALA. NH LA. NH Educ. Media Assn. NEA. Boys Scouts of Amer. Troup 31: Com. Westmoreland Bible Church: Deacon. **Activities:** 10, 12; 17, 20, 21; 63 **Addr.:** P.O. Box 55, Charlestown, NH 03603.

Special Subjects/Services: 50. Adult educ.; 51. Advert./Mktg.; 52. Aerosp.; 53. Agric.; 54. Area std.; 55. Arts/Hum.; 56. Autom.; 57. Bibl./Prtg.; 58. Bio. sci.; 59. Bus./Fin.; 60. Chem.; 61. Copyrt.; 62. Documtn.; 63. Educ.; 64. Engin.; 65. Env.; 66. Eth. grps.; 67. Film; 68. Food/Nutr.; 69. Geneal.; 70. Geo.; 71. Geol.; 72. Handcpd.; 73. Hist.; 74. Int. frdm.; 75. Info. sci.; 76. Insr.; 77. Law; 78. Legis.; 79. Math./Comp. sci.; 80. Med.; 81. Metals; 82. Nat. resrcs.; 83. Newsp.; 84. Nuc. sci.; 85. Oral hist.; 86. Petr./Energy; 87. Pharm.; 88. Phys./Astr./Math.; 89. Readg.; 90. Relig.; 91. Sci./Tech.; 92. Soc. sci.; 93. Telecom.; 94. Transp.; 95. (other).

Who's Who in Library and Information Services

Eshelman, Larry (Ja. 31, 1938, Mechanicsburg, PA) Dir., East. ON Reg. Lib. Syst., 1977–, Asst. Dir., 1967–76; Lib. Dev. Consult., PA State Lib., 1966–67. **Educ.:** Lycoming Coll., 1956–60, BA (Hist.); Rutgers Univ., 1960–63, MLS. **Orgs.:** Can. LA. ON LA: Guilde des Srvs. en Lang. Fr. (Ch., 1981). Dirs. of ON Reg. Lib. Systs.: Ch. (1980–82). LA of Ottawa: Cnclr., Vice–Ch., Ch. (1969–71). **Pubns.:** "French Adult Book Selection," *ON Lib. Review* (Je. 1975); various articles, reviews. **Activities:** 9, 13; 17, 24 **Addr.:** Suite 6, 200 Cooper St., Ottawa, ON K2P 0G1 Canada.

Eshelman, William Robert (Ag. 23, 1921, Oklahoma City, OK) Pres., Scarecrow Press, 1979–; Ed., Wilson Lib. Bltn., Assoc. Ed., Gen. Pubns., The H. W. Wilson Co., 1968–78; Univ. Libn., Prof., of Bibl., Bucknell Univ., 1965–68; Coll. Libn., Los Angeles State Coll., 1959–65. **Educ.:** Chapman Coll., 1940–43, AB (Eng.); Univ. of CA, Los Angeles, 1948–50, AM (Eng.); Univ. of CA, Berkeley, 1950–51, BLS. **Orgs.:** ALA: Com. on Accred. (1976–78); Cncl. (1971–75); ORD Sci. Acq. Std. (1967–68); Ed. Com. (1964–66); ACRL, CHOICE, Ed. Bd. (1966–71); Pub. Com. (1964–67); various other orgs. **Honors:** ALA, Lib. Pers., Awd., 1961. **Pubns.:** "The NCLIS Proposal," *Wilson Lib. Bltn.* (Mr. 1974); "Audio-Visual Aids: Fallout from the McLuhan Galaxy," *NY Times Bk. Rev.* (My. 6, 1973); "College Libraries," *Ency. Americana;* "Social Responsibility and the Library Press," *Wilson Lib. Bltn.* (My. 1972); Various other articles. **Activities:** 1; 17, 19, 37; 67, 74 **Addr.:** 74 Seventh St., Edison, NJ 08837.

Espinosa, Silvia Delgado (Havana, Cuba) Asst. Ref. Libn., LA State Univ., 1977–; Asst. Sci. Libn., 1974–77; Sr. Sci. Libn., 1970–74. **Educ.:** Univ. of Havana, Dr. (Pharmacy); LA State Univ, MS (LS). **Orgs.:** ALA: Cncl. (1978–82); ACRL/Sci. Tech. Sect.; IRT; LIRT. LA LA. SWLA. Other orgs. AAUP. AAUW. Natl. Assn. of Cuban Amer. Women. Natl. Org. of Women. Other orgs. **Honors:** Speaker, AZ PR-WHCLIS Conf., 1978. **Pubns.:** Various speeches and panel presentations. **Activities:** 1, 5; 25, 31, 39; 56, 66, 74 **Addr.:** 8738 Norfolk Dr., Baton Rouge, LA 70809.

Espo, Harold Lee (Ja. 23, 1953, Providence, RI) Deputy Exec. Dir., ALA/ACRL, 1978–; Ref. Inst. Libn., Cornell Univ., 1977–78; Asst. to the Libn., Earlham Coll., 1976–77. **Educ.:** Earlham Coll., 1971–75, BA (Pol. Sci.); Indiana Univ., 1975–76, MLS. **Orgs.:** ALA: ACRL. **Honors:** Beta Phi Mu. **Pubns.:** Cont. "Periodicals for College Libraries," CHOICE (1976–78). **Activities:** 1, 12; 17, 31 **Addr.:** ACRL/ALA, 50 East Huron St., Chicago, IL 60611.

Esposito, Michael A. (D. 26, 1939, Troy, NY) Sr. Libn., NY State Dept. of Soc. Srvs., 1978–; Adj. Ref. Libn., Rensselaer Polytech. Inst., 1970–; Sr. Libn., Lib. Plng., NY State Lib., 1975–78, Asst. Libn., Serials Sect., 1972–74. **Educ.:** Russell Sage Coll., 1961–70, BS (Bus. Admin.); SUNY, Albany, 1970–72, MLS. **Orgs.:** ALA. SLA. NY LA. Cap. Dist. LA. NY State Interagency Info. Grp.: Prog. Ch. (1980–81). **Activities:** 12, 13; 17, 31, 39; 92 **Addr.:** 189 Kent St., Albany, NY 12206.

Esquibel, Sandra J. (Jl. 13, 1942, Hartford, WI) Assoc. State Libn., Info. Srvs., NM State Lib., 1980–, Assoc. State Libn., State Agency Srvs., 1979–80, Info. Srvs. Coord., 1973–79; Tech. Srvs. Dept. Head, Mesa Pub. Lib., 1971–73; Adult Srvs. Libn., Enoch Pratt Free Lib., 1965–68. **Educ.:** Wisconsin State College, Stevens Pt., 1960–64, BS (Hist.); Columbia Univ., 1964–65, MSLS. **Orgs.:** NM LA: Secy (1972–73); Spec. Com. on Oral Hist. (1974–75). Southwest. LA: Adv. Com., Oral Hist. Proj. (1978–). Oral Hist. Assn. **Activities:** 9, 13; 24, 32, 39; 85 **Addr.:** New Mexico State Library, P.O. Box 1629, Santa Fe, NM 87503.

Estabrook, Leigh Stewart (My. 1, 1942, Washington, DC) Assoc. Prof., Lib. Consult., Syracuse Univ., 1978–; Asst. Prof., Simmons Coll., 1971–77; Soviet and E. European Biblgphr., Notre Dame Univ., 1969–70. **Educ.:** Northwestern Univ., 1960–64, AB (Hist.); Simmons Coll., 1967–69, MSLS; Boston Univ., 1973–80, PhD (Soc.). **Orgs.:** ALA. AALS. **Pubns.:** Ed., *Libraries in Post-Industrial Society,* (1977); "Job Seekers in a Buyer's Market", *Lib. Jnl.* (1973); Jt auth., "The Impact of Social Change of the Library" *Lib. Trends* (1979); "Emerging Trends in Community Library Services," *Info. Socty.* (1978); Video case studies (1974). **Activities:** 9, 11; 24, 26, 41; 51, 92 **Addr.:** 39 Melville Ave., Dorchester, MA 02124.

Estes, David E. (Jy. 23, 1917, Atlanta, GA) Head, Spec. Colls., Emory Univ. Lib., 1972–; Ref. Libn., 1954–62; Docum. Libn., 1946–54. **Educ.:** Berry Coll., 1934–39, AB (Jnlsm.); Emory Univ., 1945–46, BS (LS); 1949–51, MA (Pol. Sci.). **Orgs.:** GA LA: Pres. (1969–71); various coms. ALA: Cncl. (1968–75); COA (1973–74). SELA: Exec. Bd. (1975–). Metro, Atlanta LA. GA Hist. Socty.: Bd. of Cur. (1976–); Lib. Com. (Ch., 1976–). Atlanta Hist. Socty.: Bd. of Dir. (1963–75). Metro Atlanta Boys Clubs: Bd. of Dir. (1978–). **Honors:** ODK, GALA Disting. Srv. Awd., 1977. **Pubns.:** Ed., *Special Collections in Southeastern Libraries* (1978); Ed., *Lucy M. Stanton, Artist* (1976); Various other articles. **Activities:** 1, 2; 15, 18, 36 **Addr.:** 258 Heaton Park Dr., Decatur, GA 30030.

Estes, Glenn E. (Ag. 17, 1934, Akron, OH) Assoc. Prof. (LS), Univ. of TN, 1967–; Asst. Prof., Clarion State Coll., 1966–67; Libn., Akron Pub. Schs., 1962–66; Tchr., 1956–62. **Educ.:** Univ. of Akron, 1952–56, BA (Eng.); Kent State Univ., 1961–65, MLS. **Orgs.:** ALA: Pub. Com. (1974–77; Ch., 1979–81); AASL, Exec. Com. (1971–79); ALSC; various awds. coms. (1972–80). TN LA. SELA. E. TN LA: Pres. (1973–74). **Honors:** Beta Phi Mu.; Kent State Univ., Sch. of LS, Disting. Alum. Awd., 1972. **Pubns.:** Jt.-ed., *Media Center Facilities Design* (1978); Ed. *Sch. Media Qtly.* (1971–79); "Bringing Language and Reading Together Through Children's Literature," *TN Educ.* (Fall 1972); "Bicentennial Highlights" (Column) *Sch. Media Qtly.* (1975–76). **Activities:** 10, 11; 21, 39, 48; 55, 57, 89 **Addr.:** Graduate School of Library & Information Science, University of Tennessee, Knoxville, TN 37916.

Estes, Mark E. (Jl. 18, 1950, Topeka, KS) Libn., Holme, Roberts & Owen, 1980–; Law Libn., U. of LaVerne Coll. of Law, 1978–80; Ref. Libn., U. of Denver Coll. of Law, 1977–78. **Educ.:** Ottawa Univ. (KS), 1968–72, BA (Pol. Sci.); Univ. of Denver, 1973–77, JD/MLL. **Orgs.:** AALL. South. CA Assn. of Law Libns.: Secy. (1979–80). CO Consortium of Law Libs.: Secy./Treas. (1977). **Pubns.:** "The Southern California Association of Law Libraries 1979 Salary Survey," *Law Lib. Jnl.* (1972). **Activities:** 12; 17, 39; 77 **Addr.:** Holme, Roberts & Owen, 1700 Broadway, Denver, CO 80290.

Esteves, Roberto (Je. 19, 1943, Hackensack, NJ) Dir., SFPL Comm. Ctr., San Francisco Pub. Lib., 1977–; Dir., CA Video Resrc. Proj., 1974–77, Resrch. Libn., Bay Area Ref. Ctr., 1969–74. **Educ.:** Montclair State Coll., 1961–65, BA (Eng.); Drexel Univ., 1967–69, MLS. **Orgs.:** ALA: Cnclr. (1972–76). CA LA. Bay Area Video Coal.: Pres. (1978–80). CA Post-Secondary Educ. Comsn. Title I Adv. Com. **Pubns.:** Jt. auth., *Video & Cable Communications, Guidelines for Librarians,* (1974); Ed., *CVRP Patch Panel,* (1974–77); various videotapes. **Activities:** 9; 32; 72, 93 **Addr.:** San Francisco Public Library, Communications Center, 3150 Sacramento St., San Francisco, CA 94115.

Estrella, Roberto L. (F. 12, 1929, PR); Dir., Educ. and Educ. Tech. Dept., Sacred Heart Univ., 1975–; Prof., Dir., Educ. Media Ctr., Med. Sci. Campus, Univ. of PR, 1972–75; Prof., Dir., Humacao Reg. Coll., 1970–71; Assoc. Prof., 1968–69; Assoc. Prof., Actg. Dir., AV Ctr., Univ. of PR, 1967–68; Assoc. Prof., Utilization Resrch. Ctr., 1963–67; Various other positions. **Educ.:** Univ. of PR, 1945–51; IN Univ., 1955–56, MS (AV Educ.); various wkshps. **Honors:** ACTE, PR Chap., Anl. Price Plaque, 1973; Phi Delta Kappa. **Pubns.:** "La Flora de Puerto Rico," (film) (19–); Transls. **Activities:** 10; 24, 32, 46; 63, 93 **Addr.:** University of the Sacred Heart, Education and Educational Technology Department, P.O. Box 12383, Loíza Station, Santurce, PR 00914.

Etheridge, Virginia (N. 24, 1933, Grenada Cnty., MS) Ref. Asst., Catlgr., Cncl. on For. Rel., 1963–; Gen. Libn., Donnell Ref. Lib., NY Pub. Lib., 1961–63; Msc. Lib., 1959–61. **Educ.:** MS South. Coll., 1951–55, BMEd; CO State Coll., 1957 (Msc. Supv.); LA State Univ., 1958–59, LSMS. **Orgs.:** SLA: Soc. Sci. Div. Prog. Plan. Conf. (1977); Ch., Teller's Com. (1973); Ch., Soc. Sci. Grp., NY Chap. (1971–72). **Activities:** 9, 12; 20, 39; 54 **Addr.:** 58 East 68 St., New York, NY 11375.

Ettel, Wolfgang H. (Jl. 31, 1932, Dvur Kralove, Czechoslovakia) Head, Washington DC Ofc., Gesellschaft für Info. Und Dokum. (Socty. for Info. and Docum.), 1978–; Head, Washington DC Ofc., Inst. für Documentationwesen (W. Grmn. Inst. for Docum), 1971–78; Dir., Sci. Affairs, OECD, Paris, France, 1968–71; Dyestuff Div., Hoechst (Chem. Corp., W. Grmn), 1960–68. **Educ.:** Tech. Univ., Munich, 1950–60, PhD (Chem.). **Orgs.:** ASIS. Natl. Micro. Assn. **Pubns.:** "Der Informationskrieg," *Nachrichten für Dokum.* (Ap. 1979); "Aussichten und Risiken im Informationsgeschaeft," *Nachrichten für Dokum.* (F. 1979); Rpts. on US Sci. and Tech. Info. avail. from Gesellschaft für Info. und Dokum., W. Grmn. **Activities:** 3, 4; 15, 17, 24; 78, 91, 95-Info. Policy. **Addr.:** Society for Information and Documentation, Suite 680, 1990 M Street, N.W., Washington, DC 20036.

Ettelt, Harold J. (Jl. 5, 1940, Brooklyn, NY) Asst. Dean for Lrng. Resrcs., Columbia–Greene Cmnty. Coll., 1975–; Ref.-–Docums. Libn., CT Coll., 1972–73; Ref. Libn., SUNY, Brockport, 1971–72. **Educ.:** William F. Paterson Coll., 1965–69, BA (Soc. Sci.); Rutgers Univ., 1970–71, MLS. **Orgs.:** Southeast. NY Lib. Resrcs. Cncl.: Trustee. **Pubns.:** "Book Use at a Small (Very) Community College Library," *Lib. Jnl.* (N. 15, 1978); "In Reply to Centralization versus Departmentalization," *Periodically Speaking* (Spr. 1979). **Activities:** 1; 15, 17 **Addr.:** Columbia–Greene Community College, P.O. Box 1000, Hudson, NY 12534.

Etter, Constance L. (Jl. 20, 1943, Litchfield, IL) Libn., Ofc. of the Audit. Gen., State of IL, 1979–; Interlib. Coop. Consult., Kaskaskia Lib. Syst., 1976–78; Gen. Consult., Ref. Consult., Cumberland Trail Lib. Syst., 1975–76, 1974–75, Tech. Srvs. Dir., 1971–73; Libn., Alton Meml. Hosp., Sch. of Nursing, 1968–70; Serials Libn., St. Louis Univ., 1967–68. **Educ.:** South. IL Univ., Edwardsville, 1961–65, BA (Eng.); Univ. of IL, 1966–67, MS (LS). **Orgs.:** ALA. **Honors:** Beta Phi Mu, 1967. **Pubns.:** Auth. and ed., *Datebook* (1974–77). **Activities:** 9, 12; 17, 24, 41; 59, 77, 78 **Addr.:** Office of the Auditor General, 509 S. Sixth St., Springfield, IL 62701.

Ettlinger, John R. Turner (D. 18, 1925, Tunbridge Wells, Kent, UK) Prof., Dalhousie Univ., 1969–; Col. Libn., 1966–69; Cur., Annmary Brown Meml., Brown Univ. Lib., 1963–66; Head, Spec. Cols., 1954–63. **Educ.:** Oxford Univ., 1943–44, 1947–49, BA MA (Hist.); McGill Univ., 1952–53, BLS. **Orgs.:** ALA. Can. LA. Atlantic Provs. LA. Halifax LA. Bibl. Socty. Bibl. Socty. of Amer. Bibl. Socty. of Can. **Activities:** 1, 11; 15, 26, 45; 57 **Addr.:** School of Library Service, Dalhousie Univ., Halifax NS B3H 4H8 Canada

Eubanks, Jacqualyn Karen (Ap. 17, 1938, Chicago, IL) Asst. Prof., CUNY, Brooklyn Coll., 1966–; Info. Srv. Libn., Amer. Assn. of Advert. Agencies, 1965–66; Army Libn., USDA Baumholder, Germany, 1963–65. **Educ.:** Univ. of Chicago, 1955–59, AB (Hum.), 1959–63, MA (LS); Columbia Univ., 1967–69, MA (Higher Educ. Admin.). **Orgs.:** Com. of Small Mag. Eds. and Publshrs.: Bd. (1976–79). LA of CUNY: Various coms. (1968–). ALA: SRRT (Coord., 1971–72); Sect. Cncl.; various coms. (1967–). **Pubns.:** Ed., *Alternatives In Print* (1980); "Book Fairs Are Peace Work," *Bookmark* (Spr. 1981). **Activities:** 1, 7 **Addr.:** Brooklyn College, Library Department, Brooklyn, NY 11210.

Euster, Joanne R. (Ap. 7, 1936, Grants Pass, OR) Univ. Libn., Loyola Univ., New Orleans, 1977–; Dir., Lib-Media Ctr., Edmonds Cmnty. Coll., 1973–77; Asst. Libn., 1968–73. **Educ.:** Portland State Coll., 1960–65, BA (Hum.); Univ. of WA, 1965–68, MLS, 1975–77 (MBA); ARL, Consult. Trng. Prog., 1979. **Orgs.:** ALA: LAMA, Women Admin. Disc. Grp: (Ch., 1979–); ACRL, Const. and By-laws Com. (1978–); LITA; LRRT. LA LA: Int. Frdm. Com. (1979–). SWLA. Metro. Educ. Media Assn. **Pubns.:** "A Women's Profession in Academia: Problem and Proposal," *New Horizons for Acad. Libs.* (1979); "The MBA in Library Land," *LLA Bltn.* (Spr. 1979); "The Washington Library Network as a Management Information System," *PNLA Qtly.* (Spr. 1978); "Election '76" (TV Series) (1976). **Activities:** 1; 17, 22, 34; 56, 59, 74 **Addr.:** Loyola University Library, 6363 St. Charles Ave., New Orleans, LA 70118.

Evans, Calvin D. (Mr. 23, 1931, Northern Arm, NF) Asst. Libn., Pub. Srvs., Univ. of AB Lib., 1979–; Head, Hum. and Soc. Sci. Div., Univ. of Guelph, 1973–79; Head, Per. Div. Meml. Univ. of NF, 1968–73; Catlgr., 1967–68. **Educ.:** Dalhousie Univ., 1952, BA (Phil.); Pine Hill Dvnty. Hall, 1955, MDiv (Theo.); Univ. of Toronto, 1967, BLS, 1969, ThM, (Theo.). **Orgs.:** Can. LA: Can. Assn. of Coll. and Univ. Libs. (Dir., 1979–80; Pres., 1980–81); Acad. Status Com. (1974–79). Can. Assn. of Univ. Tchrs.: Com. on Prof. Libns. (Ch., 1976–79). Bibl. Socty of Can. Hum. Assn. of Can. **Pubns.:** Librarians and Caut: Historical Overview and Future Directions," *CAUT Bltn.* (Mr. 1976); "Henry Winton," and other contribs. *Dict. of Can. Biog.* (1977). **Activities:** 1, 17, 34, 39; 55, 56, 90 **Addr.:** Cameron Library, University of Alberta, Edmonton, AB T6G 2J8 Canada.

Evans, Charles Whitney (Jn. 16, 1930, San Diego, CA) Assoc. Prof., Univ. of MS, 1973–; Asst. Prof., Univ. of KY, 1967–73; Libn., San Diego Pub. Lib., 1964–67; Prin. Libn., Alameda Cnty. Lib., 1962–64. **Educ.:** San Diego State Coll., 1948–52, AB (Econ.); Univ. of CA, 1955–56, MLS, 1960–69, DLS. **Orgs.:** ALA. AALS. Cncl. on Lib. Tech. Assts. AAUP; AMA. **Honors:** Beta Phi Mu; Phi Delta Kappa. **Pubns.:** *Middle Class Attitudes and Public Library Use* (1970); "The Evolution of Paraprofessional Library Employees," *Advncs. in Libnshp.* (1979); "A History of Community Analysis in American Librarianship," *Lib. Trends* (Ja. 1976); "Paraprofessional Library Employees" (pamphlet) (1977). **Activities:** 9, 11; 17, 26, 35; 51, 59 **Addr.:** P.O. Box 471, University, MS 38677.

Evans, Edwin Ben (Jl. 7, 1909, Bakersfield, CA) Retired; Dir., Instructional Mat., Kern Jt. Union HS Dist., 1935–72. **Educ.:** Stanford Univ., 1931, AB (Pol. Sci.), 1934, AM (Pol. Sci.); Univ. of Oslo, Norway, 1934–35 (Hist.); Univ. of CA, 1939 (Cert. in Librnshp.). **Orgs.:** AASL: Dir. (1946–48; 1953–55). Sch. LA of Ch. (Pres. 1948–49; VP 1947–48; Dir. 1949–50). CA LA (Second VP 1947–48; Exec. Brd. 1943–44). Phi Delta Kappa (Pres., Alpha Rho Field Chap. 1943–44; Del. to Nat. Cncl., 1946). Various other orgs. Univ. of CA Sch. of Libnshp. (Adv. Cncl. 1955–58). Univ. of South. CA Sch. of Lib. Sci. (Adv. Brd. 1961–67). Kern Sch. Fed. Credit Union (Pres. 1940–45). **Pubns.:** "Ally of the Gifted," *Sat. Review* (N. 1, 1958); "The School Library," *ALA Bltn.* (F. 1956); "What Are You Doing in Recruiting?" *ALA Bltn.* (N. 1946); Jt. auth., "When You are Asked to Speak," *ALA Div. of Libs. for Chld. and Young People* (O. 1948); Jt. auth., "Needed: A School Lib. Consult. Srvc." *CA Jnl. of Second. Educ.* (My. 1950); various other articles. **Activities:** 10, 11; 17, 26; 63 **Addr.:** 2524 Cedar St., Bakersfield, CA 93301.

Evans, G. Edward (Ja. 5, 1937, Huntingdon, PA) Prof., Univ. of CA, 1968–; Catlgr., IL State Univ., LA, 1965–68; Acq./Serials, CA State Univ., Hayward, 1962–65; Reserve Bk., Univ. of MN, 1959–62. **Educ.:** Univ. of MN, 1955–59, BA (Anthro), 1959–61, MA (Anthro), 1961–62, MALS; Univ. of IL, 1966–68, PhD (LS). **Orgs.:** ALA. CA LA. SLA. AAUP. Amer. Antiquity Assn. **Honors:** National Science Fndn., Resrch. Asstshp.,

PROFESSIONAL ACTIVITIES: Institutions: 1. Acad. lib.; 2. Arch.; 3. Assn.; 4. Fed./Gvt. lib.; 5. Inst. lib.; 6. Mfr./Suppl.; 7. Milit. lib.; 8. Musm.; 9. Pub. lib.; 10. Sch. lib.; 11. Sch. of lib. sci.; 12. Spec. lib.; 13. State lib.; 14. (other). **Functions/Activities:** 15. Acq./Col. dev.; 16. Adult srvs.; 17. Admin.; 18. Apprais.; 19. Archit./Bldgs.; 20. Cat./Class.; 21. Chld. srvs.; 22. Circ.; 23. Cons./Pres.; 24. Consult.; 25. Cont. ed.; 26. Educ. lib. sci.; 27. Ext. srvs.; 28. Fund/Grants; 29. Gvt. pubs.; 30. Indx./Abs.; 31. Instr. lib. use; 32. Media srvs.; 33. Micro.; 34. Netwks./Coop.; 35. Persnl.; 36. PR; 37. Publshg.; 38. Recs. mgt.; 39. Ref. srvs.; 40. Repro.; 41. Resrch.; 42. Review.; 43. Secur.; 44. Serials; 45. Spec. col.; 46. Tech. srvs.; 47. Trustees/Bds.; 48. YA srvs.; 49. (other).

1958–59; Cncl. of Lib. Resrcs., Flshp., 1972; Fulbright, Flshp., 1974. **Pubns.:** *Introduction to Technical Services* (1976); *Management Techniques for Librarians* (1980); *Developing Library Collections,* (1979); *Bibliography of Language Arts Materials for Native North Americans,* (1979); extensive lib.-related articles. **Activities:** 1, 11; 16, 18, 20; 62, 67 **Addr.:** Graduate School of Library and Information Science, 120 Powell Library, University of California, Los Angeles, CA 90024.

Evans, M. Gwynneth (Ja. 4, 1940, Toronto, ON) Head, Ref. and Bibl. Sec., Nat. Lib. of Can., 1977–, Head, Gen. Ref. Sec., 1975–77, Ref. Libn., 1975, Bibgphr., 1974–75. **Educ.:** Univ. of Toronto, 1958–61, BA (Fr.); Simmons Coll., 1973–74, MSLS; Ontario Second. Sch. Cert. in Educ., 1963–64. **Orgs.:** Can. LA. Bibl. Socty. of Can.: Cnclr. (1976–79); Ch., Local Arranges. Colloquium III, Bibl. Socty. of Can. (1978). Assn. for Can. Stds. **Honors:** Beta Phi Mu, 1974. **Pubns.:** *Women in Federal Politics* (1975); reviews. **Activities:** 1, 4; 15, 31, 39; 54, 55, 92 **Addr.:** Reference and Bibliography Section, National Library of Canada, 395 Wellington St., Ottawa, ON K1A 0N4, Canada.

Evans, Max J. (My. 11, 1943, Lehi, UT) Asst. Dir., Arch. Div., State Hist. Socty. of WI, 1977–; Asst. Church Libn., Archvst., Hist. Dept., Church of Jesus Christ of Latter-day Sts., 1975–77; Archvst., 1971–75. **Educ.:** UT State Univ., 1961–62, 1965–66; Univ. UT, 1967–68, BS (Hist.); UT State Univ., 1969–71, MS (Hist.); Univ. UT, 1975–76 (Hist.); Univ. of WI, 1978–80 (Hist.); Amer. Univ., Mod. Arch. Admin., 1974, Cert. **Orgs.:** SAA: Finding Aids Com. (1973–76); Autom. Com. (1976–); Natl. Info. Task Force, 1979–. Conf. of Intermt. Archvsts.: Founding Mem.; Nsltr. Ed. (1976). Midwest Arch. Conf. Spindex User's Ntwk.: Nsltr. Ed. West. Hist. Assn. UT Hist. Socty. Mormon Hist. Assn. **Pubns.:** "Handling photographs in the LDS Church Archives," *Amer. Archvst.* (Ap. 1977); "William C. Staines," *UT Hist. Qtly* (Fall 1975); Jt.-auth., "Preserving Mormon Manuscripts," *MSS.* (Sum. 1975); "The Stephen Post Collection," *BYU Stds.* (Fall 1973). **Activities:** 2; 17, 45; 56, 92, 73-Hist. **Addr.:** 816 State St., Madison, WI 53706.

Evans, Peter A. (O. 4, 1929, Ross, CA) Libn., Univ. of CA, Berkeley, 1975–; Head Libn., CA Hist. Socty., 1969–74; Eng. Tchr., Yuba Coll., 1962–68; Las Plumas HS, 1961–62. **Educ.:** Univ. of CA, Berkeley, 1947–51, BS (Forestry); San Francisco State Coll., 1959–61, MA (Eng.); San Jose State Coll., 1968–69, MLS. **Orgs.:** SLA: Educ. Com. (1976–78); Prog. Com. (1979–80). **Pubns.:** *The First Hundred Years: a descriptive bibliography of Calif. Hist. Soc. pubs. 1871–1971* (1971); *Directory of selected forestry-related bibliographic data bases* (1979); "The gentle row," *San Francisco Examiner and Chronicle* (F. 15, 1976); "Marin County shipwrecks" *Point Reyes Hist.* (1977). **Activities:** 1; 15, 17, 39; 65, 82, 91 **Addr.:** 6 Hillcrest Rd., Berkeley, CA 94705.

Evans, Richard A. (Ag. 29, 1923, Wilkes-Barre, PA) Lib. Dir., U.S. Naval Acad., 1967–; Group Supvsr., Ctrl. Lab. Lib. Grp., Applied Phys. Lab., The Johns Hopkins Univ., 1963–67; Mgr., Tech. Info. Ctr., HRB-Singer, Inc., 1957–63; Ref. Libn., U.S. Govt., 1951–57. **Educ.:** King's Coll., 1946–50, BA (Soc. Stds.); Univ. of Syracuse, 1950–51, MSLS. **Orgs.:** SLA. ALA. **Activities:** 1, 4; 17, 24 **Addr.:** 346 Sheffield Rd., Severna Park, MD 21146.

Evans, Robert L. (N. 10, 1922, Omaha, NB) Owner, Pres., Eastin Phelan Distr. Corp., 1968–; Vice Pres., Sales Mgr., 1968–74; Vice Pres., Mgr., Hooker Glass and Paint Co. of IA, 1962–65. **Educ.:** Drake Univ., 1940–41; State Univ. of IA, 1941–47, BA (Gen. Sci.). **Orgs.:** ALA: Exhibitors RT (Vice-Pres., 1978–79). Fin. Secur. Life Insr. Co. (Moline, IL): Dir., Ch. of Bd. Life Secur. of IA (Davenport): Vice-Pres., Bd. Regency Fin. Grp., (Davenport): Dir., Ch. of Bd. **Activities:** 6; 32; 67, 95-Videocassettes. **Addr.:** 1235 West Fifth St., Davenport, IA 52808.

Evans, Roy W. (Mr. 18, 1926, Johnston City, IL) Assoc. Prof. (LS), Univ. of MO, 1968–; Instr., Instr. Mtrls., South. IL Univ., 1958–68; Libn., Rich Twp. HS (IL), 1954–58; Tchr., Libn., Newton (IL) HS, 1951–54. **Educ.:** South. IL Univ., 1946–50, BS (Educ.); George Peabody Coll., 1951–56, MA (LS); South. IL Univ., 1958–68, PhD. **Orgs.:** AALS. MO LA. AECT. **Pubns.:** "Extension Classes as a Source of Recruitment," *Off-Campus Credit Programs: The Quality Issue* (Jl. 1979); "John Dewey and Audio Visual," MO AECT (Fall 1977). **Activities:** 11; 25, 26, 27; 50, 75 **Addr.:** 105-B Stewart Hall, University of Missouri, Columbia, MO 65211.

Evans, Ruth Anne (My. 18, 1924, Schenectady, NY) Asst. Libn., Schaffer Lib., Union Coll., 1961–; Ref. Libn., Union Coll. Lib., 1956–61; Asst. Catlgr., 1952–56; Asst. Catlgr., Colgate Univ. Lib., 1948–52. **Educ.:** Smith Coll., 1942–46, AB (Hist.); Columbia Univ., 1947–48, BS (LS). **Orgs.:** ALA. NY LA. Capital Dist. Lib. Cncl. for Ref. and Resrch. Resrcs. (Trustee 1974–80; Pres., 1975–79). Phi Beta Kappa: Union Coll. Chap. (VP, 1978); Upper Hudson Assn., Prog. Com. (1979–80). **Honors:** Union Coll. Alum. Cncl., Fac. Merit. Srus. Awd., 1975. **Activities:** 1; 15, 23, 45; 57, 85 **Addr.:** Schaffer Library, Union College, Schenectady, NY 12308.

Evans, Sally Romer (Ja. 4, 1928, Chicago, IL) Msc. Libn., Amherst Coll., 1976–; Catlgr., 1972–76; Catlgr., Auerbach Corp. Lib., 1967–69; Biblgrph., McGraw-Hill Pub. Co., 1966–67; Asst., Philadelphia Union Lib., 1965–66; Asst. Catlgr., Atheneum of Philadelphia, 1964–65; Msc. Catlgr., Oberlin Coll. Lib., 1960–64; Docum. Asst./Msc. Libn./Ref. Libn., Princeton Univ. Lib., 1955–60. **Educ.:** Oberlin Coll., 1945–49, BA (Eng.); Simmons Coll., 1950–57, MS(LS). **Orgs.:** ALA. Msc. LA: New Eng. Chap., Cont. Educ. Com. (1977–). New England LA. New England Tech. Srvcs. Libns.: VP (1978–79); Pres. (1979–80). **Addr.:** Vincent Morgan Library, Music Center, Amherst College, Amherst, MA 01002.

Evensen, Richard H. (Mr. 18, 1929, Boston, MA) Proj. Coord., Natl. Lib. Srv. for the Blind and Phys. Handcpd., 1973–; Sr. Job Anal., First Natl. Bank of Boston, 1969–73, Job Anal., 1965–69. **Educ.:** Harvard Coll., 1949–53, AB, cum laude (Pol. Sci.); Boston Univ., 1953–54, MA (Pol. Sci.); Cath. Univ. of Amer., 1976–81, MSLS. **Orgs.:** Rehab. Info. RT. ALA. Amer. Assn. of Workers for the Blind: Natl. Pubn. Bd. (1979–81); Lib. Srv. Interest Grp., Ch. (1977–79); Ch.-Elect (1975–77); DC–MD Chap. (Bd. of Dirs., 1980–83). Braille Athrty. of N. Amer.: NLS/BPH Rep., US–UK Liaison Com. (Ch., 1980–). Natl. Braille Assn.: Reader–Transcriber Registry (1978–); Site Finding Com. (1980–). Assn. for Educ. of the Visually Handcpd.: Various ofcs. Various other orgs., ofcs. **Honors:** Amer. Fndn. for the Blind, Charles Brown Medal, 1957. **Pubns.:** "Cassette Braille Evaluation," *Educ. of the Visually Handcpd.* (forthcoming); jt. auth., "Research Topic: Developing Information Service Aids and Programs for Handicapped Individuals," *Drexel Qtly.* (Fall 1980); jt. auth., "Services Are 500 Percent Better," *Amer. Libs.* (Je. 1979); jt. auth., "Equalizing Information Access by Handicapped Persons," *ASIS Procs.* (1979); "Braillist, Braille Technology, Braille Readers and Braille," *NBA Bltn.* (Win. 1978–79). **Activities:** 4, 9; 17, 41; 72 **Addr.:** National Library Service for the Blind and Physically Handicapped, 1291 Taylor St. N.W., Washington, DC 20542.

Evensen, Robert Lloyd (S. 29, 1945, Chicago, IL) Creative Arts Libn., Brandeis Univ., 1974. **Educ.:** Roosevelt Univ., 1964–67, BA (Fine Arts); Univ. of Chicago, 1970–74, MALS. **Orgs.:** Msc. LA: Ch., New England Chap. (1977–78); Program Ch. (1976–77). Art Libs. Socty./N. Amer. **Honors:** Del. for the MA Gov. Conf. on Lib. and Info. Srvs., 1978–79. **Activities:** 1; 15, 39; 55 **Addr.:** Creative Arts Section, Goldfarb Library, Brandeis University, Waltham, MA 02254.

Everitt, Cynthia Ann (O. 9, 1945, Bremerton, WA) Freelnc. Consult., Univ. of UT Med. Ctr., 1980–; Map Libn., Univ. of TX, El Paso, 1974–77; Libn., El Paso Archlg. Socty., 1972–73; Ref. Libn., Soc. Sci., Hum., TX A and M Univ. Lib., 1968–70. **Educ.:** Dickinson State Coll., 1964–67, BS (Elem. Educ., Art); Brigham Young Univ., 1977–79, MLS. **Orgs.:** SLA: Geo. and Maps Div., Chap. Mem. Ch. West. Assn. Map Libns.: Hosplty. Com., 1980 Mid-winter Mtg. Assn. of Amer. Geographers. UT State Hist. Socty. **Pubns.:** "Black on White Mimbres Pottery—a Bibliography," *The Artifact* (1973); "A Preliminary Report on Black Mesa (Arizona) Firehearths," *Transactions* (1974); Jt. Auth., "The Cruz Tarin Paleo Site," *AWANYU* (1974); "Paleo-Indian Bison Kill Sites in North America—a Bibliography," *The Artifact* (1975); "Security in Map Collections," *Lib. Trends* (Spr. 1981). **Activities:** 1, 12; 15, 17, 24; 55, 70, 92 **Addr.:** 609 7th Ave., Salt Lake City, UT 84103.

Everts, Irma Dee (Ja. 3, 1921, Shelbyville, MO) Assoc. Libn., San Antonio Coll., 1961–, Asst. Libn., 1961–72; Asst., San Antonio Pub. Lib., 1950–52; Norman (OK) HS Libn., 1945–46. **Educ.:** Univ. of OK, 1934–39. **Orgs.:** TX LA: Treas. Bexar Cnty. LA. TX Jr. Coll. Tchrs. Assn. Cosmo Internatl. Women in Comm. Zonta Internatl. Delta Psi Omega. **Pubns.:** Producer, "The Library Hour" (radio) (1970–); "The Library Hours," *Coll. Radio* (1975); "The Library Hour," *Jr. Coll. Messenger* (1976); "The Library Hour," *Lib. Jnl.* (1974). **Activities:** 1, 9; 31, 32, 39; 55, 72, 93 **Addr.:** San Antonio College Library, 1001 Howard St., San Antonio, TX 78234.

Ewald, Robert B. (N. 21, 1938, Lexington, VA) Desc. Cat. Spec., Lib. of Congs., 1978–; Head, Misc. Langs. Cat. Sect., 1972–78; Descr. Cat., Grmn. Langs., 1968–73; Catlgr., Harvard Div. Sch. Lib., 1961–66. **Educ.:** Hampden-Sydney Coll., 1957–61, BA (Classics); Harvard Univ., 1961–64, STB (Theo.); Simmons Coll., 1964–66, MS (LS). **Orgs.:** ALA. **Pubns.:** Ed., *The Research Paper Guide* (1970). **Activities:** 1, 4; 20; 90 **Addr.:** 130 Twelfth St., S.E., Washington, DC 20003.

Ewick, Charles R. (S. 13, 1937, Shelbyville, IN) Dir. IN State Lib., 1978–; Dir., Rolling Prairie Libs., 1972–78; Asst. Dir., IN State Lib., 1968–72; Consult., IN State Lib., 1966–68. **Educ.:** Wabash Coll., 1955–62, BA (Eng.); IN Univ., 1965–66, MA (LS). **Orgs.:** ALA. IN LA. **Activities:** 9, 13; 17, 34; 78 **Addr.:** Indiana State Library, 140 N. Senate Ave., Indianapolis, IN 46204.

Eyman, David Harry (O. 15, 1937, Lancaster, OH) Dir. of Libs., Juniata Coll., 1978–; Dir. of Libs., Northeast. OK State Univ., 1975–78; Head Libn., Findlay Coll., 1974–75; Ref. Libn., Asst. to the Dir., Ctrl. MI Univ., 1970–72. **Educ.:** OH Univ., 1966, AB (Hist.), 1966–67, MA (Amer. Hist.); Univ. of MI, 1967–69, AMLS, 1971–75, PhD (LS). **Orgs.:** ALA: ACRL, AV Com. (1976–). PA LA. Beta Phi Mu. **Pubns.:** "Library Budgets in the Independent Liberal Arts College," *Liberal Educ.* (Fall 1979). **Activities:** 1; 17 **Addr.:** Library, Juniata College, Huntingdon, PA 16652.

Eyster, George Warren (Mr. 24, 1925, Harrisburg, PA) Dir., Div. of Con. Educ., Morehead State Univ., 1969–; Dir., Appalachian Adult Educ. Ctr., Morehead State Univ., 1969–77; Asst. Supt., Dir., Adult Educ., Amer. Sch. Fndn. de Mexico, 1963–69; Dir., Youth Actv. and Spec. Projs., The Mott Fndn., Flint Bd. of Educ., 1953–63. **Educ.:** Univ. of MI, 1952–52, MA (Sch. Admin.); 1947–50, BS (Psy.); Eastern MI Univ., 1954–56, MS (Cmnty. Educ.); MI State Univ., 1956–60, Spec. (Adult Educ.). **Orgs.:** ALA: Ofc. of Lib. Srvc. to the Disadv. Natl. Cmnty. Educ. Assn.: Bd. (1970–71); Pubns. Com. (Ch., 1972). Natl. Assn. for Pub. and Cont. Adult Educ.: various coms. Adult Educ. Assn. Intl. Reading Assn. **Pubns.:** The Community School Center Development Act," *Cmnty. Educ. Jnl.* (Mr./Ap. 1974); "ETV" Utilization in Adult Education," *Adult Leadership* (D. 1976); "Interagency Collaboration..The Keystone to Community Education." *Cmnty. Educ. Jnl.* (S./O. 1975). **Activities:** 1; 41; 50, 89 **Addr.:** Division of Continuing Education, Bureau of University and Regional Services, Morehead State University, Morehead, KY 40351.

Ezell, Charlaine Louise (F. 15, 1950, St. Louis, MO) Reg. Prog. Coord., Daniel Boone Reg. Lib., 1971–. **Educ.:** Univ. of MO, 1968–71, BA (LS), 1972–73, MA (LS). **Orgs.:** MO LA: Chlds. Srvs. RT (Ch., 1978–79); PR Com. (Ch., 1979–80). ALA: ALSC, Natl. Parks Jt. Com. (Ch., 1980–81), Chlds. and YA Bk. Sel. Com. (1973). Natl. Heritage Trust. Beta Phi Mu. Delta Kappa Gamma. AAUW: Lcl. Branch (Secy., 1974–78). **Activities:** 9; 16, 17, 36; 55, 63, 67 **Addr.:** 303 Loch Ln., Columbia, MO 65201.

Ezzell, Joline Ridlon (N. 19, 1944, Fall River, MA) Head, Serials Dept., Duke Univ., 1980–, Asst. Head, 1976–80, Asst. Head, Acq., 1971–76, Actg. Head, Bibl. Unit, Acq., 1971, Actg. Head, ILL, 1970–71. **Educ.:** Univ. of ME, 1962–66, BA (Latin); Univ. of NC, 1966–68, MA, 1969–70, MLS. **Orgs.:** NC LA. ALA: RTSD/Serials Sect., Lib. Sch. Educ. Com. (1979–81). **Honors:** Phi Beta Kappa, 1965; Beta Phi Mu, 1970. **Activities:** 1; 17, 44 **Addr.:** Serials Dept., Duke University Library, Durham, NC 27706.

F

Fabian, Merle (F. 21, 1938, Baltimore, MD) Head Libn., Can. Embassy, 1974–; Sr. Ref. Libn., US Civil Srv. Cmsn., 1966–74; Resrcs. Ofcr., Gvtl. Affairs Inst., 1963–66; Ref. Libn., San Francisco Pub. Lib., 1962–63. **Educ.:** Syracuse Univ., 1955–59, AB (Am. Std.); Cath. Univ., 1960–62, MSLS. **Orgs.:** DC LA: Ed., *DC Libraries* (1966–67); Bd. of Dir. (1979–81). Can. LA. ALA. **Honors:** Phi Beta Kappa, 1960; Beta Phi Mu, 1962. **Activities:** 4; 17, 36; 54, 77, 92 **Addr.:** Canadian Embassy Library, 1771 N St. N.W., Washington, DC 20036.

Fadlalla, Gerald J. (Ag. 17, 1943, Olean, NY) Lib. Dir., Glen Rock (NJ) Pub. Lib., 1973–; Head Gen. Ref. Dept., Jersey City (NJ) Free Pub. Lib., 1973; Asst. Dir. and Ref. Libn., Englewood (NJ) Lib., 1971–73; Dir., Salamanca (NY) Pub. Lib., 1970–71. **Educ.:** St. Bonaventure Univ., 1961–65, BA (Hist.); Univ. of Pittsburgh, 1965–66 MLS. **Orgs.:** ALA. NJ LA: Persnl. Admin. Com. (1979–); Lib. Dev. Com. (1979–). Lib. PR Cncl. **Honors:** Beta Phi Mu, 1966. **Activities:** 9; 16, 17, 35 **Addr.:** Glen Rock Public Library, 315 Rock Rd., Glen Rock, NJ 07452.

Fagan, George V. (O. 4, 1917, Philadelphia, PA) Prof. of LS and Head Libn., Charles Leaming Tutt Lib., CO Coll., 1969–; Prof. of Hist. and Dir. of Acad. Libs., U.S. Air Frc. Acad., 1955–69; Lectr. in Hist., Univ. of CO, 1959–68; Lectr. in Hist., Univ. of Denver, 1962–63. **Educ.:** Temple Univ., 1936–40, BS, 1940–41, MA; Univ. of PA, 1946–54, PhD (Hist.); Univ. of Denver, 1957, MALS. **Orgs.:** CO State Com. for Natl. Lib. Wk: Exec. Dir. (1959–63). ALA. Bibl. Ctr. for Resrch.: Fin. Com. (1962–69). CO LA: Exec. Com. (1964–67). CO Springs Fine Arts Ctr. Org. of Amer. Histns. Amer. Hist. Assn. Air Hist. Fndn. **Pubns.:** *Geography and National Power* (1953); "Philip Washburn, A Thorough Colorado Man," *CO Mag.* (1972); "F.D.R. and Naval Limitations," *U.S. Nvl. Inst. Procs.* (1955). **Activities:** 1; 17; 75, 85 **Addr.:** 1408 N. Cascade Ave., Colorado Springs, CO 80907.

Faibisoff, Sylvia G. (New York, NY) Ch., Dept. of LS, North. IL Univ., 1978–; Assoc. Prof. and Co-Dir., Univ. of AZ, Grad. Sch., 1976–78; Asst. Prof., Univ. of IL Grad. Sch., 1975–76; Exec. Dir., S. Ctrl. Resrch. Lib. Cncl., 1968–75; Dept. Head, Ctrl. Serials Rec. Dept., Cornell Univ. Libs., 1961–68. **Educ.:** Hunter Coll., 1941, BA (Hist., Pol. Sci.); West. Rsv. Univ., 1942, BLS; Case-West. Rsv., 1968, MLS, 1975, PhD (LS). **Orgs.:** ALA: NY State Chap. (Cnclr., 1974); RASD, Com. on Coop. Ref. (Ch., 1973); various coms. AALS: Cncl. of Deans and Dirs. (1978–); Com. on the Org. of Constn. and Bylaws (1978–). IL LA: Com. on Cont. Educ. (1979–81). ASIS: Spec. Interest Grp., Nu-

Special Subjects/Services: 50. Adult educ.; 51. Advert./Mktg.; 52. Aerosp.; 53. Agric.; 54. Area std.; 55. Arts/Hum.; 56. Autom.; 57. Bibl./Prtg.; 58. Bio. sci.; 59. Bus./Fin.; 60. Chem.; 61. Copyrt.; 62. Documtn.; 63. Educ.; 64. Engin.; 65. Env.; 66. Eth. grps.; 67. Film; 68. Food/Nutr.; 69. Geneal.; 70. Geo.; 71. Geol.; 72. Handcpd.; 73. Hist.; 74. Int. frdm.; 75. Info. sci.; 76. Insr.; 77. Law; 78. Legis.; 79. Math./Comp. sci.; 80. Med.; 81. Metals; 82. Nat. resrcs.; 83. Newsp.; 84. Nuc. sci.; 85. Oral hist.; 86. Petr./Energy; 87. Pharm.; 88. Phys./Astr./Math.; 89. Readg.; 90. Relig.; 91. Sci./Tech.; 92. Soc. sci.; 93. Telecom.; 94. Transp.; 95. (other).

meric Data Bases (Nsltr. Ed., 1977–78, 1980–81). AZ LA: Consult. (1978). Various other orgs., ofcs. Amer. Cncl. for the Advnc. of Women in Higher Educ.: IL Chap. (Consult., 1978–79). IL Inst. for Env. Qual.: Consult. (1975). Ctr. for the Std. of Info. and Educ.: Consult. (1974–75). **Honors:** Natl. Assn. of State and Lcl. Histns., Natl. Awd. of Merit. **Pubns.:** *A Bibliography of Newspapers in Fourteen New York Counties* (1978); *Changing Times: Changing Libraries* (1976); contrib. ed., *The ASLA Report on Interlibrary Cooperation* (1976); *An Introduction to Information and Information Needs: Comments and Readings* (1973); "Functions and Services of Libraries," *Bookmark* (1978); various articles, mono. (1965–76). **Activities:** 1, 11; 15, 26, 34; 56, 75, 92 **Addr.:** Department of Library Science, Northern Illinois University, DeKalb, IL 60115.

Faigel, Martin J. (My. 14, 1938, Lawrence, MA) Univ. Biblgphr., Univ. of AL Lib., 1977–; Fr. and Italian Biblgphr., Univ. of VA Lib., 1972–77; Tchr., Eng. as second lang., Centro di Studi Americani, Rome, Italy, 1967–68; Resrch. Ed., McGraw-Hill Book Co., 1966–67; Chief Libn., Villa I Tatti: The Harvard Univ. Ctr. for Italian Renaissance Studies, 1964–66; Asst. to the Libn., Houghton Lib., Harvard Univ., 1962–64; Asst. to the Couns. to the Dir. for the Col., Widener Lib., 1961–62. **Educ.:** Harvard Coll., 1955–59, AB (Hist.); Univ. of CA, Berkeley, 1968–70 (Italian), 1970–72, MLS; Univ. Cattolicà, Milan, Italy, 1967, Dipl. **Orgs.:** ALA: RTSD/Resrc. Sect., Nom. Com. (1978–79); Consult., Coll. Dev. Com. (1979–81); Sub-com. on Reg. Col. Dev. Inst. (1979–81); ACRL/Ch., West. European Spec. Sect. (1979–80); Bd. of Dir. (1979–80); Prog. Plng. Com. (1980–81). AL LA: Bibl. Com. (1978–80). **Honors:** Phi Beta Kappa, 1959; Beta Phi Mu, 1972. **Pubns.:** "Research Tools for the Study of Modern Italy", *European Std. Nsltr.* (Ap./My. 1977, Sum. 1977); "Berenson Library", *Encyc. of Lib. and Info. Sci.*, vol. 2 (1969); "Two States of a Bodoni Type Specimen", *The Book Collector* (Sum. 1964); Contrib. *A Directory of Virginia Library Resources,* (1976); Transl., Alberti, Leon Battista: *Ippolito e Lionora,* (1970). **Activities:** 1; 15, 17, 46; 55, 57, 92 **Addr.:** University of Alabama Library, P.O. Box S, University, AL 35486.

Fain, Elaine (S. 8, 1929, Chicago, IL) Asst. Prof., Sch. of Lib. Sci., Univ. of WI, Milwaukee, 1975–; Lect., Lib. Sch., Univ. of WI, Madison, 1967–73, Resrch. Asst., Dept. of Urban and Reg. Plng., 1965–67; Ref. Libn., Credit Un. Natl. Assn., 1962–65. **Educ.:** Univ. of IL, 1946–49, BS (Jnlsm.); Univ. of CA, Berkeley, 1951–52, BLS; Univ. of WI, 1965–72, PhD (Educ.). **Orgs.:** SLA. ALA. **Honors:** Univ. of WI, Milwaukee, Fromkin Resrch. Awd., 1978, Grad. Sch. Resrch. Awd., 1977. **Pubns.:** "The Library and American Education," *Lib. Trends* (Win., 1978); "Selection and Soapboxes," *Wilson Lib. Bltn.* (O., 1977). **Activities:** 11; 27; 64, 67, 93 Deceased.†

Fairchild, Constance Ashmore (Ag. 27, 1938, Freeport, IL) Asst. Ref. Libn., Univ. of IL, 1966–; Serials Libn., Univ. of Lagos, Nigeria, 1964–65; Serials Catlgr., Univ. of IL 1961–63. **Educ.:** Univ. of IL, 1956–60, AB (Hist.), 1960–61, MS (LS). **Orgs.:** ALA. IL State Hist. Socty. Sierra Club. **Pubns.:** Reviews. **Activities:** 1; 39, 42; 55, 92 **Addr.:** 2707 Lawndale, Champaign, IL 61820.

Fair-Spaulding, Judy H. (O. 6, 1940, Rapid City, SD) Customer Srvs., Gvt. Spec., Lockheed DIALOG Info. Retrieval Srv., 1979–; Dir., J. Hugh Jackson Lib., Stanford Univ., 1978–79; Dir., Lib., Urban Inst., Washington, DC, 1972–78; Head, Gvt. Docum. Dept., Stanford Univ. Libs., 1967–71, Libn., 1963–67. **Educ.:** Stanford Univ., 1958–62, AB (Eng.); Univ. of CA, Berkeley, 1962–63, MLS. **Orgs.:** SLA. ASIS. **Honors:** Cncl. on Lib. Resrcs., Acad. Lib. Mgt. Prog. Intern, 1974–75. **Pubns.:** "Microform Management," *Special Libraries; A Reader* (1979); "The Microform Reading Room, Parts 1–5," *Micro. Review* (1973–75). **Activities:** 14-Info. Srv. Vendor; 29, 49-Instr.; 62 **Addr.:** 1111 Morse Ave. #134, Sunnyvale, CA 94086.

Fake, Elizabeth C. (Ja. 26, 1946, Huntington, WV) Exec. Dir., Socty. for Scholarly Publshg, 1980–; Proj. Dir., Capital Syst. Grp., Inc., 1977–; Resrch. Asst., Univ. of VA Lib., 1972–75; Tchr., St. Mary's Cnty, MD, 1967–69. **Educ.:** Mary Washington Coll., 1963–67, BA (Art Hist.); Univ. of MD, 1976–76, MLS; Cert., 1977–81, Hlth. Sci. Libn. I. **Orgs.:** ASIS. Assoc. Info. Mgrs. Socty. for Scholarly Publshg.: Bd. of Dirs. (1978–81). Phi Kappa Phi. **Pubns.:** Jt. auth., *The Impact of Behavioral and Technical Information Interventions on R&D Productivity–A Final Report* (1979); "Automatic Ordering of Reprints," *Improving the Dissemination of Scientific and Technical Information* (N. 1978). **Activities:** 4, 12; 24, 29, 37; 56, 75, 80 **Addr.:** 15516 Straughn Dr., Laurel, MD 20810.

Falconer, Joan O. (Mr. 3, 1930, Schenectady, NY) Msc. Libn., Appalachian State Univ., 1977–; Msc. Dept. Libn., SUNY, Albany, 1974–77; Msc. Libn., CT Coll., 1968–70; Various positions in Circ. and Ref., Msc. Div., New York Pub. Lib., 1960–66; Msc. Catlgr., Columbia Univ., 1958–60. **Educ.:** Cornell Univ., 1947–51, BA; Columbia Univ., 1951–55, MA (Msclgy.); Univ. of Chicago, 1955–57, MA (LS); Columbia Univ., 1957–69, PhD (Msclgy.). **Orgs.:** Msc. LA: SE Chap., Exec. Bd. (1979), Nsltr. Ed. (1979–). Intl. Assn. of Msc. Libs. Amer. Msclgl. Socty. **Honors:** Phi Beta Kappa, 1951; Beta Phi Mu, 1957; Fulbright–Hayes Flwshp., 1953–54; AAUW, Flwshp., 1966–67. **Pubns.:** "Music in the Lilly Library: Handel, Opera, and Latin Americana," *Notes* (S. 1972); "The Second Berlin Song School in America," *Msc. Qtly.* (Jl. 1973); "Do-It-Yourself Music Binding," *Wilson Lib. Bltn.* (D. 1973). **Activities:** 1, 9; 15, 20, 39; 55 **Addr.:** Music Library, Greer Hall, Appalachian State University, Boone, NC 28608.

Falgione, Joseph F. (O. 4, 1931, Pittsburgh, PA) Assoc. Dir., Ctrl. Reader Srvs., Carnegie Lib. of Pittsburgh, 1973–, Coord. of Adult Srvs., 1969–73, Coord. of Dist. Srvs., 1963–69, Ref. Asst., 1961–63. **Educ.:** Duquesne Univ., 1949–54, BS (Msc.); Carnegie Lib. Sch., 1956–57, MLS. **Orgs.:** PA LA: Pres. (1973–74). ALA. PA Interlib. Delivery Syst.: Secy. (1978–79). **Honors:** Univ. of Pittsburgh, Carnegie Lib. Sch., Disting. Alumn., 1969. **Activities:** 9; 15, 17, 19; 56, 89 **Addr.:** 307 Burlington Rd., Pittsburgh, PA 15221.

Falk, Joyce Duncan (Jl. 26, 1938, Pecos, TX) Database Coord. and Ref. Libn., Univ. of CA, Irvine, 1981–; Dir., Amer. Bibliographical Ctr; Exec. Ed. of *Hist. Abs., Amer.: Hist. and Life,* Clio Bibl. Series, Dir. of the lib. and of online srvs., ABC-Clio, Inc., 1974–81; Lectr., Dept of Hist. CA State Univ., Fullerton, 1972–74, Instructor, Dept of Hist. Mt. St. Mary's Coll., Los Angeles, 1965–68, Lectr, Dept of Hist. CA State Coll., Los Angeles, 1967. **Educ.:** Univ. of NM, 1956–60, BA (Hist.); Univ. of South. CA, 1960–69, PhD (Hist.); Univ. of CA, Los Angeles, 1971–72, MLS. **Orgs.:** ASIS. ALA: RASD/Hist. Sect. (Ch., 1980–81); Bibl. & Indexes Com. (1975–79); Publns. Com. (1978–82); ACRL, Publns. Com. (1978–80); Srch. Com., Ed., *Coll. & Resrch. Libs.* (1979–80). Amer. Socty. of Indxrs.: Bd. of Dir. (1977–78). Assn. for the Bibl. of Hist. Assn. for Comp. and the Hum. Phi Alpha Theta. Phi Kappa Phi. Amer. Hist. Assn. Amer. Socty. for Eighteenth-Century Std. **Honors:** West. Socty. for Fr. Hist., Cert. of Merit, 1977, 1978. **Pubns.:** "Theatre Ex Machina: Using the Computer for Theatre Research," *Theatre Journal* (1981); "Controlled and Free Vocabulary Indexing of the ABC-Clio Databases in History," in *Proc. of the Conference on Databases in the Humanities and the Social Sciences* (1980); "Computer-assisted Production of Bibliographic Databases in History," *The Indexer,* (1981); "Research Opportunities at the Theatre Institute Library, Barcelona," *Performing Arts Resrcs.* (1978); "The Theatre Institute Library of Barcelona," *Spec. Libs.* (1978). **Activities:** 1; 17, 39, 49–OnLine 50, Searching, 54, 92 **Addr.:** 164 Esplanade, Irvine, CA 92715.

Falk, Julia Ferguson (Ja. 27, 1928, Shenandoah, IA) Vice Ch., State Lib. Comsn. of IA, 1979–. **Educ.:** Univ. of IA, 1945–49, BA (Psy.), 1952–53. **Orgs.:** IA Lib. Trustees Assn. Exec. Bd.: Treas. (1975–79); Dist. Rep. (1971–75). IA LA: Int. Frdm. Com. IA Gov. Conf. on Libs. and Info. Srvs.: Del. (1979). Shenandoah Pub. Lib. Bd. of Trustees: Pres. (1975–79). AAUW. Univ. of IA Parents Assn. **Activities:** 4, 9; 47; 74, 85 **Addr.:** 1304 Southmoreland, Shenandoah, IA 51601.

Falkner, Ralph Victor, Jr. (D. 15, 1938, Coffeyville, KS) Supvsr., Lab. Systs. Sect., Baxter-Travenol Labs., Inc., 1977–; Sci. Info. Spec., Univ. of MO, Columbia Sch. of Med. 1975–77, Resrch. Spec., 1973–75, Acq. Prgmr., Columbia Lib., 1967–70. **Educ.:** MA Inst. of Tech., 1956–57, (pre-engi); Univ. of MO, 1962–65, BA (zlgy.), 1965–67, MA (zlgy.), 1971–73, MALS, 1977, MS (pharmgy.). Certs. of completion I.B.M. Educ. Ctr., St. Louis, MO, 1969; Cert., Data Proc. Operations Management seminar, Univ. of Chicago Ctr. for Cont. Educ., 1978; Cert., Hewlett-Packard Disc-based RTE Operating Systs., Rolling Meadows, IL, 1979. **Orgs.:** Med. LA. SLA. AAAS. **Pubns.:** Jt. Ed., *Diabetes Mellitus Drug Interaction Guide* (Jt. auth., "A Computer-Based Drug Information System" *Med. Electronics Digest* (2:4-5, 1977); Paper presented SLA Conf. (1976). **Activities:** 12; 56, 57, 87 **Addr.:** 946 N.W. Holcomb Mundelein, IL 60060.

Fall, James Edward (F. 18, 1939, New York, NY) Dir., Tech. Srvs Grp., Columbia Univ. Libs., 1980–, Dir., Lib. Tech. Support Grp., 1973–80, Head, Prcs. Dept., 1970–73, Asst. Head, Acq. Div., 1964–70; Libn., NASA Goddard Inst. for Space Std., 1962–64. **Educ.:** Brown Univ., 1956–60, BA (Eng. Lit.); Rutgers Univ., 1960–62, MLS. **Orgs.:** ALA. **Activities:** 1; 17, 46 **Addr.:** 201 E. 15th St., Apt. 4 F, New York, NY 10003.

Fallon, Margaret Sanders (Mr. 26, 1952, Clinton, IL) Libn., White & Williams, 1979–; Asst. Libn., Kirkland & Ellis, 1977–79; Asst. Libn., Westinghouse, 1976. **Educ.:** Coll. of Notre Dame of MD, 1970–74, BA (Eng.); Univ. of MD, 1974–75, MLS. **Orgs.:** AALL. Grt. Philadelphia Law Lib. Assn.: Inst. Comm. SLA. **Pubns.:** "Non-verbal Communication in Library Question Negotiation," in *Knowledge and Its Organization,* (1976). **Activities:** 12; 17, 20, 39; 77 **Addr.:** Library, White & Williams, 1234 Market St., Philadelphia, PA 19107.

Fallon, Robert Patrick (Ja. 24, 1951, New York, NY) Libn./Assoc. Mgr., Prudential Insr. Co., Corporate Ofc., 1978; Asst. Ref. Libn., Fairleigh Dickinson Univ., Rutherford Campus, 1978; Libn., Herald News Ed. Lib., 1975–78. **Educ.:** Univ. of VT, 1969–73, BA, magna cum laude (Hist.); St. John's Univ., 1974–75, MLS. **Orgs.:** SLA: Insr. Div.; NJ Chap. Prudential Insr. Co. Lib. Netwk. Com. St. John's Univ. Lib. Adv. Com. **Honors:** Beta Phi Mu, 1975. **Pubns.:** "Resource Information Booklet," *Prudential Pubns.* (1979); "Library User's Guide," *Prudential Pubns.* (1980). **Activities:** 12; 17, 39, 41; 76, 95-Mgt., Persnl. **Addr.:** 177 W. Pierrepont Ave., Rutherford, NJ 07070.

Fallsgraff, Sr. Rose (Jl. 31, 1915, Syracuse, NY) Lib. Media Spec., Rome Cath. HS, 1970–; Tchr., Albany NY Diocesan Schs. **Educ.:** Coll. of St. Rose, BA (Eng., Latin), MS (Eng., Educ.); SUNY, Albany, 1971, MLS. **Orgs.:** Cath. LA: HS Sect. (Nsltr. Ed., 1975–); Syracuse Chap., Past Treas. (1973–75), Ch. (1975–77), Nsltr. Ed. (1975–). Ctrl. NY LA. Srs. of Saint Joseph of Carondelet. **Activities:** 10; 31, 48 **Addr.:** 808 Cypress St., Rome, NY 13440.

Falsone, Anne Marie (My. 20, 1937, New York City, NY) Asst. Comsn., Ofc. of Lib. Srvs., CO Dept. of Educ., 1976–, Supvsr., ESEA IV–B, 1975–76, Consult., Sch. Libs., 1972–75; Asst. Head, Hist. Dept., Memphis Pub. Lib., 1971–72. **Educ.:** Memphis State Univ. 1955–59, BS (Educ.), 1963–68, MS (Hist.); Vanderbilt Univ., 1965–69, MLS. **Orgs.:** ALA: ASCLA (Pres., 1981–82). West. Cncl. of State Libs.: Pres. (1978). Netwk. Adv. Com. to Lib. of Congs. Chief Ofcrs. of State Lib. Agencies: Networking Com. (Ch., 1978–80). CO Gvrs. Comsn. on Pub. Telecom. CO Gvrs. Comsn. on Pub. Broadcasting. **Activities:** 10, 13; 17, 24, 39; 56, 78, 93 **Addr.:** Colorado State Library, 1362 Lincoln, Denver, CO 80203.

Famera, Karen McNerney (O. 29, 1941, Binghamton, NY) Msc. Catlgr., NY Pub. Lib., Resrch. Libs., 1981–; Libn., Amer. Msc. Ctr., Inc., 1976–80; Msc. catlgr., City Coll. of NY, 1973–76. **Educ.:** Eastman Sch. of Msc., Univ. of Rochester, 1960–64, BM (Theory); Yale Sch. of Msc., 1964–67, MM (Perf.); Queens Coll., 1972–73, MLS. **Orgs.:** Msc. LA. Sonneck Socty. Intl. Horn Socty. **Pubns.:** *Contemporary Concert Music by Women: A Directory of the Composers and Their Works* (1981); *Catalog of the American Music Center Library, vol. 2: Chamber music* (1978); *National Endowment for the Arts Composer/Librettist Program Collection at the American Music Center* (1979); *Library Association of the City University of New York Directory* (1975–1976). **Activities:** 2, 12; 15, 20, 39; 55 **Addr.:** 600 W. 111th St., New York, NY 10025.

Fancher, Evelyn P. (Marion, AL) Dir. of Libs., TN State Univ., 1976–, Coord. of LS Curric., 1975–76, Head, Circ. ILL Dept., LS Instr., 1973–75, Head, Ref. Dept., LS Instr., 1964–65, Docum. and Biblgphr., 1962–64, 1966–72; Circ. Libn., LS Instr., 1972–73, Dir., Lib. Media Ctr., Council HS, Huntsville, 1959–62; Tech. Asst., AL A&M Univ., 1956; Tchg. position, 1950–56. **Educ.:** AL State Univ., 1942–46, BS (Nat. Sci.); Atlanta Univ., 1961, MSLS; George Peabody Coll., 1967–69, EdS (LS), 1975, PhD (LS). **Orgs.:** ALA: ACRL/TN Chap. (Ch., 1981–82); Sci. and Tech. Com. (1979–80); Urban Univs. Com. (1978–79). TN LA. SELA. Mid. TN LA: Adv. Bd. Various other orgs. Phi Delta Kappa. AAUW: Exec. Bd. (Secy., 1975–77). **Pubns.:** "Univeristy Curriculum Reforms: Faculty and Librarian Collaboration," *TN Libn.* (Sum./Fall 1974); "Educating Ethnic Minorities: An American Challenge," *The Negro Educ. Review* (Ja. 1974); Jt. auth., "Continuing Education Programs for Librarians in Tennessee–A Survey," *TN Libn.* (Sum. 1972); "College Admission Practices and the Negro Student," *The Negro Educ. Review* (Ap. 1971); "Good Teachers, A Renaissance?" *TASCD Jnl.* (Spr. 1979); Various other articles. **Activities:** 1, 10; 17, 26, 31; 63, 66, 91 **Addr.:** Director of Libraries, Tennessee State University, Nashville, TN 37203.

Fang, Josephine Riss (Ap. 3, 1922, Saalfelden, Salzburg, Austria) Prof., Grad. Sch. of Lib. and Info. Sci., Simmons Coll., 1970–; Head, Acq. Dept., Boston Coll. Libs., 1968–69; Adj. Lectr., Sch. of Lib. and Info. Sci., Univ. of MD, 1966–68; Assoc. Prof., Dept. of LS, Cath. Univ., 1963–68; Ed., Corpus Instrumentorum, Inc., 1967–68; Resrch. Ed., *New Cath. Encyc.,* Cath. Univ., 1963–67; Ed., *Guide to Cath. Lit.,* Cath. LA, 1961–63; Spec. Catlgr. for Farmington Plan, Cath. Univ., 1951–54; various prof. positions, 1941–50. **Educ.:** Univ. of Vienna, 1940–47, Absolutorium (Eng.); Univ. of Graz, 1947–48, PhD (Eng.); Cath. Univ. of Amer., 1951–54, MSLS. **Orgs.:** ALA: Intl. Lib. Educ. Subcom. (Ch., 1978–); IRRT, E. Asia, Area Ch. (1976–80), Ch. (1980–81), Vice–Ch. and Ch.-Elect (1979–80); various coms.; ACRL, Cont. Educ. Com. (Rep., 1978–); African and Asian Sect. (Secy., 1976–79); various coms. (1972–74). AALS: Various coms., ofcs. (1973–). IFLA: Various coms., ofcs. (1977–). SLA: Various coms., ofcs. (1972–76). Various other orgs., ofcs. AAUP: Simmons Coll. Chap., Exec. Bd. (1972–77), VP (1974–75), Pres. (1975–76). AAUW. **Honors:** Beta Phi Mu, 1973; Marion and Jasper Whiting Fndn., Awd., 1974; Cncl. on Lib. Resrcs., Flwshp., 1977–78; Simmons Coll. Resrch. Fund, Awds., 1972, 1975; other hons. **Pubns.:** *International Guide to Library, Archival and Information Science Associations* (1976, 1980); *Handbook of National and International Library Associations* (1973); "International and Comparative Librarianship: A Current Assessment," *Bowker Anl.* (1981); "IFLA Conference on Manila," *Bowker Anl.* (1981); "China, People's Republic of," *ALA World Encyc. of Lib. and Info. Srvs.* (1980); various articles, presentations (1973–). **Activities:** 11; 15, 23, 26; 54, 95-Intl. and compar. libnshp. **Addr.:** Graduate School of Library and Information Science, Simmons College, 300 The Fenway, Boston, MA 02115.

PROFESSIONAL ACTIVITIES: Institutions: 1. Acad. lib.; 2. Arch.; 3. Assn.; 4. Fed./Gvt. lib.; 5. Inst. lib.; 6. Mfr./Suppl.; 7. Milit. lib.; 8. Musm.; 9. Pub. lib.; 10. Sch. lib.; 11. Sch. of lib. sci.; 12. Spec. lib.; 13. State lib.; 14. (other). **Functions/Activities:** 15. Acq./Col. dev.; 16. Adult srvs.; 17. Admin.; 18. Apprais.; 19. Archit./Bldgs.; 20. Cat./Class.; 21. Chld. srvs.; 22. Circ.; 23. Cons./Pres.; 24. Consult.; 25. Cont. ed.; 26. Educ. lib. sci.; 27. Ext. srvs.; 28. Fund/Grants; 29. Gvt. pubs.; 30. Indx./Abs.; 31. Instr. lib. use; 32. Media srvs.; 33. Micro.; 34. Netwks./Coop.; 35. Persnl.; 36. PR; 37. Publshg.; 38. Recs. mgt.; 39. Ref. srvs.; 40. Repro.; 41. Resrch.; 42. Review.; 43. Secur.; 44. Serials; 45. Spec. col.; 46. Tech. srvs.; 47. Trustees/Bds.; 48. YA srvs.; 49. (other).

Fannon, Elizabeth Lazear (D. 3, 1929, Tampa, FL) Head, Docum. Col., Cleveland Pub. Lib., 1976–, Asst. Head, Bus. Info., 1973–76; Head, Bus., Sci. and Indus., Jacksonville Pub. Lib., 1966–73, Reader's Consult., 1962–65; Ref. Libn., NC State Lib., 1961–62; Asst. Head, Ref. Dept., St. Petersburg Pub. Lib., 1953–60; Libn., Fernandina Beach HS, 1951–53. **Educ.:** FL State Univ., 1947–51, BA (LS), 1960–61, MA (LS). **Orgs.:** ALA. OH LA. **Honors:** Beta Phi Mu. **Activities:** 9; 29, 39 **Addr.:** 3780 Northampton Rd., Cleveland Heights, OH 44121.

Fant, Cheryl Nadine (O. 9, 1949, Mound Bayou, MS) Libn., Memphis City Schs., 1980–; Lib. Dir., Rutledge Jr. Coll., 1979–80; Asst. Libn., Lane Coll., 1976–79; Resrch. Asst., Resrch. Ctr., Atlanta Univ., 1975–76; Proj. Coord., Neighborhood Info. Ctrs. Projs., Atlanta Pub. Lib., 1973–75; Consult., various projs., 1973–. **Educ.:** LeMoyne-Owen Coll., 1969–72, BA (Soc. Sci.); Atlanta Univ., 1972–73, MSLS; Certificate-Archives and Records Management/Emory University (Participant in the twelth annual Georgia Archives Institute) **Orgs.:** ALA. SELA. TN LA. SAA. Natl. Assn. for the Advnc. of Colored People. Natl. Geographic Socty. **Activities:** 1, 12; 17, 24, 41; 66, 85, 89 **Addr.:** 3308 Formosa Rd., Memphis, TN 38109.

Fant, Handy Bruce (N. 21, 1903, Abbeville, SC) Retired; Archvst., Natl. Hist. Pubns. Comsn., 1956–73; Archvst., Natl. Arch., 1946–56, Archvst., State Dept. Recs., 1940–41; Hist. Instr., Afton Ctrl. Sch., 1933–37; Actg. Asst. Prof., Amer. Hist., Univ. of ME, 1929–30; Eng. Instr., Lanier HS for Boys, 1924–28. **Educ.:** Univ. of GA, 1920–24, AB (Hist., Eng.); Mercer Univ., 1925–27, AM (Eng.); Harvard Univ., 1928–30, AM (Hist.). **Orgs.:** SAA: *Amer. Archvst.* News Notes Ed. (1956–59); Fellow (1974–). Assn. for Documentary Ed. Intl. Cncl. on Arch. Amer. Hist. Assn. South. Hist. Assn. GA Hist. Socty. VT Hist. Socty. **Honors:** GA Hist. Socty., Essay Prize, 1931. **Pubns.:** "Carl Ludwig Lokke, 1897–1960," *Amer. Archvst.* (Jl. 1960); "In Memoriam, Richard George Wood, 1900–1967," *Amer. Archvst.* (Ap. 1967); articles, *Dictionary of American History* (1940); various articles, *Dictionary of NC Biography* (1979) ed., "Levi Woodbury's Week in Vermont, May 1819," *VT Hist.* (1966); various hist. articles (1931–59, 1981). **Activities:** 2, 4; 37, 39; 62 **Addr.:** 8110 White's Ford Way, Rockville, MD 20854.

Farace, Virginia Kapes (Mrs. Frank) (Jl. 10, 1945, Hazleton, PA) Lib. Dir., Boynton Beach City Lib., 1970–; Ref./Gvt. Docum. Libn., Hazleton Area Pub. Lib., 1968–70. **Educ.:** Rider Coll., 1963–67, BA (Jnlsm., Eng. Lit.); Rutgers Univ., 1967–68, MLS. **Orgs.:** Palm Beach Cnty. LA: Pres. (1979–80); Pres.-Elect (1978–79); Bylaws Rev. Com. (1980–81); FL LA: Cit. and Awds. Com. (1978); Stans. Rev. Subcom. (1981). SELA. ALA. Alpha XI Delta: Palm Beach Alum. Chap. **Honors** Palm Beach Cnty. LA, Leadership and Srv., 1980; B'nai B'rith, FL State Assn., Merit. Srv., 1980. **Pubns.:** Ed., *Library Resources in Palm Beach County, Florida* (1979). **Activities:** 9; 16, 17, 19; 85 **Addr.:** Boynton Beach City Library, 208 S. Seacrest Blvd., Boynton Beach, FL 33435.

Farber, Evan Ira (Je. 30, 1922, New York, NY) Head Libn., Earlham Coll., 1962–; Chief, Serials and Binding Div., Emory Univ. Lib., 1955–62; Libn., State Tchrs. Coll., Livingston, AL, 1953–55; Asst. (part-time), Docum. Dept., Univ. of NC Lib., 1951–53. **Educ.:** Univ. of NC, Chapel Hill, 1940–44, AB (Pol. Sci.), 1949–51, MA (Pol. Sci.), 1951–53, BSLS; Princeton Univ., 1945–47, Grad. Std. (Pol. Sci.). **Orgs.:** ALA: Cncl. (1969–71, 1979–); Coll. Libs. Sect. (Ch., 1968–69); ACRL (Pres., 1978–79). IN LA: Leg. Com. (1965–72); LSCA Title III Adv. Cncl.; Coll. and Univ. Sect. (Ch., 1974–75). Adv. Com. on ARL ILL Std. (1973). IN Cvl. Liberties Un. Richmond (IN) Civic Thea. **Honors:** St. Lawrence Univ., Doctor of Humane Letters, 1980. **Pubns.:** *The Academic Library: Essays in Honor of Guy R. Lyle* (1974); *Classified List of Periodicals for the College Library*, 5th ed. (1972); Contrib., "Title IIa–A Bargain at the Price: A Symposium" *Jnl. of Acad. Libnshp.* (S. 1979); jt. auth., "Collection Development from a College Perspective: A Comment and a Response," *Coll. & Resrch. Libs.* (Jl. 1979); "Library-Faculty Communication Techniques," *Proceedings from Southeastern Conference on Approaches to Bibliographic Instruction* (1978); Numerous other articles on lib. topics. **Activities:** 1; 17, 24, 31; 95-Pers. **Addr.:** Lilly Library, Earlham College, Richmond, IN 47374.

Farhat, Fred (S. 24, 1925, Inglewood, CA) Mgr., Lib. Srvs., Kaiser Aluminum and Chemical Corp. Ctr. for Tech., 1970–; Chief Libn., Atomics Intl., 1962–69, Supvsr., Lib., Hughes Aircraft Co., 1959–62, Chief Libn., Rocketdyne, 1956–59, Libn. II, Detroit Pub. Lib., 1952–1956. **Educ.:** Pomona Coll., 1946–49, BA (Liberal Arts); Syracuse Univ., 1950–52, MS (LS). **Orgs.:** SLA. ASIS. AAAS. **Activities:** 12; 17; 60, 81, 91 **Addr.:** 487 St. Francis Dr., Danville, CA 94526.

Farkas, Andrew (Ap. 7, 1936, Budapest, Hungary) Dir. of Libs. & Prof. of LS, Univ. of N. FL, 1970–; Asst. Mgr., Walter J. Johnson, Inc., 1967–70; Chief Biblgphr. & Asst. Head, Acq. Dept., Univ. of CA, Davis, 1965–67, Gift & Exch. Libn., 1962–65. **Educ.:** Eotvos Lorand Univ. of Law, Budapest, 1954–56 (Law); Occidental Coll., 1957–59, BA (Fr.); Univ. of CA, Berkeley, 1961–62, MLS; Univ. of CA, Davis, 1963–65 (Italian); Univ. of FL (Educ.), 1976–77. **Orgs.:** ALA: LAMA/BES. FL LA. SELA. Duval Cnty. LA. Alpha Mu Gamma. **Honors:** Univ. of CA, Berkeley, Lib. Sch., Della J. Sisler Awd., 1962. **Pubns.:** Adv. Ed., *Opera Biographies* (1977); "Profile of the Library Job Seeker," *Lib. Jnl.* (F. 15, 1972); "On the Drawing Board: A New University Library," *FL Libs.* (Fall, 1971); other articles. **Activities:** 1; 17, 24, 26; 55, 57, 63 **Addr.:** University of North Florida, Library, P. O. Box 17605, Jacksonville, FL 32216.

Farkas–Conn, Irene S. (S. 26, 1928, Budapest, Hungary) VP and Managing Partner, Arthur L. Conn & Assocs., Ltd., 1978–; Indp. Consult., Lib. Mgt. and Info. Systs. Plng., 1966–78; Coord. for Plng., Douglas Lib., Chicago State Univ., 1971–75; Consult., Med. Info. Proj., Univ. of Chicago Clinics, 1962–69; Info. Retrieval Proj. Plng., Case West. Rsv. Univ., 1960–62; Biochem. Resrch. Assoc., Rockefeller Univ. and Case West. Rsv. Univ., 1949–59. **Educ.:** Barnard Coll., 1947–48, AB (Chem.); Bryn Mawr Coll., 1948–49, MA (Organic Chem.); Univ. of Chicago, 1967, MA (LS). **Orgs.:** ASIS: Chicago Chap. (Ch., 1970); Natl. Dir. (1972–75); Pubns. Com. (1972–74); Exec. and Fin. Com. (1975); Com. on Coms. (Ch., 1975–76); Intl. Rel. Com. (Ch., 1980–); Oper. Plng. Task Frc. (1977–79). SLA. U.S. Natl. Com. for the Intl. Fed. of Docum. Amer. Inst. of Chem. Engins.: Natl. Prog. Com., Mgt. Sci. Sect. (Ch., 1979–); Mgt. Div. (Dir., 1980–82). **Honors:** Phi Beta Mu; ASIS, Watson Davis Awd., 1977–. **Pubns.:** Various articles on biochem., info. sci., LS, sps. **Activities:** 14-Consult. firm; 17, 25, 38; 86, 93 **Addr.:** Arthur L. Conn & Associates, Ltd., 1469 E. Park Pl., Chicago, IL 60637.

Farley, Janice Skinner (Jl. 3, 1945, Corbin, KY) Admin., Arrowhead Lib. Syst., 1974–; Serial Biblgrphr., OH State Univ., 1971–74; Ext. Libn., Rock Cnty. Lib. Srvs., 1969–71. **Educ.:** Berea Coll., 1962–66, BA (Eng.); Univ. of KY, 1968–69, MS (LS); various cont. educ. crs., 1974–79. **Orgs.:** WI Assn. of Pub. Libns.: Ch.–Elect (1981); Secy. (1975, 1976). WI LA: Awds. and Hons. Com. (Ch., 1980); Natl. Lib. Week (Ch., 1977). ALA. Assn. of Rock Cnty. Libns. AAUW. **Addr.:** 316 S. Main St., Janesville, WI 53545.

Farley, John J. (Mr. 19, 1920, New York, NY) Prof., Sch. of Lib. and Info. Sci., SUNY, Albany, 1967–, Dean, Prof., 1967–77; Assoc. Prof., Ch., Dept. of LS, Queens Coll., CUNY, 1960–67. **Educ.:** Catholic Univ., 1937–40, BA (Eng.); Columbia Univ., 1949–50, MA (Eng., Compar. Lit.), 1950–53, MSLS. NY Univ., 1958–64, PhD (Educ.). **Orgs.:** ALA. NY LA. AALS. **Honors:** NY Univ., Fndrs. Day Awd., 1964. **Pubns.:** *Introduction to Library Science* (1969). **Activities:** 10, 11; 17; 74, 92 **Addr.:** School of Library and Information Science, State University of New York at Albany, 1400 Washington Ave., Albany, NY 12222.

Farley, Judith R. (Ja. 15, 1946, Philadelphia, PA) Ref. Libn., Lib. of Congs., 1978, Biblgrphr., 1968–78. **Educ.:** Cath. Univ. of Amer., 1963–67, AB (Eng. Lit.); Drexel Univ., 1967–68, MS (LS). **Orgs.:** ALA: Cncl.-at-lg. (1976–80, 1981–84); Com. on Plng. (Ch., 1980–81). Exec. Bd. (1981–85). DC LA. Lib. of Congs. Prof. Empl. Gld., AFSCME 2910, AFL–CIO. **Honors:** Phi Beta Kappa, 1967. **Pubns.:** "Enoch Pratt Free Library and Black Patrons," *Jnl. of Lib. Hist.* (Fall 1980); "A Week at LC," *MS Libs.* (Sum. 1980). **Activities:** 4; 15, 16, 39; 55, 57, 95-Trade uns. **Addr.:** Apt. N–404, 1301 Delaware Ave. S.W., Washington, DC 20024.

Farley, Richard Alan (Ja. 17, 1918, Highbridge, WI) Dir., Natl. Agr. Lib., 1974–; Dir. of Libs., McGill Univ., 1972–74; Dir. of Libs., KS State Univ., 1963–72. **Educ.:** Northland Coll., 1936–40, BA (Arts and Sci.); Univ. of WI, 1940–41, BLS; Univ. of IL, 1951–52, MS (LS), 1952–67, PhD (LS). **Orgs.:** ALA. ASIS. **Activities:** 4; 17; 91 **Addr.:** 1902 Wooded Ct., Adelphi, MD 20783.

Farmann, Kathleen E. (Ag. 21, 1920, Addison, NY) Law Libn., Univ. of Notre Dame, 1966–; Asst. Dir. of Resrch. Srvs., OH State Univ., 1962–66; Law Libn., HI Supreme Ct., 1961–62; Asst. Law Libn., OH State Univ., 1957–61; Assoc. Attorney, Covington and Burling, 1945–53. **Educ.:** Trinity Coll., 1937–41, AB (Hist.); Cath. Univ., 1942–45, JD; Univ. of WA, 1956–57, MLL. **Orgs.:** OH Reg. Assn. of Law Libs.: Past Pres. AALL. DC Bar Assn. **Activities:** 12; 49-Law libn.; 77 **Addr.:** Notre Dame Law Library, P.O. Box 535, Notre Dame, IN 46556.

Farmann, Stanley Lester (Ag. 29, 1931, Raymond, WA) Assoc. Law Libn., Univ. of Notre Dame Law Sch., 1966–; Biblgphr., Engin. Libn., OH State Univ., 1962–66; Circ. Libn., Univ. of HI, 1961–62; Admin. Asst. to Dir. of Libs., OH State Univ., 1958–61. **Educ.:** Univ. of WA, 1949–53, BS (Swedish), 1956–57, MSLS. **Orgs.:** AALL: Nom. Com. (1970). **Activities:** 1, 14-Law sch. lib.; 15, 20, 39; 77 **Addr.:** Notre Dame Law School Library, Box 535, Notre Dame, IN 46556.

Farmer, Frances (D. 5, 1909, Keysville, VA) Prof. Emeritus, Law Lib. Consult., Univ. of VA Law Sch., 1979–, Consult. to Dir., Oceans Ctr., 1976–79, Law Libn., Prof., 1942–76; Law Libn., Univ. of Richmond, 1934–42. **Educ.:** Westhampton Coll., 1927–31, BA (Hist.); Univ. of Richmond, 1931–33, LLB (Law); Columbia Univ. Lib. Sch., Sums. 1938–39. **Orgs.:** AALL: Pres. (1959–60); numerous ofcs. VA State Bar Assn. Ord. of the Coif. **Honors:** Phi Beta Kappa; Univ. of Richmond, Natl. Alum. Awd., 1977. **Pubns.:** Jt. auth., *Manual of Legal Bibliography* (1947); Numerous articles in *Law Lib. Jnl.* **Activities:** 10; 17, 24, 32; 75, 77 **Addr.:** University of Virginia Law School, University of Virginia N. Grounds, Charlottesville, VA 22901.

Farrell, Lois C. (N. 5, 1919, Indianapolis, IN) Head, Nat. Resrcs. Lib., Univ. of CA, Berkeley, 1969–; Prog. Dir., Vision Info. Ctr., Countway Lib. of Med., Harvard Univ., 1967–69; Tech. Info. Spec., Lawrence Livermore Lab., 1965–67; Sci. Biblgrphr., SUNY, Binghamton, 1963–65. **Educ.:** DePauw Univ., 1936–40, AB (Bot.); Univ. of CA, Berkeley, 1940–42, MA (Bot.); Univ. of MI, 1962–63, MALS. **Orgs.:** SLA: San Francisco Bay Reg. Chap. (Pres., 1980–81). ASIS. CA Botanical Socty. **Honors:** Phi Beta Kappa, 1940; Beta Phi Mu, 1963. **Pubns.:** Jt. ed., *Guide to Sources for Agricultural and Biological Research* (1981). **Activities:** 1; 15, 39; 58, 65, 82 **Addr.:** Natural Resources Library, 40 Giannini Hall, University of California, Berkeley, CA 94720.

Farrell–Duncan, Howertine L. (S. 29, 1945, Omaha, NE) Libn./Supvsr. Ref., Hlth. Sci. Lib., Howard Univ., 1978–; Church Libn., Bethesda First Bapt. Church, 1976–; Ref. Libn., Natl. Lib. of Med., 1969–78, Assoc. (Intern), 1968–69. **Educ.:** Mncpl. Univ. of Omaha, 1963–67, BS (Educ.); Univ. of OK, 1967–68, MLS; Med. LA, 1970, Cert. **Orgs.:** SLA. CSLA. Church Lib. Cncl. Natl. Cap. and Suburban Areas. Med. LA: Mid-Atl. Reg. Grp. Alpha Kappa Alpha Sorority. **Pubns.:** "Selected Reference Aids for Small Medical Library," *Bltn. Med. LA* (Ap. 1970); "Working Through Sorrow and Death with Children," *Bethesda First Bapt. Church Nsltr.* (Ap. 1978); "Working Through Grief and Sorrow," *Bethesda First Bapt. Church Nsltr.* (Jl.–Ag. 1978); various reviews, (1979–80). **Activities:** 1, 4; 17, 32, 39; 58, 80, 90 **Addr.:** Health Sciences Library, Howard University, Washington, DC 20059.

Farrington, Jean Walter (Ap. 25, 1948, Ann Arbor, MI) Asst. Head, Circ., Van Pelt Lib., Univ. of PA, 1979–; Head, Non-print Rsv. and Per. Srvs., SUNY, Albany, 1979; Head, Per., Micro. & Rsv., 1978–79; Head, Serials Dept., 1976–78; Head, Per. Unit, 1975–76; Serials Catlgr., 1973–75. **Educ.:** St. Lawrence Univ., 1966–70, BA (Eng.); Simmons Coll., 1970–72, MLS; SUNY, Albany, 1973–75, MA (Eng.). **Orgs.:** ALA: ACRL (Non-Print Ed. Brd. 1980–); RTSD (Serials Sect., Com. to Study Serial Records, 1980–81); LAMA. SUNY LA: Secy. (1975–76); First VP (1976–77); Pres. (1977–78). **Pubns.:** "How to Select a Microfilm Reader," *Serials Libn.* (1980); Co-ed., "Women's Periodicals" *Serials Review* (1980); Ed., "Newsletters", *Serials Review* (1979–). **Activities:** 1; 17, 33, 44; 55, 72 **Addr.:** 221 Martroy Le., Wallingford, PA 19086.

Farris, Alice Hild (D. 24, 1940, Washington, DC) Instr. (part-time), Chapman Coll. R. E. C., Warren AFB, 1974–; Freelnc. Consult., 1972–; Coord., Instr. Resrcs., WY Dept. of Educ., 1966–72; Libn. A, Ext. Div., VA State Lib., 1963–66. **Educ.:** Roanoke Coll., 1958–62, AB (Eng.); Univ. of Denver, 1962–63, MALS. **Orgs.:** ALA: Cncl. (1969–72); AASL, Nom. Com. (Ch., 1971–72). WY Instr. Media Assn.: Exec. Secy. (1969–71). AAUW. **Activities:** 10, 13; 17, 24, 32; 63 **Addr.:** 1101 Taft Ave., Cheyenne, WY 82001.

Farrow, Mildred H. (Ap. 8, 1919, W. Palm Beach, FL) Asst. Libn., A.G. Bush Lib., Univ. of Chicago, 1962–; Asst. Libn., Guilford Coll., 1949–60; HS Libn., Tarboro City Schs., 1945–49; Sch. Libn. Murphy (NC) City Schs., 1942–45. **Educ.:** Asheville Normal Tchrs. Coll., 1935–39, BS (Elem. Educ.); Geo. Peabody Coll. for Tchrs., 1941–42, BSLS; Univ. of NC, 1955–59, MSLS; Univ. of Chicago, 1960–69, Cert. of Advnc. Std. **Orgs.:** ALA. SLA. **Honors:** Beta Phi Mu. **Pubns.:** *History of Guilford College Library, 1837–1955* (1960). **Activities:** 1, 12; 15, 20, 46; 59, 95-Mgt. org. and indus. Rel. **Addr.:** 1450 E. 55th Pl., Apt. 1025, Chicago, IL 60637.

Faruquee, Atauar (O. 9, 1931, Tangail, Bangladesh) Trng. Coord., State Lib. of PA, 1972–, Consult., 1970–72; Dir., Cartert (NJ) Pub. Lib., 1967–70; Prin. Libn., Belleville (NJ) Pub. Lib., 1966–67. **Educ.:** Oglethorpe Univ., 1958–60, BA (Pol. Sci.); Emory Univ., 1960–61, MA (Pol. Sci); Pratt Inst., 1963–64, MA (LS). **Orgs.:** NJ LA: Nom. Com. (1969). PA Pub. Lib. Cert. Com.: Ch. **Pubns.:** "How to Develop A Legislative Workshop" in *Libraries in the Political Process;* "Community Calendar of Events," *Wilson Lib. Bltn.* (N. 1971). **Activities:** 25, 26; 63 **Addr.:** Atauar Faruquee, 2605 Cranberry Cir., Harrisburg, PA 17110.

Fasana, Paul James (Jl. 20, 1933, Bingham Canyon, VT) Assoc. Dir., Prep. Srvs., Resrch. Libs., NY Pub. Lib., 1979–; Chief, Prep. Srvs., 1971–78; Asst. to the Dir., Columbia Univ. Libs., 1966–71, Asst. Coord. of Cat., 1964–66. **Educ.:** Univ. of CA, Berkeley, 1959, BA (Lang/Lit.), 1959–60, MLS. **Orgs.:** ALA: Cncl. (1970–73); RTSD (Pres., 1976–77; Bd. 1970–74); ISAD (Bd. 1971–74). ASIS: Cncl. (1971–74). **Honors:** NY Tech. Srvs. Libns., Awd. of Merit, 1978. **Pubns.:** *Future of the Catalog* (1979); *Collaborative Library Systems Development* (1971); "Impact of national developments on Library Tech Services," *Jnl. of Lib. Autom.* (1974); "Serials Data Control: current problems and prospects," *Jnl. of Lib. Autom.* (1976); "Systems Analysis," *Lib. Trends* (1973). **Activities:** 14-Resrch. lib.; 15, 20, 23; 95 **Addr.:** 325 W. 52nd St., Apt. 1G, New York, NY 10019.

Special Subjects/Services: 50. Adult educ.; 51. Advert./Mktg.; 52. Aerosp.; 53. Agric.; 54. Area std.; 55. Arts/Hum.; 56. Autom.; 57. Bibl./Prtg.; 58. Bio. sci.; 59. Bus./Fin.; 60. Chem.; 61. Copyrt.; 62. Documtn.; 63. Educ.; 64. Engin.; 65. Env.; 66. Eth. grps.; 67. Film; 68. Food/Nutr.; 69. Geneal.; 70. Geo.; 71. Geol.; 72. Handcpd.; 73. Hist.; 74. Int. frdm.; 75. Info. sci.; 76. Insr.; 77. Law; 78. Legis.; 79. Math./Comp. sci.; 80. Med.; 81. Metals; 82. Nat. resrcs.; 83. Newsp.; 84. Nuc. sci.; 85. Oral hist.; 86. Petr./Energy; 87. Pharm.; 88. Phys./Astr./Math.; 89. Readg.; 90. Relig.; 91. Sci./Tech.; 92. Soc. sci.; 93. Telecom.; 94. Transp.; 95. (other).

Fasick, Adele M. (Mr. 18, 1930, New NY) Prof., Univ. of Toronto, 1971–; Asst. Prof., Rosary Coll., 1970–71. **Educ.:** Cornell Univ., 1947–51, AB (Eng. Lit.); Columbia Univ., 1953–56, MA (Eng.), MLS; Case Western Reserve Univ., 1967–70, PhD (LS). **Orgs.:** ALA: ALSC, Resrch. Com. (Ch., 1977–). Can. Assn. of Lib. Sch.: Pres. (1980–82). Can. LA: Conv., Ed. Bd., *Can. Lib. Jnl.* (1978–). **Pubns.:** *What Should Libraries Do for Children?* (1978); *Children Using Media; Reading and Viewing Preferences Among the Users and Non-Users of the Regina Public Library* (1977); "Research and Measurement in Library Services to Children," *Can. Lib. Jnl.* (O. 1978); "Parents and Teachers View Library Service to Children" *Top of the News* (Spr. 1979). **Addr.:** Faculty of Library Science, 140 St. George St., Toronto, ON M5S 1A1, Canada.

Fass, Evelyn M. (Jl. 30, 1922, Syracuse, NY) Asst. Mgr., Tech. Info. Srvs., Inst. for Defense Anal.; Asst. Libn., Info. Requirements and Anal., Asst. Libn. for Reader Srvs., 1968; Acting Chief, Open Lib., 1967–68, Ref. Libn., 1966–67; Libn., Hist. Eval. and Resrch. Org., 1963–66. **Educ.:** Syracuse Univ., 1939–43, BA (Eng.), 1943–44, BSLS; Various courses, automation, on-line srvcs., and mgt., 1967–. **Orgs.:** SLA: Dir., Wash., DC Chap., 1979–81. **Honors:** Beta Phi Mu; Phi Beta Kappa. **Pubns.:** "Government Information Services; or Of Needles and Haystacks," *Drexel Lib. Qtly.* (1974). **Activities:** 12; 17, 29, 39; 74, 91, 92 **Addr.:** Institute for Defense Analyses, 400 Army Navy Drive, Arlington, VA 22202.

Fast, Louise A. (Ja. 16, 1949, Montreal, PQ) Cust. Srv. Mgr., Micromedia Ltd., 1974–; Adult Srv. Libn./Cmnty. Srv. Ofcr., Brampton Pub. Lib., 1972–74. **Educ.:** Bishop's Univ., 1966–70, BA (Hist., Pol. Sci.); Univ. of Toronto, 1970–72, MLS. **Orgs.:** Can. Assn. of Spec. Libs. & Info. Srvs.: Toronto Chap., Prog. Coord. (1976/77); Vice Ch. (1977/78); Ch. (1978/79); Past Ch. (1979/80). Indexing & Abst. Socty. of Can.: Lcl. Conf. Ch. (1980). Assn. of Women Exec. Girl Guides of Canada: Div. Camp Adv. (1973–78); Natl. Camp Com. (1978–). **Honors:** Girl Guides of Canada, Thanks Badge, 1979. **Activities:** 6; 17, 24, 29, 33; 59, 62, 75 **Addr.:** Micromedia Limited, 144 Front Street West, Toronto, ON M5J 1G2 Canada.

Fast, Viktor (F. 22, 1941, Poland) Libn. & AV Co-ord., L.P. Miller Comprehensive Sch., 1970–; Tchr., Prince Albert Collegiate Inst., 1966–68; Tchr., Viscount HS, 1965–66. **Educ.:** Univ. of SK, 1960–65, BA (Chem.), 1968–69, BEd, BA (Educ., Eng.); Univ. of West. ON, 1969–70, MLS. **Orgs.:** Wapiti Reg. Lib., Exec. Mem. (1971–). SK Lib. Dev. Bd.: Exec. Mem. (1975–). Can. LA. Can. Assn. of Sch. Libs. Other orgs. SK Tchrs. Assn.: Cnclr. (1975, 1976). SK Tchrs. Fed.: Comm. Com. (1975). **Activities:** 9, 10; 17, 47, 48 **Addr.:** Library, L.P. Miller Comprehensive School, Box 2650, Nipawin, SK S0E 1E0 Canada.

Fatcheric, Jerome P. (Ag. 29, 1948, Syracuse, NY) Mgr., Info./Docum., Miles Pharmaceuticals, 1980–; Sr. Info. Sci., Schering Corp., 1975–80; Asst. Libn., AMP, Inc., 1974–75. **Educ.:** Hobart Coll., 1966–70, BA (Bio.); Syracuse Univ., 1972–74, MLS. **Orgs.:** ASIS. SLA. Drug Info. Assn. Natl. Micro. Assn. **Honors:** Beta Phi Mu. **Pubns.:** "Survey of Users of a Medium-Sized Technical Library," *Spec. Libs.* (My./Je. 1975). **Activities:** 12; 17, 30, 38; 56, 58, 80 **Addr.:** 2050 Huntington Tpke., Trumbull, CT 06611.

Fatzer, Jill (F. 26, 1943, W. Palm Beach, FL) Head, Ref. Dept., Univ. of DE Lib., 1981–; Actg. Head, Ref. Srvs. Dept., Gen. Libs., Univ. of TX, 1980–81, Bus. Ref. Libn., 1978–80; Dir. of Resrch., Info. Unlimited, 1973–78; Assoc. Instr., Sch. of LS, Univ. of CA, Berkeley, 1974–75; Libn. II, Sci. and Docum. Dept., San Francisco Pub. Lib., 1970–72, Libn. I, Per. Dept., 1968–70. **Educ.:** Newcomb Coll., Tulane Univ., 1960–64, BA (Phil.); Univ. of CA, Berkeley, 1967, MLS. **Orgs.:** Austin OLUG: Secy.–Treas. (1980). Socty. of Univ. of TX Libns.: Prof. Actv. Com. (Ch., 1978–79); Mem. Com. (Ch., 1980–81). SLA: TX Chap., Assns. Liaison Com. (1979–80); Prog. Com. (1980–81); Austin Area Lcl. Prog. Plng. Com. (Ch., 1980–81). TX LA: Coll. and Univ. Div., Coop. Com. (Ch., 1979–80). **Pubns.:** "Automated Serials Check-in and Binding Procedures at the San Francisco Public Library," *ASIS Procs.* (1969). **Activities:** 1; 17, 31, 39; 51, 59, 91 **Addr.:** 206 Elderfield Rd., Newark, DE 19713.

Faull, Sandra K. (D. 26, 1950, Bradford, PA) Docums. Libn., NM State Lib., 1978–; Pub. Srvs./Docums. Libn., Asst. Prof., Stockton State Coll., NJ, 1975–78; Head, Docums. Dept., Kearney State Coll., NE, 1973–75. **Educ.:** Wilson Coll., 1968–72, AB (Hist.); Univ. of Denver, 1972–73, MALS; Univ. of NM, 1979– (Pub. Admin.). **Orgs.:** NM LA: Vice-Ch. (1979–80). Gvt. Docums. Assn. of NJ: Treas. (1976–77); VP, Pres. (1977–78). ALA: GODORT (Secy., Admin. and Org. Task Force, 1976–77; Asst. Coord., 1977–78; Ch., Deposit. Docu. Com. of Fed. Docu. Task Force, 1978–). Girl Scouts Sangre de Cristo Cncl.: Santa Fe Neighborhood Ch. (1978–79); Prog. Com. (1979–). Bus. and Prof. Women Capital City Club: Secy., (1979–80). **Pubns.:** Co-complr., *Cumulative Title Index to U.S. Public Documents, 1789–1976,* (1979); "Unit Profile of Government Documents Round Table," *Amer. Libs.* (F., 1980); "Cost and Benefits of Federal Depository Status for Academic Research Libraries," *Docums. to the People* (Ja., 1980); Jt. auth., "Ode to Government Publications," (videotape NM State Lib.) (1979). **Activities:** 1, 13; 29, 31, 39; 59, 78, 92 **Addr.:** 155-E Calle Ojo Feliz, Santa Fe, NM 87501.

Faunce, Stephen S. A. (Jl. 18, 1933, Denver, CO) Syst. Engin., Intl. Bus. Machines, 1968–; Head Libn., Interamer. Univ., Bayamon, PR, 1966–68, Asst. to Head Libn., Med. Sch. Lib., WA Univ., 1965–66. **Educ.:** Univ. of MN, 1955–58, BA (Psy.), 1964–65, MALS; IV Curso de Filologia Española, Malaga. C.S.I.C., 1969, Dip. **Orgs.:** SALALM. ASIS. REFORMA. Sociedad de Bibtcrs. de PR. Assn. for Computational Ling. Assn. de ling. y filologos de Amer. Latina. **Pubns.:** Jt. auth., *MARCAL, Manual para la automatizacion de las reglas de catalogacion para America Latina* (1976, 1978). **Addr.:** Condominio Palma Real 11J, Calle Madrid #2, Miramar, Santurce, PR 00907.

Faust, Mary Proctor (Ja. 2, 1929, Omaha, NE) Dir. of Lib. Srvs., N. Haven Meml. Lib., 1978–, Asst. Dir., 1976–78, Ref. Libn., 1973–76; Asst. Head, Circ., Univ. of Notre Dame, 1951–52. **Educ.:** Univ. of MN, 1946–50, BS; South. CT State Coll., 1965–70, MLS. **Orgs.:** CT LA: Adv. Com. on Lib. Line Srvs. (1979); Exec. Bd., Prog. for Educ. Grants (1977–78); Cont. Educ. Sect. (Ch., 1976–77). New Eng. LA; Com. on Cont. Educ. (1978–79); LEAP (Lib. Exch. Aids Patrons): VP (1979–80). ALA. **Honors:** Rotary Club of N. Haven, Guest Speaker Awd. **Activities:** 9; 15, 17, 28; 50, 56, 63 **Addr.:** North Haven Memorial Library, North Haven, CT 06473.

Fawcett, John T. (N. 27, 1943, IA City, IA) Supvsr. Archvst., Presidential Libs., Natl. Arch., 1976–; Supvsr. Archvst., Lyndon B. Johnson Lib., 1974–76, AV Archvst., 1972–74. **Educ.:** Univ. of IA, 1962–66, BA (Hist.); Univ. of TX, 1972–76 (Pol. Sci.). **Orgs.:** SAA. Amer. Pol. Sci. Assn. Org. of Amer. Histns. **Activities:** 2; 17, 41; 56, 85 **Addr.:** Office of Presidential Libraries (NL), 8th & Pennsylvania Ave., N.W., Rm. 103, Washington, DC 20408.

Fawcett, Patrick James (O. 10, 1950, Lancaster, Lancashire, Eng) Systs. Coord., Libs., Univ. of MB, 1980–; Asst. Med. Libn., Univ. of MB Libs., 1979–80, Pub. Srvs. Libn., 1973–79; Dir., Cat. Dept., Midland Book Ctr., 1972–73; Italian Biblgphr., Univ. of AB Libs., 1970–71. **Educ.:** Univ. of AB, 1967–70, BA (Eng.); 1971–72, BLS. **Orgs.:** Can. Hlth. Libs. Assn.: Exec. Com. (1978–). MB LA: Dir. (1972–74). ASIS. Can. Assn. Info. Sci. Mensa Socty. Count Dracula Socty. **Pubns.:** Ed., *Manitoba Library Association Bulletin* (1972–74); Ed., *Bibliotheca Medica Canadiana,* (1979–); "Personal filing systems revisited," *Ear Nose and Throat Jnl.* (S., 1978); "Librarian/Dean communication," *Bltn. of the Med. Lib Assn.* (Ja., 1980); radio script. **Addr.:** Elizabeth Dafoe Library, University of Manitoba, Winnipeg, MB R3T 2N2, Canada.

Fayen, Emily Gallup (F. 9, 1941, Newton, NJ) Dir., Lib. Autom., Dartmouth Coll. Libs., 1979–, Dir., OL Pilot Proj., 1979; Syst. Anal., Norris Cotton Cancer Ctr., 1977–79; Consult., US Gvt., 1972–77. **Educ.:** Univ. of MD, 1961–63, BS (Math, Phys.); Amer. Univ., 1965–70, MPA (Info. Sci.). **Orgs.:** Association of Computing Manufacturers ASIS. Assn. of Comp. Mfrs. **Honors:** ASIS, Best Bk. of 1974, 1975. **Pubns.:** jt. auth., *Information Retrieval On-Line* (1974); "On-Line Personal Bibliographic Retrieval System," *ACM/SIGIR Proceedings* (Sum. 1978); "Experimental On-Line Catalog for the Dartmouth College Libraries," (Ap. 1980). **Activities:** 1, 12; 49-Comp. Srvs.; 56 **Addr.:** Baker Library, Dartmouth College, Hanover, NH 03755.

Feagley, Ethel M. (Ja. 22, 1894, Jersey City, NJ) Retired; Assoc. Prof., Sch. of Lib. Srv., Columbia Univ., 1959–61, Assoc. Libn. and Assoc. Prof., Tchrs. Coll. Lib., 1932–59; Instr., Drexel Lib. Sch., 1931; Sch. Libn., Cheltenham HS, 1926–31. **Educ.:** State Normal Sch. (PA), 1918–20, Dip. (Eng.); Tchrs. Coll., Columbia Univ., 1925–26, BS (Eng.), Sch. of Lib. Srv., 1927–30, BS (LS), Tchrs. Coll., 1936–38, MA (Educ.). **Orgs.:** ALA. Wilson Lib. Bltn.: Sch. Lib. Sect. (Ed., 1934–35). Women's Fac. Club, Columbia Univ. Riverside Church. **Pubns.:** *International Guide to Educational Documentation, 1955–1960* (1963); "Preparation of Pupils and Teachers for Effective Library Service: Teachers," *The Library in General Education* (1943); "Library Consultant Services as Developed at Teachers College, Columbia University," *Assn. of Spec. Libs. and Info. Burs. Rpt. of Procs.* (1936). **Activities:** 11, 12; 31, 39; 57, 62 **Addr.:** 106 Morningside Dr., New York, NY 10027.

Featheringham, Tom R. (D. 17, 1942, Massillon, OH) Assoc. Prof., Comp.–Info. Sci., NJ Inst. of Tech., 1975–; Assoc. Fac. Mem., Rutgers PhD Prog. in Mgt., 1978–; Sr. Resrch. Asst., Univ. of Pittsburgh, 1974–75; Consult., Comp. Cmnd. and Cntrl. Co., 1970–71; Assoc. Resrch. Anal., Univ. of Dayton Resrch. Inst., 1968–70. **Educ.:** Kent State Univ., 1960–64, BS (Math.); Univ. of Pittsburgh, 1972–75, PhD (Info. Sci.). **Orgs.:** ASIS. Assn. for Comp. Mach. Inst. of Electrical and Electronic Eng.: Comp. Socty. AAAS. **Pubns.:** "Paperless Publishing and Potential Institutional Change," *Schol. Publshg.* (O. 1981); jt. auth., "Libraries and Communication-Information Technology," *Cath. Lib. World* (Ap. 1979); "Computerized Conferencing and Human Communication," *IEEE Transactions on Prof. Comm.* (D. 1977); "Computer Conferencing and Its Potential for Business Management," *Data Comms.* (Je. 1977); jt. auth., "Systems Problem Solving and the Error of the Third Kind," *Theory and Decisions* (F. 1975); jt. auth., "Systemic Hypothesis Testing and the Error of the Third Kind," *Bhvl. Sci.* (O. 1974); various articles, sps., presentations (1974–79). **Activities:** 11, 14-Sch.-comp. sci.; 24, 26, 41; 56, 75, 91 **Addr.:** 11 Whitcomb Rd., East Windsor, NJ 08520.

Feathers, Ruth E. (S. 27, 1954, Butler, PA) Prof. Asst., ALA/AASL, 1979–; Lib. Media Spec., Wilkinsburg Sch. Dist. (PA), 1977–79. **Educ.:** State Univ. Coll. of NY, Oswego, 1972–76, BS (Educ., Eng.); Univ. of Pittsburgh, 1976–77, MLS. **Orgs.:** ALA: AASL. PA Sch. Libns. Assn.: Lib. Promo. Com. (1978–79). Cncl. for Sch. Libns. NEA/PSEA; Kappa Delta Pi. **Activities:** 10; 21, 31, 32 **Addr.:** American Association of School Librarians, 50 East Huron St., Chicago, IL 60611.

Fechter, Claudia Zieser (Mr. 14, 1931, New York, NY) Librn., Jewish Cmnty. Fed., 1973–; Suburban Temple, 1976–; Libn., Glen Oak Sch., 1971–73; Libn., in charge, St. John Cantius, 1970–71; Libn., Beachwood HS, 1969–70. **Educ.:** Western Reserve Univ., 1948–52, AB (Pol. Sci.), 1952–53 (LS); Columbia Univ., 1950–52 (Pol. Sci). **Orgs.:** Jewish LA: Pres (1976–78), VP (1974–76). Jewish Bk. Cncl.: Ch. (1975–1979). Temple Emanu El Sisterhood: Bd., (1965–1978). Leag. of Women Voters. **Activities:** 5, 10; 15, 16, 20; 66, 90 **Addr.:** 2541 Richmond Rd., Beachwood, OH 44122.

Federici, Yolanda D. (Ag. 8, 1910, Chicago, IL) Consult., Chld. Books, 1977–; Consult., Chld. Bk. Promo., Follett Publshg. Co., 1977; Chld. Matrls. Spec., Chicago Pub. Lib., 1974–77; Supvsr., Ctrl. Chld., 1970–74; Dir.,Chld. Bk. Fest., 1969–74; Dir., Lib. Prom., Follett Publshg., 1964–69; Work with Chld., Chicago Pub. Libs., 1931–64. **Educ.:** Univ. of Chicago, 1939–40; Northwestern Univ., 1949–52. **Orgs.:** ALA: Cnclr. (1973–76); CSD, Bd. of Dir. (1971–72); Newbery-Caldecott Com. (1954, 1962). IL LA: Chld. Libns. Sect. (Ch., 1955–56). Chicago Lib. Club: VP (1966–67); Treas. (1962–63). *Bltn. of the Ctr. for Chld. Books,* Adv. Com. (1948–64, 1970–); Member of Advisory Com. to Ed. Other orgs. Women's Intl. Leag. for Peace & Frdm.: Jane Addams Juv. Bk. Awd. (1975–). Friends of Amer. Writers: Juv. Bk. Awd. Com. (1977–79). US, UNICEF: Chicago Educ. Com. (1976–77). Girl Scouts of America: Chicago Chap., HQ Prog. Com. (1962–64). **Honors:** IL LA, Chld. Libn. Sect., Davis Cup for Disting. Srv. to Children in IL, 1977; Chicago Chld. Readg. RT Awd. for Disting. Lib. Srvs. to Child., 1980. **Pubns.:** "Children's Libraries," *IL Libs.* (1960–66); Ed., "Children's Services," *IL Libs.* (D. 1960–66); Intro., "Nineteenth Century Children's Periodicals" (1977). **Activities:** 9; 21, 24, 37; 51, 57, 67 **Addr.:** 1130 S. Michigan Av., Apt. 1210, Chicago, IL 60605.

Fedunok, Suzanne (Ap. 23, 1945, Pittsburgh, PA) Math/Phys. Libn., Columbia Univ., 1977–; Head Libn., Mathematical Reviews, 1975–77, Libn., 1969–75. **Educ.:** Bryn Mawr Coll., 1963–67, AB (Pol. Sci/Fr.); Univ. of MI, 1967–69, MA (Asian Std.), 1970–73, AMLS. **Orgs.:** SLA: MI Chap., Hosplty. Com. (1974–76); Phys.-Astr.-Math Div., Awds. Com. (1978); Nom. Com. (1977); *Bltn.* co-ed. (1978–80). NY Lib. Club. Friends of Columbia Libs. Friends of Bryn Mawr Lib. Bryn Mawr Coll. Alum. Assn.: Ann Arbor Chap. (Pres., 1975–77); Sel. Com. (1978–81); Class Pres. (1972–77); Class Collector (1977–). Asia Socty. Archlg. Inst. of Amer. Natl. Org. for Women. **Pubns.:** Articles and oral presentations. **Activities:** 1, 12; 15, 17, 30; 88, 91 **Addr.:** Mathematics Library, 303 Mathematics Building, Columbia University, New York, NY 10027.

Feehan, Patricia Ellen (Jl. 20, 1945, Grand Rapids, MI) Statewide Chld. Consult. for Pub. Libs., 1978–; Asst. Coord. of Chld. Srvs., Kent Cnty. Lib., 1973–78; Dir., Martinsville Pub. Lib., 1971–73; Libn., Gaines Twp. Lib., 1969–71. **Educ.:** Grand Rapids Jr. Coll., 1963–65, AA; West. MI Univ., 1966–67, BA (Eng.), 1967–68, MLS. **Orgs.:** ALA: ALSC, Newbery-Caldecott Com. (1979–80). OR LA: PR (Ch., 1981–82). OR Educ. Media Assn.: Fall Conf. Prog. Plng. Com. (1979). Pac. N.W. LA: Young Readrs. Choice Ballot (Ch., 1980). Puppeteers of Amer. Columbia Assn. of Puppeteers. **Pubns.:** Ed., *Children's Service Gnusletter.* **Activities:** 9, 13; 21, 24, 48 **Addr.:** 100 W. 13th, Eugene, OR 97401.

Feehan, Paul G. (My. 18, 1935, Springfield, MA) Coord., Lib. Instr., Univ. of Miami Lib., 1969–. **Educ.:** FL State Univ., 1957–62, BA (Eng.), 1966–67, MS (LS). **Orgs.:** FL LA: Mem. Com. (1970–72); Int. Frdm. (1974–76). Dade Cnty. Lib. Assn.: Mem. Ch. (1974–77). Friends of Univ. Lib.: Prog. Ch. (1978–). FL Gvrs. Conf. on Libs.: Reg. Co-Ch. (1978). Natl. Book Critics' Circle. Common Cause: Dist. Del. (1976). **Honors:** Beta Phi Mu, 1969. **Pubns.:** *Library Resources for the Miccosukee Indians* (1975); *A Bibliography of Materials on the Seminole Indians* (1974); "Separate Undergraduate Libraries: A Dying Breed?" *FL Libs.* (Ja./F. 1978); "Buying Votes," *New Times* (D. 10, 1976); "A Bibliography on the Lumbee Indians of North Carolina," *ERIC* (1978); Videotape. **Activities:** 1; 22, 24, 31; 50, 57, 66 **Addr.:** University of Miami Library, Coral Gables, FL 33124.

Feeney, Karen E. (Ja. 13, 1945, Long Beach, CA) Sci. Ref. Libn., Biblgphr., Sci. & Engin. Lib., Univ. of CA, San Diego, 1975–, Serials Catlgr., 1974–75; Hum. Catlgr., Biblgphr., Univ. of CA, Irvine, 1967–74. **Educ.:** Univ. of CA, Santa Barbara, 1962–66, BA (Hist.); Univ. of CA, Los Angeles, 1966–67, MLS.

Orgs.: SLA: Dir., San Diego Chap. (1979–80); Secy. (1980–81). CA LA. **Activities:** 1; 15, 31, 39; 60, 64, 88 **Addr.:** Science and Engineering Library C-075-E, University of California, San Diego, La Jolla, CA 92093.

Feeney, Mary Elizabeth (S. 18, 1918, Kansas City, MO) Libn., Yale Med. Lib., Yale Univ., 1977–; Dir., New Eng. Reg. Med. Lib. Srvc., Harvard Univ., 1970–77; Assoc. Libn., NY Acad. of Med., 1963–70; Asst. Libn., Coll. of Phy., Philadelphia, 1962–63; Libn., Hospital, Univ. of PA, 1952–62. **Educ.:** Coll. of St. Elizabeth, 1936–39 (Eng.); Univ. of PA, Philadelphia, 1946–47, AB (Eng./Soc.); Univ. of PA, 1947–49 (Libnshp.). **Orgs.:** Med. LA. Cath. LA. New Eng. Reg. Med. Lib. Adv. Com. (1977–). Amer. Psyth. Assn.: Consult., Search Com. (1979–). Bryn Mawr Hosp. Lib.: Consult. (1954–69). **Activities:** 1, 12; 17, 27 **Addr.:** Yale Medical Library, 333 Cedar St., New Haven, CT 06510.

Feinberg, Hilda (Atlanta, GA) Mgr., Lib. and Info. Srvs., Revlon Resrch. Ctr., 1955–; Adj. Assoc. Prof., Pratt Inst., 1972–; Adj. Assoc. Prof., Queens Coll., 1972–. **Educ.:** Univ. of GA, 1934–37, BS Summa cum laude (Chem.), 1938, MS (Chem.); Columbia Univ., 1966–72, MLS, DLS. **Orgs.:** SLA. Med. LA. Amer. Socty. Indxrs.: Secy. ASIS. Socty. of Cosmetic Chem.: Head, Lib. Com. Amer. Chem. Socty. Natl. Micro. Assn.: Head, Lib. Com. Drug Info. Assn. **Honors:** Beta Phi Mu, 1972; Phi Beta Kappa, 1938. **Pubns.:** *Title Derivative Indexing* (1973); Jt. auth., *Book Catalogs;* (1973); articles. **Addr.:** 1685 Ocean Ave., Brooklyn, NY 11230.

Feiner, Arlene M. (Mr. 23, 1937, Spring Green, WI) Coord. of Serial Actv. and Women Std. Biblgrphr., Loyola Univ., Chicago, 1979–; Head Libn., Jesuit Sch. of Theo., 1972–79; Coord. of Pers., Jesuit-Krauss-McCormick Lib., 1975–79; Asst. Dir., Bellarmine Sch. of Theo., 1971–72; Libn., Acad. of the Holy Cross, 1967–70; Preliminary Catlgr., Lib. of Congs., 1965–67; Asst. Libn., Univ. of MD, Munich, 1962–64. **Educ.:** Alverno Coll., 1956–59, BA (Hist.); Rosary Coll., 1970–71, MALS; various addl. crs., 1967–76. **Orgs.:** ALA: RTSD. ATLA. NLA: IL Chap. (Bd., 1979–80). Chicago Cluster of Theo. Schs.: Libns. Cncl. (Vice-Ch., 1977–78); Serials Com. (Ch., 1977–79); Tech. Srvs. Libn. for Chicago Un. Cat. in Relig. (1978–79). **Pubns.:** "Women–An Inquiry Approach," *Procs.: ATLA Conf.* (1980); "A China Report/Libraries," *Loyola Univ. Lib. Nsltr.* (1980). **Addr.:** 336 W. Wellington Ave., #2102, Chicago, IL 60657.

Feinglos, Susan J. (Ap. 23, 1949, Montreal, PQ) OL Srvs. Coord., Duke Med. Lib., 1980–, Ref. Libn., ILL Coord., 1978–80, Ref. Libn., 1976–78, Libn. for the Duke Ctr. for the Study of Aging and Human Dev., 1973–76; Asst. Med. Libn., Montreal Chld. Hosp., 1972–73. **Educ.:** McGill Univ., 1966–70, BA (Art Hist.), 1970–72, MLS. **Orgs.:** Med. LA: Cert. Exam Review Com. (Ch., 1982–83); Med. LA 1980 Mid-Atl. Reg. Mtg., Cont. Educ. Com. (Ch.). SLA. NC OL UG. AAUP. **Pubns.:** "Searching the Literature of Aging Gerontology Reference Sources," *Educ. Grntlgy.* (1978); *Library Newsletter for the Duke Ctr. for the Study of Aging Keyword Index to Training Resources in Aging* (1973–76). **Activities:** 12; 34, 39, 49-Comp. srch.; 80, 91, 95-Grntlgy. **Addr.:** 20 Scott Pl., Durham, NC 27705.

Feingold, Karen E. (Ap. 10, 1947, Miami, FL) Indp. Consult, in Info. Prog. and Srvs. Plng. and Futures Resrch., 1980–; Resrch. Mgr., Info. Prods., Kalba Bowen Assocs., 1979–80; Mgr., Tech. Info. Srvs., Intel Corp., 1978–79; Mgr., Corp. Lib., Digital Equipment Corp., 1976–78; Head, Career Resrcs. Ctr., Baker Lib., Harvard Bus. Sch., 1975–76, Ref. Libn., 1974–75; Libn., Ctr. for Std. in Educ. and Dev., Harvard Grad. Sch. of Educ., 1971–73. **Educ.:** Univ. of Miami, 1966–68, BA (Span.); Simmons Coll., 1971–73, MSLS. **Orgs.:** SLA. ASIS: New Eng. Chap., Prog. Com. (Ch., 1977–78). Assoc. Info. Mgrs. **Pubns.:** Jt. auth., "A Survey of Library User Demands in an Industrial Corporate Library," *Quantitative Measurements and Dynamic Library Services* (1978); "Information on Lifestyle and Career Planning," *Harvard Bus. Review* (Ja.-F. 1976); "Library and Information Services for Improving Organizations and the Professions" (discuss. guide for WHCOLIS) (1979); Various other pubns., articles, and oral presentations. **Activities:** 1, 12; 17, 24, 41; 56, 59, 75 **Addr.:** 2451 Brickell Ave., No. 14D, Miami, FL 33129.

Feinler, Elizabeth Jocelyn (Mr. 2, –, Wheeling, WV) Sr. Info. Sci., Telecom. Sci. Ctr., SRI Intl., Menlo Park, CA, 1975–, Mgr., ARPANET Netwk. Info. Ctr., 1973–, Head, Lit. Resrch. Sect., 1960–72; Asst. Ed., *Chemical Abs.*, Chemical Abs. Srv., 1958–60; Biochem., Shuman Chemical Co., 1957. **Educ.:** W. Liberty State Coll., Wheeling, BS (Chem.); Purdue Univ., Grad. Std. (Biochem.). **Orgs.:** ASIS. Intl. Fed. for Info. Pres. WHCOLIS: Del.-at-large (1979). Inst. of Electrical and Electronics Engins. **Pubns.:** Ed., *ARPANET Resource Handbook* (yearly); Ed., *ARPANET Protocol Handbook* (1978); Ed., *ARPANET Directory* (yearly); Jt. auth., "An Experimental Network Information Center Name Server, NICNAME," *Proceedings of 4th Berkeley Conference on Distributed Data Management and Computer Networks* (1979); Various other articles. **Activities:** 12; 34, 37, 41; 56, 75, 93 **Addr.:** Rm. J221, SRI International, 333 Ravenswood Ave., Menlo Park, CA 94025.

Feinman, Valerie (Jackson) (Je. 28, 1937, Hamilton, ON) Serials Acq. Libn., Adelphi Univ., 1970–; Serials Catlgr., Columbia Univ., 1969–70; Indxr., Srch., and Biomed. Com. Netwk., Upstate Med. Ctr., 1967–69, Ed., Un. List (NY State), 1965–67; Phys. Libn., Syracuse Univ., 1964–65. **Educ.:** McMaster Univ., 1963, BA (Sci. Std.); Syracuse Univ., 1966, MS (LS). **Orgs.:** ALA: ACRL. Nassau Cnty. LA. AAUP. **Honors:** Beta Phi Mu. **Pubns.:** Ed., *Union List of Serials/NYS* (1966, 1967); *Central New York Union List of Serials* (1968); "Dilemmas and Consequences of Converting Periodicals Holdings to Microformat," *Serials Libn.* (Fall 1979); "Attic to Annex and After," *Serials Libn.* (1981); "Security in an Off Campus Book Storage Facility," *Lib. and Arch. Secur.* (forthcoming); various papers (1980). **Activities:** 1; 15, 33, 44; 56, 88 **Addr.:** 119 Schenck Ave., Great Neck, NY 11021.

Feldick, Peggy Riha (Je. 14, 1951, Bismarck, ND) Ref. Libn., Macalester Coll. Lib., 1978–; Asst. Ref. Libn., Gvt. Docum. Libn., Anoka Cnty. Lib., 1973–78; Libn., Ramsey Cnty. Mental Hlth. Ctr., 1973. **Educ.:** Coll. of St. Catherine, St. Paul, MN, 1969–73, BA (Eng., LS); Univ. of WI, Madison, 1976–77, MALS. **Orgs.:** MN LA: Gvt. Docum. RT (Ch., 1979–80). Coop. Libs. in Cnsrtm.: Ill Com. (1978–). **Activities:** 1, 9; 29, 31, 39; 70, 95-State hist. srcs. **Addr.:** 3624 35th Ave. S., Minneapolis, MN 55406.

Feldman, Iris S. (My. 22, 1947, Brooklyn, NY) Sch. Libn., Lawrence Sch., Brookline, MA, 1969–. **Educ.:** Queens Coll. of CUNY, 1964–68, BA (Early Childhood Educ.); Syracuse Univ., 1968–69, MSLS. **Orgs.:** ALA: ALSC, Film Eval. Com. (1973–79), Lib. Srvs. to Preschoolers and their Parents (1972–73), Boy Scouts Adv. Com. (1978–). **Honors:** Phi Beta Kappa, 1967; Beta Phi Mu, 1969. **Pubns.:** "Recycle," *Start Early For An Early Start* (1976); jt. auth., "Sex Role Stereotyping in the School" (handbook) (1975). **Activities:** 10; 21, 31, 48; 63, 67 **Addr.:** Lawrence School Library, 27 Francis St., Brookline, MA 02146.

Feldman, Laurence M. (O. 3, 1940, Cleveland, OH) Branch Libn., Univ. of MA, 1974, Branch Libn., Bio. Scis. Lib., 1974–81, Branch Libn., Phys. Scis. Lib., 1971–74; Libn., Engin. and Appld. Sci. Lib., Yale Univ., 1968–71. **Educ.:** Univ. of AZ, 1964–67, BA (Oriental Std.); Univ. of MI, 1967–68, AMLS. **Orgs.:** SLA. **Pubns.:** "Short Bibliography on Faster Than Light Particles (Tachyons)," *Amer. Jnl. Phys.* (1974); "Selected Bibliography on Optical Spatial Filtering," *Optical Engin.* (1972); *PathFinders* (1971–75). **Activities:** 1; 15, 17, 39; 58, 70, 88 **Addr.:** University of Massachusetts, Morrill Biological Sciences Library, Amherst, MA 01003.

Feldman, Mary K. (Jl. 21, 1920, Sapulpa, OK) Chief, HQ Srvs. Br., Lib. Srvs. Div., U.S. Dept. of Transportation, 1979–; Instr., Dept. of Lib. and Info. Sci., Cath. Univ. of Amer., 1978–; Chief, Cat. Sect., 1973–79; Catlgr., 1972–73; Head, Tech. Srvs., Trinity Coll., Lib., Washington, DC, 1964–72; Ref. Libn., Georgetown Univ., 1970–72; Indexer, *The New Catholic Encyc.*, 1964–66; Catlgr., U.S. Book Exch., 1964. **Educ.:** Monte Cassino Jr. Coll., 1937–39, AA; Cincinnati Cons. of Msc., 1939–41; Univ. of MD, College Park, 1960–63, BSc (Educ.); Catholic Univ., 1963–64, MSLS; Catholic Univ., 1975, Cert. **Orgs.:** Cath. LA: Ch., Legis. Com. (1969–72); Secy., (1967–68) (WA-MD Unit); Ch., Coll. and Sem. Sect., (1979–80). ALA: Mem. Ch., DC, (1968–72). DC LA: Secy. (1969–71). ASIS. SLA: Secy., DC Chap. (1977–78); Secy./Treas., Transp. Grp. (1973–74); Pres., (1974–75); Secy., Documtn. Grp. (1975–77). Phi Kappa Phi; Beta Phi Mu. **Pubns.:** Ed., *Inter-Com* (Newsletter, DC LA) (1971); Ed., *Alum. Forum* (Cath. Univ.) (1973–); other newsletters. **Activities:** 1, 4; 20, 26, 39; 57, 94 **Addr.:** 7117 Poplar Avenue, Takoma Park, MD 20012.

Feldman, Rayma J. (Jl. 1, 1929, Louisville, KY) Owner, info. spec., Seatrack, Maritime Info. Srvs., 1972; Adj. Lect., Queens Coll., Grad. Dept. of LS, 1972–. **Educ.:** Brooklyn Coll., 1946–50, BA Magna cum Laude (Math.); Queens Coll., 1970–72, MLS. **Orgs.:** ASIS. SLA. Assn. of Marine Libns. Pi Mu Epsilon. **Honors:** Queens Coll., S.R. and Anita R. Shapiro Awd. for Excel. in LS Std., 1972; Phi Beta Kappa, Beta Phi Mu. **Activities:** 4, 12; 15, 17, 30, 49; 94 **Addr.:** Seatrack, 97 Oxford Blvd., Great Neck, NY 11023.

Feldman, Sari (My. 29, 1953, Monticello, NY) Libn., Onondaga Cnty. Pub. Lib., Syracuse, NY, 1980–; Dir., Onondaga Free Lib., 1979–80; Libn., I Cook Meml. Lib., Libertyville, IL, 1977–79. **Educ.:** SUNY, Binghamton, 1970–73, BA (Eng.); Univ. of WI, 1976–77, MA (LS). **Orgs.:** ALA. NY LA. Women Lib. Workers. Women's Info. Ctr. Syracuse, NY. **Honors:** Beta Phi Mu. **Pubns.:** *Drugs: A Multimedia Source book for Young Adults* (1979); Reviews. **Activities:** 5, 9; 16, 27, 48; 80 **Addr.:** Onondaga Cnty Public Library, 335 Montgomery, Syracuse, NY 13202.

Feldman, Susan E. (F. 14, 1947, New York, NY) Partner, Information Assoc. of Ithaca, 1981–; Freelnc. writer on lib. educ., 1979–81; Mgt. intern, Cuesta Coll., 1978–79, Ref. Libn. and Instr., 1976–79, YA and Ref. Libn., Tompkins Cnty. Pub. Lib., 1972–75. Instr., Syracuse Univ., Sch. of info. Sci., 1975; Coord. of AV Resrcs., S. Ctrl. Resrch. Lib. Cncl., 1970–71; Tech. Info. Spec., Natl. Tech. Info. Srvs., 1968–70. **Educ.:** Cornell Univ., 1963–67, BA (Ling); Univ. of MI, 1967–68, AMLS; NY Pub. Libns. Cert., 1972, CA Cmnty. Coll. Libn. Cert., 1976. **Orgs.:** Lib. and Media People: Pres. and Org., (1977–1979), Chld. and YA Srvs. Sect., First VP and pres. elec., (1974–1975), NY LA. ASTS. Sierra Clb.: Finger Lakes Grp., Secy. (1972–1975). Brahms Orch., Cornell Univ. **Honors:** Beta Phi Mu, 1968–. **Pubns.:** Jt. auth.; "Bibliography of Newspapers in 14 counties of New York State," *NY Hist.* (1971 and 1972). **Activities:** 1, 9; 26, 39 **Addr.:** 109 Randolph Rd., Ithaca, NY 14850.

Feldman, T. K. (O. 23, 1934, Paterson, NJ) Dir., Lit. Arts Dept., Jewish Cmnty. Ctr. of Grt. Washington, 1973–, Ed., 1970–72; Asst. Pubcty. Dir., WERE, 1956–58. **Educ.:** OH Univ., 1952–56, BS (Jnlsm.). **Orgs.:** Assn. of Jewish Libs. Cncl. of Jewish Libns. Assn. of Jewish Ctr. Workers. **Activities:** 14-Soc. srv. agency; 15, 17, 49-Programming; 95-Holocaust, Israel, Zionism. **Addr.:** Kass Judaic Library, Jewish Community Center of Greater Washington, 6125 Montrose Rd., Rockville, MD 20852.

Felicetti, Barbara Whyte (Mr. 31, 1947, New York, NY) Dir., Info/motion, 1977–. **Educ.:** Boston Univ., 1966–69, BA (Gvt.); SUNY, Albany, 1975–76, MLS. **Orgs.:** ALA. SLA. ASIS. Assoc. Info. Mgrs. **Pubns.:** "Information for Fee and Information for Free: The Information Broker and the Public Librarian" *Pub. Lib. Qtly.* (Spr. 1979); Regular contrib. to the *Jnl. of Fee-Based Info. Srvs.* **Activities:** 14-For-profit co.; 24, 41, 49-full range of information services; 59, 65, 95-energy. **Addr.:** Info/motion, 214 W. Mountain Rd., Lenox, MA 01240.

Feller, Judith M. (Ag. 29, 1939, Philadelphia, PA) Docums. Libn., E. Stroudsburg State Coll., 1970–; Ref. Libn., Temple Univ., 1966–70; Ref. Libn., E. Stroudsburg State Coll., 1963–65. **Educ.:** Univ. of PA, 1957–61, BA (Creat. Wrtg.); Drexel Univ., 1962–63, MLS; Rutgers Univ., 1972–73. **Orgs.:** PA LA: Spec. Com. on Gvt. Docums., Mem. Ch. (1975); Gvt. Docums. Round Table, Ch., (1976–77); 1977 Annual Conf., Ch., Local Arrang. Com. ALA: ACRL: Bd. of Dir. (1973–76); Secy. (1979–). **Activities:** 1; 29, 31, 39; 55, 63 **Addr.:** Library, East Stroudsburg State College, East Stroudsburg, PA 18301.

Fellows, Barbara Goodwin (S. 20, 1927, Boston, MA) Asst. Dir., Main Lib., Pub. Lib. of Columbus and Franklin Cnty., 1980–, Head, Bus. & Tech Div., 1973–80; Libn., PA Div., Carnegie Lib. of Pittsburgh, 1968–72. **Educ.:** Radcliffe Coll., 1945–49, AB (Soc. Rel.); Univ. of Pittsburgh, 1966–68, MLS; Sorbonne, Univ. of Paris, 1949–50, Cert. (Fr. Civ.); Miami Univ., Exec. Dev. Prog. for Lib. Admin., 1978, Cert. **Orgs.:** ALA: Pub. Docum. Com. (1976–77); Subcom. on Census Use (Ch., 1976–77); GODORT, Fed. Docum. Task Force, Work Grp. on Census Use (Ch., 1978). OH LA. Franklin Cnty. LA. **Honors:** Beta Phi Mu, 1968. **Activities:** 9; 15, 17, 39; 59, 91, 92 **Addr.:** 4660 Ralston St., Columbus, OH 43214.

Fenelon, Patricia Suzanne (O. 12, 1934, Davenport, IA) Univ. Biblgphr., IN Univ., S. Bend, 1979–; Acq. Head, 1976–79; Coll. Lib., Asst. Head, Univ. Notre Dame, 1975–76, Ref., 1969–75. **Educ.:** Cardinal Stritch Coll., 1952–56, BA (Hist.); Columbia Univ., 1966–69, MLS; Univ. of Notre Dame, 1969–80, PhD (Eng.). **Orgs.:** SLA. NLA. Natl. Cncl. Tchrs. of Eng. IN Univ., S. Bend, Fac. Senate: Curric. Com. (Ch., 1976–7); Student Affairs Com. (Secy., 1979–80). **Honors:** Univ. of Notre Dame, Zahm Travel Grant, 1977. **Pubns.:** "Faulkners Mayday," S. Bend Tribune (Ja. 1980); "Shirely," N. IN Hist. Socty. *Courthouse News* (N. 1978); "Rare Religious books in Americana Collection IUSB," *NET* (My. 1978). **Activities:** 1; 15, 20, 26; 57, 77, 90 **Addr.:** 301 Parkovash, S Bend, IN 46617.

Feng, Cyril C. H. (D. 1, 1937, Hongchow, China) Dir., Hlth. Sci. Lib., Univ. of MD, 1977–; Deputy Dir., Assoc. Prof., Univ. of Miami, Sch. of Med. Lib., 1973–77; Head, Readers' Srvs., Asst. Prof., 1972–73; Acq. Libn., 1967–72; Basic Sci. Br. Libn., 1965–67. **Educ.:** Tamkang Coll. of Arts and Scis., Taiwan, 1957–61, BA (Lit.); Univ. of KY, 1963–65, MSLS. **Orgs.:** State of MD: Lib. Ntwk. Plng. Com. (1978–). Med. LA: Recruit. Com. (1974–76). SLA: Pres., FL Chap. (1976–77). Cong. of Acad. Lib. Dir., MD: Exec. Brd. (1979–). Biomed. Comm. Ntwk.: Secy./Treas. (1979–). Univ. of MD, Baltimore: Acad. Cncl. (1977–); Ch., Culture Enrichment Com. (1979–). Univ. of Miami, Sch. of Med.: Curr. Com. (1969–71); Computer Com. (1968–70). Comprehensive Cancer Ctr. of the State of FL: Educ. Com. (1976–77). **Pubns.:** Jt. Auth., "Using Computerized Literature Searches to Produce Faculty Publications Lists," *Med. LA Bltn.* (1979); Jt. auth., "Excerpta Medica Abstracting Journals," *Med. LA Bltn.* (Ap. 1977); "An Invitation to MEDLINE," *Miami Med.* (O., 1974); "Recommendation for Procedural Change in PRINT OFF-LINE Command," *Lib. Ntwk./MEDLARS Tech. Bltn.* (Ag. 1974); Jt. auth., "Evaluation of MEDLINE Service by User Survey," *Med. LA Bltn.* (O. 1974). **Activities:** 1, 12; 17, 24, 27, 36; 75, 80 **Addr.:** University of Maryland, Health Sciences Library, 111 South Greene St., Baltimore, MD 21201.

Fenichel, Carol Hansen (Ja. 3, 1935, Davenport, IA) Dir. of Libs., Philadelphia Coll. of Pharm. and Sci., 1980–; Asst. Prof., University of KY, 1979–80, Assoc. Libn., Med. Coll. of PA, 1973–77, Consult., AUERBACH Assoc., Inc., 1972–73. **Educ.:** Bryn Mawr Coll., 1953–57, BA (Chem), Drexel Univ., 1976–79, PhD (Info. Sci.), Med. LA., Cert., 1978–. **Orgs.:** Med. LA.: Oral

Special Subjects/Services: 50. Adult educ.; 51. Advert./Mktg.; 52. Aerosp.; 53. Agric.; 54. Area std.; 55. Arts/Hum.; 56. Autom.; 57. Bibl./Prtg.; 58. Bio. sci.; 59. Bus./Fin.; 60. Chem.; 61. Copyrt.; 62. Documtn.; 63. Educ.; 64. Engin.; 65. Env.; 66. Eth. grps.; 67. Film; 68. Food/Nutr.; 69. Geneal.; 70. Geo.; 71. Geol.; 72. Handcpd.; 73. Hist.; 74. Int. frdm.; 75. Info. sci.; 76. Insr.; 77. Law; 78. Legis.; 79. Math./Comp. sci.; 80. Med.; 81. Metals; 82. Nat. resrcs.; 83. Newsp.; 84. Nuc. sci.; 85. Oral hist.; 86. Petr./Energy; 87. Pharm.; 88. Phys./Astr./Math.; 89. Readg.; 90. Relig.; 91. Sci./Tech.; 92. Soc. sci.; 93. Telecom.; 94. Transp.; 95. (other).

hist. com. (Ch. 1979–80). ASIS: (Curric. Com. (Ch. 1979–80); Philadelphia Chap. (Ch. 1974–75). Miquon Sch.: Secy. (1966–67). Natl. Org. for Women. **Honors:** ASIS, Elaine D. Kaskela Awd., 1974; ASIS, Chap. of the Yr., 1975. **Pubns.:** Ed., *Changing Patterns in Information Retrieval* (1974); Jt. Ed., *Women in Medicine: A Bibliography of the Literature about Women Physicians* (1977); "Size and Scope of the Biomedical Literature," *ASIS Proc.* (1975); "Editing the Permuterm Subject Index," (1971); "Daughters of Science: An Oral-History Project on Women In Medicine," (1978). **Addr.:** Joseph W. England Library, Philadelphia College of Pharmacy and Science, 42d St. and Woodland Av., Philadelphia, PA 19104.

Fenn, Dan Huntington, Jr. (Mr. 27, 1923, Boston, MA) Dir., John F. Kennedy Lib., 1971–; Lectr., Harvard Bus. Sch., 1969–. **Educ.:** Harvard Univ., 1940–46, BA (Gvt.), 1946–48, AM (Gvt.). **Orgs.:** Oral Hist. Assn. New Eng. Archvsts. **Activities:** 2, 4; 15, 17, 36; 50, 59, 92 **Addr.:** John F. Kennedy Library, Boston, MA 02125.

Fennell, Doris Pauline (S. 20, 1925, Brantford, ON) Educ. Ofcr., Mnstry. of Educ., 1966–; Lib. Coord., Toronto Township, 1964–66; HS Libn., Etobicoke Bd. of Educ., 1962–64, Elem. Sch. Tchr. **Educ.:** McMaster Univ., 1948–51, BA (Geog.); Univ. of Toronto, 1961–62, BLS, 1973, MLS, 1970, MEd; Spec. in Sch. Libnshp.; Spec. Educ. Cert. **Orgs.:** Can. Sch. LA: Pres. (1979–80). Intl. Assn. of Sch. Libnshp.: Can. Bd. Member (1975–76). ON LA. Other orgs. ON Film Assn. Assn. for Media and Tech. in Educ. in Can. Chld. Recreational Reading Cncl.: Secy. (1968–74). Royal ON Musm. **Honors:** Univ. of Toronto Fac. LS, Ref. Srvs. Prize, 1962; Can. Centennial Medal, 1967. **Pubns.:** Jt. Auth., *Cataloguing for School Libraries* (1970); "Education for School Librarians," *IPLO Quarterly* (Ap. 1975); "School Libraries in Ontario," *ON Lib. Review* (Je. 1969); "Resource Centre Assessment," *Media Message* (1978); Jt. auth., "Libraries in Canadian schools," *Librarianship in Canada, 1946–1967; essays in honour of Elizabeth Homer Morton,* (1968); other articles. **Activities:** 10, 13; 20, 21, 26; 63, 89 **Addr.:** Ministry of Education, Ontario, Mowat Block, Queen's Park, Toronto, ON M7A 1L2 Canada.

Fennell, Janice C. (Je. 29, Roanoke, VA) Dir. of Libs., GA Coll., 1978–; Instr., Lib. Media, Univ. of Ctrl. FL, 1974–76, Resident Ctr. Lib. Coord., 1972–74; Sci. Ref. Libn., FL State Univ., 1971–72; Circ. Libn., Sci. Lib., Univ. of GA, 1967–71. **Educ.:** James Madison Univ., 1959–62, BS (Hist.); FL State Univ., 1966–67, MLS, 1976–78, PhD (LS). **Orgs.:** GA LA: Task Force on GA LA-ACRL Status (1979–80). ALA. **Honors:** Beta Phi Mu. **Pubns.:** Jt. comp., *The Black Experience: A Bibliography of Bibliographies 1970–75* (1978); "The Woman Academic Library Administrator: A Career Profile," *Research Issues on Women in Librarianship* (1981); "Where Is 'Womanagement' In Librarianship?" *Columns* (Spr. 1980); Contrib., "Back on the Job," *In-Basket Simulation Techniques: A Sourcebook* (1978); Contrib., "Monday Morning Bedlam in the Science Library," *In-Basket Simulation Techniques: A Sourcebook* (1978). **Activities:** 1, 10; 17, 22, 26; 63 **Addr.:** Ina Dillard Russell Library, Georgia College, Milledgeville, GA 31061.

Fenske, David Edward (Je. 26, 1943, Sheboygan, WI) Head, Msc. Lib., IN Univ., 1974–, Assoc. Msc. Libn., 1971–74; Asst. Msc. Libn. & Admin. Asst., Univ. of WI, 1967–71. **Educ.:** Univ. of WI, 1961–65, BM (Msc. Educ.), 1965–73, PhD (Msclgy.). **Orgs.:** Msc. LA: Bd. of Dir. (1975–77); Midwest Chap., Ch. (1979–). IN Univ. Libns. Assn.: Pres. (1973–74); Treas. (1972–73). Amer. Msclgl. Socty., Midwest Chap. **Pubns.:** "Budget Resources in Ten Major Music Libraries" *InULA Qtly.* (Sum. 1978); "Contrapuntal Textures in the String Quartets, Op. 51, No. 1, and Op. 67 of Johannes Brahms" *Music East and West: Essays in Honor of Walter Kaufmann.* **Activities:** 1, 14-Music Library; 15, 17, 26; 55 **Addr.:** Music Library, Indiana University, Bloomington, IN 47401.

Fenske, Ruth Elizabeth (S. 29, 1945, Menomonie, WI) Asst. Prof., Grad. Sch. of Lib. Srv., Univ. of AL, 1981–; Ref. Libn., Med. Ctr. Lib., Univ. of MI, 1978–81; Assoc. Dir., Hlth. Affairs Lib., E. Carolina Univ., 1976–78; Spec. Projs. Libn., Hlth. Sci. Lib., Univ. of WI, 1970–76; Trainee, Sch. of Med. Lib., Washington Univ., 1969–70. **Educ.:** Willamette Univ., 1963–67, BA (Math); Univ. of WI, Madison, 1967–69, MALS; Washington Univ., 1969–70, Cert. (Comp. Libnshp.); Univ. of MI, 1978–, PhD Cand. **Orgs.:** Med. LA: Cont. Educ. Com. (1974–78); Recert. Com. (1977–78); Com. on Srvys. and Stats. (1980–). SLA. ASIS: WI Chap. (Secy., 1973–75). ALA. Various other orgs. **Honors:** Beta Phi Mu, 1969. **Pubns.:** "Correlations between National Library of Medicine Classification Numbers and MeSH Headings," *Bltn. of Med. LA* (Ap. 1972); "Section N: Audiovisual Services," *Basic Library Management for Health Science Librarians* (1975). **Activities:** 11, 12; 17, 26, 46; 80 **Addr.:** Graduate School of Library Service, University of Alabama, P.O. Box 6242, University, AL 35486.

Fenster, Valmai Ruth (Je. 17, 1939, Nelson, NZ) Asst. Prof., Univ. of WI Lib. Sch., 1979–, Lectr., 1967–79; Catlgr., Univ. of WI Meml. Lib., 1966–67; Catlgr., Univ. of Canterbury, NZ, 1965–66; Catlgr., Univ. of IL, 1963–64. **Educ.:** Univ. of Canterbury, NZ, 1957–59, BA (Eng.), 1960, MA, hons. (Eng.); Univ. of IL, 1961–63, MS (LS); Univ. of WI, 1971–76, PhD (LS). **Orgs.:** ALA: IRRT (Ch., 1972–74). WI LA. AALS. Amer. Prtg. Hist. Assn. **Honors:** Beta Phi Mu, Boyd Awd., 1963; Phi Kappa Phi. **Pubns.:** "Women's Contributions to the Library School," *University Women: A Series of Essays* (1980); "Linda Anne Eastman," *Notable American Women: The Modern Period: A Biographical Dictionary* (1980); "Public Documents in Library Education at the University of Wisconsin Library School, 1895-1939," *Gvt. Pubns. Review* (1980); "Wisconsin Library Bulletin Celebrating its 75th Anniversary," *WI Lib. Bltn.* (N.–D., 1979); "Mary Emogene Hazeltine," *Dictionary of American Library Biography* (1977). **Activities:** 1, 11; 20, 26; 55 **Addr.:** University of Wisconsin Library School, 600 N. Park St., Madison, WI 53706.

Fenstermann, Duane W. (Ja. 25, 1939, Greeley, IA) Acq. Libn., Head of Tech. Srvs., Luther Coll. Lib., 1969–, Acq. Libn., 1966–81; Asst. Cur., Josiah C. Trent Col. in the Hist. of Med., Duke Univ. Med. Ctr. Lib., 1965. **Educ.:** Univ. of Dubuque, 1956–58; Morningside Coll., 1958–61, BA (Phil.); Duke Univ., 1961–64, MDiv (Theo.); Univ. of NC, 1964–66, MS (LS). **Orgs.:** IA LA: Exec. Bd. (1980–83). ALA: ACRL; RTSD; LITA. Midwest Arch. Conf. IA Hist. Mtrls. Prsrvn. Socty. Winneshiek Cnty. Hist. Socty. Natl. Model Railroad Assn. **Honors:** IA Hist. Recs. Adv. Bd., Bd. Mem., 1979–82. **Pubns.:** *Northeast Iowa Union List of Serials* (1978); various papers. **Activities:** 1, 2; 15, 23, 46; 56, 69, 94 **Addr.:** Luther College Library, Decorah, IA 52101.

Fenton, Ann D. (D. 21, 1946, Tampa, FL) Sr. Libn., Orlando Pub. Lib., 1969–. **Educ.:** Univ. of S. FL, 1964–68, BA (Elem. Educ., LS); FL State Univ., 1968–69, MSLS. **Orgs.:** ALA. FL LA: Chld. and Sch. Caucus (Ch., 1980). **Pubns.:** Jt. auth., *Reference Books for Children* (1981); jt. auth., *Index to Children's Songs* (1979). **Activities:** 9; 21 **Addr.:** 3407 S. Crystal Lake Dr., Orlando, FL 32806.

Fenton, Calvin D. (F. 7, 1939, West Carthage, NY) Libn., NY Milit. Acad., 1966–, Asst. Libn., 1963–66. **Educ.:** SUNY, Albany, 1958–62, BA (Soc. Std.), 1962–63, MLS. **Orgs.:** ALA. NY LA. SAA. **Activities:** 10; 17, 31, 32 **Addr.:** New York Military Academy, Academy Ave., Cornwall-on-Hudson, NY 12520.

Fenton, Elaine P. (N. 3, 1948, Abbeville, SC) Circuit Libn., U.S. Ct. of Appeals, 1981–; Libn., GA State Lib., 1972–80. **Educ.:** Emory Univ., 1966–70, BA (Pol. Sci.), 1971–72, MLn (LS). **Orgs.:** GA LA: Docum. Com. (1978–). Atlanta Law Libs. Assn.: VP (1973); Pres. (1974). AALL. **Honors:** AALL, Schol., 1979. **Activities:** 4; 15, 17; 77, 78 **Addr.:** Library - U.S. Court of Appeals, 56 Forsyth St. N.W., Atlanta, GA 30303.

Fenton, Peter Low (N. 2, 1941, Providence, RI) Dir., Robbins Lib. (Arlington, MA) 1980–; Dir. of Libs., Boston State Coll., 1974–80; Dir. of Libs., Elmira Coll., 1969–74; Head Libn., Franklin Pierce Coll., 1968–69; Staff Assoc., Cncl. for the Advnc. of Small Colls., 1967–68; Asst. Per. Libn., Bucknell Univ., 1966–67. **Educ.:** Bowdoin Coll., 1960–64, BA (Eng.); Columbia Univ., 1965–66, MS (LS). **Orgs.:** ALA: ACRL. New Eng. LA. New Eng. Lib. Bd.: Panel of Cnclrs. (1975–). Conf. of Chief Libns. of Pub. Higher Educ. Inst.: VP (1977); Pres. (1978); Ch., Legis. Liason Com. (1979–). Other orgs. Harvard Musical Assn. Highlands Yacht Club. **Pubns.:** Jt. auth., "A Cloud of Unknowing," *Amer. Libs.,* (Je. 1975); "The Fenway Library Consortium After Two Years," *Bulletin of the Special Library Association - Boston Chapter,* (My.-Je. 1977); "The Learning Center as Business," *The Bookmark,* (Ja.-F. 1972); Contrib., "Zero Growth: When is NOT-Enough Enough? A Symposium," *Jnl. of Acad. Libnshp.,* (N. 1975). **Activities:** 1; 17, 34, 41; 56, 57 **Addr.:** Robbins Library, Arlington, MA 02174.

Fenwick, Sara Innis (D. 25, 1908, Lima, OH) Prof. Emeritus, Grad. Lib. Sch., Univ. of Chicago, 1974–, Prof., 1956–74; Visit. Prof., Univ. of South. CA, 1975–76; Tchr., Libn., Lab. Sch., Univ. of Chicago, 1949–56; Head, Work with Chld., Gary (IN) Pub. Lib., 1946–49; Asst. to Dir., Work with Chld., Enoch Pratt Free Lib., 1944–46; Young People's Libn., Osterhout Free Lib., Wilkes-Barre, PA, 1931–44. **Educ.:** West. Rsv. Univ., 1931–39, BA (Eng., Classics); Univ. of Chicago, 1948–51, MALS. **Orgs.:** ALA: Chld. Srvs. Div. (Pres., 1971–72); AASL (Pres., 1962–63). Intl. Readg. Assn.: Com. on Readg. and Libs. (Ch., 1973–74). AAUW. Pi Lambda Theta. **Honors:** Australian LA and US State Dept., Fulbright Sr. Lectr., 1964; Chicago Area Readg. Assn., Cara Awd., 1973; Chicago Area Chld. Readg. RT, Anl. Awd., 1974. **Pubns.:** *Library Services for Children in Schools and Public Libraries in New Zealand* (1975); Jt. ed., *Differentiating the Media* (1975); *School and Public Library Services for Children in Australia* (1966); Ed., *A Critical Approach to Children's Literature* (1966); "Scholarly Research about Historical Children's Books," *Lib. Trends* (Spr. 1979); various other articles. **Activities:** 9, 10; 21, 32, 48; 63, 75, 89 **Addr.:** 6909 9th St. S., St. Petersburg, FL 33705.

Ferens, Mariley B. (Jl. 18, 1949, San Diego, CA) Libn., NW Fed. Reg. Cncl. Lib., 1978–, Lib. Tech., 1972–78. **Educ.:** Westmont Coll., Santa Barbara, 1967–71, BA (Psy.); Univ. of WA, Seattle, 1976–77, MLS. **Orgs.:** SLA: Pac. NW Chap., Prog. Com. (1979–80), Pubcty. Com. (1978–79). **Activities:** 4, 12; 15, 17, 39; 77, 78, 92 **Addr.:** NW Federal Regional Council Library, M.S. 132 Arcade Plaza Bldg., 1321 Second Ave., Seattle, WA 98101.

Ferguson, Chris Duane (Mr. 13, 1951, Saginaw, MI) Soc. Sci. Biblgphr., Univ. of CA, Irvine, 1981–; Ref.-Biblgphr. and Coord. for Bibl. Instr., Univ. of MS, 1979–. **Educ.:** Saginaw Valley State Col., 1969–73, BA (Hist.); SUNY, Binghamton, 1973–79, PhD (Hist.); Univ. of TX, 1979–80, MLS. **Orgs.:** ALA: RASD/Hist. Sect., Bibl. and Indexes Com. (1980–); 1981 Prog. Com.; ACRL/Bibli. Instr. Sect., Educ. for Bibl. Instr. Com. (1980–81); ANSS/Bibli. Com. (1981–). MS LA. SELA. Amer. Hist. Assn. **Honors:** Beta Phi Mu, Outstan. Student, 1980. **Pubns.:** "The Binghamton Manuscript of Petrarch" *Manuscripta* (1981). **Pubns.:** "Clio and the Computer: Trading the Typewriter for the Computer Terminal" *AHA Newsletter* (JE 1981); "Taming the Serials Budget" *Technicalities* (Jl. 1981). **Activities:** 1; 15, 31, 39; 55, 92 **Addr.:** University Library, University of California, Irvine, CA 92713.

Ferguson, Douglas K. (Jl. 4, 1939, Detroit, MI) Mgr., OL Cat. Projs., Resrch. Libs. Grp., 1979–; Head, Data Srvs. Prog., Stanford Univ. Libs., 1972–79; Mgr., Documtn. Srvs., SPIRES-BALLOTS, Stanford Comp. Ctr., 1969–71; Jr. Spec., Inst. of Lib. Resrch., Univ. of CA, Berkeley, 1968–69. **Educ.:** Macalester Coll., 1956–60, BA (Phil., Pol. Econ.); Univ. of CA, Berkeley, 1966–67, MLS; Stanford Univ., Univ. of CA, Berkeley, 1973–78, Grad. std. in mktg., comm., info. sci. **Orgs.:** ASIS. ALA. AAAS. Assn. for Comp. Mach. Various other orgs. **Honors:** UC Prof. Schs. Fellow-India, 1967–68. **Pubns.:** Jt. auth., *Attitudinal and Other Correlates of Values* (1979); jt. auth., *Demographics of Values* (1979); ed., *System Scope for Library Automation and Information Retrieval* (1971); "Social Science Data Files, the Research Library and the Computing Center," *Drexel Lib. Qtly.* (Ja. 1977); "Marketing Online Services in the University," *OL Mag.* (Jl. 1977); Various other articles and pubns. **Activities:** 1, 12; 24, 34, 39; 51, 56, 92 **Addr.:** 1801 Rose St., Berkeley, CA 94703.

Ferguson, Elizabeth (Ja. 27, 1906, Willoughby, OH) Libn., Inst. of Life Insr., 1944–69; Ref. Libn., Lima (OH) Pub. Lib., 1930–43; Tchr., spec. libs. crs., Pratt Inst., Univ. of HI, Univ. of MI, 1959–75. **Educ.:** Middlebury Coll., Oberlin Coll., 1923–27, BA (Eng. Lit); West. Rsv. Univ., 1929–30, BS in LS. **Orgs.:** SLA: Pres. (1952–53); Insr. Div. (Ch., 1946–48, 1961–62); various other coms. ALA: Com. on Accred. (1969–71). CNLIA: Ch. (1953–55); Trustee (1955–62). YWCA of the City of New York. Natl. Cncl. on the Aging: Lib. and Exec. Coms. (1959–68). **Honors:** SLA, Hall of Fame, 1970; Case West. Rsv. Univ. Sch. of LS, 75th Anniv. Hon., 1979. **Pubns.:** Ed., *Sources of Insurance Statistics* (1965); *Income, Resources and Needs to Older People: A Bibliography* (1964); "Council of National Library Associations," *International Encyclopedia of Library and Information Science* (1971); "Public Relations in Special Libraries," *Public Relations for Libraries* (1973); "They Need to Be Trained on the Job," *Special Librarianship: A New Reader* (1980); various articles. **Activities:** 11, 12; 26, 36, 39; 76 **Addr.:** 105 E. 24th St., New York, NY 10010.

Ferguson, J. Ray (Jl. 10, 1943, Thomaston, GA) Assoc. Law Libn., Washington Univ. Sch. of Law, 1976–; Asst. Law Libn., TX Tech Univ. Sch. of Law, 1974–75. **Educ.:** Mercer Univ., 1961–65, AB (Soclgy., Eng.), Walter F. George Sch. of Law, 1965–68, JD (Law); Univ. of WA, 1973–74, MLL (LS). **Orgs.:** Mid-Amer. Assn. of Law Libs. AALL: Place. Com. (1977–); State, Ct. and Cnty. Law Libs. Spec. Interest Sect. (1980–); Acad. Law Libs., Spec. Interest Sect. (1980–); Exhibits Com., 1980 AALL Anl. Mtg., Co-Ch. Southwest. Assn. of Law Libs.: Nom. Com. (1976–77); Place. Com. (Ch., 1977–). **Honors:** Phi Alpha Delta. **Pubns.:** Jt. auth., *Federal Consumer Protection: Laws, Rules, and, Regulations* (1979, 1980 supplementation); reviews. **Activities:** 1, 12; 15, 17; 77 **Addr.:** Washington University, Law Library, Campus Box 1120, St. Louis, MO 63130.

Ferguson, John W. (N. 4, 1936, Ash Grove, MO) Dir. of Libs., Mid-Continent Pub. Lib., 1981–, Assoc. Dir. of Libs., 1964–80; Asst. Libn., Pub. Libs. of Springfield and Greene Cntys., 1961–64. **Educ.:** Southwest MO State Coll., 1954–58, BS (Geol., Geo.); Univ. of OK, 1961–62, MLS. **Orgs.:** ALA. MO LA. Northwest MO Lib. Netwk.: Bd. Mem. MO Lib. Film Coop.: Bd. Mem. Various other orgs. **Activities:** 9; 17, 27, 34; 67, 72, 93 **Addr.:** 3820 Stonewall Ct., Independence, MO 64055.

Ferguson, Paul F. (F. 16, 1925, Danvers, MA) Dir. of Law Lib., St. Mary's Univ. of San Antonio, 1966–; Libn., Essex Cnty. (MA) Law Lib., 1953–66. **Educ.:** Harvard Coll., 1942–47, AB (Gvt.); Boston Univ., 1949–53, JD (Law); Our Lady of the Lake Univ., San Antonio, 1968–70, MS in LS. **Orgs.:** TX LA. AALL. **Activities:** 1, 14; 77 **Addr.:** St. Mary's University School of Law, Law Library, One Camino Santa Maria, San Antonio, TX 78284.

Ferguson, Richard Dimitri, Jr. (S. 29, 1933, Richmond, IN) Pres., Appld. Info. Sci. and Tech., 1978–; Assoc. Dean, Dir., Comm. Resrch. Ctr., Boston Univ., Sch. of Pub. Comm., 1975–78; Dir., Syst. Plng. and Dev., Boston City Hosp., Patient Info. Syst. Proj., 1974–75; Asst. to Pres., Syst. Dev., Tufts Univ., 1972–74; Supvsr., Stats. Comp. Prog. Grp., Harvard

PROFESSIONAL ACTIVITIES: Institutions: 1. Acad. lib.; 2. Arch.; 3. Assn.; 4. Fed./Gvt. lib.; 5. Inst. lib.; 6. Mfr./Suppl.; 7. Milit. lib.; 8. Musm.; 9. Pub. lib.; 10. Sch. lib.; 11. Sch. of lib. sci.; 12. Spec. lib.; 13. State lib.; 14. (other). **Functions/Activities:** 15. Acq./Col. dev.; 16. Adult srvs.; 17. Admin.; 18. Apprais.; 19. Archit./Bldgs.; 20. Cat./Class.; 21. Chld. srvs.; 22. Circ.; 23. Cons./Pres.; 24. Consult.; 25. Cont. ed.; 26. Educ. lib. sci.; 27. Ext. srvs.; 28. Fund/Grants; 29. Gvt. pubs.; 30. Indx./Abs.; 31. Instr. lib. use; 32. Media srvs.; 33. Micro.; 34. Netwks./Coop.; 35. Persnl.; 36. PR; 37. Publshg.; 38. Recs. mgt.; 39. Ref. srvs.; 40. Repro.; 41. Resrch.; 42. Review.; 43. Secur.; 44. Serials; 45. Spec. col.; 46. Tech. srvs.; 47. Trustees/Bds.; 48. YA srvs.; 49. (other).

Univ./MA Inst. of Tech., Cambridge Proj., 1971–72; Staff Info. Sci., EDUCOM, 1968–70; Info. Spec., Bolt, Beranek, and Newman, 1967–68; Comp. Prog., Honeywell E.D.P., 1963–67. **Educ.:** Boston Univ., 1961, AB (Soclgy.); Simmons Coll., 1969, MS (LS); Boston Univ., 1970, MS (Comm. Resrch.); Harvard Bus. Sch., 1970–71, (Syst.); Boston Univ., 1980, PhD (Info. Sci.). **Orgs.:** ASIS: Info. Anal. and Eval. Spec. Interest Grp. (Ch., 1979). Socty. for the Soc. Std. of Sci. Assn. for Comp. Mach. **Activities:** 12, 14-Consult.; 24, 41, 49-Comp.-based systs.; 56, 91, 95-Comm. resrch. **Addr.:** 314 Oakland St., Wellesley Hills, MA 02181.

Ferguson, Stephen (My. 27, 1947, Camden, NJ) Cur. of Rare Bks., Princeton Univ. Lib., 1975–; Libn., Scottish Rite Musm., Lexington, MA, 1974–75; Spec. Consult., John Hay Lib., Brown Univ., 1974, Asst. Biblgphr., John Carter Brown Lib., 1970–74. **Educ.:** Bowdoin Coll., 1965–69, AB (Phil.); Rutgers Univ., 1976–78, MLS; Brown Univ., 1969–70, Relig. Std. **Orgs.:** ALA: ACRL/Rare Bks. and Mss. Sect. (Secy., 1980–81). Bibl. Socty. of Amer. Frnds. of the Princeton Univ. Lib.: Treas. (1978–). **Honors:** Phi Beta Kappa, 1969. **Pubns.:** "The Codigo Brasiliense...," *Inter-Amer. Review of Bibl.* (Ap. 1974). **Activities:** 1; 45; 55, 57 **Addr.:** Princeton University Library, Princeton, NJ 08540.

Fern, Alan M. (O. 19, 1930, Detroit, MI) Dir. for Spec. Cols., Lib. of Congs., 1978–, Dir., Resrch. Dept., 1976–78, Chief, Prints and Photographs Div., 1973–76, Asst. Chief, 1964–73. **Educ.:** Univ. of Chicago, 1948–50, BA (Gen. Educ.), 1950–60, MA, PhD (Art Hist.); Courtauld Inst., Univ. of London, Eng., 1954–55, Fulbright Fellow. **Orgs.:** Grolier Club. Amer. Antiq. Socty. Baltimore Bibliophiles. DC LA. Coll. Art Assn. Print Cncl. of Amer.: Pres. (1969–71). **Honors:** Belgian Gvt., Chevalier - Ordre de La Couronne, 1980. **Pubns.:** Jt. auth., *Revolutionary Soviet Film Posters* (1974); *Leonard Baskin* (1970); *Word and Image* (1969); jt. auth., *Art Nouveau* (1960); *A Note on the Eragny Press* (1957); various articles. **Addr.:** Special Collections, Research Services, Library of Congress, Washington, DC 20540.

Fern, Lois (O. 2, 1934, Detroit, MI) Freelnc. Biblgphr., Ed., Tchr., 1972–; Ref. Libn., US Info. Agency, 1963–71; Asst. Ref. Libn., Univ. of Chicago Lib., 1959–61; Asst. Managing Ed., *Jnl. of Gen. Educ.*, Univ. of Chicago Press, 1956–59. **Educ.:** Univ. of Chicago, 1951–54, BA (Gen. Std.), 1956–61, MALS. **Orgs.:** DC LA: Prog. Com. (Ch., 1967–68); Bd. of Dirs. (1968–70); Ref. RT (Coord., 1969–73). ALA: Subj. Spec. Sect. (Secy., 1967–70). Fed. Lib. Com.: Task Force on Pub. Rel. (Ch., 1968–72). Frdm. to Read Fndn. Amer. Cvl. Liberties Un. **Honors:** US Info. Agency, Merit. Hon. Awd., 1967. **Pubns.:** "On Foreign Soil; Some Embassy Libraries of Washington," *DC Libs.* (Win. 1970). **Activities:** 1, 4; 26, 39, 41; 54, 55, 92 **Addr.:** 3605 Raymond St., Chevy Chase, MD 20015.

Fernald, Anne Conway (My. 28, 1951, Brooklyn, NY) Dir. of HARFAX Databases, Harper & Row Publishers, Inc., 1980; Head, Resrch. Dept., Warner Eddison Associates Inc., 1977–80; Managing Dir., Select Press Bk. Srv., 1976–77; Dir. of Approval Prog., Yankee Book Peddler, Inc 1976; Catlgr., Univ. of MA, 1974–76. **Educ.:** SUNY, Plattsburgh, 1969–72, BA (Bhvl. Sci.); Columbia Univ., 1973, MSLS; Univ. of NH, 1976–77, Bus. Admin. **Orgs.:** ALA: ACRL, New Eng. Chap. (Secy.-Treas., 1975–77). **Activities:** 1; 15, 24, 41; 51, 56, 59 **Addr.:** 59 Lakewood Rd., South Weymouth, MA 02190.

Fernández-Caballero, Carlos (F. 24, 1937, Minas, Paraguay) Dir., Univ. of PA, Natl. EMS Info. Clearinghouse, 1973–78; Prof., LS, Natl. Univ. of Asuncion, 1971–73; Supvsr., Tech. Srvs., Prince William Cnty. (VA) Pub. Lib. 1969–71. **Educ.:** Natl. Univ. of Cordoba, Argentina, 1961–63, Dipl. (LS); Syracuse Univ., 1967–68, MS (LS). **Orgs.:** SALALM. Asociación de Bibtcr. Graduados de la República Argentina. Asociación de Bibtcr. del Paraguay. Latin Amer. Std. Assn. Inst. de Ling. Guaraní del Paraguay. Asociación de Prof. de Lengua Guaraní del Paraguay. **Honors:** Phi Delta Kappa. **Pubns.:** *The Paraguayan Bibliography*, (1970–75). **Activities:** 1, 12; 17, 30, 41; 54, 63, 80, 92 **Addr.:** 246 West Upsal St. #F-403, Philadelphia, PA 19119.

Fernandez-Caballero, Marianne (O. 11, 1946, Washington, DC) Catlgr., Temple Univ., 1975–; Supvsr. of Reg. Photocopy and TWX, Coll. of Physicians of Philadelphia, 1973–75; Libn., Amer. Sch. of Asuncion, 1971–73; Catlgr., Lib. of Congs. Shared Cat. Div., 1968–71. **Educ.:** Mary Washington Coll., 1964–68, BA (Pre-Frgn. Srv.); Drexel Univ., 1973–75, MS (LS). **Orgs.:** ALA. SALALM. **Honors:** Alpha Phi Sigma, Phi Sigma Iota, Pi Gamma Mu; Beta Phi Mu. **Pubns.:** "Problemas en la Biblioteca de un Colegio Bilingue," *Bibliotecologia y Doc. Paraguaya* (1972); "Libraries in Paraguay," *SALALM Nsltr.* (Ja. 75). **Activities:** 1; 20, 25, 46; 54, 57, 92 **Addr.:** 246 West Upsal St. #F-403, Philadelphia, PA 19119.

Fernando, Sriani (Jl. 26, 1940, Colombo, Sri Lanka) Head, Chld. Dept., W. Vancouver Meml. Lib., 1978–, Libn., 1975–78. **Educ.:** Univ. of Ceylon, 1959–63, BA (Eng.); Univ. of BC, 1973–75, MLS. **Orgs.:** Can. LA: Bk. of the Yr. for Chld. Com. (1979–83). Can. Assn. of Chld. Libns.: Secy./Treas. (1978–79). BC LA; Pac. NW LA: BC Rep. for Young Readrs. Choice Awd. **Pubns.:** Reviews. **Activities:** 9; 15, 17, 21 **Addr.:** West Vancouver Memorial Library, 1950 Marine Dr., West Vancouver, BC V7V 1J8 Canada.

Ferrall, J. Eleanor (Ja. 11, 1925, Lima, OH) Ref. Libn., AZ State Univ., 1969–; Head, Tech. Srvs., Scottsdale Pub. Lib., 1963–69. **Educ.:** Heidelberg Coll., 1943–47, AB (Eng.); AZ State Univ., 1970–73, MA (Educ.). **Orgs.:** AZ LA: Ch., AZ Highways 50 Year Indexing Com. SWLA: PreConf. Plng. Com. (1976). **Activities:** 1; 15, 39, 41; 92 **Addr.:** University Library, Arizona State University, Tempe, AZ 85281.

Ferrall, Rebecca Tahyi (O. 18, 1948, Zanesville, OH) Head of Tech. Srvs., Fed. Bur. of Investigation Acad. Lib., 1977–; Ref. Libn., Popltn. Ref. Bur., 1977; Asst. to Lib. Dir., Tidewater Comnty. Coll., 1973–76. **Educ.:** Wittenberg Univ., 1966–70, BA (Eng. and Hist.), Catholic Univ., 1976–77, MLS; SUNY, Binghamton, 1970–71, (Eng. Lit), Univ. of Exeter, Exeter, England, 1969, (Eng. Lit). **Orgs.:** ALA. SLA. DC LA. WHCOLIS. Smithsonian Resident Assoc., Amer. Film Inst., Fed. Bur. of Investigation Acad. Ed. Bd. **Honors:** Beta Phi Mu Mem. 1977. **Pubns.:** "Effective Library Research" (slide-tape) (1978); Special Libraries Assn. *Reference Update 1980*, "Criminal Justice" (1980); "Arson Information: Who, What, Where," *FBI Law Enforcement Bulletin* (My. 1981). **Activities:** 4, 12; 17, 31, 46; 77, 92 **Addr.:** 2818 Cambridge Dr., Woodbridge, VA 22192.

Ferrell, Dorothy Anne (Perkins) (N. 6, 1914, Nicholasville, KY) Head cat. & class., Mary Baldwin Coll., 1960–; Libn., Covenant Presby. Church, 1962–; Libn., C. & O. Sch. of Nursing, Clifton Forge, VA, 1957–75; Libn., Clifton Forge HS, 1947–1960; Libn., Versailles HS, 1946–47. **Educ.:** Univ. of KY, 1933–37, AB (LS); George Peabody Coll., 1947–49, MA (LS); Univ. of VA, 1948, (AV). **Orgs.:** VA LA. SELA. ALA. Daughters of the Amer. Revolution. AAUW. Beta Sigma Phi Sorority. **Activities:** 1; 20, 31, 39; 56, 63 **Addr.:** 1001 Selma Blvd., Staunton, VA 24401.

Ferrier, Douglas M. (O. 12, 1943, Dallas, TX) Acq. Libn., Univ. of AR, Little Rock, 1979–; Spec. Col. Catlgr., Univ. of TX, Arlington, 1978–79; Asst. Univ. Archvst., 1975–78; Reg. Archvst., TX State Arch., 1973–75. **Educ.:** Univ. of TX, Austin, 1965–71, BA (Hist.); Univ. of TX, Arlington, 1971–72, MA (Hist./Arch.); N. TX State Univ., 1975–78, MLS. **Orgs.:** ALA. SAA: Reg. Act. Com. AR LA. Socty. of Southw. Archvsts.: Exec. Brd. **Pubns.:** Jt. auth., *Inventory of County Records–Delta County Courthouse* (1975); Jt. auth., *Inventory of County Records–Coleman County Courthouse* (1975); *Inventory of County Records–Camp County Courthouse*, (1975); *Inventory of County Records–Rains County Courthouse*, (1975). *Inventory of County Record-Hood County Courthouse*, (1974). **Activities:** 1, 2; 15, 18, 44 **Addr.:** 625 Skyline Dr., North Little Rock, AR 72116.

Ferstl, Kenneth Leon (My. 31, 1940, Richland Center, WI) Asst. Prof., Sch. of Lib. & Info. Sci., N. TX State Univ., 1978–, Lect., 1975–78; Assoc. Instr., Grad. Lib. Sch., IN Univ., 1973–74; Instr., N. TX State Univ., 1969–72; Head, Tech. Srvs. Div., Asst. Dir., Oshkosh (WI) Pub. Lib., 1967–69; Instr., Lib. Sch., Univ. of WI 1965–67. **Educ.:** N. TX State Univ., 1959–63, BMsc. (Msc.); Univ. of WI, 1964–66, MS in LS, IN Univ., 1972–75, PhD (LS). **Orgs.:** ALA: PLA, Human Srvs. Com. (1977–79); RASD, Com. on Lib. Srvs. to an Aging Popltn. (Ch., 1977–80). Cath. LA: Parish Cmnty. Lib. Sect., Adv. Bd., (1979–81). CLENE: Pubn. Com. (1978–80). TX LA: Cont. Educ. Com. (Ch., 1979–80); Cncl. (1979–80). Adult Educ. Assn. of the USA. Natl. Cncl. on the Aging. Natl. Book Leag. Grntlgcl. Socty. **Honors:** Beta Phi Mu. **Pubns.:** *Public Librarians and Service to the Aging: A Study of Attitudes* (1978); "Indiana Libraries and Services to the Elderly...." *Focus on IN Libs.*, (Win. 1974); "On Serving Older Americans: Some Perspectives for Librarians." *Focus on IN Libs.*, (Spr.-Sum. 1975); *TX Lib. Jnl.*, Ed. (1979–); "Public Librarian Support for the 'Library's Responsibility to the Aging'." *Lib. Sch. Review*, (1979); Other articles. **Activities:** 9, 11; 16, 20, 25; 50, 72, 95-Grntlgy. **Addr.:** P.O. Box 13256, North Texas State University, Denton, TX 76203.

Fesenmaier, Stephen Lee (D. 1, 1949, Minneapolis, MN) Head, Film Srvs., WV Lib. Comsn., 1978–; Ch. Emeritus, Univ. Film Socty., Univ. of MN, 1975–78, Ch., 1972–75; Info. Spec., Tela-Ad Mfr. Co. 1977–78. **Educ.:** Univ. of MN, 1968–71, BA magna cum laude (Phil.), 1977–78, MALS; Cert. (Univ.-Cmnty. Video), 1978. **Orgs.:** WV LA: Int. Frdm. Com. (1978–79). Educ. Film LA. WV Zoopraxographers. Amer. Film Inst. Appalachian Literary Leag. **Pubns.:** "Films on West Virginia and Appalachia," *Goldenseal* (Spr. 1979); "Mindscape," Clmn. in *Appalachian Illustrated Intelligencer* (Fall 1979); "Filmmaking in West Virginia," *WV Art News* (Fall 1979); "Films in the Mountains," *Film Lib. Qtly* (Sum. 1980); "The Filmmaker as 'Anti-Therapist'," *Film/Psychology Review* (Sum./Fall 1980). Various film programmings. **Activities:** 9, 13; 15, 32, 46; 55, 67, 74 **Addr.:** 3108 Virginia Ave. S.E., Charleston, WV 25304.

Fessenden, Ann T. (O. 4, 1951, Norman, OK) Tech. Srvs. Libn., Univ. of MS Law Lib., 1978–. **Educ.:** Univ. of OK, 1969–74, BA (Jnlsm.), 1975–77, MLS; Univ. of MS, 1979– (Law). **Orgs.:** AALL: Dupl. Exch. Com. (1979–). Southeast. Assn. of Law Libs.: Nsltr. Com. (1979–). MS LA: Int. Frdm. Com. (1981–). Amer. Bar Assn.: Student Div. **Pubns.:** *Guide to Basic Oklahoma Legal Research* (1978); "S.E.A.L.L. Briefs," *Southeast. Law Libn.* (1979–). **Activities:** 1, 12; 20, 44, 46; 77 **Addr.:** University of Mississippi Law School Library, University, MS 38677.

Fetros, John G. (Ag. 19, 1932, Billings, MT) Head of Acq., San Francisco Pub. Lib., 1974–, Head of Gen. Ref., 1972–74, Ref. Libn., Hist. Dept., 1969–72, Ref. Libn., Sci. Dept., 1964–69. **Educ.:** Univ. of CA, Berkeley, 1950–54, BS (Bus.); Univ. of South. CA, 1963–64, MLS. **Orgs.:** West. Assn. of Map Libs. **Pubns.:** *Dictionary of Factual and Fictional Riders and Their Horses* (1979); *This Day in Sports* (1974); "State and Local Atlases," *Bltn., West. Assn. Map Libs.* (Mr. 1972); "Cooperative Picture Searching and Collection Development", *Spec. Libs.* (My./Je. 1971); "Observations on Biographical Assignments," *The Soc. Std.* (Mr. 1973); other articles. **Activities:** 9; 15, 16, 17; 55, 59, 70 **Addr.:** 3220 24th St., Sacramento, CA 95818.

Fetzer, Mary Kathleen (Jl. 6, 1942, Spring Valley, IL) Docum. Libn., Rutgers Univ., 1969–. **Educ.:** IL State Univ., 1960–64, BA (Eng.); Rutgers Univ., 1969–70, MLS, 1973–76, MA (Pol. Sci.). **Orgs.:** ALA: GODORT, Intl. Docum. Task Force, Work Grp. on Bibl. Control of IGO Documtn. (Ch., 1979–). Gvt. Docum. Assn. of NJ: Intl. & Foreign Docum. Task Force (Ch., 1978–). **Pubns.:** *United Nations Documents and Publications: A Research Guide*, (1976). **Activities:** 1; 29, 39; 78, 92 **Addr.:** 501 Lindsley Dr., 2F, Morristown, NJ 07960.

Feuer, Sylvia (Ja. 22, 1917, New York, NY) Extramural Coord., Cleveland Hlth. Sci. Lib., 1969–. **Educ.:** West. Rsv. Univ., 1935–39, BA (Soclgy.); Case West. Rsv. Univ., Sch. of LS, 1966–69. **Orgs.:** Med. LA: Hosp. Lib. Sect., PR Com. (1978–); Hosp. Lib. Impact Com. (1976–78); Rittenhse. Awds. Com. (1976–79); N.E. OH Chap. (Ch., 1973–74); Midwest Reg. Grp. **Honors:** Med. LA, Ida and George Elliot Awd., 1978; Cleveland Hlth. Sci. Lib., Apprec. Awd., 1978; Beta Phi Mu. **Pubns.:** "The Circuit Rider Librarian," *Bltn. of the Med. LA* (1977); *Health-Related Agencies: A Directory of Selected Agencies Serving the Greater Cleveland Area* (1978). **Activities:** 1, 12; 24, 25, 27 **Addr.:** Allen Memorial Library, 11000 Euclid Ave., Cleveland, OH 44106.

Few, John E. (S. 9, 1942, San Diego, CA) Ref. Libn., City Coll. of San Francisco; Libn., Hassard, Bonnington, Rogers and Huber; Fac., Sch. of Lib. and Info. Std., Univ. of CA, Berkeley. **Educ.:** Univ. of San Francisco, 1969, BS (Theo.); Rosary Coll., 1970–71, MALS. **Orgs.:** AALL. North. CA Assn. of Law Libns. Private Law LA. Flwshp. of Reconciliation. Frnds. of Calligraphy. **Addr.:** Hassard, Bonnington, Rogers & Huber, 44 Montgomery St., San Francisco, CA 94104.

Feye-Stukas, Janice (N. 2, 1943, Columbus, NE) Lib. Spec., Consult., Ofc. of Pub. Libs. and Interlib. Coop., MN Dept. of Educ., 1976–; Branch Head, Hennepin Cnty. (MN) Lib., 1973–76; Branch Head, Minneapolis Pub. Lib. and Info. Ctr., 1970–73; Asst. Branch Libn., Kansas City Pub. Lib., 1969–70; Libn. I, Denver Pub. Lib., 1966–67. **Educ.:** Midland Lutheran Coll., Fremont, NE, 1961–65, BA (Eng. Lit.); Univ. of Denver, 1965–66, MALS. **Orgs.:** ALA: Awds. Com. (Ch., 1979–82); LAMA, Stats. for State Lib. Agencies Com. (Ch., 1978–80); ASCLA, Gen. Consults. Discuss. Grp. (Ch., 1977–78); PLA, Nom. Com. (1979–80); SRRT; various other coms. MN LA: Ref. and Adult Srvs. (Ch., 1974–75). Amer. Natl. Stans. Inst.: Z39.7 Subcom. on Stans. for Lib. Stats. (1977–). **Pubns.:** Jt. ed., *Minnesota Public Library Trustees Handbook* (1977). **Activities:** 9, 13; 17, 24, 34 **Addr.:** 301 Hanover Bldg., 480 Cedar St., St. Paul, MN 55101.

Fichtenau, Lane E. (Ja. 30, 1936, Eugene, OR) Asst. Law Libn., Adams-Pratt Oakland Cnty. Law Lib., 1977–, Tech. Srvs. Libn., 1975–76; Hum. Ref., FL State Univ. Lib., 1965–66; Hum. Ref., Univ. of WA Lib., 1960–64. **Educ.:** Lewis and Clark, 1954–58, BA (Span.), Univ. of WA, 1958–60, MLS; AALL Certified Law Libn., 1978. **Orgs.:** OH Reg. Assn. Law Libs.: Secy. (1979–80); VP/Pres. Elect (1980–81). MI Assn. Law Libs.: PR Ch. (1979–80). AALL. **Activities:** 4, 9; 20, 39; 77 **Addr.:** Adams-Pratt Oakland County Law Library, Oakland County Court House, 1200 North Telegraph Rd., Pontiac, MI 48053.

Fick, John Shaffer (S. 18, 1950, Jefferson City, MO) Asst. Dir., Acad. Support Ctr., Univ. of MO-Columbia, 1974–, Interim Dir., 1978–80, Asst. Ed., 1973–74. **Educ.:** Univ. of MO, 1968–72, BS (Educ.), 1974–76, MEd (Higher and Adult Educ.); NCATE, 1972, Accredited Life Cert. (Eng. and Jnlsm.). **Orgs.:** Cnsrtm. of Univ. Film Ctr.: Sel. and Eval. Com. (1973–). MO AECT: Treas. (1979–); Mem. Ch. (1980–); Student 8mm Film Fest. (Co-Ch., 1979). EFLA. AECT: Conv. Eval. (1978). Natl. Cncl. of Tchrs. of Eng. **Honors:** Phi Delta Kappa. **Pubns.:** "Educational Media Leadership Conference," *MO Jnl. of Instr.* (Win. 1978); contrib., *Educational Film Locator* (1978, 1980); various sps. **Activities:** 5, 10; 15, 17, 20; 50, 67 **Addr.:** University of Missouri-Columbia, Academic Support Center, 505 E. Stewart Rd., Columbia, MO 65211.

Ficke, Eleanore R. (N. 30, 1937, Milford, NE) Exec. Dir., CLENE, Inc., 1979–; Ref. Libn. II, Univ. Lib., George Washington Univ., 1977–79; Sci. Ref. Libn., Fenwick Lib., George Mason

Special Subjects/Services: 50. Adult educ.; 51. Advert./Mktg.; 52. Aerosp.; 53. Agric.; 54. Area std.; 55. Arts/Hum.; 56. Autom.; 57. Bibl./Prtg.; 58. Bio. sci.; 59. Bus./Fin.; 60. Chem.; 61. Copyrt.; 62. Documtn.; 63. Educ.; 64. Engin.; 65. Env.; 66. Eth. grps.; 67. Film; 68. Food/Nutr.; 69. Geneal.; 70. Geo.; 71. Geol.; 72. Handcpd.; 73. Hist.; 74. Int. frdm.; 75. Info. sci.; 76. Insr.; 77. Law; 78. Legis.; 79. Math./Comp. sci.; 80. Med.; 81. Metals; 82. Nat. resrcs.; 83. Newsp.; 84. Nuc. sci.; 85. Oral hist.; 86. Petr./Energy; 87. Pharm.; 88. Phys./Astr./Math.; 89. Readg.; 90. Relig.; 91. Sci./Tech.; 92. Soc. sci.; 93. Telecom.; 94. Transp.; 95. (other).

Univ., 1974–77; Lib. Tech., Career Conditional, US Geol. Srvy. Lib., Denver, 1972–74. **Educ.:** NE Wesleyan Univ., 1954–60, BA (Eng.); Univ. of Denver, 1971–74, MALS; George Washington Univ., 1977–81, MA. **Orgs.:** AAAS: Comp. and Comm. Sect. ALA: RASD, Prof. Dev. Com. (Ch., 1979–81; ACRL. DC LA: Mem. Com. (Ch., 1977–78). VA LA: Cont. Educ. Com. (1974–75). Various other orgs. **Honors:** Beta Phi Mu, International Library Science Honor Society Membership. **Pubns.:** A Study of Microfiche as an Alternative to the Reserve Room Function ERIC ED 114 045 1974; Ficke, Eleanore R., and Ficke, John F., 1977, Ice on rivers and lakes–a bibliographic essay: U.S. Geological Survey Report of Water Resources Invest. 77–95, 176 p. 1977; A Walking Tour of The University Library, George Washington University 1978. **Activities:** 1, 3; 25, 31, 39; 50, 63, 70 **Addr.:** 11310 Fairway Ct., Reston, VA 22090.

Fidler, Leah Josephine (O. 23, 1932, Glenville, WV) Acq. Libn., Marshall Univ., 1969–, Biblgphr., 1967–69, Asst. Catlgr., 1964–67, Instr., Dept. of LS, 1962–64; Head Libn., Alderson-Broaddus Coll., 1957–62; Asst. Libn., Glenville State Coll., 1955–57; Libn., Tygart Valley HS, 1954–55. **Educ.:** Glenville State Coll., Glenville, WV, 1950–54, AB (Educ.); IN Univ., 1960, MLS. **Orgs.:** WV LA: Pres. (1972–73); various coms. SELA: Resrcs. and Tech. Srvs. Libs. (secy., 1976–78); Spec. Col. Compendium Proj. (1977–78). ALA. AAUP. AAUW. Delta Kappa Gamma. Cabell Wayne Hist. Socty. Various other orgs. **Honors:** Beta Phi Mu, 1960; WV LA, Outstan. and Dedicated Srv. to Libs. and Libnshp., 1976. **Pubns.:** "Special Collections in Libraries of West Virginia," *Special Collections in Libraries of the Southeast* (1978). **Activities:** 1; 15, 44, 46; 63 **Addr.:** 1228 7th St., Huntington, WV 25701.

Fidoten, Robert Earl (O. 21, 1927, New York, NY) Dir., Info. Syst. Glass Grp., PPG Industries, 1971–; Mgr., Resrch. Staff Srvs., 1964–71; Chief Libn., Republic Aviation Corp., 1956–64; Chief Libn., Martin Marietta Corp., 1956–56. **Educ.:** NY Univ., 1944–49, BA; Univ. of Pittsburgh, 1965–71, PhD (Info. Sci.); Harvard Univ., 1950–52 (Educ.); Pratt Inst., 1949–50, BLS. **Orgs.:** Intl. Comsn. on Glass: Ch., Sub-Com. Docu. and Info. Retrieval (1973–77). SLA: Pres., Pittsburgh Chap.; Ch., Annual Conf. (1973). ASIS: Ch., Pittsburgh Chap. Civil Srvs. Comsn., Township of O'Hara: Secy. (1979–). **Honors:** Beta Phi Mu. **Pubns.:** "The Impact of Computer and Automation on the Management of Engineering Index, Inc.," (1971); "Current Awareness," *Ency. of Lib. and Info. Sci.* (1970). **Activities:** 12; 36; 56, 75 **Addr.:** Information Systems, Glass Group, PPG Industries, One Gateway Center, Pittsburgh, PA 15222.

Field, Carolyn Wicker (N. 5, 1916, Melrose MA) Coord., Ofc. of Work with Chld., Free Lib. of Philadelphia, 1953–; Cnty. Libn., New Castle Cnty. Free Lib., Wilmington, DE, 1950–53, Head of Chld. Work, Wilmington Inst. Free Lib., 1946–50, Recreation Worker, Amer. Red Cross, Eng., 1944–45; Field Worker, Cuyahoga Cnty. Lib., 1943–44; Instr., Sch. of LS, Simmons Coll., 1942–43; Hostess Libn., Boston YMCA, 1940–42; Chld. Libn., New York Pub. Lib., 1938–40. **Educ.:** Simmons Coll., 1934–38 BS (Lib Sci). **Orgs.:** ALA: Child. Services Division, (Pres., 1959–60); Com. on Liaison With Natl. Org. Serving the Child (Ch., 1967–74); Com. on Natl. Plng. For Spec. Col. (Ch., 1964–70). Newbery Caldecott Study Com. (Ch.); Radio and TV Com. PA LA: Pres. (1970–71). Natl. Cncl. of Tchrs. of Eng.: Comsn. on Reading (1970–73); Com. on Censorship and Bias in the Elem. Sch. (1973–76). Philadelphia Chld. Reading RT, Ch. (1965–). **Honors:** Grolier Socty. Inc., Awd., 1963; Disting. Daughter of PA, 1974; Simmons Coll. Grad. Sch. of LS, Alum. Achiev. Awd., 1975; B.A. Bergman Awd., 1979. **Pubns.:** *Subject Collections in Children's Literature*, (1969); Various articles. **Activities:** 9, 11; 21, 36, 45; 72, 74, 85 **Addr.:** 1A Manheim Gardens, Philadelphia, PA 19144.

Field, Jean (Jl. 12, 1936, Boston, MA) Mgr., Info. and Lib. Srvs., Honeywell Info. Syst. Inc., 1971–, Software Cntrl. and Cust. Support Spec., 1970–71; Dept. Supvsr., Acq. Cat. Libn., GTE-Sylvania, 1968–70; Asst. Engin. Libn., MA Inst. of Tech., 1966–68. **Educ.:** Wellesley Coll., 1954–58, BA (Biblical Hist.); Simmons Coll., 1960–62, MSLS. **Orgs.:** SLA. Assn. for Info. Mgrs. Assn. for Info. Sci. Indus. Tech. Info. Mgrs.' Grp.: Mgt. Com. (1979–80). Various other orgs. Assn. for Comp. Mach. Inst. for Electrical and Electronics Engins. **Pubns.:** "Marketing Information Services in Industry," Natl. Info. Conf. and Exposition (1979). **Activities:** 12; 17, 24, 49-Documtn. cntrl.; 56, 59, 93 **Addr.:** Information and Library Services, MS 423, Honeywell Information Systems Inc., 200 Smith St., Waltham, MA 02154.

Field, Judith J. (S. 30, 1939, Bucyrus, OH) Head, Gen. Ref. Dept., Flint Pub. Lib., 1972–; Resrch. Assoc., Univ. of MI Inst. for Intl. Cmrce., 1971–72, Head Libn., 1969–71; Assoc. Libn., Univ. of MI Grad. Sch. of Bus. Admin., 1966–69; Asst. Libn., Univ. of MI Nat. Sci. Lib., 1965–66; Lib. Mgr., West. Electric/Bell Telephone Labs., 1962–65. **Educ.:** Univ. of MI, 1961, BBA (Bus. Adm.), 1963, AMS (LS), 1969, MBA (Bus. Adm.). **Orgs.:** CLENE: Bd. of Dir. (1979–82). SLA: Educ. Com. (1977–80, Ch. 1977–78); Rep. to CLENE (1977–80); Ch., Mem. Com., Lib. Mgt. Div., (1977–79); Bd. of Dir. (1975–77); Ch., Bus. & Finance Div. (1972–74). **Honors:** SLA, John Cotton Dana Lect., 1974. **Pubns.:** *Bibliography of International Finance* (1971). **Activities:** 9; 17 **Addr.:** General Reference Dept., Flint Public Library, Flint, MI 48502.

Field, Sr. Mary (Ja. 17, 1918, Wisconsin Dells WI) Two-year leave of absence, 1981–; Chief Libn., Rosary Coll., 1964–81, Ref. Libn., 1960–64, Tchr. and Libn., Sinsinawa Dominican HS Libs., 1945–60. **Educ.:** Rosary Coll., 1937–39, BA; Univ. of WI, 1939–40, MA; Rosary Coll., 1955–60, MALS. **Orgs.:** Cath. LA: Pubn. Com. (Ch., 1979–81); Local unit (Sect., 1962–63). Pvt. Acad. Libs. of IL: Secy. and Treas. (1979–80). ALA. IL LA. **Honors:** Kappa Delta Pi, (1940). **Activities:** 1; 15, 17, 35; 90, 92 **Addr.:** Rosary College Library, 7900 West Division St., River Forest, IL 60305.

Field, Oliver Thoburn (N. 3, 1912, Aberdeen, WA) Assoc. Prof., Univ. of Denver Grad. Sch. of Libnshp. and Info. Mgt., 1969–; Asst. Prof., Univ. of IL Grad. Sch. of Lib. Sci., 1965–69; Chief, Tech. Srvs. Div., Air Univ. Lib. Maxwell Air Force Base, 1958–65; Chief, Cat. Br., 1954–58; Head, Automotive Hist. Dept., Detroit Pub. Lib., 1953–54; Lib. Consult. U.S. Info. Ctrs., Bonn, 1952–53; Chief, Tech. Srvs. U.S. High Commission for Germany, 1948–52; Chief, Tech. Srvs. Assoc. Coll. of Upper NY, Plattsburgh, 1947–48; various other positions in ref. **Educ.:** Reed Coll., 1932–35, BA (Lit.); Univ. of WA, 1935–37, BA; Columbia Univ., 1969, DLS. **Orgs.:** ALA: Ch., Subj. Heading Com. (1961–62); Ch., Dewey Awd. Com. (1967–68); Desc. Cat. Com. (1967–72, 1974–78). **Honors:** Beta Phi Mu, 1969. **Pubns.:** Contrib., *America Houses, A Study of the U.S. Information Center Program in Germany* (1953); Contrib. *American Peoples Encyclopedia* (1957). **Activities:** 11; 17, 20, 29 **Addr.:** Graduate School of Librarianship and Information Management, University of Denver, Denver, CO 80210.

Fielders, Margaret Grant (N. 22, 1914, Philadelphia, PA) Prof. of LS, Ch. of LS Dept., OH Dominican Coll., 1955–; Libn., La Salle Coll. Prep, La Salle Coll., 1947–54; Med., Hosp., Film Libn., US Army, 1942–45; Chld. Libn., 1938–42, Wyomissing Pub. Lib., 1945–46. **Educ.:** PA State Coll. at Kutztown, 1931–35, BS (LS, Eng., Educ.); Temple Univ., 1950–51 (Hist. Educ.); Drexel Univ., 1946–47, BS (LS); Bread Loaf Sch. of Eng., Middlebury, VT, 1958–62, MA (Eng.), 1971–74, MLitt; St. John's Coll., Oxford Univ., 1978, (Anglo-Irish Lit.). **Orgs.:** ALA. Cath. LA: Adv. Bd. (1955–). OH LA: Bd. of Dir. (1974–77); Archvst. (1974–); OH Educ. Lib. Media Assn. Rocky Fork-Headley Hunt; OH Dominican Coll.: (Honors Com. Ch., 1960–72). **Honors:** OH Dominican Coll., Fac. Dev. Grants, 1975–78. **Pubns.:** "The Honors Program at Ohio Dominican," *Natl Honors Review* (1970); Guest Ed., *Protean Qtly.* (D. 1972); *Restoration of Holy Cross Abbey* Super-8 mm film/tape (1974); *Simple Processing of library materials* slide/tape (1975); *The Electronic Library: OCLC and Ohio Dominican College* Videotape (1977); other articles. **Activities:** 11; 24, 25, 26; 50, 63, 75 **Addr.:** 6079 Clark State Rd., Columbus, OH 43230.

Fielding, Kenneth Richard (D. 6, 1938, Black River, NY) Asst. Lib. Dir., Steele Meml. Lib., 1968–; Dir., East Rochester Pub. Lib., 1967–68; Adult Srvs. Libn., Jervis Lib., Rome, NY, 1964–67, Gen. Srvs. Libn., 1963–64. **Educ.:** Univ. of WI, 1960–63, BA Honors (Eng.); Syracuse Univ., 1963–65, MSLS. **Orgs.:** ALA: Video srvs. (1977–). Toastmasters Intl. **Pubns.:** "Video and the Library–An Uncertain Collaboration," *Educ. and Indus. TV* (Ap. 1981). "How to Prevent Censorship: Cultivate Local Politicians," *Amer. Libs.* (N. 1976); "A Co-operative Effort: A Library and a Cable Station Produce TV Shows," *Cable Libs.* (Ag. 1978); various videotapes. **Activities:** 9; 17, 28, 32; 55, 66, 86 **Addr.:** Steele Memorial Library, One Library Plz., Elmira, NY 14901.

Fields, Dorothy J. (D. 31, 1942, Miami, FL) Fndr., Chief Archvst., Black Arch., Hist. and Resrch. Fndn. of S. FL, Inc, 1977–; Tchr., Sch. Libn., Dade Cnty. Pub. Sch., 1964. **Educ.:** Spelman Coll., 1960–64, BA (Educ.); C.W. Post Coll., 1965, Cert. (LS); Univ. of North. CO, 1973–74, MA (Curric. and Instr.); Emory Univ., 1977, Cert. (Arch. Admin.). **Orgs.:** SAA: Eth. Heritage Com. (1977–78); Women's Caucus (1977–78). Hist. Assn. of South. FL. FL Hist. Socty. **Honors:** Beta Tau Zeta Chap., Zeta Phi Beta Sorority, Inc, Humanitarian of the Yr., 1978. **Pubns.:** *Julia's Daughters, A History of Women in Miami, Florida* (1980). **Activities:** 2; 15, 16, 41; 62, 66, 86 **Addr.:** Black Archives, History & Research Foundation of South Florida, Inc., 5400 N.W. 22nd Ave., Miami, FL 33142.

Fifer, Susan Melinda (Ja. 23, 1948, Stockton, CA) Asst. Libn., Natl. Geographic Socty., 1980–; Circ. Libn., 1975–80; Resrch., Logistics Mgt. Inst., 1971–73; Tchr., Colorado Springs, CO, 1970–71. **Educ.:** Univ. of NE, 1966–70, BS (Eng.); Univ. of MD, 1974, MLS; Cath. Univ.; Geo. Washington Univ. **Orgs.:** ALA. SLA: Geo. and Map Div., Ch. (1978), Vice-Ch. (1977). DC LA: Secy. (1981–83); Mem. Com. (1976). Smithsonian Assoc. AAUW. **Honors:** Beta Phi Mu. **Activities:** 1, 12; 22, 34, 36; 54, 70, 83 **Addr.:** 501 Slaters Ln. 916, Alexandria, VA 22314.

Figueras, Myriam (D. 12, 1928, Camaguey, Cuba) Actg. Chief, Columbus Meml. Lib., Org. of Amer. States, 1979–, Head Ref. Libn., 1976–78, Head Indxr., Serial Pubn. Sect., 1972–75, Indxr. OAS Docum., 1961–71. **Educ.:** Univ. of Havana, 1946–50, PhD, 1959–60, LS; Catholic Univ., 1962–67, MLS. **Orgs.:** ALA. DC LA. Corcoran Gallery of Art. Smithsonian Inst. **Activities:** 14-Intl. org.; 22, 39; 54, 95-Latin Amer. **Addr.:** 5550 Columbia Pike, Apt. 293, Arlington, VA 22204.

Fikes, Robert, Jr. (Je. 18, 1949, Birmingham, AL) Sr. Asst. Libn., San Diego State Univ., 1981–; Asst. Libn., San 1977-81; Instr., Univ. of VA, 1976–77; Tchg. Asst. in Hist., Univ. of MN, 1970–73. **Educ.:** Tuskegee Inst., 1967–70, BS, (Hist.); Univ. of MN, 1970–76, MA (Hist.), MALS, 1973–76, PhD Cand. (Hist.). **Orgs.:** NLA: Prof. Welfare Com. (1979–). CA LA: Palomar Chap. CA State Coll. and Univ. Libs. **Pubns.:** "Jose De Acosta's Window on the New World," *Américas* (Je.-Jl. 1978); "Military Recruitment in Subsaharan Africa," *Jnl. of Ethnic Std.* (Spr. 1978); "User Charges: A Debate in Search of a Premise," *News Notes of CA Libs.* (1978); numerous other articles and reviews on Afro-American and African hist. and lit. **Activities:** 1; 31, 39, 41; 66 **Addr.:** University Library, San Diego State University, San Diego, CA 92182.

Filion, Louise (D. 6, 1945, Montréal, PQ) Chief, Retrospective Natl. Bibl., Bibl. Natl. du PQ, 1978–; Dir., Télécat/Unicat, 1975–78, Catlgr., Official Pubns., 1969–75. **Educ.:** Univ. de Montréal, 1959–67, BA, 1967–69, BA (LS), 1972–74, MALS. **Orgs.:** ASTED. Corp. des Bibtcrs. Prof. du PQ: Com. de Discipline (1978–). Can. LA. **Pubns.:** *Class. des Pubns. Govt. du PQ* (1974); "La Bibliographie du Québec 1821–1967," *Bltn. Bibl. Natl. du PQ* (S. 1979); "Classification des Publications Gouvernementales du PQ," *Bltn. Bibl. Natl. du PQ* (1973). **Activities:** 13; 20, 34, 46; 56, 57, 75 **Addr.:** 48 Joyce #19, Outremont, Montréal, PQ H2V 1S6 Canada.

Filion, Paul-Emile, SJ. (Ag. 9, 1922, Montréal, PQ) Asst. Vice-Rector, Dir. of Libs., Concordia Univ., 1976–; Coord. of Lib. Syst., Univ. du PQ, 1971–76; Head Libn., Laurentian Univ., Sudbury, 1960–70; Instr. in LS, Univ. de Montréal, 1957–60; Head Libn., Jesuit Semy., Montréal, 1957–60; Dir., Sci. Lab., Tafari Makonnen Sec. Sch., Addis Ababa, Ethiopia, 1948–51. **Educ.:** Univ. de Montréal, 1948, BA; Jesuit Semy., 1949, Licn. (Phil.), 1958, Licn. (Theo.); Columbia Univ., 1957, MSc (LS). **Orgs.:** ASTED: 2nd VP (1970); Montreal Chap. (Pres., 1959). Can. LA: 2nd VP (1965–66). ALA: Com. on Accred. Visit. Team (1966–). Assn. of Univs. and Colls. of Can.: Lib. Com. (1974–78). Various other orgs. Société can. d'hist. orale. Assn. des écrivains canadiens: VP (1981–82). Corp. of Prof. Libns. of PQ, Pres. (1981–83). Natl. Lib. of Can.: Adv. Bd. (1981–84). **Honors:** Univ. of West. ON, LL.D. (Honoris causa), 1972; Univ. Laval, D.U.L. (Honoris causa), 1969; Gvt. of Can., Can. Medal, 1967. **Pubns.:** Ed., *CACUL Newsletter* (1963–71); "Finies les -thèques," *L'administration budgétaire des bibliothèques* (1972); "Biblo-Québec en l'an 2000," *Bltn. de l'ACBLF* (1969); "University Libraries before and after Williams," *Librarianship in Canada, 1946 to 1967* (1968); "Une enquête de bibliothèque universitaire," *Institut sur les enguêtes de bibliothèques* (1965). **Activities:** 1; 17 **Addr.:** Concordia University Library, 1455 de Maisonneune Blvd. W., Montreal, PQ H3G 1M8 Canada.

Filipak, Grace Markowitz (Je. 12, 1952, New York, NY) Sr. Resrch. Anal., Marsh and McLennan, Inc., 1980–, Resrch. Anal., 1977–80, Libn., 1976–77; Libn., MONY, 1975–76. **Educ.:** Queens Coll., 1970–74, BA, cum laude (Eng.), 1974–76, MLS; St. John's Univ., 1977. **Orgs.:** SLA: Adv. Cncl. (1977–78); Insr. Div. (Ch., 1977–78). Law Libn. Assn. of Grt. NY. Socty. of Insr. Resrch.: Resrch. Srcs. Com. (Vice-Ch., 1979–81). **Pubns.:** *Sources of Insurance Statistics* (1981); contrib., *Insurance Periodicals Index* (1977–81). **Activities:** 12; 38, 39, 41; 56, 59, 76 **Addr.:** Marsh & McLennan, Inc., 1221 Ave. of the Americas, National Statistical Group, New York, NY 10020.

Filstrup, E. Christian (My. 9, 1942, Hollywood, CA) Chief, Oriental Div., NY Pub. Lib., 1978–, First Asst., Oriental Div., 1975–78. **Educ.:** Haverford Coll., 1960–65, BA (Pol. Sci.); Harvard Univ., 1965–67, MA (Mid. East); Columbia Univ., 1973–74, MLS. **Orgs.:** Mid. East Libns. Assn.: Ed. (1978–). ALA: ACRL/Asian & African Sect. (Vice Ch./Ch. elect 1978–81). Mid. East Std. Assn. **Honors:** Phi Beta Kappa, 1965, Beta Phi Mu, 1974. **Pubns.:** "North Africa and the Middle East" in *American Book World Geography* (1979); "Islamic Cats in the Middle East", *Portland Review* (Fall 1979); "The Norths go South," *The State* (Ag. 1978); "The alphabet of things in the art of Walter Hatke," *World Order* (Fall 1977); Reviews. **Activities:** 1; 15, 35, 39; 90, 95-Middle East. **Addr.:** Oriental Division, New York Public Library, Fifth Ave. & 42d St., New York, NY 10018

Finch, C. Herbert (N. 8, 1931, Boise City, OK) Asst. Univ. Libn., Cornell Univ., 1972–; Archvst., Labor Mgt. Documen Ctr., NY State Sch. of Indus. and Labor Rel., 1970–76, Cur. Univ. Archvst., Col. of Reg. Hist. and Univ. Arch., 1967–72 Assoc. Arch., 1964–67; Fld. Rep., Univ. of KY Lib., 1961–64 **Educ.:** OK Bapt. Univ., 1953, BA; South. Bapt. Theo. Semy. 1957, BD; Univ. of KY, 1959, MA, 1965, PhD (Hist.). **Orgs.** Mss. Socty. ARL: Com. on Access to Mss. and Rare Bks. SAA Cncl. (1969–73); Exec. Com. (1972–73); Awd. Com. (1973–74) Prog. Com. (Ch., 1977); Mss. and Spec. Col. Com., Ch.; Urban Arch. Com., Ch. Amer. Hist. Assn. Org. of Amer. Histns. Natl Arch. Adv. Cncl. (1975–80). NY State Labor Hist. Assn.: Treas Various other orgs. **Honors:** SAA, Fellow, 1969. **Pubns.** "Deaccessioning" *Documtn. Nsltr.* (Fall 1980); "The Problem o

PROFESSIONAL ACTIVITIES: Institutions: 1. Acad. lib.; 2. Arch.; 3. Assn.; 4. Fed./Gvt. lib.; 5. Inst. lib.; 6. Mfr./Suppl.; 7. Milit. lib.; 8. Musm.; 9. Pub. lib.; 10. Sch. lib.; 11. Sch. of lib. sci.; 12. Spec. lib.; 13. State lib.; 14. (other). **Functions/Activities:** 15. Acq./Col. dev.; 16. Adult srvs.; 17. Admin.; 18. Apprais.; 19. Archit./Bldgs.; 20. Cat./Class.; 21. Chld. srvs.; 22. Circ.; 23. Cons./Pres.; 24. Consult.; 25. Cont. ed.; 26. Educ. lib. sci.; 27. Ext. srvs.; 28. Fund/Grants; 29. Gvt. pubs.; 30. Indx./Abs.; 31. Instr. lib. use; 32. Media srvs.; 33. Micro.; 34. Netwks./Coop.; 35. Persnl.; 36. PR; 37. Publshg. 38. Recs. mgt.; 39. Ref. srvs.; 40. Repro.; 41. Resrch.; 42. Review.; 43. Secur.; 44. Serials; 45. Spec. col.; 46. Tech. srvs.; 47. Trustees/Bds.; 48. YA srvs.; 49. (other).

Confidentiality in a College Archives," *Amer. Archvst.* (Jl. 1968); "Ezra Cornell," *Americana Encyclopedia* (1968); "Administrative Relationships in a Large Manuscript Repository," *Amer. Archvst.* (Ja. 1971); "New York Medical Archives in the Upstate Area," *NY State Jnl. of Med.* (Je. 15, 1971); "Gifts Appraisals and Taxes," *Bltn. Cornell Univ. Libs.* (My.–Je. 1974); various articles, reviews. **Activities:** 1, 2; 17, 28, 45; 54, 73 **Addr.:** Cornell University Libraries, Ithaca, NY 14853.

Finch, Mildred E. (D. 01, 1948, Spartanburg, SC) Dir. of Tech. Srvs., Cnty. of Henrico Pub. Lib., 1977–, Tech Srvs. Libn., Richland Cnty. Pub. Lib. Columbia, SC 1975–77, Tech Srvs. Libn., Spartanburg (SC) Cnty. Pub. Lib. 1971–75. **Educ.:** Transylvania Univ., 1966–70, BA (Hist); Univ. of KY, 1970–71, MSLS. **Orgs.:** ALA. SELA. VA LA. AAUW. Beta Sigma Phi. **Honors:** Beta Sigma Mu. **Pubns.:** "Improving Working Relationships: The Media Specialist and the School Administrator," *Southeast. Libn.* (Win. 1971). **Activities:** 9; 15, 20, 46; 55, 56 **Addr.:** County of Henrico Public Library, 1000 N. Laburnum Ave., Richmond, VA 23223.

Findly, Sarah Elizabeth (Ap. 2, 1908, Winfield, KS) Retired, 1977–; Dean, Sch. of Libnshp., Univ. of OR, 1973–74, Prof. of Libnshp., 1968–77, Head Ref. Libn., 1947–68, Ref. Libn., 1937–47, Sr. Asst., Circ. Dept., 1935–37, Ref. Dept., 1934–35; Tchr., Geneva, IA, 1929–33. **Educ.:** Drake Univ., 1925–29, AB (Hist.); Univ. of IL, 1933–34, BSLS; Univ. of MI, 1942–45, AM in LS. **Orgs.:** ALA: Cncl. (1965–69). Pac. NW LA: 2nd VP (1967–69); Lib. Educ. Div. (Ch., 1970–73). OR LA: Pres. (1950–51). AALS. Various other orgs. Wesley Fndn., Univ. of OR: Exec. Bd. (Ch., 1975–78). Altrusa Club of Eugene. AAUP. First Untd. Meth. Church. **Honors:** Pac. NW LA, Hon. Life Mem., 1976; OR LA, Hon. Life Mem., 1974; Phi Beta Kappa. **Pubns.:** "Relationship between PNLA and PNBC: an Ad Hoc Committee Report," *PNLA Qtly.* (Jl. 1966); "Newspapers on Microfilm," *Univ. of OR Lib., Occasional Paper No. 2* (1963); "Checklist of Books and Pamphlets Relating to the Pacific Northwest," *PNLA Qtly.* (Jl. 1966; O. 1965; Ja. 1965; O. 1963); "A Bibliography of Bibliographies of Instructional Aids to Learning," *Univ. of OR Curric. Bltn.* (1947); various other articles. **Activities:** 1, 11; 26, 29, 39; 55, 83, 92 **Addr.:** 860 E. 39th Ave., Eugene, OR 97405.

Fine, Catherine K. (N. 6, 1940, Elizabeth, NJ) Prog. Mgr., CA Data Base for Mono., CA Lib. Athrty. for Syst. and Srvs., 1979–; Proj. Mgr., CO Title Locator File, Denver Pub. Lib., 1978–79; Libn., ILL, 1977–78; Libn., Soclgy. and Bus., 1970–72. **Educ.:** South. CT State Coll., 1963–65, BA (Fr.); Pratt Inst., 1967–68, MLS. **Orgs.:** ALA. SLA. ASIS. Amer. Recs. Mgt. Assn. **Honors:** Phi Beta Mu, 1968. **Pubns.:** *Elements of a Versatile Microfiche Reader* (1979). **Activities:** 9, 12; 33, 34, 38; 56, 59, 62 **Addr.:** California Library Authority for Systems and Services, 1415 Koll Cir., Suite 101, San Jose, CA 95112.

Fine, Sara F. (Mr. 23, 1931, Pittsburgh, PA) Assoc. Prof., Univ. of Pittsburgh, 1975–; Asst. Prof., 1975–78; Couns. Psy., Shadyside Hosp., 1970–73; Couns. Consult., Pittsburgh-Mt. Oliver Intermediate Unit, 1973–75; Prog. Dir., Psychological Measurements, Inc., 1970–75. **Educ.:** Univ. of Pittsburgh, 1945–48, AB (Eng.), 1967–69, MA (Couns.), 1970–75, PhD (Couns.). **Orgs.:** ALA: YASD. Amer. Persnl. and Guid. Assn. Amer. Coll. Persnl. Assn. Natl. Cncl. on Family Rel. Socty. for Intercultural Educ. Trng. and Resrch. **Pubns.:** "Communication Processes" In *Librarian as a Learning Consultant;* (1976); "The Library Needs of the Adolescent": *Cath. Lib. World* (O. 1977); *Career Collections Development and Counseling;* (1980); "Technology and the Human Factor," in *Proceedings of the Conference on the Governance and Structure of Library Networks;* (1979); "The Librarian as Youth Counselor;" *Drexel Lib. Qtly.* (Ja. 1978); in *Library Literature: The Best of 1978;* (1979); Other articles. **Addr.:** 606 LIS Building, School of Library and Information Sciences, University of Pittsburgh, Pittsburgh, PA 15260.

Fingerote, Barbara Gail (N. 15, 1948, Winnipeg, MB) Resrch. Libn., IBM Canada Ltd., 1978–; Freelnc. Resrch., 1977–78; Libn., Bibl. Ctr., Metro. Toronto Lib. Bd., 1975–77; Libn., Serials-Acq., Robarts Lib., Univ. of Toronto, 1974–75; Catlgr., Boro. of York Pub. Lib., 1973–74; Libn., MB Dept. of Mines Resrcs. and Env. Mgt., 1972–73. **Educ.:** Univ. of Winnipeg, 1966–69, BA (Eng.); Univ. of West. ON, 1970–72, MLS. **Orgs.:** SLA: Toronto Chap., Co-Prog. Ch. (1980–81) Dir. Ed. (1975–76); Hosplty. Com. (1978–); Dir. Com. (1980–81). Can. LA: Toronto Chap., Can. Assn. for Spec. Libs. and Info. Srvs., Secy. (1978–79, 1979–80), Dir. (1980–81). Can. Assn. Info. Sci.: Toronto Chap. Bd. ALA. Various other orgs. Ward Six Cmnty. Org. Toronto Pub. Lib. Citizen's Com. Yorkville Pub. Lib. Bldg. Com. **Pubns.:** Reviews. **Activities:** 12; 17, 41; 51, 56, 59 **Addr.:** IBM Canada Limited, Dept. 776 - 1185 Eglinton Ave. E., Don Mills, ON M3C 3C6 Canada.

Fingerson, Ronald L. (Je. 15, 1933, Billings, MT) Dean, Lib. and Lrng. Resrcs., Univ. of WI-Whitewater, 1981–; Assoc. Prof., Sch. of LS, Emporia State Univ., 1971–81, Head, Serials Dept., Univ. of IA Libs., 1968–70, Mss. Libn., 1966–68, Spec. Col. Libn., 1964–66, Ref. Libn., 1964. **Educ.:** Univ. of IA, 1957–61, BA (Eng.); Univ. of MN, 1962–63, MALS; Univ. of IA, 1968, MFA (Eng.); KS State Univ., 1979, PhD (Educ.). **Orgs.:** KS LA: Treas. (1979–); Exec. Com. (1979–). AALS. SLA. AECT. Various other orgs. **Pubns.:** "The Library Binding Manual," *Lib. Scene* (Win. 1973); "The Library Science Library: A Necessary Duplication," *Jnl. of Educ. for Libnshp.* (Fall 1973); "Start with One," *Lib. Scene* (Win. 1972); "Treasures of the University Libraries," *Iowan Mag.* (Spr. 1968); Various other articles. **Activities:** 1, 11; 25, 26, 41; 56, 63, 93 **Addr.:** Library and Learning Resources, University of Wisconsin-Whitewater, Whitewater, WI 53190.

Fink, Eleanor E. (Jl. 3, 1944, Bridgeport, CT) Ch., Ofc. of Visual Resrcs., Natl. Musm. of Amer. Art, 1976–, Slide and Photograph Libn., 1973–76; Slide Cur., American Univ., 1971–73. **Educ.:** Elmira Coll., 1963–67, BA (Writing, Lang.); American Univ., 1970–73, MA (Medvl. Art). **Orgs.:** ARLIS/NA: Visual Resrcs. Ch. (1976). SLA. Coll. Art Assn. Georgetown Univ. Fac. Art Apprec. Grp.: Art Apprec. Ch. (1978); Washington Print Club. **Pubns.:** "Computer-Assisted Retrieval of Slides and Photographs of the National Collection of Fine Arts," *Procs. of the Arch. Autom. Symp.* (1980); "A Thesaurus for American Works of Art," *Procs. of the Fifth Intl. Conf. on Comps. and the Hum.* (1981); "Subject Access to Reproductions of American Works of Art," "Procs. of the Fourth Intl. Conf. on Comps. and the Hum.," (1979); oral presentations. **Activities:** 2, 4; 17, 20, 26; 55, 56, 62 **Addr.:** Office of Visual Resources, National Museum of American Art, 8th and G Sts., N.W., Washington, DC 20560.

Fink, Michael (Mr. 15, 1939, Long Beach, CA) Assoc. Prof., Musicology, Univ. of TX, San Antonio, 1975–; Prof. Staff, SWRL Educ. Resrch. Dev., 1971–75; Visit. Asst. Prof., CA State Univ., Fullerton, 1970. **Educ.:** Univ. of South. CA, 1956–60, BM (Msc.); New Eng. Cnsvty., 1960–62, MM (Msc.); Univ. of South. CA, 1970–77, PhD (Msc.). **Orgs.:** Msc. LA. Coll. Msc. Socty. Intl. Musicological Socty. Amer. Musicological Socty. **Pubns.:** "Pierre Boulez: A Selective Bibliography," *Current Musicology* (1972); "Anton Webern: A Supplement to a Basic Bibliography," *Current Musicology* (1973); "The Autobiography and Early Diary of Alfred Einstein," *Musical Qtly.* (Jl. 1980); "Rovigo, Francesco," *New Grove's Dictionary* (1980) *Music Analysis: An Annotated Bibliography* (1972). **Activities:** 1; 24, 41; 55 **Addr.:** Division of Music, University of TX, San Antonio, San Antonio, TX 78285.

Fink, Norman (Mr. 4, 1943, Noranda, PQ) Dir.-Gen., Bib. ctrl. de prêt de l'Abitibi-Témiscaminque, 1976–; Prof., Coll. du Nord-Ouest, 1975–76; Coord. of Libs., Comm Scolaire Rouyn-Noranda, 1966–75. **Educ.:** Coll. de Rouyn, 1956–64, BC (Hum.); Univ. de Montréal, 1965–66, BLS, 1971–72, MLS. **Orgs.:** Can. LA. ASTED. Conseil de la Culture de l'Abitibi-Témiscaminque: Pres. (1979–). **Pubns.:** "Les centres régionaux de documentation, une nouvelle dimension des bibliothèques scolaires," *Bltn. de l'A.C.B.L.F.* (Mr. 1972); "Documentation et information en milieu scolaire," *Documtn. et bibs.* (S. 1976). **Activities:** 9; 17, 24, 34 **Addr.:** Bibliothèque centrale de prêt A.T., C.P. 266, 19 Eleventh St., Noranda, PQ 19X 5A6 Canada.

Finkelstein, Norman H. (N. 10, 1941, Chelsea, MA) Actg. Dir. of Lib. Srvs., Brookline (MA) Pub. Schs., 1979–, Coord. of AV Comm., 1973–79; AV Coord., Brookline HS, 1970–73. **Educ.:** Boston Univ., 1959–63, BS (Educ.), 1963–64, EdM (Educ. Media); Hebrew Coll., Brookline, 1957–61, BJEd (Educ.). **Orgs.:** AECT: Natl. Com. on the Future (1977–78). MA Assn. for Educ. Comm. and Tech.: Bd. of Dirs. (1976–77). MA Assn. for Educ. Media: Bd. of Dirs. (1977–78); Leg. Com. (Ch., 1977–78). MA AV Equipment State Contract Com. **Pubns.:** "The Audiovisual Supermarket," *FOCUS* (N. 1976); "Communications through Media," *Lrng. Resrcs.* (My. 1975); "Gone 'Fiching," *AV Instr.* (S. 1977); "Books 'n Kids," *Media Forum* (D. 1977). **Activities:** 10; 17, 32; 67, 75, 93 **Addr.:** Department of Library Services, Brookline Public Schools, 115 Greenough St., Brookline, MA 02146.

Finkelston, Candace (Ag. 13, 1948, Chicago, IL) Ref. Libn./Asst. Prof., St. Louis Cmnty. Coll., 1973–; Catlgr./Ref. Libn., Our Lady of the Lake Univ., 1972–73; Art and Msc. Ref. Libn., San Antonio Pub. Lib., 1971. **Educ.:** Elmhurst Coll., 1966–70, BA (Soclgy.); Rosary Coll., 1970–71, MA (LS). **Orgs.:** ALA: ASCLA, ByLaws Com., Lib. Srv. to Blind & Phys. Handcpd. (1980–82). Grt. St. Louis Lib. Club: Bd. of Dirs. Natl. Educ. Assn. Natl. Women's Pol. Caucus. **Activities:** 1; 16, 31, 39; 72, 91, 92 **Addr.:** Library, St. Louis Community College at Meramec, St. Louis, MO 63122.

Finkler, Norman (Jl. 20, 1920, Philadelphia, PA) Retired, 1980–; Dir. Emeritus, Dept. of Pub. Libs., Montgomery Cnty., MD, 1969–80, Deputy Dir., 1962–69; Asst. Coord., Work with Adults, Free Lib. of Philadelphia, 1959–62, Branch Libn., 1957–59, Libn. II, Soc. Sci. and Hist. Dept., 1953–57; Libn., Asst. Prof. of Eng., DE Valley Coll., 1946–53. **Educ.:** Temple Univ., 1937–42, BS (Eng. Educ.); Drexel Univ., 1946–49, BSLS; Univ. of PA, 1949–56, AM (Amer. Cvlztn.). **Orgs.:** ALA: Notable Bks. Cncl. (1960–64); Subscrpn. Bks. Com. (1956–62). MD LA: Ed. Com. (Ch., 1965–68). DC LA: Prog. Com. (1965–66). Metro. Washington Cncl. of Gvts. **Honors:** Sligo-Branview Cmnty. Assn., Awd. of Merit, 1977. **Pubns.:** "Montgomery County Library: Bethesda," *Lib. Jnl. Spec. Rpt. #8* (1979). **Activities:** 9; 17, 19, 35; 78, 92 **Addr.:** 3904 Byrd Rd., Kensington, MD 20795.

Finlayson, Janet L. (My. 5, 1938, Lennoxville, PQ) Head Libn., MacDonald Campus, McGill Univ., 1979–, Tech. Srvs. Libn., 1972–79, Serials Libn., 1969–72; Libn., Chateauguay Valley Reg. HS, 1967–69. **Educ.:** McGill Univ., 1955–59, BSc (Home Econ.), 1964–65, BLS. **Orgs.:** Can. LA. Corp. of Prof. Libns. of PQ. Assn. of McGill Univ. Libns. **Activities:** 1; 17; 58, 68, 91 **Addr.:** Library, MacDonald Campus of McGill University, 21,111 Lakeshore Rd., Ste. Anne De Bellevue, PQ H9X 1C0 Canada.

Finley, Vera Lewis (S. 13, 1948, Montgomery, AL) Head of Tech. Prcs., Harrison Cnty. Lib. Syst., 1979–; Head Catlgr., Xavier Univ., 1973–79; Catlgr., Duke Univ., 1971–73. **Educ.:** Fisk Univ., 1966–70, BA (Span.); Atlanta Univ., 1970–71, MSLS. **Orgs.:** ALA. SWLA. LA LA: Int. Frdm. Com. (1979–80). Alpha Kappa Alpha. **Activities:** 1, 9; 17, 20, 46; 55, 56 **Addr.:** 224 17th St. #10, Gulfport, MS 39501.

Finnegan, Nancy S. (Ag. 15, 1950, Toledo, OH) Public Services Specialist, OCLC Lib., 1980–; Ref. Libn., Columbus Tech. Inst., 1978–80; Visit. Asst. Prof., Kent State Univ. Sch. of LS, 1979–, Ref. Libn., Pub. Lib. of Columbus and Franklin County 1973–78. **Educ.:** Adrian Coll., 1968–71, BA (Earth Sc.), Univ of MI, 1972, AMLS, Med. LA, Grade I Cert., 1972. **Orgs.:** OH LA: Asst. Coord., Inf. Org. Retrieval & Srvs. Div. (1980–); Ch., OH Dupl. Exch. Task Force (1979); (Mem.-at-large, 1979–1980). Franklin Cnty. LA: Pres. (1980–81). OLUG: Co-initiator (1979); Strg. Com. (1979–1980). Columbus Area Lib. and Info. Cncl. of OH: Comp. Info. Srv., Adv. Com. (1978–); Ch. (1980). Various other orgs. Alpha Chi Natl. Hon. Socty. Sigma Alpha Iota Natl. Msc. Fraternity. **Pubns.:** "Special Libraries and Databases: A State of the Art Report," *Special Libraries* (Ap. 1981); Ed., *Ohio Duplicate Exchange List* (1979); "Would A Computer Help?" slide-tape, (1978). **Activities:** 1, 11; 26, 31, 39; 56, 75, 91 **Addr.:** OCLC Library, P.O. Box 7777, Dublin, OH 43017.

Finnegan, Shonnie (Marchand M.) (O. 9, 1931, Washington, DC) Univ. Archvst., SUNY, Buffalo, 1967–. **Educ.:** Trinity Coll., Washington, DC, 1949–53, BA (Eng.); Cath. Univ., 1953–55, MA (Eng.); Cert. Inst. on Mod. Arch. Admin., Natl. Arch., 1968. **Orgs.:** SAA: Cncl. (1978–); Coll. and Univ. Arch. Com., (1968–, Ch., 1974–77); Prog. Com. (1971, 1972, Ch., 1974); Resol. Com., (Ch., 1977). Five Assoc. Univ. Libs.: Spec. Col. Com. (1968–70). Mss. Socty. Org. of Amer. Histns. Other orgs. AAUP: Cncl. (1979–); Nom. Com. (1974); Ad Hoc Acad. Frdm. Investigating Com. (1974); Com. on Hist. of the Assn. (1979–); SUNY at Buffalo Chap./Pres. (1972–74); VP (1970–72). **Honors:** SAA, Fellow, 1975; SUNY, Chancellor's Awd. for Excel. in Libnshp., 1979. **Activities:** 1, 2; 15, 17, 45; 85 **Addr.:** University Archives, 420 Capen Hall, SUNY at Buffalo, Buffalo, NY 14260.

Finnel, Soma W. (F. 17, 1925, Brooklyn, NY) Dir., Oceanside Free Lib., 1978–; Dir., Merrick Lib., 1972–78, Adult Srvs. Libn., 1968–72; Queens Boro. Pub. Lib., 1966–68. **Educ.:** Brooklyn Coll., 1942–46, BA (Pol. Sci.); Long Island Univ., 1963–66, MS (LS). **Orgs.:** Lib. Dirs., Nassau Lib. Syst.: Exec. Bd. (1978–82). Long Island Lib. Resrcs. Cncl.: Secy. (1980–81). Nassau Cnty. LA. NY LA. Adelphi Univ. Coll. Adv. Com. Bellmore-Merrick HS Dist. Adult Educ. Adv. Com. W. Nassau Mental Hlth. Clinic Assn. Natl. Cncl. of Jewish Women: VP (1956–60). **Pubns.:** Ed., *Oceanside Free Library Prose and Cons* (1978–); "On the Bookshelves," *Oceanside Beacon* (1980–). **Addr.:** Oceanside Free Library, Davison Ave., Oceanside, NY 11510.

Finnemore, Mary Alison (O. 27, 1924, Montreal, PQ) Chief, Lib. Grp., Pulp & Paper Resrch. Inst. of Can., 1953–; Asst. Libn., Shawinigan Water & Power Co., 1951–53; Asst. Libn., Sch. of Cmrce., McGill Univ., 1949–51, Asst. Libn., Cat. Dept., 1948–49. **Educ.:** McGill Univ., 1942–46, BA (Arts), 1946–47, BLS. **Orgs.:** Can. LA. PQ LA. SLA. Corp. of Prof. Libns. of PQ. **Activities:** 12; 20, 39, 41; 65, 86, 91 **Addr.:** Pulp & Paper Research Institute of Canada, 570 St. John's Blvd., Pte. Claire, PQ H9R 3J9 Canada.

Finnerty, Sandra J. (My. 19, 1946, Boston, MA) Head of Tech. Prcs., Springfield (MA) City Lib., 1978–; Tech. Srvs. Libn., West. Reg. Pub. Lib. (MA) Syst., 1976–78; Catlgr., Univ. Microfilms, 1974–75. **Educ.:** Univ. of MA, 1964–68, BA (Educ.); Univ. of MI, 1973–74, AMLS. **Orgs.:** MA LA: Tech. Srvs. Sect., Secy./Treas. (1978–81). ALA. **Activities:** 9; 20, 46 **Addr.:** Springfield City Library, 220 State St., Springfield, MA 01103.

Finnigan, Georgia Logan (Ag. 6, 1943, Rochester, NY) Pres., Info. Store, 1979–; Partner, Info. Unlimited, 1971–78; Libn., Shell Dev. Co., 1970–71; Libn., Univ. of NC, 1967–70. **Educ.:** Mary Washington Coll. of Univ. of VA, 1961–65, BA (Hist.); Univ. of NC, 1965–66, MSLS; Pepperdine Univ., 1980, MBA. **Orgs.:** Info. Indus. Assn. SLA: Educ. Com. (1979); Bltn. (1970–71). San Francisco OL Users Grp.: Ch. (1979–80). Amer. Mktg. Assn. San Francisco Chamber of Cmrce. **Pubns.:** "The Incredible Information Explosion," *MAC/West. Advert. News* (N. 29, 1979); "Instant Invormation," *San Francisco Bus.* (S. 1978); "Nontraditional Information Service," *Spec. Libs.* (My. 1976); "Document Delivery," *OL* (Ja. 1978). **Activities:** 14-Bus.;

Special Subjects/Services: 50. Adult educ.; 51. Advert./Mktg.; 52. Aerosp.; 53. Agric.; 54. Area std.; 55. Arts/Hum.; 56. Autom.; 57. Bibl./Prtg.; 58. Bio. sci.; 59. Bus./Fin.; 60. Chem.; 61. Copyrt.; 62. Documtn.; 63. Educ.; 64. Engin.; 65. Env.; 66. Eth. grps.; 67. Film; 68. Food/Nutr.; 69. Geneal.; 70. Geo.; 71. Geol.; 72. Handcpd.; 73. Hist.; 74. Int. frdm.; 75. Info. sci.; 76. Insr.; 77. Law; 78. Legis.; 79. Math./Comp. sci.; 80. Med.; 81. Metals; 82. Nat. resrcs.; 83. Newsp.; 84. Nuc. sci.; 85. Oral hist.; 86. Petr./Energy; 87. Pharm.; 88. Phys./Astr./Math.; 89. Readg.; 90. Relig.; 91. Sci./Tech.; 92. Soc. sci.; 93. Telecom.; 94. Transp.; 95. (other).

17, 36, 49-Mktg. and prod. dev.; 59, 75, 77 **Addr.:** 235 Montgomery St. #800, San Francisco, CA 94104.

Finzi, John Charles (Mr. 27, 1920, Campiglia Marittima, Italy) Dir., Cols. Dev. Ofc., Lib. of Congs., 1979–, Asst. Dir., 1966–78, Coord., Dev. and Org. of Col., 1964–66, Dir., Pub. Law 480 Prog., S. Asia, New Delhi, 1961–64, Head, European Exch. Sect., 1959–61, Head, Orientalia Exch. Sect., 1958–59, Biblgphr., 1958, Intern, 1957. **Educ.:** Univ. of Rome, 1937–38, (Belles Lettres); Univ. of CA, Los Angeles, 1944–45, BA (Hist.), 1944–45, MA (Hist.), 1945–50, (Hist.); Univ. of CA, Berkeley, 1956–57, MLS. **Orgs.:** ALA. Indian LA. DC LA. **Honors:** Phi Beta Kappa; Beta Phi Mu. **Pubns.:** *Oscar Wilde and His Literary Circle: A Catalog of Manuscripts in the William Andrews Clark Library* (1967); *Report of a Survey of the National Central Library, Florence* (1968); various articles. **Activities:** 4; 15, 17, 23; 54, 92 **Addr.:** 2700 Virginia Ave., N.W., Washington, DC 20037.

Firth, Margaret A. (Mr. 21, 1919, Lawrence, MA) Libn., Beverly Hosp., 1975–; Libn., USM Corp., 1945–75; Libn., Celanese Corp., 1942–45; Libn. Asst., Clark Univ., 1941–42. **Educ.:** Univ. of MA, 1936–40, BA (Eng.); Simmons Coll., 1940–41, BSLS. **Orgs.:** SLA: numerous coms. Med. LA. Gld. of Beverly Artists. Beverly Coll. Clb. **Honors:** SLA, Sci. Tech. Div. Awd. of Hon., 1955. **Pubns.:** *Scientific and Technical Awards in the U.S. and Canada 1900–54* (1954). **Activities:** 12; 15, 16, 17; 80 **Addr.:** Beverly Hospital Library, Herrick St., Beverly, MA 01915.

Fischer, Eugene T. (Ag. 19, 1944, New Orleans, LA) Dir., Campbell Cnty. Pub. Lib., 1973–. **Educ.:** Tulane Univ., 1962–66, BA (Pol. Sci.); LA State Univ., 1971–72, MSLS. **Orgs.:** ALA: PLA, AV Com. (1979–81). SELA: Mem. Com. (1979–). VA LA: Exec. Dir. (1977–). **Pubns.:** "The Public's Library?" (videotape) (1978). **Activities:** 9; 32, 39, 47; 61, 67, 85 **Addr.:** Box 310, Rustburg, VA 24588.

Fischer, Margaret T. (Jl. 10, 1924, New York, NY) Bus. Consult., Mgt. Decisions, 1975–; Chief of Resrch., Link Resrcs., Inc., 1981–; Mgr., Data Srvs. Div., R. R. Bowker Co., 1973–75; Dir., Info. Srvs., Xerox Corp., 1972–73; Mgr., Info. Prcs. Dept., Time Inc., 1958–72; Jnlst., *Time, Life, Sports Illustrated,* Time Inc., 1946–58; various positions as resrc. lectr., 1964–76. **Educ.:** Bucknell Univ., 1942–46, BA (Eng.). **Orgs.:** ASIS: Pres. (1977), Cnclr. (1971–74). SLA. The Fndn. Ctr. Bucknell Univ. Bd. of Trustees. **Honors:** ASIS, Pres. Plaque, 1977; Phi Beta Kappa, 1946. **Pubns.:** Ed.-in-chief, *Online Database Rpt.* (1979–); dir., ed., *Electronic Info. Prog. Rpts.* (1980–); ed. adv. bd., Chemical Abs. Srvs.; various articles. **Activities:** 11, 12; 17, 24, 37, 47; 56, 75 **Addr.:** Management Decisions, 44 Taconic Rd., Greenwich, CT 06830.

Fischier, Adrienne Grace (Jl. 23, 1933, New York, NY) Libn., The Harvard Lib. in NY, 1981–; Asst. to the Dir. of Libs., Mercy Coll., 1980–81; Libn., Gen. Socty. of Mech. and Tradesmen, 1974–80. **Educ.:** Brooklyn Coll., 1951–60, BA (Engl. Lit.); Pratt Inst., 1969–72, MLS. **Orgs.:** Metro. Ref. and Resrch. Agency: Small Libs. Disc. Grp. (1975–76). ALA. SLA: Musms., Arts, Hum. Div. (1976–); NY LA. **Activities:** 9; 15, 17, 22; 50, 55 **Addr.:** 19 Gracecourt, 2 B, Brooklyn, NY 11201.

Fischler, Barbara Brand (My. 24, 1930, Pittsburgh, PA) Actg. Dir. of Libs., IN Univ.-Purdue Univ. at Indianapolis, 1981–; Prof. (part-time), IN Univ. Sch. of Lib. & Info. Sci., 1972–; Couns., Coord., Tchr., IN Univ. Sch. of Lib. & Info. Sci. Prog., IN Univ.-Purdue Univ. at Indianapolis, 1972–, Pub. Srvs. Libn., 1976–81, Circ. Libn., 1970–76; Actg. Libn., Undergrad. Lib., IN Univ., 1963–63, Asst. Libn., 1961–63. **Educ.:** Wilson Coll., 1948–52, AB (Msc.); IN Univ., 1952–54, MM (Msc.), 1957–64, MALS, 1980–, Spec. Degree (Lib. Mgt.). **Orgs.:** ALA. IN LA: Coll. and Univ. Div. (Ch., 1977–78). SLA. IN Gvr.'s Conf. on Libs. and Info. Srvs.: Core Com. and Prog. Ch. (1976–78). Various other orgs. Pi Kappa Lambda. **Honors:** Ctrl. IN Area Lib. Srvs. Athrty., Outstan. Srv. Awd., 1979; Beta Phi Mu, 1963. **Activities:** 1, 11; 17, 26, 39; 55, 91 **Addr.:** University Libraries, Indiana University/Purdue University at Indianapolis, 815 W. Michigan St., Indianapolis, IN 46202.

Fish, James H. (F. 21, 1947, MA) State Libn., MA State Lib., 1980–; Dir., Robbins Lib., Arlington, MA, 1977–80; Dir., Leominster (MA) Pub. Lib., 1972–77; Dir. of Libs., Levi Heywood Meml. Lib., Gardner, MA, 1971–72. **Educ.:** Univ. of MA, 1964–68, BA (Hist.); IN Univ., 1968–71, MLS; Anna Maria Coll., 1976–80, MBA (Bus. Admin.). **Orgs.:** MA LA: Educ. Com., Ch., Exec. Bd. (1980–81). New Eng. LA. Ctrl. MA Reg. Lib. Syst. Adv. Cncl.: Ch. (1974); Vice-Ch. (1973). Grt. Boston Pub. Lib. Admins.: Pres. (1978). **Honors:** Beta Phi Mu, 1971. **Pubns.:** *An Analysis of Arlington, Massachusetts and its Robbins Library* (1978); *An Analysis of the Community and the Public Library of Leominster, Massachusetts* (1976); "Community Analysis," *Bay State Libn.* (Sum. 1978). **Activities:** 9, 13; 15, 16, 17 **Addr.:** 10 Minot St., Reading, MA 01867.

Fishbein, Meyer H. (My. 6, 1916, New York, NY) Dir., Milit. Arch. Div., Natl. Arch., 1976–80, Dir., Recs. Apprais. Staff, 1973–76, Archvst., 1940–73; Adj. Prof., American Univ., 1977–. **Educ.:** American Univ., 1941–50, BS (Hist.), 1950–54, MA (Hist.), 1954–62, (Econ. Hist.). **Orgs.:** Intl. Cncl. on Arch.: Com. on Autom. (Ch., 1972–80); Sem. Dir., Eng., Ivory Coast (1973, 1977, 1980). SAA: Cncl. (1979–83); Com. on Mech. Readable Recs. and Autom. Techq. (1972–76). Org. of Amer. Histns. Soc. Sci. Hist. Assn. Bus. Hist. Conf. Cosmos Club. **Honors:** SAA, Fellow, 1965; Natl. Arch., Commendable Srv. Awds. 1965, 1968, 1973. **Pubns.:** Ed., *The National Archives and Statistical Research* (1973); *Early Business Statistical Operations of the Federal Government* (1953); *The Censuses of Manufactures: 1810–1890* (1963); "Archival Remains for Research and Development During the Second World War," in *World War II: An Accounting of its Documents* (1976); "ADP and Archives: Selected Publications on Automatic Data Processing," *Amer. Archvst.* (Ja. 1975); other articles. **Activities:** 2; 15, 25, 41; 50, 56 **Addr.:** 5005 Elsmere Ave., Bethesda, MD 20014.

Fisher, Alan J. (Ap. 9, 1946, Wichita, KS) Coll. Dev. Libn., CO Coll., 1977–. **Educ.:** CO Coll., 1965–68, BA (Pol. Sci.); Univ. of Denver, 1971–72, MALS; Univ. of NE, 1975–76, MBA. **Orgs.:** ALA. CO LA. **Pubns.:** "Expanding OCLC Applications in Small and Medium Sized Libraries," *CO Libs.* (S. 1979); "Inflation, Efficiency and Collection Development," *Co Libs.* (Mr. 1980). **Activities:** 1, 12; 15, 17; 56, 59 **Addr.:** 908 Ellston St., Colorado Springs, CO 80907.

Fisher, Alice J. Ref. Libn., Volun. Coord., Santa Monica Pub. Lib., 1977–; Ref. Libn., Beverly Hills Pub. Lib., 1976–77; Freelnc. Resrch., 1975–; Libn., Art Resrch. Lib., CBS TV Netwk., Los Angeles, 1975–76. **Educ.:** Rutgers Univ., 1942–46, LittB (Jnlsm.); Univ. of South. CA, 1973–75, MSLS. **Orgs.:** CA LA. CA Socty. of Libns.: Com. on Lib. Resrch. (1975). Beta Phi Mu: Beta Chap. Dir. (1980–1983), Schol. Com. (Ch., 1980–). ALA. Leag. of Women Voters. Women's Intl. Leag. for Peace and Frdm. **Pubns.:** *Health Care in the 70's: A National Crisis* (1974); reviews. **Activities:** 9; 16, 39, 41; 66, 72 **Addr.:** 723 N. Oakhurst Dr., Beverly Hills, CA 90210.

Fisher, Becky R. (O. 12, 1937, St. Louis, MO) Asst. Prof. in Educ., Peru St. Coll., 1981–; Asst. Prof., Ctrl. MI Univ., 1978–81; Asst. Prof., AR State Univ., 1976–77. **Educ.:** Harris Tchrs. Coll., 1957–69, BS (Educ.); Univ. of MO, 1971–74, MS (Instr. Media), PhD (Curric. & Instr.). **Orgs.:** ALA. AECT. AAUW. MI Assn. of Tchr. Educ. MI Assn. for Media Educ. **Pubns.:** "Teaching is Giving," *The Principal*; "Words Can Be Fun," *The Reading Clinic*; "Using Literature to Teach Science," *Jnl. of Resrch. in Teaching Sci.*; Cassette Tape "Use of Literature to Teach Seventh Grade Biology". **Activities:** 14-School of Educ.; 26, 41, 42; 63 **Addr.:** Apt. B-4, Peru St. Coll., Peru, NE 68421.

Fisher, Ilo D. (O. 18, 1913, Springfield, OH) Sci. Libn., Wittenberg Univ., 1973–79, Spec. Proj. Libn., 1967–73, Head, Tech. Srvs., 1965–67, Chief Libn., 1946–65, Head, Cat. & Order Dept., Warder Pub. Lib., 1943–46. **Educ.:** Wittenberg Univ., 1931–35, AB (Eng.); Univ. of IL, 1939–40, BS in LS, 1947–51, MS (LS). **Orgs.:** Friends of Warder Pub. Lib.: Pres. (1967–69). Friends of Lib. Geneal. Resrch. Grp.: Coord. (1967–). OH LA: Dir. (1973–76). SLA: Pres., Dayton Chap. (1967–68). Other orgs. Altrusa Intl.: Pres., lcl. club (1973–74). Women's Natl. Book Assn. **Honors:** Clark Cnty. Mental Hlth. Assn., Pres. Awd., 1973. **Pubns.:** *The Coming of Age of a College Library* (1978); "Dard Hunter, Master Craftsman", *Type & Press,* (Ap. 1975); "The Library: Hub of Learning," *The Clearing House,* (O. 1963); "A College Librarian Speaks Her Mind," *OH LA Bltn.* (Ja. 1961); "Books in a Communicative Environment," *Rub-Off,* (Mr./Ap. 1959); reprinted in *Of, By and For Librarians, Second Series* (1974); Other articles. **Activities:** 1, 9; 18, 39, 41; 50, 57, 69 **Addr.:** 5747 Detrick Jordan Rd., Springfield, OH 45502.

Fisher, Janet S. (Ap. 3, 1943, Wyandotte, MI) Asst. Dean for Lrng. Resrcs., Coll. of Med., E. TN State Univ., 1978–, Asst. Libn., 1975–78; Ref. Libn., Coll. of Med., Univ. of UT, 1971–75; Ref. Libn., Coll. of Med., Univ. of MD, 1969–71; Asst. Libn. for Cat., Bowman Gray Sch. of Med., 1967–69. **Educ.:** Jacksonville (AL) State Univ., 1961–65, BA (Eng., Bio.); FL State Univ., 1965–66, MSLS; Med. LA, 1978, Cert. **Orgs.:** Med. LA: Hlth. Sci. Libs. Tech. Com. (Ch., 1979–80). TN LA: Spec. Libs. Sect. (Ch., 1980–81); Leg. Netwk. (Reg. Coord., 1979–80). SELA: Spec. Lib. Sect. (Secy., 1979–80). Southeast. Reg. Med. Lib. Prog.: Adv. Com. (1978–). Various other orgs. AAUP. TN Ctr. for Human Values and the Hlth. Sci. Appalachian Hist. of Med. Socty. E. TN State Univ. Coll. of Med. Speakers Clb. **Pubns.:** "A Health Sciences Libraries Consortium in a Rural Setting," *Bltn. Med. LA* (Ap. 1978); "Forum–What Is Special about the Special Library," *TN Libn.* (Fall 1979); "Online Database Education," Eric Pubn. (Je. 1979); MEDLINE (videotape, Univ. of UT) (1974). **Activities:** 1, 12; 17, 24; 80 **Addr.:** Medical Library, East Tennessee State Univeristy, Box 23290A, Johnson City, TN 37614.

Fisher, Kim N. (Jl. 14, 1948, Washington, DC) Head, Humanities Div., OK St. Univ. Lib., 1981–; Serials Libn., VA Cmwlth. Univ., 1978–81, Gvt. Docum. Libn., 1975–77, Visit. Instr., Univ. of KY Coll. of LS, 1974; Asst. Ref. Libn., VA Cmwlth Univ., 1972–75. **Educ.:** Univ. of KY, 1966–70, BA (Eng.), 1971–72, MA (LS); VA Cmwlth Univ., 1980–81, MA (Eng.). **Orgs.:** ALA: ACRL. **Pubns.:** "The KWOC Index or There is Light at the End of the Tunnel," *Documents to the People* (Mr. 1977). **Activities:** 1; 29, 39, 44; 55 **Addr.:** 1015 Preston, Stillwater, OK 74074.

Fisher, Marshall (O. 11, 1943, Chicago, IL) Ref. Libn., William Rainey Harper Coll., 1979–; Catlgr., 1968–79; Catlgr./Ref., Bogan Jn. Coll., 1967. **Educ.:** Wright Jr. Coll., 1962–63, AA; Chicago Tchrs. Coll., 1963–65, BEd (Educ.); Rosary Coll., 1966–67, MA (LS). **Orgs.:** ALA. IL LA. **Pubns.:** Jt. auth., "Copyright and ownership of College-developed materials," *New Directions for Community Colleges* (Sp. 1975). **Activities:** 1; 31, 39 **Addr.:** Harper College Library, Algonquin & Roselle Rds., Palatine, IL 60067.

Fisher-Fleming, Shirley D. (Jl. 31, 1926, Douglas, Isle of Man, UK) Educ. Media Coord., Sch. Dist. #35, Langley, 1974–, Uplands and Belmont Elem. Sch., 1973–74. **Educ.:** Univ. of BC, 1971, BA (Eng.), 1972–73, Libnshp.; 1973, Prof. Tchg. Cert. **Orgs.:** BC Sch. LA: Reviews Coord. Can. LA. Pac. Instr. Media Assn. **Honors** Delta Kappa Gamma. Univ. of BC Sch. of Libnshp., Ruth Cameron Gold Medal, 1973. **Activities:** 10; 20, 21, 32; 63, 67 **Addr.:** Resource Centre, School District #35, 19740 - 32nd Ave., Langley, BC V3A 4S1 Canada.

Fishman, Jack (Ja. 22, 1924, New York, NY) Asst. Lib. Dir., Free Pub. Lib. of Woodbridge, 1966–, Adult Srvs. Coord., 1966; Supvsr., Info. Desk, Brooklyn Pub. Lib., 1964–66, Ref. Libn., 1961–63. **Educ.:** NY Univ., 1946–49; Univ. of ID, 1950–51, BA (Soclgy.); Pratt Inst., 1961–63, MLS. **Orgs.:** ALA: Adult Srvs. Div., Atlantic City Conf. (Prog. Ch., 1969); Legis. Com. (Ch., 1969). NJ LA: PR Com. (Ch., 1969–70); Conf. Ch. (1971–72); Nom. Com. (Ch., 1972); *NJ Libs.* Ed. (1966–71). **Activities:** 9; 16, 17, 21; 50, 72, 89 **Addr.:** Free Public Library of Woodbridge, George Frederick Plz., Woodbridge, NJ 07095.

Fishman, Joel Harris (S. 13, 1946, New York, NY) Law Libn., Allegheny Cnty. Law Lib., 1977–; Asst. Law Libn., Seton Hall Univ. Law Sch., 1973–77. **Educ.:** Hunter Coll., 1963–67, BA (Hist.); Univ. of WI, 1967–69, MA (Hist.), 1969–77, PhD (Hist.); Queens Coll., 1972–73, MLS; AALL, 1980, Cert. Law Libn. **Orgs.:** AALL. State Ct. and Cnty. Law Libs.: Stans. Com. (Ch., 1977–80); Stats. Com. (Ch., 1980–81). PA LA: Adult Srvs. Com. (VP/Pres-Elect, 1980–81). West. PA Law LA: VP (1979). Amer. Socty. for Legal Hist. **Honors:** Phi Alpha Theta, 1966. **Pubns.:** *Acquiring a Pennsylvania Law Library* (1980); *The Legislative History of the 1980 Pennsylvania Divorce Law* (1981); various articles. **Activities:** 12; 17, 33; 77 **Addr.:** Allegheny County Law Library, 921 City - County Bldg, Pittsburgh, PA 15219.

Fite, Alice Emily (S. 7, 1929, New York, NY) Exec. Dir., AASL, 1974–; Assoc. Prof., Towson Univ., 1971–75; Media Spec., Montgomery Cnty. Pub. Schs., 1967–74; Sch. Libn., Searingtown Elem. Sch., 1964–66. **Educ.:** Wheaton Coll., 1946–48; Bob Jones Univ., 1948–49, BS (Eng., Sec. Educ.); Columbia Univ., 1949–51, MS (Lib. Srv.). **Orgs.:** ALA: AASL. Chicago Socty. of Assn. Execs. Amer. Socty. of Assn. Execs. **Pubns.:** "A Supervisors Commitment to Quality Media Programs," *Sch. Lib. Jnl.*; "Media Center Services for Development of Reading Skills," *Sch. Media Qtly.* (Fall 1973); Contrib., *ALA World Encyc. of Lib. and Info. Srvs.* (1980); Contrib., *Excellence in School Media Programs* (1980); "AASL Notes," Qtly. clmn. *Sch. Media Qtly.* (1980). **Activities:** 10, 11; 17, 26, 32; 63, 89, 93 **Addr.:** 50 E. Huron, Chicago, IL 60611.

FitzGerald, Ardra F. (My. 7, 1938, York, PA) Sr. Info. Spec., Lit. Resrch., Lib. & Resrch. Info. Srvs., SRI Intl., 1972–; Ref. Libn., CA State Polytech. Univ., 1969–72; Lit. Srchr., SRI Intl. 1968–69; Lit. Srchr., Lockheed Missiles & Space Co., 1966–68; Tech. Libn., Link Grp., General Precision, Inc., 1963–64; Libn., MI Med. Srv., 1962–62. **Educ.:** Wayne State Univ., 1956–62, BA (Soclgy.); San Jose State Univ., 1964–66, MA (Libnshp); Coll. of Notre Dame, CA, 1975–79, MBA (Bus.); CA Cmnty. Coll. Lifetime Teaching Cred., 1970; Trng. in Online Sch. **Orgs.:** SLA. ASIS. Alpha Beta Alpha: Treas. of chap. (1966). **Pubns.:** *Fundamentals of Systems Analysis,* 2nd ed. (1981); "Computerized Literature Searching," *LeCourt* (Spr. 1976). **Activities:** 12; 17, 24, 49-Lit. Srch.; 59, 64, 91 **Addr.:** Reference/Search Service AG020, Library & Research Information Services, SRI International, 333 Ravenswood Ave., Menlo Park, CA 94025.

Fitzgerald, Dorothy A. (S. 6, 1949, Sydney, NS) Libn., The Can. Lib. of Fam. Med., The Lib. Srv. of the Coll. of Fam. Physicians of Can., 1974–. **Educ.:** Mt. Saint Vincent Univ., BA (Soc. Sci.); Dalhousie Univ., 1972–74, MLS; Med. LA, 1974, Cert. **Orgs.:** Can. Hlth. Libs. Assn.: ON Corresp., Nsltr. (1978–81); Nom. Com. (1981); Confer. Prog. Ch. (1982). Med. LA: Upstate NY and ON Chap. (1979–81) Mem. at Large. Toronto Med. Libs. Grp. World Org. of Natl. Colls. Acads., and Acad. Assns. of Gen. Practitioners/Fam. Physicians.: Bibl. Com. The Coll. of Fam. Physicians of Can. **Honors:** Dept. of Fam. Med., Univ. of West. ON, Hon. Lectr., 1979. **Pubns.:** "Basic library list for family medical centres," *Can. Fam. Physician* (1980); "Searching the medical literature," *Can. Fam. Physician* (1980); "Using the medical library to best advantage," *Family Practice Manual* (forthcoming); Ed., *FAMLI* (1980–). **Activities:** 1, 12; 27, 30, 39; 80 **Addr.:** Canadian Library of Family Medicine,

PROFESSIONAL ACTIVITIES: Institutions: 1. Acad. lib.; 2. Arch.; 3. Assn.; 4. Fed./Gvt. lib.; 5. Inst. lib.; 6. Mfr./Suppl.; 7. Milit. lib.; 8. Musm.; 9. Pub. lib.; 10. Sch. lib.; 11. Sch. of lib. sci.; 12. Spec. lib.; 13. State lib.; 14. (other). **Functions/Activities:** 15. Acq./Col. dev.; 16. Adult srvs.; 17. Admin.; 18. Apprais.; 19. Archit./Bldgs.; 20. Cat./Class.; 21. Chld. srvs.; 22. Circ.; 23. Cons./Pres.; 24. Consult.; 25. Cont. ed.; 26. Educ. lib. sci.; 27. Ext. srvs.; 28. Fund/Grants; 29. Gvt. pubs.; 30. Indx./Abs.; 31. Instr. lib. use; 32. Media srvs.; 33. Micro.; 34. Netwks./Coop.; 35. Persnl.; 36. PR; 37. Publshg.; 38. Recs. mgt.; 39. Ref. srvs.; 40. Repro.; 41. Resrch.; 42. Review.; 43. Secur.; 44. Serials; 45. Spec. col.; 46. Tech. srvs.; 47. Trustees/Bds.; 48. YA srvs.; 49. (other).

Who's Who in Library and Information Services

Medical Bldg., University of Western Ontario, London, ON N6A 5C1 Canada.

Fitzgerald, Florence E. (Je. 16, 1921, Minneapolis, MN) Ext. Srvs. Libn., Fullerton Pub. Lib., 1975–, AV Libn., 1972–75, Catlgr., 1965–72; Med. Ref. Libn., VA Hosp., Ann Arbor, MI, 1953–54; Sr. Srv. Libn., Univ. of MI, 1949–50; Med. Ref. Libn., VA Reg. Ofc., Chicago, 1948–49; Ed. Asst., ALA, 1946–47; Dental Libn., Marquette Univ., 1943–46. **Educ.:** Coll. of St. Catherine, 1939–43, BS (LS); CA State Univ., Fullerton, 1973–75, MS (LS). **Orgs.:** CA LA: South. CA PR Chap. (1975–76). Santiago Lib. Syst.: PR Com. (Ch., 1978–). **Activities:** 1, 4; 16, 20, 36; 72, 80, 95-I&R. **Addr.:** 15349 San Bruno Dr., LaMirada, CA 90638.

Fitzgerald, Sr. M. Alexius, I.H.M. (D. 15, 1926, Brooklyn, NY) Media Gen., Tchr., St. John the Evangelist, Silver Spring, MD, 1972–; Media Generalist, Tchr., St. Mary of the Assumption, Upper Marlboro, MD, 1958–72; Tchr., Cath. schs., 1947–58. **Educ.:** Marywood Coll., 1944–54, BS (Educ.), 1964–70, MS (Elem Educ.); West. MD Coll., 1975–78, Lib. Cert.; Univ. of MD, Baltimore, 1977. **Orgs.:** Cath. LA: DC Chap., Ch. (1974–76, 1978–80); Vice-Ch. (1977). MD Educ. Media Org. Montgomery Cnty. Film Fest. Com. Natl. Cath. Educ. Assn. **Activities:** 1, 10; 17, 20, 32; 67 **Addr.:** St. John the Evangelist School, 10201 Woodland Dr., Silver Spring, MD 20902.

Fitzgerald, Michael Joseph (Mr. 2, 1936, Providence, RI) Chief Catlgr. and Head, Cat. and Serials Divs., Harvard Col. Lib., 1976–, Chief Catlgr., and Head, Cat. Div., 1971–, Catlgr., 1965–71; Cat. Asst., Brown Univ., 1960–65. **Educ.:** Providence Coll., 1953–57, AB (Eng.); Brown Univ., 1958–60, Simmons Coll., 1962–64, MSLS. **Orgs.:** New Eng. Tech. Srvs. Libns.: (Ch., 1967–68). ALA: Descr. Cat. Com. (Ch., 1976–78); Intl. Cat. Consultation Com. (1976–80); AACR 2 Introductory Prog. Com. (1977–79). **Honors:** Fulbright Schol., 1957–58. **Addr.:** 26 Yerxa Rd., Arlington, MA 02174.

FitzGerald, Patricia A. (Je. 14, 1949, Elmira, NY) Assoc. Ref. Libn., Univ. of DE, 1978–; Actg. Chem. Libn., Syracuse Univ., 1978, Geol. Libn., 1972–78. **Educ.:** Syracuse Univ., 1967–71, BA (Geol.), 1971–75, MSLS. **Orgs.:** ALA. DE OLUG: Ch. (1979–). SLA. **Pubns.:** *Doing Research: A Beginning Library Research Strategy* (1981). **Activities:** 1; 15, 31, 39; 60, 64, 91 **Addr.:** Reference Dept., University of Delaware Library, Newark, DE 19711.

Fitzgerald, Ruth Carpenter (Ja. 18, 1935, South Haven, MI) Asst. Prof., Lib.–Media, Ctrl. MI Univ., 1980–; Media Spec., Linden Cmnty. Schs., 1976–79; Reg. Educ. Media Ctr. Dir., Berrien Cnty. Intermediate Sch., 1975–76; Media Dir., Dowagiac Union Schs., 1974–75; Media Spec., Edwardsburg Pub. Schs., 1971–74; Catlgr., Niles Pub. Lib., 1970–71; Libn., Jackson Cmnty. Coll., 1968–70; Libn., Albion Pub. Schs., 1964–68; Tchr., Parma West. Schs., 1962–64. **Educ.:** West. MI Univ., 1952–61, BS (Eng.), 1964–68, MSL; Univ. of MI, 1969–, doctoral cand. **Orgs.:** MI Assn. for Media in Educ.: Conf. Com. Ch. (1977); Pres.-elect (1979); Pres. (1980); Bd. of Dir. (1974–1976). MI Assn. for Sch. Libns.: Secy. (1973). ALA: AASL. AECT. MI Educ. Assn. Natl. Educ. Assn. Phi Delta Kappa. MI Assn. of Middle Sch. Educ. **Honors:** Beta Phi Mu, 1967. **Pubns.:** "Video - High Voltage Learning" *Media Spectrum* (3rd Quarter, 1979). **Activities:** 10; 24, 32, 48, 49; 63 **Addr.:** 4151 Louis Dr., Flint, MI 48507.

Fitzgerald, Tom (My. 25, 1946, Brooklyn, NY) Dir. of Advert., H.W. Wilson Co., 1979–; Mid. Sch. Prin., Fiedel Sch., Glen Cove, NY, 1978; Tchr., Monroe-Woodbury Jr. HS, 1972–78; Prod. Mgr./Pubcty., *Sociological Abstracts*, 1970–71. **Educ.:** Richmond Coll., CUNY, 1971, BA (Eng.); New Paltz State Univ., 1974, MA (Eng.), 1976, MS (Educ. Admin.). **Orgs.:** ALA: ERT (Mem. Ch., 1980–81). **Activities:** 6; 36, 37; 51 **Addr.:** The H.W. Wilson Company, 950 University Ave., Bronx, NY 10452.

Fitzgibbons, Shirley A. (My. 5, 1936, Camden, NY) Asst. Prof., Coll. of Lib./Info. Srvs., 1975–; Adjunct Fac., Rutgers, State Univ. of NJ, 1973–75; Sch. Libn., West Genesee Ctrl. Schs., Syracuse, NY, 1963–67; Sch. Libn., Liverpool Ctrl. Schs., Liverpool, NY, 1961–63. **Educ.:** SUNY, Oswego, 1954–58, BS (Educ.); Syracuse Univ., 1964, MSLS; Rutgers, State Univ. of NJ, 1972–76, PHD (Lib. Sci.). **Orgs.:** AALS Conf. Plng. Com., Resrch. Pres. Co-Ch. (1977–78); Gvt. Rel. Com. (1978–80); ALA: AASL; ALSC (Ch. of ad hoc Com. Pub. Com. 1978–79); YA Srvs. Div., Ch., Resrch. Com. (1979–80); Resrch. Com. (1976–). MD Educ. Media Org.: Secy., Bd. of Dir. (1977–78); Graham Media Prog. Awards Com. (1978–79). Intl. Assn. of Sch. Libns. Chld. Lit. Assn. **Honors:** Beta Phi Mu, 1964; Kappa Delta Pi, 1958; Adv. Plng. Com. to MD Gov. Conf. on Libs. and Info. Srvcs., 1977–78. **Pubns.:** Cont., "Citation Analysis in the Social Sciences", *Collection Development in Libraries*, (1980); "Professionalism and Ethical Behavior," *Sch. Media Qtly.* (W. 1980); "Code of Ethics," *1977 ALA Yrbk.* (1977); "Children's Literature in the U.S. in the 1970's," (1979). **Activities:** 1, 10, 11; 21, 39, 48; 63, 74, 92 **Addr.:** College of Library and Information Services, University of Maryland, College Park, MD 20742.

FitzPatrick, Arthur (F. 14, 1927, Calgary, AB) Head, Info. Syst., AB Resrch. Cncl., 1957–; Engin. Instr., South. Inst. of Tech., 1956–57; Sr. Partner, A. FitzPatrick, Consult. Engin., 1954–57; Asst. Prod. Mgr., Robinson Mach. & Supply Ltd., 1951–54. **Educ.:** Univ. of AB, 1945–49, BSc (Chem.), 1954–56, MA (Psy.), 1968–71, MSc (Math.), 1953–55, PEng, (Mech. Eng.). **Orgs.:** AB Info. Retrieval Assn.: Ch. (1980–81). Adv. Bd. on Sci. and Tech. Info.: (1978–81). Assn. of Prof. Engin., Geologists, and Geophysicists. Psychologists Assn. of AB. **Pubns.:** *Gasoline Marketing in the Context of the Oil Industry*, (1978); oral presentations. **Activities:** 14-Resrch. Cncl.; 24, 41; 91 **Addr.:** Information Systems, Alberta Research Council, Terrace Plz., 4445 Calgary Trail South, Edmonton, AB T6H 5R7 Canada.

Fitzpatrick, Kelly (Ag. 10, 1928, Washington, DC) Dir., Spec. Col., Mt. St. Mary's Coll., 1979–, Dir., Phillips Lib., 1972–79; Libn., Hebron Acad., Hebron, ME, 1969–72. **Educ.:** Mt. St. Mary's Coll., 1951, BS (Econ.); Wesleyan Univ., 1958, MA (Hist., Phil.); Univ. of ME, 1971, MLS. **Orgs.:** Cath. LA: Pres. (1981–83). MD Ctr. for Autom. Prcs.: Exec. Bd. (1974–). Natl. Cncl. of Lib. and Info. Assns.: AACR2 Com. (1979–). ALA: Leg. Netwk. (1976–). Various other orgs. **Pubns.:** *MALCAP Union List of Serials Holdings* (1976); Reviews. **Activities:** 1, 10; 15, 17, 24; 55, 90, 93 **Addr.:** Albatross Hall, 30 Altamont Ave., Thurmont, MD 21788.

Fitzpatrick, Lois A. (Mr. 27, 1952, Yonkers, NY) Dir., Carroll Coll. Lib., 1979–, Actg. Dir., 1979, Ref. Libn., 1976–79; Libn. I, Yonkers Pub. Lib., 1975–76. **Educ.:** Mercy Coll., 1970–73, BS (Soclgy.); Pratt Inst., 1974–75, MLS. **Orgs.:** ALA. MT LA: Nom. Com. (1979); Ad Hoc Com. Pub. Lib. Stans. (1980–); Resols. (1981). Pac. NW LA. MT Gvr.'s Pre-White Hse. Conf.: Plng. Com., Strg. Com., Arrange. Com. (Ch., 1977–78). Soroptimist Intl. of Helena. **Activities:** 1; 15, 17, 31 **Addr.:** Carroll College Library, Helena, MT 59610.

Fitzpayne, Elizabeth Fainsod (Ja. 1, 1942, Cambridge, MA) Assoc. Sci. Libn., Brandeis Univ., 1981–, Sr. Readers' Srvs. Libn., 1976–81; Libn., Inverclyde and Bate Coll. of Nursing, 1975–76; Asst. Libn., Univ. of Strathclyde, 1970–71; Asst. Libn., Brunel Univ., 1968–69; Parkes Catlgr., Univ. of Southampton, 1967–68. **Educ.:** Radcliffe Coll., 1959–63, BA (Hist.); Univ. Coll. London, 1966–67, Dip. Lib.; UK LA, 1969, Assoc. **Orgs.:** New Eng. OLUG: Com. on Mgt. (Ch., 1979–). ALA: ACRL. SLA. New Eng. LA. **Activities:** 1; 39; 75, 91 **Addr.:** Gerstenzang Science Library, Brandeis University, South St., Waltham, MA 02254.

Fitzsimmons, Richard (Mr. 21, 1943, Scranton, PA) Dir. of the Lib., Worthington Scranton Campus, PA State Univ., 1968–; Asst. Ref. Libn., Univ. of Scranton, 1966–68; Libn., St. Pius X Semy., 1970–71; Asst. Dir., Bur. of Urban Lib. Resrch., 1971–73. **Educ.:** Univ. of Scranton, 1961–65, BS (Bus. Admin.); Univ. of Pittsburgh, 1965–66, MLS, 1971–74, PhD (LS); Temple University, 1969–71 (Voc. Ed.). **Orgs.:** ALA: Mem. Com.; RASD, Nom. Com. AALS; Middle Atl. Reg. Lib. Ref.: Bd. of Dir. (1976). PA LA: Pres. (1977–78); VP (1976–77); Gen. Ch., 1974 Conf.; Bd. of Dir. (1970–); other orgs. AAUP. Amer. Vocational Assn. Untd. Nations Assn. of Grt. Scranton: VP. Redev. Athrty. of Wyoming Cnty.: Secy.; other orgs. **Honors:** Beta Phi Mu; PA State Univ., Outstan. fac. mem. of the yr. **Activities:** 1; 17, 25, 28; 59, 78, 82 **Addr.:** Falls, PA 18615.

Flack, Shirley J. (Ja. 15, 1934, Mitchell, NE) Lib. Dir., Scottsbluff Pub. Lib./N.W., NE Reg. Lib. Syst., 1968–, Asst. Libn., 1960–67, Chld. Libn., 1953–54. **Educ.:** NE West. Coll., 1952–53. **Orgs.:** NE LA: Pres. (1979–80); Secy. (1973–74); Pub. Lib. Sect. (Ch., 1970–72). Mt. Plains LA: Secy. (1977–78); Pub. Lib. Sect. (Ch., 1969–70, 1974–75). Panhandle Lib. Netwk. Adv. Cncl.: Secy. (1970–80). NE Pre-White Hse. Conf. on Libs. and Info. Srvs.: Plng. Com. (1978–79). Various other orgs. NE Com. for the Hum. Panhandle Press: Bd. of Dirs. (1975–78). Adult and Cont. Educ. Assn. of NE: Bd. of Dirs. (1975–76). Scotts Bluff Cnty. Volun. Bur.: Bd. of Dirs. (1972–76). **Activities:** 9; 17, 21, 36; 50, 66 **Addr.:** Scottsbluff Public Library, 1809 Third Ave., Scottsbluff, NE 69361.

Flake, Chad J. (D. 28, 1929, Snowflake, AZ) Cur., Spec. Col., Brigham Young Univ., 1957–, Docum. Libn., 1955–57, Asst. Ref., 1953–54. **Educ.:** Brigham Young Univ., 1951–53, BA (Eng., Hist.); Denver Univ., 1953–54, MALS. **Orgs.:** ALA. UT LA: a Past Pres. UT Hist. Assn. Mormon Hist. Assn. **Honors:** Mormon Hist. Assn., Best Mormon Bk. of 1978, 1979; John Whitmer Hist. Assn., Best Mormon Bk. of 1978, 1978; Coll. and Resrch. Libs., Best Ref. Bk. in Relig., 1979. **Pubns.:** *A Mormon Bibliography, 1830–1930* (1978); Jt. auth., *The Brescia Dante* (1975); "Source Review of Stanley P. Hirshon's Lion of the Lord," *Dialogue* (1970); "The Newell Whitney Collection," *BYU Std.* (1971); "The Death of a Son," *Manuscripts* (1973); Various other articles and reviews. **Activities:** 1, 11; 15, 39, 45; 57, 75, 90 **Addr.:** Curator, Special Collections, Brigham Young University, Lee Library, Provo, UT 84601.

Flanagan, Cathleen Coyla (Ap. 21, 1945, St. Paul, MN) Asst. Prof., Grad. Sch. of Educ., Univ. of UT, 1976–; Grad. Tchg. Asst., Grad. Sch. of LS, Univ. of IL, 1971–76; AV Libn., Marriott Lib., Univ. of UT, 1969–71. **Educ.:** Carleton Coll., 1963–65 (Eng.); Univ. of IL, 1965–67, AB (Fr.), 1967–69, MSLS, 1971–76, PhD (LS). **Orgs.:** ALA: Cncl. (1972–75); JMRT (Exec. Bd., 1971–74). AECT. UT LA: Int. Frdm. Com. (Ch., 1978–79). UT Educ. Media Assn. AAUW. Wasatch Mt. Clb. UT Heritage Fndn. Phi Delta Kappa. Various other orgs. **Honors:** Phi Beta Kappa. Beta Phi Mu. **Pubns.:** *Books and Other Print Materials* (1980); Comp., *Utah Governor's Conference on Library and Information Services–Conference Final Report* (1979); jt. auth., *American Folklore: A Bibliography 1950–74* (1977); "Use of Commercial Sound Recordings in Scholarly Research," *ARSC Jnl.* (Fall 1979); "Aubertus Miraeus: An Early Belgian Librarian," *Jnl. of Lib. Hist.* (O. 1975); Various other articles and Sound-Slide presentations. **Activities:** 11; 15, 31, 39; 63 **Addr.:** 5772 South 1615 East, Salt Lake City, UT 84121.

Flanagan, Leo Nelson Lawrence (Je. 21, 1939, Pittsburgh, PA) Reg. Coord., Reg. One Coop. Lib. Srv. Unit, 1978–; Consult., RI LA, 1977–78; Asst. Dir., Pawtucket Pub. Lib., 1974–77; Reg. Coord., North. Interrel. Lib. Syst., 1973–74. **Educ.:** Wheeling Coll., 1957–61, AB (Eng.); Brown Univ., 1961–67, MA (Eng.); Simmons Coll., 1972–73, MLS. **Orgs.:** CT LA: Persnl. Com. (Ch., 1980–81); Legis. Com. (Vice-Ch., 1980). CT State Film Adv. Com.: Ch. (1981). New Eng. LA: Coop. Lib. Agencies Sect. (1980–81). Current Std. in Libnshp.: Ed. Bd. (1978–81). **Honors:** RI LA, Anl. Tribute Awd., 1978; Reg. One Coop. Lib. Srv. Unit, Spec. Bd. Cmdn., 1979; Beta Phi Mu, 1973. **Pubns.:** Jt. auth., *Directory of Connecticut Libraries and Media Centers* (1980); ed., *History of Pawtucket 1635–1976* (1976); "Defending the Indefensible," *Lib. Jnl.* (O. 15, 1975); "Sleeping Giant Awakens: Library Unions," *Wilson Lib. Bltn.* (F. 1974); various other articles. **Activities:** 12; 17, 27, 34; 56, 67, 95-ILL. **Addr.:** Region One CLSU, 267 Grand St., Waterbury, CT 06702.

Flanders, Bruce L. (My. 9, 1954, Lawrence, KS) Head, State Docum. and ILL, State Lib. of KS, 1978–. **Educ.:** Univ. of KS, 1972–77, BA (Eng., Geo.); Univ. of IL, 1977–78, MS (LS). **Orgs.:** KS LA: GODORT (Secy./Treas., 1980–). **Pubns.:** *Statistical Data in Kansas State Documents* (1981); *Selected U.S. and Kansas Publications for School and Public Libraries* (1980); "State Documents in Kansas: Automated Bibliographic Control," *Docum. to the People* (My. 1980). **Activities:** 13; 20, 29, 34 **Addr.:** State Library of Kansas, 3rd Floor, State Capitol, Topeka, KS 66612.

Flanders, Frances Vivian (S. 18, 1908, Howe, OK) Retired, 1973–; Dir., Ouachita Par. Pub. Lib., 1946–73; Org., Dir., Trail Blazer Lib. Syst., 1970–73. **Educ.:** Mansfield Female Coll., 1925–27; Northwest. LA Univ., 1927–29, AB (Eng., Soc. Sci.); LA State Univ., 1934–36, BS (LS). **Orgs.:** LA LA: Treas. (1937–38); Pres. (1950–51); Modisette Awd. Com., Ch.; LA State Lib. Adv. Cncl. SWLA: Mem. Ch. (1940). ALA: Geneal. Com. (1960). Daughters of Amer. Revolution: VP Gen. (1977–80). Natl. Socty. Daughters of Fndrs. and Patriots of Amer. Natl. Socty. of Colonial Wars: Natl. VP (1980–82). Colonial Dames of the XVII Century. Various other orgs. **Honors:** LA LA, Essae M. Culver Awd., 1973. **Pubns.:** Various articles. **Activities:** 9, 14-Syst.; 17, 24; 69 **Addr.:** 1703 N. Third St., Monroe, LA 71201.

Fleckner, John A. (Ag. 28, 1941, Oak Park, IL) Archvst., State Hist. Socty. of WI, 1971–; Prog. Ofcr., Resrch. Cols., Natl. Endow. for the Hum., 1978. **Educ.:** Colgate Univ., 1959–63, BA (Hist.); Univ. of WI, 1963–65, MA (Hist.), 1970, MA (Indian Std.), 1971–, PhD Cand. **Orgs.:** SAA: Prog. Com. (Co-Ch., 1981); Ed. Bd. (1977–1980); Natl. Conf. on Hist. Recs. Priorities (1977). Midwest Arch. Conf.: Cncl. (1979–81); Ed. Bd. (1974–77). **Honors:** Phi Beta Kappa. **Pubns.:** "Cooperation as a Strategy for Archival Institutions," *Amer. Archvst.* (O., 1976); "Poverty and Relief in 19th Century Janesville," *WI Mag. of Hist.* (Sum. 1978); *Archives and Manuscripts: Surveys* (1977); "Records Surveys: A Multi-purpose Tool for the Archivist: Introduction," *Amer. Archvst.* (1979); "The Records Program of the NHPRC," *Midwest. Archvst.* (1978); various other articles. **Activities:** 2; 17, 28, 34; 73 **Addr.:** Archives Division, State Historical Society of Wisconsin, 816 State St., Madison, WI 53711.

Fleeman, Mary Grace (Moore) (Ag. 24, 1947, Morgantown, WV) Sr. Catlgr., George Washington Univ. Law Lib., 1980–; Serials Catlgr., Univ. of OK, 1979–80; Cat. Libn., Frostburg State Coll., 1974–79; Asst. Exch. and Gift Libn., Serials Catlgr., U.S. Geol. Srvy., 1971–74. **Educ.:** Allegheny Coll., 1965–69, BS (Math); Univ. of NC, 1969–71, MSLS; Frostburg State Coll., 1977–79, MSM (Mgt.). **Orgs.:** ALA. DC LA. AALL. AAUW. **Honors:** Beta Phi Mu, 1971. **Pubns.:** "Availability and Acceptability of Serial Records in the OCLC Data Base," *Serials Libn.* (1981–82); index, *Allegany County–A History* (1976). **Activities:** 1; 20, 44, 46; 59, 77, 88 **Addr.:** 4923 McCall St., Rockville, MD 20853.

Fleitas, Nina H. (Je. 25, 1950, Philadelphia, PA) Law Libn., Blitman & King, 1979–; Law Libn., Melvin & Melvin, 1978–79; Law Libn., Hancock, Estabrook, Ryan, Shove & Hust, 1973–78. **Educ.:** Syracuse Univ., 1973–80, BA (Geo.), 1975–, MLS, 1980. **Orgs.:** Assn. of Law Libs. of Upstate NY: Pres. (1977–79), Secy. (1975–76). AALL: Co-Ch., Lcl. Arrang. (1978). SLA. **Activities:** 12; 15, 20, 38; 77, 78

Special Subjects/Services: 50. Adult educ.; 51. Advert./Mktg.; 52. Aerosp.; 53. Agric.; 54. Area std.; 55. Arts/Hum.; 56. Autom.; 57. Bibl./Prtg.; 58. Bio. sci.; 59. Bus./Fin.; 60. Chem.; 61. Copyrt.; 62. Documtn.; 63. Educ.; 64. Engin.; 65. Env.; 66. Eth. grps.; 67. Film; 68. Food/Nutr.; 69. Geneal.; 70. Geo.; 71. Geol.; 72. Handcpd.; 73. Hist.; 74. Int. frdm.; 75. Info. sci.; 76. Insr.; 77. Law; 78. Legis.; 79. Math./Comp. sci.; 80. Med.; 81. Metals; 82. Nat. resrcs.; 83. Newsp.; 84. Nuc. sci.; 85. Oral hist.; 86. Petr./Energy; 87. Pharm.; 88. Phys./Astr./Math.; 89. Readg.; 90. Relig.; 91. Sci./Tech.; 92. Soc. sci.; 93. Telecom.; 94. Transp.; 95. (other).

Fleming, Erin Patricia Lockhart (D. 27, 1939, Hamilton, ON) Lect., Fac. of LS, Univ. of Toronto, 1971–; Head, Bibl. Ctr., Metro. Toronto Ctrl. Lib., 1964–69. **Educ.:** McMaster Univ., 1957–60, BA (Lang & Lit); Univ. of Toronto, 1963–64, BLS, 1966–70, MLS; Univ. of London, 1975–77, MA (Hist. and Anal. Bibl.), PhD in prog. **Orgs.:** Bibl. Socty. Bibl. Socty. of Can. Can. LA. **Honors:** Canada Cncl., Resrch. Grant, 1973; Univ. of London, Cowley Medal, 1977. **Pubns.:** "A Bibliography of Ontario Directories to 1867", *ON Lib. Rev.* (Je. 1975); "A Study of Pre-Confederation Ontario Bookbinding," *Papers of the Bibl. Socty. of Canada* (1972). **Activities:** 39, 45; 55, 57, 95-Canadiana. **Addr.:** Faculty of Library Science, University of Toronto, 140 St. George St., Toronto, ON M5S 1AN Canada.

Fleming, John Zinn (S. 5, 1941, Lewistown, PA) Ref. libn., Asst. Prof., Edinboro State Coll., 1970–; Msc. Lib. Asst. Instr., Univ. of IL, 1967–70. **Educ.:** Juniata Coll., 1959–63, BS (Msc. Educ.); Univ. of Pittsburgh, 1966–67, MLS. **Orgs.:** Msc LA. Msc. LA PA Chap., Co-Fndr. (1973); Mem. Com. (1974–76). AAUP. **Pubns.:** Weekly radio programs (1973–1979). **Activities:** 1; 15, 20, 32; 55, 67, 95 **Addr.:** Box 60, 310 Plum St., Edinboro, PA 16412.

Fleming, June D. (Je. 24, 1931, Little Rock, AR) Dir. of Libs., City of Palo Alto, CA, 1968–; Libn. II, Mtn. View, CA, 1967–68; Chief Libn., Philander Smith Coll., 1960–67; Libn., Dunbar HS, 1955–56. **Educ.:** Talladega Coll., Talladega, AL, 1949–53, BA (Psy.); Drexel Univ., 1953–54, MLS; Stanford Univ. Grad. Sch. of Bus., 1973, Cert. **Orgs.:** CA LA: Pres. (1977). ALA. Delta Sigma Theta Sorority. Soroptimist Intl. **Activities:** 1, 9; 17, 35; 72 **Addr.:** 250 Hamilton Ave., Palo Alto, CA 94301.

Fleming, Lois DeLavan (Ja. 25, 1928, Toledo, OH) Lib. Admin., Leon Cnty. Pub. Lib. Syst. 1978–; Pub. Lib. Consult., FL State Lib., 1972–78; Cmnty. Srvs. Libn., Palm Beach Cnty. Pub. Lib. Syst., 1970–72; Asst. Libn., Instr., Strozier Lib., FL State Univ., 1965–67. **Educ.:** FL State Univ., 1950, BA (Jnlsm.), 1965, MLS, 1968, Advnc. Mstrs. Degree (LS). Univ. of UT, 1968–69, Post Grad. Std. (Educ. Psy.); FL State Univ., 1976–, Doct. Prog. (Adult Educ.). **Orgs.:** ALA: RASD, Adult Srvs. Com. (1978–80); PLA, Alternative Educ. Progs. Sect. (Ch., 1978–79); Crs. by Newsp. Proj. Adv. Com. (1978–). CLENE: Adv. Bd. (1978–81). SELA. FL LA: Bd. of Dirs. (1978–81); various coms. Various other orgs. FL Cncl. on Aging. FL Hist. Socty. Natl. Assn. of Parlmts. World Future Socty. Various other orgs. **Honors:** Beta Phi Mu. **Pubns.:** Ed., *Adult Basic Education and Public Library Service* (Conf. Proceedings) (1974); "Adult Services," *ALA Yearbook* (1979); "Library Services to the Older Adult," *Catholic Lib. World* (D. 1978); "The State Library's Role in the Literacy Effort," *Drexel Lib. Qtly.* (Win. 1979); "Public Libraries and School Media Centers: Partners in the Big Picture," *Sch. Media Qtly.* (Fall 1978); various other articles, wkshps., and oral presentations. **Activities:** 9; 17, 24, 26; 50, 89 **Addr.:** Rt. 3, Box 162, Quincy, FL 32351.

Fleming, Thomas B. (N. 14, 1948, Philadelphia, PA) Chief, Law Branch, US Dept of Cmrc. Lib., 1973–, Law Libn., 1972–73. **Educ.:** Rockford Coll., 1968–71, BA (Hist.); Case Western Reserve Univ., 1971–72, MSLS. **Orgs.:** AALL: Law Lib. Jnl. (1977–78). Law Libns. Socty. of Washington, DC: Treas. (1975–78). ASIS. **Honors:** US Dept of Cmrc., Outstan. Perf. 1976, 77, 78, 79; Beta Phi Mu. **Activities:** 4; 15, 17, 24; 59, 77, 78 **Addr.:** U.S. Department of Commerce Library, Law Branch, Rm. 1894, 14th & Constitution Ave, N.W., Washington, DC 20230.

Flemister, Wilson N. (Ag. 15, 1939, Atlanta, GA) Head Libn., Interdenominational Theo. Ctr., 1969–, Actg. Libn., 1968–69, Asst. Libn. for Tech. Srvs., 1965–68. **Educ.:** Clark Coll., 1957–59, 1961–63, BA (Msc.); Atlanta Univ., 1964–65, MS (LS); Candler Sch. of Theo., Emory Univ., 1968–70, 1972–73, MDiv, 1975, Cert. (Admin. and Mgt. of Arch. Cols.). **Orgs.:** ATLA: Bd. of Dirs. (1972–75); Bd. of Microtext (1972–76). GA LA. Meth. Libns. Flwshp.: Pres. (1969–72). Amer. Theo. Assn. **Pubns.:** "Annotated List of Dissertations on the Life and Work of Martin Luther King, Jr.," *Jnl. of the Interdenominational Theo. Ctr.* (Spr. 1977). **Addr.:** Interdenominational Theological Center, 671 Beckwith St. S.W., Atlanta, GA 30314.

Flener, Jane G. (Ja. 3, 1920, Hopkinsville, KY) Assoc. Dir. of Libs., Univ. of MI, 1976–; Assoc. Univ. Libn., Univ. of CA, Berkeley, 1973–76; Asst. Dir. of Libs., IN Univ., 1963–73. **Educ.:** George Peabody Coll., 1939–45, BS, BS in LS, MA (Eng.); IN Univ., 1958–63, EdD (Higher Educ.). **Orgs.:** ALA: ACRL, Bd. of Dir. (1976–80). IFLA: Secy., Univ. Libs. Sect. (1977–81). IN LA: Pres. (1970). SLA. **Pubns.:** Jt. auth., "Copyright–One Year Later: A Symposium," *Jnl. of Acad. Libnshp.* (Jl., 1979); "Personalizing Personnel", *Jnl. of Acad. Libnshp.* (Mr., 1975); "Staff Participation in Management of Large University Libraries", *Coll. & Resrch. Libs.* (Jl., 1973). **Activities:** 1; 17 **Addr.:** 818 Hatcher Graduate Library, The University of Michigan, Ann Arbor, MI 48109.

Flesher, Lorna J. (O. 31, 1945, Everett, WA) Law Libn., CA Dept. of Transp., 1976–, Sr. Libn., 1971–76; Libn. I and II, CA State Lib., Gvt. Pubns., 1968–71. **Educ.:** Humboldt State Coll., 1963–67, BA (Soclgy.); Univ. of CA, Berkeley, 1967–68, MLS. **Orgs.:** SLA: Sierra NV Place. (1977–78). AALL. North. CA Assn. of Law Libs. **Activities:** 12, 13; 17, 30, 41; 77, 94 **Addr.:** California Dept. of Transportation, Legal Div. Library, 1120 "N" St. Rm. 1315, Sacramento, CA 95814.

Fletcher, Homer L. (My. 11, 1928, Salem, IN) City Libn., San Jose Pub. Lib., 1970–; City Libn., Vallejo Pub. Lib., 1965–70; City Libn., Arcadia Pub. Lib., 1959–65; Head Libn., Ashland Pub. Lib., 1956–59. **Educ.:** IN Univ., 1949–53, AB (Hist.); Univ. of IL, 1953–54, MS (LS). **Orgs.:** ALA: Int. Com. (1967–72). CA LA: Pub. Lib. Sect. (Pres., 1967). Pub. Lib. Execs. of Ctrl. CA: Pres. (1980–81). Rotary Club. **Honors:** Phi Beta Kappa, 1953. **Addr.:** San Jose Public Library, 180 W. San Carlos St., San Jose, CA 95113.

Fletcher, Janet (Mr. 20, 1938, New York, NY) Ed., The Book Review, *Lib. Jnl.*, 1972–. **Educ.:** City Coll. of NY, 1964–68, AB (Eng. Lit.). **Orgs.:** ALA: Notable Books Cncl. (1979–81). Natl. Book Critics Circle. **Honors:** Phi Beta Kappa, 1968. **Activities:** 14-Prof. Jnl.; 42 **Addr.:** 10 Sheridan SQ #11A, New York, NY 10014.

Fletcher, Marilyn P. (Ag. 3, 1940, El Dorado, AR) Serials Acq. Libn., Univ. of NM Gen. Lib., 1981–, Serials Catlgr., 1980–81; Univ. of Southwest. LA, 1977–79; Head, Serials Cat. Team, Univ. of NM, 1973–77, Head, Serials Dept., 1970–73; Catlgr., Sandia Labs. Tech. Lib., 1968–70; Acq. Libn., Univ. of NM, 1965–68. **Educ.:** Gulf Park Coll., 1958–60, AA (Liberal Arts); Centenary Coll., 1960–62, BS (Bus. Admin.); LA State Univ., 1964–65, MS (LS). **Orgs.:** ALA. SWLA: Schol. Com. (1971); Coll. and Univ. Int. Grp. (Secy., 1976–78). NM LA: Schol. Com. Ch. (1968–71); Coll., Univ. and Spec. Lib. Div. (Ch., 1970); Treas. (1973–74); Constn. and Bylaws Com. (1972). LA LA. AAUP. AAUW. Civitan Intl. **Honors:** Beta Phi Mu, 1965. **Pubns.:** *Science Fiction Story Index 1950-1979* (1981); jt. auth., "More Staff for No Money" *NM Libs. Nsltr.* (F. 1976); reviews. **Activities:** 1; 20, 44, 46; 75 **Addr.:** 10429 Karen N.E., Albuquerque, NM 87111.

Fletcher, Marjorie Amos (Jl. 10, 1923, Easton, PA) Dir. of Arch. and Oral Hist., Amer. Coll., 1975–, Fac., 1972–, Resrch. Libn., 1968–75. **Educ.:** Bryn Mawr Coll., 1942–46, BA (Econ.). **Orgs.:** SLA: Pres. Phila. Chap. (1978); Dir., Insurance Div. (1979–80). Oral Hist. Assn. SAA: Oral Hist. Com. (1976–). Hobson Pittman House and Meml. Gallery, Bryn Mawr Coll.: Ch. (1979–). **Pubns.:** *Acquisitions in the Special Library: Print and Nonprint* (1976); *The Open University, The External Degree and Nontraditional Study* (1972); "The Open University of Great Britain: Its Influence on Nontraditional Education in the United States," *Drexel Lib. Qtly.* (Ap. 1975); Film strip and audiocassette, *The Catalog., Multimedia and the Special Library* (1973). **Activities:** 2, 14; 17, 23, 41; 50, 59, 75, 85 **Addr.:** Archives and Oral History, The American College, Bryn Mawr, PA 19010.

Flick, Frances Josephine (Ag. 17, 1916, Maryville, MO) Acq. Libn., Sci. Biblgphr., Univ. of AZ, 1969–; Head Libn., Natl. Animal Disease Ctr., 1961–69; Ref. Libn., Univ. of IA, 1956–61; Forestry Biblgphr., US Dept. of Agr. Lib., 1947–56; Engin. Resrch. Libn., Carrier Corp., Syracuse, 1945–47; Engin. and Docum. Libn., LA Polytech. Inst., 1944–45; Ref. and Cat., Des Moines Pub. Lib., 1940–44. **Educ.:** IA State Univ., 1936–39, BS (Forestry); Syracuse Univ., 1941–43, BS (LS); Comp. Applications in Libs., Univ. of IL, 1967, Cert. **Orgs.:** SLA. AZ LA: Spec. Libns. Grp. (Vice Ch., 1975–76). AAUW. **Activities:** 1, 4; 15, 20, 39; 65, 82, 91 **Addr.:** University of Arizona Library, Tucson, AZ 85716.

Flitton, Marilyn G. (Mr. 21, 1922, Halifax, NS) Freelnc. resrchr., biblgphr., cmplr., 1976–; Resrch. Assoc., Simon Fraser Univ., 1973–76; Instr., Vancouver Cmnty. Coll., 1970–71; Instr., Simon Fraser Univ., 1966–67. **Educ.:** McGill Univ., 1939–42, BA; Simon Fraser Univ., 1972–73, MA (Eng.); Univ. of BC, 1961–62 (Eng.); Prof. Tchg. Cert. **Orgs.:** Indx. & Abs. Socty.: Reg. Dir. (1977–80). Bibl. Socty. of Can.: Indxr. to the Socty. (1979–80). Assn. of Can./PQ Lit.: Bibl. com. (1976–78). **Pubns.:** *Index to Canadian Monthly & National Review 1872–1882* (1976); "Annual Bibl. of Can. Literature," *The Jnl. of Commonwealth Lit.* (D. 1978, D. 1979). **Activities:** 1, 2; 30, 41; 55, 57 **Addr.:** 2766 West First Ave., Vancouver, BC V6K 1H3 Canada.

Flood, Barbara Joyce (S. 4, 1931, New York, NY) Dir., Info. Sci. Inst. and Socty., 1975–; Asst. Prof. of Info. Sci., Drexel Univ., 1966–75; Tech. Writer, Dental Resrch. Lab, Univ. of PA, 1964–65; Asst. Ed., Biological Abs., 1961–64. **Educ.:** Wellesley Coll., 1949–53, BA (Psy.); Columbia Coll. of Physicians & Surgeons, 1958–60, (Med.); Drexel Univ., 1965–66, MS (Info. Sci.); Temple Univ., 1967–71, Ed.D. (grp. & Soc. processes). **Orgs.:** ASIS: Ch., Const. & Bylaws (1972–74); Ch., SIG Tech./Info./Socty. (1972–73); ProtoSIG Writing/Editing/Publishing (1977–78); Task Force on SIGs (1975–76). Natl. Info. Retrieval Colloquium: Ch. (1971–72), Pres. (1972–73). AAAS. **Honors:** Phi Kappa Phi, 1967; Beta Phi Mu, 1967. **Pubns.:** Jt. ed., "Recent advances in indexing," *Drexel Lib. Qtly.* (Ap. 1972); "Teaching abstracting and indexing," *Jnl. Amer. Socty. Info. Sci.* (1972); "Aggrevation quotient: search time/use time," *Proc. Amer. Socty. Info Sci.* (1973); "Management training emphasizing evaluation," *ASIS SIG Newsletter ED.-1:* (1974); "Broadcasting vs. narrowcasting: the user as receiver and sender of information," *Proc. Amer. Socty. Info. Sci.* (1975); Other articles. **Activities:** 6; 24, 26, 30; 75, 80, 91 **Addr.:** 521 South 24th St., Philadelphia, PA 19146.

Flores, Fay F. (D. 25, 1946, Prince Albert, SK) Lib. Dir., Aguadilla Reg. Coll., PR, 1978–; Ref. Libn., Edmonton Pub. Lib., 1975–77; Catlgr., Aguadilla Reg. Coll., 1973–77; Head, Pub. Srvs., Cayey Univ. Coll., 1970–73; Serials Libn., Univ. of Calgary, 1968–69. **Educ.:** Univ. of Calgary, 1964–67, BA (Hist.); Univ. of BC, 1967–68, BLS. **Orgs.:** ALA. Sociedad de Bibliotecarios de PR. Assn. of Caribbean Univ. and Resrch. Libs. **Addr.:** Biblioteca, Colegio Regional de Aguadilla (UPR), P.O. Box 160, Ramey, PR 00604.

Flores, John G. (Boston, MA) Dir., Lib. Media Srvs., Watertown (MA) Pub. Sch., 1978–, AV Media Spec., 1973–78, Tchr., 1972–73; Adj. Prof., Dept. of Educ. Media, Boston State Coll., 1974–. **Educ.:** Boston State Coll., 1969–71, BS (Educ.); Boston Univ., 1972–73, MEd (Educ. Media); Boston Coll., 1975–77, (Educ. Admin.); Boston State Coll., 1977–78, Cert. Advnc. Std. (Educ. Admin.). **Orgs.:** ALA: AASL. AECT. MA Assn. for Educ. Media: Prof. Stan. Ch. (1980–). New Eng. Educ. Media Assn. Natl. Educ. Assn. MA Tchrs. Assn. Assn. for Supvsn. and Curric. Dev. Watertown Tchrs. Assn.: First VP (1975–77). **Addr.:** Watertown Public Schools, 30 Common St., Watertown, MA 02172.

Flores, Robert J. (Jl. 26, 1927, Albany, NY) Chief, Bur. of Reg. Lib. Srvs., NY State Lib., 1967–, Actg. Dir. of Lib. Dev., 1974–76, Assoc. Lib. Supvsr., Ext., 1963–67, Sr. Lib. Supvsr., Ext., 1957–63, Asst. Lib. Supvsr., 1956–57, Jr. Libn., 1950–56. **Educ.:** Siena Coll., 1945–49, AB (Eng.); SUNY, Albany, 1949–50, MS (LS); Univ. of MD, 1968, Cert. (Lib. Admin. Dev. Prog.). **Orgs.:** NY LA: Schol. and Rcrt. Com. (Ch., 1958–59). ALA: Person-to-Person Rcrt. Netwk. (1958–68); NY State Ch. (1964); Lib. Admin. Div., Cert. Com. (1965–68). Albany Lib. Sch. Alum. Assn.: Pres. (1965–66). NY State Pub. Libns. Cert. Exam. Com.: Secy. (1964–67). Various other orgs. Town of Colonie (NY) Hist. Socty.: Pres. (1980); Dir. (1981–). **Pubns.:** Ed., *The Bookmark* (1964–65). **Activities:** 9, 13; 17, 27, 34; 78 **Addr.:** 13 Comely Ln., Latham, NY 12110.

Flott, Nancy L. (Je. 8, 1932, Wichita, KS) Dir., KS Educ. Dissemination/Diffusion Syst., Resrc. Component, KS State Dept. of Educ., 1975–, Info. Spec., Proj. Communicate, 1973–75; Sch. Lib. Media Spec., USD #345, Topeka, KS, 1963–73; Sch. Libn., Lab. Sch., Emporia State Univ., 1960–63. **Educ.:** Emporia State Univ., 1950–54, BS (LS, Math), 1960–62, MS (LS); KS State Univ., 1973–76, PhD (Adult Educ.). **Orgs.:** Assn. for Info. Mgrs. KS Assn. for Sch. Libns. KS Online Grp. AAUW: Topic Ch.; Phi Delta Kappa. **Addr.:** KEDDS Resources, Kansas State Department of Education, 120 E. 10th, Topeka, KS 66612.

Flower, Kenneth Earl (My. 14, 1952, Burlington, VT) Chief, Ref. Srvs., MA State Lib., 1980–; Co-Chief, 1979–80, Ref. Libn., 1977–79. **Educ.:** St. Lawrence Univ., 1970–74, AB (Gvt.); Simmons Coll., 1975–77, MS (LS); Northeast. Univ., 1979–, MPA Cand. (Pub. Admin.). **Orgs.:** SLA: Boston Chap., Manual Rev. Com. (1979–81). Boston Grp. of Gvt. Libs.: VP (1981–82); Bylaws (1980–81); Dir. (1980–81). Boston Lib. Cnsrtm.: Readr. Srvs. (1978–80); Acq. (1980–82). **Honors:** Beta Phi Mu. **Pubns.:** Contrib., *Guide to Massachusetts Legislative and Government Research* (1981); *A Guide to Mass. Genealogical Material in the State Library of Massachusetts* (1979). **Activities:** 12, 13; 15, 17, 39; 62, 77, 78 **Addr.:** Reference Services, Massachusetts State Library, 341 State House, Boston, MA 02133.

Flower, Mrs. M. A. (Bridgeport, CTk) Head, Nursing Lib., McGill Univ., 1978–, Info Coord., Sch. of Nursing Resrch. Unit, 1976–78; Libn., ON Med. Assn., 1972–76. **Educ.:** McGill Univ., 1935–39, BA (Eng & Phil.); Univ. of Toronto, 1968–69, BLS, 1975, MLS; Cert. of Med. Libnshp., Med. LA, 1975. **Orgs.:** Med. LA: Med. Socty. Libs. Grp. (Secy. 1973–74, Ch. 1974–75); Can. Grp. (Ch.-Elect, 1976–77, Ch., 1977–78); Surveys and Stats. Com. (1979–). Can. LA: Stats. Com. (1979–). Can. Hlth. Libs. Assn.: Pres. (1977–79). Can. Inst. of Sci. and Tech. Info.: Adv. Com. on the Hlth. Sci. Resrc. Ctr. (1979–). Other orgs. **Pubns.:** "Hospital Libraries–who cares?," *ON Med. Rev.* (May 1974); Jt. auth., "Canadian standards for hospital libraries," *Canad. Med. Assn. Jnl.* (May 1975); "Toward hospital library standards in Canada", *Bltn. Med. LA* (July 1978); "Canadian Health Library Project: working notes", *Bibliotheca Medica Canadiana* (1979); "Canadian Health Libraries Association," *Canadian Library Handbook,* (1979); other articles. **Activities:** 1, 12; 17, 24, 25; 50, 80, 92 **Addr.:** Nursing Library, Wilson Hall, McGill University, 3506 University St., Montreal, PQ H3A 2A7 Canada.

Flowers, Helen F. (Ag. 10, 1931, Elizabethtown, KY) Lib. Media Spec., Bay Shore HS, 1965–; Adj. Asst. Prof., Palmer Grad. Lib. Sch., Long Island Univ., 1976–; Libn., Ashley Hall, Charleston, SC, 1962–64; Tchr., St. Andrews HS, Charleston, SC, 1956–61; Asst. Libn., Army Lib. Srv., 1955–56. **Educ.:** Peabody Coll. for Tchrs., 1951–54, BA (Eng. Educ.); Columbia Univ., 1961–62, MSLS; 1964–65; Hofstra Univ., 1977–79, Admin. Cert. (Educ. Admin.), 1979–80, Prof. Dip. (Educ. Admin.), 1980–, Doct. Cand. (Educ. Admin.). **Orgs.:** Intl. Assn. of Sch. Libnshp.

PROFESSIONAL ACTIVITIES: Institutions: 1. Acad. lib.; 2. Arch.; 3. Assn.; 4. Fed./Gvt. lib.; 5. Inst. lib.; 6. Mfr./Suppl.; 7. Milit. lib.; 8. Musm.; 9. Pub. lib.; 10. Sch. lib.; 11. Sch. of lib. sci.; 12. Spec. lib.; 13. State lib.; 14. (other). **Functions/Activities:** 15. Acq./Col. dev.; 16. Adult srvs.; 17. Admin.; 18. Apprais.; 19. Archit./Bldgs.; 20. Cat./Class.; 21. Chld. srvs.; 22. Circ.; 23. Cons./Pres.; 24. Consult.; 25. Cont. ed.; 26. Educ. lib. sci.; 27. Ext. srvs.; 28. Fund/Grants; 29. Gvt. pubs.; 30. Indx./Abs.; 31. Instr. lib. use; 32. Media srvs.; 33. Micro.; 34. Netwks./Coop.; 35. Persnl.; 36. PR; 37. Publshg.; 38. Recs. mgt.; 39. Ref. srvs.; 40. Repro.; 41. Resrch.; 42. Review.; 43. Secur.; 44. Serials; 45. Spec. col.; 46. Tech. srvs.; 47. Trustees/Bds.; 48. YA srvs.; 49. (other).

ALA: AASL, Pubn. Com. (1975–76). NY LA: Exhibits Com. (1976); Pubn. Com. (1976); Sch. Lib. Media Sect., Awds. Ch. (1979–80); Exec. Bd. (1980–82). Suffolk Cnty. LA: Pres. (1971–72); Exec. Bd. (1966–73, 1975). AAUP. Amer. Educ. Resrch. Assn. **Honors:** Phi Delta Kappa. **Pubns.:** Various sps. **Activities:** 10, 11; 17, 26, 32; 55 **Addr.:** 401 E. Main St., Apt. A-7, Bay Shore, NY 11706.

Fluckiger, Adrienne N. (Ag. 28, 1926, Branford, CT) Head of Chld. Srvs., Syosset Pub. Lib., 1968–; Chld. Libn., Seaford Pub. Lib., 1963–68. **Educ.:** Middlebury Col., 1943–47, BA (Soclgy.); Long Island Univ., 1963–67, MLS. **Orgs.:** ALA: Newbery-Caldecott Com. (1978). NY LA. Nassau Cnty. Lib. Assn.: VP (1980); Pres. (1981); Chld. Srvs. Div. (Pres., 1974). **Honors:** Beta Phi Mu. **Activities:** 9; 21; 67 **Addr.:** 3964 Marilyn Dr., Seaford, NY 11783.

Flynn, Barbara L. (O. 3, 1943, Chicago, IL) Head, AV Ctr., Chicago Pub. Lib., 1969–. **Educ.:** Loyola Univ., 1964–69, BA (Comm.); Rosary Coll., 1970–71, MA (LS); Loyola Univ., 1981–, MA Cand. (Theo.). **Orgs.:** ALA: PLA, AV Com. (1975–78); ASCLA, AV Com. (1977–78). Ofc. of Lib Srv. to Disadv.: Adv. Com. (1977–78). Coal. on Lib. Srv. to Hearing Impaired: Pres. (1979–80). Chicago Jr. Assn. Cmrce. and Indus.: Bd. of Dirs. (1977). **Pubns.:** "Deaf Are Being Heard," *Film News* (O. 1979); "Film Programming/Western Civilization," *Film News* (O. 1972); reviews. **Activities:** 9; 17, 32, 39; 67, 72, 93 **Addr.:** Chicago Public Library - AV Center, 78 E. Washington St., Chicago, IL 60631.

Flynn, Kathryn Jean (D. 11, 1920, Buhl, MN) Dir., Neenah Pub. Lib., 1963–; Lib. Dir., Shorewood Pub. Lib., 1953–63; Asst. Libn./Catlgr., Milwaukee-Downer Coll., 1950–53; Instr., Cat., Univ. of WI, Milwaukee, 1960–61, 1956–58. **Educ.:** Milwaukee - Downer Coll., 1938–42, BA (Eng.); Univ. of WI, Madison, 1949–50, BLS. **Orgs.:** ALA. WI LA: Pres., Pub. Lib. Sect. (1967–68); Ch., Sch. Com. (1959). Fox Valley LA: Pres. (1966). Fox Valley Lib. Cncl.: Secy. (1978–79). Univ. of WI Lib. Sch. Alum. Assn.: Pres. (1969–70). Lawrence Univ. Alum. Assn. Woman's Tuesday Club, Neenah, WI: Secy. (1978–80). Altrusa Club of Neenah-Menasha, WI. **Honors:** Beta Phi Mu, 1959. **Activities:** 9; 17, 35, 42 **Addr.:** Neenah Public Library, 240 E. Wisconsin Ave., Neenah, WI 54956.

Flynn, Neil C. (Jl. 28, 1923, St. Paul, MN) Dir., Lake Cnty. (IN) Pub. Lib., 1979–; Exec. Dir., Lewis & Clark Lib. Syst. (IL), 1976–79; Dir., Northwest Reg. Lib. (MN), 1975–76; Assoc. Dir., Wilmington & New Castle Cnty. Libs. (DE), 1971–75. **Educ.:** Univ. of MN, 1966–69, BA (Hist.), 1969–71, MA (LS). **Orgs.:** ALA. IN LA. SLA. IL Lib. Syst. Dir. Org.: Presiding Ofcr. (1979). Rotary Intl. Kiwanis. **Activities:** 9; 17, 34; 56, 93 **Addr.:** Lake County Public Library, 1919 West Lincoln Hwy., Merrillville, IN 46410.

Flynn, Roger R. (My. 11, 1939, Chicago, IL) Asst. Prof., Coord., Undergrad. Prog., Mgr., Corp. Lab, Univ. of Pittsburgh, 1980–, Lectr., 1977–80. **Educ.:** Villanova Univ., 1959–62, BA (Phil.); IL Inst. of Tech., 1972–73, MST (Comp. Sci.); Univ. of Pittsburgh, 1974–78, PhD (Info. Sci.). **Orgs.:** ASIS. AALS. Assn. for Comp. Mach. **Pubns.:** Jt. auth., "Network Topology: Functions of Existing Networks," *The Structure and Governance of Library Networks* (1980); jt. auth., "Reply to the SLC Report," *Lib. Acq.: Prac. and Theory* (1980); "The University of Pittsburgh Study of Journal Usage: A Summary Report," *Serials Libn.* (1979); jt. auth., "On the Strength of Belief Systems," *Intl. Jnl. of Gen. Systs.* (1978). **Activities:** 11; 26, 34; 56, 75, 93 **Addr.:** University of Pittsburgh, SLIS, Pittsburgh, PA 15260.

Fobes, Hazel Weaver (Ag. 16, 1915, Charlottesville, VA) Pres., Frnds. of Chapel Hill (NC) Pub. Lib. (Volun.), 1981–; Ref. Libn., Amer. Lib. in Paris, 1965–68; Head Libn., Amer. Intl. Sch., New Delhi, India, 1960–64; Libn., Hollin Hall Elem. Sch., Alexandria, VA, 1957–60; Resrch. Libn., Docmlst., Fletcher Sch. of Law and Diplomacy, 1941–42; Libn., Fluvanna Cnty. (VA) HS, 1935–41. **Educ.:** Westhampton Coll., Univ. of Richmond, 1931–35, BA (Lit.); Univ. of VA, 1935–37, (LS); Indiana Univ., Sum. 1970, Intl. Libs. **Orgs.:** ALA. Frnds. of Chapel Hill Pub. Lib. AAUW. Unesco Cmnty. Srv., Unesco House, Paris: Fndr., Dir. (1972–78). Intl. Women's Yr.: Del. (1975). **Honors:** Unesco Cmnty. Srv. *Review,* Dedication in Bianl. Lit. Pubn., Win. 1977. **Pubns.:** "Why an International Women's Year?" Unesco Cmnty. Srv. *Review* (Win. 1975); "The Family in the Balance," *Review* (Sum. 1976); "Let's Relate to the UN Field Staff Member and his Family," *Unesco Field Staff Letter* (Fall 1978); "A Library Handbook for Volunteers" (handbk.) (1958). **Activities:** 10, 12; 21, 41, 48; 54, 89 **Addr.:** 739 Gimghoul Rd., Chapel Hill, NC 27514.

Fody, Barbara A. (Mr. 17, 1953, Bronx, NY) Mgr., Lib. Srvs., Blyth Eastman Paine Webber, 1980–; Head Libn., Paine Webber Jackson and Curtis, 1978–80, Asst. Libn., 1976–78. **Educ.:** Molloy Coll., 1970–74, BS (Bio.); St. John's Univ., 1974–76, MLS. **Orgs.:** SLA: Downtown Luncheon Com. (Co-Ch., 1980); NY Chap. Audit Com. (1980–); SLA NY Chap. Dir., Ed. Staff (1979–80), Co-Ed. (1981–). **Activities:** 12; 15, 17, 18; 59 **Addr.:** Blyth Eastman Paine Webber, Library, 1221 Ave. of the Americas, New York, NY 10020.

Fogarty, Catherine B. (F. 14, 1913, Liverpool, Eng.) Libn., Grey Nuns of the Sacred Heart Motherhse. Complex, 1975–; Tchr., various Cath. schs., 1960–74; Prod. Asst. Dir., Brit. Info. Srvs., NY, 1957. **Educ.:** D'Youville Coll., 1968, BS (Eng.); Villanova Univ., 1972, MA (Eng.), 1981–, MLS Cand.; various crs. **Orgs.:** ALA. Cath. LA. PA LA. **Activities:** 1 **Addr.:** Grey Nuns Motherhouse Library, Quarry Rd., Yardley, PA 19067.

Fogarty, Nancy Clark (Je. 13, 1944, Greensboro, NC) Head Ref. Libn., Univ. of NC, Greensboro, 1976–; Asst. Ref. Libn., 1970–76; Asst. Ref. Libn., Univ. of NC, Chapel Hill, 1969–70; Eng. Tchr., Walter Hines Page Sr. HS, Greensboro, NC, 1966–68. **Educ.:** Univ. of NC, Greensboro, 1962–66, BA (Eng); Univ. of NC, Chapel Hill, 1968–69 MLS; Univ of NC, Greensboro, 1974–80 MA (Comm.). **Orgs.:** SELA. NC LA: Sec. VP and Ch. of Mem. (1971–1973). Guilford Lib. Club. Beta Phi Mu: Epsilon Chap. (Secy. Treas., 1971–73). Sch. of LS, Univ. of NC, Chapel Hill Alum. Assn.: Pres., (1976–1977). AAUP. **Honors:** Univ. of NC, Greensboro Fac. Resrch. Cncl. Resrch. Grant, 1971. **Activities:** 1; 31, 34, 39; 74, 93 **Addr.:** Walter Clinton Jackson Library, UNC-Greensboro, Greensboro, NC 27412.

Fogerty, James E. (Ja. 26, 1945, Minneapolis, MN) Deputy State Archvst., MN Hist. Socty., 1979–, Field Dir., 1977–79, Dir., Reg. Resrch. Ctrs., 1976–77. **Educ.:** Coll. of St. Thomas, 1963–67, BA (Hist.); Univ. of MN, 1968–70, MLS. **Orgs.:** SAA: Oral Hist. Com. (1975–); Basic Wkshps. Adv. Com. (1978–); Res. Arch. Actv. Com. (1975–79). Midwest Arch. Conf.: Secy.-Treas. (1977–). Oral Hist. Assn. Amer. Assn. for State and Local Hist. Phi Alpha Theta. **Pubns.:** Jt. auth., *Manuscripts Arrangement and Preservation for Local Historical Societies* (1980); "Minnesota Regional Research Centers," *MN Hist.* (Spr. 1974); Various other pubns. and articles on hist. socty. work; Reviews. **Activities:** 2; 17, 34; 59, 85, 94 **Addr.:** Minnesota Historical Society, Research Center, 1500 Mississippi St., St. Paul, MN 55101.

Fogleman, Marguerite Flint (Jl. 3, 1926, Alexandria, VA) Assoc. Libn., Reese Lib., Augusta Coll., 1967–, Asst. Libn., 1965–67; Asst. Libn., Wilmington (NC) Coll. Lib., 1964–65, Actg. Libn., 1963–64; Asst. Libn., Wilmington (NC) Pub. Lib., 1961–63; Serials Libn., LA State Univ., 1957–59; Lib. Asst., Kennedy Vets. Admin. Hosp. Lib., Memphis, 1951–52; Catlgr., Cossitt Pub. Lib., Memphis, 1950–51; Cat. position, 1948–50. **Educ.:** LA State Univ., 1943–47, BS (Home Econ.), 1947–48, BSLS, 1974, MLS. **Orgs.:** ALA. SELA. SC LA. Ctrl. Savannah River Area LA: Pres. (1970–71); Un. List of Serials (Ch., 1977–79); various other coms. LSU Alum. Assn. Alpha Chi Omega. Phi Upsilon Omicron. Richmond Cnty. Hist. Socty. Various other orgs. **Honors:** Beta Phi Mu. **Pubns.:** Ed., comp., *C.S.R.A. Union List of Serials* (1979); "Local History in the Small College Library," *RQ* (Fall 1971) "Some Notes on Richmond County Libraries Established Before 1900," *Richmond Cnty. Hist.* (Sum. 1971). **Activities:** 1; 17, 20, 44 **Addr.:** 706 Woodlawn Ave. W., North Augusta, SC 29841.

Foise, Arthur D. (F. 1, 1915, Brooklyn, NY) Retired 1974–; Sr. Libn., Brooklyn Pub. Lib. 1967–74; Chief Libn., Mercantile Lib. of NY 1957–61; Chief Libn., Gen. Socty. of Mechanics & Tradesmen of NY, 1953–57. **Educ.:** Brooklyn Coll., 1933–37, BA (Hist.); Columbia Univ., 1953–55, MSLS. **Orgs.:** ALA. Staten Island Inter-Branch Lib. Com.: Vice Ch. (1976–). MENSA. Amer. Red Cross. **Pubns.:** Reviews. **Activities:** 9, 14-Private lib.; 17, 39 **Addr.:** 82 Jules Dr., Staten Island, NY 10314.

Folcarelli, Ralph J. (O. 5, 1928, Philadelphia, PA) Prof., Palmer Grad. Lib. Sch., 1980–, Actg. Dean, 1979–80; Prof., 1978–79; Asst. VP for Acad. Affairs, Long Island Univ., 1976–78; Prof., Palmer Grad. Lib. Sch., 1963–76. **Educ.:** Kutztown State Coll., 1964–51, BS LS; Rutgers Univ., 1955–58, MLS; NY Univ., 1965–72, PhD (Ed. Comm.). **Orgs.:** ALA. Assn. of Educ. Comm. and Tech. NY LA. Suffolk Cnty. Lib. Assn. Film Lib. Info. Cncl. Huntington (NY) Pub. Lib.: Trustee. Long Island Lib. Resrcs. Cncl.: Trustee. **Honors:** Kappa Delta Pi. **Pubns.:** Reviews; Jt. auth., "Microforms," *Lib. Trends* (1976). **Activities:** 10, 11; 26, 33, 47; 74, 89, 93 **Addr.:** 117 Bay Dr., Huntington, NY 11743.

Foley, David W. (O. 21 1919, Bowmanville, ON) Assoc. Prof., Lrng. Resrcs., Richland Cmnty. Coll., Decatur, IL, 1974–; Tech. Srvs. Libn., Pub. Srvs. Libn., South. AB Inst. of Tech., 1969–74; Assoc. Prof., LS, Sch. of LS, Univ. of AB, 1967–69; Chief Biblgphr., Chief Libn., Univ. of MB, Winnipeg, 1961–67; Asst. Chief Libn., Univ. of Toronto, 1954–61; Asst. Libn., Prin. Catlgr., Royal Milit. Coll., Kingston, ON, 1950–54. **Educ.:** McMaster Univ., 1939–42, BA (Eng.); Univ. of Toronto, 1946–47, 1947–48, BLS; Univ. of MI, 1948–50, AMLS. **Orgs.:** Can. LA: Resrch. Sect. (Ch., 1957–58); Pres. (1964–1965); Can. Assn. of Coll. and Univ. Libs., Nom. Com. (Ch., 1969–70). ALA: ALA/Can. LA Liaison Com. (1964–65). **Pubns.:** "Metropolitan Library Service in Toronto," *MB LA Bltn.* (Mr. 1962); "New Directions for Canada's Libraries," *Can. Lib.* (S. 1964); "Neighbors Around the Pole," *MB LA Bltn.* (Fall 1965); "From the Baltic to the Caucasus; A Visit to Libraries in the Soviet Union," *Can. Lib.* (N. 1965); "The Canadian Library Association as Publisher," *Librarianship in Canada, 1946-1967* (1968); various other articles, poems. **Activities:** 1; 17, 39, 46; 55, 57, 92 **Addr.:** Learning Resources Center, Richland Community College, 2425 Federal Dr., Decatur, IL 62522.

Foley, Harriet Elizabeth (Fealy) (Ag. 11, 1935, Franklin, OH) Head of Media Ctrs., Carlisle Lcl. Sch. Dist., 1962–; Fr. tchr., libn., Carlisle HS, 1961–63; Tchr., Carlisle Elem. Sch., 1957–61. **Educ.:** Coll. of Mt. St. Joseph, 1953–57, AB (Educ.); Univ. of KY, 1958–61, MS (LS); NDEA Inst. in Sch. Lib. Prog., Kent State Univ., 1965. **Orgs.:** OH Educ. Lib. Media Assn.: Conf. treas. (1978). OH Assn. of Sch. Libns.: Ch., Stans. Com.; Reg. Dir. (1968–70); Secy. (1970–71); Treas. (1973–75). OH LA. ALA/AASL. Carlisle Fed. Credit Un.: Bd. of Dirs. (Secy. 1962–). Franklin Area Hist. Socty.: VP (1965); Secy. (1966, 1968); Bd. of Dirs. 1967–68). Natl. Educ. Assn. OH Educ. Assn. **Pubns.:** Jt. auth., *The teachers quick guide to copyright - photocopying* (1979); Centennial Booklet for St. Mary Parish, Franklin, Ohio 1868–1968; "Convention session report," *OH Media Spectrum* (Win. 1980); "Media Expo 1969", *OH Assn. of Sch. Libns. Bltn.* (My. 1969); "Come to the fair," *OH Assn. of Sch. Libns. Bltn.* (My. 1965). **Activities:** 10; 17, 20, 48; 61, 69 **Addr.:** P.O. Box 345, Franklin, OH 45005.

Foley, Kathy A. (Mr. 18, 1949, New York, NY) Chief Libn., Houston Post, 1979–; Libn., Superior Oil Co., 1978–79; Asst. Libn., Houston Post, 1974–78. **Educ.:** Univ. of Dallas, 1967–71, BA (Hist.); Cath. Univ., 1971–73, MLS. **Orgs.:** SLA: TX Chap., Cont. Educ. Com. (1978–80). Houston OLUG: Pres. (1980). **Activities:** 12; 17, 39; 83 **Addr.:** Houston Post Library, Houston, TX 77001.

Foley, Margaret M. (Mr. 2, 1925, Troy, NY) Asst. Dir., Schenectady Cnty. Pub. Lib., 1966–, Head, Circ., 1954–66, Branch Libn., 1951–54; YA Libn., Albany Pub. Lib., 1949–51. **Educ.:** Coll. of St. Rose, 1943–47, BA (Soc. Std.); SUNY, Albany, 1947–51, MS in LS. **Orgs.:** ALA. NYLA: Pub. Lib. Sect. Mem. Ch. (1976–79). Hudson Mohawk LA: Pres. (1970–72), Bd. (1972–74), Secy. (1958–60). **Activities:** 9; 16, 17 **Addr.:** 33 Sylvan Ave., Latham, NY 12110.

Foley, Patricia H. (D. 31, 1941, Manitowoc, WI) Head, Bus. Lib., Univ. of IA, 1979–; Bus. Ref. Libn., Univ. of NE, Omaha, 1977–79; Ref. Libn., NM State Univ., 1975–76; Lib. Tech., State Hist. Socty. of WI, 1972–75; Lib. Tech., Univ. of WI Meml. Lib., 1968–69. **Educ.:** Univ. of WI, Madison, 1961–64, 68, BA (Intl. Rel.), 1972–74, MALS; Univ. of WI, Ireland, 1969–71, (Celtic Lang.); Univ. of NE, Omaha, 1978–79, (Bus. Admin.); Univ. of IA, 1980–, (Bus. Admin.). **Orgs.:** ALA: ACRL; LAMA/Mid. Mgt. Div. IA LA: Coll. and Univ. Sect., Spr. Conf. Com. (1980). NLA: News Ed., *Natl. Libn.;* Bibl. Com.; Prof. Welfare Com. (1976–79). **Pubns.:** *Newstart Workbook* (1977–79). **Activities:** 1, 12; 15, 17, 39; 51, 59, 92 **Addr.:** Business Library, Phillips Hall, University of Iowa, Iowa City, IA 52242.

Folk, Charlotte H. (Ap. 12, 1943, Camp Forrest, TN) Libn. and Resrc. and Media Spec., GA Ctr. for Cont. Ed. Lib., Univ. of GA Libs., 1981–, Head, Cat. Dept., 1979–81, Head, Serials Cat., 1976–79; Serials Catlgr., Columbia Univ. Libs., 1975–76; Asst. Catlgr., Un. Theo. Semy. Lib., 1973–75. **Educ.:** Mary Baldwin Coll., Staunton, VA, 1961–65, BA (Eng. Lit.); Queens Coll. of CUNY, 1971–73, MLS. **Orgs.:** ALA. SELA: Presented tutorials on AACR2 (1979). GA LA: Presented wkshp. on AACR2 (1979). **Honors:** Beta Phi Mu. **Pubns.:** Comp., *The Black Experience in America: A Selected Bibliography of Resources in the Union Theological Seminary Library, New York, New York* (1975); "The Researcher Researched: An Interview with Richard B. Harwell," *The Southeast. Libn.* (Win. 1979). **Activities:** 1; 20, 44, 46; 55, 91, 92 **Addr.:** 408-4 Springdale St., Athens, GA 30606.

Follick, Edwin Duane (F. 4, 1935, Glendale, CA) Dean, Student Affairs, Cleveland Chiro. Coll., Los Angeles, CA, 1976–; Dir., Educ. and Admis., 1974–, Libn., 1969–74; Pvt. Prac., Canoga Park, CA, 1972–; Libn., Sec. Admin., Jr. Coll., Los Angeles City Schs., 1957–. **Educ.:** Pasadena City Coll., 1954, AA (Hum.); CA State Univ., Los Angeles, 1956, BA (Soc. Sci.); Pepperdine Univ., 1957, MA (Soc. Sci.); St. Andrews Intercollegiate Univ., London, Eng., 1958, DTheo, PhD (Soclgy., Relig.); CA State Univ., Los Angeles, 1961, MA (Educ.); State of CA, Libnshp. Cred., 1963; Univ. of South. CA, Los Angeles, 1963, MS (LS), 1964, MEd (Instr. Mtrls.); Blackstone Law Sch., 1966, LLB, 1967, JD; Univ. of South CA, Los Angeles, 1969, Advnc. MEd (Educ. Admin.); Cleveland Chiro. Coll., Los Angeles, CA, 1972, DC; Pepperdine Univ., 1977, MPA; Acad. Theatina, Pescara, Italy, 1978, PhD (Ecclesiastical Law); other CA creds. **Orgs.:** ALA: AASL. AALL. Los Angeles Sch. LA: Legal Com. (1972–73). Natl. Geo. Socty. Natl. Bd. of Chiro. Examiners: Jurisprudence Com. (Ch., 1972–76). Natl. Educ. Assn. Assoc. Clinical Sci. Com.: Ch. (1976–). **Honors:** Phi Delta Kappa; St. Andrews Intercollegiate Univ., London, Doctor of Lit. honoris causa, 1968; London Coll., PhD honoris causa, 1973. **Pubns.:** "The Chiropractic Profession in Historical Perspective," *Digest of Chiro. Econ.* (My.–Je. 1974); "Is Chiropractic Education a Part of Higher Learning?" *Digest of Chiro. Econ.* (Jl.–Ag. 1976); "Extended Day Chiropractic Education: Is It a Part of Creative Higher Learning?" *Digest of Chiro. Econ.* (S.–O. 1976); "The Doctor of Chiropractic in a Professional/Educational Perspective," *Digest of Chiro. Econ.* (N.–D. 1976); "The Law and Chiropractic," *Digest of Chiro. Econ.* (My.–Je. 1979). **Activities:** 1, 10;

Special Subjects/Services: 50. Adult educ.; 51. Advert./Mktg.; 52. Aerosp.; 53. Agric.; 54. Area std.; 55. Arts/Hum.; 56. Autom.; 57. Bibl./Prtg.; 58. Bio. sci.; 59. Bus./Fin.; 60. Chem.; 61. Copyrt.; 62. Documtn.; 63. Educ.; 64. Engin.; 65. Env.; 66. Eth. grps.; 67. Film; 68. Food/Nutr.; 69. Geneal.; 70. Geo.; 71. Geol.; 72. Handcpd.; 73. Hist.; 74. Int. frdm.; 75. Info. sci.; 76. Insr.; 77. Law; 78. Legis.; 79. Math./Comp. sci.; 80. Med.; 81. Metals; 82. Nat. resrcs.; 83. Newsp.; 84. Nuc. sci.; 85. Oral hist.; 86. Petr./Energy; 87. Pharm.; 88. Phys./Astr./Math.; 89. Readg.; 90. Relig.; 91. Sci./Tech.; 92. Soc. sci.; 93. Telecom.; 94. Transp.; 95. (other).

17, 24; 77, 80, 90 **Addr.:** West Valley Chiropractic Health Center, 7022 Owensmouth Ave., Canoga Park, CA 91303.

Follmer, Diane E. (IA) Supvsr., Info. Resrch., Pub. Rel. Dept., 3M Co., 1968–; Consumer Resrch., Pillsbury Co., 1967–68; Tchg. Asst., Univ. of Pittsburgh, 1966–67; Educ. Data Prcs. Resrch., Univ. of IA, 1965–66. **Educ.:** Univ. of IA, 1965, BA (Eng. Educ.); Univ. of Pittsburgh, 1967, MS (Info. Sci.) **Orgs.:** ASIS: Conf. Ch., Anl. Mtg. (1979); MN Chap. (Pres., 1973–74); Conf. and Mtgs. Com. (1976–). Assn. of Info. Dissemination Ctrs.: Natl. Secy. (1971–72). People, Inc.: VP (1975–). **Honors:** Beta Phi Mu. **Pubns.:** "Foreward," *Information Choices and Policies; Proceedings of the ASIS Annual Meeting* (1979); various local pubns. **Activities:** 14-Indus.; 17, 41, 49-Arch.; 59, 95-Pub. rel. **Addr.:** 3M Company, 3M Center, 225-5N-04, St. Paul, MN 55144.

Folter, Siegrun Heinecke (Germany) Acq. Libn., Pierpont Morgan Lib., 1978–79; Head catlgr., Msc. Lib., Univ. of IL, 1977–78, Microfilm catlgr., 1973–77; Instr. of Grmn., Providence Coll., 1967–69; Instr. of Grmn., Howard Univ., 1965–67. **Educ.:** Univ. of Rochester, 1958–61, MA (Fr.); Univ. of KS, 1961–65, MA, PhD (Grmn.); Univ. of IL, 1970–72, MS (LS). **Orgs.:** Intl. Assn. of Msc. Libs.: Microfilm Com. (1975–1979). Msc LA: Microform Com. (1975–1979); Midw. Chapt.; Grt. New York Chap. IL Msc. Libs.: Co-Ch. (1975–1976). Mod. Lang. Assn. **Honors:** Delta Phi Alpha, 1962; Beta Phi Mu, 1972. **Pubns.:** Ed., *Library of Congress, Classification Class M: Music and Books on Music* (1978); "Library Restrictions on the Use of Microfilm Copies," *Fontes Artis Musicae* (1977, no. 4). **Activities:** 1, 14; 15, 17, 20; 55, 57, 95 **Addr.:** 1320 Langdon Ln., Mamaroneck, NY 10543.

Fomerand, Raissa (Ja. 10, 1945, Brooklyn, NY) Libn., Keeper of Rare Bks. and Prints, Sleepy Hollow Restorations, 1974–; Instr., Pratt Inst. Grad. Sch. of Lib. and Info. Sci., 1979–; Head Libn., Reg. Plan Assn., 1972–74. **Educ.:** Brooklyn Coll., 1963–67, BA (Fr. Lit.); Pratt Inst., 1967–69, MLS; Inst. d'Etudes Francaises, Aix-en-Provence, France, 1965–66, Dip. (Fr. Lit. and Art). **Orgs.:** ARLIS/NA: East. Reg. Rep. Bd. SLA. Coll. Art Assn. Amer. Hist. Print Socty. **Pubns.:** *Arlis/NY Archives Checklist* (1977); ed., *Decor. Arts Trust Nsltr.* (1979–80); abstctr., *RILA* (1975–80). **Activities:** 8, 11; 24, 41, 45; 55, 93 **Addr.:** 222 Martling Ave., Tarrytown, NY 10591.

Foner, Harold Bernard (Jl. 23, 1923, New York, NY) Trustee, Brooklyn Pub. Lib., 1977–. **Educ.:** NY Univ., 1942–48, BA, MA (Gvt.); Brooklyn Law Sch., 1948–50, JD (Law), 1950–56, LLM (Law). **Orgs.:** ALA: ALTA. NY LA. Brooklyn Pub. Lib.: Law Com. Brooklyn Bar Assn.: Mncpl. Affairs. and Legis. Com. (Ch., 1978–). **Honors:** NY City Police Dept., Hon. Legion, 1980; NYC Boro. Pres., Cit., 1980. **Activities:** 9; 17, 47; 77, 78 **Addr.:** 160 E. 38th St., New York, NY 10016.

Fontaine, Janet O. (S. 11, 1927, New York, NY) Head, Acq. and Col. Dev., Auraria Lib., 1980–, Coord. of Spec. Srvs., 1977–80, Head Circ., 1975–77; Circ. Libn., Metro. State Coll. Lib., 1969–75. **Educ.:** Swarthmore Coll., 1945–47; Univ. of Chicago, 1947–51, MA (Human Dev.); Univ. of Denver, 1968–69, MA (LS). **Orgs.:** CO LA: Coll. and Univ. Div., Ch. (1976–77), Ch.-Elect (1975–76); Autom. Circ. Systs. (Panel Mem., 1979); Exec. Bd. (1976–77); Prog. Com., Anl. Conv. (1975–77); Spring Prog. C&U (Ch., 1975–76). ALA. Mt. Plains LA. Univ. of Denver Grad. Sch. of Lib. and Info. Mgt. Alum. Assn. **Honors:** Beta Phi Mu, 1969. **Pubns.:** "Check-List for an On-Line Circulation System," *CO Libs.* (Je. 1979). **Activities:** 1; 15, 22, 49-Moving a lib.; 61, 92 **Addr.:** Acquisitions Department, Auraria Library, Lawrence at 11th St., Denver, CO 80204.

Fontaine, Sue (Jeane) (Je. 28, 1928, IA) Pub. Info. Ofcr., PR Consult., WA State Lib., 1977–; Resrch. Proj. Asst., Sch. of LS, Univ. of MO, 1976–77; PR Dir., Tulsa City-Cnty. Lib. Syst., 1970–76; Consult., LA State Lib., 1963–65, PR Dir., 1960–63; Various positions as Writer-producer in mass media, 1949–60, 1968–70. **Educ.:** Univ. of IA, 1944–47, BA (Jnlsm.); Univ. of MO, 1976–77, MLS; Univ. of IA, Cert. (Jnlsm.). **Orgs.:** ALA: Natl. Lib. Week Com. (Ch., 1978–81); Ad Hoc Com. on WHCOLIS (1976–80); Lib. Admin. Div./PR Sect. (Ch., 1975–76). WA LA: PR Forum, Strg. Com. (1978–81); Conf. PR-Pubcty. Com. (1977–80). Pac. NW LA. PR Socty. of Amer. Women in Comm. Inc. **Honors:** Beta Phi Mu. **Pubns.:** Jt. ed., *Communications for the Humanities* (1974); "Off the Wall: An AV 'How to'," *Prepare: The Library Public Relations Handbook* (1978); "Public Relations for Small Libraries" (trng. manual) (1977); "PR Tick-Click: Public Relations for Public Libraries" (AV) (1976); Various articles and ed. of various nsltrs. **Activities:** 9, 13; 24, 25, 36; 51 **Addr.:** Washington State Library, AJ 11, Olympia, WA 98504.

Fonvielle, Yvonne (Ap. 30, 1937, Chicago, IL) Law Libn., Assoc. Prof. of Law, South. Univ. Law Sch., 1978–; Law Libn., Assoc. Prof. of Law, NC Ctrl. Univ., 1977–78; Attorney, Criminal Defense Div., NY Legal Aid Socty., 1974–75; US Frgn. Srv. Ofcr., Vice Consul, US Dept. of State, 1963–70. **Educ.:** Fisk Univ., 1954–55; Univ. of Chicago, 1955–58, BA (Rom. Lang. and Lit.); Pratt Inst., 1975–77, MLS; Univ. of Chicago, 1971–74, JD (Law); The Sorbonne, 1959, Cert. (Fr.); Columbia Univ., 1960–62, MA (Tchg. Eng. as Frgn. Lang., Span.). **Orgs.:** AALL: Frgn., Compar., and Intl. Law Com. (1979–80). SLA. Baton Rouge LA. **Activities:** 1; 17; 77 **Addr.:** P.O. Box 10854, Baton Rouge, LA 70813.

Foos, Donald Dale (Mr. 11, 1929, Chicago, IL) Sr. Ed., Admin., Libs. Unlimited Inc., 1980–; Pres., Lib. Systs. Inc., 1977–80; Dean and Prof., Grad. Sch. of LS, LA State Univ., 1971–79; HEA Title II-B Fellow, FL State Univ., 1969–71; Admin. Asst. to the Dean, Asst. Prof., Admin. Ofcr., Sch. of LS, SUNY, Geneseo, 1968–69; Lectr., Lib. Consult., Coll. of LS, Univ. of KY and KY Dept. of Libs., 1967–68; Dir., El Paso Pub. Lib., 1966–67; Lib. Consult., Proj. Ofcr., LSCA Title II, AL Pub. Lib. Srv., 1962–66. **Educ.:** Univ. of AL, 1961–62, AB (Pol. Sci.); FL State Univ., 1963–64, MS (LS), 1969–70, MS (Adult Educ.), 1969–70, Advnc. Mstrs. (LS), 1969–71, PhD (LS); South. Univ., 1976–78, MEd (Comm. and Instr. Tech.). **Orgs.:** ALA: Hammond Jury Awd. (Ch., 1967–68); Com. on Accred. Visit. Teams (1975–76). SLA: LA Chap. (Pres., 1973–74). ASIS: Educ. Com. (1974–76). SWLA: Cont. Educ. for Lib. Staffs Adv. Grp. (Ch., 1974–76); Pub. Lib. Interest Grp. (Ch., 1976–78). Various other orgs., coms. **Honors:** Phi Delta Kappa. **Pubns.:** *The Role of the State Library in Adult Education* (1973); "LSU Graduate School of Library Science," *Encyc. of Lib. and Info. Sci.* (1975); jt. auth., "Continuing Education and Institutes as a Function of Interlibrary Cooperation," *Lib. Trends* (O. 1975); "Aksel G.S. Josephson, 1860-1966, Precursor," *Procs. of Fourth Lib. Hist. Sem.* (1971). **Addr.:** 5758 S. Gallup St. #308, Littleton, CO 80120.

Foote, Lynne (Mr. 21, 1949, Auburn, NY) Dir., CO Tech. Ref. Ctr., 1978–; Info. Spec., Univ. of Pittsburgh, 1975–78. **Educ.:** PA State Univ., 1967–71, BA (Eng.); Univ. of Pittsburgh, 1974, MLS. **Orgs.:** SLA. ASIS. Rocky Mt. OLUG: Prog. Ch. Info. Indus. Assn. **Activities:** 14-Info. broker; 17, 39; 51, 64, 91 **Addr.:** Colorado Technical Reference Center, Campus Box 184 Norlin Library, Boulder, CO 80309.

Foran, Bryan Patrick (D. 12, 1946, Sudbury, ON) Info. Srvs. Libn., Saskatoon Pub. Lib., 1977–, YA Srvs. Libn., 1978–79; Asst. Chief Libn., Wheatland Reg. Lib., 1975–76. **Educ.:** Laurentian Univ., 1964–68, BA (Hist.); Univ. of AB, 1974–75, BLS. **Orgs.:** Can. LA. Saskatchewan LA: 2nd vp (1981–83); Int. Frdm. Com.; YA Caucus (Pres., 1980–81). Can. Hist. Assn. Com. on Can. Labour Hist. Access: The Can. Com. for the Right to Pub. Info. **Pubns.:** Ed., *The Conserver Society: An Annotated Resource Guide. . .* (1979); Ed., *Something to Chew On: Canadian Fiction for Young Adults* (1979). **Activities:** 9; 16; 57, 74 **Addr.:** Saskatoon Public Library, 311 - 23rd St. East, Saskatoon, SK S7K 0J6 Canada.

Forbes, James D. (S. 13, 1949, Trail, BC) Cur., Trail City Arch., 1977–. **Educ.:** Univ. of BC, 1967–71, BA (Hist.); 1971–73, Dip. (Plng.). **Orgs.:** Assn. of BC Archvsts.: VP (1979–80); Arch. Act Com. (1979). Assn. of Can. Archvsts. BC Hist. Assn. **Orgs.:** Heritage Canada: Rep. BC/Yukon Reg. Cncl. Trail Hist. Socty.: Pres. (1977–79). **Pubns.:** Ed., *Historical Portraits of Trail* (1980). **Activities:** 2; 15, 23, 37; 55, 62, 63 **Addr.:** Trail City Archives, 1394 Pine Ave., Trail, BC V1R 4E6 Canada.

Force, Ronald W. (S. 7, 1941, Sioux City, IA) Asst. Dir. for Pub. Srvs., WA State Univ., 1979–; Head, Educ. Lib., OH State Univ., 1972–78, Head, Engin. Libs., 1970–72, Asst. Head, Dept. Libs., 1968–72. **Educ.:** IA State Univ., 1959–63, BS (Entomology); Univ. of MN, 1966–68, MALS; OH State Univ., 1974–75, MS (Nat. Resrcs.). **Orgs.:** ALA. WA LA. **Pubns.:** *A Guide to the Literature of Biomedical Engineering* (1972); "Access to Alternative Catalogs," *Coll. and Resrch. Libs.* (My. 1979). **Activities:** 1; 17; 56, 82 **Addr.:** Washington State University Libraries, Pullman, WA 99163.

Force, Stephen E. (Jl. 22, 1948, Morristown, NJ) Supusg. Libn., Queens Borough Pub. Lib., (Jamaica, NY.) 1980–; Admin. Asst., Rutgers Grad. Sch. of Lib. and Info. Sci., 1978–80, Co-adj. Prof., 1977–80; Adult Srvs. Libn., Morris Cnty. Free Lib., 1976. **Educ.:** Seton Hall Univ., 1966–70, BS (Bus. Admin.); Rutgers Univs., 1975–76, MLS, 1976– (LS). **Orgs.:** ALA. NJ LA: Educ. for Libnshp. (1977–); Del. to NJ Gvrs. Conf. (1979). **Honors:** Beta Phi Mu, 1976; Prize for paper, NJ Gvrs. Conf. 1979. **Activities:** 9, 11; 16, 17, 26; 56, 78, 95 **Addr.:** 163 Park Ave., Teaneck, NJ 07666.

Ford, Barbara J. (D. 5, 1946, Dixon, IL) Docum. Libn., Univ. of IL, Chicago Circle, 1979–, Asst. Docum. Lib., 1975–79, Dir., Soybean Insect Resrch. Info. Ctr., IL Natural Hist. Srvy., 1973–75. **Educ.:** IL Wesleyan Univ., 1964–68, BA (Hist. and Educ.), Tufts Univ., 1968–69, MA (Intl. Rel.), Univ. of IL, 1972–73, MS (LS). **Orgs.:** ALA: Cnclr. (1980–84), Lippincott Awd. Jury (1979–80), Mem. Promo. Task Force (1977–79), GODORT. IL LA.: Exec. Bd. (1980–84). SLA: IL Chap. Pubcty. Com. Ch. (1977–79). ASIS. Various other orgs. AAUP. **Honors:** Beta Phi Mu. **Pubns.:** "Government Publications in Humanistic Research and Scholarship", *New Horizons for Academic Libraries* (1979); "Reaching the Undergraduate with Government Publications: a Case Study in Bibliographic Instruction", (1978), "Revising the Consumer Price Index", *Government Publications Review,* (1977); "Foreign Country Information in United States Government Publications", *International Studies Notes,* (1977); "The Literature of Arthropods Associated with Soybeans." *IL Natural Hist. Survey Biological Notes* (1975). **Activities:** 1; 29, 31, 39; 78, 92 **Addr.:** Documents Department, Library, Box 8198, University of Illinois at Chicago Circle, Chicago, IL 60680.

Ford, Mark Robert (Jl. 6, 1923, Bethlehem, PA) AV Mgr., Electronic Systs. Div., AFSC, 1963–; AV Archvst., Aerosp. Med. Div., 1959–63; Chief, Accessions Branch, US Air Force Film Depos., 1955–59; Archvst., Natl. Arch., 1951–55. **Educ.:** Lehigh Univ., 1946–50, BA (Hist., Gvt.); New Eng. Sch. of Law, 1964–68, JD (Law). **Orgs.:** SAA: AV Com. (1955–). Smithsonian Assn. Air Force Hist. Assn. Info. Film Producers of Amer.: Boston Chap. (Pres., 1971–72). **Honors:** ESD/Acq. Support Div., Sustained Superior Performance, 1968; ESD/Directorate of Mgt. Srvs., Outstan. Performance, 1979; Delta Theta Phi. **Pubns.:** Film Resrch., "NBC Victory at Sea," (1952); "Scientific and Engineering Retention," Motion Pic. (1979). **Activities:** 2, 4; 17, 29, 32; 61, 67, 93 **Addr.:** 82 Menotomy Rd., Arlington, MA 02174.

Ford, Ray Douglas (D. 11, 1944, Washington, DC) Libn., Milton I. Swimmer, Plng. & Design, Beverly Hills, CA, 1980–; Asst. Libn., Marquand Lib., Princeton Univ., 1978–80; Asst. Coll. Libn., Univ. of South. CA, 1976–78; Biblgphr., Hennessey & Ingalls, Inc., 1975–78. **Educ.:** Univ. of CA, Santa Barbara, 1971–73, BA (Art Hist.), 1973–75, MA (Art Hist.); Univ. of South. CA, 1975–76, MSLS. **Orgs.:** ARLIS/NA. Socty. of Archit. Histns. **Pubns.:** Contr., *Magill's Bibliography of Literary Criticism,* (1979); CA Univ., Santa Barbara. Art Galleries. *European Drawings by Minor Old Masters of the Sixteenth, Seventeenth and Eighteenth Centuries,* (1975); *A Medieval Miscellany: Romanesque and Early Gothic Metalwork,* (1974). **Activities:** 1, 12; 15, 17, 45; 55 **Addr.:** 9100 Wilshire Blvd., Beverly Hills, CA 90213.

Ford, Robert B. (N. 27, 1935, Miami, FL) Chief Libn., Medgar Evers Coll., 1975–, Actg. Chief Libn., 1971–75; Serials and Per. Libn., Queensborough Cmnty. Coll., 1968–70; Mono. and Serials Catlgr., Engin. Societies Lib., 1967–68; Ref. Libn., North Bellmore (NY) Pub. Lib., 1969–72; Libn. for Fed. Proj., Miami Jackson Sr. HS, 1966–67; Libn., Richmond Elem. Sch., 1963–66; Asst. Libn., Dorsey Jr. HS, 1961–65. **Educ.:** Bethune-Cookman Coll., 1952–55, BA (Sp. & Drama); NY Univ., 1956–58, MA (Dramatic Arts Educ.); Pratt Inst., 1958–59, MLS; Rutgers Univ., 1974–, PhD in prog. (LS); Univ. of MD, Lib. Admin. Dev. Prog., 1973. **Orgs.:** LA City Univ. of NY: Treas. (1971–73). NY LA: Bd. of Dir., Coll. & Univ. Libs. Sect. (1979–81). ALA: Coll. Libs. Sect. Ad Hoc Com. on Goals (1972–74); Nom. Com. (1974–75). AAUP. Alpha Phi Alpha. **Pubns.:** Contrib., *What Black Librarians Are Saying* (1972); Contrib., *Handbook of Black Librarianship* (1977); "Title IIa - a bargain at the price: a symposium," *Jnl. of Acad. Libnshp.* (S. 1979); "Help for the decision-maker: a decision-process model", *The Bookmark* (Spr. 1979). **Activities:** 1, 12; 17, 20, 33; 56, 66, 75 **Addr.:** Medgar Evers College Library, 1150 Carroll St., Brooklyn, NY 11225.

Ford, Stephen W. (S. 7, 1924, Detroit MI) Lib. Dir., Grand Valley State Col., 1962–; Head of Ord. Dept., Univ. of MI, 1954–62; Chief of Serials Div., South. IL Univ., 1953–54; Asst. Libn., Lawrence Univ., 1949–53. **Educ.:** Wayne State Univ., 1942–48, AB (Hist); Univ. of MI, 1948–49, AMLS. **Orgs.:** ALA. American Natl. Stans. Inst., Z39: Subcom. 16, (Ch.). Beta Phi Mu: Intl. Pres. (1965). **Honors:** Phi Kappa Phi, 1949. **Pubns.:** *The Acquisition of Library Materials* (1978); Assistant Ed., *Library Resources and Technical Services* (1957–59; 1962–65). **Activities:** 1; 15, 17; 55, 57 **Addr.:** 3346 Coit St., N.E., Grand Rapids, MI 49505.

Ford, Virginia A. (Ja. 15, 1934, Springfield, OH) Lit. Resrch. Anal., Aerosp. Corp., 1971–; Asst. Libn., Atl. Richfield Co., 1969–71; Admin./Persnl. Ofcr., U.S. Air Frc., 1957–69. **Educ.:** Otterbein Coll., 1951–55, BA (Fr.); Immaculate Heart Coll., 1969, MALS. **Orgs.:** SLA: South. CA Chap. (Treas., 1978–80); Sci-Tech News, Bus. Mgr. (1980–). **Activities:** 12; 20, 30, 46; 52, 56, 91 **Addr.:** The Aerospace Corporation, The Charles C. Lauritsen Library, P.O. Box 92957, Los Angeles, CA 90009.

Foreman, Gertrude Evelyn (Ag. 8, 1932, York, NE) Assoc. Prof., Libn., Bio-Med. Lib., Univ. of MN, 1979–, Asst. Prof., Libn., 1973–78, Instr., Libn., 1971–73; Resrch. Fellow, Libn., Northlands Reg. Med. Prog., 1970–71. **Educ.:** Univ. of MN, 1962–67, BA (Hum.), 1968–70, MALS; Immanuel Sch. of Nursing, Omaha, 1950–53, RN. **Orgs.:** ALA: Machine-Assisted Ref. Sect., Measur. of Srv. Com. (1978–80). Med. LA: Com. on Bibl. Projs. and Problems (Ch., 1975–76); Anl. Conf. Strg. Com. (1976). ASIS: MN Chap. (Pres., 1978–79; Secy., 1976–77). MN LA: Ref. Div. (Ch., 1976–77). Various other orgs. AAUP. **Pubns.:** "Online Search Aids," *OL* (O. 1977); jt. auth., "The Use of Computer Technology to Aid Research-in-Progress," *Jnl. of Clinical Comp.* (1977); jt. auth., "BIOSIS Previews and MEDLARS–A Biomedical Team," *OL* (Ja. 1977); jt. auth., "Evaluation of Library Service to Rural Physician Associate Program Students," *Bltn. of Med. LA* (O. 1976); "Use of Multiple Databases in Bibliographic Services," *Bltn. of Med. LA* (Ja. 1976); Various other articles and ERIC docum. **Activities:** 1; 15, 31, 39; 58, 80 **Addr.:** Bio-Medical Library, Diehl Hall, University of Minnesota, Minneapolis, MN 55455.

PROFESSIONAL ACTIVITIES: Institutions: 1. Acad. lib.; 2. Arch.; 3. Assn.; 4. Fed./Gvt. lib.; 5. Inst. lib.; 6. Mfr./Suppl.; 7. Milit. lib.; 8. Musm.; 9. Pub. lib.; 10. Sch. lib.; 11. Sch. of lib. sci.; 12. Spec. lib.; 13. State lib.; 14. (other). **Functions/Activities:** 15. Acq./Col. dev.; 16. Adult srvs.; 17. Admin.; 18. Apprais.; 19. Archit./Bldgs.; 20. Cat./Class.; 21. Chld. srvs.; 22. Circ.; 23. Cons./Pres.; 24. Consult.; 25. Cont. ed.; 26. Educ. lib. sci.; 27. Ext. srvs.; 28. Fund/Grants; 29. Gvt. pubs.; 30. Indx./Abs.; 31. Instr. lib. use; 32. Media srvs.; 33. Micro.; 34. Netwks./Coop.; 35. Persnl.; 36. PR; 37. Publshg.; 38. Recs. mgt.; 39. Ref. srvs.; 40. Repro.; 41. Resrch.; 42. Review.; 43. Secur.; 44. Serials; 45. Spec. col.; 46. Tech. srvs.; 47. Trustees/Bds.; 48. YA srvs.; 49. (other).

Forester, James Lawrence (Ap. 14, 1935, Cord, AR) Libn., LA State Univ., Eunice, 1966–; Ord. Libn., LA State Univ., Baton Rouge, 1965–66; Instr., Univ. of New Orleans, 1960–64. **Educ.:** AR Coll., 1952–55, BSE (Hist.); George Peabody Coll. for Tchrs., 1960, MALS; LA State Univ., 1960–64, Hist. **Orgs.:** ALA. SWLA. LA LA: Fed. Rel. Com.; Nom. Com.; Audit Com. LA Hist. Assn. Alpha Psi Omega. Phi Alpha Theta. **Activities:** 1; 15, 17, 34; 69, 92 **Addr.:** LeDoux Library, Louisiana State University at Eunice, Eunice, LA 70535.

Forgay, W. Arthur (My. 15, 1925, Lampman, SK) Educ. Consult., Sch. Libs., SK Dept. of Educ., 1970–; Libn., Martin Collegiate, Regina, SK, 1969–70; Prin., Estevan Collegiate, Estevan, SK, 1956–69. **Educ.:** Univ. of SK, 1947–49, BEd (Math. and Sci.); Univ. of BC, 1964–65, BLS. **Orgs.:** Can. LA. Can. Sch. LA: Pres. (1978–79). SK Assn. of Educ. Media Specs. Intl. Bd. on Bks. for Young People. Regina Assn. for the Mentally Retarded: Pres. (1976–78). **Activities:** 10, 13; 24; 63 **Addr.:** Department of Education, 2220 College Ave., Regina, SK S4P 3V7 Canada.

Forget, Louis J. S. (Ag. 13, 1941, Bearn, PQ) Dir., Lib. Syst. Ctr., Natl. Lib. of Canada, 1979–, Asst. Dir., Syst., R&P Branch, 1974–79, Head, Lib. Syst. Anal. Sect., 1973–74, Syst. Libn., 1969–73, Subj. Anal., 1964–69. **Educ.:** Univ. of Montreal, 1959–63, BA (Arts & Sci.), 1963–64, BBibl (LS). **Orgs.:** Can. LA. ALA. ASTED: Cnclr. (1969–70; 1973–74). Can. Assn. for Info. Sci.: Dir. (1972–73). Data Prcs. Inst. Mgt. Consult. Inst. Inst. for Gen. Mgt. **Pubns.:** Jt. auth., *Le format MARC canadien* (1975); Jt. auth., "Evaluation of the DOBIS system for use in Canada," *Can. jnl. of info. sci.* (My. 1977); "L'automatisation de la Bibliographie nationale du Canada: Canadiana," *Documentation et bibliothèques,* (D. 1974, Mr. 1975); "Bibliographie sur l'automatisation dans les bibliothèques," Association canadienne des bibliothécaires de langue française, *Bltn.* (Je. 1971); "Le système de numérotation normalisée internationale du livre (international standard book numbering, ou ISBN)," Association canadienne des bibliothécaires de langue française, *Bltn.* (S. 1970); other articles, reviews, oral presentations. **Activities:** 1, 14-Natl. libs.; 17, 34, 46; 56, 75, 91 **Addr.:** Library Systems Centre, National Library of Canada, 395 Wellington St., Ottawa, ON K1A 0N4 Canada.

Forgie, Donald John (F. 15, 1927, Toronto, ON) Assoc. Prof., Fac. of LS, Univ. of Toronto, 1968–; Dir. of Econ. and Bus. Resrch., ON Paper Co., 1953–68; Resrch. Econ., McLaren Advert. Ltd., 1950–53; Nvl. Info. Ofcr., Royal Can. Navy, 1949–50. **Educ.:** Univ. of Toronto, 1945–49, BA Honours (Econ.), 1955, MCom (Bus. Admin.); Univ. of West. ON, 1971, MLS. **Orgs.:** AALS. Can. Assn. of Lib. Schs. Can. LA. ON LA. Other orgs. Niagara Dist. Airport Cmsn.: Past Ch., Honorary Life Mem. **Honors:** Untd. Nations, Can. Winner, Intl. Essay Competition and Schol., 1950. **Pubns.:** "Videotex Research and Development: The Canadian Context and Contribution," *Can. Jn. of Info. Sci.* (Je. 1981); "Toward Effective Utilization of Educational Communications Resources," *CJIS* (My. 1978); Jt. auth., "Designing a Learner-Centered Environment", *Continuous Lrng.* (My.-Je. 1971); Key-Word Retrieval Prog., (Comp. Prog.) (1974). **Activities:** 11; 19, 32, 41; 59, 75, 92, 93 **Addr.:** Faculty of Library Science, University of Toronto, 140 St. George St., Toronto, ON M5S 1A1 Canada.

Fork, Donald J. (My. 27, 1938, Beaver Falls, PA) Ch., Dept. of Educ. Media & Dir., Instr. Support Srvs., Coll. of Educ., Temple Univ., 1977–79; Asst. & Assoc. Prof., 1972–; Resrc. Spec./Libn., Pasadena Sch. Dist., 1967–70, Tchr., 1964–67. **Educ.:** CA State Univ. at Los Angeles, 1960–62, BA (Liberal Arts), 1962–70, MA (Hist.); Immaculate Heart Coll., 1969–70, MA (LS); Univ. of Pittsburgh, 1970–74, PhD (Lib/Info Sci.); PA Dept. of Educ. Prof. Certs., LS, Instr. Media Spec., 1971–75. **Orgs.:** Intl. Assn. of Sch. Libnshp.: Ed., *IASL Nsltr.* (1977–). Intl. Visual Litcy. Assn.: Pres. (1981–). ALA: AASL, Resrch. Com. (1978–). PA Sch. Libns. Assn.: Prof. Stan. Com. (1978); Comm. Com. (1979); Tech. Com. (1981). **Honors:** Beta Phi Mu, 1971; Phi Delta Kappa, 1981. **Pubns.:** Jt. ed., *Exploration and Interpretation: Theoretical Approaches to the Study of Visual Literacy and Visual Learning* (1978); Jt. ed., *People to Contact for Visiting School Libraries/Media Centers.* (1977); "Audiovisual Production in Support of Higher Education," *Cath. Lib. World* (1978); "Approaches to the Study of Visual Literacy: A Brief Survey for Media Personnel," *PA Media Review* (1977); Future Trends in Educational Technology: Perspectives from the U.S.A. Slide/Tape (1977). **Activities:** 14-Coll. of Educ.; 17, 26, 32, 49; 63, 95 **Addr.:** Department of Educational Media, College of Education, Temple University, Philadelphia, PA 19122.

Forman, Dorothy J. (Ja. 26, 1919, Detroit, MI) Sr. Ref. Libn., Resrch. Labs., General Motors, Corp., 1977–, Ref. Libn., 1969–77, Libn., Fisher Body Div., 1968–69, Libn., Ternstedt Div., 1961–68. **Educ.:** Wayne State Univ., 1937–41, BA (LS). **Orgs.:** SLA: MI Chap., Pres. (1955–56). Engin. Soctys. of Detroit. **Pubns.:** "How to approach the reference question," *Spec. Libs.* (O. 1955); "various speeches". **Activities:** 12; 39, 49-ILL; 64, 75, 91 **Addr.:** Research Laboratories, General Motors Corporation, General Motors Technical Center, Warren, MI 48090.

Forman, Jack (N. 16, 1942, Rochester, NY) Ref./Instr. Srvs. Libn., San Diego State Univ. Lib., Ref./Bibl. Srvs. Libn., Mesa Coll. Lib., 1981–; Dir. of Lib. Srvs., Univ. for Humanistic Std., 1979–81; Reg. Srvs. Libn., East. MA Reg. Lib. Syst., 1973–78; Asst. Coord. Adult-YA Srvs., Branch Libn., Free Pub. Lib. of Woodbridge, NJ, 1967–73. **Educ.:** Univ. of Rochester, 1960–64, BA; Rutgers Univ., 1966–67, MLS. **Orgs.:** ALA: JMRT (Ch., 1970–72); YASD Best Bks. for Young Adults (1974–78); Ref. and Subscrpn. Bk. Review Com. (1975–). CA LA. **Pubns.:** "Young Adult Literature," *ALA Yearbook* (1978); "Biography for Children: More Facts, Less Fiction," *Sch. Lib. Jnl.* (S. 1972); "YA Selection Material: A Second Opinion," *SLJ* (S. 1978); Reviews. **Activities:** 1, 9; 32, 39, 48; 50, 67, 74 **Addr.:** 5708 Baltimore Dr., #396, La Mesa, CA 92041.

Forrest, Carl Edward (S. 18, 1936, Buffalo, NY) Lib. Consult., Polish Cmnty. Ctr. of Buffalo, 1978–; Dir. of Libs., Niagara Univ., 1970–77; Catlgr., SUNY, Buffalo, 1968–70; Cat. Libn., Canisius Coll., 1960–67; Asst. Catlgr., Iona Coll., 1960; Libn., Cranwell Sch., 1959–60. **Educ.:** Canisius Coll., 1954–58, BA (Eng.); Cath. Univ., 1958–59, MS (LS). **Orgs.:** ALA: ACRL. NY LA: Mem. Com. (1972). Cath. LA: Pubns. Com. (1964). **Honors:** Beta Phi Mu, 1960. **Pubns.:** Reviews. **Activities:** 1, 12; 17, 24, 46; 50, 55, 66 **Addr.:** 97 Gardenwood Ln., Buffalo, NY 14223.

Forrest, Kathryn S. (Ja. 9–, Johnson Cnty., IN) Assoc. Dir. of the Lib., San Jose State Univ., 1973–81; Head, Sci./Tech. Div., OR State Univ., 1971–73; Asst. Lib. Dir., Univ. of CA, Riverside, 1969–71; Head, Bio-Agr. Lib., 1961–69. **Educ.:** IN Ctrl. Univ., 1941–44, BA (Eng., Hist.); Univ. of South. CA, 1958, MS (LS). **Orgs.:** SLA: Bio. Sci. Div. (Ch., 1968/69); Lib. Mgt. Div. (Ch., 1979/80). ALA: ACRL. CA LA: Coll. & Resrch. Libs. **Honors:** Beta Phi Mu. **Activities:** 1, 2; 15, 17, 25; 56, 59, 95-Couns. **Addr.:** 1946 Rosebud Ct., San Jose, CA 95128.

Forsee, Joe B. (O. 25, 1949, Fulton, KY) Dir., Div. of Pub. Lib. Srvs., 1980–; MS Lib. Comsn., 1978–80, Asst. Dir. for Admin., 1976–78, Consult. III, 1976; Dir., Interlib. Coop., KY Dept. of Lib. and Arch., 1973–76, Assoc. Reg. Libn., 1972–73. **Educ.:** Murray State Univ., 1967–71, BSLS; Univ. of KY, 1971–72, MSLS, CEUs for insts. in persnl. mgt., syst. charting, media util. **Orgs.:** ALA. SELA. COSLA. GLA. Various MALA coms. Frnds. of Handcpd. Readers. State Energy Task Force. Alpha Beta Alpha. **Honors:** MS LA, Cert. of Apprec., 1979. **Pubns.:** "A Report on the White House Conference," *The Packet* (N.-D. 1979); "LSCA Advisory Council," *The Packet* (S. 1978); "Anyone for Rebuttal?" *MS Lib. News* (Jl. 1978); "Grants, MLC and Me," *CLAM OL* (D. 1977); "Programmed Reference" (oral presentation) (1973). **Activities:** 4, 13; 17 **Addr.:** 500 Three Oaks Bend #7, Stone Mountain, GA 30083.

Forsman, Carolyn D. (D. 10, 1943, New York, NY) Consult., 1979–; Lect., Univ. of MD Col. of Lib. & Info. Srvs., 1976–78; Chief, Telephone Ref. Srv., DC Pub. Lib., 1974–76; Head of Ref., Vallejo Pub. Lib., 1967–69. **Educ.:** New York Univ., 1960–64, BA (Math.); Univ. of CA, Berkeley, 1964–65, MLS; Univ. of MD, 1969–72. (LS). **Orgs.:** ALA: Cnclr. (1978–82); Policy Monitoring Com. (1980–82); Com. on Com. (1979–80); Ch., Const. & By-Laws Com. (1977–79); Com. on Org. (1970–75); YASD, Resrch. Com. (1971–1976). ASIS. Alliance of Info. Referral Srvs.: Prof. Adv. Bd., (1973–1975). **Honors:** Beta Phi Mu, 1965. **Pubns.:** Ed., *Magazine Industry Market Place* (1979); Consult. Ed., *Sources* (1978–); Contrib., *Media and the Young Adult: A Selected Bibliography,* 1950–72. (1977); "Crisis Information Services to Youth," *Sch. Lib. Jnl.* (Mr. 1972); "Information and Referral Services: A Resource Guide," in *Information for the Community* (1976). **Activities:** 9, 11; 24, 31, 37, 39, 44, 48 **Addr.:** 104 W 76 St., New York, NY 10023.

Forsyth, Joseph (Ag. 15, 1942, Washington, Cnty. Durham, Eng) Dir. of Lib. Srvs., Gvt. of AB, 1978–, Lib. Dev. Ofcr., 1970–78; Ref. Libn., Calgary Pub. Lib., 1966–70; Div. Libn., N. Yorkshire Cnty. Lib., Eng., 1964–66. **Educ.:** Univ. of London, 1975–76, MA (LS); Newcastle Sch. of Libnshp., 1962–63, ALA; 1971, FLA. **Orgs.:** LA (UK). Can. LA. LA of AB. ALA. **Pubns.:** *Bibliography of Government Publications Relating to Alberta,* (1972); "Alberta Scene," *PNLA Qtly.* (Sum. 1979); "Working Paper for Serving the Public in Rural Areas," *Lib. Assoc. of AB Bltn.* (Jl. 1969). **Activities:** 9, 13; 17, 24, 34; 78 **Addr.:** Alberta Culture, Library Services, 16214-114 Ave., Edmonton, AB T5M 2Z5 Canada.

Forsyth, Pamela I. (S. 19, 1948, Virden, MB) Chief Libn., Charlottetown Confed. Ctr. Pub. Lib., 1976–; Bkmobile Supvsr., PE Prov. Lib., 1972–75; Catlgr., Xavier Coll. Lib., 1970–72. **Educ.:** Brandon Univ., 1966–69, BA (Eng.); Univ. of Toronto, 1969–70, BLS; Labour Coll. of Can., 1979. **Orgs.:** Can. LA: Prison Lib. Com. (1979). Atl. Prov. LA: VP for PE (1979–81); Mem. Com. (1974–75); Int. Frdm. (1979–80). PE Sch. LA. PE Pub. Srv. Assn.: Secy. (1977–81); Ch., Educ. Com. (1974–80); Human Rights Com. (1977–79); Constn. Com. (1977–78). **Activities:** 9; 15, 16, 17; 50, 74, 89 **Addr.:** Confederation Centre Public Library, Box 7000, Charlottetown, PE C1A 1G7, Canada.

Forth, Stuart (Ag. 13, 1923, Manistee, MI) Dean of Univ. Libs., PA State Univ., 1973–; Dir. of Libs., Prof. of Lib. Sci., Univ. of KY, 1965–73; VP for Std. Affairs, 1968–70; Assoc. Dir. of Libs., Univ. of KS, 1961–65; Undergraduate Libn., 1959–61; Ref. Libn., Seattle Pub. Lib., 1956–59; Asst. to Dir. of Libs., OR State Univ., 1952–54, Catlgr., 1950–52. **Educ.:** Univ. of MI, 1946–49, BA (Hist.), 1949–50, MALS; Univ. of WA, 1954–59, PhD (Hist.). **Orgs.:** ALA: ACRL (Ch., Univ. Libs. Sect., 1967–68; Ch., Acad. Status Com., 1969–71). PA LA: Pres. (1979–80). **Activities:** 1; 15, 17, 45 **Addr.:** University Libraries, The Pennsylvania State University, University Park, PA 16802.

Fortier, Jan Marie (My. 5, 1946, Los Angeles, CA) Head Libn., Pacific Univ., 1978–; Tech. Srvs. Libn., Univ. of Portland, 1976–78, Spec. Srvs. Libn., 1973–76; Catlgr., Fort Vancouver Reg. Lib., 1973. **Educ.:** Portland State Univ., 1966–68, BA (Eng.); Temple Univ., 1969–70, MA (Eng.); Univ. of OR, 1973, MLS. **Orgs.:** Pac. NW LA. OR LA. NW Assn. of Pvt. Colls. and Univs. Portland Area Spec. Libns.: Ch. (1979–80). **Activities:** 1; 15, 17, 28 **Addr.:** 6937 N. Fiske, Portland, OR 97203.

Fortin, Jean Luc (N. 20, 1940, St Jean Port Joli, PQ) Chief Libn., Gvt. du PQ, Ministere du Loisir, de la Chasse et de la Peche, 1976–; Head Ref. Libn., Assemblee Natl. du PQ, 1975–76; Head, Bibl. Sect., Bib. Natl. de Cote D'Ivoire, 1973–75; Ref. Libn., Assemblee Natl. du PQ, 1971–73, Head, Cat. Sect., 1970–71; Serials Bibl. Cntrl. and Inventory, Univ. LaVal, 1968–70, Ord. Dept., 1965–68, Cat. Dept., 1964–65. **Educ.:** Univ. de Montréal, 1963–64, BLS. **Orgs.:** Corp. of Prof. Libns. of PQ: Empl. Com. (1977–). ASTED: Com. de Rel. Intl. (1977–81). Can. Assn. Info. Sci.: Anl. Conf. Prog. Com. (1980–81). **Pubns.:** Ed., *Bibliographie de la Cote D'Ivoire* (1974–75). **Activities:** 1, 13; 15, 29, 39; 65, 78, 82 **Addr.:** 2300 Chapdelaine 106, Sainte-Foy, PQ G1V 1N1 Canada.

Fortney, Lynn Marjorie (My. 19, 1950, Macon, GA) Head Med. Libn., Asst. Prof., Hlth. Sci. Lib., Univ. of AL, 1975–, Med. Ref. Libn., 1973–75; Grad. Asst., Atlanta Pub. Lib., 1972–73. **Educ.:** Grinnell Coll., 1968–72, BA (Amer. Std.); Emory Univ., 1972–73, MLS; Med. LA, 1975, Cert. **Orgs.:** Med. LA. AL LA: Hlth. Sci. Libns.' RT (Mdrtr., 1977–79). South. Reg. Grp. of Med. LA: Secy.-Treas. (1978–79). Pilot Intl. **Honors:** Beta Phi Mu, 1973. **Activities:** 1, 12; 15, 17; 80 **Addr.:** Health Sciences Library, University of Alabama, Box 6331, University, AL 35486.

Fortney, Virginia J. (Ag. 27, 1932, Salina, KS) Head, Info. Srvs. Dept., Bell Telephone Labs., 1980–, Grp. Supvsr., Comp. Info. Srv., 1976–77, Grp. Supvsr., Tech. Lib., 1971–76, Ref. Libn., 1969–71. **Educ.:** KS State Univ., 1950–52 (Bio. Sci.); Rutgers Univ., 1963–68, BA (Psy.), 1968–69, MLS. **Orgs.:** SLA: NJ Chap., 1st VP & Pres.-Elect (1979/80); 2nd VP & Prog. Ch. (1978/79); Ch., Educ. Com. (1977/78). **Activities:** 12; 17, 34, 49-Comput. Info. Syst.; 56, 75, 93 **Addr.:** 95 Mountain View Rd., Warren, NJ 07060.

Fortson-Jones, Judith L. (Ja. 6, 1943, Summerville, SC) Cons. Spec., NE State Hist. Socty., 1977–; Instr., Concordia Coll., 1972–76; Resrch., Admin. Assoc., Univ. of WI, 1967–70. **Educ.:** Baylor Univ., 1961–65, BA (Eng.); Univ. of WI, 1966–67, MA (Eng.). **Orgs.:** Amer. Inst. for Cons. of Hist. and Artistic Works. SAA. Midwest Arch. Conf. **Pubns.:** "Preservation of Paper," *The Cornerstone* (My.-O. 1980); "When Disaster Strikes," *Countyline* (N. 1980); various presentations. **Activities:** 2; 23, 25 **Addr.:** 1736 Harwood, Lincoln, NE 68502.

Fortune, Joan S. (My. 13, 1947, Newark, NJ) Info. Srvs. Mgr., Amer. Critical Care, Div. of Amer. Hosp. Supply Corp., 1977–; Supvsr., Tech. Info., G.D. Searle, 1976–77; Supvsr., Biochem. Lit. & Data, 1975–76; Info. Sci., 1974–75. **Educ.:** Cath. Univ., 1965–69, BA (Chem.); Univ. of WI, 1969–70, MS (Org. Chem.); Univ. of Chicago, 1977–81, MBA (Fnc. & Mktg.). **Orgs.:** Assoc. Info. Mgrs.; ASIS. Amer. Chem. Socty.; Chem. Notation Assn. **Honors** Phi Beta Kappa. Beta Gamma Sigma. **Pubns.:** Jt. auth., "An Integrated Computer Network in Pharmaceutical Technology," *Pharm. Tech.* (1980); Jt. auth., "AMANDA: A Computerized Document Management System," *MIS Qtly.* (1980); Jt. auth., "Effect of beta-galactosidase inhibitors on lysosomal enzyme activities in cultured skin fibroblasts." *Lab. Investigation,* (1975); Jt. auth., "Effect of beta-galactosidase inhibitors on acid hydrolases from cultured fibroblasts." *Fed. Proc.,* (1974); Jt. auth., "Serum proteins and alkaline phosphatase levels in patients with tuberous sclerosis." *Amer. Jnl. of Mental Deficiency,* (1974). **Activities:** 12; 17, 38, 49; 56, 60, 80, 87 **Addr.:** Arnar-Stone Laboraties Inc., 1600 Waukegan Rd., McGaw Park, IL 60085.

Foster, Donald L. (Mr. 7, 1928, Chicago, IL) Assoc. Prof. of Libnshp., Univ. of NM, 1964–; Catlgr., Univ. of IL Lib., 1961–64; Inst., NM State Univ., 1958–59; Msc. Tchr., Sheffield HS, 1956–58. **Educ.:** De Paul Univ., 1946–50, BMus (Msc.), 1952–53, MMus (Msc.); Univ. of IL, 1960–61, MS (LS). **Orgs.:** ALA. AAUP. **Pubns.:** *Managing the Catalog Department* (1975) *Prints in the Public Library* (1973) Various articles. **Activities:** 1; 17, 20, 41; 55, 63, 90 **Addr.:** 12104 Baja Dr., Albuquerque, NM 87111.

Foster, Eloise C. (Mr. 28, 1943, Wilmington, DE) Dir., Lib. of the Amer. Hosp. Assn. Asa S. Bacon Meml., 1978–; Mgr.,

Special Subjects/Services: 50. Adult educ.; 51. Advert./Mktg.; 52. Aerosp.; 53. Agric.; 54. Area std.; 55. Arts/Hum.; 56. Autom.; 57. Bibl./Prtg.; 58. Bio. sci.; 59. Bus./Fin.; 60. Chem.; 61. Copyrt.; 62. Documtn.; 63. Educ.; 64. Engin.; 65. Env.; 66. Eth. grps.; 67. Film; 68. Food/Nutr.; 69. Geneal.; 70. Geo.; 71. Geol.; 72. Handcpd.; 73. Hist.; 74. Int. frdm.; 75. Info. sci.; 76. Insr.; 77. Law; 78. Legis.; 79. Math./Comp. sci.; 80. Med.; 81. Metals; 82. Nat. resrcs.; 83. Newsp.; 84. Nuc. sci.; 85. Oral hist.; 86. Petr./Energy; 87. Pharm.; 88. Phys./Astr./Math.; 89. Readg.; 90. Relig.; 91. Sci./Tech.; 92. Soc. sci.; 93. Telecom.; 94. Transp.; 95. (other).

1975–78, Head, Southeast. Reg. Med. Lib. Prog., A.W. Calhoun Med. Lib., Emory Univ., 1973–75, Various positions, 1969–73. **Educ.:** PA State Univ., 1961–65, BS; Emory Univ., 1968–69, MLN. **Orgs.:** ALA: ASCLA, Stan. Review Com. (1978–80). Med. LA: Bd. of Dir. (1980–). SLA: Bio. Sci. Div. (Secy.-Treas., 1977–1980). Other orgs. Intl. Hosp. Fed.: Std. Com. on Docum. and Info. Handling. ASIS. Hlth. Sci. Comm. Assn. **Honors:** Med. LA. Cert. Grade I. 1969; Ida and George Eliot Prize 1980; Beta Phi Mu; Phi Kappa Phi; Pi Lambda Theta. **Pubns.:** Various articles. **Activities:** 1, 12; 17, 24, 34; 75, 80, 95-Hlth. Admin. **Addr.:** Library of the American Hospital Association, 840 N. Lake Shore Dr., Chicago, IL 60611.

Foster, Harry E. (Ap. 28, 1926, Jefferson City, MO) Head Libn., Anne Arundel Cmnty. Coll., 1961–; Spec. Asst., VA Musm. of Fine Arts, 1960–61; Tech. Couns., MD State Dept. of Educ., 1954–60; Catlgr., Enoch Pratt Free Lib., 1951–53. **Educ.:** Dartmouth Coll., 1947–50, BA (Art Hist.); Columbia Univ., 1950–51, MSLS. **Orgs.:** MD LA: Div. of Coll. and Resrch. Libs. (Ch., 1962–63). MD Congs. of Acad. Libns.: Exec. Bd. (1977–). Readg. Reform Fndn. ALA. Cncl. for Basic Educ. **Pubns.:** "The Media Religion," *Amer. Libs.* (O. 1974); "The Debasement of School Libraries," *Cncl. for Basic Educ. Bltn.* (My. 1974); "Here's One Reason Johnny Can't Read," *Baltimore Sun* (Jl. 25, 1976). **Activities:** 1; 15, 20; 89 **Addr.:** Riquewihr, Crownsville, MD 21032.

Foster, Joan (My. 3, 1931, New York, NY) Dir., Wilton Lib. Assn., 1979–; Dir., Jr. Srvs., Danbury Pub. Lib., 1974–79; Libn., Untd. Nations Intl. Sch., New York, 1973–74. **Educ.:** Brooklyn Coll., 1952, BA (Eng., Gvt.); Pratt Inst., 1971–73, MLS. **Orgs.:** Southwest. CT Lib. Cncl.: Prog. Com. (1980–81). Fairfield Lib. Admins. Grp. ALA. CT LA. **Honors:** Beta Phi Mu, 1973. **Pubns.:** "Urban Poetry for Children," *RQ* (Sum. 1974); *Reader in Children's Librarianship* (1979); reviews, TV interviews. **Activities:** 9; 16, 17, 42 **Addr.:** Curiosity Ln., West Redding, CT 06896.

Foster, M. Anne (Ja. 11, 1949, Montreal, PQ;) Coord., Comp. & the Law, Can. Law Info. Cncl., 1979–; User Srvs., QL Syst. Ltd., 1977–79; Ref. Libn., Univ. of Toronto, 1973–77. **Educ.:** Queen's Univ., 1967–71, BA (Eng./Fr.); Univ. of Strathclyde, Glasgow, 1971–72, Dip Lib. **Orgs.:** AALL: Spec. Com. on Networking (1979–). Can. Assn. for Info. Sci.: Toronto Chap., Exec. Com. (1978). Can. Assn. of Law Libns. Libns. Assn., Univ. of Toronto: Pres. (1974/75); Exec. Com. (1975/76). Univ. of Toronto, Fac. Assn.: Exec. Com. (1975/76); Negotiating Com. (1975/76). **Pubns.:** "Automated Legal Research: A Manual for QL Users," *CLIC Wkg. Paper No. 5* (1980); Co-ed., "Applications of Computer Technology to Law (1969–78): A Selected Bibliography," *CLIC Wkg. Paper No. 4* (1980); "CLIC Service Centres - Ready to meet the Practitioners," *National (CBA)* (S. 1979); "From stone tablets to cathode-ray tubes in one difficult step," *CALL Newsletter* (My. 1979); "QL Systems Ltd.: A survey of its retrieval system", *Proceedings*, ASIS, (1977); oral presentations. **Activities:** 14-Resrch. Ctr.; 17, 24, 41; 56, 77, 78 **Addr.:** Canadian Law Information Council, 112 Kent St., Suite 2010, Place de Ville, Tower "B", Ottawa, ON K1P 5P2, Canada.

Foster, Saba L. (Jl. 2, 1920, New Haven, CT) Chief Libn., Natl. Life Insr. Co., 1975–; Coll. Textbk. Ed., Houghton Mifflin Co., 1969–74; Mag. Ed., Park St. Church, 1962–69. **Educ.:** Wheaton Coll., 1938–42, BS (Econ., Bus.); Simmons Coll., 1974–75, MLS. **Orgs.:** VT LA: Treas. (1979). SLA. AALL. VT State Adv. Cncl. AAUW: VT Div. (Pres., 1973–75). **Activities:** 5, 12; 17, 39, 41; 59, 76, 77 **Addr.:** The Library, National Life Insurance Company, Montpelier, VT 05602.

Fouser, Jane G. (F. 18, 1942, Chicago, IL) Sr. Resrch. Anal., Continental IL Natl. Bank, 1978–; Libn., Untd. Charities of Chicago, 1974–78; Ref. Libn., Medline Anal., Northwestern Univ., 1971–74. **Educ.:** Lake Forest Coll., 1961–64, BA; MI State Univ., 1964–65, MA; Rosary Coll., 1970–71, MALS. **Orgs.:** SLA: IL Chap., Treas./Bd. Mem. (1979–1981). Small Spec. Lib. Discuss. Grp. Co-organizer (1977). **Activities:** 12; 39, 41; 59 **Addr.:** Continental Illinois National Bank, Information Services RC 3040, 231 S. LaSalle St., Chicago, IL 60693.

Fouty, Gary C. (O. 21, 1946, Urbana, IL) Head, Ref. Dept., IA State Univ. Lib., 1978–, Ref. Libn., 1973–78. **Educ.:** Dartmouth Coll., 1964–68, AB (Bio.); Univ. of WA, 1968–71, MS (Compar. Physio.); Univ. of Chicago, 1971–72, MA (LS). **Orgs.:** ALA. **Pubns.:** Jt. auth., "A Mathematical Model for Estimating the Effectiveness of Bigram Coding," *Info. Prcs. and Mgt.* (1976). **Activities:** 1; 39; 58 **Addr.:** Iowa State University Library, Ames, IA 50011.

Fowle, Donald Wallace (Ap. 25, 1929, Boston, MA) Libn., Thea. Col., New York Pub. Lib., 1967–, Libn., Gen. Lib., Lincoln Ctr., 1965–67. **Educ.:** Harvard Coll., 1946–50, BA (Hist. & Lit.), 1950, MAT (Tchg.), 1951; Yale Sch. of Drama, 1953–58, MFA (Playwrighting), Rutgers Univ., 1963–64, MLS; Army Lang. Sch., 1952–53, Cert. (Russ.). **Orgs.:** Thea. LA. Amer. Film Inst.: Terminology Com. Libns. Local 1930, D.C. 37, AFSCME:: Shop Steward (1968–). Armstead-Johnson Fndn. for Thea. Resrch.: Bd. (1976–). Carol Dye Awd. Fund, Yale Drama Sch.: Ch. (1962–). **Pubns.:** "List of American Premieres, 1967–1974," in *Notable Names in the American Theatre*, (1975); "Theatre, Film, & Dance Bibliography," *Funk & Wagnall's Encyclopedia* (1972); "American Premieres, 1967–1974" *Players Mag.* (1968–1974); Several Produced Plays. **Activities:** 2, 9; 15, 20, 41, 45; 55, 62, 67 **Addr.:** Theatre Collection, The New York Public Library, 111 Amsterdam Ave., New York, NY 10014.

Fowler, Bonnie Shaw (Je. 13, 1953, Baltimore, MD) Head, Chld. Dept., Forsyth Cnty. Pub. Lib., 1977–. **Educ.:** Wake Forest Univ., 1971–75, BA (Phil.); Univ. of Chicago, 1975–76, AM (LS). **Orgs.:** ALA: Newbery-Caldecott Com. (1980). NC LA: Chld. Srvs. Sect. (Prog. Ch., 1980–81). SELA: Sch. and Chld. Sect. (Secy., 1981–82). **Pubns.:** "Reactions by a Recent Library School Graduate," *Children's Services of Public Libraries* (1978); "Toddler's Storytime," *NC Libs.* (Sum. 1980); "Outreach: Advantages for the Disadvantaged," *Pub. Libs.* (Fall 1978). **Activities:** 9; 15, 21, 39 **Addr.:** Forsyth County Public Library, 660 W. Fifth St., Winston-Salem, NC 27101.

Fowler, Karla Fingerson (Jl. 13, 1950, Madison, WI) Head Libn., Media Spec., Olympia Tech. Cmnty. Coll., 1975–; Prog. Coord., Cable TV/Comms., Univ. of WI - Ext., 1973–75. **Educ.:** Univ. of WI, 1968–72, BA (Radio-TV-Film), 1972–74, MA (LS). **Orgs.:** Cmnty. Coll. Libns. and Media Specs.: WA State Pres. (1980–81); Pres.-Elect (1979–80); Secy.-Treas. (1977–79). AECT. NW Coll. and Univ. Cncl. for the Mgt. of Educ. Tech. WA LA: Strg. Com., PR Forum (1979–). WA State Info. Cncl. **Honors:** Beta Phi Mu. **Pubns.:** "The Issue is...Image: Communication and College Identity," *NW/MET Bltn.* (S. 1980); "Wire We Here: Basic Information about Cable," *WI Lib. Bltn.* (Ja.–F. 1975); jt. auth., "Get 'Plugged in' to Cable TV," *WI Jnl. of Educ.* (N.–D. 1973); "Citizen Cable TV Programming," *Proceedings, National Cooperative Cable TV Conference* (My.–Je. 1973); various slide tape shows. **Activities:** 1; 17, 32, 39; 50, 67, 93 **Addr.:** Olympia Technical Community College, 2011 Mottman Rd. S.W., Olympia, WA 98502.

Fowlie, E. Leslie (F. 10, 1928, Chatham, ON) Chief Libn., Toronto Pub. Lib., 1979–; Dir., Calgary Pub. Lib., 1973–78; Chief Libn., St. Catharines Pub. Lib., 1968–73; Libn., The Archts. Collaborative, 1967–68; Libn., Assn. of Univs. and Colls. of Can., 1963–67; Deputy Head Libn., Univ. of AB, Ext. Lib., 1960–63. **Educ.:** Queen's Univ., Kingston, ON, 1949–53, BA, hons. (Pol. Sci.); Univ. of Toronto, 1959–60, BLS. **Orgs.:** Can. LA: Treas. (1972–73). ON LA. ALA. AB LA: Pres. (1978). Inst. of Prof. Libns. of ON: Pres. (1971–72). **Pubns.:** Ed., *I P L O Bltn.* (1972–73); Ed., *Univ. Affairs* (1966–67); Asst. Ed., *Univ. Affairs* (1963–66). **Activities:** 9, 12; 17, 19, 25 **Addr.:** Toronto Public Library, 40 Orchard View Blvd., Toronto, ON M4R 1B9 Canada.

Fox, Barbara S. (My. 5, 1935, Fillmore, NY) Col. Dev. Libn., James Madison Univ., 1978–, Asst. Acq. Libn., 1974–78; Libn., W. Irondequoit HS, Rochester, NY, 1958–60; Bus. Libn., Eastman Kodak Co., 1957–58. **Educ.:** SUNY, Coll. at Geneseo, 1953–57, BS (Educ.), 1960–62, MLS. **Orgs.:** VA LA: Mem. Com. (1976–77); Reg. VI (Ch., 1979); State Cncl. (Mem., 1979). ALA: ACRL, VA Chap. SELA. **Pubns.:** "Library Displays on a Shoestring," *Southeast. Libn.* (N. 1979). **Activities:** 1; 15 **Addr.:** Madison Memorial Library, James Madison University, Harrisonburg, VA 22807.

Fox, Dexter L. (Jl. 28, 1946, Cincinnati, OH) Chief, Cat. Sect., US Army Lib., 1981–; Libn., US Army Env. Hygiene Agency, 1975–81; Lib. Tech. Univ. of MD, 1971–75; Consult., Ideamatics, Inc., 1976–. **Educ.:** OH Univ., 1964–68, BFA (Graph. Arts); Univ. of MD, 1972–74, MLS. **Orgs.:** SLA: Env. Info. Div. ASIS. Med. LA. **Activities:** 1, 4; 17, 20, 39; 60, 65, 95-Toxicology. **Addr.:** US Army Library, 1A518 Pentagon, Washington, DC 20310.

Fox, George A. (Ap. 23, 1924, Chicago, IL) Dir. of Lrng. Srvs., Prairie State Coll., 1966–; Dir. of Libs., Joliet Jr. Coll. and HS, 1954–66. **Educ.:** Knox Coll., 1946–50, BS (Geol.); Univ. of IL, 1953–54, MS (LS). **Orgs.:** IL Assn. of Sch. Libns. ALA. AECT. Midwest Assn. of Libns. Other orgs. Natl. Educ. Assn. Veterans of Frgn. Wars. MOOSE. **Pubns.:** *A Multimedia Survey of the Community College Libraries of the State of Illinois* (1970); various articles. **Activities:** 1, 2; 17, 41; 63, 67 **Addr.:** 237 Willow Ln., New Lenox, IL 60451.

Fox, Herbert S. (Ap. 11, 1929, Edmonton, AB) Assoc. Libn., CA State Univ., Fresno, 1969–. **Educ.:** Concordia Coll. and Semy., 1947–51, BA; Univ. of BC, 1968–69, BLS; Concordia Semy., 1951–54, Theo. Dip. **Orgs.:** West. Assn. of Map Libs.: Pres. (1972–73). **Pubns.:** "Classification and Cataloging Scheme for a Small Map Library," *West. Assn. of Map Libs. Info. Bltn.* (N. 1972); "The Reorganization of WAML," *West. Assn. of Map Libs. Info. Bltn.* (Je. 1978). **Activities:** 1; 39; 70 **Addr.:** The Library, California State University, Fresno, Fresno, CA 93740.

Fox, James R. (Je. 30, 1950, Dayton, OH) Law Libn., Assoc. Prof., Dickinson Sch. of Law, 1976–; Media Tech., Natl. Ctr. on Educ. Media and Mtrls. for the Handcpd., 1973–75. **Educ.:** Otterbein Coll., 1968–72, BA (Hist.); OH State Univ., 1972–74, JD (Law); Drexel Univ., 1976–78, MS (LS); AALL, Cert. Law Libn., 1979. **Orgs.:** AALL: AV Com. (1976–1978); Ch., AV/Micro. SIS. Grt. Philadelphia Law Lib. Assn. Amer. Std. Assn. Amer. Bar Assn. **Pubns.:** Reviews, "Delivering Educational Materials for the Handicapped" slide/tape (1975). **Activities:** 12; 17, 32; 77 **Addr.:** Dickinson School of Law, 150 S. College St., Carlisle, PA 17013.

Foy, Kathleen M. (Ja. 19, 1912, Souris, MB) Head Libn., Montreal Chld. Lib., 1976–; Chld. Libn., R. G. Dawson Lib., Mt. Royal, PQ, 1967–76; Chld. Libn., McLaughlin Pub. Lib., Oshawa, ON, 1961–67. **Educ.:** Univ. of MB, 1929–32, BA; McGill Univ., BLS; 1960, Elem. Tchg. Cert. **Orgs.:** PQ LA. Can. LA. **Pubns.:** Jt. auth., "Children of Immigrants and Multi-Ethnic Heritage," *Lib. Trends* (Fall 1980). **Activities:** 9, 10; 21, 25; 50, 66, 72 **Addr.:** Montreal Children's Library, 3835 Sewell St., Montreal, PQ H2W 1W1 Canada.

Foyle, James K. (N. 20, 1929, Grindstone, PA) Asst. Prof., Univ. of Denver, Grad. Sch. of Libnshp., 1980–, Actg. Dean, 1979–79, Asst. Prof. and Asst. Dean, 1968–78; Head, Tech. Prcs., IN Univ. Reg. Campus Libs., 1966–68; Admin. Asst., Instr., Div. of LS, IN Univ., 1963–66; Asst. Ref. Libn., PA State Univ., 1961–63. **Educ.:** PA State Univ., 1953–57, AB (Soc. Std.); Univ. of WI, 1957–58 (Eur. Hist.); IN Univ., 1958–61, MA (LS). **Orgs.:** AALS: Conf. Com. (1977–78). CO LA: Ch., Coll. and Univ. Sect. (1971–72). ALA: Ref. and Sub. Books Bltn. (1974–78); Dir., LED/Tchrs. Sect. (1973–76). Univ. of Denver: Senate (1971–75); Grad. Cncl. (1975–79). **Activities:** 17, 26, 39; 56, 92 **Addr.:** 4395 E. Arapahoe Pl., Littleton, CO 80122.

Fraley, Ruth Ann (O. 16, 1942, Peekskill, NY) Head, Hawley Lib., SUNY, Albany, 1979–; Head, Tech. Srvs., Schenectady Cnty. Cmnty. Coll., 1973–79; Lib.-Media Spec., Schenectady Pub. Sch., 1966–72. **Educ.:** SUNY, Albany, 1960–64, BA (Soc. Std.), 1964–66, MSLS; NY State Sch. Lib. Media Spec., 1966, Cert. **Orgs.:** NY LA: Resrcs. and Tech. Srvs. Sect. (Pres., 1979–80; Treas. 1976–78: First VP, Pres-elect 1978–79). SUNY/OCLC Network Adv. Com.: Vice Ch., (1979–81). Com. to Coord. AACR2 in NY: Ch., (1979–). Mohawk Hudson LA: Bd. (1979–81); other orgs. **Pubns.:** "Publishers vs. Wholesalers: Ordering Dilemma", *Lib. Acq.: Practice and Theory* (vol 3 no 1 1979); "AACR2 What will it do to you?," *NYLA Bltn.* (S. 1979); "How to Use a Law Library" (videotape) (1977). **Activities:** 1, 10; 17, 24, 46; 77 **Addr.:** 29 Roslyn Dr., R.D. 1, Ballston Lake, NY 12019.

Frame, Ruth Rhea (O. 19, 1916, Frederick, OK) Deputy Exec. Dir., ALA, 1973–, Exec. Secy., Lib. Admin. Div., 1967–73; Asst. State Libn., MI State Lib., 1964–67, Consult., 1957–63. **Educ.:** Ctrl. State Coll., Edmond, OK, 1933–37, BA (Msc.); George Peabody Coll., 1938–39, BS in LS; Syracuse Univ., 1955, Cert. (AV); Univ. of MD, 1971, Cert. (Lib. Admin.). **Orgs.:** ALA. Frdm. to Read Fndn. Frnds. of Libs. USA. Amer. Natl. Stan. Inst.: ALA rep. (1979–80); Com. Z 39, Task Force on Z 39, Actv. and Future Directions (1978). **Pubns.:** *Certification of Public Librarians in the United States, 2d ed.* (1972); "ALA and Nonprint Media," *Educ. Media Yrbk.*, (1978); "Mediation, Arbitration, and Inquiry," *ALA Yrbk.*, (1979). **Activities:** 3, 14; 17, 35; 76 **Addr.:** American Library Association, 50 E. Huron, Chicago, IL 60611.

Francis, Derek R. (S. 26, 1941, Winnipeg, MB) Head Coll. Libn., Kwantlen Coll., 1981–; Head, Tech. Srvs., Douglas Coll., 1971–; Asst. Prof., Sch. of Libnshp., Univ. of BC, 1969–71; Sci./Tech. Libn., Univ. of MB, 1967–69; Can. Colombo Plan Lib. Adv., Khon Kaen Univ., Thailand, 1965–67. **Educ.:** Univ. of MB, 1958–62, BID (Design); Univ. of BC, 1963–64, BLS. **Orgs.:** Can. LA. Can. Lib. Trustees Assn. BC LA. Grt. Vancouver Lib. Fed.: Bd. of Dir. (Ch., 1977–). Richmond Pub. Lib. Bd.: Ch. (1974–). **Pubns.:** "Is this trip really necessary?," *Can. Lib.* (Jl. 1968); "University librarians: shepherds of books or disseminators of information," *Can. Lib. Jnl.* (Mr.-Ap. 1969). **Activities:** 1, 9; 24, 46, 47 **Addr.:** Kwantlen College Libraries, P.O. Box 9030, Surrey, BC V3T 5H8, Canada.

Franck, Jane P. (Ja. 11, 1921, Akron, OH) Dir., Tchrs. Coll. Lib., Columbia Univ., 1977–; Libn. & Admin. Ofcr., Ford Fndn., 1968–77; Archvst. & Spec. Col. Libn., City Coll., 1966–68, 1960–66; Lect., Pratt Inst. Lib. Sch., 1963–68; Catlgr., City Coll., 1949–54; First Asst., Msc. Lib., Columbia Univ., 1946–49, Ref./Circ. Asst., 1943–46. **Educ.:** Hofstra Univ., 1938–42, BA cum laude (Grmn. & Fr. Lit.); Columbia Univ., 1943, BS (LS), 1949, MA (Msclgy.); City Univ., 1967–69, (Msclgy.); Various seminars, 1968–. **Orgs.:** ALA: ACRL/Educ. Bhvl. Sci. Sect., Nom. Com. (1979); Stan. Com. (1978–81); Intl. Rel. Com. (1978–79). SLA: NY Chap., Musm., Arts and Hum. Div. (Ch., 1973–75). Msc. LA: Archvst. (1967–1979). IFLA: Stats. and Stan. Com. (1971). Other orgs. Amer. Musicological Socty. Amer. Civil Liberties Un. Common Cause. **Pubns.:** Jt. auth., *ALA Criteria to be used in the Selection of Candidates to represent ALA Abroad* (1979); Jt. auth., *ALA International Relations Policy*, (1978); "Report on the work of the Committee on Statistics and Standards of the International Federation of Library Associations (IFLA)," *Spec. Libs.* (F. 1975); Jt. ed., *Code for Cataloging Music and Phono Records.* (1958). **Addr.:** Teachers College Library, Box 69, Columbia University, 525 West 120th St., New York, NY 10027.

Franckowiak, Bernard M. (Je. 2, 1934, Angelica, WI) Dean and Prof., Grad. Sch. of Libnshp. and Info. Mgt., Univ. of

PROFESSIONAL ACTIVITIES: Institutions: 1. Acad. lib.; 2. Arch.; 3. Assn.; 4. Fed./Gvt. lib.; 5. Inst. lib.; 6. Mfr./Suppl.; 7. Milit. lib.; 8. Musm.; 9. Pub. lib.; 10. Sch. lib.; 11. Sch. of lib. sci.; 12. Spec. lib.; 13. State lib.; 14. (other). **Functions/Activities:** 15. Acq./Col. dev.; 16. Adult srvs.; 17. Admin.; 18. Apprais.; 19. Archit./Bldgs.; 20. Cat./Class.; 21. Chld. srvs.; 22. Circ.; 23. Cons./Pres.; 24. Consult.; 25. Cont. ed.; 26. Educ. lib. sci.; 27. Ext. srvs.; 28. Fund/Grants; 29. Gvt. pubs.; 30. Indx./Abs.; 31. Instr. lib. use; 32. Media srvs.; 33. Micro.; 34. Netwks./Coop.; 35. Persnl.; 36. PR; 37. Publshg.; 38. Recs. mgt.; 39. Ref. srvs.; 40. Repro.; 41. Resrch.; 42. Review.; 43. Secur.; 44. Serials; 45. Spec. col.; 46. Tech. srvs.; 47. Trustees/Bds.; 48. YA srvs.; 49. (other).

Denver, 1980–; Assoc. Prof., Univ. of WA, 1976–79; Dir., Bur. of Sch. Lib. Media Prog., WI Dept. Pub. Instr., 1975–76, Supvsr., Sch. Lib., 1968–75; Libn., Ripon HS, 1962–68; Libn., Kimberly HS, 1959–62. **Educ.:** Univ. of WI, 1955–59, BS (Bio.); George Peabody Coll., 1965–68, MLS; Univ. of WI, 1969–75, PhD (Educ., Admin.). **Orgs.:** CLENE: Adv. Bd. WI Assn. of Sch. Libns.: Pres. (1969–70). WA LA: Cont. Educ. Com. (1977–79). ALA: AASL (Pres., 1973–74), Stans. Implementation Com., Ch., Stans. Task Frc.; Stdg. Com. on Lib. Educ. (1980–83); various other coms. Various other orgs. Univ. of Denver Grad. Cncl. Assoc. Info. Mgrs. **Honors:** WI LA, Spec. Srv. Awd., 1976. **Pubns.:** *School Library Media Programs and the National Program for Library and Information Services* (1975); jt. ed., *Cataloguing, Processing, Administering A-V Materials: A Model for Wisconsin Schools* (1974); "Networks, Databases, and Media Programs: An Overview," *Sch. Media Qtly.* (Fall 1977); "School Library Media Programs: 1975 Annual Report Shows Ten Years of Progress," *WI Lib. Bltn.* (N.–D. 1976); ed. com., *Sch. Media Qtly.* **Activities:** 10, 11; 17, 24, 26; 58, 63, 75 **Addr.:** Graduate School of Librarianship and Information Management, University of Denver, University Park, Denver, CO 80208.

Frank, Agnes T. (Budapest, Hungary) Chief Med. Libn., St. Vincent's Hosp. (NY), 1974–; Dir. of Med. Libs., French & Polyclinic Med. Sch. & Hlth. Ctr., 1970–74; Dir. of Med. Lib., NY Med. Coll.-Metrop. Hosp. Div., 1968–70; Lit. Resrchr., Montefiore Hosp., 1966–68; Ref. Asst., NY Acad. of Med. Lib., 1964–66. **Educ.:** Columbia Univ., 1964, MLS; Cert. in Med. Libnshp., 1966. **Orgs.:** Med. LA: NY Reg. Grp. **Activities:** 12; 17; 56, 58, 80 **Addr.:** 372 Central Park West, Apt. 16 A, New York, NY 10025.

Frank, Anne Baldwin (F. 13, 1937, San Francisco, CA) Assoc. Libn., Cat. Dept., Univ. of CA, Irvine, 1966–; Ref. and Bkmobile. Libn., Lib. Assn. of Portland OR, 1964–66, Libn. I, Acq. Dept., Univ. of CA, Berkeley, 1961–62. **Educ.:** Univ. of CA, Berkeley, 1954–58, BA (Hist.), 1960–61, MLS. **Orgs.:** CA LA: Tech. Srvs. Chap. (Secy., 1980, 2nd VP, 1981). Intellectual Freedom Com., (1981). Natl. Libns. Assn. South. CA Tech. Processes Grp. ALA. Orange Cnty. LA. CA St. Empl. Assoc. **Activities:** 1; 20, 31, 46; 55, 90 **Addr.:** Catalog Department, The University Library, University of California, P.O. Box 19557, Irvine, Irvine, CA 92713.

Frank, Bernice C. (Ja. 3, 1923, Powell River, BC) Law Lib., Burroughs Corp. 1972–. **Educ.:** West. Coll. for Women, 1941–45, BA (Hist.); Wayne State Univ., 1970–72, MSLS. **Orgs.:** AALL: Lcl. Arrang. Ch. for Natl. Conv. (1982). OH. Reg. Assn. of Law Libs.: Treas. (1977); VP (1978), Bd. Mem. (1979). MI. Assn. of Law Libs.: Place. Coord. (1979–80). **Activities:** 12, 14; 15, 17, 39; 61, 77, 78 **Addr.:** Legal Activity Library, Burroughs Corporation, Burroughs Pl., Detroit, MI 48232.

Frank, Christine D. (Je. 17, 1950, Buffalo, NY) Dir., Lrng. Resrc. Ctr., Rush Univ., 1977–; Head, Multimedia Srvs., Lib. of the Hlth. Sci., Univ. of IL, Med. Ctr., Chicago, 1975–77, Multimedia Ref. Libn., 1973–75. **Educ.:** SUNY, Buffalo, 1968–72, BA (Eng.), 1972–73, MLS. **Orgs.:** Hlth. Educ. Comms. Assn.: Biomed. Libs. Sect. Ch., 1981–82. Med. LA. **Pubns.:** "PLATO IV," *Netwk.* (1977); "Selection Tools for Health Education Media," *IL Libs.* (1976). **Addr.:** Learning Resource Center, Rush University, 600 S. Paulina St., Chicago, IL 60612.

Frank, Ilene B. (O. 22, 1945, Detroit, MI) Assoc. Libn., Univ. of S. FL, 1974–. **Educ.:** Univ. of MI, 1963–67, BSD (Painting), 1968–74, AMLS; Univ. of S. FL, 1981–, MFA. **Orgs.:** ARLIS/NA: SE Chap. Msc. LA: SE Chap. Untd. Fac. of FL: State VP (1977–79); Treas. (1979–80). Coal. of Labor Un. Women. **Pubns.:** Reviews. **Activities:** 1; 15, 30, 39; 55, 92 **Addr.:** The Library (L1B110) University of South Florida, Tampa, FL 33620.

Frank, Nathalie D. (Ja. 28, 1918, St. Petersburg, Russia) Assoc. Prof., Pratt Inst. Grad. Sch. of Lib. & Info. Sci., 1968–78; Dir., Info. & Lib. Srvs., Stewart, Dougall & Associates, 1965–67; Head, Resrch. Lib., Geyer, Morey, Ballard, Inc., 1944–65. **Educ.:** Barnard Coll., 1939, BA (Fr.); Columbia Univ., 1941, MS (LS). **Orgs.:** ALA. Amer. Socty. of Indxrs.: Nom. Com. (Ch., 1972–73). ASIS. SLA: Elec. Com. (Ch., 1950–51); Advert. Div. (Secy., 1949–50); NY Chap., Advert. Grp. (Ch., 1946–47); Dinner Com. (Ch. 1947–48); Consult. Com. (1979–). Advert. Women of NY: Educ. Com. (1948/49, 1952/53); Resrch. Com. (1967/68). Edit. Freelancers Assn. **Pubns.:** "Selection Aids for Marketing and Communications," *Spec. Libs.*, (My./Je. 1964); *Market Analysis; a Handbook of Current Data Sources*, (1964); *Data Sources for Business and Market Analysis*, (1969); "Who, What, When, Where," *Bookletter*, (Feb. 3, 1975); reprinted in *Harper's Magazine*, (May 1975); "After the *Statistical Abstract* - What?," *RQ*, (Spr. 1975); other articles. **Activities:** 12; 17, 26, 30; 51, 57, 59 **Addr.:** 120 Vermilyea Ave., New York, NY 10034.

Frank, Robyn Claire (Jl. 28, 1945, Washington, DC;) Chief, Food and Nutr. Info. Ctr., US Dept. of Agr., 1978–, Tech. Info. Spec., 1973–78; Asst. Proj. Dir., Educ. Resrcs. Ctr., ASIS, 1971–73; Resrch. Asst., Pub. Sch. of DC, 1969–71. **Educ.:** Univ. of MD, 1963–67, BS (Home Econ.), 1970–72, MLS. **Orgs.:** ASIS: Spec. Int. Grp. on Info. Srvs. to Educ. (Ch., 1980). SLA: Food and Nutr. Sect. **Honors:** US Dept. of Agr., Young Exec. Com., 1976. **Pubns.:** "Survey of Information Needs of Educational Information Specialists" *ERIC*, (1972); "On-line access to human nutrition information", *On-line Review*; Slide/Tape - "All About ERIC" (1971). **Activities:** 4, 12; 15, 17, 39; 63, 68 **Addr.:** Food and Nutrition Information Center, National Agricultural Library Building, Rm. 304, Beltsville, MD 20705.

Franke, Eileen M. (F. 23, 1930, St. Louis, MO) Bk. Sel. Coord., St. Louis Pub. Lib., 1970–, Head, Educ. Dept., 1965–70, Ref. Dept. Asst., 1960–65, Readers' Adv. Asst., 1957–60. **Educ.:** Webster Coll., Webster Groves, MO, 1948–52, AB (Span. Lit.); St. Louis Univ., 1953–55, MA (Span. Lit.); Univ. of MI, 1957–59, AMLS. **Orgs.:** ALA: SORT, Strg. Com. (1965–66). Cath. LA: Grt. St. Louis Unit (Secy., 1969–71; Pubcty. Ch., 1977–79; Co-Ed. of Nsltr., 1978–). MO LA: Cert. Com. (1965–70). SLA: St. Louis Chap. (Empl. Ch., 1978–79; PR Ch., 1972–75). Various other orgs. **Honors:** Beta Phi Mu, 1960. **Activities:** 9; 15 **Addr.:** Book Selection Coordinator, St. Louis Public Library, 1301 Olive, St. Louis, MO 63103.

Frankel, Norman (Ap. 22, 1947, New York, NY) Ref./Instr. Libn., West. MI Univ., 1981–; Visit. Lectr., Queen's Univ., Sch. of Lib. and Info. Std., Belfast, North. Ireland, 1981–; Dir., LS Lib., West. MI Univ., 1978–81; Judaica Libn., Buffalo Bd. of Jewish Educ., 1978; Dir., Nursing Sch. Lib., Buffalo Gen. Hosp., 1971–77. **Educ.:** SUNY, Buffalo, 1965–69, BA (Pol. Sci.), 1970–71, MLS, 1971–72, MA (Media Std.), 1973–76, MA (Pol. Sci.). **Orgs.:** ALA: Ref. and Subscrpn. Bks. Review Com. (1980–82); LS Libns. Discuss. Grp. Brit. LA. Intl. Std. Assn. Royal Untd. Srvs. Inst. for Defense Std. **Pubns.:** *Political Science Serials: An Annotated Bibliography* (forthcoming); contrib., *Magazines for Libraries* (1982); bk. review ed., *Terror Watch* (1978–80); reviews. **Activities:** 1, 11; 17, 41, 42; 54, 75, 92 **Addr.:** 1416 Oak St., Kalamazoo, MI 49008.

Franklin, Ann York (N. 22, 1923, Friendship, TN) Lib. Consult., Jefferson Cnty. Pub. Sch., 1971–; Visiting Libn., 1966–71; HS Libn., Durrett HS, 1961–66. **Educ.:** Univ. of Louisville, 1940–44, AB (Chem.); Nazareth Coll., 1957–59, MSLS; Spalding Coll., 1970–71, MA Ed. **Orgs.:** AASL: Cert. of Sch. Media Spec. (1974–78). Sch. Lib. Media Prog. of Year (1979–80). KY LA: Treas. (1966–68); Ed. of *KLA Bltn.* (1973–79); KY Sch. Media Assn.: Ed. of *KASL Bltn.* (1964–65); Secy. (1965–66); Pres. (1970–73); KY Filmstrip Com. (1973–75); Cert. of Sch. Media Libn. Com. (1979–80). KY AV Assn.: Treas. (1972–73). KY Dept. of Educ.: Dev. of Stan. for Sch. Media Libns. (1971–73); Cert. of Sch. Media Pers. (1972–73); Gov. Pre-White House Conf.: (1978–79). **Honors:** KY LA, Outstanding Sch. Libn., 1964. **Pubns.:** "School Library Certification Requirements: 1978 Update," *Sch. Lib. Jnl.* (D. 1978); "Capsule Certification Comparison," *Southeast. Libn.* (1976); "School Library Certification Requirements - Phase II," *Sch. Lib. Jnl.* (D. 1973); "School Library Certification Requirements", *Sch. Lib. Jnl.* (D. 1972). **Activities:** 10; 23, 24, 32; 63, 75, 89 **Addr.:** 1820 Knollwood Rd., Louisville, KY 40207.

Franklin, Hardy R. (My. 9, 1929, Rome, GA) Dir., DC Pub. Lib., 1974–; Asst. Prof., LS Dept., Queens Coll., 1971–74; Sr. Cmnty. Coord., Brooklyn Pub. Lib., 1956–68; Tchr.-Libn., Rockdale Cnty. Bd. of Educ., 1950–53. **Educ.:** Morehouse Coll., 1950, BA (Soclgy.); Atlanta Univ., 1956, MSLS; Rutgers Univ., 1971, PhD (LS). **Orgs.:** ALA: Cncl. (1979–82); Com. on Prog. Eval. and Support (1979–81); PLA Nom. Com. (Ch., 1978–79). DC LA. Exec. Flwshp.: D.C. Conv. WHCOLIS: Del. (1979). Cath. Univ. of America: Bd. of Visitors (1980). Howard Univ. Press: Com. on Mgt. & Oper. (1980). **Honors:** DC Pub. Sch. Libns. Assn., Disting. Pub. Srv., 1979; Natl. Endowment for the Hum., Grant, 1970. **Pubns.:** "The Relationship of Disadvantagement to Library Services," (June 1975); Jt. auth., *The Illinois Minorities Manpower Project - An Evaluative Study*, (1975); "Reaching the Nonuser," *Wilson Lib. Bltn.* (May 1967); other reports, oral presentations. **Addr.:** District of Columbia Public Library, Office of the Director, 901 G Street, N.W., Washington, DC 20001.

Franklin, Ralph W. (Ag. 20, 1937, Ojus, FL) Dir., Whitworth Coll. Lib., 1977–; Bibl. Syst. Consult., WA State Lib., 1974–76, Netwk. Consult. (under contract), 1971–74; Asst. Prof., Dean of Students, Grad. Lib. Sch., Univ. of Chicago, 1971–74; Asst. Chief, Tech. Srvs. and Dev., WA State Lib., 1970–71; Cur. of Spec. Col. Asst. Prof. of Amer. Lit., Middlebury Coll., 1968–70; Asst. Prof. of Eng., Univ. of WI, 1964–66; Tchg. Asst., Northwestern Univ., 1963–64. **Educ.:** Univ. of Puget Sound, 1955–59, BA (Eng.); Northwestern Univ., 1959–64, MA (Eng.), PhD (Amer. Lit.); Univ. of Chicago, 1967–68, MALS. **Orgs.:** ALA: ASCLA, Pubns. Com. (1978–79); ASLA, Interlibrary Coop. Com. (1975–76). WA Lib. Netwk.: Cat. Stans. Com. (Ch., 1978–); Autom. Applications Com. (1978–). Cncl. on Lib. Resrcs.: Working Grp. on MARC Format Review (1979–). WA LA. Various other orgs. **Pubns.:** Jt. auth., *The ASLA Report on Interlibrary Cooperation* (1976); Jt. auth., "The Washington Library Network," *Spec. Libs.* (F. 1976); "Conjectures on Rarity," *Lib. Qtly.* (O. 1974); Various pubns. and articles on Amer. lit. **Activities:** 1, 13; 17, 34, 46; 55, 56, 57 **Addr.:** Whitworth College Library, Spokane, WA 99251.

Franklin, Robert Dumont (S. 15, 1908, Memphis, TN) Freelnc. Consult. and Lectr., 1973–; Dir., Jefferson-Madison Reg. Lib., Charlottesville, 1971–73; Dir., Toledo Pub. Lib., 1956–70, Asst. Dir., 1946–56; Dir., Shelby Cnty. Libs., Memphis, 1938–46; Dir., Amer. Merchant Marine Lib., 1936–38; Ref., Circ. Depts., New York Pub. Lib., 1934–36; Evening Libn., Lib. Sch. Lib., Columbia Univ., 1933–34. **Educ.:** Southwest. Coll., Univ. of TN, 1926–33, BA (Hist.); Columbia Univ., 1933–34, BSLS. **Orgs.:** ALA: Cncl. (1950s). OH LA: Pres. (1954–55). **Pubns.:** Numerous articles in *LJ* (1937–68); *The Tee-Pee* (nsltr.) (1947–69); Numerous slide talks on lib. pub. and staff rel. **Activities:** 9, 11; 17, 24, 36; 95-Pubcty. **Addr.:** *Ex Libris* 2716 Northfields Rd., Charlottesville, VA 22901.

Fransiszyn, Marilyn D. (Montréal, PQ) Mss. and Ref. Libn., Osler Lib., McGill Univ., 1972–, Catlgr., 1970–71. **Educ.:** Univ. de Montréal, 1963–67, BA (Hist.); McGill Univ., 1968–70, MLS. **Orgs.:** Can. LA. Can. Hlth. Libs. Assn. Assn. of Libns. in the Hist. of the Hlth. Sci.–Can. corresp., *The Watermark.* Assn. of Can. Archvsts. Bethune Fndn.: Secy. (1971–78). Can. Socty. for the Hist. of Med. **Pubns.:** "Osler Library Fiftieth Anniversary Exhibition", *Osler Lib. Nsltr* (Je. 1979); "The Age of Acupuncture", *Osler Lib. Nsltr.* (Je. 1973); "Norman Bethune and his friends", *Osler Lib. Nsltr.* (Je. 1972). **Activities:** 1, 2; 39, 45; 80 **Addr.:** Osler Library, 3655 Drummond St., Montréal, PQ H3G 1Y6 Canada.

Frantz, John C. (Ag. 25, 1926, Seneca Falls, NY) City Libn., San Francisco Pub. Lib., 1977–; Consult., Pahlavi Natl. Lib., Teheran, Iran, 1975–76; Exec. Ch., Natl. Bk. Com., New York City, 1970–75; Dir., Brooklyn Pub. Lib., 1967–70; Dir., Lib. Srvs. and Construct. Act, US Ofc. of Educ. 1961–67; Dir., Green Bay, (WI) Pub. Lib., 1958–61. **Educ.:** Syracuse Univ., 1950–52, AB, BS (Eng.), MLS. **Orgs.:** ALA. Amer. Readg. Cncl.: Exec. Bd. Bks. for Youth: Exec. Bd. Lib. of Congs. Ctr. for the Bk.: Natl. Adv. Bd. Various other orgs. Coffee House Clb. **Activities:** 9; 17; 74, 78, 89 **Addr.:** San Francisco Public Library, Civic Center, San Francisco, CA 94102.

Frantz, Ray W., Jr. (Ag. 17, 1923, Princeton, KY) Univ. Libn., Univ. of VA, 1967–; Dir. of Libs., Univ. of WY, 1962–67; Asst. Dir., OH State Univ., 1960–62; Dir. of Lib., Univ. of Richmond, 1955–60. **Educ.:** Univ. of NE, 1948, AB (Hist., Eng.); Univ. of IL, 1949, MS (LS), 1955, PhD (Eng.). **Orgs.:** ALA: Awds. Com. (1972–73). Assn. of Southeast. Resrch. Libs.: Ch. (1974–75). ARL: Pres. (1978). **Activities:** 1; 15, 17, 45; 73 **Addr.:** General Office, Alderman Library, University of Virginia, Charlottesville, VA 22901.

Frappier, Gilles J. C. (F. 13, 1931, Papineauville, PQ) Dir. and Secy.-Treas., Ottawa Pub. Lib., 1979–; Assoc. Parliamentary Libn., Lib. of Parliament, Ottawa, 1970–79; Dir., Sci. Libs., Univ. of Montreal, 1969–70; Supvsr., Engin. Libs., Canadair Ltd., 1963–69; Libn., Untd. Aircraft of Canada Ltd., 1959–63; Branch Libn., Pulp and Paper Resrch. Inst. of Canada, 1957–59; Libn., Baie Comeau Cmnty. Assn., 1955–57. **Educ.:** Univ. of Ottawa, 1945–54, BA BPh 1954–55, BLS; McGill Univ., 1957–60, (LS). **Orgs.:** SLA: Pres. (1973–74). Corp. of Prof. Libns. of PQ. Can. LA. Assn. of Parliamentary Libns. in Canada: Secy. other orgs. Inst. of Pub. Admin. of Can. Can. Micro. Socty.: Secy.-Treas. (1972–73). Jr. Cham. of Cmrce., Baie Comeau and Longueuil: Pres. (1956–57; 1961–62). **Activities:** 4, 9; 17; 77, 78 **Addr.:** Ottawa Public Library, 120 Metcalfe St., Ottawa, ON K1P 5M2 Canada.

Frase, Robert W. (Ja. 1, 1912, Chicago, ILY) Exec. Dir., Amer. Natl. Stan. Com. Z39, 1978–; Asst. Exec. Dir. & Econ., Natl. Comsn. on New Tech. Uses of Copyrighted Works, 1975–78; Dir., Lib. Stats. Proj., ALA, 1973–74; VP & Econ., Amer. Assn. of Publshrs., 1950–72. **Educ.:** Univ. of WI, 1929–34, AB (Econ.); Harvard Univ., 1934–35, 1937–38, AM (Pol. Econ.). **Orgs.:** ALA. **Honors:** Guggenheim Foundation, Fellow, 1948–49. **Pubns.:** Jt.-auth., *Books and the Mass Market* (1953); Jt. auth., *Launching Social Security* (1970); Jt.-auth., *Book Publishing in the U.S.S.R.* (1971); *Library Funding and Public Support* (1973); "Five Years of Struggle for Federal Funds," *Publshrs. Weekly* (Ja. 21, 1974). **Activities:** 3; 56, 57, 62, 61, 62, 75, 78, 92 **Addr.:** ANSC Z39 Admin-E106, National Bureau of Standards, Washington, DC 20234.

Fraser, Jeanmarie Lang (Mr. 26, 1954, Jersey City, NJ) Coord. of Online Srvs., Univ. of MO, 1978–; Ref. Libn., IN State Lib., 1977–78. **Educ.:** Univ. of MO, 1972–76, AB (Pol. Sci.), 1976–77, MA (LS), 1980–, (Pub. Admin). **Orgs.:** ALA. Ctrl. MO OLUG: Ch., co-fndr. MO LA: Comp. and Info. Tech. Com. **Honors:** Beta Phi Mu. **Activities:** 1; 15, 31, 39; 56, 75, 92 **Addr.:** 202 E Ellis Library, University of Missouri-Columbia, Columbia, MO 65201.

Fraser, M(eta) Doreen E. (Je. 8, 1915, Grenfell, SK) Asst. Prof., Admin. Asst., Dalhousie Univ. Sch. of Lib. Srv., 1972–80; Hlth. Sci. Libn., Dalhousie Univ. Fac. of Med., 1962–72; Biomed. Libn., Univ. of BC, 1953–64. **Educ.:** Univ. of AB, 1932–36, BA (Eng., Hist.); Univ. of Toronto, 1936–37, BLS; Columbia Univ., 1953, Cert. (Med. Bibl.); Med. LA Cont. Educ. Workshops. **Honors:** Med. LA, Fellow, 1980. **Pubns.:** Jt. auth., *Information Needs of Physiotherapists in Community General Hospitals with*

Special Subjects/Services: 50. Adult educ.; 51. Advert./Mktg.; 52. Aerosp.; 53. Agric.; 54. Area std.; 55. Arts/Hum.; 56. Autom.; 57. Bibl./Prtg.; 58. Bio. sci.; 59. Bus./Fin.; 60. Chem.; 61. Copyrt.; 62. Documtn.; 63. Educ.; 64. Engin.; 65. Env.; 66. Eth. grps.; 67. Film; 68. Food/Nutr.; 69. Geneal.; 70. Geo.; 71. Geol.; 72. Handcpd.; 73. Hist.; 74. Int. frdm.; 75. Info. sci.; 76. Insr.; 77. Law; 78. Legis.; 79. Math./Comp. sci.; 80. Med.; 81. Metals; 82. Nat. resrcs.; 83. Newsp.; 84. Nuc. sci.; 85. Oral hist.; 86. Petr./Energy; 87. Pharm.; 88. Phys./Astr./Math.; 89. Readg.; 90. Relig.; 91. Sci./Tech.; 92. Soc. sci.; 93. Telecom.; 94. Transp.; 95. (other).

Who's Who in Library and Information Services

Suggested Physiotherapy Working Collections for Hospitals under 500 Beds, (1981); "Attitudes-Attitudes-Attitudes" *Can. Inst. of Relig. and Grntlgy. Nsltr.* (March 1979) (April 1979); "The MLA Certification Examination: an overview. Response #4." *Can. Hlth. Libs. Assn. Nsltr.* (Win. 1979); "Your Health-My Health-Everyone's Health!," *Biblioteca Medica Canadiana,* (1979); other books and articles. **Activities:** 12; 17, 24, 26; 80 **Addr.:** 830 McLean St., Apt. 24, Halifax, NS B3H 2T8 Canada.

Frautschi, Barbara A. (O. 14, 1932, Toledo, OH) Tech. Info. Lib. Dev. and Oper., Sherex Chem. Co., 1979–; Spec. Lib. Projs. and Market Anal., Ashland Chem. Co., 1976–78; Spec., Mgt. Policies, Battelle Columbus Labs., 1975–76, Sr. Proj. Leader, 1967–74, Info. Spec., 1955–66. **Educ.:** Coll. of Wooster, 1950–54, BA (Chem.). **Orgs.:** ASIS; SLA. Amer. Chem. Socty. Assn. for Women in Sci. **Honors:** Columbus Tech. Cncl., Tech. Woman of the Yr., 1974; ASIS, Ctrl. OH Chap., Awd. of Recog., 1974. **Activities:** 12; 17, 49-Lit. srchs.; 59, 60 **Addr.:** Technical Information, Sherex Chemical Co., Inc., P.O. Box 646, Dublin, OH 43017.

Frazier, John Peden, III (O. 19, 1939, Hartford, CT) Sr. Tech. Libn., Chem. Engin., Argonne Natl. Lab., 1974–; Ref. Libn., Math. Biblgphr., SUNY, Binghamton, 1973–74, Biblgphr. for Math. and Sci., 1970–73; Resrch. Chem., Sylvania Electric Products, 1966–70. **Educ.:** Bethany Coll., 1960–63, BS (Chem.); TX Tech. Coll., 1963–66, MS (Physical Chem.); Univ. of Pittsburgh, 1971–74, MLS. **Orgs.:** SLA. Chicago OLUG: Mem. Ch. (1979–80); Pres., Ch. (1980–81). Chicago Lib. Club. Amer. Chem. Socty. Amer. Inst. of Chem. Engin. **Honors:** Beta Phi Mu, 1974; Sigma Xi, 1976. **Pubns.:** "An Introduction to DOE/RECON and NASA/RECON", *Sci-Tech News* (1978); other articles, bibliographies, technical reports, oral presentations. **Addr.:** TIS-205-L101, Argonne National Laboratory, Argonne, IL 60439.

Frear, Ruth A. (N. 30, 1945, Utica, NY) Head, Comp.-Aided Ref. Srvs., Univ. of UT, Marriott Lib., 1979–, Head, Non-Print Ref. Srvs., 1971–80, Orig. Catlgr., 1969–71. **Educ.:** Westminster Coll., 1964–68, BA (Grmn.); Case West. Rsv. Univ., 1968–69, MS (LS); Univ. of UT, 1976–77, Prof. Cert. (Mgt.). **Orgs.:** ALA: LITA, Ed. Bd. (1977–79); Mem. Com. (1980–). AECT: Bd. of Dirs., Info. Systs. Div. (1977–80). UT LA: Int. Frdm. Com. (1974–76). UT Coll. Lib. Cncl.: Non-Print Media Com. (Ch., 1979–80). **Honors:** Beta Phi Mu. **Pubns.:** "Son of Kaiparowits," *Sierra* (Ap. 1978); "Coal Plant Planners Eye Southern Utah," *High Country News* (My. 6, 1977). **Activities:** 1; 17, 39, 49-Online Srch.; 56, 65, 82 **Addr.:** 315 Marriott Library, University of Utah, Salt Lake City, UT 84112.

Fréchette, Edmée (Je. 5, 1930, Victoriaville, PQ) Bibtcr., Bib. Mncpl., Montreal, 1959–; Bibtcr., Bib. Natl., 1951–54; Bibtcr., Bib. de Rosemont, 1949–50. **Educ.:** Coll. Saint-Maurice, 1946–49; Univ. de Montréal, 1949–51, Dip. (Bibliotheconomie). **Orgs.:** ASTED. L'Assn. des bibtcrs. du PQ. **Pubns.:** *Bio-bibliographie - Pierre Baillargeon* (1949). **Activities:** 9; 20, 41, 46; 62 **Addr.:** 3555 rue Berri, app. 615, Montréal, PQ H2L 4G4 Canada.

Frederick, Ronald Dean (My. 19, 1944, Oklahoma City, OK) Dir. of Pub. Srvs., Coll. St. Benedict and St. John's Univ. Lib., 1980–; Lib. Dir., Coll. of St. Benedict, 1977–80; Ref. Libn., IN State Univ., 1972–77. **Educ.:** Univ. of OK, 1963–67, BA (Hist.), 1967–68, MA (Intl. Rel.); Univ. of MI, 1970–72, AMLS; Univ. of MN, 1979–80. **Orgs.:** Ctrl. MN Lib. Exch.: Adv. Com. (Ch., 1979–). MN LA: Multi-Cnty./Multi-Type Coops, (Conv., 1980). ALA. ASIS. Cub Scout Leader. Par. Treas. **Activities:** 1, 12; 34, 39, 49-Online databases; 56, 75, 93 **Addr.:** College of St. Benedict, St. Joseph, MN 56374.

Fredericka, Theresa M. (My. 11, 1951, Warren, OH) Lib. Media Consult., OH Dept. of Educ., 1980–; Lib. Media Consult., KY Dept. of Educ., 1978–80; Elem. Libn., Deer Park Cmnty. Schs., 1977–78; HS Libn., Findlay City Schs., 1973–76. **Educ.:** Bowling Green State Univ., 1969–73, BS (Eng., LS); Univ. of KY, 1976–77, MSLS. **Orgs.:** ALA: LAMA/PR Sect., Nom. Com. (1981–82), John Cotton Dana Awd. Com. (1981–83), PR Srvs. to Libs. (Ch., 1980–81); AASL, NY Conf. (Prog. Ch., 1980). Natl. Assn. of State Educ. Media Profs.: Secy. (1981). KY LA: PR Ch. (1978–80). OH Educ. Lib. Media Assn.: Bd. of Dirs. (1980). Various other orgs. **Honors:** Beta Phi Mu, 1978. **Pubns.:** "The Case For Creative Programming in School Library Media Centers" *PR Recipe Book* (forthcoming); creator, performer, "The Picadilly Pickle Parade" cable TV show (1979–80); "National Library Week in Review," *KY Lib. Bltn.* (S. 1980); "Senior Send Off," *OH Assn. Sch. Libn. Bltn.* (O. 1976). **Activities:** 10; 24, 32, 36; 63 **Addr.:** 337 E. Beck St., Columbus, OH 43206.

Fredericksen, Richard B. (My. 5, 1937, Milwaukee, WI) Dir., Lister Hill Lib. of the Hlth. Sci., Univ. of AL, Birmingham, 1978–; Hlth. Sci. Libn., Meml. Univ. of NF, 1971–78; Head Libn., Socty.-Univ. Lib., Univ. of CA, San Diego, 1969–71, Head of Cat., Biomed. Lib., 1968–69. **Educ.:** Univ. of CA, Los Angeles, 1959–63, AB (Psy.); Univ. of South. CA, 1965–67, MLS; Med. LA, 1973, Cert. (Med. Libnshp., Grade I). **Orgs.:** Med. LA: Ed. Consult. for *Bltn. of Med. LA* (1977–); Natl. Prog. Com. (1981); Can. Grp. (Ch., 1975–77). SLA. AL LA. **Pubns.:** "Subject Cataloging Practices in North American Medical School Libraries," *Bltn. Med. LA* (O. 1976); "Centralization-Decentralization; Survey of Canadian Medical School Libraries," *Hlth. Sci. Libs. in Can.* (Ja. 1976); "New Library Buildings: The Health Sciences Library of Memorial University of Newfoundland," *Bltn. of Med. LA* (Jl. 1979); Ed., *Assn. of Acad. Hlth. Sci. Lib. Directors News* (1980–); Ed., *CHLA Nsltr.* (1976–78). **Activities:** 1, 12; 17, 19, 41; 58, 75, 80 **Addr.:** Lister Hill Library of the Health Sciences, University Station, University of Alabama in Birmingham, Birmingham, AL 35294.

Free, Opal Moore (O. 17, 1922, Ivan, FL) Univ. Libn., Head, Spec. Col., FL State Univ., 1974–, Head, Cat. Dept., 1969–74, Asst. Libn., Docum. Dept., 1965–68; Libn. GS-9, Ref., Serials, Acq. of Clasfd. Docum., Air Univ. Lib., Maxwell Air Force Base, Montgomery, and Tyndall Air Force Base, Panama City, FL, 1949–58 and 1959–62; **Educ.:** FL State Coll. for Women, Tallahassee, 1941–45, BA (Eng., LS); FL State Univ., 1956–57, MALS, 1967–68, Advnc. Mstrs. (LS). **Orgs.:** FL LA: Com. on Bylaws and Manual (1976–78). American Library Association. SELA. Pilot Clb. of Tallahassee. **Honors:** Beta Phi Mu, 1958. **Pubns.:** Ed., *A Dissertation Bibliography: Florida* (1979); *The Use of Government Publications in the Documents and Maps Division of Florida State University Library* (1957); "Commercial Reprints of Federal Documents: Their Significance and Acquisition," *Spec. Libs.* (Mr. 1969); "The Acquisition of Materials Difficult to Locate and Acquire" (oral presentation) (1977). **Activities:** 1, 4; 20, 29, 39; 57, 74, 95-Rare bks. **Addr.:** 6260 Crawfordville Rd., Tallahassee, FL 32304.

Freed, J. Arthur (N. 11, 1929, Los Angeles, CA) Head Libn., Univ. of CA Los Alamos Scientific Lab., 1970–, Asst. Head Libn., 1967–70, Pub. Srvs. Libn., 1966–67, Libn., Main Lib., 1960–66, Order Libn., 1959–60, Asst. Rpt. Libn., 1958–59; Sr. Libn., 1st Asst. Branch Libn., Brooklyn Pub. Lib., 1957–58, Adult Srvs. Libn., 1956–57. **Educ.:** Univ. of CA, 1947–51, AB (Anthro.), 1952, 54–56, MA (Anthro.), 1955–56, MLS. **Orgs.:** SLA: various div. and chap. coms. NM LA. J. Robert Oppenheimer Meml. Com. **Activities:** 12; 17; 64, 84, 91 **Addr.:** University of California, Los Alamos Scientific Laboratory, P.O. Box 1663 MS-362, Los Alamos, NM 87545.

Freedman, Annetta R. (O. 21, 1918, Grafton, WV) Dir., Media Srvs., Andover (MA) Pub. Schs., 1969–, HS Libn., 1960–68; Tchr., Schs. in WV and PA, 1940–57; Visit. Lectr., Fitchburg State Coll., 1976–77; Visit. Lectr., North. Essex Cmnty. Coll., 1977. **Educ.:** OH State Univ., 1936–40, BS (Educ.); Boston Univ., 1964–68, MS (Educ.); WV Univ., Univ. of MI, 1940–79. **Orgs.:** ALA. MA Assn. Educ. Media: Treas. (1978–80). AECT. N. Shore Sch. Libns. Natl. Educ. Assn. Natl. Cncl. of Eng. Tchrs. Natl. Cncl. of Soc. Std. **Honors:** Ency. Brittanica, Sch. Lib. Media Prog. of the Yr., Runner-up, 1978. **Activities:** 10; 26, 32, 46 **Addr.:** Andover Public Schools, 36 Bartlet St., Andover, MA 01810.

Freedman, Maurice J. (N. 14, 1939, Newark, NJ) Assoc. Prof., Sch. of Lib. Srv., Columbia Univ., 1977–; Coord., Tech. Srvs., Branch Libs., NY Pub. Lib., 1974–77; Dir., Tech. Srvs., Hennepin Cnty. Lib., 1969–74; Mgr., Lib. Prcs., Info. Dynamics Corp., 1968–69; Exec. Asst., Prcs. Dept., Lib. of Congs., 1967–68, Admin. Officer, 1966–67, Asst. Head, African-Asian Exch. Sect., 1966, Spec. Rcrt., 1965–66. **Educ.:** Rutgers Univ., 1957–61, BA (Phil.); Univ. of CA, Berkeley, 1964–65, MLS; Rutgers Univ., 1976–, PhD Cand. (LS). **Orgs.:** ALA: Ad Hoc Com. to Redraft a Natl. Info. Policy Statement (Ch. 1978); Cncl. (1977–81); LITA, Bd. of Dirs. (1976–79); LITA, Pres. (1977–78); RTSD, Nom. Com. (1976–77); various other coms. AALS. ASIS. NY LA. Various other orgs. **Honors:** ALA, LITA, Awd. for Achvmt. in Lib. and Info. Tech., 1981; Beta Phi Mu, 1965. **Pubns.:** Jt. auth., *Public Libraries in San Diego* (1981); "Opening a Catalog," *Closing the Catalog* (1980); jt. ed., *The Nature and Future of the Catalog* (1979); jt. ed., *Regional Processing Center* (1978); jt. auth., *Bibliographic Resources Integration* (1978); various articles. **Activities:** 9, 11; 22, 24, 46; 56 **Addr.:** 158 Landsdowne Ave., Westfield, NJ 07090.

Freedman, Phyllis D. (F. 25, 1938, San Juan, PR) Mncpl. Ref. Libn., Orlando Pub. Lib., 1973–, ILL Libn., 1971–73, Libn. in Bus. Dept., 1969–71. **Educ.:** Univ. of FL, 1956–60, BA (Educ.); FL State Univ., 1968–69, MSLS. **Orgs.:** SLA: Dir. (1976–80); State Bltn. Ed. (1981–). Cncl. of Plng. Libns. FL LA. **Honors:** Beta Phi Mu. **Addr.:** Municipal Reference Library, City Hall, 400 S. Orange, Orlando, FL 32801.

Freeland, Robert Frederick (D. 20, 1919, Flint, MI) Libn., Helix HS, 1952–; Coll. Libn., Linda Vista Bible Coll., 1970–; Libn. and AV Coord., Edison Inst.-Greenfield Vlg. Sch., 1950–52, Msc. Dir., Carson City (MI) Pub. Sch., 1948–50, Msc. supvsr., Warren (MI) Consolidated Schs., 1946–48. **Educ.:** MI State Univ. 1940; East. MI Univ., 1942, BS (Msc.); Univ. of MI 1951, Univ. of South. CA, 1948, MS (Lib.-Educ.); San Diego State Univ., (Lib.-Educ.); Lib., Gen. Sec., Jr. Coll., Admin. Certs. **Orgs.:** CA LA: Palomer Chap. (Pres.). CA Media & Lib. Educ. Assn. Msc. LA of South. CA. American Legion. Christian Reformed Church: Cncl. Natl. Educ. Assn. CA Tchrs. Assn. **Honors:** Linda Vista Bible Coll., Dr. of Lit., 1973. **Pubns.:** "Book and Media Aids to the Teaching of Music," *The Sch. Musician,* (Monthly). **Activities:** 10, 11 **Addr.:** 4800 Williamsburg Ln., 223, La Mesa, CA 92041.

Freeman, Carla (My. 14, 1949, Washington, DC) Pres., InfoMgt., 1979–; Libn., Resrc. Plng. Assoc., 1978–79. **Educ.:** Univ. of AZ, 1973–77, BA (Hist.), 1977–78, MLS. **Orgs.:** SLA: Ed., Nsltr., Nat. Resrcs. Div. (1978–); Univ. of AZ, Student Chap., (Ch., 1977–78). DC LA. Natl. Assn. of Women Bus. Owners. **Activities:** 12; 24, 38, 49-Creating, org. spec. libs. **Addr.:** InfoManagement, 4204 38th St. N.W., Washington, DC 20016.

Freeman, Doris Lund (Ag. 13, 1929, Plentywood, MT) Proj. 81 Coord., Upper Merion Area Sch. Dist., 1977–; Sch. Libn., 1971–77; Trustee, Montgomery Cnty.–Norristown Pub. Lib., 1969–78; Founder/Trustee, Wolfsohn Meml. Lib., Upper Merion Twp., 1960–74. **Educ.:** Univ. of MT, 1946–50, BA (Eng.); Villanova Univ., 1969–71; MSLS. **Orgs.:** PA Sch. Libns. Assn.: Legis. Com. (Ch., 1975–76). PA LA: Lib. Dev. Com. (Ch. 1981–). Assn. Supvsn. Curric. Dev. ALA: ALTA, AASL. Delta Kappa Gamma. Natl. Educ. Assn. **Honors:** Upper Merion Jaycees, Disting. Srv. to Cmnty., 1977. **Pubns.:** "A Word to Trustees" clmn. *PA. LA Bltn.* (1961–69); Reviews. **Activities:** 9, 10; 17, 36, 47; 63, 78, 89 **Addr.:** 582 Hansen Rd., King of Prussia, PA 19406.

Freeman, Elsa Sloane Dir. of Libs., U.S. Dept. of Housing & Urban Dev., 1956–; Head Libn., U.S. Ofc. of Geo. Lib., Dept. of Interior, 1951–56; Asst. Libn., U.S. Navy Dept., Bur. of Ordnance, 1949–51; Asst. Chief Circ. Sect., U.S. Dept. of Agr. Lib., 1941–49. **Educ.:** Columbia Univ., 1940, BA; 1941, MS. **Orgs.:** FLC: Exec. Advisory Council, FEDLINK-1980, Chm. Task Force on Acquisition of Library Materials. ALA: Com. Ch. SLA: Pres. of Wash., DC Chap., Com. & Div. Ch. ASIS. Other orgs. Christ Episcopal Church, Alexandria, Virginia: Vestry (1976–79), Bd. of Christ. Educ. Performing Arts Assn. of Alexandria: Bd. of Gvrs. (1976–). North. VA Fine Arts Assn. Columbian Toastmistress: Charter Pres. (1959–60). **Honors:** Phi Beta Kappa; Beta Phi Mu; HUD Spec. Achieve. Awd., 1976, 1978, 1979. **Pubns.:** "The HUD Library and Information Division" *The Bowker annual of library and book trade information,* (1974); HUD's Library: a national resource, *Cncl. of Plng. Libns. Nsltr.* (June 1974); "Grade structure of field librarians and technicians panel," in *Federal Interagency Field Librarians Workshop* (1975); "Selected publications from HUD," *DEA News* (Fall 1975); "Promoting the use and insuring access to HUD publications," *Gvt. Pubns. Review,* (1975); other articles, reviews, oral presentations. **Activities:** 4, 12; 17, 34; 75, 91, 92 **Addr.:** U.S. Department of Housing & Urban Development, 451-7th St., S.W., Washington, DC 20410.

Freeman, Jan Guest (F. 11, 1938, Lawton, OK) Head Libn., Redmond Cmnty. Lib., 1979–; YA Coord., King Cnty. Lib. Syst., 1968–79; Asst. Ref. Libn., Grt. Falls Pub. Lib., 1967–68. **Educ.:** Univ. of WA, 1956–66, BA (Slavic Std.), 1966–67, MLS. **Orgs.:** ALA: YASD, Best Bks. for YA (Ch., 1979); Bd. of Dirs. (1978); Sel. Films for YA Ed. (1976). WA LA: Chld. and YA Srv. Interest Grp. (Pres., 1973–74). **Activities:** 9; 16, 17, 48; 55, 67, 74 **Addr.:** Redmond Community Library, 15810 N.E. 85th, Redmond, WA 98052.

Freeman, Jane L. (F. 13, 1936, Chester, SC) Dir., Abbot Vincent Taylor Lib., Belmont Abbey Coll., 1975–; Head, Mktg. Info. Ctr., Coca-Cola, 1974–75, Sr. Info. Spec., Tech. Info. Ctr., 1969–74; Lect., Div. of Libnshp., Emory Univ., 1973–74. **Educ.:** NC State Univ., 1953–57, BChE (Chem. Engin.); PA State Univ., 1958–60, MS (Chem. Engin.); Emory Univ., 1968–69, MLn (Libnshp.). **Orgs.:** NC LA. SC LA. SELA. SLA: S. Atl. Chap.: (VP, Pres.-Elect, 1974–75). AAUW. Parent-Tchr. Org., Westchester Sch.: Pres. (1972–73). **Pubns.:** "The Benedictine Collection," *Crescat* (Fall 1979). **Activities:** 1; 15, 16, 17 **Addr.:** 1203 Cambridge St., Gastonia, NC 28052.

Freeman, Michael Stuart (N. 10, 1946, Brooklyn, NY) Dir. of Lib. Srvs., The Coll. of Wooster, 1981–; Chief, Dept. of Ref. Srvs., Dartmouth Coll., 1978–81, Asst. Chief, 1975–78; Soc. Sci. Libn., IL Wesleyan Univ., 1971–75. **Educ.:** Brooklyn Coll., CUNY, 1964–68, BA (Hist.); Univ. of WI, 1968–70, MA (Hist.), 1970–71, MALS. **Orgs.:** ALA: RASD/Hist. Sect., Com. on Bibl. and Indexes (1977–79); Goals and Objectives Com. for Plng. (1979–). New Eng. LA: Bibl. Com. (1976–78); Coll. Lib. Sect. (Vice Ch., 1979–). Acad. Libns of NH: Ch. (1978–79). NH Gvr. Conf. on Lib. and Info. Srvs.: Del. (1978). Various other orgs. **Pubns.:** Jt. auth., *Guide to Newspaper Indexes in New England* (1978); "Published Study Guides: What They Say about Libraries," *Jnl. of Acad. Libnshp.* (N. 1979); "Guide to the Bibliographic Sources on Film Literature," *RQ* (Sum. 1974); "Researching Historical Problems: An Introduction to Basic Resources" (slide-tape) (1976); Reviews. **Activities:** 1; 17, 31, 39 **Addr.:** Andrews Library, The College of Wooster, Wooster, OH 44691.

Freeman, Patricia E. (N. 30, 1924, ElDorado, AK) Indp. Sch. Lib. Media Ctr. Consult., 1967–; Sch. Libn., Albuquerque Pub. Schs., 1964–67; Base and Tech. Libn., US Air Force, Barksdale, 1948–49; Libn., Univ. of CA, Berkeley, 1946–47. **Educ.:** Centenary Coll., 1940–43, BA (Art); LA State Univ., 1945–46, BSLS; CA State Univ., Fullerton, 1959–61 (Educ.); Univ. of NM, 1964–74 (Educ.); N. TX State Univ., 1974 (LS); George Peabody

PROFESSIONAL ACTIVITIES: Institutions: 1. Acad. lib.; 2. Arch.; 3. Assn.; 4. Fed./Gvt. lib.; 5. Inst. lib.; 6. Mfr./Suppl.; 7. Milit. lib.; 8. Musm.; 9. Pub. lib.; 10. Sch. lib.; 11. Sch. of lib. sci.; 12. Spec. lib.; 13. State lib.; 14. (other). **Functions/Activities:** 15. Acq./Col. dev.; 16. Adult srvs.; 17. Admin.; 18. Apprais.; 19. Archit./Bldgs.; 20. Cat./Class.; 21. Chld. srvs.; 22. Circ.; 23. Cons./Pres.; 24. Consult.; 25. Cont. ed.; 26. Educ. lib. sci.; 27. Ext. srvs.; 28. Fund/Grants; 29. Gvt. pubs.; 30. Indx./Abs.; 31. Instr. lib. use; 32. Media srvs.; 33. Micro.; 34. Netwks./Coop.; 35. Persnl.; 36. PR; 37. Publshg.; 38. Recs. mgt.; 39. Ref. srvs.; 40. Repro.; 41. Resrch.; 42. Review.; 43. Secur.; 44. Serials; 45. Spec. col.; 46. Tech. srvs.; 47. Trustees/Bds.; 48. YA srvs.; 49. (other).

Coll., 1973–75, EdS (LS). **Orgs.:** Friends of Sch. Libs., Inc.: Ch. (1979–). ALA: LAMA. TX LA. TX Assn. of Sch. Libns.: Conv. Swap Shop Ch. (1979). AAUW: Albuquerque Branch, (Bd., 1972–74); Dallas Branch, Bd. (1976–). Goals for Dallas: Environment Task Force Achieve. Com. (1977–). Hist. Prsrvn. Leag. Natl. Trust for Historic Prsrvn. Other orgs. **Honors:** AAUW, Flwshp. Honoree (1978); Dallas Indp. Sch. Dist., Volun. Awd. for Outstan. Srv., 1978. **Pubns.:** *Pathfinder: An Operational Guide for the School Librarian (Harper & Row)* (1975); "Index to Research in School Librarianship, 1960–1974," *ERIC* (1976). **Activities:** 10; 17, 21, 24; 63 **Addr.:** 6216 Junius St., Dallas, TX 75214.

Freeman, Peter L. (Ap. 9, 1938, Fort William, ON) Chief Libn., Supreme Ct. of Can., 1980–; Law Libn., Univ. of AB, 1970–80. **Educ.:** Univ. of MB, 1954–58, BA, 1958–62, LLB; Univ. of WA, 1969–70, MLLS. **Orgs.:** AALL. Can. ALL. Can. Bar Assn. Amer. Bar Assn. Can. Inst. For The Admin. of Justice. Can. Std. of Parlmt. Grp. **Activities:** 1, 4; 15, 17; 77, 78 **Addr.:** Library, Supreme Court of Canada, Wellington St., Ottawa, ON K1A 0J1 Canada.

Freeman, Robert R. (Ja. 1, 1936, Rochester, NY) Deputy Dir., Env. Sci. Info. Ctr., Natl. Oceanic and Atmospheric Admin., 1975–, Chief, Tech. Info. Div., 1972–75, Chief, Scientific Info. Syst. Branch, 1969–72; Proj. Mgr., Documtn. Resrch. Prog., Amer. Inst. of Phys., 1965–68; Asst. Dir., Documtn. Resrch., Ctr. for Appld. Ling., 1965–68; Chief, Info. Syst. Dev., Amer. Meterological Socty., 1963–65; Resrch. Assoc., Chemical Abs. Srv., 1959–63. **Educ.:** Univ. of Rochester, 1953–57, BS (Chem.); MA Inst. of Tech., 1957–59, MS (Indus. Mgt.); Univ. of WA, 1974–75, Cert. (Pub. Admin. and Policy). **Orgs.:** ASIS: Potomac Valley Chap. (Ch., 1971–72). Amer. Socty. for Pub. Admin. Amer. Oceanic Org. **Honors** US Dept. of Cmrce., Silver Medal for Merit. Fed. Srv., 1978. **Pubns.:** Jt. auth., "A Policy for Access to an International Database, Aquatic Sciences and Fisheries Abstracts," *Proceedings of ASIS* (1979); Jt. auth., "SAM'S CLUB: Computer Conferencing as a Tool in the Management of an International Information System," *North American Networking* (1979); "Ocean and Environmental Information: Theory, Policy, and Practice of Knowledge Management," *Marine Policy* (1977); Numerous other articles and rpts. **Activities:** 4, 12; 17; 65, 75 **Addr.:** Environmental Science Information Center, National Oceanic and Atmospheric Administration, 11400 Rockville Pike, Rockville, MD 20852.

Freiband, Susan J. (N. 28, 1942, Brooklyn, NY) Proj. Dir., Hertzberg Circus Proj., Asst. Prof. of Intercult. Std., Inst. for Intercult. Std. and Resrch., Our Lady of the Lake Univ., 1979–, Asst. Prof., Lrng. Resrcs. Cert. Prog., 1978–79, Asst. Prof. of Lib. and Media Sci., 1975–78. **Educ.:** Univ. of CA, Santa Barbara, 1961–64, BA (Bio.); Our Lady of the Lake Coll., 1966–67, MS (LS); Rutgers Univ., 1969–73, PhD (Lib. Srv.). **Orgs.:** ALA. TX LA: Cont. Educ. Com. (1977–79). SLA: TX Chap., Cont. Educ. Com. (1978–79). AAUP. **Honors:** Natl. Endow. for the Hum., Pub. Lib. Prog. Grant, 1981. **Pubns.:** "Evaluation of Reference Collections in Public, Community Colleges and High School Libraries," *Col. Mgt.* (Win. 1980); "Oral History for Adults in Public Libraries," *Cath. Lib. World* (1979); "Reference Service and Evaluation in Colombian University Libraries," *Unesco Bltn. for Libs.* (1978); "Library Planning in the Interamerican Library School Curriculum," *Jnl. of Educ. for Libnshp.* (1976); "Latin American Children's Literature, a Bibliography of Bibliographies," *Intl. Lib. Review* (1976); various other articles. **Activities:** 9, 11; 16, 26, 41; 55, 66, 95-Intercult. Std. **Addr.:** Institute for Intercultural Studies and Research, Our Lady of the Lake University, 411 S.W. 24th St., San Antonio, TX 78285.

Freiburger, Gary A. (O. 27, 1949, Chicago, IL) Syst. and Autom. Libn., Hlth. Sci. Lib., Univ. of MD, 1980–; Ref. Libn., Loyola-Notre Dame Lib., Baltimore, MD, 1979–80; Ref. Libn., Salisbury State Coll., Salisbury, MD, 1977–79; Ref. Libn., Barber-Scotia Coll., Concord, NC, 1975–77. **Educ.:** Northwest. Univ., 1967–71, BMsc (Theory, Composition); Univ. of TX, Austin, 1973–74, MLS. **Orgs.:** ALA. ASIS. MD LA: JMRT (Pres., 1980–81); Acad. Div. (Secy., 1979–80). **Activities:** 1; 17, 39; 56 **Addr.:** 151 Hammershire Rd., Reisterstown, MD 21136.

Freides, Thelma K. (F. 26, 1930, New York, NY) Head, Readers Srvs., SUNY, Coll. at Purchase, 1978–; Soc. Sci. Libn., Swarthmore Coll., 1975–78; Assoc. Prof., Sch. of Lib. Srv., Atlanta Univ., 1967–75; Gvt. Docum. Libn., Emory Univ., 1966–67; Ref. Libn., Wayne State Univ., 1960–66. **Educ.:** Hunter Coll., 1948–52, BA (Pol. Sci.); Yale Univ., 1952–55, MA (Intl. Rel.); Univ. of MI, 1958–60, MA (LS). **Orgs.:** Pub. Affairs Info. Srv.: Trustee, (1976–). Bhvl. and Soc. Sci. Libn.: Ed. Bd. (1978–). ALA: RASD, (Pres., 1971–73); Prog. Com. (1978–79); Consult., *Choice* (1976–): SLA: Stats. Com. (1978–79); Rep. to ALA ILL Com. (1977–79); other orgs. and coms. **Pubns.:** *Literature and Bibliography of the Social Sciences* (1973); "Publishing Under Pressure", *Bhvl. and Soc. Sci. Libn.* (Win. 1979); "Guide to Information Sources on Federal Agencies," *News for Tchrs. of Pol. Sci.* (Sum. 1978); "Bibliographic Gaps in the Social Science Literature," *Spec. Libs.* (F. 1976); "Bibliographies in the Social Sciences: Characteristics of Retrospective Bibliography," *RQ* (Fall 1971); other articles, reviews. **Activities:** 1; 26, 31, 39; 54, 78, 92 **Addr.:** Library, SUNY College at Purchase, Purchase, NY 10577.

Freitag, Wolfgang Martin (O. 27, 1924, Berlin, Germany) Sr. Lectr. on Fine Arts, Libn., Fine Arts Lib., Harvard Univ., 1964–, Assoc. Univ. Libn. for Resrcs. and Acq., 1965–67; Chief, Undergrad. Lib. Div., Stanford Univ., 1962–64; Libn., Gordon McKay Lib., Harvard Univ., 1960–62, Subj. Catlgr., Harvard Coll. Lib., 1955–60; Ed., Ref. Works, Droemer Knaur-Verlag, Munich, 1953–55; Ref. Libn., Prog. Mgr., US Info. Ctr. Lib., Frankfurt, 1950–53. **Educ.:** Albert Ludwigs Univ., Germany, 1944–50, PhD (Eng.); Simmons Coll., 1951–52, 55–56, MSLS. **Orgs.:** ALA: RTSD, Intl. Pubns. Com. (1960–62); ACRL/Subj. Spec. Sect. (Ch., 1970–72), Art Subsect. (Ch., 1969–70). ARLIS/NA: Ch. (1980–81); various coms. IFLA. ARLIS/UK. Coll. Art Assn. Amer. Prtg. Hist. Assn. **Honors:** Fulbright Fellow, 1968; Cncl. on Lib. Resrcs. Fellow, 1975. **Pubns.:** Ed., "Fine Arts," *Books for College Libraries* (1975); "The Selection of Periodicals for Art Libraries," *Art Lib. Jnl.* (Sum. 1976); "Early Uses of Photography in the History of Art," *Art Jnl.* (Win. 1979–80); "Training the Librarian for Rapport with the Collection," *Lib. Trends* (Ja. 1975); Ed., *Fine Arts Lib. Nsltr.* (1967–71); Various other articles and oral presentations. **Activities:** 1, 8; 15, 17, 32; 55, 57, 62 **Addr.:** Fine Arts Library, Harvard University, Fogg Art Museum, Cambridge, MA 02173.

Freitas-Obregon, Brenda J. (Ja. 29, 1953, Honolulu, HI) Chld. Libn. III, Ewa Beach Cmnty./Sch. Lib., 1976–; Chld. Libn., III, Aina Haina Cmnty. Lib., 1976; YA Libn. IV, HI State Lib., 1976, Chld. Libn. II, 1975–76. **Educ.:** Univ. of HI, Manoa, 1970–73, BA (Eng.), 1973–75, MLS. **Orgs.:** ALA: JMRT; ALSC. HI LA: Chld. and Youth Sect. (Secy. 1976–77/1978–79); Tech. and Gen. Srvs. (Vice-Ch. 1979–80, Ch. 1980–81); JMRT Liason (1979–82); HI Assn. of Sch. Libns. **Honors** H. W. Wilson Co., John Cotton Dana PR Awd., 1977. **Activities:** 9; 21 **Addr.:** Ewa Beach Community/School Library, 91-950 North Rd., Ewa Beach, HI 96706.

Freivogel, Elsie Freeman (D. 12, 1930, Rochester, NY) Dir., Acad. and Curric. Dev., Educ. Div., Natl. Arch. and Recs. Srv., 1973–, Asst. to Pub. Info. Officer, 1971–73; Asst. Cur., Mss., Arch. of Amer. Art, Smithsonian Inst., 1970–71; Head, Mss. Div., Washington Univ. Libs., 1965–71; Instr. Eng., KS State Univ., 1964–65; HS Tchr. **Educ.:** SUNY, Albany, 1948–52, AB, magna (Eng., Amer. Hist.); Boston Univ., 1955, MA (Eng. Lit.). **Orgs.:** SAA: Cncl. (1973–77); Exec. Com. (1976–77); Com. on Status of Women, Ch. Mid Atl. Arch. Conf. Amer. Assn. State and Lcl. Hist. Org. of Amer. Histns. **Honors:** SAA, Fellow, 1975. **Addr.:** 1731 Harvard St., N.W., Washington, DC 20009.

French, Beverlee A. (Mr. 18, 1949, Lansing MI) Head, Sci. & Engin. Lib., Univ. of CA, San Diego, 1981–; Ref. Libn., Biomedical Lib., 1975–; Cat. Libn., Ctrl. Lib., 1973–75. **Educ.:** Univ. of CA, Berkeley, 1969–71, AB (Soc. Sci.), 1972–73, MLS; Med. LA Cert. in Med. Libnshp., 1977. **Orgs.:** ALA: ACRL Med. LA: Intl. Coop. Com. (1979). Libns. Assn. of the Univ. of CA: Statewide Exec. Bd. (1977–78). **Honors:** Univ. of CA, Berkeley, Phi Beta Kappa, 1971. **Pubns.:** Chapter in "The Fourth generation: research libraries and community information," *In New Horizons for Academic Libraries, Proceedings of the ACRL 1978 National Conference* (1979); "Health Information in San Diego," *CA Libn* (Ja. 1978). **Activities:** 1; 31, 39, 49-Computerized Literature Searching; 58, 80 **Addr.:** Science and Engineering Library, University of California, San Diego, La Jolla, CA 92093.

French, Linda Louise Morgan (F. 3, 1938, Denver, CO) Mgr., Corporate Tech. Lib., Comp. Sci. Corp., 1976–; Supvsr., Tech. Info. Ctr., McDonnell Douglas Corp., 1973–74, Catlgr./Grp. Leader, 1971–73; Info. Spec., Tech. Info. Ctr., TRW Systs. Grp., 1966–71; Ref. Libn./Indxr., Pac. Aeronautical Lib., 1957–66. **Educ.:** CA State Univ., 1976, BA (Hist., Urban Std.). **Orgs.:** SLA: South. CA Chap., various coms., chs. ASIS: Los Angeles Chap. (Secy., 1969). Assn. for Comp. Mach. Inst. of Electrical and Electronics Engins. Ninety Nines. **Pubns.:** Cmplr., *Permuted Index to American Rocket Society Papers* (1968); cmplr., *Permuted Index to National Aeronautical Electronics Conference* (1967). **Activities:** 12; 17; 56, 59, 93 **Addr.:** Corporate Library, 650 N. Sepulveda Blvd., El Segundo, CA 90245.

Frese, Anne Marie (Chicago, IL) Head Lib., Niles Cmty. Lib., 1966–, Other positions, 1958–66. **Educ.:** Univ. of Budapest, Hungary, West. MI Univ., MLS. **Orgs.:** MI LA: Ref. Div., Trustee (1975–78), Pub. Lib. Div. Sect. (1969–71), PR Bd. (1969–71). ALA. Four Flags Area Hist. Comsn.: Trustee (1978), Berrien Cnty. Bicentennial Comsn.: Comsn. (1976–77), Fort St. Joseph Restoration Comsn.: Comsn. (1974–78), Four Flags Area Bicentennial Cmsn.: VP. (1974–76). **Activities:** 9; 15, 16, 17 **Addr.:** Niles Community Library, 620 E. Main St., Niles, MI 49120.

Fretwell, Gordon E. (Ja. 16, 1937, Adrian, MI) Assoc. Dir., Pub. Srvs., Univ. Lib., Univ. of MA, Amherst, 1970–; Head, Pub. Srvs., Ctrl. Univ. Lib., Univ. of CA, San Diego, 1965–70; Head of Circ., Law Lib., Univ. of MI, 1962–65. **Educ.:** MI State Univ., 1954–59, BA (Soc. Sci.); Univ. of MI, 1960–64, MALS; Univ. of MA, 1977–80, MPA (Pub. Admin.). **Orgs.:** ALA: ACRL, New Eng. Chap. Amer. Socty. for Pub. Admin. **Pubns.:** *Association of College and Research Libraries. Annual Salary Survey, 1978–79* (1980). **Activities:** 1; 17, 35, 43; 56, 61, 77 **Addr.:** Box 216, Leverett, MA 01054.

Freudenthal, Juan R. (S. 11, 1937, Santiago, Chile) Assoc. Prof., Simmons Coll. Grad. Sch. of Lib. and Info. Sci., 1972–; Spec. Coll. Libn., SUNY, Binghamton, 1968–69; Head of Ref., Hamilton Coll., 1966–68. **Educ.:** Univ. of Concepciòn, Chile, 1957–60, Title (Jnlsn.); Syracuse Univ., 1965–66, MSLS; Univ. of MI, 1969–72, PhD (LS). **Orgs.:** ALA: ACRL/Bibl. Instr. Sect. (1978–); RASD Bibl. Com. (1974–). SALALM: Bibl. Com., (1973–); Exec. Bd. (1975–1978). AALS. ARLIS/NA. AAUP. **Honors:** Beta Phi Mu, 1972; Univ. of MI, Edmon Low Student Awd., 1972; Univ. of Cairo, Egypt, Fulbright Prof., 1979–80. **Pubns.:** *Index to Anthologies of Latin American Literature in English Translation* (1977); "The National Library in Chile, 1813–1978", *LIBRI* (1978); "Public Libraries in Latin America," *Encyclopedia of Library and Information Science* (1978); "The Slide as a Communication Tool," in *Expanding Media.* (1977). **Activities:** 1, 12; 26, 31, 45; 54, 55, 57 **Addr.:** Simmons College, Graduate School of Library and Information Science, 300 The Fenway, Boston, MA 02115.

Freund, Alfred L. (D. 23, 1929, Bayshore, NY) Dir., Ramapo Catskill Lib. Syst., 1972–; Dir., Plainedge Pub. Lib., 1963–72; Ref. and YA Libn., Hicksville Free Lib., 1961–63. **Educ.:** City Coll. of NY, 1950–54, BA (Hist.); Pratt Inst., 1959–61, MLS. **Orgs.:** NY State Comsn. Com. on Lib. Dev. NY State LSCA Adv. Cncl.: Ch. (1979–82). Pub. Lib. Syst. Dirs. Org.: Ch. (1977–79). NY LA: Pub. Lib. Sect. (Pres., 1977). ALA. **Activities:** 9; 17, 24; 50 **Addr.:** 24 Pond Hill Ave., Warwick, NY 10990.

Freund, Clare E. (Gleiwitz, Germany) Libn., Eastman Kodak Resrch. Labs., 1962–; Resrch. Libn., Time Inc., 1951–62. **Educ.:** Univ. of PA, Bucknell Univ., 1946–50, AB (Soc. Std.); Drexel Univ., 1950–51, MS (LS). **Orgs.:** SLA: Rcrt. Ch. Upstate NY chap. (1964–65); Place. Ch., 1966–70); Rochester Reg. Resrch. Lib. Cncl.: Acq. Com. **Honors** Delta Kappa Gamma, 1950; Phi Beta Kappa, 1950. **Pubns.:** "Guide to Photographic Information", *5 PSE Handbook of Photographic Science & Engineering* (1973); "Catalog on Microfiche at the Eastman Kodak Libraries," *Spec. Libs.* (N. 1977). **Activities:** 12; 15, 20, 46; 91, 95-On line searching. **Addr.:** Eastman Kodak Research Library, Bldg. 83, Rochester, NY 14650.

Freve, Reay Howie (F. 8, 1932, Glasgow, Scotland) Chief Libn., Colchester-E. Hants Reg. Lib., 1975–; Rotch Libn., MA Inst. of Tech., 1966–73, Asst. Libn., 1961–66, Lib. Asst., Vancouver Pub. Lib., 1957–61. **Educ.:** Assoc. of the LA, London, Eng., 1956. **Orgs.:** Can. LA. Jt. Reg. Lib. Bds. Assn. of NS: Dir. (1978–81). Atl. Prov. LA. NS LA: Nom. Com. (1979–80). Natl. Cncl. of Women. Taxpayers for Safe Economical Energy. **Activities:** 9; 17, 39, 47 **Addr.:** R.R. #6, Truro, NS B2N 5B4 Canada.

Frew, Martha Gale (Ag. 21, 1925, Fremont, OH) Libn., Media Spec., Acad. Notre Dame, DC, 1979–; Elem. Sch. Libn., Seneca E. Pub. Sch., 1970–73; Elem. Sch. Libn., Norwalk Pub. Sch., 1966–70; Libn., Pleasant HS, 1963–66; Chld. Libn., Maui Cnty. Free Lib., 1960–62; Chld. Libn., DE Cnty. Dist. L (OH), 1955–60; Chld. Libn., E. Cleveland Pub. Lib., 1950–55. **Educ.:** OH Univ., 1945–47, BS (Educ.); IA State Univ., 1943–45; Case West. Rsv. Univ., 1949–50, MS (LS). **Orgs.:** ALA. OH LA: Jr. Libn.; Sch. Libn.; Prog. Com. (1957–58); Secy. (1953–54). Metro. WA Indp. Sch. Libn. AAUW. Common Cause. Amer. Cvl. Liberties Un. **Activities:** 9, 10; 21, 31, 32 **Addr.:** 1662 Carlyle Dr., Apt. E, Crofton, MD 21114.

Frey, Emil F. (Mr. 10, 1927, Zuerich City, Switzerland) Prof. of Lib. Sci., 1980–, and Dir., Univ. of TX Med. Branch Lib., 1973–; Dir., Hlth. Sci. Ctr. Lib., SUNY, Stony Brook, 1969–73; Assoc. Dir., Mayo Clinic Lib., 1964–69; Admin. Libn., Duke Univ. Hlth. Sci. Lib., 1962–64. **Educ.:** William Jennings Bryan Univ., 1953–57, BA (Hist.); Univ. of TN, 1957–59, MA (Grmn.); Univ. of NC, 1961–62, MS in LS. **Orgs.:** Med. LA: Bylaws Com. (Ch., 1977–80). Houston Area Resrch. Lib. Cnsrtm.: Pres. (1978–80). Intl. Socty. for the Hist. of Med. **Honors:** Univ. of TX Med. Branch, Leone Awd. for Admin. Excel., 1979. **Pubns.:** "Medicine in Seventeenth-Century France," *Bookman* (Ja. 1980); "Saints in Medical History," *Clio Medica* (S. 1979). **Activities:** 1, 12; 17, 24, 49-Hist. of Med.; 58, 80, 91 **Addr.:** The University of Texas Medical Branch Library, Galveston, TX 77550.

Frey, Judith L. (S. 29, 1944, Evanston, IL) Head, Lib. Tech. Srvs., Seattle Pub. Schs., 1974–; Acq. Libn., Head, Order & Prcs., King Cnty. Lib. Syst., 1972–74; Serials Libn., Seattle Pub. Lib., 1971–72. **Educ.:** Mundelein Coll., 1961–65, BA (Eng.); West. WA State Univ., 1965–67, MA (Eng.); Univ. of WA, 1969–70, MA (LS). **Orgs.:** ASIS: Pac. NW Chap. (Ch. 1979–80; Mem. Ch. 1974–75). WA LA: Cont. Educ. Com. (1973–74). SLA: Pac. NW Chap., Educ. Com. (1971). WA State Gvrs. Conf. Bus. and Prof. Women: PR, Univ. Club (1978). **Activities:** 9, 10; 20, 46; 56, 75 **Addr.:** 3837 E. Ames Lake Dr. N.E., Redmond, WA 98052.

Frick, Elizabeth Anne (Ap. 3, 1936, Ottawa, ON) Head of User Srvs., Univ. of CO, CO Springs, 1976–; Ref. Libn., Earl-

Special Subjects/Services: 50. Adult educ.; 51. Advert./Mktg.; 52. Aerosp.; 53. Agric.; 54. Area std.; 55. Arts/Hum.; 56. Autom.; 57. Bibl./Prtg.; 58. Bio. sci.; 59. Bus./Fin.; 60. Chem.; 61. Copyrt.; 62. Documtn.; 63. Educ.; 64. Engin.; 65. Env.; 66. Eth. grps.; 67. Film; 68. Food/Nutr.; 69. Geneal.; 70. Geo.; 71. Geol.; 72. Handcpd.; 73. Hist.; 74. Int. frdm.; 75. Info. sci.; 76. Insr.; 77. Law; 78. Legis.; 79. Math./Comp. sci.; 80. Med.; 81. Metals; 82. Nat. resrcs.; 83. Newsp.; 84. Nuc. sci.; 85. Oral hist.; 86. Petr./Energy; 87. Pharm.; 88. Phys./Astr./Math.; 89. Readg.; 90. Relig.; 91. Sci./Tech.; 92. Soc. sci.; 93. Telecom.; 94. Transp.; 95. (other).

Who's Who in Library and Information Services

ham Coll., 1972–76; Assoc. Libn. for Ref. Col., Olin Lib., Cornell Univ., 1972, Ref. Libn., M.P. Catherwood Lib., 1970–71, Asst. Libn., Cat., 1967–69. **Educ.:** Univ. of Toronto, 1954–58, BA (Honours) (Phil., Eng.); Syracuse Univ., 1966–68, MSLS. **Orgs.:** CO LA. ALA: ACRL/Coll. Lib. Sect., Nom. Com. (1980–) *Choice* Ed. Bd. (1981–). Rocky Mt. OUG: Nom. Com. (1979); Treas. (1981–). Assn. for Experiential Educ.: Ed. Consult., *Jnl. of Experiential Educ.,* (1977–80). Multiple Scelerosis Socty.: Southeast. CO Chap., (Exec. Bd., 1979–). **Honors:** Cncl. on Lib. Resrcs., Lib. Srv. Enhancement Prog. Grant, 1977–78; Earlham Coll., Prof. Dev. Grant, 1976. **Pubns.:** *Library Research Guide to History: Illustrated Search Strategy and Sources* (1980); "Information Structure and Bibliographic Instruction", *Jnl. of Acad. Libnshp.* (Sept. 1975); "Periodicals for College Libraries", *Choice* (1974–); "Some of My Best Friends are Faculty," *CO Libs.* (June, 1978); Reviews. **Activities:** 1; 15, 17, 24, 31, 39, 41, 42; 77, 78, 92 **Addr.:** Library, University of Colorado, Colorado Springs, Colorado Springs, CO 80907.

Fridley, Bonnie Jean (Ap. 29, 1941, Youngstown, OH) Srch. Anal., Sch. of Aerosp. Med., Brooks AFB, TX, 1979–; Med. Libn., VA Hosp., San Antonio, TX, 1977–79; Spec. Proj. Libn., Sch. of Aerosp. Med., Brooks AFB, TX, 1977–77. **Educ.:** OH State Univ., 1961–63, BS (Physical Therapy); Univ. of TX, 1975–76, MLS. **Orgs.:** Med. LA: S. Ctrl. Reg. Cont. Educ. Com. Ch. (1980–). SLA. ALA. TALON (Natl. Lib. of Med. Reg. IX): Hosp. Libns. Com., (1979); HOLSA (Hlth. Orient. Lib. San Antonio): Pres. (1980). **Honors:** Med. LA, Rittenhouse Awd., 1976; Beta Phi Mu, 1976; Phi Kappa Phi, 1976. **Activities:** 4, 12; 36, 39; 52, 80, 91 **Addr.:** Aeromedical Library (TSK-1), School of Aerospace Medicine, Brooks AFB, TX 78235.

Frieden, Charles L. (F. 25, 1941, West Bend, IA) Dir. of Circ. Srvs., Univ. of VA, 1978–, Asst. Dir. of Circ. Srvs. 1972–78; Serials Libn., Coe Coll., 1969–72. **Educ.:** Mankato State Univ., 1960–63, BA (Pol. Sci., Bus.); Univ. of IA, 1965–67, MA (Pol. Sci.), 1968–69, MALS. **Orgs.:** ALA. VA LA: Coop. Progs. Com. (1978); *VA Libn. Nsltr.* (Bus. Ed.). **Pubns.:** Jt. auth., *Reference-Information Services in Iowa Libraries* (1969). **Activities:** 1; 22 **Addr.:** Alderman Library, University of Virginia, Charlottesville, VA 22901.

Friedman, Arthur Lewis (S. 10, 1947, Brooklyn, NY) Media Libn., Nassau Cmnty. Coll., 1978–; Dir., Instr. Support Srvs., Sch. of Educ., Brooklyn Coll., 1973–78; Asst. Dir., AV & Curric. Mtrls. Ctr., Defiance Coll., 1972–73. **Educ.:** Defiance Coll., 1967–69, AB (Phys. Sci.); IN Univ., 1969–70, MSinED (AV Comm.); Queens Coll., 1975–78, MLS. **Orgs.:** Nassau Cnty. Lib. Assn.: Coll. & Univ. Libs. Div., (VP 1979; Pres. 1980; Secy. 1981–82). Long Island Media Cnsrtm.: Rec. Secy. (1979–82). AECT: Div. of Instr. Dev. **Honors:** Beta Phi Mu, 1979. **Activities:** 1; 15, 32, 39 **Addr.:** Nassau Community College Library, Stewart Ave., Garden City, NY 11530.

Friedman, Elaine S. (Je. 14, 1951, New York NY) Head, Cat. Maintenance Div., Univ. of MI Lib., 1978–81, Cat. Info. Libn., 1976–78, Subj. Catlgr., 1975–76, Asst. Libn. and Catlgr., SUNY Binghamton Lib., 1974–75. **Educ.:** SUNY, Binghamton, 1968–72, BA, Summa cum Laude, (Eng. and Hum.); Univ. of MI, 1973–74, AMLS. **Orgs.:** ALA: LAMA, Mid. Mgt. Discuss. Grp. (1978–), (Vice Ch., 1979–80); JMRT, Students to ALA Com. (1976). **Honors:** Beta Phi Mu, 1974; Phi Beta Kappa, 1972. **Pubns.:** "Library Applications of Computer Output Microfilm: An Annotated Bibliography," *Spec. Libs.* (D., 1977); "Patron Access to OnLine Cataloging Systems: OCLC in the Public Service Environment," *Jnl. of Academic Librarianship* (Jl. 1980). **Activities:** 1; 17, 38, 46 **Addr.:** 3C Hibben Apts., Faculty Rd., Princeton, NJ 08540.

Friedman, Joan M. (N. 30, 1949, New York, NY) Cur., Rare Books, Yale Ctr. for Brit. Art, 1976–; Asst. Resrch. Libn., 1975–76; Asst. Resrch. Libn., Beinecke Rare Book & Ms. Lib., 1974–75. **Educ.:** Radcliffe Coll., 1967–71, BA (Art Hist.); Courtauld Inst. of Art, Univ. of London, 1971–73, MA (Art Hist.); Columbia Univ., 1973–74, MSLS. **Orgs.:** ALA: ACRL (Rare Book and Mss. Sect., Ch. preconf., 1978; Vice-Ch., Ch.-Elect, 1980–81). Bibl. Socty. of Amer. Bibl. Socty. (London). Grolier Club. **Pubns.:** *Color Printing in England 1486–1870* (1978); "Every lady her own drawing master," *Apollo* (Ap. 1977). **Activities:** 1; 15, 41, 45; 55, 57 **Addr.:** Yale Center for British Art, Box 2120 Yale Station, New Haven, CT 06520.

Friedman, Martha O. (Ag. 14, 1927, Texarkana, AR) Hist. & Phil. Libn., Assoc. Prof., Univ. of IL, 1966–; Biblgphr., Instr., 1965–66. **Educ.:** Univ. of MO, 1947–50, BJ (Jnlsm.), 1958–64, AM (Hist.); Univ. of IL, 1964–65, MSLS. **Orgs.:** ALA: ACRL: Acad. Status Com. (1981–83). The Lib. Assn. London. AAUP: Pres. (1978–80); First VP (1976–78); Cncl. (1973–); Exec. Com. (Ch. 1978–80); Univ. of IL Chap. (Pres., 1971–73); IL Conf. of AAUP Chap. (Pres., 1972–76). **Addr.:** 304 West Florida Ave., Urbana, IL 61801.

Friedman, Roberta G. (O. 11, 1946, Brooklyn, NY) Sr. Law Libn., Fed. Rsv. Bank of NY Law Lib., 1975–; Ref. Libn., Brooklyn Law Sch. Lib., 1971–75. **Educ.:** Hunter Coll., 1963–67, BA (Anthro.); Univ. of MD, 1970–71, MLS; Amer. Inst. of Banking, 1978–81, Cert. (Banking). **Orgs.:** Law LA of Grt. NY: Pres. (1981–82); VP (1980–81); Exec. Bd. Dir. (1978–80). **Activities:** 1, 4; 30, 39, 41; 77, 78, 95-Banking. **Addr.:** Federal Reserve Bank of New York Law Library, 33 Liberty St., New York, NY 10045.

Friedman, Susanna Ruth (Stern) (O. 28, 1924, Baytown, TX) Head Libn., Hyman Judah Schachtel Lib., Congregation Beth Israel, 1970–; Sch. Libn., S. TX Hebrew Acad., Houston, 1974–; Head Libn., Cantor Rubin Kaplan Lib., Congregation Beth Yeshurun, 1965–70; Tchr., Houston Indp. Sch. Dist., 1953, 1959–61; Br. Libn., Pelly, TX (Harris Cnty), 1941–43. **Educ.:** Lee Jr. Coll., 1943–47, AA; Univ. of TX, 1947–49, BA (Arts and Sci.), 1971–73, MLS, Elem. and HS Tchr. Certs., 1960, Sch. Libn. Cert., 1968; Sam Houston Univ., Lib. Media Spec./ Multi-Ethnic Endorsement 1978; Prof. Cert., 1979. **Orgs.:** AJL: Rec. Secy. (1975–78); Schol. Com. (1971–75); Synagogue, Sch. and Ctr. Div. (VP, 1976–78; Pres. 1978–80); SW Reg. Chap., (Pres. 1976–). Lrng. Resrc. Prog. Dir. of TX. B'nai B'rith Women: VP/Various coms. (1953–71). Hadassah: Houston Chap., Cncl. (1973–78). Marcus Levinson ZOA. Jewish Natl. Fund: Bd. (1978–81). TX Jewish Hist. Scty.: Bd. (1980–82). Other orgs. **Honors:** Elsie Hart (BBW) Awd. **Pubns.:** "Painter of Human Souls," *AJL Bltn.* (Win. 1979); "Southern Artist," *AJL Bltn.* (Spr. 1979); "Chaim Goldberg, the Artist," *AJL Bltn.* (Win. 1978); "Audiovisuals in the Jewish Library," *AJL Bltn.* (Spr. 1978); "The Jewish Sabbath" Slide tape presentation (1978); Other articles. **Activities:** 10, 12; 16, 17, 21; 63, 69, 90 **Addr.:** 10911 Rampart Ave., Houston, TX 77096.

Fries, Mary A. (My. 13, 1924, Chehalis, WA) Chld. Libn., Moore Branch, Tacoma Pub. Lib., 1978–, Head, Chld. Dept., 1958–78, Chld. Libn., 1947–58; Asst. Libn., Port Angeles Pub. Lib., 1946–47. **Educ.:** Marylhurst Coll., 1941–45, BA (Hist.); Univ. of WA, 1945–46, BALS. **Orgs.:** ALA. Pac. NW LA. WA LA. The Mountaineers. Audubon Socty. **Activities:** 9; 21, 39 **Addr.:** 620 No. C, Tacoma, WA 98403.

Friesen, Ronald D. (Ap. 8, 1945, Winkler, MB) Sch. lib. Coord., West. Sch. Div., 1974–80; Tchr.-libn., Boundary Sch. Div., 1970–73; Tchr., MB Schs., 1966–69. **Educ.:** Univ. of MB, 1962–65, BA (Gen.), 1965–66, Cert. Ed. (Eng.); 1970, BEduc, 1970; Univ. of AB, 1973–74, BLS. **Orgs.:** MB LA: Pres. (1978–79); Dir. (1975–76). Can. LA: Cncl. (1978–79). MB Sch. Lib. and AV Assn. Can. Sch. LA. S. Central Reg. Pub. Lib.: Vice-Ch., Bd. of Trustees (1978–). Mensa Canada. MB Tchrs. Socty.: Lcl. div. VP (1977–78). Amer. Mensa Libn. Spec. Int. Grp. **Pubns.:** "A Selective Survey of Canadian Mennonite Fiction," *Moccasin Telegraph* (Sum., 1976); other articles and reviews. **Activities:** 10; 17, 24, 32; 63 **Addr.:** Box 1316, Morden, MB R0G 1J0 Canada.

Friesner, Virginia G. F. ("Vee") (Ap. 20, 1949, Dodge City, KS) Dir., Lib. Dev. Div., KS State Lib., 1978–, Hum. Biblgphr., KS State Univ. Lib., 1976–78, Asst. Hum. Libn., 1973–76, Sci. Catlgr., 1972–73. **Educ.:** KS Wesleyan Univ., 1967–71, BA (Eng.); Univ. of IL, 1971–72, MLS; KS State Univ., 1974–78, MA (Eng.). **Orgs.:** KS LA: Ed., *KLA Nsltr.* (1978–80); Pubcty. and Pubns. Com. (Ch., 1978–80); JMRT (Ch., 1977–78). Mt. Plains LA: Cont. Educ. Com. (1976–80); Tech. Srvs. Sect. (Pres., 1980–82). ALA. NLA. Various other orgs. **Honors:** Beta Phi Mu. **Pubns.:** Jt. auth., "Sequential Analysis: A Methodology for Monitoring Approval Plans," *Coll. and Resrch. Libs.* (Jl. 1979). **Activities:** 1, 13; 24, 25, 34; 55, 56 **Addr.:** Rt. 1 Box 7, St. George, KS 66535.

Frisbie, Richard (N. 27, 1926, Chicago, IL) Pres., N. Suburban Lib. Syst., 1979–81; Treas., 1978–79; Pres., Arlington Heights Meml. Lib., 1973–79, Treas., 1971–73, Bd. mem., 1967–. **Educ.:** Univ. of Chicago, 1944–45; Univ. of AZ, 1945–48, BA (Jnlsm.). **Orgs.:** ALA. IL LA. **Activities:** 9, 14-Lib. Syst.; 47 **Addr.:** 631 N. Dunton Ave., Arlington Heights, IL 60004.

Frissell, Barbara L. (F. 15, 1927, San Francisco, CA) Head, Col. Mgt. and Resrcs. Dev., Old Dominion Univ., 1980–; Asst. to Univ. Libn., Univ. of HI, 1978–80, Head, Acq./Srch. Sect., 1969–77. **Educ.:** Univ. of CA, Berkeley, 1944–48, BA (Psy.); Univ. of HI, 1967–69, MLS; Univ. of South. CA, 1977–78, Doct. Prog. **Orgs.:** ALA. HI LA: Coll. and Univ. Sect. (Secy., 1971–72). VA LA. **Activities:** 1; 15, 17 **Addr.:** University Library, Old Dominion University, Norfolk, VA 23508.

Fritsche, Johanna Elizabeth (New York, NY) Msc. Libn., Sonoma State Univ., 1963–; Sr. Libn.,-Msc. Dept., Oakland Pub. Lib., 1953–62; Indust. Rel. Libn., Union Carbide and Carbon Corp., 1946–50; Ref. Asst., Pentagon Lib., 1944–46; Libn., Notre Dame Coll. of Staten Island, 1940–44. **Educ.:** Hunter Coll., 1932–36, BA (Latin); Columbia Univ., 1939–40, BS LS; Univ. of Lausanne, 1962, (Fr.). **Orgs.:** Msc. LA: Ch., North. CA Chap. (1975–77). CA LA. **Honors:** Phi Beta Kappa, 1936. **Activities:** 1, 9; 20, 32, 39; 95-Music. **Addr.:** 865 Sonoma Ave., Santa Rosa, CA 95404.

Frohmberg, Katherine A. (My. 29, 1949, Cleveland, OH) Systs. Libn., Oberlin Coll., 1979–; Tech. Libn., R and D Assocs., 1976–79; Tech. Libn., Value Engin., 1975–76. **Educ.:** Pomona Coll., 1967–71, BA (Math.); Univ. of South. CA, 1973–75, MLS. **Orgs.:** ALA. ASIS: Various coms. Natl. Org. for Women. **Pubns.:** "Research on the Impact of a Computerized Circulation System on the Performance of a Large College Library," *Reports to NSF on Grant No. IST–78–10821*; various papers. **Activities:** 1, 12; 22, 41, 46; 56, 91 **Addr.:** Oberlin College Library, Oberlin, OH 44074.

Fromm, Roger W. (F. 12, 1933, Buffalo, NY) Coll. Archvst./Ref. Libn., Bloomsburg State Coll., 1974–; Assoc. Libn., NY State Hist. Assn., 1970–74; Prin., Amer. Sch., Benghazi, Libya, 1968–69; Tchr., Escola Inglesa de Luanda, Angola, 1967–78. **Educ.:** OH Wesleyan Univ., 1951–55, BA (Soc. Sci.); Univ. of VT, 1960–66, MEd (Educ.); Rutgers Univ., 1969–70, MLS; Univ. of Scranton, 1977–80, MA (Hist.); Mod. Arch. Inst., Natl. Arch., 1979, Cert. **Orgs.:** ALA. PA LA: Resrch. Mtrls. Com. (1978–); Arch. Com. (1979–). SAA. Mid-Atl. Reg. Arch. Conf. **Honors:** Beta Phi Mu; Phi Alpha Theta. **Pubns.:** "Tuesday Morning Live–Personality and Bibliographic Instruction," *Directions for the Decade: Library Instruction in the 1980's* (1981); reviews. **Activities:** 1, 2; 31, 39; 92 **Addr.:** Andruss Library, Bloomsburg State College, Bloomsburg, PA 17815.

Frommeyer, L. Ronald (S. 2, 1935, Cincinnati, OH) Head, Acq. Dept., Univ. of Cincinnati Libs., 1977–; Dean, Univ. Lib., Wright State Univ., 1972–76, Staff Asst., Ofc. of Provost, 1976–77, Assoc. Dir., 1971–72. **Educ.:** Athenaeum of OH, 1954–57, BA (Phil.); Western Reserve Univ., 1961–65, MSLS. **Orgs.:** ALA. Cath. LA. OH LA: Mem. Ch. (1971–72). OCLC: Bd. of Trustees (1974–77); Secy. to Bd. (1975–77). **Activities:** 1; 15, 17, 46 **Addr.:** Central Library, Univ. of Cincinnati, Cincinnati, OH 45221.

Frosch, Paula (F. 25, 1935, New York, NY) Libn., Metro. Musm. of Art, 1973–; Dlr. in Mss., 1972–73; Asst. to Bk. Dlr., Ursus Bks., 1972. **Educ.:** Vassar Coll., Adelphi Univ., 1951–54, AB (Phil.); Columbia Univ., 1969–72, MS (LS). **Orgs.:** ALA. SLA. ARLIS/NA: NY Chap., Cat. Com.; Acq. Com.; Awds. Com. **Activities:** 8; 20, 39, 42; 55 **Addr.:** 15 W. 75 St., New York, NY 10023.

Frost, Carolyn Olivia (O. 17, 1940, New York, NY) Assoc. prof., Sch. of LS University of MI, 1977–; Instr., Univ. of OR, 1972–73; Cat. libn., Univ. of OR Med. Sch., 1971–72, Instr., Univ. of IL - Chicago, 1964–68. **Educ.:** Howard Univ., 1957–61, BA (Grmn.), Univ. of Chicago, 1962–64, MA (Grmn.), Univ. of OR, 1970–71, MLS, Univ. of Chicago, 1973–77, PhD (LS). **Orgs.:** ALA. AALS. MI LA. **Honors:** Phi Beta Kappa, 1960; Fulbright Scholar, 1961. **Pubns.:** "The Use of Citations in Literary Research," *Lib. Qtly.* (O. 1979); "Teaching the Cataloging of Non-Book Media," *Jnl. of Educ. for Libnshp.*; "The Bodleian Catalogs of 1674 and 1738," *Lib. Qtly.* (Jl. 1976). **Activities:** 11; 20 **Addr.:** School of Library Science, University of Michigan, Ann Arbor, MI 48104.

Frost, Judith G. (F. 24, 1946, Columbus, OH) Assoc. Libn., Cleveland Musm. of Art, 1975–; Head Libn., Baltimore Musm. of Art, 1971–75. **Educ.:** Colby Coll., 1964–68, BA (Art Hist.); Univ. of Denver, 1969–71, MA (LS). **Orgs.:** SLA. ARLIS/NA: Reg. Rep. to Exec. Bd. (1976); Stan. Com. (1973–); MD., Washington, VA Chap. (Ch., 1974–75); OH Chap. (Ch. 1976–77). **Activities:** 12; 17, 22, 39; 55 **Addr.:** Library, Cleveland Museum of Art, Cleveland, OH 44106.

Frost, Tamara U. (Ag. 23, 1947, Munich, W. Germany) Chief, Cat. Dept., Stanford Univ. Libs., 1980–; Head, Cat. Dept., SUNY, Buffalo, 1977–80; Coord., Mono. Cat., TX A&M Univ., 1976–77, Serials Catlgr., 1974–76; Admin. Libn., US Army Spec. Srvs. Lib. Prog., Europe 1970–73. **Educ.:** Univ. of Akron, 1965–69, BA (Eng., Grmn.); Univ. of Denver, 1969–70, MALS; TX A&M Univ., 1974–77, MA (Eng.). **Orgs.:** ALA: LAMA/ Persnl. Admin. Sect., Com. on Econ. Status, Welfare and Fringe Benefits (1978–82); Com. on Accred., Site Visitation Mem. (1979–); ACRL. SUNY Libns. Assn. OCLC, Inter-Netwk. Qual. Cntrl. Cncl.: Rep. of FAUL (1977–80). **Pubns.:** Reviews. **Activities:** 1; 17, 20 **Addr.:** Catalog Department, Stanford University Libraries, Stanford, CA 94305.

Frost, William John (Ap. 26, 1939, Virginia, MN) Ref. Col. Libn., Bloomsburg State Coll., 1972–; Admin. Asst., Rutgers Univ., 1970–72. **Educ.:** Old Dominion Univ., 1964–66, BA (Eng.); Rutgers Univ., 1969–70, MLS; Univ. of Scranton, 1972–77, MA (Eng.). **Orgs.:** PA LA: Ch., Lib. Instr. Com . (1979–); Ch., W. Branch Chap. (1975–76). ALA. Assn. of PA State Coll. and Univ. Prof.: Ch., Bloomsburg Fac. Assn. Mem. Com. (1977–1980); Sec. (1981–). AAUP. **Pubns.:** College Library Instruction/College Instruction: A Review of the Literature, (1979). **Activities:** 1; 31, 39 **Addr.:** Harvey A. Andruss Library, Bloomsburg State College, Bloomsburg, PA 17815.

Fry, Bernard M. (O. 24, 1915, Bloomfield, IN) Dean, Grad. Lib. Sch., IN Univ., 1967–; Dir., Clearinghouse for Fed. Sci. and Tech. Info., 1963–67; Deputy Head, Ofc. of Sci. Info. Srv., Natl. Sci. Fndn., 1959–63; Member & Director, Tech. Info. Srv., Atomic Energy Cmsn., 1947–58. **Educ.:** IN Univ., 1933–37, AB (Hist.), 1938–39, MA (Pol. Sci.); Cath. Univ., 1950–52, MS (LS); American Univ., 1960–67, Doct. work (Pub. Admin.). **Orgs.:** ASIS: Past-Pres. (1967). ALA: Cncl. (1980–83). SLA: Ch., Sci-Tech Div. (1953–54). **Honors:** ASIS, Info. Sci. Book-of-the Yr. Awd., 1978; Beta Phi Mu, 1967; Phi Delta Kappa, 1939. **Pubns.:** Jt.

PROFESSIONAL ACTIVITIES: Institutions: 1. Acad. lib.; 2. Arch.; 3. Assn.; 4. Fed./Gvt. lib.; 5. Inst. lib.; 6. Mfr./Suppl.; 7. Milit. lib.; 8. Musm.; 9. Pub. lib.; 10. Sch. lib.; 11. Sch. of lib. sci.; 12. Spec. lib.; 13. State lib.; 14. (other). **Functions/Activities:** 15. Acq./Col. dev.; 16. Adult srvs.; 17. Admin.; 18. Apprais.; 19. Archit./Bldgs.; 20. Cat./Class.; 21. Chld. srvs.; 22. Circ.; 23. Cons./Pres.; 24. Consult.; 25. Cont. ed.; 26. Educ. lib. sci.; 27. Ext. srvs.; 28. Fund/Grants; 29. Gvt. pubs.; 30. Indx./Abs.; 31. Instr. lib. use; 32. Media srvs.; 33. Micro.; 34. Netwks./Coop.; 35. Persnl.; 36. PR; 37. Publshg.; 38. Recs. mgt.; 39. Ref. srvs.; 40. Repro.; 41. Resrch.; 42. Review.; 43. Secur.; 44. Serials; 45. Spec. col.; 46. Tech. srvs.; 47. Trustees/Bds.; 48. YA srvs.; 49. (other).

auth., *Publishers and Libraries: A Study of Scholarly and Research Journals,* (1976); Jt. auth., "Journal Publisher Practices and Attitudes on Article Copying: Summary of a Survey," *IEEE Transactions on Prof. Comm.* (N., 1977); "Research Conducted in Library Schools," *Info. Storage and Retrieval* (My. 1973); Ed., *Info. Prcs. and Mgt.* (1968–); Ed., *Gvt. Pubns. Review,* (1973–); other books. **Activities:** 11, 12; 24, 26, 37; 56, 75, 93 **Addr.:** 3649 E. Third St., Bloomington, IN 47401.

Fry, James W. (My. 8, 1939, Canton, OH) Deputy State Libn. for Tech. Srvs., State Lib. of OH, 1975–; Head, Reg. Campuses Tech. Srvs. Div., OH State Univ. Libs., 1969–75. **Educ.:** Milligan Coll., 1962–66, BA (Hist.); IN Univ., 1968–69, MLS; OH State Univ., 1969–71, MA (Soc. Hist.). **Orgs.:** ALA: ASCLA/Interlib. Coop. Com. (1979–81); RTSD/Tech. Srvc. Dir. of Prcs. Ctrs. Discuss. Grp. (Ch., 1978–79); LAMA/Mem. Rep. for OH (1977–79). OH LA. OH Hist. Socty. Socty. of OH Archvsts. **Pubns.:** "Technical Services in the Small Library" (1980); *A Feasibility Study for Consolidating and/or Coordinating Technical Procedures in Beaver County Pennsylvania Libraries,* (1977); "Technical Services and Centralized Processing for the Rural Public Library: An overview," *Lib. Trends* (Spr., 1980); Jt. auth., "State Library Agency Organization and Services," *Lib. Trends,* (Fall, 1978); "Library Services Act and Library Services and Construction Act, 1956–1973: A Legislative History," *Lib. Trends,* (Jl., 1975); Other pubns. **Activities:** 1, 13; 22, 35, 46; 56, 90, 93 **Addr.:** The State Library of Ohio, 65 South Front St., Columbus, OH 43215.

Fry, Roy H. (Je. 16, 1931, Seattle, WA) Coord. of Bibl. Srvs., E.M. Cudahy Meml. Lib., Loyola Univ., 1976–; Biblgphr. For Bus. & Pol. Sci., Lewis Towers Lib., 1975–76; Circ. Libn., E.M. Cudahy Meml. Lib., 1974–75; Bibl. Srvs. Libn., 1973–74; Head Ref. Libn., 1967–1973; Evening Ref. Libn., 1965–1967; Libn., Mark Morris Jr.-Sr. HS, Longview, WA, 1961–1964; Libn. & AV Coord., Zillah Pub. Sch., 1960–61. **Educ.:** Univ. of WA, 1953–59, BA (Asian Std.); BA (Anthr.); West. MI Univ., 1961–65, MA (LS); Northeast. IL Univ., 1971–1973, MA (Pol. Sci.); Additional courses at Univ. of VT, Univ. of Denver, Univ. of IL at the Med. Ctr. **Orgs.:** NLA: Bd. (1975–1976); Nom. Com. (1980–81); IL Chap., Const. Com. (1978–1979); Elect. Com. (1979); Bd. (1979–). Asian/Pac. Amer. Libns. Assn. Midwest Arch. Conf. ALA: ACRL; GODORT; LIRT; IRRT. IL LA. Pi Sigma Alpha; Midwest Pol. Sci. Assn. **Activities:** 1; 29, 31, 39; 66, 92, 95 **Addr.:** 10059 D Frontage Rd., Skokie, IL 60077.

Fry, Stephen Michael (Ja. 5, 1941, Boise ID) Head, Msc. Lib., Univ. of CA, Los Angeles, 1975–; Assoc. Msc. Libn., Northwestern Univ., 1972–75, Msc. Libn. and Assoc. Prof. of Msc., Indiana Univ. of PA, 1970–72, Msc. Libn., Univ. of CA, Riverside, 1967–70. **Educ.:** Univ. of CA, Riverside, 1959–63, BA (Msc); Claremont Grad. Sch., 1964–65, MA (Msc.); Univ. of South. CA, 1965–69, MSLS. **Orgs.:** Msc. LA: Bd. of Dir. (1979–81); Amer. Msc. Proj. Com. (1975–76); Ch., Pubcty. Com. (1970–72). Intl. Assn. of Msc. Libs. Amer. Musicological Socty. Guild of Carillonneurs in N. Amer.: Ch., Lib. Com. (1973–78). **Pubns.:** Ed., *The Life and Times of Sadakichi Hartmann, 1867–1944.* (1970); *Directory and Index of Special Music Collections in Southern California Libraries.* (1970); *A Manual for the Classification and Cataloging of Bell and Carillon Literature.* (1974); "The Anton Brees Carillon Library at the Bok Singing Tower." *GCNA Bulletin.* (N., 1972); "New Reference Books" column, *Notes* (1975–79). **Activities:** 1, 2; 15, 17, 24; 55, 95 **Addr.:** Music Library, Schoenberg Hall, University of California, Los Angeles, CA 90024.

Fry, Thomas K. (O. 17, 1948, Terre Haute, IN) Actg. Head Coll. Lib., Univ. of CA, Los Angeles, 1979–, Head Pros. Sect., Coll. Lib., 1977–79, Asst. Ch. Acq. and Serials Dept., CA State Univ., Northridge, 1974–76, Catlgr., 1973–74. **Educ.:** CA State Univ., Northridge, 1968–70, BS (Bus. Admin.); Univ of CA, Los Angeles, 1972–73, MLS; Cert. of Specialization, Univ of CA, Los Angeles, Grad. Sch. of Lib. and Info. Sci., 1972–73. **Orgs.:** ALA: ACRL. CA Lib. Assn.: Col. Dev. Chap. (Ch. 1977). South. CA Tech. Pres. Grp. Sierra Club: Los Angeles Chap., Mountaineering Trng. Com. (1977). **Honors:** Univ. of CA Los Angeles Grad. Sch. of Lib. and Info. Sci. Alum. Assn. Cert. of Apprec., 1979. **Pubns.:** Guest Ed., *CA Libn.* (Ap. 1977); *Use of Selection Tools,* ERIC (1974). **Activities:** 1; 15, 17, 31 **Addr.:** College Library UCLA, Los Angeles, CA 90024.

Fu, Paul S. (S. 7, 1932, Shen-Yang, Liao-Ning, China) Law Libn., Supreme Court of OH Law Lib., 1972–; Assoc. Prof. and Law Libn., OH North. Univ. Coll. of Law, 1971–72, Asst. Prof. and Law Libn., 1969–71; Lect. and Asst. Law Libn., Detroit Coll. of Law, 1968–69. **Educ.:** Soochow Univ. Law School, Taiwan, China, 1956–60, LLB (Law); Univ. of IL Coll. of Law, 1961–62, MCL (Law); Villanova Univ., 1966–68, MSLS. **Orgs.:** AALL: State, Court, and Cnty. Law Libs. Sect. (Ch., 1977–78). OH Reg. Assn. of Law Libs.: AV Com. (Ch., 1974–75). ALA. Amer. Socty. of Intl. Law. Amer. Trial Lawyers Assn.: Fac. Member (1971–). **Pubns.:** "One Law Librarian to Another," *Nsltr. of State and Court Law Libs. of the US and Canada,* (Spr. 1976). **Activities:** 13; 17; 77 **Addr.:** Supreme Court of Ohio Law Library, 30 E. Broad St., Columbus, OH 43215.

Fu, Tina Cheng (Kiang-si, China) Asst. Dir., Pub. Srvs., Univ. of WI, Oshkosh, 1979–; Pub. Srvs. Libn., 1969–79. **Educ.:** Taiwan Normal Univ., 1958–61, BA (Eng./Ed.); Marquette Univ., 1963–65, MA (Eng.); Univ. of WI, Madison, 1966–68, MALS. **Orgs.:** ALA: Equal Employment Oppor. Subcom. (1977–); Louise Giles Minority Sch., jury (1980–). WI LA. Assn. of Univ. of WI Fac.: Elec. Com. (1979). Univ. of WI, Oshkosh Fac. Senate: Exec. Com. (1977–79). **Pubns.:** Contrib. to Chinese newspapers (1972–). **Activities:** 1; 15, 17, 39 **Addr.:** Public Services Division, Libraries & Learning Resources, University of WI, Oshkosh, Oshkosh, WI 54901.

Fudge, Lucretia L. (Je. 28, 1937, Kansas City, MO) Prog. Coord., Maui Pub. Lib., 1979–; Sch. Lib. Srvs. Spec., Dept. of Educ., Hawaii, 1975–79; Media Spec., Ewa Beach Comnty. Sch. Lib., 1971–75; Sch. Libn., Iliahi Sch., Wahiawa, HI, 1970–71. **Educ.:** Univ. of KS, Lawrence, 1956–59, BS (El. Educ.); Univ. of South. CA, 1976–78, DLS; Univ. of HI, 1966–67, MLS. **Orgs.:** HI LA: Pres. (1980–81). ALA: Assn. for Educ. in Comm. and Tech. HI Assn. of Sch. Libns. Soroptimist Intl.: Comm. Srvcs., Ch. (1980). Toastmasters Intl.: Sgt. at Arms (1980–81). **Activities:** 9, 10; 21, 24, 36; 63 **Addr.:** P.O. Box 302, Wailuku HI 96793.

Fuller, Fredrick Lee, Jr. (My. 17, 1953, Selma, AL) Info. Srvs. Libn., AL Pub. Lib. Srv., 1978–; Asst. Libn., Univ. of Montevallo, 1975–78. **Educ.:** Univ. of AL, 1972–74, BA (Hist.), 1974–75, MLS. **Orgs.:** ALA. SELA. AL LA: Int. Frdm. Com.; JMRT Exec. Cncl. **Activities:** 13; 39, 41; 69, 74 **Addr.:** 6063-3 Monticello Dr., Montgomery, AL 36117.

Fuller, Kathleen Brain (O. 18, 1938, Hull, Eng) Info. Spec., Ferro Corp., 1980–; Info. Spec., B.F. Goodrich, 1977–80. **Educ.:** Case Western Reserve Univ., 1956–60, BA (Chem.), 1974–77, MS, in LS. **Orgs.:** ASIS: Secy. (1978–79). Mather Coll. Alum. Bd., Case Western Reserve Univ.: Schol. Com. (1978–80). **Activities:** 12; 15, 20, 39; 59, 60, 64 **Addr.:** 2877 Winthrop Rd., Cleveland, OH 44120.

Fuller, Nancy Fay (S. 23, 1945, Oxford, MS) Libn., Sch. of Pharmacy, Univ. of MS, 1976–; Prof., Head Libn., State Tech. Inst. at Memphis, 1974–76, Asst., Assoc. Prof., Asst. Libn., 1969–74; Pers. Libn., George Peabody Coll. for Tchrs., 1968–69. **Educ.:** Wood Jr. Coll., 1963–65, (Liberal Arts); Univ. of MS, 1965–67, BAE (Sec. Educ.), 1967–68, MLS. **Orgs.:** MS LA: Rcrt. Com. (1977–78, 1979–80). SELA. ALA. Amer. Assn. of Colls. of Pharmacy: Libs.-Educ. Resrcs. Sect., Nom. Com. (1978–79), Ad Hoc Handbk. Com. (1979–80). Various other orgs. Kappa Delta Pi. **Activities:** 1, 12; 17, 31, 39; 63, 87, 91 **Addr.:** Box 1511 Chickasaw Rd., Oxford, MS 38655.

Fullshire, Lynn C. (Ap. 6, 1948, Rockville Centre, NY) Sr. Law Libn., Dir., Supreme Court Law Lib. (Suffolk), 1974–; Acq. Libn., Manhattan Coll., 1971–74. **Educ.:** Univ. of CO, 1968–70, BA (Eng.); Long Island Univ., 1970–71, MS (LS); Manhattan Coll., 1973–77, MA (Eng.); Cert. Law Libn., AALL, 1977. **Orgs.:** AALL: Supreme Court Lib. Stan. Law Lib. Assn. of Grt. NY. Long Island Lib. Resrcs. Cncl. NY State Ofc. of Court Admin.: Lib. staffing & stan. com. **Activities:** 12, 13; 17, 39, 41; 77 **Addr.:** Supreme Court Law Library, 10th J.D., Rm. 210, Court House, Griffing Avenue, Riverhead, NY 11901.

Fulmer, Russell Francis (N. 28, 1946, Birmingham, AL) Coord. of Tech. Srvs., Jackson Metro. Lib. Syst., 1974–; Catlgr., Univ. of AL, 1971–74. **Educ.:** Dickinson Coll., 1964–68, BA (Hist., Russ. and E. European Std.); Univ. of AL, 1970–72, MLS. **Orgs.:** ALA. SELA. MS LA: JMRT (Ch., 1979). Southeast. Lib. Netwk.: Data Base Qual. Cntrl. Com. (1980). Easter Seals of MS. St. Andrews Cathedral (Episcopal): Lib. Com. (Ch.). **Honors:** Beta Phi Mu, 1975. **Pubns.:** Gen. contrib., *MS Libs.* (1979–); Jt. ed., *CLAM OL* (1978). **Activities:** 1, 9; 20, 23, 46; 56 **Addr.:** Jackson Metropolitan Library System, 301 N. State St., Jackson, MS 39201.

Fulton, June H. (My. 26, 1943, Berwyn, IL) Dir., Mid-East. Reg. Med. Lib. Srv., Coll. of Physicians of Philadelphia, 1976–, Actg. Assoc. Dir., 1975–76, Asst. Dir., 1972–75, Head, Reg. Ref. Dept., 1971–72; Life and Env. Sci. Subj. Spec., Lib., Univ. of AL, Huntsville, 1969–70; Asst. Acq. Libn., Univ. of NC, Greensboro, 1967–68. **Educ.:** Univ. of NC, Greensboro, 1961–65, BA (Hist.); Univ. of NC, Chapel Hill, 1966–67, MSLS. **Orgs.:** Med. LA: Srvys. and Stats. Com. (1981–82); Cert. Examination Admin. Com. (1977–78, 1978–79); Philadelphia Reg. Grp. Univ. of NC Lib. Sch. Alum. Assn. **Pubns.:** "The Mid-Eastern Regional Medical Library Service," *Natl. Lib. of Med. News* (Jl.–Ag. 1978); "MERMLS Offers Outreach Services from College Library," *Fellow's Forum* (Ja. 1978). **Activities:** 12, 14-Reg. med. lib.; 24, 27, 34; 80, 95-Hlth. sci. **Addr.:** Mid-Eastern Regional Medical Library Service, College of Physicians of Philadelphia, 19 S. 22nd St., Philadelphia, PA 19103.

Funabiki, Ruth Patterson (Jl. 28, 1950, Indiana, PA) Cat. Libn., WA State Univ., 1978–; Cat. Libn., Univ. of ID, 1977–78; Msc. Catlgr., SUNY, Stony Brook, 1974–77; Asst. Libn., Curric. Mtrls., IN Univ. of PA, 1974. **Educ.:** IN Univ. of PA, 1968–72, BS (Msc. Educ.); Kent State Univ., 1972–73, MLS. **Orgs.:** ALA. Msc. LA: Pac. NW Chap. (Secy.-Treas., 1978–81). Msc. OCLC Users Grp. Pac. NW LA. Delta Omicron. Kappa Delta Pi. **Pubns.:** *Music OCLC Users Group Tagging Workbook and Reference Manual* (F. 1980). **Activities:** 1; 20, 34, 39; 56, 95-Msc. **Addr.:** Holland Library, Washington State University, Pullman, WA 99164.

Funk, Elizabeth A. (Ag. 17, 1938, Pottstown, PA) Lib. Dev. Adv., State Lib. of PA, 1975–, Lib. Dev. Asst., 1966–75; Sr. HS Libn., Cumberland Valley Sch. Dist., 1961–62. **Educ.:** Juniata Coll., 1956–60, BA (Hist.); Drexel Univ., 1960–64, MLS. **Orgs.:** ALA: HRLSD Mem. (1977–79); ASCLA/LSIES Nom. (1977–79); ASCLA/LSIES Plng. (1979–81). PA LA: Mem., PR, Schol., Cont. Educ., Awds., and Nom. Com. **Activities:** 5, 13; 24, 25; 72, 95 **Addr.:** State Library of Pennsylvania, Bureau of Library of Library Development, Box 1601, Harrisburg, PA 17105.

Funk, Grace E. (Ap. 20, 1924, Saskatoon, SK) Libn., Harwood Elem. Sch., Vernon, BC, 1971–; Libn., Harwood Demonstration Sch. Lib. Proj., 1971–75; Libn., BX and Okanagan Landing Elem. Schs., 1969–71; Libn., S. Rutland Elem. Sch., 1967–69; Libn., Tchr., Rutland Jr. Sr. Sec. Sch., 1960–66; Libn., Tchr., Enderby HS, 1957–60; Tchr., Armstrong HS, 1949–50; Tchr., Agassiz HS, 1947–49. **Educ.:** Univ. of SK, 1945, BA magna cum laude (Eng.); Univ. of BC, 1967, BLS, 1977, MLS. **Orgs.:** Can. LA: Ed. Bd., *Can. Mtrls.* (1978–); Can. Sch. Lib. Assn. (Cncl., 1978–). BC Sch. Libns. Assn.: Ed., *BCSLA Review. Srv.* (1976–); Ed., *Bkmark* (1969–70); Treas. (1965–66); Secy. (1962–63). BC LA. BC Tchrs.' Fed. Can. Coll. of Tchrs. Delta Kappa Gamma. **Pubns.:** "Haunted Bookshop," *BC Lib. Qtly.* (Ap. 1966); "Science Fiction," *BC Tchr.* (Ap. 1965); "Studying the Novel: An Approach to *Lord of the Flies,*" *BC Eng. Tchr.* (Je. 1965); Reviews. **Activities:** 10; 15, 17, 21; 63 **Addr.:** Rural Route No. 1, Lumby, BC V0E 2G0 Canada.

Funkhouser, Richard L. (Ap. 13, 1934, Lafayette, IN) Sci. Libn., Purdue Univ., 1975–, Math. Sci. & Geosci. Libn., 1969–75, Engin. Libn., 1966–69; Libn. & Visit. Prof., Indian Inst. of Tech., Kanpur, India, 1964–66; Engin. Libn., Purdue Univ., 1958–64. **Educ.:** IN Univ., 1952–56, BSEd (Soc. Sci.), 1956–57, MA (LS). **Orgs.:** SLA: IN Chap. Treas. (1967–69); Pres.-Elect (1972–73); Pres. (1973–74). SLA: Phy.-Astr.-Math. Div., Treas. (1974–76); Ch.-Elect (1976–77); Ch. (1977–78); Schol. Com. (1975–78, Ch. 1977–78). ALA. **Pubns.:** *A Guide to the Literature of Electrical and Electronics Engineering* (1970). **Activities:** 1; 15, 17, 39; 88, 91 **Addr.:** Purdue University Libraries, West Lafayette, IN 47907.

Funn, Courtney H. (N. 30, 1941, Baltimore Cnty., MD) Dir. of the Lib., Bowie State Coll., 1969–; Asst. Prof., Msc./Actg. Dir., 1967–70; Fine Arts Spec., Provident Hosp., Baltimore, 1968–69. **Educ.:** Fisk Univ., Nashville, TN, 1959–63, BA (Msc.); Columbia Univ., 1965–67, MA (Msc.); Univ. of MD, College Park, 1970–71, MLS. **Orgs.:** ALA; MD LA: Ad- Hoc Legis. Com. (1977–78); Fed. Rel. Com. (1975–76); DC LA; ASIS; Extensive Library Assn. mem. AAUW: Mem. Com. (1976–78); Hist. (1979). **Honors:** Beta Phi Mu; Kappa Delta Pi. **Pubns.:** "Beyond the Work Week: Some Creative Uses of Leisure Time," *MD LA* (Je. 1974); "A Guide to Libraries of State Colleges," *MD LA* (1975). **Activities:** 1, 9; 17, 24, 32; 55, 59, 63 **Addr.:** 6523 Rolling Ridge Dr., Capitol Heights, MD 20027.

Furlong, Robert E. (Ap. 21, 1941, Chicago, IL) Grp. Supvsr., Indian Hill and Indian Hill W. Tech. Lib., Comp. Info. Lib., Bell Telephone Labs., 1976–, Grp. Supvsr., Pubns. and Tech. Prcs. Grp., 1971–76; Head, Tech. Srvs., Riverside (CA) Pub. Lib., 1969–71; Branch Head, Fresno Cnty., CA, 1965–69. **Educ.:** Bradley Univ., 1959–63, BA (Chem.); Univ. of IL, 1963–65, MSLS. **Orgs.:** SLA. ALA: SORT. Dupage Libns. Assn.: VP, Pres.-Elect (1980–82). CA LA: Conf. Ch. (1968). **Activities:** 12; 17, 41; 64, 91, 93 **Addr.:** Bell Telephone Labs, Technical Library, Warrenville - Naperville Rd., Naperville, IL 60566.

Furlow, Karen Lynne (O. 2, 1947, New Orleans, LA) Corp. Libn., McDermott, Inc., 1980–; ILL Libn., Ref., Howard-Tilton Meml. Lib., Tulane Univ., 1970–80. **Educ.:** LA State Univ., 1964–68, BA (Psy.), 1968–70, MS (LS); Tulane Univ., 1970–73, MEd (Admin.), 1976–, MBA, in prog. **Orgs.:** ALA: ACRL; LAD, Friends of Libs. Com. (1976–78, 1978–80); RASD, Coop. Ref. Srvs. Com. (1977–79); Facts on File Awd. Com. (1979–81); Info. Retrieval Com. (1973–75, 1975–77). LA LA. SWLA. Kappa Delta Pi: Pres., Epsilon Beta Chap., (1973–74). LSU Lib. Sch. Alum. Assn. Friends of the Tulane Univ. Lib. Tulane Univ. Women's Assn. **Honors:** Beta Phi Mu; Kappa Delta Pi, Compatriot in Educ. Awd., 1976. **Pubns.:** Contrib., *Friends of the Library* (1980); "Friends of the Library", *Coll. and Resrch. Libs.* (Jl. 1975); "Friends of the Library", *Just Friends* (1975); "On Trial: Free Photocopy for SOLINET Libraries in Louisiana", *Some Current Reprographic Concerns Related to Interlibrary Loan,* (1977). **Activities:** 1; 31, 34; 61 **Addr.:** 117 Raspberry St. E., Metairie, LA 70005.

Furness, Reginald J. (Ap. 7, 1928, Burlington, VT) Asst. Law Libn., Boston Univ. Sch. of Law, 1954–. **Educ.:** Boston Univ., 1948–50, AA, 1950–52, JD (Law). **Orgs.:** AALL. Law Libns. of New Eng.: Pres., Vice Pres., Treas. (1973–79). **Activities:** 1, 14-Law; 39; 77 **Addr.:** Boston University, School of Law Library, 765 Commonwealth Ave., Boston, MA 02215.

Special Subjects/Services: 50. Adult educ.; 51. Advert./Mktg.; 52. Aerosp.; 53. Agric.; 54. Area std.; 55. Arts/Hum.; 56. Autom.; 57. Bibl./Prtg.; 58. Bio. sci.; 59. Bus./Fin.; 60. Chem.; 61. Copyrt.; 62. Documtn.; 63. Educ.; 64. Engin.; 65. Env.; 66. Eth. grps.; 67. Film; 68. Food/Nutr.; 69. Geneal.; 70. Geo.; 71. Geol.; 72. Handcpd.; 73. Hist.; 74. Int. frdm.; 75. Info. sci.; 76. Insr.; 77. Law; 78. Legis.; 79. Math./Comp. sci.; 80. Med.; 81. Metals; 82. Nat. resrcs.; 83. Newsp.; 84. Nuc. sci.; 85. Oral hist.; 86. Petr./Energy; 87. Pharm.; 88. Phys./Astr./Math.; 89. Readg.; 90. Relig.; 91. Sci./Tech.; 92. Soc. sci.; 93. Telecom.; 94. Transp.; 95. (other).

Fusaro, Jan Barre (F. 7, 1925, Detroit, MI) Cmnty. Fac., Metro State Univ., 1972–; Proj. Coord., MN Higher Educ. Coord. Bd., 1970–71; Libn., Anoka-Ramsey Cmnty. Coll., 1965–70. **Educ.:** Univ. of MN, 1943–49, BA (Chem., Math), 1950–51, MA (Grmn. Lang. and Lit.), 1951–53, BSLS, 1968, PhD (Grmn. Lang. and Lit.); Stephens Coll., 1968, Media Inst. **Orgs.:** ALA. MN Assn. of Cont. Adult Educ. **Honors:** MN LA, MN Libn. of the Yr., 1968; Metro State Univ., Tchg. Excel. Awd., 1977, 1980. **Pubns.:** Numerous articles in jnls. such as *RQ, Lrng. Today, AV Jnl.* (Univ. of MN). **Activities:** 1; 49-Tchg.; 55, 63 **Addr.:** Metro State University, 121 Metro Sq. Bldg., 7th and Robert Sts., St. Paul, MN 55101.

Fuseler, Elizabeth A. (Je. 15, 1947, Philadelphia, PA) Lib. Dir., U.S. Merchant Marine Academy, 1981–; Lib. Dir., TX A&M Univ., Galveston, 1975–81; Libn., NOAA, NE Fisheries Ctr., 1974–75; Head Catlgr., Marine Bio. Lab., Woods Hole, 1973–74; Dept. Head Libn., Bio. Lib., Univ. of PA, 1969–73. **Educ.:** Coll. of William and Mary, 1965–68, AB (Bio. Educ.); Drexel Univ., 1970–72, MS (LS); Univ. of Houston, Clear Lake City, 1978–81, MS (Env. Mgt.). **Orgs.:** Intl. Assn. of Marine Sci. Libs.: Pres. (1979–80). TX LA: Resrch. Com. (1978–80, Ch. 1978–79). ALA. SWLA. Other orgs. AAUW: Corres. Secy. (1979–80). Galveston Hist. Fndn. AAUP. Env. Mgt. Assn. **Honors:** US Dept. of Cmrce., Unit Cit., 1975. **Pubns.:** Red tide bibliography 1974. **Activities:** 1, 12; 15, 17, 35; 58, 65, 82 **Addr.:** 200 Lexington, #8F, Oyster Bay, NY 11771.

Fussler, Herman H. (My 15, 1914), Philadelphia, PA) Martin A. Ryerson Disting. Srv. Prof., Grad. LS, Univ. of Chicago, 1948–; Dir., Univ. Lib., Univ. of Chicago, 1948–71, Science Lib. to Assoc. Dir. of the Lib., 1943–47, Head, Dept. Photographic Reprodct; Asst. Dir. Info. Div., Metallurgical Proj., Univ. of Chicago 1936–45. **Educ.:** Univ. of NC, 1931–35, AB (Math.), 1935–36, ABLS, Univ. of Chicago, 1941, MA (LS), 1948, PhD (LS). **Orgs.:** ALA: Cncl., Com. on Natl. Un. Cat., Photoreproduction. ARL: Bd. of Dir. (1961–64) (1970–71). Natl. Lib. of Med.: Bd. of Regents (1963–67). Natl. Adv. Comsn. on Libs. Ctr. for Resrch. Libs.: Bd. of Dir.: (1950–67), Ch. (1960–61). **Honors:** Amer. Acad. Arts and Sci., Fellow, 1976; AAAS, Fellow, 1968; ALA, Melvil Dewey Medal, 1954; ALA, Ralph Shaw Awd., 1976. **Pubns.:** *Research Libraries and Technology* (1973), *Patterns in the Use of Books in Large Research Libraries* (1969), "Current Research Library Issues," Monash Univ., Australia (Occas. Papers), (1978); "Contemporary Issues in Bibliographical Control," *Lib. Qtly,* (1977); Other books and articles. **Addr.:** Graduate Library School, The University of Chicago, Chicago, IL 60637.

Futas, Elizabeth (My. 8, 1944, New York, NY) Asst. Prof., Div. of Libnshp., Emory Univ., 1977–; Ref. Libn., Queens Coll., 1968–76; Adj. Lectr., Grad. Sch. of Lib. and Info. Sci., Rutgers Univ., 1974–77; Catlgr., Ford Fndn., 1967–68. **Educ.:** Brooklyn Coll., 1961–65, AB (Pol. Sci.); Univ. of MN, 1965–66, MALS; Rutgers Univ., 1974–80, PhD (LS). **Orgs.:** ALA: Cncl. (1978–82); Com. on the Status of Women in Libnshp. (1977–82); Task Force on Women (1974–81). Feminist Action Alliance. **Pubns.:** *Library Acquisition Policies and Procedures* (1977); Ed. Bd., *Serials for Libraries* (1979); "Searching Sequence for College Libraries," *Col. Bldg.* (1979); "MBO: History of an Idea," *LACUNY Jnl.* (Fall 1976). **Activities:** 1; 15, 20, 39; 95-Women's std. **Addr.:** Emory University, Division of Librarianship, Atlanta, GA 30322.

Fuxa, Mary A. (My. 28, 1923, Minneapolis, MN) Elem. Sch. Libn., Fargo Pub. Schs., 1963–, Tchr., 1946–63; Tchr., Staples (MN) Pub. Schs., 1943–46. **Educ.:** Moorhead State Univ., 1941–43, 1950–53, BS (Elem. Educ.); Univ. of MN, 1963–66, (LS minor); Purdue Univ., 1968–69, MS (Educ. Media). **Orgs.:** ALA: Treatment of Minority Grps. in Lib. Bks. and Other Instr. Mtrls. Com. (1970–73); AASL (Dir., Region IV, 1974–76). ND LA: Secy. (1973–75); Sch. Lib. Sect. (Ch., 1971–72). Natl. Educ. Assn. ND Educ. Assn. Delta Kappa Gamma. **Activities:** 10; 21, 31, 32 **Addr.:** 402 15th Ave. S., Fargo, ND 58103.

Fyan, Loleta Dawson (My. 14, 1894, Clinton, IA) Retired, 1961–; State Libn., MI State Lib., 1941–61; Secy., MI State Bd. for Libs., 1941–61; Libn., Wayne Cnty. Lib., Detroit, 1921–41; Ref. Asst., Detroit Pub. Lib., 1920–21. **Educ.:** Wellesley Coll., 1911–15, BA (Bot., Msc.); West. Rsv. Univ., 1919–20, Cert. (LS). **Orgs.:** ALA: Pres. (1951–52). MI LA: Pres. (1934–35). Amer. Assn. of State Libs.: Pres. (1960–61). AALS. **Activities:** 9, 13; 17 **Addr.:** 2700 Burcham Dr., #537, East Lansing, MI 48823.*

Fyfe, Janet Hunter (Ap. 29, 1929, Blantyre, Scotland) Prof., Sch. of Lib. & Info. Sci., Univ. of West. ON, 1970–; Head, Dept. of Bibl. & Book Sel., Murray Meml. Lib., Univ. of SK, 1966–70, Coord. of Branch Libs., 1965–66; Ref. Libn., Univ. of SK, Regina, 1963–65; Sr. Asst. Libn., Univ. of St. Andrews, Scotland, 1959–63, Asst. Libn., 1958–59; Branch Libn., Borough of Heston & Isleworth Pub. Libs., 1957–58. **Educ.:** Univ. of Edinburgh, 1947–50, MA; Univ. of Guelph, 1971–76, PhD (Hist.); 1957, ALA; 1960, FLA. **Orgs.:** Assn. of Can. Archvsts. LA (UK). Can. LA. SK LA: Cnclr. (1964–66); Ch., Bltn. Com. & Ed., *SK Lib.,* (1966–70). Other orgs. Amer. Hist. Assn. Conf. on British Std. Can. Assn. for Scottish Std. Scottish Labour Hist. Socty. Other orgs. **Honors:** Inst. for Advnc. Std. in the Hum., Univ. of Edinburgh, Visit. Resrch. Flwshp., 1979. **Pubns.:** Ed., *Autobiography of John McAdam (1806-1883), with Selected Letters* (1980); *Directory of Special Collections in Canadian Libraries,* (1968); "The Scottish Volunteers with Garibaldi," *Scottish Hist. Review* (O. 1978); "The North British Review: Advocate of Italian Independence," *Scottish Tradition* (1976); "Herder in English," *Stechert-Hafner Book News* (N. 1969); "Scottish Collections in Canadian Libraries," *Lib. Review* (Aut. 1965). **Activities:** 2, 11; 15, 41, 45; 55, 85, 92 **Addr.:** 1083, Richmond St., London, ON N6A 3K3 Canada.

G

Gabbert, Gretchen Wilhelmina (D. 9, 1941, Sioux Falls, SD) Libn., Jack G. Raub Co., 1980–; Libn., St. Anthony HS, 1973–80; Libn., Santa Ana Pub. Lib., 1971–; Archvst., Pac. Mutual Life Insn., 1979–. **Educ.:** CA State Univ., Fullerton, 1966–69, BA (Fr.); Univ. of South. CA, 1969–71, MS (LS); Alliance Française, Paris, 1964–65, Dipl. (Fr.). **Orgs.:** ALA. CA LA. SLA. ASIS. Los Angeles Cnty. Msm. of Art. Univ. of S. CA Alum. Assn. **Pubns.:** Slide tape programs. **Activities:** 9, 10; 31, 39, 48; 55, 76, 95-French. **Addr.:** 206 Maui Ave., Santa Ana, CA 92704.

Gabrielian, Leon (Jl. 17, 1933, Tehran, Iran) Slavic Cat. Libn., Univ. of CA, Los Angeles, 1973–, Acq. Libn., 1966–72; Russ. Transl., Translavic Assoc., 1960–62. **Educ.:** Maryville Coll., 1955–60, BA (Grmn.); Univ. of CA, Los Angeles, 1960–64, MA (Slavic Lang.), 1964–66, MLS. **Orgs.:** ALA. CA LA. Libn. Assn. of Univ. of CA. Amer. Assn. for the Advnc. of Slavic Std. **Pubns.:** Trans., *Organization of Work Therapy in the Neuropsychiatric Hospital* (1960); "The Saltykov-Shchedrin State Public Library," *CA Libn.* (O. 1977); Trans., "The Rarest Reprint" *Jnl. of Lib. Hist.* (Ap. 1973); "Russian Revolutionary Literature on Microfilm," *UCLA Libn.* (Mr.–Ap. 1978); "Russian History & Culture on Microfilm," *UCLA Libn.* (F. 1979). **Activities:** 1; 15, 20, 46; 92 **Addr.:** 6029 S. La Cienega Blvd., Los Angeles, CA 90056.

Gadula, Marie Anne (S. 26, 1951, Toronto, ON) Libn., McLeod Young Weir Ltd., 1979–; Libn., Marsh and McLennan Ltd., 1976–79. **Educ.:** Univ. of Waterloo, 1970–74, HBA (Hist., Fine Arts); Univ of Toronto, 1974–76, MLS. **Orgs.:** SLA: Toronto Chap., PR Rep. (1979–80). Can. LA. **Activities:** 12; 38, 39, 41; 59, 77, 86 **Addr.:** McLeod Young Weir Ltd., P.O. Box 433, Commercial Union Tower, Toronto Dominion Centre, Toronto, ON M5K 1M2 Canada.

Gaeddert, Barbara Knisely (Mr. 29, 1942, Sandusky, OH) Assoc. Cat. Libn. II, Univ. of KS, 1974–; Acq. Libn., Univ. of IA, 1972–74, Msc. Catlgr., 1970–72; Readers Srvs. Libn., Deere and Co. Lib., 1965–67. **Educ.:** Oberlin Coll., 1960–64, (Math.); Case West. Rsv. Univ., 1964–65, MSLS. **Orgs.:** ALA. KS LA. Msc. LA. **Honors:** Beta Phi Mu. **Pubns.:** "The Classification and Cataloging of Sound Recordings," *Msc. LA Tech. Pubn.* (1977). **Activities:** 1; 20, 44; 92 **Addr.:** Rural Rte. #3, Baldwin City, KS 66006.

Gaertner, Donell J. (S. 30, 1932, St. Louis, MO) Dir., St. Louis Cnty. Lib., 1968–, Asst. Dir., 1964–68, Admin. Asst., 1957–64. **Educ.:** Washington Univ., 1950–54, AB (Econ.); Univ. of IL, 1954–55, MLS. **Orgs.:** MO LA: Pres. (1964–65); Ch., MO Lib. Network Corp. Com. (1981). ALA: Com. on Accred. (1975). **Honors:** Beta Phi Mu, 1955; Omicron Delta Gamma, 1954. **Activities:** 9; 17 **Addr.:** St. Louis County Library, 1640 So. Lindbergh Blvd., St. Louis, MO 63131.

Gagne, Gerard J. (Ja. 5, 1922, Thompson, CT) Assoc. Univ. Libn., Tech. Srvs. Southeast. MA Univ., 1976–; Acq. Libn., 1971–76, Lib. Dir., Assumption Coll., 1967–71. **Educ.:** Assumption Coll., 1962–65, BA (Educ.) Univ. of Pittsburgh, 1967–69 MLS (LS). ARL Mgt. Skills Inst., 1978. **Orgs.:** ALA: ACRL. CLENE. **Activities:** 1; 15, 17, 46 **Addr.:** 718 Russells Mills Rd., So. Dartmouth, MA 02747.

Gaines, Abner J. (Mr. 31, 1923, Atlantic City, NJ) Rare Bks., Spec. Cols. Libn., Univ. of RI, 1977–, Assoc. Univ. Libn., 1971–77, Assoc. Libn. Readers Srvs., 1963–71; Chief Biblgphr., Temple Univ., 1958–63; Libn., S. Asia Reg. Std. Lib., Univ. of PA, 1952–58; Head, Ref. Dept., NJ State Lib., 1950–51, Sr. Libn., 1947–50. **Educ.:** Univ. of WI, 1940–43, Assoc. (Intl. Rel.); Univ. of MI, 1943–44, AB (Hist.); Columbia Univ., 1946–47, BSLS; Univ. of PA, 1948–51, MA (Hist.). **Orgs.:** ALA. New Eng. LA. RI LA. Frdm. to Read Fndn. RI Hist. Socty. Pettasquamscutt Hist. Socty. Amer. Cvl. Liberties Un. AAUP. **Pubns.:** "Recruiting for Librarianship," *Wilson Lib. Bltn.* (1951); "New Jersey," *Britannica Book of the Year* (1951); various bk. reviews, *Lib. Jnl.* (1947–51); ed. bd., *Micro. Review* (1972–73). **Activities:** 1; 15, 45; 55, 57, 74 **Addr.:** 116 Biscuit City Rd., Kingston, RI 02881.

Gaines, Ervin James (D. 8, 1916, New York, NY) Dir., Cleveland Pub. Lib., 1974–; Dir., Minneapolis Pub. Lib., 1964–74; Asst. Dir., Boston Pub. Lib., 1958–64. **Educ.:** Columbia Univ., 1936–42, BS (Eng.), 1946–47, MA (Eng.), 1947–52, PhD (Lit.). **Orgs.:** ALA: Cncl.; Int. Frdm. Com. (Ch., 1966–67). OH LA: Legis. Com. Urban Libs. Cncl.: Exec. Dir. (1973–77). Intl. Assn. of Metro. Libs. **Pubns.:** Various articles. **Activities:** 9; 17 **Addr.:** Cleveland Public Library, 325 Superior Ave., Cleveland, OH 44114.

Gaines, James Edwin, Jr. (F. 21, 1938, Dalton, GA) Head Libn., VA Military Inst., 1976–; Lib. Dir., Birmingham-Southern Coll., 1968–74; Asst. Libn. for Tech. Srvs., Antioch Coll., 1965–68; Asst. to the Head of Pub. Srvs., Univ. of Cincinnati Lib., 1964–65; Tchr., Marist Coll. HS, 1961–62. **Educ.:** Emory Univ., 1957–61, AB (Eng.), 1962–64, MLS; FL State Univ., 1974–76, PhD (LS). **Orgs.:** ALA. ACRL. SELA. VA LA: Ch., Coll. and Univ. Sect., (1979–80). South. Assn. of Coll. and Sch.: Visiting Com., (1974–). **Honors:** Beta Phi Mu, 1976. **Pubns.:** "Financial Aspects of Reclassification," in *Reclassification: Rationale and Problems; Proceedings . . . ,* (1968); "Reclassification in the Libraries of the Great Lakes Colleges Association," *Coll. and Resrch. Libs.* (Jl. 1968). **Activities:** 1; 17, 46 **Addr.:** Preston Library, Virginia Military Institute, Lexington, VA 24450.

Gaines, Robert F. (Ap. 26, 1942, Murfreesboro, TN) Head Libn., Docum. and Micro. Div., Univ. of NC, Greensboro, 1974–; Asst. Prof. (Hist.), Tusculum Coll., 1966–72. **Educ.:** Vanderbilt Univ., 1960–64, BA (Hist.), 1964–66 M.A.T. (Hist.) Univ. of TN, Knoxville, 1967–73 (Hist.), 1973–74, MSLS. **Orgs.:** NC LA: Exec. Bd. (1976–77); Docum. Sect. (Ch., 1976–77); Govt. Rel. Com. (1978–79); Lib. Resrcs. Com. (1980–81). ALA: RASD, Outstand. Ref. Bks. Com. (1976–78); GODORT, Constn. Com. (1977–78). NC Gov. Conf. on Lib. and Info. Srvs.: Display Comm. (Ch., 1978). **Pubns.:** "Recent Developments In Depository Systems For State Government Publications," *Documents To The People,* (N. 1978); "A North Carolina State Documents Depository System: An Update," *NC Libs.* (Spr. 1978). Reviews. **Activities:** 1; 29, 33, 49-Online Srch.; 78, 80 **Addr.:** Jackson Library, University of North Carolina, Greensboro, NC 27412.

Gaines, Willene J. (S. 19, 1936, Columbus, GA) Chief, Tech. Srvs. Branch, US Dept. of Cmrc. Lib., 1970–; Catlgr., US Dept. of Hlth., Educ., Welfare Lib., 1966–69; Catlgr. and Ref. Libn., VA State Coll., 1958–66. **Educ.:** Prairie View A & M Coll., 1953–57, BA (Eng.); Atlanta Univ., 1957–58, MSLS. **Orgs.:** ALA. Fed. Lib. and Info. Netwk: Taskforce on OCLC Error Reports (1979–80). Potomac Tech. Procs. Libns. Assn.: Bd. (1977–78). Washington Chap., National Epicurean's Inc.: Pres. (1972–1976). **Activities:** 1, 4; 15, 20, 29; 59, 63 **Addr.:** U.S. Dept. of Commerce Library, Washington, DC 20230.

Gaiser, Rosemary (Ap. 6, 1948, Cincinnati, OH) Head, Sci. and Indus. Dept., Pub. Lib. of Cincinnati, 1977–; Head, Cincinnati Reg. Lib. for the Blind and Phys. handcpd., 1974–77, Libn., Gvt. and Bus. Dept., 1971–74. **Educ.:** Univ. of Cincinnati, 1966–70, BM (Msc.); Univ. of KY, 1970–71, MSLS. **Orgs.:** SLA. **Activities:** 9; 15, 17, 39; 91 **Addr.:** Public Library of Cincinnati, 800 Vine St., Cincinnati, OH 45202.

Gal, Imre (D. 1, 1917, Alberti, Hungary) Prof., Dir. of Libs., Bloomfield Coll., 1968–; Resrch., Dept. Head, Manhattan Coll., 1959–68; Attorney at Law, Budapest Bar Assn., Hungary, 1941–50. **Educ.:** Royal Hungarian Univ., Budapest, 1941, LLB, JD; CT State Coll., 1959, MS; Columbia Univ., 1959, Cert.; NY Univ., 1971, PhD (Pol. Sci., Intl. Law); MD Univ., 1971, Cert.; Rutgers Univ., 1971, Cert. **Orgs.:** Amer. Socty. of Intl. Law. Amer. Mgt. Assn. ALA. NJ LA. AAUP. Amer. Pol. Sci. Assn. Intl. Std. Assn. Socty. of Syst. Resrch. **Honors:** NY Univ., Outstan. Schol., Fndrs. Day Cert., 1972. **Pubns.:** "The Function of UNCITRAL in the Progressive Development of the Law of International Trade," micro. (1972); *The Development of American-Hungarian Diplomatic Relations* (1963); "The Commercial Law of Nations and the Law of International Trade," *Cornell Intl. Law Jnl.* (1972); "History Repeat Itself," *Bltn.* (1969). **Addr.:** Bloomfield College Library, 467 Franklin St., Bloomfield, NJ 07003.

Gale, Sarah E. (Boston, MA) Head, Acq. Dept., IN State Univ. Lib. (Terre Haute), 1978–; Head, Srch. Dept., Univ. of PA Lib., 1969–78, Ref. Libn., Univ. of PA Lib., 1966–69, Ref. Libn., Univ. of Rochester, 1963–66. **Educ.:** Mount Holyoke Coll., 1957–61, AB cum laude (Fr.); Univ. of MI, 1961–63, MA (LS). **Orgs.:** ALA: RTSD, Pre-Order and Pre-Cat. Bibl. Srch. Disc. Grp. (Ch., 1979–80). **Activities:** 1; 15 **Addr.:** Cunningham Memorial Library, Indiana State University, Terre Haute, IN 47809.

Galejs, John E. (Jy. 18, 1927, Sinole, Latvia) Asst. Dir. for Resrcs., IA State Univ. Lib., 1974–, Asst. Dir. for Resrcs. and Tech. Srvs., 1969–74, Coord., Resrcs. Dev., and Head, Serials Dept., 1968–69, Head, Serials Dept., 1962–68. **Educ.:** Univ. of MN, 1951–53, BA (Intl. Rel.), 1953–55, MA (Intl. Rel.), 1957–58 MALS. **Orgs.:** ALA: RTSD, Policy and Research Com. (1980–81), Lib. Mtrls. Price Index Com. (1973–79). IA LA: Srv. to Non-User Com. (1977–79). IA Hist. Mtrls. Pres. Socty. AAUP. Assn. for the Adv. of Baltic Stds. **Pubns.:** "Application of the Micrographic Catalog Retrieval System in the Iowa State University Library," *Lib. Resrcs. and Tech. Srvs.,* (Fall, 1971); "Economics of Serials Exchange," Lib. Resrcs. and Tech. Srvs.

PROFESSIONAL ACTIVITIES: Institutions: 1. Acad. lib.; 2. Arch.; 3. Assn.; 4. Fed./Gvt. lib.; 5. Inst. lib.; 6. Mfr./Suppl.; 7. Milit. lib.; 8. Musm.; 9. Pub. lib.; 10. Sch. lib.; 11. Sch. of lib. sci.; 12. Spec. lib.; 13. State lib.; 14. (other). **Functions/Activities:** 15. Acq./Col. dev.; 16. Adult srvs.; 17. Admin.; 18. Apprais.; 19. Archit./Bldgs.; 20. Cat./Class.; 21. Chld. srvs.; 22. Circ.; 23. Cons./Pres.; 24. Consult.; 25. Cont. ed.; 26. Educ. lib. sci.; 27. Ext. srvs.; 28. Fund/Grants; 29. Gvt. pubs.; 30. Indx./Abs.; 31. Instr. lib. use; 32. Media srvs.; 33. Micro.; 34. Netwks./Coop.; 35. Persnl.; 36. PR; 37. Publshg.; 38. Recs. mgt.; 39. Ref. srvs.; 40. Repro.; 41. Resrch.; 42. Review.; 43. Secur.; 44. Serials; 45. Spec. col.; 46. Tech. srvs.; 47. Trustees/Bds.; 48. YA srvs.; 49. (other).

(Fall, 1972); Reviews. **Activities:** 1; 15, 17, 45; 54, 92 **Addr.:** Iowa State University Library, Iowa State University, Ames, IA 50011.

Gallagher, Barbara A. (My. 2, 1937, Chicago, IL) Head, Lib. Srvs., Amer. Chem. Socty., 1960–; Docum. Anal., Armour and Co., 1959–60. **Educ.:** St. Xavier Coll., 1955–59, BA (Chem.). **Orgs.:** SLA: DC Chap., Pic. Grp. (Treas., 1978–). **Pubns.:** "Searching US Government Documents," *Advances in Chemistry Series* (1961). **Activities:** 12; 17, 39; 60, 75, 91 **Addr.:** American Chemical Society, Library, 1155 – 16th St., N.W., Washington, DC 20036.

Gallagher, Connell Bernard (My. 13, 1944, Brooklyn, NY) Univ. Archvst., Cur. of Mss., Univ. of VT, 1978–; Arch. Asst., Univ. of IL 1977–78; Mss. Libn., Univ. of VT, 1970–78; Arch. Asst., State Hist. Socty. of WI, 1969–70. **Educ.:** Pace Coll., 1963–66, BA (Eng.); Univ. of WI, 1966–70 MA (Eng.); Univ. of IL, 1977–78, MS (LS). Ohio Hist. Socty., 1971, Cert. (Arch. Admin.). **Orgs.:** VT LA: Pres. (1980); VP (1979). New Eng. Archvsts: Secy. (1979–). SAA: Various Coms. (1972–). ALA. Ctr. For Resrch. on VT: Exec. Bd., (1978–). **Honors:** Beta Phi Mu. **Pubns.:** Contrib., *Look Around St. George and Shelburne, Vermont* (1975); Contrib., *A Union List of Local Documents: Champaign, Urbana and Champaign County, Illinois* (1979). **Activities:** 1; 45; 55, 57 **Addr.:** Bailey/Howe Library, University of Vermont, Burlington, VT 05405.

Gallagher, D. Nora (Mr. 23, 1918) Dir. of Libs., Adelphi Univ., 1963–, Libn., 1946–63, Actg. Libn., 1945–46, Circ. Libn., 1944–45; Lib. Asst., Hunter Coll., 1943–44. **Educ.:** Hunter Coll., 1937–41, AB (Eng.); Columbia Univ., 1941–43, BLS; Fordham Univ., 1946–50 (Hist.); City of NY Grad. Ctr., 1971–75 (Info. Sci.). **Orgs.:** Nassau Cnty. LA: Pres. (1952–54). NY LA: Coll. and Univ. Div. (Pres., 1961–62); Cncl. (1962–63). ALA: AV Com. (1965–67); Ref. Srv. Div. Com. on Wilson Indxs. (1952–72); Rcrt. Com. (1951). Long Island Lib. Resrcs. Cncl.: Bd. Trustees (1965–71); Pres. (1970–71). Various other orgs. Nassau Cnty. Hist. Socty. Soroptimist Intl. Long Island Bk. Collectors. **Activities:** 1; 17 **Addr.:** 708 Westbury Ave., Westbury, NY 11590.

Gallagher, Rev. Dennis Joseph, O.S.A. (Mr. 30, 1935, Bryn Mawr, PA) Asst. Prof., LS, Couns., Resident Students, Villanova Univ., 1975–, Dir., Resident Students, Malvern Prep. Sch., 1970–72, Libn., Tchr., Couns., 1969–72; Tchr., Libn., Austin Prep. Sch., 1966–69, Dir. of Readg. Srvs., 1965–69, Dir., AV, 1965–67; various asst. libn. positions, 1961–69. **Educ.:** Villanova Univ., 1956–60, BA (Phil.); Cath. Univ. of Amer., 1972–75, PhD (Admin.); Villanova Univ., 1961–65, MSLS; Augustinian Coll., DC, 1965, MA (Relig. Educ.); Cmwlth. of PA, 1972, Cert. (Sch. Libnshp.); Villanova Univ., Amer. Mgt. Assn., 1978–79, Cert. (Bus. Mgt.). **Orgs.:** ALA. AALS. Augustinian Educ. Assn. Cath. LA: Coll. and Univ. Sect., Newmann Chap. (Ch., 1979–), East. PA Unit, Vice-Ch., Secy. (1977–79); Lib. Educ. Div. (Secy.-Treas., 1977–79). Intl. Readg. Assn. Villanova LS Alum. Assn.: Treas. (1969–72). **Pubns.:** *The Emerging Role of the College Librarian in the Context of Selected Innovative Educational Practices as Perceived by a Selected Sample of Librarians and Teachers* (1975). **Activities:** 11; 15, 17, 20; 55, 63, 75 **Addr.:** Graduate Dept. of Library Science, Villanova University, Villanova, PA 19085.

Gallagher, Marian Gould (Ag. 29, 1914, Everett, WA) Retired; Law Libn., Univ. of WA, 1944–81; Prof. (Law), 1953–; Assoc. Prof. (Law), 1948–53; Asst. Prof. (Law), 1944–48; Law Libn., Instr. (Law), Univ. of UT, 1939–44. **Educ.:** Whitman Coll., 1931–32; Univ. of WA, 1932–37, AB, LLB, 1937–39, MLS. **Orgs.:** AALL: Pres. (1954–55). ALA. WA LA. Pac. Northwest LA. WHCOLIS: Adv. Com. (1976–). Amer. Bar Assn.: Legal Educ. and Admis. to the Bar Sect., Accred. Com. (1975–79), Cncl. (1979–). WA State Bar Assn. Seattle-King Cnty. Bar Assn. Amer. Bar Fndn.: Flw. **Honors:** Univ. of WA, Sch. of Libnshp., Disting. Alum., 1970; AALL, Disting. Srv. Awd., 1966; Whitman Coll., Merit Alum Awd., 1981; Order of the Coif; U.S. Pres.'s Adv. Com. on Libs. (1967–68). **Activities:** 1, 12; 17; 77 **Addr.:** 1000 8th Ave., Seattle, WA 98104.

Galligan, Sara A. (Je. 18, 1949, Oak Park, IL) Head Ref. Dept., Univ. of MI, Dearborn Lib., 1976–, Ref. Libn., 1972–76. **Educ.:** MI State Univ., 1967–71, BA (Soc. Sci.); Wayne State Univ., 1971–72, MSLS; Univ. of MI, 1977–80, MPA (Pub. Admin.). **Orgs.:** MI LA: Ref. Caucus (Ch., 1980). ALA: Coop. Ref. Srvs. Com. (1978–82). State WHCOLIS: West. Wayne Cnty. (Del., 1979). **Honors:** Phi Beta Kappa, 1971; ALA, JMRT, Shirley Olofson Meml., 1976. **Pubns.:** "Infopass: Some Organizational Concerns of a Local Cooperative Reference Program," ERIC (1980); "Reference Department Policy Statement," ERIC (1977). **Activities:** 1; 17, 31, 39; 63, 75, 92 **Addr.:** University of Michigan, Dearborn Library, 4901 Evergreen, Dearborn, MI 48128.

Gallinger, Janice (S. 2, 1925, Melrose, MA) Consult., 1981–; Coll. Libn., Plymouth State Coll., 1965–81; Asst. Libn., Erie Cnty. Tech. Inst., 1957–65; Remedial Elem. Tchr., Leslie-Dearborn Sch., 1955–56; Admin. Asst., U.S. Frgn. Srv., Rangoon, 1950–55. **Educ.:** Tufts Univ., 1944–48, AB (Hist.); Carnegie Inst. of Tech., 1956–57, MLS. **Orgs.:** Acad. Libns. of NH: Ch. (1970) Bylaws Com. (1970). ALA: Cncl. (1970–73); ACRL, AV Com. (1971–73). New Eng. Lib. Info. Netwk.: Exec. Com. (1974–77, 1978–79). NH State Adv. Cncl. on Libs. Various other orgs. **Honors:** Beta Phi Mu. **Pubns.:** Ed., *Project Mediabase* (1979); *Educational Media Selection Centers and Academic Libraries* ERIC (1974); "The Reasons for Media," audio tape rec. (1972). **Activities:** 1; 17, 19, 32 **Addr.:** 11 Rogers St., Plymouth, NH 03264.

Gallivan, Marion F. Van Orsdale (D. 2, 1940, Buffalo, NY) Branch Mgr., Erie Cnty. Lib. Syst., 1981–; Curric. Libn., Gannon Univ., 1978–80; Ref. Libn., Behrend Coll. of PA State, 1978–79; Asst. Dir., Mercer Cnty. Lib., Trenton, NJ, 1974–77; various lib. positions, Buffalo and Erie Cnty. Pub. Lib., 1963–74. **Educ.:** Syracuse Univ., 1958–62, BA (Hist., LS), 1958–59, MSLS; Gannon Univ., 1978–81, MBA. **Orgs.:** ALA: Chld. Srvs. Div., Print and Poster Eval. Com. (Ch., 1974–77); Resrch. and Dev. Com. (1971–74). PA LA: Lib. Dev. Com. (1980–). PA Citizens for Better Libs.: Bd. (1980–). Frnds. of the Erie Cnty. Lib.: Pres. (1978–80). AAUW. Natl. Org. for Women. Leag. of Women Voters. **Honors:** Beta Phi Mu. **Pubns.:** *Fun for Kids, An Index to Children's Craft Books* (1981); "Research in Children's Services, An Annotated Bibliography," *Top of the News* (Ap. 1974). **Activities:** 9; 16, 17, 27; 59, 74, 93 **Addr.:** 427 Colleen Dr., Erie, PA 16505.

Galloway, Linda Bennett (Dixon, KY) Dir. of Media Srvs., Wayne Cnty. (NC) Schs., 1971–; Libn., Goldsboro (NC) Schs., 1967–71; Lib. Coord., Webster Cnty (KY) Schs., 1961–67; Ed., Hist. Div., 15th Army, Bad Nauheim (Germ.), 1945–46; Libn., US Army, (Rheims, Fr.) 1944–45. **Educ.:** Stephens Coll., 1934–36, AA, Univ. of IL, 1936–38, AB, (Hist.); 1938–39, BLS; Vanderbilt Univ., 1948–49, MA (Hist.). **Orgs.:** NC Assn. of Sch. Libns. ALA. SE LA. Educ. Media Assn. Walnut Creek (NC) Cntry. Club. American Red Cross Delta Kappa Gamma: Lcl. Chap. (Secy., 1978–80). Daughters of the American Revolution: Secy. (1970–72). **Pubns.:** *Andrew Jackson, Jr., Son of a President* (1966); various articles. **Activities:** 10; 17, 19, 24 **Addr.:** 105 Wooten Point Rd., Goldsboro, NC 27530.

Galloway, R. Dean (F. 26, 1922, Dinuba, CA) Lib. Dir., CA State Coll., Stanislaus, 1960–; Head, Tech. Srvs., Humboldt State Coll., 1958–60; Libn., Inst. for Admin. Affairs, Univ. of Tehran, 1956–58; Acq. Libn., Humboldt State Coll., 1950–56. **Educ.:** Humboldt State Coll., 1941–47, AB (Soc. Sci.); Univ. of South. CA, 1949–50, MS (LS); Univ. of CA, Berkeley, 1972–75 (LS). **Orgs.:** ALA. ASIS. CA LA. AAUP. CA Fac. Assn. **Pubns.:** Ed., *Hunted Down* (1975); "Rowena Granice," *Pac. Histn.* (Spr. 1980); "Status or Stasis," *Amer. Libs.* (Je. 1979); "ILL Can Be Cost Effective," *LJ Spec. Rpt.* (1979); "Library Cooperation at the Grass Roots," *Jnl. of Acad. Libnshp.* (1979). **Activities:** 1; 15, 17, 41 **Addr.:** California State College, Stanislaus, Turlock, CA 95380.

Galloway, Sarah Beth (Mr. 17, 1935, Crescent, OK) Lib. Dir., Roswell Pub. Lib., 1980–; Coord., Pub. Srvs., Davis Cnty. Lib., 1971–80; Cat. Dept., Univ. of UT, Marriott Lib., 1970–71; Tchr., Rigby and Bonneville HS, 1956–65. **Educ.:** UT State Univ., 1953, 1956–60, BS (Fam. Life); Brigham Young Univ., 1976–78, MLS; States of ID, UT, Basic Prof. Sec. Tchg. Cert. **Orgs.:** ALA. Mt. Plains LA. UT LA: PR Com. (Ch., 1978–79). Pecos Valley LA: Pres. Various other orgs. **Honors:** Beta Phi Mu, 1978. **Activities:** 9; 17, 36, 39; 68 **Addr.:** Box 524, Roswell, NM 88201–0524.

Galneder, Mary H. (Je. 29, 1936, Detroit, MI) Map Libn., Cartographic Lab., Univ. of WI, 1965–; Map Libn., Morris Lib., South. IL Univ., 1961–65. **Educ.:** Wayne State Univ., 1955–59, BA (Geo.); South. IL Univ., 1960–63, MA (Geo.); Univ. of WI, 1966–71, MLS. **Orgs.:** West. Assn. Map Libs. Assn. of Can. Map Libs. SLA: Geo. and Map Div., *Bltn.* Bk. Review Ed. (1969–); Ch.-Elect, Prog. Ch. (1970–71); Ch. (1971–72); Hons. Com. (Ch., 1979–80). Madison Area Lib. Cncl.: Bd. of Dirs. (1972–73); Bd. Secy. (1973). Amer. Congs. on Surveying and Mapping. **Honors:** SLA, Geo. and Map Div., Hons. Awd. for Outstan. Achvmt., 1978. **Pubns.:** Jt. auth., "Maps and Map Collections," *Nonprint Media in Academic Libraries* (1975); "The Recataloging/Reclassification Project at the Map and Air Photo Library, University of Wisconsin-Madison," *SLA Geo. and Map Div. Bltn.* (Je. 1977); jt. auth., "Anglo-American State and Provincial Thematic Atlases: A Survey and Bibliography," *Can. Cartographer* (Je. 1969). **Activities:** 1, 12; 15, 17, 20; 70 **Addr.:** Map Library, Science Hall, University of Wisconsin, 550 N. Park St., Madison, WI 53706.

Galvin, Hoyt R. (F. 26, 1911, Pleasantville, IA) Lib. Bldg. Consult., 1956–; Interim Dir., Pub. Lib. of Columbus and Franklin Cnty. (OH), 1978–79; Interim Dir., Atlanta Pub. Lib., 1976; Dir., Pub. Lib. of Charlotte and Mecklenburg Cnty. (NC), 1940–70. **Educ.:** Simpson Coll., 1928–32 BA (Phys.); Univ. of IL, 1932–34 BS (LS). Brookings Inst. Ctr. for Adv. Std., 1966–67 Cert. (Urban Std.). **Orgs.:** ALA: Second VP (1969–70); Lib. Admin. Div., Pres. (1965–66). SELA: Pres. (1962–64). NC LA: Pres. (1942–43). AL LA: Pres. (1939–1940). Rotary: Charlotte, NC: Pres. (1949–50). Jaycees. NC Adult Educ. Assn.: Pres. (1957–58). **Honors:** SELA, Outstand. Pub. Libn. Awd., 1970. Simpson Coll. Alum. Achvmt. Awd., 1970. Natl. Conf. of Christians and Jews, Cert. of Recog. **Pubns.:** *The Small Public Library Building* (1959). Ed., *Planning a Library Building: the Major Steps* (Conf. Procs.) (1955). "Public Library Buildings," *Lib. Jnl.* (Anl., 1968–78). "Films in Public Libraries, pt. II," *Lib. Jnl.* (O. 15, 1947). **Activities:** 1, 9; 19 **Addr.:** 2259 Vernon Dr., Charlotte, NC 28211.

Galvin, Thomas J. (D. 30, 1932, Arlington, MA) Dean, Prof., Sch. of Lib. and Info. Sci., Univ. of Pittsburgh, 1974–; Assoc. Dir., Sch. of LS, Simmons Coll., 1962–74, Asst. Dir. of Libs., 1959–62; Dir., Abbot Pub. Lib. (Marblehead, MA), 1956–59; Ref. Libn., Boston Univ. Lib., 1954–56. **Educ.:** Columbia Univ., 1950–54 AB (Eng.); Simmons Coll., 1954–56 S.M. (LS); Case West. Rsrv. Univ., 1966–73, PhD (LS). **Orgs.:** ALA: Pres. (1979–80); RASD, Com. on Wilson Indexes (Ch., 1974–76), Ref. and Subscrpn. Bks. Rev. Com. (Ch., 1974–76); Cncl. (1974–81); LED, Pres. (1974–75). ASIS. SLA. Freedom to Read Fndn.: Bd. of Dir. (1978–80). Various other orgs. AAUP. Tennessee Squires. **Honors:** Case West. Rsrv. Univ., Disting. Alum., 1979; Simmons Coll., Alum. Achvmt. Awd., 1978; ALA, Isadore Gilbert Mudge Cit., 1972; Beta Phi Mu; Other honors. **Pubns.:** Jt. ed., *Excellence in School Media Programs* (1980); Jt. ed., *The Structure and Governance of Library Networks* (1979); Jt. ed., *The On-line Revolution* in Libraries (1978); Jt. ed., Library Resource Sharing (1977); *The Case Method in Library Education* (1973); other monographs; numerous *Jnl.* articles; Twenty Unpubl. Consult. Rpts. **Activities:** 1, 9; 17, 26, 39; 63, 75 **Addr.:** School of Library and Information Science, University of Pittsburgh, LIS Bldg., 135 North Bellefield, Pittsburgh, PA 15260.

Gamaluddin, Ahmad Fouad M. (O. 4, 1935, Cairo, Egypt) Prof. (LS), Clarion State Coll., 1970–; Catlgr., Cleveland Publ. Lib., 1967; Intern., Harvard Univ. Lib., 1964–65, Head, Mss. Dept., Egyptian Natl. Lib., 1957–63. **Educ.:** Cairo Univ. (Egypt) 1953–57 BA (LS), West. MI Univ., 1965–66 MSLS; Univ. of Pittsburgh, 1968–1973, PhD. HS of Foreign Langs. Cairo, 1958–63, Dipl. (Russ.). **Orgs.:** PA School Libns. Assn.: Stud. Com. (1978–). AALS: Liason to Clarion State Coll. (1975–). ALA. PA LA: Northwest Chap. (PR Ch., 1976–78). Univ. of Pittsburgh, Sch. of Lib. Sci.: Alum. Bd. of Dir. (1979–). Pittsburgh Reg. Lib. Ctr.: Trustee (1977–). **Pubns.:** "LMTA In Pennsylvania: Pandora's Box or Panacea," *Lrng. and Media* (Sum. 1976). **Activities:** 1, 9; 17, 20, 26; 63, 89 **Addr.:** School of Library Science, Clarion State College, Clarion, PA 16214.

Gambee, Budd Leslie (N. 16, 1917, Auburn, NY) Prof. (LS), Univ. of NC, 1963–; Visit. Lectr. (LS), Univ. of MI, 1962–63; Assoc. Prof. (LS), SUNY Albany, 1958–61; Asst. Prof. (LS), Ball State Univ., 1951–58; Chief AV Libn., WV Univ. Lib., 1948–51; Various positions, Detroit Pub. Lib., 1943–48; Ref Libn., Aurora (IL) Pub. Lib., 1941–43. **Educ.:** Univ. of Rochester, 1937–40, BA with Distinction (Eng.); Univ. of MI, 1940–41, BA (LS), 1945–49, MA (LS), 1957–1963, PhD (LS). **Orgs.:** ALA: LHRT (Ch., 1977–78); Lib. Educ. Div./Tchrs. Sect. (Secy.-Treas., 1968–69); Schol. and Awds. Com. (Ch., 1973–74). SELA. AALS. NCLA: Schol. Com. (1976–78); Com. on Educ. for Libnshp. (Ch., 1972–74), Secy., 1970–72). NC Art Socty. Chapel Hill Hist. Socty. **Honors:** Beta Phi Mu, 1963; Fulbright Lectrshps, LS, Cairo (1952–53) and Tehran (1974–75). **Pubns.:** *Return Engagement: The Role of American Librarians at the Second International Library Conference, London, 1877* (1977). *Non-Book Materials as Library Resources* (1967); *Frank Leslie and His Illustrated Newspaper* 1855–1860. (1964). Jt.-auth., "Impressions of the Centenary", *Jnl. of Lib. Hist.* (Spr. 1978). Other articles. **Activities:** 1, 10; 32, 33, 45; 57, 67, 70 **Addr.:** School of Library Science, University of North Carolina, Chapel Hill, NC 27514.

Ganning, Mary Kay Daniels (Je. 15, 1944, Orange, NJ) Sr. Bibl. Systs. Spec., Lib. of Congs., 1978–, Sr. Libn. Info. Systs. Spec., 1977–78, Libn., Info. Syst. Spec., 1974–77, Sr. Info. Systs. Resrch. Anal., 1969–74, Info. Systs. Resrch. Anal., 1968–69, Intern, 1967–68. **Educ.:** Bucknell Univ., 1962–66, BA (Eng.); Rutgers Univ., 1966–67, MLS; Inst. for Advnc. Tech., 1979. **Orgs.:** ALA: RTSD, Bk. Cats. Com. (1971–73, 1973–75); ISAD, Prog. Plng. Com. (1974–76)/Reprodct. of Lib. Mtrls., Ad Hoc Subcom. for Microfilming Cat. Cards (1972–74); RTSD/RASD/LITA MARBI, LC Liaison to Com. (1978–80). ASIS. Potomac Tech. Prcs. Libns. Lib. of Congs. Prof. Assn. Intl. Platform Assn. **Honors:** Beta Phi Mu, 1967. **Pubns.:** "Library of Congress Cataloging Distribution Service, 1901–1976," *Lib. Resrcs. & Tech. Srvs.* (Fall 1977); "The Catalog: Its Nature and Prospects," *Jnl. of Lib. Autom.* (Mr. 1976); "Automated Serials Control: National and International Considerations," *JOLA* (Je. 1975); "Library Automation–A State-of-the-Art Review," *LC Info. Bltn.* (1973); jt. auth., "Library of Congress Bibliographic Record Printing and Distribution System," *Current State of Catalog Card Reproduction* (1975). **Activities:** 4; 17, 49-Data admin.; 56 **Addr.:** 1805 Roxboro Pl., Crofton, MD 21114.

Ganss, Dawn Sloan (Ag. 28, 1931, Philadelphia, PA) Head Libn., Westfield HS, 1970–; Libn., N. Plainfield HS, 1970; Libn., Scotch Plains HS, 1968–69; Sub., Scotch Plains Sch. Dist., 1964–68; Tchr., Roosevelt Jr. HS, NB, 1953–55. **Educ.:** Douglass Coll., 1949–53, BA (Eng.); Rutgers Univ., 1972–75, MLS; NJ Tchr. Cert. (Eng., Hist.); 1980, NJ Supvisory. Cert. **Orgs.:** NJ

Special Subjects/Services: 50. Adult educ.; 51. Advert./Mktg.; 52. Aerosp.; 53. Agric.; 54. Area std.; 55. Arts/Hum.; 56. Autom.; 57. Bibl./Prtg.; 58. Bio. sci.; 59. Bus./Fin.; 60. Chem.; 61. Copyrt.; 62. Documtn.; 63. Educ.; 64. Engin.; 65. Env.; 66. Eth. grps.; 67. Film; 68. Food/Nutr.; 69. Geneal.; 70. Geo.; 71. Geol.; 72. Handcpd.; 73. Hist.; 74. Int. frdm.; 75. Info. sci.; 76. Insr.; 77. Law; 78. Legis.; 79. Math./Comp. sci.; 80. Med.; 81. Metals; 82. Nat. resrcs.; 83. Newsp.; 84. Nuc. sci.; 85. Oral hist.; 86. Petr./Energy; 87. Pharm.; 88. Phys./Astr./Math.; 89. Readg.; 90. Relig.; 91. Sci./Tech.; 92. Soc. sci.; 93. Telecom.; 94. Transp.; 95. (other).

Educ. Media Assn.: Corres. Secy. (1981–82); Pubns. Ch. (1979–81); Prof. Dev. Com. (1980–81); Pubcty. Ch. (1978–79); EMA/NJ LA Sch. PR Com. (Ad Hoc Co-Ch., 1981–82). Un. Cnty. Educ. Media Assn.: Prog. VP (1978–79); Pres. (1979–80); Exec. Bd. (1980–81). NJ State Task Force for Networking. Westfield HS Parent-Tchr. Org. **Honors:** ALA, John Cotton Dana Awd. for PR, 1980. **Activities:** 10, 13; 17, 32, 34; 63, 75, 95-Curric. **Addr.:** Westfield High School Library, Westfield, NJ 07090.

Gant, Margaret Delgatty (Ap. 23, 1941, Flin Flon, MB) Libn. Garden City Sch. Sys., 1981–; Libn., Holcomb Cmnty. Sch., 1979–81; Libn., St. Agnes Sch., 1976–78; Dir., Vermillion Pub. Lib. 1973–76. **Educ.:** Univ. of SD 1972–77, BS (LS). **Orgs.:** KS LA. KS Lib. Ntwk. Auth. Cncl. (1979). SD Pub Libns.: Pres. (1975–76); Legis. Com. (1974–75) SD Int. Frdm. Com.: Co.-Ch. (1978). Various other orgs. **Honors:** Vermillion City Cncl., Citn. for Lib. Srvs., 1976; Garden City School Board, Citn. for Outstanding Srvs to Community. **Pubns.:** Jt.-auth., "Vermillion Public Library - Five Year Plan," 19–. Jt.-auth., "Bibliography of South Dakota," (1976). "Coalition for Fact," (Censorship Newspaper) (1978). Various other pubns. **Activities:** 9, 10; 17, 21, 36; 74, 78 **Addr.:** 1212 Pinecrest, Garden City, KS 67846.

Gantt, Mildred Myrtle (N. 11, 19–, Gantt, AL) Lib. Dir., E. Hill Bapt. Church, Tallahassee, 1966–; Ref. Libn., Appalachian State Tchrs. Coll., 1965; Prof., LS, FL State Univ., 1965; Assoc. Prof., LA Polytech. Inst., 1949–64; Libn., Marianna HS, 1947–49; Prof., LS, George Peabody Coll. Sum. 1948, 1949; Libn., Ouachite Par. HS, Monroe, LA, 1937–38; Libn., Andalusia HS, 1927–37. **Educ.:** Howard Coll., 1924–27, AB (Eng.); LA State Univ., 1935–37, BS (LS); George Peabody Coll., 1945–47, MS (LS). **Orgs.:** ALA. AL LA. LA LA. FL LA. AAUW. **Honors:** Delta Kappa Gamma. **Pubns.:** "Wouldn't You Like to be a Librarian?" *Wilson Lib. Bltn.* (Je. 1955); reviews. **Activities:** 10, 11; 20, 21, 22; 63, 90 **Addr.:** 1110 Brandt Dr., Tallahassee, FL 32308.

Gapen, D. Kaye (Jl. 1, 1943, Mitchell, SD) Dean of Libs., Univ. of AL, 1981–; Asst. Dir. for Tech. Srvs., IA State Univ., 1977–81; Instr. & Head, Quick Editing, OH State Univ., 1974–77, Instr. & Asst. Head, Quick Editing, 1972–74; Gen. Catlgr., Coll. of William & Mary, 1971–72. **Educ.:** Univ. of WA, 1970, BA (Soclgy.), 1971, MLS. **Orgs.:** ALA: LITA, Prog. Plng. Com. (1978–); Ch. (1979–81). IA LA: RTSD/Vice Ch., Ch. elect). IA OCLC Users Grp.: Exec. Com. (1979–). OCLC: Bd. of Trustees (1978–86). Other orgs. AAUP. **Pubns.:** Jt. ed., *Closing the Catalog: Proceedings of the LITA Institutes,* (1979); "OCLC Network Impact on Work Flow and Productivity" in *OCLC: Its Impact on Librarianship,* (1978); Preface to *OCLC Impact & Use* (1977); Jt. auth., "Library Booktheft, a Case Study" *Coll. and Resrch. Libs.* (March 1977); Jt. auth., "A Cost Analysis of the OCLC On-Line Shared Cataloging System in the Ohio State University Libraries", *Lib. Resrcs. & Tech. Srvs.,* (Sum. 1977); Jt. auth., "Management and Use: OCLC and Technical Services at the Ohio State University Libraries", *Lib. Resrcs. and Tech. Srvs.,* (Sum. 1977); Other articles; reviews. **Activities:** 1; 15, 17, 20; 56, 59, 75 **Addr.:** Amelia Gayle Gorgas Library, Box S, University of Alabama, University, AL 35486.

Garber, Marion Harriett (Je. 20, 1921, Charleston, SC) Libn., Med. Lib., Oak Ridge Assoc. Univ., 1974–, Inf. Ofcr., 1970–73, Assoc. Lib. Supvsr., 1957–70, Libn., 1950–57. **Educ.:** Temple Univ., 1939–43, BA (Psych.); Drexel Univ., 1946–47, BS in LS; Teaching Cert., TN, 1974. **Orgs.:** ALA. TN LA. E. TN LA. **Pubns.:** Ed., *Clinical Uses of Radionuclides* (1972). **Activities:** 12; 17, 39; 58, 80 **Addr.:** Medical Library, Oak Ridge Associated Universities, P.O. Box 117, Oak Ridge, TN 37830.

Garcia, Emanuel Ernest (O. 24, 1954, Philadelphia, PA) Policy Adv. for Arts and Hum., Inst. for Sci. Info., 1978–, Transl., 1977–78, Bibl. Resrchr., 1975–77. **Educ.:** Univ. of the State of NY, BS (LS); Inst. for Psychoanalytic Psychotherapy, 1979–. Swarthmore Coll., 1972–74; Trinity Coll., Univ. of Dublin, 1974–75; Temple Univ., 1977–79. **Orgs.:** ASIS. MLA. Assn. for Comps. and the Hums. **Pubns.:** "Citation Indexing in the Humanities," *Eds. News* (Spr. 1979). Various talks. **Activities:** 12; 17, 30, 36; 55, 75, 92 **Addr.:** Emanuel E. Garcia, 1407 S. 13th St., Philadelphia, PA 19147.

Garcia, June Marie (S. 12, 1947, Bryn Mawr, PA) Lib. Ext. Srvs. Admin., Phoenix Pub. Lib., 1981–, Actg. Lib. Ext. Srvs. Admin, 1980–81, Branch Libn., Cholla Branch, 1977–80, Branch Libn., Mesquite Branch, 1975–77; Head, Ref. Dept., Plainfield (NJ) Pub. Lib., 1972–75; Head, Ref. Dept., New Brunswick (NJ) Pub. Lib., 1970–72. **Educ.:** Douglass Coll., 1965–69, BA (Hist.); Rutgers Univ., 1969–70, MLS. **Orgs.:** ALA: PLA, Starter List for New Branch Cols. Com. (1976–80), Resrch. Com. (1980–); ALA Mem. Rcrt. Task Force (1980–). AZ LA: Conf. Com. (1977; Ch., 1979); Mem. Recs. (Ch., 1980). ACLU. **Honors:** Beta Phi Mu. **Activities:** 9; 15, 17, 27; 74 **Addr.:** 3601 W. Las Palmaritas, Phoenix, AZ 85021.

Garcia, Lana Cheryl Caswell (Ja. 5, 1949, Wichita Falls, TX) Law Libn., Resrch. Spec., E. TX Legal Srvs., Inc., 1978–; Law Libn., Orgain, Bell, & Tucker, 1977–78; Inst. of Eng., Lamar Univ., 1973–75; Asst. Ref. Libn., Moffett Lib. Midwestern State Univ., 1971–72. **Educ.:** Midwestern State Univ., 1967–71, BSE (Eng.); 1971–73, MA (Eng.); Univ. of TX, 1975–77, MLS. **Orgs.:** AALL: Rela. with Publshrs. and Dealers Com. (1979–1980). Amer. Assn. of Legal Srvs. Libns. **Pubns.:** "Supreme Court Law Clerks: An Annotated Bibliography," *Law Lib. Jnl.* (Ag., 1977); "A Survey of Legal Services Librarians - Salaries and Benefits," *Amer. Assn. of Legal Srvs. Libns. Nsltr.* (Spr., 1980). **Activities:** 12, 14; 17, 24, 41; 77 **Addr.:** East Texas Legal Services, Inc., 527 Forsythe, P.O. Box 2552, Beaumont, TX 77701.

Gardi, Robert K. (My. 25, 1926, China) Inst. Lib. Consult., IN State Lib., 1968–; Asst. Libn., Peru (IN) Pub. Lib., 1968. **Educ.:** Natl. Univ. of Pol. Sci., 1945–49, BA (Jnlsm.); IN Univ., 1965–68, MLS. **Orgs.:** ALA. Intl. Y's Men's Club. Amer. Correct. Assn.: Lib. Sect. **Pubns.:** "Survey of Institutional Library Service Programs in USA," *ALA Bltn.* (1969); "Institutional Library Service at the State Level," *ALA Bltn.* (S. 1970); ed., "Institutional Library Services," *Portion Focus* (S. 1971); "Please Don't Shut the Door! The Library Service and Construction Act," *AHIL Qtly.* (Sum.–Fall 1974). **Addr.:** Indiana State Library, 140 N. Senate Ave., Indianapolis, IN 46204.

Gardiner, George L. (My. 3, 1933, Cambridge, MA) Dean of the Lib., Prof., Oakland Univ., 1972–; Dir. of Libs., Central State Univ., 1970–72; Ref. Libn. in Hum., IL State Univ., 1967–70; Asst. to Exec. Sec., LAD, ALA, 1967. **Educ.:** Fisk Univ., 1960–63, AB (Mod. Lang.); Univ. of Chicago, 1963–67, MLS, 1969, CAS (LS). **Orgs.:** ALA. ASIS. MI LA. MI Lib. Cnsrtm.: Ch. of Bd. (1978–79). IL Afro-Amer. Hist. Com., (1970). OH State Lib. Cncl. on Fed. Prog. (1970–72). Normal (IL) Pub. Lib.: Bd. (1967–70). Corn Belt Library Bd. (IL) (1968–70). **Honors:** Amer. Missionary Assn., 1st Prize, Natl. Essay Contest, 1963. **Pubns.:** *A Bibliography of the Published Writings of Charles S. Johnson* (1960); "The Empirical Study of Reference," *Coll. and Resrch. Libs.* (S. 1969); "Computer Assisted Indexing in the Central State University Library", *Occasional Papers of the Univ. of IL, Grad. Sch. of LS* (O. 1975). **Activities:** 1; 17, 34; 56, 75 **Addr.:** Kresge Library, Oakland University, Rochester, MI 48063.

Gardner, Charles A. (F. 21, 1930, Tucson, AZ) Dir. of Libs. Hastings Coll. (NB), 1965–; Ref. Libn., WA State Univ. Libs., 1962–65; Instr. Mtrls. Libn., Supvsr., Elem. Sch. Libs., Tucson (AZ) Pub. Schs., 1957–62; Ref. Libn. U.S. Air Frc. Acad. (CO), 1955–57. **Educ.:** Univ. of AZ, 1947–51, BA (Eng. Educ.); Univ. of Denver, 1952–53, MA (LS). **Orgs.:** ALA: Cncl. (1970–72), Ref. and Subscr. Bks. Rev. Com. (1971–74). NB LA: Pres., 1976–77. Mt. Plains LA. Frdm. to Read Fndn. AAUP. Amer. Civil Liberties Assn. **Pubns.:** *Special, Comprehensive, or Unique Collections Located in Nebraska Libraries,* (State Docum.) (1973); "Libraries in Ireland: a Sabbatical View," *NB LA Qtly.* (1975); "Building a Professional Library in the High School," *Readg. Improvement* (1964); **Activities:** 1; 15, 17, 44; 63, 74, 92 **Addr.:** 422 West 11th St., Hastings, NE 68901.

Gardner, Jane Elizabeth (Ag. 2, 1947, Upper Darby, PA) Field Srv. Libn. for Chld. Srvs., SC State Lib., 1979–; Youth Srvs. Coord., Yakima Valley Reg. Lib., 1973–77; Chld. Coord., N. Ctrl. Lib. Dist. (PA), 1970–73. **Educ.:** Dickinson Coll., 1965–69, BA (Hist./Rel.); Univ. of WA, 1969–70, M Libr. **Orgs.:** ALA: CSD, Srv. to the Disadvantaged (1976–1977); Stan. Com. Task Force on Chld. Srvs. (1972–1973); Srv. to Chld. (1975–1977); PLA. WA LA: Exec. Bd. (1975–1977). Chld. and YA Srvs. Sect. Bd. (1974–1975). PA LA. SC LA. **Pubns.:** "Walter de la Mare's Stories for Children: An Analyses of Variant Texts," *The Pvt. Lib.* (Autumn, 1978); Contrib., *Penquin Companion of Children's Literature.* **Activities:** 9, 13; 21, 24 **Addr.:** 1500 Senate Street, Post Office Box 11469, Columbia, SC 29211.

Gardner, Joseph (Tony) A. (Jl. 4, 1943, San Luis Obispo, CA) Sr. Asst. Libn., CA State Univ., Northridge, 1974–. **Educ.:** CA State Univ., Northridge, 1964–67, BA (Hist.); Univ. of CA, Los Angeles, 1971–73, MLS; Univ. of AZ, 1967–69, MA (Mid. E. Std.). **Orgs.:** NLA: Cert. Stand. Com. (1978–); CA Chap., (VP/Pres. Elect, 1979–80; Pres., 1980–). **Pubns.:** Reviews. **Activities:** 1; 15, 20, 44; 92 **Addr.:** Catalog Dept., Library, California State University, Northridge, CA 91330.

Gardner, Richard Kent (D. 7, 1928, New Bedford, MA) Prof., Lib. and Info. Sci., Univ. of CA, Los Angeles, 1977–; Ed., *Choice,* ACRL, 1972–77, 1963–66; Dir., Prof. titulaire, Ecole de Bibliothéconomie, Univ. de Montréal, 1970–72, Assoc. Prof., 1969–70; Assoc. Prof., Sch. of LS, Case West. Rsv. Univ., 1968–69, Lectr., 1966–68; Libn., Marietta Coll., 1959–63; Lib. Adv., MI State Univ. Adv. Grp. in Pub. Admin., Gvt. of Viet-Nam, Saigon, 1957–58; Asst. Libn., Case Inst. of Tech., 1955–57. **Educ.:** Middlebury Coll., 1946–50, AB (Arts); Case West. Rsv. Univ., 1955, MS (LS), 1968, PhD; Univ. de Paris, 1953–54, Dip. Litt. **Orgs.:** Can. Assn. of Coll. and Resrch. Libs.: Com. to Rev. Can. Univ. Lib. Stans. (1970–72). CALS: Com. to Estab. Guidelines for Can. Doct. Progs. in LS (1969–70). ALA: ACRL, Pubns. Com. (1967–71), various coms.; Lib. Educ. Div., Legis. Com. (1968–69); RTSD/Serials Sect., Dupl. Exch. Un. Com. (1962–63); Acq. Sect., Policy and Resrch. Com. (1968–70). AALS. Various other orgs. Lake Placid Educ. Fndn.: Forest Press Com. (1972–); Vice-Ch. (1977–). Russell Pub. Lib., Middletown, CT: Trustee (1974–77). **Honors:** Sch. of LS, Case West. Rsv. Univ., Disting. Alum., 1979; Phi Beta Kappa, 1950; Beta Phi Mu, 1955. **Pubns.:** Jt. auth., *Bibliography of Periodicals Published in Vietnam* (1959); *The Cataloging and Classification of Books; With the Vietnamese Decimal Classification. Phuong Phap tong ke va phan loai sach; voi Phuong phap thap phan Viet-Nam* (1959); *Opening Day Collection* (1967); "Reference," "Music," *Books for College Libraries* (1967); *Library Collections: Their Origin, Selection, and Development* (1981); various bks., articles. **Activities:** 11; 15, 26, 42; 55, 57 **Addr.:** Graduate School of Library and Information Science, University of California, Los Angeles, CA 90024.

Gardner, Roberta Joan (Ap. 12, 1932, NYC, NY) Dir., Info. Srvs., Moody's Investors Service, 1980–; Mgr., Info. Srvs., Dun and Bradstreet, 1978–80; Mgr., Lib. Srvs., 1976–78, Libn., 1970–76; Dir. Lib. Srvs., Bus. Intl., Inc 1965–70. **Educ.:** Queens Coll., 1949–51, 1959–62 BA (Econ.); Pratt Inst., 1962–64, MLS. City Univ. of NY, 1972–76, Cert. (Info. Sci.). **Orgs.:** Assoc. Info. Mgrs.: Natl. Info. Conf. Exhibit (Nice) IV (Ch., 1979–80). SLA: Bus. and Finance Grp. (Ch., 1976). Fncl. Comm. Socty. Pubcty. Club of NY. **Honors:** Beta Phi Mu. **Pubns.:** "Leverage in the Information Manager's Career," *Info. Mgr.* (My. 1979); "Ten Commandments for Library Customers," *Spec. Libs.* (Jy. 1975); Contrib. Ed., *D&B Rpts.*; "Information Managers Seek Job Clarity," *Info. World* (Ap. 1979). **Activities:** 12; 17, 36, 49; 51, 59 **Addr.:** Information Services, Moody's Investors Service, 99 Church St., New York, NY 10007.

Gardner, Stan A. (S. 16, 1949, Tonasket, WA) Dir. Learn, Res. Ctr., Co. Mtn. Coll. 1980–; Dir. KS City Sub-Reg. Lib. for the Blind & Phys. Hndcpd. 1979–80; Dir., Lib. Srvs., Pioneer Cmnty. Coll., 1976–79; Asst. Film Consult., AV Educ. Film Lib., Univ. of MI, 1974–75. **Educ.:** Ctrl. WA Univ., 1968–72, BA (Soc. Sci., Educ.); Univ. of MI, 1974–75, AMLS. West. WA Univ., 1973–74 (Media). **Orgs.:** Colorado Lib. Assoc.; Sci. Fict. Res. Assoc.; Royal Order of Deep Silence; ALA. SLA. Sword and Shield Club: Pres. (1978–80). Bite the Mountain: Instigator (1979–80). **Pubns.:** "Academia," (Colmn.) *Sword & Shield Nsltr.* (1979). "Dreams," *Sword & Shield Nsltr.* (Ap. 1979). "Friends are a Marvelous Part of Living" (slide/tape) (1974). "Parallel Worlds" (slide/tape) (1979). **Activities:** 1, 9; 17, 27, 36; 51, 56, 72 **Addr.:** Colorado Mountain College, L.R.C., Leaderville, CO 80461.

Gardner, Trudy A. (S. 17, 1940, Washington, DC) Instr., Dept. Info. Sci., Univ. of MO, 1977–, Instr., Dept. Family & Cmnty. Med., 1973–77. **Educ.:** Temple Univ., 1961–62, BA (Fr. & Eng.); Univ. of MO, 1970–73, MA (LS), 1977–, PhD cand. (Higher Educ.). **Orgs.:** SLA: Mid MO Chap., (1977–78); Pres. (1976–77). Med. LA. ASIS. **Honors:** Beta Phi Mu, 1973. **Pubns.:** "Consumer Health Information Needs and Access Through Existing Indexes: Results of a Study," *RQ* (Sum. 1981); "The Effect of Online Data Bases on Reference Policy," *RQ* (Fall, 1979); "The Inadequacy of Interdisciplinary Subject Retrieval, *Spec. Libs.* (My./Je., 1977). **Activities:** 11, 12; 26, 30, 39; 80, 91 **Addr.:** School of Library & Informational Science, 113-D Stewart Hall, Columbia, MO 65211.

Gardner, William M. (D. 16, 1932, Cleveland, OH) Dir. of Libs., Marquette Univ., 1974–; Assoc. Dir. for Plng. and Dev., Univ. of KY Libs., 1974, Asst. Dir. for Tech. Srvs., 1966–74, Agr. Libn., 1965–66; Asst. Acq. Libn., Cornell Univ., 1963–64, Cat. Ref. Libn., 1960–63. **Educ.:** John Carroll Univ., 1951–55, BS (Eng.); Case West. Rsv. Univ., 1960, MSLS. **Orgs.:** WI LA. ALA. **Activities:** 1; 17 **Addr.:** Marquette University Memorial Library, 1415 W. Wisconsin Ave., Milwaukee, WI 53233.

Garen, Robert John (F. 10, 1938, Chatham, ON) Coord., Srv. to Shut-ins and Retirees, Detroit Pub. Lib., 1981–, Chief, Film Dept., 1973–81, Asst. to PR Coord., 1970–73; Writer/Planner, Motion Pic., Jam-Handy Prodct., 1968–70; Ext. Libn., Wayne State Univ., 1967–68; Ref. Libn., Univ. of Windsor, 1964–67. **Educ.:** Univ. of Windsor, 1959–63, BA (Eng.); Univ. of Toronto, 1963–64, BLS. **Orgs.:** ALA: MI Cnclr. (1979–82); Mem. Com. (MI Ch., 1980–81). MI LA. Prof. Org. of Libns., Detroit Pub. Lib. Assn. of Prof. Libns. of Detroit Pub. Lib. **Pubns.:** Producer, "Detroit City" multi-media show (1974); producer, "Sing-Along History of America" multi-media show (1976); producer, "Sing-Along History of Old Detroit (1890–1920)" multi-media show (1973–75); various presentations, wkshps., prod. consults. **Activities:** 1, 9; 24, 32, 36; 67, 93 **Addr.:** Utley Branch Library, 8726 Woodward Ave., Detroit, MI 48202.

Garfield, Eugene (S. 16, 1925, New York, NY) Pres., Fndr., Bd. Ch., Inst. for Sci. Info., 1956–; Staff Member, Mach. Indexing Proj., Johns Hopkins Univ., 1951–53; Chem., Columbia Univ., 1950–51; Resrch. Chem., Evans Resrch. & Dev. Corp., 1949–50. **Educ.:** Columbia Univ., 1947–49, BS (Chem.), 1953–54, MS (LS); Univ. of PA, 1958–61, PhD (Structural Ling.). **Orgs.:** Info. Indus. Assn.: Pres. (1972–74). ASIS: Pres., Delaware Valley Chap.; Ch., 1970 Natl. Conv.; Inst. of Info. Sci. (London): Fellow. Rockefeller Univ. Cncl. AAAS: Cncl. (1970–73); Fellow; Ch. of Sect. "T". Grolier Socty.: Fellow. **Honors:** Div. of Chem. Info. Sci., Amer. Chem. Socty., Info. Sci. Awd., 1977; Info. Indus. Assn., Hall of Fame Awd., 1977; ASIS, Best Info. Sci. Book of 1977, ASIS Awd. of Merit, 1975. **Pubns.:**

PROFESSIONAL ACTIVITIES: Institutions: 1. Acad. lib.; 2. Arch.; 3. Assn.; 4. Fed./Gvt. lib.; 5. Inst. lib.; 6. Mfr./Suppl.; 7. Milit. lib.; 8. Musm.; 9. Pub. lib.; 10. Sch. lib.; 11. Sch. of lib. sci.; 12. Spec. lib.; 13. State lib.; 14. (other). **Functions/Activities:** 15. Acq./Col. dev.; 16. Adult srvs.; 17. Admin.; 18. Apprais.; 19. Archit./Bldgs.; 20. Cat./Class.; 21. Chld. srvs.; 22. Circ.; 23. Cons./Pres.; 24. Consult.; 25. Cont. ed.; 26. Educ. lib. sci.; 27. Ext. srvs.; 28. Fund/Grants; 29. Gvt. pubs.; 30. Indx./Abs.; 31. Instr. lib. use; 32. Media srvs.; 33. Micro.; 34. Netwks./Coop.; 35. Persnl.; 36. PR; 37. Publshg.; 38. Recs. mgt.; 39. Ref. srvs.; 40. Repro.; 41. Resrch.; 42. Review.; 43. Secur.; 44. Serials; 45. Spec. col.; 46. Tech. srvs.; 47. Trustees/Bds.; 48. YA srvs.; 49. (other).

Essays of an Information Scientist, Vol 1-3 (1977, 80); *Citation Indexing - Its Theory and Application to Science, Technology, and Humanities.* (1979); Various articles. **Activities:** 6; 17, 37, 41; 55, 91, 92 **Addr.:** Institute for Scientific Information, 3501 Market St., University City Science Center, Philadelphia, PA 19104.

Gargan, William Michael (Ap. 18, 1950, Brooklyn, NY) Hum. Libn., Brooklyn Coll., 1979–; Libn., Brooklyn Pub. Lib., 1976–79; Adj. Lectr., Kingsborough Cmnty. Coll., 1973–74. **Educ.:** Kingsborough Cmnty. Coll., 1968–70, AA (Liberal Arts); SUNY, Stony Brook, 1970–72, BA (Eng.); Columbia Univ., 1972–73, MA (Eng.), 1974–76, MS (LS). **Orgs.:** NY LA. Oral Hist. Assn. ALA: Lcl. Arrange. Subcom. (1979–); SR RT (1979–); ACRL. LA CUNY: Pubns. Com. (1979–); Instr. Com. (1979–); Exec. Com. (Brooklyn Coll. Del., 1979). Mod. Lang. Assn. James Joyce Socty. **Pubns.:** "Whose Problem?" *SRRT Nsltr.* (Je. 1979); "Unions and Problem Patrons," *Lib. Jnl.* (Ja. 15, 1979); *Popular Songs In Collections: An Index to Rock, Folk-Rock, Soul and Disco* (forthcoming); "Photo Essay: Pier Reading," *Moody St. Irregulars: A Jack Kerouac Nsltr.* (Spr. 1979); "Jack Kerouac: Biography and Criticism, a Working Bibliography," *Moody St. Irregulars: A Jack Kerouac Nsltr.* (Win.–Spr. 1980). **Activities:** 1, 9; 15, 31, 39; 55, 56, 85 **Addr.:** Brooklyn College Library, Bedford Ave. and Ave. H, Brooklyn, NY 11210.

Garganta, Narciso Merioles (S. 18, 1932, Philippines) Dir., Med. Lib., Burbank Cmnty. Hosp., 1979–; Lib. Asst., VA Med. Ctr., Brentwood, CA, 1978–79; Curric. Dev. Spec., RCA Resrc. Ctr., 1972–77; Med. Libn., Milton Lib. of Legal Med., 1970–72. **Educ.:** Arellano Univ., Manila, Philippines, 1952–56, BSE (Eng. & LS); Pratt Inst.,1970–71, MLS; Org., Mgt. & Srvs. of Small Hosp. Lib., 1979; Pub. Libns. Prof. Cert., NY, 1975. **Orgs.:** Med. LA: Hosplty. Com. (1973). Med. Lib. Grp. of S. CA, AZ. NY Reg. Grp., Med. LA. NY Geneal. Socty. **Pubns.:** Managing Ed., *Intl. Micro. Jnl. of Legal Med.* (1970). **Addr.:** 513 North Ave. 50, Los Angeles, CA 90042.

Garner, Jane (O. 23, 1937, Port Lavaca, TX) Rare Books and Mss. Libn., Nettie Lee Benson Latin Amer. Col., Univ. of TX, 1975–; Ref. Libn., 1966–75. **Educ.:** Victoria Coll., 1955–57, AA (Eng.); Univ. of TX, 1957–59, BA (Eng.); 1964–69, MLS; Natl. Arch., Cert., Intro. to Modern Arch. Admin., 1979. **Orgs.:** ALA: RTSD/Reprodct. of Lib. Mtrls. Sect. (Ch., 1976/77); Bd. of Dir. (1976/77); other coms. SALALM: Member-at-large, Exec. Bd. (1973–1976); Ch., Jt. Com. on Reprodct. of Latin Amer. Matrls. (1975–1977); Ch., Constn. and Bylaws Com. (1979–1982); Ch., Ad hoc Com. on SALALM Arch., (1978–). Socty. of Univ. of TX Libns. Socty. of SW Archvsts. Other orgs. **Pubns.:** Cmplr., *Archives and Manuscripts on Microfilm in the Nettie Lee Benson Latin American Collection; a Checklist* (1980); Ed., *Final Report and Working Papers,* 17th SALALM (1975); Jt. auth., "Provisional List of Dissertations on Latin American Topics, 1971," *Newsletter,* Latin Amer. Std. Assn., (S. 1973); Ed., "Significant Acquisitions of Latin American Materials, Decennial Cumulation, 1961/62 - 1970/71," *Final Report and Working Papers,* 16th SALALM (1973). **Activities:** 1; 33, 39, 45; 54 **Addr.:** Benson Latin American Collection, Sid Richardson Hall 1.108, University of Texas General Libraries, Austin, TX 78712.

Garodnick, Judith S. (O. 13, 1947, New York, NY) Ed.-in-Chief, Bk. Div., R. R. Bowker Co., 1979–, Exec. Ed., 1978–79, Acq. Ed., 1976–78, Ed. Supvsr., 1974–76; Ed., Gen. Pubns. Dept., H. W. Wilson Co., 1970–74. **Educ.:** Russell Sage Coll., 1964–68, BA (Amer. Hist.); NY Univ., 1968–69, MA (Urban Hist.); SLA, 1978, Cert. (Gvt. Docum.). **Orgs.:** ALA: RASD/Machine-Assisted Ref. Sect., 1981 Conf. Prog. Com. "Delivery of Computerized Information Services to the Home"; Lib. and Info. Lit., Mem. Initiative Grp., Task Frc. on Info. Needs of the Lib. Prof.; Ad Hoc Com. on Bus. Support for Libs. NJ Gvr.'s Conf. for WHCOLIS: SLA Del. (1978). SLA. Assn. of Amer. Publshrs.: Libs. Com.; Assn. of Amer. Publshrs./ALA Jt. Com., 1981 Adult Litcy. Prog., Co-Ch. NJ Gvr.'s Conf. on Chld. and Youth Srvs., Del. (D. 1981). Palisades Nat. Assn. Fortune 500 Women in Bus. Club. Frnds. of Fort Lee Pub. Lib. Women in Comms. **Activities:** 14-Publshg. co.; 17, 26, 39; 57, 75, 93 **Addr.:** 1 Wall St., Ft. Lee, NJ 07024.

Garoogian, Andrew (Ja. 10, 1928, Brooklyn, NY) Ref. Libn., Brooklyn Coll. Lib., 1966–; Sr. Libn., Soc. Sci. Div., Brooklyn Pub. Lib., 1962–66. **Educ.:** Brooklyn Coll., 1948–50, 1958–60, BA (Pol. Sci.); Pratt Inst., 1960–62, MLS; Brooklyn Coll., 1967–74, MA (Pol. Sci.). **Orgs.:** LA CUNY. **Pubns.:** *Deinstitutionalization and the Care of the Developmentally Disabled: A Select Bibliography, 1961–1981* (forthcoming); *School Desegregation and "White Flight": A Select Bibliography* (1980); jt. auth., *Child Care Issues for Parents and Society: A Guide to Information Sources* (1977); "Making Book at the Reference Desk," *Lib. Jnl.* (Je. 15, 1978); "Freebie Cards Get Free Documents," *UNABASHED Libn.* (Spr. 1974); "Pamphlet Power," *LA CUNY Jnl.* (Spr. 1974). **Activities:** 1; 39; 68, 78, 92 **Addr.:** Brooklyn College Library, Reference Division, Brooklyn, NY 11210.

Garralda, John C. (S. 13, 1934, Elko, NV) Dir., Lib. Srv., West. State Coll. of CO, 1975–; Dir., Libs., KS State Coll. of Pittsburg, 1969–75, Asst. Prof., LS, 1967–69, Serials, Docum. Libn., 1963–67. **Educ.:** KS State Coll. of Pittsburg, 1953–56, BS (Eng.); Univ. of Denver, 1963, MA (Libnshp.). **Orgs.:** CO LA: Coll. and Univ. Div. (Pres., 1980). ALA. CO Educ. Media Assn. Pathfinder Reg. Lib.: Vice Ch. (1979–80). **Activities:** 1; 15, 17, 45; 65, 74, 93 **Addr.:** Savage Library, Western State College, Gunnison, CO 81230.

Garrawaway, Martha F. (F. 10, 1941, Ellisville, MS) Dir., Lrng. Resrcs., Abilene Indp. Schs., 1972–, HS Libn., 1970–71; Jr. High Libn., Petal Schs., 1969–70; Serials Libn., Delta State Coll., 1966–68; Jr. High Libn., Holly Springs, MS, 1963–65; HS Libn., W. Tallahatchie HS, 1962–63. **Educ.:** Univ. of South. MS, 1960–62, BS (LS), 1963–66, MS (LS); Abilene Christ. Univ., 1975–76 (Supvsn.). **Orgs.:** ALA: AASL. Lrng. Resrcs. Ctr. Prog. Dirs. of TX. TX LA: Plng. Com. (1976–79); Legis. Com. (1978–79). TX Assn. of Sch. Libns.: Secy.; Treas. (1976–77). TX State Tchrs. Assn. Abilene Educ. Assn. TX Intl. Readg. Assn. **Honors:** Kappa Delta Pi; Phi Delta Kappa; Delta Kappa Gamma. **Activities:** 10; 17, 21, 32; 56, 63 **Addr.:** 4301 S. 20th, Abilene, TX 79605.

Garrett, Laura (Ja. 4, 1926, Normal, IL) Libn., State Farm Insr. Co., 1978–, Asst. Libn., 1968–78, Catlgr., 1967–68. **Educ.:** IL State Univ., 1969–73, BS (LS). **Orgs.:** SLA: Ch.-Elect (1980–81), Ch. (1981–82); IL Chap., Bd. (1980–82). AALL: PR Com. (1980–81). **Pubns.:** Indxr., *Monthly-Best's Review Mag.* (1976–); indxr., *Insr. Pers. Anl. Indx.* (1976–). **Activities:** 12; 15, 17, 20; 59, 76, 77 **Addr.:** State Farm Insurance Cos., Corporate Library, E-5, One State Farm Plz., Bloomington, IL 61701.

Garrett, Sarah Ann Mathews (N. 25, 1928, Racine, WI) Supvsr., Info. Ctr., Gulf Oil Exploration and Prod. Co., 1980–; Asst. Ref. Libn., NM State Univ., 1975–80. **Educ.:** Univ. of WI 1946–50, BS (Occupational Therapy); OH State Univ., 1960–67, MS (Home Econ., Foods, Nutr.); CA State Univ., Fullerton, 1973–75, MS (LS). **Orgs.:** NM LA: Pres. (1980). SLA. West. Assn. Map Libs. NM Adv. Cncl. on Libs. AAUW: NM State Univ. (Corporate Del., 1979–80). Altrusa: Las Cruces Branch, Bd. of Dirs. (1978–80). **Honors:** Phi Kappa Phi, 1975. **Pubns.:** Jt. auth., "The National Program to Microfilm Agricultural Documents," *Coll. & Resrch. Libs.* (N. 1980); "You're Welcome" slide-tape (1976). **Activities:** 1, 12; 17, 38, 39; 58, 86, 91 **Addr.:** Gulf Oil Exploration and Production Co., P.O. Box 2619, Casper, WY 82602.

Garrison, Guy G. (D. 17, 1927, Akron, OH) Dean, Prof., Sch. of Lib. and Info. Sci., Drexel Univ., 1968–; Dir., Lib. Resrch. Ctr., Prof., Univ. of IL, 1962–68; Head, Reader Srvs., Kansas City (MO) Pub. Lib., 1960–62; Asst. Libn., Oak Park Pub. Lib., 1954–58. **Educ.:** Baldwin-Wallace Coll., 1946–50, BA (Eng.); Columbia Univ., 1953–54, MS (LS); Univ. of IL, 1958–60, PhD (LS). **Orgs.:** ASIS. PA LA: Nom. Com. (Ch., 1973–74). AALS: Exec. Bd. (1970–73, 1974–78); Pres. (1976–77); various coms. ALA: Lib. Admin. Div., Com. on Compar. Lib. Org. (1963–66); Lib. Educ. Div., Resrch. Com. (1965–70); Resrch. Clearinghse., Adv. Com. (1966–67); Cncl. (1973–77); various coms. Cncl. of Comm. Soctys.: Secy.-Treas. (1980–82). **Honors:** Cncl. on Lib. Resrcs., Flwshp., 1973; Baldwin-Wallace Coll., Ritter Awd. for Srv. in Libnshp., 1979. **Pubns.:** Ed., *Total Community Library Service* (1973); ed., *Studies in Public Library Government, Organizations, and Support* (1969); ed., *The Changing Role of State Library Consultants* (1968); jt. auth., *Library Resources in the North Country Area of New York State* (1966); *A Statewide Reference Network for Wisconsin Libraries* (1964); various articles. **Activities:** 9, 11; 16, 17, 26; 50, 63, 89 **Addr.:** School of Library and Information Science, Drexel University, Philadelphia, PA 19104.

Garrison, Lora D. (O. 18, 1934, Cleburne, TX) Assoc. Prof., Rutgers Univ., 1972–. **Educ.:** Fullerton State Coll., 1968–69, BA (Hist.); Univ. of CA, Irvine, 1969–72, PhD (Hist.). **Orgs.:** ALA: Com. on Accred. (1978–80). Berkshire Conf. of Women Histns. **Pubns.:** *Apostles of Culture: The Public Library and American Society* (1979). **Activities:** 14-Univ. Dept.; 26 **Addr.:** 320 Lawrence Ave., Highland Park, NJ 08904.

Garry, Loraine Spencer (Jl. 16, 1937, Halifax, NS) Pres., Spencer Garry Consults., 1975–; Libn., Regis. Nurses Assn. of ON, 1976–80; Lectr., Fac. of LS, Univ. of Toronto, 1975–76; Lectr., Fac. of Lib. Srv., Dalhousie Univ., 1973–75; Sci. and Med. Lib., Univ. of Toronto, 1971–73; Cent. Coll. of Appld. Arts and Tech., 1967–71; Fac. of Dvnty., McGill Univ., 1963–65; Acq. Dept., Univ. of Toronto Lib., 1961–63. **Educ.:** McGill Univ., 1955–59, BA, hons. (Eng.), 1960–61, BLS; Univ. of Toronto, 1967–71, MLS. **Orgs.:** Can. LA: Cncl.; Info. Srvs. Sect. (Ch., 1970–72); various coms. Inst. of Prof. Libns. of ON. Can. Assn. of Lib. Schs.: Secy.-Treas. (1974–75). ON LA. Inst. of Pub. Admin. of Can. Univ. Women's Club: N. Toronto Branch (Prog. Conv., 1977–78). Women for Pol. Action. **Pubns.:** Ed., *Canadian Libraries in Their Changing Environment* (1977); cmplr., *Northern Ontario: A Bibliography* (1968); "Human Relations Management in Libraries," *APLA Bltn.* (1974); "Librarians and Their Career Choice," *IPLO Qtly.* (1974); "Canadian Library Associations," "Recruitment and Selection," *Canadian Libraries in Their Changing Environment* (1977). **Activities:** 11, 12; 24, 26, 41; 50, 78, 92 **Addr.:** Spencer Garry Consultants, P.O. Box 1213, Campbellford, ON K0L 1L0 Canada.

Garten, Edward Dale (F. 19, 1948, Hinton, WV) Dir., Univ. Libs., TN Tech. Univ., 1981–; Dir. of Libs./Media Srvs., North. State Coll., 1980–81; Asst. to Dir., Moorhead State Univ., 1977–79; Admin. Asst., Univ. of Toledo, 1975–77; Asst. Libn., Mary Manse Coll., 1974–75. **Educ.:** Concord Coll., 1964–67, BS (Educ.); Kent State Univ., 1973–74, MLS; Meth. Theo. Sch., 1969–72, MDiv (Relig.); Meth. Theo. Sch. and OH State Univ, 1969–72, MA (Educ.); Univ. of Toledo, 1975–77, PhD (Admin. Higher Educ.). **Orgs.:** ALA: LAMA. Amer. Assn. for Higher Educ. MN State Univ. Syst.: Chancellor's Task Force on Prof. Dev. (1979–80). Amer. Assoc. Univ. Admins. **Pubns.:** "Theory as Friend in Media Management," *Educ. Tech.* (Spr. 1980); "A state-wide study of consultation and intervention with governance structures," *Connexion* (1979); "Skills and competencies for effective consultation and intervention: an Ohio study," *Connexion* (1979); "The university as moral community," *Critique.* (1977); Reviews. **Activities:** 1; 15, 17, 25, 49; 63, 90, 92 **Addr.:** University Libraries, Tennessee Technological University, Cookeville, TN

Gartenfeld, Ellen S. (My. 28, 1938, New York, NY) Netwk. Coord., Cmnty. Hlth. Info. Netwk., Mt. Auburn Hosp., 1977–; Head of Readers' Srvs., SUNY, Stony Brook, Hlth. Sci. Lib., 1973–77; Per. Libn., Hebrew Univ.-Hadassah Hosp., 1969–72; Head of Readers' Srvs., Med. Resrch. Lib. of Brooklyn, 1961–69. **Educ.:** Univ. of Rochester, 1955–59, BA (History); Columbia Univ., 1959–61, MSLS. **Orgs.:** Med. LA: Ed. Com. (1977–79, Ch., 1979–80). N. Atl. Hlth. Sci. Libns.: Regis. Com. (Ch., 1977–78). N.E. Reg. Med. Lib. Adv. Com.: Educ. Com. (1979–80). ALA. **Pubns.:** "The Community Health Information Network," *Lib. Jnl.* (O. 1978); Jt. auth., *The Public Library System as a Dissemination Network for Health Information.;* "Community Access to Hospital Libraries" in *Hospital Library Management.* (1980). **Activities:** 1, 14-Network; 24, 34, 39; 80, 95 **Addr.:** 281 Walden St., Cambridge, MA 02138.

Gartland, Joan W. (D. 24, 1941, Brooklyn, NY) Libn., Tannahill Resrch. Lib., Greenfield Village and Henry Ford Musm., 1978–; Head Ref. Libn., Univ. of Detroit, 1975–77, Ref. Dept., 1969–75; Registrar, Oriental Inst. Musm., Univ of Chicago, 1967–69. **Educ.:** Barnard Coll., 1959–63, BA (Hist.); Univ. of Chicago, 1963–68, MA (Egyptology); Univ. of MI, 1970–71, MA (LS). **Orgs.:** MI LA. ALA. SLA. **Honors:** Phi Beta Kappa, 1963; Beta Phi Mu, 1973. **Pubns.:** Contrib., *Reference Resources: A Systematic Approach* (1976); "Downstairs at Fairlane," The Herald (Edison Institute) (Sum., 1979); Reviews. **Activities:** 1, 8; 39; 55, 92 **Addr.:** Tannahill Research Library, Greenfield Village and Henry Ford Musuem, Dearborn, MI 48121.

Garvey, Jeffrey M. (S. 7, 1950, New York, NY) Libn., Mercy Hosp. of Watertown, 1974–. **Educ.:** Colgate Univ., 1968–72, BA (Hist.); Syracuse Univ., 1973–74, MSLS. **Orgs.:** Med. LA: Bylaws Com., Hosp. Lib. Sect. (1977–). SLA. Hay Memorial Lib., Sackets Harbor, NY: Bd. of Trustees (1978–). NY and NJ Reg. Med. Lib.: Com. on Com. (1976–77); Subcom. on Reg. Plan (1978–). Hlth. Resrcs. Cncl. of Ctrl. NY: Ch., (1976–77); Strg. Com. (1975–). **Pubns.:** Ed., *Union List of Serials, Basic Unit Libraries, Central New York* (1979). **Activities:** 5, 12; 17; 80 **Addr.:** 101 East Main St., Sackets Harbor, NY 13685.

Garvey, Mona C. (N. 1, 1934, Omaha, NB) Pub. Rel. Consult., M. G. Assocs., 1977–; Pub. Rel. Libn., Chattahoochee Valley Reg. Lib., 1974–78; Media Spec., Hebrew Acad. of Atlanta, 1969–72; Adult Srvs. Libn., Brooklyn Pub. Lib., 1967–68. **Educ.:** Clarke Coll.; Univ. of IA, 1952–56, BA (Art); Atlanta Univ., 1966–67, MSLS. **Orgs.:** ALA: LAMA/Pub. Rel. Sect., Pubn. Com. (1979–81), Ad Hoc Inst. Plng. Com. (1979–81); Natl. Lib. Wk. Com. (1978–81). **Pubns.:** *Library Public Relations* (1980); *Teaching Displays* (1972); *Library Displays* (1969); "Display 6 Pack" (multimedia display) avail. from M.G. Assocs. (1974). **Activities:** 9, 10; 24, 36, 37; 51 **Addr.:** 251 Peachtree Way N.E., Atlanta, GA 30305.

Garvin, Andrew P. (Jl. 24, 1945, New York City, NY) Pres., FIND/SVP, 1970–; VP, Four Elements, Inc., 1968–69. **Educ.:** Yale Univ., 1963–67, BA (Pol. Sci.); Columbia Univ., 1967–68, MS (Jnlsm.). **Orgs.:** Info. Indus. Assn.: Bd. of Dirs. (1979). Amer. Mktg. Assn. SLA. Amer. Mgt. Assn. St. Elmo Socty.: Treas. Natl. Info. Conf. and Exposition: Ch. (1979). **Pubns.:** *How to Win with Information (or Lose Without It)* (1980); "Welcome to the Information Revolution," *Plng. Review* (Mr. 1979). **Activities:** 12; 17, 37, 41; 51, 93 **Addr.:** FIND/SVP, 500 5th Ave., New York, NY 10036.

Garvin, Jewel H. (Jl. 27, 1910, Haralson, GA) Univ. Libn., Univ. of FL, 1975–, Assoc. Libn., 1960–75; Dir., Ocala Pub. Lib., 1951–60; Branch Libn., Atlanta Pub. Lib., 1950–51; various positions, 1933–50. **Educ.:** FL State Coll. for Women, 1928–32, AB (Frgn. Lang.); Emory Univ., 1932–33, BS (LS). **Orgs.:** FL LA: Pub. Lib. Sect., Head, Secy./Treas.; various coms. Med. LA: Hosplty. Com. (1970–71); South. Grp. (Secy./Treas., 1974–75). Leag. of Women Voters. AAUP. **Pubns.:** Various articles. **Activities:** 1, 9; 17, 22, 23; 80, 85, 89 **Addr.:** University Station, Box 12546, Gainesville, FL 32601.

Garypie, Renwick (My. 21, 1932, Massapequa, NY) Dir., Oxford Pub. Lib., 1976–; Dir., Genesee Cnty. Lib., 1969–76; Dir.,

Special Subjects/Services: 50. Adult educ.; 51. Advert./Mktg.; 52. Aerosp.; 53. Agric.; 54. Area std.; 55. Arts/Hum.; 56. Autom.; 57. Bibl./Prtg.; 58. Bio. sci.; 59. Bus./Fin.; 60. Chem.; 61. Copyrt.; 62. Documtn.; 63. Educ.; 64. Engin.; 65. Env.; 66. Eth. grps.; 67. Film; 68. Food/Nutr.; 69. Geneal.; 70. Geo.; 71. Geol.; 72. Handcpd.; 73. Hist.; 74. Int. frdm.; 75. Info. sci.; 76. Insr.; 77. Law; 78. Legis.; 79. Math./Comp. sci.; 80. Med.; 81. Metals; 82. Nat. resrcs.; 83. Newsp.; 84. Nuc. sci.; 85. Oral hist.; 86. Petr./Energy; 87. Pharm.; 88. Phys./Astr./Math.; 89. Readg.; 90. Relig.; 91. Sci./Tech.; 92. Soc. sci.; 93. Telecom.; 94. Transp.; 95. (other).

Sioux City Pub. Lib., 1967–69; Dir., Ingham Cnty. Pub. Lib., 1962–67. **Educ.:** Hamilton Coll., 1950–54, AB (Lib. Arts); Univ. of MI, 1954–56, AMLS. **Orgs.:** ALA. MI LA: Legis. Com. (1979–). Detroit Suburban Libns. RT. Oxford Cncl. of the Arts: Treas. (1976–). **Activities:** 9; 17, 19, 26 **Addr.:** 618 Oxford Oaks Ct., Oxford, MI 48051.

Gasaway, Laura N. (F. 24, 1945, Searcy, AR) Dir., Law Lib., Prof. of Law, Univ. of OK, 1975–; Law Libn., Univ. of Houston, 1973–75, Asst. Law Libn., 1971–73, Cat., Circ. Libn., 1968–71. **Educ.:** TX Woman's Univ., 1963–67, BA (Gvt.), 1967–68, MLS; Univ. of Houston, 1968–73, JD (Law). **Orgs.:** AALL: Southwest. Chap. (Pres., 1974–76). Educ. Com. (1971–76); Nom. Com. (1974–75, 1979–80); Copyrt. Com. (1979–82). SLA: Educ. Com. (1978–81); TX Chap. (Pres., 1973–74). Natl. Comsn. on Libs. and Info. Sci.: Adv. Com. on the Natl. Pers. Syst. (1977–80). Assn. of Amer. Law Schs.: Com. on Libs. (1974–77). State Bar of TX. **Honors:** Univ. of OK, Calvert Law Fac. Awd., 1978, 1981. **Pubns.:** "Management Comparable Worth: A Post-Gunther Overview," *Georgetown Law Jnl.* (1981); *American Indian Legal Materials: A Union List* (1979); *Legal Protection for Computer Programs* (1980); "Management Techniques Using Traditional Library Records," *Law Lib. Jnl.* (1977); "Women in Special Libraries," *Special Librarianship: A Reader* (1980). **Activities:** 1, 12; 17; 77 **Addr.:** Law Center Library, University of Oklahoma, 300 Timberdell Rd., Norman, OK 73019.

Gaskill, Lula M. (Ja. 14, 1920, Ingraham, IL) Head Libn., Allerton Pub. Lib., 1957–. **Orgs.:** Lincoln Trail Libns. Assn.: Pres. (1976). IL LA: PR Ch. (1976). ALA. Interagency Cncl.: Srv. Dir. Ch. Hist. Prsrvn. Bd.: Ch. **Honors:** Amer. Bus. Womens Assn., Boss of the Yr., 1975. **Activities:** 9; 36; 50, 55 **Addr.:** 201 N. State, Monticello, IL 61856.

Gates, Francis Law Libn., Prof. of Law, Columbia Univ. Law Lib., 1975–; Law Libn., Prof., Legal Bibl., Sch. of Law Lib., Univ. of South. CA Law Ctr., 1973–74, Law Libn., Asst. Prof., Legal Bibl., 1972–73, Assoc. Law Libn., Asst. Prof., Legal Bibl., 1970–72; Resrch. Attorney, CA Cont. Educ. of the Bar, Univ. Ext., Univ. of CA, Berkeley, 1965–69, Proj. Supvsr., OEO Legal Srvs. Attorneys Trng. Prog., 1966–68, Law Libn., 1960–69; Ref. Libn., Soc. Sci. Ref. Srvs., Univ. of CA Lib., Berkeley, 1954–60; various positions as consult., 1960–. **Educ.:** Univ. of CA, Berkeley, 1952, AB (Pol. Sci., Sp.), 1954, BLS; San Francisco Law Sch., 1963, JD; 1963, Admitted to CA Bar; 1963, Admitted to Prac. before Fed. Cts.; 1966, Admitted to Prac. before U.S. Supreme Ct. **Orgs.:** ALA: PLA. Law Libns. Assn. of Grt. NY. NY Tech. Srvs. Libns. AALL: Pres. (1980–81); VP, Pres.-Elect (1979–80); Exec. Bd. (1975–77); AALL Exec. Bd. to AALS Libs. Com. (Liaison, 1975–77); Law Lib. Netwk. Com. Exec. Bd. (Bd. Liaison, 1979–80); AALL Pres. Ad Hoc Com. (1978–79); various coms., ofcs. Various other orgs. AAUP. Jt. Com. of the Assn. of the Bar of the City of New York, Columbia Univ. Law Sch., NY Univ. Law Sch. (1977–80). State Bar of CA: Various coms. Amer. Bar Assn.: Various coms. Various other orgs. **Honors:** Phi Beta Kappa; Univ. of South. CA Law Ctr., Coif, Hon., 1973. **Pubns.:** Supvsg. ed., *CEB Legal Srvs. Gazette* (S. 1966–S. 1968); "Selection of Personnel in Law Libraries," *Law Lib. Jnl.* (1969); "Legal Bibliography of Current Social Problems: The Environment, Race Relations, and Poverty," *Law Lib. Jnl.* (1971); "Social Science Research Sources," *How to Find the Law* (1976); "175 Years of Service," *Boston Bar Jnl.* (N. 1980); various articles. **Addr.:** 560 Riverside Dr., Apt. 17–M, New York, NY 10027.

Gatlin, Nancy L. (Fb. 2, 1946, New Albany, MS) Libn., South. Coll. of Optometry 1974–, Cat. Libn., 1971–74. **Educ.:** Univ. of MI, 1964–68, BA (Eng.); Vanderbilt Univ., 1977–79, MLS. **Orgs.:** SLA: Bd. of Dir. (1978–80). Assn. of Visual Sci. Libns.: Ch. (1978–80). Assn. of Memphis Area Hlth. Sci. Libs.: Ch. 1980. Med. LA. **Activities:** 1; 17, 24, 32; 58, 80, 88 **Addr.:** Southern College of Optometry, 1245 Madison Ave., Memphis, TN 38104.

Gatner, Elliott S. M. (O. 24, 1914, New York City, NY) Dir., Emeritus, Libs., Long Island Univ., 1981–, Dir., Libs., Exhibitions, Long Island Univ. Press, 1976–; Prof., Long Island Univ., 1964–, Actg. Dir., 1975–76, Assoc. Dir., 1965–75; Asst. to Provost, 1964–65, Asst. Dir., Libs., 1961–64, Assoc. Prof., Hist., 1956–63, various positions in lib., tchg., admin., 1936–61. **Educ.:** Long Island Univ., 1936, BA (Eng., Hist.); Coll. of the City of New York, 1939, MS (Eng., Educ.); Columbia Univ., 1947, BS (Coll., Univ. Libs.), 1975, EdD (Higher and Adult Educ.). **Orgs.:** ALA. Long Island Arch. Conf. NY State Hist. Socty. Amer. Educ. Std. Assn. Acad. Libs. of Brooklyn: Pres. (1967–69). Various other orgs. Long Island Univ. Alum. Assn.: Exec. Secy. (1939–41). Long Island Univ.: Com. on Coms.; Fac. Review Com.; Univ. Sen. (1964–70); Ofc. of Plng., Mstr. Plng. Com., Freshman Orien. Prog. (Dir., 1961–64); various coms., ofcs. Mod. Lang. Assn. of Amer. Coll. Eng. Assn. Various other orgs. **Honors:** Long Island Univ., Chrt. Day Awd. "For Devoted and Disting. Srv.," 1973; Long Island Univ., Alum. Awd., 1975. **Pubns.:** Contrib. ed., *A Bibliography of American Educational History* (1975); "Introductory Essay on the Study of Educational History," *A Brief History of Education* (1963); *Higher Education in the French-Speaking Countries of Black Africa* (1969); *Challenge and Response: The Community College* (1975); *Long Island: The History of a Relevant and Responsive University, 1926–1968* (1974); various bks., reviews. **Activities:** 1; 17, 28, 37; 55, 57, 94 **Addr.:** General Delivery, Bellerose, NY 11426.

Gattin, Leroy M. (Je. 4, 1944, Benton, AR) Coord., Ext., AR State Lib., 1979–; Libn., Dir., Mid-AR Reg. Lib., 1973–79; Dir., Poplar Bluff Pub. Lib., 1971–73; Lib. Supvsr., Poplar Bluff Pub. Schs., 1966–71. **Educ.:** Univ. of Ctrl. AR, 1962–66, BS (Hist., LS); Univ. of MO, 1971–73, MA (LS). **Orgs.:** AR LA: VP (1978); Pres. (1979). SW LA: Constn.-Bylaws Com. ALA: Branch Lib. Starter List Com. (1980); Mem. Com. (1976–80). **Activities:** 9, 13; 24, 27, 47; 67, 78, 93 **Addr.:** 2603 Denise, Benton, AR 72015.

Gaughan, Thomas Michael (N. 24, 1946, Camden, NJ) Dir., Lib., Bard Coll., 1980–; Persnl. Libn., Univ. of IL, 1978–80, Asst. Persnl. Libn., 1977–78; Soc. Sci. Info. Spec., Hamline Univ., 1974–77. **Educ.:** Trenton State Coll., 1965–69, BA (Hist.); Montclair State Coll., 1971–73, MA (Persnl.); Rutgers Univ., 1973–74, MLS. **Orgs.:** ALA: Ref. and Subscrpn. Bks. Review Com. (1980–); ACRL, Persnl. Ofcrs. Discuss. Grp. (1977–); RASD, Nom. Com. (1981–). MN LA. IL LA. AAUP. **Pubns.:** "Resume Essentials for the Academic Librarian," *Coll. & Resrch. Libs.* (Mr. 1980); jt. auth., "Socialization of Library School Students....," *Jnl. of Educ. for Libnshp.* (Spr. 1979); "Book Reviews: Producers and Consumers," *ARLIS/NA Nsltr.* (My. 1979); ed., "In Review," *RQ* (1976–79); various reviews in *Lib. Jnl., C&RL, RQ*. **Activities:** 1; 17, 35, 39 **Addr.:** Box 916, Bard College, Annandale-on-Hudson, NY 12504.

Gaulke, Mary Florence (S. 24, 1923, Johnson City, TN) Supvsr., Libs., Roseburg Pub. Schs., 1973–; Supvsr., Libs., Medford Pub. Sch., 1970–72; Instr., Psy., Remedial Readg., South. OR Coll., 1970–72; Lib. Consult., Douglas Cnty. Educ. Dist., 1964–66. **Educ.:** OR State Univ., 1961–63, BS (Home Econ.); Univ. of OR, 1968–70, MS (LS), 1968–70, PhD (Spec. Educ.); various crs. **Orgs.:** ALA. Pac. NW LA. OR LA: Lib. Dev. Com. (1974–76). South. OR Lib. Fed.: Secy. (1970–72). Ord. of East. Star: Worthy Matron (1956–57). Delta Kappa Gamma: Omicron Chap. (VP, 1979–80). OR Educ. Media Assn. Lane-Douglas Reg. LA. **Pubns.:** *Handbook for Library Skills* (1971); *Library Program Guide* (1976). **Activities:** 11; 21 **Addr.:** 3373 Riverside Properties, Star Rte. Box 60, Canyonville, OR 97417.

Gaver, Mary Virginia (D. 10, 1906, Washington, DC) Prof. Emeritus, Rutgers Univ., 1971–; Consult., Brodart Fndn., 1965–; Assoc. Prof., Prof., Rutgers Univ., 1954–71; Assoc. Prof., Trenton State Coll., 1942–54. **Educ.:** Randolph-Macon Woman's Coll., 1923–27, AB (Eng., Msc.); Columbia Univ., 1930–32, BSLS, 1937–38, MSLS. **Orgs.:** ALA: Pres. (1966–67); AASL, Pres. (1959–60). NJ LA: Pres. (1954–55). Women's Natl. Bk. Assn. CSLA: Pres. (1974–76). AAUW. LWV. Young Womens' Christ. Assn. **Honors:** Women's Natl. Bk. Assn., Constance Lindsay Taylor Awd., 1973; AASL, Baker and Taylor, Pres. Awd., 1980; Herbert Putnam Hon. Awd., 1963; Rutgers Resrch. Cncl. Awd., 1963; other hons. **Pubns.:** *Effectiveness of Elementary School Library Services* (1962); *Patterns of Development of Elementary School Libraries* (1969); *Elementary School Library Collection* (1965–75). **Activities:** 10, 11; 21, 24, 26 **Addr.:** 300 Virginia Ave., Danville, VA 24541.

Gavryck, Jacquelyn A. (Ap. 28, 1930, Elmira, NY) Assoc. Libn., SUNY, Albany, 1967–; Visit. Instr., SUNY, Sch. of Lib. and Info. Sci., 1975–; Asst. Libn., Russell Sage Coll., 1965–67; Asst. Libn., Hudson Valley Cmnty. Coll., 1963–65. **Educ.:** SUNY, Albany, 1947–51, BA (Eng.), 1952–54, MA (Eng.), 1962–67, MLS; Rensselaer Polytech. Inst., 1976, PhD (Comm.). **Orgs.:** ALA: ACRL/East. NY Chap. (Secy., 1979–81). Cap. Dist. Lib. Cncl.: Wrtg. and Resrch. Interest Table (Fndr., 1979–). SUNY Libns. Assn.: Nsltr. Ed. (1974–76); Persnl. Policies Com. (1977–79). State Univ. Sen. Com. on Persnl. Policies (1974–76). Cordialettes Chorus. **Honors:** Phi Delta Kappa, 1979. **Pubns.:** "Teaching Concept Identification Through Use of the *Thesaurus of ERIC Descriptors," Online* (Ja. 1980); "Shaping the Library's In-House Publications Policy," *Wilson Lib. Bltn.* (D. 1979); "Computer-Based Reference Services, a Course Taught by Practitioners," *Online* (Ap. 1978); "The SUNY Librarians' Faculty Status Game," *Jnl. of Acad. Libnshp.* (Jl. 1975); "State Secrets Made Public: the Albany Plan," *Lib. Resrcs. & Tech. Srvs.* (Win. 1973). **Activities:** 1, 11; 15, 31, 39; 75, 92, 93 **Addr.:** State University of New York, Albany Library, ULB 16, 1400 Washington Ave., Albany, NY 12222.

Gay, Elizabeth Kirk (O. 25, 1946, Lexington, KY) Asst. to Ctrl. Lib. Dir., Los Angeles Pub. Lib., 1979–, Subj. Dept. Mgr.-Sci. & Tech., 1976–79, Sr. Libn. Felipe de Neve Branch, 1974–76, Sr. Libn. Srv. to Shut-Ins, 1971–74, Libn. I-Sci. & Tech. Dept., 1971–71, SCAN Libn., 1969–71. **Educ.:** Vanderbilt Univ., 1964–68, BA (Eng.); Univ. of CA, Berkeley, 1968–69, MLS. **Orgs.:** CA LA: Int. Frdm. Com. (1976–79, Ch., 1978); CA Socty. of Libns. (Pres. 1975); Gvt. Rel. Com. (1975, 1978); NewCals Div., (VP, 1971); Grievance Com. (Ch. 1979, 1980). SLA: South. CA Chap. Adv. Bd. (1969–70). ALA. **Honors:** City of Los Angeles, Cert. of Cmdn. from Mayor, 1974. **Pubns.:** "Harm - In the Mind or in the Matter?" *CA Libn.* (Ap.-Jl. 1971). **Activities:** 9; 17, 49-Volun.; 74, 83, 91 **Addr.:** 800 W. First St. #806, Los Angeles, CA 90012.

Gaynon, David Bruce (N. 26, 1950, Chicago, IL) Info. Mgt. Consult., 1981–; Archvst., Cur. of Mss., N.E. MN Hist. Ctr., 1977–81; Intern, Cmrcl. Rec. Ctr., Recs. Mgt. Srvs., 1977; Archvst., IL State Arch., 1975–76. **Educ.:** Northwest. Univ., 1970–73, BA (Hist.); Case West. Rsv. Univ., 1973–74, MS (LS); 5th Anl. Wkshp. on Coll. and Univ. Arch., 1974, Cert. (Arch.); IL State Univ., 1967–81, MA (Hist.); various crs. **Orgs.:** SAA. Midwest Arch. Conf. Assn. of Recs. Mgrs. and Admins. Socty. of Can. Archvsts. **Honors:** Phi Alpha Theta. **Pubns.:** *Bibliography of Genealogical Reference Materials at Northeast Minnesota Historical Center* (1979); *Descriptive Inventory of the Archives of the State of Illinois* (1978); "Problems of Provenance in the General Assembly Records," *For the Rec.–Nsltr. of the IL State Arch.* (Ap. 1976); "Evolution and History of the Illinois Land Records," *For the Rec.–Nsltr. of the IL State Arch.* (N. 1975). **Activities:** 1, 2; 39, 45, 46; 54, 69, 85 **Addr.:** 3410 W. Foster Ave., Chicago, IL 60625.

Geahigan, Priscilla Cheng (Hong Kong) Head, Ref. Dept., Asst. Prof. (LS), Krannert Mgt. and Econ. Lib. Purdue Univ., 1977–; Actg. Head Ref. Libn., Oberlin Coll., 1977, Ref. Libn., 1970–77. **Educ.:** Hong Kong Bapt. Coll., 1963–67, BA; Ctrl. MI Univ., 1967–68, MA; Wayne State Univ. 1968–1970, MSLS. **Orgs.:** ALA. ASIS: IN Chap., (Secy., Treas., 1978–79). **Activities:** 1; 15, 31, 39; 59, 77, 92 **Addr.:** Krannert Library, Purdue University, West Lafayette, IN 47907.

Gearin, Louvan B. (Jl. 5, 1917, St. Louis, MO) Sch. libn., Hixson Jr. High, Webster Groves District, 1953–; Libn., Lincoln Inst., Lincoln Ridge, KY, 1950–53. **Educ.:** Fisk Univ., 1933–37, BA (Eng.); Atlanta Univ., 1947–48, BSLS; Univ. of MI, 1952–54, AMLS. **Orgs.:** St. Louis Suburban Sch. Libns.: Pres. (1960–62). MO Assn. of Sch. Libns.: Pres. (1966–67). Grt. St. Louis Lib. Club: Exec. Com. (1954–56). ALA: YASD Dir., (1974–77); Lib. Educ. Com. (1974–77); AASL Educ. Com. (1978–81). Webster Groves Assn. of Classroom Tchrs.: Tchr. Admin. Bd. Com. (1974–76). AAUW. **Pubns.:** "Combining Services for YAs", *Sch. Lib. Jnl.* (N. 1976). **Activities:** 10 **Addr.:** 11999 Villa Dorado Dr. Apt. C, St. Louis, MO 63141.

Geary, James W. (Ja. 13, 1945, Fort Myers, FL) Assoc. Prof., Lib. Admin., Asst. Dean, Acad. Affairs, Kent State Univ., 1977–; Dir., Amer. Hist. Resrch. Ctr., Univ. Archvst., 1977–, Fac.–Staff Coord., 1976–78, Archvst., Amer. Hist. Resrch. Ctr., 1975–77. **Educ.:** SUNY, Buffalo, 1966–69, BA (Hist., Pol. Sci.); Kent State Univ., 1969–71, MA (Hist.), 1971–76, PhD (Hist.), 1976–78, MLS; Arch.-Lib. Inst., OH Hist. Socty., 1975, Cert. **Orgs.:** ALA: JMRT, Arch. Com. (1978–79); SRRT; (Prog. Com. (Ch., 1978–79); SAA: Com. on Arch.–Lib. Rel.; Task Frc. on Arch. Slide–Tape Prog. (Ch., 1978–79); various other coms. Socty. of OH Archvsts.: Cncl. (1979–). OH Netwk. of Amer. Hist. Resrch. Ctrs.: Arrange. and Descr. Com. (1975–). OH Acad. of Hist.: Jt. Com. of OH Acad. of Hist.–Socty. of OH Archvsts. Org. of Amer. Histns. Immigration Hist. Socty. **Pubns.:** "A Fading Relationship: Library Schools and Preappointment Archival Education Since 1973," *Jnl. of Educ. for Libnshp.* (Sum. 1979); "Clement L. Vallandigham Views the Charleston Convention," *OH Hist.* (Spr. 1977); ed. adv. bd., *Socty. of OH Archvsts. Nsltr.* (1980–); various presentations. **Activities:** 1, 2; 17, 34, 45 **Addr.:** East Liverpool Campus, Kent State University, 400 E. 4th St., East Liverpool, OH 43920.

Geary, Kathleen A. (O. 28, 1939, Pittsfield, MA) Freelnc. Info. and Dev. Srvs. Consult., Self-Empl., 1979–; Exec. Secy., VT LA, 1978–79; Lib. Dir., Fletcher Free Lib., 1963–79. **Educ.:** Trinity Coll., 1957–61, BA (Eng., Span.); Simmons Coll., 1961–63, MLS (Lib. and Info. Sci.); St. Michael's Coll., 1978–79, MATESL; VT Dept. of Educ., Certs. (Media Generalist, Eng. Tchr., Readg. Tchr.); various crs. **Orgs.:** Champlain Valley LA: Pres. 1964; PR Dir. (1963); various coms., ofcs. New Eng. LA: Nom. Com. (1964, 1968–69); Outrch. Rap Session Grp. Leader (1971); various ofcs. VT LA: Bd. (Pres., Ch., 1965–67); various coms., ofcs. Zonta Club of Burlington: Secy. (1970–71); Pubcty., PR Com. Ch. (1972); various ofcs. Various other orgs. Leag. of Women Voters. Chittenden Cnty. Hist. Socty.: Com. on Hist. Sites (Ch., 1969–71). Burlington Hist. Sites Com.: Secy. (1970–80). Simmons Coll. Grad. Sch. of Lib. and Info. Sci. Alum. Assn.: Fund Dr. Plng. Com. (1969–70); Fund Dr. Team (1969–71); Bd. (Pres., Ch., 1973–74). Various other orgs. **Pubns.:** Cmplr., ed., *Vermontiana Checklist* (1976); *Outreach Directory I* (1972); "History of The Vermont Library Association," *Encyc. of Lib. and Info. Sci.* (forthcoming); "Insurance for Libraries," *VT Libs.* (N. 1971); "History of The Champlain Valley Library Association," *VT Libs.* (D. 1970); various articles. **Activities:** 9; 19, 24, 28; 51, 89 **Addr.:** 47 S. Williams St. #107, Burlington, VT 05401.

Gebhard, Patricia A. (Ja. 25, 1926, Minneapolis, MN) Ref. Libn., Coord., Lib. Instr., Univ. of CA, Santa Barbara, 1971–, Systs. Libn., 1969–71, Ref. Libn., 1962–69, Cat. Libn., 1961–62; Libn., Amer. Girls Acad., Uskudar, Istanbul, Turkey, 1960–61; Libn., S. Jr. HS, Roswell, NM, 1956–59; Asst. Libn., Base Lib., Walker Air Frc. Base, 1955–56; various libn. positions, 1951–55. **Educ.:** Oberlin Coll., 1944–48, AB (Art Hist.); Mills Coll., 1948–50, MA (Art Hist.); Univ. of MN, 1954, BS (LS). **Orgs.:** ALA: ACRL/Ref. Sect.; LIRT. CA Clearinghse. on Lib. Instr. Univ. of CA, Santa Barbara, Libns. Assn. **Pubns.:** Jt. auth., *Li-*

PROFESSIONAL ACTIVITIES: Institutions: 1. Acad. lib.; 2. Arch.; 3. Assn.; 4. Fed./Gvt. lib.; 5. Inst. lib.; 6. Mfr./Suppl.; 7. Milit. lib.; 8. Musm.; 9. Pub. lib.; 10. Sch. lib.; 11. Sch. of lib. sci.; 12. Spec. lib.; 13. State lib.; 14. (other). **Functions/Activities:** 15. Acq./Col. dev.; 16. Adult srvs.; 17. Admin.; 18. Apprais.; 19. Archit./Bldgs.; 20. Cat./Class.; 21. Chld. srvs.; 22. Circ.; 23. Cons./Pres.; 24. Consult.; 25. Cont. ed.; 26. Educ. lib. sci.; 27. Ext. srvs.; 28. Fund/Grants; 29. Gvt. pubs.; 30. Indx./Abs.; 31. Instr. lib. use; 32. Media srvs.; 33. Micro.; 34. Netwks./Coop.; 35. Persnl.; 36. PR; 37. Publshg.; 38. Recs. mgt.; 39. Ref. srvs.; 40. Repro.; 41. Resrch.; 42. Review.; 43. Secur.; 44. Serials; 45. Spec. col.; 46. Tech. srvs.; 47. Trustees/Bds.; 48. YA srvs.; 49. (other).

brary Skills ERIC (1979); jt. auth., *Library Research* ERIC (1978); "Networking in the Microcosm: Reference Referrals," *RQ* (Spr. 1978); "How to Evaluate Library Instructional Programs," *CA Libn.* (Ap. 1976); jt. auth., "Survey of Local Newspapers in California," *CA Libn.* (Ja. 1975); various articles. **Activities:** 1; 31, 39 **Addr.:** 895 E. Mountain Dr., Santa Barbara, CA 93108.

Gecas, Judith Gaskell (O. 22, 1945, Littlefork, MN) Head, Pub. Srvs., Univ. of Chicago Law Lib., 1980–, Ref. Libn., 1977–79; Law Libn., Sonnenschein Carlin Nath and Rosenthal, 1974–76. **Educ.:** Carleton Coll., 1963–67, BA (Eng. Lit.); Univ. of Chicago, 1971–75, MA (LS); DePaul Univ., 1975–80, JD (Law). **Orgs.:** AALL. Chicago Assn. of Law Libs. Amer. Bar Assn. IL State Bar Assn. Chicago Bar Assn. **Activities:** 1; 17, 22, 39; 77 **Addr.:** University of Chicago Law Library, 1121 E. 60th St., L206, Chicago, IL 60637.

Geddes, Andrew (O. 2, 1922, Flushing, NY) Dir., Nassau Lib. Syst., 1964–, Deputy Dir., 1963–64; Actg. Persnl. Dir., Queensboro. Pub. Lib., 1960–61, Chief, Ext. Srvs., 1961–63, 1956–60, Admin. Asst., 1955–56; Branch Libn., Brooklyn Pub. Lib., 1952–55, Asst. Branch Libn., 1952; various tchg. positions at univ. lib. schs., 1967–69. **Educ.:** Hofstra Univ., 1946–50, BA (Hist.); Columbia Univ., 1950–51, MLS; NY Univ., 1955–58, various certs. (Job Analysis, Work Simplification, Org. Plng., Performance Stans.). **Orgs.:** ALA: PLA (Pres., 1970–71); various coms., chs. (1951–). NY LA: Pres. (1967–68); various coms., chs. (1951–). Lib. PR: Treas. (1961–63); various coms., chs. (1960–). NY Lib. Club: Treas. (1957–60); various coms., chs. (1955–57). Various other orgs. Melvil Dui Chowder and Marching Assn. Hofstra Alum. Assn. Columbia Alum. Assn. **Pubns.:** *Fiscal Responsibility and the Small Public Library* (1978); *Securing a New Library Director* (1979); 30 std. of libs., lib. opers., bldg. progs., (1963–80); various articles in *Lib. Jnl., Amer. Libs., Can. LA Procs., NY LA Bltn., ALTA Nsltr., RQ*, others. **Activities:** 13; 17 **Addr.:** 29 Patten Ave., Oceanside, NY 11572.

Gehres, Eleanor M. (F. 18, 1932, Riverside, NJ) Instr., CO Hist., Metro. State Coll., 1975–; Head, West. Hist. Dept., Denver Pub. Lib., 1974–; Prog., Grants Coord., CO State Lib., 1973–74; Visit. Asst. Prof., Univ. of Denver Grad. Sch. of Lib., 1971–73; Elem. Sch. Libn., Denver Pub. Schs., 1961–71; various tchg. positions, 1952–61. **Educ.:** Univ. of VA, 1948–52, BA (Eng.); Univ. of Denver, 1968, MA (Libnshp.), 1972, MA (Hist.), Univ. of Denver, 1980–, Ph.D. (Higher Educ.); 1980–, Cert. (Mgt.); various sems. **Orgs.:** ALA. Mt. Plains LA. SLA. CO Bibl. Proj.: Adv. Com. (1976–80). Various other orgs. CO Hist. Grp.: Secy.-Treas.; Pres. (1976–). Untd. Profs. in Educ.: Norfolk Cnty. Educ. Assn. (Secy., 1954–59); VA Educ. Assn. Statewide Com. on Integration (1958–59); Denver Classrm. Tchrs. Assn. (Bldg. Rep., 1963–67); Sch. Bldg. Com. (Ch., 1968–71). AAUP. CO Women's Coll.: Pres. Adv. Bd. (1976–). Various other orgs. **Pubns.:** "Mountaineering: Climbing Colorado's Peaks," *Trail and Timberline* (O. 1970); various curric. guides, wkshps., radio and TV interviews. **Activities:** 9, 12; 17, 36, 45; 54, 73 **Addr.:** 935 Pennsylvania St., Denver, CO 80203.

Gehringer, Michael E. (N. 5, 1950, Philadelphia, PA) Pres., FDR ONLINE INC., 1981–; Asst. libn. for Resrch. Srvs., Supreme Court of the US, 1978–81; Ref. Spec., American-British Law Div., Law Lib., Lib. of Congs., 1976–78; Ref. Libn., Robert J. White Law Lib., Catholic Univ., 1975–76, Catlgr., 1974–75. **Educ.:** Duquesne Univ., 1968–72, AB (Eng.); Catholic Univ., 1972–74, MSLS, 1974–79, JD (Law). **Orgs.:** AALL: (Vice-ch./Ch.-elect, Gvt. Docum. Spec. Int. Sect, 1978–79; Ch., 1980–81). Law Libns. Socty. of Washington, DC: Bd. of Dir. (1978–1981). Amer. Bar Assn. **Honors:** Beta Phi Mu. **Pubns.:** Ed., "Questions and Answers" *Law Lib. Jnl.* (1977–). **Activities:** 1, 4; 17, 29, 39; 77, 78 **Addr.:** FDR ONLINE, Inc., 510 Fifth Street, N.W., Washington, DC 20001.

Gehringer, Susan M. (O. 29, 1952, Reading, PA) Catlgr., Reading Pub. Lib., 1978–, Ref./Gvt. Docs. Libn., 1976–78, Branch Asst., 1974–76. **Educ.:** Kutztown State Coll., 1970–74, BS (Lib. Educ.); Drexel Univ., 1975–77, MS (LS). **Orgs.:** ALA. PA LA: Secy., Chld., Young Peoples & Sch. Libns. Div., (1979–80). Middle Atl. Reg. LA: Conf. Lcl. Arrange. Ch. (1979). **Activities:** 9; 20, 21, 39; 56 **Addr.:** Reading Public Library, 5th & Franklin Sts., Reading, PA 19602.

Geiger, Richard G. (S. 13, 1946, Los Angeles, CA) Chief Libn., *San Jose Mercury News*, 1980–; Libn., *San Francisco Chronicle*, 1976–80; Libn., Natl. Maritime Musm., 1975–76. **Educ.:** Univ. of CA, Santa Barbara, 1964–70, BA (Art, Bio.); Univ. of CA, Los Angeles, 1973–75, MLS (Lib., Info. Sci.). **Orgs.:** SLA: Bay Area Chap. (Advert. Ch., 1979–); Newsp. Div. (Bus. Mgr., 1980–). Blue Water Cruising Club. San Francisco Folk Club. **Activities:** 12; 17, 37, 41; 83 **Addr.:** San Jose Mercury News, Library, 750 Ridder Park Dr., San Jose, CA 95190.

Geil, Wilma Jean (My. 24, 1939, Pittsburgh, PA) Assoc. Msc. Libn., Univ. of IL, 1963–. **Educ.:** Swarthmore Coll., 1957–61, BA (Msc.), Univ. of IL, 1961–67, MS (LS), 1965, MM (Msclgy.) (1967). **Orgs.:** Intl. Assn. of Msc. Libs. Msc. LA: various coms. Amer. Msclgy. Socty. Sonneck Socty.: Secy. (1976–p.) **Pubns.:** Asst. Dir., *Resources of American Music History* (1980); "American Sheet Music in the Walter N. H. Harding Collection at the Bodleian Library, Oxford" Msc. LA *Notes* (Je. 1978). **Activities:** 1; 15, 31, 39; 55, 95 **Addr.:** Music Library, 2136 Music Building, 1114 W. Nevada, Urbana, IL 61801.

Geiser, Elizabeth A. (Phillipsburg, NJ) VP, Gale Resrch. Co., 1976–; Adj. Prof., Univ. of Denver, 1977; Dir., Univ. of Denver Publ. Inst., 1976–; Sr. VP, R. R. Bowker Co., 1972–75, VP, Mktg., 1970–74, Dir., of Mktg., 1968–70, Sales Mgr., 1960–67; Lectr., Radcliffe Coll. Publ. Procs. Course, 1967–74. **Educ.:** Hood Coll., 1947, AB (Mod. Langs.). **Orgs.:** ALA: Exhibits RT, (Pres., 1967–69; Bd. of Dir., 1969–71). AAP: Libs. Com. (Ch., 1973–74); Educ. for Publ. Com. (1975–79); Frankfurt Bk. Fair Adv. Com. (1968). **Honors:** Hood Coll., Alum. Achvmt. Awd., 1972. **Pubns.:** "Tools of the Trade," *Manual of Bookselling* (1968); "New Talent for the Publishing Field," *Antiquarian Bookman* (My. 29, 1978). **Activities:** 6, 14; 17; 95-Intl. Mktg. **Addr.:** Gale Research Co., 150 East 50th St., New York, NY 10022.

Gelfand, Morris A. (Je. 1, 1908, Bayonne, NJ) Prof. Emeritus, Queens Coll., Grad. Sch. of Lib. and Info. Std., 1976–, Ch., Dept. of LS, 1970–76, Chief Libn., 1946–70; Fulbright Lectr. and Lib. Consult., Univ. of Rangoon, 1958–59; Consult. for Unesco, Ford Fndn., Rockefeller Fndn., U.S. Agency for Intl. Dev., Overseas, 1962–77. **Educ.:** NY Univ., 1929–33, BS (Econ.); Columbia Univ., 1932–34, BS (LS); NY Univ., 1960, PhD (Higher Educ.). **Orgs.:** ALA: ACRL. Bibl. Socty. of Amer. NY LA: VP (1968–69). ASIS. Amer. Prtg. Hist. Assn.: Trustee; Educ. Com. (Ch., 1978–). **Pubns.:** *University Libraries for Developing Countries* (1968); various articles, reviews; contrib. to various bks. **Activities:** 1, 4; 17, 19, 24; 57, 78 **Addr.:** Stone House, 35 Post Dr., Roslyn Harbor, NY 11576.

Gelinas, Jeanne L. (Ag. 14, 1933, Holyoke, MA) Prin. Libn., Golden Valley Cmnty. Lib., Hennepin Cnty. (MN) Lib. 1975–; Asst. Dir., Ref. Bridgeport Pub. Lib., 1974–75; Head, Ext., Knoxville-Knox Cnty. Pub. Lib., 1972–74; Asst. Prof. (LS), Univ. of TN, 1971–72; Asst. Dir., Ferguson Lib. (Stamford, CT), 1967–71. **Educ.:** Coll. of St. Catherine, 1950–54, BA (Fr., LS) Case-Western Resrv. Univ., 1965–66 MLS. Univ. of Poitiers, Fr., 1954–55 (Fr.). **Orgs.:** ALA: Notable Bks. Cncl; LAMA Lib. Org. and Mgt. Sect. (Ch., 1978–79). MN LA: Rep. at Lg. (1976–78). SLA. Metro. Cncl.: Comm. Adv. Com. (1976–78). **Honors:** Beta Phi Mu; Phi Beta Kappa. Fulbright Schol., 1954–55. **Activities:** 9; 15, 35, 39; 50, 55, 90 **Addr.:** Hennepin County Library, 7009 York Ave. S., Edina, MN 55435.

Gélinas, René (Ja. 12, 1946, Grand'Mère, PQ) Agent de Dev. Ped., Min. de l'Educ. du PQ, 1981–; Cnslr. Péd. en Moyens d'Enseignement, Comsn. Scol. Rég. Louis-Fréchette, 1972–81; Bibtcr., Comsn. Scol. Rég. Orléans, 1971–72; Enseignant, Comsn. Scol. Rég. de la Mauricie, 1968–70. **Educ.:** Sém. Ste-Marie, 1967, BA; Univ. d'Ottawa, 1970–71, BLS; Univ. Laval, 1979, Bac. d'ens. sec. **Orgs.:** ASTED. Can. LA. Corp. des Bibtcrs. Prof. du PQ. **Pubns.:** *Méthode et Techniques de Travail* (1976); *Liste Sélective de Périodiques* (1976); *Un guide d'Organisation* (1981). **Activities:** 10; 17, 32, 46 **Addr.:** 826, Boul. Méthot, St-Nicolas-Est., PQ G0S 3L0 Canada.

Gell, Marilyn Killebrew (Ag. 23, 1944, Chickasha, OK) Pres., Gell and Assocs., 1981–; Dir., WHCOLIS, 1979–81; Sr. Resrch. Assoc., King Resrch. Inc., 1978–79; Chief of Lib. Progs., Metro. Washington Cncl. of Gvts., 1973–77; Dept. Head, Arlington Cnty. Pub. Lib., 1969–73; Libn., NJ State Lib., 1968–69. **Educ.:** Univ. of Dallas, 1962–66, BA (Eng. Lit.); N. TX State Univ., 1966–68, MLS; Harvard Univ., 1977–78, MPA (Pub. Admin.). **Orgs.:** ALA. SLA. ASIS. **Honors:** N. TX State Univ., Disting. Alum., 1979. **Pubns.:** "Washington and Beyond: The White House Conference on Library and Information Services," *Sch. Media Qtly.* (Fall 1979); "The Politics of Information," *Lib. Jnl.* (S. 15, 1979); "User Fees I: The Economic Argument," *Lib. Jnl.* (Ja. 1, 1979); "User Fees II: The Library Response," *Lib. Jnl.* (Ja. 15, 1979); "Cooperative Planning in Action: The Washington Experiment," *Spec. Libs.* (Jl. 1976); various other articles. **Activities:** 4; 17, 24; 78, 89 **Addr.:** Gell and Assocs., Arlington, VA 22207.

Gellatly, Peter (F. 16, 1923, Scone, Scotland) Ed. and Consult., *The Serials Librarian, Library and Archival Security & Topics in Technical Services*, Haworth Press, 1977–; Head, Serials, Univ. of WA Libs., 1970–77, Serials Libn., 1959–77, Biblgphr., 1954–59. **Educ.:** Univ. of BC, 1945–50 BA (Langs.); Univ. of WA, 1953–54, ML (LS). **Orgs.:** ALA: Various ofcs. Can. LA. Pac. NW LA: Various ofcs. **Honors:** Beta Phi Mu. **Pubns.:** *The Management of Serials Automation* (1981); *Sex Magazines in the Library Collection* (1980); jt.-auth., *Guide to Magazine and Serials Agents* (1975); various articles. **Addr.:** 310 Third St., New Westminster, BC V3L 2R9 Canada.

Geller, Lawrence D. (My. 29, 1940, Newark, NJ) Archvst. of Plymouth, MA, 1978–; Vist. Prof. in Arch. Mgt., Bridgewater State Coll., 1969–; Dir., Pilgrim Socty. Lib. and Musm., 1969–77; Prof. of Hist., James Madison Univ., 1965–69. **Educ.:** Middlebury Coll., 1959–62, BA (Hist.); New York Univ., 1962–65, MA (Hist.); Roosevelt Univ., 1971–73, PhD (Hist., Arch.). **Orgs.:** SAA: Mncpl. Arch. New Eng. Archvsts. Socty. of Archit. Histns. Amer. Hist. Assn. **Honors:** Fellow, Royal Socty. of Arts (London), 1975. **Pubns.:** *The Books of the Pilgrims* (1976); *The Architecture of Elegance* (1975); *The Arthur Lord Collection in the Pilgrim Society Library; Elder William Brewster and The First New England Library.* **Activities:** 2, 13; 17, 19, 20, 23; 62, 95-Mncpl. Gvt. **Addr.:** 13 Vernon St., Plymouth, MA

Gellert, Charles Lawrence (Ja. 26, 1946, Brooklyn, NY) Head of Ref. Unit, Motion Pic. & Snd. Rec. Branch, Natl. Arch., 1980–, Archvst. AV Arch. Div., 1978–80, Arch. Head of Ref. & Prsrvn. Unit, Mach. Readable Arch. Div., 1977; Archvst.-Mach. Readable Arch. Div., 1973–77. **Educ.:** Univ. of Chicago, 1962–66, BA (Hist.); NY Univ., 1966–70, MA (Hist.). **Orgs.:** SAA: Mach. Readable Recs. Com. (1973–75); Aural & Graphic Recs. Com. (1979–). Mid-Atl. Reg. Arch. Conf. Org. of Amer. Histns. Amer. Jewish Hist. Socty. **Pubns.:** *Catalog of Machine Readable Records in the National Archives of the United States* (1975). **Activities:** 2; 17, 18, 20, 49; 56, 67 **Addr.:** Motion Picture & Sound Recording Branch (NNVM), National Archives and Records Service, Washington, DC 20408.

Gellert, Roberta Holder (My. 1, 1939, Newark, NJ) Consult., Self-empl., 1980–; Coadj., Grad. Sch. of Lib. and Info. Srvs., Rutgers Univ., 1978–80; Sr. YA Libn., Greenburgh Pub. Lib., 1973–75; Dir., Ardsley Pub. Lib., 1972–73; Libn., NY Pub. Lib., 1968–72. **Educ.:** Bryn Mawr Coll., 1957–61, AB (Phil., Pol. Sci.); Columbia Univ., 1967–68, MS, PhD (LS); various crs. **Orgs.:** ALA: YASD, Org. Com. (Ch., 1979–); Re-eval. of Goals and Objectives Com. (1977–78); TV Com. (1971–73). Westchester LA: YA and Chld. Libn. (Ch., 1974–75). **Activities:** 9, 11; 17, 26, 48; 63 **Addr.:** Lewis Rd., Irvington, NY 10533.

Genaway, David C. (My. 29, 1937, Elmira, NY) Univ. Libn., Youngstown State Univ., 1980–; Assoc. Dean, Libs. and Lrng. Resrcs., East. KY Univ., 1976–; Libn., Waite Meml. Lib., Univ. of MN, 1972–76; Lib. Dir., Dakota State Coll., 1969–71; Asst. Prof., Peabody Lib. Sch., Vanderbilt Univ., 1967–69; Instr., Ctrl. WA State Univ., 1965–67; Descr. Cat. Libn., Andrews Univ., 1963–64; Spec. Educ. Tchr., Niles Excep. Sch., 1961–62; Tchr., Flint Jr. Acad., 1960–61; various positions as consult. **Educ.:** Atl. Un. Coll., 1955–60, BA; Andrews Univ., 1960–64, MA; Univ. of MI, 1964–65, AMLS; Univ. of MN, 1971–75, PhD (LS); various crs. **Orgs.:** KY LA: Bd. (1978–79); Acad. Lib. Sect. (Ch., 1978–79). SLA: KY Chap., Bd. (1979–80). Ctrl. WA State Univ. Lib. Staff Assn.: Past Pres. (1965–66). ASIS. Various other orgs. Microprcs. Users Grp.: Fndr. (1979–). Pilots Assn. of Libns.: Fndr. (1977). Mensa. **Pubns.:** "Bar Coding and the Librarian Supermarket; an Analysis of Advertised Vacancies," *Lib. Jnl.* (F. 1, 1978); "Quasi-Departmental Libraries," *Coll. & Resrch. Libs.* (My. 1977); "Multi-media Resources, a Unified Approach," ERIC; "The Job Market in the Southeast: Analysis of S.E.L.A. Library Vacancies Advertised in the National Library Journals," *The Southeast. Libn.* (Sum. 1978); "General Aviation: An Overview and Subjective, Synoptic, Summary of Sources," *Lib. Jnl. Spec. Rpt. No. 6* (1978); various bk. reviews. **Activities:** 1, 5; 17, 24; 52, 56, 59 **Addr.:** 530 W. Regency Cir., Canfield, OH 44406.

Genesen, Judith L. (Mr. 12, 1932, Chicago, IL) Ref. Libn., Chicago Transit Athrty. Lib., 1974–; Ref. Libn., Jt. Ref. Lib., 1971–74; Libn., Lab. Sch. HS Lib., 1965–70. **Educ.:** Univ. of Chicago, 1947–51, (Liberal Arts); 1961–65, AM (LS). **Orgs.:** SLA: Pres., IL Chap. (1981–82); Cont. Educ. Com. (1978–1980); Pres.-Elect and Ch., Prog. Com. (1980–81); Ch., Career Guid. and Affirmative Action Com. (1976–1978). Chicago Lib. Club: Secy. (1976–1977). Chicago Lib. Syst.: Cont. Educ. Com. (1979–80). IL Reg. Lib. Cncl.: Subcom. on Col. Dev., Conv., Bus. Interest Sub. Grp. (1977–1979). Transp. Resrch. Bd.: Com. on Transit Info. Exch. (1977–). **Activities:** 12; 15, 38, 39; 59, 94 **Addr.:** P.O. Box 3555, Merchandise Mart Plz., Chicago, IL 60654.

Gennett, Robert G. (Mr. 1, 1937, New York, NY) Assoc. Libn., Lafayette Coll., 1965–; Ref. Libn., NY Pub. Lib., 1961–64. **Educ.:** Queens Coll., 1955–59, BA (Hist.); Columbia Univ., 1959–61, MLS. **Orgs.:** ALA. ACRL - Delaware Valley Chap., Dir.-at-large, (1976–78). Amer. Friends of Lafayette: Secy.-Treas., (1971–). **Activities:** 1; 17, 45 **Addr.:** David Bishop Skillman Library, Lafayette College, Easton, PA 18042.

Gensel, Susan Lee (My. 2, 1941, Los Angeles, CA) Mktg. Dir., Head Libn., Cold Spring Harbor Lab., 1978–, Head Libn., 1972–77; Sci. Ref. Libn., Univ. of CA, Riverside, 1971–72, Head, Serials Tech. Prcs., Autom. and Systs. Libn., 1964–71; Adj. Asst. Prof., Anl. Serials Crs., Long Island Univ. **Educ.:** Univ. of CA, 1958–64, BA (Eng. Lit.); Univ. of South. CA, 1970–71, MLS. **Orgs.:** SLA: Bio. Sci. Div. (Pres., 1979–80); Long Island Chap. (Pres., 1976–77). Long Island Lib. Resrcs. Cncl.: Bd. of Trustees (Pres., 1975–76). ALA. Med. LA. Various other orgs. **Pubns.:** Jt. ed., *Cell Index 1974–77* (1978); jt. ed., *Nassau-Suffolk Un. List of Serials* (1975); ed., *SLA Bio. Sci. Div. Nsltr.* (1973–75); *Black Theatre; An Annotated Bibliography and Commentary* (1974); *Flora and Fauna of Cold Spring Harbor's Wetlands, Sandspit, and Inner Harbor. Bibliography* (1972). **Activities:** 2, 12; 15, 17, 26; 55, 58, 75 **Addr.:** Cold Spring Harbor Laboratory, The Library, P.O. Box 100, Cold Spring Harbor, NY 11724.

Special Subjects/Services: 50. Adult educ.; 51. Advert./Mktg.; 52. Aerosp.; 53. Agric.; 54. Area std.; 55. Arts/Hum.; 56. Autom.; 57. Bibl./Prtg.; 58. Bio. sci.; 59. Bus./Fin.; 60. Chem.; 61. Copyrt.; 62. Documtn.; 63. Educ.; 64. Engin.; 65. Env.; 66. Eth. grps.; 67. Film; 68. Food/Nutr.; 69. Geneal.; 70. Geo.; 71. Geol.; 72. Handcpd.; 73. Hist.; 74. Int. frdm.; 75. Info. sci.; 76. Insr.; 77. Law; 78. Legis.; 79. Math./Comp. sci.; 80. Med.; 81. Metals; 82. Nat. resrcs.; 83. Newsp.; 84. Nuc. sci.; 85. Oral hist.; 86. Petr./Energy; 87. Pharm.; 88. Phys./Astr./Math.; 89. Readg.; 90. Relig.; 91. Sci./Tech.; 92. Soc. sci.; 93. Telecom.; 94. Transp.; 95. (other).

Gentz, William H. (My. 10, 1918, Cokato, MN) Pubns. Dir., CS LA, Ed., *Church and Synagogue Libs.*, 1977–; various positions in bk. publshg, including Bk. Ed., The Seabury Press, The Genesis Proj., Friendship Press. **Educ.:** Univ. of MN, 1935–39, BA (Jnlsm.); Luther Theo. Semy., 1941–45, MTh (Theo.). **Orgs.:** CS LA: Pres. (1976–77). Luth. Church LA: Fndn. Mem. **Pubns.:** *The Religious Writers Marketplace* (1980); *Careers Opportunities in Religion* (1979). **Activities:** 12; 37; 90 **Addr.:** 300 E. 34th St. (9C), New York, NY 10016.

Geoffroy, Melba Y. (Ap. 20, 1926, Bronaugh, MO) Dir., Winchester (IN) Cmnty. Lib., 1979–; Dir., Mishawaka (IN) Pub. Lib., 1974–78, Asst. Dir., 1972–74, Libn., 1969–72. **Educ.:** Univ. of KS, 1944–48, BS (Educ.), 1949–51, MS (Eng.-Educ.); West. MI Univ., 1972–74, MLS. **Orgs.:** ALA: PLA, Org. Com. (1977–81). IN LA. Legis. Com. (1976–78). Bus. and Prof. Women. Altrusa. AAUW: All Lcl. Ofcs. **Activities:** 9; 17, 36; 50, 78 **Addr.:** Winchester Community Library, Winchester, IN 47394.

George, Mary W. (Ja. 23, 1948, Ann Arbor, MI) Head, Ref. Dept., Princeton Univ. Lib., 1980–; Ref. Libn. & Bibl. Univ. of MI Lib., 1972–80, Lect., Sch. of LS, 1976–80, Asst. ILL Libn., 1970–72. **Educ.:** Univ. of MI, 1965–69, BA (Eng.); 1969–70, AMLS, 1972–75, MA (Eng.). **Orgs.:** ALA: ACRL Plng. Com. (1976–80); Constn. & Bylaws Com. (Ch. 1978–80); Cncl. (1981–85). Bibl. Instr. Sect., Policy & Plng. Com. (Ch. 1978–80). MI LA: Ch., Acad. Div., (1978–79); Ch., Ref. Sect., (1977–78); Cont. Educ. Com. (1976–78). Mod. Lang. Assn. of America: Adv. Bd., Bibl. Rev. Proj. (1978–80). Univ. of MI Alum. Assn.: Bd. of Dir., (1976–79). Univ. of MI: Sen. Assembly (1978–80); Com. on the Econ. Status of the Fac. (1976–79); Rules Com. (1978–80). **Honors:** Beta Phi Mu, 1975. **Pubns.:** Jt. auth., *Michigan Library Association Workshop Manual* (1977); Contrib., *The Complete Stylist and Handbook* (1980); Contrib., *Bibliographic Instruction Handbook* (1979); jt. auth., "The Bibliography and Research Methods Course in American Departments of English," *Literary Resrch. Nsltr.* (Win. 1979); "Things We Weren't Taught in Library School," in *Putting Library Instruction in Its Place: In the Library and in the Library School,* (1978); Reviews. **Activities:** 1; 26, 31, 39; 55, **Addr.:** Princeton University Library, Princeton, NJ 08544.

George, Melvin R. (F. 20, 1937, Grove City, MN) Univ. Libn. and Dir. of Lrng. Srvs., Northeast. IL Univ., 1974–; Visit. Lctr. (LS), Rosary Coll. 1967–; Coll. Libn., Elmhurst Coll., 1965–74; Libn., St. Louis Park (MN) Pub. Schs., 1960–65. **Educ.:** St. Cloud State Univ., 1955–59 BS (Lang. Arts), 1960, MA (Eng.); Univ. of MN, 1963–65 MA (LS); Univ. of Chicago, 1971–1979 PhD (Educ.). **Orgs.:** IL LA: Pres. (1976–77). IL Assn. of Coll. and Resrch. Libs.: Ch. (1973). ALA: ACRL, *Choice* Ed. Bd. (Ch., 1975–78). Cncl. of Dirs. of State Univ. Libs. in IL: Ch. (1978–79). IL Reg. Lib. Cncl.: Bd. of Dir. (1972–75). IL State Lib.: Adv. Com. (1973–). **Pubns.:** "Small Academic Libraries," *Multitype Library Cooperation,* (1977); "Durkheim and Weber in Wonderland, or Building Environmental Collections for the Real World," *Information Resources in the Environmental Sciences* (1973); "Budget Planning," *Cath. Lib. Wld.* (Ap. 1977); "More than Survival for Academic Libraries Too," *Cath. Lib. Wld.* (S. 1977). **Activities:** 1; 17, 24, 26; 50, 63, 95-Lib. Bldgs. **Addr.:** University Librarian, Northeastern Illinois University, 5500 N. St. Louis Ave., Chicago, IL 60625.

George, Shirley H. (D. 29, 1938, Elgin, IL) Admin. Libn., Maywood Pub. Lib., (IL), 1975–; Head of Reader's Srv. and Ref. Dept., Helen M. Plum Meml. Lib., Lombard, IL, 1973–75; Ref. Libn., Elmhurst (IL) Pub. Lib., 1971–73. **Educ.:** Valparaiso Univ., 1956–60, BA (Eng.); Univ. of MN, 1969, MA (LS). **Orgs.:** ALA. IL LA: Ch., Intl. Frdm. Com. (1976–77); Dir., Intl. Frdm. Proj. (1977–78). Lib. Admin. Conf. of North. IL, Treas. (1979–80). Maywood Cham. of Cmrce.: Bd. of Dirs. (1977–). IL WHCOLIS: Del. (1978). **Activities:** 9; 15, 17, 35; 74, 75, 78 **Addr.:** 580 Mitchell, Elmhurst, IL 60126.

Georgenson, Gail S. (F. 5, 1950, Cincinnati, OH) Resrch. Libn., Space Imagery Ctr., Lunar and Planetary Lab., Univ. of AZ, 1976–; Resrch. Asst., Dept. of Agr., Univ. of AZ, 1975–76. **Educ.:** OH Univ., 1968–72, BS (Gen. Std.); Univ. of AZ, 1973–75, MLS. **Orgs.:** AZ State LA: Conf. Plng. Com. (1976). SLA: Bltn. Ed. (1978); Chap. Pres. (1979). Assn. of Recs. Mgrs. and Admins.: Educ. Com. (Ch., 1979–80). Planned Parenthood of South. AZ: Exec. Bd. (1978–79); Nsltr. Ed. (1977–78). Com. on Status of Univ. Women. Univ. of AZ Grad. Lib. Sch.: Long Range Plng. Com. (1979–80). **Activities:** 12; 17, 23, 38; 52, 67, 88 **Addr.:** Space Imagery Center, Lunar & Planetary Laboratory, University of Arizona, Tucson, AZ 85721.

Georgi, Charlotte (Pittsburgh, PA) Chief Libn., Grad. Sch. of Mgt. Lib., Univ. of CA, Los Angeles, 1959–; Chief, Bus. Admin. and Soc. Sci. Div., Univ. of NC, 1957–59, Libn., Grad. Sch. of Bus. Admin., 1955–57; Assoc. Prof., Integrated Arts, Stephens Coll., 1943–54. **Educ.:** SUNY, Buffalo, 1938–42, BA magna cum laude (Eng.); 1942–43, MA (Comp. Lit); Univ. of NC, 1954–55, MS (LS); Grad. work in Integrated Arts, Univ. of WI, 1947–49. **Orgs.:** ALA. CALA. SLA: Natl. Bd. of Dir., (1967–71); Ch., Bus. & Finance Div., (1964–66). AAUP: Secy., UCLA Chap., (1969–78). Los Angeles Com. of Bus. and Prof. Women: Bd. of Dir. (1975–81). **Honors:** Phi Beta Kappa, Beta Phi Mu; Phi Chi Theta; Pi Lambda Theta. **Pubns.:** Jt. cmplr., Sources of Commodity Prices (1960); *Statistics Sources* (1962, 1965, 1971); *The Literature of Executive Management* (1963); jt. ed., *Encyclopedia of Business Information Sources* (1965, 1970, 1976, 1980); *The Arts and the World of Business* (1973, 1979); Articles and reviews. **Activities:** 1, 12; 17, 39, 42; 55, 59 **Addr.:** Graduate School of Management, University of California, Los Angeles, CA 90024.

Gerard, Helene L. (Ja. 30, 1932, Brooklyn, NY) Sch. Lib. Media Spec., Westhampton Beach, 1970–; Libn., Bd. of Coop. Educ. Srvs., 1968–70. **Educ.:** Smith Coll., 1949–53, BA (Pol. Sci.); Long Island Univ., 1966–71, MLS. **Orgs.:** NY LA: Legis. Com. (1978–79). Suffolk Cnty. LA: Sch. Liaison to Bd. (1979–80); Legis. Com. (Rep., 1979–80); Schol. Com. (1975). Suffolk Sch. Lib. Media Assn.: Bd. (1975); Pres. (1976); Bd., various coms. (1977–79). Oral Hist. Assn. New Eng. Assn. of Oral Hist. **Pubns.:** "And We're Still Here: 100 Years of Small Town Jewish Life," *Long Island Forum* (O. 1981); *A History of the Westhampton Free Library in Westhampton Beach, New York* (1971); "The Past is Still Present," *Media and Methods* (N. 1977); "Remembrance of Things Past-Orally," *NY LA Bltn.* (Mr. 1978). **Activities:** 10; 15, 17, 21; 55, 78, 85 **Addr.:** Box 146, Remsenburg, NY 11960.

Gercken, Richard (Ja. 5, 1933, Jacksonville, FL) Dir., Great Falls Pub. Lib., 1977–; Hum. Libn., Univ. of MT Lib., 1973–77, Head Ref. Libn., 1969–73; various positions, NY Pub. Lib., 1964–69. **Educ.:** Univ. of Notre Dame, 1951–54, AB (Mod. Lang.); Univ. of CA, Los Angeles, 1962–64, MLS (Lib. Srv.). **Orgs.:** Pac. NW LA. MT LA: Pres. (1980). Frdm. to Read Fndn. **Honors:** Phi Delta Kappa, Frnd. of Educ., 1979. **Activities:** 9; 16, 21, 42; 55, 67, 90 **Addr.:** Great Falls Public Library, 2nd Ave. N. & 3rd St., Great Falls, MT 59401.

Gerdes, Rev. Neil W. (O. 19, 1943, Moline, IL) Libn., Asst. Prof., Chicago Theo. Semy., 1980–; Lib. Prog. Dir., Chicago Cluster of Theo. Schs., 1976–80; Libn., Asst. Prof., Meadville/Lombard Theo. Sch., 1973–; Ed. Asst., *Lib. Qtly.*, 1973–74; Instr. of Hum.,-Tuskegee Inst., 1971–73. **Educ.:** Univ. of IL, 1961–65, AB (Hist./Eng.); Harvard Univ., 1965–68, STB (Relig.); Columbia Univ., 1970–71, MA (Educ. Admin.); Univ. of Chicago, 1973–75, AM (LS). **Orgs.:** ALA. ATLA. Chicago Area Theo. LA: Secy. (1976–79). Collegium of Liberal Relig. Schol.: Secy.-Treas., (1975–). Hyde Park - Kenwood Cncl. of Churches and Synagogues: Exec. Com. (1977–). **Pubns.:** Ed., *Cluster Union List of Periodicals* (1979). **Activities:** 1; 17; 90 **Addr.:** 5701 S. Woodlawn Ave., Chicago, IL 60637.

Gerhardt, Lillian Noreen (S. 28, 1932, New Haven, CT) Ed.-in-Chief, *Sch. Lib. Jnl.*, 1971–, Bk. Review Ed., 1966–71; Assoc. Ed., *Kirkus Reviews,* 1962–66; Head, Ref., Meriden Pub. Lib., 1958–61, Asst. Ref. Libn., 1955–58; Storyteller, Libn., New Haven Free Pub. Lib., 1954–55; Instr., Columbia Univ. Sch. of Lib. Srv., 1969–72. **Educ.:** South. CT State Coll., 1950–54, BS (LS); Univ. of Chicago Grad. Lib. Sch., 1961–62. **Orgs.:** ALA: Cnclr.-at-Lrg. (1976–80); ALSC, Pres. (1978–79); Past Pres. (1979–80). NY LA. Women's Natl. Bk. Assn.: NY Chap. (Bd. of Mgrs., 1972–75). Natl. Bk. Critics Cir. **Honors:** South. State Coll., Div. of LS, Disting. Alum., 1978. **Pubns.:** Ed., *Issues in Children's Book Selection* (1973); sr. ed., compilation coord., *Children's Books In Print* (1969); sr. ed., compilation coord., *Subject Guide to Children's Books In Print* (1969); various articles, edshps., reviews, *Sch. Lib. Jnl.* (1966–). **Activities:** 9, 10; 21, 37, 42 **Addr.:** *School Library Journal,* R.R. Bowker Co., 1180 Ave. of the Americas, New York, NY 10036.

Gerhardt, Stephen L. (My. 17, 1930, Iowa Falls, IA) Mktg. Rep., C.L. Systs., Inc., 1979–; Head, of Cmnty. Rel., New Orleans Pub. Lib., 1978–79; Dir., Puget Sound Cmnty. Coll. Lib. Coop., 1972–77; Dir., of Instr. Resrcs., Shoreline Cmnty. Coll., 1966–72. **Educ.:** Cascade Coll., 1948–52, BA, (Educ.); Univ. of WA, 1963–65, ML. **Orgs.:** ALA: LITA, Distribution and Exch. Com. (1978–80). LA LA. SWLA. U.S. Coast Guard Resrv.: Unit Cmndg. Ofcr. (1969–70). Northwest Assn. of TV Arts and Sci. **Honors:** Phi Delta Kappa. Beta Phi Mu. **Pubns.:** "Sabbatical - Or How to Manipulate the System for Fun and Profit," *Pac. Northwest LA Qtly.* (Spr. 1977); "Creative Librarianship in New Orleans," *Film Lib. Qtly.* (1978); Producer, Host, "Community Bulletin Board" (Wkly Cable TV Series) (1976); Jt.-producer, Jt.-Host, "Election '76" - (Cable TV Series) (1976). **Activities:** 1, 9; 22, 34, 36; 56, 93 **Addr.:** 6 Captain Dr., #245, Emeryville, CA 94608.

Gericke, Paul William (Ap. 8, 1924, St. Louis, MO) Dir. of the Lib., New Orleans Bapt. Theo. Semy., 1965; Pastor Various Bapt. Churches, 1955–64. **Educ.:** Washington Univ., 1946–49, BS (Elect. Engin.); South. Bapt. Theo. Semy., 1958–60, BD (Theo.); New Orleans Bapt. Theo. Semy., 1960–64, ThD (Pastoral Mnstry.); Univ. of New Orleans, 1970–72, MA (LS). **Orgs.:** ATLA. SWLA. Natl. Religious Broadcasters. Amer. Radio Relay Leag. **Pubns.:** *Crucial Experiences in the Life of D. L. Moody* (1978); *Sermon Building* (1973); *The Ministers Filing System* (1971); *The Preaching of Robert G. Lee* (1967). **Activities:** 1; 15, 31, 32; 90 **Addr.:** New Orleans Baptist Theological Seminary, 3939 Gentilly Blvd., New Orleans, LA 70126.

Gerity, Louise P. (Jl. 29, 1933, Honolulu, HI) Ref. Libn., Lewis and Clark Coll. Lib., 1963–; Catlgr., Portland State Coll., 1962–63; Chld. Libn., Lib. of HI, 1959–62; Chld. Libn., NY Pub. Lib., 1957–58. **Educ.:** Reed Coll., 1951–55, BA (Lit.); Columbia Univ., 1955–57, MS (Lib. Srv.). **Orgs.:** Pac. NW LA: Exec. Bd. (1978–80). OR LA: Schol. Com. (Ch., 1971); Treas. (1972–74); Cont. Educ. Com. (Ch., 1975–77); Natl. Lib. Week (Ch., 1977–78); Exec. Bd. (1978–80). ALA: Mem. Com. (1970–74); GODORT, Micro. Task Frc. (Co-Coord., 1974); ACRL/Bldg. and Equip. Sect., various coms. Univ. of WA: Career Dev. and Assess. Ctr. for Libns.: Strg. Com. (1980–). **Honors:** Cncl. on Lib. Resrcs., Lib. Srv. Enhancement Prog., 1976–77. **Activities:** 1, 9; 21, 29, 39 **Addr.:** Lewis & Clark College Library, 0615 S.W. Palatine Hill Rd., Portland, OR 97219.

Germain, Claire M. (S. 22, 1951, Chaumont, Fr.) Sr. Ref. Libn. and Lectr., Duke Univ., Law Lib., 1977–. **Educ.:** Univ. de Paris III, Sorbonne Nouvelle, 1968–71, Licence-ès-Lettres (Germ.); Univ. de Paris XII, 1969–74, LLB; LA State Univ., 1974–75, MCL (Law); Univ. of Denver, 1977, MLL (Law Libnshp.). **Orgs.:** AALL: Com. on Frgn. and Intl. Law (1978–), Ch. (1981–), Com. on the Index to Frgn. Legal Periodicals (1979–). Intl. Assn. of Law Libs. Duke Univ. Libs.: Exec. Com. of the Lib. Asm. (1979–). **Honors:** Max-Planck-Inst. (Germ.), Resrch Flw., Guest Libn., 1980; Beta Phi Mu. **Pubns.:** "European Community Law—A Selective Bibliography of Publications in English, French and German with Annotations," *Intl. Jnl. of Law Libs.* (D. 1980); "Current Research Sources in French Law," *Intl. Jnl. of Law Libs.* (N. 1979); "France: Libraries of Law and Librarians," *Law Lib. Jnl.* (Spr. 1979). **Activities:** 29, 31, 41; 77, 78 **Addr.:** Law Library, Duke University, Durham, NC 27706.

Gerritts, Judy Ann (O. 18, 1939, Appleton, WI) Chief Libn., *San Francisco Examiner,* 1979–; Chief Libn., Miami News, 1976–79; Sr. Resrch. Libn., Xerox, 1969–76; Chief Libn., *Houston Chronicle,* 1967–69. **Educ.:** Marquette Univ., 1954–61, AF (Hist., Eng.); Univ. of Vienna, Vienna, Austria, 1960; Univ. of WI, 1965–66, MA (LS). **Orgs.:** SLA: CT Valley Chap., Pres., Secy., Treas.; Newsp. Div., Autom. Com., Nsltr. Bus. Mgr. **Honors:** Beta Phi Mu, 1966. **Activities:** 5, 12; 17, 33, 39; 56, 62, 83 **Addr.:** San Francisco Examiner Library, 110 5th St., San Francisco, CA 94103.

Gersack, Dorothy Hill (O. 24, 1910, Livingston, IL) Archvst. U.S. Natl. Arch., 1936–1975; Catalgr., Univ. of IL, 1933; 1934–36; Asst. Chld. Libn., Warder Pub. Lib. (Springfield, OH), 1931–31; Circ. and Ref. Libn., Danville (IL) Pub. Lib., 1933–34. **Educ.:** Wittenberg Univ., Western Coll., Univ. of IL, 1928–32 BS (Educ.); Univ. of IL, 1932–1933 BS (LS), 1934–1936 MS (LS). George Washington Univ., 1939–41 (Law). **Orgs.:** ALA: RAST/Hist. Sect., Bd. of Dir. SAA: *News Notes* (Ed., 1960–68). Univ. of IL Lib. Sch. Assn.: Pres. (1941–46). Bethesda (MD) Fire Board: Archvst., Hist. (1966–68), Procedures Com. (1969–70), Secy. (1970–75). Citizens Com. (Oakmont, MD): Fiscal Rev. Com. (1957–58), Ordinance Rev. Subcom. (1967–68). Many other orgs. **Honors:** Beta Phi Mu., SAA Flw., 1967. **Pubns.:** *National Crime Reporting, 1930–1967* (1973). "Colonial, State and Federal Court Records, A Survey," *Amer. Archvst.* (Ja. 1973). "Research Use of Federal Court Records," (Audio Tape) (U.S. Fed. Recs. Ctr., Chicago, File 64-19) (1971). Many lectrs. and presented papers. **Activities:** 1, 2; 18, 20, 38; 62, 69, 77 **Addr.:** P.O. Box 645, Ruidoso Downs, NM 88346.

Gerson, Gordon M., Sr. (O. 2, 1936, New York, NY) Dept. Mgr., Info. Srvs. Dept., C.A.C.I., Inc., 1979–; Deputy Chief, Comp. Systs. Div., Defense Comms. Agency, 1975–79; Assoc. Prof., Comp. Sci., U.S. Air Frc. Acad., 1972–75, Asst. Prof., 1971–72. **Educ.:** U.S. Nvl. Acad., 1954–58, BS (Gen. Engin.); Univ. of MI, 1963–65, MSE (Electrical Engin.); Univ. of TX, Austin, 1969–71, PhD (Comp. Sci.). **Orgs.:** ASIS: Jnl. (Referee, 1973–). Assn. for Comp. Mach. Inst. for Electrical and Electronics Engins. **Honors:** Defense Comms. Agency, Defense Merit. Srv. Medal, 1979; U.S. Air Frc. Acad., Merit. Srv. Medal, 1975. **Pubns.:** "Cliqueing; A Technique for Forming Maximally Connected Clusters," *Jnl. of The Amer. Socty. for Info. Sci.* (1975); "An Automatic Classification and Retrieval System for U.S. Patents," *Info. Retrieval* (1972). **Activities:** 24, 30; 56, 70, 75 **Addr.:** 10913 Knights Bridge Ct., Reston, VA 22090.

Gertzog, Alice (Ap. 30, 1934, NY, NY) Dir., Meadville Pub. Lib., 1975–; Archvst., Crawford Cnty. Hist. Socty., 1972–75; Ref. Libn., New Haven Pub. Lib., 1968–72; Acq. Libn., New Haven Coll. Lib., 1965–68; Acq. Libn., Econ. Growth Ctr., Yale Univ., 1964–65, Info. Consult., NASA (Washington DC), 1963, Ref. Libn., Univ. of NC Lib., 1960–62. **Educ.:** Antioch Coll., 1951–55 AB (Lit.); Catholic Univ. 1958–60, MSLS. **Orgs.:** ALA: PLA, Northwest Chap. (Ch.). PA LA: Bd. Mem.; Nom. Com. **Pubns.:** "Chapter XI; Conversations on Libraries," *Lib. Jnl. Spec. Rpt.* 12, (19–). **Activities:** 1, 9; 16, 17, 39; 50, 74, 92 **Addr.:** Meadville Public Library, 848 North Main St., Meadville, PA 16335.

Gervino, Joan Dir., Lib. Srvs., Amer. Bankers Assn., 1973–; Libn., DC Bar Assn., 1972–73; Libn., Fed. Deposit Insr. Corp., 1967–72. **Educ.:** Mt. Holyoke Coll., 1962–66, AB (Eng. Lit.); Rutgers Univ., 1966–67, MLS. **Orgs.:** Law Libns. Socty., DC: Treas. (1978–79). SLA: Bus. and Fin. Div., Ch. (1980–81), Ch.-Elect (1979–80), Bank Libs. Cir. (Coord., 1977); WA Chap. Prog.

PROFESSIONAL ACTIVITIES: Institutions: 1. Acad. lib.; 2. Arch.; 3. Assn.; 4. Fed./Gvt. lib.; 5. Inst. lib.; 6. Mfr./Suppl.; 7. Milit. lib.; 8. Musm.; 9. Pub. lib.; 10. Sch. lib.; 11. Sch. of lib. sci.; 12. Spec. lib.; 13. State lib.; 14. (other). **Functions/Activities:** 15. Acq./Col. dev.; 16. Adult srvs.; 17. Admin.; 18. Apprais.; 19. Archit./Bldgs.; 20. Cat./Class.; 21. Chld. srvs.; 22. Circ.; 23. Cons./Pres.; 24. Consult.; 25. Cont. ed.; 26. Educ. lib. sci.; 27. Ext. srvs.; 28. Fund/Grants; 29. Gvt. pubs.; 30. Indx./Abs.; 31. Instr. lib. use; 32. Media srvs.; 33. Micro.; 34. Netwks./Coop.; 35. Persnl.; 36. PR; 37. Publshg.; 38. Recs. mgt.; 39. Ref. srvs.; 40. Repro.; 41. Resrch.; 42. Review.; 43. Secur.; 44. Serials; 45. Spec. col.; 46. Tech. srvs.; 47. Trustees/Bds.; 48. YA srvs.; 49. (other).

Ch., Pres.-Elect. (1981–82), Soc. Sci. Grp., Ch. (1979–80), Prog. Ch., Ch.-Elect (1978–79), Nom. Com. (1978–79). AALL. Metro. WA Cncl. of Gvts.: Lib. Cncl. Assoc. Info. Mgrs. **Pubns.:** "Business and Banking Information Sources," *Law Lib. Jnl.* (N. 1977). **Activities:** 12; 17; 59, 77, 78 **Addr.:** American Bankers Association, Library, 1120 Connecticut Ave., N.W., Washington, DC 20036.

Gesterfield, Kathryn J. (Ap. 3, 1915, Minatare, NE) Dir., IL State Lib., 1975–, Consult., 1970–75; Dir., Champaign Pub. Lib., 1962–69; Dir., Scottsbluff Pub. Lib. **Educ.:** Univ. of Denver, 1938–39, AB (LS); Univ. of IL, 1960–61, MSLS. **Orgs.:** IL LA. ALA: RASD, Bd. (1969–71); LAMA/Stats. Sect., Stats. for SLA (1980–), 2nd VP (1968–69), Pub. Lib. Sect. (Ch., 1963–64); Exec. Bd. (1975–). **Addr.:** 209 Circle Dr., Springfield, IL 62703.

Ghali, Raouf S. (Ap. 10, 1941, Cairo, Egypt) Assoc. Dental Libn., NY Univ., Med. Ctr. Lib., 1977–, Asst. Libn., Dental Ctr. Lib., 1972–77, Asst. to Head, Cat. Dept., Bobst Lib., 1969–77; Head Libn., Giza Educ. Zone Pub. Lib., Cairo, Egypt, 1958–69. **Educ.:** Cairo Univ., 1954–58, BA (LS); Pratt Inst., 1970–72, MLS; NY Univ., 1976–78, MPA (Pub. Admin.). **Orgs.:** ALA. NY LA. Med. LA. **Honors:** Beta Phi Mu. **Pubns.:** *Classified List of Selected Books for School Libraries* (1969); 5 articles in Arabic, *Lib. World* (1960–69). **Activities:** 1; 17, 35, 46; 80 **Addr.:** 169–04 73rd Ave., Flushing, NY 11366.

Ghausi, Marilyn (Ag. 12, 1937, New York, NY) Musm. Archvst., Detroit Inst. of Arts, 1978–; Archvst., Amer. Psyt. Assn., 1973–76; Asst. Archvst., Butterick Arch., 1971–72. **Educ.:** Pratt Inst., 1956–59, BS (Art Educ.); NY Univ., 1971, MA (US Hist./Art Hist.); Cert., Arch. Admin., Natl. Arch., Amer. Univ., 1973. **Orgs.:** SAA: Intl. Arch. Affairs Com. MI Arch. Assn. **Pubns.:** *From the Inside: The Archives of the Detroit Inst. of Arts 1883-1945* (1980); *Summary Inventory, Museum Archives of the Detroit Inst. of Arts* (1979). **Activities:** 2; 18, 19, 23, 41; 55 **Addr.:** Detroit Institute of Arts, Detroit, MI 48108.

Gherman, Paul M. (S. 10, 1942, Detroit, MI) Asst. Dir., Admin. Srvs., IA State Univ., 1977–; Persnl. Ofcr., PA State Univ., 1974–77; Circ. Libn., Wayne State Univ., 1971–74. **Educ.:** Wayne State Univ., 1962–66, BA (Eng.); Univ. of MI, 1970–71, MALS. **Orgs.:** ALA: ACRL, Discuss. Grp. of Persnl. Ofcrs., Discuss. Grp. of Staff Dev. Ofcrs. Amer. Socty. of Persnl. Admins.: Cyclone Country Chap., Secy.-Treas. **Pubns.:** "Post Masters Internship Program," *Lib. Jnl.* (Je. 15, 1980); "Implementing an Integrated Personnel System," *Jnl. of Acad. Libnshp.* (S. 1980). **Activities:** 1; 17, 19, 35 **Addr.:** 163 Library, Iowa State University, Ames, IA 50011.

Gholston, Howard Donald (Ag. 20, 1927, Lorenza, TX) Supvsr., Tech. Lib., Chevron Resrch. Co., 1961–; Asst. Libn., E. R. Squibb, 1955–61. **Educ.:** Univ. of TX, Austin, 1948–50, BS (Chem.), 1950–53, MA (Biochem.), 1953–54 (Lib. Sch.). **Orgs.:** SLA: San Francisco Bay Reg. Chap., Dir. (1964–66), Pres. (1970–71), Petr. Div. (Ch., 1972–73). Amer. Chem. Socty. **Pubns.:** Jt. ed., *Dictionary of German Chemical Abbreviations* (1966); asst. ed., *Unlisted Drugs* (1955–59); ed., *Unlisted Drugs* (1960–61). **Activities:** 12; 17; 60, 64, 86 **Addr.:** Chevron Research Co., 576 Standard Ave., Richmond, CA 94805.

Giaquinta, C. (Carolyn) Joyce (D. 12, 1942, Alton, IL) Gen. Docum. Libn., Gvt. Pubns. Dept., Univ. of IA Libs., 1980–; Mss. Libn., State Hist. Socty. of IA, 1974–80. Head Libn., 1971–74, Libn., 1965–66. **Educ.:** Univ. of IL, 1959–63, BA (Hist.); Univ. of IA, 1967–69, MA (LS). **Orgs.:** IA LA: Johnson Brigham Plaque Com. (Ch., 1977–80); Exec. Bd. (1980–83). SAA. Midwest Archs. Conf. IA Hist. Mtrls. Prsrvn. Socty. IA Lcl. Hist. and Musm. Assn. Faith Bapt. Church. IA Hist. Recs. Adv. Bd.: Secy. (1976–80). **Pubns.:** "The State Historical Society of Iowa," *Encyc. of Lib. and Info. Sci.* (1980); "The Irish-Preston Papers, 1832–72," *Annals of IA* (Fall 1978); "Patriotic Envelopes," *The Palimpsest* (N.–D. 1974). **Activities:** 2, 13; 15, 23, 45; 55, 70, 85 **Addr.:** 445 Upland, Iowa City, IA 52240.

Gibbons, Virginia Harris (Ag. 12, 1946, Plymouth, IN) Cat. Mgt. and Mktg. Sect. Libn., Northwest. Univ., 1981–; Serials Libn., Princeton Univ., 1980–81, Cat. Maintenance Libn., 1979–80, Team Leader, Near E. Team, Cat. Div., 1976–78, Serials Catlgr., Cat. Div., 1974–76. **Educ.:** Allegheny Coll., 1964–68, BA (Fr.); Univ. of CA, Berkeley, 1972–73, MLS. **Orgs.:** ALA. Mid. E. Libns. Assn.: VP; Com. Ch. (1976–77). Mid. E. Std. Assn. **Pubns.:** "A Bibliography of Middle Eastern Statistical Documents," *Mid. E. Std. Assn. Bltn.* (My. 31, 1974). **Activities:** 1; 17, 20, 44; 54, 56 **Addr.:** Catalogue Management & Marketing Section, Northwestern University Library, Evanston, IL 60202.

Gibbs, Donald L. (D. 3, 1942, Richmond, CA) Latin Amer. Bibl., Univ. of TX, 1972–, Circ., Acq. Libn., Latin Amer. Coll., 1968–72. **Educ.:** OK State Univ., 1960–64, BA (Sp., Fr.); Univ. of TX 1965–68, MA (Latin Amer. Stds.), 1969–79, PhD (Hist.). **Orgs.:** Sem. on the Acq. of Latin Amer. Lib. Mtrls. (SALALM): Rapporteur Gen. (1976–77); Subcom. on Coop. Acq. (Ch., 1979–80); Gifts and Exch. Subcom., (1975–); Acquisitions Com. (1979–). Latin American Stds. Assn. **Honors:** Fulbright Flwshp., Bolivia, 1964. **Pubns.:** Jt.-auth., "Provisional list of dissertations on Latin American topics...," *Latin Amer. Stds. Assn. Nsltr.* (1974–); comp. "Latin American History: Selected Reference Sources," *Latin American Culture Studies: Information and Materials for Teaching About Latin America.* (1977); "The Archives of Cuzco," *Research Guide to Andean History: Bolivia, Chile, Ecuador, Peru.* (Duke Univ. Press) (1981); various presented papers. Reviews. **Activities:** 1; 15, 45; 54, 57 **Addr.:** 8217 Renton Dr., Austin, TX 78758.

Gibbs, Jane Frances (Mr. 6, 1913, Lincoln, NE) Sub., Cleveland Pub. Lib., 1978–, Catlgr., Retired, 1973–78; Med. Lib. Libn., Cleveland Clinic Fndn., 1971–73; Libn., Cleveland Musm. of Nat. Hist., 1962–71; Catlgr. of Rare Bks., Natl. Lib. of Med., 1944–62; Gen. Adult Asst., Cleveland Hts. Pub. Lib., 1940–44; Catlgr., Ref. Libn., Canton Pub. Lib., 1936–40. **Educ.:** Miami Univ., OH, 1931–35, AB (Hist., Eng.); Case West. Rsv. Univ., 1935–36, BS (LS). **Orgs.:** SLA: Cleveland Chap. (Treas., 1969–70). OH LA. ALA: RTSD, Conv. Com. Lcl. Arrange. Ch., 1950), Pubcty. Com. North. OH Tech. Srvs. Libns.: Chrt. Mem.; Ch. (1952). Various other orgs., ofcs. Bus. and Prof. Women's Club of Cleveland. **Activities:** 4, 12; 20, 39, 45; 80, 82, 91 **Addr.:** 2600 Traymore Rd., University Heights, Cleveland, OH 44118.

Gibbs, Margareth Strout (Ag. 23, 1939, La Salle, IL) Consult., Info. Network Srvs., IL Valley Lib. Syst., 1977–; Interlib. Coop. Coord., Starved Rock Lib. Syst., 1975–76; Dir. of Quality Control, Bobbie Sue Div. of Unishops, Inc., 1970–73. **Educ.:** Univ. of IL, 1973–74, BA (Rhetoric); 1974–75, MSLS. **Orgs.:** ALA: RASD, Coop. Ref. Com. (1978–80). IL LA. NLA. **Honors:** Beta Phi Mu, 1975. **Activities:** 14-Multi-Type Lib. Syst.; 15, 17, 39; 69, 85 **Addr.:** 1310 La Fayette St., La Salle, IL 61301.

Gibbs, Robert Coleman (Ag. 27, 1930, Bath, NC) Asst. Univ. Libn., For Ref. and Info. Srvs., Auburn Univ. Libs., 1976–; Asst. to the Dir., 1968–76; Serials Acq. Libn., PA State Univ., 1964–68; Asst. Acq. Libn., Univ. of FL, 1960–64; Gifts and Exch. Libn., 1958–60. **Educ.:** Duke Univ., 1948–52 AB (Hist.); Univ. of NC, 1957–58, MSLS. **Orgs.:** ALA. AL LA: Various Coms. SELA. AAUP. **Honors:** Beta Phi Mu. **Pubns.:** "Periodicals Reevaluation Project," Proc. Southeast. LA Conf. (1972). **Activities:** 1; 15, 17, 35 **Addr.:** 1238 Juniper Dr., Auburn, AL 36830.

Gibbs, Ruth B. (F. 2, 1943, Taylorville, IL) Assoc. Univ. Libn., Resrch. and Instr. Srvs., Univ. of CA, Los Angeles, 1979–; Head, Access Srvs., Columbia Univ., 1974–77, Head, Circ. Dept., 1971–74, Asst. Head, Bus. Lib., 1969–71. **Educ.:** Valparaiso Univ., 1961–65, BA (Pol. Sci.); Univ. of MI, 1967–69, MALS. **Orgs.:** ALA: ACRL; LAMA; RASD; LIRT. CA ACRL. CA Clearinghse. on Lib. Instr. Natl. CLSI Users' Grp.: Acad. Sect. (Ch., 1979–81). Assn. of Acad. Women, Univ. of CA, Los Angeles. Frnds. of the Univ. of CA, Los Angeles Lib. South. CA Tech. Prcs. Grp. **Pubns.:** "The UCLA Stack Annex: Help for the Library's Space Problems," *Univ. of CA, Los Angeles, Libn.* (S. 1980); "Library Service to Undergraduates: Directions for the 1980's," *Univ. of CA, Los Angeles, Libn.* (F. 1981). **Activities:** 1; 17 **Addr.:** Research & Instructional Services, University of California, Los Angeles, Library, 405 Hilgard, Los Angeles, CA 90024.

Giblin, James C. (Jl. 8, 1933, Cleveland, OH) Ed. and Publshr., Houghton Mifflin/Clarion Bks., 1979–; Sr. VP, Ed.-in-Chief, Clarion Bks., Seabury Press, 1967–79; Ed., Lothrop, Lee and Shepard Co., Inc., 1962–67. **Educ.:** Case West. Rsv. Univ., 1951–54, AB (Eng., Dramatic Arts); Columbia Univ., 1954–55, MFA (Drama). **Orgs.:** ALA: Int. Frdm. Com. (1980–). Chld. Bk. Cncl., Inc.: Bd. of Dirs. (1971–74, 1975–78); Pres. (1976). Socty. of Chld. Bk. Writers: Bd. of Dirs. (1975–). Natl. Cncl. of Tchrs. of Eng. **Pubns.:** "Honesty vs. 'Acceptability': How Does an Editor Decide?" *Top of the News* (Spr. 1979); "Conversations in Cuba," *Sch. Lib. Jnl.* (S. 1978). **Activities:** 6; 21, 37; 74 **Addr.:** Houghton Mifflin/Clarion Books, 52 Vanderbilt Ave., New York, NY 10017.

Giblon, Della L. (O. 16, 1945, Scottsbluff, NE) Publ. Srvs. Dir., Leon Cnty. Pub. Lib., 1980–; Cmnty. Rel. Libn., Leon Cnty. Pub. Lib., 1977–80. Head, Infor. Srvs., 1975–77; Instr. (LS), FL State Univ., 1974–80; Head, Ad. Srvs., Leon Cnty. Pub. Lib., 1971–75. **Educ.:** Univ. of CA, Santa Barbara, 1964–67, BA (Fr., Eng.); Univ. of CA, Los Angeles, 1967–68 Tchng. Cert. (Fr.) FL State Univ., 1969–71, MSLS, 1971–73, AMD (LS). **Orgs.:** CLENE.-SELA: Ref. and Adult Srvs. Sect. (Ch., 1976–78). FL LA: Bd. of Dir. (1978–80); Ch. of Various Interest Grps. ALA: RASD, Adult Lib. Mtrls. Com. (Ch., 1979–81), Various other Coms.; ASCLA, Lib. Srvs. to the Unserved Disc. Grp. (Ch., 1976–79); LAMA/Pub. Rel. Sect., Pub. Rel. and Libs. Com. (1979). Various other orgs. Tallahassee Garden Club: Sasangua Garden Circle (Pres., 1977). Killearn Ladies Club: Book Review Group. World Future Socty.: Tallahasee Chap. (Secy., 1979–). Beta Phi Mu: Gamma Chap. (FL State Univ.) (Pres., 1976–77). **Pubns.:** Ed., *Adult Services Issue* RQ (Spr. 1979) Ed., *Florida Libraries* (FL LA Jnl.) (Spr. 1978–). "Who, What, When, How About Adult Services," *Southeast. Libs.* (1975); "Public Relations with a P for Practicality," *FL Libs.* (1973); Other colmns. **Activities:** 9, 11; 16, 36, 39; 50, 51, 89 **Addr.:** Leon County Public Library, 1940 N. Monroe St., Tallahassee, FL 32303.

Gibson, Barbara H. (My. 3, 1941, Concord, NH) Dir. of Lib. Srvs., The Vlg. Lib., 1973–, Coord., Srvs. to Chld. and YA, 1971–73, Branch Libn., 1970–71; Curric. Lab. Libn., Ctrl. CT State Coll., 1965–70. **Educ.:** Wheelock Coll., 1959–63, BS (Early Chld. Educ.); South. CT State Coll., 1970, MLS; various crs. **Orgs.:** CT LA: Chld. Srvs. Sect. (Ch., 1975–77). New Eng. LA. ALA. Cap. Reg. Lib. Cncl.: Pres. (1977–79). Town and Gown Film Circuit: Admin. Libn. (1973–). **Pubns.:** Jt. auth., "Work with Children in Connecticut," *CT Libs.* (1975). **Activities:** 9; 15, 17 **Addr.:** The Village Library, 71 Main St., Farmington, CT 06032.

Gibson, Charles Mac (Ag. 14, 1946, Lubbock, TX) Corp. Libn., Roy M. Huffington, Inc., 1981–; Syst. Coord., Rice Univ., 1979–81; Coord. of Circ. Srvs., 1977–79; Soc. Sci. Ref. Libn., 1974–77; Tchr., Ch., Eng. Dept., Roosevelt Indep. Sch. Dist., 1969–73. **Educ.:** TX Tech. Coll., 1964–68, BA (Hist.); 1968–69, MA (Hist.); Univ. of TX, 1973–74, MLS; Univ. of Houston, 1976–81, MBA. **Orgs.:** ASIS. TX LA: Spec. Libs. Div., Sec./Treas. (1976–77); Pres. (1977–78). SLA: Cont. Educ. Com. (1974–77); *TX List* Ed. Adv. Bd. (1978–); Liaison with TX LA (1975–77). Houston OLUG: Treas. (1978–79). TX Folklore Socty. Amer. Folklore Socty. **Pubns.:** "Fondren Online with All Systems 'Go'," *The Flyleaf* (S. 1979); "User Oriented Serials List," *TX Spec. Libs. Bltn.* (F. 1977); Reviews. **Activities:** 1; 17, 22, 34; 56, 75, 92 **Addr.:** 13126 Ferry Hill, Houston, TX 77015.

Gibson, Claude E. (Ap. 25, 1935, Tuskegee, AL) Dir., Info. Resrcs. and Recs. Mgt., Grumman Aerosp. Corp., 1980–, Mgr., Info. and Rec. Srvs., 1970–80, Chief Libn., 1968–70, Asst. Chief Libn., 1963–68; Lit. Resrch. Spec., Space Tech. Labs., 1961–63; Asst. Libn., Ryan Aeronautical Co., 1958–61; Tech. Rpts. Anal., Goodyear Atomic Corp., 1957–58. **Educ.:** Rensselaer Polytech. Inst., 1953–57, BS (Chem.); Univ. of South. CA, 1958–62, MS (LS); various crs. **Orgs.:** SLA: Long Island Chap., Pres. (1977–78), Treas. (1974–76); various coms., ofcs. Inst. of Electrical and Electronic Engin. **Pubns.:** Contrib., *Encyc. of Lib. and Info. Sci.* (1968). **Activities:** 12; 17, 33, 38; 52, 56, 75 **Addr.:** 41 Landing Rd., Huntington, NY 11743.

Gibson, Eleanor Beatrice (Mr. 8, 1905, London, Eng.) Lib. Consult.; Tech. Supvsr., Un. Cat. Comp. Proj., CT State Lib., 1968–71; Lib. Adv., Carrier Corp., 1968–70, Head Libn., 1947–67; Libn., Resrch. Div., Aetna Life and Casualty, 1928–42. **Educ.:** Cornell Univ., 1923–27, AB (Fr.); Syracuse Univ., 1954–57, MS (LS). **Orgs.:** SLA: NY Chap. (Pres., 1959–60), various coms.; Metals/Mtrls. Div. (Natl. Ch., 1961–62). ASIS: Upstate NY Chap. (Org., 1968). West Hartford Art Leag. Amer. Legion. CT Acad. of Fine Arts. **Honors:** SLA, Hall of Fame, 1968; SLA Metals/Mtrls. Div., Hons. Awd., 1968; Pi Lambda Sigma, 1957; Beta Phi Mu, 1958. **Pubns.:** Ed., *Guide to Metallurgical Information* (1965); various articles. **Activities:** 4, 12; 24, 41, 46; 55, 81, 91 **Addr.:** Leighton Hill Rd., Wells River, VT 05081.

Gibson, Elizabeth (Liz) Ellen (Je. 5, 1942, Sacramento, CA) Systs., Autom. Consult., CA State Lib., 1975–, CLSA Prog. Dir., 1977–80, Asst. Systs. Anal., 1970–75. **Educ.:** Univ. of CA, Davis, 1960–64, AB (Eng., Math.), 1964–65, Sec. Tchg. Cred. (Eng.); Univ. of CA, Berkeley, 1969–70, MLS (Libnshp.). **Orgs.:** ALA. CA LA. SLA. **Honors:** CA Lib. Srvs. Bd., Resol. of Cmdn., 1980. **Pubns.:** *BIBCON 360, Volume 1: A File Management System for Bibliographic Records Control* (1972); "BIBCON-A General Purpose Software System for MARC-Based Book Catalog Production," *Jnl. of Lib. Autom.* (D. 1973); "Evaluation of Automated Circulation Systems," *News Notes of CA Libs.* (1976). **Activities:** 9, 13; 24, 31, 49-Systs. analysis, autom.; 56, 93 **Addr.:** 4974 Daru Way, Fair Oaks, CA 95628.

Gibson, Harold R. (S. 12, 1937, McMinnville, OR) Dir. of Libs., Pac. Med. Ctr., 1975–; Dir., Visual Sci. Info. Ctr., Univ. of CA and Pac. Med. Ctr., 1969–; Dir. of Libs., Pac. Univ., 1962–68. **Educ.:** Linfield Coll., 1959, BA (Eng.); Univ. of Portland, 1961, MLS, Univ. of CA, 1968, MLS. **Orgs.:** Med. Lib. Assn. SLA. Assn. of Visual Sci. Libns. Fndr. AAAS. Amer. Acad. of Optometry: Sect. on Info. (Ch., 1966–71). **Honors:** Amer. Optometric Assn., Auxiliary Grant, 1973. **Pubns.:** Ed., *Vision Index* (1971–1977). **Activities:** 1, 12; 17, 30, 34; 75, 80 **Addr.:** 310 Rugby Ave., Kensington, CA 94708.

Gibson, Mary Jane (Lexington, KY) Ref. Spec., Lib. of Congs., 1963–. **Educ.:** Transylvania Coll., 1941–45, AB (Fr.); LA State Univ., 1962–63, MLS. **Orgs.:** ALA. SLA. Amer. Socty. of Indxrs. DC LA. **Pubns.:** Comp., *Portuguese Africa; a Guide to Official Publications* (1967); Comp., "United States of America National Bibliographical and Abstracting Services and Related Activities," *RQ* (anl.). **Activities:** 4; 15, 39; 54, 57 **Addr.:** 2401 H St., N.W., Apt. 806, Washington, DC 20037.

Gibson, Robert Stansill (Ag. 1, 1925, Richmond Cnty., NC) Asst. Prof. and Coord. of the LS Prog., Radford Univ., 1970–, Asst. Prof. of LS & Pub. Srvs. Libn., 1964–69; Assoc. Libn., Louisburg Coll., 1963–64; Asst. Soc. Sci. Libn., Univ. of GA, 1961–63; Dir., Appalachian Wesley Fndn., 1958–60; Pastor, NC Meth. Conf., 1952–58; Tchr., Spartanburg Jr. Coll., 1949–50. **Educ.:** High Point Coll., 1946–48, (Eng.); Duke Univ., 1948–49, AB (Educ.), 1950–53, MDiv (Relig.); FL State Univ., 1960–61, MA (LS), 1969–70, Adv. Masters (LS). **Orgs.:** VA Educ. Media Assn., VA LA. SELA. ALA. AAUP. Natl. Educ. Assn. Grove

Special Subjects/Services: 50. Adult educ.; 51. Advert./Mktg.; 52. Aerosp.; 53. Agric.; 54. Area std.; 55. Arts/Hum.; 56. Autom.; 57. Bibl./Prtg.; 58. Bio. sci.; 59. Bus./Fin.; 60. Chem.; 61. Copyrt.; 62. Documtn.; 63. Educ.; 64. Engin.; 65. Env.; 66. Eth. grps.; 67. Film; 68. Food/Nutr.; 69. Geneal.; 70. Geo.; 71. Geol.; 72. Handcpd.; 73. Hist.; 74. Int. frdm.; 75. Info. sci.; 76. Insr.; 77. Law; 78. Legis.; 79. Math./Comp. sci.; 80. Med.; 81. Metals; 82. Nat. resrcs.; 83. Newsp.; 84. Nuc. sci.; 85. Oral hist.; 86. Petr./Energy; 87. Pharm.; 88. Phys./Astr./Math.; 89. Readg.; 90. Relig.; 91. Sci./Tech.; 92. Soc. sci.; 93. Telecom.; 94. Transp.; 95. (other).

United Meth. Church. **Honors:** Beta Phi Mu, 1961. **Pubns.:** "Instruction in Library Use," *Radford Review* (Fall, 1971); "Library Science at Radford College," *Mediagram* (Ap., 1976). **Addr.:** 108 Hammett Ave., Radford, VA 24141.

Gibson, Robert W., Jr. (Mr. 15, 1923, Canova, SD) Head, Lib. Dept., General Motors Resrch. Labs, 1965–; Asst. Libn., IBM-Thomas J. Watson Resrch. Ctr., 1962–65; Asst. Supvsr. Libn., Battelle Meml. Inst., 1944–62; Chem., Maytag Washing Machine Co., 1944. **Educ.:** Yankton Coll., 1940–44, BA (Chem.); OH State Univ., 1945–49. **Orgs.:** SLA: Dir., Past Pres. ALA. CLENE. Engin. Index, Inc.: Trustee. MICCLE. Amer. Chem. Socty. AAAS. **Pubns.:** "How the Engineer Can Best Use His Library," *SAE paper* (1978); *Japanese Scientific and Technical Literature.* **Activities:** 12; 17; 75, 81, 94 **Addr.:** General Motors Research Laboratories Library, General Motors Technical Center, Warren, MI 48090.

Gibson, Sarah Scott (Mr. 2, 1932, Harrisburg, PA) Asst. Dean, Matthew A. Baxter Sch. of Lib. and Info. Sci., Case West. Rsv. Univ., 1979–, Asst. Prof., 1975–, Libn., 1975–77; Asst. Prof., Sch. of LS, Univ. of MI, 1972–73; Asst. Catlgr., Denison Univ., 1958–69. **Educ.:** Smith Coll., 1949–53, AB (Hist.); Case West. Rsv. Univ., 1967–68, MS (LS), 1968–72, MA (Art Hist.), 1968–75, PhD (Lib., Info. Sci.). **Orgs.:** ALA. SLA. ARLIS/NA. **Pubns.:** "Some Characteristics of the Exchange Literature of Regional Scientific Societies," *Lib. Resrch.* (Ap. 1980); "Sources of Humanist and Secular Iconography 16th–18th Centuries: A Preliminary Bibliography," *Spec. Libs.* (Sum. 1981). **Activities:** 1, 12; 20, 26, 29; 55, 57, 73 **Addr.:** Matthew A. Baxter School of Library and Information Science, Case Western Reserve University, Cleveland, OH 44106.

Gibson-MacDonald, Norma E. B. (O. 26, 1949, Toronto, ON) Libn., Agr. Canada, 1978–; Libn., Intl. Jt. Comsn., 1975–78; Libn., Atmospheric Environment Srv., 1974–75. **Educ.:** York Univ., 1967–72, BA (Hist.), 1972–73, MA (Hist.); Univ. of West. ON, 1973–74, MLS. **Orgs.:** SLA: Dir., Environmental Info. Div. Great Lakes Environmental Info. Sharing: Founding Mem. Can. LA. **Activities:** 4; 15, 39; 58, 65, 91 **Addr.:** Library, Research Station, Agriculture Canada, Vineland Station, ON L0R 2E0 Canada.

Giefer, Gerald J. (S. 9, 1925, St. Paul, MN) Libn., Water Resrcs. Ctr., Univ. of CA, Berkeley, 1959–; Catlgr., Air Frc. Acad., 1955–59; Asst. to Dir., Lib. Sch., Univ. of MN, 1953–55; Asst. Libn., Highlands Univ., 1951–53. **Educ.:** St. Thomas Coll., 1946–50, BA (Eng. Lit.); Univ. of MN, 1950–51, BS (LS). **Orgs.:** SLA. **Pubns.:** Cmplr., *Bibliography of Current Literature on Water Resources Development and Water Rights (1955–1963)* (1964); cmplr., *Bulletins and Reports of California State Water Agencies* (1963); ed., *California Water Project, 1955–1961* (1967); *Sources of Information in Water Resources, an Annotated Guide to Printed Materials* (1976); jt. auth., *Water Publications of State Agencies* (1972); various rpts., bibls., indxs. **Activities:** 1, 12; 17; 65, 82 **Addr.:** Water Resources Center Archives, Rm. 40, N. Gate Hall, University of California, Berkeley, CA 94720.

Giesbrecht, Herbert (Ag. 5, 1925, Wohldemfuerst, Kuban, South Russia) Coll. Libn., Mennonite Brethren Bible Coll., 1955–. **Educ.:** Univ. of BC, 1945–48, BA (Eng., Math.), 1948–49, Cert. (Sec. Sch. Tchg.); San Francisco State Univ., 1956, MA (Educ.); Univ. of MN, 1967, MLS; Univ. of MB, 1978, MA (Eng.). **Orgs.:** Prairie Relig. LA. Can. LA. SAA. Christ. Libns. Flwshp. **Honors:** Beta Phi Mu, 1968. **Pubns.:** *The Mennonite Brethren: A Bibliographic Guide to Information* (1971); jt. auth., *We Recommend: Recommendations and Resolutions of the General Conference of Mennonite Brethren Churches* (1978); "Christian Approach to Teaching the Liberal Arts," *Christianity Today* (S. 2, 1966); various articles. **Activities:** 1, 2; 15, 20, 30; 55, 66, 90 **Addr.:** The Library of the Mennonite Brethren Bible College, 77 Henderson Hwy., Winnipeg, MB R2L 1L1 Canada.

Giesbrecht, Josephine Area Coord., Lib. Srvs. (ON), Can. Dept. of Agr., 1978–; Ed., *Canadiana,* Natl. Lib. of Can., 1960–77. **Educ.:** Univ. of BC, 1951–53, BA (Hist.); McGill Univ., 1953–54, BLS. **Orgs.:** Can. LA. Can. Assn. of Spec. Libs. and Info. Srvs. SLA. Bibl. Socty. of Can. **Pubns.:** *"Canadiana": Canada's National Bibliography, Description and Guide* (1978); "Current national bibliography: CANADIANA," *Natl. Conf. on the State of Can. Bibl., 1974,* Proc. (1977). **Activities:** 4, 12; 17, 39; 58, 60, 91 **Addr.:** Library, Research Institute, Agriculture Canada, University Sub P.O., London, ON N6A 5B7 Canada.

Gilbert, Christine Bell (Je. 30, 1909, Brooklyn, NY) Retired; Assoc. Prof., LS, Grad. Lib. Sch., Long Island Univ.; Libn., Manhasset Pub. Schs., 1947; Libn., Lincoln Sch., Tchrs. Coll., Columbia Univ., 1934–47; various tchg. positions. **Educ.:** Mt. Holyoke Coll., 1928–32, BA; Columbia Univ., 1933–34, BLS, 1945, MA. **Orgs.:** ALA: Newberry-Caldecott Com. Assn. for Childhood Educ. **Pubns.:** Jt. cmplr., *Best Books for Children* (1978, 1981); "Reading and Study Guide for New Book of Knowledge," *Booklists* (1979–80); various bk. reviews in *Parents Mag., Instr., Sch. Lib. Jnl., Childhood Educ.* **Addr.:** Star Rte. 70, Box 79L, Great Barrington, MA 01230.

Gilbert, Donna Jean Peter (Ja. 22, 1930, Urbana, IL) Print Media Spec., Westerville N. HS, 1977–; Non-Print Media Spec., 1975–77; Libn., Jones Jr. HS, 1970–75; Branch Libn., Turkey, US Army, 1967–68. **Educ.:** Univ. of IL, 1947–69, BS (Soc. Std.); 1969–70, MSLS; OH State Univ., 1970–73, MA (Educ. Comm.), 1979–80, Cert. (Supvsn.). **Orgs.:** ALA: AASL. OH Educ. Lib./Media Assn.: Int. Frdm. (Ch., 1978–80). Altrusa Intl.: Pres., Delaware, OH Club (1979–80). AAUW. **Activities:** 4, 10; 21, 32, 48; 74, 74 **Addr.:** 59 N. Washington St., Delaware, OH 43015.

Giles, Janice Fisher (Ag. 1, 1949, Galesburg, IL) Head, Chld. Srvs., Pekin Pub. Lib., 1978–; Chld. Libn., Heatherdowns Branch, Toledo-Lucas Cnty. Pub. Lib., 1972–76, Asst. Chld. Libn., Sanger Branch, 1972. **Educ.:** Univ. of IL, 1967–71, BA (Thea. Art), 1971–72, MLS. **Orgs.:** ALA. IL LA: Chld. Libns. Sect. (1980–). AAUW. **Pubns.:** Reviews. **Activities:** 9; 20, 21, 31 **Addr.:** Pekin Public Library, 301 S. 4th St., Pekin, IL 61554.

Gilheany, Rosary Scacciaferro (O. 2, 1929, New York, NY) Dir., Lib. and Info. Srvs., Untd. Hosps. Med. Ctr., 1972–; Assoc. Libn., Acad. of Med. of NJ, 1962–72; Asst. Libn., Contl. Insr. Cos., 1954–61; Libn., Regis HS, 1954; Catlgr., NY Hist. Socty., 1951–53. **Educ.:** Barnard Coll., 1945–49, AB (Hist.); Columbia Univ., 1951, MS (LS); 1967, Med. Libn. Cert.; Rutgers Univ. Mgt. Dev. Prog. 1979, Cert.; Natl. Lib. of Med. Online Srvs. Trng., 1979–81. **Orgs.:** Med. LA. Hlth. Sci. LA of NJ: Bd. (1977–); NJ LA. Cosmopolitan Biomedical Lib. Cnsrtm.: Ch. (1976–78). Fam. Srv. Bur., Nutley. Natl. Trust for Hist. Prsrvn. Leag. of Women Voters of Nutley. AAUW. **Honors:** Natl. Lib. of Med., Grant, 1978; Untd. Hosps. of Newark Med. Ctr., Srv. Awd., 1977. **Pubns.:** *Children's Health Audiovisuals Materials Project Catalog* (1981); "The Hospital in Newark, 1862–1903," *NJ Hist.* (1966); ed., *HSLANJ* (Nsltr.) (1978–); "Libraries–Hospitals, NJ–Manpower," pictorial (1976). **Activities:** 12; 17; 80 **Addr.:** 21 De Vausney Pl., Nutley, NJ 07110.

Gill, Bernard Ives (My. 16, 1921, Winnebago, IL) Head Libn., Moorhead State Univ., 1950–; Ref. Asst., Milwaukee Pub. Lib., 1949–50; Tchr., Bensenville (IL) Pub. Schs., 1946–47. **Educ.:** Univ. of IL, 1940–43, AB (Soclgy.), 1948–49 MS (LS). **Orgs.:** ALA. MN LA. AAUP. Natl. Educ. Assn. **Activities:** 1, 2; 15, 17, 19; 55, 70, 82 **Addr.:** Box 325, Hillsboro, ND 58045.

Gill, Suzanne (Lutz) (Je. 30, 1941, Quincy, IL) Instr., LS, Univ. of MO, 1981–; Coord., Lib. Tech. Asst. Prog., St. Louis Cmnty. Coll., 1981–; Consult., Owner, Info. Resrc. Consults., 1977–; Instr., Lib. Tech. Asst. Prog., St. Louis Cmnty. Coll., 1974–; Actg. Coord., Lib. Tech., Cuyahogha Cmnty. Coll., 1972–74; Coord., Lib. Tech. Asst. Prog., St. Louis Cmnty. Coll., 1970–72; Coord., Lib Tech. Asst. Prog., Univ. of Toledo Cmnty. and Tech. Coll., 1967–70; Libn., Pkwy. Sch. Dist., 1963–66. **Educ.:** Fontbonne Coll., 1959–63, BA (Hist.); Univ. of MI, 1966–67, MALS. **Orgs.:** SLA. Cncl. on Lib./Media Tech.: Pubns. (Ch., 1979–); Educ. (1970–74). MO LA: Lib. Educ. Com. (1979–); Lib. Educ. and Manpower (1974–76); Assn. of Recs. Mgrs. and Admins.: St. Louis Chap., Educ. Com., Ch. Various other orgs. Clayton Twp. Republican Club. Amer. Legion Auxiliary: Kirkwood Post. Post 624 Cub Scout: Den Leader (1975–77, 1979–81). **Honors:** Pi Gamma Mu, 1963. **Pubns.:** *File Management and Information Retrieval Systems* (1981); *Bibliography on Library/Media Technical Assistants* (1977); "New Directions for Library Paraprofessionals?" *Wilson Lib. Bltn.* (Ja. 1981); "Education and Information Trends," *ARMA Qtly.* (Jl. 1980). **Activities:** 12; 24, 26, 38; 62, 63, 75 **Addr.:** Information Resource Consultants, 11920 Hargrove, St. Louis, MO 63131.

Gilles, Debra L. (N. 4, 1954, Chippewa Falls, WI) Med. Libn., Howard Young Med. Ctr., 1977–. **Educ.:** Univ. of WI, 1972–76, BA (Psy.); Univ. of Denver, 1976–77, MA (LS); Med. LA, 1977, Cert. **Orgs.:** WI Hlth. Sci. LA: Treas., Mem. Ch. (1978–). Midwest Hlth. Sci. Lib. Netwk.: State Rep. (1979–). North. WI Hlth. Sci. Libs. Coop.: Cnsrtm. Coord. (1978–). Med. LA: Hosp. Lib. Sect., Nom. Com. (1980–); Midwest Reg. Grp., Exec. Com. Oneida Cnty. Hlth. Resrc. Com.: Secy. (1980–). **Activities:** 12; 17, 39; 80 **Addr.:** R. 1, Box 43-8, Woodruff, WI 54568.

Gillespie, David M. (Ag. 19, 1938, Webster Springs, WV) Lib. Dir., Glenville State Coll., 1968–; Libn., St. Michaels HS, 1965–66; Libn., Hampshire Cnty. HS, 1964–65. **Educ.:** Glenville State Coll., 1961–64, AB, cum laude (LS); IN Univ., 1966–67, MLS; FL State Univ., 1975–80, PhD (LS). **Orgs.:** WV LA: Exec. Bd. (1980–81); Pres. (1979–80); VP (1978–79); Coll. and Univ. Sect. (Ch., 1971–72, 1976–77). SE LA: WV Mem. Ch. (1978–82). ALA. Tri-State ACRL. Glenville State Alum. Assn.: Pres. (1981–82). WV Hist. Socty. AAUP. Rotary Club of Glenville WV: Pres. (1971–72). **Honors:** Beta Phi Mu, 1979. **Pubns.:** *Index to Poetry, Ballads and Songs in West Virginia Hillbilly–1956–79* (1980); *Obituary Index–Glenville Democrat–1935–79* (1980); "A Citation-Entry Analysis of the Literature on Prison Libraries," *AHIL Qtly.* (Spr. 1968); "A Bibliography of Virginia Library History," *Jnl. of Lib. Hist.* (Ja. 1971); "President's Message," *WV Libs.* (1980); various articles. **Activities:** 1; 17, 30, 37; 57, 63 **Addr.:** Robert F. Kidd Library, Glenville State College, Glenville, WV 26351.

Gillespie, John T. (S. 25, 1928, Thunder Bay, ON) Dean, Palmer Grad. Lib. Sch., C. W. Post Ctr., Long Island Univ., 1980–, Prof., 1977–80, Dean, Prof., 1971–76, Assoc. Prof., 1963–72, Adj. Asst. Prof., 1960–63; Sch. Libn., Roslyn Sch. Dist., 1957–63; Sch. Libn., Hicksville Sch. Dist., 1956–57; Tchr., Prin., BC Pub. Schs., 1949–55; various positions as visit. prof., pub. sch. tchr., sch. libn., wkshp. coord. **Educ.:** Univ. of BC, 1944–48, BA (Eng., Hist.), 1949, Sec. Cert. (Educ.); Columbia Univ., 1955–57, MS (LS); Hunter Coll., 1958, Cert. (Educ.); NY Univ., 1965–70, PhD (Educ. Comm.). **Orgs.:** ALA: Subscrpn. Bk. Bltn. Com. (1978). NY LA: Sch. Lib. Sect., Pres. (1963), Past VP. Nassau/Suffolk Sch. LA: Pres. (1961); VP (1960). Ctrl. NY LA Cncl. Various lib. sch., univ. coms. **Honors:** C. W. Post Ctr., Long Island Univ., Pres. Outstan. Achiever Awd., 1976; Phi Delta Kappa; Kappa Delta Pi. **Pubns.:** *Creating A School Media Program* (1973); *Introducing Books* (1970); *Juniorplots* (1966); *Library Learning Laboratory* (1969); *A Model School District Media Program* (1977); various bks., articles, reviews, sps. **Activities:** 10, 11; 26, 48; 56, 63, 75 **Addr.:** 360 E. 72 St., Apt. A1212, New York, NY 10021.

Gillet, Lloyd (My. 12, 1936, Chicago, IL) Pres., Bd. of Trustees, Niles Pub. Lib. Dist., 1978–, Treas., 1976–78. **Educ.:** IL State Univ., 1959, BS (Bio.); Northeast. IL Univ., 1966, MS (Bio.). **Orgs.:** ALA: ALTA. IL LA. **Honors:** IL Grt. Tchr. Socty., "IL Grt. Tchr.," 1972. **Pubns.:** "Remedial Course in College Biology," *Jnl. of Coll. Sci. Tchg.* (Ja. 1976). **Activities:** 9; 47 **Addr.:** 6958 Hamilton Dr., Niles, IL 60648.

Gillette, Catherine Hall (O. 25, 1951, Painesville, OH) Pub. Srvs. Libn., Cleveland-Marshall Law Sch., 1978–; Dir., Stark Cnty. Law LA, 1975–78. **Educ.:** OH Wesleyan Univ., 1970–74, BA (Pol. Sci.); Case West. Rsv. Univ., 1974–75, MLS. **Orgs.:** AALL: Mem. Com. (1980); Recrt. Com. (1976–78). OH Reg. Assn. of Law Libs.: VP/Pres. Elect (1980–82); Mem. Com. (Ch., 1979–80). SLA. OH WHCOLIS: Del. (1977). **Activities:** 12; 17, 35, 39; 77, 78 **Addr.:** Cleveland Marshall College of Law, E. 18th and Euclid Ave., Cleveland, OH 44115.

Gillette, Gerald Wayne (F. 17, 1928, Labette, KS) Resrch. Histn., Presby. Hist. Socty., 1963–; Ref. Libn., Princeton Theo. Semy., 1958–63; Asst. Libn., Rsvs. Dept., Univ. of Chicago, 1953–57. **Educ.:** Park Coll., 1946–50, AB (Soc. Sci.); Princeton Theo. Semy., 1950–53, BD (Theo.); Univ. of Chicago, 1953–58, MA (Church Hist.); Rutgers Univ., 1960–62, MLS (Lib.). **Orgs.:** ATLA: Archvst. (1976–); various coms. Presby. LA: Exec. Com. SAA. **Pubns.:** Assoc. ed., *Jnl. of Presby. Hist.* (1963–); various articles in *Jnl. of Presby. Hist., Procs. of the ATLA, Vanguard, Drexel Lib. Qtly., Princeton Semy. Bltn.* **Activities:** 4, 12; 15, 16, 17; 85, 90 **Addr.:** Presbyterian Historical Society, 425 Lombard St., Philadelphia, PA 19147.

Gillfillan, Nancy M. (Ja. 8, 1942, Robinson, IL) Owner, Mgr., The Bk. Barn, 1980–; Instr., IL Valley Cmnty. Coll., 1977–; Instr., LS, Ext. Libn., IN State Univ., 1966–69; Ref. Libn., Kansas City (MO) Pub. Lib., 1964–66. **Educ.:** Univ. of IL, 1960–64, AB (Eng.), 1964–66, MS (LS); Univ. of Denver, Out-of Print/Antiq. Bk. Wkshp., 1980. **Orgs.:** ALA/Natl. Univ. Ext. Assn. Jt. Com. (1968–70). Assn. for Fld. Srvs. in Tchr. Educ.: Pub. Info. Com. (1968); Resrch. Com. (Ch., 1969); Exec. Bd. (1969). ALA. Adult Educ. Assn. of IN: Co-Ed., *Adult Horizons* (1967–69); Bd. of Dirs. (1967–69). Bur. Cnty. Home Hlth. Srvs. IL Fed. of Womans Clubs. Princeton IL Untd. Meth. Women. Princeton Evening Womans Club. various orgs. **Pubns.:** "Ellie Offcampus Solves Her Library Dilemma," *The New Campus* (Spr. 1969); "Guidelines Established for Extension Libraries," *Adult Horizons* (N. 1968); Ed., *IL Homemakers Ext. Fed. Nsltr.* (1978–80). **Activities:** 1, 14-Bk. Dealer; 16, 26, 27; 50 **Addr.:** R.R. 1, Walnut, IL 61376.

Gillham, Virginia Ann Caskie (My. 22, 1941, Hamilton, ON) Head, Docum. and Media Resrcs., McLaughlin Lib., Univ. of Guelph, 1975–; Head, Circ., 1973–75; Resrv. Libn., 1972–73; Cat. Libn., Univ. of North. CO, 1970–72. **Educ.:** McMaster Univ. 1959–62, BA (Eng.), Univ. of IL, 1969–70, MSLS. Univ. of Toronto, 1962–63, Tchr. Cert. **Orgs.:** Can. LA: Can Assn. for Info. Sci. ALA: ACRL SLA. OLA. CODOC (ON Coop. Docums. Grp.): Ch. (1978–79, 1980–), Exec. Mem. (1977–80). Can. Figure Skating Assn.: Natl. Judge (1977–), Judge (1960–). **Pubns.:** "The Guelph Document System," *Gvt. Pubns. Rev.* (1980); Ed., "High Interest Canadian Government Publications," (column), *Gvt. Pubns.* Rev. (1978–); Reviews; Various presented papers. **Activities:** 1; 17, 29, 39; 56, 62, 78 **Addr.:** McLaughlin Library, University of Guelph, Guelph, ON N1G 2W1 Canada.

Gilliam, Dorothy Jane (Mr. 24, 1940, Charlotte, NC) Head, Cat. Dept., Un. Theo. Semy., VA, 1968–; Catlgr., Princeton Theo. Semy., 1965–68. **Educ.:** Mars Hill Jr. Coll., 1958–60, AA; Wake Forest Univ., 1960–62, BA (Relig.); Japan Intl. Christ. Univ., 1962–63; Southeast. Bapt. Theo. Semy., 1963–64; Univ. of NC, 1964–65, MS (LS). **Orgs.:** ATLA: Cat. and Class. Com. (Ch., 1970–71); Exec. Com. (1971–73); Nom. Com. (Ch., 1977–78). **Honors:** Beta Phi Mu, 1965. **Activities:** 1, 12; 20, 46; 90 **Addr.:** Union Theological Seminary Library, 3401 Brook Rd., Richmond, VA 23227.

PROFESSIONAL ACTIVITIES: Institutions: 1. Acad. lib.; 2. Arch.; 3. Assn.; 4. Fed./Gvt. lib.; 5. Inst. lib.; 6. Mfr./Suppl.; 7. Milit. lib.; 8. Musm.; 9. Pub. lib.; 10. Sch. lib.; 11. Sch. of lib. sci.; 12. Spec. lib.; 13. State lib.; 14. (other). **Functions/Activities:** 15. Acq./Col. dev.; 16. Adult srvs.; 17. Admin.; 18. Apprais.; 19. Archit./Bldgs.; 20. Cat./Class.; 21. Chld. srvs.; 22. Circ.; 23. Cons./Pres.; 24. Consult.; 25. Cont. ed.; 26. Educ. lib. sci.; 27. Ext. srvs.; 28. Fund/Grants; 29. Gvt. pubs.; 30. Indx./Abs.; 31. Instr. lib. use; 32. Media srvs.; 33. Micro.; 34. Netwks./Coop.; 35. Persnl.; 36. PR; 37. Publshg.; 38. Recs. mgt.; 39. Ref. srvs.; 40. Repro.; 41. Resrch.; 42. Review.; 43. Secur.; 44. Serials; 45. Spec. col.; 46. Tech. srvs.; 47. Trustees/Bds.; 48. YA srvs.; 49. (other).

Gilliam, Susanne Phelps (D. 13, 1943, Lexington, KY) Cat. Libn., Univ. of Cincinnati, Hlth. Sci. Libs., 1981–; Libn., CORVA Hlth. Plng. Agency, 1978–81; Spec. Consult., North. KY Area Dev. Dist., Citizens Com. on Youth, Cincinnati, OH, 1979–80; Instr., North. KY Univ., 1978–79; Libn., Moyer Elem. Sch., 1973–78; Circ. Libn., Thomas More Coll., 1973–74; Tchr., Covington Jr. HS, 1971–73; Libn., Belmont Jr. HS, 1969–71; Instr., Univ. of KY, 1967–69; Libn., Ashland Elem. Sch., 1966–67. **Educ.:** Univ. of KY, 1965, BA (Arts, Sci.), 1969, MA (Eng.), 1975, MS (LS). **Orgs.:** SLA: Cincinnati Chap. (Treas., 1980–81). Cincinnati Area Hlth. Sci. Libns. Assn.: Treas. (1980–81). **Honors:** Beta Phi Mu; Chi Delta Phi. **Pubns.:** "Looking for Something," *PHI Plng. for Hlth. Issues* (Sum. 1980). **Activities:** 10, 12; 21, 31, 38; 80 **Addr.:** 204 Levassor Ave., Covington, KY 41014.

Gillies, Ellen M. (Ap. 7, 1918, Worcester, MA) Med. Libn., Lib. Prof., Dana Med. Lib., Univ. of VT, 1965–, Per. Libn., 1947–48; Libn., Pan American Airways, 1944–45. **Educ.:** Simmons Coll., 1935–39, BLS. **Orgs.:** Med. LA. SLA. N. Atl. Hlth. Sci. Libs. **Activities:** 1, 12; 17; 80 **Addr.:** Dana Medical Library, University of Vermont, Burlington, VT 05405.

Gillies, Thomas D. (O. 18, 1920, South Bend, WA) Dir., Linda Hall Lib., 1974–, Serials Libn., Assoc. Dir., 1953–73; Visit. Instr., Univ. of WA, Sch. of Libnshp., 1962–64; Asst. Libn., Willamette Univ., 1948–50. **Educ.:** Univ. of MI, 1938–42, BA (Eng.); Cornell Univ., 1946–47, MA (Amer. Lit.); Columbia Univ., 1947–48, BS in LS. **Orgs.:** ALA. Pac. NW LA. AAAS. **Activities:** 12; 17, 26, 44; 57, 91 **Addr.:** 2510 Grand, Kansas City, MO 64108.

Gilligan, Janet M. (My. 1, 1944, Niagara Falls, NY) Asst. Ref. Libn., CO State Univ., 1977–, Asst. Serials Catlgr., 1972–77. **Educ.:** Niagara Univ., 1962–66, BA (Eng.); Univ. of MI, 1966–67, MA (Eng.); 1967, NY State Tchrs. Cert. Univ. of MI, 1969–71, MLS. **Orgs.:** ALA: RASD, Bibl. Com. (Ch., 1979–80), Hist. Sect., Bibl. and Indxs. Com. (1979–81); LI RT, Natl. Prog. Std. Task Frc. (1980–). CO LA: Educ. Com. (Ch., 1977–78); CO LA/Mt. Plains LA Jt. Conf. (Lcl. Arrange. Ch., 1979). Leag. of Women Voters, Fort Collins, CO: Unit Ch. (1973–75); Human Resrcs. Com. (Co-Ch., 1974–75); Housing Com. (Ch., 1975–76); Urban Crisis Com. (Ch., 1978–). Amer. Cvl. Liberties Un.: Larimer Cnty. Chap. (Secy., 1973–75). **Honors:** Delta Sigma Delta, 1965. **Pubns.:** "Problems in Evaluating Librarians as Faculty," *CO Acad. Lib.* (Spr. 1973); jt. auth., "CLA 1978 Annual Conference: An Evaluation," *CO Libs.* (Je. 1979); various reviews, *Serials Review.* **Activities:** 1; 31, 39, 42 **Addr.:** Colorado State University Libraries, Fort Collins, CO 80523.

Gillis, Robert Peter (N. 3, 1946, Lindsay, ON) Chief, Manpower and Soc. Dev. Recs., Pub. Arch. of Can., 1977–, Head, Trade and Comms. Recs., 1975–77, Sr. Archvst., Nat. Resrc. Recs., 1973–75, Archvst., Pre-confed. Sect., 1970–73; Park Histn., Algonquin Park, ON Mnstry. of Nat. Resrcs., 1968–70. **Educ.:** Trent Univ., 1968–69, BA, hons. (Hist.); Queen's Univ., 1969–70, MA (Hist.); Carleton Univ., 1970, Cert. (Arch. Principles). **Orgs.:** Assn. Can. Archvsts.: Constn. Review Com. (Ch., 1979–). East. ON Archvsts.' Assn.: Pres. (1979–80). Can. Hist. Assn.: Pubns. Com. (Ch., 1973–79). Org. of Amer. Histns. Forest Hist. Socty.: Bd. of Dirs. (1979–). Soc. Sci. Fed.: Com. of Schol. Eds. (1973–79). **Honors:** Forest Hist. Socty., Theodore Blegen Awd., 1974; Gvt. of Can., Queen Elizabeth II Jubilee Medal, 1977. **Pubns.:** *"For the Purposes of the Dominion": A Guide to Federal Records Relating to the Economic and Social Development of Western Canada, 1870–1936* (1980); "Ottawa, 1870–1930: The Death of the Industrial City," *Planning the Federal Capital Region* (1978); "The Ottawa Lumber Barons and the Conservation Movement, 1880–1914," *Jnl. of Can. Std.* (F. 1974); *Inventory to Provincial, Local and Territorial Records in the Public Archives of Canada* (1971); *Inventory to 19th Century Pre-Confederation Papers in the Public Archives of Canada* (1972). **Activities:** 2; 15, 17, 38; 66, 75, 82 **Addr.:** Public Archives of Canada, 395 Wellington St., Ottawa, ON K1A 0N3 Canada.

Gillmore, Sally Gearhart (Ap. 19, 1936, Washington, DC) Libn., Mayfield Mid. Sch. Lib., 1963–, Adj. Asst. Prof., Kent State Univ., 1967–; Libn., Southington Lcl. Sch., 1962–63; Asst. Libn., Euclid HS, 1961–62. **Educ.:** Coll. of William and Mary, 1954–58, BA (Math.); Kent State Univ., 1958–62, MA (LS). **Orgs.:** Mayfield Educ. Assn.: Pres. (1975–78). OH LA: Bd. of Dirs. (1974–77); Int. Frdm. Com. (Ch., 1981–82). OH Educ. Lib. Media Assn.: Conv. Com. (Lcl. Arrange. Ch., 1980). ALA: YASD, Mem. Com. Delta Kappa Gamma. Beta Phi Mu: Adv. Cncl. (1978–). West Geauga Bd. of Educ. (1980–83). **Pubns.:** Reviews. **Activities:** 10, 11; 15, 26, 48; 74, 89 **Addr.:** 13043 Fairfield Trail, Chesterland, OH 44026.

Gilman, Lelde B. (My. 20, 1938, Riga, Latvia) Head, Acq. Div., Biomed. Lib., Univ. of CA, Los Angeles, 1979–, Serials Libn., 1973–78, Trng. Coord., Grad. Progress in Med. Libnshp., 1967–73; Ref. Libn., Multnomah Cnty. Pub. Lib., 1966–67; Med. Libn., Samuel Merritt Hosp. Med. Lib., 1964–65. **Educ.:** Univ. of CA, Berkeley, 1956–60, AB (Pol. Sci.), 1962–64, MLS. **Orgs.:** ALA. ASIS. Med. LA: Vital Notes Participatory Panel (1973–). Med. Lib. Grp. of South. CA and AZ. **Activities:** 1, 12; 15, 17, 44; 56, 58, 80 **Addr.:** Acquisitions, Biomedical Library / Center for the Health Sciences, University of California, Los Angeles, CA 90024.

Gilman, Nelson J. (Mr. 30, 1938, Los Angeles, CA) Dir., Asst. Prof. of Med. Educ., Norris Med. Lib., Univ. of South. CA, 1971–; Assoc. Dir., Pac. SW Reg. Med. Lib. Srv., UCLA Biomed. Lib., 1969–71, Asst. Biomed. Libn., 1967–69, Asst. to the Biomed. Libn., 1966–67; Asst. to the Univ. Libn., UCLA, 1965–66, Lib. Admin. Intern, 1964–65. **Educ.:** Univ. of South. CA, 1955–59, BS (Educ.), 1959–60, MS (Educ.); Univ. of CA, Berkeley, 1963–64, MLS. **Orgs.:** Assn. of Acad. Hlth. Sci. Lib. Dir.: (Bd. of Dir., 1980–; Com. on the Dev. of Stan. & Guidelines, Ch., 1979). Med. LA: Bd. of Dir. (1977–79); Ad Hoc Com. on MLA Grp. Structure, (1975–77); Med. Sch. Libs. Grp., (Ch., 1971–72). Med. Lib. Grp. of South. CA & AZ: Adv. Cncl., (1976–77). SLA: Bio. Sci. Div. Nom. Com. (Ch., 1973–74). Excerpta Medica: Adv. Bd. (1979–). Med. Lib. Schol. Fndn.: Bd. of Dir. (1971–); Ch., Schol. Awd. Com., (1977–). UCLA Adv. Cncl. on Educ. for Lib. & Info. Sci. (1972–80). **Pubns.:** "Continuing education and library services for physicians in office practice," Med. LA *Bltn.* (O. 1979); "NLM plus WESRAC equals UCASS," in: *Buying New Technology* (LJ Special Report #4) (1978); "Review of resource grant applications at the National Library of Medicine: Discussion," Med. LA *Bltn.* (Ja. 1973); "Library services for health professionals," *CA Libn.* (Ap. 1972); "The Pacific Southwest Regional Medical Library Service," *CA Med.* (O. 1971). **Activities:** 1; 17, 19, 28; 80, 87, 91 **Addr.:** Norris Medical Library, Health Sciences Campus, University of Southern California, 2025 Zonal Ave., Los Angeles, CA 90033.

Gilmer, Wesley, Jr. (S. 24, 1928, Cincinnati, OH) State Law Libn., Cmwlth. of Ky, 1976–; Fac., East. Ky Univ., 1980–81; Actg. Ch., Paralegal Std. Dept., Midway Coll., 1979–80, Fac., 1977–80; Asst. Law Libn., Fac., Coll. of Law, Univ. of Cincinnati, 1967–76; Gen. Prac. of Law, Danville, KY, 1952–67. **Educ.:** Univ. of Cincinnati, 1945–49, BA (Pol. Sci.), 1948–50, JD (Law); Univ. of KY, 1969–72, MSLS. **Orgs.:** AALL: *Law Lib. Jnl.* Com. (1971–75). KY Bar Assn.: Cont. Legal Educ. Com. (1977–); Paralegal Com. (1981–). Amer. Coll. of Legal Med.: *Jnl. of Legal Med.* Ed. Bd. (1975–77). **Honors:** AALL, Cert. of Competence in Law Libnshp., 1971. **Pubns.:** *Legal Research, Writing and Advocacy: A Sourcebook* (1978); Rev., *Cochran's Law Lexicon, The Law Dictionary* (1973); *Guide to Kentucky Legal Research: A State Bibliography* (1979); *Legal Research, Writing and Advocacy, Paralegal Instructor's Manual* (1979); "Scanning the Legal Literature," clmn. *Jnl. of Legal Med.* (1975–77); various articles. **Activities:** 1, 12; 17, 31, 39; 77, 80 **Addr.:** State Law Library, Rm. 200 State Capitol, Frankfort, KY 40601.

Gilner, David Jonathan (My. 26, 1948, Brooklyn, NY) Head, Pub. Srvs., Hebrew Union Coll.–Jewish Inst. of Rel., 1980–, Judaica Libn., 1978–80; Visit. Inst. in Judaic Stds., Wilmington Coll., 1973–74. **Educ.:** Emory Univ., 1966–70, BA (Rel.), 1970–72, MA (Bible). Hebrew Union Coll., 1972– (Bible); Univ. of IL, 1976–77, MS (LS). **Orgs.:** Assn. of Jewish Libs.: Conv. Exhibits com. (1979). AAUP. So ty of Bibical Lit.: Consult. on Bibical and Ancient Near East. Law (co-conv., 1976–78); Grp. on Bibical Law and Comp. Stds. (strg. com., 1978–79). **Honors:** Beta Phi Mu; Pi Delta Epsilon. **Activities:** 1; 20, 39, 44; 90 **Addr.:** 2543 Moorman Ave., Cincinnati, OH 45206.

Gilpin, Dorothea Hayman (Ag. 26, 1921, Davenport, IA) Media Dir., Warren Twp. HS, 1967–; Libn., Cmnty. Consolidated Sch. Dist, Palatine, IL, 1965–67; Tchr., IL Valley Unit Dist., Chilliocothe, IL, 1955–65. **Educ.:** Eureka Coll., 1938–41; 1957–59, BA (Eng.); Univ. of IL, 1964–67, MSLS. **Orgs.:** IL Pub. Lib. Trustees Assn.: Exec. Bd. (1969–75); Secy. (1973–75). Palatine Pub. Lib. Dist.: Trustee (1967–80); Treas. (1968); Pres. (1970–71; 1976–80); Policy Ch. (1970–76). ALA. IL LA. Amer. Fed. of Tchrs. **Activities:** 9, 10; 26, 32, 47; 63, 75 **Addr.:** 915 East Pratt Dr., Palatine, IL 60067.

Gilreath, Charles L. (Ag. 4, 1945, Canadian, TX) Head, Autom. Info. Retrieval Srv., TX A&M Univ. Libs., 1977–; Ref. Libn., 1973–77. **Educ.:** Univ. of TX, 1965–67, BA (Eng.); 1967–69, MA (Eng.); 1971–73, MLS. **Orgs.:** TX LA: Ch., Ref. RT (1976–78). ALA: Ref. & Subscrpn. Books Review Com., (1977–); RASD/Machine Asst. Ref. Sect., (Org. Com., 1977–78); ACRL/Nom. Com. (1979); Ch., Nom. Com., Sci. & Tech. Sect. (1979); Oberly Awd. Com. (1978–). **Honors:** Assoc. of the Natl. Agr. Lib., Awd. of Spec. Recog., 1977; Phi Kappa Phi, 1973. **Pubns.:** *Cain Online User's Guide* (1976); *Agricola User's Guide* (1979); "Agricola: Multipurpose Data Base for Agricultural and Life Sciences Libraries," *Serials Libn.* (Fall, 1978); "Effective Training: The Key to Efficient Retrieval," *Jnl. of NAL Assoc.* (O./D. 1977); "Faculty Governance: The Texas A&M Case," *TX Lib. Jnl.* (Sum. 1975). **Addr.:** Automated Information Retrieval Service, Texas A&M University Libraries, College Station, TX 77843.

Gilroy, Dorothy A. (Anthon, IA) Chief Resrch. Libn., Univ. Afflt. Cincinnati Ctr. for Dev. Disorders 1978–; Libn., St. Francis Semy., 1970–78. **Educ.:** Univ. of North. IA, 1947–53, BA (Educ.); Univ. of Cincinnati, 1968–70, MEduc.; Univ. of KY, 1975–77; MSLS. Med. LA Cert., 1977. **Orgs.:** Cath. LA: Grtr. Cincinnati Chap. (1973–79). Cincinnati Area Hlth. Sci. LA: Const. Com. (Ch., 1979–80). SLA. MLA. Various civic, church, and Sch. Orgs. and Ofcs. **Honors:** Kappa Delta Phi; Beta Phi Mu. **Activities:** 1, 12; 15, 17, 41; 72, 80, 92 **Addr.:** Research Library, University Affiliated Cincinnati Center for Developmental Disorders, Elland & Bethesda Aves., Cincinnati, OH 45229.

Gilson, Preston A. (My. 7, 1947, Salina, KS) Dir., Lrng. Resrcs., Lincoln Coll., 1972–; Patients' Libn., Ctrl. State Hosp., 1970–72). **Educ.:** Grinnell Coll., 1965–69, AB (Classical lang.); Univ. of OK, 1969–71, MLS. **Orgs.:** ALA. IL LA. IL ACRL: Exec. Bd. (1978–1980). Sangamon Valley Acad. Lib. Cnsrtm.: Ch. (1976). Kiwanis: VP (1980). **Activities:** 1; 17, 31, 39; 55, 59, 75 **Addr.:** McKinstry Library, 700 North Ottawa St., Lincoln, IL 62656.

Gimmi, Robert D. (My. 20, 1942, Philadelphia, PA) Head Cat. Libn., Shippensburg State Coll., 1968–; Elem. Sch. Libn., South. Huntington Cnty. Schs., 1966–67. **Educ.:** Shippensburg State Coll., 1960–64, BS (Biol.); Drexel Univ., 1964–66, MSLS. **Orgs.:** ALA. Potomac Tech. Prcs. Libns. Sigma Pi: Chap. Dir. (1971–). **Activities:** 1; 20, 39, 45; 58, 60, 91 **Addr.:** Library, Shippensburg State College, Shippensburg, PA 17257.

Ginader, George Hall (Ap. 5, 1933, Buffalo, NY) Pres., WHALGIN Assocs., 1980–; Dir., Info. Resrc. Ctr., Morgan Stanley and Co., Inc., 1970–80; Exec. Dir., SLA, 1967–70; Chief Libn., NY Stock Exch., 1966–67; Mgr., NY Cham. of Cmrce. and Indus., 1964–66; Actg. Cur., Auto. Ref. Col., Free Lib. of Philadelphia, 1961–64. **Educ.:** Allegheny Coll., 1951–55, BA (Hist., Pol. Sci.); Drexel Univ., 1961–64, MSLS. **Orgs.:** Assn. of Recs. Mgrs. and Admins.: NY Chap. (Treas., 1974–75). Admin. Mgt. Socty. Natl. Micro. Assn. SLA: Pres. (1981–82); Advert. and Mktg. Div. (Ch., 1979–80); Bus. and Fin. Div. (Ch., 1975–76); Com. on Coms. (Ch., 1976–79); *What's New in Advertising and Marketing* Ed. (1967–69). Cranbury (NJ) Hist. and Prsrvn. Socty. Sons of Amer. Revolution. **Pubns.:** Various articles, *Spec. Libs.* **Activities:** 12, 14-Consult. Prac.; 17, 24, 38 **Addr.:** 45 S. Main St., Cranbury, NJ 08512.

Gitler, Robert Laurence (My. 1, 1909, New York City, NY) Univ. Libn. Emeritus, Gleeson Lib., Univ. of San Francisco; 1977–; Adv., Consult., Univ. Libn., Sophia Univ., Tokyo, Japan, 1977, 1979, 1981–; Emeritus Fac., Fromm Inst. Lifling Lrng., Univ. of San Francisco, 1976, Univ. Libn., Prof., Gleeson Lib., 1967–75; Dir., Prof., George Peabody Coll., Lib. Sch., 1964–67; Dir., Prof., Dept. Lib. Educ., SUNY, Geneseo, 1962–64; various univ. positions as consult., 1962; Fndn. Dir., Prof., Japan Lib. Sch., Keio Univ., Tokyo, Japan, 1952–56; Dir., Sch. of Libnshp., Univ. of WA, 1946–51; Sum. Fac., Sch. of Lib. Srv., Columbia Univ., 1946–47; various positions as prof., admin., libn., 1930–46. **Educ.:** Univ. of CA, Berkeley, 1927–30, BA (Hist., Gvt.), 1930–31, Grad. Cert. (Libnshp.); Columbia Univ., 1938–39, MS (Grad. Fac. Subjs., LS). **Orgs.:** ALA: Lib. Educ., Exec. Secy. (1956–60); Accred. Ofcr. (1956–60); JMRT (Pres., 1938–39). CA LA: Golden Gate Dist. (Pres., 1968–69). Various accred. visits. Intl. Hse. of Japan: Lib. Plng. Com. (1953–54). Univ. of San Francisco Fac. Assn.: Fac. Lib. Com. (1967–75). Univ. of San Francisco: Pres. Adv. Cncl. (1974–75); Inst. of Asian/Pac. Std., Adv. Com. (1976–). Various other orgs. **Honors** Beta Phi Mu, Disting. Srv. to Libnshp., 1961; Keio Univ., Tokyo, Japan, Hon. PhD, 1956; Japan LA, Disting. Srv. Awd., 1961; Imperial Household, Emperor of Japan, Ord. of the Rising Sun, 4th Merit, 1961. **Pubns.:** *Library Report: Education for Librarianship at the University of Hawaii; A Study of the Present Status and Potential for Development* (1961); various articles in *Lib. Jnl., ALA Bltn., Jnl. of Lib. Educ., Jnl. of Lib. Hist., Coll. & Resrch. Libs., Jr. Coll. Jnl., Toshokan Kai, Toshokan Zasshi* (Japanese jnls.). **Addr.:** 222 Willard N. #301, San Francisco, CA 94118.

Gitner, Fred J. (N. 28, 1951, New York, NY) Libn., Dir., Fr. Inst./Alliance Française, 1976–; Asst. Mgr., Catlgr., Christopher P. Stephens, Bookseller, 1975–76. **Educ.:** Hamilton Coll., 1969–73, AB (Mod. Lang.); Rutgers Univ., 1973–75, MLS; Middlebury Coll., 1973–76, MA (Fr.). **Orgs.:** ALA. NY LA. SLA: Musms., Arts, Hum. Div., NY Chap., Mem. Secy. (1979–80), Secy.-Treas. (1980–81). ASTED. **Pubns.:** "French Institute/Alliance Française Library: Past, Present and Future," *Argus* (Ja.–F. 1978); *French-Language Materials for Children: A Guide to Information and Sources* (1979, 1980). **Activities:** 12; 15, 17, 39; 54, 55, 66 **Addr.:** French Institute/Alliance Francaise Library, 22 E. 60th St., New York, NY 10022.

Gittelsohn, Marc (Mr. 7, 1929, San Francisco, CA) Head, Cluster Undergrad. Lib., Univ. of CA, San Diego, 1971–; Actg. Asst. Univ., Libn., 1979–80; Head, Moffitt Undergrad. Lib., Univ. of CA, Berkeley, 1969–71; Head, Agr. Sci. Lib., 1965–69; Asst. in Admin., 1964–65; Head, Agr. Lib., 1962–64; Head, Morrison Lib., 1958–62; Intern in Admin., 1956–58. **Educ.:** Univ. of CA, Berkeley, 1946–50, BA (Hist.); Univ. of WI, 1950–51 (Hist.); Univ. of CA, Berkeley, 1955–56, MLS. **Orgs.:** ALA. CA LA: Cnclr. (1970–1973); Ch., Com. on Chap. (1972); Palomar Chap. (Pres. 1976). Univ. of CA (San Diego), Libns. Assn.: Pres. (1975). **Honors:** Phi Beta Kappa, **Pubns.:** Reviews. **Activities:** 1; 31, 39, 49-Undergrad. Libs. **Addr.:** Cluster Undergraduate Library (C-075), University of California, San Diego, La Jolla, CA 92093.

Gittens, Anthony Edgar (D. 25, 1944, Brooklyn, NY) Dir., Black Film Inst., Univ. of DC, 1976–; Prog. Assoc., Ofc. of

Special Subjects/Services: 50. Adult educ.; 51. Advert./Mktg.; 52. Aerosp.; 53. Agric.; 54. Area std.; 55. Arts/Hum.; 56. Autom.; 57. Bibl./Prtg.; 58. Bio. sci.; 59. Bus./Fin.; 60. Chem.; 61. Copyrt.; 62. Documtn.; 63. Educ.; 64. Engin.; 65. Env.; 66. Eth. grps.; 67. Film; 68. Food/Nutr.; 69. Geneal.; 70. Geo.; 71. Geol.; 72. Handcpd.; 73. Hist.; 74. Int. frdm.; 75. Info. sci.; 76. Insr.; 77. Law; 78. Legis.; 79. Math./Comp. sci.; 80. Med.; 81. Metals; 82. Nat. resrcs.; 83. Newsp.; 84. Nuc. sci.; 85. Oral hist.; 86. Petr./Energy; 87. Pharm.; 88. Phys./Astr./Math.; 89. Readg.; 90. Relig.; 91. Sci./Tech.; 92. Soc. sci.; 93. Telecom.; 94. Transp.; 95. (other).

Coll. Dev., Fed. City Coll., 1973–76, Dir., Proj. START Reg. Team, 1972–73; Ed., Writer, Black Child Dev. Inst., 1971–72; Ed., Writer, Day Care and Child Dev. Cncl. of Amer., Inc., 1970–71; various consult. positions. **Educ.:** Howard Univ., 1965–68, BA (Eng., Phil.); Un. Grad. Sch., 1974–76, PhD (Urban Std.); various grad. crs. **Orgs.:** EFLA. Intl. Film Sems.: Adv. Bd. Washington Area Filmmakers Leag. Amer. Film Inst. Mayor's Art and Hum. Task Force. **Honors:** Lorton Reformatory, Chancellor Williams Awd. for Cmnty. Srv.; Natl. Assn. of Schs. of Pub. Affairs and Admin., Fellow; Natl. Inst. for Mental Hlth., Fellow. **Pubns.:** "The Black Film Institute," *Sightlines* (Spr. 1979); "Black Films for Young Children," *Essence Mag.* (O. 1979). **Activities:** 10; 32; 67 **Addr.:** Black Film Institute, Learning Resources, University of the District of Columbia, Carnegie Bldg., 8th & K Sts., NW, Washington, DC 20001.

Gittings, Barbara (Jl. 31, 1932) Coord., Gay Task Frc., ALA, SRRT, 1971–. **Orgs.:** ALA: SRRT, Gay Task Frc., Natl. Gay Task Frc.: Bd. of Dirs. (1973–). PA Cncl. for Sexual Minorities. Sr. Action in a Gay Env.: Adv. Bd. **Honors:** Integrity, Anl. Awd., 1976; Natl. Gay Hlth. Coal., Jane Addams-Howard Brown Meml. Awd., 1979; Gay Acad. Un., Spec. Recog. Awd., 1979. **Pubns.:** Jt. auth., *Censored, Ignored, Overlooked, Too Expensive? How to Get Gay Materials Into Libraries. A Guide to Library Selection Policies for the Non-Librarian* (1979); cmplr., *A Gay Bibliography* (1980); jt. auth., "Lesbians and the Gay Movement," *Our Right to Love: A Lesbian Resource Book* (1978); "Combatting the Lies in the Libraries," *The Gay Academic* (1978); cmplr., "Where to Get Help and Information," "Suggested Reading," *We Speak For Ourselves: Experiences in Homosexual Counseling* (1977); various papers. **Activities:** 12; 15, 24, 37; 55, 92 **Addr.:** P.O. Box 2383, Philadelphia, PA 19103.

Giuliano, Vincent G. (N. 17, 1929, Detroit, MI) Head, Org. Comms. Tech. Grp., Arthur O. Little, Inc., 1972–; Fndn. Dean, Prof., Sch. of Info. and Lib. Std., SUNY, Buffalo, 1967–72; Sr. Prof. Staff, Arthur Little, Inc., 1959–67. **Educ.:** Univ. of MI, 1948–52, AB (Math.), Univ. of MI, 1952–56, MS (Math.); Harvard Univ., 1956–59, PhD (Appld. Sci.). **Orgs.:** ASIS. IEEE. **Pubns.:** *Into the Information Age* (1978); various articles. **Activities:** 12; 75, 93 **Addr.:** Arthur Little, Inc., Acorn Park, Cambridge, MA 02140.

Givens, Johnnie E. (S. 7, 1925, Pleasant View, TN) Consult., Metrics Resrch. Corp., 1979–; Exec. Dir., SELA, 1977–79; Head Libn., Austin Peay State Univ., 1958–76, Asst. Libn., 1946–57. **Educ.:** Austin Peay State Univ., 1942–46, BS (Eng.); Peabody Coll., 1947–49, BS in LS; Univ. of Chicago, 1954–57, AM (LS). **Orgs.:** ALA: Com. on Prog. Eval. (1977–79); Cncl. (1977–80); ACRL Com. on Appointments (1973) and Nom. (Ch., 1974); Ad Hoc Com. to Revise the 1959 Stan. for Coll. Libs. (Ch., 1973–75); Com. on Plng. (1980–82). SELA: Nom. Com. (1973–74). TN LA. Southeast. Lib. Network: Bd. of Dir. (1973–75; Vice Ch., 1974–75). Other orgs. TN Higher Educ. Comsn.: Adv. Com. for Study on Acad. Libs. (1973–76). TN State Lib. and Arch.: Lib. Adv. Cncl. (1973–78 Ch., 1976–77). Kappa Delta Pi. South. Assn. of Coll. and Sch.: Task Force to Revise Reg. Stan. for Acad. Libs. (1973–76). **Honors:** Cncl. on Lib. Resrcs., Flwshp., 1970–71; Beta Phi Mu. **Pubns.:** Jt. auth., "College Libraries in Tennessee", *TN Libn.,* (Win., 1968); "The Use of Resources in the Learning Experience", *Advances in Librarianship* (1974); Jt. auth., "Accrediting Agencies and Library Cooperation in Education", *Lib. Trends,* (O., 1975); Jt. auth., "The Academic Library Development Program," *Coll. and Resrch. Libs.,* (Ja., 1977); "The Public and Private Senior Colleges", *Resources of South Carolina Libraries* (1976); Other articles, reviews. **Activities:** 3, 14; 17, 19, 24; 51, 63, 86 **Addr.:** Metrics Research Corporation, P.O. Box #895, Tucker, GA 30084.

Gladish, Mary Louise (My. 15, 1920, Prospect, TN) Bibl. Resrch. Srvs. Libn., Vanderbilt Univ. Med. Ctr. Lib., 1980–, Head Ref. Libn., 1976–80, Med. Resrch. Libn., 1964–76. **Educ.:** Univ. of TN, 1937–41, BS (Home Econ.); Univ. of NC, 1943–44, MSPH (Pub. Hlth. Educ.); Univ. of Chicago, 1947–48, MA (Adult Educ.); Emory Univ., 1964, Cert. (Med. Libnshp.); George Peabody Coll., 1966, MLS; Med. LA, 1967, Cert. Rank II. **Orgs.:** Med. LA: Med. Lib. Educ. Sect. (Ch., 1980–81); Curric. Com. (Ch., 1972–73). TN LA: Spec. Libs. Sect. (Ch., 1969–72); Fin. Com., Bd. (1973–75). Mid-State LA: Adv. Cncl. (1972–76, 1980–81). Nashville Lib. Club: Pres. (1976–77); Exec. Com. (1974–78). Women's Natl. Bk. Assn. **Honors:** Delta Kappa Gamma, 1962–70; Kappa Delta Pi, 1965; Beta Phi Mu, 1967; Pi Lambda Theta, 1948. **Pubns.:** Jt. rev., *Eileen R. Cunningham's Classification for Medical Literature* (1967); jt. auth., "Origin of the Terms 'Mongolism' and 'Down's Syndrome,'" *Jnl. of Pediatrics* (Ap. 1966). **Activities:** 1, 12; 26, 39, 41; 58, 80, 91 **Addr.:** Vanderbilt University Medical Center Library, Nashville, TN 37232.

Gladysz, Margean A. (F. 28, 1928, Kalamazoo, MI) Docum. Libn., Kalamazoo Pub. Lib., 1981–; Consult. for Media Srvs., Kalamazoo Pub. Sch., 1975–, Libn., 1968–75; Libn., Comstock Pub. Sch., 1967–68. **Educ.:** West. MI Univ., 1943–46, BA (Hist.), 1965–67, MLS. **Orgs.:** ALA. MI Assn. for Media in Educ.: Noms. (1977). Beta Phi Mu: Pres. (1975). **Pubns.:** "Facilitating the Positive Image... A Materials Examination Center in Action," *Media Spectrum* (1977); reviews. **Activities:** 10; 17, 24, 42; 63, 89 **Addr.:** 275 West Michigan, Galesburg, MI 49053.

Glanz, Lenore Marie (S. 16, 1933, Chicago, IL) Dir., Lib. and Info. Resrc. Ctr., Natl. PTA, 1981–; Head, Resrch. Dept., World Book - Childcraft Intl., 1980–81; Resrch. Libn., 1967–79; Asst. Ed., 1963–67; Ed. Resrchr., 1961–63; Libn., Ref. Dept., Chicago Pub. Lib., 1960–61; Couns., Dean's Ofc., Univ. of IL, 1955–59. **Educ.:** Univ. of IL, 1951–54, BA (Hist.); 1954–57, MA (Hist.); 1959–60, MS in LS; Loyola Univ., 1962–72, PhD (Hist.). **Orgs.:** SLA: *The Informant,* Ed. (1974–78); Asst. Ed., (1967–68). IL LA. Chicago Lib. Club. Loyola Univ. Alum. Assn.: Exec. Bd. (1973–). Chicago Cncl. on Frgn. Rel.: Forum Stng. Com.; VP, Strg. Com. (1981–82). **Pubns.:** "Chapter Newsletters - A Survey," *Spec. Libs.* (Je. 1978); various articles *World Events* (1976–); reviews. **Activities:** 12; 17, 39, 41, 49; 73, 72 **Addr.:** The National PTA, 700 N. Rush St., Chicago, IL 60611.

Glasby, Dorothy Joens (Je. 3, 1927, Blue Island, IL) Asst. Chief, Serials Recs. Div., Lib. of Congs., 1981–, Conser Opers. Coord., 1977–81, Head, Eng. Lang. Serials Cat. Sect., 1976–77, Head, Serials Cat. Sect., 1968–76, Asst. Head, Serials Sect., Descr. Cat. Div., 1967–68. **Educ.:** Thornton Jr. Coll., 1946–48, Dip.; Elmhurst Coll., 1948–50, BS (Bio.); Northwest. Univ., 1951–53, MA (Eng. Lit.); Univ. of IL, 1957–59, MS (LS). **Orgs.:** ALA: RTSD/Serials Sect. (Vice-Ch./Ch. Elect, 1981–), Ad Hoc Com. to Std. Serials Cat. (1974–76). **Honors:** Lib. of Congs., Rcrt. Prog. for Outstan. Lib. Sch. Grads., 1959; Beta Phi Mu, 1958. **Pubns.:** "Serials in 1978," *Lib. Resrcs. & Tech. Srvs.* (Sum. 1979); "Serials in 1979," *Lib. Resrcs. & Tech. Srvs.* (Sum. 1980); asst. ed., serials sect., *Lib. Resrcs. & Tech. Srvs.* (1975–81); "Year's Work in Serials, 1980," *Lib. Resrcs. & Tech. Srvs.* (Sum. 1981). **Activities:** 4; 20, 44, 46 **Addr.:** 3612 Thornapple St., Chevy Chase, MD 20815.

Glasco, Ingrid, T. M. (Ap. 29, 1935, Schweinfurt, Bavaria, Germany) Coord./Ed., PA Union List of Serials/PRLC, 1980–; ILL/Ref. Libn., Univ. of Pittsburgh, 1974–80, Serials Libn., Fine Arts Lib., 1971–73). **Educ.:** SUNY, Buffalo, 1965–69, BA (Grmn.); Univ. of Pittsburgh, 1969–71, MA (Art Hist.), 1971–73, MLS, 1978–, PhD in prog. (LS). **Orgs.:** ALA. Pittsburgh On-Line Users Forum. Assn. of Univ. Libns. West. PA Conservancy. Natl. Trust for Hist. Prsrvn. **Activities:** 1, 14-Networks; 34, 39, 44; 55, 57, 74 **Addr.:** Hillman Library, Univ. of Pittsburgh, Pittsburgh, PA 15260.

Glascock, Mary A. (Ja. 1, 1952, Flushing, NY) Libn., Salvation Army Arch. Resrch. Ctr., 1978–; Lib. Asst., Harcourt Brace Jovanovich, 1977–78. **Educ.:** Long Island Univ., 1969–73, BA (Hist.); Queens Coll., 1975–77, MLS; Univ. of Chicago, 1973–74, MA (Hist). **Orgs.:** SLA: NY Chap. (Secy., 1981–82); Pubcty Com. (1980–81); Janus sem. com. (1981); Lib. Liaison. Com. (1979–80). Lib. Liaison Com., (1979–80); Lib. Assn. Liaison, (1978–79). NY Lib. Club. Queens Hist. Socty.: Bd. of Trustees, Dir. of Lib. Srvs., (1977–). **Activities:** 12; 15, 45, 46; 57, 90, 92 **Addr.:** Salvation Army Archives and Research Center, 145 W. 15 St., New York, NY 10011.

Glascoff, Elisabeth Ann (S. 23, 1943, Milwaukee, WI) Docum. Libn., Gvrs. State Univ., 1973–; Nursing Sch. Libn., Meth. Hosp. Sch. of Nursing, Madison, WI, 1970–71; Asst. Indxr./Ed., Air Univ. Lib., 1966–69. **Educ.:** Univ. of WI, 1964–65, BA (Hist.), 1965–66, MA (LS); Univ. of Chicago, 1976–80, CAS (LS). **Orgs.:** ALA: State Docum. Work Grp. on State Checklists (1976); Fed. Docum. Task Frc. Com. on Distributive Autom. Rec. Prcs. (1980–). IL LA: GODORT (Treas., 1977–81); Liaison to ALA/GODORT (1978–80). Chicago Acad. Lib. Cncl.: Docum. Subcom. (1980–); Serials Subcom. (1975–76, 1981–). **Pubns.:** Ed., *IL LA GODORT Nsltr.* (1977–). **Activities:** 1; 20, 29 **Addr.:** University Library, Documents, Governors State University, Park Forest South, IL 60466.

Glaser, June E. (Ag. 23, 1934, Newark, NJ) Libn., Eastman Dental Ctr., 1976–; Libn., AV, Serials, Rochester Gen. Hosp., 1974–76; various other positions, 1956–63. **Educ.:** Univ. of MI, 1952–56, BA (Eng.); Harvard-Radcliffe Prog., 1957–58, Cert. (Bus. Admin.); SUNY, Geneseo, 1973–74, MLS; Med. LA, 1974, Med. Libn., Grade I. **Orgs.:** Med. LA: Upstate NY and ON Chap., Ch. (1980–81), Vice-Ch., Ch.-Elect (1979–80), Treas. (1978–79), Cncl. (1981–84). Rochester Reg. Resrch. Lib. Cncl.: Cont. Educ. Com. (1980–). Monroe Cnty. Lib. Syst.: Marion McGuire Meml. Com. (1980–). NY and NJ Reg. Med. Lib.: Adv. Plng. Com., AV Subcom. (1977–79). Harvard Bus. Sch. Club of Rochester: Pubcty. and Arrange., Ch.; Bd. of Dirs. Rochester Area Libs. in Healthcare: Ch. (1975–76). **Activities:** 1; 15, 17, 39; 80 **Addr.:** Basil G. Bibby Library, Eastman Dental Center, Rochester, NY 14620.

Glasgow, Kathleen Goodwin (Ja. 14, 1953, Niagara Falls, NY) Admin. Anal., Hooker Chem., 1976–. **Educ.:** State Univ. Coll. of NY, Geneseo, 1971–74, BA (Eng.); SUNY, Buffalo, 1976–78, MLS; 1978, Cert. in Recs. Mgt. **Orgs.:** SLA: Upstate NY Chap. (Prog. Ch., 1979–80). Assn. of Recs. Mgrs. and Admins.: Mem. VP (1979–80); Grt. Rochester Chap. **Pubns.:** "The Documentation Manager," *Info. and Recs. Mgt.* (S. 1979); various sps. **Activities:** 12; 24, 33, 38; 56, 62 **Addr.:** Hooker Chemical, M.P.O. Box 8, Niagara Falls, NY 14302.

Glasgow, Vicki L. (N. 15, 1947, Nashville, TN) Ref. Libn., Biomed. Lib., Univ. of MN, 1979–; Biomed. Ref. Libn., Brown Univ., 1977–79; Head, Serials Srvs., Houston Acad. of Med.-TX Med. Ctr. Lib., 1974–77; Ext. Libn., 1972–74. **Educ.:** Vanderbilt Univ., 1965–69, BA (Psy.); Univ. of NC, 1970–71, MSLS; Univ. of MN, 1979–, (Bio.); Cert. of Internship in Biomed. Librnshp., Univ. of CA, Los Angeles, 1971–72. **Orgs.:** Med. LA: Oral Hist. Com. (1977–79); Med. Lib. Tech. Com. (1973–1976). S. Ctrl. Reg. Grp. Med. LA: Plng. Com. Anl. Meeting (1973). Amer. Inst. of Bio. Sci. **Honors:** Med. LA, Rittenhouse Awd., 1972. **Activities:** 1, 12; 27, 39, 44; 58, 80, 91 **Addr.:** 1109 W. Iowa, St. Paul, MN 55108.

Glass, Mary Ellen (Mr. 31, 1927, Reno, NV) Head, Oral Hist. Proj., Univ. of NV, Reno, 1964–. **Educ.:** Univ. of NV, Reno, 1957–62, BA (Hist., Pol. Sci.), 1962–65, MA (Hist.). **Orgs.:** Oral Hist. Assn.: Various coms. Conf. of Intermt. Archvsts.: Various coms. West. Hist. Assn. NV Hist. Socty. **Pubns.:** *Silver and Politics in Nevada, 1892–1902* (1970); *Water for Nevada, The Reclamation Controversey, 1886–1902* (1966); "The Silver Governors, Immigrants in Nevada Politics," *NV Hist. Socty. Qtly.* (Fall–Win. 1978); "Hot Summer in the Sierra . . .," *CA Hist. Socty. Qtly.* (Win. 1972); "The Newlands Reclamation Project . . .," *Jnl. of the W.* (Ja. 1968); various other articles in west. hist. jnls. **Activities:** 1; 15, 45; 85 **Addr.:** University Library, University of Nevada-Reno, Reno, NV 89557.

Glasser, Barbara Robin (O. 9, 1935, Brooklyn, NY) Head Libn., Cantor Rubin Kaplan Meml. Lib., Cong. Beth Yeshurun, 1970–. **Educ.:** Brooklyn Coll., 1953–59, BA (Bio.); Univ. of NC, 1962–69, MLS; Lib. Fellow, 1967–69. **Orgs.:** ALA. AJL. CSLA. TX LA. **Honors:** Untd. Synagogue of America, Solomon Schecter Awd., Outstan. Cong. Lib., 1975–77; 1977–79. **Pubns.:** "Hyman E. Finger Resource Center & the Rubin Kaplan Mem. Lib.," *Assn. of Jew. Lib* (Win. 1976). **Addr.:** Cantor Rubin Kaplan Memorial Library, Cong. Beth Yeshurun, 4525 Beechnut Blvd., Houston, TX 77096.

Glasser, Sylvia B. (Ap. 21, 1924, Brooklyn, NY) Prin. Libn., Brooklyn Pub. Lib., 1979–, Supvsg. Libn., 1970–79, Sr. Libn., 1968–70, Libn., 1967–68. **Educ.:** Brooklyn Coll., 1940–44, BA (Psy.); Pratt Inst., 1962–67, MLS. **Orgs.:** ALA. NY LA. Jewish Libns. Caucus. **Activities:** 9; 17 **Addr.:** 2507 E. 23 St., Brooklyn, NY 11235.

Glassmeyer, Anita Tschida (D. 8, 1933, Beach, ND) Media Libn., AZ Hlth. Sci. Ctr. Lib., Univ. of AZ, 1973–; Asst. Libn., Pub. Srvs., AZ Med. Ctr. Lib., 1972–73, Asst. Pub. Srvs. Libn., 1971–72. **Educ.:** Mercy Hosp. Sch. of Nursing, 1955, Dip. (Nursing); State of CO, 1955, Regis. Nurse; Univ. of Denver, 1966–68, BA (Grmn.), 1968–69, MA (Libnshp.); Univ. of TN Med. Units, 1970–71, Cert.; Med. LA, 1972, Grade II Cert. **Orgs.:** Hlth. Educ. Media Assn. SLA. Med. Lib. Grp. of South. CA and AZ. AZ State LA: Spec. Libs. Div., Secy. (1977), Pres. (1979), Cont. Ed. Com. (1980–). Hlth. Sci. Comm. Assn. **Pubns.:** "Armchair Education: Audiovisual Programs for CME Credit in the University of Arizona Health Sciences Center Library," *AZ Med.* (Ap. 1980); "Audiovisual Programs for Nurses in the University of Arizona Health Sciences Center Library," *AZ Nurse* (1980). **Activities:** 1, 12; 15, 17, 32; 80, 87, 92 **Addr.:** Arizona Health Sciences Center Library, University of Arizona, Tucson, AZ 85724.

Glatt, Carol R. (New York, NY) Lib. Consult., Freelnc. Writer, 1980–; Mgr., Ctrl. Files, Lib., Cncl. of Jewish Feds., 1978–80; Dir., Lib. Srvs., E. Orange Gen. Hosp., 1973–78; Ref. Libn., New Trier Twp. HS, 1968–69. **Educ.:** Columbia Univ., 1955–59, BS (Hebrew Lit.); Drexel Univ., 1963–66, MSLS; Med. LA, 1975, Cert. (Med. Libnshp.); Rutgers Univ., 1978–80, MA (Indus. Rel., Human Resrcs. Dev.). **Orgs.:** Hlth. Sci. LA of NJ: Pres. (1978); Secy. (1976). Med. LA: NY Reg. Grp., Pubcty. Com. (Ch., 1976–77), Legis. Com. (1977–78). **Pubns.:** "Information Please," *Amer. Jnl. of Nursing* (Ap. 1978); bk reviewer, *Lib. Jnl.;* various sps., wkshps. **Activities:** 12; 24, 35, 38; 80, 90 **Addr.:** 21 Forester Dr., Princeton, NJ 08540.

Glazer, Frederic J. (F. 20, 1937, Portsmouth, VA) Dir., WV Lib. Comsn., 1972–; Dir., Chesapeake Pub. Lib., 1967–72; Libn., Kirn Meml. Lib., 1964–67. **Educ.:** Columbia Univ., 1950–54, BA (Econ.), 1963–64, MLS. **Orgs.:** ALA: Mem. Com. (Gen. Ch., 1974–77). SE LA. WV LA: Exec. Bd., Ex-Officio Mem. **Honors:** U.S. Ofc. of the Exec., Pres. Cert. of Apprec., 1968; U.S. Dept. of Hlth., Educ. and Welfare, Reg. III Outstan. Citizen's Awd., 1977; WV LA, Dora Ruth Parks Awd., 1979. **Pubns.:** *Public Library Construction* (1977); "Instant Libraries," *Lib. Jnl.* (D. 1, 1972); "Selling The Library," *Lib. Jnl.* (Je. 1, 1974); "The Better Life" multi-media presentation (1973); "LSCA/Star Years" multi-media presentation (1981). **Activities:** 13; 17, 19, 24; 72, 78, 93 **Addr.:** West Virginia Library Commission, Science & Cultural Center, Charleston, WV 25305.

Glazier, Edwin E. (Je. 29, 1947, St. Louis, MO) Quality Spec., RLG, Inc., 1981–; Head, Serials Cat., and Coord., Title II-C Serials Conversion Proj., Univ. of MI, 1979–81; Serials Catlgr., 1976–79, Mono. Catlgr., 1970–76. **Educ.:** MI State Univ., 1965–69, BA (Classics); Univ. of MI, 1969–70, MA (LS). **Orgs.:**

PROFESSIONAL ACTIVITIES: Institutions: 1. Acad. lib.; 2. Arch.; 3. Assn.; 4. Fed./Gvt. lib.; 5. Inst. lib.; 6. Mfr./Suppl.; 7. Milit. lib.; 8. Musm.; 9. Pub. lib.; 10. Sch. lib.; 11. Sch. of lib. sci.; 12. Spec. lib.; 13. State lib.; 14. (other). **Functions/Activities:** 15. Acq./Col. dev.; 16. Adult srvs.; 17. Admin.; 18. Apprais.; 19. Archit./Bldgs.; 20. Cat./Class.; 21. Chld. srvs.; 22. Circ.; 23. Cons./Pres.; 24. Consult.; 25. Cont. ed.; 26. Educ. lib. sci.; 27. Ext. srvs.; 28. Fund/Grants; 29. Gvt. pubs.; 30. Indx./Abs.; 31. Instr. lib. use; 32. Media srvs.; 33. Micro.; 34. Netwks./Coop.; 35. Persnl.; 36. PR; 37. Publshg.; 38. Recs. mgt.; 39. Ref. srvs.; 40. Repro.; 41. Resrch.; 42. Review.; 43. Secur.; 44. Serials; 45. Spec. col.; 46. Tech. srvs.; 47. Trustees/Bds.; 48. YA srvs.; 49. (other).

ALA. Thea. LA. **Activities:** 1; 20, 44 **Addr.:** RLG, Inc., Hanford, CA 94305.

Gleason, Virginia Lee (Casey) (S. 7, 1923, Buckhannon, WV) Coord., Chld. Srvs. Springfield-Greene Cnty (MO) Pub. Lib. 1956–; Ref. Libn., Univ. of IA, 1955–56; Chld. Libn., San Diego (CA) Pub. Lib., 1952–53; Libn., Superior Ctrl. HS (WI), 1949–50; Circ. Libn., Northwest. Univ., 1946–49. **Educ.:** WV Wesleyan Coll., 1941–45, AB Magna cum Laude (Eng.); Columbia Univ. 1945–46, BLS; Northwest. Univ., 1946–1949 MA (Eng). **Orgs.:** MO State Lib.: Chld. and YA Bk. Sel. Com. (1969–). MO LA: Chld. Srvs. RT (Ch., 1974–76). Springfield Area Libns. Assn.: VP (1969–70); Secy. (1980–81). PTA City Cncl.: Readg. and Lib. Ch. (1972–74). St. Paul United Meth. Church: Lib. Com. (Ch., 1970–). Springfield Area Puppeteers Assn. **Pubns.:** "Schmidt Storytelling Collection," *SHOW-ME LIBS.* (Ag. 1979); "Children's Book Shelf," (Wkly. Clmn.) Springfield (MO) Leader and Press (S. 1979–). **Activities:** 1, 9; 21, 22, 39 **Addr.:** 1710 E. Latoka St., Springfield, MO 65804.

Gleaves, Edwin S. (F. 28, 1936, Nashville, TN) Prof., Ch., Dept. of LS, George Peabody Coll., Vanderbilt Univ., 1967–, Dir., Prof., Sch. of Lib. and Info. Sci., 1975–79, Dir., Progs. for Educ. Support Persnl., 1974–75, Dir., Assoc. Prof., 1967–73, Sum. Fac., Dir. Designate, 1967, Asst. Prof., Eng., 1966–67; Head Libn., Asst. Prof., Eng., David Lipscomb Coll., 1964–65; Ref. Libn., Bus. and Sci. Dept., Atlanta Pub. Lib., 1961; various positions as visit. prof., consult., 1965–80. **Educ.:** David Lipscomb Coll., 1954–58, BA (Eng.); Emory Univ., 1958–60, MA (Libnshp.), 1960–64, PhD (Eng.); Escuela Normal del Estado, Saltillo, Mex., 1962, Dip. (Span.). **Orgs.:** TN LA: VP, Pres.-Elect (1970–71); Pres. (1971–72); Interim Pres. (1972–73); Exec. Com. (1973–74); Com. on Staff Dev. and Rcrt. (Ch., 1980–81). ALA: IRRT (Area Ch. for Latin Amer., 1980–81), Exec. Bd. (1972–73); Com. on Accred., Grad. Lib. Educ. Progs. (Eval., 1973–); various ofcs., coms. SALALM: Task Frc. on the Asst. of Nicaraguan Libs. (1968–70). AALS: Spec. Com. on Latin Amer.-N. Amer. Rel. (Co-Ch., 1980–81). Various other orgs. Wilderness Socty. TN Trails Assn. George Peabody Coll.: Cncl. on Persnl. Policy (Ch., 1977–78); Peabody Coll. Fac. (Ch., 1978–79); Univ. Srch. Com. for the Peabody Actg. Dean (Ch., 1979); Univ. Srch. Com. for the Peabody Dean (1980); Coll. Com. on Curric. and Educ. Progs. (Ch., 1980–81). Vanderbilt Univ. Fac. Sen.: Com. on External Affairs (Ch., 1980–81). **Honors:** Univ. of Costa Rica, Fulbright Lectr., 1971. **Pubns.:** Ed., *Guía de fuentes de información en las humanidades y las ciencias sociales* (1971); jt. auth., *Microformulation: A Selective Bibliography on Microforms, 1970–75* ERIC; transl., "Libraries in Paraguay," *Encyc. of Lib. and Info. Sci.* (1977); "Drury, F.K.W.," *Dictionary of American Library Biography* (1978); ed., spec. Latin Amer. issue, *Leads* (Sum. 1981); various mono., articles in Eng. and Span., reviews, rpts. **Activities:** 1, 11; 26, 33, 42; 54, 74 **Addr.:** Dept. of Library Science, George Peabody College for Teachers, Vanderbilt University, Nashville, TN 37203.

Gleim, David E. (Ap. 29, 1947, Owensboro, KY) Head, Mono. Cat., Wilson Lib., Univ. of NC, 1977–, Sci. Catlgr., 1976–77; Serial Catlgr., Strozier Lib., FL State Univ., 1973–76. **Educ.:** Brescia Coll., 1969–71, BA (Hist.); Univ. of KY, 1972–73, MS (LS). **Orgs.:** ALA. NC LA. **Pubns.:** Jt. auth., "The Case for Not Closing the Catalog," *Amer. Libs.* (Mr. 1979); jt. auth., "The Implementation of AACR 2: Some Questions," *RTSD Nsltr.* (S.–O. 1980). **Activities:** 1; 20; 56 **Addr.:** Catalog Dept., Wilson Library 024A, University of North Carolina, Chapel Hill, NC 27514.

Glenister, Peter G. (S. 24, 1943, Halifax, NS) Cat. Libn., Mt. Saint Vincent Univ., 1968–. **Educ.:** Saint Mary's Univ., 1960–67, BA (Eng.), 1967–68, BEd (Educ.); Dalhousie Univ., 1969–71, MLS (Lib. Srv.). **Orgs.:** Can. LA. Atl. Prov. LA: *APLA Bltn.* Ed. (1975–80); Pubns. Com. (Conv., 1980–81). Halifax LA: Secy.-Treas. (1976–77). Can. Assn. of Univ. Tchrs. NS Confederation of Univ. Fac. Assns.: Secy. (1977–78). **Activities:** 1; 20, 39, 46 **Addr.:** 1669 Larch St., Halifax, NS B3H 3X2 Canada.

Glidden, Iris Olsen (D. 4, 1917, Winchester, WI) Dir., Lib., Media Srvs., West Bend Pub. Sch., 1970–; Head Libn., West Bend HS, 1962–70; Actg. Fac., Kenwood Lib., Univ. of WI, 1961–62. **Educ.:** Northland Coll., Univ. of WI, 1935–38, 1958–62, BA (Eng., LS); Univ. of WI, 1968–71, MA (LS); various crs. **Orgs.:** WI LA: Int. Frdm. Com. WI Sch. Lib. Media Assn.: Past Pres. (1971–72). WI AV Assn.: Bd. Lib. Cncl. of Metro. Milwaukee: Sch. Task Frc. Various other orgs. AAUW: State Educ. Ch. Univ. of WI, Milwaukee Alum. Assn. WI Acad. of Sci., Arts and Letters. **Honors:** WI Assn. of Sch. Libns., Sch. Libn. Of The Yr., 1975. **Pubns.:** "Legislation That Rings Bells for School Librarians," *WI Lib. Bltn.* (Jl. 1972); "Automation for Media Centers?" *WI Lib. Bltn.* (My. 1977); "Wisconsin Audiovisual Association, Conference 1977," *WI Lib. Bltn.* (Ja. 1978). **Activities:** 10; 15, 17, 20; 63, 67, 74 **Addr.:** West Bend Public Schools, 697 S. 5th Ave., West Bend, WI 53095.

Glogoff, Stuart J. (D. 11, 1948, Trenton, NJ) Head, Circ. Dept., Univ. of DE Lib., 1981–; Asst. Head, Lending Srvs., PA State Univ., 1977–81, Undergrad. Ref. Libn., 1974–77. **Educ.:** Univ. of Cincinnati, 1966–70, BA (Hist.), 1970–72, MA (Mod. Eur. Hist.), IN Univ., 1973, MLS. **Orgs.:** ALA: ALA/LAMA Stats. for Circ. Com. (1981–82). DE LA. SLA. PALA: PR Media Eval. Com, (1977–78); PA Reg. Lib. Ctr., Instr. Mtrls. Com., (1976–77). **Pubns.:** "Using Statistical Tests to Evaluate Library Instruction," *Jnl. Acad Libnship* (Ja. 1979); "Cannons Bibliography of Library Economy and its Role in the Development of Bibliographic Tools in Librarianship," *Jnl. Lib Hist.* (Win. 1977). "Copyright and a Reserve Reading Room: From Menace to office Routine," *Collection Mgt.* (Win. 1979/actually Ag. 1981). **Activities:** 1; 22, 31, 39; 65, 91, 92 **Addr.:** University of Delaware Library, Newark, DE 19711.

Glover, Peggy D. (O. 5, 1931, Vancouver, WA) Coord., Free Lib. of Philadelphia, 1970–, Head, Cmnty. Srvs., Adult, YA, 1965–70, Head, Tech. Lib., DISC, DOD, 1961–65, Adult Srvs. Libn., 1960–61; Base Libn., U.S. Air Frc., Eng., Germany, 1956–60; Adult, YA Libn., Enoch Pratt Free Lib., 1954–56. **Educ.:** Pomona Coll., 1951–53, BA (Eng. Lit.); Carnegie Inst. of Tech., 1953–54, MLS. **Orgs.:** ALA: Cncl. (1973–75); Publshg. Com. (1979–81); Booklist Adv. Bd. (1975–76; 1978–79); ASD, Adult Lib. Com. (Ch., 1971–73); RASD, Srvs. to Adults Com. (Ch., 1978–80); PLA, Rpt. Com. (1977–79). PA LA. Adult Educ. Assn. PA Assn. of Adult Cont. Ed. **Pubns.:** "Planning for the Future," *Top of the News* (N. 1972); "Beyond the First R," *Wilson Lib. Bltn.* (My. 1976); "The Philadelphia Story: Adult Literacy Program at the Free Library of Philadelphia," ERIC (Ap. 1979); "Adult Education and the Free Library of Philadelphia," *Cath. Lib. World* (Jl.–Ag. 1979). **Activities:** 4, 9; 15, 16, 17; 50, 75, 89 **Addr.:** Office of Work with Adults/Young Adults, The Free Library of Philadelphia, Logan Sq., Philadelphia, PA 19103.

Gluckstein, Fritz P. (Ja. 24, 1927, Berlin, Germany) Coord. for Vetny. Affairs, Natl. Lib. of Med., 1966–; Chief, Microbio. Branch, Smithsonian Sci. Info. Exch., 1963–66; Veterinary Anal., US Dept. of Agr., 1957–63. **Educ.:** Univ. of MN, 1953, BS (Vetny. Med.); 1955, DVM; Dipl., Amer. Coll. of Vetny. Preventive Med., 1966; Fellow, Royal Socty. of Hlth. (London), 1968. **Orgs.:** Med. LA. Amer. Vetny. Med. Assn. Amer. Pub. Hlth. Assn. **Pubns.:** Contrib., *Diseases of Public Health Significance in the Biology of the Laboratory Rabbit* (1974); Jt. auth., "The Laboratory Animal Data Bank (LADB)," *Procs. of Internatl. Symposium on Animal Health and Disease Data Banks* (1979). **Activities:** 4; 24, 49-Info. Col. and Retrieval; 95-Vetny. Med. **Addr.:** National Library of Medicine, Bethesda, MD 20209.

Gnat, Jean M. (D. 14, 1929, Milwaukee, WI) Head, Tech. Opers., IN Univ., Purdue Univ., 1976–, Head, Acq., 1975–76, Serials Acq., 1969–75; Branch Libn., Milwaukee Pub. Lib., 1961–62. **Educ.:** Univ. of IL, 1956–57, BA (Soclgy., Psy.), 1957–58, MS (LS). **Orgs.:** ALA. IN LA. Econ. Club of Indianapolis. **Honors:** Beta Phi Mu, 1958. **Activities:** 1; 17, 20, 46; 56, 75 **Addr.:** Technical Services, University Library IUPUI, 420 Blake St., Indianapolis, IN 46260.

Gnat, Raymond E. (Ja. 15, 1932, Milwaukee, WI) Dir., Indianapolis-Marion Cnty. Pub. Lib., 1972–, Asst. Dir., 1963–72; Subj. Libn., Milwaukee Pub. Lib., 1958–63; Catlgr., Univ. of IL, 1956–58. **Educ.:** Univ. of WI, 1950–54, BBA (Bus.); Univ. of IL, 1956–58, MS (LS); IN Univ., Purdue Univ., Indianapolis, 1981, MPA (Pub. Admin.). **Orgs.:** ALA. IN LA: Pres. (1980). Bibl. Socty. of Amer. Indianapolis Lit. Club. Rotary. **Activities:** 9; 17, 24; 56, 57 **Addr.:** 40 E. Saint Clair St., Indianapolis, IN 46204.

Gobble, Richard L. (Ja. 11, 1922, Albia, IA) Dir. of Lib., Ft. Lewis Coll., 1967–; Head Un. Cat., US Dept of Hlth., Educ., Welfare, 1967; Catlgr., Shared Cat., Libs. of Congs., 1966–67; Chief, Cat., US AFA, 1955–66; Head Libn., Univ. of North. CO, 1951–55; Docum. Lib., Denver Pub. Lib., 1950–51. **Educ.:** Univ. of Denver, 1946–49, BSBA (Econ); 1949–50, MA (LS). **Orgs.:** CO LA. **Activities:** 1; 15, 17, 35 **Addr.:** 1616 Forest, Durango, CO 81301.

Godbout-Mercure, Micheline (Ja. 17, 1940, Sherbrooke, PQ) Chef, Srvs. Tech., Radio-PQ, 1978–; Bibtcr., Srv. Tech., Ctrl. des Bibs., 1974–78; Bibtcr., Srv. Tech., Univ. de Sherbrooke, 1965–74. **Educ.:** Univ. d'Ottawa, 1969–70, Bac. (Bib.); Univ. de Sherbrooke, 1956–60, Bac. (Péd.). **Orgs.:** ASTED: Cnsl. d'Admin. (1976–77). Corp. des Bibtcrs. Prof. du PQ. **Activities:** 1, 12; 20, 32, 46; 56, 63, 93 **Addr.:** 5485 Mennereuil, St-Léonard, PQ H1S 1S7 Canada.

Goddard, Susan W. (O. 24, 1944, St. Catharines, ON) Head Libn., Fac. of Dentistry, Univ. of Toronto, 1978–, Asst. Libn., 1974–78; Libn., F.W. Minkler Lib., 1968–73; Libn., Univ. of Toronto, Fac. of LS, 1968, Libn., Dept. of Bk. Sel., 1966–67. **Educ.:** Univ. of Toronto, 1962–65, BA (Eng.), 1965–66, BLS, 1972–76, MLS. **Orgs.:** Can. LA: Toronto Med. Libs. Grp. Libns. Assn. of Univ. of Toronto. CHLA. **Activities:** 1, 12; 15, 17, 39; 63, 80 **Addr.:** Faculty of Dentistry Library, 124 Edward St., Toronto, ON M5G 1G6 Canada.

Godden, Irene P. (N. 1, 1932, Braunschweig, Germany) Asst. Dir., Tech. Srvs., CO State Univ., 1979–; Asst. Dir., Tech. Srvs., Howard Univ., 1976–78; Head, Bibl. Recs., CA State Univ., 1972–74; Ref. Libn., Los Angeles Pub. Lib., 1970–72. **Educ.:** Brooklyn Coll., CUNY, 1964–68, BA (Grmn., Compar. Lit.); Univ. of CA, Los Angeles, 1969–70, MLS, 1968–74, MA (Grmn.). **Orgs.:** ALA. CO LA. CA LA: Coll. and Resrch. Chap. (Secy.-Treas., 1973); Col. Dev. Libns. Chap. (South. CA Coord., 1972–74). NLA: *Natl. Libn.* Bibl. Ed. (1979–). Univ. of CA Lib. Schs. Alum. Assn.: Pres. (1976). **Honors:** Beta Phi Mu. **Pubns.:** Jt. auth., "Colorado State University Joins the Research Libraries Group: Plus or Minus for Resource Sharing in Colorado?" *CO Libs.* (D. 1980); jt. auth., "Improving Approval Plan Performance: A Case Study," *Lib. Acq.* (S. 1980); "A Firing at Rio Hondo," *CA Libn.* (Jl. 1972); *Basic Reference Sources for Business Students* bibl. (1973). **Activities:** 1; 46 **Addr.:** Colorado State University, William E. Morgan Library, Fort Collins, CO 80523.

Godfrey, (Mrs.) Florence Lewis (My. 29, 1917, Fairmount, WV) Consult., 1981–; Adult Srvs. Libn., Cherry Hill Free Pub. Lib., 1970–81; Libn., Tech. Srvs., Mercer Cnty. Lib., 1969–70; YA Libn., Free Lib. of Philadelphia, 1967–69; various secy. positions, 1941–67. **Educ.:** WV Univ., 1939, BA (Jnlsm.); Drexel Univ., 1966, MSLS. **Orgs.:** NJ LA: Int. Frdm. Com. (1978–80). ALA. CS LA: DE Valley Chap. (Pres., 1978–79). Church Lib.: Lib. Com. (Head, 1976–). **Pubns.:** Various Bibls., articles. **Activities:** 5, 9; 16, 20, 42; 90, 93 **Addr.:** 523 Estate Rd., Maple Shade, NJ 08052.

Godfrey, Lois Erwin (Mr. 26, 1928, Cambridge, MA) Asst. Head Libn., Los Alamos Sci. Lab., 1963–, Asst. Branch Libn., 1959–63, Tech. Lit. Srch., 1956–59, Tech. Lib. Sect. Leader, 1954–55; Ref. Libn., Johns-Manville Resrch. Ctr., 1950–54. **Educ.:** Simmons Coll., 1947–50, BS (LS). **Orgs.:** SLA: Exec. Bd., Chap. Cabinet Ch. (1976–77), Ch.-Elect (1975–76); Rio Grande Chap. (Pres., 1959–60, 1972–73), Exec. Bd. (1958–61, 1971–74); various ofcs., coms. NM LA: Pres. (1978–79); Nom. Com. (Ch., 1979–80); various ofcs. NM Lib. and AV Educ. Cncl.: Secy. (1969–71). NM Adv. Cncl. on Libs. Various other orgs. Leag. of Women Voters of Los Alamos: Nsltr. Ed. (1968–69); Fin. Ch. (1972–73); Pres. (1974–75). AAAS. **Honors:** SLA, Sci.-Tech. Div., Pubns. Awd., 1963. **Pubns.:** Jt. ed., *Dictionary of Report Series Codes* (1962, 1973). **Activities:** 12; 17, 31, 34; 74, 91 **Addr.:** 156 Tunyo, Los Alamos, NM 87544.

Godoy, Alicia F. (F. 27, 1917, Matanzas, Cuba) Lang. Libn., Miami-Dade Pub. Lib. Syst., 1961–; Circ. Libn., Bib. Natl. José Marti, 1960–61. **Educ.:** Univ. of Habana, 1938–41 PhD. Library Science. University of Havana 1959–60 MA (LS). **Orgs.:** ALA. Reforma. Lat. Amer. Stds. Assn. FL LA. Other orgs. Cuban Women's Club. Edgar Allan Poe Socty. **Honors:** Cuban Women's Club, Cert. of Appreciation, 1974. Miami Sr. HS Adult Educ., Cert. of Appreciation, 1974. Premio Anual del Liceo Cubano, Gran Orden Martiana, 1976. Cruzada Educativa Cubana, Premio Juan J. Remos, 1977. **Activities:** 9; 16 **Addr.:** Miami-Dade Public Library, 1 Biscayne Blvd., Miami, FL 33132.

Godsey, James M. (N. 26, 1947, Bloomington, IN) Dir., Huntington City-Twp. Pub. Lib., 1976–. **Educ.:** Univ. of MN, 1966–70, BS (Eng.); IN Univ., 1973–76, MLS. **Orgs.:** ALA: LAMA; PLA (1977–). IN LA: Cmnty. Srvs. Div. (Ch., 1981–82). Tri-Cnty. LA: Pres. (1979–81); Ch.-Elect (1982); Vice-Ch. (1981). Tri-ALSA Lib. Coop.: Bd. (1978–); Past Pres. (1978); Legis. Com. (Ch., 1981). **Activities:** 9; 15, 17, 36 **Addr.:** Huntington Public Library, 44 E. Park Dr., Huntington, IN 46750.

Godwin, Frances L. (Elliott) (My. 13, 1920, Colorado City, TX) Libn./Media Dir., - Colorado HS, 1962–, 1945–48, 1942–43; Libn., Pecos HS, 1941–42. **Educ.:** TX Woman's Univ., 1937–41, BA (LS); Hardin-Simmons Univ., 1967–69, MEd (Guid. Couns.). **Orgs.:** TX LA. TX Assn. of Sch. Libns. ALA: AASL. AECT. Other orgs. Order of the Eastern Star: Worthy Matron (1955–56). Order of the Rainbow for Girls: Mother Adv. (1957–66). Social Order of the Beauceant: Pres. (1977–78). Delta Kappa Gamma: VP (1980–81). Other orgs. **Activities:** 10, 11; 32, 48; 63 **Addr.:** 735 East 16th St., Colorado City, TX 79512.

Goecks, Margaret D. (My. 20, 1927, Milwaukee, WI) Dir. of Lib. Srvs., Sch. Dist. of Menomonee Falls, WI, 1978–; Libn., East HS, Menomonee Falls, 1969–78; Libn., North HS, 1966–69; Libn., Milwaukee Pub. Lib., 1950–58. **Educ.:** Marquette Univ., 1945–49, PhD (Eng.); Western Reserve Univ., 1949–50, MS (LS). **Orgs.:** ALA. WI LA. **Activities:** 10; 15, 17, 20 **Addr.:** P.O. Box 68, Menomonee Falls, WI 53051.

Goehlert, Robert U. (D. 1, 1948, Springfield, MA) Libn. for Econ., Pol. Sci., Forensic Stds., IN Univ., 1974–. **Educ.:** Univ. of MA, 1966–70, BA (Pol. Sci., Russ.) IN Univ., 1970–72, MA (Pol. Sci.), 1974–76, MLS, 1972– (Pol. Sci.). **Orgs.:** ALA: ACRL, Cont. Educ. Com. (1978–80)/Law and Pol. Sci. Sect., Mem. at Lg. (1979–81). ASIS. **Honors:** Beta Phi Mu. **Pubns.:** *Congress and Law-Making: Researching the Legislative Process* (1979); "Computor Programming in Library Education," *Jnl. of Educ. for Libnshp.* (Spr. 1980); "Effect of Loan Policies on Circulation Recalls," *Jnl. of Acad. Libnshp.* (My., 1979); "Doctoral dissertations in Political Science: Finding Them in U.S. Universities," *Tchng Pol. Sci* (Ja., 1979); Other articles and bibls. **Activities:** 1, 4; 24, 29, 41; 59, 78, 92, 95-Pol. Sci. **Addr.:** Indiana University Library, Bloomington, IN 47405.

Goehner, Donna Marie (Mr. 9, 1941, Chicago, IL) Acq., Serials, Unit Coord., West. IL Univ., 1975–, Pers. Dept. Head, 1974–75, Curric. Lab. Libn., 1968–73; Resrch. Assoc., Univ. of

Special Subjects/Services: 50. Adult educ.; 51. Advert./Mktg.; 52. Aerosp.; 53. Agric.; 54. Area std.; 55. Arts/Hum.; 56. Autom.; 57. Bibl./Prtg.; 58. Bio. sci.; 59. Bus./Fin.; 60. Chem.; 61. Copyrt.; 62. Documtn.; 63. Educ.; 64. Engin.; 65. Env.; 66. Eth. grps.; 67. Film; 68. Food/Nutr.; 69. Geneal.; 70. Geo.; 71. Geol.; 72. Handcpd.; 73. Hist.; 74. Int. frdm.; 75. Info. sci.; 76. Insr.; 77. Law; 78. Legis.; 79. Math./Comp. sci.; 80. Med.; 81. Metals; 82. Nat. resrcs.; 83. Newsp.; 84. Nuc. sci.; 85. Oral hist.; 86. Petr./Energy; 87. Pharm.; 88. Phys./Astr./Math.; 89. Readg.; 90. Relig.; 91. Sci./Tech.; 92. Soc. sci.; 93. Telecom.; 94. Transp.; 95. (other).

IL, 1966. **Educ.:** South. IL Univ., 1959–63, BS (Eng.); Univ. of IL, 1965–66, MS (LS), 1973–74, CAS (LS); South. IL Univ., PhD prog. **Orgs.:** ALA: ACRL. IL LA. IL ACRL: Comms. Com. (Ch., 1979). **Honors:** Beta Phi Mu, 1966. **Pubns.:** Cmplr., *A Directory of College and Research Librarians in Illinois* (1979). **Activities:** 1; 15, 44, 46; 57, 63, 75 **Addr.:** 600 Meadow Dr., Macomb, IL 61455.

Goerdt, Arthur L. (Ja. 13, 1912, Dyersville, IA) Assoc. Prof. of Eng., St. Mary's Univ., 1957–; Dir., House of Std., 1957–63; Libn., Tchr., HS in MO, WI, MI, TX, 1935–57. **Educ.:** Univ. of Dayton, 1932–35, BS (Educ.); Our Lady of the Lake Univ., 1937–42, BS (LS); 1943–50, MEd, (Eng.). **Orgs.:** Cath. LA: Pres. (1959–61). Natl. Cncl. of Tchrs. of Eng. S. Ctrl. Mod. Lang. Assn. Conf. on Coll. Composition and Comm. San Antonio Cncl. of Tchrs. of Eng.: Pres. **Honors:** Cath. LA, Life mem., 1963. **Pubns.:** *Campus Unrest* (1970); various articles. **Activities:** 1, 10; 24, 31, 32; 55, 89, 93 **Addr.:** St. Mary's University, San Antonio, TX 78284.

Goerler, Raimund E. (O. 17, 1948, Wilhelmshaven, W. Germany) Univ. Archvst., OH State Univ., 1978–; Mss. Spec., The West. Rsv. Hist. Socty., 1976–78; Lectr., Amer. Hist., Cuyahoga Cmnty. Coll., 1975–76; Resrch., Writer, OH Bicent. Comsn., 1974–75. **Educ.:** SUNY, Buffalo, 1966–70, BA (Hist.); Case West. Rsv. Univ., 1970–75, MA, PhD (Arch., Hist.); 1973, Cert. of Intl. Wkshp. on Coll. and Univ. Arch. **Orgs.:** Socty. of OH Archvsts.: Exec. Cncl. (1980–). SAA: Coll. and Univ. Arch. Grp. (1978). Assn. of Recs. Mgrs. and Admins. OH State Univ. Lib.: Exhibits Com. (1979–); Paper Prcs. Com. (1979–). **Honors:** Phi Beta Kappa, 1970. **Pubns.:** *The Johnson–Humrickhouse Memorial Museum: A History* (1981); "Land Speculating in the Western Reserve," *West. Rsv. Hist. Socty. Bltn.* (Ap. 1978); "Lincoln's Gadfly: Clement L. Vallandigham," *West. Rsv. Hist. Socty. Bltn.* (Mr. 1977); various bk. reviews, *The Amer. Archvst., The Midwest. Archvst., OH Hist., Jnl. of Amer. Std., Greenville Press Reprint Reviews;* "The Tom L. Johnson Papers," *West. Rsv. Hist. Socty. Bltn.* (D. 1976); "Family Psychology and History," *The Psychohist. Review* (D. 1975); various papers. **Activities:** 2, 5; 15, 17, 38; 55 **Addr.:** 209 Converse Hall, The Ohio State University, 2121 Tuttle Park Pl., Columbus, OH 43210.

Goetz, Arthur H. (My 29, 1928, NY, NY) Admin., Wicomico Cnty. Free Lib., 1978–; Dir., Pub. Lib. of Johnston and Smithfield Cntys., 1974–78; Libn., Coastal Carolina Cmnty. Coll., 1971–74. Warrant Ofcr., U.S. Marine Corps., 1945–67. **Educ.:** Adelphi Univ., 1968–70, BBA (Bus. Admin.); Pratt Inst., 1970–71, MLS. **Orgs.:** MD LA: Prog. Com. (1979–80). Salisbury Cham. of Cmrc.: Tourism, Conv. Com. (1978–80). Rotary: Bd. of Dirs. (1974–80). **Honors:** Beta Phi Mu. **Pubns.:** "General Revenue Sharing," *Amer. Libs.* (My. 1978); "Books in Peril," *Wilson Lib. Bltn.* (Ja. 1973); Rx fo PR in Public Libraries (16mm sound, color film, 15 min.) (1978); "Self Study of the Public Library of Johnston County & Smithfield and its Service Area." (1977); Jt.–Auth., "Getting books faster and cheaper: a jobber acquisition study," *Public Libraries,* (Winter, 1980); Jt.–auth. "Solar power in the Public Library," *Public Libraries,* (Summer, 1981). **Activities:** 9; 17, 36, 47 **Addr.:** Wicomico County Free Library, P.O. Box 951, Salisbury, MD 21801.

Goetz, Rita D. (Ag. 4, 1948, New York City, NY) Ed., Bio. and Agr. Index, H. W. Wilson Co., 1975–, Asst. Ed., 1974–75, Indxr., 1972–74. **Educ.:** Hunter Coll., CUNY, 1966–70, BA (Bio.); Queens Coll., CUNY, 1970–72, MLS. **Orgs.:** ALA. SLA. ASIS. Amer. Musm. of Nat. Hist. Smithsonian Inst. NY Zoological Socty. **Activities:** 14; 30, 37; 58, 68, 87 **Addr.:** Editor, Biological & Agricultural Index, H. W. Wilson Co., 950 University Ave., New York City, NY 10452.

Goheen, Patricia A. (D. 10, 1929, Dayton, OH) Asst. Dir., Pub. Srvs., FL State Univ., 1978–; Cust. Rep., CLSI, 1977–78; Mgr., Tech. Info. Ctr., Xerox Corp., 1975–77; Asst. Prof., Sch. of LS, Case Western Reserve Univ., 1970–75. **Educ.:** Purdue Univ., 1947–51, BS (Span.); Queens Coll., 1957–58, MED; Pratt Inst., 1961–62, MSLS; Case Western Reserve Univ., 1966–69, PhD (LS). **Orgs.:** ALA. ASIS. FL LA. SELA. **Activities:** 1; 17; 56 **Addr.:** 2731 Blairstone Rd. Apt. 170, Tallahassee, FL 32301.

Gold, Leonard Singer (Jl. 3, 1934, Brooklyn, NY) Asst. Dir. for Jewish, Oriental and Slavonic Std., NY Pub. Lib., 1980–, Chief, Jewish Div., 1971–, Libn., 1966–71; Tchr., Hugim HS, Haifa, Israel, 1961–63; HS Tchr., Kiryat Hayim, Israel, 1960–61. **Educ.:** Brooklyn Coll., 1951–54; McGill Univ., 1954–56, BA; Columbia Univ., 1964–66, MS (Lib. Srv.); NY Univ., 1963–75, MA (Eng.), PhD (Hebrew). **Orgs.:** AJL: VP (1972–74); Pres. (1974–76). Cncl. of Arch. and Resrch. Libs. in Jewish Std.: Pres. (1978–). Natl. Jewish Welfare Bd.: Jewish Bk. Cncl., Exec. Bd. (VP, 1980–); Lib. Com. (Ch., 1974–). Assn. of Jewish Std. **Pubns.:** "Judaica and Hebraica in Book Catalogs," *Jewish Bk. Anl.* (1977–78); "Abraham Solomon Freidus," *Std. in Bibl. and Booklore* (Win. 1973–74); "Judaica," *East Central and Southeastern Europe: A Handbook of Library and Archival Resources* (1976); assoc. ed., *Jewish Bk. Anl.* (1980–). **Activities:** 1, 9; 15, 17, 20; 54, 55 **Addr.:** Jewish Division - Rm. 84, The New York Public Library, 5th Ave. & 42nd St., New York, NY 10018.

Gold, Renee L. (Jl. 18, 1948, New York, NY) Asst. Ed., *Wilson Lib. Bltn.,* 1979–; Libn., NY City Bd. of Educ., 1978–79; Resrch. Libn., J. Walter Thompson, 1970–72. **Educ.:** City Coll. of NY, 1964–68, BA (Hist.); Queens Coll., 1975–78, MLS. **Orgs.:** ALA. SLA. **Honors:** Beta Phi Mu. **Activities:** 6, 12, 14; 37, 39, 42 **Addr.:** Wilson Library Bulletin, H. W. Wilson Company, 950 University Ave., Bronx, NY 11452.

Goldberg, Kenneth Paul (Ja. 13, 1949, Rochester, NY) Ed. Asst., Metals Info. Dept., Amer. Socty. for Metals, 1981–; Pub. Srvs. Libn., Cleveland Inst. of Art, 1978–81, Ref. Libn., 1973–78; Lectr. on Cleveland Archit. and Hist., 1973–. **Educ.:** Syracuse Univ., 1966–70, BA, cum laude (Art Hist.); SUNY, Binghamton, 1970–72, MA (Art Hist.); Syracuse Univ., 1972–73, MLS. **Orgs.:** ARLIS/NA: Fndr.; OH Chap. (Secy./Treas., 1978–). Cleveland Area Metro. Libs. Syst.: Resrcs. Com. (1979–81); ILL Com. (1979–81). West. Rsv. Archit. Histns.: Secy. (1978–); Secy.-Treas. (1979–81). SLA. Cleveland Encyc. Archit. Com. Park Synagogue Couples Club. Cleveland Jewish Singing Socty. **Honors:** State Lib. of OH, Resrc. Guide to Hum. in OH, 1979; Phi Mu Alpha Sinfonia, 1968. **Pubns.:** Reviews. **Activities:** 1, 12; 22, 39, 45; 55, 61, 70 **Addr.:** Metals Information Dept., American Society for Metals, Metals Park, OH 44073.

Goldberg, Robert L. (My. 2, 1924, Chicago, IL) Dir. of Lib. Srvs., William Paterson Coll., 1975–; Adj. Prof., Rutgers Univ., 1970–; Dean of Admin., SUNY, Coll. at Old Westbury, 1967–71; Mgt. Consult. to Libs., Nelson Assoc., VP 1960–67; Managing Ed. of Curr. Mtrls., Sci. Resrch. Assoc., 1955–60; Dir. of Adult Educ., Jewish Comnty. Ctr. of Baltimore, 1954–55; Tchr., George Fox Jr. HS, 1950–54. **Educ.:** St. John's Coll., 1946–50, BA (Lib. Arts); Georgetown Univ., 1950–53, MA (Hist.); Rutgers Univ., 1972–75, PhD (LS). **Orgs.:** ALA. NJ Cncl. of State & Univ. Libns., VP/Pres. elect (1979). NJ Cncl. of Univ. and Coll. libns.: Pres. (1980); Exec. N.J. Com. on Inter-lib. Coop. NJ Bd. of Higher Educ. Chancellor's Task Force on libs. (1978–1980). **Pubns.:** *A Systems Approach to Library Program Development* (1976). **Activities:** 1; 18, 25, 27; 56, 57, 60 **Addr.:** 5 Dupont Ave., White Plains, NY 10605.

Goldberg, Thresa Cutler (Ap. 21, 1928, Toledo OH) Head, Sanger Branch, Toledo Lucas Cnty Pub. Lib., 1974–, First Asst., Branch, 1970–74. **Educ.:** Univ. of Toledo, 1940–45 BA (Fr.); Univ. of MI, 1969–70 MLS. OH State Univ., Adv. Middle Mgt. Sem., 1976–77; Miami Univ. Mgt. Sem., 1978. **Orgs.:** ALA. OH LA: Div. VI, Persnl. Functions (Coord., 1977). **Pubns.:** "The changing role of Supportive Staff," *OH LA Bltn.* (Ap. 1977). "Fringe Benefits and Wage Profile of Ohio Libraries," *OH Libs. Nsltr.* (Ap. 1976). **Activities:** 9; 16, 17, 39; 55, 66 **Addr.:** Sanger Branch Library, 2753 W. Central Ave., Toledo, OH 43606.

Goldberger, Judith M. (Teresi) (D. 18, 1948, Chicago, IL) Freelnc. Ed., Writer, Reviewer, 1975–; Chld. Bk. Reviewer, *ALA Booklist,* 1973–75; Chld. Libn., Skokie Pub. Lib., 1973; Resrc. Coord., Playboy Fndn., 1971–72. **Educ.:** Roosevelt Univ., 1966–70, BA hons. (Eng.); Univ. of Chicago, 1971–73, MA (LS). **Orgs.:** Socty. of Chld. Bk. Writers. ALA: Newbery-Caldecott Com. (Liaison mem., 1978); Notable Bks. Com. (Liaison Com., 1978). Cir. Pines Ctr. **Pubns.:** *The Looking Glass Factor* (1979); "Judy Blume: Target of the Censor," *Int. Frdm. Nsltr.* (My. 1980); "Johnny's Reading *'Jaws',*" *Chicago Sun-Times* (Mr. 10, 1976); "Evaluating High/Low Books: A Reviewer's Perspective," *High/Low Handbk.* (1981). Reviews. **Activities:** 14-Self-empl.; 37, 42; 55, 63, 89 **Addr.:** 6733 N. Newgard, Chicago, IL 60626.

Golden, Fay Ann (Ja. 24, 1930, Lynn, MA) Dir., Liverpool Pub. Lib., 1975–, Chld. Libn., 1971–75; Adj. Prof., Syracuse Univ. Sch. of Info. Std., 1970–76; Chld. Consult., Onondaga Lib. Syst., 1970–71; Sch. Libn., Baldwinsville Ctrl. Schs., 1970. **Educ.:** Tufts Univ., 1947–51, AB (Drama); Cornell Univ., 1967, M.Ed.; Syracuse Univ., 1968–70, MSLS. **Orgs.:** ALA: Lib. Admin. Div., Women Admins. Std. Grp. (1978–79), Stats. Com. for Circ. Srvs. (1979–81), Stdg. Com. on Lib. Educ. (1982–83). NY LA: Pub. Libs. Sect., Legis. Std. Com. (1977–). Libns. Unlimited: Pres. (1975–76, 1978–79). NY State Gvr.'s Conf. on Libs.: Del. (1978). Amer. Cvl. Liberties Un.: Syracuse Chap. Reg. Conf. Hist. Agencies. **Honors:** Beta Phi Mu, 1970. **Activities:** 9, 11; 17, 21, 26; 95-Storytel. **Addr.:** Liverpool Public Library, Tulip and 2nd Sts., Liverpool, NY 13088.

Goldenberg, Steven L. (Ja. 19, 1947, New York, NY) Coord., Vid. Srvs., Seattle Pub. Lib., 1979–; Coord., Vid. Srvs., Port Washington Pub. Lib., 1975–79; Media Consult., Bur. of Lib. Ext., 1974–75; Libn., Enosburg Falls HS, 1972–74. **Educ.:** SUNY, Buffalo, 1964–69, BS (Indus. Engin.), 1969–71, MLS. **Orgs.:** ALA: Vid. and Cable Comms. Sect. **Activities:** 9, 10; 32; 85, 93 **Addr.:** Seattle Public Library, 1000 4th Ave., Seattle, WA 98104.

Goldhor, Herbert (F. 8, 1917, Newark, NJ) Dir., Lib. Resrch. Ctr., Grad. Sch. of LS, Univ. of IL, 1975–; Dir., Grad. Sch. of LS, 1962–78; Dir., Pub. Lib., Evansville (IN) & Vanderburgh Cnty., 1952–61; Asst. Prof./Assoc. Prof., Lib. Sch., Univ. of IL, 1946–51. **Educ.:** Newark Coll., Rutgers Univ., 1932–35, BA (Econ.); Columbia Univ., 1937–38, BSLS; Univ. of Chicago, 1939–42, PhD (LS). **Orgs.:** ALA. IL LA. IN LA. Amer. Civil Liberties Un. **Honors:** Phi Beta Kappa, Beta Phi Mu. **Pubns.:** Jt. auth., *Practical Administration of Public Libraries* (1962); *An Introduction to Scientific Research in Librarianship* (1972). **Activities:** 9, 11; 16, 41, 49 **Addr.:** 410 David Kinley Hall, University of Illinois, 1407 W. Gregory Dr., Urbana, IL 61801.

Goldman, Brenda Chasen (NY, NY) Assoc. Libn., Msc., Tufts Univ., 1980–; Asst. Libn., Msc., Tufts Univ., 1973–80; Catlgr., Mount Holyoke Coll., 1968–71. **Educ.:** Brandeis Univ., AB Cum Laude (Msc.); Simmons Coll., 1967–68, SM (LS). Univ. of CA, Berkeley, (Msc. Hist.) New Eng. LA, 1979, Cert. (Persnl. Mgt.). **Orgs.:** Msc. LA: Msc. Lib. Admin. Com. (1976–78; Ch., 1978–); Finance Com. (1981–); Plng. and Prog. Com., Natl. Mtg. (1978) /New Eng. Chap., Ch. (1980–81). ALA: LAMA/Stats. Sect., Com. on Stats. for Nonprint Media, 1979–. New Eng. LA: Techr. Srvs. Libns., Prog. Com. (1975). AAUP. Amer. Mscological Soc. **Activities:** 1; 15, 17, 20; 55 **Addr.:** Tufts University Library, Medford, MA 02155.

Goldman, Myla K. (S. 9, 1947, Washington, DC) Consult., Self-empl., 1979–; Consult., Pan Amer. Hlth. Org., 1978–79; Info. Spec., Herner and Co., 1977–78; Consult., Consejo Nacional de Ciencia y Tecnologia, 1974–76; Dir., Info. Ctr., Ctr. de Info. Metalurgica, Mexico; Libn., Brown and Bain, Law Firm, Phoenix, AZ; Consult., U.S. Dept. of Cmrce., DC; Libn., Amer. Grad. Sch. of Intl. Mgt. **Educ.:** Univ. of AZ, 1965–69, BA (Lang.); Univ. of TX, Austin, 1969–70, MLS; Amer. Grad. Sch., 1972–73, MIM (Intl. Mgt.). **Orgs.:** SLA: Sci. Tech. Com. (1977); Pres. **Pubns.:** *Latin America: Economic History and Conditions; An Annotated Bibliography* (1973); jt. auth., "Capacitacion tecnica: una solucion parcial al problema de personal," *Jornadas Mex. de Biblioteconomia* (1976); "Technical Information Services in Mexico," *Spec. Libs.* (S. 1978); various std. in Span. (1975–76). **Activities:** 1, 12; 15, 24, 41; 54, 59, 91 **Addr.:** 6016 N. 10 Ave., Phoenix, AZ 85013.

Goldschmidt, Eva Maria (Je. 2, 1921, Munich, Germany) Assoc. Ed., Frgn. Lang. Indx., Pub. Affairs Info. Srv., 1976–, Asst. Ed., 1973–76; Ref. Libn., NY Pub. Lib., 1969–73; Admin. Secy., Walter E. Meyer Resrch. Inst. of Law, 1967–69; various positions, C. Haedke and Co., Inc., 1956–67; Resrch. Writer, Dept. of Pub. Info., Untd. Nations, 1946–49; Resrch. Anal., Ofc. of Strategic Srvs., 1944–45. **Educ.:** Manchester Coll., 1939–43, BA (Hist.); Univ. of Chicago, 1943–44, MA (Hist.); Columbia Univ., 1967–69, MLS. **Orgs.:** ALA. Amer. Socty. of Indxrs. Amer. Arbit. Assn.: Arbit. (1966–). Appalachian Mt. Club. Adironadack Mt. Club. NY, NJ Trail Conf. **Honors:** Beta Phi Mu. **Pubns.:** Ed., *Champion of a Cause: Essays and Addresses on Librarianship* (1971); "Archibald MacLeish: Librarian of Congress," *Coll. & Resrch. Libs.* (1969); "Pioneer Professional: Friedrich Adolf Ebert (1791–1834), Librarian to the King of Saxony," *Lib. Qtly.* (1970). **Activities:** 12; 30, 39; 54, 59, 92 **Addr.:** 41 W. 83rd St., New York, NY 10024.

Goldsmith, Maxine K. (Ap. 25, 1947, Tarrytown, NY) Libn., NJ Dept. of Higher Educ., 1978–; Libn., NJ Div. of Criminal Justice, 1976–77; Pers. Libn., NJ State Lib., 1971–76; Ref. Libn., McGraw-Hill, Inc., 1970–71. **Educ.:** Russell Sage Coll., 1965–69, BS (Soc. Sci.); Rutgers Univ., 1969–70, MLS (Lib. Srv.). **Orgs.:** SLA: Princeton-Trenton Chap., Bus. Mgr. (1978–81); Dir. (1977–78); Treas. (1975–77). Ewing Twp. (NJ): Dem. Committeewoman (1977–). B'nai B'rith Women: Judea Chap., VP (1979–81); Secy. (1977–79). **Pubns.:** *Going to College in NJ* bibl. (1978, 1980); *Program Evaluation* (1979); indxr., *Popular Periodicals Index* (1975–). **Activities:** 13; 15, 20, 31 **Addr.:** 10 Tall Tree Ct., Trenton, NJ 08618.

Goldstein, Charles M. (Chicago, IL) Chief, Comp. Tech. Branch, Lister Hill Natl. Ctr. for Biomed. Comms., Natl. Lib. of Med., 1974–; Tech. Dir., Data Base Syst., Informatics, 1973–74; Chief, Info. Syst. Branch, NASA Lewis Resrch. Ctr., 1969–73, Sci., Physicist, 1955–69. **Educ.:** Purdue Univ., 1947–53, BS (Aero. Engin.), 1953–54, MS (Mech. Engin.); Univ. of Gottingen, W. Germany, 1954–55 (Math., Phys.); Case West. Rsv. Univ., 1957–69 (Grad. Phys.). **Orgs.:** ASIS: Stans. Com. (1979–). ALA. Natl. Fed. of Abs. and Indexing Srvs.: New Tech. Subcom. AAAS. **Honors:** Fulbright Grant to W. Germany, 1954; Natl. Inst. of Hlth., Dir.'s Awd., 1977. **Pubns.:** "The Potential Impact of Optical Disk Technology on Libraries and Online Services," *Telecommunications in Libraries* (1981); "Library Automation: Design Aspects for Collection Management and Control," *Col. Mgt.* (1981); "User Cordial Interface," *Online Review* (1978). **Activities:** 4, 14-R&D; 41; 56, 75 **Addr.:** LHNCBC/CTB, Bldg. 38A Rm. 8N803, 8600 Rockville Pike, Bethesda, MD 20902.

Goldstein, Cynthia Higginbotham (Ja. 9, 1945, St. Louis, MO) Chief, Tech. Srvs., Rudolph Matas Med. Lib., Tulane Univ. Sch. of Med., 1978–, Acq. Libn., 1973–78, Admin. Asst., Lab. of Env. Med., 1971–73. **Educ.:** Drury Coll., 1962–66, BA (Fr.); LA State Univ., 1974–76, MLS; Med. LA, 1976–81, Grade I Cert. **Orgs.:** Med. LA: Schol. Com. (1981–84). S. Ctrl. Reg. Med. Lib. Prog. (TALON): Com. on the Coop. Acq. of Mono. (1979–81); Lcl. Arrange. for 1980 Jt. Reg. Mtg., Regis. Com., Ch. **Honors:** Beta Phi Mu, 1976; Mortar Bd., 1966; Alpha Lambda Delta, 1963. **Pubns.:** "A Study of Weeding Policies in Eleven TALON Resource Libraries," *Bltn. Med. LA* (Jl. 1981); "Preservation Goals and Tips Aired at Oklahoma Seminar," news note

PROFESSIONAL ACTIVITIES: Institutions: 1. Acad. lib.; 2. Arch.; 3. Assn.; 4. Fed./Gvt. lib.; 5. Inst. lib.; 6. Mfr./Suppl.; 7. Milit. lib.; 8. Musm.; 9. Pub. lib.; 10. Sch. lib.; 11. Sch. of lib. sci.; 12. Spec. lib.; 13. State lib.; 14. (other). **Functions/Activities:** 15. Acq./Col. dev.; 16. Adult srvs.; 17. Admin.; 18. Apprais.; 19. Archit./Bldgs.; 20. Cat./Class.; 21. Chld. srvs.; 22. Circ.; 23. Cons./Pres.; 24. Consult.; 25. Cont. ed.; 26. Educ. lib. sci.; 27. Ext. srvs.; 28. Fund/Grants; 29. Gvt. pubs.; 30. Indx./Abs.; 31. Instr. lib. use; 32. Media srvs.; 33. Micro.; 34. Netwks./Coop.; 35. Persnl.; 36. PR; 37. Publshg.; 38. Recs. mgt.; 39. Ref. srvs.; 40. Repro.; 41. Resrch.; 42. Review.; 43. Secur.; 44. Serials; 45. Spec. col.; 46. Tech. srvs.; 47. Trustees/Bds.; 48. YA srvs.; 49. (other).

Lib. Jnl. (O. 1, 1980). **Activities:** 1, 12; 15, 45, 46; 80 **Addr.:** Rudolph Matas Medical Library, Tulane University School of Medicine, 1430 Tulane Ave., New Orleans, LA 70112.

Goldstein, Doris M. (Mr. 11, 1942, Somerville, NJ) Dir., Lib. & Info. Srvs. Ctr. for Bioethics, Kennedy Inst. of Ethics, Georgetown Univ., 1973–; Instr., Bowie State Coll., 1969–72; Catlgr., Lib. of Congs., 1968–69; Instr., Haile Selassie I Univ. & Tefari Makonnen Sch. (Peace Corps), Ethiopia, 1966–68. **Educ.:** Univ. of NE, 1960–64, BA (Grmn.), 1964–66, MA (Grmn.); Univ. of MD, 1972–73, MLS, Goethe Univ., Frankfurt, W. Germany, 1964, Cert. (Grmn.). **Orgs.:** SLA: Bio. Sci. Grp. (Treas. 1974–76); Adv. Cncl., Wash. DC Chap. (1976–77). Med. LA. ASIS. **Honors:** Beta Phi Mu, 1973; Phi Beta Kappa, 1964; Delta Phi Alpha, 1964; Alpha Lambda Delta, 1961. **Pubns.:** Jt. Auth., "Bioethics: The Moral Frontiers of Science." *Library Journal Special Report #6: Collection Development,* (1978); "Additional Resources in Bioethics." *Encyclopedia of Bioethics* (1978); Bioethics: A Guide to Information Source, (1981). **Activities:** 1, 12; 15, 17, 30; 55, 77, 80 **Addr.:** 5000 Andrea Avenue, Annandale, VA 22003.

Goldstein, Harold (O. 3, 1917, Norfolk, VA) Dean, Sch. of LS, FL State Univ., 1967–; Prof. (LS), Univ. of IL, 1959–67; Dir., Davenport (IA) Pub. Lib., 1954–59; Dir. of Libs., U.S. Info. Srv., Colombo, (Sri Lanka) 1951–53; Asst. Prof., Univ. of MN, Duluth, 1949–51. **Educ.:** Univ. of MD, 1939–42, BS (Educ.) Columbia Univ., 1946–47, BS (LS), 1947–48, MA (Educ.), 1948–49, EdD (Educ.). **Orgs.:** ALA: Resrch. Com., (1978–80); Cncl. (1979–82); Ed. Com. (1973–76); Legis. Com. (1972–76). FL LA. AECT. **Pubns.:** Ed., *Milestones to the Present* (1978); jt. auth., *State Library Policy* (1971); "Radio-TV and the Library," *Encyclopedia of Library and Information Science* (1978). **Activities:** 9, 11; 16, 26, 41; 50, 63, 92 **Addr.:** Library, Florida State University, Tallahassee, FL 32306.

Goldstein, Marianne (Ja. 8, 1927, Hirshberg, Germany) Ref. Libn., SUNY, Buffalo, 1966–. **Educ.:** Boston Univ., 1945–49, BA (Latin Amer. Stds.); SUNY, Geneseo, 1964–66, MLS. **Orgs.:** ALA: Prog. Ch., West. European Spec. Sect. (1977). SUNY LA; Delegate, 1973–75. AJL. Assn. of Jewish Std. **Pubns.:** *A Survey of Library Resources in Judaic Studies in the FAUL and SUNY Cener Libraries, ERIC* (1976); Jt. auth., "Using A Sample Technique to Describe Characteristics of a Collection," *Coll. and Resrch. Libs.* (My. 1977); *Library Research in Spanish, French and German Literature* (1979); slides with cassettes. **Activities:** 1; 15, 31, 39; 54, 55, 57 **Addr.:** Lockwood Memorial Library, Reference Department, State University of New York at Buffalo, Amherst, NY 14260.

Goldstein, Melvin Shepard (N. 28, 1918, New York, NY) Dir., Intl. Oper., Israel Bond Org., 1962–; Admin. Vice Ch., Untd. Jewish Appeal, 1951–61; Asst. Secy., European Exec. Cncl., Amer. Jewish Jt. Distribution Com., Paris, 1941–51. **Educ.:** New York Univ., 1942, BA (Econ.); Pratt Inst., 1970, MLS. **Orgs.:** NY LA. ALA. Beta Phi Mu: Dir. New York Univ. Club. **Pubns.:** *Collective Bargaining in the Field of Librarianship* (1969). **Activities:** 9, 12; 17; 66 **Addr.:** 710 Park Ave. (Apt 8A), New York, NY 10021.

Goldstein, Rachael Keller (Ja. 15, 1938, New York, NY) Head, Hlth. Sci. Lib., Columbia Univ., 1979–; Lib. Dir., Mt. Sinai Sch. of Med., 1973–79, Assoc. Dir., Lib., 1971–73, Head, Cat., 1969–72, Cat. Lib., 1964–69. **Educ.:** Barnard Coll., 1955–59, AB (Hist.); Columbia Univ., 1959–60, MS (Lib. Srv.). **Orgs.:** Med. LA: Std. Grp. on Med. LA's Role in the Educ. Prcs. for Hlth. Sci. Libns. (1980–81); Com. on Status and Econ. Interests of Hlth. Sci. Lib. Persnl. (Ch., 1980–81); NY Reg. Grp. (Grp. Ch., 1978–79), Exec. Bd. (1971–73, 1977–78, 1979–80), Prog. Com. (Ch., 1970–71); various coms., ofcs. Assn. of Acad. Hlth. Sci. Lib. Dirs.: Com. on Med. Educ. (1979–81); Prog. Com. (1978–79). NY Tech. Srvs. Libns. Cncl. of Chief Libns., CUNY: Various coms. Biomed. Comm. Netwk.: Bd. of Dirs. (1976–78); Nom. Com. (1979). NY Metro. Ref. and Resrch. Lib. Agency: Bd. of Trustees (1980–); Resrc. Dev. Com. (1975–80). Med. Lib. Ctr. of NY: Bd. of Dirs. (1975–76); Libns. Adv. Bd. (1973–76). Various other orgs. **Pubns.:** "The Levy Library: A Center for Learning Resources," *Mt. Sinai Alum. Spectrum* (1975); jt. auth., "The Status of Women in the Administration of Health Science Libraries," *Bltn. Med. LA* (O. 1975); "Women and Health Sciences Librarianship: An Overview," *Bltn. Med. LA* (Jl. 1977); "The Art of Non-Reading: Information Media and Quality Evaluation," *Hlth. Comm. Informatics* (1979); jt. auth., "Organizing Library Audiovisual Services to Support Continuing Education," *Mt. Sinai Jnl. of Med.* (Jl.–Ag. 1979); various articles. **Addr.:** Health Sciences Library, Columbia University, 701 W. 168 St., New York, NY 10032.

Gollata, James A. (Ag. 18, 1945, Manitowoc, WI) Dir., Lib. Srvs., Mount Senario Coll., 1974–. **Educ.:** Univ. of WI, Oshkosh, 1964–69, BS (Eng., Phil.), 1971–73, MA (LS). **Orgs.:** Indianhead Fed. Lib. Syst. Multitype Lib. Coop. Syst.: Strg. Com. (1980–). WI LA. WI Assn. of Acad. Libns. Indianhead LA: Pres./Elect (1980); Pres. (1981). Ladysmith Cmnty. Players: Pres., (1975–). Flambeau Valley Arts Assn., Bd. of Dir., (1977–). **Pubns.:** Reviews. **Activities:** 1; 15, 17, 39; 55, 57, 63 **Addr.:** Mount Senario College, College Ave. W., Ladysmith, WI 54848.

Goltz, Eileen A. (S. 13, 1937, Peterborough ON Can.) Asst. Libn. and Head, Pub. Docum. Dept., Laurentian Univ. Lib., 1975–; Head Libn., Espanola Pub. Lib., 1974–75. **Educ.:** Laurentian Univ., 1969–73 BA (Hons.) (Hist. Soclgy.) Univ. of West. ON, 1973–74, MLS. **Orgs.:** ON LA. Can. LA. ON Archlg. Assn. ON Hist. Socty. **Pubns.:** "Historical Resources in the Turks and Caicos and in the Caymen Islands," *Caribbean-Ctrl. Amer. Resrch.* Guide (1980); "Espanola: The History of a Pulp and Paper Town," *Laurentian Univ. Rev.* (Jn. 1974). **Activities:** 1; 15, 17, 29; 62, 92 **Addr.:** Box 700, Massey, ON Canada.

Goman, LaVerne Pruden (F. 23, 1918, Glenrock, WY) Adj. Assoc. Prof., Univ. of Puget Sound, 1963–; Sch. Libn., Annie Wright Sch., 1964–; Asst. Libn., Univ. of Puget Sound Lib., 1952–63; Resrv. Libn., OR State Univ., 1941–44. **Educ.:** Doane Coll., 1934–38, AB (Sp.); Univ. of WA, 1940–41, ABLS; Univ. of NE, 1938–39, (Eng., Sp.). **Orgs.:** ALA. WA Lib. Media Assn.: Jt. Com. on Cert. SW WA Lib. Media Cnsrtm.: Secy. (1977). Christ Episcopal Church: Clerk of Vestry, Nsltr. Ed. (1979–80). Puyallup Parent Teacher Assn.: Pres. (1955–58). **Activities:** 10, 14-Sch. of Educ.; 26 **Addr.:** University of Puget Sound, 1500 North Warner, Tacoma, WA 98416.

Gonce, Nancy C. (My. 21, 1939, Birmingham, AL) Coord., Spr. Prog., Coop. Campus Mnstry., Univ. of N. AL, 1980–; Libn., Riverbend Ctr. for Mental Hlth., 1974–80; Fld. Rep., AL Pub. Lib. Srv., 1966–68, Area Libn., 1961–66; Reader Adv., Friedman Lib., 1960–61. **Educ.:** Univ. of AL, 1957–61, BS (LS); George Peabody Coll., 1961, MS (LS). **Orgs.:** AL LA: Trustees Div., Cp. Frnds. (1969); Plng. Com. (1979); Legis. Com. (1981). SE LA. ALA. WHCOLIS: Del. Various other orgs. Rural Hlth. Assn.: Adv. Bd. AL Women's Pol. Caucus. Lauderdale Cnty. Hlth. Cncl. AAUW: Branch Pres.; Branch Legis. Ch.; Branch VP; State VP; Women's Cp. Legis. Ch. Various other orgs. **Honors:** Colbert-Lauderdale Chap., Natl. Assn. of Soc. Workers, Citizen of Yr., 1978; TN Valley Unit, Natl. Assn. of Soc. Workers, Citizen of Yr., 1978. **Activities:** 12; 17; 80, 92 **Addr.:** 213 Colonial Dr., Florence, AL 35630.

Gonnami, Tsuneharu (F. 26, 1940, Tokyo, Japan) Japanese Libn., Ref. Srvs., Asian Stds. Lib., Univ. of BC, 1969–; Libn., Resrch. and Tech. Lib., Meidensha Co., Tokyo, 1962–69. **Educ.:** Japan Lib. Sch., Keio Univ., Tokyo, 1958–62, BLS. **Orgs.:** Can. LA. Mita Socty. of Lib. and Info. Sci., Tokyo. Assn. for Asian Stds.: Com. on East Asian Libs., Sub-com. on Japanese Mtrls. (1978–). **Activities:** 1, 12; 15, 17, 39; 55, 57, 75 **Addr.:** Asian Studies Library, The University of British Columbia, 2075 Westbrook Mall, Vancouver, BC V6T 1W5 Canada.

Gontrum, Barbara Sutton (My. 18, 1950, Greencastle, IN) Dir., Univ. of MD, Law Lib., 1979–; Assoc. Libn., Duke Univ. Law Sch. Lib., 1977–79, Ref. Libn., 1975–77; Libn., Taft, Stettinius and Hollister, 1973–74. **Educ.:** Purdue Univ., 1968–72, BA (Pol. Sci.); Univ. of IL, 1972–73, MLS; Duke Univ., 1975–78, JD. **Orgs.:** AALL. NC Bar Assn. **Honors:** Phi Beta Kappa; Beta Phi Mu. **Pubns.:** "Researching the Law of Products Liability," *Jnl. of Prods. Liability* (1979). **Activities:** 1; 17; 77 **Addr.:** University of Maryland Law School Library, 20 N. Paca St., Baltimore, MD 21201.

González, Armando Eugenio (Ap. 24, 1921, Havana, Cuba) Asst. Chief, Hisp. Law Div., Lib. of Congs., 1977–, Sr. Legal Spec., 1968–77, Legal Spec., 1967–68; Circ. Libn., Law Lib., Columbia Univ., 1965–67; Srv. Engin., R.E. Foote, Inc., 1960–64; Vice-Secy., Legal Couns., Godoy-Sayán, S.A. Havana, Cuba, 1956–60; various positions as attorney, Havana, Cuba, 1954–60. **Educ.:** Inst. of Havana, 1936–39, BA; Univ. of Havana, 1939–43, LLD; Columbia Univ., 1964–65, MLS. **Orgs.:** AALL. Law Libns. Socty. of DC. SLA. SALALM. Amer. Bar Assn.: Com. on Intl. Assocs. **Pubns.:** Jt. ed., *Basic Latin American Legal Material, 1970–75* (1977); "Law Materials," *Cuban Acquisitions and Bibliography* (1970); "Group Roles in American Legal History. Part IV: People of Spanish Descent," *69 Law Lib. Jnl.* (1976); "The Role of Latin America Legal Material in the Social Science Research Library," *64 Law Lib. Jnl.* (1971); various bk. reviews, *Intl. Jnl. Law Libs.* **Addr.:** 10201 Grosvenor Pl., 709, Rockville, MD 20852.

Gonzalez, Nelly S. (Jl. 1, 1930, Cochabamba, Bolivia) Latin Amer. Biblgphr., Asst. Prof. of Lib. Admin., Univ. of IL, 1978–; Latin Amer. Biblgphr., Instr. in Lib. Admin., Serials Dept., 1976–78; Libn., Clinica de la Mujer, Bolivia, 1974–75. **Educ.:** Univ. Mayor de San Andres, Bolivia, 1947–49, BS (Pol. Sc. & Phil.); 1949–53, JD (Law); Univ. of IL, 1971–73, MSLS; Univ. of MI, 1960, Dipl. **Orgs.:** SALALM: Ch., Jt. Com. on Ofcl. Pubns.; Subcom. on Oper. Bolivian Amer. Fund: PR Com. Bolivian Fed. of Prof. and Univ. Women. Latin Amer. Std. Assn. Midwest Assn. for Latin Amer. Std. **Honors:** Beta Phi Mu, 1975. **Activities:** 1; 15, 17, 44; 54, 57, 66 **Addr.:** University of Illinois Library, Room 324; Latin American Collection Development, Urbana, IL 61801.

Gonzalez, Silvia A. (La Habana Cuba) Chief, Pub. Srvs., Law Lib., Univ. of CA, Davis, 1974–; Docum. Libn., 1969–; Acq. Libn., 1969–74; Catlgr., 1967–69. **Educ.:** Colegio Corazon de Maria, Cuba, 1947–52, BA (Letters); Univ. de La Habana, Cuba, 1952–59, Dr. at Law (Law); KS State Teachers Coll., 1965–1967, MSLS. **Orgs.:** ALA: ACRL/ Law & Pol. Sci. Sect. (Mem. at large, 1974–75); Ch., Nom. Com. (1979–80). AALL: Asst. Coord. of Stats. (1977–); Stats. Com. (1970–77); Frgn. & Intl. Law Com. (1975–76; 1969–70); Memb. Com. (1969–70). Cuban Bar Assn. in Exile. **Pubns.:** *Interim Index to Library of Congress Class KF, Law of the United States* (1968); Cmpl., "List of basic law materials for Columbia & Costa Rica" in *Union List of Basic Latin American Legal Materials* (1970); "Statistical Survey of Government Law Libraries," *Law Lib. Jnl.* (1973); "Statistical Survey of Law Libraries Serving a Local Bar," *Law Lib. Jnl.* (1976, 1977, 1978); other articles. **Activities:** 1, 12; 15, 22, 29; 62, 77, 78 **Addr.:** 4414 Vista Way, Davis, CA 95616.

Gooch, William DeWitt (My. 20, 1935, Fort Worth, TX) Asst. State Libn., TX State Lib., 1971–; Dir., Ector Cnty. Lib., 1966–71; Dir., Tom Green Cnty. Lib., 1963–65; Ext. Dir., Amarillo Pub. Lib., 1958–62. **Educ.:** N. TX State Univ., 1954–58, BA (Lib. Srv.); Univ. of OK, 1962–63, MLS. **Orgs.:** TX LA: Pub. Lib. Div., Ch.; Natl. Lib. Week State Ch. SW LA: SLICE Prog., Ch. ALA. **Activities:** 9, 13; 17, 19, 24 **Addr.:** Texas State Library, P.O. Box 12927, Capitol Station, Austin, TX 78711.

Good, Eleanor M. (Lin) (Jy. 30, Manchester, Eng.) Assoc. Libn., Queen's Univ. Lib., 1978–, Asst. Chief Libn., 1972–78; Head, Acq. Div., 1959–72; Head, Dept. of Hist., Coll. Libn., Redland Coll. (Eng.), 1946–49. **Educ.:** Bedford Coll., Univ. of London, 1939–43, BA Hons (Hist.), Univ. of London, Cambridge Univ., 1946–46 (Hist.). Dipl. in Educ., 1st Class Hons., 1943–44 (LS). **Orgs.:** Can. LA. Ont. Cncl. on Univ. Affairs. Soc. Sci. and Hum. Resrch. Cncl. of Can.: Com. on Resrch. Resrcs. **Honors:** Can., Queen Elizabeth II Jubilee Medal, 1978. Can. Red Cross Socty., Long Srvs. Awd. **Activities:** 1; 15, 17, 35; 61, 92, 95-Status of Women. **Addr.:** 153 Brock St., Kingston, ON K7L 4Y8 Canada.

Goodding, Martha C. (My. 5, 1940, Kansas City, MO) Dir., Patients and Prof. Libs., St. Joseph State Hosp., 1976–, Dir., Patients Lib., 1970–76, Asst. Libn., Prof. Lib., 1968–70, Actv. Aide, 1958–68. **Educ.:** Univ. of MO, 1965–68, BA (Soclgy.), 1968–71, (Soc. Psy.); MO West. State Coll., 1969–71, Tchr. Cert. (Soc. Std.). **Orgs.:** MO LA: Outrch. RT (Ch., 1977). St. Joseph Area Lib. Coop.: Pres. (1977–79). NW MO Lib. Netwk.: Bd. (1979–81). Hlth. Sci. Lib. Grp. of Grt. Kansas City. **Activities:** 5; 17, 27; 80 **Addr.:** Patient Library, St. Joseph State Hospital, P.O. Box 263, St. Joseph, MO 64502.

Goodemote, Rita La Tour (Jersey City, NJ) Assoc. Dir., Lib. Info. Ctr., Schering-Plough Pharm. Resrch. Div., 1953–; Anal. Chem., Hoffmann-La Roche, 1943–49; Anal. Chem., Mallinckrodt, 1941–43. **Educ.:** Coll. of St. Elizabeth, Convent Station, NJ, 1937–41, AB (Bio. Chem.); Columbia Univ., 1952–53, MLS. **Orgs.:** SLA: Pharm. Sect., Secy. (1958–59), Ch. (1962–63); NJ Chap., Secy. (1959–61), Pres. (1966–67); various coms. Drug Info. Assn.: Anl. Conf. (Hosplty. Ch., 1975–76). ASIS. Med. LA. **Pubns.:** "Planning Online Search Service for a Pharmaceutical Company," *Sci. and Tech. Libs.* (Fall 1980); "Impact of OTC Efficacy Review on the Industry," *Drug Info. Jnl.* (Ap.–S. 1976). **Activities:** 12; 17; 60, 80, 87 **Addr.:** Library Information Center, Schering-Plough Pharmaceutical Research Div., 60 Orange St., Bloomfield, NJ 07003.

Gooden, Carole Yvonne Laferne (S. 4, 1942, Kingston, Jamaica, W. Indies) Libn., Team Coord., St. Joseph HS, 1978–; Sr. Tchr., Libn., St. Andrew Tech. HS (Kingston, Jamaica), 1965–78. **Educ.:** Univ. of NB, 1960–64, BSc (Bio.), Columbia Univ., 1969–70, MS (LS). Univ. of the W. Indies, 1964–65 (Educ.). **Orgs.:** Jamaica LA: Sch. Lib. Sect. (Secy., 1976–77). St. Croix LA: VP. (1979–80). **Pubns.:** Jt.-auth., *School Library Standards for Jamaica* (1971); Contrib., *Suggestions for Teacher-Librarians* (1977). **Activities:** 10; 31, 32, 48; 89, 91 **Addr.:** St. Joseph High School, P. O. Box 517, Frederiksted, St. Croix, U.S. Virgin Islands, 00840.

Goodfellow, Marjorie E. (Jn. 12, 1938, Sherbrooke, PQ) Lib. Consult., 1973–; Asst. Univ. Libn., Pub. Srvs., Sir George Williams Univ., 1968–73; Chief Libn., United Aircraft of Can. Ltd., 1963–68; Asst. Libn., Bell Telephone Co. of Can., 1961–63; Asst. Libn., Dept. of Citizenship and Immigration, Can., 1960–61. **Educ.:** Bishop's Univ. 1955–59 BA (Hist.); McGill Univ., 1959–60, BLS, 1963–67, MLS. **Orgs.:** Corp. of Prof. Libns. of PQ: Bd. of Dir. (1969–71); Admis. Com. (1968–72; Ch., 1969–71). Can. LA: Com. on Use of Prof. Staff (Ch., 1966–67). SLA: Montreal Chap. (Pres., 1966–67), 1969 SLA Conf. (Deputy Ch., 1962–69). Sherbrooke and Dist. Univ. Women's Club: Pres., (1978–80). The East. Twps. Heritage Fndn.: Educ. Com. (Ch., 1978–80). English-speaking Townshippers Assn. Inc.: VP (1979–80). **Honors:** Comsn. des Bib. du PQ, Mem. 1978–84. **Pubns.:** Wkly. Clmn. on Lcl. Hist., *The Record* (1979–); "Library Consulting, a view from Quebec," *QLA Bltn.* (Ap., My., Jn., 1975). **Activities:** 1, 12; 17, 24, 39; 55, 64, 69 **Addr.:** P.O. Box 1135, Sherbrooke, PQ J1H 5L5 Canada.

Goodhart, Lillian B. (Mr. 16, 1907, New York, NY) Volun. Church Libn., New Brunswick Presby. Church, 1973–; Retired, 1970–; Admin. Asst. to Libn., Rutgers Univ., Alexander Lib., 1968–70, Head, Pers. Dept., 1956–68, Head Catlgr., Douglass Coll., 1947–56; Catlgr., Yale Law Sch. Lib., 1946–47; Catlgr.

Special Subjects/Services: 50. Adult educ.; 51. Advert./Mktg.; 52. Aerosp.; 53. Agric.; 54. Area std.; 55. Arts/Hum.; 56. Autom.; 57. Bibl./Prtg.; 58. Bio. sci.; 59. Bus./Fin.; 60. Chem.; 61. Copyrt.; 62. Documtn.; 63. Educ.; 64. Engin.; 65. Env.; 66. Eth. grps.; 67. Film; 68. Food/Nutr.; 69. Geneal.; 70. Geo.; 71. Geol.; 72. Handcpd.; 73. Hist.; 74. Int. frdm.; 75. Info. sci.; 76. Insr.; 77. Law; 78. Legis.; 79. Math./Comp. sci.; 80. Med.; 81. Metals; 82. Nat. resrcs.; 83. Newsp.; 84. Nuc. sci.; 85. Oral hist.; 86. Petr./Energy; 87. Pharm.; 88. Phys./Astr./Math.; 89. Readg.; 90. Relig.; 91. Sci./Tech.; 92. Soc. sci.; 93. Telecom.; 94. Transp.; 95. (other).

Worcester Pub. Lib., 1944–46; various lib. positions, Enoch Pratt Free Lib., 1934–44; Sch. Libn., East. HS, 1929–31. **Educ.:** Goucher Coll., 1924–28, AB (Eng.); Columbia Univ., 1928–29, BS (LS), 1952, MA (Eng.). **Orgs.:** NJ LA: Various coms., sects. MD LA. ALA. CS LA. Common Cause. Leag. of Women Voters. **Activities:** 1, 9; 20, 29, 44; 57, 62, 90 **Addr.:** 3 Redcliffe Ave., Apt. 3-A, Highland Park, NJ 08904.

Goodhartz, Gerald (O. 23, 1938, New York, NY) Head Libn., Kaye, Scholer, Fierman, Hays and Handler, 1970–; Head Libn., Keatinge and Sterling, 1969–70; Head Libn., Rosenman Colin Freund Lewis and Cohen, 1965–69; Lib. Asst., Cravath, Swaine and Moore, 1961–65; Night Ref. Asst., Assn. of the Bar of the City of New York, 1956–61. **Educ.:** City Coll. of New York, 1957–61, (Cvl. Engin.); AALL, 1966, Cert. **Orgs.:** Law LA of Grt. NY. AALL. SLA. ALA. Various other orgs. **Activities:** 12; 15, 17, 39; 56, 77 **Addr.:** Kaye, Scholer, Fierman, Hayes & Handler, 425 Park Ave., New York, NY 10022.

Goodkind, Joan Carol (O. 27, 1938, Los Angeles, CA) Chief, Acq. Div., NY Pub. Lib., 1975–; Lib. Systs. Anal., Columbia Univ., 1969–71; Libn., Inst. for Lib. Resrch., Univ. of CA, Los Angeles, 1966–68. **Educ.:** Univ. of CA, Los Angeles, 1955–63, BA (Eng. Lit.), 1963–64, MLS. **Orgs.:** ALA: Col. Dev. Com. (1978–80); RTSD/Assn. of Amer. Publshrs. Jt. Com. (1977–80). **Activities:** 12; 15, 17; 56 **Addr.:** Acquisition Division, New York Public Library, 5th Ave. & 42nd St., New York, NY 10018.

Goodman, Delena Ella (Ag. 16, 1918, Mt. Olive, IL) Libn., Anderson Coll. Sch. of Theo., 1952–; Dir., Relig. Educ., Church of God, Oklahoma City, OK, 1948–50; Dir., Relig. Educ., Church of God, Decatur, IL, 1945–47. **Educ.:** Anderson Coll., 1941–45, BS; Oberlin Sch. of Theo., 1950–52, MA; Univ. of IL, 1953–54, MS (LS). **Orgs.:** ATLA: Rec. Secy. (1972–75); Anl. Conf. Com. (1979–81). Chicago Area Theo. LA. IN Coop. Lib. Srvs. Athrty. Park Pl. Church of God, Anderson, IN. **Activities:** 2; 90 **Addr.:** School of Theology Library, Anderson College, Anderson, IN 46011.

Goodman, Helen C. (N. 14, 1920, New York, NY) Lib. Coord., Gadsden Sch. Dist., Anthony, NM, 1974–; Resrch. & Spec. Proj. Libn., El Paso Pub. Lib., 1973–74; Coord. of Pub. Srvs., 1969–72, Acq. Libn., 1966–69; Catlgr., Univ. of CO Libs., 1963–66. **Educ.:** Queens Coll., 1943–47, BA (Econ.); Pratt Inst., 1947–48, MLS. **Orgs.:** ALA. Border Reg. LA: Pres. (1975). NM LA. Hadassah: Charter Pres. of Bus. & Prof. Grp. **Honors:** Job Corps, Awd. for training students as lib. volun., 1972. **Pubns.:** Jt. auth., *Audio visual cataloging manual* (1980); "Volunteers in El Paso," *Lib. Jnl.* (My. 1972); "Spanish book selection in a bilingual community," *TX Lib. Jnl.* (Sum., 1971). **Activities:** 9, 10; 17, 21, 49-Volun.; 50, 66, 89 **Addr.:** 408 Chermont Dr., El Paso, TX 79912.

Goodman, Henry James Abraham (Jy. 21, 1917, Toronto, ON Can.) Prof. (Educ.), Univ. of Calgary, 1964–; Soc. Stds. Dept. Head, Tchr., Vancouver (BC) Pub. Schs. 1951–62. **Educ.:** Univ. of BC, 1940–44, BA Hons. (Hist.), 1944–46, MA (Hist.); Harvard Univ., 1946–48, 49–50 MEd.; Univ. of CA, Los Angeles, 1962–64, 1967–68 Ed.D. Univ. of BC, Tchr. Trng. Dipl., 1944–45 (Sec. Educ.) **Orgs.:** ASIS: West. Can. Chap. (Treas., 1977–79). Can. Assn. Info. Sci. Assn. Ed. Media and Tech. in Canada. AECT. Other orgs. AAAS. Amer. Educ. Resrch. Assn. **Honors:** Various guest lectrshps. **Pubns.:** "Media Program Evaluation," *AB Lrng. Resrcs. Jnl.* (1977); "Technology and Teacher Education *ATA Mag.* (Ja.-F. 1974); "Prospective Metamorphoses of the Roles of Public Information Utilities in a Global Information Network," *Can. Jnl. of Info. Sci.* (My. 1976); "Planning and Plans for National Library and Information Services," *Ency. of Lib. and Info. Sci.* (1977); other articles, presented papers. **Activities:** 14-Univ. fac.; 24, 26, 32; 63, 75, 93 **Addr.:** Education Tower, University of Calgary, 2920 24th Ave. N.W., Calgary, AB T2L 0Z6 Canada.

Goodman, Marcia McCay (Jn. 30, 1927, Tulsa, OK) Assoc. Prof. (Bibl.), Hist. of Sci. Libn., Univ. of OK Libs., 1973–. **Educ.:** Univ. of OK, 1970, BA (Hist., Fr.), 1973, MALS. **Orgs.:** ALA: ACRL; RTSD. Southwest. LA. OK LA: Prntg. Arts RT, Secy. (1978–79). Midwest Junto of the Hist. of Sci. **Honors:** Beta Phi Mu. **Pubns.:** Jt. ed., *The Catalogue of the History of Science Collections of the University of Oklahoma Libraries* (1976); *Short-Title Catalog of the History of Science Collections, University of Oklahoma Libraries* (1961–); *Chronological Listing of the Short-Title Catalog of the History of Science* (1964–). **Activities:** 1; 45; 95-Hist. of Sci. **Addr.:** History of Science Collections, University of Oklahoma Libraries, Norman, OK 73019.

Goodman, Marie Cleckner (F. 23, 1924, Harrisburg, PA) Lib., Media Spec., DC Pub. Schs., 1967–; Volun. Libn., St. Pius X Lib., Blessed Sacrament Church, 1960–66; Freelnc. Ed., Indexing, Self-empl., 1959–67; Chief, Resrc. Sect., U.S. Ofc. of Geo., Interior Dept., 1956–59; Head, Map Acq. Sect., Lib. of Congs., 1947–56. **Educ.:** Coll. of Notre Dame of MD, 1943–45, BA (Fr., Span.); Case West. Rsv. Univ., 1946–47, BSLS; various crs. **Orgs.:** SLA: Geo. and Map Div., Chap. and Natl. Ofcs. (1953–59). ALA. DC Assn. of Sch. Libns.: Prog. Ch. (1972–75); VP (1975–77). Intl. Fed. of Cath. Alum. **Honors:** SLA, Geo. and Map Div., Hons. Outstan., 1955; Delta Epsilon Sigma; Delta Kappa Gamma. **Pubns.:** Jt. auth., *Marketing Maps of the U.S.* (1952); ed., *Map Collections in the U.S. and Canada* (1954); "Acquisitions Notes," *Lib. of Congs. Info. Bltn.* (1954–56); "Maps of Interest to Teachers," series *Jnl. of Geo.* (1954–56). **Activities:** 15, 21, 31; 57, 63, 70 **Addr.:** 3259 Van Hazen St. N.W., Washington, DC 20015.

Goodman, Rhonna Appel (S. 21, 1945, Boston, MA) Supvsg. YA Libn., Staten Island Branches, NY Pub. Lib., 1978–, AV Libn., 1977–78, Sr. YA Libn., 1970–73. **Educ.:** OH Wesleyan Univ., 1963–65; Boston Univ., 1965–67, BA (Pol. Sci.); Pratt Inst., 1967–68, MLS. **Orgs.:** NY LA: Chld. and YA Srvs. Sect., Pres. (1979–80), VP (1978–79). ALA: YASD, TV Com. (Ch., 1975–77), Lcl. Arrange. (1980–). **Pubns.:** Jt. auth., "The library as a Showcase for Teenage Talent," *Bookmark* (Win. 1978); jt. auth., "A Basic Library for Liberated Children," *MS* (Spr. 1970); "A 20th Century Visual Encyclopedia," *Film Lib. Qtly.* (Spr. 1970). **Activities:** 9, 13; 24, 48; 72, 89 **Addr.:** Staten Island Borough Office, 10 Hyatt St., Staten Island, NY 10301.

Goodpaster, Howard Thomas (My. 12, 1917, Winchester, KY) State Archvst. and Dir., Cmwlth. of KY Dept. of Lib. and Archs., Div. of Arch. and Recs. Mgt., 1971–, Deputy State Archvst. and Dir., 1967–70; Regis. and Admin. Srv. Ofcr., East. State Hosp., 1965–66. **Educ.:** Univ. of KY, 1936–40, BS, 1965 (Hist.); 1978, Cert. Recs. Mgr. **Orgs.:** Assn. of Recs. Mgrs. and Admins.: Louisville Chap. (Pres., 1978–79). SAA: Session on Court Recs. (Ch., 1976). Natl. Assn. of State Archs. Recs. Admins.: Prog. Com. (Ch., 1977–79). KY Micro. Assn.: Bd. (1976–80). KY Cncl. of Archvsts. **Honors:** Assn. of Recs. Mgrs. and Admins., Recs. Mgr. of the Yr. Awd., 1976–77; Assn. of Recs. Mgrs. and Admins., Chap. Mem. of the Yr. Awd., 1979. **Pubns.:** Jt. auth., *Records Management Handbook - Files and Filing* (1971); *Court Records of Kentucky* (1978); *Records Centers* (1976). **Activities:** 2, 13; 33, 38, 41; 62, 69, 75 **Addr.:** 1 Timberlawn Ln., Frankfort, KY 40601.

Goodrich, Jeanne D. (O. 8, 1949, Walla Walla, WA) Dir., Lib. Dev. Div., NV State Lib., 1979–; Dir., Idaho Falls Pub. Lib., 1973–79; Coord., Ext. Srvs., Fort Vancouver Reg. Lib., 1972–73. **Educ.:** ID State Univ., 1967–71, BA (Eng.); Univ. of OR, 1971–72, MLS. **Orgs.:** ALA: RASD, Persnl. Dev. Com. (1980–); Cncl. (1977–79). ID LA: Pres. (1978–79); Pub. Libs. Div. (Ch., 1976–77). Pac. NW LA. NV LA. AAUW: Cmnty. Rel. Area Rep. (1978–79). CA LA. **Honors:** ID LA, Libn. of the Yr., 1975–76. **Pubns.:** "Idaho State Report," *ALA Yrbk.* (1977, 1978, 1979); "Idaho Falls Public: A New Building for Some Old Friends," *ID Libn.* (Jl. 1978). **Activities:** 9, 13; 17, 24, 34 **Addr.:** 2618 Gordon, Minden, NV 89423.

Goodrich, Marilyn W. (Ap. 3, 1935, Little Falls, NY) Sch. Libn., Rolling Ridge Elem., 1973–; Sch. Libn., Limona Elem., 1971–72; Sch. Libn., Upper Dublin Jr. High, 1969–71; Sch. Libn., Newton Sr. High, 1964–65; Sch. Libn., Fonda-Fultonville Sr. High, 1957–61. **Educ.:** SUNY, Geneseo, 1953–57, BS (Educ., Lib. Educ.); Univ. of MO, Kansas City, 1973–74, MA (Elem. Educ.). **Orgs.:** Gvr.s' Conf. on Lib. and Info. Srvs.: Del. (1979). KS Assn. of Sch. Libns.: Pres. (1979–80); VP (1978–79). ALA: AASL, Bd. of Dirs; EBC/AASL SLMPY Awd. Com. (Ch., 1982). Natl. Educ. Assn.: KS and Olathe Chap., Bicent. Com. (1975–76). Delta Kappa Gamma: Beta Omega Chap., 1st VP. **Honors:** Olathe Tchr. of the Yr., 1979. **Pubns.:** "President's Corner," *KS Assn. of Sch. Libns. Nsltr.* (Je. 1979–D. 1979). **Activities:** 10; 21, 31; 63 **Addr.:** 11902 W. 143rd Terr., RR. #8, Box 82, Olathe, KS 66062.

Goodrum, Charles A. (Jl. 21, 1923, Pittsburg, KS) Wrtg., Consult., Self-empl., 1978–; Dir., Plng. and Dev., Lib. of Congs., 1977–78, Asst. Dir., Congsnl. Resrch. Srv., 1970–77, Coord., Resrch., 1963–70, various positions, 1949–63. **Educ.:** Princeton Univ., Wichita State Univ., 1941–46, BA (Amer. Hist.); Columbia Univ., 1948–49, BS. **Pubns.:** *Treasures of the Library of Congress* (1980); *The Library of Congress* (1974); contrib., *Lib. Jnl., Spec. Libs., Wilson Lib. Jnl., New Yorker, Atl., Christ. Sci. Monitor,* other pubns.; *Dewey Decimated* (1977); *Carnage of the Realm* (1979); Contrib., *Murderess Ink* (1979). **Activities:** 4; 17, 24; 56 **Addr.:** 2808 Pierpont St., Alexandria, VA 22302.

Goodwater, Leanna K. (S. 2, 1950, Spokane, WA) Biblgphr., Ref. Libn., Univ. of Santa Clara, Orradre Lib., 1975–. **Educ.:** San Jose State Univ., 1968–72, BA (Eng.), 1972–74, MA (Libnshp.). **Orgs.:** ALA: ACRL (1974–). CA Acad. and Resrch. Libns. Intl. Horn Socty. **Honors:** Phi Kappa Phi, 1972; Beta Phi Mu, 1974. **Pubns.:** *Women in Antiquity: An Annotated Bibliography* (1975); "Afterbeats," *The Horn Call* (O. 1980). **Activities:** 1; 15, 39 **Addr.:** Orradre Library, University of Santa Clara, Santa Clara, CA 95053.

Goodwin, Willard (Mr. 10, 1948, Baltimore, MD) Libn., Hum. Resrch. Ctr. Cat. Dept., Gen. Libs. Univ. of TX, Austin, 1978–. **Educ.:** Un. Coll., 1965–72, BA (Eng.); Univ. of CA, Santa Barbara, 1972–74, MA (Eng.); Univ. of CA, Los Angeles, 1976–78, MLS (Bibl.). **Orgs.:** ALA: ACRL/Rare Bks. and Mss. Sect.; RTSD/Serials Sect. Socty. of Univ. of TX Libns.: Secy. (1979–80); VP/Pres.-Elect (1981–82). Frnds. of the Univ. of CA, Los Angeles Lib. Frnds. of the Un. Coll. Lib. Natl. Poetry Fndn. **Pubns.:** "Library-Publisher Synergy (and) Maintaining Serials Sanity," *Amer. Libs.* (Jl.–Ag. 1980); "Ebullient History Seminar Palliates Library Myopia," *AL* (My. 1980); "Dallas Discovered," *AL* (Je. 1979); various photographs, *Gen. Libs. Nsltr. Univ. of TX* (1979–). **Activities:** 1; 20, 37, 45; 55, 57 **Addr.:** P.O. Box 7414, Austin, TX 78712.

Goodyear, Mary L. (Mr. 4, 1952, Independence, MO) Head of Ref., Wichita State Univ., 1981–; Ref. Libn., Stephens Coll., 1979–81; Coord., Data Base Srvs., Univ. of MO, 1976–79; Lib. Consult., RLDS Church, Independence, MO, 1976. **Educ.:** Graceland Coll., 1970–74, BA (Relig., Soclgy.); Univ. of MO, 1975, MA (LS), 1979–81, MS (Pub. Admin.). **Orgs.:** ALA: RASD/Machine-Assisted Ref Sect., Com. on Data Base Prods. and Srch. Srv. Vendors (1978–81); LAMA/Lib. Org. and Mgt. Sect., Budgeting, Fin., and Costs Com. (1981–). MO LA: Women in Libs. Com., Ch.; Comp. and Info. Tech. Com., Ch. MO ACRL. Ctrl. MO OLUG. MO State Women's Pol. Caucus: Pres. **Pubns.:** Ed. bd., *Graceland Monos.*; jt. auth., "Training for Interpersonal Relations in the Information Transfer Process," *Procs. of the 43rd ASIS Anl. Mtg.* (1980); jt. auth., "Acquisitions and Records Management: Help Where It is Needed," *Lib. Acq. Prac. and Theory* (1977); jt. auth., "The Inadequacy of Interdisciplinary Subject Retrieval," *Spec. Libs.* (My.–Je. 1977). **Activities:** 1, 2; 17, 38, 39; 56, 75, 90 **Addr.:** 7677 E. 21st, Wichita, KS 67206.

Goolsby, D. Linda (S. 26, 1940, Omaha, NB) Libn., Rawlins Middle Sch., 1975–; Libn., Coronado HS (CO Springs, CO), 1968–75; Ref. Libn., Littleton (CO) Pub. Lib., 1967–68. **Educ.:** Wayne State (NB) Coll. 1958–66, BAE (Bus. Educ.); Denver Univ., 1966–67, MA (LS); Univ. of CO, 1970–75 (Lib. Media); Univ. of WY, 1975– (Educ.). **Orgs.:** ALA: AASL. Natl. Educ. Assn.: WY Educ. Assn., WY Instr. and Prof. Dev. Cmsn. (1978–80). WY LA: Sch. Lib. Media Sect. **Activities:** 10; 32, 48; 63 **Addr.:** Rawlins Middle School, Brooks & Harshman Sts., Rawlins, WY 82301.

Gorchels, Clarence C. (Ag. 26, 1916, Oshkosh, WI) Dir., Libs., West. OR State Coll., 1966–; Dir., Libs., CA State Univ., Dominguez Hills, 1963–66; Dir., Libs., Ctrl. WA State Univ., 1960–63; Various positions, Columbia Univ., 1958–60; Various positions, WA State Univ., 1945–58. **Educ.:** WI State Univ., 1936–40, BS (Eng.); Univ. of WI, 1944–45, BLS (Libnshp.); Columbia Univ., 1950–52, MS (Libnshp.), 1958–60, DLS (Lib. Admin.). **Orgs.:** ALA: Cncl. (1956–57); LAMA/Lib. Org. and Mgt. Sect. (Ch., 1957), Stats. Com. (Ch., 1956–57); ACRL/Educ. and Bhvl. Sci. Sect. (Ch., 1978–80); various coms. Pac. Northwest LA: Vice-Ch. (1958). Cncl. of WA State Libns.: Ch. (1962–63). CA Acad. Libns.: Secy. (1964–66). **Pubns.:** *A Land-Grant University Library* (1972); "Librarian of 3,000,000 Wet Square Miles," *Amer. Libs.* (O. 1978); "Of New Libraries and Futuristic Libraries," *Coll. & Resrch. Libs.* (Jl. 1964); "Centralized Services in New Central Washington Building," *Coll. & Resrch. Libs.* (S. 1962); various other articles. **Activities:** 1, 11; 17, 26, 37; 56, 63, 92 **Addr.:** 342 Stadium Dr. S., Monmouth, OR 97361.

Gordon, Barbara Bingham (O. 21, 1924, Washington, PA) Head, Forest Resrcs. Lib., Univ. of WA, 1972–; Prin. Investgtr., WESTFORNET contract, 1978–81; Ref. Libn., Gen. Motors Resrch. Labs. Lib., 1968–71; Sci. Libn., Oakland Univ., 1966–68; Tech. Libn. and Staff Bio., Space Defense Corp. 1964–66; Supvsr, Chlds. Zoo, Detroit Zoological Park, 1947–49. **Educ.:** Univ. of MI, 1942–46, BA, Zlgy., 1963–66 MA (LS). Oakland Univ., 1967–68, Cert. (Comp.). **Orgs.:** ALA: ACRL, Bd. of Dir. (1975–77)/Agr. and Bio. Sci. Sect., Ch. (1975–77), Secy. (1973–75), Goals and Structures Com. (1978–81). SLA: Various Ofcs. Pac. Northwest LA. Marine Tech. Socty.: Educ. Com. (1966–72), Buoy Tech. Com. (1966–68), Man's Underwater Activities Com. (1966–68). Leag. of Women Voters: Various Ofcs. Socty. of Women Engin. **Honors:** Partners of the Amers., WA State Chap., and Org. for Tropical Stds., Grant for Std. Tour of 27 Latin Amer. Libs., 1974. **Pubns.:** "The University of Washington's Participation in PACFORNET as a Contractor," *New Horizons for Academic Libraries* (1979); "Modern Scientific and Technical Information Services for Forest Pathology," *West. Intl. Forest Disease Work* Conf. (1978); Jt. auth., "Census of a population of the red-backed Salamander," *Amer. Midland Naturalist* (Mr. 1948). **Activities:** 1, 12; 17, 39, 49; 58, 82, 91 **Addr.:** Forest Resources Library AQ-15, University of Washington, Seattle, WA 98195.

Gordon, Ruth I. (My. 13, 1933, Chicago, IL) Coord., IMC Lib. Srvs., Ofc. of the Lassen Co. Supt of Sch., 1977–; Supvsg. Libn., Portola Valley Sch. Dist., 1973–77; Lectr., Dir. of Lib. Practicum, Univ. of San Francisco, 1970–75; Tchr., Dept. of Defense Sch., Aviano, Italy, 1962–66; Tchr., Portola Valley Schs., 1956–62. **Educ.:** Tufts Univ., 1950–54, AB magna cum laude (Eng., Classics, Hum.); Brown Univ., 1954–55, AM (Amer. Civ.); Univ. of CA, Berkeley, 1966–74, MLS, PhD (LS). **Orgs.:** ALA: ALSC, Newbery-Caldecott-Com. (1979); Notable Children's Books Com. (1978; Ch. 1979). Assn. of Chld. Libns. of North. CA: Pres. (1976). CA Media Libns. Educ. Assn. Book Club of CA. Friends of the Earth. Sierra Club. Prtg. Hist. Socty. **Honors:** Beta Phi Mu, 1967; J. Morris Jones Fund Awd., 1979. **Pubns.:** "Aprizing Prizes," *Sch. Lib. Jnl.* (Mr. 1980); reviews. **Activities:** 10; 17, 21, 24; 72, 74 **Addr.:** 2270 Sloat Blvd., San Francisco, CA 94116.

PROFESSIONAL ACTIVITIES: Institutions: 1. Acad. lib.; 2. Arch.; 3. Assn.; 4. Fed./Gvt. lib.; 5. Inst. lib.; 6. Mfr./Suppl.; 7. Milit. lib.; 8. Musm.; 9. Pub. lib.; 10. Sch. lib.; 11. Sch. of lib. sci.; 12. Spec. lib.; 13. State lib.; 14. (other). **Functions/Activities:** 15. Acq./Col. dev.; 16. Adult srvs.; 17. Admin.; 18. Apprais.; 19. Archit./Bldgs.; 20. Cat./Class.; 21. Chld. srvs.; 22. Circ.; 23. Cons./Pres.; 24. Consult.; 25. Cont. ed.; 26. Educ. lib. sci.; 27. Ext. srvs.; 28. Fund/Grants; 29. Gvt. pubs.; 30. Indx./Abs.; 31. Instr. lib. use; 32. Media srvs.; 33. Micro.; 34. Netwks./Coop.; 35. Persnl.; 36. PR; 37. Publshg.; 38. Recs. mgt.; 39. Ref. srvs.; 40. Repro.; 41. Resrch.; 42. Review.; 43. Secur.; 44. Serials; 45. Spec. col.; 46. Tech. srvs.; 47. Trustees/Bds.; 48. YA srvs.; 49. (other).

Who's Who in Library and Information Services

Gordon, Thelma Stone (N. 18, 1930, Boston, MA) Art, Msc. Libn., Pic. Spec., Westport Pub. Lib., 1967–; various libn., tchg. positions, 1963–65; Exec. Secy., Mem., Bd. of Dirs., Assoc. Women Investors, 1959–62; various art exhibitions, 1955–72. **Educ.:** Univ. of Bridgeport, 1969, BA (Art); South. CT State Coll., 1972, MLS; various crs. **Orgs.:** SLA: Bd. of Dirs. (1979); Pic. Div., Ch. (1978); Ch.-Elect (1977); various ofcs. ARLIS/NA: Natl. Conf. (Panelist, 1977); CT Rep. (1975). CT LA: Adult Srvs. Sect., Ch. (1974), Co-Ch. (1973). ALA. Amer. Assn. of Pic. Profs. Westport Weston Arts Cncl. Frnds. of Msc. **Pubns.:** "The Westport Public Library Picture Collection," *ARLIS Nsltr.* (Sum. 1978). **Activities:** 9; 15, 16, 45; 55 **Addr.:** 32 Lincoln St., Westport, CT 06880.

Gordon, Vesta Lee (N. 11, 1942, Charlottesville, VA) Dir., Lib. Srvs., St. Johns River Cmnty. Coll., 1977–; Spec. Cols. Libn., Archvst., VA Cmwlth. Inst., 1975–77; Asst. Cur., Mss. Dept., Univ. of VA Lib., 1972–75, Mss. Catlgr., 1966–72. **Educ.:** Hollins Coll., 1960–64, AB (Hist.); FL State Univ., 1964–65, MS (LS); Univ. of VA, 1978, MA (Hist.). **Orgs.:** ALA: ACRL/Rare Bks. and Mss. Sect., Exec. Com. (1975–78), Mss. Col. Com. (Ch., 1976–78). Mid-Atl. Reg. Arch. Conf.: VA Rep. (1976–77). SAA. FL LA. Frnds. of the Libs. of Putnam Cnty. FL: Anl. Bk. Sale (Ch., 1980–). Putnam Cnty. Hist. Socty. **Honors:** Beta Phi Mu, 1965. **Pubns.:** "What's So Special about Special Collections," *V.C.U. Mag.* (Win. 1976); jt. auth., "A Chronological Catalog: Virginia's Approach," *The Amer. Archvst.* (O. 1970); *A Guide to the Microfilm Edition of the Letter Book, 1688–1761, of the Company for the Propagation of the Gospel in New England* (1969). **Activities:** 1, 2; 17, 23, 45; 55, 61, 92 **Addr.:** 512 Mulholland Dr., Palatka, FL 32093.

Gordon, William Robert (S. 24, 1936, Pratt, KS) Dir., Prince George's Cnty. Lib., 1977–; Dir., Arrowhead Lib. Syst., Virginia, MN, 1966–77; Head Libn., Pocatello (ID) Pub. Lib., 1963–66; Asst. Libn., Renton (WA) Pub. Lib., 1962–63. **Educ.:** Baker Univ., 1954–57, 1959–60, BA (Soclgy.); Univ. of KS, 1960–61 (Soclgy.); Univ. of Denver, 1961–62, MA (LS); ID State Univ., 1964–65 (Eng.). **Orgs.:** ALA: LAMA, Budget and Fin. Com. (1981–83); Joseph Lippincott Awd. Jury (Ch., 1980–81). ID LA: Pub. Libs. Div. (Ch., 1965–66). **Addr.:** Prince George's County Library, Hyattsville, MD 20782.*

Gorecki, Danuta M. (Wojnar) (Je. 29, 1922, Lwow, Poland) Law Catlgr., Univ. of IL, 1974–; Assoc. Prof. of Lib. Admin.; Lawyer, Cracow, Poland, 1952–68. **Educ.:** Jagiellonian Univ., Cracow, Poland, 1945–52, ML (Law); 1966, PhD (Roman Law); Univ. of IL, 1971–73; Cert. AALL, 1976, MLS. **Orgs.:** AALL: Com. on Forgn., Intl. and Comp. Law (1975–80). **Pubns.:** "The Commission of National Education and Civic Revival through Books in Eighteenth-Century Poland," *Jnl. of Lib. Hist.* (1980); *Roman Law: A Selected Bibliography of Book Written in English:* (1978); "The Zatuskis' Library of the Republic in Poland" *Jnl. of Lib. Hist.* (O. 1978); "The Development of Public Libraries in Poland" *Jnl. of Lib. Hist.* (Ja. 1976); "Heraclean Land Tax Reform: Objectives and Consequences," *Byzantine Std.,* (1977); other books and articles. **Activities:** 1; 20, 24, 41; 77, 92 **Addr.:** Univ. of Illinois Library, 1408 W. Gregory Dr., Urbana, IL 61801.

Gorman, Michael (Mr. 6, 1941, Witney, Oxfordshire, UK) Dir., Tech. Srvs. Depts, Univ. of IL, 1977–; Prof. of Lib. Admin. & Dept. Afflt., Grad. Sch. of LIS, Univ. of IL, 1977–; Head Bibl. Stan. Ofc., British Lib., 1974–77; Bibl. Consult., British Lib. Plng. Secret., 1972–74; Head of Cat., British Natl. Bibl., 1969–72, Author Cat. Rev., 1967–69. **Educ.:** Assoc. of the British LA, 1964–66. **Orgs.:** ALA: RTSD, Ch. Margaret Mann Com. (1981–82); LITA, Ch., Intl. Mechanisation Consultation Com. (1979–). IFLA: Com. on Cat. (1976–79); Working Grp. on ISBD-G and ISBD-M (1969–76). Jt. Strg. Com. for the Rev. of AACR, (1976–). Lib. Assn./British Lib.: Com. on the Rev. of the AACR (1974–78). **Honors:** ALA RTSD, Margaret Mann Cit., 1975. British LA, Fellow (FLA), 1978. **Pubns.:** *Concise AACR 2* (1981); jt. ed., *Anglo American cataloguing rules,* 2nd ed. (1978); *Format for machine readable cataloguing of motion pictures* (1973); other books, articles, papers, and reviews. **Activities:** 1, 14-Natl. Lib.; 17, 20, 41; 95 **Addr.:** University of Illinois Library, Urbana, IL 61801.

Gorman, Robert Marshall (Mr. 13, 1949, Miami, FL) Libn., KS Newman Coll., 1977–; Libn., GA Milit. Coll., 1972–77. **Educ.:** Miami-Dade Cmnty. Coll., 1967–69, AA; FL State Univ., 1969–71, BA (Hist.); Emory Univ., 1971–72, MLn (Libnshp.); GA Coll., 1973–75, MA (Hist.). **Orgs.:** KS LA: Int. Frdm. Com. (Ch., 1979–); Coll. and Univ. Libs. Sect. (Secy.-Treas., 1980–81). Pvt. Acad. Libns. of KS: Ch. (1980–81). KS Lib. Netwk.: Task Frc. on Un. List of Serials (1980–). ALA. **Honors:** Mt. Plains LA, One-to-One Cont. Educ. Grant, 1978. **Pubns.:** "Racial Antisemitism in England: The Legacy of Arnold Leese," *Wiener Lib. Bltn.* (1977). **Activities:** 1; 17 **Addr.:** Kansas Newman College, 3100 McCormick Ave., Wichita, KS 67213.

Gormly, Mary (O. 14, 1919, San Francisco, CA) Assoc. Libn., Ref., CA State Univ., Los Angeles, 1962–; Anthro. Archvst., Pac. NW Archlg. Arch., Univ. of ID, 1976; Instr. in Art, CA State Univ., Los Angeles, 1973; Libn., Asst. Cur., Amerind Fndn., 1959–62. **Educ.:** Univ. of WA, 1941–43, 1946–47, BA (Anthro.); Mex. City Coll., 1947–48, MA (Anthro.); Univ. of WA, 1958–59, MSLS (Libnshp.); various crs. **Orgs.:** SALALM: Com. on Bibl. (1978–). West. Hist. Assn. Socty. for CA Archlg. Amer. Anthro. Assn. Latin Amer. Std. Assn. Pac. Coast Cncl. on Latin Amer. Std.: Secy., Exec. Com. (1976–). AAUP: CA State Univ.: Los Angeles Chap., Secy.-Treas. (1974–76), Del.-at-Lg. (1977–). Various other orgs. **Honors:** Beta Phi Mu, 1960; Amer. Socty. of Aerosp. Educ., Aerosp. Ambassador, 1979; Air Frc. Assn., Excep. Srv. Awd. for Aerosp. Educ., 1979. **Pubns.:** *Resources for Latin American Studies* (1977); "Spanish Documentary Material Pertaining to the Northwest Coast Indians," *Davidson Jnl. of Anthro.* (1955); "Tlingits of Bucareli Bay, Alaska (1774–1792)," *NW Anthro. Resrch. Notes* (1971); "Early Culture Contact on the Northwest Coast, 1774–1795," *NW Anthro. Resrch. Notes* (1977); various bk. reviews, *Amer. W. Mag., Lib. Jnl.* (1962–70). **Activities:** 1; 15, 31, 39; 54, 70, 92 **Addr.:** John F. Kennedy Memorial Library, California State University, Los Angeles, 5151 State University Dr., Los Angeles, CA 90032.

Gosebrink, Jean E. Meeh (My. 29, 1941, Rochester, NY) Proj. Dir., African Std. Info. Resrcs. Dir. Proj., African Std. Assn., 1980–; Area Spec., African Std., IN Univ. Libs., 1974–78; Supvsr., Hist., Geneal. Dept., Ref. Libn., St. Louis Pub. Lib., 1972–73; Ref. Libn., Biblgphr., African Sect., Lib. of Congs., 1970–72. **Educ.:** Marymount Coll., 1959–63, BA (Eng. Lit.); Univ. of CA, Los Angeles, 1968–69, MA (African Std.); IN Univ., 1969–70, MLS. **Orgs.:** ALA: ACRL. African Std. Assn.: Arch. Libs. Com. **Pubns.:** "Sources for Contemporary Southern Africa," *Southern Africa: The Continuing Crisis* (1979); *Sources for African Studies* (1978); "Bibliography and Sources for African Studies," *Africa* (1977); ed., *A Bibliography of Africana in the Lilly Library* (1977); jt. cmplr., *Periodicals and Other Serials for African Studies Currently on Subscription in the Indiana University-Bloomington Libraries* (1976); various articles. **Activities:** 1, 9; 15, 39, 41; 54, 92 **Addr.:** 3533a Wyoming, St. Louis, MO 63118.

Gosling, William Arthur (Ja. 13, 1943, Newport, RI). Asst. Univ. Libn. for Tech. Srvs., Duke Univ. Libs., 1976–; Prog. Mgr., CIP, Lib. of Congs., 1971–76, Admin. Ofcr., MARC Dev. Ofc., 1970–71, Descr. Catlgr., Natl. Union Cat. of Mss. Cols., 1969–70. **Educ.:** Bates Coll., 1961–65, BA (Hist.); Univ. of Pittsburgh, 1965–66, MLS. **Orgs.:** ALA: RTSD, Pres. (1978–80), Bk. Dir.–Lib. Rels. Com. (1976–78), AAP–RTSD Jt. Com. (1975–78). Unvsl. Serials and Bk. Exch.: Treas. (1979–80. Amer. Natl. Stands. Inst., Z39: Subcom. 45, Stand. Lib. Identifier (Ch.). **Honors:** Beta Phi Mu. U.S. Army, Bronze Star, 1968. **Activities:** 1, 4; 17, 23, 46 **Addr.:** 4339 Berini Dr., Durham, NC 27705.

Goslinga, Marian (Je. 2, 1939, Rotterdam, Netherlands) Intl. Affairs Libn., FL Intl. Univ., 1974–; Assoc. Cat. Libn., CA State Univ., Fresno, 1969–74. **Educ.:** Univ. of the Americas, Mexico City, 1956–65, BA (Pol. Sci.); Univ. of CA, Berkeley, 1966–68, MA (Lat. Amer. Hist.), 1968–69, MLS. **Orgs.:** SALALM: Com. on Bibl.; Subcom. on Cuban Bibl. (1974–). Assn. of Caribbean Univ. and Resrch. Libs.: Com. on Bibl. (1977–). Assn. of Caribbean Std. **Pubns.:** Bibliographer, *Caribbean Review,* 1977–. **Activities:** 1, 5; 15, 20, 30; 54, 57, 92 **Addr.:** Florida International University, Miami, FL 33199.

Gosner, Pamela W. (Je. 14, 1941, Montclair, NJ) Head, Chld. Srvs., Maplewood Meml. Lib., 1971–; Asst. Chld. Libn., Bloomfield Pub. Lib., 1969–71; Asst. Libn., Newark Musm. Lib., 1964–66. **Educ.:** Bradford Jr., 1959–61; Smith Coll., 1961–63, BA (Art Hist.); Rutgers Univ., 1966–69, MLS (Lib. Srv.). **Orgs.:** NJ LA. Bloomfield Env. Action Com. Co-fndr. (1969–71). Socty. of Archit. Histns. **Pubns.:** "More on Children's Services," *NJ Libs.* (Mr. 1981); *Historic Architecture of the U.S. Virgin Islands* (1971); *Caribbean Georgian* (forthcoming); "Library Services to Young Persons: Denmark," *NJ Libs.* (Win. 1970); "Maya Architecture" slide presentation (1974); various nsltrs., news releases (1969–). **Activities:** 9; 17, 21, 36; 55 **Addr.:** Maplewood Memorial Library, 51 Baker St., Maplewood, NJ 07040.

Goss, Marie Clarke (Jl. 23, 1911, New York, NY) Pres., METRONET Bd. of trustees, 1979–81 Retired; Pres., Bd. of Trustees, Metro. Lib. Srv. Agency, 1977–80; Trustee, Minneapolis Pub. Lib. & Info. Ctr., 1971–83, Pres., 1974–77; Pres., Frnds. of the Minneapolis Pub. Lib., 1968–71; Pres., Frnds. of MN Libs., 1976–80. **Educ.:** George Washington Univ., 1929–33, BA (Educ., Bot.). **Orgs.:** MN LA: Legis. com. (1974–75); Lib. Trustee Assn. (Secy., 1975–77; VP, 1977–80); Pub. Lib. Div., Telecom. com. (1978). Ofc. of Pub. Libs. and Interlib. Coop. Formula Com. (1978). Gvrs. Conf. on Libs. and Info. Srvs.: Del. (1978). Minneapolis Socty. of Fine Arts: Bd. (1974–77). Science Musm. of MN: Bd. (1976–82); Cmty. Rel. com. (1977–82). Metro Cmnty. Coll. Fndn. for Urban Higher Educ.: Bd. (1977–83). Citizens Leag. of Metro area. **Honors:** MN LA, Trustee of the Yr., 1977; Frnds. of the Minneapolis Pub. Lib., Honorary mem., 1978. **Activities:** 9, 14; 34, 47; 56, 78 **Addr.:** 4846 Thomas Ave. S., Minneapolis, MN 55410.

Gossage, Wayne (Je. 13, 1926, Bellingham, WA) Co-fndr. and Prin., Gossage Regan Assocs., Inc., 1980–; Lib. Dir., Bank St. Coll. of Educ., 1967–80; Asst. Libn., Tchrs. Coll., Columbia Univ., 1964–67; Dir., Warner Lib. of the Tarrytowns, NY, 1956–63; Head, Adult Srvs., Levittown Pub. Lib., 1954–55; Asst. Head, Adult Srvs., East Orange Pub. Lib., 1951–54. **Educ.:** Univ. of WA, 1943–49, BS (Psy.); Columbia Univ., 1950–51, MS (Libnshp.), 1963–69, MA (Higher Educ. Admin.). **Orgs.:** ALA: Scarecrow Press Awd. for Lib. Lit. (Jury Mem., 1975–76); ACRL/Educ. and Bhvl. Sci. Sect. (Ch., 1975–76), Bd. of Dirs. (1974–76), various coms., ofcs; RASD, Notable Bks. Cncl. (1961–62), Wilson Indxs. Com. (Ch., 1978–80). SLA: Soc. Sci. Div. (Ch., 1975–76); various ofcs. CLENE: Adv. Com. (1979–81). ASIS. NY LA: Resrcs. and Tech. Srvs. Sect. (2nd VP, 1974–75); Coll. and Univ. Libs. Sect. (Pres., 1978–79). Hist. Socty. of the Tarrytowns, NY: VP (1960–61). Columbia Univ., Sch. of Lib. Srv. Alum. Assn.: Pres. (1977–78). Alum. Fed. of Columbia Univ.: Alum. Trustee Nom. Com. (1975–79); Columbia Sen. Com. on Libs. (Alum. Rep., 1977–79); Com. on the Qual. of Student Life, Libs. Subcom., Ch. Harvard Lib. in New York, Bd. of Trustees (1978–). **Honors:** Jr. Cham. of Cmrce. of Tarrytowns, NY, Disting. Cmnty. Srv. Awd., 1962; Cncl. on Lib. Resrcs., Flwshp., 1978–79. **Pubns.:** "Joint Use of Collections," *Amer. Libs.* (F. 1970); "The American Library College Movement to 1968," *Educ. Libs. Bltn.* (Sum. 1975); "Psychology," "Psychiatry and Mental Health," *Update 80: Selected Recent Works in the Social Sciences* (1980). **Activities:** 1, 9; 15, 17, 24; 63, 75, 92 **Addr.:** Gossage Regan Associates, Inc., 15 W. 44th St., New York, NY 10036.

Goss-Coleman, Anne S. (S. 3, 1942, Warren, PA) Head, Hlth. Sci. Lib., Ohio Univ., 1977–; Cood., Tech. Prcs., Med. Coll. of Georgia, 1974–77, Tech. Prcs. Libn., Hlth. Sci. Lib., Univ. of UT, 1970–74, Actg. Head, Cat., Alden Lib., OH Univ., 1968–70; Asst., Cat., Alden Lib. OH Univ., 1966–68. **Educ.:** Grove City Coll., 1960–64, BA (Hist.); Syracuse Univ., 1964–66, MSLS. Emory Univ., 1971, Med. LA Cert. **Orgs.:** Med. LA. OH Hlth. Info. Org. Acad. Lib. Assn. of OH. OH Acad. of Sci. **Honors:** Phi Beta Mu. **Pubns.:** "Synergism among Special Librarians," *Spec. Libs.* (S. 1975); Producer and Publshr., "MEDOC: A computerized index to U.S. government documents in the medical and health sciences." (1975). **Activities:** 1; 15, 17, 24, 28, 34; 80 **Addr.:** Health Sciences Library, Ohio University, Athens, OH 45701.

Gothberg, Helen M. (Ap. 5, 1930, Casper, WY) Assoc. Prof., Grad. Lib. Sch., Univ. of AZ, 1974–; Asst. Prof., Sch. of Educ., Univ. of CO, 1973–74; Consult., CO State Lib., 1971–72; Head Libn., Ctrl. WY Coll., 1968–70; Sch. Libn., C Y Jr. HS, 1963–68; Tchr., Natrona Cnty. HS, 1962–63; Catlgr., Natrona Cnty. Pub. Lib., 1956–62. **Educ.:** Univ. of CO, 1948–56, BA (Eng. Lit.); Univ. of CA, Berkeley, 1959–62, MLS (Libnshp.); Univ. of Denver, 1971–72, Cert. (Advnc. Std., Libnshp.), 1972–74, PhD (Comm.). **Orgs.:** AALS: Cont. Ed. Com. (1976–79). ALA: Cncl. (1976–78); Mem. Promo. Task Frc. (1978); RASD, Cont. Ed. Com. (1977–79). AZ State LA: Exec. Bd. (1977–78); various coms. AAUP. **Pubns.:** *Feasibility Study on Institutional Library Service. Final Report* (1979); *Training Library Communication Skills: Development of Three Video Tape Workshops: Final Report* ERIC (1977); *A Comparison of Two Teaching Methodologies for a Course in Basic Reference: Final Report* ERIC (1977); "A Study of the Audio-Tutorial Approach to Teaching Basic Reference," *Jnl. of Educ. for Libnshp.* (Win. 1978); "Immediacy: A Study of Communication Effect on the Reference Process," *Jnl. of Acad. Libnshp.* (Jl. 1976); various articles, vid. and audio cassettes. **Addr.:** Graduate Library School, College of Education, University of Arizona, 1515 E. 1st St., Tucson, AZ 85721.

Gothia, Sr. Blanche (O. 27, 1930, Port Arthur, TX) Media Coord., St. Agnes Acad., 1969–; AV Dir., 1967–69; Prin., St. Anthony's Cathedral Sch., 1965–67; Tchr., 1964–67; Tchr., TX Schs., 1950–64. **Educ.:** Dominican Coll., 1960, BA (Eng.); TX Woman's Univ., 1973, MLS. **Orgs.:** ALA. Amer. Film Inst. AECT: Co-Ch., TX Legis. Com. (1970–). Cath. LA: Adv. Bd. HS Sect. (1979–1983); other orgs. Houston Area Film Tchrs. Assn.: Co-Dir. (1973–75). **Activities:** 10; 17, 48; 63 **Addr.:** Saint Agnes Academy, 9000 Bellaire Blvd., Houston, TX 77036.

Gottselig, Leonard J. (Ag. 18, 1943, Regina, SK Can.) Chief Libn., Glenbow-Alberta Inst., 1972; Legis. Libn., Legis Lib. of SK, 1967–71. **Educ.:** Univ. of Waterloo 1962–66 BA (Hist.); Univ. of Regina, 1967–71 BA Hon. (Hist.). Univ. of WA, 1967–72 MLS. **Orgs.:** Can. LA: Bd. and Cncl. (1973–74). LA of AB: Govt. Pubn. Com. (1972–73). SLA. Alpine Club of Can.: Calgary Sect. (Ch., 1978–79). Intl. Cncl. of Mus. Can. Hist. Assn. **Activities:** 2, 12; 15, 17, 18; 55, 70 **Addr.:** Glenbow-Alberta Institute, 9th Ave. and 1st St. S.E., Calgary, AB T2G 0P3 Canada.

Goudy, Allie Wise (N. 21, 1949, Saluda, SC) Msc. Libn., West. IL Univ., 1976–; Instr., Msc., Wilson Coll., 1974–75. **Educ.:** Converse Coll., 1969–72, BM (Voice Performance); Univ. of MD, 1975–76, MLS. **Orgs.:** Msc. LA: Natl. Mem.; Midwest Chap. (Secy.-Treas., 1979–81), Bibl. Instr. Com. (1978–), Prog. Com. (1979), Mem. Com. Ch. Msc. OCLC Users. Grp. Natl. Assn. of Tchrs. of Singing. **Pubns.:** "The Culmination of the Lied: Hugo Wolf's Italienisches Liederbuch," *NATS Bltn.* (1980); "A Bibliography: Fine Arts Materials from Foreign Countries," *Cath. Lib. World* (O. 1979); "Music Education Faculty: A Study of Their Library Use," *IL Lib.* (O. 1980). **Activities:** 1, 12; 15, 20, 39; 55 **Addr.:** 1801 Riverview Dr., IL 61455.

Special Subjects/Services: 50. Adult educ.; 51. Advert./Mktg.; 52. Aerosp.; 53. Agric.; 54. Area std.; 55. Arts/Hum.; 56. Autom.; 57. Bibl./Prtg.; 58. Bio. sci.; 59. Bus./Fin.; 60. Chem.; 61. Copyrt.; 62. Documtn.; 63. Educ.; 64. Engin.; 65. Env.; 66. Eth. grps.; 67. Film; 68. Food/Nutr.; 69. Geneal.; 70. Geo.; 71. Geol.; 72. Handcpd.; 73. Hist.; 74. Int. frdm.; 75. Info. sci.; 76. Insr.; 77. Law; 78. Legis.; 79. Math./Comp. sci.; 80. Med.; 81. Metals; 82. Nat. resrcs.; 83. Newsp.; 84. Nuc. sci.; 85. Oral hist.; 86. Petr./Energy; 87. Pharm.; 88. Phys./Astr./Math.; 89. Readg.; 90. Relig.; 91. Sci./Tech.; 92. Soc. sci.; 93. Telecom.; 94. Transp.; 95. (other).

Goudy, Frank William (Jl. 17, 1949, Canton, IL) Assoc. Prof., Ref. Libn., West. IL Univ., 1977–; Ref., Gvt. Docum. Libn., Los Angeles Cnty. Pub. Lib. Syst., 1974–77; Libn. V, Lincoln Lib., 1972–73; Tchr., Chandlerville HS, 1971–72. **Educ.:** IL Coll., 1967–71, BA (Hist.); Sangamon State Univ., 1972–73, MA (Pol. Std.); Univ. of South. CA, 1973–74, MSLS, 1975–81, DLS. **Orgs.:** IL LA. West. IL Reg. Std.: Adv. Com. **Pubns.:** Jt. auth., "Battered Wives: A Bibliography," *Cath. Lib. World* (Ap. 1981); "The Local Public Works Program: Impact on Public, School and Academic Libraries," *Pub. Lib. Qtly.* (Spr.–Sum. 1981); "General Revenue Sharing and Public Libraries: An Estimate of Fiscal Impact," *Lib. Qtly.* (Ja. 1982); "The Local Public Works Program: Success for Libraries in the Northwest?" *Pac. NW LA Qtly.* (Sum. 1980); "General Revenue Sharing Support for Libraries," *The Bowker Annual of Library and Book Trade Information* (1980); various articles. **Activities:** 1; 31, 39; 51, 59 **Addr.:** Western Illinois University Libraries, Macomb, IL 61455.

Gould, Linda J. (Ap. 7, 1938, Boston, MA) Coord., Col. Dev. and Mgt. Ofc., Univ. of WA Libs., 1980–, Head, Pol. Sci. Lib., 1974–80; Libn., Hist. and Gvt. Dept., Seattle Pub. Lib., 1972, Chld. Libn., 1970–72. **Educ.:** Boston State Tchrs. Coll., 1955–58 (Educ.); Univ. of Chicago, 1959 (Hist.); Univ. of WA, 1965–66, BA (Hist.), 1969–70, MLS. **Orgs.:** ALA. WA LA. **Pubns.:** *Eighty Years of Service: A History of the Children's Department, Seattle Public Library* (1971); "Symposium on Books on Asia," *Top of the News* (Ja. 1973); "Library Development and Education for Librarianship in Israel," *PNLA Qtly.* (Spr. 1971); "India: A Guide to Books for Children," *Top of the News* (Ja. 1973). **Activities:** 1; 15, 17; 54, 92 **Addr.:** 4805 - 38th Ave. N.E., Seattle, WA 98105.

Gould, Martha B. (O. 8, 1931, Claremont, NH) Asst. Cnty. Libn., Washoe Cnty. Lib., 1977–; Pub. Srvs. Libn., 1974–1979; Actg. Dir. Pub. Srvs. & Ref. Libn., NV State Lib., 1972–74; Chld. libn. & Sr. Chld. Libn., Los Angeles Pub. Lib., 1960–72; Consult., NM State Lib., 1959–60; Admin. Lib. Srvs. Act demonstration reg. lib. proj., Pawhuska, OK, 1958–59; Chld. libn., New York Pub. Lib., 1956–58. **Educ.:** Univ. of MI, 1949–53, BA (Educ.); Simmons Coll., 1954–56, MS (LS); Univ. of Denver Lib. Sch., Cmnty. Analysis Resrch. Inst., 1978, Cert. **Orgs.:** ALA: Dir., IFRT (1977–79); IFC (1979–83). NV LA: Pub. Info. (Ch. 1972–73); Int. Frdm. (Ch. 1975–78); Gvt. Rel. (Ch. 1978–79); VP, Pres. Elect (1980); Pres. (1981). Untd. Jewish Appeal: Bd. of Dir. Temple Sinai: Bd. of Trustees. North. Nevadans for ERA: Bd. of Dir. RSVP: Bd. of Dir. **Honors:** Nevada State Library Letter of commendation 1973; Washoe County Bd. of Commissioners Resolution of Appreciation, 1978; Nevada Library Association Special Citation for work done in Intellectual Freedom 1978. **Pubns.:** Jt. cmplr., *Bibliography of mining in Nevada and the West* (1974); Cmplr., *A selected bibliography on censorship and obscenity* (1974); Cmplr., *Drug abuse & venereal disease: a bibliog. for young people* (1974). **Activities:** 9; 17, 21, 34; 56, 74, 78 **Addr.:** Washoe County Library, P.O. Box 2151, Reno NV 89505.

Gourley, Janet H. (O. 16, 1931, Lowell, MA) Chld. Libn., Welles-Turner Meml. Lib., 1981–, 1972–81, Actg. Dir., 1981; Chld. Libn., Boston Pub. Lib., 1971–72; Libn., Albert Church Brown Lib., 1966–70; Chld. Libn., Providence Pub. Lib., 1959–66. **Educ.:** Brown Univ., 1949–53, BA (Fr. Lit.); Simmons Coll., 1956–57, MS (LS). **Orgs.:** CT LA: Chld. Srvs. Sect., Prog. Ch. (1976–78), Comm. Ch. (1978–79), Vice-Ch. (1979–80). Cap. Reg. Lib. Cncl.: Chld. RT (Booklist Ch., 1979). Hist. Socty. of Glastonbury: Rec. Secy. Natl. Alum. Schs. Prog.: Brown Univ. Interviewer. **Pubns.:** "One to One and Group Parent Support Activities," *Sch. Lib. Jnl.* (Ap. 1980). **Activities:** 9; 17, 21, 36 **Addr.:** Welles-Turner Memorial Library, 2407 Main St., Glastonbury, CT 06033.

Govan, James F. (My. 9, 1926, Chattanooga, TN) Univ. Libn., Univ. of NC, 1973–; Head Libn. & Lect. in Hist., Swarthmore Coll., 1965–73; Head Libn. & Prof. of Hist., Trinity Univ., 1961–65; Pub. Srvs. Libn., Univ. of AL, 1955–61. **Educ.:** Univ. of the South, 1948, BA (Hist.); Emory Univ., 1955, MA (Libnshp.); Johns Hopkins Univ., 1960, PhD (Hist.); Inst. of Hist. Resrch., Univ. of London, 1951–52. **Orgs.:** ALA: Cncl. (1971–72); ACRL, Bd. of Dir. (1971–72); Com. on Inst. and Use of Libs. (Ch. 1968–70); Com. on Accred. (1972–75); Adv. Com. on Coop. with Prof. and Educ. Org. (Ch., 1969–72). NC LA. SELA. ARL: Bd. of Dir. (1980), Com. on Prsrvn. (1976–). Other orgs. **Honors:** Phi Beta Kappa, 1948; Beta Phi Mu, 1955. **Pubns.:** "The University of North Carolina Library," *Encyclopedia of Library and Information Science* (1977); "The Better Mousetrap: External Accountability and Staff Participation," *Lib. Trends* (Fall, 1977); "North Carolina: James Davis, *The Office and Authority of a Justice of the Peace,*" *Thirteen Colonial Americana* (1977); "The Present and Future Status of ALA Accreditation," *KY LA Bltn.* (Win. 1978); "Implications for Research Libraries," *Minutes of Ninety-Fourth Meeting,* ARL (1979); Other articles. **Activities:** 1, 11; 17, 24, 34; 55, 56, 75 **Addr.:** Louis Round Wilson Library, University of North Carolina at Chapel Hill, Chapel Hill, NC 27514.

Goyer, Doreen S. (Je. 26, 1930, Detroit, MI) Soc. Sci., Hum. Resrch. Assoc. IV, Libn., Popltn. Resrch. Ctr., Univ. of TX, 1971–; Asst. Prof., Span., SW TX State Univ., 1966–70; Asst. Prof., Mod. Langs., IN State Univ., 1964–66; Tchr., Jefferson HS, 1958–60. **Educ.:** Wayne State Univ., 1951–53, BA (Span.); FL State Univ., 1960–63, MA (Span.); Univ. of TX, Austin, 1970–71, MLS (Acad. Lib.). **Orgs.:** Assn. of Popltn./Fam. Plng. Libs. and Info. Ctrs. Intl.: 2nd VP (1980–81); Bd. of Dirs. (1978–80). Popltn. Assn. of Amer. **Honors:** U.S. Gvt., Fulbright Grant in Spain, 1963; Phi Kappa Phi, 1962; Sigma Delta Pi, 1961; Pi Delta Phi, 1962. **Pubns.:** *International Population Census Bibliography, Revision and Update: 1945–1977* (1980); *National Population Censuses, 1945–1976: Some Holding Libraries* (1979); "Censuses–The Librarian's Nightmare," *Procs. 10th Anl. Conf. APLIC* (1977); "Censuses Printed and Computer Stored," *Procs. 10th Anl. Conf. APLIC* (1978). **Activities:** 1, 12; 15, 41, 45; 57, 92 **Addr.:** Population Research Center, 1800 Main Bldg., Univ. of Texas, Austin, TX 78712.

Grabowski, John Joseph (Ja. 15, 1949, Cleveland, OH) Assoc. Cur., Mss., West. Rsv. Hist. Socty., 1977–, Eth. Arch. Spec., 1971–77, Pic. Spec., 1973–77; various positions as consult. **Educ.:** Case West. Rsv. Univ., 1967–71, BA (Hist.), 1971–77, MA, PhD (Hist., Amer. Hist.). **Orgs.:** Socty. of OH Archvsts.: VP (1977–78); Pres. (1978–80); *Nsltr.* Managing Ed. (1979–). SAA: Com. on Eth. Arch. (1975–79). Org. of Amer. Histns. **Honors:** Phi Beta Kappa, 1971. **Pubns.:** Jt. auth., *Polish Americans and Their Communities in Cleveland* (1976); assoc. cmplr., *Ethnic Groups in Ohio; An Annotated Bibliographic Guide* (1975); "From Progressive to Patrician: George Bellany and Hiram House Social Settlement, 1896–1914," *OH Hist.* (Win. 1977–78); "Ethnic Research in Cleveland," *The Immigration Hist. Nsltr.* (My. 1977); "Ethnic Collections of the Western Reserve Historical Society," *IL Libs.* (Mr. 1975); "Michael P. Kniola: Polish Entrepreneur," *West. Rsv. Hist. Socty. News* (My. 1977); various articles, papers, lects. **Activities:** 2, 3; 15, 33, 45; 66, 70, 95-Photographs. **Addr.:** Western Reserve Historical Society, 10825 E. Blvd., Cleveland, OH 44106.

Grace, Mrs. Loranne (N. 17, 1941, Frederic, WI) Pers. Libn., McKee Lib., South. Missn. Coll., Collegedale, TN, 1970–; Libn., Mid. E. Coll., Beirut, Lebanon, 1969–70; Serials Libn., Walla Walla Coll., 1967–69; Tchr.-Libn., Blue Mt. Acad., 1964–67. **Educ.:** Walla Walla Coll., 1960–64, BA (Hist.); Univ. of WA, 1965–68, MLS. **Orgs.:** ALA. SE LA. TN LA. Chattanooga Area LA. **Activities:** 1; 15, 20, 44; 56, 63 **Addr.:** McKee Library, Southern Missionary College, Collegedale, TN 37315.

Grady, Agnes M. (F. 8, 1934, Spokane, WA) Cat. Libn., OR State Univ. Lib., 1970–. **Educ.:** Univ. of WA, 1965–69, BA (Grmn.), 1969–70, MLS (Libnshp.); Univ. of OR, 1977–78, MA (Law, Pol. Sci., Hist.). **Orgs.:** Pac. NW LA. ALA: RTSD; LITA; ACRL. ASIS: Pac. NW Chap., *Points Northwest* Ed. (1979–81), Ch.-Elect. **Pubns.:** "AACR2 Name Authority Project at Oregon State University Library," *Alternative Cat. Nsltr.* (D. 1980); "Divided Catalogs: A Selected Bibliography," *Lib. Resrcs. & Tech. Srvs.* (Spr. 1976). **Activities:** 1; 20, 29, 46; 56, 77 **Addr.:** 701 N.W. 29th St., Corvallis, OR 97330.

Graf, John A. (S. 12, 1917, Providence, RI) Sr. Cat. Libn., Newark Pub. Lib., 1962–; Sr. Bus. Libn., Newark Bus. Lib., 1958–62; Sr. Educ. Libn., Newark Pub. Lib., 1954–58, Jr. Libn., Educ. Dept., 1951–54; various tchg. positions, 1941–47. **Educ.:** Univ. of MN, 1938–40, BS (Soc. Std.), 1940–41, (Eng., Latin); Columbia Univ., 1949–53, MS (LS); 1959, NJ Prof. Libns. Cert.; 1977, NJ Educ. Media Spec. Cert.; 1977, NJ Sec. Sch. Tchrs. Cert. **Orgs.:** ALA. NJ LA: PR Com. (1951). NY LA. Univ. of MN Alum. Assn. **Honors:** Newark Pub. Lib., Cert. for 30 Yrs. of Srv., 1978. **Activities:** 9, 12; 20, 39; 55, 59, 63 **Addr.:** 761 Mt. Prospect Ave., Newark, NJ 07104.

Graf, Thomas H. (D. 15, 1940, Milwaukee, WI) Supervisory Archvst., Natl. Arch., 1980–, Archvst., 1973–80. **Educ.:** Marquette Univ., 1967–70, BA (Hist., Pol. Sci.), 1971–72, MA (Hist.). **Orgs.:** SAA: Gvt. Recs. Prof. Afnty. Grp.; Ref. Access and Outrch. Prof. Afnty. Grp. Natl. Arch. Asm.: Com. on Access and Release. Natl. Class. and Mgt. Socty. **Honors:** Phi Alpha Theta; Pi Sigma Alpha. **Activities:** 2; 38 **Addr.:** Rm. 18W, National Archives Bldg., 8th St. & Pennsylvania Ave., N.W., Washington, DC 20408.

Graham, Aileen Wheeldon (Ja. 3, 1928, Brownville, NE) Dir., Lib. Media Srvs., Pub. Sch. Dist., Manhattan, KS, 1975–, Jr. HS Media Spec., 1967–75; Asst. Libn., Peru State Coll., 1956–68; HS Libn., Fairbury Pub. Sch., 1954–56. **Educ.:** Peru State Coll., 1944–48, AB (Educ.); Univ. of MN, 1950–54, MS (LS); KS State Univ., 1976–77, MS (Educ. Admin.). **Orgs.:** ALA. KS Assn. of Sch. Libns.: Dist. IV Dir.; various other ofcs. KS LA. Delta Kappa Gamma: Eta Chap., Pres. KS Sch. Lib. Media Dir.: Past Pres. **Pubns.:** Ed., *Manhattan KS Nsltr.* (1978–80). **Activities:** 10; 17, 20, 32 **Addr.:** Library Media Services, Manhattan Public Schools, 2031 Poyntz Ave., Manhattan, KS 66502.

Graham, Beverly Mae (Mr. 26, 1951, Edmonton, AB) Asst. Libn., McGill Univ., 1977–; Libn., SIDA Trng. Ctr., 1976; Asst. Libn., Wizara Ya Uchumi, Tanzania, 1972–75. **Educ.:** Univ. of AB, 1968–71, BA (Hist.), 1971–72, BLS; McGill Univ., 1976–77, MLS, 1976–78, Cert. of Proficiency in Fr. **Orgs.:** SLA: East. Can. Chap., *Bltn.* Ed. (1978–80); Nom. Com. (1980–81). Assn. of McGill Univ. Libns.: Secy. (1980–81). **Activities:** 1; 31, 39, 46; 51, 59 **Addr.:** Reference Dept., Howard Ross Library of Management, McGill University, 1001 Sherbrooke St. W., Montreal, PQ Canada.

Graham, Clarence R. (F. 28, 1907, Louisville, KY) Managing Dir., The Filson Club (Hist.), 1979–; Visit. Assoc. Prof., Dept. of LS, Univ. of KY, 1963; Co-fndr., Consult., Free Neighborhood Colls. Prog., 1947; Dir., Louisville Free Pub. Lib., 1942–77; Dir., Natl. Coll. of Educ., 1936–42; Asst. to Libn., Louisville Free Pub. Lib., 1935–36; Libn., Parkland Jr. HS, 1930–34; various positions as lib. consult., 1952–65. **Educ.:** Univ. of NC, 1924–27 (Eng.); Univ. of Louisville, 1934, AB (Eng.); Case West. Rsv. Univ., 1935, BS (LS); Northwest. Univ., 1937–38 (Educ.); Spalding Coll., 1977, LLD. **Orgs.:** ALA: Pres. (1950–51). SE LA: Pres. (1948–50). KY LA: Pres. (1946–47); KY Libs. Cert. Bd. (1943–50). Filson Hist. Club. Arts Club. Rotary. **Honors:** Beta Phi Mu; Younger Women's Club of Louisville, Citizens Laurate, 1947. **Pubns.:** *First Book of Public Libraries* (1959); various articles in prof. jnls. **Activities:** 1, 9; 17, 21, 46; 55, 67, 69 **Addr.:** The Filson Club, Inc., 118 W. Breckinridge St., Louisville, KY 40203.

Graham, Elaine (Mr. 29, 1952, Long Beach, CA) Head, PSRMLS Consult. and Trng. Sect., Univ. of CA, Los Angeles, 1981–; Med. Libn., Kaiser Permanente Med. Ctr., 1976–81. **Educ.:** Univ. of CA, Los Angeles, 1969–73, BA (Fr.), 1974–76, MLS; Med. LA, 1976–81, Cert. **Orgs.:** Med. Lib. Grp. of South. CA and AZ: Schol. Com. (Ch., 1979); Nsltr. Com. (1980–81); Exch. Com. (1978–79, 1980–81) Nsltr. Ed. (1981–82); Salary Srvy. Com. Med. LA. **Activities:** 12; 15, 17, 39; 80 **Addr.:** PSRMLS Consulting & Training Section, University of California Los Angeles Biomedical Library Center for the Health Sciences, Los Angeles, CA 90024.

Graham, Heather F. (S. 14, 1943, Belfast, North Ireland) Area Libn., E. Kildonan-Transcona, Winnipeg Pub. Lib., 1979–, Branch Libn., 1979; Asst. Libn., Transcona Pub. Lib., 1965–79. **Educ.:** Univ. of MB, 1961–65, BA (Gen. Arts); Univ. of AB, 1972–73, BLS. **Orgs.:** Can. LA. MB LA: Pres. (1977–78); 1st VP (1976–77); Treas. (1974–76). MB Sch. Lib. and Visual Assn. MB Assn. of Lib. Techs. **Pubns.:** "Canadian Children's Illustrators; A...Selected Bibliography," *MB LA Bltn.* (S. 1979). **Activities:** 9; 16, 17, 39 **Addr.:** Winnipeg Public Library, Henderson Branch, 1044 Henderson Hwy., Winnipeg, MB R2K 2M5 Canada.

Graham, Lee O. (My. 28, 1943, Frederick, OK) Libn., N.E. HS, Oklahoma City Pub. Schs., 1981–; Libn., N.W. Classen HS, 1980–81, Media Eval. Consult., 1978–80, Libn., Classen HS, 1971–78, Libn., Eisenhower Jr. HS, 1966–69. **Educ.:** Ctrl. State Univ., 1961–66, BA (Eng.), 1966–73, MEd (Sch. Admin.); Univ. of OK, 1973–76, MLSc (LS). **Orgs.:** ALA: Nom. Com.; IFRT (1979–80); AASL (1977–). Oklahoma City Assn. of Sch. Libns.: Pres. (1977–78). OK LA: Int. Frdm. Com. Co-Ch. (1980–81), Ch. (1979–80, 1981–82); Lib. Dev. Com. (1977–81). OK Dept. of Libs.: Netwk. Adv. Cncl. (1980–81). OK Fed. of Tchrs.: 1st VP (1980–). Labor Cncl. of Ctrl. OK, AFL-CIO: Sergeant-at-Arms (1979–81); Pub. Empls. Com. (Ch., 1980–81). **Activities:** 10; 15, 32, 48; 63, 74, 78 **Addr.:** 4132 N.W. 61st Terr., Oklahoma City, OK 73112.

Graham, Peter S. (My. 26, 1939, NY, NY) Head, Bk. Acq., Columbia Univ. Libs., 1981–; Syst. Ofcr., IN Univ. Libs., 1979–81; Sr. Syst. Anal., Resrch. Libs. Grp., 1975–78; Instr. (Eng.), York Coll. (PA), 1973–75; Mgr., Syst. Prog., Comp. Ctr., Columbia Univ., 1966–69. **Educ.:** Columbia Univ., 1964–69, BA (Eng.), 1969–70, MA (Eng.); Oxford Univ. (UK) 1970–72, BPhil (Eng.); IN Univ. 1979–80, MLS. **Orgs.:** ALA: RTSD, Tech. Srvs. Costs Com. (1977–81), Ch. (1980–81); ACRL; LITA, *Jnl. of Lib. Autom* (Ed. Bd., 1978–). Bibl. Socty. Amer. Prtg. Hist. Assn. Renaissance Socty. of Amer. **Honors:** Phi Beta Kappa; Beta Phi Mu. **Pubns.:** "Terminals and Printers for Library Use," *Jnl. of Lib. Autom.* (D. 1977). **Activities:** 1; 34, 46, 49-Syst. Dev.; 55, 56, 57 **Addr.:** 202 Butler, Columbia University, New York, NY 10027.

Graham, T. Garth (F. 27, 1942, Ottawa, ON) Deputy Mnstr., Dept. of Lib. and Info. Resrcs., Gvt. of Yukon, 1980–, Dir., 1977–80, Dir., Lib. Srvs. and Arch. Branch, 1967–77. **Educ.:** Univ. of West. ON, 1964, BA; Univ. of BC, 1967, BLS; Univ. of Toronto, 1974, MLS. **Orgs.:** Can. LA. AK LA. Natl. Lib. Adv. Bd.: Bibl. and Comms. Netwk. Com. Bibl. Database for North. Can.: Mgt. Com. Various other orgs. Assn. of Can. Univs. for North. Std. **Pubns.:** "Libraries in the Yukon," *Canadian Libraries in their Changing Environment* (1977); "Yukon Settlements: A String of Beads Along a Road Pattern," *Human Settlements and Renewable Resources North of Sixty* (1979); "Yukon," *Canadian Annual Review of Politics and Public Affairs, 1979* (1980). **Addr.:** Library and Information Resources, Government of Yukon, Whitehorse YT Y1A 2C6 Canada.

Grainger, William Keith (D. 17, 1922, Paso Robles, CA) Coll. Libn., Pasadena City Coll., 1959–; Asst. Libn., Bakersfield Coll., 1954–59; Libn., Compton HS, 1953–54; Asst. Libn., Compton Coll., 1947–53. **Educ.:** Bakersfield Jr. Coll., 1940–42, AA (Eng.); Univ. of CA, Berkeley, 1942–43, BA (Gen. Curric.), 1946–47, BLS, Univ. of South CA, 1958, MLS. **Orgs.:** ALA. CA

PROFESSIONAL ACTIVITIES: Institutions: 1. Acad. lib.; 2. Arch.; 3. Assn.; 4. Fed./Gvt. lib.; 5. Inst. lib.; 6. Mfr./Suppl.; 7. Milit. lib.; 8. Musm.; 9. Pub. lib.; 10. Sch. lib.; 11. Sch. of lib. sci.; 12. Spec. lib.; 13. State lib.; 14. (other). **Functions/Activities:** 15. Acq./Col. dev.; 16. Adult srvs.; 17. Admin.; 18. Apprais.; 19. Archit./Bldgs.; 20. Cat./Class.; 21. Chld. srvs.; 22. Circ.; 23. Cons./Pres.; 24. Consult.; 25. Cont. ed.; 26. Educ. lib. sci.; 27. Ext. srvs.; 28. Fund/Grants; 29. Gvt. pubs.; 30. Indx./Abs.; 31. Instr. lib. use; 32. Media srvs.; 33. Micro.; 34. Netwks./Coop.; 35. Persnl.; 36. PR; 37. Publshg.; 38. Recs. mgt.; 39. Ref. srvs.; 40. Repro.; 41. Resrch.; 42. Review.; 43. Secur.; 44. Serials; 45. Spec. col.; 46. Tech. srvs.; 47. Trustees/Bds.; 48. YA srvs.; 49. (other).

LA. Natl. Educ. Assn. CA Tchrs. Assn. Amer. Assn. for Higher Educ. Assn. of CA Cmnty. Coll. Admin. **Honors:** Beta Phi Mu. **Activities:** 1; 17 **Addr.:** Pasadena City College Library, 1570 E. Colorado Blvd., Pasadena, CA 91106.

Grainger-Inselburg, Shirley J. (S. 5, 1937, London, Eng.) Dir., Dana Biomed. Lib., Dartmouth Coll., 1971–; Dir. for Tech. Srvs., Univ. of CT Hlth. Sci. Lib., 1970–71; Leverhulme Resrch. Asst., Royal Socty. of Med., London, 1968–70; Deputy Libn., Chief Asst. Libn., Assistant Librarian, Assistant to the Librarian King's Coll. Hosp., Med. Sch., Univ. of London, 1960–68; Visit. Libn., Univ. of Miami Sch. of Med., 1965–67. **Educ.:** Northwest. Polytech. Sch. of Libnshp., London, 1959–60, ALA (Libnshp.), 1960–61, Advnc. std.; Additional courses. **Orgs.:** Med. LA: Rcrt. Com. (1965–67). NH Hosp. Libn. Assn.: Pres. (1971–73) N. Atl. Hlth. Sci. Libs.: Ch. (1975–76). New Eng. Reg. Med. LA Grp.: Ch. (1972–73). **Pubns.:** "Development of hospital library services in New England: New Hampshire," *NERMLS News*, (F. 1972); "Horse and Buggy Medicine," *Dartmouth Med. Sch. Alum. Mag.* (Fall 1979); Various speeches, other articles. **Activities:** 1, 12, 14; 17, 32, 45; 58, 65, 80 **Addr.:** Dana Biomedical Library, Dartmouth College, Hanover, NH 03755.

Gralapp, Marcelee Gayl (N. 2, 1931, Winfield, KS) Lib., Arts Dir., Boulder Pub. Lib., 1966–; Visit. Fac., KS State Tchr.'s Coll., 1965; Visit. Fac., Univ. of Denver, 1965–67; Assoc. Libn., Boulder Pub. Lib., 1959–66; Chld. Libn., Laurence Pub. Lib., 1957–59; Chld. Libn., Hutchison Pub. Lib., 1952–57. **Educ.:** KS State Tchrs. Coll., 1952, BA (LS); Univ. of Denver, 1963, MA (LS); CO Univ., 1966, Audit., Mncpl. Gvt. and Admin. **Orgs.:** ALA. CO LA: Legis. Com. Mt. Plains LA. State Plan for Lib. Dev.: Ch. Pub. Lib. Guidelines Com. Mem. Boulder Ctr. for Visual Arts: Bd. City Staff Liaison (Boulder) Arts Adv. Com. Boulder Asm. on the Arts and Hum.: Bd. Various other orgs. **Honors:** CO, Gvr.'s Awd. for Arts, 1981; Delta Kappa Gamma. **Activities:** 9; 17, 32, 34; 55, 56, 93 **Addr.:** Boulder Public Library, 1000 Canyon Blvd., P.O. Drawer H, Boulder, CO 80306.

Gramka, Billie Jean (Jl. 18, 1951, Mobile, AL) Cat. Libn., Biomed. Lib., Univ. of S. AL, 1978–; Sci., Tech. Ref. Libn., Cook Lib., Univ. of South. MS, 1977–78; Asst. Libn., Faulkner State Jr. Coll., 1975–77. **Educ.:** Auburn Univ., 1969–73, BS (Geo.); FL State Univ., 1974–75, MS (LS); Med. LA, 1980, Cert. **Orgs.:** Med. LA: South. Reg. Grp. AL LA. OCLC Hlth. Sci. User Grp. AL Hlth. Libs. Assn. **Honors** Beta Phi Mu, 1975. **Activities:** 1, 12; 20, 46; 58, 80 **Addr.:** Biomedical Library, 312 Library Bldg., University of South Alabama, Mobile, AL 36688.

Grams, Theodore Carl William (S. 29, 1918, Portland, OR) Prof., Head, Prcs. Srvs., Lib., Portland State Univ., 1952–; Libn., U.S. Bonneville Power Admin., 1951–52, Acct., 1948–50, Land Title Asst., 1939–45. **Educ.:** Univ. of WA, 1945–47, BA (Econ.); Harvard Law Sch., 1947–48; Univ. of South. CA, 1950–51, MS (LS). **Orgs.:** ASIS: OR Chap., Bd. of Gvrs. (1977–78). SLA: OR Chap., Com. on Progs. (1979). Portland Area Spec. Libns.: Pres. (1954–55). ALA. Hub-Cmnty. Action Prog.: Bd. of Dirs. (1967–70). Proj. ABLE (A Better Living for Elderly): Bd. of Dirs. (1972–74). Area Agency on Aging: Adv. Cncl. (1974–75). City-Cnty. Comsn. on Aging of Portland and Multnomah Cnty. OR: Treas.; Comsn. (1975–80). **Honors:** Beta Phi Mu, 1953; HEW Fellow, 1968–69. **Pubns.:** Jt. ed., *Special Collections in Libraries of the Pacific Northwest* (1979); jt. ed., *Information Roundup; Proceedings, 4th Mid-Year Meeting, American Society for Information Science* (1975); *Textbook Classification: Class LT* (1968); *Allocation of Joint Costs of Multiple-Purpose Projects* (1952). **Activities:** 1; 17, 46; 56, 57, 75 **Addr.:** 1000 S.W. Vista Ave., Portland, OR 97205.

Grandbois, Mildred May (My. 26, 1906, Minneapolis, MN) Dir. of Mktg. and Customer Srv., Cumulative Index to Nursing & Allied Health Literature, 1978–, Ed., 1956–77; Med. Libn., Glendale Adventist Med. Ctr., 1956–68; Libn., Voice of Prophecy & Ed., VOP News, 1952–55; Secy. to Dir., Spanish Voice of Prophecy Broadcast, 1944–51; Tchr., private sch. and coll., 1929–43. **Educ.:** Andrews Univ., 1925–29, BA (Romance Lang.); Sorbonne, Paris, 1930; Univ. of MI, 1933, MA (Lang.); Univ. of South. CA, 1953, MS (LS). **Orgs.:** ALA. SLA. Med. LA. Med. Lib. Grp. of South. CA. **Activities:** 1, 12; 17, 24, 30; 58, 80, 95-Nursing & Allied Health. **Addr.:** 1570 E Chevy Chase, Glendale, CA 91206.

Grande, Paula G. (Mr. 1, 1949, New York, NY) Libn., Coopers and Lybrand, Actuarial and Benefits Consult. Div., 1978–; Asst. Libn., William M. Mercer, Inc., 1975–78; Claims Rep., Soc. Secur. Admin., 1970–72. **Educ.:** Queens Coll., CUNY, 1966–70, BA (Fr.), 1972–74, MLS. **Orgs.:** SLA: Insr. Div., Treas. (1978–81), Secy. (1981–82). **Pubns.:** Indxr., *Insurance Periodicals Index* (1977–); contrib., *Insurance and Employee Benefits Literature* (1979–). **Activities:** 12; 30, 39, 41; 59, 76, 78 **Addr.:** Coopers & Lybrand, 1251 Ave. of the Americas, New York, NY 10020.

Grande, Sally (Sara) (Jy. 26, 1951, Louisville, KY) Systems Consult., INFOMART, 1981–, Coord., Educ. and Trng., 1980–81, ON Territory Mktg., 1978–79, PQ and East. Can. Territory, 1977–78, Cust. Srvs. Mktg., Action Desk, 1975–76. **Educ.:** Marymount Manhattan, 1968–72, BA (Phil.) Drexel Univ. 1974–75, MSc (LS). **Orgs.:** Can. Assn. for Info. Sci.: Toronto Chap., Chief Exec. (1977–78); Exec. Bd. (1979–). SLA. **Activities:** 6; 26, 36, 49-Database Dev.; 75 **Addr.:** INFOMART, Village by the Grange, 122 St. Patrick St., Toronto, ON M5T 2X8 Canada.

Granese, Mary A. (Ap. 28, 1914, Wakefield, MA) Docum. Libn., MIT Lincoln Lab., 1951–; Chem., Melrose Labs., 1943–51; Libn., Burroughs-Wellcome Co., 1942–43; Lit. Searcher, General Chemical Co., 1939–42; Asst. Libn., US Rubber Co., 1937–38. **Educ.:** Radcliffe Coll., 1932–36, AB (Chem.); Columbia Univ., 1939–43. **Orgs.:** SLA. ASIS. Radcliffe Club of Boston. MIT Women's League. **Activities:** 1, 12; 15, 17, 20; 52, 88, 91 **Addr.:** 26 Franklin St., Wakefield, MA 01880.

Granger, Mary Smith (Ja. 8, 1909, Elmira, NY) Retired; st Dir., ON Coop. Lib. Syst., Wayne Cnty. Lib. Syst., 1961–64; 1st Libn., Westbury Cmnty. Ctr. Lib., 1947–56; Libn., Oyster Bay Pub. Lib., 1944–47; Libn., Brooklyn Pub. Lib., 1932–43. **Educ.:** Elmira Coll., 1926–30, BA (Latin, Math.); Columbia Univ., 1937, BS (Pub. Libs.), 1948, MA (Pub. Libs.). **Orgs.:** ALA. NY LA. The Granger Homestead Socty. Inc.: VP (1979). Newark Wayne Cmnty. Hosp. Auxillary: Holly Twig (1979). **Activities:** 9; 17; 50 **Addr.:** 422 E. Ave., Newark, NY 14513.

Granick, Lois W. (Mr. 5, 1932, Weatherford, OK) Dir., Psy. Abs. Info. Srv., Amer. Psy. Assn., 1979–; Exec. Ed., Psy. Abs., 1974–; Consult., Info. Sci., 1973–74; Dir., Autocode, Autocomp, Inc., 1972–73. **Educ.:** Univ. of NM, 1949–51 (Msc.). **Orgs.:** Natl. Fed. of Abs. & Indexing Srvs.: Bd. of Dir. (1977–); Pres.-Elect (1979); Pres. (1980). Assn. of Info. and Dissemination Ctrs.: Plng. Com. (1980–81). ASIS. Documtn. Abs., Inc.: Bd. of Dir. (1978–80). Intl. Cncl. of Sci. Unions: Abs. Bd. (1974–). **Activities:** 6, 12; 17, 30, 37; 56, 57, 93 **Addr.:** 5414 Center St., Chevy Chase, MD 20815.

Granito, Charles E. (N. 14, 1937, Brooklyn, NY) Pres., Chem. Info. Mgt. Inc., 1975–; Consult., C. G. Assocs., 1973–75; Dir., Chem. Info. Systs., Inst. for Sci. Info., 1969–72. **Educ.:** Univ. of Miami, 1960, BS (Chem.), 1962, MS (Organic Chem.). **Orgs.:** ASIS. Amer. Chem. Socty.: Div. of Chem. Info., Ch., Secy. Drug Info. Assn. Chem. Notation Assn.: Pres. (1969). Inst. for Info. Scis. (London). SLA. AAAS. NY Acad. of Sci. **Pubns.:** "Wiswesser Chemical Line Notation - An Introduction," *The Merck Index* (1976); "Substructure Search and Correlation in the Management of Chemical Information," *Naturwissenschaften* (1973); various other articles. **Activities:** 12; 17, 24; 75 **Addr.:** Chemical Information Management Inc., P.O. Box 2740, Cherry Hill, NJ 08034.

Grant, Frances Louise (Ja. 22, 1937, Lordsburg, NM) Assoc. Prof., CA State Univ., Chico, 1979–; Info. Prcs., Lockheed Missiles & Space Co., 1976–79; Resrch. Info. Anal., 1975–76; Info. Retrieval Syst. Asst., 1972–75; Mtls. & Prcs. Anal., 1972; Resrch. Asst., Amer. Justice Inst., 1971–72. **Educ.:** San Jose State Coll., 1971, BA (Soclgy.); San Jose State Univ., 1974, MA (Educ.); Univ. of South. CA, 1977– (Educ.); CA Tch. Cred., 1972; CA Cmnty. Coll. Cred., 1979. **Orgs.:** ASIS. Assn. for Comp. Mach: Educ. Spec. Interest Grp. AECT. SLA. **Pubns.:** "Calm of Paperwork," *Datamation* (O. 1979). **Addr.:** Center for Information & Communication Studies, California State University, Chico, Chico, CA 95926.

Grant, George E. (S. 17, 1941, Portsmouth, VA) Grp. Supvsr.–Lib. Netwk. Support, Bell Labs., Holmdel, NJ, 1977–; Grp. Supvsr.–Tech. Lib., Bell Labs., Columbus, OH, 1969–77; Ref. Libn., Bell Labs., Greensboro, NC, 1967–69. **Educ.:** Wagner Coll., 1962–66, BA (Eng.); Rutgers Univ., 1966–67, MLS. **Orgs.:** ASIS: Ctrl. OH Chap. (Ch., 1974). SLA. **Pubns.:** "Columbus Technical Library," *Planning The Special Library* (1972). **Activities:** 12; 17, 37, 46; 56, 91, 93 **Addr.:** Bell Laboratories Rm. 2G110, Crawfords Corner Rd., Holmdel, NJ 07733.

Grant, Joan (O. 19, 1945, Milwaukee, WI) Dir. of Col. Mgt., New York Univ., 1980–; Dir., Fogelman Lib., New Sch. for Soc. Resrch., 1978–79; Head, Acq. Dept., Univ. of Louisville Lib., 1973–78; Instr., Univ. of KY Sch. of LS, 1976–77. **Educ.:** Univ of MI, 1963–66, BA (Pol. Sci.), 1967–69, AMLS; Univ of Louisville, 1970–80 MA (Higher Educ). **Orgs.:** ALA: ACRL/Col. Lib. Sect. Prog. Plng. 1980 Conf. (1979–80). NY LA. **Pubns.:** Jt. auth., "Vendor Performance Evaluation," *Jnl. of Acad. Libnshp.* (N. 1978). **Activities:** 1; 15, 17, 27; 63 **Addr.:** 224 E. 7th St. Apt. 6, New York, NY 10009.

Grant, Juanita G. (Jl. 25, 1930, Princeton, WV) Dir. of Lib., Averett Coll., 1967–; Dir. of Lib., Judson Coll., 1964–67; Asst. Libn., Carson-Newman Coll., 1960–64; Asst. Libn., Nichols State Coll., 1958–59; Libn., Spec. Srvs., U.S. Army, Germany and France, 1956–58; Libn., Roanoke Rapids HS, 1953–56. **Educ.:** Concord Coll., 1950–53, BS (Eng.); Univ. of NC, 1953–55, BS (LS); Johns Hopkins Univ., 1969–70, MLA (Liberal Arts); various crs. **Orgs.:** ALA. VA LA. SELA. Danville Pub. Lib.: Lib. Adv. Com. (1978–). VA Cncl. Higher Educ.: Lib. Adv. Com. (1976–78). Amer. Hist. Assn. Danville Hist. Assn. Danville Musm. of Fine Arts and Hist.: Lib. Com. (Ch., 1975–). Various other orgs. **Honors:** Phi Delta Kappa. **Activities:** 1; 15, 17 **Addr.:** Blount Library, Averett College, 344 W. Main St., Danville, VA 24541.

Grant, Mildred Bricker (Ag. 26, 1915, Kansas City, MO) Ref. Libn., Asst. Prof., Hunt Meml. Lib., Fort Valley State Coll., 1974–; Spec. Libn., Ofc. of Indus. Dev. Std., Univ. of MO, 1969–70; Self-empl., Co-owner, Co-oper., Nestland Poultry Farm, 1953–69; Mgt. Asst., Fed. Pub. Housing, Reg. VII, Seattle, 1946–48. **Educ.:** Univ. of MO, 1934–40, BS, PA (Pol. Sci.), 1969–71, MA (LS). **Orgs.:** ALA: RASD; ACRL. SE LA. GA LA: Educ. for Libnshp. Com. (1979–81). Frdm. to Read Fndn. **Honors:** Sigma Delta Pi, 1939; Beta Gamma Sigma, 1940; Beta Phi Mu, 1971. **Pubns.:** Cmplr., *Indexes to the Competitor* (1978); jt. auth., "Some Notes on the Capital 'N'," *Phylon* (D. 1975); "Ballad of the Black Mother," poem *Crisis* (Jl. 1976). **Activities:** 1; 31, 39; 92 **Addr.:** 501 Forrest Dr., Fort Valley, GA 31030.

Grantier, John R. (Jy. 30, 1937, Utica, NY) VP, Tech. Srvs., Coutts Lib. Srvs., 1969–; Head, Acq., Serials Dept., York Univ., 1966–69; Asst. Chief, Acq. Dept., Washington Univ., 1964–66. **Educ.:** Coll. of William and Mary, 1955–59 AB (Hist.); Case West. Resrv. Univ., 1961–62, MSLS. **Orgs.:** ALA: **Activities:** 6 **Addr.:** 736 Cayuga St., Lewiston, NY 14092.

Grasmick, Charles Richard (Rocky Ford, CO) Dir., Joplin Pub. Lib., 1981–; Campus Libn., Metro. Tech. Cmnty. Coll., 1974–81; Dir., Lawton Pub. Lib., 1973–74; Dir., Eau Claire Pub. Lib., 1969–73; Dir., Plains and Peaks Pub. Lib., 1968–69. **Educ.:** CO State Univ., 1964–67, BA (Hist.); Univ. of Denver, 1967–68, MA (LS). **Orgs.:** ALA. NE LA: Treas. (1980–81). Omaha Metro. Libns. Assn.: Pres. (1981). Indianhead Lib. Dist., WI: Pres. (1972). Rotary: Educ. Com. (1969–). Toastmasters: Pres. (1960–74). NE Consistory. **Honors:** Phi Alpha Theta, 1966. **Activities:** 1, 9; 16, 17, 19; 59, 63, 75 **Addr.:** 2442 E. 12th St., Joplin, MO 64801.

Gration, Selby U. (Mr. 17, 1930, Summit, NJ) Dir., Libs., SUNY, Coll. at Cortland, 1968–; Dir. of Lib., RI Coll., 1962–68, Asst. Libn., 1961–62; Libn., Barrington Coll., 1958–61. **Educ.:** Barrington Coll., 1948–52, BA (Biblical Std.); Gordon Dvnty. Sch., 1952–55, BD (Theo.); Simmons Coll., 1958–59, MS (LS). **Orgs.:** ALA. SUNY Libns. Assn. S. Ctrl. Resrch. Lib. Cncl.: Trustee (1969). Volun. Fam. Couns. Srv.: Bd. of Dirs. (Pres., 1980). **Pubns.:** "Reference Bibliographers in the College Library," *Coll. & Resrch. Libs.* (Ja., 1974). **Activities:** 1; 17, 26, 35; 90 **Addr.:** Memorial Library, SUNY, College at Cortland, P.O. Box 2000, Cortland, NY 13045.

Grattan, Robert, III (Ag. 21, 1940, Ashland, VA) Dir., Lrng. Resrcs. Ctr., J. Sargeant Reynolds Cmnty. Coll., Parham Campus, 1981–, Assoc. Prof., 1976–; Instr., Eng., Fr., VA Cmwlth. Univ., 1968–73; Lang. Lab. Dir., Coll. of Petr. and Minerals, Dhahran, Saudi Arabia, 1965–67; Instr., Eng., Berlitz Lang. Sch., Versailles, France, 1960–61. **Educ.:** Randolph Macon Coll., 1957–62, BA (Eng., Fr.); Univ. of Richmond, 1964–65, MA (Eng.); Univ. of TX, Austin, 1974–75, MLS (Acad. Lib.). **Orgs.:** ALA. VA LA. Radio Amat. Satellite Corp. Amat. Radio Resrch. and Dev. Corp. **Activities:** 1; 15, 34, 49-Online srvs.; 55, 56, 75 **Addr.:** 107 Howard St., Ashland, VA 23005.

Gratz, Delbert L. (Mr. 5, 1920, Richland Twp., Allen Cnty., OH) Libn., Bluffton Coll., 1950–. **Educ.:** Bluffton Coll., 1938–42, AB (Hist.); Ohio State Univ., 1942, 1945, MA (Hist.); Univ. Bern, (Switzerland) 1948–50 Dr.Phil. (Hist.); Univ. of MI, 1951–52, AMLS. **Orgs.:** OH Coll. Assn.: Lib. Sect. (Ch., 1964). Christian Libns. Flwshp.: Bd. (1975–); Ch. (1981); Prog. Ch. (1980). Swiss Cmnty. Hist. Socty.: Bd. (1953–); Pres. (1974–79). **Honors:** Pro Helvetia, Zurich, Switzerland, Flwshp.; Bapt. Theo. Semy., Rüschlikon ZH, Switzerland, Visit. Schol., 1964–65, 1971–72, 1979; Fullbright Resrch Grant, 1971–72. **Pubns.:** *The Bernese Anabaptists* (1953); "Mennonite Genealogical Research," *World Conf. on Recs.* (1969). **Activities:** 1, 2; 17, 41, 45; 69, 70, 90 **Addr.:** R 2, Box 89, 8990 Augsburger Rd., Bluffton, OH 45817.

Graubart, Marilyn S. (Ag. 2, 1936, Kansas City, MO) Mgr. Lib. Srvs., Diamond Shamrock Corp., 1980–; Supvsr., Corp. Lib., Diamond Shamrock Corp., 1978–80, Tech. Info. Anal., SCM Corp., 1975–78. **Educ.:** Barnard Coll., 1954–58, BA (Psy.); Case Western Reserve Univ., 1973–75, MLS. **Orgs.:** SLA. ASIS: Treas., North. OH Chap. (1979–80). Hadassah. **Activities:** 12; 17, 36, 39; 51, 59, 64 **Addr.:** Diamond Shamrock Corporation, Corporate Library, PO Box 348, Painesville, OH 44077.

Graves, Ann R. (O. 7, 1925, Orange, TX) Ref. Libn., TX State Lib., 1964–; Libn., Tulane Univ., 1964. **Educ.:** Univ. of TX, 1942–45, BA (Eng.); LA State Univ., 1963–64, MLS. **Orgs.:** ALA. TX LA. SLA. SWLA. **Addr.:** Texas State Library, 1201 Brazos, P.O. Box 12927 Capitol Station, Austin, TX 78711.

Graves, Dan Wesley (Mr. 12, 1920, Mt. Hope, KS) Dir., Libs., Clarion State Coll., 1965–; Assoc. Dir., Franklin and Marshall Coll., 1962–65; Chief Acq. Libn., Univ. of MI Law Lib., 1961–62, Biblgphr., Head, Gift and Exch., 1954–61; Head, Circ. Dept., Univ. of Wichita, 1953–54; Catlgr., Univ. of KS, 1951–53; Photoreprodct. Lab. Libn., Serials Asst., Univ. of IL, 1949–51; Head Libn., Willamette Univ., 1944–49. **Educ.:** Univ. of Denver,

Special Subjects/Services: 50. Adult educ.; 51. Advert./Mktg.; 52. Aerosp.; 53. Agric.; 54. Area std.; 55. Arts/Hum.; 56. Autom.; 57. Bibl./Prtg.; 58. Bio. sci.; 59. Bus./Fin.; 60. Chem.; 61. Copyrt.; 62. Documtn.; 63. Educ.; 64. Engin.; 65. Env.; 66. Eth. grps.; 67. Film; 68. Food/Nutr.; 69. Geneal.; 70. Geo.; 71. Geol.; 72. Handcpd.; 73. Hist.; 74. Int. frdm.; 75. Info. sci.; 76. Insr.; 77. Law; 78. Legis.; 79. Math./Comp. sci.; 80. Med.; 81. Metals; 82. Nat. resrcs.; 83. Newsp.; 84. Nuc. sci.; 85. Oral hist.; 86. Petr./Energy; 87. Pharm.; 88. Phys./Astr./Math.; 89. Readg.; 90. Relig.; 91. Sci./Tech.; 92. Soc. sci.; 93. Telecom.; 94. Transp.; 95. (other).

1939–40, BA (LS); Univ. of MI, 1954–58, MA (Amer. Hist.); PA State Univ., 1972, Cert. (Mgt. Trng.). **Orgs.:** OR LA: Legis. and Lib. Stans. Com. (1946–47); Cert. Com. (1947–48); various coms. PA LA: NW Chap. (Ch., 1966–68); Coll. and Resrch. Libs. Div. (Ch., 1969–70); various coms., ofcs. SLA. ACRL.: Tri-State Chap., VP (1968–69), Pres. (1969–70). Various other orgs. Reg. Cncl. for Intl. Educ.: Com. on Lib. Resrcs. (1969–70). **Pubns.:** Cmplr., coll. and univ. stats., *Coll. and Resrch. Libs.* (1949–55). **Activities:** 1, 2; 15, 17, 19; 74, 85, 92 **Addr.:** Box 627, Clarion, PA 16214.

Graves, Deborah Ann (F. 20, 1948, Dexter, ME) Branch Libn., Coventry Vlg. Lib., Cleveland Hts.–Univ. Hts. Pub. Lib., 1979–; Chld. Libn., Brooklyn Lib., Cuyahoga Cnty. Pub. Lib., 1978–79, Chld. Libn., Maple Hts. Reg. Lib., 1977–78; Chld. Libn., Lewiston Pub. Lib., 1974–77; Chld. Libn., Auburn Pub. Lib., 1972–73. **Educ.:** Univ. of ME, 1966–70, BA (Amer. Hist.); Case West. Rsv. Univ., 1973–74, MSLS. **Orgs.:** ALA: ALSC, Com. for Sel. of Chlds. Bks. from Other Cultures (1979–). OH LA. CSLA. Cleveland Wholistic Hlth. Ctr. **Honors:** Beta Phi Mu. **Pubns.:** Jt. ed., *Ctrl. ME Lib. Dist. Chld. Srvs. Nsltr.* (1975–77). **Activities:** 9; 16, 17, 21; 54, 89 **Addr.:** 3075 Meadowbrook, Cleveland Heights, OH 44118.

Graves, Frances M. (S. 7, 1919, Sacramento, CA) Libn., Luther Burbank Sr. HS, 1975–; Coord., Lib. Cred. Prog., CA State Univ., Sacramento, 1976–; Libn., Various CA Jr. HS, 1969–75; Catlgr., Hartford Semy. Fndn. Lib., and Librarian, Kit Carson Jr. HS, 1956–69; Catlgr., St. Mary's Coll. Lib., 1955–56. **Educ.:** Sacramento Jr. Coll., 1937–39 SS (Math Educ.); St. Mary of the Wasatch, 1939–40, Sacramento State Coll., 1950–51, BA (Eng, Math); Rosary Coll., 1954–55, MA (LS). **Orgs.:** ALA. Cath. LA. CA LA. SLA. Other orgs. Natl. Educ. Assn. CA Tchrs. Assn. Sacramento Tchrs. Assn. **Activities:** 10, 11; 26, 48; 57 **Addr.:** 1016 Dolores Way, Sacramento, CA 95816.

Graves, Fred Hill (F. 11, 1914, Rockdale, TX) Visit. Lectr., Sch. of Lib. Srv., Columbia Univ., Sums., 1979–81. Head Libn., Cooper Un. for the Advnc. of Sci. and Art, 1960–79; Asst. Prof., Grad. Sch. of Lib. Srv., Rutgers Univ., 1954–60; Asst. to Dean, Sch. of Lib. Srv., Columbia Univ., 1952–54; Chief Libn., TX A and I Univ., 1945–51. **Educ.:** SW TX State Univ., 1931–35, BA (Eng., Educ.); Columbia Univ., 1951–54, MS (Lib. Srv.), 1973, Advnc. Cert. (Libnshp.). **Orgs.:** ALA. NY LA. NY Tech. Srvs. Libns.: Pres. (1964–65). **Activities:** 1, 11; 17, 20, 26; 57 **Addr.:** 360 E. 55 St., New York, NY 10022.

Graves, Karen J. (N. 23, 1936, Watonga, OK) Asst. Prof., Head, Educ. Srvs., Univ. of TN Ctr. for the Hlth. Scis. Lib., 1977–; Libn., City of Memphis Hosp., 1974–77; Clinical Libn., Dept. of Med., Univ. of TN, 1973–74. **Educ.:** Univ. of OK, 1955–59, BS (Med. Tech.); Univ. of MD, 1970–71, MSLS. Univ. of TN, Postgrad. Trng. for Hlth. Sci. Libns., 1972–73, Cert.; Med. LA., 1975–, Cert. **Orgs.:** Med. LA: Hlth. Sci. Lib. Technicians Com. (1979–82); Ch. (1981–82). South. Reg. Grp., Cont. Educ. Com. (Ch., 1980–82). TN LA: Nom. Com. (1978–79). TN Hlth. Sci. LA: Bylaws Com. (1977). Assn. of Memphis Area Hlth. Sci. Libs. (Ch., 1976–77). AAUP. **Honors:** Beta Phi Mu; Lambda Tau. **Pubns.:** Jt.-auth., "Hospital library consortia: Vital Component for Hospital-Wide Education. *Jnl. Cont. Educ. Nursing* (Sept.-Oct. 1978); Jt. auth., "Introduction to the University of Tennessee Center for the Health Sciences Library" (Prog. Lesson for PLATO) (1978); ed., *Periodicals Holdings List* (Assn. of Memphis Area *Hlth. Sci.* Libs.) (1976). **Activities:** 1, 12; 17, 31, 32; 58, 60, 80 **Addr.:** UTCHS Library, 800 Madison Ave., Memphis, TN 38163.

Graves, Lessie Louise (H.) (N. 8, 1908, Halls Hill, VA) Retired, 1976–; Tchr., Sch. of LS, NC Ctrl. Univ., 1971–76; Jr. HS Libn., Ctrl. Jr. HS, Cleveland, 1964–71; Asst. Head, Hough Branch, Cleveland Pub. Lib., 1960–64, Per. Readg. Rm. Libn., 1956–60; Libn., Tchr., Campbell St. HS, 1949–56; Libn., Tchr., GA Bapt. Coll., 1944–49; Ref. Libn., Morgan Coll., 1940–42; various other prof. positions. **Educ.:** WV State, 1927–30, AB (Eng.); McGill Univ., 1932, Cert. (LS); Univ. of IL, 1934, BS (LS), 1952, MS (LS), 1969, Cert. Adv. Std. **Orgs.:** ALA: AASL. AECT. SLA. L'Un. Intl. de la Marionette. Puppeteers of Amer. Amer. Gld. of Organists. **Honors:** Beta Phi Mu, 1970. **Pubns.:** Jt. auth., *Bibliography of the Biological Sciences* (1962). **Activities:** 1, 10; 15, 17, 22 **Addr.:** 2029 Braddish Ave., Baltimore, MD 21216.

Graves, Sid F., Jr. (My. 11, 1946, Memphis, TN) Dir., Carnegie Pub. Lib. of Clarksdale and Coahoma Cnty., MS, 1976–; Dir., S. MS Reg. Lib., 1973–76; Instr., Eng., Univ. of MS, 1969–72; Visit. Lectr., Univ. of AL Lib. Sch., 1979. **Educ.:** Millsaps Coll., 1964–68, BA (Eng.); Univ. of MS, 1969–71, MA (Eng.); Peabody Coll., 1972–73, MLS. **Orgs.:** MS LA: Pub. Lib. Sect. (Ch., 1975–76). SELA: NW Reg. (Ch., 1977–78); Bicent. Com. Coahoma Cnty. Cham. of Cmrce. **Honors:** MS LA, Past Pres. Awd., 1976; MS LA, Outstan. Achvmt. Awd., 1980. **Pubns.:** Ed., *Report of a Planning Conference for Solar Technology Information Transfer* (1978). **Addr.:** P.O. Box 280, Clarksdale, MS 38614.

Gray, Beverly Ann (Ag. 3, 1940, Boston, MA) Head, African Sect., African and Mid. East. Div., Lib. of Congs., 1972–; Head, African Std. Lib., Boston Univ., 1967–72; Africana Biblgphr., Harvard Coll. Lib., 1965–67. **Educ.:** Simmons Coll., 1958–62, BA (Econ.); Columbia Univ., 1962–64, MA (Pol. and Gvt.), 1962–64, Cert. (African Std.), 1964–65, MLS. **Orgs.:** ALA: ACRL/Asian and African Sect., Nom. Com. (1980). African Std. Assn.: Arch.-Libs. Com., Ex-officio Mem. Lib. of Congs.: Task Frc. on Goals, Org., and Plng. Mid.-Atl. Reg. Africanist Assn. African-Amer. Women's Assn. **Pubns.:** *Uganda; Subject Guide to Official Publications* (1971); *Nigerian Petroleum Industry; A Guide* (1978); "A Selected Directory of Sources Specializing in Current Africana," *A Current Bibl. on African Affairs* (Je.–Jl. 1970); "Area Studies and the African Field," *Frgn. Acq. Nsltr.* (Spr. 1971); various sps., reviews. **Activities:** 4; 15, 39; 57 **Addr.:** Rm. 1040-C, Adams Bldg., Library of Congress, Washington, DC 20540.

Gray, Dorothy A. (N. 11, 1926, Milwaukee, WI) Head, Ref. Dept., Univ. of Louisville Ctrl. Lib., 1976–; Prin. Ref. Libn., Head, Ref. Dept., Northwest. Univ. Lib., 1969–74; Ref. Libn., OH State Univ. Libs., 1963–69; Jr. Catlgr., Wellesley Coll. Lib., 1953–56. **Educ.:** Univ. of WI, 1944–48, BA (Zlgy.), 1948–49, MLS. **Orgs.:** ALA: ACRL. KY LA. **Pubns.:** Jt. auth., *Science and Engineering Literature* (1976); contrib., *Sources of Information in the Social Sciences* (1974); contrib., *Serial Bibliographies in the Humanities and Social Sciences* (1969). **Activities:** 1; 30, 31, 39; 58, 93 **Addr.:** 5406 Nimitz Ct., Louisville, KY 40214.

Gray, Dorothy Pollet (D. 17, 1945, Billings, MT) Educ. Liaison Ofcr., Lib. of Congs., 1977–, Ref. Spec., 1975–77, Ref. Libn., Bibl., 1972–75. **Educ.:** Univ. of Rochester, Univ. of CO, 1964–69, BA (Msc., Soclgy.); Syracuse Univ., Sch. of Info. Std., 1971–72, MSLS. **Orgs.:** ALA: Intl. Rel. RT (Mem. Ch. 1978–); Nsltr. Ed. (1980–). SLA: Mgt. Div. (Audit., 1978–79). **Pubns.:** Jt. ed., *Sign Systems for Libraries* (1979); "You Can Get There From Here," *Wilson Lib. Bltn.* (F. 1976); jt. auth., "Talking Books and the Local Library," *Lib. Jnl.* (S. 15, 1974); jt. auth., "Those Missing Readers: The Visually and Physically Handicapped," *Cath. Lib. World* (My.–Je. 1975). **Activities:** 4, 9; 16, 36, 39; 72, 92, 93 **Addr.:** 3656 Gunston Rd., Alexandria, VA 22302.

Gray, E. Maurine (S. 2, 1943, Galveston, TX) Lib. Dir., Beaumont Pub. Lib. Syst., 1966–; Part-time Prof., Sch. of LS, Sam Houston State Univ., 1976; Jr. HS Libn., Caddo Par. Sch. Bd., Shreveport, LA, 1966. **Educ.:** N.E. LA State Univ., 1962–66, BA (Eng. Educ.); N. TX. State Univ., 1968–69, MLS. **Orgs.:** ALA: JMRT (Secy.–Treas., 1972–73). SWLA: Exec. Bd. (1974–75). TX. Mncpl. Libns. Assn. VP (1970–71); Pres. (1971–72). TX LA: Pres. (1974–75); Legis. Com. (Ch., 1978–81). Various other orgs. Beaumont Civic Opera. Phi Mu Fraternity, Beaumont Alum.: Pres. (1978–80). Altrusa Intl. Amer. Cancer Socty. Various other orgs. **Honors:** Sch. of Lib. and Info. Srv., N. TX State Univ., Disting. Alum., 1980; Beta Phi Mu. **Pubns.:** *Beaumont Libraries–Then and Now* (1976); *History of Medicine in Beaumont, Texas* (1969). **Activities:** 9; 17; 78 **Addr.:** 485 Longmeadow Dr., Beaumont, TX 77707.

Gray, Helen Rodd (Ag. 4, 1920, Windsor, ON Can.) Sr. Libn. for Hist. and Pol. Sci., Simon Fraser Univ. Lib., 1969–; Gen. Ref. Libn., Simon Fraser Univ. Lib., 1966–68. Gen. Libn., Catlgr., New Westminster Pub. Lib. 1962–65. **Educ.:** Univ. of Toronto, 1939–43 BA (Hons.) (Eng.); Fletcher Sch. of Intl. Law & Dipl., Tufts Univ., 1944–45, AM. Univ. BC, 1961–62, BLS. **Orgs.:** Can. LA BC LA. Can. Hist. Assn. Can. Bibl. Assn. **Activities:** 1; 15, 31, 39 **Addr.:** 2610 Colwood Dr., North Vancouver, BC V7R 2R1 Canada.

Gray, Jane E. (Ja. 5, 1928, Oak Park, IL) Dir., Lib. Dev., State Lib. of IA, 1977–; Interlib. Coop. Consult., DuPage Lib. Syst., 1975–77; Head Libn., Batavia Pub. Lib., 1973–75; Head Libn., Judson Coll., 1969–73; Libn., Acq., North. IL Univ., 1968–69; Head of Adult Srvs., Pawtucket Pub. Lib., 1967–68. **Educ.:** Elmhurst Coll., 1945–49, BA (Eng.); Univ. of RI, 1967–68, MLS. **Orgs.:** ALA: ASLA, Plng. Com. (1979–81). IA LA: Guidelines Com. (1980–81). **Activities:** 13; 17, 24, 34 **Addr.:** 224 1/2 Sixth St., West Des Moines, IA 50265.

Gray, Karen S. (D. 12, 1943, Decatur, IL) Asst. Exec. Dir., Gt. River Lib. Syst., 1972–; Consult., Cumberland Trail Lib. Syst., 1970–72; Jr. HS Libn., Rochelle, IL, 1968–70. **Educ.:** East. IL Univ., 1963–67, BS in Ed (Soc. Sci.); Univ. of IL, 1967–68, MS (LS). **Orgs.:** IL LA: Pub. Lib. Sect. Bd. of Dir. (1975–76). ALA. State Lib. of IL: Adv. Com. on Srv. to the Blind & Physically Handcpd. (1976–). WHCOLIS: Prog. Ch. (1978). **Pubns.:** "Looking into the Public Libraries of the People's Republic of China," *IL Libs.* (S. 1980); "Serving the Special Student," *IL Libs.* (S. 1978). **Activities:** 14-Syst. HQ; 15, 17, 24; 50, 72 **Addr.:** Great River Library System, 515 York, Quincy, IL 62301.

Gray, Phyllis A. (Ja. 2, 1926, Boston, MA) Lib. Dir., Miami Beach Pub. Lib., 1978–, Asst. Lib. Dir., Lib., 1976–78; Admin. Libn., Miami-Dade Pub. Lib. Syst., 1969–76; Lib. Dir., Cmrce. Pub. Lib., 1961–68. **Educ.:** Barry Coll., 1943–47, PhB (Hist.); Cath. Univ., 1948–50, MS (LS); Barry Coll., 1976–79, MBA. **Orgs.:** ALA. FL. LA: Treas. (1976–78). Dade Cnty. LA: Pres. (1957–58). Women in Gvt. Srv. Barry Coll. Alum. Assn.: Pres. (1972); Dir. (1980). Amer. Socty. for Pub. Admin. **Activities:** 9; 17, 25, 31; 55 **Addr.:** 54 Park Dr. #6, Bal Harbour, FL 33154.

Gray, Randall J. (S. 30, 1949, Santa Monica, CA) Libn., Adams, Duque and Hazeltine, 1976–; Asst. Libn., O'Melveny and Myers, 1974–76. **Educ.:** CA State Univ., Northridge, 1967–72, BA (Eng.); Univ. of CA, Los Angeles, 1972–74, MLS, 1974, Cert. (Law Libnshp.); AALL, 1980, Cert. **Orgs.:** South. CA Assn. of Law Libs.: VP/Pres.-Elect (1981–82); Pres. (1982–83); Consult. Com. (Ch., 1981); Spec. Com. on Exch. of Dupls. (Ch., 1976). AALL: Pvt. Law Libs. Spec. Interest Sect., Pubns. Com. (Ch., 1980). SLA: Lib. Mgt. Div. ASIS. Various other orgs. Amer. Mgt. Assn. **Pubns.:** "Information Systems for Litigation Support," *The Private Law–New Information Functions* (1981); "Effective Administration: Better Decisions through Information," *The Legal Admin.* (N. 1981); "Off the Shelf," *Los Angeles Daily Jnl.* (Ja. 23, 1974); contrib., "Internship: A University of California and Los Angeles County Law Library Joint Venture," *Law Lib. Jnl.* (Ag. 1974). **Activities:** 12; 17; 77 **Addr.:** Adams, Duque & Hazeltine, 523 W. Sixth St., Los Angeles, CA 90014.

Grayson, Bessie Rivers Assoc. Prof., Sch. of Lib. Media, AL A and M Univ., 1981–, Asst. Prof., 1969–81; Asst. Catlgr., Asst. Prof. of LS, AL State Univ., 1966–69; Asst. Libn., Asst. Prof. of LS, Philander Smith Coll., 1963–66; Tchr., McIntypre Elem. Sch., 1959–63; Libn., Hale Cnty. Trng. Sch., 1952–59; Prin., Tchr., Sidney Chapel Jr. HS, 1947–52; Tchr., John Essex Jr. HS, 1945–47; Asst. Prin., Tchr. Myrtlewood Jr. HS, 1944–45. **Educ.:** AL State Univ., 1950, BS (Educ.), 1954, MEd., Cert. (Soc. Std., Eng.); AL Univ., 1965, MSLS; George Peabody Coll., PhD Cand. **Orgs.:** AL LA. AL Instr. Media Assn.: Outrch. Com. (Ch., 1969). AL Educ. Assn.: Mem. Com. (Ch., 1969). AAUW. Cncl. of Tchrs. Educ. Various other orgs. **Honors:** Phi Delta Kappa; Outstan. Educ. Awd., 1973; NAACP, Outstan. Srv. Awd., 1976; Oakwood Church, Outstan. Srv. Awd., 1978. **Pubns.:** "A Black Librarian's Challenge to the Publisher's World," *What Black Librarians are Saying* (1972); "National Library Week: A Focus on Education," *AL Libns.* (Ap. 1969); "Comprehensive Requirements. ALA Schools," *Jnl. of Educ. for Libnshp.* (Fall 1977). **Addr.:** Alabama Agricultural and Mechanical University, School of Library Media, Normal, AL 35762.

Graziano, Eugene E. (Ag. 10, 1927, Pittsburgh, PA) Asst. Univ. Libn. - Srvs., Univ. of CA, Santa Barbara, 1965–; Resrch. Info. Spec., Lockheed Missles & Space Co., 1961–65; Chief Sci. Libn., South. IL Univ., Carbondale, 1959–61, Asst. Sci. Libn., 1958–59; Head Libn., Emporia (KS) Pub. Lib., 1957–58; Head Libn., Parsons (KS) Pub. Lib., 1956–57; Head Libn., Duncan (OK) Pub. Lib., 1956–56. **Educ.:** Univ. of OK, 1948–51, BA (Phil.), 1954–56, MA (Phil.); Carnegie Lib. Sch., Pittsburgh, 1953–54 (LS); KS State Tchrs. Coll., Emporia, 1958–58 (LS); San Jose State Coll., 1963–65, Tchg. Cred.; Univ. of MD, 1969, Cert. (Lib. Mgt.). **Orgs.:** Total Interlib. Exch.: Pres. (1969). Amer. Civl Liberties Un. Great Books Discuss. Grps. **Pubns.:** *Language - Operational - Gestalt Awareness* (1975); various articles. **Activities:** 1, 9; 16, 17, 19, 41; 75, 91 **Addr.:** 6815 Pasado Rd., Goleta, CA 93017.

Grazier, Margaret Hayes (D. 19, 1916, Denver, CO) Prof., Div. of LS, Wayne State Univ., 1965–; Head Libn., Groves HS, Birmingham (MI), 1961–65, Head Libn., Derby Jr. HS, 1956–61; Asst. Prof., Grad. Lib. Sch., Univ. of Chicago, 1954–56; Asst. Prof., Coll. of Libnshp., Univ. of Denver, 1948–52, Chief, Pub. Srvs. Div., 1946–48; Lib. Consult., W. K. Kellogg Fndn., Battle Creek, 1945–46; Libn., Lake Forest HS, 1942–45; various other lib. positions. **Educ.:** Univ. of North. CO, 1934–37, BA (LS); Univ. of Denver, 1937–38, Dip. (LS); Univ. of Chicago, 1952–54 (LS). **Orgs.:** ALA: Cncl. (1960–64, 1972–74); Com. on Resrch. (1970–76); AASL (2nd VP, 1970–71), Media Prog. Dev. Unit (Head, 1973–76), Afflt. Asm. (1980–81). AALS: Mem. Com. (Ch., 1979–81). MI Assn. for Media in Educ.: Pres. (1981). MI LA. Various other orgs. Assn. for Supvsn. and Curric. Dev. AAUP. Amer. Cvl. Liberties Un. Common Cause. **Pubns.:** "Preparation of the School Librarian," *Education for Librarianship: Design of Curriculum for Library Schools* (1971); *High School Library in Transition* (1967); "The Curriculum Consultant Role of the School Library Media Specialist," *Lib. Trends* (Fall 1979); "The Elementary and Secondary Education Act, Title II," *Lib. Trends* (Jl. 1975); "A Role for the Media Specialist in the Curriculum Development Process," *Sch. Media Qtly.* (Spr. 1976). **Activities:** 10, 11; 21, 41, 48; 63, 74, 89 **Addr.:** 18300 Parkside, Detroit, MI 48221.

Greaves, F. Landon (Ja. 19, 1938, Ferriday LA) Lib. Dir., Southeast. LA Univ., 1969–; Head, Sci. and Tech. Div., 1966–69. **Educ.:** LA Tech. Univ., 1956–61, BS (Bus. Admin.); LA State Univ., 1964–66, MS (LS); FL State Univ., 1971–73, PhD, (LS). **Orgs.:** ALA. LLA: Pres. (1980–81). SWLA. Phi Kappa Phi. Kiwanis: Pres. (1980–81). **Activities:** 1; 17 **Addr.:** Box 302 University Station, Hammond, LA 70402.

Grebey, Betty H. (Mr. 28, 1933, Sonestown, PA) Lib. Coord., Downingtown Area Sch. Dist., 1965–; Lectr. (LS), Villanova Univ., 1965–; Libn., Coatesville HS, 1959–65; Libn., Nurnberg (Germ.) Elem. Sch., 1958–59, Tchr., 1957–58; Libn., West Chester State Coll., 1956–57. **Educ.:** Kutztown State Tchrs. Coll., 1953–57, BS (LS); Drexel Univ., 1960–63, MSLS, 1975 (Lib. Admin.). **Orgs.:** ALA: AASL–RTSD, Cat. of Chld. Mtrls., 1974–; ERT, Stans. Com. (1980–). PA LA: Com. on Dues. Structure (Ch., 1976–77). PA Sch. Libns. Assn.: Exhibits Com. (Ch.,

PROFESSIONAL ACTIVITIES: Institutions: 1. Acad. lib.; 2. Arch.; 3. Assn.; 4. Fed./Gvt. lib.; 5. Inst. lib.; 6. Mfr./Suppl.; 7. Milit. lib.; 8. Musm.; 9. Pub. lib.; 10. Sch. lib.; 11. Sch. of lib. sci.; 12. Spec. lib.; 13. State lib.; 14. (other). **Functions/Activities:** 15. Acq./Col. dev.; 16. Adult srvs.; 17. Admin.; 18. Apprais.; 19. Archit./Bldgs.; 20. Cat./Class.; 21. Chld. srvs.; 22. Circ.; 23. Cons./Pres.; 24. Consult.; 25. Cont. ed.; 26. Educ. lib. sci.; 27. Ext. srvs.; 28. Fund/Grants; 29. Gvt. pubs.; 30. Indx./Abs.; 31. Instr. lib. use; 32. Media srvs.; 33. Micro.; 34. Netwks./Coop.; 35. Persnl.; 36. PR; 37. Publshg.; 38. Recs. mgt.; 39. Ref. srvs.; 40. Repro.; 41. Resrch.; 42. Review.; 43. Secur.; 44. Serials; 45. Spec. col.; 46. Tech. srvs.; 47. Trustees/Bds.; 48. YA srvs.; 49. (other).

1975–). Lrng. Resrcs. Assn: Lib. Interest Grp. (Pres., 1978–79). Various other coms. and ofcs. Aircraft Owners and Pilots Assn; Kappa Delta Pi. **Pubns.:** Centralized Processing for School Libraries (Bibliography avail. from AASL) (1970, 1972). **Activities:** 10, 11; 20, 26, 48 **Addr.:** Downingtown Area School District, 445 Manor Ave., Downingtown, PA 19335.

Grebis, Edward Joseph (Jy. 26, 1939, Windber, PA) Dist. Media Supvsr., Northfield Pub. Schs., 1978–; Media Generalist, Northfield Jr. HS, 1968–78; Sci. Instr., Cathedral HS (St. Cloud, MN), 1967–68. **Educ.:** Catholic Univ., 1960–62 BA, (Phil.) Mankato State Univ., 1976, MS (Instr. Media and Tech.). **Orgs.:** MN Educ. Media Org.: Nsltr. Ed. (1970–76). Ofc. of Pub. Libs. and Interlib. Coop.: Adv. Cncl. (1977–81). **Activities:** 10, 13; 17, 32, 40; 63, 67, 93 **Addr.:** Northfield Public Schools, 1400 S. Division St., Northfield, MN 55057.

Grech, Anthony Paul (Jl. 16, 1930, New York, NY) Libn., Assn. of the Bar of the City of New York, 1967–, Ref. Libn., 1965–67, Asst. Ref. Libn., 1958–65. **Educ.:** Manhattan Coll., 1949–52, BBA (Bus. Admin.); Columbia Univ., 1960–61, MLS; AALL, 1961, Cert. Law Libn. **Orgs.:** AALL: Exec. Bd. (1980–83); *Law Lib. Jnl.* (1962–63); Pubns., Vice-Ch. (1974–75), Ch. (1975–76); Frgn. and Compar. Law (1971–73); various ofcs. Law LA of Grt. NY: Bd. of Dirs. (1960–61, 1962–63); Pres. (1967–68); various ofcs. Assn. of Law Libs. of Upstate NY: Bd. of Dirs. (1977–78). ALA. Various other orgs. The Supreme Ct. Hist. Socty. Natl. Micro. Assn. Bibl. Socty. of Amer. Bibl. Socty. of Univ. of VA. **Honors:** AALL, Joseph L. Andrews Bibl. Awd., 1967; Beta Phi Mu. **Pubns.:** Jt. cmplr., "Selected Bibliography on Human Rights," *Human Rights Reader* (1979); "Malta," *Constitutions of the Countries of the World* (1971); jt. cmplr., "A Bibliography of Selected Materials on International Financing and Investment," *International Financing and Investment* (1964); jt. cmplr., "Bibliographies," *Lawyer's Guide to International Business Transactions* (1963); jt. cmplr., *Reference Use of Official Documents* (1962); various bibls., articles. **Activities:** 12; 17, 33, 45; 57, 77 **Addr.:** Association of the Bar of the City of New York, 42 W. 44 St., New York, NY 10036.

Greear, Yvonne (Etnyre) (Je. 19, 1921, Austin, TX) Asst. Dir. for Pub. Srvs., Univ. of TX, El Paso, 1972–; Dir., Ref. Srvs., TX West. Coll., 1964–71; Visit. Lect., Grad. Sch. LS, Univ. of TX, Austin, 1968, 69; Ref. Libn., Spec. Srvs. Lib., Fort Bliss, TX, 1963–64; Libn., Resrch. & Dev. Lib., El Paso Nat. Gas Co., 1957–62. **Educ.:** Univ. of TX, 1944–48, BFA (Radio Brdcasting); 1957–62, MLS. **Orgs.:** TX LA: Exec. Bd., Rep-at-Large (1974–77); various coms. SLA: TX Chap. Pres. (1961–62); various coms. Border Reg. LA: Pres. (1975–76); various coms. Amer. Name Socty. El Paso Cnty. Hist. Socty.: Bd. of Dir. (1973–75). **Honors:** Border Reg. LA: Libn. of the Yr., 1968. **Pubns.:** "The Name of the Game: Street Names," *S. Ctrl. Names Inst.* (1977); "Antelope, Buffalo, Deer & Tiger in the Street," *S. Ctrl. Names Inst.* (1974); "At the Corner of Pecan & Congress," *S. Ctrl. Names Inst.* (1973); "The Search for John Claude White, C.I.E." *NOVA* (Jan/Mar. 1973). **Activities:** 1; 17, 22, 39; 55, 70, 82 **Addr.:** Library, Univ. of Texas at El Paso, El Paso, TX 79968.

Green, Arminda Ruth Cole (Ap. 30, 1922, Bogue Chitto, MS) Instr., Lib. Tech., Macomb Cnty. Cmnty. Coll., 1971–; Libn., Bloomfield Hills Schs.; Ref. Libn., Samford Univ., 1949–50; Asst. Prof., Wayland Coll., 1948; Tchr., Canton HS, 1943–45. **Educ.:** MS Coll., 1939–43, BA (Eng.); LA State Univ., 1949 (LS); Wayne State Univ., 1969–70, MSLS; Univ. of MI, 1964, Sec. Cert.; State of MI, 1977, Cert. **Orgs.:** ALA. Macomb Cnty. Cmnty. Coll.: Lib. Tech. Adv. Com. (1972–79). MI Lib. Media Tech. Grp. Metro. Detroit CLENE. Amer. Angus Assn. U.S. Air Frc. Acad. Parents Assn. Kirk in the Hills Presby. Church. **Activities:** 1, 10; 31, 39; 77 **Addr.:** 5934 Blandford Rd., Bloomfield Hills, MI 48013.

Green, Charlotte (N. 15, 1924, New York, NY) Info. Supvsr., The Halcon SD Grp. Inc., 1975–; Asst. Sci. Libn., Queens Coll., 1972–74. **Educ.:** Queens Coll., 1942–45, BS (Chem.); Long Island Univ., 1966–69, MS (LS). **Orgs.:** SLA. ASIS. **Pubns.:** "Nonprofessional Library Workers in the Science Libraries in Industry," *Spec. Libs.* (O. 1970); jt. auth., "Composition of the Deoxypentose Nucleic Acids of Four Genera of Sea Urchin," *Jnl. of Bio. Chem.* (1952); jt. auth., "Composition of the Deoxyribonucleic Acid of Salmon Sperm," *Jnl. of Bio. Chem.* (1951); jt. auth., "Human Deoxypentose Nucleic Acids - Composition of Human Deoxypentose Nucleic Acids," *Nature* (1950); jt. auth., "Nucleotide Composition of Pentose Nucleic Acids," *Jnl. of Bio. Chem.* (1950); various articles in chem. **Activities:** 12; 17, 30, 39; 60, 64 **Addr.:** Halcon SD Group Inc., 2 Park Ave., New York, NY 10016.

Green, David Edward (Je. 22, 1937, Adrian, MI) Assoc. Libn. for Col. Mgt., Grad. Theo. Un. Lib., 1977–, Actg. Dir., 1976–77, Head, Access Srvs., 1970–76, Ref. Libn., 1969–70. **Educ.:** Harvard Coll., 1960, BA (Ling.); Church Dvnty. Sch. of the Pac., 1963, BD; Univ. of CA, Berkeley, 1969, MLS. **Orgs.:** ATLA: Bd. Dirs. (1970–72); Statistician (1975–). Univ. of CA Lib. Sch. Alum. Assn.: Bd. of Dirs. (1980–). Presby. LA: Pres. (1967–68). **Honors:** Beta Phi Mu. **Pubns.:** Various transls. **Activities:** 1; 15, 17, 39; 90 **Addr.:** Graduate Theological Union Library, 2400 Ridge Rd., Berkeley, CA 94709.

Green, Douglas A. (F. 17, 1925, Gilmer, TX) Doct. Cand., E. TX State Univ., 1978–; 1980, EdD (Ed. Tech.); Dir. of Libs., Ambassador Coll., 1976–78; Dir. of Lib., Laredo State Univ., 1975–76; Ch. of Lrng. Resrcs., Richland Cmnty. Coll., 1973–75; Dir., of Lrng. Resrcs., Bee Cnty. Coll., 1968–73; Chief Biblgphr., Univ. of AR, 1963–67; Sch. Libn., TX schs., 1951–63. **Educ.:** N. TX State Univ., 1949–50, BA (LS); E. TX State Univ., 1950–51, MA (Hist.); LA State Univ., 1967–68, MS (LS); E. TX State Univ., 1978–80, EdD (Educ. Tech.). **Orgs.:** ALA. TX LA. **Pubns.:** "An Index to Collected Essays on Educational Media and Technology" (1981). **Activities:** 1; 15, 17, 46; 56, 63, 93 **Addr.:** 1210 Monroe St., Commerce, TX 75428.

Green, E. Alice (S. 20, 1916, KS) City Libn., Amarillo Pub. Lib., 1947–; Ast. Libn., 1943–47; Gen. Asst., 1941–43; Gen. Asst., TX State Lib., 1939–41; Libn., TX Military Coll., 1938–39. **Educ.:** OK Univ., 1937–38 (LS). **Orgs.:** TX LA: Ch., Lib. Dev. Com. (1945–46; 59–60); Ch., Pub. Lib. Div. (1952–53; 73–74); Ch., Local Arrange. 1970 Conf. TX Mncpl. Libns. Assn.: Secy./Treas. (1966–67). SWLA. ALA. Altrusa Club. Cham. of Cmrce. TX Mncpl. Leag.: Dir. (1977–78; 1978–79). **Honors:** TX LA: TX Libn. of the Yr., 1977. **Activities:** 9; 17 **Addr.:** 3704 Clearwell, Amarillo, TX 79109.

Green, James N. (D. 18, 1947, Los Angeles, CA) Rare Bk. Biblgphr., Spec. Col., Regenstein Lib., Univ. of Chicago, 1981–; Cur. of Rare Books, New Eng. Hist. Geneal. Socty., 1976–81. **Educ.:** Oberlin Coll., 1965–69, AB (Eng.); Yale Univ., 1969–72, MPhil (Eng.); Columbia Univ., 1975–76, MS (LS). **Orgs.:** Bibl. Socty. of Amer. Amer. Prtg. Hist. Assn. ALA: ACRL/Mss., Local arrange., Boston Conf. (1980); Cont. Ed. Com. (1979–82). Athenaeum Grp. **Activities:** 14-Resrch. Lib.; 15, 20, 45; 57, 69, 95-History. **Addr.:** Special Collections, Regenstein Library, University of Chicago, Chicago, IL 60637.

Green, Judith Gibson (Ap. 19, 1941, New York, NY) Head, Cat. and Class., Can. Inst. for Sci. and Tech. Info., 1980–, Libn., Systs. Dev., 1979–80, Catlgr., Head, Tech. Rpts. Sect., 1975–78; Asst. Libn., Educ. Lib., Univ. of NB, 1972–74. **Educ.:** Carleton Coll., 1958–62, BA; Univ. of West. ON, 1970–71, MLS. **Orgs.:** Can. LA. Can. Assn. Info. Sci. **Honors:** Phi Beta Kappa, 1962. **Activities:** 12; 17, 20, 46; 75, 88, 91 **Addr.:** 3 Davidson Dr., Ottawa, ON K1J 6L7 Canada.

Green, Julian Wiley (O. 13, 1946, Rochester, NY) Head Libn., Geol. Sci. Lib., Harvard Univ., 1979–; Geol. Sci. Libn., Univ. of NC, 1978–79; Map Spec., Dartmouth Coll. Lib., 1975–77. **Educ.:** Dartmouth Coll., 1964–68, BA (Soclgy.), 1973–77, MA (Geol.); Univ. of NC, 1977–78, MS (LS). **Orgs.:** ALA. SLA. Geosci. Info. Socty. Geol. Socty. of Amer. Assn. of Geosci. for Intl. Dev. **Honors:** Univ. of Rochester, Dept. of Geol., Golden Brachiopod, 1973; Harvard Univ., Bryant Flwshp., 1981. **Activities:** 11 **Addr.:** 43 Floral St., Newton Highlands, MA 02161.

Green, Kerry (F. 26, 1951, Toledo, OH) Admin., Electronic Arts Intermix, 1980–; Dir. of AV Srvs., William Paterson Coll. of NJ, 1977–80; Libn., NY Botanical Garden, 1974–77; Actg. Dir., Lib., NY Zoological Socty., 1974–75. **Educ.:** Miami Univ., OH, 1969–73, BA (Eng.); Queens Coll., 1973–75, MLS; NY Univ., 1975–79, MA (Film); New Sch. for Soc. Resrch., 1979–80 (Langs.). **Orgs.:** EFLA. Film Lib. Info. Cncl. NY Metro. Ref. and Referral Agency: Media Libns. RT. AECT. Amer. Film Inst. Natl. AV Assn. Amer. Film Fest. NY: Juror (1979–80). **Pubns.:** "Services for the Handicapped - What the A-V Professional Can Do," *Media and Methods* (Mr. 1980); "What's New in Italian Animation: The World of Bruno Bozzetto," *Film Lib. Qtly.* (1980); "The Special Pleasures of Going to the Movies in Rome," *NY Times* (Ja. 11, 1981). **Activities:** 1; 17, 24, 32; 55, 67 66. **Addr.:** 821 Rte. 9W, Nyack, NY 10960.

Green, Nancy W. (Je. 14, 1947, Bemidji, MN) Libn., Amer. Numismatic Assn., 1979–. **Educ.:** Univ. of MN, 1965–69, BA (Soclgy.); Univ. of Denver, 1975, MA (LS). **Orgs.:** SLA. CO LA: Spec. Col. RT. **Honors:** Beta Phi Mu, 1975. **Pubns.:** "Bookmarks," clmn. *The Numismatist.* **Activities:** 12; 17, 20, 45; 55, 92, 95-Numismatics. **Addr.:** American Numismatic Association, P.O. Box 2366, Colorado Springs, CO 80901.

Green, Rosa F. (Fb. 16, 1910, Carlisle, KY) Head Libn., Valley HS (Louisville, KY), 1954– Libn., Parkland Jr HS (Louisville, KY), 1934–43. **Educ.:** KY Wesleyan Coll.; Univ. of KY, 1928–32 (Eng.); Univ. of KY, 1955–59, (LS). **Orgs.:** ALA. KY LA. Louisville Lib. Clb. Jefferson Cnty. Sch. Media Assn. Nazareth Coll. Alum. Assn. **Honors:** KY LA, Outstand. Media Libn., 1975. **Pubns.:** "A tribute," *KY LA Bltn.* (1962). **Activities:** 10; 32, 48; 63 **Addr.:** 827 Melford Ave., Louisville, KY 40217.

Green, Sue Bailey (My. 28, 1915, Camilla, GA) Retired, 1978–; Educ. Media Spec., Newark Pub. Schs., 1961–78; Resrch. Assoc., Sch. of Educ., Rutgers Univ., 1960–61; Sch. Libn., Montclair, NJ, 1956–57; Chld. Libn., East Orange Pub. Lib., 1952–56. **Educ.:** Asbury Coll., 1933–36, AB (Eng., Fr.); Emory Univ., 1937–39, MA (Eng. Lit.); Columbia Univ., 1951–53, MS; NJ Dept. of Educ., Certs. (Educ. Media Spec., Tchr., Prof. Libn.). **Orgs.:** ALA. Educ. Media Assn. of NJ. Assn. of Sch. Libns.: Pres. (1962). Natl. Retired Tchrs. Assn. Various other orgs. NJ Sch. Media Assn.: Lib. Dev. Com. (1970–75). Newark Pub. Schs.: Various of CS., coms. Natl. Educ. Assn. **Pubns.:** *Using Libraries as an Educational Resource and Tool* (1961); *Where to Find It* (1975). **Activities:** 9, 10; 17, 21, 32; 56, 63, 66 **Addr.:** P.O. Box 234, Cranford, NJ 07016.

Greenaway, Emerson (My. 25, 1906, Springfield, MA) Dir. Emeritus, Free Lib. of Philadelphia, 1969–; Dir., 1951–69; Dir., Enoch Pratt Free Lib., (Baltimore), 1945–51; Libn., Worcester (MA) Free Lib., 1940–45; Libn., Pub. Lib. (Fitchburg, MA), 1937–40; Asst. Libn., Pub. Lib. (Hartford, CT), 1930–37. Visit. Lectr., Kent State Univ., Drexel Univ., Columbia Univ., Simmons Coll. **Educ.:** MA Agr. Coll., 1923–27, BSc (Educ.); Univ. of NC, 1934–35 AB (LS). **Orgs.:** ALA: Pres. (1957–58), VP (1956–57), 2d VP (1945–46); Legis. Com. (Ch., 1959–65); Intl. Rel. Com. (1965–70). Mem., Amer. Del. of Libns. to the Soviet Union, 1961. Amer. Philosophical Socty.: Lib. Com. (1968–). Natl. Bk. Com.: Ch. (1962). Tracy Meml. Lib.: Trustee (1979–). ALA, Lippincott Awd., 1955, Centennial Cit., 1976. PA LA, Disting. Srv. Awd., 1960. Drexel Grad. Lib. Sch., Disting. Achvmt. Awd., 1965; several honorary doct. **Pubns.:** Various pubns. **Activities:** 9, 13; 16, 17, 24; 50, 63, 78 **Addr.:** North Pleasant St., New London, NH 03257.

Greenberg, Bette R. (Jl. 22, 1937, Chicago, IL) Head Libn., Ref. Dept., Yale Med. Lib., 1965–, Catlgr., 1965–67. **Educ.:** Univ. of MO, 1955–57; Univ. of Pittsburgh, 1957–59, BA (Psy.), 1964–65, MLS. **Pubns.:** *How to Find Out in Psychiatry* (1978); *Index to Scientific Writings in Creativity* (1974–75); "Evaluation of a Clinical Medical Librarian Program at the Yale Medical Library," *Bltn. Med. LA* (1978); "MEDLINE Demand Profiles: An Analysis of Requests for Clinical and Research Information," *Bltn. Med. LA* (1977); "William Shakespeare: Medico-Psychological and Psychoanalytic Studies on His Life and Works: A Bibliography," *Intl. Review of Psychoanalysis* (1974). **Activities:** 1; 17, 39, 49-Comp. srch. srv.; 80, 95-Psyt. **Addr.:** Reference Department, Yale Medical Library, 333 Cedar St., New Haven, CT 06510.

Greenberg, Emil (Ap. 7, 1910, New York, NY) Consult., Coll. Org. and Plng., Prof. Emeritus, CUNY, 1976–; Prof. of Eng., Boro. of Manhattan Cmnty. Coll., 1974–76, Chief Libn., 1971–74, 1964–68, Ch., Lib. Tech. Prog., 1968–74; Dir., AV Srvs., City Univ. Div. of Tchr. Educ., 1948–64; Supvsr., Radio-TV Ctr., Brooklyn Coll., 1949–52; Ref. Asst., Chief Circ. Libn., Brooklyn Coll. Lib., 1946–48; various coll. lectr. and coll./univ. libs. positions, 1932–. **Educ.:** NY Univ., 1932, BA, cum laude (Phil.), 1936, MA (Eng.); Columbia Univ., 1941, BLS hons. **Orgs.:** ALA: ACRL/Jr. Coll. Lib. Sect., Stans. and Criteria Com. (1966). Cncl. on Lib. Tech. AAUP. Various cmnty. and coll. orgs., coms. and actv. **Honors:** Boro. of Manhattan Cmnty. Coll., Decennial Srv. Medal, 1973; Educ. Facilities Labs., Grant for Srvy. of New Media Installations, 1965. **Pubns.:** Jt. auth., *Reading for Pleasure Series 1-4* (1949–51); *Social Science References* (1940); *Guide to Research Sources in Education* (1941); *Guide to Research Sources in English and American Literature* (1942); ed., cmplr. of various other bks. **Activities:** 1, 11; 16, 17, 24; 50, 51, 93 **Addr.:** 3099 Brighton 6 St., Brooklyn, NY 11235.

Greenberg, Esther (My. 25, 1923, New York, NY) Coord. of Lib. Systs., Case West. Rsv. Univ., 1974–, Head Catlgr. and Asst. Head of Tech. Srvs., 1968–74; Head Catlgr., Case Inst. of Tech., 1965–68, Actg. Head of Cat., 1964–65, Asst. Catlgr., 1963–64. **Educ.:** NY Univ., 1940–44, BS (Home Econ. and Bio.); West. Rsv. Univ., 1960–63, MSLS; various sems. and wkshps. **Orgs.:** ALA: Com. on Tech. Srvs. Costs (1977–); Com. on Stats. for Tech. Srvs. (1976–). various other coms., ofcs. TriState ACRL: Dir. (1973–74); Nom. Com. (Ch., 1974); Lcl. Arrange. Ch. (1973). North. OH Tech. Srvs. Libns.: Prog. Ch. (1971); Dir. (1972–73). Acad. LA of OH: Org. Com. (Ch., 1973); Exec. Bd. (1974–75). AAUP. OCLC Users Cncl.: Exec. Bd. (1978–79). NEOMAL Serials Com.: Ch. (1980–). **Honors:** Cncl. on Lib. Resrcs., Fellow, 1973; Beta Phi Mu. **Pubns.:** "Innovative Designs for Acquisitions and Cataloging Departments As a Result of Library Automation," *ERIC* (1974); "Automated Cataloging - the State of the Art," *Med. LA Bltn.* (Ja. 1976); "The Management Review and Analysis Program," *Jnl. of Acad. Libnshp.* (Ja. 1976); "OCLC - Seven Years of Library Change," *CA Libn.* (Ja. 1977); jt. auth., "Locally Distributed Access to the OCLC Data Base," *ASIS Conf. Procs.* (My. 1979). **Activities:** 1; 34, 41, 46; 56, 75 **Addr.:** Case Western Reserve University Libraries, 11161 East Blvd., Cleveland, OH 44106.

Greenberg, Lenore R. (O. 9, 1950, New York, NY) Resrch. Libn., Human Resrcs. Ctr., 1977–; Dir., Libs., NY Chiro. Coll., 1975–77; Asst. Libn., Temple Beth-El, Great Neck, NY, 1974–75. **Educ.:** Harpur Coll., SUNY, Binghamton, 1969–72, BA (Eng. Lit.); SUNY, Albany, 1973–74, MLS. **Orgs.:** ALA: ASCLA; Rehab. Info. RT, (Secy., Pres., 1979–). **Pubns.:** Ed., *Meeting the Challenges of Employment in the Rehabilitation Process* (1980); *Guess Who's Coming to Work: Annotated Bibliography of Materials on Employment of Handicapped Workers* (1981); contrib., *Magazines for Libraries* (4th ed.); "Dealing with Disabilities," *Lib. Jnl.* (D. 1, 1980–Ag. 1981); jt. ed., *Exch.* (1977–); various articles. **Activities:** 12; 15, 39, 41; 72 **Addr.:** Research Library, Human Resources Center, Albertson, NY 11507.

Special Subjects/Services: 50. Adult educ.; 51. Advert./Mktg.; 52. Aerosp.; 53. Agric.; 54. Area std.; 55. Arts/Hum.; 56. Autom.; 57. Bibl./Prtg.; 58. Bio. sci.; 59. Bus./Fin.; 60. Chem.; 61. Copyrt.; 62. Documtn.; 63. Educ.; 64. Engin.; 65. Env.; 66. Eth. grps.; 67. Film; 68. Food/Nutr.; 69. Geneal.; 70. Geo.; 71. Geol.; 72. Handcpd.; 73. Hist.; 74. Int. frdm.; 75. Info. sci.; 76. Insr.; 77. Law; 78. Legis.; 79. Math./Comp. sci.; 80. Med.; 81. Metals; 82. Nat. resrcs.; 83. Newsp.; 84. Nuc. sci.; 85. Oral hist.; 86. Petr./Energy; 87. Pharm.; 88. Phys./Astr./Math.; 89. Readg.; 90. Relig.; 91. Sci./Tech.; 92. Soc. sci.; 93. Telecom.; 94. Transp.; 95. (other).

Who's Who in Library and Information Services

Greenberg, Marilyn Werstein (O. 29, 1937, Brooklyn, NY) Fac., CA State Univ., Los Angeles, 1974–; Fac., Univ. of South. CA, 1970–74; Tchr.-Libn., Joyce Kilmer Elem. Sch., 1965–67. **Educ.:** Brooklyn Coll., 1955–60, BA (Eng.); Univ. of Chicago, 1967–69, MA (LS), 1970–81, PhD (LS). **Orgs.:** ALA. CA. Media and Lib. Educ. Assn. CA LA. **Pubns.:** Contrib., *Media and the Young Adult* (1977); Contrib., *Libraries and Young Adults,* (1979); "Desirable Outcomes of a Course in Children's Literature," *CA Libn.* (Ja. 1974); Jt. auth., "Don't Underrate Service to Children," *CA Libn.* (Ap. 1976); "A New Library Services Credential Program," *CA Sch. Libs.* (Win. 1975); Other articles. **Activities:** 10; 26; 72 **Addr.:** School of Education, California State University, Los Angeles, Los Angeles, CA 90032.

Greenberg, Stuart (O. 6, 1949, Baltimore, MD) Chief, Class. and Cat. Branch, U.S. Gvt. Prtg. Ofc., 1977–, Libn., 1976–77; Assoc. Libn., Baltimore Hebrew Coll., 1973–76. **Educ.:** Yeshiva Univ., 1967–71, BA (Soclgy., Hist.); Univ. of MD 1973–74, MLS. **Orgs.:** ALA: GODORT; FLRT. **Pubns.:** *Pub. Docums. Highlights* (Regular Clmn.). **Activities:** 4; 17, 20, 29 **Addr.:** 11612 Lockwood Dr., Silver Spring, MD 20904.

Greene, Ellin Peterson (S. 18, 1927, Elizabeth, NJ) Assoc. Prof., Dean of Students, The Univ. of Chicago, Grad. Lib. Sch., 1980–; Visit. Prof., Chld. Lit. Spec., Natl. Coll. of Educ., 1976–77; Coadj. Fac., Rutgers Univ., Grad. Sch. of Lib. and Info. Std., 1967–79; Storytel. Spec., Asst. Coord., Chld. Srvs., NY Pub. Lib., 1965–67, Chld. Spec., Bronx Boro., 1964–65, Asst. Grp. Work Spec., 1959–64; various libn. positions, Free Pub. Lib., Elizabeth, NJ, 1953–59; various positions as guest lectr. **Educ.:** Douglass Coll., 1953, AB (Soclgy., Econ.); Rutgers Univ., 1955–57, MLS (Lib. Srv.), 1976–79, EdD (Creat. Arts Educ.). **Orgs.:** Natl. Assn. For The Prsrvn. and Perpet. of Storytel.: Bd. of Dirs. ALA: ALSC, AV Com., Ch., Newbery-Caldecott Com. (1976), R and D Com. (Ch., 1981–82); various other coms. Various other orgs. Auths. Gld. AAUP. Rutgers Univ. Adv. Cncl. on Chld. Lit. Arrow Bk. Club, Natl. Ed. Bd.: Schol. Bk. Srvs. **Honors:** Psi Chi, 1953; Douglass Socty., Disting. Alum., 1981. **Pubns.:** *Story Telling: Art and Technique* (1977); *A Multi-Media Approach to Children's Literature* (1977); "Nursery Rhyme," *World Book Encyc.;* "Storytelling," *World Book Encyc.; Films for Children* (1966); various bks., sps., articles. **Activities:** 1, 9; 21, 24, 26; 55, 63 **Addr.:** The University of Chicago, Graduate Library School, 1100 E. 57th St., Chicago, IL 60637.

Greene, Gladys Y. (Moore) (Mr. 8, 1911, Brooklet, GA) Dir. of the Lib./Lrng. Resrc. Ctr., Bethune-Cookman Coll., 1980–, Chief, Readers Srvs., Ref., 1970–77, Acq., Ref. Libn., 1967–70; Libn., Itinerant, Volusia Cnty. Bd. of Pub. Instr., 1966–67; Libn., Volusia Cnty. Cmnty. Coll., 1958–1966; Ext. Libn. II, Univ. of MI, 1957–58; Libn. 1-12, St. Lucie Cnty. Bd. of Pub. Instr. (FL), 1949–1956. **Educ.:** GA Normal Coll., 1933–35, Jr. Dip.; TN State A & I Univ., 1940–1942, BS (Eng., Math.); Atlanta Univ., 1946–48, BSLS, 1951–53, MSLS; Univ. of MI, 1956–61, MA (Educ.). **Orgs.:** ALA: ACRL; RTSD; LITA. Volusia Cnty. Lib. Bd.: (Vice Ch., 1979). Phi Delta Kappa: E. Ctrl. FL Chap. (Treas., 1977–1979). Alpha Kappa Alpha Sorority. **Honors:** Phi Delta Kappa, E. Ctrl. FL, Plaque for Srv., 1979; Alpha Kappa Alpha; Volusia Cnty. Cncl., Cert. of Apprec., 1976; Dept. of Educ. (FL), Cert. of Apprec.; Alpha Kappa Alpha Sorority, Inc., Margaret Davis Bowen Awd. for Outstan. Srv. to the Cmnty. **Pubns.:** "History of the Negro Branch of the Bulloch County Library (Regional)," *GA State Tchrs. Assn. Bltn.* (1944); "A Longitudinal Study of Library Use, Harrison Rhodes Memorial Library," *Bethune-Cookman Coll. Rsrch. Bltn.* (F. 1970). **Activities:** 1, 9; 17, 32, 39 **Addr.:** 128 N. Adams St., Daytona Beach, FL 32014.

Greene, Jon S. (Jl. 22, 1942, Los Angeles, CA) Head Libn., Archit. and Urban Plng. Lib., Univ. of CA, Los Angeles, 1974–; Admin. Mgr./Prod. Ed., Academic Media Publishing Co., 1970–74; Soc. Sci. Biblgphr., Honnold Lib., Claremont Coll., 1969–70; Cat. Libn., Los Angeles Cnty. Law Lib., 1968–69; Cat. Libn., Los Angeles Cnty. Gen. Hosp. Med. Lib., 1967–68; Acq./Ref. Libn., Coll. Lib., Univ. of E. Africa, Dar es Salaam, Tanzania, 1964–66. **Educ.:** Earlham Coll., 1960–64, BA (Pol. Sci.); Univ. of South. CA, 1966–68, MSLS; Univ. of CA, Los Angeles, 1978–80, Cert. (Indus. Rel./Persnl. Mgt.). **Orgs.:** Cncl. of Plng. Libns.: (Bd., 1978–1980; Treas., 1981–1983). ARLIS/NA. SLA: South. CA Chap., (Consult. Com., 1975–1980; student chap. liaison, 1980). CA LA: Int. Frdm. Com. (1970–72). Other orgs. **Pubns.:** Ed., *Standard Education Almanac* (1970–73); Ed., *Yearbook of Higher Education* (1970–73); Jt. ed., *Directory of Scholarly Publishing and Research Opportunities* (1971); Ed., *Grantsmanship: Money and How to Get It* (1973). **Activities:** 1, 12; 17, 31, 39; 55, 92 **Addr.:** 12625 Appleton Way, Los Angeles, CA 90066.

Greene, Philip E. N., III (D. 7, 1943, New York, NY) VP, EBSCO Subscrpn. Srv., 1981–, Gen. Mgr., 1978–81, Reg. Sales Mgr., 1975–78; Reg. Sales Mgr., Unvsl. Per. Srv., 1971–75; VP, Turner Subscrpn. Agency, 1968–71. Guest Lectr., various univs., 1969–80. **Educ.:** Rutgers Univ., 1962–66, BA (Eng.); West. New Eng. Coll., 1967. **Orgs.:** NJ LA: Exhibits Com. (1979–80). ALA: ERT (1969). Penn Sch. LA. NJ Hlth. Scis. LA. Rumson Bd. of Educ. Delta Kappa Epsilon: Intl. Bd. of Dirs. and Fndrs. **Pubns.:** "The Three-Way Responsibility: Dealer - Publisher - Library," *Management Problems in Serials Work* (1974); various sps. **Activities:** 1, 5; 24; 59, 75, 78 **Addr.:** EBSCO Subscription Services, EBSCO Bldg., Red Bank, NJ 07701.

Greene, Richard L. (S. 28, 1942, Bonnaventure, PQ) Dir., Hum. Soc. Sci. Lib., Univ. de Montreal, 1977–; Dir., Redpath Lib., McGill Univ., 1972–77; Plng. Resrch. Ofcr., Conf. of Rector, 1970–71; AUCC Libn., Assn. of Coll. and Univ. of Can., 1965–71. **Educ.:** Univ. de Montreal, 1965–66, BLS; McGill Univ., 1973–75, MLS. **Orgs.:** Can. LA: Can. Assn. of Coll. and Univ. Libs., Ed. ASTED: Treas. ALA: ACRL. **Activities:** 1; 17 **Addr.:** Bibliotheque des Sciences Humaines et Sociales, Universite de Montreal, 3150, Rue Jean Brillant, Suite 2145, Montreal, PQ H3C 3J7 Canada.

Greene, Richard O. (Ja. 2, 1949, Syracuse, NY) Reg. Lib. Dir., Mid-MS Reg. Lib. Syst., 1976–; Dir., Pub. Libs., Oktibbeha Cnty. (MS) Lib. Syst., 1974–76. **Educ.:** Eisenhower Coll., 1968–72, BS (Art Hist.); Syracuse Univ., 1973–74, MLS. **Orgs.:** MS LA: Pub. Lib. Sect. (Ch., 1977); Long Range Plng. Com. (1977–80). N. Ctrl. White House Conf. (Ch., 1978–79). SELA: Mem. Com. ALA: Mem. Com. Cnsrt. for Lib. Autom. in MS. Socty. of MS Archvsts. **Activities:** 2, 9; 17, 19, 24; 55, 56, 78 **Addr.:** Mid-Mississippi Regional Library System, 201 S. Huntington St., Kosciusko, MS 39090.

Greene, Richard O. (Ap. 15, 1948, Columbus, OH) Mgr., Bibl. Maintenance Sect., OCLC, Inc., 1978–; Asst. to Deputy State Libn. for Tech. Srvs., State Lib. of OH, 1976–78, Catlgr., 1973–76. **Educ.:** OH State Univ., 1966–71, BA (Eng.); Case West. Rsv. Univ., 1972–73, MSLS. **Orgs.:** ALA. OH LA: Div. III (Coord., 1979–80). **Activities:** 1; 20, 34, 46 **Addr.:** 1081 Hardesty Pl. E., Columbus, OH 43204.

Greener, Barbara R. (My. 31, 1927, New York, NY) Head, Msc. Lib., Chief of Subj. Reader Srvs., Queens Coll., 1972–, Msc. Libn., 1950–72. **Educ.:** Brooklyn Coll., 1944–49, BA (Rom. Lang., Msc.); Pratt Inst., 1949–50, BLS. **Orgs.:** Msc. LA. LA CUNY: Ch. (1963). **Activities:** 1; 15, 17, 39; 55 **Addr.:** Queens College Music Library, Flushing, NY 11367.

Greenfield, Jane W. (O. 5, 1941, New York, NY) Coord. of Adult Srvs., Evanston Pub. Lib., 1979–, ILL Coord., 1978–79, Readers' Asst., 1975–78; Adult Srvs. Libn., Cook Meml. Lib., 1968–70; Adult Srvs. Libn., NY Pub. Lib., 1964–67. **Educ.:** Univ. of Rochester, 1959–63, BA (Hist.); Simmons Coll., 1963–64, MS (LS). **Orgs.:** ALA: RASD, ILL Com. (1980–); LAMA/Persnl. Admin. Sect., Staff Dev. Com. (1980–). IL LA. **Activities:** 9; 16 **Addr.:** 2627 Reese Ave., Evanston, IL 60201.

Greenfield, Judith C. (F. 16, 1935, Stamford, CT) Chld. Libn., Rye Free Readg. Rm., 1974–; Lib. Media Spec., Washington Ave. Sch., 1973–74; Ref. Libn., Klapper Lib., Queens Coll., 1966–70; Catlgr., Biblgphr., Natl. Lib. of Med., 1960–61; Head, Cat. Dept., Watertown (MA) Pub. Lib., 1959–60. **Educ.:** Brown Univ., 1952–56, BA (Hist.); Simmons Coll., 1957–60, MLS; NY Univ., 1964–70, MA (Eng.). **Orgs.:** ALA. NY LA: Speaker Spr. Conf. Westchester LA: Chld. and YA Srvs. Sect. (1981); Chld. Srvs., Adv. Bd. (1976–78, 1980–); Tech. Srvs., Adv. Bd. (1978–). Brown Univ.: Alum. Schs. Prog. (Reg. Dir., 1978–81). Amer. Fld. Srv.: Student Exch., Reg. Screening Com. (1981). Fam. Interest Resrc. and Srv. Team, Rye (1981–). **Pubns.:** "The New Library," *Brown Alum. Monthly* (S. 1958). **Activities:** 9, 10; 17, 21, 46; 89 **Addr.:** 539 Oakhurst Rd., Mamaroneck, NY 10543.

Greengrass, Alan R. (D. 6, 1942, New York, NY) Resrch. Mgr., NY Times Info. Srv., 1981–; Ed., Pubns., The Info. Bank, 1980–81, Deputy Managing Ed., 1975–79; Staff Asst., Info. Srvs., *The NY Times,* 1967–75. **Educ.:** Columbia Univ., 1959–63, AB (Gvt.), 1963–65, MA (Gvt.), 1965–68, MLS (Libnshp.). **Orgs.:** Amer. Socty. of Indxrs.: Pres. Pro. Tem. (1968–69). ASIS. **Activities:** 12; 30, 37; 75, 83 **Addr.:** New York Times Information Service, 1719A Rte. 10, Parsippany, NJ 07054.

Greenwald, Camille Duer (Ap. 9, 1951, Cleveland, OH) Resrch. Libn., Columbia Gas Syst. Srv., Corp., 1980–; Mgr., Lib. Info. Srvs., Duphar Labs., 1978–80; Drug Info. Libn., OH State Univ. Hosps. 1977; Drug Info. Libn., Case West. Rsv. Univ., 1974–77. **Educ.:** Ursuline Coll., 1970–73, BA, magna cum laude (Eng.); Case West. Rsv. Univ., 1973–74, MSLS. **Orgs.:** SLA: PR (Ch., 1980–81). Mid. OH Hlth. Scis. Libs. Org.: VP (1979–81). Amer. Gas Assn.: Lib. Srvs. Com. (1980–). **Activities:** 12; 17, 39, 41; 64, 87, 91 **Addr.:** Research Library, Columbia Gas System Service Corp., 1600 Dublin Rd., Columbus, OH 43215.

Greenwood, Anna Starbuck (My. 13, 1923, Glendale, CA) Media Spec., Montgomery Cnty. Pub. Schs., 1962–, Tchr., 1961–62; Tchr., Wiseburn Sch. Dist., 1956–61; Tchr., Torrance Unfd. Sch. Dist., 1953–56. **Educ.:** Univ. of South. CA, 1947–53, AB (Eng.); Cath. Univ., 1962–66, MSLS. **Orgs.:** Church Lib. Cncl. CSLA. Montgomery Cnty. Educ. Media Specs.: Pres. (1973–74); VP (1972–73); Secy. (1971–72). MD Educ. Media Assn. Natl. Genealogical Socty. MD Genealogical Socty. Assn. for State and Lcl. Hist. **Activities:** 10, 14-Church; 20, 21, 22; 69, 86, 90 **Addr.:** New Hampshire Estates Elementary School, 8720 Carroll Ave., Silver Spring, MD 20903.

Greenwood, Blair (N. 11, 1933, Salmon Arm, BC) Coord., Instr. Media, N. Vancouver Sch. Dist., 1975–; Educ. Media Coord., Langley Sch. Dist., 1963–75. **Educ.:** Univ. of BC, 1960, BA (Eng., Hist.), 1960–62, MA (Hist.); Univ. of Toronto, 1970–72, MLS. **Orgs.:** BC Sch. Libns. Assn.: Pres. (1976–77). Can. Sch. Libns. Assn. Visual Litcy. Assn. **Activities:** 10, 11; 17, 21, 32; 57, 63, 67 **Addr.:** Curriculum Services Centre, School District 44, 135 W. 12th St., North Vancouver, BC V7M 1N2 Canada.

Greer, Barbara F. (F. 20, 1950, Louisa, KY) Reg. Libn., KY Dept. of Lib. and Arch., FIVCO Reg. Lib., 1979–, KENCLIP Libn., Dist. 4, Univ. of KY, 1978–79; KENCLIP Libn., Dist. 3, East. KY Univ., 1974–77; Reg. Libn., N. Cumberland Valley Reg. Lib., 1972–74. **Educ.:** Univ. of KY, 1967–71, BA (Soclgy.), 1971–72, MSLS. **Orgs.:** KY LA: Pub. Lib. Sect., Schol. Com. (Ch., 1977–79). SE LA. ALA. Richmond (KY) Bus. and Prof. Women's Club: Pres. (1976–77). Reality, Attitude, Potential: Treas. (1977). Save Our Reusable Trash: Secy.-Treas. (D. 1979–). **Honors:** Phi Beta Kappa; Beta Phi Mu; Olofson Awd., 1981. **Activities:** 9, 13; 24 **Addr.:** FIVCO Regional Library, Box 370, Louisa, KY 41230.

Greer, Brian J. (S. 19, 1942, Loma Linda, CA) Dir., Coll. Lib., Palmer Coll. of Chiro., 1977–; Dir., Ofc. of Lib. Dev., State Lib. Cmsn. of IA, 1976–77; Dir., Kemper Newton Reg. Lib., 1972–76; Chief Pub. Srv. Libn., Charles H. Taylor Meml. Lib., 1970–72. **Educ.:** Brigham Young Univ., 1964–65, BA (Hist.), 1966–70, MLS; Coll. of William & Mary, 1970–72, Cert. (Higher Educ. Admin.). **Orgs.:** ALA: PLA, Legis. Com. (1975–79); ASLA, Grantsmanship Com. (1977–80). Med LA: Ed. Com. for MLA Bltn. (1981–82). Chiro. Lib. Cnsrtm.: Ch. (1979–). **Activities:** 1, 9; 17, 19, 24; 58, 78, 80 **Addr.:** Palmer College Library, 1000 Brady St., Davenport, IA 52803.

Greer, Nancy B. (O. 13, 1942, Pittsburgh, PA) Grp. Mgr., Tech. Srvs., Solar Energy Resrch. Inst., 1978–; Head, Cat. Maintenance Dept., Denver Pub. Lib., 1972–78; Asst. Libn., West. Electric Co., Engin. Resrch. Ctr., 1970–72; Elem. Sch. Tchr., Pittsburgh Pub., Parochial Schs., 1965–68. **Educ.:** Carlow Coll., 1960–65, BA (Span.); Univ. of Pittsburgh, 1968–69, MLS. **Orgs.:** ALA. ASIS. SLA: Rocky Mt. Chap. Bylaws Com. (Ch., 1974–76), *Rocky Mt. Chap. Bltn.* Ed. (1975–76), Pres. (1976–77), No-host Conf. Com. (1977); Documtn. Div., Com. for Name Change and Scope (1977–78); Cent. Chap. (ASIS Liaison, 1979–80). Denver Art Musm. Denver Symph. Assn. Animal Protection Inst. Common Cause. **Honors:** Beta Phi Mu, 1969; Denver Pub. Lib., Outstan. Empl. of the Yr., 1977. **Activities:** 9, 12; 39, 46; 64, 91 **Addr.:** Solar Energy Information Center, Solar Energy Research Institute, 1617 Cole Blvd., Golden, CO 80401.

Greer, Roger C. (Ap. 29, 1928, Pilot Mound Twp., MN) Dean, Prof., Sch. of lib. and Info. Mgt., Univ. of South. CA, 1979–; Dir., Commentary Analysis Resrch. Inst. Prof., Grad. Sch. of Libnshp., Univ. of Denver, 1977–78; Prof., Sch. of Inf. Std., Syracuse Univ., 1972–76; Dean, 1968–72; Asst. Dean, 1967–68; Dir. of Libs., State Univ. Coll., Potsdam, 1964–67; Instr., Sch. of Lib. Srv., Rutgers Univ., 1960–64; Asst. Prof. and Head, LC Cat. and Card Prep. Dept., Purdue Univ. Lib., 1957–60. **Educ.:** St. John's Univ., MN, 1950–54, BA (Hist.); Columbia Univ., 1954–55, (Hist.); Rutgers Univ., 1956, MLS, 1960, PhD (LS), 1964. **Orgs.:** ALA: Cnclr. (1971–75); Ref. Srvs. Div., Ch., Bibl. Com., (1969–74); Dir. (1970–72); CA LA: Cont. Educ. Com. (1979). LRRT (Dir. 1970–72); LED (Ch., 1971–72). ASIS. SLA. Other orgs. **Pubns.:** *Illustration Index* 4th Ed. (1977); "National Bibliography" in *Lib. Trends,* (Ja. 1976); Reports. **Activities:** 11; 17, 25, 26; 57 **Addr.:** School of Library and Information Management, University of Southern California, University Park, CA 90007.

Greey, Kathleen M. (My. 8, 1937, Princeton, NJ) Educ. Libn., Portland State Univ. Lib., 1968–; Libn., Lit. Dept., San Francisco Pub. Lib., 1963–67; Ref. Libn., Wethersfield Pub. Lib., 1960–63. **Educ.:** OR State Coll., 1954–56, 1957–59, BA (Educ.); Univ. of Denver, 1959–60, MA (Libnshp.). **Orgs.:** Pac. NW LA: Ref. Div. (Ch., 1977–79). SLA. OR LA. **Honors:** Phi Kappa Phi. **Activities:** 1, 12; 31, 39; 63 **Addr.:** 1717 S.W. Park Ave. Apt. 1108, Portland, OR 97201.

Grefrath, Richard Warren (Ag. 7, 1946, Greenwich, CT) Ref. Libn. Univ. of NV Lib., 1978–; Ref. Libn., Pac. Luth. Univ. Lib., 1973–78. **Educ.:** Carnegie Inst. of Tech., 1964–66, (math.); New York Univ., 1966–68, BA (Eng.); Temple Univ., 1970–72, MA (Eng.); Univ. of MD, 1972, MLS. **Orgs.:** ALA. NV LA. CA LA. 101st Airborne Div. Assn. Amer. Civil Liberties Un. **Honors:** Phi Beta Kappa, 1969; Phi Kappa Phi; Sigma Delta Omicron; Beta Phi Mu. **Pubns.:** "Classical Myths for Children," *PNLA Qtly.* (1978); "War Information Centers in the U.S. During World War II," *Lib. Hist. Review,* (S. 1974); "A Study of Citations to 308 Journal Articles in Chemistry Published in 1963," *Journal of Chemical Documentation;* (1974); "Will the Real Librarian Please Stand Up?–An Informal Look at how we've been portrayed in the Occupational Outlook Handbook", *Technicalities* (Je 1981); "Don't Break that Run!–Trimming the Reference Serials Budget," *High Roller* (My/Je 1980). Reviews. **Activities:** 1; 17, 39, 42; 55, 67, 74 **Addr.:** Reference Dept., University of Nevada Library, Reno, NV 89557.

PROFESSIONAL ACTIVITIES: Institutions: 1. Acad. lib.; 2. Arch.; 3. Assn.; 4. Fed./Gvt. lib.; 5. Inst. lib.; 6. Mfr./Suppl.; 7. Milit. lib.; 8. Musm.; 9. Pub. lib.; 10. Sch. lib.; 11. Sch. of lib. sci.; 12. Spec. lib.; 13. State lib.; 14. (other). **Functions/Activities:** 15. Acq./Col. dev.; 16. Adult srvs.; 17. Admin.; 18. Apprais.; 19. Archit./Bldgs.; 20. Cat./Class.; 21. Chld. srvs.; 22. Circ.; 23. Cons./Pres.; 24. Consult.; 25. Cont. ed.; 26. Educ. lib. sci.; 27. Ext. srvs.; 28. Fund/Grants; 29. Gvt. pubs.; 30. Indx./Abs.; 31. Instr. lib. use; 32. Media srvs.; 33. Micro.; 34. Netwks./Coop.; 35. Persnl.; 36. PR; 37. Publshg.; 38. Recs. mgt.; 39. Ref. srvs.; 40. Repro.; 41. Resrch.; 42. Review.; 43. Secur.; 44. Serials; 45. Spec. col.; 46. Tech. srvs.; 47. Trustees/Bds.; 48. YA srvs.; 49. (other).

Gregg, Alice Elizabeth (F. 24, 1920, Lambert, MT) Interim Dir. of Libs., Loma Linda Univ. Lib., 1980–, Assoc. Dir., 1971–79, Ch., Dept. of Tech. Srvs., 1965–80, Head of Acq., 1963–65. **Educ.:** Walla Walla Coll., 1939–45, BA (Eng.); Univ. of South. CA, 1959–62, MSLS. **Orgs.:** ALA. Med. Lib. Grp. of S. CA. Christ. Libns. Assn. Loma Linda Univ. Fac. Women's Club. Loma Linda Bk. Club. **Pubns.:** "Tell It to the World," *Adventist Heritage* (Win. 1977); "SDA Periodical Index," *Jnl. of Adventist Educ.* (Sum. 1977). **Activities:** 1; 15, 17 **Addr.:** Loma Linda University Library, 4700 Pierce St., Riverside, CA 92515.

Greggs, Elizabeth M. (N. 7, 1925, Delta, CO) Asst. Coord., Chld. Srvs., King Cnty. Lib., 1978–; Reg. Chld. Coord., 1968–78; Coord., Chld. Srvs., Renton Pub. Lib., 1962–68, Dir., 1961–62. **Educ.:** Univ. of Denver, 1946–48, AB (LS). **Orgs.:** Puget Sound Cncl. for Rev. Chld. Media: Ch. (1974–75), Exec. Bd. (1975–). ALA: Boy Scout Adv. Com. (1973–78; Ch., 1976–78); Newbery Caldecott Com. (1978–79); Mem. Com. (1978–); ALSC, Exec. Com. (1978–). Other orgs. and ofcs. Boy Scouts of Amer.: Kloshee Dist., Adv. Com. (Ch., 1975–78); Seattle Cncl., Adv. Com. (1975–78). **Honors:** Boy Scouts of Amer., Service to Youth Awd., 1971, Awd. of Merit, 1977. **Pubns.:** Ed. *Cayas Nsltr.* (WA LA) (1971–74); Film Reviews. **Activities:** 9; 21, 24 **Addr.:** 800 Lynnwood N.E., Renton, WA 98056.

Gregor, Dorothy Deborah (Ag. 15, 1939, Dobbs Ferry, NY) Assoc. Univ. Libn. for Tech. Srvs., Univ. of CA, Berkeley, 1980–; Head, Serials Dept., 1976–, Tech. Srvs. Libn., Pub. Hlth. Lib., 1973–76, Asst. to Assoc. Univ. Libn. for Tech. Srvs., 1975; Consult., John Wesley Cnty. Hosp., Los Angeles, CA, 1972; Ref. Libn., Sci. and Tech. Div., Univ. of HI, 1971–72; Dept. Libn., Pub. Hlth. Lib., Univ. of CA, Berkeley, 1969–71; Ref. Libn., Medical Center Lib., Univ. of CA, San Francisco, 1968–69. **Educ.:** Occidental Coll., 1957–61, AB (Phil.); Univ. of HI, 1961–63, MA (Phil.); Univ. of TX, 1966–68, MLS; Univ. of CA, Berkeley, 1974–76, Cert. (Lib. Mgt.). **Orgs.:** Med. LA: Prog. Com. (1979); Mem. Com. (Ch., 1973–75); Ad Hoc Com. to Std. MLA Grp. Structure (1975–77). North. CA Med. Lib. Grp: VP (1973); Pres. (1974). ALA. **Honors:** Phi Beta Kappa, 1960; Phi Kappa Phi, 1963. **Pubns.:** Jt. auth., "Planning Serials Cancellations and Cooperative collection Development in the Health Sciences," *Med. LA Bltn.* (O. 1975); *Feasibility Study of Cooperative Collecting of Exotic Foreign Language Serial Titles Among Health Sciences Libraries in California* (1974). **Activities:** 1; 17, 44, 46; 80 **Addr.:** University of California, 245 Main Library, General Library, Berkeley, CA 94720.

Gregorian, Vartan (Ap. 7, 1935, Tabriz, Iran) Pres., New York Pub. Lib., 1981–; Dean, Fac. of Arts and Scis., Univ. of PA, 1974–80, Provost, 1973–74, Prof., Hist., 1972–80; Prof., Hist., Univ. of TX, 1968–72; Assoc. Prof., Hist., San Francisco State Coll., 1962–68. **Educ.:** Stanford Univ., 1958, BA, 1964, PhD (Hist.). Amer. Hist. Assn. Far West. Slavic. Conf. Mid. East. Std. Assn. Assn. Advnc. Slavic Std. **Honors:** Univ. of PA, Hon MA, 1972; Guggenheim Fellow, 1971–72; . Awd., 1971; other hons. **Pubns.:** *The Emergence of Modern Afghanistan* (1969); "Russia, Armenia, and the Armenians," *Impact of Russia on Asia* (1973); "Mahmud Tarzi and Saraj-ol-Akhbar," *Mid. East. Jnl.* (1967); other bks., articles. **Activities:** 9, 14-Resrch. lib.; 73 **Addr.:** New York Public Library, 5th Ave. and 42nd St., New York, NY 10018.*

Gregory, Helen Patricia Byrne (F. 27, 1939, Toledo, OH) Toledo-Lucas Cnty. Pub. Lib. 1981–; Chld. libn., Albion Pub. Lib., 1973–; Adjunct Instr., Albion Coll., 1974–77; Branch libn., Toledo-Lucas Cnty. Pub. Lib., 1968–73. **Educ.:** Univ. of Toledo, 1957–61, BEd (Eng.); PA State Univ., 1962–64, MA (Theat. Arts); Univ. of MI, 1976–78, AMLS. **Orgs.:** ALA: Newbery/Caldecott Com. (1978–79); Newbery Com. (1982–83). MI LA: Chld. Srvs. RT Inst., Lcl. Arrange. (Ch., 1978); Prog. Ch. (1976); Discuss. Leader, (1974 & 75). **Pubns.:** "Sing Me a Story," *Sch. Lib. Jnl.* (S. 1979); "Darth Vader, Macbeth's Witches, Charlie Brown & Assorted Clowns," *MI Libn.* (Sum. 1978); "Telestory", *MI Libn.* (Win. 1975); reviews; TV storyteller (1968–69). **Activities:** 9, 14-Sch. of Educ.; 21, 42, 48; 55, 63, 95-Chld. Thea. **Addr.:** 1301 Barnes, Albion, MI 49224.

Gregory, Melissa Ritter (F. 11, 1933, Streator, IL) Serials/Acq. Libn., Argonne Natl. Lab., 1968–; Libn, Comms. Div., Motorola, Inc., 1962–68; Engin. Libn., Farm Equip., Intl. Harvester Co., 1959–62; Libn., Lyons Twp. HS, 1957–58; Libn., Ela-Vernon Twp. HS, 1955–57. **Educ.:** IL State Univ., 1951–55, BS (Educ.); Univ. of IL, 1957–59, MS (LS). **Orgs.:** SLA. Coll. of DuPage Lib. Tech. Asst. Adv. Bd. (1971–). Vlg. of Willowbrook (IL): Lib. Com. (1978–80). Willowbrook Pub. Lib. Dist.: Bd. of Trustees (Pres., 1980–). **Activities:** 9, 12; 15, 26, 47; 64, 84, 91 **Addr.:** Technical Information Services -Bldg. 203, Argonne National Laboratory, 9700 S. Cass Ave., Argonne, IL 60439.

Gregory, Ruth W. (F. 20, 1910, West Point, NE) Lib. Consult./Libn. Emeritus, Waukegan Pub. Lib., 1976–, Head Libn., 1939–76; Actg. Libn., Stevens Point Pub. Lib., 1938–39. **Educ.:** Univ. of NE, 1929–33, BA (Eng.); Univ. of WI, 1937–38, BLS. **Orgs.:** IL LA: Pres. (1947–48). ALA: PL Div. (Pres., 1955). IL State Lib. Adv. Com.: Titles I and II (1967–76). AAUW. Lake Cnty. Crippled Chld. Clinic. **Honors:** IL LA, Libn. Cit., 1976; Lake Cnty. Mental Hlth. Socty., Anl. Awd., 1965; AAUW, Educ. Fndn. Name Grant Awd., 1980. **Pubns.:** Jt. auth., *Public Libraries in Cooperative Systems* (1971); *Anniversaries and Holidays* 3d ed., (1975); "Federal Funds and Library Development in Illinois," *IL Libs.* (Je. 1980). **Activities:** 9; 16, 19, 24; 50, 74 **Addr.:** 2035 Walnut St., Waukegan, IL 60087.

Gregory, Vicki Lovelady (F. 13, 1950, Chattanooga, TN) Head, Tech. Srvs., Auburn Univ. at Montgomery, 1978–; AV Libn., 1976–78. **Educ.:** Univ. of AL, 1968–71, AB (Hist.), 1971–73, MA (Hist.), 1973–74, MLS. **Orgs.:** AL LA: Conv. Lcl. Arrange. (Ch., 1978–79); JMRT (Secy. 1977–78). SELA. ALA. **Honors:** Phi Alpha Theta. **Activities:** 1; 15, 32, 46 **Addr.:** Library, Auburn University at Montgomery, Montgomery, AL 36193.

Greig, Peter E. (Jn. 27, 1944, Montreal PQ) Union Lists of Newsps. Libn., Newsp. Div., Natl. Lib. of Can. 1981–; Secy., Com. on Bibliographical Srvs. for Can. (Natl. Lib. Adv. Bd.), 1975–81, Head, Bibl. Sect., 1974–76; Indxr., Lib. of Parlmt., 1971–73; Burgon Bickersteth Lib. Flw., Massey Coll., 1969–71. **Educ.:** Queen's Univ., 1963–67, BA (Hist., Eng.); Univ. of Toronto, 1968–69 BLS; Inst. of Bibl. and Textual Criticism, Univ. of Leeds (UK) 1973–74, MA. **Orgs.:** Bibl. Socty. of Can.: Index Com. (Ch., 1970–73); Indxr. to the Socty., (1973–79); Stnd. Com. on the *Bibliography of Canadian Bibliographies,* (Ch., 1978–). Indexing and Abstr. Socty. of Can.: Pres. (1977–78); Liaison to the Socty. of Indxrs. (UK), (1978–). Society of Indexers (UK). **Pubns.:** "IASC/SCAD Activities, June 1978 to January 1980," *The Indxr.* (Ap. 1980); "The I and A Reference Shelf," *IASC/SCAD Nsltr.* (F. 1978; My. 1978); "The Indexing and Abstracting Society of Canada," IASC/SCAD Nsltr. (My. 1978); Various indxs. and other pubns. **Activities:** 4; 30; 57 **Addr.:** 402-235 Bay St., Ottawa, ON K1R 5Z2 Canada.

Greisser, Harriet (Je. 2, 1948, Texarkana, TX) Resrch. Libn., Agency for Instr. TV, 1978–; Libn., Haskins Labs., 1974–77; Bibl. Asst., Univ. Microfilms, 1972–74. **Educ.:** Univ. of MI, 1966–71, AB (Hist.), 1971, AM (LS). **Orgs.:** ALA: LITA/Vid. and Cable Comms. Sect., Comms. Com. (1979–81); SRRT/Task Frc. on Alternatives in Print (1979–). SLA: Telecom. Provisional Div. (1978–). **Pubns.:** *Survey of Library Facilities at Telecommunications and Educational Research Organizations* (1978). **Activities:** 12; 39, 41, 45; 63, 92, 93 **Addr.:** Agency for Instructional Television, P.O. Box A, Bloomington, IN 47402.

Gremillion, Virginia P. (O. 3, 1937, Alexandria, LA) Ref. Libn., Tucson Pub. Lib., 1965–; Eng. Tchr., Libn., Rapides Par./Glenmora HS, 1960–64; Bkmobile. Libn., LA State Lib., 1959–60. **Educ.:** Northwest. State Coll., 1956–59, BA (Eng., Educ., LS); LA State Univ., 1965, MS (LS). **Orgs.:** ALA: Newbery-Caldecott Com. (1973). SWLA: Young People's Interest Grp. (1976). AZ LA. **Pubns.:** Annotated bibl., AZ sect., *Southwestern Children's Books* (1976); reviews. **Activities:** 9, 11; 21, 39, 42; 57, 65, 66 **Addr.:** Wilmot Branch Library, 530 N. Wilmot Rd., Tucson, AZ 85711.

Gremling, Richard C. (My. 24, 1917, Toledo, OH) Lit. Sci., Ortho Pharm. Corp., 1981–, Supvsr., Lit. Srvs., 1973–81, Libn., 1966–73; Chief Libn., ITT Fed. Labs., 1964–66; Chief Libn., Lockheed Electronics, 1961–64. **Educ.:** Univ. of Toledo, 1934–38, BS (Bio., Chem.); West. Rsv. Univ., 1939–40, MSLS. **Orgs.:** Amer. Documtn. Inst.: Dir. SLA: Chap. Pres.; Sci. Tech. Div., Ch. **Activities:** 5, 12; 17, 24, 44 **Addr.:** Ortho Pharmaceutical Corp., U.S. Hwy. 202, Raritan, NJ 08869.

Griba, Walter (D. 30, 1935, Kamsack, SK) Dir., AV Ctr., Simon Fraser Univ., 1966–; Sci. Illustrator, Univ. of BC, 1960–66. **Educ.:** Vancouver Sch. of Art, 1960–61. **Orgs.:** Media Exch. Coop. of BC: Pres. (1979–80). AECT. Media Tech. Assn. of BC. Assn. Media Tech. & Educ. in Canada. Socty. Motion Picture & TV Engin. Audio Engin. Socty. Natl. Assn. Educ. Broadcasting. **Pubns.:** Slide progs. and audio documentaries. **Activities:** 5, 12; 17, 24, 32; 63, 70, 88 **Addr.:** 2853 West 15 Ave., Vancouver, BC V6K 3A1 Canada.

Gribbin, John Hawkins (S. 22, 1920, Charleston, SC) Dir. of Libs., Univ. of MO, 1977–; Lib. Dir., Tulane Univ., 1966–76; Assoc. Univ. Libn., Univ. of NC, 1961–66; Libn., Natl. Acad. of Sci.-Natl. Resrch. Cncl., 1955–61; Assoc. Libn., Rice Univ., 1953–54; Geol. Libn. and Instr., Lib. Sch., Univ. of TX, 1950–51; Docum. Libn., Univ. of MO, 1947–49. **Educ.:** Univ. of NC, 1938–42, AB (Chem.); Univ. of CA, Berkeley, 1946–51, MLS; Univ. of Chicago, 1951–58, PhD (LS). **Orgs.:** Assn. of Southeast. Resrch. Libs.: Ch., (1971–73). Southeast. Lib. Network: Ch., Bd. of Dir. (1972–73). **Honors:** SELA, Rothrock Awd., 1978. **Pubns.:** Ed., *Scientific & Technical Societies of the U.S. and Canada, 7th ed.* (1961); Ed., *Industrial Research Laboratories of the United States, 11th ed.* (1960); "Factors in the Organization of SOLINET," *Coll. & Resrch. Lib. News* (F. 1975); "SOLINET: the Million-dollar Beginning," *Southeast. Libn.* (Fall 1974); "Interlibrary Cooperation and Collection Building," *The Academic Library: Essays in Honor of Guy R. Lyle* (1974); Other articles. **Activities:** 1; 17; 56, 95-Networks. **Addr.:** University of Missouri-Columbia Libraries, Columbia, MO 65201.

Grieb, Lyndal Claude (Jn. 12, 1940, Doniphan, MO) Librarian II, Memphis and Shelby Cnty. (TN) Pub. Lib., 1973–; Actg. Head, Hist. Dept., Kansas City, Pub. Lib. 1970–72; Eng. Tchr., Kansas City, Sch. Dist., 1966–68. **Educ.:** Univ. of MO, 1958–61, Southwest MO State Univ., 1963–66, BSEd (Eng.) Univ. of MO, 1970–72, MLS. **Orgs.:** TN LA: Legis. Com. (1979–); Nsltr. Ed. (1979–). ALA. **Honors:** Beta Phi Mu. **Pubns.:** *The Operas of Gian Carlo Menotti, 1937–1972: A Selective Bibliography,* (1974). **Activities:** 9; 39; 55, 67 **Addr.:** 135 N. Montgomery, Memphis, TN 38104.

Grieder, Elmer Moery (Ag. 14, 1909, Dubuque, IA) Assoc. Dir. of Libs., Emeritus, Stanford Univ., 1949–; Univ. Libn., WV Univ., 1947–49; Asst. Libn., Grad. Sch. of Pub. Admin., Harvard Univ., 1938–46; Asst. to the Dir. of Libs., 1946–47; Prof. & Dir., Inst. of Libnshp., Ankara Univ., Turkey, 1955–57. **Educ.:** Univ. of Dubuque, 1926–30, BA (Hist.); Columbia Univ., 1935–36, BS (LS); Harvard Univ., 1939–47, AM (Hist.). **Orgs.:** CA LA: Pres., Golden Gate Dist. (1953–54). ALA: Cnclr. (1961–62). SLA. **Pubns.:** Various articles. **Activities:** 1; 15, 17 **Addr.:** 17 Pearce Mitchell Pl., Stanford, CA 94305.

Griffel, Eugene B. (Jl. 23, 1931, Brooklyn, NY) Dir., Mideast. MI Lib. Coop., 1966–; Head Libn., Elmwood Park Pub. Lib., 1963–66; Ref., Branch, Assoc. Libn., Willoughby-Eastlake Pub. Lib., 1961–63. **Educ.:** Brooklyn Coll., 1950–54, BA; Case West. Rsv. Univ., 1960–61, MSLS. **Orgs.:** ALA. MI LA. Flint Area LA. **Honors:** Flint Area LA, Libn. of the Yr., 1979. **Activities:** 9; 17, 34 **Addr.:** 2106 Pierce, Flint, MI 48503.

Griffen, Agnes M. Hallanger (Ag. 25, 1935, Fort Dauphin, Madagascar) Dir., Montgomery Cnty. Dept. of Pub. Libs., Rockville, MD, 1981–; Deputy Lib. Dir., Tucson Pub. Lib., 1974–81; Lectr., Grad. Lib. Sch., Univ. of AZ, 1979, 1975–76; Deputy Libn., Staff and Prog. Dev., King Cnty. Lib. Syst., 1971–74, Inst. Libs. Coord., 1968–71, Area Chld. Libn., 1965–68. **Educ.:** Pac. Luth. Univ., 1953–57, BA (Eng.); Univ. of WA, 1964–65, M.Libnshp.; various crs. **Orgs.:** ALA: Cnclr.-at-Lg. (1972–76); Cncl. Orien. Com. (Ch., 1977–80); Equal Empl. Oppt. Subcom. (Ch., 1974–75, 1977–78); PLA, Pres. (1981–82), Dir.-at-Lg. (1977–81), Stans. Com. WA LA: State Title IV Adv. Cncl. (Ch., 1969–70); WA State Adv. Cncl. on Libs., Equitable Srvs. Task Frc. (1971–72). SRRT of WA State: Org./Clerk (1970–71). Pac. NW Luth. Church LA: Co-Fndr. (1958–63). Various other orgs. King Cnty. Untd. Way: Cncl. of Plng. Afflts., Bd. (1973–74). Exec. Women's Cncl. of South. AZ. Natl. Org. for Women. AZ Hum. Cncl.: Secy. (1979–80). **Pubns.:** "Equal Employment Opportunity Principles and Affirmative Action Practices in Library Supervision," *Supervision of Employees in Libraries* (1979); "The Future Is Yours, The Future Is Ours; An Introd. to Library/Information Futures," *Educational Technology-The Alternative Futures* (1977); "On Communicating with Supervisors," *UNABASHED Libn.* (1977); "Some Insights into Access: The Problem of Prison Libraries," *IL Libs.* (S. 1974); "Personnel and Employment: Affirmative Action," *The ALA Yrbk.* (1978); various articles. **Activities:** 9, 11; 17, 26, 35; 56, 72, 92 **Addr.:** Montgomery County Dept. of Public Libraries, 99 Maryland Ave., Rockville, MD 20850.

Griffin, Marie Elizabeth (Picker) (F. 3, 1919, New York, NY) Libn., Inst. of Jazz Std., Rutgers Univ., 1979–, AV Catlgr., Libs., 1969–79; Tchr., Maxson Jr. HS, 1967–69; Sub. Tchr., 1946–67. **Educ.:** Rutgers Univ., 1960–67, BA, highest hons. (Eng.), 1969–73, MLS; various crs., wkshps. **Orgs.:** Msc. LA: Autom. Com. (1979–); Prog. Participant (1980). ALA: RTSD, AV Com. (1980–); LITA, Prog. Participant (1980). Assn. for Rec. Snd. Cols.: Prog. Participant (1979). Msc. OCLC Users Grp.: Speaker (1979). Piscataway Twp. Cvl. Rights Comsn. Leag. of Women Voters of Piscataway. Amer. Fld. Srv.: Piscataway Chap. Natl. Assn. of Parlmts. **Honors:** Natl. Endow. for the Hum., Grant, 1978, 1979. **Pubns.:** Various articles, *Rutgers Libs. Nsltr.* **Activities:** 1, 2; 34, 46; 55 **Addr.:** 21 Lake Park Dr., Piscataway, NJ 08854.

Griffin, Mary Ann (Mr. 6, 1946, Hazleton, PA) Dir. of the Lib., Xavier Univ. and Edgecliff Coll. at Xavier Univ., 1979–; Consult. to the Pres. (Dev.), Unity Coll., 1978; Head, Circ. and Bldg. Srvs., Tufts Univ. Lib., 1974–77. **Educ.:** PA State Univ., 1964–67, BS (Math. Educ.), 1967–70, MA (Germ.); Simmons Coll 1973–74, MS (LS), 1976–80, DA (Lib. Admin.). German Script Course, Archvs. of the Moravian Church, 1975. **Orgs.:** Grtr. Cincinnati Lib. Cnsrtm.: Pres. (1981–82), Treas. (1979–80). OHIONET: ILL Adv. Cncl. (1979–80); Instr. and Trng. Cncl. (1980–81). Simmons Coll. Sch. of LS Governing Bd.: Secy. (1975–77). ALA: ACRL. Acad. Lib. Assn. of OH. AAUP: Sect./Pres. Elect, Xavier Univ. **Pubns.:** Jt.-auth., "Adding to Knowledge of Document Exposure Counts in Three Academic Libraries," *Quantitative Measurement and Dynamic Library Service* (1978); "The ORLIS Plan and GCLC," *Update: GCLC* (Mr. 1980); Ed., *The Simmons Librarian* (Alum. Nsltr.) (1978–81). **Activities:** 1; 17 **Addr.:** Xavier University Library, Victory Pkwy. and Dana Ave., Cincinnati, OH 45207.

Griffin, Mary Frances (Ag. 24, 1925, Cross Hill, SC) Lib. Consult., SC State Dept. of Educ., 1966–; Libn., Greenville Cnty. Sch. Dist., 1952–66; Libn., Lee Cnty. Sch. Dist., 1951–52; Tchr.-Libn., Johnston Training Sch., 1947–51. **Educ.:** Benedict Coll., 1943–47, BA (Eng.); IN Univ., 1954–57, MSLS; additional coursework at SC State Coll., Atlanta Univ., VA State Coll. **Orgs.:**

Special Subjects/Services: 50. Adult educ.; 51. Advert./Mktg.; 52. Aerosp.; 53. Agric.; 54. Area std.; 55. Arts/Hum.; 56. Autom.; 57. Bibl./Prtg.; 58. Bio. sci.; 59. Bus./Fin.; 60. Chem.; 61. Copyrt.; 62. Documtn.; 63. Educ.; 64. Engin.; 65. Env.; 66. Eth. grps.; 67. Film; 68. Food/Nutr.; 69. Geneal.; 70. Geo.; 71. Geol.; 72. Handcpd.; 73. Hist.; 74. Int. frdm.; 75. Info. sci.; 76. Insr.; 77. Law; 78. Legis.; 79. Math./Comp. sci.; 80. Med.; 81. Metals; 82. Nat. resrcs.; 83. Newsp.; 84. Nuc. sci.; 85. Oral hist.; 86. Petr./Energy; 87. Pharm.; 88. Phys./Astr./Math.; 89. Readg.; 90. Relig.; 91. Sci./Tech.; 92. Soc. sci.; 93. Telecom.; 94. Transp.; 95. (other).

ALA. SELA: Secy. (1978–80). SCLA: Plng. Com. (1970–72); Secy. (1979). SC Assn. of Sch. Libns.: Adv. Com. (1978–). Assn. for Curr. Dev.: Recog. Com. (1978–80). AAUW. Les Escapeés. **Honors:** Natl. Cncl. of Negro Women: Columbia Sect., Cert. of Living the Legacy Awd., 1980. **Activities:** 10 **Addr.:** P.O. Box 1652, Columbia, SC 29202.

Griffin, Richard E. (D. 14, 1942, Hartford, CT) Asst. Exec. Dir., SLA, 1976–, Mgr., Mem. Dept., 1972–76; Head, LTP Info. Srvs., ALA, 1971–72; Asst. Libn., Lib. for the Blind and Phys. Handcpd., CT State Lib., 1968–70; Asst. Libn., Rsv. Bk. Rm., LA State Univ., 1968. **Educ.:** Tulane Univ., 1964–66, BA (Eng.); LA State Univ., 1967–68, MS (LS). **Orgs.:** SLA: Copyrt. Com. (1976–79). ASIS. Amer. Bk. Awds.: Hist. Nom. Com. (1980). **Pubns.:** "SLA, 1977-80," *Bowker Anl.* (1980); "SLA Salary Survey–1979," *Spec. Libs.* (D. 1979). **Activities:** 3; 17, 35 **Addr.:** 28 Lawrence Ln., Harrison, NY 10528.

Griffin, Richard G. (Je. 24, 1927, Tampa, FL) Dir. of Lib. Srvs., Fayetteville State Univ., 1981–; Admin. Libn., U.S. Merchant Marine Acad., 1979–80; Dir. of Libs., NY Inst. of Tech., 1959–80; Asst. Libn., Knoxville Coll., 1957–58; Univ. Libn., TX South. Univ., 1954–57. **Educ.:** Morehse. Coll., 1945–49, AB (Hist.); Atlanta Univ., 1949–50, MSLS. **Orgs.:** ALA: Black Caucus Pubns. (Ch., 1977–). SLA: ed., *The Rpt.* (1980); Engin. and Tech. Div. TX LA: Coll. Div. (Secy., Treas., 1956). Concerned Citizens for Sch. Bd. Elec., Westbury (NY). Westbury Dem. Club. **Honors:** NY Inst. of Tech., Man of The Yr., 1976. **Pubns.:** Jt. auth., *Computerized Information Retrieval: A User Manual* (1977). **Activities:** 1; 15, 17, 24; 59, 63, 91 **Addr.:** Chesnutt Library, Fayetteville State University, Fayetteville, NC 28301.

Griffis, Rev. Barbara M. (O. 26, 1919, Johnson City, NY) Subj. catlgr., Soc. Sci. II Soclgy., Lib. of Congs., (1980–), Asst. Cat. Ed., Natl. Un. Cat. Pubn. Proj., 1976–80; Col. Dev. Libn., Un. Theo. Semy., 1975–76, Head, Circ. Srvs., 1972–75, Head Ref. Libn., 1965–72; Libn., Vice Prin. and Tchr., Aleppo Coll. for Girls, Syria, 1954–58. **Educ.:** Univ. of Cincinnati, 1938–42, BS (Educ.); Un. Theo. Semy., 1947–50, MDvnty., 1958–59, MSacred Theo.; Columbia Univ., 1963–65, MS, hons. (LS); Long Island Univ., 1974–76, MA, hons. (Soclgy.). **Orgs.:** ALA. Pres., TLA. Amer. Fed. of State, Cnty. and Mncpl. Empls. Lib. of Congs. Prof. Assn. Washington Litcy. Cncl.: Tutor (1979–). Potomac Assn. of the Ctrl. Atl. Conf., Untd. Church of Christ. **Pubns.:** "The Way to Move Mountains," *Summary of Procs., 28th Anl. Conf., ATLA* (1974); "A Proposed Role for ATLA: a Study of Faculty Status for Theological Librarians," *Summary of Proc., 27th Anl. Conf., ATLA* (1973); jt. auth., "The Reference Collection of the Missionary Research Library," *Occasional Bltn. from the Missn. Resrch. Lib.* (Jl. 17, 1961). **Activities:** 1, 4; 15, 20, 39; 57, 90, 92 **Addr.:** 2800 Quebec St. N.W., Apt. 1040, Washington, DC 20008.

Griffis, Joan Elizabeth (My. 19, 1938, Portland, OR) Media Coord., Portland Pub. Schs., 1973–; Media Spec., Medford Sr. HS, 1971–73; Supvsr. of Tchr. Trng., Cmnty. Coll. of Amer. Samoa, 1970–71; Instr. of Tchr. Trng., Feleti Sch. of Amer. Samoa, 1968–70; TV Tchr., Dept. of Educ., Pago Pago, Amer. Samoa, 1966–68; Sp. and Eng. Tchr., Hayward Unfd. Sch. Dist., 1963–66; Sp., Span., Eng. Tchr., ElDorado Un. HS Dist., 1960–62. **Educ.:** Willamette Univ., 1956–60, BA (Sp., Drama); San Jose State Coll., 1962–66, MA (Instr. Mtrls., TV); Portland State Univ., 1971–74; Certs. (Educ. Media, Sch. Admin., Sec. Tchg.). **Orgs.:** ALA: Lib. Educ. Com. (1980–81); Mem. Promo. Task Frc. (1981); AASL, Dir. Bd. (1976–79), Awd. Sel. Com. (Pres., 1980), Sch. Lib. Media Prog. of the Yr. Com. (1980), Intl. Rel. Com. (1976–77). OR LA. AECT. Amer. Radio Relay Leag. OR Educ. Media Assn.: Bd. (1972–75). **Honors:** Delta Kappa Gamma. **Pubns.:** "How to Be a Winner: The School Library Media Program of the Year Award," *Sch. Media Qtly.* (Sum. 1980); "AV Materials: Can They Be More Creative and Innovative?" *Cath. Lib. World* (O. 1979). **Activities:** 10; 17, 32, 48; 63, 93 **Addr.:** Portland Public Schools, P.O. Box 3107, Portland, OR 97208.

Griffith, Belver C. (Mr. 28, 1931, Hampton, VA) Prof., Info. Sci., Drexel Univ., 1969–; Assoc. in Comms., Annenberg Sch., Univ. of PA NSF Proj. of Sci. Info., 1966–67; Dir. and Prin. Investigator, Exch. in Psy., Amer. Psy. Assn., 1966–69, Assoc. Dir. and Prin. Investigator, 1961–66; Resrch. Assoc., Edward R. Johnstone Trng. and Resrch. Ctr., 1960–62; Mem., Tech. Staff, Bell Telephone Labs., 1956–57. **Educ.:** Univ. of VA, 1948–51, BA (Psy.); Univ. of CT, 1953, MA (Psy.), 1957, PhD (Psy.). **Orgs.:** ASIS: Awds. Com. (1979). AAAS. NATO: Sci. Affairs Div. (Consult., 1976–). Natl. Insts. of Hlth.: Biomed. Comms. Std. Sect. (1976). Natl. Info. Retrieval Colloquium: Bd. of Dirs. (1976). **Honors:** Sigma Xi; Drexel Univ., Rsrch. Awd., 1980; Univ. Coll. London, Sch. of Lib. and Info. Arch., Hon. Rsrch. Fellow, 1975–76; Univ. of Sussex, Hon. Fellow, 1975–76. **Pubns.:** Ed., "Improving Library Services to Users: Some Research Approaches," *Drexel Lib. Qtly.* (Ja. 1971); "Research Prospects and Problems in Education for Library and Information Science" AALA conf. on cassette (1972); "An Empirical Examination of Bradford's Law and the Scattering of Scientific Literature," *Jnl. of ASIS* (1978); "Interlibrary Loans: Impact of the New Copyright Law," *Jnl. of ASIS* (1978); ed., *Key Papers in Information Science* (1980); various other bks., articles. **Activities:** 11; 24, 26, 41; 75, 91, 92 **Addr.:** School of Library and Information Science, Drexel University, Philadelphia, PA 19104.

Griffith, Susan C. (Jn. 7, 1951, Grand Rapids, MI) Dir., Prog. Resrcs., Coop. Chld. Bk. Ctr., 1978–; Asst. Libn., 1977–78; Head Tchr., Salvation Army Day Care Ctr. (Chicago), 1974–76; Elem. Sch. Libn., Kenowa Hills Sch. Dist., (MI) 1973–74. **Educ.:** Ctrl. MI Univ., 1969–73, BS (Educ.); Univ. of WI, 1976–78, MA (LS). **Orgs.:** ALA: ALSC, Notable Chld. Bk. Com. (1980–82). WI LA: Chld. and YA Srvs. Sect. (Bd. of Dir. (1979–80). Women Lib. Workers: Natl. Coord. (1980–81). Natl. Assn. for the Educ. of Young Chld. **Pubns.:** Jt.-auth., "Readable Wisconsin for Children," *WI Lib. Bulletin* March-April 1978 and 1980. **Activities:** 9, 13; 16, 21, 25; 55, 63, 74 **Addr.:** Cooperative Children's Book Center, 600 N. Park St., Madison, WI 53706.

Griffiths, Suzanne N. (Jl. 4, 1925, Syracuse, NY) Classics Libn., Univ. of IL, 1965–, Asst., Rare Bk. Rm., 1960–65. **Educ.:** Syracuse Univ., 1943–47, AB (Eng.); Queens Univ., ON, 1945–46; Syracuse Univ., 1948–49, MA (Eng.); Univ. of IL, 1958–60, MSLS. **Orgs.:** ALA. IL LA. **Activities:** 1; 15; 55 **Addr.:** RR 1, Box 134, Urbana, IL 61801.

Grigg, Dorothy Claire (Jl. 9, 1924, Shelby, NC) Head Catlgr., NC Dept. of Cult. Resrcs., Div. of State Lib., 1962–; Asst. Cat. Libn., NC State Lib., 1959–62; Ord. Libn., Winthrop Coll. Lib., 1954–59; Jr. Asst. Cat. Libn., Woman's Coll. Univ. NC, 1952–54, Asst. Libn., Ref. and Ord. Dept., 1951–52; Ord. Libn., Greensboro Pub. Lib., 1950–51; Libn., Shelby Pub. Lib., 1947–49; Asst. Libn., Rockingham Cnty. Lib., (Leaksville, NC), 1946–47. **Educ.:** Univ. of NC, 1941–45, BA (Eng.), 1945–46, BSLS. **Orgs.:** ALA. SELA. NC LA. E. African Wild Life Socty. **Activities:** 13; 15, 20 **Addr.:** S-2 Country Club Homes, Raleigh, NC 27608.

Grigg, Virginia Caffee (Mr. 5, 1924, Baltimore, MD) Chief, Bureau of Lib. Dev., State Lib. FL, 1972–, Actg. State Libn., 1972–72; Consult., Assoc. Consults. in Educ., 1971; Chief, Bureau of Lib. Dev., State Lib. of FL, 1969–70, Consult., Bureau of Lib. Dev., 1963–69; Instr., Sch. of LS, FL State Univ., 1960–63; Asst. Libn., Leon Cnty. (FL) Pub. Lib., 1955–59; Libn., Tochwotten Branch, Providence (RI) Pub. Lib., 1953–55. **Educ.:** Randolph-Macon Womans Coll., 1941–45, AB; Univ. of NC, 1948–49, BLS. **Orgs.:** ALA: ASCLA/Index of State Libs. Actv. Com. (1978–80); Nom. Com. (Exec. Com. 1977–78); LAD/Sect. on Bldgs. and Equipment, Nom. Com. (1975–76). SELA: Pub. Libs. Sect. (Ch., 1976–78); Interstate Coop. Com. (Ch., 1974–76). FL LA: Pub. Libs. Sect. (Ch., 1966–67); Cit. and Awds. Com. (1976–77). Amer. Socty. for Pub. Admin., Mem. Com. (Ch., 1979–80); Awd. Com., Nom. Com. (Ch., 1978–79). **Honors:** Amer. Socty. for Pub. Admin., N. FL Chap., Pub. Admin. of the Yr., 1976. **Pubns.:** Ed., *FL State Lib. Nsltr.* (1963–65); Ed., *FL Lib. Dir. with Stats.* (1963–65). **Activities:** 9, 13; 24; 95-Library Development. **Addr.:** 2500 Harrimon Cir., Tallahassee, FL 32312.

Griggs, Beatrice E. (S. 16, 1933, Seneca Falls, NY) Assoc., Bur. of Sch. Libs., State Educ. Dept., Albany, NY, 1970–; Lib. Spec., Reg. Ctr. for Instr. Mtrls., 1969–70; Libn., Sand Creek Jr. HS, 1968–69; Libn., Colonie Ctrl. HS, 1966–68; Libn., Lakeshore Rd. Elem. Sch., 1958–66; Libn., Moravia Elem. Sch., 1954–58. **Educ.:** State Univ. Tchrs. Coll., Geneseo, 1950–54, BS (Educ., LS); State Coll. of Educ., Oswego, 1958–63, MS (Educ.); Syracuse Univ., 1967–69, MLS. **Orgs.:** NY LA: Cont. Ed. Com. (Ch., 1980–81); Bur. of Sch. Libs. Liaison (1970–). ALA: AASL, Pres. Awd. Com. (1978–79), Dallas Conf. Com. (1978–79), Media Ctr. Facilities Com. (1975–78), Pubns. Com. (1973–75). East. NY Sch. Lib. Media Assn.: Pres. (1968–70). Onondaga-Oswego Sch. Libns. Assn.: Pres. (1960–61). Various other orgs. Bus. and Prof. Women's Club: Status of Women Com. (Ch., 1979–80). NY State Sum. Sch. of the Arts: Sch. of Thea. (Admin. Dir., 1979–81). **Honors:** Delta Kappa Gamma. **Pubns.:** Ed., *News and Notes* (1977–80). **Activities:** 10, 13; 17, 24, 32 **Addr.:** 22 Knob Hill Rd., Loudonville, NY 12211.

Griggs, H. K., Sr. (Mr. 26, 1910, Reidsville, NC) Retired 1974–; Prin., Reidsville Sr. HS., 1969–74; Prin., Washington HS, 1948–69; Prin., Branch St. Sch., 1945–48; Tchr., 1936–40. **Educ.:** Shaw Univ., 1929–34; Univ. of MI, 1945–48. **Orgs.:** Rockingham Cnty. Lib. Bd. (1968–86); Ch. (1976–81). NC Trustee Assn.: Ch. (1979–81). ALA: ALTA. SELA: SELTA. NAACP. Boy Scouts of America. YMCA. Natl. Educ. Assn. Various other orgs. **Activities:** 9; 47; 63 **Addr.:** 1713 Courtland Ave., Reidsville, NC 27320.

Griggs, John B. (S. 4, 1935, Lincoln, NE) Dir., Lloyd Lib. and Musm., 1972–; Ref. Libn., Cincinnati Pub. Lib., 1966–72; Engin. Libn., Purdue Univ. Libs., 1963–66; Ref. Libn., Milwaukee Pub. Lib., 1960–63. **Educ.:** Univ. of WI, 1953–57, BA (Lang.); Univ. of KY, 1960–61, MS (LS). **Orgs.:** SLA. OH LA. **Activities:** 12; 24, 39; 58, 64, 87 **Addr.:** c/o Lloyd Library and Museum, 917 Plum St., Cincinnati, OH 45202.

Grigsby, Gary L. (Ja. 27, 1945, Marshall, MO) KCMW-FM Msc. Dir./Record Libn., Ctrl. MO State Univ., 1976–; Camdenton, MO, Jr & Sr High Choral Msc., 1972–74. **Educ.:** Univ. of MO, 1963–68, BS (MusEd); Ctrl. MO State Univ., 1973– MA in progress (MusHistLit); Life Tchg. Cert., MO, K-12 Vocal Msc., 1968. **Orgs.:** Msc. LA. Amer. Musicological Socty. Msc. Educ. Natl. Conf. MO Msc. Educ. Assn. **Pubns.:** *Music periodical index, 1946–1948: a computer assisted sort of a selected group of music periodicals in English.* (1981). **Activities:** 1, 12; 15, 30, 49; 55, 61, 93 **Addr.:** Central Missouri State University, P.O. Box 669, Warrensburg, MO 64093.

Grilikhes, Sandra B. (New York, NY) Dir., Annenberg Sch. of Comms. Lib., Univ. of PA, 1969–; Head, Audio, Cult. Actv., Exhibition, Rsv. Bk. Facility, Temple Univ., 1965–69, Head, Ambler Campus Lib., 1961–65; Asst. Head, Film Lib., NY Pub. Lib., 1958–60. **Educ.:** Queens Coll., 1954–58, BA (Hist. of Art, Archit.); Columbia Univ., 1958–60, MS (LS); Bryn Mawr Coll., 1960–61 (Hist. of Art). **Orgs.:** SLA: Comms./Telecom. Div. AAUP. Inst. for Non-Verbal Comm. Rsrch. Amer. Film Inst. **Honors:** Spec. Poetry Consult. to the Bicent., 1975–76. **Pubns.:** *On Women Artists: Poems, 1975-80* (1981); *Landing on the Blue Plain* (1978); *City Poems* (1977); *Body/With Words* (1976); *Sea Agon* (1976); various other pubns. **Activities:** 1, 9; 15, 16, 39; 55, 67, 93 **Addr.:** Annenberg School of Communications, Univ. of Pennsylvania, 3620 Walnut St., Philadelphia, PA 19104.

Grills, Caroline Margaret (Je. 4, 1936, Washington, DC) Dir. of Pubns., Amer. Anthropological Assn., 1981–; Mgr. of Micro. & Back Issues, Amer. Chem. Socty., 1976–81, Head of Prod., Assn. for Supvsn. & Curric. Dev., 1973–76. **Educ.:** Univ. of KS, 1956–59, BA (Radio-TV); Univ. of CA, Los Angeles, 1971, (Scriptwriting); Various positions in TV and publshg. **Orgs.:** Natl. Micro. Assn.: Stan. Com. on Color Microfilm (1979–); Stan. Com. on Terminology (1978–79); Publn. Com. (1979–). Intl. Micro. Congress: Publn. Bd. (1979–). ASIS. Amer. Chem. Socty. Socty. of Photographic Engin. and Sci. Com. on Photographic Papers Sem. (1979–p.). **Honors:** Natl. Micro. Assn., Dele. WACOLIS, 1979. **Pubns.:** Jt. auth. *"Micropublishing in the 80's"* (1980); *"Micrographics Technology"* (1976); "Microblock: A New Method of Presenting Text for Visual Communications," *Jnl. of Micro.* (N.-D. 1979); "Uncapping Handicapped Persons Via Micrographics," *Bltn. of The Amer. Socty. for Info. Sci.* (Ap. 1979); various papers. **Activities:** 12; 17, 32, 33, 37; 60, 91, 95 **Addr.:** 8984 Watchlight Ct., Columbia, MD 21045.

Grimes, Carolyn Ruocco (Jl. 18, 1945, Salina, KS) Pres., Bd. of Trustees, Clinton Pub. Lib., 1979–81; VP, Clinton Cnty. Assn. of Pub. Libs. Inc. 1976–; VP, Bd. of Trustees, Clinton Pub. Lib., 1977–79; various clerical positions. **Educ.:** Susquehanna Univ., 1963–67, AB (Eng., Fr.); Montclair State Coll., 1967 (Readg.). **Orgs.:** IA LA. IA Lib. Trustees Assn.: Treas. (1980–). ALA: ALTA. **Honors:** Lib. Club, Montclair HS, Natalie Armstrong Awd. for Lib. Srv., 1963. **Activities:** 9; 47 **Addr.:** 530 30th Ave. N., Clinton, IA 52732.

Grimm, L. Emily (Mr. 2, 1939, Carlisle PA) Ref. Libn., Univ. of Cincinnati, 1971–; Resrch. Resrcs. Libn., Bowling Green State Univ. Lib., 1967–70; Asst. Catlgr., Lafayette Coll. Lib., 1963–67. **Educ.:** Dickinson Coll., 1957–61, BA (Fr.) cum laude; Univ. of IL, 1961–63, MS LS. Univ. of Pittsburgh, 1970–71 (LS). **Orgs.:** ALA. ASIS: South. OH Chap., PR Ch., 1979–80. OH LA. Acad. LA of OH. AAUP. **Pubns.:** "An Academic Librarian Looks at Staff Orientation and Training," *OH Lib. Assn Bltn.* (Jy. 1978). **Activities:** 1; 20, 39, 49-Online Srching.; 62, 63, 75 **Addr.:** 5400 Hamilton Ave., Apt. 309, Cincinnati, OH 45224.

Grimshaw, Polly Swift (S. 14, 1931, Baltimore, MD) Libn. for Anthro., Soclgy., Cur. of Folklore Col., IN Univ. Lib., 1965–; Libn., Free Lib. of Philadelphia, 1958–59. **Educ.:** Univ. of MO, 1949–53, BA (Anthro.); Drexel Univ., 1957–58, MS (LS). **Orgs.:** ALA: ACRL Com. on Appts. (1977), Com. on Noms. (1978)/Anthro. Sect., Noms. Com. (Ch., 1976–77). Amer. Sociological Assn.: Archs. Com. (1971–73). Amer. Folklore Socty. Cntrl. States Anthro. Assn. **Pubns.:** *Motif-Index to Folk Literature. Bibliography and Abreviations* (1975); "Indiana Folklore; An Annotated Bibliography, 1962–72," *IN Folklore* (1973). **Activities:** 1; 54, 92 **Addr.:** E 760 Indiana University Libraries, Bloomington, IN 47401.

Grimsted, Patricia Kennedy (O. 31, 1935, Elkins, WV) Resrch. Assoc., Harvard Univ., Russ. Resrch. Ctr., Ukrainian Resrch. Inst., 1974–; Visit. Resrch. Prof., Warsaw Univ., Inst. of Hist., 1981–82, 1979, 1977; Visit. Resrch. Schol., Acad. of Sci. of the USSR, 1978, 1976, 1973; Resrch. Assoc., Columbia Univ., Russ. Inst., 1969–74; Assoc. Prof., Amer. Univ., 1971–72; Lectr., Univ. of MD, 1968–70; Assoc., Russ. Resrch. Ctr., Harvard Univ., 1967–68, 1964; Lectr., Dept. of Hist., Bucknell Univ., 1965–67; various positions as fellow, prof., 1958–70. **Educ.:** Univ. of CA, Berkeley, 1955–57, BA (Hist.), 1957–64, MA, PhD (Russ. Hist.). **Orgs.:** SAA: Com. on Intl. Arch. Affairs (1971–). Intl. Cncl. on Arch. Amer. Hist. Assn.: Com. on Adams and Beer Prizes (1970–73). Amer. Assn. for the Advnc. of Slavic Std. Baltic Std. Assn. **Honors:** SAA, Waldo Giffor Leland Prize, 1973; NEH, Resrch. Grant, 1972–; Amer. Cncl. of Learned Soctys., Resrch. Grant, 1969, 1972. **Pubns.:** *Archives and Manuscript Repositories in the USSR: Estonia, Latvia, Lithuania, and Belorussia* (1981); *Archives and Manuscript Repositories in the USSR: Moscow and Leningrad. Supplement I* (1976); *Archives and Manuscript Repositories in the USSR: Moscow and Lenin-*

PROFESSIONAL ACTIVITIES: Institutions: 1. Acad. lib.; 2. Arch.; 3. Assn.; 4. Fed./Gvt. lib.; 5. Inst. lib.; 6. Mfr./Suppl.; 7. Milit. lib.; 8. Musm.; 9. Pub. lib.; 10. Sch. lib.; 11. Sch. of lib. sci.; 12. Spec. lib.; 13. State lib.; 14. (other). **Functions/Activities:** 15. Acq./Col. dev.; 16. Adult srvs.; 17. Admin.; 18. Apprais.; 19. Archit./Bldgs.; 20. Cat./Class.; 21. Chld. srvs.; 22. Circ.; 23. Cons./Pres.; 24. Consult.; 25. Cont. ed.; 26. Educ. lib. sci.; 27. Ext. srvs.; 28. Fund/Grants; 29. Gvt. pubs.; 30. Indx./Abs.; 31. Instr. lib. use; 32. Media srvs.; 33. Micro.; 34. Netwks./Coop.; 35. Persnl.; 36. PR; 37. Publshg.; 38. Recs. mgt.; 39. Ref. srvs.; 40. Repro.; 41. Resrch.; 42. Review.; 43. Secur.; 44. Serials; 45. Spec. col.; 46. Tech. srvs.; 47. Trustees/Bds.; 48. YA srvs.; 49. (other).

grad (1972); *The Foreign Ministers of Alexander I: Political Attitudes and the Conduct of Russian Diplomacy, 1801–1825* (1969); "The Fate of Early Records in Lviv Archives: Documentation from Western Ukraine under Polish Rule to 1772," *Slavonic and E. European Review* (forthcoming); various articles, cats. **Activities:** 1, 12; 24, 41, 42; 54, 57 **Addr.:** Harvard Ukrainian Research Institute, 1583 Massachusetts Ave., Cambridge, MA 02138.

Grisham, Frank Phillips (Ag. 28, 1928, Birmingham, AB) Dir., Assoc. Prof. (Bibl.), Vanderbilt Univ. Lib., 1968–; Assoc. Dir. Jt. Univ. Libs., Assoc. Prof. (Bibl.), 1967–68; Asst. Dir. Jt. Univ. Libs., Assoc. Prof. (Bibl.), 1965–1967; Libn. Dvnty. Lib. Assoc. Prof. Dvnty. Sch., 1956–64; Dir., of Relig. Life, Birmingham-South. Coll., 1954–56; Assoc. Mnstr., McCoy Meth. Church (Birmingham, AB), 1954–56; Libn., Relig. Sect., Jt. Univ. Libs., 1952–54. **Educ.:** Birmingham-South. Coll., 1946–49, AB (Hist.); George Peabody Coll., 1956–58, MLS; Vanderbilt Univ., 1949–52, MDiv (Church Hist.). **Orgs.:** ALA. ARL: Bd. of Dir. (1977–80); Ofc. of Mgt. Stds. Adv. Com. (1977–). SELA: Exec. Bd. (1971). Southeast. Lib. Ntwk. (SOLINET): Bd. of Dir. (1977–82, Ch., 1978–79). TN LA: Pres. (1976) Other orgs. and Ofcs. Family and Chld. Srvs.: Bd. of Dir. (1978). Civic Com. on Pub. Educ.: Past Pres. Ordained Meth. Mnstr. **Honors:** Delegate, WHCOLIS, 1979. **Activities:** 1; 17, 24, 34; 56, 75, 90 **Addr.:** Vanderbilt University Library, 419 21st Ave. S., Nashville, TN 37203.

Grisso, Karl M. (My. 22, 1937, Sidney, IN) Assoc. Prof./Ref. and Col. Dev. Libn., East. IL Univ., 1969–; Asst. Libn., Hanover Coll., 1967–69; Head, Gvt. Docums., Pub. Lib., Ft. Wayne and Allen Cnty., 1962–67. **Educ.:** Manchester Coll., 1955–59, BS (Hist.); IN Univ., 1960–62, AM (Hist.), 1964–66, AM (LS); Univ. of IL, 1972–80, PhD (Educ.). **Orgs.:** ALA. Amer. Hist. Assn. Org. of Amer. Histns. IL State Hist. Socty. Amer. Assn. for Higher Educ. **Honors:** Kappa Delta Pi; Phi Kappa Phi; Phi Delta Kappa; Beta Phi Mu. **Activities:** 1; 15, 17, 39; 57, 92 **Addr.:** 2424 Village Rd., Charleston, IL 61920.

Groen, Frances K. (Brantford, ON) Life Sci. Area Libn., McGill Univ., 1973–; Cur., Hist. of Med., Univ. of Pittsburgh, 1969–73, Sr. Info. Libn., 1968–69; Tech. Srvs. Libn., Acq., Stanford Univ., 1963–67; Ref. Libn., Univ. of Toronto, 1961–62. **Educ.:** Univ. of Toronto, 1959, BA, 1961, BLS; Univ. of Pittsburgh, 1973, MA. (Hist. and Phil. of Sci.) **Orgs.:** Assn. of Can. Med. Colls.: Spec. Resrc. Com. on Med. Sch. Libs., Ch. (1976–78). Can. Assn. of Info. Sci.: Bd. of Dir. (1979–). Med. LA: Intl. Coop. Com. (1977–; Ch., 1978–79); Anl. Mtg. Prog. Com. (1979–81); Various other ofcs. Can. Inst. for Sci. and Tech. Info.: Adv. Com. on the Hlth. Sci. Resrcs. Ctr. (Ch., 1978–80). Various other orgs. AAAS. Amer. Assn. for the Hist. of Med. ASTD. **Honors:** Beta Phi Mu. **Pubns.:** Reviews. **Activities:** 1, 12; 15, 17, 19; 75, 80, 91 **Addr.:** Medical Library, McGill University, 3655 Drummond St., Montreal, PQ H3G 1Y6 Canada.

Groendyke, Judith Kay (My. 20, 1940, Pella, IA) Head, Bibl. Srch., Univ. of IA, 1973–, Catlgr., 1968–73. **Educ.:** Central Coll., 1958–62, BA (Eng.); Univ. of IA, 1965–68, MA (LS). **Orgs.:** IA LA. ALA. Frnds. of the Univ. of IA Libs. **Activities:** 1; 15, 20, 46; 56 **Addr.:** 922 E. College, Iowa City, IA 52240.

Groot, Elizabeth H. (Ja. 22, 1922, Buitenzorg, Java, Dutch E. Indies) Mgr., Tech. Info. Srvs., Schenectady Chems., Inc., 1973–; Resrch., Schenectady Bur. of Mncpl. Resrch., 1967–71; Chem., Un. Oil Co. of CA, 1942–47. **Educ.:** Univ. of Chicago, 1939–42, BS (Chem.); SUNY, Albany, 1974–78, MLS (Lib. and Info. Sci.). **Orgs.:** ASIS. SLA. Amer. Chem. Socty. **Pubns.:** "A Comparison of Library Tools for Monograph Verification," *Lib. Rsrcs. & Tech. Srvs.* (Ap.–Je. 1981); "International Coden Directory," *Micro. Review* (Mr.–Ap. 1978); "Unique Identifiers for Serials: 1977 Update," *The Serials Libn.* (Spr. 1978); "Unique Identifiers for Serials: An Annotated, Comprehensive Bibliography," *The Serials Libn.* (Fall 1976). **Activities:** 12; 17, 39; 56, 59, 60 **Addr.:** Schenectady Chemicals, Inc., 2750 Balltown Rd., Schenectady, NY 12309.

Groover, Eloise T. (F. 14, 1918, Leesburg, GA) Retired, 1981–; Admin., Sch. Lib. Media, FL Dept. of Educ. 1964–81; Instr., Sch. of LS, FL State Univ., 1961–64; Libn., Miller Cnty. HS, 1952–61, Tchr., 1939–52. **Educ.:** GA State Coll. for Women, 1935–39, AB (Eng.); FL State Univ., 1955, MS (LS). **Orgs.:** ALA. AECT. FL Assn. for Media in Educ. SELA. Various other orgs. Delta Kappa Gamma. FL Assn. of Sch. Libns.: Exec. Secy. (1964–73). FL LA: Chld. and Young People's Sect. (Ch., 1966–77). Assn. of State Sch. Lib. Supvsrs.: Ch. (1965–66). Various other orgs. **Honors:** Beta Phi Mu. **Activities:** 11, 14-State Educ. Agency; 25, 26; 63 **Addr.:** 1711 Country Club Dr., Tallahassee, FL 32301.

Grosch, Audrey N. (Ja. 10, 1934, Minneapolis, MN) Prof., Dir., Lib. Srvs. Div., Lib. Syst. Dept., Univ. of MN Libs., 1978–, Consult., 1965–, Assoc. Prof., Systs. Div., 1974–78, Asst. Prof., 1969–74, Instr., 1965–69. **Educ.:** Univ. of MN, 1952–55, BA (Fr., Hist.), 1955–56, MA (LS). **Orgs.:** ASIS: Past Pres. (1979); Pres. (1978); Pres.-Elect (1977); Cnclr. (1975–76). SLA: Various coms. (1958–73). Assn. for Comp. Mach.: Twin Cities Chap. (Exec. VP, 1979–80). Data Prcs. Mgt. Assn. Intl. Shooter Dev. Fund: Bd. of Dirs. (1978–80). Natl. Rifle Assn.: Collegiate Prog. Com. (1977); Intl. Competitions Com. (1977–78). **Honors:** SLA, Prof. Awd., 1977; SLA, John Cotton Dana Lectr., 1972. **Pubns.:** *Minicomputers in Libraries* (1979); "Library Automation," *Anl. Review of Info. Sci. and Tech.* (1976); various articles, (1965–). **Activities:** 1; 24, 34, 46; 56, 62, 75 **Addr.:** 17210 Cedarcrest Dr., Eden Prairie, MN 55344.

Grose, B. Donald (Ja. 13, 1943, West Plains, MO) Dir., of Lib. Srvs., IN Univ.–Purdue Univ., Ft. Wayne, 1975–; Asst. Dir., Libs., Univ. of MO, Columbia, 1973–75, Asst. to the Dir. of Libs., 1971–73, Acq. Libn., 1970–71. **Educ.:** Southwest MO State Univ., 1965–67, BA (Eng.), Univ. of KY, 1967–69, MA (Eng.), 1969–70, MSLS; Univ. of MO, 1973–79 PhD (Theat. Hist.). **Orgs.:** ALA. Thea. LA. Amer. Socty. for Thea. Resrch. Amer. Thea. Assn. Semiotic Socty. of Amer. **Pubns.:** Jt.-auth., *A Selected & Annotated Bibliography for Secondary School Teacher & Student* (1976); *The Antiquarian Booktrade* (1972); "Theatre Arts in the High School Library," *Hoosier Sch. Libs.* (O. 1976); "Job Enrichment in the Academic Library," Jnl. of Acad. Libnshp. (M. 1976); "The Teasdale-Rossetti Ghost," *RQ* (Sp. 1973). **Activities:** 1; 17; 55 **Addr.:** Walter E. Helmke Library, Indiana University-Purdue University at Fort Wayne, 2101 Coliseum Blvd. E., Fort Wayne, IN 46805.

Grose, Rosemary Fullerton (My. 26, 1946, Springfield, MO) Dir. of Media Srvs., Leo Jr.-Sr. HS, 1977–; Assoc. Fac., IN Univ.,-Purdue Univ., 1975–80; Supvsr. of Elem. Sch. Libs., Fulton Pub. Sch., 1971–75; Language Arts Tchr., Anderson Jr. HS, 1967–70. **Educ.:** SW MO State Univ., 1964–67, BS in Educ (Eng.); Univ. of MO, 1970–71, MA (LS). **Orgs.:** ALA: AASL. AECT. Assn. for IN Media Educ.: Dist. Dir. (1979–81); Young Hoosier Book Awd. Com. (1976–1979); Conf. Plng. Com. (1979–80). Ft. Wayne LA. Natl. Educ. Assn. IN State Tchrs. Assn. E. Allen Educ. Assn. Delta Kappa Gamma. **Honors:** Beta Phi Mu. **Activities:** 10; 32, 48 **Addr.:** 7518 Hope Farm Rd., Ft. Wayne, IN 46815.

Gross, Alice (N. 20, 1926, Chicago, IL) Corporate Libn., Joseph E. Seagram and Sons, Inc., 1973–; Head Libn., Distilled Spirits Cncl. of U.S., 1971–72; Head Libn., Ogilvy and Mather, Advert., 1966–71; Head Libn., Warwick, Welsh and Miller, 1958–64. **Educ.:** Hunter Coll., 1946–50, BA (Econ., Eng.); Columbia Univ., 1950–52, MLS. **Orgs.:** SLA. ALA. ASIS. Socty. of Wine Educs. Les Amis du Vin. Sommelier Socty. **Pubns.:** Article in *Food Sci. and Tech.* (F. 1978); various articles in pubns. on alchl. beverage indus. **Activities:** 12; 17; 51, 68 **Addr.:** 47 E. 87th St., New York, NY 10028.

Gross, Dean Cochran (F. 21, 1922, Waterville, OH) Lib. Dir., Norfolk Pub. Lib., 1977–; Dir., Citizens Lib., (Washington, PA), 1973–76; State Libn., KS State Lib., 1971–73; Dir., Harrisburg and Dauphin Cnty. Pub. Lib., 1966–71. **Educ.:** Miami Univ., 1941–47, BA (Hist.); Drexel Univ., 1951–52, MS (LS). **Orgs.:** ALA. VA LA. SELA. Norfolk Rotary Club. Torch Club. **Activities:** 9; 16, 27, 34; 55, 78, 89 **Addr.:** 6138 Ivor Ave., Norfolk, VA 23502.

Gross, Dorothy-Ellen (Je. 13, 1949, Buffalo, NY) Head Libn., Assoc. Prof. of Bibl., Barat Coll., 1980–, Asst. Libn., 1977–79, Tech. Srvs. Libn., 1975–77. **Educ.:** Westminster Coll., 1967–71, BA (Christ. Educ.); McCormick Theo. Semy., 1971–75, MDiv; Rosary Coll., 1974–75, MALS; Kent State Univ., 1977, Cert.; Univ. of IA, 1980, Cert. (Bus. Ref.). **Orgs.:** Chicago Area Theo. LA: Treas. (1978–); Com. on Bibl. Inst., Ch.; Futures Com. ALA. Pvt. Acad. Libs. of IL: Vice-Ch. (1981); Ch. (1982). Libras: Futures Com. (1981). AAUP. **Activities:** 1; 15, 17, 31; 50, 75, 90 **Addr.:** 649 Chip Ct., Gurnee, IL 60031.

Gross, Richard F. (Ap. 16, 1940, Castine, ME) Lib. Dir., Lewiston Pub. Lib., 1971–; Eng. Instr. and Libn., ME Maritime Acad., 1969–71; Eng. Tchr., Traip Acad., 1967–68; Amer. Hist. Tchr., Mid. Pac. Inst., Honolulu, 1966–67; Eng. Tchr., Radford HS, Honolulu, 1965–66; Eng. Tchr., Hampden Acad. (ME), 1963–65; Eng. Tchr., Orono HS (ME), 1962–63. **Educ.:** Univ. of ME, Orono, 1958–62, BS (Eng.), 1962–64, MAT (Eng.), 1969–71, MLS; PA State Univ. (Eng.). **Orgs.:** ME LA: Treas. (1972–74); VP (1974–76); Pres. (1976–78); Past Pres. (1978–80). New Eng. LA: Bibl. Com. (1974–76). ALA: PLA, Leg. Com. (1979–81). Lewiston/Auburn Rotary Club. Androscoggin Valley Untd. Way. Litcy. Voluns. of ME: Bd. of Dirs. (1978–81). Ctrl. ME Lib. Dist.: Exec. Bd. (Ch., 1973–77). Various other orgs. **Honors:** Androscoggin Cnty. Untd. Way, Campaign Anl. Awd., 1978. **Pubns.:** Ed., *Historic Lewiston: Franco - American Origins* (1976); ed., *Historic Lewiston: A City in Transition* (1977). **Activities:** 9; 17, 24, 42; 50, 55, 69 **Addr.:** Lewiston Public Library, 105 Park St., Lewiston, ME 04240.

Grosshans, Maxine Z. (S. 16, 1941, Pittsburgh, PA) Head, Ref. Srvs., Univ. of MD Law Sch., 1974–; Libn., Venable, Baetjer and Howard, 1969–74; Asst. Catlgr., Biddle Law Lib., Univ. of PA, 1968–69; Asst. Libn., Contl. Natl. Amer. Grp., 1964–68. **Educ.:** Univ. of Pittsburgh, 1959–63, BA (Pol. Sci.); Univ. of Chicago, 1963–69, MA (LS). **Orgs.:** Law Libns. Socty. of DC. Baltimore Legal Info. Sci. Spec. AALL. Pvt. LA. **Honors:** Alpha Delta Pi. **Activities:** 1; 34, 39, 41; 77, 78 **Addr.:** Marshall Law Library, University of Maryland School of Law, 20 N. Paca St., Baltimore, MD 21201.

Grossman, David G. (F. 22, 1954, New York, NY) Mktg. Rep., Syst. Dev. Corp., 1979–; Supvsr., Scientific Srvs., Travenol Labs., 1979; Info. Spec., Richardson Co., 1977–79. **Educ.:** Univ. of MI, 1971–75, BA (Jnlsm.); 1975–77, AMLS. **Orgs.:** ASIS: Mem. Com. (1979–81). Assoc. Info. Mgrs.; Chicago OLUG: Ch. (1978–79). SLA. **Activities:** 6, 12; 39, 49-Online Services; 56, 62, 75 **Addr.:** SDC Search Service, 625 N. Michigan Ave., Suite 500, Chicago, IL 60611.

Grossman, George S. (My. 31, 1938, Poltar, Czechoslovakia) Prof. of Law & Law Libn., Northwestern Univ. Law Sch., 1979–; Prof. of Law & Law Libn., Univ. of MN, 1973–79; Prof. of Law & Law Libn., Univ. of UT, 1968–73; Tech. Prcs. Law Libn., Univ. of PA, 1966–68. **Educ.:** Univ. of Chicago, 1957–61, BA (Honors), (Intl. Rel.); Stanford Law Sch., 1963–1966, LLB (Law); Brigham Young Univ., 1969–71, MA (LS). **Orgs.:** AALL: Ch., Com. on Job Security, (1970–72); Co-Ch., Com. on Ethics, (1972–73); Co-Ch., Com. on Index to Legal Per., (1977–78); Co-Ch., Spec. Com. on the Indexing of Legal Lit. (1978–79). Assn. of Amer. Law Schs.: Com. on Libs. (1975–1977). **Pubns.:** *The Sovereignty of American Indian Tribes* (1979); Contrib., *How to Find the Law* (1976); *Clinical Legal Education: An Annotated Bibliography* (1974); *Bibliographic Control in Law and the Environment* (1972); articles and reviews. **Activities:** 1, 12; 17, 19, 24, 31; 77 **Addr.:** Northwestern University Law Library, 357 E. Chicago Ave., Chicago, IL 60611.

Grossmann, Maria (Je. 12, 1919, Vienna, Austria) Libn., Harvard Dvnty. Sch., 1979–, 1965–74; Libn. for Col. Dev., Harvard Univ. Lib., 1974–79. **Educ.:** Smith Coll., 1940–42, BA (Hist.); Radcliffe Coll., 1942–43, MA (Hist.); Harvard Univ., 1943–44, PhD (Hist.); Simmons Coll., 1953–56, MLS. **Orgs.:** ATLA: Pres. (1969); Bd. of Microtext (1975–). ALA. Amer. Socty. for Church Hist. Renaissance Socty. of Amer. Amer. Socty. for Reformation Std. Luther Gesellschaft. **Honors:** Amer. Phil. Socty., Flwshp., 1964; Amer. Cncl. of Learned Socty., Flwshp., 1964; Deutsche Forschungsgemeinschaft, Flwshp., 1965; ATLA, Flwshp., 1965. **Pubns.:** *Humanism in Wittenberg, 1485-1517* (1975); "Wittenberg Printing, Early Sixteenth Century," *Sixteenth Century Essays and Std.* (1970); various other articles. **Activities:** 1; 15, 17; 90 **Addr.:** Harvard Divinity School, 45 Francis Ave., Cambridge, MA 02138.

Groth, Paul E. (Jl. 14, 1942, Winterset, IA) Div. VP, deHaen Info. Systs., Micromedex, Inc., 1978–; Tech. Info. Spec., Fed. Drug Admin., Bur. of Drugs, 1976–78; Assoc. Prof., Clinical Pharm., Creighton Univ., 1974–76; Assoc. Coord., Oper. Srvs., NE Reg. Med. Prog., 1970–74. **Educ.:** Univ. of IA, 1963–67, BS (Pharm.), 1967–70, MS (Hosp. Pharm.). **Orgs.:** Drug Info. Assn.: Secy. (1979–81). Amer. Socty. of Hosp. Pharmacists. Med. LA. NE Socty. of Hosp. Pharmacists. Amer. Pub. Hlth. Assn. **Pubns.:** Jt. auth., "Lactulose – Important Foreign Drugs," *Hosp. Pharm.* (F. 1975); jt. auth., "Suspected Reactions to Gamma Benzene Hexachloride," *Jnl. of the Amer. Med. Assn.* (D. 1976); jt. auth., "Scabies: Transcutaneous Poisoning During Treatment," *Pediatrics* (Ap. 1977); jt. auth., "Drug Reaction Alerts," *Amer. Jnl. of Hosp. Pharm.* (Jl. 1977); jt. auth., "Drug Evaluation Data – Prazosin," *Drug. Intelligence and Clinical Pharm.* (Jl. 1978); various presentations, articles. **Activities:** 14-Publshr.; 15, 33, 37; 60, 80, 87 **Addr.:** deHaen Information Systems, Micromedex, Inc., 2750 S. Shoshone St., Englewood, CO 80110.

Grotzinger, Laurel Ann (Ap. 15, 1935, Truman, MN) Dean & Chief Resrch. Ofcr., Grad. Coll., West. MI Univ., 1979–, Prof., 1968–, Assoc. Prof., 1966–68, Asst. Prof., 1964–66; Asst. Libn. & Inst., IL State Univ., 1958–62. **Educ.:** Carleton Coll., 1953–57, BA (Eng.); Univ. of IL, 1957–58, MS (LS), 1962–64, PhD (LS). **Orgs.:** ALA: Lib. Hist. RT (Secy.-Treas., 1973–74); Ref. and Subscrpn. Books Com. AALS: Ed. Bd., *Jnl. of Educ. for Libnshp.* (1973–77). MI LA: Mem. Com. (1966–69). Beta Phi Mu: Kappa Chap. (Pres. 1967–68). Cncl. of Grad. Schs. in US. Phi Beta Kappa: Southwest. MI Assn. (Pres. 1977–78). AAUP: West. MI Univ. Chap. (Exec. Com., 1968–70). Frdm. to Read Fndn. **Honors:** Pi Delta Epsilon, 1956. **Pubns.:** *The Power and the Dignity: Librarianship and Katharine Sharp* (1966); "Alberta L. Brown, 1894–" in *Special Delivery: a Collection of Papers, 1974–77* (1978); "Dewey's 'Splendid Women' and Their Impact on Library Education" in *Milestones to the Present, Papers from Library History Seminar V* (1978); "Faculty Duties and Responsibilities" in *The Administrative Aspects of Education for Librarianship: A Symposium* (1975); six biographies in *Dict. of Amer. Lib. Biog.* (1978); various articles, reviews, oral presentations. **Activities:** 1, 11; 17, 39, 41; 91 **Addr.:** 2729 Mockingbird Dr., Kalamazoo, MI 49008.

Grove, Lynn Albert (Jy. 12, 1938, Carbondale, IL) Cur., Quaker Col., Coll. Archvst., Wilmington Coll. of Ohio, 1979–; Head Libn., McKendree Coll., 1968–77; Asst. Catlgr., Coll. of Wooster, 1964–68. **Educ.:** McKendree Coll. 1956–60, AB (Eng.-Jnlsm.); Univ. of Denver, 1963–64, MA (LS). Emory Univ. and GA Dept. of Arch., 1976, Cert. (Arch. Mgt.). **Orgs.:** ALA. SAA. Socty. of GA Archvsts. Midwest Arch. Conf. **Activities:** 1, 2; 23, 45, 46; 69, 90 **Addr.:** Pyle Center, Box 1173, Wilmington College, Wilmington, OH 45177.

Special Subjects/Services: 50. Adult educ.; 51. Advert./Mktg.; 52. Aerosp.; 53. Agric.; 54. Area std.; 55. Arts/Hum.; 56. Autom.; 57. Bibl./Prtg.; 58. Bio. sci.; 59. Bus./Fin.; 60. Chem.; 61. Copyrt.; 62. Documtn.; 63. Educ.; 64. Engin.; 65. Env.; 66. Eth. grps.; 67. Film; 68. Food/Nutr.; 69. Geneal.; 70. Geo.; 71. Geol.; 72. Handcpd.; 73. Hist.; 74. Int. frdm.; 75. Info. sci.; 76. Insr.; 77. Law; 78. Legis.; 79. Math./Comp. sci.; 80. Med.; 81. Metals; 82. Nat. resrcs.; 83. Newsp.; 84. Nuc. sci.; 85. Oral hist.; 86. Petr./Energy; 87. Pharm.; 88. Phys./Astr./Math.; 89. Readg.; 90. Relig.; 91. Sci./Tech.; 92. Soc. sci.; 93. Telecom.; 94. Transp.; 95. (other).

Grove, Pearce S. (S. 21, 1930, Augusta, GA) Dir. of Libs., West. IL Univ., 1975–81; Lib. Dir., East. NM Univ., 1966–75; Asst. Dir. of Libs., KS State Univ., 1964–66; Head Libn., CO Women's Coll., 1961–64; Acq., Serials Libn., Asst. Prof., Univ. of IL, Chicago, 1960–61; Instr., Asst. Libn., Univ. of IL, Urbana, 1958–60. **Educ.:** Univ. of FL, 1956, BA (Hist.), 1957, MED; Univ. of IL, 1958, MSLS; East. NM Univ., 1970 (Educ. Admin.). **Orgs.:** ALA: ACRL/Bd./Univ. Libs. Sect., Prog. Com., Ch.; Nom. Com., Ch. IL LA. IL ACRL: Pres.-Elect. Various other orgs. Phi Delta Kappa: Schol. Com., Ch. U.S. Nvl. Rsv. Assn. Univ. of IL Alum. Assn. **Honors:** Phi Kappa Phi; Border Reg. LA, Ref. Awd., 1975. **Pubns.:** "Nonbook Materials," *Law Lib. Jnl.* (N. 1972); "Standards for the Bibliographic Control of Nonprint Media," *The Bowker Anl.* (1972); "Bibliographic Control–Who's Responsible," *Library and Media Marriage or Divorce* (1977); jt. auth., *Systems and Standards for the Bibliographic Control of Nonprint Media* (1975); *Nonprint Media in Academic Libraries* (1975); various other bks., articles. **Activities:** 1, 2; 17, 19, 24; 56, 83 **Addr.:** 620 Western Ave., Macomb, IL 61455.

Grove, R. Genevieve (Ap. 2, 1912, WA) Docum. Libn., Univ. of WA Law Lib., 1968–, Cat. Libn., 1953–65; Cat. Libn., Univ. of WA Lib., 1963–64. **Educ.:** Univ. of WA, BA (Gen. Std.), 1952–53 MA (LS). **Orgs.:** AALL: Mem. Com., Rcrt. Com. ALA. Univ. of WA Fac. Club: House Com. **Activities:** 1, 12; 20, 29; 77 **Addr.:** Law Library, University of Washington, Seattle, WA 98105.

Grover, Mark L. (Jn. 26, 1947, Malad, ID) Latin Amer. Stds. Libn., Brigham Young Univ., 1973–. **Educ.:** Brigham Young Univ., 1968–71, BA (Hist.), 1971–73, MLIS; IN Univ., 1978–79, MA (Hist.). **Orgs.:** Sem. on the Acq. of Latin Amer. Lib. Mtrls. (SALALM): Bibl. Com. (1976–). Reforma. Latin Amer. Stds. Assn. **Honors:** Phi Kappa Phi; Beta Phi Mu. **Pubns.:** "Index to Volume 83," *Amer. Hist. Rev.* (D. 1979); "The Mexican American in Utah: A Bibliography," *UT Libs.* (Spr. 1975). **Activities:** 1; 15, 39, 41; 54, 66, 73 **Addr.:** Harold B. Lee Library, Brigham Young University, Provo, UT 84602.

Grover, Robert J. (O. 27, 1942, LaPorte, IN) Asst. Dean, Sch. of Lib. and Info. Mgt., Univ. of South. CA, 1976–; Assoc. Instr., Grad. Lib. Sch., IN Univ., 1976; Libn., Oak Park/River Forest HS, 1970–74; Media Srvs. Coord., Westville Pub. Schs., 1968–70. **Educ.:** Ball State Univ., 1961–65, BA (Eng.); IN Univ., 1968–70, MLS, 1974–76, PhD (LS). **Orgs.:** ALA: ALSC, Film Eval. Com. (1980–82); AASL. CA Media and Lib. Educs. Assn.: South. Sect. (Pres., 1981), Resrch. Com. (Co-Ch., 1978–80). Amer. Ctr. of Films for Chld.: Exec. Bd. (1979–). CA LA: Chld. Srvs. Chap. Various other orgs. Cub Scouts. **Honors:** Beta Phi Mu, 1970; Pi Lambda Theta, 1976. **Pubns.:** Ed., *Children's Film International* (1979–80); "A Qualitative and Quantitative Study of Children's Film Reviews," *Top of the News* (Spr. 1981); "Library Media Programming and Learning: A Summary of Major Research," *CMLEA Jnl.* (Spr. 1980). **Activities:** 11; 17, 21, 25 **Addr.:** 633 W. Kelso St., Inglewood, CA 90301.

Grover, Robert J. (O. 27, 1942, LaPorte, IN) Dean, Sch. of LS, Emporia State Univ., 1981–; Asst. Dean, Sch. of Lib. and Info. Mgt., Univ. of South. CA, 1979–81, Asst. Prof., 1976–81; Libn., Oak Park and River Forest HS, 1970–74. **Educ.:** Ball State Univ., 1961–65, BA (Eng.); IN Univ., 1968–70, MLS, 1974–76, PhD (LS). **Orgs.:** ALA: ALSC, Film Eval. Com. (1980–); AASL. CA Media and Lib. Educs. Assn.: South. Sect. (Pres., 1980–81), Resrch. Com. (Co-Ch., 1978–80), Schol. Ch. (1978–79). IL Assn. of Sch. Libns.: Pubns. Com. (Ch., 1973–75). KS LA. Various other orgs. Amer. Ctr. of Films for Chld.: Exec. Bd. (1979–). KS Assn. for Educ. Comms. Tech. **Honors:** Beta Phi Mu, 1970; Pi Lambda Theta, 1976. **Pubns.:** Jt. auth., "A Study of Children's Film Reviews," *Top of the News* (Spr. 1981); *Media: Resources for Discovery* (1974); ed., *Chld.'s Film Intl.* (1977, 1979–80); jt. auth., "Research on Media and Learning: A Preliminary Report of the CMLEA Research Committee," *CMLEA Jnl.* (Spr./Sum. 1979); "Library Media Programming and Learning: A Summary of Major Research," *CMLEA Jnl.* (Spr. 1980). **Activities:** 11; 26 **Addr.:** School of Library Science, Emporia State University, 1200 Commercial, Emporia, KS 66801.

Grubel, Margaret Johnson (Mr. 30, 1923, Winchester, NH) Sch. Lib. Media Spec., Sauquoit Valley Ctrl. Sch., 1970–, Tchr., Home Econ., 1945–48. **Educ.:** Univ. of NH, 1941–45, BS (LA); Syracuse Univ., 1971–74, MLS. **Orgs.:** Ctrl. NY LA. NY LA. ALA. **Honors:** Phi Upsilon Omicron; Kappa Delta; Beta Phi Mu. **Activities:** 10; 21, 31, 32; 63 **Addr.:** 9453 Paris Hill Rd., Sauquoit, NY 13456.

Gruben, Karl T. (N. 17, 1951, Pampa, TX) Libn., Vinson and Elkins, 1977–; Catlgr., TX State Law Lib., 1975–77. **Educ.:** Univ. of TX, 1969–73, BA (Hist.), 1973–77, MLS; S. TX Coll. of Law, 1978–. **Orgs.:** TX LA: SL Div. Pres. (1978); Cnclr. (1980–83). AALL. Southwest. Assn. Law Libs. Beta Phi Mu: Beta Eta Chap. (Treas., 1980). Alum. Assn., Univ. TX GSLS: Pres. (1980–82). **Pubns.:** "Annotated Bibliography of Texas Legal Materials," *Law Lib. Jnl.* (Spr. 1981). **Activities:** 12; 17, 39; 77 **Addr.:** Library, Vinson & Elkins, Houston, TX 77002.

Gruhl, Andrea Morris (D. 9, 1939, Ponca City, OK) Trustee, Howard Cnty. Pub. Lib. Syst., 1979–; Volun., Natl. Gallery of Art Lib., 1978–80; Exec. Bd., Lib. Tech. Com., Baltimore Reg. Plng. Cncl., 1976–79; Art Hist. Resrch., Joseph Alsop, 1972–74; various ref. libn. and cat. positions, 1968–79. **Educ.:** Wesleyan Coll., 1957–61, BA (Educ.); Univ. of MD, 1967–68, MLS; Johns Hopkins Univ., 1969–70, M (Liberal Arts); Univ. of MD, 1968, 1970–72, M (Art Hist.). **Orgs.:** ARLIS/NA: Pubn. Exhibit Coord. (1980–82). Amer. Socty. of Indxrs. MD LA: Trustee Div. (VP, Pres.-Elect, 1981–83). ALA: Trustee Div. Frnds. of the Howard Cnty. Pub. Lib.: Pres. (1976). **Honors:** Beta Phi Mu, 1968; Kappa Delta Epsilon, 1961. **Pubns.:** *Annotated Bibliography of Books in the General Reference Department, McKeldin Library, University of Maryland, That List and/or Locate Newspapers and/or Magazines* (My. 1972); *Annotated Bibliography of Member Publications Exhibited at 8th Annual Conference, Art Libraries Society of North America* (Ja. 1980); *Annotated Bibliography of Member Publications Exhibited at 9th Annual Conference, Art Libraries Society of North America* (F. 1981); *Learning Vacations* (1978). **Activities:** 4, 5; 39, 41, 47; 55, 57 **Addr.:** 5990 Jacob's Ladder, Columbia, MD 21045.

Grunder, Henry D. (S. 16, 1937, Medina, OH) Cur. of Rare Bks., Coll. of William and Mary, 1967–80; Asst. Cur., Spec. Cols., Northwest. Univ., 1965–67. **Educ.:** Miami Univ., 1955–60, BA (Eng.); Univ. of MI, 1960–62 (Law); Miami Univ., 1962–64, MA (Eng.); Univ. of Chicago, 1963–65, AM (LS); Coll. of William and Mary, 1979–80, Advnc. Cert. (Higher Educ. Admin.), Doct. Cand. **Orgs.:** ALA: ACRL. Amer. Assn. for Higher Educ. Assn. for the Std. of Higher Educ. **Activities:** 1; 17, 23, 45; 59 **Addr.:** 234 Christopher Wren Rd., Williamsburg, VA 23185.

Grundt, Leonard (S. 5, 1936, Brooklyn, NY) Prof., Lib. Dept., Nassau Cmnty. Coll., 1975–, Dir. of Lib., 1967–75, Deputy Dir. of Lib., 1966–67, Asst. Prof., Lib. Dept., 1965–66; Asst. Resrch. Spec., Grad. Sch. of Lib. Srv., Rutgers Univ., 1964–65; Resrch. Libn., Boston Pub. Lib., 1962–63. **Educ.:** Brooklyn Coll., 1954–58, BA (Econ.); Columbia Univ., 1958–60, MS (Lib. Srv.); Rutgers Univ., 1961–64, PhD (Lib. Srv.). **Orgs.:** ALA. AECT. NY LA. Nassau Cnty. LA: Coll. and Univ. Libs. Div. (Pres., 1981). Various other orgs. AAUP. Amer. Cvl. Liberties Un. SUNY Cncl. of Head Libns.: Ch. (1978–79). **Honors:** Brooklyn Coll., Dept. of Econ. Awd., 1958; Phi Beta Kappa, 1958; Beta Phi Mu, 1960. **Pubns.:** *Efficient Patterns for Adequate Library Service in a Large City* (1968); jt. ed., *Research on Library Service in Metropolitan Areas* (1967); "Conserving Library Energy," *Wilson Lib. Bltn.* (F. 1974); "Community Colleges in New York State and Their Libraries," *Bookmark* (Ja. 1972); "Cooperation Limited," *Essays for Ralph Shaw* (1975); various other articles. **Activities:** 1; 17, 39, 42; 63 **Addr.:** 12 Commander Vic Ln., Nesconset, NY 11767.

Grundy, Robert (Bob) S. (My. 6, 1950, Houston, TX) Attorney, Law Libn., Conoco Inc. Legal Dept., Law Lib., 1979–; Head, Ref. Dept., Univ. of Houston Law Lib., 1978–79, Pub. Srv./Serials, Asst. Ref. Libn., 1975–77, Ref. Libn., 1975; Legal Lib. Consult., Shell Oil Co., 1974. **Educ.:** Earlham Coll., 1969–73, BA (Phil.); Case West. Rsv. Univ., 1973–74, MSLS; Univ. of Houston, 1974–79, JD. **Orgs.:** SW Assn. of Law Libs.: Ed., *SWALL Bltn.* (1975–77); VP, Pres.-Elect., Prog. Ch. (1980–81). AALL: Autom. and Sci. Dev., Spec. Interest Sect. (Ch., 1981). Houston Area Law Libns.: Strg. Com. (1978). **Honors:** Jt. Chap. Mtg., SW and Pac. Assn. of Law Lib., Speaker's Plaque, 1977; Case West. Rsv. Univ., Sch. of LS, Co-winner, Jesse Hauk Shera Awd, 1974. **Pubns.:** Various sps. **Activities:** 1, 12; 15, 39, 44; 56, 77, 86 **Addr.:** Conoco Inc., Law Library-Ste. 1614, P.O. Box 2197, Houston, TX 77252.

Grunow, Millie H. (O. 16, 1931, Bedford Cnty., TN) Med. Libn., Deaconess Hosp., 1972–; Coord., Tech. Srvs., Univ. of Evansville Lib., 1970–72; Head, Cat. Dept., WV Inst. of Tech. Lib., 1967–70. **Educ.:** George Peabody Coll., 1949–53, BA (Soc. Stds.) 1953–55, MA (LS). **Orgs.:** Med. LA: Midwest Chapter; Exec. Com. (1975–1979), Prog. Ch., Spr. Mtg., (1977), Prog. Guide Update (Ch. 1976–79). Midwest Hlth. Sci. Lib. Ntwk.: Consortia Formation and Dev. Com. (1978–81); IN St. Rep. to MHSLN (1981–). IN LA. Various other orgs. **Honors:** IN Gov.'s Conf. on Libs. and Info. Srv., Delegate, 1978. **Activities:** 5, 12; 17, 34, 39; 80, 95-Nursing Allied Hlth. **Addr.:** Health Science Library, Deaconess Hospital, 600 Mary St., Evansville, IN 47747.

Guagliardo, Victoria Elizabeth (Je. 17, 1949, Tulsa, OK) Chld. Libn., Pioneer Multi Cnty. Lib., 1977–; Readers Srvs. Asst., Tulsa City Cnty. Lib., 1974–77, Chld. Asst., 1971–74. **Educ.:** Univ. of Tulsa, 1967–71, BS (LS); Univ. of OK, 1974–75, MLS. **Orgs.:** SWLA. OK LA: Chld. Awd. Com. (1979–82); Sequoyah Ch. (1981–82); Right to Read Ch. (1978–79). Frnds. of Day Care Tulsa. **Activities:** 9; 21, 48 **Addr.:** 331 North Bdwy, Shawnee, OK 74801.

Guasco, Jean Ackers (Mrs. Dante V.) (Lancaster, OH) Consult., 1976–; Chief Libn., McGraw-Hill, Inc., 1960–75, Assoc. Libn., 1954–60, Ref. Libn., 1953–54; Asst. Libn., Ft. Jay Post, 1st Army Ref. Lib., 1951–53; Circ. Libn., Univ. of CT, 1949–51; Libn., Rogers Jr. HS, 1946–48; Tchr., Mifflin HS, 1942–46. **Educ.:** Capital Univ., 1939–40; OH State Univ., 1941–43, BS (Educ.), 1943–45, MA (Educ.); Columbia Univ., 1951–53, MS (Lib.). **Orgs.:** ALA. ASIS. SLA: Awds. Com. (Ch., 1966–67); Publshg. Div. (Ch., 1968–69); NY Chap. (Dir., 1964–66), Publshg. Grp. (Ch., 1966–67). **Honors:** Beta Phi Mu. **Addr.:** Apt. 7C, 300 Gilkeson Rd., Pittsburgh, PA 15228.

Guay, Alice Helen (Jn. 25, 1946, Trani, Barrie, Italy) Sect. Head, Frgn. and Intl. Official Pubns., Natl. Lib. of Can., 1976–; Ref. Docums. Libn., 1973–75, Srch. Libn., Location Sect., Natl. Lib. of Can., 1972–73; Libn., Sir George Williamson Med. Lib., Civic Hosp., 1970–72. **Educ.:** Univ. of Ottawa, 1963–66, BA (Eng.), 1969–70, BLS, McGill Univ., 1975–76, MLS. **Orgs.:** Can. LA: Can. Assn. of Spec. Libs. and Info. Srvs. (Workshp. Coord., 1979). Assn. of Intl. Libs. **Activities:** 4, 12; 15, 17, 39; 54, 78, 92 **Addr.:** Alice Guay, Foreign and International Official Publications Sections, National Library of Canada, Ottawa, ON K1A 0N4 Canada.

Gubman, Nancy (O. 26, 1948, New York, NY) Head Libn., NY Univ., Courant Inst. of Math. Scis., 1976–, Asst. Libn., 1975–76. **Educ.:** Syracuse Univ., 1965–68; NY Univ., 1968–69, BA (Hist.); Columbia Univ., 1973–75, MSLS. **Orgs.:** SLA: PAM Div. Awds. Com. (1981); PR Com. (1978–80), Bltn. Ed. ASIS. **Pubns.:** "Collection Organization in a Mathematical Research Library" ERIC (1978). **Activities:** 1; 15, 17, 20; 88 **Addr.:** New York University, Courant Institute - Library, 251 Mercer St., New York, NY 10012.

Gudgen, Gretta H. S. (Ag. 14, 1911, Pittsburg, KS) Circ. Libn., Pittsburg State Univ., 1966–; Tchr., Pittsburg Pub. Schs., 1946–66. **Educ.:** KS State Tchrs. Coll., 1929–32, BS (Elem. Educ.); Pittsburg State Univ. (KS), 1966–70, MS (Educ., LS). **Orgs.:** ALA. KS LA: Constn. Rev. Com. (1972). **Honors:** Kappa Delta Pi; Phi Delta Kappa. **Activities:** 1; 22 **Addr.:** 417 W. Adams, Pittsburg, KS 66762.

Guedon, Mary Scholz (Je. 22, 1945, Berkeley, CA) Ref. Libn., Coll. of Notre Dame (CA), 1980–; Asst. Ref. Libn., Univ. of Santa Clara, 1973–80; Catlgr., Carroll Coll., 1970–72. **Educ.:** Univ. of CA, Davis, 1963–67, BA (Art Hist.); Univ. of CA, Berkeley, 1969–70, MLS; San Jose State Univ., 1974–79, MA (Art Hist.). **Orgs.:** CA LA. ARLIS/NA. **Honors:** Phi Beta Kappa, 1967; Beta Phi Mu, 1970. **Activities:** 1; 31, 39 **Addr.:** Library, College of Notre Dame, Belmont, CA 94002.

Guenther, Charles (John) (Ap. 29, 1920, St. Louis, MO) Tchr.-consult., 1976–; Adj. asst. prof., St. Louis Univ., Metro. Coll., 1977–78; Supvsr. libn., Defense Mapping Agency Aerospace Ctr., St. Louis, MO, 1957–75; Supv. cartographer, Asst. chief, lib., USAF Aero. Chart & Info. Ctr., St. Louis, MO, 1943–57. **Educ.:** Harris Tchrs. Coll., 1938–40, AA (Eng., langs.); Webster Coll., 1973–74, BA, MA (Eng); St. Louis Univ., 1976–78, (Hisp. lang). **Orgs.:** SLA: Grt. St. Louis Chap. Pres. 1969/70; VP, 1968/69; (Pubcty. Ch., Natl. Conv., 1964). Grt. St. Louis Lib. Club: Cncl. (1978–81). Poetry Socty. of America: Midwest reg. VP (1977–). MO Writers' Gld.: Pres. (1973–74); VP (1971–73). St. Louis Writers' Gld. Pres. (1976–77). St. Louis Poetry Ctr.: Ch., Bd. of chancellors (1965–72); pres. (1974–76). **Honors:** South. IL Univ., Edwardsville, Doct. of Humane Letters, 1979, Webster Review, Transl. Prize, 1979; Poetry Socty. of Amer., James Joyce Awd., 1974; Repub. of Italy, Commander, Order of Merit of the Italian Repub., 1973; Other awds. **Pubns.:** *Modern Italian Poets* (1961); *Paul Valery in English* (1970); *Phrase / Parapharase* (1970); *High Sundowns: Twelve poems of death and resurrection, from the Spanish of Juan Ramon Jimenez* (1974); *Voices in the Dark* (1974); reviews; other poems, articles, transls., Poetry rec. for the Lib. of Congs., Arch. of Recorded Poetry and Lit., (1972). **Activities:** 4, 12; 17, 24, 37; 55, 70, 74 **Addr.:** 2935 Russell Blvd., St. Louis, MO 63104.

Guerette, Normand (Ja. 30, 1939, Cabano, PQ) Dir. des Bibs., Mnstry. de l'Energie et des Resrcs., 1979–; Dir. de la Bib., Mnstry. des Richesses Nat., 1976–79; Dir. des Srvs. Tech., Univ. du PQ, Rimouski, 1970–76; Dir. des Srvs. Tech., Cegep de Rimouski, 1967–70. **Educ.:** 1966–70, BLS. **Orgs.:** Corp. des Bibtcrs. Prof. du PQ: Bd. ASTED. Can. LA. SLA. Various other orgs. **Pubns.:** *Le Service du Catalogue* (1971). **Activities:** 13; 17, 27, 33; 56, 64, 75 **Addr.:** Ministère de l'Energie et des Ressources, 1530, Blvd. de l'Entente, Québec, PQ G1S 4N6 Canada.

Guider, Geneva L. (F. 25, 1915, Lenoir City, TN) Head Libn., El Paso HS, 1949–, Libn., Prof Lib., El Paso Pub. Schs., 1947–49; Libn., Bearden HS, 1944–47; Libn., Gibbs HS, 1942–44; Tchr. and Prin., Martel Sch., 1938–42. **Educ.:** TN Tech. Univ., 1934–37, BS (Hist.); George Peabody Coll., 1940–41, BS (LS); Univ. of TX at El Paso, 1954–55, MA (Educ.). **Orgs.:** ALA. Border Reg. LA. Trans. Pecos LA: Vice-Ch. (1951). TX State Tchrs. Assn. El Paso Tchrs. Assn. **Honors:** Alpha Delta Kappa. **Activities:** 10; 15, 17, 48 **Addr.:** 2312 Arizona Ave., El Paso, TX 79930.

Guidinger, Delmar John (Jl. 18, 1948, Columbus, NE) Libn./Dir., Liberal Meml. Lib., 1974–. **Educ.:** Hastings Coll., 1966–70, BA (Hist.); Emporia State Univ., 1973–74, MLS. **Orgs.:** KS LA: Nom. Com. Mt. Plains LA. ALA. SW KS Area Cncl. of Libns.: Secy (1981); Pres. (1982). **Activities:** 9; 16, 17, 39 **Addr.:** 416 S. Purdue, Liberal, KS 67901.

PROFESSIONAL ACTIVITIES: Institutions: 1. Acad. lib.; 2. Arch.; 3. Assn.; 4. Fed./Gvt. lib.; 5. Inst. lib.; 6. Mfr./Suppl.; 7. Milit. lib.; 8. Musm.; 9. Pub. lib.; 10. Sch. lib.; 11. Sch. of lib. sci.; 12. Spec. lib.; 13. State lib.; 14. (other). **Functions/Activities:** 15. Acq./Col. dev.; 16. Adult srvs.; 17. Admin.; 18. Apprais.; 19. Archit./Bldgs.; 20. Cat./Class.; 21. Chld. srvs.; 22. Circ.; 23. Cons./Pres.; 24. Consult.; 25. Cont. ed.; 26. Educ. lib. sci.; 27. Ext. srvs.; 28. Fund/Grants; 29. Gvt. pubs.; 30. Indx./Abs.; 31. Instr. lib. use; 32. Media srvs.; 33. Micro.; 34. Netwks./Coop.; 35. Persnl.; 36. PR; 37. Publshg.; 38. Recs. mgt.; 39. Ref. srvs.; 40. Repro.; 41. Resrch.; 42. Review.; 43. Secur.; 44. Serials; 45. Spec. col.; 46. Tech. srvs.; 47. Trustees/Bds.; 48. YA srvs.; 49. (other).

Guidry, George J., Jr. (N. 13, 1922, Plaquemine, LA) Lib. Dir., LA State Univ., 1974–, Assoc. Dir., 1964–74, Asst. Dir., 1962–64. **Educ.:** LA State Univ., 1940–47, BS (Educ.) 1947–48, MA (Educ.) 1948–49 BSLS. **Orgs.:** ALA. SWLA. LA LA. Assn. of Southwest. Resrch. Libs.: Pres. (1978–79). Amer. Legion: Cmndr. Jaycees: Past State VP. United Givers: Baton Rouge. (Past Bd. Mem.). Resrv. Ofcrs. Assn.: Baton Rouge Chap., (Past Pres.). **Activities:** 1; 17; 63 **Addr.:** Louisiana State University Library, Baton Rouge, LA 70803.

Guilbault, Oscar R. (D. 14, 1931, Woonsocket, RI) Dir., Rockville Pub. Lib., 1973–; Head, Reader Srvs., U.S. Nvl. War Coll., 1970–73; Reader Srvs. Libn., Providence Coll., 1968–70; Coord., North. Interrelated Lib. Syst., 1967–68. **Educ.:** Providence Coll., 1955–59, AB (Eng.); Univ. of RI, 1965–67, MLS. **Orgs.:** RI LA: Schol. Com. (1969–71); Exec. Com. (1972). RI Cnsrtm. of Acad. Libs.: Resrc. Sharing Com. (1972). CT State Lib. Srv. Ctr., Willimantic: Adv. Bd. of Gvrs., Exec. Com. (1974–75, 1980–82). East. CT LA: Exec. Com. (1975–77, 1980–82). CT State Bd. of Acad. Awds.: Fac. Com. (1981–82). **Activities:** 1, 9; 17, 35, 36; 59 **Addr.:** Red Oak Hill, Willington, CT 06279.

Guilbeault, Claude (Ap. 23, 1948, Valleyfield PQ) Head Libn. Bib., CEGEP Bois-de-Boulogne 1979–; Head Libn., Bib. Emile-Nelligan, Laval, PQ, 1976–79; Head, Pub. Srvs., Bib. Champlain, Univ. of Moncton, 1974–75, Head, Gvt. Docum., 1971–74; Indxr. Lib. of Parlmt., Ottawa, 1970–71. **Educ.:** Coll. de Valleyfield, 1960–69, BA; Univ. of Ottawa, 1969–70, BLS; 1970–74, MLS. **Orgs.:** Can. LA. ASTED. Corp. des Bibtcrs. Prof. de PQ. **Pubns.:** *Inventaire Général des Sources Documentaires sur les Acadiens,* V. II (19–). **Activities:** 1; 17; 50 **Addr.:** 708 Marier, Ste-Thérèse, PQ J7E 3Y4 Canada.

Guilfoyle, Marvin C. (Ap. 30, 1945, Greenville, MI) Dir., Pub. Srvs., Univ. of Evansville, 1979–; Asst. Dir., Pub. Srvs., Northeast. OK State Univ., 1978–79; Docum. Libn., Univ. of OK, 1973–78. **Educ.:** Ctrl. MI Univ., 1963–67, BSEdu (Hist., Msc.), 1968–74, MA (Hist.); West. MI Univ., 1972–73, MSL (Libnshp.). **Orgs.:** ALA. **Pubns.:** "Government Documents Practicum," *Gvt. Pubns. Review* (1978); *Microform Centralization Project* (1976); jt. auth., "Guidelines For The Acquisition, Control," *Micro.* (1977). **Activities:** 1; 29, 31, 33; 63 **Addr.:** Clifford Library & Learning Resources, University of Evansville, P.O. Box 329, Evansville, IN 47702.

Guillaume, Sandra A. (N. 27, 1937, Ottawa, ON) Archvst., Multicult. Hist. Socty. of ON, 1977–; Asst. Archvst., Univ. of Toronto Arch., 1974–77; Asst. Univ. Archvst., McGill Univ. Arch., 1970–74; Supvsr., Pvt. Mss. Sect., Arch. of ON, 1961–67, Staff, 1959–61. **Educ.:** Sir George Williams Univ., 1956–58, BA (Hist.); McGill Univ., 1958–59, (Hist.); Carleton Univ., 1959, Cert. (Arch. Admin.). **Orgs.:** Assn. of Can. Archvsts.: Mem. Com. (1975–76, 1978–81). Toronto Area Archvsts. Grp. SAA. Assn. des Archvsts. du PQ. Can. Assn. for the Advnc. of Netherlandic Std.: Constn. Com. (1979–81). Can. Hist. Assn. Can. Socty. for the Hist. and Phil. of Sci. ON Hist. Socty. **Pubns.:** "Some Sources for Genealogical Research in Ontario," *World Conf. on Recs. Procs.* (1969); "Problems Faced by Archivists Dealing with the Historical Resources of Science and Technology in Canada," *Sci., Tech. and Can. Hist.* (1980). **Activities:** 2; 17, 39; 66 **Addr.:** Multicultural History Society of Ontario, Suite 602, 77 Grenville St., Toronto, ON M5S 1B3 Canada.

Guité, Paul Vilbon (D. 2, 1933, Waterville, ME) Asst. Chief, Printed Arch. Branch, Natl. Arch., 1975–, Libn., 1969–75; Libn., Univ. of ME, Portland-Gorham, 1967–68; Asst. Libn., Windham Coll., 1965–67; Libn., Univ. of Notre Dame, 1964–65. **Educ.:** Univ. of Notre Dame, 1953–57, BA; Georgetown Univ., 1957–60, MA (Amer. Hist.); Simmons Coll., 1963–64, MS (LS). **Orgs.:** SAA. ALA. Intl. Cncl. on Arch. **Pubns.:** "Writings on Archives, Historical Manuscripts, and Current Records: 1976 and 1977," *Amer. Archvst.* (Jl. 1978, Jl. 1979); reviews. **Activities:** 2, 4; 23, 29, 45; 62, 75, 92 **Addr.:** 4601 N. Park Ave., # 216, Chevy Chase, MD 20015.

Gull, Cloyd Dake (Je. 17, 1915, Lorain, OH) Pres., Cloyd Dake Gull and Assocs., Inc., 1969–; WA Rep., Docum. Systs., Inc., 1968–69; Liaison Ofcr., Natl. Libs. Task Frc. on Autom., Natl. Lib. of Med., 1967–68; Prof., Grad. Lib. Sch., IN Univ., 1964–67; Consult. Anal., Gen. Electric Info. Systs. Oper., 1958–63; various admin. positions, 1954–58, 1945–52; Tech. Anal., Documtn. Inc., 1952–54; Per. Libn., NC State Coll., 1939–42. **Educ.:** Allegheny Coll., 1932–36, AB (Liberal Arts); Univ. of MI, 1936–37, ABLS, 1937–39, AMLS. **Orgs.:** ASIS: Pres. (1959–60). ALA: Cnclr. (1962–65). SLA: IN Chap. (Pres., 1966–67). Intl. Fed. for Documtn.: US Natl. Com. (Ch., 1960–63). **Honors:** Phi Beta Kappa; Phi Kappa Phi, 1937. **Pubns.:** "A Punched Card Method for the Bibliography, Abstracting and Indexing of Chemical Literature," *Jnl. of Chem. Educ.* (O. 1946); "The Compilation and Production of Indexes to Catalogs and Bibliographies by Punched Card Machines" typescript and microfilm (1947); "An Electronic Information System for the Library of Congress" (O. 1959); "The Impact of Electronics upon Cataloguing Rules," *Intl. Conf. on Cat. Prins., Paris, 1961* (1963); "Structure of Indexing Authority Lists," *Lib. Resrcs. & Tech. Srvs.* (Fall 1966); various articles, rpts., reviews. **Activities:** 4, 12; 24, 26, 46; 64, 75, 91 **Addr.:** 4200 Dresden St., Kensington, MD 20795.

Gullion, Susan L. (O. 30, 1940, Pittsburgh, PA) Asst. Biomed. Libn. for Tech. Srvs., Biomed. Lib., Univ. of CA, Los Angeles, 1979–, Head, Cat.-Bindery Div., 1968–79, Asst. Head, 1966–68, Grad. Training Prog. in Biomed. Libnshp., 1964–65. **Educ.:** Carnegie-Mellon Univ., 1958–62, BS (Tech. Wrtg. and Ed.); Univ. of Pittsburgh, 1962–64, MLS. **Orgs.:** Med. LA: Cert. Exam. Review Com. (1977–80). ALA. Med. Lib. Grp. of South. CA and AZ. **Activities:** 1, 12; 17, 46; 80 **Addr.:** Biomedical Library, Center for the Health Sciences, University of California, Los Angeles, CA 90024.

Gumb, Raymond Daniel (O. 20, 1938, Atlanta, GA) Prof., Comp. Sci., CA State Univ., Northridge, 1979–; Assoc. Prof., Comp. and Info. Sci., Temple Univ., 1971–80; Asst. Prof., Phil., Lafayette Coll., 1970–71; Comp. Consult., Self-empl., 1967. **Educ.:** MA Inst. of Tech., 1956–60, BS (Indus. Mgt.); Emory Univ., 1965–67, MA (Phil.); Lehigh Univ., 1967–70, PhD (Phil.). **Orgs.:** Assn. for Comp. Mach. Assn. for Comput. Ling. Assn. for Symbolic Logic. Socty. for the Phil. of Sci. Psychotherapy and Ethics. **Honors:** U.S. Natl. Comsn. for the Intl. Un. of the Hist. and Phil. of Sci., Travel Grant, 1979; Fndn. for the Advnc. of Interdisciplinary Std., Resrch. Grant, 1978. **Pubns.:** *Rule-Governed Linguistic Behavior* (1972); *Evolving Theories* (1980); "Metaphor Theory," *Reports on Mathematical Logic* (1978); "A Mechanized Proof Procedure for a Family of Free Intensional Logics," *IJCAI* (1977); jt. auth., "Logical Techniques for Pinpointing Inconsistencies in the Knowledge Base," *ASIS* (1978). **Activities:** 1; 26, 37; 56, 75 **Addr.:** Computer Science Dept., California State University, Northridge, CA 91330.

Gundry, Leslie D. (Ap. 6, 1942, Dubuque, IA) Dir. of Libs., Bryn Mawr Hosp., 1973–; Ref. Libn. and Biblgphr., Univ. of PA, 1968–73; Ref. Libn., Columbus Pub. Lib., 1965–67. **Educ.:** Macalester Coll., 1958–62, BA (Hist.); Drexel Univ., 1967–68, MS (LS); 1976, Cert. (Med. Libnshp.). **Orgs.:** Med. LA. **Honors:** Beta Phi Mu, 1968. **Pubns.:** Cmplr., *Medicine and Society* (1972); *Guide to Science and History of Science Resources in the Philadelphia Area* (1970). **Activities:** 12; 17, 39, 41; 58, 80 **Addr.:** Medical Library, The Bryn Mawr Hospital, Bryn Mawr, PA 19010.

Gunhold, Ruellen C. (Jl. 9, 1950, Calgary, AB) Coord., Chld. Srvs., Calgary Pub. Lib., 1980–; Chld. Srv. Spec., 1977–80; Elem. Sel. Libn., Calgary Bd. of Educ., 1976–77. **Educ.:** Univ. of Calgary, 1968–71, BFA (Drama Dsgn.); Brigham Young Univ., 1974–75, MLS. **Orgs.:** Can. LA. Can. Assn. of Chld. Libns. LA of AB: Chld. Interest Grp. (Pres., 1980). **Honors:** Calgary Cable TV, Producer of the Year, 1979; Calgary Cable TV, Year of the Child Awd., 1978. **Activities:** 9; 17, 21, 36 **Addr.:** Children's Services, Calgary Public Library, 616 Macleod Trail S., Calgary, AB T2G 2M2 Canada.

Gunn, Margaret H. (Ag. 1924,–, Wichita Falls, TX) Asst. Prof. (LS), Delta State Univ., 1967–; Sch. Libn., Houston (TX) Indep. Sch. Dist., 1965–67, Chld. Libn., Jackson (MS) Mncpl. Lib., 1963–65, Assistant Librarian, Mississippi College Library, 1954–62. **Educ.:** Baylor Univ., 1937–41 BA (Eng.); TX Woman's Univ., 1963–65 MLS. **Orgs.:** MSLA: Various coms. SELA: Various coms. Chld. Lit. Assn.: AAUW. **Pubns.:** "146,000 Books - What Next?" *MS Lib. News* (Jn. 1974); "Only a Ten-Minute Walk!" *MS Lib. News* (D. 1974); "IRC Spells Learning," *MS Lib. News* (Sum. 1979); "Internationalism in Children's Literature," *MS Lib. News* (Fall 1979). **Activities:** 1, 11; 21, 48 **Addr.:** Delta State University, Cleveland, MS 38733.

Gunn, Sharon M. (F. 7, 1941, Detroit, MI) Branch Chld. Libn., Chicago Pub. Lib., 1976–81; Elem. Sch. Libn., Lexington Pub. Schs., 1963–65. **Educ.:** Univ. of MI, 1959–63, BA (Hist.), 1963–64, MALS. **Orgs.:** ALA: ALSC Rec. Eval. (Ch., 1981). **Pubns.:** Jt. auth., "It's About Time," *Sch. Lib. Jnl.* (S. 1979). **Activities:** 9; 21 **Addr.:** 2678 Briardale Woods Way, NE, Atlanta, GA 30345.

Gunn, Thomas H. (D. 22, 1940, Pelham, NC) Lib. Dir., Assoc. Prof., Jacksonville Univ., 1977–; Dir., Cmnty. Coll. Libnship. Prog., Appalachian State Univ., 1976–77, Asst. Prof., Msc. Libn., 1972–75; Asst. Libn., Rockingham Cmnty. Coll., 1969–71; Instr., VA Episcopal Sch. and Bolles Sch., 1963–69. **Educ.:** High Point Coll., 1959–63, BS (Msc.); Univ. of NC, Greensboro, 1969–71, MEd (LS). George Peabody Coll. for Tchrs., 1971–72, MLS. Univ. of MI, 1975–77 (LS). **Orgs.:** ALA: Frnds. of the Lib. Frnds. of the Jacksonville Univ. Lib. SELA. **Honors:** Beta Phi Mu. **Activities:** 1, 12; 15, 17, 36; 55, 61, 63 **Addr.:** Carl S. Swisher Library, Jacksonville University, Jacksonville, FL 32211.

Gunning, Kathleen (S. 13, 1947, New Bedford, MA) Head of Ref. and Col. Dev., Univ. of Houston, Ctrl. Campus, 1981–; Cncl. on Lib. Resrcs. Acad. Lib. Mgt. Intern, Univ. of WI, 1980–81; Head of Ref., Brown Univ., 1978–80, Ref. Libn., 1975–78, ILL Libn., 1974–75. **Educ.:** Brown Univ., 1965–69, BA, cum laude (Compar. Lit.); Univ. of RI, 1973–74, MLS. **Orgs.:** RI LA: VP (1978); Pres. (1979); Past-Pres. (1980). Resrch. Lib. Grp.: Pub. Srvs. Com. (1980). ALA: LAMA; RASD; ACRL. N. Atl. Hlth. Sci. Libs. Assn. Various other orgs. **Honors:** Phi Beta Kappa, 1969; Univ. of RI Outstan. Alum. Awd., 1980. **Pubns.:** "Increasing the Reference Librarian's Participation in the Research Process," *Jnl. of Acad. Libnshp.* (S. 1978); "Finding and Utilizing New Information Resources in the Academic Institution," *Essays from the New Eng. Acad. Libns. Wrtg. Sem.* (1980). **Activities:** 1; 15, 17, 39; 55, 91, 92 **Addr.:** 1711 Albans Rd., Houston, TX 77005.

Gunning, Kathryn McPherson (Je. 20, 1947, Norman, OK) Info. Spec., 1979–; Media Spec., Sacramento Pub. Lib., 1974–79. **Educ.:** Univ. of CA, Los Angeles, 1967–69, BA (Pol. Sci.); Univ. of Denver, 1972–73, MA (LS). **Orgs.:** Sacramento Area Media Educ.: Ch. (1978). CA LA: N. CA A-V Chap., Co-Fndr.; Ch. (1978). Women Lib. Workers: River City Chap., Fndr., Ch. (1977–78). Natl. Org. for Women. Sacramento Women's Network: Bd. (1979–); Nsltr. Ed. (1980). **Honors:** Beta Phi Mu, 1973. **Pubns.:** Ed., *California/Washington Videocassette Catalog* 1979; reviews; videotapes. **Activities:** 9; 24, 32, 34; 56, 67, 93 **Addr.:** 3028 Marshall Way, Sacramento, CA 95817.

Gupta, Anand Kumar (N. 19, 1940, Auraiya, Uttar Pradesh, India) Asst. Prof., LS, Jackson State Univ., 1975–; Lectr., LS, Aligarh Muslim Univ., India, 1969; Resrch. Schol. in Documtn., Documtn. Resrch. and Trng. Ctr., Bangalore, India, 1966–69; Sr. Documtn. Asst., Indian Natl. Sci. Documtn. Ctr., New Delhi, India, 1964–65; Assoc. Ed., *Insdoc List of Current Scientific Literature,* 1964–65; Assoc. Ed., *Bibliography of Scientific Publications of South and South East Asia,* 1964. **Educ.:** Banaras Hindu Univ., Varanasi, India, 1958–61, BSc (Phys., Math., Geol.); Univ. of Delhi, India, 1963–64, M Lib Sc; Univ. of Pittsburgh, 1969–70, MLS; various crs. **Orgs.:** ASIS. ALA. MS LA: Spec. Libs. Sect. (Ch., 1981); Long-Range Plng. Com. (Co-Ch., 1980); Autom. and Netwk. RT, Task Force (1979–80); Lib. Educ. Com. (1980); Int. Frdm. Com. (1979). Natl. Geo. Socty. MS Musm. of Arts. **Pubns.:** Jt. ed., *Free Book Service for All: An International Survey* (1968); "Scattering of Articles by Indian Authors," *Annals of Library Science and Documentation* (1965); "Interpolation of Basic Subjects in Colon Classification," *Library Science with a Slant to Documentation* (1968); various articles. **Activities:** 11; 20, 25, 26, 56, 57, 61 **Addr.:** 3150 Robinson Rd., Apt. 313, Jackson, MS 39209.

Gurievitch, Grania Balfour (Ag. 13, 1940, New York, NY) Producer, Dir., Consult. in Educ. Media, TOGG Films, 1971–; Freelnc. Assoc. Film Producer, NY, Mex., Austria, 1964–71; Resrch. Asst., Inst. des Hautes Etudes, Paris, 1962–64. **Educ.:** Sarah Lawrence Coll., 1958–62, BA (Liberal Arts); Inst. des Etudes Pol., Paris, 1962–63. **Orgs.:** EFLA. Assn. for Indp. Vid. and Filmakers. Syracuse Univ. Div. of Dept. of Educ., Ctr. on Human Policy, Media Consult. Earth Metabolic Dsgn. Inc.: Media Consult. **Honors:** EFLA, Blue Ribbon, 1979; EFLA, Red Ribbon, 1979; EFLA, Blue Ribbon, 1976; Intl. Rehab. Film Fest., 1st Prize; other film awds. **Pubns.:** numerous films. **Activities:** 24, 49–Media Prod. **Addr.:** TOGG Films Inc., 630 9th Ave., New York, NY 10036.

Gurnee, Rita Mae (S. 6, 1922, Allentown, PA) Sci. Ref. and Occup. Info. Libn., Mt. San Antonio Coll., 1959–; Asst. Libn., Electro Data Corp., 1957–59; Ref. Libn., Pasadena Pub. Lib., 1952–57. **Educ.:** Univ. of South. CA, 1948–51, BA (Eng.), 1951–52, MLS. **Orgs.:** CA LA: Docum. Com. (Ch., 1956); Ref. Libns. RT (Pres., 1957). SLA: South. CA Chap. (Pres. Elect, 1981–82), Sci. and Tech. (Ch., 1974), Educ. Com. (Ch., 1975). Univ. of South. CA Lib. Sch. Alum. Assn.: Pres. (1963); Secy. (1977). Various other orgs. Beta Phi Mu: Beta Chap. (Pres., 1961–62). AAUW. Mt. San Antonio Coll. Reg. Arts Cncl. Univ. of South. CA Gen. Alum. Assn.: Bd. of Gvrs. (1980–). **Addr.:** The Library, Mt. San Antonio College, 1100 N. Grand Ave., Walnut, CA 91789.

Gurner, Richard (Ap. 12, 1929, Cambridge, MA) Lib. Admin., Polaroid Corp., 1978–, Serials Libn., 1970–75. **Educ.:** Boston Univ., 1949–56, AB (Eng.), 1956–58, MA (Eng.); Simmons Coll., 1974–1975, MLS. **Orgs.:** SLA: Serials Com. (1980). 128 Libns. Grp.: Pres. (1980–81). Natl. Micro. Assn. Natl. Cncl. of Tchrs. of Eng. **Activities:** 5; 15, 17, 24; 60, 75, 88 **Addr.:** Polaroid Corporation Library, P.O. Box 150, Cambridge, MA 02139.

Guss, Carolyn (Je. 11, 1910, Indianapolis, IN) Prof. Emeritus, IN Univ., 1942–, Prof., 1942–; Libn., Tchr., Amo HS, 1935–42; Tchr., Kingman HS, 1929–35. **Educ.:** Butler Univ., 1926–29, BA (Latin, Eng.); IN Univ., 1942–52, MS (Educ.), EdD (Educ.). **Orgs.:** EFLA: Pres. (1961). AV Instr. Dirs.: State (IN) Pres. (1947). AECT: Bd. of Dirs. (1968–70). Delta Kappa Gamma: Intl. Pres. (1964–66). Comsn. on Intl. Film Events: Bd. of Dirs. (1970–). **Honors:** AECT, Disting. Srv. Awd., 1977; Delta Kappa Gamma, Natl. Achvmt. Awd., 1963. **Pubns.:** Jt. auth., *Guides to Educational Media* (1971); "Monthly Film Evaluations," *Educ. Screen* (1942–55). **Activities:** 1; 20, 49-Eval. and sel.; 63 **Addr.:** 10155 E. St. Rd. 46, Bloomington, IN 47401.

Gustow, Hazel (S. 24, 1917, Philadelphia, PA) Lib. Dir., Philadelphia Coll. of Art, 1965–; Asst. Ed., Holiday Mag., 1946–57. **Educ.:** Temple Univ., 1935–38, BS (Educ.); Drexel Univ., 1963–64, MLS. **Orgs.:** Tri-State Coll. Lib. Coop.: Bd. of Dir. ARLIS/NA. ALA: ACRL. **Activities:** 1; 15, 17; 55 **Addr.:**

Special Subjects/Services: 50. Adult educ.; 51. Advert./Mktg.; 52. Aerosp.; 53. Agric.; 54. Area std.; 55. Arts/Hum.; 56. Autom.; 57. Bibl./Prtg.; 58. Bio. sci.; 59. Bus./Fin.; 60. Chem.; 61. Copyrt.; 62. Documtn.; 63. Educ.; 64. Engin.; 65. Env.; 66. Eth. grps.; 67. Film; 68. Food/Nutr.; 69. Geneal.; 70. Geo.; 71. Geol.; 72. Handcpd.; 73. Hist.; 74. Int. frdm.; 75. Info. sci.; 76. Insr.; 77. Law; 78. Legis.; 79. Math./Comp. sci.; 80. Med.; 81. Metals; 82. Nat. resrcs.; 83. Newsp.; 84. Nuc. sci.; 85. Oral hist.; 86. Petr./Energy; 87. Pharm.; 88. Phys./Astr./Math.; 89. Readg.; 90. Relig.; 91. Sci./Tech.; 92. Soc. sci.; 93. Telecom.; 94. Transp.; 95. (other).

Philadelphia College of Art, Broad and Spruce Sts., Philadelphia, PA 19102.

Guthrie, Vera Grinstead (O. 5, 1930, Glasgow, KY) Head, Dept. of LS and Instr. Media, West. KY Univ., 1958–; Libn., Vine Grove Sch., 1957–58; Libn., Reddick Schs., 1954–56; Libn., Glasgow HS, 1953–54; Tchr., Barren Cnty. Schs., 1949–51. **Educ.:** West. KY State Coll., 1948–53, AB (Math., LS); Univ. of KY, 1956–57, MSLS, 1970–73, EdD (Curric. Instr.). **Orgs.:** KY LA: Pres. (1969). SE LA: Mem. Com. (1976–78). ALA: AASL, Prog. Plng. Com. (1980). AAUW: Pres. (1960–61); Treas. (1959); VP (1979–80). Altrusa Club of Bowling Green: Secy. (1972); Treas. (1978–80). **Honors:** AAUW, KY State Div., Gift to Endow., 1973–74. **Pubns.:** "Jesse Stuart's Childrens Books," *Jesse Stuart* (1977); "Elementary School Library Media Centers in Kentucky," *KY Sch. Media Nsltr.* (Ja. 1974); "Communications on Public Relations," *KY Sch. Lib. Consult. Nsltr.* (1972). **Activities:** 10, 11; 20, 21, 46 **Addr.:** 1660 Normal Dr., Bowling Green, KY 42101.

Guy, Wendell A. (Ag. 30, 1940, New Haven, CT) Dir., Pharm. Std. Ctr., A&M Schwartz Coll. of Pharm., Long Island Univ., 1972–; Prod. Mgr., McGraw Hill; Libn., Brooklyn Pub. Lib. **Educ.:** Trinity Coll., 1958–62, BA (Hist.); Pratt Inst., 1962–65, MLS; New Sch., MA (Psy.). **Orgs.:** Med. LA. Hlth. Sci. Comm. Assn. Amer. Assn. of Colls. of Pharm.: Lib./Educ. Resrcs. Sect., Instr. Resrcs. Com., Ch. Acad. Libs. of Brooklyn: Pres. (1976). **Honors:** Kappa Delta Pi. **Pubns.:** "Introduction to the Intl. Pharm. Abs." slide/tape; various sps., papers. **Activities:** 1, 12; 17, 32, 49-Instr. Dev.; 63, 80, 87 **Addr.:** 464 Clinton Ave., Brooklyn, NY 11238.

Guydon, Janet Hawkins (S. 20, 1949, Oneida, AR) Head, W.E.B. DuBois Branch Lib., Gary Pub. Lib., 1981–, Catlgr., Ref., Info. Ctr., 1978–81, Head, Cont. Educ. for Staff, Ref., 1976–78, Deputy Asst. Dir. for Branch Opers., 1975–76, Branch Libn., 1972–75. **Educ.:** Ouachita Bapt. Univ., 1967–71, BSE (Educ., LS); Univ. of IL, 1971–72, MSLS; Purdue Univ. 1979– (Comp. Sci.). **Orgs.:** ALA: Black Caucus, Caribbean Task Frc. IN LA: Autom. Tech. Div. Univ. of IL. Alum. Assn. Ouachita Bapt. Univ. Alum. Assn. Univ. of IL Grad. LS Sch. Alum. Assn. **Activities:** 9, 12; 15, 20, 39; 66, 77, 92 **Addr.:** W.E.B. DuBois Branch Library, Gary Public Library, 1835 Broadway, Gary, IN 46407.

Gwinn, Nancy E. (Ag. 19, 1945, Sheridan, WY) Assoc. Dir. of Prog. Coord., Resrch. Libs. Grp., 1980–; Prog. Ofcr., Cncl. on Lib. Resrcs., Inc., 1979–80; Info. and Pubns. Ofcr., 1975–79; Libn., Congs. Ref. Ctrs., Lib. of Congs., 1971–75, Sr. Ref. Spec. 1970–71, Spec. Recruit, Lib. of Congs., 1969–70. **Educ.:** Univ. of WY, 1963–67, BA (Eng.); Univ. of MI, 1968–69, AMLS. Oxford Univ. (Eng.), Fulbright Schol., 1967–68. **Orgs.:** ALA: ACRL, Cont. Educ. Com. (1978–80); RASD, Pubn. Com. (Ch., 1977–), MARS Exec. Com. (1980–), Ref. and Subscrpn. Bks. Rev. Com. (1974–78). DC LA: Pres. (1979–80). LC Prof. Assn.: Pres. (1971). SLA. Various other ofcs. **Honors:** Univ. of WY, Phi Beta Kappa, Phi. Kappa Phi; Univ. of MI, Disting. Alum. Awd., 1971; Beta Phi Mu. **Pubns.:** "Academic Libraries and Undergraduate Education: The CLR Experience," Coll. & Resrch. Libs. (Ja. 1980); Jt.-auth., "Mastering the Information Revolution: CLR's Bibliographic Service Development Program," *Lib. Jnl.* (S. 15, 1979); Jt.-auth., "Bibliographic Service Development: A New CLR Program," *Jnl. of Lib. Autom.* (Jn. 1979); "A National Periodicals Center," *Lib Jnl.* (N. 1, 1978); "CLR and Preservation," *Coll. and Resrch. Libs.* (Mr. 1981); Various other articles. **Activities:** 14-Fndn.; 17, 37, 42 **Addr.:** Research Libraries Group, Jordan Quadrangle, Stanford, CA 94305.

Gwyn, Ann S. (F. 15, 1935, Hong Kong) Spec. Col. Libn., Johns Hopkins Univ. Lib., 1981–; Head, Spec. Cols., Tulane Univ. Lib., 1976–81; Asst. Head, Spec. Cols., 1972–75, Rare Book Libn. and Mss. Catlgr., 1968–72. **Educ.:** Univ. of St. Andrews (Scotland), 1956, MA (Hist.), Univ. of London, 1967, MLS. **Orgs.:** ALA. SAA. Mss. Socty.: Conv. Plng. Com. (1979). LA Hist. Recs. Adv. Comsn. (1976–79). **Pubns.:** *Catalogue of the Lafcadio Health Coll., Tulane Lib.,* (1977); "The Wisdom Coll. of Wm. Faulkner," *Manuscripts* (Sp. 1980); "Friends of the Library," *Coll. & Resrch. Libs.* (Jy. 1975); Contrib. *Friends of Libraries* (1980). **Activities:** 1; 15, 35, 45; 55, 57 **Addr.:** Milton S. Eisenhower Library, Johns Hopkins University, Baltimore, MD 21218.

Gyorgyey, Ferenc (Mr. 14, 1925, Budapest, Hun.) Hist. Libn., Yale Univ. Med. Lib., 1968–, Asst. Hist. Libn., 1967–68, Sr. Catlgr., 1965–67, Catlgr., 1960–65. **Educ.:** Univ. of Budapest, 1943–48, Absol, (Hist., Art Hist.); South. CT Coll., 1958–60, MLS; Yale Univ., 1963–67, MA, (Med. Hist.). **Orgs.:** Med. LA: Hist. of Med. Gp. Assn. of Libns. in Hist. of Health Sci. Amer. Assn. for Hist. of Med. Beaumont Med. Club. Fellow, Jonathan Edwards Coll. (Yale). **Pubns.:** Various articles. **Activities:** 1; 17, 39, 45; 55, 73, 80 **Addr.:** Historical Library, Yale Medical Library, 333 Cedar St., New Haven, CT 06510.

H

Haas, Elaine S. (Jl. 27, 1918, Brooklyn NY) Pres., Tech. Lib. Srvs. 1962–; Asst. Prof., Manhattan Cmnty. Coll., 1964–65; Asst. Libn., Sci. Lib., Queens Coll., 1963–64. **Educ.:** Hunter Coll., 1935–39, AB (Chem.); Columbia Univ., 1962–63, MLS; City Univ. NY, 1972–75. **Orgs.:** SLA. ALA. ASIS. SAA. Assn. Amer. Musm. **Activities:** 6; 20, 24, 46; 59, 91 **Addr.:** Technical Library Service, 130 Fifth Ave., New York, NY 10011.

Haas, Eva L. (Je. 23, 1926, Brno, Czech.) Chief, Base Lib. Mgt. Branch, US Air Force, Europe, 1977–; Base Libn., Rhein Main Air Base, Germany, 1960–77; Base Libn., Bordeaux AB, France, 1956–58; Libn., Lockheed Aircraft Corp., 1954–56. **Educ.:** Univ. of South. CA, 1947, 1947–49, MA (Int. Rel.), 1952–53, MS (LS). **Orgs.:** ALA: FLIRT. IFLA. **Honors:** Beta Phi Mu. **Activities:** 4; 17, 24, 46; 54, 75 **Addr.:** HQ USAFE/DPSL, Box 8358, APO New York NY 09012.

Haas, Marilyn L. (N. 19, 1931, Columbus, OH) Ref. Libn., SUNY, Buffalo, 1967–. **Educ.:** Univ. of MO, 1948–51, BA (Soclgy.); SUC, Geneseo, 1964–67, MLS. **Orgs.:** ALA: ACRL/Anthro. Sect. (Ch., 1978). **Pubns.:** "Anthropology: A Guide To Basic Sources," *Ref. Srvs. Review* (O./D. 1977); "A Basic Guide to Reference Sources for the Study of the North American Indian," *Ref. Srvs. Review* (Jl./S. 1979). **Activities:** 1; 15, 39; 66 **Addr.:** Lockwood Memorial Library, SUNY at Buffalo, Buffalo, NY 14260.

Haas, Pamela B. (D. 22, 1948, Tucson, AZ) Asst. Libn. for Arch. and Photographic Coll., Amer. Musm. Nat. Hist., 1980–, Photographic Col. Libn., 1978–80, Ref. Libn., 1976–78; Interlib. Loan Libn., Pfizer Pharmaceuticals, 1975–76, Archaeological Photographer, AZ State Musm. 1972. **Educ.:** Univ. of AZ, 1966–70, BA (Anthro.); Columbia Univ., 1974–75, MSLS. **Orgs.:** SLA: Tellers' Com. (1976–77); Ch., MAH Group, NY, (1979–80), Socty. for the Bibl. of Nat. Hist. ALA: ACRL (Anthro.-Soclgy. Sect., Vice-Ch., 1981–82). Archons of Colophon. Socty. for the Anthro. of Visual Com. Socty. for Amer. Archlg. Amer. Socty of Picture Prof.: Nwsltr. Com. (1979–80). **Honors:** Beta Phi Mu. **Pubns.:** *Visits of Inspection: Northwest Coast Photographs by Edward Dossetter* (1981); "Additional Reading," *Nat. Hist. Magazine* (1977); "Rare and endangered animals and plants," exhibit, Grolier Club, (1977); "Museum Photography: Rarities from the Photographic Collection," exhibit, Amer. Natl. Hist. Musm, (1979). **Activities:** 2, 8; 17, 20, 23; 55, 58, 92 **Addr.:** American Museum of Natural History Library, Central Park West at 79th St., New York, NY 10024.

Haas, Warren J. Pres., Cncl. on Lib. Resrcs., 1978–; VP for Info. Srvs., Univ. Libn., Columbia Univ., 1972–77, Dir. of Libs., 1970–72; Dir. of Libs., Univ. of PA, 1966–69; Assoc. Dir. of Libs., Columbia Univ., 1961–66; Lib. Consult., Cncl. of Higher Educ. Inst. of NY, 1959–60; Acq. Libn., Asst. Libn., Johns Hopkins Univ., 1952–59; Head, Branch Libs., WI) Pub. Lib., 1950–52. **Educ.:** Wabash Coll., 1948, BA, Univ. of WI, 1950, BS (LS). **Orgs.:** ALA: Intl. Rel. Com., Adv. Com. on Liaison with Japanese Libs. cncl.; Lib. of Congs. Ctr. for the Bk.: Adv. Com. ARL: Pres. Ctr. for Resrch. Libs.: Pres. other orgs. Comsn. on the Hum.: mem. Amer. Cncl. of Learned Societies: Com. on Resrch. Libs. Natl. Enquiry Into Scholarly Comm.: Strg. Com. Visit. Coms., various colls. and univs. other orgs. **Honors:** Phi Beta Kappa, 1948. **Pubns.:** "Managing Change," *Japanese and U.S. Research Libraries at the Turning Point,* (1977); "Organizational Structures to Meet Future Bibliographic Requirements," *Prospects for Change in Bibliographic Control,* (1977); "Future Prospects," *American Libraries as Centers of Scholarship* (1978); "Managing Our Academic Libraries: Ways and Means," *New Horizons for Academic Libraries* (1979); Jt. auth., "Managing the Information Revolution," *Lib. Jnl.* (S. 15, 1979); other articles. **Activities:** 14-Fndn. **Addr.:** Council on Library Resources, Suite 620, One Dupont Cir., NW, Washington, DC 20036.

Haase, Ingrid Monika (S. 5, 1940, Berlin-Charlottenburg, Germany) Ref. Libn., Head, Off Campus Libs., Univ. of Ottawa, 1976–; Tech. Srvs. and Branch Libs., Colchester-E. Hants Reg. Lib., 1975–76; Comp. Cat., Univ. of Göttingen, 1974–75; Adult Srvs., Colchester-E. Hants Reg. Lib., 1972–73; Tchg., 1963–69. **Educ.:** Mt. St. Vincent Univ., 1958–63, BA; Dalhousie Univ., 1970–72, MLS; Mt. St. Vincent Univ., 1980, BEd. **Orgs.:** Atl. Prov. LA: Secy-Treas. (1973). Can. LA: Can. Assn. Spec. Lib. Info. Srvs., Exec. Com.; Cont. Educ. Com. (1979–81); Can. Assn. of Coll. and Univ. Libs. Amnesty Intl. **Pubns.:** "Canadian Librarian in Germany," *APLA Bltn.* (1977); reviews. **Activities:** 1, 9; 16, 25, 27; 50, 55, 90 **Addr.:** 2240 Halifax Dr., Apt. 1403, Ottawa, ON K1G 2W8 Canada.

Habel, Sue A. (N. 10, 1946, Hamilton OH) Asst. Div. Chief Hist. Div., Brooklyn Pub. Lib., 1978–, Libn. Hist. Div., 1975–78, Libn. Art and Msc. Div., 1972–75, Libn. Brighton Beach Branch, 1971–72. **Educ.:** OH St. Univ., 1966–69, BA (Art Hist.); Pratt Inst., 1970–71, MLS. **Orgs.:** SLA: Hosplty. Com. NY LA Women Lib. Wkers. Natl. Org. of Women. **Honors:** Beta Phi Mu, 1971. **Pubns.:** *Dictionary of Amer. Biography* (two entries) 1980; *Metro Union List of Serials* (Rev. Com.) 1980. **Activities:** 9, 12; 16, 17, 39; 55, 70, 90 **Addr.:** Brooklyn Public Library, History Division, Grand Army Plz., Brooklyn, NY 11238.

Haber, Walter H. (Je. 19, 1928, New York, NY) Dir., Baldwin Pub. Lib., 1970–; Dir., New Milford Pub. Lib., 1965–70; Gen. Libn., Great Neck Lib., 1964–65. **Educ.:** New York Univ., 1948–52, BS (Bus.); Pratt Lib. Sch., 1963–64, MLS. **Orgs.:** Lib. PR Cncl.: VP, Pres. (1972–75). Mid-Bergen Fed.: Exec. Secy. (1966); Ch., Grant Com. (1967). NJ LA: Ch., Legis. Com. (1969). Bergen/Passaic Co. LA: Pres. (1967–68). Other orgs. **Honors:** Beta Phi Mu, 1964. **Pubns.:** *Survey of County Library System for Hunterdon County, N.J.* (1971); *Building Survey & Construction Consultation, Basking Ridge, N.J.* (1973); *Library Development Plan for Hillsborough Township, N.J.* (1973). **Addr.:** Baldwin Public Library, Baldwin, NY 11510.

Haberland, Jean (Ag. 8, 1929, Philadelphia, PA) Head, Fiction/Fine Arts/Virginiana Sections, Arlington Cnty. Dept. of Libs., 1973–; Sr. Media Spec./Inst. of Lib. Sci., Univ. of DC, 1971–73; Reg. Libn. for AS, Eastern Mass. Reg. Lib. System, Boston, 1968–71; Cmnty. Libn., Montgomery Cnty. Dept. Libs., 1965–68; Head, Bookmobile Div., Prince Georges Cnty. Mem. Lib. MD, 1963–65. **Educ.:** Converse Coll., 1952, BA (Lib. Arts), Catholic Univ. 1963, MSLS; American Univ., 1955–57 (Comm). **Orgs.:** ALA. DC LA: Ch., Book Review Group, (1966). MD LA: Mem. Com., (1967). **Honors:** Beta Phi Mu. Theta Signa Phi. **Pubns.:** *Color, and how to use it* (1959). Reviews. **Addr.:** 7821 Sycamore Dr., Falls Church, VA 22042.

Hacker, Harold S. (Jl. 9, 1916, Buffalo, NY) Dir. Emeritus, Rochester Pub. Lib. and Monroe Cnty. Lib. Syst., 1978–, Dir., 1954–78; Dir., Grosvenor Lib., Buffalo, NY, 1952–54; Deputy Dir., Erie Cnty. Pub. Lib., 1948–52; various positions, Buffalo Pub. Lib. and Grosvenor Lib., 1941–48. **Educ.:** Canisius Coll., 1933–37, BA (Hist., Phil.); Univ. Buffalo, 1937–41, BLS. **Orgs.:** ALA: LAD, Sect. Lib. Org., Ch. (1962–64); Cnclr. (1965–69). NY LA: Pres. (1946–47) NY St. Assn. Lib. Bd.: Secy. (1951–61); Treas. (1950–70). Consult. Gen. WHCLIS: NY Del. Rochester Area Educ. TV Assn.: Pres. (1961–67). NY St.: Comsn. Educ. Com. Lib. Dev. (1967–70); Comsn. Educ. Com. Pub. Lib. Srv. (V Ch., 1956–57). **Honors:** Lib. Trustees Fndn. NY, Velma K. Moore Mem. Awd. for Distin. Srv. at St. Level, 1963; Rochester Musm. and Sci. Ctr., Civic Medal Awd., 1977; Canisius Coll., Doc. of Humane Letters, 1976; NY LA, Hon. Life Memshp., 1978. **Pubns.:** "Implementing Network Plans in New York State" in *Interlibrary Communications and Information Networks,* (1971). **Activities:** 9, 13; 17, 24, 34; 93, 95-Non-Print Media-Planning. **Addr.:** 1077 East Ave., Rochester, NY 14607.

Hackman, Larry J. (N. 3, 1942, Glasgow, MO) Dir., Hist. Rec. Grant Prog., Natl. Arch., 1975–; Dir. of Spec. Prog., John F. Kennedy Lib., 1974–75, Sr. Archvst. for Domestic and Pol. Affairs, 1971–74; Dir., John F. Kennedy Oral Hist. Prog., Natl. Arch., 1968–70. **Educ.:** Univ. of MO, 1960–64, AB (Hist.), 1964–65, MA (Hist.); Harvard Univ., 1970–71, MPA. **Orgs.:** SAA: Prog. Com. (1975, 1978, ch. 1982); Com. Col. Personal Papers; Com. Reg. Arch. Affairs. Oral Hist. Assn.: Pres. Com. Eval. Oral Hist. (1976–78). Mid-Atl. Reg. Arch. Assn.: Strg. Com. (1977–79); Prog. Com. (Ch., 1980). Amer. Assn. for St. and Local Hist. Org. of Amer. Hist. **Honors:** Harvard Univ., Littauer Flw. in Pub. Admn., 1970; Natl. Arch., Commendable Srv. Awd., 1978. SAA Flw., 1980. **Pubns.:** "The Historical Records Program: The States and the Nation", *The Amer. Archvst.* (Ja. 1980); "Oral History and the Consumer Interest", *Oral Hist. Review* (1978); Co-Auth., "The NHPRC and a Guide to Manuscript and Archival Materials in the United States", *The Amer. Arch.* (Ap. 1977); Exec. prod., "A Stroke of the Pen" (1975), Film. **Activities:** 1, 2; 17, 28, 45; 55, 56, 78 **Addr.:** National Historical Publications and Records Commission, National Archives Service, Washington, DC 20408.

Hackney, Mary Martha (Ap. 28, 1921, Fort Worth, TX) Supvsr., Ref. Ctr., Fort Worth Pub. Lib., 1980–, Supvsr., Readers Adv. Srvs., 1978–80, Supvsr., Bus. and Tech. Dept., 1975–78, Asst. Supvsr., Gen. Ref. Dept., 1971–75. **Educ.:** TX Woman's Univ., 1938–42, BS (Art), 1970–73. **Orgs.:** TX LA: Com. for Int. Frdm. (1974–76). Jr. Leag. of Fort Worth, TX. **Honors:** Beta Phi Mu. **Activities:** 9; 16; 59, 74, 91 **Addr.:** 4913 Pershing Ave., Fort Worth, TX 76107.

Hadgin, Ellis (F. 5, 1938, High Point, NC) Dir. of Lib., Coll. of Charleston, NC, 1971–; Dir. of Lib., New Milford Pub. Lib., 1970–71; Job Dev., Comnty. Improvement Cncl., 1969–70; Div. of Lib., Martinsville Mem. Pub. Lib., 1967–69. **Educ.:** High Point Coll., 1962–65, BA (Eng./Hist.); Univ. of NC, 1965–67, MSLS; Cent. MI Univ., Charleston, NC, 1976– (Mgt.). **Orgs.:** ALA. SC LA. AECT NLA. **Pubns.:** "Yes Virginia, There Is No Santa Claus:" *VA Libn.* (1969). "Library Resources in SC" *SC Libn.* (1976). "Interview with John Thomas, President, National Librarians Association," *Amer. Lib.* (Je. 1976). "Orphans Without a Home," *Lib. Jrnl.* (Se. 1, 1977). "Metropolitan Consortia: Some Observations." *SC Libn.* (1978). **Addr.:** 161 King St., Charleston, SC 29401.

Hadidian, Dikran Y. (Je. 9, 1920, Aintab, Turkey) Libn. and Prof. of Bibl., Pittsburgh Theo. Sem., 1966–; Libn., Hartford Semy. Fndn., 1957–66; Instr., Sweet Briar Coll., 1952–55. **Educ.:**

PROFESSIONAL ACTIVITIES: Institutions: 1. Acad. lib.; 2. Arch.; 3. Assn.; 4. Fed./Gvt. lib.; 5. Inst. lib.; 6. Mfr./Suppl.; 7. Milit. lib.; 8. Musm.; 9. Pub. lib.; 10. Sch. lib.; 11. Sch. of lib. sci.; 12. Spec. lib.; 13. State lib.; 14. (other). **Functions/Activities:** 15. Acq./Col. dev.; 16. Adult srvs.; 17. Admin.; 18. Apprais.; 19. Archit./Bldgs.; 20. Cat./Class.; 21. Chld. srvs.; 22. Circ.; 23. Cons./Pres.; 24. Consult.; 25. Cont. ed.; 26. Educ. lib. sci.; 27. Ext. srvs.; 28. Fund/Grants; 29. Gvt. pubs.; 30. Indx./Abs.; 31. Instr. lib. use; 32. Media srvs.; 33. Micro.; 34. Netwks./Coop.; 35. Persnl.; 36. PR; 37. Publshg.; 38. Recs. mgt.; 39. Ref. srvs.; 40. Repro.; 41. Resrch.; 42. Review.; 43. Secur.; 44. Serials; 45. Spec. col.; 46. Tech. srvs.; 47. Trustees/Bds.; 48. YA srvs.; 49. (other).

Amer. Univ. of Beirut, 1939–44, BA (Relig.); Hartford Theo. Sem., 1946–48, BD; Columbia Univ., 1959–60, MS LS. **Orgs.:** ATLA. Pittsburgh Reg. Lib. Ctr. Pittsburgh Bibl. Socty. of Biblical Lit. Socty. for New Testament Std. **Pubns.:** Ed., *Bibliographia Tripotamopolitana;* Ed., *Pittsburgh Theological Monograph Series: and Pittsburgh Original Texts and Translations Series;* "Seminary Libraries" in *Encyc. of Lib. and Info. Sci.* (1979); "Richardson, Ernest Cushing" in *Encyc. of Lib. and Info. Sci.* (1978). **Activities:** 1; 15, 24; 57, 90 **Addr.:** Pittsburgh Theological Seminary, 616 N. Highland Ave., Pittsburgh, PA 15206.

Hadley, Alice E. (N. 11, 1949, Miami, FL) Station Libn., U.S. NAVCAMS WESTPAC GUAM, 1979–; Libn. III, Nieves M. Flores Meml. Lib., 1977–79. **Educ.:** Stetson Univ., 1967–74, BA (Hist.); FL State Univ., 1974–75, MS (LS). **Orgs.:** ALA. GU Lib. Media Assn.: PR (1978–80). Gvr.'s WHCOLIS: Del. (1978). Conf. on Lib. Coop. in Micronesia: Del. (1979). Amer. Assn. Of State and Lcl. Hist. GU Film Socty.: Treas. (1979–80). Trust Territory WHCOLIS 1978. **Activities:** 4, 9; 16, 17, 20; 74 **Addr.:** P.O. Box 10437, Sinajana, GU 96910.

Haertle, Robert Joseph (My. 26, 1929, Milwaukee, WI) Head/Col. Dev., Marquette Univ. Meml. Lib., 1978–, Head, Acq. Dept., 1966–78, Admin. Asst., 1963–66, Readers Srvs. Staff, 1959–63. **Educ.:** St. Francis Semy., 1949–53; Marquette Univ., 1953–54, BA (Phil.), 1954–56, MA (Phil.); Univ. of IL, 1958–59, MS (LS). **Orgs.:** ALA. **Honors:** Beta Phi Mu. **Pubns.:** "Coordinating Collections in the Milwaukee Area," *Lib. Jnl. Spec. Rpt.* (No. 9). **Activities:** 1; 15, 34 **Addr.:** 520 E. Homre St., Milwaukee, WI 53207.

Haeuser, Michael J. (Jl. 5, 1943, LaCrosse, WI) Head Libn., Linfield Coll., 1976–; Reader's Srvs. Libn., Knox Coll., 1973–76. **Educ.:** Univ. of WI, 1970, BA (Hist.), 1972, MA (Hist.), 1973, MLS. **Orgs.:** ALA. OR LA. N.W. LA. Amer. Hist. Assn. **Honors:** Natl. Endow. for the Hum., Sum. Flw., 1978; West. St. Hum. Conf., Participant, 1977; Lilly Fndn., Participating Libn., 1975. **Pubns.:** "Curriculum Reform: A Role for Librarians" in *New Horizons for Academic Libraries* (1979); "Curriculum Planning, Library Instruction and the Academic Librarians" *Lib. Trends* (Sum. 1980). **Activities:** 1; 17, 31, 35; 63, 92 **Addr.:** Linfield College, McMinnville, OR 97128.

Haffner, Barbara (N. 5, 1925, Oak Park, IL) Lib. Dir., Bedford Park Pub. Lib., 1977–; Spec. Proj. Libn., Suburban Lib. Syst., 1967–76. **Educ.:** Beloit Coll., 1943–47, BA (Eng.); Rosary Coll., 1962–67, MLS. **Orgs.:** Chicago Lib. Club. IL LA. ALA. Daughters of the Amer. Revolution. **Addr.:** Bedford Park Public Library, 7816 W. 65th Pl., Bedford Park, IL 60501.

Hafner, Arthur Wayne (Je. 1, 1943, Fort Wayne, IN) Dir. of Libs., Chicago Coll. of Osteopathic Med., 1980–; Dir., Educ. Resrcs., Univ. of MN, Sch. of Med. (Duluth), 1971–79. **Educ.:** Purdue Univ., 1961–65, BS (Math.); Univ. of MN, 1965–67, MS (Math.), 1969–70, MA (LS), 1970–74, PhD (LS); Med. LA Cert. **Orgs.:** Med. LA. **Pubns.:** Various articles. **Activities:** 1, 12; 17, 34, 41; 80 **Addr.:** Alumni Memorial Library, Chicago College of Osteopathic Medicine, 5200 S. Ellis Ave., Chicago, IL 60615.

Hafter, Ruth Anne (Ap. 18, 1935, New York, NY) Lib. Dir., Sonoma State Univ., 1978–; Head Libn., St. Mary's Univ., 1968–75; Asst. Educ. Libn., Harvard Univ., 1967–68; Supvsr. of Sch. Libs., Halifax Cnty. Sch. Bd., 1966–67. **Educ.:** Brandeis Univ., 1952–56, BA, cum laude (Hist.); Columbia Univ., 1961–63, MLS; Harvard/Radcliffe, 1956–57, Cert. (Bus. Admin.). **Orgs.:** CA ACRL: Vice Ch., Ch.-Elect (1980–). Sonoma Lib. Cnsrtm.: Ch. (1980–). ALA: Com. on Accred.; Fld. Site Com. (1979–). CA Women in Higher Educ. Sonoma Cnty.: Comsn. on the Status of Women (1980–). **Pubns.:** *Acadian Education in Nova Scotia* (1970); "The Performance of Card Catalogs," *Lib. Resrch.* (N. 1979); "An Analysis of User Success with the Card Catalog," *Info. Prcs. and Mgt.* (N. 1979). **Activities:** 1, 10; 17, 24, 26; 56, 66, 86 **Addr.:** 1019 San Francisco Way, Rohnert Park, CA 94928.

Hage, Christine C. (N. 26, 1949, Detroit, MI) Head of Adult Srvs., Avon Twp. Pub. Lib., 1981–; Lib. Dir., Shelby Twp. Lib., 1977–81; Head of Adult Srvs., Troy Pub. Lib., 1971–77. **Educ.:** Oakland Univ., 1967–70, (Eng.); Univ. of MI, 1970–71, AMLS. **Orgs.:** ALA. MI LA: Ch., JMRT (1973–74); Secy/Treas. Pub. Lib. Div. (1974–75); Prog. Ch. (1977); Ref. Caucus, Ch. (1981–82). Troy Comnty. Educ. Cncl.: Bd. of Dirs. Cultural Arts Cncl.: (Shelby) PR Ch. **Pubns.:** "Notes on Networks," *MI Libn.* (Sum. 1976); Pub. Lib. Ed., *MI Libn.* (1974–75). **Addr.:** 1893 Ludgate Ln., Rochester, MI 48063.

Hagedorn, Dorothy L. (S. 4, 1929, McKeesport, PA) Head, Sci. Engin. Div., Tulane Univ., 1971–; Head, Adult Srvs., New Orleans Pub. Lib., 1968–71, Head, Bus. and Sci., 1964–68; Tech. Info. Spec., Lawrence Radiation Lab., 1961–64. **Educ.:** Seton Hill Coll., 1946–50, BA (Bio.); Fordham Univ., 1950–51, MS (Bio.); Columbia Univ., 1953–56, MS (LS). **Orgs.:** ALA. AAUP. **Activities:** 1; 15, 39; 91 **Addr.:** Howard-Tilton Memorial Library, Tulane University, New Orleans, LA 70118.

Hagelstein, Robert Philip (D. 15, 1942, New York City, NY) Pres., Greenwood Press, 1973–, VP, 1970–73; Prod. Mgr., Johnson Reprint Corp., 1965–68, Ed. in Chief, 1968–70. **Educ.:** Long Island Univ., 1960–64, BA (Lit.); New York Univ., Various. **Orgs.:** SLA. ASIS. Info. Indust. Assn. Aldwych Press (London): Dir. **Pubns.:** Various articles. **Activities:** 6; 17 **Addr.:** Greenwood Press, 88 Post Rd. West, Westport, CT 06881.

Hagemeyer, Alice L. (F. 22, 1934, Mitchell, NE) Libn. for the Deaf, DC Pub. Lib., 1976–, Srch. Unit Head, 1965–76. **Educ.:** Gallaudet Coll., 1952–57, BS (LS); Univ. of MD, 1974–76, MLS. **Orgs.:** ALA: Lib. Srv. to the Deaf Ad Hoc Com. (1976–78); ASCLA Lib. Srv. to the Deaf Sect. Ch. (1980–81), Pubns. Com. Ch. (1979–); Intl. Yr. of Disabled Persons Com. Consult. (1980–82); PLA. WHCOLIS: Del. (1979). MD Gvr. Conf. on Lib. and Info. Srvs.: Del. (1978). Amer. Deafness and Rehab. Assn. Metro. Washington Cncl. of Gvt.: Libns. Com., Ch., Task Force Com. on Lib. Srv. to the Deaf (1977–). **Honors:** Phi Kappa Phi, 1976; Beta Phi Mu, 1976. **Pubns.:** *Deaf Awareness Handbook for Public Librarians* (1975); *The Public Library Talks to You* (1975); *A Deaf Person's Quick Guide to Washington, D.C.* (1976); "Librarian for the Deaf," *Amer. Libs.* (Je. 1976); "Lifestyles of Handicapped Individuals - Making It," filmstrip (1978). **Activities:** 9; 22, 24, 36; 50, 66, 72 **Addr.:** 2930 Craiglawn Rd., Silver Spring, MD 20904.

Hagloch, Susan Beard (My. 5, 1948, Akron, OH) Cnty. Ext. Libn., Tuscarawas Cnty. Pub. Lib., 1977–; Nursing Sch. Libn., Akron Gen. Med. Ctr., 1975–76. **Educ.:** Univ. of Akron, 1966–70, BA Educ (Eng.); Kent State Univ., 1974–75, MLS. **Orgs.:** ALA: Pub. Lib. Assn. (1980). OH LA: Mtrls. Eval. Div. (1978–80). Kent State Univ., Alum. Assn., Sch. of LS: Secy. (1979–80). Biblio Clan: Pres. (1980–81). Dover (OH) Hist. Socty.: Hist. Re-creations Com. (1979). **Pubns.:** Reviews. **Activities:** 9, 14-Cnsrtm.; 15, 27, 34; 50 **Addr.:** 310 East Second St., Dover, OH 44622.

Hahn, Anne A. (N. 8, 1950, Key West, FL) Asst. Ref. Libn., VA Milit. Inst., 1977–80; Assoc. Libn., Cath. Theo. Un., 1975–76; Asst. Libn., Luth. Theo. Semy., SC, 1974–75; Libn., Kenmare HS, 1973–74. **Educ.:** Kirkland Coll., 1968–72, AB (Anthro.); Univ. of SC, 1972–73, MA (LS). **Orgs.:** ALA. VA LA: Reg. VI (Ch.-Elect, Ch., 1978–80); Pub. Docum. Forum, Nom. Com. (1979). **Honors:** Beta Phi Mu, 1975. **Activities:** 1; 29, 31, 39; 61, 64, 91 **Addr.:** 310 E. Michigan Ave., #2, Urbana, IL 61801.

Hahn, Arlene Clara (N. 26, 1928, Frachville, PA) Admin. Libn., Yongsan Lib., Seoul, Korea, 1980–; Dir., Lib. Srv. Ctr., U.S. Army, Seoul, Korea, 1977–79; Readers Adv., Yongsan Lib., Seoul, Korea, 1975–76. **Educ.:** Kutztown State Coll., 1946–50, BS (Educ., LS); George Peabody Coll., 1951–54, MA (LS); Univ. of South. CA (Seoul Campus), 1975–77, MSEd. **Orgs.:** ALA: Armed Frcs. Libns. Sect. Federally Empl. Women: Secy. (1979). Royal Asiatic Socty. U.S. 8th Army Ofcrs. Club. U.S. Embassy Club, Seoul. **Honors:** ALA, John Cotton Dana Pub. Awd., (1967–69, 1971–72, 1975). **Activities:** 9; 17, 36, 46; 50, 63, 74 **Addr.:** 99 S. Main St., Mahanoy City, PA 17948.

Hahn, Ellen Zabel (O. 9, 1945, Stoneham, MA) Chief, Gen. Reading Rooms Div., Lib. of Congs., 1978–, Asst. Chief, Network Dev., Div. for the Blind & Phys. Handcpd., 1975–78; Asst. Chief, Branches & Ext., Chicago Pub. Lib., 1974–75, Head, Dept. for the Blind and Phys. Handcpd., 1972–74; Dir., Blind and Physically Handcpd. Div., KS State Lib., 1970–72. **Educ.:** Washburn Univ., 1965–69, BA (Fr.); KS State Tchrs. Coll., 1969–70, ML (LS). **Orgs.:** ALA: RASD, Com. on Performance Improvement for Ref. Libns. (1979–); LAMA, Com. on Labor Rel. for Mgrs. (1979–). Washington Area Metro. Cncl. of Gvts.: Libns. Tech. Com. (1978–). Martin Luther King Pub. Lib.: Lib. Srvs. and Construction Act Adv. Cncl. (1976–78). **Pubns.:** "Serving Blind and Physically Handicapped Readers: A Shared Responsibility," *Information Reports and Bibliographies* (1978); "Library Services to the Blind and Physically Handicapped: Local Commitment," *IL Libs.* (S. 1975); "Services to the Blind and Handicapped: The Unmet Need," *KS Lib. Bltn.* (41:2). **Activities:** 4, 9; 17, 34, 39; 72 **Addr.:** 11663 Newbridge Ct., Reston, VA 22091.

Hahn, Susanne (F. 21, 1941, Philadelphia, PA) Head Libn., Schnader, Harrison, Segal & Lewis, 1976–; Ref./Circ. Libn., Villanova Law School Lib., 1973–76. **Educ.:** Univ. of PA, 1959–62, BA (Eng.), Villanova Univ., 1974–76, MSLS. **Orgs.:** AALL. Grt. Philadelphia Law LA: Secy. (1979–80); Exec. Brd. (1976–77). **Activities:** 12; 15, 20, 39; 77 **Addr.:** Schnader, Harrison, Segal & Lewis, 1719 Packard Bldg., Philadelphia, PA 19102.

Haikalis, Peter D. (Jl. 23, 1934, Decatur, IL) Head, Ref. Srvs., J. Paul Leonard Lib., San Francisco State Univ., 1979–; Coadj. Fac., Grad. Sch. of Lib. and Info. Srv., Rutgers Univ., 1978; Ref. Libn., Firestone Lib., Princeton Univ., 1977–79; Asst. Prof. of Russ., Univ. of CA, Riverside, 1967–75. **Educ.:** Washington Univ., St. Louis, 1955–57, BA (Hist.); Univ. of PA, 1964–67, PhD (Slavic Lang. and Lit.); Univ. of CA, Los Angeles, 1975–77, MLS. **Orgs.:** ALA: RASD; ACRL/Univ. Libs. Sect., Strg. Com. (1979–82). CA LA. **Pubns.:** *Reading Contemporary Russian* (1979); *Real Estate: A Bibliography and Union List of Materials in the California State University and College Libraries* (1981). **Activities:** 1; 17, 31, 39; 56 **Addr.:** J. Paul Leonard Library, San Francisco State University, 1630 Holloway, San Francisco, CA 94132.

Hail, Christopher (Je. 15, 1938, Cheyenne, WY) Asst. Libn., Frances Loeb Lib., Grad. Sch. of Dsgn., Harvard Univ., 1971–; Map Rm. Asst., Harvard Coll. Lib., Harvard Univ., 1967–71. **Educ.:** Princeton Univ., Univ. of CA, Berkeley, 1956–59, 1961–65, AB (Archit.). **Orgs.:** ARLIS/NA. Cncl. of Plng. Libns.: Secy. (1979–81). **Activities:** 1; 17, 39; 55, 65 **Addr.:** Harvard University, Frances Loeb Library, Graduate School of Design, Gund Hall, Cambridge, MA 02138.

Hajnal, Peter I. (Jl. 23, 1936, Budapest, Hungary) Head, Gvt. Pubn. Sect., Univ. of Toronto Lib., 1975–, Actg. Head, Serials Cat. Sect., 1974–75; Assoc. Libn./Docmlst., Dag Hammarskjold Lib., Untd. Nations, 1970–74; Libn., Univ. of Toronto Lib., 1968–70. **Educ.:** New Sch. for Soc. Resrch., 1966, BA (Comp. Lit.); Columbia Univ., 1966–68, MS (LS). **Orgs.:** ALA: GODORT Work Grp. on IGO Documentation (Ch., 1978–79). Assn. of Intl. Libs. Libns. Assn. of the Univ. of Toronto. Can. Inst. of Intl. Affairs. Assn. of Former Intl. Civil Servants. Univ. of Toronto Fac. Assn. **Pubns.:** "Collection development: United Nations material," *Gvt. Pubn. Review* (1981); *Guide to United Nations Organization, Documentation and Publishing* (1978); *The United Nations and its Publications; a Bibliographical Guide* (1976); "UNBIS and UNDOC," *Docum. to the People* (Mr. 1979); "MARC and CODOC; a Case Study in Dual Format Use.," *Jnl. of Lib. Autom.* (D. 1977). **Activities:** 1, 12; 29, 41; 54, 62, 92 **Addr.:** 255 Glenlake Ave., Apt. 603, Toronto, ON M6P 1G2 Canada.

Haladus, Rev. Victorian James, O.F.M. (O. 25, 1933, Cleveland, OH) Libn, Instr. Media, Padua Franciscan HS, 1962–. **Educ.:** John Carroll Univ., Quincy Coll., 1951–57, BA (Phil.); Rosary Coll., 1962–68, MA (LS); St. Joseph Semy. Teutopolis (IL), 1959–61, STB (Theo.). **Orgs.:** Cath. LA: N.E. OH Unit Ch. (1977–79); Vice-Ch. (1975–77); Past Pres. (1979–81); HS Rep. (1971–77); Nsltr. Ed. (1975–77). OH LA. Assn. of AV Techns. Knights of Columbus. Clowns of Amer. **Honors:** Knights of Columbus, Past Grand Knight, 1974. **Activities:** 10; 32, 48 **Addr.:** Padua Franciscan High School, 6740 State Rd., Parma, OH 44134.

Halbrook, Barbara (Ag. 16, 1946, Salem, MO) Assoc. Dir., WA Univ. Med. Lib., 1978–, Asst. Libn. for Pub. Srvs., 1976–78, Head of Ref., 1972–76, ILL Libn., 1969–72. **Educ.:** Univ. of MO, 1964–69, AB (LS). **Orgs.:** Med. LA: ILL and Resrc. Sharing Com. (1980); Midcontl. Chap. Hlth. Educ. Netwk.: Nom. Com. (Ch., 1981). St. Louis Med. Libns. Grp. Univ. of MO Alum. Assn. AAAS. **Pubns.:** Jt. auth., "Selection and Acquisition Manual Development," *Bltn. Med. LA* (Ja. 1979); jt. auth., "A Clinical Librarian's Program," *Bltn. Med. LA* (Ap. 1976). **Activities:** 1, 12; 17, 34; 56, 80 **Addr.:** Medical Library, Washington University, 4580 Scott Ave., St. Louis, MO 63110.

Halcums, Robert E. (S. 10, 1952, Portsmouth, VA) Branch Libn., VA Beach Pub. Lib. Syst., 1977–; Branch Libn., Portsmouth Pub. Lib., 1976–77. **Educ.:** Old Dominion Univ., 1970–74, BS (Acct.); LA State Univ., 1975–76, MLS. **Orgs.:** ALA: JMRT, Pubcty. Dir. (1977–79), Prof. Dev. Grant Com. (1980–81); PLA, Starter List Com. (1979–80); SRRT (1979–81). VA LA: JMRT, Pres. (1978); Prog. Ch. (1977). **Honors:** ALA, 3M/JMRT Prof. Dev. Grant Recipient, 1978; **Activities:** 9; 17 **Addr.:** Virginia Beach Public Library System, Kempsville Branch, 832 Kempsville Rd., Virginia Beach, VA 23464–2793.

Halda, Diana C. (Mr. 22, 1918, Wellman, IA) Supvsr., Tech. Prcs., Twp. HS Dist. 214, Mt. Prospect, IL, 1974–; Head libn., Prospect HS, 1971–74; Libn., Maine South HS, 1964–71; Libn., Richmond (VA) Pub. Sch., 1963–64. **Educ.:** Coe Coll., 1937–41, BA (Msc.); Rosary Coll., 1965–68, MALS; VA Commonwealth Univ., 1960–63, (LS). **Orgs.:** ALA. IL LA. Libns. of Chicagoland. AAUW. **Honors:** Beta Phi Mu, 1968. **Pubns.:** "Technical processing - library cooperation," *IL Libs.* (S. 1976). **Activities:** 10; 20, 46, 48; 63 **Addr.:** 1131 S. Seminary Ave., Park Ridge, IL 60068.

Hale, Charles Edward (Ap. 13, 1938, Albion, NY) Lib. Dir., Millikin Univ., 1976–; Dir. U.S.O.E. Inst., IN Univ. Grad. Lib. Sch., 1973–74; Dir., Lrng. Resrcs. Ctr., Lees Jr. Coll., 1970–73; Tchr., Lowell Pub. Sch. Syst., 1960–62. **Educ.:** Hope Coll., 1958–60, BA (Hist., Pol. Sci.); Univ. of KY, 1969–70, MSLS; IN Univ., 1973–76, PhD (LS). **Orgs.:** ALA: ACRL. IL LA. IL Assn. of Coll. and Resrch. Libns.: Secy/VP-Elect (1978–79). Sangamon Valley Acad. Lib. Cnsrtm.: Ch. (1978–79). Various other orgs. Westminster Presby. Church. Cent. Lab. Sch. Decatur Optimists Club. Rolling Prairies Lib. Syst.: Exec. Bd. (1978–). **Honors:** Beta Phi Mu; Lees Jr. Coll., Grad. Class, Outstan. Fac. Srv. Awd., 1972; Lees Jr. Coll. Fac., Pres. Fac. Srv. Cit., 1973. **Pubns.:** Various articles. **Activities:** 1; 15, 17, 31; 61 **Addr.:** Millikin University, Decatur, IL 62522.

Hale, Martha L. (N. 30, 1942, Pittsburgh, PA) Lect. & Assoc. Dir., Cmnty. Anal. Resrch. Inst., Sch. of Lib. and Info. Mgmt., Univ. of South. CA, 1979–; Assoc. Dir., Cmnty. Anal.

Special Subjects/Services: 50. Adult educ.; 51. Advert./Mktg.; 52. Aerosp.; 53. Agric.; 54. Area std.; 55. Arts/Hum.; 56. Autom.; 57. Bibl./Prtg.; 58. Bio. sci.; 59. Bus./Fin.; 60. Chem.; 61. Copyrt.; 62. Documtn.; 63. Educ.; 64. Engin.; 65. Env.; 66. Eth. grps.; 67. Film; 68. Food/Nutr.; 69. Geneal.; 70. Geo.; 71. Geol.; 72. Handcpd.; 73. Hist.; 74. Int. frdm.; 75. Info. sci.; 76. Insr.; 77. Law; 78. Legis.; 79. Math./Comp. sci.; 80. Med.; 81. Metals; 82. Nat. resrcs.; 83. Newsp.; 84. Nuc. sci.; 85. Oral hist.; 86. Petr./Energy; 87. Pharm.; 88. Phys./Astr./Math.; 89. Readg.; 90. Relig.; 91. Sci./Tech.; 92. Soc. sci.; 93. Telecom.; 94. Transp.; 95. (other).

Resrch. Inst., Univ. of Denver, 1977–78. **Educ.:** Univ. of NH, 1960–64, BA (Hist.); Syracuse Univ., 1975–77, MLS; Univ. of S. CA, 1979–, PhD (Pub. Admin.) in progress. **Orgs.:** ALA. CA LA. **Honors:** Beta Phi Mu. **Pubns.:** *County Census Data for Library Planning* (1978); "Research in Action-User Studies & Census Data–A Tool for Decision-Making," *Pub. Libs.* (Sum. 1978); "Community Analysis: Overview, Thanks & CARI," *DIKTA* (Fall 1978). **Activities:** 11; 24, 25, 26; 50, 92, 95-Public Administration. **Addr.:** 1444 S. Irena, Redondo Beach, CA 90277.

Hale, Robert G., ESr. (Ap. 20, 1934, Waterbury, CT) Educ. Consult., Coord. Lrng. Resrcs. Tech. Unit, CT St. Dept. Educ., 1981–. Dir. of Instr. Media, Branford Pub. Sch., 1972–81, Dir., Elem. Sec. Educ. Title III Proj., 1968–72, Tchr., Indus. Educ., 1958–66. **Educ.:** Tchr. Coll. of CT, 1952–56, BS (Indus. Educ.); Ctrl. CT St. Coll., 1962–66, MS (Indus. Educ.); Syracuse Univ., 1966–67, 6th Yr. (Educ. Admn.). **Orgs.:** AECT: Natl. Mem. Com. (Ch., 1977); Del. Cncl. (Ch.); Bd. Dir.; Pubn. Coord. Com.; Cncl. Steering Com. (Ch., 1978). CT Educ. Media Assn.: Mem. Com. (Ch., 1976); Prof. Rights Resp. Com. (Ch., 1978); Bd. Dir. New England Educ. Media Assn.: Various com. ALA. AASL. Amer. Indus. Arts Assn. CT Comsn. on Cable Telecom.: Coord. Com. (Ch.). Cable TV Adv. Cncl., Cmnty. TV Syst., Inc.: Treas. **Honors:** Epsilon Pi Tau. Phi Delta Kappa, 1967; Madison Jaycees, CT, Disting. Srv. Awd., 1978. **Pubns.:** *Educational Media in Special Education* (1980); "Data Processing & Inventory Control", *AV Instr.* (1971). **Activities:** 10; 17, 26 **Addr.:** 76 Fairview Dr., Madison, CT 06443.

Hale, Ruth Carlton (F. 16, 1934, Griffin, GA) Head, Bibl. Srvs. Div., GA Inst. of Tech. Lib., 1979–, Head, Info. Exch. Ctr., 1971–79, Interlib. Srvs. Libn., 1966–71, Gen. Std. Libn., 1965; Hum. Ref. Libn., Univ. of TX 1956–65. **Educ.:** Univ. of AR, 1951–55, BSE (Educ.); Columbia Univ., 1955–56, MS (LS). **Orgs.:** ALA. SELA. GA LA. **Pubns.:** *Secretary's Survival Kit; an Interlibrary Loan Manual* (1973). **Activities:** 1; 17, 34, 39; 91 **Addr.:** 2204 Peachtree Rd., N.W., Apt. C-1, Atlanta, GA 30309.

Hales, Dorothy G. (S. 24, 1912, Baltimore, MD) Dir., Sequoyah Reg. Lib., 1970–; Assoc. Dir., Mid. GA Reg. Lib., 1968–70, Admin. Asst., 1964–68, Ref. Libn., 1955–64. **Educ.:** Johns Hopkins Univ., 1929–33, BS (Grmn., Fr.), 1934–36, MA (Grmn. Langs.); Peabody Coll., 1963–64, MA (LS). **Orgs.:** ALA. SELA. GA LA: Mem. Com. (1971–73); Handbk. Com. (1980–81). N. GA Assoc. Libs.: Vice–Ch. (1980); Ch. (1981–). Canton Bus. and Prof. Women's Club. **Honors:** Beta Phi Mu. **Activities:** 9; 15, 17, 24 **Addr.:** Sequoyah Regional Library, 400 E. Main St., Canton, GA 30114.

Hales, John Daniel, Jr. (N. 7, 1949, Giessen, Germany) Dir. of Libs., Suwannee River Reg. Lib., 1976–; Ref. Libn., Jacksonville Pub. Lib., 1974–76. **Educ.:** Univ. of KY, 1967–71, BS (Acct.), 1972–73, MSLS. **Orgs.:** ALA: PRS Pubns. (1979–); PLA/Small and Medium-Size Lib. Sect., Rural Lib. Srvs. Com. (1981–) FL LA: PR Caucus (Ch.–Elect, 1979–). Duval Cnty. LA: VP (1976). **Honors:** Beta Phi Mu, 1973. **Pubns.:** "Legislative Tips, Local," "PR Bookshelf: A Select Bibliography," *PR Handbook for Florida Libraries* (1980); "Reaching The Rural," *FL Libs* (N./D. 1977). **Activities:** 9; 17, 36 **Addr.:** Suwannee River Regional Library, 207 Pine Ave., Live Oak, FL 32060.

Haley, Marie V. (S. 20, 1933, Sioux City IA) Lib. Media Dist. Dir., Sioux City Cmnty. Sch., 1968–, Lib. Media Coord., E. HS, 1960–68; Libn., Washington HS (Cherokee, IA), 1958–60; Libn., Harlan HS (Harlan, IA), 1956–58. **Educ.:** Briar Cliff Coll., 1951–55, (Soc. Sci. LS) Univ. of IA, 1966–69, MA (LS). **Orgs.:** IA Educ. Media Assn.: Pres. (1972–74) Various com. ALA: AASL, Supvsr. Sect. (Ch.); Bd. Mem. (1978–79), Affiliate Asm. (1978–80). Delta Kappa Gamma, St. Pubcty. Ch. (1975–79). Quota Club. Briar Cliff Coll. Alum. Assn.: Pres., Bd. Mem. Sioux City Tchrs. Credit Union: Bd. Mem. **Honors:** Briar Cliff Coll., Alum. of the Yr., 1967; Outstan. Young Woman of the Yr., 1965; Sioux City Tchrs. Credit Union, Milton Delzell Awd., 1977. **Activities:** 10; 17, 32; 63, 89 **Addr.:** Sioux City Community Schools, 1221 Pierce St., Sioux City, IA 51105.

Hall, Alan Craig (Mr. 9, 1954, Marietta, OH) Dir., Delphos (OH) Pub. Lib., 1977–. **Educ.:** WV Univ., 1972–76, BS Ed (Educ.); Case Western Reserve Univ., 1976–77, MSLS. **Orgs.:** OH LA: Secy., Div. V; Com. for NW OH Reg. Conf. (1977, 1979). ALA. West. OH Reg. Lib. Dev. Syst.: Secy. (1978); Pres. (1979). Delphos Lions Club. First Untd. Presby. Church: Libn. **Honors:** Del., OH WHCOLIS, 1978. **Pubns.:** *Obituaries in Delphos, OH 1960–1980* (1980); "From the Bookshelf," *Delphos Herald* (monthly column). **Activities:** 1, 9; 17, 39, 47; 63, 69 **Addr.:** Delphos Public Library, 309 W. 2nd St., Delphos, OH 45833.

Hall, Alice Marion (O. 2, 1918, New York, NY) Head Cat., Lafayette Coll., 1959–; Head Cat., Baldwin-Wallace Coll., 1951–59; Asst. Cat., FL St. Univ., 1946–51; Asst. Cat., Canton Pub. Lib. (OH), 1943–44 Libn., Canton Twp. HS, 1942–43. **Educ.:** St. Univ. of NY at Fredonia, 1936–39, BS (Educ.); St. Univ. of NY at Geneseo, 1939–40, BLS; Univ. MI, 1944–46, AMLS. **Orgs.:** ALA: Elect. Com. (1953); ACRL. AAUP: Lafayette Chap., Secy. (1962). **Activities:** 1; 17, 20, 44 **Addr.:** 3777 Fleetwood Dr., Easton, PA 18042.

Hall, Alison Janet Byron (Je. 17, 1939, Watford, Hertfordshire, Eng.) Msc. Catlgr., Carleton Univ. Lib., 1981–, Msc. Libn., 1974–81, Hum. Cat. Team Leader, 1972–74; Catlgr., Ottawa Pub. Lib., 1968–72; Catlgr., Inner London Educ. Athrty., Eng., 1967–68; Catlgr., City of London Lending Libs., 1966–67; Libn., Arch. Dept., City of Westminster Pub. Libs., London, Eng., 1965–66. **Educ.:** Carleton Univ., 1972–79, BA, BMus (Msc.). Assoc. of the LA (UK), 1961–64. **Orgs.:** LA (UK). Can. LA. Msc. LA. Can. Assn. of Msc. Libs.: Bd. of Dir. (Secy., 1977–78); Cat. Com. (1979–); Rep., Repertoire Internationale d'Iconographie Musicale (1979–). **Pubns.:** *Palestrina: An Index to the Casimiri, Kalmus, and Haberl Editions* (1980). **Activities:** 1; 20; 55, 95-Msc. **Addr.:** 2590, Fox Hollow Crescent, Gloucester, ON K1T 1X4 Canada.

Hall, Ann Bowman (Ashland, KY) Libn., Natl. Marine Fisheries Srv.; Libn., Bardstown City Sch. (KY), Libn., Nelson Cnty. Sch., KY, Cat., Univ. KY. **Educ.:** Univ. of KY, AB (LS). **Orgs.:** SLA. NC LA. Intl. Assn. of Marine Sci. Lib. and Info. Ctrs.: Secy. **Pubns.:** Various bibl. on fish and marine life. **Activities:** 4; 49-One-person library; 58, 82, 91 **Addr.:** National Marine Fisheries Service, Southeast Fisheries Center, Beaufort Laboratory, Beaufort, NC 28516.

Hall, Blaine H. (D. 12, 1932, Wellsville, UT) Hum. Libn., Brigham Young Univ., 1972–, Instr. of Eng., 1963–72; Eng. Tchr., Clearfield HS, 1960–61. **Educ.:** Brigham Young Univ., 1958–60, BS (Eng.), 1961–65, MA (Amer. Lit.), 1966–71, MLS. **Orgs.:** UT LA: Pres. Elect. (1980–81); Ed., *UT Libs* (1972–75); Ed. Bd. (1972–75). Mt. Plains LA: Ed., *MPLA Nsltr.* (1977–); Exec. Bd. ALA. UT Coll. Lib. Cncl.: Pub. Srv. Com. (Ch., 1976–77). Chld. Lit. Assn. of UT: Org. Com. Orem (Utah) Pub. Lib.: Bd. of Trustees (1979–). **Honors:** ALA, ALA/H. W. Wilson Per. Awd. for *UT Lib.*, 1977; Mt. Plains LA, Prof. Dev. Grant Awd., 1979. **Pubns.:** Co. Auth., *Using the Library: The Card Catalog* (1971); "UCLC and Library Cooperation in Utah," *UT Lib.* (Fall 1978); "Whitmore - More Than a Whit More," *UT Lib.* (Fall 1974). **Activities:** 1; 15, 37, 39; 55, 74 **Addr.:** Blaine H. Hall, Harold B. Lee Library, Brigham Young University, Provo, UT 84057.

Hall, Danelle L. (F. 9, 1939, Oklahoma City, OK) Gvt. Docum. Libn., Oklahoma City Univ. Lib., 1970–; HS Libn., Wallkill (NY) Ctrl. Sch., 1966–67; Spec. Educ. Tchr., Leptondale Elem., 1963–65; HS Eng. Tchr., Wallkill Ctrl. Sch., 1962–63; HS Eng. Tchr., Bucklin (KS), 1960–61. **Educ.:** Northwest. State Coll., OK, 1956–60, BA (Eng.); Univ. of OK, 1969–70, MLS. **Orgs.:** OK LA: Natl. Lib. Week Com. (1975–76); OK LA Gvr.'s Mansion Lib. Com. (1976–77). **Pubns.:** "When You Don't Find It in the Monthly Catalog," *OK Libn.* (Jl./O. 1979); "Child Abuse Bibliography," *OK Libn.* (Ap. 1979); "Training of Aides for Information Centers," *OK Libn.* (O. 1977); "Paraprofessional Training of Aides for American Indian Information Centers," *Wilson Lib. Bltn.* (My. 1977); "Legend of Robbers' Roost," *Old Timers News* (Fall 1974). **Activities:** 1; 29 **Addr.:** Dulaney Browne Library, Oklahoma City University, 2501 N. Blackwelder, Oklahoma City, OK 73106.

Hall, David (D. 16, 1916, New Rochelle, NY) Cur., Rodgers and Hammerstein Arch. of Rec. Snd., NY Pub. Lib., 1980–, Head, 1967–80; Pres., Composers Recs., Inc., 1963–67; Msc. Ed., *Stereo Review Mag.*, 1956–62; Visit. Fulbright Lectr., Univ. of Copenhagen, 1955–56; Musical Dir., Classics, Mercury Rec. Corp., 1948–55; Msc. Prog. Annotator, NBC, 1942–48; Advert. Dept. Copywriter, Columbia Recs., 1941–42. **Educ.:** Yale Univ., 1936–39, BA (Psy.); Columbia Univ., 1939–40 (Psy.). **Orgs.:** Assoc. for Rec. Snd. Cols.: Jnl. Ed. (1968–71); Bd at Lg. (1975–77); 1st VP (1977–79); Pres. (1979–). Intl. Assn. of Msc. Libs. Intl. Assn. of Snd. Archs. Amer.–Scan. Fndn.: Trustee (1968–80). Natl. Msc. Cncl.: Bd. (1969–79). **Honors:** Finnish Gvt., Ord. of the Finnish Lion, 1st Class, 1970. **Pubns.:** *The Record Book* (1940); "The Rodgers and Hammerstein Archives of Recorded Sound," *Assn. for Rec. Snd. Cols. Jnl.* (1974). **Activities:** 9, 12; 15, 17, 47; 55, 95-Snd. recs. **Addr.:** 155 Catalpa Rd., Wilton, CT 06897.

Hall, Deanna Morrow (Je. 4, 1941, Wadena, SK) Mgr., Tech. Info. Resrcs., GA-Pac. Corp., 1976–, Tech. Info. Spec., 1969–76; Ed., Ctr. for Info. Srvs., 1966–67; Ed. Asst., Chem. Abs., 1962–66. **Educ.:** Univ. of SK, 1959–62, BA (Chem.); Case Western Resrv. Univ., 1968–69, MSLS. **Orgs.:** ASIS: SIG/Mgt., Ch.-Elect (1980–81); Pac. NW Chap. (Secy./Treas., 1972). SLA: Forestry/Forest Prod. Sect. (Ch., 1977–78). Amer. Chem. Socty.: Portland Sect. Centennial Com. (Ch., 1974–76); Spec. Com. on Div. Structures (1980–81). Tech. Assn. of the Pulp and Paper Indus.: Info. Mgt. Com. (Ch., 1975); Exec. Com. (1981). **Pubns.:** "A generalized flowchart for the use of ORBIT and other on-line interactive bibliographic search systems," *Jnl. Of The Amer. Socty. For Info. Sci.* (Ja.-F. 1976); "Information Management: A Revolutionary Decade," *TAPPI* (F. 1980); "Using The Technical Literature: One Company's Approach," *TAPPI* (Ja. 1972). **Activities:** 12; 17, 39, 49-Lit. Srchg.; 60, 64, 91 **Addr.:** Georgia-Pacific Corporation, P. O. Box 105041, Atlanta, GA 30348.

Hall, Edward B. (N. 10, 1928, Mt. Stering, KY) Admin., Annapolis and Anne Arundel Cnty. Lib., 1971–; Dir., Washington Cnty. Free Lib., 1962–71; Dir., South. MD Reg. LA, 1959–62; Branch Libn., Free Lib. of Philadelphia, 1956–59. **Educ.:** Univ. of KY, 1947–51, AB (Hist.), 1953–54, MSLS. **Orgs.:** MD LA: Legis. and Plng. Com., Ch. **Honors:** Beta Phi Mu; Phi Alpha Theta. **Activities:** 9; 17, 47; 78 **Addr.:** Library Headquarters, Anne Arundel County Public Library, 5 Harry S. Truman Pkwy., Annapolis, MD 21401.

Hall, Edward James (Mr. 31, 1935, Boston, MA) Catlgr., Lib. Admin., Kent State Univ., 1973–, Asst. Archvst., 1978–79, Geo. and Urban Std. Libn., 1973–78. **Educ.:** Boston Univ., 1953–57, BA (Hist.); SUNY, Albany, 1972–73, MLS; Univ. of VT; SLA: Cert. in Lib. Admin., Cert. in Cat. Non-Print Mtrls. **Orgs.:** ALA: Gvt. Docum. Task Force on Microfilms. SLA. Geosci. Info. Socty.: Geol. Guidebooks Com. **Activities:** 1, 2; 20, 29, 39; 54, 70, 80 **Addr.:** 635 Woodside Dr., Kent, OH 44240.

Hall, Ellen Francine (Ap. 25, 1947, Minneapolis MN) Lib. Dir., Presentation Coll., 1977–; Dept. Head, Sci. Lib., Univ. of MO (Columbia), 1976–77, Co-Dept. Head, Sci. Lib., 1971–76; Staff Libn., Sci. and Tech., St. Paul Pub. Lib., 1970–71. **Educ.:** Univ. of MN, 1965–69, BA (Eng.), 1969–70, MA (LS); Med. LA, 1971, Cert. Grade I. **Orgs.:** Med. LA. Mid-Continental Reg. Med. Lib. Grp.: By-Laws Com. (1979–). SD LA. Mt. Plains LA. Daniel Boone Reg. Lib. Bd. (Columbia, MO): Trustee (1976–77). Aberdeen City Plng. Comsn.: Ch. (1981–). Jt. City–Cnty. Plng. Comsn., Vice Ch. (1981). **Activities:** 1; 17, 31, 39; 80, 90, 95-Nursing. **Addr.:** Presentation College, Aberdeen, SD 57401.

Hall, Frances Hunt (Jl. 14, 1919, Panama City, Panama) Libn., NC Supreme Court Lib., 1977–; Libn., Assoc. Prof., South. Meth. Univ. Law Sch., 1975–77; Asst. Libn./Assoc. Prof., Univ. of IL Law Sch., 1973–74; Assoc. Libn./Assoc. Prof., Univ. of VA Law Sch., 1972–73; Asst. Prof., Univ. of NC Sch. of LS, 1968–72; Docum. Libn., Asst. Ref. Libn., Univ. of NC, Greensboro, 1966–68; Asst. Law Libn., Univ. of Chicago, 1963–66; Asst. Law Libn., Univ. of NC, 1959–63. **Educ.:** Univ. of NC, Greensboro, 1936–40, BA (Hist.); Univ. of NC, Chapel Hill, 1954–59, MA (Hist.), JD, MSLS. **Orgs.:** ALA: Ref. & Subscrpn. Bk. Review Com. (1971–76). AALL. SLA. NCLA. Other orgs. Assn. NC Bar Assn. NC State Bar. **Honors:** Beta Phi Mu. **Pubns.:** *Cases and Materials on Librarianship and the Law* (1971); various articles. **Activities:** 1, 13; 17, 20, 39; 77 **Addr.:** N.C. Supreme Court Library, P.O. Box 28006, Raleigh, NC 27612.

Hall, Halbert Weldon (O. 29, 1941, Waco, TX) Spec. Formats Libn., TX A&M Univ. Lib., 1970–; Serials Libn., Sam Houston State Univ. Lib., 1967–70; Bio. Tchr., West Indp. Sch. Dist., 1964–65. **Educ.:** Univ. of TX, Austin, 1960–64, BA (Bio.); N. TX State Univ., 1966–67, MLS. **Orgs.:** ALA: Cncl. (1976–79). TX LA: Chap. Cnclr. (1976–79); Pubns. Com. (1974–75). Sci. Fiction Resrch. Assn.: Bd. of Dirs. (1973–79); Lib. Com. (1976–77). **Pubns.:** *Science Fiction Book Review Index, 1923-1973* (1975); *SFBRI: Science Fiction Book Review Index* (1974–); "Serials '74: A Review," *Lib. Resrcs. & Tech. Srvs.* (Sum. 1975); "Science Fiction in Libraries," *OK Libn.*, (O. 1978); "Announcing The Future: Science Fiction at Texas A&M Univ.," *TX Lib. Jnl.* (D. 1974). **Activities:** 1 **Addr.:** Library - Special Formats, Texas A&M University, College Station, TX 77843.

Hall, Henry Palmer, Jr. (O. 1, 1942, Beaumont, TX) Coord. of Instr. Resrcs., St. Mary's Univ., 1980–, Dir., Acad. Lib., 1978–, Asst. Dir., Pub. Srvs., 1978, Col. Dev. and Ref., 1977–78; Instr., Univ. of TX, Austin, 1973–77. **Educ.:** Lamar Univ., 1960–64, BS (Sp.); Defense Lang. Inst., 1966, Cert. (Vietnamese); Univ. of TX, Austin, 1973–74, MA (Eng.), 1975–76, MSLS. **Orgs.:** ALA. TX LA: Pubns. Com. (1978–); Univ. Div., Coll. and Resrch. Grants Com. (1978–). TX Cncl. of Lib. and Info. Netwks.: Exec. Bd. Cncl. of Resrch. and Acad. Libs. of the San Antonio Area: VP. **Honors:** Alpha Psi Omega. **Pubns.:** "Personnel Administration in the College Library," *College Librarianship* (1980). **Activities:** 1, 2; 15, 17, 32; 55, 59, 63 **Addr.:** 4826 Rockford, San Antonio, TX 78249.

Hall, Holly (D. 30, 1946, Kearny, NJ) Head, Spec. Cols., Washington Univ. Libs., 1981–, Chief, Rare Bks. and Spec. Cols., 1976–81, Actg. Chief, 1975–76, Head, Mss. Div., 1971–75. **Educ.:** Wittenberg Univ., 1964–68, BA (Eng.); Leeds Univ. (Eng.), 1968–69, MA (Eng.); Natl. Arch. and Recs. Srvs., 1971, Cert. (Arch. Admin.). **Orgs.:** SAA: Lcl. Arrange. Com. (1973). Midwest Arch. Conf.: Cncl. (1975–77); Ed. Bd. (1975–78); Nom. Com. (Ch., 1978–79); Prog. Com. (1979–80). **Activities:** 1; 15, 23, 45; 55, 57 **Addr.:** Special Collections, Washington University Libraries, St. Louis, MO 63130.

Hall, Homer J. (D. 12, 1911, Uniontown, PA) Visit. Investigator, NSF Proj. Dir., Rutgers Univ. Grad. Sch. of Lib. and Info. Std., 1977–; Tech. Info. Anal., Resrch. Chem., Exxon Co., 1935–76, Proj. Mgr., Gvt. Contract Resrch., Gvt. Resrch. Labs., 1968–76, Spec. Ed., Sr. Anal., Tech. Info. Div., 1958–67, Patent Com., Gen. Secy., Patent Div., 1948–57, Exploratory Resrch. Div., Grp. Head, Tech. Adv. to Legal Dept., 1937–48. **Educ.:** Marietta Coll., 1927–31, AB (Bio., Chem.); OH State Univ., 1931–35, MS, PhD (Chem.). **Orgs.:** ASIS: Spec. Interest Grp. on Info. Anal. and Eval. (Ch.–Elect, 1981). Wainwright Ctr. for Dev. of Human Resrcs.: Trustee (1979–); Dir. (1970–79); Leader (1969–71). Un. Cnty. (NJ) Cult. and Heritage Com. AAAS: Natl. Cnclr. (1973–79). Amer. Inst. of Chems.: Bd. of Dirs., Ch.; Natl.

PROFESSIONAL ACTIVITIES: Institutions: 1. Acad. lib.; 2. Arch.; 3. Assn.; 4. Fed./Gvt. lib.; 5. Inst. lib.; 6. Mfr./Suppl.; 7. Milit. lib.; 8. Musm.; 9. Pub. lib.; 10. Sch. lib.; 11. Sch. of lib. sci.; 12. Spec. lib.; 13. State lib.; 14. (other). **Functions/Activities:** 15. Acq./Col. dev.; 16. Adult srvs.; 17. Admin.; 18. Apprais.; 19. Archit./Bldgs.; 20. Cat./Class.; 21. Chld. srvs.; 22. Circ.; 23. Cons./Pres.; 24. Consult.; 25. Cont. ed.; 26. Educ. lib. sci.; 27. Ext. srvs.; 28. Fund/Grants; 29. Gvt. pubs.; 30. Indx./Abs.; 31. Instr. lib. use; 32. Media srvs.; 33. Micro.; 34. Netwks./Coop.; 35. Persnl.; 36. PR; 37. Publshg.; 38. Recs. mgt.; 39. Ref. srvs.; 40. Repro.; 41. Resrch.; 42. Review.; 43. Secur.; 44. Serials; 45. Spec. col.; 46. Tech. srvs.; 47. Trustees/Bds.; 48. YA srvs.; 49. (other).

Secy. (1970–80). **Pubns.:** *User Values in the Selection of Information Services* (1977); *Profile Study of Air Pollution Control Activities in Foreign Countries* (1971); "Patterns in the Use of Information," *Jnl. of ASIS* (Mr. 1981); "Patterns in Information Analysis: Why Be Different," *Oak Ridge Natl. Labs. Symp. Procs.* (S. 1980); "Time as an Ally in Technology - an Enemy in Politics," *Chem.* (Ag. 1975). **Activities:** 11; 24, 41 **Addr.:** 310 Prospect Ave., Cranford, NJ 07016.

Hall, Jack (O. 12, 1947, Lowell, MA) Coord. of Media Srvs., Grt. Lowell Reg. Vocational Tech. Sch. Dist., 1973–; Admin. Asst., Dept. of Bldg. and Housing, Louisville (KY), 1972–73. **Educ.:** Curry Coll., 1966–70, BA (Hist.); Spalding Coll., 1971–72, MA (LS). **Orgs.:** ALA: AASL, Amer. Vocational Assn. Jt. Com. (Ch., 1979–80). AECT. New Eng. Educ. Media Assn.: Media Prog. in Vocational Schs., Ch. MA Educ. TV. Vocational Competency Testing Prog. **Pubns.:** Jt. auth., *Vocational Technical Core Collection* (1981); *Construction Trades Bibliography* (1976); "Needs Assesment, A Crucial Factor in Vocational-Technical Library Development," *NEEMA* (Win. 1979); "This Vo-tech School Finds Many Uses for Video," *Indus. and Educ. TV* (O. 1979); "Jack of All Trades or Motivation for Media Center Usage," *NEEMA* (Win. 1979); various instr. tapes for vocational educ. **Activities:** 10; 15, 17, 32; 67, 93, 95-Vocational educ. **Addr.:** 7 Chickering Ct., Andover, MA 01810.

Hall, Janice M. (Jl. 21, 1948, Columbus, GA) Pers. Libn., St. Petersburg Jr. Coll., 1971–. **Educ.:** Univ. of FL, 1966–70, BA (Eng.); FL State Univ., 1970–71, MS (LS); Univ. of S. FL, 1972–78, MA. **Orgs.:** SELA. FL LA: Int. Frdm. Com. (Ch., 1974–75); Nom. Com. (1976). Lib. Adv. Com., Safety Harbor (FL). **Honors:** Phi Kappa Phi; Beta Phi Mu. **Activities:** 1; 22, 33, 44; 55, 74, 89 **Addr.:** St. Petersburg Jr. College, Clearwater, 2465 Drew St., Clearwater, FL 33519.

Hall, John Brown (Mr. 28, 1942, Toledo, OH) Asst. Prof., Sch. of Lib. and Info. Sci., Drexel Univ., 1972–; Assoc. Libn., Albion Coll., 1971, Tech. Srvs. Libn., 1968–70, Readers Srvs. Libn., 1966–68; Consult. Libn., Starr Cmwlth., Marshall (MI), 1968. **Educ.:** Bowling Green State Univ., 1961–65, BA (Bus., Eng., LS); West. MI Univ., 1965–66, MS (LS); FL State Univ., 1970–72, PhD (LS). **Orgs.:** ALA: ACRL, Acad. Status Com. (1973–77), Ad Hoc Salary Srvy. Advnc. Com. (1974–77), Rep. to ALA Collective Bargaining Com. (1976–79), Cont. Educ. Com. (1978–81), *Coll. & Rsrch. Libs.* Ed. Bd. (1980–). AALS. PA LA: Coll. and Rsrch. Div., Lib. Dev. Com. (1973–76, 1979–81). AAUP. Beta Phi Mu: Schol. Dev. Com. (Ch., 1975); Nom. Com. (1978). **Honors:** Drexel Univ., Lindback Awd. for Disting. Tchg., 1977; Phi Kappa Phi, 1973. **Pubns.:** Jt. auth., "Library Services and the Open University," *Drexel Lib. Qtly.* (Ap. 1975); jt. auth., "Mediated Approaches to Library Instruction," *Drexel Lib. Qtly.* (Ja. 1980). **Activities:** 17, 26, 46 **Addr.:** School of Library & Information Science, Drexel University, Philadelphia, PA 19104.

Hall, John D. (S. 3, 1944, Abingdon, VA) Head, Orig. Cat., Univ. of Houston Libs., 1978–, Catlgr., Asst. Prof., 1976–78; Asst. Prof. of Grmn. Ling., Univ. of VA, 1970–73. **Educ.:** Davidson Coll., 1961–64, AB (Grmn., Russ.); Princeton Univ., 1965–69, MA (Ling.); Univ. of Bonn, 1964–65, (Grmn.); Free Univ. Berlin, 1967–68, (Ling.); Univ. of Pittsburgh, 1975–76, MLS. **Orgs.:** ALA: RTSD. Mod. Lang. Assn. Ling. Socty. of Amer. Natl. Endow. for the Hum.: Grant Proposal Eval. (1980–). **Honors:** Davidson Coll., Phi Beta Kappa, 1964; Univ. of Pittsburgh, August Alpers Awd., 1977; Fulbright Flwshp., 1964. **Pubns.:** Jt. auth., "The Use of Personnel and Bibliographic Resources for Cataloging By OCLC Participating Libraries," *Lib. Res. and Tech. Srvs.* (Spr. 1980). **Activities:** 1; 20, 44, 46; 55, 95-Ling. **Addr.:** Cataloging Dept., M. D. Anderson Library, University of Houston Central Campus, Houston, TX 77003.

Hall, Joseph H. (Je. 2, 1933, Orlando, FL) Libn., Covenant Theo. Semy., 1970–, Asst. Libn., 1968–70; Head, Serials and Binding, Univ. of IA, 1967–68, Catlgr., 1964–67. **Educ.:** Calvin Coll., 1957–60, AB (Eng. Lit.); Univ. of MI, 1963–64, AMLS; Covenant Semy., 1968–70, MDiv; Concordia Semy., 1970–74, ThD. Presby. Hist. Socty. Amer. Socty. of Church Hist. **Activities:** 1, 12; 15, 17; 90 **Addr.:** 826 Crestland Dr., Ballwin, MO 63011.

Hall, Louise McG. (Ja. 4, 1920, Scotland Neck, NC) Head, Hum. Ref. Dept., Univ. of NC, 1957–, Actg. Univ. Libn., 1973; Actg. Libn., Amer. Sch. of Classical Std., Athens, Greece, 1966; Asst. Head, Ref. Dept., Univ. of NC, 1953–57, Ref. Libn., 1947–53; Ref. Libn., Army Map Srv., 1944–47; Asst. Head, Un. Browsing Room, Univ. of IL, 1941–44. **Educ.:** St. Mary' Coll., 1936–38; Univ. of NC, 1938–40, AB (Hist.), 1940–41, BS in LS; Univ. of IL, 1941–44, MA (LS). **Orgs.:** ALA. SELA. NC LA. Archlgl. Assn. of Amer. AAUP. NC Archlgl. Socty.: Exec. Bd. (1975–76). **Pubns.:** Ed., *Medieval and Renaissance studies ... selected reference works...* (1974); "Bibliographical control of microforms," *Southeast. Libn.* (Win. 1970). **Activities:** 1; 39 **Addr.:** Humanities Reference Department, University of North Carolina, Wilson Library 024 A, Chapel Hill, NC 27514.

Hall, Margaret S. (Ap. 27, 1948, St. Paul, MN) Asst. Libn., Hennepin Cnty. Law Lib., 1980–, Tech. Srvs. Libn., 1975–1980; Serials Libn., Univ. of MN Law Lib., 1974–75, Cat. Lib. Asst., 1972–74. **Educ.:** Univ. of MN, 1967–70, BA (Eng.), 1970–72, MA (LS), 1973–, (Amer. Std.). **Orgs.:** ALA. AALL.: Rel. Pubshr. Com. (1977–78). MN LA. MN Assn. of Law Lib.: VP (1976–77); Co-ed. Nsltr. (1977–); Cont. Educ. Com. (1977–). MN Hist. Socty. **Honors:** Beta Phi Mu. **Activities:** 12; 15, 20, 46; 77 **Addr.:** Hennepin County Law Library, C-2451 Government Center, Minneapolis, MN 55487.

Hall, Mary A. (Je. 18, 1930, Great Bend, KS) Asst. Dir. for Pub. Srvs., Prince George's Cnty. Meml. Lib. Syst., 1969–; Admin. Coord., KS Info. Circuit, Topeka Pub. Lib., 1967–69, Head, Adult Srvs., 1963–66, Head, Ext. Srvs., 1960–62; Pub. Lib. Consult., KS State Lib., 1959–60; City Libn., Pub. Lib., Manhattan (KS), 1958–59; Ext. Srvs./Asst. Head Libn., Jackson Cnty. Pub. Lib., Independence (MO), 1954–58. **Orgs.:** ALA: LAMA (Pres., 1980–81)/Persnl. Admin. Sect., Racism and Sexism Awareness Trng. Com. (Ch., 1976–79), Staff Dev. Com. (Ch., 1973–74). KS LA: Pres. (1965–66). **Pubns.:** Contrib., *Library Management without Bias* (1981); "Performance Appraisal, Part 1," *Pub. Libs.* (Spr. 1978); "Performance Appraisal, Part 2," *Pub. Libs.* (Sum., 1978); "First County-wide Tel-Med in Maryland," *MD State Med. Jnl.* (Mr. 1981). **Activities:** 9; 17, 27, 35 **Addr.:** Prince George's County Memorial Library System, 6532 Adelphi Rd., Hyattsville, MD 20782.

Hall, Nancy M. (Mr. 16, 1929, Montreal, PQ) Dir., Pub. Lib. Srv., Etobicoke Pub. Lib., 1979–; Asst. Dir., Scarborough Pub. Lib., 1976–79, Div. Head, 1973–76, Acq. Coord., 1970–73. **Educ.:** Univ. of Toronto, 1948–52, BA (Hist.), 1952–53, BLS. **Orgs.:** Can. LA. ON LA. **Activities:** 9; 17, 47; 56, 74, 93 **Addr.:** Etobicoke Public Library, Box 501, Etobicoke, ON M9C 5G1 Canada.

Hall, Ronald J. (Je. 6, 1946, Toronto, ON) Head, Info. and Promo., Addiction Resrch. Fndn., 1979–, Head, Info. Srvs., 1977–79, Libn., 1971–77, Docmlst., 1970–71. **Educ.:** Univ. of Toronto, 1965–70, BSc. **Orgs.:** Libns. and Info. Spec. in Addictions: Exec. (1978–80). Substance Abuse Libns. and Info. Spec. Can. LA. Can. Addictions Fndn. **Pubns.:** Ed., *Disulfiram in the Treatment of Alcoholism: An Annotated Bibliography* (1978); Ed., *The Ethical Pharmaceutical Industry and Some of Its Economic Aspects* (1977). **Activities:** 4, 12; 17, 34, 36; 57, 62, 92 **Addr.:** Addiction Research Foundation, 33 Russell St., Toronto, ON M5S 2S1 Canada.

Hall, Sandra K. (Sandy) (N. 26, 1943, Sydney, Australia) Dir., Spec. Srvs., The AZ Daily Star, 1979–, Chief Libn., 1973–79; Tchr., 1965–70. **Educ.:** Univ. of Sydney, 1961–63, BA (Educ.); Univ. of AZ, 1968–69, MEd; 1972, MLS; Univ. of Sydney, 1964 Diploma in (Educ.); Univ. of AZ, 1971–72, MLS. **Orgs.:** AZ LA. Lib. Assn. of Australia. CLENE. SLA: Bd. of Dirs. (1980–81); Newsp. Div., Ch. (1979–80), Secy./Treas. (1977–78), Dir. (1976–77); Educ. Com. (1977–80), Auto. Com. (1975–78); Bltn. Ed., Lib. Mgt. Div. (1977–78); Various other com. Amer. Records Mgt. Assn. Exec. Women's Cncl. of South. AZ. Leag. of Women Voters. World Future Socty. Amer. Hum. Assn. **Honors:** Univ. of AZ, Cmnty. Educ. Awd., 1979; Beta Phi Mu. **Pubns.:** *Handbook on Picture librarianship* "Press Libraries", (1980); Public Relations for Special Libraries", *SLA/Lib. Mgt. Div. Bltn.* (Win. 1979); "Microfilm at the Arizona Daily Star," *Proceedings of the Australasian Micrographics Congress,* (1978). **Activities:** 12; 83 **Addr.:** 4502 Hacienda del Sol, Tucson, AZ 85718.

Hall, Sylvia Dunn (Je. 21, 1949, Kewanee, IL) Dir. of Lib. Dev., State Lib. of PA, 1981–; Asst. Dir., South. Tier Lib. Syst., 1978–81; Div. Head, Tech. Srvs., Corpus Christi Pub. Lib., Acq. & Budget, 1976–78; Syst. Coord., San Antonio Major Resrc. Ctr., San Antonio Pub. Lib., 1975–76, Branch Libn., 1973–75; Libn., Holding Inst., Laredo, TX, 1972–73. **Educ.:** Rockford Coll., 1967–71, BA (Span.); N. TX State Univ., 1971–72, MLS; Univ. of TX at San Antonio, 1975–80, MA (Bicult. Biling. Std.). **Orgs.:** ALA. NY LA: Concerns of Women RT (Ch., 1979–80). TX LA: Natl. Lib. Week Com. (1975). S. Ctrl. Ref. & Resrch. Lib. Cncl.: Plng. & Adv. Com. (Ch., 1979–81). AAUW. Bus. and Prof. Women. **Pubns.:** Ed., *Pub. Lib. Qtly.* (1981–); "Brief annotated bibliography of nonbook materials on the Mexican-American," *TX Lib. Jnl.* (O. 1973); "Summer is sea-monstrously fun!" *TX Lib. Jnl.* (D. 1974); "Cooperation Improving Service in the San Antonio System," *TX Libs.* (Spr., 1976). **Activities:** 9, 14-Pub. Lib. Syst.; 17, 24, 28; 56, 66, 89 **Addr.:** State Library of Pennsylvania, Harrisburg, PA 17120.

Hall, Vivian S. (S. 11, 1923, Newcomb, TN) Geol. Libn., Univ. of KY, 1963–; Libn., Actg. Head, SE Cmnty. Coll., 1962–63; Tchr., Benham and Cumberland Elem. Sch., 1956–62. **Educ.:** Univ. of KY, 1960–62 (Educ.), 1964–66, (LS); various wkshps. **Orgs.:** SLA. SELA. Geosci. Info. Socty.: Pres. (1976–77); VP (1975–76). KY LA: Pres. (1976); VP (1975). **Honors:** KY LA, Spec. Libs. Sect., Outstan. Libn., 1975. **Pubns.:** *Environmental Geology: A Selected Bibliography* (1975). jt. cmplr., "Bibliography of the Kentucky Geological Survey, 1839 through 1978," *KY Geol. Srvy., Series XI, Info. Circular 2* (1980); jt. auth., "The ABC's of Proposal Writing," *Southeast. Libn.* (Win. 1980); jt. auth., "Proposal Writing for Librarians," *KY LA Bltn.* (Spr. 1980); cmplr., *An Eastern Gas Shale Bibliography Selected Annotations, Gas, Oil, Uranium, Etc.* (1980); "Library - Information Center Profile," *SLA, KY Chap. Bltn.* (Mr., 1976); various other articles. **Activities:** 1, 12; 15, 17, 22; 57, 70, 71 **Addr.:** Geology Library, 100 Bowman Hall, University of Kentucky, Lexington, KY 40506.

Hallam, Arlita (Warrick) (Je. 28, 1944, Peoria, IL) Dir., Pub. Srvs., Abilene Pub. Lib., 1978–; Sales Dir., Grp. 5 Dev. Co., 1978; Exec. Dir., Fort Crevecoeur, Creve Coeur, IL, 1977; Reg. Coord., IL Bicent. Comsn., 1974–76; Dir., Fondulac Dist. Lib., 1967–74; Dir., Normal Pub. Lib., 1965–67. **Educ.:** IL State Univ., 1961–65, BS (Eng., LS); Univ. of IL, 1965–68, MS (LS). **Activities:** 9; 17, 35, 36; 51, 66 **Addr.:** RR 7, Box 293, Abilene, TX 79605.

Hallerberg, Gretchen Anne (D. 10, 1949, Jacksonville, IL) Head Med. Libn., Cleveland Clinic, 1981–; Dir., Med./Surgical Lib., Univ. Hosps. of Cleveland, 1977–81; Adj. Prof., Case West. Rsv. Univ. Sch. of LS, 1978–80; Col. Dev. Coord., St. Paul Campus Libs., Univ. of MN, 1976–77; Ref. Libn., Allen Meml. Med. Lib., Cleveland Hlth. Sci. Lib., 1975–76, Ref. Libn., Hlth. Ctr. Lib., 1973–75. **Educ.:** Valparaiso Univ., 1967–70, BS (Bio.); Case West. Rsv. Univ., 1970–72, MS (Bio.), 1972–73, MSLS; Med. LA 1975, Cert. **Orgs.:** Med. LA: Prog. Com., 1975 Anl. Mtg.; Northeast. OH Chap., Treas. (1974, 1975, 1978); VP (1979); Pres. (1980). SLA. **Activities:** 12; 15, 26, 39; 80 **Addr.:** Medical Library, Cleveland Clinic, 9500 Euclid Ave., Cleveland, OH 44106.

Halligan, John T. (Ag. 1, 1933, Lynn, MA) Libn., Sacramento City Coll., 1968–; Libn., Fallbrook (CA) HS, 1965–68; Libn., Cambridge (MA) Pub. Schs., 1964–65; Libn., Carlsbad (CA) HS, 1960–64. **Educ.:** Northeast. Univ., 1952–54; Boston Univ., 1954–56, BS (Jnlsm.); Boston Tchrs. Coll., 1958–59, MEd (Educ.); Long Island Univ., 1960–63, MLS; Sacramento Cnty. Rsv. Acad. Sheriff's Dept., 1974. **Orgs.:** SLA. Poet Tree, Inc. Los Rios Fed. of Tchrs. **Pubns.:** "The King Who Died in San Francisco," *CA Hwy. Ptl. Mag.* (N. 1980); columnist, "Background Books," *Sacramento Bee* (1980–); various articles, reviews. **Activities:** 1; 15, 39, 41; 85, 93 **Addr.:** 2409 Sixth Ave., Sacramento, CA 95818.

Halliwell, Dean Wright (Jl. 26, 1924, Estevan, SK) Univ. Libn., Univ. of Victoria, 1960–; Asst. Libn., Univ. of SK, 1957–60, Canadiana Libn., 1955–57; Coord., Ref. Srvs., Cuyahoga Cnty. Pub. Lib., 1952–55, Bkmobile Libn., 1949–52. **Educ.:** Univ. of SK, 1939–43, BA (Eng.), 1945–48, MA (Eng.); Univ. of Toronto, 1948–49, BLS. **Orgs.:** Can. LA: Pres. (1971–72). Can. Assn. of Coll. & Univ. Libs.: Pres. (1967–68). BC LA: Pres. (1965–66). ALA: Cnclr. (1979–82). **Honors:** Gvt. of Canada, Queen's Silver Jubilee Medal, 1977. **Activities:** 1; 18 **Addr.:** University of Victoria, P.O. Box 1800, Victoria, BC V8W 2Y3 Canada.

Halloran, Joseph G. (Je. 10, 1920, Richmond Hill, NY) Dir., Syosset Pub. Lib., 1963–; Branch Admin., Yonkers Pub. Lib., 1961–63; Dir., Mentor Pub. Lib., 1958–61; Ref. Asst., Detroit Pub. Lib., 1955–58; Ref. Asst., Queensborough Pub. Lib., 1950–55. **Educ.:** Brooklyn Coll., 1950, AB (Fr.); Columbia Univ., 1955, MLS. **Orgs.:** ALA. Nassau Cnty. LA: Pres. (1967–68). **Pubns.:** Various articles. **Activities:** 9; 17, 35, 39; 50, 74, 92 **Addr.:** Syosset Public Library, 225 So. Oyster Bay Rd., Syosset, NY 11791.

Hallowitz, Mildred F. (F. 24, 1920, Brailow, Ukraine, U.S.S.R.) Assoc. Libn., Hist. of Med. Dept. and Col., Hlth. Sci. Lib., SUNY, Buffalo, 1974–, Serials Libn., 1970–73, Head, Pre-Cat. and Verification Sect., Tech. Srvs., 1969–70, Sr. Catlgr., 1966–68. **Educ.:** Hunter Coll., 1936–40, AB (Msc., Grmn.); State Univ. Coll., Geneseo, 1962–65, MLS; NY Cert. Pub. Libn. **Orgs.:** Med. LA. Assn. of Libns. in the Hist. of Med. Socty. for the Soc. Hist. of Med. (London). Buffalo and Erie Cnty. Med. Hist. Socty.: Cncl. (1975–); Pres.-Elect (1980). **Activities:** 1; 15, 20, 39 **Addr.:** 294 Hendricks Blvd., Buffalo, NY 14226.

Halman, Ruth B. (Je. 8, 1941, New York, NY) Ref. Libn., Univ. of CA (Riverside), 1967–, Head, Ref. Srv., 1975–80. **Educ.:** Wheeling Coll., 1959–63, BA (Hist.); Univ. of South. CA, 1966–67, MSLS. **Orgs.:** ALA. CA LA. CA Acad. Resrch. Libns. **Activities:** 1; 17, 31, 39 **Addr.:** Reference Dept., University Library, University of California, Riverside, CA 92507.

Halperin, Michael (Ap. 18, 1940, New York, NY) Head, Ref. Dept., Drexel Univ., 1975–, Bus. Admin. Libn., 1971–75, Govt. Docum. Libn., 1970–71. **Educ.:** Washington Coll., 1959–63, BA (Hist.); Temple Univ., 1965–67, MA (Hist.); Drexel Univ., 1967–68, MSLS, 1974–76, MBA. **Pubns.:** "Measuring Students Preferences for Library Service," *Lib. Qtly.* (1980); "Cluster Sampling Reference Transactions," *RQ* (1978). **Activities:** 1; 39; 59 **Addr.:** Drexel University Lib., Philadelphia, PA 19104.

Halpern, Meyer W. (Jl. 1, 1920, Romania) Law Libn., Marin Cnty. Law Lib., 1969–; Asst. Law Libn., San Francisco Cnty. Law Lib., 1967–69. **Educ.:** Univ. of Buffalo, 1937–41; Lincoln Univ. Sch. of Law, 1967–71; AALL, 1975 (Law Lib. Admin.), 1977, Cert. Law Libn. **Orgs.:** AALL. ALA. **Activities:** 9, 12; 17, 24, 35; 77 **Addr.:** Marin County Law Library, C–33 Hall of Justice, San Rafael, CA 94903.

Special Subjects/Services: 50. Adult educ.; 51. Advert./Mktg.; 52. Aerosp.; 53. Agric.; 54. Area std.; 55. Arts/Hum.; 56. Autom.; 57. Bibl./Prtg.; 58. Bio. sci.; 59. Bus./Fin.; 60. Chem.; 61. Copyrt.; 62. Documtn.; 63. Educ.; 64. Engin.; 65. Env.; 66. Eth. grps.; 67. Film; 68. Food/Nutr.; 69. Geneal.; 70. Geo.; 71. Geol.; 72. Handcpd.; 73. Hist.; 74. Int. frdm.; 75. Info. sci.; 76. Insr.; 77. Law; 78. Legis.; 79. Math./Comp. sci.; 80. Med.; 81. Metals; 82. Nat. resrcs.; 83. Newsp.; 84. Nuc. sci.; 85. Oral hist.; 86. Petr./Energy; 87. Pharm.; 88. Phys./Astr./Math.; 89. Readg.; 90. Relig.; 91. Sci./Tech.; 92. Soc. sci.; 93. Telecom.; 94. Transp.; 95. (other).

Who's Who in Library and Information Services

Halporn, Barbara (D. 14, 1938, Amsterdam, MO) Libn. for Phil., Classics, Hist. of Sci., and Psy., IN Univ. Libs., 1969–, Rare Bks. Catlgr., Lilly Lib., 1968–69, Gifts Libn., 1966–68. **Educ.:** Univ. of MO, 1956–60, AB (Eng.); IN Univ., 1960–66, MA (LS), 1971–75, MA (Classics). **Orgs.:** ALA: ACRL/West. European Spec. Sect., Resrch. and Pubns. Com. (1980–82). Amer. Philological Assn. Socty. for the Hist. of Ancient Med. Amer. Prtg. Hist. Assn. **Honors:** Cncl. on Lib. Resrcs., Advnc. Std. Flwshp., 1976–77. **Pubns.:** "Libraries and Printers in the Fifteenth Century," *Jnl. of Lib. Hist.* (1981); "The Reluctant Publisher," *Schol. Publshg.* (1979). **Activities:** 1; 15, 39, 45; 57 **Addr.:** E 1060 Main Library, Indiana University, Bloomington, IN 47405.

Halporn, Roberta (S. 9, 1927, Brooklyn, NY) Dir., Ctr. for Thanatology Resrch. and Educ., 1980–; Pres., Highly Spec. Promos., Inc., 1977–; Sales Mgr., Hlth. Sci. Pub. Corp., 1971–76; Sales Mgr., Riverside Press, 1964–71; Tchr., NY City Bd. of Educ., 1954–64. **Educ.:** NY Univ., 1945–49, BA (Eng., Psy.), 1949–51, MA (Educ.), 1968, Cert. (Direct Mail, Sales Promo.); Jewish Educ. Com., 1970, Cert. (Operating a Small Lib.); Med. LA, 1972, Cert. (Text Cat. Sem.); CSLA, 1974, Cert. (AV Cat.), 1978, Cert. (Arch. Prsrvn.). **Orgs.:** ALA. CSLA. Med. LA. Publshrs. Lib. Mktg. Grp.: Treas. (1967–72); Pres. (1974). Fndn. of Thanatology. Forum on Death Educ. and Couns. Natl. Hospice Org. Assn. for Gravestone Std. **Pubns.:** *How To Create a Small Thanatology Library and Make It Grow* (1981); *The Thanatology Library* (1977); *Lessons From the Dead, The Cemetery as a Classroom for the Study of the Life Cycle* (1980); cmplr., ed., *Hospice Objectives: Attainment Through Administration* (forthcoming); cmplr., ed., *The Hospice Concept* (1977); various articles, presentations, ed. of various bks., pubns. **Activities:** 12; 15, 20, 24; 57, 80, 92 **Addr.:** 391 Atlantic Ave., Brooklyn, NY 11217.

Halsey, Richard Sweeney (Ap. 8, 1929, Los Angeles, CA) Dean, Sch. of Lib. and Info. Sci., SUNY, Albany, 1980–, Assoc. Prof., 1973–79; Asst. Prof., Sch. of Lib. Sci., 1972–73; Info. Sci., Univ. of Toronto, Cent. Midwestern Reg. Educ. Lab., 1968–69; Dir. of Lrng Resrcs., Sch. Dist. of Univ. City, MO, 1965–68, Chief, AV Dept., Washington Univ., 1962–65. **Educ.:** New England Cnsvty., 1948–52, BMsc, 1952–1954, MMsc; Simmons Coll., 1960–62, SMLS; Case Western Resrv., Univ., 1969–72, PhD (Lib. and Info. Sci.). **Orgs.:** ALA: Ch., Ref. and Sub. Books Rev. Com. (1975–79); *Booklist* Ed. Adv. Brd. (1972–79); Dartmouth Award Com., (1976–79). AALS: Ch., 1974 Conf. Prog. Com. Eastern NY Sch. Lib. Media Assn. NY LA: Pres., Lib. Educ. Sect. (1979–80); Leg. Com., Secy. (1980–81). Common Cause: Steering Com. Coord. 28th Cong. Dist., NY State (1979). **Honors:** Pi Kappa Lambda. **Pubns.:** *Reference Books for Small and Medium-Sized Libraries* (1979); *Purchasing an Encyclopedia: 12 Points to Consider* (1979); *Classical Music Recordings for Home and Library* (1976); Jt. auth., "Biographical Dictionaries," *Booklist* (My. 1974); "Classical Recordings for Children," *Booklist* (Ap. 1974). **Activities:** 11; 17, 25, 26; 50, 78, 89 **Addr.:** 239 Juniper Dr., Schenectady, NY 12306.

Halverson, Eric Gordon (Ja. 2, 1949, Hardin, MT) Proj. Dir., Fish/Wildlife Ref. Srv., 1979–; TALINET Info. Spec., Univ. of Denver, 1978–79; Dir., Wash. Carnegie Lib., 1976–78; Asst. Dir., Paducah (KY) Pub. Lib., 1974–76. **Educ.:** Univ. of OK, 1967–71, BS (Soc./Std.); Univ. of KY, 1973, MSLS; Cmnty. Anal. Inst., Univ. of Denver, 1978. **Orgs.:** NLA. ALA. CO LA. Amer. Civil Liberties Un. **Honors:** Commonwealth of KY, KY Col., 1976. **Activities:** 9, 12; 15, 17, 45; 56, 67 **Addr.:** 2444 South York Ave., Denver, CO 80210.

Hamann, Edmund G. (Ap. 25, 1933, New York, NY) Coll. Libn., Suffolk Univ., 1975–; Serials & Acq. Spec., Harvard Univ., 1973–74; Serials Libn., Cat. Maintenance Libn., Cornell Univ., 1966–72; Serials Libn., Univ. of NH, 1961–66; Cat. Libn., Univ. of Auckland, NZ, 1959–61; Catlgr., Univ. of MI Law Lib., 1956–59. **Educ.:** Hamilton Coll., 1951–55, BA (Hist.); Univ. of MI, 1955–59, MA (LS), MA (Hist.). **Orgs.:** ALA: RTSD/Serials Sect. (Ch., 1971). New Eng. LA. MA LA. **Pubns.:** "The Clarification of Some Obscurities Surrounding the Imprisonment of Richard Grafton in 1541 and 1543," *Bibl. Socty. of America, Papers,* (1958); "Out-of-print Periodicals; the U.S.B.E. As a Source of Supply," *Lib. Resrcs. & Tech. Srvs.,* (Win. 1972); "Expansion of the Public Card Catalog in a Large Library," *Lib. Resrcs. & Tech. Srvs.* (Fall 1972); "Access to Information; a Reconsideration of the Service Goals of a Small Urban College Library" in *New Horizons for Academic Libraries, Papers Presented at the First National Conference of the Association of College and Research Libraries* (1979); Jt. auth., "OCLC and the One-Room Library," *SLA Boston Chap. News Bltn.* (1978). **Activities:** 1; 17 **Addr.:** Suffolk University, College Library, Beacon Hill, Boston, MA 02114.

Hambleton, Ann Collins Beardsley (Ap. 10, 1951, Midland, TX) Asst. Libn. for Admin., Univ. of TX Law Sch. Lib., 1978–; Asst. Libn., Univ. of KS Law Sch. Lib., 1975–77; Acq. Libn., TX State Law Lib., 1973–75. **Educ.:** Our Lady of the Lake Coll., 1969–72, BA (Gvt.); Univ. of TX, Austin, 1973–75, MLS, 1977–78, MA (Gvt.). **Orgs.:** AALL: Com. on Rel. with Publshrs. and Dlrs. Southwest. Assn. of Law Libs.: Mem. Com. ALA: LAMA/Bldgs. and Equip. Sect. **Pubns.:** Cmplr., *A Bibliography of Legal Tapes and Cassettes* (1974); "State Law Library: an Introduction," *TX Chap. SLA Bltn.* (Ja. 1976). **Activities:** 1, 12; 17, 19, 29; 77, 92 **Addr.:** University of Texas School of Law, Tarlton Law Library, 2500 Ted River, Austin, TX 78705.

Hambleton, James E. (Ag. 24, 1947, New York, NY) Dir., State Law Lib., 1981–; Asst. Libn. for Pub. Srvs., Univ. of TX Law Lib., 1978–81; Consult., Mead Data Ctrl., 1977–78; Assoc. Libn., Arnold and Porter, 1976–78; Libn., Hamel, Park, McCabe and Saunders, 1975–76; Ref. Libn., Suffolk Univ. Sch. of Law, 1971–75. **Educ.:** Middlebury Coll., 1965–69, BA (Russ.); Univ. of MI, 1970–71, MALS; George Washington Univ., 1975–78, JD (Law). **Orgs.:** AALL. State Bar of TX. **Pubns.:** Cmplr., *Noter-Up* (1979–); contrib., *Problem Book, Fundamentals of Legal Research* (1980); "JURIS: Legal Information in the Department of Justice," *Law Lib. Jnl.* (My. 1976). **Activities:** 1, 12; 17, 31, 39; 77, 78 **Addr.:** State Law Library, Supreme Court Bldg., P.O. Box 12367, Capitol Station, Austin, TX 78711.

Hamby, Sharon (D. 14, 1943, Memphis, TN) Dir., Boston Coll. Law Lib., 1979–; Consult., Legal Srvs. Inst., 1979; Ref. Libn., Harvard Law Lib., 1975–78; Actg. Libn., Lamont Lib., Harvard Univ., 1974–75, Asst. Libn., 1971–73, Admin. Asst. 1969–71; Rsvs. Libn., Bus. Lib., Columbia Univ., 1968–69, Asst. Circ. Libn., 1966–68. **Educ.:** South. Meth. Univ., 1961–65, BA; Columbia Univ. 1965–66, MLS; Harvard Law Sch., 1975–79, JD. **Orgs.:** AALL. Amer. Assn. of Zoological Parks and Aquariums. MA Bar Assn. **Activities:** 1; 17; 77 **Addr.:** Boston College Law Library, 885 Centre St., Newton, MA 02159.

Hamdy, Mohamed Nabil (Cairo, Egypt) Assoc. Prof., Sch. LS, Univ. of Denver, 1972–; Head Cat. Dept., Hillman Lib., Univ. of Pittsburgh, 1968–71, Cat., 1966–68, Bibl. Searcher, 1965–66; Searcher, Univ. of MN Lib. (1964–65); Head, Legal Depos. & Purchasing, Natl. Lib. of Egypt, 1958–63; Ref. Libn., 1957–58. **Educ.:** Cairo Univ., 1954–57, BA (LS); Univ. of MN, 1963–65, MA (LS); Univ. of Pittsburgh, 1965–72, PhD (LS), 1965–66, Adv. Cert. (LS). **Orgs.:** ALA. AALS: Resrch. Com. (1976–78); Liaison Rep. (1979–). Middle E. Libns. Assn. (1975–). CO Assn. Intl. Educ. (1978–). Mt. Plains LA: (1972–). CO LA: (1973–). CO Muslim Socty.: Plng. Com. (Ch., 1977–79); Trustee (1980–82). **Pubns.:** Reviews. *The Concept of the Main Entry in the Anglo-American Cataloging Rules; ...* (1973); "Trends and Issues in Cataloging and Classifying Arabic Materials" in *Cataloging and Classification of Non-Western Library Materials: Concerns, Issues, and Practices;* "Main Entry and AACR Revision: Review and Recommendations" *UT Libs.* (Fall 1978); Ed., *"Egyptian Pubns. Bltn.,"* (1959–63); jt. ed., "The Arab Bibliography; Publications of the U.A.R. (Egypt) 1962," *The Arab Lib.* (Je. 1963). **Activities:** 1, 11; 20, 26, 46; 56, 75 **Addr.:** Graduate School of Librarianship & Information Management, University of Denver, Denver, CO 80208.

Hamer, Collin Bradfield Jr. (S. 3, 1939, New Orleans, LA) Head, LA Div. & City Arch., New Orleans Pub. Lib., 1968–, Ref. Libn., Bus. & Sci. Div., 1966–67. **Educ.:** Univ. of New Orleans, 1960–63, BA (Psy.); LA State Univ., 1964–66, MS (LS). **Orgs.:** LA LA: Docum. Com. (1975–79, Ch. 1977–79); LA Un. Cat. Com. (1976–79); Pubn. Com. (1974–77). Friends of the Arch. of LA: Bd. (1978–); Treas. (1979–81). Socty. of SW Archvsts. Geneal. Resrch. Socty. of New Orleans: Bd. of Dir. (1969–75); 2nd VP (1973–74), 1st VP (1979–80). LA Hist. Assn. **Pubns.:** "Records of the City of Lafayette (1833–1852) in the City Archives Department of the New Orleans Public Library," *LA Hist.* (Fall 1972); "Records of the City of Jefferson (1850-1870) in the City Archives Department of the New Orleans Public Library," *LA Hist.* (Win. 1976). **Activities:** 2, 9; 17, 33, 45; 69, 83 **Addr.:** 219 Loyola Ave., New Orleans, LA 70140.

Hamill, Geneva Staples (Je. 4, 1918, Lynn, MA) Cat. Libn., Boston Univ. Sch. of Theo., 1967–; Assoc. Libn., Gordon Coll., 1963–65; Tchr., Augusta Cnty. VA, 1942–62. **Educ.:** Gordon Coll., 1938–42, BA (Biblical Std.); Boston Univ. Sch. of Theo., 1965–67, MRE (Relig. Educ.). **Orgs.:** ATLA: Conf. Com. (1979–). New Eng. Theo. LA: Ch. (1973). **Pubns.:** A Unit of Curriculum resource material for junior highs (1970); "Stand in my shoes," *Adult leader* (My., 1979); "We pioneered with Paul," *Intl. Jrl. of Relig. Educ.* (D. 1953). **Activities:** 1, 9; 20, 21, 22; 63, 89, 90 **Addr.:** 745 Commonwealth Ave., Boston, MA 02215.

Hamilton, Beth Alleman (Ap. 3, 1927, Stewartstown, WV) Sr. Info. Sci., Triodyne Inc. Consult. Engin., 1979–; Exec. Dir., IL Reg. Lib. Cncl., 1972–78; Sci. Libn., Assoc. Prof., Univ. of IL at Chicago Circle, 1969–72; Visit. Asst. Prof., Univ. of IL, (1977–1978); Visit. Lect., Rosary Coll., (1970–1971); Various other positions. **Educ.:** WV Univ., 1944–48, BS (Chem.); Rosary Coll., 1966–69 MALS; Univ. of Chicago, 1971–77, CAS (LS). **Orgs.:** IFLA: Stdg. Com. Sci. Tech. (1977–78); Stdg. Com. Interlending (1977–79). SLA: Netwking Com. (Ch., 1977–78). ALA: ACRL, Urban Univ. Lib. Com. (1974–76); ASLA, Interlib. Coop. Com. (1975–78); Libns. Lg. Day (Ch. 1976). IL LA. Chicago Lib. Club. ASIS various com. in all orgs. Amer. Chem. Socty.: Chem. Exposition (1950–52). Arlington Heights Dist. 25 Sch. Bd.: (1967–1969). **Honors:** Beta Phi Mu, 1969. **Pubns.:** Jt. Ed., *As Much to Learn as to Teach: Essays in Honor of Lester Asheim* (1979); Jt. Ed., *Multitype Library Cooperation* (1977); "The Role of Special libraries in Networking," *Lib. Acq. Prac. and Theory* (Spr. 1979); "Principles, Programs, and Problems of a Metropolitan Multitype Library Cooperative," *Spec. Lib.* (Ja. 1976); Jt.-Ed., *Libraries and Information Centers in the Chicago Metropolitan Area* (1973); Jt.-Ed., *Union List of Serial Holdings in Illinois Special Libraries* (1977). **Activities:** 1, 12; 15, 26, 34; 60, 75, 91 **Addr.:** 2420 Fir St., Glenview, IL 60025.

Hamilton, Fae Kooper (Jl. 17, 1949, Passaic, NJ) Lib. Systs. Spec., NELINET, 1980–, Mem. Srvs. Libn., 1978–80; Head, LC Cat. Sect., MA Inst. of Tech., 1976–78; Asst. Head, LC Cat. Sect., Wayne State Univ., 1974–76; Asst. Libn., Tech. Srvs., Dutchess Cmnty. Coll., 1973–74. **Educ.:** Queens Coll., 1968–71, BA (Psy.); Univ. of MI, 1971–73, AMLS. **Orgs.:** ALA. **Honors:** Beta Phi Mu, 1973; Phi Beta Kappa. **Pubns.:** Reviews. **Activities:** 14-Network; 25, 34, 46; 56 **Addr.:** NELINET, Inc., 385 Elliot St., Newton, MA 02164.

Hamilton, Linda Catherine (D. 4, 1950, Fremont, NE) Chld. Libn., Pub. Lib. Syst. (Holdrege, NE), 1978–. **Educ.:** Univ. of NE, 1968–72, BS (Elem. Educ.); Univ. of MO, 1976–77, MA (LS). **Orgs.:** NE LA: JMRT (VP, 1979–80); Sch., Chld. and Young People's Sect. (Sec./Treas., 1980–81). Mt. Plains LA. ALA. AAUW.: Prog. VP (1979–80). Bus. and Prof. Women's Club: Finance Com. (1979–80). **Activities:** 9; 21 **Addr.:** Public Library System, 604 East Ave., Holdrege, NE 68949.

Hamilton, Linda K. (My. 13, 1945, Waukegan, IL) Mgr., Col. Oper., Univ. Microfilms Intl., 1979–, Mgr., Bibl. Srvs., 1977–79; Asst. Dir., MI Lib. Cnsrtm., 1975–77; Head, Cat. Dept., Wayne State Univ., 1973–76; Sect. Head, LC Prcs., MI State Univ., 1969–73. **Educ.:** MI State Univ., 1963–66, BA (Pol Sci.); Univ. of MI, 1967–68, AMLS; MI State Univ., 1970–72, MBA (Mgt.). **Orgs.:** ALA. ASIS. MI LA: Ch., Acad. Sect. (1976–77); Ch., Int. Frdm. Com. (1973–75); ARL: Adv. Com., Bibl. Control of Mtrls. in Micro. (1979–). **Pubns.:** *The Library of Congress Shelflist, a user's guide to the microfiche edition* (1979); *Searching on the OCLC on-line system* (1977); "Bibliographic support for micropublications," *Univ. Microfilms Intl. Nsltr.* (Win. 1978); "OCLC in Michigan," *Mich. Libn.* (Sum. 1976); Ed., *MLA Intellectual Freedom Newsletter* (1974–77). **Activities:** 1, 6; 20, 33, 34 **Addr.:** University Microfilms International, 300 N. Zeeb Rd., Ann Arbor, MI 48106.

Hamilton, Nancy J. (S. 13, 1948, Toronto, ON) Sr. Libn., Mncpl. Ref. Lib., Metro Toronto Lib. Bd., 1970–. **Educ.:** Queen's Univ., 1966–69, (Eng., Hist.); Univ. of Toronto, 1969–70, BLS. **Orgs.:** SLA: Toronto Chap., Place. Ch. (1975–77); Mem. Ch. (1977–78). Univ. Womens Club. **Activities:** 9, 12; 29, 36, 39; 92, 94 **Addr.:** Municipal Reference Library, Metropolitan Toronto Library Board, City Hall, Toronto, ON M5H 2N1 Canada.

Hamilton, Susan Sprague (Ag. 29, 1943, Seattle, WA) Librarian, Our Lady of Fatima Sch., 78–; Libn., Holy Family Sch., 1977–78; Dir., Chem., Bio. Lrng. Ctr., Tuskegee Inst., 1975–77. **Educ.:** Mills Coll., 1961–63; George Washington Univ., 1963–65, AB (Eng., Educ.); Auburn Univ., 1971–74, MA (Eng.); Emory Univ., 1967–68, 1974–75, MLn (LS). **Orgs.:** Cath. LA. ALA. SWLA. LA LA: Modisette Awd. Com. (1980–81); Hosp. Com. (1979–80). Lafayette Parish Sch. Libns.: Pres. (1980–81); Finance Com. (1979–80). AAUW: Tuskegee Branch, Secy. (1972–73); Cmnty. Rel. (Ch., 1971–72). Frnds. Lafayette Pub. Lib. Village Sch. (Auburn, AL): Sch. Bd. (1976–77). **Honors:** Lafayette Jaycees, Outstan. Young Educ., 1979; Beta Phi Mu. **Pubns.:** "Work motivation of Alabama librarians," *The AL Libn.* (1976); sps. **Activities:** 10; 21, 32, 48; 63, 74 **Addr.:** 204 Stephanie Ave., Lafayette, LA 70503.

Hamlin, Arthur T. (F. 8, 1913, Haverhill, MA) Dir. of Libs. and Prof., Emeritus, Temple Univ., 1969–, Dir. of Libs., 1968–79; Dir. of Libs., Univ. of Cincinnati, 1956–68; Exec. Secy., ALA, ACRL, 1949–56; Asst. Libn., Univ. of PA, 1945–49. **Educ.:** Harvard Coll., 1930–34, AB (Lit.), Harvard Grad. Sch., 1936–38; Columbia Univ., 1938–39, BS in LS. **Orgs.:** ALA: Cncl. and many other com.; ACRL; LAD Various com. Bibl. Socty. Amer. PA LA. **Honors:** Fulbright Lect., Univ. of Pavia (Italy), 1962; Fulbright Resrch. Schol., Univ. of Birmingham (Eng.) 1966–67; Cit. Gvt. of Italy, Aid to flooded Florentine Libs., 1967. **Pubns.:** *The University Library in the United States: Its Origins and Development* (1981); *Harvard in Cincinnati* (1969); various articles. **Addr.:** R. D. #1, Box S-650, Wiscasset, ME 04578.

Hamlin, Jean Boyer (My. 6, 1932, Portobello, Scotland) Libn., Rutgers Univ., 1976–; Chief of Coll. Dev., Temple Univ. Lib., 1968–75, Asst. Head, Cat. Dept., 1966–67; Asst. Libn., ON Inst. for Std. in Educ., 1965–66; Catlgr.-in-Charge, Secondary Sch. Lib., Toronto Brd. of Educ., (1962–64). **Educ.:** Univ. of Toronto, 1956–61, BA (Fr.), 1961–62, BLS; Cert. in Libnshp. LA of Australia. **Orgs.:** ALA: ACRL/Univ. Libs. Sect., Ch., (1979–80); RTSD/Resrcs. Sect./Coll. Dev. Com. Ch. (1977–78); Ch., (1979–80); Esther J. Piercey Awd. Jury, (1972–73). NJ LA: Pubns. Com. (1977–79). PA LA. Frdm. to Read Fndn. AAUP. **Honors:** ON LA: Lib. Sch. Std. Prize, 1962. Cncl. on Lib. Rescs.: Acad. Lib. Mgt. Internship, 1975. **Pubns.:** Collection development, *ALA Yearbook* (1976, 1977). Selection tools - What's available? *Cath. Lib. World,* (1976). **Activities:** 1; 15, 17, 46; 58, 65, 92 **Addr.:** John Cotton Dana Library, Rutgers University, 185 University Ave., Newark, NJ 07102.

PROFESSIONAL ACTIVITIES: Institutions: 1. Acad. lib.; 2. Arch.; 3. Assn.; 4. Fed./Gvt. lib.; 5. Inst. lib.; 6. Mfr./Suppl.; 7. Milit. lib.; 8. Musm.; 9. Pub. lib.; 10. Sch. lib.; 11. Sch. of lib. sci.; 12. Spec. lib.; 13. State lib.; 14. (other). **Functions/Activities:** 15. Acq./Col. dev.; 16. Adult srvs.; 17. Admin.; 18. Apprais.; 19. Archit./Bldgs.; 20. Cat./Class.; 21. Chld. srvs.; 22. Circ.; 23. Cons./Pres.; 24. Consult.; 25. Cont. ed.; 26. Educ. lib. sci.; 27. Ext. srvs.; 28. Fund/Grants; 29. Gvt. pubs.; 30. Indx./Abs.; 31. Instr. lib. use; 32. Media srvs.; 33. Micro.; 34. Netwks./Coop.; 35. Persnl.; 36. PR; 37. Publshg.; 38. Recs. mgt.; 39. Ref. srvs.; 40. Repro.; 41. Resrch.; 42. Review.; 43. Secur.; 44. Serials; 45. Spec. col.; 46. Tech. srvs.; 47. Trustees/Bds.; 48. YA srvs.; 49. (other).

Hamlin, Omer Jr. (Jl. 16, 1930, Tollesboro, KY) Dir., Med. Ctr. Lib. and Comm. Syst., Univ. of KY, 1969–81, Dir., Med. Ctr. Lib., 1963–69, 1981–, Asst. Med. Libn., 1962–63; Libn., Milligan Coll., 1959–62. **Educ.:** Milligan Coll., 1952–56, AB (Relig.); Univ. of KY, 1958–59, MSLS. **Orgs.:** Med. LA: Gifts and Exchange (1965–68); Legis. (1971–73). SLA. SELA. KY LA. Hlth. Sci. Comm. Assn.: Sect. Functions Com. (1973–74). Assn. Biomed. Comm. Dir. **Honors:** KY Lib. Trustee Assn., Outstand. Spec. Libn., 1965. **Pubns.:** "University of Kentucky Health Sciences Learning Center," *Biomed. Comm.* (S. 1979); "New Concepts of Media and Their Management at the University of Kentucky Medical Center," *Drexel Lib. Qtly.* (Ap. 1971). **Activities:** 1; 17, 32, 34; 80, 93 **Addr.:** Omer Hamlin, Jr., 3405 Westridge Circle, Lexington, KY 40502.

Hammargren, Betty Lou Cecilia (D. 17, 1926, Kilkenny, MN) Cat. Libn. II, Minneapolis Pub. Lib. and Info. Ctr., 1958–; Church Lib. Consult., Twin City Metro. Area, 1960–; Branch Asst. Libn., Minneapolis Pub. Lib. and Info. Ctr., 1955–58, Asst. Libn., Ref. Dept., 1954–55; Cat. Libn., Ramsey Cnty. Lib., 1953; Cat. Libn., Univ. of Notre Dame, 1950–53; Cat. Libn., Univ. of Santa Clara, 1948–50. **Educ.:** Coll. of St. Catherine, 1944–48, BS (LS); Univ. of Notre Dame, 1949–50; Mankato State Univ., 1979. **Orgs.:** Cath. LA: Par. Sect., Ch. (1967–68), Secy. (1979–81); MN-Dakota Unit, Par. Sect., Ch. MN LA. CSLA: Pres. (1972–73); VP (1971–72). ALA. Amer. Legion Auxiliary. Daughter of the Un. Vets. Coll. of St. Catherine Alum. Assn.: Bd. of Dirs. (1974–76). St. Joseph's Hosp. Auxiliary. **Pubns.:** Various articles. **Activities:** 9, 12; 15, 20, 24; 55, 56 **Addr.:** 1440 Randolph Ave., St. Paul, MN 55105.

Hammer, Donald P. (D. 16, 1921, Pottsville, PA) Exec. Dir., LITA, ALA, 1973–; Assoc. Dir. for Lib. and Info. Systs., Univ. of MA, 1972–73; Head, Lib. Systs. Dev., Purdue Univ. Libs., 1963–71, Head, Serials Unit, 1959–65; Bookstack Libn., Univ. of IL Lib., 1955–58; Law Libn. and Exch. Libn., PA State Lib., 1950–55. **Educ.:** Kutztown State Coll., 1944–48, BS (Educ.); George Peabody Coll., 1953–55, MLS; Univ. of Pittsburgh, 1970, Cert. (Info. Sci.). **Orgs.:** ALA: LITA, VP/Pres.-Elect. ASIS. **Honors:** Beta Phi Mu, 1948. **Pubns.:** Ed., *The Information Age: Its Development, Its Impact* (1976); ed., *Indiana Seminar on Information Networks Procs.* (1972); *ANSI/Z39 Tech. Report Number Standard* (STRN) Z39.23–1974 (1974); "Continuing Education–the Endless Pursuit of Knowledge," *Special Librarian: A New Reader* (1980); "Machine Applications," *Serial Publications in Large Libraries* (1970); various other articles. **Activities:** 1, 13; 25, 46; 56, 75, 93 **Addr.:** Library and Information Technology Association, American Library Association, 50 E. Huron St., Chicago, IL 60611.

Hammer, Leonard (Ap. 30, 1929, New York, NY) Dir., Steele Mem. Lib., 1974–; Dir., John McIntire Pub. Lib., 1965–74; Dir., Shelter Rock Pub. Lib., 1962–65; Admin. Asst., Gt. Neck Lib., 1958–62. **Educ.:** Brooklyn Coll., 1946–50, BA (Econ.); Columbia Univ., 1953–55, MSLS. **Orgs.:** ALA: Mem. Com. (1975–). NY LA. OH LA. Rotary Int.: Dir. (1975–78). Economic Opportunity: Pres. (1965–73). **Pubns.:** TV Programs. **Activities:** 9; 17, 19, 24; 75, 78, 93 **Addr.:** 1655 Scarsdale Rd., Pine City, NY 14871.

Hammer, Louise K. (M. 11, 1924, Hellertown, PA) Lib./Media Dir., Chicago Met. Baptist Assn., 1978–; Asst. Prof., Purdue Univ., Dept. of Educ., 1965–72; Research libn., Wabash Valley Educ. Ctr., 1967–68; Ref. Libn., Purdue Univ. Libs., 1964–65; Asst. Libn., Undergraduate Lib., Univ. of IL, Urbana, IL, 1957–58; Libn., Camp Hill HS, 1951–1955. **Educ.:** Kutztown State Coll., 1944–48, BS (Educ.); Vanderbilt Univ., 1951–55, MLS. **Orgs.:** ALA: YASD–Best Books for Young Adults (1969). **Honors:** Beta Phi Mu, 1955. Kappa Delta Pi, 1947. **Pubns.:** Reviews. **Activities:** 10, 12; 17, 20, 32; 63, 90 **Addr.:** 203 Stafford Dr., Wheeling, IL 60090.

Hammer, Mary M. (Mr. 2, 1943, Wellsville, KS) Libn. II, Holland Lib., WA State Univ., 1975–; Ref. Libn., Salem (OR) Pub. Lib., 1974–75; Asst. Libn., Neill Pub. Lib., Pullman (WA), 1973–74. **Educ.:** Ottawa Univ., 1961–65, BS (Educ.); IN Univ., 1967–68, MLS. **Orgs.:** WA LA. Pac. NW LA. Lib. Staff Assn.: Pres. (1979–80). WA State Univ. Sen.: Rep. (1980–82). **Pubns.:** "Search Analysts as Successful Reference Librarians," *Bhvl. and Soc. Scis. Libn.*, (Spr. 1981); *World of Women: A Selective List of Current Resources* (1977–80). **Activities:** 1; 15, 39, 49-Comp. lit. srch.; 55, 56, 92 **Addr.:** N.W. 900 Clifford St., Pullman, WA 99163.

Hammer, Sharon A. (Jl. 26, 1938, Seattle, WA) Asst. Dir. of Libs., Undergrad. Lib. Srvs., Univ. of WA, 1978–, Actg. Univ. Libs. Persnl. Ofcr., 1980–81; Dir., WA Reg. Lib. for the Blind and Phys. Handcpd., Seattle Pub. Lib., 1974–78, Dir., Handcpd./Elderly Lib. Prog., 1972–74. **Educ.:** Univ. of WA, 1969, BA (Hist.), 1971, MLS; WA State Tchg. Cert. **Orgs.:** ALA: Cncl. Orien. Com. (1978–79); Chap. Cnclr. (1975–79); ACRL, Undergrad. Libns. Discuss. Grp. (1978–); ASCLA, Exec. Bd. (1977–79); various coms. Pac. NW LA. WA LA: Exec. Bd. Nom. Com. (Ch., 1981); Exec. Bd. (1974–79); various other coms. **Pubns.:** "Consumer Outreach," *Info. Rpts. and Bibls.* (1978); "Radio Reading–A Logical Form of Library Service," *Hlth. and Rehab. Lib. Srvs. Div. Jnl.* (Fall 1976); "Goals for Service Improvements at the Washington Regional Library for the Blind and Physically Handicapped," *Braille Rpt.* (Spr. 1976); various other articles. **Activities:** 1, 9; 17, 31, 49-Outrch.; 72 **Addr.:** Odegaard Undergraduate Library, DF-10, University of Washington, Seattle, WA 98195.

Hammerschmidt, Alma Loretta, Sr. (N. 28, 1917, St. Louis, MO) Libn., St. Joseph's Acad., 1977–; Libn., Sts. John & James Elem. Sch., 1973–76; Libn., Our Lady of Lourdes Elem. Sch., 1972–73; Tchr., 1942–72. **Educ.:** Fontbonne Coll. & De Paul Univ., 1939–53, BS (Educ.); Univ. of Notre Dame, 1958–63, MA (Theo.); State of MO Pub. Sch. Life Cert., 1975; State of MO Lib. Cert. **Orgs.:** ALA. MO Assn. of Sch. Libns. MO LA. Cath. LA: Grt. St. Louis Chap. (Treas., 1974–79; Secy., 1979–81). Other orgs. Sr. of St. Joseph of Carondelet: Prov. Finance Com. (1977–). Police Cmnty. Rel. Grp. St. Louis Gene. Socty. **Honors:** Natl. Sci. Fndn. grant, 1966–67. **Pubns.:** "Vacation Opportunities," *The Cath. Messenger* (1962). **Activities:** 10; 15, 17; 90 **Addr.:** Saint Joseph's Academy, 2307 South Lindbergh Blvd., Saint Louis, MO 63131.

Hammerstein, Gretchen G. (Jl. 13, 1937, Indiana, PA) Lib. Dir., Groton Pub. Lib., 1974–; Libn., Holy Apostles Coll., 1972–74; Ref. Libn., Greenwich Lib., 1972; Libn., Len E. Coe Lib., 1972. **Educ.:** Wells Coll., 1955–59, BA (Chem.); South. CT State Coll., 1975, MLS; Univ. of CT, Inst. for Pub. Srv., 1974– (Pub. Admin.). **Orgs.:** Southeast. CT Lib. Assn.: Pres. (1974); Bd. (1975). CT LA: Ref. and Adult Srvs., Exec. Com. (1972–73). CT Women in Libs.: Co-fndr. (1972); Prog. Coord. (1972, 1974). All Souls Unitarian Church. Middlefield Assn. Indian and Colonial Resrch. Ctr, Inc.: Bd. of Trustees (1978–). CT Assn. for Cont. Educ.: Exec. Bd. (1974–75); Pubns. Com. (Ch., 1975). **Honors:** Bus. and Prof. Women's Club, Woman of the Yr., 1980. **Pubns.:** Cassette tapes, "Sexism in Childrens' Literature" (1973). **Activities:** 9; 17, 19, 47 **Addr.:** Groton Public Library, Rte. 117, Groton, CT 06340.

Hammitt, Margaret Read (Ag. 23, 1938, Perth Amboy, NJ) Elem. Libn., Chadron Pub. Sch. (NE), 1968–, Spec. Educ. Tchr., 1968; Various positions tchg. **Educ.:** OH Wesleyan Univ., 1955–59, BA (Elem. Educ.); Rutgers Univ., 1959–61, MEd; Univ. of MI, 1966–67, AMLS. **Orgs.:** ALA. Mt. Plains LA. NE Educ. Media Assn.: Reg. Coord. (1979–1981). NE LA: Film Com. (1974); Int. Frdm. Com. (1977–79). NE Educ. Assn.: Pres., Neg. (Ch.), Secy. Local Assn. AAUW: St. Pres. (1978–80); Pres. Elect (1977–78); Topic (Ch., 1975–77). NE State Adv. Cncl. on Libs., 1979–. Beta Sigma Phi. **Honors:** Gvr's. Conf. on Lib. Srvs., Del. **Activities:** 10; 21; 63, 89 **Addr.:** 630 Pine Crest Dr., Chadron, NE 69337.

Hammock, Janice D. (S. 1, 1943, Seattle, WA) Coord. of Cat., WA State Lib., 1976–, Syst. Libn., 1972–76, Catlgr., 1969–72, Resrch. Asst. to Head, Tech. Srvs., 1968–69; Math. Tchr., Bellingham (WA) Sch. Dist., 1965–67. **Educ.:** Univ. of WA, 1961–65, BS (Math.), 1967–68, MLibr; Tchg. Cert., WA State, 1961–67. **Orgs.:** WA LA: Tech. Srvs. Int. Grp. (Vice-Ch., 1980–81; Pres.-Elect. 1981–82). Pac. NW LA. ALA. **Honors:** Beta Phi Mu. **Activities:** 13; 20, 34; 56, 88 **Addr.:** Washington State Library, AJ-11, Olympia, WA 98504.

Hammond, Jane L. (Nashua, IA) Law Libn. & Prof. of Law, Cornell Univ., 1976–; Law Libn., Prof. of Law, Villanova Univ., 1965–76, 1962–1975, Asst. Law Libn., 1954–62; Cat., Harvard Law Lib., 1952–54. **Educ.:** Univ. of Dubuque, 1950; BA; Columbia Univ., 1952, MSLS; Villanova Univ., 1965, JD (Law). **Orgs.:** AALL: Pres. (1975–76); Secy., (1965–70); Chm. Com. on Index to Legal Per., (1970–74); Program Ch., Annual Meeting, (1971–80); Cncl. of Nat. Lib. and Info. Assn.: Ch., (1979–80); Secy., (1970–72). ALA. SLA. Assn. of Amer. Law Sch.: Exec. Com., (1977). H.W. Wilson Co.: Adv. Com. on the Index to Legal Per., (1979–). **Activities:** 1, 12; 17; 77 **Addr.:** Cornell Law Library, Myron Taylor Hall, Ithaca, NY 14853.

Hammond, Wayne G. (F. 11, 1953, Cleveland, OH) Asst. Libn., Chapin Lib., Williams Coll., 1976–. **Educ.:** Baldwin-Wallace Coll., 1971–75, BA (Eng.); Univ. of MI, 1975–76, AMLS. **Orgs.:** ALA: ACRL. **Pubns.:** Jt. auth., *Book Decoration in America 1890–1910* (1981); "Samuel Butler: A Checklist of Works and Criticism," *Samuel Butler Nsltr.* (Sum. 1980); "Addenda to 'J.R.R. Tolkien: A Bibliography," *Bltn. of Bibl.* (Jl.–S. 1977). **Activities:** 1; 20, 39, 45; 55, 57 **Addr.:** Chapin Library, Williams College, P.O. Box 426, Williamstown, MA 01267.

Hamrell, Susan H. (S. 20, 1949, Long Island City, NY) Comp. Srvs. Libn., McGill Univ. Med. Lib., 1980–; Engin. Libn., Duke Univ., 1979–80, Radiology Libn., 1978; Med. Libn., Cedars-Sinai Med. Ctr., 1972–77. **Educ.:** Adelphi Univ., 1968–71, BS (Educ.); Univ. of South. CA, 1971–72, MS (LS); Med. LA cert., 1975. **Orgs.:** Med. LA. SLA. Montreal Medline Users Grp.: Ch. **Activities:** 1, 12; 31, 39; 56, 80 **Addr.:** Medical Library, McGill University, 3655 Drummond St., Montreal, PQ H3G 1Y6 Canada.

Han, Chin-Soon (N. 7, 1942, Seoul, Korea) Head Libn., Bon Secours Hosp., 1979–; Traffic Mgr., Msc. Libn., ABC, WAKR, Akron, OH, 1972–78; Head Libn., CBS Radio, Seoul, Korea, 1965–67. **Educ.:** Ewha Women's Univ., Seoul, Korea, 1961–65, BA (LS); Univ. of South. CA, 1968–71, MSLS; various crs. **Orgs.:** Med. LA. Northeast. Cnsrtm. for Hlth. Info. MA Hlth. Sci. Libns. Assn. Cath. LA. Various other orgs. **Activities:** 5, 12; 16, 25, 41; 58, 80, 87 **Addr.:** Medical Library, Bon Secours Hospital, 70 East St., Methuen, MA 01844.

Hand, M. Dorcas (D. 21, 1951, Charlottesville, VA) Libn., St. John's Lower Sch., Houston, 1978–. **Educ.:** Wellesley Coll., 1969–73, BA (Hist. of Art); SUNY, Albany, 1977–78, MLS. **Orgs.:** ALA: AASL. TX LA. TX Assn. of Sch. Libns. **Pubns.:** Reviews. **Activities:** 10; 20, 21, 22 **Addr.:** St. John's School, Lower Library, 2401 Claremont, Houston, TX 77019.

Hande, D'Arcy Kevin (D. 14, 1951, Langenburg, SK) Staff Archvst., SK Arch. Bd., 1974–; Arch. Asst., Prov. Arch. of AB, 1973–74. **Educ.:** Univ. of SK, 1969–72, BA (Pol. Sci.); Arch. Dipl. from Pub. Arch. of Canada & Can. Hist. Assn. Course, 1975. **Orgs.:** Assn. of Luth. Archvsts. & Histns. in Canada: Pres., (1977–79); Ed. of nsltr. (1977–). Luth. Church in America: Ctrl. Canada Synod, Archvst. (1974). SK Geneal. Socty.: Pres. (1972–73). AB Geneal. Socty.: Treas. (1973–74). **Activities:** 2; 15, 16, 30; 69, 85, 90 **Addr.:** Central Canada Synod Archives, c/o Lutheran Theological Seminary, 114 Seminary Crescent, Saskatoon, SK S7N 0X3 Canada.

Handlin, Oscar (S. 29, 1915, New York, NY) Dir. of the Univ. Lib., Harvard Univ., 1979–, Carl H. Pforzheimer Univ. Prof., 1972–, Charles Warren Prof. of Hist., 1965–72, Winthrop Prof. of Hist., 1962–65, Prof. of Hist., 1954–62, Assoc. Prof. of Hist., 1948–54, Asst. Prof., 1940–48. **Educ.:** Brooklyn Coll., 1930–34, BA (Hist.); Harvard Univ., 1934–40, AM, PhD (Hist.). **Orgs.:** NY Pub. Lib.: Trustee. Boston Broadcasters, Inc.: Ed. Bd. (Ch.). Amer. Acad. of Arts and Sciences. **Honors:** Pulitzer Prize in Hist., 1951; LL.D., Colby Coll., 1962; Litt.D., Brooklyn Coll., 1972; LL.D., Boston Coll., 1975; other hon. degrees. **Pubns.:** *Truth in History* (1979); *The Uprooted* (1951); *Boston's Immigrants* (1941); *Wealth of the American People* (1975); *Facing Life: Youth and Family in American History* (1971); other books and articles. **Activities:** 1; 17; 73 **Addr.:** Harvard University Library, Wadsworth House, Cambridge, MA 02138.

Handy, Catherine (My. 10, 1932, Holyoke, MA) Ref. Libn., Westfield State Coll. Lib., 1969–; Libn., L. P. Wilson Sch., 1965–69; Tchr., Longmeadow, MA Jr. HS, 1954–56; Tchr., New Salem Acad., 1953–54. **Educ.:** Univ. of MA, 1949–53, BA (Educ., Rom. Lang.); South. CT State Coll., 1963–65, MSLS; various courses, 1967–69. **Orgs.:** ALA: AASL; ACRL; RASD. MA Tchrs. Org. Acad. Fed., Westfield State Coll. NEA. **Pubns.:** "Your Library", (slide tape prog.); Various bibl. inst. pubs. **Activities:** 1; 31, 39, 44; 63, 92 **Addr.:** 61 Woodland Dr., Old Saybrook, CT 06475.

Hane, Paula J. (Je. 22, 1949, St. Cloud, MN) Ref./ILL Libn., SUNY Coll. at Purchase Lib., 1974–; Libn. trainee, Yonkers Pub. Lib., 1973. **Educ.:** St. Cloud State Coll., 1967–69, (Eng. Lit.); Univ. of MN, 1969–71, BA (Eng. Lit.); Columbia Univ., 1973, MS (LS); NY Univ., 1975–79, MA (Eng. Lit.). **Orgs.:** ALA: ACRL. SUNY Libns. Assn.: Pub. Info. & Comm. Com. (1977–). Westchester Libns. Assn.: Coll. Lib. Sect. (Exec. Bd., 1976–77, 1978–83; Ch., 1981–82; Secy./Treas., 1979–). METRO: Coop. Acq. Prog. Strg. Com. (1978–80; Ch., 1979–80). **Activities:** 1; 15, 31, 39; 55, 61 **Addr.:** The Library, State University of New York College at Purchase, Purchase, NY 10577.

Hanes, Fred W. (Ag. 21, 1920, Vandalia, IL) Dir. of Libs., Univ. of Texas, El Paso, 1974–; Dean of Lib. Srvcs., IN State Univ., 1958–74; Col. Libn., Humboldt State Coll., 1967–68; Visiting Prof. and Libn., Univ. of the Punjab, Lahore, W. Pakistan, 1961–63. **Educ.:** Earlham Coll., 1938–42, AB (Eng.); IN Univ., 1950–51, MALS. **Orgs.:** ALA. TX LA. Border-Regional Lib. Assn. Southwestern LA. AMIGOS Bibl. Cncl.: Brd. of Trustees (1977–). SWLA. Various other Orgs. **Pubns.:** *Program Requirements for General Library Building at Indiana State University* (1968); *Introductory Material for American Literary Manuscripts* (1960); *Building Program, Central Library Building, University of Texas at El Paso* (1980); various articles. **Activities:** 1; 17, 34, 35; 56, 57, 75 **Addr.:** The University of Texas at El Paso, Director of Libraries, El Paso, TX 79968.

Hanff, Peter Edward (Ja. 23, 1944, Jacksonville, FL) Coord., Tech. Srvs., Bancroft Lib., Univ. of CA, Berkeley, 1970–; Asst. to Coord., Info. Syst., Lib. of Congs., 1968–69, Intern, Spec. Rcrt. Prog., 1967–68; Rare Bk. Catlgr., Zeitlin and Ver Brugge, Booksellers, 1966–67. **Educ.:** Univ. of CA, Santa Barbara, 1962–66, BA (Eng.); Univ. of CA, Los Angeles, 1966–67, MLS; Columbia Univ., Inst. on Lib. Cons., 1978. **Orgs.:** ALA: ACRL/Rare Books and Mss. Sect. (Ch., 1979–80; Prog. Ch., 1980–81). Amer. Prtg. Hist. Assn. Intl. Wizard of Oz Club: Pres. (1977–). Book Club of CA: Bd. of Dir. Colophon Club, San Francisco: Mem. Ch. (1980–). Roxburghe Club. **Honors:** Lilly Lib., IN Univ., Flwshp. in Rare Bks., 1969–70. **Pubns.:** *Introduction to By The Candelabra's Glare, a facsimile of book by L. F. Baum* (1981); *Bibliographia Oziana, a concise bibliographical checklist of Oz books* (1976); "Music in The Bancroft Library," *Cum Notas Variorum* (Mr. 1981); "L. Frank Baum: Success and Frustration," *Baum Bugle* (Win. 1977); speeches. **Activities:** 1; 15, 17,

Special Subjects/Services: 50. Adult educ.; 51. Advert./Mktg.; 52. Aerosp.; 53. Agric.; 54. Area std.; 55. Arts/Hum.; 56. Autom.; 57. Bibl./Prtg.; 58. Bio. sci.; 59. Bus./Fin.; 60. Chem.; 61. Copyrt.; 62. Documtn.; 63. Educ.; 64. Engin.; 65. Env.; 66. Eth. grps.; 67. Film; 68. Food/Nutr.; 69. Geneal.; 70. Geo.; 71. Geol.; 72. Handcpd.; 73. Hist.; 74. Int. frdm.; 75. Info. sci.; 76. Insr.; 77. Law; 78. Legis.; 79. Math./Comp. sci.; 80. Med.; 81. Metals; 82. Nat. resrcs.; 83. Newsp.; 84. Nuc. sci.; 85. Oral hist.; 86. Petr./Energy; 87. Pharm.; 88. Phys./Astr./Math.; 89. Readg.; 90. Relig.; 91. Sci./Tech.; 92. Soc. sci.; 93. Telecom.; 94. Transp.; 95. (other).

Who's Who in Library and Information Services

39, 45; 57 **Addr.:** Coordinator, Technical Services, The Bancroft Library, University of California, Berkeley, CA 94720.

Hankamer, Roberta A. (S. 7, 1937, Sandusky, OH) Libn., Grand Lodge of Masons in MA, 1971–; Dean of Students, Bryant & Stratton, 1965–71; Asst. Dean Women, Instr., Bridgewater State Coll., 1964–65; Asst. Dean Women, Lect., Lawrence Univ., 1961–64. **Educ.:** Denison Univ., 1955–59, BA Honors (Eng.); IN Univ., 1959–61, MSEd (Couns.); Simmons Coll., 1971–74, MSLS; Prsrvn. Workshop, Soc. Law Lib., 1980. **Orgs.:** SLA: Boston Chap., Manual Revision Com. (Ch. 1979–); Musms., Arts & Hum. Div., Memb. Ch.; Secy.-Treas (1976–). ALA. MA LA. New Eng. LA. MENSA. New Eng. Hist. Geneal. Socty. Sierra Club. **Pubns.:** *A Short List of Books on Freemasonry* (1980). **Activities:** 12; 17, 23, 45; 55, 69 **Addr.:** 55 Magazine St. - 19, Cambridge, MA 02139.

Hanke, Maxine K. (St. Petersburg, FL) Dir., Mid-Atl. Reg. Med. Lib. Prog., Natl. Lib. of Med., 1979–, Col. Control Ofcr., 1974–79, Asst. to Assoc. Dir., Extramural Progs., 1964–67, Head, Loan and Stack Sect., 1961–64, Head, Ed. Sect., 1960–61. **Educ.:** Univ. of Portland, 1951–55, AB (Rom. Lang.); Univ. of WA, 1957–58, MLS. **Orgs.:** Med. LA. DC LA. MD Assn. of Hlth. Sci. Libns. DC Hlth. Sci. Info. Netwk. Metro. Washington Cncl. of Gvts. **Pubns.:** "Library Statistics of Schools in the Health Sciences," *Bltn. Med. LA* (1966; 1967); "Training at the Post-Graduate Level for Medical Librarians," *Bltn. Med. LA* (Ja. 1980); various speeches. **Activities:** 1, 4; 17, 24, 25; 56, 63, 80 **Addr.:** National Library of Medicine, 8600 Rockville Pike, Bethesda, MD 20209.

Hankins, Frank D. (Mr. 1, 1922, Harlingen, TX) Libn. (Dir.), Del Mar Coll., 1958–; Asst. Libn., Wichita Pub. Lib., 1955–58; Libn., Parsons Pub. Lib., 1952–55; Branch Libn., Multnomah Cnty., 1951–52. **Educ.:** Univ. of TX, Austin, 1949, BJ (Jnlsm.), 1950–51, MLS. **Orgs.:** TX LA: Pres. (1966–67); Int. Frdm. Com., Ch.; Dist. 4, Ch.; Admin. RT (Ch., 1978–79). ALA. SWLA. TX Jr. Coll. Tchrs. Assn.: Lrng. Resrcs. Sect., Ch. AAUP. TX Jazz Fest. Socty.: Schol. Ch. (1977–). **Activities:** 1; 15, 17, 39 **Addr.:** 721 Crestview Dr., Corpus Christi, TX 78412.

Hankinson, Frances (Mr. 29, 1906, Brooklyn, NY) Retired, 1972–; Tchr. of Lib., McKee Voc. and Tech. HS, 1949–72, Lib. Asst., 1936–49. **Educ.:** Cornell Univ., 1923–27, BA (Eng./Greek); Columbia Univ., 1933–34, BS (LS); summer courses, Tchrs. Coll., N.Y. Univ., Middlebury Coll., Columbia Univ. **Orgs.:** ALA. NY City Sch. Libns. Assn.: Secy. (1951–); VP (1942–43). Staten Island Tchrs. Assn: Ch., Lib. Com. (1941–43). Delta Kappa Gamma: Mem. Ch. Women's Class, 1927, Cornell Univ.: VP (1977–). The American Recorder Socty. Other orgs. **Addr.:** 101 Daniel Low Terrace, Apt. 4J, Staten Island, NY 10301.

Hankinson, Margery Ann (N. 7, 1949, Cleveland, OH) Media Spec., Lexington Jr. HS, 1975–; Media Spec., Geneva Sec. Sch., 1972–74. **Educ.:** Denison Univ., 1967–71, BA (Eng.); Kent State Univ., 1971–72, MLS; Univ. of VA, 1974–75, EdS (Educ. Media). **Orgs.:** N. Ctrl. OH Educ. Lib. Media Assn.: Pres. (1977–78). OH Educ. Lib. Media Assn.: Nom. (1978); Mem. (1981); Stan. (1980, 1979). Phi Delta Kappa. OH Educ. Assn. Lexington Tchrs. Assn. **Pubns.:** "Audio Visual Elective," *OH Media Spectrum* (Spr. 1979). **Activities:** 10; 31, 32, 48; 63, 89 **Addr.:** 360 Oxford Rd., Lexington, OH 44904.

Hanks, Dorothy Moss (Mrs. John B.) (Ja. 12, 1913, Texarkana, TX) Retired, 1972; Asst. Prof. of LS, LA Tech Univ., 1970–72; Asst. Prof. of LS, Northwestern State Univ., 1965–70; Libn., CE Byrd HS, 1952–65; Med. Libn., Vets. Admin. Hosp., 1950–51; Dir., Shreve Meml. Lib., 1936–38; Dir. of Lib., Centenary Coll., 1933–36. **Educ.:** Centenary Coll., 1933, BA; Univ. of NC, 1934, BA (LS); Univ. of Chicago, 1944; LA State Univ., 1962; Northwestern State Univ., 1963, 1968–69. **Orgs.:** ALA: AASL. LA Assn. of Sch. Libns.: LA LA.: Treas. (1967–68). Pres. (1965–66). Coll. Tchrs. of Lib. Sci., LA. LA Tchrs. Assn. Assn. for Supvsn. and Curric. Dev. Friends of Centenary Coll. Lib. **Pubns.:** Reviews. **Activities:** 10, 11; 26, 31, 42; 63, 75, 85 **Addr.:** 7457 Camelback Dr., Box 5602, Shreveport, LA 71105.

Hanks, Ellen Todd (S. 6, 1939, Middletown, CT) Col. Dev., Sr. Ref. Libn., Univ. of TX Hlth. Sci. Ctr., San Antonio, 1981–, Head Ref. Libn., 1975–81; Asst. Prof., Grad. Sch. of LS, Univ. of TX at Austin, 1976–79; Dir., Lrng. Resrcs. Ctr., Univ. of TX Hlth. Sci. Ctr., San Antonio, 1974–75; Instr., Med., Dental Bibl. Cur., Lister Hill Lib. of the Hlth. Sci., Univ. of AL in Birmingham, 1971–74; Asst. Prof., Spec. for Info. Srvs., Human Resrcs. Dev. Ctr., Tuskegee Inst., 1970; Instr., Auburn Univ., 1968–70. **Educ.:** Univ. of TX, Austin, 1957–61, BA (Anthro.), 1966–69, MLS; Auburn Univ., 1970, (Educ. Admin.); Natl. Lib. of Med., 1970, MEDLARS Trainee. **Orgs.:** Med. LA: *MLA Bltn.*, Consult. Ed. Panel (1979–81). SLA: TX Chap., Schol. Com. (1980–83), San Antonio Subgrp., CE Com. (1978–), Pre-Regis. Ch. (Spr. 1979 Mtg.). San Antonio OLUG. Hlth. Oriented Libs. of San Antonio: Cont. Ed. Com. (Ch., 1976–77). Various other orgs. El Gato Club of San Antonio. **Activities:** 1; 15, 26, 39; 80, 87, 91 **Addr.:** 4023 Dunmore, San Antonio, TX 78230.

Hanna, Alfreda H. (Ap. 28, 1932, New Rockford, ND) Admn. Libn., Bethany Nazarene Coll. 1979–, Asst. Libn., 1960, 1966–79; Admn. Libn., Fed. Aviation Agency, 1964–66; Asst. Libn., Civil Aeromed. Resrch. Inst.; Adm. Libn., William Beaumont Gen. Hosp., 1961–63. **Educ.:** Bethany Nazarene Coll. 1950–55, BA (Eng. Lit.); Univ. of OK, 1959–60, MA (LS). **Orgs.:** ALA: Chap. Cnclr. (1981–84). SLA: OK Chap., Pres. (1971–72). OK LA: Pres. (1976–77); Exec. Bd. (1975–78). Natl. Endow. Hum.: OK Image, Exec. Bd. (1977–80). SWLA: Exec. Bd. (1976–77, 1981–). AMIGOS Com. Cat. Qual. Control: (1979–81). Phi Delta Lamda Secretary (1968–69). **Honors:** Beta Phi Mu, 2nd Intl. Contest Lib. Jnlsm., 1960. Phi Delta Lamda: Secy. (1968–69). Univ. OK, Grace E. Herrick Awd., 1960. Bethany Nazarene Coll., Alum. B Awd. **Pubns.:** "President's postings," *OK Libn.* (1976, 1977); "Councilor's Corner" *OK Libn.* (1981–). **Activities:** 1, 4; 15, 17, 29; 58, 90, 95-Humanities. **Addr.:** R. T. Williams Library, Bethany Nazarene College, 4115 N. College, Bethany, OK 73008.

Hanna, Mary Ann (Ag. 8, 1920, Greencastle, IN) Head Educ. Srvs. Prog., MI Dept. of Educ. State Lib. Srvs, 1976–80; Head Consult. Sect., MI State Lib., 1972–76, Head Sch. Lib. Consult., 1965–72, Sch. Lib. Consult., 1960–65. **Educ.:** DePauw Univ., 1938–42, AB (Eng. Lit.); Univ. of IL, 1943–44, BS (LS); Western MI Univ., 1969, MSL. **Orgs.:** ALA: YASD, Pres. (1969–71). AECT. MI LA. MI Assn. for Media in Educ. PEO Sisterhood. **Honors:** AECT, Region V Edgar Dale Awd. for MI, 1979; Kappa Alpha Theta. **Activities:** 2, 10, 13; 17, 24, 32; 61, 63, 74 **Addr.:** Michigan Dept. of Education, State Library Services, Box 30007, Lansing, MI 48909.

Hanna, Peggy J. (Ag. 7, 1947, Conway, SC) Media Coord., Charleston Cnty. Sch. Dist., 1977–, Lib. Media Spec., 1969–77. **Educ.:** Columbia Coll., 1965–69, BA (LS); Appalachian State Univ., 1975–77, MAT (AV Educ.). **Orgs.:** ALA. SC Assn. of Sch. Libns. AECT. SC Assn. of Curric. Dev. **Activities:** 10; 17, 24, 32; 63, 67 **Addr.:** 3 Chisolm St., Charleston, SC 29401.

Hannaford, Claudia Lee (S. 29, 1929, Portsmouth, OH) Lib. Dir., St. Michael's in the Hills Epi. Ch., 1979–; Instr., Schuylkill Bus. Inst., 1978–79; Media Catlgr., Erie Met. Lib. 1973–76; Recordings Libn., Greenville, OH, Pub. Lib., 1962–1965. **Educ.:** Wilmington Coll., 1947–51, BS (Educ.). **Orgs.:** Cncl. of Nat. Lib. and Info. Assns.: Brd. of Dir.; Cncl. CSLA: Pres. (1973–74); Natl. Conf. Ch., (1972–73), Ed., Official Jrnl., (1970–72, 1974–75); Exec. Bd. (1968–). *Cath. LA. Luth. Church LA.* National Bus. Educ. Assn. **Honors:** ALA, John Cotton Dana Pub. Awd., 1970. **Pubns.:** *Standards for Church and Synagogue Libraries:* (1977). Jt. auth., *Promotion Planning All Year 'Round, CSLA Guide No. 2* (1975). "The Story Hour," in MEDIA: Lib. Srvcs. Jrnl. (1974). "Once Upon a Time...," in SPECTRUM: Int. Jrnl. of Rel. Educ. Vol. 49, No. 3 (1973). "Letters to a Would-Be Librarian" in *Baptist Leader,* (N. 1974); "Libraries in Partnership" in *MEDIA: Library Services Jnl.,* (Jan/Feb/Mar 1974); other articles. **Activities:** 9, 12; 17, 26, 36; 90 **Addr.:** 4684 Brittany Rd., Ottawa Hills, Toledo, OH 43615.

Hannaford, William E., Jr. (Ag. 15, 1940, Worcester, MA) Head of Acq., Middlebury Coll., 1978–; Actg. Asst. Dean for Col. Dev., Univ. of NM, 1977–78, Hum. Biblgphr., 1975–77; Asst. Prof. (Phil.), IL State Univ., 1970–73. **Educ.:** Univ. of NH, 1964–66, BA (Phil.); Univ. of CO, 1966–72, MA (Phil.), 1966–72, PhD (Phil.); Univ. of IL, 1974–75, MS (LS). **Orgs.:** ALA. Amer. Phil. Assn. **Honors:** Cncl. on Lib. Resrcs., Fellow, 1979; Beta Phi Mu, 1975. **Pubns.:** "Toward a Theory of Collection Development," *Col. Dev.* (1980); Jt. auth., *Introduction to Psychology* (1974); "Perspectives on Diffusion: Descriptive and Prescriptive," *So. Sci. Educ. Cnsrtm. Nsltr.* (N. 1973); "A Short Bibliography of Philosophy Books for Public Libraries," *ERIC* (1978). **Activities:** 1; 15, 17, 39; 55, 57, 63 **Addr.:** Middlebury College Library, Middlebury College, Middlebury, VT 05770.

Hanns, Stephen J. (S. 20, 1951, Toronto, ON) Head, Adult Srvs., Willand Pub. Lib., 1981–; Chief Libn., Hanover Pub. Lib., 1977–81. **Educ.:** Univ. of Toronto, 1971–75, BA (Hist.), 1975–77, MLS. **Orgs.:** ON LA. Can. LA. Chld. LA. **Activities:** 9; 17, 20, 39 **Addr.:** Willand Public Library, 140 King St., Willand, ON L3B 3J3 Canada.

Hanrath, Linda G. (Ag. 22, 1949, Chicago, IL) Corp. Libn., Wm. Wrigley Jr. Co., 1978–; Bkmobile. Libn., Arlington Heights Meml. Lib., 1977–78; Outrch. Libn., Indian Trails Pub. Lib., 1975–77; Tchr., Notre Dame HS For Girls, 1971–75. **Educ.:** Rosary Coll., 1967–71, BA (Hist.), 1972–74, MALS. **Orgs.:** SLA. SAA. Chicago Lib. Club: Secy. (1979–80). Lib. Admin. Conf. of North. IL: Chld. Srvs. (Treas., 1978–). **Honors:** Beta Phi Mu. **Activities:** 9, 12; 27, 36, 39; 59, 68 **Addr.:** Wm. Wrigley Jr. Company, 410 N. Michigan Ave., Chicago, IL 60611.

Hansard, James W. (My. 2, 1936, Charleston, AR) Dir. of Libs., AR St. Univ., 1978–, Assoc. Libn., 1965–78, Ch., Div. of LS, 1965–80, Acq. Libn., 1964–65; Dir. of Lib., Memphis Univ. Sch., 1960–64. **Educ.:** AR St. Tchr. Coll., 1956–58, BSE (Soc. Std.) LA St. Univ., 1960–66, MS (LS). **Orgs.:** ALA. AR LA: Pres. N.E. AR LA: Pres. SELA **Pubns.:** "ERIC? Who," *AR Libs* (Spr. 1970); "Cut to Fit," *Lib. Resrc. Tech. Srvs.* (Win. 1970). **Activities:** 1, 10; 15, 17, 35; 63, 82, 85 **Addr.:** Box 273, Arkansas State University, Jonesboro, AR 72467.

Hansberry, Verda R. (Ag. 19, 1919, Sterling, CO) Asst. City Libn., Seattle Pub. Lib., 1975–, Actg. City Libn., 1975, Dept. Head, Circ. Srvs., 1966–74, Mobile Branch Libn., 1958–65. **Educ.:** Univ. of Denver, 1935–38, BS (LS). **Orgs.:** WA LA: Pres. (1979–81); ILL Proc. Com. (Ch., 1973); WA State Adv. Cncl. on Libs. Pac. NW LA: Circ. Sect. (Secy., 1973). Ref. and Subscpr. Books Review Com. (1972–1973); Circ. Srvs., (Secy., 1975–76); Nom. Com., Circ. Srvs., (Ch., 1974). **Honors:** Disting. Srv. Awd., City of Seattle, 1976. **Activities:** 9; 16, 17, 22 **Addr.:** 5603 30th Ave., S. W., Seattle, WA 98126.

Hansen, Andrew M. (Mr. 25, 1929, Storm Lake, IA) Exec. Dir., RASD, ALA, 1971–, Exec. Secy., ALTA, ALA, 1973–78, Exec. Secy., PLA, ALA, 1976–78; Instr., Sch. LS, Univ. IA, 1967–71; Libn., Sioux City (IA) Pub. Lib., 1963–67; Visit. Prof., IN St. Univ., 1966; Libn., Bismarck (ND) Pub. Lib., 1957–63. **Educ.:** Univ. of Omaha, 1947–51, BA (Math.); Univ. of MN, 1955–56, 1962, MA (LS); Univ. of IA, 1968–71, (Educ.). **Orgs.:** ND LA: VP, Pres. (1958–59); Secy., Treas. (1962–63). IA LA: VP, Pres. (1966–68); Pubn. Bd. (Ch., 1970–71). ALA: LED, Beta Phi Mu Awds. Com. (1970–71). **Activities:** 9, 14-Library Association; 16, 17, 39; 50 **Addr.:** Reference and Adult Services Division, American Library Association, 50 East Huron St., Chicago, IL 60611.

Hansen, Irene F. (Mr. 22, 1930, Clintonville, WI) Media Spec., Hatch Elem. Sch., 1968–; Tchr., WI Elem. Schs., 1953–56. **Educ.:** Univ. of WI, Milwaukee, 1948–53, BS (Elem. Educ.); Rosary Coll., 1967–71, MALS. **Orgs.:** IL Assn. for Sch. Libs.: Awds. Com. (1976–78). IL Assn. for Media in Educ.: Rev. Com. (1978–); Stan. Com. (1979–). IL LA. ALA. Oak Park Tchrs. Assn. IL Educ. Assn. Natl. Educ. Assn. **Pubns.:** "Individualized Library Instruction Boosts Student Interest," *IASL News for You* (D. 1972). **Addr.:** 720 S. Harvey, Oak Park, IL 60304.

Hansen, Joanne J. (Mr. 13, 1933, Arcadia, MI) Coord. Sci./Tech. Div., Eastern MI Univ., 1965–; Tchr./Libn., Centro Colombo Americano, 1964–65; Huron Valley Sch., 1956–64; Tchr., Pontiac Sch. **Educ.:** Eastern MI Univ., 1951–55, BMusEd; Case-Western Reserve, 1959–62, MSLS; Eastern MI Univ., 1963, MA (Geog.). **Orgs.:** SLA: MI Chap., (Secy., 1974–75; Pres.-Elect, 1975–76; Pres., 1976–77). Washtenaw Cnty LA: Secy. (1966–67); VP (1967–68); Pres. (1968–69). MI Map Socty. Western Assn. of Map Libns. Delta Kappa Gamma: Beta Chap. VP (1974–76). MI Academy of Sci. Arts & Letters: Ann Arbor Chap. Mu Phi Epsilon: Secy. (1972–73). **Activities:** 1; 31, 34, 39; 70, 91 **Addr.:** Center of Educational Resources, Eastern Michigan University, Ypsilanti, MI 48197.

Hansen, Lois N. (D. 24, 1920, Boise, ID) Continuations Libn., ID St. Univ., 1976; Instr., Sch. LS, Univ. OR, 1976; Dir., Biomed. Comm. for ID, 1974–75; Reg. and Ext. Libn., Boise Pub. Lib., 1973–74; Acq. Libn., Glendale Cmnty. Coll. (AZ), 1968–71; Adult Srvs. Coord., Phoenix (AZ) Pub. Lib., 1966–68; Libn., U.S. Air Force Hosp. and Wiesbaden AFB (Germany), 1962–65. **Educ.:** Univ. ID, 1938–42, BA (Eng.); Univ. South. CA, 1944–45, BS (LS); Univ. of London, 1959, (Eng. Lit.); Univ. Denver, 1971–72, 6th Yr. (Adv. Cert.) (LS). **Orgs.:** ALA. Pacific N. W. LA: Various Offices Frdm. to Read Fndn. ID LA: Various offices. **Pubns.:** "Computer-Assisted Instruction in Library Use: an Evaluation," *Drexel Lib. Qtly.* (Jl. 1972). **Activities:** 1, 12; 22, 31, 39 **Addr.:** Idaho State University, Campus Box 8293, Pocatello, ID 83209.

Hansen, Margaret Kane (N. 6, 1946, Washington, DC) INFORM Libn., Minneapolis Pub. Lib., 1979–; Libn., Env. Lib. of MN, 1978–79; Lib. Dir., Comptroller of the Currency, Natl. Banks, 1975–76; Sr. Ref. Libn., US Treas. Dept., 1970–75. **Educ.:** Emory and Henry Coll., 1964–68, BA (Hist.); Univ. of MD, 1969–70, MLS. **Orgs.:** MN LA. MN OLUG: Plng. Com. SLA: Bus. Div. Leag. of Women Voters. **Activities:** 9, 12; 24, 39, 41; 51, 59 **Addr.:** INFORM, Minneapolis Public Library and Information Center, 300 Nicollet Mall, Minneapolis, MN 55401.

Hansen, Ralph W. (My. 14, 1927, New York, NY) Assoc. Univ. Libn., Boise St. Univ., 1979–; Chief, Acq. Dept., Univ. Archvst., Stanford Univ. Lib., 1967–79, Univ. Archvst., Mss. Librn. 1962–67; Univ. Archvst., Mss. Libn., Brigham Young Univ., 1956–62, Asst. Ref. Libn., 1953–56. **Educ.:** Brigham Young Univ., 1947–51, AB (Hist.), 1951–54, MA (Hist.); Univ. of CA (Berkeley), 1967–1970, MLS; Harvard-Radcliffe, Inst. on Arch. Prsrvn., 1956. **Orgs.:** ALA. ID LA. Pacific N. W. LA. SAA. Palo Alto Hist. Assn.: City Hist. (1963–67), Pres. (1970–71). **Pubns.:** Various. **Activities:** 1, 2; 15, 17, 23; 61 **Addr.:** 712 W Highland View Dr, Boise, ID 83702.

Hanson, Agnes O. (Mr. 1, 1905, Northfield, MN) Archvst., Libn., Episcopal Diocese of OH, 1978–; Head, Bus. Info. Dept., Cleveland Pub. Lib., 1956–73, Ref. Libn., Bus. Info. Dept., 1938–56; Catlgr., Resrch. Lab. Lib., Gen. Motors Corp., 1934–38; Catlgr., Actg. Libn., Peter White Pub. Lib., Marquette, MI, 1930–33; Asst. and Sr. Reviser, Lib. Sch., Univ. of WI, 1929–30; Catlgr., East Chicago, IN, 1928–29. **Educ.:** St. Olaf 1922–27, BA Coll., 1922–27, BA, cum laude (Hist.); Univ. of WI,

PROFESSIONAL ACTIVITIES: Institutions: 1. Acad. lib.; 2. Arch.; 3. Assn.; 4. Fed./Gvt. lib.; 5. Inst. lib.; 6. Mfr./Suppl.; 7. Milit. lib.; 8. Musm.; 9. Pub. lib.; 10. Sch. lib.; 11. Sch. of lib. sci.; 12. Spec. lib.; 13. State lib.; 14. (other). **Functions/Activities:** 15. Acq./Col. dev.; 16. Adult srvs.; 17. Admin.; 18. Apprais.; 19. Archit./Bldgs.; 20. Cat./Class.; 21. Chld. srvs.; 22. Circ.; 23. Cons./Pres.; 24. Consult.; 25. Cont. ed.; 26. Educ. lib. sci.; 27. Ext. srvs.; 28. Fund/Grants; 29. Gvt. pubs.; 30. Indx./Abs.; 31. Instr. lib. use; 32. Media srvs.; 33. Micro.; 34. Netwks./Coop.; 35. Persnl.; 36. PR; 37. Publshg.; 38. Recs. mgt.; 39. Ref. srvs.; 40. Repro.; 41. Resrch.; 42. Review.; 43. Secur.; 44. Serials; 45. Spec. col.; 46. Tech. srvs.; 47. Trustees/Bds.; 48. YA srvs.; 49. (other).

1927–28, BS (LS); Univ. of MI, 1936–41, Advnc. MA (LS); Columbia Univ., 1933, grad. stds.; other courses. **Orgs.:** ALA. SLA: Cleveland Chap. (Pres., 1946–47); Bus. & Finance Div. (Ch., 1950–51), Bltn. Ed. (1950–51); Secy. (1953–4); Rep. SLA, ASLIB Conf. London (1954). AAUW. Cleveland Cncl. on World Affairs. Frnds. of Cleveland Musm. of Art. West. Resrv. Hist. Socty. Other orgs. **Honors:** SLA, Hall of Fame Awd., 1974; Amer. Mktg. Assn., Cleveland Chap., Cit., 1973; St. Olaf Coll., Disting. Alum. Awd., 1975. **Pubns.:** *Executive and Management Development for Business and Government: A Guide to Information Sources* (1976); "The Business Library: Its Services & Functions," *OH State Univ. Bltn. of Bus. Resrch.*, (Ap. 1968); "Commercial and Technical Library Service in Great Britain," *Spec. Libs.* (Ja. 1955); other articles. **Activities:** 2, 12; 15, 17, 39; 51, 57, 59 **Addr.:** 2938 South Moreland Blvd., Cleveland, OH 44120.

Hanson, Charles D. (N. 2, 1944, Whitehall, WI) Head Libn., N. Baltimore (OH) Pub. Lib., 1977–; Ch., Ref. Dept., Findlay Pub. Lib., 1975–76; Instr. Srvs. Libn., Aquinas Coll., 1973–75; Libn.-Media Coord., Wanwatosa Pub. Sch., 1968–71. **Educ.:** Eau Claire State Univ., 1962–66, BA (Eng.); Univ. of WI, Milwaukee, 1968–70, MA (LS); Bowling Green State Univ., 1976–78, PhD (Eng.). **Orgs.:** ALA. OH LA: Reg. Plng. Com. (1980). Chld. Lit. Assn. Toledo Musm. of Art. Scan. Club. **Pubns.:** "Visions: School-Public Library Cooperation," *Jnl. of Amer. Sec. Educ.* (S. 1978); "Poems and Critique," *Poet and Critic* (1979). **Activities:** 1, 9; 17, 25, 39; 50, 55, 63 **Addr.:** 519 Putnam St., Findlay, OH 45840.

Hanson, Eugene Russell (S. 4, 1926, Bertrand, NE) Prof. of Lib. Sci., Shippensburg State Coll., 1970–; Head Libn., Minot State Coll., 1964–66; 1969–70; Head Tech. Processes, Wayne State Coll., 1961–63; Head Libn., Southern State Coll., 1957–61. **Educ.:** Chadron State Coll., 1949–53, BA (Eng., Hist.); Univ. of Denver, 1954–57, MALS; Univ. of Pittsburgh, 1966–74, PhD (Lib., Info. Sci.). **Orgs.:** ALA: RTSD (Catlg. Com., 1973–77); LITA; ACRL; AASL. PA Sch. LA. AALS. Cumberland Cnty. Sch. LA. Tri-Cnty. Sch. LA. Company of Military Hist. **Honors:** Beta Phi Mu. **Pubns.:** Jt. auth., "Catalog and Cataloging," *Encyclopedia of Lib. and Info. Sci.* (1970). **Addr.:** 33 Country Club Rd., Carlisle, PA 17013.

Hanson, Nancy Ann Baker (O. 15, 1933, Albany, OR) Med. Libn., Wuesthoff Meml. Hosp., 1973–; Admin. Libn., Nvl. Resrch. Lab., USRD, 1971–73; Chief, Lib. Div., PAF Base, FL, 1971; Asst. to Libn., Kennedy Space Ctr.-NASA Lib., 1970–71; Chief, Lib. Srv., U.S. Vets. Admin. Hosp., 1966–69, 1962–64; Libn., Lead, Aerosp. Lib., Boeing Co., 1964–65; Sr. Libn., Chld. Srvs., LA, Portland, OR, 1958–61. **Educ.:** Williamette Univ., 1951–55, AB (Hist.); Univ. of WA, 1956–58, ML (Libnshp.); various crs., sems. **Orgs.:** Med. LA: South. Reg., Cont. Educ. Com. (1980–81). FL Med. Libns. Assn. **Honors:** U.S. Vets. Admin. Hosp., Superior Performance Awd., 1964. **Activities:** 12; 17, 32, 39; 58, 80, 91 **Addr.:** Medical Library, Wuesthoff Memorial Hospital, P.O. Box 6, Rockledge, FL 32955.

Hanson, Polly (Pauline M.) (S. 20, 1927, Danville, IL) Dir., Whatcom Cnty. Lib. Syst., 1978–, Asst. Dir., Pub. Srvs., 1975–78; Head, Issaquah Branch Lib., King Cnty. Lib. Syst., 1972–75, Chld. Libn., Mercer Island Branch. **Educ.:** Univ. of MI, BA (Eng., Hist.); Univ. of WA, MLibnshp. **Orgs.:** ALA. Pac. NW LA. WA LA: Int. Frdm. Com. (Ch.). Whatcom Hist. Assn. Allied Arts of Whatcom Cnty. **Activities:** 9; 17 **Addr.:** Whatcom County Library System, 5205 Northwest Rd., Bellingham, WA 98225.

Hanson, Roger K. (N. 24, 1932, Aneta, ND) Dir. of Libs., Univ. of UT, 1973–, Assoc. Dir. of Libs., 1972–73; Dir. of Libs., Univ. of ND, 1969–72; Asst. to Dir. of Libs., Univ. of MN, 1967–69. **Educ.:** Mayville State Coll., 1957–61, BS in Ed. (Math, LS); Univ. of Denver, 1964–66, MALS; Brigham Young Univ., 1976–78, MPA (Pub. Admin). **Orgs.:** ALA: LAMA, Cost, Acct. & Budgeting Com. (1977–81). Mt. Plains LA. UT LA: Pres. (1979–80). **Honors:** Mayville State Coll., Outstan. Alum. Awd., 1974. **Activities:** 1; 17, 19, 34 **Addr.:** Marriott Library, University of Utah, Salt Lake City, UT 84112.

Hanson, Sally L. (Je. 28, 1922, Hancock, MI) Dir., Libs., Valley City Pub. Sch., 1967–; Fingal Pub. Schs., 1965–66; Valley City Pub. Lib., 1964–65. **Educ.:** Suomi Coll., 1940–42, AA; North. MI Univ., 1942–44, BA (Hist.); Univ. of OR, 1968–71, MLS. **Orgs.:** ND LA. ND Educ. Assn.: Media Sect. ALA. Mt. Plains LA. Valley City Bus. and Prof. Women's Clubs. Our Savior's Luth. Church. **Honors:** Delta Kappa Gamma. **Activities:** 10; 32, 48; 63 **Addr.:** 1416 Chautauqua Blvd., Valley City, ND 58072.

Hanway, Wayne E. (S. 6, 1948, Lincoln, NE) Dir., Cattermole Meml. Lib., 1974–. **Educ.:** Univ. of NE, 1966–70, BA (Pol. Sci.); Univ. of IA, 1973–74, MA (LS). **Orgs.:** IA LA: Empl./Empl. Rights and Resp. Com. (1976–77); AV Com. (1979–). IA JMRT: Affl. Rep. (1975–77); Ch. (1978). ALA. Fort Madison Lions Club. **Activities:** 9; 15, 16, 17 **Addr.:** Cattermole Memorial Library, 614 7th St., Fort Madison, IA 52627.

Hanzas, Barbara (Mrs. Peter) (Ag. 9, 1927, Cleveland, OH) Libn., Dir., Woodruff Meml. Lib., 1972–; various other positions. **Educ.:** Middlebury Coll., 1945–49, BA (Amer. Lit.); West. Rsv. Univ., 1952–53, MSLS. **Orgs.:** ALA. CO LA. Mt. Plains LA. Various lcl. orgs. **Activities:** 9; 17, 20; 61, 73, 77 **Addr.:** Woodruff Memorial Library, P.O. Box 479, La Tunta, CO 81050.

Harbaugh, Margaret A. (S. 9, 1947, Houston, TX) Asst. Libn., McLennan Cmnty. Coll., 1974–; Instr., Lib. Srvs., San Antonio Coll., 1973–74. **Educ.:** Univ. of Houston, 1966–70, BA (Eng.); Univ. of TX, 1972–73, MLS. **Orgs.:** TX LA: Mem. Com. (1976–1978; Ch., 1981–82). TX Reg. Grp. of Catlgrs. and Clasfrs.: Ch. (1979–80). ALA: RTSD Cncl. of Reg. Grps. (1979–80). Altrusa, Intl. **Activities:** 1; 20, 39, 46; 56 **Addr.:** 1400 College Dr., Waco, TX 76708.

Harber, Philip Keith (S. 1, 1932, Birmingham, UK) Lib. Consult., Toronto Bd. of Educ., 1980–; Libn., Field Worker, Lakeshore Sch. Bd., Lindsay Place HS, Pointe Claire, PQ, 1976–80; Asst. Libn., Tchr., 1969–76; Tchr., Harrison Coll., Barbados, 1959–69. **Educ.:** Christ's College, Cambridge Univ., 1952–55, MA (Mod. Lang.); Univ. of NB, 1970–72, BEd (Educ.); Simmons Coll., 1973–76, SM (LS). **Orgs.:** ON LA. ON Sch. LA. Can. Sch. LA. ASIS. Amer. Assn. of Tchrs. of Span. and Portuguese. **Honors:** Beta Phi Mu, 1976. **Activities:** 10; 20, 21, 48 **Addr.:** 2441 Winthrop Crescent, Mississauga, ON L5K 2A8 Canada.

Harbord, Heather Anne (Liverpool, Lancashire, UK) Chief Libn., Coquitlam Pub. Lib., 1977–; Chief Libn., Dartmouth Reg. Lib., NS, 1970–77; Chief Libn., Wheatland Reg. Lib., SK, 1967–70; Asst. Reg. Libn., Wapiti Reg. Lib., SK, 1966–67. **Educ.:** Edinburgh Univ., 1957–60, MA (Soc. Anthro); Univ. of BC, 1965–66, BLS; Lib. Assoc. of Great Britain, 1960–63, ALA. **Orgs.:** Atl. Prov. LA: Pres. (1973–74). NS LA: Pres. (1974–75). Can. LA: Cnclr. (1967–70); Ombudsman (1973–75); Can. Assn. of Pub. Libs. (Pres., 1979–80). BC LA: Dir. (1979–80). **Activities:** 1, 9; 17, 35, 47; 50, 70, 95-Popular Literature. **Addr.:** Coquitlam Public Library, Administrative Headquarters, 901 Lougheed Hwy, Coquitlam, BC V3K 3T3 Canada.

Hardesty, Larry Lynn (Ag. 8, 1947, Hyannis, NE) Head of Ref. Dept., Dir., CLR-NEH Grant Proj., DePauw Univ., 1975–; Asst. to the Lib. Dir., Dir. of the Lib. Lrng. Prog., Kearney State Coll., 1975–75, Coord. of User Srvs., 1974–75, Asst. Ref. Libn., 1973–74; Soc. Worker, NE, 1971–72. **Educ.:** Kearney State Coll., 1965–69, BA in Educ. (Hist.), 1969–71, MS in Educ. (Hist.); Univ. of WI, 1973–74, MLS; IN Univ., 1976–78, MS in Educ. (Instr. Syst. Tech.), 1976–, Cand. for PhD (LS). **Orgs.:** ALA: ACRL/Coll. Libs. Sect., Ch., Ad Hoc Com. on Stan. and Guidelines (1979–); Bibl. Instr. Sect. IN LA. **Honors:** Beta Phi Mu, 1975. **Pubns.:** Jt. auth., "Application of Instructional Development to Mediated Library Instruction," *Drexel Lib. Qtly.* (Ja. 1980); *Use of Slide/Tape Presentations in Academic Libraries* (1978); Jt. auth., "Evaluating Library-Use Instruction," *Coll. & Resrch. Libs.* (Jl. 1979); "Use of Slide-Tape Presentations in Academic Libraries," *Jnl. of Acad. Libnshp.* (Jl. 1977); "The Academic Library: Unused and Unneeded?" *Lib. Scene* (Mr. 1976); oral presentations. **Activities:** 1; 24, 32, 39; 63, 92 **Addr.:** Roy O. West Library, DePauw University, Greencastle, IN 46135.

Hardin, Mary Una (Ja. 19, 1943, Gainesville, TX) Head, OK Telecomm. Interlib. Syst./info. Srvs., 1968–; ILL Libn., OK Dept of Libs., 1967–68, Pub. Lib. Consult., 1966–67. **Educ.:** OK State Univ., 1961–64, BA (Soc. Sci.); Univ. of OK, 1964–66, MLS. **Orgs.:** ALA: RASD, Exec. Bd. (Secy., 1981–82),/MARS, Strg. Com. (1966–67), Exec. Bd. (1978–80); ASCLA, Info. Needs of State Gvt. Discuss. Grp. (Ch., 1979–80). OK LA: ILL Com. (Ch., 1972–77); Ref. Div. (Secy., 1973–74). SWLA. Sierra Club. Parent Tchrs. Assn. AAUW. Leag. of Women Voters. **Pubns.:** Jt. auth., "Training Remote Profilers," *Online* (Jl. 1978); "Oklahoma Libraries and the New Copyright Law," *OK Libn.* (Ap. 1978); Contrib., *Some Reprographic Concerns Related To Interlibrary Loan* (1977); Jt. auth., "Oklahoma's Interlibrary Loan Code," *OK Libn.* (Jl. 1976). **Activities:** 9, 13; 15, 34, 39 **Addr.:** Oklahoma Department of Libraries, 200 N.E. 18th St., Oklahoma City, OK 73105.

Hardin, Sue Hunt (S. 18, 1929, Monroe, LA) Dir. of Media Srvs., Irmo (SC) HS, 1972–; Instr., Univ. of SC, 1970–72; Media Spec., Keenan Jr. HS, Columbia, SC, 1969–70; Media Spec., Euclid Jr. HS, Littleton, CO, 1968–69; Media Spec., Alameda Jr. HS, Denver, CO, 1967–68; Media Spec., W. Monroe (LA) Jr. HS, 1964–67; Media Spec., Lenwil Elem. Sch., W. Monroe, LA, 1963–64; Media Spec., W Monroe (LA) HS, 1959–63; Tchr., LA schs., 1950–59. **Educ.:** LA Coll., 1946–50, BA (Sp. Educ.); Univ. of Denver, 1960–62, MA (Libnshp.); Univ. of SC, 1975–77, EdD (Educ. Admin.); NE LA State Univ., 1956–59, Cert. (LS). **Orgs.:** ALA: AASL. SC Assn. of Sch. Libns. SC LA. SC HS Lib. Media Assn.: Exec. Secy. (1977–80). **Pubns.:** *Guidelines for the Establishment of District Level Media Centers* (1977). **Activities:** 10; 32, 48 **Addr.:** P.O. 730 B Ave., West Columbia, SC 29169.

Harding, Bruce C. (Jl. 12, 1925, Sioux Falls, SD) Consult. on Arch. Microfilm and Recs. Disposition, 1981–; Recs. Ofcr., WA State Univ., 1975–81; Chief, Reg. 5 Arch. Branch, Natl. Arch. & Recs. Srv., 1969–75; Univ. Archvst., OH State Univ., 1965–69; Archvst., MI Hist. Comsn. 1961–65; Archvst. OH Hist. Socty., 1957–61. **Educ.:** Ctrl. WA Univ., 1947–49, BEd (Soc. Sci.); WA State Univ., 1949–51, MA (Hist.); Radcliffe Coll., Hist. Admin., 1955; American Univ., Arch. Admin., 1960; Univ. of IL, Chicago Circle, Cons. Prsrvn., 1964. **Orgs.:** Assn. of Recs. Mgrs. & Admin.: Pres. (1969–70). SAA: Ch., Prog. Com. (1964). WA LA. Inst. of Cert. Recs. Mgrs. Other orgs. Neill Pub. Lib.: Trustee (1977–78). Whitman Cnty. Hist. Socty.: Pres. (1979–80). WA Hist. Recs. Adv. Bd. **Honors:** SAA, Fellow, 1971; Assn. of Recs. Mgrs. & Admin., Record Mgr. of the Yr., 1971. **Pubns.:** *A Records Management Manual for Michigan Municipalities* (1964); "Federal-University Relationship," *The Amer. Archvst.* (Jl. 1968); "What Can I Do Besides Teach?" *Jnl. of Coll. Place.* (O.-N. 1969); "Archives Program Cuts Out the Junk," *Coll. & Univ. Bus.* (O. 1970); "A New Research Source: Regional Archives Branches," *Amer. Libs.* (Mr. 1971). **Activities:** 2; 24, 33, 38, 47; 69, 73, 85 **Addr.:** NE 1105 Myrtle St., Pullman, WA 99163.

Harding, Thomas Spencer (F. 24, 1910, Gaines, NY) Libn. Emeritus, Washburn Univ. of Topeka, 1975–, Coll. Libn., 1966–75; Libn., Evansville Coll., 1948–66; Libn., MO Valley Coll., 1946–48; Libn., Univ. Coll., Northwestern Univ., 1937–42. **Educ.:** Univ. of Buffalo, 1929–33, BA summa cum laude (Hist.), 1933–37, BSLS; Univ. of Chicago, 1936–39, MA, 1951–57, PhD (Hist.); NY Prof. Lib. Cert., 1936. **Orgs.:** ALA: Elec. Com., (1942). IN LA: Ch., Col. & Univ. Libs. Sect. (1951). KS LA. AAUP. **Honors:** Phi Kappa Phi, 1963; Dialectic & Philanthropic Lit. Societies, Univ. of NC, Hon. mem., 1978. **Pubns.:** *College Literary Societies: their contribution to higher education in the United States, 1815-1876* (1971); "College Literary Societies and their libraries," *Lib. Qtly.* (Ja., Ap. 1959); "Carleton B. Joeckel" and "M. Llewellyn Raney," *Dict. Amer. Lib. Biography* (1978); reviews. **Activities:** 1; 15, 17, 19; 50, 57, 92 **Addr.:** 2120 High, Apt. A, Topeka, KS 66611.

Hardison, Osborne B. (O.B.) (O. 22, 1928, San Diego, CA) Dir., Folger Shakespeare Lib., 1969–; Prof., Eng. and Compar. Lit., Univ. of NC, 1966–69. **Educ.:** Univ. of NC, 1945–50, BA, MA (Eng. Lit.); Univ. of WI, 1950–53, PhD (Eng. Lit.). **Orgs.:** Indp. Resrch. LA: Ch. (1974–76). Mod. Lang. Assn. Renaissance Socty. of Amer. Milton Socty. **Honors:** Hon. degrees: Rollins Coll., Amherst Coll., Georgetown Univ.; Cavaliere Ufficiale della Republica Italiana, 1975; Medvl. Acad. of Amer., Charles Homer Hasking Gold Medal, 1969; other hons. **Pubns.:** Producer, "The Mystery of Elche" film and videotape; *Entering the Maze: Identity and Change in Modern Culture* (1981); various pubns. **Activities:** 12; 17; 55 **Addr.:** 201 E. Capitol St., Washington, DC 20003.

Hardisty, A. Pamela (Winnipeg, MB) Indp. Lib. Consult. and Bibliographical Resrch., 1980–; Asst. Parliamentary Libn., Lib. of Parlmt., 1962–80; Asst. Dir., Ref. Branch, Natl. Lib. of Canada, 1953–62; Ref. Libn., Toronto Pub. Libs., 1947–53. **Educ.:** Univ. of Manitoba, 1938–41, BA; Univ. of Toronto, 1946–47, BLS, 1954, MLS. **Orgs.:** Can. LA. Can. ALL: Pres. (1975–77); Treas. (1971–73). LA of Ottawa-Hull. Inst. of Prof. Libns. of ON: Pres. (1965–66). Zonta Club of Ottawa. **Honors:** Beta Phi Mu. **Pubns.:** *Publications of the Canadian Parliament, a detailed guide* (1974); "Brief History of Official Publishing And Distribution Policies in Canada," *Can. ALL Nsltr.* (N.-D. 1978); "Canadian Parliamentary Publications," *Can. ALL Nsltr.* (Jl.-O. 1977); "Some Aspects of Canadian Official Publishing," *Gvt. Pubn. Review* (Fall 1973). **Activities:** 4, 12; 17, 20, 39; 77, 78 **Addr.:** 3340 ALbion Rd., Ottawa, ON K1V 8V5 Canada.

Hardnett, Carolyn Judy (Ag. 12, 1947, Washington, DC) Libn., Chicago Tribune Press Srv., 1976–; Secy., Lib. Asst., 1970–76. **Educ.:** Hampton Inst., 1965–68 (Home Econ., Educ.); various SLA sems., 1977, 1979, 1980. **Orgs.:** DC SLA: Comms. Com. (1979–81). SLA: Positive Action Liaison (1981–82); Newsp. Div. Hosplty. Com., HI Conf. (Co-Ch., 1979), DC Conf. (Ch., 1980). Metro. WA Caucus of Black Libns.: Mem. Com. (1981); Corres. Secy. (1982). DC Newsp. Libns. Grp.: Jt. Org. (1978). Various other orgs. **Activities:** 12; 17, 39; 83 **Addr.:** Chicago Tribune Press Service, 1707 H St., N.W., 9th Floor, Washington, DC 20006.

Hardy, Floyd C. (Ag. 27, 1933, Pleasant Hill, NC) Dir. of Lib. Srvs., Cheyney State Coll., 1979–; Head Libn., Del. Tech. & Com. Coll., 1973–79; Docum. Libn. Rutgers Univ., 1968–73; Sci. Libn., NY Univ., 1966–68. **Educ.:** NC Cent. Univ., 1952–56, BA (Amer. Hist.); Univ. of MI, 1959–61, MALS, NY Univ., 1968–77, PhD (Higher Educ.). **Orgs.:** ALA. DE LA: Pres., Coll. & Resrch. Libs. Div., 1975–76. Tri-State Coll. Lib. Coop.: Treas., (1975–76). **Activities:** 1; 17 **Addr.:** L.P. Hill Library, Cheyney State College, Cheyney, PA 19319.

Hardy, M. Catherine (Ja. 5, 1938, Watertown, MA) Libn., Media Spec., Norton Mid. Sch., 1973–; Circ. Libn., RI Jr. Coll., Knight Campus, 1972–73; Libn., N.E. Metro. Reg. Vocational-Tech. Sch., 1970–72; Libn., Woburn Pub. Schs., 1965–70. **Educ.:** Univ. of NH, 1955–61, BA (Eng. Lit.); Syracuse Univ., 1969–72, MS (LS); Univ. of RI, MA Cand. (Bus. Admin.). **Orgs.:** MA Educ. Media Assn. ALA. Bristol Cnty. Educs. Assn. MA Tchrs. Assn. The Players. **Honors:** Beta Phi Mu, 1971. **Activities:** 10; 17, 31, 48; 59, 63 **Addr.:** 244 Hillside Ave., Pawtucket, RI 02860.

Hare, Ann T. (Atlanta, GA) Lib. Dir., Lander Coll., 1968–; Asst. Libn./Catlgr., Columbia Theo. Semy., 1959–68, Actg. Head

Special Subjects/Services: 50. Adult educ.; 51. Advert./Mktg.; 52. Aerosp.; 53. Agric.; 54. Area std.; 55. Arts/Hum.; 56. Autom.; 57. Bibl./Prtg.; 58. Bio. sci.; 59. Bus./Fin.; 60. Chem.; 61. Copyrt.; 62. Documtn.; 63. Educ.; 64. Engin.; 65. Env.; 66. Eth. grps.; 67. Film; 68. Food/Nutr.; 69. Geneal.; 70. Geo.; 71. Geol.; 72. Handcpd.; 73. Hist.; 74. Int. frdm.; 75. Info. sci.; 76. Insr.; 77. Law; 78. Legis.; 79. Math./Comp. sci.; 80. Med.; 81. Metals; 82. Nat. resrcs.; 83. Newsp.; 84. Nuc. sci.; 85. Oral hist.; 86. Petr./Energy; 87. Pharm.; 88. Phys./Astr./Math.; 89. Readg.; 90. Relig.; 91. Sci./Tech.; 92. Soc. sci.; 93. Telecom.; 94. Transp.; 95. (other).

Who's Who in Library and Information Services

Libn., 1966–67; Asst. Libn., Berry Coll., 1965–66. **Educ.:** N. GA Coll., 1953–57, BA (Eng.); Emory Univ., 1957–58, MLn; Univ. of SC, 1975–79, MBA. **Orgs.:** SC LA: Constn. and By-Laws Com. (1978–79); Coll. and Univ. Sect. (Vice Ch./Ch.-Elect, 1981–). ALA. SELA. AAUP. **Activities:** 1; 15, 17, 29 **Addr.:** Jackson Library, Lander College, Greenwood, SC 29646.

Harfst, Linda Lovgren (N. 5, 1949, Mora, MN) Proj. Dir., Southwest. OH Rural Libs., 1977–; Dir., LeSueur-Waseca Reg. Lib., 1974–77. **Educ.:** Bethel Coll., 1967–71, BA (Eng.); Univ. of MN, 1971–72, MA (LS). **Orgs.:** OH LA: ILL Ad Hoc Com. (1979). ALA. US Figure Skating Assn. Amer. Swedish Inst. **Activities:** 9, 14-Multitype syst.; 17, 24, 28; 50, 67 **Addr.:** SWORL (Southwestern Ohio Rural Libraries), 22 1/2 W. Locust, Wilmington, OH 45177.

Hargrave, Victoria E. (Ag. 22, 1913, Ripon, WI) Libn. Emeritus, MacMurray Coll., 1978–, Head Libn., 1947–78; Head Libn., Ripon Coll., 1944–46; Ext. Libn., IA State Coll., 1938–44. **Educ.:** Ripon Coll., 1930–34, AB (Latin & Grmn.); Univ. of WI, 1937–38, Dipl. (LS); Univ. of Chicago, 1946–47, MA (LS). **Orgs.:** ALA: ACRL/Coll. Lib. Sect. (Secy. 1959–60); Bhvl. Sci. Sect. (Secy. 1973–75); RASD/Hist. Sect. Mem.-at-large (1975–78); Cncl. (1952–55). IL LA. Midw. Arch. Conf. AAUP. AAUW. Univ. of IL Grad. Lib. Sch.: Adv. Cncl. (1962–64). **Pubns.:** "Comparison of reviews of books in the social sciences in general and scholarly periodicals," *Lib. Qtly.* (Jl. 1948); "Library publications and the college librarian," *ILA Record* (Ap. 1956). **Activities:** 1, 2; 15, 17, 39 **Addr.:** 141 Caldwell St., Jacksonville, IL 62650.

Hargrove, Marion Hanson (Ag. 5, 1941, Lexington, KY) YA Age Level Spec., Prince George's Cnty. Meml. Lib., 1972–, YA Libn., 1969–72. **Educ.:** Transylvania Coll., 1959–63, AB (Hist.); Univ. of KY, 1968, MSLS, 1963–65, Tchg. Sec. Cert. (Hist.). **Orgs.:** ALA: YASD, Best Books (1975–79), Bd. (1971), Nom. Com. (1980), Biog. Rev. Com. (1979–81). MD LA: Adult-YA Srvs. Div., Prog. Plng. Com. (1979–81). Prince George's Cnty. Mem Lib. Staff Assn.: Corres. Secy. (1971). **Honors:** Prince George's Cnty. Mem Lib., Cert. of Cmdn., 1977. **Pubns.:** "Young Adult Literature," *ALA Yrbk.* (1979–81). **Activities:** 9; 17, 42, 48; 89 **Addr.:** Prince George's County Memorial Library System, Bowie Branch, 15210 Annapolis Rd., Bowie, MD 20715.

Harig, Katherine Jean (Richardson) (D. 31, 1946, Painesville, OH) Branch Libn., Light St. Branch, Enoch Pratt Free Lib., 1977–; Resrch. Asst.-Continuing Educ. Recog. Proj., CLENE, 1975–77; Branch Libn., US Spec. Srvs. Lib., HQ V Corps, Frankfurt Germany, 1971–74. **Educ.:** Lake Erie Coll., 1965–69, BA (Eng./Pre-Med.); Cath. Univ., 1969–71, MSLS. **Orgs.:** ALA: PLA; ASCLA/Impaired Elderly Sect. (1979–). MD LA. CLENE: Recog. for Lib. Educ. (1977–). Baltimore City Mayor's Jr. Exec. Com. (1979–). **Honors:** Beta Phi Mu, 1971. **Pubns.:** Jt. auth., *Model Continuing Education Recognition System In Library And Information Science* (1979). **Activities:** 1, 9; 16, 25, 27; 50, 55, 92 **Addr.:** 9621 Pastora Pl., Columbia, MD 21045.

Haring, Jacqueline Kolle (Jl. 29, 1915, Brooklyn, NY) Mss. Cur., Knox Coll., 1978–; Archvst., 1976–78, Cur. of Spec. Coll., 1965–76. **Educ.:** Vassar Coll., Univ. of MI, 1933–37; AB (Eng.); Univ. of IL, 1967, (Arch. Admin.). **Orgs.:** SAA: Many Com. (1971–73); Coll. and Univ. Com. (1979); Prog. Com. Midwest Arch. Conf. (1972). Amer. Musm. Assn. Amer. Assn. for State and Lcl. Hist. Mss. Socty. **Pubns.:** "The College Arrangement," *IL Libs.* (1975). "Dear Archivist," MAC Nwsltr. (1972–78). Reviews. **Activities:** 2; 17, 18, 20, 23; 55, 61 **Addr.:** Archives, Knox College, Galesburg, IL 61401.

Harken, Shelby Elaine (My. 6, 1947, Minot, ND) Head Catlgr., Univ. of ND, 1969–. **Educ.:** Univ. of ND, 1965–69, BS (LS, Fr.), 1969–71, MA (LS). **Orgs.:** ND LA. AAUW: Secy. (1969–71); Parlmt. (1978–); Pres. (1976–77); State Histn. (1980–82). **Activities:** 1; 20, 38, 44 **Addr.:** Chester Fritz Library, University of North Dakota, Grand Forks, ND 58202.

Harkins, Anna W. (Ag. 20, 1926, Pittsburgh, PA) Asst. Dir. Lib. Srvs., Pittsburgh Bd. of Educ., 1974–, Supvsr., Lib. Srvs., 1966–74, Libn.-Tchr., 1952–66. **Educ.:** PA State Univ., 1948–52, BS (Educ.); Univ. of Pittsburgh, 1953–55, MEd (Educ.), 1964–65, MSLS. **Orgs.:** ALA: Newbery/Caldecott Com. (1969); Mag. Com. (1970); Best Books for YA Com. (1980). PA LA: Chld. Young People & Sch. Libns. (1968); Awds. Com. (1976–77). PA Sch. Libns. Alum. Assn., Grad. Lib. Sch., Univ. of Pittsburgh, Exec. Bd. (1975–78); Ch. (1976). Admin. Women in Educ.: Budget; Nom. Coms. (1976–78). Pittsburgh Admin. Assn.: Soc. Com. (1974–79). **Honors:** Pi Lambda Theta, 1951; Disting. Daughter, Univ. of Pittsburgh, 1976; PA Gvr. Conf. on Libs. and Info. Srvs., Del., 1977–78. **Activities:** 10; 17 **Addr.:** Pittsburgh Board of Education, Library Services, 327 Hazelwood Ave., Pittsburgh, PA 15207.

Harkness, Mary Lou (Ag. 19, 1925, Denby, SD) Dir. of Libs., Univ. of S. FL, 1968–, Actg. Dir. of Libs., 1967–68, Head Catlgr., 1958–67; Consult. in Cat., Natl. Lib. of Nigeria, 1962–63; Head Catlgr., GA Inst. of Tech., 1953–57, Asst. Catlgr., 1952–53; Asst. Catlgr., CA State Polytech. Coll., 1950–52; Jr. Catlgr., Law Lib., Univ. of MI, 1948–50. **Orgs.:** ALA. SELA. FL LA: Mem.-at-large, Exec. Bd. (1974–76). Southeast. Lib. Network: Bd. of Dir. (1977–80). Friends of the Lib. of Hillsborough Cnty.: Pres. (1974/75); Exec. Bd. (1972–76). **Honors:** NE Wesleyan Univ. Alum. Achvmt. Awd., 1972. **Activities:** 1; 17, 20 **Addr.:** 13511 Palmwood Ln., Tampa, FL 33624.

Harlan, Donna B. (D. 19, 1926, Columbus, OH) Archvst./Ref. libn., IN Univ., South Bend, 1978–; Interim Exec. Secy., RTSD, ALA, 1978; Head Libn., IN Univ., South Bend, 1966–77; Staff and Trng. Ofcr., Univ. of Pittsburgh Libs., 1965–66; Deputy Exec. Secy., Head of the Prcs. Ctr., Head of Ref. Srvs., Consult., WV Lib. Comsn., 1962–65; Consult., MI State Lib., 1959, 1957; Cat. Libn., Fed. Resrv. Bank of Chicago, 1953–54; Branch Libn., Ref. Libn., Racine (WI) Pub. Lib., 1952. **Educ.:** Stephens Coll., 1944–46, AA (Aviation); Morris Harvey Coll., 1946–48, AB (Pol. Sci.); Columbia Univ., 1948–50, MS (LS); NY Cert. Exam. for Libns., 1960; courses. **Orgs.:** ALA: RTSD/Serials Sect., Dupl. Exch. Union Com. (1978–80); Mem. Com. (1963–65). Amer. Lib. Socty.: VP (1976–79); Secy.-Treas., Exec. Bd. Secy. (1970–76). State of IN Area 2 Lib. Srvs. Athrty.: Exec. Com. (1975–77); Plng. Comsn. (1973–75). IN LA: Various coms. AAUP: IN Conf. (VP, 1980–81); IN Univ., South Bend Chap. (Pres., 1980–81, 1974–75). City of South Bend Mayor's Comsn. on the Status of Women: Pres. (1976–77). **Activities:** 1, 2; 23, 39, 45; 54, 78, 92 **Addr.:** 1015 Hudson Ave., South Bend, IN 46616.

Harlan, Robert D. (Ag. 4, 1929, Hastings, NE) Prof. and Assoc. Dean, Sch. of Lib. and Info. Std., Univ. of CA, Berkeley, 1976–, Asst. Prof., Assoc. Prof., 1963–76; Asst. Prof., Univ. of South. CA, 1960–63; Lectr., Univ. of MI, 1958–59. **Educ.:** Hastings Coll., 1947–50, BA (Hist.); Univ. of MI, 1955–56, MALS, 1957–58, MA (Hist.), 1958–60, PhD (LS). **Orgs.:** ALA. CA LA: Cncl. (1974–76); Lib. Hist. Com. (Ch., 1973–76). AALS: Stats. Com. (Ch., 1964). Socty. of CA Archvsts. Amer. Socty. for Eighteenth-Century Std. Amer. Prtg. Hist. Assn. Bk. Club of CA: Ed. Com. (1978–). Bibl. Socty. of Amer. Various other orgs. **Honors** ACRL, Resrch. Grant, 1963, 1965. **Pubns.:** *The Colonial Printer: Two Views* (1978); *Bibliography of the Grabhorn Press 1957-66 and Grabhorn-Hoyem 1966-73* (1977); *John Henry Nash: The Biography of a Career* (1970); jt. auth., "Trends in Modern American Book Publishing," *Lib. Trends* (1978); "The San Francisco Public Library's Kuhl Memorial Collection," *Bk. Club of CA Qtly. Nsltr.* (1977); various other articles. **Activities:** 1, 11; 26, 37, 45; 57, 74 **Addr.:** University of California, School of Library and Information Studies, Berkeley, CA 94720.

Harlow, Aileen W. (Mr. 24, 1924, Ithaca, NY) Media Libn., Dir., AV Srvs., Housatonic Cmnty. Coll., 1966–; Libn., Stratford LA, 1965–66; Sub. Tchr., Milford Pub. Schs., 1963–65. **Educ.:** Montclair State, 1942–46, BA (Eng.); South. CT State Coll., 1968–75, MLS; various crs. **Orgs.:** CT Higher Educ. TV Assn.: Secy. (1979–81). CT LA. ALA. Cmnty. Coll. Assn. for Instr. and Tech. Congs. of CT Cmnty. Colls. Amer. Assn. of Women in Cmnty. and Jr. Colls. **Activities:** 1; 16, 20, 32; 50, 67 **Addr.:** Housatonic Community College, 510 Barnum Ave., Bridgeport, CT 06608.

Harlow, Neal (Je. 11, 1908, Columbus, IN) Retired, 1969–; Dean, Grad. Sch. of Lib. Srv., Rutgers Univ., 1961–69; Libn., Univ. of BC, 1951–61; Head, Dept. Spec. Col., Asst. Univ. Libn., Univ. of CA, Los Angeles Lib., 1945–51; CA State Lib., 1938–45; Bancroft Lib., Univ. of CA, Berkeley, 1934–38. **Educ.:** Univ. of CA, Los Angeles, 1932, EdB (Hist.); Univ. of CA, Berkeley, 1933, Cert (LS), 1949, MA (LS). **Orgs.:** ALA: Exec. Bd.; various coms.; ACRL (Pres., 1963–64). Can. LA: Pres. (1960–61); Exec. Bd.; various coms. **Honors:** Moravian Coll., Hon. LHD, 1967. **Pubns.:** *Maps and Surveys of the Pueblo Lands of Los Angeles* (1976); *Maps of San Francisco Bay from Spanish Occupation to 1846* (1950); various articles. **Activities:** 1, 11; 17, 19, 26 **Addr.:** P. O. Box 26101, Los Angeles, CA 90026.

Harmeling, Deborah (D. 24, 1946, Covington, KY) Head Libn., Mt. St. Mary Semy., 1975–; Circ./Ref. Libn., Thomas More Coll., 1973–75; Hist. Tchr., Villa Madonna Acad., 1970–73. **Educ.:** Thomas More Coll., 1966–70, BA (Hist. Sec. Educ.); Univ. of KY, 1970–74, MLS. **Orgs.:** Grt. Cincinnati Lib. Cnsrtm.: Pres (1979–80); Secy. (1975–76); Long Range Plng. Com., Ed. of Nsltr. (1978–). Acad. Lib. Assn. of OH. OH Assn. of Theo. Libs. AAUP. Amer. Benedictine Acad. **Pubns.:** Jt. auth., "Thomas Jefferson" and "John L. Sibley," *Dict. of Amer. Lib. Biog.* **Activities:** 1; 15, 17, 23; 90 **Addr.:** Mt. St. Mary Seminary Library, 6616 Beechmont Ave., Cincinnati, OH 45230.

Harmon, E. Glynn (N. 4, 1933, Hollister, CA) Prof., Grad. Sch. of Lib. and Info. Sci., Univ. of TX, 1970–; Asst. and Assoc. Prof., Univ. of Denver, 1966–70; Ref. and Admin. Libn., Lectr. in Gvt., Chico State Univ., 1965–66; Resrch. Assoc., Case West. Rsv. Univ., 1964–65. **Educ.:** Univ. of CA, Berkeley, 1958–60, BA (Pol. Sci.), 1960–61, MA (Pub. Admin); Case West. Rsv. Univ., 1964–65, MLS, 1967–70, PhD (Info. Sci.); SW TX Univ., 1971–73, MBA. **Orgs.:** Med. LA. ASIS: SIG–Educ. (Ch., 1973–74). Data Prcs. Mgt. Assn. ALA. World Futures Socty. **Honors:** Beta Phi Mu, 1965. **Pubns.:** *Human Memory and Knowledge* (1973); "Education for Information Science," *Anl. Review of Info. Sci.* (1976); "Evolution of Information Science," *Jnl. of ASIS* (Jl.–Ag. 1971). **Activities:** 11, 12; 17, 26, 34; 59, 75, 80 **Addr.:** Graduate School of Library and Information Science, Box 7576 University of Texas, Austin, TX 78712.

Harms, Louise I. (Je. 25, 1924, Birmingham, AL) Dir. of the Lib., TN Wesleyan Coll., 1965–, Asst. Libn., Assoc. Prof. of Eng., 1964–65; Tchr. of Eng., Sweetwater (TN) HS, 1963–64; Admin. Libn., Depot Libn., Field Libn., Spec. Srvs. Div., US Army, Europe, 1951–63; Head Catlgr., Asst. Prof. of LS, Coll. of Educ., Univ. of AL, 1948–51; First Catlgr., Univ. of AR, 1947; Head Catlgr., Allegheny Coll., 1946–1947; Asst. Libn., Coll. of Educ., Univ. of AL, 1944–45. **Educ.:** Univ. of AL, 1941–44, BS in Ed (LS, Soc. Sci.); George Peabody Coll., 1945–46, BS in LS. **Orgs.:** TN LA: Finance Com. (1975–76). SELA. ALA. Alpha Beta Alpha. AAUP. Vets. of Frgn. Wars, Ladies Aux. **Honors:** Univ. of AL, Tchr. of the yr., 1951. **Pubns.:** "The Cataloging of Tests and Measurements," *Lib. Jnl.* (Ap., 1951). **Activities:** 1, 11; 17, 20, 26 **Addr.:** 112 Hickory Ln., Sweetwater, TN 37874.

Harms, Sally L. (Ag. 4, 1947, Ord, NE) Dir., Hlth. Sci. Lib., St. Luke's Methodist Hosp., 1970–. **Educ.:** Univ. of NE (Lincoln), 1965–69, BA (Hist.); Univ. of IA, 1969–70, MLS. **Orgs.:** Med. LA: Cont. Educ. Com. (1978–); Midwest Reg. Grp., Exec. Com. (1977–80), VP, Pres. Elect (1980), Finance Com. Midwest Hlth. Sci. Lib. Netwk.: Cncl. Governing Bd. (1975); Educ. Com. (Ch., 1977–). Educ. Telecomm. Cnsrtm.: Bd. (1978–). YWCA: Cedar Rapids, IA, Bd. Dir. (1979–); Finance Com. (1979–); Steering Com. (1980–). Jr. League Cedar Rapids: Grantsmanshp. Com. (VCh., 1979–80). Untd. Way Linn Cnty.: Bd. (1975–78); Budget Com.; Appeals Com. (Ch.). **Activities:** 12; 17, 32, 39; 63, 80 **Addr.:** Health Science Library, St. Luke's Methodist Hospital, 1026 A Ave. N.E., Cedar Rapids, IA 52402.

Harmsen, Tyrus G. (Jl. 24, 1924, Pomona, CA) Coll. Libn., Occidental Coll., 1959–; Catlgr., Dept. of Mss., Henry E. Huntington Lib., 1948–59. **Educ.:** Stanford Univ., 1941–47, AB (Hist.), 1949–50, MA (Hist.); Univ. of MI, 1947–48, ABLS. **Orgs.:** ALA: ACRL/Rare Books and Mss. Sect. Zamorano Club: *Hoja Volante* (Ed., 1954–64). Rounce and Coffin Club: Treas. (1955–). **Honors:** Cncl. on Lib. Resrcs., Fellow, 1969; Eng.-Speaking Un., Los Angeles, Travel grant 1975. **Pubns.:** *The Plantin Press of Saul and Lillian Marks* (1960); "Zamorano Club: Fifty Years," *The Zamorano Club: the First Half century* (1978); "Three Unpublished Letters by Robinson Jeffers," *Robinson Jeffers Nsltr.,* (D. 1976); "John Robinson Jeffers, Student at Occidental College," *Robinson Jeffers Nsltr.* (Mr., 1978); "Foreword," *Ward Ritchie, Printer:* (1980); other articles, reviews. **Activities:** 1; 17, 45; 57 **Addr.:** Occidental College Library, 1600 Campus Rd., Los Angeles, CA 90041.

Harned, Robert Laurence (My. 4, 1944, Des Moines, IA) Ref. Libn. and Exhibits Coord., Univ. of PA, Van Pelt Lib., 1973–, Cat. Libn., 1969–73, Head, - Rosengarten Rsv. Rm., 1968–69; Cat. Libn., Lib. of Congs., 1967–68. **Educ.:** Univ. of HI, 1962–66, BBA (Bus. Admin.), 1966–67, MLS, Univ. of PA 1979–, (Archaeology). **Orgs.:** ALA. **Pubns.:** Ed., *Philex Calendar,* (1978). **Activities:** 1, 4; 20, 39; 55, 67 **Addr.:** 2029 Walnut St., Philadelphia, PA 19103.

Harney, Robert F. (Mr. 5, 1939, Salem, MA) Acad. Dir., Multicult. Hist. Socty. of ON, 1977–; Prof. of Hist., Univ. of Toronto, 1971–, Co.-Dir., Ethnic Std. Prog. **Educ.:** Harvard Univ., 1956–60, AB (Hist. & Lit.); Univ. of CA, Berkeley, 1961–66, PhD (Hist.). Amer. Italian Hist. Socty.: Cncl. Can. Italian Hist. Socty.: Pres. Centro Scuola E Cultura Italiana. *Intl. Jnl. of Oral Hist.:* Ed. Bd. (1980–). **Honors:** Univ. of Toronto, Connaught Flshp., 1975. **Pubns.:** *The Italian Immigrant Woman in North America* (1978); *Italians in Canada* (1978); "The Padrone System & The Sojourner in the Canadian North, 1880-1915," *Pane E. Lavoro* (1980); "Boarding and Belonging," *Urban Hist. Review* (Fall 1978). **Activities:** 2, 12; 15, 37, 41; 66, 85 **Addr.:** Multicultural History Society of Ontario, 43 Queen's Park Crescent East, Toronto, ON M5S 2C3 Canada.

Harnsberger, Therese (Coscarelli) (Ap. 13, Muskegon Hts., MI) Med. Lib. Consult., 1978–; Med. Libn. and Tumor Registrar, Alhambra Cmnty. Hosp. 1975–79; Tumor Regis. Huntington Meml. Hospt., 1979; Ref. Libn., LA Cmnty. Coll., 1972; Libn., District, Covina Valley Sch. Syst. (CA), 1962–67, Jr. HS Libn., 1959–62; Los Angeles Cmnty. Colls.; Libn., CA St. Col., Los Angeles, 1956-59; Libn. and Lib. Consult. San Marino HS, 1952–56. **Educ.:** Marymount, 1951-52 BA (Hon) (Eng.); Univ. S. CA, 1952–53, MSLS, Univ. CA (Los Angeles), 1960–61. **Orgs.:** Med. LA CA LA: Sch. Libns., Legis. Com. (Ch., 1957–59). Med. LA S. CA: Educ. Com. (1976–). Assn. Sch. Libns. for Chlds. Lit. So. CA. Assn. Law Libns., 1979. Amer. Nutr. Assn. Amer. Fed. Tchrs. Natl. Educ. Assn. Alhambra Hist. Socty. **Honors:** Grad. Schol., Univ. of So. CA. Libn. Sch., 1952–53; Pi Lambda Theta. **Pubns.:** "Publicizing the High School Library," *Wilson Lib. Bltn.* (Mr. 1957). **Activities:** 1, 12; 16, 20, 24; 50, 80 **Addr.:** 2809 W. Hellman Ave., Alhambra, CA 91803.

Haro, Roberto P. (S. 9, 1936, Sacramento, CA) Acad. Asst. to the Vice Chancellor, Univ. of CA, Berkeley, 1979–, Assoc. Dir., Prof. Dev. Prog., 1975–78; Asst. Univ. Libn., Univ. of South. CA, 1971–75; Libn., Lect., Coll. of Lib. and Info Srvs., Univ. of MD, 1969–71; Head, Inst. of Gvt. Affairs Lib., Univ. of CA, Davis, 1965–69. **Educ.:** Univ. of CA, Berkeley, 1954–58, BA

PROFESSIONAL ACTIVITIES: Institutions: 1. Acad. lib.; 2. Arch.; 3. Assn.; 4. Fed./Gvt. lib.; 5. Inst. lib.; 6. Mfr./Suppl.; 7. Milit. lib.; 8. Musm.; 9. Pub. lib.; 10. Sch. lib.; 11. Sch. of lib. sci.; 12. Spec. lib.; 13. State lib.; 14. (other). **Functions/Activities:** 15. Acq./Col. dev.; 16. Adult srvs.; 17. Admin.; 18. Apprais.; 19. Archit./Bldgs.; 20. Cat./Class.; 21. Chld. srvs.; 22. Circ.; 23. Cons./Pres.; 24. Consult.; 25. Cont. ed.; 26. Educ. lib. sci.; 27. Ext. srvs.; 28. Fund/Grants; 29. Gvt. pubs.; 30. Indx./Abs.; 31. Instr. lib. use; 32. Media srvs.; 33. Micro.; 34. Netwks./Coop.; 35. Persnl.; 36. PR; 37. Publshg.; 38. Recs. mgt.; 39. Ref. srvs.; 40. Repro.; 41. Resrch.; 42. Review.; 43. Secur.; 44. Serials; 45. Spec. col.; 46. Tech. srvs.; 47. Trustees/Bds.; 48. YA srvs.; 49. (other).

(Hist.), 1958–59, MA (Hist/Pol. Sci.), 1961–1962, MLS, 1975–79, PhD (Interdisciplinary). **Orgs.:** REFORMA. ALA. Assn. of Mexican Amer. Educ. West. Gvtl. Resrch. Assn. **Pubns.:** *Latin Americana Research in the U.S. and Canada* (1971); *Developing Library and Information Services for Americans of Hispanic Origin* (1981); "Viva la Evolucion," *Amer. Libs.* (Je. 1979); "Toward a Typology of Ethnic Studies," *Jnl. of the Socty. of Eth. and Spec. Std.* (Fall, 1980); "Library Services for College Students," *Social Responsibilities And Libraries* (1976); other books and articles. **Activities:** 1, 9; 17, 24, 34; 66, 75, 92 **Addr.:** 925 Madison St., #4, Albany, CA 94706.

Harper, Helen R. (Je. 18, 1919, Sewickley, PA) Elem. Libn., Moon Area Sch. Dist., 1970–, Jr. High Libn., 1967–70; Chld. Lit. Instr., PA State Univ., 1969–72. **Educ.:** Juniata Coll., 1937–41, BS cum laude (Sci.); Univ. of Pittsburgh, 1966–80, MLS, Ad. Cert., Elem. Cert., Geneva Coll., 1975–76, PhD (LS) 1981. **Orgs.:** ALA. Cncl. of Sch. Libns.: Prog. Com. (1975–1979). PA Sch. Libns. Assn. ALA. Doct. Guild, Univ. of Pittsburgh: Comm. Com.; By-Laws Com. AAUW: Branch Pres. (1963–65), State Bd. (1965–66). Untd. Presby. Church: Elder (1975–77). Natl. Educ. Assn. PA Educ. Assn. **Pubns.:** "Christmas Reading," *Interview* (Win. 1977); other articles. **Activities:** 10; 15, 17, 31; 63, 89 **Addr.:** 98 Valentine Rd., Coraopolis, PA 15108.

Harper, Laura Griffith (Mr. 21, 1946, Monroe, LA) Assoc. Prof., Ref.–Biblgphr., and Head, Online Srch. Srvs., Univ. of MS Lib., 1979–, Sr. Libn., Ref. Dept., 1971–78; Ref. Libn., Trail Blazer Pilot Lib. Syst., 1970–71; Asst. to the Dir., Ouachita Parish Pub. Lib., 1969–70. **Educ.:** LA St. Univ. (Baton Rouge), 1964–68, BS (Educ.), 1968–69, MLS. **Orgs.:** ALA: RASD, Bibl. Com. (1978–8), Mach. Asst. Ref. Sect., Nom. Com. 1978–79) Data Base Prods. Com. (1981–). MS LA: JMRT, Afflt. Cncl. (Del., 1978), Booth Com. (Ch., 1977), Prog. Com. (1977–78); Aut. Netwk. RT, Search Anal. Gr. (Ch., 1978–79), Secy./Treas. (1980). Various other com. Bibl. Retrieval Srvs., Inc., User Bd. (1978–80). **Pubns.:** "A Comparative Review of BRS, Dialog, and Orbit", *Ref. Srvs. Review* (Ja.–Mr. 1981); "Searching ECER on BRS", *DATABASE* (Je. 1979). **Activities:** 1; 31, 39; 56, 63, 75 **Addr.:** Reference Dept., University of Mississippi Library, University, MS 38677.

Harper, Lois M. (Ap. 25, 1930, Dundas, ON) Asst. to Coord., Lrng. Resrcs., Scarborough Bd. of Educ., 1973–; Tchr.-Libn., St. Andrews P.S., Scarborough, 1968–73; Itinerant Tchr.-Libn., Scarborough Bd. of Educ., 1965–67; Tchr., Bendale P.S., Scarborough, 1958–65; Tchr., Hamilton Bd. of Educ., 1952–58. **Educ.:** McMaster Univ., 1949–51, BA (Soclgy.); 1965–66, Spec. (Sch. Libnshp.); Univ. of BC, 1967–68, BLS. **Orgs.:** ON Sch. LA. Can. LA. Can. Sch. LA. Fed. of Women Tchrs. of ON. **Honors:** Scarborough-E. York Readg. Cncl., Readg. Cncl. Awd., 1975. **Activities:** 10; 17, 24, 31; 63, 89 **Addr.:** Professional Library—Level 2, Scarborough Board of Education, Scarborough, ON M1P 4N6 Canada.

Harper, Shirley F. (D. 11, 1926, Sauk Centre, MN) Dir., Martin P. Catherwood Lib., Libn., NY State Sch. of Indust. and Labor Rel., Cornell Univ., 1975–; Libn., Indust. Rel. Ctr., Univ. of Chicago, 1949–75. **Educ.:** Univ. of MN, 1944–47, (Liberal Arts); Univ. of Chicago, 1947–49, MA (LS), additional courses, 1963–65. **Orgs.:** ASIS: Ch., Chicago Chap. (1970). SLA: Pres., IL Chap. (1965–66); Ch., Div. Rel. Com. (1952–54); Ch., Persnl. Com. (1965–69); Ch., 1975 Conf. Com. Com. of Indust. Rel. Libns.: Ch. (1953, 1969, 1973, 1981). Indust. Rel. Resrch. Assn. World Future Socty. **Honors:** SLA, Prof. Awd., 1967. **Pubns.:** *ILR Thesaurus*, working draft (1977); Jt. ed., *Performance Appraisal, Research and Practice* (1962); "The Universal Decimal Classification," *Amer. Docum.* (O. 1954); Jt. auth., "Industrial Relations–A Case Study of Specialized Communication Involving Several Groups" *Amer. Docum.* (O. 1953). **Activities:** 1, 12; 17; 92 **Addr.:** Martin P. Catherwood Library, 237 Ives Hall, Cornell University, Ithaca, NY 14853.

Harpole, Patricia Chayne (N. 14, 1933, Two Harbors MN) Chief, Ref. Lib., MN Hist. Socty., 1977–, Asst. Chief Libn., 1972–77, Head, Ref. Div., 1971–77, Ref. Libn., 1970–71, Asst. Ref. Libn., 1963–70. **Educ.:** Univ. of MN 1951–55, BA (Fine Arts); Univ. of Denver, 1961–62, MA (LS); Amer. Univ., Inst. of Geneal. Resrch., 1971. **Orgs.:** MN LA: Secy. (1974–76); Bd. Dir. (1974–76); VP/Pres. Elect (1979–82); Lib. Plng. Dev. Com. (1972–77); Various other com. MN Geneal. Socty.: Founder; Ch. (1968); Pres. (1969–70); Ed. Pubns. (1969–73). ALA. SLA. Women's Ctr., YWCA: Bd. Dir. (1975–81); Pres. Bd. (1977–79). Women Hist. Midwest: Steering Com. (1973); Co-ed., Bltn. (1973–74). Amer. Swedish Inst. Bus. Prof. Women St. Paul. **Honors:** WHCOLIS, Del., 1979; Gvr. Conf. Libs., Del., 1978. **Pubns.:** Ed., *MN Genealogist* (1969–73); Co-ed., *Minnesota Territorial Census 1850* (1972); "Selected Periodical Articles on Minnesota," *MN Libs.* (1975–); "Brief Biographies of Other Minnesota Women", in *Women of Minnesota* (1977). **Activities:** 2, 12; 39, 41, 45; 69, 83, 95-Local History. **Addr.:** Minnesota Historical Society, 690 Cedar St., St. Paul, MN 55101.

Harrar, H(elen) Joanne (My. 9, 1935, Seattle, WA) Dir. Lib., Univ. of MD, 1975–; Assoc. Dir. Lib., Univ. of GA, 1971–75; Libn., Prof. LS, Winthrop Coll., 1963–70; Asst. to Dir., Resrch. Asst., Columbia Univ. Lib., 1961–63; Mem., Adj. Staff, Rutgers Univ. Lib., 1961–63. **Educ.:** Oberlin Coll., 1957, BA; Rutgers Univ., 1960, MLS, 1962, PhD. **Orgs.:** ALA: RASD (Pres., 1980–81); Budget Com. (1980–82); ACRL Constn. and Bylaws Com. (1980–82). DC LA. **Honors:** Beta Phi Mu. **Pubns.:** Ed., *S. East. Libn.* (1972–75). **Activities:** 1; 17 **Addr.:** McKeldin Library, University of Maryland, College Park, MD 20742.*

Harrell, Charles B. (Ag. 27, 1940, Decatur, TX) Assoc. Univ. Libn., Univ. of TX, Arlington, 1977–, Asst. Univ. Libn., 1975–77, Docu. Libn., 1969–75, Asst. Ref. Libn., 1968–69. **Educ.:** Univ. of TX, Arlington, 1963–67, BA (Eng.); LA State University, 1967–68, MSLS; N. TX State Univ.; 1975–80, PhD (in prog.); (Lib. Sci.) **Orgs.:** ALA. TX LA: Cnclr. (1980–83); Plng. Com., (1978–80); Dist. Local Arrange., (1977–79); Dist. Treas. (1972–73), (1973–74). Anl. Conf. lcl. Arrange. (1982). Awds. Com (1981–82). Alpha Phi Omega: Adv., (1969–); Ch. Adv. Com. (1976–). Fort Worth Corral, Westerners Intl. Sheriff, (1979–80). **Honors:** Beta Phi Mu. **Pubns.:** *An Automated Library Circulation System: A Justification* (1978). *An Automated Library Circulation System:* (1979). *Inventory of County Records, Delta County Courthouse, Cooper, Texas* (1976). "A Comparison of Joe Christmas and Martin Eden, *Arlington Review* (1966). "Plato's Educational Philosophy" (1966). **Activities:** 1, 2; 17, 35, 36; 56, 61, 62 **Addr.:** The University of Texas at Arlington Library, P.O. Box 19497 UTA, Arlington, TX 76019.

Harrell, Yvonne (Jl. 24, 1937, Ahoskie, NC) Tchr. of Lib., John M. Coleman I.S., 1968–; Ref. Libn., Howard Univ., 1963–64; Tchr./Libn., Robert L. Vann HS, 1959–62. **Educ.:** NC Coll. at Durham, 1955–59, BA cum laude (Eng./LS); Columbia Univ., 1970–71, MLS; Hunter Coll., 1969, (Fr./Eng.); Queensboro Cmnty. Coll., 1974–76, (Span.); Howard Univ., 1962–64, (Eng.). **Orgs.:** NY City Sch. Libns. Assn.: Soc. Ch. (1976–78); Exec. Com. (1973–75); Rep. from Dist. (1971–73). ALA. Columbia Univ. Sch. of Lib. Srv. Alum. Assn. NY LA. NY State Untd. Fed. of Tchrs. Amer. Fed. of Tchrs. Grad. Fac. Alum. of Columbia Univ. Natl. Educ. Assn. **Addr.:** Post Office Box 1045, Corona Station, Elmhurst, NY 11373.

Harrer, Gustave Adolphus (D. 30, 1924, Durham, NC) Dir. of Libs., Univ. of FL, 1968–; Dir. of Libs., Boston Univ., 1960–68; Asst. Dir. for Ctrl. Srvs., Stanford Univ., 1958–60, Chief, Acq. Div., 1957–58; Assoc. Ord. Libn., Univ. of TN, 1955–57, Asst. Ord. Libn., 1954–55; Asst. Prof., Millsaps Coll., 1949–51. **Educ.:** Univ. of NC, 1941–48, AB (Grmn.), 1948–49, MA (Grmn.), 1951–53, PhD (Germanic Langs.); Univ. of IL, 1953–54, MSLS; Rutgers Univ., 1958, Carnegie Proj. in Advnc. Lib. Admin. **Orgs.:** ALA: Cncl. (1968–71); various coms. ARL: Bd. of Dirs. (1973–76). Assn. of Caribbean Univ., Resrch. and Inst. Libs: Exec. Cncl. (1973–76); Pres. (1977–78). **Activities:** 1; 15, 17, 46 **Addr.:** 2815 N.W. 29th St., Gainesville, FL 32605.

Harrington, Anne W. (Je. 18, 1926, Philadelphia, PA) Med. Staff Libn., Chester Cnty. Hosp., 1977–. **Educ.:** Univ. of PA, 1944–48, BA (Bact.); Villanova Univ., 1974–77, MSLS. **Orgs.:** SLA. Med. LA. Wilmington Friends Sch.: Secy.; Ch., Instr. Com. AAUW. Socty. of Friends. **Activities:** 12; 15, 17, 39; 80, 91 **Addr.:** 1117 Talleyrand Rd., West Chester, PA 19380.

Harrington, Charles W. (Jl. 29, 1923, Miami, FL) Head of Acq., Watson Lib., Northwestern State Univ., 1977–; Parish Libn., St. Mary Parish Lib., 1975–77; Head Libn., Centenary Coll., 1962–75; Lib. Consult., Univ. of Concepcion, Chile, 1967–69; Libn. in Trng., Queens Borough Pub. Lib., 1961–62; Dir., US Dept. of State Binational Ctrs., Guatamala, Dominican Republic, 1947–51. **Educ.:** Coll. of William & Mary, 1941–43; Univ. of NC, 1943–44, BA (Pol. Sci.); Harvard Bus. Sch., 1944–45, Cert.; Univ. of NM, 1951–53, MA (Inter-Amer. Affairs); Tulane Univ., 1953–60, (Hist.); LA State Univ., 1960–61, MS (LS). **Orgs.:** ALA. LA LA: Acad. Libs. Sect. (Ch., 1965, 1973). SWLA. Ozark Socty. Sierra Club. **Pubns.:** "The Louisiana Literary Award, A Thirty-Year View," *LA LA Bltn.* (Sum. 1980); "Directory of Publishers of Louisiana Materials," *LA LA Bltn.* (Fall 1981); "Library Consulting–Chile Style," *LA LA Bltn.* (Fall, 1969). **Activities:** 1; 15, 34, 36; 55, 65, 74 **Addr.:** Watson Library, Northwestern State University, Natchitoches, LA 71457.

Harrington, Sue Anne (Ja. 10, 1927, Tulsa, OK) Head, Serials Prcs., Assoc. Prof. Bibl., Univ. of OK Lib., 1978–, Coord., Serials Prcs., Asst. Prof. of Bibl., 1977–78, Serials Cat., 1974–77, Cat., July 1972–74, Cat., Instr., 1968–72. **Educ.:** Univ. of OK, 1944–48, BA (LS, Eng.), 1967–68, MLS. **Orgs.:** OK LA: Tech. Srvs. Div., V CH. (1973–74), Ch. (1974–75); Nom. Com. (1977); Mem. Com. (1977–78); Various other com. Beta Phi Mu: Secy./Treas. (1969–70); Nom. Com. (1972–73); Pres. (1976–77). ALA. SWLA. Various other orgs. AAUP. Higher Educ. Alum. Assn. of OK. Univ. of OK: Faculty Appeals Bd. (1978–82); Univ. Bk. Exch. (1978–81, Ch. 1979–80); Univ. Com. on Discrimination (1976–78). **Honors:** Delta Phi Alpha, 1971. **Pubns.:** "ISBD Workshop," *OK Libn.* (Spr. 1975); "Successive Entry Cataloging of Serials", *Univ. OK Lib. Bltn.* (Spr. 1973); "Serials: National Trends–Local Implications," *Univ. of OK Lib. Bltn.* (Sum. 1975); "OU Serials Data Updated," *Univ. of OK Lib. Bltn.* (Sum. 1976); "Bizzell Library Serials Area Reorganized," *Univ. of OK Lib. Bltn.* (Fall 1977). **Activities:** 1; 17, 33, 44; 83, 95-Current Periodicals. **Addr.:** Head, Serials Processing, University of Oklahoma Libraries, Norman, OK 73019.

Harrington, Thomas Roger (S. 23, 1950, Natchez, MS) Media Libn., Gallaudet Coll. Lib., 1975–, Asst. Libn., 1974–75. **Educ.:** Emory Univ., 1968–70; Gallaudet Coll., 1970–73, BS (LS); Univ. of MD, 1973–74, MLS. **Orgs.:** ALA: HRLSD, Stan. for Lib. Srvs. to the Deaf Subcom. (1977–79); ASCLA/Ch., Plng., Org. and Bylaws, Lib. Srv. to the Deaf Sect., (1980–82). Phi Alpha Pi: VP (1978–79); Pres. (1979–80). **Honors:** Phi Eta Sigma, 1974. **Pubns.:** Complr., *Mediagraphy on Deafness and the Deaf* (1979). **Activities:** 1, 12; 17, 32, 39; 72 **Addr.:** Gallaudet College Library, 7th Street and Florida Ave. N.E., Washington, DC 20002.

Harris, Addie (F. 22, 1923, Yazoo City, MS) Ref. Libn./Subj. Spec., Inst. of Lib. Resrcs. and Afro-Amer. Std., Governors State Univ., 1974–. **Educ.:** Governors State Univ., 1971–72, BA (Ethnic Std.); Univ. of IL, 1973–74, MLS; Union Grad. Sch., 1975–77, PhD. **Orgs.:** ALA: Black Caucus. SAA. Midwest Arch. Conf. Afro-American Hist. RT. Assn. for the Study of Afro-Amer. Life and Hist. Afro-American Geneal. and Hist. Socty. of Chicago. Afro-American Hist. and Geneal. Socty., Inc. **Pubns.:** Reviews, videorecording. **Activities:** 1; 39, 45; 66, 69, 85 **Addr.:** University Library, Governors State University, Park Forest South, IL 60466.

Harris, Alice D. (Jl. 10, 1930, Brooklyn, NY) Resrc. Mtrls. Spec., East-West Popltn. Inst., 1969–, West. Lang. Cat., 1965–69; Branch Libn., Cat., Rutgers Univ., 1964–65; Ref. Libn., Cat., Paramus, NJ Pub. Lib., 1960–62; Bus. Libn., Newark Bus. Lib., 1956–58; Libn. I, Free Lib. of Philadelphia, 1953–56. **Educ.:** Russell Sage Coll., 1947–51, BA (Amer. Cvlztn.); Drexel Univ., 1953–56, MS (LS); Univ. of HI, 1971–75, MA (Geo.); Univ. of PA, 1953–53. **Orgs.:** HI LA. SLA. Assn. of Popltn. Family Plng. Lib. and Info. Ctr., Intl.: Bd. Dir. (1976–). Popltn. Assn. of Amer. **Honors:** Phi Kappa Phi, 1956; Beta Phi Mu, 1971. **Pubns.:** "The East-West Population Institute Library", *HLA Bltn.* (Je. 1971). **Activities:** 5; 17, 39, 45; 54, 92 **Addr.:** East-West Population Institute, Resource Materials Collection, East-West Center, 1777 East-West Rd., Honolulu, HI 96848.

Harris, Carolyn L. (N. 17, 1947, Austin, TX) Head, Prsrvn. Dept., Col. Univ. Libs., 1981–; Manu. Catlgr., Con. Coord., Human. Resrch. Ctr., 1973–81; Libn., U.S.A.A. Insurance Corp., 1971–72; Spec. Col. Libn., Southwestern Univ., 1970–71. **Educ.:** Univ. of TX, Austin, 1965–69, BA (Art Hist.); 1969–70, MLS, Inst. for the Dev. and Admin. of Pres. Prog. for Lib. Materials, 1978. **Orgs.:** ALA: ACRL (Rare Bks. and Manu. Sect.); RTSD (Prsrvn. of Lib. Mat. Sect.). Beta Phi Mu: Secy./Treas. (1978–79). **Pubns.:** "Mass Deacidification," *Lib. Jrnl.* (Jl. 1979); "A Check-list of Emblem Books at the Humanities Research Center," *Lib. Chron.;* Reg. Ed. of Con. Admin. *Nsltr.* (1979–); Reviews. **Activities:** 1, 12; 23, 36, 45; 55, 57 **Addr.:** Columbia University Libraries, New York, NY 10027.

Harris, Diana Cohen (My. 23, 1951, Canton, OH) Admn. Asst., Lib. Dev. Div., St. Lib. of OH, 1978–, Asst. to the St. Libn., 1974–78, Asst. Coord., OH Gvr. Conf. on Lib. and Info. Srv., 1973–74. **Educ.:** OH St. Univ., 1969–72, BS (Eng., Educ.); Kent St. Univ., 1972–73, MLS. **Orgs.:** OH LA: Pub. Rel. Com. Anl. Conf. (Ch., 1980); Exec. Bd. (Rep. Div. VI, 1978–79); Div. VI (Secy., 1977–78); Task Force Recruit., Interviewing (Co. Ch., 1977–78); various other coms. ALA: ASCLA; Task Force Min. Qualifications Libns. (1978–79). ASIS: Ctrl. OH Chap. Franklin Cnty. LA: Nom. Com. (1976–77); Record. Secy. Intl. Assn. of Bus. Comm.: Columbus Chap., Dir. (1978–79). **Pubns.:** "Ohio Delegation to White House Conference Reviews Recommendations," *The OH Lib. Trustee,* (Ap. 1980); "Affirmative Action and Hiring: Guidelines for Recruitment and Selection," *OH Lib. Assn. Bltn.* (O. 1978); "National Library Week in Ohio Is Great! 10-4, Good Buddy," *OH Media Spectrum* (My. 1977); "An Invitation from The State Library of Ohio," *OH Lib. Assn. Bltn.* (Ja. 1976). **Addr.:** Coord., OH White House Conf., The State Library of Ohio, 65 S. Front St., Columbus, OH 43215.

Harris, Hammon Rand (F. 13, 1946, Bakersfield, CA) Coord. of Adult Srvs., Chicago Lib. Syst., 1979–; Head, Henry Legler Branch, Chicago Pub. Lib., 1978–79; Libn. II, IL Reg. Lib. for the Blind and Phys. Handcpd., 1977–78; Spec. Srvs. Consult., Kaskaskia Lib. Syst., 1976–77. **Educ.:** Univ. of Tulsa, 1964–69, BA (Creat. Wrtg.); Univ. of West. ON, 1973–75, MLS. **Orgs.:** IL LA. Chicago Lib. Club. ALA: Hlth. and Rehab. Lib. Srvs. Div., Bylaws Com. (1978–79). Chicago Men's Gathering. Chicago WHCOLIS. Lions of IL: Com. of Agencies (1978). **Activities:** 9, 13; 16, 17, 24; 50, 72 **Addr.:** 3505 W. Sunnyside Ave., Apt. C-2, Chicago, IL 60625.

Harris, Ira W. (Ap. 14, 1924, Ossining, NY) Dean, Grad. Sch. of Lib. Std., Univ. of HI, 1976–, Asst. Dean, 1969–75, Dir., Undergrad. Lib., 1966–69, Resrch. Assoc., 1965–66; Instr., Rutgers Univ., 1962–65; Asst. Libn., NJ Inst. of Tech., 1958–62; Ref., Adult Srvs. Libn., Newark Pub. Lib., 1957–58. **Educ.:** Univ. of Detroit, 1943–44 (Engin.); Univ. of PA, Penn Acad. of Fine Arts, 1947–49, 1949–52, (Fine Arts); Pratt Inst., 1949–52, BID (Indus. Dsgn.); Rutgers Univ., 1955–57, MLS, 1962–66, PhD (Libnshp.). **Orgs.:** ALA: State Chap. Cnclr. (1972–73); Cnclr.-at-

Special Subjects/Services: 50. Adult educ.; 51. Advert./Mktg.; 52. Aerosp.; 53. Agric.; 54. Area std.; 55. Arts/Hum.; 56. Autom.; 57. Bibl./Prtg.; 58. Bio. sci.; 59. Bus./Fin.; 60. Chem.; 61. Copyrt.; 62. Documtn.; 63. Educ.; 64. Engin.; 65. Env.; 66. Eth. grps.; 67. Film; 68. Food/Nutr.; 69. Geneal.; 70. Geo.; 71. Geol.; 72. Handcpd.; 73. Hist.; 74. Int. frdm.; 75. Info. sci.; 76. Insr.; 77. Law; 78. Legis.; 79. Math./Comp. sci.; 80. Med.; 81. Metals; 82. Nat. resrcs.; 83. Newsp.; 84. Nuc. sci.; 85. Oral hist.; 86. Petr./Energy; 87. Pharm.; 88. Phys./Astr./Math.; 89. Readg.; 90. Relig.; 91. Sci./Tech.; 92. Soc. sci.; 93. Telecom.; 94. Transp.; 95. (other).

Lg. (1973–77). AALS: Task Frc. on WHCLIS Implications (1979–80); Prog. Com. (1981); Dean and Dirs. Cncl. (1975–). HI LA: Int. Frdm. Com. (Ch., 1965–67); Pres. (1970–71). NJ LA: Coll.-Univ. Sect. (Secy., 1960–61). Various other orgs. **Honors:** Cncl. on Lib. Resrcs., Flwshp., 1974. **Pubns.:** "Scholars in Residence," *Essays For Ralph Shaw* (1975); "The GSLS Placement Report: Familiar Patterns," *HI LA Jnl.* (1980); "Hawaii Library Association," *Encyc. of Lib. and Info. Sci.* (1973); *A Study of Computer-Based Reader Services and The Educational Requirements of Librarians* (1974). **Activities:** 1, 11; 15, 26, 39; 50, 56, 63 **Addr.:** Graduate School of Library Studies, University of Hawaii at Manoa, 2550 The Mall, Honolulu, HI 96822.

Harris, Jeanne Gail (N. 29, 1953, Chicago, IL) Consult. Div., Resrch. Admin., Arthur Andersen & Co., 1980–, AIS Resrch. Admin, 1978–80; Admin. Srvs. Libn., 1977–78. **Educ.:** Washington Univ., 1971–74, AB (Eng. Lit., Art Hist.); Univ. of IL, 1975–76, MS (LS). **Orgs.:** SLA: Mem. Dir. Com. (Ch., 1981). ASIS. Assn. of Comp. Users. Kappa Kappa Gamma. **Honors:** Beta Phi Mu. **Activities:** 12; 17, 24, 41; 56, 59, 93 **Addr.:** Consulting Division Research, Arthur Andersen & Co., 33 West Monroe St., Chicago, IL 60602.

Harris, Joan S. (S. 4, 1929, Middletown, OH) Lib. Dir., Winnetka Pub. Lib. Dist., 1974–; Actg. Dir., Fort Lauderdale Pub. Lib., 1972–73, Head, Adult Srvs., 1970–72, Libn. III, 1966–70. **Educ.:** Univ. of Cincinnati, 1950–53, BA (Eng.); FL State Univ., 1961, Tchr. Cert.; George Peabody Coll., 1965–66, MLS. **Orgs.:** ALA: Pub. Lib. Sect., Legis. Com. (1975–81); RASD/Hist. Sect., Geneal. Com. IL LA. Lib. Admins. Conf. of North. IL. Amer. Cvl. Liberties Un. Leag. of Women Voters. AAUW. **Activities:** 9; 16, 17, 35 **Addr.:** 1100 Pine St. #D, Glenview, IL 60025.

Harris, June Crowe (My. 16, 1947, Athens, GA) Map Spec., Detroit Pub. Lib., 1979–; Asst. Libn., Univ. of MI, 1977–79; Asst. Map Cur., William L. Clements Lib., 1977–78; Map Cur., Univ. of GA, 1970–76. **Educ.:** Univ. of GA, 1965–69, BA (Geo.), 1969–70, MEd (Geo.); Univ. of MI, 1976–1977, AMLS; SLA Cont. Educ. Sem. on Grantsmanship, 1978. **Orgs.:** SLA: Geo. & Map Div., Stan. Com. (Ch., 1979–); Assoc. Ed., *Bltn.* (1971–76); Nom. Com. (1978). West. Assn. of Map Libs. SALALM. OCLC Users Grp.: Acting Treas., Ch., Nom. Com. (1979–). MI Map Socty.: Secy. (1977–79). Southeast. Assn. of Amer. Geographers. **Pubns.:** *Selected Map Acquisitions at the University of Georgia* (1974–1976); *Sanborn atlas sheets in the Map Collection, Univ. of Georgia* (1975); *List of Air Photo Indexes for Georgia in the Univ. of Georgia Map Collection* (1975). **Activities:** 1, 9; 15, 20, 24; 70 **Addr.:** History & Travel Dept., Detroit Public Library, 5201 Woodward Ave., Detroit, MI 48202.

Harris, Karen H. (Ja. 25, 1934, Detroit, MI) Assoc. Prof., LS, Univ. of New Orleans, 1970–; Instr. Mtrls. Libn., Orleans Par. Pub. Schs., 1967–70; Admin. Ref. Libn., Wayne State Univ., 1964–66. **Educ.:** Wayne State Univ., 1951–57, BA (Econ.), 1964–66, MEd (LS). **Orgs.:** ALA: AASL. **Honors:** Houston Pub. Lib., Harriet Dickson Reynolds Endowment Speaker, 1980; ALA, Outstan. Ref. Book, 1978. **Pubns.:** Jt. auth., *Books for the Gifted Child* (1980); Jt. auth., *Notes from a Different Drummer; A Guide to Juvenile Fiction Portraying the Handicapped* (1977); Jt. auth., "The Library Media Specialist as a Mainstreaming Facilitator," *Sch. Media Qtly.* (Fall 1980); Jt. auth., "Materials for Educating Nonhandicapped Students about Their Handicapped Peers," *Tchg. Exceptional Chld.* (Fall 1980); Jt. auth., *The Special Child in the Library* (1976); other articles, filmstrips. **Activities:** 10, 11; 26; 63, 72, 95-Gifted youth. **Addr.:** College of Education, University of New Orleans, Lakefront, New Orleans, LA 70122.

Harris, Margaret J. (S. 15, 1930, Mansfield, PA) Reg. Libn., Cuyahoga Cnty. Pub. Lib., 1971–; Visit. Asst. Prof., Kent State Univ. Sch. of LS, 1978–; Branch Libn., Cuyahoga Cnty. Pub. Lib., 1966–71, YA Libn., 1964–66. **Educ.:** Coll. of Wooster, 1948–52, BA (Fr.); Case Western Reserve Univ., 1963–64, MS in LS. **Orgs.:** ALA: PLA Starter List (1978–80); YASD Mem. (1976–79); Publshrs. Liason (1980–82); Ofc. for Lib. Persnl. Resrcs. (1980–82). Mayfield Hts. Cham. of Cmrce. **Honors:** Case Western Reserve University, Lubrizol Awd., 1964. **Activities:** 9, 11; 17, 26 **Addr.:** 1600 Rydalmount Rd., Cleveland Hts., OH 44118.

Harris, Marinelle Marie (Ja. 3, 1930, Weatherford, OK) Serials Libn., Al Harris Lib., Southwest. OK State Univ., 1969–; Assoc. Ref. Libn., TX Tech Univ., 1968–69; Head, Ref. Dept. and Pub. Srvs., Wilmington Inst. Free Lib., 1967–68; Ref. Libn., Univ. of IA, 1961–67; Tchr., Weatherford (OK) HS, 1951–52. **Educ.:** OK City Univ., 1951, BMsc.; Univ. of OK, 1961, MLS. **Orgs.:** OK LA: Constn. and by-Laws (1971); Arch. Com. (1976–77); Coll. and Univ. Div. (1969–); Tech. Srvs. Div. (1969–). SW LA. Southwest. OK State Univ.: Fac. Sen. (1976–79); VP (1978–79). Higher Educ. Alum. Cncl. of OK. Natl. Trust for Hist. Prsrvn. AAUP. **Activities:** 1; 23, 30, 44 **Addr.:** 1004 North Bryan, Weatherford, OK 73096.

Harris, Martha Jane (D. 29, 1926, Milton, WV) Dir. of AV, Ft. Pierce Ctrl. HS, 1976–; Dir., Youth Srvs., St. Lucie-Okeechobee Reg. Lib., 1975–76, Chld. Libn., 1965–70; Elem. Sch. Libn., Lakeside Elem. Sch., 1960–64. **Educ.:** Indian River Cmnty. Coll., 1972–73; FL State Univ., 1973–74, BA (LS), 1974–75, MS (LS). **Orgs.:** ALA. SELA. FL LA: Cit. and Awds. Com. (1978); Cont. Educ. Com. (1979–80). FL Assn. for Media in Educ. AAUW. Classroom Tchrs. Assn. **Honors** Beta Phi Mu, 1975. **Activities:** 9, 10; 21, 32, 48 **Addr.:** Ft. Pierce Central High School, 1101 Edwards Rd., Fort Pierce, FL 33450.

Harris, Mary Arden (Mr. 3, 1926, Monroe, NC) Prog. Spec., Media Ctrs., Charlotte-Mecklenburg Schs., 1977–; Sch. Lib. Media Spec., 1973–77, Curric. Coord., 1972–73, Tchr., 1960–72. **Educ.:** Winthrop Coll., 1960, BA (Eng.), 1970, MAT (LS); Appalachian State Univ., 1981, EdS (Admin.). **Orgs.:** ALA: AASL. NC LA: Various coms. (1979–81). NC Assn. of Sch. Libns.: Dir. (1977–81). Mecklenburg LA: Secy. (1978); VP (1980–81); Pres. (1981–82). Alpha Delta Kappa: Upsilon Chap., Pres. (1972–74); State Pres. Cncl., Secy. **Honors** Phi Kappa Phi, 1970; Phi Delta Kappa. **Activities:** 10; 17, 21, 32 **Addr.:** 149 Benbow Ln., Charlotte, NC 28214.

Harris, Mary Belle (N. 11, 1916, Barnesville, OH) Retired, 1980–; Libn., Fairfax Cnty. Pub. Sch., 1976–80, Tchr., 1937–65. Libn., 1965–68, Media Spec., Area II, 1974–76, Libn., 1972–74, Asst. Supvsr. of Libs., 1969–72. **Educ.:** Asbury Coll., 1935–43, AB (Educ.); George Washington Univ., 1952–64, MA (Educ.); Univ. of MI, 1970, AMLS. **Orgs.:** ALA. VA Educ. Assn. Assn. of Sch. Libns. Fairfax Cnty. Daughters of Amer. Rev. **Activities:** 10; 15, 21 **Addr.:** 2516 NW 21st Ave., Gainesville, FL 32605.

Harris, Patricia R. (F. 12, 1948, Rome, Italy) Assoc. OERI, US Educ. Dept., 1981–; Consult., 1979–80; Asst. to Exec. Dir., ALA, 1975–79, Asst. to Dir., Ofc. for Int. Frdm., 1972–75; Asst. Ref. Libn., Princeton Univ., 1970–71. **Educ.:** Randolph-Macon Woman's Coll., 1965–69, BA (Hist.); Univ. of NC, 1969–70, MS (LS). **Orgs.:** ALA: GODORT. **Pubns.:** *Librarians, Censorship and Intellectual Freedom* (1972); "The ALA Council," *ALA Yrbk.* (1976–79); reviews. **Activities:** 1, 3; 24, 41; 74, 78 **Addr.:** 1721 Luzerne Ave., Silver Spring, MD 20910.

Harris, Richard J. (Ag. 15, 1948, Bournemouth, Hampshire, Eng.) Tech. Srvs. Libn., East. VA Med. Sch., 1975–. **Educ.:** Glassboro State Coll., 1966–71, BA (Eng.); Rutgers Univ., 1973–75, MLS; Med. LA cert., 1978. **Orgs.:** Med. LA: Mid-Atl. Reg. Grp., Prog. Com. (1981). Hlth. Sci. OCLC Users Grp. Tidewater Hlth. Sci. Libns.: Ch. (1976–77). **Activities:** 1, 12; 15, 20, 44 **Addr.:** Eastern Virginia Medical School Library, P.O. Box 1980, Norfolk, VA 23501.

Harris, Robert (Ag. 21, 1936, Glasgow, Scotland) Exec. Dir., Mgt. Adv. Cncl., BC Colls. and Prov. Insts., 1980–; Lib. Consult., Ofc. for Lib. Coord., Mnstry. of Educ., 1976–80; Asst. Dir., Educ. Plng., BC Med. Ctr., 1974–76; Chief Libn., BC Inst. of Tech., 1967–74; Head, Circ. Div., Univ. of BC Lib., 1962–67. **Educ.:** Univ. of BC, 1955–59, BA (Phys.), 1961–62, BLS, 1972–79, MLS. **Orgs.:** Can. LA: Resrch. and Spec. Libs. Sect. (Exec. Mem., 1966–67); Tech. Colls.-Insts. Com. (Ch., 1967–68); Can. Assn. of Coll. and Univ. Libns. (Ch., 1970–72); Mem. Com. (1977–80). Assn. of BC Libns.: Treas. (1967–68). BC LA: Pres. (1971–72). Can. Vocational Assn. Univ. of BC, Dept. of Adult Educ.: Fld. Adv. Com. (1977–78). **Honors:** BC LA, Helen Gordon Stewart Awd., 1979. **Pubns.:** "Faculty Collective Bargaining in B.C. Community Colleges," *PACE Nsltr.* (Ja. 1979); "New Directions in Library Services for Adult Basic Education," *The Open Door, BCLTA Nsltr.* (D. 1979). **Activities:** 1, 13; 17, 24, 34; 50, 61, 89 **Addr.:** Management Advisory Council, 7671 Alderbridge Way, Richmond, BC V7X 1Z9 Canada.

Harris, Robert Alvord (F. 15, 1946, Detroit, MI) Lib. Dir., Bellwood Pub. Lib., 1980–; Lib. Dir., Bartlett Pub. Lib., 1978–80; Branch Head, Chicago Pub. Lib., 1977–78, Gvt. Docum. Libn., 1975–77. **Educ.:** Univ. of MO, 1963–65, BA (Math.); Univ. of MI, 1969, MA (LS). **Orgs.:** ALA: PLA, Small and Medium Sized Lib. (1981). IL LA: 1976 Conf. Regis. Ch. Chicago Lib. Club: Treas. (1975–76); Secy. (1976–77). Lib. Admin. Conf. of North. IL: Salary Survey Ch. (1980–81). YMCA Indian Guides. **Honors:** Beta Phi Mu, 1969; Phi Kappa Phi, 1969. **Pubns.:** *LACONI Salary Survey* (1980, 1981). **Activities:** 9; 16, 17 **Addr.:** 304 N. Worth, Elgin, IL 60120.

Harris, Rodger S. (Ja. 24, 1932, Milwaukee, WI) Head, Cat. Dept., Univ. of NC, 1973–, Geol./Zlgy. Libn., 1971–72. **Educ.:** Univ. of WI, 1949–53, BS (Geol.), 1953–55, MS (Geol.); Univ. of OK, 1970–71, MLS. **Orgs.:** ALA. SELA. NC LA. **Pubns.:** "Is Another National Network the Best Answer?," *NC Libs.* (Win. 1979). **Activities:** 1; 20, 41; 82, 86 **Addr.:** Wilson Library 024 A, University of North Carolina at Chapel Hill, Chapel Hill, NC 27514.

Harris, Sarah Lucille (O. 27, 1915, Evanston, WY) Asst. Dir., Salt Lake City Pub. Lib., 1952–, Head, Circ. Dept., 1949–52, Asst. in Circ. Dept., 1943–49; Libn., Judge Meml. HS, 1939–43. **Educ.:** Westminster Coll., Salt Lake City, 1934–36, AA; Univ. of UT, 1936–38, BA (Eng.); Univ. of Denver, 1945–47, BS in LS. **Orgs.:** ALA. Mt. Plains LA: Treas. (1955–56). UT LA: Sec.-Treas. (1951–52); VP (1956–57); Pres. (1957–58). Zonta Intl.: Secy., Pres., Salt Lake Club (1963–64). Delta Kappa Gamma. **Activities:** 9; 17, 35 **Addr.:** 136 Lincoln St., Salt Lake City, UT 84102.

Harris, Susan C. (D. 20, 1944, Alexandria, LA) Head, Info. Srvs. Sect., NifTAL Proj., Univ. of HI, 1979–, Biblgphr., Dept. of Agronomy, 1977–78; Tchr., Sacred Hearts Acad., 1967–68. **Educ.:** Univ. of CO, 1962–64, Univ. of HI, 1964–66, BA (Eng. Lit.), 1975–76, MLS. **Orgs.:** SLA. Agri. Comm. in Educ. **Pubns.:** Ed., *Planning an Internat'l Network of Inoculation Trials* (1979); Jt. auth., *Select Bibliography of Centrosema, Desmodium and Stylosanthes* (1981); "Mutual Advantages: Biological Partners in Development," *Agenda*; Jt. auth., *A Selected Bibliography of Soil P and Phosphate Fertilization for the Tropics* (1981). **Activities:** 12, 14-Docum. Ctr.; 17, 27, 37; 54, 62, 91 **Addr.:** Dept. of Agronomy and Soil Sci (NifTAL), University of Hawaii, Honolulu, HI 96822.

Harris, Thomas J. (Ag. 14, 1948, Mt. Carmel, IL) Asst. Dir., Cumberland Trail Lib. Syst., 1974–; Spec. Srvs. Libn., 1972–74. **Educ.:** East. IL Univ., 1968–71, BS (Educ.), 1971–72, MS (LS); IN Univ., 1980– (LS). **Orgs.:** IL LA: AV Com. (Ch., 1980). EFLA. **Activities:** 13; 15, 17, 32; 56, 67 **Addr.:** Cumberland Trail Library System, 12th & McCawley Sts., Flora, IL 62839.

Harris, Winifred E. (Betty) Hanafi (Ap. 14, 1936, 'Nkana, N. Rhodesia) Dir., Lrng. Resrcs. Ctrs., Fraser Valley Coll., 1974–; Chief Libn., Centennial Coll., 1972–74; Supvsr., Hum. and Soc. Sci. Branch Libs., Queens Univ., 1970–72; Dir. of Libs., St. Lawrence Coll., 1969–70; Chief Libn., Sch. of Bus., Algonquin Coll., 1967–69. **Educ.:** Carleton Univ., 1966, BA (Eng.); Univ. of Toronto, 1969, BLS. **Orgs.:** BC Un. Cat.: Mgt. Com. (Ch., 1981–). BC LA: Dir. (1976–78). Cncl. of Post-Sec. Lib. Dir. of BC: Vice-Pres./Secy. (1977–79); Pres. (1979–81). Can. LA: Cmnty. and Tech. Coll. Sect., C.A.C.U.L. (Ch., 1974–76). Various other orgs. and ofcs. Fraser Valley Coll. Fac. and Staff Assn.: Pres. (1977–78). **Pubns.:** Reviews. **Activities:** 1; 17 **Addr.:** Fraser Valley College, 34194 Marshall Rd., Abbotsford, BC V2S 5E4 Canada.

Harrison, Alice Willis (Ja. 8, 1929, CO) Head Libn., Atl. Sch. of Theo., 1978–, Assoc. Libn., 1972–77; Lect., Dalhousie Univ. Sch. of Lib. Srv., 1971, 1978–; Libn. in Boys and Girls Room, Carnegie Lib. of Pittsburgh, 1962–70; Lect., University of IL Grad. Sch. of LS, 1959–60; Media Spec., Elem. Sch., Evanston, IL, 1957–59; Asst. Libn., Film Cncl. of America, 1954–55; Film Libn., Art and Music Dept., Evanston Pub. Lib., 1951–54. **Educ.:** Northwestern Univ., 1946–52, BS (Educ.); Univ. of IL, 1955–57, MS (LS); Atl. Sch. of Theo., 1977– (Theo.). **Orgs.:** ATLA. Bibl. Socty. of Can. Can. LA. Atl. Prov. LA: Cons. Com. (1978–). Other orgs. Intl. Inst. For Cons. of Hist. and Artistic Works. Visual Arts NS. **Honors:** Beta Phi Mu, 1957; Atl. Prov. LA, Alberta Letts Meml. Flwshp., 1976; Jamaica Gvt. Arch., Trng. Internship, 1977; Halifax LA, Disting. Srv. Awd., 1979. **Pubns.:** "Alberta Letts Memorial Fellowship," *Jamaica Lib. Bltn.* (1977); "Bulldog Clips: Conservation of Library Materials," *APLA Bltn.* (1977–81); "The First Alberta Letts Fellowship: A Report," *APLA Bltn.* (Mr. 1979); "Inspiring Conservation Programmes By Canada's Atlantic Provinces," *Lib. Scene* (Je. 1980); "Ecumenism in Action: The Library of the Atlantic School of Theology," *Bltn. of the Assn. of British Theo. and Phil. Libs.* (N. 1980); various papers. **Activities:** 1, 12; 15, 17, 23; 55, 57, 90 **Addr.:** Atlantic School of Theology, 640 Francklyn St., Halifax, NS B3H 3B5 Canada.

Harrison, Annie W. (S. 27, 1928, Powhatan, VA) Libn., Saint Paul's Coll., 1979–, Act. Dir., Lrng. Resrcs. Ctr., 1977–79, Actg. Libn., 1975–77, Asst. Libn., 1957–75; Libn., Nottoway Cnty. (VA) HS, 1955–56; Tchr.-Libn., Powhatan Cnty. (VA) HS, 1949–55. **Educ.:** VA State Univ., 1945–49, BS (Educ.); Syracuse Univ., 1958–63, MS (LS); Catholic Univ., 1976–79, Post Masters Cert. (LS). **Orgs.:** VA LA: Ch., Region II, (1979–80). SELA. ALA. **Honors:** Beta Phi Mu. **Activities:** 1; 15, 17, 32 **Addr.:** Lawrenceville, VA 23868.

Harrison, Dennis I. (My. 26, 1941, Cleveland, OH) Cur. of Mss., West. Reserve Hist. Socty., 1970–, Asst. Cur., 1969, Mss. Prcs., 1968–69. **Educ.:** Heidelberg Coll., 1959–65, AB cum laude (Hist., Grmn.); West. Reserve Univ., 1965–68, MA (Hist.); Case Western Reserve Univ., 1968–75, PhD (Hist.). **Orgs.:** SAA. Socty. of OH Archvsts.: Pres. (1975–76); VP (1974); Cncl. (1972–73); Ch., Legis. Com. (1976–). **Pubns.:** Reg. Ed., *Guide to Manuscripts Collections and Institutional Records in Ohio* (1974). **Activities:** 14-Hist. Socty.; 15, 17, 45; 63, 73 **Addr.:** The Western Reserve Historical Society, 10825 East Blvd., Cleveland, OH 44125.

Harrison, Donald F. (My. 24, 1928, Philadelphia, PA) Supvisory Archvst., Natl. Arch., 1970–; Milit. Histn., Dept. of the Army, 1960–70. **Educ.:** Univ. of PA, 1945–49, AB (Eng.); Georgetown Univ., 1969–76, PhD (Hist.). **Orgs.:** SAA: Lcl. Arrang. (Ch., 1970, 1976). Mid-Atl. Reg. Arch. Conf.: Ofcr., Ed. Nsltr. (1972–). Intl. Assn. for Soc. Sci. and Info. Sci. Tech.: Processed Produced Data Com. (Ch., 1976–). Inter-Univ. Sem. for the Std. of Armed Forces and Socty. Amer. Milit. Inst. Org. of Amer. Histns. **Honors:** Natl. Arch., Commendable Srv. Awd., 1976. **Pubns.:** "Glossary For Archivists," *Amer. Archvst.* (Jl.

PROFESSIONAL ACTIVITIES: Institutions: 1. Acad. lib.; 2. Arch.; 3. Assn.; 4. Fed./Gvt. lib.; 5. Inst. lib.; 6. Mfr./Suppl.; 7. Milit. lib.; 8. Musm.; 9. Pub. lib.; 10. Sch. lib.; 11. Sch. of lib. sci.; 12. Spec. lib.; 13. State lib.; 14. (other). **Functions/Activities:** 15. Acq./Col. dev.; 16. Adult srvs.; 17. Admin.; 18. Apprais.; 19. Archit./Bldgs.; 20. Cat./Class.; 21. Chld. srvs.; 22. Circ.; 23. Cons./Pres.; 24. Consult.; 25. Cont. ed.; 26. Educ. lib. sci.; 27. Ext. srvs.; 28. Fund/Grants; 29. Gvt. pubs.; 30. Indx./Abs.; 31. Instr. lib. use; 32. Media srvs.; 33. Micro.; 34. Netwks./Coop.; 35. Persnl.; 36. PR; 37. Publshg.; 38. Recs. mgt.; 39. Ref. srvs.; 40. Repro.; 41. Resrch.; 42. Review.; 43. Secur.; 44. Serials; 45. Spec. col.; 46. Tech. srvs.; 47. Trustees/Bds.; 48. YA srvs.; 49. (other).

1974); "Developments in Air Mobility," *Army Aviation Digest* (Je. 1969). **Activities:** 2; 15, 18, 39 **Addr.:** 5020 South 22nd St., Arlington, VA 22206.

Harrison, Harriet W. (S. 18, 1939, Norfolk, VA) Head, Prcs. Sect., Motion Picture, Broadcasting & Recorded Sound Div., Lib. of Congs., 1979–, Head, Prcs. Unit, Motion Picture Sect., 1974–79, Catlgr., 1969–74, Intern, 1968–69. **Educ.:** Southwest. Coll., 1957–61, BA (Hist.); Georgetown Univ., 1961–65, MA (Intl. Rel.); Univ. of CA, Los Angeles, 1967–68, MLS. **Orgs.:** SAA: Com. on Aural & Graphic Recs. (1974–). Intl. Fed. of Film Arch.: Cat. Comsn. (1974–; Ch., 1980). **Pubns.:** Jt. auth., *Film Cataloging* (1979); Jt. Auth., *The George Kleine Collection of Early Motion Pictures in the Library of Congress* (1980); "Cataloging Motion Picture Film: a Descriptive Bibliography," *Amer. Archvst.* (Ap. 1976). **Activities:** 2, 4; 20, 32, 45; 67, 95-Broadcasting. **Addr.:** Motion Picture, Broadcasting & Recorded Sound Division, Library of Congress, 10 1st St., S.E., Washington, DC 20540.

Harrison, James Orion, Jr. (O. 5, 1944, Atlanta, GA) Head Ref. Libn., GA South. Coll., 1978–, Proj. Libn., Lib. Srv. Enhancement Prog. Grant Cncl. on Lib. Resrc., 1977–78, Circ. Libn., 1975–77, Ref. Libn., 1973–75 Cat., 1972–73, Asst. to the Dir. of Lib., 1970–1972. **Educ.:** GA St. Univ., 1967–69, AB (Eng.); Emory Univ., 1969–70, MLn (LS). **Orgs.:** ALA: Lib. Instr. RT, Memshp. Task Force (1979). SELA. GA LA. AAUP. **Honors:** Beta Phi Mu. **Pubns.:** *The Organization of Information in the Field of Biology and How to Get to It* (ERIC Document, 1980). **Activities:** 1; 17, 31, 39 **Addr.:** P.O. Box 7547, Statesboro, GA 30458.

Harrison, Karen A. (Mr. 28, 1947, Toronto, ON) Libn., Twp. of Delhi Pub. Lib., 1974–; Cur., ON Tobacco Musm., 1979–; Ref. Libn., Brantford Pub. Lib., 1973–74; Tech. Srvs., Law Socty. of Upper Can., 1972–73; Cmnty. Srvs. Libn., Toronto Pub. Libs., 1969–71. **Educ.:** Univ. of West. ON, 1965–68, BA (Hist., Pol.); Univ. of Toronto, 1969–73, BLS, MLS. **Orgs.:** Can. LA. ON LA: Pubcty., PR Com. ON Musm. Assn. **Activities:** 8, 9; 17 **Addr.:** Township of Delhi Public Library, 192 Main St., Delhi, ON N4B 2M2 Canada.

Harrison, Rose H. (Ag. 13, 1946, Ashland, KY) Asst. Dir., ILL Ctr., CT State Lib., 1980–, ILL Libn., 1973–80, Ref. Libn., 1969–73. **Educ.:** Univ. Of KY, 1964–68, BA (Phil.), 1968–69, MLS. **Orgs.:** CT LA. ALA. New Eng. LA. **Activities:** 13; 24, 34; 62 **Addr.:** Connecticut State Library/ Interlibrary Loan Center, 90 Washington St., Hartford, CT 06106.

Harrison, Susan B. (N. 11, 1943, Philadelphia, PA) Automated Systs. Coord., Free Lib. of Philadelphia, 1980–, Acq. Libn., 1973–80, Asst. Head, Acq., 1972–73, Libn., Acq., 1968–72, Ref. Libn., 1967–68. **Educ.:** Ursinus Coll., 1961–65, BA (Eng.); Drexel Univ., 1966–67, MSLS. **Orgs.:** ALA: BKdealer Rel. Com. (Ch., 1978–80); Reprodct. Lib. Mtls. Pubns. Com. (1976–77); Assn. Amer. Publshr./ALA RTSD Jt. Com. (1979–), ch. (1980–81). OCLC: Aut. Acq. Adv. Com. PA LA. **Activities:** 9; 15 **Addr.:** 3308 Warden Dr., Philadelphia, PA 19129.

Harrison, Thomas Demetrius (My. 25, 1923, Brunswick, GA) Dir., Haverford Sch. Instruc. Media Ctr., 1964–; Head Libn., Helen Kate Furness Free Lib. (Wallingford, PA), 1961–64. **Educ.:** Emory Univ., 1946–48, AB (Eng.), 1948, AM (Eng.); Villanova Univ. 1959–60, MS (LS); Rutgers Univ., 1967–69, MLS. **Orgs.:** ALA. Natl. Assn. Educ. Broadcasters. PA LA. Mid. Atl. Film Bd. AECT. Franklin Inst. **Honors:** Phi Beta Kappa, 1948; Beta Phi Mu; Cum Laude Socty., 1964. **Pubns.:** Contrib., *Work Simplification in Public Libraries* (1965). **Activities:** 9, 10; 17, 20, 48; 55, 67, 91 **Addr.:** The Haverford School IMRC, 440 W. Lancaster Ave., Haverford, PA 19041.

Harsaghy, Fred Joseph, Jr. (S. 16, 1916, New York, NY) Lect., Mgt. Pol. Sci., Univ. New Haven, 1977–79; Tchr., Spec. Educ. and Adult Educ., Dunbury Sch., 1975–81; Prof. and Chief Libn., York Coll., City Univ. New York, 1972–74; Area Dir. Lib., Prof., Inter Amer. Univ., PR, 1969–72; Dir. Lib. Srvs., Coll. Petro. Minerals, Dhahran, Saudi Arabia, 1965–69; various tchg. positions, Danbury HS and Danbury State Coll., 1961–65; various positions in Japan and Saudi Arabia, 1949–60. **Educ.:** New York Univ. 1948, BA, 1953, MPA, 1965, PhD; Columbia Univ., 1954, MLS. **Orgs.:** ALA. SLA. Assn. Caribbean Univ. and Resrch. Lib. AAUP Amer. Socty. Pub. Admn. AAAS. Natl. Educ. Assn. Other prof. soctys. **Addr.:** Box 8897, Candlewood Hills, New Fairfield, CT 06810.

Harshe, Florence E. (O. 16, 1917, Lima, OH) Retired, 1980–; Dir., South. Adirondack Lib. Syst., 1959–80; Dir., NY State Reg. Lib. Srv. Ctr., 1957–59, Asst. Dir., Head of Adv. Srvs., 1951–57; Head, Ord. Dept., Lib. of HI, 1949–51, Head, Circ. Dept., 1947–49; Head, Circ. Dept., Lima Pub. Lib., 1943–47, N. Branch Libn., 1941–43. **Educ.:** OH State Univ., 1935–39, BS (Educ.); Case West. Rsv. Univ., 1940–41, BS (LS). **Orgs.:** NY LA: Cncl. (1957–60, 1962); Adult Srvs. Sect. (Pres., 1962); Schol. Com.; Pub. Lib. Sect. (Secy., 1978–79). ALA: Lib. Ext. Sect., Treas.; Mem. Com. Cap. Dist. Lib. Cncl.: Trustee (1967–70); various coms. NY Bd. Regents Prof. Libn. Examinations Com. NY Pub. Lib. Syst. Dir.: Com. Various other orgs. AAUW: Bd. Bus. and Prof. Women's Assn. **Honors:** St. Lawrence Univ., N. Country Citizen's Awd., 1958. **Pubns.:** "Processing Procedures at the Watertown Regional Library Service Center," *Jnl. of Cat. and Class.* (O. 1955); "Small Libraries Progress Together in the Watertown Region," *ALA-PLD Rpt.* (N. 1956); "One New Idea Per Year," *Lib. Jnl.* (Ap. 1, 1958); "Are Public Relations Poor Relations," *Bookmark* (J. 1959); "Profile of the South Adirondack Library System," *Bookmark* (O. 1963). **Activities:** 9; 16, 17, 27; 50 **Addr.:** Loughberry Rd., Saratoga Springs, NY 12866.

Hart, Carol Suzanne (Je. 9, 1941, Wyandotte, MI) Sr. Info. Mgr., Kappa Syst., Inc., 1978–, Proj. Mgr., Cancer Info. Clearinghouse, 1978–80, Sr. Libn., Cancer Info. Clearinghouse, 1976–78. **Educ.:** Univ. of MD, 1969–72, BA (Eng.); 1974–75, MLS, 1973–74, (Eng.). **Orgs.:** ALA: LAMA. ASIS. Med. LA. DC LA. Natl. Assn. of Female Execs. **Pubns.:** Jt. auth., "The Coordinated Development of Health-Related Clearinghouse Vocabularies: A Proposed Technique," *ASIS Procs.* (O. 1979). **Activities:** 12; 17, 24, 46; 75, 80, 92 **Addr.:** Kappa Systems, Inc., 7910 Woodmont, Suite 1300, Bethesda, MD 20014.

Hart, Earl Durwood (Je. 14, 1939, Durham, NC) Assoc. Prof. of LS, Univ. of New Orleans, 1968–; Libn., Acq. Dept., E. Carolina Univ., 1964–66; Libn., N. Broughton HS, Raleigh Pub. Sch. (NC), 1963–64; Libn., Tarboro HS, 1961–63. **Educ.:** E. Carolina Univ., 1958–61, BS (Hist.), 1962–64, MA (Educ.); George Peabody Coll., 1966–67, MLS; LA St. Univ., 1977– (Media). **Orgs.:** ALA. Cath. LA. AECT: Int. Frdm. Com.; LA Chap., Leadershp. Com.; LA LA. LA Assn. Sch. Libn.: Exec. Bd. Phi Delta Kappan. **Pubns.:** *Populus: A Bibliography of World Literature: 1964–1974* (1976); jt. auth., *Guidelines for School libraries* (1978). **Activities:** 10, 11; 20, 32; 63 **Addr.:** Univ. of New Orleans, College of Education, New Orleans, LA 70122.

Hart, Eldon C. (Mr. 1, 1915, Plain City, UT) Retired, 1980–; Dir. of Auxiliary Srvs., Ricks Coll., 1964–80; Phys. Libn., Univ. of IL, 1960–63; Bus. Mgr., Ricks Coll., 1942–59, Libn., 1940–53. **Educ.:** Brigham Young Univ., 1934–38, AB (Bus.); Univ. of IL, 1938–40, BS, MA (LS), 1959–64, PhD (LS). **Orgs.:** ALA. ID LA: Pres. **Addr.:** 151 North First East, Rexburg, ID 83440.

Hart, George Charles (Mr. 1, 1945, Indianapolis, IN) Latin Amer. Biblgphr., OH State Univ., 1973–; Catlgr., Cleveland Pub. Lib., 1973; Peace Corps Volun., Brazil, 1967–69. **Educ.:** IN Univ., 1963–67, BA (Span.), 1969–72, MA (Portuguese), 1970–73, MLS, 1977– (Span., Portuguese). **Orgs.:** SALALM: Com. on Bibl. (1974–77); Subcom. on Bibl. Tech. (Ch., 1976–79). Mod. Lang. Assn. of Amer.: Portuguese Sect., *MLA Intl. Bibl.* (1974–79). AAUP. Latin Amer. Stds. Assn. Midw. Assn. for Latin Amer. Stds. **Honors:** Cncl. on Lib. Resrcs., CLR Adv. Std. Fellow, 1977; OH State Univ. Grad. Sch., Small Grant, 1976; OH State Univ. Libs., Libs. Resrch. Grant, 1975. **Pubns.:** Jt.-trans., Xavier, F.C., *Christian Agenda* (1970); Trans., Traba, M., "The Monumental I of Anais Nin," *Under the Sign of Pisces* (Win. 76); "Camões em Inglês," *Ocidente* (N. 1972); Contrib., *MLA International Bibliography* (1974–78); Contrib., *Hispanic American Periodicals Index* (1975). **Activities:** 1, 12; 15, 31, 39; 54, 55, 95–Frgn. Langs. **Addr.:** Acquisition Department, The Ohio State University Libraries, 1858 Neil Avenue Mall, Columbus, OH 43210.

Hart, Marion L. (S. 5, 1942, Richmond, VA) Asst. VP, Info. Srvs., Untd. VA Bank, 1971–; Ref. Libn., Reynolds Metals Co., 1964–71. **Educ.:** Mary Washington Coll., 1959–62, BA (Psy.); Univ. of NC, 1969–71, MS in LS; VA Sch. of Bank Mgt., Univ. of VA, 1977–79. **Orgs.:** SLA: Pres., VA Chap. (1979–80); Dir., Bus. & Finance Div. (1978–80); Dir., VA Chap. (1972–74). VA LA. Natl. Assn. of Bank Women: Prog. Com. (1978). **Honors** Co-Valedictorian, VA Sch. of Bank Mgt., 1979. **Pubns.:** Jt. auth., *Statistical Information Sources; a guide for financial institutions* (1979). **Activities:** 12; 17, 39, 42; 59, 77, 95-Banking. **Addr.:** United Virginia Bank, P.O. Box 26665, Richmond, VA 23261.

Hart, Robert Allan (F. 17, 1930, Dallas, TX) Lib. Dir., Santa Barbara Pub. Lib., 1965–; Lib. Dir., Lompoc Pub. Lib., 1962–65; Admin. Asst., Anaheim Pub. Lib., 1959–62. **Educ.:** TX Tech. Univ., 1948–54, BBA (Mktg.); Univ. of South. CA, 1956–57, MLS. **Orgs.:** CA LA: Pres. (1979); Treas. (1970–73). **Activities:** 9; 16, 17 **Addr.:** Santa Barbara Public Library, P.O. Box 1019, Santa Barbara, CA 93102.

Hart, Thomas L. (Mr. 7, 1938, Auburn, IN) Prof., FL State Univ., 1971–; Asst. Prof., Ball State Univ., 1966–71; Asst. Prof., Purdue Univ., 1965–66; Mtrls. Ctr. Dir., Kokomo-Cente Twp. Sch., IN, 1960–65. **Educ.:** Ball State Univ., 1956–60, BS (Elem. Educ.), 1960–63, MA (Admin.); Case Western Reserve Univ., 1961–64, MSLS, 1965–74, PhD (LS). **Orgs.:** ALA; AASL: Prof. Dev. Com., Ch. (1974–79). AALS: Ed. Bd., *Jnl. of Educ. for Libnshp.* (1977–81). IN Sch. Libns. Assn.: Treas. (1969–71). IN LA: Lib. Educ. (Ch. 1969). FL Assn. for Media in Educ.: Bd. (1974–75); Pres. (1976–77); VP (1977–78). Other orgs. Natl. Assn. for Barbershop Singing in Amer. First Christ. Church: Elder (1978–80). Untd. Fund. **Honors:** IN Sch. Libns. Assn., Media Man of the Yr., 1965. **Pubns.:** *Multi-Media Reviews and Selection Sources* (1975); *Instruction in School Media Center Use* (1978); "Dare to Integrate," *AV Instr.* (O. 1976); "Integration of Multimedia Collections–A Potpourri of Theory and Practice," *Sch. Media Qtly.* (Fall 1976); "Florida Governor's Conference," slide-tape presentation (1978). **Activities:** 11; 31, 32, 48; 56, 63, 78 **Addr.:** School of Library Science, Florida State University, Tallahassee, FL 32306.

Hartbank, Betty R. (My. 23, 1921, Tolono, IL) Head, Ref. Dept., Booth Lib., East. IL Univ., 1967–, Serials Libn., 1966–67, Lab. Sch. Libn., 1956–66; Ref. Libn., Univ. of Notre Dame Lib., 1955–56. **Educ.:** Univ. of IL, 1954, BS (Psy.), 1955, MS (LS). **Orgs.:** ALA. IL LA. Assn. for Humanistic Psy. Univ. Prof. of IL. **Pubns.:** Jt. auth., *A Selected Bibliography on Constitutional Conventions* (1970). **Activities:** 1; 39 **Addr.:** Reference Department, Booth Library, Eastern Illinois University, Charleston, IL 61920.

Harter, Stephen Paul (O. 9, 1941, Canton, OH) Assoc. Prof., Univ. of S. FL, 1974–; Instr., Amer. Coll. for Girls, Istanbul, 1966–69; Head, Math. Dept., W. Jr. HS, Maple Heights, OH, 1964–66. **Educ.:** OH State Univ., 1959–63, BS (Math.), 1963–64, MA (Math. Educ.); Univ. of Chicago, 1969–70, AM (LS), 1970–75, PhD (LS). **Orgs.:** ALA: RASD/MARS, Educ. and Trng. Com. (1980–). ASIS: Educ. Com. (1978–); Doct. Forum Com. (1976–78; Ch., 1978). AALS. FL LA. Other orgs. AAAS. **Honors:** Beta Phi Mu, 1971. **Pubns.:** Jt. auth., *Research Methods in Librarianship* (1980); Jt. complr., *Directory of Computer Applications in Florida Libraries* (1979); "An Assessment of Instruction Provided by Library Schools in On-Line Searching," *Info. Prcs. and Mgt.* (1979); Jt. auth., "Circulation, Reference, and the Evaluation of Public Library Service," *RQ* (Win., 1978); "Statistical Approaches to Automatic Indexing," *Drexel Lib. Qtly.* (Ap., 1978); other articles. **Activities:** 11; 26, 39, 41; 56, 75 **Addr.:** Library, Media and Information Studies, University of South Florida, Tampa, FL 33620.

Hartin, J(ohn) S(ykes) (O. 26, 1916, Columbus, MS) Prof., Sch. of LS, Univ. of MI, 1975–, Dir. of Libs., 1947–75; Chief, Pub. Srvs., Swarthmore Coll., 1945–47; Libn., Sch. of Msc., Univ. of MI, 1943–45. **Educ.:** Univ. of MS, 1935–39, BA (Eng., Fr.); Univ. of MI, 1939–40, ABLS, 1940–42, AMLS, 1952–53, AM (Eng.), 1952–56, PhD (LS). **Orgs.:** ALA: Cncl. (1960–63); Subscrpn. Bks. Com. (1950–54). MS LA. SELA. Phi Kappa Phi. Univ. of MI Assn. LS Alum.: Pres. (1945–46). **Honors:** Beta Phi Mu. **Activities:** 11; 26; 55, 57 **Addr.:** Box 25, University, MS 38677.

Hartje, George N. (S. 24, 1924, St. Louis, MO) Dir. of Libs., Head, Div. of Libs. & Musm., NE MO State Univ., 1964–; Supvsr. Tech. Srvs., St. Louis Pub. Lib., 1960–63, Chief, Cat. & Order Dept., 1956–60, Asst. Chief, Cat. & Order Dept., 1955–56, Catlgr., 1953–55; Cat.-in-Charge, Reclassification, Washington Univ., 1950–53, Asst. Chief, Acq. Dept., 1950. **Educ.:** Harris Jr. Coll., 1941–43, AA (Engin.); Washington Univ., 1945–47, AB (Eng.); Univ. of IL, 1948–50, MS (LS); Univ. of MO, 1970–71, (Higher & Adult Educ.). **Orgs.:** MO ACRL: Pres. (1968). MO LA: Arch. Com. (Ch., 1975–76); Pres. (1973–74). ALA: RTSD/Acq. Sect., Bylaws Com. (1967–69); Conf. Prog. Com. (1964); Serials Sect., Nom. Com. (1963). SAA. Other orgs. Kirksville Kiwanis Club: Pres. (1975). Hist. Socty. of MO. St. Charles Cnty. Hist. Socty. **Honors:** Amer. Bus. Women's Assn., Emerald City Chap., Boss of the Yr., 1978; Kirksville Kiwanis Club, Kiwanian of the Yr., 1974. **Pubns.:** *Missouri Library Association 1970–75* (1975); "Parameters of Developing and Managing a Library Collection," *Col. Mgt.* (My. 1980); "Factors Affecting Collection Development in Academic Libraries," *Show-Me Libs.* (O./N. 1978); "Staff Development at NMSU," *Show-Me Libraries,* (Ag. 1978); "Missouri Library Association." *Encyc. of Lib. & Info. Sci.* (1976); other articles. **Activities:** 1, 2; 15, 17, 26; 50, 63 **Addr.:** Rural Route 6, Box 316, Kirksville, MO 63501.

Hartman, Ann L. (Ag. 19, 1948, Carlisle, PA) Ed., Libs. Unlimited, 1981–; Head, Pub. Srvs., Natl. City Pub. Lib., 1978–81; Instr. Srvs./Ref. Libn., San Diego City Coll., 1978–79; Ref. Libn., Coronado Pub. Lib., 1978–79; Consult., Adult Educ. Ctr., 1978–79. **Educ.:** Millersville State Coll., 1966–73, BS (Educ.); Univ. of Pittsburgh, 1975–76, MLS; CA Cmnty. Coll. Cred. **Orgs.:** ALA. CA LA: Palomar Chap. (Pres., 1981–82). **Activities:** 9; 16, 17, 32 **Addr.:** 1607 Gilpin St., Denver, CO 80218.

Hartman, Eleanor C. (Je. 1, 1928, Cleveland, OH) Musm. Libn., Los Angeles Cnty. Musm. of Art, 1964–; Ref. Libn., Los Angeles Pub. Lib., 1962–64. **Educ.:** West. Resrv. Univ., 1946–51, BA (Span.); Univ. of CA, Los Angeles, 1960–62, MLS; Univ. of MI, Tchg. Eng. as a Frgn. Lang., 1951, Cert. **Orgs.:** ARLIS/NA. ALA. Coll. Art Assn. **Activities:** 12; 15, 17 **Addr.:** Art Research Library, Los Angeles County Museum of Art, 5905 Wilshire Blvd., Los Angeles, CA 90036.

Hartman, Matthew (D. 14, 1941, New York, NY) Head, Serials Cat. Unit, Univ. of BC, 1971–; Serials Catlgr., NY Pub. Lib., 1967–70; Libn., NY Herald-Tribune, 1965–66. **Educ.:** Queens Coll., 1964–68, BA (Eng.); Columbia Univ., 1969–71, MS (LS). **Orgs.:** Can. LA. BC LA. **Pubns.:** Managing ed., *Jnl. of the Can. Lib. Sci. Socty.* (1978–); Managing ed., "Canadian Library Progress" (1974–77); reviews. **Activities:** 1; 17, 20, 24, 26, 33, 37 **Addr.:** 3738 W. 37 Ave., Vancouver, BC V6N 2V9 Canada.

Special Subjects/Services: 50. Adult educ.; 51. Advert./Mktg.; 52. Aerosp.; 53. Agric.; 54. Area std.; 55. Arts/Hum.; 56. Autom.; 57. Bibl./Prtg.; 58. Bio. sci.; 59. Bus./Fin.; 60. Chem.; 61. Copyrt.; 62. Documtn.; 63. Educ.; 64. Engin.; 65. Env.; 66. Eth. grps.; 67. Film; 68. Food/Nutr.; 69. Geneal.; 70. Geo.; 71. Geol.; 72. Handcpd.; 73. Hist.; 74. Int. frdm.; 75. Info. sci.; 76. Insr.; 77. Law; 78. Legis.; 79. Math./Comp. sci.; 80. Med.; 81. Metals; 82. Nat. resrcs.; 83. Newsp.; 84. Nuc. sci.; 85. Oral hist.; 86. Petr./Energy; 87. Pharm.; 88. Phys./Astr./Math.; 89. Readg.; 90. Relig.; 91. Sci./Tech.; 92. Soc. sci.; 93. Telecom.; 94. Transp.; 95. (other).

Hartman, Ruth Dahlgren (My. 26, 1916, Wilton, ND) Head Docum. Libn., Ctrl. WA Univ., 1965–; Ref. Libn., Fresno State Coll., 1961–65; Circ., Ref., Univ. of NV, 1960–61; Libn., Glendale Pub. Lib., 1956–60. **Educ.:** Minot State Coll., 1947–51, BS (Ed. Art); Univ. of MI, 1953–60, AMLS. **Orgs.:** ALA: GODORT, State Docum. Task Force (Coord., 1976–78). WA LA. West. Assn. of Map Libns. AAUW. AAUP. **Honors:** Kappa Delta Pi. **Pubns.:** Reviews. **Addr.:** 1213 Vuecrest Ave., Ellensburg, WA 98926.

Hartmetz, Walter J. (Jud) (Ap. 14, 1941, Wichita, KS) Lib. Dir., N. Kansas City Pub. Lib., 1979–; Lib. Dir., Cass County (MO) Pub. Lib., 1976–78; Lib. Dir., Miami (OK) Pub. Lib., 1971–76. **Educ.:** Wichita State Univ., 1959–69, BA (Hist.); Emporia State Univ., 1970–71, MLS. **Orgs.:** ALA. MO LA: VP, Pres.-Elect, Pub. Lib. Div. (1979–81). NW MO Lib. Network: VP (1979–80). **Activities:** 9; 17 **Addr.:** North Kansas City Public Library, 715 East 23rd Ave., North Kansas City, MO 64116.

Hartner, Elizabeth Pearsall (N. 6, 1910, Corning, NY) Consult., 1975–; Mgr., Tech. Anal., KASC, Univ. of Pittsburgh, 1965–75; Consult., IL Inst. of Tech., 1963–64; Jr. Fellow, Mellon Inst., 1960–62; Staff, Physical Metallurgy, E.C. Bain Resrch. Lab., US Steel, 1956–58; Index Ed., *Chem. Abs. Srv.,* 1954–55, Abstctr., 1953–58; Resrch. Engin., Metallurgy, 1931–46. **Educ.:** Carnegie-Mellon Univ., 1927–31, BS (Sci.), 1936–37, MS (Chem.); 1931–42, (Physical Metall.); Univ. of Pittsburgh, 1965–67, (LS). **Orgs.:** ASIS: Ch., Pittsburgh Chap. (1975–76); Ch., Nom. Com. (1977); Ed., *PGHASIS,* (1979–80). AAAS. Amer. Chem. Socty. **Pubns.:** *An Introduction to Automated Literature Searching* (1981); "Electron Microscopy Across the World," *Metal Progress* (Je. 1963); "New Electron Metallography," *Metal Progress* (Mr. 1962). **Activities:** 12; 24, 30, 42; 64, 81, 91 **Addr.:** 119 Harlow St., Pittsburgh, PA 15218.

Hartness-Kane, Ann (Chicago, IL) Asst. Head Libn., Benson Latin Amer. Col., Univ. of TX, 1978–; Pub. Srvs. Libn., 1975–78; Head, Latin Amer. Serials Cat., 1974–75; Cat. Libn., Latin Amer. Serials, 1970–74; Cat. Libn., Salt Lake City Pub. Lib., 1969–1970. **Educ.:** Univ. of TX, 1954–58, BA (Eng.); 1958–61, MLS; Latin Amer. Std. and Span., Cornell Univ., 1967–68. **Orgs.:** SALALM: Exec. Bd., Member at large (1979–); Ch., Ed. Bd., (1978–); Com. on Resrch. (Ch., 1975–76). Latin Amer. Std. Assn. **Pubns.:** *Subject Guide to Statistics in the Presidential Reports of the Brazilian Provinces, 1830–1889* (1977); "Hispanic American Periodicals for Libraries," *Serials Libn.* (Fall 1979); "Latin American Periodicals for Libraries," *Serials Libn.* (Fall 1978). **Activities:** 1, 12; 17, 31, 39; 54 **Addr.:** 8712 Tallwood Drive, Austin, TX 78759.

Hartong, Dorothea H. (Ja. 23, 1944, Pittsburgh, PA) Libn., N. Canton Jr. HS, 1979–; Libn., Spring Hill Jr. HS, 1978–79; Libn., Mercy Sch. of Nursing, 1974–78; Med. Libn., Timken Mercy Hosp., 1974–77; Lib. Coord., Tuslaw Lcl. Sch. Dist., 1972–74; Libn., Alliance (OH) Sr. HS, 1968–69. **Educ.:** OH North. Univ., 1962–66, BA (Math.); Kent State Univ., 1969–70, MLS, 1974–79, MEd (Media Sup.). **Orgs.:** OH Educ. Lib. Media Assn. Stark County Libns.: Pres. (1978–79). Canton-Massillon Area Hlth. Scis. Libns. Assn.: Pres. (1977–79). Summit Cnty. Sch. Media Spec. OH Educ. Assn. Natl. Educ. Assn. OH Cncl. of Tchrs. of Math. **Pubns.:** "Mathematics: A Bibliography," *OASL Bltn.* (1970). **Activities:** 10, 12; 21, 48; 63, 80 **Addr.:** 604 Jackson Ave. N.W., Massillon, OH 44646.

Hartsook, Pieter (Je. 11, 1947, National City, CA) Asst. Dir., Sci. and Tech., Howard Univ., 1981–; Proj. Mgr., Mgt. Support and Info. Syst., Info. Plng. Assn., 1978–81; Tech. Srvs. Libn., Maharishi Intl. Univ., 1978; Proj. Dir./Coord., World Plan Exec. Cncl. - USA, 1974–78; Lib. Dir., Maharishi Intl. Univ., 1973–74. **Educ.:** Univ. of CA, Berkeley, 1972, BA (Bio. Sci.), 1972–73, MLS, 1973–74, 6th Yr. Cert. (Lib. Admin.). **Orgs.:** ALA. ASIS. DC LA. Mensa. **Activities:** 1; 17, 24, 34; 56, 91 **Addr.:** Assistant Director - Science and Technology, University Libraries, P.O. Box 708, Howard University, Washington, DC 20059.

Hartz, Fred R. (Mr. 31, 1933, Annville, PA) Libn., DeSoto Correctional Inst. Lib., 1980–; Med. Libn., Warren (PA) State Hosp., 1977–80; Dir., Media Ctr., E. Penn Sch. Dist., 1975–76; Asst. Prof., Ch., Dept. of LS, Trenton State Coll., 1964–74; Dir., Pub. Lib. of Willingboro, NJ, 1960–64; Head, Campus Branch & Circ. Libn., Rider Coll.; Sr. Libn., Bur. of Law and Legis. Ref., State Lib. of NJ, 1960; Milit. Ed., US Army, 1958–60; Sch. Libn., Pennsbury Schs., 1954–58. **Educ.:** Kutztown State Coll., 1950–54, BS (LS); Syracuse Univ., 1957–63, MSLS; Drexel Univ., 1966–68; Temple Univ., 1968–70; Occidental Univ. of St. Louis, 1975–77, PhD (Educ. Media). **Orgs.:** Med. LA: Pittsburgh Reg. PA LA. AAUP: Secy.-Treas., Rider Coll. Chap. (1962–63). **Honors:** Beta Phi Mu, 1963. **Pubns.:** *Warren State Hospital 1880–1980: A Psychiatric Centennial* (1981); *I Sometimes Wish God Had Freddie Hood: A Case History in Psychiatry and Law* (1979); "Racial Delusion: Psychopathology and Legal Anti-Semitism of Luther, Wagner, and Hitler," *Legal Med. Qtly.* (S. 1979); "Preparing the Library Policies and Procedures Manual for the Medical Library," *IL Libs.* (O. 1979); "Origin, Development, and Present State of the Secondary School Library as a Materials Center" in *Instructional Materials Centers: Selected Readings* (1969); other articles. **Activities:** 1, 12; 20, 26, 37; 74, 77, 92 **Addr.:** Library, DeSoto Correctional Institution, Arcadia, FL 33821.

Hartz, Mary K. (F. 6, 1943, Ann Arbor, MI) Libn., User Srvs., Bur. of Soc. Sci. Resrch., 1977–; Catlgr., Recs., WGMS, RKO Gen., 1977; Consult., Biblgphr., Natl. Acad. of Sci., 1977; Ed., Info. Indus. Assn., 1977. **Educ.:** Univ. of MD, 1962–65, BA (Hist.), 1975–76, MLS. **Orgs.:** ASIS. SLA: Soc. Sci. **Pubns.:** *Information Sources Directory* 1st ed. (1977). **Activities:** 12; 15, 39, 41; 63, 92 **Addr.:** 10717 Seneca Spring Way, Gaithersburg, MD 20760.

Harvey, Carl G. (Jl. 5, 1944, Lethbridge, AB) Libn., Hudson's Bay Oil and Gas Co. Ltd., 1977–; Libn., Sci. Div., Univ. of Calgary, 1975–77; Env. Std. Libn., Univ. of Waterloo, 1971–74, Libn., Engin., Math, Sci. Lib., 1970–71. **Educ.:** Univ. of AB, 1962–66, BSc (Physical Geog.), 1969–70, BLS; Univ. of Toronto, 1974–75, MLS. **Orgs.:** Assn. of Can. Map Libs.: Secy. (1972–73); Treas. (1973–74). Can. LA. Can. Assn. of Spec. Libs. & Info. Srvs.: Calgary Chap., (Secy. 1977). Calgary OLUG: Prog. Coord. (1978–80). Other orgs. South. AB Inst. of Tech.: Lib. Arts Adv. Com. (1978–81). **Activities:** 12; 17, 39, 49-On-line searching; 70, 86, 91 **Addr.:** Hudson's Bay Oil and Gas Company Limited, 700 Second St. S.W., Calgary, AB T2P 0X5 Canada.

Harvey, Donald F. (S. 13, 1939, St. John's, NF) Pres., Can. Lib. Trustees Assn., Can. LA, 1980–; Ch., NF Pub. Libs. Bd. **Educ.:** Queen's Theo. Coll., 1958–63 (Theo.). **Orgs.:** Can. LA: Trustee Div. Can. Sch. Trustees Assn.: Table Ofcr. (1974–76). Kiwanis Club of St. John's. **Honors:** NF Sch. Trustees Assn., Life Mem., 1977; Can. Sch. Trustees Assn., Life Mem., 1978. **Activities:** 47 **Addr.:** 150 LeMarchant Rd., St. John's, NF A1C 2H2 Canada.

Harvey, Elizabeth R. (F. 3, 1945, Philadelphia, PA) Dir., Schlow Meml. Lib., 1976–, Chld. Libn., 1973–76; Cnty. Libn., Clearfield (PA) Cnty. Lib., 1972; Chld. Libn., Free Lib. of Philadelphia, 1968–72. **Educ.:** Oberlin Coll., 1963–67, BA (Hist.); Drexel Univ., 1967–68, MSLS. **Orgs.:** PA LA: Treas. (1979–81); Exec. Com. (1979–81); Bd. of Dir. (1978–79); Secy.-Treas., Juniata Conemaugh Chap.; Secy., Chld., YA and Sch. Libns. Div. ALA: PLA/Small and Medium sized libs. sect. (Secy., 1978–79). **Honors:** Phi Beta Kappa, 1967; Beta Phi Mu, 1968. **Activities:** 9; 17 **Addr.:** Schlow Memorial Library, 100 E. Beaver Ave., State College, PA 16801.

Harvey, John Frederick (Ag. 24, 1921, Maryville, MO) Intl. Lib. Consult., 1980–; Visit. Prof. of Lib. and Info. Sci., Mottahedin Univ., Tehran, Iran, 1978–80; Consult., 1976–78; Dean of Lib. Srvs., Hofstra Univ., 1974–76; Dean of Lib. Srvs., Univ. of NM, 1972–74; Fndr. and Tech. Dir., Iranian Docum. Ctr. and Tehran Book Prcs. Ctr., 1968–71; Ch., Dept. of LS, Fac. of Educ., Univ. of Tehran, 1967–68; Dean and Prof., Grad. Sch. of LS, Drexel Univ., 1958–67; Head Libn., State Coll., Pittsburg, KS, 1953–58; other positions. **Educ.:** Dartmouth Coll., 1940–43, AB (Eng.); Univ. of IL, 1943–44, BSLS; Univ. of Chicago, 1945–49, PhD (LS). **Orgs.:** ALA: Cncl. (1958–62); ACRL, Exec. Bd. (1958–62); LAMA, Exec. Bd. (1975–78); LED Exec. Bd. (1964–66); Com. on Resol. (1962–63); Lib. Hist. RT; IRRT; LRRT. ASIS: Exec. Cncl. (1963–65). Archons of Colophon. AALS. Other orgs. AAUP. Dartmouth Coll. Alumni Assn: N. Country Club (Pres. 1977–78). Univ. of Chicago Alum. Assn.: Pres. NY Chap. (1975–76). Ed., *Church and Synagogue Libs.* (1980). Ed., *Data Processing in Coll. and Pub. Libs.* (1966). **Honors:** Eisenhower Exch. Flwshp. Bd., US Embassy, Tehran, 1970–71. **Pubns.:** "James T. Gerould," "Harriet B. McPherson," "F. L. D. Goodrich," "Hans Peter Luhn", *Dict. of Amer. Lib. Biog.,* (1977); Ed., *Comparative and International Library Science,* (1977); Jt. auth., "University Library Search and Screen Committees," *Coll. and Resrch. Libs.* (Jl. 1976); "University of New Mexico Libraries," *Encyc. of Lib. and Info. Sci.* (1977); "Southwest Academic Library Consortium," *Intl. Lib. Review* (O. 1975); other books and articles. **Activities:** 1, 11; 17, 24, 26; 75, 80 **Addr.:** 603 Chanteclair House, 2 Sophoulis St., Nicosia 136, Cyprus.

Harvey, Lois M. (O. 1, 1918, Genoa, IL) Ref. Libn., Wethersfield Pub. Lib., 1966–; Dir., Hallandale Pub. Lib., 1964–66. **Educ.:** Univ. of IL, 1936–40, BS (Educ.); Univ. of Miami, 1964–69; various crs. in LS, lit. and sci. **Orgs.:** CSLA. CT LA. 1st Presby. Church of Hartford. **Honors:** Hallandale, FL, Woman of the Yr. Awd., 1965. **Activities:** 9; 15, 22; 50 **Addr.:** 554 Silas Deane Hwy., Wethersfield, CT 06109.

Harvey, Mary Louise (Ag. 2, 1924, South Bend, IN) Acq. Libn., Boston Univ. Pappas Law Lib., 1973–; Catlgr., Univ. of Nairobi, Kenya, 1971–72. **Educ.:** Univ. of MI, 1959, BA, 1965, MLS. **Activities:** 1; 15, 20; 77 **Addr.:** 137 Marlborough St., Boston, MA 02116.

Harvey, Robert Duncan (Fe. 9, 1919, Brooklyn, NY) Head Libn. and Prof. of Lib. Sci., SW MO State Univ., 1959–; Head of Ref. and Spec. Srvs., Northwestern Univ., 1956–59; Asst. Director, Pub. Srvs., Univ. of VT, 1950–56. **Educ.:** Wesleyan Univ., 1937–41, BA (Govt.); Columbia Univ., 1949–50, MSLS. **Orgs.:** ALA. MO LA. MO Assn. of Coll. and Resrch Libs.: Pres., (1968–69). SW MO Lib. Network Adv. Cncl.: Vice-Ch., (1977–78). MO State Tchrs Assn. **Pubns.:** *Special Resources of Southwest Missouri Libraries,* Rev. ed. (1971); *Missouri Handbook for School Library Services* (1964). **Activities:** 1; 17, 26, 34 **Addr.:** 821 E. Delmar St., Springfield, MO 65807.

Harvie, J. Patrick B. (Ap. 19, 1943, Toronto, ON) Cnty. Libn., Wellington Cnty. Pub. Lib., 1975–; Chief Libn., Parry Snd. Pub. Lib., 1973–75. **Educ.:** Queen's Univ., 1964–66, BA (Phil.), 1967–69, MA (Phil.); Univ. of West. ON, 1972–73, MLS. **Orgs.:** ON LA. Cnty. and Reg. Municipality Libns.: Secy. (1979–80). **Activities:** 9; 15, 17, 39; 55 **Addr.:** Wellington County Public Library, RR #1, Fergus, ON N1M 2W3 Canada.

Harvill, Melba S. (Ja. 22, 1933, Bryson, TX) Dir. of Libs., Midwestern State Univ., 1973, Ref. Libn., 1967–73. **Educ.:** N. TX State Univ., Denton, 1951–54, BA (Hist.), 1954–55, 1967–68, MA (Hist.); North Texas State University, Denton, Texas MLS 1973; North Tx State Univ., 1980–, Cert. Aduc. Study (LS). **Orgs.:** TX LA: College/Univ. Div., Mem. Com., (1977–78); Plng. Com., (1978–80). TX Cncl. of State Univ. Libns. Phi Alpha Theta, Tau Gamma Chapter, MSU: Secy., (1978–79); VP (1979–80). Senior-Junior Forum. Pub. Ch.; Exec. Brd. Northside Girls' Club Brd. of Dir. Met. Bus. and Prof. Women's Club: Ch., Com. on Status of Women; Woman of the Yr. Nom., (1979), Pres., 1980. Ch., Nat. Bus. Women's Week, (1978). TX Fed. BPW and Dist. X Dir. (1981–82). **Honors:** Beta Phi Mu, 1974. Alpha Lambda Delta, 1971. **Pubns.:** "The Election of 1864: The Campaign and Its Issues," *MSU Faculty Forum Papers* (1979). **Activities:** 1; 17, 31, 39; 56, 92 **Addr.:** Route 2, Box 187, Iowa Park, TX 76367.

Harvin, Janice Marie (My. 5, 1924, Alto, TX) Dir., Resrch. Med. Lib., Univ. TX, M.D. Anderson Hosp., 1966–; Dir., Med. Lib., Univ. AR Med. Ctr., 1960–66; Ref. Libn., Natl. Lib. of Med., 1957–60; Ref. Libn., Vanderbilt Univ. Med. Lib., 1956–57; Ref. Libn., Univ. NE Coll. of Med. Lib., 1955–56; Cat. Libn., Univ. MD Med. Lib., 1949–55; Cat. Libn., Vanderbilt Univ. Med. Lib., 1947–49. **Educ.:** Stephen F. Austin State Univ., 1940–43, BA (Eng., Biol.); George Peabody Coll., 1943–45, BSLS. **Orgs.:** SLA: Bio. Sci. Div. (Treas., 1975–76). Med. LA: Various coms., ofcs. (1947–75). **Pubns.:** Ed., "Code for the Training and Certification of Medical Librarians," *Bltn. Med. LA* (O. 1964); jt. auth., "Health Science Library Resources in Texas," *Survey of Texas College and University Facilities* (1968); "The Library as a Laboratory: from Concern to Involvement," *Continuing Education for Nursing, Tools and Techniques* (1968); "The Lateral Truth is That the Real Reference Problem Is So Tired It Can't Stand Up; A Vignette," *RQ* (Fall 1966); "International Cancer Research Data Bank," *Shared Services, Shared Ideas; Procs. of the 4th Anl. Mtg. S. Ctrl. Reg. Grp. Med. LA* (1976); various other articles. **Activities:** 1, 12; 17, 20, 39; 80 **Addr.:** 3515 Deal St., Houston, TX 77025.

Harwell, Richard Barksdale (Je. 6, 1915, Washington, GA) Retired, 1980–, Cur. of Rare Bks. and Mss., Univ. of GA, 1975–80; Dir. of Libs., GA South. Coll., 1970–75; Coll. Libn., Smith Coll., 1968–70; Coll. Libn., Bowdoin Coll., 1961–68; Assoc. Exec. Dir., Exec. Secy., ACRL, ALA, 1957–61; Dir., Pubns., VA State Lib., 1956–57; Dir., Southeast. Interlib. Resrch. Facility, 1954–56; other lib. positions, 1938–54. **Educ.:** Emory Univ., 1937, AB, 1938, BLS. **Orgs.:** ALA. GA LA. SE LA. Grolier Club. GA Hist. Socty. South. Hist. Socty. Amer. Antiq. Socty. **Honors:** New Eng. Coll., DLitt, 1966; Phi Beta Kappa. **Pubns.:** Confederate Music (1950); *The Confederate Hundred* (1964); *Hawthorne and Longfellow* (1966); *Brief Candle: The Confederate Theatre* (1973); Ed., *Coll. and Resrch. Libs.* (1962–63); other books, articles, reviews. **Addr.:** P.O. Box 607, Washington, GA 30673.

Harwood, James Lawrence (D. 17, 1938, Huntington, WV) Archvst., Natl. Arch. of the U.S., 1969–; Grad. Tchg. Asst., WV Univ., 1966–69, Flw. of the WV Col., 1967–68. **Educ.:** Marshall Univ., 1960–63, BA (Hist.), 1964–67, MA (Hist.); WV Univ., 1966–69 (Hist.). **Orgs.:** SAA. **Pubns.:** Various NARS micro. pubns. on Revolutionary War fin. (1976). **Activities:** 2; 18, 23, 39; 59 **Addr.:** National Archives, Washington, DC 20408.

Harwood, Judith Ann (O. 10, 1938, Montreal, PQ) Undergrad. Libn., South. IL Univ., Carbondale, 1972–, Serials Catlgr., 1969–70; Tech. Srvs. Libn., Parkland Coll., 1967–69; Asst. Educ. Libn., Univ. of IL, 1965–67. **Educ.:** Univ. of ND, 1956–60, BA (Eng.); Univ. of IL, 1964–65, MS (LS); South. IL Univ., Carbondale, 1974–81, PhD (Educ.). **Orgs.:** ALA: ACRL/Bibl. Instr. Sect., Resrch. Com. (1979–81). IL LA: IL ACRL, Bibl. Instr Com. (1976–78), Exec. Com. (1978–80). **Activities:** 1; 17, 31, 39 **Addr.:** Undergraduate Library, Southern Illinois University at Carbondale, Carbondale, IL 62901.

Hary, Edith Lydia (S. 18, 1922, Woonsocket, RI) Dir., ME Law & Legis. Ref. Lib., 1971–; Law & Legis. Ref. Libn., ME State Lib., 1947–71. **Educ.:** Bates Coll., 1943–47, BA (Hist./Gvt.); Simmons Coll., 1949–50, MS (LS). **Orgs.:** AALL. Law Libns. of New Eng.: Pres. (1956–58). ME LA. Hubbard Free Lib., Hallowell, ME: Trustee (1964–); Clerk (1974–). ME Arch. Adv. Bd.: Secy. (1976). ME Judicial Cncl.: Lay mem. (1959–). ME Bd. of Bar Examiners: Lay mem. (1976–). **Honors:** AAUW, State of ME Cit., 1967; Univ. of ME, LLD, 1975; ME Bar Assn., Disting. Srv. Awd., 1976; Westbrook Coll., Deborah Morton Socty., 1978.

PROFESSIONAL ACTIVITIES: Institutions: 1. Acad. lib.; 2. Arch.; 3. Assn.; 4. Fed./Gvt. lib.; 5. Inst. lib.; 6. Mfr./Suppl.; 7. Milit. lib.; 8. Musm.; 9. Pub. lib.; 10. Sch. lib.; 11. Sch. of lib. sci.; 12. Spec. lib.; 13. State lib.; 14. (other). **Functions/Activities:** 15. Acq./Col. dev.; 16. Adult srvs.; 17. Admin.; 18. Apprais.; 19. Archit./Bldgs.; 20. Cat./Class.; 21. Chld. srvs.; 22. Circ.; 23. Cons./Pres.; 24. Consult.; 25. Cont. ed.; 26. Educ. lib. sci.; 27. Ext. srvs.; 28. Fund/Grants; 29. Gvt. pubs.; 30. Indx./Abs.; 31. Instr. lib. use; 32. Media srvs.; 33. Micro.; 34. Netwks./Coop.; 35. Persnl.; 36. PR; 37. Publshg.; 38. Recs. mgt.; 39. Ref. srvs.; 40. Repro.; 41. Resrch.; 42. Review.; 43. Secur.; 44. Serials; 45. Spec. col.; 46. Tech. srvs.; 47. Trustees/Bds.; 48. YA srvs.; 49. (other).

Pubns.: Jt. auth., *Legislative process in Maine* (1973); "Depository libraries in Maine," *Bltn., ME LA* (1962); other articles. Activities: 4, 13; 17, 31; 77, 78 Addr.: State House, Station 43, Augusta, ME 04333.

Harzfeld, Lois A. (My. 7, 1932, New York, NY) Lect., Univ. of CA, Berkeley, Sch. of Lib. and Info. Stds., 1973–; Sub. Ref. Libn., Peralta Cmnty. Coll., 1975–; Ref. libn., Skyline Coll., 1974–80; Libn., Meiklejohn Cvl. Liberties Inst., 1971–73; Ref. Libn., Univ. of CA, Davis, 1970–71. **Educ.:** Univ. of MI, 1949–53, BA (Soclgy.), 1953–55, MA (Soclgy.); Univ. of CA, Berkeley, 1969–1970, MLS. **Orgs.:** CA LA: CA Socty. of Libns., Com. Prof. Stan. (1979). **Honors:** Phi Beta Kappa, 1953. **Pubns.:** *Periodical Indexes in the Social Sciences and Humanities: A Subject Guide* (1978). **Activities:** 11; 31, 39 **Addr.:** 5329 Miles Ave., Oakland, CA 94618.

Haselden, Clyde L. (Ag. 26, 1914, Latta, SC) Libn. Emeritus, Lafayette Coll., 1980–, Libn., 1959–80; Libn., Baldwin-Wallace Coll., 1950–59; Libn., Parsons Coll., 1947–50; Ref. Asst., Univ. of AR, 1939–43. **Educ.:** Furman Univ., 1934–38, BA (Hist.); Columbia Univ., 1938–39, BSLS; Univ. of Chicago, 1946–47, MALS. **Orgs.:** ALA: ACRL (College Sect., Ch. Bldg. Com, 1965–67); DE Chap. of ACRL: Pres., (1954–56). AAUP. **Honors:** Phi Beta Kappa. **Activities:** 1; 17, 19, 24 **Addr.:** 1921 Washington Blvd., Apt. B12-S, Easton, PA 18042.

Haselhuhn, Ronald Paul (Jl. 10, 1933, Dallas, IA) Assoc. Prof., Sch. of LS, Emporia State Univ., 1971–; Asst. Prof., IN State Univ., 1970–71; Assoc. Prof., St. Cloud State Univ., 1961–69; Asst. Libn., US Air Force Acad., 1959–61. **Educ.:** Omaha Univ., 1953–58, BFA (Art); Denver Univ., 1958–59, MA (LS); Univ. of MN, 1962–69, PhC (Higher Educ.). **Orgs.:** ALA: GODORT (Asst. Coord. 1979–). Mt. Plains LA. KS LA: GODORT (Ch. 1979–). **Activities:** 1, 13; 17, 29 **Addr.:** 719 West, Emporia, KS 66801.

Haselwood, E. LaVerne (Jl. 19, 1933, Barnard, MO) Prof., Univ. of NE, Omaha, 1963–, Gvt. Docum. Libn., 1963–66; Jr.-Sr. HS Libn., Lewis Ctrl. Cmnty. Schs., Council Bluffs, IA, 1961–63; Jr. HS Libn., Omaha Pub. Sch., 1960–61. **Educ.:** Univ. of Omaha, 1957–60, BS (Educ.); Univ. of Denver, 1961–63, MA (LS); Univ. of NE, Lincoln, 1967–72, PhD (Educ. Admin.). **Orgs.:** NE LA: Pres. (1981–82). Metro. Lib. Network Adv. Cncl. NE Lib. Comsn. NE State Adv. Cncl. on Libs.: Ch. (1980). Omaha Metro. Libns. Club: Pres. (1979–80). Other orgs. Phi Delta Kappa. AAUP. **Honors:** Univ. of NE at Omaha, Finalist, Grt. Tchr. Awd., 1977. **Pubns.:** Contrib., *Guide for Establishing, Developing and Evaluating School Media Programs* (1975); Jt. auth., "A Factorial Study of Library Media Proficiencies," *Intl. Jnl. of Instr. Media* (1980–81). **Activities:** 1, 10; 26, 31, 39; 63 **Addr.:** College of Education, University of NE at Omaha, Omaha, NE 68182.

Hasija, Gian C. (S. 16, 1941, D. G. Khan, W. Pakistan) Med. Libn., Jersey Shore Med. Ctr., 1973–; Libn., Springdales Sch., New Delhi, India, 1968–69; Libn., Ctrl. Secret. Lib., Mnstry. of Educ., New Delhi, 1959–68. **Educ.:** Agra Univ., New Delhi, India, 1964, BA (Arts); Glassboro State Coll., 1972–73, MA (LS); Cert., LS, Aligar Muslim Univ., Aligarh, India, 1959–59; Cert., Elem. Fr., New Delhi Sch. of Frgn. Lang., 1960–61. **Orgs.:** Med. LA. Monmouth Biomed. Info. Cnsrtm. Hlth. Sci. Lib. Assn. of NJ. **Activities:** 12; 17, 30, 32; 61, 67, 80 **Addr.:** Jersey Shore Medical Center, 1945 Corlies Ave., Neptune, NJ 07753.

Haskell, John Duncan, Jr. (Ja. 3, 1941, Providence, RI) Assoc. Libn., Coll. of William and Mary, 1978–; Ed., Comm. for a New England Bibl., Inc., Boston, 1972–78; Libn., Univ. of MD, Baltimore Cnty., 1965–69. **Educ.:** Univ. of RI, 1958–62, AB (Eng.); Rutgers Univ., 1963–64, MLS (Lib. Sci.); George Washington Univ., 1969–71 (Amer. Studies), M. Phil (1972), PhD (1977). **Orgs.:** ALA: ACRL (Pub. Com. 1979–83). VA LA. Bibl. Socty. of Amer. Bibl. Socty. of the Univ. of VA. Amer. Std. Assn. Org. of Amer. Hist. **Pubns.:** Jt. auth., *New Hampshire: A Bibliography of Its History* (1979); *Maine: A Bibliography of Its History* (1977); Reviews, various articles. **Activities:** 1; 17, 35; 54, 57 **Addr.:** Earl Gregg Swem Library, College of William and Mary, Williamsburg, VA 23185.

Haskell, Peter C. (F. 9, 1939, Providence, RI) Dir. of the Lib., Franklin and Marshall Coll., 1977–81; CLR Mgt. Intern, IN Univ., Bloomington, 1976–77; Assoc. Univ. Libn., Colgate Univ., 1973–76; Asst. Circ. Libn., Cornell Univ., 1970–73; Cat./Ref. Libn., 1968–70. **Educ.:** Bowdoin Coll., 1957–61, BA (Govt.); Rutgers Univ., 1967–68, MLS. **Orgs.:** ALA: ACRL (Stan. and Accred. Com. (1978–81). NLA. PA LA: Treas., Coll. and Resrch. Div. (1980); Ch., Bldg. and Equip. Sect. (1980). AAUP. **Pubns.:** Ed., *Sign Systems for Libraries* (1979). **Activities:** 1; 17 **Addr.:** Box 545, Barnstable, MA 02630.

Haskin, Susan Myrnette (Atlanta, GA) Fed. Grants Coord., State Lib. of MI, 1976–, Head, Blind and Phys. Handcpd. Lib., 1966–76, Ord. Libn., 1964–66; Tchr., Lansing Sch. Dist., 1961–62. **Educ.:** MI State Univ., 1961, BA (Educ.); West. MI Univ., 1964, MA (LS). **Orgs.:** ALA: Cncl. (1979–81); Scarecrow Press Awd. Jury (1974–75); ASCLA: Bd. (1978–81); Hlth. and Rehab. Lib. Srvs. Div., Pres. (1977–78), Bd. (1974–77); Lib. Srv. for the Blind RT, Ch. (1972–73), Bd. (1971–74), Treas. (1967–69). MI Lib. Cnsrtm. Exec. Cncl. (1979–). KY, OH, MI Reg. Med Lib. Netwk. Exec. Com. (1979–). State of MI Task Frc. on ILL: Ch. (1980). MI LA: Int. Frdm. Com. (1973–74). Amer. Assn. of Workers for the Blind: State Chap. (VP, 1975–76). MI Braille Transcribers Srv.: Adv. Com. (1972–75). WKAR-FM Radio Talking Bk.: Strg. Com. (1972–74). Christ. Rec. Braille Fndn.: Adv. Bd. (1969–74). **Honors:** Amer. Cncl. of the Blind, Robert S. Bray Awd., 1978; MI LA, Walter H. Kaiser Awd., 1973; Beta Phi Mu. **Pubns.:** Various articles. **Activities:** 13; 24, 28, 34 **Addr.:** State Library Services, P.O. Box 30007, Lansing, MI 48909.

Haskins, Katherine Wheldon (O. 2, 1950, New York, NY) Serials Libn., Art Inst. of Chicago, 1981–, Catlgr., 1979–81; Libn., Nelson Gallery of Art, 1978–79; Serials Libn., Metro. Musm. of Art, 1976–78; Serials Re-Class Libn., Carnegie Pub. Lib., 1975–76. **Educ.:** Univ. of Pittsburgh, 1969–71, AB (Chinese lang.), 1972–73, MLS; Washington Univ., 1973–75, MA (Art Hist.). **Orgs.:** ARLIS/NA: Ed., *Serials Reviews*, Arlis Nsltr.; Cat. Adv. Com. (1980–81); Mdrtr., Cat. and Indx. Spec. Int. Grp. (1979–80). Metro. Musm.: Educ. Assm. (Secy. 1977–78). **Honors:** Beta Phi Mu, 1974. **Activities:** 8; 20, 44, 46; 55, 56 **Addr.:** Libraries, The Art Institute of Chicago, Michigan Ave. at Monroe, Chicago, IL 60603.

Hassan, Khan M. (My. 4, 1941, Fatehpur, UP, India) Asst. Libn./AV Srvs., ID State Univ., 1977–; Serials and AV Libn., Alfred State Coll., 1973–77; Jr.-Sr. HS Libn., Walton (NY) Ctrl. Sch., 1972–73; HS Libn., Salmon River Schs., Ft. Covington, NY, 1971–72. **Educ.:** Univ. of Karachi, 1959–63, BSc (Geol.), 1963–65, MSc (Geol.); Univ. of West. ON, 1969–70, Post-Grad. Dipl. (LS); State Univ. Coll., Geneseo, 1970–71, MLS, 1973–76, 6th Year Spec. (Media Mgt.). **Orgs.:** ID LA: Schol. and Awds. Com. (1979–). ID Educ. Media Assn.: Mem. Com. (Ch., 1979–80); Pres. (1981–82). Consrtm. of Univ. Film Ctrs.: Data Bank Com. (1977–79); Transp. Com. (Ch., 1979–81). Friends of 10, Inc. Toastmasters Intl. **Pubns.:** Ed., *Media Directory* (1976); "New Spirit in Leadership," *Moments In Media*, (Ja., 1981); Jt. ed., *A Union List of Serials In Three Alfred Libraries* (1975); "Uses of Television for Instruction," *Medium* (Fall, 1980); "Northern Rockies Consortium for Higher Education," *NW/MET Bulletin* (May, 1980); other articles. **Activities:** 1; 15, 17, 32; 67, 75, 95-Instr. Tech. **Addr.:** Audio Visual Services, Idaho State University, Campus Box 8064, Pocatello, ID 80009.

Hasse, Glenn Edwin (N. 5, 1941, Nicollet, MN) Chief Libn., Vets. Admin., 1973–; Supvsr., Lib. AV Ctr., Bemidji (MN) State Univ., 1970–73. **Educ.:** Mankato State Univ., 1960–63, BS (Elem. Educ.), 1969–71, MS (LS); St. Cloud State Univ., 1972–77, EdS (Info. Media); Immanual Luth. Coll., 1960–63, Dipl. (Relig.). **Orgs.:** Hlth. Educ. Media Assn. Med. LA. ND LA. Tri-Coll. Univ. ILL Com.: Pres. (1976–77). Valley Med. Network: Treas. (1977–78). **Activities:** 4, 12; 17, 24, 27; 56, 70, 80 **Addr.:** Veterans Administration Medical Center, Fargo, ND 58102.

Hastings, Joy L. (D. 7, 1946, Long Beach, CA) Mgr., Info. Ctr. Hunt-Wesson Foods, Inc., 1978–; Ref. Coord., Santiago Lib. Syst., 1974–78; Bus. Libn., Santa Ana Pub. Lib., 1971–74. **Educ.:** CA State Univ., Fullerton, 1964–69, BA (Geo.); Univ. of South. CA, 1969–71, MSLS. **Orgs.:** SLA. Orange Cnty. LA: Rec. Secy. (1978–). **Activities:** 12; 17, 38, 41; 59, 68 **Addr.:** Hunt-Wesson Foods, Inc., Information Center, M.S. 506, Fullerton, CA 92634.

Haswell, Hollee (My. 4, 1948, Albany, NY) Libn., The Sleepy Hollow Restorations, Inc., 1981–; Libn., Worcester Art Musm., 1978–81; Art and Msc. Libn., Forbes Lib., 1973–78. **Educ.:** Russell Sage Coll., 1970–72, BA (Fine Arts); Simmons Coll., 1972–73, MLS. **Orgs.:** ALA: ACRL. ARLIS/NA: New Eng. Chap., Charter Mem.; By-law and Nom. Com. (1973–74); Treas. (1976–77); Vice-Ch., Ch. (1979–81). **Honors:** Beta Phi Mu, 1973. **Activities:** 8, 9; 17, 39, 41; 55 **Addr.:** The Sleepy Hollow, Restorations, Inc., 150 White Plains Rd., Tarrytown, NY 10591.

Hatch, Lucile (Mr. 25, 1913, Walla Walla, WA) Prof. Emeritus, Grad. Sch. of Libnshp. and Info. Mgt., Univ. of Denver, 1978–, Prof., 1965–78, Actg. Dean, 1966–68, Assoc. Prof., 1956–65; Libn., Sharples Jr. HS, Seattle, 1955–56; Visit. Asst. Prof., Sch. of Libnshp., Univ. of WA, 1954–55; Libn., Sharples Jr. HS, 1952–54; Libn., Lincoln HS, Tacoma, 1951–52; Tchr., Libn., Various HS, 1935–51. **Educ.:** State Coll. of WA, 1930–35, MA (Frgn. Lang.); Univ. of Denver, 1944–46, BS (LS); Univ. of OR, 1953–54, MEd (Educ.); Columbia Univ., 1969–1970, Advnc. Std.; Univ. of CA, Grad. Work. **Orgs.:** ALA: Cncl. (1962–63); Comsn. on a Natl. Plan for Lib. Educ.; AASL, Dir. for Reg. V, Bd. of Dirs. (1960–62); Lib. Educ. Div., Tchrs. Sect. (Ch., 1970–71); YASD, Pres. (1962–63); various ofcs. AALS. CO LA. CO Educ. Media Assn.: Bd. of Dirs. (1976–77). Other orgs. and coms. Natl. Educ. Assn. Amer. Assn. of Higher Educ. **Honors:** Phi Beta Kappa, 1935; CO Educ. Media Assn., Life Mem., 1976; Mt. Plains LA, Disting. Srv. Awd., 1977; Frnds. of the Denver Pub. Lib., Nell I. Scott Awd. for Outstan. Contrib. to Lib. Srv., 1979. **Pubns.:** "Our Foreign Students Comment," *Jnl. of Educ. for Libnshp.* (Sum. 1964); "Training the Young Adult Librarian," *Lib. Trends* (O. 1968); "Public Libraries in Finland," *Jnl. of Lib. Hist.* (O. 1971); "The National Diet Library, the National Library of the Philippines, and the Singapore National Library," *Jnl. of Lib. Hist.* (O. 1972); "Upgrading Performance Through PPBS in School Media Centers," *Lib. Trends* (Ap. 1975); other books, articles. **Activities:** 10, 11; 17, 26, 32; 95-Chld. Lit. **Addr.:** 2350 East Iliff Ave., Apt. 4, Denver, CO 80210.

Hatcher, Danny R. (S. 16, 1947, Murray, KY) Deputy Dir. for Lib. Oper., Country Msc. Fndn., Inc., 1979–, Dir., Country Msc. Fndn. Lib. Media Ctr., 1974–79, Archvst., 1972–73, various other positions in same place. **Educ.:** Murray St. Univ., 1970, BA (Hist., Pol. Sci.); George Peabody Coll., 1972, MA (LS). **Orgs.:** Assoc. Record. Sound: Legal Com. (Ch. 1979–); Bd. Dir. (1977–79). TN Lib. Legis Netwk.: Med. TN Coord. (1978–). Msc. LA: Finance Com. (1978–); Prog. Com. (1974). TN LA: SLA Sect., Nom. Com. (1978). Various other orgs. and coms. **Honors:** Beta Phi Mu. **Pubns.:** Various historical pubns. and music pubns. Ed., *TN Libn.* (1974–77); Bk. Review Ed., *Jnl. Country Msc.* (1972); Speeches. **Activities:** 12; 17 **Addr.:** Country Music Foundation, 4 Music Square E., Nashville, TN 37203.

Hatcher, Karen A. (Je. 1, 1941, Waukesha, WI) Head of Cat. Dept., Assoc. Prof., Univ. of MT 1978–, Cat., 1968–78; Tech. Prcs. Dept., NM Highlands Univ., 1967–68; Spec. Srvs. Libn., Germany, 1964–66. **Educ.:** Univ. of WI (Milwaukee), 1959–63, BS (Eng.); Univ. of WI (Madison), 1963–64, MS (LS). **Orgs.:** MT LA: Acad. Spec. Lib., Ch. (1967–77); MT Auth. Com. (Ch. 1973–76); Cont. Educ. Com. (1978–). Pacific N.W. LA: Acad. Div., V Ch. (1979–). ALA. **Pubns.:** Jt. Auth., *Frenchtown Valley Footprints* (1976). **Activities:** 1; 20, 44, 46; 69, 85 **Addr.:** University of Montana Library, Missoula, MT 59812.

Hatfield, Brenda Garibaldi (Jl. 26, 1943, New Orleans, LA) Assoc. Dir. of Instr. Resrcs., New Orleans Pub. Sch., 1978–, Libn. for Prof. Lib., 1977–78; Actg. Head of Circ., Main Lib., Head, Norman Mayer Lib., New Orleans Pub. Lib., 1976–77; Coord. of Reader Srvs., Hamilton Pub. Lib., Canada, 1975–76, Branch Head, Mt. Lib., 1974–75, Chld. Srvs. Coord., 1973–74; Tchr., 1965–68. **Educ.:** Univ. of New Orleans, 1961–65, BA (Span.); Univ. of Toronto, 1971–73, MLS; Univ. Nacional de Mexico, 1964; Howard Univ., 1965. **Orgs.:** LA AECT: Bd. of Dirs. (1980–). LA LA: Exec. Cncl. of Sch. Libns. Sect. Grt. New Orleans Metro. Educ. Media Org.: Treas. (1979–80); Exec. Bd. (1980–); Pres. (1981). New Orleans Lib. Club: Secy. (1978–79). Other orgs. Sigma Gamma Rho Sorority. **Honors:** Beta Phi Mu. **Activities:** 10; 17, 32; 63, 67, 95-Educ. TV. **Addr.:** Instructional Resource Center, New Orleans Public Schools, 4300 Almonaster Ave., New Orleans, LA 70126.

Hatfield, Frances S. (F. 2, 1922, Tennille, GA) Dir. of Lrng. Resrcs., Sch. Bd. of Broward Cnty., FL, 1947–; Tchr., Ft. Lauderdale HS, 1943–47. **Educ.:** FL State Coll. for Women, 1939–43, BS (Sci. Educ.); FL State Univ., 1948–49, MA (LS). **Orgs.:** FL Assn. of Sch. Libns.: Bd.; Pres. (1966–67); other ofcs. FL AV Assn.: Pres. (1955–56). FL Assn. for Media in Educ. ALA: Cncl. (1969–72; 1974–78); Com. on Org. (1973; Ch., 1974–75); AASL (Pres., 1971–72). FL Educ. Assn. FL Assn. of Supvsrs. of Media: Pres. (1978–79). Natl. Educ. Assn. Soroptimist Club of Ft. Lauderdale: Pres. (1968–69). Various other orgs. **Honors:** Women in Comm., Ft. Lauderdale, Woman of the Yr. in Educ., 1977; Beta Phi Mu. **Pubns.:** Jt. auth., *The School Media, District Director* (1981); "Broward County, Florida, Program," *Lib. Trends* (Ap., 1968); Ed., "Media Center," *Instr. Mag.* (N. 1970); "Electronic Security Systems Do Work," *Sch. Lib. Jnl.* (N. 1979). **Activities:** 10; 17, 25, 32; 63, 67, 75 **Addr.:** Director of Learning Resources, Broward County Schools, 1320 S.W. 4th St., Ft. Lauderdale, FL 33312.

Hattery, Lowell H. (My. 26, 1916, VanWert, OH) Publshr. and Ed., Lomond Pubn., Inc. 1966–; Prof., Amer. Univ. 1948–78. **Educ.:** OH Univ., 1936, AB (Soc. Sci.); Syracuse Univ., 1936–38; Amer. Univ., 1938–39, PhD (Pub. Admn.). **Orgs.:** ALA. ASIS. Amer. Socty. for Pub. Admn.: Sci. Tech. in Gvt. Sect. (Ch.). **Honors:** AAAS, Flw. **Pubns.:** *Technological Change in Printing and Publishing* (1973); Co-Ed., *Reprography and Copyright Law* (1964); *Information and Communication in Biological Science* (1961); "Managing the Impact of Computers in the Federal Government," *The Bureaucrat* (Sum. 1978); Ed., *Info. Retrieval & Lib. Auto.* (1965–). **Activities:** 6, 11; 37; 56, 75 **Addr.:** R.D. #4, Mt. Airy, MD 21771.

Hauck, Linda Cznadel (D. 13, 1950, Cleveland, OH) Admin., Somerset Cnty. Lib. Syst., 1980–; Sub. Libn., NASA Wallops Flight Ctr. Tech. Lib., 1979–80; Bks. Libn., Rutherford B. Hayes Presidential Ctr. Lib., 1976–79; Resrch. Asst., Lib. Resrch. Ctr., Univ. of IL, 1975–76. **Educ.:** Kalamazoo Coll., 1969–73, BA (Hist.); SUNY, Albany, 1973–74, MLS; Friedrichs-Alexander Univ., W. Germany, 1971–72 (Archlg.). **Orgs.:** ALA: JMRT, Arch. Com. (1979–; Ch., 1980–); PLA/Small and Medium-sized Libs. Sect., Plng. Com. for the PLA Conv. (1981–83). **Activities:** 2, 9; 17, 45; 55, 69 **Addr.:** Somerset Cnty. Lib. Syst., E. Prince William St., Princess Anne, MD 21853.

Hause, Aaron H. (My. 4, 1936, Brooklyn, NY) Docum., Serials, Maps Libn., East. MT Coll. Lib., 1978–, Actg. Dir., Lib. Srvs., 1979–80, Docum., Serials, Maps Libn., 1978–79; Soc. Sci. Acq. Libn., Univ. of AZ Lib., 1977–78, Head Docum. Libn.,

Special Subjects/Services: 50. Adult educ.; 51. Advert./Mktg.; 52. Aerosp.; 53. Agric.; 54. Area std.; 55. Arts/Hum.; 56. Autom.; 57. Bibl./Prtg.; 58. Bio. sci.; 59. Bus./Fin.; 60. Chem.; 61. Copyrt.; 62. Documtn.; 63. Educ.; 64. Engin.; 65. Env.; 66. Eth. grps.; 67. Film; 68. Food/Nutr.; 69. Geneal.; 70. Geo.; 71. Geol.; 72. Handcpd.; 73. Hist.; 74. Int. frdm.; 75. Info. sci.; 76. Insr.; 77. Law; 78. Legis.; 79. Math./Comp. sci.; 80. Med.; 81. Metals; 82. Nat. resrcs.; 83. Newsp.; 84. Nuc. sci.; 85. Oral hist.; 86. Petr./Energy; 87. Pharm.; 88. Phys./Astr./Math.; 89. Readg.; 90. Relig.; 91. Sci./Tech.; 92. Soc. sci.; 93. Telecom.; 94. Transp.; 95. (other).

1975–77; Docum. Libn., Hofstra Univ. Lib., 1968–75; Sr. Ref. Libn., Queens Borough Pub. Lib., 1966–68. **Educ.:** New York Univ., 1954–57, BA (Hist., Pol. Sci.); Pratt Inst., 1965–66, MLS; New York Univ., 1980, MA (Pol.). **Orgs.:** ALA: ACRL/Law and Pol. Sci. Sect., Elect. Com. (Ch., 1970–71, 1973–74); GODORT. SLA: NY Chap., Soc. Sci. Sect., Goals Com. (1974). MT LA: Gvt. Docum. RT, Liaison to ALA (1980). Amer. Pol. Sci. Assn. **Activities:** 1, 4; 17, 29, 39; 54, 77, 92 **Addr.:** 30 Almadin Rd., Apt. #A-4, Billings, MT 59101.

Hausman, Patricia R. (Ag. 10, 1949, Ft. Worth, TX) Ref. Libn., Jackson Lib., Univ. of NC, 1976–80; Bibgphr. & Supvsr., Illinet Ofc., Univ. of IL, 1973–75. **Educ.:** Coll. of William & Mary, 1967–71, AB (Fine Arts); Univ. of MI, 1971–72, AMLS. **Orgs.:** SELA. ALA: Instr. RT, Prog. Com. (1978–79). NC LA: JMRT (Secy.-Treas., 1977–79). **Pubns.:** Reviews. **Activities:** 1; 34, 39, 42; 55, 59 **Addr.:** 305 Hempstead Rd., Williamsburg, VA 23185.

Hausrath, Donald Craig (F. 19, 1934, Ames, IA) Reg. Lib. Consult., Asia, Intl. Comm. Agency, 1978–, Chief, Lib. Srvs. Staff, 1975–77; Lib. Dev. Ofcr., US Info. Agency, 1971–75; Dir., Cosumnes River Coll., 1969–71; Dir., Kalamazoo Valley Cmnty. Coll., 1968–71. **Educ.:** Univ. of IA, 1959–61, AB (Eng.); Univ. of CA, 1963–64, MLS; Univ. of MD, 1977–78, (Mgt. and Info. Sci.); Lib. Admin. Dev. Prog., 1978; Frgn. Srv. Inst., Country Std. Prog., 1971, 1975; Intl. Flow of Info.-Trans Pac. Conf. Participant, 1979. **Orgs.:** ASIS. ALA: IRRT, Ch. of SE Asian Sect. (1978–). SLA. Amer. Frgn. Srv. Assn. **Honors:** US Info. Agency, Jefferson Flwshp., 1977–78. **Pubns.:** "U.S. International Communication Agency Library Program," *Bowker Anl.* (1981); "International Communication Agency," *Encyc. of Lib. and Info. Sci.* (1980); various articles, workshops. **Activities:** 4, 12; 17, 24, 25; 75, 92, 95-International Librarianship. **Addr.:** U.S. International Communication Agency, ECA/CL, Washington, DC 20547.

Hauth, Allan C. (Jl. 30, 1947, Cleveland, OH) Ref. Coord., Jackson Metro. Lib., 1975–. **Educ.:** Univ. of Akron, 1971–73, BA (Psy.); Univ. of KY, 1973–74, MLS. **Orgs.:** MS LA. SELA. Ctrl. MS Lib. Cncl.: Vice-Ch. (1977–78); Ch. (1978–79). **Activities:** 9; 16, 31, 39; 50, 57, 83 **Addr.:** Jackson Metropolitan Library System, Jackson, MS 39201.

Havener, Ralph S. (O. 31, 1925, Moline, IL) Dir. of Arch., Univ. of MO Syst., 1969–; Prof. of Hist., Blackhawk Coll., 1963–69; Local Recs. Archvst., IL State Arch., 1959–63; Asst. Archvst., WI State Arch., 1957–59. **Educ.:** Univ. of Miami, 1947–49, BA (Hist./Gvt.); Univ. of WI, 1949–50, MA (Hist.), 1954–57, (Hist.); Arch. Mgt. Inst., Natl. Arch., Cert., 1961. **Orgs.:** SAA: Coll. & Univ. Arch. Com. (1970–). Midwest Arch. Conf.: Strg. Com. (1972); Prog. Com. (1974–76). Assn. of St. Louis Area Archvsts.: Cncl. (1979–). Sch. of Lib. & Info. Sci., Univ. of MO: Adv. Cncl. (1978–). Univ. Recs. & Arch. Com.: Secy. (1969–). **Pubns.:** *Understanding American Government* (1959); "A View of the Local Records Act," *IL Libs.* (Je. 1962); "University of Missouri Archives Program," *Show-Me Libs.* (Ja. 1974). **Activities:** 2; 15, 17, 20; 55, 62, 85 **Addr.:** University of Missouri-UMCA, 701 Lewis Hall, Columbia, MO 65211.

Havens, Shirley E. (New York, NY) Sr. Ed., *Lib. Jnl.*, R. R. Bowker Co., 1957–; Admn. Secy. to the Libn., Carnegie Endow. for Intl. Peace, 1954–57; Exec. Secy. to Secy., Mental Hlth. Film Bd., 1952–54; Admn. Asst. to Bursar, Columbia Univ., 1947–52. **Educ.:** Hunter Coll., 1943–47, BA (Eng.); Columbia Univ., 1947–52, (Eng. Jnlsm.). **Orgs.:** ALA: ASCLA, Resrch. Pubn. Com. (1975–79); Pub. Com. (1979–81); H. W. Wilson Lib. Per. Awd. Jury (1971); Int. Frdm. RT Awd. Com. (1976). Pres. Com. Employ. Handcpd.: Lib. Com. (1963–). New York Lib. Club: Ed., *Bltn.* (1965–67). Scarecrow Press Lib. Lit. Awd. Jury: 1978. **Honors:** Pres. Com. on Empl. of the Handcpd., Cmdn., 1969; Phi Beta Kappa, 1947. **Pubns.:** Ed. of Arch. Issues *Lib. Jnl.* (D. 1962–66); articles and editorials in *Lib. Jnl.* (1963–); "Bruce Joffe's Private Library," *Sch. Lib. Jnl.* (My. 1963); "Church Library Buildings," *Protestant Church Bldgs. & Equipment* (N. 1964). **Activities:** 5, 9; 19, 23, 37, 42; 57, 72, 74 **Addr.:** Library Journal, R. R. Bowker Co., 1180 Ave. of the Americas, New York, NY 10036.

Haviland, Virginia (My. 21, 1911, Rochester, NY) Chief, Chld. Lit. Ctr., Lib. of Congs., 1963–; Readers Adv. for Chld., Boston Pub. Lib., 1952–63, Branch Libn., 1948–52, Chld. Libn., 1939–48. **Educ.:** Cornell Univ., 1929–33, BA (Econ., Math.); Boston Pub. Lib. Trng. Prog., 1934–40. **Orgs.:** DC LA. Auths. Gld. PEN. **Honors:** Grolier Fndn., Grolier Awd., 1974; Cath. LA, Regina Medal, 1974; Lib. of Congs., Disting. Srv. Awd., 1974. **Pubns.:** Comp., *Children and Literature* (1973); Ed., *Children's Literature: A Guide to Reference Sources* (1967, 1972, 1977); *The Travelogue Storybook of the Nineteenth Century* (1949); "Books for America's Children: 1776-1976," *Children's Literature in Education* (Spr. 1978); "Summary and Proposals for the Future," *Lib. Trends* (Spr. 1979); other articles. **Activities:** 2, 4; 26, 37, 39; 95-Chld. Lit. **Addr.:** Children's Literature Center, Library of Congress, Washington, DC 20540.

Havlice, Patricia Pate (F. 2, 1943, Cleveland, OH) Freelnc., 1969–; Sr. Ref. Libn., IN Univ., Gary, 1969–70; Jr. Ref. Libn., OH State Univ., 1967–68; Adult Srvs. Libn., Cuyahoga Cnty. Pub. Lib., 1966–67. **Educ.:** Ursuline Coll. for Women, 1961–65, BA (Eng.); Univ. of MI, 1965–66, MALS. **Pubns.:** *World Painting Index* (1977); *Index to Literary Biography* (1975); *Index to Artistic Biography* (1973). **Activities:** 30, 37, 41 **Addr.:** 1803 Neptune Ln., Houston, TX 77062.

Havlik, Robert James (O. 13, 1925, Chicago, IL) Univ. Engin. Libn., Univ. of Notre Dame, 1980–, Asst. Dir. for Tech. Srvs., 1973–80; Consult., Info. Storage and Retrieval, Auerbach Assoc. Inc., 1972–73; Dir. of Libs., Nova Univ., 1967–72; Resrch. Lib. Spec., US Ofc. of Educ., 1963–67; Tech. Libn., Linde Div. Union Carbide Corp., 1955–63; Asst. Ref. Libn., Purdue Univ., 1953–55; Exch. Libn., Iowa State Coll., 1951–53. **Educ.:** IL Inst. of Tech., 1943–49, BS ChE (Chem. Engin.); Univ. of IL, 1950–51, MSLS; Univ. of South. CA, 1970, Cert. (Info. Sci.). **Orgs.:** SLA: Nom. Com. (1965–66); Resrch. Com. (1974–77); FL Chap., (Ch. 1971–72); West. NY Sect., Bd. of Dirs. (1963); Treas. (1961–63). ALA: ACRL. Abraham Lincoln Grp. of DC: Pres. (1965–67). Buffalo, NY Civil War RT: Pres. (1961–63). **Pubns.:** "Program analysis and planning for a project to complete current library backlogs in a five-year period utilizing the INCOLSA/OCLC Cataloging system" *ACRL SPEC KIT #52* (Mr. 1979); "Abraham Lincoln and the Technology of "Young America,"" *Lincoln Herald* (Spring 1977); Jt. auth., "History and Development of Special Library Standards," *Lib. Trends,* (O., 1972); "Nova University's Libraries, a new approach to education," *FL Libs.* (Mr. 1969); "The Role of Special Libraries in the United States," *Spec. Libs.* (Ap. 1968); Other articles, reviews. **Activities:** 1, 12; 17, 46; 62, 75, 91 **Addr.:** University of Notre Dame Engineering Library, Notre Dame, IN 46556.

Hawbaker, A. Craig (Ap. 8, 1951, Des Moines, IA) Ctrl. Ref. Libn., Bus. and Econ., Univ. of AZ Lib., 1977–; Dir. of User Srvs. and Lib. Lrng. Prog., Kearney State Coll., 1977, Instr. Srvs. Libn., Circ., 1975–77. **Educ.:** Drake Univ., 1969–73, BS (Mktg.); West. MI Univ., 1974–75, MSL. **Orgs.:** ALA. AZ LA. AZ OLUG: Secy.-Treas. (1980–). NE Ctrl. Lib. Network: Treas. (1976–77). **Honors:** Beta Phi Mu. **Pubns.:** *Kearney State College Library Survey* ERIC (1976). **Activities:** 1; 31, 39, 49-Online bibl. srchg.; 56, 59, 92 **Addr.:** Central Reference Department, University of Arizona Library, Tucson, AZ 85721.

Hawes, Grace M. (F. 4, 1926, Cumberland, WI) Arch. Spec., Hoover Inst., Stanford Univ., 1976–. **Educ.:** San Jose St. Univ., 1959–63, BA (LS), 1964–71, MA (Hist.). **Orgs.:** SAA. Socty. of CA Archvsts. Women in Hist. Resrch. **Pubns.:** *The Marshall Plan for China: Economic Cooperation Administration, 1948–1949* (1977). **Activities:** 2; 20, 22, 39; 54, 92 **Addr.:** 410 Sheridan Ave., #220 Palo Alto, CA 94306.

Hawkins, Andrea E. (Ja. 1, 1948, Springfield, MO) Dir., Joplin Pub. Lib., 1979–; Chief, Consult. Srvs. Div., WA State Lib., 1978–79; Coord. of Lib. Resrcs., MO State Lib., 1974–78; Ref. Libn., Springfield-Greene Cnty. Lib., 1972–74; YA Srvs. Libn., Thomas Jefferson Lib. Syst., 1971–72. **Educ.:** American Univ., 1970, BA (Eng.); Univ. of MD, 1970–71, MLS. **Orgs.:** ALA: LAMA/Stats. Sect. (Vice Ch., Ch.-Elect 1979–81); ASCLA/State Lib. Agency Sect. (Ch., 1978–79); LAMA/Staff Dev. Com., (1975–79; Ch. 1978–79). Jefferson City Persnl. Mgt. Assn.: Prog. Com., (1975–76). **Pubns.:** "Role Identity Crisis of the Library Whatchamacallit," *Show-Me Libs.* (D. 1978); "Supervisors – The Weak Link?" *Show-Me Libs.* (Ag. 1977); *A Library Or Information Science Career: What's in it For You?* (1977); Jt. ed., *Staff Development Bibliography,* (1976). **Activities:** 9, 13; 24, 25, 35; 50, 59 **Addr.:** 1526 Connecticut, Joplin, MO 64801.

Hawkins, B. Elizabeth (F. 2, 1942, Vancouver, BC) Spec. Proj. Ofcr., Natl. Lib. of Can., 1976–, Info. Coord., Cat., 1973–76, Chief, Canadiana Acq. Div., 1966–73. **Educ.:** Carleton Univ., 1960–63, BA (Psy.); Univ. of Toronto, 1963–64, BLS, Hons. **Orgs.:** Can. LA. Can. Assn. of Spec. Libs. and Info. Srvs. **Activities:** 1, 4; 17, 34 **Addr.:** National Library of Canada, 395 Wellington St., Ottawa, ON K1A 0N4 Canada.

Hawkins, Jo Anne W. (N. 28, 1938, El Paso, TX) Head Libn., Circ. Srvs. Dept., Univ. of TX, Austin, 1975–, Head Libn., Inter-Lib. Srv., 1973–75, Head Libn., Inter-Lib. Borrowing, Ref. Dept., 1969–73, Ref. Libn., 1967–69. **Educ.:** Univ. of TX, Austin, 1957–60, BSA (Art), 1963–66, MLS. **Orgs.:** ALA: LAMA, Opers. Resrch. Com. (1979–81). TX LA: Coll. and Univ. Lib. Div., Ad Hoc Com. on Acad. Status (Ch., 1978–79). Socty. of Univ. of TX Libns.: Pres. (1974). TX Assn. of Coll. Tchrs. **Pubns.:** Jt. auth., *The Status of Status – The Status of Librarians in Texas Academic Libraries* ERIC (Mr. 1980). **Activities:** 1; 17, 22, 34; 56, 61 **Addr.:** Circulation Services Dept., The General Libraries, P.O. Box P, The University of Texas at Austin, Austin, TX 78712-7330.

Hawkins, John J. (Jl. 16, 1932, Somerville, MA) Head Libn., Bunker Hill Cmnty. Coll., 1973–; Dir. of Libs., Bentley Coll., 1969–73, Asst. Dir. of Lib., 1959–69. **Educ.:** St. John's Coll., 1949–53, AB (Phil.); Simmons Coll., 1957–59, SM (LS); State Coll. at Boston, 1967, MEd (Educ.). **Orgs.:** MA Conf. of Chief Libns. in Pub. Higher Educ. Inst.: Exec. Bd. (1977–78); Secy. (1978–79); VP (1979–80); Pres. (1980–81). Cncl. of Libns./Lrng. Resrc. Dir.: VP (1978–77); Pres. (1977–79). ALA: ACRL, New Eng. Chap. State Adv. Cncl. on Libs. MA Bd. of Reg. Cmnty. Coll.: Task Force on Lrng. Resrc. Stan. (Secy., 1978–81). **Activities:** 1; 17, 31, 32; 63, 72 **Addr.:** Bunker Hill Community College, New Rutherford Ave. & Gilmore Bridge, Boston, MA 02129.

Hawkins, Marilyn E. (O. 21, 1951, Pasco, WA) Pub. Info. Coord., King Cnty. Lib. Syst., 1977–; Prog. Writer, Evergreen Safety Cncl., 1976–77; Pub. Info. Spec., Seattle City Light, 1974–76. **Educ.:** WA State Univ., 1971–73, BA (Hum.); Univ. of WA, 1974–76 (Eng.). **Orgs.:** ALA: PR Srvs. to Libs. Com. (Prog. Ch., 1981); JMRT, Pubcty. Com. (1981). WA LA: PR Forum Com. (1980–). Intl. Assn. of Bus. Comm./Pac. NW. Seattle Women in Advert. Seattle/King Cnty. Mncpl. Leag. **Honors:** 3M/JMRT, Prof. Dev. Grant, 1981; ALA and H.W. Wilson Co., John Cotton Dana Lib. PR Awd., 1980; Intl. Assn. of Bus. Comm., Pacesetter Awds., 1978, 1980. **Pubns.:** "Seattle's Bookmobile Metamorphosis," *Wilson Lib. Bltn.* (Mr. 1980). **Activities:** 9; 28, 36, 40; 51, 55 **Addr.:** King County Library System, 300 - 8th Ave. N., Seattle, WA 98109.

Hawkins, Ronald Arthur (S. 30, 1940, Lincoln, NB) Catlgr./ILL Libn., Untd. Theo. Semy., 1970–; Hum. - Ref. Libn., Univ. of NB, 1968–70. **Educ.:** Phillips Univ., 1959–63, AB (Liberal Arts), 1963–67, M Div (Theo.); Univ. of OK, 1967–68, MLS. **Orgs.:** ATLA. OH Theo. Libns.: Secy. (1976–78). Dayton Miami Valley Cnsrtm.: Exec. Com. (1976–77). Eagles Inc.: Bd. Pres. (1973–75). **Activities:** 1, 12; 16, 20, 34; 55, 56, 90 **Addr.:** 24 Vassar Dr., Dayton, OH 45406.

Haworth, Kent M. (F. 11, 1946, Vancouver, BC) Chief, Audio and Visual Recs. Prog., Prov. Arch. of BC, 1972–. **Educ.:** Univ. of BC, 1964–68, BA (Hist.); Univ. of Victoria, 1973–75, MA (Hist.); Pub. Arch. of Canada Arch. Course. **Orgs.:** Assn. of Can. Archvsts.: Pubn. Com. (1978–79); VP (1979–80); Pres. (1980–81). Assn. of BC Archvsts.: Nsltr. ed. (1977–79). **Pubns.:** "Local Archives: Responsibilities & Challenges for Archivists," *Archivaria* (Win. 1976–77). **Activities:** 2; 17, 23, 36; 62, 75, 78 **Addr.:** Provincial Archives of British Columbia, Victoria, BC V8V 1X4 Canada.

Hay, Charles C., III (N. 12, 1944, Miami, FL) Archvst., East. KY Univ., 1976–; Mss. Cur., Univ. of KY Lib., 1971–76; Instr. in Hist., Madisonville Cmnty. Coll., 1968–69. **Educ.:** FL State Univ., 1965–67, BA (Hist.), Univ. of KY, 1967–71, MA (Hist.). **Orgs.:** SAA: Coll. and Univ. Arch. (1976–). Assn. of Records Man. and Admin.: Nwsltr Ed. (1979–). KY Cncl. on Arch.: Nwsltr Ed. (1978–). Organ. of Amer. Hist. South. Hist. Assn. **Pubns.:** Cont., *Dictionary of American Biography* (1977). **Activities:** 2; 18, 39, 46; 63, 86, 93 **Addr.:** University Archives, Eastern Kentucky University, Richmond, KY 40475.

Haycock, Kenneth R. (F. 15, 1948, Hamilton, ON) Coord., Lib. Srvs., Vancouver Sch. Bd., 1976–; Educ. Consult., Can. Chld. Lit. Proj., Methuen Publshrs., 1975–77; Educ. Media Consult., K–13, Wellington Cnty. ON Bd. of Educ., 1972–76; Head, Lrng. Media Ctr., Colonel By Sec. Sch., Carleton ON Bd. of Educ., 1970–72; Assoc. Tchr., Sch. Libnshp., Fac. of Educ., Queen's Univ., 1970–72; Tchr., Head Libn., Glebe Collegiate Inst., Ottawa ON Bd. of Educ., 1969–70; various tchg. positions. **Educ.:** Univ. of West. ON, 1965–68, BA (Pol. Sci.), 1968–69, Dip. (Educ.); Univ. of Ottawa, 1973, MEd (Fndns.); Univ. of MI, 1974, AMLS; BC Prof. Tchg. Cert., Category 6; ON Tchg. Certs., Permanent HS Cert., Endorsed for Advnc. Class., Permanent Elem. Sch. Tchr. Cert., Stan. 4. **Orgs.:** ALA: AASL (Can. Rep., 1973–75); YASD. ON LA: Sch. Libs. Div., Legis. Action Grp. (Ch., 1975–76). Can. LA: Pres. (1977–78); Bd. of Dirs. (1974–75); Cncl. (1974–81); various ofcs., coms. Can. Sch. LA: Pres. (1974–75); Awds. Jury (Ch., 1975–76); various ofcs., coms. various other orgs. Vancouver Schs. Coord. Assn.: Pres. (1979–80); Treas. (1978–79). Vancouver Cmnty. Coll.: Tchr. Asst. Adv. Com. (1977–80); Lib. Tech. Prog. Adv. Com. (1979–81). Univ. of BC: Musm. of Anthro., Tchr. Adv. Com. (1977–80). ON Sec. Sch. Tchrs. Fed.: Cncl., Dist. 39 (1972–76), Branch 10 (Pres., 1972–76). various other orgs. **Honors:** Can. Sch. LA, Margaret B. Scott Awd. of Merit, 1979; Phi Delta Kappan, Leaders in Educ. Panel, 1981; Gvr.-Gen. of Can., Silver Jubilee Medal, 1977; Univ. of MI Beta Phi Mu Awd., 1976; other hons. **Pubns.:** *Sears List of Subject Headings: Canadian Companion* (1978); *Free Magazines for Teachers and Libraries* (1977); *Security–Secondary School Resource Centres* (1975); *Index to the Contents of Moccasin Telegraph* (1975); *Free Magazines for Teachers and Libraries* (1974); various chaps., pamphlets, articles, sps., rpts., reviews, edshps. **Activities:** 10; 17, 24, 31; 50, 63, 89 **Addr.:** 6871 Shawnigan Pl., Richmond, BC V7E 4W9 Canada.

Haycraft, Howard (Jl. 24, 1905, Madelia, MN) Ch. of Bd., H.W. Wilson Co., 1967–, Pres., 1953–67, VP, 1940–53, Staff, 1929–40; Staff, Univ. of MN Press, 1928–29. **Educ.:** Univ. of MN, 1928, AB. **Orgs.:** ALA: RT on Lib. Srv. to the Blind (Ch., 1968–69). Forest Press: Dir. (1951–68); Pres. (1961–62). Mystery Writers of Amer.: Pres. (1963). US Pres. Com. for Empl. of the Handcpd.: Mem. (1963–74). **Honors:** ALA, Spec. Centennial Cit., 1976; ALA, Francis Joseph Campbell Cit., 1966; Gustavus Adolphus Coll., LHD, 1975; Univ. of MN, Outstand. Achvmt. Awd., 1954. **Pubns.:** *American Authors 1600-1900* (1938);

PROFESSIONAL ACTIVITIES: Institutions: 1. Acad. lib.; 2. Arch.; 3. Assn.; 4. Fed./Gvt. lib.; 5. Inst. lib.; 6. Mfr./Suppl.; 7. Milit. lib.; 8. Musm.; 9. Pub. lib.; 10. Sch. lib.; 11. Sch. of lib. sci.; 12. Spec. lib.; 13. State lib.; 14. (other). **Functions/Activities:** 15. Acq./Col. dev.; 16. Adult srvs.; 17. Admin.; 18. Apprais.; 19. Archit./Bldgs.; 20. Cat./Class.; 21. Chld. srvs.; 22. Circ.; 23. Cons./Pres.; 24. Consult.; 25. Cont. ed.; 26. Educ. lib. sci.; 27. Ext. srvs.; 28. Fund/Grants; 29. Gvt. pubs.; 30. Indx./Abs.; 31. Instr. lib. use; 32. Media srvs.; 33. Micro.; 34. Netwks./Coop.; 35. Persnl.; 36. PR; 37. Publshg.; 38. Recs. mgt.; 39. Ref. srvs.; 40. Repro.; 41. Resrch.; 42. Review.; 43. Secur.; 44. Serials; 45. Spec. col.; 46. Tech. srvs.; 47. Trustees/Bds.; 48. YA srvs.; 49. (other).

Twentieth Century Authors (1942); *British Authors before 1800* (1952); *Books for the Blind* (1972); other ref. bks.; mysteries and detective stories. **Activities:** 6; 37, 39 **Addr.:** 18-01 Meadow Lakes, Hightstown, NJ 08520.*

Hayden, Elizabeth L. (N. 29, 1924, Cecilia, KY) Supvsr. of Pub. Srvs., Lansing Pub. Lib., 1961–; Head Libn., Albion Pub. Lib., 1956–61; Supvsr. of Chld. Work & Ext., Muncie Pub. Lib., 1954–56; Branch Libn., S. Bend Pub. Lib., 1949–54, Branch Asst., 1947–49. **Educ.:** Univ. of KY, 1943–46, AB (Eng. Lit.), 1946–47, BS in LS; Univ. of MI, 1959–61, AM in LS. **Orgs.:** ALA: Cncl. (1974–78); Resol. Com. (1976–77). MI LA: Exec. Bd. (1974–78); Ch., Legis. Com. (1972–73 & 1973–74); Second VP (1971–72); Treas. (1969 & 1970). AAUW: Treas. (1964–66). Delta Kappa Gamma: First VP (1972–73), Treas. (1973–80). Pilot Club: Pres. (1979–80). **Honors:** MI LA: Libn. of the Yr., 1973; Beta Phi Mu. **Activities:** 9; 17, 21, 27; 78, 89 **Addr.:** Lansing Public Library, 401 S. Capitol, Lansing, MI 48914.

Hayden, Florence Marie (D. 10, 1931, Beaumont, TX) Acq. Libn., Sam Houston State Univ., 1970–. **Educ.:** Sam Houston State Univ., 1967–69, BS (Educ.); LA State Univ., 1969–70, MA (LS); TX A&M Univ., 1974–79, PhD (Educ. Admin.). **Orgs.:** TX LA. ALA. Sam Houston Lib. Alum. Assn. Phi Delta Kappa. AAUP. AAUW. TX Assn. of Coll. Tchrs.: State Secy.–Treas. (1980–81). **Activities:** 1, 11; 15, 17, 26; 63, 75, 92 **Addr.:** 115 Willow Bend, Huntsville, TX 77340.

Hayes, Florence C. (Ag. 8, 1928, Hermosa Beach, CA) Assoc. Serials Libn., Cornell CONSER Proj. Dir., Cornell Univ. Libs., 1975–, Serials Catlgr., Mann Lib., 1974–75, Gifts and Exch./Serials Libn., 1971–74. **Educ.:** Pomona Coll., 1945–49, BA (Span.); Syracuse Univ., 1969–70, MS (LS). **Orgs.:** ALA: RTSD/Serials Sect., Policy and Resrch. Com. (1981–); ACRL. **Honors:** Phi Beta Kappa. **Activities:** 1; 20, 44, 46 **Addr.:** Serials Dept., Cornell University Libraries, Ithaca, NY 14853.

Hayes, Franklin D. (Mr. 31, 1946, Florence, AL) Pers. Libn., Harding Univ., 1975–; Libn., Freed-Hardeman Coll., 1973–75. **Educ.:** Florence State Univ., 1972, BS (Hist.); George Peabody Coll., 1972–73, MLS (Acad. Libs.). **Orgs.:** AR LA: Constn. Com. (1980–81). **Activities:** 1; 44 **Addr.:** 14 Mohawk Dr., Searcy, AR 72143.

Hayes, Hazel S. (Mr. 13, 1896, Clinton, IN) Retired, 1975–; Med. Libn. and Consult., Ingalls Meml. Hosp., 1968–75; Dir., Allegan Pub. Lib., 1967–68; Dir., Herrick Pub. Lib., 1953–66; Head Libn., Clinton Pub. Lib., 1946–53; Tchg., Bus., 1914–44. **Educ.:** IN State Tchrs. Coll., 1946–53, BA (Eng.); Univ. of IL, 1952–53, MSLS. **Orgs.:** MI LA: Treas. (1958–60). MI State Lib.: Adv. Com. (1959–61). ALA. Various orgs. **Honors:** MI LA, Libn. of Yr., 1967. **Addr.:** 69 Park, Apt. 202, Park Forest, IL 60466.

Hayes, L. Susan (D. 6, 1948, Ypsilanti, MI) Info. Spec., Gould Inc., S.E.L. Comp. Systs. Div., 1977–; Ref. Libn., FL Atl. Univ., 1973–77. **Educ.:** Albion Coll., 1970, BA (Grmn.); Wayne State Univ., 1972, MSLS. **Orgs.:** SLA: FL Chap. (Pres., 1977–78). ASIS. Broward Cnty. LA: Treas. (1979–80). FL LA. **Pubns.:** "The Reference Interview for Online Searching," *Bltn. FL SLA* (O. 1980). **Activities:** 12; 17, 39, 46; 56, 64 **Addr.:** Gould Inc., S.E.L. Computer Systems Div., 6901 W. Sunrise Blvd., Ft. Lauderdale, FL 33313.

Hayes, Robert M. (D. 3, 1926, New York, NY) Dean, Grad. Sch. of Lib. and Info. Sci., Univ. of CA, Los Angeles, 1975–, Prof., 1964–75, Dir., Inst. of Lib. Resrch., 1966–70; VP, Sci. Dir. and Pres. of the Advanced Info. Syst. Co., 1959–64. **Educ.:** Univ. of CA, Los Angeles, 1947, BA (Math.), 1949, MA (Math.), 1952, PhD (Math.). **Orgs.:** ASIS: Pres. (1967–68). ALA: ISAD (Pres., 1968–69, 1969–70). AAAS: VP (1969–70); Sect. T (Ch., 1970–71). Amer. Documen. Inst.: Pres. (1962–63). Assn. for Comput. Mach.: Assoc. Ed., Jnl. (1960–70). Sigma Xi. **Honors:** U.S. Natl. Com. Intl. Fed. for Documtn., Member; Assn. for Comp. Mach., ACM Lect., 1967–68; ASIS, Disting. Lectr., 1968–69; Univ. of IL, Windsor Lectr., 1968–69; Phi Beta Kappa. **Pubns.:** Jt. auth., *Information Storage and Retrieval: Tools, Elements, Theories* (1963); Jt. auth., *Handbook of Data Processing for Libraries* (1970, 1975). **Activities:** 11; 26; 75 **Addr.:** University of California-Los Angeles, 405 Hilgard Ave., Los Angeles, CA 90024.

Hayes, Sherman L. (Ag. 4, 1948, Fowler, KS) Asst. to the Dir., Chester Fritz Lib., Univ. of ND, 1977–; Admin. Coord., Atlanta Pub. Lib., 1976–77; Asst. to the Dir., Kalamazoo Pub. Lib., 1973–76; Libn., IN Vo Tech Coll., Columbus, 1971–73. **Educ.:** Univ. of IA, 1966–70, BA (Hist.); IN Univ., 1970–71, MLS; West. MI Univ., 1973–75, MBA (Mgt.). **Orgs.:** ALA: LAMA, LOMS Budgeting, Acct. & Costs Com. (Ch., 1976–78); LOMS, Insr. for Libs. Com. (Ch., 1979–). **Honors:** Phi Beta Mu, 1971; Betta Gamma Sigma, 1975. **Pubns.:** *Primer of Business Terms Related to Libraries* (1978); Ed., *Library Budgets - A Collection* (1977). **Activities:** 1; 17 **Addr.:** Chester Fritz Library, University of North Dakota, Grand Forks, ND 58202.

Hayes, William F. (D. 25, 1931, Brazil, IN) Dir., Boise Pub. Lib., 1966–; Asst. Dir., Kokomo (IN) Pub. Lib., 1965–66, Head, Tech. Prcs., 1963–65. **Educ.:** KS State Coll., 1962; Univ. of Denver, 1963. **Orgs.:** ALA: Cncl. (1971–76). Pac. NW LA: Pres. (1980–81). ID LA. Miss ID Schol. Pageant. Boise Lions Club. **Activities:** 9; 17 **Addr.:** Boise Public Library, 715 S. Capitol Blvd., Boise, ID 83702.

Hayko, Mary (Ag. 23, 1952, Pittston, PA) Mgr., Non-Jnl. Oper., Inst. for Sci. Info., 1980–; Libn., MERIT Ctr., Temple Univ., 1977–80; Libn., Frgn. Lang. Ofc., Philadelphia Sch. Dist., 1976–77. **Educ.:** SUNY, Binghamton, 1970–74, BA (Span., Art Hist.); Rutgers Univ., 1974–75, MLS; Univ. of Madrid, 1972. **Orgs.:** ASIS. SLA. Natl. Org. for Women. **Honors:** Phi Beta Kappa, 1974. **Activities:** 6; 17, 30; 75 **Addr.:** Non-Journal Operations, Institute for Scientific Information, 3501 Market St., Philadelphia, PA 19104.

Haymond, Jay M. (O. 11, 1933, Cedar City, UT) Coord. of Col. & Resrch., UT State Hist. Socty., 1971–; Assoc. Prof. of Hist., Dixie Coll., 1965–69. **Educ.:** Brigham Young Univ., 1951–64, BSMS (Hist.); Univ. of UT, 1969–71, PhD (Hist.). **Orgs.:** SAA: Oral Hist. (1975–79); Local Arrang. (Ch. 1977). Conf. of Intermountain Archvsts.: Cncl. (Ch. 1973–80). UT LA: Histn. (1976–77); PR (1979–80). Forest Hist. Socty.: Awd. Com. (1978). Mormon Hist. Assn.: Awd. Com. (1976). **Honors:** State of UT, Outstan. Pub. Emp., 1977. **Pubns.:** Contrib. Ed., *Fabulous Gold and Where To Find It* (1975); "Oral History," *Genealogical Jnl.* (S. 1977); "Natural Resources in Emery County" in *Emery County - Reflections on It's Past and Future* (1979); "Bear River," and "Sevier River," *Rolling Rivers* (1980). **Activities:** 2, 14-St. Hist. Socty.; 17; 73, 85 **Addr.:** Utah State Historical Society, 300 Rio Grande, Salt Lake City, UT 84101.

Haynes, Donald (O. 8, 1934, Fieldale, VA) State Libn., VA State Lib., 1972–, Dir., Lib. Srvs., 1969–72; Libn., Asst. Prof., Univ. of VA, Wallops Island, 1966–69; Mss. and Ref. Asst., Univ. of VA, Charlottesville, 1963–65; Tchr., VA pub. schs., 1960–62. **Educ.:** Univ. of VA, 1960, BA; Univ. of NC, 1966, MLS. **Orgs.:** ALA. COSLA. VA LA. SELA. Other orgs. VA Hist. Recs. Adv. Bd.: Ch. (1976–). VA Hist. Landmarks Comsn. Ctrl. VA Educ. TV: Bd. (1972–). VA Hist. Socty. **Honors:** Beta Phi Mu. **Pubns.:** Ed., *Virginiana in the Printed Book Collections of the Virginia State Library* (1975). **Activities:** 13 **Addr.:** Virginia State Library, Richmond, VA 23219.*

Haynes, Jean E. (Je. 18, 1924, Wellsville, NY) AV and Adult Srvs. Consult., Chautauqua-Cattaraugus Lib. Syst., 1966–; Adult Srvs. Libn., Brooklyn Pub. Lib., 1962–66. **Educ.:** OH State Univ., 1943–48, BA (Soclgy.); Columbia Univ., 1961–62, MS (LS). **Orgs.:** ALA. NY LA: Film/Video RT (Pres. 1977, Exec. Com. (1979–80), Secy. 1979–80). Film Lib. Info. Cncl. NY State Cncl. on the Arts: Film Panel (1976, 1977, 1978). **Pubns.:** "Film Service To The Elderly," *Lib. Trends* (Sum. 1978); "Freedom To View," *The Bookmark* (Fall 1977). **Addr.:** Chautauqua-Cattaraugus Library System, 106 West 5th St., Jamestown, NY 14701.

Haynes, Robert Vaughn (N. 28, 1929, Nashville, TN) Dir. of Libs., Univ. of Houston Ctrl. Campus, 1977–, Interim Dir., 1976–77, Prof. of Hist., 1967–, Actg. Dir., Afro-Amer. Std., 1969–71, Visit. Prof., Black Std. Consult., Univ. of AL, 1970; Dir., Inst. of Cultural Understanding, 1971. **Educ.:** Millsaps Coll., 1952, BA (Hist.); Peabody Coll., 1953, MA (Hist.); Rice Univ., 1959, PhD (Hist.). **Orgs.:** ALA. TX LA. SWLA. Amer. Hist. Assn. Org. of Amer. Histns. South. Hist. Assn. Amer. Std. Assn. Other orgs. **Honors:** Danforth Assoc., 1969. **Pubns.:** *A Night of Violence: The Houston Mutiny and Riot of 1917* (1976); *The Natchez District and the American Revolution* (1976); *Blacks in White America Before 1865* (1972); "Life on the Early Mississippi Frontier: The Case of Matthew Phelps," *Jnl. of MS Hist.* (F. 1977); "American Blacks," *Muslim Peoples: A World Ethnographic Survey* (1978); other articles, reviews. **Activities:** 1; 17; 55 **Addr.:** 2010 Banks, Houston, TX 77098.

Haynie, Altie Virginia (N. 28, 1949, Prattville, AL) Head Cat. Libn., Pan Amer. Univ., 1977–, Cat. Libn., 1973–77. **Educ.:** Univ. of Montevallo, 1968–72, BA (Eng.); George Peabody Coll., 1972–73, MLS. **Orgs.:** ALA. TX LA: Cont. Ed. Com. (1979–81). SW LA: Ad Hoc Com. on Mex. Projs. (1976–). Valley LA. Hidalgo Cnty. Hist. Socty. Valley African Violet Socty. **Pubns.:** Cmplr., *Nuestras bibliotecas son sus bibliotecas* (1979). **Activities:** 1; 20; 95-Photography. **Addr.:** 202 Montevideo, Apt. 2, Edinburg, TX 78539.

Hays, Carl H. (Ap. 11, 1938, Des Moines, IA) Assoc. Dir. for Tech. and Autom. Srvs., University of MD, 1977–; Asst. Dir. for Tech. Srvs., IN Univ. Reg. Campus Libs., 1969–77; Ref. Libn., Wayne State Coll., 1964–68. **Educ.:** Univ. of North. IA, 1955–61, AB (Elem. Educ.); Univ. of Denver, 1963–64, AM (LS); Univ. of WI, 1968–69, Spec Cert (LS). **Orgs.:** ALA. **Activities:** 1; 17, 46 **Addr.:** Rm. 1106 McKeldin Library, University of MD College Park, College Park, MD 20742.

Hays, Dick W. (O. 7, 1933, Holtville, CA) Deputy Asst. Secy., Ofc. of Libs. and Lrng. Tech., Dept. of Educ., 1980–; Assoc. Deputy Comsnr., Bur. of Elem. and Sec. Educ., Ofc. of Educ., 1975–76, Assoc. Comsnr., Ofc. of Libs. and Lrng. Resrcs., 1973–79, Asst. Comsnr. for Spec. Concerns, 1970–73. **Educ.:** Univ. of Redlands, 1953–56, BA; Univ. of CA, Los Angeles, 1958–59, MPA; MI State Univ., 1960–61, Adv. Grad. Std.; Univ. of CA, 1961–62, Doct. prog. Amer. Pol. Sci. Assn. Amer. Socty. for Pub. Admin. **Pubns.:** "The Governance of Library Networks' Reactions," *The Structure and Governance of Library Networks* (1979); "The Federal Government and the Library Trustee," *Library Trustee* (1978). **Activities:** 4; 17, 28; 63, 78 **Addr.:** Education Department, 400 Maryland Ave., S.W., Room 3600, ROB-3, Washington, DC 20202.

Hays, Joy K. (Ja. 29, 1929, St. Louis, MO) Libn., Shelby (NC) HS 1979–; Media Coord., Cleveland Cnty. Tech. Inst., 1975–76; Ref. Libn., Gardner-Webb Coll., 1973–75; Libn., San Juan Sch. (PR), 1966–69. **Educ.:** N. West. Univ., 1947–50, BS (Sp.); Drexel Univ., 1967–73, MSLS. **Orgs.:** NC LA: Schol. Com. (1974–). ALA. SELA. Phi Delta Kappa. **Activities:** 1, 10; 15, 17, 39 **Addr.:** 205 Lakewood Dr., Rt 3, Kings Mountain, NC 28086.

Hays, Mary J. (Mr. 28, 1946, Oakland, CA) Libn., Cooley, Godward, Castro, Huddleson and Tatum, 1979–; Libn., Brobeck, Phleger and Harrison, 1972–79. **Educ.:** Univ. of San Francisco, 1964–68, BA (Fr.). **Orgs.:** SLA. AALL. North. CA Assn. of Law Libs.: Nom. Com. (Ch., 1981–82). **Activities:** 12; 15, 17, 39; 77 **Addr.:** Cooley, Godward, Castro, Huddleson & Tatum, 1 Maritime Plz., 20th Floor, San Francisco, CA 94111.

Haythorn, Joseph Denny (Mr. 16, 1947, Chicago, IL) Law Libn. & Assoc. Prof of Law, Whittier Coll. Sch. of Law, 1976–; Ref. Law Libn., Univ. of Puget Sound Sch. of Law, 1975–76; Ref. Law Libn., Univ. of Denver, 1976. **Educ.:** DePauw Univ., 1965–69, BA (Hist.); Univ. of Puget Sound, 1973–75, JD (Law); Univ. of WA, 1975–76, MLL (Libnshp.); Chapman Coll., 1971–73, MA (Hist.). **Orgs.:** AALL: various coms. South. CA Assn of Law Libns.: Ch., Place. WA LA. WA State Bar. Amer. Bar Assn. **Activities:** 1, 12; 17, 39; 77, 78 **Addr.:** 5353 West Third St., Los Angeles, CA 90020.

Hayton, E. Elise (O. 14, 1944, Montreal, PQ) Coord. of Circ. Srvs., McMaster Univ., 1977–, Bus. Libn., 1973–77; Asst. Libn., Imperial Oil Ltd., 1970–71. **Educ.:** McGill Univ., 1961–65, BSC (Bio.); Univ. of Toronto, 1971–73, MLS. **Orgs.:** Can. LA. ON LA: Ed., *OCULA Cncl. Nsltr.* (1978–); OCULA Cnclr. (1980–82). SLA. **Honors:** SLA, Toronto Chap., Kathleen Reeves Meml. Prize, 1973. **Activities:** 1, 12; 17, 22, 34; 56, 59 **Addr.:** Mills Memorial Library, McMaster University, Hamilton, ON L8S 4L6 Canada.

Hayum, Renate (Ja. 29, 1930, Tübingen, Germany) Actg. Managing Libn. II, Quick Info. Ctr./Pers., Seattle Pub. Lib., 1981–, Sr. Asst. Managing Libn., 1967–81. **Educ.:** Reed Coll., Univ. of WA, 1948–1952, BA (Bus. Admin.), 1966–68, MS (Libnshp.). **Orgs.:** ALA. Pac. NW LA: NW Bibl. Com. (1970–74). WA LA. **Activities:** 9; 16, 17, 39; 56, 75, 92 **Addr.:** 1405 East John St. #6, Seattle, WA 98112.

Hayward, Edward Beardsley (Ja. 21, 1916, Rutland, VT) Dir., Hammond Pub. Lib., 1954–; Asst. Libn., Racine Pub. Lib., 1948–54. **Educ.:** Middlebury Coll., 1934–38, AB (Lit.), 1938–39, MA (Lit.); Univ. of IL, 1946–47, BLS. **Orgs.:** ALA. IN LA: Pres. (1966). IN Coop. Lib. Srvs. Athrty.: Pres. (1979–80). Hammond Hist. Socty.: Pres. (1962). **Pubns.:** *Hammond Indiana's American Bicentennial Yearbook* (1976). **Activities:** 9; 17; 50, 55 **Addr.:** Hammond Public Library, 564 State St., Hammond, IN 46320.

Hayward, Olga Hines (Alexandria, LA) Prof. of LS, Ref. Libn., South. Univ., 1980–, Soc. Sci. Libn., 1973–79, Ref. Libn., 1948–73; Branch Libn., New Orleans Pub. Lib. Syst., 1947–48; Head Libn., Grambling Coll., 1944–46. **Educ.:** Dillard Univ., 1937–41, AB (Soc. Sci.); Atlanta Univ., 1943–44, BS (LS); Univ. of MI, 1953–59, MA (LS); LA State Univ., 1975–77, MA (Hist.). **Orgs.:** SLA: LA Chap., Pres. (1978–79), Secy., Treas. (1975–76). LA LA. ALA. LA Episcopal Diocese Cmnty. Srv.: Bd. (1972–78). **Pubns.:** *A Bibliography of Southern University Graduate Theses, 1959-1971* (1972); "Special Libraries in Louisiana," *Bltn. LA LA* (Sum. 1979); "Bibliography of Works By and About Whitney Moore Young," *Bltn. of Bibl.* (Jl. 1974). **Activities:** 1; 31, 34, 39; 92 **Addr.:** 1632 Harding Blvd., Baton Rouge, LA 70807.

Hazeltine, Robert Earl (My. 30, 1916, Fremont, OH) Retired, 1979–; Dir., Ashtabula Cnty. Dist. Lib., 1966–79; Dir., Portsmouth (OH) Pub. Lib., 1960–66; Head, Tech. Prcs., Canton (OH) Pub. Lib., 1955–60; Catlgr., Bowling Green State Univ., 1950–55. **Educ.:** Univ. of Akron, 1946–49, AB (Eng.); Case West. Resrv. Univ., 1949–50, MSLS; Wayne State Univ., Inst. on Lib. Bldgs., 1968; Miami Univ., Exec. Dev. Prog. for Lib. Admin., 1970. **Orgs.:** ALA: State Rep., Rcrt. Com. (1964–69). OH LA: Rcrt. Com. (Ch., 1964–66). North. OH Catlgrs.: Ch. (1955–56). Northeast. OH LA: Pres. (1973–75). Ashtabula Area Dev. Assn.: Bd. of Trustees (1969–). Kiwanis. **Pubns.:** Reviews. **Activities:** 1, 9; 15, 17, 20 **Addr.:** 811 Myrtle Ave., Ashtabula, OH 44004.

Healey, James S. (Jl. 14, 1931, Chicago, IL) Prof., LS, Dir., Sch. of LS, Univ. of OK, 1975–; Assoc. Prof., LS, Univ. of RI, 1968–75; Chief, Div. of Ext. Srvs., RI Dept. of Lib. Srvs., 1967–68; City Libn., New Bedford, MA, 1961–67. **Educ.:** Stonehill Coll., 1950–55, AB (Eng.); Simmons Coll., 1955–58, MS

Special Subjects/Services: 50. Adult educ.; 51. Advert./Mktg.; 52. Aerosp.; 53. Agric.; 54. Area std.; 55. Arts/Hum.; 56. Autom.; 57. Bibl./Prtg.; 58. Bio. sci.; 59. Bus./Fin.; 60. Chem.; 61. Copyrt.; 62. Documtn.; 63. Educ.; 64. Engin.; 65. Env.; 66. Eth. grps.; 67. Film; 68. Food/Nutr.; 69. Geneal.; 70. Geo.; 71. Geol.; 72. Handcpd.; 73. Hist.; 74. Int. frdm.; 75. Info. sci.; 76. Insr.; 77. Law; 78. Legis.; 79. Math./Comp. sci.; 80. Med.; 81. Metals; 82. Nat. resrcs.; 83. Newsp.; 84. Nuc. sci.; 85. Oral hist.; 86. Petr./Energy; 87. Pharm.; 88. Phys./Astr./Math.; 89. Readg.; 90. Relig.; 91. Sci./Tech.; 92. Soc. sci.; 93. Telecom.; 94. Transp.; 95. (other).

(LS); Columbia Univ., 1969–73, DLS. **Orgs.:** ALA. SWLA. OK LA. AALS. **Honors:** AALS, Resrch. Awd., 1979; OK LA, Cert. of Apprec., 1979; RI LA, Cert. of Apprec., 1975. **Pubns.:** *John E. Fogarty: Political Leadership for Library Development* (1974); "Accreditation from the Other Side," *Jnl. of Educ. for Libnshp.* (F., 1981); "Research and the *reader's guide*," *Serials Libn.* (Ja. 1978); "John E. Fogarty," "William E. Foster," *Dictionary of American Library Biography* (1977); "Invitation to a Smoke-Filled Room," *Wilson Lib. Bltn.* (My., 1975); other articles. **Activities:** 11; 17, 26, 34 **Addr.:** School of Library Science, University of Oklahoma, Norman, OK 73019.

Healy, Sr. Frances Dir., Hlth. Sci. Lib., Providence Hosp., 1973–; Asst. Libn., St. Joseph Coll., Emmitsburg, MD, 1966–73; Dir. of Nursing, Sacred Heart Hosp., Cumberland, MD, 1964–65; Asst. Dir. of Nursing, Providence Hosp., Detroit, MI, 1960–64. **Educ.:** Cath. Univ., 1944, BS in N (Nursing), 1946, MSNE (Nurs. Educ.), 1967, MSLS; RN, 1944; Cert. Hlth. Sci. Libn., 1975–. **Orgs.:** ALA: AASL Leg. Com. (1981–82). SLA. Med. LA. Libn. Div. of Hosp. Cncl., Natl. Capital Area: ch. (1979). **Pubns.:** *A Check-list of Rochester, N.Y. Imprints for the Years 1855–58, With a Historical Introduction* (1966); *A Study of the Cost of Educating a Student in a Basic Professional Degree Program in Nursing* (1945). **Activities:** 5; 17, 34; 80 **Addr.:** 1150 Varnum St., N.E., Washington, DC 20017.

Heaney, Ellen (Je. 6, 1949, Regina, SK) Head, Chld. Dept., New Westminster Pub. Lib., 1974–; Chld. Libn., Vancouver Pub. Lib., 1972–74. **Educ.:** Univ. of SK, Regina, 1966–70, BA (Fr.); Univ. of AL, 1971–72, BLS; Univ. of SK, 1970, Biling. Dipl. **Orgs.:** Can. LA: Can. Assn. of Chld. Libns. (Ch., 1978–79). BC LA: Rec. Secy. (1980–81). Soroptimist Intl. of New Westminster. Vagabond Players. **Honors:** LA of AB, Pub. Libs. Awd., 1972. **Pubns.:** Reviews. **Activities:** 9; 15, 21, 48 **Addr.:** New Westminster Public Library, 716 Sixth Ave., New Westminster, BC V3M 2B3 Canada.

Heaney, Howell J. (Jl. 7, 1917, Beacon, NY) Rare Bk. Libn., Free Lib. of Philadelphia, 1971–; Adjunct Prof., Sch. of Lib. and Info. Sci., Drexel Univ., 1962–; Bibl., Rare Bk. Dept., Free Lib. of Philadelphia, 1955–71; Libn., Private Lib. of Thomas W. Streeter, 1947–55; Ref. Libn., Univ. of NH, 1946–47, Order Libn., 1942. **Educ.:** Cornell Univ., 1935–39, AB (Govt.), 1938–40 (Law), 1940–41, MA (Comp Lit.): Columbia Univ., 1941–42, BS (LS). **Orgs.:** ALA: ACRL, Secty., Rare Bk. Sect., Assn. Coll. and Resrch. Libs., (1967–68); Ch., Nom. Com., (1972–73). AALS. Bibli. Socty. Bibli. Socty. of Amer., Pub. Com., (1969–75). PA LA. Amer. Antiquarian Socty. Grolier Club. Philobiblon Club: Secy. (1966–78), VP (1978). **Honors:** Phi Beta Kappa, 1938. **Pubns.:** *The Pennsylvania German Fraktur of The Free Library of Philadelphia* (1976); "A Century of Early American Children's Books in German, 1738–1837," *Phaedrus* (1979); "Thomas W. Streeter, Collector, 1883–1965," *Papers of the Bibl. Socty. of Amer.* (1971); other articles. **Activities:** 9, 11; 45 **Addr.:** 341 W. Mt. Airy Ave., Philadelphia, PA 19119.

Heanue, Anne A. (Fe. 7, 1940, Fort Oglethorpe, GA) Asst. to the Dir., Washington Office, ALA 1979–; Libn., Deloitte Haskins & Sells, 1977–79. **Educ.:** Dunbarton Coll. of Holy Cross, 1959–62, BA (Hist.); Georgetown Univ., 1964–66, MA (Hist.); Catholic Univ., 1974–76, MSLS. **Orgs.:** ALA. ASIS. SLA. Law Libns. Socty., Washington, DC. Alexandria VA Spec. Educ. Adv. Com.: Ch., (1978–79). Alexandria VA League of Women Voters: Bd. of Dir., (1966–78). **Honors:** Pi Gamma Mu 1962; Beta Phi Mu, 1976. **Activities:** 12; 17, 34, 39; 59, 72, 77 **Addr.:** Assistant to the Director, Washington Office, American Library Association, 110 Maryland Ave., N.E., Washington, DC 20002.

Heaphy, MaryAnne (Mr. 7, 1944, Syracuse, NY) Dir., Baldwinsville Pub. Lib., 1980–; Dir., Solvay Pub. Lib., 1979–80; Dir., Marcellus Free Lib., 1976–79. **Educ.:** LeMoyne Coll., 1963–66, BA, magna cum laude (Soviet Area Std.); Syracuse Univ., 1977, MLS; various courses. **Orgs.:** ALA: PLA/Small-Med. Size Libs. Sect. ALTA, Pubcty. Com. (1979–81), Persnl. Policies/Practices Task Force (1980–81). NY LA: Pub. Lib. Sect., Small Libs. Com. (Ch., 1980–81). Libns. Unlimited of Onondaga Cnty. **Pubns.:** Contrib., *American Reference Books Annual* (1980–); Contrib., *Pub. Lib. Trustee* (1979–); Contrib., NY LA BLTN. **Activities:** 9; 17, 36, 47 **Addr.:** Baldwinsville Public Library, 43 Oswego St., Baldwinsville, NY 13027.

Heaps, Irene D. (Ag. 25, 1921, School Cnty., PA) Libn., Hershey Pub. Lib., 1946–; Asst. Ref., Reading Pub. Lib., 1945–46; Libn., Monongahela Pub. Lib., 1943–44. **Educ.:** Kutztown State Coll., 1939–43, BS (LS); Albright Coll., 1945. **Orgs.:** Frnds. of the Hershey Pub. Lib.: Secy. (1963–81). PA LA: S. Ctrl. Chap. (Secy., 1977). ALA. Hershey Bus. and Prof. Women. **Activities:** 9; 16, 22, 36; 63, 65, 90 **Addr.:** 671 S. Harrison St., Palmyra, PA 17078.

Heard, Frances Schouler (D. 5, 1909, Elkton, MD) Trustee, Panhandle Reg. Lib. Syst., 1977–; Trustee, Kootenai Cnty. Free Lib. Dist., 1976–; various positions teaching Eng. in Univ. **Educ.:** Wellesley Coll. 1926–30, BA (Eng.); Johns Hopkins Univ. 1932–35, PhD (Eng.). **Orgs.:** ID LA: Legis. Com. (1979–). ALA. Natl. Citizens. Pub. Libs. Leag. Women Voters: St. Educ. (Ch. 1970–72). AAUW ID Hist. Socty. East. WA Geneal. Socty. **Honors:** WHCOLIS, ID Del., 1979; ID Gvr's. Conf., Plng. Com., 1978. **Pubns.:** Ed., *Queen Anne's County, MD* (1950); "Did Thomas Warton Borrow from Himself," *Mod. Lang. Notes* (1936); "Notes on 18th Century Dramas," *Mod. Lang. Notes* (1937); Various other articles. **Activities:** 9; 47 **Addr.:** Route 3 Box 41, Hayden Lake, ID 83835.

Hearder-Moan, Wendy P. (Je. 16, 1947, Hamilton, ON) Libn./Exec. Secy., Hamilton Law Assn., 1979–; Libn./Admin., Middlesex Law Assn., 1978–79. **Educ.:** McMaster Univ., 1965–69, BA (Fr., Eng.); Univ. de Montpellier, 1969–71, L.és L (Fr.); McMaster Univ., 1971–73, MA (Fr.); Univ. of West. ON, 1976–77, MLS. **Orgs.:** Can. LA. ON LA: Ch. (1979); Gvt. Pubs. Com. (1978–). Can. ALL. **Pubns.:** "Canadian Librarians and Access to Government Information," *Can. Lib. Jnl.* (D. 1977). **Activities:** 12; 17, 29, 39; 74, 77, 78 **Addr.:** Hamilton Law Association, 50 Main St. E., Hamilton, ON L8N 1E9 Canada.

Hearne, Betsy G. (O. 6, 1942, Wilsonville, AL) Ed., Chld. Bks., *Booklist*, ALA, 1973–; Instr., Chld. lit., Univ. of IL, Chicago, 1970–71; Reviewer, Chld. Bks., *Booklist*. ALA, 1968–69; Chld. Libn., Univ. of Chicago Lab. Schs., 1967–68; Chld. Libn., Wayne Cnty. Pub. Lib., 1964–65. **Educ.:** Coll. of Wooster, 1960–64, BA (Hist.); Univ. of Chicago, 1965–68, MA (LS), 1979–, Doct. in Progress. **Orgs.:** ALA: Notable Bks. Com., Consult.; Newbery - Caldecott Awd. Com.; Mildred Batchelder Com. (1973–77). Chld. Readg. RT. **Honors:** Judge, Natl. Bk. Awds. (1975); ALA, Agnes Sayer Klein Awd. for Grad. Std., (1979). **Pubns.:** *Choosing Books for Children: A Commonsense Guide* (1980); *Home* (1977); *South Star* (1979); "A Reviewer's Story," *Lib. Qtly.* (Ja. 1981); "The American Connection," *Signal* (Ja. 1980); various reviews, eds. **Activities:** 9, 10; 21, 37; 63, 74, 89 **Addr.:** American Library Association, 50 E. Huron St., Chicago, IL 60611.

Hearne, Mary Glenn (D. 11, 1927, Athens, AL) Supvsg. Libn., Nashville Room, Pub. Lib. of Nashville/Davidson Cnty., 1966–; Tchr./Libn., Phelps Sch., Malvern, PA, 1958–65; Libn., David Lipscomb Coll., 1951–58. **Educ.:** Florence State Tchrs. Coll., 1945–46; Univ. of AL, 1946–48, BS (Hist.), 1948–49, MA (Hist.); George Peabody Coll., 1951–52, MALS, 1973–74, EdS (LS). **Orgs.:** Nashville Lib. Club: Pres. (1977–78). Mid-State LA: Exec. Com. (1970's). TN LA: Treas. (1980–81). Women's Natl. Book Assn.: Pres. (1980–82). TN Hist. Socty: VP (1979–81). Inter-Musm. Cncl. of Nashville. **Honors:** Beta Phi Mu. **Pubns.:** Jt. auth., *Authors Of Nashville And Davidson County* (1974); *Nashville Authors* (1973); Ed., *Paragraphs from Nashville History* (1972–1978); Reviews. **Activities:** 9, 12; 36, 37, 45; 57, 69, 86 **Addr.:** 3838 Granny White Pike, Nashville, TN 37204.

Heath, Susan L. (Jl. 13, 1943, Flint, MI) Ref., Col. Dev. Libn. Nicolet Coll., 1971–; Dir.-Criminal Justice Ref. and Info. Ctr., Univ. of WI Law Sch., 1969–71; Ref. Libn., and Bus. Sci. Div., Madison Pub. Lib., 1967–69; Circ., ILL Libn., Univ. of MI Law Lib., 1966–67. **Educ.:** Univ. of MI, 1961–65, BA (Amer. Stud.); 1965–66, MA (LS). **Orgs.:** ALA: Int. Frdm. Com. (1979–83). WI LA: Int. Frdm. Com. (Ch., 1976–79); Nom. Com. (Ch., 1979); Assn. Acad. Lib. Div., Secy., Treas. (1978, Ch. elect, 1980; ch., 1981); Exec. Bd. (1980–81). WI Int. Frdm. Coal.: Pres. (1978–80). Rhinelander Pub. Lib.: Bd. of Trustees (1973–1977). **Pubns.:** Jt. Ed., *Intellectual Freedom: Guidelines to help protect the free access to information* (1979). **Activities:** 1; 15, 39, 45; 74, 95-Women's Studies. **Addr.:** Nicolet College - Learning Resources Center, Lake Julia Campus, Rhinelander, WI 54501.

Heathfield, Cynthia A. (Ap. 2, 1951, Detroit, MI) Chief Libn., Vets. Admin. Med. Ctr., San Francisco, CA, 1981–; Med. Libn., 1977–81; Med. Libn., Vets. Admin. Med. Ctr., Hampton, VA, 1976–77; Med. Libn., Hampton Inst. Sch. of Nursing, 1976–77. **Educ.:** Univ. of S. FL, 1969–73, BA (Interdisciplinary Soc. Sci.); 1974–76, MA (LS); Med. LA, 1976, Cert. **Orgs.:** Med. LA. Vets. Admin. Lib. Netwk.: Task Frc. on Lib. Staffing (1980). **Activities:** 4, 12; 15, 34, 39; 80 **Addr.:** 3215 Clement St. #102, San Francisco, CA 94121.

Heaton, Gwynneth T. (Toronto, ON) Head, Sci. and Med. Lib., Univ. of Toronto, 1970–; Head of Acq., SUNY, Binghamton, 1967–70, Asst. to Dir., 1966–67; Acq. Libn., Jackson Lib. of Bus., Stanford Univ., 1961–66. **Educ.:** Univ. of Toronto, 1955–59, BA (Hist.), 1959–60, BLS, 1974, MLS. **Orgs.:** ON LA. Can. LA. Can. Hlth. Libs. Assn. Can. Assn. for Info. Sci. Other orgs. Assn. of Can. Med. Coll.: Spec. Resrcs. Com. for Med. Sch. Libs. (Ch., 1980–82). **Honors:** Beta Phi Mu. **Pubns.:** "Weeding gun," *OH Media Spectrum* (My. 1980); ""Gun" Eases Weeding," *Feliciter* (F. 1980); "Computers and Acquisitions," *Lib. Resrcs. and Tech. Srvs.* (Sum. 1970). **Activities:** 1; 17; 80, 91 **Addr.:** Science and Medicine Library, 7 Kings College Circle, University of Toronto, Toronto, ON M5S 1A5 Canada.

Hébert, Françoise M. T. (Ja. 29, 1947, Ottawa, ON) Exec. Dir., Natl. Lib. Div., Can. Natl. Inst. for the Blind, 1976–; Spec. Asst., Natl. Libn. of Can., 1974–76; Chief Libn., Dept. of Secy. of State for Can., 1970–74. **Educ.:** Univ. Laval, 1963–67, BA; Univ. of Ottawa, 1967–68, BLS; Univ. of Toronto, 1973–74, MLS. **Orgs.:** Can. LA: Treas. (1979–81); Copyrt. Com. (1972–; Ch., 1981–). IFLA: RT on Libs. for the Blind (Secy., 1979–). Book and Per. Dev. Cncl.: Vice–Ch. (1981–). **Pubns.:** Jt. auth., *Copyright and Materials for the Handicapped* (1981). **Activities:** 4, 12; 17, 28, 36; 61, 72 **Addr.:** National Library Division, Canadian National Institute for the Blind, 1929 Bayview Ave., Toronto, ON M4G 3E8 Canada.

Hébert, John R. (Mr. 2, 1943, Houma, LA) Asst. Chief, Hispanic Div., Lib. of Congs., 1974–, Ref. Libn., Geo. and Map Div., 1969–74; Asst. to the Dean, Grad. Sch., Georgetown Univ., 1968–69. **Educ.:** Univ. of Southwest. LA, 1961–65, BA (Hist.); Georgetown Univ., 1965–72, MA, PhD (Hist.). **Orgs.:** SALALM: Bibl. Com. (1977–; Ch., 1979–); Gifts and Exch. Subcom. (1977–; Ch., 1978–). Latin Amer. Std. Assn.: Scholarly Resrcs. Com. (1978–79). Conf. on Latin Amer. Hist.: Microfilm Com. (1977). Socty for Span. and Portuguese Hist. Std.: Lcl. Arrang. (Ch., 1979); Exec. Com. (1981–). Inter Amer. Cncl.: Secy. (1977–78). Other orgs. **Honors:** Jr. Cham. of Cmrce., Outstan. YOung Men of America, 1966, 1976. **Pubns.:** *Panoramic Maps of Anglo-American Cities; A checklist* (1974); Contrib., *Latin American Publications Available by Gift and Exchange I and II* (1977–78); "Maps by Ephraim George Squier," *Qtly. Jnl. of the Lib. of Congs.* (Ja. 1972); "The Hispanic Collections of the Library of Congress," *The Fed. Linguist* (1976); "Mapping the Road to Santa Fé, 1825–1827," *Terrae Incognitae* (1976); other articles. **Activities:** 4; 15, 17, 41; 54, 57 **Addr.:** Hispanic Division, Library of Congress, Washington, DC 20540.

Hecht, James M. (O. 27, 1949, McKees Rocks, PA) Dir., Hoyt Lib., Kingston, PA, 1975–; Ref./ILL Libn., Reading (PA) Pub. Lib., 1973–75. **Educ.:** Univ. of Pittsburgh, 1967–71, BA (Hist.), 1971–73, MLS. **Orgs.:** PA LA: Bd. of Dir. (1978–79, 1980–81); 2nd VP (1980–81); Ch., NE Chap. (1978–79); Ch., Tech. Arrang. Com., Conf. (1977). Luzerne Intermediate Unit #18, Adv. Cncl.: Pub. Libs. Rep. (1976–80). Northeast. PA Bibl. Ctr.: Secy., Bd. of Dir. (1977–78). Pre-Gvrs. Conf. on Libs.: Plng. Com. (1977). Cmnty. Concert Assn. of Wyoming Valley. **Honors:** Beta Phi Mu, 1973. **Pubns.:** "Library Service to the Handicapped and Elderly," *PA LA Bltn.* (May 1977). **Activities:** 9; 17, 28, 35; 50, 74, 89 **Addr.:** The Hoyt Library, 284 Wyoming Ave., Kingston, PA 18704.

Hecht, Judith Nell (Mr. 16, 1938, Allentown, PA) Info. Spec., Univ. of Dayton Resrch. Inst., 1973–. **Educ.:** Alfred Univ., 1954–58, BS (Nursing); Columbia Univ., 1959, Pub. Hlth. Cert.; Univ. of Dayton, 1977, MA (Amer. Std.); Univ. of KY, 1978, MSLS. **Orgs.:** SLA: Ctrl. OH Chap., Pres.–Elect (1981–82), Treas. (1979–81), Secy. (1975–76). Miami Valley Assn. Hlth. Sci. Libs.: Pres. (1979–80). ASIS. **Honors:** Beta Phi Mu, 1978. **Activities:** 12; 15, 17, 39; 52, 64, 91 **Addr.:** University of Dayton Research Institute, 300 College Park Ave., Dayton, OH 45469.

Hecht, Rachel Rebekah (S. 21, 1936, Brooklyn, NY) Libn., US Dept. of Justice, Tax Div., 1977–; Asst. Ref. Libn., Davis, Graham & Stubbs; Libn., US Court of Appeals, DC Circuit, 1970–74; Asst. Libn., Covington & Burling, 1967–70; Libn., DC Pub. Schs., 1963–67; Libn., NYC Pub. Schs. **Educ.:** Cornell Univ., 1953–57, BA (Econ.); Columbia Univ., 1960–61, MSLS; Fletcher Sch. of Law & Diplomacy, 1957–58, AM (Intl. Econ.). **Orgs.:** AALL. SLA. DC LA. **Honors:** US Dept. of Justice, Spec. Achiev. Awd., 1979. **Pubns.:** "Survey of Federal Court Libraries," *Law Lib. Jnl.* (My. 1974); "Collecting and Keeping Federal Documents," *Law Lib. Jnl.* (F. 1970); oral presentations. **Activities:** 4, 10; 17, 31, 39; 77, 78 **Addr.:** Tax Division, Rm. 4335 Main, U.S. Department of Justice, Washington, DC 20530.

Hecht, Richard (S. 11, 1924, New York, NY) Sr. Libn., NY Pub. Lib., 1968–. **Educ.:** Columbia Univ., 1963–67, BS (Lit.); Pratt Inst., 1967–68, MLS; Lockheed Resrch. Lab., 1980, Dialog Sem. Amer. Film Fest.: Juror (1968–74). Inst. for Intl. Educ. **Pubns.:** *No Crystal Stair* (1975); Film script, "Ding Dong, the Witch Is Dead" (1969). **Activities:** 9; 16, 17, 27; 50, 63, 72 **Addr.:** P.O. Box 245, New York, NY 10156.

Heck, Linda Ann (O. 14, 1950, Portsmouth, VA) Hlth. Libn., Camino Real Hlth. Syst. Agency, Inc., 1976–. **Educ.:** Coll. of William & Mary, 1970–72, BA (Anthro.); Univ. of TX, 1974–76, MLS. **Orgs.:** SLA: TX Chap., Lcl. Plng. Grp. Liaison (1978–80). Med. LA. Hlth.-oriented Libs. of San Antonio: Secy. (1978–80); Union List Com. (1980). ALA. **Honors:** *Organizing & Maintaining A Document Collection In A Health Systems Agency* (1978); Jt. auth., *Economic Anthropology: A Working Bibliography* (1973). **Activities:** 4, 12; 15, 29, 46; 80, 95 **Addr.:** 4619 Villa Nava, San Antonio, TX 78233.

Heck, Thomas F. (Jl. 10, 1943, Washington, DC) Head, Msc./Dance Lib., OH State Univ., 1978–; Asst. Msc. Libn., WI Cnsvty. of Msc., 1977–78; Asst. Prof. of Msc. Lit., John Carroll Univ., 1974–75; Asst. Prof. of Msc. Lit., Case Western Reserve Univ., 1971–74. **Educ.:** Univ. of Notre Dame, 1961–65, BA (Liberal Arts); Yale Univ., 1965–70, PhD (Msclgy.); Univ. of South. CA, 1976–77, MLS. **Orgs.:** Msc. LA. Intl. Assn. of Msc. Libs. ALA. Amer. Msclgl. Socty. Guitar Fndn. of Amer.: Archvst. (1973–). **Honors:** Fulbright Fellow, Vienna, Austria, 1968–69. **Pubns.:** *Franz Schubert: Sixteen Songs with Guitar Accompaniment* (1980); *Mauro Giuliani: Oeuvres choisies pour guitare* (1973); Contrib., *Grove's Dict. of Msc. and Musicians,* (1981); *Computerized catalog of guitar music in the Archive of the Guitar Fndtn. of America* (1978–); various articles in msc. jnls., re-

PROFESSIONAL ACTIVITIES: Institutions: 1. Acad. lib.; 2. Arch.; 3. Assn.; 4. Fed./Gvt. lib.; 5. Inst. lib.; 6. Mfr./Suppl.; 7. Milit. lib.; 8. Musm.; 9. Pub. lib.; 10. Sch. lib.; 11. Sch. of lib. sci.; 12. Spec. lib.; 13. State lib.; 14. (other). **Functions/Activities:** 15. Acq./Col. dev.; 16. Adult srvs.; 17. Admin.; 18. Apprais.; 19. Archit./Bldgs.; 20. Cat./Class.; 21. Chld. srvs.; 22. Circ.; 23. Cons./Pres.; 24. Consult.; 25. Cont. ed.; 26. Educ. lib. sci.; 27. Ext. srvs.; 28. Fund/Grants; 29. Gvt. pubs.; 30. Indx./Abs.; 31. Instr. lib. use; 32. Media srvs.; 33. Micro.; 34. Netwks./Coop.; 35. Persnl.; 36. PR; 37. Publshg.; 38. Recs. mgt.; 39. Ref. srvs.; 40. Repro.; 41. Resrch.; 42. Review.; 43. Secur.; 44. Serials; 45. Spec. col.; 46. Tech. srvs.; 47. Trustees/Bds.; 48. YA srvs.; 49. (other).

views. **Activities:** 1, 2; 15, 17, 41; 55 **Addr.:** O.S.U. Music/Dance Library, 1813 N. High St., Columbus, OH 43210.

Hecklinger, Ellen Louise (S. 29, 1925, Long Beach, CA) Libn., Tchr., Long Beach Schs., 1961–; Lib. Asst., Univ. of MI, 1959–60; Tchr., Redlands Pub. Schs., 1949–59. **Educ.:** Univ. of Redlands, 1948, AB (Eng.); Mex. City Coll., Mex., 1955 (Grad. Work); Univ. of MI, 1961, AM (Eng.), 1967, AMLS. **Orgs.:** Long Beach Sch. Libr. Assn. ALA. Univ. of MI Alum. Assn. Natl. Educ. Assn. Long Beach Tchrs. Assn. CA Tchrs. Assn. Various other orgs. **Pubns.:** "Night Souls," *Pegasus XII* (1955); "After Rain," *Midland Poetry Review* (Win. 1953); "It is Gone," *Midland Poetry Review* (Spr. 1954); "How Well History Records," *Natl. Poetry Anthology* (Mr. 1953). **Activities:** 10; 21, 31; 63 **Addr.:** 315 Junipero #5, Long Beach, CA 90814.

Heckman, Florence E. (Ap. 28, 1938, Kutztown, PA) Ref. Libn., Natl. Sci. Fndn., 1966–; Libn., Natl. Referral Ctr. for Sci. and Tech., 1964–66; Descr. Catlgr., Lib. of Congs., 1963–64. **Educ.:** Gettysburg Coll., 1956–60, BA (Lang.); Cath. Univ., 1963–64, MS (LS). **Orgs.:** SLA. Phi Sigma Iota. **Honors:** Natl. Sci. Fndn., Spec. Achvmt. Awd., 1970; Beta Phi Mu. **Activities:** 4, 12; 31, 34, 39; 63, 64, 91 **Addr.:** 1111 Army-Navy Dr., Apt. A1408, Arlington, VA 22202.

Heckman, Lucy T. (Je. 9, 1954, New York, NY) Cat. Libn., St. John's Univ. Lib., 1977–. **Educ.:** St. John's Univ., 1972–76, BA (Eng.), 1976–77, MLS; Adelphi Univ., 1978–81, MBA. **Orgs.:** ALA. Natl. Libn. Assn. Beta Phi Mu. AAUP. Fac. Assn. **Pubns.:** "Review of Coping with the OCLC Cataloging Subsystem," *Coll. and Resrch. Lib.* (Mr. 1979); "New York Magazine," *Serials Review* (Ja./Mr. 1980); "Harper's Magazine," *Serials Review* (Ja./Mr. 1981); reviews. **Activities:** 1; 15, 20, 31; 55, 59, 67 **Addr.:** 100-50 223 St., Queens Village, NY 11429.

Hedderick, Alice Marie (Je. 13, 1922, Waterloo, ON) Libn., Anglican Church of Can., 1965–; Catlgr., Univ. of Toronto, 1963–65. **Educ.:** Univ. of West. ON, 1939–44, BA (Eng.); Univ. of Toronto, 1962–63, BLS, 1968–73, MLS. **Orgs.:** ON LA. Can. LA: Can. Assn. of Spec. Lib. and Info. Srvs. **Activities:** 5, 12; 15, 20, 39; 90, 92 **Addr.:** Anglican Church of Canada, 600 Jarvis St., Toronto, ON M4Y 2J6 Canada.

Hedin, Bonnie J. (Mr. 4, 1947, Cleveland, OH) Instr., Head of Tech. Prcs., St. Cloud State Univ., 1976–; Ref. Libn., Evansville (IN) Pub. Lib., 1972–75. **Educ.:** Univ. of MN, 1965–69, BA (Soclgy.); Univ. of IL, 1971–72, MS (LS). **Orgs.:** ALA. MN LA: Cont. Educ. Com. (1980–81). MN Educ. Media Org. AECT. **Activities:** 1, 9; 20, 26, 39; 75, 92 **Addr.:** 103 Centennial, St. Cloud State University, St. Cloud, MN 56301.

Hedlin, Ethel W. (Edie) (Ag. 28, 1944, Girard, KS) Archvst., Grants Anal., Natl. Hist. Pubns. and Rec. Comsn., Natl. Arch. and Rec. Srv., 1979–; Corp. Archvst., Wells Fargo Bank, 1975–79; Inst. Rec. Spec., OH Hist. Socty., 1972–75, State Arch. Spec., 1970–72. **Educ.:** Radford Coll., 1962–66, BA (Hist.); Duke Univ., 1969, MA (Hist.), 1974, PhD (Hist.). **Orgs.:** SAA: Bus. Arch. Com. (Ch., 1975–77); Nom. Com. (1977–78); Prog. Com. (1976); Constn. and ByLaws Rev. Com. (1980–81); Bus. Arch. Wkshp. (Instr., 1978–). Mid-Atl. Reg. Arch. Conf.: Lcl. Arrange. Com. (1980); Prog. Com. (1981). Socty. of GA Archvsts. **Honors:** AAUW, Coretta Scott King Awd., 1969. **Pubns.:** *Business Archives: An Introduction;* "Access to Business Archives," *GA Arch.* **Activities:** 2; 24, 28 **Addr.:** National Historical Publications & Records Commission, National Archives Bldg., Washington, DC 20408.

Hedman, Kenneth Wesley (F. 15, 1940, Karlstad, MN) Assoc. Dir. of Libs., Univ. of Texas, El Paso, 1979–; Asst. Dir. of Libs., Western IL Univ., 1976–79; Asst. Dir. of Libs., Univ. of TX, El Paso, 1973–76, Asst. Dir. for Tech. Srvcs., 1972–73. **Educ.:** Cent. WA State Univ., 1960–62, Univ. of TX, El Paso, 1963–65 BS (Educ.), Univ. of WA, 1968–69, MLS, Univ. of TX, El Paso, 1973–77, MA (Pol. Sci.). **Orgs.:** Midst. Acad. LA: Co-chair (Prog. Com., 1979). ALA: ACRL (Univ. Libs. Sect., Nom. Com., 1979–80). Border Reg. LA: Pres., (1972–73). TX LA: Dist. 6, Pres., (1975–76). **Pubns.:** "Is the Second Master's Degree Really Needed?," Nat. LA (1979); Ed.: *Directions;* Nsltr. of Western IL Univ. Libs. (1976–79). **Addr.:** University Library, The University of Texas at El Paso, El Paso, TX 79968.

Hedrick, David T. (F. 14, 1942, Bristol, VA) AV Libn., Gettysburg Coll., 1976–, Circ. Libn., 1972–76. **Educ.:** Emory and Henry Coll., 1960–64, BA (Hist.); Univ. of Denver, 1971–72, MA (Lib., Info. Sci.). **Orgs.:** Assoc. Coll. Libs. of Ctrl. PA: Strg. Com. (Ch., 1976–77). On-Line AV Catlgrs.: Treas. (1980–). **Activities:** 1; 17, 19, 32; 67, 70, 86 **Addr.:** RD 7, Box 104, Hoffman Rd., Gettysburg, PA 17325.

Heemstra, Linda R. (Ap. 28, 1943, Troy, OH) Dir., Bay Cnty. Lib. Syst., 1974–, Asst. Dir., 1974–74; Asst. Dir., Bay City Libs., 1972–73; Cmnty. Srvs. Libn., Bay City Pub. Lib., 1971–72; Head Libn., Bay City Ctrl. HS, 1965–67. **Educ.:** Bowling Green State Univ., 1961–65, BS (Educ./LS); Univ. of MI, 1966–68, AMLS. **Orgs.:** MI LA: Syst. RT (Secy., 1975–76; Vice-Ch., 1978–79); Coop. Caucus (Ch. 1979–80). ALA. Bay Med. Ctr.: Bd. (1978–81). Bay Chorale: Bd., Secy. (1977–78). Bay Cnty. Bicentennial Com.: Bd. (1976). **Activities:** 9; 16, 17, 22, 34, 35, 36 **Addr.:** Bay County Library System, 307 Lafayette Ave., Bay City, MI 48706.

Heer, Lynn C. (Jl. 13, 1943, Nashville, TN) Head, Ref. and Info. Srvs., State Lib. of OH, 1976–; Ref. Libn., Fed. Trade Comsn., 1975–76; Libn., TN Correct. Dept., 1972–73; Ref. Libn., Univ. of TN, 1971–72. **Educ.:** Mid. TN State Univ., 1961–65, BS (Bus. Admin.); George Peabody Coll., 1967–68, MLS; Miami Univ., 1978–79 (Exec. Dev. Prog. for Lib. Admins.). **Orgs.:** SLA: Cont. Ed. Com. (Ch., 1977–79); Ctrl. OH Chap. (Pres.-Elect, 1980–81; Pres., 1981–82); Natl. Educ. Com. (1980–83). Ctrl. OH ASIS. **Pubns.:** "Information for Decision Making," REF. LIBN. (forthcoming); "Using the Federal Register," *OH Media Spectrum* (Spr. 1979). **Activities:** 13; 15, 25, 39; 56, 59, 92 **Addr.:** State Library of OH, 65 S. Front St., Columbus, OH 43215.

Hehman, Jennifer L. (S. 30, 1950, Terre Haute, IN) Slide Cur., Slides & Prints Col., Hist. of Art Dept., OH State Univ., 1978–; Asst. Slide Libn., Slide Lib., Fine Arts Dept., IN Univ., 1976–78. **Educ.:** IN State Univ., 1968–73, AB (Art & Art Hist.); IN Univ., 1974–76, AM (Art Hist.), 1977–80, MLS. **Orgs.:** ARLIS/NA: Visual Resrcs. Com. (1974–); OH Chap. Coll. Art Assn.: Visual Resrcs. Com. (1976–). OH State Univ. Women's Fac. Club: Bowling Com. (1978–79; Ch., 1979–80). AAUP. Mid-America Coll. Art Assn. **Pubns.:** 'How to Look at a Print' Art Exhibition & Cat. & Telecast (1972); *IN Univ. Lib. Video Tape Catalog-Manual of Instruction* (1979). **Activities:** 1, 12; 32, 45; 50, 55, 95-Slides and Photographs. **Addr.:** 204 Hayes Hall, History of Art Department, Ohio State University, 108 North Oval Mall, Columbus, OH 43210.

Heilman, Mary M. (D. 27, 1922, New York, NY) Ref. Supvsr., E. I du Pont de Nemours & Co. Tech. Lib., 1966–, Libn., Photo Prod. Dept., 1954–66, Asst. Libn., Marshall Lab., 1950–54; Various other positions for same co. **Educ.:** Douglass Col., 1940–44, BS (Chem.); Drexel Univ., 1951–54, MLS. **Orgs.:** SLA. ASIS. Amer. Chem. Socty.: Div. Chem. Infor. **Activities:** 12; 15, 31, 39; 59, 60, 91 **Addr.:** 2 Colony Blvd., Apt. 110A, Wilmington, DE 19802.

Heim, Fern V. (Ja. 10, 1916, Stamford, NE) Assoc. Dir./Coord. Metro Ntwk. NE Lib. Comsn., 1966–; Coord. Northern Libr. Ntwk, 1966–72; Dir., Resrch Lib., B.F. Goodrich Res. Ctr., 1946–59; Head of Cir., Univ. of NE, 1945–46, Head of Per. Div., 1942–45. **Educ.:** Univ. of NE, 1937, BS (Math.); Columbia Univ., 1941–49, MLS. **Orgs.:** SLA: Ch., Chem. Sect. ALA. NE LA. United Meth. Women: Conf. Pres. (1967–68). YWCA: Sch. Com. **Honors** Iota Sigma Pi, 1935, Phi Beta Kappa, 1937. **Activities:** 1, 9, 12; 22, 24 **Addr.:** Nebraska Library Commission, 1420 P St., Lincoln, NE 68508.

Heim, Kathleen McEntee (Jl. 29, 1948, Chicago, IL) Asst. Prof., Univ. of IL Grad. Sch. of Lib. and Info. Sci., 1978–; Lectr., Tchg. Asst., Univ. of WI Lib. Sch., 1976–78; Dir. of Pub. Srvs., Rebecca Crown Lib., Rosary Coll., 1972–76; Ref. Libn., Elmhurst Coll., 1971–72; Math. Tchr., Martin Sch., 1970–71. **Educ.:** Univ. of IL, 1965–69, BA (Eng.); Marquette Univ., 1969–70, MA (Eng.); Univ. of Chicago, 1971–72, MA (LS); Univ. of WI, 1976–78, PhD (LS). **Orgs.:** ALA: Cent. Celebration Com. (1976); ERA Task Frc. (1979); stdg. com. on the Status of Women in Libnshp. (Ch., 1980–82). IL LA. Women Lib. Workers. Natl. Org. for Women. Leag. of Women Voters. Citizens Against Vietnam Involvment. **Pubns.:** Jt. auth., *The Role of Women in Librarianship 1876–1976* (1979); "Professional Education: Some Comparisons," *As Much to Learn As to Teach* (1979); jt. ed., *Emerging Patterns of Community Service Library Trends* (1979); jt. auth., "A Profile of the ALA Membership," *Amer. Libs.* (D. 1980); "Women in Librarianship, Status of," *ALA Yrbk.* (1979–81); "Sex, Salaries, and Library Support," *Lib. Jnl.* (Mr. 15, 1979, Ja. 1, 1980, S. 15, 1981); various articles. **Activities:** 9, 11; 16, 17, 29; 50, 92, 95-Women in Libnshp. **Addr.:** University of Illinois/ Graduate School of Library and Information Science, 410 David Kinley Hall, 1907 W. Gregory Dr., Urbana, IL 61801.

Heinemann, Luba (Ag. 29, 1943, Lviv, Ukraine) Mem. Srvs. Coord., SOLINET, 1981; Catlgr., Asst. Prof., LS, Alma Coll., 1979–81. **Educ.:** Univ. of Rochester, 1961–65, BA (Latin); IN Univ., 1977–78, MLS. **Orgs.:** MI Acad. of Sci., Arts and Letters: Lib. Sci. Sect. (Ch., 1979–81). NLA: Treas. (1980–81). MI LA. ALA. Matinee Musicale of the Natl. Fed. of Msc. Clubs, Muncie, IN: Pres. (1973–74); Prog. Ch. (1971–73). **Pubns.:** "Some Notes on Soviet Librarianship," *MI Academician* (Spr. 1981). **Activities:** 1; 20, 31, 39; 55, 66, 75 **Addr.:** 2841 Windy Hill Rd., Apt. 1149, Marietta, GA 30067.

Heinrich, Dorothy L. (Jl. 8, 1920, New London, WI) Spec. Cols. Libn., Univ. of WI, Green Bay, 1971–. **Educ.:** Univ. of WI, Green Bay, 1971–75, BA (Hum.); Univ. of WI, Madison, 1977–79, MA (Lib. Arch.); various crs. **Orgs.:** WI LA. Midwest Arch. Conf. SAA. **Honors:** Univ. of WI, Green Bay, Excel. in Cmnty. Outrch., 1978–79. **Pubns.:** "Establishing an Ethnic Collection in a Small Institution," *Midwest. Archvst.* (N. 1, 1977). **Activities:** 1, 2; 31, 38, 39; 66, 69, 73 **Addr.:** Library Learning Center—Rm. 705, University of WI, Green Bay, WI 54301.

Heinritz, Fred J. (Mr. 1, 1931, Piqua, OH) Prof., LS, Div. of LS and Instr. Tech., South. CT State Coll., 1967–, Asst. Dir. of Div., 1974–79; Asst. Prof., Sch. of LS, Univ. of NC, 1963–67; Sch. Libn., Santa Monica Unfd. Sch. Dist., 1960–61; Sci. Libn., Univ. of CA, Los Angeles, 1958–60; Tchr., Cincinnati Pub. Schs., 1956–57; Fld. Scout Exec., Boy Scouts of Amer., Cleveland, 1952–1953; various sum. positions tchg. LS at univ. level, 1970–74. **Educ.:** Univ. of Cincinnati, 1948–52, BA (Eng.), 1955–56, BS (Educ.); Rutgers Univ., 1957–58, MLS, 1961–63, PhD (LS). **Orgs.:** ALA: Bd. of Eds., *Coll. and Resrch. Libs.* (1969–73). Sierra Club. CT Forest and Parks Assn. **Pubns.:** Jt. auth., *Scientific Management of Library Operations* (1966); "Compound Growth in Libraries," *Essays For Ralph Shaw* (1975); "Using the Computer for Library Random Sample Selection," *Coll. and Resrch. Libs.* (My. 1979); "Decision Tables: A Tool for Librarians," *Lib. Resrcs. and Tech. Srvs.* (Win. 1978); "Modern Scientific Management in the Academic Library," *Jnl. of Acad. Libnshp.* (Jl. 1975); various articles, reviews. **Activities:** 11; 26; 56, 57, 91 **Addr.:** Division of Library Science and Instructional Technology, Southern CT State College, New Haven, CT 06515.

Heins, Ethel L. (Ap. 9, 1918, New York, NY) Ed., *The Horn Book Mag.*, 1974–, and Adjunct Prof., Simmons College Ctr. for Std. of Child. Lit., 1975–; Instr. Matrls. Spec., Lexington (MA) Pub. Sch., 1962–74; Chld. Libn., Boston Pub. Lib., 1955–62; Chld. Libn., NY Pub. Lib., 1938–43; Lect., Boston Coll. Grad. Sch. of Educ., 1968–70. **Educ.:** Douglass Coll., 1934–38, BA (Eng. & LS); Columbia Univ., 1939, (LS); Harvard Grad. Sch. of Educ., 1964. **Orgs.:** ALA: ALSC, Newbery-Caldecott Com. (1969–73); Bk. Eval. Com. (1970–73); Mildred L. Batchelder Awd. Com. (Ch., 1971; 1978); New Eng. LA: Caroline Hewins Lectr. Com. (1963–67); MA LA.; AASL, Early Childhood Educ. Com. (Ch., 1972–74). Friends of IBBY. Natl. Cncl. of Tchrs. of Eng. Chld. Lit. Assn. Intl. Resrch. Socty. for Chld. Lit. **Honors:** Rutgers Univ. Grad. Sch. of Alum. Assn. Cit., 1979; Lib. Std. **Pubns.:** Contrib., *Book Reviewing* (1978); "Literature Bedeviled," *The Horn Bk. Mag.* (Je. 1974); "For Listening Children," *The Horn Bk. Mag.* (D. 1957); "From the Mixed-up Files of Mrs. Basil E. Frankweiler' and Nineteen Other Books...," *Harvard Mag.* (D. 1975); "Storytelling Through Art: A Guide to Picture Books for Children," *Harvard Mag.* (D. 1976); other articles, reviews. **Activities:** 26, 42, 49-Ed.; 95-Chld. and YA Lit. **Addr.:** 29 Hope St., Auburndale, MA 02166.

Heins, Paul (F. 15, 1909, Boston, MA) Lect., Simmons Coll. Ctr. for the Study of Chld. Lit., 1975–; Ed., *The Horn Book Mag.*, 1967–74; Tchr., English HS, Boston, 1946–67; Tchr., HS of Cmrce., Boston, 1934–46. **Educ.:** Harvard Coll., 1927–31, AB (Eng.); Boston Tchrs. Coll., 1931–32, MEd (Eng.); Oxford Univ., 1954–55. **Orgs.:** ALA: Newbery-Caldecott Com. (1969, 1981); Caroline M. Hewins Schol. Com. (1975–78); H.C. Andersen Awd. Nom. Com. (Ch., 1978). New Eng. LA. Chld. Lit. Assn. Intl. Resrch. Socty. for Chld. Lit. **Pubns.:** Transl., *Snow White* (1974); Ed., *Crosscurrents of Criticism* (1977); "Out on a Limb with the Critics," *Horn Book Mag.* (Je. 1970); "Coming to Terms with Criticism," *Horn Book Mag.* (Ag. 1970); Jt. auth., "Reviewing and Criticism in the *Horn Book Magazine,*" *Bomen over Boek en Jeugh* (1977); other books and articles. **Activities:** 14-Grad. Sch. for Chld. Lit. Publshg.; 37, 42; 95-Chld. and YA Lit. **Addr.:** 29 Hope St., Auburndale, MA 02166.

Heintz, Robert L. (My. 22, 1942, Pipestone, MN) Media Dir., Spencer Cmnty. Schs., 1966–; Libn., Cedar Falls Cmnty. Schs., 1964–66; Display Mgr., Montgomery Ward and Co., 1962–64. **Educ.:** Univ. of North. IA, 1960–66, BA (LS); Ctrl. MO State Univ., 1968–70; MS (Educ.); various grad. crs. **Orgs.:** ALA. IA Educ. Media Assn. AECT. IA State Educ. Assn. Assn. for Supvsn. and Curric. Dev. **Activities:** 10; 15, 17, 32; 64, 92 **Addr.:** 519 E. 4th St., Spencer, IA 51301.

Heinz, Catharine Frances (Anaheim, CA) Dir. and VP, Broadcast Pioneers Lib., 1971–; Libn., Tele. Info. Off., 1959–71; Libn., Mutual Life Ins. Co. of NY, 1956–59; Dir., Asst. Dir., Hosp. Lib. Bureau United Hosp. Fund of NY 1948–56; Med. Libn., U.S. Naval Hosp. (Brooklyn, NY), 1947; 1947–48; Newspr. Class., Jrnlism. Lib., Columbia Univ., 1946–47; Sch. Dept. Libn., Orange Cnty. Free Lib. (Santa Ana, CA) 1942–43. **Educ.:** Rosary Coll., 1937–41, BALS; Columbia Univ., 1952, MSLS. **Orgs.:** ALA: Hosp. Libs. Div., Pres. (1950–51); Pub. Rel. Srvcs. to Libs. Radio-Tele. Film Fest. (1966–67); Ch., Hosp and Inst. Lib. Awd. Com. (1966–67). SLA: Ch., Com. on Standards for Hosp. Libs. (1949–52); Ch. Pub. Rel. Com. (1959–61); Hosp. Chap. New York City (1947–48); Exec. Ed. Greater NY Dir. (1963) Secy., New York City Chap. (1962–63). Amer. Women in Radio and Tele: Ch., Industry Info. Com (1964–66); Ch. NY Chap. Mem. Com. (1968–69). Nat. Broadcasters Club: Gov. (1972–75). **Pubns.:** Jt. Auth., *Objectives and Standards for Hospital Libraries* (1953). Ed., *Broadcast Pioneers Lib. Reports* (1975–). "Women Radio Pioneers," Jrnl. of Pop. Culture (1978). "Broadcast Pioneers Library" *Stechert Macmillan News* (1979). **Activities:** 2, 12; 17, 39, 45; 54, 84, 93 **Addr.:** Broadcast Pioneers Library, 1771 N St., N.W., Washington, DC 20036.

Heinzkill, John Richard (My. 31, 1933, Appleton, WI) Head, Hum. Sect., Univ. of OR Lib., 1967–; Ref. Libn., WA Univ., 1964–67. **Educ.:** St. John's Univ., Collegeville, MN,

Special Subjects/Services: 50. Adult educ.; 51. Advert./Mktg.; 52. Aerosp.; 53. Agric.; 54. Area std.; 55. Arts/Hum.; 56. Autom.; 57. Bibl./Prtg.; 58. Bio. sci.; 59. Bus./Fin.; 60. Chem.; 61. Copyrt.; 62. Documtn.; 63. Educ.; 64. Engin.; 65. Env.; 66. Eth. grps.; 67. Film; 68. Food/Nutr.; 69. Geneal.; 70. Geo.; 71. Geol.; 72. Handcpd.; 73. Hist.; 74. Int. frdm.; 75. Info. sci.; 76. Insr.; 77. Law; 78. Legis.; 79. Math./Comp. sci.; 80. Med.; 81. Metals; 82. Nat. resrcs.; 83. Newsp.; 84. Nuc. sci.; 85. Oral hist.; 86. Petr./Energy; 87. Pharm.; 88. Phys./Astr./Math.; 89. Readg.; 90. Relig.; 91. Sci./Tech.; 92. Soc. sci.; 93. Telecom.; 94. Transp.; 95. (other).

1951–55, BA; Univ. of MI, 1963–64, AMLS. **Orgs.:** ALA: ACRL. **Pubns.:** *Film Criticism: an Index to Critics' Anthologies* (1975); "Characterisics of References in Selected Scholarly English Literary Journals," *Lib. Qtly.* (1980); "Addenda to Woods' Bibliography of Sir Winston Churchill," *Bibl. Socty. Amer.* Papers (1978); "Introducing Nonverbal Communication," *RQ* (1972). **Activities:** 1; 30, 39, 41; 55, 67, 75 **Addr.:** 2161 Hilyard St., Eugene, OR 97405.

Heise, George Franklin (Jl. 30, 1934, Murphysboro, IL) Assoc. Dir. of Indx. Srv., The H. W. Wilson Co. 1972–, Admn. Asst., Asst. Dir. of Indx. Srv., 1967–72; Acq. Libn., West. IL Univ., 1965–67, Doc. Libn., 1964–65; Head Educ. & Training, IL St. Lib., 1964; Consult., IL St. Lib. and Dir. of West. IL Reg. Lib., 1962–63; Bkmobile Libn. & Head of Bkmobile Srv., South. IL Reg. Lib., (Carbondale) (1959–61). **Educ.:** South. IL Univ. (Carbondale), 1952–57, BA (Gov), 1959–61, MA (Gov); George Peabody College, 1961–62, MA (LS). **Orgs.:** ALA: ACRL, Nom. Com. (1975); PLA; LAMA; various other div. Amer. Socty. Indx.: Nom. Com. (Ch. 1971). ASIS: Tech. Prog. Com. (1978); Metro. NY Chap., Ch. (1975–76), Nom. Com. (1974, 1979); various other coms. SLA: Bus. Finance Div., Doc. New York Library Club. New York Tech. Srv. Libn. **Honors:** Beta Phi Mu. **Activities:** 1; 17; 57, 75 **Addr.:** 110 Vreeland Ave., Bergenfield, NJ 07621.

Heiser, Jane C. (S. 20, 1943, Worcester, MA) Litcy. Resrc. Libn., Enoch Pratt Free Lib., 1979–, Coord. Volun. Srvs., 1975–79; Head Libn., Moss Pt. City Lib., 1974–74; Lib. Consult., Singing River Hosp., 1974–74; Asst. Law Libn., Cat., Marquette Univ., 1970–1972. **Educ.:** Anna Maria Coll., 1961–65, BA (Eng.); Univ. of WI (Milwaukee), 1969–70, MALS; Litrcy. Volun. of Amer. 1977–, Trainer's Cert. **Orgs.:** Litcy. Volun. Amer.: Voting Mem. (1977–). ALA: LAD; RASD; PLA, AEPS (Ch. 1979–81). MD LA: YASD, Prog. Com. (1976–81), Pres. (1980–81). Pres. elect (1979–80). V.Pres.–Pres. elect. (1981–82); Basic Educ. and Litcy. Com., ch. (1979–81); MD St. Dept. of Educ.: Resrc. person (1976–). MD Assn. Pub. Supported Cont. Educ. Montgomery Cnty. Gov., Ofc. Family Resrc.: Resrc. person (1979–). **Honors:** WHCOLIS, Del., 1979. **Pubns.:** *Literacy Sources: An Annotated Check List for Tutors and Librarians* (1981). **Activities:** 9; 15, 16; 50, 63, 89 **Addr.:** Enoch Pratt Free Library, 400 Cathedral Street, Baltimore, MD 21201.

Heiser, W(alter) Charles, S. J. (Mr. 16, 1922, Milwaukee, WI) Libn., Dvnty. Lib., St. Louis Univ., 1955–; Instr. in Latin, St. Louis Univ. HS, 1947–50. **Educ.:** St. Louis Univ., 1940–45, AB (Phil), 1945–47, AM (Latin), 1950–55, STL (Theo.); Catholic Univ., 1955–58, MS (LS). **Orgs.:** Cath. LA. ATLA. Cath. Theo. Socty. of Amer. **Pubns.:** "Theology Digest Book Survey," *Theo. Digest* (1963–). **Activities:** 1; 17, 20, 39; 90 **Addr.:** Divinity Library, 3655 West Pine Blvd., Rm. 0616, St. Louis, MO 63108.

Heiserman, Glenn R. (O. 12, 1936, Monroe, MI) Dist. Media Spec., ARAMCO Sch., 1980–; Instr. Cat., Univ. of OR (Eugene), 1979; Media Spec., Intl. Sch. of Kuala Lumpur, 1976–78. **Educ.:** Univ. of MI, 1960–63, BS, MS (Bio.); Univ. of OR, 1966–70, MLS. **Orgs.:** ALA. **Activities:** 10; 17, 21; 56, 63, 95-Arabian Overseas Schools. **Addr.:** Arabian American Oil Company, PO Box 8588, Dhahran, Saudi Arabia.

Heitz, Thomas R. (D. 20, 1940, Kansas City, MO) Chief, Lib. Srvs., State of NY, Dept. of Law Lib., 1980–; Dir., Law Libs., BC Law Lib. Fndn., 1974–79; Asst. Law Libn., Univ. of Puget Snd., Sch. of Law, 1972–73. **Educ.:** Univ. of KS, 1958–62, BA (Hum.); Univ. of MO, 1962–65, JD; Univ. of WA, 1972–73, M Law Libr. **Orgs.:** Can. ALL: Com. on Law Socty. Pubns. (Ch., 1976–77). AALL: Spec. Interest Sect., Autom. and Sci. Dev. (Ch., 1978–80). Amer. Bar Assn.: Sect. of Legal Econ. and Ofc. Prac., Lib. Com. (Ch., 1977–78). Amer. Judicature Socty. **Pubns.:** *British Columbia Legislative Digest* (1978–79); "Legal Information vs. Legal Advice," *Reference and Information Services: A Reader* (1978). **Activities:** 4, 12; 15, 17, 39; 56, 75, 77 **Addr.:** Dept. of Law Library, State of NY, The Capitol, Albany, NY 12224.

Helburn, Judith Horwitz (Je. 3, 1938, Milwaukee, WI) Volun. Libn., Temple Beth Israel Lib., 1978–; Ed., *Prac. Law Bks. Review,* 1978–; Dir., Lib. Mgt. and Srvs., 1977–; Spec. Proj. Libn., Coord. of Pubns., Tarlton Law Lib., Univ. of TX, 1978–80; Actg. Head Chld. Libn., Madison Pub. Lib., 1965; Med. Proj. Asst., Univ. of WI Med. Lib., 1965; Sch. Libn., Madison Pub. Schs., 1960–64. **Educ.:** Univ. of WI, 1956–60, BS, hon. (Educ.), 1962–65, MSLS. **Orgs.:** AALL. AJL. Southwestern Law Libs. Assn.: Un. List of Frgn. Legal Per. Rev. (Ch., 1981). Austin Lib. Comsn.: Secy. (1976–79). Leag. of Women Voters: Bd., Com. Ch. (1975–76; 1970–72). All Austin Coop. Nursery Sch.: Pres., Bd. (1971–73). **Honors:** Phi Kappa Phi, 1960; Beta Phi Mu, 1965. **Pubns.:** Jt. rev., *Legal Novels: an Annotated Bibliography* (1979); Jt. rev., *Basic Lists for Texas Law Libraries* (1979); "Law Library Consulting," *What Else You Can Do With a Library Degree* (1980); "Law Librarian as a Consultant: a Panel," *Law Lib. Jnl.* (Fall 1979); "Law Library Consultant: Help When You Need It," *Legal Econ.* (Mr.–Ap. 1981). **Activities:** 14-Consult., Ed.; 24, 37, 42; 57, 77, 95-Aging. **Addr.:** Library Management & Services, 5914 Highland Hills Dr., Austin, TX 78731.

Held, Charles Holborn (Ja. 26, 1929; Detroit, MI) Head Libn., Albion Coll., 1965–; Assoc. Prof. of Lib. Sci., Univ. of Western Ont., 1970–71; Instr. of Lib Sci., Wayne State Univ., 1963–65; Libn., Fordson HS, 1954–63. **Educ.:** Albion Coll., 1946–50, AB (Hist); Univ. of MI, 1950–51, AMLS; Wayne State Univ., 1963–69, PhD (Lib Sci). **Orgs.:** ALA. NLA. Rotary: Pres. of Albion Club (1975). **Honors:** Phi Delta Kappa. **Pubns.:** "Apologia Pro William B. Silber," *Io Triumphe* (Je. 1972). "The President Who Was Hissed," *Albionian* (1976). **Activities:** 1, 11; 17, 26, 31; 63, 74, 85 **Addr.:** 1155 Rivers Bend, Albion, MI 49224.

Helfman, Richard (Jl. 2, 1923, New York, NY) Engin./Sci. Libn., Cooper Union, 1978–; Head of Ref., Engin. Socty. Lib., 1967–78, Asst. Ref. Libn., 1961–67; Asst. Ref. Libn., E. Meadow Pub. Lib., 1960–61; Adult Srvs. Libn., Brooklyn Pub. Lib., 1958–60. **Educ.:** Brooklyn Coll., 1953–58, BA (Psy.); Rutgers Univ., 1958–60, MLS. **Orgs.:** SLA. **Activities:** 12; 64, 81, 91 **Addr.:** 303 W. 66 St. #5D-E, New York, NY 10023.

Helguera, Byrd S. (D. 14, 1927, Buchanan, VA) Assoc. Dir. and Asst. Dir. for Pub. Srvs., Vanderbilt Univ. Med. Ctr. Lib., 1970–; Pub. Srvs. Libn., 1966–69; Consult., Univ. Nacl., Bogotá, Colombia, 1970. **Educ.:** Mary Washington College of Univ. of VA, 1944–48, BA (Span.); George Peabody Coll., 1965–66, MLS; Univ. of NC (Chapel Hill), 1949–50, (Span.). **Orgs.:** Med. LA: Ed. Com., *Bltn.,* 1981–. Mid-TN Hlth. Sci. Libn.: Pres. (1978–79). Nashville Lib. Club. League of Women Voters: Nashville Chap., Com. for Century III Wkshp. (1979–80). **Honors:** AAUW Coll. Fac. Prog., 1965. **Pubns.:** Speeches. **Activities:** 1, 12; 17, 22, 39; 80 **Addr.:** 2309 Sterling Rd., Nashville, TN 37215.

Hellard, Ellen G. (Ag. 22, 1943, Richmond, KY) Dir., Fld. Srvs., Dept of Lib. and Arch., 1976–; Reg. Libn., Bluegrass N. Reg. Lib., 1966–76. **Educ.:** Berea Coll., 1961–65, BA (Eng., Msc.); Univ. of KY, 1965–66, MS (LS). **Orgs.:** KY LA: Pub. Lib. Sect. (Ch., Vice-Ch., Secy., 1970–74); Legis. Ch. (1979–80); Mem. Ch. (1981); SELA rep. (1981–82). ALA: ASCLA, Gen. Consult. Grp. (Ch., 1980), State Lib. Agency, Plng. Com. (1981). Woodford Cnty. JayceeEttes: Secy. (1967–69). **Activities:** 9, 13; 17, 24, 47; 55, 62, 78 **Addr.:** Dept. of Library & Archives, P.O. Box 537, Frankfort, KY 40602.

Heller, Adelia O. (Ja. 15, 1933, Tripoli, Lebanon) Supvsr., Docum. Prcs. Sect., TN Valley Athrty., 1976–; Asst. Chief, Cat. Div., Copyrt. Ofc., Lib. of Congs., 1972–76, Head, Ed. and Pub. Sect., 1968–72, Asst. Head, 1966–68. **Educ.:** George Washington Univ., 1955–62, BA (Pol. Sci.). **Orgs.:** Natl. Micro. Assn. ASIS: E. TN Chap., Secy.-Treas. (1980–81); Natl. Mgt. Assn. **Pubns.:** "A Management and Engineering Data System—Active and Archival," *Gvt. Data Systs.* (Je. 1977). **Activities:** 4, 12; 17, 38, 46; 56, 61, 75 **Addr.:** 206 Land Oak Dr., Rte. 37, Knoxville, TN 37922.

Heller, Dawn Hansen (Ag. 11, 1932, Green Bay, WI) Media Srvs. Coord., Dist. 208, Riverside, IL, 1972–; Head Libn., Riverside-Brookfield HS, 1969–72, Ref. Libn., 1965–69; Instr., Triton Coll., 1973–76. **Educ.:** Carleton Coll., 1950–54, AB (Eng.); Rosary Coll., 1964–66, MALS, Nat. Coll. of Educ., 1979–81, (Educ. Admin). **Orgs.:** IL LA: Pres. (1978–79). IL Assn. for Media in Educ.: Pres. (1976–77). ALA: Elect. Com. (1978); LAMA; AASL. Assn. for Educ. Comm. and Tech. Nat. Sch. Pub. Rel. Assn. **Pubns.:** Ed. *IL Libs.* (S. 1978). Co.-publshr., *Library Insights, Promotion, and Programs.* "So What about Networks," *Sch. Lib. Jrnl.,* (D. 1978). "Media Gets the Message: An Inservice Program," for IL Office of Educ., (1978). Educ. Cassette Prog. **Activities:** 10, 13; 17, 32, 36; 63 **Addr.:** 516 S. Ashland Ave., La Grange, IL 60525.

Heller, James S. (Ap. 11, 1950, Detroit, MI) Head Libn., US Dept. of Justice, Cvl. Div. Lib., 1980–; Dir., Reader Srvs., George Washington Univ. Law Lib., 1977–80. **Educ.:** Univ. of MI, 1967–71, BA (Soc. Stds.); Univ. of San Diego, 1973–76, JD, cum laude; Univ. of CA, Berkeley, 1976–77, MLS. **Orgs.:** AALL: Copyrt. Com. (1980–81). Law Libns. Socty. of Washington, DC: Cont. Educ. Grants Com. (1980–81). Com. of Lib. and Info. Assns.: Ad Hoc Com. on Copyrt. Law and Implementation. State Bar of CA. Bar Assn. of DC. **Activities:** 1, 4; 17, 39; 77 **Addr.:** 2308 41st St., N.W., #1-B, Washington, DC 20007.

Heller, Linda Hall (My. 21, 1951, El Reno, OK) Libn., Aucilla Christian Acad., K-12, 1980–; Libn., Cardinal Newman HS, 1979–80; Libn., Head of Chld. Dept., Stillwater Pub. Lib., 1977–78; Coord. of Lib. Srvs., Garber (OK) Pub. Sch., 1973–74. **Educ.:** OK State Univ., 1969–73, BS (Lib. Educ.), 1974–76, MS (Educ. Media), Grad. work towards an EdD, 1976–77; Lib. Teaching Cert., OK, FL. **Orgs.:** ALA. OK LA: Sequoyah Chld. Book Awd. Com. (1978). AECT: Del. to reg. conf. FL LA. AAUW: Bd. Alpha Chi Omega. **Activities:** 9, 10; 21, 32, 48 **Addr.:** 3013 Godfrey Pl., Tallahassee, FL 32308.

Heller, Susan J. (Ja. 25, 1928, New York City, NY) Reg. Libn., U.S. Dept. of Housing and Urban Dev., 1978–; Libn., 1976–78; Adult Srv. Libn., Rockville Centre Pub. Lib., 1972–74. **Educ.:** Hunter Coll., CUNY, 1944–48, BA (Msc.); Long Island Univ., 1968–72, MLS. **Orgs.:** NY LA. SLA. Law Libns. Assn. of Grt. NY. **Honors:** U.S. Dept. of Housing and Urban Dev., Reg. II, NY, Cert. of Spec. Achvmt., 1980. **Activities:** 4, 12; 15, 17, 39; 65, 77, 92 **Addr.:** U.S. Dept. of Housing & Urban Development, Regional Library Rm. 1304, 26 Federal Plz., New York, NY 10278.

Hellum-Berman, Bertha D. (N. 1, 1911, El Paso, TX) Lib. Consult., 1972–; Cnty. Libn., Contra Costa Cnty., 1954–72 and Alameda Cnty., 1964–69; Lib. Consult., CA State Lib., 1952–54; Parish Libn., Jefferson Parish Lib., 1950–52; Demonstration Libn., LA State Lib., 1949–50; Cnty. Libn., El Dorado Cnty. Lib., 1947–49; City Libn., Monterey Pub. Lib., Calif. 1937–46; Chief of Branches, Sacramento City Free Lib., 1934–37. **Educ.:** Univ. of TX, Univ. of CA, Berkeley, 1930–33, AB, 1933–34, Cert. (LS). **Orgs.:** ALA: various coms. CA LA: Past Pres. (1963). Pub. Lib. Exec. of Ctrl. CA: Past Pres. (1970–71). League of Women Voters. AAUW. Conf. of CA Hist. Societies. CA Hist. Socty. Other orgs. **Honors:** Assembly of the State of California (legislature) Resolution of Appreciation for services to the people of Contra Costa County and the state 1974; Resolution of Appreciation from Contra Costa County Board of Supervisors, 1972. **Pubns.:** *A Study of the California Section of the California State Library* (1979); "Friends of County Libraries," *Friends of the Lib.* (1962); various articles. **Activities:** 9, 13; 17, 19, 24; 73, 78 **Addr.:** 1525 Cottonwood Ct. #2, Walnut Creek, CA 94595.

Helmer, Dona J. (Ag. 25, 1948, Miles City, MT) Dir., Nenana Pub. Lib. (AL), 1979; Asst. Prof. LS, S. E. MO St. Univ., 1979–79; Head, Youth Srvs., City Cnty. Lib. Missoula, 1978–79; Libn., Jorden Valley HS 1975–76; Coord., Spec. Events Chld., Spokane Pub. Lib., 1974–75. **Educ.:** Univ. of WI (Whitewater), 1966–70, BS (Eng., Hist.); North. IL Univ., 1970–72, MA (Hist.); North. IL Univ., 1972–75, MA (LS). **Orgs.:** ALA: YASD, Com. Revise Fic. Coll. Bound (1979–80); ALSC, Orgs. Bylaws Com. (1979–81); Newbery Bk. Awd. Com. (1981). MT LA: Com. Implement Lib. Stan. (1978–79) Pacific N. W. LA. Asm. Lit. Adlsnt.: Bd. Dir. (1976–78). Natl. Story Leag. Phi Alpha Theta: Nu Beta Chap., Hist. (1968–69). Puppeteers Amer. **Honors:** MT LA, Cont. Educ. Awd., 1979. **Pubns.:** Reviews. **Activities:** 9, 10; 21, 26, 48; 55, 67, 89 **Addr.:** Box 215, Nenana, AL 99760.

Helmick, Aileen B. (St. George, KS) Instr., Ctrl. MO State Univ., 1979–; Lrng. Resrcs. Dir., Sedalia Jr. High/Middle Sch., 1973–79; Adj. Instr., Ctrl. MO State Univ., 1978–79; Instr., OK State Univ., 1966–68. **Educ.:** Marymount Coll., 1947–51, AB (Psy.); KS State Univ., 1957, MS (Educ.); Ctrl. MO State Univ., 1976, EdS (Lrng. Resrcs.); MO Tchg. Cert. **Orgs.:** ALA. MO LA: Lib. Dev. (1979). MO Sch. LA: Treas. (1977–78); Schol. (1975–77). **Honors:** Phi Kappa Phi, Phi Delta Kappa. **Activities:** 10, 14-Lib. Educ.; 17, 25, 26; 50, 63 **Addr.:** 318 Johnson, Warrensburg, MO 64093.

Helmuth, Ruth W. (Ag. 29, 1918, Cleveland, OH) Adj. Prof. of LS, Matthew A. Baxter Sch. of Info. and LS, 1970–, Univ. Archvst., Case West. Rsv. Univ., 1967–, Univ. Archvst., 1964–67. **Educ.:** Radcliffe Coll., 1935–39, AB (Hist.); Smith Coll., 1939–40, MA (Hist.). **Orgs.:** SAA: Cncl. (1973–77); VP (1979–80); Pres. (1980–81). Socty. of OH Archvsts.: Secy.-Treas. (1968–72). **Honors:** SAA, Fellow, 1974; Socty. of OH Archvsts., Spec. Cit., 1974. **Activities:** 2, 11; 17, 25, 26; 63 **Addr.:** Case Western Reserve University, Cleveland, OH 44106.

Helsley, Alexia Jones (S. 9, 1945, Louisville, KY) Supvsr., Ref. and Resrch. Div., SC Dept. of Arch. and Hist., 1976–, Asst. Ref. Archvst., 1972–76, Archvst., 1969–72. **Educ.:** Furman Univ., 1963–67, BA (Hist.); Univ. of SC, 1967–, MA (Hist.), PhD cand. (Pol. Sci.), Inst. for Modern Arch. Admin., 1978. **Orgs.:** SAA: Access Subcom. of Ref., Access and Outreach Prof. Afnty. Grp. (Ch., 1979–). SC Hist. Socty. **Pubns.:** "Black Confederates," *SC Hist. Mag.* (Jl. 1973). **Activities:** 2; 36, 39, 41; 69 **Addr.:** South Carolina Department of Archives and History, P.O. Box 11,669, Columbia, SC 29211.

Helvey, Mary Sewell (N. 26, 1917, Keystone, WV) Cat. Dept. Head, Davidson Col. Lib., 1976–, Asst. Cat., 1966–76; Asst. Libn., Asst. Prof. of LS, Concord Coll., 1946–66. **Educ.:** Concord Coll., 1934–38, AB (Math); Univ. of NC (Chapel Hill), 1947–49, BS (LS). **Orgs.:** NC LA. Mecklenburg Cnty. LA. SELA. **Activities:** 1; 20, 22, 39 **Addr.:** Box 842, Davidson, NC 28036.

Hemingway, Luella Butler (D. 26, 1940, Baton Rouge, LA) Asst. Libn., San Jose State Univ., 1978–. **Educ.:** San Jose State Univ., 1974–76, BA (Soclgy.); Univ. of CA, Berkeley, 1976–77, MLS. **Orgs.:** ALA: Black Caucus (1979–). CA LA: CA State Univs. and Colls. Libns. Chap. (Secy.-Treas., 1980–). SLA: Lib. Mgt. Div., Mem. Com. (1980). **Activities:** 1; 15, 31, 39; 56, 77, 92 **Addr.:** San Jose State University, Library, San Jose, CA 95127.

Hemmes, Diane Carolyn (Ja. 30, 1951, Staten Island, NY) Dir., Libs., St. Catherine's Sch., 1978–; Lower Sch. Libn., Rye Country Day Sch., 1975–78; Chld. Libn., Albany Pub. Lib., 1974–75. **Educ.:** SUNY, Oswego, 1968–72, BA (Sp., Thea.); SUNY, Albany, 1974–75, MLS. **Orgs.:** ALA: AASL, Early Chld. Educ. Com. (1980–82). Natl. Assn. of Indp. Schs.: Richmond Area Libns. (Ch., 1980–81). Natl. Assn. for the Prsrvn. and Per-

PROFESSIONAL ACTIVITIES: Institutions: 1. Acad. lib.; 2. Arch.; 3. Assn.; 4. Fed./Gvt. lib.; 5. Inst. lib.; 6. Mfr./Suppl.; 7. Milit. lib.; 8. Musm.; 9. Pub. lib.; 10. Sch. lib.; 11. Sch. of lib. sci.; 12. Spec. lib.; 13. State lib.; 14. (other). **Functions/Activities:** 15. Acq./Col. dev.; 16. Adult srvs.; 17. Admin.; 18. Apprais.; 19. Archit./Bldgs.; 20. Cat./Class.; 21. Chld. srvs.; 22. Circ.; 23. Cons./Pres.; 24. Consult.; 25. Cont. ed.; 26. Educ. lib. sci.; 27. Ext. srvs.; 28. Fund/Grants; 29. Gvt. pubs.; 30. Indx./Abs.; 31. Instr. lib. use; 32. Media srvs.; 33. Micro.; 34. Netwks./Coop.; 35. Persnl.; 36. PR; 37. Publshg.; 38. Recs. mgt.; 39. Ref. srvs.; 40. Repro.; 41. Resrch.; 42. Review.; 43. Secur.; 44. Serials; 45. Spec. col.; 46. Tech. srvs.; 47. Trustees/Bds.; 48. YA srvs.; 49. (other).

pet. of Storytel. Richmond Cncl. on Educ.: Lib. Com. (1981–). **Honors:** Alpha Psi Omega, 1969. **Pubns.:** *Annotated Reading Lists of Selected Independent Schools, Vol. 2: 5th through 8th grade* (forthcoming); various reviews, *Voice of Youth Advocates* (1980–). **Activities:** 10; 20, 21, 48; 55, 56 **Addr.:** St. Catherine's School, 6001 Grove Ave., Richmond, VA 23226.

Hemming, J. Terry (N. 25, 1948, Pocatello, ID) Circ. Libn., Brigham Young Univ. Law Lib., 1978–, Acq. Libn., 1973–78, Cat. Libn., 1972–73. **Educ.:** Brigham Young Univ., 1969–73, BA (Pol. Sci.), 1975–78, MLS; 1979, Cert. Law Libn. **Orgs.:** AALL: Com. on Rel. with Pubshrs. and Dlrs. (1976–). UT Coll. Lib. Cncl.: Pub. Srvs. Com. (Ch., 1980–82). UT LA: Spec. Lib. Sect. (1979–). **Pubns.:** Ed., *Abs. of Bk. Reviews in Current Legal Pers.* (1980–); Pubshr., *Pubns. Clearing Hse. Bltn.* (1978–1981). **Activities:** 12; 22, 36, 39; 59, 77, 92 **Addr.:** Brigham Young University, Law Library, Provo, UT 84602.

Hemphill, B. Franklin (Ja. 21, 1936, Lincoln, NE) Asst. Dir., Baltimore Cnty. Pub. Lib., 1964–, Admin. Asst., 1961–63. **Educ.:** Univ. of NE, 1955–59, BA (Eng. Phil., Anthro.); Rutgers Univ., 1959–60, MS, LS; Salisbury State Coll., 1979, Cert. (Energy Audit.). **Orgs.:** ALA: Ch., Archit. for Pub. Libs. Com. (1974–77). MD LA: Ch., Anl. Prog. Com. (1965); Ch., Nom. Com. (1967). **Pubns.:** "New Concepts in Baltimore County, *Wilson Lib. Bltn.* (1981); *Minilibraries (Reading Centers)* (1976); "Lessons of a Fire," *Lib. Jnl.* (Mr. 1966); "When Bigger Isn't Better," *Lib. Jnl.* (D. 1979). **Activities:** 9; 17, 19, 24 **Addr.:** 1809 Landrake Rd., Towson, MD 21204.

Hempleman, Barbara Florence (Mr. 3, 1925, Bellevue, PA) Lib. Dir., Warren Wilson Coll., 1978–; Ref. Libn., Atlanta Univ., 1974–78; Lectr., Emory Univ., Div. of Libnshp., 1973–74; Asst. Prof., Hist., Warren Wilson Coll., 1966–69, 1954–56. **Educ.:** Coll. of Wooster, 1947, AB (Hist.); NY Univ., 1953, MA (Hist.); Atlanta Univ., 1973, MLS; various crs. **Orgs.:** ALA. NC LA: Int. Frdm. Com. (1980–). West. NC LA: VP, Pres. Elect (1981). Young Women's Christ. Assn.: Bd. of Dir. (1979–80). **Honors:** Beta Phi Mu, 1974. **Pubns.:** Various articles in Presby. Church pubns. **Activities:** 1; 17, 39; 74, 92 **Addr.:** Warren Wilson College Library, Swannanoa, NC 28778.

Hench, John Bixler (F. 21, 1943, Colorado Springs, CO) Alden Porter Johnson Resrch. & Pubn. Ofcr., Amer. Antiq. Socty., 1977–, Ed. of Pubns., 1973–77; Asst. Prof. of Hist., Mankato State Coll., 1970–73. **Educ.:** Lafayette Coll., 1961–65, AB (Hist.); Clark Univ., 1965–70, AM (Hist.), 1979, PhD (Hist.). **Orgs.:** Assn. for the Bibl. of Hist. Amer. Cncl. of Learned Societies: Conf. of Secretaries (1977–). Amer. Hist. Assn. Org. of Amer. Histns. **Pubns.:** Jt. ed., *The Press and the American Revolution* (1980); "Massachusetts Printers and the Commonwealth's Newspaper Advertisement Tax of 1785," *Procs. of the Amer. Antiq. Socty.* (Ap. 1977). **Activities:** 14-Indp. resrch. lib.; 33, 37, 41; 55, 56, 57 **Addr.:** American Antiquarian Society, 185 Salisbury St., Worcester, MA 01609.

Henderson, Carol C. (O. 25, 1938, Columbus, OH) Deputy Dir., Washington Ofc., ALA, 1979–; Assoc. Dir., 1977–79, Asst. Dir., 1975–77; Asst. Libn. for Pub. Srvs., George Mason Univ., 1972–75, Ref. and Circ. Libn., 1969–72. **Educ.:** OH State Univ., 1958–60, BA (Eng.), Cath. Univ., 1967–68, MSLS. **Orgs.:** ALA. DC LA: Nat. Lib. Week Com. (1975–77); Legis. Com., (1979). VA LA: Second VP (1974); Ch., Coll. and Univ. Sect. (1972); Ch. ad hoc VLA Dev. Com., (1974–75); Ch. Mem. Com., (1974); Lib. Com. Cons. for Cont. Higher Educ. in North. VA (1973–75). Task Force on Interlibrary Loan; VA State Cncl. of Higher Educ. and VA State Lib., (1975). Com. for Full Funding of Educ. Programs: VP (1978–). Higher Educ. Group of Washington DC: Treas., (1979–80). **Honors:** Beta Phi Mu. **Pubns.:** Jt. auth., "Legislation Affecting Librarianship in 1977, 78, 79, 80" *Bowker Annual of Lib. & Book Trade Info.* (1978, 79, 80, 81). "ALA Washington Notes," *Wilson Lib. Bltn.*, (1976–77). Ed., *ALA Washington Nwsltr.*, (1977–). Ed., *Legis. Report of the ALA Washington Office* (1977–). Ed., George Mason Univ. *Lib. Notes* (1972–75). **Activities:** 1; 17, 36; 78 **Addr.:** ALA Washington Office, 110 Maryland Ave., N.E., Box 54, Washington, DC 20002.

Henderson, Douglas A. (Jl. 16, 1950, Washington, DC) Pers. Dept. Head, Clark Cnty. Lib. Dist., 1976–. **Educ.:** Univ. of S. FL, 1972–75, MA (Eng.); FL State Univ., 1975–76, MLS. **Orgs.:** ALA. NV LA: South. Dist., Secy.-Treas. U.S. Hang Gliding Assn. **Activities:** 9; 32, 33, 44; 56 **Addr.:** Clark County Library District, 1401 E. Flamingo Rd., Las Vegas, NV 89109.

Henderson, George Fletcher (F. 17, 1936, Kingston, ON) Asst. Archvst., Queen's Univ. Arch., 1974–, Gvt. Docum. Libn., 1962–74. **Educ.:** Queen's Univ., 1955–59, BA Hon. (Hist.), 1959–64, MA (Hist.); McGill Univ., 1961–62, BLS. **Orgs.:** Assn. of Can. Archvsts. Can. Oral Hist. Assn. Assn. of Recorded Sound Col. Kingston Hist. Socty.: Corres. Secy. (1978–). **Pubns.:** *Federal Royal Commissions in Canada, 1867-1966: A checklist* (1967); "The Royal Commission Collection at Queen's University Library," *Douglas Lib. Notes* (Spr. 1968); "The first Canadian census," *Douglas Lib. Notes* (Spr. 1969); "Joseph Scriven: Canadian Hymn-Writer," *Douglas Lib. Notes* (Aut. 1969); Jt. auth., "Queen's progress towards computerized access to government publications," *CACUL Nsltr.* (IV (6)); other articles. **Activities:** 2; 15, 32, 39; 67, 85 **Addr.:** Queen's University Archives, Kathleen Ryan Hall, Queen's University, Kingston, ON Canada.

Henderson, James Wood (Je. 6, 1917, Carthage, MO) Proj. Dir., Dict. Cat. of the Resrch. Libs., NY Pub. Lib., 1977–, Andrew W. Mellon Dir. of the Resrch. Libs. 1963–77, Asst. to the Dir., 1959–63, Chief, Acq. Div., 1953–59, Head, Entry Investigation Sect., 1951–53; Head, Cat. Sect., NY State Lib., 1949–51; Lectr., Pratt Inst. Lib. Sch., 1955–60. **Educ.:** Univ. of OK, 1935–39, BA (Letters), 1939–41, MA (Eng.); Columbia Univ., 1947–48, BSLS; NY Univ., 1950–58, MPA. **Orgs.:** NY LA. ALA. Mss. Socty. Grolier Club. **Honors:** Phi Beta Kappa. **Pubns.:** Jt. ed., *Library Catalogs, Their Preservation and Maintenance by Photographic and Automated Techniques* (1968); "Consulting in Union-Management Relations," *Lib. Trends* (Win. 1980); Jt. auth., "The Librarian as Conservator," *Lib. Qtly.* (Ja. 1970); "Introduction," *Dict. Cat. of The Resrch. Libs. of The NY Pub. Lib.* (1979–). **Activities:** 17, 23, 46 **Addr.:** 175 West 12th St., Apt. 2 D, New York, NY 10011.

Henderson, Katherine Slocum (Ja. 26, 1935, Carmel, CA) Lib. Dir., Clark Cnty. Law Lib., 1972–; Legal Resrch. Asst., 1970–72; HS and Elem. Sch. Tchr., 1964–68. **Educ.:** Univ. of CA, Berkeley, 1954–57, BA (Eng.); Univ. of Santa Clara, 1968–72, JD (Law); Univ. of Denver, 1978–79, MLL; CA Stan. Elem. Teaching Cred., 1968; Spec. Tchr. in Reading Cert., 1968; Cert. Law Libn., AALL, 1979. **Orgs.:** AALL: West. Pac. Chap. South. CA Assn. of Law Libs. NV LA. NV State Adv. Cncl. on Libs.: Spec. Lib. Rep. (1975–82). **Pubns.:** *Researching the Law in Nevada* (1974); *Accredited Law School Library Minimum Collection and Estimated Start Up Costs* (1979). **Addr.:** Clark County Law Library, 200 E. Carson Ave., Las Vegas, NV 89101.

Henderson, Kathryn Luther (Jl. 12, 1923, Champaign, IL) Assoc. Prof., Univ. of IL Grad. Sch. of Lib. Sci., 1965–; Head Catlgr., McCormick Theo. Semy., 1956–65, Circ. Libn., 1953–56; Serial Catlgr., Univ. of IL, 1950–53. **Educ.:** Univ. of IL, 1940–44, BA (Hist.), 1946–48, BS (LS), 1948–51, MS (LS). **Orgs.:** ASIS. ALA: Subj. Headings Com. (Ch., 1966–67); Com. on Cat. of Chld. Mtrls. (1969–71); RTSD, Elec. Com. (Ch., 1960–62); various coms. IL LA: Cat. and Class. Sect. (Ch., 1956–57). ATLA: ATLA/ALA Cat. Code Rev. Com. (Consult., 1962–66); Cat. and Class. Com. (Ch., 1959–62); various coms. Beta Phi Mu: Fndn.; 1st Natl. Secy. AAUP. **Honors:** Beta Phi Mu. **Pubns.:** Ed., *Major Classification Systems: the Dewey Centennial* (1977); Ed., *MARC II Records and their Users* (1971); Ed., *Trends in American Publishing* (1968); "Treated with a Degree of Uniformity, and Common Sense: Descriptive Cataloging in the United States: 1876–1975," *Lib. Trends* (Jl. 1976); "Serial Cataloging Revisited," *Serial Pubns. in Large Libs.* (1970). **Activities:** 11; 20, 26, 46 **Addr.:** 1107 E. Silver St., Urbana, IL 61801.

Henderson, Madeline M. (S. 3, 1922, Merrimac, MA) Consult., 1979–; Mgr., ADP Info. Anal., Natl. Bur. of Stan., 1978–79, Chief, Comp. Info. Sect., 1975–78, Staff Asst. Comp. Usage Info., 1972–75, Data Prcs. Applications Anal., 1964–72; Resrch. Anal., Natl. Sci. Fndn., 1956–62. **Educ.:** Emmanuel Coll., 1940–44, AB (Chem.); American Univ., 1975–77, MPA (Pub. Admin.). **Orgs.:** ASIS. ALA: Tech. Stds. for Lib. Autom. Com. (1975–). Fed. Lib. Com.: Ch., Task Force on Autom. (1970–75). Amer. Natl. Stan. Inst.: Z-39 Com. on Lib. Work (Rep., 1975–79). NY Acad. of Sci. AAAS: Sect. T (Secy., 1978–). Amer. Chem. Socty.: Com. on Copyrt. (Ch., 1978–80). **Honors:** Pi Alpha Alpha, 1977; Dept. of Cmrce., Sci. & Tech. Fellow, 1971. **Pubns.:** Jt. ed., *Electronic Communication: Technology & Impacts* (1980); Contrib., *The Federal Sector in the Information Age: Its Development, Its Impact* (1976); "Copyright Impacts of Future Technology," *Jnl. of Chem. Info. and Comp. Sci.* (My. 1976); Jt. auth., "Federal Library Cooperation," *Lib. Trends* (O. 1975); other articles. **Activities:** 4; 17, 24, 34; 56, 61, 93 **Addr.:** 5021 Alta Vista Rd., Bethesda, MD 20014.

Henderson, Mary Emma S. (Ap. 16, 1923, Ben Hill Cnty., GA) Head Libn., Abraham Baldwin Agri. Coll., 1969–, Asst. Libn., 1967–69; Libn., Irwin Cnty. HS, 1958–67. **Educ.:** GA State Coll. for Women, 1939–43, AB (Eng.); FL State Univ., 1963–67, MLS, 1976–77, AMD (LS). **Orgs.:** ALA: ACRL. GA LA. **Honors:** Beta Phi Mu. **Activities:** 1; 15, 17, 35 **Addr.:** 110 South Apple St., Ocilla, GA 31794.

Henderson, Roberta Marie (Jl. 27, 1929, Mosinee, WI) Ref. Libn., Assoc. Prof., North. MI Univ., 1971–; Tutor, Nkozi Tchr. Trng. Coll., Nabusanke, Mpigi, Uganda, 1968–70; Libn., Ankara Amer. HS, Ankara, Turkey, 1966–68; Tchr., Libn., Zama Amer. HS, Camp Zama, Japan, 1963–66; Libn., Frankfurt Amer. HS, Frankfurt, Germany, 1959–63; Libn., Prescott Jr. HS, 1958–59; Tchr., Libn., Clark Air Base, 1956–57; Libn., Ashland (WI) HS, 1955–56; various positions as tchr., libn., 1951–55. **Educ.:** Univ. of WI, Stevens Point, 1947–51, BS (Eng., Bio.); Univ. of WI, Madison, 1957–58, MS (LS); North. MI Univ., 1974–75, MA (Eng.); Univ. of Denver, 1979–80, CAS (Libnshp., Info. Sci., Env. Sci.); various crs. **Orgs.:** ALA. AAUP. **Honors:** GSLIM, Univ. of Denver, Title II–B Flwshp., Advnc. Std. Prog., 1979; N.D.E.A. Flwshp., Sum. Inst., 1967; Phi Kappa Phi. **Pubns.:** "Locating Materials in Periodicals and Documents" slide/tape (1977); "Library Materials for Literature Students" slide/tape (1979). **Activities:** 1, 10; 26, 31, 39; 55, 65 **Addr.:** 433 E. Ridge Apt. A, Marquette, MI 49855.

Henderson, Rosemary N. (Jl. 15, 1936, Coffeyville, KS) Dir., Lrng. Resrcs., Coffeyville Cmnty. Jr. Coll., 1968–; Assoc. Prof., Libnshp., Univ. of ND, 1967–68. **Educ.:** Stephens Coll., 1954–56, AA; TX Wesleyan Coll., 1957–59, BS (Soc. Sci.); Emporia State Univ., 1966–67, ML (Libnshp.); KS Univ., 1973–76, EdD (Higher Educ. Admin.). **Orgs.:** ALA: ACRL/Cmnty./Jr. Coll. Sect. (Ch., 1975–76); ALA Nom. Com. (1979); Archvst./Histn., Cmnty./Jr. Coll. Sect. (1978–). KS LA: Cncl. (1970–74; 1978–); Mem. Ch. KS ALA (1978–). Mt. Plains LA: Coll. & Univ. Sect. (Ch., 1973–74). **Pubns.:** Reviews. **Activities:** 1; 17 **Addr.:** 2205 West 2nd, Coffeyville, KS 67337.

Henderson, Ruth (D. 8, 1943, Jackson, MI) Asst. Msc. Libn., Msc. Catlgr., The City Coll., CUNY, 1970–. **Educ.:** Alma Coll., 1962–66, BA (Eng.); Univ. of MI, 1968–69, MMus, 1969–70, AMLS. **Orgs.:** Msc. LA: Cat. Com. (1973–81); Autom. Com. (1976–81); Pubns. Cncl. (1975–1980). Msc. OCLC Users Grp.: REMUS Com. (Ch., 1980–). Intl. Assn. of Msc. Libs. **Pubns.:** Ed., *Msc. Cat. Bltn.* (1974–80). **Activities:** 1, 12; 20; 55 **Addr.:** Music Library, The City College, 138th St. at Convent Ave., New York, NY 10031.

Henderson, Sallie (Ap. 16, 1942, St. Louis, MO) Dir., Scenic Reg. Lib., 1975–, Asst. Dir., 1970–74, YA Libn., 1965–70. **Educ.:** Univ. of MO, 1960–64, BA; Rutgers Univ., 1964–65, MLS. **Orgs.:** MO LA: Pres. (1981–82); VP (1980–81); Legis. Ch. (1977–79); Pub. Lib. Div. (Pres., 1976). Un. Area Cham. of Cmrce. **Pubns.:** "Bookmobile Service: Still Important to Scenic Regional Library," *Show-Me Libs.* (Ap. 1980). **Activities:** 9; 16, 17, 36 **Addr.:** Scenic Regional Library, 11 S. Washington, Union, MO 63084.

Henderson, William T (O. 5, 1929, IL) Binding and Prsrvn. Libn., Univ. Lib., Univ. of IL, 1965–; Acq. Asst., McCormick Theo. Semy. Lib., 1957–65. **Educ.:** Univ. of IL, 1947–51, BS (Floriculture); McCormick Theo. Semy., 1953–57, MDiv (Theo.); Univ. of Chicago, 1957–60, MALS. **Orgs.:** IL LA: Resrcs. and Tech. Srvs. Sect. (Ch., 1964–65). ALA: RTSD/Serials Sect., Nom. Com. (1972). ATLA. **Pubns.:** "Serials Binding–A Librarian's View," *Serials Publications in Large Libraries* (1970). **Activities:** 1; 17, 23, 44 **Addr.:** 1107 E. Silver, Urbana, IL 61801.

Hendricks, Donald D. (N. 3, 1931, Flint, MI) Dean of Lib. Srvs., Univ. of New Orleans, 1978–; Prof. and Dir. of Lib. and Dir., Univ. of TX S. West. Med. Sch., S. Ctrl. Reg. Med. Lib. Prog., 1970–78; Dir. of Libs., Sam Houston St. Univ., 1966–70; Head Libn., Millikin Univ., 1960–63. **Educ.:** Univ. of MI, 1954, AB (Pol. Sci); 1954–55, AMLS; Univ. of IL, 1963–66, PhD (LS). **Orgs.:** ALA: Ctrl. Prsc. Com. (1967–69, Ch. 1968–71); Cnclr. Lg. (1971–72); Com. Resrch. (1974–78); Cncl. (1975–79); various other coms. Med. LA: Prog. Com. (Ch. 1974); Com. Prob. Netwk. Interfacing (1976–77); many other coms. TX LA: many coms. Univ. IL LS Alum. TX Inf. Exch. various other orgs. and coms. Bibl Socty. (London). Bibl. Socty. of Amer. Grolier Club. Kiwanis Club: Huntsville, Pres. (1969–70). **Pubns.:** "Advances in Medical Librarianship" in *Advances in Librarianship* (1979); Ed., *Medical Library Statistics, 1975–76* (1977); Ed., *Medical Library Statistics, 1974–75* (1976); *A Report on Library Networks* (Occasional Paper, 1973); jt. ed., *Proceedings: Medical Libraries, Needs and Services* (1972); various monographs and articles. **Activities:** 1; 17, 34, 45; 56, 57, 70 **Addr.:** Earl K. Long Library, University of New Orleans, Lake Front, New Orleans, LA 70148.

Hendrickson, Linnea M. (My. 29, 1944, Marinette, WI) Asst. Libn., Penn State Univ., 1976–; Assoc. Fac., Pima Cmnty. Coll., 1975–76; Instr., Coll. of Ganado, 1973–75; Caseworker, NY City Dept. Soc. Srvs., 1967–68; Volun., VISTA, U.S. Gvt., 1966–67. **Educ.:** Univ. of MI, 1962–66, BA (Hist.); Univ. of MA, 1969–71, MAT (Eng., Educ.); Univ. of AZ, 1971–73, MA (Eng.), 1975–76, MLS. **Orgs.:** ALA. PA LA. **Pubns.:** Jt. auth., *Bibliographic Instruction: A Handbook* (1980). **Activities:** 1; 31, 39; 63, 92 **Addr.:** E108 Pattee Library, Penn State University, University Park, PA 16802.

Hendrickson, Norma K. R. (S. 13, 1936, Morris, MN) Subj. Cat., Library of Congress 1979–; Agent at the Lib. of Cong., Northwest. Univ. Lib. Africana Proj., 1978–79; Cat. Ed., Cook Cnty. Law Lib. (Chicago), 1974–78; Sr. Descr. Cat., Lib. of Cong., 1968–74, Descr. Cat., 1966–68; Ref. Libn., Fairfax Cnty. Pub. Lib. (VA) 1965; Law Cat., Univ. of Chicago Law Lib., 1963–65; Circ. and Ref. Libn., Univ. of Chicago Educ. Lib., 1962–63; Jr. Soc. Sci. Libn., OK St. Univ. Lib., 1959–62. **Educ.:** Concordia Coll., 1954–58, BA (Eng. Lit.); Univ. of MI, 1958–59, AMLS; Univ. of WI–Madison, Sum. 1956, (LS). **Orgs.:** ALA. AALL. Law Libn. Socty. of Washington, D.C. IL LA. Lutheran Church LA. Boy Scouts of Amer.: Pack Com. Mem. Pack 1086. **Activities:** 4; 20; 77 **Addr.:** 12306 Greenhill Drive, Silver Spring, MD 20904.

Hendrix, Wilma P. (Mr. 14, 1925, Trenton, TN) Coord. of Pub. Srvs., Memphis State Univ., 1973–, Ref. Libn., 1967–73, Branch Libn., 1966–67; Tchr., Shelby Cnty., 1961–66. **Educ.:** Memphis State Univ., 1957–61, BS (Educ.); George Peabody Coll., 1964–66, MLS. **Orgs.:** ALA: LAMA, Com. Coll. & Univ.

Special Subjects/Services: 50. Adult educ.; 51. Advert./Mktg.; 52. Aerosp.; 53. Agric.; 54. Area std.; 55. Arts/Hum.; 56. Autom.; 57. Bibl./Prtg.; 58. Bio. sci.; 59. Bus./Fin.; 60. Chem.; 61. Copyrt.; 62. Documtn.; 63. Educ.; 64. Engin.; 65. Env.; 66. Eth. grps.; 67. Film; 68. Food/Nutr.; 69. Geneal.; 70. Geo.; 71. Geol.; 72. Handcpd.; 73. Hist.; 74. Int. frdm.; 75. Info. sci.; 76. Insr.; 77. Law; 78. Legis.; 79. Math./Comp. sci.; 80. Med.; 81. Metals; 82. Nat. resrcs.; 83. Newsp.; 84. Nuc. sci.; 85. Oral hist.; 86. Petr./Energy; 87. Pharm.; 88. Phys./Astr./Math.; 89. Readg.; 90. Relig.; 91. Sci./Tech.; 92. Soc. sci.; 93. Telecom.; 94. Transp.; 95. (other).

Who's Who in Library and Information Services

Stats. (1979, 80); RASD, Stan. Com. (1979, 80). SLA: VP, Pres.-Elect, Mid-South Chap. (1979–80). SELA. TN LA. **Activities:** 1; 17, 33, 39 **Addr.:** 4700 Priscilla Ave., Memphis, TN 38128.

Hendry, Barbara L. (S. 4, 1930, W. Palm Beach, FL) Chief, Tech. Srvs. Div., Air Force, Simpson Hist. Resrch. Ctr., 1980–; Chief, Docum. Systs. Branch, Air Univ. Lib., 1978–80, Indxr., Chief Indexing Systs. Branch, 1969–77; Serials Libn., Los Alamos Scientific Lab., 1959–68. **Educ.:** FL State Univ., 1947–51, AB (Eng.), 1958–59, MA (LS). **Orgs.:** SLA: Cont. Educ. Com. (1970–74). **Activities:** 4, 12; 30, 33, 46; 52, 56, 74 **Addr.:** Air Force, Simpson Historical Research Center, Montgomery, AL 36108.

Hendsey, Susanne B. (Mr. 19, 1936, Providence, RI) Lib. Dir., Fed. Trade Comsn., 1979–, Deputy Libn., 1972–79; Sr. Asst. Libn., Bus. and Pubns. Admin., Cornell Univ., Grad. Sch., 1967–72; Head, Mgt. Bus. Admin. Lib., Univ. of CT, 1965–66. **Educ.:** Univ. of CT, 1954–60, BA (Eng.); Univ. of MI, 1966–67, MLS. **Orgs.:** Law Libns. Socty. of Washington DC: Bd. of Dir. (1980–81). AALL. SLA. DC LA. **Honors:** Beta Phi Mu, 1967; Fed. Trade Comsn., Supervisory Merit Awd., 1980. **Pubns.:** Jt. Auth., "US and Canadian Business and Banking Information Sources," *Law Lib. Jnl.* (N. 1977); "Questions and Answers," *Law Lib. Jnl.* (My. 1974); Jt. Auth., "Selected Sources of Data for Marketing Analyses," *Demand Analyses for Marketing Decisions* (1973). **Activities:** 4; 17, 39; 59, 77, 78 **Addr.:** Federal Trade Commission Library, 6th and Pennsylvania Ave., N.W., Washington, DC 20580.

Heneghan, Mary A. (D. 12, 1926, Somerville, MA) Reg. Admin., East. MA Reg. Lib. Syst., 1972–; Reg. Liaison, MA Bur. of Lib. Ext., 1971–72; Lib. Consult., Arthur D. Little, Inc., 1967–71; Head, Ref.-Per. Micro., Providence Pub. Lib., 1963–67; Ref. Asst., 1954–63; Visit. Fac., Syracuse Univ. Lib. Sch., 1966, 1967, 1971; Libn., Sch. of Nursing, Georgetown Univ., 1952–54. **Educ.:** Boston Coll., 1945–48; Simmons Coll., 1949–52, SB (LS); Cath. Univ., 1952–55, MS (LS). **Orgs.:** ALA: Cncl., (1973–77); PLA Goals, Guidelines and Stan. Com. (1973–79); Strg. Com. for Dev. of Process for Stan. (1978–79). MA LA: Ad Hoc Com. to Study State Aid Statutes; Exec. Bd. New Eng. LA. Women's Natl. Bk. Assn. Women's Educ. and Indus. Un. Simmons Coll. Alum. Assn.: various coms., **Pubns.:** "Conversations on Libraries," LJ Special Report #16; "Telephone and mag. selections," *RQ* (Spr. 1972); "Developing a model for continuing education and personnel development in libraries," *Lib. Trends* (Jl. 1971). **Activities:** 9; 17, 24, 34 **Addr.:** 1580 Mass. Ave., Cambridge, MA 02138.

Henes, Elizabeth Mary (Ja. 18, 1920, Liverpool, NY) Ref. Libn., Syracuse Univ. Lib., 1967–, Per. Libn., 1966–67, Back Sets-Acq., 1965–66, Actg. Serials Libn., 1964–65, Asst. Serials Libn., 1958–63, Asst. Order Libn., 1947–57; Tchr.-Libn., Truxton (NY) Ctrl. Sch., 1943–46. **Educ.:** Syracuse Univ., 1938–42, AB (Eng. Educ.), 1942–43, MA (Eng. Educ.), 1951, MS in LS. **Orgs.:** ALA. NY LA. Friends of the Liverpool Pub. Lib. Syracuse Univ. Libns. Asm. Phi Beta Kappa: Kappa of NY Chap. (Pres., 1978–79). AAUP. **Honors:** Beta Phi Mu. **Activities:** 1; 31, 33, 39 **Addr.:** 208 Tamarack St., Liverpool, NY 13088.

Hengen, Jamie Lynn (Ap. 25, 1955, Biloxi, MS) Asst. Dir., Biloxi Pub. Lib., 1978–. **Educ.:** Univ. of S. AL, 1973–77, BA (Hist.); FL State Univ., 1977–78, MS (LS). **Orgs.:** ALA. SELA. MS LA. Altrusa Club of Biloxi. **Pubns.:** "Service to the Disadvantaged," *MS Libs.* (Aut. 1979). **Activities:** 9; 15, 17, 36 **Addr.:** 203 Miramar Ave., Biloxi, MS 39530.

Heninger, Irene Callen (F. 2, 1923, Jerome, ID) Dir., Kitsap Reg. Lib., 1971–; Asst. Prof., Sch. of Libnshp., Univ. of WA, 1968–71; Asst. Libn., Ghld. Libn., Twin Falls (ID) Pub. Lib., 1965–68. **Educ.:** Barnard Coll., 1947, AB (Eng.); Columbia Univ., 1954–55, MLS. **Orgs.:** WA LA: Second VP (1975–77); WA Lib. Network: Exec. Cncl. Cont. Educ. com. (1975–77). ALA. Pac. NW LA: Pres. (1979–80); Chld. and YA Div. (Ch., 1974–75). Amer. Civil Liberties Un. Leag. of Women Voters. Common Cause. **Activities:** 9, 11; 17, 19, 21 **Addr.:** Kitsap Regional Library, 1301 Sylvan Way, Bremerton, WA 98310.

Henington, David M. (Ag. 16, 1929, El Dorado, AR) Dir., Houston Pub. Lib., 1967–; Asst. Dir., Dallas Pub. Lib., 1962–67; Dir., Waco Pub. Lib., 1958–62; Head, Lit. and Hist. Dept., Dallas Pub. Lib., 1958; YA Libn., Brooklyn Pub. Lib., 1956–58. **Educ.:** Univ. of Houston, 1947–51, BA (Hist.); Columbia Univ., 1955–56, MSLS. **Orgs.:** ALA: PLA (Pres., 1966–67); Lib. Admin. Div./PR Sect., Bd. TX LA: Pres. (1968). Rotary Club of Houston. **Honors:** TX LA, Libn. of the Yr., 1976; Houston Bar Assn., Liberty Bell Awd., 1976. **Activities:** 9; 17 **Addr.:** 6225 San Felipe Rd., Houston, TX 77057.

Henke, Dan (F. 18, 1924, San Antonio, TX) Prof. of Law & Dir., Legal Info. Ctr., Hastings Coll. of the Law, Univ. of CA, 1970–, Prof. of Law & Law Libn., Univ. of CA at Berkeley, 1959–70; Head, Bur. of Law & Legis. Ref., State of NJ, 1956–59; Asst. to Law Libn., Univ. of WA, 1955–56; Attorney, San Antonio, Texas, 1952–55. **Educ.:** Georgetown Univ., 1940–43, BS (Frgn. Srv.), 1947–51, JD; Univ. of WA, 1955–56, MLL (LS). **Orgs.:** ASIS. AALL: Ch., Com. on Rel. with Pubshrs. (1968–69); Ch., Law Lib. Jnl. Com. (1966–67); Pres., West. Pac. Chap. (1976–77). Natl. Micro. Assn. ALA: ACRL/Law & Pol. Sci. Sect. (Ch., 1974–75); Intl. Frdm. Com. (1974–75). Amer. Bar Assn.: Sci. and Tech. Sect./Educ. Com. (Ch., 1979–). State Bar of CA: Com. on Comp. and Law (Ch., 1975–76). Other orgs. **Honors:** Order of the Coif, 1962; Beta Phi Mu, 1956; Purple Heart; Bronze Star, US Army-Italy 1945. **Pubns.:** *California Legal Research Handbook* (1971); *California Law Guide* (1976); "Law Library Salaries," *Law Lib. Jnl.* (1970); "State Legal Publications," *Law Lib. Jnl.* (1960); Jt. auth., *Anglo-American Law Collections, University of California, Berkeley & Davis* 1970–1979 Supplement. **Activities:** 1, 12; 17, 19, 24; 59, 75, 77 **Addr.:** Legal Information Center, Hastings College of the Law, University of California, 200 McAllister St., San Francisco, CA 94102.

Henke, Esther Mae (Ap. 4, 1925, Orlando, OK) Head, Lib. Srvs. Branch, OK Dept. of Lib., 1956–, Field Libn., 1953–55; Cnty. Libn., Ray Cnty. Lib. (Richmond, MO), 1948–51, Bkmobile Libn., 1947–48. **Educ.:** Univ. of OK, 1944–47, BA (LS), 1952–53, MA (Hist.). **Orgs.:** ALA: Fed. Rel. Coord. (1957–). SWLA. OK LA. OK Women's Posse of the West.: Sheriff. Soroptomist Intl. Club of Okla. City: Pres. (1965–1973). **Honors:** OK LA, Disting. Srv. Awd., 1971–; Theta Sigma Phi Byliners Awd., Outstan. Woman of the Yr. 1966. **Addr.:** 4316 Woodland Drive, Oklahoma City, OK 73105.

Henkle, Herman H. (Mr. 26, 1900, Colorado Springs, CO) Retired, 1969–; Exec. Dir., The John Crerar Lib., 1963–69, Libn., 1947–65; Dir., Prcs. Dept., Lib. of Congs., 1942–47; Dean, Sch. of LS, Simmons Coll., 1937–42; Assoc., Sch. of LS, Univ. of IL, 1936–37; Jr. Libn., Bio. Lib., Univ. of CA, Berkeley, 1931–35. **Educ.:** Whittier Coll., 1924–28, AB (Sci.); Univ. of CA, Berkeley, 1929–33, MS (LS); Univ. of Chicago, 1935–36 (LS). **Orgs.:** ALA: Various coms., bd. appts. (1933–). SLA: Pres. (1945–46); various coms., bd. appts. (1935–). ASIS: Fndr.; Pres. (1958). AAAS. UNESCO: SE Asian Conf. on Documtn. (Amer. Rep., 1961); Consult. on Sci. Libs., Pakistan (1961). **Honors:** Whittier Coll., Alum. Awd. for Prof. Achvmt. in Libnshp., 1961; Whittier Coll., Hon. LittD, 1961; Amer. Socty. for Metals, Hon. Life Mem., 1961; SLA, Hall of Fame, 1971. **Pubns.:** *Report and Recommendations for Establishing National Science Libraries and Information Centers in Pakistan* (1966) various tech. rpts. based on consult. srvys. (1969–74). **Activities:** 1, 12; 17, 20, 24; 58, 60, 64 **Addr.:** 2801 King Dr., Apt. 1901, Chicago, IL 60616.

Henley, Atha Louise (My. 17, 1927, Marshall, MO) Vetny. Med. Libn. and Libn. II, Auburn Univ., 1970–; Libn., Div. Plant Indus., FL St. Dept. Agr., 1966–70; Sci. Libn., Univ. FL, 1960–66; Libn. Pharm. Bacteriology, OH St. Univ., 1955–60. **Educ.:** MO Valley Coll., 1945–49, BA (Hist.); Univ. CA, Berkeley, 1954–55, 1956, MLS. **Orgs.:** AL LA: Coll. Univ. Spec. Lib. Div., V Ch. (1976–77), Ch. (1977–78); Hlth. Sci. Libns. RT, Nom. Com. (1979–80). Med. LA: Vetny. Med. Lib. Grp., Ch. (1974), Ad Hoc Com. Basic List Vetny. Mtls. (Ch., 1976–78), Com. Survey Vetny. Lib. (1978). SLA: AL Chap., Recruit. (Ch., 1973–74); various other coms. Assn. Amer. Vetny. Coll. **Pubns.:** "Organization and Compilation of a Basic List of Veterinary Medical Serials," *Jnl. Vetny. Med. Educ.* (Fall 1978); "A Basic List of Veterinary Medical Serials," (letter) *Bltn. Med. Lib. Assn.* (O. 1979). **Activities:** 1; 17, 31, 39; 58, 80, 95-Veterinary Medicine. **Addr.:** Veterinary Medical Library, Auburn University, Auburn, AL 36849.

Henn, Barbara J. (Ag. 2, 1936, Indianapolis, IN) Asst. Acq. Libn., IN Univ., 1980–, Tech. Srvs. Libn.-Bus., 1978–80, Acq. Libn.-RCL, 1968–78; Ref. Libn.-Krannert, Purdue Univ., 1967–68. **Educ.:** Concordia Tchrs. Coll., 1954–58, BS (Educ.); IN Univ., 1966–67, MLS. **Orgs.:** ALA. IN LA. IN Univ. Libns. Assn.: VP (1973–74). Beta Phi Mu: Chi Chap., Pres. (1973–74); Exec. Bd. (1974–75). **Pubns.:** "RCL Central Services," in *ULA Qtly.* (Fall 1978); Reviews. **Activities:** 1; 15, 39, 46; 59, 63, 92 **Addr.:** 4407 Kinser Dr., Bloomington, IN 47401.

Henne, Frances E. (O. 11, 1906, Springfield, IL) Prof. Emeritus, Sch. of Lib. Srv., Columbia Univ., 1975–, Lect., 1975–77, Prof., 1961–75, Assoc. Prof., 1954–61, Assoc. Prof., Grad. Lib. Sch., Univ. of Chicago, 1949–54, Assoc. Dean, Dean of Students, Asst. Prof., 1946–50, Instr., 1942–46; Libn., Univ. HS, Univ. of Chicago, 1939–42; Ref. and Circ. Libn. NY State Coll. for Tchrs., Albany, 1935–38. **Educ.:** Univ. of IL, 1926–29, AB (Eng.), 1934, MA (Eng.); Columbia Univ., 1934–35, BSLS; Univ. of Chicago, 1949, PhD (LS). **Orgs.:** ALA: Nom. Com. (1959–60); Cncl. (1965–69); AASL, Bd. (1945–47); Ch. (1948–49); ALSC; LED, Bd. of Dir. (1965–69). AALS. Intl. Assn. of Sch. Libnshp. Cncl. of Natl. Lib. Assn.: Jt. Com. on Lib. Educ. (1959–64). Other orgs. and coms. AAUP. Chld. Lit. Assn. Women's Natl. Book Assn. Bronte Socty. **Honors:** ALA, Lippincott Awd., 1963; ALA, Centennial Cit., 1976; Beta Phi Mu, Beta Phi Mu Awd., 1978; AASL and Baker and Taylor Co., President's Awd., 1979. **Pubns.:** *The Library World and the Publishing of Children's Books* (1976); "American Society as Reflected in Children's Literature" *Society and Children's Literature* (1978); Jt. auth., *Planning Guide for the High School Library Program* (1951); Jt. ed., *Youth, Communication and Libraries* (1949); "Crucial Issues in School Library Development and Professional Education" in *Intl. Assn. of Sch. Libnshp. Conf. Procs.* (1976); other books and articles. **Activities:** 10, 11; 21, 26, 48 **Addr.:** 345 East 50th St., New York, NY 10022.

Hennessy, Charlene C. (Ap. 26, 1928, Avoca, PA) Coord., Lib. Srvs., Cnty. of Delaware, 1978–; Org. of Co. Lib. Syst., Consult., Louis T. Klauder & Sons, 1974–76; Serials Libn., Villanova Univ., 1957–59; Asst. Libn., PA Railroad, 1955–57. **Educ.:** Marywood Coll., 1945–49, BA (LS); Villanova Univ., 1976–77, MSLS. **Orgs.:** ALA. PLA. Delaware Cnty. LA. SLA. Grt. Philadelphia Law LA. AAUW. **Activities:** 9; 17, 28, 34 **Addr.:** Delaware County Library Services, Court House, Media, PA 19063.

Hennings, LeRoy, Jr. (Ag. 17, 1936, Mt. Kisco, NY) Dir., Martin Cnty. Pub. Lib., 1968–; ILL Libn., FL State Univ., 1968; Libn., Bus. Sci. and Tech. Dept., Miami Pub. Lib., 1966–67; Libn. Acq., Ref. Depts., Miami Dade Jr. Coll., 1964–65; Dept. Libn., Engin. and Phys. Lib., Univ. of Miami, 1962–63; Sch. Libn., Tchr., Glades Cnty. Sch. Syst., 1961–62. **Educ.:** Univ. of Miami, 1955–60, AB (Hist.); FL State Univ., 1963–64, 1968, MS (LS). **Orgs.:** ALA. LA. FL LA. **Activities:** 9; 17, 39, 46; 59, 74, 75 **Addr.:** 610 Old Dixie Hwy. #222, Jensen Beach, FL 33457.

Henricks, Duane Edward (N. 21, 1935, Valley City, ND) Docum./Ref. Libn., Kent Lib., SE MO State Univ., 1970–; Ref. Libn., Univ. of North. IA, 1964–65; Ref. Libn., Seattle Pub. Lib., 1964. **Educ.:** Valley City State Tchrs. Coll., 1953–57, BS Educ. (Art & Eng.); Univ. of Denver, 1963–64, MA (LS); Univ. of ND, 1962–63. **Orgs.:** ALA. MO LA. **Pubns.:** "Historic preservation," *Show-Me Libs.* (S. 1979). **Activities:** 1; 29, 39; 55 **Addr.:** 1030 Broadway, Cape Girardeau, MO 63701.

Henry, Alice C. (D. 20, 1947, Waukesha, WI) Resrc. Spec., WI Info. Srv., 1978–; Libn., Cmnty. Rel., Soc. Dev. Comsn., Milwaukee Cnty., 1971–78. **Educ.:** Univ. of WI, 1966–70, BA (Soclgy.), 1970–71, MA (LS). **Orgs.:** SLA: Soc. Sci. Div., Soc. Welfare Sect. (Secy., 1975–76). Info. and Ref. Providers of WI: Comms. Com. (1980–82). Lib. Cncl. of Metro. Milwaukee: Long Range Plng. Com., Coop. Prcs. Subcom. (1975); Elec. Com. (1978). **Activities:** 14-Info. and ref. srv.; 49-Info. and ref.; 92 **Addr.:** Wisconsin Information Service, 161 W. Wisconsin Ave., Rm. 7071, Milwaukee, WI 53203.

Henry, Anne Harris (Jl. 17, 1926, Miami, FL) Archvst., Natl. Hist. Pubns. and Recs. Comsn., Natl. Arch. and Recs. Srv., DC, 1974–; Ed. Asst., Frgn. Broadcast Info. Srv., 1973–74; Archvst., Natl. Hist. Pubns. Comsn., Natl. Arch. and Recs. Srv., 1952–57. **Educ.:** TX Coll. of Arts and Indus., 1947–49, BA (Hist., Gvt.); various grad. crs. in hist. **Orgs.:** Assn. for Documentary Ed. Natl. Arch. Asm. SAA. Socty. for Hist. in the Fed. Gvt. Amer. Cvl. Liberties Un. South. Hist. Assn. Ctr. for Env. Educ. Common Cause. Natl. Trust for Hist. Prsrvn. Various other orgs. **Honors:** Gen. Srvs. Admin., Natl. Arch. and Recs. Srv., Commendable Srv. Awd., 1979; Pi Gamma Mu, 1957; Alpha Chi, 1948. **Pubns.:** Prin. contrib., *Archives and Manuscripts Finding Aids: Directory of Archives and Manuscript Repositories* (1978); ed. asst., *Guide to Archives and Manuscripts in the United States* (1961); jt. cmplr., *List of Photographs Made by the Office of War Information at the United Nations Conference on International Organization, San Francisco, 1945 (Record Group 208)* (1953). **Activities:** 2; 37, 41; 63 **Addr.:** P.O. Box 686, Glen Echo, MD 20812.

Henry, Bruce Ward (Mr. 30, 1943, Glendale, CA) Staff Asst., Co. Recs. Mgt. Offc. Hughes Aircraft Co., 1981–; Corp. Archvst., Atlantic Richfield Co., 1979–81; Asst. Cur., Amer. Mss., Huntington Lib., 1970–79. **Educ.:** Whittier Coll., 1961–65, BA (Hist.); Univ. of South. CA, 1967–75, PhD (Hist.). **Orgs.:** Socty. of CA Archvsts.: Cncl., (1977–79). SAA: Steering Com.; Bus. Arch. Group (1979). **Activities:** 2; 17; 59 **Addr.:** 2285 Las Lunas St., Pasadena, CA 91107.

Henry, Clarice R. (Mr. 25, 1921, New York, NY) Libn., Art Spec., Hewlett-Woodmer Pub. Lib., 1979–; Libn., Sterling's Mags., 1976–79; Adjunct Lectr., Queens Coll., 1974–76. **Educ.:** Queens Coll., 1969–73, BA (Latin Amer. Std., Rom. Langs.), 1974–75, MLS, 1975–76, MA (Art Hist.). **Orgs.:** ARLIS/NA: Acq. Com. (1980–81). Amer. Prtg. Hist. Assn. Nassau Cnty. LA. **Honors:** Phi Beta Kappa, 1973. **Pubns.:** "Art Doc/NY" Vid. interviews with artists (1974). **Activities:** 9; 15, 20, 39; 55 **Addr.:** 790 Garden Dr., Franklin Square, NY 11010.

Henry, Diane V. (Ap. 15, 1947, Washington, DC) AV Chief, DC Pub. Lib., 1975–, AV Libn., 1972–75, Lcl. Hist. Libn., 1967–72. **Educ.:** Howard Univ., 1965–69, BA (Hist., Gvt.); Drexel Univ., 1971–72, MLS. **Orgs.:** Washington Film Cncl.: Bd. (1979–80). EFLA: Film Juror (1977–). Cncl. on Intl. Non-Thea. Events: Film Juror (1979–). **Pubns.:** "Film Service of the DC Public Library," *Bookmark* (Fall 1977). **Activities:** 9; 15, 32, 42; 67, 93 **Addr.:** 1447 Bangor St. S.E., Washington, DC 20020.

Henry, Eugene Baker, Jr. (My. 13, 1917, Birmingham, AL) Head Libn., Newport Pub. Lib., 1971–. **Educ.:** US Nvl. Acad., 1935–39, BS (Electrical Engin.); George Washington Univ., 1967–68, MS (Intl. Affairs); Univ. of RI, 1969–70, MLS. **Orgs.:** RI LA. New Eng. LA. ALA. Rotary. **Activities:** 4, 9; 15, 17 **Addr.:** Newport Public Library, Newport, RI 02840.

PROFESSIONAL ACTIVITIES: Institutions: 1. Acad. lib.; 2. Arch.; 3. Assn.; 4. Fed./Gvt. lib.; 5. Inst. lib.; 6. Mfr./Suppl.; 7. Milit. lib.; 8. Musm.; 9. Pub. lib.; 10. Sch. lib.; 11. Sch. of lib. sci.; 12. Spec. lib.; 13. State lib.; 14. (other). **Functions/Activities:** 15. Acq./Col. dev.; 16. Adult srvs.; 17. Admin.; 18. Apprais.; 19. Archit./Bldgs.; 20. Cat./Class.; 21. Chld. srvs.; 22. Circ.; 23. Cons./Pres.; 24. Consult.; 25. Cont. ed.; 26. Educ. lib. sci.; 27. Ext. srvs.; 28. Fund/Grants; 29. Gvt. pubs.; 30. Indx./Abs.; 31. Instr. lib. use; 32. Media srvs.; 33. Micro.; 34. Netwks./Coop.; 35. Persnl.; 36. PR; 37. Publshg.; 38. Recs. mgt.; 39. Ref. srvs.; 40. Repro.; 41. Resrch.; 42. Review.; 43. Secur.; 44. Serials; 45. Spec. col.; 46. Tech. srvs.; 47. Trustees/Bds.; 48. YA srvs.; 49. (other).

Henry, Linda J. (My. 10, 1943, West Plains, MO) Archvst./Recs. Mgr., Amer. Pyst. Assn., 1981–; Archvst., Natl. Arch. for Black Women's Hist., 1978–81; Archvst., Schlesinger Lib., Radcliffe Coll., 1973–78; Libn., Univ. of MO, St. Louis, 1972–73, Instr. of Hist., 1966–71. **Educ.:** Univ. of MO, 1961–65, BS (Educ.); 1965–66, MA (Hist.); Natl. Arch. Inst. in Arch. Admin., 1974. **Orgs.:** SAA: Com. on Col. Personal Papers & Mss. (1977–79); Co-ed., Women's Caucus Nsltr. (1978). Amer. Assn. for State and Lcl. Hist. Mid-Atl. Reg. Arch. Conf. Assn. of Recs. Mgrs. and Admin. **Pubns.:** "Collecting Policies of Special Subject Repositories," *Amer. Archvst.* (Winter 1980); "Florence A. Blanchfield," *Notable Amer. Women* (1980). **Activities:** 2, 12; 17, 20, 39; 55, 66, 73 **Addr.:** American Psychiatric Association, 1700 18th St. N.W., Washington, DC 20009.

Henry, Marjorie R. New York, NY) Libn. II, Hist. and Maps, Seattle Pub. Lib., 1972–; Libn. I and II, Mncpl. Ref. Lib., Seattle, 1968–72. **Educ.:** Black Mt. Coll., 1940–42, Univ. of MN, 1945–48, BA (Eng. Lit.); Univ. of WA, 1966–68, MLS. **Orgs.:** West. Assn. of Map Libs.: Secy. (1979–80). WA LA. Pac. NW LA. SLA. 33rd Legis. Dist. Dem. Precinct Org. **Activities:** 9; 15, 39, 45; 70, 92 **Addr.:** History Department, Seattle Public Library, 1000 Fourth Ave., Seattle, WA 98104.

Henry, Mary Brigid (Mr. 13, 1948, Phillipsburg, NJ) Bus. Mgr., *NJ Libs.*, NJ LA, 1979–; Head, Cat. Maintenance Sect., Rutgers Univ. Lib., 1974–78, Supvsr., Law Lib. Conversion, 1974. **Educ.:** Douglass Coll., 1966–70, BA (Russ.); OH State Univ., 1970–72, MA (Slavic Lang.); Rutgers Univ., 1972–74, MLS. **Orgs.:** ALA. **Honors:** Phi Beta Kappa, 1969; Russ. Hon. Socty., 1970; Beta Phi Mu. **Pubns.:** "Closing the Card Catalog," *NJ Libs.* (O. 1978). **Activities:** 3; 17, 37 **Addr.:** 11 Deer Path, Holmdel, NJ 07733.

Henry, Mary K. (Je. 28, 1950, Chicago, IL) Hum. Biblgphr. and Ibero-Amer. Libn., Bobst Lib., NY Univ., 1978–; Span. and Portuguese Catlgr., Meml. Lib., Univ. of WI, Madison, 1975–78; Lib. Dir., CEDE Lib., Univ. de los Andes, Bogotá, Colombia, 1972–75. **Educ.:** Univ. of Pittsburgh, 1968–71, BA (Eng., Compar. Lit.); 1971–72, MLS; Univ. of WI, Madison, 1976–78, MA (Ibero-Amer. Std.). **Orgs.:** ALA; Sem. on the Acq. of Latin Amer. Lib. Mtrls. Latin Amer. Std. Assn. Conf. on Latin Amer. H Hist. Mod. Lang. Assn. **Activities:** 1; 15, 39; 54, 66 **Addr.:** Bobst Library, New York University, 70 Washington Sq. S., New York, NY 10012.

Henry, Nell Murray (Mr. 4, 1921, Columbia, MS) Trustee, AR St. Lib. 1971–; Trustee, Searcy Pub. Lib., 1955. **Educ.:** Univ. of MS, 1941–43, BA (Elem. Educ.). **Orgs.:** AR LA: Trustee Div., Ch. (1974), Legis. Com. (1977–), VCh. (1980); Cont. Educ. (1977–79); various other com. SWLA: Trustee Div., Secy. (1978–80). ALA: ALTA, Prog. Com. (1975–, Ch., 1980), Legis. Com. (1978–80), St. Assn. Com. (1974–76); various other com. Various other orgs. AAUW. White Cnty. Arts Cncl. AR Dem. Com. AR Geneal. Assn. **Activities:** 9, 13; 47 **Addr.:** 109 N. Olive St., Searcy, AR 72143.

Henry, Ray, Jr. (D. 5, 1951, Pontiac, MI) Ed., *Ulrich's Intl. Pers. Dir.*, 1981–; Ed., Life Insr. Index, Univ. Microfilms Intl., 1979–81. **Educ.:** Univ. of MI, 1970–76, BMusA (Performance); Simmons Coll., 1977–78, MS (LS). **Orgs.:** Msc. LA. MI LA: Int. Frdm. Com. (1979–80). Amer. Socty. of Indxrs. Amer. Gld. of Organists. **Activities:** 14-Publshg.; 30, 33, 37; 55, 76 **Addr.:** R.R. Bowker Co., 1180 Ave. of the Americas, New York, NY 10036.

Hensel, Janet W. (D. 14, 1923, Cleveland, OH) Head, Tech. Srvs., New Brunswick Free Pub. Lib., 1974–; Sch. Lib. Sub., Educ. Dept., Newark, NJ, 1974; Catlgr., Corporate Info. Ctr., Sea-Land Srvs., Inc., 1972–73; Cat. Libn., Essex Cnty. Coll., 1971; Cat. Libn., Rose Meml. Lib., Drew Univ., 1966–71; Sch. Libn., Claude O. Markoe Sch., Frederiksted, St. Croix, VI, 1966; Cat. Libn., Mohawk Valley Cmnty. Coll., 1962–65; NY Lib. Trustee, Town of Ulster Pub. Lib., Ulster Cnty., NY, 1961–62; Cat., Ref. Libn., Resrch. and Dev. Lab. Lib., Intl. Bus. Machines Corp., 1959–62; various positions as libn., 1946–59. **Educ.:** Allegheny Coll., 1941–45, BA (Eng. Lit.); Syracuse Univ., 1945–46, BS (LS); NY Prof. Libn. Cert.; 1966, NJ Prof. Libn. Cert.; various crs. **Orgs.:** ALA. NY LA. NJ LA: Sec. Tech. Srvs. Div. (1980–); Conf. Com. (1980–81). New Brunswick Tercentennial Com.: Art Com. (1980); Lit. Com. (1980). **Pubns.:** "New Brunswick Children's Library," *NJ Libs.* (F. 1981); Ed., *Lib. Lantern–New Brunswick Lib. mag.* (1974–78); "Community Calendar–New Brunswick, NJ," (1980–); Ed. Staff, *NJ Libs.* (1980–81). **Activities:** 1, 9; 20, 36, 46; 55, 56, 75 **Addr.:** Technical Services Dept., New Brunswick Free Public Library, 60 Livingston Ave., New Brunswick, NJ 08901.

Henselman, Frances Wood (S. 2, 1917, Emmett, ID) Exec. Dir., City of Long Beach Pub. Corp. for the Arts, 1979–; Dir. of Lib. Srvs., City of Long Beach, 1968–78, Asst. Libn., 1953–68, Other prof. positions. **Educ.:** Univ. of CA, Los Angeles, 1937–39, BA (Pol. Sci.); Univ. of South. CA, 1939–43, BS (LS); Univ. of CA, Los Angeles, 1965–66, MA (Pub. Admin); additional courses and workshops. **Orgs.:** ALA: Ch., PR Sect. (1965–66); Ch., Persnl. Admin. Sect. (1973); Cncl. (1973–76). CA LA: Ch., several coms. & sects., Cncl. SLA. Pub. Lib. Exec. Assn. Other orgs. Leag. of Women Voters. NAACP. Long Beach Cham. of Cmrce. Amer. Civil Liberties Un. Other orgs. **Honors:** USC Lib. Sch. Alum. Assn., Alum. of the Year, 1977; Psi Sigma Alpha, 1939. **Activities:** 9, 14-Mncpl. Arts Coord. Agency; 17; 50, 55 **Addr.:** 253 Belmont Ave., Long Beach, CA 90803.

Hensen, Steven Lee (Ja. 30, 1944, Oak Park, IL) Sr. Mss. Catlgr., Mss. Div., Lib. of Congs., 1976–; Mss. Catlgr., Yale Univ. Lib., 1971–76; Resrch. Asst., State Hist. Socty. of WI, 1969–71; Mss. and Arch. Asst., Univ. of Chicago Lib., 1967–69. **Educ.:** Univ. of WI, 1962–67, BA (Eng.), 1969–71, MA (LS). **Orgs.:** Mid-Atl. Reg. Arch. Conf. Cncl. of Natl. Lib. and Info. Assns.: Jt. Com. on Spec. Cat., SAA Mem. SAA: Task Frc. on Natl. Info. Systs.; Strg. Com. on Descr. **Pubns.:** "The Journals of Sir John Henry Lefroy," *Yale Univ. Lib. Gazette,* (Ja. 1974); "A Gold Rush Diary," *Mss.* (Spr. 1974). **Activities:** 1, 2; 20, 30, 45; 56 **Addr.:** Manuscript Division, Library of Congress, Washington, DC 20540.

Hensley, Barbara Smith (O. 1, 1947, Amarillo, TX) Resrch. Anal., Info. Spec., Univ. of MO, 1978–; Libn., Meadow Hts. HS, 1977–78. **Educ.:** Austin Coll., 1966–70, BA (Eng., Hist.); Washington Univ., St. Louis, MO, 1971–74, MA (Urban Affairs); Univ. of MO, 1978–80, MA (LS). **Orgs.:** SLA: Dir. Com. (Co-ch., 1980–81). Ctrl. MO OLUG: Secy.-Treas. (1981–83). **Pubns.:** *Index to American Journal of Agricultural Economics* (1981); "The Instruction of Online and Manual Searching at the University of Missouri," *Pub. Utils. Div. Nsltr.* (1980); "Adaptation and Implementation of a Computerized Retrieval System," *Pub. Utils. Div. Nsltr.* (1980); "Agricultural Economics Serials," *Serials Review* (O. 1981); various papers. **Activities:** 1, 12; 15, 17, 24; 53, 56, 57 **Addr.:** 2046 S. Wellington, Springfield, MO 65807.

Hensley, Charlotta C. (O. 7, 1942, E. Liverpool, OH) Head, Serials Dept., Univ. of CO Libs., 1970–, Serials Catlgr., 1969–70; Cat. Libn., Mars Hill Coll., 1968–69. **Educ.:** Maryville Coll., TN, 1960–64, BA (Eng. Lit.); Univ. of NC, 1967–68, MSLS; Univ. of CO, 1977–80, PhD. **Orgs.:** ALA: Cncl. Com. on Plng. (1979–81); RTSD/Amer. Natl. Stan. Inst. Z39 (Alt. Rep., 1979–81); RTSD Pres. (1981–82); Bd. of Dirs. (1977–79); Plng. Com. (Ch., 1977–79; Secy. 1975–77); Serials Sect./Policy and Resrch. Com. (1977–79); Large Resrch. Libs. Discuss. Grp. (Ch. 1975–76). CO LA. Mt. Plains LA. Phi Delta Kappa. **Honors:** Beta Phi Mu, 1968. **Pubns.:** "'We Have Fired Our Computer...,'" *CO Acad. Lib.* (Fall 1970). **Activities:** 1; 17, 44, 46; 63 **Addr.:** 1385 Edinboro Dr., Boulder, CO 80303.

Henson, James R. (O. 27, 1937, Arkansas City, KS) Consult., CA State Lib., 1979–; Dir., Peninsula Lib. Syst., 1974–79; Mgr., Los Angeles Reg. Ofc., Richard Able and Co., 1973–74; Acq. Libn., CA State Univ., Northridge, 1972–73. **Educ.:** Univ. of South. CA, 1955–60, BS (Bus. Admin.), 1971–72, MS (LS). **Orgs.:** CA LA: Lib. Stans. Com. (Ch., 1976–78). South. CA Tech. Prcs. ALA: Golden Gate Mem. Dist., Ch. Daly City Lions Club: Secy.-Treas. (1977–78); Spec. Events (1976). **Pubns.:** *Copyright Practices in Commercial Organizations* (1964); *Administration of a Public Library Cooperative System* (1978); *Functions and Proceedures in Acquisitions* (1972). **Activities:** 9, 13; 15, 17, 24; 59 **Addr.:** 1519 Spinnaker Ln., Half Moon Bay, CA 94019.

Henson, Llewellyn L., III (Jl. 14, 1937, Hyammis, MA) Dir. of Lib., FL Inst. of Tech. 1972–, Assoc. Dir. of Libs., 1971–72; Admn. Libn., US Army Spec. Srvs. (Europe), 1970–71. **Educ.:** Univ. of SC, 1958–61, BA (Span.); FL St. Univ., 1969–70, MLS, 1978–80, PhD (LS). **Orgs.:** ALA. FL LA. SELA. FL Assn. Media Educ. Natl. Assn. of Under Water Instr. **Activities:** 1, 4; 17, 32, 35; 64, 91, 92 **Addr.:** Florida Institute of Technology, Melbourne, FL 32901.

Henson, Pamela M. (Ag. 15, 1948, Jersey City, NJ) Histn., Oral Hist. Proj., Smithsonian Inst. Arch., 1974–, Resrch. Aide, Ofc. of Musm. Prog., 1973–74. **Educ.:** George Washington Univ., 1967–71, BA (Amer. Cvlztn.), 1972–75, MA (Amer. Cvlztn.). Oral Hist. Assn. Oral Hist. in the Mid-Atl. Reg.: Pres. (1980–81). Org. of Amer. Histns. Amer. Std. Assn. **Pubns.:** "Mary Agnes Chase" and "Harold Fred Dorn," *Dict. of Amer. Biog.* (1980); "Oral History at the Smithsonian," Oral History Assn *Nsltr.* (F. 1979); "The Study of Children's Play in the U.S.," *Chesapeake Amer. Std. Qtly.* (Spr. 1973). **Activities:** 2, 4; 15, 41, 45; 55, 58, 85 **Addr.:** Smithsonian Institution Archives, A&I 2135, Washington, DC 20560.

Hepner, John C. (S. 28, 1946, Harlingen, TX) Ref. Libn., TX Woman's Univ., 1974. **Educ.:** Univ. of TX, Austin, 1967–70, BA (Eng.), 1971–74, MLS; TX Southmost Coll., 1965–67, AA (Biology). **Orgs.:** TX LA: Ch.-elect, Ref. RT (1979–81); Ch., Bib. Com., Ref. RT (1979–80). Ref. RT Rep. Cncl. of State and Reg. Groups. Ref. and Adult Srvs. Div. ALA. Southwestern LA. Socty. of Southwestern Archvsts. Denton Bach Sty.: Bd. of Dir., (1979). **Activities:** 1; 31, 39; 55 **Addr.:** Texas Woman's University Library, P.O. Box 23715, TWU Station, Denton, TX 76201.

Hepting, Edward M. (Mr. 20, 1949, Philadelphia, PA) Staff Libn., E.W. Rhodes Mid. Sch., 1973–. **Educ.:** La Salle Coll., 1967–71, BA (Eng., Educ.); Drexel Univ., 1971–73, MLS. **Orgs.:** ALA. PA LA. Assn. of Philadelphia Sch. Libns.: Corres. Secy. PA Sch. LA. Various other orgs. Drexel Univ. Alum. Assn. La Salle Coll. Un. Assn. PA Fed. of Tchrs. Philadelphia Fed. of Tchrs. **Activities:** 10, 11; 15, 20, 21 **Addr.:** E.W. Rhodes Middle School IMC, 29th and Clearfield Sts., Philadelphia, PA 19132.

Herb, Elizabeth D. (Ap. 30, 1933, Summit Station, OH) Media Spec., Brookhaven HS, Columbus Pub. Sch., 1973–. **Educ.:** OH Dominican Coll., 1967–73, BS (Educ. Media Elem. Educ.); OH State Univ., 1973–75, MA (ED C&F). **Orgs.:** ALA: AASL. OH Educ. Lib. Media Assn.: Lcl. Arrang. Ch. (1979). Natl. Educ. Assn. OH Cncl. of Tchrs. of Eng. OH Educ. Assn. Columbus Educ. Assn.: Lib. Rep., Jt. Cncl. with Columbus Bd. of Educ. (1973, 74, 75). **Honors:** Phi Delta Kappa, 1979. **Pubns.:** "Building a New School Library–Getting from the Old to The New," *OH Media Spectrum,* (Ja. 1977); multi-media presentation (1976). **Activities:** 10; 22, 32, 48 **Addr.:** 4727 Harlem Rd., New Albany, OH 43054.

Herbel, Patricia F. (S. 20, 1936, Grafton, ND) Lib. Srvs. and Elem. Curric. Coord., Dept. of Pub. Instr., 1977–; Libn., Hebron Pub. Sch., 1971–77; Rock Lake Pub. Sch., 1960–71. **Educ.:** Mayville State Coll., 1954–61, BF (Elem. Educ., Phys. Educ., LS); various crs. **Orgs.:** ALA: AASL. ND LA. VFW Auxilary. AML Auxilary. **Activities:** 10, 13; 17, 24; 49-Info., retrival srvs.; 63, 75 **Addr.:** Library, Dept. of Public Instruction, Bismarck, ND 58505.

Herd, Janice M. (F. 14, 1947, Northampton, PA) Romance Lang./Social Sci. Libn., Libr. of Congs., 1973–; Bi-lingual Aid to the Ambassador, Embassy of Ecuador, Washington, D.C., Prelim. Catlgr., Lib. of Congs., 1972–73. **Educ.:** Moravian Coll., 1965–69, BA (Span.); American Univ., 1969–72, MA (Latin Amer. Std.); Catholic Univ., 1975–76, MLS; Cent. MI Univ., 1979–80, MBA. **Orgs.:** ALA. DC LA. Amer. Socty. of Indexers. SALALM: Bibl. Com. Latin Amer. Std. Assn. Inter-Amer. Cncl.: Secy. (1976); VP (1977). Intl. Std. Assn. Socty. of Fed. Linguists: Pub. Com. **Pubns.:** Ed. *Mass Media in/on Cuba and the Caribbean Area* (1979); Ed. *Automobile Industry in Latin America* (1980). **Activities:** 4, 12; 30, 37, 39 **Addr.:** 4640 South Thirty-sixth St., Arlington, VA 22206.

Heriard, Robert T. (F. 15, 1948, New Orleans, LA) Ref. Libn., Univ. of New Orleans, 1974–. **Educ.:** Univ. of New Orleans, 1970–72, BA (Fine Arts); LA State Univ., 1973–74, MLS. **Orgs.:** ALA. ARLIS/NA. LA LA: JMRT (Ch., 1978–79). **Honors:** Beta Phi Mu, 1974. **Pubns.:** Jt. Ed., *LA LA Bltn.* (1980–). **Activities:** 1; 39 **Addr.:** Earl K. Long Library, University of New Orleans, Lakefront, New Orleans, LA 70148.

Herkness-Brown, June Rickard (D. 15, 1935, Flushing, NY) Catlgr., Arco/Polymer, Inc., 1981–; Lib. Dir., Huntingdon Valley Pub. Lib., 1977–79; Lib. Dir., Ridley Twp. Pub. Lib., 1972–77; Ref. Libn., Marple Pub. Lib., 1971–72. **Educ.:** Coll. of William and Mary, 1953–57, AB (Pol. Sci.); Drexel Univ., Grad. Sch. of Lib. and Info. Sci., 1969–71. **Orgs.:** ALA. PA LA: Adult Srvs. Sect. (Ch., 1975–77). DE Cnty. Libns. Assn.: PR (Ch., 1975–77). Delta Delta Delta: Pres. (1964–66). **Honors:** 1956; Beta Phi Mu, 1971. **Activities:** 9, 12; 16, 17, 20; 50, 89, 92 **Addr.:** 56 S. Sproul Rd., Broomall, PA 19008.

Herling, John P. (Jl. 17, 1917, Madison, WI) Chief Libn., Ch., Lib. Dept., Brooklyn Coll., CUNY, 1974–; Dir., Libs., Cleveland State Univ., 1968–74; Asst. Dir. of Libs., SUNY, Buffalo, 1963–68; Libn., Lummus Co., 1961–63, Acq. Libn., Ref. Libn., Engin. Soctys. Lib., 1953–61; Info. Asst., NY Pub. Lib. Resrch. Lib., 1946–50; Engin., Circ. Asst., Univ. of MI, 1941–44. **Educ.:** Univ. of WI, 1934–38, BA (Eng.), Lib. Sch., 1937–38, Dip.; 1950–51, MA (Eng.). **Orgs.:** ALA. NY LA. **Pubns.:** Jt. Ed., *Measuring the Quality of Library Service* (1974); various articles. **Activities:** 1; 17 **Addr.:** 5 Clearland Ave., Carle Place, NY 11514.

Herman, Edward (S. 28, 1949, Brooklyn, NY) Asst. Docum. Libn., SUNY, Buffalo, 1977–; Ref. Libn., Queens Borough Pub. Lib., 1972–76. **Educ.:** Hunter Coll., 1967–71, BA (Hist.); Queens Coll., 1972–74, MLS; Hunter Coll., 1979, MA (Hist.). **Orgs.:** ALA: GODORT, Adv. Mgr., *Docum. to the People* (1978–). Jewish Libns. Caucus: Prog. Ch. (1977–). **Pubns.:** *Jewish Americans and Their Backgrounds: Sources of Information* (1976); "Information Handling Systems' Checklist of State Publications: Two Viewpoints," *Docum. to the People* (N. 1978); "Directory of Government Document Dealers and Jobbers, 1979," *Docum. to the People* (Jl. 1979). **Activities:** 1; 29, 31, 39; 92 **Addr.:** Government Documents Department, Lockwood Memorial Library, State University of New York at Buffalo, Amherst, NY 14260.

Herman, Elizabeth S. (Jl. 22, 1922, Los Angeles, CA) Assoc. Libn., Cat. Libn., Resrch. Lib., Univ. of CA, Los Angeles, 1972–, Head, Copycat. Sect., 1969–72, Continuations Cat. Libn., 1967–69, Asst. Libn., Univ. Elem. Sch. Lib., 1965–66. **Educ.:** Univ. of CA, Los Angeles, 1939–43, BA (Psy.); Univ. of South. CA, 1962–64, MSLS; various courses, UCLA and USC, 1965–. **Orgs.:** ALA: Cnclr. (1979–84); RTSD, Bd. of Dir. (1979–84); Cat. and Class. Sect., Exec. Com. (1977–80); Cat. Code Revision Com., Subcom. on Rules for Cat. Mach.-readable Data Files, Ch.; Descriptive Cat. Com., Subcom. on Rules for Cat. Mach.-readable Data Files (1970–74); Resrcs. Sect. Micropubshg. Com., Bibl. Control of Microforms Subcom., CCS liaison (1978–79). ARLIS/

Special Subjects/Services: 50. Adult educ.; 51. Advert./Mktg.; 52. Aerosp.; 53. Agric.; 54. Area std.; 55. Arts/Hum.; 56. Autom.; 57. Bibl./Prtg.; 58. Bio. sci.; 59. Bus./Fin.; 60. Chem.; 61. Copyrt.; 62. Documtn.; 63. Educ.; 64. Engin.; 65. Env.; 66. Eth. grps.; 67. Film; 68. Food/Nutr.; 69. Geneal.; 70. Geo.; 71. Geol.; 72. Handcpd.; 73. Hist.; 74. Int. frdm.; 75. Info. sci.; 76. Insr.; 77. Law; 78. Legis.; 79. Math./Comp. sci.; 80. Med.; 81. Metals; 82. Nat. resrcs.; 83. Newsp.; 84. Nuc. sci.; 85. Oral hist.; 86. Petr./Energy; 87. Pharm.; 88. Phys./Astr./Math.; 89. Readg.; 90. Relig.; 91. Sci./Tech.; 92. Soc. sci.; 93. Telecom.; 94. Transp.; 95. (other).

NA. Libns. Assn. of the Univ. of CA. Assn. of Acad. Women, UCLA. Other orgs. Palm Socty. San Diego Zoological Socty. **Honors:** Beta Phi Mu. **Pubns.:** "Bibliographic control of Machine-readable data files," in *Report of the Conference on Cataloging and Information Services for Machine-Readable Data Files* (1978). **Activities:** 1; 20, 39, 44; 55, 67 **Addr.:** Research Library, Technical Services Dept., University of California, 405 Hilgard Ave., Los Angeles, CA 90024.

Herman, Gertrude Becker (Je. 20, 1915, Fond du Lac, WI) Assoc. Prof., Univ. of WI, Madison Sch. of LS, 1973–, Asst. Prof., 1968–73; Libn., Madison Pub. Schs., 1965–67; Libn., Tchr., Fieldston Sch., NY, 1941–65; Asst. Chld. Libn., NY Pub. Lib., 1938–41; Tchr., Marshfield (WI) HS, 1936–38. **Educ.:** Univ. of WI, 1936, BS magna cum laude (Eng.); Columbia Univ., 1942, BS (LS); Univ. of WI, 1968, MS (LS), 1968, Spec. in Libnshp. **Orgs.:** ALA: ALSC/Coord., Priority II: Eval. of Media (1979–81); Nominee, Caldecott Awd. Com. (1981); Laura Ingalls Wilder Awd. Com. (1980); Batchelder Awd. Com. (1972); Newbery-Caldecott Awds. Com. (1970). WI LA. AALS. Coop. Chld. Book Ctr.: Exec. Bd. (Ch. 1974–76). AAUP. WI Acad. of Sci., Arts and Letters. **Pubns.:** "Chapbooks, Star Wars, and Other Entertainments," *Sch. Lib. Jnl.* (Fall 1979); "Footprints on the Sands of Time: Biography for Children," *Chld. Lit. in Educ.* (Sum. 1978); "The Wisconsin Cooperative Children's Book Center," *Phaedrus* (Fall 1976); "Folklore Studies–A Selected Bibliography: A Suggested Basic Reference Collection for Academic Libraries," *Choice* (November 1976); "Folktales for Children," *Drexel Lib. Qtly.* (O. 1976); other articles, reviews. **Activities:** 11; 21, 26, 32; 95-Chld. Lit. **Addr.:** Library School, University of Wisconsin-Madison, 600 North Park St., Madison, WI 53706.

Herman, Leslie (F. 12, 1953, San Antonio, TX) Libn., Comp. Aided Opers., Radar Systs. Grp., Hughes Aircraft Co., 1979–; Libn., Planetary Image Facility, Jet Propulsion Lab., 1978–79, Libn., Viking Flight Team, 1977–78. **Educ.:** Univ. of CA, Irvine, 1971–75, BA (Compar. Lit.); CA State Univ., Fullerton, 1976–77, MS (LS). **Orgs.:** SLA. Data Prcs. Libns. Assn. CA State Univ., Fullerton, Grad. LA. **Activities:** 12; 17, 24, 37; 52, 56, 75 **Addr.:** Computer Aided Operations Library, Hughes Aircraft Co., P.O. Box 92426, M.S. R1/B207, Los Angeles, CA 90009.

Herman, Steven J. (O. 23, 1941, New York City, NY) Chief, Col. Mgt. Div., Lib. of Cong., 1977–, Asst. Netwk. Support, 1973–77; Head, Lib. for Blind and Handicpd., NJ St. Lib., 1969–73; Dir., Highland Park Pub. Lib., (NJ), 1965–69. **Educ.:** City Coll. of New York, 1959–63, BS (Psy.); Rutgers, 1963–64, MLS. **Orgs.:** ALA. **Activities:** 4; 17, 39 **Addr.:** 8506 Rosewood Dr., Bethesda, MD 20014.

Hernandez, Marilyn J. (Je. 29, 1948, Toronto, ON) Hlth. Libn., MB Dept. of Hlth., 1977–; Chief Catlgr., Univ. of Winnipeg Lib., 1974–77, Catlgr., 1973–74; Libn., Imperial Oil Ltd., 1973. **Educ.:** Univ. of Toronto, 1967–71, BSc (Hon.) (Psy.), 1971–73, MLS. **Orgs.:** Med. LA, Can. LA. MB LA. Can. Hlth. Libs. Assn. MB Hlth. Libs. Assn. (Pres., 1981–82). **Pubns.:** Jt. ed., *Winnipeg: A Centennial Bibliography* (1974). **Activities:** 12, 13; 15, 17, 20, 39; 80 **Addr.:** Anna E. Wells Memorial Library, Manitoba Dept. of Health, 202 - 880 Portage Avenue, Winnipeg, MB R3G 0P1 Canada.

Hernandez, Mary Fallon (S. 8, 1925, Waterbury, CT) Dir., Lib., Coll. of Mt. St. Vincent, 1974–; Dir., Lib. Media Ctr., Baldwin Sch., 1968–73; Chief Libn., Quinsigamond Cmnty. Coll., 1964–68; Dir., Libs., Mithras, Inc., Microwave Assn., 1960–64. **Educ.:** Clark Univ., 1953–59, BS (Psy.); Simmons Coll., 1957–60, MLS. **Orgs.:** ALA. NY LA: Pubns. Ch. (1979–). Cath. LA: Exec. Cncl. (1976–77). **Activities:** 1, 12; 15, 17, 32; 92 **Addr.:** College of Mt. St. Vincent, Riverdale Ave., Riverdale, Bronx, NY 10471.

Hernandez, Ramon R. (F. 23, 1936, Evanston, IL) Dir., McMillan Meml. Lib., WI Rapids, WI, 1975–; Dir., T.B. Scott Free Lib., Merrill, WI, 1970–75; Dir. of Youth Work, WI Conf., Untd. Church of Christ, 1964–70; Co-Pastor, St. Stephen, UCC, 1960–64. **Educ.:** Elmhurst Coll., 1954–57, BA (Hist.); Eden Theo. Semy., 1958–62, BD (Hebrew Std. & Educ.); Univ. of WI, Madison, 1969–70, MA (LS). **Orgs.:** ALA: RASD Coop. Ref. Srv. (1974–76). WI LA: Tech. Srvs. Sect., (Ch., 1976); Lib. Admin. RT (Ch. 1976–77); VP (1979); Pres. (1980). WI Lib. Film Circuit: Pres. (1978–82). WI Valley Lib. Assn. Riverview Hospital Corp.: Bd. of Dirs. (1979–). WI Rapids Twins Prof Baseball Club: Bd. of Dirs., (1979–). WI Hist. Recs. Prsrvn. Cmsn. Rotary Club of Merrill, WI: Pres. (1974–75). Other orgs. **Honors:** Beta Phi Mu, 1971; Rotary Club of Merrill, WI, Cmnty. Srv. Awd., 1975; WI LA, McMillan Lib. named WI Lib. of Yr., 1979. **Pubns.:** "Compact Media Service to Young Adults," *WI Lib. Bltn.* (Jl.-Ag. 1975); "Federal Grant Applications for Small Libraries," *WI Lib. Bltn.* (Ja.-F. 1976). **Activities:** 2, 9; 17, 35, 36; 55, 69, 90 **Addr.:** McMillan Memorial Library, 490 E. Grand Ave., Wisconsin Rapids, WI 54494.

Hernandez, Tamsen MacWatt (S. 10, 1946, Suffern, NY) Dir., Info. Srv., The Conf. Bd., Inc., 1975–, Sr. Info. Spec., Mgt., 1973–75, Sr. Info. Spec., Econ., 1972–73, Info. Spec., 1969–72. **Educ.:** NY Univ., 1965–68, BA (Hist.); Columbia Univ., 1968–69, MLS. **Orgs.:** SLA. ASIS. **Activities:** 12; 17, 37, 39; 56, 59, 93 **Addr.:** Information Service, The Conference Board, Inc., 845 3rd Ave., New York, NY 10022.

Herndon, Leon (S. 30, 1924, Charlotte, NC) Assoc. Libn., Pub. Srvs., Jas. B. Duke Meml. Lib., Johnson C. Smith Univ., 1979–; Head, Cat., Sheppard Lib., MA Coll. of Pharm., 1978–79; Asst. Dir., Head, Tech. Srvs., Univ. of Pittsburgh, 1972–78; Head, Cat., Med., Dentistry Lib., Med. Coll. of WI, 1971–72. **Educ.:** Hamilton Coll., 1944–48, AB (Pol. Sci., Hist.); Columbia Univ., 1956–58, MS (LS). **Orgs.:** ALA: ACRL. SLA. NC LA. Med. LA. **Activities:** 1, 12; 15, 17, 20; 56, 75 **Addr.:** 3829 Selwyn Ave., Charlotte, NC 28209.

Hernon, Peter (Ag. 31, 1944, Kansas City, MO) Assoc. Prof., Grad. Sch. of Lib. and Info. Sci., Simmons Coll., 1981–, Asst. Prof., 1978–81; Assoc. Instr., Grad. Lib. Sch., IN Univ., 1975–78; Ref. Libn., Univ. of NE at Omaha, 1971–75. **Educ.:** Univ. of CO, 1963–66, BA (Hist.), 1966–68, MA (Hist.); Univ. of Denver, 1970–71, MA (LS); IN Univ., 1975–78, PhD (LS). **Orgs.:** ALA. AALS. New Eng. LA. **Honors:** Beta Phi Mu, 1978. **Pubns.:** *Microforms and Government Information* (1981); *Use of Government Publications by Social Scientists* (1979); Jt. auth., *Municipal Government Reference Publications and Collections* (1978); "Academic Library Reference Service for the Publications of Municipal, State, and Federal Government," *Gvt. Pubn. Review* (1978); other articles. **Activities:** 1, 11; 29, 39, 41; 92 **Addr.:** Graduate School of Library and Information Science, Simmons College, Boston, MA 02115.

Herold, Jean (Jl. 30, 1924, Jennings, MO) Ref. Libn., Univ. of TX, 1964–; Libn., Lamar Jr. HS, 1962–64; Tchr., Brentwood Elem. Sch., 1958–61. **Educ.:** Washington Univ., 1940–42; Univ. of TX, 1955–58, BA (Eng.), 1961–64, MLS. **Orgs.:** ALA. TX Assn. of Coll. Tchrs. Austin Pub. Lib.: Comsn. Heritage Socty. of Austin. Natl. Trust for Hist. Prsrvn. Smithsonian Assoc. **Honors:** Phi Beta Kappa, 1958. **Pubns.:** "Survey of Political Science Reference Sources," *Ref. Srvs. Review* (Ja./Mr. 1977); "Survey of Political Science Reference Sources," *Ref. Srvs. Review* (Ja./Mr. 1978); "Texas Monthly," *Serials Review* (Ja./Mr. 1977); Reviews. **Activities:** 1; 39; 92 **Addr.:** Box 7048, Austin, TX 78712.

Heron, David Winston (M. 29, 1920, Los Angeles, CA) Senior libn. Hoover Inst., 1980–; Sr. Lecturer, Univ. of CA, Berkeley, 1978–79; Univ. Libn., Univ. of CA, Santa Cruz, 1974–78; Emeritus, 1979; Dir. of Libs., Univ. of KS, 1968–74; Ref. Libn., Univ. of CA, Los Angeles, 1948–52; Libn., Amer. Embassy, Tokyo, 1952–53; Staff Asst., to the Libn.; Univ. of CA, Los Angeles, 1953–55, Asst. to the Dir., Stanford Univ. Lib., 1955–57. **Educ.:** Pomona Coll., 1938–42, AB (Eng.); Univ. of CA, Berkeley, 1946–48, BLS; Univ. of CA, Los Angeles, 1949–51, MA (Pol. Sci.). **Orgs.:** ALA: Exec. Brd. (1970–74); Cncl. (1962–64; 1967–70); ARL: Brd. of Dir., (1974). NV LA: Pres., (1964–66). CA LA. AAUP: Secy/Treas., Santa Cruz Chap. (1976–78). Roxburghe Club of San Francisco. Book Club of CA. **Honors:** U.S. Dept of State, Fulbright Fellowship, 1963. **Pubns.:** Ed., *ACRL Monographs* (1966–69). Ed., *A Unifying Influence, Essays of R.C. Swank* (1981). "Freezing Books to Save Them", *CA Living (San Francisco Examiner/Chronicle)* (N. 18, 1979); "Waiting for the Genie," *Jrnl. of Acad. Libnshp.,* (N., 1978). "Short Shoelaces: Machlup Looks at Library Statistics," *AAUP Bltn.* (N., 1977). "Univ. of KS Libs.", *Encyclopedia of Lib. and Info. Sci.* (1975). "On Building a Library," *Books and Lib.,* (Mr., 1973). **Activities:** 1, 4; 17, 23, 26; 55, 92, 93 **Addr.:** 120 Las Lomas Rd., Aptos, CA 95003.

Heron, Susan Jane (D. 8, 1948, Indianapolis, IN) Lib. Coord., Resrch. Libs. Grp., Inc., 1978–; Auto-Graphics, Inc., 1977–78; Tech. Srvs. Libn., Ctr. for the Study of Youth Dev., 1976–77; Catlgr., Univ. of Louisville, 1974–76. **Educ.:** IN Univ., 1967–71, BA (Fr.), 1971–74, MLS. **Orgs.:** ALA. ARLIS/NA. **Activities:** 12; 20, 34, 46; 56 **Addr.:** Research Libraries Group, Inc., Box 3727, Stanford, CA 94305.

Heroux, Marlene Sue (S. 17, 1948, Philadelphia, PA) Serials Libn., SUNY; Binghamton, 1979–; Ser. Cat. Libn., Univ. of VT, 1975–79; Serials Catlgr., Univ. of NE, 1974–75; Cat. Libn., CO State Univ., Ft. Collins, 1973–74. **Educ.:** SUNY, Albany, 1968–70, BA (Soc.), 1971–72, MLS. **Orgs.:** ALA: RTSD (Serials Sect. Ch., 1980–81). VT LA: Nom. Com. (1979–80). New England LA. Univ. of VT, Friends of the Lib. Green Mountain Club. Triple Cities Hiking Club. **Pubns.:** Assoc. Ed., *Serials Review;* reviews. **Activities:** 1; 17, 20, 44; 56 **Addr.:** Glenn G. Bartle Library, State University of New York at Binghamton, Binghamton, NY 13901.

Herrgesell, Ronald H. (Jl. 3, 1938, New Rochelle, NY) Corporate Libn., Agway Inc., 1975–. **Educ.:** Dutchess Cmnty. Coll., 1959–62, AA (Liberal Arts); State Univ. Coll., Oneonta, NY, 1962–64, BA (Pol. Sci.); Syracuse Univ., 1968–71, MS (Educ.), 1973–74, MS (LS). **Orgs.:** SLA: Upstate NY Chap. Ctrl. NY Lib. Resrcs. Cncl.: Finance Com. (Ch., 1979–80); Prof. Dev. Com., (Ch., 1976–77; VP, 1979–80, 1980–81). Libns. Unlimited, Onondaga Cnty.: VP (1978–79). Common Cause in NY State 32/33 Congsnl. Dist. (Area Coord., 1974–75). **Pubns.:** Jt. Ed., *1980 Directory, Onondaga County, Library Resources and Resource People* (1980). **Activities:** 12; 17 **Addr.:** 509 Balsam St., Liverpool, NY 13088.

Herrick, Kenneth R. (N. 10, 1939, Chicago, IL) Dir. of Libs., Univ. of HI (Hilo), 1976–; Head, Col. Dev., Univ. of WI (Parkside), 1973–76, Actg. Dir. of Libs., 1973, Acq. Libn., 1969–73. **Educ.:** Colorado Coll., 1962–65, BA (Hist.); Univ. of HI, 1968–69, MLS. **Orgs.:** ALA.: Cncl. (1981–); ACRL, Mem. Com. (1977–79) Nom. Com. (1981–82). HI LA: Exec. Com. (1981–); Fall Conf. (Co-Chair, 1978). St. Hist. Socty. of WI. **Honors:** Beta Phi Mu, 1969. **Activities:** 1; 15, 19, 31 **Addr.:** Library, University of Hawaii at Hilo, Hilo, HI 96720.

Herring, Billie Grace (N. 16, 1932, Flatonia, TX) Assoc. Prof., Univ. of TX, 1968–; Libn., Harris Sch., 1962–67; Libn., Fly Jr. HS, 1961–62; Dir., Educ., Westminister Church, Austin, TX, 1956–57; Parish Worker, First Luth. Church, Austin, TX, 1953–56. **Educ.:** Univ. of TX, 1949–53, BS (Elem. Educ.), 1961–68, MLS, 1971–74, PhD (Educ. Tech.). **Orgs.:** TX AECT: VP (1980–81); Secy. (1978–80); Exec. Bd. (1978–); Bd. of Dir. (1976–); Cert. Com. (Ch., 1977–80). ALA: Cncl. of Reg. Grps. (1980–81); various coms. TX LA: Catlgrs. RT (Ch., 1980–81); Awds. Com. (1978–79). AECT: Hist. and Arch. (Ch., 1979–82); Reg. VII (Secy., 1979–80). Various orgs. Trinity Presby. Church: Ruling Elder (1978–). AAUW: Histn. (1971–73). Travis Audubon Socty. N. Amer. Simulation and Gaming Assn.: Conf. Adv. Bd. (1979–80). **Pubns.:** *Cataloging and Classification* (1975); *Designing a Study of Available Resources in Special Education* (1975); "Alice Sinclair Harrison," *Dictionary of Amer. Lib. Biog.* (1978); "Many-Linked Chain of Bibliographic Control," *AV Instr.* (N. 1978); "Needs," "Software," *How Now Brown Cow: Texas Educational Communications* (1975). **Activities:** 11; 20, 21, 32; 63 **Addr.:** Graduate School of Library and Information Science, University of Texas, Box 7576, Austin, TX 78712.

Herring, Jack W. (Ag. 28, 1925, Waco, TX) Prof. of Eng. and Dir., Armstrong Browning Lib., Baylor Univ., 1959–; Asst. Prof., AZ State Univ., 1955–59; Assoc. Prof., Grand Canyon Coll., 1951–55; Tchg. Asst., Univ. of PA, 1950–51; Instr., Howard Coll., 1948–50. **Educ.:** Baylor Univ., 1942–47, BA (Eng.), 1947–48, MA (Eng.); Univ. of PA, 1950–58, PhD (Eng.). **Orgs.:** Waco Lib. Club. Mod. Lang. Assn. AAUP. **Honors:** Margaret Root Brown Ch. of Robert Browning Std., 1973. **Pubns.:** *The Old Schoolfellow: The Artistic Relationship of Two Robert Brownings* (1972); "The Counter-Reformation," "Anabaptists and Baptists," *A Milton Encyc.* (1978). **Activities:** 12; 45; 55 **Addr.:** Armstrong Browning Library, Box 6336, Waco, TX 76706.

Herron, Margie Eleanor (Ja. 26, 1941, Alken, SC) Dir. of Field Srvs., SC State Lib., 1975–, Field Srv. Libn., 1966–75; Ext. Libn., Aiken-Bamberg-Barnwell-Edgefield Reg. Lib., 1964–66. **Educ.:** Winthrop Coll., 1959–63, BA (Hist.); Rutgers Univ., 1963–64, MLS; Comm. Mgt., & Change Sem., Syracuse Univ., 1970; Social Action Wkshp. on Rural Lib. Srvs., Univ. of WI, 1972. **Orgs.:** ALA. SELA. SC LA: Secy. (1968–69); Ch., Pub. Lib. Sect. (1967–68); Pubcty. Com. (1978–). **Addr.:** Senate Plz., Apt. 6C, Columbia, SC 29201.

Hersch, Robert C. (Mr. 17, 1941, New York, NY) Head Libn., Asst. Prof. Hist., Methodist Coll., 1978–; Visit. Dir. Lib., Tusculum Coll., 1977–78; Asst. Prof. Hist., W. GA Coll., 1968–76. **Educ.:** St. Univ. NY (Binghamton), 1958–62, BA (Hist.); St. Univ. NY (Buffalo), 1962–64, MA (Hist.), 1964–74, PhD (Hist.); George Peabody Coll., 1976–77, MLS; Arch. Wkshop., Case West. Reserve Univ., 1978, Cert. **Orgs.:** ALA. SAA. NC LA. Cape Fear LA. SELA. Sullivan Cnty. (TN) Hist. Socty. Fayetteville Arts Cncl. Assn. Hist. E. NC. GA Assn. Hist.: Careers Com. (1975). **Honors:** Beta Phi Mu, 1977; Atlanta Pub. Sch., Cert. Educ. Contrib., 1974. **Pubns.:** "Slavery and the Development of the South Prior to 1850," *W. GA Coll. Stud. in the Social Sciences* (Je. 1969); "Weapons and Technical Expertise," *SECOLAS Annals* (1976). **Activities:** 1; 17, 31, 39; 54, 55, 92 **Addr.:** Davis Memorial Library, Methodist College, Fayetteville, NC 28301.

Herscher, Rev. Irenaeus Joseph O.F.M. (Mr. 11, 1902, Guebwiller, Haute-Alsace, France) Art Cu. and Archvst., St. Bonaventure Univ., 1971–; Libn., 1937–71, Prof. of Ancient Lang., 1934–40, Asst. Libn., 1934–37; Prof. of Phil., St. Stephen Phil. Croghan, 1932–33; Master of Clerics, 1932–33; Asst. Pastor, 1932–33. **Educ.:** St. Bonaventure Univ., 1925–29, BA, 1929–30, MA (Theo.), Catholic Univ., 1930–31, STB (Theo.), Columbia Univ., 1934, MLS; Univ. of Chicago Grad. Sc. of Lib. Sci.; St. Bonaventure Univ., 1969, Litt. D. (Honorary). **Orgs.:** ALA. Cath. LA. WNY Cath. Lib. Conf. Franciscan Educ. Conf.: Treas. (1947–). **Pubns.:** *Checklist of Franciscan Literature* (1958). *Preliminary Checklist of Franciscan Literature* (1952). *Franciscana: Bibliography of Works in English on St. Francis* (1953). *Marian Index of Holy Name Province* (1950). Contributer to numerous periodicals. **Activities:** 1, 2; 23, 24, 39, 45; 57, 58, 90 **Addr.:** Friedsam Memorial Library, St. Bonaventure University, St. Bonaventure, NY 14778.†

Hersey, David F. (Ja. 7, 1928, Canal Zone, Panama) Pres., Smithsonian Sci. Info. Exch., 1972–, Assoc. Dir., VP, 1961–71; Clinical Lab. Ofcr., US Air Force, 1952–60. **Educ.:** Trinity Univ., San Antonio, TX, 1944–48, BS (Bio.); Washington Univ., 1948–51, PhD (Microbio.); Bd. Cert., Amer. Acad. of Mibrobio., 1952. **Orgs.:** ASIS. Intl. Cncl. of Scientific Un.: Natl. Com., Abs. Bd. (1977–). Amer. Socty. of Microbio. Amer. Acad. of Microbi-

PROFESSIONAL ACTIVITIES: Institutions: 1. Acad. lib.; 2. Arch.; 3. Assn.; 4. Fed./Gvt. lib.; 5. Inst. lib.; 6. Mfr./Suppl.; 7. Milit. lib.; 8. Musm.; 9. Pub. lib.; 10. Sch. lib.; 11. Sch. of lib. sci.; 12. Spec. lib.; 13. State lib.; 14. (other). **Functions/Activities:** 15. Acq./Col. dev.; 16. Adult srvs.; 17. Admin.; 18. Apprais.; 19. Archit./Bldgs.; 20. Cat./Class.; 21. Chld. srvs.; 22. Circ.; 23. Cons./Pres.; 24. Consult.; 25. Cont. ed.; 26. Educ. lib. sci.; 27. Ext. srvs.; 28. Fund/Grants; 29. Gvt. pubs.; 30. Indx./Abs.; 31. Instr. lib. use; 32. Media srvs.; 33. Micro.; 34. Netwks./Coop.; 35. Persnl.; 36. PR; 37. Publshg.; 38. Recs. mgt.; 39. Ref. srvs.; 40. Repro.; 41. Resrch.; 42. Review.; 43. Secur.; 44. Serials; 45. Spec. col.; 46. Tech. srvs.; 47. Trustees/Bds.; 48. YA srvs.; 49. (other).

Who's Who in Library and Information Services

o. Scientific Resrch. Socty. of Amer. **Pubns.:** "Information on Research and Development: Growth of Science and Technology in the U.S.," *UNESCO Jnl. of Info. Sci. Libnshp. and Arch. Admin.* (1980); "Information Systems for Research in Progress" in *Anl. Review of Info. Sci. and Tech.* (1978); "Preface" in *Info. Srvs. on Resrch. in Progress, A Worldwide Inventory* (1978); "Indexing and Retrieval of Thanatology Research in a Computerized Data Base of Ongoing Research" in *Communicating Issues of Thanatology* (1976); "Information Networks: A Look at Future Needs and Improvements" in *Info. Systs. and Netwks.* (1975); other articles. **Activities:** 6, 14-Info. Resrcs.; 39, 41, 46; 62, 75, 91 **Addr.:** Smithsonian Science Information Exchange, Room 300, 1730 M St., N.W., Washington, DC 20036.

Hershcopf, Richard D. (Ap. 9, 1922, New York, NY) Assoc. Dir. of Libs. for Pub. Srvcs., CO State Univ., 1968–; Head Libn., Western State Coll. in CO, 1961–68; Ref. and Per. Libn., Bradley Univ., 1959–61. **Educ.:** Brooklyn Coll., 1939–43, BA (Hist.), Univ. of WI, 1946–51, MA (Hist.), 1957–59, MALS. **Orgs.:** ALA: ACRL (Legis. Com., 1980–81). CO LA: Exec. Brd., 1965–66; 1974–76. AAUP. **Honors:** Cncl. on Lib. Resrcs., Study Flwshp, 1976. **Pubns.:** "The Undergraduate Library and the Subject Divisional Plan: Problems and Prospects," New Horizons for Acad. Libs. (1979). **Activities:** 1; 17 **Addr.:** Colorado State University Libraries, Fort Collins, CO 80523.

Hershey, Johanna (Ap. 9, 1947, The Hague, Netherlands) Head of Cat., Johns Hopkins Univ., 1977–; Netwk. Coord., MI Lib. Cnsrtm., 1976–77; Head, Pub. Cat. Info. Sect., Univ. of MI, 1974–76, Descr. Cat., 1971–74. **Educ.:** Vassar Coll., 1964–68, AB (Latin); Univ. of MI, 1968–69, MA (Latin), 1970–71, MLS. **Orgs.:** ALA. MD LA. Potomac Tech. Prcs. Libns. OCLC: PALINET rep., OCLC Adv. Com. on Cat. Other orgs. **Pubns.:** "Impact of the AACR 2 on cataloging at the Johns Hopkins University," *Alternative Cat. Nsltr.* (F. 1979). **Activities:** 1; 17, 20, 34, 46 **Addr.:** The Milton S. Eisenhower Library, The Johns Hopkins University, Baltimore, MD 21218.

Hershman, Virginia L. (Ja. 31, 1930, Lafayette, IN) Lib. Media Prof., Purdue Univ., 1978–, Instr., 1968–78; Tchr., Rensselear HS, 1951–55. **Educ.:** Purdue Univ., 1947–51, BS (Lang. Arts), 1966–68, MSEd (Media Sci.). **Orgs.:** Assn. of IN Media Educs.: Secy. (1980–81). ALA: AASL, Facilities Com. (1976–80). AECT. **Pubns.:** "Indiana and the 1975 Standards for District Media Programs," *Hoosier Sch. Libs.* (Ap. 1976); "The Effective Utilization of Media Support Personnel," *IN Media Jnl.* (Fall 1979). **Activities:** 11; 26, 31 **Addr.:** Library Media and Instructional Development, 118 Matthews Hall, Purdue University, W. Lafayette, IN 47907.

Herstein, Sheila R. (S. 22, 1942, New York, NY) Assoc. Prof., Ref., City Coll., CUNY Lib., 1964–. **Educ.:** Brooklyn Coll., 1959–63, BA (Eng.); Columbia Univ., 1963–64, MLS; CUNY, Grad. Sch., 1972–80, PhD (Hist.). **Orgs.:** ALA: ACRL/BIS, Cont. Educ. Com. (1981–83). LA CUNY: Pres. (1975–76); Lib. Instr. Com. (Ch., 1978–). NY LA. SLA. Amer. Hist. Assn. Org. of Amer. Histns. Coord. Com. for Women in the Hist. Prof. Amer. Prtg. Hist. Assn. **Pubns.:** Jt. Auth., *United States of America: a bibliography* (1981); "Team Teaching and Bibliographic Instruction," *The Bookmark* (Fall 1979); Gen. Ed., Amer. Continent Volumes, *World Bibliographical Series.* **Activities:** 1; 31, 39; 56, 66, 92 **Addr.:** 8001 Bay Pkwy., Brooklyn, NY 11214.

Herther, Nancy K. (Ja. 19, 1951, St. Paul, MN) Resrch. Consult., Yamaha Motor Corp., Resrch. and Dev., 1979–; Sub. Libn., Minneapolis Pub. Lib., 1978–; Head Libn., Asst. Prof., Northwestern Coll. of Chiro., 1977–78. **Educ.:** Univ. of MN, 1969–74, BA (Amer. Std., Hist.), 1975–77, MA (LS, Adult Educ.); various crs. **Orgs.:** ALA: RASD, Bus. Ref. Srvs. Com. (1980–82). MN LA: Int. Frdm. Com. (Ch., 1977–78). SLA. MN Assn. for Cont. Adult Educ.: Dir.-at-Lg. (1981–82). Adult Educ. Assn. of USA. Amer. Cvl. Liberties Un. MN Cvl. Liberties Un. Univ. of MN: Lib. Sch. Cncl. (1976–77); Com. on the Eval. of Instr., Lib. Sch. (1976–77); Grad. Lib. Sci. Students Assn., Pres. (1976–77), *Nsltr.* Ed. (1976). **Pubns.:** Ed., Contrib., *Intellectual Freedom in Minnesota: The Continuing Problem of Obscenity* (1979); "Library Free-lancing: A Personal Experience," *RQ* (Win. 1979); Reviews. **Activities:** 9, 12; 24, 39; 50, 59, 64 **Addr.:** 1309 E. 24th St. #3, Minneapolis, MN 55404.

Hertz, Sylvia (Je. 7, 1927, Latrobe, PA) Pers., Ref. Libn., Scarsdale Pub. Lib., 1974–; Libn., Jewish Cmnty. Ctr., 1976–79. **Educ.:** Univ. of MN, 1945–49, BA (Gvt.); Columbia Univ., 1971–74, MS (LS). **Orgs.:** ALA. NY LA. Westchester Cnty. LA. **Activities:** 1, 9; 15, 39, 44; 83, 90, 92 **Addr.:** 14 Dupont Ave., White Plains, NY 10605.

Hervey, Norma J. (O. 28, 1935, Akron, OH) Assoc. Libn., Head of Tech. Srvs., Gustavus Adolphus Coll., 1981–; Head of Cat., Univ. of AR, 1980–81; Head of Tech. Srvs., St. Bonaventure Univ., 1976–80, Cat. Libn., 1972–76, Ref. Srvs, 1970–72. **Educ.:** Univ. of Akron, 1952–56, BA (Hist.); SUNY, Geneseo, 1971–72, MLS; St. Bonaventure Univ. 1973–80, MA (Hist.). **Orgs.:** ALA: ACRL. Western NY/ON ACRL; RTSD. Cattaraugus Cnty. Mental Hlth Assn.: Bd. of Dirs. (1964–70). Olean Human Rights Org.: Bd. of Dirs. (1960–64). **Honors:** Phi Alpha Theta, 1955. **Activities:** 1; 20, 31, 46; 75 **Addr.:** Library, Gustavus Adolphus College, St. Peter, MN 56082.

Heslin, James J. (Je. 15, 1916, Cambridge, MA) Dir., Libn., NY Hist. Socty., 1960–, Assoc. Dir., 1958–60, Asst. Dir., 1956–58; Asst. Dir., Univ. of Buffalo Libs., 1955–56; 1st Asst., Amer. Hist. Div., New York Pub. Lib., 1953–54; Lectr., Columbia Univ., 1959–68. **Educ.:** Boston Coll., 1949, BS (Hist.); Boston Univ., 1949, MA (Hist.), 1952, PhD (Hist.); Columbia Univ., 1954, MS (LS). **Orgs.:** Bibl. Socty. of Amer.: 2nd VP; Pres. (1972–73). Grolier Club. Amer. Hist. Assn. Amer. Assn. for State and Lcl. Hist. Amer. Antiq. Socty. Sleepy Hollow Restorations, Inc.: Trustee. NY State Hist. Assn., Trustee. Other orgs. **Pubns.:** Jt. auth., *Keepers of the Past* (1965); *Museum and Education* (1968). **Activities:** 14-Resrch. lib.; 17, 39 **Addr.:** New York Historical Society, 170 Central Park West, New York, NY 10024.*

Hess, Alma M. (Je. 6, 1928, Baton Rouge, LA) Dir., Libs., St. Martin's Protestant Episcopal Sch., 1972–; Libn., Orleans Par. Sch. Syst., 1965–72; Libn., Peabody Demonstration Sch., 1959–60; Libn., Jt. Univs. Lib., 1958–59. **Educ.:** LA State Univ., 1945–49, BS (Hist., Gvt.); George Peabody Coll., 1958–60 (LS); Univ. of New Orleans, 1969–71, MEd (Curric., Instr., LS). **Orgs.:** ALA. LA LA. SW LA. **Honors:** Phi Kappa Phi; Delta Kappa Gamma. **Pubns.:** "Disaster Strikes the Library," *The Lib. Connection* (Fall 1980); "Agenda for Action: Teacher Library Planning," *LA LA Bltn.* (Sum. 1973). **Activities:** 10; 15, 17, 31 **Addr.:** St. Martin's Protestant Episcopal School, 5309 Airline Hwy., Metairie, LA 70003.

Hess, Edward Jorgen (F. 18, 1925, Hamburg, IA) Asst. Univ. Libn. for Pub. Srvs., Univ. of South. CA, 1976–, Asst. Prof., 1970–76, Lectr., 1969–70; Asst. Libn. and Chief of Pub. Srvs., CA State Univ., Northridge, 1967–69, Asst. Libn., Chief, Tech. Srvs., 1966–67; Lib. Dir., Lompoc Pub. Lib., 1965–66; Lib. Supvsr., of Tech. Srvs., San Diego State Univ., 1961–63, Lib. Supvsr. of Pub. Srvs., 1959–61; other lib. positions. **Educ.:** Peru State Coll., 1946–49, BA (Soc. Sci., Sec. Educ.); Univ. of South. CA, 1954, MA (Pol. Sci.), 1957, MS (LS), 1963–70, PhD (LS). **Orgs.:** CA LA: Cnclr. (1975–77); Com. on Alt. to Fee Charging (Ch., 1979). ALA: ACRL. ASIS. SLA: San Diego Chap., Mem. Ch. (1961–62). Other orgs. Sierra Club. Natl. Trust for Hist. Prsvn. West. Photographic Collectors Assn. Friends of the Chinatown Lib. **Honors:** Kappa Delta Pi, 1949; Beta Phi Mu, 1957. **Pubns.:** "The Report of the Joint Committee on the Master Plan for Higher Education: Its Implications for Public Libraries," *CA Libn.* (Ja. 1974); *BCN: On-Line Information Retrieval for the Masses?* ERIC (1974); *Library Trustees' Views of Their Duties and Responsibilities* ERIC (1974); "The Politics of Planning Information Services," *Info. and Politics, Procs. of the ASIS Anl Mtg.* (1976); "Information Management and the Charrette," *Info. Mgmt. in the 1980's, Procs. of the ASIS Anl Mtg.* (1977); other articles. **Activities:** 1; 17 **Addr.:** 517 North Vista Bonita Ave., Glendora, CA 91740.

Hess, James A. (Je. 6, 1917, Columbus, OH) VP, Bd. of Trustees, E. Brunswick Pub. Lib., 1981–, Pres., Bd. of Trustees, 1966–81. **Educ.:** Mt. Union Coll., 1934–38, BS (Bio.); Natl. Trng. Sch. for Scout Execs., 1938. **Orgs.:** ALA: ALTA: Pres. (1979–80). NJ Lib. Trustee Assn. (VP, 1978–80). N. Brunswick (NJ) Kiwanis Club. **Honors:** ALA, Trustee Cit., 1976; NJ LA, Trustee of the Yr., 1976. **Pubns.:** Jt. auth., *Securing a New Library Director* (1979); "The American Library Trustee Association," *ALA Yrbk.* (1980). **Activities:** 9, 12; 35, 36, 47; 50, 58, 66 **Addr.:** 91 Farms Road Cir., East Brunswick, NJ 08816.

Hess, Mrs. Joyce R. (F. 4, 19–, Shreveport, LA) Art Libn., Univ. of TX, Austin, 1967–. **Educ.:** TX Christ. Univ., Ft. Worth, 1962–66, BA (Art); Univ. of TX, 1966–69, MLS. **Orgs.:** ARLIS/NA. TX LA. Laguna Gloria Art Musm. Heritage Socty. **Addr.:** 908 Red Bud Trail, Austin, TX 78746.

Hess, Stanley William (Jl. 9, 1939, Bremerton, WA) Head Libn., Spencer Art Ref. Lib., Nelson Gallery, Atkins Musm., 1980–; Assoc. Libn. for Photographs & Slides, Cleveland Musm. of Art, 1973–80; Supvsr., Photographs & Slides, Seattle Art Musm., 1964–73. **Educ.:** Olympic Coll., 1958–60; Univ. of WA, 1960–64, BA (Gen. Art); Case Western Reserve Univ., 1973–76, MSLS. **Orgs.:** SLA: Pic. Div. (Ch., 1979–80; Dir., 1980–82). ARLIS/NA. Art Libs. Socty.-OH. Coll. Art Assn. of Amer. Amer. Assn. of Musms. **Honors:** Beta Phi Mu, 1976. **Pubns.:** Contrib., *Hanbook on Picture Librarianship* (1981); Jt. ed., *Directory Of Art Libraries And Visual Resource Collections In North America* (1978); *An Annotated Bibliography of Slide Library Literature* (1978); "Art libraries & visual resource collections in North America," *ARLIS-ANZ News* (Ag. 1979); Adv. Com., *Slide Buyers Guide* (1976). **Activities:** 8, 12; 15, 17, 32; 55, 63 **Addr.:** 216 W. 51st Terr., Kansas City, MO 64112.

Hess, Stephen Harrill (Ag. 26, 1947, Salt Lake City, UT) Dir., Instr. Media Srvs., Univ. of UT, 1979–, Dir., Educ. Media Ctr., 1976–78, Asst. Dir., 1974–76, Supvsr., Campus Media Srvs., 1973–74. **Educ.:** Univ. of UT, 1968–74, BS (Hist.), 1973–74, MEd (Educ. Media), 1974–78, PhD (Educ. Admin.). **Orgs.:** EFLA: Bd.; Pres. (1979–81). AECT: Instr. Dsgn. Div. (1974–81). Cnsrtm. of Univ. Film Ctrs.: Sel./Eval. Com. (Ch., 1974–81). **Honors:** Phi Delta Phi; Phi Delta Kappa. **Pubns.:** "The Comparative Value of EFLA and Film Libraries and Distributors," *Procs. of CUFC Mtgs.* (Fall 1979); "Analysis of the 100 Most Rented Film Lists," *CUFC Leader* (Spr. 1979); *The Tools for the Selection and Evaluation Audio Visual Software Materials* (1977); *Film Damage Its Causes and Cures* (1976). **Activities:** 1, 10; 17, 32, 37; 57, 63, 67 **Addr.:** Instructional Media Services, 207 Milton Bennion Hall, University of Utah, Salt Lake City, UT 84112.

Hessel, William Herman (Ap. 3, 1933, Menominie, WI) Sem. Libn., Andrews Univ., 1976–; Libn. (Ch., Dept. of Pub. Srvs), Loma Linda Univ., 1971–76; Libn., Bible Tchr., Grand Ledge Acad., La Sierra Campus 1969–71; Rel. Tchr., Andrews Univ., 1959–68; Min., WI Conf. of Seventh-day Adv., 1956–59. **Educ.:** Andrews Univ., 1956, BA (Rel.), MA (Anc. Hist.); 1966, BD, Univ. of MI., 1967, AMLS. **Orgs.:** ATLA. Bibl. Socty. of Amer. Chicago Area Theo. LA. **Activities:** 1, 12; 15, 26, 39; 57, 90 **Addr.:** 209 N. George, Berrien Springs, MI 49103.

Hesselgrave, Sherman (O. 23, 1952, Moline, IL) Libn., Msc. & Art Dept., Carnegie Lib. of Pittsburgh, 1976–. **Educ.:** Allegheny Coll., 1970–74, BA (Msc./Chem); Univ. of IL, 1975–76, MSLS. **Orgs.:** Msc. LA.: PA Chap., Treas., Ch., Pubn. Com. Pittsburgh Cham. Singers: Treas. **Honors:** Beta Phi Mu, 1976. **Pubns.:** Ed., *MLAPa-Duckles Union List* (1980). **Activities:** 9; 15, 39; 55, 77, 80 **Addr.:** Carnegie Library of Pittsburgh, 4400 Forbes Ave., Pittsburgh, PA 15213.

Hesslein, Shirley (S. 2, 1918, New York, NY) Dir., Lockwood Meml. Lib., 1981–; Assoc. Dir., Hlth. Sci. Lib., SUNY, Buffalo, 1971–81, Ref. Libn., 1969–71; Libn., Dept. of Health, Nassau Cty., NY, 1967–69. **Educ.:** Wellesley Coll., 1936-38; Barnard Coll. 1938–40, AB (Chem); Tchrs. Coll., Columbia Univ., 1940–41, MA (Sci. Educ.); Rutgers Univ., 1964–67, MLS. **Orgs.:** ALA. Med. LA: Relevance Grp., Co-Ch. (1975–76); Bibl. and Info. Srvcs. Assessment Com. (1977–78); Ad Hoc Com. to Develop a Statement of Goals (1978–80). SLA. Upstate NY and ON Reg. Grp./Med. LA (Secy./Treas. 1969–71; Vice-Ch., 1975–76; Ch., 1976–77). West. NY Hlth. Sci. Libn.: Exec. Com., (1974–). State University of NY SUNY LA. Amer. Acad. of the Hist. of Dent. Buffalo & Erie Co. Hist. Socty. Med. Sect. Amer. Assn. of Dental Sch. **Honors:** SUNY, Chancellor's Awd. for Excellence in Libnshp., 1977. School of Info. and Lib. Std., SUNY/Bflo, Libn. of the Year, 1977. Beta Phi Mu, 1967. **Pubns.:** Nassau Cnty Hlth Dept. Lib., Pub. Hlth. Reports, (My. 1969); reviews. **Activities:** 1, 11; 15, 17, 39; 80 **Addr.:** Lockwood Memorial Library, SUNY at Buffalo, Buffalo, NY 14260.

Hessler, David William (My 9, 1932, Oak Park, IL) Prof. of Lib. Sci. and Dir. of Instrl. Strategy Srvs. of Sch. of Educ. and Lib. Sci., Univ. of MI, 1977–; Assoc. Prof. of Educ., West. MI Univ., 1974–77; Dir. of Instr. Srvs, Univ. of SC, 1973–74; Dir. of Sch. Libs., Ann Arbor Pub. Sch., 1966–67; Assoc. Dir., AV Educ. Ctr. of Univ. of MI, 1960–65. **Educ.:** Univ. of MI, 1951–55, BA (Econ./Geog.), 1959–61, MA (Admin); MI State Univ., 1969–72, PhD (Instrl. Dev.); West. MI Univ., 1967–68. **Orgs.:** ALA: LITA; ACRL; Television Com. (1979); AASL. MI AV Assn. (Secy/Treas. 1960–65). AECT. AALS. Univ. MI Grad. "M" Club. Univ. of MI and MI State Univ Alum. Assn. **Honors:** Phi Delta Kappa. Phi Kappa Phi. **Pubns.:** "Creativity with the Projected Image" in *Creativity With Media* (1977); Jt. auth., *Student Production Guide* (1975); "Technology and the Learner," in *Acad. Forum Series* (1975); "Michigan Exemplary Media Programs" in *Highlights of Sch. Using Educ. Media* (1968); filmstrips. **Activities:** 11; 24, 26, 32; 63, 67, 93 **Addr.:** The University of Michigan, Ann Arbor, MI 48109.

Hester, Helen W. (Ja. 5, 1928, Rustburg, VA) Libn., Merck Sharp and Dohme Resrch. Labs., 1965–, Lab. Tech., 1951–65. **Educ.:** Randolph-Macon Woman's Coll., 1946–50, AB (Liberal Arts); Rutgers Univ., 1963–65, MLS. **Orgs.:** SLA: Bltn. Ed. (1971–73); Mem. Ch. (1970–71). ASIS: NJ Chap., Chrt. Mem., Hosplty. Com. (1979–80). **Activities:** 12; 15, 39, 46; 58, 60, 87 **Addr.:** Merck Sharp and Dohme Research Laboratories, Library, Bldg. 80, Box 2000, Rahway, NJ 07065.

Hettich, Helen S. (Ja. 14, 1918, Hartford, CT) Dir., Lib., Upsala Coll., Wirths Campus, 1979–; Head Libn., Sparta HS, 1959–79; Libn., Franklin HS, 1957–59; Bkmobile. Srv. to Schs., Sussex Cnty. Lib., 1956–57; Readr. Assistance, Asst. Circ. Dept., E. Orange Pub. Lib., 1949–51; Consult., Info. Srvs., Savings Banks Life Insr. Fund, 1948–49; Libn., Burton Bigelow Org., 1945–47; Asst. Libn., *McCall's Mag.*, 1943–45; Libn., Lipton Foods, Contl. Foods Resrch. Dept., 1944. **Educ.:** Smith Coll., 1935–39, BA (Eng.); Columbia Univ., 1941–42, BS (LS); Rutgers Univ., 1958–59, Cert. (NJ Media Spec.), 1969–70, Persnl. Cert. **Orgs.:** ALA: AASL. NJ LA. NJ Educ. Media Assn.: Exec. Bd., Pres. (1962–72). Sussex Cnty. Sch. Media Assn.: Fndr.; Pres.; various coms.; various orgs. Natl. Educ. Assn. NJ Educ. Assn. Delta Kappa Gamma: Epsilon Chap., Fndr., Pres. (1959–61); State VP. (1961–63). Soroptimist Intl. of Sussex Cnty.: Dir.; Awds. Com. **Honors:** NJ Dept. of Educ., Innovation Mini-Grant, 1972–73; NJ Sch. Media Assn. Lib. Dev. Com., Recog., Model Lib. for Observation, 1975. **Activities:** 1, 10; 17, 31, 32; 50, 55, 63 **Addr.:** Upsala College, Wirths Campus, R.D. 3, Box 138A, Sussex, NJ 07461.

Special Subjects/Services: 50. Adult educ.; 51. Advert./Mktg.; 52. Aerosp.; 53. Agric.; 54. Area std.; 55. Arts/Hum.; 56. Autom.; 57. Bibl./Prtg.; 58. Bio. sci.; 59. Bus./Fin.; 60. Chem.; 61. Copyrt.; 62. Documtn.; 63. Educ.; 64. Engin.; 65. Env.; 66. Eth. grps.; 67. Film; 68. Food/Nutr.; 69. Geneal.; 70. Geo.; 71. Geol.; 72. Handcpd.; 73. Hist.; 74. Int. frdm.; 75. Info. sci.; 76. Insr.; 77. Law; 78. Legis.; 79. Math./Comp. sci.; 80. Med.; 81. Metals; 82. Nat. resrcs.; 83. Newsp.; 84. Nuc. sci.; 85. Oral hist.; 86. Petr./Energy; 87. Pharm.; 88. Phys./Astr./Math.; 89. Readg.; 90. Relig.; 91. Sci./Tech.; 92. Soc. sci.; 93. Telecom.; 94. Transp.; 95. (other).

Heumann, Karl F. (Mr. 3, 1921, Chicago, IL) Dir. of Pub. Exec. Ed., Fed. of Amer. Socty. for Exper. Bio., 1966–; Dir., Office of Docum., Nat. Acad. of Sci., 1959–66; Res. Dir., Chem. Abstracts, 1955–59; Dir., Chem-Biol. Coord. Ctr., Natl. Acad. of Sci., 1952–55. **Educ.:** IA State Univ., 1938–43, BS MS (Chem), Univ. of IL, 1947–51, PhD (Chem. Lit.). **Orgs.:** ASIS: Pres. (1959). Amer. Chem. Socty. Div. Chem. Info: Ch. (1960). Cncl. of Biol. Ed.: Ch. (1974–75). Fed. Int. de Docum.: VP (1961–64). **Activities:** 37; 58, 60, 75 **Addr.:** FASEB, 9650 Rockville Pike, Bethesda, MD 20014.

Heutte, Frederic A. (S. 29, 1927, Fall River, MA) Msc. Libn., Fine Arts Libn., Univ. of MD, 1958–; Readers Adv., DC Pub. Lib., 1953–58. **Educ.:** Univ. of Miami, 1949–51, AB (Msc.); Cath. Univ., 1951–56, MA (Msclgy.), 1955–65, MSLS. **Orgs.:** Msc. LA: Ch., Chesapeake Chap. (1960–64; 1979); Ed. Staff, *Notes* (1958–67); Circ. Mgr., *Notes Suppl.* (1952–61). Amer. Msclgl. Socty.: Secy., Grt. Washington Chap. (1958–60). Natl. Assn. of Pastoral Musicians. **Honors:** BMI Young Composer's Awd., 1st Prize for Choral Work, 1952. **Pubns.:** *Mass in Honor of St. Gregory* (1966). **Activities:** 1, 9; 15, 20, 39; 55 **Addr.:** 1600 Newton St. N.E., Washington, DC 20018.

Hevelone, Dorothy G. (Mrs. Maurice S.) (O. 31, 1910, Omaha, NE) Ch., Bd. of Trustees, Beatrice Pub. Lib., 1970, Trustee, 1964–. **Educ.:** Univ. of NE, 1932, BS (Educ.). **Orgs.:** NE LA: NE Lib. Dev. Com. (1968–); Fed. Legis. Com.; various coms. ALA: ALTA/Jury on Cits. (Ch., 1975); Nom. Com. (1976); Endow. Com. (1976); Action Dev. Com. (1979–82); various coms. Univ. of NE Alum. Assn.: VP. (1952); Bd. (1949). Univ. of NE Fndn.: Chancellors Club; Pres. Club. **Honors:** ALA, Trustee Cit., 1980; Univ. of NE Alum. Assn., Disting. Srv. Awd., 1980; NE LA, Trustee Cit., 1975; Beatrice Cham. of Cmrce., Salute to Women Cultural Awd., 1975. **Addr.:** 705 North Eighth Street, Beatrice, NE 68310.

Hewison, Nancy S. (F. 7, 1950, Lewiston, ME) Asst. Prof./Head of Ref., Univ. of OR Hlth. Sci. Ctr. Lib., 1979–; Sr. Asst. Libn./Head of Ref., Tufts Univ. Med. & Dental Lib., 1976–79; Evening Ref. Libn., New Hampshire Coll., 1976–76; Libn., Deryfield Sch., 1974–76; Libn., Spaulding HS, 1972–74. **Educ.:** Univ. of NH, 1968–72, BA (Soclgy.); Simmons Coll., 1973–75, MS (LS); Cert. of Med. Libnshp., Med. LA, 1976; Prof. Cert., Sch. Libn., NH, 1975; various courses. **Orgs.:** Med. LA. Pac. NW Grp. of Med. LA. N. Atl. Hlth. Sci. Libns.: Prog. Com. (1977–78). New Eng. Reg. Med. Lib. Adv. Cncl.: Hosp. Lib. Stan. Com. (1979). Other orgs. **Honors:** Bus. and Prof. Women, Rochester NH Chap., Young Career Woman, 1974; Phi Beta Kappa, 1972; Phi Kappa Phi, 1972; Alpha Kappa Delta, 1972; Pi Gamma Mu, 1972. **Activities:** 1; 17, 27, 39; 80, 91, 95-Nursing. **Addr.:** University of Oregon Health Sciences Center Library, P. O. Box 573, Portland, OR 97207.

Hewitt, Joe A. (O. 13, 1938, Newton, NC) Assoc. Univ. Libn. for Tech. Srvs., Adjunct Assoc. Prof. of LS, Univ. of NC, 1975–; Head, Cat. Dept., Univ. of CO, 1972–75; Coord., CO Acad. Libs. Book Prcs. Ctr., 1970–72; Head, Serials Dept., Univ. of CO, 1968–70. **Educ.:** Univ. of NC, 1956–60, BA (Hist.), 1964–66, MSLS; Univ. of CO, 1968–75, PhD (Educ.). **Orgs.:** ALA: RTSD/Resrcs. Sect., Policy and Resrch. Com. (1975–78); LRRT, Strg. Com. (1976–79). CO LA: Ch., Coll. and Univ. Div. (1973–74). NC LA. SELA. **Pubns.:** *OCLC: Impact and Use* (1977); "The Impact of OCLC," *Amer. Libs.* (My. 1976); "The Case for not closing the catalog," *Amer. Libs.* (Mr. 1979). **Activities:** 1; 15, 17, 46 **Addr.:** Wilson Library 024 A, University of North Carolina, Chapel Hill, NC 27514.

Hewitt, Julia F. (O. 4, 1929, Schuylerville, NY) Mgr., Main Lib., Gen. Elect. Co., 1979–, Ref. Libn., 1965–79, Catlgr., 1961–65. **Educ.:** SUNY, Albany, 1947–51, BS (Bus. Educ.), 1962–64, MLS. **Orgs.:** SLA: Upstate NY Chap. Bltn. Ed. (1965–66); Secy. (1967–68). Hudson Mohawk LA: Brd. of Dir. (1971–74). Capital Dist. Lib. Cncl.: Trustee (1980–85). AAUW. **Honors:** PI Omega PI, 1950. **Pubns.:** "Factors Influencing the Growth and Development of the Industrial Library" in *Social and Political Aspects of Librarianship* (1965). **Activities:** 12; 15, 17, 39; 59, 64, 81 **Addr.:** General Electric Co., Main Library Bldg. 2, 1 River Rd., Schenectady, NY 12345.

Hewitt, Marylouise Mann (F. 27, 1935, Reading, PA) Ed., *Education Index*, H. W. Wilson Co, 1973–, Asst. Ed., 1971–73, Indxr., 1961–71; Ref. Libn., Equitable Life Assurance Socty., 1960–61; Asst. Libn., Compton Advert. Agency, 1959; Dir., Port Jervis, Pub. Lib., 1958; HS Libn., Liberty Ctrl. Sch., 1956–58. **Educ.:** Kutztown, State Tchrs. Coll., 1952–56, BS (LS); State Univ. Coll., Geneseo, 1957–58, (LS). **Orgs.:** ALA. NY Lib. Club. **Activities:** 6; 17, 30, 37; 63 **Addr.:** H. W. Wilson Co., 950 University Ave., Bronx, NY 10452.

Hewitt, (Mrs.) Vivian D. (F. 17, 1925, New Castle, PA) Chief Libn., Carnegie Endowment for Int. Peace, 1963–; Libn., Rockefeller Fndn., 1955–63; Resrchr., Asst. to Dir. Readers' Ref. Srvc., Crowell-Collier Publ. Co., 1953–55; Sr. Asst. Libn., Homewood Br., Carnegie Lib., 1947–49, Sr. Asst., Spec. Worker, Wylie Ave. Br., Carnegie Lib., 1944–47; Instr. Libn., Sch. of Lib. Srvc. Atlanta Univ., 1949–51, Sr. Asst. Libn., Carnegie Lib., 1944–49. **Educ.:** Geneva Coll., 1939–43, BA (Fr. Psy.), Carnegie Inst. of Tech., 1943–44 BSLS, Univ. of Pittsburgh, 1947–48. **Orgs.:** SLA: Pres. (1978–79); NY Chap. ALA: Black Caucus, African & Carribean Task Force (1972–). NY Lib. Club. Archons of Colophon, NY. IFLA: SLA Del. Alpha Kappa Alpha. **Honors:** ALA; Black Caucus Awd., 1978; Geneva Coll., LHD 1979. Univ. of Pittsburgh, Distinguished Alumna Award, 1978. **Pubns.:** Contrib., *The Black Librarian in America* (1970). Contrib., *What Black Librarians are Saying* (1972). Contrib., *New Dimensions for Academic Library Service* (1975). "Special Libraries" (1978, 1979); other books and articles. **Activities:** 12; 17, 39; 54 **Addr.:** Carnegie Endowment for International Peace, 30 Rockefeller Plz. - 54th Floor, New York, NY 10020.

Heyman, Berna L. (Ja. 18, 1945, Chicago, IL) Head of Bibl. Srvs., Coll. of William and Mary, 1979–, Head, Cat. Dept., 1977–79, Asst. Head, Cat. Dept., 1972–77; Head, Cat. Dept., Univ. of MO, St. Louis, 1969–72; Asst. Law Libn., Coll. of William and Mary, 1968–69; Catlgr., MA Inst. of Tech., 1967–68. **Educ.:** Washington Univ., 1962–66, AB (Eng. Hist.); Simmons Coll., 1966–67, MSLS. **Orgs.:** ALA: LITA Prog. Plng. Com.; Co-ch., Autom. Acq. Inst. (1979–80); ACRL/Coll. Sect., Cont. Educ. Com. (1978–80). Potomac Tech. Prcs. Libns.: VA Rep. (1977–79). VA LA: Local Arrang. Ch. (1978); ALA/SELA Mem. Com. (1976–77). DC LA. **Pubns.:** "Annotated Bibliography on Performance Appraisal," Coll. Lib. Info. packet (1980). **Activities:** 1; 17, 34, 46; 56, 75 **Addr.:** Earl Gregg Swem Library, College of William and Mary, Williamsburg, VA 23185.

Heyman, Sister Jerome (D. 15, 1914, Chicago, IL) Libn., Edgewood Coll., 1953–; Libn., Catholic HS (Oklahoma City), 1950–53; Libn., Visitation HS (Chicago), 1941–50. **Educ.:** Rosary Coll., 1933–37, BA (LS); Univ. of IL, 1941–47, MS (LS); SD, Life Cert., 1940. **Orgs.:** ALA. Cath. LA. WI LA: Memshp. Com. (1975–78). Madison Area Lib. Cncl.: Bd. Dir. (1968–72, 1974–76, 1978–80); Recog. Com. (1976–). WI Assn. Acad. Libns.: Memshp. Com. (1976); Com. Acad. Status Tenure (1972–74). **Activities:** 1; 15, 17, 39; 63, 90 **Addr.:** Edgewood College, 855 Woodrow St., Madison, WI 53711.

Heyman, Juliane M. (Mr. 25, 1925, Danzig, Free City) Pres., Aspen Intl. Consul.; Consul., Checchi & Co., 1979; Peace Corps., Senegal & Washington 1979; USAID, Mauritania, 1978, Inter. Food Pol./Resrch Inst. 1978; Lib. Adv., USAID, El Salvador, 1969–70; Asst. Proj. Off., Dev. Assoc., 1975–77. **Educ.:** Columbia Univ., 1943–46, BA (Intl. Rel); Univ. of CA, Berkeley, 1946–49, MA (Intl. Rel), MLS. **Orgs.:** ALA. Socty. of Intl. Dev.: VP.-Assn. of Asian Std. Aspen Inst. for Human. Std. **Pubns.:** *Nepal - Sociology* (1956). *Pakistan Politics* (1956). "Mauritania: An annotated Bibliography of Bib.," *Current Bibl. of African Aff.* (1978–79). "Libraries in Vietnam," *UNESCO Bltn. for Libs.* (O. 1959). "Training for South Asian Peace Corps Projects," *Asian Stds. Nwsltr.* (1963). **Addr.:** 2727 - 29th St., Apt. 406, Washington, DC 20008.

Heyneman, Alan Lionel (Mr. 14, 1924, San Francisco, CA) Assoc. Treas., Admin., Univ. of Rochester, 1974–, Dir. of Persnl., 1964–73; Chief, Persnl. Ofc., NY Pub. Lib., 1955–64; various admin., prof. positions, Lib. of Congs., 1949–55; Adj. Prof. Libnshp., Mgt., St. John Fisher Coll., 1974–76; Adj. Prof. Libnshp., Mgt., Rutgers Univ., 1960–61. **Educ.:** Univ. of CA, Berkeley, 1948, AB (Econ., Eng.), 1949, BLS (Libnshp.). **Orgs.:** NY LA: Various coms., ofcs. (1955–73). ALA: Various divs., coms., ofcs. (1949–72). Coll. and Univ. Persnl. Assn.: Various coms.; Dir., Secy.-Treas. (1964–74). Natl. Assn. of Coll. and Univ. Bus. Ofcrs.: Various coms. (1973–). **Honors:** Coll. and Univ. Persnl. Assn., Creative Achvmt. Medal, 1972. **Pubns.:** Various articles in prof. jnls. **Activities:** 1; 17, 24, 32; 57, 61, 62 **Addr.:** The University of Rochester, Rochester, NY 14627.

Heynen, Jeffrey W. (Ap. 14, 1942, New York, NY) Pres., Info. Interchange Corp., 1980–, Coord., Micro. Proj., Assn. of Resrch. Libs., 1981–; Micropublshg. Projs. Dir., Congsnl. Info. Srv., 1974–80; Exec. VP., Redgrave Info. Resrcs., 1972–74; Sr. Ed., Greenwood Press, Inc., 1968–72. **Educ.:** Swarthmore Coll., 1960–64, BA; Univ. of WI, 1964–66, MA (Hist.); London Sch. of Econ., 1968–69, PhD work; Univ. of London, Birkbeck Coll., 1969–70, PhD work. **Orgs.:** ALA: RTSD/Reprodct. of Lib. Mtrls. Sect. (Ch., 1979–80). Natl. Micro. Assn.: Stans. Bd. (1979–). Amer. Natl. Stans. Inst.: ANSI Com. PH5, Micro. (1979–). Intl. Org. for Standardization: Tech. Com. 171, Micro. (1979–). **Pubns.:** Various articles, rpts. **Activities:** 6; 30, 33, 37 **Addr.:** 503 11th St. S.E., Washington, DC 20003.

Hiatt, Peter (O. 19, 1930, New York, NY) Dir. and Prof., Sch. of Libnshp., Univ. of WA, 1974–; Dir., Cont. Educ. Prog. for Lib. Persnl., West. Interstate Comsn. for Higher Educ., 1970–74; Dir., IN Lib. Std., IN Univ. & IN State Lib., 1968–70; Assoc. Prof., Grad. Lib. Sch., Consult. IN State Lib., 1963–68. **Educ.:** Colgate Univ., 1948–52, BA (Hist.); Rutgers Univ., 1955–57, MLS; 1959–62, PhD (LS). **Orgs.:** ALA: PLA, Educ. for Pub. Libns. Com. (Ch., 1979–80); Goals, Guidelines & Stan. Com. (Ch., 1976–79); LED (Pres., 1972–74); ASD (Pres., 1970–71). IN LA: Ref. Sect. (Ch., 1965–67). NJ LA. AALS: Bd. of Dir. (1976–78). **Honors:** AALS, Outstan. Srv., 1978. **Pubns.:** "The Impact of Continuing Education on Library Change" in *The Evaluation of Continuing Educ. for Professionals* (1979); "Margaret E. Monroe: Concepts, Methods and Impact" in *The Service Imperative for Libraries* (1981); Ed., *The Indiana Library Studies* (1970); Jt. ed., *Public Library Services for the Functionally Illiterate: A Survey of Practice* (1967); "A Delivery System for Library Continuing Education" in *The Assessment & Development of Professionals: Theory and Practice* (1976); other articles, slide-tape shows. **Activities:** 25, 26, 41 **Addr.:** 19324 8th Ave., N.W., Seattle, WA 98177.

Hiatt, Robert Miller (O. 9, 1942, Columbus, OH) Asst. to Dir. for Cat., Lib. of Congs., 1971–, Catlgr., Shared Cat. Div., 1968–71. **Educ.:** OH State Univ., 1960–64, BSEd (Fr.); Columbia Univ., 1967–68, MS (LS). **Orgs.:** ALA: RTSD, Reprinting Com. (1971–75); Nom. Com. (1975); Resrcs. Sect., Nom. Com. (1976); Cat. Code Revision Com. (1976–78). Jt. Strg. Com. for Rev. of AACR: LC Deputy Rep. (1975–78). Lib. of Congs. Prof. Assn. Sigma Pi Fraternity. **Honors:** Beta Phi Mu, 1968; Lib. of Congs., Merit. Srv. Awd., 1978. **Pubns.:** "Anglo-American Cataloguing Rules," *ALA Yrbk.* (1976); "AACR 2: Implementation Plans," *Lib. of Congs. Info. Bltn.* (N. 17, 1978); Ed., *Cat. Srv. Bltn.* (1975–). **Activities:** 4; 17, 20 **Addr.:** Library of Congress, Processing Services, Washington, DC 20540.

Hibbert, R. June (Je. 14, 1937, Belfast, North. Ireland) Head, Tech. Srvs., Brantford Pub. Lib., 1976–; Catlgr., Ref. Libn., 1967–75; Catlgr., Ref. Libn., N. Bay Pub. Lib., 1962–65; Cmrcl. Info. Ofcr., Metal Box Co., London, 1959–61. **Educ.:** Assoc. of the LA, Grt. Britain, 1958–59. **Orgs.:** Can. LA. **Activities:** 9; 15, 20, 46 **Addr.:** 9 Queen St., St. George, ON N0E 1N0 Canada.

Hibbs, Jack E. (Ja. 14, 1933, Toledo, OH) Resrch. Libn., Univ. of Akron, 1974–; Libn., Firelands Campus, Bowling Green State Univ., 1969–74; Libn., Northwood HS Toledo, 1965–69; Tchr., Whitmer HS Toledo, 1964–65. **Educ.:** Univ. of Toledo, 1956–60, BEduc (Soc. Sci.), 1966–69, MA (LS). **Orgs.:** ALA: ACRL. OH LA. Acad. LA of OH. OH Friends of the Lib.: Trustee (1974–); Pres. (1978). AAUP. **Pubns.:** "A History of the Toledo Public Library, 1873–1964," *NW OH Qtly.* (1975); reviews. **Activities:** 1, 10; 15, 31, 39; 63, 75, 92 **Addr.:** 205 Filmore Ave., Cuyahoga Falls, OH 44221.

Hibler, James P. (S. 3, 1948, Detroit, MI) Lib. Dir., Independence Twp. Lib., 1979–; Head Libn., John F. Kennedy, Jr. Lib., 1979; Ref. Libn., Univ. of MI, Dearborn, 1978; Libn., Archvst., Market Opinion Resrch. Co., 1977–78. **Educ.:** Univ. of MI, 1966–71, BA (Hist., Elem. Educ.); Wayne State Univ., 1972–74, MA (Hist.), 1975, MSLS. **Orgs.:** ALA. SAA. MI LA. MI Arch. Assn. Clarkston Area Jaycees. Independence Twp. MI Week Com. Midwest Arch. Conf. **Activities:** 2, 9; 15, 17, 21 **Addr.:** Independence Township Library, 6495 Clarkston Rd., Clarkston, MI 48016.

Hickey, Damon Douglas (O. 30, 1942, Houston, TX) Assoc. Lib. Dir. and Cur. of the Friends Hist. Col., Guilford Coll., 1975–; Actg. Cur. of Rare Books, Duke Univ. Lib., 1973–74; Presby. Mnstr. prior to 1973. **Educ.:** Rice Univ., 1960–65, BA (Phil.); Princeton Theo. Semy., 1965–68, MDiv; Univ. of NC, 1974–75, MS (LS); Cert. in Clinical Pastoral Care, Inst. of Relig. & Human Dev., 1968–69. **Orgs.:** ALA: ACRL/Coll. Lib. Sect., Com. on Cont. Educ. (1976–77). SELA. NC LA: Dir., Coll. & Univ. Sect. (1975–77). Beta Phi Mu: Epsilon Chap. Rep. (1978–80); VP and Pres.-Elect (1981–82). NC Friends Hist. Socty.: Nsltr. ed. (1978–). Friends Hist. Assn. (Philadelphia). Friends Hist. Socty. (London). **Pubns.:** "Mary Wollstonecraft and *The Female Reader,*" *Eng. Lang. Notes,* (D. 1975); "The Friends of the Duke University Library," *NC Libs.* (Fall 1976); "The Impact of Instructional Technology on the Future of Academic Librarianship" in *Acad. Libs. by the Year 2000:* (1977); Book Review Ed., *The Southern Friend: Jnl. of the NC Friends Hist. Socty.* (1978–); Assoc. Ed., *NC Libs.* (1977–78). **Activities:** 1; 17; 90, 92 **Addr.:** Friends Historical Collection, Guilford College Library, Greensboro, NC 27410.

Hickey, Thomas B. (Jl. 30, 1947, Buffalo, NY) Sr. Resrch. Sci., OCLC, 1977–, Syst. Anal., 1977; Sci. Ref. Libn., The John Crerar Lib., 1970–73. **Educ.:** SUNY, Stony Brook, 1965–69, BS (Phys.); SUNY, Geneseo, 1969–70, MLS; Univ. of IL, 1973–77, PhD (LS). **Orgs.:** ALA. ASIS. Assn. for Comp. Mach. **Honors:** Beta Phi Mu. **Pubns.:** "Derived Search Keys for Government Documents," *Info. Prcs. and Mgt.* (1979); "Automatic Detection of Duplicate Monographic Records," *Jnl. of Lib. Autom.* (1979); various rpts. **Activities:** 3; 34, 41; 56, 75, 93 **Addr.:** Office of Research, OCLC, 6565 Frantz Rd., Dublin, OH 43017.

Hickok, Beverly (O. 31, 1919, San Francisco, CA) Head Libn., Inst. of Transp. Std., Univ. of CA, Berkeley, 1948–; Ref. Libn., Docum. Dept., Gen. Lib., Univ. of CA, Berkeley, 1947–48; Tchr., Bell Gardens Jr. HS, 1943–44. **Educ.:** Univ. of CA, Berkeley, 1938–41, BA (Hist.); Univ. of CA, Los Angeles, 1941–42 (Gen. Sec. Educ.) Univ. of CA, Berkeley, 1946–47, BLS. **Orgs.:** SLA: Transp. Div. (Ch., 1956–57), Transp. Resrch. Coord. Com. (Secy., 1973–78); San Francisco Chap. (Pres., 1957–58). **Pubns.:** *Transportation Systems Management: A Selected Bibliography for Transportation Planners and Engineers* (1978); "The Management of Transportation Information: Accomplishments and Prospects," *ITS Review* (N. 1978). **Activities:** 1, 12; 17, 35, 39; 64, 65, 94 **Addr.:** Institute of Transportation Studies, 412 McLaughlin Hall, University of California, Berkeley, CA 94720.

PROFESSIONAL ACTIVITIES: Institutions: 1. Acad. lib.; 2. Arch.; 3. Assn.; 4. Fed./Gvt. lib.; 5. Inst. lib.; 6. Mfr./Suppl.; 7. Milit. lib.; 8. Musm.; 9. Pub. lib.; 10. Sch. lib.; 11. Sch. of lib. sci.; 12. Spec. lib.; 13. State lib.; 14. (other). **Functions/Activities:** 15. Acq./Col. dev.; 16. Adult srvs.; 17. Admin.; 18. Apprais.; 19. Archit./Bldgs.; 20. Cat./Class.; 21. Chld. srvs.; 22. Circ.; 23. Cons./Pres.; 24. Consult.; 25. Cont. ed.; 26. Educ. lib. sci.; 27. Ext. srvs.; 28. Fund/Grants; 29. Gvt. pubs.; 30. Indx./Abs.; 31. Instr. lib. use; 32. Media srvs.; 33. Micro.; 34. Netwks./Coop.; 35. Persnl.; 36. PR; 37. Publshg.; 38. Recs. mgt.; 39. Ref. srvs.; 40. Repro.; 41. Resrch.; 42. Review.; 43. Secur.; 44. Serials; 45. Spec. col.; 46. Tech. srvs.; 47. Trustees/Bds.; 48. YA srvs.; 49. (other).

Hicks, Donna M. (My. 2, 1941, Duluth, MN) Head, Pop. Srvs., Northbrook Pub. Lib., 1977–; Libn., Ref. Dept., Univ. of MN, 1965–71. **Educ.:** Hamline Univ., 1959–63, BA (Art, Grmn.); Univ. of MN, 1963–65, MLS. **Orgs.:** ALA. IL LA. **Activities:** 9; 16, 36 **Addr.:** Northbrook Public Library, 1201 Cedar Ln., Northbrook, IL 60062.

Hicks, Doris Askew (My. 24, 1926, Sulphur Springs, TX) Dir., Dept. of Lrng. Resrcs.-Rochester City Sch. Dist., 1973; Sch. Libn., Madison H.S. Rochester City Sch. Dist., 1969–73; Sch. Libn., Macedonia Sch., Texarkana, TX, 1961–69; Multi-Sch. Libn., Bowie Co., Boston, TX, 1954–61. **Educ.:** Bishop Coll., 1946–48, BA (English); Univ. of TX, Austin, 1954–59, MLS (LS); Cert. in Supvsn. & Admin., 1975. **Orgs.:** Grt. Rochester Area Sch. Media Specs., Prog. Com. (1979). NY LA, Exec. Bd. (1978). Sch. Lib. Media Sect. of NY LA, Pres. (1978). ALA/AASL Unit Head (1979–80). Rochester Tchrs. Assn. NY Tchrs. Assn. Delta Kappa Gamma. **Honors:** AASL and Encyc. Britannica Sch. Lib. Media Prog. of Year Awd., 1975. **Pubns.:** "Management of Nonprint School Library Materials from Selection to Circulation," *Cath. Lib. World,* (Ap. 1978). **Activities:** 10; 15, 20, 24 **Addr.:** 131 West Broad St., Rochester, NY 14608.

Hicks, Mary Ellen (Je. 1, 1938, Syracuse, NY) Syst. Libn., Syracuse City Sch. Lib. Syst., 1981–; Lib. Media Spec., Bellevue Sch., 1973–81; Church Libn., Univ. Church, 1967–70; Pub. Libn., Merritt Island Pub. Lib., 1966–67. **Educ.:** Syracuse Univ., 1956–60, AB (Eng., LS), 1960–62, MSLS; various crs. **Orgs.:** ALA. NY LA. Ctrl. NY Media Specs. **Activities:** 10; 31, 34, 46; 63 **Addr.:** 311 Cooper Ln., Dewitt, NY 13214.

Hieb, Louis A. (Ap. 11, 1939, Carlsbad, NM) Head Spec. Col. Libn., Univ. of AZ Lib., 1978–; Asst. Prof., Dept. of Anthr., WA State Univ., 1972–78; Ref. & Acq. Libn., Princeton Theo. Semy., 1965–68. **Educ.:** Grinnell Coll., 1957–61, BA (Soclgy.); Yale Univ., 1961–65, BD (Relig.); Rutgers Univ., 1965–67, MLS; Princeton Univ., 1968–72, PHD (Anthro.). **Orgs.:** AZ LA. **Pubns.:** "The Ritual Clown: Humor and Ethics," in *Forms of Play of Native North Americans* (1979); "Masks and Meaning: A Contextual Approach to the Hopi tüvi kü," in *Ritual Symbolism and Ceremonialism in the Americas* (1979); "Rhythms of Significance: Towards a Symbolic Analysis of Dance in Ritual," in *New Dimensions in Dance Research: Anthropology and Dance—The American Indian* (1974). **Activities:** 1, 2; 15, 17, 45; 66, 91, 92 **Addr.:** The University of Arizona Library, Tucson, AZ 85721.

Hiebing, Dorothea R. (Mr. 16, 1944, Oak Park, IL) Pub. Lib. Consult. and Cont. Educ., WI Div. Lib. Srvs., 1979–; Dir., N. W. Reg. Lib., 1976–79; Resrch. Assoc., Sch. LS, Univ. Denver, 1975–76; Dir., Middle Sch. Media Ctr., 1970–73. **Educ.:** Univ. WI, 1964–64, BS (Educ.); Rosary Coll., 1968–69, MA (LS) Univ. Denver, 1975–76, MPA. **Orgs.:** ALA: ASCLA, Cont. Educ. Com. (Ch., 1979); LAMA/PAS Bd. Sec. (1982–). Midwest Fed. LA: Cont. Educ. Com. (1979–81). MN Hum. Cmsn.: 1978–80. **Activities:** 9, 13; 17, 25; 55 **Addr.:** 4817 Sheboygan #220, Madison, WI 53705.

Higbee, Joan Florence (Ja. 1, 1945, Washington, DC) Libn., Lib. of Congs., 1976–; Instr., Fr., Johns Hopkins Univ., 1968–72; Asst. d'anglais, Lycee Frederic Chopin, Nancy, France, 1967–68. **Educ.:** Sorbonne, Paris, France, 1962–63, Cert. of Presence; George Washington Univ., 1963–67, BA (Fr.); Univ. de Nancy, France, 1967–68, Cert. of Presence (Resrchr. in Residence); Johns Hopkins Univ., 1968–75, MA, PhD (Rom. Langs.); Cath. Univ. of Amer., 1975–76, MS (LS). **Orgs.:** DC LA: Nom. Com. (Ch., 1981). ALA: Cnclr.-at-Large (1980–84); ACRL/West. European Specs. Sect., Resrch. and Pubns. Com. (1980–82); SRRT, Lib. Un. Task Force (Coord., 1980–); RASD; RTSD. Assn. des bibtcrs. français. Mod. Lang. Assn. Socty. of Fed. Lings.: VP. (1979–81); Ed. Bd. (1979–81); Prog. Com. (1978–80). The Johns Hopkins Univ.: Strg. Com. (1978–). **Honors:** Beta Phi Mu; Fulbright Travel Grant, 1967–68; French Gvt., Tchg. Flwshp., 1967–68. **Pubns.:** Two Chaps. in, *Léon Gontran Damas, 1912–1978* (1979); Chap. in, *La critique générative* (1973); "French Resources of the Library of Congress: An Interim Report," *West. European Specs. Sect. Nsltr.* (1980); "Oral and Written Languages of Senegal: Cultures in Transition," *The Fed. Ling.* (1979). **Activities:** 4; 20, 41, 45; 54, 57 **Addr.:** 13 N. Bedford St., Arlington, VA 22201.

Higdon, Thomas David (Mr. 7, 1930, Walters, OK) Dir., Univ. of AZ Hlth. Sci. Ctr. Lib., 1976–, Asst. Libn., 1975–76; Head Cat. Libn., Houston Acad. Med., TX Med. Ctr. Lib., 1972–75; Head, Tech. Srvs., TX Tech. Univ., Sch. of Med., 1971–72; Head Cat. Libn., Univ. of AZ Med. Ctr. Lib., 1965–71; Asst. Cat. Libn., Univ. of CA, Los Angeles, Biomed. Lib., 1960–64; Cat. Libn., Los Angeles Cnty. Med. Assn. Lib., 1958–60. **Educ.:** Univ. of OK, 1948–51, 1955–57, BA (Hist.); Columbia Univ., 1957–58, MS (LS). **Orgs.:** Med. LA: Prog. and Conv. Com. (Ch., 1980–81); Nom. Com. (1980); Bibl. Problems and Projs. Com. (1969–70). AZ LA: Spec. Libs. Div. (Pres., 1980–81). **Activities:** 1, 12; 15, 17, 20; 80 **Addr.:** University of AZ Health Sciences Center Library, Tucson, AZ 85724.

Higginbotham, Barbra Buckner (Ap. 12, 1946, Dallas, TX) Head, Orig. Cat., Columbia Univ., 1979–, Asst. Head, Orig. Cat., 1977–78; Tech. Srvs. Libn., US Customs Srv. Lib., 1974–76; Catlgr., US Dept. of Transp. Lib., 1973–74; Catlgr., RI Coll. Lib., 1971–73; Chld. Libn., Chicago Pub. Lib., 1969–70. **Educ.:** Centenary Coll. of LA, 1964–68, BA (Eng.); Columbia Univ., 1968–69, MLS, 1978–, DLS Cand. **Orgs.:** ALA: GODORT, Cat. Manual Com. Bk. Leag. of NY. NY Tech. Srvs. Libns. NY Lib. Club. **Activities:** 1; 17, 20 **Addr.:** 320 Butler Library, Columbia University, New York, NY 10027.

Higginbotham, Prieur Jay (Jl. 16, 1937, Jackson Cnty., MS) Lcl. Hist.-Spec. Cols. Spec., Mobile Pub. Lib., 1973–, Head, Lcl. Hist. Dept., 1973–80; Tchr., Mobile Cnty. Pub. Schs., 1962–73. **Educ.:** Univ. of MS, 1955–62, BA (Pre-Law); various crs. **Orgs.:** AL LA. Smithsonian Socty. Natl. Geo. Socty. Intl. Platform Assn. **Honors:** LA Hist. Assn., L. Kemper Williams Prize, 1978; Inst. Fr. de Washington, Gilbert Chinard Prize, 1977; AL LA, Non-fiction Bk. Awd., 1979; Mobile Hist. Dev. Comsn., Elizabeth B. Gould Awd., 1981. **Pubns.:** *Old Mobile—Fort Louis de la Louisiane, 1702–1711* (1977); *A Voyage To Dauphin Island, 1720* (1974); "Origins of the Franch-Alabama Conflict, 1704," *AL Review* (Ap. 1978); "The Chaumont Concession," *Jnl. of MS Hist.* (N. 1974); "Fast Train Russia," *Dalmi Vostok* (Jl. 1981). **Activities:** 9; 45 **Addr.:** 60 N. Monterey St., Mobile, AL 36604.

Higgins, (K.) Elaine (Ja. 14, 1942, Long Beach, CA) Cat. Libn., Univ. of MT, 1971–. **Educ.:** Univ. of CA (Berkeley), 1962–65, AB (Ling.); Univ. of South. CA, 1970–71, MSLS. **Orgs.:** ALA. Pacific N.W. LA. MT. LA.: Doc. Div., (Ch., 1977–78); Acad. Div. (Secy., 1975–76); MT Auth. Athrty. File Com. (1979–). Church and Synagogue LA. Lutheran Church LA. Univ. MT LA: Various offices. Lutheran Women's Missionary Leag.: VP (1978–79). West. MT Geneal. Socty. MT Regis. of Interpreters for the Deaf. **Honors:** Alpha Mu Gamma, 1964. **Pubns.:** "St. Helens: an Initial Bibliography" *PNLA Qtly.* (Fall 1980). "A Volcanic Saga: St. Helens Bibliography, pt. II" *PNLA Qtly.* (Win. 1981). Contents for Chapter 6, AACR," *PNLA Qtly.* (Win. 1974–75). **Activities:** 1; 20, 29, 49-Theses & Dissertations; 95-Foreign languages & translation. **Addr.:** Mansfield Library, University of Montana, Missoula, MT 59812.

Higgins, Judith H. (White Plains, NY) Dir., Lrng. Resrcs. Ctr., Valhalla, NY HS, 1969–; YA Libn., Mamaroneck Free Lib., 1967–69; Reporter, *Life* Mag. **Educ.:** Simmons Coll., BS (Pubshg.); Columbia Univ., 1964–67, MLS; 1972–77, DLS. **Orgs.:** ALA: AASL/Intl. Rel. Com. (1979–); AASL/Amer. Sch. Couns. Assn. Jt. Com. (1979–). Intl. Assn. of Sch. Libns. NY LA: Ref. Com. (1978–). Sch. Lib. Media Spec. of Southeast. NY: Pres. (1971–72). **Honors:** Beta Phi Mu, 1967. **Pubns.:** *Energy: A Multimedia Guide for Children and Young Adults* (1979); Column "Paperbacks" *Tchr.* (1968–81); various articles. **Activities:** 10; 15, 32, 39; 63, 67, 89 **Addr.:** 83 Greenridge Ave., White Plains, NY 10605.

Higgins, Matthew J. (My. 1, 1938, Clonmel, Ireland) Chief, Plng., Dev., RI Dept. of State Lib. Srvs., 1978–; Dir., Greenville Pub. Lib., 1975–78. **Educ.:** Univ. of CT, 1961–66, BA (Hist.); Trinity Coll., 1968–74, MA (Hist.); Univ. of RI, 1973–74, MLS; Simmons Coll., 1975–80, DA (Lib. Admin.). **Orgs.:** ALA: Archit. for Pub. Libs. Com., Subcom. for Lib. Educ. New Eng. LA: Com. for Lib. Educ. RI LA. **Pubns.:** "Nelinet Automation Study Report," *RI LA Bltn.* (S. 1981); "Public Libraries: The Price of Survival," *RI LA Bltn.* (N. 1977); Ed., *RI LA Bltn.* (1977–78). **Activities:** 13; 17, 19, 34; 56, 63, 69 **Addr.:** RI Dept. of State Library Services, 95 Davis St., Providence, RI 02907.

Higgins, Patricia J. (Miami, FL) Head, Tech. Srvs., Maricopa Cnty. Law Lib., 1978–, Law Lib. Tech., 1977–78; Law Libn., Dir., OK City Univ., 1972–76; Acq. Libn., Amer. Bar Fndn., 1966–72. **Educ.:** Loyola Univ., Chicago, 1958–67, BS (Eng. Lit.); Rosary Coll., 1967–70, MA (LS); various crs. **Orgs.:** AALL. AZ LA. **Activities:** 1, 4; 15, 17, 20; 77 **Addr.:** Maricopa County Law Library, 101 W. Jefferson St., Phoenix, AZ 85003.

High, Bruce C., III (Ja. 13, 1943, Tallahassee, FL) Dean of the Fac. and Libn., The Baylor Sch., 1967–69, 1970–; Head Libn., Richard Bland Coll., Coll. of William and Mary, 1969–70; Tchr. in various HS. **Educ.:** Emory and Henry Coll., 1959–63, BA (Eng. & Pol. Sci.); Univ. of NC (Chapel Hill), 1963–64, 1968, MS (LS). **Orgs.:** ALA: AASL; ACRL; RASD, Ref. Subscrpn. Bks. Com. (1974–75). Chattanooga Area LA: VP, Pres. TN LA: Int. Frdm. Com. (Ch., 1975). SELA: Int. Frdm. Com. (1973–75). Chattanooga Adult Educ. Cncl.: Bd. Dir. (1973–75). Chattanooga Arts Cncl. Blue Key Natl. Hon. Frat. Allied Arts Fund of Greater Chattanooga: Educ. Div. (Ch.). **Honors:** TN Conf. on Lib. and Info. Sci., Del., 1978. **Activities:** 10; 17 **Addr.:** The Baylor School, Chattanooga, TN 37401.

Highfield, Betty Jane (Je. 24, 1917, Chicago, IL) Dir., Coll. Lib., N. Park Coll., 1944–, Asst. Libn., 1939–44. **Educ.:** Rockford Coll., 1933–37, BA (Hist.); Univ. of IL, 1938–39, BS, 1942–47, MS (LS). **Orgs.:** ALA: Cncl. (1960–64); RASD, Arch. Com. (Ch., 1970–71); ACRL/Coll. Lib. Sect., Exec. Bd (1974–76), Nom. Com. (1974–75). IL LA: Coll. and Ref. Sect., Bd. (1952); various coms. ATLA: Exec. Bd. (1959–61). Swedish Pioneer Hist. Socty.: Exec. Bd (1971–75, 1978–81); Arch. Com. (Secy., 1975–). **Honors:** Beta Phi Mu. **Activities:** 1; 17 **Addr.:** 1585 Ridge Ave. #404, Evanston, IL 60201.

Highfill, William Carl (Ag. 12, 1935, Hontubby, OK) Univ. Libn., Auburn Univ., 1973–; Dir. of Lib., E. TX State Univ., 1969–73; Asst. Libn., Coop. Fac. Mem., Dept. of LS, KS State Tchrs. Coll., 1962–65; Tchr.–Libn., Chase Cnty. Cmnty. HS, 1959–62; Tchr.–Libn., Isabel HS, 1957–59; Visit. Instr., Dept. of Libnshp., KS State Tchrs. Coll., Sum. 1966, Sum. 1968. **Educ.:** OK Bapt. Univ., 1953–57, AB (Eng.); KS State Tchrs. Coll., 1958–61, MS (LS); Univ. of IL, 1969, PhD (LS). **Orgs.:** ALA. AL LA: Pres. (1979–80). Southeast. Lib. Netwk.: Bd. of Dirs. (1976–79). SELA. **Honors:** Phi Delta Kappa; Phi Kappa Phi; Beta Phi Mu. **Activities:** 1; 17, 34, 41 **Addr.:** Ralph Brown Draughon Library, Auburn University, Auburn, AL 36849.

Highum, Clayton D. (D. 7, 1932, Fargo, ND) Dir., Libs., IL Wesleyan Univ., 1972–; Dir., Undergrad. Lib., South. IL Univ., 1969–72; Dir., Libs., Parkland Coll., 1967–69; Resrch. Assoc., Lib. Sch., Univ. of IL, 1966–67; Libn., Cols. and Srvs., FL Atl. Univ., 1963–66; Asst. Libn., HS Instr., Mora Pub. Schs., 1956–61. **Educ.:** State Coll., Mayville, ND, 1952–56, BS (Eng.); State Coll., St. Cloud, MN, 1960, MS; Univ. of IL, 1962–63, MS (LS). **Orgs.:** IL LA: Exec. Bd.; Pres.-elect, Pres. (1981–83). IL ACRL: Pres.-Elect, Pres. (1975–77); Exec. Bd.; Secy. State Lib. Adv. Com. for Acad. Libs.: Ch. State Lib. Adv. Com. on Autom.: Ch. Various other orgs. Natl. Educ. Assn. MN Educ. Assn. IL Wesleyan Univ.: Various coms., ofcs. AAUP. **Pubns.:** *The Illinois Library Materials Processing Center: A Study* (1980); *Centralized Processing for Public Libraries in Illinois* (1967); "Cataloging for Document Retrieval at Florida Atlantic University," *Coll. & Resrch. Libs.* (My. 1964); ed., "Participating Program Planning and Management for Libraries," *IL Libs.* (Je. 1978); various wkshps., sems. **Activities:** 1; 17, 24 **Addr.:** Library, Illinois Wesleyan University, Bloomington, IL 61701.

Hiland, Leah F. (D. 30, 1932, Lebanon, IN) Asst. Prof., Univ. of North. IA, 1972–; Asst. Prof., Univ. of IA, 1969–72; Libn., Homewood-Flossmoor HS, 1962–66; Libn., Nurnberg Amer. HS, 1960–62; Libn., Merrillville HS, 1955–59. **Educ.:** IN Univ., 1951–55, BS (Soc. Std.), 1959–60, MALS, 1966–73, PhD (Sch. Libnshp.). **Orgs.:** ASIS. ALA: AASL, Vid. Comm. Com. (1979–81). IA Educ. Media Assn.: Legis. Com. (1977–80); Prof. Dev. Com. (1974–76). Phi Delta Kappa: Univ. of North. IA Resrch. Rep. (1977–80). Univ. of North. IA Untd. Fac.: AAUP/Natl. Educ. Assn. Resrch. Com. (1980–81). **Honors:** Beta Phi Mu; Pi Lambda Theta. **Activities:** 10, 11; 26, 31, 39; 56, 63, 92 **Addr.:** Department of Library Science, University of Northern Iowa, Cedar Falls, IA 50613.

Hildebrant, Darrel D. (Ap. 5, 1947, Beach, ND) Prog. Coord., Vet. Meml. Lib., 1971–; Dir., Dickinson Pub. Lib., 1969–71. **Educ.:** Dickinson State Coll., 1965–69, BS (Lang. LS). **Orgs.:** Mt. Plains LA: Nom. Com. (1979). ND LA: Ch., Pub. Lib. Sect., Bi Centennial Com. (1975); Exec. Bd., ND Gvr. Conf. on Libs. (1978); VP/Pres. elect, Chld. RT (1980). ALA: John Cotton Dana Lib. PR Com. (1980); Toys, Games and Reaba. Com. (1979–81). Puppeteers of America: Liaison to ALA. **Honors:** US Jaycees, Outstan. Young Man of 1979, 1979. **Activities:** 9; 21, 24, 48; 55 **Addr.:** Veterans Memorial Library, 520 Ave. A East, Bismarck, ND 58501.

Hilferty, Sr. Joseph Leona (Ag. 24, 1908, Philadelphia, PA) Chief Libn., Mt. St. Joseph Acad., 1974–; Head Media Spec., Archbishop Kennedy HS, 1970–74; Head Media Spec., York Cath. HS, 1949–70. **Educ.:** Chestnut Hill Coll., 1940, AB (Eng.); Villanova Univ., 1947, MA (Eng.), 1954, BSLS, 1972, MSLS. **Orgs.:** Cath. LA: Neumann Chap. (Pres., 1977–79, 1979); Nlstr. Ed. (1970–). Natl. Cath. LA. ALA. PA LA. PA Sch. LA. **Activities:** 10; 32, 48 **Addr.:** Mt. St. Joseph Academy, Wissahickon & Stenton Ave., Flourtown, PA 19031.

Hilgert, Earle (My. 17, 1923, Portland, OR) Coord., Col. Dev. Jesuit-Kraus-McCormick Lib., 1975–; Prof. of Bibl., Biblical Std., McCormick Theo. Semy., 1972–; Actg. Gen. Dir., Jesuit-Kraus-McCormick Lib., 1980–81; Prof. Lectr., New Testament, Univ. of Chicago, 1976–78; Visit. Lectr., New Testament, Lib. Consult., Pac. Theo. Coll., Fiji, 1975; Ref. Libn., McCormick Theo. Semy., 1969–75; VP., Acad. Admin., Andrews Univ., 1966–69, Prof., New Testament, 1960–69; Lectr. to Assoc. Prof., New Testament, Adventist Theo. Semy., 1952–60; various positions as instr., hist., 1947–52. **Educ.:** Walla Walla Coll., 1942–45, BA (Hist.); Adventist Theo. Semy., 1945–46, MA (Church Hist.), 1952–55, BD (Dvnty.); Univ. of Basel, Switzerland, 1956–62, ThD (New Testament); Univ. of Chicago, 1969–70, MA (LS). **Orgs.:** ATLA: Com. on Pubn. (1980–); Com. on Accred. Stans. (Ch., 1973–76). Chicago Cluster of Theo. Schs.: Com. on Lib. Col. Dev. (Ch., 1975–80). Chicago Area Theo. LA: Ch. (1972–73). Chicago Socty. of Biblical Resrch.: Pres. (1980–81). The Philo Inst.: Dir. (1976–). Socty. of Biblical Lit. Socty. of New Testament Std. **Honors:** Beta Phi Mu, 1971. **Pubns.:** *The Ship and Related Symbols in the New Testament* (1962); "Calvin Ellis Stowe:Pioneer Academic Librarian," *Lib. Qtly.* (1980); "Annual Bibliographies on Philo Judaeus," *Studia Philonica 1–5* (1972–78); Jt. Ed., *Essays on Theological Librarianship* (1980); "Johann Froben and the Basel University Scholars," *Lib. Qtly.* (1971); various articles. **Activities:** 1, 5; 15, 26, 37; 57, 73, 90 **Addr.:** Jesuit-Krauss-McCormick Library, 1100 E. 55th St., Chicago, IL 60637.

Special Subjects/Services: 50. Adult educ.; 51. Advert./Mktg.; 52. Aerosp.; 53. Agric.; 54. Area std.; 55. Arts/Hum.; 56. Autom.; 57. Bibl./Prtg.; 58. Bio. sci.; 59. Bus./Fin.; 60. Chem.; 61. Copyrt.; 62. Documtn.; 63. Educ.; 64. Engin.; 65. Env.; 66. Eth. grps.; 67. Film; 68. Food/Nutr.; 69. Geneal.; 70. Geo.; 71. Geol.; 72. Handcpd.; 73. Hist.; 74. Int. frdm.; 75. Info. sci.; 76. Insr.; 77. Law; 78. Legis.; 79. Math./Comp. sci.; 80. Med.; 81. Metals; 82. Nat. resrcs.; 83. Newsp.; 84. Nuc. sci.; 85. Oral hist.; 86. Petr./Energy; 87. Pharm.; 88. Phys./Astr./Math.; 89. Readg.; 90. Relig.; 91. Sci./Tech.; 92. Soc. sci.; 93. Telecom.; 94. Transp.; 95. (other).

Hill, Barbara M. (S. 19, 1924, Keene, NH) Libn., Sheppard Lib., MA Coll. of Pharm. and Allied Hlth. Sci., 1969–, Assoc. Libn., 1958–69, Asst. Libn., 1952–58; Chld. Libn., Keene (NH) Pub. Lib., 1947–52; Tchr., Thayer HS, 1946–47. **Educ.:** Keene Tchrs. Coll., 1946, BEd (Sci., Math.); Simmons Coll., 1952, MS (LS). **Orgs.:** Drug Info. Assn. Med. LA: Cont. Educ. Com. (1967–69); Pharm. Grp. Ch. (1965–66). SLA: Pharm. Div., Ch. (1973/74); Bio. Sci. Div., Nom. Com. (1963–65); Boston Chap., Sci.-Tech. Grp. Secy. (1960–61); Nom. Com. (1965, 1975–76, 1981); Educ. Com. (1979–80). Amer. Assn. of Coll. of Pharm.: Libs. and Educ. Resrcs. Sect.: Del. to House of Del. (1979–80, Ch.-Elect, 1981–82). AAUP. **Honors:** Kappa Delta Pi, Rho Chi Society. **Pubns.:** *Recent Advances in the Literature of Pharmacy* (1968, 1973, 1975); "Serials in a Special Library," *Lib. Resrcs. & Tech. Srvs.* (Win. 1962). **Activities:** 1; 15, 17, 31; 75, 87, 91 **Addr.:** Sheppard Library, Massachusetts College of Pharmacy and, Allied Health Sciences, 179 Longwood Ave., Boston, MA 02115.

Hill, Deane White (O. 11, 1921, Ingraham, IL) Dir., Instr. Mtrls. Ctr., Sch. of Educ., Univ. of WI, 1979–; Dir., Lib., Arya-Mehr Univ. of Tech., Iran, 1977–79; Ch., Lrng. Resrc. Ctr., Lincoln Land Cmnty. Coll., 1968–77; Coord., Lib. Srvs., Champaign Cmnty. Schs. Dist. 4, 1958–68. **Educ.:** Univ. of IL, 1939–43, BA (Liberal Arts), 1948–50, MSLS; E. W. Ctr., Inst. on Asian Std., Univ. of HI, 1963. **Orgs.:** ALA: Cncl. (1973–76). IL LA: Bd. (1973–76); Prog. Ch. (1979); Conf. Secy. (1971–72). WI LA. **Activities:** 1, 10; 17; 63 **Addr.:** Instructional Materials Center, 225 N. Mills, Madison, WI 53706.

Hill, Edwin L. (Jl. 15, 1936, Des Moines, IA) Spec. Col. Libn., Univ. of WI (La Crosse), 1968–; Asst. Ref. Libn., West. IL Univ., 1966–68. **Educ.:** North. AZ Univ., 1962–64, BA (Eng.); Rutgers Univ., 1965–66, MLS; Univ. of WI (La Crosse), 1974–78, MS (AV). **Orgs.:** SAA. Univ. of WI Syst. Arch. Cncl. Midwest Arch. Conf. Photographic Hist. Socty. Amer. **Pubns.:** "Libraries and the small press" in *Toward a Further Definition,* (1981). **Activities:** 1, 2; 15, 23, 45; 55, 85, 95-Local History. **Addr.:** Special Collections Dept., Murphy Library, University of Wisconsin - La Crosse, La Crosse, WI 54601.

Hill, Esther Lugo (Ja. 15, 1921, Yauco, PR) Lib. Dir., Inter-Am. Univ. (Bayamón), 1979–; Lib. Dir., Inter-Am Univ. (Fort Buchanan) 1975–79; Ref. Libn., Cat., Univ. of PR (Rio Piedras), 1965–72. **Educ.:** Inter-Am Univ. at (San Germán), 1948–50, BS (Psyc.); Syracuse Univ., 1950–1952, MSLS. **Orgs.:** ALA. Socty. Bibtcr. de PR. **Activities:** 1; 15, 17, 20, 25; 55, 63, 92 **Addr.:** Tintillo St. #10, Bayamón, PR 00619.

Hill, Fred E. (F. 11, 1936, Buhl, ID) Asst. Prof., Instr. Tech., St. Cloud State Univ., 1977–; Admin. Consult., IN Univ., 1976–77, Mgr., AV Ctr., 1974–76. **Educ.:** UT State Univ., 1971–73, BS cum laude (Pol. Sci.), 1973–74, MEd (AV, Admin. LS); IN Univ., 1974–77, EdD (Instr. Tech. Comm.). **Orgs.:** Amer. Socty. for Trng. and Dev. AECT. MN Educ. Media Org. Phi Kappa Phi: St. Cloud State Univ. Fac. Sel. Com. Coll. of Educ. Strategic Long-Range Plng. Com.: Ch. **Pubns.:** "ASTD's Organizational Media Management Survey," *The Communicator* (1979); "Utilization of Audio-Visuals Materials in Vocational Eduction" filmstp., handbk. (1974). **Activities:** 1; 26, 32, 40; 63, 75, 93 **Addr.:** Center for Library/AV Education, CH30 St. Cloud State University, St. Cloud, MN 56301.

Hill, George R. (Jl. 12, 1943, Denver, CO) Assoc. Prof., Msc., Msc. Biblgphr., Baruch Coll., CUNY, 1973–; Fine Arts Libn., Univ. of CA, Irvine, 1972–73; Asst. Msc. Libn., NY Univ., 1971–72; Libn. I, Msc. Div., NY Pub. Lib., 1966–70. **Educ.:** Stanford Univ., 1961–65, AB dept. hon. (Msc.); Univ. of Chicago, 1965–66, AM (LS); NY Univ., 1966–75, PhD (Musicology). **Orgs.:** Intl. Assn. of Msc. Libs. Assn. for Rec. Snd. Cols. ALA. Amer. Musicological Socty. Msc. LA: Bd. of Dir. (Secy., 1978–); Pub. Srvs. Interest Grp. (Co-ch., 1979–81); Com. on Sel. and Acq. (1972–81); Com. on Mem. (1966–68). **Honors:** Deutscher Akademischer Austauschdienst, Resrch. Awds., 1970–71, 1977; Beta Phi Mu, 1966. **Pubns.:** Jt. Auth., "Music Price Indexes: 1980 Update," *Notes* (Mr. 1981); Jt. Auth., "Music Price Indexes: 1979 Update," *Notes* (Mr. 1980); Jt. Auth., "Price Indexes, Foreign and Domestic Music," *Notes* (Mr. 1979); "Music Publishers' Catalogues," *Notes* (1977–); "Forthcoming Meetings," *Amer. Musicological Socty. Nsltr.* (1978–); various articles, reviews. **Activities:** 1, 2; 15, 17, 39; 55, 57 **Addr.:** Box 838, Madison Sq. Station, New York, NY 10159.

Hill, Graham Roderick (Ap. 4, 1946, Richmond, Surrey, England) Univ. Libn., McMaster Univ., 1979–, Assoc. Univ. Libn., Col. Dev., 1973–79. **Educ.:** Univ. of Newcastle upon Tyne, 1965–68, Hon. BA (Eng. Lang., Lit.) Lancaster Univ., 1968–69, MA (Lit. and Socty.), Univ. of West. ON, 1970–71, MLS. **Orgs.:** Assn. of Resrch. Lib. Can. Assn. of Resrch. Lib. Cncl. of ON Univ. Lib. **Honors:** Cncl. on Lib. Resrc., Acad. Lib. Mgt. Intern Prog., 1977. **Activities:** 1; 17 **Addr.:** Mills Memorial Library, McMaster University, 1280, Main St. W., Hamilton, ON L8S 4L6 Canada.

Hill, Janet Swan (S. 11, 1945, Tulsa, OK) Head, Cat. Dept., Northwestern Univ. Lib., 1977–; Head, Cat. Unit, Geo. and Map Div., Lib. of Congs., 1975–77, Map Cat., 1971–75, Spec. Rcrt., 1970–71. **Educ.:** Vassar Coll., 1964–67, BA magna cum laude (Geol.); Univ. of Denver, 1969–70, MA (Libnshp.). **Orgs.:** SLA. West. Assn. of Map Libs. ALA: RTSD/Cat. and Class. Sect., Com. on Cat.: Desc. and Access. (Secy. 1980–); Map and Geo. RT (Nom. Com., 1981). IL LA. **Honors:** Lib. of Congs., Meritorious Srv., 1975; Beta Phi Mu, 1970. **Pubns.:** "The Northwestern Africana Project: An Experiment in Decentralized Bibliographic and Authority Control," *Coll. & Resrch. Libs.* (1981); "Developments in Map Cataloging at the Library of Congress," *Spec. Libs.* (Ap. 1977); "Alternatives to the Card Catalog Committee, Northwestern University Library," *Alternative Cat. Nsltr.* (D. 1980). **Activities:** 1, 4; 17, 20, 46; 70 **Addr.:** Catalog Department, Northwestern University Library, Evanston, IL 60201.

Hill, John Davis (Jl. 19, 1920, Vinita, OK) Sci. Ref. Libn., Univ. of NE, 1977–; Geol., Geophys. Libn., Univ. of CA, Los Angeles, 1970–76; Tchr., Boulder Pub. Schs., 1961–68; Phys. Sci. Instr., Univ. of CO, 1960–61. **Educ.:** Univ. of OK, 1938–40, 1942–43, BS (Phys.); Univ. of NM, 1951–56, MS (Geol.); Univ. of Denver, 1969–70, MA (Libnshp.). **Orgs.:** SLA: Positive Action Com. (1978–82). NE LA: Spec. and Inst. Sect. (Ch., 1979–80). Geosci. Info. Socty. ALA. **Pubns.:** "Devonian Stratigraphy of the Ely Area," *Geology of East Central Nevada* (1960). **Activities:** 1, 12; 15, 31, 39; 64, 70, 91 **Addr.:** Reference Department, Library, University of Nebraska at Omaha, Omaha, NE 68182.

Hill, Linda L. (Ja. 7, 1936, Tulsa, OK) Tech. Info. Srvs. Mgr., Cities Service Co., 1979–; Head, Bus. Tech. Dept., Tulsa City - Cnty. Lib., 1972–79. **Educ.:** Baker Univ., 1954–58, BA (Bio.); Univ. of MI, 1969–71, MLS. **Orgs.:** SLA: Bus. Finance Div. (Secy. 1978–79); OK Chap. (Pres., 1974–75, Dir., 1977–80). ASIS. AMIGOS: Exec. Bd. (1981–84). Netwk. Adv. Com., OK: (1979–81). Adv. Cncl., OK Pubns. Clearhse.: (1978–79). **Honors** Beta Phi Mu, 1971. **Activities:** 9, 12; 17, 34, 39; 59, 86, 91 **Addr.:** Rt. 6, Box 496A, Tulsa, OK 74127.

Hill, Malcolm K. (F. 12, 1950, Cooperstown, NY) Dir., Pottsville Free Pub. Lib. & Pottsville Lib. Dist. Ctr., 1977–; Asst. Lib. Dir., Haverhill Pub. Lib., 1976–77, Ref. Libn., 1973–76. **Educ.:** Harvard Coll., 1967–71, AB (Eng.); Simmons Coll., 1972–73, MSLS. **Orgs.:** ALA. PA LA. MA LA: Exec. Brd., (1976–77). Pottsville PA Kiwanis Club: 2nd VP (1979–80). **Pubns.:** Reviews. **Addr.:** Pottsville Free Public Library, 3rd & Market St., Pottsville, PA 17901.

Hill, Marnesba D. (Mr. 30, 1913, La Crosse, WI) Prof. and Chief Libn., Herbert H. Lehman Coll., 1976–, Assoc. Libn., 1967–76, Educ. Libn., 1958–67; Libn., Spec. Col., Atlanta Univ., 1947–58. **Educ.:** Langston Univ., 1939–40, BS (Elem. Educ.); Atlanta Univ., 1946–47, BLS; Univ. of London Sch. of Libnshp., 1952–53 (Arch. Admin.); Columbia Univ. Tchrs. Coll., 1960–63, MA (Guid. and Persnl.). **Orgs.:** ALA: Natl. Lib. Week Com. (1967–70); ACRL. LA of the City Univ. of New York: VP (1967–69). Archons of Colophon: Ch., Mem. Com. (1977–78). Kappa Delta Pi: VP, Grt. New York Chap. (1972–74). **Pubns.:** *Puerto Rican Authors: a Biobibliographic Handbook* (1974). **Activities:** 1; 17, 41, 45; 57, 66 **Addr.:** Herbert H. Lehman College Library, Bedford Park Blvd. West, Bronx, NY 10468.

Hill, May Davis (Je. 29, 1922, Louisburg, NC) Cur. of Photo., (Assoc. Archvst.) Univ. of MI, Ann Arbor, 1974–; Visiting Lectr./Resrch Cur., Univ. of MI, Ann Arbor, 1972–74; Asst. Cur., Prints and Drawings, Philadelphia Musm. of Art, 1967–72; Acting Cur. of Prints, Princeton Univ., Art Musm., 1966–67; Art Libn., Cur. and Keeper of Prints and Drawings, Univ. of NC, 1958–66, Libn., Registrar, Cur. (Pr. and Drawings), NC Musm. of Art, Raleigh, 1955–58, Visiting Lectr., Peace Coll., Raleigh, NC, 1956–57, Gen. Coll. Libn., Univ. of NC, Chapel Hill, 1952–55. **Educ.:** Univ. of NC, Chapel Hill, 1941–43, BA (Art & Hist.), 1943–44, MA (Art Hist.), 1951–55, BS (Lib. Sci.); NY Univ. Inst. of Fine Arts, 1944–47, 1962–63, (Fine Arts). **Orgs.:** SAA: Com., Aur. & Graphic Records. MI Arch. Assn.: Prog. Ch., (1979–80). Women's Resrch. Club, Univ. of MI., Print Club of NC Brd, (1962). Collectors' Club of NC. Women of the Univ. Faclty, Univ. of MI. NC State Art Socty: Secy., (1955–58). Musm. Assn. of NC: VP (1965–66). **Honors:** Phi Beta Kappa, Beta Phi Mu, 1943–55. Belgian Amer. Educ. Fdn., Flwshp, 1962. **Pubns.:** *Arts of the Fin de Siècle: Elegant Objects and Images,* (Catalog) (1966). *Forain,* (Catalog) (1966). *Telltale Photographs: The Stoner Railroad Collection* (1981). *The William Hayes Ackland Memorial Art Center* Chapel Hill, (1962). *Mediaeval Art* (Catalog) (1961). Various Art and Photography Articles. **Activities:** 1, 2; 18, 20, 45; 55, 92 **Addr.:** 191 Baldwin Ln., Birmingham, MI 48009.

Hill, Robert L. (D. 4, 1943, Malone, NY) Actg. Dir., Savitt Med. Lib., Univ. of NV, 1980–; Ref. Libn., CA State Univ., Fullerton, 1978–80; Med. Libn., King Abdul Aziz Milit. Hosp., Tabuk, Saudi Arabia, 1975–77; Med. Ref. Libn., Los Angeles Cnty. Med. Assn. Lib., 1973–75. **Educ.:** Univ. of MD, 1965–68, BA (Psy.); Univ. of South. CA, 1972–74, MLS, MPA (Pub. Admin.). **Orgs.:** Med. LA. Med. Lib. Grp. of North. CA. North. NV Med. Lib. Grp. **Pubns.:** *Bibliography–Intellectual Freedom/California Library Association* (1972); "MEDLINE" 8 mm film (1973). **Activities:** 1, 12; 15, 17, 39; 75, 80, 92 **Addr.:** Savitt Medical Library, School Of Medicine / University of Nevada, Reno, NV 89557.

Hill, Sara Inger (D. 21, 1940, Wichita, KS) Dir., Med. Lib., OU-Tulsa Med. Coll. Lib., 1980–; Dir. of Med. Lib., St. Luke's Hosp. of Kansas City, 1971–80; Ref. Libn., KS Reg. Med. Prog., Univ. of KS Med. Lib., 1968–71; Asst. Law Libn., Univ. of KS Law Lib., 1964–68. **Educ.:** OK State Univ., 1959–62, BA (Hist.); Simmons Coll., 1963–64, MS (LS); Univ. of KS, 1964–68, (Law). **Orgs.:** SLA: Bio. Sci. Div. (Ch., 1981–82), Nom. Com. (Ch., 1975–76); Heart of America Chap., Bd. of Dir., (1976–77); Pres. (1970–71). Med. LA: Hosp. Lib. Stan. and Practices Com. (Ch., 1979–80); Nom. Com., (1979–80); Prog. and Conv. Com. (Ch., 1978–79). Kansas City Lib. Network: Ch. (1978). Kansas City Metro. Lib. Network: Plng. Com. (Ch., 1979–). Other orgs. and coms. Jr. Leag. of Kansas City: Prof. Grp. (Ch., 1972–73). Pi Beta Phi Jr. Alum. Club. Kansas City Ski Club: Bd. of Dir. (1975–78); various coms. MO Mansion Prsrvn., Inc.: Speakers Bureau (Ch., 1979–). **Honors:** Pi Alpha Theta, 1961; Gvr. Conf. on Libs. and Info. Srvs., 1978; WHCOLIS, MO Alt., 1979. **Pubns.:** *Basic Medical Librarianship* (1970). **Activities:** 5, 12; 56, 58, 80 **Addr.:** OU-Tulsa Medical College Library, 2808 S. Sheridan, Tulsa, OK 74129.

Hill, Susan M. (N. 7, 1939, Lebanon, PA) Libn., Lib. Dir., Natl. Assn. of Broadcasters, 1973–; Libn., Free Pub. Lib. of Woodbridge, 1969–73; Tchr., 1962–68. **Educ.:** PA State Univ., 1957–61, AB (Eng.); Columbia Univ., 1961–62, MA (Eng. Educ.); Rutgers Univ., 1968–69, MLS. **Orgs.:** SLA: Telecom. Div. (Ch., 1977–79), Bylaws Com. (Ch., 1980–81), Nom. Com. (Ch., 1980–81); Advert. and Mktg. Div. Mem. Com. (Ch., 1976–77); Washington, DC Chap., Place. Com. (Ch., 1980–81); Soc. Sci. Div. Ref. Update, 1976 Conf., Telecom. Sect., Co-ch. ALA. DC LA. Amer. Women in Radio and TV. **Honors:** Beta Phi Mu, 1969. **Pubns.:** "SLA Prepares for Leadership Role in the 80's: Report of 1980 SLA Annual Conference," *Bltn. of the Amer. Socty. for Info. Sci.* (Ag. 1980); Asst./Assoc. Ed., *NJ Libs.* (1969–71). **Activities:** 12; 17, 39; 51, 93 **Addr.:** Library, National Association of Broadcasters, 1771 N St., N.W., Washington, DC 20036.

Hill, Suzanne Kovacs (F. 18, 1942, San Fernando, CA) Dir., Lib. Srvs., Lrng. Resrcs. Div., Catonsville Cmnty. Coll., 1980–, Asst. Head, 1975–80, Coord., Readrs. Srvs., 1971–75, Ref. Libn., 1970–71. **Educ.:** Univ. of TX, 1959–63, BA (Eng.), 1963–69, MLS; Johns Hopkins Univ., 1975–80, MLA (Liberal Arts). **Orgs.:** ALA: ACRL. MD LA: Acad./Resrch. Lib. Div., Secy., Prog. Ch. (1975–78); 2nd VP., Prog. Ch. (1978–79); ByLaws Ch. (1977); Nom. Ch. (1980). AAUP. Mod. Lang. Assn. **Pubns.:** "Library Services to the Handicapped at CCC," *The Crab* (F. 1981). **Activities:** 1; 17, 31 **Addr.:** Catonsville Community College, 800 S. Rolling Rd., Baltimore, MD 21228.

Hill, William W. (Mr. 30, 1937, Huntington, NY) Owner, Cross Hill Books, 1976–; Spec. Coll. Libn., Colby Coll., 1969–76; Media Spec., Hauppague HS, 1968–69. **Educ.:** St. Michael's Coll., 1955–59, BA (Eng. Lit.); Long Island Univ., 1966–68, MS (LS); Long IS Univ., Hofstra Univ., 1968–69, (Educ.). **Orgs.:** ALA: ACRL/Rare Books and Mss. Sect. New Eng. LA. Friends of Lib., Patten Free Lib. Bibl. Socty. of America. Amer. Prtg. Hist. Assn. **Pubns.:** "Laurence Housman in Books: A Checklist," *Colby Lib. Qtly.* (Je. 1973). **Activities:** 1, 6; 18, 24, 45 **Addr.:** P.O. Box 798, 866 Washington St., Bath, ME 04530.

Hillard, James Milton (S. 27, 1920, Nortonville, KY) Dir. of Lib. Srv., The Citadel, 1957–; Assoc. Libn., US Military Acad., 1955–57; Dir. of Lib., Meriden (RT) Pub. Lib., 1953–57; City Libn., Fort Smith (AR) Pub. Lib., 1950–53; Asst. Libn., Summit (NJ) Pub. Lib., 1948–50. **Educ.:** OH Univ., 1940–43, 1946–47, BA (Hist.); Univ. of IL, 1947–48, MLS. **Orgs.:** ALA. SELA. SC LA: Secy. (1960–61), Treas. (1965–77). Optimist Club. Exchange Club. **Pubns.:** *Where to Find What* (1975); *Where to Find More* (1977); various articles. **Activities:** 1; 17, 39 **Addr.:** 203 Caroline Blvd., Isle of Palms, SC 29451.

Hillard, Jane E. (Je. 28, 1952, Toronto, ON) Libn., MacKimmie Matthews, Barr. and Sol., 1979–; Consult., ON Comsn. on Frdm. of Info. and Individual Privacy, 1977–78. **Educ.:** Univ. of Toronto, 1971–75, BA (Eng. Lit.), 1975–77, MLS. **Orgs.:** AALL: Lcl. Arrange. Com. (1977; 1979). Can. ALL. Foothills LA: Secy. (1979–80). **Pubns.:** *Freedom of Information and Individual Privacy: A Selective Bibliography* (1978); "A Brief Bibliography on Freedom of Information," *Can. Law Info. Cncls. Legal Mtrls. Letter* (My. 1978). **Activities:** 12; 15, 17, 20; 59, 77, 78 **Addr.:** 3111–34th Ave. S.W., Calgary, AB T3E 0Z1 Canada.

Hillman, Kathy Ann Robinson (Mrs. John R.) (Ag. 5, 1951, Sonora, TX) Acq. Libn., Baylor Univ., 1980–, Asst. Acq. Libn., 1976–80; Sch. Libn., Schleicher Cnty. Indp. Sch. Dist., 1974–76. **Educ.:** Baylor Univ., 1969–73, BA (Oral Comm.); N. TX State Univ., 1974–76, MLS. **Orgs.:** TX LA. AAUP. Zeta Phi Eta: Reg. Dir. (1976–). **Honors:** Beta Phi Mu. **Activities:** 1, 10; 15, 24, 46; 55, 90, 93 **Addr.:** 8505 Oakdale, Waco, TX 76710.

Hillman, Missy (O. 24, 1945, Pittsburgh, PA) Spec. Asst. to the Natl. Libn., Natl. Lib. of Can., 1978–; Libn., Transport Canada Trng. Inst., 1975–78; Ref. Libn., Env. Canada, 1974–75; Asst. Libn., Univ. of Ottawa Lib. Sch., 1971–74. **Educ.:** Univ. of Pittsburgh, 1963–67, BA (Fr.); McGill Univ., 1967–69, MLS. **Orgs.:** Can. LA: Cont. Educ. Coord. Grp. (1978–); Local Arrang. Com.,

PROFESSIONAL ACTIVITIES: Institutions: 1. Acad. lib.; 2. Arch.; 3. Assn.; 4. Fed./Gvt. lib.; 5. Inst. lib.; 6. Mfr./Suppl.; 7. Milit. lib.; 8. Musm.; 9. Pub. lib.; 10. Sch. lib.; 11. Sch. of lib. sci.; 12. Spec. lib.; 13. State lib.; 14. (other). **Functions/Activities:** 15. Acq./Col. dev.; 16. Adult srvs.; 17. Admin.; 18. Apprais.; 19. Archit./Bldgs.; 20. Cat./Class.; 21. Chld. srvs.; 22. Circ.; 23. Cons./Pres.; 24. Consult.; 25. Cont. ed.; 26. Educ. lib. sci.; 27. Ext. srvs.; 28. Fund/Grants; 29. Gvt. pubs.; 30. Indx./Abs.; 31. Instr. lib. use; 32. Media srvs.; 33. Micro.; 34. Netwks./Coop.; 35. Persnl.; 36. PR; 37. Publshg.; 38. Recs. mgt.; 39. Ref. srvs.; 40. Repro.; 41. Resrch.; 42. Review.; 43. Secur.; 44. Serials; 45. Spec. col.; 46. Tech. srvs.; 47. Trustees/Bds.; 48. YA srvs.; 49. (other).

1979 Conf. Can. Assn. of Spec. Libs. and Info. Srvs.: Ottawa Area Chap., Pubcty. and PR Ch. (1974–76). Cncl. of Fed. Libs.: Ch., Com. on Cont. Educ. (1977–79). Can. Assn. for Info. Sci.: Local Arrang. Com., Conf. (1977). **Activities:** 4; 17, 41 **Addr.:** National Library of Canada, 395 Wellington St., Ottawa, ON K1A 0N4 Canada.

Hillman, Stephanie (S. 19, 1935, Los Angeles, CA) Asst. Univ. Libn., CA State Univ., Fresno, 1968–, Head, Acq. Dept., 1966–68, Head, Pers. Dept., 1961–66, Sr. Ref. Libn., 1960–61, Jr. Ref. Libn., 1958–60. **Educ.:** Univ. of CA, Los Angeles, 1955–57, BA (Liberal Arts); Univ. of CA, Berkeley, 1957–58, MLS. **Orgs.:** ALA: Mem. Promo. Task Force (1978–). CA Gvrs. Conf. on Lib. and Info. Srvs.: Del. (1979). Area Wide Lib. Netwk.: Cncl. (1976–). Fresno Area Lib. Cncl.: Secy.-Treas. (1971–73); Ch. (1974–76). CA LA: Ctrl. Sierra Lib. and Media Assn., Pres. (1975); Exec. Bd. (1976); Nsltr. Ed. (1977, 1980); various coms. Natl. Endow. for the Hum. Japanese-Amer. Proj., San Joaquin Valley Lib. Syst., Adv. Com. (1979–80). **Activities:** 1; 17, 31, 36 **Addr.:** CA State University, Fresno, CA 93740.

Hillman, Thomas A. (My. 31, 1943, Kingston, ON) Archvst., Pub. Arch. of Can., 1974–, Libn., 1969–74. **Educ.:** Sir George Williams Univ., 1964–67, BA (Can. Hist.); McGill Univ., 1967–69, MLS. **Orgs.:** Assn. Can. Archvsts. East. ON Archvsts. Assn. **Pubns.:** *Catalogue of Census Returns on Microfilm, 1666–1881* (1981). **Activities:** 2, 4; 38, 39, 41 **Addr.:** 404 Edgewood Ave., Ottawa, ON K1Z 5K5 Canada.

Hillmann, Diane Ileana (D. 28, 1948, Paterson, NJ) Head, Tech. Srvs., Cornell Law Lib., 1979–, Asst. Catlgr., 1977–79; Serials Catlgr., Syracuse Univ., 1975–77. **Educ.:** Syracuse Univ., 1966–71, BS (TV/Radio), 1973–77, MLS. **Orgs.:** AALL: On-line Bibl. Srvs. Spec. Int. Sect., (Ch., 1979–80). Natl. Org. for Women: Tompkins Cnty. Chap. (Secy., 1979–). **Addr.:** Cornell Law Library, Myron Taylor Hall, Ithaca, NY 14853.

Hillmer, Margaret Patricia Hall (Mr. 17, 1936, Cirencester, Gloucestershire, Eng.) Dir., Tiffin-Seneca Pub. Lib., 1980–, Head, Ref. Dept., 1979–80; Admin. Asst., Heidelberg Coll., Water Qual. Lab., 1978–79. **Educ.:** London Acad. of Msc. and Dramatic Art, London, Eng., 1955, ALAM (Sp.); Heidelberg Coll., 1976, AB (Eng., Hist.); Univ. of MI, 1976–77, AMLS. **Orgs.:** ALA. OH LA: NW OH Reg. Plng. Com. NW Lib. Dist.: Area Resrcs. Subcom., Staff Dev. Subcom. Tiffin Leag. of Women Voters: Pres. (1981–83). OH Leag. of Women Voters: Intl. Rel. (Ch., 1973–75). **Honors:** Beta Phi Mu, 1978. **Activities:** 9; 15, 17 **Addr.:** Tiffin-Seneca Public Library, 77 Jefferson St., Tiffin, OH 44883.

Hills, Bethany P. (F. 20, 1949, Paoli, IN) Dir., Lib. Srvs., White Settlement Pub. Lib., 1977–; Ref. Libn., Fort Worth Pub. Lib., 1976–77; Med. Libn., St. Joseph Hosp., Wichita, 1975–76. **Educ.:** West. KY Univ., 1967–72, BA (LS), 1972–74, MLS. **Orgs.:** Med. LA. ALA. TX LA. **Activities:** 9, 12; 15, 17, 39; 80 **Addr.:** 100 Meadow Park Dr., Fort Worth, TX 76108.

Hills, Margarette Constance Kasper (Ag. 26, 1928, Chicago, IL) Dir., Christian Heritage Coll. Lib., 1979–; Cat. and Ref. Libn., Christian Heritage Coll. Lib., 1975–79; Lectr., San Diego State Univ., 1977; Chicago City Coll., 1969; Lib. Dir., MacCormac Jr. Coll., 1966–70; Writer, Ed., Rschr, World Book Encyclopedia, 1958–64; Tech. Writer, Automatic Electric Co., 1956–58; Rsch. Ed., American Peoples Encyclopedia, 1953–56. **Educ.:** Aurora Coll., 1944–47, BA (Eng.); Rosary Coll., 1965–66, MALS; Indiana Univ., 1968–1971 Phd. Cand. (Info. Sci.). **Orgs.:** SLA: Pres., San Diego Chap. (1979–80). San Diego Greater Met. Area Lib. Cncl.: Acq. Com. (1979–80). **Honors:** Beta Phi Mu. **Activities:** 1, 5; 20, 31, 39; 55, 90, 92 **Addr.:** 5610 Bolivar, San Diego, CA 92139.

Hills, Virginia Carter Head Libn., Natl. Geographic Socty., 1943–. **Educ.:** Radford Coll., 1938–42, BS (Eng.); Cath. Univ., 1948–51, BS (LS). **Orgs.:** SLA. ALA. ASIS. CLENE. Other orgs. Zonta Intl. Socty. of Woman Geographers. Assn. of Amer. Geographers. AAUW. **Activities:** 12; 17; 54, 70, 83 **Addr.:** National Geographic Society, Washington, DC 20036.

Hillsamer, Mark O. (Ja. 12, 1940, Manistee, MI) Head Libn., St. Albans Sch., 1966–. **Educ.:** Manchester Coll., 1958–62, BA (Pol. Sc. & Econ.); American Univ., 1965–70, MA (Intl. Affairs); Columbia Univ., 1975–76, MS in LS. **Orgs.:** ALA: AASL Prog. Com. (1979–). DC LA. Metro. Washington Indp. Sch. Lib. & Assoc. Indp. Sch. Media Srvs.: Strg. Com. (1976–). **Honors:** Columbia Univ., R. Krystyna Dietrich Awd., 1976. **Addr.:** St. Albans School, Mass. & Wisc. Aves., N.W., Washington, DC 20016.

Hilt, Gerri L. (D. 14, 1938, Aurora, IL) Dir., Resrch., Russell Reynolds Assn., 1980–; Head, Mktg. Lib., *Chicago Tribune,* 1978–80; Resrch. Libn., Arthur Meyerhoff Assn., 1967–78. **Educ.:** North. IL Univ., 1957–61, BA (Eng.), 1967, MLS. **Orgs.:** SLA: Various coms. **Activities:** 12; 17; 59 **Addr.:** Russell Reynolds Association, 200 S. Wacker, Suite 3600, Chicago, IL 60606.

Hilton, Robert Chadwick (Ag. 28, 1935, Boston, MA) Dir., Cary Meml. Lib., 1967–; Asst. Libn., Fitchburg Pub. Lib., 1962–67; Asst. Libn., Waltham Pub. Lib., 1960–62. **Educ.:** Boston Univ., 1956–58, AB (Classics); Simmons Coll., 1958–80, MS, DA (LS); Tufts Univ., 1969–73, AM (Classics). **Orgs.:** ALA: Local Hist. Com. (1976–). New Eng. LA. MA LA: State Aid Com. (1977–). Carlisle Hist. Cmsn.: Vice-Ch. (1978–). Lexington Rotary Club: Histn. (1978–). **Pubns.:** "Performance Evaluation of Library Personnel," *Spec. Libs.* (N. 1978); "Public Support for Library Service...," *Lib. Jnl.* (Je. 1978). **Activities:** 1, 9; 16, 17, 19; 50, 55, 92 **Addr.:** Box 93, Carlisle, MA 01741.

Hilton, Ruth B. (O. 9, 1926, Detroit, MI) Msc. Libn./Assoc. Cur., New York Univ., 1968–; Asst. Msc. Libn., Cornell Univ., 1958–68. **Educ.:** Cornell Univ., 1943–47, AB (Msc.); Syracuse Univ., 1964–67, MLS. **Orgs.:** Msc. LA: Treas. (1969–76); Finance Com. (1969–75; Ch. 1969–74). Intl. Assn. of Msc. Libs. Cncl. of Natl. Lib. Assns.: Msc. LA rep. (1970–77); Sec/Treas., Exec. Bd. (1975–77). RILM Abstracts: Consult., (1969–75). Amer. Musicological Socty. Sonneck Socty. Amer. Msc. Ctr. Amer. Inst. for Verdi Std.: Libn., Bd. Mem. (1976–). **Pubns.:** *An index to early music in selected anthologies* (1978). **Activities:** 1; 15, 20, 39, 46; 55 **Addr.:** Music Library, New York University, 70 Washington Sq. So., New York, NY 10012.

Hiltz, Starr Roxanne (S. 7, 1942, Little Rock, AR) Prof., Ch., Soclgy., Upsala Coll., 1969–; Resrch. Anal., Prudential Insr., 1967–69. **Educ.:** Vassar Coll., 1960–63, AB (Soclgy.); Columbia Univ., 1963–69 MA, PhD (Soclgy.). **Orgs.:** Assn. for Comp. Mach.: SIGSOC (Vice-ch., 1979–81). **Honors:** Natl. Sci. Fndn., Fac. Flwshp., 1976; Natl. Inst. of Mental Hlth., Resrch. Flwshp., 1974. **Pubns.:** Jt. Auth., *Computer-Mediated Communication Systems: Status and Evaluation* (1982); Jt. Auth., *The Network Nation; Human Communication Via Computer* (1978); *Creating Community Services for Widows* (1976); Jt. Auth., "The Electronic Journal: A Progress Report," *Jnl. Amer. Socty. Info. Sci.* (1981); "Operational Trials of the Electronic Information Exchange System: Feedback from the Members," *Telecom. Policy* (Je. 1979). **Activities:** 1; 17, 24, 41; 93 **Addr.:** 1531 Golf St., Scotch Plains, NJ 07076.

Hilyard, Stevens W. Lib. Dir., Pittsburg State Univ., 1976–; Coll. Libn., New Eng. Coll., 1966–76; Asst. Libn., Grand Valley State Coll., 1965–66. **Educ.:** Bowdoin Coll., 1962, AB (Eng.); Univ. of MI, 1964, AMLS; Boston Univ., 1975–, EdD (Educ. in progress media). **Orgs.:** ALA: ACRL, LAD. KS LA: Coll. and Univ. Lib. Sect. New Eng. LA: Exec. Bd., Cncl. (1971–73; 1975–76). NH LA: Treas. (1968–69); Exec. Bd. (1971–74, 1975–76); Spec. and Subj. Col. Com. (Ch., 1968–76). Other orgs. **Activities:** 1; 17 **Addr.:** University Library, Pittsburg State University, Pittsburg, KS 66762.

Himelfarb, Laurence A. (Ap. 3, 1952, New York, NY) Lib. Dir., Southeastern Univ. Lib., 1981–; Libn., Metro. WA Cncl. of Gvts., 1979–81, Asst. Libn., 1978–79; Liaison, Info. Ofcr., Cath. Univ., Sch. of Lib. Sci., 1976–77. **Educ.:** George Washington Univ., 1970–74, BA (Hist.); Cath. Univ., 1976–78, MS (LS). **Orgs.:** DC LA: Bd. of Dir. (1980–). Washington-Baltimore Interlib. Users Assn.: Bd. (1979–81). SLA: Geo. and Map Div., Pubns. Com. (Ch., 1980). Law Libns. Socty. of DC. **Honors:** Beta Phi Mu, 1978. **Pubns.:** Various reviews. **Activities:** 12; 15, 17, 39; 65, 70, 94 **Addr.:** 24 Philadelphia Ave., Takoma Park, MD 20912.

Himmelsbach, Carl J. (Ag. 20, 1925, Lackawanna, NY) Lib. Dir., Morrill Meml. Lib., 1973–; Libn., Ledgemont Lab., 1962–73; Libn., Spec. Metals, Inc., 1959–62. **Educ.:** Kenyon Coll., 1948–50, AB (Hist.); Univ. of RI, 1973–73, MLS. **Orgs.:** SLA: Transl. Com. ALA. **Pubns.:** *A Guide to Scientific & Technical Journals in Translation* (1969, 1972); *Three Super-Alloys: An Annotated Bibliography* (1960). **Activities:** 9, 12; 17, 24, 49-Transl.; 60, 81, 88 **Addr.:** 452 Taunton St., Wrentham, MA 02093.

Hinckley, Ann T. (My. 25, 1933, Ogden, UT) Head, Ref. Dept., Univ. of CA, Los Angeles, 1973–, Asst. Head, Ref. Dept., 1970–73, Ref. Libn., 1967–70, ILL, 1964–67. **Educ.:** Stanford Univ., 1951–55, BA (Eng. Lit.); Univ. of CA, Los Angeles, 1963–64, MLS. **Orgs.:** ALA. UCLA Assn. of Acad. Women: Pres. (1975–76). **Pubns.:** Jt. auth., *The Effective Reference Librarian* (1981); "The Reference Librarian," *C&RL News* (Mr. 1980); reviews. **Addr.:** Reference Department, University Research Library, University of California, Los Angeles, Los Angeles, CA 90024.

Hindman, Jane (Ferguson) (Je. 22, 1905, Philadelphia, PA) Chap. Coord., Cath. LA, 1973–, Asst. to Exec. Dir., 1963–73; Asst. Libn., Holy Family Coll., 1960–63; Libn., A Lincoln HS, 1950–60; Libn., Benj. Franklin HS, 1940–50; Libn., Theo Roosevelt HS, 1930–40. **Educ.:** Drexel Univ., 1923–24, Cert. (LS); Temple Univ., 1924–29, BS (Educ.). **Orgs.:** Cath. LA. CSLA. **Pubns.:** *An Ordinary Saint* (1977); *Elizabeth Anne Seton* (1976); *Mathew Carey; Pamphleteer for Freedom* (1960); Ed., *Cath. World* (1960–70); various articles. **Activities:** 10; 25, 36, 37; 90 **Addr.:** The Mermont (207), Bryn Mawr, PA 19010.

Hindmarsh, Douglas P. (Mr. 19, 1941, Provo, UT) Dir., Ref. Srvs., UT State Lib., 1979–, Asst. Head, Ref. Srvs., 1977–79; Actg. Coord., Pub. Srvs., Salt Lake Cnty. Lib. Syst., 1976–77, Info. Ctr. Dept. Head, 1974–76, Branch Libn., 1974; Catlgr., Brigham Young Univ., 1968–73. **Educ.:** Brigham Young Univ., 1959–65, BA (Eng.), 1965–68, MLS. **Orgs.:** ALA: RASD, Notable Bks. Cncl. (1978–82). SLA. Mt. Plains LA: Schol. Com. (1978); State Lib. Sect., Nom. Com. (1978, 1980); Reg. White Hse. Conf. Com. (1978); Prof. Dev. Grants Com. (Ch., 1979–82). UT LA: New Perspectives RT (Ch., 1978); various coms. Various orgs. Lions Club. UT Acad. of Sci., Arts and Letters. Adult Educ. Assn. of UT. **Honors:** Beta Phi Mu. **Pubns.:** *Utah State Governmental Agency Libraries and Information Centers* (1978); Ed. Adv. Bd., *The Indx to US Gvt. Pers.* Ed., *Horsefeathers* (1978–). **Activities:** 9, 13; 17, 20, 39 **Addr.:** UT State Library, Reference Services, 2150 S. 300 W., Suite 16, Salt Lake City, UT 84115.

Hinds, Vira C. (Ja. 3, –, Cuba) Assoc. Prof., Educ./Psy. Libn., City Coll., City Univ. of NY, 1970–; Supvsr., Curric. Readg. Room, Tchrs. Coll., Columbia Univ., 1969–70, Ref. Libn., Chief of AV Dept., 1968–69; Sch. Libn., PS 175 Manhattan, 1967–68. **Educ.:** City Coll. of NY, 1959–66, BA cum laude (Eng.); Columbia Univ., 1966–67, MLS, Tchrs. Coll., 1968–70, MA (Educ.), 1970–76, EdD (Educ.). **Orgs.:** Alum. Assn., Columbia Univ. Sch. of Lib. Srv.: Bd. of Dir. (1970–73); Pres. (1972–73). ALA: Ref. & Subscrpn. Books Review Com. (1977–79). NY Metro. Ref. & Resrch. Lib. Agency: Educ. & Psy. Libns. Discuss. Grp. Columbia Univ.: Alum. Senator (1975–77); Alum. Trustee Nom. Com. (1974–79). Lincoln Hall: Bd. of Mgrs. (1979–). **Pubns.:** *Open Education: A CUNY Union List* (1977). **Activities:** 1; 15, 31, 39; 50, 63 **Addr.:** 106-A East Hill Dr., Somers, NY 10589.

Hines, Erma Gaye (N. 12, –, Marion, OH) Libn., Montessori Child Enrichment Ctr., 1979–; Chld. Libn., New London Pub. Lib.; Libn., Lexington Pub. Lib.; Libn., Richland Cnty. Musm.; Libn., Church of the Cross. **Educ.:** Ohio State Univ.; Univ. of UT. **Orgs.:** OH Gvr. Cncl. for Lib. and Info. Srvs. CSLA: Exec. Bd., PR. Mansfield Art Ctr.: Docent. Richland Cnty. Musm.: Docent. **Activities:** 2, 9; 21; 55, 63 **Addr.:** Hartland Farms, Hartland Center RD #1, Collins, OH 44826.

Hinkemeyer, Joan (Redlands, CA) Ref. Libn., Energy/Env. Info. Ctr., Denver Pub. Lib., 1978–; Sch. Libn., Englewood Pub. Sch. (CO) 1968–77; Cat., Univ. CA Los Angeles, 1974–75; Ref. Libn., Littleton (CO) Pub. Lib. 1968–74. **Educ.:** Coll. of St. Benedict (MN), 1954–58, BA (Msc.); Univ. Denver, 1959–63, MA (Msc.), 1966–67, MA (LS). **Orgs.:** ALA. CA LA. CO LA: Asst. Ed., *CO Libs.* **Pubns.:** "Popular psychology books for young adults", *CA Libn.* (D. 1976). **Activities:** 9; 16, 39, 48; 55, 65, 82 **Addr.:** Denver Public Library, 1357 Broadway, Denver, CO 80203.

Hinkle, John E. (S. 23, 1934, Ponca City, OK) Cont. Educ. Coord., OK Dept. of Lib., 1977–, Consult., Outreach and Inst., 1972–77; Dir., Choctaw Nation Multi-Cnty. Lib., 1969–72; Sch. Libn., Boise City Sch. (OK), 1966–68. **Educ.:** Phillips Univ., 1953–57, BA (Msc. Educ.); Univ. of OK, 1968–69, MLS. **Orgs.:** CLENE: Cncl. (1979–80); Adv. Com. (1978–81). SWLA: Cont. Educ. S. W. Lib. Com. (1977–81). ALA: ASCLA, Cont. Educ. Com. (1979–81). OK LA: Cont. Educ. Com. (Adv., 1974–); Right to Read Com. (Adv., 1972–); Various other com. OK Adult Educ. Assn. Various other orgs and com. OK City Lit. Cncl. Adv. Com.: (1974–). **Pubns.:** "Library Service to Shut-ins through the use of Volunteers Pub." (SWLA, Slide/Tape) (1972). **Activities:** 13; 24, 25, 27; 50, 89, 95-Institutions. **Addr.:** Oklahoma Department of Libraries, 200 N.E. 18th St., Oklahoma City, OK 73105.

Hinkle, Regina A. (Jn. 7, 1951, Cullman, AL) Corp. Libn., South. Natl. Gas Co., 1976–, Circ. Libn., Bob Jones Univ., 1973–75. **Educ.:** Bob Jones Univ., 1969–73, BA (Hist.); Univ. of AL, 1975–76, MLS. **Orgs.:** SLA. ALA. Birmingham Assn. of Law Libns. Univ. of AL Alum. Assn. Jefferson Cnty. Young Republicans. **Activities:** 1, 12; 15, 20, 31; 59, 77, 86 **Addr.:** Southern Natural Gas Co., P. O. Box 2563, Birmingham, AL 35202.

Hinnov, Ann (S. 12, 1949, Geislingen, Germany) Libn., Allendale Mutual Insr. Co., 1973–. **Educ.:** Univ. of CT, 1967–71, BA (Eng.); Univ. of RI, 1972–73, MLS. **Orgs.:** SLA: RI Chap., Bltn. Ed. (1980), Pres. Elect and Prog. Ch. (1976–77), Pres. (1977–78). New England OLUG. RI LA. New England Lib. Bd. Panel Cnclr. (1975–78). Univ. RI Sch. LS Adv. Com. (1979–80). **Activities:** 12; 15, 17, 39; 59, 76 **Addr.:** Allendale Mutual Ins. Co., Allendale Pk., P.O. Box 7500, Johnston, RI 02919.

Hinton, Frances (Mr. 19, 1922, Atlanta, GA) Chief, Prcs. Div., Free Lib. of Philadelphia, 1975–, Head, Cat. Dept., 1962–75; Catlgr., 1955–62, Head, Cent. YA Dept., 1953–55; Catlgr., Kauai Pub. Lib., 1949–53, YA Libn., S. Bend Pub. Lib., 1948–49; Head, Loundes-Echols Reg. Lib., 1945–48; Ref. and YA Libn., NY Pub. Lib., 1943–45. **Educ.:** Agnes Scott Coll., 1938–42, BA (Eng.); Univ. of NC, 1942–43, BSLS. **Orgs.:** ALA: Cat. and Class. Sect., Pol. and Resrch. Com. (1969–74); Cat. Code Rev. Com. (1974–78); AACR (Jt. Steering Com.); Deputy Rep. (1974–78); ALA Rep. (1978–83); Ch. (1981–83) Dec. Class Ed. Pol. Com. (1966–78); Ch. (1969–75). PA LA. **Pubns.:** "Dewey 17: A review," *Lib. Resrcs. and Tech. Srvcs.* (1966). "Progress on Code Revision" (1975), (1976), (1977). "Dewey Decimal Classification," *Libra* (1975–76); "Anglo-American Cataloging Rules Revision," *Cath. Lib. World* (My./Je. 1977).

Special Subjects/Services: 50. Adult educ.; 51. Advert./Mktg.; 52. Aerosp.; 53. Agric.; 54. Area std.; 55. Arts/Hum.; 56. Autom.; 57. Bibl./Prtg.; 58. Bio. sci.; 59. Bus./Fin.; 60. Chem.; 61. Copyrt.; 62. Documtn.; 63. Educ.; 64. Engin.; 65. Env.; 66. Eth. grps.; 67. Film; 68. Food/Nutr.; 69. Geneal.; 70. Geo.; 71. Geol.; 72. Handcpd.; 73. Hist.; 74. Int. frdm.; 75. Info. sci.; 76. Insr.; 77. Law; 78. Legis.; 79. Math./Comp. sci.; 80. Med.; 81. Metals; 82. Nat. resrcs.; 83. Newsp.; 84. Nuc. sci.; 85. Oral hist.; 86. Petr./Energy; 87. Pharm.; 88. Phys./Astr./Math.; 89. Readg.; 90. Relig.; 91. Sci./Tech.; 92. Soc. sci.; 93. Telecom.; 94. Transp.; 95. (other).

Activities: 9; 15, 20, 23 **Addr.:** 105 W. Walnut Ln., Philadelphia, PA 19144.

Hinz, James A. (F. 21, 1938, Fairmont, MN) Prop., F. Thomas Heller Rare Books, 1981–; Hum. Libn., Swarthmore Coll., 1972–80; Catlgr., Wm. P. Wreden, Bookseller, 1972; Resrch. Asst., Fndn. for Reformation Resrch., 1965–67. **Educ.:** Northwestern Coll., 1956–58; Concordia Sr. Coll., 1958–60, BA (Classics); Concordia Semy., 1961–66, MDiv (Church Hist.); Stanford Univ., 1967–71, AM (Hist.). **Orgs.:** The Philobiblon Club. Bibl. Socty. of Amer. Amer. Prtg. Hist. Assn. Amer. Socty. for Reformation Resrch. Renaisance Socty. of Amer. Hist. of Sci. Socty. **Pubns.:** *Handlist of Printed Books in the Simmlersche Sammlung* (1976); Ed., *Will Petersen: Stone Prints 1963-1976* (1976); Ed., *Sidney Chafetz: Literary Portraits* (1979); "Reformation and the Beginnings of Biblical Philology," *Bltn. of the Lib., Fndn. for Reformation Resrch.* (1970); "Toward the Control of Bibliography for the Study of the 16th Century," *Bltn. of the Lib., Fndn. for Reformation Resrch.* (1971). **Activities:** 1; 15, 31, 49-Exhibits; 55, 57, 90 **Addr.:** 308 E. 79th St., New York, NY 10021.

Hirsch, Felix Edward (F. 7, 1902, Berlin, Prussia, Germany) Prof. Emeritus, Trenton State Coll., 1972–, Libn. and Prof. of Hist., 1955–72; Libn. and Prof. of Hist., Bard Coll., 1936–55; Adjunct Prof. of LS, Drexel Univ., 1963–68; Ed., Natl. Zeitung and Berliner Tageblatt, Berlin, Germany, 1924–33. **Educ.:** Univ. of Berlin and Heidelberg, Germany, 1920–24, PhD (Hist.); Columbia Univ., 1935–40, BS (LS). **Orgs.:** ALA: Cncl. (1953–57); ACRL, Ch., Com. on Stan. (1957–63). NJ LA: Exec. Bd. (1958–61); 2nd VP (1962–63); Pres., Coll. and Univ. Sect. (1959–60). Amer. Cncl. on Germany: Bd. of Dir. (1952–56). **Honors:** Bard Coll., Bard Medal, 1961; Pres., Fed. Repub. of Germany, Commanders Cross, Order of Merit, 1973. **Pubns.:** *Stresemann; ein Lebensbild* (1978); "The Scholar as Librarian," *Lib. Qtly.* (1939); "College Libraries, today and tomorrow," *AAUP Bltn.* (S. 1966); "Standards for Libraries," Issue editor, *Lib. Trends* (O. 1972); "Library Standards," *Encyc. of Lib. and Info. Sci.* (1975); other articles. **Activities:** 1, 11; 17, 39, 42; 54, 73, 83 **Addr.:** 14 Pershing Ave., Trenton, NJ 08618.

Hirshon, Arnold (D. 8, 1950, New York, NY) Asst. Head, Cat. Dept., Duke Univ., 1978–; Head, OCLC Sect., Cat. Dept., Wayne State Univ., 1976–78, Asst. Head, 1974–76. **Educ.:** SUNY, Plattsburgh, 1968–72, BA (Eng.); IN Univ., 1973–74, MLS; Wayne State Univ., 1976–78, MPA (Pub. Admin.). **Orgs.:** ALA: RTSD Bd. of Dir. (1979–82); Ch., Cat. Maintenance Discuss. Grp. (1979); Rep., Bd. of Dir., LITA (1979); Ch., Role of the Prof. in Tech. Srvs. Discuss. Grp. (1977–78); Ch., Pre-Order and Pre-Cat. Bibl. Search Discuss. Grp. (1977–78); Ch., Bylaws Com. (1977–79). NC LA. AAUP. **Pubns.:** Ed., *RTSD Newsletter* (1979–82); "The Scope, Accessibility, and History of Presidential Papers," *Gvt. Pubn. Review* (1974); "Recent Developments in the Accessibility of Presidential Papers and Other Presidential Historical Materials," *Gvt. Pubn. Review* (1979); "What's in a Name?" *MI Libn.* (1977). **Activities:** 1; 15, 17, 20, 46; 55, 56, 77 **Addr.:** Box 9184 - Duke Station, Durham, NC 27706.

Hirst, Donna L. (Ag. 31, 1948, Charlestown, SC) Tech. Srvs. Libn., Univ. of IA Law Lib., 1977–, Acq. Libn., 1976–77. **Educ.:** Oklahoma City Univ., 1966–70, BA (Soclgy.); OK Univ., 1970–71, MPH (Human Ecol.); Univ. of IA, 1974–76, MA (LS). **Orgs.:** AALL: Schol. Com. (1979–); Rel. With Pubshrs. and Dlrs. (1977–79); Tech. Srvs. Spec. Interest Sect. (1979–); On-Line Bibl. Srvs. Spec. Interest Sect. (1979–). Mid-Amer. Assn. of Law Libs.: Com. on Resrc. Sharing (1980–). Amer. Cvl. Liberties Un. Natl. Org. of Women. **Honors:** Beta Phi Mu, 1976. **Pubns.:** *Report on Automated Cataloging for the Law Library* (1979); "Computerized Cataloging in Law Libraries: OCLC and RLIN Compared," *Law Lib. Jnl.* (Win. 1980). **Activities:** 1, 12; 15, 44, 46; 56, 57, 77 **Addr.:** Law Library, University of IA, Iowa City, IA 52242.

Hisle, Wendell Lee (Mr. 26, 1950, Danville, KY) Lib. Dir., Lexington Tech. Inst., 1976–; Libn., Media Spec., Henderson Cmnty. Coll., 1973–76. **Educ.:** Ripon Coll., 1967–69; Berea Coll., 1969–71, BA (Eng./Drama); Univ. of KY, 1972–73, MS (LS). **Orgs.:** KY LA: Acad. Lib., Ch. Elect (1980), Prog. Plng. (1978–80), Treas. (1976); Prog. Dev. Com. (1979–80); Cmnty. and Jr. Coll. RT, Ch. (1979–80, 1975–76) Various other com. KY Assn. Comm. Tech.: VP, Pres. Elect (1980). AECT. ALA. SELA. Sigma Alpha Epsilon Fraternity. **Honors:** Phi Kappa Phi, 1971. **Activities:** 1; 17, 25, 32; 59, 80, 91 **Addr.:** Lexington Technical Institute, Library, Cooper Drive, Lexington, KY 40506.

Hiss, Sheila Mary (My. 7, 1949, Evanston, IL) Asst. Libn., N. FL Jr. Coll., 1977–; Libn., Art and Msc. Dept., Jacksonville Pub. Lib., 1974–76. **Educ.:** Mundelein Coll., 1967–71, BA (Hist.); Loyola Univ., Rome, Italy, 1969–70; IN Univ., 1972–73, MLS. **Orgs.:** ALA. FL LA. Handweavers Gld. of Amer. **Honors:** Beta Phi Mu. **Pubns.:** "The Mansion" film (1979). **Activities:** 1; 20, 32, 39; 63, 93 **Addr.:** 731 Suwannee Ave., Live Oak, FL 32060.

Hitchcock, Jennette E(liza) (Je. 1, 1910, Woodbury, CT) Chief Libn. Emerita, Cat. Div., Stanford Univ. Libs., 1973–, Chief Libn., Cat. Div., 1958–73; Head, Subj. Cat. Div., Yale Univ. Lib. 1952–58, Catlgr., 1931–52. **Educ.:** Smith Coll., 1927–31, BA (Premed.); Univ. of Chicago, 1938, MA (LS). **Orgs.:** ALA: Cncl. (1966–70); Cat. and Class. Sect. (Ch., 1964–65), Awd. of the Margaret Mann Cit. Com. (Ch., 1962–63), Nom. Com. (1961–62), Cat. Policy and Resrch. Com. (Ch., 1960–61); Div. of Cat. and Class., Nom. Com. (1952–53). CA LA: Coll., Univ. and Resrch. Libs. Sect. (Secy., 1961). North. CA Tech. Prcs. Grp. NY Reg. Cat. Grp. **Pubns.:** Jt. Auth., "Yale Meets Its Catalog," *Coll. & Resrch. Libs.* (Jl. 1951); "Selection and Standards of Subject Headings for Use in University Libraries," *Jnl. of Cat. and Class.* (D. 1952); "The Yale Library Classification," *Yale Univ. Lib. Gazette* (Ja. 1953); "Objective Subjectivity: Four-Year Report on Starred Subject Cards," *C&RL* (Ja. 1959); "Works Entered Under Title," *Working Papers: Inst. Cat. Code Rev., McGill Univ.* (1960); various bk. reviews. **Activities:** 1; 20; 91 **Addr.:** 200 Leeder Hill Dr., Apt. 311, Hamden, CT 06517.

Hitt, Gail D. (D. 27, 1935, NY) Dir., Inst. Resrch., Fordham Univ., 1980–, Asst. Dean for Cont. Educ., 1978–80; Head Libn., Minneapolis Coll. of Art & Design, 1977–78; PHILSOM Coord., Washington Univ. Sch. of Med. Lib. 1976–77; Asst. Chief Libn., AIAA Tech. Info. Srv., 1968–71; Acq. Libn., SUNY Maritime Coll., 1965–68. **Educ.:** Univ. of Rochester, 1953–57, BA (Eng.); Rutgers Univ., 1963–65, MLS. **Orgs.:** ALA: ACRL. SLA. ARLIS/NA. **Honors:** Phi Beta Kappa, 1956. **Pubns.:** "Information as a Communicable Disease" (1980); "Information Resources for Adult Students" (1978); Jt. ed., *Censorship News* (1979–); "PHILSOM II" videotape (1977). **Activities:** 1, 12; 15, 16, 17; 50, 74, 75 **Addr.:** 178 Beach St., City Island, NY 10464.

Hitt, Samuel (N. 13, 1921, Prescott, AR) Dir., Hlth. Sci. Lib., Univ. of NC, 1976–; Exec. Dir., Houston Acad. of Med., TX Med. Ctr. Lib., 1972–76; Dir. of Libs., Univ. of CT Hlth. Ctr., 1965–71; Assoc. Dir. for Tech. Srvs., Univ. of MO, 1958–65, various positions, 1951–58. **Educ.:** Univ. of MO, 1946–47, BA (Eng.); Emory Univ., 1950–51, MA (LS). **Orgs.:** Med. LA: Pres. (1974–75); Pubn. Panel (Ch., 1978–81). Assn. of Acad. Hlth. Sci. Lib. Dirs.: Pres. (1979–80). Reg. Med. Lib., Region IV: Reg. Adv. Com. (Ch., 1979–80). ALA. Other orgs. Assn. of Amer. Med. Coll. **Activities:** 1, 11; 17, 26; 80 **Addr.:** Damascus Church Rd., Route 3 Box 254, Chapel Hill, NC 27514.

Hixon, Don L. (Ag. 9, 1942, Columbus, OH) Fine Arts Libn., Univ. of CA, Irvine, 1974–; Ref. Libn., 1968–74. **Educ.:** CA State Univ., Long Beach, 1960–65, BA (Msc.), 1967–68, MA (Msc.); Univ. of CA, Los Angeles, 1966–67, MS LS. **Orgs.:** Msc. LA: So. CA Chap., Ch., (1977–78). Intl. Assn. of Msc. Libs. Intl. Msclgy. Socty. Amer. Msclgy. Socty. **Pubns.:** *Nineteenth-Century American Drama,* (1977). *Women in Music:* (1975). *Music in Early America* (1970). Reviews. **Activities:** 1; 15, 20, 39; 55, 57, 67 **Addr.:** 9392 Mayrene Dr., Garden Grove, CA 92641.

Hlava, Marjorie M. K. (Je. 9, 1946, Manistee, MI) Pres., Access Innovations, Inc., 1979–; Mgr. for Info., Tech. Application Ctr., Univ. of NM, 1975–79, Info. Dir., Natl. Energy Info. Ctr. Afflt. 1978; Asst. Libn., Bio. Lib., Univ. of WI, 1965–67. **Educ.:** Univ. of WI, 1964–70, BS (Bot.); Univ. of NM, 1975–79, (MPA & IS); Sec. Educ. Cert. WI. **Orgs.:** SLA: Long-Range Plng. Com., Ch. (1980–81); Spec. Tech. Com. (1980); Career Com. (1978); Proj. Com. (1977); VP, Pres.-Elect, Chap. (1979–80), Pres. (1980–81). ASIS: SIG Energy Env. Info., Secy./Treas. SWLA: OLUG (Ch., 1977–80). Natl. Online Circuit: Strg. Com. (1978–79); Ch. (1979–80). Various other orgs. West. Info. Netwk. Energy: Educ. Ch. (1979, 1980); Anl. Mtg. Ch. (1979, 1980). **Pubns.:** Ed., "Search Corner," *Online Review* (D. 1979); jt. auth., "Coal Information: How to Find It," Procs. ASIS Mtg. (1979); "Online Systems", *Info. Mgr.* (N. D. 1979); "National Online Circuit," *Info. Mgr.* (S. O. 1979); jt. auth., "Effective Search Strategies," *Online Review* (Je. 1979); many other pubns. **Activities:** 6; 24, 30, 38, 49-Online Searching as Literature Reviews; 56, 62, 75 **Addr.:** Access Innovations, Inc., P.O. Box 40130, Albuquerque, NM 87196.

Hlavaty, Anna Marie (O. 12, 1949, Bay City, TX) Lrng. Resrcs. Spec., J.B. Passmore Elem. Northside Indp. Sch. Dist., 1974–, Libn., 1974–76; Libn., Holmes HS, Sum. 1975; Libn., E. T. Wrenn Jr. HS, 1972–74. **Educ.:** Our Lady of the Lake Coll., 1968–72, BA (Hist., Grmn.); Univ. of TX, San Antonio, 1974–77, MA (Educ.); 1970–72, Provisional All-Level Libn. Cert.; 1977, Prof. All-Level Lrng. Resrcs. Spec.; various crs. **Orgs.:** ALA: ALSC, Filmstp. Eval. Com. (1976–80); JMRT, Mem. Mtg. Com. (1979). Cath. LA: Chld. Sect. Bd. (1979–81). AECT. TX LA: Rcrt. Com. (1977); Cont. Ed. Com. (1979–81). Various other orgs. TX Assn. For Supvsn. and Curric. Dev.: Mem. Com. (1979); Nsltr. Com. (1979). Our Lady of the Lake Alum. Assn.: Corres. Secy. (1978–79). Univ. of TX at San Antonio Alum. Assn.: Treas. (1979). Camp Fire: Leader (1979–80). **Honors:** Dept. of Educ., Fulbright Cult. Grant, Exch. Libn. in Can., 1979. **Activities:** 10, 14-Church; 21, 22, 32; 63, 67, 90 **Addr.:** Northview Tower, #212, 7039 San Pedro, San Antonio, TX 78216.

Ho, Carol T. (D. 13, 1928, Peking, China) Med. Libn., St. Clair Mem. Hosp., 1973–, Ref. Libn., West. PA Reg. Med. Prog. Lib. Syst., 1970–73. **Educ.:** Scripps Coll., 1948–52, BA (Bio.); Univ. of Pittsburgh, 1962–68, MLS. Med. LA, 1976 and 1983, Cert. **Orgs.:** Med. LA.: Pittsburgh Reg. Grp., Nom. Com. (1973–74), Treas. (1975–76, 1976–77). **Honors:** Beta Phi Mu, 1969. **Activities:** 5, 14-Hospital library; 15, 17, 39; 80, 91 **Addr.:** Health Sciences Library, St. Clair Memorial Hospital, 1000 Bower Hill Rd., Pittsburgh, PA 15243.

Ho, Don T. (S. 4, 1922, Shanghai, China) Libn., Piscataway & S. Plainfield Tech. Libs., Bell Labs., 1979–, Libn., Piscataway & Centennial Park Tech. Libs., 1976–79, Libn., Murray Hill Tech. Lib., 1969–76, Libn., Holmdel Tech. Lib., 1963–69; Head Libn., 3M Co., 1959–63; Ref. Libn., Asst. Libn., W. R. Grace & Co., 1955–59; Tech. Libn., Jefferson Chem. Co., 1952–55, Abs., 1951–52. **Educ.:** Natl. Tsing Hua Univ., Peking, China, 1945–49, BSc (Chem.); Drexel Inst. of Tech., 1950–51, MS (LS). **Orgs.:** SLA: Secy.-Treas., Chem. Sect. (1962–63); Rep. to ALA's Lib. Tech. Prog. (1966–72); Rep. to ANSI Sect. Com. Z85 on Lib. Equipment and Supplies (1966–); MN Chap., Dir. (1961–62), Chap. Consul. (1961–63); NJ Chap., Dir. (1966, 1978); Pres. (1967–68); Ch., Nom. Com. (1969–70). Amer. Chem. Socty. Assn. for Comp. Mach. **Activities:** 12; 17, 24, 49-Design & Plng.; 56, 91, 93 **Addr.:** Bell Laboratories, 6 Corporate Pl., Piscataway, NJ 08854.

Ho, James (Ag. 2, 1935) Asst. Dir., Howard Univ. Libs., 1968–; Engin. & Archit. Libn., Univ. of KS, 1966–68. **Educ.:** Natl. Taiwan Univ., 1953–57, BA (Econ.); Natl. Chengchi Univ., 1957–60, MA (Jnlsm.); South. IL Univ., 1960–62, MS (Mass Comm); Univ. of OK, 1964–66, MLS; Howard Univ., 1969–70, MA (Econ.). **Orgs.:** ALA. SLA. **Pubns.:** *Black Engineers in the United States* (1974); *Guide to Mechanical Engineering Literature* (1972). **Activities:** 1; 15, 39, 44; 59, 64, 91 **Addr.:** Howard University Libraries, 500 Howard Place, N.W., Washington, DC 20059.

Ho, Kwai Yiu (Ag. 2, 1942, Hong Kong, UK) Ed., Micromedia Limited, 1975–, Admn., Resrch. Dir., Brandon Univ., 1971–74. **Educ.:** South China Univ., 1961–65, BA (Hon.) (Soclgy.); Univ. of AB, 1969–71, MA (Soclgy.); Univ. of West. ON, 1974–75, MLS; Control Data Inst., 1976, (Comp. Prog.). **Orgs.:** Can. LA. Condominium Assn. for York Reg.: VP (1979–80). York Condominium Corp. 272: VP (1976–80). **Pubns.:** Ed., *Canadian Business Index* (1975–); Ed., *Canadian News Index* (1977–); "The Willingness to Intervene: Differing Community Characteristics," *Social Problems* (1974); "Free-lance Indexing and Index Publishing as Career Altenatives for Librarians," *What Else You Can Do With a Library Degree* (1980). **Activities:** 6; 37; 56, 59, 83 **Addr.:** 52 Glen Cameron Rd., Thornhill, ON L3T 1P6 Canada.

Hoadley, Irene Braden (S. 26, 1938, Hondo, TX) Dir. of Libs., TX A&M Univ., 1974–; Asst. Dir. of Libs., OH State Univ., 1973–74, Libn. for Gen. Admin. and Resrch., 1966–73; Grad. Asst. Dept. of LS, Univ. of MI, 1964–66; Head, Circ. Dept., KS State Univ. Lib., 1962–64; Catlgr. Univ. Lib., Sam Houston State Tchrs. Coll., 1961–62. **Educ.:** Univ. of TX, 1956–60, BA (Eng.); Univ. of MI, 1960–61, AMLS; KS State Univ., 1962–65, MA (Hist.); Univ. of MI, 1964–67, PhD (LS). **Orgs.:** ALA: Cncl. (1975–78); Com. on Accred. (1975–77); ACRL; JMRT; various coms. TX LA: Exec. Bd. (1978–81); Coll. and Univ. Libs. Div., Ch. (1977–78), VP (1976–77); various coms., ofcs. Ctr. for Resrch. Libs.: Nom. Com. (1975–76). ARL: Bd. of Dirs. 1978–81). Various other orgs. SWLA. Adv. Com. for a Natl. Distribution Syst. for Newly Processed Mtrls. and ILLs (Cleveland). Protean Ed. Bd. OH State Univ.: Various coms. **Honors:** Scarecrow Press Awd. for Lib. Lit., 1971; Univ. of MI, Disting. Alum., 1976. **Pubns.:** Jt. auth., "To Be or Not To Be: An Academic Library Research Committee," *Jnl. of Acad. Libnshp.* (Mr. 1976); jt. auth., *An Automated On-Line Circulation System: Evaluation, Development, Use* (1973); jt. ed., *Quantitative Methods in Librarianship: Standards, Research, Management* (1972); *The Undergraduate Library* (1970); "The Year of Upheaval," *OH LA Bltn.* (Ap. 1973); various other articles, sps. **Activities:** 1; 17, 46 **Addr.:** Rte. 5, Box 1048, College, TX 77840.

Hoagland, Sister Mary Arthur (My. 12, 1915, New York, NY) Dir. Lib. Media Srvcs, Archdiocese of Philadelphia, 1965–; Prof., Villanova Univ., 1964–81; Tchr.-Libn., Bishop McDevitt HS, 1959–65; St. Alice Elem. Sch., 1951–59; Tchr., Diocese of Philadelphia, 1939–51. **Educ.:** Immaculata Coll. (part-time), 1939–53, AB (Eng.); Marywood Coll., 1958–63, MSLS; Villanova, Temple, Fordham and Columbia Univ. (Eng., Educ., Admin., Lib. Sci.). **Orgs.:** Cath. LA: Pres. (1977–1978). PA LA: Board Mem. (1979–1980). ALA: AASL. Lib. Dev. Com. (1965–71). PA Sch. Lib. Assn. Natl. Cncl. Tchrs. Eng. **Honors:** Cath. LA, Cert. of Merit, 1977. **Pubns.:** "Diocesan Media Center Library Supervisor," *Cath. Lib. World* (1975). "School Library Volunteers" (1976). "Test. at General Subcommittee on Education, 1969–" (1973). **Activities:** 10, 11; 24, 35, 42; 63, 89, 90 **Addr.:** Archdiocese of Philadelphia, Superintendent of Schools Office, 222 N. 17th St., Philadelphia, PA 19103.

Hoar, Lore M. C. (Jl. 5, 1949, Trochu, AB) Pres., Consolidated Info. Consults., 1977–; Catlgr., Univ. of Calgary, 1976–77, Hum. Ref. Libn., 1974–75, Med. AV Libn., 1972–74. **Educ.:** Univ. of Calgary, 1967–70, BA (Eng.); Univ. of AB, 1971–72, BLS. **Orgs.:** Can. LA. Can. Assn. of Spec. Libs. and Info. Srvs. **Activities:** 14-pvt. consult.; 15, 17 **Addr.:** Consolidated Information Consultants Ltd., 2404 Langriville Dr. S.W., Calgary, AB T3E 5G8 Canada.

PROFESSIONAL ACTIVITIES: Institutions: 1. Acad. lib.; 2. Arch.; 3. Assn.; 4. Fed./Gvt. lib.; 5. Inst. lib.; 6. Mfr./Suppl.; 7. Milit. lib.; 8. Musm.; 9. Pub. lib.; 10. Sch. lib.; 11. Sch. of lib. sci.; 12. Spec. lib.; 13. State lib.; 14. (other). **Functions/Activities:** 15. Acq./Col. dev.; 16. Adult srvs.; 17. Admin.; 18. Apprais.; 19. Archit./Bldgs.; 20. Cat./Class.; 21. Chld. srvs.; 22. Circ.; 23. Cons./Pres.; 24. Consult.; 25. Cont. ed.; 26. Educ. lib. sci.; 27. Ext. srvs.; 28. Fund/Grants; 29. Gvt. pubs.; 30. Indx./Abs.; 31. Instr. lib. use; 32. Media srvs.; 33. Micro.; 34. Netwks./Coop.; 35. Persnl.; 36. PR; 37. Publshg.; 38. Recs. mgt.; 39. Ref. srvs.; 40. Repro.; 41. Resrch.; 42. Review.; 43. Secur.; 44. Serials; 45. Spec. col.; 46. Tech. srvs.; 47. Trustees/Bds.; 48. YA srvs.; 49. (other).

Hoare, Colin G. D. (Jl. 4, 1940, Southampton, Eng.) Supvsr., Sci. Documtn., Hoffmann-La Roche (Canada), 1975–; Info. Ofcr., Ayerst Lab., 1964–75. **Educ.:** Exeter Univ., 1959–62, BSc (Chem.); Concordia Univ. (Montreal), 1976–80, DLS. **Orgs.:** SLA: East. Can Chap., Copyrt. Ch. (1977–80). ASIS. Drug Inf. Assn. **Activities:** 12; 30, 39, 41; 58, 80, 87 **Addr.:** Medical Department, Hoffmann-La Roche Ltd., 1000 Bvld Roche, Vaudreuil PQ J7V 6B3 Canada.

Hoare, Valerie E. (S. 1, 1929, Ottawa, ON) Branch Libn., Srvys. and Mapping Branch, Energy, Mines and Resrcs., Can., 1972–; Reg. Libn., Protestant Sch. Bd. of the Ottawa Valley, 1970–72. **Educ.:** Carleton Univ., 1964–68, BA (Span.); McGill Univ., 1968–70, MLS (Lib.); Carleton Univ., 1971–74, BA hons. (Geo.). **Orgs.:** Can. LA. SLA. Ottawa LA. Cncl. of Fed. Libs. Heritage Can. Ottawa Humane Socty. Can. Nature Fed. **Activities:** 4; 15, 17; 70, 91 **Addr.:** Library, Surveys and Mapping Branch, Energy, Mines and Resources Canada, 615 Booth St., Ottawa, ON K1A 0E9 Canada.

Hoban, Mary Frances A. (S. 24, 1946, New York, NY) Mgr. Prof. Dev., SLA, 1977–; Exec. Asst. to Dean of Lib., New York Univ., 1974–77, Resrch. Asstshp., 1971–74; Place. Dir., Molloy Coll., 1969–71. **Educ.:** Molloy Coll., 1963–67, BA (Hist.); Fordham Univ., 1967–69, MA (Hist.); New York Univ., 1971–76, PhD (Org. Bhv.). **Orgs.:** SLA. CLENE: Secy. Advert. Women of N.Y.: Netwk. Com.; Women in Success Com., Ch. (1979–80). Pi Lambda Theta: VP (1979–81). Cncl. on the Cont. Educ. Unit. **Pubns.:** "Salary Survey," *Spec. Lib.* (D. 1979); "An Activist Approach to Continuing Educ," *Spec. Lib.* (N. 1979); "New York University: A Users Survey," *Resrc. in Educ.* (S. 1977); ed., "Professional Development Series". **Activities:** 1, 3; 17, 25, 28; 50, 55, 63 **Addr.:** Special Libraries Association, 235 Park Ave. South, New York, NY 10003.

Hobbins, Alan John Townson (Jl. 23, 1944, Bolton, Eng.) Head, ILL, McLennan Lib., McGill Univ., 1976–, Instr. Srvs. Libn., 1970–76, Ref. Libn., 1968–70. **Educ.:** McGill Univ., 1963–66, BA (Hist.), 1966–68, MLS. **Orgs.:** Can. LA: ILL Com. (1979–). Can. Assn. of Coll. and Univ. Libs.: Instr. Srvs. Wkshp. Com. (1975). **Pubns.:** "Le Pret entre Bibliotheque," *Documtn. et Bib.* (Mr. 1979); "Interlibrary Loan in the Large Library," *OLA Bltn.* (D.–D. 1978); "Seminars and Assignments," *Acadenne Library Instruction* (1975); "The Library, The Professor and the Student," *Lrng. and Dev.* (N. 1974). **Activities:** 1; 17, 34, 39 **Addr.:** 3833 Oxford, Montréal, PQ H3A 1Y1 Canada.

Hobbs, Brian E. (Ag. 5, 1942, Calgary, AB) Head, Bibl. Verification Div., Univ. of AB Lib., 1974–. **Educ.:** Univ. of AB, 1960–63, BA (Eng.); McGill Univ., 1964–65, BLsc (LS). **Orgs.:** Can. LA. LA of AB. **Activities:** 1; 15, 46; 57 **Addr.:** University of Alberta, Library, Bibliographic Verification, Edmonton, AB T6G 2J8 Canada.

Hobbs, Kathleen (O. 19, 1918, Toronto, ON) Ref. Libn., Concordia Univ., 1976–. **Educ.:** McGill Univ., 1935–39, BSc (Chem.), 1974–76, MLS. **Orgs.:** SLA. Can. LA. Corp. of Prof. Libns. of PQ. Univ. Women's Club. Can. Club: Pres. (1963–64). **Activities:** 1; 15, 31, 39; 60, 64, 71 **Addr.:** 129 Thornton Ave., Montreal, PQ H3P 1H7 Canada.

Hobson, Kitty A. (My. 22, 1922, Vienna, Austria) Archvst., Hist. Libn., Oshkosh Pub. Musm., 1974–; Archvst., Hist. Libn., WI Conf. Untd. Meth. Church, 1972–; Libn., Trinity Luth. Church, Oshkosh, 1971. **Educ.:** Univ. of WI, 1967–70, BA (Hist.), 1970–71, MA (LSC); Arch. Wkshp., Sem. on Hist. Photographs, 1978. **Orgs.:** SAA: Relig. Arch. Afnty. Grp. (1979–80). Winnebago Cnty. Archeological and Hist. Socty.: Secy. (1978–79). **Pubns.:** Various lects., wkshps, slide presentations (1974–81). **Activities:** 2; 17, 41, 45; 55, 69, 90 **Addr.:** Oshkosh Public Museum, 1331 Algoma Blvd., Oshkosh, WI 54901.

Hoch, Minnie B. (S. 30, 1913, Pittsburgh, PA) Dir., Bard Lib., Cmnty. Coll. of Baltimore, 1975–, Asst. Dir., Tech. Srvs., 1961–75. **Educ.:** Univ. of Pittsburgh, 1930–34, BA (Hist.); Carnegie Lib. Sch., 1934–35, BS (LS); Columbia Univ., 1940–41, MS (LS). **Orgs.:** MD Acad. Lib. Ctr. for Autom. Prcs.: Bd. of Dir. (1974–79). Cncl. of Lib. Acad. Dirs. Oral Hist. Assn. MD LA: Coll. and Resrch. Div. (Secy., 1966–67); Schol. Com. (1966–68); Nom. Com. (1972–73). MD Assn. of Cmnty. and Jr. Colls. New Org. of Women. AAUP: CCB Chap. (Pres., 1975–76). MD Cmnty. Colls.: Cncl. of Resrc. Dirs. **Pubns.:** Jt. Auth., *Australia, the New Customer* (1945); various articles, reviews. **Activities:** 1; 15, 17, 20; 74, 86, 92 **Addr.:** Community College of Baltimore, 2901 Liberty Hts. Ave., Baltimore, MD 21215.

Hock, Paula C. (D. 2, 1950, Bloomsburg, PA) Branch Libn., Salt Lake City Pub. Lib., 1974–. **Educ.:** East. Nazarene Coll., 1968–72, BA (Psy.); Simmons Coll., 1973–74, MS (LS). **Orgs.:** Mt. Plains LA: JMRT, Vice-ch. (1980–81), Ch. (1981–82). ALA. Frdm. to Read Fndn. UT LA: Pub. Lib. Sect., Strg. Com. (1977–78); New Perspectives RT (Vice-ch., 1978–79, 1980–81); Jr. Mems. Grassroots Grants (Coord., 1979–80); Int. Frdm. Fund, Fund Raising Strg. Com. (1980–81). **Addr.:** Chapman Branch Library, 577 S. 900 W., Salt Lake City, UT 84104.

Hock, Randolph E. (D. 11, 1944, Chestertown, MD) DIALOG Rep., Lockheed Info. Syst., 1978–; Data Srvs. Libn., Univ. of PA, 1973–74; Asst. Sci. Libn., MA Inst. of Tech., 1971–73. **Educ.:** Salisbury State Coll., 1962–66, BS (Phys. Sci.); Univ. of MD, 1970–71, MLS; Temple Univ., 1974–78, MA, PhD (Relig.). **Orgs.:** ASIS. ALA. Socty. for the Sci. Std. of Relig. Amer. Acad. of Relig. **Honors:** Beta Phi Mu, 1971. **Pubns.:** "Providing Access to Externally Available Bibliographic Data Bases in an Academic Library," *Coll. and Resrch. Libs.* (My. 1975); "Publically-Available Online Databases in the Humanities," *Conf. on Databases in the Hum. and Soc. Sci., Procs.* (1979). **Activities:** 6; 25, 36; 62, 75, 90 **Addr.:** DIALOG Information Services, 200 Park Ave., Suite 332E, New York, NY 10017.

Hocker, Margaret Louise (S. Carrollton, KY) Prof. Emeritus, Univ. WI (La Crosse), 1978–, Assoc. Prof., 1961–78, ch. (LS) (1967–76), Asst. Prof., 1954–61, Ref. Libn., 1950–54, Ref. Libn.; Univ. Cincinnati, 1947–49; Libn., Central City (KY), 1943–47. **Educ.:** West. KY Univ., 1930–32, AB (Eng.); Univ. KY, 1944–46, BLS; Univ. MI, 1949–50, AMLS. **Orgs.:** ALA. WI LA. AAUW: Local Schol. Com. (Ch., 1961–68); Flwshp. Com. (1969–72). Delta Kappa Gamma: Treas. (1962–64). **Honors:** Beta Phi Mu. AAUW, Name Hon. Grant, 1975. **Pubns.:** "Punched Card Charging System for A Small College Library," *Coll. Resrch. Lib* (Mr. 1958). **Activities:** 1, 11; 26, 31, 39; 57, 63, 75 **Addr.:** 1225 Park Ave., La Crosse, WI 54601.

Hockersmith, Charles Edwin (N. 12, 1947, Shippensburg, PA) Lib. Admin., Cecil Cmnty. Coll., 1981–; Lib., Media Spec., Newark HS (DE), 1977–81; Lib., Media Spec., Christiana HS (Newark, DE) 1973–77. **Educ.:** Shippensburg St. Co., 1969–73, BS (Eng., LS); Univ. of Delaware, 1978–80, MA (Comm.). **Orgs.:** ALA: LITA, Video Cable Comm. NAB. **Pubns.:** Contrib., *Guidelines: Media Programs for Delaware Schools* (1977). **Activities:** 10; 32, 41, 48; 63, 75, 93 **Addr.:** Cecil Community College, 1000 North East Rd., North East, MD 21901.

Hodge, M. Patricia (Ja. 12, 1926, Pennsdel, PA) Libn., Exxon Corp., Med Dept., REHD Lib., 1966–; various positions in industry. **Educ.:** Rutgers Univ. 1958–65, BA (Hist.), 1965–66, MLS. **Orgs.:** SLA: NJ Chap., Pres. (1971–72) Med. LA. ASIS. Lions Club - Auxiliary: Som'l NJ., Pres. (1950). Raritan Valley Grange #153: Lect. (1979–). **Honors:** Beta Phi Mu, 1966. **Activities:** 12; 15, 30, 38; 65, 80, 95-Toxicology. **Addr.:** Exxon Corp.-Medicine: Environ. Health Dept., REHD Library, PO Box 235, E. Millstone, NJ 08873.

Hodge, Patricia A., R.S.M. (Pittsburgh, PA) Lib. Dir., Trinity Coll. (Burlington, VT), 1977–; Assoc. Dir., Dept. Educ., Holy Cross Hosp. (Ft Lauderdale), 1976–77; Head Libn., Carlow Coll., 1972–76, Actg. Ch., Dept. Eng., 1967–70; Instr., Dept. Eng., 1963–70. **Educ.:** Carlow Coll., 1957, BA (Eng.); Duquesne Univ., 1964, MA (Eng.); Villanova Univ., 1971, MSLS. **Orgs.:** ALA: ACRL. Women's Natl. Bk. Assn.: Exec. Bd. (Secy., 1979–); Natl. Treas. (1979–); Bd. Dir. (1977–). New Eng. LA. VT LA. Natl. Cncl. Tchrs. Eng. Chittenden Cnty. Hist. Assn. **Honors:** Delta Kappa Gamma. **Pubns.:** Reviews. **Activities:** 1; 17, 31; 63 **Addr.:** Trinity College, Colchester Ave., Burlington, VT 05401.

Hodge, Ruth E. (Ap. 27, 1937, Caledonia, VA) Chief, Tech. Srvs. Branch, US Army Milit. Hist. Inst., 1981–; Chief, Cat. and Prcs. Sect., US Army War Coll. Lib., 1975–80, Sr. Catlgr., 1974–75, Catlgr., 1971–74. **Educ.:** Lycoming Coll., 1954–58, BS (Bus., Exec. Sci.); Shippensburg State Coll., 1969–71, MSLS; various crs. **Orgs.:** ALA. SLA. CS LA. Assn. for the Std. of Afro-Amer. Life and Hist. Y's Menette: Carlisle's Club Pres. (1977–78); PA State Reg. Dir. (1979–81). **Honors:** Carlisle Barracks, Fed. Woman of the Year, 1980; Carlisle Barracks, Fed. Supvsr. of the Year, 1979. **Activities:** 4, 7; 17, 20, 46; 66, 73, 75 **Addr.:** Technical Services Branch, US Army Military History Institute, Carlisle Barracks, PA 17013.

Hodges, Judith L. (Jl. 10, 1939, Montreal, PQ, Can.) Libn., TN Hosp. Assn., 1975–; Libn., Loss Control, Inc., 1973–75; Libn., N.side Hosp. (Atlanta), 1971–72; Libn., MA Hosp. Assn., 1968–70; Adult Srvs. Libn., Brooklyn Pub. Lib., 1961–64. **Educ.:** Simmons Coll., 1957–61, BSc (LS); Emory Univ., 1970–73, MLn (LS). Med. LA, 1974, Cert. (grade 1 level). **Orgs.:** Med. LA: Hlth. Sci. Lib. Tech. Com. (1978–81). TN Hlth. Sci. LA: Staff Liaison. **Honors:** Beta Phi Mu, 1973. **Pubns.:** "Aids for the medical library in the small hospital" *TN Libn.* (Spr. 1973); "Library News," *TN Hosp. Times* Column (1976–). **Activities:** 12; 17, 24, 39; 80 **Addr.:** Tennessee Hospital Association, 500 Interstate Blvd., S. Nashville, TN 37210.

Hodges, Lois Foight (N. 13, 1930, Pittsburgh, PA) Coord., Chld. Srvs., Schenectady Cnty. Pub. Lib., 1978–; Lib. Media Spec., Greenfield Elem. Sch., 1975–78; Libn., Chld. Srvs., Schenectady Cnty. Pub. Lib., 1969–74. **Educ.:** Univ. of Pittsburgh, 1948–52, BA (Eng.), 1956–57, MA (Eng. Lit.), 1966–68, MLS. **Orgs.:** ALA. NY LA. Amer. Recorder Socty.: Chap. Pres. (1977–80). **Pubns.:** "Best Picture Books for Children," *Early Educ. Rpt.* (1971–75, 1979). **Activities:** 9, 10; 15, 17, 21; 57, 63, 89 **Addr.:** Schenectady County Public Library, Liberty and Clinton Sts., Schenectady, NY 12305.

Hodges, T(erence) Mark (Je. 18, 1933, Sheffield, Eng.) Dir., Med. Ctr. Lib., Vanderbilt Univ., 1972–; Assoc. Dir., A. W. Calhoun Med. Lib., Emory Univ., 1970–72; Dir., New England Reg. Med. Lib. Srvc., Harvard Univ., 1967–70; Head of Circ. Srv., Countway Lib. of Med., Harvard Univ., 1964–67; Sr. Libn., Lang. and Lit. Div., Brooklyn Pub. Lib., 1961–63; Circ. Libn., Swarthmore Coll., 1960–61; Ref. Libn., Hamilton Coll. Lib., 1957–60; Branch Libn., Sheffield (Eng.) Pub. Lib., 1956–57. **Educ.:** Univ. of OK, 1963–69, BLS; Leeds (Eng.) Coll. of Cmrce., Sch. of Libnshp., 1955–56, ALA (LS). **Orgs.:** Med. LA: Parlmt. (1978–) and numerous coms. ALA: Ref. & Subscrpn. Bk. Review Com. (1977–78). S. East. Reg. Med. Lib. Prog.: Adv. Com. (1970–). LA of Great Britain. AAUP. **Pubns.:** "TWX and Interlibrary Loans," *Bltn. Med. Lib. Assn.* (Jl. 1976); "NERMLS and the Community Hospital," *Bltn. Med. Lib. Assn.* (Jl. 1970); "NERMLS: The First Year," *Bltn. Med. Lib. Assn.* (O. 1969). **Activities:** 1, 14-Medical; 17, 24, 34; 58, 68, 80 **Addr.:** Medical Center Library, Vanderbilt University, Nashville, TN 37232.

Hodges, Thelma Floy (F. 25, 1918, Martinsville, IN) Assoc. Libn., Christ. Theo. Semy., 1950–; Tchr.-Libn., Richland Twp. Sch., Newtown IN, 1947–50; Tchr., Various IN schs., 1940–47. **Educ.:** IN Univ., 1935–39, AB (Latin), 1942–47, MA (Latin); Butler Univ., Christ. Theo. Semy., 1961–66, MA (New Testament). Univ. of IL, 1951–52, (LS). **Orgs.:** ATLA. Theta Phi: Beta Chap. (VP 1974–75). Ctrl. IN Litcy. Cncl.: Treas. (1968–70). **Honors:** Christ. Theo. Semy. Alum. Assn., Disting. Srv., 1973. **Pubns.:** Poem "Books," *Wilson Lib. Bltn.* (1953); reviews. **Activities:** 1; 20, 39; 90 **Addr.:** Christian Theological Seminary Library, 1000 West 42nd St., Indianapolis, IN 46208.

Hodgman, Suzanne L. (Jl. 16, 1925, Chicago, IL) Bib. for Ibero-Amer. Std., Univ. of WI, Madison, 1965–; Latin Amer. Spec. in Acq., Univ. of FL Libs., 1960–65; Ref. Libn., San Antonio, Pub. Lib., 1959–60. **Educ.:** Univ. of NM, 1945–57; BA (Inter-Amer. Affairs), Tulane Univ., 1948–50, MA (Latin Amer. Std.); Univ. of TX, Austin, 1958–60, MLS; National Univ. of Mexico, 1946. **Orgs.:** SALALM: Nom. Com. (1975), Mem. Ch. (1978–80), Exec. Bds. (1977–80). Exec. Secy. (1980–); Latin Amer. Microform Proj.: Exec. Bd. (1975–77; 1980–82). Latin Amer. Std. Assn.: Com. on Scholarly Resrcs. (1978–82). Midwest Assn. of Latin Amer. Std. Conf. on Latin Amer. Hist. **Pubns.:** Ed., *Microfilming Projects Nwsltr,* (1964–). **Activities:** 1; 15; 54 **Addr.:** Memorial Library, University of Wisconsin, Madison, WI 53706.

Hodgson, James S. (Ap. 26, 1942, Detroit, MI) Acq. Libn., Fine Arts Lib., Fogg Art Musm., Harvard Univ., 1967–. **Educ.:** Brown Univ., 1960–64, AB (Indp., Inter Disciplinary Std.) Simmons Coll., 1965–66, MSLS. **Orgs.:** ARLIS/NA: Stans. Com. (1979–); Bk. Awds. Com. (Ch., 1977). **Pubns.:** Contrib. Ed., *ARLIS/NA Nsltr.* (1976–77). **Activities:** 1, 8; 15, 39; 55, 67 **Addr.:** Fine Arts Library, Fogg Art Museum, Harvard University, Cambridge, MA 02138.

Hodina, Alfred J. (N. 26, 1923, Linz, Austria) Head, Sci.-Engin. Lib., Univ. of CA, Santa Barbara, 1973–; Chief, Procurement Sect., Natl. Agr. Lib., 1972–73, Chief, Cat. Sect., 1971–72; Lectr. and Dir. of Admis., Sch. of Lib. and Info. Srvs., Univ. of MD, 1967–70; Systs. Spec., Asst. to Dir. of Libs., Univ. of Houston Lib., 1965–67; Sci. Info. Spec., Rensselaer Polytech. Inst. Lib., 1964–65, Serials and Ref. Spec., 1963–64; various tchg. positions. **Educ.:** SUNY, Albany, 1955–60, BS (Phys.), 1961–62, MS (Phys.); Univ. of WA, 1962–63 (Oceanography); SUNY, Albany, 1963–64, MLS; Rensselaer Polytech., 1964–65 (Mgt. Sci.); Univ. of Houston, 1966–67 (Comp. Sci.); various certs. **Orgs.:** ALA. SLA. Amer. Meteorological Socty.: Santa Barbara–Ventura Chap. **Honors:** Sigma Pi Sigma. **Pubns.:** *Reader in Science Information* (1973); "An Online Component in an Interdisciplinary Course on Information Resources for Science and Engineering Students," *Online Review* (1978); "Counting U.S. Government Documents," *TX Lib. Jnl.* (1966). **Activities:** 1, 11; 17, 39, 41; 56, 75, 91 **Addr.:** Sciences-Engineering Library, University of California, Santa Barbara, CA 93106.

Hodnette, Milton G(ardner), Jr. (Ag. 23, 1918, Denver, CO) Sr. Catlgr., OH Univ. Lib., 1980–, Head, Cat. Dept., 1978–80, Head, Tech. Srvs. Div., 1975–78, Head, Cat. Dept., 1969–75; Coord., NV Ctr. for Coop. Lib. Srvs., 1968–69; Head Catlgr., Catlgr., Chico State Coll. Lib., 1958–68; Docum. Libn., CA State Polytech. Coll. Lib., 1954–58; Mncpl. Ref. Libn., Denver Pub. Lib., 1952–54, Libn., Docum. Dept., 1951–54. **Educ.:** CO Coll., 1938–42, BA (Span.); Univ. of Denver, 1950–51, MA (LS), 1942–43, (Educ.); Univ. of CO, 1949, (Span.); Univ. of CA, 1945–46, (Russ.); Stanford Univ., 1944–45, (Russ.). **Orgs.:** Acad. Libns. Assn. of OH. ALA. OCLC: Cat. Adv. Com. (1970–74); Serials Adv. Com. (1971–74). OH LA: Info. Org. (1970–); Retrieval and Srv. Div., Coord. (1974); Asst. Coord. (1973). Other orgs. **Activities:** 1; 20, 34, 46; 55, 56 **Addr.:** 49 Pomeroy Road, Athens, OH 45701.

Hodosy, Kenneth G., Jr. (Ap. 27, 1950, Buffalo, NY) Dir., Orchard Park Pub. Lib., 1980–; Asst. Libn., Grand Island Meml. Lib., 1978–80; Sr. Libn., Grt. Lakes Lab., SUNY, Buffalo, 1977–78, Asst. to Head, Ctrl. Tech. Srvs., 1976–77; Chief, Lib. Srvs., Base Lib., KS Air Base, 1975–76. **Educ.:** SUNY, Buffalo, 1969–73, BA (Classics), 1973–74, MLS; various crs. **Orgs.:** SLA:

Special Subjects/Services: 50. Adult educ.; 51. Advert./Mktg.; 52. Aerosp.; 53. Agric.; 54. Area std.; 55. Arts/Hum.; 56. Autom.; 57. Bibl./Prtg.; 58. Bio. sci.; 59. Bus./Fin.; 60. Chem.; 61. Copyrt.; 62. Documtn.; 63. Educ.; 64. Engin.; 65. Env.; 66. Eth. grps.; 67. Film; 68. Food/Nutr.; 69. Geneal.; 70. Geo.; 71. Geol.; 72. Handcpd.; 73. Hist.; 74. Int. frdm.; 75. Info. sci.; 76. Insr.; 77. Law; 78. Legis.; 79. Math./Comp. sci.; 80. Med.; 81. Metals; 82. Nat. resrcs.; 83. Newsp.; 84. Nuc. sci.; 85. Oral hist.; 86. Petr./Energy; 87. Pharm.; 88. Phys./Astr./Math.; 89. Readg.; 90. Relig.; 91. Sci./Tech.; 92. Soc. sci.; 93. Telecom.; 94. Transp.; 95. (other).

Upstate NY Chap. NY LA. Libns. Assn. of the Buffalo and Erie Cnty. Pub. Lib.: PR Com. (1979–80). **Pubns.:** "Some Applications of Marketing Techniques to a Small Town Library," *Lib. Jnl.* (Mr. 1981). **Activities:** 9; 17, 35, 36; 51 **Addr.:** Orchard Park Public Library, S-4570 S. Buffalo St., Orchard Park, NY 14127.

Hodowanec, George V. (N. 5, 1935, Ukraine) Dir., Emporia St. Univ., 1975–; Prof., Drexel Univ., 1969–74; Chief Libn., Cambria-Somerset Lib. Syst., 1967–69; Dir., Carteret Pub. Lib., 1965–67; Math Tchr.; Plymouth-Whitemarsh HS (PA), 1963–65; Cat., Temple Univ., 1962–63; Ref. Libn., Free Lib. Philadelphia, 1960–62. **Educ.:** Temple Univ., 1954–58, BS (Math, Msc.); Drexel Univ., 1959–60, MS (LS); Temple Univ., 1969–72, EdD (Comm., Educ. Media); Pittsburgh Univ., 1968–69, (Adv. Cert. LS). **Orgs.:** ALA: ACRL, Com. Appt. Nom. (1978–80), Stan. Accred. Com. (1979–). AALS. Mt. Plains. LA. KA LA. Emporia LA. Lyons Srvc. Org. **Honors:** Plymouth - Whitemarsh (PA) HS, Merit. Tchr. Awd., 1965. **Pubns.:** Ed. *The May Massee Collection: Creative Publishing for Children, 1923–1963* (1979); "Analysis of Variables Which Help to Predict Book and Periodical Use," *Lib. Acq.: Prac. and Theory* (Spr. 1980); "Library User Behavior," *Coll. Mgt.* (Sum./Fall 1979); "An Acquisition Rate Model for Academic Libraries," *Coll. & Resrch. Libs.* (N. 1978); "Is the Media Specialist Multi-media Trained?" *PLA Bltn.* (Mr. 1974); Reviews. **Activities:** 1; 17, 41 **Addr.:** 2032 Huntington Road, Emporia, KS 66801.

Hoduski, Bernadine Esther Abbott (Ja. 27, 1938, New Deal, MT) Prof., Staff Mem. for Lib. and Distribution Srvs. US Cong., Jt. Com. on Prtg., 1974–; Head Libn., US Env. Protection Agency Reg. VII, 1970–74; Serial Cat., Univ. of MO (Kansas City), 1969–70; Head, Gvt. Docum. Dept., Ctrl. MO St. Univ., 1965–69. **Educ.:** Avila Coll., 1955–59, BA (Hist., Eng.); Univ. of Denver, 1964–65, MA (LS). **Orgs.:** ALA: GODORT, Doc. Cat. Com. (Ch., 1974–); RTSD, Cat. Com. Descrip. and Access (1979–); SRRT, Task Force Gvt. Pubs. (Ch., 1970–72); various other com. IFLA: Official Pubs. Com. (1978–). AALL: Rep. to IFLA. DC LA. Various other com. and orgs. Women's Pol. Caucus. AAUP: CMSU Chap. (Exec. Bd., 1968–69). Amer. Civil Liberties Union. Natl. Prsrvn. Socty. **Honors:** ALA, James Bennett Childs Awd. for Disting. Contr. to Doc. Libnshp., 1977; U.S. Env. Protection Agency, EPA Bronze Medal for Cmdn. Srv., 1973. **Pubns.:** *Environmental Services, A Bibliography* (1973); "Federal Libraries and Intellectual Freedom", in *Intellectual Freedom Manual* (1974); "The Federal Depository System: What Is Its Basic Job?," *Drexel Lib. Qtly.* (Ap. 1974) "Documents to the People" in *RQ* (1973); Co-Ed., Doc. to the People (1972–73); Ed., Gvt. Pubs. Review (Fed. Sect.) (1974–) Various speeches. **Addr.:** 129 3rd St., N.E., Washington, DC 20002.

Hoeber, Mary L. (Jl. 28, 1949, Rutland, VT) Tech. Prcs. Libn., Missn. Coll., 1977–; Chld. Libn., Santa Clara Cnty., 1977; Ref. Libn., W. Valley Coll., 1975–77; Libn., Amer. Indian Lib., Univ. of CA, Los Angeles, 1974–75. **Educ.:** CA State Univ., Northridge, 1971–72, BA (Eng.); Univ. of CA, Los Angeles, 1972–74, MLS; 1972–74 Cert. (Nonbk. Libnshp.). **Orgs.:** ALA: LITA; RTSD. CA LA: North. CA Tech. Prcs. Grp. **Pubns.:** Jt. Auth., *Catalog of Sanborn Fire Insurance Maps at California State, Northridge* (1972). **Activities:** 1; 20, 34, 46; 56, 75, 93 **Addr.:** Mission College, 3000 Mission College Blvd., Santa Clara, CA 95054.

Hoefer, Margaret J. (Jl. 28, 1909, Brooklyn, NY) Lbn., Mktg. Lib., Harris Corp., 1981–; Brevard Cnty. (FL) Lib. Bd., 1977–; Libn., Golden Hills Acad., Ocala, FL, 1972–74; Asst. Prof., Readers Srvs., Suffolk Cnty. Cmnty. Coll., 1969–72; Head, Ref. Dept., Nassau Cmnty. Coll., 1967–69; Dir., Emma S. Clark Meml. Lib., Setauket, NY, 1965–67; Head, Ref. Srvs., Smithtown (NY) Lib., 1963–65; Head Libn., Woodlawn Jr. HS, 1962–63; Cnty. Libn., Carroll Cnty. Pub. Lib., 1958–62; other lib. positions. **Educ.:** KS State Coll., 1928–32, BS in Ed (Eng.); CO State Coll., 1938–39, MA (Eng.); Univ. of Denver, 1941–43, BS in LS. **Orgs.:** ALA: ALTA; IRRT. FL LA: Friends and Trustees Caucus. Brevard Assn. for the Advancement of the Blind. Natl. Braille Assn. Brevard Art Ctr. & Musm. Amer. Assn. of Retired Persons. Other orgs. **Activities:** 9; 16, 39, 47; 50, 55, 61 **Addr.:** 839 S.E. Edgewood Dr., Palm Bay, FL 32905.

Hoefler, Barbara Burton (Ap. 8, 1920, Cleveland, OH) Head Libn., Assoc. Prof., HI Pac. Coll., 1974–; Engin. Libn., Hawaiian Electric Co., Inc., 1973–74; Resrch. Consult., 1971–73; Head Libn., Maui Cmnty. Coll., 1969–71; Mncpl. Libn., Mncpl. Ref. Lib., City and Cnty. of Honolulu, 1966–69; Libn., Pineapple Resrch. Inst. of HI, 1963–66; Libn., Sch. of Dentistry, Case West. Rsv. Univ., 1962–63, Asst. Regis., Sch. of Med., 1953–60. **Educ.:** Flora Stone Mather Coll., 1938–42, AB (Eng.); Case West. Rsv. Univ., 1962, MS (LS). **Orgs.:** SLA. HI LA: Exec. Bd. (1963–64, 1979–81), Spec. and Ref., Ch., Int. Frdm., Ch. Frnds. of the Lib. of HI. Assoc. of Univ. of HI Libs. Soroptimist Intl.: Dir. (1968–69); VP (1971). AAUP. HI Hist. Assn. **Honors:** Beta Phi Mu. **Pubns.:** "From the Campus, Maui Community College," *Maui News* (Mr. 7, My. 30, 1970); "Mini Operation for a Maxi Move," *HI LA Jnl.* (Je. 1971); various articles. **Activities:** 1, 12; 15, 17, 44; 55, 59, 92 **Addr.:** P.O. Box 2805, Honolulu, HI 96803.

Hoehn, Philip (O. 23, 1941, Poplar Bluff, MO) Map Libn., Univ. of CA at Berkeley, 1980–, Head, Map & Atlas Div., Bancroft Lib., 1969–80, Asst. Libn., Gen Ref. Srv., 1967–69. **Educ.:** Univ. of CA, Los Angeles, 1959–63, AB (Geog.); Univ. of CA, Berkeley, 1965–67, MLS. **Orgs.:** SLA: Geography & Map Div., Mem. Com. (1978–79). West. Assn. of Map Libs.: Pres. (1976–77); VP (1975–76); Secy. (1974–75); Pubn. Com. (1977–). CA LA. Assn. of Can. Map Libs. **Pubns.:** *Union List of Sanborn Fire Insurance Maps Held by Institutions in the United States and Canada* v.1 (1976); "The Dakin Publishing Co. and its Fire Insurance Maps," *West. Assn. of Map Libs. Info. Bltn.* (1976); "The Bancroft Library Map Collection," *West. Assn. of Map Libs. Info. Bltn.* (1976). **Activities:** 1; 15, 20, 39; 70 **Addr.:** Map Room-Library, Univ. of Calif., Berkeley, CA 94720.

Hoey, Evelyn L. (Ag. 28, 1919, Estill, SC) Dir., Med. Lib., SUNY Upstate Med. Ctr., 1971–, Acting Dir., Med. Lib., 1969–70, Assoc. Libn. for Admin., 1966–69; Info. Spec., General Electric Co., 1962–66; Chief, Docu. Lib., Rome Air Dev., Ctr., 1960–62; Plant Libn., Union Carbide Corp., 1949–60; Army Libn., U.S. Army Spec. Srvcs., 1946–49; Chief Libn., Subsistence Resrch. & Dev. Lab., U.S. Quartermaster Corps, 1944–46. **Educ.:** Meredith College, 1935–39, BS (Gen. Sci.); Simmons Coll., 1939–40, BSLS. **Orgs.:** Upstate NY and ON Reg. Med. LA: Ch. (1979–80). Med. LA: Legis. Com. (1972–73). **Pubns.:** "The Upstate Medical Center Library: A Decade of Progress," *Syracuse Med. Alum. Assn., Alum. News* (1970); "Establishing a Medical Library Technology Program - The SUNY Experience," *Bltn. of the Med. Lib. Assn.* (1969); other articles, reviews. **Activities:** 1; 17, 34; 58, 80, 87 **Addr.:** Medical Library, SUNY Upstate Medical Center, 766 Irving Ave., Syracuse, NY 13210.

Hoffman, Alice M. (Je. 17, 1929, Brooklyn, NY) Assoc. Prof., PA St. Univ., 1966–; Bibl., Union Lib. Cat., 1953–54. **Educ.:** Earlham Coll., 1947–51, AB (Hist.); PA St. Univ., 1959–65, MA (Hist.). **Orgs.:** Oral Hist. Assn.: Secy., Pres., VP, Nom. Com., Ethics Com. Univ. Coll. Labor Educ. Assn.: East. Rep. to Bd. **Pubns.:** "Introduction," *Working Women Roots, An Oral History Primer* (1979); "Who Are the Elite and What is a Non-Elitist?," *Oral Hist. Review,* (1976); "Validity and Realiability in Oral History," *Today's Sp.* (Win. 1974); "Oral History in the United States," *Jnl. of Lib. Hist.* (Jl. 1971); "Oral History in Great Britain," *Jnl. of Lib. Hist.* (Jl. 1971); "Basic Problems in Oral History," in *The Fourth National Colloquium on Oral History,* (1970). Other articles and media presentations. **Activities:** 2; 50, 85 **Addr.:** Penn. State Univ. Graduate Center, 259 Radnor-Chester Rd., Radnor, PA 19087.

Hoffman, Andrea C. (F. 15, 1949, Boston, MA) Asst. Dir., Head, Resrc. and Resrch. Div., Columbia Univ., 1978–; Dir., Kresge Ctr. for Tchg. Resrc., Lesley Coll., 1973–77. **Educ.:** Boston Univ., 1967–69, BA (Russ.); IN Univ., 1969–71, MA (Slavic Lang., Lit.); Simmons Coll., 1971–73, MS (LS); Simmons Coll., 1977–78, DA (LS). **Orgs.:** ALA. **Pubns.:** "Collection Development Programs in Academic Libraries: An Administrative Approach," *The Bk.mark* (Spr. 1979); "Monograph duplication in the Kresge Ctr. for Teaching Resources" in *Quantitative Measurement and Dynamic Library Service* (1978). **Activities:** 1; 15, 17; 63 **Addr.:** Teachers College Library, 525 W 120th St., N.Y., NY 10027.

Hoffman, David Martin (Jl. 6, 1943, Brooklyn, NY) Chief Libn., Newsday, 1970–; Head Adult Srvs. Libn., Levittown Pub. Lib., 1967–70; Libn., Brooklyn Pub. Lib., 1964–67. **Educ.:** City Coll. of New York, 1960–64, BA (Ling.); Pratt Inst., 1964–65, MLS. **Orgs.:** Motor Vehicle Documtn. Arch.: Dir. (1979–). Socty. of Automotive Histns. SLA. Temple Sinai. **Activities:** 2, 12; 15, 17, 45; 83, 94 **Addr.:** Newsday, Long Island, NY 11747.

Hoffman, David R. (S. 28, 1934, Brownwood, TX) Dir., Lib. Srvs. Div., State Lib. of PA, 1981–, Coord., Interlib. Coop., 1975–81; Dir., Lib. Manpower Study, Univ. of WI Ext., 1974–75; State Libn.; Dept. State Libn, Coord., Lib. Dev., MT State Lib., 1968–73; Asst. Dir., IRO; Head Tech. Info., Lib Techn. Proj, ALA, 1963–68; Admin. Asst., WI Free Lib. 1959–63. **Educ.:** Davis and Elkins Coll., 1952–54, BA (Eng.); Western Reserve Univ., 1954–55, MSLS. **Orgs.:** ALA: Int. Rel. Com. (1969–71); Cncl. (1971–72); Nom. Com. (1972–73). Assn. of State Lib. Agencies: VP (1972–73). Pacific Northwest Bibl. Ctr.: Board (1970–71); Pres. (1971–73). **Honors:** Cncl. on Lib. Resrcs., Flwshp, 1970. **Pubns.:** *1976 Inventory of Pennsylvania Library Cooperative Organizations* (1977). *1978 Inventory of Pennsylvania Library Cooperative Organizations* (1979). Ed., *WI Lib. Bltn.* (1959–63). Ed., *MT Nwsltr.* (1970–73). **Activities:** 13; 17, 34 **Addr.:** PO Box 247, Harrisburg, PA 17108.

Hoffman, Diane J. (Jl. 16, 1943, Rahway, NJ) Mgr., User Educ. and Resrch., Inst. for Sci. Info., 1980–, Mgt., Comm., 1977–79, Lectr., Prof. Educ., 1975–77, Supvsr., Customer Srvcs., 1974–75; Sci. Ref. Libn., SUNY-OSWEGO, 1971–1974; Asst. Libn., Nat. Sci. Lib., Syracuse Univ., 1968–71. **Educ.:** Syracuse Univ., 1962–66, BA (Eng. Lit.), 1969–71, MSLS. **Orgs.:** ALA. ASIS. SLA: Info. Tech. Div. Mem., Ch. (1975–78); Treas. (1977–78); Pub. Rel. (1978–79); Secy. (1979–81). AAAS. **Activities:** 6; 17, 26, 30; 51, 75, 91 **Addr.:** Institute for Scientific Information, University City Science Center, 3501 Market St., Philadelphia, PA 19104.

Hoffman, Herbert H. (Ja. 22, 1928, Berlin, Germany) Ed., Pubshr., Headway Pubns., 1976–; Cat. Libn., Santa Ana Coll., 1970–. **Educ.:** CA State Univ., Los Angeles, 1957–59, BA (Eng.); Univ. of South. CA, 1959–60, MS (LS). **Orgs.:** ASIS. South. CA OLUG. **Pubns.:** Jt. Cmplr., *Spoken World Poetry Index* (1981); *Workmarc: A Record Format for Works in Analytic Catalogs* (1980); *Cuento Mexicano Index* (1978); *Simple Library Bookkeeping* (1978); Jt. Auth., *Introduction to Quantitative Research Methodology for Librarians* (1978); various monos., articles. **Addr.:** Headway Publications, 1700 Port Manleigh Cir., Newport Beach, CA 92660.

Hoffman, Kathryn J. (N. 1, 1948, Cleveland, OH) Head, Cat. Srvs., Houston Acad. of Med., TX Med. Ctr. Lib., 1975–, Col. Dev. Libn., Serials Catlgr., 1973–75. **Educ.:** Case West. Rsv. Univ., 1967–71, BA (Hist.); Univ. of IL, 1971–73, MSLS. **Orgs.:** Med. LA: Lib. Stan. and Prac. Com. (1980–). Hlth. Sci. OCLC Users Grp.: Secy.-Treas. (1979–). Houston Area Resrch. Lib. Cnsrtm.: Tech. Srvs. Com. (1979–). **Activities:** 1, 12; 20, 25, 46; 80 **Addr.:** Houston Academy of Medicine Texas Medical Center Library, Jesse H. Jones Library Bldg., Houston, TX 77030.

Hoffman, Kathryn Jean Ross (Je. 3, 1949, Newark, NJ) Ref. Libn., Fairfax Cnty. Pub. Lib., 1978–. **Educ.:** Marietta Coll., 1967–71, BA (Hist.); PA State Univ., 1971–73, MA (Art Hist.); Univ. of IL, 1976–77, MS (LS). **Orgs.:** ALA. VA LA. Fairfax Cnty. Empls. Assn. **Honors:** Alpha Xi Delta. **Pubns.:** Jt. auth., "Historical Review of the U.S. Grades and Standards for Grain," *IL Agr. Econ.* (Ja. 1976). **Activities:** 9; 16, 39, 41; 55, 92 **Addr.:** 8704 Parliament Dr., Springfield, VA 22151.

Hoffman, Mary Ann (Je. 15, 1924, Downers Grove, IL) Coord. of Spec. Col. & Srvs., Hlth. Sci. Lib., Wright State Univ., 1979–; Libn., St. Elizabeth Med. Ctr., 1969–79; Asst. Libn., Miami Valley Hosp., 1964–69. **Educ.:** Mills Coll./Univ. of Louisville, 1948, BA (Bio.); Wright State Univ., 1975–79, MA (Hist.). **Orgs.:** Med. LA: Nom. Com. (1978); Ad Hoc Com. to Dev. a Statement of Goals (1978–); Prog. and Conv. Com. (1981–); Hosp. Lib. Int. Grp. (Treas., 1976–77. KY-OH-MI Reg. Med. Lib.: Org. Com. (1977–78). Miami Valley Assn. of Hlth. Sci. Libs.: Vice-Ch. (1974–75); Ch. (1975–77). SAA. Other orgs. OH Acad. of Med. Hist. **Honors:** Phi Alpha Theta, 1978. **Activities:** 1, 12; 23, 27, 45; 52, 80 **Addr.:** Health Sciences Library, Wright State University, 3640 Colonel Glenn Highway, Dayton, OH 45431.

Hoffman, William J. (S. 2, 1922, Glidden, WI) Dir., Learning Resrcs., Mt. San Antonio Coll., 1975–; Asst. Dean, College Srvs., Johnson Cnty. Com. Coll., 1969–75; Prog. Of., USOE/HEW, 1967–68; Head Libn., Maryvale HS, 1962–67. **Educ.:** Lakeland Coll., 1946–50, BA (Hist.); Univ. of WI, 1950–51, MS (Eng.); Univ. of Denver, 1960–63, MA (Libnshp.). **Orgs.:** ALA: ACRL (Ch., Community and Jr. Coll., 1972). AZ State LA: Pres. Elect, (1967). KS LA: (1969–75). Amer. Assn. Educ. Comm. and Tech. Task Force, Comm. Coll. Standards (1971–72). **Activities:** 1, 10; 17, 24; 55, 63, 93 **Addr.:** 1212 Shasta Dr., West Covina, CA 91791.

Hoffmann, Christa F. B. (Je. 9, 1936, Berlin, Germany) Bibli. Data Base Coord., Univ. of NE (Lincoln) 1979–, Prcs. Dept. Head, 1975–79, Asst. Ref. Libn., 1973–75; Hum. Libn., West. MI Univ., 1971–73; Catlgr., Sr., IN Univ., 1968–70. **Educ.:** Wilmington Coll., 1961–65, BA cum laude (Eng.), IN Univ., 1965–68, (LS); 1970–71, (Compar. Lit.). **Orgs.:** OCLC, Inc: Interntwk. Qual. Cont. Cncl. (1978–). ALA: Cat. Com. Descrip. Access (1980–81). NE LA. **Activities:** 1; 20, 34, 46; 55 **Addr.:** Love Library Rm 106, University of Nebraska - Lincoln Libraries, Lincoln, NE 68502.

Hoffmann, Ellen (Jl. 28, 1943, Cape Girardeau, MO) Asst. Dir., Pub. Srvs., York Univ., 1978–, Ref. Dept., 1971–78; Cross Campus Lib., Yale Univ., 1968–71, Cat. Dept., 1966–68. **Educ.:** Univ. of WI, 1961–65, BA (Compar. Lit.), 1965–66, MA (LS). **Orgs.:** ALA: Ref. and Subscrpn. Bks. Review Com. Can. LA. **Pubns.:** "Reference Librarians and Performance Appraisal," *Proceedings of the CACUL Syposium on the Reference Interview* (1969). **Activities:** 1; 17, 39 **Addr.:** 310 Scott Library, York University, 4700 Keele St., Downsview, ON M3J 2R2 Canada.

Hoffmann, Frank William (My. 2, 1949, Geneva, NY) Asst. Prof., Sam Houston State Univ., 1979–; Libn., Patient Lib., Woodville State Hosp., 1976–79; Ref. Libn., Northland Pub. Lib., 1976–78; Ref. Libn., Carlow Coll., 1974–76; Ref. Libn., Cnty. Bkmobile. Libn., Memphis Pub. Lib., 1972–74. **Educ.:** IN Univ., 1967–71, BA (Hist.), 1972, MLS; Univ. of Pittsburgh, 1974–77, PhD (LS). **Orgs.:** ALA. SLA. AALS: Mem. Com. (1981–). SLA: TX Chap. (1979–); Advert. Mgr. (1981–). Jnl. of Pop. Culture. Bijou Natl. Film Socty. **Pubns.:** *The Literature of Rock, 1954–1978* (1981); *The Development of Library Collections of Sound Recordings* (1979); "Music for the Bubblegum Set," *Sch. Lib. Jnl.* (O. 1975); "Popular Music Collections and Public Libraries," *Southeast. Libn.* (Win. 1974); "Record Store Adds Computerized Reference Service," *Rec. Digest.* (1978); various articles. **Activities:** 9, 12; 15, 17, 29; 55, 74, 83 **Addr.:** School of Library Science, Box 2236, Sam Houston State University, Huntsville, TX 77341.

PROFESSIONAL ACTIVITIES: Institutions: 1. Acad. lib.; 2. Arch.; 3. Assn.; 4. Fed./Gvt. lib.; 5. Inst. lib.; 6. Mfr./Suppl.; 7. Milit. lib.; 8. Musm.; 9. Pub. lib.; 10. Sch. lib.; 11. Sch. of lib. sci.; 12. Spec. lib.; 13. State lib.; 14. (other). **Functions/Activities:** 15. Acq./Col. dev.; 16. Adult srvs.; 17. Admin.; 18. Apprais.; 19. Archit./Bldgs.; 20. Cat./Class.; 21. Chld. srvs.; 22. Circ.; 23. Cons./Pres.; 24. Consult.; 25. Cont. ed.; 26. Educ. lib. sci.; 27. Ext. srvs.; 28. Fund/Grants; 29. Gvt. pubs.; 30. Indx./Abs.; 31. Instr. lib. use; 32. Media srvs.; 33. Micro.; 34. Netwks./Coop.; 35. Persnl.; 36. PR; 37. Publshg.; 38. Recs. mgt.; 39. Ref. srvs.; 40. Repro.; 41. Resrch.; 42. Review.; 43. Secur.; 44. Serials; 45. Spec. col.; 46. Tech. srvs.; 47. Trustees/Bds.; 48. YA srvs.; 49. (other).

Hofmann, Anne J. (D. 6, 1951, New York, NY) Supvsg. Branch Libn., NY Pub. Lib., 1970–. **Educ.:** H. H. Lehman Coll., CUNY, 1969–72, BA (Hist.); Queens Coll., CUNY, 1972–73, MLS. **Orgs.:** ALA: ALSC. NY LA: Pub. Libs. Sect.; Chld. and YA Srvs. Sect. Bronx LA. The Marble Hill Neighborhood Improvement Corp. The City of NY Bronx Cmnty. Plng. Bd. # 8: Com. on Libs. and Cult. Affairs (Vice-Ch., 1978–). **Honors:** Marble Hill Neighborhood Improvement Corp., Good Citizen, 1979, 1980; New York City Youth Bd., Sum. Prog. Grant for Clason's Point Branch Lib., 1980. **Activities:** 9; 17, 21; 78, 89 **Addr.:** 57 Adrian Ave., Marble Hill, NY 10463.

Hofstad, Richard Joseph (S. 27, 1926, Minneapolis, MN) Athen. Libn., Ctrl. Srvs. Bk. Sel. Libn., Minneapolis Pub. Lib., 1980–, Acq. Libn., 1962–80, Asst. Head, Lit. Dept., 1959–62, Libn. II, Sci. and Tech. Dept., 1956–59; LC Liaison Libn., US Dept. of Agr., 1955–56; Soc. Sci. Libn., Univ. of Notre Dame, 1954–55; Acq. Libn., Georgetown Univ., 1951–54. **Educ.:** Univ. of MN, 1944–49, BS (Eng. Educ.), 1950–51, BS (LS); various crs. **Orgs.:** ALA: ACRL. **Activities:** 9; 15, 23, 45 **Addr.:** 4047 Dupont Ave. N., Minneapolis, MN 55412.

Hogan, Alan D. (D. 5, 1938, Cleveland, OH) Asst. Dir., Syst. & Prcs., Univ. of Toledo, 1970–; Syst. Autom. Libn., Wright State Univ., 1966–70; Assoc. Libn., SUNY, Binghamton, 1963–66. **Educ.:** John Carroll Univ., 1957–61, AB (Classics); Case Western Reserve Univ., 1962–63, MS in LS. **Orgs.:** Acad. LA of OH: Exec. Bd. (1974–75). ALA. ASIS: Ch., Spec. Int. Grp. on Lib. Autom. and Networks (1974–75). AAUP: Chap. Exec. Com. (1967–68); Chap. Secy./Treas. (1968–70). **Pubns.:** "Acceptance of cataloging contributed by OCLC members" in *OCLC a National Library Network* (1979). **Activities:** 1; 17, 46; 56, 75 **Addr.:** 2344 Crossbough, Toledo, OH 43614.

Hogan, Daniel E. (Ag. 30, 1931, Brownville, ME) Lib., Media Content Spec., Medfield Pub. Schs., 1979–, Dir., Media Srvs., 1973–79, Supvsr., Sch. Libs., 1971–73. **Educ.:** Boston Univ., 1956–57, BS (Educ.); State Coll. at Bridgewater, MA, 1973, MEd (Libnshp.). **Orgs.:** ALA: AASL. MA Assn. for Educ. Media. Natl. Educ. Assn. MA Tchrs. Assn. **Activities:** 10; 17, 21, 26; 63, 95-Photography. **Addr.:** 4 Meade Ave., Medfield, MA 02052.

Hogan, James William (Ag. 13, 1938, London, Eng.) Univ. Libn., Brock Univ., 1970–, Circ. Libn., Serials Libn., Actg. Univ. Libn., 1967–70; Libn., Hong Kong Gvt. Ofc., London, Eng., 1964–67; Libn., Ctrl. Ref. Lib., Westminster City Libs., London, Eng., 1963–64. **Educ.:** London Univ., 1956–59, BA (Hons) (Geo.), 1962–63, Postgrad. Dip. (Libnshp.); LA (UK), ALA. **Orgs.:** Niagara Reg. Lib. Syst.: Reg. Adv. Com. (1968–). Niagara Coll. of Arts & Applied Tech.: Lib. Tech. Prog., Adv. Com. (1968–; Ch., 1975–78). UNICAT/TELECAT: Mgt. Com. (1974–; Vice Ch. 1976–). ON Cncl. of Univ. Libs.: Secy. (1973–74); Vice Ch. (1975–76). Other orgs. Archlg. Inst. of Amer., Niagara Chap.: Treas. (1968–69), Pres. (1976–78). Torch Club, St. Catharines Chap.: Treas. (1974–77); Pres. (1977–78). **Activities:** 1; 17, 34; 70, 71 **Addr.:** Brock University Library, St. Catharines, ON L2S 3A1 Canada.

Hogan, Lawrence J. (Je. 5, 1926, Toronto, ON) Volun. Trustee, Scarborough Pub. Lib. Bd., 1977–. **Orgs.:** Can. Lib. Trustee Assn. ON LA: Trustee. Scarborough Bd. of Educ.: Trustee. **Activities:** 9, 13; 17 **Addr.:** 14 Chestnut Cresent, Scarborough, ON M1L 1Y5 Canada.

Hogan, Patricia Marie (Chicago, IL) Head libn, Itasca Pub. lib., 1981–; Info. Libn., Computer Coord., N. Suburban Lib. Syst., 1975–81; Head, Dept. of Public Srvs., Schaumburg Township Pub. Lib., 1972–75; Instr., LTA Prog., Coll. of DuPage, 1975; Indexer, Newbank, 1973. **Educ.:** Rosary Coll., BA (Eng./Germn); Univ. of Chicago, 1966–67, MA (Eng.); Rosary Coll., 1971–72 MALS. **Orgs.:** ALA: ALA Cncl. Mem. at lg. (1980–84); Ref. and Subs. Books Review Com. (1973–77); Guest Review (1978); LAMACSS Ch. (1980–81). IL LA: By-Laws and Revisions Com. (1973–75); Publicity and Pub. Rel. for 1978 ILA Conf. IL Reg. Lib. Cncl.: Sub. Com. on Human Resrcs. (1975–78). Midwest CLSI Users Group. IL OCLC User's Group. **Honors:** IL State Lib., Lib. Sci. Flwshp, 1971. Beta Phi Mu, 1972. **Pubns.:** Compiler, *Directory of Human Resources* (1979) "Perspectives on Community," IL Libs. (N. 1979). Jt. Auth. "Examining the 'in' Groups," *Cath. Lib. World* (Ap. 1978). Lib. Sci. articles, Micropedia sect. Britannica 3 (1976). Reviews. **Activities:** 11; 17, 24, 42; 55, 56 **Addr.:** 500 W. Irving Park Itasca, IL 60143.

Hogan, Sharon Anne (Mr. 17, 1945, Santa Barbara, CA) Asst. to the Dir., Univ. of MI, 1979–; Bibl. Inst. and Ref. 1974–79; Verticle File Libn., 1971–74, Audio Room Libn., 1968–70. **Educ.:** Coll. of William and Mary, 1963–67, AB (Hist.), Univ. of MI, 1968, AMLS. **Orgs.:** ALA: ACRL/Bibl. Inst. Sect. Ch., (1979–80); Bibl. Instr. Sect. Educ. Com., Ch. (1977–79); RASD Bibl. Com. (Ch., 1976–78). MI Lib. Consortium: Task Force on Ref. Bibl. Data. Bases (1977–78). **Pubns.:** *Training and Education of Library Instruction Librarians", Lib. Trends* (Sum. 1980); "Reaching Graduate Students: Techniques and Administration," in *Faculty Involvement in Library Instruction* (1976); "Things We Weren't Taught in Library School" *Conf. on Lib. Orientation for Acad. Libs.* (1978). **Activities:** 1; 17, 31, 39; 55 **Addr.:** Harlan Hatcher Library, University of Michigan, Ann Arbor, MI 48109.

Hogan, Shirley Louthan (Ag. 23, 1934, Akron, OH) Freelnc. Writer, Resrchr., Interviewer, 1978–; Archvst., CA State Arch., 1977–78; Libn., Sacramento Pub. Lib., 1970–77; Lib. Consult., WV Lib. Comsn., 1967–68. **Educ.:** OH State Univ., 1952–57, BA (Hist.); Case West. Rsv. Univ., 1957–58, MS (LS); Univ. of WI, MA (Hist.); MI State Univ., PhD (Hist.). **Orgs.:** SAA. West. Hist. Assn. Org. of Amer. Histns. Amer. Assn. for State and Lcl. Hist. CA Hist. Socty. **Activities:** 2, 9; 24, 30, 41; 57, 72, 92 **Addr.:** 2221 19th Ave., Sacramento, CA 95822.

Hogan, Thomas H. (Jl. 8, 1944, Summit, NJ) Pres., Plexus Pubshg., Inc., 1977–; VP, Data Courier, Inc., 1973–77; Mktg. Mgr., BIOSIS, 1971–73; Mktg. Mgr., IEEE, 1970–71. **Educ.:** LeMoyne Coll., 1962–66, BA (Eng.); Univ. of Louisville, 1973–77, MBA (Bus.). **Orgs.:** ASIS. **Pubns.:** Jt. auth, *Online Searching: A Primer* (1981); "News retrieval services–growing but where are they headed?" *Online Review* (S. 1979); News ed., *Online Review.* **Activities:** 6; 17; 58, 75 **Addr.:** Plexus Publishing, Inc., Box 550, Marlton, NJ 08053.

Hohhof, Bonnie N. (Je. 3, 1950, Medina, OH) Lib. Mgr., Motorola Inc., 1977–; Resrch. Libn., Gould Inc., 1974–77; Newsp. Supvsr., Northwest. Univ., 1972–73. **Educ.:** Northwest. Univ., 1968–72, BA (Pol. Sci.); Rosary Coll., 1973–74, MSLS, 1978–, CAS (Lib. Mgt.). **Orgs.:** SLA. **Activities:** 12; 17; 59, 64, 93 **Addr.:** Motorola Inc., 1301 E. Algonquin, Schaumburg, IL 60196.

Hoke, Elizabeth Conklin (Ag. 9, 1924, Washington, DC) Coord., Chlds. Srvs., Montgomery Cnty. Pub. Lib., 1978–, Asst. Coord., 1978, Asst. Cmnty. Libn., Reg. Chlds. Libn. **Educ.:** Univ. of Rochester, 1941–45, BA with High Hon. (Eng.); Univ. of MD, 1966–67, MLS. CT Coll., San Diego St. Univ., Catholic Univ., 1957–76. **Orgs.:** DC LA: Chld. and YA (Ch., 1975–76, 1979–80). MD LA. ALA. **Honors:** Phi Beta Kappa, 1945; Delta Phi Alpha, 1945. **Activities:** 9; 21, 25, 36; 55, 72, 89 **Addr.:** 5700 Ridgefield Rd., Bethesda, MD 20816.

Hoke, Elizabeth G. (O. 24, 1917, Hartford, CT) Chief Libn., Wadsworth Athen., 1964–. **Educ.:** Smith Coll., 1935–39, AB (Eng.); Univ. of MN, 1962–63, MA (LS). **Orgs.:** CT LA. ARLIS/NA. Univ. Club of Hartford. **Activities:** 8; 15, 17, 20; 55 **Addr.:** Auerbach Art Library, Wadsworth Atheneum, 600 Main St., Hartford, CT 06103.

Hoke, Shelia Wilder (Jl. 15, Greensboro, NC) Lib. Dir., S. West. OK St. Univ., 1969–, Cat., 1963–69; Spec. Srvs. Libn., US Army, Bavaria, Ger., 1958–59; Chlds. Libn., Enoch Pratt Free Lib., 1955–58. **Educ.:** Univ. KS, 1950–51 AB (Hist.), BS (Educ.); Univ. WI, 1954–55, MLS; S. West. OK St. Univ., 1976, M.Ed. **Orgs.:** ALA. SWLA. OK LA: Tech. Srvs. Div., Lib. Educ. Div., Coll. Div., Arch. Com. (1979); Recruit. Com. (1977). Delta Kappa Gamma: Lambda Chap., Pres. (1981–); V Ch. (1979); Resrch. Ch. (1979) Other com. AAUW: Weatherford Chap., Pres. (1981–); VP (1979–81). **Honors:** Phi Alpha Theta, 1948. **Activities:** 1; 17 **Addr.:** Southwestern Oklahoma State University, Weatherford, OK 73096.

Holahan, Paulette (Mrs. John M.) (My. 25, 1934, New Orleans, LA) Pub. Inf. Ofcr., LA Supreme Court, 1977–; Pub. Info. Ofcr., Orleans Parish Prison, 1976–77. **Educ.: Orgs.:** NCLIS (1980). ALA: ALTA, Bd. Dir. (1976–), Reg. VP (1976–); Action Dev. Com. LA LA: Legis. Act. Com. New Orleans Pub. Lib.: Ch. Bd. Dir. (1978–). Many orgs. **Honors:** LA LA Modisette Awd., outstanding service as lib. trustee, 1980; WHCOLIS, 1979; Gvr. Conf. Lib. Inf. Sci., 1979. **Pubns.:** Ed. various pubns. **Activities:** 9, 13; 28, 47 **Addr.:** 6417 Fleur de Lis Dr., New Orleans, LA 70124.

Holbrook, Carol R. (N. 13, 1933, Los Angeles, CA) Head, Ref. Dept., Univ. of MI Lib., 1979–, Head, Current Serials Srv., 1977–79, Assoc. Libn., Sel. Ofc., 1975–77, Libn., Ctr. for Resrch. on Econ. Dev., 1967–75. **Educ.:** Univ. of CA, Riverside, 1955–56, AB (Eng. Lit.); Univ. of MI, 1965–67, MALS. **Orgs.:** ALA: ACRL. RASD. MI LA. **Honors:** Beta Phi Mu, 1967. **Pubns.:** Jt. auth., "Position Classification at Michigan: Another Look," *Coll. and Resrch. Libs.* (v. 40, no. 3). **Activities:** 1; 15, 39, 42; 54, 92 **Addr.:** Reference Department, Harlan Hatcher Graduate Library, University of Michigan, Ann Arbor, MI 48109.

Holden, Harley Peirce (Ag. 18, 1937, Shirley, MA) Cur., Harvard Univ. Arch., 1971–, Asst. Cur., 1970–71, Asst., 1960–70. **Educ.:** Boston Univ., 1956–60, AB (Hist.), 1963–65, AM (Hist.); Simmons Coll., 1965–67, SM (LS); Harvard-Radcliffe Inst. on Hist. and Arch. Mgt., 1960, Cert.; Amer. Univ. Natl. Arch. Inst. on Arch. Mgt., 1966, Cert. **Orgs.:** SAA: Com. on Coll. and Univ. Arch. (1970–). New Eng. Archvst. Arch. of Amer. Art: Ch., New Eng. Adv. Com. Intl. Cncl. on Arch. Wheaton Coll.: Lib. Vist. Com. (1976–); Arch. Com. (1978–). Middlesex Canal Assn.: Bd. of Dir. (1963–78); Arch. Com. (1968–). Harvard Univ. Musms. Cncl. Bay State Hist. Leag.: Bd. of Dir. (1977–80). **Honors:** Phi Alpha Theta, 1965; Phi Beta Kappa, 1978; Harvard Meml. Socty., 1972. **Pubns.:** "Clifford K. Shipton," *Amer. Archvst.* (Jl., 1974); "Benton MacKaye: The Shirley Influence," *The Living Wilderness* (Ja./Mr. 1976); "Benton MacKaye, 1879–1975," *Appalachia* (Je. 1976); "Student Records: The Harvard Experience," *The American Archivist* (O. 1976); "The Harvard University Archives: A Source of Cambridge History," *Cambridge Hist. Socty.: Procs.* (1978); other articles. **Addr.:** Horse Pond Rd., Shirley Center, MA 01465.

Holder, Vivian D. (O. 1, 1937, Ruston, LA) Libn., Liberia Bapt. Theo. Semy., 1980–; Catlgr., New Orleans Bapt. Theo. Semy., 1978–79; Libn., Bapt. Theo. Semy., Rüschlikon, Switzerland, 1969–76; Cat. Asst., S. West. Bapt. Theo. Semy., Fort Worth, TX, 1967–68; Admn. Libn., Un. Par. Lib., Farmerville, LA, 1965–67; Ref. Libn., Lib. U.S.A., New York World's Fair, 1965; Admn. Libn., Caldwell Par. Lib., Columbia, LA, 1963–65. **Educ.:** LA Polytech. Inst., 1955–59, BA (Eng., Educ.); LA State Univ., 1963–64, MS (LS); New Orleans Bapt. Theo. Semy., 1976–78, MDiv, MRE (Theo. Couns.). **Orgs.:** ATLA. N.E. Reg. LA (LA): Ch. (1966–67). St. Charles Ave. Bapt. Church, New Orleans, LA: Lib. Com. (1978–). Volun. Srv., South. Bapt. Hosp. (New Orleans, LA): Gift Shop Staff (1979–). **Activities:** 12, 14-Theo. Lib.; 17, 20, 31; 54, 90 **Addr.:** Liberia Baptist Theological Seminary, P.O. Box 1778, Monrovia, Liberia West Africa.

Holicky, Bernard H. (S. 1, 1937, Cleveland, OH) Dir. of Lib. Srvs., Assoc. Prof. of LS, Purdue Univ., Calumet, 1966–; Asst. Ref. Libn., Purdue Univ., W. Lafayette, 1963–66; Acq. Libn., Cornell Univ. Law Lib., 1961–63. **Educ.:** OH Univ., 1955–59, AB (Gvt.); Case Western Reserve Univ., 1959–61, MSLS. **Orgs.:** IN LA: Ch., Coll. & Univ. Div. (1972); Ch., Schol. & Loan Fund (1976–78); Dir.-at-Large (1978–79). ALA. IN Film Cncl. Frdm. to Read Fndn. Other orgs. Amer. Civil Liberties Un. **Pubns.:** "The Microbook Library," *Focus on IN Libs.* (Fall 1973); "Recommend A Dirty Book," *Focus on IN Libs.* (Spr. 1972); "Loan Agreements Among Lake County Academic Libraries," *Focus on IN Libs.* (Je. 1971); Reviews. **Activities:** 1; 17 **Addr.:** 7218 Ontario Ave., Hammond, IN 46323.

Holladay, Janice W. (Ja. 1, 1937, Beckley, WV) Head, Ref. Dept., Rush Rhees Lib., Univ. of Rochester, 1981–, Actg. Head, Sci. and Engin. Lib., 1980–81, Asst. Head, Sci. and Engin. Lib., 1977–79; Lib. Dir., Taylor Instrument's Lib., 1974–77; Info. Spec., Xerox Corp., 1972–74. **Educ.:** Univ. of TN, 1956, BS (Chem.); St. Univ. of NY (Geneseo), 1970–72, MLS. **Orgs.:** SLA: NY Chap., VP (1979–80), Pres. (1980–81). Rochester Area Online Users Grp.: Org. Grp., Coord. (1978–79). ALA: ACRL. **Honors:** Phi Kappa Phi, 1959. **Pubns.:** "Small Libraries: Keeping the Professional Position Professional," *Spec. Libs.* (Ja. 1981). "Toxicity, Toxicology Handling & Disposal of Se, SeO2 & H2Se," *Xerox Rept #x77–04131* (Jl. 1973); "Bibliography of Waterless LRthography," *Xerox Rept #77–04126* (D. 1973). Various speeches and lectures. **Activities:** 1; 15, 17, 39; 56, 64, 91 **Addr.:** Rush Rhees Library, University of Rochester, Rochester, NY 14627.

Holland, Edna C. (D. 15, 1921, Antigo, WI) Head Libn., Gail Borden Pub. Lib. Dist., 1962–; Field Libn., WI Div. for Lib. Srvs., 1960–62; Head Libn., Antigo Pub. Lib., 1947–60; Chldn. Libn., 1944–47. **Educ.:** Northland Coll., 1939–45, BA (Eng.); Case-Western Resrv. Univ., 1947–51, BSLS. **Orgs.:** WI LA. ALA: Mem. Ch. for 12 (1969–73). IL LA: Lib. Legis. and Dev. Com (1973); VP, Pres. Elect (1974–75); Pres. (1975–76). N. Suburban Lib. Syst.: Reg. Advis. Com (1968–72). Zonta Club of Elgin: Pres. (1969–71); Secy (1973–75). First Congretional Church: Deaconess (1965–66). **Honors:** IL LA, Libn. of the Year, 1977. **Activities:** 9; 17, 35, 36; 66, 68, 80 **Addr.:** Gail Borden Public Library District, 200 N Grove Ave., Elgin, IL 60120.

Holland, F. Alleene (Ag. 18, 1939, Okemah, OK) Lib./Media Spec., C. A. Taylor Elem. Sch., 1976–; Lib. Media Spec., Lexington Elem. Sch., 1974–76. **Educ.:** Univ. of SC, BA (Elem. Educ.), 1973–74, MLS. **Orgs.:** SC Assn. of Sch. Libs.: Pres. (1980–81); Mem. Ch. (1976–79); Contact Ch. (1974–76). SC LA: Plng. Com. (1979–80); YA, Chld. Strg. Com. (1978–79). ALA. Natl. Educ. Assn. SC Educ. Assn. Brooklyn-Cayce Educ. Assn. **Activities:** 10; 21, 32, 36; 63 **Addr.:** 501 Nottingham Rd., Columbia, SC 29210.

Holland, Harold Edward (Jl. 16, 1924, Nashville, TN) Dir. of Libs., Pepperdine Univ., 1981–; Assoc. Prof., LS, Univ. of MO, 1977–81, Asst. Prof., 1967–77; Visit. Assoc. Prof., LS, Pahlavi Univ., 1977–78; Ch., Dept. of LS, Appalachian State Univ., 1965–67; Asst. Prof., LS, Univ. of OK, 1963–64; Sr. Libn., Aerospace Corp., 1960–63; Libn., Pepperdine Coll., 1958–61. **Educ.:** David Lipscomb Coll., 1941–43; Harding Coll., 1943–45, BA (Eng.); Vanderbilt Univ., 1946–47, (Sci.); Harding Coll., 1954–55, MA (Relig.); Columbia Univ., 1955–57 MS (LS), 1964–65, 1976, DLS; Univ. of South. CA, 1961–62, (LS). **Orgs.:** SLA: Dir., OK Chap., (1963–64); Grt. St. Louis Chap., Treas. (1972–73); Pres.-Elect (1973–74); Pres. (1974–75); Mid-MO Chap., Treas. (1976–77). ALA. MO LA. AALS. Hymn Socty. of Amer. Disciples of Christ Hist. Socty. **Pubns.:** "The Hymnody of the Churches of Christ," *The Hymn* (O. 1979); "Academic Libraries and the History of Science," Univ. of IL Grad. Sch. of Lib. Sci. *Occasional Papers* (Ja. 1968); "Teaching Dictionary Use," *RQ* (Fall 1966). **Activities:** 11; 25, 26, 41; 57, 90, 91 **Addr.:** Pepperdine Univ., Malibu, CA 90265.

Special Subjects/Services: 50. Adult educ.; 51. Advert./Mktg.; 52. Aerosp.; 53. Agric.; 54. Area std.; 55. Arts/Hum.; 56. Autom.; 57. Bibl./Prtg.; 58. Bio. sci.; 59. Bus./Fin.; 60. Chem.; 61. Copyrt.; 62. Documtn.; 63. Educ.; 64. Engin.; 65. Env.; 66. Eth. grps.; 67. Film; 68. Food/Nutr.; 69. Geneal.; 70. Geo.; 71. Geol.; 72. Handcpd.; 73. Hist.; 74. Int. frdm.; 75. Info. sci.; 76. Insr.; 77. Law; 78. Legis.; 79. Math./Comp. sci.; 80. Med.; 81. Metals; 82. Nat. resrcs.; 83. Newsp.; 84. Nuc. sci.; 85. Oral hist.; 86. Petr./Energy; 87. Pharm.; 88. Phys./Astr./Math.; 89. Readg.; 90. Relig.; 91. Sci./Tech.; 92. Soc. sci.; 93. Telecom.; 94. Transp.; 95. (other).

Holland, Jane Dizer (Mr. 1, 1950, Valparaiso, IN) Libn., Fulbright and Jaworski, 1977–, Asst. Libn., 1974–76; ILL Libn., Univ. of OK, 1973–74. **Educ.:** IN Univ., 1968–72, AB (Hist.), 1972–73, MLS. **Orgs.:** AALL: Rel. with Publshrs. and Dlrs. (1979–80). Southwest. Assn. of Law Libs. Houston Area Law Libns.: Place. Ofcr. (1980–81). **Honors:** Phi Beta Kappa, 1972. **Activities:** 12; 15, 17, 39; 77 **Addr.:** Fulbright and Jaworski, Bank of the Southwest Bldg., Houston, TX 77002.

Holland, Mary Kathryn (My. 20, 1949, Avoca, PA) Asst. Prof., LS, AV Comms., Kutztown State Coll., 1981–; Asst. Prof.–Lib./Media, Univ. of NE, Omaha, 1978–81; Asst. Instr., E. TX State Univ., 1976–78; Tchr., Petersburg Pub. Sch., 1972–75. **Educ.:** Coll. of William and Mary, 1969–72, BA (Sec. Educ.); E. TX State Univ., 1975–76, MLS, 1976–78, EdD. **Orgs.:** ALA. NE LA: Anglo Amer. Cat. Rules II Org. and Implementation Com. (1979–80). AECT. NE Educ. Media Assn. **Honors:** Kappa Delta Pi; Phi Delta Kappa. **Pubns.:** "A Factorial Study of Library Media Proficiencies," *Intl. Jnl. of Instr. Media* (Ja. 1981); "Literature for Adolescents and Self-Concept," *Prejudice Project;* "CAI and ET-ERIC," *Natl. Conf. on CAI Conf. Papers* (My. 1978); "OCLC-Simulation," CAI prog. (1977); "The Use of ERIC" movie (1977). **Activities:** 10, 11; 20, 26, 32; 56, 63, 75 **Addr.:** 80 S. Elm. #D, Kutztown, PA 19530.

Holland, Maurita Peterson (Mr. 5, 1944, Sault Ste. Marie, MI) Head, Tech. Libs., Univ. of MI, 1974–, Ref. Libn., Engin.-Transp. Lib., 1972–73; Ref. Libn., Ann Arbor Pub. Lib., 1968–70. **Educ.:** Univ. of MI, 1962–65, BMsc. (Msc. Lit.), 1965–66, MALS. **Orgs.:** SLA: Engin. Div., (Secy./Treas., 1978–80). Assn. of Info. Mgrs. Amer. Socty. for Engin. Educ.: Engin. Libs. Div., Program Ch., (1978–79); Accred. Com., (1979–). **Pubns.:** Jt. auth., "Information resources in engineering courses," *Engin. Educ.* (N. 1979); "Serials cuts vs. public service: a formula," *Coll. & Resrch. Libs.* (N. 1976); "Library facilities for technical research," videotape (1980); "Online bibliographic data bases–can they help you?" videotape (1977). **Activities:** 1; 17, 31, 39; 64, 91, 94 **Addr.:** Engineering-Transportation Library, University of Michigan, Ann Arbor, MI 48109.

Hollander, Patricia A. (Ag. 27, 1942, Brooklyn, NY) Lib. Dir., Catskill Pub. Lib., 1978–. **Educ.:** Skidmore U.W.W., 1974–75, BA (LS); SUNY, Albany, 1975–77, MLS. **Orgs.:** Greene Cnty. LA: Pres. (1981–82). ALA. NY LA. Litcy. Voluns. of Amer. **Honors:** Beta Phi Mu. **Pubns.:** Ed., African Sect., *Magazines for Libraries* (1978); Jt. auth., "Contrasts: Black and White Women," *Black Collegian* (F. 1980). **Activities:** 9; 16, 17, 20; 50, 74, 89 **Addr.:** Catskill Public Library, 1 Franklin St., Catskill, NY 12414.

Holleman, Belva Bise (O. 22, 1928, Uniontown, PA) Elem. Libn., Rocky Hill Sch., Knoxville, TN, 1972–. **Educ.:** Coll. of St. Francis, Joliet, IL, 1966–70, BA (Eng.); Univ. of TN, 1971–74, MSLS, 1975–79, EdD (Curric. & Instr.). **Orgs.:** ALA. E. TN LA: Pres. (1978–79). TN LA. Intl. Reading Assn. TN Educ. Assn. E. TN Educ. Assn. Natl. Educ. Assn. **Honors:** H. W. Wilson–ALA, John Cotton Dana Awd., 1975. **Pubns.:** "Pet Lending," *Sch. Media Qtly.* (Win. 1977); 3 30-min. radio progs. on sch. libs., (1979–). **Activities:** 10; 21, 24; 55, 63 **Addr.:** 5405 Riverbend Dr., Knoxville, TN 37919.

Holleman, Curtis P. (Ja. 22, 1944, Grand Rapids, MI) Libn. for Col. Dev., South. Meth. Univ., 1976–, Ref. Libn., 1973–76; Asst. Prof., Park Coll., 1967–70. **Educ.:** Hope Coll., 1961–65, BA (Eng.); Univ. of KS, 1965–67, MA (Eng.); Univ. of TX, 1971–73, MLS. **Orgs.:** ALA. TX LA. Interuniv. Cncl.: Acq. Com. (Ch., 1978–79). **Honors:** Phi Kappa Phi, 1973; Beta Phi Mu, 1973. **Pubns.:** "A Distinguished Press Approval Plan for Academic Libraries of Medium Size," *Procs. of Fourth Intl. Conf. on Approval Plans and Col. Dev.* (1980). **Activities:** 1; 15 **Addr.:** 7305 Dalewood Ln., Dallas, TX 75214.

Holleman, Marian I. (Jl. 23, 1923, Toronto, ON) Univ. Libn., Assoc. Prof., Lib. Sci., Univ. of San Diego, 1973–; Head Libn., San Diego Coll. for Women, 1969–73, Catlgr., 1964–69; Libn., Bishop's Sch., Toronto, 1962–64; Libn., Acad. of Med. 1947–61. **Educ.:** Univ. of Toronto, 1941–45, BA hons. (Hist.), 1945–48, BLS, MA (LS, Hist.); Med. LA, 1951, Cert. (Med. Libnshp.). **Orgs.:** SLA: Toronto Chap., Past Pres.; San Diego Chap., Past Pres.; Bltn. Ed.; Bd. of Dirs. Med. LA: Conv. Ch. (1959). Victoria Coll. Alum. **Honors:** Murray Gottlieb Prize Essay Awd., 1957. **Pubns.:** Ed., *Sci. Mtgs.* (1962–); various articles (1950–69). **Activities:** 1; 17, 31; 55, 80 **Addr.:** University of San Diego, James S. Copley Library, Alcala Park, San Diego, CA 92110.

Hollenhorst, Sr. Bernice (S. 15, 1929, St. Cloud, MN) Head Libn., St. Mary's Coll., Notre Dame, IN, 1975–. **Educ.:** St. Mary's Coll., 1960, BA (Hist.); Rosary Coll., 1967, MALS. **Orgs.:** ALA. IN LA. Cath. LA. IN Coop. Lib. Srvs. Athrty.: Bd. of Dirs. (1976–); Mem.-at-Large, Exec. Com. (1978–81). **Activities:** 1; 17, 39 **Addr.:** Saint Mary's College Library, Notre Dame, IN 46556.

Holley, Edward Gailon (N. 26, 1927, Pulaski, TN) Dean, Sch. of LS, Univ. of NC, 1972–; Dir. of Libs., Univ. of Houston, 1962–71; Educ., Phil. & Psy. Libn., Univ. of IL, 1957–62; Asst. Libn., David Lipscomb Coll., 1949–51. **Educ.:** David Lipscomb Coll., 1946–49, BA magna cum laude (Eng.); George Peabody Coll., TN, 1949–51, MA (LS); Univ. of IL, 1951–52, 1956–61, PhD (LS). **Orgs.:** ALA: Legis. Com. (1976–78, Ch., 1976–77); Pubn. Bd. Ch. (1975–); VP (1973–74); Pres. (1974–75); Exec. Bd. (1973–76); Ed., *ACRL Pubn. in Libnshp.* (1969–72). TX LA: Pres. (1971). AALS. NCLA. Other orgs. Kappa Delta Pi. Phi Kappa Phi. Disciples of Christ Hist. Socty.: Bd. of Trustees (1973–). AAUP. **Honors:** ALA, Scarecrow Press Awd., 1964; Beta Phi Mu; Visit. Schol., Univ. of HI, 1978. **Pubns.:** *Charles Evans, American Bibliographer,* (1963); *Raking the Historic Coals; The ALA Scrapbook of 1876* (1967); Jt. auth., *Resources of South Carolina Libraries* (1976); "ALA at 100" in *ALA Yrbk.* (1976); "What Lies Ahead for Academic Libraries" in *Acad. Libs. by the Year 2000,* (1977); other books, articles, reviews. **Activities:** 1, 11; 17, 35; 61, 78 **Addr.:** 100 Manning Hall 026-A, University of North Carolina, Chapel Hill, NC 27514.

Holley, Robert Paul (M. 1, 1944, Toledo, OH) Asst. Dir. for Tech. Srvs., Univ. of UT, 1980–; Asst. to Head Libn., Cat. Dept., Yale Univ., 1975–79, Head Soc. Sci. Sect., Subj. Cat. Div., 1974–75, Soc. Sci. Catlgr., 1973–74. **Educ.:** Xavier Univ., 1962–65, 1966–67, AB (Fr., Latin), Yale Univ., 1967–71, PhD, (Fr.); Columbia Univ., 1972–73, MLS; Univ. de Lyon, 1965–66, (Fr.). **Orgs.:** ALA: RTSD (Ch., Prof. in Acad. Resrch. Tech. Srvs. Discuss. Grp. (1978–80); Catlg. and Class. Sect., Subj. Anal. Com. (1979–); ACRL; LITA. UT LA. **Honors:** Woodrow Wilson Fellowship, 1967. Columbia Univ., Tauber–Begner Awd. in Tech. Srvs, 1974. **Pubns.:** "Processing OCLC MARC subscription tapes at Yale University, *Jrnl. of Lib. Auto.* (Mr. 1979). "A Modest proposal on modern literature collection development" Jrnl. of Acad. Libnshp. (My. 1979). **Activities:** 1; 46; 55, 56 **Addr.:** Marriott Library, University of Utah, Salt Lake City, UT 84112.

Holli, Melvin G. (F. 22, 1933, Ishpeming, MI) Prof., Dir. Urban Hist. Col., Univ. IL (Chicago), 1966–; Cur., MI Hist. Col., Univ. MI, 1960–63. **Educ.:** N. MI Univ., 1954–57, BA (Hist.); Univ. MI, 1961–66, PhD (Hist.). **Orgs.:** SAA. Amer. Hist. Assn. Org. Amer. Hist. Swedish Pioneer Socty. Finnish Amer. Hist. Socty.: Ed. Bd. **Honors:** Woodrow Wilson Fndn., Flwsh., 1958; Natl. Endowment Hum., NEH Flwsh., 1969–70; Fulbright, Prof. (Finland), 1978. **Pubns.:** *Reform in Detroit* (1969); *The Ethnic Frontier* (1977); "Detroit: Locked in the Past," *Mid W. Qtly.* (Spr. 1978); "French Detroit", *IN Soc. Sci. Qtly.* (Spr. 1976); Ed. Film: "Polish Army in Russia 1944," (1977). **Activities:** 1; 15; 66, 92 **Addr.:** Dept. of History, University of Illinois, Chicago, IL 60680.

Hollingsworth, Anne E. (Ap. 5, 1951, Quanah, TX) Media Consult., TX State Lib., 1977–81; Media Libn., S. TX Lib. Supt., 1974–77. **Educ.:** Univ. of TX, 1969–73, BA (Eng.), 1973–74, MLS, 1978–, MBA, 1981. **Orgs.:** ALA: JMRT (Pres., 1980–81); Exec. Bd. (1977–78, 1979–80). TX LA: Cncl. (1977–78, 1979–80); JMRT (Pres., 1977–78); Plng. Com. (Ch., 1979–80). AECT. TX Assn. for Educ. Tech: Exec. Com. (1978–80). **Honors:** Beta Phi Mu; Phi Kappa Phi. **Pubns.:** Jt. auth., *A Librarian's Planning Handbook 1979: In Search of Texas Treasures* (1979); "Flick On-Films Come to South Texas" *TX Libs.* (Fall, 1976); Reviews. **Activities:** 9, 13; 24, 25, 32, 36; 51, 63, 67 **Addr.:** 7122 Wordhollow #17, Austin, TX 78731.

Holloway, George Martin (N. 28, 1923, Hickory, NC) Head, Com. Srvs., Free Lib. of Philadelphia, 1973–, Head, Reg. Film Ctr., 1966–73, Head, Educ. Films Dept., 1959–66, Libn. II, 1953–58; Asst. Libn., Hill Sch., Pottstown, PA 1950–53. **Educ.:** Univ. of NC, 1942, 1946–48, BA (Radio Prod.); Drexel Univ., 1949–50, MSLS. **Orgs.:** ALA: AV Com. Booklist Film Preview Sub-Com. (1960–67). PLA, AV Com. (1973–76). PA LA: AV Com. Ch. (1963–65). Film Lib. Info. Cncl.: Brd. of Dir. (1968–72). Middle Atlantic Film Board. Adult Educ. Cncl. of Philadelphia. **Activities:** 10; 17, 24 **Addr.:** 58 W. Tulpehocken St., Philadelphia, PA 19144.

Holloway, Jean A. (F. 16, 1920, Dorchester, MA) Resrc. Ctr. Libn., Sch. of LS, Univ. of WI, Milwaukee, 1980–; Asst. Libn., V Brown Deer Pub. Lib., 1974–80; Lib. Dir., Wissahickon Valley Pub. Lib., 1966–72; Lib. Dir., Topsfield Town Lib., 1960–63. **Educ.:** Simmons Coll., 1938–39; Univ. of WI-Milwaukee, 1975–78, BS (Eng.), 1979–80, MLS; MA Cert. for Small Pub. Lib., 1961. **Orgs.:** WI LA. **Activities:** 1, 11; 15, 20, 39; 56, 74, 75 **Addr.:** School of Library Science, University of Wisconsin - Milwaukee, Mitchell Hall P.O. Box 413, Milwaukee, WI 53201.

Holly, James Francis (Je. 9, 1915, Pittsburgh, PA) Consult., 1973–, Dean, Lib. Srvs., Evergreen State Coll., 1969–73; Libn., Assoc. Prof., Macalester Coll., 1959–69; Assoc. Libn., Asst. Prof., Univ. of Omaha, 1957–59; Circ., Carnegie Lib., Pittsburgh, 1941–42. **Educ.:** PA State Coll., 1939, BA, 1951, MA; Carnegie Inst. of Tech., 1941, BSLS. **Orgs.:** ALA: ACRL, Midw. Acad. Libns. Conf. (Ch., 1963–65). WA LA. Pac. NW LA. AAUP. Amer. Civil Liberties Un. **Addr.:** 3004 Cloverfield Dr. S.E., Olympia, WA 98501.

Holm, Blair I. (D. 3, 1935, Miller, SD) Chld. Libn., Colton Pub. Lib., 1980–; Libn., Chld. Libn., Riverside Pub. Lib., 1977–80; Branch Libn., Chino Branch, San Bernardino Cnty. Lib., 1970–74. **Educ.:** Mt. San Antonio Jr. Coll., 1957–61, AA (Liberal Arts); CA State Polytech. Univ., Pomona, 1966–70, BS (Soc. Sci.); Univ. of South. CA, 1970–76, MSLS. **Orgs.:** CA LA: Chld. Srvs. Chap. Inland Lib. Syst.: Chld. Srvs. Com. (Vice-Ch., 1980–81, Ch., 1981–82); PR Com. South. CA Cncl. On Lit. For Chld. And Young People. **Activities:** 9; 21, 36 **Addr.:** 4057 Oakwood Pl., Riverside, CA 92506.

Holman, Anna L. (Ap. 1, 1927, Kinburn, ON) Libn.-in-charge, Educ. Lib., Univ. of West. ON, 1972–; Supvsr. of Libs., Ottawa Bd. of Educ., 1965–72; Chief of Pub. Srvs., Carleton Univ. Lib., 1961–65; Asst. Libn., Leamington Pub. Lib., 1953–61. **Educ.:** Carleton Univ., 1947–49, BA (Arts); McGill Univ., 1949–50, BLS. **Orgs.:** ON LA: Secy. Treas., ON Coll. and Univ. LA (1977–79); Cnclr. (1972–73). **Pubns.:** Reviews. **Activities:** 1; 17; 63 **Addr.:** Apt. 1109, 1 Grosvenor St., London, ON N6A 1Y2 Canada.

Holman, William R. (S. 7, 1926, Oklahoma City, OK) Prof., Grad. Sch. of LS, Univ. of TX, 1978–, Head Libn., Hum. Resrch. Ctr., 1967–78; Dir., San Francisco Pub. Lib., 1960–67; Dir., San Antonio Pub. Lib., 1957–60; Dir., Rosenberg Lib., Galveston, 1955–57; Head Libn., Pan American Coll., 1951–55. **Educ.:** Univ. of OK, 1946–49, BS (Hist & Soc. Sci.); Univ. of IL, 1950–51, MLS. **Orgs.:** ALA: Cncl. (1964–67), Ch., Pub. Info. Com. (1964–66); Friends of the Lib. Com. (1957–60). TX LA: Ch., Legis. Com. (1956–58). Book Club of CA: Bd. of Dir. (1961–67). Roxburgh Club. Grolier Club. **Pubns.:** *Library Publications* (1965); "Friends of the Library in Metropolitan Libraries," *Friends of the Lib.* (1962); *Bookplates for Libs.* (1968); "Eric Gill, Master of Letter Forms," *The Lib. Chronicle* (N. 1970); "Rosenberg Library...," *Lib. Jnl.* (Mr. 15, 1957). **Activities:** 1, 9; 17, 23, 37 **Addr.:** 4509 Balcones, Austin, TX 78731.

Holmer, Susan E. (S. 27, 1948, San Francisco, CA) Ref. Coord., Peninsula Lib. Syst., 1981–; Ref. Libn., Modesto-Stanislaus Cnty. Pub. Lib., 1979–81; Outrch. Libn., Peninsula Lib. Syst., 1977–79; Libn., Burlingame Pub. Lib., 1976–77. **Educ.:** San Francisco State Univ., 1971–75, BA (Art Hist.); San Jose State Univ., 1975–76, MLS. **Pubns.:** "Outreach Services: The Library is For Everyone," *Prime Times* (Win. 1978); "Reaching Out to The Aged: How a Public Library Outreach Program Serves The Elderly," *Aging Mag.* (S.–O. 1979); "Sharing Outreach: How One Program Serves Several Communities," *News Notes of CA Libs.* (1978); "Volunteering For The Library," *Prime Times* (Sum. 1978); "When The Money Runs Out: San Mateo County Cities Sustain Library Outreach Services," *West. City* (S. 1978); reviews. **Activities:** 9; 15, 37, 39 **Addr.:** Peninsula Library System, 55 W. 3rd Ave., San Mateo, CA 94403.

Holmes, Jeanne Maiden (F. 10, 1922, Dayton, OH) Consult., 1979–; Deputy Dir. for Resrc. Dev., Natl. Agri. Lib., 1975–79, Chief, Analysis Div., 1971–75, Chief, Div. of Cat. and Recs., 1962–71, various positions, 1952–62. **Educ.:** George Washington Univ., 1943, BA (Eng.); Columbia Univ., 1952, MS (LS). **Orgs.:** ALA: various coms. (1952–). Coastal GA Hist. Socty.: Col. Org. (1979–). **Honors:** Beta Phi Mu; US Dept. of Agri. Spec. Merit Awd., 1966; Superior Srv. Awd., 1968, 1974. **Activities:** 4, 8; 17, 30, 46; 55, 58 **Addr.:** P.O. Box 416, Sea Island, GA 31561.

Holmes, Jill M. (N. 30, 1940, Tulsa, OK) Educ. Libn., OK State Univ. Lib., 1967–; Libn., US Army Spec. Srvs., Ulm and Munich, Germany, 1965–67; Asst. Phys. Sci. Libn., OK State Univ., 1963–65. **Educ.:** N. TX State Univ., 1958–61, BS (Elem. Educ.); OK State Univ., 1980, BA (Grmn.); TX Women's Univ., 1961–63, MLS. **Orgs.:** ALA. OK LA. Natl. Educ. Assn. OK Educ. Assn. Natl. Women's Std. Assn. Women in Grmn. **Honors:** Alpha Chi, 1960. **Pubns.:** "Education: A Selected Bibliography of Reference Sources," *OK Libn.* (1980); Clmnst., *Educ. Libs.* (1981–); "What a bon voyage: Special Services Libraries," *OK Libn.* (1968); "Library of Congress career subject headings," *RQ* (1977); "A bibliography of bibliographies of tests and assessment instruments," *Educ. Libs.* (1979). **Activities:** 5; 15, 31, 39; 63, 92 **Addr.:** Library, Social Sciences Division, Oklahoma State University, Stillwater, OK 74078.

Holmes, Robert R. (My. 31, 1922, NJ) Lib. Consult., 1980–; Dir. Cat. Mgt., Prod. and Pubn., Lib. of Congs., 1978–80, Asst. Dir., Prcs. Dept., 1969–78, Chief, Subj. Cat. Div., 1967–69, Asst. Chief, Subj. Cat. Div., 1961–67, Head, E. European Accessions Index, 1958–61, Head, European Exch. Sect., 1956–58, Head, Amer. and British Exch. Sect., 1954–56, other positions, 1952–54. **Educ.:** George Washington Univ., 1940–47, AB (Eng. Lit.); Columbia Univ., 1947–48, MA (Eng. Lit.), 1948–49, 1951–52, MS (LS). **Orgs.:** ALA. Southeast. Univ.: Trustee (1977–). Frnds. of the Lighthouse Musm., St. Simons, Island, GA: Pres. (1981–). **Honors:** Beta Phi Mu, 1967. **Addr.:** Cottage 340, PO Box 416, Sea Island, GA 31561.

Holmes, Rose F. (Je. 10, 1918, Madison, WI) Supvsr., Media Prcs. Srvs., Madison Metro. Sch. Dist., 1965–; Libn., Proviso Twp. HS (Maywood, IL), 1965; Libn., US Air Force, Truax Field, Madison, WI, 1961–63; Libn., RCA Whirlpool, St. Joseph, MI, 1957–58. **Educ.:** Univ. of WI, 1935–39, BS (Eng.), 1939–40, MA (LS). **Orgs.:** ALA. WI LA: Tech. Srvs. Sect., Secy./Treas. (1972); WI Sch. Lib. Media Assn.: Pres. (1977). Univ. of WI Lib. Sch. Alum. Assn.: Mem. Ch. (1975). Madison

PROFESSIONAL ACTIVITIES: Institutions: 1. Acad. lib.; 2. Arch.; 3. Assn.; 4. Fed./Gvt. lib.; 5. Inst. lib.; 6. Mfr./Suppl.; 7. Milit. lib.; 8. Musm.; 9. Pub. lib.; 10. Sch. lib.; 11. Sch. of lib. sci.; 12. Spec. lib.; 13. State lib.; 14. (other). **Functions/Activities:** 15. Acq./Col. dev.; 16. Adult srvs.; 17. Admin.; 18. Apprais.; 19. Archit./Bldgs.; 20. Cat./Class.; 21. Chld. srvs.; 22. Circ.; 23. Cons./Pres.; 24. Consult.; 25. Cont. ed.; 26. Educ. lib. sci.; 27. Ext. srvs.; 28. Fund/Grants; 29. Gvt. pubs.; 30. Indx./Abs.; 31. Instr. lib. use; 32. Media srvs.; 33. Micro.; 34. Netwks./Coop.; 35. Persnl.; 36. PR; 37. Publshg.; 38. Recs. mgt.; 39. Ref. srvs.; 40. Repro.; 41. Resrch.; 42. Review.; 43. Secur.; 44. Serials; 45. Spec. col.; 46. Tech. srvs.; 47. Trustees/Bds.; 48. YA srvs.; 49. (other).

Who's Who in Library and Information Services

Area Lib. Cncl. **Pubns.:** *Cataloging, Processing, Administering AV Materials; a model for Wis. Schools* (1972); *Organizing Audiovisual Instructional Materials* (1970); "Madison Public Schools' Automated Library Processing System," *WI Lib. Bltn.* (S. 1970); "Madison Public Schools' ALPS and OCLC," *WI Lib. Bltn.* (N. 1978). **Activities:** 10; 15, 20, 32, 46; 56, 63 **Addr.:** 2802 Wimbledon Way, Madison, WI 53713.

Holmgren, Edwin Surl (Je. 13, 1934, Rock Springs, WY) Dir., Branch Lib. Syst., NY Pub. Lib., 1971–; Asst. Dir. for Gen. Admin. and Tech. Srvs., Rochester Pub. Lib., 1965–70; Asst. Dir., New Orleans Pub. Lib., 1962–65; Lib. Consult., Charles M. Upham Assoc. Inc. for Royal Thai Highway Dept., Bangkok, Thailand, 1960–62; Asst. Dir., Actg. Dir., Summit Free Pub. Lib., (1957–60); Ref. Asst., Gary Pub. Lib., (1956–57). **Educ.:** Stanford Univ., 1952–55, AB (Eng.); Univ. of IL, 1955–56, MS (LS). **Orgs.:** ALA. NY LA. SLA. Thai LA. Amer. Assn. of Musms. Amer. Socty. for Pub. Admin. **Honors:** Beta Phi Mu, 1956; Phi Beta Kappa, 1955. **Addr.:** The Branch Library System, The New York Public Library, 8 East 40th St., New York, NY 10016.

Holoch, S. Alan (D. 5, 1947, Farmer City, IL) Assoc. Dir. Law Lib., Adj. Asst. Prof. Law, Univ. of South. CA 1978–, Head, Tech. Srvs. Dept., 1973–75, Ref. Libn., 1971–73. **Educ.:** Washington Univ. (St. Louis), 1965–69, AB (Fr.); Univ. of South. CA, 1970–71, MSLS, 1975–78, JD. **Orgs.:** AALL: Educ. Com. (1978–). South. CA Assn. Law Libs.: Pres. (1980–81). SLA: Soc. Sci. Div. CA St. Bar Assn. Los Angeles Cnty. Bar Assn. **Honors:** Beta Phi Mu, 1971. **Pubns.:** Jt. Cmplr., *Medical Malpractice Insurance and Its Alternatives* (1975); "Index, Volume 11," *The Intl. Lawyer* (1976–1977); Jt. Cmplr., *Comparative Constitutional and Administrative Law* (1979); Jt. Cmplr., *Attorney Specialization and Certification: An Annotated Bibliography* (1978). **Activities:** 1, 12; 17, 39, 41; 77, 78, 95-International Organizations. **Addr.:** Law Library, University of Southern California, University Park, Los Angeles, CA 90007.

Holst, Ruth M. (S. 22, 1947, Fond du lac, WI) Med. Libn., Columbia Hosp., 1970. **Educ.:** Univ. WI (Milwaukee) 1965–70, BS (Educ.), 1970–73, MS (LS). **Orgs.:** Med. LA: Hosp. Lib. Impact Com. (Ch., 1978–81). SLA. WI Hlth. Sci. Libns. Assn.: Secy. (1979–80). Cncl. Hlth. Sci. Lib.: Pres. (1978–79); Record. Secy. (1975–77). Mid W. Hlth. Sci. Lib. Netwk.: Ref. Com. (1977–80); Cnsrtm. Dev. Com. (1978–80). Various other orgs. and coms.). **Pubns.:** Assoc. ed., *Hospital Library Management* (due 1982). **Activities:** 5, 12; 15, 17, 39; 80 **Addr.:** Columbia Hospital, Medical Library, 2025 E. Newport Ave, Milwaukee, WI 53211.

Holsworth, Patricia L. (My. 2, 1937, Emporia, KS) Reg. Libn., Cuyahoga Cnty. Pub. Lib., 1977–, Head, Adult Srvs., Fairview Park Reg. Branch, 1975–77, Branch Libn., Bay Village Branch, 1971–75, Head, Adult Srvs., Brook Park Branch, 1970–71. **Educ.:** Anderson Coll., 1954–58, BS (Math.); Case Western Reserve Univ., 1969–70, MSLS. **Orgs.:** ALA. OH LA: Div. VI Secy. (1974); Reg. Mtgs. Local Ch. (1980). **Activities:** 9; 16, 35, 36 **Addr.:** 27485 Hollywood Dr., Westlake, OH 44145.

Holt, Barbara Cornwell (Mr. 31, 1950, Enumclaw, WA) Assoc. Libn., Perkins, Coie, Stone, Olsen & Williams, 1976–; Instr., Highline Cmnty. Coll., 1978–. **Educ.:** Kalamazoo Coll., 1968–72, BA (Hist.); Univ. of WA, 1974–75, MLS. **Orgs.:** AALL: Place. Com. (1978–80). SLA: Nwsltr. Ed., Pac. NW Chap. (1978–81). **Honors:** Beta Phi Mu. **Activities:** 12; 15, 39, 46; 77 **Addr.:** Perkins, Coie, Stone Olsen & Williams, 1900 Washington Bldg., Seattle, WA 98101.

Holt, Constance Wall (S. 9, 1932, Cleveland, OH) Ref. Libn., Univ. of WI (Oshkosh), 1980–; Ref. Libn., Wayne State Univ., 1977–80; Dir., Abington Coop. Lib. Cncl., 1976. **Educ.:** OH State Univ., 1950–54, BS (Bus. Adm.), Syracuse Univ., 1970–72, MS (Higher Educ.), NY SUNY Coll., Geneseo, 1976–77, MLS. **Orgs.:** ALA: ACRL. MI White House Conf. on Libs. and Info. Sci., (1979). Wayne State Univ. Libn. Assembly: V-Ch. (1978–79). AAUP. Nicolet Coop. Assn.: Brd. of Dir. (1978–80). **Honors:** Alpha Lambda Delta, 1951. Beta Gamma Sigma, 1954. Wayne St. Univ. Merit Award, 1979. **Pubns.:** *Political Science: A guide to library resources for undergraduates.* (1979. *Urban Research Resources: Detroit* (1979). *Undergraduate Psychology Guide* (1978). *Community Resources File* (1976). **Activities:** 1; 22, 31, 39; 59, 63, 92 **Addr.:** 3410 W. Silver Spring Dr., Milwaukee, WI 53209.

Holt, David Earl (My. 17, 1928, Magna, UT) Dir. of Libs., Austin Pub. Lib., 1967–; Dir., Waco-McLennan Cnty. Lib., 1965–67; Dir., Hayner Pub. Lib., 1963–65. **Educ.:** Brigham Young Univ., 1955–57, BA (Msc.), 1957–58, MA (Msc.); Emory Univ., 1962–63, MLN. **Orgs.:** TX LA. SWLA. ALA. **Activities:** 9; 17, 19, 24; 56, 75, 93 **Addr.:** Austin Public Library, 800 Guadalupe P.O. Box 2287, Austin, TX 78768.

Holt, June Celestine (Boston, MA) Libn. III, MA Rehab. Comsn. 1980–, Resrch. Anal., 1978–80, Resrch. Asst., 1976–78. **Educ.:** Boston State Coll., 1968–75, BA (Eng. Lit.); Simmons Coll., 1975–78, MLS. **Orgs.:** SLA: Boston Chap. Info. Ctr. Indiv. with Disabilities: Bd. of Trustees (1980). Boston Grp. of Gvt. Libns. Boston Biomed. Lib. Cnsrtm. **Pubns.:** "A Model Library: Community and Commission Benefit," *Jnl. of Rehab.* (Mr.-Ap. 1973). **Activities:** 4, 12; 15, 17, 22; 72, 92 **Addr.:** Library, Massachusetts Rehabilitation Commission, 20 Providence St., Room 331, Boston, MA 02116.

Holt, Raymond M. (Je. 3, 1921, San Bernardino, CA) Lib. Consult., 1970–; City Libn., Pomona Pub. Lib., 1950–70; Ref. Libn., Fullerton Pub. Lib., 1947–50. **Educ.:** Univ. of Redlands, 1938–42, AB (Hist.), Univ. of Southern CA, 1946–47, BSLS. **Orgs.:** CA LA. ALA: LAMA; LITA; ASCLA; PLA; various other orgs. Pacific Northwest Lib. Assn. Southern CA Local Hist. Cncl.: Pres., (1968–71). **Pubns.:** *Wisconsin Library Building Handbook* (1979). "Libraries," *Handbook of Building Security Planning and Design* (1978). *An Architectural Strategy for Change* (1976). *Focusing Library Service on the Economic Community* (1971). "Buildings," *The ALA Yearbook* (1976-). **Activities:** 1, 9; 17, 19, 24 **Addr.:** P.O. Box 745, Del Mar, CA 92014.

Holt, Wendy M. (F. 7, 1944, Reading, PA) Assoc. Libn., R and D Ctr. Lib., Carpenter Tech. Corp., 1978–; Asst. Catlgr., Reading Pub. Lib., 1973–78, Asst. Ref. Libn., 1966–72. **Educ.:** Albright Coll., 1962–66, AB (Grmn.); Drexel Univ., 1967–68, MS (LS). **Orgs.:** ASIS. SLA. Berks Cnty. LA: Pres. (1981–82). Early Amer. Socty. Hist. Socty. of Berks Cnty. Amer. Iron and Steel Inst.: Steel Libns. and Info. Ctrs. Indus. Mgt. Club. **Pubns.:** Jt. auth., "1st Continental Regiment/1st Pennsylvania Regiment Flag," *Milit. Collector and Histn.* (Spr. 1975). **Activities:** 12; 15, 20, 39; 60, 81, 91 **Addr.:** Carpenter Technology Corp., R & D Center Library, P.O. Box 662, Reading, PA 19603.

Holter, Charlotte S. (Je. 24, 1925, Frederick, MD) Supvsr. of Lib. Media Srvs., Bd. of Educ. of Frederick Cnty., 1972–; Dept. Ch., Libn., Gvr. Thomas Johnson HS, 1966–72; Libn., Frederick HS, 1962–64; Libn., New Midway Sch., 1964–66. **Educ.:** Hood Coll., 1942–46, AB (Soc., Psy.); Univ. of MD, 1969–72, M Educ (Admin./Tech.); Fellow in Prog. for Admin. in Curric. Tech., 1970–72. **Orgs.:** ALA. MD LA. MD Educ. Media Org. Educ. Media Assn. of Frederick Cnty.: Pres. Other orgs. Delta Kappa Gamma. **Pubns.:** Contrib., *Media Center Facility Design for Maryland Schools* (1975). **Activities:** 10; 17, 20, 24 **Addr.:** 5933 Holter Rd., Jefferson, MD 21755.

Holton, Tommy S. (D. 7, 1947, DeKalb, MS) Dir., Instr. Media Ctr., Dillard Univ., 1977–, Asst. Ref. Libn., 1976–77. **Educ.:** Dillard Univ., 1966–70, BA (Soclgy.); New Orleans Bapt. Theo. Semy., 1972–74, MRE (Soc. Work); Atlanta Univ., 1975–76, MSLS. **Orgs.:** ALA. LA AECT. LA LA: JMRT, Mem.-at-large (1978–81). SLA: LA Chap., Empl. Coord. (1977–80); Bd. of Dir. (1978–80); Secy./Treas. (1980–81); VP/Pres. Elect (1981–82). Other orgs. Alpha Phi Alpha Fraternity. American Legion. Dillard Univ. Alum. Assn. Jefferson Parish Cmnty. Dev. Agency. Other orgs. **Pubns.:** "Business is a Priceless Profession" slide program (1980); "Get a Piece of the Action: Free Enterprise" slide program (1981). **Activities:** 1; 17, 32; 63, 90, 92 **Addr.:** Instructional Media Center, Dillard University, New Orleans, LA 70122.

Holtz, Virginia H. (Jl. 6, 1932, Milwaukee, WI) Dir., Prof., Ctr. for Hlth. Sci. Lib., Univ. of WI, 1971–, Assoc. Libn., 1967–71, Ref. Libn., Outrch. Srvs., 1956–67. **Educ.:** WI State Coll., 1951–54, BA (Eng., Soclgy.); Univ. of WI, 1955–56, MSLS. **Orgs.:** Assn. of Acad. Hlth. Sci. Lib. Dirs.: Pres. (1981–82); Exec. Bd. (1980–83). Med. LA: Exec. Com. (1977–79); Bd. of Dirs. (1976–79); Comm. Com. (1980–); Pubn. Panel (1979–82); various coms. Madison Area Lib. Cncl.: Pres. (1972); Bd. (1971–73); Interlib. Rel. Com. (Ch., 1973). WI Assn. of Acad. Libns.: Exec. Bd. (1972); Lib. Dev. and Legis. Com. (1977). Various other orgs. Hlth. Plng. Cncl.: Pub. Info. and Educ. Com. (1972–). Midwest HSLN: Asm. Ch. (1979–80); Ref. Srvs. Plng. Subcom. (Ch., 1974–76); Ad Hoc Long Range Plng. Com. (1974–76). Various other orgs. **Pubns.:** "Medical Library Service," *WI Lib. Bltn.* (Mr.-Ap. 1969); ed., *WI Med. Libns. Nsltr.* (1968–71); ed., *Basic Library Management for Health Science Librarians* (1970); jt. auth., "Planning for Meaningful Change in Libraries and Library Networks: A First Step," *Bltn. of the Med. LA* (1976); contrib., "Medical Libraries, Measurement and Evaluation," *ALA World Encyc. of Lib. and Info. Srvs.* (1980); various articles. **Activities:** 1, 12; 17, 34; 61, 80 **Addr.:** University of Wisconsin, Center for Health Sciences Library, 1305 Linden Dr., Madison, WI 53562.

Holtze, Sally Holmes (O. 26, 1952, Des Moines, IA) Freelance Writer and Chlds. Bk. Critic; Copyed. Chlds. Bk. Dept., Macmillan Publshg. Co., Inc. 1978–79; Asst. Ed., Bk. Review., The Horn Bk. Mag., 1975–77. **Educ.:** Mt Holyoke Coll., 1971–74, BA (Eng.). **Orgs.:** ALA New Eng. LA. Frnds. New York Pub. Lib. **Pubns.:** "A Second Look: *Come By Here,*" *Horn Bk.* (F. 1980) Introductions to Gregg Press Reprints of *Cautionary Tales; Nurse Matilda.* **Activities:** 30, 37, 42; 89 **Addr.:** 45 Gramercy Park, New York, NY 10010.

Holz, Gloria Jean (O. 16, 1941, Black Creek, WI) Circ. Srvs. Libn., Law Lib., Univ. of WI, 1968–; Tchr., Mukwonago (WI) Union HS, 1965–67; Tchr., Kaukauna (WI) HS, 1964–65. **Educ.:** Lakeland Coll., 1960–64, BA (Eng., Grmn.); Univ. of WI, 1967–69, MA (LS). **Orgs.:** AALL: Contemporary Soc. Problems Com. (1975–76); Contemporary Soc. Problems Spec. Int. Sect. (1976–). **Activities:** 1, 13; 17, 22, 34; 77, 78 **Addr.:** Law Library, University of Wisconsin-Madison, Madison, WI 53706.

Holzberlein, Deanne B. (Oklahoma City, OK) Asst. Prof. of LS, Ball State Univ., 1979–; Sci. Ref./Cat. Libn., Principia Coll., 1974–78; Head, Gvt. Docum. Dept., St. Louis Pub. Lib., 1971–73; Instr., Instr. Media, South. IL Univ., Edwardsville, 1964–69. **Educ.:** OK State Univ., 1949–53, BS (Pol. Sci.); Univ. of OK, 1957–59, MLS; Univ. of MI, 1961–71, PhD (Lib. Sci.); Univ. of OK, 1962–66, (Pol. Sci.). **Orgs.:** ALA: AASL; LITA; RTSD; RASD; GODORT. IN LA. IL LA. SLA. Friends of the Earth. Intl. Solar Energy Socty. Sierra Club. Common Cause. **Pubns.:** "List of Items to which currently subscribed by Federal depository libraries in Missouri" (1973–74); Bibls. on gvt. docum. in *Docum. to the People* (1973–74); "St. Louis public library depository," *Gvt. Pubn. Review* (Spr. 1974); reviews. **Activities:** 1, 11; 20, 26, 29, 30; 75, 86, 91 **Addr.:** Department of Library Science, Ball State University, Muncie, IN 47306.

Homan, J. Michael (Ag. 16, 1947, Portland, OR) Head, Inf. Srvs., Corp. Tech. Lib., The Upjohn Company, Kalamazoo, MI 49001, 1979–; **Educ.:** Head, Info. Srvs., Pacific Southwest Reg. Med. Lib. Srv. Univ. of CA, Los Angeles, Biomed. Lib., 1974–79, Info. Spec., 1972–74. **Educ.:** Lewis & Clark Coll., 1965–69, BA (Hist./Bio.), Univ. of Chicago, 1969–71, MA (LS), Univ. of CA, Los Angeles, 1971–72, Cert. (Med. Libnshp). **Orgs.:** Med. LA: Ch., Scho. Com. (1979–80). SLA. Med. Lib. Grp. of South. CA and AZ: Ch.: Nom. Com. (1976); Prog. Ch.: (1978–79); Pres.-Elect: (1978–79). Nat. Lib. of Med. **Honors:** Univ. of Chicago, USPHS Flwshp., 1969. Univ. of CA, Los Angeles, USPHS Flwshp., 1971. **Pubns.:** "CE31: Basic Media Management" *Med. LA* (1979). "Audiovisual Reference Sources," *Intro. to Ref. Socs. in the Hlth Sci.* (1980). "CE 51: ONLINE Search Optimization" *Med LA* (1980). **Activities:** 1, 12; 17, 35, 39; 56, 58, 80 **Addr.:** Corporate Technical Library, The Upjohn Company, Kalamazoo, MI 49001.

Homes, Nellie M. (Jl. 24, 1898, Warren Cnty., IA) Libn. Emerita, Cottey Coll., 1966–; Hist. Sect., KS City Pub. Lib., 1968–70; Geo., Hist., Univ. of MO, 1966–68; Libn., Cottey Coll., 1945–66; Ref. Libn., Beloit Coll., 1939–45; Asst. in Lib., Flora Stone Mather Coll., West. Rsv. Univ., 1926–39; Cleveland Pub. Lib., 1920–26. **Educ.:** West. Rsv. Univ., 1918–19, BS (LS); Case West. Rsv. Univ., 1947, MA (Hist.). **Orgs.:** ALA: ACRL/Coll. Sect. (Secy., 1942–46); Jr. Coll. Sect. (Ch., 1954–55). MO LA: Pres. (1955–1956); MO ACRL (Secy., Vice Ch., Pres, 1950–53). Third Master Plan for Post Sec. Educ. in MO. Frnds. of the Nevada (MO) Pub. Lib.: Treas. (1977–81). Altrusa Intl. AAUW. **Honors:** MO LA, Past Pres. Awd., 1975; Cottey Coll. Alumn. Assn., Alumn. Srv. Awd., 1977; Beta Phi Mu, MO LA, Awd. of Merit, 1979. **Addr.:** 204 South Tucker, Nevada, MO 64772.

Homeyard, Marjorie A. (Jl. 19, 1940, Butler, PA) Deputy Head/Mtrl. Selector, US Navy Gen. Lib. Srvs., 1977–, Nvl. Reg. Libn., San Diego, 1974–77; Libn., Nvl. Station, San Diego, CA, 1973–74; Libn., US Navy Fleet Actv., Yokosuka, Japan, 1971–73. **Educ.:** Millersville State Coll., 1958–62, BE (Eng./LS); Drexel Univ., 1963–69, MLS. **Orgs.:** ALA: PLA/Armed Forces Libns. Sect. (Pres., 1980–81); FLRT. **Honors:** Beta Phi Mu. **Activities:** 4, 7; 15, 17; 74 **Addr.:** 2910 Blackshear, Pensacola, FL 32503.

Hommel, Claudia (Ja. 27, 1950, Paris, France) Arch. Consult., 1981–; Dir. of Mus. Arch., Detroit Inst. of Arts, 1978–81; Self-employed Consult., Find-File Systs., 1977–; Libn., Wayne Cnty. Fed. Libs., 1977–78; Arch. Tech., Arch. of Labor Hist., 1974–77. **Educ.:** Antioch Coll., 1967–72, BA (Hist.); Wayne State Univ., 1973–75, MSLS. **Orgs.:** SAA: Desc. Afnty. Grp.; Bus. Arch. Afnty. Grp. Amer. Assn. of Musms. Belmont Conf. on Mus. Arch.: Planner. **Pubns.:** "A Model Museum Archives," *Mus. News* (N.-D. 1979); "Guide to the Max Shachtman Collection," Tamiment Library (1981). **Activities:** 2, 12; 17, 24, 45; 55, 85, 92 **Addr.:** 17666 Manderson, Detroit, MI 48203.

Honhart, Frederick Lewis (O. 29, 1943, San Diego, CA) Dir., Univ. Arch. and Hist. Col., MI State Univ., 1979–, Asst. Dir., 1974–79; Fld. Rep., OH Hist. Socty., 1972–73. **Educ.:** Coll. of Wooster, 1962–64; Wayne State Univ., 1964–66, BA (Hist.); Case West. Rsv. Univ., 1966–72, MA, PhD (Amer. Hist.). **Orgs.:** SAA. Midwest Archs. Conf.: Prog. Com. (Ch., 1982). MI Arch. Assn.: Secy.-Treas. (1977–81). Amer. Hist. Assn. Org. of Amer. Histns. **Pubns.:** "Sources of Forest History," *Jnl. of Forest Hist.* (Jl. 1979); ed., *A Guide to the Michigan State University Archives and Historical Collections* (1976); asst. ed., *A Guide to Manuscript Collections and Institutional Records in Ohio* (1974). **Activities:** 2; 15, 17, 26; 67, 85 **Addr.:** University Archives and Historical Collections, Michigan State University, East Lansing, MI 48824.

Honza, Sr. Julian (S. 6, 1923, Ennis, TX) Coord., Lrng. Resrcs. Cert. Prog., Our Lady of the Lake Univ., 1980–, Libn., 1969–80. **Educ.:** Our Lady of the Lake Coll., BA (Eng.), MSLS. **Orgs.:** ALA. Bexar Cnty. LA. Cath. LA. **Activities:** 1, 11; 39, 44; 59, 63, 95 **Addr.:** 411 S.W. 24th St., San Antonio, TX 78285.

Hood, Joan S. (My. 10, 1938, Pittsburgh, PA) Head, Lib. Srvs., Pensacola Jr. Coll., Warrington Campus, 1978–, Head,

Special Subjects/Services: 50. Adult educ.; 51. Advert./Mktg.; 52. Aerosp.; 53. Agric.; 54. Area std.; 55. Arts/Hum.; 56. Autom.; 57. Bibl./Prtg.; 58. Bio. sci.; 59. Bus./Fin.; 60. Chem.; 61. Copyrt.; 62. Documtn.; 63. Educ.; 64. Engin.; 65. Env.; 66. Eth. grps.; 67. Film; 68. Food/Nutr.; 69. Geneal.; 70. Geo.; 71. Geol.; 72. Handcpd.; 73. Hist.; 74. Int. frdm.; 75. Info. sci.; 76. Insr.; 77. Law; 78. Legis.; 79. Math./Comp. sci.; 80. Med.; 81. Metals; 82. Nat. resrcs.; 83. Newsp.; 84. Nuc. sci.; 85. Oral hist.; 86. Petr./Energy; 87. Pharm.; 88. Phys./Astr./Math.; 89. Readg.; 90. Relig.; 91. Sci./Tech.; 92. Soc. sci.; 93. Telecom.; 94. Transp.; 95. (other).

Tech. Srvs., 1975–78, Libn., Milton Ctr., 1972–74, Circ. Libn./Ref. Libn., 1969–71. **Educ.:** PA State Univ., 1956–59, BA (Eng. Lit); Carnegie Inst. of Tech., 1959–60, MLS. **Orgs.:** ALA. FL LA: Secy., Jr. Coll. Sect. (1979). W. FL LA: Pres. (1975–76). Parents Without Partners. AAUW. **Honors:** Phi Beta Kappa, 1959. **Addr.:** 4645 Treeline Dr., Pensacola, FL 32504.

Hood, Lawrence E. (Mr. 24, 1945, Long Beach, CA) Acq. Libn., Brigham Young Univ. Law Lib., 1978–, Serials Libn., 1973–78. **Educ.:** Brigham Young Univ., 1971, BA (Hist.), 1978, MLS; AALL, 1979, Cert. (Law Libn.). **Orgs.:** AALL: West. Pac. Chap. Wasatch Front Area Law Libns.: 1980 Law Firm Libns. Sem. (Fac. Mem.). **Pubns.:** Ed., *Abstracts of Book Reviews in Current Legal Periodicals* (1974–79). **Activities:** 1, 12; 15, 23, 34; 69, 77, 78 **Addr.:** Brigham Young University, Law Library, Provo, UT 84602.

Hood, Mary Dullea (Ja. 3, 1947, Fargo, ND) Instr., Legal Resrch., Paralegal Inst., Univ. of Santa Clara, 1976–81, Head, Pub. Srvs., Heafey Law Lib., 1978–, Ref. Libn., 1976–78. **Educ.:** Coll. of Notre Dame, 1965–68; Univ. of Santa Clara, 1968–70, BA (Soc. Sci.), 1971–75, JD (Law); San Jose State Univ., 1976–79, MLS. **Orgs.:** AALL. North. CA Assn. of Law Libs.: Strg. Com. (1980); Ch., Const. & Bylaws, (1980–81); VP, Pres.-Elec. (1981). CA State Bar. City of Santa Clara Cvl. Srv. Commsn. **Activities:** 1, 12; 15, 31, 39; 77, 78 **Addr.:** Heafey Law Library, University of Santa Clara, Santa Clara, CA 95053.

Hood, Mary E. (Ja. 19, 1915, Sautee, GA) Asst. Libn., Assoc. Prof. of LS, N. GA Coll., 1947–; Tchr., GA HS, 1935–47. **Educ.:** Piedmont Coll., 1933–35, AB (Eng., Fr.); George Peabody Coll., 1947, BLS, 1964, MLS; Emory Univ. & GA Dept. of Arch. & Hist., 1978, Cert. **Orgs.:** ALA. SELA. GA LA: Stan. Com. (1975–76). Delta Kappa Gamma. **Activities:** 1; 20 **Addr.:** 405 North Hall Rd., Dahlonega, GA 30533.

Hook, Carolyn A. (O. 31, 1942, Murray, UT) Head, Educ. Lib., Washington St. Univ., 1970–; Asst. Dir., Moscow-Latah Cnty. Lib. Syst., 1969–70; Chld. Libn., San Jose Pub. Lib., 1967–69. **Educ.:** San Jose St. Univ., 1963–65, BA with Honors (Eng.), 1965–72, MA (LS); Univ. of South. CA, 1974–81, MPA, 1979, PhD (LS) 1981; San Jose St. Univ., 1965. **Orgs.:** Pacific N.W. LA. ALA. **Honors:** Epsilon Eta Sigma, 1965. **Pubns.:** "Moscow's Summer Reading Club", *The Idaho Libn.* (1970). **Activities:** 1; 17, 39; 50, 63, 89 **Addr.:** 961 North Grant St., Moscow, ID 83843.

Hook, Robert D. (My. 13, 1939, Susanville, CA) Pub. Srvs. Libn., Univ. of ID Lib., 1968–; Info. Desk Libn., San Jose Pub. Lib., 1966–68. **Educ.:** Chico St. Coll., 1960–64, BA (Soc. Sci.); San Jose St. Coll., 1964–68, MA (LS); Univ. of South. CA, 1974–76, MPA 1974–1980 PhD Lib Sci. **Orgs.:** ALA. Pacific N.W. LA: Circ. Div. (Ch., 1977–79). ID LA: Acad. Div., Secy. (1969–70), V. Ch. (1978–79), Ch. (1979–80); ALA Cnclr. (1979–); Fed. Rel. Coord. (1979–); Coop. Com. (1973–75). CA LA. **Pubns.:** "59 Footnotes......Survey of Library Hours and their use in selected Pacific Northwest Libraries, with Richard J. Beck," *PNLA Qtly.* (Spr. 1974); "Idaho State Report," *ALA Yrbk.* (1979, 1980) other articles *ID Libn.* and *ID Bkmark.* **Activities:** 1; 17, 22 **Addr.:** 961 N. Grant St., Moscow, ID 83843.

Hoornbeek, Lynda C. (Jl. 12, 1933, Springfield, IL) Ref. libn., Franklin Park Pub. Lib., 1978–; Subs. libn., Bloomingdale Pub. Lib., 1977–78; Head Libn., Winfield Pub. Lib., 1974–77; Lib. Coord. Subs., Glen Ellyn Sch. Dist. #41, 1973–74. **Educ.:** Univ. of IL, 1951–55, BA (Soclgy.); Cornell Univ., 1955–56, MEd (Educ.); Univ. of South. CA, 1971–73, MLS; Pac. Sch. of Relig., Univ. of CA, Berkeley, 1954. **Orgs.:** IL LA: Cont. Educ. (1975–76). ALA. AAUW. **Honors:** Beta Phi Mu. **Activities:** 9, 10; 16, 20, 39; 63, 92 **Addr.:** Franklin Park Public Library, 9618 Franklin Ave., Franklin Park, IL 60131.

Hootkin, Neil Marc (Je. 20, 1951, Milwaukee, WI) Spec. Col. Libn., Med. Coll. of WI, 1980–; Asst. Libn., Murphy Med. Lib., Milwaukee Cnty. Med., 1978–79; Cat. U.S. Intl. Trade Comsn., 1977–78; Libn., Sampson Lib., 1974–77. **Educ.:** Univ. of WI (Milwaukee), 1969–73, BA (Soclgy.), 1974–75, MA (LS). **Orgs.:** SLA: WI Chap./Lib. Mgt. Div.; Musm., Arts, and Hum. Div.; Chap. Bltn. Ed. (1978–80). Alpha Epsilon Pi–Mu Epsilon fraternity. **Activities:** 1, 12; 23, 33, 45; 80 **Addr.:** Todd Wehr Library, Medical College of Wisconsin, P.O. Box 26509, 8701 W. Watertown Plank Rd., Milwaukee, WI 53226.

Hoover, Austin (O. 29, 1938, Polk Cnty., AR) Univ. Archvst., NM State Univ., 1974–; Dir., Lib. Dev. Srvs. Unit, CO State Lib., 1972–74, Consult., Grants Coord. Unit, 1971; Field Consult., Field Srvs. Div., TX State Lib., 1969–70. **Educ.:** Little Rock Univ., 1959–63, BA (Hist., Pol. Sci.); Univ. of TX, El Paso, 1964–67, MA (Hist.); Univ. of Denver, 1968–69, MA (Libnshp.); Natl. Arch. and Recs. Srv., Inst. in Mod. Arch. Admin., 1974, Cert. (Arch. Mgt.). **Orgs.:** SAA. Socty. of SW Archvsts.: Bd. (1980–); Awds. Com. (1976–78). NM LA: Co-Ch., Mem. and Awds. Com. (1979–80); Ch., Lcl. and Reg. Hist. RT (1977). Border Reg. LA: Pres. (1979); Bd. (1970, 1975). Other orgs. West. Hist. Assn. Hist. Socty. of NM: VP (1981–). Dona Ana Cnty. Hist. Socty. **Honors:** Phi Alpha Theta, 1963; Beta Phi Mu, 1969. **Pubns.:** Ed., *Rio Grande History* (1974–); Reviews. **Addr.:** University Archives, New Mexico State University Library, Box 3475, Las Cruces, NM 88003.

Hoover, James L. (Je. 15, 1945, Oklahoma City, OK) Asst. Law Libn., Columbia Univ., 1978–; Assoc. Law Libn., Univ. of OK, 1975–78; Asst. Law Libn., St. Louis Univ., 1974–75. **Educ.:** Univ. of OK, 1963–67, BA (Pol. Sci.); 1973, JD (Law); Univ. of WA, 1973–74, MLL (Libnshp.). **Orgs.:** AALL: Vice Ch., Prog. Com. (1978). Southwest. Assn. of Law Libs.: Vice Pres. (1977–78). SLA. Law Lib. Assn. of Grt. NY. MO Bar Assn. **Pubns.:** *American Indian Legal Materials: a union list* (1980). **Addr.:** Columbia Univ. Law Library, 435 W. 116th St., New York, NY 10027.

Hoover, John D. (O. 22, 1937, Clinton, ON) Asst. Dir. of Libs./Col. Dev., Univ. of West. ON, 1972–, Col. Anal., 1971–72, Libn.-in-Charge, Bus. Lib., 1963–71. **Educ.:** Univ. of West. ON, 1957–61, BA (Hist.), 1961–70, MA (Hist.); McGill Univ., 1962–63, BLS. **Orgs.:** ON LA. Can. LA. ALA. **Activities:** 1; 15, 17 **Addr.:** The University of Western Ontario, London, ON N6A 3K7 Canada.

Hoover, Ryan E. (Je. 1, 1942, Columbus, OH) Mgr., Life Sci. Info. Srvs., SDC Srch. Serv., 1978–; Head, Comp.-Aided Ref. Srvs., Univ. of UT Libs., 1976–78, Life Sci. Ref. Libn., 1973–76, Life Sci. Cat., 1970–73. **Educ.:** OH State Univ., 1960–65, BS (Bio.); Case West. Resrv. Univ., 1969–70, MSLS; Univ. of UT, 1976–78, Cert. (Mgt.). **Orgs.:** ASIS: Ch.-Elect, Los Angeles Chap. South. CA OLUG. **Pubns.:** Ed. and jt. auth., *The Library and Information Manager's Guide to Online Services* (1980); "Computer-Aided Reference Services in the Academic Library," *Online* (O. 1979); "A Comparison of Three Commercial Online Vendors," *Online* (Ja. 1979); "Patron Appraisal of Computer-Aided On-Line Bibliographic Retrieval Services," *Jnl. Lib. Autom.* (D. 1976). **Activities:** 6, 14; 49-Online srvs.; 58, 65, 68 **Addr.:** SDC Search Service, 2500 Colorado Ave., Santa Monica, CA 90406.

Hope, Dorothy H. (Jl. 20, 1938, GA) Cat. Libn., Univ. of Louisville, 1974–81. **Educ.:** Wesleyan Coll., 1958–62, AB (Hist.); Univ. of KY, 1973–74, MA (LS); Med. LA, 1976, Cert. **Orgs.:** ALA: ACRL/Nom. Com., Sci. and Tech. Sect. (1979–81). Med. LA: Nom. Com., Hlth. Sci. AV Grp. (1979–80); Bylaws Com. (1980). KY LA: Secy., Spec. Libs. Sect. (1979–80). AAUP. **Pubns.:** Jt. Auth., "Biomedical journal holdings: a multi-subject approach," *Spec. Libs.* (My./Je. 1976). **Activities:** 1, 12; 20, 25, 26; 58, 75, 80 **Addr.:** 1930 SW 19th Way, Gainesville, FL 32608.

Hope, Nelson W. (O. 17, 1916, Maysville, OK) Tech. Resrch. Libn., Garrett Turbine Engine Co. (Phoenix, AZ), 1966–; Asst. Libn., General Atomic (San Diego, CA), 1960–66; Ref. Spec., General Electric Co. (Richland, WA), 1955–60; various positions as engin. **Educ.:** Univ. of OK, 1936–41, BA (Engin., LS); AZ St. Univ., 1966–1970, MA (Educ.), 1970–74, Ed D. **Orgs.:** SLA: Sci. Meetings Com. (Ch., 1967–70). **Pubns.:** "Aren't 100 Legs Enough?" *Adult Leadership* (Ap. 1961); "Needle in a Haystack," *Coll. and Resrch. Lib.* (Mr. 1963); "Some Thoughts on the Changing Image of the Librarian," *Jnl. Educ. Libnshp.* (Win. 1963); "Vocabulary of a Technology Librarian," *Jnl. Educ. Libnshp.* (Win. 1962); "Check List for Classified Documents," *Spec. Lib.* (F. 1966); other pubns. **Activities:** 12; 15, 17, 39; 64, 75 **Addr.:** Engineering Library, Garrett Turbine Engine Co., 111 South 34th St., P.O. Box 5217, Phoenix, AZ 85010.

Hopewell, Helen Jeanene (Ap. 18, 1925, Birmingham, AL) Per. Libn., Air Univ. Lib., 1960–, Ref. Libn., 1957–60, Bk. Circ. Libn., 1953–57. **Educ.:** Univ. of AL, 1942–46, BA (Soclgy.); FL St. Univ., 1952–53, MA (LS). **Orgs.:** SLA. AL LA. **Pubns.:** *Union List of Military Periodicals* (1960); Co-Ed., *Union List of Foreign Military Periodicals* (Prelim. Ed.) (1957). **Activities:** 4; 39, 41, 44; 52, 57, 74 **Addr.:** 1243 Adell St., Prattville, AL 36067.

Hopkins, Frances L. (Jl. 4, 1930, Yorktown Heights, NY) NEH/CLR Proj. Coord., Franklin & Marshall Coll., 1979–, Ref./Instr. Libn., 1975–78; Design Resrcs. Libn., Armstrong Cork Comp., 1973–74. **Educ.:** Franklin & Marshall Coll., 1961–68, BA (Phil.), Drexel Univ., 1968–74, MSLS, 1979, (LS); Univ. of MD, 1978, Cert. (Lib. Admin. Dev.). **Orgs.:** ALA: ACRL (Cont. Educ. Com.); RASD; Lib. Instr. RT. Nat. LA: Secy. (1978–80). PA LA.: Ch., S. Cent. Chap., State Bd. (1978–79). Philadelphia Area Ref. Libn. Info. Exch. AAUP. **Honors:** Beta Phi Mu, 1974. **Pubns.:** "General Classification Theory–a Review of Classification Research Group Work," *Lib. Resrcs. & Tech. Serv.* (1973). *Coll. Libnshp.* (1980) "Lib. Instr." in *Coll. Libnshp.* **Activities:** 1; 31, 39; 55 **Addr.:** Fackenthal Library, Franklin & Marshall College, Lancaster, PA 17604.

Hopkins, Jean Baker (Ap. 29, 1930, Los Angeles, CA) Med. Libn., ID Falls Consolidated Hosp., 1971–; Lib. Aide, ID Falls HS, 1970–71. **Educ.:** Stanford Univ., 1947–51, BA (Educ.); ID St. Univ. (Ext.), 1967–71. ID Sec. Tchg. Cert., 1971. **Orgs.:** Med. LA. ID Hlth. Info. Assn.: Secy. (1976); Pres.-Elect (1978); Pres. (1979, 1980). ID LA. **Honors:** ID Gvr. Conf., Del., 1978. **Activities:** 5; 17, 34, 39; 80 **Addr.:** 193 Tenth St., Idaho Falls, ID 83401.

Hopkins, Judith (Jl. 15, 1934, Wilkes-Barre, PA) Head, Orig. Cat. Sect., Ctrl. Tech. Srvs., State Univ. NY (Buffalo), 1977–, Adj. Prof. (LS), 1980–; Asst. Prof. Sch. LS, Univ. MI, 1974–77; Instruc., Sch. LS, Univ. IL, 1973–74; Bibl. Ed., OCLC, inc., 1970–72; Asst. Head, Cat. Dept., Yale Law Lib., 1965–67; Cat., Mt. Holyoke Coll. Lib., 1957–65. **Educ.:** Wilkes Coll., 1951–55, AB (Hist.); Univ. IL, 1955–57, MSLS, 1967–70, Cert. Adv. Stud., 1972–73. **Orgs.:** ALA: RTSD, Cat. Class. Section Exec. Com. (mem. 1982–, Secy. 1975–77), Subj. Anal. Com. (1972–75), Nom. Com. (Ch., 1978–79), Cat. Asian African Mtls. (1979–); LITA, Nom. Com. (1974), Bd. Dir. (1976–78) Liaison To RTSD Filing Com. (1979–81); Various other com. and div. NY LA. AALS. OCLC, Inc. Users Cncl. Many other com. and orgs. Amer. Civil Liberties Union. Amnesty Intl. **Honors:** Beta Phi Mu, 1957. Higher Educ. Act of 1965 title IIB Flwshp., 1969–70. **Pubns.:** *Index to Chapter 6 (1974) AACR* (1975); Co.-ed., Manual for OCLC Catalog Card Production (1972); "The Ohio College Library Center," *LRTS* (Sum. 1973); Ed., Nsltr. MI Chap. ASIS (1974–77). **Activities:** 1, 11; 20, 26 **Addr.:** Cataloging Dept., Lockwood Library Bldg., SUNY at Buffalo, Amherst, NY 14260.

Hopkins, Karen Ann (Ag. 22, 1948, Bath, NY) Mgr., Media Srvs., Natl. Tech. Inst. for the Deaf, 1979–; Tchr. Gates-Chili Ctrl. HS, 1970–79. **Educ.:** SUNY Coll., Brockport, 1966–69, BA (Eng.); SUNY Coll., Geneseo, 1972–74, MLS; SUNY Coll., Brockport, 1977–79, Cert. Advnc. Std. (Educ. Admin.). **Orgs.:** ALA: Lib. Srv. to Deaf, Vice-Ch. and Ch.-elec. (1981) Pubns. Com. (1980–81); ASCLA, AV Com. (1980, 1981). Rochester AV Assn. Rochester Resrcs. Cncl. **Activities:** 1, 12; 32, 45; 72 **Addr.:** National Technical Institute for the Deaf, 1 Lomb Memorial Dr., Rochester, NY 14623.

Hopkins, Monroe (Ap. 4, 1926, Houston, TX) Libn., William Woods Coll., 1967–; Ch., Jt. Libs., Westminter, William Woods Coll., 1971–; Libn., Hannibal-LaGrange Coll., 1958–67; Asst. Libn., Belmont Coll., 1957–58; Libn., Bremton-Parker Coll., 1956–57. **Educ.:** Hannibal-LaGrange Coll., 1951–52, AA; Univ. of MO, 1953–55, BA (LS, Hist.); George Peabody Coll., 1957–59, MA (LS). **Orgs.:** ALA: ACRL, Natl. Lib. Week Com. (1964–67). MO ACRL: Ch. (1963). Ordained Bapt. Minister. Callaway Cnty. (MO) Lib. Bd. Daniel Boone Reg. Lib. Bd. **Honors:** William Woods Coll., Disting. Tchg. Awd., 1972. **Activities:** 1; 15, 26, 47 **Addr.:** William Woods College, Fulton, MO 65251.

Hopp, Ralph H. (O. 24, 1915, Cook, NE) Dir., Inst. of Tech. Libs., Univ. of MN, 1978–, Dir. of Lib. Dev., 1976–78, Dir. of Libs., 1971–76, Univ. Libn. & Assoc. Dir., 1953–71; Agr. & Sci.-Tech. Libn., Univ. of NE, 1951–53; Resrch. Libn., Battelle Meml. Inst., 1946–49; Resrch. Ed., Bituminous Coal Resrch., Inc., 1944–45; Resrch. Fellow, Mellon Inst. of Indust-Resrch., 1943–44. **Educ.:** Peru State Tchrs. Coll., 1934–35, 1937–38, Tchg. Cert. (Educ.); Univ. of NE, 1938–43, BS (Chem. Engin.); Univ. of IL, 1949–51, MS (Libnshp.), 1956, PhD (Libnshp.). **Orgs.:** MN LA. ARL: Pres., (1974–75); Bd. of Dirs., (1972–76); ALA: Lib. Tech. Prog. Adv. Com. (Ch.); LAD/Bldgs. & Equipment Sect., (Ch.); Lib. Org. & Mgmt. Sect., (Ch.); ACRL/Univ. Libs. Sect., (Ch.). Unvsl. Serials & Book Exch., Inc.: Pres. (1980); Bd. of Dirs. (1979–81); other orgs. **Honors:** Beta Phi Mu, Fulbright Lect., Turkey, 1962–63. **Pubns.:** *Enjoying the active life after fifty* (1979); "Librarians and science literature," *Kütüpaneciligin Sesi* (N. 1963). **Activities:** 1; 17; 91 **Addr.:** 1341 Keston St., St. Paul, MN 55108.

Hopper, Mildry S. (Jl. 22, 1908, Tacoma, WA) Chief, Clasfd. Lib., National Defense Univ., 1977–, Cat. and Ref., Clasfd. Lib., Indus. Coll. Armed Forces 1973–76; Transl., Maritime Admn., 1960–73; Cat., Natl. Lib. Med., 1954–60. **Educ.:** Univ. Puget Sound 1926–29, BA (Fren., Ger.); Univ. of WA, 1930–31, MA (Fren. Span.); Univ. of WA, 1937–38, BA (LS). **Orgs.:** ALA. Girl Scouts: Leader (1954–64); Scandinavian Exch. Proj. (1959). **Honors:** Maritime Admn., Outstan. Performance, 1963, 1967, 1968. **Pubns.:** Various. **Activities:** 1, 4; 17, 20, 39; 54, 80 **Addr.:** 3713–35th St. N.W., Washington, DC 20016.

Hopson, Rex C. (Je. 12, 1933, Mound, TX) Asst. Prof. of Libnshp., Univ. of NM, 1967–; Libn., Albuquerque Pub. Sch., 1966–67; Libn., Panama CZ Sch., 1963–66. **Educ.:** Baylor Univ., 1950–54, BA (Eng.); Southwest. Bapt. Theo. Semy., 1954–56, MRE (Relig. Educ.); George Peabody Coll., 1959–60, MA (Eng.); Univ. of Denver, 1965–68, MA (Libnshp.). **Orgs.:** NM LA. NM Hist. Socty. Albuquerque Hist. Socty. **Pubns.:** *Adobe: A comprehensive bibliography* (1979). **Activities:** 1; 39; 73, 85 **Addr.:** University of New Mexico, Albuquerque, NM 87106.

Hopwood, Susan H. (Ap. 12, 1946, Boston, MA) Ref. Libn., Marquette Univ., 1980–; Ref. Libn., Capital Univ., 1974–80; Circ. Head, Case West. Rsv. Univ., 1972–74. **Educ.:** Skidmore Coll., 1964–68, BA (Eng.); Case West. Rsv. Univ., 1971–74, MSLS. **Orgs.:** ALA. WI LA. **Pubns.:** *Foundations in Wisconsin: A Directory* (1980). **Activities:** 1; 31, 36, 39 **Addr.:** Memorial Library, Marquette University, 1415 W. Wisconsin Ave., Milwaukee, WI 53233.

Hordusky, Clyde Walter (Ja. 23, 1937, Union City, PA) Docum. Spec., State Lib. of OH, 1969–; Sel. Ofcr., Case Western

PROFESSIONAL ACTIVITIES: Institutions: 1. Acad. lib.; 2. Arch.; 3. Assn.; 4. Fed./Gvt. lib.; 5. Inst. lib.; 6. Mfr./Suppl.; 7. Milit. lib.; 8. Musm.; 9. Pub. lib.; 10. Sch. lib.; 11. Sch. of lib. sci.; 12. Spec. lib.; 13. State lib.; 14. (other). **Functions/Activities:** 15. Acq./Col. dev.; 16. Adult srvs.; 17. Admin.; 18. Apprais.; 19. Archit./Bldgs.; 20. Cat./Class.; 21. Chld. srvs.; 22. Circ.; 23. Cons./Pres.; 24. Consult.; 25. Cont. ed.; 26. Educ. lib. sci.; 27. Ext. srvs.; 28. Fund/Grants; 29. Gvt. pubs.; 30. Indx./Abs.; 31. Instr. lib. use; 32. Media srvs.; 33. Micro.; 34. Netwks./Coop.; 35. Persnl.; 36. PR; 37. Publshg.; 38. Recs. mgt.; 39. Ref. srvs.; 40. Repro.; 41. Resrch.; 42. Review.; 43. Secur.; 44. Serials; 45. Spec. col.; 46. Tech. srvs.; 47. Trustees/Bds.; 48. YA srvs.; 49. (other).

Reserve Univ., 1968–69, Acq. Libn., 1964–68, Ref. Libn., 1963–64. **Educ.:** Grove City Coll., 1954–58, BA (Eng.); Case Western Reserve Univ., 1960–63, MSLS. **Orgs.:** SLA: Ed., Cleveland Chap. Bltn. (1967–68). OH LA: Dir., Div. 3 (1978–79). ALA: Ch., Constn. Com. GODORT (1978–). **Pubns.:** Ed., *Ohio Documents; a list of publications of state agencies* (1970–). **Activities:** 12, 13; 29, 33, 41; 78 **Addr.:** 503 E. Cooke Rd., Columbus, OH 43214.

Horecky, Paul L. (S. 8, 1913, Trutnov, Czechoslovakia) Retired, 1977–; Visit. Prof., Hokkaido Univ., Sapporo, Japan, 1979–80; Sr. Resrch. Fellow, Inst. for Sino-Soviet Std., George Washington Univ., 1978–79; Chief, Slavic and Ctrl. European Div., Lib. of Congs., 1972–77, Asst. Chief, 1958–71, Slavic and E. European Anal. Spec. 1951–58; Resrchr., Russian Resrch. Ctr., Harvard Univ., 1949–51; Trial Attorney, Pubns. Ed., US Ofc. of Chief of Counsel, Nuremberg, Germany, 1947–49. **Educ.:** Prague Univ., 1931–36, Dr. Jur. (Law, Pol. Sci.); Sorbonne, Paris, 1933–34 (Intl. Law); Harvard Univ., 1949–51 MA (Soviet Area Std. Prog.). **Orgs.:** ALA: Exec. Com., Slavic and E. European Subsect. (1966–67). Amer. Assn. for the Advnc. of Slavic Std.: Lib. and Documen. Com. (1970–73). Pol. Sci. Assn. Harvard Club, Washington D.C. Cosmos Club. Amer. Cncl. of Learned Societies and Soc. Sci. Resrch. Cncl.: Jt. Com. on East. Europe (1971–75); Resrch. and Lib. Resrcs. Adv. Com. (Ch., 1970–72). Amer. Cncl. on Educ. Task Force on Lib. and Info. Resrcs. (1975). **Pubns.:** *East Central and Southeastern Europe: A Handbook of Library and Archival Resources in North America* (1976); Ed., *A Guide to Yugoslav Libraries and Archives* (1975); *East Central Europe: A Guide to Basic Publications* (1969); *Southeastern Europe: A Guide to Basic Publications* (1969); Jt. Cmplr., *Basic Russian Publications: An Annotated Bibliography on Russia and the Soviet Union* (1962); Other books and articles. **Activities:** 2, 5; 15, 17, 41; 54, 57, 92 **Addr.:** 2207 Paul Spring Rd., Alexandria, VA 22307.

Horn, Andrew H. (Jl. 22, 1914, Ogden, UT) Prof. Dean Emer., Univ. of CA, Los Angeles, 1978–; Prof., Dean, 1959–78; Coll. Libn., Occidental Coll., 1957–59; Univ. Libn., Prof. of Libnshp., Univ. of NC, Chapel Hill, 1954–57; Asst. Assoc. Univ. Libn., Univ. of CA, Los Angeles, 1951–54, Univ. Arcvst., 1950–57, Asst. Head, Head, Dept. of Spec. Coll., 1948–51. **Educ.:** Univ. of CA, Los Angeles, 1935–37, BA (Hist.), 1937–40, MA (Hist.); American Univ., 1951, Cert. in Arch.; 1951. Univ. of CA, Los Angeles, 1940–43, PhD (Hist.); Univ. of CA, Berkeley, 1947–48, BLS. **Orgs.:** ALA: Cncl. (1957–58; 1969–72). **Activities:** 1, 11; 17, 26, 45; 54, 57, 73, 92 **Addr.:** 1919 Alpha Rd., Glendale, CA 91208.

Horn, David Emmett (Jl. 1, 1937, Laconia, NH) Archvst., DePauw Univ., Untd. Meth. Church of IN, 1974–; Arch. and Ref. Libn., MT State Univ., 1971–74; Tchr., Libn., Newman Prep. Sch., Boston, 1959–69. **Educ.:** St. Anselm Coll., 1954–59, AB (Phil.); Boston Univ., 1966–68, MA (Hist.); Cert., Inst. in Archival Libnshp., Univ. of OR, 1969–70, MLS. **Orgs.:** SAA: Midwest Arch. Conf. NW Archvsts.: Strg. Com. (Ch., 1972–74). Socty. of GA Archvsts.: Ed. Bd. (1975–77). **Pubns.:** *Copyright, Literary Rights, and Ownership: A Guide for Archivists* (1978); "Who Owns Our History?," *Lib. Jnl.* (Ap. 1, 1975); "A Church Archives: the United Methodist Church in Indiana," *GA Arch.* (Fall 1980). **Activities:** 1, 2; 17, 38, 45; 55, 61, 75 **Addr.:** DePauw University Archives, Greencastle, IN 46135.

Horne, Alan John (Ap. 22, 1931, Ilford, Essex, UK) Head, Ref. Dept., Robarts Lib., Univ. of Toronto, 1981; Asst. Libn., Reader Srvs., 1971–81; Libn., Commonwealth Inst., London, UK, 1959–71; Asst. Libn., Royal Inst., London, UK, 1954–59. **Educ.:** Univ. of London, 1956–60, BA Hon (Eng.); Lib. Assn. of Grt. Britain, 1952–56, ALA. **Orgs.:** Can. LA. ON LA. **Pubns.:** *Margaret Atwood: An Annotated Bibliography* (1980). **Activities:** 1; 17, 23 **Addr.:** University of Toronto Library, Toronto, ON M5S 1A5 Canada.

Horne, Ernest Lincoln (Ag. 9, 1926, Boston, MA) Sr. Cat. Libn., Gen. Motors Resrch. Labs., 1961–; Catlgr., Detroit Pub. Lib., 1957–61, Ref. Asst., 1954–57. **Educ.:** Harvard Coll., 1944–48, AB (Hist.); Simmons Coll., 1952–54, MS (LS). **Orgs.:** SLA: MI Chap., Treas. (1958–61); (1962–63); Dir. (1965–66); Ch., Ad Hoc Com. of the MI Partners of the Americas (1976–); Trans. Div., Secy.-Treas. (1968–69); Ch.-Elect (1969–70); Ch. (1970–71). ASIS. Algonquin Club. Sierra Club. **Pubns.:** Ed., *Directory of Transportation Libraries and Information Centers* (1969). **Activities:** 12; 20, 44, 46; 81, 91, 94 **Addr.:** General Motors Corporation, Research Laboratories Library, General Motors Technical Center, Warren, MI 48090.

Horner, James W., Jr. (Ja. 24, 1914, Sioux Falls, SD) Retired, 1980, Sr. Resrch. Chem., 1978–80; Grp. Leader, Tech. Info., Ashland Chem. Co., 1967–78; Grp. Leader, Tech. Info., Archer Daniels Midland Co., 1960–67, Resrch. Chem., 1946–60; Resrch. Chem., various cos., 1940–46. **Educ.:** Univ. of MN, 1931–35, BCh (Chem.), 1935–40, PhD (Organic Chem.). **Orgs.:** ASIS: Secy., Ctrl. OH Chap. (1979–80). SLA. Amer. Chem. Socty. **Pubns.:** "Planning the new library: Archer Daniels Midland Company Research Library," *Spec. Libs.* (Ja. 1964); "Report of the Literature Review Committee. Annual review of the literature on fats, oils, and detergents," *Jnl. of American Oil Chem. Socty.* (1960–65); a patent (1961). **Activities:** 12; 39; 60 **Addr.:** 96 Daniel Dr., Westerville, OH 43081.

Horner, Richard Wilson (Ja. 12, 1928, Windsor, ON) Libn., Detroit Bapt. Theo. Semy., 1980–; Ref. Libn./Asst. Prof., Bapt. Bible Coll. of PA, 1974–80; Fac. Mem., Eng. Dept., Bob Jones Univ., 1970–74; Assoc. Prof. of Eng., Bapt. Bible Coll. of PA, 1968–70. **Educ.:** Gordon Coll., 1953, AB (Eng.); Univ. of RI, 1963–68, MA (Eng.); Grace Theo. Semy. IN, 1953–55, MDiv (Theo.); Univ. of West. ON, 1975–80, MLS. **Orgs.:** Southeast. PA Theo. LA. ATLA. Christ. Libns. Flwshp. Mod. Lang. Assn. Natl. Cncl. of Tchrs. of Eng. **Activities:** 1, 5; 15, 17, 39; 55, 62, 90 **Addr.:** c/o Detroit Baptist Theological Seminary, 4801 Allen Rd., Allen Park, MI 48101.

Horner, William C. (Ap. 2, 1929, Pittsburgh, PA) Syst. Libn., NC State Univ., 1970–; Sci. Engin. Libn., Tufts Univ., 1965–70. **Educ.:** Univ. of Pittsburgh, 1950–52, BBA (Acct.), 1963–64, MLS. **Orgs.:** ASIS. SLA: Dir., Boston Chap. (1967–68); Dir., Carolinas Chap. (1973–74). Assn. for Computational Ling. AAUP: Treas., NC State Chap. (1977–78). Amer. Socty. for Engin. Educ.: Ch., Engin. Libs. Div., New Eng. Sect. (1968–69). AAAS. Other orgs. **Pubns.:** "Computer Processing of OCLC Archive Tapes," *Jnl. of Lib. Autom.* (Mr. 1979); Jt. auth., "Periodical Prices: A Comparison of Local and National Averages," *Lib. Acq.: Prac. and Theory* (Win. 1978); "The Use and Economics of Computer-Generated Microfiche Catalogs," *NC Lib.* (Win. 1975). **Activities:** 1; 17, 24, 49-Computer Systems; 56, 75 **Addr.:** 2110 D. H. Hill Library, North Carolina State University, Raleigh, NC 27650.

Horny, Karen Louise (Ap. 22, 1943, Highland Park, IL) Asst. Univ. Libn. for Tech. Srvs. Northwestern Univ. Lib., 1971–; Core Libn., Northwestern Univ. Lib., 1968–71; Asst. Core Libn., 1966–68. **Educ.:** Brown Univ., 1961–65, AB (Fr.); Univ. of MI, 1965–66, AMLS. **Orgs.:** ALA: RTSD (Pres. 1980–81); Cncl. of Reg. Groups, (Ch., 1976–78). IL LA: Resrcs. and Tech. Srvs. Sect. (Exec. Com. Mem.-at-Large, 1976). Freedom to Read Fndn. **Honors:** Phi Beta Kappa, 1965; Beta Phi Mu, 1966; Phi Kappa Phi, 1966. **Pubns.:** "NOTIS-3 (Northwestern On-line Total Integrated System)," *Lib. Resrcs. and Tech. Srvcs.* (Fall 1978). "Automation of Technical Services: Northwestern's Experience," *Coll. and Resrch. Libs.* (S. 1974). Reviews. **Activities:** 1; 17, 46; 56 **Addr.:** Assistant University Librarian for Technical Services, Northwestern University Library, Evanston, IL 60201.

Horodecka, Oxana (My. 26, 1944, Sianik, Ukraine) Sr. Descr. Cat., Lib. of Congs., 1968–. **Educ.:** Syracuse Univ., 1962–66, BA (Hist.); 1966–68, MSLS. **Orgs.:** ALA. Lib. of Congs. Prof. Assn. Socty. of Fed. Ling. **Activities:** 4; 20 **Addr.:** 3114 Wisconsin Ave. N. W., Apartment #602, Washington, DC 20016.

Horowitz, Harvey P. (Jl. 9, 1935, New York, NY) Libn., Hebrew Union Coll., 1963–. **Educ.:** Univ. of CA, Los Angeles, 1958–61, BA; Univ. of South. CA, 1961–63, MLS. **Orgs.:** AJL: Pres. (1978–80). *West. States Jewish Hist. Qtly.*: Contrib. Ed. (1969–). **Pubns.:** Reviews. **Activities:** 1; 15, 17, 31; 66, 90 **Addr.:** Hebrew Union College-J1R, Frances-Henry Library, 3077 University Ave., Los Angeles, CA 90007.

Horowitz, Marjorie Brailove (O. 7, 1927, Philadelphia, PA) Sch. Libn., Glenfield Middle Sch., 1977–; Sch. Libn., Other NJ schs., 1966–77. **Educ.:** Wellesley Coll., 1945–49, BA (Eng.); Columbia Univ., 1961–66, MLS, 1972–80, Cert. of Advnc. Libnshp. **Orgs.:** Essex Cnty. Sch. Lib. Media Assn.: VP (1969–72). Educ. Media Assn. of NJ: Prog. Com. (1970–72, 1981–). ALA. Montclair Educ. Assn.: Rep. (1971–). NJ Educ. Assn. Natl. Educ. Assn. **Honors:** Beta Phi Mu, 1967. **Activities:** 10; 15, 17, 21; 63 **Addr.:** 10 Prospect Ave., Montclair, NJ 07042.

Horrell, Ruth C. (N. 4, 1909, Ava, IL) Church Libn., First Untd. Meth. Church, Pasadena, CA, 1970–; Sec. Sch. Libn., Pontiac (IL) Twp. HS, 1957–70; Libn., Arcola Cmnty. HS, 1956–57; Tchr., W. Frankfort (IL) City Schs., 1942–56. **Educ.:** South. IL Univ., Carbondale, 1930–52, BS (Elem. Educ.); Univ. of IL, 1955–60, MS (LS); West. MI Univ., 1968; IL Normal Univ., 1967. Natl. Retired Tchrs. Assn. Women's City Club. Ladies of the Lions Den. **Honors:** Pontiac (IL) Twp. HS, Plaque for Outstan. Srv., 1970. **Pubns.:** "Influence of TV on Reading of Children," *Sch. Lib. Jnl.* (S. 1955). **Activities:** 12; 49; 89, 90 **Addr.:** 932 East Elm Ave., San Gabriel, CA 91775.

Horrocks, Norman (O. 18, 1927, Manchester, Eng.) Prof. and Dir. Sch. of Lib. Srv., Dalhousie Univ., 1972–, Assoc. Prof. and Asst. Dir., 1971–72; Tchg. Flw., Instr. and Asst. Prof., Sch. of LS, Univ. of Pittsburgh, 1963–71; Ext. Lect., Prog. Cert. of Lib. Assts., St. Lib. PA, 1966–71; Sum. Sch. Fac., Sch. of LS, Univ. HI, 1969; Tech. Libn. and Info. Ofcr., St. Lib. of West. Australia, 1956–63; Lect. in Libnshp., Perth Tech. Coll., 1961–63; Libn., British Cncl., Cyprus, 1954–55; various positions, Manchester Pub. Lib., Eng., 1943–45, 1950–54. **Educ.:** Univ. of West. Australia, 1957–60, BA (Hist.); Univ. of Pittsburgh, 1963–64, MLS, 1964–70, PhD (LS); Sch. of Libnshp., Manchester, Engl., 1948–50, FLA; Lib. Assn. of Australia, 1957, ALAA. **Orgs.:** ALA: Cncl. (1972–81); Exec. Bd. (1977–81); Intl. Rel. Com. (1973–75, Ch. 1974–75); various other com. AALS: Ed. Bd. (Ch., 1971–76); various other com. Beta Phi Mu: Natl. Treas. (1968–71). Can LA: Sec. VP (1978–80); Cont. Educ. Coord. Grp. (Ch., 1976–78); various other com. Lib. Assn. UK. Lib. Assn. Australia. Many other orgs. and com. Banook Canoe Club: Nsltr. Ed. (1978–79). **Honors:** Beta Phi Mu, 1964; W.H. Brown Prize, 1949; Atl. Prov. Lib. Assn. Merit Awd., 1979. **Pubns.:** Ed. *The Great Bibliographers Series* (1974–); numerous articles contributed to the library press (1955–79). Many editorshps. and adv. bds. for jnls. and nsltrs. **Activities:** 11; 26, 29, 37; 54 **Addr.:** School of Library Service, Dalhousie University, Halifax, NS B3H 4H8 Canada.

Horst, Stanley E. (Je. 23, 1934, Lebanon, PA) Assoc. Dir., North. IL Univ., Coll. of Law Lib., 1979–; Assoc. Law Libn., Lewis Univ., Coll. of Law, 1974–79; Head, Tech. Srvs., Northwestern Univ. Sch. of Law Lib., 1972–74. **Educ.:** PA State Univ., 1951–55, BA; Univ. of WI, 1965–67, MLS. **Orgs.:** AALL: Ch., Job Secur., Remuneration & Empl. Prac. Com. (1973–74). Chicago Assn. of Law Libs. Intl. Assn. of Law Libs. **Activities:** 1, 12; 15, 17; 77, 78 **Addr.:** Northern Illinois University, College of Law Library, Glen Ellyn, IL 60137.

Hortin, Larry L. (Jl. 13, 1934, Evanston, WY) Lib. Dir., Provo City Lib., 1970–; Order Supvsr., Brigham Young Univ., 1969–70; Sch. Libn., Boulder City Jr. Sr. HS, 1962–69. **Educ.:** Brigham Young Univ., 1958–61, BS (Psy.); Univ. of OR, 1965–67, MS (LS). **Orgs.:** UT LA: Ch., Pub. Lib. Com.; Ch., Legis. Com.; By-Laws Com. Adult Educ. Assn. of UT: Bd. of Dir. **Activities:** 9, 10 **Addr.:** 3675 N 500 E, Provo, UT 84601.

Horton, Forest Woody, Jr. (O. 26, 1930, CA) Exec. Dir., Fed. Info. Syst. Locator Task Force, Exec. Ofc. of the Pres., 1978–; Dir. of Info. Mgt., Comsn. on Fed. Paperwork, 1975–78; Visit. Prof., Univ. of MD, 1974–75; Dir., Info. Mgt., Pres. Spec. Trade Rep., 1972–74; Dir., Mgt. Info. Syst., Env. Protection Agency, 1970–72; Asst. Dir., Mgt. Syst., US AID Mission to S. Vietnam, 1969–70; Asst. Dir., Info. Syst. Div., Ofc. of Mgt. and Budget, 1965–67; Mgt. Anal., Oper. Resrch. Anal., Analytical Statistician, US Gvt., 1956–65. **Educ.:** Univ. of CA, Berkeley, 1947–50, BA (Arts & Sci); Univ. of CA, Los Angeles, 1950–51, MA (Liberal Arts); Columbia Univ., 1951–52; Univ. of Lausanne, Switzerland, 1966–67, Dr (Sci. Econ., Pub. Admin.). **Orgs.:** Assoc. Info. Mgrs.: Exec. Com. (1978–). Assn. for Syst. Mgt. ASIS. Socty. for Mgt. Info. Syst. **Honors:** U.S. Government (20 years of civil service), 4 Outstanding Service Awards and Certificates of Achievement; 5 Sustained Superior Service Awards; 2 Letters from former Presidents of the United States. **Pubns.:** Ed., *The Information Resource* (1979); *Information Resources Management: Concept and Cases* (1979); *How to Harness Information Resources: A Systems Approach* (1974); *Reference Guide to Advanced Management Techniques* (1972); various articles. **Activities:** 14-Gvt.; 17, 24, 29; 56, 75, 78 **Addr.:** Apt. B901, 500 - 23rd St. N.W., Washington, DC 20037.

Horton, Janet S. (Ja. 22, 1928, Frankfort, IN) Asst. Prof., IN State Univ., 1971–; Head, Undergrad. Lib., IN Univ., 1963–67, Asst. Circ. Libn., 1961–63. **Educ.:** Univ. of KY, 1945–47; IN Univ., 1958–60, BA (Fr.), 1960–61, MA (LS), 1967–75, PhD (LS). **Orgs.:** IN LA: Cont. Educ. Com. (1979–80). ALA. Vigo Cnty. Mental Hlth. Assn. Amer. Contract Bridge Leag. Kappa Alpha Theta Alum. Assn. IN Univ. Alum. Assn.: Bd. (1968–71). **Honors:** Phi Beta Kappa; Phi Sigma Iota; Beta Phi Mu. **Pubns.:** "The High School Graduate and the College Library," *Hoosier Sch. Libs.* (O. 1977); "Library Skills in College: the Heritage of High School," *IN Media Jnl.* (Spr. 1979). **Activities:** 1; 15, 17, 25, 39; 74 **Addr.:** Dept. of Library Science, Reeve Hall 337, Indiana State University, Terre Haute, IN 47809.

Horton, Mary A. (S. 4, 1950, Fremont, OH) Instr. Dept. Med. Lib. Sci., Univ. of OK Hlth Sci. 1977–79; Med. Transcriptionist, Univ. of OK. Hlth Sci. Ctr., Pul. Disease, 1976–77; Med. Libn., Richmond Heights Gen. Hosp., 1974–76. **Educ.:** Mary Manse Coll., 1968–72, BA (Soc. Std.); Case Western Rsrv. Univ., 1972–73, MSLS; Med. LA., 1976–83 Cert. **Orgs.:** Med. LA: Hosp. Lib. Sect.; Patient Educ. Com. (1975–77). Health Sci. Libn. of Northwestern OH. Satellites, Med. Coll. of OH. Toledo Musm. of Art. **Honors:** Kappa Gamma Pi, 1972. Beta Phi Mu, 1979. Phi Delta Gamma, 1973. **Pubns.:** Jt. auth. "A Suggested Current Literature and Reference Library for the Respiratory and Chest Physical Therapist;" Various articles for Med. LA, OK Chap. **Activities:** 1, 12; 15, 20, 39; 58, 80 **Addr.:** 135 Partridge Ln., Perrysburg, OH 43551.

Horton, Stanley W. (My. 24, 1948, Fort Lewis, WA) Dir., Lib., CO Northwest. Cmnty. Coll., 1977–; Head, Tech. Srvs., Univ. of SC, 1975–77; Catlgr., Jamestown Coll., 1973–75. **Educ.:** Univ. of WA, 1966–71, BA (Hist.), 1972–73, MLS. **Orgs.:** ALA. CO LA. Three Rivers Reg. Lib. Srv. Syst.: Governing Bd. (Pres.). CO Gvrs. Conf. on Lib. and Info. Srvs.: Del. (1979). **Activities:** 1; 31, 35, 46 **Addr.:** CNCC Box 723, Rangely, CO 81648.

Horton, Weldon Joe (Ap. 11, 1941, Denton, TX) Dir. of Lrng. Resrcs., Midland Coll., 1979–; Dir. of Lib. Srvs., Cooke Cnty. Coll., 1974–79; Asst. Libn. for Pub. Srvs., Lee Coll., 1972–74; Libn., Seminole Jr. HS, 1970–72. **Educ.:** N. TX State Univ., 1963–66, BA (Hist.), 1969–70, MLS, 1976–79, PhD (LS);

Special Subjects/Services: 50. Adult educ.; 51. Advert./Mktg.; 52. Aerosp.; 53. Agric.; 54. Area std.; 55. Arts/Hum.; 56. Autom.; 57. Bibl./Prtg.; 58. Bio. sci.; 59. Bus./Fin.; 60. Chem.; 61. Copyrt.; 62. Documtn.; 63. Educ.; 64. Engin.; 65. Env.; 66. Eth. grps.; 67. Film; 68. Food/Nutr.; 69. Geneal.; 70. Geo.; 71. Geol.; 72. Handcpd.; 73. Hist.; 74. Int. frdm.; 75. Info. sci.; 76. Insr.; 77. Law; 78. Legis.; 79. Math./Comp. sci.; 80. Med.; 81. Metals; 82. Nat. resrcs.; 83. Newsp.; 84. Nuc. sci.; 85. Oral hist.; 86. Petr./Energy; 87. Pharm.; 88. Phys./Astr./Math.; 89. Readg.; 90. Relig.; 91. Sci./Tech.; 92. Soc. sci.; 93. Telecom.; 94. Transp.; 95. (other).

Cooke Cnty. Coll., Cert. in Comp. Oper., 1979. **Orgs.:** TX LA: Dist. 18 Treas. (1980). Natl. Libns. Assn. Midland Cnty. Lib. Bd. **Pubns.:** "Bibliographic Problems With Materials Relating to Emergency Medical Care, Including a Bibliography of Books," *EMT Jnl.* (D. 1978); "The Painless, Professional Library Tour," *UNABASHED Libn.* (N. 23, 1977); "From Problems to Opportunities," *Lrng. Today* (Sum. 1975); "Grand Old Lady of the Bayou," *Media; Lib. Srvs. Jnl.* (1975). **Activities:** 1; 17, 18, 32; 56, 57 **Addr.:** Midland College, 3600 N. Garfield, Midland, TX 79701.

Horvath, David (Ap. 16, 1951, Erie, PA) Asst. Cur., Univ. of Louisville Photographic Arch., 1978–; Intern, Pic. Col., MO Hist. Socty., 1977–78; Ed., Amer. Home Missionary Socty. Papers, Microfilming Corp. of Amer., 1975–76. **Educ.:** Mercyhurst Coll., 1969–73, BA (Amer. Hist.); Cooperstown Grad. Prog., SUNY, Oneonta, 1975–76, MA (Musm. Std.); Natl. Arch. Cert., Advnc. Arch. Admin.; Presrvn. of Still Photographs, 1980. **Orgs.:** SAA: Aural & Graphics Recs. Com. (1980–). KY Cncl. on Arch. Image Access Socty. **Pubns.:** "The Red Scare in Erie, Pennsylvania 1918–1920," *Jnl. of Erie Std.* (Spr. 1974); Traveling exhibition "Photographic View of Kentucky Women, 1880–1930" (1980). **Activities:** 1, 2; 23, 39, 45; 55, 62, 95-Photography. **Addr.:** Photographic Archives, Belknap Campus, Univ. of Louisville, Louisville, KY 40208.

Horvath, Patricia M. (Ap. 10, 1952, Carlisle, PA) Asst. Law Libn., Univ. of Pittsburgh Law Lib., 1977–; Elem. Libn., Greenwood Sch. Dist., 1974–76. **Educ.:** Shippensburg State Coll., 1970–74, BS (Elem. Educ., LS); Univ. of Pittsburgh, 1976–77, MLS. **Orgs.:** AALL. West. PA Law LA: Pres. (1979–80); Exec. Bd. (1981–82). Assn. of Univ. Libs.: Salary Srvy. Com. (1980–81). **Activities:** 1; 22, 33, 34; 77, 78 **Addr.:** University of Pittsburgh Law Library, 408 Law Building, 3900 Forbes Ave., Pittsburgh, PA 15260.

Horwath, Daniel Owen (Jl. 26, 1950, St. Paul, MN) Asst. Dir., Clinton Pub. Lib., 1978–; YA Libn., S. St. Paul Pub. Lib., 1977–78. **Educ.:** Univ. of MN, 1968–74, BA (Eng.), 1975–77, MA (LS); Cmnty. Analysis Wkshp., 1978. **Orgs.:** ALA. IA LA: JMRT (1978–). Volun. Srvs. for Clinton Cnty. S. St. Paul Civic Art Comsn. Univ. of MN Twin Cities Student Assn.'s Telecomm. Corp. **Activities:** 9, 12; 16, 17, 22; 51, 56, 93 **Addr.:** 2114 N. 2nd St., Clinton, IA 52732.

Horwitz, Marsha Victoria (Ja. 16, 1942, Detroit, MI) Actg. Chief Libn., Tech. Srvs., City Coll. of NY, 1981–, Asst. Chief Libn., 1979–81, Chief, Cat. Div., 1975–79, Head, OCLC Unit, 1974–75, Catlgr., 1968–74. **Educ.:** Wayne State Univ., 1959–63, BA (Grmn.); Columbia Univ., 1963–66, MA (Grmn. Lit.), 1966–68, MSLS. **Orgs.:** ALA. NY LA: Bibl. Control Com. (1978–). NY Tech. Srvs. Libns.: Recording Secy. (1978–79). SUNY/OCLC Quality Control Com. **Honors** Phi Beta Kappa, 1963. **Activities:** 1; 17, 20, 46 **Addr.:** City College Library, Convent Avenue at 138th St., New York, NY 10031.

Hosel, Harold Victor (Ag. 25, 1947, Teaneck, NJ) Head of Gen. Ref., Libn. III, Adj. Asst. Prof. of LS, Univ. of MO, 1978–; Coord. of Lib. Instr., Gen. Lib. Univ. of CA, Riverside, 1977–78; Asst. Libn. for Reader Srvs., Burling Lib., Grinnell Coll., 1973–77. **Educ.:** Springfield Coll., 1966–69, BA (Hist.); Univ. of IA, 1972–73, MA (LS), 1970–74, MA (Relig.). **Orgs.:** ALA: ACRL; LAMA; RASD. CA LA: Chap. of Acad. & Resrch. Libns. CA Clearinghouse on Lib. Instr. (South): Treas., Exec. Com., Strg. Com., Stan. Task Force (1977–78). Libns. Assn. of Univ. of CA, Riverside: Com. on Lib. Plng. & Policies, (Ch., 1977–78). IA Regents' Univ. Consultation on Relig. and Pub. Educ. **Activities:** 1, 11; 17, 31, 39; 90, 95-Amer. History. **Addr.:** General Reference, 202B Ellis Library, University of Missouri, Columbia, MO 65201.

Hoskin, Adele (Jl. 7, 1947, Cleveland, OH) Chief Libn., Eli Lilly & Co., 1979–, Asst. Dept. Head, 1978–79, Supvsr., Lib. Srvs., 1977–78, Sr. Ref. Libn., 1971–77. **Educ.:** Hiram Coll., 1965–69, BA (Chem.); Univ. of Chicago, 1969–71, MA (LS); IN Univ., MBA. **Orgs.:** SLA. IN Coop. Lib. Srvs. Athrty.: Treas. (1978–79). **Activities:** 12; 20, 34, 39; 87, 91 **Addr.:** Eli Lilly & Co., Scientific Library, 307 E. McCarty St., Indianapolis, IN 46285.

Hoskin, Irene L. (Ag. 2, 1924, London, Eng.) Branch Coord., Grt. Victoria Pub. Lib., 1975–; Libn.-in-Charge, Thunder Bay Pub. Lib., Arthur St. Lib., 1971–73; Asst. Prov. Libn., SK Prov. Lib., 1969–71, Lib. Consult., 1968–69. **Educ.:** Univ. of SK, 1964–67, BA with Distinction, (Eng., Fr.); Univ. of BC, 1967–68, BLS. **Orgs.:** Can. LA. BC LA: Dir. (1979–80); Corres. Secy. (1980–81). Inst. of Victoria Libns.: VP (1976–77); Educ. (1977–78). Frnds. of the Prov. Musm. **Activities:** 9, 13; 17, 24, 25; 50, 72, 89 **Addr.:** Greater Victoria Municipal Library, 794 Gates St., Victoria, BC V8W 1L4 Canada.

Hostetter, Alice Wagner (F. 20, 1928, Hamilton, OH) Assoc. Prof., Dept. of Lib. Sci., Millersville State Coll., 1968–, Libn. Campus School, 1960–68; Libn. Cncl. Rock Sch. Dist., Newtown, Bucks Conty., 1950–60. **Educ.:** Millersville SC, 1946–50, BS (Eng. Lib. Sci.); Columbia Univ., 1953–57, MS LS; MI State Univ., 1970–71, Ed. Spec. (Instr. Tech.). **Orgs.:** ALA. PA Sch. LA: Prof. Stan. Com.; Nom. Comm. (1971–). AECT. PA Lrng. Resrcs. Assn. Nat. Educ. Assn. PA State Educ. Assn. AAUP. **Activities:** 10, 11; 21, 26, 48; 63, 75, 89 **Addr.:** 109 E. Charlotte St., Millersville, PA 17551.

Houck, Michael Paul (Ja. 30, 1951, Baltimore, MD) Med. Libn., Greater Baltimore Med. Ctr., 1979–; Libn., Johns Hopkins Univ. Sch. Med. Dept. of Radiology, 1977–79. **Educ.:** Washington and Lee Univ., 1969–73, BA (Eng.); Catholic Univ. of Amer., 1975–76, MLS. **Orgs.:** ALA. MD LA. Med. LA. MD Assn. Hlth. Sci. Libns.: Bylaws Com. (Ch. 1979–80). Baltimore Cnsrtm. for Resrc. Sharing: Vice Ch. (1979–80). **Honors:** Beta Phi Mu, 1978. **Addr.:** 1106 Overbrook Rd., Baltimore, MD 21239.

Houdek, Frank G. (D. 22, 1948, Long Beach, CA) Libn., Lawler, Felix & Hall, 1979–; Lect., UCLA Grad. Sch. of Lib. & Info. Sci., 1978–; Ref. Libn., Los Angeles Cnty. Law Lib., 1975–79. **Educ.:** Univ. of CA, Los Angeles, 1967–71, BA (Psy.), 1974–76, MLS, 1971–74, JD (Law). Certified Law Libn., 1979, AALL. **Orgs.:** AALL. South. CA Assn. of Law Libs.: Nsltr. Ed. (1978–80), Pres. (1981–82). SLA. State Bar of CA. **Pubns.:** *The Freedom of Information Act: A Comprehensive Bibliography of Law Related Materials* (1978); "Sports & the Law: A Comprehensive Bibliography of Law Related Materials," *COMM/ENT* (Spr. 1979); "The Federal Election Campaign Act & Its Amendments: A Selected Legal Bibliography with Annotations," *Law Lib. Jnl.* (Spr. 1979); "Automated Legal Research at the Los Angeles County Law Library," *Los Angeles Bar Jnl.* (Jl. 1977); "Admission to the Bar: An Annotated Bibliography of Law Review Articles, 1966–1976," *Bar Examiner* (1977). **Activities:** 11, 12; 17, 26, 39; 77 **Addr.:** Lawler, Felix & Hall, 700 S. Flower St., 31st Floor, Los Angeles, CA 90017.

Hough, Carolyn Adele (Jl. 5, 1940, Providence, RI) Mgr., Lib. Srvs., MI Osteopathic Med. Ctr., 1971–; Asst. Libn., Petersburg (VA) Pub. Lib., 1969–70; Indxr./Ed., *Book Review Digest*, H.W. Wilson Co., 1968–69; Ref. Libn., Detroit Pub. Lib., 1963–68. **Educ.:** Univ. of NH, 1958–62, BA (Eng.); Simmons Coll., 1962–63, MS (LS); MEDLINE training, Natl. Lib. of Med., 1977. **Orgs.:** ALA: Dupls. Exch. Com. (1981–83). Med. LA: Finance Com. (1977–79). SLA. Sci. Book & Serial Exch.: Exec. Bd. (1976–). Metro. Detroit Med. Lib. Grp.: Exec. Bd. (1973–75); Treas. (1974–75). Phi Kappa Phi. **Honors:** Phi Beta Kappa. **Pubns.:** Jt. Auth., descriptive brochure, Sci. Book & Serial Exch. (1976). **Activities:** 5, 12; 17, 24, 39; 80 **Addr.:** 525 Fourth St., Ann Arbor, MI 48103.

Hough, Leslie S. (O. 2, 1946, Springfield, OH) Archvst., William Russell Pullen Lib., GA State Univ., 1977–; Co-Dir., OH Labor Hist. Proj., OH Hist. Socty., 1975–77. **Educ.:** Olivet Nazarene Coll., 1965–69, BA (Hist.); Univ. of VA, 1969–70, MA (Hist.), 1972–75, PhD (Hist.). **Orgs.:** SAA: Labor Arch. Com., (1975–79). Socty. of GA Archvsts.: Secy. (1978–79); Pres. (1979–). Amer. Hist. Assn. South. Labor Std. Assn.: Secy.-Treas., (1977–80). Coal Miners Resrch. Assn.: Secy., (1976–78). **Activities:** 1, 2; 15, 17, 45; 66, 78, 95-Labor. **Addr.:** Southern Labor Archives, Georgia State University, Atlanta, GA 30303.

Hough, Raymond Leigh (O. 15, 1942, Cincinnati, OH) Coord., Sci. Bk. and Serials Exch., 1976–; **Educ.:** Wayne State Univ., 1971, BA (Chem.), 1971–73, MA (Chem.); Univ. of MI, 1974–81, PHD (Chem.). **Orgs.:** Sci. Bk. & Serials Exch.: Exec. Com. (1976–). Amer. Chem. Socty. **Pubns.:** Reviews. **Activities:** 6; 15, 24; 60, 80, 91 **Addr.:** 525 Fourth St., Ann Arbor, MI 48103.

Hough, William E., III (D. 20, 1930, Cincinnati, OH) Head Libn., Lebanon Valley Coll., 1970–; Head Libn., Univ. of Dubuque, 1966–70; Head Libn., King's Coll. (NY), 1959–66. **Educ.:** King's Coll. (NY), 1955, BA (Math); Dallas Theo. Semy., 1959, THM (Theo.); Columbia Univ., 1965, MSLS; Philadelphia Coll. of Bible, 1952, Dip. **Orgs.:** ALA. PA LA: Nom. Com. (1978). Assoc. Coll. Libs. of Central PA: Ch., Strg. Com. (1974–75). Interlibrary Delivery Srv. of PA: Bd. (1973–79); Pres. (1976–78). **Activities:** 1; 17, 34, 46 **Addr.:** Lebanon Valley College Library, Annville, PA 17003.

Houk, Judith Ann (F. 2, 1935, Muncie, IN) Chief Exec. officer, Lib. Rpts. and Resrch. Srv., Inc., 1981– Pres., 1972–; Supvsr., Lib. Srvs. to St. Agencies, CO St. Lib., 1978–81; Ref., Doc. Libn., CO St. Lib., 1976–78; Syst. Libn., Ctrl. CO Pub. Lib. Syst., 1968–72; Reg. Libn., Inter-County Reg. Plng. Cmsn., 1967–68; Libn., Westminster (CO) Pub. Lib., 1964–1967; Ref. Libn., Branch Libn., US Air Force Inst. of Tech., 1963–1964. Other Lib. positions. **Educ.:** IN Univ., 1956–58, BA (Hist.), 1958–59, MA (LS). **Orgs.:** ALA: Cnclr. Lg. (1972–1976). CO LA: Pres. (1967–68); Exec. Secy. (1970–72). SLA. Mt. Plains LA. **Honors:** Phi Beta Kappa, 1958; Beta Phi Mu, 1959. **Pubns.:** *Public Libraries in the Denver Metropolitan Area: A Plan and Program for Library Development to 1985.* (1968); *Classification System for Ohio State Documents* (1962); "Libraries involved in government," *Amer. Libs.* (Ap. 1970). **Activities:** 6, 13; 17, 29, 39; 56, 75 **Addr.:** 4140 West 80th Pl., Westminster, CO 80030.

House, Emelyn B. (MI) US Docum. Libn., Univ. of MI Law Lib., 1973–, Biblgphr., 1969–73. **Educ.:** Univ. of MI, 1961–70, AB (Amer. Cult.), 1970–71, AMLS. **Orgs.:** AALL: Ch., Gvt. Docum. Spec. Int. Sect. (1977–78); Ch., Gvt. Docum./SIS Com. on Legis. Hist. Proj. (1978–81). MI Assn. of Law Libs.: Pres. (1980–81); Exec. Bd. (1977–78). Gvt. Docum. RT of MI. **Honors:** Beta Phi Mu. **Activities:** 1; 15, 29, 39; 78 **Addr.:** The Law Library, The University of Michigan, Ann Arbor, MI 48109.

Housel, James Robert (F. 16, 1917, Cripple Creek, CO) Retired, 1980–; Lib. Dir., City of Ontario, CA, 1959–80; Head Libn., Monterey Park Pub. Lib., 1956–59; Dir., First Reg. Lib. of MS, 1952–56; Head Libn., Ellensburg Pub. Lib., 1950–52; Circ. and Ref. Asst., Richmond (CA) Pub. Lib., 1948–50; Machinist, Bercut-Richards Cannery, 1946–48. **Educ.:** Univ. of WY, 1937–41, BA (Pub. Admin.); Univ. of CA, Berkeley, 1947–48, BS (LS); Univ. of South. CA, 1971, MS (LS). **Orgs.:** CA LA. ALA. Inland Lib. Syst. Pub. Lib. Execs. Assn. of South. CA. Various other orgs. Amer. Legion. Masons. ON Cham. of Cmrce. Elks. Various other orgs. **Activities:** 9; 17, 19, 24; 50, 74, 85 **Addr.:** P.O. Box 855, Ontario, CA 91761.

Houser, Florence (N. 6, 1923, Worcester, MA) Chief of Ref. and Acq. Srvs., Assoc. Prof., Kingsborough Cmnty. Coll., 1973–, Head, Tech. Srvs., 1967–73, Acq. & Ref. Libn., Col. Builder, 1964–67; Evening Libn., NY City Cmnty. Coll., 1960–64; Tchr. of Lib., Lafayette HS, 1957–58; Circ. & Ref. Libn., Long Island Univ., 1948–55; Catlgr. & Ref. Libn., Equitable Life Assurance Socty., 1947–48; Asst. Libn. & Resrchr., Schenley Distillers Corp., 1945–47. **Educ.:** Brooklyn Coll., 1940–44, BA (Soclgy.-Psy.); Columbia Univ., 1944–46, BS in LS; Brooklyn Coll., 1949–53, (Soclgy.); Hebrew Union Coll., 1971–73, MA (Educ.); NYC Bd. of Educ., Cert. in Chld. Lit., 1958. **Orgs.:** LA of the City Univ. of NY. NY Lib. Club. **Activities:** 1; 15, 16, 38; 91 **Addr.:** Kingsborough Community College of the City University of N.Y., 2001 Oriental Blvd., Brooklyn, NY 11235.

Houser, L. (Ap. 25, 1922, Ashland, IL) Assoc. Prof., Univ. of Toronto, 1969–; Asst. Prof., Rutgers Univ., 1966–69. **Educ.:** Washington Univ., 1946–49, AB; Univ. of IL, 1955–57, MS (LS); Rutgers Univ., 1964–68, PHD (LS). **Orgs.:** Inst. of Prof. Libns. of ON: Pres. (1971–72). Can. LA: Stat. Com. (Ch., 1972–75). **Pubns.:** Jt. auth., *Search for A Scientific Profession* (1968); Jt. auth., "Introduction a Significant Statistics Component into a Library Science Research Methods Course," *Jnl. of Educ. for Libnshp.* (Win. 1978); Jt. auth., "The Knowledge Base for the Administration of Libraries," *Lib. Resrch.* (Aut. 1979); Jt. auth., "Library Administration Literature: A Bibliometric Measure of Subject Dispersion," *Lib. Resrch.* (Win. 1980). **Activities:** 15, 26, 41; 75, 92, 95-Bibliometrics. **Addr.:** Faculty of Library Science, University of Toronto, Toronto, ON M5S 1A1 Canada.

Housman, Edward M. (Ap. 28, 1932, Brooklyn, NY) Mgr., Info. Srvs., GTE Labs., 1970–; Info. Spec., US Army Electronics Cmnd., 1955–70. **Educ.:** Brooklyn Coll., 1950–53, BA (Chem.); Columbia Univ., 1953–54, MS (Jnlsm.). **Orgs.:** ASIS: Cnclr.; SIG Ch. Assn. of Info. and Dssm. Ctrs.: Stan. Com. Inst. of Electrical and Electronics Engins. **Honors:** ASIS, Best SIG Pubn. of Yr., 1968. **Pubns.:** *Selective Dissemination of Information, ARIST* (1972); *Impact of an SDI Service on a large R & D Installation* (1968); Speeches. **Activities:** 5, 12; 17; 56, 93 **Addr.:** Information Services, GTE Laboratories, 40 Sylvan Rd., Waltham, MA 02154.

Houston, Guyla Ann Bond (F. 27, 1938, Washington, D.C.) Head Acq. Libn., OK St. Univ., 1975–, Serials Acq. Libn., 1963–75. **Educ.:** St. Petersburg Jr. Coll., 1956–58, AA; FL St. Univ., 1958–60, BA; LA St. Univ., 1961–63, MS (LS). **Orgs.:** ALA. OK LA: Auto. RT (1978–); Pubn. Com. (1979–). **Honors:** Beta Phi Mu, 1964. **Pubns.:** *Thomas Edward Lawrence, a checklist of Lawrenciana, 1915–1965* (1967), and supplements (1970, 1975, 1978). **Addr.:** P. O. Box 564, Stillwater, OK 74074.

Hovda, Mary Lou (Ag. 8, 1927, Tyler, MN) Head Libn., Northwest. Coll., 1972–; Admin. Libn., Metro. Cmnty. Coll., 1967–72; Asst. Libn., Northwest. Coll., 1964–67. **Educ.:** Northwest. Coll., 1948–1953, BA (Bible); Macalester Coll., 1959–62, BA (Eng.); Univ. of MN, 1962–64, MA (LS). **Orgs.:** Assn. of Christ. Libns., Inc.: Secy. (1976–77). ALA. **Activities:** 1; 15, 17, 45; 59, 90, 92 **Addr.:** 339 N. Finn St., St. Paul, MN 55104.

Hove, Nancy Virginia Paysinger (N. 8, 1946, Newberry, SC) Coord., Media Field Srvs., GA Dept of Educ., 1977–; Visit. Prof., Emory Univ., Div. of Libnshp., 1976–77, Visit. Lect., 1976; Head Lib. Media Spec., Briarcliff HS, DeKalb Cnty., GA, 1970–76. **Educ.:** Agnes Scott Coll., 1964–68, BA (Hist/Pol. Sci.); Emory Univ., 1968–69, MLN (LS); Univ. of GA, 1972–75, 6th yr. (Educ. Admin.), 1975–, EdD in progress (Educ. Admin.). **Orgs.:** Metro. Atlanta LA: VP (1975–76); Pres. (1976–77). ALA: AASL, Ad Hoc Supvsrs. (1979–80); Stan. (1980–81). GA LA: Ex-officio Mem. of Bd. (1977–). GA Assn. of Instr. Tech. Delta Kappa Gamma. Kappa Delta Pi. **Honors:** Beta Phi Mu, 1970. **Activities:** 13; 17, 24, 32 **Addr.:** 156 Trinity Ave. S.W., Atlanta, GA 30303.

Hover, Leila M. (N. 1, 1932, Brooklyn, NY) Libn., Holy Name Hosp., Teaneck, NJ, 1978–; Clinic Supvr., Planned Parenthood, 1962–64; Ofc. Nurse & Admin., 1951–61. **Educ.:** Empire State Coll., 1976–77, BS (Hum.); Rutger Univ., 1977–78, MLS. **Orgs.:** Med. LA. SLA: NJ Chap., Prog. Com. (1978–); Dir., Exch. List (1979–). Hlth. Sci. Lib. Assn. of NJ. **Pubns.:** "The Independ-

PROFESSIONAL ACTIVITIES: Institutions: 1. Acad. lib.; 2. Arch.; 3. Assn.; 4. Fed./Gvt. lib.; 5. Inst. lib.; 6. Mfr./Suppl.; 7. Milit. lib.; 8. Musm.; 9. Pub. lib.; 10. Sch. lib.; 11. Sch. of lib. sci.; 12. Spec. lib.; 13. State lib.; 14. (other). **Functions/Activities:** 15. Acq./Col. dev.; 16. Adult srvs.; 17. Admin.; 18. Apprais.; 19. Archit./Bldgs.; 20. Cat./Class.; 21. Chld. srvs.; 22. Circ.; 23. Cons./Pres.; 24. Consult.; 25. Cont. ed.; 26. Educ. lib. sci.; 27. Ext. srvs.; 28. Fund/Grants; 29. Gvt. pubs.; 30. Indx./Abs.; 31. Instr. lib. use; 32. Media srvs.; 33. Micro.; 34. Netwks./Coop.; 35. Persnl.; 36. PR; 37. Publshg.; 38. Recs. mgt.; 39. Ref. srvs.; 40. Repro.; 41. Resrch.; 42. Review.; 43. Secur.; 44. Serials; 45. Spec. col.; 46. Tech. srvs.; 47. Trustees/Bds.; 48. YA srvs.; 49. (other).

ent Learner & The Academic Library: Access & Impact" in *New Horizons for Academic Libraries: ACRL 1978* (1979). **Activities:** 12; 15, 17, 39; 80 **Addr.:** 2 Mountain Run, RD 3, Boonton, NJ 07005.

How, Sarah E. (Ag. 1, 1951, Saskatoon, SK) Head, Geo. and Geophys. Lib., Univ. of CA, Los Angeles, 1981–; Ref. Libn., Univ. of IL, Chicago Circle Campus, 1980–81; Prog. Ofcr., ACRL, ALA, 1980; Ed. Mgr., *Jnl. of Geol.,* Univ. of Chicago Press, 1978–79. **Educ.:** Mt. Holyoke Coll., 1969–71; Univ. of PA, 1972–75, BA (Eng.) Magna Cum Laude; Univ. of Chicago, 1977– (LS). **Orgs.:** ALA: ACRL; MAGERT. SLA: Geo. and Map Div. Chicago Map Socty. Amer. Com. for Irish Stds. **Pubns.:** Pic. Ed., *ALA World Encyclopedia of Library and Information Services* (1980); Interim Ed., *College & Research Libraries News* (My.-Ag. 1980). **Activities:** 1, 12; 39; 70, 91 **Addr.:** Geology-Geophysics Library, 4697 Geology Bldg., University of California, Los Angeles, CA 90024.

Howard, Alison (Ja. 30, 1939, Worcester, MA) Optometry Libn., Univ. of CA, Berkeley, 1969–. **Educ.:** Swarthmore, 1956–60, BA (Bio.); Univ. of CA, Berkeley, 1968–69, MLS. **Orgs.:** Med. LA. North. CA Med. Lib. Grp. Assn. of Visual Sci. Libns.: Ch. (1974–75). Amer. Acad. of Optometry: Sect. on Optometric Educ., Prog. Com. (1975). **Activities:** 1, 12; 15, 30, 39; 80 **Addr.:** Optometry Library, University of California, Berkeley, CA 94720.

Howard, Alma L. (Jl. 8, 1927, Detroit, MI) Consult., Bus. Hist., Indp. Archvst. and Resrchr., 1978–; Pub. Info. Ofcr., Kitsap Reg. Lib., 1977–78; Dir., E. Detroit Meml. Lib., 1971–76; Lib. Dir., Detroit Country Day Sch., 1968–71. **Educ.:** MI State Univ., 1945–48, BA (Jnlsm.); Univ. of MI, 1965–68, MA (LS). **Orgs.:** SAA. Assn. of Recs. Mgrs. and Admins. **Activities:** 14-Indp.; 24, 38, 41; 75, 86 **Addr.:** 5709 35th Ave. N.E., Seattle, WA 98105.

Howard, Anna Lila (S. 15, 1918, Ashland, KY) Dir. of Hlth. Sci. Libs., Marshall Univ., 1975–; Med. Libn., South. IL Univ., 1970–75, Asst. Sci. Libn., 1964–70; Libn., Mead Corp., 1949–63; Dir. of Inst. Libs., Commonwealth of KY, 1944–48. **Educ.:** Univ. of MN, 1941–43, BS (LS); Columbia Univ., 1948–49, MS (LS). **Orgs.:** Med. LA. SLA. WV LA. Altrusa Intl. AAUW. **Activities:** 1, 12; 17, 34; 58, 80, 91 **Addr.:** 1313 Lexington Ave., Ashland, KY 41101.

Howard, Corliss Mays (Ja. 19, 1927; St. Louis, MO) Coord., Lib. Resrcs., State Dept. of Educ., Fed. Prog. Div., 1974–; Master Counslr., Mgr., Little Rock Skills Ctr., 1971–74; Master Counslr., Employment Security Div., 1965–71; Teacher, VPrincipal, Vocational Couns. AR Pub. Sch., 1947–65. **Educ.:** A.M.&N. Coll. (Univ. of AR), Pine Bluff, 1944–47, BA (Soc. Std.); Syracuse Univ., 1948–53, MA (Counsel.); Univ. of Cent. AR, Univ. of AR, Little Rock, 1974–76 (Cert. Lib. Sci.). **Orgs.:** ALA: AASL. AAVA. AR LA: Leg. Com., (1977–78); Treas., (1979–80). AR AV Org. Nat. Educ. Assn. AR Educ. Assn. AR State Brd. of Higher Educ. Post Secondary Educ. Plng. Comsn. AAUW: Br. Pres. (1967–69); First VP (1965–67); Secy. (1963–65); Div. Bd. (1967–69); State Div. Leg. Ch. (1975). **Honors:** AR Pre-White House Conf. on Lib. and Info. Srvs., Del., 1978; Natl. Del., 1979. **Pubns.:** "Here to Stay," *Women in the AR Labor Force* (M., 1978). **Activities:** 4, 13; 15, 28, 32; 63, 66, 89 **Addr.:** State Coordinator, Library Resources, Federal Programs Division, 1209 E. Twin Lakes Dr., Little Rock, AR 72205.

Howard, Donald H. (Mr. 20, 1941, Nampa, ID) Hist. & Relig. Libn., Brigham Young Univ., 1969–; Catlgr., Wesleyan Univ., 1967–69; Docum. & Maps Libn., Brigham Young Univ., 1965–67, Asst. Circ. Libn., 1964–65. **Educ.:** Univ. of ID, 1959–63, BA (Hist.); Univ. of CA, Berkeley, 1963–64, MLS. **Orgs.:** UT LA. ATLA. Mormon Hist. Assn. **Activities:** 1; 15, 31, 39; 69, 90, 92 **Addr.:** 4224 HBLL, Brigham Young University, Provo, UT 84602.

Howard, Edward Neal (Ja. 22, 1920, Carlisle, IN) Dir., Vigo Cnty. Pub. Lib., 1968–; Asst. Dir., Bur. of Pub. Discuss., IN Univ., 1966–68; Asst. Dir., Monroe Cnty. (IN) Pub. Lib., 1964–66. **Educ.:** IN Univ., 1961–65, AB (Eng.), 1966–68, MA (LS). **Orgs.:** ALA: Cncl. (1975–79); Pubshg. Com. (1975–78). IN LA: Ed., Focus on IN Libs. (1966–70); Legis. Com. (1979–). IN Com. for the Hum.: Charter Mem. (1971–75). Wabash Valley Press Club: Bd. of Dirs., Ch., Mem. Com. (1977–). Untd. Way of the Wabash Valley: Ch. of Bd. (1977). IN State Lib.: Cont. Educ. Adv. Com. (1979–). Other orgs. **Honors:** IN Lib. Trustees Assn., Libn. of the Yr., 1969; Phi Beta Kappa, 1965; John Cotton Dana Pubcty. Awd., H.W. Wilson Co., 1969; Terre Haute Jaycees, Disting. Srv. Awd., 1975. **Pubns.:** *Local Power And The Community Library* (1978); "The Orbital Organization," *Lib. Jnl.* (My. 1, 1970); "Toward Ppbs In The Public Library," *Amer. Libs.* (Ap. 1971). **Activities:** 9; 17, 36; 92 **Addr.:** Vigo County Public Library, One Library Sq., Terre Haute, IN 47807.

Howard, Elizabeth E. (Ag. 14, 1935, Chicago, IL) Sch. Libn., Hillside Sch., Dist. 93, 1972–; Adj. Fac., Grad. Sch. of LS, Rosary Coll., 1976–78; Intermediate Grade Tchr., Hillside Sch., Dist. 93, 1958–71. **Educ.:** Rosary Coll., 1953–57, BA (Econ.); Loyola Univ., 1966–68, MEd (Curric., Guid.); Rosary Coll., 1971–72, MALS. **Orgs.:** ALA. **Honors:** Beta Phi Mu, 1972. **Activities:** 10; 15, 20, 21 **Addr.:** Hillside School, District 93, 4804 W. Harrison, Hillside, IL 60162.

Howard, Elizabeth Fitzgerald (D. 28, 1927, Baltimore, MD) Asst. Prof., WV Univ., 1978–; Visit. Lectr., Univ. of Pittsburgh, 1976–78; Ref./Per. Libn., Pittsburgh Theo. Semy., 1974–77; Resrc. Libn., Episcopal Diocese of Pittsburgh, 1972–74; Chld. Libn., Boston Pub. Lib., 1952–1956. **Educ.:** Radcliffe Coll., 1944–48, AB (Hist.); Univ. of Pittsburgh, 1970–77, MLS, PHD (LS). **Orgs.:** ALA: Ref. & Subscrpn. Bk Reviews Com. (1978–); Lib. Srvs. to Rural Poor & Appalachian Peoples (1979–). Beta Phi Mu: Secy., Natl. Assn. (1979–80). WVLA. ATLA. **Activities:** 11; 21, 26, 48 **Addr.:** 919 College Ave., Pittsburgh, PA 15232.

Howard, Helen Arlene (S. 7, 1927, Kingston, ON) Assoc. Prof., Fac. of LS, Univ. of Toronto, 1977–; Dir. of Libs., Sir George Williams Univ., 1967–73, Head of Pub. Srvs., 1964–67; Fndr. and Libn.-in-Charge, Montreal Engin. Co., 1958–64; Libn.-in-Charge, Newsprint Assn. of Canada, 1957–58; Head, Ref. Dept., Redpath Lib., McGill Univ., 1956–57. **Educ.:** Queen's Univ., 1945–48, BA (Fr., Grmn.); McGill Univ., 1955–56, BLS, 1964–67, MLS; Rutgers Univ., 1973–76, PhD; Lib. Admin. Prog., Univ. of MD, 1967. **Orgs.:** ALA: ALA/CLA Jt. Com. (1970–71; Ch., 1970–72). AALS: Mem. Com. (1980–); Nom. Com. (1979–). Can. LA: Nom. Com. (1979–); Cnclr. (1972–73). Can. Assn. of Coll. and Univ. Libs. Other orgs. and coms. U.S. Book Exch.: Bd. of Dir. (1972–73). Arctic Inst. of N. Amer.: Lib. Working Grp. (1968–70). Univ. of Toronto Fac. Assn. **Honors:** Cncl. on Lib. Resrcs., Flwshp., 1973. **Pubns.:** *Administrative Integration of Information Resources and Services in Universities in Canada and the United States* (1974); "Innovation in University Organization: the Communication Model," *Jnl. of Acad. Libnshp.* (1980); "The Relationship Between Background of Experience and Training of Online Searchers and Search Results," *Procs. of the 1980 Anl. Conf. of the Can. Assn. for Info. Sci.* **Activities:** 11; 17, 24, 35; 64, 75, 91 **Addr.:** University of Toronto, Faculty of Library Science, 140 St. George St., Toronto, ON M5S 1A1 Canada.

Howard, Joseph Harvey (Ja. 15, 1931, Olustee, OK) Asst. Libn. for Procs. Srvs., Lib. of Congs. 1976–; Asst. Dir., Catlg., 1975–76, Chief, Ser. Record Div., 1972–75, Chief, Desc. Catlg. Div., 1968–72, Asst. Chief, Desc. Catlg. Div., 1967–68; Chief, Cat. Dept., Washington Univ., 1965–67; Assoc. Dir. of Pub. Srvs., Univ. of CO, 1959–63, Circ. Libn., 1958–59. **Educ.:** Univ. of OK, 1948–52, BME (Mus. Educ.); 1956–57, MLS. **Orgs.:** ALA: RTSD, Mann Cit. Com., Ch. (1979–80); Cat. Pol. and Resrch Com. (1976–); Brd. of Dir., (1977–). Assn. of Resrch. Libs.: Task Force on Bib. Cont., (1978–). Dec. Class. Ed. Pol. Com., OCLC Task Force on AACR 2/Auth. Cont., Consult. (1979–). **Honors:** Univ. of OK Lib. Sch. Alum., Awd. for Outstanding Cont. to Libnshp., 1979. **Pubns.:** *Malay Manuscripts:* (1966). "Main Entry for Serials," *Lib. of Cong. Info. Bltn.* (1974). **Activities:** 1, 4; 17, 34, 46; 56, 75 **Addr.:** 336 M St., S.W., Washington, DC 20024.

Howard, Milo B. Jr. (O. 21, 1933, Montgomery, AL) Dir., AL Dept. of Arch. and Hist., 1967–, Asst. Dir., 1965–67, Archvst., 1958–65. **Educ.:** Auburn Univ., 1951–55, BA (Hist.), 1957–60, MA (Hist.). **Orgs.:** AL LA. SAA. AL Hist. Assn.: Treas (1959–); Pres. (1965–66). **Honors:** AL Acad. of Honor, 1975. **Pubns.:** Jt. auth., *Memoire Justificatif of the Chevalier Montaut de Monberault* (1965); Jt. auth., *Minutes Journals and Acts of the General Assembly of British West Florida* (1978). **Activities:** 2, 12; 17†

Howard, Pamela F. (F. 22, 1953, San Diego, CA) Ref. Libn., Latin Amer. Lib., Tulane Univ., 1980–; Libn., Santa Monica Pub. Lib., 1980; Asst. Ref. Libn., Univ. of CA, Los Angeles, 1979–80. **Educ.:** San Diego State Univ., 1971–75, BA (Latin Amer. Std.), MA (Latin Amer. Std.); Univ. of CA, Los Angeles, 1977–79, MLS. **Orgs.:** SALALM: Rapporteur (1979); Lcl. Arrange. (Coord., 1981). CA LA. **Pubns.:** *Wife Beating: a Selected, Annotated Bibliography* (1978); Transl., "Historia de la Población de la Parroquia de San Miguel Duenas," *Mesoamér.* (Je. 1981); various articles in *SALALM Nsltr.* **Activities:** 1; 15, 39, 49-Gifts and Exch.; 54, 66 **Addr.:** Latin American Library, 7001 Freret St., Tulane University, New Orleans, LA 70118.

Howard, Sandra L. (F. 18, 1948, Pittsburgh, PA) Lib. Srv. Mgr., Netwk. Coord., Pittsburgh Reg. Lib. Ctr., 1978–; Coord. of Tech. Srvs., Cmnty. Coll. of Allegheny Cnty., 1977–78; Tech. Srvs. Libn., Butler Cnty. Cmnty. Coll., 1976–76; Cult. Libn., Cncl. of Three Rivers Amer. Indian Ctr., 1974–76. **Educ.:** PA State Univ., 1966–70, BA (Eng.); Univ. of Pittsburgh, 1973–74, MLS. **Orgs.:** ALA. **Activities:** 1, 14-Network; 17, 34, 46; 55, 56, 75 **Addr.:** PRLC, Beatty Hall, Chatham College, Pittsburgh, PA 15232.

Howatt, Sr. Helen Clare (Ap. 5, 1927, San Francisco, CA) Lib. Dir., Holy Names Coll., 1977–; Jr. HS Math Tchr., St. Cecilia Sch., San Francisco, 1971–77; Sch. Lib., St. Monica Sch., 1969–71; Sch. Lib., St. Augustine Sch., 1964–69; Prin., St. Mary School, 1960–63; Prin., St. Monica Elem. Sch., 1957–60. **Educ.:** Holy Names Coll., 1955, BA (Hist.); CA Stan. Tchg. Cred., 1955; Univ. of South. CA, 1972, MSLS; CA Gen. Sch. Srvs. Cred. in Libnshp., 1962; Cert. for Advnc. Std., Inst. for Sch. Libns., 1966. **Orgs.:** ALA. CA LA. Cath. LA: North. CA Unit Elem. Sch. Coord. (1971–72). Archdiocese of Los Angeles: Curric. Com. for Span. Speaking Chld. (1962–63). **Pubns.:** Contrib., *Calculator Math* (1978). **Activities:** 1; 17, 31; 55, 90 **Addr.:** 3500 Mountain Blvd., Oakland, CA 94619.

Howder, Murray L. (Ag. 10, 1932, Washington, DC) Dir., Lrng. Resrcs. Ctr., Washington Intl. Coll., 1981–; Mgr. Info. Srvs., Natl. Clearhouse for Biling. Educ., 1979–81; Assoc. Proj. Mgr., ERIC Prcs. & Ref. Facility, 1977–79, Acq. Libn., 1971–79; Asst. Dir., ARL, 1969–71; Assoc. Prof./Acq. Libn., Gallaudet Coll., 1968–69; Asst. Prof./Brigade Libn., US Nvl. Acad., 1967–68; Sr. Ed./Catlgr./Transl., Lib. of Congs., 1959–67. **Educ.:** George Washington Univ., 1950–54, BA (Gvt.); Univ. of Edinburgh, 1954, Cert. (Hist.); Middlebury Coll., 1958–60, MA (Russ.); Cath. Univ., 1961–68, MS (LS); Army Lang. Sch., 1955–56, Cert. (Russ.). **Orgs.:** DC LA: Secy. (1974–76); VP/Pres, 1979–81). ALA: Chap. Rel. Com. (1981–84); Ch., GODORT (1979–80). Socty. of Fed. Ling.: Pres. (1963–67). Cncl. of Comm. Societies: Secy./Treas. (1977–79). **Honors:** Slavic Honor Socty., 1965. **Pubns.:** "Subject Analysis" in *Anl. Review of Inf. Sci. & Tech.* (1977); "Library Surveys" in *Resrch. Libs.* (1971); "Preparing Documents for Users," *Resrcs. in Educ.* (1973); "Translation of French Chemical Texts," *Jnl. of Chem. Documen.* (My. 1970). **Activities:** 12; 15, 17, 49-Computer Services; 55, 63, 75 **Addr.:** 3711 Livingston St., N.W., Washington, DC 20015.

Howdle, Susan F. (Ja. 28, 1949, Milwaukee, WI) Libn., Quarles and Brady Law Firm, 1975–, Asst. Libn., 1973–75. **Educ.:** Univ. of WI, 1967–71, BA (Letters, Sci.), 1971–73, MLS. **Orgs.:** AALL. Lib. Cncl. of Metro. Milwaukee. SLA. **Activities:** 12; 15, 39, 41; 77 **Addr.:** Quarles & Brady, 780 N. Water St., Milwaukee, WI 53202.

Howe, Helen E. (Jl. 21, 1925, Philadelphia, PA) Head Libn., Pedagogical Lib., Sch. Dist. of Philadelphia, 1973–, Asst. Libn., 1965–73; Dietitian, Sch. Dist. of Philadelphia, 1947–65. **Educ.:** PA State Univ., 1943–47, BS (Home Econ.); Drexel Univ., 1963–66, MSLS. **Orgs.:** ALA: ACRL. Educ. Libns. Assn. **Activities:** 5, 12; 15, 17, 35; 63 **Addr.:** Wynnewood Park Apts., 13A, Wynnewood, PA 19096.

Howe, Peggy O. (N. 24, 1928, Fairfield, AL) Pub. Info. Ofcr., NC Dept. of Cultural Resrcs., 1970–; Staff writer, *The Raleigh Times,* 1967–70; Ed., *The Ware Shoals Life,* 1951–54; Pub. Info. Ofcr., U.S. Steel, 1949–51. **Educ.:** Univ. of AL, 1945–49, AB (Jnlsm.); IN Univ., 1965 (writing); other courses. **Orgs.:** NC LA: PR Com. (1977–78). SELA. ALA: LAMA, Secy., PR Srvs. to Libs. (1980–82); White House Conf. PR Com. (1976–78); PR Com. to State Libs. (1977–). NC Assn. of Gvt. Info. Ofcrs.: Secretary, (1974–75); Secretary (1977), V. Pres. 1978, Pres. (1979). Raleigh PR Socty.: Publicity Chm. (1978); Secretary (1979); Exec. Board (1980–). **Honors:** Raleigh Public Relations Society, Annual PR Awd., 1977, Disting. Achvmt. Awd., 1980; State Empl. Combined Campaign, "Outstanding Ch. Awd.," 1979; John Cotton Dana–ALA–LAMA–PR, 1978. **Activities:** 13; 36 **Addr.:** N.C. Dept. of Cultural Resources, 109 E. Jones St., Raleigh, NC 27611.

Howell, Barbara Judith (Ap. 4, 1949, Brookline, MA) Dir., Info. Ctr., Harvard Jt. Ctr. for Radiation Therapy, 1979; Info. Spec., Pfizer, Inc, 1976–77, Asst. Libn., 1974–76; Dir. of Lib., St. Elizabeth's Hosp., 1973–74. **Educ.:** Univ. of MA, 1967–71, BA (Psy.), Simmons Coll., 1972–73, MS (LS). **Orgs.:** ASIS. **Pubns.:** "Those Anti-Doctor Books," *NEJM* (Ap., 1975). **Activities:** 1, 12; 17, 39; 80, 84 **Addr.:** Information Center, Harvard Joint Center for Radiation Therapy, 50 Binney St., Boston, MA 02115.

Howell, Bradley Sue (Jl. 15, 1933, McKinney, TX) Media Coord., San Jacinto K-6 Elem. Sch., 1960–; Tchr., TX Hist., Mineral Wells Jr. HS, 1957–58; Tchr., Lang. Arts/Soc. Std., Hood Jr. HS, 1955–56. **Educ.:** Southern Meth. Univ., 1951–55; BS (Educ.), E. TX State Univ., 1962–68, MLS. **Orgs.:** AASL: "Student Involvement in the Media Program" Com. (1972–76). Amer. Lib. Srvs. to Cldn.: Ch., Local Arr. Dallas Conf. (1979); Newbery Com. (1980). Mildred Batchelor Awd. Com. (1981–83). Dallas Assn. of Sch. Libns.: VP (1975–76) Pres. (1976–77). Texas Association of School Librarians Chairman, Nominations Committee 1977–78. TX LA: Dist. V, Treas. (1975–76); Ch. (1977–78); Nat. Lib. Week Com. (1977–78). Delta Kappa Gamma. Pres. Eta Zeta Chap., (1976–78); Ch., Exhibits Alpha State (1975). Comsn. on Arch. and Hist.: Ch., N. TX Conf. United Meth. Church (1972–75; 1976–80). **Pubns.:** "Student Involvement in the Media Program," *TX Lib. Jrnl.* (D. 1973). **Activities:** 10; 21 **Addr.:** 722 Ridgeway Street, Dallas, TX 75214.

Howell, John B. (O. 25, 1925, Greer, SC) Dir., MS Coll. Lib., 1960–; Circ. Libn., Univ. of GA, 1958–60; Asst. Libn., Clemson Univ., 1954–58; Ref. Libn., VA Polytech. Inst., 1953–54; Acq. Libn., Emory Univ., 1946–51. **Educ.:** Furman Univ., 1942–45, BA (Eng.), 1945–46, BA, LS, Univ. of IL, 1952–53, MS (LS). **Orgs.:** ALA: State Mem. Ch. (1964–66). SELA: Treas. (1972–74); Pres., (1976–78). MS LA: Treas.

Special Subjects/Services: 50. Adult educ.; 51. Advert./Mktg.; 52. Aerosp.; 53. Agric.; 54. Area std.; 55. Arts/Hum.; 56. Autom.; 57. Bibl./Prtg.; 58. Bio. sci.; 59. Bus./Fin.; 60. Chem.; 61. Copyrt.; 62. Documtn.; 63. Educ.; 64. Engin.; 65. Env.; 66. Eth. grps.; 67. Film; 68. Food/Nutr.; 69. Geneal.; 70. Geo.; 71. Geol.; 72. Handcpd.; 73. Hist.; 74. Int. frdm.; 75. Info. sci.; 76. Insr.; 77. Law; 78. Legis.; 79. Math./Comp. sci.; 80. Med.; 81. Metals; 82. Nat. resrcs.; 83. Newsp.; 84. Nuc. sci.; 85. Oral hist.; 86. Petr./Energy; 87. Pharm.; 88. Phys./Astr./Math.; 89. Readg.; 90. Relig.; 91. Sci./Tech.; 92. Soc. sci.; 93. Telecom.; 94. Transp.; 95. (other).

(1966–67); Pres., (1970). **Pubns.:** Ed., *Special Collections in Libraries of the Southeast* (1978); Ed., *SC Libn.* (1956–58); Ed., *MS Lib. News* (1972–76); Cont. Ed., *Southeastern Libn.* (1979–). **Activities:** 1; 17, 37 **Addr.:** Mississippi College Library, P.O. Box 127, Clinton, MS 39056.

Howell, Katherine E. (Jl. 28, 1920, Rome, GA) Dir., New Hanover Cnty. Pub. Lib., Wilmington, NC, 1956–; Asst. Libn., Wilmington Pub. Lib., 1954–56; Catlgr., Carnegie Lib., Rome, GA, 1950–52; Ref. Libn., Long Beach (CA) Pub. Lib., 1947–48. **Educ.:** Converse Coll., 1937–41, BA (Soclgy.); Emory Univ., 1946, BA (LS). **Orgs.:** NC LA: Dir. (1966–67); Ch., Persnl./Com., Pub. Lib. Sect. (1968–69). SELA. ALA. Hist. Wilmington Fndn.: Bd. of Trustees (1972–). Lower Cape Fear Hist. Socty.: Bd. (1963–69). Hist. Presrvn. Socty. of NC: Reg. VP (1970–). **Addr.:** 10 S. 5th Ave., Wilmington, NC 28401.

Howell, Margaret Anderson (Ja. 16, 1936, Penrose, CO) Head, Spec. Col., Univ. of MO, 1974–, Lib. Sci. Libn., 1968–74; Ext. Libn., Daniel Boone Reg. Lib., 1959–62. **Educ.:** SW MO State Univ., 1953–57, BS (Educ.); Univ. of IL, 1958–59, MS (LS). **Orgs.:** ALA. MO LA: Arch. Com. (1975–79; Ch. 1976–79). **Pubns.:** *English Dissent; A Catalogue to an Exhibition of Eighteenth Century Pamphlets* (1979). **Addr.:** 402 Elmer Ellis Library, University of Missouri-Columbia, Columbia, MO 65201.

Howell, Marvin E. (D. 28, 1925, Manila, AR) Ref. Libn., Sacramento City Coll., 1978–; Dir. of Lib. Srvs., Sacramento City Coll., 1967–78; Consult. in Sch. Lib. Srvs.; CA State Dept. of Educ., 1963–67; Coord. of Instr. Matls., Orange Un. Sch. Dist., 1961–63; Tchrs., 1947–61. **Educ.:** Harding Univ., 1945–48; BA (Bio.); George Peabody Coll. of Vanderbilt Univ., 1949–50; MA (Sch. Adm.), Univ. of Southern CA, Los Angeles, 1961–62, MS LS. **Orgs.:** ALA. CA Assn. of Sch. Libns. CA LA.: Cncl. (1974–76). Sacramento Area LA. Lib. Admin. Assn. of Northern CA. Prof. Educ. Grp. of CA. Comstock Club. Sacramento Book Collectors Club. **Honors:** Phi Delta Kappa. Alpha Psi Omega. **Pubns.:** *School Libraries in California,* (1968). "Should school libraries be open at night?" *CA Educ.* (1963). "Should School Libraries be Open at Night," *Educ. Digest* (1965). **Activities:** 1, 4, 10; 15, 39, 44; 63, 83 **Addr.:** 7513 Collingwood St., Sacramento, CA 95822.

Howell, Mary Gertrude (My. 25, 1932, Wenona, IL) Head Tech. Info. Srv. Dept., Cyanamid Med. Resrch. Div., 1971–; Head Lit. Srvs. Dept., Lederle Labs., 1967–70, Sr. Lit. Chem., 1959–67. **Educ.:** Univ. IL, 1950–54, BS (Chem.); MA Inst. of Tech., 1955–59, PhD (Organic Chem.). **Orgs.:** ASIS. Drug Info. Assn. Amer. Chem. Socty.: Div. Chem. Info. Div. Comps. in Chem. Pharm. Mfr. Assn.: Assoc. Sci. Info. Subsect., Strg. Com. (1974–77). Com. on Chem. Info. Natl. Resrch. Cncl. Natl. Acad. Sci. **Pubns.:** *Formula Guide to NMR Literature Data Volume 1 and 2* (1965, 1966); "Status of Chemical Information," *Jnl. Chem. Doc.* (1973); various other pubns. in chem. **Activities:** 12; 17, 39, 46; 58, 60, 80 **Addr.:** Cyanamid Medical Research Division, Pearl River, NY 10965.

Howland, Margaret E. C. (Je. 6, 1927, Northampton, MA) Dir. of Lrng. Resrcs., Greenfield Cmnty. Coll., 1968–; Libn., Univ. of MA Lib., 1968; Libn., Travelers Resrch. Ctr., Inc., 1962–68; Libn., Factory Insurance Assn., 1961–62; Law Catlgr., CT State Lib., 1961; Libn., Combustion Engin., Inc., 1957–61. **Educ.:** Hofstra Univ., 1947–49, BA (Phil.); South. CT State Coll., 1960–72, MSLS; Univ. of MA, 1974–79, MPA (Pub. Admin.) **Orgs.:** SLA: CT Valley Chap., Secy.; VP; Pres. MA Conf. of Chief Libns.: Secy.; VP; Pres. MA Cncl. of Lib./Lrng. Resrc. Dir.: Secy.; VP; Pres. MA Admin. in Cmnty. Coll.: Ch., Const. Com. **Pubns.:** Contrib., *Learning Resources and the Instructional Program in Community Colleges* (1980); Contrib., *Directory of Subject Strengths in Connecticut* (1967). **Activities:** 1, 13; 17, 24, 45; 95-Public Admin. **Addr.:** Greenfield Community College, One College Dr., Greenfield, MA 01301.

Howrey, Mary M. (Ja. 31, 1950, Chicago, IL) Lib. Dir., Aurora Coll., 1980–; Soclgy./Anthrop./Geo. Libn., North. IL Univ., 1979–80; Media Spec., Joliet Twp. HS, 1978–79; Media Spec., Plainfield HS, 1975–78. **Educ.:** Moraine Valley Cmnty. Coll., 1968–70, AA; IL State Univ., 1970–72, BSEd (Soclgy., LS), 1972–77, MS (Soclgy.); Rosary Coll., 1975–78, MLS. **Orgs.:** ALA. IL LA. LIBRAS (Cnsrtm. of Chicago-area private liberal arts coll.): Ch., New Directions Com. 1980–); Secy. (1981–82). IRLC: Dir. of Human Resrcs. in Libs. Com. (1980–81). IL Educ. Assn. Amer. Sociological Assn. Amer. Socty. of Indxrs. **Honors:** Beta Phi Mu, 1978. **Pubns.:** "Professionalism of Librarians," *IL Libs.* (My. 1978). **Activities:** 1; 17; 92 **Addr.:** 216A Dee Rd., North Aurora, IL 60542.

Howser, Ray E. (Je. 3, 1923, IL) Oper. Mgr., Resrc. Sharing Alliance of W. Ctrl. IL, 1981–; Exec. Dir., IL Valley Lib. Syst., 1970–81, Asst. Dir., 1966–70; Asst. Dir., Peoria Pub. Lib., 1959–66, Coord. of Grp. Srvs., 1955–59, Chief AV Dept., 1952–55. **Educ.:** Drake Univ., 1946; Univ. of IL, 1947–49, BS (Pub. Admin.), 1949–51, MSLS. **Orgs.:** ALA: State Ch., Rcrt. Network (1964–66). IL LA: Treas. (1976); Ch., Legis. Lib. Dev. Com. (1980); Ch., Rcrt. Com. (1964–66); Mem. Com. (1955). CLENE. IL State Lib. Adv. Com.: Mem. (1979–81). **Honors:** IL LA, Libn. of the Yr., 1980. **Pubns.:** Various articles. **Activities:** 13, 14-Multi-Type Lib. Syst.; 17, 34; 78 **Addr.:** Illinois Valley Library System, Pekin, IL 61554.

Hoyland, Christine June (Je. 17, 1943, Doncaster, Yorkshire, England) Film Eval./Progmr., Mississauga Pub. Lib., 1976–; Film Libn., Burlington Pub. Lib., 1973-76. **Educ.:** York Univ., 1975, (Fine Art/Film). **Orgs.:** ON Film Assn.: Bd. Pubns Subcom. (1979–); Nsltr. Advert. Mgr. (1979–). ON LA: Int. Frdm. Subcom. (1978). Educ. Film LA: Juror, Amer. Film Fest. (1978, 1979). Can. Filmmakers Distribution Ctr.: Bd. of Dir.; Secy. (1978). **Pubns.:** Contrib., *The Film User's Guide to Canadian Short Films* (1978); "Reviewing Reviews," *Nsltr. Called Fred* (D. 1976); "Another Gruelling Grierson," *Nsltr. Called Fred* (S. 1978); other reviews. **Activities:** 9; 15, 32, 42; 67 **Addr.:** Mississauga Public Library, 110 Dundas St. West, Mississauga, ON L5B 1H6 Canada.

Hoyle, Karen Nelson (Boston, MA) Curator and Assoc. Prof., Univ. of MN, 1967–; Asst. Libn., Tchr., John Marshall Sr. HS, (1961–63); Libn., Amer. HS, Augsburg, Germany, 1964–65; Elem. Sch. Libn., Anoka-Hennepin Sch. Dist., 1966–67. **Educ.:** St. Olaf Coll., 1954–58, BA (Eng.); Univ. of CA, Berkeley, 1964, MLS; Univ. of MN, 1971, MA (Scan. Area Std.), 1975, PhD (LS). **Orgs.:** ALA: Mildren L. Batchelder Awd. (Ch., 1978); Natl. Plng. of Spec. Col. (1969–75); Caldecott Awd. (1980); Notable Chld.'s Books (1971–75). IFLA: Secy. (1979–). RT of Libs. Rep. Documen. Ctrs. for Resrch. in Chld. Lit. Socty. for the Advancement of Scan. Std. Chld. Lit. Assn.: Lcl. Ch., 1981 Conf. Intl. Resrch. Socty. for Chld. Lit. **Pubns.:** Many articles in *Twentieth Century Children's Writers* (1978); "Images of Pluralism in Children's Literature," *MN Conf. on Ethnic America Procs.* (1978); "Virginia Lee Burton," "Natalie Savage Carlson," and "Marguerite Lofft De Angeli" in *American Women Writers* (1979); "A Children's Classic: Millions of Cats" *Mss.* (Fall 1979); "Children's Literature Research Collections, University of Minnesota" *Mss.* (Fall 1979); other articles. **Activities:** 1; 49-Chld. lit. Resrch. **Addr.:** CLRC, 109 Walter Library, U of MN, Minneapolis, MN 55455.

Hoyt, Anne Kelley (Mr. 31, 1919, Muskogee, OK) Dir., Curric. Mtrls. Lab., OK State Univ. Lib., 1974–; Assoc. Prof., LS, OK State Univ., 1969–74; Asst. Libn., Instr., Northeast. State Coll., 1966–69; Educ. Div. Libn., NM State Univ. Lib., 1965–66; Libn., Jr. HS, Springdale, AR, 1957–64; Libn., OK State Tech., 1948–50; Libn., Washington Cnty. Lib., Fayetteville, AR, 1946–47; Libn., Bacone Coll., 1943–45; Branch Libn., Pub. Lib., Muskogee, OK, 1942–43. **Educ.:** Univ. of AR, 1938–42, BA (Eng.), 1942–62, MEd (Educ.); LA State Univ., 1964–65, MS (LS). **Orgs.:** ALA: OK mem. Ch. (1972–74). SWLA. AR LA. OK LA: Secy. (1968–69); Lib. Educ. Div. (Ch., 1974, 1979); Awds. Com. (Ch., 1975); Resol. Com. (Ch., 1977). **Honors:** Beta Phi Mu. **Pubns.:** *Melt-Down of the Melting Pot: Materials for Multicultural Education in the Curriculum Materials Laboratory of Oklahoma State University* (1980); *Bibliography of the Cherokees* (1969); Jt. auth., "Now Upon a Time: A Look at the Curriculum Materials Laboratory at OSU," *OK Libn.* (O. 1980); Jt. auth., *Oklahoma Fact and Fancy: A Selected Annotated Graded Bibliography for Schools* (1968). **Addr.:** 625 S. Monroe, Stillwater, OK 74074.

Hoyt, Beryl E. (Scranton, IA) Retired; Ed. Libn., Div. Lib. Srvs., WI Dept. Pub. Instruc., 1966–80; Pubns. Libn., Racine (WI) Pub. Lib., 1956–65; Asst. to the Chief, ALA Publshg. Srvs., 1953–56; Head Libn., Simpson Coll., 1944–53; Head Libn., Dakota Wesleyan Univ., 1943–44; Head Libn., IN Ctrl. Coll., 1937–40. **Educ.:** Simpson Coll., 1932–36, AB (Eng.); Univ. IL, 1936–37, BS (LS); Northwest. Univ., 1940–42, MA (Relig.). **Orgs.:** ALA: Cncl. (1949–53); RASD, Pubns. Adv. Com. (1966–68); Ed. Guides to Lit. (1967–69); LAD, Recruit. Mtls. Com. (1966). IA LA: Coll. Sect. (Ch., 1948–49). WI LA: VP (1963–64); Pres. (1964–65); Exec. Bd. (1965–66); Mem. Com. (1958–59, 1965–69); Various other com. WI Reg. Writers' Assn. WI Flwshp. Poets. AAUW: Chicago Branch, Bltn. Ed. (1955). Madison Area Writers. **Honors:** WI LA, Cit. Merit, 1969; Simpson Coll., Alum. Achvmt. Awd., 1967; WI St. Jnl., Madison, Know Your Madisonian Cit., 1972. **Pubns.:** Ed., Books Around the Globe (1960); Various poetical wks.; "Discovering the Community," *Jnl. Educ. Libnshp* (Spr. 1969); Various articles in *Amer. Libs.*; Ed., *WI Lib. Bltn. and Channel DLS* (1966–80). **Activities:** 13; 37 **Addr.:** 4218 Tokay Blvd., Madison, WI 53711.

Hryciw, Carol A. (F. 23, 1946, Fall River, MA) Head, Tech. Srvs., James P. Adams Lib., RI Coll., 1977–, Asst. Libn., Cat., 1975–77. **Educ.:** Brown Univ., 1964–68, BA (Latin & Greek); Univ. of MI, 1968–70, MA (Classical Std.); Simmons Coll., 1973–75, MS (LS). **Orgs.:** ALA: Mem. Promo. Task Force for RI (Ch., 1976–1978); Mem. Com. (1978–1980); Reg. Ch. for New Eng. (1978–1980); ACRL, New Eng. Chap., Ch., Mem. Com. (1979–81). New Eng. Tech. Srvs. Libns.: Nom. Com. (1975). RI LA. Classical Assn. of New Eng. **Pubns.:** *John Hawkes: an Annotated Bibliography* (1977); "Teaching a Mini-Course on OCLC: a Personal Perspective," *RI LA Bltn.* (F. 1981). **Activities:** 1; 17, 20, 46 **Addr.:** 552 Woodman St., Fall River, MA 02724.

Hsieh, Rebecca Tung (F. 21, 1938, China) Coord. of Pub. Srvs., Instr. Tech. Ctr., Essex Cmnty. Coll., 1980–, AV Libn., 1978–80; Libn., Sheppard Pratt Hosp., 1975–78; Lang. Instr., Towson State Univ., 1975–81. **Educ.:** Univ. of Evansville, 1958–59, BA (Eng.); Cath. Univ., 1974–75, MLS; Drexel Univ., 1979, Cert. **Orgs.:** ALA: ACRL/Cmnty. and Jr. Coll. Libs. Sect., Srvs. to Disadv. Students Com. (1980–82). MD Educ. Media Org. Chinese-Amer. LA. MD LA: 1981 Conf. Plng. Com.; AV Div., Fund Raising Com. (Co-ch.). Other orgs. Org. of Chinese-Amer. Assn. of Chinese Schs.: Ed., Nsltr. (1978–79). **Activities:** 1, 10; 17, 32, 39; 67 **Addr.:** 601 Stacy Ct., Baltimore, MD 21204.

Hsu, Martha Russell (S. 6, 1941, Wheeling, WV) Assoc. Libn., Cornell Univ., 1975–, Sr. Asst. Libn., 1972–75, Asst. Libn., 1967–72. **Educ.:** Coll. of Wooster, 1959–63, BA (Grmn. Lit.); Cornell Univ., 1964–66, MA (Grmn. Lit.); Univ. of MI, 1966–67, AMLS. **Activities:** 1; 39 **Addr.:** Reference Department, Olin Library, Cornell University, Ithaca, NY 14853.

Htway, Khin K. (D. 12, 1936, Rangoon, Burma) Ref. Libn., Howard Univ. Lib., 1977–; Inf. Spec., Hlth. Care, Capital Syst. Grp., 1976–77; AV Cat., George Washington Univ., 1975–76; Mem. Rec. Libn., Amer. Socty. Pub. Admn., 1974–75; Announcer, Voice of Amer., 1975–78 (part time). **Educ.:** Univ. of Rangoon, 1953–57, BA (Soc. Sci.), 1957–58, BA (Hon.) (Psy.), 1960–62, MA (Psy.); Univ. MD, 1973–74, MLS; Med. Libn. Cert., I, 1973–74. **Orgs.:** Med. LA. Dist. Columbia LA. **Activities:** 1; 15, 20, 39; 62, 80, 92 **Addr.:** 4113 Conger St., Wheaton, MD 20906.

Hu, David Y. (D. 23, 1916, Kiangsu Prov., China) E. Asian Biblgphr., Assoc. Prof. of Lib. Admin., OH State Univ. Lib., 1971–; Cur. of E. Asian Col., Washington Univ. Lib., 1964–71; Catlgr. & Resrch. Asst., Yale Univ. Lib., 1960–64; Asst. Catlgr., Columbia Univ. E. Asian Lib., 1958–60. **Educ.:** Natl. Ctrl. Univ., China, 1938–42; Columbia Univ. Lib. Srv., 1958–60. **Orgs.:** Assn. for Asian Std.: Com. on E. Asian Libs. Assn. For Chinese Libs. **Pubns.:** "Current Bibliographical Sources on East Asia," *Frgn. Acq. Nsltr., Assn. of Resrch. Libs.* (Fall 1979); "Problem of cataloging Chinese books," *Jnl. of Lib. & Info. Sci.* (Ap. 1977); "The East Asian studies in the Ohio State University," *Bltn. of Chinese Std. in the USA,* (O. 1977); "The East Asian Collection in the Ohio State University," *Bltn. of the Com. on E. Asian Libs., The Assn. for Asian Std.,* (O. 1978); other articles. **Addr.:** Ohio State University Library, 1858 Niel Ave., Columbus, OH 43210.

Hu, Shu Chao (S. 4, 1932, Hsinyu, Kiangsi, China) Prof. of LS, St. Francis Coll. of PA, 1979–, Assoc. Prof. of LS, 1975–79, Asst. Prof. of LS, 1971–75, Instr., 1967–71; Cat., E. Asian Lib., Columbia Univ., 1966–67. **Educ.:** Natl. Taiwan Univ., 1953–57, BA (Law); Natl. Chengchi Univ., 1957–60, LLM (Pol. Sci.); Columbia Univ., 1963–65, MA (Amer. Gvt.); Villanova Univ., 1965–66, MLS; FL State Univ., 1974–77, PhD (LS); Univ. of Pittsburgh, 1968–70, Advnc. Cert. (LS). **Orgs.:** ALA. AALS. Pittsburgh Reg. Lib. Ctr.: Alt. Mem., Bd. of Trustees (1975–). Laurel Highlands Hlth. Sci. Lib. Cnsrtm.: Ch., Serials Com. (1979–). Other orgs. Assn. for Asian Std. AAUP. Amer. Pol. Sci. Assn. **Pubns.:** *The Development of the Chinese Collection in the Library of Congress* (1979); *American Politics: A Collection of Essays* (1977); *American Presidents: Their Life and Times* (1973); "Former Presidents Acts of China and the United States: A Comparison," *The China Tribune* (Ap. 10, 1978); "Wang Yun-wu, The Greatest Contributor to Chinese Libraries," *Biog. Lit.* (S. 1979); other articles. **Activities:** 1, 4; 15, 17, 39; 54, 77, 92 **Addr.:** 612 Ashcroft Ave., Cresson, PA 16630.

Huang, C. K. (D. 29, 1927, Chang-i, Shantung, China) Dir., Hlth. Sci. Lib., Prof. of Med. Com., SUNY, Buffalo, 1970–, Assoc. Dir., 1969–70; Head Libn., East Asian Lib., Univ. of KS, 1968–69; Head Libn., E. Asian Lib., Univ. of Rochester, 1965–68. **Educ.:** Far Eastern Univ., 1959–61, BA (Econ.); Univ. of MI, 1964, AMLS; Stanford Univ., 1963, (Data Process.) **Orgs.:** Med. LA: Ch., Int. Coop. Com. (1976–77); Ch., Ad Hoc Com. to Study Int. Exch. and Redist. (1978–80); Nom. Com., (1979); Ch., Couningham Intl. Flwshp Sub-Com. (1975–76). Med. Hist. Socty. of Western NY: VP (1978–79); Pres. (1979–80). NY and NJ Reg. Med. Lib.: Ch., Adv. and Plng. Com. (1979–80). Buffalo Acad. of Med. Biomed. Com. Network: Vice Ch. and Ch.-Elect (1979–80). **Honors:** SUNY, Chancellor's Award for Excellence in Libnshp, 1979. **Pubns.:** "Asian-American Special Librarians" in *Opportunity for Minorities in Librarianship* (1977); "Physical Facilities of Medical School Libraries in the United States 1966–75; A Statistical Review," *Bltn. of Med. LA* (Ap. 1976); "The Delivery of Information Services in a Health Sciences Library," *The Bookmark* (1977); "Developing an East Asian Collection: Requirements and Problems," *The Lib. Qtly.* (Ap. 1970). **Activities:** 1, 13; 17; 58, 80, 87 **Addr.:** 57 Treebrooke Ct., Williamsville, NY 14221.

Huang, George W. (Ap. 20, 1936, Miao Li, Taiwan, Rep. of China) Prof. of Educ., CA State Univ., Chico, 1969–; Teaching Fellow, Instr., Univ. of ID, 1967–69; Libn., NM Highlands Univ., 1963–67; Libn., Taipei Amer. Sch., Taiwan, 1962–62; Acq. Libn., Nat. Cent. Lib., Taiwan, 1959–60. **Educ.:** Nat. Taiwan Normal Univ., 1955–59, BA (LS); Vanderbilt Univ., 1962–63, MA (LS); NM Highlands Univ., 1964–67, MEd; Univ. of ID, 1967–69, PhD (Educ.). **Orgs.:** ALA. Chinese LA: (Pres. 1980; VP 1979; Ed. of Nsltr. 1977–78). CA Med. and Lib. Educ. Assn. CA Tchr. Assn. Toastmaster Int., Ishi Club, Chico, CA: Pres. (1974).

PROFESSIONAL ACTIVITIES: Institutions: 1. Acad. lib.; 2. Arch.; 3. Assn.; 4. Fed./Gvt. lib.; 5. Inst. lib.; 6. Mfr./Suppl.; 7. Milit. lib.; 8. Musm.; 9. Pub. lib.; 10. Sch. lib.; 11. Sch. of lib. sci.; 12. Spec. lib.; 13. State lib.; 14. (other). **Functions/Activities:** 15. Acq./Col. dev.; 16. Adult srvs.; 17. Admin.; 18. Apprais.; 19. Archit./Bldgs.; 20. Cat./Class.; 21. Chld. srvs.; 22. Circ.; 23. Cons./Pres.; 24. Consult.; 25. Cont. ed.; 26. Educ. lib. sci.; 27. Ext. srvs.; 28. Fund/Grants; 29. Gvt. pubs.; 30. Indx./Abs.; 31. Instr. lib. use; 32. Media srvs.; 33. Micro.; 34. Netwks./Coop.; 35. Persnl.; 36. PR; 37. Publshg.; 38. Recs. mgt.; 39. Ref. srvs.; 40. Repro.; 41. Resrch.; 42. Review.; 43. Secur.; 44. Serials; 45. Spec. col.; 46. Tech. srvs.; 47. Trustees/Bds.; 48. YA srvs.; 49. (other).

Pubns.: "The Evaluation of Lib. Services," *Jnl. of Lib. and Info. Sci.*, (O. 1978). "Mottos, Songs and Lifetime Employment," *The Asianist* (1979). "School Media Programs and the 'Back to Basic' Movement," *CMLEA Jrnl.* (1978). "Chiang Ching-Kuo: New President of Republic of China," (1978). "Chinese Mythology: A Bibliography," *Chinese LA Nwsltr.*, (D. 1977). **Activities:** 11; 26 **Addr.:** Department of Education, California State University, Chico, Chico, CA 95929.

Huang, Sam B. (N. 6, 1937, Chia-Yi, Taiwan) Asst. Law Libn., McKusick Law Lib., Univ. of SD, 1981–, Adq. Libn., 1978–81; Lib. Tech., Libn., Soc. Work Lib., Howard Univ., 1971–78. **Educ.:** Soochow Univ., Taipei, Taiwan, 1957–62, LLB (Law); Howard Univ., 1970–72, MCJ (Compar. Law); Cath. Univ. of Amer., 1972–74, MSLS; George Washington Univ., 1975–77, MCL (Compar. Law). **Orgs.:** MN Assn. of Law Libs. AALL. **Honors:** Univ. of SD, Empl. of the Month, N. 1979. **Activities:** 1, 12; 15, 17, 46; 77 **Addr.:** McKusick Law Library, Law School, The University of SD, Vermillion, SD 57069.

Huang, Su-Lee (Je. 30, 1935, Kaohsiung, Taiwan, China) Assoc. Libn. for Tech. Srvs., Cleveland Musm. of Art Lib., 1980–, Head Catlgr., 1974–79, Oriental Catlgr., 1969–73; Chinese Catlgr., Harvard Yenching Lib., 1962–64. **Educ.:** Natl. Taiwan Univ., 1953–57, BA (Eng.); Univ. of WI, 1959–60, MS (Eng.); Simmons Coll., 1960–62, MS (LS). **Orgs.:** ARLIS/NA: Cat. & Indexing Syst. Spec. Int. Grp. (1974–79). Resrch. Libs. Grp.: Art and Archit. Prog. Com. (1980–). Com. on E. Asian Libs. **Activities:** 1, 5; 15, 20, 46; 55, 56, 92 **Addr.:** The Library of The Cleveland Museum of Art, 11150 East Blvd., Cleveland, OH 44106.

Huang, Theodore S. Dir. of Libs., Fairleigh Dickinson Univ., 1969–81; Dir. of Lib., Tri-State Coll., 1968–69; Branch Libn., Queens Borough Pub. Lib., 1961–64. **Educ.:** Natl. Fuh Tan Univ., Shanghai, China, 1943–47, BA (Soclgy.); Rutgers Univ., 1959–61, MLS, 1964–67, PhD (LS). **Orgs.:** ALA. ASIS. NJ LA. New York Lib. Club. **Honors** Beta Phi Mu. **Pubns.:** *Efficacy of Citation Indexing* (1967); Jt. auth., *Administration and Change* (1969); Jt. auth., *Essays for Ralph Shaw* (1975); "JCC/LRTS, 1948–1964: One Man's View," *Lib. Resrcs. and Tech. Srv.* (Win. 1967); Contrib., "Zero Growth: When Is Not-Enough Enough?," *Jnl. of Acad. Libnshp.* (N. 1975). **Activities:** 1, 12; 17, 26, 41; 54, 55, 75 **Addr.:** 605 Cumberland Ave., Teaneck, NJ 07666.

Huang, Theresa C. Reg. Libn., Brooklyn Pub. Lib., 1978–, Branch Libn., Asst. Branch Libn., Dist. Libn., Dist. Chld. Srvs. Spec., Chld. Libn., 1960–78; Catlgr., Harvard Univ., 1958–60. **Educ.:** Natl. Taiwan Univ., 1951–55, BA (Frgn. Lang. & Lit.); Syracuse Univ., 1956–58, MSLS. **Orgs.:** ALA: ALA-CSD Com. on Chld. Books on Asia (1965–66); Com. on Eval. of Lib. Tools, (1968–71); Adv. Com. to the ALA Ofc. for Lib. Srv. to the Disadv. (1975–77); ALA-Chld. Book Cncl. Jt. Com. (1976–80); PLA Srv. to Chld. Com. (1980–); ALSC/Preschl. Service and Parent Educ. Com. (1981–). **Pubns.:** Jt. complr., *Asia: A Guide to Books for Children* (1966). **Activities:** 1, 9; 17, 21, 41; 55, 59, 75 **Addr.:** 605 Cumberland Ave., Teaneck, NJ 07666.

Hubbard, Abigail (Je. 21, 1949, Lincoln, NE) Resrch. Anal., Resrch. Div., Legis. Cncl., State of NE, 1981–; Asst. Prof. Biblgphr., Univ. of NE, 1979–81, Asst. Prof., Law Lib., 1978–79, Instr., Biblgphr., 1977–78. **Educ.:** Dana Coll., 1967–71, BS (Soc. Sci.); N. TX State Univ., 1975–76, MLS; Univ. of NE, Lincoln, 1979–81, MEd (Educ. Admin.), 1980–, PhD (Educ. Admin.) in progress. **Orgs.:** ALA. NE OLUG: Prog. Ch. (1980–81). NE LA: Nom. Com. (Ch. 1980–81). Lincoln LA: Pres. (1980–81). **Pubns.:** "An Analysis of Effective Management Information Searching: A Comparison of Three Major Bibliographic Databases," *2nd Natl. Online Mtg., Proc.* (1981); "Online Research for State Legislatures," *Online '81, Proceedings* (1981); "User Subaccount Codes," *BRS Bulletin* (O. 1981). **Activities:** 4, 12, 13; 17, 39, 49-online retrieval; 56, 63, 78 **Addr.:** 1101 D St. #C5, Lincoln, NE 68502.

Hubbard, Frances Joyce (Ap. 21, 1918, East Orange, NJ) Lib. Media Spec., Nonnewaug HS, 1976–; Admn. Asst., Trng. Assoc., Capitol Reg. Educ. Cncl. 1975–76; Lib. Dir., Southington Pub. Lib., 1973–75; Chlds. Libn., Perrot Mem. Lib., Greenwich, CT, 1972–73, Asst. Coord. WK. Cld., Enoch Pratt Free Lib., 1971–72; Dir. Chld. Srvs., Nashua Pub. Lib. (NH), 1968–71. **Educ.:** Radcliffe Coll., 1937–40, AB (Msc.); Simmons Coll., 1966–68, MS (LS); South. CT St. Coll., 1976–82, Tchg. Cert.; Sacred Heart Univ., 1979–81, MAT (Hum. Educ.). **Orgs.:** ALA. New Eng. LA. New Eng. RT Chlds. Libns. (V. Ch., 1969–70). New Eng. Media Asst. Chlds. Lit. Assoc. CT LA. AAUW. Intl. Readg. Assn. CT Educ. Assn. Puppeteers of Amer.: Liason with ALA (1971–72). **Pubns.:** Various radio and television broadcasts. **Activities:** 9, 10; 16, 21, 24; 55, 63, 85 **Addr.:** 24 Clubhouse Dr., Woodbury, CT 06798.

Hubbard, Lee L. (My. 15, 1931, San Diego, CA) Dir., Carlsbad Pub. Lib. and Musm., 1978–; Dir., Park Cnty. Lib., 1976; Map Libn., Univ. of Wash. Libs., 1970–76; City Libn., Handley Lib., VA. 1966–70; Art-Arch.-Musc. Libn., Univ. of MO Lib., 1962–66; Arch. Libn., Univ. of TX Lib., 1958–62. **Educ.:** Univ. of Chicago, 1949–50, 1951–53, (Anth.); Univ. CA, Berkeley, 1950–51, 1953–56, AB (Gen. Std.), 1956–58, MLS; Univ. of AZ Arch. Field Sch., 1952, 1955; Cambridge Univ. 1953. **Orgs.:** NM LA. **Pubns.:** *Old Buildings & Battlefields of Southeast England* (1961). "Indefensible: Flanagan, censors" *Lib. Jrnl.* (1976), "Maps for use" *Bltn., Geog. and Map Div., SLA*, (1975). "Crater hunting" (Western Assn. of Map Libs. Info.) *Bltn.*, June (1975). "More on Gore" *Lib. Jrnl.* (1975). **Activities:** 1, 9; 15, 19, 20; 54, 70, 91 **Addr.:** Carlsbad Public Library, 101 S. Halagueno, Carlsbad, NM 88220.

Hubbard, Marlis M. (F. 9, 1944, Hopewell, VA) Libn. in charge of the Guidance Info. Ctr., Concordia Univ., 1979–; Campus Libn., Vanier Coll., 1977–79; Libn., Lorain Pub. Lib., 1971–76. **Educ.:** Univ. of MO at Kansas City, 1966–69, BA (Psy.); KS State Tchrs. Coll., 1970–71, ML (Libnshp.). **Orgs.:** Corp. of Prof. Libns. of PQ. Can. LA. Career Info. Resrc. Adv. Grp. **Pubns** *Blueprint for a Guidance Information Centre* (1981). **Activities:** 1, 12; 17, 20, 31; 63, 95-Career plng. **Addr.:** 4819 Melrose Av., Montreal, PQ H3X 2P4 Canada.

Hubbard, Mary Kathryn (O. 16, 1948, Belleville, IL) Lib. Mgr., Brown & Root, Inc., 1981–; Lib. Mgr., Turner, Collie and Braden Inc., 1973–81; Libn., Browning-Ferris Indus., 1973; Libn., Rice Univ., 1970–72; Libn., Univ. of St. Thomas, 1967–69. **Educ.:** Univ. of St. Thomas, 1966–70, BA (Art Hist.); Sam Houston State Univ., 1979–81, MLS. **Orgs.:** SLA: TX Chap., Mem. Ch. (1978–79), Srvy. Com. (Ch., 1980–81); Sam Houston Student Chap. (Pres., 1980–81). ALA. ASIS. **Activities:** 12; 17; 64, 65, 91 **Addr.:** Brown & Root, Inc., PO Box 3, Houston, TX 77001.

Hubbard, Taylor (Terry) E. (Mr. 15, 1939, Burlington, VT) Soc. Sci. Libn., Assoc. Prof., CO St. Univ., 1980–; Ch., Lib. Tech. Asst. Prog., Tanana Valley Cmnty. Coll., 1977–79; Instr. Libn., Asst. Prof., AK (Fairbanks), 1976–79; Ref. Libn., Asst. Libn., St. Univ. NY (Stony Brook) 1973–76; Ref. Libn., Dutchess Cmnty. Coll., 1969–73. **Educ.:** Univ. VT 1963–66, BA (Hist.); Univ. CA (Los Angeles), 1969–70, MLS; San Francisco St. Coll., 1967–68, MA (Hist.). **Orgs.:** AK LA: AK Rep. to Pacific N. W. LA; N. Chap. (Pres. 1976–77). ALA: IFRT, Mem. Com. (1974–76). Pacific N. W. LA: Bd. Dir. (1979–80). St. Univ. NY LA: Pub. Inf. Com. (Ch. 1973–76). Dutchess Cnty. Rural Dev. Corp.: Bd. Dir. (1970–71). **Honors:** ALA, Excel. Nsltr. Publshg., 1979. **Pubns.:** "History of Faculty Status for SUNY Librarians," ERIC (1974); "Fairbanks LTA Program," *Sourdough* (v. 16 1979); Ed., *Sourdough* (AK LA) (1979–80); Ed., *CO Libs.* (1980–); various lib. instr. mtls. **Activities:** 1; 92 **Addr.:** Social Sciences Library, Colorado State Univ., Fort Collins, CO 80523.

Hubbard, William J. (Jl. 17, 1941, Grand Rapids, MI) Dir., Lib. Srvs., VA State Lib., 1980–; User Srvs. Libn., VA Tech, 1975–80; Circ. Libn., SUNY, Fredonia, 1973–75; Contract Libn., Xerox Corp., 1971–72. **Educ.:** Dartmouth Coll., 1959–63, AB (Anthro.); SUNY, Geneseo, 1971–72, MLS. **Orgs.:** ASIS: Secy., Carolinas Chap. (1977–80). ALA: Bldgs. for Coll. & Univ. Libs. (1981–83). SELA: Interstate Coop. Com. (Ch., 1981–82). VA LA. **Pubns.:** *Stack Management: A Practical Guide to Shelving and Maintaining Library Collections* (1981); "Development & Administration of a Large Off-Campus Shelving Facility," in *New Horizons for Academic Libraries* (1979); Jt. auth., "A Political Prescription for the Market Place Realities Affecting Interactive Literature Searching-A User's View," in *Information & Politics: Proceedings of the ASIS Annual Meeting* (1976). **Activities:** 1, 13; 17, 34; 56 **Addr.:** Virginia State Library, 12th & Capitol, Richmond, VA 23219.

Hubbard, Willis M. (S. 18, 1940, Monmouth, IL) Dir., Stephens Coll., 1977–; Head Libn. and Dir. of Inst. Resrch. and Plng., Eureka Coll., 1972–77, Head Libn., Asst. Prof. Pol. Sci., 1968–72; Asst. Soc. Sci. Libn., South. IL Univ., 1967–68, Asst. Sci. Libn., 1963–67. **Educ.:** Monmouth Coll., 1958–62, BA (Lit.); Univ. of IL, 1962–63, MS (LS); South. IL Univ., 1964–68, MA (Pol. Sci.). **Orgs.:** ALA: ACRL Bd. Mem. (1979–84); ACRL/Coll. Lib. Sect., Vice Ch., Ch. Elec. (1979–81); Coll. and Univ. Lib. Stats. Com. (1977–1981). MO LA: Lib. Educ. and Manpower Com. (1977–79). MO Lib. Netwk.: Bd. Ch. (1980–81), Mem. (1979–81). Mid–MO Lib. Netwk.: VP (1980–82), Treas. (1979–80). **Honors:** Pi Sigma Alpha, 1968; U.S. Jaycees, Hon. Life Mem., 1977. **Pubns.:** *Library Costs and Services* (1979); Various speeches. **Activities:** 1; 17, 32, 39; 91, 92 **Addr.:** 609 Maplewood Dr., Columbia, MO 65201.

Hubble, Gerald Blaine (Ap. 21, 1934, Eubank, KY) Dir. of the Lib., Rockhurst Coll., 1973–; Dir. of the Lib., Stephens Coll., 1967–73; Asst. Libn., Berea Coll., 1961–67. **Educ.:** Berea Coll., 1953–61, BA (Econ.); Univ. of KY, 1961–63, MS (LS). **Orgs.:** ALA. Natl. Libns. Assn. Mt.-Plains LA. **Activities:** 1; 17, 33, 43 **Addr.:** Rockhurst College Library, 5225 Troost Ave., Kansas City, MO 64110.

Huber, Donald L. (S. 19, 1940, Columbus, OH) Libn., Trinity Luth. Semy., 1978–; Libn., Evang. Luth. Theo. Semy., 1973–78, Instr., Church Hist., 1969–72. **Educ.:** Capital Univ., 1958–62, AB (Math.); Evang. Luth. Theo. Semy., 1962–66, BD (Theo.); Duke Univ., 1966–71, PhD (Relig.); Univ. of MI, 1972–73, AMLS. **Orgs.:** ATLA: Publn. Com. (1974–76; Ch., 1975–76). OH Theo. Libns.: Ch. (1975–77). Amer. Socty. of Church Hist. Luth. Hist. Conf.: Bd. of Dir. (1976–; Treas., 1978–). **Honors:** Univ. of MI Sch. of LS, Margaret Mann Awd., 1973. **Pubns.:** "Timothy Cutler: The Convert as Controversialist," *Hist. Mag. of the Protestant Episcopal Church* (D. 1975). **Activities:** 1; 15, 17; 90 **Addr.:** Trinity Lutheran Seminary, 2199 E. Main St., Columbus, OH 43209.

Huber, George K. (D. 11, 1939, Washington, DC) Msc. Libn., Swarthmore Coll., 1973–, Head, Spec. Col., 1967–73, Asst., Circ. Dept., 1964–67. **Educ.:** Univ. of PA, 1957–62, BA (Msc.); Drexel Univ., 1962–64, MLS. **Orgs.:** Msc. LA. Amer. Musical Instrument Socty. **Pubns.:** "Recent books," *Amer. Musical Instrument Socty., Jnl.* (1975–80). **Activities:** 1; 15, 20, 22; 55 **Addr.:** Daniel Underhill Music Library, Swarthmore College, Swarthmore, PA 19081.

Hucks, Herbert, Jr. (Je. 2, 1913, Conway, SC) Archvst., Wofford Coll., 1966–, Libn., 1953–66, Assoc. Libn., 1947–53; Tchr., Sr. HS, Greensboro, NC, 1935–42. **Educ.:** Wofford Coll., 1930–34, AB (Fr., Grmn.); Emory Univ., 1934–35, MA (Fr.), 1946, BALS; GA Dept. of Arch. & Hist., Emory Univ., 1967, Cert. (Arch. Inst.). **Orgs.:** ALA. SC LA: Pres. (1952). SAA. SELA: Exec. Bd. (1956–60). Natl. Educ. Assn. Retired Ofcrs. Assn. Civitan Club of Spartanburg. Sons of the Amer. Revolution. **Honors:** Phi Beta Kappa, Wofford Coll., Plaque for 15 years srv., 1978; SC LA, Hon. Life Mem. **Pubns.:** Ed., *SC Libn.* (1959–70); various articles. **Activities:** 1, 2; 38; 73, 90 **Addr.:** P.O. Box 5193, Spartanburg, SC 29304.

Hudgens, Jan Butler (D. 28, 1934, McCook, NE) Asst. Acq. Libn., Long Island Univ., Brooklyn Ctr., 1977–; Asst. Cur., Prints, NY Hist. Socty., 1961–77. **Educ.:** Fort Hays KS State Univ., 1952–56, BA (Soclgy., Eng.); Pratt Inst., 1973–75, MLS. Green Mt. Club. Appalachian Mt. Club. Sierra Club. Natl. Wildlife Fed. Amer. Fed. of Tchrs. **Activities:** 1, 12; 15; 55 **Addr.:** 30–61 48th St., Astoria, NY 11103.

Hudnut, Sophie K. (N. 30, 1938, Detroit, MI) Resrch. Sci., DIALOG Info. Srvs., Inc., 1978–; Tech. Info. Spec., Syst. Consult. Inc., 1976–78; Supvsr., Indexing, Aerospace Corp., 1966–71, Lit. Resrch. Anal., 1964–66; Lib. Resrch. Anal., Rocketdyne, 1961–63. **Educ.:** AZ State Univ., 1956–59, BS (Chem.), 1959–62, MS (Chem.); Univ. of CA, Los Angeles, 1963–64, MLS. **Orgs.:** SLA: Chap., Hosplty. Com. (1965–66, Ch., 1967); Dir. Ch. (1971–72); Conv. Com. (1967). ASIS. **Honors:** Beta Phi Mu. **Pubns.:** Ed., *Directory of Special Libraries in Southern California* (1972); Ed., *Supplement* (1974). **Activities:** 6, 12; 17, 25, 49-Online info. retrieval; 60, 81, 91 **Addr.:** 19971 Lindenbrook, Cupertino, CA 95014.

Hudon, Marcel (Jl. 23, 1925, Montauban, PQ) Dir., Rare Bk. Rm. Theses and Livres Rares, Univ. Laval, 1976–, Dir., Bib. Gen., 1969–76, Bibtcr., Sci. de l'Admin., 1966–69, Bibtcr., Fac. des Sci., 1963–66, Bibtcr., 1947–63. **Educ.:** Univ. Laval, 1943–45, BA (Hum.); Cath. Univ., 1960–61, MS (LS). **Orgs.:** Corp. des Bibtcrs. Prof. du PQ: Admin. (1970–72); Com. Ad Hoc sur la Révision du Mode d'Élec. (Pres., 1971); various coms. and ofcs. ASTED: Cnsl. (1961–65); 2nd VP (1969–70); 1st VP (1970–71). various ofcs. Assn. du Persnl. Admin. et Prof. de l' Univ. Laval: VP (1979–). Various other orgs. **Honors:** Beta Phi Mu. **Pubns.:** Jt. auth., *Le Bibliothéque de l'Université Laval* (1962); "D'Hier à Aujourd Hui," *Au Fil des Événements* (1969); "Point de Non-Retour," *Bltn. de Assn. Can. Bibtcrs. Lang. Fr.* (1972); various articles. **Activities:** 1; 17, 20, 45; 55 **Addr.:** 1373, Emilien Rochette, Ancienne-Lorette, PQ G2E 2T6 Canada.

Hudson, Alice C. (Mr. 17, 1947, Oak Ridge, TN) Chief, Map Div., NY Pub. Lib., 1981–, First Asst., Map Div., 1978–81, Map Ref. Libn./Catlgr., 1970–78. **Educ.:** Middle TN State Univ., 1967–69, BA (Geo.); Peabody Coll. for Tchrs., 1965–67, 1969–70, MLS. **Orgs.:** SLA: Geo. and Map Div., Lib. of Congs. Liaison Com. (Ch., 1980–81); NY Chap., Geo. and Map Grp. (Ch., 1975–77; Secy., 1973–75). ALA: Map and Geo. RT (Ch., 1982–83). New York Map Socty.: Pres. (1980). **Honors:** Beta Phi Mu, 1970. **Pubns.:** "Conversion to Automated Cataloging at the Map Division, NYPL," *Spec. Libs.* (F. 1976); Reviews. **Activities:** 9, 14-Resrch. Lib.; 15, 39, 45; 70 **Addr.:** Map Division, NYPL, 5th Avenue & 42d St., New York, NY 10018.

Hudson, Dale L. (Jl. 11, 1930, Sumrall, MS) Head, Msc. Lib., FL State Univ., 1972–; Libn. II, Msc. Div., NY Pub. Lib., 1968–72; Msc. Fac., Milligan Coll., TN, 1960–63; Msc. Fac., Great Neck (N/Y/) Cultural Ctr., 1963–66. **Educ.:** Millsaps Coll., 1947–50, BA, (Music); Univ. of South. MS, 1950–51, BM, 1951–52, MM; Rutgers Univ. 1966–68, MLS; post-grad. study, FL State Univ., 1958–60, Music. **Orgs.:** Msc. LA: Pubns. Com. (1979–); SE Chap.: Exec. Bd. (1974–75, 1980–82; Ch., 1979). FL LA. **Pubns.:** Asst. Ed., Msc LA *Notes*, (1971–72); Columnist, Msc. LA *Notes*, (1969–72). **Activities:** 1, 14-Research; 15, 17, 39; 95-Music. **Addr.:** Music Library, MSN 090, Florida State University, Tallahassee, FL 32306.

Hudson, Gary Austin (Mr. 29, 1938, Spencer, IA) Acq. Libn., SD State Univ., 1977–; Wayne State Coll., 1976–77, Ref. Libn., 1971–75; Instr. of Eng., IA Lakes Com. Coll., 1968–71; Asst. Prof. of Eng., Morningside Coll., 1967–68. **Educ.:** Univ. of Northern IA, 1956–60, BA (Eng.); Univ. of Northern CO, 1963–65, MA (Eng.); Emporia State Univ., 1969–72, MLS. **Orgs.:** ALA. SD LA: Intel. Freedom Com., (1979–) Conv. Ex-

Special Subjects/Services: 50. Adult educ.; 51. Advert./Mktg.; 52. Aerosp.; 53. Agric.; 54. Area std.; 55. Arts/Hum.; 56. Autom.; 57. Bibl./Prtg.; 58. Bio. sci.; 59. Bus./Fin.; 60. Chem.; 61. Copyrt.; 62. Documtn.; 63. Educ.; 64. Engin.; 65. Env.; 66. Eth. grps.; 67. Film; 68. Food/Nutr.; 69. Geneal.; 70. Geo.; 71. Geol.; 72. Handcpd.; 73. Hist.; 74. Int. frdm.; 75. Info. sci.; 76. Insr.; 77. Law; 78. Legis.; 79. Math./Comp. sci.; 80. Med.; 81. Metals; 82. Nat. resrcs.; 83. Newsp.; 84. Nuc. sci.; 85. Oral hist.; 86. Petr./Energy; 87. Pharm.; 88. Phys./Astr./Math.; 89. Readg.; 90. Relig.; 91. Sci./Tech.; 92. Soc. sci.; 93. Telecom.; 94. Transp.; 95. (other).

hibts Ch. (1978). NE LA: Int. Frdm. Com., (1976–77). **Honors:** Beta Phi Mu, 1973. **Activities:** 1; 15, 39, 46; 55, 67, 74 **Addr.:** 1001 Parkway Blvd., Brookings, SD 57006.

Hudson, Patricia H. (Ap. 11, 1948, Monroe, MI) Archvst., Monroe Cnty. Hist. Comsn., 1974–. **Educ.:** East. MI Univ., 1966–69, BS (Pol. Sci.); Wayne State Univ., 1970–72, MA (Hist.); East. MI Univ., 1969–70, Tchg. Cert. **Orgs.:** MI Archival Assn.: Exec. Com. (1976–79); Pres. (1980–82); Jt. ed., nsltr. (1978–). Mid-West Arch. Conf. SAA. Geneal. Socty. of Monroe Cnty., MI. **Pubns.:** "Lone Archivist" column *Open Entry* (1978–); Reviews. **Activities:** 2; 15, 20; 69, 73 **Addr.:** Monroe County Historical Commission Archives, Monroe, MI 48161.

Hudson, Phyllis Janecke (Ag. 16, 1933, Rock Island, IL) Ref. Libn., Coord. of Online Srch. Srvs., Univ. of Ctrl. FL, 1980–, Ref. Libn., Coord. of Lib. Instr., 1974–80, Assoc. Libn., Catlgr., 1973–74, Assoc. Libn., Head of Circ., 1972–73; Asst. Libn., Instr., Univ. of IL, Educ. & Soc. Sci. Lib., 1970–72. **Educ.:** Univ. of IL, 1962–65, BA (Eng.), 1968–70, MS (LS). **Orgs.:** Univ. of IL Lib. Fac. Assn.: Com. on Const. & By-Laws (1971–72). ALA: ACRL/Bibl. Instr. Sect., Cont. Educ. Com. (1977–78). FL LA: Caucus on Lib. Orien. & Bibl. Instr. (Ch., 1978–79); ACRL (Secy. 1979–80). Other orgs. Untd. Fac. of FL: Ch., Women's Rights Com. (1977–79); Univ. of Ctrl. FL Chap. (VP, 1977–78; Treas. 1978–80). Univ. of Ctrl. FL: Fac. Senate Rep. (1975–76). Seminole Cnty. Chap. Natl. Org. of Women: Secy. (1979–80). **Honors:** Univ. of IL Grad. Sch. of LS, Libn.-in-Residence, 1977; Univ. of Ctrl. FL, Prof. Dev. Leave, 1978. **Pubns.:** "LOBI News," *FL Libs.* (My./Je. 1978–); "Librarians Denied Salary Equity," *FL Libs.* (N./D. 1978); "Equal Pay Issue at FTU" *FL Libs.* (My./Je. 1978); "Report From Loex" *FL Lib.* (Ja./F. 1978); "Copyright Conference" *FL Lib.* (S./O. 1977). **Activities:** 1; 22, 31, 39; 56, 63, 92 **Addr.:** 1510 Glastonberry Rd., Maitland, FL 32751.

Hudson, Saundra H. (Jl. 9, 1940, Kansas City, MO) Pres., Bd. of Trustees, Univ. City Pub. Lib., 1975–; Asst. Libn., MO Inst. of Psyt., 1967–; Libn., Harper & Row Publshr., 1964–66; Jr. Lit. Sci., Portland Cement Assn., 1962–63. **Educ.:** Univ. of MO, 1959–62, BA (Romance Lang.). **Orgs.:** St. Louis Med. Libns.: Pres. (1968–69); Exec. Com. (1970–71); Ed., Un. List of Serials (1977). St. Louis Reg. Lib. Network: Cncl. (1979–81). MO LA: Lib. Educ. and Manpower Com. (1977–79). Metro. Area Trustee Lib. Trustees. **Activities:** 9, 12; 27, 39, 47; 80, 95-Psyt. **Addr.:** 7531 Gannon, University City, MO 63130.

Hudson, Wilma J. (Ja. 29, 1916, Walnut Grove, MO) Media Spec., Zionsville Middle Sch., 1968–; Media Spec., Eagle Elem., 1966–68; Eng. Tchr., 1963–66, 1943–1947; Free-lance ed., Bobbs-Merrill Co., 1959–63; Sp. Instr., Butler Univ., 1942–43; Eng. & Sp. Tchr., 1937–42. **Educ.:** Drury Coll., 1932–36, AB (Eng., Msc.); Washington Univ., 1936–37, MA (Eng.); Butler Univ., 1966–67, Lib./AV Cert. **Orgs.:** IN Sch. Libns. Assn.: Arch. Com. (1970–74). Assn. IN Media/Educ.: Area bd. mem. ALA: AASL. Psi Iota Xi. Delta Delta Delta. AAUW. **Pubns.:** *Dwight D. Eisenhower: Young Military Leader* (1970); *J. C. Penney: Golden Rule Boy* (1972); *Harry S. Truman: Missouri Farm Boy* (1973). **Activities:** 10; 31 **Addr.:** 10550 Zionsville Rd., Zionsville, IN 46077.

Huemer, Christina G. (My. 24, 1947, Orange, NJ) Fine Arts Biblgphr., Columbia Univ., 1980–; Art Libn., Oberlin Coll., 1976–80; Indxr., *Art Index*, H. W. Wilson Co., 1975–76; Asst. Fine Arts Libn., Cornell Univ., 1970–75. **Educ.:** Mt. Holyoke Coll., 1965–69, BA (Art Hist.); Columbia Univ., 1969–70, MS (LS); Cornell Univ., 1971–75, MA (Art Hist.). **Orgs.:** ARLIS/NA: Midwest Reg. Rep. (1977–79). ALA. **Activities:** 1; 15, 39; 55 **Addr.:** Avery Architectural and Fine Arts Library, Columbia University, New York, NY 10027.

Huestis, Jeffrey C. (Ja. 3, 1949, Berkeley, CA) Coord., Resrch. Info. Srvs., Inst. of Wood Resrch., MI Tech. Univ., 1978–; Tech. Writer, Smart/Isley Archit., Inc., 1974–78; Eng. Tchr., US Peace Corps, Nepal, 1972–73. **Educ.:** Univ. of S. CA, 1966–71, BA (Comp. Lit); Univ. of NC, 1974–78, MSLS; MI Tech. Univ., 1979–, (Comp. Sci.). **Orgs.:** ALA. SLA: Forestry/Forest Products Sect. (Ch., 1981–82). ASIS. **Honors:** Beta Phi Mu, 1979. **Activities:** 12; 17, 39; 56, 58, 60, 64 **Addr.:** Research Information Center, Institute of Wood Research, Michigan Technological University, Houghton, MI 49931.

Hueting, Gail P. (My. 10, 1949, Belleville, IL) Coord. of Hum. Cat., Univ. of IL Lib., 1976–; Catlgr., Pius XII Meml. Lib., St. Louis Univ., 1973–76. **Educ.:** Knox Coll., 1967–71, BA (Grmn. Area Std.); Univ. of IL, 1971–73, MS (LS), 1976–80, MA (Grmn.). **Orgs.:** ALA: ACRL; RTSD. **Honors:** Univ. of IL, Resrch. grant to travel to Grmn. Dem. Repub., 1981. **Pubns.:** Reviews. **Activities:** 1; 20, 45; 54, 55, 57 **Addr.:** Original Cataloguing Department, 246 Library, University of Illinois, 1408 W. Gregory Dr., Urbana, IL 61801.

Huff, James Ellen, S.C.N. (F. 23, 1904, Rose Hill, KY) Rare Bks. Libn., Lib. Dir. Emeritus, Spalding Coll., 1970–, Dir., 1946–70, Libn., Fac. in LS, 1937–58; HS Libn., Tchr., St. Andrew Sch., 1938–45; Elem. Sch. Tchr., Libn., Sacred Heart, 1933–36. **Educ.:** Nazareth Jr. Coll., 1922, Cert.; Spalding Coll., 1932–37, BA (Eng.); Coll. of St. Catherine, 1936–38, BS in LS; Univ. of OK, 1969, (Media); various insts. **Orgs.:** ALA: AV Com. SELA: Assoc. Coll. and Ref. Cath. LA: Mem. Com. (1967–69, Ch.). KY LA: Coll. & Ref. Sect., Ch. AAUP. AAUW. Amer. Assn. of Retired Persons. KY Assn. of Older Persons. **Honors:** KY LA, Trustees Sect., Outstan. Acad. Libn., KY, 1972. **Pubns.:** Reviews. **Activities:** 1, 10; 15, 24, 45; 50, 66, 90 **Addr.:** Spalding College, 839 South Fourth St., Louisville, KY 40203.

Huff, Margaret Farris (O. 23, 1925, Danville, KY) Dean, Lrng. Resrc. Ctr., Orangebury-Calhoun Tech. Coll., 1977–, Libn., 1968–77; Asst. Libn., Calhoun Cnty. Pub. Lib., 1967–68; Tchr., Cameron (SC) HS, 1963–66; Asst. Libn., Vets. Admin., Columbia, 1948–49. **Educ.:** Mary Baldwin Coll., 1943–45; Univ. of NC, 1945–47, BA (Hist.), 1947–48, BS (LS). **Orgs.:** SC LA: Secy. (1977). SELA. ALA. SC Lrng. Resrcs. Persnl.: Pres. (1975). SC Tech. Educ. Assn. **Honors:** Phi Beta Kappa, 1947. **Activities:** 1; 17, 31 **Addr.:** 111 Dantzler Ave., St. Matthews, SC 29135.

Huff, William Howard (My. 29, 1922, Detroit, MI) Asst. Dir. for Col. Dev. and Prsrvn., Univ. of IL Lib., 1954–, Head, Col. Dev. & Prsrvn. Dept., 1978–80, Serials Libn., 1957–58; Serials - Acq. Libn., Univ. of IL Lib., Chicago, Navy Pier, 1954–57; Asst. Ref. Libn., Northwestern Univ., 1950–54. **Educ.:** Univ. of MI, 1946–49, AB (Eng. Lit.), 1949–50, AMLS. **Orgs.:** ALA: RTSD/Serials Sect. (Ch., 1967–68); Asst. Ed. for "Serials," *Lib. Resrcs. & Tech. Srvs.* IL LA. Frdm. to Read Fndn. *Serials Libn.:* Ed. Bd. (1976–). AAUP. **Pubns.:** "Serials," *ALA Yearbook* (1975–80); "The National Periodicals Center," *Cath. Lib. World* (F. 1978); "The Periodical Collection in Times of Tight Budgets," *IL Libs.* (F. 1978); "Serial Subscription Agencies," *Lib. Trends* (Ap. 1976); "Annuals," *Encyc. of Lib. and Info. Sci.* (1968); Other articles. **Activities:** 1; 15, 17, 44; 57, 74 **Addr.:** 611 W. Oregon, Urbana, IL 61801.

Huffstetler, Joy K. (Jl. 21, 1929, White Deer, TX) Info. Ctr. Analysis II, Fossil Energy Info. Ctr., Oak Ridge Natl. Lab., 1973–. **Educ.:** Univ. of TN, 1946–49, BA (Eng.), 1971–72, MLIS. **Orgs.:** SLA: South. Appalachian Chap., Pres., (1980–81); Nom. Com. (Ch., 1978); Treas. (1975–76). ASIS: E. TN Chap. (Mem. Ch., 1978–79, 1979–80). Oak Ridge Cmnty. Playhouse. Oak Ridge Arts Cncl.: Dir. (1968–72). **Pubns.:** *Environmental Compliance Program Handbooks* (1980–81); *Energy/Environmental Terminology Index* (1976). **Activities:** 12; 30, 49-data base bldg.; 64, 65, 91 **Addr.:** 136 Orchard Le., Oak Ridge, TN 37830.

Huggens, Gary D. (S. 24, 1950, Woodbury, NJ) Systs. Anal., Zimmerman & Assocs., Inc., 1981–; Entry Ed. Libn., Natl. Serials Data Prog., Lib. of Congs., 1976–81, Intern, 1978–79; Instr./Ref. Libn., GA State Univ., 1975–76. **Educ.:** Univ. of MI, 1968–72, BA (Grmn. lit.), 1973–75, AMLS; Albert Ludwigs Univ., W. Germany, 1970–71 (Grmn. lit.); Gallaudet Coll., 1979–81 (Amer. Sign Lang.). **Orgs.:** Lib. of Congs. Prof. Assn.: Pres. (1981). Metro Atlanta Lib. Assn.: Second VP and Mem. Ch. (1976). Lib. Sci. Student Org., Univ. of MI: Pres. (1973). **Honors:** Lib. of Congs., Merit. Srv. Awd., 1979; Univ. of MI, Edmon Low Student Awd., 1974. **Activities:** 1, 4; 20, 34, 44; 72, 74 **Addr.:** Zimmerman & Associates, Inc., 7700 Leesburg Pike, Su. 420, Falls Church, VA 22043.

Hughes, Dorothy Swaringen (S. 17, 1928, Alcoa, TN) Libn., Seattle Trust and Savings Bank, 1977–; Resrch. Asst., Sch. of Info. and Comp. Sci., GA Inst. of Tech., 1973–75. **Educ.:** Meredith Coll., 1945–49, AB (Eng.); Emory Univ., 1951–52, MLS. **Orgs.:** SLA: Pac. NW Chap. (PR Ch., 1980–81). **Activities:** 12; 56, 59, 75 **Addr.:** 2707 68th Ave. S.E., Mercer Island, WA 98040.

Hughes, Evelyn Marie Hill (S. 9, 1920, Morgantown, WV) Libn., Sch. of Nursing, Sewickley Valley Hosp., 1968–; Catlgr., Asst. Catlgr., Med. Ctr. Lib., WV Univ., 1959–67; Sub. Tchr., Maple Hts., OH, 1955–58; Foods Resrch. Lab., Purity Bakeries, 1943–44; Home Econ. Tchr., Wayne Cnty. HS, 1942–43. **Educ.:** WV Univ., 1938–42, BS (Home Econ.), 1954–58, MS (Home Econ. Educ.), 1962–70, MA (Educ., LS). **Orgs.:** Med. LA: Pittsburgh Reg. Grp. Natl. Leag. for Nursing. PA Leag. for Nursing. **Honors:** Kappa Delta Pi, 1966. **Activities:** 1, 10; 20, 31, 39; 80, 95-Nursing. **Addr.:** School of Nursing, Sewickley Valley Hospital, Sewickley, PA 15143.

Hughes, Geraldine (Mr. 31, 1918, Burgessville, ON, Can.) Dir., Lib. Tech. Prog., Sheridan Coll., 1970–, Head, Readers' Srvs., Mackinac Coll., 1968–70, Head, Tech. Srvs., 1965–68; Tchr., London Bd. of Educ. 1939–51. **Educ.:** Univ. of West. ON, 1951, BA (Psy.); Univ. of MI, 1968 AMLS; London Tchrs. Coll., 1939 Tchg. cert. **Orgs.:** Can. LA: Com. Lib. Tech. (1979–). ON Assn. of Lib. Tech. Instr.: Pres. (1977–79). ALA. SLA. Med. LA. **Honors:** Beta Phi Mu, 1968. **Activities:** 1, 11; 20, 26; 50, 57, 63 **Addr.:** Library Techniques Program, Sheridan College, Trafalgar Rd., Oakville, ON L6H 2L1 Canada.

Hughes, J. Marshal (Ap. 2, 1945, Concord, NC) Head, Tech. Lib. Div., Nvl. Surface Weapons Ctr., 1979–; Libn., Natl. Aeronautics and Space Admin., 1967–79. **Educ.:** Campbell Univ., 1963–67, BS (Eng.); George Peabody Coll., 1968–69, MLS; FL State Univ., 1971–72, AMS (LS), 1972–75, PhD (LS). **Orgs.:** ALA. Amer. Socty. of Info. Specs. SLA. VA LA. VA Micro. Assn. **Honors:** Beta Phi Mu, 1968; NASA Career Dev. Prog. for Ctr. Empls., 1978. **Pubns.:** "A Tour of the Library - By Audiotape," *Spec. Libs.* (Volume 65); "The Technical Library of the Langley Research Center," *VASLA* (Mr. 1974). **Activities:** 4; 17, 24, 26; 56, 75, 74 **Addr.:** Technical Library Division, Mailstop X-20, Naval Surface Weapons Center, Dahlgren, VA 22448.

Hughes, M. Virginia (Jl. 31, 1920, Baltimore, MD) Prin. libn., Lib. Consult., CA State Lib., 1957–; Consult. in Work with Schs., Enoch Pratt Free Lib., 1953–57, Branch Libn., 1952–53; Dependent Schs. Libn., US Army, France, Germany, 1951–52; Armed Forces Libn., US Army, Germany, Hawaii, US, 1945–51; Jr. Coll. Monmouth Jr. Coll., 1944–45; Tchr. Libn., Baltimore City Schs., 1940–44. **Educ.:** Goucher Coll., 1936–40, AB (European Hist.); Columbia Univ., 1941–44, BS (LS). **Orgs.:** ALA: "Books Worth Their Keep" (1955–56). Assn. of Sch. Libns., MD: Bd. of Gvrs. (1953–57). MD LA: Rcrt. Com. (1956). CA LA: Stan. Com. (1965); Cclr. (1982–84). **Pubns.:** Coord., *California Library Trustees and Commissioners "TOOL KIT"* (1981); "Demonstrating Bookmobile Service," *Wilson Lib. Bltn.* (My. 1959); "Public Relations and a Bookmobile," *News Notes of CA Libs.* (Fall 1960). **Activities:** 9, 13; 21, 24, 27, 47; 89 **Addr.:** 4795 Monterey Way, Sacramento, CA 95822.

Hughes, Sue Margaret (Ap. 13, –, Cleburne, TX) Dir., Moody Lib., Baylor Univ., 1980–, Acq. Libn., 1964–79, Asst. in Pub. Srvs., 1960–64. **Educ.:** Univ. of TX, 1945–49, BBA; TX Woman's Univ., 1959–60, MLS. **Orgs.:** ALA: RTSD Reprinting Com. (Secy., 1975–76); Dupl. Exch. Un. (1969–74; Ch, 1971–74). SWLA. TX LA: Dist. III (Lcl. Ch., 1975). Beta Phi Mu. AAUP: Baylor Chap. (Pres., 1979–80). AAUW. Baylor Univ.: Sen. (1974–). Delta Kappa Gamma Socty. Intl. Other orgs. **Honors:** AAUW, Outstan. Woman of the Yr., Waco Branch, 1978. **Activities:** 1; 15, 17, 46 **Addr.:** Moody Memorial Library, Baylor University, Box 6307, Waco, TX 76706.

Hughes, Susan Kutscher (N. 24, 1946, San Antonio, TX) Decision Support & Info. Srvs., 1981–; Info. Resrcs. Coord., Mobil Producing TX and NM Inc., 1979–81; Libn., McKinsey and Co. Inc., 1977–79; Tech. Libn., City of Houston, Dept. of Aviation, 1975–76; Head, Fine Arts Dept., Houston Pub. Lib., 1970–72. **Educ.:** Trinity Univ., 1963–67, BA (Drama, Sp.); Univ. of TX, Austin, 1967–68, MLS; Univ. of TX, San Antonio, 1973–75, grad. work in Env. Mgt. **Orgs.:** SLA: TX Chap. (2nd VP, 1979–81), Pubns. Com. (Ch., 1980–81); Petr. Div. (Ch.-Elect, 1981–82). ASIS. Houston OLUG. **Pubns.:** Ed., *TX SLA Chap. News* (1979–80); ed., *TX Chap. SLA Bltn.* (1979–81). **Activities:** 12; 15, 17, 41; 59, 64, 86 **Addr.:** P.O. Box 6068, San Antonio, TX 78209.

Hughes, Suzanne J. (Ja. 11, 1943, Brownsville, TX) Coord. Info. Svrs., LA Legis. Cncl., 1970–; Tchr., Spring Branch Jr. HS, Houston, TX, 1964–67. **Educ.:** Univ. of TX, 1960–64, BA (Hist.); LA State Univ., 1967–70, (Hist.); TX Teaching cert., 1964. **Orgs.:** LA LA. SLA. LA Gvt. Info. Ntwk: Steering Com. (Ch., 1979–). Natl. Assn. for State Info. Syst. Natl. Conf. of State Legis.: Legis. Ref. Libn. Staff Sect. (Ch., 1977–78); Legis. Info. Needs Com. (1976–; Vice ch., 1979–81); Legislative Info. Syst. Task Frc. (1979–); Bill Status Task Frc. (1977–). **Pubns.:** "Spotlight on Special Libraries: Librarians Aid Lawmakers," *LA LA Bltn.* (Ja. 1980). **Activities:** 13; 17, 34, 39; 75, 77, 78 **Addr.:** Louisiana Legislative Council, P.O. Box 44012, Baton Rouge, LA 70804.

Hughey, Elizabeth (House) (F. 2, 1916, Robersonville, NC) Retired, 1980–; Chief, State and Pub. Lib. Srvs. Branch, US Ofc. of Educ., 1968–80, Lib. Ext. Spec., Lib. Srvs. Bureau, 1965–68; State Libn., NC State Lib., 1956–65; Secy. and Dir., NC Lib. Comsn., 1950–56, Field Libn., 1946–50; Libn., BHM Reg. Lib., Washington, 1941–46; HS Libn., 1938–41. **Educ.:** Atl. Christ. Coll., 1932–36, AB (Eng.); Peabody Coll., 1937–38, BS (LS). **Orgs.:** ALA. NC LA. SELA. Bus. and Prof. Women; Delta Kappa Gamma. **Honors:** Atl. Christ. Coll., DLitt. **Activities:** 4, 9 **Addr.:** 8013 Greeley Blvd., Springfield, VA 22152.*

Huisman, Gary Brant (Ap. 8, 1940, Grand Haven, MI) Libn., Covenant Coll., 1966–. **Educ.:** Calvin Coll., 1959–63, AB (Msc.); West. MI Univ., 1965–66, MSL. **Orgs.:** ALA.: ACRL, Legis. Corres. (1976–1978). Christian Libn. Flwshp.: Pubn. Com. (1969–70). Assn. for the Advnc. of Christ. Scho. **Activities:** 1; 15, 17 **Addr.:** Kresge Memorial Library, Covenant College, Lookout Mountain, TN 37350.

Hukill, Jane Ellet (F. 12, 1933, Benton Harbor, MI) Lib. Dir., Brandywine Coll. of Widener Univ., 1967–. **Educ.:** Univ. of MI, 1950–54, BA (Eng.); Villanova Univ., 1970–73, MSLS. **Orgs.:** DE LA: Pres. (1975–76); VP (1974–75); Secy. (1972–74). Mid. Atl. Reg. Lib. Fed.: Exec. Bd. (1979–); Pres. (1980–81, 1981–82). Tri-State Coll. Lib. Coop.: Bd. of Dir. (1969–). DE Lib. Cnsrtm. Other orgs. AAUP. Middle States Assn. Consult. **Activities:** 1; 17, 31, 34; 59 **Addr.:** Box 7139, Concord Pike, Brandywine College of Widener University, Wilmington, DE 19803.

Hulbert, Linda Ann (N. 10, 1947, Racine, WI) Coll. Dev. Libn., SUNY Upstate Med. Ctr., 1977–; Med. Ref. Libn., Hlth. Sci. Lib., Univ. of IA, 1973–77. **Educ.:** Washington Univ., 1965–69, BA (Eng./Educ.); Univ. of IA, 1971–73, MA (LS).

PROFESSIONAL ACTIVITIES: Institutions: 1. Acad. lib.; 2. Arch.; 3. Assn.; 4. Fed./Gvt. lib.; 5. Inst. lib.; 6. Mfr./Suppl.; 7. Milit. lib.; 8. Musm.; 9. Pub. lib.; 10. Sch. lib.; 11. Sch. of lib. sci.; 12. Spec. lib.; 13. State lib.; 14. (other). **Functions/Activities:** 15. Acq./Col. dev.; 16. Adult srvs.; 17. Admin.; 18. Apprais.; 19. Archit./Bldgs.; 20. Cat./Class.; 21. Chld. srvs.; 22. Circ.; 23. Cons./Pres.; 24. Consult.; 25. Cont. ed.; 26. Educ. lib. sci.; 27. Ext. srvs.; 28. Fund/Grants; 29. Gvt. pubs.; 30. Indx./Abs.; 31. Instr. lib. use; 32. Media srvs.; 33. Micro.; 34. Netwks./Coop.; 35. Persnl.; 36. PR; 37. Publshg.; 38. Recs. mgt.; 39. Ref. srvs.; 40. Repro.; 41. Resrch.; 42. Review.; 43. Secur.; 44. Serials; 45. Spec. col.; 46. Tech. srvs.; 47. Trustees/Bds.; 48. YA srvs.; 49. (other).

Orgs.: Med. LA: Mem. Com. (1979–81); Upstate NY/ON Reg. Grp., Med. LA. SUNY LA. **Pubns.:** "Evaluation of an approval plan," *Coll. and Resrch. Libs.* (N. 1978); "One Man's Tsuris...," *Lib. Jnl.* (S. 1977); "Tattle tape machinery," *Jnl. of the Amer. Med. Assn.* (Je. 1978). **Activities:** 1; 15, 44; 80 **Addr.:** State University of New York, Upstate Medical Center, Library, 766 Irving Ave., Syracuse, NY 13210.

Huleatt, Richard S. (Ag. 13, 1931, Boston, MA) Pres., Info. Intelligence Inc., 1979–; Mgr., Lib. Srvs., Armour Resrch. Ctr., 1976–80; Consult., 1975–76; Tech. Info. Mgr., Stone & Webster Engin. Corp., 1968–75; Chief Libn., General Dynamics, 1967–68; Tech. Info. Mgr., Lab. for Electronics, Inc., 1960–67; Data Coord., Raytheon, 1957–60. **Educ.:** Boston Univ., 1949–51. **Orgs.:** AZ LA: Lib. Dev./Legis. Com. (1979/80). SLA: Boston Chap. (Pres., 1971–72); AZ Chap. (Pres., 1978); Networking Com. (1979–80). AZ Gvrs. Conf. on Lib. and Info. Srvs.: Del. AZ OLUG. Other orgs. **Pubns.:** "Rx for Acquisitions Hangups," *Spec. Libs.* (F. 1973); "The Publisher as Vendor - Special Library," *The serials Librarian: Acquisition Case Book* (1975); News Ed., *Online Mag.* (1979–80); "Finishing the Online Search," *Online* (Ap. 1979); "Online Use of Chemical Abstracts: a Primer for Beginning Chemical Searchers," *Database* (D. 1979); Other articles. **Activities:** 6; 24, 37; 59, 80, 91 **Addr.:** Information Intelligence Incorporated, P.O. Box 31098, Phoenix, AZ 85046.

Huling, Willadean (Jl. 14, 1946, Ontario, OR) Instr. Mtrls. Ctrs., Dir., Sch. Dist. #15, 1968–. **Educ.:** Treasure Valley Cmnty. Coll., 1964–66, AS (Gen.); Univ. of OR, 1966–68, BS (LS), 1968–71, MLS. **Orgs.:** ALA OR Educ. Media Assn. East. OR Lib. Assn. Snake River LA: Pres. (1972–74). Vale Area Educ. Assn.: Secy./Treas. (1969–70); VP (1970–71); Pres. (1971–72). Natl. Educ. Assn. OR Educ. Assn. Various other orgs. **Honors:** Acad. of Amer. Educ., Outstand. Educ. in Amer., 1973–74; Phi Lambda Theta, 1977; Beta Phi Mu, 1968. **Activities:** 10; 15, 17, 20, 21, 22, 31, 32 **Addr.:** Rt. 3 Box 614, Ontario, OR 97914.

Hull, Barbara (My. 10, 1949, New York, NY) Lib. Media Spec., Samuel Gompers Vocational HS, 1980–; Lib. Media Spec., Queens Vocational HS, 1980–81; Lib. Media Spec., N.Y.C. Bd. of Educ., 1974–; Ref. Libn., Queens Borough Pub. Lib., 1972–74. **Educ.:** Queens Coll., 1966–70, BA (Soclgy.), 1971–72, MLS; New York Inst. of Tech., 1978– MA in progress (Comm); Certs., Pub. Libn., Lib. Media Spec., NY State. **Orgs.:** New York City Sch. Libns. Assn.: Secy. (1977–79). New York Lib. Club: Cncl. (1978–82). NY LA: Pres., NY LA JMRT (1976–77); NY LA/ Baker and Taylor Grassroots Grant Com. (1978). ALA: AASL; RASD; YASD; RASD, Wilson Index Com. (1979–82); JMRT, nom. com. (1981–82). Other coms. Untd. Fed. of Tchrs. **Honors:** ALA, JMRT, Shirley Olofson Awd., 1974; Beta Phi Mu. **Activities:** 10; 31, 39, 48; 95-Vocational/Tech./Applied Sci. **Addr.:** 455 Southern Blvd., Bronx, NY 10455.

Hull, David C. (F. 29, 1940, New Malden, Surrey, Eng.) Div. Head, Sci. and Vetny. Sci., Univ. of Guelph, 1979–, Div. Head, Vetny. Sci., 1975–79, Libn., Spec. Col., 1973–75; Libn., Assoc. Lead Mfrs. Ltd., 1967–70. **Educ.:** Univ. of Guelph, 1958–63, BASc (Chem.); Univ. of West. ON, 1971–73, MLS; ON Coll. of Educ., 1963–64, Tchg. Cert. **Orgs.:** Med. LA: Vetny. Med. Grp., Com. on Un. List of Serials (1979–). Can. Hlth. Libs. Assn. Intl. Assn. of Agr. Libns. & Docmlsts. Vetny. Hist. Socty. **Pubns.:** *Union List Of Periodicals Not Indexed In Index Medicus Held By Veterinary Colleges Of Canada And U.S.A.* (1980). **Activities:** 1; 17, 39; 58, 95-Vetny. Med., Agr. **Addr.:** Science and Veterinary Science Division, University of Guelph Library, Guelph, ON N1G 2W1 Canada.

Hull, John J. (Je. 7, 1921, Presque Isle, ME) Serials Libn., Asst. Acq. Libn., Univ. of NH, 1975–, Asst Order Libn., 1967–75; Libn., Newmarket (NH) HS, 1965–67; Libn., Epping (NH) HS, 1964–65. **Educ.:** MA St. Coll., 1940–43; Univ. NH, 1946–47, BA (Eng.), 1967–68, MED (Educ.); Simmons Coll., 1973–75, MSLS. **Orgs.:** New Eng. Sch. LA: Pres. (1966–67). New Eng. LA. NH LA. New Eng. Tech. Srvs. Libns. New Eng. Serials Srv. Task Force: Ch. (1977–78). NH Coll. and Univ. Cncl.: Serials Com. (Ch., 1977–). **Pubns.:** *Atherosclerosis* (M.I.T. Pathfinder Prog.) (1973); *Ludwig van Beethoven, Life & Works* (M.I.T. Pathfinder Prog.) (1974). **Activities:** 1; 15, 34, 44; 55, 74, 92 **Addr.:** Dimond Library, Serials Division, University of New Hampshire, Durham, NH 03824.

Hulton, Clara A. (Ap. 10, 1919, Sharon, PA) Libn., FL Correctional Inst., 1971–; Asst. Coord. of Chld. Srvs., New York Pub. Lib., 1967–71, Branch Libn., 1965–67, Chld. Libn., 1963–65, YA Libn., 1949–63; Chld. Libn., Manhasset (NY) Pub. Lib., 1946–49; Libn., Dun & Bradstreet, 1945–46; Chld. Libn., New York Pub. Lib., 1943–45. **Educ.:** Lake Erie Coll., 1936–38; Mt. Holyoke Coll., 1938–40, AB (Eng.); Carnegie-Mellon Univ., 1942–43, BLS; Columbia Univ., Pratt Inst., 1944–45; 1964–65 (LS). **Orgs.:** ALA: Ch., Best Books for Chld. (1960–70, 1971); Ch., Mildred Batchelder Awd. Com., (1972); Lib. Srv. to Prisoners Com. (1977–). NY LA: Ch., Recordings for Chld. Com. (1969–71). FL LA: Outreach Caucus (1973–). SELA. AAUW: 2nd VP, Ocala Chapter (1978–80). Leag. of Women Voters: Bd., Ocala Branch (1971–74). Soroptimist Intl.: Pres., Ocala Branch (1978–80). **Activities:** 5, 9; 16, 21, 48; 50, 89, 95-Bibliotherapy. **Addr.:** 2817 S.E. 4th St., Ocala, FL 32670.

Hulton, John G., Jr. (O. 25, 1922, Latrobe, PA) Dir., Lrng. Resrcs., Ctrl. FL Cmnty. Coll., 1971–; Assoc. Prof., LS, Pratt Inst., 1963–71; Coord. of Branches, Richmond Borough, New York Pub. Lib., 1961–63, Various positions, 1949–61. **Educ.:** Washington & Jefferson Coll., 1940–43, BA (Econ.); Harvard Univ., 1946–48, MA (Hist.); Columbia Univ., 1950–51, MS (LS). **Orgs.:** ALA. FL LA. FL Assn. for Media in Educ. **Honors:** Phi Beta Kappa, 1943. **Activities:** 1; 17 **Addr.:** Central Florida Community College, P.O. Box 1388, Ocala, FL 32678.

Humbertson, Jane Vinton (F. 14, 1931, Richmond, VA) Lib. Dir., Hagerstown Jr. Coll., 1963–; Tech. Srvs. Libn., West. MD Coll., 1954–62. **Educ.:** Washington Coll., 1949–53, BA (Hist.); Carnegie Mellon Univ., 1953–54, MLS. **Orgs.:** ALA. MD LA. Cumberland Valley Lib. Assn.: Treas. (1978–); Secy. (1976–78). Zonta Intl. of Hagerstown: Secy. (1976–78). **Activities:** 1; 15, 17, 31; 63, 64, 92 **Addr.:** Hagerstown Junior College Library, 751 Robinwood Dr., Hagerstown, MD 21740.

Humel, Joyce A. (Mr. 4, 1948, Cleveland, OH) Dir., Rolling Hills Consolidated Lib., 1977–, Branch Libn., 1977; Outrch. Asst., Little Dixie Reg. Libs., 1975–77. **Educ.:** Georgetown Univ., 1965–67; OR State Univ., 1970–71, BA (Soc. Sci.); Univ. of MO, 1975–77, MLS. **Orgs.:** ALA. MO LA: Int. Frdm. Com. (Ch., 1980–81). NW MO Lib. Netwk.: Treas. (1978–79); Pres. (1979–80). **Activities:** 9; 17, 27 **Addr.:** 501–A N. Belt, St. Joseph, MO 64506.

Hummel, Frances Cope (My. 13, 1911, Ann Arbor, MI) Resrch. Libn., Coord., Ctrl. Retrieval Alcolac, Inc., 1971–; Lit. Srchr., Libn., Indxr., Fibers Div., Allied Chem. Corp., 1965–71; Libn., Hawaiian Sugar Planters Assn., 1963–64; Libn. I, New York Pub. Lib., 1962–63. **Educ.:** Wayne Univ., 1926–28; Univ. of MI, 1928–30, BS (Chem.), 1930–31, MS (Chem.); Columbia Univ., 1960–62, MS (LS); Cert. Med. Libn., 1971. **Orgs.:** VA LA: Ch., Spring workshop, (1971). SLA: Secy., Baltimore Chap. (1972–73). ASIS: Treas., Chesapeake Bay Chap. (1977). Amer. Chem. Socty.: Mem. Ch., MD Sect. (1975–78); Secy. (1979, 1980, 1981); Natl. Women Chem. Com. (1977–79). **Honors:** Phi Beta Kappa, Phi Kappa Phi. **Pubns.:** Various articles on nutrition. **Activities:** 9, 12; 15, 16, 17; 57, 58, 60 **Addr.:** 9627 Whiteacre Rd., Columbia, MD 21045.

Hummel, Janice A. (Ag. 10, 1952, Albuquerque, NM) Reg. Ref. Libn., South. MD Reg. LA, 1976–. **Educ.:** SUNY, Stony Brook, 1970–74, BA (Econ.); Univ. of MD, 1975–77, MLS. **Orgs.:** MD LA: Adult/YA Srvs. Div. ALA: RASD, Cncl. of State & Reg. Grp. (Ch., 1980–81); RASD Bd. (1980–81). **Honors:** Gvrs. Task Force on State Docum., 1979. **Activities:** 9; 16, 34, 39; 75 **Addr.:** Southern Maryland Regional Library Association, PO Box 1069, LaPlata, MD 20646.

Hummel, Ray O., Jr. (O. 22, 1909, Lincoln, NE) Scholar-in-Residence, VA Commonwealth Univ., 1975–; Asst. State Libn., VA State Lib., 1948–75; Asst. Prof., Univ. of MN Lib. Sch. and Chief Cat. Libn., Univ. of MN, 1946–48; Rare Bk. Catlgr., Folger Shakespeare Lib. 1936–46; Libn., Washington Cathedral, 1940–42; Instr., Cath. Univ., 1938–42. **Educ.:** Univ. of NE, 1926–30, AB (Hist.), 1930–32, MA (Hist.); Univ. of IA, 1932–33; Univ. of NE, 1933–34 PhD (Hist.); Univ. of MI, 1935–36, ABLS. **Orgs.:** VA LA: Pres. (1957–58). ALA: Cncl. (1950–54, 1956–59). SELA: Ref. Adult Srvs. Sect., Ch. (1968–70). Jt. Com. on Lib. Educ.: Ch. (1960). **Pubns.:** *Portraits and Statuary of Virginians* (1977); *More Virginia Broadsides* (1975); *Southeastern Broadsides Before 1877* (1971); *Virginia Local History, A Bibliography* (1971); *List of Places in 19th Century VA Directories* (1960). **Activities:** 1, 13; 17, 18, 45; 57, 73 **Addr.:** 5107 Sylvan Rd., Richmond, VA 23225.

Humnicky, Virginia Avis (S. 27, 1923, Carroll Cnty., IN) Retired, 1981; Ext. Libn., IN Univ., Sch. of Med. Lib., 1979, Info. Srvs. Libn., 1978–79, Coord. for Hlth. Sci. Libs. in IN, 1973–78, Ext. Libn., 1969–73. **Educ.:** Purdue Univ., 1966, BA (Sch. Media); IN Univ., 1966–69, MLS. **Orgs.:** SLA: Chap. Cabinet (1975–77); IN Chap., Dir. at Large (1973–74); Pres. (1976–77) Consult. Ofcr. (1977–). Med. LA: Midwest Reg. Grp. IN LA. Midwest HSLN: Educ. Plng. Com. (1977–); Arch. Com. (1979–). AAUP: Lcl. Chap., Nom. Com. (1979); VP (1979–81); IN Conf., Com. W. Plng. Com., IN Gvrs. Conf., on Libs. and Info. Srvs: Spec. Libs. Rep. (1977–78). **Pubns.:** Contrib. ed., *Basic Library Management for Health Science Librarians* (1975); "The Evolution of a Health Science Library Network in Indiana," *Lib. Occurent* (F. 1974); "Network Perspectives - Indiana. Midwest Health Science Library Network," *Resrcs.* (Win. 1975–76); Actg. Ed., *IN Slant,* (1975–76). **Activities:** 1, 12; 24, 27, 34; 58, 80, 91 **Addr.:** Indiana University School of Medicine Library, 1100 W. Michigan St., Indianapolis, IN 46223.

Humphrey, David C. (S. 13, 1937, Rochester, NY) Archvst., Lyndon Baines Johnson Lib., 1977–; Archvst., Ofc. of Presidential Libs., Natl. Arch. and Recs. Srv., 1976–77; Asst. Prof. of Hist., Carnegie-Mellon Univ., 1968–76, Instr., 1965–68. **Educ.:** Princeton Univ., 1955–59, BA (Hist.); Harvard Univ., 1959–60, MAT (Tchg./Hist.); Northwestern Univ., 1960–68, MA PhD (Hist.); Family and Cmnty. Hist. Summer Trng. Inst., 1975, Cert. Org. of Amer. Histns. TX State Hist. Assn. **Honors:** Amer. Assn. for State and Lcl. Hist., Cert. of Cmdn., 1977; NJ Hist. Socty., William Adee Whitehead Awd., 1974; Natl. Endow. for the Hum., Resrch. Grant, 1971–72. **Pubns.:** *From King's College to Columbia, 1746–1800* (1976); "Dissection and Discrimination: The Social Origins of Cadavers in America, 1760–1915," *Bltn. of the NY Acad. of Med.* (S. 1973); reprinted in *Essays on the History of Medicine* (1976); "Anglican 'Infiltration' of Eighteenth Century Harvard and Yale," *Hist. Mag. of the Protestant Episcopal Church,* (S. 1974); "The King's College Medical School and the Professionalization of Medicine in Pre-Revolutionary New York," *Bltn. of the Hist. of Med.* (Sum. 1975); "King's College and the American Revolution," *Columbia Lib. Columns* (My. 1976); Other articles, reviews. **Activities:** 2, 4; 39, 45; 54 **Addr.:** Lyndon Baines Johnson Library, Austin, TX 78705.

Humphrey, Helen C. (Jl. 12, 1917, Harrison Cnty., KY) Lib. Media Spec., Westside Elem. Sch., 1965–; Tchr., Harrison Cnty. HS, 1962–64; Tchr., Cynthiana HS, 1952–62, 1945–46; Prog. Dir., Girl Scout Cncl., St. Petersburg, FL, 1942–43; Tchr., Connersville HS, 1940–42. **Educ.:** KY Wesleyan Coll., 1935–39, AB (Eng.); Univ. of KY, 1964–65, MS (LS). **Orgs.:** ALA: AASL. KY LA. KY Sch. Media Assn. Ctrl. KY Sch. Media Assn. Natl. Educ. Assn. KY Educ. Assn. Harrison Cnty. (KY) Educ. Assn. KY Hist. Socty. **Honors:** Beta Phi Mu. **Activities:** 10; 15, 17, 20; 63, 89 **Addr.:** Westside Elementary School Library Media Center, Route 6 Box 288, Cynthiana, KY 41031.

Humphrey, Virginia Shea (D. 12, 1949, Rochester, NY) Volun. Indxr., Ballston Spa (NY) Pub. Lib., 1979–; Dir., Johnstown (NY) Pub. Lib., 1972–79. **Educ.:** SUNY, Buffalo, 1967–71, BA (Eng.); SUNY, Albany, 1971–72, MLS. **Orgs.:** ALA. NY LA. Tryon Lib. Assoc.: Secy. (1978–80). SUNY, Albany, Sch. of Lib. and Info. Sci. Alum. Assn. Mohawk Valley Chorus. Amer. Rabbit Breeders Assn. SUNY, Buffalo Alum. Assn. **Activities:** 9; 16, 30, 39; 55, 67, 69 **Addr.:** RD 5 Fairground Ave., Ballston Spa, NY 12020.

Humphreys, Carlos (N. 29, 1951, Ysleta, TX) Pub. Srv. Libn., El Paso Com. Coll., Valle Verde, 1976–; Ref. and Audiovisual Asst. El Paso Pub. Lib., 1974–75, Ref. and Ext. Srvs Asst. 1973–74. **Educ.:** Univ. of TX, El Paso, 1969–75, BA (Mass Comm.); Univ. of AZ, 1975–76, MLS. **Orgs.:** REFORMA: El Paso Chap.: Pres. (1979–80), VP (1978–79). REFORMA: Nat. Brd. (1978–79). Border Reg. LA. Concilio de El Paso: Secy. (1980). Assn. of Mexican-Amer. Educ. Pol. Action Com. (1977–80). Prof. Assn. of Coll. Educ. (1979–80). TX State Tchrs. Assn. (1979–80). **Honors:** Beta Phi Mu, 1977. **Activities:** 1, 9; 17, 31, 39; 66, 92 **Addr.:** 8000 Lowd Ave., El Paso, TX 79907.

Humphreys, Nancy K. (Je. 24, 1946, Erie, PA) (Bus., Econ. Bibl., Info. Srvs. Libn., Univ. of WI (LaCrosse), 1976–. **Educ.:** Wittenberg Univ., 1964–66; Temple Univ., 1967–69, BA (Eng.); Univ. of WI (Madison), 1969–70, MA (Eng.), 1970–71, MS (Econ.); Univ. of SC, 1975–76, ML (LS). **Orgs.:** ALA. WI Women Lib. Wkrs. **Honors:** Beta Phi Mu, 1977. **Pubns.:** "Ethiopia: Trapped by Foreign Aid," *The Nation* (Je. 1973); reviews. **Activities:** 1; 15, 30, 39; 51, 59, 92 **Addr.:** Murphy Library, University of Wisconsin LaCrosse, LaCrosse, WI 54601.

Humphreys, Richard H. (Jl. 12, 1930, Ashland, KS) Assoc. Prof., Libn., DE Law Sch., 1975–; Asst. Prof., Asst. Dean, Univ. of Detroit Law Sch., 1970–75; Hse. Couns., Tulsa Crude Oil, 1968–70; Sales, Tamko Asphalt, 1963–68. **Educ.:** Univ. of KS, 1948–52, AB (Pol. Sci.); Univ. of Tulsa, 1965–68, JD (Law); Wayne State Univ., 1974–75, MSLS (Lib.). **Orgs.:** DE LA: Pres. (1981–82). AALL. Grt. Philadelphia Law LA: Exec. Bd. (1980–81). Gvrs. Task Frc. on Lib. Coop. OK Bar Assn. **Honors:** Univ. of Detroit Student Bar, Outstan. Tchr., 1975. **Pubns.:** "Library Needs for Sole Practitioner/Small Firm Libraries," *NY Law Jnl.* (Mr. 1979); fac., "Michigan Continuing Legal Education," *Oil and Gas* (1974); ed., *AALL Nsltr.* (1979–82). **Activities:** 1; 17, 35, 41; 77, 82, 86 **Addr.:** Delaware Law School, Box 7475, Concord Pike, Wilmington, DE 19803.

Humphries, Beverly H. (Jl. 3, 1930, Gatesville, TX) Libn., Lewis & Clark Cmnty. Coll., 1970–; Libn., Monticello Coll., 1965–70; Per. Libn., Davenport Pub. Lib., 1957–59; Serials & Docum. Libn., TX A. & M. Univ., 1954–57. **Educ.:** N. TX State Univ., 1948–50, BS (Educ., LS); South. IL Univ., Edwardsville, 1969–71, MS (Educ. Admin.). **Orgs.:** IL Ctrl. Educ. Network: Bd. of Dir. (1980–). IL ACRL: Bd. of Dir. (1980–). ALA: ACRL, Cont. Educ. Com. (1977–79). South. IL Lrng. Resrcs. Coop.: Ch. Elect (1980–). Grt. Alton Concept Assn. Zonta. **Activities:** 1; 17; 95-Instr. TV. **Addr.:** Lewis & Clark Community College, Godfrey, IL 62035.

Humphry, James, III (Jl. 21, 1916, Springfield, MA) VP, H. W. Wilson Co., 1968–; Chief Libn., Metro. Musm. of Art, 1957–68; Bus. Mgr., Colby Coll. Press., Colby Coll., 1954–57, Libn. & Prof. of Bibl., 1947–57; Chief, Map Div., NY Pub. Lib., 1946–47. **Educ.:** Harvard Univ., 1935–39, AB (Econ.); Columbia Univ., 1939–41, MS (LS). **Orgs.:** ALA: Cncl. (1959–63; 1967–69); ACRL (Pres., 1967–68); Ad Hoc Subcom. on Goals, Priorities & Structures (1973–). SLA: Ch., Nom. Com., (1971–72). ASIS. NY Lib. Club: Pres. (1965–66). Other orgs.

Special Subjects/Services: 50. Adult educ.; 51. Advert./Mktg.; 52. Aerosp.; 53. Agric.; 54. Area std.; 55. Arts/Hum.; 56. Autom.; 57. Bibl./Prtg.; 58. Bio. sci.; 59. Bus./Fin.; 60. Chem.; 61. Copyrt.; 62. Documtn.; 63. Educ.; 64. Engin.; 65. Env.; 66. Eth. grps.; 67. Film; 68. Food/Nutr.; 69. Geneal.; 70. Geo.; 71. Geol.; 72. Handcpd.; 73. Hist.; 74. Int. frdm.; 75. Info. sci.; 76. Insr.; 77. Law; 78. Legis.; 79. Math./Comp. sci.; 80. Med.; 81. Metals; 82. Nat. resrcs.; 83. Newsp.; 84. Nuc. sci.; 85. Oral hist.; 86. Petr./Energy; 87. Pharm.; 88. Phys./Astr./Math.; 89. Readg.; 90. Relig.; 91. Sci./Tech.; 92. Soc. sci.; 93. Telecom.; 94. Transp.; 95. (other).

Amer. Assn. of Musms.: Lib. Grp. (Ch., 1965). Arch. of Amer. Art: Trustee (1967–77); Ch., Adv. Com. (1967–79). Archons of Colophon. Assn. of Amer. Publshrs.: Libs. Com., (1976–80). Other orgs. **Pubns.:** *Library of Edwin Arlington Robinson* (1950); Jt. Ed., Fitzgerald's *Rubaiyat* (1959); Contrib., *Amer. Heritage Dict.* (1970); "Museum Libraries" *Encyc. of Educ.,* (1971); various articles. **Activities:** 1, 6, 12; 17, 24, 47; 51, 55 **Addr.:** The H. W. Wilson Company, 950 University Ave., Bronx, NY 10452.

Humphry, John A. (Jl. 21, 1916, Springfield, MA) Exec. Dir., Forest Press, Publshr. of the Dewey Decimal Classification, 1977–; Asst. Com. of Educ. for Lib., NY State Educ. Dept., 1967–77; Dir., Brooklyn Pub. Lib., 1964–67; Exec. Dir., Springfield Lib. and Musm. Assn., 1960–64, Dir., Springfield City Lib., 1948–64; Dir., of Book Processing, Enoch Pratt Free Lib., 1946–48. **Educ.:** Harvard Coll., 1935–39, AB (Econ.), 1942–43; Columbia Univ., 1940–41, BS LS. **Orgs.:** ALA: Cncl., (1960–64); ACRL. NY LA: Legis. Com., (1965). MA LA: Pres., (1957–58). Western MA Lib. Club. New England LA: Bd. of Dirs., (1953–54). Cncl. on Lib. Resrcs.: Bd. of Dirs., (1968–). MA Bd. of Lib. Comsns.: Secy., (1957–64). Metro. Ref. and Resrch. Lib. Agency: Bd. of Dirs., (1965–67). **Pubns.:** *Library Service in Louisiana, Keeping Pace with Progress in the State* (1968); *Library Cooperation, The Brown University Study of University, School and Community Library Coordination in Rhode Island* (1963). **Activities:** 9, 13; 17, 20, 24; 57, 75, 78 **Addr.:** Forest Press, 85 Watervliet Ave., Albany, NY 12206.

Hund, Flower L. (Ap. 29, 1928, Kansas City, MO) Econ. and Bus. Libn., Ctrl. MO State Univ., 1981–; Lib. Dir., Cincinnati Country Day Sch., 1978–81; Asst. Libn., Pembroke Country Day Sch., 1976–78. **Educ.:** Vassar Coll., 1946–50, BA (Econ.); Univ. of MO, Kansas City, 1972–1976, MA (Educ.); Emporia State Univ., 1976–78 MLS; Univ. of Denver, 1980– Advnc. Std. (LS). **Orgs.:** ALA. MO LA. SLA: Cincinnati Chap. (Secy., 1980–81). Grt. Cincinnati Lib. Cnsrtm.: Dir. (1979–81); Secy. (1980–81); Exec. Bd. (1980–81). Frnds. of Art, Nelson-Atkins Gallery. Cincinnati Nature Ctr. **Honors:** Phi Kappa Phi, 1976. **Activities:** 1, 10; 34; 56, 59 **Addr.:** 804 Tyler St., Warrensburg, MO 64093.

Hunger, Charles H. (Ag. 4, 1931, OH) Dir., AV Srvs., Kent State Univ., 1974–, Assoc. Dir., 1967–74, Supvsr., Film Ctr., 1964–67. **Educ.:** Kent State Univ., 1955–59, BS Ed (Bus./Hist.), 1961–65, MEd (Media); Grad. work, Syracuse, MI State, IN Univ. **Orgs.:** Cnsrtm. of Univ. Film Ctrs.: Pres. (1979–80). AECT. OH Educ. Lib./Media Assn.: Bd. of Dir. (1977–85). Kent Kiwanis: Pres. Kent Free Lib.: Bd. of Dirs. (1977–85). **Pubns.:** "Locally Produced Instructional Materials and the Classroom Teacher," *AV Instr.* (Mr. 1972); multi-media prod. **Activities:** 10; 32; 67 **Addr.:** 330 University Library, Kent State University, Kent, OH 44242.

Hunsberger, Charles W. (S. 25, 1929, Elkhart, IN) Dir. of Libs., Clark Cnty. Lib. Dist., 1971–; Dir., Monroe Cnty. Lib., IN, 1964–71; Libn., Peabody Free Lib., IN, 1962–64. **Educ.:** Bethel Coll., 1947–52, BA (Lit.); IN Univ., 1964, MLS. **Orgs.:** NV Cncl. on Libs.: Ch. (1978–81). NV LA. ALA. Rotary. Pub. Radio Station: Bd. of Dir. **Pubns.:** "Library Consolidation," *NV Gvt. Today* (Fall, 1974). **Activities:** 9; 17, 34, 36 **Addr.:** 1401 E. Flamingo Rd., Las Vegas, NV 89109.

Hunsberger, Willard D. (Jl. 19, 1926, Souderton, PA) Asst. Dir. Lib. Srvs., IN Univ.-Purdue Univ. at Ft. Wayne, 1968–; Head Libn., IN Inst. of Tech., 1964–68; Asst. Prof., LS, TX Woman's Univ., 1963–64; Head Libn., Govt. of Guam Sch., 1959–63. **Educ.:** Goshen Coll., 1946–50, BA (Soc. Sci.); Temple Univ., 1953–55, (Educ.); FL State Univ., 1957–59, (LS). **Orgs.:** IN LA: Ch., Coll. & Univ. Com. (1973–74); Ch., Tech. Srvs. Com. (1974–75); Ch., Int. Frdm. Com. (1968–70). **Pubns.:** *Clarence Darraw: A Bibliography* (1981); *Franconia Mennonites and War* (1951); "Censorship and Delinquency," *Focus on IN Libs.* (Je. 1968). **Activities:** 1; 15, 17 **Addr.:** Indiana Univ.-Purdue Univ., Library - 2101 Coliseum Blvd., Fort Wayne, IN 46805.

Hunsucker, Alice E. (D. 27, 1933, Salinas, CA) Asst. VP & Mgr., Wells Fargo Bank, 1971–; Chief Libn., Bank of America, 1956–71. **Educ.:** San Jose State Coll., 1951–55, (Educ.). **Orgs.:** SLA: Chap. Dir. (1976–77); Pubcty. Ch. (1972); Hosplty. Ch. (1976); Prog. Ch. (1977); Nom. Ch. (1980); Bus & Finance Div. (Co–Ch., Prog. Com., 1971). ASIS. Assoc. Info. Mgrs. **Activities:** 12; 15, 17, 36; 59 **Addr.:** Library - Wells Fargo Bank, 475 Sansome St., San Francisco, CA 94163.

Hunt, Charles Amoes (Ja. 21, 1950, Montclair, NJ) Eng. Instr., Libn., Kiddy Coll. Eng. Sch., Kimitsu City Chiba Pref., Japan, 1979–; Ref. Libn., CA St. Univ., Fullerton, 1979; Head, Data Prcs. Dept., Tech. Lib., Atlantic Richfield Co., Los Angeles, CA, 1978–79; Branch Lib. Head, Anaheim Pub. Lib., 1978; Branch Lib. Head, Chicago Pub. Lib., 1976–78, Asst. Branch Lib. Head, 1975–76; Asst. to Ed., Ref. and Subscrpn. Bk. Review Com., ALA, 1975; PR, Graph. Dsgn. Asst., Montclair Pub. Lib., 1974. **Educ.:** Rutgers Univ., 1969 (Comp. Prog.); MA Inst. of Tech. Bus. Sch., 1969, Comp. Prog. Cert.; Doane Coll., 1969–73, BA (Eng.); Syracuse Univ., 1974–75, MLS; Midwest Cnsrtm. for Urban Tchr. Educ., 1973, CUTE (Prog. Cert.). **Orgs.:** ALA: Ref. and Subscrpn. Bks. Com. (Reviewer, 1975–79); JMRT. Chicago Lib. Club. Frdm. to Read Fndn. Natl. Black Caucus. **Activities:** 1, 9; 16, 36, 42; 56, 66, 89 **Addr.:** Kiddy College English School, 1845 Minamikoyasu, Kimitsu City, Chiba Pref., 299-11 Japan.

Hunt, Deborah S. (D. 22, 1952, Alameda, CA) Acting Govt. Pub. Libn., Univ. of NV, Reno, 1979–, Asst. Govt. Pub. Libn., 1978–79, Asst. Ref. Libn., 1977–78, Asst. Govt. Pub. Libn.(.5ETE), 1977–78; Lib. Consult., 1976–77. **Educ.:** Univ. of CA, Berkeley, 1971–75; AB (Span.), 1975–76, MLS. **Orgs.:** NE LA: Pubcty. Dir., (1980); Ch., NE Govt. Docum. Interest, Grp, (1979). CA LA: Ed., CA Clearinghouse on Lib. Instr. Nwsltr. (1978). **Pubns.:** "Publicizing the Government Publications Collection," *Unabashed Libn.* (1979). **Activities:** 1; 29, 31, 39; 56, 78 **Addr.:** Government Publications Dept., University of Nevada Library, Reno, NV 89557.

Hunt, Diana E. (Jl. 12, 1944, Toronto, BC) Chief Libn., Russell & DuMoulin, Barristers & Solicitors, 1978–; Chief Libn., McCarthy & McCarthy, 1973–78; Chief Libn., Ctr. of Criminology, Univ. of Toronto, 1971–73; Ref. Libn., Glendon Coll., York Univ., 1968–71; Ref. Libn., Main Lib., Univ. of Toronto, 1966–68. **Educ.:** Univ. of Toronto, 1961–65, BA (Soclgy.), 1965–66, BLS; York Univ., 1969–73, MA (Soclgy.). **Orgs.:** Can. ALL: Treas. (1977–79); Secy. (1979–81); VP (1981–83). AALL: Mem. Com. (1976–77); Conf. Plng. Com. (1976–77). SLA. **Honors:** Beta Phi Mu, 1966. **Activities:** 12; 17, 39, 41; 77, 78 **Addr.:** Russell & DuMoulin, Barristers & Solicitors, 1700-1075 West Georgia St., Vancouver, BC V6E 3G2 Canada.

Hunt, Donald R. (N. 5, 1921, Richmond, IN) Dir. of Libs., Univ. of TN, 1976–; Dir. of the Lib., San Jose State Univ., 1972–76; Assoc. Dir. of Libs., OR State Univ., 1955–72; Ref. Libn., WA State Univ., 1954–55. **Educ.:** Univ. of Cincinnati, 1940–42, (Engin.); Univ. of CO, 1946–50, BA (Hist.), 1950–51, MA (Hist.); Stanford Univ., 1951–53 (Hist.); Univ. of MI, 1953–54, MALS. **Orgs.:** ALA: ACRL; LITA. TN LA. SELA. Phi Kappa Phi. **Honors:** Phi Alpha Theta, 1950; Phi Kappa Phi, 1954. **Activities:** 1; 17, 39 **Addr.:** Library, The University of Tennessee, Knoxville, TN 37916.

Hunt, Florine E. (Ag. 11, 1928, Richmond, VA) Corp. Libn., Pub. Srv. Electric and Gas Co., 1955–; Child Welfare Caseworker, City of Norfolk, VA, 1950–52; Adj. fac., Rutgers Univ., 1974–75. **Educ.:** Richmond Prof. Inst., Coll. of William & Mary, 1945–49, BS (Soc. Sci.); Rutgers Univ., 1954–55, MLS. **Orgs.:** SLA: Pub. Util. Div. (Ch.-Elect, Ch. 1972–1974); NJ Chap. Dir. (1960–1962), Treas. (1958–1960), Archvst. (1972–). Amer. Gas Assn.: Lib. Srvs. Com. **Pubns.:** *Public Utilities Information Sources* (1965); "Information: Production, Transmission and Distribution," *Amer. Gas Assn. Monthly* (F. 1976); "Problems in Research and Reference Services," *Amer. Gas Assn. Monthly* (F. 1973). **Activities:** 12; 17; 59, 64, 95-Pub. Utilities. **Addr.:** Public Service Electric and Gas Company, 80 Park Plaza P3C, Newark, NJ 07101.

Hunt, Gary A. (O. 13, 1944, Pasadena, CA) Head of Arch. & Spec. Col., OH Univ. Lib., 1979–; Mss. Asst., Boston Univ. Lib., 1976–79; Instr. in Eng., Univ. of MA, Boston, 1970–75. **Educ.:** Univ. of CA, Berkeley, 1962–66, AB (Eng.); Brandeis Univ., 1966–76, PhD (Eng.); Simmons Coll., 1976–79, MLS. **Orgs.:** ALA. SAA. Acad. Lib. Assn. of OH. **Pubns.:** "'A Reality That Can't Be Quite Definitely Spoken:' Sexuality in THEIR WEDDING JOURNEY," *Std. in the Novel* (Spr. 1977); "Manuscript Solicitation for Libraries, Special Collections, Museums, and Archives," *Lib. Jnl.* (D. 15, 1978). **Activities:** 1; 17, 28, 45; 55, 57 **Addr.:** Department of Archives & Special Collections, Ohio University Library, Athens, OH 45701.

Hunt, James Robert (My. 5, 1925, West Brownsville, PA) Dir., Pub. Lib. of Cincinnati and Hamilton Cnty., 1971–; State Libn., HI Dept. of Educ., 1971, Actg. Deputy Supt. of Educ., 1970–71, State Libn., 1964–70; Asst. State Libn., MI State Lib., 1962–64; Head, Ctrl. Srvs., Wayne Cnty. (MI) Lib., 1960–62, Admin. Asst. to Libn., 1958–60, Bkmobile Libn., 1956–57. **Educ.:** Univ. of Detroit, 1951, PhB, 1955, MA (Pol. Sci.); Univ. of MI, 1959, AMLS. **Orgs.:** ALA: Assn. of State Lib. Agencies (VP, 1971–72; Pres., 1972–73). HI LA: ALA rep. (1964–68). OH LA. State Bd. of Lib. Examiners. Cincinnati Hist. Socty.: Bd. (1972). Amer. Socty. for Pub. Admin.: Honolulu Chap. (Secy., 1966). **Pubns.:** Various articles. **Activities:** 9, 13 **Addr.:** 800 Vine St., Cincinnati, OH 45202.*

Hunt, Judith Lin (Ja. 13, 1945, Kansas City, MO) Univ. Libn., Univ. of Bridgeport, 1980–, Dir. of Lib. Srvs., 1978–80, Head, Ref. Dept., 1976–78; Soc. Sci. Ref. Lib. & Biblgphr., Queens Coll., 1972–76. **Educ.:** Univ. of Miami, 1963–67, BA (Lat. Am. Hist.); Queens Coll., 1970–72, MLS; New York Univ., 1972–74, MA (Brit. Hist.). **Orgs.:** Fairfield Lib. Admin. Grp.: VP (1980–). Southwest. CT Lib. Cncl.: Bd. of Trustees (1979–); Treas. (1980–). ALA: ACRL. CT LA. Victorian Socty. in Amer.: Art Nouveau Chap. **Honors:** Beta Phi Mu, 1971. **Pubns.:** "Philanthropy and Pietism in English Education, 1700 to ca. 1815," *CORE: Collected Original Resources in Education* (O. 1980). **Activities:** 1; 17, 34, 39; 54, 55, 92 **Addr.:** University of Bridgeport, Magnus Wahlstrom Library, 126 Park Ave., Bridgeport, CT 06602.

Hunt, Margaret Mary (Peggy) (N. 29, 1934, Gary, IN) Media Libn., Curric. Coord., Hobart Twp. Cmnty. Sch. Corp., 1975–, Tchr., 1970–75. **Educ.:** IN Univ. NW, 1952–70, BS (Elem. Educ.), 1970–72, MS (Elem. Educ.); Cert. in Sch. Lib. and A-V, K-12 1973–74; IN State Univ., 1976–80 EdS (Educ. Admin., and Suprvsn.). **Orgs.:** ALA. Assn. for IN Media Educ. Lake Cnty. Pub. Lib. Bd.: (1978–82). AAUW. Assn. for Supvsn. and Curric. Dev. Intl. Reading Assn. **Honors:** Post Tribune Newspaper, Gary-Hobart, Educ. Progress Maker, 1979. **Pubns.:** *Elementary Media Curriculum Guide K-6* (1980); Ed., *Elementary Mathematics Curriculum Guide* (1978); Ed., *Elementary Reading Curriculum Guide K-6* (1978). **Activities:** 9, 10; 17, 21, 32; 63, 75, 89 **Addr.:** 103 Fraser Ln., Hobart, IN 46342.

Hunt, Mary Alice (Ap. 14, 1928, Lima, OH) Assoc. Prof., Sch. of LS, FL State Univ., 1974–, Asst. Prof., 1961–74, Instr. & Libn., 1955–61, Exec. Secy., 1953–55. **Educ.:** FL State Univ., 1946–50, AB (Jnlsm.), 1952–53, MA (LS); IN Univ., 1970–73, PhD (LS). **Orgs.:** ALA: ALSC Film Eval. Com. (Ch. 1978, 1979); Newberry-Caldecott Com. (1974–75, 1979–80). FL LA: Exec. Cncl., Dir. (1975–77). Beta Phi Mu: Dir., Exec. Bd. (1976–79); VP, Pres. Elect (1979–81). **Honors:** FL State Univ., Fac. Dev. Grant, 1970. **Pubns.:** Jt. auth., *Multimedia Indexes, Lists and Review Sources* (1975); "Randolph Caldecott: The Children Remember," *FL Lib.* (Ja.-F. 1979); Jt. auth., "Survey of L.S. Ph.D. Graduates of three Universities," *Jnl. of Educ. for Libnshp.* (Win. 1979); "Ten Trends in Films for Children," *FL Media Qtly.* (Spr. 1979); "Locating Information Using Media Indexes" (lrng. module). **Activities:** 10, 11; 21, 32, 48; 67 **Addr.:** 1603 Kolopakin Nene, Tallahassee, FL 32301.

Hunt, Suellyn (My. 9, 1942, Rockville Center, NY) Persnl. & Trng. Mgr., Rochester Pub. & Monroe Cnty. Lib. Syst., 1977–, Trng. Coord., 1973–76, Exec. Asst. to Lib. Dir., 1969–73; Bkmobile Libn., Suffolk Coop. Lib. Syst., 1968; Libn. Trainee, Vets. Hosp., 1968; Asst. Branch Libn., Cleveland Pub. Lib., 1964–67. **Educ.:** State Univ. Coll., Geneseo, 1960–64, BS (LS); Syracuse Univ., 1967–69, MLS. **Orgs.:** ALA. NY LA: Subcom. on Civil Srv., Persnl. Admin. Com. (1979–); NYLA: Ad Hoc Com. on Cont. Educ. (1977–79); Legis. Com. (1974–77); Ch., Pub. Lib. Sect., Nom. Com., (1975–76); Pres., Pub. Lib. Sect. (1974–75); Cncl., Sect. Rep. (1974–75). Amer. Socty. for Trng. & Dev.: Genesee Valley Chap., Exec. Bd., (1977–79); ASTD, GVC, Conf. Plng. Com. (1979); Ch., Conf. Reg. Com. (1979); Ch., Nom. Com. (1978); Ch., Audit Com. (1978); Ch., Hosplty. Com. (1976–78). Canandaigua Yacht Club: Bd. of Gvrs. (1976–79); Ch. (1978–79). **Honors:** Natl. Mental Hlth. Assn. & Pres. Com. on Empl. of Handcpd., Empl. of the Yr., 1979; Beta Phi Mu, 1969. **Pubns.:** "Learn for Job, Self, Library: Human Resource Development; The Broad Scope of Training," *WI Lib. Bltn.* (N.-D., 1975). **Activities:** 9; 24, 25, 35; 50, 72, 78 **Addr.:** Monroe County & Rochester Public Library, 115 South Ave, Rochester, NY 14604.

Hunter, Ann Gail (N. 8, 1949, Milwaukee, WI) Corp. Libn., Anheuser-Busch Co., Inc., 1976–; Catlgr., MacMurray Coll., 1973–76; Dir. of Lib., Univ. of WI, Wausau Ctr., 1972–73. **Educ.:** Univ. of WI, 1967–71, BA (Eng.), 1971–72, MA (LS). **Orgs.:** St. Louis Reg. Lib. Network: Delivery Syst. com. (1979–). SLA: St. Louis Metro Area, Mem. at Large (1979–). Grt. St. Louis Lib. Club. AAUW: St. Louis Chap., Educ. Fndn. Com. **Pubns.:** "Busch, Bud & Books," *Show-Me Libs.* (My. 1979); "Anheuser-Busch," *Business & Finance Div. Newsletter SLA* (Spr. 1978); reviews. **Activities:** 12; 15, 17, 20; 60, 68 **Addr.:** Anheuser-Busch Companies, Inc., Corporate Library, P.O. Box 1828 Bechtold Station, St. Louis, MO 63118.

Hunter, Doris A. (Ag. 24, 1920, Hartford, CT) Retired, 1981–; Chief, Tech. Srvs., US Army Milit. Hist. Inst., 1970–81; Dir., Lib. Prog., US Army, HI and Korea, 1964–69; Ref. Libn., US Army, Europe, 1959–64. **Educ.:** Univ. of PA, 1938–42, AB (Eng.); Columbia Univ., 1954–55, MSLS; Trinity Coll., Hartford, CT, 1942–43, Cert. (Educ.). **Orgs.:** ALA. SLA. **Honors:** Commandant's Awd. for Merit. Srv., 1981. **Activities:** 1, 4; 17, 39, 46; 74 **Addr.:** P.O. Box 117, Boiling Springs, PA 17007.

Hunter, Dorothea (Je. 24, 1926, Detroit, MI) Lib. Media Spec., Berry Elem. Sch., 1968–; Libn., Bellevue Elem. Sch., 1948–68. **Educ.:** Wayne State Univ., 1944–48, AB (Educ.), 1962, MEd (Lib. Sci.), additional courses. **Orgs.:** ALA: Cldns. Srvs. Div., Local Arr., Ch. (1977); ALSC, Newbery-Caldecott Awds. Com. (1979–80); MI Assn. of Sch. Libns.: Prog. Com. (1969–70). MI LA. Wayne State Lib. Sci. Alum. Assn.: Bd. of Dir. (1972–78). ALSC, Filmstp Evaluation Com. (1980–83). Nat. Educ. Assn. League of Women Voters. **Activities:** 10; 21, 31, 32; 63, 66 **Addr.:** 1920 Thornhill Pl., Detroit, MI 48207.

Hunter, Fern Lorene (O. 17, 1900, Harrison Cnty., IN) Church Libn., Ctrl. Christ. Church, Orlando, FL, 1977–; Ref. Libn., Indust. Coll. of the Armed Forces, 1964–69; Resrch. Libn., US Combat Dev. Agency, 1962–63; Resrch. Libn., US Army Ordnance Bd., 1956–62; Ref. Libn., Indust. Coll. of the Armed Forces, 1948–56; Ref., Indx. & Abs. Libn., Vets. Admin., 1947–48; Ref. and Class., Ext. Div. Lib., IN Univ., 1930–43. **Educ.:** Butler Univ., 1919–23, AB (Eng. & Hist.); IN Univ., 1927–28 (Eng.). **Orgs.:** CSLA: FL Chap. (Pres.). VP). AAUW. **Pubns.:** Reviews. **Activities:** 4, 12; 20, 39, 42; 50, 89, 90 **Addr.:** 1483 Westgate Dr., Apt. UU 4, Kissimmee, FL 32741.

PROFESSIONAL ACTIVITIES: Institutions: 1. Acad. lib.; 2. Arch.; 3. Assn.; 4. Fed./Gvt. lib.; 5. Inst. lib.; 6. Mfr./Suppl.; 7. Milit. lib.; 8. Musm.; 9. Pub. lib.; 10. Sch. lib.; 11. Sch. of lib. sci.; 12. Spec. lib.; 13. State lib.; 14. (other). **Functions/Activities:** 15. Acq./Col. dev.; 16. Adult srvs.; 17. Admin.; 18. Apprais.; 19. Archit./Bldgs.; 20. Cat./Class.; 21. Chld. srvs.; 22. Circ.; 23. Cons./Pres.; 24. Consult.; 25. Cont. ed.; 26. Educ. lib. sci.; 27. Ext. srvs.; 28. Fund/Grants; 29. Gvt. pubs.; 30. Indx./Abs.; 31. Instr. lib. use; 32. Media srvs.; 33. Micro.; 34. Netwks./Coop.; 35. Persnl.; 36. PR; 37. Publshg.; 38. Recs. mgt.; 39. Ref. srvs.; 40. Repro.; 41. Resrch.; 42. Review.; 43. Secur.; 44. Serials; 45. Spec. col.; 46. Tech. srvs.; 47. Trustees/Bds.; 48. YA srvs.; 49. (other).

Hunter, Gregory S. (S. 7, 1953, Los Angeles, CA) Archvst., Untd. Negro Coll. Fund, Inc., 1978–; Asst. to the Archivist, Chase Manhattan Bank, 1977–78. **Educ.:** St. John's Univ., 1971–75, BA (Hist.); NY Univ., 1975–, MPhil (Hist.), MA (Hist.); NY Univ., 1977–78, Cert. (Arch. Mgt.). **Orgs.:** SAA: Bus. Arch. Prof. Afnty. Grp. (1979–). Mid-Atlantic Reg. Arch. Conf: Lcl. Arrange. Grp. (1981). Metro. NY Archvst. RT. Org. of Amer. Hist. Bus. Hist. Conf. **Pubns.:** "United Negro College Fund Establishes History Project," *The Archvst. Hist.* (Spr. 1979). **Activities:** 2; 17, 28; 59, 66, 85 **Addr.:** United Negro College Fund, Inc., 500 East 62nd St., New York, NY 10021.

Hunter, Isabel (Mr. 4, 1930, St. John, NB) Dir., Hlth. Sci. Lib., Meml. Univ. of NF, 1979–; Dir. Hlth. Sci. Lib., Shadyside Hosp., Pittsburgh, PA, 1973–79; Consult., Reg. Med. Prog., Pittsburgh, PA, 1971–73. **Educ.:** Fairmont State Coll., 1965–69, BA (Fr.); Univ. of Pittsburgh, 1969–71, MLS; RN, Royal Victoria Hosp. **Orgs.:** Med. LA. Can. Hlth. Libs. Assn. Assn. of Can. Med. Coll.: Spec. Resrc. Com. (Secy., 1980–82). **Activities:** 1; 80 **Addr.:** Health Sciences Library, Memorial University of Newfoundland, St. John's, NF A1B 3V6 Canada.

Hunter, James Jerome (D. 12, 1946, Akron, OH) Lib. Dir., Dispatch Prtg. Co., 1974–. **Educ.:** Kent State Univ., 1964–69, BA (Pol. Sci.), 1972–73, MLS. **Orgs.:** Columbus Area Info. Cncl. of OH: Bd. of Trustees. SLA: Ctrl. OH Chap. (Secy., 1977). ALA. Columbus Cham. of Cmrce.: Reg. Info. Srv., Bd. of Trustees. Press Club of Ctrl. OH. **Pubns.:** Columbus, OH article, *Colliers Encyc.* (1981); OH article, *World Book* (1981). **Activities:** 12; 17, 30, 41; 56, 83, 93 **Addr.:** Library, Columbus Dispatch, 34 S. 3rd St., Columbus OH 43216.

Hunter, M. Darlene (Mr. 8, 1939, Scioto Cnty., OH) Libn./Media Spec., Grove City HS, 1972–; Libn., Columbus Pub. Schs., 1964–72; Eng. tchr., Scioto Cnty. Schs., 1960–64; Instr., OH Univ., 1978. **Educ.:** OH State Univ., 1956–60, BS (Educ.); Case-West. Resrv. Univ., 1962–64, MS (LS); OH State Univ., 1975–77, cert. (Supvsn.). **Orgs.:** OH Educ. Lib. Media Assn.: Conf. Com. (1966, 1972, 1979, 1980); VP (1980); Treas. (1978–80). OH LA: Int. Frdm. Com. (1976–77; Ch., 1978). Franklin Cnty. LA: Pres. ALA: AASL, Int. Frdm. Com. (Ch., 1979–81). Delta Kappa Gamma. OH Educ. Assn. Natl. Educ. Assn. **Honors:** Beta Phi Mu, 1964. **Pubns.:** "Reading Preferences of Students Enrolled in Grove City High School," *OH Media Spectrum* (Win. 1979). **Activities:** 10; 15, 20, 24, 31; 58, 74, 91 **Addr.:** 2541 Vernal Dr., Grove City, OH 43123.

Hunter, Robert J. (Ja. 2, 1947, Dumont, NJ) Dir., Haddon Heights Pub. Lib., 1977–; Asst. Dir., Dixon Homestead Lib., 1972–75. **Educ.:** Washington Coll., 1965–69, AB (Hist.); Univ. of RI, 1969–70, MA (Hist.); Rutgers Univ., 1975–76, MLS. **Orgs.:** NJ LA: Trustee Rel. Com. (Ch.). **Honors:** Beta Phi Mu. **Activities:** 9; 17 **Addr.:** Haddon Heights Public Library, 608 Station Ave., Haddon Heights, NJ 08035.

Huntley, William Robert (Ap. 7, 1928, Spindale, NC) Asst. Chief, Descr. Cat. Div., Lib. of Congs., 1972–, Head, Preliminary Cat. Sect., 1963–72, Asst. Head, 1962–63. **Educ.:** Univ. of NC, 1958, AB (Lang.); Cath. Univ., 1958–63, (LS). **Orgs.:** SLA. Lib. of Congs. Prof. Assn. Kiwanis: Secy. (1976–79); Pres. (1980–81). BPO Elks. **Honors:** Lib. of Congs., Meritorious Srv. Awd., 1977. **Activities:** 4; 17, 20, 35 **Addr.:** 4215 Flam St., Oxon Hill, MD 20022.

Hunt-McCain, Pearl O. (Prince George, VA) Libn., Boston Redev. Athrty., 1977–; Catlgr., Monthly Cat., US Govt. Prtg. Ofc., 1974–75; Ref. Anal., Indus. Rel. Ctr., Univ. of MN, 1972–73; Preliminary Catlgr., Lib. of Congs., 1971–72. **Educ.:** VA State Univ., 1963–67, BS (LS); Simmons Coll., 1975–76, MS (LS). **Orgs.:** SLA. Cncl. of Plng. Libns.: Mem. Com., Ch. **Pubns.:** *Public Administration in City Government* (1976). **Activities:** 12; 15, 39, 41; 65, 66, 94, 95-Urban Plng. **Addr.:** Boston Redevelopment Authority Library, Boston City Hall - 9th floor, Boston, MA 02201.

Huq, A. M. Abdul (F. 1, 1931, Mymensingh, Bangladesh) Assoc. Prof., St. John's Univ., 1973–; Asst. Prof., Dalhousie Univ., 1971–73; Univ. Libn., Agr. Univ., Bangladesh, 1962–64; Univ. Libn., Engin. Univ., Pakistan, 1961–62; Libn., Inst. of Bus. Admin., Univ. of Karechi, 1957–61; Asst. Libn., US Info. Serv., Bangledesh, 1954–57. **Educ.:** Univ. of Dacca, Bangladesh, 1949–51, BCom (Bus.Admin.), 1951–53, MCom (Bus. Admin.); Carnegie-Mellon Univ., 1957–58, MLS; Univ. of Pittsburgh, 1967–70, PhD (LS). **Orgs.:** SLA. AALS. ALA. LA of Bangladesh. **Honors:** Beta Phi Mu, 1970. **Pubns.:** Jt. auth., *Librarianship and the Third World: An Annotated Bibliography of Selected Literature on Developing Nations, 1960–75* (1977); "A Report on the Library Situation in India and Bangladesh," *LEADS* (S. 1976); "Problems and Prospects in the Organization of Bengali Materials," *Libri* (Mr. 1979); Other articles. **Activities:** 1, 12; 20, 34, 46; 56, 59, 75 **Addr.:** 60-61 251st St., Little Neck, NY 11362.

Hurlbert, Bruce M. (S. 26, 1936, Indianapolis, IN) Asst. Dir. of Univ. Libs., VA Commonwealth Univ., 1973–; Asst. Dir. for Tech. Srvcs., FL Atl. Univ., 1971–72, Coord. of Prcs. for Tech. Srvs., 1970–71, Head of Cat. Dept., 1969–70, Cat. Libn., 1969, Ref. Libn., 1968. **Educ.:** The Citadel, 1955–59, BA (Hist.); FL State Univ., 1967–68, MSLS. **Orgs.:** ALA: ACRL; LAMA, Equipment Com. (1979–81). SELA. VA LA. **Honors:** Phi Alpha Theta, 1958. **Activities:** 1; 17, 32, 46; 55, 56, 61 **Addr.:** Cabell Library, Virginia Commonwealth University, 901 Park Ave., Richmond, VA 23284.

Hurowitz, Robert (S. 6, 1940, Revere, MA) Head, Syst. Ofc., Stanford Univ. Libs., 1981–, File Mgr., Cat. Dept., 1975–80, Cat. Libn., 1968–74. **Educ.:** Middlebury Coll., 1958–62, BA (Russ.); Univ. of CA, Berkeley, 1962–68, MLS, Sec. Sch. Tchg. Cred. **Orgs.:** ALA. ASIS. **Pubns.:** "Bibliographic Links at Stanford University Libraries," *Cat. and Class. Qtly.* (V. 1, no. 1). **Activities:** 1; 17, 41; 56, 75 **Addr.:** Systems Office, Stanford University Libraries, Stanford, CA 94305.

Hurr, Doris Smith (O. 18, 1949, Fayetteville, NC) Asst. Dir., Cumberland Cnty. Pub. Lib., 1977–, Actg. Dir., 1979, Coord. of Info. Srvs., 1975–77, State and Local Hist. Libn., 1971–74. **Educ.:** Saint Andrews Presby. Coll., 1967–71, BA (Hist.); Emory Univ., 1974–75, MLn (LS). **Orgs.:** Cape Fear LA: VP (1976–77); Pres. (1977–78); Nom. Com. (1978–79). NC LA: Pub. Lib. Sect. Persnl. Com. (1979–81); Ref. and Adult Srvs. Sect. (VP/Pres. Elect., 1979–81). SELA. ALA: JMRT Mem. Mtg. Com. (1979–80). Arts Cncl. of Fayetteville/Cumberland Cnty. Fayetteville Musm. of Art. Fayetteville Symph. Orch. Assn.: Bd. of Dir. (1977–81). Jr. Leag. of Fayetteville (1980–). **Pubns.:** "Resources for Local History and Genealogy in North Carolina Public Libraries," *NC Geneal. Socty. Jnl.* (Ja. 1975). **Activities:** 9; 17, 35, 36; 50, 55, 63 **Addr.:** 2619 Huntington Rd., Fayetteville, NC 28303.

Hurrey, Katharine C. (Ja. 5, 1928, Washington, DC) Dir., South. MD Reg. LA, 1968–, Admin. Asst., 1965–67; Bkmobile Libn., Calvert Cnty. Pub. Lib., 1962–65. **Educ.:** Hollins Coll., 1945–49, AB (Psy.); Univ. of MD, 1966–67, MLS; Lib. Admin. Dev. Prog., Univ. of MD, 1970; Other sems. **Orgs.:** MD LA: 2nd VP & Prog. Ch. (1975–76); 1st VP (1978–79); Pres. (1979–80). ALA: PLA/Rcrt. Task Force (1979–80); Chap. Rel. Com. (1978–80). MD Assn. of Pub. Lib. Admin. Secy. (1970–71). MD Adv. Cncl. on Libs. Calvert Cnty. Bd. of Educ.: Pres. (1969–73). World Future Socty. Amer. Mgt. Assn. Amer. Assn. of Sch. Admin. **Honors:** MD LA, MD LA Awd., 1978. **Activities:** 9, 14-Reg.; 17, 24, 34; 72, 78 **Addr.:** Southern Maryland Regional Library Assn., P.O. Box 1069, LaPlata, MD 20646.

Hurt, Charlene Schmidt (Ag. 10, 1940, St. Louis, MO) Univ. Libn., Washburn Univ. of Topeka, 1979–, Actg. Univ. Libn., 1977–79, Asst. Libn. Readers' Srvs., 1976–77, Cat. Libn., 1974–76. **Educ.:** Culver Stockton Coll., 1964, BA (Eng., Hist.); Emporia St. Univ., 1973–74, MLS; Univ. KS, 1977–79, MPA. **Orgs.:** ALA: Instr. Use of Lib. Com. Mt. Plains LA: MPLA Pre-Reg. White House Conf. KS LA: Sec. VP (1977–78); RTS (Ch., 1976–77). KS OLUG: Strg. Com. (1978). KS Lib. Netwk. Auth. Cncl.: Governance Task Force (1979). KS Com. Hum.: St. Strg. Com. Hum. Prog. (1979). KS Dept. Educ.: Field Adv. Grp. (1978–79). **Honors:** ALA, JMRT, Shirley Olafson Mem. Awd. 1979; Mt. LA, Cont. Educ. Grant, 1978–79. **Activities:** 1; 17, 31, 39; 63, 92 **Addr.:** Mabee Library, Washburn University of Topeka, Topeka, KS 66621.

Hurt, Charlie Deuel, III (S. 20, 1950, Charlottesville, VA) Asst. Prof., McGill Univ., 1981–; Lectr., Univ. of WI–Madison, 1980–81; Tchg. Asst., 1978–80; Engin. Libn., Univ. VA, 1975–78, Autom. Libn., 1975–77, Env. Sci. Libn., 1973–74. **Educ.:** Univ. VA, 1968–72, BA (Eng. Relig. Std.); Univ. of KY, 1974–75, MSLS; Univ. of WI-Madison, 1981, PhD. (LS). **Orgs.:** ALA. ASIS. **Pubns.:** "An Examination of Differences Between Two Studies of Highly Cited Old Papers," *Jnl. of ASIS.* "Author Productivity and Subject Breadth in Engineering Publications," *ERIC.* "Engineering Libraries–A Suggestion for Financial Survival," *Engin. Educ.* "A Correlation Study of the Journal Article Productivity of Environmental Scientists," *Info Prcs. and Mgt.* **Activities:** 11, 12; 24, 26, 41; 56, 75, 91 **Addr.:** Graduate School of Library Science, McGill University, 3459 McTavish St., Montreal, PQ H3A 1Y1 Canada.

Hurtt, Betty D. (N. 22, 1946, Birmingham, AL) Libn., Woman's Missn. Un., 1977–. **Educ.:** Samford Univ., 1966–69, AB (Soclgy.); IN Univ., 1969–70. **Orgs.:** SLA. AL LA. Socty. of AL Archvsts. Assoc. Info. Mgrs. **Activities:** 5, 12; 17, 32, 39; 90 **Addr.:** Woman's Missionary Union, SBC, 600 N. 20th St., Birmingham, AL 35203.

Hurwitz, Gloria Holland (S. 4, 1947, Portsmouth, VA) Coord., Lrng. Resrc. Fac., Med. Col. of VA Campus, VA Commonwealth Univ., 1974–, Plng. Libn., 1973–74; Circ. Libn., 1970–73. **Educ.:** Mary Washington Coll., 1965–69, BA (Pol.); Univ. of NC, 1969–70, MSL; VA Commonwealth Univ., 1973–76, MBA. **Orgs.:** Hlth. Sci. Com. Assn.: Rep. to the Med. LA (1979–80); Bd. of Dirs., Biomed. Lib. Sect. Rep. (1977–79); Ch., Ad Hoc Cont. Educ. Com. (1978–79). Med. LA: Ch., Stdg. Com. on Lib. Stan. and Prac., Subcom. on AV (1978–80). Mid-Atlantic Reg. Med. LA: Local Arrange. Ch. (1976–77). VA LA: Exec. Brd. (1979–80), Ch., Com. on Coms. (1979–80), Prog. Ch., Coop. Prog. Com. (1978–79). Other orgs. and coms. Biomed. Lib. Review Com. **Honors:** Phi Kappa Phi, 1977. **Pubns.:** "Profile, Data and Management of Two Learning Resource Centers, 1970–1978" (1979); "Profile, Data and Management of Two Learning Resource Centers, 1970–78," *Bltn. of Med. LA* (1979); "Management of A Learning Resource Center," *Jrnl. of Med. Educ.* (1979). **Activities:** 1; 17, 32; 58, 59, 80 **Addr.:** Visual Education Department, Medical College of Virginia Campus, Virginia Commonwealth University, MCV Box 62, Richmond, VA 23298.

Hurwitz, Johanna Frank (O. 9, 1937, New York, NY) Chld. Libn., Great Neck Lib., 1978–; Resrc. Coord., Calhoun Lrng. Ctr., 1968–75; Lect. in LS, Queens Coll., 1965–68; Chld. Libn., NY Pub. Lib., 1959–64. **Educ.:** Queens Coll., 1955–58, BA (Eng.); Columbia Univ., 1958–59, MLS. **Orgs.:** ALA. NY LA. Nassau LA. Amnesty Intl. Writer's Guild, P.E.N. **Honors:** Phi Beta Mu, 1966. **Pubns.:** "Will the Real Peter Rabbit Please Stand Up," *Sch. Lib. Jnl.* (Ap. 1969); "A Letter from the Past," *Horn Book* (D. 1976); "E is for Easy, E is for Enormously Difficult," *Lang. Arts* (Ap. 1978); *Busybody Nora* (1976); *Law of Gravity* (1978). **Activities:** 9, 10; 21, 26 **Addr.:** 10 Spruce Pl., Great Neck, NY 11021.

Hurych, Jitka M. (F. 3, 1942, Brno, Czechoslovakia) Coord., Comp. Ref. Srvs., North. IL Univ., 1981–, Ref. Libn. and Srch. Anal., 1973–81, Instr., Russ., 1969–71, Lib. Tech. Asst., 1968–69; Instr., Russ. and Czech, Sch. of Econ., Czechoslovakia, 1964–67. **Educ.:** Purkyne Univ., Czechoslovakia, 1959–64, MA (Russ. and Czech Lang. and Lit.); North. IL Univ., 1971–73, MA (LS). **Orgs.:** IL LA. ALA. Chicago OLUG. **Pubns.:** Jt. auth., "An In-Depth Analysis of a Term Paper Clinic Held at NIU," *IL Libs.* (Mr. 1978); jt. auth., "Is There a Future for the End User in Online Bibliographic Searching?" *Spec. Libs.* (O. 1981); various reviews, *Lib. Jnl., Reprint Bltn.* **Activities:** 1; 31, 39, 49-Online Srch.; 95-Russ. Lang.-Transl. **Addr.:** General Reference Dept., Northern Illinois University Library, DeKalb, IL 60115.

Husband, Janet G. (Jl. 4, 1942, Pittsburgh, PA) Acq. Libn., Thomas Crane Pub. Lib., Quincy, MA, 1973–; Ed. and Place. Asst., MA Bureau of Lib. Ext., 1973; Book Sel., Libn. II, Free Lib. of Philadelphia, 1967–70, Ref. Libn., 1967. **Educ.:** Univ. of Pittsburgh, 1962–66, BA (Eng.); Rutgers Univ., 1966–67, MLS. **Orgs.:** ALA: New Branch Starter List Com. (1981–83). MA LA: Ed., *Bay State Letter* (1981–); Conf. Com. (1978–81); PR Com. (1974–75). New Eng. LA. **Honors:** Beta Phi Mu. **Pubns.:** "Reserve Book Survey at the Free Library," *PA LA Bltn.* (My. 1968); Reviews. **Activities:** 9, 13; 15, 17, 27; 50, 57, 92 **Addr.:** 317 Hancock St., Braintree, MA 02184.

Husbands, Charles William (S. 10, 1939, Beatrice, NE) Syst. Libn., Harvard Univ. Lib., 1976–; Syst. Libn., Harvard Coll. Lib., 1967–76, Lib. Intern, 1965–67; Asst. Mgr., DeWolfe and Fiske Co., 1962–65. **Educ.:** Amherst Coll., 1957–61, BA (Msc.); Simmons Coll., 1965–67, MS (LS). **Orgs.:** ALA: MARBI Com. (1973–77). ASIS: Tech. Prog. Ch., Anl. Mtg. (1975). Amer. Natl. Stan. Inst.: Com. Z39 Subcoms. (1974–). **Activities:** 1; 56 **Addr.:** Harvard University Library, Cambridge, MA 02138.

Huston, Catherine C. (Mr. 15, 1905, Brooklyn, NY) Cmnty. Arch., Sisters of St. Dominic, Blauvelt, NY, 1969–; Dir. of Lib., Dominican Coll. of Blauvelt, 1947–69, Instr., 1938–53; Tchr., Several Schs., 1925–47. **Educ.:** Hunter Coll., 1924–41, BA (Math, Sci.); Fordham Univ., 1941–44, MS (Educ.); St. John's Univ., 1954–56, MLS; Columbia Univ., 1963; Villanova Univ., 1953–54, (LS). **Orgs.:** SAA. Metro. Arch. Dominican Sister Archvst. Rockland Cnty. (NY) Hist. Socty. **Honors:** Dominican Coll. of Blauvelt, Dr. of Humane Letters, 1976. **Pubns.:** "Xerography in Cooperative Projects," *Cath. Lib. World* (N. 1961). **Activities:** 2, 12; 15, 17, 41; 62, 69, 86 **Addr.:** Sisters of St. Dominic of Blauvelt, Rockland Cnty., Blauvelt, NY 10913.

Huston, Esther L. (Jl. 10, 1934, Chicago, IL) Sr. Libn., Law Lib., CA State Lib., 1979–; Libn., CA Sect., CA State Lib., 1977–79; Ref./Doc. Libn., Sacramento Pub. Lib., 1971–77; Asst. to the Director, Ewha Womans Univ. Lib., Seoul, 1968–71; Ref./Docu. Libn., Colorado Coll., 1964–67. **Educ.:** Manchester Coll., 1952–56, BS (Elem. Educ.), Univ. of IL, 1963–64, MS LS. **Orgs.:** CA LA: Secy. Govt. Publ. Chap. (1975–77). ALA. SLA. **Activities:** 4, 9; 17, 29, 39; 54, 77, 73 **Addr.:** Law Library, California State Library, P.O. Box 2037, Sacramento, CA 95809.

Huston, Mary M. (F. 10, 1950, Minneapolis, MN) Ref. Libn., Evergreen State Coll., 1980–; Asst. Prof. of Lib. Admin., Univ. of IL, 1978–80; Assoc. Libn., Univ. of Ctrl. FL, 1977–78; Ref. Libn., Univ. of HI - Hilo Coll., 1973–76. **Educ.:** Hamline Univ., 1967–71, BA (Amer. Std.); Univ. of HI, 1971–72, MLS; Goddard Coll., 1976–77, MA (Women and Lit.); Univ. of IL, Cert. of Adv. Study pending, 1981–. **Orgs.:** ALA: ACRL/Bibl. Instr. Sect., Coop. Com. (1979–81). AAUP. **Pubns.:** "Fee or Free: the Effect of Charging on Information Demand," *Lib. Jnl.* (S. 15, 1979); "Educational Aspirations of Twentieth Century American Females: A Bibliographic Essay," *Bhvl. and Soc. Sci. Libn.* vol. 1, no. 2.; Jt. auth., "User-Computer Interface Design for Information Systems: A Review," *Lib. Resrch.* vol. 2, no. 1; computer programs. **Activities:** 1; 31, 39, 41; 56, 75, 92 **Addr.:** Evergreen State College Library, Olympia, WA 98505.

Special Subjects/Services: 50. Adult educ.; 51. Advert./Mktg.; 52. Aerosp.; 53. Agric.; 54. Area std.; 55. Arts/Hum.; 56. Autom.; 57. Bibl./Prtg.; 58. Bio. sci.; 59. Bus./Fin.; 60. Chem.; 61. Copyrt.; 62. Documtn.; 63. Educ.; 64. Engin.; 65. Env.; 66. Eth. grps.; 67. Film; 68. Food/Nutr.; 69. Geneal.; 70. Geo.; 71. Geol.; 72. Handcpd.; 73. Hist.; 74. Int. frdm.; 75. Info. sci.; 76. Insr.; 77. Law; 78. Legis.; 79. Math./Comp. sci.; 80. Med.; 81. Metals; 82. Nat. resrcs.; 83. Newsp.; 84. Nuc. sci.; 85. Oral hist.; 86. Petr./Energy; 87. Pharm.; 88. Phys./Astr./Math.; 89. Readg.; 90. Relig.; 91. Sci./Tech.; 92. Soc. sci.; 93. Telecom.; 94. Transp.; 95. (other).

Hutcheson, Mary (Ag. 3, 1917, Danielsville, GA) Libn., Texaco Resrch. Ctr., Beacon, NY, 1957–; Post Libn., Fort Knox, KY, 1955–57; Cmnd. Libn., US Army, Frankfurt, Germany, 1952–55; Post Libn., US Army Lib. Srv., TN, Germany, 1943–52; Libn., Sue Bennett Coll., 1940–43; Church Libn., Fishkill Untd. Meth. Church, 1960–. **Educ.:** Sue Bennett Coll., 1935–37; Emory Univ., 1937–1939, BA (Amer. Hist.); LA State Univ., 1939–40, BS (LS). **Orgs.:** SLA. CSLA. **Activities:** 4, 12; 44; 74, 90 **Addr.:** P.O. Box 35, Fishkill, NY 12524.

Hutchinson, Barbara Jane (D. 17, 1940, Neptune, NJ) Head Ref. Libn., NM State Univ. Lib., 1978–; Ref. Libn., Princeton Univ. Lib., 1976–78, Circ. Libn., 1974–76; Behvl. Sci. Libn., Nova Univ. Libs., 1971–73; Assoc. Libn., FL Atl. Univ. Lib., 1968–70; Asst. Libn., Monmouth Coll. Lib., 1966–68. **Educ.:** Drew Univ., 1958–62, BA (Pol. Sci.); Rutgers Univ., 1966, MLS. **Orgs.:** ALA: ACRL/Univ. Libs. Sect, Prog. Com. (1980–81). NM LA: Secy. (1980–). Border Reg. Lib. Assn.: Exec. Bd. (Mem.–at–Large, 1979–80). NM State Univ. Adv. Cncl. on Admin. Policy: Alternate Mem. (1979–). **Honors:** Beta Phi Mu, 1966. **Activities:** 1; 17, 31, 39; 56, 73 **Addr.:** 1705 Anita Dr., Las Cruces, NM 88001.

Hutson, Jean Blackwell (S. 7, 1914) Asst. Dir., Col. Mgmt. and Dev.: Black Culture, The Schomburg Ctr. for Resrch. in Black Culture, 1980–, Chief, 1972–80, Cur., 1949–72; Lect., Adjunct Assoc. Prof., Hist. Dept., City Coll. of NY, 1962–71; Asst. Libn., Univ. of Ghana, 1964–65; Sr. Libn., Woodstock Branch, NY Pub. Lib., 1949. **Educ.:** Univ. of MI, 1931–34; Barnard Coll., 1935, BA, 1936, MALS; Columbia Univ., 1941, Tchrs. Cert., New Sch. of Social Resrch., 1948–52, African Race Rel. **Orgs.:** ALA. NAACP. Nat. Urban League Guild. African Std. Assn. Black Acad. of Arts and Letters. **Honors:** Delta Sigma Theta, 1934. **Pubns.:** *Harlem, A Cultural History* (1969); "The Schomburg Collection," *Freedom Ways* (1963); reviews. **Addr.:** 2255 Fifth Ave., New York, NY 10037.

Huttner, Marian A. (Ap. 10, 1920, Minneapolis, MN) Asst. Dir., Cleveland Pub. Lib., 1976–; Head, Ctrl. Lib. Sub. Depts., Minneapolis Pub. Lib., 1969–75, Head, Soclgy. Dept., 1967–69, Adult Grp. Consult., 1964–67. **Educ.:** Macalester Coll., 1937–41, BA summa cum laude, (Hist.); Univ. of MN, 1941–42, BS (LS). **Orgs.:** ALA: Ch., Coop. Ref. Srvs. Com. OH LA. MN LA: Secy. (1963–67). Vanderburgh Presby. Church: Trustee (1961–68); Elder (1969–71). **Pubns.:** *Program for Branches, 1976–1980: Buildings* (1976); "Branches to Rebuild Cities," *Lib. Jnl.* (Ja. 15, 1977); "Measuring & Reducing Book Losses," *Lib. Jnl.* (F. 15, 1973); other articles. **Activities:** 9; 17 **Addr.:** Cleveland Public Library, 325 Superior, Cleveland, OH 44114.

Huyck, Sr. Margaret L., C.S.J. (Ap. 4, 1918, Baton Rouge, LA) Sch. Lib. Consult., 1975–; Libn., St. Joseph Academy, New Orleans, 1966–75; Tchr./libn., Cath. High, New Roads, LA, 1964–66; Tchr./libn., McNicholas High, Cincinnati, OH, 1962–64; Libn., St. Joseph Jr. Coll., New Orleans, 1956–62; Tchr./libn., McNicholas High, 1948–56. **Educ.:** Athenaeum of OH, 1938–46, BS Educ (Math.); Xavier Univ., 1948–53, M Ed (Admin.); LA State Univ., 1952–58, MSLS. **Orgs.:** Cath. LA: Ch., Elect. Com. (1974); Ed. (1975–77); By-laws, (1977–). Cath. LA, Baton Rouge Unit: HS Sect. (Ch., 1964–66); New Orleans Unit, Treas. (1967–69); Awd. Com. Ch. (1975–); VP (1979–81), Pres. (1981–83). LA LA. LA Assn. of Sch. Libns. **Honors:** Archdiocese of New Orleans, Outstan. lib. srv. to Archdiocesan sch., 1972. **Pubns.:** Jt. auth., *Guidelines For School Libraries* (1979); "ESEA Title II Funds And Local CLA Unit Efforts Produce Professional services," *Cath. Lib. World* (Ap. 1975). **Activities:** 10; 24; 63, 88 **Addr.:** 1200 Mirabeau Ave., New Orleans, LA 70122.

Huyda, Richard J. (Winnipeg, MN) Dir., Natl. Photography Col., Pub. Arch. Canada, 1975–, Head, Hist. Photographs Sect., 1964–75. **Educ.:** Univ. of MN, 1964, MA (Hist.). **Orgs.:** Assn. of Can. Archvsts. Can. Musms. Assn. **Pubns.:** *Camera in The Interior: H.L. Hime Photographer* (1975); "Photographs and Archives in Canada," *Archivaria* (Win. 1977–78); oral presentations. **Activities:** 2; 17, 41, 45; 55, 62, 95-Photography. **Addr.:** National Photography Collection, Public Archives Canada, 395 Wellington St., Ottawa, ON K1A 0N3 Canada.

Hycnar, Barbara J. Asst. Libn., Tech. Srvs., Northwest. Univ. Sch. of Law Lib., 1980–; Asst. Cat. Libn., Univ. of IL, Chicago, 1968–80. **Educ.:** Univ. of WI, 1961–65, BA (Span.); Univ. of MI, 1967–68, AMLS. **Orgs.:** IL LA. AALL. ALA: RTSD/Cat. and Class. Sect., Nom. Com. (1979–80). **Honors:** Phi Beta Kappa, 1964; Phi Kappa Phi, 1964; Beta Phi Mu, 1968. **Activities:** 1; 20, 46

Hyde, E. Clarendon (Je. 8, 1915, Columbia, MO) Libn. III, Univ. of MO, 1974–, Jr. Libn., 1957–74; Jr. Libn., Univ. of CO, 1955–57; Clergyman, 1940–53. **Educ.:** Univ. of MO, 1933–37, AB (Grmn.); Union Theo. Semy., 1937–40, MDiv (Church Hist.); Univ. of MN, 1953–55, MA (LS). **Orgs.:** ALA: Margaret Mann Cit. Com. (1977); ACRL. MO LA. MO ACRL. NAACP. Natl. Assn. for the Self-Supporting Active Ministry. Amer. Civil Liberties Un. Common Cause. **Honors:** Phi Beta Kappa, 1937; Beta Phi Mu, 1955; Eta Sigma Phi, 1935. **Activities:** 1; 20; 90 **Addr.:** 509 Thilly Ave., Columbia, MO 65201.

Hyland, Anne Meade (Je. 29, 1946, Eureka, CA) Dist. Media Coord., Northeast. Lcl. Schs., 1978–; State Supvsr., Sch. Media Prog., OH Dept. of Educ., 1976–78; Resrc. Spec., Mexican-American ofc., Toledo Pub. Sch., 1971–74, Elem. Lib. Supvsr., 1970–71 & 1974–76; Jr. HS Libn., Monroe (MI) Pub. Sch., 1968–70. **Educ.:** Bowling Green State Univ., 1964–68, BS Ed (Eng. & LS); Univ. of Toledo, 1971–78, Ms E (Ed. Media), Ph D (Curric.). **Orgs.:** OH Educ. Lib. Media Assn.: Bd. of Dir. (1975–); Ch., Pubns. com.; Ed., OH Media Spectrum Co-Ch., 1979 Anl. Conf. ALA: AASL, ESOL Task Force (1978). AECT: *A V Instr.* Adv. Bd. (1976–79). Church work. Natl. Cncl. on Basic Educ. Assn. for Supvsn. and Curric. Dev. Pi Lambda Theta. Phi Delta Kappa. **Honors:** John Cotton Dana lib. PR Awd., ALA, 1975. **Pubns.:** "Library Instruction in Schools" in *Pub. Lib. User Educ.* (1981); *OH Sch. Lib. Media Test* (1978); "Recent Directions in Educating the Library User," *Progress in Educating the Lib. User* (1978); "First Round Draft Choice for Middle School Teaching Team," *Middle Sch. Jnl.* (Je. 1976); Several ERIC pubns. **Activities:** 10; 24, 31, 32; 63 **Addr.:** 236 E. Clearview, Worthington, OH 43085.

Hyland, Barbara (N. 7, 1942, Sherbrooke, PQ) Mgr., Info Globe, Globe and Mail, 1980–; Mgr., Sales & Mktg., Micromedia Ltd., 1976–80; Freelance Libn., 1967–76; Libn., Bus. Ref., Toronto Pub. Lib., 1965–67. **Educ.:** Bishop's Univ., Lennoxville, PQ, 1959–63, BA (Hist./Eng.); Univ. of Toronto, 1964–65, BLS. **Orgs.:** SLA. Can. Assn. for Info. Sci.: Toronto Chap. Exec. (1980–81). Young People's Theatre. **Activities:** 6, 12; 17, 33, 37; 51, 56, 59 **Addr.:** 444 Front St. West, Toronto, ON M5V 2S9 Canada.

Hyland, Rosemary E. (F. 20, 1951, Philadelphia, PA) Adult Srvs. Libn., Ridley Twp. Pub. Lib., 1977–. **Educ.:** W. Chester St. Coll., 1969–73, BA (Eng.); Drexel Univ., 1976–77, MS (LS). **Orgs.:** ALA. PA LA: Adult Srvs. Div., Cnty. Pub. Div., Secy. Treas. (1978–79). DE Cnty. LA: Secy. Treas. (1979–81). **Honors:** Beta Phi Mu. **Activities:** 9; 16, 39, 48 **Addr.:** Ridley Twp. Public Library, MacDade Blvd. & Morton Ave., Folsom, PA 19033.

Hyman, Ferne B. (Ag. 17, 1926, Pittsburgh, PA) Coord., Col. Dev., Rice Univ., 1979–, Hum. Ref. Libn., 1971–79, Gifts and Exchs. Libn., 1968–71; Instr. LS, Univ. of TX, Austin, 1972–. **Educ.:** Univ. of CA, Los Angeles, 1944–49, BA, hons. (Pol. Sci.); Univ. of IL, 1965–69, MSLS; Loyola Univ., Los Angeles, 1970, MA (Hist.). **Orgs.:** ALA. TX LA: Info. and Educ. Com. (1978–). Houston Ctr. for the Hum. **Honors:** Beta Phi Mu, 1967. **Pubns.:** Jt. auth., *Reports of Cases Decided by Chief Justice Chase* (1972); "Library Explorations: A Unique Experience," *Flyleaf* (1973); "User-oriented Serials List: A Progess Report," *SLA Bltn. #2* (1976). **Activities:** 1; 15, 31, 39; 63, 92 **Addr.:** Fondren Library, Rice University, Box 1892, Houston, TX 77001.

Hyman, Henry Anthony (Tony) (My. 13, 1939, Los Angeles, CA) Dir. of Educ. Comm., Steuben-Allegany BOCES, 1972–; Instr., Ithaca Coll., 1971–72; Tchr., Watsonville HS, 1965–68. **Educ.:** San Jose State Coll., 1962–65, BA (Soc. Sci.); IL Inst. of Tech., 1968–69, MS (Soclgy.); Tchrs. Coll., Columbia Univ., 1969–71, EdD (Curric.). **Orgs.:** Assn. of Lib. Dir. and Planners: Exec. Com. (1979–). NY Educ. Comm. Assn. NY Educ. Comm. Dir. Assn. AECT. Other orgs. **Honors:** OH State Awd., 1977. **Pubns.:** Jt. auth., *Skills for Life: Effective Integration of the Mentally Retarded into the Community* (1980); *Handbook of American Cigar Boxes* (1979); "Filmmaking in High School," *Media & Methods* (1973); photographs, videotape. **Activities:** 1, 14-Reg. Media Lib.; 15, 17, 34; 67, 93 **Addr.:** Steuben-Allegany BOCES Media Center, RD #1, Bath, NY 14891.

Hyman, Karen D. (N. 26, 1946, Camden, NJ) Head, Ref. Srvs., Cherry Hill Free Pub. Lib., 1980–, Ref./Grants Libn., 1975–80; Dir., Gloucester Twp. Lib., 1973–74. **Educ.:** Douglass Coll., 1964–68, AB (Russ. Std.); Drexel Univ., 1972–73, MS (LS). **Orgs.:** ALA: LITA. NJ LA: Exec. Bd. (1981–). Libs. Unlimited: Nsltr. Ed. (1979–). Beta Phi Mu: Secy. (1979–80). **Activities:** 9; 28, 34, 39; 59 **Addr.:** 224 Westover Dr., Cherry Hill, NJ 08034.

Hyman, Richard Joseph (F. 11, 1921, Malden, MA) Dir., Grad. Sch. of Lib. and Info. Std., Queens Coll. of the City Univ. of NY, 1977–, Prof., 1968–81; Lib. Assoc., NY Univ. Lib., 1963–68. **Educ.:** Harvard Coll., 1939–42, AB (Hist. Lit.); Columbia Univ., 1965–69, DLS (Lib. Sci.); Harvard Univ., 1948, MBA; Columbia Univ., 1961–62, MLS; U.S. Navy School of Oriental Lang., Boulder, CO, 1942–43, Dip. (Japanese Lang. & Lit.). **Orgs.:** ALA: ACRL. AALS. LA of the City Univ. of NY: Ed. Brd. (1977–). NY LA: Bd. Dirs., Lib. Educ. Sect., (1974–77); Nom. Com. (1978–79). Beta Phi Mu, NY Chap.: VP (1974–75); Pres., (1975–76). Phi Beta Kappa. **Pubns.:** *Shelf Classification Research: Past, Present-Future* (1980); *Analytical Access: History, Resources, Needs* (1978); "AACR Under Attack," *Lib. Jrnl.* (Mr. 1977); "In Response to Community Needs," *The Bookmark* (1972); other articles. **Activities:** 1, 11; 20, 26, 39; 50, 55, 63 **Addr.:** Graduate School of Library and Information Studies, Queens College, Flushing, NY 11367.

Hymes, Judith Irvin (S. 20, 1941, Blossburg, PA) Dir. of Tech. Srvs. and Cat., Bayamón Univ. Tech. Coll., Univ. PR, 1972–; Dir. of Tech. Srvs. and Cat., Cayey Univ. Coll., Univ. PR, 1970–72; Acq. Libn., Inter Amer. Univ. (San Germán, PR), 1967–70; Dir. of Elem. Sch. Libs., Manheim Ctrl. Sch. Dist. (Manheim, PA), 1963–67. **Educ.:** Mansfield St. Coll., 1959–63, BS (LS, Hist.) Drexel Univ., 1964–67, MS (LS). **Orgs.:** ALA. Socty. de Bibtcr. Tioga Co. (PA) Hist. Socty. Natl. Geneal. Socty. New England Hist. Geneal. Socty. **Activities:** 1, 10; 15, 20, 21 **Addr.:** Calle Esteban González 869, Río Piedras, PR 00925.

Hynes, Arleen M. (My. 3, 1916, Sheldon, IA) Pres., Biblther. RT, 1976–; Libn., Bibltherist., Circ. Lib., St. Elizabeths Hosp., 1970–80. **Educ.:** The College of St. Catherine, 1938–40, BS (LS); Assn. for Poetry Therapy, 1970–74, CPT (Poetry Ther.). **Orgs.:** ALA: Bibliother. Com. (Ch. 1977–80). Natl. Educ. Cncl. on Creative Therapies: Adv. Bd. (1979–80). **Honors:** St. Elizabeths Hosp. (Washington, D.C.), 1st Dorothea Lynde Dix Awd., 1977. **Pubns.:** Jt. Ed., *Proceedings of the Fourth Bibliotherapy Round Table* (1978); "The Goals of Bibliotherapy" in *The Arts in Psychotherapy* (1980); "Bibliotherapy and the Aging," *The Cath. Lib. World* (1979). **Activities:** 4, 5; 17, 49-Bibliotherapy Training; 95-Bibliotherapy. **Addr.:** St. Benedict's, St. Joseph, MN 56374.

Hyslop, Marjorie R. (Mr. 24, 1908, Cleveland, OH) Consult. on Info. Sci., 1971–; Dir. of Metals Info., Amer. Socty. for Metals, 1967–70, Assoc. Dir., Documen. Srv., 1963–67, Managing Ed., *Metal Progress*, 1950–63. **Educ.:** OH State Univ., 1926–30, BA (Metallurgy). **Orgs.:** ASIS: Natl. Secy. (1966–68). Natl. Fed. of Abs. and Indx. Srvs.: Bd. of Dir. (1958–70). SLA: Various coms. Amer. Socty. for Metals: Secy., Documen. Com. (1953–71). **Honors:** Phi Beta Kappa; SLA, Metals/Mtrls. Div., Honors Awd., 1969; SLA, Prof. Awd., 1970. **Pubns.:** *A Brief Guide to Sources of Metals Information* (1973); Ed., *Pioneering in Steel Research* (1975); various articles. **Activities:** 12; 24, 30, 39; 64, 81, 91 **Addr.:** 17262 Chillicothe Rd., Chagrin Falls, OH 44022.

I

Iamele, Richard Thomas (Ja. 29, 1942, Newark, NJ) Libn., Los Angeles Cnty. Law Lib., 1980–, Asst. Libn., 1978–80, Asst. Ref. Libn., 1977–78, Asst. Catlgr., 1971–77; Catlgr., Univ. of South. CA, 1967–71. **Educ.:** Loyola Univ. of Los Angeles, 1959–63, BA (Hist.); Univ. of South. CA, 1965–67, MSLS; Southwest. Univ. Sch. of Law, 1972–76, JD. **Orgs.:** ALA. South. CA Assn. of Law Libs.: Mem. & Dir. Com. (1977–78). AALL: Cat. (1971–76); Dir. Com. (1977–78); Const. and Bylaws (1980–); Spec. Com. on Cert., Educ. and Stan. (1980–). Cncl. of CA Cnty. Law Libns.: VP (1980–81); Pres. (1981–82). Amer. Bar Assn. State Bar of CA. **Pubns.:** "Library of Congress Subject Heading Modification and Development of the Subject Authority File at Los Angeles County Law Library," *Law Lib. Jnl.* (F. 1975). **Activities:** 12, 14; 17, 35; 77, 78 **Addr.:** Los Angeles County Law Library, 301 West First St., Los Angeles, CA 90012.

Ibach, Robert Daniel, Jr. (D. 31, 1940, Lynch, NE) Dir. of Lib., Grace Coll. and Grace Theo. Semy., 1976–. **Educ.:** Detroit Bible Coll., 1959–63, BRE (Theo.); Grace Theo. Semy., 1963–66, BD (Theo.), 1966–69, ThM (Old Testament); IN Univ., 1974–75, MLS. **Orgs.:** ATLA. IN Coop. Lib. Srvs. Athry.: Dir.-at-Lg. (1978–79). Amer. Sch. of Oriental Resrch.: Assoc. Trustee (1978–80). Near E. Archlg. Socty.: Dir. (1979–81). Socty. of Biblical Lit. **Pubns.:** Various articles on archlg. **Activities:** 1; 15, 17, 31; 90, 95-archaeology. **Addr.:** Library, Grace Theological Seminary, Winona Lake, IN 46590.

Iddins, Mildred L. (Fountain City, TN) Libn., Carson-Newman Coll., 1944–1981; Army Libn., Ft. Oglethorpe, GA, 1943–44; Tchr./Libn., Dandridge HS, 1941–43; Tchr., Roane Cnty. HS, 1937–41; Tchr., Bell House Sch., 1936–37. **Educ.:** Carson-Newman Coll., 1933–36, BA (Eng.); George Peabody Coll., 1939–41, BS (LS). **Orgs.:** ALA. SELA. TN LA. AAUW. Monday Lit. Club. Mod. Lit. Club. **Addr.:** 403 Russell St., Jefferson City, TN 37760.

Idema, Celene E. (S. 22, 1925, Grand Rapids, MI) Head, MI Hist./Geneal., Grand Rapids Pub. Lib., 1977–, Head, Chld. Dept., 1973–77, Chld. Libn., 1962–73. **Educ.:** Mary Washington Coll., 1945–47, AB (Art); Univ. of MI, 1958–62, AMLS; Grand Rapids Jr. Coll., 1943–45, AA (Art). **Orgs.:** ALA: Lippincott Awd. Jury (1975). MI LA: Chld. Srvs. RT (Ch. 1973). CSLA. MI Arch. Assn. Grand Rapids Libn. Club: Pres. (1970). Women's Natl. Bk. Assn.: Grand Rapids Chap. (Pres., 1979). Delta Kappa Gamma. Natl. Trust Hist. Prsrvn. MI Nature Assn. Hist. Socty. MI. **Honors:** MI LA, Loleta Fyan Awd., 1965. Beta Phi Mu. **Activities:** 9; 23, 41, 45; 69, 85, 92 **Addr.:** Grand Rapids Public Library, 60 Library Plz., N.E., Grand Rapids, MI 49504.

Iffland, Carol D. (O. 28, 1946, Lawrence, MA) Syst. Dev. Consult., Bur Oak Lib. Syst., 1981–, Interlib. Coop. Coord., 1979–81, Chld. Consult., 1979–79; Dir. of Chld. Srv., Woodridge Pub. Lib., 1972–77; Chld. Libn., La Grange Pub. Lib., 1969–72. **Educ.:** Univ. of MI, 1964–68, BA (Russ.), 1968–69, MALS.

PROFESSIONAL ACTIVITIES: Institutions: 1. Acad. lib.; 2. Arch.; 3. Assn.; 4. Fed./Gvt. lib.; 5. Inst. lib.; 6. Mfr./Suppl.; 7. Milit. lib.; 8. Musm.; 9. Pub. lib.; 10. Sch. lib.; 11. Sch. of lib. sci.; 12. Spec. lib.; 13. State lib.; 14. (other). **Functions/Activities:** 15. Acq./Col. dev.; 16. Adult srvs.; 17. Admin.; 18. Apprais.; 19. Archit./Bldgs.; 20. Cat./Class.; 21. Chld. srvs.; 22. Circ.; 23. Cons./Pres.; 24. Consult.; 25. Cont. ed.; 26. Educ. lib. sci.; 27. Ext. srvs.; 28. Fund/Grants; 29. Gvt. pubs.; 30. Indx./Abs.; 31. Instr. lib. use; 32. Media srvs.; 33. Micro.; 34. Netwks./Coop.; 35. Persnl.; 36. PR; 37. Publshg.; 38. Recs. mgt.; 39. Ref. srvs.; 40. Repro.; 41. Resrch.; 42. Review.; 43. Secur.; 44. Serials; 45. Spec. col.; 46. Tech. srvs.; 47. Trustees/Bds.; 48. YA srvs.; 49. (other).

Orgs.: ALA: AASL; ALSC; ASCLA; PLA. IL LA: Chld. Libn. Sect., Ed., *Crier Nsltr.* (1975–77); IAME; PLS; SLSS; Conf. Prog. Com. (1980). Lib. Admn. Conf. North. IL: Chld. Srvs. Sect., Pres. (1981–82), Treas. (1974–76), Adv. Bd. (1979–), Ed., "Rainbow of Resrc" (1975–77) Chld. Readg. RT. Lib. Media Assn. Other orgs. Girl Scouts of the US: DuPage Cnty. Cncl. (1951–); various offices. **Honors:** Lions Club of Woodridge, Cert. for Srv. to the Deaf, 1976; Beta Phi Mu 1969. **Pubns.:** "Partnership in Service," *IL Lib.* (D. 1980); Ed., "Rainbow of Resources," *Lib. Admn. Conf. of North. IL* (1975–77); "Mainstreaming," *IL Lib.* (D. 1976); "Acorn," *Bur Oak Lib. Syst.* (1979); "Children's Crier, *IL LA Otly. Nsltr.* (1975–77). **Activities:** 9, 14-Library system; 24, 25, 34; 63, 72, 89 **Addr.:** Bur Oak Library System, 405 Earl Rd., Shorewood, IL 60436.

Iglar, Jon L. (Ja. 27, 1928, Pittsburgh, PA) Lib. Dir., Calumet Coll., 1965–; Instr., Univ. of IL Grad. Lib. Sch., 1967–68; Circ. Libn., Univ. of Chicago Harper Lib., 1964–65; Circ. Libn., Univ. of Chicago Law Lib., 1962–64. **Educ.:** St. Francis Coll., Loretto, PA, 1953, AB (Phil., Eng.); St. Francis Semy., 1953–56, (Theo.); Rosary Coll., 1962–64, MALS; Univ. of IL, 1967–69, CAS (LS); Calumet Coll., 1977–79, BS (Acct.). **Orgs.:** ALA. Cath. LA. **Activities:** 1; 17; 63, 68, 90 **Addr.:** 1412 Elliott Dr., Munster, IN 46321.

Ihrig, Alice Bennett (Ag. 19, 1921, St. Paul, MN) Dir., Civic and Cult. Progs., Moraine Valley Cmnty. Coll., 1977–; Various speaking, tchg., wrtg. positions. **Educ.:** Univ. of MN, BS (Biochem.). **Orgs.:** ALA: Cncl.; Exec. Bd. (1974–79); Com. Org.; Policy Manual Rev. Com.; Space Needs Com.; various other coms. IL LA: Pres. IL Lib. Trustees Assn.: Pres. Various other orgs. Leag. of Women Voters (IL): Pres.; Constn. Rev., Ch. Natl. Mncpl. Leag.: Bd. S W Young Men's Christ. Assn., Bd. IL Mental Hlth. Plng. Bd.: Ch. Various other orgs. **Honors:** IL LA, Spec. Awd.; ALA, ALTA, Trustee Yr.; Oak Lawn Cham. Cmrce., Citizen Yr., 1970. **Pubns.:** "Trustees," *ALA Yearbook;* ed., *Pub. Lib. Trustee, Cornerstones.* **Activities:** 14-Cmnty. Srvs.; 24, 25, 36; 50, 55 **Addr.:** 9322 S. 53rd Ave., Oak Lawn, IL 60453.

Ikena, Richard Joseph (D. 24, 1932, Baltimore, MD) Med. Libn., Eglin Reg. Hosp., Eglin AFB, FL, 1979–; Asst. Med. Libn., DC Gen. Hosp., 1970–79; Physics Libn., Cath. Univ., 1968–70; HS Libn., Marian HS, Mishawaka, IN, 1967–68; Soc. Sci. Libn., Cath. Univ., 1964–67; Chld. & Vision Sect. Libn., Prince Georges Cnty., MD, 1963–64; Tchr., Howard Cnty., MD, 1957–60. **Educ.:** Loyola Coll., Baltimore, MD, 1954, AB (Eng.); Cath. Univ., 1961–63, MS (LS); Med. Lib. Cert., 1975. **Orgs.:** Med. LA: Vice Ch., Milit. Med. Spec. Int. Grp. (1980–). **Honors:** Beta Phi Mu, 1963. **Activities:** 1, 12; 15, 17, 39; 80, 88, 92 **Addr.:** 137 Lincolnshire Dr., Niceville, FL 32578.

Ilacqua, Anne Kennedy (Je. 30, 1940, Boston, MA) Libn. II, Biblgphr., Boston Univ., 1978–; Ref. Libn., Providence Pub. Lib., 1973–78. **Educ.:** Stonehill Coll., 1958–62, AB (Eng.); Univ. of RI, 1970, MLS. **Orgs.:** ALA. RI LA. New Eng. On-Line Searchers Grp. New Eng. Lib. Info. Netwk.: Gvt. Docum. Task Force. **Activities:** 1; 15, 39, 49-on-line bibl. srch.; 92 **Addr.:** 71 Forest St., Providence, RI 02906.

Imai, Margaret K. (S. 7, 1952, Tokyo, Japan) Proj. Dir., Libn., Ronalds-Reynolds & Co. Limited, 1978–; Resrch. Libn., Needham, Harper & Steers Can., 1977–78; Libn., Can. Broadcasting Corp., 1976–77. **Educ.:** Univ. of Toronto, 1970–74, BA with honors (Hist.), 1975–77, MLS. **Orgs.:** SLA: Consult. Ch. (1979–80); Student liason (1977–78) Can. LA. Can. Assn. of Info. Sci. Fac. of LS Alum. Assn., Univ. Toronto: Student liason (1977–1979). Prof. Mktg. Resrch. Socty.: Conf. Com. (1979–80). **Pubns.:** "Bibliography of Basic Advertising Texts," *Stimulus Mag.* (D. 1977); "Tools of Information Searching," *PMRS Imprints* (Je. 1978); Speeches. **Activities:** 12; 24, 39, 41; 51, 59 **Addr.:** Ronalds-Reynolds & Company Limited, 154 University Ave., Toronto, ON M5H 3B1 Canada.

Imbrie, Agnes E. (Ag. 10, 1919, New York, NY) Libn., Los Angeles Cnty. Hlth. Dept., 1952–; Libn., Los Angeles Cnty. Gen. Hosp., 1946–51. **Educ.:** Grove City Coll., 1937–41, AB (Latin-Grmn.); Univ. of South. CA, 1942–43, BS (LS). **Orgs.:** SLA. Med. LA. Bus. & Prof. Women's Club. **Activities:** 12; 15, 34, 41; 58, 68, 80 **Addr.:** Los Angeles County Health Dept., 313 N. Figueroa St., Los Angeles, CA 90012.

Imhoff, Kathleen R. T. (S. 9, 1945, Superior, WI) Syst. Libn. for Pub. Srvs., Broward Cnty. Lib., 1980–; Dir., Chattahoochee Valley Reg. Lib., 1978–80; Dir. of Bur. of Pub. Coop. Lib. Srvs., Div. of Lib. Srvs., State of WI, 1974–78; Head of Mobile Info. Srvs., Atlanta Pub. Lib., 1973–74; Dir., Horseshoe Bend Reg. Lib., 1968–73. **Educ.:** Valparaiso Univ., 1965–67, BA (Eng.); Univ. of WI, 1967–68, MA (LS). **Orgs.:** ALA: Pub. Lib. Systs. Sect. (Pres., 1981); John Sessions Meml. Awd. Com. (Ch., 1981). Soroptomists. **Pubns.:** "Inter-Library Cooperation," *Cath. Lib. World* (My.–Je. 1978); "Labor Collections and Services in Public Libraries throughout the United States," *RQ* (Win. 1977). **Activities:** 9, 13; 17, 24, 34 **Addr.:** Broward County Library - Administration Bldg. D, 1301 Copans Rd., Pompano, FL 33064.

Immroth, Barbara Froling (Orange, NJ) Asst. Prof., GSLIS, Univ. of TX (Austin), 1980–; Dir. Lib. Srvs., Ctrl. Catholic HS, 1975–80; Instr., Univ. Pittsburgh External Std. Prog., 1975–77; Instr., St. Lib. PA, Lib. Asst. Trng., 1973; Indxr., Ency. Lib. Inf. Sci., 1971–75; Sub. Libn., Carnegie Lib. Pittsburgh, 1968–75; Libn., NDEA Sum. Inst. Sch. Libns., Univ. Denver, 1966. **Educ.:** Brown Univ., 1964, BA (Span.); Univ. Denver, 1965, MA (LS); Duquesne Univ., 1975, Sch. Cert.; Univ. Pittsburgh, 1980, PhD (LS). **Orgs.:** ALA: ALSC, Newbery Caldecott Com. (1979); Int. Frdm. Com. (1978–80); AASA Sub-com. PA LA: Sch. Libns. Assn.; Nom. Com. (1980). Pittsburgh Bibliophiles. TX LA: Ch., Com. on Int. Frdm. and Prof. Resp. **Honors:** Beta Phi Mu. Univ. Schol., Univ. of Pittsburgh. **Pubns.:** Jt. auth., "The New Role of Librarians as Professionals: A Literature Review," in *The Information Society;* jt. auth., "Interim Index to Volumes 1 to 5" in *Encycl. of Lib. and Info. Sci.;* reviews. **Activities:** 10; 39, 48; 63, 74 **Addr.:** 2633 Barton Hills Dr., Austin, TX 78704.

Ince, David L. (D. 28, 1941) Dir. of the Lib., Assoc. Prof., Valdosta St. Coll., 1977–; Asst. Prof. LS and Asst. Dir. of Tech. Srvs., NM St. Univ. (Las Cruces), 1974–77; Instr. LS, Head, Adm Srv. Dept., Univ. of NM (Albuquerque), 1972–74; Spec. Asst., Admin. Srvs., Univ. of TX (Austin), 1970–72. **Educ.:** TX A & I Univ., 1960–64, BA (Psyc.); Univ. of TX (Austin), 1968–70, MLS. **Orgs.:** ALA. SELA. GA LA: Coll. Univ. Div. (Ch., 1978–81). N. Valdosta Rotary Club: Bd. of Dir. (1978–79). Big Brothers/Big Sisters of S. GA: Pres. (1980). **Pubns.:** Jt. ed., *Central Georgia/South Georgia Associated Libraries Union List of Serials* (1979); Ed., *Georgia Union List of Serials* (1981). **Activities:** 1; 17, 26, 32 **Addr.:** Valdosta State College Library, Valdosta, GA 31601.

Ingraham, Alice L. (Ag. 1, 1952, Quakertown, PA) Dir., John Stewart Meml. Lib., Wilson Coll., 1979–; Head, Ref., Wilmette Pub. Lib., 1976–79. **Educ.:** Albright Coll., 1970–74, AB (Hist.); Rosary Coll., 1974–76, MA (LS). **Orgs.:** ALA. Tri-Cnty. Sch. Libns. Interlib. Delivery Srv.: By-laws Com. (1980–). Assoc. Coll. Libs. of Ctrl. PA: Gen. Policies Com. (1979–). AAUW. **Activities:** 1; 17; 74, 90 **Addr.:** John Stewart Memorial Library, Wilson College, Chambersburg, PA 17201.

Ingraham, Leonoor Swets (F. 23, 1941, Hilversum, Netherland) Head Circ. & Spec. Projects, Univ. of OR Hlth. Sci. Ctr. Lib., 1980–, Head, Pub. Srvs., 1977–79, Coord., Col. Dev., Acq. Libn., 1973–77; Acq. Libn., Boise State Univ., 1970–71; Catlgr./Serials Libn., Fine Arts Lib., Harvard Univ., 1967–69. **Educ.:** Scripps Coll., 1960–62, BA (Art Hist.); Simmons Coll., 1965–67, MS (LS); Med. LA Cert. Grade I, 1976–81. **Orgs.:** Med. LA: Status and Econ. Int. of Hlth. Sci. Lib. Persnl. (1978–80); Recert. Com. (1980–); Pac. NW Reg. Chap., Legis. Com. (Ch., 1980–). City Club of Portland. Portland Art Musm. Docents. **Honors:** Cncl. on Lib. Resrcs., Hlth. Sci. Acad. Lib., Natl. Lib. of Med., Mgt. Internship, 1979–80. **Activities:** 1, 12; 15, 17, 22 **Addr.:** 2676 S.W. Talbot Rd., Portland, OR 97201.

Ingram, Charles Dean (D. 29, 1928, Lawton, OK) Acq. Libn., Al Harris Lib., Southwest. OK State Univ., 1973–; Acq. Libn., OK City Univ., 1968–73, Docum. Libn., 1965–68; Asst. Libn. for Pub. Srvc., Univ. of OK Med. Ctr. Lib., 1963–65; Asst. Acq. Libn., Univ. of OK, 1962–63. **Educ.:** OK City Univ., 1946–49, (Art); Univ. of OK, 1949–51, BFA (Art), 1960–63, MLS. **Orgs.:** OK LA: Coll. & Univ. Div. (Ch., 1968); Const. & By-Laws Com. (Ch., 1971); Auditing Com. (Ch., 1972). Socty. of N. Amer. Artists. Higher Educ. Alum. Cncl. of OK. AAUP. Southwest. OK State Univ. Fac. Sen. **Honors:** Beta Phi Mu. **Activities:** 1; 15, 30, 46 **Addr.:** 1304 Lark, Weatherford, OK 73096.

Ingram, John E. (Ap. 23, 1945, Jersey City, NJ) Resrch. Archvst., Colonial Williamsburg Fndn., 1979–; Mss. Prcs., Brown Univ., 1976–79. **Educ.:** Fordham Univ., 1963–68, AB, AM (Russ.); Brown Univ., 1968–77, PhD (Slavic); Natl. Arch. and Recs. Srv., Intro. Archival Mgt., 1978, Cert. **Orgs.:** SAA. Mid-Atl. Reg. Arch. Conf. Natl. Micro. Assn. Amer. Assn. of Tchrs. of Slavic and E. European Lang. **Activities:** 2, 8, 14; 15, 20, 45; 55, 70 **Addr.:** Colonial Williamsburg Foundation, P.O. Box C, Williamsburg, VA 23187.

Ingram, LouElla L. (Ag. 25, 1918, Union, WV) Libn., US Court of Claims, US Court of Customs & Patent Appeals, 1967–; Ref. Libn., US Dept. of Justice Main Lib., 1946–48, Circ. & Asst. Ref. Libn., 1943–46; Libn. I, Brooklyn Pub. Lib., 1941–43. **Educ.:** Univ. of CA, Berkeley, 1940, AB (Fr, Eng, Hist); Columbia Univ., 1941, BS (LS). **Orgs.:** AALL. **Activities:** 4; 17, 20, 39; 77, 78, 91, 95-Patents. **Addr.:** US Court of Claims, US Court of Customs & Patent Appeals, 717 Madison Place, N.W., Washington, DC 20005.

Ingram, Sara (O. 20, 1943, Cincinnati, OH) Consult. in Data Prcsg. Prac, Peat, Marwick, Mitchell & Co., 1981–; Mgr., Info Srvs., Burson-Marsteller, 1978–80; Libn., Staff Exec., Amer. Assn. Advert. Srvs., 1969–78. **Educ.:** Murray St. Univ., 1962–65, BA (Eng.); FL St. Univ., 1965–66, MLS. **Orgs.:** SLA: Advert. Mktg. Div., Ch. Elect (1979–80). ASIS. Assn. Info. Mgrs. **Activities:** 12; 17, 41; 51, 59, 92 **Addr.:** 666 Pelham Rd., New Rochelle, NY 10805.

Inman, Harvey J. (O. 5, 1946, Paris, IL) Catlgr., Decatur (IL) Pub. Lib., 1978–; Catlgr., Parkland Coll. Lib., 1977–78. **Educ.:** East. IL Univ., 1964–68, BS in Ed. (Hist.), 1970–71, MA (Hist.); Univ. of IL, 1976–77, MS (LS). **Orgs.:** ALA: RTSD. IL LA: Resrcs. and Tech. Srvs. Sect., Exec. Bd. (Mem.-at-Large, 1981). Decatur Pub. Lib. Staff Assn.: VP (1979). **Honors:** Beta Phi Mu. **Activities:** 1, 9; 16, 20, 32; 63, 92 **Addr.:** Decatur Public Library, 247 E. North St., Decatur, IL 62523.

Inouye, Patricia C. (Ag. 17, 1949, Indianapolis, IN) US Libn., Univ. of CA (Davis), 1976–. **Educ.:** CA St. Univ. (Chico), 1967–71, BA (Phil.) Univ. of Denver, 1974–75, MA (LS). **Orgs.:** ALA: GODART CA LA: Cnclr. (1980–1983); Gov. Pubns. Chap. (Ch., 1979). **Honors:** Beta Phi Mu. **Activities:** 1, 9; 29, 36, 39; 65, 78, 86 **Addr.:** Government Documents Dept., Shields Library, University of California, Davis, CA 95616.

Inskip, Anita L. (D. 18, 1935, Hanover, PA) Coord., Lib.-Media Srvs., Cncl. Rock Sch. Dist., 1966–, Libn., Wrightstown Elem. Sch., 1971–74, Libn., Cncl. Rock HS, 1969–71, Libn., Cncl. Rock Intermediate Sch., 1964–67, Libn., Cncl. Rock HS, 1960–64, Libn., Biglerville HS 1957–60. **Educ.:** Millersville State Coll., 1953–57, BS (LS); Syracuse Univ., 1958–61, MSLS. **Orgs.:** ALA. PA Sch. Libns. Assn.: Supvsrs. Com. (1980). Bucks Cnty. Sch. Libns. Assn.: Pres. (1965–68, 1970–72, 1976–78). Cncl. Rock Educ. Assn. PA State Educ. Assn. Natl. Educ. Assn. Delta Kappa Gamma Socty: Alpha Nu Chap. (1st VP., 1978–80; Pres., 1980–82). DE Valley Supvsn. and Curric. Dev. Adv. Bd. **Honors:** Beta Phi Mu, 1961. **Activities:** 10; 17, 24, 32 **Addr.:** 1292 Hi-View Dr., Southampton, PA 18966.

Intner, Sheila (Mr. 27, 1935, Chicago, IL) Asst. Prof., Div. of Lib. and Info. Mgt., Emory Univ., 1981–; Adjunct Lectr., Queens Coll., CUNY, 1980–81; Coord., Autom. Srvs., Grt. Neck Lib., 1978–81, Msc. Libn., Head, Msc. Dept., 1976–78, Asst. to Head, Tech. Srvs., 1976. **Educ.:** Northwestern Univ., 1952–55, BA (Econ.); Queens Coll., CUNY, 1973–76, MLS; Columbia Univ., 1976–, DLS Cand. **Orgs.:** ALA. AALS. Msc. LA. NY LA: CLSI East. Reg. Pub. Acad. and Spec. Lib. Users Grp., Strg. Com. (Secy., 1979–). Grt. Neck Lib. Staff Assn. **Addr.:** 2742 Parkview Dr. NE, Atlanta, GA 30345.

Ippolito, Andrew V. (Mr. 6, 1930, New York, NY) Dir. of Lib. and Resrch., Newsday Inc. 1965–; Dir., Merrick Lib., 1962–65; Dir., N. Babylon Pub. Lib., 1960–62; Dir., Lindenhurst Mem. Lib., 1959–60. **Educ.:** Georgetown Univ., 1953–55, BS (Frgn. Srv.); Pratt Inst. Lib. Sch., 1958–59, MS (LS); C. W. Post, 1975– (Educ.). **Orgs.:** SLA: Spec. Lib. Com. (Ch., 1968–70); Newsp. Div., Dir. (1966–67), Auto. Com. (Ch., 1977–); NY Chap., Newsp. Div., Ch. (1966–67, 1971–75). Nassau Cnty. LA: Exec. Bd. (1964, 1972–74); Pres. (1978). Queens Sch.: Ch. of the Bd. (1974–76); Mem. of the Exec. Bd. (1973–). **Honors:** Amer. Mgt. Assn., Contrib. Srvs. AMA Sem., 1972–73; SLA, Newsp. Div., Apprec. Prof. Excel. and Leadership Div. Ch., 1968. **Pubns.:** *Special Equipment for Special Libraries* (1972); Ed., Publ., "Automated Libraries" (Ag. 1967); "Library Without Books," *SCLA DATA* (Win. 1968). **Activities:** 12; 32; 83 **Addr.:** Newsday Library, Long Island, NY 11747.

Ireland, Leland R. (Mr. 8, 1949, Vandalia, IL) Dir., Pub. Lib. Syst. (Holdrege, NE), 1977–; Interlib. Coop. Consult., North. IL Lib. Syst., 1975–77; First Asst., Bus., Sci. & Tech. Div., Rockford Pub. Lib., 1974–75. **Educ.:** Augustana Coll., 1967–71, BA (Msc.); North. IL Univ., 1973–74, MALS. **Orgs.:** ALA. NELA: Legis. Com. (Ch., 1977–80); Pub. Lib. Sect. (Ch. 1979–80). NE Educ. Media Assn. Mt. Plains LA. **Activities:** 9; 17, 34, 39 **Addr.:** Public Library System, 604 East Ave., Holdrege, NE 68949.

Ireland, Norma Olin (Mr. 27, 1907, Wadsworth, OH) Dir., Ireland Indexing Srv., Freelnc. Indexing, Lib. Resrch., Geneal. Bus., 1938–; Co-owner, Ireland Bk. and Lib. Srv., 1942–50; Actg. Head, Educ. Lib., Assoc. Prof., Sch. of Lib. Srv., Univ. of South. CA, 1938; Actg. Head, Ref. Dept., 1st Asst. to Libn., Glendale Pub. Lib., 1937–38; Actg. Head, Loan Dept., Pomona Coll. Lib., 1936–37; Instr., Univ. of Akron, 1936, Rsv. Rm. Libn., Ref. Libn., 1929–36. **Educ.:** Univ. of Akron, 1924–28, BA (Pol. Sci.); West. Rsv. Univ., 1928–29, BS (LS); 1970, Cert. Geneal. Resrch. **Orgs.:** Amer. Socty. of Indxrs. ALA: JMRT (Coord., 1936–37); Exec. Bd. (1939–40); PR Com. (1939–42); Pubcty. Com., Jr. Subcom. (1938–39). SLA: South. CA Chap., Pubcty. Com. (Ch., 1938–39). OH LA: OH Jr. Mems. (Secy.-Treas., 1934–36). Socty. of Mayflower Descendants. CT Socty. of Genealogists. West. Rsv. Univ. Lib. Sch., South CA Alum. Daughters of the Amer. Revolution. Various orgs. **Honors:** Fallbrook Cham. of Cmrce., Spec. Cert., 1976; Univ. of Akron, "A-Awd." for Disting. Alum., 1979; AAUW, Hon. as One of 3 Outstan. Women of Fallbrook, 1973; Alpha Phi Gamma; other hons. **Pubns.:** *Index to America, 19th Century* (forthcoming); *Index to America, 18th Century* (1976); *Index to America, 17th Century* (1978); *Index to America, 20th Century* (forthcoming); 6-article series on geneal. indexing, *Tri-State Trader* (O.–N. 1976); various bks., reviews, bibls., pamphlets, indxs., ed. projs. **Activities:** 14-Indexing Srv.; 30, 42; 69 **Addr.:** 2237 Brooke Rd., Fallbrook, CA 92028.

Irick, Robert L. (Ag. 14, 1930, Competition, MO) Pres., Chinese Mtrls. Ctr., Hong Kong, 1978–; Pres., Chinese Mtrls. Ctr., Inc., 1973–; Partner, Bkstore, 1977–79; Adj. Prof., Natl.

Special Subjects/Services: 50. Adult educ.; 51. Advert./Mktg.; 52. Aerosp.; 53. Agric.; 54. Area std.; 55. Arts/Hum.; 56. Autom.; 57. Bibl./Prtg.; 58. Bio. sci.; 59. Bus./Fin.; 60. Chem.; 61. Copyrt.; 62. Documtn.; 63. Educ.; 64. Engin.; 65. Env.; 66. Eth. grps.; 67. Film; 68. Food/Nutr.; 69. Geneal.; 70. Geo.; 71. Geol.; 72. Handcpd.; 73. Hist.; 74. Int. frdm.; 75. Info. sci.; 76. Insr.; 77. Law; 78. Legis.; 79. Math./Comp. sci.; 80. Med.; 81. Metals; 82. Nat. resrcs.; 83. Newsp.; 84. Nuc. sci.; 85. Oral hist.; 86. Petr./Energy; 87. Pharm.; 88. Phys./Astr./Math.; 89. Readg.; 90. Relig.; 91. Sci./Tech.; 92. Soc. sci.; 93. Telecom.; 94. Transp.; 95. (other).

Chengchi Univ., 1977–78, Adj. Assoc. Prof., 1976–, Adj. Prof., 1974–75; Partner, Taiwan Enterprises Co., 1970–; Res. Dir., CA St. Intl. Progs., 1965–. **Educ.:** S.W. MO St. Univ., 1948–55, BA (Hist.) Harvard Univ., 1955–71 MA (E. Asian Stud.), PhD (Hist., Lang.); Yale Univ., 1951–53, Cert. (Chinese). **Orgs.:** Assn. Asian Stud.: Com. E. Asian Libs. Intl. Assn. Oriental Libns. **Pubns.:** Various articles, guides rel. to Chinese lang. **Activities:** 6; 17, 37, 39; 54, 55, 57 **Addr.:** 1716 Ocean Ave., Suite 103, San Francisco, CA 94112.

Irvine, Betty Jo (Jl. 13, 1943, Indianapolis, IN) Fine Arts Libn., IN Univ., 1969–, Asst. Fine Arts Libn., 1968–69, Fine Arts Slide Libn., 1966–68. **Educ.:** IN Univ., 1962–66, AB Distinction (Art Hist.), 1969, MLS, Doct. Cand., LS. **Orgs.:** ALA: ACRL, Art Sect., Nom. Sect. (Ch., 1972–73), Ch. (1978–79). ARLIS/NA: Stan. Com. (1974–76); Nom. Com. (1979). SLA: IN Chap., Secy. (1973–74). Coll. Art Assn.: Natl. Strg. Com. Slides Photographs (1971–76). Midwest Art Hist. Socty. IN Cncl. Tchr. Eng.: Media Com. (1971–74). **Honors:** Cncl. on Lib. Resrc., Ofcr. Grant, 1971; Pi Lambda Theta, 1973; Beta Phi Mu, 1977. **Pubns.:** *Slide Libraries: A Guide for Academic Institutions, Museums & Special Collections* (2d ed.) (1979); *Slide Libraries: A Guide for Academic Institutions and Museums* (1974); "Bibliographic Instruction for Graduate Art History Students," *Art Lib. Jnl.* (1979); "Organization & Mgt. of Art Slide Collections," *Lib. Trends* (1975); "Slide Classification: A Historical Survey," *Coll. & Resrch. Lib.* (1971); Reviews. **Activities:** 1; 17, 31, 41; 55, 67, 95-Nonprint Media. **Addr.:** Fine Arts Library, Indiana University, Bloomington, IN 47405.

Irving, Ophelia M. (Ap. 4, 1929, Gadsden, AL) Asst. Chief Info. Srvs. Sect., NC St. Lib., 1968–; Head Libn., St. Augustine's Coll., 1961–68, Cat., 1955–61; Libn., Spencer Jr. HS (Columbus, GA), 1954–55; Libn., Ctr. HS (Waycross, GA), 1951–54. **Educ.:** Clark Coll., 1947–51, AB (Soc. Sci.); Atlanta Univ. and Syracuse Univ., 1954–58, MLS; Drexel Inst. of Tech., (LS); NC Dept. Arch. Hist., Geneal. Cert., 1976; NC Dept. Persnl., Mgt. Cert., 1977. **Orgs.:** ALA. SELA: Nom. Com. (1971–72); Lib. Educ. Com. (1970–72). NC LA: Dir. (1972–74). NC OLUG. Alpha Kappa Alpha: Raleigh Chap., Black Heritage Com. (Ch., 1970–73). YWCA. **Activities:** 1, 13; 17, 29, 39; 56, 69, 92 **Addr.:** 533 East Lenoir St., Raleigh, NC 27601.

Irwin, Barbara Smith (Jl. 15, 1939, Atlantic City, NJ) Lib. Dir., NJ Hist. Socty., 1979–, Ref. Libn., 1977–79. **Educ.:** Douglass Coll., 1976, BA (Amer. Std.); Rutgers Univ., 1977, MLS. **Orgs.:** NJ LA: Hist. and Bibl. Sect., Pres., VP. (1980–82). Leag. of Hist. Soctys. of NJ: Del. (1979–82). Northeast Docum. Cons. Ctr.: Adv. Bd. (NJ Del., 1981–84). Westfield Meml. Lib.: Trustee (1980–83). NJ Folklore Socty.: Rec. Secy. (1979–80). **Honors:** Beta Phi Mu, 1977; Franklin Twp., NJ, Cult. Arts Srv. Awd., 1974. **Pubns.:** Jt. Auth., *New Jersey Folklore Bibliography* forthcoming; "New Jersey Folklore: An Annotated Bibliography," *NJ Folklore* (Spr. 1979); "Pine Barrens Folklore: A Selective Bibliography," *NJ Folklore* (Spr. 1979). **Activities:** 12, 13; 15, 23, 45; 69 **Addr.:** NJ Historical Society, 230 Broadway, Newark, NJ 07104.

Irwin, Janet Marie (My. 17, 1947, Vancouver, WA) Head, Circ. Srvs., Lib. Assn. Of Portland, 1978–; Branch Libn., 1974–78, Libn. I, 1970–74. **Educ.:** West. MI Univ., 1967–69, BA (Hist.), 1969–70, MLS; Port Huron Jr. Coll., 1965–67, AA (Hist.). **Orgs.:** Pacific NW LA: Circ. Div. (Vice Ch., 1979–81; Ch., 1981–83) OR LA: Treas. (1981–83); Auto. Com. (1978–80); Legis. Com. (1975–77). **Activities:** 9; 16, 22, 34; 56, 78 **Addr.:** 4420 S.E. Belmont #12, Portland, OR 97215.

Isaacs, Nancy B. (Ja. 20, 1930, Springfield, MA) Dir., Lib., Lasell Jr. Coll., 1975–; Catlgr., Gutman Lib., Harvard Univ., 1974–75; Prog. Dir., Lib. Tech., Lasell Jr. Coll., 1972–77. **Educ.:** Swarthmore Coll., 1947–51, BA (Eng.); Yale Univ., 1952–53, MA (Tchg.); Simmons Coll., 1970–72, MS (LS). **Orgs.:** MA Assn. of Jr. Coll. Libns.: Coord. (1975–). Weston Pub. Lib.: Bd. of Lib. Trustees (Ch., 1975–76). New Eng. LA. ALA. MA LA: Tech. Srvs. Sect., Prog. Com. (1979–), PR Com. (1975–76), Educ. Com. (Ch., 1973–74). **Honors:** Beta Phi Mu, 1972. **Activities:** 1; 20; 63 **Addr.:** Zero Bay State Rd., Weston, MA 02193.

Isaacson, David Kent (My. 18, 1943, Gary, IN) Asst. Head of Ref. and Hum. Libn., West. MI Univ., 1978–, Gen. Ref. Libn., 1973–78. **Educ.:** IN Univ., 1961–65, AB with Honors (Eng.); Claremont Grad. Sch., 1965–66, MA (Amer. Studies); Univ. of IL, 1973, MLS. **Orgs.:** MI LA: Int. Frdm. Com. (1978–). ALA. MI Acad. of Arts, Letters and Sci. AAUP: Various offices at West. MI Univ. (1977–78). Pop. Cult. Assn. Midwest Pop. Cult. Assn. **Honors:** Phi Beta Kappa, 1965; Beta Phi Mu, 1973. **Pubns.:** "Let's Talk Turkey: A Librarian Criews Fowl to Libraryese," *Wilson Lib. Bltn.* (S. 1978); "Our Motto-Service With a Difference," *the Unabashed Libn.* (29, 1978); "Positive Facial Regarding as a Technique in the Reference Interview," *Jnl. Acad. Libnshp.* (N. 1979); "The Academic Library in a 'Schooled' Society," *Jnl. of Acad. Libnshp.* (Mr. 1978). **Activities:** 1; 26, 31, 39; 55, 74, 95-Literature. **Addr.:** Reference Dept., Waldo Library, Western Michigan University, Kalamazoo, MI 49008.

Isacco, Jeanne M. (Ag. 22, 1946, Ellwood City, PA) Dir., Branch Srvs., Cuyahoga Cnty. Pub. Lib., 1980–81; Head User Support Sect., Lib. of Congs., 1979–80; Chief, Rec. Branch, Gvt. Prtg. Ofc., 1974–79; State Planner, Ofc. of the Gvr., VA, 1973–74; Ref. Libn., VA Cmwlth. Univ., 1972–73; Ref. Libn., Free Lib. of Philadelphia, 1969–72. **Educ.:** Wheeling Coll., 1964–68, BA (Hist.); Univ. of Pittsburgh, 1968–69, MLS. **Orgs.:** ALA: Cncl. (1980–84); GODORT (Ch., 1980–82); Fed. Docum. Task Force. Coord. (1977–79), Asst. Coord. (1975–77), Educ. Task Force (Asst. Coord., 1979–80). **Pubns.:** "Helpful Hints for Ordering From GPO," *Docum. to the People* (Ja. 1975). **Activities:** 9; 17, 27; 56, 75 **Addr.:** 3174 E. Overlook Rd., Cleveland Hts., OH 44118.

Isché, John P. (N. 2, 1919, Brooklyn, NY) Dir., Div. of Libs., LA St. Univ. Med. Ctr., 1959–; Assoc. Dir., J. Hillis Miller Hlth. Ctr., Univ. of FL, 1957–59; Med. Socty. Co. Kings, Brooklyn, 1938–47. **Educ.:** Taylor Univ., 1947–50, AB; Pratt Inst., 1950–51, MLS; Med. Libn., 1955, Cert. **Orgs.:** LA LA: Secy., Pres. Med. LA: Bd. of Dir., Treas. **Activities:** 1; 17; 80 **Addr.:** Louisiana State University Medical Center, 1542 Tulane Ave., New Orleans, LA 70112.

Ishaq, Mary Rush (Minneapolis, MN) Asst. Head, Hum. Ref. Dept., Univ. of NC Lib., 1969–; Libn., Ames Lib. of S. Asia, Univ. of MN, 1964–68, Libn., Ctr. for Intl. Rel. and Area Std., 1962–64. **Educ.:** Univ. of MN, 1960, BA cum laude (Span., Pol. Sci.), 1967, cum laude MA (LS); Osmania Univ., Hyderabad, India, 1961–62; various crs. **Orgs.:** ALA. NC OLUG: Fndn. Com. (1977). Assn. of Libns. at Univ. of NC: Secy. (1976). **Pubns.:** Jt. Auth., "Library and Research Consultations: A Service for Graduate Students," *RQ* (Win. 1978); various bibl. guides. **Activities:** 1; 39; 54, 55, 57 **Addr.:** University of NC, Louis Round Wilson Academic Affairs Library, Chapel Hill, NC 27514.

Ishimoto, Carol F. (F. 6, 1926, San Jose, CA) Head, Union Cat. Srv. Off., Harvard Univ. Lib., 1980–, and Head, Cat. and Prcs. Dept., Harvard Coll. Lib., 1973–, Cat., 1960–73; Cat., Univ. of PA Lib., 1958–60; Ref. Libn., Lamont Lib., Harvard Coll., 1955–57, Admn. Asst., Cat. Dept., Widener Lib., Harvard Coll., 1950–55; Asst. Instr., Simmons Coll. Lib. Sch., 1948–49. **Educ.:** Simmons Coll., 1944–48, BS (LS). **Orgs.:** ALA: RTSD, Cncl. Reg. Grp. (VCh., Ch., 1970–72), Cat. Sect. (VCh., Ch., 1973–75), Nom. Com. (Ch., 1973–74), Cat. Code Rev. Com. (1974–76), Tech. Srvs. Dir. Lg. Lib. (Ch., 1976–77), Margaret Mann Cit. Com. (1976–77); various other coms. New England LA. Jnl. of Acad. Libnshp.: Ed. Bd. (1974–78). Cncl. on Lib. Resrc.: Bibl. Srv. Dev. Prog. Com. (1978–). **Honors:** Cncl. on Lib. Resrc., Flwshp. 1971–72. **Pubns.:** "National Program for Acquisitions and Cataloging: its Impact on University Libraries," *Coll. & Resrch. Lib.* (1973); translated into Japanese, *Gendai no Toshokan* (1973); "Cataloging and Classification," *ALA Yrbk* (1976). **Activities:** 1; 17, 24, 46 **Addr.:** Harvard College Library, Cambridge, MA 021؍8.

Iskenderian, Marguerite (New York, NY) Msc. Catlgr., Brooklyn Coll., CUNY, 1972–. **Educ.:** Oberlin Coll., 1962–67, BM (Piano); Northwestern Univ., 1967–70, MM (Msc. Hist.); Rosary Coll., 1970–71, MLS. **Orgs.:** Msc. LA: Cat. Com. (1980–); Pubns. Cncl. (1980–); Constn. Rev. Com. (1979–). LA CUNY: Pubns. Com. (Ch., 1979–80); Inst. Com. (1972); *LACUNY Dir.* Ed. (1979–80). **Pubns.:** Cmplr., Ed., *Music Cataloging Bulletin Index/Supplement to Volumes 6–10* (1980); Ed., *Music Cataloging Bulletin, Volume II* (1980–). Ed., *Urban Academic Librarian,* (Spr. 1981). **Activities:** 1; 20; 55 **Addr.:** 737 E. 32 St., Brooklyn, NY 11210.

Isley, Doris Natelle (O. 18, 1929, Jacksonville, FL) Mgr., Info. Srvs. Div., MS Resrch. and Dev. Ctr., 1967–; Adj. Prof. of LS, Univ. of MS, 1975–; Asst. Prof., City Plng. Prog., GA Inst. of Tech., 1964–66, Sch. of Arch. Libn., 1959–66; UNESCO Tech. Expert, Mid. E. Tech. Univ. (Ankara, Turkey), 1958–59; Sch. of Arch. Libn., GA Inst. of Tech., 1953–57; Asst. Branch Libn., Atlanta Pub. Lib., 1952–53. **Educ.:** FL St. Univ., 1947–51, BA (Soc. Sci. and Hist.), 1951–52, MA (LS). **Orgs.:** Consort. for Lib. Auto. in MS: (1974–78, Pres., 1975). SELA. ALA. SLA. ASIS. MS LA: Various coms., Various other orgs. **Honors:** Beta Phi Mu. **Pubns.:** *A Manual for Small Planning Agency Libraries* (1966); *Bibliography on the Control of Roadside Development* (1955); "R & D Center Information Services Division Has Varied Collections for Public Use," *MS Lib. News* (Mr. 1968); "The Literature of Zoning," *GA Local Gov. Jnl.* (My. 1955); various speeches. **Activities:** 1, 12; 17, 19, 24; 55, 59, 93 **Addr.:** 5025 Wayneland Dr., Apt. L-8, Jackson, MS 39211.

Isman, Bonnie Jane (S. 1, 1946, Topeka, KS) AV Spec., A. Richards Jr. HS, U.S. VI, 1979–; Resrch. Libn., VI Bur. of Lib. and Musms., 1976–79; Adult Srv. Libn., Jones Lib., 1972–76. **Educ.:** Univ. of KS, 1964–68, BA (Span.); Univ. of MD, 1971–72, MLS; Univ. of Cordoba, Argentina, 1969; Univ. of the Repub., Montevideo, Uruguay, 1968. **Orgs.:** VI LA: Pres. (1980–). St. Croix LA: Pres. (1979–); Nsltr. Ed. (1977–79). Assn. Caribbean Univ. Resrch. Libs.: Micro. Com. (Secy., 1977–79). ALA: SRRT, (Clearinghse. Writer, 1978–80). W. End Food Coop (St. Croix): Treas. (1980–). Amherst Cable Adv. Com. (MA): Ch. (1974–75). Women's Info. Proj. (MA): Coord. (1973–74). **Honors:** U.S. Dept. of State, Fulbright-Hays Grant, 1968. **Pubns.:** *Library Resources in The U.S. Virgin Islands* (1978); jt. auth., *Virgin Islands Demonstration Library Network Study: Test Phase* (1979); jt. auth., *Virgin Islands Demonstration Library Network Study–Exploring Library Networks in Remote Disadvantaged Areas* (1978); "Whose Community Librarian?" *SRRT Nsltr.* (Ag.–S. 1979); "The Virgin Islands Demonstration Library Network Study," *The Serials Libn.* (Sum. 1978); various other pubns. **Activities:** 9, 10; 16, 32, 34; 50 **Addr.:** P.O. Box 2765, Frederiksted, St. Croix, U.S. VI 00840.

Isom, Bill V. (Jl. 25, 1981, Dongola, IL) Circ. Libn., Assoc. Prof., East. IL Univ. Lib., 1967–, Asst. Circ. Libn., 1964–67; Asst. Educ. Libn., South. IL Univ., 1957–64; Asst. Circ. Libn., Fort Wayne Pub. Lib. 1955–56; Asst. Mail Ref. Libn., IL State Lib., 1956–57; Asst. Circ. Libn., Fort Wayne Pub. Lib., 1955–56; Sch. Libn., Tchr., Thebes HS, 1952–53, 1949–50. **Educ.:** South. IL Univ., 1945–49, BS (Educ.); Univ. of IL, 1953–55, MS (LS); South. IL Univ., 1958–61, MS Ed (Sec. Educ.). **Orgs.:** IL LA. ACRL. **Honors:** Phi Kappa Tau; Phi Beta Kappa; Kappa Delta Pi. **Activities:** 1; 22 **Addr.:** 2605 5th St., Charleston, IL 61920.

Ison, John E. (Ja. 11, 1943, Denver, CO) Dir., Durango Cnty. Pub. Lib., 1978–; Budget Consult., CO Dept. Educ., 1976–78; Admin. Asst., CO State Lib., 1970–76. **Educ.:** CO State Univ., 1961–66, BS (Bus. Admin.); various grad. crs. **Orgs.:** ALA. CO LA: Pub. Lib. Div. (Ch., 1978–80). Durango Fine Arts Cncl. Durango Lions Club. **Activities:** 9; 16, 17, 35; 75, 82, 91 **Addr.:** Durango Public Library, 1188 2nd Ave., Durango, CO 81301.

Ivanochko, Robert W. E. (Ag. 31, 1944, Yorkton, SK) Lib. Consult., SK Prov. Lib., 1971–. **Educ.:** Univ. of SK, 1962–67, BA (Eng.); Univ. of MI, 1968–71, MLS; various lang. progs. **Orgs.:** ALA: ACRL/SEES, Nom. Com. Can. LA: Cncl. (1975–76). SK LA: Pres. (1975–76). Can. Assn. of Slavists. Can. Eth. Std. Assn. **Pubns.:** various bibl. **Activities:** 9, 13; 24, 27, 45; 54, 55, 66 **Addr.:** 1410 College Ave., Regina, SK S4P 1B3 Canada.

Ives, Sidney E. (N. 28, 1925, Orlando, FL) Rare Bks. Libn., Univ. of FL, 1980–; Acq. Biblgphr., Houghton Lib., Harvard Univ., 1964–79. **Educ.:** Harvard Univ., 1947–49, AB (Eng.); various crs. **Orgs.:** Bibl. Socty. of Amer.: Pubns. Com. Grolier Club. Club of Odd Volumes. **Pubns.:** *Houghton Library Reports XXX–XXXVI* (1979–80); *The Trial of Mrs. Leigh Perrott* (1980); various articles. **Activities:** 1; 15, 17, 28 **Addr.:** 531 Library W., The University of FL, Gainesville, FL 32611.

Ivey, Robert D., Jr. (F. 8, 1936, Miami, FL) Libn., *Gainesville Sun,* 1976–; Lib. Asst., Lincoln Mid. Sch., 1974–76; Lib. Asst., IFAS, Univ. of FL, 1970–72; Libn., WA Univ., 1964–70. **Educ.:** Univ. of FL, 1953–57, BA (Hist.); Univ. of MN, 1960–63, MA (LS). **Orgs.:** SLA: Autom./Tech. Com. **Addr.:** 4401 S.W. 13 St., Apt. J, Gainesville, FL 32608.

Ivy, Karen E. (Ap. 2, 1946, Vallejo, CA) Libn., Coopers and Lybrand, 1976–; Libn. II, San Jose Pub. Lib., 1971–73, Libn. I, 1969–71. **Educ.:** Univ. of CA, Berkeley, 1963–67, BA (Eng.), 1967–68, MLS. **Orgs.:** SLA: Assoc. Bltn. Ed. (1978–80); San Francisco Bay Reg. Chap., Mailing Com. (Ch., 1980–81). Mensa. **Honors:** Phi Beta Kappa. **Activities:** 12; 17, 39, 45; 59, 77 **Addr.:** Coopers & Lybrand, 333 Market St., San Francisco, CA 94105.

Iwetz, Sr. Marie Cecile (D. 29, 1916, E. Orange, NJ) Media Spec., Our Lady of the Valley (Orange) HS, 1973–, Tchr., Libn., 1969–73; Tchr., Libn., Bishop McGuinness HS, NC, 1968–69; Relig. Tchr., Libn., Archbishop John Carroll HS, PA, 1967–68; Tchr., Libn., Pius X HS, PA, 1960–67; Tchr., John W. Hallahan HS, 1958–60; various tchg. positions in PA, Washington, DC, 1937–58. **Educ.:** Chestnut Hill Coll., 1937–54, AB (Eng., Soc. Std.); Cath. Univ. of Amer., 1958–66, MSLS (Eng.); Univ. of PA, (Educ. Media); State of NC, 1968, Cert. (Sec. Eng. Tchr., Libn.); Cmwlth. of PA, 1969, Cert. (Comprehensive Eng.); State of NJ, 1971, Cert. (Tchr. of Eng., Libn.). **Orgs.:** Cath. LA: North. NJ Chap. (Pres., 1979–81); Adv. Cncl. (1970–81). Educ. Media Assn. of NJ. Essex Cnty. Sch. Media Assn. Natl. Cath. Educ. Assn. NJ Tchrs. of Sec. Schs. Natl. Cncl. of Tchrs. of Eng. **Honors:** Mid. States Assn. of Colls. and Sec. Schs., Recog. of Outstan. Srv. Certs., 1973, 1975, 1976; Archdio. of Newark Ofc. of Educ., Cert. of Prof. Dev., 1976. **Pubns.:** "Comment on: Teacher/Librarian Relations," *Cath. Lib. World* (O. 1978); "Ho Chi Minh: An Aftermath," *Asia* (Win. 1971). **Activities:** 10; 17, 32, 48; 55, 75, 90 **Addr.:** 518 Valley St., Orange, NJ 07050.

Izbicki, Walter John (Mr. 6, 1949, Norwich, CT) HS Libn., Woodstock Acad., 1976–; Elem. Sch. Libn., Coventry Pub. Sch., 1974–76. **Educ.:** Univ. of CT, 1967–71, BA (Hist.); Univ. of RI, 1973–74, MLS; RI Coll., 1975–78, MEd (Instr. Tech.). **Orgs.:** ALA. New Eng. LA. CT LA. East. CT LA. CT Army Natl. Grd. **Honors:** Beta Phi Mu, 1980; Holt Meml. Awd., 1977–80. **Activities:** 9, 10; 16, 39, 48; 63, 74, 92 **Addr.:** 5 Mile River Rd., E. Putnam, CT 06260.

Izumo, Patsy M. (Je. 24, 1934, Paia, HI) Dir., Multimedia Srvs. Branch, Ofc. of Instr. Srvs., HI State Dept. of Educ., 1974–, Prog. Spec., Sch. Lib. Srvs., 1966–74; Vice-Prin., Admin. Trainee, Puuhale Sch./Kuhio Sch., 1955–66; Sch. Libn., various schs., 1961–65; Classrm. Tchr., various schs., 1957–61. **Educ.:** Univ. of HI, 1952–56, BEd (Elem. Educ., Lib. Std.), 1956–57, 5th yr. (Elem. Educ., Lib. Std.), 1967, MEd (Educ. Admin., Couns.,

PROFESSIONAL ACTIVITIES: Institutions: 1. Acad. lib.; 2. Arch.; 3. Assn.; 4. Fed./Gvt. lib.; 5. Inst. lib.; 6. Mfr./Suppl.; 7. Milit. lib.; 8. Musm.; 9. Pub. lib.; 10. Sch. lib.; 11. Sch. of lib. sci.; 12. Spec. lib.; 13. State lib.; 14. (other). **Functions/Activities:** 15. Acq./Col. dev.; 16. Adult srvs.; 17. Admin.; 18. Apprais.; 19. Archit./Bldgs.; 20. Cat./Class.; 21. Chld. srvs.; 22. Circ.; 23. Cons./Pres.; 24. Consult.; 25. Cont. ed.; 26. Educ. lib. sci.; 27. Ext. srvs.; 28. Fund/Grants; 29. Gvt. pubs.; 30. Indx./Abs.; 31. Instr. lib. use; 32. Media srvs.; 33. Micro.; 34. Netwks./Coop.; 35. Persnl.; 36. PR; 37. Publshg.; 38. Recs. mgt.; 39. Ref. srvs.; 40. Repro.; 41. Resrch.; 42. Review.; 43. Secur.; 44. Serials; 45. Spec. col.; 46. Tech. srvs.; 47. Trustees/Bds.; 48. YA srvs.; 49. (other).

Guid.), 1967–68, MEd (Educ. Comms. and Tech.). **Orgs.:** HI Assn. of Sch. Libns.: Pres.; VP; various coms. ALA: AASL, Sch. Fac. Mtrls. Sel. Com. HI Assn. for Supvsn. and Curric. Dev.: Bd. HI LA. Other orgs. Delta Kappa Gamma Socty. Intl.: State Pres.; State Corresp. Secy.; State Com. Ch. Pi Lambda Theta: Pres.; VP; Com. Ch. Zonta Intl.: Various ofcs. **Pubns.:** Various reviews. **Activities:** 14-State Dept. of Educ.; 17, 24, 32; 75 **Addr.:** Multimedia Services Branch, 641 18th Ave., Honolulu, HI 96816.

J

Jackson, Adele M. (O. 15, 1918, N. Garden, VA) Assoc. Dir., South. Univ. Lib., 1976–, Actg. Dir., 1974–75, Assoc. Dir., 1970–74, Dir. of Tech. Prcs., 1966–70, Catlgr., 1955–66, Acq. Libn., 1953–55; Lib. Asst., MI State Lib., 1951–52; Dir., Negro Srvs. Branch, LA State Lib., 1948–51; Various other lib. positions, 1946–48. **Educ.:** VA State Coll., 1934–38, AB (Sec. Educ.); Univ. of MI, 1945–46, ABLS. **Orgs.:** ALA: Black Caucus (Exec. Bd., 1978–80); Awds. Com. (1979–82). SWLA. LA LA. LA Gvr.'s Conf. on Lib. and Info. Srvs. (1978). Various other orgs. Intl. Hosplty. Fndn. of Baton Rouge. Young Women's Christian Assn. Baton Rouge Arts and Hum. Cncl. LA's Intl. Educs. **Pubns.:** Comp., *Louisiana Documents–Peoples, Places, Publications* (1975). **Activities:** 1, 13; 17, 20, 29 **Addr.:** 2066 79th Ave., Baton Rouge, LA 70807.

Jackson, Arlyne (Mr. 22, 1944, New Haven, CT) Assoc. Libn., M.I.T., 1979–; Info. Spec., Arthur D. Little, Inc., 1977–79; Ref. Libn., Baker Lib., Harvard Bus. Sch., 1970–77; Biblgphr., Project Intrex, Barker Lib., M.I.T., 1970–70. **Educ.:** Howard Univ., 1962–66, BA (Fr.); Simmons Coll., 1969–70, SM (LS). **Orgs.:** ALA: RASD, Wilson Indexes Com. (1972–76). SLA. **Pubns.:** 1)"Information Sources on Business Writing and Speaking," *Harvard Bus. Review* (My., Je. 1976); 2)"Small Business Development and Management," *Harvard Bus. Review* (S., O. 1977); Contrib., *Intl. Encyc. Higher Educ.* (1977). **Activities:** 1, 12; 17, 39; 59, 77, 92 **Addr.:** Dewey Library, E53-180, MIT, Cambridge, MA 02139.

Jackson, Audrey Nabor (Jl. 10, 1926, New Orleans, LA) Retired; Sch. Libn. Grades K-12, Chaneyville Sch., 1955–81. **Educ.:** South. Univ., 1951, BA (Soc. Sci., LS), 1966, MEd (Admin., Supvsn.). **Orgs.:** ALA: AASL-Amer. Vocational Assn. Jt. Com. (1979–82); Black Caucus (Exec. Bd., 1978–). LA LA. SWLA. Natl. Educ. Assn. Futurma Soc. Clb. E. Baton Rouge Par. Assn. of Educs. LA Assn. of Educs. Various other orgs. **Activities:** 10; 17, 31, 49-All srvs.; 63, 66 **Addr.:** Rte. 3 Box 143, Zachary, LA 70791.

Jackson, Bernice McGee (Ja. 11, 1923, Warrenton, MO) Dir., Lawton Pub. Lib., 1975–; Cnty. Libn., San Patricio Cnty., TX 1973–75; Dir., Requirements and Distribution, US Air Force Film Lib. Ctr., 1959–69. **Educ.:** Dominican Coll., San Rafael, CA, 1949–51, BS (Chem.); Univ. of MO, 1970–71, MA (LS). **Orgs.:** ALA. SWLA. OK LA: Pub. Lib. Div. (Ch.-Elect, 1981). Altrusa: Dir. (1981). Bus. and Prof. Women. Lawton Women's Forum. **Honors:** Amer. Bus. Women, St. Louis, MO, Woman of the Year, 1966. **Activities:** 9; 17, 28, 34; 55, 56, 78 **Addr.:** P.O. Box 551, Lawton, OK 73502.

Jackson, Bryant H. (Ag. 2, 1923, Los Angeles, CA) Assoc. Univ. Libn., IL State Univ., 1982–, Assoc. Dir., 1965–81, Serial Catlgr., 1960–64; Head, Tech. Srvs., Pittsburg State Univ., KS, 1951–60; Libn., KS Wesleyan Univ., 1950–51; Tchr., Bishop HS, 1946–49. **Educ.:** Univ. of Redlands, 1941–45, BA (Hist.); Univ. of CA, Los Angeles, 1945–46 (Educ.); Univ. of South. CA, 1949–50, MSLS; Univ. of IL, 1962–69, (LS). **Orgs.:** ALA: ACRL. IL LA. IL ACRL. McLean Cnty. LA. AAUP. **Honors:** Phi Delta Kappa; Alpha Beta Alpha. **Activities:** 1; 17 **Addr.:** 303 Oakdale Ave., Normal, IL 61761.

Jackson, Clara O. (Jl. 5, 1915, New York, NY) Assoc. Prof., Sch. of Lib. Sci., Kent State Univ., 1963–; various other positions in education. **Educ.:** Univ. of MN, 1933–37, BS; Columbia Univ., 1957–58, MS, 1958, MSLS. **Orgs.:** ALA: Status of Women in Libnshp. (1979–80); ALSC, Newbery Awd. Com. (1980); AASL, Netwking. Com. (1979–80). Other orgs. Assoc. for Early Chldhd., Intl. Natl. Cncl. of Tchrs. of Eng. Other orgs. **Honors:** Phi Beta Kappa, 1937. **Pubns.:** *A Bibliography of Afro-American and Other American Minorities Represented in Library. . .* (1970); *Supplement* (1972); *Building a Children's Literature Collection* (1974); articles in various journals; reviews. **Activities:** 1, 11; 25, 26, 44; 63, 74, 95-Children's Literature. **Addr.:** Kent State University School of Library Science, Kent, OH 44242.

Jackson, Elisabeth Schell (Je. 8, 1940, New York, NY) Actg. Law Libn. and Dir. of Admin., Georgetown Univ. Law Ctr., 1977–; Law Libn., Antioch Sch. of Law, 1974–77, Clinical Law Biblgphr., 1973–74; Dir. of Tech. Srvs., US Ofc. of Econ. Oppt., 1966–73; Catlgr., Harvard Med. Lib., 1964–65. **Educ.:** Drew Univ., 1958–61; Howard Univ., 1960; Hofstra Univ., 1962–63, BA (Psy.); Simmons Coll., 1963–64, MS (LS). **Orgs.:** AALL: AV Com. (1975–76); Schol. Com. (1979–80). Law Libns. Socty. of Washington, DC: Rec. Secy. (1977–79); Const. Rev. Com. (Ch., 1979–81). SLA. **Activities:** 1, 4; 17, 20, 46; 77, 80, 92 **Addr.:** Georgetown University Law Library, 600 New Jersey Ave., N.W., Washington, DC 20001.

Jackson, Eugene B(ernard) (Je. 18, 1915, Frankfort, IN) Prof. of LS, Grad. Sch. of LS, Univ. of TX, Austin, 1971–; Prof. Consult. in Indus. Info. Systs., 1974–; Dir. of Lib. Srvs. and Info. Retrieval, Corp. HQ, IBM, 1965–71; Head, Lib. Dept., Gen. Motors Resrch. Labs., 1956–65; Chief, Div. of Resrch. Info., U.S. Natl. Adv. Com. for Aeronautics, 1952–56; Chief, Div. of Aeronautical Intelligence, 1950–52; Head, Resrch. Info. Sect., Ofc. of Quartermaster Gen., R & D Div., U.S. Army, 1949–50; various lib. positions, 1938–49. **Educ.:** Purdue Univ., 1933–37, BS (Sci.); Univ. of IL, 1937–38, BSLS, 1938–42, MALS. **Orgs.:** ALA: Lib. Tech. Proj. Adv. Com. (Ch.). ASIS: TX Chap. (Pres., 1974–75). SLA: Pres. (1961–62); Bd. of Dirs. (1953–56, 1960–63); Sci.-Tech. Div. (Ch., 1950–52). IFLA. Intl. Fed. for Documtn.: U.S. Natl. Com. for FID, Natl. Acad. of Sci. (Ch., 1970–72). Various other orgs. Engin. Index, Inc.: Pres. (1968–73). Amer. Inst. of Aerosp. Sci. **Pubns.:** Ed., *Special Librarianship: A New Reader* (1980); Jt. auth., *Industrial Information Systems* (1978); "Special Libraries in 1980 as Seen in 1961 and 1978," *Sci.-Tech. News* (Ap. 1979); Jt. auth., "The Industrial Special Library Universe," *Jnl. of ASIS* (My. 1977); Jt. auth., "Quantitative Measures of Library Service in the 'Fortune 500' Industrial Corporations," *Soc. Sci. Data File Dir.* (1976); numerous other articles, rpts., and reviews on lib. topics. **Activities:** 11, 12; 24, 26, 30; 64, 75, 91 **Addr.:** P.O. Box 7576, Austin, TX 78712.

Jackson, Frances O. (N. 2, 1932, Hilo, HI) Univ. Archvst., Univ. of HI, Manoa, 1968–; Ref. Libn., HI State Lib., 1968; Self-empl. Histn., 1963–68; State Parks Histn., State of HI, 1961–63. **Educ.:** Stanford Univ., 1951–54, BA (Anthro.); Univ. of HI, 1954–58, MA (Hist.); Univ. of CA, Berkeley, 1964–66, MLS; Univ. of Denver, 1969, Cert. (Arch. Admin.). **Orgs.:** HI LA: Coll. and Univ. Sect. (Ch., 1971–72). SAA. Hawaiian Hist. Socty.: Pres. (1971–74); Jnl. Ed. (1974–80). HI Musms. Assn.: Secy. (1971). **Pubns.:** *National Parks in Hawaii—50 Years, 1916–1966* (1966); Jt. Auth., *Old Honolulu. A Guide to Oahu's Historic Buildings* (1969); "Bombs in a National Park," *Hawaiian Jnl. Hist.* (1976); "Military Use of Haleakala National Park," *Hawaiian Jnl. Hist.* (1972); "University of Hawaii Archives," *HI LA Jnl.* (1969). **Activities:** 1, 2; 17, 41, 45; 55, 73, 86 **Addr.:** University of HI at Manoa Archives, Sinclair Library Rm. 305, 2425 Campus Rd., Honolulu, HI 96822.

Jackson, Harriett Davis (O. 21, 1928, Ripley, MS) Branch Libn., Memphis/Shelby Cnty. Lib., 1966–; Libn., Shelby Cnty. Schs., 1963–66; Libn., S. Tippah HS, 1960–63. **Educ.:** MS State Coll. for Women, 1945–49, BS (Educ.); Univ. of MS, 1960–63, MLS. **Orgs.:** ALA. SELA. TN LA. **Activities:** 9; 15, 17, 39 **Addr.:** Parkway Village Branch Library, 4655 Knight Arnold Rd., Memphis, TN 38118.

Jackson, Joseph Abram (O. 17, 1933, Brewton, AL) Prof., Dir. of Libs., Univ. of TN, Chattanooga, 1973–; Actg. Dean of Libs., Univ. of AL, 1969–72, Head of Sci. Lib., 1963–69, Catlgr., 1955–63. **Educ.:** Samford Univ., 1950–54, AB (Soc. Sci.); Peabody Coll., 1954–55, MALS. **Orgs.:** ALA. SELA. AL LA: Pres. (1970–71). Phi Delta Kappa. **Honors:** Beta Phi Mu. **Pubns.:** *Masonry in Alabama, a Sesquicennial History* (1970). **Activities:** 1; 17, 20, 24; 56, 91, 92 **Addr.:** 318 Arrow Dr., Signal Mountain, TN 37377.

Jackson, Leveda (McGlorie) (Jl. 1, 1934, Okmulgee, OK) Media Spec., Parkton Sch., 1979–; Instr., Fayetteville State Univ., 1979; Tchr., Brill Elem. Sch., 1978; Asst. Catlgr., Prairie View A. and M. Univ., 1974–78; Readrs. Srvs. Libn., Fisk Univ., 1972–74, Asst. Catlgr., 1965–72; Asst. Ref. Libn., FL A. and M. Univ., 1963–65. **Educ.:** Tuskegee Inst., 1952–57, BS (Bio. Sci.); Univ. of OK, 1962–63, MSLS; Prairie View A. and M. Univ., 1974–77, MEd (Elem. Educ.). **Orgs.:** NC State LA. Robeson Cnty. Media Specs. Assn. NC Educ. Assn. Delta Sigma Theta Sorority: Secy. (1979–81). **Honors:** Phi Delta Kappa. **Activities:** 10; 21, 32, 48 **Addr.:** 1641 Banbury Dr., Fayetteville, NC 28304.

Jackson, Lorraine Sano (Ag. 27, 1945, Boulder, CO) Lib. Dir., S. Brunswick Pub. Lib. 1978–; Libn., The Cmnty. Sch., 1977–78; Dir., Upper Saddle River Pub. Lib., 1970–76; Asst. Dir., New Milford Pub. Lib., 1968–70. **Educ.:** Univ. of CO, 1963–67, BA (Asian Stud.) Univ. of MI, 1967–68, MLS; various mgt. courses. **Orgs.:** ALA. NJ LA: Exec. Com., Corres. Secy.; Adult and YA Sect., VP, Pres.; Intl. Frdm. Com., Secy., VCh.; Lib. Dev. Com.; Conf. Com.; Ref. Sect.; Admn. Sect. Lib. PR Cncl.: Exec. Com. Mem.-at-Lg.; Treas. Bergen-Passaic LA: VP, Pres., various coms. Mid-Bergen Fed. Libs.: various coms. Lib. S. Middlesex: Pres. Appalachian Mt. Club: NY Chap., Secy. (1979–80). Amer. Canoe Assn. Town Hist. Socty. Bergen Cnty. Ofc. Aging: Educ. Com. **Activities:** 9; 15, 16, 17; 50, 74 **Addr.:** South Brunswick Public Library, Kingston Ln., Monmouth Jct., NJ 08852.

Jackson, M. Virginia (S. 23, 1923, Talladega Springs, AL) Asst. Prof., Ref. Biblgphr., Mervyn H. Sterne Lib., Univ. of AL, 1973–; Resrch. Chem., South. Resrch. Inst., 1948–72. **Educ.:** Univ. of AL, 1944–48, BS (Chem.), 1972–73, MLS. **Orgs.:** ALA: RASD/Machine-Assisted Ref. Sect., Educ. and Trng. Com. (1978–80). SELA: 1980 Conv. Com. (Prog. Ch., 1978–80). AL LA. Amer. Chem. Socty. **Pubns.:** *History of the Alabama Section of the American Chemical Society* (1977); *Genetic Engineering and the Recombinant DNA Controversy: a Historical Bibliography, 1973-1977* (1977); *Space shuttle–1981; a Bibliographic Guide* (1981). **Activities:** 1; 15, 39; 60, 75, 91 **Addr.:** 3120A Napoleon Ct., Birmingham, AL 35243.

Jackson, Margaret A. (Ag. 8, 1946, Lynn, MA) Head, Tech. Srvs., Univ. of MO, 1977–; Mgr., Blackwell N. Amer., 1975–77; Tech. Srvs. Libn., Harvard Univ. Libs., 1972–75; Supvsr., Proj. INTREX, MA Inst. Tech., 1970–72. **Educ.:** Salem State Coll., 1964–68, AB (Eng.); Simmons Coll., 1968–69, MSLS. **Orgs.:** ALA: RTSD/RS, Chief Col. Dev. Ofcrs. of Medium-sized Resrch. Libs. Discuss. Grp. (Ch., 1979–80). OCLC: Acq. Subsyst. Dev. Adv. Com. (1978–80). **Activities:** 1; 15, 17, 46 **Addr.:** 1017 Crestland Ave., Columbia, MO 65201.

Jackson, Mary E. (N. 20, 1949, Oshkosh, WI) Head, ILL Dept., Univ. of PA Libs., 1978–, Head, Serials Dept., 1977–78, Head, Rosengarten Rsv., 1974–77, Libn., Srchg. Dept., 1973–74; Jr. Catlgr., Drexel Univ. Lib., 1971–73. **Educ.:** Carroll Coll., 1967–71, BA (Soclgy., Grmn.); Drexel Univ., 1971–73, MSLS. **Orgs.:** Philadelphia Reg. ILL Grp.: Co-Ch., Co-Fndr. (1979–). ALA: RASD, ILL Com. 1980–82), ILL Discuss. Grp. (Co-Ch., 1981–); ACRL; RTSD/SS, Nom. Com. (1978). Christ Church, Philadelphia, PA. Beta Phi Mu: Sigma Chap., Nom. Com. (Ch., 1980), Exec. Com. (1981–). Univ. of PA Libs.: Libns. Asm. (Secy., 1975–77), Exec. Com. (1974–75). PALINET Org. Com. **Honors:** Alpha Kappa Delta, 1971. **Activities:** 1; 17, 34, 39; 61 **Addr.:** Interlibrary Loan Dept., University of PA Libraries, 3420 Walnut St., Philadelphia, PA 19104.

Jackson, Meliza W. (Ja. 15, 1950, Washington, DC) Patients' Libn., West. Psyt. Inst. and Clinic, 1980–; Sch. Libn., Tchr., Pittsburgh Pub. Schs., 1978–79; Libn., Carnegie Lib. of Pittsburgh, 1976–78. **Educ.:** RI Coll., 1970–72, BS, BA (Soclgy., Elem. Educ.); Univ. of Pittsburgh, 1975–76, MLS. **Orgs.:** ALA: ASCLA. State Lib. Inst. Libns.: Anl. Mtg., Plng. Com. (1981). Natl. Affiliation for Litcy. Advnc.: Grt. Pittsburgh Cncl. (VP, 1981). **Honors:** Bessie F. Anathan Fndn., Pittsburgh, Resrch. Grant. **Activities:** 5; 16, 21, 48; 63, 80, 89 **Addr.:** Western Psychiatric Institute and Clinic, 3811 O'Hara St., Pittsburgh, PA 15261.

Jackson, Miles Merrill (Ap. 28, 1929, Richmond, VA) Prof., Grad. Sch. of Lib. Std., Univ. of HI, 1975–; Assoc. Prof., SUNY, 1969–75; Dir. of Libs., Atlanta Univ., 1964–69; Asst. Supt. for Lib. Srvs., Dept. of Educ., Amer. Samoa, 1962–64; Lib. Dir., Hampton Inst., 1958–62; Ref. Libn., Free Lib. of Philadelphia, 1956–58. **Educ.:** VA Un. Univ., 1951–55, BA (Eng., Soc. Sci); Drexel Univ., 1955–56, MS (LS); Syracuse Univ., 1971–74, PhD (Comm.). **Orgs.:** ALA: Cncl. (1977–81). ASIS. AALS. HI LA. Other orgs. East-West Ctr. Alum. Assn.: Bd. of Dir., HI Chap., (1979–82). LSCA Adv. Cncl.: Ch. (1980–82). **Honors:** US State Dept., Fulbright Prof., Univ. of Tehran, 1968–69; Cncl. on Lib. Resrcs., Travel grant, 1978; Beta Phi Mu, Harold Lancour Awd., 1977; Ford Fndn., Non-western Travel Awd., 1969. **Pubns.:** *Comparative and International Librarianship,* (1970); *International Handbook of Contemporary Developments in Librarianship* (1981); *Bibliography of Negro History and Culture U. of Pittsburgh Press* (1969); various articles. **Activities:** 11; 75, 92, 93 **Addr.:** Graduate School of Library Studies, University of Hawaii at Manoa, Honolulu, HI 96822.

Jackson, Nancy G. (Ap. 23, 1943, Fort Wayne, IN) Head, Post-Cat. Sect., Desc. Cat. Div., Lib. of Congs., 1980–, Descr. Catlgr., 1967–80. **Educ.:** Concord Coll., 1961–65, BA (Eng.); Univ. of NC, 1965–67, MSLS; George Washington Univ., 1970–73, MA (Eng.). **Orgs.:** ALA. DC LA. LC Prof. Assn: *LC Prof. Assn. Nsltr.* (Jt. Ed., 1975); Nom. Com. (1977). **Honors:** Beta Phi Mu. **Activities:** 1, 4; 17, 20; 55 **Addr.:** 2401 Calvert St., N.W. Apt. 213, Washington, DC 20008.

Jackson, Paul T. (N. 21, 1935, Traverse City, MI) Owner, Pubshr., Consult., P. S. Enterprises, 1972–; Acct. Exec., Mgt. Recruiters, 1979–80; Sales and Mktg. Rep., Callender, II, 1977–79; Purchasing Agent, Tri-Cnty. Cmnty. Wkshp. and Trng. Ctr., 1977; Exec. Dir., Untd. Way, Canton, IL, 1975–77; Performing Arts Libn., Oakland Univ., Rochester, MI, 1968–72; Info./Mtrls. Mgr., Richmond Org., 1967–68; Actg. Head, Asst. Head, Rodgers and Hammerstein Arch. of Rec. Snd., Lincoln Ctr. Resrch. Lib., 1965–66; various positions as consult. **Educ.:** East. MI Univ., 1954–58, BS (Educ., Eng., Msc.); Colgate Rochester Dvnty. Sch., 1958–59 (Phil., Hist.); Univ. of MI, 1963–65, MA (Lib. and Info. Sci., Comm.); various crs., sems. **Orgs.:** Intl. Assn. of Snd. Arch. Msc. LA: Admin. Com. Assn. for Rec. Snd. Cols.: Pres.-Elect/VP. (1969–72); Corres. Secy. (1965–69); Contrib. Ed., *ARSC Jnl.* (1968–78); Legal Com. (Ch., 1980–). Rochester, MI Symph. Anchorage Symph. Orch. Peoria Breakdown. Phi Mu Alpha Sinfonia: Past Pres. **Pubns.:** *Interview Manual* (1981); *Collectors' Contact Guide* (1973–74; 1975); *Sound Search; Recording Occasional Papers* (1976); various articles, reviews, presentations. **Activities:** 12, 14-Consult. info., Org. Dev.; 24, 37, 41; 51, 57, 59 **Addr.:** P.S. Enterprises, 1627 Moody Ct., Peoria, IL 61604.

Special Subjects/Services: 50. Adult educ.; 51. Advert./Mktg.; 52. Aerosp.; 53. Agric.; 54. Area std.; 55. Arts/Hum.; 56. Autom.; 57. Bibl./Prtg.; 58. Bio. sci.; 59. Bus./Fin.; 60. Chem.; 61. Copyrt.; 62. Documtn.; 63. Educ.; 64. Engin.; 65. Env.; 66. Eth. grps.; 67. Film; 68. Food/Nutr.; 69. Geneal.; 70. Geo.; 71. Geol.; 72. Handcpd.; 73. Hist.; 74. Int. frdm.; 75. Info. sci.; 76. Insr.; 77. Law; 78. Legis.; 79. Math./Comp. sci.; 80. Med.; 81. Metals; 82. Nat. resrcs.; 83. Newsp.; 84. Nuc. sci.; 85. Oral hist.; 86. Petr./Energy; 87. Pharm.; 88. Phys./Astr./Math.; 89. Readg.; 90. Relig.; 91. Sci./Tech.; 92. Soc. sci.; 93. Telecom.; 94. Transp.; 95. (other).

Jackson, Rebecca Jane (Jl. 29, 1933, Erie, PA) Owner-Mgr., Info. Profs., 1978–, Freelnc., 1976–78; Acq. Libn., Univ. of CO, Denver, 1975–76; Supvsr. of Tech. Srvs. Metro. State Coll., 1968–75; Med. and Nursing Libn., Mercy Hosp., Denver, 1963–68; Libn., Lord Mfr. Co., Erie, PA, 1961–63; Resrch. Libn., Erie Resistor Corp., 1959–60; Jr. and Sr. High Libn., Lewistown (PA) Sch. Dist., 1957–59. **Educ.:** PA State Univ., 1951–53, 1955–57, BA (Liberal Arts, Hist.); Univ. of Denver, 1964–67, MLS. **Orgs.:** SLA: Place. Com. (Ch., 1978–); Anl. Conf. Local Rep. (1976); Sci.-Tech. Div. Nom. Com. (1976–77). CO LA. ALA. Mt.-Plains LA. Various other orgs. Amer. Mgt. Assn. **Pubns.:** "The Metropolitan State College Library," *The Columbine* (Ja.-F. 1971). **Activities:** 12, 14-Info. broker-consult.; 15, 17, 20; 56, 59, 91 **Addr.:** Information Professionals, 800 Washington St., No. 209, Denver, CO 80203.

Jackson, Richard H. (F. 15, 1936, New Orleans, LA) Head, Americana Col., Msc. Div., New York Pub. Lib., 1965–. **Educ.:** Loyola Univ., New Orleans, 1955–58, BMSc (Organ); Tulane Univ., 1959–62, MA (Msclgy.); Pratt Inst., 1965–68, MLS. **Orgs.:** Msc. LA. Sonneck Socty. Amer. Musicological Socty. Amer. Msc. Ctr. Natl. Sheet Msc. Socty. **Pubns.:** *United States Music: Sources of Bibliography and Collective Biography* (1973); *U.S. Bicentennail Music 1* (1977); various other articles on msc. **Activities:** 9, 14-Resrch. lib.; 15, 23, 39; 95-Msc. **Addr.:** The New York Public Library at Lincoln Center, New York, NY 10023.

Jackson, Ruth L(illian) (Whitlock) (Mr. 9, 1916, Indianapolis, IN) Auth., Freelnc. Indxr., 1971–; Ref. Libn., Mt. Pleasant Pub. Lib., Pleasantville, NY, 1969–71; Biblgphr. on Spec. Projs. (part-time), Engin. Soctys. Lib., NYC, 1966–68, Asst. Libn., Ctrl. Ofc. Lib., Ford Motor Co., 1964–65; Libn., Engin. Staff Lib., GM Tech. Ctr., 1959–64; Ref. Libn., Bur. of Ships Tech. Lib., U.S. Navy, 1950–52; Descr. Catlgr., Army Med. Lib., U.S. Army, 1948–50; Various other lib. positions, 1937–48. **Educ.:** Univ. of IL, 1933–37, BA with hons. (Grmn.), 1937–38, BSLS, 1938–41, MALS; State of NY, 1970, Pub. Libns. Prof. Cert. **Orgs.:** SLA: Prof. Consults. Com. (1960–64); TX Chap., Pubns. Com. (1977), Constn. and Bylaws Com. (1974–75). ALA. Protestant Episcopal Church. **Pubns.:** Jt. auth., *Industrial Information Systems* (1978); *Author Headings for the Official Publications of the State of Wisconsin* (1954); Jt. auth., "Characterising the Special Library Universe," *Jnl. of ASIS* (Ja. 1980); Jt. auth., "The Personnel, Material, and Financial Resources of the Library Systems of 311 Industrial Corporations," ERIC Rpt. (1978); Jt. auth., "The Industrial Special Library Universe," *Jnl. of ASIS* (1977); various other articles and rpts. **Activities:** 9, 12; 20, 30, 39; 64, 90, 91 **Addr.:** 8512 Silver Ridge, Austin, TX 78759.

Jackson, Ruth Moore (S. 27, 1938, Potecasi, NC) Assoc. Prof. and Coord., LS Prog., VA State Univ., 1976–, Interim Ch., Dept. of LS and Educ. Media, 1978–79, Asst. Prof. and Coord., LS Pros., 1976–77; Visit. Lectr., Grad. Lib. Sch., IN Univ., 1971–72; Visit. Catlgr., Monroe Cnty. Pub. Lib., Bloomington, IN, 1971; Ref. Libn., VA State Univ., 1968–70, Actg. Ref. Libn., 1966–67, Asst. Educ. Libn., 1964–65. **Educ.:** Hampton Inst., Hampton, VA, 1956–60, BS (Bus.); Atlanta Univ., 1964–65, MSLS; IN Univ., 1967–71, 1975–76, PhD (LS). **Orgs.:** ALA: ACRL. AECT. ASIS. WHCOLIS. Various other orgs. Amer. Mgt. Assn. Boy Scouts of Amer. Kappa Delta Pi. Beta Phi Mu. **Pubns.:** Jt. auth., "100 Years of Personnel Concerns; Problems and Perspectives," *A Century of Service for Librarianship in the U.S. and Canada* (1976), "Legislative Support for Library Services in Virginia" *Libraries in the Political Process* (1981). **Activities:** 14-acad. dept.; 17, 26, 41; 62, 95-Lib. mgt. **Addr.:** Box 35, Department of Library Science and Educational Media, Virginia State University, Petersburg, VA 23803.

Jackson, Susan Kathryn (S. 29, 1949, Ramsgate, Kent, Eng.) Tech. Libn., Amer. Can Co., Princeton Resrch. Ctr., 1978–; Sr. Lit. Sci., Merck, Sharp and Dohme, Rahway, NJ, 1974–78; Lit. Resrch., Lubrication Lab., Imperial Coll., London, 1974; Asst. Grp. Tech. Info. Ofcr., Brit. Aluminium, Gerrards Cross, Bucks, 1972–73. **Educ.:** Imperial Coll., London, 1968–71, BS (Chem.); City Univ., London, 1971–72, MS (Info. Sci.). **Orgs.:** Inst. of Info. Scis. ASIS. SLA. **Pubns.:** "Online Retrieval of Chemical Patent Information," *Jnl. Chem. Info. Comp. Sci.* (1977); "Format Layout and Bibliographic Preservation of Microforms," *NRCd Bltn.* (1973). **Activities:** 12; 17, 39, 46; 60, 75, 91 **Addr.:** American Can Co., Princeton Research Center, P.O. Box 50, Princeton, NJ 08540.

Jackson, W(illis) Carl (My. 20, 1923, Beverly, MA) Dean of Univ. Libs., IN Univ., 1973–; Dir. of Libs., PA State Univ., 1965–72; Assoc. Dir. of Libs., Univ. of CO, 1963–65; Chief Acq. Libn., Univ. of MN, 1957–63; Head, Acq. Dept., Univ. of IA, 1955–57, Head, Order Dept., 1954–55; Asst. Order Libn., Univ. of TN, Knoxville, 1952–54. **Educ.:** FL State Univ., 1948–51, AB (Hist.); 1951–52, MA (LS); Certs. from inst., workshops, etc. **Orgs.:** ALA: Cncl.; RTSD, Pres. (1969–70); Bd. of Dir., ACRL, Bd. of Dir. (1965–70). Midwest Reg. Lib. Network: Bd. of Dir., Exec. Com. (1975–). ARL: Ch., Fed. Resrcs. Com. Ctr. for Resrch. Libs.: Cncl. (1973–). SALALM. Other orgs. AAUP: Del. to Anl. Conf. (1956, 1959, 1961). Grolier Club. US Power Squadron: Exec. Ofcr., Salt Creek Squadron. Bloomington Yacht Club: Bd. of Gvrs. Other orgs. **Honors:** PA LA, Disting. Srv. Awd., 1972; Gvr. of KY, KY Colonel, 1979; FL State Univ., Carl Jackson Schol., 1979; Beta Phi Mu, 1957. **Pubns.:** Various articles. **Activities:** 1; 15, 17, 24; 56, 57, 74†

Jackson, William Vernon (My. 26, 1926, Chicago, IL) Prof., LS, Univ. of TX (Austin), 1976– Assoc. Prof., Span., Portuguese, Vanderbilt Univ., 1970–76; Prof., LS, George Peabody Coll., 1970–76; Prof., LS, Univ. of Pittsburgh, 1966–70; Assoc. Prof., Span., Portuguese, Univ. of WI, 1963–65; Assoc. Prof., LS, Univ. of IL, 1958–62, Asst. Prof., LS, 1952–58; Spec. Rcrt., Lib. of Congs., 1951–52. **Educ.:** Northwest. Univ., 1945, BA, summa cum laude,; Harvard Univ., 1948, MA; Univ. of IL, 1951, MS (LS); Harvard Univ., 1952, PhD. **Orgs.:** ALA: Endow. Funds Trustee (1977–); IRRT (Ch., 1965–66); various coms. AALS. SALAM: Pres. (1977–78); various coms. Various other orgs. Beta Phi Mu: Pres. (1955–56). **Honors:** Phi Beta Kappa; Sigma Delta Pi; Phi Lambda Beta. **Pubns.:** *Catalog of Brazilian Acquisitions of Library of Congress, 1964–74* (1977); *Steps Toward the Future Development of a National Plan for Library Services in Colombia* (1971); *Resources of Research Libraries* (1969); *The National Textbook Program and Libraries in Brazil* (1967); *Library Guide for Brazilian Studies* (1964); many other pubns. **Activities:** 1; 26; 54, 55, 63 **Addr.:** School of Library Science, Univ. of Texas, Box 7576, Austin, TX 78712.

Jacob, Louis A. (Ap. 25, 1927, Cleveland, OH) Head, South. Asia Sect., Asian Div., Lib. of Congs., 1972–; Head, Asian Ref. Dept., Univ. of PA, 1968–72; Biblgphr. for S. Asia, Univ. of CA, Berkeley, 1959–68. **Educ.:** Case West. Rsv. Univ., 1952–55, AB (Soc. Sci.); Univ. of CA, Berkeley, 1955–61, MA, MLS (S. Asian Std.). Assn. for Asian Std.: Adv. Com., Bibl. of Asian Std. (Ch., 1971–). **Addr.:** Southern Asian Section, Asian Division, Library of Congress, Washington, DC 20540.

Jacobius, Arnold J. (Ag. 2, 1916, Augsburg, Germany) Exec. Dir., Bibl. Consult., Academia Bk. Exhibits, 1979–, Field Dir., Overseas Ofc., Lib. of Congs., Wiesbaden, Germany, 1966–79, Head, Aerospace Med. Bibl. Proj., 1959–66, Biblgphr., Sci. Tech. Div., 1953–59. **Educ.:** Univ. of Milano and Pavia, Columbia Univ., 1934–42, BS (Chem.); NY Univ., Columbia Univ., 1947–55, MA (Grmn.), PhD (Grmn.), MSLS; Lib. of Congs., 1951–52, Intern Prog. **Orgs.:** ALA. Intl. Astronautics Fed. **Honors:** Lib. of Congs., Awd. for Superior Srv., 1979; NY Univ., Fndrs. Day Achvmt. Awd., 1956. **Pubns.:** Ed., *Aerospace Medicine and Biology Bibliography* (1956–66); *Carl Zuckmayer: Eine Bibliographie* (1971); "Chemistry in the 15th Edition of Dewey," *Jnl. of Cat. and Class.* (Fall 1951); "Cataloging the Private Library of Adolf Hitler," *LC Info. Bltn.* (Ap. 27, 1953); Abs. in *Aerospace Med.* (1958–66). **Activities:** 1; 15, 17, 24; 51, 57, 91 **Addr.:** 4036 Poplar St., Fairfax, VA 22036.

Jacobs, Alma S. (N. 21, 1916, Lewistown, MT) State Libn., MT State Lib., 1973–; Chief Libn., Great Falls Pub. Lib., 1954–73, Cat. Libn., 1946–54. **Educ.:** Talladega Coll., 1934–38, BA (Soclgy.); Columbia Univ., 1941–42, MSLS. **Orgs.:** Pac. NW LA: Pres. (1957). MT LA: Pres. (1960). ALA: Exec. Bd. (1964–68). Cmnty. Chest. Young Women's Christ. Assn.: Exec. Bd. (1959–61). MT Adv. Com. to the U.S. Cvl. Rights Comsn. Gvrs. Com. on Status of Women. **Honors:** MT State Univ., Doctor of Letters, 1962; Mt. Holyoke, S. Hadley, MA, Doctor of Humane Letters, 1968; MT LA, Libn. of the Yr., 1968. **Pubns.:** *The Negro in Montana, 1800–1945, a Selective Bibliography* (1970); "What Is the Role of the Small Public Librarian in the Political Process," *OK Libn.* (Je. 1954); "The Small Public Library and Service to Labor," *MN Libs.* (S. 1954); "Problems of Small and Medium-Sized Public Libraries in Adult Education Programs," *PNLA Qtly.* (Jl. 1964); "Montana Chooses Federations of Libraries," *Lib. Trends* (Ja. 1965). **Activities:** 9, 13; 17, 19, 34; 50, 55, 89 **Addr.:** 1205 Highland, Helena, MT 59601.

Jacobs, Geraldine M. (Mr. 4, 1925, Preston, ID) Lib. Dir., Madison Lib. Dist., 1961–; HS Libn., Madison HS (Rexburg, ID), 1953–58. **Educ.:** Univ. of ID, 1943–47, BA (Eng.); 1950–51 (LS). **Orgs.:** ID LA: Pres. (1979–80); Pub. Lib. Div., Pres. (1954–55). Pacific N.W. LA. Rexburg Fed. Women's Club: Pres. **Honors:** ID LA, Outstan. Libn. of Yr., 1978. **Addr.:** Madison Library District, 73 N. Center, Rexburg, ID 83440.

Jacobs, Roger F. (Ja. 1, 1938, Detroit, MI) Libn., Supreme Ct. of the U.S., 1978–; Law Libn., Prof., Law, South. IL Univ., 1973–77; Law Libn., Prof., Law, Univ. of Windsor, 1967–73; Law Libn., Univ. of Detroit, 1962–67. **Educ.:** Univ. of Detroit, 1959–62, AB (Hist.); Univ. of MI, 1962–64, AMLS; Univ. of Detroit, 1964–70, JD. **Orgs.:** AALL: Pres. (1981–82). Can. ALL: Pres. (1971–73). Mid-Amer. Assn. of Law Libs.: Pres. (1974–75). **Honors:** South. IL Univ. Sch. of Law, Sr. Class Awd., 1976; Univ. of MI Sch. of LS, Disting. Alum., 1980. **Pubns.:** Jt. auth., *Illinois Legal Resource* (1977); ed., *Memorials of Supreme Court Justices* (1981). **Activities:** 4; 17; 77 **Addr.:** Supreme Court of the U.S., Washington, DC 20543.

Jacobsen, Edward T. (Jl. 22, 1922, Chicago, IL) Dir. of Libs., Winona State Univ., 1953–; Ref. Libn. & Asst. Prof., LS, SD State Coll., 1951–53. **Educ.:** Ripon Coll., 1940–43, 1946, AB (Hist.); Univ. of OK, 1947–49, MA (Hist.); Univ. of WI, 1949–51, MA (LS); Univ. of Chicago, 1960–61, Grad. Work. **Orgs.:** ALA. MN LA: Exec. Bd. (1968–70); Plng. & Dev. Com. (1970–73). Southeast. Libs. Coop.: Bd. (1974–80), Pres. (1979–80). Minitex: Adv. Bd. (1972–73). MN Dept. of Educ.: Adv. Cncl. on Lib. Srv. (1973–76). **Activities:** 1; 15, 17, 23; 63, 77, 91 **Addr.:** 1767 W. Mark, Winona, MN 55987.

Jacobsen, LaVonne (S. 29, 1946, St. Paul, NE) Ref. and Map Libn. San Francisco State Univ. Lib., 1972–, **Educ.:** Univ. of WA, 1964–68, BA (Anthro.), 1968–70, MA (Anthro.); Univ. of OR, 1971–72, MLS. **Orgs.:** West. Assn. Map Libns.: Secy. (1974–75); Nom. Com. SLA: San Francisco Bay Area Chap., Educ. Com. (1978–80). Women Lib. Workers: Bay Area Chap. Coord. (1975–77). **Pubns.:** "Map Resources in San Francisco," *West. Assn. Map Libns. Bltn.* (Spr. 1975). **Activities:** 1; 29, 31, 39; 54, 70, 92 **Addr.:** San Francisco State University Library, San Francisco, CA 94132.

Jacobson, Betty L. (D. 20, 1926, St. Louis, MO) Libn., Univ. Club, 1979–; Docmlst., Mnstry. Éduc. (Gabon), 1977–78; Consult. Libn., W. R. Grace Co., 1976–77; Head, Pub. Srv., Univ. CO, 1971–74. **Educ.:** Univ. CO, 1965–68, BA (Amer. Stud.) Univ. Denver, 1969–71, MA (LS) Troy St. Univ., 1974–75, MPA. **Orgs.:** SLA.: DC Chap. ALA. Smithsonian Assoc. AAUW. **Pubns.:** "Women's Work: A job description," *Lib. Jnl.* (v. 96, 1971); "Microfiche: Friend or Foe," *Amer. Lib.* (Jl. 1971); "Bell & Howell Briefcase Reader," *Micro Review* (v. 2, 1973). **Activities:** 1, 12; 36, 41; 59 **Addr.:** University Club, 1135 16th St. N.W., Washington, DC 20036.

Jacobson, Dena F. (S. 5, 1916, Syracuse, NY) Libn., Msc. Libn., Cur., Hailperin Col. of Judaica, Duquesne Univ. Lib., 1967–; Ref. Libn., Msc. Div., Carnegie Lib. of Pittsburgh, 1945–67; Ref. Libn., Msc. and Art Div., Syracuse Pub. Lib. 1944–45. **Educ.:** Syracuse Univ., 1933–36, BMus (Msc., Piano), 1936–37 (P.G. Msc.), 1943–44, BS (LS); NY State, 1943, Cert. (Sch. Msc. Tchr.). **Orgs.:** Msc. LA. Intl. Assn. of Msc. Libs. AJL. Sigma Alpha Iota Alum.: Pittsburgh Chap. (Pres., 1979–). Hadassah. **Addr.:** Duquesne University Library, Reference Dept., Pittsburgh, PA 15219.

Jacobson, Lillian E. (Ag. 23, 1919, Fingal, ND) Retired, 1980–; Lib. Dir., Valley City State Coll., 1965–80, Campus Sch. Libn., 1956–80; Circ. Libn., North. IL State Coll., 1951–56. **Educ.:** Valley City State Tchrs. Coll., 1936–40, BA (Eng.); Univ. of Denver, 1945–47, BS (LS). **Orgs.:** ALA. ND LA. NDEA. Natl. Educ. Assn. **Honors:** Delta Kappa Gamma. **Activities:** 1; 17 **Addr.:** 252 2nd Ave. S.W., Valley City, ND 58072.

Jacobson, Nancy Crown (F. 9, 1931, Los Angeles, CA) Dir., Meml. Hall Lib., Andover, MA, 1974–, Asst. Dir., 1971–74; Libn., W. Elem. Sch., 1967–71; Libn., E. Jr. HS, 1966–67. **Educ.:** Univ. of CA, Berkeley, 1949–52, AB (Hist., Pol. Sci.); Simmons Coll., 1966–70, MLS. **Orgs.:** MA LA: Bd. (1974–). WHCOLIS. New Eng. LA. ALA. Andover Hist. Socty. Leag. of Women Voters. **Pubns.:** "Junior High School Reading/Media Use Survey" indexed in ERIC (1970). **Addr.:** Memorial Hall Library, Elm Sq., Andover, MA 01810.

Jacobstein, J. Myron (J. 27, 1920, Detroit, MI) Prof. of Law, Law Libn., Stanford Univ., 1963–; Prof. of Law, Law Libn. Univ. of CO, 1959–63; Assoc. Law Libn., Columbia Univ., 1955–59; Asst. Law Libn., Univ. of IL, 1952–55. **Educ.:** Wayne State Univ. 1942–46, BA (Econ.); Columbia Univ., 1949–50, MLS; IL Inst. of Tech., Chicago-Kent Coll. of Law, 1952–55, JD (Law). **Orgs.:** AALL: Pres. (1978–79). ALA. CA LA. Amer. Bar Assn. Amer. Socty. of Intl. Law. **Pubns.:** *Fundamentals of Legal Research* (1981); Jt.-ed., *Law Books in Print* (1976). **Activities:** 1; 17; 61, 63, 77 **Addr.:** Law Library, Stanford University, Stanford, CA 94305.

Jacque, Sylvie N. (Ja. 13, 1953, Paris, France) Assoc. Libn., Untd. Nations, Translation Div., 1980–; Asst. Libn., Untd. Nations Lib., 1978–80; Documtn. Ctr. Asst., Untd. Nations Ctr. on Transnatl. Corps., 1976–78. **Educ.:** Univ. of Paris, Nanterre, 1970–73, BA (Eng.), 1973–74, MA (Eng.); Univ. of MI, 1975, MLS. **Orgs.:** SLA. **Addr.:** United Nations Headquarters, Rm. 1262, New York, NY 10017.

Jaeger, James Gordon (Je. 26, 1941, Morrison, IL) Head, Nonfiction Srvs., Joliet Pub. Lib., 1980–; Pub. Srvs. Libn., Kankakee (IL) Cmnty. Coll., 1979–80; Head Libn., Kankakee Pub. Lib., 1977–79; Head Libn., Mitchell Pub. Lib., Hillsdale, MI, 1970–77; Reader's Adv., Monroe Cnty. (MI) Lib. Syst., 1969–70; Ref. Libn., Catlgr., Enoch Pratt Free Lib., 1964–68. **Educ.:** Blackburn Coll., Carlinville, IL, 1959–63, BA (Hist.); IN Univ., 1963–64, MLS; MI State Univ., 1976, Cert. (Fncl. Mgt. and Plng.). **Orgs.:** ALA. IL LA. MI LA: Pubcty. Com. (1976–77); Systs. RT (Secy., 1976–77). **Pubns.:** Jt.-ed., *Michigan Materials: Books and Other Media in the Monroe County Library System* (1971). **Activities:** 1, 9; 15, 17, 20; 55, 59, 92 **Addr.:** 1657 E. River St., Kankakee, IL 60961.

Jaeger, Sally J. (N. 23, 1935, Bound Brook, NJ) Head Libn., W. Flint Branch, Flint Pub. Lib., 1971–, Librn., Downtown Branch, 1969–71. **Educ.:** Univ. of MI (Flint), 1967, AB (Hist.); Univ. of MI, 1967–69, AMLS; Univ. of MI, 1971–77, AM (Hist.). **Orgs.:** Flint Area LA: Secy., VP, Pres., Flint Pub. Lib. Staff Assn.: VP, Pres., Schol. Com. MI LA: Int. frdm. Com. ALA. Natl.

PROFESSIONAL ACTIVITIES: Institutions: 1. Acad. lib.; 2. Arch.; 3. Assn.; 4. Fed./Gvt. lib.; 5. Inst. lib.; 6. Mfr./Suppl.; 7. Milit. lib.; 8. Musm.; 9. Pub. lib.; 10. Sch. lib.; 11. Sch. of lib. sci.; 12. Spec. lib.; 13. State lib.; 14. (other). **Functions/Activities:** 15. Acq./Col. dev.; 16. Adult srvs.; 17. Admin.; 18. Apprais.; 19. Archit./Bldgs.; 20. Cat./Class.; 21. Chld. srvs.; 22. Circ.; 23. Cons./Pres.; 24. Consult.; 25. Cont. ed.; 26. Educ. lib. sci.; 27. Ext. srvs.; 28. Fund/Grants; 29. Gvt. pubs.; 30. Indx./Abs.; 31. Instr. lib. use; 32. Media srvs.; 33. Micro.; 34. Netwks./Coop.; 35. Persnl.; 36. PR; 37. Publshg.; 38. Recs. mgt.; 39. Ref. srvs.; 40. Repro.; 41. Resrch.; 42. Review.; 43. Secur.; 44. Serials; 45. Spec. col.; 46. Tech. srvs.; 47. Trustees/Bds.; 48. YA srvs.; 49. (other).

Libns. Assn.: MI Chap., Secy. Univ. Mich Alum. Assn.: Secy. (1977–78); VP (1978–79); Pres. (1979–80). Altrusa Intl.: Treas. (1978–79). **Activities:** 9; 25, 36, 39; 65, 90, 92 **Addr.:** 715 S. Franklin, Flint, MI 48503.

Jaeggli, Evelyn K. (Mr. 27, 1923, San Benito, TX) Dir., Butt-Holdsworth Meml. Lib., 1971–; Reg. Libn., Tulsa City-Cnty. Lib., 1971, Branch Libn., 1966–71. **Educ.:** Mex. City Coll., 1946–48, BA (Latin Amer. Std.); Univ. of OK, 1968–69, MLS. **Orgs.:** TX LA: Dist. 10 (Pres., 1972–75); Cont. Educ. Com. (1977–78); Legis. Com. (1979–81). Zonta Intl. Leag. of Women Voters. **Activities:** 9; 15, 16, 17 **Addr.:** 505 Water St., Kerrville, TX 78028.

Jaffarian, Sara (S. 7, 1915, Haverhill, MA) Lib. Consult., 1956–; Coord. of Instr. Mtrls. and Srvs., Lexington (MA) Pub. Schs., 1961–; Dir. of Libs., Seattle Pub. Schs., 1960–61; Dir. of Libs., Greensboro (NC) Pub. Schs., 1953–60; Libn., Quincy (MA) Pub. Schs., 1943–53; Visit. Instr., Sum. Sessions, various grad. lib. schs., 1956–. **Educ.:** Bates Coll., 1933–37, BA (Hist., Gvt.); Simmons Coll., 1943–47, BSLS; Boston Univ., 1953–57, MEd (AV Educ.); Harvard Univ., 1962–70, Educ. Crs.; Univ. of South. CA, 1968, Info. Sci. **Orgs.:** ALA: Cncl. (1962–66); Natl. Lib. Week Com. (Ch., 1960); AASL (Dir., 1954–56; Secy., 1956–57). New Eng. LA: Dir. (1962–64); various com. chs. MA Sch. Lib. Assn.: Pres. (1964–66). New Eng. Sch. Lib. Assn.: VP-Pres. Elect (1952–53); various com. chs. (1947–53). Various other orgs. MA Tchrs. Assn. Natl. Educ. Assn. Ord. of East. Star. Assn. for Supvsn. and Curric. Dev. Various other orgs. **Honors:** Encyc. Britannica, Sch. Lib. Awd., 1964; Phi Delta Kappa; Pi Lambda Theta; Bates Key. **Pubns.:** Ed., *Every School Needs a Library* (1953); "The Library-centered School" in *Tchg. in a World of Change* (1966); "The Library Is a Media Center" in *Current Trends in Educ.* (1971); various articles and ed. of issues in lib. jnls. (1943–77); reviews. **Activities:** 10, 11; 17, 24, 32; 63 **Addr.:** 58 Bateman St., Haverhill, MA 01830.

Jaffe, Lawrence L. (Ap. 26, 1947, Harrisburg, PA) Libn., Downingtown Sch. Dist., 1972–; Libn., Wissahickon Sch. Dist., 1970–72. **Educ.:** Millersville State, 1967–70, BS (LS); Villanova Univ., 1972–74, MLS; 1978–80, Lib. Supervisory Cert. **Orgs.:** PA Sch. Libns. Assn.: Promos. Com. (1979–). PA LA. PA Citizens for Better Libs. Natl. Educ. Assn. PA State Educ. Assn. **Activities:** 10 **Addr.:** 577 Gravel Pike, Gratersford, PA 19426.

Jaffe, Steven (S. 7, 1928, New York, NY) Libn., Consolidated Edison Co., 1970–; Chief Libn., US Nvl. Appld. Sci. Lab., 1960–70; Libn., Pollack Lib., Yeshiva Univ., 1952–60. **Educ.:** Yeshiva Coll., 1948–52, BA (Hist.); Columbia Univ., 1952–53, MA (European Hist.), 1956–58, MLS. **Orgs.:** SLA: Pub. Util. Div. (Ch., 1977–78; Secy.-Treas., 1975–76); Milit. Libns. Div. (Secy., 1968). US Nvl. Inst. Photographic Socty. of Amer. Edison Camera Club. **Activities:** 1, 12; 17, 24, 39; 64, 65, 91 **Addr.:** Consolidated Edison Co., Rm. 1650–S, Technical Library, 4 Irving Pl., New York, NY 10003.

Jaffee, Cyrisse (O. 2, 1953, New York, NY) Asst. Ed., Chld. Bks., Addison-Wesley Publshg. Co., 1980–; YA Libn., Morse Inst. Pub. Lib., 1979–80; Asst. Prof., Salem State Coll., 1979; Lib. Consult., Jr. Leag. of Boston, 1978; Catlgr., YA Libn., Parlin Meml. Lib., 1976–79; Mobile Branch Libn., Bennett Pub. Lib., 1974–76; Chld. Libn., Somerville Pub. Lib., 1974–75; various consult. positions. **Educ.:** SUNY, Binghamton, 1970–73, BA (Eng. Lit., Hist., Medvl. Std.); 1973, Cert. (Medvl. Std.); Simmons Coll., 1974–75, MLS with hons. **Orgs.:** ALA. New Eng. LA. Women Lib. Workers. YA Bk. Review Grp. Women's Writing Gld. Natl. Org. of Women. **Honors:** Phi Beta Kappa, 1973; Beta Phi Mu, 1975. **Pubns.:** "More Pain than Pleasure: Teen Romances," *Sch. Lib. Jnl.* (Ja. 1979); "Strange Brew: A Rock Music Bibliography," *Sch. Lib. Jnl.* (Ag. 1980); "Chelsea Warning," *Wilson Lib. Bltn.* (S. 1978), "Don't Agonize, Organize! And Other Thoughts on Libraries Today," *Kliatt Bk. Guide* (My. 1979); various bk. reviews, wkshps. **Activities:** 6; 21, 37, 48; 55, 74 **Addr.:** Assistant Editor, Children's Books/Addison-Wesley, Reading, MA 01867.

Jagoe, Katherine Pearson (Kippy) (Mr. 15, 1944, Denton, TX) Head, TX and Dallas Hist. and Arch. Div., Dallas Pub. Lib., 1979–, Libn., Col. Dev. and Resrc. Sharing, Northeast TX Lib. Syst., 1974–79; Archvst., Jagoe Abs. Co., 1972–74; Asst. Ref. Libn., TX Christ. Univ., 1966–72. **Educ.:** N. TX State Univ., 1962–66, BA hons. (Lib. Srv.), 1972–74, MLS; various crs., sems. **Orgs.:** ALA: JMRT, Anl. Conf. Soc. (Ch., 1979). TX LA: Conf. Plng. Com. (1967); JMRT (Vice-ch., 1977–78; Ch., 1978–79); Arch. RT (Ch., 1980–81); Int. Frdm. Pre-conf. (Discuss. Leader, 1979). Socty. of Southwest Archvsts.: Mem. Com. (1980–81). various org. Chld. of the Amer. Revolution: TX Socty. (State Pres., 1961–62); Natl. Socty. (Corres. Secy., 1962–63). Alpha Beta Alpha: Treas. (1965). Alpha Lambda Sigma: Secy. (1965–66); Pres. (1972–73). N. TX State Univ., Sch. of Lib. and Info. Sci. Alum. Socty. various org. **Honors:** Beta Phi Mu; TX LA, Outstan. New Libn. of TX, 1979; Press Club of Dallas, Headliner, 1980, 1981; TX Hist. Comsn., Cert. of Cmdn. for Disting. Srv. in the Fld. of Hist. Prsrvn., 1980. **Pubns.:** Jt. Ed., *Texas History Award—Winning Essays* (1977); historical articles, *Denton Rec.–Chronicle* (Mr. 16 and Ag. 6, 1975); "Texas on Film," *Film: a Dallas Public Library Perspective* (1981); Interviewer, "Fred H. Minor," (N. TX State Univ. Oral Hist. Col.) (1973). **Activities:** 2, 9; 17, 24, 36; 56, 83, 85 **Addr.:** 13340 Kit Ln., #B–12, Dallas, TX 75240.

Jagusch, Sybille A. (F. 16, 1941, Elbing, Germany) Chld. Lit. Spec., Baltimore Cnty. Pub. Lib., 1969–80. **Educ.:** Pädagogische Hochschule, Bielefeld, Fed. Republic of Germany, 1960–63, BA (Educ.); Univ. of MD, 1968–69, MLS. **Orgs.:** ALA: ALSC, Caldecott Com. (1980–81), H.C. Andersen Jury, (US Rep., 1979–81), Sel. of Frgn. Chld. Bks. (1974–78), Intl. Rel. Com. (1973–78), Batchelder Awds. Com. (1971–73); ACRL (1981–). Frnds. of IBBY. Intl. Resrch. Socty. for Chld. Lit.: (Secy., 1978–). **Pubns.:** "Bibliotheksdienste für das zweisprachige Kind in den USA. Ein historischer Abriss," *Bücher für ausländische Kinder* (1979); "The Hans Christian Andersen Awards," *Top of the News* (Sum. 1980); Assoc. Ed., *Phaedrus, An Intl. Jnl. of Chld. Lit. Resrch.* (1978–). **Activities:** 9; 21, 45 **Addr.:** 3 Chesham Ct., Cockeysville, MD 21030.

Jahoda, Gerald (O. 22, 1925, Vienna, Austria) Prof. of LS, FL State Univ., 1963–; Head, Lib. and Syst., Anal., Tech. Info. Div., Esso Resrch. & Engin. Co., 1957–63. **Educ.:** New York Univ., 1945–47, BA (Chem.); Columbia Univ., 1951–52, MS (LS), 1953–60, DLS. **Orgs.:** ASIS: Cnclr. (1964–65); Ch., Educ. Com. (1965–68). ALA. FL LA. Amer. Cncl. of the Blind: Lib. Com. **Pubns:** Jt. auth., *The Librarian and Reference Queries* (1980); *Information Storage & Retrieval Systems for Individual Researchers* (1970); various articles. **Activities:** 11; 30, 39; 72, 91 **Addr.:** School of Library Science, Florida State University, Tallahassee, FL 32306.

Jahoda, Gerald (O. 22, 1925, Austria) Prof., Sch. of Lib. Sci., FL State Univ., 1963–; Head, Syst. Resrch. and Lib., Tech. Info. Div., Esso Resrch. and Engin. Co., 1957–63; Grp. Leader, Tech. Info. Ctr., Colgate-Palmolive Co., 1953–57; Chem. Libn., Univ. of WI, 1952–53. **Educ.:** NY Univ., 1947, AB (Chem.); Columbia Univ., 1952, MS (LS), 1960, DLS. **Orgs.:** ALA: ASCLA, Resrch. Com. (1980–)/LSBPH, Stan. Eval. Com. (1979–81). Amer. Cncl. of the Blind: Lib. Com. (1977–). **Pubns.:** Jt. Auth., *The Librarian and Reference Queries: A Systematic Approach* (1980); "Suggested Goals for Public Library Service to Physically Handicapped Persons," *RQ* (Win. 1980). **Activities:** 11; 26 **Addr.:** School of Library Science, FL State University, Tallahassee, FL 32306.

Jaillite, Joyce Ann (S. 5, 1948, Marion, KS) Dir., Med-MO Lib. Netwk., 1982–; Head Ref. Libn., Pickler Meml. Lib., NE MO State Univ., 1978–81; Head Libn., Kirtley Lib., Columbia Coll, 1975–78; Tchr., Libn., Harwood Sch., 1970–72. **Educ.:** Ctrl. Meth. Coll., 1966–70, AB (Eng., Relig., Educ.); Univ. of MO, 1973–75, AM (LS). **Orgs.:** ALA: ACRL; RASD; LITA; IFRT; LIRT; JMRT (MO Afflt. Cncl. Rep., 1978–80). SLA: Mid-MO Chap. (Secy.-Treas., 1977–78; Pres.-elect., 1978–79; Pres., 1979–80); Educ. Div., *Educ. Libs.* (Bus. Mgr., 1980–). MO LA: Legis. Com. (1975–78); MO ACRL (Pres., 1981–82); JMRT (Secy., 1977–78); various com. Chld. and YA Bk. Sel. Com. of MO. AAUW. Natl. Org. for Women. Untd. Meth. Church. Beta Phi Mu: Psi Chap. (Secy., 1977–78). various org. **Activities:** 1; 31, 39, 49-Data Base Srch.; 56, 63, 74 **Addr.:** Mid-Missouri Library Network, Daniel Boone Regional Library, P.O. Box 1267, Columbia, MO 65205.

Jakubiak, Victoria Mary (My. 23, 1938, Newark, NJ) Educ. Media Spec., Vailsburg HS, 1977–; Tchr., Eng. as Sec. Lang., Dept. of Adult Educ., Newark Bd. of Educ., 1976–, Textbk. Coord., Textbk. Lib., 1974–77; Ref. Libn., Newark Pub. Lib., 1970–72; Sch. Libn., Newark Sch. Syst., 1968–74; Tchr., John Adams Jr. HS, 1964–66; Tchr., Clinton Place Jr. HS, 1962–64; Tchr., Hillside Ave. Sch., 1961–62. **Educ.:** Rutgers Univ., 1956–60, BA (Hist.); Columbia Univ., 1960–61, MA (Tchg. of Soc. Std.); NY Univ., 1964–66, MA (Hist.); Pratt Inst., 1966–68, MLS; Permanent NJ Sec. Tchrs. Cert.; Sch. Libn. Cert.; Prof. Libn. Cert.; Educ. Media Spec. Cert. **Orgs.:** ALA. NJ Sch. Media Assn. Newark Sch. Libns. Assn.: VP. (1971–73); Pres. (1973–75). Essex Cnty. Sch. Lib. Media Assn. AAUW. Newark Tchrs. Assn. Natl. Educ. Assn. NJ Educ. Assn. various org. **Honors:** Beta Phi Mu. **Activities:** 10; 15, 32, 48 **Addr.:** 51 Marsac Pl., Newark, NJ 07106.

James, Billy Michael (O. 14, 1944, Beaumont, TX) Chief, Hlth. Sci. Lib., US Pub. Hlth. Srv. Hosp., 1971–; Asst. Libn., Fortier Sr. HS, 1967–70. **Educ.:** LA State Univ., 1962–67, BA (Soc. Std., Educ.), 1970–71, MS (LS); Med. LA, 1974 Cert. of Med. Libnshp. **Orgs.:** Med. LA. **Honors:** Beta Phi Mu; Phi Kappa Phi; Kappa Delta Pi. **Activities:** 4, 14-Hosp.; 22, 39, 46; 80 **Addr.:** US Public Health Service Hospital, Health Sciences Library, 210 State St., New Orleans, LA 70118.

James, Henry, Jr. (Ag. 16, 1917, New York, NY) Dir. of Libs., Sweet Briar (VA) Coll., 1972–; Libn., Briarcliff Coll., 1966–72; Libn., Lamont Lib., Harvard Univ., 1960–66; Head of Adult Srvs., Ferguson Lib., Stamford, CT, 1956–60; PR, Brooklyn Pub. Lib., 1952–56. **Educ.:** Yale Univ., 1936–40, BA (Eng.); Stanford Univ., 1940–42, MA (Eng.); Columbia Univ., 1950–52, MLS, 1960, CAS (LS) 1972. **Orgs.:** ALA. VA LA: Ed., *VA Libn.* (1973–75). Lynchburg Area Lib. Coop.: Ch. (1977–78). Yale Clb. of NY. **Pubns.:** "The U.S. Information Libraries," *Lib. Qtly.* (Ap. 1953). **Activities:** 1; 15, 34, 37 **Addr.:** Sweet Briar College Library, Sweet Briar, VA 24595.

James, Janet Markley (O. 30, 1936, Tulsa, OK) Head Libn., Watsonville HS, 1969–; Elem. Libn., San Ramon Valley VSD, 1967–69. **Educ.:** Univ. of CA, Berkeley, 1954–58, BA (Eng.), 1965–67, MLS **Orgs.:** CA Assn. of Media Lib. Educs. Pajaro Valley Fed. of Tchrs. **Pubns.:** Indxr., *The Ballad as Song* (1969); Jt. indxr., *Tunes to the Child Ballads* (Volume 4). **Activities:** 10; 15, 17, 20 **Addr.:** 1117 Bay St., Santa Cruz, CA 95060.

James, John (My. 24, 1932, London, UK) WCVM Libn., Univ. of SK, 1969–, Vetny. Med. Libn. 1969–, Catlgr., 1967–69. **Educ.:** Univ. of SK, 1961–64, BA (Sci.); Univ. of BC, 1966–67, BLSc (Lib.). **Orgs.:** Can. LA: Can. Assn. of Spec. Libs. and Info. Srvs. Amer. Med. Assn.: Vetny. Chap. **Activities:** 1; 17, 39; 80 **Addr.:** WCVM Library, University of Saskatchewan, Saskatoon, SK S7N 0W0 Canada.

James, John E. (My. 30, 1937, Philadelphia, PA) Supvsr., Lib. Srvs., Wyeth Lab., Inc., 1969–; Mgr. Ed., Inst. for Sci. Info., 1967–69; Chief Libn., Philco-Ford Corp., 1961–67; Per. Libn., Villanova Univ., 1960–61. **Educ.:** Villanova Univ., 1955–59, BS (Bio.), 1959–60, MS (LS); Drexel Univ., 1967–71, MS (Info. Sci.). **Orgs.:** SLA: Philadelphia Chap., Com. Lib. Dev. (1979–80); Treas. (1978–79). Med. LA. PA LA. **Activities:** 12; 17, 24, 26; 75, 87, 91 **Addr.:** Library Services, Wyeth Laboratories Inc, King of Prussia Rd. and Lancaster Pike, Radnor, PA 19087.

James, Lillie B. (F. 10, 1946, Kingstree, SC) Lib. Media Spec., Prince George's Cnty. Pub. Schs., 1969–; Libn., Florence Pub. Schs., 1967–69. **Educ.:** SC State Coll., 1963–67, BS (LS); NC Ctrl. Univ., 1969–72, MSLS. **Orgs.:** MD LA. Educ. Media Assn. of Prince George's Cnty. ALA. MD Educ. Media Org. Natl. Educ. Assn.: Media Adv. Com. **Activities:** 10; 21, 32 **Addr.:** 2515 R St. S.E. #224, Washington, DC 20020.

James, Olive C. R. (D. 4, 1929, New York, NY) Chief, Loan Div., Lib. of Congs., 1980–; Chief, Gen. Ref. Dept., Stanford Univ. Libs., 1977–80; Adjunct Asst. Prof., Div. of Libnshp., Queens Coll., CUNY, 1975–76, Head, Gen. Ref. Dept., 1973–76, Ref. Libn., 1966–73; Catlgr., Rev., Supvsr., Queens Boro. Pub. Lib., 1963–66; Freelnce. Ed., McGraw-Hill Encyc. Co., 1963. **Educ.:** City Coll. of New York, 1946–50, BS magna cum laude (Rom. Lang.); Rutgers Univ., 1964–65, MLS; 1973, Cert. (Lib. Admin. Dev. Prog.); various crs. **Orgs.:** ALA: Com. on Accred. (Site Visitor, 1980–); ACRL/BIS, Exec. Cncl. (1977–81), Actv. Com. for 1990 (1981–); RASD, ILL Com. (1980–); LAMA (Legis. Asm. Rep., 1979–80); Joseph Lippincott Awd. Jury (1977–78). LA CUNY: Nom. Com.; Ref. Resrcs. Com. Metro (NY): Sem. and Com. on Personal Access (Prog. Ch., 1977). **Honors:** Beta Phi Mu, 1966; Sigma Delta Pi; 1952; Pi Delta Phi, 1951. **Pubns.:** Asst. Ed., *City Coll. Alum.* (1950–52). **Activities:** 1, 4; 17, 34, 39; 54, 55, 67 **Addr.:** Loan Division, Library of Congress, Washington, DC 20540.

James, R. Scott (N. 1, 1943, Oxford, Eng.) Dir. of Recs., City Archvst., City of Toronto, 1975–, Supvsr. of Arch., 1967–75. **Educ.:** Univ. of Wales, 1962–65, BA with honors (Hist.); London Univ., 1965–66, PGCE (Educ.); Dalhousie Univ., 1966–67, MA (Incomplete) (Hist.). **Orgs.:** Assn. of Can. Archvsts.: Cons. Com. (Ch., 1975–76). SAA: Local Arrange. Com. (1974). Toronto Area Archvsts. Grp: Fndr.; Secy. (1973–76); Ontario's Heritage Proj. Ed. Bd. (Ch., 1976–). Can. Hist. Assn. Toronto-Amsterdam Artist Exch. Com. ON Assn. of Art Galleries. Intl. Inst. for Cons. Various other orgs. **Pubns.:** "The Historical Photograph," *Archivaria* (Win. 1976–77); "Cleaning Glass Negatives," *Can. Archvst.* (1974); "The City of Toronto Archives," *Urban Hist. Review* (1973). **Activities:** 2; 17; 55, 75, 95-Hist. **Addr.:** City of Toronto Archives, City Hall, Toronto, ON M5H 2N2 Canada.

James, Seymour W. (O. 12, 1922, Jamaica, W. Indies) Chief, Ref. and Bibl. Sect. Dag Hammarskjold Lib., Untd. Nations, 1971–; Visit. Lectr., Grad. Sch. of Lib. and Info. Sci., Pratt Inst., 1972–77; Libn., UN Econ. Comsn. for Africa, 1964–68; Cur. and Head, Educ. Div., NY Univ. Libs., 1960–64; Libn., Amer. Inst. of Banking, NY, 1959–60. **Educ.:** Fordham Univ., 1947–50, BS magna cum laude (Sci.); NY Univ., 1950–52, MA (Sci. Educ.); Columbia Univ., 1957–59, MLS, 1963–64, Doct. Std. (LS). **Orgs.:** ALA: RASD, Stans. Com. (1976–78). SLA. **Pubns.:** Jt. auth., *An Annotated Bibliography of School Law* (1964); various papers and speeches. **Activities:** 11, 14-Intl. org.; 17, 39; 56 **Addr.:** 1022 Cramer Ct., Baldwin, NY 11510.

James, Stephen Elisha (My. 19, 1942, Montgomery, AL) Asst. Prof., Atlanta Univ., 1976–; Asst. Dir., Urban Srvs., Cleveland Pub. Lib., 1972–73, Branch Libn., 1971–72, Outrch. Libn., 1970–71. **Educ.:** Case West. Rsv. Univ., 1967–70, BA (Eng., Soclgy.), 1970–71, MSLS; various grad. crs. **Orgs.:** ALA. AALS: Constn. and Bylaws Com. (1979–). GA LA. Acad. of Mgt. Mensa: Libns. Spec. Interest Grp. (1978–). **Honors:** ALA, Goals Awd., 1971; OH Hse. of Reps., Cmdn., 1971. **Pubns.:** Jt. Ed., *Measuring The Quality of Library Service* (1974); "Survival Instructions for Inner-City Librarians," *IN Right to Read Conf. Proc.* (1972); "Breaking into the Non-Establishment," *OH Lib. Bltn.* (Ap. 1972); Jt. Auth., "The Changing Role of Supportive

Special Subjects/Services: 50. Adult educ.; 51. Advert./Mktg.; 52. Aerosp.; 53. Agric.; 54. Area std.; 55. Arts/Hum.; 56. Autom.; 57. Bibl./Prtg.; 58. Bio. sci.; 59. Bus./Fin.; 60. Chem.; 61. Copyrt.; 62. Documtn.; 63. Educ.; 64. Engin.; 65. Env.; 66. Eth. grps.; 67. Film; 68. Food/Nutr.; 69. Geneal.; 70. Geo.; 71. Geol.; 72. Handcpd.; 73. Hist.; 74. Int. frdm.; 75. Info. sci.; 76. Insr.; 77. Law; 78. Legis.; 79. Math./Comp. sci.; 80. Med.; 81. Metals; 82. Nat. resrcs.; 83. Newsp.; 84. Nuc. sci.; 85. Oral hist.; 86. Petr./Energy; 87. Pharm.; 88. Phys./Astr./Math.; 89. Readg.; 90. Relig.; 91. Sci./Tech.; 92. Soc. sci.; 93. Telecom.; 94. Transp.; 95. (other).

Staff" slide/tape (1976); "Public Library Outreach" slide/tape (1976). **Activities:** 11; 26; 59, 61, 74, 94 **Addr.:** Atlanta University, School of Library and Information Studies, 223 Chestnut St. S.W., Atlanta, GA 30314.

Jameson, Elizabeth (Betty) (O. 5, 1926, Greene County, AR) Med. Libn., Alton Meml. Hosp., 1975–; Sub. Libn., Alton Sch. Dist., 1972–75; Instr., Lib. Sci., Lewis and Clark Cmnty. Coll., 1972–74; Libn., Clio Sch. Dist., 1968–71. **Educ.:** Bob Jones Univ., 1947–51, BA (Bible); Univ. of MI, 1965–68, MA (LS). **Orgs.:** Med. LA. ILLINET. Areawide Hosp. Lib. Cnsrtm.: Prog. Proj. (Ch.). **Activities:** 12; 15, 20, 39; 80 **Addr.:** Alton Memorial Hospital, Alton, IL 62002.

Jamison, Carolyn C. (Ja. 26, 1948, Ellerbe, NC) Ref./Docum. Libn., Appalachian State Univ., 1980–; Asst. to the Vice Chancellor for Acad. Affairs, 1979–80, Gvt. Docum. Libn., 1972–79. **Educ.:** Univ. of NC, 1966–70, AB (Hist.), 1970–71, MSLS. **Orgs.:** ALA: RASD, Bibl. Com. (1975–76). NC LA: Docum. Sect. (Treas. 1975–76; Vice-Ch.-Ch. Elect 1978–79, Ch. 1979–80). SELA. Phi Delta Kappa. **Activities:** 1; 29, 31, 39; 55 **Addr.:** Appalachian State University, Boone, NC 28608.

Jamison, JoAnna (D. 1, 1948, Tulsa, OK) Libn., Dallas Baptist Coll., 1975–; Chld. Libn. Dallas Pub. Lib. 1971–74. **Educ.:** OK State Univ., 1967–70, BS (Home Econ.); N. TX State Univ., 1971–76, MLS. **Orgs.:** TX LA: Local Info. (Ch., 1980). ALA. SWLA. Phi Kappa Phi. Apha Lambda Delta. Omicron Nu. Mu Kappa Tau. Various other orgs. **Activities:** 1; 20, 39, 46; 50, 77, 90 **Addr.:** 942 Green Rock, Duncanville, TX 75137.

Janaske, Paul C. (Jl. 28, 1920, Shamokin, PA) Dir., Div. of Lib. Prog., US Ofc. of Educ., 1976–, Prog. Mgr., Lib. Resrch. and Demonstrations, 1967–76; Asst. Branch Chief, Fed. Clearinghouse for Sci. and Tech. Info., 1964–67; Exec. Dir., Amer. Docum. Inst., 1963–64; Info. Spec., Amer. Inst. Bio. Sci., 1961–63; Asst. to Libn., Ctrl. Intelligence Agency, 1951–61; Head, Srv. Div., Kent State Univ., 1949–51. **Educ.:** Dickinson Coll., 1938–42, BS (Bio.); Columbia Univ., 1949, MS (LS). Phi Kappa Sigma. **Pubns.:** Ed., *Information Handling and Science Information* (1962); Ed., *Automation and Scientific Communication* (1963). **Activities:** 4 **Addr.:** Division of Library Programs, US Office of Education, 7th & D Sts. S.W., ROB #3, Washington, DC 20202.*

Janes, Dorothy (Je. 30, 1921, Montréal, PQ) Ref. Libn., Law Lib. Univ. of Toronto 1971–, Catlgr., Robarts Lib., 1969–71. **Educ.:** Victoria Univ. Univ. of Toronto, 1949–53, BA (Grm., Eng., Fr.); Univ. of Toronto, 1968–69, BLS. **Orgs.:** Libns. Assn. of the Univ. of Toronto. Can. ALL: Secy. (1975–77). AALL. Frnds. House Lib. (Quakers) Toronto. **Pubns.:** *Women and the Law; A Bibliography* (1979). **Activities:** 1; 22, 31, 39; 77 **Addr.:** University of Toronto Law Library, Toronto, ON M4E 2W8 Canada.

Janiak, Jane M. (Ja. 10, 1947, Brooklyn, NY) Chief Libn., Port Athrty. of NY and NJ, 1974–, Asst. Chief Libn., 1973–74, Staff Libn., 1972–73; Libn., Econ. Anal., Caltex Petroleum Co., 1971–72; Acg. Lib. Supvsr., Shell Oil Co. 1968–71. **Educ.:** Fordham Univ., 1964–68, BA (Eng.); Columbia Univ., 1968–70, MSLS. **Orgs.:** SLA: NY Chap., Tech. Sci. Grp. (Ch. 1976); Intl. Affairs Sect., Soc. Sci Grp. (Secy., Treas. 1978–80); Transp. Div. (Ch., 1981–82). ALA. Assoc. Info. Mgr. **Activities:** 12; 17, 39, 49-Computer Applications; 64, 94, 95-Urban Affairs. **Addr.:** Port Authority of New York and New Jersey, Library - 54 North, One World Trade Center, New York, NY 10048.

Jann-Ferreira, Cheryl R. (S. 19, 1949, Chicago, IL) Lib., Lrng. Ctr. Dir., LaGrange Dist. #105, 1977–; Dist. Libn., Dist. #127 1/2, Chicago Ridge, 1976–77; Libn., Chicago Pub. Schs., 1974–76; Tchr., Dist. #152 1/2, Hazel Crest, 1971–73. **Educ.:** Andrews Univ., 1966–71, BA (Hist., Pol. Sci.); Chicago State Univ., 1973–75, MSEd (Media, Comm., LS). **Orgs.:** ALA: AASL; JMRT. IL Educ. Assn. Natl. Educ. Assn. **Honors:** Phi Delta Kappa. **Activities:** 10; 15, 17, 20; 63, 82, 89 **Addr.:** District #105, 1001 S. Spring Ave., LaGrange, IL 60525.

Janowski, Bronislaw (Mike) (N. 23, 1913, Tarnopol, Poland) Admn. Libn., Evangeline Parish Lib., 1962–; Asst. Libn., Allen Parish Lib., 1959–62; Tchr., St. Mary Sch. (Orange, TX), 1958–59. **Educ.:** S. West. Univ., 1949–52, BS (Educ.); LA State Univ. Lib. Sch. 1957–59, MS (LS); Tchr. Coll. Dip. in Poland, 1930–35. **Orgs.:** ALA: ALTA, Int. Frdm. Com. (1976–); Pubns. Com. (1980–). LA LA: Pub. Lib. Sect., Ch. (1964); Chap. Cnclr. to ALA (1976–79). SWLA. LA State Lib. Adv. Com. on Netwk. Dev., 1980–. Ville Platte Rotary Intl.: Pres. (1967). **Honors:** LA Farm Bur., Frd. Awd., 1976; Gamma Pi Awd. **Activities:** 9 **Addr.:** 505 Maple, Oakdale, LA 71463.

Jansen, Guenter Alfred (S. 19, 1930, Philadelphia, PA) Instr., Suffolk Cnty. Cmnty. Coll., 1980–; Secy., Treas., Bellport Travel, Inc., 1976–; Dir., Suffolk Coop. Lib. Syst., 1967–76; City Libn., New Orleans Pub. Lib., 1965–67; Dir., Mobile Pub. Lib., 1961–65, Asst. Dir., 1960–61; Head, Ext. Dept., Cedar Rapids Pub. Lib., 1958–60, Serials Cat., Lib. of Cong., 1957–58; various other positions. **Educ.:** Univ. of PA, 1948–55, AB (Eng.); Drexel Univ., 1955–56, MS (LS). **Orgs.:** ALA. NY LA: Pres. (1973–74). **Activities:** 9; 17, 19, 24 **Addr.:** 12 Station Rd., Bellport, NY 11713.

Janzen, Mary E. (March 23, 1943, Hillsboro, KS) Sr. Achvst., NEA Mss. Prcs. Grant, Chicago Hist. Socty., 1980–; Actg. Cur. of Spec. Col., Morris Lib., South. IL Univ., 1978–80; Mss. Resrch. Spec., Univ. of Chicago, 1970–78; Instr., Knoxville Coll., 1967–68. **Educ.:** Bethel Coll., 1961–65, BA (Hist.); Univ. of Chicago, 1965–67, MA (Hist.), 1967–72, ABD (Hist.). **Orgs.:** SAA: Com. on Sci. and Tech. (1976–79). Midwest Arch. Conf.: Cncl. (1981–83). Amer. Hist. Assn. **Honors:** Woodrow Wilson Natl. Flwshp. Fndn., Woodrow Wilson Flwshp. (1965). **Pubns.:** *A Guide to the James Franck Papers* (1976); various other articles. **Activities:** 2; 15, 17, 28, 45; 91 **Addr.:** Chicago Historical Society, Clark St. at North Ave., Chicago, IL 60614.

Jaques, Thomas Francis (D. 25, 1938, Crowley, LA State Libn., LA State Lib., 1975–, Assoc. State Libn., MS Lib. Comsn., 1974–75, Pub. Lib. Consult., 1973–74; Asst. Par. Libn., Rapides Par. Lib., 1971–73. **Educ.:** Univ. of Southwest. LA, 1960, BA (Mgt.); LA State Univ., 1968–69, MSLS. **Orgs.:** LA LA. SWLA. ALA. COSLA. **Activities:** 9, 13; 17, 24 **Addr.:** 12348 E. Sheraton Ave., Baton Rouge, LA 70815.

Jaquith, F. Luree (My. 31, 1936, Chicago, IL) Lib. Media Spec., Lexington Pub. Schs., 1965–; Guest Lectr., Boston Univ., 1968–69; Tchg. Staff, Higher Educ. Inst., West. MI Univ., Sum. 1968; Tchr., IL Pub. Schs., 1956–62. **Educ.:** IL State Univ., 1963, BS (Elem. Educ.); West. MI Univ., 1963–65, MALS. **Orgs.:** ALA: Grolier Fndn. Jury (1974); ALSC, Film Eval. Com. (1979–), Eval. of Sch. Media Progs. (1975–79); Chld. Srvs. Div., Newbery-Caldecott Com. (1971); AASL (Rec. Secy., 1971–72). **Honors:** Beta Phi Mu, 1965. **Pubns.:** Bk. reviews, *Appraisal* (1978–). **Activities:** 10; 21, 31, 32 **Addr.:** Bowman Elementary School, Philip Rd., Lexington, MA 02173.

Jarboe, Linda S. (Ag. 13, 1941, San Fernando, CA) Lib. Coord. Tech. Srv., Burbank Pub. Lib., 1979–, Lib. Coord. Ref. Srv., 1976–79, Lib. Coord., Buena Vista Branch, 1973–76, Sr. Libn., 1972–73, Libn., 1969–72. **Educ.:** Immaculate Heart Coll., Los Angeles, 1959–65, BA (Hist.), 1968–69, MALS, 1965–66, Elem. Tchg. Cred. **Activities:** 9; 15, 16, 46 **Addr.:** Burbank Public Library, 110 N. Glenoaks Blvd., Burbank, CA 91503.

Jarboe, Wilford A. (Mr. 20, 1916, Tell City, IN) Supvsr., Media Ctrs., Evansville-Vanderburgh Sch. Corp., 1947–; Prin., Harwood Sch., 1941–47; Prin., Lincoln City Sch., 1939–41. **Educ.:** Univ. of Evansville, 1934–39, BS (Hist.); IN Univ., 1949–51, MS (AV Admin.); Wayne State, 1966, (TV Comm.). **Orgs.:** ALA: YASD, Film Sel. (1979–81). AECT. Assn. IN Media Educ. Past Pres. **Honors:** AV Instr. Dir. of IN, Srv. Awd., 1970; Evansville Vanderburgh Pub. Lib., Merit. Srv. Awd., 1978. **Activities:** 9, 10; 17, 31, 48; 63, 67 **Addr.:** 4600 Kratzville Rd., Evansville, IN 47710.

Jardine, Patricia Jane (N. 9, 1931, Fredericton, NB) Head Libn., NB Cmnty. Coll., 1968–, Instr., Libn., 1966–68; Tchr., City of Moncton Sch. Bd., 1963–66; Acad. Instr. Cont. Ed., Dept. of Educ., 1960–62. **Educ.:** NB Tchrs. Coll., 1948–50, Class I Licn.; Univ. of Moncton, 1969, BEEd (Tchg.), 1972, BA; Univ. of NB, 1974, BEd; Simmons Coll., 1975–80, MS (LS); Univ. of Moncton, 1978–81, MEd (Admin.). **Orgs.:** Can. LA: Can. Assn. of Coll. and Univ. Libs. Atl. Prov. LA. NB Sch. Lib.-Media Cncl. ALA. Can. Coll. of Tchrs. Univ. Women's Club. Bus. and Prof. Women's Club: Schol. Com.; Prog. Com.; PR Com. Univ. of NB Alum. **Activities:** 1, 10; 15, 16, 17; 56, 64, 91 **Addr.:** 97 Waverley Ave., Moncton, NB E1C 7T8 Canada.

Jarmak, Sandra B. (Ja. 29, 1951, Sanford, ME) Lib. Dir., Pittsfield Pub. Lib., 1978–; Asst. Libn., Gardiner Pub. Lib., 1974–78. **Educ.:** Bates Coll., 1969–73, BA (Soclgy.). **Orgs.:** ALA. ME LA: Bd. of Cert. (Ch., 1980–); Legis. Strg. Com. (1980). Small Pub. LA: Secy. (1979–); Exec. Bd. (1979–). **Activities:** 9; 17 **Addr.:** RFD 2, Box 204, Tildon, NH 03276.

Jaros, Rod (Je. 13, 1939, Waterbury, CT) Dir., Lib. Media Srvs., Horace Greeley HS, 1970. **Educ.:** Fairfield Univ., 1957–61, BSS (Eng.); Trinity Coll., 1964, MA (Eng.); Pratt Inst., MLS. **Orgs.:** Sch. Libns. of Southeast. NY: Pres. (1977–78). NY LA: Sch. Lib. Media Sect. (2nd VP, 1980–81). NY Gvrs. Conf. on Libs.: Del. (1978). **Activities:** 10; 17, 32, 34 **Addr.:** Library Media Services, Horace Greeley High School, Chappaqua, NY 10514.

Jaroslow, Sylvia Walter (Ja. 14, 1920, New York, NY) AV Supvsr., Ocean Cnty. Lib. Syst., Tom's River, NJ, 1981–; Msc. Consult., 1977–81; AV Supvsr., Prog. Coord., Paterson Free Pub. Lib., 1970–81; Instr. Msc. Instr., Baroque Instruments, Adult Educ. Ctrs., 1965–70; Prof. Musician, Double Bass, St. Louis and Kansas City Symph. Orchs., Boston Pops, varied instrumental ensembles 1942–65; Instrumental Tchr., Conductor, Girls' Vocational HS. **Educ.:** Julliard Sch. of Msc., 1942–44; Brooklyn Coll., BA (Msc., Educ.); Pratt Inst., 1970, MLS; 1973, Cert. Harvard Univ., (Inst. in Arts Admin.) Amer. Recorder Socty., Tchrs. Cert. **Orgs.:** NJ LA. Msc. LA. Coal. for Arts and Hum. of NJ. Amer. Fed. of Musicians. Grt. Paterson Arts Cncl. Amer. Recorder Socty. **Pubns.:** *Book of Intradas—Melchior Frank* (1965). **Activities:** 9; 15, 17, 24; 55, 67, 93 **Addr.:** 160 Overlook Ave., Hackensack, NJ 07601.

Jarred, Ada Nell Delony (Ap. 14, 1937, Ruston, LA) Head Libn., LA State Univ., Alexandria, 1977–, Sr. Libn., Instr. of Bks. and Libs., 1973–76; Asst. Libn., Cat. Div., LA State Univ., Baton Rouge, 1972–73, Visit. Prof., Sch. of LS, Sum. 1972; various lib. positions, 1963–70; Cat. Libn., Emory Univ. Lib., 1962–63; Dir. of Reader Srvs., LA Coll. Lib., 1959–62. **Educ.:** LA Coll., Pineville, 1959, BA (Eng. Educ.), Univ. of Denver, 1961, MALS. **Orgs.:** ALA. SWLA. LA LA: Un. Cat. Com. (1967–70); Adv. Com. on Pubns (1975–78); Anl. Conf. Pubcty. Com. (1975). AAUW. Alexandria Musm. and Visual Arts Ctr. **Activities:** 1; 17, 31, 46; 55 **Addr.:** 5515 Mildred, Alexandria, LA 71301.

Jarrell, James R. (Je. 26, 1940, Greensboro, NC) Asst. Acq. Libn., Univ. of NC, Greensboro, 1970–; Ref. Libn. (part-time), Bennett Coll., 1970–74; Asst. Libn./Coord. of AV, Greensboro City Schs., 1968–69; Tchr., Leonia (NJ) Pub. Schs., 1966–68; Tchr., School City of Gary (IN), 1963–66. **Educ.:** Winston-Salem Tchrs. Coll., 1959–63, BS (Educ.); Atlanta Univ., 1969–70, MSLS; ACRL Cert., 1974–75, (Lib. Mgt. Internship); Univ. of NC, Greensboro, 1970–74, (Educ. Media). **Orgs.:** ALA: Adv. Com. for Coretta Scott King Awd. (1970–74). NC LA: Ch., Lib. Resrc. Com. (1975–77), Secy., Coll. & Univ. Sect. (1973–75). Guilford Lib. Club: Pres. (1979–80). Winston-Salem State Univ. Alum. Assn.: Pres. (1975–77). Neo Black Socty.: Adv. (1977–79). **Honors:** Winston-Salem State Univ., Alum. Recog. Awd., 1973. **Pubns.:** "Bennett Women: Past, Present, and Future," *Bennett Belle Ringer* (Je., 1973). **Activities:** 1, 10; 15, 21, 39; 55, 66, 89 **Addr.:** 2114 Byrd St., Greensboro, NC 27401.

Jarrett, Gladys W. (F. 6, 1916, Barnesville, GA) Chief Libn., York Coll. of the City Univ. of NY, 1974–, Head, Pub. Srvs. Div., 1972–74, Head, Cat. Sect., 1967–72, Ref., Acq. Libn., Pace Univ., 1964–67 Cat. Dept., Brooklyn Pub. Lib., 1961–62; Head, Cat. Div., NC Agr. Tech., 1957–61. **Educ.:** Hunter Coll., 1932–36, BA (Span.); Columbia Univ., 1936–37, MA (Span.) Univ. NC, 1960, (LS); Pratt Univ., 1962–63, MLS; City Univ. NY, 1974–75, Comp. Sci. **Orgs.:** ALA: ACRL, Com. on Stan. & Accred. (1976, 1977); Secy. (1977); Com. on Budget and Finance (1979–81). Beta Phi Mu: Theta Chap., VP (1976, 1977); Pres. (1978, 1979). LA City Univ. New York: Pres. (1972–73); Exec. Cncl. (1972–74); Com. Prog. Social Act. (Ch., 1973–76); various other coms. New York Lib. Club. New York Tech. Srv. Libns. Various other orgs. Modern Hum. Resrch. Assn. Untd. Negro Coll. Fund. **Honors:** Beta Phi Mu, 1963; Archons of Colophon, 1976. **Pubns.:** Ed., *The American Indian - Then and Now* (ERIC) (1975); reviews. **Activities:** 1; 17, 35, 39; 70 **Addr.:** 315 West 70th St., New York, NY 10023.

Jarvi, Edith T. (My. 12, 1921, Toronto, ON) Prof., Univ. of Toronto, 1964–; Head, Ref. Dept., Windsor Pub. Lib., 1954–63. **Educ.:** Univ. of Toronto, 1947–49, BA, 1963–64, MLS. **Orgs.:** Can. LA. ON LA. SLA. Can. Assn. Info. Sci. Other orgs. Can. Inst. for Intl. Affairs. **Honors:** Univ. of Toronto, Alum. Jubilee Awd., 1979. **Pubns.:** *Access to Can. Govt. Pubns. in Can. Academic & Public Libraries* (1976); Jt. auth., *Canadian Selection* (1977). **Activities:** 9, 11; 16, 29, 39; 92 **Addr.:** Univ. of Toronto, Faculty of Library Science, 140 St. George St., Toronto, ON M5S 1A1 Canada.

Jason, Nora H. (Ja. 15, 1936, Schenectady, NY) Proj. Leader, Fire Resrch. Info. Srvs., Natl. Bur. of Stan., 1971–; Admin. Libn., Spec. Srvs. Libs., Nellingen and Munich, W. Germany, 1967–70; Catlgr., CA State Univ., Sacramento, 1966–67; Elem. Sch. Libn., Clinton Sch. Dist., 1964–65. **Educ.:** SUNY, Albany, 1960–64, BA (Soc. Std.), 1965–66, MLS. **Orgs.:** SLA. ASIS. ALA: European Div. Zonta Intl. Stan. Com. for Women: Pres. (1978). **Honors:** Dept. of Cmrce., Bronze Medal Awd., 1977; Natl. Aeronautics and Space Admin., Cert. of Recog., 1979. **Pubns.:** Ed., *Fire Investigation Handbook* (1980); *Fire Research Publications* (1973–). **Activities:** 4; 17, 39, 41; 64, 76 **Addr.:** National Bureau of Standards, Bldg. 224, Rm. B250, Washington, DC 20234.

Jasper, James M. (Ag. 20, 1929, Kingman, KS) Head, Tech. Srvs., Oxnard Pub. Lib., 1980–, Head, Adult/Tech. Srvs. 1977–80, Head, Adult Srvs., 1975–77, Ref. Libn., 1973–75; Dir., Newton Free Lib., 1966–73; Cat. Libn., Baker Univ., 1968–69; Head Catlgr., Acq., Upper IA Univ., 1967–68; Head, Tech. Srvs., Saskatoon Pub. Lib., 1966; Coord., Srvs., Johnson Cnty. Pub. Lib., 1964–66; various libn., admin. positions, 1960–64. **Educ.:** KS Univ., 1947–50 (Fine Arts); MO Valley Coll., 1952–54, BS (Bus. Admin.); Emporia State Univ., 1959–60, MS (LS). **Orgs.:** KS LA: Pub. Lib. Com. (Ch., 1972–73). ALA: LITA. Assn. Childhood Educ. Intl. **Activities:** 9; 15, 16, 20 **Addr.:** Oxnard Public Library, 214 S. C St., Oxnard, CA 93030.

Jax, John Joseph (Je. 17, 1935, Cazenovia, WI) Dir., Lib., Asst. Dean Lrng. Resrcs., Univ. of WI, Stout, 1971–, Asst. Libn., Circ., 1968–71; Indxr. Abs., ERIC, Univ. of IL, 1967–68; Circ., Ref. Libn., Univ. of WI, 1959–66. **Educ.:** Univ. of WI, LaCrosse, 1954–58, BA (Hist.); Univ. of WI, Madison, 1958–59, MS (LS); Univ. of IL, 1967–68, CAS (LS). **Orgs.:** ALA. WI LA: Pres. (1981). WI AV Assn. WHCOLIS: Del. (1979). Assn. of Univ. of

PROFESSIONAL ACTIVITIES: Institutions: 1. Acad. lib.; 2. Arch.; 3. Assn.; 4. Fed./Gvt. lib.; 5. Inst. lib.; 6. Mfr./Suppl.; 7. Milit. lib.; 8. Musm.; 9. Pub. lib.; 10. Sch. lib.; 11. Sch. of lib. sci.; 12. Spec. lib.; 13. State lib.; 14. (other). **Functions/Activities:** 15. Acq./Col. dev.; 16. Adult srvs.; 17. Admin.; 18. Apprais.; 19. Archit./Bldgs.; 20. Cat./Class.; 21. Chld. srvs.; 22. Circ.; 23. Cons./Pres.; 24. Consult.; 25. Cont. ed.; 26. Educ. lib. sci.; 27. Ext. srvs.; 28. Fund/Grants; 29. Gvt. pubs.; 30. Indx./Abs.; 31. Instr. lib. use; 32. Media srvs.; 33. Micro.; 34. Netwks./Coop.; 35. Persnl.; 36. PR; 37. Publshg.; 38. Recs. mgt.; 39. Ref. srvs.; 40. Repro.; 41. Resrch.; 42. Review.; 43. Secur.; 44. Serials; 45. Spec. col.; 46. Tech. srvs.; 47. Trustees/Bds.; 48. YA srvs.; 49. (other).

WI Facs. WI Lib. Cnsrtm.: Ch. (1977). **Honors:** Beta Phi Mu, 1968. **Pubns.:** *A Library Conference Planning Manual* (1981); "Textbook Rentals—An Educational Syndrome," *WI Jnl. of Educ.* (Ja. 1973); "COM (Computer Output Microfiche) In Libraries" videocassette (1976). **Activities:** 1; 17, 19 **Addr.:** 401 12th Ave., W., Menomonie, WI 54751.

Jay, Hilda Lease (D. 29, 1921, Indianapolis, IN) Dir. of Media Srvs., Ridgefield (CT) HS, 1958–; Instr., Univ. of Bridgeport, CT, 1979–; Instr., Univ. of CT, 1977–; Chld. Rm., Bridgeport Pub. Lib., 1942–44. **Educ.:** IN Univ., 1945, BS (Educ., LS); Danbury State Coll., 1960, MS (Educ.); Univ. of Bridgeport, 1964, Sixth Yr. Prof. Dip. (Spec. Std.); NY Univ., 1970, EdD (Supvsn., Curric.). **Orgs.:** ALA: AASL. AECT: Sch. Media Specs., Bd. Dirs. (1981–). CT Educ. Media Assn.: Pres. (1975–77); Secy. (1979–80). CT Sch. LA: Exec. Bd. (1963–66, 1970–76); Lib. Skills Com. (Ch., 1964–66). Various other orgs. Natl. Educ. Assn. Assn. for Supvsn. and Curric. Dev. **Honors:** Girl Scouts, Thanks Badge, 1956. **Pubns.:** *Stimulating Student Search: Classroom/Library Media Teacher Techniques* (1981); Ed., *Back to Basics with Media* (1978); Ed., *School Library/Media Center, A Primary Force for Equity of Educational Opportunity* (1979); Jt. auth., *Report on School Instruction in Library Skills in Connecticut* (1964); "Buggin Library Materials," *WI Assn. of Sch. Libns. Communique* (My. 1974); "Surveillance System for School Media Centers," *Wilson Lib. Bltn.* (Mr. 1974); various other articles and slide presentations. **Activities:** 10, 11; 26, 31, 48; 63, 75 **Addr.:** P.O. Box F, Sandy Hook, CT 06482.

Jay, Margaret Ellen (Mr. 23, 1946, Bridgeport, CT) Media Spec., Montgomery Cnty. (MD) Pub. Schs., 1969–. **Educ.:** IN Univ., 1964–68, BS (Elem. Educ.), 1968–69, MS (Elem. Educ.); Kent State Univ., 1978–80, PhD (Curric., Instr.). **Orgs.:** ALA: Stdg. Com. on Lib. Educ.; AASL. AECT. Montgomery Cnty. Educ. Media Specs. Assn.: Exec. Bd. (1972–78). OH Educ. Lib. Media Assn. Assn. of Supvsn. and Curric. Dev. **Pubns.:** *Involvement Bulletin Boards and Other Motivational Reading Activities* (1976); various articles. **Activities:** 10; 21, 31, 32; 95-Curric. support. **Addr.:** P.O. Box F, Sandy Hook, CT 06482.

Jay, Peggy Pres., Info. and Comm. Specs., Inc., 1981–; Proj. Mgr., Solar Energy Resrch. Inst., Resrch.-in-Progress Data Base, 1980–81; Ed., Lexicographer, Indxr.-Info. Handling Srvs., 1977–79; Freelnc. Photographer, Rocky Mt. News, 1977–78; Tchr., Introductory Jnlsm., Univ. of CO Sch. of Jnlsm., 1977–78; Thea. Critic–*Boulder Daily Camera,* 1977–78; Tchr., Eng. Natl. Coll. of Bus., 1976–77; Asst. Ed., Libs. Unlimited, 1976; Bk. Reviewer, *The Denver Post,* 1975–76; various positions in lib., 1970–76. **Educ.:** Pasadena Playhouse Coll. of Thea. Arts, 1965–67, BTA (Thea. Arts); Univ. of Denver, 1971–72, MA (LS); Univ. of CO, 1976–81, MA (Jnlsm.). **Orgs.:** ASIS. Women in Comm., Inc. Women's Rsrcs., Unlimited. **Honors:** Kappa Tau Alpha; Alpha Psi Omega. **Pubns.:** *Photojournalism and Photojournalists: An Annotated and Descriptive Bibliography to 1980* (forthcoming); various articles. **Activities:** 12; 24, 30, 37; 55, 56, 57, 58 **Addr.:** Information & Communication Specialists, Inc., PO Box 10445, Denver, CO 80210.

Jayatilleke, Rajasinghe A. (Ja. 6, 1932, Gampaha, West. Prov., Sri Lanka) Asst. Prof., Sci. Libn., Brooklyn Coll., CUNY, 1978–; Consult., Abs./Indexing, New York City Bd. of Educ., 1977; ERIC Coord., Libn., Tchrs. Coll., Columbia Univ., 1969–77 Med. Libn., Staten Island Hosp., 1968; Actg. Chief Libn., Univ. of Ceylon, Colombo, 1967–68, Campus Libn., 1960–67; Resrch. Ofc. in Nematology, Tea Resrch. Inst. of Ceylon, Colombo, Ceylon, 1959–60; Asst. Prof., Zlgy., Univ. of Ceylon, 1957–59; various tchg. positions in Ceylon, 1957–59. **Educ.:** Univ. of Ceylon, Colombo, Ceylon, 1953–57, BSc hons. (Zlgy.); Deutsches Kultur Inst., Colombo, Sri Lanka, 1959–61, Cert. (Grmn.); Columbia Univ., 1962–63, MS (LS), 1976–, PhD (LS). **Orgs.:** Ceylon LA: VP (1966–67); Secy. (1964–65); Fndn. Mem. (1962–). LA CUNY: Alternate Del. (1980–81). Ceylon Assn. for the Advnc. of Sci. Royal Socty. of Hlth. of London: Fellow (1971). **Honors:** UNESCO, Fellow, Sem. in Sci. Documtn., 1963; London Inst. for Appld. Resrch., DSc, honoris causa, 1973. **Pubns.:** Jt. Cmplr., *Union List of Scientific Periodicals in Ceylon* (1971); "Acephaline Gregarines of the Ceylon Earthworm, Pheretima Peguana Rosa," *Ceylon Jnl. of Sci.* (Ag. 1957); Jt. Cmplr., *Directory of Information Sources on the Disadvantaged* (1972); Cmplr., *Human Relations in the Classroom* (1972, 1973–75). **Activities:** 1; 26, 31, 39; 56, 91 **Addr.:** 157 E. Hamilton Ave., Englewood, NJ 07631.

Jaynes, Phyllis E. (Ja. 11, 1938, Flint, MI) Dir. of User Srvs., Dartmouth Coll., 1980–, Engin. & Bus. Admin. Libn., 1971–80; Sci. & Engin. Libn., Haile Sellassie I Univ., Ethiopia, 1968–71; Supvsr. of Lib. Oper., General Motors Inst., 1964–68, Ref. Libn., 1960–64; Asst. Ref. Libn., Genesee Cnty. Lib., Flint, MI, 1959–60. **Educ.:** SW MO State, 1955–58, BS (Bus.); Rutgers Univ., 1958–59, MLS. **Orgs.:** SLA: Ch., Nom. Com., Bus. & Finance Div. (1979–80); Ch., Coll. & Univ. Bus. Libs. RT (1977–78). New Eng. LA. ALA: Pres., JMRT (1966); AV Com. (1967). Quota Intl.: Pres., Upper Valley Chap. (1979–80). **Honors:** ARL, Consult. Trng. Prog., 1979. **Pubns.:** Oral presentations. **Activities:** 1; 17, 24, 39; 51, 59, 64 **Addr.:** Baker Library, Dartmouth College, Hanover, NH 03755.

Jebb, Marcia (O. 11, 1934, Manchester, NH) Asst. Univ. Libn. for Pub. Srvs., Cornell Univ., 1975–, Ref. Libn., 1968–75; Assoc. Ref. Libn., Temple Univ., 1962–65, 1965–68. **Educ.:** Colby Coll., 1951–55, AB (Fr.); George Washington Univ., 1959–60, MA (Fr.); Simmons Coll., 1961–62, MLS; Univ. de Lyons, 1955–56, (Diplôme Fr.). **Orgs.:** ALA. NY LA: Ref. Com. (1974–75). Resrch. Libs. Grp.: Shared Resrcs. Com. (1980–); Col. Mgt. and Dev. Com. (1980–). **Pubns.:** *Microforms in the Five Associated University Libraries: a reference guide and Union List* (1973); *Racism and restructuring: an annotated bibliography* (1969); "Bibliographic control of microforms," *Drexel Lib. Qtly.* (Ja. 1976). **Activities:** 1; 17, 39, 42; 57 **Addr.:** 201 Olin Library, Cornell University, Ithaca, NY 14853.

Jeffcott, Janet Bruhn (D. 5, 1939, Madison, WI) Tech. Libn., Madison Area Tech. Coll., 1968–. **Educ.:** Univ. of WI, 1958–62, BA (Eng.), 1967–68, MALS. **Orgs.:** ASIS: WI Chap. (Treas., 1977). ALA. WI LA: WI Lib. Dev. and Legis. Com. (1976); Nom. Com. (1978). Madison Area Lib. Cncl.: Secy. (1976); Cmnty. Rel. Com. (1977–); Lib. Prac. Com. (1978–). Various other orgs. Amer. Vocational Assn. WI Assn. of Vocational Adult Educ. **Pubns.:** *Welding Literature* (1969); "Computer Produced Library Catalogs," *AVA Jnl.* (Ap. 1975); "Book Catalog by Computer," *WI Lib. Bltn.* (Mr.-Ap. 1975); Dsgn. and Dev. of more than 40 OL databases (1976–79). **Activities:** 1; 17, 30, 49-OL database dsgn.; 56, 64, 91 **Addr.:** Madison Area Technical College, 211 North Carroll St., Madison, WI 53703.

Jefferson, Lila R. (S. 23, 1953, Monroe, LA) ILL Libn., Abilene Pub. Lib., 1976–. **Educ.:** Northeast LA Univ., 1971–74, BA (Eng. Educ.); LA State Univ., 1974–75, MLS. **Orgs.:** ALA. TX LA: ILLRT, Nom. Com. (Ch., 1980), Mem. Com. (1979–80); JMRT, Dist. Rep. to Dist. 1 (1979), Cnclr. (1980). AAUW. **Activities:** 9; 34 **Addr.:** Abilene Public Library, Interlibrary Loan, 202 Cedar, Abilene, TX 79601.

Jefferson, Mary Evelyn (My. 9, 1921, Danville, VA) Asst. Libn., Assoc. Prof., Averett Coll., 1976–; Instr., Libn., Danville Cmnty. Coll., 1974–76; Assoc. Prof., Assoc. Libn., Stratford Coll., 1957–74. **Educ.:** Univ. of NC, 1955–57, AB (Eng.); Univ. of VA, 1959–61, MA (Eng.); Univ. of NC, 1966–68, MS (LS). **Orgs.:** ALA. SELA. VA LA. AAUP. **Honors:** Phi Beta Kappa, 1957; Phi Delta Kappa. **Activities:** 1; 31, 39; 55 **Addr.:** 169 Hawthorne Dr., Danville, VA 24541.

Jeffery, Jonathan B. (Ag. 30, 1950, New Haven, CT) Assoc. Ref. Libn., Univ. of DE, 1978–, Actg. Head, Gvt. Docum. and Maps Dept., 1980–81; Asst. Dept. Head, Ref., 1978–80, Asst. Ref. Libn., 1975–78. **Educ.:** Univ. of CT, 1968–72, BA (Psy.); South. CT State Coll., 1973–75, MLS. **Orgs.:** ALA. DE LA. ACRL: DE Valley Chap., Nom. Com. (1979). **Pubns.:** Series of bibl. articles for theme issues, *Marriage and Fam. Review* (forthcoming). **Activities:** 1; 17, 29, 39 **Addr.:** RD #1, Box 237, Landenberg, PA 19350.

Jeffs, Joseph (Jl. 1, 1924, Philadelphia, PA) Univ. Libn., Georgetown Univ., 1960–, Assoc. Libn., 1956–59, Chief, Tech. Srv., 1955–56, Ref. Libn., 1954; Asst. Libn., Dumbarton Oaks, 1953–54. **Activities:** 1; 17 **Addr.:** Univ. Libn., Georgetown University Library, Washington, DC 20057.*

Jekich, Danica (Jl. 7, 1927, Cerevic, Srem, Yugoslavia) S. Slavic Bibl., Univ. of MI Grad. Lib., 1965–. **Educ.:** Univ. of Belgrad, Yugoslavia, 1948–53, Dip. (History of Art); Univ. of MI, 1960–62, MA (Hist. of Art), 1964–65, MALS. **Orgs.:** Amer. Assn. for the Advnc. of Slavic Std. **Activities:** 1; 15, 20; 55 **Addr.:** University of MI, University Library, Ann Arbor, MI 48109.

Jelin, Victor A. (O. 18, 1916, Petrograd, Russia) Lib. Com., Rochester Frnds. Mtg., 1978–; Libn., First Universalist Church, Rochester, NY, 1972–75; Asst. Libn., Coll. of Ceramics, SUNY, Alfred, 1968–69; Asst. Libn., Sch. of Prtg., Rochester Inst. of Tech., 1967. **Educ.:** Univ. of Brussels, Belgium, 1935–39, BS (Physiol.); Hunter Coll., CUNY, 1954–62, MA (Bio.); Univ. of Chicago, 1964–68, MA (LS). **Orgs.:** ALA. Socty. for Gen. Syst. Resrch. AAAS. **Pubns.:** "The 'Instrumental' Use of Libraries. A Study of the Intellectual Origins of the Modern Industrial Libraries," *LIBRI* (1972); "Studies in Operational Analysis. III. Reductionism in Biology," *General Systems* (1974); "Studies in Operational Analysis. IV. Systems Theory and Operational Analysis," *Proc. of the Socty. for GL. Syst. Resrch.* (1976). **Activities:** 3; 16; 75, 90, 95–Theory of Knowledge. **Addr.:** Scientific Translations, P.O. Box 1369, Rochester, NY 14603.

Jenkins, Barbara Williams (Ag. 17, 1934, Union, SC) Head Libn., Assoc. Prof., SC State Coll., 1962–; Ref. and Docum. Libn., 1958–62, Circ. Libn., 1956–58. **Educ.:** Bennett Coll., Greensboro, NC, 1951–55, BA (Eng., LS); Univ. of IL, 1955–56, MSLS; Rutgers Univ., 1971–79 PhD (LS). **Orgs.:** ALA: Cncl. (1978–82); ACRL, Stans. and Accred. Com. (1977–81); Black Caucus (Treas., 1976–80). SELA: Coll. Sect. (Dir., 1978–80). SC LA: Coll. Sect. (Vice-Ch., 1979–80). 1890 Lib. Dirs. Org.: Pres. (1979–80). Various other orgs. The Links, Inc. Delta Sigma Theta. NAACP. Williams Chapel AME Church. **Pubns.:** Contrib. *South Carolina's Blacks and Native Americans* (1977). **Activities:** 1; 17, 24; 75 **Addr.:** P.O. Box 1565, South Carolina State College, Orangeburg, SC 29117.

Jenkins, Darrell L. (Ag. 12, 1949, Roswell, NM) Admin. Srvs. Libn., South. IL Univ., 1977–; Actg. Head, Ref. Dept., NM State Univ., 1977, Asst. Serials Libn., 1976–77, Asst. Cat. Libn., 1975–76, Asst. Ref. Libn. 1974–75, Educ./Psy. Div. Libn. 1973–74, Asst. Educ. Psy. Gift Acq. Libn. 1972–73, Actg. Sci. Div. Libn. 1972. **Educ.:** East. NM Univ., 1967–71, BA (Soc. Std.); Univ. of OK, 1971–72, MLS; NM State Univ., 1974–76, MA (Pub. Admin.). **Orgs.:** ALA: ACRL/Educ. and Bhvl. Sci. Sect. Exec. Com. (1976–79), Problems of Access and Cntrl. of Educ. Mtrls. Com. (Ch., 1976–79); LAMA/Pub. Admin. Sect., Com. on Persnl. Dynamics for Supvsrs. (1979–80). IL LA. ASIS. South. IL LA: Pres. (1979–). **Honors:** Beta Phi Mu, 1972. Phi Kappa Phi, 1971; Univ. Chap. Pres. (1981–82). **Pubns.:** Various reviews, speeches, and pubns. **Activities:** 1; 17, 35, 49-staff dev.; 56, 63 **Addr.:** Morris Library, Southern Illinois University at Carbondale, Carbondale, IL 62901.

Jenkins, Glen Pierce (Ag. 14, 1929, Pomona, CA) Rare Bk. Libn., Archvst., Cleveland Hlth. Sci. Lib., 1972–; Assoc. Tchr., Olver Wendell Holmes Elem. Sch., 1966–68. **Educ.:** Scripps Coll., 1947–51, BA (Liter.); Case Western Reserve Univ., 1969–72, MSLS; Cont. Educ. Courses, 1975, 1978. **Orgs.:** SAA. Socty. of OH Archvsts.: Rare Bks. Com. (1975–). Assn. of Libns. in the Hist. of the Hlth. Sci. Amer. Assn. for the Hist. of Med. Handerson Med. Hist. Socty. OH Musms. Assn. **Pubns.:** "Women physicians and Woman's General Hospital" in *Medicine in Cleveland and Cuyahoga County 1810–1976* (1977); "Volunteers in special collections," *Watermark* (Jl. 1979); "The Archives at the Library," *Bltn. of the Cleveland Med. Lib.* (O. 1977); Reviews. **Activities:** 1, 11; 26, 45; 55, 58, 80 **Addr.:** Howard Dittrick Museum of Historical Medicine, Cleveland Health Sciences Library, 11000 Euclid Ave., Cleveland, OH 44106.

Jenkins, Sadie J. (Je. 3, 1944, Colquitt, GA) Talking Bk. Ctr. Libn., Tri-Cnty. Reg. Lib., 1976–; Libn., Talking Bk. Ctr., Chestatee Reg., 1975–76; Branch Libn., Adult Srvs. Libn., Albany-Dougherty Pub. Lib., 1970–75; Tchr., Sponsor, Sch. Newsp., Greenfield Acad., 1968–69; Tchr., Sumner Elem., 1967–68; Libn., Poulan Public Lib., 1957; various consult. positions. **Educ.:** Berry Coll., 1963–67, BA (Eng.); Emory Univ., 1971–72, MLn (Libnshp.); various crs., wkshps., sem. **Orgs.:** GA LA: Pubcty. Com. (Ch., 1977–79); RT for the Blind and Phys. Handcpd. (Nsltr. Ed., 1975–77). Coosa Valley LA: VP (1978–79); Pres. (1979–80). ALA: ASCLA/LSBPH, Bd. (1978–79). South. Conf. of Libns. for the Blind and Phys. Handcpd.: Ch. (1977); DIKTA Ed. (1979); Natl. Mtrls. Sel. Conf., Washington DC: (Rep., 1976). GA Fed. of the Blind. GA Dem. Com.: Comm. Com.; Affirmative Action Com. Coosa Valley Area Plng. and Dev. Comsn., Title XX: Bd.; Cncl. on Aging. Young Democrats of GA: Natl. Committeewoman (1979–80); Cmnty. Rel. (Ch., 1978–79); Nsltr. Ed. (1978–79); Young Democrats Conv., Rome GA (Prog. Ch., 1979). various org. **Honors:** Gvrs. Com. on Empl. of the Handcpd., Letter of Cmdn., 1977; Awd. for Oustan. Talking Bk. Ctr. in GA, 1978–79, 1979–80. **Pubns.:** "Georgia's Subregionals: An Update," *DIKTA.* **Activities:** 9; 17, 24, 36; 72 **Addr.:** 606 Broad, Rome, GA 30161.

Jenkinson, Judith (Ap. 9, 1943, Monroe, MI) Libn., Ketchikan HS, 1975–; Libn., White Cliff Elem. Sch., 1972–75; Libn., Alcona Cmnty. HS, 1969–72; Elem. Tchr., Alcona Cmnty. Schs., 1966–68. **Educ.:** MI State Univ., 1964–66, BA (Educ.); Univ. of MI, 1968–69, AMLS. **Orgs.:** ALA: Int. Frdm. Com. AK LA: Exec. Bd. LA: Pres. (1975). Natl. Educ. Assn. AK Educ. Assn. Ketchikan Educ. Assn. **Activities:** 10; 15, 17, 20; 63 **Addr.:** Ketchikan High School, 2610 4th Ave., Ketchikan, AK 99901.

Jenks, Arlene I. (N. 10, 1928, Montpelier, VT) Media Spec., Butte Elem. Sch., Matanuska-Susitna Boro. Schs., 1980–, Media Spec., Palmer HS, 1977–80; Media Spec., Fairbanks N. Star Boro. Sch., 1972–77; Media Spec., Delta/Ft. Greeley Schs., 1968–72. **Educ.:** State Tchrs. Coll., Oneonta, NY, 1946–50, BS (Educ.); Syracuse Univ., 1967–73, MS (LS). **Orgs.:** ALA: AASL. Int. Frdm. Com. AK LA: (1980). Mat-Su LA: Secy.-Treas. (1979–80, 1980–81). Natl. Educ. Assn. AK Educ. Assn. **Honors** Beta Phi Mu. **Activities:** 10; 15, 21, 22; 63, 74 **Addr.:** P.O. Box 908, Wasilla, AK 99687.

Jenner, Elizabeth V. (Ja. 11, 1946, Budapest, Hungary) Head Libn., Ref. Lib., Can. Broadcasting Corp., 1976–, Libn., 1972–76; Libn., N. York Pub. Lib., 1969–71. **Educ.:** Univ. of BC, 1965–68, BA (Pol. Sci.), 1968–69, BLS. **Orgs.:** SLA: Telecom. Div. (Ch.-Elect/Ch., 1979–81). Can. LA. **Activities:** 12; 15, 39, 41; 93 **Addr.:** Canadian Broadcasting Corp., Reference Library, P.O. Box 500, Station A, Toronto, ON M5W 1E6 Canada.

Jennerich, Edward John (O. 22, 1945, Brooklyn, NY) Ch., Dept. of LS, Baylor Univ., 1974–; Libn., Westinghouse Jr.-Sr. HS, Pittsburgh (PA) Pub. Schs., 1970–74; Admin. Intern, Ofc. of the Assoc. Provost, Univ. of Pittsburgh, 1973; Evening Libn., Fairleigh Dickinson Univ., 1968–70; Tchr., Rahway (NJ) HS, 1967–70. **Educ.:** Trenton State Coll., 1963–67, BA (U.S. Hist., LS); Drexel Univ., 1967–70, MSLS; Univ. of Pittsburgh, 1971–74, PhD (Higher Educ. Admin., LS). **Orgs.:** ALA: OLPR (Adv. Bd., 1980–82); AASL; Lib. Educ. Com. (1979–81). AALS. TX LA. Amer. Assn. of Univ. Admins.: Bd. of Dirs. (1980–82); Reg. Coord. (1975–). AAUP: Proj. Ch. (1977–78). **Pubns.:** "The Art of the Reference Interview," *IN Libs.* (Spr. 1981); "Compe-

Special Subjects/Services: 50. Adult educ.; 51. Advert./Mktg.; 52. Aerosp.; 53. Agric.; 54. Area std.; 55. Arts/Hum.; 56. Autom.; 57. Bibl./Prtg.; 58. Bio. sci.; 59. Bus./Fin.; 60. Chem.; 61. Copyrt.; 62. Documtn.; 63. Educ.; 64. Engin.; 65. Env.; 66. Eth. grps.; 67. Film; 68. Food/Nutr.; 69. Geneal.; 70. Geo.; 71. Geol.; 72. Handcpd.; 73. Hist.; 74. Int. frdm.; 75. Info. sci.; 76. Insr.; 77. Law; 78. Legis.; 79. Math./Comp. sci.; 80. Med.; 81. Metals; 82. Nat. resrcs.; 83. Newsp.; 84. Nuc. sci.; 85. Oral hist.; 86. Petr./Energy; 87. Pharm.; 88. Phys./Astr./Math.; 89. Readg.; 90. Relig.; 91. Sci./Tech.; 92. Soc. sci.; 93. Telecom.; 94. Transp.; 95. (other).

tencies for Department Chairpersons: Myths and Realities," *Lib. Educ.* (Spr. 1981); "The Forgotten Stepchildren: Branch Campus Libraries" in *Making Cooperation Work* (1979); "Teaching the Reference Interview," *Jnl. of Educ. for Librnshp.* (Fall 1976); various other articles, speeches, and wkshps. **Activities:** 1, 11; 17, 26, 39; 63, 74 **Addr.:** Department of Library Science, Baylor University, Waco, TX 76706.

Jennings, John Melville (O. 22, 1916, James City Cnty., VA) Dir. Emeritus, Consult., VA Hist. Socty., 1979–, Dir., Libn., 1958–78, Libn., 1948–53; Cur. of Mss., Coll. of William and Mary, 1946–47, Cur., Rare Bks., 1939–43. **Educ.:** Coll. of William and Mary, 1934–38, BA (Pol. Sci.); Amer. Univ., 1947–48, MA (Hist. Arch. Admin.). **Orgs.:** SAA. Amer. Antiq. Socty. AAAS. MA Hist. Socty. **Honors:** Coll. William and Mary, LLD, 1968; SAA, Fellow, 1963. **Pubns.:** *The Library of the College of William and Mary, 1693-1793* (1968); ed., *VA Hist. Socty. Bltn.*; contrib., various bibl., hist., arch. jnls. **Activities:** 2, 14-Pvt. lib.; 45; 55 **Addr.:** Virginia Historical Society, P.O. Box 7311, Richmond, VA 23221.*

Jennings, Margaret Stone (Ap. 20, 1947, New York, NY) Info. Spec., Capital Syst. Grp., Inc., 1980–; Tech. Info. Spec., Lib. of Congs., 1979; Ed./Conf. Dir., Washington Resrchrs., 1978–79; Prog. Coord., Info. Indus. Assn., 1978; Tech. Prog. Asst., ASIS, 1975–77. **Educ.:** Radcliffe Coll., 1965–69, BA (Grmn. Lit.); Radcliffe Publshg. Proc. Course, 1969. **Orgs.:** ASIS: Spec. Int. Grp. on Arts & Hum., Nsltr. Ed. (1978–79), Ch. (1979–). Assn. for Comp. and the Hum. Mod. Lang. Assn. of America. Amer. Mensa Limited. Amer. Assn. for the Advnc. of the Hum. **Pubns.:** Ed., *Library and Reference Facilities in the Area of the District of Columbia* (1979); Ed., *Researcher's Guide to Washington* (1979); Ed., *Washington Information Workbook* (1979); "Sarah Kadec–the 'Information Manager'," *The Info. Mgr.* (Mr./Ap., My./Je. 1979); "Universal Access: An Achievable Information Future," *Comm. Tomorrow* (Fall/Win. 1978); other articles. **Activities:** 12, 14-Indus.; 29, 37, 49-Ed./Writing; 55, 75 **Addr.:** 6373 Barefoot Boy, Columbia, MD 21045.

Jennings, Nancy Elizabeth (Ap. 16, 1939, Kingston, ON) Data Archvst., Pub. Arch., 1975–. **Educ.:** Carleton Univ., 1969–72 (Arts, Soclgy.), 1976–77 (Arch.). **Orgs.:** Assn. Can. Archvsts.: Past Mem. Ch. (1978–80). IASSIST. Alum. Fund and Info. Cncl. Can. Addictions Fndn. **Pubns.:** *The Machine Readable Archives - An Overview of Its Operations and Procedures* (1980); *Drug Use Files* (1978); "Children By The Number: the Machine Readable Archives Salutes the Year of the Child," *Archvst.* (N.–D. 1979). **Activities:** 2, 4; 15, 18, 41; 56, 80, 92 **Addr.:** Public Archives of Canada, Machine Readable Archives, 395 Wellington St., Ottawa, ON K1A 0N3 Canada.

Jennings, Vincent (New York, NY) Docum., Map Libn., Hofstra Univ. Lib., 1976–; Gvt. Docum. Libn., Montclair State Coll., 1969–76; Ref. Libn., N. York Pub. Lib., 1967–68; Instr., Eng. as 2nd Lang., Coll. of Engin., Saudi Arabia, 1966–67. **Educ.:** Fordham Univ., 1956–61, AB (Eng. Lit.); 1961–64, MA (Eng. Lit); Pratt Inst., 1965–66, MLS; Univ. of South. CA, 1970 (Inst. on Lib. Autom. and Info. Retrieval). **Orgs.:** ALA: GODORT, Audit Com. (1980–81); ACRL, Legis. Com. (1981–82); MAGERT. Gvt. Docum. Assn. of NJ: Conv. (VP., 1975). Long Island Lib. Resrcs. Cncl: Com. on Gvt. Info. (1977–). AAUP. **Pubns.:** Reviewer, *Ref. and Subscrpn. Bks. Reviews* (1979–); *Choice* (1977–); Contrib., *NJ Libs., Documents to the People.* **Activities:** 1; 29, 31, 39; 70 **Addr.:** 45 W. 81 St., New York City, NY 10024.

Jensen, David P. (Mr. 27, 1938, Middletown, OH) Tech. Info. Spec., US Env. Protection Agency, 1980–82; Dir., Lib. Srvs., Greensboro Coll., 1970–78; Ref. Libn., Univ. of NC, 1968–70. **Educ.:** Greensboro Coll., 1962–65, BA (Hist.); Univ. of NC, 1967–68, MSLS. **Orgs.:** NC LA: Coll. and Univ. Sect. (Ch., 1975–77). ALA: ACRL. Beta Phi Mu: Epsilon Chap. (Pres., 1971–73). **Pubns.:** "Status and Future Needs of College and University Libraries in North Carolina," *NC Libs.* (Win. 1978); "North Carolina," *ALA Yearbook* (1976–78); Assoc. Ed., *NC Libs.* (1972–78). **Activities:** 1; 15, 17, 39 **Addr.:** 105–A Sue Ann Ct., Carrboro, NC 27510.

Jensen, Dennis F. (Jl. 14, 1938, Brooklyn, NY) Lib. Mgr., Standard & Poor's Corp., 1975–; Serials Libn., F. H. LaGuardia Cmnty. Coll., 1972–75; Asst. Libn., St. Univ. NY (Farmingdale), 1970–72. **Educ.:** Brooklyn Coll., 1957.-62, BA (Eng.) St. John's Univ., 1968–70, MLS. **Orgs.:** SLA: NY Chap., Bus. Finance Grp., VCh., Ch.-Elect (1979–80); Ch. (1980–81). ALA. City Univ. New York Libns. Assn. St. Univ. NY Libns. Assn.: Del (1971–72). **Activities:** 12; 17; 59 **Addr.:** Library, Standard & Poor's Corporation, 25 Broadway, New York, NY 10004.

Jensen, Doris J. (Je. 28, 1927, Poughkeepsie, NY) Ref. Spec., Lib. of Congs., Law Lib., 1978–; Ref. Libn., Cornell Univ., Law Lib., 1976–78, Catlgr., 1968–76. **Educ.:** Vassar Coll., 1945–48, AB (Fr.); Syracuse Univ., 1967–68, MLS. **Orgs.:** AALL. Law Libns. Socty. of Washington, DC. **Activities:** 1, 4; 20, 31, 39; 77, 78 **Addr.:** Law Library, Library of Congress, Washington, DC 20540.

Jensen, Mary Ann (N. 24, 1936, Milwaukee, WI) Cur., Thea. Col., Princeton Univ., 1966–; Asst. Dir., WI Ctr. for Thea. Resrch., 1963–66. **Educ.:** Lawrence Coll., Milwaukee-Downer Coll., 1954–58, BA (Thea.); Univ. of WI, 1962–63 (Thea.). **Orgs.:** Thea. LA: Exec. Bd. (1980–83). CNLIA. Amer. Socty. for Thea. Resrch.: Exec. Bd. (1969–72). **Pubns.:** *Let Joy Be Unconfined: a Catalog of a Ballet Exhibition* (1980); "The William Seymour Theatre Collection," *Spec. Cols.* (1981); Ed., *Amer. Socty. for Thea. Resrch. Nsltr.* (1969–72). **Activities:** 5, 12; 15, 17, 23; 55 **Addr.:** Theatre Collection, Princeton University Library, Princeton, NJ 08544.

Jensen, Mary Louise (Je. 14, 1949, Brunswick, ME) Msc. Libn., Asst. Prof., E. Carolina Univ., 1976–; Asst. Hum. Libn., Miami Univ., 1974–76, Catlgr., 1972–74. **Educ.:** Hiram Coll., 1967–71, BA (Msc.); Univ. of Pittsburgh, 1971–72, MLS. **Orgs.:** Msc. LA: Southeast. Chap. NC LA. ALA. SELA. **Activities:** 1, 12; 15, 17, 39; 55 **Addr.:** Music Library, School of Music, E. Carolina University, Greenville, NC 27834.

Jensen, Patricia E. (Ap. 1, 1929, Portland, ME) Prof. of LS, Grad. Lib. Sch., Univ. of RI, 1977–; Lib. Dir., Educ. Resrc. Ctr., 1975–77; Prof. of LS, S. CT State Coll., 1968–75; Media Dir., Ctr. Sch., New Canaan, CT, 1963–68. **Educ.:** Colby Coll., 1946–50, BA (Psy. Soc.), Univ. of NH, 1957–60, MEd (Educ. Admin.), 1960–61, MEd (Elem. Educ.); S. CT State Coll., 1963–69, MSLS; **Orgs.:** ALA: AASL (Bd. of Dirs., 1979–). AECT. New Eng. Sch. LA: Pres. (1972). New Eng. Educ. Media Assn.: Past Pres.; Bd. of Dirs. (1979–). AAUP. **Pubns.:** Contrib., *Excellence in School Media Programs* (1980); "Learning to Use the Library" Study Skills Series (1973). **Activities:** 10, 11; 17, 20, 32; 56, 63 **Addr.:** Graduate Library School, University of Rhode Island, Kingston, RI 02879.

Jensen, Raymond Allan (Ag. 5, 1926, Portland, ME) Asst. Dir., Tech. and Info. Transfer, Ofc. of Water Resrch. and Tech. U.S., Dept. of the Interior, 1979–, Coord., Mgr., 1967–79; Exec. Secy., Natl. Fed. of Sci. Abs. and Indexing Srv. 1959–66. **Educ.:** Bowdoin Coll., 1944–48, AB (Math., Phys.); Univ. of MD, Catholic and Amer. Univs., 1948–58, (Math.). **Orgs.:** ASIS. AAAS. Geosci. Info. Socty. Amer. Water Resrcs. Assn. **Honors:** ASIS, Outstan. Info. Sci. Nonprint Media Awd., 1978; Amer. Socty. of Mech. Engins., Film Fest. Grand Prize for Best Instr. Mtrls. for Mech. Engin. Educ., 1979. **Pubns.:** *An Overview of the Water Resources Scientific Information Center* (1978); "U.S. Engineering Information Services and the Role of the Water Resources Scientific Information Center," *Jnl. of Inst. of Engins.* (Australia) (N.-D. 1974). "Where Do We Go From Here?" film (1978). **Activities:** 12, 14-Natl. ctr.; 17, 30, 41; 65, 82, 95-Water resrcs. **Addr.:** Technology and Information Transfer, Office of Water Research and Technology, U. S. Department of the Interior, Washington, DC 20240.

Jensen, Wilma Mary W. (Je. 11, 1916, Hopkins, MN) Exec. Secy., Lutheran Church LA., 1963–; Secy., Bd. of Amer. Missions, Augustana Lutheran Church, Minneapolis, 1957–62; Libn.-Secy., Donavon-Lovering-Boyle, Contractors, 1951–56; Couns., Univ. of CA, Berkeley, 1943–47; Asst. Libn., Ref. Lib., Univ. of MN, 1940–43. **Educ.:** Gustavus Adolphus Coll., St. Peter, MN, 1934–38, BA (Eng.); Univ. of MN, 1939–40, BSLS; Certs. for various sems. and crs. **Orgs.:** Lutheran Church LA: Pres. (1962). Church and Synagogue LA: Pres. (1971–72); Bd. of Dirs. (1967–78). MN Adv. Cncl. on Lib. Srvs.: Bd. Mem. (1973–76). Cncl. of Natl. Lib. and Info. Srvs.: Cnclr. (1979–). Various other orgs. Lutheran Student Assn. of Amer.: Natl. Adv. (1946–47). **Honors:** Gustavus Adolphus Coll., Disting. Alum. Awd, 1974. **Pubns.:** *The Church Library: Organization and Administration* (1963, rev. 1980); *The Library Serves the Church School* (1970); *The Library Serves the Educational Program of the Congregation* (1973); "So–You Are A Church Librarian!" *Lutheran Libs.* (1963); various other articles, wkshps., and oral presentations on church libs. **Activities:** 12; 17, 26, 27; 50, 90 **Addr.:** Lutheran Church Library Association, 122 West Franklin Ave., Minneapolis, MN 55404.

Jernigan, Dr. William W. (Mr. 4, 1935, Savannah, GA) VP for Lrng. Resrcs. and Instr., Oral Roberts Univ., 1972–, Dir. of Extended Sessions, 1969–, Dir. of Lrng. Resrcs. and Lib., 1967–72, Dir. of Libs., 1965–67; Asst. Libn., Trevecca Nazarene Coll., Nashville, 1965. **Educ.:** Trevecca Nazarene Coll., 1957, AB (Theo.); Nazarene Semy., Kansas City, 1960, BD; George Peabody Coll., Nashville, 1961, MALS; Univ. of Tulsa, 1972, EdD (Educ.). **Orgs.:** Med. LA. OK LA. SWLA. Kiwanis of Tulsa. Amer. Assn. of Higher Educ. Amer. Mgt. Assn. First Untd. Methodist Church. **Pubns.:** "Learning Resources Center is Built Around Instruction," *Coll. and Univ. Bus.* (N. 1965); "Oral Roberts Favors 'Futuristics'," *Lib. Jnl.* (D. 1966); "One Who DAI-Red–A Dial Access System," *Wilson Lib. Bltn.* (F. 1970); "Dial Access at Oral Roberts University," *EPIE* (Je. 1971). **Activities:** 1; 17 **Addr.:** Oral Roberts University, 7777 South Lewis, Tulsa, OK 74171.

Jeschke, Channing R. (D. 28, 1927, Buffalo, NY) Libn., Prof. of Theo. Bibl., Pitts Theo. Lib., Emory Univ., 1971–; Libn., Assoc. Prof., Berkeley Dvnty. Sch., 1966–71. **Educ.:** Oberlin Coll., 1945–49, BA (Hist.); Yale Univ. Dvnty. Sch., 1949–52, BD (Ch. Hist.); Dvnty. Sch., Univ. of Chicago, 1966, PhD (Church Hist.); Columbia Univ., 1966–67, MS with Honors (LS). **Orgs.:** ATLA: Com. on Pubns. (1972–75, Ch., 1974–75); Bd. of Dir. (1975–78). Meth. Libns. Flwshp. Untd. Church of Christ. Hist. Socty. of the Evangelical and Reformed Church. **Honors:** Assn. of Theo. Sch. in the U.S. and Can., Study Grant, 1978. **Pubns.:** "The Lutherana Collection at the Pitts Theology Library," *Ex Libris* (O. 1978); "A Premier Theological Collection," *Ex Libris* (O. 1975). **Activities:** 1; 15, 17; 90 **Addr.:** Pitts Theology Library, Emory University, Atlanta, GA 30322.

Jeter, Ann H. (Je. 1, 1953, Torrance, CA) Libn., Hughes and Hill, 1979–; Asst. Libn., Johnson Swanson and Barbec, 1978–79. **Educ.:** Drake Univ., 1971–74, BA (Hum.); N. TX State Univ., 1974–75, MLS. **Orgs.:** AALL. Southwestern ALL: Pvt. Law Libs. (1979–81). Dallas ALL: Pres. (1981); 1st VP., Pres.-Elect (1980); 2nd VP (1979). **Activities:** 12; 15, 30, 39; 77 **Addr.:** Hughes & Hill, 1000 Mercantile Dallas Bldg., Dallas, TX 75201.

Jett, Don W. (Ag. 10, 1936, Knoxville, TN) Assoc. Prof., Head, Ag.-Vet. Med Libn., Univ. of TN, 1981–; Assoc. Prof., Head, Sci.-Engin. Libn., 1974–81, Sci. Libn., 1963–74, Ref. Libn., 1960–63. **Educ.:** Univ. of TN, 1955–60, BS (Transp.); FL State Univ., 1960–63, MSLS. **Orgs.:** SLA: South. Appalachian Chap. (Treas., 1967; Consult. Ofcr., 1971–). TN LA: *TN Libn.* (Bus. Mgr., 1965–67); Spec. Libs. Sect. (Ch., 1967–69). SELA. Geosci. Info. Socty. **Pubns.:** *Mysore University of Agricultural Sciences: A Report on the Library* (1968). **Activities:** 1, 12; 17, 24, 39; 60, 88, 91 **Addr.:** Agriculture-Veterinary Medicine Library, A113 Veterinary Hospital, University of Tennessee, Knoxville, TN 37916.

Jette, Jean-Paul (Je. 16, 1946, St. Hyacinthe, PQ) Dir., Vetny. Lib., Univ. De Montreal, 1971–. **Educ.:** Seminaire De St. Hyacinthe, 1960–67, BAC (Arts); Ecole de Bibliotheconomie, Univ. de Montreal, 1969–71, BAC (Bibl.), 1975–79 Mstrs. (Bib.). **Orgs.:** Assn. des Bib. de la Sante du Can. Intl. Assn. of Agr. Libs. and Docmlsts. Med. LA: Pres. (1980–81); Vetny. Med. Sect. (Secy.-Treas., 1979–80). Assn. Interamericana de Bibtcrs. y Docmlsts. Agricolas. **Pubns.:** "Caracteristiques de la Litterature Veterinaire de Langue Française," *MV Quebec* (N. 1979). **Activities:** 1; 17; 80 **Addr.:** 1455 Demeulles, St-Hyacinthe, PQ J2S 6Z3 Canada.

Jewell, John Huttsell (My. 13, 1940, Kansas City, MO) Coord., Ref. Srvs., Fresno Cnty. Free Lib., 1976–, Sci. Libn., 1970. **Educ.:** Univ. of KS, 1958–61, BA (Eng.); Univ. of Denver, 1968–69, MA (Libnshp.). **Orgs.:** SLA. CA LA. AAAS. **Honors:** Beta Phi Mu; Phi Beta Kappa. **Activities:** 9; 39; 91 **Addr.:** Fresno County Free Library, 2420 Mariposa, Fresno, CA 93721.

Jimenez, Margarita (D. 18, 1928, Barcelona, Spain) Dir., Readrs. Srvs., Univ. of PR Med. Sci. Campus, 1972–, Org. of Small Lib., Dept. of Hlth., Geriatric Sect., 1964. **Educ.:** Univ. of PR, 1948–52, BA (Hist.), 1970–71, MLS (Lib.); 1980, Advnc. Trng. Medline. Univ. of PR Sch. of Dentistry: Curric. Com. (1979–). **Honors:** Phi Alpha Theta, 1953. **Pubns.:** "State Department Consular Dispatches 1868," *Historia* (O. 1952); "Notes and Documents, Lares Revolution," *Historia* (O. 1953); cmplr., *Bibliography: Dr. Jose Oliver Gonzalez* (1971). **Activities:** 1; 22, 36, 39; 75, 80 **Addr.:** University of Puerto Rico, Medical Sciences Campus Library, GPO Box 5067, Rio Piedras, PR 00936.

Jimenez, Regina A. (Jl. 12, 1945, San Francisco, CA) Head Libn., San Francisco Univ. HS, 1978–; Ref. Libn., Marin Cnty. Lib., 1974–78, Film-Bkmobile. Libn., 1972–74, Branch Lib. Supvsr., 1970–72. **Educ.:** Univ. of CA, Berkely, CA State Univ., Sonoma, 1965–70, BA (Phil., Msc.); Univ. of CA, Berkeley, 1974–75, MLS, 1975, Cert. (Law Libnshp.); Med. LA, 1976, Cert. (Med. Libnshp.). **Orgs.:** ALA: AASL. CA LA. Bay Area Sch. Libns. Assn. Natl. Assn. of Indp. Schs. CA Assn. of Indp. Schs. **Honors:** Beta Phi Mu. **Activities:** 9, 10; 15, 17, 39; 55, 77, 80 **Addr.:** 15 Aureo Way, Fairfax, CA 94930.

Jimerson, Randall C. (Ap. 9, 1949, Ann Arbor, MI) Univ. Archvst., Univ. of CT, 1979–; Archvst., Yale Univ., 1977–79; Asst. Archvst., Univ. of MI, 1976–77. **Educ.:** Earlham Coll. 1967–71, BA (Lit.-Hist.); Univ. of MI, 1971–77, MA, PhD (Hist.); NHPRC Inst. Ed. of Hist. Doc., 1978 Cert. **Orgs.:** SAA. New England Archvst.: Nsltr. ed. (1980–). Amer. Assn. for State and Local Hist. South. Hist. Assn. **Pubns.:** Ed., *Guide to the Microfilm Edition of Temperance and Prohibition Papers* (1977); "The Papers of Three Hiram Binghams," *Yale Univ. Lib. Gazette* (O. 1979); "Civil War Memoirs", *Ency. of South. Hist.* (1979). **Activities:** 1, 2; 15, 17, 45; 95-History. **Addr.:** Historical Manuscripts & Archives, University of Connecticut Library, Storrs, CT 06268.

Jizba, Laurel (S. 22, 1949, Quito, Ecuador) Assoc. Libn., Spec. Asst., Autom. Prcs. Dept., IN Univ. Libs., 1972–, Asst. Libn., Latin American Catlgr., 1974–77, Asst. Libn., Libn. for Latin American Docum., 1972–74. **Educ.:** Univ. of NE, 1968–71, BA (Latin Amer. Std.); Univ. of Pittsburgh, 1971–72, MLS; IN Univ., 1975–; various workshops. **Orgs.:** ALA: LITA. IN LA: Co-Ch., Statewide Mem. Com. (1978–79); VP, Pres. Elect. Dist. V (1980–81). SALALM: Jt. Com. on Official Pubns. (1975–); Lcl. Arrange. Com. (1976–). Ohio Valley Grp. of Tech. Srv. Libns.: Lcl. Arrange. Com. (1979). Other orgs. Latin Amer. Std. Assn.

PROFESSIONAL ACTIVITIES: Institutions: 1. Acad. lib.; 2. Arch.; 3. Assn.; 4. Fed./Gvt. lib.; 5. Inst. lib.; 6. Mfr./Suppl.; 7. Milit. lib.; 8. Musm.; 9. Pub. lib.; 10. Sch. lib.; 11. Sch. of lib. sci.; 12. Spec. lib.; 13. State lib.; 14. (other). **Functions/Activities:** 15. Acq./Col. dev.; 16. Adult srvs.; 17. Admin.; 18. Apprais.; 19. Archit./Bldgs.; 20. Cat./Class.; 21. Chld. srvs.; 22. Circ.; 23. Cons./Pres.; 24. Consult.; 25. Cont. ed.; 26. Educ. lib. sci.; 27. Ext. srvs.; 28. Fund/Grants; 29. Gvt. pubs.; 30. Indx./Abs.; 31. Instr. lib. use; 32. Media srvs.; 33. Micro.; 34. Netwks./Coop.; 35. Persnl.; 36. PR; 37. Publshg.; 38. Recs. mgt.; 39. Ref. srvs.; 40. Repro.; 41. Resrch.; 42. Review.; 43. Secur.; 44. Serials; 45. Spec. col.; 46. Tech. srvs.; 47. Trustees/Bds.; 48. YA srvs.; 49. (other).

Honors: Midwest Univ. Cnsrtm. for Intl. Act., Travel Grant, 1975; Beta Phi Mu. **Pubns.:** "Bibliographic and Information Gathering Activities of Three Central Banks of the Caribbean," *Final Report and Working Papers, 21st SALALM* (1976); "Colombian Belles Lettres Collections in Selected United States Libraries," *Final Report and Working Papers, 20th SALALM* (1975). **Activities:** 1; 17, 20; 56 **Addr.:** Automated Processing Department, Indiana University Libraries, Bloomington, IN 47405.

Job, Amy Grace (Mr. 8, 1942, Orange, NJ) Head of Cat., Adj. Prof., William Paterson Coll., Wayne, NJ, 1968–; Catlgr., State Univ. Coll., Potsdam, NY, 1965–67. **Educ.:** Montclair (NJ) State Coll., 1960–64, BA (Educ., Soc. Std.); Rutgers Univ., 1964–65, MLS; Montclair State Coll., 1976–78, MEd (Educ. Media). **Orgs.:** ALA. NJ LA: Coll. and Univ. Sect. (Secy.-Treas., 1980–81); Bicentennial Com. (Vice-Ch., 1975–76). Natl. Educ. Assn. Pi Lambda Theta. William Paterson Coll. Fac. Women. **Pubns.:** Jt. auth., "Rotation and Revolution," *Instr.* (1965); reviews. **Activities:** 1; 20, 31, 42; 56, 63, 70 **Addr.:** 5 Navajo Trail, West Milford, NJ 07480.

Jobin, Françoise (D. 18, 1938, Montreal, PQ) Prof., Tech. de la Documtn., Cegep Lionel-Groulx, 1970–; Responsable/Srvs. Tech., Coll. Bathurst, NB, 1968–70; Responsable/Bib., Ecole N.D. de Bonsecours, 1966–68; Libn., Brit. Inst., Univ. de Paris, 1964–66; Bibtcr., Comsn. Scol., Outremont, 1960–62. **Educ.:** Univ. de Montreal, 1959–60, Dip. (Tech. Support), 1972–74, M Bibl. **Orgs.:** Assn. Can. des Sci. de L'Info.: Montreal Sect. (Exec. Secy., Pres., 1977–78). ASTED: Com. des Tech. de la Documtn. Corp. des Bibtcrs. Prof. PQ: Bur. (Ch., 1980–81); Com. de Formation Prof. des Pubns. d'ARGUS. Assn. des Archvsts. du PQ. **Pubns.:** Collaborator, *Livre, Bibliothèque et Culture Québécoise* (1972); "Bilan Sommaire des Activités du Comité De formation Professionnelle de la CBPQ," *ARGUS* (S.–O. 1978); "La Formation Professionnelle en France," ARGUS (S.–O. 1974). **Activities:** 1; 25, 26; 50 **Addr.:** Dept. Techniques de la documentation, Cegep Lionel-Groulx, 100, rue Duquet, Ste-Thérèse, PQ J7E 3L8 Canada.

Johanson, Cynthia J. (O. 17, 1946, Warren, PA) Head, Col. Improvement Sect., Lib. of Congs., 1978–, Sr. Descr. Catlgr., 1973–78. **Educ.:** WV Univ., 1964–68, BA (Hist.); Univ. of MI, 1972–73, MALS. **Orgs.:** ALA: Status of Women in Libnshp. (1980–84); Cnclr.-at-Large (1979–83); SRRT, Task Force on Women Strg. Com. (1977–79). Lib. of Congs: Fed. Women's Prog. Com. (1974–76). Women Lib. Workers. Lib. of Congs. Prof. Gld.: Pres. (1977–78); Contract Negotiating Team (1976–78). Amer. Fed. of State, Cnty., and Mncpl. Empl.: Cncl. 26 Exec. Bd. (1976–78). **Honors:** Lib. of Congs., Merit. Srv. Awd., 1970. **Pubns.:** Various articles. **Activities:** 4; 17, 20, 39; 95-Labor-Mgmt. Rel. **Addr.:** 2137 Suitland Terr., S.E. #102, Washington, DC 20020.

John, Nancy R. (F. 1, 1948, Brooklyn, NY) Asst. Univ. Libn., Univ. of IL at Chicago Circle, 1980–, Cat. Libn., 1978–80; Catlgr., Natl. Gallery of Art, 1974–77. **Educ.:** Stanford Univ., 1965–69, AB (Psy.); Univ. of CA, Los Angeles, 1972–73, MLS, 1972–73, Cert. (Art Libnshp.). **Orgs.:** ARLIS/NA: Ch. (1976–77). ALA: RTSD/Cat. and Class. Sect., Prog. Com. (1978–79); ARLIS/NA Rep. to Cat. Code Rev. Com. (1975–78); ACRL. IL LA: Resrcs. and Tech. Srvs. Sect. Exec. Bd. (1979–80). **Pubns.:** "Art Libraries," *ALA Yrbk.* (1978–80); "Choice of Entry" AACR2 videotape (1979). **Activities:** 1, 12; 17, 20, 22; 55, 56 **Addr.:** University of Illinois at Chicago Circle, Library, P.O. 8198, Chicago, IL 60680.

John, Patricia La Caille (O. 11, 1946, Bottineau, ND) Head, Cat. Sect., Natl. Agri. Lib. Tech. Info. Syst., 1979–; Chief, Tech. Srvs., US Gen. Acct. Ofc. Lib., 1978–79, Chief, Cat. Sect., 1974–78; Actg. Prin. Catlgr., US Dept. of State Lib., 1973–74, Sr. Libn., 1970–73; Catlgr., Kennedy Lib., East. WA State Univ., 1969–70. **Educ.:** Pacific Univ., 1964–68, BA (Hist.& World Lit.); Univ. of WA, 1968–69, ML (LS); George Washington Univ., 1971–74, MA (Hist.). **Orgs.:** SLA. ALA. FEDLINK Network: Finance Com. (1978–79); Tape User's Grp. (1977–79); Cncl. on Lib. Rsrcs., Jt. Com. on Bibl. Stans. (1981–). **Honors:** Beta Phi Mu, 1970. **Activities:** 4, 12; 17, 20, 46; 54, 75, 92 **Addr.:** 539 N. Littleton St., Arlington, VA 22203.

Johns, Cecily Ann (O. 5, 1939, Wichita, KS) Dir. of Col. and Info. Srvs., Univ. of Cincinnati, 1981–, Head, Ref./Bibl. Srvs., 1979–81; Asst. to the Dir. of Libs., Ctrl. MI Univ., 1972–79, Ref. libn., 1971–72; Ref. libn., Univ. of TX, 1968–70. **Educ.:** Univ. of KS, 1957–61, BA (Eng./Fr.), 1962–67, MA (Eng.); Univ. of CA, Los Angeles, 1968–70, MLS. **Orgs.:** ALA: RASD, Cat. Use Com. (1979–81); Machine Assisted Ref. Sect., Costs and Financing Com. (1979–81); Ref. and Subscrpn. Books Review Com. (1980–82); ACRL/Bibl. Instr. Sect., Resrch. Com. (1977–79). **Pubns.:** "Faculty status and collective bargaining: their contribution to the professional status of academic librarians," *MI Libn.* (Fall 1975); "Librarianship: a female profession?" *MI Libn.* (Aut. 1972); "Library Exercises" in *Writing Objectives for Bibliographic Instruction in Academic Libraries* (1976); Ed., *Reference Services Review* (1977–80); Contrib., *Magazines for Libraries,* 3rd ed. (1978). **Activities:** 1; 15, 17, 39 **Addr.:** Central Library, University of Cincinnati, Cincinnati, OH 45208.

Johns, Claude J., Jr. (Ag. 28, 1930, Jacksonville, FL) Dean, Lib. Srvs., Univ. of North. CO, 1976–; Dir., Libs., US Air Force Acad., 1969–76, Prof., Pol. Sci., Ch. of Instr., Dept. of Pol. Sci., 1967–69, Instr. to Prof., Pol. Sci., 1961–67. **Educ.:** FL State Univ., 1952, BS (Sec. Educ., Pub. Admin.), 1952–53, MS (Pub. Admin.); Univ. of NC, 1964, PhD (Pol. Sci., Pub. Admin.), Univ. of Denver, 1975, MA (LS). **Orgs.:** ALA: Cncl. (1978–82). CO LA: Pres. (1978); Bd. of Dir. (1977–80). ASIS. Mt. Plains LA. **Pubns.:** *Union Activities in U.S. Libraries: Actors and Issues* (forthcoming); "Union Activities in American Libraries," *Encyc. of Lib. and Info. Sci.* 1981; "Staff Development Program at the University of Northern Colorado," *CO Libs.* (S. 1979); Jt. Auth., "Management Data Generated by Automated Circulation Systems: Uses and Limitations," *Amer. Socty. for Info. Sci. Proc.* (O. 1978) "PR as a Management Tool," *CO Libs.* (S. 1978); various articles, bks. **Activities:** 1; 17, 34, 35; 56, 77, 93 **Addr.:** Library Services, James A. Michener Library, University of Northern CO, Greeley, CO 80639.

Johns, Francis A. T. (My. 5, 1923, Ringwood, Eng.) Resrch. Bibl., Alexander Lib., Rutgers Univ., 1979–, Univ. Bibl., 1958–79; Various Lib. positions, Untd. Kingdom, Can., 1948–55. **Educ.:** Rutgers Univ., 1955–57, AB (Fr.), 1957–58, MLS, 1965, MA (Fr.). **Orgs.:** Grt. Britain LA.: Fellow. ALA. Bibl. Socty. of Amer. Orien. Ceramic Socty. London. AAUP. **Honors** Phi Beta Kappa. **Pubns.:** *A Bibliography of Arthur Waley* (1968); Ed., *Chinese Poems (1916)* (1965); Ed., *Pseaumes 83... (1551)* (1973); Various articles (1952–). **Activities:** 1; 15, 45; 55, 57 **Addr.:** Box 406a, R.D. 3, Somerset, NJ 08873.

Johns, Michele Ann (Ap. 28, 1954, Chicago Heights, IL) Branch Libn., Lib. of Hlth. Sci., Univ. of IL, Med. Ctr. Peoria Sch. of Med., 1980–, Ref. Libn., 1977–80. **Educ.:** Univ. of IL, 1972–76, BS (Outdoor Recreation), 1976–77, MS (LS). **Orgs.:** Med. LA. Hlth. Sci. Libns. IL. Med. LA: Midwest Reg. Grp. **Honors** Beta Phi Mu. **Pubns.:** "Application of a Computerized Literature Retrieval System in Patient Care Management: The CML Conept," *Proc. of the 4th Anl. Symp. on Comp. Applications in Med.* (1980). **Activities:** 1, 12; 15, 17, 35; 80 **Addr.:** Library of the Health Sciences, Peoria School of Medicine, P.O. Box 1649, Peoria, IL 61656.

Johnson, Anita K. (My. 12, 1947, Wilmington, DE) Lib. Dir., Notre Dame Coll., 1977–; Ref. and Adult Srvs. Libn., Mentor Pub. Lib., 1975–77; Ref. Libn., Otterbein Coll., 1971–74. **Educ.:** Wittenberg Univ., 1965–69, BA (Eng.); Case West. Rsv. Univ., 1974–75, MSLS. **Orgs.:** OH LA. Acad. LA of OH. Cath. LA: North. OH Unit. **Activities:** 1, 9; 16, 17, 39; 55, 57, 63 **Addr.:** Clara Fritzsche Library, Notre Dame College, 4545 College Rd., Cleveland, OH 44121.

Johnson, Antoinette L. (S. 24, 1926, Centralia, IL) Libn. for Syst. Dev., Dallas Pub. Lib., 1980–, Head, Cat. Div., 1977–80, Unit Head, 1973–77; ILL Libn., Mobil Resrch. Lib., 1973. **Educ.:** Univ. of TX, Austin, 1944–48, BA (Eng.); TX Woman's Univ., 1972–73, MLS. **Orgs.:** ALA: Lcl. Arrange. Com. Dallas Conf. (1979). TX LA: TX Reg. Grp. Cat. and Class. (Secy.-Treas. 1979–80). **Activities:** 9, 12; 17, 46; 56, 75 **Addr.:** Dallas Public Library, Systems Development Office, 1954 Commerce St., Dallas, TX 75201.

Johnson, B. Lamar (Je. 28, 1904, IA) Emeritus Prof. Higher Educ., Univ. of CA, Los Angeles, 1972–; Disting. Prof., Higher Educ., Pepperdine Univ., 1977–; Prof. of Higher Educ., Univ. of CA, Los Angeles, 1952–72; Consult. on higher Educ., Ministry of Sci. and Educ., Iran, 1976–77; Exec. Dir., League for Innovation in the Comnty. Coll., 1968–76; Dean of Instr. and Libn., Stephens Coll., 1932–52. **Educ.:** Univ. of MN, 1925, BS (Eng.), 1927, MA (Educ.-Eng.), 1930, PhD (Educ. and Eng.); Univ. of MI, 1931–32, (Lib. Sci.). **Orgs.:** ALA. Amer. Assn. for Higher Educ.: Pres. (1955–56). **Honors:** Univ. of MN, Outstanding Achievement Award, 1960; Univ. of CA, Los Angeles, Disting. Tchg. Awd., 1970; Amer. Assn. of Comnty. and Jr. Coll., Disting. Srv. Awd., 1972. **Pubns.:** *Islands of Innovation Expanding: Changes in the Community College,* (1969); *Starting a Community Junior College,* (1964); *General Education in Action,* (1952); jt. Auth., *The Librarian and the Teacher in General Education,* (1948); *Vitalizing a College Library,* (1939); Various other monographs. **Activities:** 1; 17 **Addr.:** 1515 Tigertail Rd., Los Angeles, CA 90049.

Johnson, Barbara Coe (Ja. 19, 1923, Detroit, MI) Dir., Libs., Harper-Grace Hosps., Harper Hosp. Div., 1956–; Med. Libn. Vets. Admin. Hosp., Palo Alto, CA, 1953–56, Patients' Libn., 1951–52; various consult. positions. **Educ.:** Bryn Mawr Coll., 1940–44, AB (Classical Archlg.); Univ. of CA, Berkeley, 1950–51, MSLS; 1959, Spec. Cert. (Med. Libnshp.). **Orgs.:** Med. LA: Pres-Elect (1974–75); Pres., (1975–76); Past Pres. (1976–77); various com. (Ch.). SLA: Various com. (Ch.). Natl. Lib. of Med.: Biomed. Lib. Review Com. (1978–82). **Pubns.:** Chap. in *Libraries in Hospitals* (1976); Chap. in *Hospital Library Management* (1981); various articles in prof. jnls.; various sp. **Activities:** 5, 12; 17; 80 **Addr.:** Harper-Grace Hospitals, Harper Hospital Div., Dept. of Libraries, 3990 John R. St., Detroit, MI 48201.

Johnson, Betty Jo (Drees) (D. 1, 1937, Sidney, OH) Head of Tech. Srvs., Stetson Univ., 1972–, Head Cat. Libn., 1970–72; Head Cat. Libn., Armstrong State Coll., 1969–70; Head Cat. Libn., Stetson Univ., 1963–69, Acq. Libn., 1961–63. **Educ.:** Stetson Univ., 1955–59, BA (Hist.), 1959–62, MA (Hist.); Columbia Univ., 1961–64, MSLS. **Orgs.:** SELA. FL LA. ALA. Volusia Cnty. LA: Pres., 1981. Leag. of Women Voters. **Honors:** Beta Phi Mu. **Pubns.:** Numerous abs. in hist. abs. pubns. **Activities:** 1; 15, 20, 46; 59, 63, 92 **Addr.:** 722 N. Arlington, DeLand, FL 32720.

Johnson, Bettye R. (Je. 10, 1939, Millry, AL) Supvsr. of Libs. and Media Ctr., Montgomery Bd. of Educ., 1976–, Libn., Capitol Heights Jr. HS, 1968–76; Libn., Robert E. Lee HS, 1967–68; Libn., AL State Univ., 1965–67; Libn., Hayneville Rd. Sch., 1963–67. **Educ.:** AL State Univ., 1957–59, 1961–63, BS (Soc. Sci., LS), 1968–69, MEd (Sec. Media); Auburn Univ., 1976–77, Cert. (Admin.); Univ. of AL, 1976–79, MLS. **Orgs.:** ALA. AL LA. AL Instr. Media Assn. Montgomery Cnty. LA. Natl. Educ. Assn. AL Educ. Assn. Montgomery Clean City Com. AL ESEA Title IV Adv. Cncl. Various other orgs. **Activities:** 10, 12; 17, 21, 32; 63, 67 **Addr.:** Montgomery Board of Education, Box 1991, Montgomery, AL 36108.

Johnson, Bruce Leon (O. 26, 1945, Minneapolis, MN) Lib. Dir., CA Hist. Socty., 1980–; Lectr., Sch. of Lib. and Info. Std., Univ. of CA, Berkeley, 1974–80; Cur., Kemble Col. on West. Prtg. and Publshg., CA Hist. Socty. Lib., 1978–; Guest Lectr., Mills Coll., Oakland, CA, 1978–79. **Educ.:** Univ. of MN, 1963–67, BA (Hist.), 1967–69, MA (Hist.); Univ. of CA Berkeley, 1971–72, MLS, 1974–80, PhD (Lib. and Info. Std.). **Orgs.:** ALA. CA LA. Bibl. Socty. of Amer. Bibl. Socty. of the Univ. of VA. Prtg. Hist. Assn. Various other orgs. Amer. Hist. Assn. Org. of Amer. Histns. Amer. Cvl. Liberties Un. **Pubns.:** Jt. auth., *Methods of Library Use: Handbook for Bibliography 1* (1978); "Labels, Lithography, and Max Schmidt," *The Kemble Occasional* (Aut. 1979); Jt. auth., "Trends in Modern American Book Publishing," *Lib. Trends* (Win. 1978); "Fictitious Nevada Imprints: The Role of Towne and Bacon," *The Kemble Occasional* (Je. 1978); "The California Library Association, 1895–1906: Years of Experimentation and Growth," *CA Libn.* (Ap. 1976). **Activities:** 11, 12; 26, 31, 45; 57, 85 **Addr.:** California Historical Society Library, 2099 Pacific Ave., San Francisco, CA 94109.

Johnson, Carol Clark (Je. 30, 1949, Minneapolis, MN) Dir., Libs., Clayton Cnty. Libs., 1980–; Branch Libn., DeKalb (GA) Lib. Syst., 1977–80; Branch Libn., Memphis/Shelby Cnty. Pub. Lib. and Info. Ctr., 1973–77. **Educ.:** FL Atl. Univ., 1970–71, BA (Eng.); FL State Univ., 1972, MS (LS). **Orgs.:** ALA. SELA. GA LA. **Activities:** 9; 15, 17, 35; 56, 67 **Addr.:** Clayton County Libraries, 124 Smith St., Jonesboro, GA 30236.

Johnson, Carol Tanzer (Ap. 2, 1945, St. Louis, MO) Mtls. Coord., Metro. Lib. Syst. (OK Cnty.), 1972–; AV Libn., Univ. of OK Hlth. Sci., 1971–72; Branch Libn., OK Cnty. Lib., 1969–71, Reference Libn., Bus. & Sci. Dept., 1969–69; Cat., E.I. du Pont De Nemours & Co., 1968–1969. **Educ.:** LA St. Univ., 1963–67, BA (Hist.); Univ. of MI, 1967–68, MALS. **Orgs.:** ALA: RASD, Notable Bk. Com. (1973–76); Ref. and Subscrpn. Com. (1975–78). OK LA: SRRT (Ch. 1974). AAUW. Okla. City Women's Resrc. Ctr. **Pubns.:** *Catalog of Audiovisual Materials, University of Okla. Health Sciences Center* (1972). **Activities:** 9; 15, 17, 34; 57, 67, 74 **Addr.:** 131 Dean A. McGee Ave., Oklahoma City, OK 73102.

Johnson, Carolyn E. (Je. 11, 1944, Hampton, VA) Lib. Dir., Pearl River Pub. Lib. (NY), 1970–, Chld. Libn., 1968–69; Chld. Libn., Greenburgh Pub. Lib. (NY), 1966–68; Asst. Chld. Libn., Flint Pub. Lib. (MI), 1964–66. **Educ.:** Fisk University, 1959–63, BA (Eng.); Univ. of WI (Madison), 1963–64, MSLS. **Orgs.:** ALA: YASD, TV Com. (1977–79); LAMA, Fines Com. (1977). NY LA: Moshier Wynkoop Awds. Com. (Ch., 1973–75). LA Rockland Cnty.: Treas. (1977–). Rockland Cnty. Pub. Libns.: Pres. (1973–75). Ramapo Catskill Lib. Syst. Dir. Assn.: Exec. Bd., Mem. Rep. (1974–). Various other orgs. and coms. AAUW: Various coms. (1973–). Alpha Kappa Alpha Sorority (1962–). **Honors:** Salvation Army, Cmnty. Srv. Cit., 1974. **Activities:** 9; 17, 35, 48; 50, 89 **Addr.:** 9-1 Granada Crescent, White Plains, NY 10603.

Johnson, Carolyn Mary (Ap. 3, 1949, Brooklyn, NY) Asst. Libn., Cat., NY Bot. Garden Lib., 1979–; Catlgr., Pace Univ. Lib., 1976–77; Ed. Asst., *ASIS Anl. Review,* 1974–75. **Educ.:** Queensboro Cmnty. Coll., 1968–70, AA (Liberal Arts); Hunter College, 1970–73, BA (Eng.); St. John's Univ., Jamaica, NY, 1973–75, MLS, 1976–80, MA (Eng.). **Orgs.:** ALA. Thoreau Flwshp., Inc. **Honors:** Beta Phi Mu, 1976. **Pubns.:** "Highlights of ...Remarks on...Libraries...in Africa," *ALA/LEADS* (Ja. 1975); "Library Display Idea," *Wilson Lib. Bltn.* (My. 1978); "How Did Samuel Johnson Define A Library?" *St. John's Univ. Grad. Eng. Nsltr.* (Fall 1979); "How Did Washington Irving Define A Library?" *St. John's Univ. Grad. Eng. Nsltr.* (Sum. 1979); "How Did S.T. Coleridge Define Himself, and Perhaps Scholars, with Respect to Library Activities?" *St. John's Univ. Grad. Eng. Nsltr.*

Special Subjects/Services: 50. Adult educ.; 51. Advert./Mktg.; 52. Aerosp.; 53. Agric.; 54. Area std.; 55. Arts/Hum.; 56. Autom.; 57. Bibl./Prtg.; 58. Bio. sci.; 59. Bus./Fin.; 60. Chem.; 61. Copyrt.; 62. Documtn.; 63. Educ.; 64. Engin.; 65. Env.; 66. Eth. grps.; 67. Film; 68. Food/Nutr.; 69. Geneal.; 70. Geo.; 71. Geol.; 72. Handcpd.; 73. Hist.; 74. Int. frdm.; 75. Info. sci.; 76. Insr.; 77. Law; 78. Legis.; 79. Math./Comp. sci.; 80. Med.; 81. Metals; 82. Nat. resrcs.; 83. Newsp.; 84. Nuc. sci.; 85. Oral hist.; 86. Petr./Energy; 87. Pharm.; 88. Phys./Astr./Math.; 89. Readg.; 90. Relig.; 91. Sci./Tech.; 92. Soc. sci.; 93. Telecom.; 94. Transp.; 95. (other).

Who's Who in Library and Information Services

(Fall 1980); various articles, reviews. **Activities:** 1, 12; 20, 30, 42; 55, 56 **Addr.:** 5916 Madison St., Ridgewood, NY 11385.

Johnson, Clifton H. (S. 13, 1921, Griffin, GA) Exec. Dir., Amistad Resrch. Ctr., 1966–; Prof. of Hist., LeMoyne Coll., 1963–66; Archvst., Fisk Univ., 1961–63; Prof. of Hist., LeMoyne Coll., 1959–61. **Educ.:** Univ. of NC, 1946–48, BA (Hist.); Univ. of Chicago, 1948–49, MA (Hist.); Univ. of NC, 1956–58 PhD (Hist.). **Orgs.:** SAA: Ethnic Hist. Com. (1977–79:. Socty. of SW Archvsts. Frnds. of the Arch. of LA: Pres. (1977); Dir. (1978–). LA Hist. Recs. Adv. Comsn. (1976–79). South. Hist. Assn. Org. of Amer. Histns. **Pubns.:** Various bks. and articles on Black hist. **Activities:** 2; 15, 17, 28; 66, 90 **Addr.:** Amistad Research Center, Dillard University, New Orleans, LA 70122.

Johnson, Corinne E. (F. 20, 1944, Valparaiso, IN) Dir., S. West. Ohio Rural Lib., 1980–, Asst. Dir., 1980; Consult., Toledo-Lucas Cnty. Lib., 1975–79; Chld. Libn., Asst. Branch Libn., Dayton & Montgomery Cnty. Pub. Lib., 1966–75. **Educ.:** IN Univ., 1961–66, AB (Ling.) Univ. of KY, 1970–71, MS (LS). **Orgs.:** ALA: PLA; ALSC, Cont. Educ. Com. (1978–). OH LA: Stan. Com. (1977–79); Org. Com. (1981). OH Educ. Lib. Media Assn. **Honors:** Beta Phi Mu, 1971. **Activities:** 9; 17, 24; 89 **Addr.:** 367 S. Beechgrove Rd., Wilmington, OH 45177.

Johnson, Donald Clay (Ag. 19, 1940, Clintonville, WI) Head, Reader Srvs. Div., Coll. of William and Mary, 1981–, Reader Srvs. Libn. 1980–81, Asst. Libn. for Reader Srvs., Natl. Univ. of Malaysia, 1972–74; Head Ref. Libn., North. AZ Univ., 1971–72; Cur. SE Asia Col., Yale Univ., 1967–70. **Educ.:** Univ. of WI, 1958–62, BA (Asian Std.); Univ. of Chicago, 1963–67, MALS; Univ. of WI, 1975–80, PhD (LS). **Orgs.:** ALA: IRRT, SE Asia Sect. (Ch., 1968–69, 1971). Assn. for Asian Std. **Pubns.:** *Index to Southeast Asian Journals, 1960–1974* (1977); *A Guide to Reference Materials on Southeast Asia* (1970); "The Bibliographical Heritage of British Southern Asia," *Libri* (1973). **Activities:** 1; 20, 31, 39; 54, 57 **Addr.:** 142 E. Marquette St., Berlin, WI 54923.

Johnson, Doris C. (New York, NY) Head, Ref. Srvs., Adelphi Univ., 1951–, Assoc. Prof. of LS, Head of Ref. Srvs., 1969–, Asst. Prof., of LS, Head of Ref. Srvs., 1963–69, Instr. of LS, Head of Ref. Srvs., 1953–63, Head, Ref. Dept., 1951–53; Head, Chld. Dept., Hempstead Pub. Lib., 1949–51. **Educ.:** Adelphi Univ., 1967–78, BA; Pratt Inst., 1948–49, CLS. **Orgs.:** ASIS. ALA: ACRL; RASD. Nassau Cnty. LA. AAUP. Amer. Cvl. Liberties Un. **Honors:** Adelphi Univ., Silver Medal Awd., 1972. **Activities:** 1; 17, 31, 39; 75, 78, 92 **Addr.:** 58 St. Pauls Rd. N., Hempstead, NY 11550.

Johnson, Dorothy E. (Newark, NJ) Asst. Dir., Bloomfield Pub. Lib., 1971–, Ref. Libn., 1952–71. **Educ.:** Douglass Coll., 1947–51, BA (LS); Rutgers Univ., 1955–58, MLS; NJ State Bd. of Educ., 1958, Prof. Libns. Permanent Cert. **Orgs.:** ALA: RTSD, Essex Cnty. NJ Chap. (Ch., 1958–60). NJ LA: VP, Pres.-Elec. (1981–82); Admin. Sect. (Pres., 1980–81); Ref. Sect. (Pres., 1960–62); various com. NJ State Lib.: Ad Hoc Com. to Std. Area Coord. Cncls. (1978). Gvrs. Conf. on Lib. and Info. Srvs.: Recorder (1979). various org. Hist. Socty. of Bloomfield, NJ. AAUW: Pres. (1970–72). Inter-Agency Cncl. of Bloomfield, NJ. Church of the Advent. various org. **Honors:** AAUW, Bloomfield Branch, Flwshp. Grant, Named in Hon. of Dorothy E. Johnson, 1974. **Activities:** 9; 17; 63 **Addr.:** Bloomfield Public Library, 90 Broad St., Bloomfield, NJ 07003.

Johnson, Edward R. (N. 29, 1940, Denver, CO) Dir. of Libs., N. TX State Univ., 1979–, Asst. Dean of Libs., PA State Univ., 1972–79; Bus. Admin. Libn., Univ. of IA, 1967–69, Ref. Libn., 1966–67. **Educ.:** Univ. of CO, 1960–64, BA (Hist.); Univ. of WI, 1965–66, MALS, 1969–72, PhD (LS). **Orgs.:** ALA: RTSD, Tech. Srv. Admins. of Medium-Sized Resrch. Libs. (1973–74), Keybd. Com. (1974–75); Com. on Accred. (Site Visitor, 1980). TX LA. SWLA. AAUP. Oral Hist. Assn. **Honors:** Beta Phi Mu, 1966. **Pubns.:** *Organization Development for Academic Libraries: An Evaluation of the Management Review and Analysis Program* (1980); "Applying 'Management by Objectives' to the University Library," *Coll. & Resrch. Libs.* (N. 1973); "Subject Divisional Organization in American University Libraries, 1939–1974," *Lib. Qtly.* (Ja. 1977); Jt. auth., "Evaluating the Impact of MRAP on Several Research Libraries: Some Thoughts on Assessment" in *Lib. Resrch. RT, 1977, Resrch. Forums Procs.* (1979); Jt. auth., "The Undergraduate Library and the Subject-Divisional Plan; Problems and Prospects" in *New Horizons for Acad. Libs.* (1979); various other articles. **Activities:** 1; 17, 39, 46; 59, 85 **Addr.:** 529 Northridge, Denton, TX 76203.

Johnson, Edwin A. (S. 24, 1916, Schenectady, NY) Dir., Libs., Valparaiso Univ., 1979–, Asst. Dir., Libs., 1977–79, Ref. Libn., 1964–77. **Educ.:** Valparaiso Univ., 1934–38, AB (Msc., Hist.); Northwestern Univ., 1938–39, MMus (Piano); West. MI Univ., 1963–64, MA (LS). **Orgs.:** ALA. IN LA. Northwest IN Area Lib. Srvs. Athrty.: Pres. (1975–77). IN State Lib. Adv. Cncl.: Ch. (1979–80). Valparaiso Rotary Club. Valparaiso Cmnty. Concert Assn. **Honors:** Pi Kappa Lambda, 1939; Beta Phi Mu, 1964. **Pubns.:** Adv., "Council Assists State Library," *Lib. Occurrent* (My. 1980); Ed. Adv. Bd., *Indx. to US Gvt. Per.* (1974–78). **Activities:** 1; 15, 17, 39; 55, 63, 92 **Addr.:** Moellering Library, Valparaiso University, Valparaiso, IN 46383.

Johnson, Eleanor (N. 13, 1923, Chicago, IL) Fld. Libn., Univ. of AZ Hlth. Sci. Ctr. Lib., 1971–; Consult. Libn., Fac. of Med., Saigon, 1967–69; Biomed. Libn., Univ. of Chicago, 1958–67; Assoc. Libn., Head of Per., NY Acad. of Med., 1951–58. **Educ.:** Univ. of Chicago, 1943–45, BLS; Univ. of MI, 1948–49, AMLS; Univ. of IL, 1969–70, Cert. Adv. Std. (LS). **Orgs.:** Med. LA: Med. Sch. Libns. Grp. (Ch., 1961–62). ALA. SLA. US Surgeon Gens. Adv. Com. on Sci. Pubns.: Libn. Mem. (1963–67). **Honors:** Phi Kappa Phi, 1949; Beta Phi Mu, 1970; Repub. of Viet Nam, Educ. and Culture Medal, 1968. **Activities:** 1, 12; 24, 34, 39; 58, 80 **Addr.:** 1227 E. Drachman St., Tucson, AZ 85719.

Johnson, Elspeth (Betts) C. (Ag. 12, 1934, Cambridge, MA) Libn., Kodiak Island Sch. Dist., 1974–; Lib. Lrng. Ctr. Dir., Glencoe Pub. Schs., 1969–74; Tchr., Northfield Dist. 39, 1962–69. **Educ.:** North. IL Univ., 1952, BS (Educ.); Natl. Coll. of Educ., 1968–69, MA (Admin.); various grad. crs. **Orgs.:** AK LA: Pres. (1977–78); Kodiak Chap. (Pres., 1976–77). Kodiak Borough Educ. Assn.: Bd. (1977–80); Pubcty. Ch. (1978, 1981). AAUW. **Honors:** AK ESEA Title IV Adv. Cncl., Lib. Rep., 1978–, Ch., State Plan, 1980–; Kappa Delta Pi. **Activities:** 10; 17, 20, 21; 63, 89 **Addr.:** P.O. Box 186, Kodiak, AK 99615.

Johnson, Garry Block (D. 6, 1940, Philadelphia, MS) Dir., Lib. Srvs., Louisville Bapt. Hosps., 1978–; Asst. Dir., Med. Lib., Norton-Chld. Hosps., 1977–78; Prin. of Sch., Libn., KY Correct. Inst. for Women, 1974–77. **Educ.:** Univ. of Louisville, 1961–62, BA (Eng.); Spalding Coll., 1974–76, MLA (LS). **Orgs.:** KY Hlth. Sci. Lib. Cnsrtm.: Pres. (1978–80). KY Socty. of Hlth. Sci. Libns.: Pres. (1981). **Activities:** 5, 12; 17, 39; 80 **Addr.:** Louisville Baptist Hospitals, Hagan Library, 810 Barret Ave., Louisville, KY 40204.

Johnson, Glenn H., Jr. (Ag. 31, 1926, Cincinnati, OH) Dir., Churchill Lib., West. New Eng. Coll., 1977–; Asst. Dir., Lib., St. Mary's Coll., MD, 1971–77; Lib. Dir., Cragmor Campus, Univ. of CO, 1965–71, Asst. Dir., Norlin Lib., 1963–65. **Educ.:** Univ. of CO, 1944–48, BA (Eng.), 1948–50, MA (Eng.); Univ. of Denver, 1956–57, MA (LS). **Orgs.:** ALA. MA LA. New Eng. LA. Coop. Libns. of Grt. Springfield. **Activities:** 1, 2; 17, 19, 39; 55, 56 **Addr.:** Churchill Library, Western New England College, 1215 Wilbraham Rd., Springfield, MA 01119.

Johnson, Goldye Kent (F. 17, 1923, Staunton, VA) Readers' Srv. Libn., Lincoln Univ., 1955–; Sch. tchr., various tchg. positions. **Educ.:** WV St. Coll., 1934–37, AB valedictorian (Eng.); Drexel Univ., 1960–61, MSLS (Soc. Stud.); Cert. in Comp. Sci., 1978–79; Stan. Normal Tchr. Cert. **Orgs.:** ALA: Delaware Valley Chap., ARCL, Bd. Tri-St. Lib. Coop.: Secy. PA LA: Awds. Com. Donegal Presby.: Self-Dev. Peoples Com.; Christ. Educ. Com. Untd. Presby. Women: Pres. Ord. East. Star: Myrtle Chap., Past Worthy Matron. **Honors:** Valedictorian of college class Natl. Hon. Socty. Awd.; Untd. Presby. Church, Loaves and Fishes Awd. **Activities:** 1, 2; 15, 19, 22; 55, 56, 93 **Addr.:** Langston Hughes Memorial Library, Lincoln University, Lincoln University, PA 19352.

Johnson, Guy M. (Je. 26, 1927, Knox Cnty., TN) Head Libn., Nichols Sch., 1975–, Ch., Hist. Dept., 1972–75, Hist. Tchr., 1954–72. **Educ.:** Duke Univ., 1949, BA (Acct.); SUNY, Buffalo, 1964, MA (Hist.). **Orgs.:** Indp. Sch. LA of West. NY: Fndr. (1979). ALA. Buffalo Cncl. on World Affairs. Buffalo World Hosplty. Assn. **Honors:** Fulbright Fndn., Proj. Grant, 1972. **Activities:** 10; 15, 17, 31; 54, 92 **Addr.:** Nichols School Library, 1250 Amherst St., Buffalo, NY 14216.

Johnson, Harlan R. (My. 5, 1939, Hettinger, ND) Assoc. Prof. of LS, North. AZ Univ., 1975–, Curric. Libn., LS Instr., 1968–74; Libn., Westside HS, Omaha, 1967–68; Tchr., Mandan (ND) HS, 1964–66; Tchr., Steele (ND) HS, 1961–64. **Educ.:** Dickinson (ND) State Coll., 1957–61, BS (Eng.); George Peabody Coll., 1966–67, MLS; Univ. of AZ, 1972–75, EdD (Sec. Educ.). **Orgs.:** AZ LA. ALA. Phi Delta Kappa. **Pubns.:** "Teacher Utilization of Instructional Media Centers in Secondary Schools," *Clearing House* (N. 1977); "Research Review: Teacher Utilization of Libraries in the Secondary Schools of Tucson District No. 1," *Sch. Media Qtly.* (Fall 1975); "The Curriculum Materials Center," ERIC/CLIS (1973). **Activities:** 10, 11; 26; 63, 75 **Addr.:** Box 5774, Northern Arizona University, Flagstaff, AZ 86011.

Johnson, Helen Christine (O. 7, 1952, Jackson, MS) Law Libn., The Coca-Cola Co., 1979–, Asst. Law Libn., 1977–79; Asst. Law Libn., Smith, Currie and Hancock, 1977. **Educ.:** Furman Univ., 1970–74, BA (Hist.); Inst. for Paralegal Trng., 1974–75; Emory Univ., 1976–77, MLS. **Orgs.:** SLA. ALA. Atlanta Law Libs. Assn.: VP (1979); Pres. (1980); Place. Ofcr. (1981). AALL. **Activities:** 12; 15, 17, 39; 77, 78 **Addr.:** The Coca-Cola Co., Law Library (NAT 19), P.O. Box Drawer 1734, Atlanta, GA 30301.

Johnson, Herbert F. (Ag. 1, 1934, St. Paul, MN) Dir. of Libs., Emory Univ., 1978–; Libn. of Oberlin, Prof., Oberlin Coll. & Pub. Libs., 1971–78; Head Libn., Assoc. Prof., Hamline Univ., 1964–71; Asst. Bus. Libn., Columbia Univ., 1961–64; Libn., US Govt., 1959–61. **Educ.:** Univ. of MN, 1957, BA (Pol. Sci.), 1959, MA (LS); Kursverksamheten Vid Lunds Univ., 1975, Betyg (Swedish). **Orgs.:** ASIS: Ch., MN Chap. (1971); Ch., North. OH Chap. (1976–77). ALA. GA LA. SELA. AAUP. Rotary Intl. Dekalb Families in Action: Bd. (1978–). **Honors:** Beta Phi Mu, 1959; Cncl. on Lib. Resrcs., Flwshp., 1974–75. **Pubns.:** "What Future Reference Librarian," *RQ* (Spr. 1971); "Information Systems Management in the Small Liberal Arts College," *Coll. and Resrch. Libs.* (vol 30, no. 6.). **Activities:** 1; 17, 24, 26 **Addr.:** R. W. Woodruff Library, Emory University, Atlanta, GA 30322.

Johnson, J. Peter (Mr. 22, 1939, Ithaca, NY) Dir., Mid. Island Pub. Lib., 1978–; Dir., Oyster Bay-E. Norwich Pub. Lib., 1972–78; Dir., Malverne Pub. Lib., 1970–72; Head, Ref., Circ., SUNY, Farmingdale, 1967–70. **Educ.:** Hofstra Univ., 1961–65, BA (Psy., Soclgy.); Long Island Univ., 1966–67, MS (LS). **Orgs.:** Nassau Cnty LA: Pres. (1978). NY LA: Legis. Com. ALA. **Activities:** 9; 17; 67, 68 **Addr.:** Middle Island Public Library, P.O. Box 426, Middle Island, NY 11953.

Johnson, James B. Jr. (O. 1, 1943, Somerville, MA) Deputy State Libn., SC State Lib., 1979–, Dir., Srvs. for the Handcpd., 1973–79; Instr., Coll. of Libnshp., Univ. of SC, 1976–77; Inst. Lib. Consult., SC State Lib., 1972–75; Milit. Srv., U.S. Marine Corps, 1970–72; Libn., LA State Penitentiary, 1968–70. **Educ.:** Univ. of New Orleans, 1961–66, BA (Hist.); LA State Univ., 1966–68, MSLS. **Orgs.:** ALA: Com. on Adoption of Stans. for Correctional Libs. (1972–73); ASCLA/Lib. Srvs. to the Blind and Phys. Handcpd. Sect., Anl. Plng. Com. (1979–80), Stans. Review Com. (1979–81); ASCLA/Lib. Srvs. to the Impaired Elderly Sect., Plng. Com. (Ch., 1979–80). SC LA: Pubns. Com. (1978–80); Jr. Mems. RT (Ch., 1973–74). SELA. South. Conf. of Libns. for the Blind and Phys. Handcpd. SC Gvr.'s Com. on Empl. of the Handcpd. **Pubns.:** *Breakthrough with Books, Louisiana State Library* (1968); "The Public Education Campaign in South Carolina," *Dikta* (Sum. 1978); "State Library Records Books for the Handicapped," *SC Libn.* (Spr. 1978); "Cassettee Books 1974–1976," *Dikta* (Fall 1977); "A Report on the Cassettee Advisory Committee," *Dikta* (Spr. 1977). **Activities:** 9, 13; 17, 36; 72, 78 **Addr.:** South Carolina State Library, P.O. Box 11469, Columbia, SC 29211.

Johnson, Jeffrey P. (D. 4, 1944, Toledo, OH) Dir., Woodlands Lib. Coop., 1980–; Ext. Srvs. Libn., US Army Lib. Frankfurt Milit. Cmnty. (W. Germany), 1974–80; Army Libn., US Army Lib. (Fulda and Bad Hersfeld, Germany), 1972–74; Libn., Toledo Lucas Cnty. Pub. Lib., 1970–72. **Educ.:** Univ. of Toledo, 1962–66, BA Cum Laude (Hist.); Univ. of MI, 1971–71, AMLS. **Orgs.:** ALA: PLA; Small and Medium Size Lib. Sect. Assoc. of State and Coop. Lib. Agencies. MLA: Coop. Caucas. **Activities:** 7, 9; 15, 16, 17, 27 **Addr.:** 1200 Arms St. #44, Marshall, MI 49068.

Johnson, JoAnn (O. 7, 1928, Mattoon, IL) Chief, Lib. Srvs., US Env. Protection Agency, Env. Resrch. Ctr. (Cincinnati), 1974–; Dir., Hlth. Sci. Lib. OH St. Univ., 1965–74; Chief Ref. Libn., N.W. Univ. Med. Sch. Lib., 1964–65; Head Libn., Amer. Meat Inst. Fndn., Univ. of Chicago, 1956–64; Ref. Libn., Federal Reserve Bank of Chicago, 1954–56; Spec. Srvs. Libn., US Army (Civilian) Stuttgart, Ger., 1952–54. **Educ.:** Denison Univ., 1946–50, BA (Soc. Sci.); Univ. of IL, 1950–50, MSLS. **Orgs.:** ASIS: numerous local offices, coms. SLA. Med. LA: Ed. Com. *Med. Lib. Bltn.* (Ch.); other offices, coms. Grt. Cincinnati Lib. Cnsrtm.: Secy., Exec. Com. (1979). OH Acad. of Med. Hist. The Nature Conservancy, 1978– OH Hist. Socty. Amer. Civil Liberties Union. **Activities:** 1, 12; 17, 19, 39; 58, 65, 80 **Addr.:** 3675 Willowlea Ct., Apt. 6, Cincinnati, OH 45208.

Johnson, Judith J. (Mr. 31, 1942, New York, NY) Cat. Dept. Head, Memphis State Univ., 1980–, Msc. Catlgr., 1978–80; Catlgr., Albright Knox Art Gallery Art Lib., 1977–78; Msc. Catlgr., Univ. of Miami, 1969–74. **Educ.:** Peabody Cnsvty. of Msc., 1959–63, BM (Msc. Educ.); Univ. of Miami, 1968–69, MM (Musicology); FL State Univ., 1974, MLS, 1974–78, PhD (Hum.). **Orgs.:** Msc. LA. Socty. for Ethnomusicology. Socty. for Asian Msc. **Honors:** Mu Phi Epsilon, 1960. **Pubns.:** *Myth, Music and Oral Tradition in the Chinese Folk Theater* (forthcoming); *A Study of Three Representative Composers of the Early French Clavecin School* (1975); "Quality Control and the OCLC Data Base," *Lib. Resrcs. and Tech. Srvs.* (Ja. 1981) "Current Musical Trends in the Peoples Republic of China," *Interdisciplina* (S. 1975); "Index to Children's Songs in School Series" comp. printout (1969). **Activities:** 1; 20; 54, 55, 56 **Addr.:** Catalog Dept., Memphis State University Libraries, Memphis, TN 38152.

Johnson, Judy Lenore (O. 16, 1944, Marshalltown, IA) Ch., Serials Div., Love Lib., Univ. of NE, 1974–; Asst. Cat., Austin Peay State Univ., 1971–74; Libn., Zama Amer. HS, Zama, Japan, 1970–71; Libn., Hays Sr. HS, 1967–70. **Educ.:** Fort Hays KS State Univ., 1962–66, BA (Eng.); Emporia State Univ., 1966–68, MLS; Univ. of NE, 1975–76, MA (Adult Educ). **Orgs.:** ALA. Mt. Plains LA. NE LA: Ch., Spec. & Inst. Libs. Sect. (1975–76). Natl. Educ. Assn. **Pubns.:** "LEOMA: Library Education Opportunities in Mid America," *NE Lib. Qtly.* (Win. 1976); reviews. **Activities:** 1; 20, 25, 44; 50 **Addr.:** Serials Division, Love

PROFESSIONAL ACTIVITIES: Institutions: 1. Acad. lib.; 2. Arch.; 3. Assn.; 4. Fed./Gvt. lib.; 5. Inst. lib.; 6. Mfr./Suppl.; 7. Milit. lib.; 8. Musm.; 9. Pub. lib.; 10. Sch. lib.; 11. Sch. of lib. sci.; 12. Spec. lib.; 13. State lib.; 14. (other). **Functions/Activities:** 15. Acq./Col. dev.; 16. Adult srvs.; 17. Admin.; 18. Apprais.; 19. Archit./Bldgs.; 20. Cat./Class.; 21. Chld. srvs.; 22. Circ.; 23. Cons./Pres.; 24. Consult.; 25. Cont. ed.; 26. Educ. lib. sci.; 27. Ext. srvs.; 28. Fund/Grants; 29. Gvt. pubs.; 30. Indx./Abs.; 31. Instr. lib. use; 32. Media srvs.; 33. Micro.; 34. Netwks./Coop.; 35. Persnl.; 36. PR; 37. Publshg.; 38. Recs. mgt.; 39. Ref. srvs.; 40. Repro.; 41. Resrch.; 42. Review.; 43. Secur.; 44. Serials; 45. Spec. col.; 46. Tech. srvs.; 47. Trustees/Bds.; 48. YA srvs.; 49. (other).

Library, University of Nebraska-Lincoln, Lincoln, NE 68588-0410.

Johnson, Julie M. (S. 30, 1947, Urbana, IL) Assoc. Med. Libn., Sch. of Med., Univ. SC, 1976–; Actg. Dir., Biomed Lib., Univ. of of S. AL, 1975–76, Biomed. Info. Spec., 1972–75; Ref. Libn., Tampa Pub. Lib., 1970–72. **Educ.:** Randolph-Macon Woman's Coll., 1965–69, AB (Art); Univ. of MD, 1969–70, MLS; Med. LA, 1972, Cert. (Med. Libn., Grade I). **Orgs.:** Med. LA: *MLA News* Ed. Com. (Ch., 1978–79); Med. Sch. Libs. Spec. Interest Grp. (Ch., 1979–80). ASIS. SC LA. Columbia Area Med. Libns. Assn.: Pres. (1978–80). Various other orgs. AAUP. **Honors:** Beta Phi Mu, 1970. **Pubns.:** Proj. Dir., *SEMPUL: South Eastern Medical Periodicals Union List* (1981); Proj. Dir., *South Carolina Union List of Medical Periodicals* (1979); Ed., *Columbia Area Medical Libraries Union List of Peridocals* (1977); Robert Mills and the South Carolina State Hospital," *Jnl. SC Med. Assn.* (Jl. 1979); "Library Services to South Carolina via the State's Two Medical Schools," *Jnl. SC Med. Assn.* (D. 1978); various speeches. **Activities:** 1, 12; 17, 24, 34; 55, 80, 95-Med. Iconography. **Addr.:** School of Medicine Library, University of South Carolina, Columbia, SC 29208.

Johnson, K. Suzanne (Je. 21, 1945, Twin Falls, ID) Biomed. Sci. Libn., CO State Univ. Libs., 1974–; Libn., Univ. of TX Med. Branch Lib. 1970–74. **Educ.:** Univ. of NE, 1963–67, BS (Med. Tech.); Univ. of MN, 1968–69, MALS; Med. LA, 1970, Cert. (Med. Libn., Grade II). **Orgs.:** Med. LA: Com. on Srvys. and Stats. (1976–79). Vetny. Med. Libns. Grp. (Ch., 1979–80). CO Cncl. of Med. Libns. **Pubns.:** *TALON-Union List* 3rd ed. (1974); "The Politics of Book Fund Allocation: A Case Study" in *New Horizons in Academic Libraries* (1979). **Activities:** 1, 12; 15, 31, 39; 80, 95-Vetny. med. **Addr.:** Libraries, Colorado State University, Fort Collins, CO 80523.

Johnson, Karl Bernard (Mr. 25, 1942, Marinette, WI) Coord., Lib. Srvs., E. Campus, Pima Cmnty. Coll., 1977–; Braille Libn., AZ State Sch. for the Deaf and Blind, 1976; Libn., Laredo Jr. Coll., 1974–76; Libn., AZ State Univ., 1968–74. **Educ.:** Univ. of AZ, 1960–64, BA (Elem. Educ.); Univ. of Denver, 1965–67, MA (Libnshp.); AZ State Univ., 1972–74, PhD (Higher Educ. Admin.). **Orgs.:** ALA: LAMA/BES, Jr. Coll., Plng. and Proc. Boy Scouts of Amer. **Activities:** 1; 17, 18, 45 **Addr.:** Pima Community College, E. Campus Library, 8202 E. Poinciana, Tucson, AZ 85730.

Johnson, Kenneth W. (Mr. 3, 1948, ON) Univ. Archvst., Trent Univ., Peterborough, ON, 1970–. **Educ.:** Trent Univ., 1966–70, BA with honors (Hist.); Trent and York Univs. 1972–77, part-time std. (Hist.); Carleton Univ., 1970, CAPA (Arch. Principles and Admin.). **Orgs.:** Assn. of Can. Archvsts.: Secy. (1976–77). Bur. of Can. Archvsts. Toronto Area Archvsts. Grp.: Vice-Ch. (1979–80). Natl. Arch. Apprais. Bd. Otonabee Reg. Cons. Athrty. **Pubns.:** "University Archives Survey," *Arch. Bltn.* (Ja. 1974); various prof. assn. briefs to gvt. and pub. **Activities:** 1, 2; 17, 38, 45 **Addr.:** Trent University Archives, Trent University, Peterborough, ON K9J 7B8 Canada.

Johnson, Lesley S. (Je. 5, 1949, Spokane, WA) Asst. Prof., VA Commonwealth Univ., 1981–; Media Spec., NE Catholic HS, 1977–81, LS Instr., Libn., Natl. Admin. Sch., Natl. Nutrition Lib., Peace Corps, 1975–77; Tech. Libn., Singer Bus. Machines, 1974–75; Info. Spec., Baltimore Cnty. Pub. Lib., 1972–73. **Educ.:** Whitman Coll., 1967–71, BA (Eng.); Univ. of NC, Chapel Hill, 1971–72, MSLS; 1975, Cmnty Coll. and Adult Educ. Tchg. Certs.; Temple Univ., 1978–81, EdD. **Orgs.:** Intl. Assn. of Sch. Libnshp.: Asst. Ed. (1978–). ALA: YASD Resrch. Com. (1981–). Cath. LA: HS sect., Bd. Dirs. (1981–). PA Sch. LA: Comm. Com. (1979–80). Girl Scouts of the USA. Catholic Church. **Pubns.:** "Audio-Visual Production...," *Catholic Lib. World* (N. 1978). **Activities:** 10, 12; 25, 41, 48; 50, 54, 63 **Addr.:** Oliver Hall, School of Education, Division of Editorial Services, Virginia Commonwealth University, Richmond, VA 23284.

Johnson, Maggie (Ja. 3, 1949, Chicago, IL) Coord., Gvt. Docum. Div., MO State Lib., 1978–, Fed. Docum. Libn., 1974–78. **Educ.:** North. IL Univ., 1967–71, BA (Hist.); Univ. of WA, 1973–74, MLS. **Orgs.:** ALA: *Docum. to the People* (Distribution Mgr., 1977–); GODORT Fed. Docum. Task Force Work Grp. on Bibl. Cntrl. (Ch., 1976–79). MO LA: Treas. (1978–79); Exec. Bd. (1978–79); Gvt. Docum. Com. (1974–). State Lib. Rep. to MIDLNET-OCLC User Grp. **Pubns.:** Various speeches on gvt. docum. **Activities:** 13; 29, 39; 59, 95-Census, gvt. **Addr.:** Missouri State Library, P.O. Box 387, Jefferson City, MO 65102.

Johnson, Margaret Ann (Ag. 11, 1948, Atlanta, GA) Head, Tech. Srvs., St. Paul Campus Libs., Univ. of MN, 1977–; Libn., St. Paul Pub. Lib., 1975–77; Market Anal., Resrch. Consult., Cntrl. Data Corp., 1973–75; Cat. Libn., Univ. of IA Lib., 1972–73. **Educ.:** St. Olaf Coll., 1966–70, BA (Eng., Grmn.); Univ. of Chicago, 1970–72, MA (LS). **Orgs.:** MN LA: Tech. Srvs. Sect. (Ch., 1980–81). ALA: ACRL 2nd Natl. Conf., Hosplty. Ch. ARLIS/NA: Twin Cities Chap. **Activities:** 1; 15, 17, 46 **Addr.:** St. Paul Campus Libraries, Univ. of MN, 1984 Buford Ave., St. Paul, MN 55108.

Johnson, Sr. Marie Inez (Je. 2, 1909, Mitchell, SD) Head, Tech. Srvs., Coll. of St. Catherine, 1974–, Dir., 1942–74, Ref. Libn., 1940–42. **Educ.:** Coll. of St. Catherine, 1925–29, BA (Eng.), 1938–39, BS (LS); Columbia Univ., 1939–40, MS (LS). **Orgs.:** ALA: Various Com. Cath. LA: Exec. Bd. (1970–76). MN LA: Various Com. AAUP. **Honors:** MN LA, Libn. of the Year, 1967; Butler Schol. for Frgn. Std., 1958. **Pubns.:** *Development of Separate Service for Young People* (1940); *Catherine McAuley Library Survey Report* (1964); *Fontbonne College Library Administrative Study* (1968); various chld. bk. reviews. **Activities:** 1; 15, 17, 21 **Addr.:** College of St. Catherine, 2004 Randolph Ave., St. Paul, MN 55105.

Johnson, Marjorie J. (New Lisbon, IN) Dir., New Castle-Henry Cnty. Pub. Lib., 1964–, Ref.-Cat. Libn., 1956–64. **Educ.:** Ball State Univ., 1952–59, BA (Eng., LS); Univ. of IL, 1959–62, MLS; Allerton Lib. Inst., Supvsn. of Empl. in Libs., 1978, Cert. **Orgs.:** IN LA: Secy. (1965–66); Ch., Ref. Div. (1962–63); Ch., Tech. Srvs. RT (1967–68). ALA. OH Valley Grp. Tech. Srvs.: Treas. (1964–65). New Castle Bus. and Prof. Women's Club: Pres. (1972–74). Altrusa Club of New Castle: Pres. (1970–72, 1977–79). Henry Cnty. Sch. for Retarded Chld.: VP (1969–70). First Christ. Church: Bd. Secy. (1966–68, 1970–71). **Honors:** New Sunnyside Sch. of New Castle Cmnty. Sch. Corp., Outstan. Citizen, 1976. **Activities:** 9; 17, 35, 36; 69 **Addr.:** New Castle-Henry County Public Library, 376 South 15th St., P.O. Box J, New Castle, IN 47362.

Johnson, Marjorie M. (D. 9, 1926, Chicago, IL) Libn., S. Branch, Evanston Pub. Lib., 1969–; Libn., Adult Srvs., Skokie Pub. Lib., 1967–69. **Educ.:** Smith Coll., 1944–48, BA (Eng. Lit.); Rosary Coll., 1963–67, MLS. **Orgs.:** IL LA. ALA. **Honors:** Beta Phi Mu. **Activities:** 9; 16, 17, 22 **Addr.:** 1600 Hinman Ave., Evanston, IL 60201.

Johnson, Mary Lu (Mr. 1, 1926, Rockford, IL) Coop. Consult., Lib. Sci., State of IL, 1976–; Lrng. Resrc. Ctr. Dir., Meridian Jr. High, Highland Elem., Monroe Ctr. Elem., 1965–; Lang. Arts Instr., Meridian Jr. High, 1963–67; Msc. Instr., Meridian Cmnty. Unit Schs., 1959–66. **Educ.:** North. IL Univ., 1959–62, BS (Msc. Educ.), 1963, Elem. Tchg. Cert., 1967–72, MA (LS). **Orgs.:** ALA. IL LA: Mem. Com. (1973); Prog. Com. (1975–76). Ogle Cnty. Assn. of Sch. Media Persnl.: Org.; Pres. (1967–68, 1973). Amer. Gld. of Organists & Choir Dirs. **Honors:** Cont. Grant, 1973. **Activities:** 10; 21, 32, 48 **Addr.:** Box 165, Stillman Valley, IL 61084.

Johnson, Millard F. (D. 26, 1941, Seattle, WA) Dir., Resrch. and Tech. Sect., WA Univ. Med. Lib., 1973–; Syst. Anal., Univ. of MD Med. Lib., 1971–73. **Educ.:** Univ. of WA, 1965–69, BS (Psy.), 1969–70, MLS; WA Univ., St. Louis, 1970–71, Cert. (Comp. Libnshp.). **Orgs.:** Med. LA: Consult. Ed. (1978–). ASIS. MO LA: Tech. Adv. Com. (Ch., 1979–). Natl. Lib. of Med.: SERLINE Adv. Com. (1979–). ANSI Z39: Serials Frequency Stan. (1980–). **Activities:** 12; 34, 41, 44; 56, 80, 85 **Addr.:** Wash. Univ. Med. School Lib., St. Louis, MO 63110.

Johnson, Minnie L. (Spartanburg, SC) Supvsr., Med. Lit., Ciba-Geigy, 1973–; Resrch. Info. Spec., E.R. Squibb, 1967–69; Tech. Info. Spec. FDA, 1966–67; Assoc. Endocrinologist, Schering, 1962–65. **Educ.:** SC State Coll. BS (Bio.); Hunter Coll., MS (Physio.); Rutgers Univ., MLS. **Orgs.:** SLA: Chap. ofcs. (1977–80). Med. LA. ALA. **Honors:** Beta Phi Mu, 1971. **Activities:** 12; 17, 30, 39; 75, 87, 91 **Addr.:** Ciba-Geigy, 556 Morris Ave., Summit, NJ 07901.

Johnson, Nancy P. (O. 7, 1949, Chicago, IL) Asst. Law Libn., Asst. Prof. of Lib. Admin., Univ. of IL Law Lib., 1976–; Asst. Law Libn., Univ. of Chicago Law Lib., 1974–76. **Educ.:** Marycrest Coll. 1967–71, BA (Soc. Sci.); Univ. of IL 1971–72, MSLS. **Orgs.:** AALL: Gvt. Docum. SIS (Ch., 1978–79). Chicago Assn. of Law Libs. Mid-Amer. Assn. of Law Libs.: Prog. Com. (Ch., 1979). **Pubns.:** *Sources of Compiled Legislative Histories: A Bibliography of Government Documents, Periodical Articles, and Books* (1979); "Pre-1920 Government Documents Literature: A Selective Bibliography," *Gvt. Pubns. Review* (1980); "Legal Periodical Usage Survey: Method and Application," *Law Lib. Jnl.* (F. 1978); "Space Consuming U.S. Government Document Available in Microform," *Microform Review* (1980). **Activities:** 1, 14-Law; 29, 39; 77, 95-Gvt. docums. **Addr.:** 104 Law Building, University of Illinois Law Library, Champaign, IL 61820.

Johnson, Niel Melvin (Jl. 28, 1931, Galesburg, IL) Archvst., Harry S. Truman Lib., 1977–; Vstg. Asst. Prof., Univ. of NE (Omaha), 1975–76; Asst. Prof., Dana College, 1969–74; Instr., Augustana Coll., 1967–69. **Educ.:** Augustana Coll., 1949–53, BA (Hist.); State Univ. of IA, 1963–67, PhD (Hist.). **Orgs.:** SAA. Midw. Arch. Conf. Amer. Assn. of State and Local Hist. Org. of Amer. Hist. Jackson Cnty. (MO) Hist. Socty. **Honors:** Concordia Hist. Inst. (St. Louis), Cmdn. for article on MO Synod, 1977. **Pubns.:** *George Sylvester Viereck: German-American Propagandist* (1972); *Portal to the Plains* (1974); "Pro-Nazi and Pro-Freud: The Paradox of George S. Viereck," *Psychoanalytic Review* (Win. 1971–72); jt. auth., "Resources at the Truman Library on Western Issues and Programs," *Gov. Pubn. Review* (Spr. 1980). **Activities:** 4; 32, 41; 85 **Addr.:** 15804 Kiger Circle, Independence, MO 64055.

Johnson, Patricia Tanner (Ap. 24, 1940, Kankakee, IL) Libn., Mary Hoge Jr. High, 1970–; Libn., Missn. HS, 1968–70; Elem. Tchr., Desoto Cnty. Indp. Sch. Dist., 1965–68; Tchr., Sopchoppy HS, 1963–65; Elem. Tchr., Hilliard Sch., 1961–62. **Educ.:** AR State Tchrs. Coll., 1958–61, BA (Eng.); FL State Univ., 1966–70, MS (LS). **Orgs.:** ALA. TX LA. TX Assn. of Sch. Libns.: Dist. Ch. (1980–81). Delta Kappa Gamma: Epsilon Phi Chap., Treas. (1978–80); 1st VP (1980–82). TX State Tchrs. Assn. Beta Sigma Phi. **Honors:** Phi Delta Kappa; Beta Phi Mu. **Activities:** 10; 17, 32, 48 **Addr.:** P.O. Box 604, Weslaco, TX 78596.

Johnson, Peter T. (Ag. 2, 1945, Redlands, CA) Lectr., Prog. in Latin Amer. Std., Biblphr. for Latin Amer., Spain and Portugal, Princeton Univ., 1978–; Ibero-Amer. Biblgphr., Assoc. Prof., Univ. of MN, 1969–78. **Educ.:** Univ. of WA, 1967, BA (Hist.); Univ. of AZ, 1968, MA (Hist.); Univ. of WI, Madison, 1969, MALS. **Orgs.:** SALALM: Exec. Bd. (1976–79); Acq. Com. (Ch., 1976–78); Subcom. on Bk. Dealer-Publshr.-Lib. Rel. (Ch., 1974–76). ALA. Latin Amer. Micro. Proj. of the Ctr. for Resrch. Libs.: Exec. Bd. (1979–80); Ch. 1979–80). Latin Amer. Std. Assn. **Pubns.:** *Source Materials for Latin American Studies at the University of Minnesota: A Selective Bibliographic Guide* 2nd rev. ed. (1977); "Academic Press Censorship Under Military and Civilian Regimes: The Argentine and Brazilian Cases, 1964–1975," *Luso-Brazilian Review* (Sum. 1978); "The Latin American Subject Specialist and Bibliographic Instruction," SALALM XIX Working Paper No. C-1, Pt. A (1976). **Activities:** 1; 15, 31; 54 **Addr.:** Princeton University Library, P.O. Box 190, Princeton, NJ 08544.

Johnson, Richard David (Je. 10, 1927, Cleveland, OH) Dir. of Libs., State Univ. Coll., Oneonta, NY, 1973–; Dir. of Libs., Claremont Colls., 1968–73; Chief, Tech. Srvs. Libn., Stanford Univ. Libs., 1967–68, Chief, Undergrad. Lib. Proj., 1964–67, Chief, Acq. Div., 1962–64, Sr. Catlgr., 1959–60 and 1961–62, Admin. Asst. to Dir., 1960–61, Ref. Libn., 1957–59; Libn., Natl. Opinion Resrch. Ctr., 1956–57. **Educ.:** Yale Univ., 1946–49, BA (Amer. Std.); Univ. of Chicago, 1949–50, MA (Intl. Rel.), 1955–57, MALS. **Orgs.:** ALA: H. W. Wilson Lib. Per. Awd. Com. (1970–71); ACRL: Pubns. in Libnshp. Ed. Bd. (1969–75); Pubns. Com. (1974–80); 1978 Natl. Conf. Prog. Com. (Ch., 1976–78); 1981 Natl. Conf. (Consult., 1979–81); LAMA, Pubns. Com. (1977–78); RTSD, Plng. Com. (1970–75; ch., 1973–75); Cat. and Class. Sect.; Policy and Resrch. Com. (Ch., 1978–80); LITA: RASD. Frdm. to Read Fndn. CA LA: Pres. (1972). Various other orgs. **Honors:** ALA, H. W. Wilson Per. Awd., 1968; Cncl. on Lib. Resrcs., Flwshp., 1972; Beta Phi Mu. **Pubns.:** Ed., *New Horizons for Academic Libraries* (1979); Ed., *Libraries for Teaching, Libraries for Research: Essays for a Century* (1977); "Academic Libraries," *ALA Yrbk.* (1976–81); "Joint Academic Libraries," *Advncs. in Libnshp.* (1975); Ed., *Coll. and Resrch. Libs.* (1974–80); Ed. for various other lib. jnls. and auth. of various other articles. **Activities:** 1; 17, 37, 46; 57, 74, 75 **Addr.:** 2 Walling Blvd., Oneonta, NY 13820.

Johnson, Richard Kent (Mr. 22, 1952, Moberly, MO) Dir., Advert. & Promo., Congressional Info. Srv., Inc., 1977–; AV Prod. Spec., Smithsonian Inst., 1974–77; Writer/Ed., Mutual Broadcasting Syst., 1974. **Educ.:** American Univ., 1970–74, BA (Comm.). **Orgs.:** SLA: DC chap., Ed. com. (1979); Advert. & Mktg. Div., conf. lcl. coord. (1979–80). ALA. Washington Bk. Publshrs. **Pubns.:** *The Removal of Pressure Sensitive Tape from Flat Paper: A Bibliography of English Titles* (1977); "Removal of Pressure Sensitive Tape from Flat Paper," video tape (1976); "Protecting Objects on Exhibition," slide/audio package (1977); "The Docent Doesn't...," video tape (1977); "Conservation Orientation for Museum Personnel," video tape series (1974–77). **Activities:** 6; 36; 51, 57, 63 **Addr.:** Congressional Information Service, Inc., 4520 East-West Hwy., Suite 800, Washington, DC 20014.

Johnson, Robert Kellogg (Jl. 27, 1913, Grand Rapids, MI) Prof., Internship Dir., Grad. Lib. Sch., Univ. of AZ, 1972–, Univ. Libn., 1964–72; Dir. of Libs., Drexel Univ., 1962–64, Asst. Dir. of Libs., 1959–62; Chief, Circ. Branch, Air Univ. Lib., 1959, Chief, Acq. Branch, 1957–58, Chief, Tech. Srvs. Div., 1953–57, Chief, Cat. Branch, 1952–53; various lib. positions, 1938–52. **Educ.:** Univ. of MT, 1935–37, BA (Mod. Langs.); Univ. of WA, 1937–38, BALS; Univ. of IL, 1940–46, MLS, 1948–57, PhD (LS). **Orgs.:** ALA: Cncl. (1969–72); ACRL, Bd. of Dirs. (1969–72), Univ. Lib. Sect. Strg. Com. (Secy., 1969–72); Stdg. Com. on Lib. Educ.; RTSD. AZ LA: Pres. (1968–69); Exec. Bd. (1965–70); Conf. Ch. (1965–66). ARL: ARL-SALALM Jt. Com. (1970–72). Various other orgs. **Honors:** Univ. of WA Sch. of Libnshp., Disting. Alum. Awd., 1973. **Pubns.:** Jt. auth., *Organization Charts of Selected Libraries: School, Special, Public, and Academic* (1973); *Instant Statistical Methods for the Librarian-Consumer in One Easy Lesson* (1979); "The Acquisition of Latin American Library Materials in ARL Libraries," *Frgn. Acq. Nsltr.* (Fall 1972); "The Acquisition of Latin American in Non-ARL SALALM Libraries," *Frgn. Acq. Nsltr.* (Spr. 1973); "The Air University Study of Libraries in Selected Military Educational Institutions," *ACRL Microcard Series* (1955–56); various other articles on lib. topics (1941–). **Activities:** 11; 34, 41, 46 **Addr.:** 3020 E. Third St., Tucson, AZ 85716.

Special Subjects/Services: 50. Adult educ.; 51. Advert./Mktg.; 52. Aerosp.; 53. Agric.; 54. Area std.; 55. Arts/Hum.; 56. Autom.; 57. Bibl./Prtg.; 58. Bio. sci.; 59. Bus./Fin.; 60. Chem.; 61. Copyrt.; 62. Documtn.; 63. Educ.; 64. Engin.; 65. Env.; 66. Eth. grps.; 67. Film; 68. Food/Nutr.; 69. Geneal.; 70. Geo.; 71. Geol.; 72. Handcpd.; 73. Hist.; 74. Int. frdm.; 75. Info. sci.; 76. Insr.; 77. Law; 78. Legis.; 79. Math./Comp. sci.; 80. Med.; 81. Metals; 82. Nat. resrcs.; 83. Newsp.; 84. Nuc. sci.; 85. Oral hist.; 86. Petr./Energy; 87. Pharm.; 88. Phys./Astr./Math.; 89. Readg.; 90. Relig.; 91. Sci./Tech.; 92. Soc. sci.; 93. Telecom.; 94. Transp.; 95. (other).

Who's Who in Library and Information Services

Johnson, Ronald W. (Jl. 18, 1945, Andalusia, AL) Legal Ref. Libn., Bur. of Natl. Affairs, Inc., 1980–; Ref. Libn., Bus. Div., Martin Luther King Meml. Lib., 1972–; Decimal Classificationist (temporary), Lib. of Congs., 1972; Grad. Asst., Lib. Sch., Univ. of MD 1970–72; Sr. Lib. Asst., Wichita (KS) Pub. Lib., 1969–70. **Educ.:** George Washington Univ., 1967, BA (Pol. Sci.); Univ. of MD, 1970–72, MLS; George Washington Univ., 1976–80, MPA (Pub. Admin.); Cath. Univ. of Amer., 1974–75, Post MLS Std. **Orgs.:** NLA: Natl. Secy. (1977–78). SLA: Bus. and Fin. Div. **Pubns.:** "Professionalism and Unionism," *Natl. Libn.* (N. 1977). **Activities:** 9, 14-Freelnc. resrch.; 16, 35, 49-labor rel.; 59, 95-Labor std. **Addr.:** 8989 Omega Ct., Springfield, VA 22152.

Johnson, Ruth Elaine (Ja. 30, 19—, Cleveland, OH) Dir., MacKenzie Meml. Pub. Lib., 1979–; Dir., Tech. Srvs., Lorain Pub. Lib., 1976–79; Head Libn., Borromeo Semy., 1972–76; Libn., Northwest Tech. Coll., 1971–72; Sr. Catlgr., Cleveland State Univ., 1969–71; Head Libn., Anchorage Cmnty. Coll., 1965–69. **Educ.:** Case West. Rsv. Univ., 1954–58, AB cum laude (Hist.), 1958–59, MSLS; Cleveland State Univ., 1973–76, JD (Law). **Orgs.:** ALA. OH LA. AK LA: State Secy. (1968–69). Mensa. **Honors:** Beta Phi Mu. **Activities:** 1, 9; 15, 17, 46; 69, 72, 77 **Addr.:** 29055 Weber Ave., Wickliffe, OH 44092.

Johnson, Sandra J. (Ag. 29, 1949, Rochester, MN) Info. Spec., Instr., Drug Info. Srv. Ctr., Univ. of MN, 1980–, Coord., Dev. Proj., Biomed. Lib., 1978–80; Ref. Libn., Abbott-Northwest. Hosp. Lib., 1976–78. **Educ.:** Univ. of MN, 1967–73, BA (Hist., Eng.), 1974–76, MALS. **Orgs.:** Hlth. Sci. Comm. Assn. Med. LA. MN Hlth. Sci. LA. MN Gvr.'s Pre-WHCOLIS (1978). Various other orgs. **Activities:** 1, 12; 25, 32, 39; 67, 80, 87 **Addr.:** DISC, 32 Appleby Hall, University of Minnesota, Minneapolis, MN 55455.

Johnson, Stephen, J. Resrch. Biblgphr., Univ. of BC, 1972–, Serials Libn., Gifts and Exch. Libn.; Undergrad. Libn., McGill Univ. Lib. **Educ.:** Univ. of Windsor, 1953–54, BA; McGill Univ., 1955–56, BLS. Fac. Assn., Univ. of BC. **Pubns.:** *Canadian Library Handbook* (Fndr.) (1979); *Directory of Canadian Reports* (1976); *Canadiana Out of Print* (1974); *Canadian Library Progress* (1973); *Canadian Serials Directory* (1972). **Activities:** 1; 44, 46; 57 **Addr.:** 4571 West 3rd Ave., Vancouver, BC V6R 1N3 Canada.

Johnson, Theodora Lucia (Ap. 27, 1918, Washington, DC) City Libn., Richmond Pub. Lib., 1971–; Reg. Supvsr., Sacramento City Lib., 1970–71; City Libn., Azusa Pub. Lib., 1962–70; City Libn., Lompoc Pub. Lib., 1960–62; Adult Srvs. Coord. Palo Alto Pub. Lib., 1959–60, Ord. Libn., 1954–59, Asst. Ref. Libn. 1953–54, Asst. Catlgr., 1952–53, Lib. Asst., 1951–52; various positions in jnlsm., 1939–51. **Educ.:** George Washington Univ., 1941, AB (Eng. Lit.); San Jose State Coll., 1953, Lib. Cert.; Univ. of South. CA, 1964, Lib. Admin. **Orgs.:** Pub. Lib. Execs. of Ctrl. CA: Pres. (1973). Metro. Coop. Lib. Syst.: Ch. (1970). Bay Area Lib. and Info. Srvs.: Ch. (1978). ALA. CA LA: Cncl. (1981–83); Finance Com. Various other orgs. Leag. of CA Cities. Assn. of Mgt. Persnl. **Activities:** 9; 17 **Addr.:** Richmond Public Library, Civic Center Plz., Richmond, CA 94804.

Johnson, Thomas Lindemann (N. 26, 1935, Annapolis, MD) Asst. Libn., S. Caroliniana Lib., Univ. of SC, 1973–. **Educ.:** Univ. of NC, 1953–57, AB (Hist.); Un. Theo. Semy., 1960–64, BD (Dvnty.); Fac. de Theo., Montpellier, France, 1962–63 (Exch. Student); Univ. of SC, 1968–71, MA (Eng.), 1972–80, PhD (Eng.); various grad. crs. **Orgs.:** SAA. SC LA. SC Hist. Socty. **Pubns.:** "James McBride Dabbs: A Portrait of the Man as Reader," *The Axis* (Mr. 1980); various bibl. lists, *First Printings of American Authors* (1978–82). **Activities:** 1, 12; 15, 23, 45; 55, 62, 69 **Addr.:** South Caroliniana Library, University of SC, Columbia, SC 29208.

Johnson, Walter W. (O. 21, 1925, Grand Rapids, MI) Lib. Dir., Huntington Beach City Lib., 1959–; Circ. Libn., Univ. of CA, Long Beach, 1957–59. **Educ.:** MI State Univ., 1945–49, BA (Art, Educ.), 1949–50, MA (Art); Univ. of South. CA, 1954–56, MSLS. **Orgs.:** Pub. Lib. Admin. of Orange Cnty.: Past Pres. (1968). Orange Cnty. Libns. Assn.: Past Pres. (1966). Pub. Lib. Execs. of South. CA. Rotary Intl.: Bd. of Dir. (1976–78). **Activities:** 9; 17, 28, 36; 55 **Addr.:** 8081 Yorktown Ave., Huntington Beach, CA 92646.

Johnson, Wayne H. (My. 2, 1942, El Paso, TX) State Libn., WY State Lib., 1978–, Chief Bus. Ofcr., Arch. & Hist. Dept., 1976–78, Chief, Admin. Srvs., 1973–76; Consult., OK Mgt. & Engin. Consult., Inc., 1972. **Educ.:** UT State Univ., 1964–68, BS (Hist.); Univ. of CO, 1969–70, MPA (Pub. Admin.); Univ. of OK, 1972, MLS. **Orgs.:** ALA. WY LA: Pres. (1976–78). Grt. Cheyenne Cham. of Cmrce. Kiwanis. Boy Scouts of Amer. **Activities:** 13; 17, 18, 35, 47; 52, 78 **Addr.:** Wyoming State Library, Supreme Court Building, Cheyenne, WY 82002.

Johnston, H. G. (Ag. 12, 1920, Ellston, IA) Jt. Dir., Bloomfield Twp. and Baldwin Pub. Lib., 1969–; Dir., Detroit Metro Resrch. Proj., 1967–68; Asst. Dir., Flint Pub. Lib., 1958–66; Libn., Owosso Pub. Lib., 1954–57. **Educ.:** St. Ambrose Coll., 1938–42, BA (Amer. Hist.); Yale Univ., 1946–48, Drama; Univ. of MI, 1949-51, AMLS. **Orgs.:** ALA: Cncl. (1969–73). MI LA: Pres. (1964–65). SLA. Rotary. **Honors:** Beta Phi Mu. **Pubns.:** *Detroit Metropolitan Library Research and Demonstration Project* (1969). **Activities:** 9; 17 **Addr.:** 5082 Buckingham, Troy, MI 48098.

Johnston, Joan Lillian (S. 9, 1926, Montreal, PQ) Ref. Libn., Lib., Univ. of Guelph, 1965–; Adult Srvs. Libn., N. York Pub. Lib., 1963–65. **Educ.:** Univ. of Toronto, 1946–50, BA (Hist.), 1961–62 BLS, 1963–70, MLS. **Orgs.:** Can. LA. ON LA. Hum. Assn. of Can.: Guelph Treas. (1979–). **Activities:** 1; 31, 39; 54, 92 **Addr.:** Library, Documentation and Media Resource Centre, University of Guelph, Guelph, ON N1G 2W1 Canada.

Johnston, Linda Mangham (N. 29, 1914, Atlanta, GA) Retired, 1977–; Libn., Fed. Rsv. Bank, Resrch. Lib., 1948–77; Libn., Atlanta Pub. Lib., 1943–48; Libn., Gillespie Park Jr. HS, 1942–43; Tchr., Muscogee Cnty. Schs., 1936–42. **Educ.:** La-Grange Coll., 1934–36, AB (Eng.); George Peabody Coll. 1941–43, BS (LS). **Orgs.:** SLA: GA Chap. (Pres., 1962–64). SELA: Spec. Lib. Sect. (Ch., 1971–74). GA LA: Spec. Lib. Sect. (Ch., 1960). Atlanta Hist. Socty. Atlanta Symph. Orch. Gld. Natl. Trust for Hist. Prsrvn. Metro. Opera Gld. **Pubns.:** "Special Libaries in Georgia," *GA Libn.* **Activities:** 12; 17; 59 **Addr.:** 119 Pharr Rd. N.W., Apt. C-4, Atlanta, GA 30305.

Johnston, Maxine (D. 21, 1928, Gillham, AR) Lib. Dir., Lamar Univ., 1980–, Assoc. Dir., 1969–80, Ref. Libn., Pub. Srvs. Div. Head, 1955–69; Asst. Libn., S. Park HS, 1953–55. **Educ.:** Lamar Univ., Sam Houston State Univ., 1946–53, BS (Lib. Srv., Eng.); Univ. of TX, 1954–58, MLS; various crs. **Orgs.:** ALA. TX LA: Dist. Ch. (1960–61); Lib. Dev. Com. (1964–66); Nom. Com. (Ch., 1965–66); Ref. RT (Vice-Ch., Ch., 1967–69). TX Info. Exch.: Bd. Ch. (1971–72). SWLA. Big Thicket Assn. Leag. of Women Voters. TX Folklore Socty. TX Assn. of Coll. Tchrs. various org. **Honors:** TX LA, Libn. of the Year, 1974; Alpha Chi; Beta Phi Mu. **Pubns.:** *A Reference Librarian Reflects on Resources, Finance and Networks* (1973); Ed., *Thicket Explorer* (1973); Jt. Auth., "Public and College Library Personnel in Texas, 1955," *TX Lib. Jnl.* (1958); Jt. Auth., "The 1969 Reference Round Table Pre-conference Institute," *TX Lib. Jnl.* (1969); Ed., *Big Thicket Assn.* (1969–). **Activities:** 1; 17, 35, 39 **Addr.:** Lamar University, Mary and John Gray Library, Box 10021 Lamar Station, Beaumont, TX 77710.

Johnston, Thomas William (N. 12, 1928, Ogden, UT) Corporate Libn., BASF Wyandotte Corp., 1974–; Resrch. Libn., Bristol Meyers Corp., 1970–74; Dir., Tech. Info. Ctr., Univ. of Rochester, 1966–70; Tech. Lib. and Patents Mgr., Sybron Corp., 1960–66; Tech. Libn., MSA Resrch. Corp., 1958–60; various positions in chem., 1953–58. **Educ.:** Brigham Young Univ., 1952, BS (Chem.); Ricks Univ., 1953, BA (Educ.); Univ. of Chicago, 1953, (Sci. Educ.); Carnegie Sch. of LS, 1958, MLS. **Orgs.:** SLA. Socty. for Early Hist. Archlg. Amer. Musm. Nat. Hist. **Pubns.:** Various pubns. on chem. **Activities:** 12; 17 **Addr.:** 37130 Judd Rd., New Boston, MI 48164.

Johnting, Wendell E. (Ag. 30, 1952, Winchester, IN) Tech. Srvs. Libn., IN Univ. Sch. of Law-Indianapolis Lib., 1975–. **Educ.:** Taylor Univ., 1970–74, AB (Eng.); IN Univ., 1974–75, MLS. **Orgs.:** IN LA: Ch., Tech. Srvs. Div. (1980–). AALL: Gvt. Docum. SIS (1979–); Online Bibl. Srvs. (1979–); Tech. Srvs. SIS (1979–). OH Reg. Assn. of Law Libs.: Legis. Com. (1978–79); Pubns. Com. (1981–). IMA Horticultural Socty.: Ch., Lib. Com. (1979–); Bd., Exec. Com. **Honors:** Beta Phi Mu, 1977–; Alpha Phi Gamma, 1974–. **Pubns.:** Ed., ORALL Newsletter (1980) **Activities:** 1, 12; 20, 29, 44; 58, 77 **Addr.:** 5917 Radnor Rd., Indianapolis, IN 46226.

Jonas, Eva S. (N. 20, 1931, Prague, Czechoslovakia) Libn., Musm. of Compar. Zlgy., Harvard Univ., 1978–, Ref. Libn., Cabot Sci. Lib., 1973–78 Libn., Inst. of Entomology, Czechoslovakian Acad. of Sci., 1963–69. **Educ.:** Charles Univ., Prague, 1963–68, RNC (Bio.), 1963–64 (LS); Harvard Univ., 1969–72, AM (Bio.). **Orgs.:** ALA. AAAS. **Pubns.:** *How to Use Biological Abstracts* (1976, 1981). **Activities:** 1; 15, 31; 91 **Addr.:** Library, Museum of Comparative Zoology, Harvard University, 26 Oxford St., Cambridge, MA 02173.

Jones, A. Kathleen (F. 4, 1922, Welland, ON) Chief Libn., Port Colborne Pub. Lib., 1964–; Co. Libn., Atlas Steels, Ltd., 1960–64; Bkmobile. Libn., St. Catharines Pub. Lib., 1954–60; Chld. Libn., Belleville Pub. Lib., 1948–52. **Educ.:** Mount Allison Univ., Sackville, NB, 1941–45, BS (Home Econ.); Univ. of Toronto, 1946–47, BLS, 1970–73, MLS. **Orgs.:** Can. LA. ON LA: Adult Srvs. (Ch., 1953–54). Assn. of Medium-sized Pub. Libs. of ON: Rec. Secy. (1976–79). Bus. and Prof. Women's Clb. Girl Guides of Can. ON Geneal. Socty. Fed. of ON Naturalists. **Activities:** 9; 16, 20, 21 **Addr.:** Port Colborne Public Library, 310 King St., Port Colborne, ON L3K 4H1 Canada.

Jones, Adrian (F. 2, 1930, London, Eng.) Dir. of Libs., Roosevelt Univ., 1969–; Actg. Dir. of Libs., Chicago State Coll., 1967–69; Asst. Ref. Libn., Univ. of Chicago, 1965–67; Asst. Libn., Weston Coll., MA, 1964–65. **Educ.:** Heythrop Coll., Chipping Norton, Eng., 1951–54, Lic. Phil. (Phil.); Sophia Univ., Tokyo, Japan, 1958–62, MA (Theo.); Univ. Coll., London, 1963–64, Sch. of Libnshp. and Arch.; Univ. of Chicago, 1965–69, CAS (Libnshp.). **Orgs.:** ALA: ACRL, Nom. Com. (1974). IL LA: Bylaws Com. (Ch., 1976–77). IL Assn. for Coll. and Resrch. Libs.: Comm. Com. (Ch., 1979–80). Chicago Acad. Lib. Cncl.: Ch. (1976–79); various other orgs. Assn. for Asian Std. **Pubns.:** Ed., "Library Automation in Illinois, *IL Libs.* (Ap. 1978). **Activities:** 1, 13; 17, 24, 34; 54, 56, 75 **Addr.:** Roosevelt University, Murray-Green Library, 430 S. Michigan Ave., Chicago, IL 60605.

Jones, Anna E. (Ja. 7, 1928, Burlington, NJ) Asst. Lib. Dir., Burlington Cnty. Lib., 1963–, Supvsg. Libn., Sr. Libn., 1951–63; Tchr., William MacFarland HS, 1948–49. **Educ.:** Trenton State Coll., 1944–48, BS (Educ.), 1950–54, BLS; Princeton Theo. Semy., 1975–80, MA (Christ. Educ.). **Orgs.:** ALA. NJ LA. **Activities:** 9; 17, 21 **Addr.:** 444 Washington Ave., Burlington, NJ 08016.

Jones, Arthur Edwin, Jr. (Mr. 20, 1918, Orange, NJ) Dir., Univ. Lib., Prof. of Eng., Drew Univ., 1955–, Asst. Prof., Eng., 1952–55, Instr., Eng., 1949–52; Instr., Syracuse Univ., 1946–49. **Educ.:** Univ. of Rochester, 1935–39, BA (Eng.); Syracuse Univ., 1939–41, MA (Eng.), 1946–50, PhD (Eng.); Rutgers Univ., 1962–64, MLS. **Orgs.:** ALA: Cncl. (1971–72); RTSD/RS (1964, 1968); ALTA: Madison Pub. Lib.: Trustee (1958–79). ATLA: VP (1960–67); Pres. (1967–). NJ LA: Various com. Natl. Cncl. of Lib. Assns.: ATLA Rep. (1969–75). Natl. Cncl. of Tchrs. of Eng. Mod. Lang. Assn. AAUP. **Honors:** NJ LA, Coll. and Univ. Libs. Sect., Disting. Lib. Srv. Awd., 1980. **Pubns.:** *Realism and Naturalism in American Fiction* (1951); Jt. Auth., *A Checklist of the Writings of John and Charles Wesley* (1961); "The Years of Disagreement," *History of American Methodism* (1964); "Presidential Address, 1968: A Steady Pressure," *Proc. of the Amer. Theo. Assn.* (Je. 1968); Reviewer. **Activities:** 1; 15, 17, 24; 55, 62, 89, 90, 91 **Addr.:** Drew University Library, Madison, NJ 07940.

Jones, Barbara (D. 4, 1946, Chicago, IL) Head, Cat., NY Univ., Bobst Lib., 1979–; Head, Bibl. Contrl., Tchrs. Coll., Columbia Univ., 1978–79; Catlgr., Univ. of Cincinnati, 1972–77. **Educ.:** Univ. of IL, 1964–68, BA (Eng.); Northwestern Univ., 1968–69, MAT (Tchg. of Eng.); Univ. of Cincinnati, 1972–77, MA (Eng.); Columbia Univ., 1977–78, MLS. **Orgs.:** ALA: Com. Mem. (1980–82); Educ. and Behvl. Sci. Sect. Bibl. Control of Educ. Mtrls. (NYLA: RTSD (Secy., 1980–82). NY Tech. Srvs. Libn.: Soc. Ch. (1979–80). Amer. Prtg. Hist. Assn.: Asst. Ed. of Nsltr. (1978–). Columbia Univ. Sch. of Lib. Srv.: Alum. Bd. (1979–80); Sec. VP (1979–80). **Honors:** Phi Beta Kappa, 1968. **Pubns.:** "The Author as Book Designer," *A Miscellany for Bibliophiles* (1979). **Activities:** 1; 17, 20, 23; 56, 57, 85 **Addr.:** 782 West End Ave. #62, New York, NY 10025.

Jones, Bertha Winona (F. 24, 1931, St. Petersburg, FL) Media Spec., Morgan E. Fitzgerald Middle Sch., 1975–; Media Spec., Dunedin Comprehensive HS, 1966–75; Tchr., Tarpon Springs Jr. HS, 1966. **Educ.:** St. Petersburg Jr. Coll., 1963–65, AA; Univ. of S. FL, 1965–66, BA (Soc. Std.), 1966–67, MA (LS), MA in progress. **Orgs.:** ALA. AECT. FL Assn. for Media in Educ.: Bd. of Dir. (1976–79); Ch., Int. Frdm. Com. (1978); Ch., Jim Harbin Student Media Fest. (1979–80); Ch., Oper. Procedures Com. (1980). Pinellas Assn. of Libns./Media Spec.: Pres. (1976); Ch., Legis. Com. (1980). Other orgs. Pinellas Cnty. Classroom Tchrs. Assn.: Fac. Rep. (1969–75/1979–80); Legis. Com. (1979–80). Natl. Educ. Assn. Natl. Assn. for Supvsn. and Curric. Dev. FL Leag. of Middle Schs. Other orgs. **Pubns.:** "Returning to the Halls of Ivy," *FL Media Qtly.* (Sum. 1979). **Activities:** 10; 20, 32, 48; 63, 78, 89 **Addr.:** Morgan E. Fitzgerald Middle School, 6410 118th Ave. North, Largo, FL 33543.

Jones, Beverly A. (N. 25, 1935, Oklahoma City, OK) Network Coord., OK Dept. of Libs., 1978–; Chief of Plng. and Dev., RI State Lib. Srvs., 1976–78, Catlgr., Head of Prcs. Ctr., 1971–75. **Educ.:** Bethany Nazarene Coll., 1952–56, BA (Lit.); Univ. of IL, 1956–58, MSLS. **Orgs.:** ALA: ASCLA/State Lib. Agency Sect., Mem. Com. (1979–). NELINET: Qual. Cntrl. Com. (1977–78). Grace Episcopal Church. Leag. of Women Voters. **Pubns.:** "OTIS in Transition: From Teletype to Telecommunications," *OK Libn.* (Jl.-O. 1979); "Performance Measures in Rhode Island Libraries," *RI LA Bltn.* (Ap. 1978). **Activities:** 13; 17, 34; 55 **Addr.:** 12300 Springwood Dr., Oklahoma City, OK 73120.

Jones, C. Lee (S. 22, 1936, Anderson, IN) Prog. Ofcr., Cncl. on Lib. Resrcs., 1978–; Hlth. Sci. Libn., Columbia Univ., 1973–78; Dir., Med. Branch Lib., Univ. of TX Med. Branch, 1967–73; Dir., Tech. Srvs., Trinity Univ., 1965–67. **Educ.:** Carleton Coll., 1954–59, BA (Soclgy.); Univ. of TX, 1963–65, MLS. **Orgs.:** ALA. Med. LA. DC LA. **Pubns.:** Ed., *National Health Planning Act: Potential for Information Service Activities* (1977); *National Periodicals Center Technical Development Program* (1978); "A Cooperative Serial Acquisition Program," *Bltn. of the Med. LA* (Ap. 1974); "Bibliographic Service Development: A New CLR Program" *Jnl. of Lib. Autom.* (Sum. 1979). **Activities:** 1; 17, 19, 34; 56, 80, 93 **Addr.:** Council on Library Resources, 1 DuPont Circle #620, Washington, DC 20036.

Jones, Catherine A. (Ap. 30, 1936, Conneaut, OH) Chief, Congsnl. Ref. Div., CRS, Lib. of Congs., 1978–; Asst. Univ. Libn., Readr. Srvs., George Washington Univ. Lib., 1973–78; Assoc.

PROFESSIONAL ACTIVITIES: Institutions: 1. Acad. lib.; 2. Arch.; 3. Assn.; 4. Fed./Gvt. lib.; 5. Inst. lib.; 6. Mfr./Suppl.; 7. Milit. lib.; 8. Musm.; 9. Pub. lib.; 10. Sch. lib.; 11. Sch. of lib. sci.; 12. Spec. lib.; 13. State lib.; 14. (other). **Functions/Activities:** 15. Acq./Col. dev.; 16. Adult srvs.; 17. Admin.; 18. Apprais.; 19. Archit./Bldgs.; 20. Cat./Class.; 21. Chld. srvs.; 22. Circ.; 23. Cons./Pres.; 24. Consult.; 25. Cont. ed.; 26. Educ. lib. sci.; 27. Ext. srvs.; 28. Fund/Grants; 29. Gvt. pubs.; 30. Indx./Abs.; 31. Instr. lib. use; 32. Media srvs.; 33. Micro.; 34. Netwks./Coop.; 35. Persnl.; 36. PR; 37. Publshg.; 38. Recs. mgt.; 39. Ref. srvs.; 40. Repro.; 41. Resrch.; 42. Review.; 43. Secur.; 44. Serials; 45. Spec. col.; 46. Tech. srvs.; 47. Trustees/Bds.; 48. YA srvs.; 49. (other).

Dir., Washington Ofc., ALA, 1972–73; Chief Ref. Libn., Ofc. Mgt. Budget, Lib., Exec. Ofc. of the Pres., 1968–72. **Educ.:** Univ. of AL, 1965, BA (Eng.); Cath. Univ. of Amer., 1969, MLS; George Washington Univ., 1980, MA (Gvt.). **Orgs.:** DC LA: Pres. (1977–78). SLA: Washington, DC Chap. (Pres.-Elec., 1980; Pres., 1981). Cath. Univ. Lib. Sci. Alum. Assn.: Pres. (1977–78). **Activities:** 1, 4; 17, 24, 39; 75, 78 **Addr.:** Congressional Reference Div., Congressional Research Service, The Library of Congress, Washington, DC 20540.

Jones, Charlotte Woodruff (Ap. 11, 1927, Kendallville, IN) Mgr., Neighborhood Srvs., Spokane (WA) Pub. Lib., 1978–, Dept. Head, Mobile Srvs.-Outrch., 1975–78, Dept. Head, Outrch. Progs., 1973–75; Serials Libn., East. WA Univ. 1968–72; Branch Libn., Spokane Pub. Lib., 1967–68; Branch Libn., Douglas Cnty. (OR) Lib., 1965–66; Admin. and Techn. Libn., McCormick-Selph Assoc. Div. of Teledyne Inc., 1960–64; various other lib. positions, 1950–54. **Educ.:** Univ. of MI, 1947–49, BS (Physical Sci.); Univ. of Pittsburgh, 1966–67, MLS. **Orgs.:** ALA: ASCLA/Lib. Srvs. to Prisoners Sect. (Ch., 1980–81); Manual on Lib. Srvs. to Shut-ins (1975–79); Resrch. and Pubns. (1975–78). **Orgs.:** WA LA: Anl. Conf. Prog. Com. (Ch., 1976); Outrch. Progs. for Essential Needs Interest Grp. (Ch., 1974–75); various coms. WA Jailers Assn. WA Assn. for Soc. Welfare. Natl. Cncl. on the Aging. **Honors:** Beta Phi Mu, 1967. **Activities:** 9; 16, 17, 27; 50, 72, 89 **Addr.:** Neighborhood Services, Spokane Public Library, W. 906 Main, Spokane, WA 99201.

Jones, Clara Stanton (My. 14, 1913, St. Louis, MO) Retired, 1978–; Dir., Detroit Pub. Lib., 1970–78; Regents' Lectr., Univ. of CA, Berkeley, Grad. Sch. of Lib. and Info. Std., 1978–79; Libn., 1944–78. Comsn., Natl. Comsn. on Libs. and Info. Sci., 1978; **Educ.:** Spelman Coll., 1930–34, AB (Eng., Hist.); Univ. of MI, 1937–38, ABLS. **Orgs.:** ALA: Pres. (1976–77); Cncl. (1972–78). MI LA. Amer. Cvl. Liberties Un. Women's Intl. Leag. for Peace and Frdm. Assn. for the Std. of Negro Life and Hist. Natl. Congs. of Negro Women. various org. **Honors:** Univ. of MI Sch. of Lib. Sci., Disting. Alum. Awd., 1971; Univ. of MI Alum., Athena Awd. for Humanitarian Srv., 1975; North. MI Univ., Hon. PhD, 1978; Wayne State Univ., Hon. PhD, 1978; Other hons. **Pubns.:** *Public Library Information and Referral Service* (1978); *The Information Society: Issues and Answers* (1978); "Survival! Politics for Libraries," *NY LA Conf. Proc.* (1971); "Public Libraries: Challenge and Change," *Lib. Jnl.* (O. 1976). **Activities:** 9; 16, 39 **Addr.:** 325 Vernon St. #404, Oakland, CA 94610.

Jones, Clifton H. (My. 29, 1949, Burbank, CA) Dir., DeGolyer Lib., Fikes Hall of Spec. Col., South. Meth. Univ., 1980–; Ms. Cur., John Hay Lib., Brown Univ., 1977–79; Ms. Cur., SD Hist. Socty., 1976–77. **Educ.:** Claremont Men's Coll., 1967–71, BA (Hist.); Univ. of OR, 1971–73, MS (Hist.); Denver Univ., 1974–75, MA (Arch., Libnshp.); Denver Univ., 1975, Cert. (Arch); Amer. Rec. Mgt. Assn., 1979, Cert. (Rec. Mgt.). **Orgs.:** ALA: ACRL/RBMS. SAA: Mss. Repositories Prof. Afnty. Grp. (Ch., 1981–83). Socty. of Southwestern Archvsts. New Eng. Archvsts.: Nom. Com. (1977–78). Lexington Grp. in Transp. Hist. West. Hist. Assn. Natl. Hist. Pubns. and Rec. Comsn. State Review Bd. of SD (1976–77). State Review Bd. of RI (1979–80). **Pubns.:** "The Huterische People: A View from the 1920's," *SD Hist.* (1976); "Manuscript Sources in Women's History," *SD Hist.* (1976); "Manuscript Sources in Religious History," *SD Hist.* (1977); "The Socialist Party of the United States, 1901–1920: A Bibliography of Secondary Sources, 1945–1974," *Labor Hist.* (Spr. 1978). **Activities:** 1, 2; 17, 38, 45; 57, 73 **Addr.:** DeGolyer Library, Southern Methodist University, Dallas, TX 75275.

Jones, David E. (N. 6, 1946, Charleston, WV) Nonprint Libn., Cnty. Coll. of Morris, 1973–. **Educ.:** Stetson Univ., 1965–68, BA (Fr.); Pratt Inst., 1972–73, MLS. **Orgs.:** NJ LA. Msc. LA. **Activities:** 1; 20, 32, 39; 67 **Addr.:** County College of Morris, Rte. 10 & Center Grove Rd., Randolph Township, NJ 07869.

Jones, David L. (N. 12, 1945, Kingston, ON) Asst. Sci. Libn., Univ. of AB, 1980–; Sr. Ref., Pub. Srvs. Libn., Humber Coll., 1971–80. **Educ.:** McMaster Univ., 1965–68, BSc (Bio.); Univ. of West. ON, 1970–71, MLS. **Orgs.:** Can. Assn. of Coll. and Univ. Libs.: Exec. Cncl. (1977–80); Treas. (1979–80); Cmnty. and Tech. Coll. Libs. Sect. (Ch., 1977–80; Secy., 1976–77). The Migraine Fndn. **Pubns.:** *Ontario Community College Librarian's Equality Campaign, 1973–75* (1975); "Community College Librarians– A Dispatch from the Front," *IPLO Qtly.* (1975); "Introduction to the Learning Resource Centre," videotape (1979). **Activities:** 1; 31, 32, 39; 58, 80, 91 **Addr.:** Cameron Library, University of Alberta, Edmonton, AB T6G 2J8 Canada.

Jones, Donna R. (Je. 23, 1948, Denver, CO) Dir., Lib. Srvs., Pioneer Meml. Lib., 1976–; Adjunct Prof., Fort Hays State Univ., 1978–79; Libn., Colby Cmnty. Coll., 1969–76; Consult., Northwest KS Lib. Syst., 1974. **Educ.:** Fort Hays State Univ., 1967–69, AB (Hist., Lib.); Emporia State Univ., 1970–72, ML (LS); various grad. crs. **Orgs.:** Thomas Cnty. LA: Pres. (1971–73); various com. Mt. Plains LA: Secy. (1974); Sect. Ch. (1972, 1979). KS LA: State Rep. (1977–81); Ch. (1975). Colby Cmnty. Coll. Fac. Assn.: Pres. (1975–76); Secy. (1974–75). KS Com. for the Hum.: Vice-Ch. (1981). Beta Sigma Phi: Com. Ch. (1979–81). **Honors:** Fort Hays State Univ., Young Alum. Awd., 1979; 3M, Prof. Dev. Grant, 1975. **Activities:** 9; 17, 24, 36; 50, 85 **Addr.:** Library Services, 375 W. 4th, Colby, KS 67701.

Jones, Dora Ann (S. 3, 1930, Morristown, SD) Spec. Col. Libn., Black Hills State Coll., 1969–; Head, Cat. Dept., Law Lib., Univ. of MN, 1962–68. **Educ.:** Mount Marty Coll., 1957–60, BA (Eng.); Cath. Univ. of Amer., 1960–62, MS (LS). **Orgs.:** ALA: ACRL. SD LA: Pres. (1980–81); Pres.-Elec. (1979–80); Finance Com. (1979–80); Docum. Com. (1972–74, 1976–79); Schol. Com. (1971–74); Acad. Sect. (Secy., 1975–76). Mt. Plains LA: Acad. Sect., Nom. Com. (1979–80), Schol. Com. (1975–77). SAA. AAUW: 1st VP. (1979–81). Queen City Bus. and Prof. Women's Club: Pres. (1976–78). Black Hills Corral of The Westerners Intl. Lawrence Cnty. Hist. Socty. **Honors:** Delta Psi Omego, 1960; Beta Phi Mu, 1962. **Pubns.:** "Business, Organization and Institution Records," In *Our Endangered Records Heritage, Report of the South Dakota Historical Records Preservation Conference* (1979). **Activities:** 1, 2; 20, 26, 45; 70, 92 **Addr.:** Case Library, Black Hills State College, Spearfish, SD 57783.

Jones, Dorothy S. (Mr. 20, 1926, Philadelphia, PA) Lib. Dir., E. Orange Pub. Lib., 1976–, Coord., Adult Srvs., 1973–76, Coord., YA Srvs., 1966–73, Asst. Coord., 1960–66, Branch Libn., 1958–59, Youth Libn., 1954–57; Sch. & Ref. Libn., New York Pub. Lib., 1951–53. **Educ.:** Upsala Coll., 1948–49, BA (Eng.); Pratt Inst., 1950–51, MLS with Honors; Cont. Educ. Units, 1976–78, (Lib. Mgt. Supvsn.). **Orgs.:** ALA: YASD, Ch., Lcl. Arrange., 1969 Conf. SLA. NJ LA: Pres. (1980–81); Mem.-at-Large (1976–79); Rec. Secy. (1975–76); Ch., Constitution & Bylaws Com. (1972–74); Chld. and Young Peoples Div. (Pres., 1969–71). Pratt Inst. Alum. Assn. Untd. Way Cncl. of the Oranges & Maplewood: VP (1979–80). Leag. of Women Voters. Mayor's Cncl. on Sr. Citizens: Secy. (1977–). E. Orange Cmnty. Educ. Adv. Cncl. **Honors** NJ Afro-American, Women of the Yr., 1957; Beta Phi Mu. **Pubns.:** Co-ch., column, "Adult Books for Young Adults," *Sch. Lib. Jnl.* (1962–66); reviews. **Activities:** 9; 16, 42, 48; 50, 89 **Addr.:** 22 Webster Pl., East Orange, NJ 07018.

Jones, Edward (Je. 22, 1948, São Paulo, Brazil) Asst. Branch Libn., Fairfax Cnty. Pub. Lib., 1977–, Ref. Libn., 1973–77. **Educ.:** American Univ., 1966–70, BA (Eng.); Univ. of MD, 1972–73, MLS. **Orgs.:** ALA. US Metric Assn. **Activities:** 9; 17 **Addr.:** 5515 Miles Ct., Springfield, VA 22151.

Jones, Elwood H. (My. 6, 1941, Nipawin, SK) Master, Otonabee Coll., Trent Univ., 1978–, Assoc. Prof. of Hist., 1975, Asst. Prof. of Hist., 1970–75; Archvst., Pub. Arch. of Can., 1964–67. **Educ.:** Univ. of SK 1959–63, BA (Hist.); Univ. of West. ON, 1963–64, MA (Hist.); Queen's Univ., Kingston, ON, 1967–70, PhD (Hist.). **Orgs.:** Natl. Arch. Apprais. Bd.: Ch. (1979); ON Ch. (1974–). Can. Hist. Assn.: Dir. (1970–73). Peterborough Hist. Socty. Can. Church Hist. Socty.: Pres. (1979–). **Pubns.:** Ed., *Arch. Appraisals* (1977); Jt.-ed., *Union List of Manuscripts in Canadian Repositories* (1968); "The Public Archives of Canada," *Prof. Pub. Srv.* (N. 1966). **Activities:** 2; 18; 95-Can. **Addr.:** Master, Otonabee College, Trent University, Peterborough, ON K9J 7B8 Canada.

Jones, Frances Mary (D. 27, 1942, Little Rock, AR) Prin. Libn., Hennepin Cnty. Lib., 1975–, Sr. Libn., 1972–75, Libn., 1970–72; Libn. II, St. Paul Pub. Lib., 1967–70; US Peace Corps, Univ. of Brasilia Lib., 1966. **Educ.:** Coll. of St. Catherine, 1960–64, BA (LS); Univ. of MN, 1977–, MA in progress. **Orgs.:** ALA: ALA/AFL-CIO Jt. Com. on Lib. Srv. to Labor Grps. (1969–74); SORT, various offices, (1974–). **Pubns.:** Ed., SORT *Bltn.* (1978–80). **Activities:** 9; 16, 17; 56, 74, 89 **Addr.:** 7414 West 22nd St., St. Louis Park, MN 55426.

Jones, Frank N. (N. 19, 1906, Reading, PA) Retired, 1973–; Lectr., Grad. Lib. Sch., Univ. of RI, 1968–73; Chief Libn., Southeastern MA Tech. Inst., 1966–73; Dir., Peabody Inst. Lib., 1957–66; Libn., Asst. Prof. Lib. Sci., OH Univ., 1949–57; lib. positions at Harvard Coll., Columbia Univ., Newburyport (MA) Pub. Lib. (1934–49). **Educ.:** Harvard Coll., 1926–30, AB (Elizabethan Lit., Bibl.), 1941, MA (Bibl., Lit.). **Orgs.:** ALA: Cncl. (1962–66); Com. MA State (Ch., 1936–40); Com. OH State (Ch., 1951–53); ACRL, Spec. Subjs. (1958–61); RTSD/Copying Methods Sect. (1961–64). MA LA: VP (1969–70); Pres. (1970–71). OH LA: Pres. (1953–54). MD LA: Pres. (1961–62). Amer. Geo. Socty.: Fellow. John Carter Brown Lib.: Assoc. **Pubns.:** *Roads Through History: a Checklist* (1966); "The Libraries of the Harvard Houses," *Harvard Lib. Bltn.* (Fall 1948). **Activities:** 1, 9; 17, 35, 39; 57, 70 **Addr.:** 8600 Skyline Dr. #1060, Dallas, TX 75243.

Jones, Frederick S. (F. 8, 1930, Chicago, IL) Admin. Asst. Head, Acq. Dept., Tufts Univ., 1970–; Admin. Asst., MA Inst. of Tech., 1969–70. **Educ.:** Yale Univ., 1948–52, BA (Soclgy., Psy., Econ.); Simmons Coll., 1968–69. **Orgs.:** ALA. New Eng. LA. Concord Free Pub. Lib.: Lib. Com., Trustee. **Activities:** 1, 9; 15, 28, 34; 56, 59, 92 **Addr.:** Tufts University Library, Medford, MA 02155.

Jones, Harold D. (Je. 26, 1911, Philadelphia, PA) Retired, 1981; Assoc. Prof., Lib. Dept., Brooklyn Coll. of CUNY, 1952–81; Head Libn., Ch. LS Dept., Fairmont (WV) State Coll., 1947–52; Libn., William Penn Chrt. Sch., Philadelphia, 1941–42; Libn., Haverford (PA) Sch., 1935–41. **Educ.:** Swarthmore Coll., 1929–33, BA (Econ.); Drexel Univ., 1934–35, BSLS; Univ. of PA, 1940, MA (Econ.); Columbia Univ., 1957–62, CAS (LS). **Orgs.:** ALA: Bldgs. for Colls. and Univs. (1979–); Equipment Com. (1976–79). IFLA: Adv. Com. on Bldgs. (1974–77); Working Grp. on Lib. Nomenclature, Lib. Bldgs. (1977–). Bibl. Socty. of Amer. NY LA: Bldg. Com. (1967–72). Various other orgs. AAUP. Gutenberg Gesellschaft. St. David's Socty. in the State of NY. Amer. Prtg. Hist. Assn. **Honors:** LA of CUNY, Cert. of Apprec., 1972. **Pubns.:** "New Trends in West German University Library Building Planning," *Coll. and Resrch. Libs.* (S. 1981); *The Development of Reference Services in Colleges for Teacher Education, 1929–58* (1963); "Book Borrowing in Academic Libraries, 1964/65–1968/69; The Trend Was Down," *ERIC Rpts.* (1978); "Postwar University Library Buildings in West Germany," *Coll. and Resrch. Libs.* (Jl. 1975); "Memo to the Building Committee," *Lib. Jnl.* (My. 1, 1971); various other articles. **Activities:** 1; 19, 24, 39; 92 **Addr.:** 160 Henry St., Brooklyn, NY 11201.

Jones, Helen Carol (Ja. 11, 1933, Richmond, VA) Asst. Prof., Ref. Libn., Pullen Lib., GA State Univ., 1976–; Asst. Ref. Libn., Univ. of SC, 1975–76; Asst. Prof., Ref. Libn., Univ. of TN, 1971–75, Asst. Prof., Cat. Libn., 1969–71. **Educ.:** Univ. of Richmond, 1950–54, BA (Hist.); FL State Univ., 1968–69, MLS. **Orgs.:** ALA. SELA. GA LA. Metro. Atlanta LA. **Honors:** Beta Phi Mu, 1969; Phi Alpha Theta, 1954. **Pubns.:** Ed., *The Atlanta Constitution: a Georgia Index* (1976–79); Ed., *Foreign Newspapers in Southeastern Libraries* 2d ed. (1972). **Activities:** 1; 30, 31, 39 **Addr.:** Reference Department, Pullen Library, 100 Decatur St., Atlanta, GA 30303.

Jones, Helen Kathryn (My. 5, 1946, Baton Rouge, LA) Asst. Dir. Pub. Srvs., Lister Hill Lib. of the Hlth. Sci., Univ. of AL, 1978–, Coord., Ref. Srvs., 1975–78, Asst. Reference Librarian 1969–75, MEDLARS Searcher 1970–72. **Educ.:** Univ. of AL, 1966–68, BA (Hist.); Case West. Rsv. Univ., 1968–69, MLS. **Orgs.:** Med. LA. AL LA. **Activities:** 1; 27, 31, 39; 80 **Addr.:** Lister Hill Library of the Health Sciences, University of AL in Birmingham, University Station, Birmingham, AL 35209.

Jones, Holway Roy (O. 11, 1922, New Orleans, LA) Head Ref. Libn., Prof., Univ. of OR, 1981–, Head Soc. Sci. Libn., Prof., 1963–80; City and Reg. Plng. Libn., Univ. of CA (Berkeley), 1955–63, Doc. Libn., 1951–54. **Educ.:** Univ. of CA (Berkeley), 1945–48, BA (Hist.), 1949–51, BLS, 1955–57, MA (Hist.). **Orgs.:** Cncl. Plng. Libn.: Treas. (1963–67); Ed. CPL Nsltr. (1971–74); Ed. Adv. Com., CPL Bibl. Index to Current Urban Doc.: Mem., Ed. Bd. (1974–). Sierra Club: Bd. Dir. (1973–76); Pubns. Com. (Ch. 1974–76); Natl. Wilderness Com. (1972–74, 1976–78); Fifth Ofcr. (1974–76). OR Wilderness Coal.: Pres. (1976–78). **Honors:** Cncl. of Plng. Libn., Distin. Srv. Awd., 1971; Sierra Club, William Colby Awd., 1977; U.S. Env. Protection Agency, Env. Qual. Awd., Region X, 1977. **Pubns.:** *John Muir and the Sierra Club: The Battle for Yosemite* (1965); Co.-auth., *City Planning: A Basic Bibliography of Sources and Trends (3rd ed)* (1972). **Activities:** 1, 12; 15, 31, 39; 59, 65, 92 **Addr.:** Reference Department, University of Oregon Library, Eugene, OR 97403.

Jones, Houston G. (Ja. 7, 1924, Caswell Cnty., NC) Cur., NC Col., Univ. of NC Lib., 1974–; Dir., NC Dept. of Arch. and Hist., 1968–74, State Archvst., 1956–68; Ch., Div. of Soc. Sci., W. GA Coll., 1955–56; Prof. of Hist., Oak Ridge Milit. Inst., 1950–53. **Educ.:** Appalachian State Univ., 1946–49, BS (Hist./Eng.); George Peabody Coll., 1949–50, MA (Hist.); Duke Univ., 1950–65, PhD (Hist.); Cert. in Arch. Admin., American Univ., 1957. **Orgs.:** SAA: Pres. (1968–69); VP (1967–68); Treas. (1961–67). Jt. Com. on the Status of the Natl. Arch.: Secy. (1967–69). N. Caroliniana Socty.: Secy.-Treas. (1975–). NC Lit. and Hist. Assn.: Secy. (1968–75); Pres. (1975–76). Amer. Assn. for State and Lcl. Hist.: Cncl. (1972–76); Secy. (1978–). Hist. Socty. of NC: Pres. (1979–80). Other orgs. **Honors:** SAA, Fellow, 1961; SAA, Walde G. Leland Prize, 1967; Amer. Assn. for State & Local Hist., Awd. of Merit, 1968; Appalachian State Univ., Disting. Alum. Awd., 1971. **Pubns.:** *Local Government Records: An Introduction* (1980); *The Records of a Nation* (1969); *For History's Sake* (1966); *Union List of North Carolina Newspapers, 1751–1900* (1963); *Bedford Brown: State Rights Unionist* (1956); various articles. **Activities:** 1; 17, 45; 73 **Addr.:** C/o North Carolina Collection, University of North Carolina Library, Chapel Hill, NC 27514.

Jones, Hugo William (Ja. 12, 1920, Long Beach, CA) Mgr., Lib. Srvs., Northrop Corp., Aircraft Grp., 1958–, Pubns. Grp. Leader, 1951–58; Partner, Graphics Prod. Kay-Christopher Advert., 1949–51; Prod. Ed., Proof Reader, Crow Pubns., 1946–48; Naval Aviator, U.S. Navy, 1941–45. **Educ.:** Univ. of AZ, 1937–39; Univ. of South. CA, 1939–41, BS (Bus. Admin.), 1961–66, MSLS. **Orgs.:** SLA: Nom. Com. (1980–81); Aerospace Div. (Ch., 1976–77); Sci.-Tech. News Bus. Mgr. (1974–80); Los Angeles Chap. (Aerospace Ch., 1975–79). ASIS: Anl. Conf. (Ch., 1973); Los Angeles Chap. (Ch., 1970). **Pubns.:** "Computerized Subscriptions and Periodicals Routing in an Aerospace Library,"

Special Subjects/Services: 50. Adult educ.; 51. Advert./Mktg.; 52. Aerosp.; 53. Agric.; 54. Area std.; 55. Arts/Hum.; 56. Autom.; 57. Bibl./Prtg.; 58. Bio. sci.; 59. Bus./Fin.; 60. Chem.; 61. Copyrt.; 62. Documtn.; 63. Educ.; 64. Engin.; 65. Env.; 66. Eth. grps.; 67. Film; 68. Food/Nutr.; 69. Geneal.; 70. Geo.; 71. Geol.; 72. Handcpd.; 73. Hist.; 74. Int. frdm.; 75. Info. sci.; 76. Insr.; 77. Law; 78. Legis.; 79. Math./Comp. sci.; 80. Med.; 81. Metals; 82. Nat. resrcs.; 83. Newsp.; 84. Nuc. sci.; 85. Oral hist.; 86. Petr./Energy; 87. Pharm.; 88. Phys./Astr./Math.; 89. Readg.; 90. Relig.; 91. Sci./Tech.; 92. Soc. sci.; 93. Telecom.; 94. Transp.; 95. (other).

Who's Who in Library and Information Services

Spec. Libs. (N. 1967); "Problems in the Handling, Maintenance and Retention of Classified Documents within the Library Environment," *Procs. of the Classified Mgt. Socty.* (1974); "AD Numbers–A Guide to Their Location," *Defense Documtn. Ctr. Digest* (S. 23, 1974). **Activities:** 12; 17, 37; 52, 62 **Addr.:** 432 30th St., Manhattan Beach, CA 90266.

Jones, James F. (Ap. 29, 1932, Brooklyn, NY) Asst. Dir. for Tech. Srvs., FL State Univ. Lib., 1967–, Msc. Libn., 1965–67, Msc. Catlgr., 1962–65. **Educ.:** FL State Univ., 1954, BMe (Msc. Educ.); OH State Univ., 1957, MA (Msc. Theory); FL State Univ., 1965, MS (LS). **Orgs.:** ALA. Msc. LA. SELA. FL LA. **Pubns.:** *Coordination of Headings in a Card Catalog* (1973); "Library Costs," *FL Libs.* (My.-Je. 1979); "The Other Half of Cataloging," *Lib. Resrcs. and Tech. Srvs.* (Sum. 1973). **Activities:** 1; 46; 55 **Addr.:** 1517 Fuller Rd., Tallahassee, FL 32303.

Jones, James V. (My. 14, 1924, Willard, OH) Dir. of Univ. Libs., Case West. Reserve Univ., 1968–; Dir. of Lib., Cleveland St. Univ., 1966–68; Dir. of Lib., St. Louis Univ., 1955–66, Asst. Dir. of Lib., 1952–55. **Educ.:** John Carroll Univ., 1946–48, BS; West. Reserve Univ., 1949–50, MSLS, Adv. Mgt. Prog., 1974–75, Cert. **Orgs.:** ALA: Cncl. (1957–61); ACRL, Com. Rel. Accred. Agencies (1962–67, Ch., 1965–66), Com. Urban Univ. Libs. (1964–66), Com. Appt. Nom. (1969, 1970); various other coms. Cath. LA: Adv. Cncl.; Schol. Com. (1958–63); various coms. MO LA: VP (1958–59); Pres. (1959–60); various coms. Many other orgs. and coms. Midw. Interlib. Ctr.: Adv. Com. Libn. (1977–65); Bd. Dir. (1960–63); Cncl. (1965–66). OH Coll. Lib. Ctr.: Bd. Trustees (1971–79); Ch. and Pres. (1972–75); Natl. Lib. Coord. Com. (1979–). many other orgs. and com. **Pubns.:** "Selected Annotated Books of 1965," *The Cath. Educ.* (Mr. 1966); "Furniture for Library Offices and Staff Work Areas," *Lib. Trends* (Ap. 1965); "55th SLA Convention Program," *Spec. Libs.* (Ap. 1964); "Vending Library Makes Progress; Research Center for Industry," *Vending Times* (O. 1961); "New Catholic Libraries: Saint Louis University," *The Cath. Lib. World* (Ap. 1960); many other articles. **Activities:** 1; 17, 24; 63 **Addr.:** Case Western Reserve University Libraries, 11161 East Blvd., Cleveland, OH 44106.

Jones, Jeannette M. (Ag. 18, 1913, Philadelphia, PA) Retired, 1981; Libn., Moorestown (NJ) HS, 1964–81; Libn., Collingswood HS, 1955–64; Tchr., Eng., Woodstown HS, 1954–55; Asst. Libn., Stevens Sch. (PA), 1947–53. **Educ.:** Hood Coll., 1931–35, AB (Eng.); Drexel Univ., 1957–61 (MSLS). **Orgs.:** Burlington Cnty. Sch. Media Assn.: Pres. (1974–76). ALA. NJ Educ. Media Assn: Rec. Secy. (1973–74); *Signal Tab* (Ed., 1974–77). Natl. Educ. Assn. NJ Educ. Assn. Delta Kappa Gamma: *Alpha Zeta State Nsltr.* (Ed., 1979–81). **Honors:** Beta Phi Mu. **Pubns.:** Editorials. **Activities:** 10; 17, 20, 31 **Addr.:** 8 S. Lakeside Dr., W., Medford, NJ 08055.

Jones, Kathryn A. (O. 21, 1952, Fernbank, FL) Cat. Libn., Mercer Univ. Law Lib., 1978–. **Educ.:** Univ. of S. FL, 1972–76, BA (Eng.); Emory Univ., 1977–78, MLn. **Orgs.:** AALL. SE Assn. of Law Libs: Nsltr. Com. (1980). AAUW. **Honors:** Phi Delta Mu. **Pubns.:** "The Card Catalog: Its History in America," *Amer. Libs.* (F. 1978); "7 1/2 x 12 1/2: the OCLC Impact on Law Libraries," *Law Lib. Jnl.* (v. 71, no. 2). **Addr.:** Mercer University Law Library, Macon, GA 31208.

Jones, Kenneth M. (Ja. 2, 1922, Charleston, WV) Dir., Instr. Media Srvs., Orange Cnty. Pub. Schs., 1966–; Guid. Dir., Glenridge Jr. HS, 1963–66; Tchr., Orange Cnty. Pub. Schs., 1957–63. **Educ.:** Marshall Univ., 1943, BA; Stetson Univ., 1960, MA (Educ. Admin. and Supvsn.). **Orgs.:** ALA. AECT. FL Assn. for Media in Educ. FL Assn. for Supvsrs. of Media. Various other orgs. Orange Cnty. Assn. of Admins. and Supvsrs. FL Assn. of Supvsn. and Curric. Dev. FL Assn. of Instr. Supvsrs. and Admins. **Pubns.:** Auth. of bk. and educ. filmstrip on FL hist. topics. **Activities:** 10, 14-District lib. media srvs.; 17, 32; 63 **Addr.:** 410 Woods Ave., Orlando, FL 32805.

Jones, Linda Gail Greene (S. 2, 1939, Asheville, NC) Acq. Libn., Cumberland Sch. of Law, Samford Univ., 1977–; Libn., Birmingham (AL) Bd. of Educ., 1975–77; Libn., Louisville (KY) Bd. of Educ., 1973–75; Libn., Dade Cnty. (FL) Bd. of Educ., 1969–73; Libn., NW AL State Jr. Coll., 1966–69. **Educ.:** Berea Coll., 1957–61, BS (Home Econ.); Appalachian State Univ., 1965–66, MA (LS). **Orgs.:** AALL. AL LA. **Addr.:** Cumberland School of Law Library, Samford University, Birmingham, AL 35229.

Jones, Margaret Palcich (O. 7, 1915, Chisholm, MN) Ref. Dept. Head, Pub. Lib., 1967–, Chld. Libn., 1963–67, Branch Libn., 1954–63. **Educ.:** IN Univ., 1963–64, (LS); Purdue Univ., 1965–67, Cert. IV (LS). **Orgs.:** IN LA: Lib. Plng. (1968). ALA: SORT, Bd. (1968–72); Secy. (1976–78). **Pubns.:** *Opinions on Collective Bargaining* (1969); Asst. Ed., *Diamond Jubilee Historical Record* (1968); "Pamphlet Classification," *RQ* (Spr. 1968). **Activities:** 9; 15, 16, 39; 59, 75, 92 **Addr.:** 8425 5th St., Highland, IN 46322.

Jones, Marianne S. (F. 21, 1949, Monroe, LA) Clinical Med. Libn., Truman Med. Ctr.-E., 1980–; Circ. Branch Chief, Univ. of KS Med. Lib., 1979–80; Branch Libn., Ouachita Parish Pub. Lib., 1975–79, Ref. Coord., 1973–75. **Educ.:** Centenary Coll., 1967–71, BS (Educ.); LA State Univ., 1971–72, MS (LS). **Orgs.:** LA LA: JMRT Ch. VP (1977–79); 2nd Vice Ch. (1979). **Pubns.:** *LLA-JMRT Nsltr.* (1977–79). **Activities:** 12; 39; 80 **Addr.:** 18026 Dover Fork, Independence, MO 64057.

Jones, Mary Chambers (Jl. 22, 1928, Aberdeen, SD) Libn.-Media Spec., Dir., Lib.-Media Ctr., Thomas Jefferson HS, Portland, OR, 1974–; Dir., Lib.-Media Ctr., John Adams HS, Portland, 1972–74; Dir., Lib.-Media Ctr., John Marshall HS, Portland, 1966–74; Libn., Multonomah Cnty. Lib., Portland, 1965–66. **Educ.:** Duchesne Coll. of the Sacred Heart, Omaha, 1946–50, BA (Eng. Lit.); Univ. of CA, Los Angeles, 1962–63, MLS. **Orgs.:** ALA: Cncl. (1978–81); AASL (Bd. of Dirs., 1971–73). OR Educ. Media Assn. OR LA. **Activities:** 10; 31, 39, 48; 55, 63, 66 **Addr.:** 3718 S.W. Hillside Dr., Portland, OR 97221.

Jones, Mary Virginia Spruill Currie (O. 8, 1954, Raleigh, NC) Mgr., Jenkins Resrch. Ctr., Bapt. Frgn. Mission Bd., 1981–; Asst. Cur. of Mss., VA Hist. Socty., 1980–81, Mss. Cat., 1979–80. **Educ.:** Univ. of NC (Chapel Hill), 1972–76, BA (Hist.), 1976–78, MA (Hist.), 1978–79, MSLS. GA Arch. Inst. 1977, Cert. **Orgs.:** SAA. SLA. VA LA. **Pubns.:** Reviews. **Activities:** 12; 20, 39, 45; 55, 69 **Addr.:** Foreign Mission Board, 3806 Monument Ave., Richmond, VA 23230.

Jones, Maxine Holmes (My. 18, 1929, St. Louis, MO) Educ. Consult., Bur. of AV Instr., Univ. of WI-Ext., 1977–, Libn., Parkway Pub. Schs., St. Louis, 1976–77; Dir. of Media, DeSoto (MO) Pub. Schs. #73, 1973–76. **Educ.:** SW MO State Univ., 1968, BS (Educ., Eng.); OH State Univ., 1972–73, MA (Media, Educ.); Univ. of WI, Madison, 1977–, PhD (Instr. Tech.). **Orgs.:** ALA. AECT: Eval. (various yrs.); Prog. Presenter (1977). WI AV Assn: Jt. ed. of jnl. (1980, 1981). Leag. of Women Voters of Jefferson Cnty., MO. **Pubns.:** "Media Port: A Library Trains 1,900 Citizens in Video," *Amer. Libs.* (Ap. 1980); "AV Services: Frills No Longer," *Amer. Libs.* (O. 1979); "Large Screen TV Projection: Variations on a Beam," *Amer. Libs.* (F. 1979). **Addr.:** 6785 Schroeder Rd., Madison, WI 53711.

Jones, Milbrey L. (N. 22, 1928, Macon, GA) Chief, Sch. Media Resrcs. Branch, US Dept. of Educ., 1978–, Educ. Prog. Spec., 1965–78; Assoc. Prof., LS Dept., James Madison Univ., 1963–65, Asst. Prof., 1956–63; Tchr., Libn., 1949–56. **Educ.:** GA Coll., 1947–49, AB (Eng.); Emory Univ., 1950–53, MA (LS); Rutgers Univ., 1963–65, PhD (LS). **Orgs.:** ALA: AASL. AECT. **Pubns.:** "School Media Programs: Progress, Obstacles, and Promising Developments" in *State-Wide Library Planning - The New Jersey Example* (1969); *Emphasis on Excellence in School Media Programs* (1969); "ESEA Title II Contributions to State Department of Education Leadership of School Media Programs" in *Essays for Ralph Shaw* (1975); *Survey of School Media Standards, 1974* (1977); "The First Year of ESEA Title IV, Part B: A Preliminary Report," *Sch. Media Qtly.* (Win., 1977); other articles. **Activities:** 10; 17 **Addr.:** Chief, School Media Resources Branch, DLP/OLLR/BESE, US Dept. of Education, 400 Md. Ave. S.W., CROB-3, Rm 3125B, Washington, DC 20024.

Jones, P. Richard (O. 23, 1926, Boston, MA) Dir., Arch., Suffolk Univ., 1966–. **Educ.:** Suffolk Univ., 1953–56, BS (Jnlsm.), 1972–74, EdM (Educ.). **Orgs.:** SAA. New Eng. Archvsts. Boston Area Archvsts. Grp. **Honors:** Alpha Phi Omega, 1970; Delta Sigma Pi, 1981. **Activities:** 2; 17, 24, 39; 85 **Addr.:** Archives, Suffolk University, Beacon Hill, Boston, MA 02114.

Jones, Plummer Alston, Jr. (O. 10, 1948, Washington, NC) Head Libn., NC Wesleyan Coll., 1976–; Msc. Tchr., Norfolk (VA) City Schs., 1970–74. **Educ.:** E. Carolina Univ., 1966–70, BM (Msc. Educ.); Drexel Univ., 1974–76, MS (LS). **Orgs.:** ALA. **Honors:** Beta Phi Mu. **Activities:** 1; 17; 55 **Addr.:** Library, North Carolina Wesleyan College, Wesleyan College Station, Rocky Mount, NC 27801.

Jones, Richard C. (Ag. 13, 1930, London, UK) Dir., N. Ctrl. Reg. Lib. Syst., 1972–, Asst. Dir., 1968–72; Branch Libn., Sudbury Pub. Lib., 1966–68; Branch Libn., Southwark Pub. Lib., 1964–66; Branch Head, Camberwell Pub. Lib., 1958–64. **Educ.:** Laurentian Univ., 1969–74, BA (Eng.); LA (UK), Assoc., 1960, Fellow, 1972. **Orgs.:** ON LA: Reg. and Pub. Lib. Div. (Vice-Ch., 1970); Can. Auth.s' Pub. Lending Right Action Grp. (Ch., 1971–72). Dirs. of ON Reg. Lib. Systs.: Treas. (1981); Secy. (1979). Anishnaube KisKantomowia/Native. Info. Srv. *ON Pub. Lib. Review:* N. ON Task Grp. Conv. (1981–). **Pubns.:** *Public Landing Right: A Survey* (1974); "The Tri-Regional Catalogue," *ON Lib. Review* (Je. 1980). **Activities:** 9, 13; 17, 26, 34; 56, 57 **Addr.:** 336 Regent St. S., Sudbury, ON P3C 4E2 Canada.

Jones, Richard Earl (Mr. 11, 1944, Camden, NJ) Msc. Libn., Univ. of WI, Milwaukee, 1977–, Reader's Adv. in Msc., Trenton State Coll., 1972–77; Asst. Head, Cat. Dept., Univ. of NC, Greensboro, 1971–72; Msc. Libn., OH Univ., 1968–70. **Educ.:** Westminster Coll. 1962–66, BMsc; OH Univ., 1966–68, MFA (Msc. Hist. and Lit.); Univ. of NC, Chapel Hill, 1970–71, MSLS. **Orgs.:** Intl. Assn. of Msc. Libs. Msc. LA: Midwest Chap., Com. on Lib. Instr. and Orien. (Ch., 1978–). AAUP. Amer. Msclgy. Socty. Civic Msc. Assn. of Milwaukee. Intl. Msclgy. Socty. Various other orgs. **Honors:** Beta Phi Mu. **Pubns.:** Ed., *Ohio University Music Library Index Series* (1968–69); Ed., *Ohio University Music Library Bulletin,* v. 1–2 (1968–69); "AACR2 and Uniform Titles in Music," *Msc. OCLC Users Grp. Bltn.* (D. 1979); Reviews. **Activities:** 1, 11; 15, 20, 39; 95-Msc. **Addr.:** 4333 N. Marlborough Dr., Shorewood, WI 53211.

Jones, Robert E. (Ap. 20, 1927, Denver, CO) Admin. Srvs. Libn., Ctrl. WA Univ., 1979–, Head, Tech. Srvs., 1971–78, Head, Cat. Dept., 1968–70; Head, Cat. Dept., East. WA Univ., 1964–67. **Educ.:** West. State Coll. of CO, 1947–51, BA (Math./Phys.); Univ. of Denver, 1957–64, MALS; Ctrl. WA Univ., 1969–71, MEd. **Orgs.:** ALA. **Pubns.:** "A Proposed Classification Schedule for a Curriculum Materials Collection," ERIC (1973); "ERIC," *Resrcs. for Tchg. and Lrng.* (Fall 1972). **Activities:** 1; 17, 46 **Addr.:** Library, Central Washington University, Ellensburg, WA 98926.

Jones, Royden R. (Ja. 18, 1944, Gladwin, MI) Chief Med. Libn., Wilford Hall Med. Ctr., Lackland Air Frc. Base, 1981–, Med. Catlgr., 1980–81; Libn., US Air Frc. Occupational and Env. Hlth. Lab., 1978–80; Lrng. Resrc. Ctr. Libn., Univ. of TX Hlth. Sci. Ctr., San Antonio, 1975–78; AV Libn., Welch Med. Lib., Johns Hopkins Univ, 1973–75. **Educ.:** Ctrl. MI Univ., 1962–66, BS (Bio.), 1969–71, MS (Bio.); Univ. of IL, 1972–73, MSLS. **Orgs.:** Med. LA. **Activities:** 1, 4; 20, 32, 39; 58, 80, 91 **Addr.:** 11627 Spring Mont, San Antonio, TX 78249.

Jones, Sarah Dowlin (S. 20, 1916, Media, PA) Libn., Goucher Coll., 1952–; Head, Ref. Dept., Univ. of PA Lib., 1949–52, Head, Math. Phys. Lib., 1947–49; Ref. Libn., Amer. Lib., London, 1945–47; Ref. Asst., Pratt Inst. Lib., 1944–45. **Educ.:** Univ. of PA, 1933–37, AB (Eng.), 1937–39, MA (Eng.), 1954, PhD (Eng.); Pratt Inst., 1943–44, BLS. **Orgs.:** ALA: Cncl. (1968–71); ACRL. MD LA. Libns. of MD Indp. Colls. and Univs.: Ch. (1973–75). Congs. of Acad. Libns. of MD. Various other orgs. AAUP. Mod. Lang. Assn. Women's Intl. Leag. for Peace and Frdm. Baltimore Bibliophiles. **Honors:** Phi Beta Kappa. **Activities:** 1; 15, 17, 39 **Addr.:** Julia Rogers Library, Goucher College, Dulaney Valley Rd., Towson, Baltimore, MD 21204.

Jones, Shirley L. (Moncton, NB) Chief Libn., Welland (ON) Pub. Lib., 1960–; Ref. Libn., St. Catharine's Pub. Lib., 1956–60, Circ. Libn., 1952–56. **Educ.:** Mt. Allison Univ., 1947–51, BA (Hist.); Univ. of Toronto, 1951–52, BLS. **Orgs.:** Can. LA. ON LA: Pub. and Reg. Libs. Div. (Cncl., 1970–76). Assn. of Medium-Sized Libs. of ON. Niagara Coll. of Appld. Arts and Tech.: Lib. Tech. Adv. Com. (Ch., 1978–). **Activities:** 9; 15, 17 **Addr.:** Welland Public Library, 140 King St., Welland, ON L3B 3J3 Canada.

Jones, Virginia Lacy (Je. 25, 1912, Cincinnati, OH) Dir., Atlanta Univ. Ctr., Robert W. Woodruff Lib., 1982–; Dean, Prof., Atlanta Univ., Sch. of Lib. and Info. Std., 1945–81, Instr., 1941–45, Cat. Libn., 1939–41; Instr. in LS, Prairie View A & M Coll., 1936–39; Libn., Louisville Mncpl. Coll., 1933–39. **Educ.:** Hampton Inst., 1929–33, BS (LS), 1935–36, BS (Educ.); Univ. of IL, 1937–38, MLS; Columbia Univ., 1941 (LS); Univ. of Chicago, 1943–45, PhD (LS). **Orgs.:** ALA: Cncl. (1946–50, 1955–59, 1967–76); Exec. Bd. (1971–76); Lib. Educ. Div., Bd. of Dirs. (1961–63); ACRL, various coms. AALS: Pres. (1967); Secy.-Treas. (1948–54); Bd. of Dirs. (1960–64); various coms. SELA: Srvy. of Southeast. Libs., Adv. Bd. (1972–75); various coms. SLA. Various other orgs. Beta Phi Mu: Bd. of Dirs. (1959–61). South. Flwshp. Fund, Inc.: Adv. Com. (1969–). Delta Sigma Theta: Natl. Lib. Com. (1950–55). GA State Bd. for the Cert. of Libns.: Vice-Ch. (1975–). Various other orgs. **Honors:** ALA, Beta Phi Mu Awd., 1980; ALA, Joseph W. Lippincott Awd., 1977; Univ. of MI, Hon. Doctor of Letters, 1979; Bishop Coll., Dallas, TX, Hon. Doctor of Humane Letters, 1979; other hons. **Pubns.:** "Virginia Lacy Jones," *Women View Librarianship* (1980); *Reminiscenses in Librarianship and Library Education...* (1979); "Library Education in Georgia," *Proceedings of the Governor's Conference on Georgia Libraries and Information Services* (1979); "Sadie Peterson Delaney," "Susan Dart Butler," *Dictionary of American Library Biography* (1978); "Library Education in the Southeast Since World War II," *Proceedings of Two Symposia Sponsored in Honor of Louis Round Wilson's 100th Birthday* (1976); various articles, reviews. **Activities:** 1, 11; 24, 25, 26 **Addr.:** 1341 Thurgood St. S.W., Atlanta, GA 30314.

Jones, William Goodrich (Ja. 12, 1941, Bryan, TX) Asst. Univ. Libn., Col. Dev. and Info. Srvs., Univ. of IL, Chicago Circle, 1980–; Head Libn., Seeley G. Mudd Lib. for Sci. and Engin., Northwestern Univ., 1977–79, Head Libn., Head Libn., Tech. Inst. Lib., 1972–77, Soc. Sci. Biblgphr., 1972; Libn., Inst. for Soc. Resrch., Univ. of MI, 1965–71, Lectr., Sch. of LS, 1969–71. **Educ.:** Princeton Univ., 1959–63, AB (Msc.); Univ. of MI, 1964, AMLS. **Orgs.:** ALA. ASIS. SLA. **Honors:** ARL, Lib. Consult. Trng. Prog., 1979. **Pubns.:** "Evaluation of the Use of MBO Procedures in a Library," *Spec. Libs.* (Jl. 1975); "How Many Reference Librarians Are Enough?" *RQ* (1974). **Activities:** 1; 17, 39; 91, 92 **Addr.:** The University of Illinois at Chicago Circle, The Library, Box 8198, Chicago, IL 60680.

Jones, Wyman H. (D. 17, 1929, St. Louis, MO) City Libn., Los Angeles Pub. Lib.; 1970–; Dir., Los Angeles Pub. Lib. Syst., 1970–; Dir., Fort Worth City/Cnty. Pub. Lib. Syst., 1964–70;

PROFESSIONAL ACTIVITIES: Institutions: 1. Acad. lib.; 2. Arch.; 3. Assn.; 4. Fed./Gvt. lib.; 5. Inst. lib.; 6. Mfr./Suppl.; 7. Milit. lib.; 8. Musm.; 9. Pub. lib.; 10. Sch. lib.; 11. Sch. of lib. sci.; 12. Spec. lib.; 13. State lib.; 14. (other). **Functions/Activities:** 15. Acq./Col. dev.; 16. Adult srvs.; 17. Admin.; 18. Apprais.; 19. Archit./Bldgs.; 20. Cat./Class.; 21. Chld. srvs.; 22. Circ.; 23. Cons./Pres.; 24. Consult.; 25. Cont. ed.; 26. Educ. lib. sci.; 27. Ext. srvs.; 28. Fund/Grants; 29. Gvt. pubs.; 30. Indx./Abs.; 31. Instr. lib. use; 32. Media srvs.; 33. Micro.; 34. Netwks./Coop.; 35. Persnl.; 36. PR; 37. Publshg.; 38. Recs. mgt.; 39. Ref. srvs.; 40. Repro.; 41. Resrch.; 42. Review.; 43. Secur.; 44. Serials; 45. Spec. col.; 46. Tech. srvs.; 47. Trustees/Bds.; 48. YA srvs.; 49. (other).

Who's Who in Library and Information Services

Chief of Branches, Dallas Pub. Lib., 1959–64, Chief, Sci. and Indus. Dept., 1958–59. **Educ.:** Adams State Coll., 1956, BA (Lit., Soc. Sci.); Univ. of IA, 1957; Univ. of TX, 1958, MLS. **Orgs.:** CA Bd. of Lib. Examiners. ALA. CA LA: Cncl. (1972–). SWLA: Pres. (1967). **Pubns.:** Jt. auth., *The Library Reaches Out* (1964); Monthly clmn., *Lib. Jnl.* (1964). **Activities:** 9; 17, 19, 24; 75 **Addr.:** Los Angeles Public Library, 630 W. Fifth St., Los Angeles, CA 90071.

Jonsberg, Judith Polansky (Je. 4, 1943, San Mateo, CA) Libn., Vinnell Corp., 1978–; Sub. Libn., City of Cmrce. Pub. Lib. 1975–76; Asst. Libn., Acad. of Motion Pic. Arts and Scis., 1972–73; Libn. I, City of Santa Monica Pub. Lib., 1970–72. **Educ.:** Univ. of CA, Berkeley, 1962–65, BA (Eng.); Univ. of CA, Los Angeles, 1969–70, MLS. **Orgs.:** SLA: South. CA Chap. **Activities:** 12; 17, 29, 41; 59, 91, 95-Gvt. Contracting. **Addr.:** Technical Services Division, Vinnell Corporation, Alhambra, CA 91802.

Joramo, Marjorie (F. 6, 1940, Owen, WI) Libn., Hennepin Cnty. Pub. Lib., 1973–; Libn., Hopkins Pub. Lib., 1970–73; Elem. Sch. Libn., Osseo Dist. 279, MN, 1968–69; Elem. Sch. Libn., LaPorte City (IA) Sch. Dist., 1965–68. **Educ.:** Univ. of North. IA, 1965, BS (Elem. Educ., Soc. Std.); George Peabody Coll., 1967, MLS. **Orgs.:** ALA: SRRT (Coord., 1978–80); YASD Int. Frdm. MN LA: Com. on Welfare of Lib. Workers (Ch., 1976–78). **Pubns.:** Comp., *Directory of Ethnic Publishers and Resource Organizations* (1978). **Activities:** 9, 10; 16, 39, 48 **Addr.:** 4715 Wingard Ln., Brooklyn Center, MN 55429.

Jordan, Anne H. (Ja. 1, 1924, El Paso, TX) Libn., Archit. and Plng. Lib., Univ. of TX, Austin, 1980–, Libn., Fine Arts Lib., 1979–80; Exec. Secy., SALALM, Benson Col., 1977–79; Asst. Acq. Libn., Wayne State Univ., 1974–77; Catlgr., Univ. of TX, Austin, 1968–69, Acq., Libn., 1967–68. **Educ.:** Univ. of TX, El Paso, 1943, BA, (Eng. Lit., Hist.); Univ. of TX, Austin, 1964–67, MLS, 1969–72, MA (Latin Amer. Std.). **Orgs.:** SALALM: Exec. Secy. (1977–). **Pubns.:** Ed., *Latin American Studies in Europe* (1979); Ed., *Multifaceted Role of the Latin American Subject Specialist* (1979); Jt. ed., *Twenty Years of Latin American Librarianship* (1978); Jt. ed., *Cannon's Bibliography of Library Economy, 1876–1920* (1976); "Mexican American Publishing Guide," *Jnl. of Mexican Amer. Hist.* (D. 1973); various other articles. **Activities:** 1; 15, 17, 39; 55, 95-Latin Amer. std. **Addr.:** 205 E. Milton, Austin, TX 78704.

Jordan, Casper LeRoy (Mr. 5, 1924, Cleveland, OH) Ctrl. Libn., Atlanta Pub. Lib., 1978–; Univ. Libn., Atlanta Univ., 1974–78, Assoc. Prof. of Lib. Srv., 1968–78; Asst. Dir., NIOGA Lib. Syst., 1961–68; Chief Libn., Wilberforce Univ., 1951–61. **Educ.:** Case Western Reserve Univ., 1943–47, AB (Hist.); Atlanta Univ., 1950–51, MS in LS. **Orgs.:** ALA. GA LA: Com. Ch. (1977–79). SELA. **Honors:** Beta Phi Mu, 1961. **Activities:** 2, 9; 17, 19, 20 **Addr.:** 1930 Honeysuckle Ln, S.W. #33, Atlanta, GA 30311.

Jordan, Hallie Adams (Ag. 6, 1941, Selma, AL) Lib. Media Spec., State of AL Dept. of Educ., 1974–; Ref. Libn., AL State Univ., 1972–74; Sch. Libn., Selma City Schs., 1970–72, Tchr., 1966–70. **Educ.:** Knoxville Coll., 1959–63, BS (Eng.); Univ. of IL, 1970–71, MLS. **Orgs.:** ALA: AASL, Admins. Awd. Com. (Ch., 1978–79). AL LA: Stans. and Cert. Com. (Ch., 1981–82); State Dept. of Educ. (Liaison, 1981–82). AL Instr. Media Assn.: Prog. Com. (Ch., 1979). Natl. Educ. Assn. AL Educ. Assn. **Activities:** 4, 10, 14-State dept. of educ.; 21, 24, 32 **Addr.:** State Dept. of Education, Educational Media Unit, 111 Coliseum Blvd., Montgomery, AL 36193.

Jordan, Katherine H. (Jl. 28, 1939, Cleveland, OH) Head, Lib. Instr. Srvs., Alexandria Campus North. VA Cmnty. Coll., 1974–, Head, Tech. Lib., Haile Selassie I Univ., 1972–74; Ref. Libn., The Urban Inst., 1970–72; Sr. Media Spec., Fed. City Coll., 1968–70; Libn., Boston Redev. Athrty., 1966–67; Ref. Asst., Boston Pub. Lib., 1964–66. **Educ.:** Wells Coll., 1957–61, AB (Eng.); Univ. of Pittsburgh, 1963–64, MLS. **Orgs.:** ALA: LIRT, Liaison Com. (Ch., 1978–79); ACRL/Bibl. Instr. Sect., Cont. Educ. Com. (1978–79). DC LA. **Pubns.:** "Books-by-Mail in Ethiopia and the 'Mailable Book,'" *The Unabashed Librarian* (Spr. 1974); "Jordan Takes Library-College to Ethiopia," *The Library-College Omnibus* (Je. 1974); Jt. auth., "Intershelving Media as a Way of Implementing the Library-College," *The Library-College Omnibus* (Je, 1975); Jt. auth., *Guide to Research: Study Guides for Students Preparing Research Papers* (1979); "The Community College Librarian as Catalyst for Curriculum Change" in *Reform and Renewal in Higher Education* (1980). **Activities:** 1; 15, 31, 39; 55, 63 **Addr.:** Library, Alexandria Campus, Northern Virginia Community College, 3001 N. Beauregard St., Alexandria, VA 22311.

Jordan, Mary K. (My. 17, 1931, Chillicothe, OH) Libn./Archvst., AAUW Educ. Fndn., 1977–; Head Libn., Natl. Educ. Assn., 1975–77, Ref. Libn., 1973–75. **Educ.:** Radcliffe Coll., 1949–53, AB (Eng. Lit.); Univ. of MD, 1970–73, MLS; Cert. in Arch. Mgt., Natl. Arch. & Rec. Svc., 1974. **Orgs.:** Beta Phi Mu: Iota Chap., VP/Pres Elect (1978–79); Pres. (1979–80). SLA. SAA. **Activities:** 2, 12; 17, 39, 46 **Addr.:** Library–AAUW Educational Foundation, Inc., 2401 Virginia Ave, N.W., Washington, DC 20037.

Jordan, Mel (F. 20, 1925, Batson, TX) Acq. Libn., Univ. of TX, Austin, 1979–; Acq. Libn., Corpus Christi State Univ., 1978–79; Acq. Libn., Oakland Univ., 1971–77; Actg. Lib. Dir., Univ. of Corpus Christi, 1970–71; Assoc. Lib. Dir., SW TX State Univ., 1967–69; Head Libn. Laredo Coll., 1966–67; Catlgr., Trinity Univ., 1965–66. **Educ.:** Univ. of TX, Austin, 1961–63, BA (Geo.), 1963–66, MLS. **Orgs.:** ALA: Ref. and Subscrpn. Bks. Review Com. (1977–79). Frdm. to Read Fndn. SALALM. TX LA: Constn. Com. (1969). MI LA: Legislative Com. (Acad. Div., 1973–74). TX Assn. of Coll. Tchrs. **Pubns.:** Jt. ed., *Cannons' Bibliography of Library Economy, 1876–1920* (1976); "Frank Patten and the Rosenberg Library," *E. TX Hist. Jnl.* (Fall 1976); "Hurricane Recovery Efforts: University of Corpus Christi Library," *TX Lib. Jnl.* (Win. 1970). **Activities:** 1; 15, 17, 30; 54, 92 **Addr.:** 205 E. Milton, Austin, TX 78704.

Jordan, Peter A. (O. 30, 1929, London, Eng.) Reg. Libn., Can. Wildlife Srv. (Edmonton), 1979–; Head, Acq., Can. Dept. of the Env. Lib. (Ottawa), 1977–79; Libn., North. Forest Resrch. Ctr., 1967–77; Catlgr., Circ. Libn., Dev. Libn., Univ. of Calgary Lib., 1964–67; Tchr./Libn., Revelstoke Sec. Sch., 1961–63. **Educ.:** McMaster Univ., 1952–55, BA (Soc. Std.); Univ. of BC, 1960–61, Dip. (Educ.), 1963–64, BLS. **Orgs.:** SLA. **Activities:** 4, 12; 15, 17, 20; 58, 65, 82 **Addr.:** Canadian Wildlife Service Library, Environment Canada, 10th Floor, 9942–108th St., Edmonton, AB T5K 2J5 Canada.

Jordan, René (Ag. 26, 1941, Batesville, AR) Head of Ext. Srvs., Knoxville-Knox Cnty. Publ. Lib., 1976–; Dir., Clinch-Powell Reg. Lib., 1973–76; Asst. Prof. of LS, Porter Lib., KS State Coll., 1969–73; Tchr., Rantoul (IL) City Schs., 1965–68. **Educ.:** Univ. of AR, 1959–63, BS (Math); Emporia State Univ., 1968–69, MLS; Univ. of UT, 1963–64, Cert. (Sec. Tchg.). **Orgs.:** E. TN LA: Pres. (1974). TN LA: Bylaws and Proc. Com. (Ch., 1978–79). SELA: Conf. Local Arrange. Com. (1976). ALA. E. TN Hist. Socty. **Pubns.:** "On Climbing Family Trees: Tennessee Genealogical Research," *TN Libn.* (Spr. 1981); "Basic Genealogical Sources," *ECHOES* (Je. 1977). **Activities:** 9; 17, 27, 35; 69 **Addr.:** Rte. 5, Box 221, Dandridge, TN 37725.

Jordan, Robert T. (Ag. 3, 1922, Chicago, IL) Prof., Univ. of the DC, 1968–; Assoc. Libn., Haile Selassie I Univ., 1972–74; Sr. Ofcr., Cncl. on Lib. Resrcs. 1960–68; Head Libn., Taft Coll., 1957–60. **Educ.:** Antioch Coll., 1939–47, BA; Univ. of CA, Berkeley, 1955–57, MLS; Univ. of IL, 1964, Wkshp. on lib. autom. **Orgs.:** ASIS. ALA: various coms. AAUP. Natl. Educ. Assn. **Pubns.:** *Tomorrow's Library* (1970); "The Library-College," *Encycl. of Educ.* (1971); Jt. auth., "Impact of the Academic Library on the Educational Program," *New Dimensions in Higher Education* (1967); Ed., *Lib.-Coll. Nsltr.* (1965–68); various other articles, speeches, ed. duties, and reviews. **Activities:** 1, 11; 25, 26, 41; 56, 67, 95-Viewdata. **Addr.:** 2687 Centennial Ct., Alexandria, VA 22311.

Jorgensen, Joan M. (N. 14, 1929, Parkston, SD) Instr., Portland Cmnty. Coll., 1978–; Media Dir., Beaverton HS, 1971–78; Instr., Portland State Univ., 1968–73; Chief Libn., BC Inst. of Tech., 1964–68. **Educ.:** East. WA State Coll., 1953–56, BA Educ. (Nat. Scis.); Univ. of WA, 1956–59, MLS; various crs., wkshps. 1965–. **Orgs.:** ALA. OR Educ. Media Assn.: Cont. Educ. (Ch., 1978–81). OR LA: Cont. Educ. Com. (Ch., 1978–81). SLA: Educ. Div. Amer. Fld. Srv.: Chap. Pres. (1973–75). Portland State Women's Assn.: Soc. Com. (Mem. Ch., 1967–71). **Pubns.:** *Fisheries Resrch. Bd. of Can., Mss. Rpt. Series #61* (Jl. 1963); cont. educ. clmn., *Interchange* (1979–80); reviews. **Activities:** 10, 14-Cmnty. coll.; 24, 25, 26; 50, 63, 75 **Addr.:** Rte. 4, Box 178, Hillsboro, OR 97123.

Jorve, Ronald M. (Ja. 8, 1930, LaMoure, ND) Asst. Dir., Lib. Resrcs. Ctr., Tech. Srvs., Amarillo Coll., 1977–; Acq. Libn., Oral Roberts Univ., 1974–76; Libn., Asms. of God Grad. Sch., 1973–74; Libn., Trinity Bible Inst., 1972–73; Acq. Libn., Whitman Coll., 1971–72; Asst. Libn., Chapman Coll., 1967–69; Sci. Ref. Libn., Humboldt State Univ., 1966–67; Acq. Libn., Princeton Theo. Semy., 1962–65. **Educ.:** Jamestown Coll., 1948–52, BS (Chem.); San Francisco Theo. Semy., 1954–55, 1956–58; MDiv (Theo.); Princeton Theo. Semy., 1958–59, ThM (Theo.); Univ. of CA, Berkeley, 1960–62, MLS (Libnshp.); Cntrl. Data Inst., 1969–70, AS (Autom.). **Orgs.:** ALA. ATLA. TX LA. SW LA. TX Jr. Coll. Tchrs. Assn. Young Men's Christ. Assn. Amarillo Coll. Alum. Assn. **Honors:** Beta Phi Mu. **Activities:** 1; 15, 20, 46 **Addr.:** Amarillo College, LRC, 2201 S. Washington, P.O. Box 447, Amarillo, TX 79178.

Jose, Jean (Mr. 28, 1935, Indianapolis, IN) Asst. Dir., IN State Lib., 1968–, Lib. Consult., 1968–76; Libn., Granville Pub. Lib., 1967–68. **Educ.:** Butler Univ., 1952–56, AB (Eng., Hist., Educ.); IN Univ., 1965–67, MLS. **Orgs.:** IN LA. ALA. WHCOLIS: Del. IN Gvr.'s Adv. Com. on Libs. and Info. Srvs. **Honors:** Beta Phi Mu; Delta Kappa Gamma. **Pubns.:** "Library Occurrent to Cease Publication," *Lib. Occurrent* (N. 1980). **Activities:** 9, 13; 17, 35, 37; 55, 56 **Addr.:** 6114 N. Ewing St., Indianapolis, IN 46220.

Jose, Phyllis Ann (Mr. 15, 1949, Detroit, MI) Lib. Dir./Cnty. Libn., Oakland Cnty. Ref. Lib., 1977–; Libn. I, Dearborn Pub. Lib., 1976–77. **Educ.:** MI State Univ., 1967–71, BA (Hist.), 1971–72, MA (Eng. as Sec. Lang.); Univ. of MI, 1973–75, MA (LS). **Orgs.:** ALA. MI LA: Leg. Com. (1977–78); PR Com. (1978–79); Int. Frdm. Com. (1981–). SLA. Gvt. Docum. RT of Ctrl. MI: Prog. Ch., Pres.-Elect (1980–81). Leag. of Women Voters. Southfield Tax Increment Fin. Athrty. Southfield Econ. Dev. Corp. **Activities:** 4, 9; 17, 29, 39; 59 **Addr.:** Oakland County Governmental Reference Library, 1200 N. Telegraph Rd., Pontiac, MI 48053.

Josel, Nathan A., Jr. (S. 28, 1941, New Orleans, LA) Dir. of Libs., El Paso Pub. Lib., 1980–; Asst. Dir., Madison Pub. Lib., 1974–79; Head, Hist. and Travel, Memphis Pub. Lib. and Info. Ctr., 1969–74; Various positions, Enoch Pratt Free Lib., 1965–69. **Educ.:** Tulane Univ., 1959–63, BA (Hist.); LA State Univ., 1963–65, MSLS. **Orgs.:** ALA: PLA Comnty. Info. Sect, Exec. Bd. (1979–81); Nom. Com. (1981); RASD/Hist. Sect. (Secy., 1974–76), Local Hist. Com. (Ch., 1974–); Ref. Resrc. File (1973–); ACRL, Com. on Priorities for *Choice* (1972). WI Gvr.'s Conf. on Libs. and Info. Sci. **Pubns.:** Contrib., *Reference Books for Small and Medium Libraries,* 3rd ed. (1979); Ed., *Local History Guidelines* (1978); "Local History: Observations on a Survey," *RQ* (Sum. 1978); "Local History Leads to Action," *WI Lib. Bltn.* (Mr.-Ap. 1976); "Ten Reference Commandments," *RQ* (Win. 1970); various other articles, speeches, and reviews. **Activities:** 9; 16, 17, 39; 69, 85, 95-Local Hist. **Addr.:** El Paso Public Library, 501 N. Oregon, El Paso, TX 79901.

Joseph, Eleanor C. (Jl. 10, 1919, Waco, TX) Head, Ref. and Info. Srvs., E. Baton Rouge Par. Lib., 1953–; Asst. Libn., Rapides Par. Lib., 1946–48; Secy., Howell-Soskin Pubns., 1943–44; Ref. Libn., New Orleans Pub. Lib., 1941–43. **Educ.:** Newcomb Coll. of Tulane Univ., 1936–40, BA (Eng. Lit.); LA State Univ., 1940–41, BSLS. **Orgs.:** Baton Rouge Lib. Clb.: Pres. (1962). ALA: Info. and Ref. Com. (1978–); Ref. and Subscrpn. Bks. Review Com. (1971). LA LA: Pub. Lib. Sect. (Ch., 1965–66); LA Lit. Awd. Com. (Ch., 1962–63); Essae M. Culver Awd. Com. (Ch., 1981–82, 1965–66). Untd. Cerebral Palsy Assn. of Grt. Baton Rouge. Untd. Cerebral Palsy Assn. of LA. **Honors:** Baton Rouge Jr. Cham. of Cmrce., Outstan. Pub. Servant Awd., 1962. **Pubns.:** "What the Patrons Ask," *Bltn. of LA LA* (Spr. 1963, Fall 1963, Sum. 1964). **Activities:** 9; 39; 95-Info. and ref. **Addr.:** 1816 Chopin Dr., Baton Rouge, LA 70806.

Joseph, Gene A. (Ap. 28, 1954, Hazelton, BC, Can.) Libn., Un. of BC Indian Chiefs, 1979–, Asst. Libn., 1978–79; Resrchr., BC Indian Bibl. Ctr., 1978–78. **Educ.:** Univ. of BC, 1976–78, BA (Hist.); Vancouver Cmnty. Coll. (Langara), 1972–75, (Can. Stud., Hist.). **Orgs.:** Orig. Peoples' LA: Pres. (1979). **Activities:** 12; 17, 39; 66 **Addr.:** Resource Centre, Union of B.C. Indian Chiefs, 3rd Floor 440 West Hastings St., Vancouver, BC V6B 1L1 Canada.

Joseph, Margaret A. (Je. 9, 1941, Urbana, IL) Asst. Dir. for Pub. Srvs., Univ. of TX, San Antonio, 1973–, Head of Ref., 1973; Sr. Asst. Libn., Soc. Sci. and Hum. Ref., Univ. of NE, 1972–73, Asst. Libn., Hum. Div., 1970–72. **Educ.:** Grinnell Coll., 1959–63, BA (Eng.); Univ. of KS, 1963–66, MA (Eng.); Columbia Univ., 1970, MSLS; Univ. of NE, 1971–73, Grad. std. in Amer. Lit. **Orgs.:** Bexar LA. ALA. TX LA. SLA. Various other orgs. UTSA Univ. Asm. **Pubns.:** Jt. auth., "A Basic Introduction to the Use of the UTSA Library," lib. instr. workbk. (1976). **Activities:** 1; 17, 31, 39; 55, 56 **Addr.:** 104 Sunnyland Dr., San Antonio, TX 78228.

Josephine, Helen B. (D. 13, 1948, IL) Proj. Dir., J. Morris Jones Awd. Psy Parity Proj., 1980–81; Dir. of Resrch., Info. on Demand, 1978–79; Ref. Libn., Solano Cnty. Pub. Lib. Vallejo, CA, 1976–78; Lib. Instr. Libn., Univ. of CA, Berkeley, 1974–76. **Educ.:** Monmouth Coll., Monmouth, IL, 1967–71, AB (Eng. Lit.); Univ. of CA, Berkeley, 1973–74, MLS. **Orgs.:** Women Lib. Workers: Bd. of Dirs. (1975–79). ALA: *RQ* (Ed., 1979–81); Com. on the Status of Women (1976–79). CA LA. Univ. of CA, Berkeley Lib. Sch. Alum. Assn.: Pres. (1977–78). **Pubns.:** "Comparable Pay for Comparable Work," *Women Lib. Workers Nsltr.* (F. 1978); "Librarians Join the Fight for Fair Pay," *Women's Agenda* (N. 1978); "Beyond Awareness: Women in Libraries Organize for Change," *Sch. Lib. Jnl.* (Jan. 1977); "Serving the Unserved Majority: The Women's Resource Librarian," *Lib. Jnl.* (J. 1974). **Activities:** 12, 14-Info. indus.; 31, 39, 49-Comp.-aided ref.; 59, 92, 95-Women's std. **Addr.:** PO Box 246, Berkeley, CA 94701.

Josey, E. J. (Ja. 20, 1924, Norfolk, VA) Chief, Bur. of Spec. Lib. Srvs., NY St. Lib., 1976–, Chief, Bur. of Acad. and Resrch. Lib., 1968–76; Assoc., Div. of Lib. Dev., NY St. Educ. Dept., 1966–68; Libn. and Assoc. Prof., Savannah St. Coll., 1959–66; Libn. and Asst. Prof., Delaware St. Coll., 1955–59; Instr. of Soc. Sci., Savannah St. Coll., 1954–55; Libn. I, Free Lib. of Philadelphia, 1953–54. **Educ.:** Howard Univ., 1946–49, AB (Hist.); Columbia Univ., 1949–50, MA (Hist.); St. Univ. NY Albany, 1952–53, MSLS. **Orgs.:** ALA: Cncl. (1970–); Exec. Bd. (1979–); Intl. Rel. Com. (Ch., 1977–78, 1976–80); Founder ALA Black Caucus; Pres. Cmsn. (1975–76); many other coms. NY LA: many coms. ASIS Assn. Coop. Lib. Orgs.: Ch. (1974–76). Assn. Study Afro-Amer. Life and Hist.: Albany Chap., Pres. (1975–76). Amer. Acad. Pol. Soc. Sci. Amer. Civil. Liberties Union. World

Special Subjects/Services: 50. Adult educ.; 51. Advert./Mktg.; 52. Aerosp.; 53. Agric.; 54. Area std.; 55. Arts/Hum.; 56. Autom.; 57. Bibl./Prtg.; 58. Bio. sci.; 59. Bus./Fin.; 60. Chem.; 61. Copyrt.; 62. Documtn.; 63. Educ.; 64. Engin.; 65. Env.; 66. Eth. grps.; 67. Film; 68. Food/Nutr.; 69. Geneal.; 70. Geo.; 71. Geol.; 72. Handcpd.; 73. Hist.; 74. Int. frdm.; 75. Info. sci.; 76. Insr.; 77. Law; 78. Legis.; 79. Math./Comp. sci.; 80. Med.; 81. Metals; 82. Nat. resrcs.; 83. Newsp.; 84. Nuc. sci.; 85. Oral hist.; 86. Petr./Energy; 87. Pharm.; 88. Phys./Astr./Math.; 89. Readg.; 90. Relig.; 91. Sci./Tech.; 92. Soc. sci.; 93. Telecom.; 94. Transp.; 95. (other).

Future Socty. Other orgs. **Honors:** WHCOLIS, Del. Lg., 1979; ALA, Joseph W. Lippincott Awd. (1980), Black Caucus Awd., Disting. Srv. Libnshp.; SUNY Albany, Alumni Awd. for Disting. Srv. Libnshp.; Shaw Univ., LHD, 1973; other honors. **Pubns.:** *The Black Librarian in America* (1970); *What Black Librarians Are Saying* (1972); *New Dimensions for Academic Library Service* (1975); jt. ed., *A Century of Service* (1976); Jt. ed., *Opportunities for Minorities in Librarianship* (1977); other pubns. **Activities:** 1, 13; 24, 25, 31; 55, 66, 92 **Addr.:** Bureau of Specialist Library Services, New York State Education Department, Cultural Education Center, Room 10C47, Empire State Plz., Albany, NY 12230.

Joy, Carol Marie Briggs (My. 10, 1944, Montclair, NJ) Bus. and Cmnty. Rel. Ofcr./Ref. Libn., 1975–; Asst. Ref. Libn., Metro. State Coll., 1970–75, Asst. Libn., Pub. and Tech. Srvs., 1969–70; Libn., Denver Equip. Co., 1967–68. **Educ.:** Univ. of WY, 1962–63; Univ. of Denver, 1963–66, BA (Grmn.), 1967–69, MA (LS), 1980–81, MBA. **Orgs.:** Beta Phi Mu: Phi Chap. (Pres., 1973–75); Adv. Asm. (1975–78). CO LA: Docum. RT (Ch., 1978–79). ALA. SLA: Docum. Div. (Lcl. Rep., 1976); Chap. Nom. Com. (Ch., 1977), Elec. Com. (1978), Prog. Com. (1979–80). Denver Concert Band. Lakewood Untd. Meth. Church Choir. Adult Educ. Cncl. of Metro. Denver. Ladies of Rotary. **Honors:** CO Cent./Bicent. Comsn. and CO LA, Grant for Pubn., 1975. **Pubns.:** jt. auth., *Colorado Local History: A Directory* (1975); lib. sketches, *Columbine* (SLA, CO Chap., Nsltr.) (1972–73); gvt. docum. clmn., *CO Libs.* (S.–D. 1978). **Activities:** 1; 29, 39, 49-Online srch.; 59, 76, 77 **Addr.:** Auraria Library, Lawrence at 11th St., Denver, CO 80204.

Joyce, Charles (Ja. 3, 1929, W. Tremont, ME) Dir., Kansas City (KS) Pub. Lib., 1978–; Dir., MA Bur. of Lib. Ext., 1973–78; Assoc. State Libn., CT State Lib., 1968–73; Dir., Morrill Meml. Lib., Norwood, MA, 1962–68. **Educ.:** Tufts Univ., 1947–51, BA (Econ.); Simmons Coll., 1954–55, MS (LS). **Orgs.:** MA LA: Ch., PR Com. (1967–68). New Eng. Lib. Bd.: Ch. (1975–77). ALA. **Pubns.:** "Goals, Myths, and Realities," *Lib. Jnl.* (O. 1, 1967); "The Suppliant Maidens," *Lib. Jnl.* (D. 15, 1961). **Activities:** 9, 13; 17, 19, 46; 55, 56, 78 **Addr.:** Kansas City, Kansas Public Library, 625 Minnesota Ave., Kansas City, KS 66101.

Joyce, Donald Franklin (N. 4, 1938, Chicago, IL) Head, Ref. Srvs./Admin. Asst. to Dir. of Libs., TN State Univ., 1981–; Cur., Vivian G. Harsh Col. of Afro-Amer. Hist. and Lit., Chicago Pub. Lib., 1960–, Head, Hall Branch, 1967–73, Asst. Head Woodlawn Branch, 1963–67, Asst. Head Bks. for Blind Dept., 1960–63. **Educ.:** Fisk Univ., Nashville, 1953–57, BA (Eng.); Univ. of IL, 1958–60, MALS; Univ. of Chicago, 1973–78, PhD (LS). **Orgs.:** ALA. IL LA. Amer. Mensa. Assn. for the Study of Afro-Amer. Life and Hist. **Pubns.:** "Project OBAC: to Teach a Black Child a Story," *IL Libs.* (Ap. 1973); "Magazines of Afro-American Throught; Can They Survive?" *Amer. Libs.* (D. 1976); "Arthur Alonzo Schomburg: a Pioneering Black Bibliophile," *Jnl. of Lib. Hist.* (Ap. 1975). **Activities:** 1, 9; 37, 41, 45; 69, 85, 95-Black std. **Addr.:** Apt. 214-Creekwood, 7439 Hwy. 70 S., Nashville, TN 37221.

Joyce, William L. (Mr. 29, 1942, Rockville Centre, NY) Asst. Dir., Rare Bks. and Mss., NY Pub. Lib., 1981–; Cur. of Mss. and Educ. Ofcr., Amer. Antiq. Socty., 1972–81; Mss. Libn., William L. Clements Lib., Univ. of MI 1968–72. **Educ.:** Providence Coll., 1960–64, BA (Hist.); St. John's Univ., 1964–66, MA (Hist.); Univ. of MI, 1966–74, PhD (Hist.). **Orgs.:** New Eng. Archvsts.: Pres., VP, Exec. Bd. (1975–79). SAA: Cncl. (1981–85); Anl. Mtg. Prog. Com. (Co-Ch., 1981); Ad Hoc Com. on Inst. Stans. (Ch., 1977–81); Anl. Mtg. Prog. Com. (1977). Am. Hist. Assn.: Prof. Div. (1978–81). MA Gvr.'s Conf. on Libs. and Info. Srvs. (1978). Natl. Endow. for the Hum. Amer. Hist. Assn. (Prof. Div., 1979–81). **Pubns.:** *Editors and Ethnicity: A History of the Irish-American Press, 1848–1883* (1976); "Three Manuscripts of Increase Mather," *Procs. of the Amer. Antiq. Socty.* (1976); "The Half-Way Covenant of 1662: Some New Evidence," *Procs. of the AAS* (1977); "The Manuscript Collections of the AAS," *Procs. of the AAS* (1979); "Introduction," *Catalogue of the Manuscript Collections of the AAS* (1979). **Activities:** 25, 45, 49-Indp. resrch. lib.; 55, 62, 83 **Addr.:** New York Public Library, 5th Ave. at 42nd St., New York, NY 10018.

Judd, Eleanor Maren (O. 6, 1945, Boston, MA) Head, Acq. Dept., Baker Lib., Harvard Bus. Sch., 1978–; Acq. Libn., 1975–78, Asst. Head, Acq. Dept., 1970–75. **Educ.:** Mount Holyoke Coll., 1963–67, AB (Hist.); Simmons Coll., 1968–70, MSLS. **Orgs.:** ALA: ACRL. **Pubns.:** Contrib., *Research in Domestic and International Agribusiness Management*, vol. 1 (1980); "For the Manager's Bookshelf," *Harvard Bus. Review* (1975–). **Activities:** 1, 12; 15, 42, 44; 57, 95-Agribus. **Addr.:** Baker Library 301, Harvard Business School, Soldiers Field, Boston, MA 02163.

Judge, Joseph M. (Je. 10, 1930, Carbondale, PA) Mgr., Tech. Info., Armstrong World Indus. Inc., 1980–; Tech. Info. Sci., Armstrong Cork Co., 1967–80, Sr. Resrch. Chem., 1958–67; Resrch. Chem., E. I. du Pont, 1955–58. **Educ.:** King's Coll., 1948–52, BS (Chem.); Univ. of Notre Dame, 1952–55, PhD (Organic Chem.). **Orgs.:** ASIS. Amer. Chemical Socty: Div. of Chemical Info. AAAS. **Activities:** 12; 17; 75, 91 **Addr.:** Technical Information Services, Armstrong World Industries Inc., Lancaster, PA 17604.

Juengling, Pamela K. (Mr. 29, 1955, Grand Forks, ND) Msc. Catlgr./Asst. Prof. (LS), North. KY Univ., 1978–. **Educ.:** Mankato State Univ., 1973–77, BS (Msc., Grmn.); SUNY, Geneseo, 1977–78, MLS. **Orgs.:** Msc. LA: Basic Msc. Lib. Com. (1980–81). KY LA. KY SOLINET Users Grp.: Prog. Com. (Ch., 1981). AAUW. **Honors:** Phi Kappa Phi. **Pubns.:** jt. cmplr., *A Basic Music Library* (1981). **Activities:** 1; 20; 55 **Addr.:** Steely Library, Northern Kentucky University, Highland Heights, KY 41076.

Juergens, Bonnie (S. 11, 1947, Denver, CO) Coord., Lib. Data Prcs., Austin Pub. Lib., 1978–; Rep., C.L. Systs., Inc., 1977–78; Lib. Liaison Ofcr., AMIGOS Bibl. Cncl., 1975–77; Asst. to Dir., Lib. Srvs., Ctrl. Admin., SUNY, 1974–75. **Educ.:** MacMurray Coll., 1965–69, BA (Russ. Area Std.); Univ. of AZ, 1970–72, MLS. **Orgs.:** ALA: LITA, Prog. Plng. Com. (Ch., 1977–79), Nom. Com., Vice-Ch., Ch.-Elect (1979–80), Ch. (1980–81) Info. Sci. and Autom. Sect. SW LA. Natl. Assn. of Women. Natl. Women's Pol. Caucus. **Pubns.:** Jt. ed., *Proceedings of the LITA Institute on Alternatives to the Card Catalog* (1979); *A Self-instructional Introduction to the OCLC Model 100 Terminal* (1976); "Circulation System Implementation: Staff Training," *Jnl. of Lib. Autom.* (S. 1979). **Addr.:** Austin Public Library, 800 Guadalupe St. Box 2287, Austin, TX 78768.

Juergensmeyer, John E. (My. 14, 1934, Stewardson, IL) Prof., Constn. Law and Pol. Sci., Judson Coll., 1963–; Sr. Partner, Juergensmeyer, Zimmerman, Smith and Leahy, Attorneys at Law, 1963–; Spec. Asst. Attorney Gen., IL, 1978–; Asst. Pub. Defender, Kane Cnty., 1964–67; Asst. State's Attorney, Kane Cnty., 1977–78; Legal Aid Ch., Elgin Bar Assn., 1964–67; Assoc. Lawyer, Kirkland, Brady, McQueen, Martin and Schnell, 1963–64; Instr., Amer. Gvt., Univ. of HI, Coll. of Gen. Std., 1959–60; Fld. Asst., Com. for Mod. Cts. in IL, 1962; Fld. Asst., People-to-People Prog., 1961–63. **Educ.:** Univ. of IL, 1955, BA; Princeton Univ., 1957, MA; 1960, PhD; Univ. of IL, 1963, JD (LLB). **Orgs.:** ALA: Endow. Fund Trustee. NCLIS (1981–82). IL LA: Attorney. Amer. Bar Assn.: Lcl. Gvt. Law Sect., Spec. Taxing Dists. Com. (1978–). Amer. Trial Lawyers' Assn. Fed. Bar Assn., Ch., Local Gvt. Law Section. IL State Bar Assn.; Ch., Municipal Law Com., Chicago Bar Assn. Various other orgs. **Pubns.:** "Special Taxing Districts: Coming or Going?" *Univ. of Richmond Law Review* (1976); "Future Development of Special Districts," *Special Districts and Other Non-Municipal Local Governments in Illinois* (1977); "The Generation Gap," *Law and Ord.* (1969); *The President, The Foundations, and the People-to-People Program* (1965); "The Campaign for the 1954 Reapportionment Amendment," *Univ. of IL Inst. of Gvt.* (1956); various articles. **Activities:** 9, 13; 77 **Addr.:** 707A Davis Rd., Suite 100, Elgin, IL 60120.

Julian, Charles A. (My. 25, 1953, Wheeling, WV) Ref. Libn., Glenville State Coll., 1980–; Catlgr., Parkersburg Cmnty. Coll., 1979–80; Libn., Moundsville Jr. HS, 1976–77; Libn., Adena HS, 1975–76. **Educ.:** Glenville State Coll., 1971–75, AB (Educ.); Univ. of Sheffield (Eng.), 1977–78, MA (Info. Std.); George Peabody Coll., 1978–79, MLS. **Orgs.:** WV LA: Coll. and Univ. Sect. (Secy., 1982); Indexing Com. (Ch., 1979–80); JMRT, Secy. (1980–), Ch. (1981). ALA. SELA. Gilmer Pub. Lib. Bd. of Trustees. Rotary. **Pubns.:** "Library Education: Anglo vs. American," *WV Libs.* (Spr. 1980); jt. ed., *WV LA Tabloid* (1980); "A Comparative Study of Subject Approaches in *C.I.J.E.* and *Education Index* with Reference to 3 Areas in Education," ERIC (1980); "An Analysis of Factors Influencing the Career Choice of Librarianship," ERIC (1981). **Activities:** 1; 22, 26, 39; 61, 63 **Addr.:** Robert F. Kidd Library, Glenville, WV 26351.

Juneau, Jocelyne Blain (Ap. 22, 1923, Montréal, PQ) Chief Libn., Ctr. de Documtn., Ctr. Hosp. Cotes-des-Neges, 1981–; Chief Libn., Ctr. Hosp. Jacques-Viger, 1975–81; Chief Libn., Hosp. de la Miséricorde, 1971–75; Dir. and Tchr., Lib. Tech. Sch., Coll. de Maisonneuve, 1969–71, Catlgr., 1966–68; Catlgr., Univ. du PQ, Montréal, 1968–69; Head, Tech. Srvs., Coll. St-Ignace Lib., 1964–66. **Educ.:** Coll. Marie-Anne, 1941–45, BA; Univ. de Montréal, 1963–64, BLS, 1970–77, MLS. **Orgs.:** ASTED. Can. LA. ALA. Med LA. Various other orgs. Good Sam Club: Prov. Dir. for Prov. PQ (1979–83). Le Cordial, Chap. of Caravaners: Pres. (1975–79). Féd. PQ de Camping et de Caravaning: Reg. dir. (1973–78). Camping Club du Can.: VP (1974–77). **Activities:** 12; 17, 20, 39; 58, 80 **Addr.:** 1668 Ave. Letourneux, PO Box 477, Montreal, PQ H1V 3M5 Canada.

Juneja, Derry C. (S. 16, 1939, Wanganui, New Zealand) Head, Cat. Dept., Cleveland Pub. Lib., 1979–, OCLC Supvsr., 1977–79, Catlgr., 1967–77; Ref. Libn., Univ. of West. ON, 1966–67; Ref. Libn., London (Eng.) Cnty. Cncl., 1962–66. **Educ.:** LA UK, 1961, Assoc. **Orgs.:** ALA. OH LA. North. OH Tech. Srvs. Libns.: Secy. (1979–81). OHIONET: Cat. Cncl. (1979–80). **Activities:** 9; 20, 46 **Addr.:** 11332 Prospect Rd., Strongsville, OH 44136.

Jung, Norman O. (My. 27, 1934, Harvey, IL) Dir. of Lib., SUNY, Old Westbury, 1976–; Head Ref. Libn., SUNY, Stony Brook, 1968–76, Circ. Libn., 1966–68; Asst. Ref. Libn., Cornell Univ., 1963–66. **Educ.:** Oberlin Coll., 1952–56, AB (Gvt.); Univ. of Chicago, 1956–59, MA (Hist.); IN Univ., 1962–63, MALS. **Orgs.:** ALA: RASD/Hist. Sect., Exec. Bd. (1973–76), Local Hist. Com. (1978–80), Nom. Com. (Ch., 1977–78). SUNY Libns. Assn. Org. of Amer. Histns. Long Island Bk. Collectors. **Activities:** 1; 17, 39, 45; 55, 57, 66 **Addr.:** 1 Cedar Hill Rd., Stony Brook, NY 11790.

Junier, Artemisia Jones (O. 21, 1921, Lexington, KY) Chief, Lib. Srv., Vets. Admin. Med. Ctr., 1974–, Patient Libn., 1949–74; Libn., Dunbar HS, 1948–49; Libn., Camp Campbell (KY), 1946–47. **Educ.:** TN State Coll., 1943, BS (Home Econ.); Atlanta Univ., 1947, BS (LS), 1959, MS (LS). **Orgs.:** ALA: ASCLA, Biblther. Com. (1963–64); Mem. Com. (1959–60). SELA. AL LA. Med. LA. Various other orgs. Imperial Ct. Daughters of ISIS. Tuskegee Civic Assn. NAACP. Bowen Untd. Meth. Church. **Pubns.:** "Bibliotherapy: Projects and Studies with the Mentally Ill Patient," *Lib. Trends* (O. 1962). **Activities:** 12; 17, 34; 80 **Addr.:** 2111 Ethel Dr., Tuskegee Institute, AL 36088.

Junion (Grisé), Gail J. (F. 21, 1947, Racine, WI) Head, Orig. Cat. Unit, Bowling Green State Univ., 1980–, Catlgr., IN Univ., 1975–80, Slide Libn., 1971–75; Slide Libn., Univ. of WI, Madison, 1970–71. **Educ.:** University of WI, Madison, 1965–69, BA (Art Hist.), 1969–70, MALS; IN Univ., 1977–, Grad. Std. (Hist.). **Orgs.:** ALA: RTSD, Com. on Cat.: Descr. and Access (1979–82); ACRL/Asian and African Sect. Exec. Com. (1979–81). ARLIS/NA: IN-IL Chap. (Secy.-Treas., 1974–76). IN Univ. Libns. Assn. African Std. Assn.: Cat. Subcom. (Ch., 1978–81). Coll. Art Assn. of Amer.: Visual Resrcs. Com. (Ch., 1974–76). **Pubns.:** "Cataloging Africana: The Problems and Guide to Solutions" (forthcoming); *Copy Photography, a resource kit* (1974). **Activities:** 1; 20, 46; 55, 66, 95-African std. **Addr.:** Original Cataloging Unit, Bowling Green State University, Bowling Green, OH 43403.

Junkins, Bobby M. (N. 1, 1946, Gadsden, AL) Lib. Dir., Gadsden Pub. Lib., 1976–, Asst. Dir., 1973–76; Tchr., Cherokee Cnty., 1969–72. **Educ.:** Jacksonville State Univ., 1965–69, BS (Educ.), 1972–73, MS (Educ.). **Orgs.:** AL LA: Pub. Lib. Div., Fed. Rel. (1980–82), Lib. Legis. Dev. (1980–82). SELA. ALA. Kiwanis. State Dem. Exec. Com. **Honors:** Gadsden Jaycees, Disting. Srv. Awd., 1979. **Activities:** 9; 17, 36; 78 **Addr.:** 254 College St., Gadsden, AL 35901.

Jurich, Mary Piliponis (Je. 24, 1927, Kewanee, IL) Semi-Retired 1977–; Chief, Inst. Srvs., Buroak Lib. Syst., 1972–77; Libn., TB Srv., Vets. Admin. Hosp., Hines, IL, 1949–72. **Educ.:** Rosary Coll., 1945–49, BALS. **Orgs.:** ALA. IL LA. DuPage LA. **Activities:** 4, 5; 15, 16, 17; 72, 77, 80 **Addr.:** 7461 Blackburn Ave., Downers Grove, IL 60515.

Juricic, Jeanne Kathen (Je. 5, 1932, Joliet, IL) Lib. Media Spec., Elwood Cmnty. Consolidated Sch., 1969–. **Educ.:** Coll. of St. Francis, 1975, BA (Elem. Educ.); 1976, Media Spec. Cert. (LS). **Orgs.:** ALA. IL LA. Lib. and Media Assn. of Grt. Will Cnty. Lkpt. Twp. Lib. Bd. Bur Oak Lib. Syst. Bd. **Activities:** 9, 10; 21, 32, 47 **Addr.:** 1832 Lincoln Ave., Crest Hill, IL 60435.

Jussim, Estelle (Mr. 18, 1927, New York, NY) Prof. for Film and Visual Comm. Simmons Coll., 1972–; Asst. Prof. for Comm. Media, Assoc. Dir. for Media Resrcs., Hampshire Coll., Amherst, 1969–72; Exec. Asst. to Dir. of Educ. Resrcs., Borough of Manhattan Cmnty. Coll., 1965–66; Subj. Catlgr., Soc. Sci., Columbia Univ., 1963–65; various positions in comm. indus., 1948–60. **Educ.:** Queens Coll., CUNY, 1943–47, BA (Art Hist.); Columbia Univ., 1960–63, MLS, 1966–69, DLS. **Orgs.:** AALS. Socty. for the Anthro. of Visual Comm. Socty. for Photographic Educ. Coll. Art Assn. **Honors** Elected to Deutsche Gesellschaft für Photographie, 1976; NY Photographical Hist. Socty., Disting. Contrib. to Hist. of Photography, 1974. **Pubns.:** *Visual Communication & the Graphic Arts* (1974); *Slave to Beauty* (1981); "The Research Uses of Visual Information," *Lib. Trends* (Ap. 1977); "The Media Age: Some Brutal Truths," *Best of Lib. Lit. for 1978–79;* various other bks., articles, and reviews on lib. film and photography topics. **Activities:** 2, 11; 26, 37, 41; 55, 67, 93 **Addr.:** P.O. Box 132, Granby, MA 01033.

Jwaideh, Zuhair E. (Je. 3, 1920, Baghdad, Iraq) Chief, Near East. and African Law Div., Law Lib., Lib. of Congs., 1959–; Ref. Libn., 1956–59; Arabic Instr., Sch. of Advnc. Intl. Std., Johns Hopkins Univ., 1949–59; Lawyer, Baghdad, Iraq, 1944–48. **Educ.:** Iraq Coll. of Law, 1939–44, LLB (Law); George Washington Univ., 1950–52, MCL (Compar. Law), 1952–1956, SJD (Law). **Orgs.:** AALL: Com. on Indx. to Frgn. Legal Pers. (Ch., 1976–). Law Libns. Socty. of DC. Intl. Assn. of Law Libs. Fed. Bar Assn. African Law Assn. in Amer. African Std. Assn. Mid. E. Std. Assn. Various other orgs. **Pubns.:** Various bks., articles, and speeches on law and legal topics. 1976. "The New Civil Code of Iraq," *George Washington Univ. Law Review*, (D. 1953). **Activities:** 4, 14-Law; 17, 24, 41; 77, 78, 95-Frgn. law. **Addr.:** Law Library, Library of Congress, Washington, DC 20540.

K

Kabelac, Karl Sanford (Jn. 30, 1942, Ithaca, NY) Mss. Libn., Univ. of Rochester Lib., 1968–, Asst. Cat. Libn., SUNY Coll., Brockport, 1964–66. **Educ.:** Auburn Cmnty. Coll., 1959–61, AA (Math); Syracuse Univ., 1961–63, AB (Hist.), 1963–64, MLS; Cooperstown Grad. Prog., SUNY Coll., Oneonta, 1966–67; 1969, MA (Amer. Folk Culture). **Orgs.:** ALA. Bibl. Socty. of Amer. Lake ON Arch. Conf. Amer. Assn. for State and Lcl. Hist. Org. of Amer. Histns. **Pubns.:** "Collecting Upstate New York Imprints," *The NY-PA Collector* (N 1977); "History of Local Press Brings Some Insights," *The Citizen* (Auburn NY) (Jy. 4, 1976); "Valentine Gill's 1832 Map of Rochester," *Univ. of Rochester Lib. Bltn.* (Sum. 1974); "First County Paper Published 175 Years Ago," *The Citizen Adv.* (Auburn NY) (Jn. 20, 1973). **Activities:** 1; 15, 39, 45; 73 **Addr.:** The University of Rochester Library, Rochester, NY 14627.

Kabler, Anne W. (Ja. 10, 1944, Lynchburg, VA) Assoc. Dir., Libs. and Lrng. Resrc. Ctrs., Med. Univ. of SC, 1975–, Assoc. Dir. of Libs., Tech. Srvs., 1973–75, Chief, Tech. Prcs., 1969–73; Pub. Welfare Worker I, Durham Cnty., 1965–67. **Educ.:** Coll. of William and Mary, 1961–65, BA (Soclgy.); Univ. of NC, 1967–69, MSLS; Med. LA, 1970, Cert., 1981, Recert. **Orgs.:** Med. LA: South. Chap., Legis. Com. (Ch., 1979–80), Nom. Com. (Ch., 1978–79), Bylaws Com. (1978–79). SC LA: Fed. Rel. Com. (1978–); Lib. Admin. Sect., Constn. and Bylaws Com. (1978), Grievance Com. (Ch., 1981–82). Med. Univ. of SC: Fac. Sen. (1977–80). **Pubns.:** "NLM's Medical Library Resource Improvement Grant for Consortia Development: A Proposed Outline to Simplify the Application Process," *Bltn. of the Med. LA* (Ja. 1980); jt. auth., "Delivery of Health-Related Information to Rural Practitioners," *Bltn. Med. LA* (O. 1981). **Activities:** 1, 12; 17, 27, 35; 80 **Addr.:** Medical University of South Carolina Library, 171 Ashley Ave., Charleston, SC 29425.

Kadanoff, Diane Gordon (Jl. 5, 1937, Everett, MA) Dir., Norwell Pub. Lib. (Norwell, MA), 1980–; Dir., Dalton Free Pub. Lib., 1979–80; Asst. Dir., Cumberland Pub. Lib., 1972–78; Sch. libn. (volun.), John Howland Sch., 1970–72; Asst. Libn., Jnlsm. Lib., Univ. of IL, 1968–69. **Educ.:** Simmons Coll., 1955–59, BS (LS); Univ. of IL, 1966–68, MS (LS). **Orgs.:** ALA: Com. on the Status of Women (1976–77); Joseph W. Lippincott Awd. Jury (1977–78); Ralph R. Shaw Awd. Jury (1978–79); Soc. Resp. RT, Action Cncl. (1974–76); Prog. Coord. (1975); Task Force on Women (Coord., 1976–78); PLA; RASD; LAMA; Int. Frdm. RT. WHCOLIS. New Eng. LA. RI Lib. Film Coop.: Exec. Bd. (1976–78). Natl. Org. of Women. **Honors:** Beta Phi Mu. **Pubns.:** "A bibliography of cartooning and related subjects" (1969); "SRRT Task Force on Women," *Sch. Lib. Jnl.* (Ja. 1977); various reviews. **Activities:** 1, 9; 15, 16, 35; 66, 74, 89 **Addr.:** 225 Flaggler Dr., Marshfield, MA 02050.

Kadec, Sarah Thomas (D. 15, 1932, Winchester, VA) Spec. Asst. to Deputy Dir., Sci. and Educ. Admin., U.S. Dept. of Agr., 1982; Deputy Dir., Ofc. of Admin., Exec. Ofc. of the Pres., 1979–81, Dir., Info. Mgt. and Srvs. Div., 1978–79; Chief, Lib. Syst. Branch, U.S. Env. Protection Agency, 1971–78; Libn., Comsn. on Gvt. Procurement, 1970–71; Consult., Israel Ctr. for Sci. and Tech. Info./Lectr., Hebrew Univ. Lib. Sch., 1969–70; Lectr./Dir., Cont. Educ. (LS), Univ. of MD, 1967–69; Head, Reader's Srvs., Appld. Phys. Lab., Johns Hopkins Univ., 1966–67; Head Libn., Booz Allen Appld. Resrch., 1963–66; Libn., 1952–63. **Educ.:** Madison Coll., 1949–52, BA (Educ., LS); Carnegie Inst. of Tech., 1960–61, MLS. **Orgs.:** Assoc. Info. Mgrs.: Exec. Adv. Com. (1977–). SLA: DC Chap. (Pres., 1976–77); Resrch. Com. (1972–74). ASIS: Pub. Affairs Subcom. (1972); Place. Com. (1972); Potomac Valley Chap. (Treas., 1971–72); various other coms. **Honors:** NC Tech. Com. Bk Awds., Excel. Awd., 1974. **Pubns.:** *Brief Guide to Sources of Consumer Information* (1973); "Some Observations on Information Management," *Online* (Ap. 1979); "Environmental Library Systems," *Spec. Libs.* (Jl. 1975). **Activities:** 4, 12; 17, 24, 26; 62, 75, 91 **Addr.:** 6 DeFoe Ct., Rockville, MD 20850.

Kadis, Averil Jordan (F. 28, 1934, Lucknow, India) Asst. Chief of PR, Enoch Pratt Free Lib., 1968–, Asst. to Adult Srvs. Coord., 1964–68, Admin. Asst., AV Dept., 1963–64, Adult Srvs. Libn., YA Libn., Gen. Ref. Dept., 1962–63; Dir., Isabella Thoburn Coll. Lib., India, 1961–62; YA Libn., Cleveland Pub. Lib., 1958–61; Chief Libn., Embassy of India, Washington, DC, 1957–58; YA Asst., Cleveland Pub. Lib., 1957–57. **Educ.:** Isabella Thoburn Coll., Lucknow, India, 1950–53, BA (Eng. Lit.); Western Reserve Univ., 1954–55, MLS; Lucknow Univ., Lucknow, India, 1953–54, MA (Eng. Lit.); Syracuse Univ., 1955–56, MA (Eng. Lit.); Smithsonian Inst., 1980, Cert. (Graphic Design). **Orgs.:** Educ. Film LA: Juror, Amer. Film Fest. (1963–64). MD LA: Int. Frdm. Com. (1965). ALA: Subcom. ALA Notable Books Cncl. (1970, 1971, 1972). Edgar Allan Poe Socty.: Ed., (1970–). Smithsonian Inst. Assoc. Citizens Plng. and Housing Assn. Friends of the Amer. Ballet Thea. **Honors:** Lib. PR Cncl., Awd. of Excel., 1978. **Pubns.:** Ed., *Mabbott as Poe Scholar; The Early Years* (1980); Ed., *Surprises and Delights from a Century of Collecting* (1978). **Activities:** 1, 9; 16, 36, 37; 57 **Addr.:** 1734 P St., N.W., Washington, DC 20036.

Kaehr, Robert E. (Jl. 2, 1942, Bluffton, IN) Coord. of Lib. Srvs., Huntington Coll., 1976–; Libn., Window Rock HS, 1968–76; Tchr., Huntington Cnty. Sch. Coop., 1965–68; Edon Sch., 1964–65. **Educ.:** Huntington Coll., 1960–65, BA (Eng.); Northern AZ Univ., 1970–72, MA (Sec. Ed.); George Peabody Coll. 1974–76, MLS; Rockford Coll.; AZ State Univ. **Orgs.:** Christ. Libns. Flwshp. Tri-Alsa INCOLSA Board of Dir. **Honors:** Phi Beta Mu, 1976. **Pubns.:** Review. **Activities:** 1; 15, 17, 20; 56, 63 **Addr.:** Huntington College, Loew Alumni Library, 2303 College Ave., Huntington, IN 46750.

Kagan, Ilse E. (S. 23, 1927, Danzig, Free City) Info. Coord., W. J. Levy Consult. Corp., 1961–; Libn., Natl. Paint Varnish & Lacquer Assn., 1952–56. **Educ.:** Oxford Univ., BA (Hon), MA; Columbia Univ., 1960, MLS. **Orgs.:** SLA: Secy., Petr. Div. Great Neck Estates Civic Assn.: Dir. Hadassah: Pres. **Activities:** 12; 17, 39, 41; 59, 86 **Addr.:** W. J. Levy Consultants Corp., 30 Rockefeller Plz., New York, NY 10020.

Kahao, Mary Jane (Jy. 17, 1924, Shanghai, China) Head, Sch. of Lib. and Info. Sci. Lib., LA State Univ., 1973–; Ref. Libn., LA State Univ., 1964–72; Other positions as Msc. Supvsr. and Payroll Clerk, 1946, 1951–55, 1957–63. **Educ.:** Newcomb Coll., 1941–45, BA (Msc.); LA State Univ., 1964, MS (LS); Simmons Coll., 1978–80 (Chlds. Lit.). **Orgs.:** Beta Phi Mu: Exec. Cncl. (1980–83); Beta Zeta Chap. (Pres., 1979–80). ALA: Ref. and Subscrpn. Bks. Com. (1978–80). LA LA: Various coms and ofcs. Msc. LA. Family Couns. Srv. of Baton Rouge: Bd. (1977–83). Friends of LA Pub. Broadcasting: Bd. (1975–). Baton Rouge Civic Symphony: Bd. (1957–60). LA State Univ. Fac. Senate (1980–83). **Honors:** Cncl. for Advance and Support of Educ., Awd. for Lumiéres, 1977, 1978. **Pubns.:** Ed., *Lumiéres,* nsltr. of LA State Univ. Lib. (1975–79); reviews. **Activities:** 1, 11; 15, 17, 45; 75 **Addr.:** School of Library and Information Science Library, Louisiana State University, Baton Rouge, LA 70803.

Kahle, Susanne Margulis (Jy. 24, 1947, Philadelphia, PA) Dir. and Msc. Libn., "Here to Make Music" pre-school prog., Sarasota, FL 1981–; Tech. Srvs. Coord., Ref. Libn., Undergrad. Lib., SUNY Buffalo, 1974–75, Serials Libn., Sci. Lib., 1973, Catlgr., Carnegie Lib. at Pittsburgh, 1971. **Educ.:** Univ. of Pittsburgh, 1965–69, BA (Msc.), 1969–71, MLS. **Orgs.:** ALA: RTSD/ Serials Sect., Dupl. Exch. Un. Com., 1973–75. **Honors:** Beta Phi Mu. **Pubns.:** Reviews. **Activities:** 1, 9; 39, 44, 46; 55 **Addr.:** 1642 Shoreland Dr., Sarasota, FL 33579.

Kahler, Mary Ellis (Ag. 2, 1919, Santiago, Chile) Field Dir., Lib. of Congs. Office, Brazil, 1978–; Chief, Hispanic Div., Lib. of Congr., 1973–78, Asst. Chief, 1971–73, Asst. Chief, Union Cat. Div., 1966–70, Chief, Ser. Record Div., 1957–66, various positions, 1950–65, Spec. Rcrt., 1949. **Educ.:** Swarthmore Coll., 1936–40, AB (Hist.); Drexel Univ., 1948–49, BLS; George Washington Univ., 1951–53, MA (Hist.); American Univ., 1958–68, PhD (Hist.). **Orgs.:** ALA: V-Ch. Ch. Ser. Seat, RTSD (1959–60); Dir. RTSD (1966–69); ALA Cnclr., 1968–72). SLA: Chap. Secy., 1964 SALALM: Ch. Com. on Policy, Resrch. and Investigation, (1975–78); Bd., (1975–77). SAA.: Awards Subcom. (1976–77). Amer. Hist. Assn. Socty. for Sp. & Portuguese Hist. Std. Latin Amer. Std. Assn.: Ch., Scholarly Resrcs. Com. (1971–74). **Honors:** Phi Beta Kappa, 1940. **Pubns.:** Ed., "Harkness Collection in the Library of Congress, Manuscripts Concerning Mexico" (1974); "Guide to the Portuguese Manuscripts of the Library of Congress" (1980); "Users of Systems" *RI*; "NST and the Union List of Serials," *LRTS*. **Activities:** 4; 15, 39, 45; 57 **Addr.:** 6395 Lakeview Dr., Falls Church, VA 22041.

Kahn, Marian (Montreal, PQ) Msc. Libn., Univ. of Ottawa, 1975–; Ref. Libn., Atmospheric Env. Srv., Env. Can., 1974–75; Ref. Asst., Med. Lib., McGill Univ., 1969–73. **Educ.:** McGill Univ., 1960–65, BMsc.; Simmons Coll., 1973–74, MLS. **Orgs.:** CAML. Msc. LA. **Pubns.:** Ed., Msc. Sect., *Touring Directory 1978–79* forthcoming; *Directory of Music Research Libraries Vol. 1; Canada and the United States* forthcoming. **Activities:** 1; 15, 17; 55 **Addr.:** Music Library, Department of Music, University of Ottawa, ON K1N 6N5 Canada.

Kaihara, Yasuto (Mr. 29, 1932, Kealia, Kauai, HI) Resrch. Libn., Univ. of HI Lib., 1966–, Hawaiian and Pac. Libn., 1963–66, Catlgr., 1959–63; Catlgr., Univ. of IL Lib., 1957–59. **Educ.:** Univ. of HI, 1950–54, BA (Psych.); Univ. of IL, 1956–58, MSLS; Univ. of HI, 1960–75, MA (Pac. Islands Std.). **Orgs.:** HI LA: Dir. (1979–81). ALA. SLA. Hawaiian Hist. Socty.: Lib. Com. (1978–). Bishop Musm. Assn. Hist. HI Fndn. **Honors:** Beta Phi Mu. **Pubns.:** Ed., *Current Hawaiiana, a quarterly bibliography,* (1970–); Complr., *Dissertations and theses, University of Hawaii at Manoa,* (1974–); reviews. **Activities:** 1; 39, 45; 54, 57 **Addr.:** Special Collections, University of Hawaii Library, 2550 The Mall, Honolulu, HI 96822.

Kaikow, Rita Ellen (Mr. 18, 1947, Brooklyn, NY) Libn., Oceanside Sr. HS, 1971–, Tchr., P.S. 214K, 1968–70. **Educ.:** Queens Coll., CUNY, 1964–68, BA (Educ.), 1968–71, MLS. **Orgs.:** ALA. NY LA. Long Island Sch. Media Assn. Frdm. to Read Fndn. NY State Untd. Tchrs. Amer. Fed. of Tchrs. **Honors:** Beta Phi Mu. **Activities:** 10; 15, 20, 46 **Addr.:** 748 Morton Ave., Franklin Square, NY 11010.

Kain, Joan P. (Middletown, NY) Asst. Libn., Kaye, Scholer, 1981–; Sr. Law Libn., NY State Dept. of Law, 1971–81. **Educ.:** Columbia Univ., BS (Govt.); Pratt Inst., 1966–69, MLS; New Sch. for Soc. Resrch., 1970–73, MA (Soc. Sci.). **Orgs.:** NY Lib. Club. Law Lib. Assn. of Grtr. NY. SLA: NY Chap., Legis. Com. (1977–78). New Sch. Alum. Assn.: Secy. (1975–77). **Activities:** 13; 17, 22; 77, 78 **Addr.:** Kaye, Scholer, Fierman, Hayes and Handler, 425 Park Ave., New York, NY 10022.

Kairoff, Arlene G. (S. 8, 1942, Los Angeles, CA) Comp. Applications Tech., Boeing Comp. Srvs., 1978–; Instr., Highline Cmnty. Coll., 1978–79; Biblgrphr., Pac. NW Bibl. Ctr., 1973–78. **Educ.:** CA State Univ., Los Angeles, 1960–64, BA (Soclgy.); Univ. of WA, 1970–72, MLS. **Orgs.:** WA Pre-WHCOLIS: Prog. Plng. Com. (1978). ASIS: WA Chap. (Prog. Ch., 1981). Pac. NW LA. WA LA: Acad. and Resrch. Libns. Interest Grp. (Ch., 1976–77). Pac. Socty. for Tech. Comms. Assn. for Women in Comp. **Activities:** 12; 24, 26, 38; 56, 62, 75 **Addr.:** Boeing Computer Services, P.O. Box 24346, Seattle, WA 98124.

Kaiser, John Robert (F. 29, 1932, Everett, PA) Coord., Col. Dev., PA State Univ., 1977–; Chief Acq. Libn., 1976–77. **Educ.:** PA State Univ., 1952–54, 1958–60, BS (Educ.), 1960–62, MA (Fr.); Columbia Univ., 1963–64, MLS. **Orgs.:** ALA: RTSD/ Resrcs. Sect., Coll. Dev. Ofcrs. of Lg. Resrch. Libs. DG (Ch., 1977–); Nom. Com. (Ch., 1979–80); Various other ofcs. PA LA: Com. on Resrch. Mtrls. (1976–78). Fr. Inst. and Alliance Fr. (NY): Adv. Com. on Fr. XX Bibl. (1964–). **Pubns.:** Chap., *Col. Dev. in Libs.* (1980); Chap., *Conference on Approval Plans* (1980); "Select Bibliography," *The Bronzes of Rembrandt Bugatti* (1979); "Baudelaire, Manet, Rossetti et Mallarme," *Bltn. Baudelairien* (Win. 1979); Other articles. **Addr.:** 1136 S. Atherton St., State College, PA 16801.

Kaiser, Ward L. (Jy. 1, 1923, Kitchener, ON) Exec. Dir., Sr. Ed., Friendship Press, Natl. Cncl. of Churches, 1977–. **Educ.:** Univ. West. ON., 1942–45, BA (Hist.); Un. Theo. Semy. 1945–49, M.Div. (Hist., Theo.). **Honors:** Wilfred Laurier Univ., Citn. of the Yr., 1968. **Pubns.:** *An Inquiry Into Racism, Ethnocentrism & Sexism in Education...* (1974); various other articles and eds. **Activities:** 6; 37; 54, 70, 90 **Addr.:** Room 772, 475 Riverside Dr., New York, NY 10027.

Káldor, Iván L. (D. 31, 1920, Beregszász, Bereg, Hungary) Prof., Sch. of Lib. and Info. Sci. SUNY, Geneseo, 1970–, Dean, 1970–80, Assoc. Prof., Interim Dean, 1967–70; Assoc. Prof. of LS, Kent State Univ., 1965–68; Aeronautics, Astronautics, and Engin. Sci. Libn., Purdue Univ. Libs., 1962–65, Asst. Serials Libn., 1960–62; Libn. and Resrch. Asst., Manchester Guardian Resrch. Lib., London, England, 1959; Asst. Libn., Readers' Srvs., Univ. of London Ctrl. Lib., England, 1957–59; Dir. of the Lib. and Tech. Info. Ofcr., Ikarusz Works Spec. Lib. and Info. Ctr., Budapest, Hungary, 1953–56. **Educ.:** Univ. of London, 1957–58, BA (Hungarian Lang. and Lit.), 1957–58, BA Honors (Russ. Lang. and Lit.), 1959–60, MA (Arch., LS); Purdue Univ., 1961–62 (Econ.); Univ. of Chicago, 1963–67, PhD (LS); LA of Great Britain, 1962, Charter (LS). **Orgs.:** AALS: Com. on ByLaws (1977–78). ALA: ACRL/Slavic and East European Subsect. (Ch., 1972); Com. on the Problems of Access and Cntrl. of Slavic and E. European Mtrls. (1972–; Ch., 1973–76, 1981–); Exec. Bd. (1972–). LA (UK). NY LA. **Pubns.:** "Recent Developments in Soviet Librarianship–the 1960s and 1970s" in *Intl. Handbook of Contemporary Devs. in Libnshp.* (1980); "Librarianship and Information Science in the People's Republic of Hungary" in *ALA World Encyc. of Lib. and Info. Srvs.* (1981); "Slavic Paleography" in *Encyc. of Lib. and Info. Sci.* (1979); Jt. auth., "Education for Academic Librarianship" in *New Dimensions for Acad. Lib. Srv.* (1975); "Faculty Governance" in *The Admin. Aspects of Educ. for Libnshp.* (1974); other books and articles. **Activities:** 1, 12; 26, 39, 41; 52, 54, 91 **Addr.:** 14 Melody Ln., Geneseo, NY 14454.

Kale, Shirley Wilmer (S. 24, 1924, Brooklyn, NY) Coord., Tech. Srvs., Asst. Prof., Bergen Cmnty. Coll., 1977–, Media Catlgr., 1970–77; Freelnc. Indxr., 1969–70; Catlgr., Musm. of Mod. Art, 1968–69. **Educ.:** Brooklyn Coll., 1941–45, BA (Fine Arts); Queens Coll., 1964–68, MLS. **Orgs.:** ARLIS/NA. NJ LA. Natl. Educ. Assn. Untd. Nations Assn. **Activities:** 1, 10; 20, 24, 46; 55, 57, 75 **Addr.:** 550 Van Buren St., Ridgewood, NJ 07450.

Kalikow, Nancy Wise (N. 2, 1952, Kansas City, MO) Lib. Info. Spec., MA Bd. of Lib. Comsn., 1980–; Asst. Dir., Robbins Pub. Lib., 1979–80; Branch Libn., Mid-Continent Pub. Lib., 1976–79; Ref., ILL Libn., Kansas City, Kansas, Pub. Lib. 1975–76. **Educ.:** Univ. of MO, 1970–73, BA (Phil.), 1973–75, MA (LS). **Orgs.:** ALA: ASCLA (1980–); LAMA Mid. Mgt. Discuss. Grp. Fndr., Ch., (1977–79); MO Rep. (1977–78); PLA/ Mem. Com. (1979–); Jr. Mem. RT (1976–77). MA LA: Leg. Com. (1979–); Pub. Rel. Com., "Lib. of Year Awd." Coord. (1979–); Conf. Prog. Com. (1979–). Boston Bus. and Prof. Women. Arlington, MA Leag. of Women Voters. **Honors:** Beta Phi Mu, 1976. **Activities:** 9, 13; 17, 25, 34; 78 **Addr.:** MA Board of Library Commissioners, 648 Beacon St., Boston, MA 02215.

Kalinsky, Karen R. (O. 19, 1945, New York, NY) Cat. Libn., Stanford Univ., 1978–, Head Libn., Math. Scis. Lib., 1972–78. **Educ.:** SUNY, Stony Brook, 1962–66, BS (Math); PA

Special Subjects/Services: 50. Adult educ.; 51. Advert./Mktg.; 52. Aerosp.; 53. Agric.; 54. Area std.; 55. Arts/Hum.; 56. Autom.; 57. Bibl./Prtg.; 58. Bio. sci.; 59. Bus./Fin.; 60. Chem.; 61. Copyrt.; 62. Documtn.; 63. Educ.; 64. Engin.; 65. Env.; 66. Eth. grps.; 67. Film; 68. Food/Nutr.; 69. Geneal.; 70. Geo.; 71. Geol.; 72. Handcpd.; 73. Hist.; 74. Int. frdm.; 75. Info. sci.; 76. Insr.; 77. Law; 78. Legis.; 79. Math./Comp. sci.; 80. Med.; 81. Metals; 82. Nat. resrcs.; 83. Newsp.; 84. Nuc. sci.; 85. Oral hist.; 86. Petr./Energy; 87. Pharm.; 88. Phys./Astr./Math.; 89. Readg.; 90. Relig.; 91. Sci./Tech.; 92. Soc. sci.; 93. Telecom.; 94. Transp.; 95. (other).

State Univ., 1966–67, MA (Math); Univ. of CA, Los Angeles, 1971–72, MLS. **Orgs.:** ALA: RTSD. **Honors:** Beta Phi Mu. **Pubns.:** Jt. auth., "Future Catalogs and Bibliographic Links at Stanford University Libraries," *Cat. and Class. Qtly.* (Fall 1980). **Activities:** 1; 20, 29; 92 **Addr.:** Green Library, Stanford University, Stanford, CA 94305.

Kalkhoff, Ann Lynn (D. 20, 1944, Chicago Hts., IL) Asst. Branch Libn./Child. Libn., Brooklyn Pub. Lib., 1980–; and Pres. & Ed., *Children's Book Review Service Inc.,* 1971–; Chld. Libn., Brooklyn Pub. Lib., 1967–80; Instr. of Chld. Lit., St. Francis Coll., Brooklyn NY, 1974–75. **Educ.:** Univ. of IL, 1962–66, BA (Hist.), 1966–67, MS (LS). **Orgs.:** ALA/ALSC: Nom. Com. (Ch., 1981); Pubns. Com. (1980–82); Newbery-Caldecott Com. (1972–73); Charles Scribner's Awd. (Ch., 1974–76); Mildred L. Batchelder Awd. (Ch. 1979); Local Arrange. (1979–80); PLA Lib. Srv. to Chld. (1977–81). NY LA: Chld. and YA Srvs. Sect., Media & Programming Com. (1973–74). **Pubns.:** "Innocent Children or Innocent Librarians," *Sch. Lib. Jnl.* (O. 1972); article also included in *Issues in Children's Book Selection* (1973). **Activities:** 9; 21 **Addr.:** 220 Berkeley Pl. #1d, Brooklyn, NY 11217.

Kalkus, Stanley (Ap. 27, 1931, Prague, Czechoslovakia) Dir., Navy Dept. Lib., 1977–; Head, Lib. Dept., Naval Underwater Syst. Ctr., 1969–77; Bibl., Lectr., Univ. of NC, 1968–69; Base Libn., Hahn Air Frc. Base (Germ.), 1963–68. **Educ.:** Classical Gymnasium, Prague, 1950, Abitur; Univ. of Chicago, 1955–59, MA (LS). Charles Univ. (Prague), 1968, Cert. **Orgs.:** ALA: PLA/Armed Frcs. Libns. Sect. (Pres., 1974). SLA: Milit. Libs. Div. (Ch., 1978). DC LA. Amer. Transl. Assn. **Pubns.:** Ed., *Navy Libraries in 1980's* (1976). **Activities:** 4; 17, 24; 74 **Addr.:** Navy Department Library, Bldg. 220, Room 220, Washington Navy Yard, Washington, DC 20374.

Kallmann, Helmut (Ag. 7, 1922, Berlin, Germany) Chief, Msc. Div., Natl. Lib. of Can., 1970–; Supvsr. of Msc. Lib., Can. Broadcasting Corp., 1962–70, Sr. Msc. Libn., Msc. Libn., 1950–62. **Educ.:** Univ. of Toronto, 1946–49, BMus (Msc.); Cert., Royal Cnsvty. of Msc., Toronto, 1948. **Orgs.:** Can. Msc. LA: Ch. (1957–58, 1967–68). Can. Assn. of Msc. Libs. Intl. Assn. of Msc. Libs.: Can. Del. (1959–71). Can. Msc. Cncl.: VP (1971–76). Bibl. Socty. of Can. Can. Folk Msc. Socty. **Honors:** Univ. of Toronto, LLD, 1971; Can. Msc. Cncl., Medal for Outstan. Srv. to Msc. in Canada, 1977. **Pubns.:** *A History of Music in Canada 1534–1914* (1960); Ed., *Catalogue of Canadian Composers* (1952); Co-ed., *Encyclopedia of Music in Canada* (1981); various articles. **Activities:** 95-Music. **Addr.:** c/o Music Division, National Library of Canada, 395 Wellington St., Ottawa, ON K1A 0N4 Canada.

Kalra, Bhupinder S. (Je. 15, 1936, Gujranwala, Panjab, India) Head Branch Libn., Niles Lib. Dist., 1973–; Adult Srvs., Niles Pub. Lib., 1970–73; Prin., Elem. Schs., Dept. of Educ., ON, 1967–69; Head, Hist. Dept., Ctrl. Sch., Jullundur Cantt, India, 1963–67. **Educ.:** Panjab Univ., India, 1954–58, BA, BT, 1963–65, MA (Hist.); Univ. of West. ON, 1969–70, MLS; Dips. in Acct., Comp. Sci. **Orgs.:** ALA: LAMA; RASD. Sikh Relig. Socty. **Activities:** 9; 15, 16, 17; 55, 63, 92 **Addr.:** 1156 S. Glenn Trail, Elk Grove Village, IL 60007.

Kalyn, Walter (Mr. 8, 1940, Hafford, SK) Libn., Thom Collegiate, 1968–; Tchr., Wilkie Sch. Unit, 1967–68; Tchr., Medstead Sch. Unit, 1962–67. **Educ.:** Univ. of SK, 1958–64, BEd; Univ. of WA, 1969–74, MLS. **Orgs.:** Can. Sch. LA: Secy. Treas. (1978–79). SK Assn. of Educ. Media Spec.: Secy. Treas. (1979–80); Ed. Com. (1975–79). SK Tchrs. Fed.: Cnclr. (1965–67). **Activities:** 10; 15, 17, 31 **Addr.:** 31 McGillivray Crescent, Regina, SK S4R 4V8 Canada.

Kamens, Harry H. (Mr. 15, 1945, Cambridge, MD) Acq. Libn., Kent State Univ. Lib., 1973–; Acq. Libn., Univ. of DE Lib., 1968–73. **Educ.:** Univ. of DE, 1963–67, BS (Acct.); Univ. of Pittsburgh, 1967–68, MLS. **Orgs.:** ALA. Acad. Libns. Assn. of OH. AAUP. **Pubns.:** "OCLC's Serials Control Subsystem," *Serials Libn.* (Fall 1978). "Serials Control and OCLC" *OCLC, a National Library Network* (1979). **Activities:** 1; 15, 44 **Addr.:** Kent State University Library, Kent, OH 44242.

Kamichaitis, Penelope Helen (S. 15, 1937, Pretoria, S. Africa) Libn., Montreal Engin. Co. Ltd., 1976–; Cat. Ref. Libn., Air Can., 1968–76; Libn., Can. Hosp. Assn., 1966–68. **Educ.:** Univ. of Natal, 1954–58, BA (Hist.); Univ. of Ottawa, 1965–66, BLS. **Orgs.:** SLA: E. Can. Chap., Prog. Com. (1970–71), Secy. (1972), Nom. Com. (1978–79). **Activities:** 12; 15, 17, 41; 64, 65, 86 **Addr.:** Montreal Engineering Co. Ltd., P.O. Box 6088, Station A, Montreal, PQ H3C 3Z8 Canada.

Kaminecki, Sharon Pyrce (Mr. 26, 1952, Chicago, IL) Mgr., Env. Info. and Recs., Stan. Oil Co. (IN), 1978–; Info. Sci., IL Inst. of Tech. Resrch. Inst., 1973–78. **Educ.:** IL Inst. of Tech., 1970–73, BS (Math.). **Orgs.:** ASIS: Mem. Com. (Ch., 1979–80); ASIS-77 Pubcty. Com. (Ch., 1977); Chicago Chap. Nsltr. Ed. (1976–78) SIG/BC Nsltr. Ed. (1981). Assn. for Comp. Mach.: Vice-Ch. (1981); Chicago Chap. (Secy., 1979); Nom. Com. (Ch., 1979). **Pubns.:** Jt. auth., "Enhancing the Retrieval Effectiveness of Large Information Systems," *NTIS* (1977); jt. auth., *Chicago Online Users Introductory Guide* (1978). **Activities:** 12; 17; 56, 65 **Addr.:** 200 E. Randoph Dr., Mail Code 3802, Chicago, IL 60601.

Kammerer, Kathryn L. (S. 23, 1927, Le Cómpte, LA) Hlth. Sci. Libn., Alta Bates Hosp., 1975–; Med. Libn., Mt. Zion Hosp., 1970–75. **Educ.:** LA State Univ., 1947–48, BA (Soclgy.), 1948–49, Cert. (Soc. Work); Univ. of CA, 1969–70, MLS. **Orgs.:** Med. LA. **Pubns.:** *Writer's Guide to Medical Journals* (1975). **Activities:** 12; 80 **Addr.:** Alta Bates Hospital, 3001 Colby Plz., Berkeley, CA 94705.

Kamper, Albert F. (F. 23, 1942, Pittsburgh, PA) Coord., Tech. Srvs., Carnegie Lib. of Pittsburgh, 1972–, Head, Bk. Ord. Ofc., 1967–72, Libn., Sci. and Tech. Dept., 1965–67. **Educ.:** Duquesne Univ., 1960–64, BA (Math., Phys.); Univ. of Pittsburgh, 1964–65, MLS. **Orgs.:** SLA. ALA. PA LA: Southwest Chap. (Ch., 1975–76); Tech. Srvs. RT (Ch., 1967–68, 1980–81). **Pubns.:** Ed., *Technical Book Review Index* (1969–); Contrib. Ed., *Serials Review* (1972–). **Activities:** 9; 34, 46; 75 **Addr.:** 427 Wimer Dr., Pittsburgh, PA 15237.

Kamra, Ramma (Ja. 22, 1935, D. G. Khan, Panjab, India) Head, Lib. Srvs., Dept. of Indian Affairs and North. Dev., 1980–, Head, Location Sect., Natl. Lib. of Can., 1975–80; Head, Bibl. Srch., Univ. of Waterloo, 1969–74; Lectr. (LS), Univ. of West. ON, 1974. **Educ.:** Panjab Univ., 1950–53, BA, hons. (Eng.); Women's Polytech., New Delhi, 1962–64, Dip. (LS); Univ. of West. ON, 1968–69, MLS. **Orgs.:** Can. LA. ALA. Can. Assn. Info. Sci. Indexing and Abs. Socty. **Activities:** 4; 17, 34, 46; 56, 66, 92 **Addr.:** Library Services, Dept. of Indian Affairs and Northern Development, Hull, PQ K1A 0H4 Canada.

Kanasy, James Emery (Mr. 13, 1927, Hungary) Chief, Tech. Info. Div. Canada Dept. of Energy, Mines and Resrcs., 1976–; Dir. of Libs. Concordia Univ., 1973–76; Assoc. Chief Libn., Univ. of Windsor, 1958–73. **Educ.:** Univ. of Windsor, 1952–56, BSc (Chem., Bio.); Univ. of MI, 1956–58, AM (LS); Univ. of Pittsburgh, 1968–71, PhD (Info. Sci.); Carleton Univ., 1978–79, Cert. (Mgmt.). **Orgs.:** ASIS. Can. Assn. Info. Sci.: Ottawa Chap. (Pres., 1979–80). ALA. Can. LA: Int. Frdm. Com. (1975–78). **Activities:** 1, 4; 17, 37; 64, 82 **Addr.:** Energy, Mines and Resources Canada, 555 Booth St., Ottawa, ON K2J 1A3 Canada.

Kane, John F. (S. 26, 1939, New Kensington, PA) Coord., Info. Srvs., Aluminum Co. of Amer., 1979–, Spec. Libn., 1969–79. **Educ.:** Univ. of Pittsburgh, 62–69, AB (Hum.). **Orgs.:** SLA: Pittsburgh Chap. (Pres., 1975–76); Metals/Mtrls. Div. (Ch., 1980–81); Com. Ch. and Assignments (1973–). The Aluminum Assn., Inc.: Aluminum Assn. Tech. Info. Com. (1979–). **Activities:** 12; 31, 36, 46; 64, 81, 91 **Addr.:** John F. Kane, Aluminum Company of America, Alcoa Laboratories, Alcoa Center, PA 15069.

Kane, Joseph P. (Mr. 17, 1937, Herkimer, NY) Libn., Panama Canal Coll., 1963–; Libn., Dunkirk Pub. Schs., 1960–61; Elem. Libn., Alexander/Pavilion Ctrl. Schs., 1959–60; Elem. Libn., Alexander/Attica Ctrl. Schs., 1958–59. **Educ.:** SUNY, Geneseo, 1954–58, BS (LS, Elem. Educ.); Syracuse Univ., 1962–63, MS (LS), 1969–70 (Higher Educ., Admin.). **Orgs.:** ALA. AAUP: Lcl. Chap., VP. Amer. Assn. of Higher Educ. Amer. Fed. of Tchrs. Amer. Fed. of Gvt. Empl. **Honors:** Phi Delta Kappa; Beta Phi Mu. **Activities:** 1, 4; 17, 20, 26 **Addr.:** Panama Canal College LRC, DoD Dependents Schools, Panama, APO Miami FL 34002.

Kane, Matthew J. (My. 30, 1946, Rochester, NY) Coord., of Dist. Srvs., Altoona Area Pub. Lib., 1976–, Asst. Dir., 1975–76, Head, Ref., 1973–75. **Educ.:** St. John Fisher Coll., 1964–68, BA (Phil.); SUNY, Geneseo, 1972–73, MLS. **Orgs.:** PA LA: Cnty. Pub. Div. (Vice Ch./Ch.-Elect, 1980–81); Consult. Libns. Org. of PA: Ch. (1977–78). PA LA: Juniata Conemaugh Chap. (Ch., 1975–77). Altoona Cont. Educ. Ctr.: Adv. Cncl. (Ch., 1978–79). Keystone Country Radio Info. Ctr. Bd. of Trustees: Fin. Com. (Ch., 1979–). **Activities:** 9; 17, 24, 27; 50, 72 **Addr.:** Altoona Area Public Library, 1600 Fifth Ave., Altoona, PA 16602.

Kane, Rita (Ap. 29, 1931, Erie, PA) Assoc. Univ. Libn. for Pub. Srvs., Univ. of CA, Berkeley, 1980–; Dept. Head, Life Sci. Libs., 1979–80, Head, Bio. Lib., 1974–78; Head, Sci. and Tech. Ref. Dept., Univ. of HI, Honolulu, 1969–73, Sci. Ref. Libn., 1967–68, Lectr., 1968–73; Lectr., Univ. of CA, Berkeley, 1974; Proj. Dir., 3-Year Nat. Lib. of Med. Grant, 1975–78. **Educ.:** Boston Univ., 1949–53, BS; Univ. of HI, 1966–67, MLS. **Orgs.:** Med. LA: Com. on Intl. Coop. (1974–76); 1979 Anl. Mtg. Prog. Ch. Northern CA Med. Lib. Grp.: Treas. (1976–77). SLA: Bio. Sci. Div. (Secy./Treas. 1975–77; Pres.-Elect 1979–80; Pres. 1980–81). ALA: Subcom. on Price Indexes (1977–). **Honors:** Beta Phi Mu, 1967. **Pubns.:** *The Literature of Public Health: A Graduate Student's Handbook* (1968); Jt. auth., *Collection Analysis Project, Final Report* (1978); "The Future Lies Ahead," *Lib. Jrnl.*; "A Directory of Libraries and Special Information Sources in Hawaii," *HI Lib. Jrnl.*; "Implications of Cost/Use Relationships for Serial Cancellations," *Procs.* Med. LA 75th Anl. Mtg. (1976). **Activities:** 1; 17, 31, 39; 58, 68, 80 **Addr.:** Room 245, The General Library, University of California, Berkeley, CA 94720.

Kaneko, Hideo (Ap. 13, 1934, Osaka, Japan) Cur., E. Asian Col., Yale Univ. Lib., 1969–, Assoc. Cur., 1968–69; Libn., E. Asian Col., Univ. of MD Lib., 1963–68; Catlgr., Sr. Catlgr., Yale Univ. Lib., 1961–63; Tchg. Flw. (Phil.), Univ. of MI, 1959–60. **Educ.:** George Fox Coll., 1955–57, BA (Soc. Std.); Univ. of MI, 1959–61, AMLS. **Orgs.:** ALA: Adv. Com. on Liaison with Japanese Libs. (1976–); ACRL, Exec. Com., Asian and African Sect. (1977–80); IRRT: Exec. Com., (1979–83). Assn. for Asian Std.: Ch., Com. on E. Asian Libs. (1979–82); Exec. Grp., Com. on E. Asian Libs. (1970–73; 1978–79). Amer. Cncl. of Learned Societies, ARL, Soc. Sci. Resrch. Cncl.: Jt. Adv. Com. on the E. Asian Lib. Prog. (1978–). Japan-U.S. Friendship Comsn.: Informal Com. on Lib. Policy (1977–78). **Pubns.:** "Cataloging and Classifying of the Japanese Language Library Materials," *Cataloging and Classification of Non-Western Materials: Concerns, Issues and Practices* (1980); "Collections in Support of Japanese Studies: Current Status," *Workshop for Japanese Collection Librarians in American Research Libraries* (1978); "Oriental Literature and Bibliography: Japanese Literature and Bibliography," *Encyc. of Lib. and Info. Sci.* Vol. 21 (1977); "Beikoku ni okeru Nihon Toshokan no genjo," *Biburosu* (1972); "On Building Collections for Japanese Studies," *Frgn. Acq. Nsltr.* (1975). **Activities:** 1; 15, 17, 45; 95-East Asia. **Addr.:** c/o East Asian Collection, Yale University Library, Box 1603A Yale Station, New Haven, CT 06520.

Kanell, Richard W. (D. 4, 1943, Pittsburgh, PA) Knoxville Br. Libn., Carnegie Lib. of Pittsburgh, 1975–80; Carrick Br. Libn., 1973–75, Adult Srvs. Consult., 1968–73. **Educ.:** Univ. of Pittsburgh, 1961–64, AB (Span.), 1964–65, MLS; Univ. of Guadalajara, Mexico, 1964 (Span.). **Orgs.:** ALA. PA LA: Ch., Southwest Chap. (1978–79). **Honors:** Beta Phi Mu. **Activities:** 9, 13; 16, 27, 47; 68, 75, 78 **Addr.:** 160 Cypress Club Dr., #609, Pompano Beach, FL 33060.

Kanely, Edna Agatha (S. 24, 1910, Baltimore, MD) Retired, 1973; Consult., Carrollton Press, Scotland ofc., 1973; 1974–75; Lib. Admin., US Gvt. Prtg. ofc., 1970–73, Lib. Sect., 1969–70, Chief, Customers Srv. Sect., 1965–69, Asst. Chief, 1951–65, other positions, 1941–51. **Educ.:** Univ. of Baltimore, 1942–58, BS (Bus. Mgt.); Cath. Univ., 1970–75, MS (LS). **Orgs.:** ALA: Ad Hoc Subcom. on Fed. Depository Legis. (1976–77). MD LA. DC LA. SLA. Arch. Assoc. MD Hist. Socty. MD Geneal. Socty. Smithsonian Assoc. Other orgs. **Honors:** Gvt. Prtg. Ofc., Outstan. Performance Awd., 1972. **Pubns.:** *Cumulative Index to Hickcox's Monthly Catalog of US Government Publications, 1885–94* (1980–81); *Cumulative Subject Index to the Monthly Catalog of US Government Publications, 1895–99* (1977); Cmplr., *Cumulative Subject Guide to US Government Bibliographies, 1924–73* (1976–77); Jt. complr., *Cumulative Subject Index to the Monthly Catalog of US Government Publications, 1900–71* (1975). **Activities:** 4, 9; 17, 29, 30; 57, 69, 75 **Addr.:** 3210 Chesterfield Ave., Baltimore, MD 21213.

Kanen, Ronald Arthur (Mr. 15, 1933, Brooklyn, NY) Chief, Bur. of Lib. Srvs., State Lib. of FL, 1969–; Head, Adult Srvs., Miami Pub. Lib., 1966–69, Head, Ext. Div., 1963–65, Branch Libn., 1959–62, Serials Libn., 1958–59, Catlgr., 1958. **Educ.:** NY State Coll. for Tchrs., Albany, 1950–54, AB (Span.); Emory Univ., 1956–57, ML (Libnshp.). **Orgs.:** ALA: Notable Books Cncl. (1969–71). FL LA: Bd. of Dir. (1976–78). Dade Cnty. LA: Pres. (1968–69). **Pubns.:** Ed., *FL Libs.* (1975–78). **Activities:** 9, 13; 15, 34, 39 **Addr.:** State Library of Florida, R. A. Gray Bldg., Tallahassee, FL 32301.

Kanies, Mary K. (Je. 6, 1924, Highmore, SD) Head Libn., St. Edward HS, 1975–, Asst. Libn., 1973–75. **Educ.:** Elgin Cmnty. Coll., 1968–71, AA; North. IL Univ., 1971–73, BS, magna cum laude (Educ.); Rosary Coll., 1974, MA (LS); 1976, Spec./Media K-12 Cert. **Orgs.:** IL LA. IL Assn. for Media in Educ. Cath. LA: North. IL Unit. St. Laurence Bd. of Educ. **Activities:** 10; 15, 17, 32 **Addr.:** 535 N. Clifton Ave., Elgin, IL 60120.

Kanner, Elliott E. (S. 14, 1929, New York, NY) Resrcs. Coord., N. Suburban Lib. Syst., 1971–; Asst. Dir., Great Falls Pub. Lib., 1965–67; Resrch. Consult., WA State Lib., 1963–65; Asst. Dir., N. Cent. Reg. Lib., Wenatchee, WA, 1958–63; Ref. Libn., MI State Lib., Lansing, 1956–58. **Educ.:** Columbia Univ., 1950–54, BS (Soc.), 1954–55, MSLS; Univ. of WI, Madison, 1967–72, PhD (Lib. Sci., Soc. Work), 1967–68, Spec. Cert. **Orgs.:** ALA: Ch., Hlth. and Rehab. Lib. Srvs. Sect. (1975–78); RASD (Aging Pop. Com.; Subscrpn. Books Com. (1963–64, 1971–75); ASCLA/LSIES Member-at-Large (1981–). MT LA: Pres., Pub. Lib. Div. (1966–67). Pacific Northwest LA: Ch., Adult Educ. Sect. (1963–64). MI LA: Ch., Rcrt. Com. (1957–58). Gerontological Socty. **Honors:** Beta Phi Mu, 1956. **Pubns.:** Various articles and reviews. **Activities:** 9; 16, 34 **Addr.:** North Suburban Library System, 200 West Dundee Rd., Wheeling, IL 60090.

Kansfield, Norman J. (Mr. 24, 1940, E. Chicago, IN) Libn., Asst. Prof., West. Theo. Semy., 1974–, Asst. Libn., 1970–74; Pastor, Second Reformed Church, Astoria, NY, 1965–68. **Educ.:** Hope Coll., 1958–62, AB (Rel.), West. Theo. Semy., 1962–65, BD (Old Testament); Un. Theo. Semy., 1965–67, STM Old Testament Univ. of Chicago, 1968–70, AM (LS), 1981, PhD (LS). **Orgs.:** ATLA: Bd. of Dir. (1978–81). Chicago Area Theo. Lib. Assn.: Pres. (1978–79). Kent-Ottawa

PROFESSIONAL ACTIVITIES: Institutions: 1. Acad. lib.; 2. Arch.; 3. Assn.; 4. Fed./Gvt. lib.; 5. Inst. lib.; 6. Mfr./Suppl.; 7. Milit. lib.; 8. Musm.; 9. Pub. lib.; 10. Sch. lib.; 11. Sch. of lib. sci.; 12. Spec. lib.; 13. State lib.; 14. (other). **Functions/Activities:** 15. Acq./Col. dev.; 16. Adult srvs.; 17. Admin.; 18. Apprais.; 19. Archit./Bldgs.; 20. Cat./Class.; 21. Chld. srvs.; 22. Circ.; 23. Cons./Pres.; 24. Consult.; 25. Cont. ed.; 26. Educ. lib. sci.; 27. Ext. srvs.; 28. Fund/Grants; 29. Gvt. pubs.; 30. Indx./Abs.; 31. Instr. lib. use; 32. Media srvs.; 33. Micro.; 34. Netwks./Coop.; 35. Persnl.; 36. PR; 37. Publshg.; 38. Recs. mgt.; 39. Ref. srvs.; 40. Repro.; 41. Resrch.; 42. Review.; 43. Secur.; 44. Serials; 45. Spec. col.; 46. Tech. srvs.; 47. Trustees/Bds.; 48. YA srvs.; 49. (other).

Acad. Lib. Assn.: Liaison with Fndns. Reformed Church Cmsn. on Hist.: Secy. (1975–). Dutch-American Hist. Cmsn.: Treas. (1973–). **Pubns.:** "Education," *Piety and Patriotism* (1976); "Every Scribe Trained for the Kingdom," *Reformed Rev.* (Fall, 1975). **Activities:** 12; 90 **Addr.:** Library, Western Theological Seminary, Holland, MI 49423.

Kantor, David (N. 2, 1915, Atlanta, GA) Lib. Consult., St. John's Cnty. Pub. Lib. Syst., 1981–; Dir. of Libs., Lib. Consult., Volusia Cnty. Div. of Libs., 1964–81; Director of Extension Services, Volusia County Public Libraries, 1962–64; Lib., Folsom Prison - California, 1949–62; Lib., Farragut College - Idaho, 1947–48; Lib., Washington State Reformatory, 1944–47; Lib., Ft. Monmouth Signal Corps Library, 1943–44; Librarian, Chemistry-Pharmacy Library - Univ. of Florida, 1941–43. **Educ.:** University of Florida (Gainesville), 1934–38, BS (Biol.); Université Libre de Bruxelles (Belgium), 1938–39, Licence Microbiology; Drexel University (Philadelphia), 1940–41, BSLS. **Orgs.:** FL LA: Pres. (1972); Pub. Lib. Div. (Ch., 1971). ALA: Hosp. and Insts. Com. (1953–58). Amer. Correct. Assn.: Correct. Educ. Com. (1955–62). **Pubns.:** *A Survey of Library Services in State Institutions of Florida* (1966); "Library Services in Correctional Institutions," *Amer. Corr. Assn. Jnl.* (1955); "Library Services in Correctional Institutions," *Correct. Educ. Jnl.* (1956). **Activities:** 9, 12; 17, 19, 47; 74, 78 **Addr.:** 7 Silk Oaks Dr., Ormond Beach, FL 32074.

Kantor, Judith Ann (Jl. 2, 1952, Burbank, CA) Univ. Elem. Sch. Libn., Univ. of CA, Los Angeles, 1977–; Chld. Libn., Santa Monica Pub. Lib., 1976–77. **Educ.:** Univ. of CA, Los Angeles, 1969–73, BA (Eng.), 1973–75, MLS. **Orgs.:** ALA. CA LA. Frdm. to Read Fndn. **Activities:** 1, 10; 15, 21, 46 **Addr.:** University Elementary School Library, 405 Hilgard Ave., Los Angeles, CA 90024.

Kantor, Paul B. (N. 27, 1938, Washington, DC) Spec. Lectr., Case Inst. Tech., 1981–; Pres., Tantalus, Inc., 1976–; Adjunct Prof. Lib. Sci., Kent State Univ., 1977–; Assoc. Prof., Lib. and Info. Sci., Case West. Rsv., 1974–76; various consult. **Educ.:** Columbia Univ., 1955–59, AB (Phy.); Princeton Univ., 1959–63, PhD (Phy.). **Orgs.:** ALA: LAMA; ACRL/Coll. and Resrch. Libs. Sect., Stats. Com. ASIS: Sig. Mgt. Amer. Stats. Assn. **Pubns.:** "The Library as an Information Utility in the University Context: Evolution and Measurement of Service," *Jnl. of the Amer. Socty. for Info. Sci.* (1976); jt. auth., "Causes and Dynamics of User Satisfaction at an Academic Library," *Col. and Resrch. Lib.* (1977); "Availability Analysis," *Jnl. of the Amer. Socty. for Info. Sci.* (1976); "Vitality, An Indirect Measure of Relevance," *Coll. Mgt.* (1978); "A Note on Cumulative Advantage Distributions," *JASIS* (1978); "Analyzing the Availability of Reference Services," *Lib. Effectiveness* (1980); various articles, papers and sp. **Addr.:** Tantalus Inc., 3257 Ormond Rd., Cleveland, OH 44118.

Kao, Angela Hui Hua (F. 7, 1937, Hu-pei, China) Orientalia Libn., U.S. Milit. Acad., 1976–; Asst. Libn., SUNY, New Paltz, 1975–76; Catlgr., Amer. Univ., 1966–67; Catlgr., Yale Univ., 1962–66. **Educ.:** Natl. Taiwan Univ., 1955–59, BA (Eng.); George Peabody Coll., 1961–62, MLS. **Orgs.:** Chin.-Amer. LA. Yeh Yu Chin. Opera Assn. Mid-Hudson Chin. Cmnty. Assn. **Pubns.:** *Catalog of the Orientalia Collection of the USMA Library* (1977). **Activities:** 4; 15, 20; 74 **Addr.:** Library, United State Military Academy, West Point, NY 10996.

Kao, Bernice C. (D. 19, 1934, Soochow, China) Head Libn., Dames and Moore, 1977–; Catlgr., AL A & M Univ., 1975; Catlgr., Univ. of FL, 1962–65; Catlgr., Cuyahoga Cnty. Pub. Lib., 1960–61. **Educ.:** Natl. Taiwan Univ., 1953–57, BA (Frgn. Langs.); Case West. Rsv. Univ., 1958–60, MLS. **Orgs.:** SLA. ASIS. Chicago OLUG. Chin.-Amer. LA. N. Suburban Lib. Syst. **Activities:** 5, 11; 15, 20, 24; 64, 65, 91 **Addr.:** Dames & Moore, 1550 Northwest Hwy., Park Ridge, IL 60068.

Kao, Mary Liu (S. 5, 1942, Yunnan, China) Dir. of Lib. Srvs., Mohegan Comnty. Coll., 1979–; Asst. Dir. of Lib. Srvs., 1970–79; Tech. Srvs. Libn., Sacred Heart Univ., 1968–70; Circ. Libn., Denison Univ., 1965–68. **Educ.:** Nat. Taiwan Univ., 1959–63, BLL (Law); TX Woman's Univ., 1963–65, MLS; Southern CT State Coll., 1975–79, MS (Instr. Tech.). **Orgs.:** ALA. CT LA. Chinese Amer. LA: Treas., New England Chap. (1979–). Assn. for Educ. Comm. and Tech. Southeastern CT Chinese Assn.: Treas. (1979). **Activities:** 1; 15, 17, 39 **Addr.:** 11 Maplewood Dr., East Lyme, CT 06333.

Kao, Yasuko W. (Mr. 30, 1930, Tokyo, Japan) Head, Cat. Div., Univ. of UT Marriott Lib., 1975, Instr. in Lib., 1960–67; Instr., Takinogawa Sr HS, 1950–57. **Educ.:** Waseda Univ., 1953–55, BA (Lit.); Univ. of Southern CA, 1958–60, MSLS; Tsuda Coll., 1947–50, Tching Cert. in Secondary Educ. **Orgs.:** ALA: LITA. Mountain Plain LA. UT LA: Rsrcs. and Tech. Srvcs. (1979). UT Asian LA: Lib. Cncl. (1978–). **Honors:** Beta Phi Mu, 1960; Univ. Flw., Waseda Univ., 1955–56. **Pubns.:** "Retrospective Conversion Project at the University of Utah Marriott Library Utah Library," (Spr. 1979). **Activities:** 1; 17, 20, 46 **Addr.:** Univ. of UT, Marriott Lib., Salt Lake City, UT 84112.

Kapecky, Michele Ann (Je. 2, 1944, Detroit, MI) Chief Libn., Detroit Free Press, 1976–; Automotive Ref. Libn., Campbell-Ewald Advert., 1974–76; Coord. Libn., TIP Srv., Detroit Pub. Lib., 1971–74, Book Sel. Libn., 1970–71. **Educ.:** Univ. of Detroit, 1962–66, BA (Hist.); Wayne State Univ., 1966–70, MLS. **Orgs.:** SLA: Ch. Audio/Visual Proj. Com., Newspaper Div. (1977–78); Ch. Ad Hoc Salary Survey and Qual. Com., Newspaper Div. (1979–80); MI Chap. Bltn. Ed. (1978–79). Detroit Hist. Socty. Detroit Women in Mgt. Nat. Micrographics Assn. **Honors:** Phi Alpha Theta, 1966. **Pubns.:** "Tip–One Year Later," (Fall 1974). "Barometric Pressure on Public Libraries" (Fall 1974). **Activities:** 2, 12; 17, 24, 35; 56, 83 **Addr.:** Detroit Free Press, 321 W. Lafayette, Detroit, MI 48231.

Kaplan, Diane E. (O. 13, 1947, Minneapolis, MN) Supvsr., Mss. Prcs., Yale Univ. Lib., 1980–; Prcs. Archvst., 1978–80, 1971–75; Archvst., Centenary Coll. of LA, 1975–78. **Educ.:** Univ. of WI, 1965–69, BA (Hist.); Univ. of MI, 1969–70, MA (Hist); various arch. insts., 1970, 1980. **Orgs.:** SAA. New Eng. Archvsts. Socty. SW Archvsts.: Exec. Bd. (1977–78). Leag. of Women Voters. **Pubns.:** Guide, micro. ed., *Papers of Henry Lewis Stimson in the Yale University Library* (1973). **Activities:** 1, 2; 33, 45 **Addr.:** Manuscripts and Archives, Yale University Library, New Haven, CT 06520.

Kaplan, Judith M. (O. 28, 1947, Brooklyn, NY) Head Libn., Amer. Fndn. for the Blind, 1975–, Ref. Libn., 1970–75. **Educ.:** SUNY, Buffalo, 1965–69, BA (Hum.); Drexel Univ., 1969–70, MLS. **Orgs.:** SLA. Cncl. for Excep. Chld. Natl. Ctr. for a Barrier-Free Env. **Honors:** Beta Phi Mu. **Pubns.:** "The M.C. Migel Memorial Library: Resources and Services," *DIKTA* (Sum. 1977); "Other Books," clmn. *Jnl. of Visual Impairment and Blindness* (1980). **Activities:** 12; 15, 17, 39; 72 **Addr.:** American Foundation for the Blind, 15 W. Sixteenth St., New York, NY 10011.

Kaplan, Rosalyn L. (Ag. 20, 1926, Boston, MA) Prog. Spec.–Info., Nat. Easter Seal Socty., 1975–; Ref. Libn., Scott Foresman & Co., 1972–75. **Educ.:** Univ. of NH, 1943–45; Univ. of Chicago, 1945–48, BA (Soc.); Rosary Coll., 1971–72, MALS. **Orgs.:** ALA: Com. to Draft Stan. for Nat. Lib. for Blind and Phys. Handcpd. (1978–79). Pres. Com. on Empl. of the Handcpd., Lib. Com. (1976–). **Activities:** 12; 17; 72 **Addr.:** National Easter Seal Society, 2023 W. Ogden Ave., Chicago, IL 60612.

Kaplan, Sylvia Y. (My. 23, 1921, Chicago, IL) Asst. Prof. of Lib. Sci., Eastern IL Univ., 1970–; Chief Libn., State of IL, Dept. of Mental Hlth., 1965–70; Libn., M. Reese Med. Ctr. Sch. of Nursing, 1963–65; Chief Libn., Instr. in Med. Bibl., Chicago Med. Sch., 1960–63. **Educ.:** Northwestern Univ. (IL), 1948–56, PhB (Lib. Arts); Rosary Coll., 1958–61, MALS; Univ. of IL, Urbana, 1964–69; Med. Lib. Cert. I (1969); Univ. of Pittsburgh, PhD cand., 1980–81. **Orgs.:** SLA. Med LA. Midwest Acad. Libns. Assn. IL LA. Cath. LA. Hadassah: Ch., Cult. Com. Nat. Semantist Org. IL Reading Cncl. **Honors:** Delta Kappa Gamma, 1979. **Pubns.:** *Multiethnic Literature,* an annotated bibl. (1981); *Glossary of Library Science and Media Terminology* (1971); reviews. **Activities:** 1, 12; 24, 26, 31; 80, 91, 92 **Addr.:** Dept. of Library Science, Eastern Illinois Library, Charleston, IL 61920.

Kapnick, Laura Beth (Je. 8, 1951, New York, NY) Mgr., Lib. Srvs., CBS News Ref. Lib., 1977–; Resrch. Libn., Consumers Un. of the US, Inc., 1975–77. **Educ.:** George Washington Univ., 1969–73, BA (Eng. Lit.); Queens Coll., 1973–74, MLS. **Orgs.:** SLA: PR Ch., Telecomm./Comm. Provisional Div. (1979–80); Asst. Bltn. Ed., Advert./Mktg. Div. (1979–80), Ed. (1980–81). **Activities:** 12; 22, 39, 41; 83, 93 **Addr.:** CBS News Reference Library, 524 West 57th St., New York, NY 10019.

Kapoor, Jagdish Chander (Ap. 1, 1923, Peshawar, India) Asst. Prof., Mono. Ord. Libn., Univ. of NH, 1975–, Resrch. Asst., Acq., 1971–75. **Educ.:** Punjab Univ. (Lahore, India) 1941–45, BA (Econ.); Islamia Coll., Peshawar, BT (Educ.); Punjab Univ., 1951 (Urdu), 1954, MA (Phil.); Univ. of NH, 1968–69, MA (Pol. Sci.); Simmons Coll., 1970–74 MS (LS). **Orgs.:** NH LA: Int. Frdm. Rep. to NH Lib. Cncl. (1976–78). ALA. New Eng. LA. **Pubns.:** Various articles, stories, poems. **Activities:** 1; 15, 46; 54, 56, 92 **Addr.:** 29 Oyster River Rd., Durham, NH 03824.

Kapsner, Oliver Leonard, OSB (Jl. 26, 1902, Buckman, MN) Retired, 1978–; Dir., Monastic Mss. Micro. Proj., St. John's Univ. (MN), 1964–71; Resrch. Catlgr., St. Vincent Coll. (PA), 1958–64; Resrch. Catlgr., Cath. Univ., 1951–58; Catlgr., St. John's Univ., 1946–50, Libn., 1939–43, Asst. Libn., 1934–39, 1925–30. **Educ.:** St. John's Univ., 1920; St. Vincent Semy., 1923–25, BA (Phil.), PhL; St. John's Semy., 1925–29, STB (Theo.); Coll. di S. Anselmo, Rome, 1930–32 (Phil.). **Orgs.:** ALA. Cath. LA. Amer. Benedictine Acad. **Honors:** Amer. Benedictine Acad., Fellow, 1975; St. Anselm's Coll., LLA, 1974; St. Vincent's Coll., LD; St. Bernard Coll., Hon. PhD; other hons. **Pubns.:** *Catholic Subject Headings* (1963); *Benedictine Bibliography* (1962, first supplement 1981); *Catholic Religious Orders* (1957); various articles, *New Cath. Encyc.* (1967), *Dizionario degli Istituti di Perfezione (Rome)* (1974–); other prof. pubns. **Activities:** 10; 20, 41; 57 **Addr.:** St. John's University Library, Collegeville, MN 56321.

Karch, Linda S. (Ap. 17, 1951, Niagara Falls, NY) Libn., Mercy Hosp., Buffalo, NY, 1975–; Libn., Buffalo & Erie Cnty. Pub. Lib., 1975; Spec. Proj. Catlgr., Hlth. Sci. Lib., SUNY, Buffalo, 1974–75. **Educ.:** SUNY Coll. at Cortland, 1969–72; SUNY, Buffalo, 1972–73, BA (Eng.), 1973–75, MLS; additional courses. **Orgs.:** ALA. Med. LA. West. NY Hlth. Sci. Libns.: Pres. (1977–78); Exec. Com. (1978–79). Reg. Med. Lib.: Com. on Com. (1977–80). Other orgs. Literacy Volun. of Amer. **Honors:** Beta Phi Mu, 1975. **Activities:** 5; 17, 20, 39; 80 **Addr.:** Mercy Hospital Medical Library, 565 Abbott Rd., Buffalo, NY 14220.

Kares, Artemis C. (S. 29, 1937, Wilmington, NC) Ref. Libn., E. Carolina Univ., 1972–; Ref. Libn., NC State Lib., 1967–69. **Educ.:** E. Carolina Univ., 1955–59, AB, BS, (Soc. Std.), 1961–62, MA Educ. (Hist.); Univ. of NC, 1966–67, MS (LS). **Orgs.:** NC LA: Secy. (1978–79). NC State Lib. Comsn. ALA: ACRL. NC OLUG. Beta Phi Mu: Epsilon Chap. (Pres., 1981–). Women's Pol. Caucus: NC Policy Cncl. (1979–). Amer. Fed. of Tchrs. Amer. Cvl. Liberties Un. **Pubns.:** Ed., *Raleigh News and Observer Index* (1967–73, 1974). **Activities:** 1; 30, 31, 39; 78, 92 **Addr.:** 501 E. Third St., Greenville, NC 27834.

Karges, Joann (F. 24, 1926, Wichita Falls, TX) Chief, Tech. Srvs., TX Christ. Univ., 1977–, Acq. Libn., 1957–77; Chief Libn., Amer. Lib. in Paris, 1953–57; Acq. Libn., Univ. of Redlands, 1952–53; Asst., Ord. Dept., Univ. of MI Lib., 1950–52. **Educ.:** TX Christ. Univ., 1943–46, BA (Eng.); Univ. of TX, Austin, 1947–48, MA (Eng.); Univ. of MI, 1948–50, MALS. **Orgs.:** ALA. TX LA: Acq. RT (Ch., 1980–81). **Activities:** 1; 15, 20, 46 **Addr.:** 2533 McCart, Fort Worth, TX 76110.

Karkhanis, Sharad (Mr. 8, 1935, Khopoli, Bombay, India) Prof. (LS), Kingsborough Cmnty. Coll., 1964–, Asst. Libn., Brooklyn Coll., 1963–64; Ref. Libn., East Orange Pub. Lib., 1960–63. **Educ.:** Univ. of Bombay, India, 1954–58 BA (Pol.); Rutgers Univ., 1960–62, MLS Brooklyn Coll. of the City Univ., 1964–66, MA (Pol.); NY Univ., 1974–78, Ph.D. (Pol.). Bombay LA, 1956–57, Dipl. (LS). **Orgs.:** ALA: RASD; Intl. Rel. RT. Lib. Assn. of City of NY: Pres. (1967–69). Asian/Pacific ALA (Pres., 1980–81, 1981–82). Prof. Staff Congs., City Univ.: Credit Un. **Honors:** LA of City Univ., Cert. of Apprec., 1972. New York Univ., Taraknath Das Awd., 1977. **Pubns.:** *Indian Politics and the Role of the Press* (1980); reviews. **Activities:** 1; 15, 37, 41; 57, 83, 92 **Addr.:** Library, Kingsborough Community College, Oriental Blvd., Brooklyn, NY 11235.

Karklins, Vija L. (Ap. 16, 1929, Riga, Latvia) Assoc. Dir. of Libs. for Bibl. Systs., Smithsonian Inst., 1975–, Chief of Tech. Srvcs., 1972–75, Head of Cat., 1969–72, Catlgr., 1965–69; Catlgr., Nat. Inst. of Hlth., 1963–65; Libn., Bio-Med. Lib., Univ. of MN, 1962–63; 1958–61; Libn., Publ. Rel. Dept., Socony Mobil Oil Co., 1957–59; Pre-Prof. Libn., Brooklyn Pub. Lib., 1955–57. **Educ.:** City College of NY, 1951–55, BA (Comp. Lit.); Columbia Univ., 1955–57, MSLS. **Orgs.:** ALA. SLA. Fed. Lib. Ntwrk: Exec. Adv. Cncl. (1979–). DC LA. **Activities:** 4, 12; 17, 34, 46; 56, 75, 91 **Addr.:** Smithsonian Institution Libraries, Museum of Natural History, 10th and Constitution Ave., N.W., Washington, DC 20560.

Karlin, Estelle R. (Boston, MA) Head Libn., Harvard Univ. Observatory, 1974–, Catlgr., 1972–74, Libn., Engin. Info. Ctr., 1967–72; Chem., Polaroid Corp., 1950–54. **Educ.:** Northeast. Univ., 1945–50, BS (Chem.); Simmons Coll., 1964–66 (LS). **Orgs.:** SLA. Newton Pub. Lib.: Trustee (1973–). **Activities:** 1, 9; 15, 17, 20; 88, 91 **Addr.:** Wolbach Library, Harvard College Observatory, 60 Garden St., Cambridge, MA 02138.

Karlson, Marjorie Elizabeth (Ap. 15, 1925, Taunton, MA) Head, Ref. Dept., Univ. of MA, Amherst, 1972–; Head, Ref. Dept., Univ. of KS Lib., 1970–72; Asst. Dir., Reader Srvs., WA Univ. Lib., 1969–70, Chief, Ref. Dept., 1956–68, Asst. Chief., 1955–56; Sr. Ref. Libn., LA State Univ. Lib., 1952–55; Ref. Asst., Rare Bk. Rm., Yale Univ. Lib., 1949–52; Catlgr., Agnes Scott Coll. Lib., 1947–48. **Educ.:** Agnes Scott Coll., 1946, BA (Eng.); Yale Univ., 1948–49, MA (Eng.); Emory Univ., 1946–47, BALS. **Orgs.:** ALA: Cncl. (1963–65); Subscrpn. Bks. Com. (1961–65); ACRL, Lib. Srvs. Com. (1965–67); Ref. Srvs. Div., Bd. (1963–65), ILL Com. (Ch., 1966–69); RASD, Bd. (1980–81), various other coms. **Honors:** Phi Beta Kappa. **Pubns.:** "The New Code," *RQ* (F. 1970); various articles in lib. pers., reviews. **Activities:** 1; 39 **Addr.:** University of Massachusetts Library, Amherst, MA

Karmazin, Sharon E. (Ag. 31, 1946, Brooklyn, NY) Asst. Dir., E. Brunswick Pub. Lib., 1979–, Head, AV and PR, 1974–79, Libn. 1969–74. **Educ.:** Douglass Coll., 1963–67, BA (Eng., Educ.); Rutgers Grad. Sch. of Lib. and Info. Std., 1967–69, MLS; NJ State Libn. Cert.; NJ State Tchr. Sec. Cert. **Orgs.:** ALA. NJ LA: PR Com. Middlesex Cnty. AV Aids Comsn.: Comsn. **Pubns.:** "Outreach on a Budget," *Lib. Trustee Nsltr.* (S.–O. 1979); "Book Theft Blues," *Lib. Trustee Nsltr.* (My.–Je. 1979); "Making Friends," *Lib. Trustee Nsltr.* (Mr.–Ap. 1979). **Addr.:** 18 Upper Brook Dr., N. Brunswick, NJ 08902.

Karon, Bernard L. (Ag. 19, 1942, St. Paul, MN) Chief Sci. Catlgr., Univ. of MN, 1967–; Hum. Catlgr., 1965–66. **Educ.:** Univ. of MN, 1960–64, BS (Bot.), 1965–65, MS (LS). **Orgs.:**

Special Subjects/Services: 50. Adult educ.; 51. Advert./Mktg.; 52. Aerosp.; 53. Agric.; 54. Area std.; 55. Arts/Hum.; 56. Autom.; 57. Bibl./Prtg.; 58. Bio. sci.; 59. Bus./Fin.; 60. Chem.; 61. Copyrt.; 62. Documtn.; 63. Educ.; 64. Engin.; 65. Env.; 66. Eth. grps.; 67. Film; 68. Food/Nutr.; 69. Geneal.; 70. Geo.; 71. Geol.; 72. Handcpd.; 73. Hist.; 74. Int. frdm.; 75. Info. sci.; 76. Insr.; 77. Law; 78. Legis.; 79. Math./Comp. sci.; 80. Med.; 81. Metals; 82. Nat. resrcs.; 83. Newsp.; 84. Nuc. sci.; 85. Oral hist.; 86. Petr./Energy; 87. Pharm.; 88. Phys./Astr./Math.; 89. Readg.; 90. Relig.; 91. Sci./Tech.; 92. Soc. sci.; 93. Telecom.; 94. Transp.; 95. (other).

ALA. SLA. Church and Synagogue Libs. Assn. Other orgs. Talmud Torah of St. Paul, MN: Bd. of Dir., Lib. Com. (Ch.). **Pubns.:** "Descriptive Cataloging," independent study course (1979); *A Botanist's Vademecum* (1966). **Activities:** 1; 20, 24, 26; 58, 75, 91 **Addr.:** 1781 Summit Ln., Mendota Heights, MN 55118.

Karp, Hazel B. (Ap. 18, 1929, Atlanta, GA) Elem. Media Spec.-Libn., Hebrew Acad. of Atlanta, 1972–. **Educ.:** Agnes Scott Coll., 1946–50, BA (Eng.); Emory Univ., 1970–72, MLn, 1980, Dip. Adv. Std. (LS). **Orgs.:** ALA. AJL: Chld. Bk. Awd. Com. (Ch., 1980–81); various other ofcs. **Honors:** Phi Beta Kappa; Beta Phi Mu. **Activities:** 10, 12; 21, 42; 66, 95-Holocaust bibl. **Addr.:** 880 Somerset Dr. N.W., Atlanta, GA 30327.

Karp, Nancy S. (Jl. 8, 1941, Detroit, MI) Sr. Assoc. Libn., Univ. of MI, 1968–. **Educ.:** Wayne State Univ., 1961–63, BS (Educ.); Univ. of MI, 1967–68, AMLS. **Orgs.:** SLA. MI/LA: GODORT. **Activities:** 1; 15, 29, 39; 59 **Addr.:** Business Administration Library, 230 School of Business, Ann Arbor, MI 48109.

Karpe, Margaret Augusta (Je. 28, 1928, Bakersfield, CA) Libn., Ctr. for Biblical Stds., 1973–; Subst. Libn., Modesto City Schs., 1970–73; Various positions as Libn. and Lib. Asst., 1961–70. **Educ.:** Denison Univ., 1945–47; Univ. of CA, Berkeley, 1947–49, BA (Zlgy.); San Jose State Univ., 1970–76, MA (LS); Various other courses. **Orgs.:** ALA. ATLA. CA LA: CA Acad. and Resrch. Libns. First Bapt. Church of Modesto. Woman's Christian Temperance Un.: Various Ofcs. **Activities:** 1, 12; 15, 17, 31 **Addr.:** Center for Biblical Studies, Inc., P. O. Box 3461, Modesto, CA 95353.

Karpel, Bernard (F. 10, 1911, Brooklyn, NY) Consult., Art Assoc., 1978–; Dir., Bicentennial Bibl. of Amer. Art, Arch. of Amer. Art, 1974–77; Chief Libn., Musm. of Mod. Art, 1943–73, Film Libn., 1943; Art Libn., 58th St. Branch, New York Pub. Lib., 1937–41. **Educ.:** City Coll. of New York, 1932, BA; Pratt Inst., 1937, BLS; Columbia Univ., 1940–41, (LS); Prof. Libn. Cert., Univ. of State of NY, 1953. **Orgs.:** ARLIS/NA. Archons of Colophon. Coll. Art Assn. Arch. of Amer. Art: Adv. Bd. Charles Burchfield Ctr.: Cncl. **Honors:** Philadelphia Coll. of Art, Awd. of Merit, 1969; MD Inst., Doctorete of Human Letters, 1976. **Pubns.:** Ed., *Art in America: a Bibliography* (1980); other bibls. **Addr.:** 3 Wilbur Rd., Poughkeepsie, NY 12603.

Karpinski, Leszek M. (S. 11, 1937, Lwow, Poland) Hum. Ref. Libn., Univ. of BC, 1969–; Libn., Royal Danish Lib., Copenhagen, 1966–67. **Educ.:** Universytet Jagiellonski, Krakow, Poland, 1957–62, MA (Eastern Std.); Univ. of BC, 1968–69, BLS. **Orgs.:** Orientalists Libn. Assn. Amer. Oriental Socty. **Pubns.:** *Religious Studies without Tears* (1972–75); *The Religious Life of Man* (1978); "Ancient Codices of the Near East" (1962). "Votive stelae from Carthage in Krakow" (1964). **Activities:** 1; 20, 31, 39; 54, 55, 90 **Addr.:** University of British Columbia Library, Humanities Division, 1956, Vancouver, BC Main Mall, V6T 1Y3 Canada.

Karr, Roger Neil (N. 18, 1950, Washington, DC) Head, Ref., Main Lib., U.S. Dept. of Justice, 1979–; Ref. Libn., Law Lib., U.S. Gen. Acct. Ofc., 1978–79. **Educ.:** Univ. of MD, 1968–72, BA (Hist.), 1975–76, MLS. **Orgs.:** AALL. **Activities:** 4; 39; 77, 78 **Addr.:** U.S. Dept. of Justice, Main Library, 10th & Pennsylvania Ave. N.W., Washington, DC 20530.

Karre, David J. (O. 11, 1949, Buffalo, NY) Head, Ref. Dept., Niagara Falls Pub. Lib., 1978–, Docum. Libn., 1975–78. **Educ.:** SUNY, Buffalo, 1967–72, BA (Fr.), 1974–75, MLS, 1977–81, MBA. **Orgs.:** NY LA: GODORT (Pres., 1980–81, 1981–82). Beta Phi Mu: Beta Delta Chap. (Pres., 1978–79). **Activities:** 9; 17, 29, 39; 51, 59 **Addr.:** Niagara Falls Public Library, 1425 Main St., Niagara Falls, NY 14305.

Karrow, Robert William, Jr. (Ag. 5, 1945, Milwaukee, WI) Cur. of Maps, Newberry Lib., 1975–, Actg. Cur. of Maps, 1974–75, Map Catlgr., 1971–74. **Educ.:** Univ. of WI, Milwaukee, 1963–68, BS (Eng.); Univ. of WI, Madison, 1970–71, MSLS. **Orgs.:** ALA: Map and geog. RT rep. to Com. on Cat.: Desc. and Access (1980–); MAGERT Nom. Com. (Ch., 1981). SLA: Geo. and Map Div., Nom. Com. (1976); Honors Com. (1978). Intl. Socty. for the Hist. of Cartography. Amer. Prtg. Hist. Assn. Prtg. Hist. Socty. **Honors:** Cncl. on Lib. Resrcs., Flwshp., 1977. **Pubns.:** "Cartobibliography," *AB Bookman's Yrbk.* (1976); "Raleigh Ashlin Skelton (1906–1970): A Bibliography," Appendix in *Maps: A Historical Survey of their Study and Collecting* (1972); Genl. ed., *Checklist of Printed Maps of the Middle West to 1900* (1981); Jt. auth., *ILA AACR2: Specialized Level Workshop: Cartographic Materials Workbook* (1980). **Activities:** 14-Indp. resrch. lib.; 20, 39, 45; 55, 57, 70 **Addr.:** The Newberry Library, 60 W. Walton St., Chicago, IL 60610.

Kars, Marjorie Irene (O. 28, 1947, Holland, MI) Dir., Hosp. Lib., Holland Comnty. Hosp., 1969. **Educ.:** Grand Valley State Coll., 1976–80, BA (Hist.). **Orgs.:** Med. LA: Ad Hoc Com. Hosp. Lib. Interest Group (1978–79); Ad Hoc Perf. Eval. Com. Hosp. Lib. Interest Group (1977–78). Western MI Hlth. Sci. Libns.: Ch. (1974–75; 1976–78). MI Hlth. Sci. LA: Exec. Brd. (1977–78); Com. to propose a State Hlth. Sci. LA (1976–77); Com., Statewide Union list of Serials (1979–80). Holland-Zeeland Info. Ntwk. **Honors:** Nat. Lib. of Med. Lib. Improvement Grant, 1973; Nat. Lib. of Med. Consort. Grant, 1979. **Activities:** 5, 12; 17, 24, 34; 80 **Addr.:** 223 West 29th St., Holland, MI 49423.

Karshner, Mary Molden (O. 12, 1950, Detroit, MI) Musm. Cur./Archvst., City of St. Clair Shores, 1980–; Arch. Asst., Walter Reuther Lib., 1979–80; Resrch. Assoc., Norwich Srvy., Univ. of E. Anglia, (Eng.), 1972–78. **Educ.:** MI State Univ., 1968–72, BA (Econ.); Wayne State Univ., 1978–81, MSLS; Cambridge Univ., 1976–78, Cert. (Lcl. Hist.). **Orgs.:** SAA. Midwest Arch. Conf. MI Arch. Assn. Amer. Assn. for State and Lcl. Hist. MI Musms. Assn. **Pubns.:** "The Clay Pipe Industry in Norwich," *Brit. Archlg. Rpts.* (1979); "The History of the Foreign Language Collection at Detroit Public Library," *Among Frnds.* (1979). **Activities:** 2, 8; 39, 41, 45; 69, 73, 85 **Addr.:** 10565 Talbot, Huntington Woods, MI 48070.

Kascus, Marie A. (Je. 2, 1943, Boston, MA) Head, Serials and Micro. Dept., Ctrl. CT State Coll., 1972–; Asst. Binding Libn., Univ. of IL, 1970–72. **Educ.:** Northeastern Univ., 1961–66, BA (Soclgy.); Univ. of IL, 1969–70, MS (LS); Simmons Coll. Sch. of LS, 1979, (Cont. Ed., Cert., Cons., Mgt. in Libs. and Arch. III). **Orgs.:** ALA: RTSD/Dupl. Exch. Un. Com. (1979–81); ACRL. New Eng. LA. CT LA. Amer. Socty. of Indxrs. Beta Phi Mu: Alpha Chap. (Secty., 1971). CT Capitol Reg. Lib. Cncl.: Com. on CT Un. List of Serials (1978–); Coord. for Reg. II Lib. (1979–). State of CT Purchasing Dept.: Spec. Adv. Com. on Binding (1975–). AAUP: CT State Coll. Chap., Libns. Col. Bargaining Contract Prep. Com. (1976); Lib. Liaison (1977). **Pubns.:** Co-ed., *CCSC Periodical Holdings* (1978, 1979); "Connecticut One Day Workshops On In-House Conservation Techniques," *Lib. Scene* (Je. 1980). **Activities:** 1; 23, 31, 33; 56, 75, 83 **Addr.:** Central Connecticut State College, Elihu Burritt Library, Serials Department, New Britain, CT 06050.

Kaser, David (Mr. 12, 1924, Mishawaka, IN) Prof., Sch. of Lib. & Info. Sci., IN Univ., 1973–; Dir. of Libs., Cornell Univ., 1968–73; Dir. of Libs., Vanderbilt Univ., 1960–68; Asst. Dir. of Libs., Washington Univ., 1959–60, Chief of Acq., 1956–59; Asst. in Exch., Univ. of MI, 1954–56; Serials Libn., Ball State Univ., 1952–54. **Educ.:** Houghton Coll., 1947–49, AB (Eng.); Univ. of Notre Dame, 1949–50, MA (Eng.); Univ. of MI, 1950–52, AMLS, 1954–56, PhD (Lib. Sci.). **Orgs.:** ALA: Cnclr. (1965–69, 1975–79); ACRL (Pres. 1968–69). Assn. of Resrch. Libs.: Exec. Brd. (1969–72). TN LA: Pres. (1968–69). Assn. Southeastern Resrch. Libs.: Ch. (1966–68). **Honors:** Beta Phi Mu. Phi Beta Kappa. Guggenheim Fellow, 1967–68. **Pubns.:** *Book for a Sixpence* (1980); *Book Pirating in Taiwan* (1969); *Library Development in 8 Asian Countries* (1969); Ed., *Books in America's Past* (1966); *Joseph Charless* (1963). **Activities:** 1; 17, 19, 26 **Addr.:** 2402 Rock Creek Dr., Bloomington, IN 47401.

Kashmere, Sr. Mary Carmela R.S.M. (Jl. 28, 1926, Scranton, PA) Acq. Libn., Coll. Misericordia, 1975–; Math. Tchr., Libn., O.L.B.S., Harrisburg, PA, 1969–75; 5th Grade Tchr., Libn., St. Ann's, Lancaster, PA, 1974–75; 5th and 6th Grade Tchr., Libn., St. Francis's, Gettysburg, PA, 1973–74. **Educ.:** Coll. Misericordia, 1961, BS (Elem. Educ.); 1967, Elem. Libn. Cert.; Villanova Univ., 1974, MSLS. **Orgs.:** Cath. LA. Mercy Higher Educ. Colloquium. **Activities:** 1, 10; 15, 17, 22 **Addr.:** College Misericordia Library, Dallas, PA 18612.

Kasinec, Edward (O. 10, 1945, New York City, NY) Libn. for Slavic Cols., Univ. of CA, 1981–; Resrch. Bibl., Libn., Harvard Ukrainian Resrch. Inst., 1973– Libn. II, Resrch. Bibl., Harvard Univ., 1978–81, Fndr., Ref. Libn. Archvst., Ukrainian Resrch. Inst. Lib., 1973–76. **Educ.:** St. John's Univ., NY, 1966, BA (Hist.); Columbia Univ., 1979, MPhil (Hist.); Univ. of IL, Slavic Lib. Inst., 1970, Cert.; Amer. Univ., Arch. Inst., 1973, Cert.; Simmons Coll., 1976, MS (LS). **Orgs.:** ALA: ACRL/Slavic and E. European Sect. (Ch., 1979–80). **Honors:** Can. Inst. of Ukrainian Std., Cat. grant, 1979. **Pubns.:** "Eighteenth-Century Russian Publications in the New York Public Library: A Preliminary Catalogue," *Bltn. NY Pub. Lib.* (1969); "Iu. O. Ivaniv-Mezhenko (1892–1969) as a Bibliographer during his Years in Kiev, 1919–1933," *The Jnl. of Lib. Hist.* (Win. 1979); "British Nineteenth-Century Travellers and Their Moscow Friends: A Note on Sources," *St. Vladimir's Theo. Qtly.* (1978); "A Bibliographical Essay on the Documentation of Russian Orthodoxy during the Imperial Era" in *Russian Orthodoxy Under the Old Regime* (1978); various articles, reviews. **Activities:** 1, 2; 15, 28, 45; 54, 57, 66 **Addr.:** University of California, Main Library, Rm. 346, Collection Development Dept., Berkeley, CA 94720.

Kasman, Dorothy Chief Libn., Coopers & Lybrand, 1958–. **Educ.:** Douglass Coll., BA; Rutgers Univ., 1958, MLS; New York Univ., 1970, MBA. **Orgs.:** SLA: Treas. (1979–82); Resrch Com. (1977–79); Publshr. Rel. Com. (Ch., 1972–76); NY Chap., 2nd VP (1965–66); Arch. Com. (1976–79); Bud. Fin. Div. (Ch., 1969–70); other coms. ASIS. New York Lib. Club. **Pubns.:** Jt. auth., "Education for Special Librarianship," *Spec. Libs.* (N. 1976). **Activities:** 12; 59 **Addr.:** Coopers & Lybrand, 1251 Ave. of the Americas, New York, NY 10020.*

Kasner, Lynn (O. 13, 1950, New York, NY) Assoc. Libn., NY Acad. of Med., 1981–; Dir., NY and NJ Reg. Med. Lib., 1978–80, Reg. Coord., 1976–78; Libn./Resrch. Assoc., NY State Nurses Assn., 1974–76. **Educ.:** SUNY, Binghamton, 1968–71, BA (Psy.); SUNY, Albany, 1972, MLS; Med. LA, 1974, Cert. **Orgs.:** ALA: ACRL. Med. LA: Prog. Com. (1982 Conv.); Legis. Com. (1977–80); Ad Hoc Com on WHCOLIS (Ch., 1978–80); NY Reg. Grp., Bylaws Com. (1981–), Cont. Educ. Com. (Upstate NY and ON Reg. Ch., 1978–80). NY LA. Various other orgs. **Honors:** Beta Phi Mu. **Pubns.:** "The Regional Medical Library Program," *Sci. and Tech. Libs.* (Win. 1980); "The WHCOLIS," *Med. LA News* (F. 1980); "The WHCOLIS," *Med. LA News* (Ag. 1979); "The NY and NJ Regional Medical Library," *Natl. Lib. of Med. NEWS* (Je. 1978); "Analysis of Select Federal Health Legislation in Relation to Nursing," *Jnl. NY State Nurses Assn.* (Je. 1976). **Activities:** 12; 17, 34, 39; 58, 80, 91 **Addr.:** The New York Academy of Medicine Library, 2 E. 103 St., New York, NY 10029.

Kasow, Harriet F. (S. 20, 1939, Brooklyn, NY) Libn., Metro. Dade Ofc. of Transp. Admin., 1979–; Serials/Ref. Libn., Hebrew Univ. of Jerusalem, 1974–78; Libn., Stono Pk. Elem. Sch., Charleston (SC), 1970–71. **Educ.:** Univ. of Miami, 1958–61, MS (Hist.); FL State Univ., 1964, MS (LS); FL State Tchg. Cert. **Orgs.:** ALA. SLA. Mid. E. LA. **Honors:** Beta Phi Mu. **Activities:** 12; 15, 16, 17; 64, 94 **Addr.:** Metro Dade Office of Transportation Administration, 44 W. Flagler St., Miami, FL 33130.

Kasper, Barbara (Mr. 2, 1935, Peru, IN) Visiting Asst. Prof., Univ. of AB, 1980–; Assoc. Instr., IN Univ., 1977–79; Dir., Delphi Pub. Lib., 1967–75. **Educ.:** IN Univ., 1974, BA (Hist.), 1975–80, PhD (Lib. Sci.). **Orgs.:** IN LA: Chldn. and Young People's Round Table, Ch. (1969); Dist. III, Ch. (1971); Nat. Lib. Week, Ch. (1972). **Honors:** Beta Phi Mu. **Pubns.:** "Is the Small Public Library Dead?" (D. 1969). **Activities:** 9, 10; 16, 21, 48; 55, 67, 74 **Addr.:** Faculty of Library Science, University of Alberta, Edmonton, AB T6G 2J4 Canada.

Kasperko, Jean Margaret (Ag. 17, 1949, Wheeling, WV) Chem. Purchasing, Resrch., Calgon Corp., 1979–, Lit. Srch., 1975–79; Comp. Sci. Libn., Univ. of Pittsburgh, 1974–75. **Educ.:** Univ. of Pittsburgh, 1968–72, BS, magna cum laude (Chem.), 1972–74, MLS; Med. LA, 1978, Cert. **Orgs.:** SLA. Pittsburgh Online Users' Forum. Mid.-East. Reg. Med. Lib. Srv.: Online Coord. Com. (1978–80). Amer. Chem. Socty. Chem. Mktg. Assn. of Pittsburgh. **Honors:** Beta Phi Mu. **Pubns.:** "Online Chemical Dictionaries: A Comparison," *DATABASE* (S. 1979). **Activities:** 12; 41; 59, 60, 86 **Addr.:** 14 Vigne Rd., Coraopolis, PA 15108.

Kass, Natalie Evans (S. 19, 1925, New Haven, CT) Asst. to Pres., Mattatuck Cmnty. Coll., 1969–; Lib. Asst., Silas Bronson Lib., 1949–50; Lib. Asst., New Haven Free Pub. Lib., 1943–49. **Educ.:** Albertus Magnus Coll. South. CT State Coll., BS (Bio. Sci.); Fairfield Univ., MA (Educ. Admin.); Grantsmanship Cert., crs. in Mgt., Cmnty. Educ. **Orgs.:** Silas Bronson Lib.: Bd. of Lib. Agts. (1970–). Assn. of CT Lib. Bds.: Pres. (1975–). CT Lib. Srv. Units Review Bd. CT State Gvr. White House/Info. Srv. Conf.: Plng. Com. **Activities:** 1, 9, 13; 25, 28, 47; 50, 63, 78 **Addr.:** 124 Gail Dr., Waterbury, CT 06704.

Kasten, Seth E. (N. 8, 1945, New York, NY) Head, User Srvs./Ref. Libn., Un. Theo. Semy. Lib., 1977–, Ref. Libn., 1976–77, Asst. Ref. Libn., 1973–76; Tech. Srvs. Libn., Manhattan Sch. of Msc., 1971–72. **Educ.:** SUNY, Binghamton, 1963–67, BA; Columbia Univ., 1967–69, MLS; Un. Theo. Semy., 1971–73, SMM (Msc.) **Orgs.:** ALA. NY Area Theo. LA: Strg. Com. (1980–). ATLA. Hymn Socty. of Amer. **Pubns.:** "Religion Periodical Indexes: A Basic List," *Ref. Srvs. Review* (Ja./Mar. 1981). **Activities:** 1; 39, 41, 45; 55, 90 **Addr.:** 700 West End Ave., Apt. 14-A, New York, NY 10025.

Kastle, Barbara W. (F. 2, 1947, Rahway, NJ) AV Consult., State Lib. of PA, 1978–; AV Libn., James V. Brown Lib., 1974–78; Adult Srv. Libn., Red Bank Pub. Lib., 1972–74. **Educ.:** Douglass Coll., 1965–69, BA (Art Hist.); Rutgers Univ., 1971–72, MLS. **Orgs.:** ALA: LITA/AV Sect., Mem. Com. PA LA: Media RT. **Honors:** Beta Phi Mu. **Activities:** 9, 13; 24, 25, 32; 67, 93 **Addr.:** 1112 Green St., Harrisburg, PA 17102.

Katan, James Thomas (Ap. 5, 1948, Oakville, ON) Chief Libn., Campbellton Cent. Lib., 1975–; Demonstration Lib. Coord., Lake ON Reg. Lib. Syst., 1973–74. **Educ.:** McMaster Univ., 1966–70, BA (Fr., Grmn.); Bonn Univ. (W. Germany), 1970–71, Cert. (Grmn.); McMaster Univ., 1971–72, MA (Grmn.); Univ. of West. ON., 1974–75, MLS. **Orgs.:** Can. LA. Atl. Prov. LA. **Pubns.:** "Children's Reading Preferences...," *Atl. Prov. LA Bltn.* (Ja. 1978); "Promotion and Public Relations for the Small Public Library," *Atl. Prov. LA Bltn.* (N. 1978). **Activities:** 9; 15, 17, 21 **Addr.:** 187 Dover St., Campbellton, NB E3N 1R3 Canada.

Katayama, Jane H. (Jl. 23, 1941, Ewa, HI) Lib. Mgr., M.I.T. Lincoln Lab., 1975–, Asst. Lib. Mgr., 1974–75, Readrs. Srvs. Libn., 1972–74, Ref. Libn., 1965–72. **Educ.:** Univ. of HI, 1959–63, EdB (Educ.); Simmons Coll., 1964–69, MS (LS). **Orgs.:** SLA. ALA. ASIS. **Activities:** 1, 12; 17, 35, 38; 56, 88, 91 **Addr.:** A-082, M.I.T. Lincoln Laboratory, 244 Wood St., Lexington, MA 02173.

PROFESSIONAL ACTIVITIES: Institutions: 1. Acad. lib.; 2. Arch.; 3. Assn.; 4. Fed./Gvt. lib.; 5. Inst. lib.; 6. Mfr./Suppl.; 7. Milit. lib.; 8. Musm.; 9. Pub. lib.; 10. Sch. lib.; 11. Sch. of lib. sci.; 12. Spec. lib.; 13. State lib.; 14. (other). **Functions/Activities:** 15. Acq./Col. dev.; 16. Adult srvs.; 17. Admin.; 18. Apprais.; 19. Archit./Bldgs.; 20. Cat./Class.; 21. Chld. srvs.; 22. Circ.; 23. Cons./Pres.; 24. Consult.; 25. Cont. ed.; 26. Educ. lib. sci.; 27. Ext. srvs.; 28. Fund/Grants; 29. Gvt. pubs.; 30. Indx./Abs.; 31. Instr. lib. use; 32. Media srvs.; 33. Micro.; 34. Netwks./Coop.; 35. Persnl.; 36. PR; 37. Publshg.; 38. Recs. mgt.; 39. Ref. srvs.; 40. Repro.; 41. Resrch.; 42. Review.; 43. Secur.; 44. Serials; 45. Spec. col.; 46. Tech. srvs.; 47. Trustees/Bds.; 48. YA srvs.; 49. (other).

Kates, Jacqueline R. (Boston, MA) Corporate Libn., Instrumentation Lab., Inc., 1969–; Paper and Ofc. Equip. Buyer, Harvard Univ., 1955–59; Asst. Dir. of Mktg. Resrch., Baird Associates, 1954–55; Admin. Asst., Arthur D. Little, Inc., 1951–54. **Educ.:** Univ. of MI, BA (Grmn.); Harvard-Radcliffe Prog., Cert. (Bus. Admin.); Simmons Sch. of Lib. Sci., 1970–73, MS (LS); Spec. Student, M. I. T., 1954, (Mktg.). **Orgs.:** SLA: Boston Chap., Nom. Com. (Ch., 1978–79). Med. LA. New Eng. LA. Route 128 Libns. MA Hlth. Sci. Libns.: Treas. (1979–80). **Honors:** Beta Phi Mu, 1973. **Pubns.:** "One Measure of a Library's Contribution," *Spec. Libs.* (Ag. 1974); "Cataloging Government Technical Reports," *Spec. Libs.* (Mr. 1974); "A Bibliography on Biomedical Engineering," *Boston Chap. SLA Nsltr.* (Mr.-Ap. 1979). **Activities:** 12; 15, 17, 20; 60, 80, 91 **Addr.:** Instrumentation Laboratory Inc., 113 Hartwell Ave., Lexington, MA 02173.

Kathman, Michael D. (D. 12, 1943, Quincy, IL) Dir. of Libs., Coll. of St. Benedict, St. John's Univ., 1980–, Lib. Dir., 1973–80; Schol.-in-Residence, Wrtg.-In-Chicago Prog., Chicago Pub. Lib., 1976–77; Dir., Pub. Srvs., St. John's Univ., 1972–73; Asst. Dir., Lrng. Resrcs., Wayne Cnty. Cmnty. Coll., 1970–72; Ref./Pers. Libn., Monroe Cnty. Cmnty. Coll., 1968–70. **Educ.:** St. Procopius Coll., 1962–66, BA (Eng.); Univ. of MI, 1966–67, AMLS, 1967–69, AM (Amer. Std.). **Orgs.:** ALA: ACRL, Prog. Com., Sec. Natl. Conf. (1980–81). City Cncl. of Cold Spring, MN. Ofc. of Pub. Libs. and ILL Coop.: Adv. Cncl. **Pubns.:** Jt. auth., "Management Problems of Student Workers in Academic Libraries," *Coll. & Resrch. Libs.* (Mr. 1978); "Librarian Finds Leave Renewing If Not Restful," *St. John's Mag.* (Spr. 1977); reviews. **Activities:** 1; 17, 34, 35; 55, 56 **Addr.:** 414 - 8th Ave. N., Cold Spring, MN 56320.

Katz, Bernard M. L. (Ja. 4, 1940, Toronto, ON) Head, Hum. and Soc. Sci. Div., Univ. of Guelph Lib., 1979–, Head, Div. of Circ. and Info. Srvs., 1978–79, Asst. Head, Div. of Circ. and Info. Srvs., 1975–78, Sr. Cat. Libn., 1973–75. **Educ.:** Univ. of Toronto, 1958–60, 1962–64, BA (Hist. and Eng.); Johns Hopkins Univ., 1964–65, MA (Creat. Wtg. and Cont. Lit.); Univ. of Toronto, 1968–69, BLS. **Orgs.:** Inst. of Prof. Libn. of ON: Coll. Bargaining Com. (1972–74). ON LA: Ed. *OLA Nsltr.* (1970–72); Educ. Action & Prof. Dev. Com. (1977–). Univ. of Toronto Lib. Sci. Alum. Assn.: Exec. Com. (1975–78). Can. LA: Copyrt. Com. (1979–); Univ. and Coll. Lib. Sect. (Exec. Mem., 1980–81). Can. Jewish Congs.: ON Reg., Educ. and Culture Com. (Vice-Ch., 1977–80; Ch., 1980). Univ. of Guelph Fac. Assn.: Constitution Com. (Ch., 1972–73); Exec. Bd. (1972–73); Salary Com. (Secty., 1975–81), Negotiating Team, 1978–); Alternatives to Collegiality Com. (1980–). **Honors:** E.J. Pratt Medal, 1964; OLA Anniv. Prize, 1969. **Pubns.:** Jt. auth., "Audio-visual media in the university library: an integrated approach to information storage and retrieval," *Media Message* (1974); jt. auth., "From the 12th to the 20th century at the flip of a card," *Teaching Forum* (My. 1975); jt. auth., "Always on Sunday–Jewish education for the 4–7 year old in a small community," *Educ. and Culture Review* (1977); "Copyright or copy wrong," *C.A.U.T. Bltn.* (1977); jt. auth., "Bibliographic Control: the challenge of an on-line public enquiry system," *Inf. in Power: OLA Conf. Papers* (1979); various sp. **Activities:** 1; 17, 31, 39; 55, 56, 61 **Addr.:** The Library, University of Guelph, Guelph, ON N1G 2W1 Canada.

Katz, Ruth M. (Jl. 11, 1937, Bridgeport, CT) Assoc. Dir., Lib. Srvs., E. Carolina Univ., 1980–; Sr. Resrch. Sci., Denver Resrch. Inst., Univ. of Denver, 1976–80, Asst. Prof., Grad. Sch. of Libnshp., 1974–76; Asst. Univ. Libn., Rutgers Univ., 1973–74; Sr. Systs. Anal., Syst. Dev. Corp., 1968–70; Phys. Sci. Ref. Spec., Lib. of Congs., 1967–68; Info. Sci., Documtn., Inc., 1965–67. **Educ.:** Clark Univ., 1955–59, AB (Chem.); Rutgers Univ., 1962–65, MLS, 1975, PhD. **Orgs.:** ALA: Cncl. (1980–84); RASD, Bd. of Dirs. (1980–84); LRRT (Ch., 1980–81); ASCLA, Stans. Review Com. (1980–82), Nom. Com. (Ch., 1981–82). ASIS: Educ. Com. (Ch., 1981–82). NC LA: Networking Com. (Ch., 1981–83); RT on the Status of Women in Libnshp. (Ch., 1981–83). CLENE. Various other orgs. Amer. Assn. for the Advnc. of Hum. Amer. Assn. for Higher Educ. Amer. Educ. Resrch. Assn. Natl. Assn. of Educ. Broadcasters. Various other orgs. **Pubns.:** *Technology as a Factor in Library Development and Educational Change* (1981); jt. auth., *Staff Training via Telecommunications: Analysis of Needs and Delivery Alternatives* (1979); "Communication Technologies and Issues: The Librarians' Need to Know," *Cath. Lib. World* (Ap. 1979); "Stand-by—Innovative Uses of Media in Libraries" videotape (1978); "Vintage—Delivering Library Services to an Aging Population" 5 videotapes, 2 slide-snd. shows, std. guide (1977); various videotapes. **Activities:** 1; 17, 26, 41; 63, 93 **Addr.:** Joyner Library, East Carolina University, Greenville, NC 27834.

Katz, William (Jl. 6, 1924, Seattle, WA) Prof., Sch. of Lib. and Info. Sci., SUNY, Albany, 1966–; Assoc. Prof., Lib. Sch., Univ. of KY, 1964–66; Asst. Ed., Ed. Dept., ALA, 1960–64. **Educ.:** Univ. of WA; Univ. of Chicago, 1960–65, PhD (LS). **Orgs.:** ALA. **Honors:** Isadore Gilbert Mudge Cit. for Ref. Libnshp., ALA, 1973; Disting. Alum. Awd., Univ. of WA, 1977; Seattle Hist. Awd. of Merit, 1965. **Pubns.:** *Introduction to Reference Work* (1982); *Magazines for Libraries* (1982); *Your Library* (1979); *Collection Development* (1980); *The Best of Library Lit* (1970–); other books and articles. **Activities:** 11; 15, 39, 44; 55, 57, 75 **Addr.:** School of Library and Information Science, Draper Hall, SUNY/Albany, Albany, NY 12222.

Kauer, Erminia U. (S. 22, 1927, Waterbury, CT) Ref./Circ./ILL Libn., E.I. DuPont, 1952–. **Educ.:** Mary Washington Coll., BS (Chem.); Columbia Univ., 1951–52, MS (LS). **Orgs.:** SLA. SC LA: Spec. Lib. Div. (Pres.-Elect, 1980–81). Ctrl. Savannah River LA: Secy. (1979–81). **Activities:** 12; 22, 34, 39; 60, 84, 91 **Addr.:** Savannah River Lab., E. I. du Pont de Nemours & Co., Inc., Aiken, SC 29801.

Kauffman, Bruce Robert (Ap. 7, 1929, Dowagiac, MI) City Libn., Boca Raton Pub. Lib., 1978–; Dir., Jackson Cnty. (MI) Lib., 1974–78; Univ. Libn., Univ. of Cincinnati, 1969–73; Coll. Libn., The Defiance Coll., 1965–68. **Educ.:** Coll. of Wooster, 1947–51, BA (Pol. Sci.); Univ. of Pittsburgh, 1963–64, MLS. **Orgs.:** OH LA: Coll. and Univ. Div. (Pres. 1970). Palm Beach Cnty. LA: VP and Pres.–Elect. (1980). **Activities:** 9; 17, 19, 34; 56 **Addr.:** Boca Raton Public Library, 200 NW 2nd Ave., Boca Raton, FL 33432.

Kauffman, Inge S. (Ap. 20, 1928, Berlin, Germany) Libn., CA Sch. of Prof. Psy., 1973–; Catlgr., Fresno Cnty. Free Lib., 1964–69; Catlgr., Univ. of TX Libs., 1955–56; Catlgr., Univ. of FL Libs., 1951–55. **Educ.:** Univ. of Tampa, 1947–50, BA (Span.); FL State Univ., 1950–51, MA (LS). **Orgs.:** Ctrl. Sierra Lib. & Media Assn.: Secy. (1979–80). Fresno Area Lib. Cncl.: Secy./Treas. (1974–75). ALA. Area Wide Lib. Network: Ch., Comp. Plng. Com. for the Network (1979–). **Activities:** 1, 12; 17, 20, 34; 92 **Addr.:** 546 E. San Ramon Ave., Fresno, CA 93710.

Kauffman, S. Blair (S. 25, 1948, St. Louis, MO) Law Libn., Natl. Judicial Coll. 1977–. **Educ.:** Univ. of MO, 1969–71, BS (Bus.) Univ. of WA, 1976–77, MLL. Univ. of MO Sch. of Law, 1971–75, JD, LLM. **Orgs.:** AALL. ALA. SLA. Amer. Bar Assn. MO Bar Assn. **Pubns.:** "Automated Legal Research for Nevada," *Inter Alia* (Ag. 1979); "Information Needs of the Judiciary," *Law Lib. Jnl.* (F. 1979). **Activities:** 1; 17; 63, 77 **Addr.:** Law Library, The National Judicial College, Reno, NV 89557.

Kaufman, Judith Leiderman (Jl. 24, 1947, New York, NY) Head, Msc. Lib., SUNY, Stony Brook, 1977–; Actg. Head, Msc. Lib., Cornell Univ., 1976; Asst. Libn., Msc. Lib., SUNY, Buffalo, 1974–76, Asst. Archvst., 1974. **Educ.:** Brown Univ., 1965–69, BA, magna cum laude (Msc.); SUNY, Stony Brook, 1969–70, MMus (Flute); SUNY, Buffalo, 1972–74, MLS. **Orgs.:** Msc. LA: Cat. Com. (Ch., 1979–), Subcom. on Msc. Other than West.-Art (1976–). Intl. Assn. of Msc. Libs.: Subcomsn. (Alternate Ch., 1979–). **Honors:** Beta Phi Mu; Phi Beta Kappa; SUNY Chancellor's Awd. for Excel. in Libnshp., 1978–79. **Pubns.:** *Recordings of Non-western Music: Subject and Added Entry Access* (Msc. LA Tech. Rpt. No. 5) (1977); "Subject Headings for Non-Western Music: Recommendations to the Library of Congress...," *Msc. Cat. Bltn.* (Jl. 1980); "A Cataloging and Classification System for Visual Resources," *Lib. Resrcs. & Tech. Srvs.* (Spr. 1979). **Activities:** 1; 15, 20, 39; 55 **Addr.:** Library W-2510, SUNY, Stony Brook, NY 11794.

Kaufman, Paula T. (Jl. 26, 1946, Perth Amboy, NJ) Bus. Libn., Columbia Univ., 1979–; Prin. Ref. Libn., Yale Univ., 1976–79; Partner, Info. for Bus., 1973–76; Info. Spec., McKinsey and Co., 1970–73; Ref. Libn., Columbia Univ., 1969–70. **Educ.:** Smith Coll., 1964–68, AB (Econ.); Columbia Univ., 1968–69, MS (LS); Univ. of New Haven, 1976–78, MBA (Bus. Admin.). **Orgs.:** SLA: Bus. and Fin. Div., Pubns. Com. (1977–). ALA. **Pubns.:** Reviews. **Activities:** 1; 17; 51, 59, 92 **Addr.:** Watson Library of Business & Economics, 130 Uris Hall, Columbia University, New York, NY 10027.

Kaufmann, Frances G. (O. 1, 1948, Hazleton, PA) Head, Access Srvs. Lehman Lib., Columbia Univ., 1978–; Head, ILL, Univ. of PA, 1974–78. **Educ.:** PA State Univ., 1966–70, BA (Fr.); Drexel Univ., 1971–73, MLS. **Orgs.:** ALA. **Honors:** Phi Beta Kappa. **Pubns.:** "The British Library Lending Division Photocopy Service, A Comparison...," *Some Current Reprographic Concerns Related to ILL* (Ap. 1977). **Activities:** 1; 22, 44, 46; 92 **Addr.:** Columbia University Lehman Library, New York, NY 10027.

Kaufmann, Shoshana (Mr. 5, 1932, Görlitz, Germany) Head, Gen. Reader Srvs., Queens Coll., 1977–, Circ. Libn., 1972–77, Gift Libn., 1967–72. **Educ.:** Columbia Univ., 1959–61, BS (Eng.), 1961–63, (Eng.); Drexel Univ., 1965–67, MLS; NY Univ., 1980–81, MA (Near East, Std.). **Orgs.:** ALA. City Univ. of New York LA. **Honors:** Beta Phi Mu, 1967. **Activities:** 1; 17, 22; 56, 72 **Addr.:** Paul Klapper Library, Queens College, Flushing, NY 11367.

Kaup, Jermain A. (Ap. 9, 1948, West Point, NE) Dir., Minot Pub. Lib., 1977–; Dir., Holdrege Pub. Lib., NE, 1973–77; Lib. Coord., NE Lib. Comnty., 1972–73. **Educ.:** Univ. of NE, 1966–70, BS (Soc. Sci); FL State Univ., 1971, MLS. **Orgs.:** ND LA: Pres., Pub. Lib. Sect. (1978–79); Ed. (1977–79); ND Pub. Lib. Plng. Com. Ch. (1979–81); Mt. Plains LA Rep. (1979–81). Mt. Plains LA. ALA: Mem. Com. Mt. Plains Reg. Rep. (1977–); John Cotton Dana PR Awd. Com. (1977–78). Minot Lions Club: Brd. of Dir. (1980–). Holdrege Lions Club: Third VP (1976–77). Knights of Columbus (1966–). **Honors:** Beta Sigma Phi. **Pubns.:** "Minot Public Library" (Mr. 1978). **Activities:** 9; 15, 17, 36; 59, 74, 92 **Addr.:** Minot Public Library, 516 2nd Ave. S.W., Minot, ND 58701.

Kauskay, Roberta Laura Bork (Jy. 14, 1916, Buffalo, NY) Dir. Media Resrcs. Ctr., Univ. of OK, 1976–, Dir., Lib. Ctr., 1966–76; Soc. Sci. Libn., 1965–66, Tchr. and Soc. Case Worker, 1939–64. **Educ.:** Elmhurst Coll., 1933–35; Washington Univ. 1935–37, BA (Eng.); Univ. of Buffalo, 1938–40, Syracuse Univ., 1963–64, Univ. of OK, 1964–65, MLS. **Orgs.:** ALA. SWLA. OK LA. Intl. Assn. of Sch. Libns. Other orgs. AAUP. Natl. Educ. Assn. AECT. Assn. for Supvsn. and Curric. Dev. **Activities:** 1, 10; 17 **Addr.:** 1621 Chestnut Ln., P.O. Box 665, Norman, OK 73070.

Kavass, Igor I. (Jl. 31, 1932, Riga, Latvia) Dir., Prof. of Law, Law Sch. Lib., Vanderbilt Univ., 1975–; Prof. of Law, Law Libn., Duke Univ., 1972–75; Prof. of Law, Law Libn., Northwest. Univ., 1970–72; Prof. of Law, Dir., Law Lib., Univ. of AL, 1968–70. **Educ.:** University of Melbourne (Australia) Sch. of Law, 1950–55, LL.B. **Orgs.:** Intl. Assn. of Law Libs.: Pres. (1977–83). AALL: Various coms. Amer. Assn. for the Adv. of Slavic Stds. Brit. Inst. of Intl. and Comp. Law. Assn. of Amer. Law Schs. **Honors:** Amer. Socty. of Intl. Law, Cert. of Merit, 1979. **Pubns.:** *United States Legislation on Foreign Relations and International Commerce, 1789–1969* (1977–78); jt. comp., *Energy and Congress: An Annotated Bibliography* (1974); *Guide to North Carolina Legal Research* (1973); *Australian Supplement to Gower's Modern Company Law* (1964); Other articles. **Activities:** 1, 12; 77 **Addr.:** Vanderbilt Law Library, Nashville, TN 37203.

Kawabata, Julie (Ag. 1, 1943, Portland, OR) Info. Broker (Owner), Northwest Info. Enterprises, 1978–; Reg. Ref. Spec., Interstate Lib. Plng. Cncl. 1977–78; Lib. Mgr., Tektronix, Inc., 1967–77. **Educ.:** Willamette Univ., 1961–65, BA (Jnlsm.); J Univ. of Portland, 1970, MLS. **Orgs.:** SLA: OR Chap., Pres., 1975–76, Bltn. Ed., 1976–79. ASIS: 1975 Midyear Mtg., Lcl. Arrang. Com. (Ch.). Assoc. Info. Mgrs. Women Entrepreneurs of OR. Amer. Mktg. Assn. **Pubns.:** Ed., *Print Samples: Electronics, Computers, & Communications* (Fall, 1980); Ed., *Directory of Libraries: ILPC* (Interstate Lib. Plng. Cncl.) (1978); Jt. ed., *Directory of Special Libraries in Oregon and Southwest Washington* (1978). **Activities:** 6; 24, 30, 39; 59, 62, 64 **Addr.:** 2383 NW 153rd, Beaverton, OR 97006.

Kawakami, Toyo S. (Ja. 14, 1916, Oroville, CA) Head, Soc. Work Lib., Asst. Head, Educ. Lib., OH State Univ., 1964–; Asst. Libn., Cincinnati Art Musm., 1959–63; Per. Libn., Lib., Univ. of Cincinnati, 1957–59, Libn., Coll. of Nursing and Hlth., 1946–57. **Educ.:** Sacramento Jr. Coll., 1933–35, AA (Latin); Univ. of CA, Berkeley, 1935–37, BA (Eng.); Univ. of MI, 1963–64, MLS. **Orgs.:** ALA: ACRL Bd. of Dirs. (1973–75)/Educ. and Bhvl. Sci. Sect. (Ch., 1974–75), Com. on Problems of Access and Cntrl. of Educ. Mtrls. (Ch., 1979–81), Nom. Com. (Ch., 1975–76); RTSD. OH LA: Mem. Com. (1969–70); Coll. and Univ. RT (Secy. 1966–67), *Nsltr.* Ed. (1967–69). ASIS: Spec. Interest Grp. in the Bhvl. and Soc. Sci. (Vice-Ch., 1973). Various other orgs., ofcs. OH State Univ. Fac. Women's Club: Pres. (1969–70). **Honors:** OH Poetry Day Assn., First and Third Prizes, 1978; First Asian Amer. Writers Conf., Awd., 1975; OH LA Bltn., Best Article of the Yr. Awd., 1974. **Pubns.:** *Acronyms in Education and the Behavioral Sciences* (1971); "The Asian Americans in Academic Libraries," *Opportunities for Minorities in Librarianship* (1977); "The Japanese in Ohio," *Ohioana Lib. Yrbk.* (1977); "An American Experience," *OH LA Bltn.* (Ap. 1974); various poems in *Yale Review, OH Poetry Review,* others. **Activities:** 1; 17, 39, 41; 63, 92 **Addr.:** 30 Orchard Ln., Columbus, OH 43214.

Kaya, Mariko (S. 5, 1936, Los Angeles, CA) Chief, Tech. Srvs. Div., Los Angeles Cnty. Pub. Lib., 1980–, Acq. Libn., 1975–80, Reg. Adult Col. Coord., 1968–75, Gvt. Pubn./Ref. Libn., 1967–68; Ref. Libn., Anaheim Pub. Lib., 1965–67; Visit. Prof. (LS), Univ. of South. CA, 1974. **Educ.:** Univ. of CA, Los Angeles, 1954–58, BA (Anthro.); Univ. of South. CA, 1963–65, MLS. **Orgs.:** ALA. CA LA: Dir. (1982–84); Tech. Srvs. Chap. (Treas., 1981). **Activities:** 9; 17, 46 **Addr.:** Los Angeles County Public Library System, 320 W. Temple St., Los Angeles, CA 90012.

Kaye, Marilyn Janice (Jl. 19, 1949, New Britain, CT) Instr., Coll. of Libnshp., Univ. of SC, 1980–; Ed. Asst., *Lib. Qtly.* 1977–79; Libn., Decatur (GA) City Schs., 1974–76. **Educ.:** Emory Univ., 1967–71, BA (Eng.), 1973–74, MLn (Libnshp.); Coll. of Libnshp., Wales, 1975; Univ. of Chicago, 1976–, PhD in progress. **Orgs.:** ALA: YASD; ALSC, Ed., ALSC Nsltr. Chld. Lit. Assn. **Honors:** Beta Phi Mu, 1975. **Pubns.:** Co-ed., *Celebrating Children's Books* (1981); "In Defense of Formula Fiction, *Top of the News* (Fall 1980); "The First Golden Age of Children's Book Publishing," *Top of the News* (Spr. 1979); "Storytelling: A Review Article," *Lib. Qtly.* (Ja. 1979); "Recurring Patterns in the Novels of M. E. Kerr," *Chld. Lit.* (1978). **Activities:** 11; 21, 48 **Addr.:** College of Librarianship, University of South Carolina, Columbia, SC 29208.

Kazanjian, Donna Siefert (My. 24, 1947, New York, NY) Libn., Handy Assocs., Inc., 1979–; Sr. Info. Anal., Info. for

Special Subjects/Services: 50. Adult educ.; 51. Advert./Mktg.; 52. Aerosp.; 53. Agric.; 54. Area std.; 55. Arts/Hum.; 56. Autom.; 57. Bibl./Prtg.; 58. Bio. sci.; 59. Bus./Fin.; 60. Chem.; 61. Copyrt.; 62. Documtn.; 63. Educ.; 64. Engin.; 65. Env.; 66. Eth. grps.; 67. Film; 68. Food/Nutr.; 69. Geneal.; 70. Geo.; 71. Geol.; 72. Handcpd.; 73. Hist.; 74. Int. frdm.; 75. Info. sci.; 76. Insr.; 77. Law; 78. Legis.; 79. Math./Comp. sci.; 80. Med.; 81. Metals; 82. Nat. resrcs.; 83. Newsp.; 84. Nuc. sci.; 85. Oral hist.; 86. Petr./Energy; 87. Pharm.; 88. Phys./Astr./Math.; 89. Readg.; 90. Relig.; 91. Sci./Tech.; 92. Soc. sci.; 93. Telecom.; 94. Transp.; 95. (other).

Bus., Inc, 1976–77; Resrch. Assoc., William E. Hill and Co., 1973–76; Asst. Libn., Dun and Bradstreet, Inc., 1969–73. **Educ.:** NY Univ., 1965–69, BA (Psy.); Columbia Univ., 1970–73, MSLS; Fordham Univ., 1974–77, MBA. **Orgs.:** SLA: NY Chap., Audit. Com. (Ch., 1977–78), Fin. Com. (1977–78), Midtown Luncheon Grp. (Ch., 1974–75). MENSA. **Honors:** NY Univ., Sandham Awd., 1969. **Activities:** 12; 15, 39, 46; 59 **Addr.:** Research Library, Handy Associates, Inc., 245 Park Ave., New York, NY 10167.

Kazlauskas, Edward John (Ja. 4, 1942, Cleveland, OH) Assoc. Dean, Univ. of South. CA, 1970–; Syst. Anal., CA State Univ., 1966–70; Acq. Libn., FL Atl. Univ., 1964–66; Asst., Undergrad. Lib., Univ. of IL, 1963–64. **Educ.:** John Carroll Univ., 1959–63, AB (Eng.); Univ. of IL, 1963–64, MS (LS); Univ. of South. CA, 1971–75, PhD (Instr. Tech.). **Orgs.:** ASIS: Anl. Conf. (Ch., 1980); Los Angeles Chap. (Ch., 1978); Intl. Rel. Com. (1980–82). South. CA Tech. Proc. Grp.: Ch. (1970). ALA. CA LA. **Pubns.:** "Use of a Minicomputer in Thesaurus Construction," *JASIS* (S. 1980); "Spanish Speaking Mental Health Research Center Bibliographic Data Base," *RQ* (Sum. 1980); "The Application of the Instructional Development Process to a Module on Flowcharting," *Jnl. of Lib. Autom.* (S. 1976); "An Exploratory Study: A Kinesic Analysis of Academic Library Public Service Points," *The Jnl. of Acad. Libnshp.* (Jl. 1976); various articles. **Activities:** 1, 11; 26, 31, 32; 56, 72, 75 **Addr.:** 4844 Escobedo Dr., Woodland Hills, CA 91364.

Kearl, Biruta Celmins (D. 24, 1948, Rome, Italy) Coord., Cent. TX Lib. Syst., 1975–; Lib. Coord., Adult Basic, Univ. of TX, Austin, 1974–75; Educ. Proj., Div. of Extension. **Educ.:** Univ. of TX, Austin, 1965–72, BFA (Art Hist.), 1973–74, MLS. **Orgs.:** ALA. TX LA: Dist. 3 Nom. Com. Ch. (1975–79); Ad Hoc PR Com., Adv. Cncl. (1977–); Cnclr. (1980–). **Pubns.:** Jt. Auth., *ABE: Guide to Library Materials* (1975); Jt. auth., "Commentary on proposing a special library" (F. 1975); Jt. auth., "Effective Introduction of Students to Networking via Projects" (Sum. 1976). **Activities:** 9, 17, 24, 25 **Addr.:** Central Texas Library System, P.O. Box 2287, Austin, TX 78768.

Kearley, David A. (F. 23, 1929, Mobile, AL) Dir., Educ. Lib., Vanderbilt Univ., 1973; Head, Grad. Lib., Univ. of AL, 1970–73, Head, Ref. Dept. Lib., 1969–70. **Educ.:** Univ. of AL, 1946–51, BA (Hist.); Peabody Coll., 1968–69, MLS; Univ. of AL, 1954–56, MA (Hist.); Gen. Theo. Sem., 1955–58, MDiv (Theo.). **Orgs.:** Nashville Lib. Club: Pres. (1979–80). TN LA: 2nd VP (1976–77). **Honors:** Beta Phi Mu, 1969; Phi Alpha Theta, 1951. **Activities:** 1; 15, 17; 63 **Addr.:** 116 Poteat Pl., Franklin, TN 37064.

Kearney, Carol A. (My. 6, 1939, Buffalo, NY) Dir., Sch. Libs., Buffalo Pub. Schs., 1973–; Visit. Lectr. (LS), SUNY Buffalo, 1978–79; Coord., Sch. Libs., W. Seneca Ctrl. Schs., 1969–73, HS Lib. Media Spec., 1971–73, Elem., Jr. HS Lib. Media Spec., 1964–71. **Educ.:** Geneseo State Tchrs. Coll., 1956–60, BS (Elem. Educ., LS); SUNY Buffalo, 1970, MS (Educ. Comm.), 1977 (Educ. Admin.). **Orgs.:** ALA: By-Laws Com. (1975). Sch. LA of West. NY: Pres. (1975). NY LA: Leg. Com. (1976–78). NY State Gov. Conf. on Libs. (1978). Other orgs. and ofcs. Delta Kappa Gamma. Lib. Info. Ntwk. Cncl. of West. NY: Ch. (1977–81). **Honors:** Amer. Bus. Women's Assn., Boss of the Yr., 1975. Sch. of Info. and LS, SUNY Buffalo, Libn. of the Yr., 1975. **Pubns.:** "Organizing For School Library Service: The District Library Supervisor," *Bookmark* (Spr. 1980). **Activities:** 10; 17, 25, 32; 63, 78, 93 **Addr.:** Room 408, City Hall, Buffalo, NY 14202.

Kearns, William K. (Ja. 17, 1928, Wilmington, OH) Assoc. Dean, Grad. Stds., Coll. of Msc., 1981–, Univ. of CO, 1965–; Cur., Ben Gray Lumpkin Col. of CO Folksongs, 1970–; Asst. Prof. (Msc.), OH State Univ., 1953–65; Asst. Prof. (Msc.) Friends Univ., 1952–53. **Educ.:** OH State Univ., 1945–52, BS (Msc.), 1952–54, MA (Msc.), Univ. of IL, 1958–65, PhD (Msclgy.). **Orgs.:** Msc. LA: Mts. and Plains Chap. Amer. Msclgy. Socty. Amer. Folklore Socty. Sonneck Socty. Coll. Msc. Socty. **Pubns.:** *A Resource Book for Music Appreciation,* (1968); *Folk Music of Colorado and the United States* (1977); "Horatio Parker," *Grove's Dict. of Msc.* (1980); "Will She Ever Return?" A Study in the Esthetic of a Popular American Song," *Msclgy. at the Univ. of CO* (1977); other articles. **Activities:** 1; 55 **Addr.:** College of Music, University of Colorado, Boulder, CO 80309.

Keaschuk, Michael J. (N. 24, 1947, Yorkton, SK) Reg. Libn., Chinook Reg. Lib., 1975–; Libn., Thompson-Nicola Lib. Syst., 1974–75; Chief Libn., Kamloops Pub. Lib., 1973–74; Reg. Libn., SE Reg. Lib., 1972. **Educ.:** Univ. of AB, 1965–68, BSc, 1968–69, BLS. **Orgs.:** SK LA: Task Frc. on Stans. (1978). SW SK Writers Proj.: Adv. Bd. (1980–81). **Activities:** 9, 14-Reg. lib.; 15, 16, 17 **Addr.:** Chinook Regional Library, 1240 Chaplin St. W., Swift Current, SK S9H 0G8 Canada.

Keasler, A. Wally (S. 23, 1950, Fort Payne, AL) Head, Bus., Sci. and Tech., Chattanooga-Hamilton Cnty. Lib., 1976–, Ref. Libn., 1973–76. **Educ.:** Univ. of TN, 1968–72, BS (Eng. Educ.), 1972–73, MSLS. **Orgs.:** SELA. TN LA: Treas. (1978–79); Fin. Com. (Ch., 1979–80). Chattanooga Area LA: Treas. (1977–78). Gvt. Docum. Org. of TN: First Ch. (1976). **Pubns.:** *Index to U.S. Dept. Agricultural Farmers' Bulletins 1751 - 2256* (1975); *Index to Home and Garden Bulletins 1-211* (1975); *Index to Agriculture Leaflets* (1976). **Activities:** 9; 16, 29, 39; 59, 91 **Addr.:** Chattanooga - Hamilton County Bicentennial Library, 1001 Broad St., Chattanooga, TN 37402.

Keating, Michael F. (Ja. 31, 1950, Cleveland, OH) Sr. Market Anal., Resrch. Mgr., Penton/IPC Publshg. Co., 1974–; Asst. Ed., *Gvt. Product News,* 1974–76; Grammatical Ed., Un. Gospel Press, 1973–74. **Educ.:** Cleveland State Univ., 1968–73, BA (Comm., Bus.); Kent State Univ., 1976–79, MLS (Bus., Ref.). **Orgs.:** SLA. ALA. Frnds. of Cleveland Pub. Lib. Amer. Fed. of TV and Radio Artists. **Pubns.:** "Sources of Information for Selling to Federal Government," *Spec. Libs.* (Ap. 1978); "Sources of Information for the Business Press Editor at the Dept. of Commerce," *Amer. Socty. of Bus. Press Ed. Notebook* (M. 1976); "Taking Stock of Two Business Services," *Ref. Srvs. Review* (Je. 1980); "Penton/IPC Library Profile," *Pubn. Div. Nsltr.* (Ap. 1980); "Selling to the Military Market with Information Sources," *Matl. Handling Distribution* (Ag. 1981). **Activities:** 12; 20, 39, 41; 51, 59, 67 **Addr.:** 10017 Lake Ave. #206, Cleveland OH 44102.

Keaveney, Sydney Starr (N. 12, 1939, Grand Rapids, MI) Prof. Art & Archit. Dept., Pratt Inst. Lib., 1966–; Libn., Fine Arts Dept., Boston Pub. Lib., 1962–66. **Educ.:** Wellesley Coll., 1957–61, BA (Art Hist.); Simmons Coll., 1962–64, MS (LS); Rutgers Univ., 1977–, PhD in progress (LS). **Orgs.:** SLA: Pres., NY Chap. (1973–74). ARLIS/NA: Ch., NY Chap. (1977). **Pubns.:** *American Painting: A Guide to Information Sources* (1974); Series Ed., "Art and Architecture Information Guides" (1972–). **Activities:** 1; 15, 17, 39; 55, 65 **Addr.:** Art and Architecture Dept., Pratt Institute Library, Brooklyn, NY 11205.

Kebabian, Paul Blakeslee (Jy. 24, 1917, Watch Hill, RI) Dir., Univ. of VT Libs., 1966–; Assoc. Dir., Assoc. Prof., Univ. of FL, Gainesville, Lib., 1963–66; Chief Cat., First Asst., Prep. Div., NY Pub. Lib., 1951–63; Ford Fndn. Prog. Spec., Lib. Dev., Univ. of Baghdad, 1961–62 Asst. to Chief, Prep. Div., NY Pub. Lib., 1948–51. **Educ.:** Yale Univ. 1934–38, AB, (Econ.); Columbia Univ., 1947–48, BS (LS). **Orgs.:** ALA: ACRL; RTSD. New Eng. Lib. Info. Ntwk.: Exec. Com. (1969–73), Fin. Com. (1978–). New Eng. Lib. Assn., various of cs. Early Amer. Indus. Assn.: Dir. (1971–), Pres., 1973–76). **Pubns.:** *American Woodworking Tools* (1978); jt.-ed., *Tools and Technologies; America's Wooden Age* (1979); various articles in libnshp. **Activities:** 1; 17, 46 **Addr.:** 11 Scotsdale Rd., South Burlington, VT 05401.

Keck, Bruce Leroy (D. 29, 1937, Minneapolis, MI) Libn., Head of Seattle Ctr., Lib. and Info. Srvs., Env. Sci. Info. Ctr., Natl. Oceanic and Atmospheric Admin., 1980–, Info. Sci. Intern, Env. Resrch. Labs., 1979, Opers. Ofcr., Ship Rainier, 1973–75, Projs. Ofcr., Ofc. of Marine Srvys. and Maps, 1971–73, Oceanographic Ofcr. Ship Fairweather, 1969–71. **Educ.:** Univ. of IL, 1958–60, BS (Geol.); Univ. of RI, 1965–69, MS (Oceanography); Univ. of WA, 1978–79, MLibr. **Orgs.:** ALA. ASIS. SLA. Amer. Chemical Socty. AAAS. Amer. Geophys. Un. Amer. Socty. of Limnology and Oceanography. **Pubns.:** "An Investigation of Recall in the ABI/Inform Data Base When Selecting by Journal," *Online Review* (1981); Jt. auth., Jt. producer, "Tidal Currents and Sedimentation in Oak Bay, Washington" motion pic. (1976). **Activities:** 4, 12; 17, 39; 64, 65, 91 **Addr.:** NOAA, EDIS, ESIC, LISD Seattle Center, Tower Bldg., 7600 Sand Point Way, N.E., Seattle, WA 98115.

Keck, Elizabeth Thatcher (My. 21, 1932, Orange, NJ) Lib. Media Spec., Chestnut Hill Mid. Sch., 1980–; TV Instr., Liverpool HS, 1977–80; Art, Msc. Libn., Onondaga Cnty. Pub. Lib., 1977. **Educ.:** Wells Coll., 1949–53, AB (Bio.); Syracuse Univ., 1973–76, MS (TV), MLS. **Orgs.:** ALA. NYLA. Ctrl. NY Media Specs. Libns. Unlimited. New Env. Assn. N. Amer. Bluebird Socty. **Honors:** Beta Phi Mu. **Activities:** 10; 21, 31, 36 **Addr.:** 113 Pine Ridge Rd., Fayetteville, NY 13066.

Keck, Jack A. (Mr. 18, 1934, Alvordton, OH) Dir., Reg. Educ. Media Ctr., 1971–; Dir., Pentaco Instr. Media Ctr., 1967–71; Coord., Campus Srv., MI State Univ. Media Ctr., 1965–67; Dist. Mgr., Ency. Brit. Films, 1961–65. **Educ.:** MI State Univ., 1957–61, BA (Soc. Std.), 1961–63, MA (Ed. Media). **Orgs.:** MI Inter. Media Assn.: Pres. (1972–73). Nat. Assn. of Reg. Media Ctrs.: Pres. (1977–78). Assn. of Educ. Comm. and Tech.: Reg. Media Ctr. Del. (1978–79). Inland Lakes Sch. Bd.: VP (1978–80). Elem./Sec. Educ. Act: Adv. Cncl. to MI Dept. of Educ. (1979–81). **Pubns.:** "The REMC Concept-How It Came About," *Media Spec.* (1979). **Activities:** 12; 17; 63 **Addr.:** Regional Educational Media Center #3, 6065 Learning Ln., Indian River, MI 49749.

Keddle, David G. (Ja. 27, 1951, Howell, MI) Dir., Med. Lib., Ingham Med. Ctr., Lansing, MI, 1973–. **Educ.:** Lansing Comnty. Coll., 1969–72, Lib. Sci.; Cent. MI Univ., 1979–. **Orgs.:** Mid-MI Hlth. Sci. LA: Ch. and Former of group (1974–79). MI Hlth. Sci. LA: AdHoc Ch. (1976–77); Exec. Brd. (1977–80). Lansing Area LA: Pres. (1979–80). Part. Lib. Adv. Com. MI State Univ. Aff. Hosp. Ch. (1979–83). Livingston Cnty. Rep. Com.: Secy (1974–78). Holt Jaycees: Board of Dir. (1979). **Activities:** 12; 17; 80 **Addr.:** Ingham Medical Center John W. Chi Memorial Medical Library, 401 West Greenlawn Ave., Lansing, MI 48909.

Keefe, Rev. Ambrose (John Francis) (F. 2, 1937, Quincy, MA) Organist/Libn., Belmont Abbey Monastery, 1981–; Catlgr., Glastonbury Abbey, 1980; Libn., Benedictine HS, 1973–79, 1969–72; Ref. Libn., Belmont Abbey Coll., 1972–73, 1964–69; **Educ.:** Boston Coll., 1954–58, BS (Hist.); Belmont Abbey Semy., 1960–64, STB; Univ. of NC, 1963–66, MSLS. **Orgs.:** ALA. Cath. LA. U.S. Cath. Hist. Socty. Church Msc. Assn. of Amer. **Honors:** Civitan, Outstan. Srv. Awd., 1979. **Activities:** 1, 10; 20, 39; 90 **Addr.:** Belmont Abbey, Belmont, NC 28012.

Keefe, Margaret Johnson (D. 10, 1941, New Britain, CT) Coord. of Pub. Srvs., Univ. of RI, 1979–; Head, Ref., 1968–79; Asst. Libn., Ref., 1964–68. **Educ.:** Albertus Magnus Coll., 1959–63, BA (Eng.), Rutgers Univ., 1963–64, MLS. **Orgs.:** ALA: ACRL. RI LA. Amer. Socty. for Engin. Educ.: Lib. Div., Anl. Prog. (Ch., 1976). **Activities:** 1, 9; 17, 31, 39; 50, 55, 75 **Addr.:** P. O. Box 283, Kingston, RI 02881.

Keefer, Alice Carolyn (Je. 19, 1947, Pittsburgh, PA) Chief, Indexing and Class., Org. of Amer. States, 1980–; Indxr., 1977–79; Ed., Lib. of Congs., 1976–77. **Educ.:** PA State Univ., 1965–69, BA (Span., Latin Amer. Std.), 1969–76, MA (Span.), 1974–76, MS (LS). **Orgs.:** SALALM. DC LA. Assn. Intl. Libns. Interamer. Cncl. **Pubns.:** *Organization of America States: Document Organization and Control* (1980); *OAS Activities in the Caribbean* (1979). **Activities:** 12; 29, 30, 33; 54, 56, 62 **Addr.:** 203 6th St S.E., Washington, DC 20003.

Keegan, Bruce J. (Ja. 12, 1942, Rockford, IL) Head Libn., Littleton HS, 1971–; Tchr., Euclid Jr. High, 1967–71; Tchr., Kamehameha Schs., 1966–67; Tchr., Rockford Pub. Schs., 1964–65. **Educ.:** Carthage Coll., 1960–64, BA (Eng.); Univ. of CO, 1966–69, MA (Eng. Lit.); Univ. of Denver, 1969–71, MA (LS). **Orgs.:** ALA. AECT. **Activities:** 10; 17, 39, 48 **Addr.:** Littleton High School Library, 199 E. Littleton Blvd., Littleton, CO 80121.

Keegan, Helen O. (O. 31, 1918, Hillside, NJ) Coord., Educ. Media, Duval Cnty. Sch. Bd., 1971–, Head Libn., Wolfson Sr. HS, 1965–71; Head Libn., Robert E. Lee Sr. HS, 1961–65. **Educ.:** Montclair State Coll., 1973–41, BA; Univ. of FL, 1964, MEd. **Orgs.:** Duval Cnty. LA: Pres. (1971–73); Treas., 1969–70. ALA. AECT. Natl. Film Mkt.: Bd. of Dir. (1978–80). **Activities:** 10; 17, 32 **Addr.:** 31 Warren St., Jacksonville, FL 32206.

Keehn, Pauline Alice (Ag. 9, 1934, Pottsville, PA) Assoc. Libn., Cat. Dept., Univ. of CA, Davis, 1970–; Biblgphr., Amer. Meteorological Socty., 1963–68. **Educ.:** George Washington Univ., 1965, BA (Russ.); Univ. of HI, 1968–69, MLS. **Orgs.:** ALA: LITA. NLA: CA Chap. CA LA. Amer. Assn. for the Advnc. of Slavic Std. Survival Intl., London. **Pubns.:** *The effect of epidemic diseases on the natives of North America; an annotated bibliography* (1978); *Bibliography on marine atlases* (1968); *Bibliography on the oceanography of the Tropical Atlantic* (1967); other bibls., transls. **Activities:** 1, 12; 20, 30, 46; 55, 62, 91 **Addr.:** P. O. Box 803, Davis, CA 95616.

Keeler, Anne G. (D. 12, 1936, New York City, NY) Head, Ext. Div., Orlando Pub. Lib., 1972–, Head Bus., Sci. and Tech. Dept., Orlando Pub. Lib., 1970–72, Osceola Cnty. Libn., Orlando Pub. Lib., 1968–70, Ref. Dept., Orlando Pub. Lib., 1967. **Educ.:** SUNY, Plattsburgh, 1954–58, BS (Elem. Educ.); FL State Univ., 1967–68, MS (LS); Cert. Univ. of MD, 1977, (Lib. Admin. Dev. Prog.). **Orgs.:** ALA. (1974–75). Southeast LA: Adult Srvs. Prog. Com. (1976–78). FL LA: RASD/Nom. Com. (1974–75); ILL Caucus (Vice-Ch., 1974–75); Outrch. Ch. (1974); Legis. and Plng. (Ch., 1978–79); Secty. (1975–76). The Greenhouse of Ctrl. FL, Inc. Secty. (1973–74). Women's Exec. Cncl.: Vice-Ch. (1974–76); Ch. (1976–78); Orlando Ctrl. Bus. Dist., Inc.: Bd. of Dirs. (1976–77); Transp. Com. (1974–76); Ch. (1975–76); Awd. Com. (1976–77). Frnds. of Channel 24 (PBS). **Honors:** Women's Exec. Com. of Orlando Ctrl. Bus. Dist., Downtown Orlando's Outstan. Woman, 1974; Beta Phi Mu, 1968; Kappa Delta Pi, 1956. **Activities:** 9; 17, 25, 27; 78, 91 **Addr.:** P.O. Box 8154, Orlando, FL 32856.

Keeley, Barbara P. (F. 4, 1934, Chicago, IL) Assoc. Prof., Oakton Cmnty. Coll., 1973–; Asst. Libn., Borg-Warner Resrch., 1972–73. **Educ.:** Mundelein Coll., 1952–56, BA (Span.); Rosary Coll., 1972–72, MALS; Univ. of WI, 1957–59, MA (Span.). **Orgs.:** ALA. IL OCLC Users' Grp.: Secy. (1978–79). **Activities:** 1; 20, 29, 46 **Addr.:** Learning Resource Center, Oakton Community College, 1600 E. Golf Rd., Des Plaines, IL 60016.

Keenan-Terenzio, Alice A. (Ag. 23, 1927, Providence, RI) Lib./Media Prog. Coord., N. Haven (CT) Pub. Schs., 1976–; Lectr. (LS), South. CT State Coll., 1975–; Lib. Media Tchr., North Haven Jr. HS, 1960–80; Libn., Tchr., Bassett Jr. HS, 1956–60; Tchr., Fair Haven Jr. HS, 1953–55. **Educ.:** Albertus Magnus Coll., 1945–49, BA (Bio., Eng.); South. CT State Coll., 1955–57, MS (LS), 1974–77, Cert. (LS). **Orgs.:** CT Sch. Lib. Assn.: Pres. (1969–70), Exec. Bd. (1964–73). CT Educ. Media Assn.: Conv. Plng. Com. (1976, 1977), Skills Com. (1978–80).

PROFESSIONAL ACTIVITIES: Institutions: 1. Acad. lib.; 2. Arch.; 3. Assn.; 4. Fed./Gvt. lib.; 5. Inst. lib.; 6. Mfr./Suppl.; 7. Milit. lib.; 8. Musm.; 9. Pub. lib.; 10. Sch. lib.; 11. Sch. of lib. sci.; 12. Spec. lib.; 13. State lib.; 14. (other). **Functions/Activities:** 15. Acq./Col. dev.; 16. Adult srvs.; 17. Admin.; 18. Apprais.; 19. Archit./Bldgs.; 20. Cat./Class.; 21. Chld. srvs.; 22. Circ.; 23. Cons./Pres.; 24. Consult.; 25. Cont. ed.; 26. Educ. lib. sci.; 27. Ext. srvs.; 28. Fund/Grants; 29. Gvt. pubs.; 30. Indx./Abs.; 31. Instr. lib. use; 32. Media srvs.; 33. Micro.; 34. Netwks./Coop.; 35. Persnl.; 36. PR; 37. Publshg.; 38. Recs. mgt.; 39. Ref. srvs.; 40. Repro.; 41. Resrch.; 42. Review.; 43. Secur.; 44. Serials; 45. Spec. col.; 46. Tech. srvs.; 47. Trustees/Bds.; 48. YA srvs.; 49. (other).

ALA: Com. on Lib. Educ.; AASL. N. Haven Educ. Assn. CT Educ. Assn. Natl. Educ. Assn. Admin. and Supvsn. Assn. Other orgs. **Activities:** 10, 11; 17, 26, 32; 63 **Addr.:** 68 Russell St., Hamden, CT 06517.

Keene, Janis C. (S. 26, 1938, St. Joseph, MO) Asst. Dir., Tulsa City-Cnty. Lib., 1976–, Bus. Mgr., 1969–76. **Educ.:** Univ. of Tulsa, 1969, BS (Bus.). **Orgs.:** OK LA: Treas. (1977–79). ALA: Prog. Eval. and Support Com. (1980–81); LAMA, Stats. Coord. Com. (1977–81)/Stats. Sect., Com. on Dev., Org., Plng., Prog. (Ch., 1979–81). Tulsa Area United Way. **Honors:** Beta Gamma Sigma. **Activities:** 9; 17, 25, 35 **Addr.:** Tulsa City-County Library, 400 Civic Center, Tulsa, OK 74103.

Kees, Stephen J. (Mr. 25, 1919, London, England) Chief Libn., Niagara Coll. of Appld. Arts and Tech., 1967–; Resrch. Libn., The ON Paper Co. Ltd., 1958–67; Deputy Libn., *The Fncl. Times,* London, Eng., 1953–57; Libn., Brit. Empl. Confederation, 1948–53. **Educ.:** Univ. of London, Eng., Sch. of Libnshp., 1937–39, 1946–1947, Lib. Assn. Flwshp. **Orgs.:** SLA: Upstate NY Chap. (Pres., 1964–65); Sci.-Tech. Div. (Ch., 1979–80). ALA: ACRL/West. NY/ON Chap., Secy. (1977–78), Dir. (1980–81). **Activities:** 1; 17; 57, 70, 91 **Addr.:** Learning Resource Centre, Niagara College, Box 1005, Woodlawn Rd., Welland, ON L3B 5S2 Canada.

Keever, Ellen Hull (Ag. 4, 1930, Marion, VA) Head, Readers' Srvs., Coll. of Wooster, 1975–; Ref. Libn., Univ. of AL, 1970–75. **Educ.:** Agnes Scott Coll., 1947–51, BA Summa Cum Laude (Eng.); Univ. of PA, 1952–54, MA (Eng.); Univ. of AL, 1970, MLS. Princeton Theo. Semy., 1954–55 (Theo.). **Orgs.:** ALA. OH LA. Acad. Lib. Assn. of OH. **Honors:** Phi Beta Kappa. **Pubns.:** "Reassessment of the Undergraduate Library," *Southeast. Libn.* (Spr. 1973); "Integrated Library Instruction on the University Campus," *Jnl. of Acad. Libnshp.* (S. 1976). **Activities:** 1; 15, 17, 39 **Addr.:** 450 E. Bowman, Wooster, OH 44691.

Kehoe, Patrick E. (N. 12, 1941, Olympia, WA) Law Libn., Amer. Univ., 1973–; Asst. Law Libn., Yale Law Sch., 1971–73; Asst. Law Libn., Univ. of Houston, 1968–71; Law Ref. Libn., Univ. of WA, 1966–68. **Educ.:** Seattle Univ., 1959–63, BCS (Finance); Univ. of WA, 1963–66, J.D., 1966–68, ML (LS). **Orgs.:** AALL: Com. on Law Lib. Jnl. (1977–). Law Libns. Socty. of Washington DC: Pres. (1979–81). WA State Bar Assn. **Pubns.:** *Cooperatives & Condominiums,* (1974); "Microforms in the Law Library," *Micros. Rev.* (1978). **Activities:** 1, 12; 17; 77 **Addr.:** Washington College of Law Library, American University, Massachusetts & Nebraska Aves., N.W., Washington, DC 20016.

Kelenson, Dora (Ja. 5, 1922, Brooklyn, NY) Libn., AFL-CIO Lib., 1974–; Ref. Libn., Prince Georges Cnty. Meml. Lib., 1969–74. **Educ.:** Coll. of the City of New York, 1938–42, BBA (Acct.); Univ. of MD, 1967–69, MLS. **Orgs.:** SLA. ALA. **Honors:** Beta Phi Mu. **Activities:** 12; 15, 17, 39; 95-Indus. rel. **Addr.:** AFL-CIO Library, 815 16 St. N.W., Washington, DC 20006.

Kell, Mary Kate (Mr. 15, 1950, Madison, WI) Asst. Law Libn., CONOCO, Inc., Law Lib., 1981–; Hd., Ref. Dept., Univ. of Houston, 1980–81; Sr. Ref. Libn., 1979–; Dir., Tuskegee Pub. Lib., 1975–76; Libn., Oak Hills Sch., 1973–74. **Educ.:** Trinity Univ., 1968–72, BA (Hist.); Univ. of TX, 1972–73, MLS, 1976–78, JD. **Orgs.:** AALL. Southwestern Assn. of Law Libs.: Pub. Com. (Ch., 1979–). ABA. **Pubns.:** *Location Guide to the Manuscripts of Supreme Court Justices* (1978). Review. "Selected Bibliography on Space Law," *Houston Jrnl. of Intl. Law* (Win. 1980). **Activities:** 1, 12; 31, 33, 39; 56, 77, 78 **Addr.:** 12418 North Garden, Houston, TX 77071.

Keller, Dean H. (My. 20, 1933, Ashtabula, OH) Head, Spec. Cols., Kent State Univ. Lib., 1979–, Cur., Spec. Cols., 1969–79, Assoc. Libn., 1967–69, Hum. Libn., 1963–66, Asst. Hum. Libn., 1958–63. **Educ.:** Kent State Univ., 1951–55, BA (Eng.) 1957–58, MA (LS). **Orgs.:** ALA: ACRL/Rare Bks. and Mss. Sect. (Exec. Com. 1979–81). Bibl. Socty. of Amer. Bibl. Socty. of the Univ. of VA. Acad. Lib Assn. of OH. Other orgs. The Rowfant Club. **Honors:** Crawford Bindery, Akron, OH, Jay Crawford Awd., 1958. Beta Phi Mu. **Pubns.:** *An Index to Plays in Periodicals* (1979); "Cooperation: The Historical Society and the Local Library," *Grand River* (Spr. 1979); "Reflections on Library Exhibits," *Undaunted Bookman* (Win. 1979); "Albion W. Tourgee, 1838–1905," *First Printings of American Authors* (1977); reviews, other articles. **Activities:** 1; 45; 55, 57 **Addr.:** Kent State University Library, Kent, OH 44242.

Keller, Michael A. (Ap. 5, 1945, Sterling, CO) Head, Msc. Lib., Univ. of CA, Berkeley, 1981–; Msc. Libn./Sr. Lectr., Cornell Univ., 1973–81; Asst. msc. libn., SUNY/Buffalo, 1970–73. **Educ.:** Hamilton Coll., 1963–67, BA (Msc.); SUNY/Buffalo, 1967–70, MA (Msclgy.); SUNY/Geneseo, 1970–71, MLS; SUNY/Buffalo, 1970–, PhD cand. (Msclgy.). **Orgs.:** Msc. LA: Bd of Dir. (1976–78); Ch., Microforms Com. (1973–76). Intl. Assn. of Msc. Libs.: Resrch. Libs. Comsn. (1973–). Amer. Musicological Socty.: Ch., Nom. Com., NYS/ON Chap (1973–76). **Pubns.:** Jt. auth., "Music Literature Indexes in Review," *Notes* (1980); Jt. auth., *An index to composers in Clarence Brenner's Bibliographical list of plays in the French Language, 1700–1789* (1979); articles on Senaillie, Guenin and Dauvergne, *New Groves Dict. of Msc. and Musicians* (1981); "Where does policy come from? a dialogue." *Cornell Univ. Libs. Bltn.* (Ja.-F. 1974); "Music serials in microform and reprint editions," *Notes,* (1973); reviews, oral presentations. **Activities:** 1; 15, 17, 24; 55, 56 **Addr.:** Music Library, Morrison Hall, University of California at Berkeley, Berkeley, CA 94720.

Keller, William Bradford (Je. 11, 1950, New Haven, CT) Head Libn., MD Hist. Socty., 1981–; Sr. Cat. Libn. and Asst. Cur., Cary Col. of Playing Cards, Beinecke Rare Book & Lib., Yale Univ., 1973–. **Educ.:** Yale Univ., 1968–72, BA (European Hist.); Columbia Univ., 1972–73, MS (LS), 1978–81, MA (Art Hist.). **Orgs.:** Bibl. Socty. of Amer. Yale Lib. Assoc. ALA. Natl. Trust for Hist. Prsrvn. The Playing Card Socty. (Britain). Natl. Arts Club. Socty. for Indus. Archlg. **Pubns.:** *A Catalogue of the Cary Collection of Playing Cards* (1981); "Richard Strauss Recording Sessions," *Antique Recs.* (1974). **Activities:** 1; 15, 20, 23, 45; 55, 57 **Addr.:** Maryland Historical Society Library, 201 W. Monument St., Baltimore, MD 21201.

Kelley, Betty H. (IN) Dir., Farmers Branch Pub. Lib., 1976–, Head, Tech. Srvs., 1974–76. **Educ.:** Franklin Coll. of IN, 1948, BA (Eng., Jnlsm.); TX Woman's Univ., 1974, MLS. **Orgs.:** ALA. TX LA. Dallas Cnty. LA: VP (1980–81); Pres. (1981–82). Pub. Lib. Admins. of N. TX: Pres. (1979). Various other orgs. Southwest. Bksellers. Assn: Dir. (1980); Treas. (1981). **Honors** Zeta Tau Alpha. **Pubns.:** "A Low-Cost, Homemade, Fully Automated Circulation and Library Cataloging System That Works," *Lib. Jnl.* (F. 1, 1979). **Activities:** 9; 17; 56, 93 **Addr.:** 212 W. Rio Grande, Garland, TX 75041.

Kelley, Cornelia A. (F. 1, 1942, Melbourne, FL) Acq. Libn., Univ. of VA, 1969–, Pers. Libn., 1966–69, Catlgr., 1966. **Educ.:** Rollins Coll., 1960–64, BA (Hist.); LA State Univ., 1964–66, MS (LS). **Orgs.:** SLA: Publshr. Rel. Com. (1978–81); Jt. SLA-Amer. Assn. of Publshrs. Com. (1979–81); Publshg. Div., Nom. Com. (Ch., 1981–82); VA Chap. (Pres., 1978–79). SELA. VA LA. Cmnty. Chld. Thea.: Pres. (1975–76); Bd. (1971–76). **Activities:** 1; 15, 17, 37; 61 **Addr.:** Alderman Library, University of Virginia, Charlottesville, VA 22901.

Kelley, Elizabeth (Jy. 10, 1946, Bloomington, IL) Dir., Maricopa Cnty. Law Lib., 1981–; Prof., Law Libn., Hamline Univ. Sch. of Law, 1974–81; Asst. Law Libn., Univ. of Akron Sch. of Law, 1973–74; Libn., Ramsey Cnty. Law Lib., 1971–73. **Educ.:** Illinois Wesleyan Univ. 1964–68, BA (Hist.); Univ. of MN, 1968–69, MA (LS); William Mitchell Coll. of Law 1969–73, JD. **Orgs.:** AALL: Mem. Com. (Co-ch., 1979–80). Phoenix Assn. of Law Libs. (1981). Amer. Bar Assn. **Pubns.:** *Legal Research for Practicing Attorneys* (1979); *Legal Research Beyond Tradition* (1981). **Activities:** 1; 77 **Addr.:** Maricopa County Law Library, 2nd Floor Superior Court Bldg., 101 W. Jefferson St., Phoenix, AZ 85003.

Kelley, Gloria A. (Ja. 20, 1931, Brooklyn, NY) Sch. Lib. Media Tchr., John St. Sch., 1956–; Tchr., NY City Sch. Dist., 1952–56. **Educ.:** St. John's Univ., 1948–52, BA (Educ., Eng.), 1956–59, MLS; Brooklyn Coll., 1954–56, Cert. (Educ.). **Orgs.:** Cath. LA: Regina Medal Awds. Com. (1980); Brooklyn-Long Island Chap. (VP-Elect, 1980–82). Long Island Sch. Media Assn.: Bd. of Dirs. (1980–81). Nassau Cnty. Area Cncl. on Sch. Lib. Networking. St. John's Univ. LS Alum.: Pres. (1970–72). Franklin Sq. Tchrs. Assn. **Honors:** St. John's Univ., LS Alum. Assn., Disting. Alum. Awd., 1981; Monroe St. Sch., Tchr. of the Yr. Awd., 1966; Parent-Tchr. Assn., Srv. Awd., 1968. **Pubns.:** Reviews. **Activities:** 10, 11; 21, 26, 34; 55 **Addr.:** John Street School, Franklin Square, NY 11010.

Kelley, Neil (O. 21, 1936, Atlanta, GA) Asst. Libn., Univ. of AR for Med. Sci., 1966–; Asst. in Charge, Grady Hosp. Lib., 1960–64; Tech. Asst., Emory Univ., A. W. Calhoun Med. Lib., 1958–60. **Educ.:** Baylor Univ., 1956–58, BA (Eng.); FL State Univ., 1964–65, MSLS; Emory Univ., 1965, Cert. (Med. Lib. Assoc., Grade 2). **Orgs.:** Med. LA: Com. on Hlth. Sci. Techs. (Ch., 1975). AR LA: Pres. (1980); Ref. Div. (Pres., 1972–73). AR Country Dance Socty. Amer. Socty. for Trng. and Dev.: AR Chap. **Honors:** Sigma Tau Delta; Beta Phi Mu. **Pubns.:** *Human Factors in Library Administration, Syllabus for CE-5* (1980); "The Biomedical Communications Network and Interlibrary Loans in Arkansas," *AR Libs.* (D. 1976); "Provision of Health Care Information: The Arkansas Network of Health Science Libraries," *AR Libs.* (1978). **Activities:** 1, 14-Health Sciences Library; 17, 25; 80 **Addr.:** 31 Hampshire Circle, Little Rock, AR 72112.

Kellman, Amy H. (D. 24, 1938, Pittsburgh, PA) Head, Chld. Dept., Carnegie Lib. of Pittsburgh, 1976–; Visit. Lectr., "Materials for Children," Sch. of Lib. and Info. Sci., 1974–76; Sch. libn. (sub.), Univ. of Pittsburgh, Churchill Area Sch. Dist., 1973–76; Resrch. Asst., Univ. of Pittsburgh, Lrng. Resrch. and Dev. Ctr., 1969–73. **Educ.:** Chatham Coll., 1956–60, BA (Eng., Drama); Univ. of CA, Berkeley, 1961–62, MLS. **Orgs.:** ALA: ALSC/Amer. V Pres. (1980–81), Bk. Eval. Com., Ch., Intl. Rel. Com. Ch., Newbery-Caldecott Com. PA LA. Pittsburgh Dance Cncl.: Bd. of Dirs. (Pres., 1972). **Pubns.:** "Wallflower and Winners: A Shuffle through Children's Dance Books," *Sch. Lib. Jnl* (O. 1973); "For Very Young Dancers: A Quick Step through Recent Books," *Sch. Lib. Jnl.* (D. 1977); "Children's Services," *ALA Yrbk.* (1978, 1979); "Children's Books and the Librarian" in *Celebrating Children's Books* (1981); various reviews in *Tchr. Mag.* **Activities:** 9; 17, 21 **Addr.:** Carnegie Library of Pittsburgh, 4400 Forbes Ave., Pittsburgh, PA 15213.

Kellogg, Patricia Ann (Jl. 16, 1945, Cleveland, OH) Supvsr., Msc. Lib. Srvs. and Prog. Arch., Can. Broadcasting Corp., 1977–; Msc. Libn., CJRT-FM, Ont. Govt. Educ. Radio, 1974–77. **Educ.:** Univ. of Miami, FL, 1963–67, Msc. B, 1967–68, MM Msclgy.; Univ. of Western Ont., 1973, MLS; Univ. of Toronto, 1970–73 (Msclgy.). **Orgs.:** Can. Assn. of Msc. Libns.: Nat. Prog. Ch. (1977–). Msc. LA. Assn. for the Study of Radio and TV Arch., Can. Assn. of Sound Archvsts. **Pubns.:** "Steven Staryk-No Profit in His Own Country," *Performing Arts in Can.* (Win. 1978). Reviews. **Activities:** 2, 12; 15, 17, 23; 55, 85 **Addr.:** Canadian Broadcasting Corp., Box 500 Station "A," Toronto, ON M5W 1E6 Canada.

Kellogg, Rebecca Anne Boone (Mr. 7, 1946, Springfield, OH) Head, Cen. Ref. Dept., Univ. of AZ Lib., 1976–; Asst. Ref. Libn., Princeton Univ., 1970–76. **Educ.:** Earlham College, Case-Western Resrv. Univ., 1964–68, BA (phil. & Hum. rel.); Univ. of NC, Chapel Hill, 1969–70, MLS. **Orgs.:** ALA: RASD, Ad Hoc Com. (1980–); Off. of Lib. Pers. Resrcs., Adv. Com., Subcom. on Equal Employment Oppor. (1977–79). Southwestern LA. AZ State LA: Anl. Conf. Prog. Coord. (1978). **Activities:** 1; 17, 39 **Addr.:** Central Reference Department, Main Library, University of Arizona, Tucson, AZ 85721.

Kelly, Ardie Lee (Ja. 19, 1932, Lynchburg, VA) Libn., The Mariners Musm., 1977–; Libn., Erskine Coll., 1974–77; Univ. of Richmond, 1967–74; Catawba Coll., 1965–67. **Educ.:** Lynchburg Coll., 1953–57, BA (Fr.); Univ. of NC, Chapel Hill, 1958–60, MSLS. **Orgs.:** Southeastern LA: Awards Com. (1978–80); Com., Compendium of Lib. Resrcs. in Southeast (1977–78). SLA. Steamship Hist. Socty. of Amer. **Activities:** 1, 12; 23, 39, 41; 55, 57, 94 **Addr.:** The Mariners Museum, Newport News, VA 23606.

Kelly, Cleo B. (Ja. 20, 1914, Clearwater, NE) Asst. Hum. Libn., Stephen F. Austin State Univ., 1973–, Asst. Ref. Libn., 1971–73, Biblgphr., 1969–71, Acq. Libn., 1966–69; Ch., Tech. Prcs., Lib., KS State Coll., Pittsburg, 1962–66; Catlgr., Lib., KS State Univ., 1960–62; Ref. Libn., SD State Univ., 1957–60; Asst. Libn., Peru State Coll., 1953–57; Tchr., 1937–52. **Educ.:** Wayne (NE) State Coll., 1938–46, BA (Educ. and Hist./Pol. Sci.); Univ. of Denver, 1952–53, MA (LS); Univ. of NE, 1951–52, (Lib. Educ.). **Orgs.:** ALA: RASD; ACRL. Mt.-Plains LA. KS LA: Exec. Cncl., Resrcs. and Tech. Srvs. Sect. Ch. (1964–65). TX LA: Cncl. (1971–72); Dist. 8, Ch. (1972). AAUP. TX Assn. of Coll. Tchrs. Univ. of Denver, Grad. Sch. of Libnshp. Alum. Assn. Univ. Prof. Women: VP (1980). **Activities:** 1; 15, 31, 39; 55, 57 **Addr.:** 315 Blount St., Nacogdoches, TX 75961.

Kelly, Elizabeth Monaco (My. 25, 19–, Chicago, IL) Assoc. Dir., Law Lib., Creighton Univ., 1973–; Libn./Prof., Wilbur Wright Coll., 1946–76; Libn./Instr., Notre Dame HS, 1943–46; Asst. Catlgr., Wright Jr. Coll., 1942–43; Catlgr., Law Lib., DePaul Univ., Sums. 1950–57. **Educ.:** Rosary Coll., 1938–42, MA (Eng.), 1942–44, BALS; DePaul Univ., 1944–47, MEduc.; AALL, 1976, Cert. **Orgs.:** ALA. AALL. MN Assn. of Law Libs. Mid Amer. Assn. of Law Libs. **Honors:** U.S. Dept. of Hlth., Educ. and Welfare, Prof. Grant, 1974; Wilbur Wright Coll., Sbtcl. Leave, 1970, Prof. Std. Leave, 1973–75. **Activities:** 1, 12; 17, 20, 46; 56, 63, 77 **Addr.:** Klutznick Law Library, Creighton University, 2500 California St., Omaha, NE 68178.

Kelly, Joanne W. (Ag. 22, 1934, Chicago, IL) Libn., Thomas Paine Elem. Sch., 1967. **Educ.:** Univ. of IL, 1964–67, BS (Elem. Educ.), 1968–70, MSLS, 1978–80, CAS (LS). **Orgs.:** ALA. IL LA. IL Assn. of Media in Educ.: Lib. Bk. Sel. Srv. (Rep., 1973–79). Univ. of IL LS Alum. Adv. Bd. (1976–80). **Honors:** Kappa Delta Pi; Beta Phi Mu; *Instr. Mag.,* Tchr. Plus, 1978. **Activities:** 10; 21, 24, 32; 63, 89 **Addr.:** 2110 Galen Dr., Champaign, IL 61820.

Kelly, Kay Med. Libn. and Coord. of Cont. Med. Educ., Burns Clinic Med. Ctr., Northern MI Hosp., 1971–; Libn., Bio-Med. Lib., Univ. of MN, 1959–71, Instr., Pub. Health and Nurse Stud. Hlth. Srvcs., 1956–59; Nurse, New Haven Visiting Nurse Assn., 1954–56. **Educ.:** Univ. of NE, 1948–53, BScN (Nursing); Univ. of MN, 1956–61 (No Thesis) (Public Hlth/Lib Sci.). **Orgs.:** SLA. Med. LA: Ed. Consultant for Bltn. (1976–78). MI Hlth. Sci. Lib. Assn.: Exec. Bd (1977–). MI State Univ.: Part. Lib. Adv. Cncl. (1978). **Pubns.:** Video Tape, "Private & Public Relations in the Hospital Libraries" (1976). **Activities:** 12; 17, 25, 39; 80 **Addr.:** The Dean C. Burns Health Sciences Library for Burns Clinic Medical Center P.C., Northern Michigan Hospitals Inc., Petoskey, MI 49770.

Kelly, Kay L. (Ja. 26, 1950, Horton, KS) Libn./Docum. Coord., Sunbelt Mining Co., 1979–; Netwk. Coord., Mid-MO Lib. Netwk., 1976–78; Branch Libn., Boonslick Reg. Lib., 1976, Bkmobile. Libn., 1973–75. **Educ.:** KS State Univ., 1968–71, BA (Eng., Sp.); Univ. of MO, 1972–73, MA (LS). **Orgs.:** SLA: Mem. Ch. (1980–81); Bltn. Ed. (1981–82). NM LA. **Pubns.:** "Mid-Missouri Library Network," *Show-Me Libs.* (Ag. 1976). **Ac-**

Special Subjects/Services: 50. Adult educ.; 51. Advert./Mktg.; 52. Aerosp.; 53. Agric.; 54. Area std.; 55. Arts/Hum.; 56. Autom.; 57. Bibl./Prtg.; 58. Bio. sci.; 59. Bus./Fin.; 60. Chem.; 61. Copyrt.; 62. Documtn.; 63. Educ.; 64. Engin.; 65. Env.; 66. Eth. grps.; 67. Film; 68. Food/Nutr.; 69. Geneal.; 70. Geo.; 71. Geol.; 72. Handcpd.; 73. Hist.; 74. Int. frdm.; 75. Info. sci.; 76. Insr.; 77. Law; 78. Legis.; 79. Math./Comp. sci.; 80. Med.; 81. Metals; 82. Nat. resrcs.; 83. Newsp.; 84. Nuc. sci.; 85. Oral hist.; 86. Petr./Energy; 87. Pharm.; 88. Phys./Astr./Math.; 89. Readg.; 90. Relig.; 91. Sci./Tech.; 92. Soc. sci.; 93. Telecom.; 94. Transp.; 95. (other).

tivities: 9, 12; 27, 34, 38; 65, 82 **Addr.:** 3312 Black Hills Rd., N.E., Albuquerque, NM 87111.

Kelly, Liam M. (Je. 7, 1935, Letterkenny, Co. Donegal, Ireland) Asst. Dir., Clerk of Corp., Boston Pub. Lib., 1972–; Asst. Dir., NELINET, 1971; Asst. to Pres., Inforonics, 1969–70; Cat., Harvard Univ., 1967–69. **Educ.:** St. Columban's Coll., Ireland, 1953–57, BA (Phil.); Boston Coll., 1963–65, BA (Eng.); Cath. Univ., 1966–67, MSLS. **Orgs.:** ASIS: New Eng. Chap. (Pres., 1973–74). New Eng. LA: Exec. Com., Finance Com. (1975–77). New Eng. Tech. Srvs. Libns.: Pres. (1976–77). Wellesley Pub. Lib.: Bd. of Trustees. Eire Socty. of Boston: VP (1976–77). MA Hist. Socty. **Honors:** Beta Phi Mu. **Pubns.:** "MARC II Based System: Studies on the Air Force Cambridge Research Library Bibliographic Processing System" (1970); "A Challenge to Leadership," *MA Libs.* (1973). **Addr.:** 20 Dean Rd., Wellesley, MA 02181.

Kelly, Richard John (S. 30, 1938, Minneapolis, MN) Ref., Bibl., Univ. of MN, 1977–; Ref. Libn., Univ. of MN, 1968–76. **Educ.:** Univ. of MN, 1960–66, BA (Eng.), 1966–68, MA (LS). **Orgs.:** ALA. MN Ctr. for Adv. Stds. in Lang., Style, and Lit. Theory. **Pubns.:** *John Berryman: A Checklist* (1972); "Letters to a Poet" in *Once in a Sycamore* (1977); "The Berryman Manuscripts," *John Berryman Stds.* (Win. 1976). "Scholarship and Poetry," *John Berryman Stds.* (Sum. 1976). Reviews. **Activities:** 1; 15, 31, 39; 55 **Addr.:** Wilson Library, University of Minnesota, Minneapolis, MN 55455.

Kelly, Robert Q. (Ap. 3, 1922, Chicago, IL) Lib. Dir., Creighton Univ. Law Sch., 1973–; Lib. Dir., DePaul Univ. Coll. of Law, 1950–73. **Educ.:** St. Mary of the Lake Univ., 1940–43, BA (Phil.); Rosary Coll., 1948–50, MA (LS); DePaul Univ., 1950–56, JD. **Orgs.:** AALL. Mid-Amer. Assn. of Law Libs.: Pres. (1978–80); Treas. (1964–66). Bibl. Socty. of Amer. Caxton Club of Chicago. **Pubns.:** "Basic Guide to Medicolegal Reference Sources," *Ref. Srvs. Review* (Jl. 1979). **Activities:** 1; 24; 77 **Addr.:** Ahmanson Law Center, 2500 California, Omaha, NE 68178.

Kelly, Virginia Marie (N. 24, 1953, Boston, MA) Sr. Rsrch. Anal., FIND/SVP, 1981–; Info. Spec., 1979–, Weekend Supvsr., Cornell Univ. Med. Lib., 1979; Libn., Tufts Univ. Med. and Dental Lib., 1973–78. **Educ.:** Northeast. Univ., 1972–74, (Psy.); Univ. of MA, Boston, 1975–77, BA Summa Cum Laude (Psy.); Columbia Univ., 1978–79, MS (LS). **Orgs.:** Med. LA. NY-NJ Reg. Med. LA: Pubcty. Com. (1979–80). Assoc. Info. Mgrs. YMCA. **Activities:** 1, 12; 17, 39, 41; 75, 80, 92 **Addr.:** FIND/SVP, 500 Fifth Ave., NY, NY 10110.

Kelm, Carol Raney (Ag. 28, 1929, Spokane, WA) Hist. Socty. of Oak Park/River Forest, 1978–; RTSD, Div. Exec. Sec., ALA, 1969–77; Cat. Dept., Chief, Smithsonian Inst. Libs., 1966–69; Asst. Cat. Libn., Joint Bank/Fund Lib., 1965–66; Subj. Catlgr.; Ser. Div. Head, Yale Univ. Lib., 1956–65; Catlgr., Univ. of CA, Davis Lib., 1953–56. **Educ.:** Reed Coll., 1947–48; WA State Univ., Pullman, 1949–52, BA (Hist.); Univ. of CA, Berkeley, 1952–53, BLS. **Orgs.:** ALA: RTSD (VP, 1968–69); Serials Sect. (Ch., 1964–65). Church and Synagogue LA. **Honors:** Phi Beta Kappa, 1952; Phi Kappa Phi, 1952; Phi Alpha Theta, 1952. **Activities:** 1; 20, 30, 46 **Addr.:** 432 N. Elmwood, Oak Park, IL 60302.

Kelton, Jon Delvey (Ag. 10, 1934, Norwood, MA) Assoc. Dir., Tech. Srvcs., Greene Cnty. Dist. Lib., 1981–; Head, Tech. Srvcs., 1979–81; Dir., Wilmington Pub. Lib., 1966–78; Head, Madisonville Br., Pub. Lib. of Cincinnati, 1963–65, Libn. I, 1959–62. **Educ.:** Hamilton Coll., 1952–56, AB (Hist.); Rutgers Univ., 1957–59, MLS. **Orgs.:** ALA: PLA (Pub. Com., 1971–72). OH LA: Stan. Com. (1977–78). **Activities:** 9; 17, 20, 39 **Addr.:** 205 1/2 N. South St., Wilmington, OH 45177.

Kelver, Ann Elkins (S. 6, 1915, Delaware City, DE) Lib. Dir., Arapahoe Reg. Lib. Dist., 1966–; Libn., Jimtown (IN) HS, 1964–65; Cost Acct., Miles Labs. (IN), 1944–62. **Educ.:** Goshen Coll., 1962–64, BS (Hist.); Univ. of Denver, 1965–66, MA, (Sec. Educ.), 1967–69, MA (LS). **Orgs.:** ALA. CO LA: Educ. Com. (1975–). Mt. Plains LA. AAUW. **Honors:** Friends of Denver Pub. Lib., Nell I. Scott Award, 1978. **Pubns.:** "Public School/Public Library Cooperation In Colorado," *CO Libs.* (S. 1975); "Sharing for Sheridan," *CO Libs.* (Mr. 1978). **Activities:** 9; 17 **Addr.:** 2305 E. Arapahoe Rd., Littleton, CO 80122.

Kemble, Harold E., Jr. (My. 19, 1940, Plainfield, NE) Cur. of Mss., RI Hist. Socty., 1979–, Bus. Archvst., 1976–79; AV Archvst., Natl. Arch. and Records Srv., Ofc. of Pres. Libs., 1970–73; Archvst., Lyndon B. Johnson Pres. Lib., 1969–70. **Educ.:** Univ. of NE, 1970, BA (Hist.); Univ. of TX, 1969–70; Cert., staff intern prog. Natl. Arch. and Records Srv., 1967–69. **Orgs.:** SAA. RI Hist. Recs. Adv. Bd., 1979–. New England Archvsts.: Bd. of Dirs. (1978–81). Northeast Docums. Cons. Ctr.: Adv. Com. (1981–). Narragansett Hist. Socty.: Bd. of Dir. (1978–79). **Activities:** 2, 4; 15, 20, 23; 55, 59, 62 **Addr.:** Rhode Island Historical Society Library, 121 Hope St., Providence, RI 02906.

Kemp, Barbara E. (Je. 6, 1944, Toledo, OH) Asst. Head, Undergrad. Lib., Univ. of MI, 1972–, Lectr., LS, Ext. Srv., 1976–, Head of Rsvs., Undergrad. Lib., 1970–72, Rsvs. Acq. Libn., Undergrad. Lib., 1968–70. **Educ.:** Northwestern Univ., 1962–66, BA (Fr.); Univ. of MI, 1968, AMLS. **Orgs.:** ALA: ACRL; RASD/Mach. Assisted Ref. Sect.; LITA. AALS. MI Data Base Users Grp.: Ch., State Strg. Com. (1979–). AAUP. **Activities:** 1; 17, 31, 39; 67, 95-Reference materials. **Addr.:** Undergraduate Library, The University of Michigan, Ann Arbor, MI 48109.

Kemp, Betty Ruth (My. 5, 1930, Tishomingo, OK) Dir., Lee Itawamba Lib. Syst., 1975–; Dir., Cherokee Reg. Lib., 1965–74; Branch Head, Dallas Pub. Lib., 1955–64; ExtraMural Loan Libn., Univ. of TX, 1952–55. **Educ.:** Univ. of OK, 1948–52, BALS; FL State Univ., 1964–65, MS (LS). **Orgs.:** ALA: PLA, Allie Beth Martin Awd. Com. (1980). MS LA: Pub. Lib. Sect. (Secy., 1977); Educ. Com. (Ch., 1978). SELA. GA LA. Various other orgs. Leag. of Women Voters. AAUW. MS Hist. Assn. Un. Meth. Women: N. MS Conf. (Secy., 1978–80). **Honors:** Beta Phi Mu. **Activities:** 9; 16, 17, 35; 69 **Addr.:** 2112 President, Tupelo, MS 38801.

Kemp, Charles H. (Ja. 27, 1939, Talihina, OK) Dir., Resrc. Ctr. OR Inst. of Tech., 1980–; Head Libn., Pacific Univ., 1972–79, Readers Srvs. Libn., 1967–72; Docum. Libn., NM State Univ., 1966–67; Army Post Libn., Korea, 1965–66. **Educ.:** Univ. of OK, 1960–64, BA (Span.), 1964–65, MLS; Univ. of WA, 1978– (Educ.). **Orgs.:** ALA. AECT. OR LA. Pac. Northwest LA. Toastmasters Intl. WA Cnty. Coop. Lib. Srvs. AAUP. Forest Grove Lib. Cmsn. **Activities:** 1; 17, 28, 32 **Addr.:** Learning Resources Center, Oregon Institute of Technology, Klamath Falls, OR 97601.

Kemp, Edward C. (O. 3, 1929, Boston, MA) Acq., Spec. Col., Univ. of OR, 1957–, Soc. Sci. librn., 1956–57, Ref. Librn., 1955–56. **Educ.:** Harvard Univ., 1947–51, AB (Fr.); Univ. of CA, Berkeley, 1951–55, MLS (Fr. Librn., Span.); Amer. Univ., Natl. Arch., 1963, Arch. Cert. **Orgs.:** ALA. SAA. Pac. Northwest LA. OR LA. West. Writers of Amer. Sheet Msc. Socty. of Amer. **Pubns.:** "Manuscript and art collections: organization, care and use," *Phaedrus* (Fall 1976); jt. auth., "James Henry Daugherty," *Imprint: OR* (Fall 1975); jt. auth., "Berta and Elmer Hader of Willow Hill," *Imprint: OR* (Spr.–Fall 1977). **Activities:** 1, 2; 15, 45, 46; 55, 57 **Addr.:** 3237 Onyx Pl., Eugene, OR 97405.

Kemp, Elaine A. (D. 14, 1940, Cottage Grove, OR) Head Cat. Libn., Univ. of OR Lib., 1976–, Cat. Libn., 1971–76. **Educ.:** Univ. of OR, 1959–62, BA (Hist.), 1968–70, MLS. **Orgs.:** ALA: ACRL; RTSD; LITA. OR LA: Nsltr. Ed., Exec. Bd. (1974–78). Pac. Northwest LA: Coll. Sect. (1971–), Tech. Srvs. Sect. (1971–). ASIS. **Honors:** Pi Lambda Theta, 1962. **Pubns.:** Jt. auth., "Berta and Elmer Hader Working Together," *Imprint: OR* (Spr.–Fall 1977); "Division of the University of Oregon Library Catalog," *Lib. RTSD* (Spr. 1976); jt. auth., "James Henry Daugherty," *Imprint: OR* (Fall 1975); Ed., *OR Lib. News* (1974–78); various essays. **Activities:** 1; 17, 20, 46; 55, 56 **Addr.:** University of Oregon Library, Eugene, OR 97403.

Kemp, Emma Jean (Jl. 18, 1951, Chicago, IL) Libn. III/Branch Head, Chicago Pub. Lib., 1968–. **Educ.:** Univ. of IL, Chicago, 1969–73, BA (Hist.); Rosary Coll., 1973–75, MALS; Med. LA, 1977, Cert. **Orgs.:** ALA: Black Caucus, Chicago Chap., Bylaws Com. (1980), Rec.-Corres. Secy. (1975–79), Com. on Stans. and Goals (Ch., 1975). IL LA. Chicago Lib. Club. Hyde Hist. Socty.: Trustee (1979–). NAACP. **Activities:** 9; 15, 16, 31; 75, 89 **Addr.:** Blackstone Branch, Chicago Public Library, 4904 S. Lake Park, Chicago, IL 60615.

Kemp, Leora M. (O. 30, 1939, San Antonio, TX) Tech. Srvs. Libn., TX State Tech. Inst., 1978–. **Educ.:** E. TX State Univ., 1958–61, BA (Eng.); Perkins Sch. of Theo., South. Methodist Univ., Dallas, TX, 1967–68, MRE (Relig. Educ.); N. TX State Univ., 1975–78, MLS. **Orgs.:** TX LA. ALA: ASCLA/Lib. Srvs. to the Deaf Sect., Pubns. Com. (Ch., 1980–). TX Socty. of Interpreters for the Deaf. TX Assn. of the Deaf. Ctrl. TX Cncl. for the Deaf: Bd. of Dir. (1979–). **Honors:** Beta Phi Mu, 1979. **Pubns.:** "Library Services for the Deaf," *TX Lib. Jnl.* (Win. 1980); "Government Publications and the Small Public Library," *TX Libs.* (Win. 1977). **Activities:** 1, 10, 12; 15, 16, 20; 50, 63, 72 **Addr.:** 405 Vance St., Waco, TX 76705.

Kemp, Thomas J. (Jl. 13, 1948, Nashua, NH) Lcl. Hist., Geneal. Libn., Ferguson Lib., 1974–; Grant Reviewer, NEH, 1978–, Consult., 1974–. **Educ.:** Brigham Young Univ., 1967–68, 1970–73, BA (Hist.), 1973–74, MLS; Columbia Univ., 1981; various crs. **Orgs.:** ALA: RASD/Hist. Sect., Geneal. Com. (1979–). New Eng. LA: Bibl. Com. (1978–). CT LA: Lcl. Hist. and Geneal. Sect. (Vice-Ch., 1980–). SAA. Org. of Amer. Hist.: US Newsp. Proj., CT Rep. (1979). Amer. Hist. Assn. Assn. for the Bibl. of Hist. Assn. for the Std. of CT Hist. **Honors:** Phi Alpha Theta, 1973. **Pubns.:** *Connecticut Researcher's Handbook* (1981); Contrib., *Genealogist's Handbook for New England Research* (1980); *The Office of Patriarch to the Church in The Church of Jesus Christ of Latter-day Saints* (1973). **Activities:** 2, 9; 23, 39, 45; 57, 69, 86 **Addr.:** Local History and Genealogy, Ferguson Library, 96 Broad St., Stamford, CT 06901.

Kemp, Toby (Mr. 28, 1940, New York, NY) Univ. Archvst., IA State Univ., 1974–. **Educ.:** Adelphi Univ., 1957–60, BA, (Drama); Univ. of IL, 1971–72, MSLS. **Orgs.:** SAA. Midwest Arch. Conf.: Cncl. (1977–79); Ed. Bd. (1979–82). IA Hist. Mtrls. Prsrvn. Socty.: Co-Fndr.; Pres. (1976–). **Honors:** Beta Phi Mu, 1973. **Pubns.:** jt. ed., *Preserving Your Historical Records: Proceedings of the Symposium* (1980); jt. ed., "Plants as Modified by Man," *IA State Jnl. of Resrch.* (F. 1981); jt. ed., "Environmental Influences on Nectar Secretion," *IA State Jnl. of Resrch.* (My. 1981); jt. cmplr., *College and University Archives: Selected Readings* (1979). **Activities:** 2; 17, 23, 39; 61, 62, 85 **Addr.:** University Archivist, 162 Library, Iowa State University, Ames, IA 50011.

Kenamore, Jane A. (Ja. 26, 1938, St. Louis, MO) Archvst., Rosenberg Lib. (Galveston, TX), 1976–, Asst. Archvst., 1976–; Tchr., 1961–76. **Educ.:** IN Univ., 1956–58; Northwest. Univ., 1958–60, AB (Hist.); Washington Univ., 1960, (Educ.); Univ. of CA, Santa Barbara, 1971–74, MA (Educ.); American Univ., 1977, Cert. (Arch. Admin.). **Orgs.:** SAA: various afnty. grps. Socty. of Southwest Archvsts.: Nom. Com. (1980); Women's Hist. Panel (Ch., 1980). SW LA: Oral Hist Grant Adv. Com. Amer. Hist. Assn. Galveston Cnty. Hist. Cmsn. **Pubns.:** Foreword, *Mier Expedition Diary* (1978); "Texas History at Rosenberg Has History of Its Own," *TX Libs.* (Spr. 1979). **Activities:** 2, 9; 15, 17, 39, 45; 69, 85 **Addr.:** Rosenberg Library, 2310 Sealy, Galveston, TX 77550.

Kendall, John Dickson (Ap. 18, 1924, Hanover, NH) Biblgphr., Amer. Std./Head, Spec. Cols., Univ. of MA, Amherst, 1969–; Head, Sel. Div., Dept of Resrcs. and Acq., Harvard Coll. Lib., 1966–69; Instr./Libn. Acq. Dept., Univ. of MN Libs., 1964–66. **Educ.:** Harvard Univ., 1941–48, AB (Hist., Lit.), 1948–50, AM (Hist.); Univ. of MN, 1951–58, MA (Eng.), 1963–65, MALS. **Orgs.:** ALA: ACRL/New Eng. Chap. SAA. New Eng. Archvsts.: Secy. (1972–76); Pres. (1980–81). New Eng. Docum. Cons. Ctr.: Adv. Cncl. (1973–80). Various other orgs. Org. of Amer. Histns. Bay State Hist. Leag.: Bd. of Dirs. (1972–75). **Honors:** Fulbright Schol., Italy, 1955–56. **Activities:** 1; 15, 23, 33 **Addr.:** University of Massachusetts Library, Amherst, MA 01003.

Kennedy, Alice Janet (My. 6, 1922, Philadelphia, PA) Ref. Libn., Biomed. Sch., Univ. of PA, 1971–, Libn., Sch. of Nursing, 1963–71; Asst. Libn., Beaver Coll., 1960–63; Libn., Sch. of Nursing, Episcopal Hosp., Philadelphia, 1956–60. **Educ.:** Beaver Coll., 1939–44, BA (Soc. Sci.); Drexel Univ., 1956–60, MS (LS). **Orgs.:** ALA. SLA: Philadelphia Chap. Med. LA: Philadelphia Chap. **Activities:** 1; 39; 58, 80 **Addr.:** Biomedical School Library, University of Pennsylvania, Philadelphia, PA 19040.

Kennedy, Ilona A. (F. 5, 1950, Montreal, PQ) Partner, Lib. and Info. Consult., 1978–; Libn., AB Labour, 1976–78; Libn., Univ. of Toronto, Sigmund Samuel Lib., 1974–75; Libn., ON Netwk. of Cmnty. Hlth. and Soc. Srvs., 1974; various tchg. positions. **Educ.:** McGill Univ., 1967–71, BA (Psy.); Univ. of Toronto, 1972–74, MLS. **Orgs.:** Can. Assn. of Spec. Lib. and Info. Srvs. Edmonton Chap., Ch. (1979–80); Vice-Ch. (1978–79). Can. LA. SLA. AB Gvt. Libs. Assn.: Vice-Ch. (1977); Secy. (1978); various coms. Mill Creek Build-A-Park: Dir. (1977–); Secy. (1978–80). **Pubns.:** Ed., *At A Glance,* nsltr. (1978–79, 1980); *An Investigation into the Development of Sci/Tech Data Bank,* consult. rpt. (1979); *Selection of an automated cataloging system for Alberta Agriculture Library,* consult. rpt. (1979). **Activities:** 12; 24; 56, 75, 92 **Addr.:** Library and Information Consultants, 10436 81 Ave., Edmonton, AB T6E 1X6 Canada.

Kennedy, James R., Jr. (Ap. 28, 1928, Detroit, MI) Ref. Libn., Earlham Coll., 1964–; Soc. Sci. Libn., Drexel Univ., 1959–64; Catlgr. & Ref. Asst., Luth. Theo. Semy., Philadelphia, 1955–59. **Educ.:** Cornell Univ., 1946–50, AB (Econ.); Columbia Univ., 1953–55, MLS. **Orgs.:** ALA. ATLA. US Tennis Assn. **Pubns.:** *Library Research Guide to Education* (1979); *Library Research Guide to Religion and Theology* (1974); "Course-Related Library Instruction," *Drexel Lib. Qtly.* (Jl.-O. 1971); "Integrated Library Instruction," *Lib. Jnl.* (Ap. 15, 1970); Jt. auth., "Structuring Facilities and Services for Library Instruction," *Lib. Trends* (Sum. 1980); other articles, reviews. **Activities:** 1; 31, 39, 42; 54, 57, 63, 90 **Addr.:** Earlham College Library, Richmond, IN 47374.

Kennedy, Joy Constance (Ja. 15, 1947, Orange, TX) Head of Ref., Arlington Hts. Meml. Lib., 1974–; Head Libn., Ela Area Pub. Lib., 1972–74. **Educ.:** Rice Univ., 1965–67; SUNY, Buffalo, 1969–71, BA (Eng.); State Univ. Coll. of NY, Geneseo, 1971–72, MS (LS). **Orgs.:** ALA: Com. on Mtrls. for Amer. Indians (1975–76); JMRT, Midwinter Act. Com. (1977–78); Afflt. Rep. for IL (1977–79). IL LA: JMRT, Sec. (1977–78); Bd. Mem.-at-Large (1976–77); Mem. Com. (1975–76). **Activities:** 9; 31, 39, 48; 50, 95-Programming. **Addr.:** 1010 N. Chicago Ave., Arlington Heights, IL 60004.

Kennedy, Kathleen A. (Camden, NJ) Col. Mgt./Educ. Libn., Glassboro State Coll., 1964–, Circ. Libn., 1964–68; Asst. Circ. Libn., Swarthmore Coll., 1963–64; Libn., Williamstown (NJ) HS, 1959–63. **Educ.:** Rutgers Univ., 1950–54, BA (Hum.); Villanova Univ., 1958–62, MS (LS). **Orgs.:** ALA: ACRL. Grt. Philadelphia Area Educ. Libns. Plng. Com. (1979–81). **Honors:**

PROFESSIONAL ACTIVITIES: Institutions: 1. Acad. lib.; 2. Arch.; 3. Assn.; 4. Fed./Gvt. lib.; 5. Inst. lib.; 6. Mfr./Suppl.; 7. Milit. lib.; 8. Musm.; 9. Pub. lib.; 10. Sch. lib.; 11. Sch. of lib. sci.; 12. Spec. lib.; 13. State lib.; 14. (other). **Functions/Activities:** 15. Acq./Col. dev.; 16. Adult srvs.; 17. Admin.; 18. Apprais.; 19. Archit./Bldgs.; 20. Cat./Class.; 21. Chld. srvs.; 22. Circ.; 23. Cons./Pres.; 24. Consult.; 25. Cont. ed.; 26. Educ. lib. sci.; 27. Ext. srvs.; 28. Fund/Grants; 29. Gvt. pubs.; 30. Indx./Abs.; 31. Instr. lib. use; 32. Media srvs.; 33. Micro.; 34. Netwks./Coop.; 35. Persnl.; 36. PR; 37. Publshg.; 38. Recs. mgt.; 39. Ref. srvs.; 40. Repro.; 41. Resrch.; 42. Review.; 43. Secur.; 44. Serials; 45. Spec. col.; 46. Tech. srvs.; 47. Trustees/Bds.; 48. YA srvs.; 49. (other).

Phi Delta Gamma. **Activities:** 1; 15, 21; 63, 92 **Addr.:** B-229, The Crossings, Glassboro, NJ 08028.

Kennedy, Mary Ellen (Fb. 28, 1939, Pittsburgh, PA) Pub. Srvs. Libn. Instr., Glenville State Coll., 1971–; Catlgr., Ref. Libn., Newport News Pub. Lib. Syst., 1970–71; Elem. Tchr., 1962–67. **Educ.:** Villa Maria Coll., 1957–61, AB (Eng.); Univ. of Pittsburgh, 1967–70, MLS; Univ. of Pittsburgh, 1977–. **Orgs.:** ALA: RASD, Ref. Subscr. Bks. Rev. Com. (1979–81). WV LA: Coll. and Univ. Sect. (1971–). AALS. Tri-State Assn. of Coll. and Resrch. Libs. (1971–). AAUW: Leg. Com. (Ch., 1979–). Delta Kappa Gamma. **Pubns.:** "Undergraduate Programs in Library Science," *WV Libs.* (Sum., 1976); "West Virginia Folklore," *WV Libs.* (Fall, 1979); "Meeting the Educational Needs of the Older Adult," ED 167-697 (1979). **Activities:** 1, 9; 26, 29, 39; 50, 55, 75 **Addr.:** 612-2 Walnut St., Glenville, WV 26351.

Kennedy, Robert A. (My. 17, 1920, Cumberland, ON) Dir., Lib. and Info. Syst. Ctr., Head, Info. Srv. Dept., Bell Labs., 1979–, Head, Lib. Oper. Dept., 1976–79, Head, Info. Syst. Dept., 1958–76; Asst. Chief Libn. (Admin.), Natl. Resrch. Cncl. of Can., 1953–58, Head, Aeronautical Lib., 1948–53, Indxr., Cat., 1946–48. **Educ.:** Trinity Coll., Univ. of Toronto, 1938–42, BA (Phil.), 1945–46, BLS. **Orgs.:** ASIS: Cnclr.-at-large (1973–76); Ed. Bd. of *Jnl.* (1961–78); Pubns. Com. (Ch., 1978–80); various coms. SLA NJ Chap. (Dir., 1965–71). ON LA: Pres. (1952–53). NATO Adv. Grp. for Aeronautical Resrch. and Dev.: Documen. Com. (Can. Del. 1953–58); Ch. (1956–57). Inst. of Electrical and Electronics Engin.: Pubns. Bd. (Consult., 1978–80). **Pubns.:** "Bell Laboratories Library Network" in *Industrial Information Systems* (1978); "Bell Laboratories Library Real-Time Loan System (BELLREL)," *Jnl. of Lib. Autom.* (1968); "Library Applications of Permutation Indexing," *Jnl. Chem. Docmtn.* (Jl. 1962); "Mechanized Title Word Indexing of Internal Reports," *Machine Indexing–Progress and Problems* (1962); Ed. Bd., *Amer. Documtn.* and *JASIS* (1961–78); various papers and sps. **Activities:** 12; 17, 34; 56, 93 **Addr.:** Bell Telephone Laboratories, Room MH 6A–320, 600 Mountain Ave., Murray Hill, NJ 07974.

Kennedy, Mrs. T. A. (Dolly) (Ja. 23, 1915, Tofield, AB) Vancouver Pub. Lib. Bd., 1974–; Tchr.; Libn.; Sch. Libn. **Educ.:** Vancouver Normal Sch.; Univ. of BC, BA, BLS. **Orgs.:** BC Lib. Trustees Assn.: Pres. (1978–80). Can. LA: BC Prov. Rep. Univ. Women's Club of Vancouver: Pres. (1972–74). Vancouver Volun. Ctr.: Bd. (1975–78). **Pubns.:** Ed., "Open Door", Nsltr. of BC Lib. Trustees' Assn. (1977–80). **Activities:** 9, 10; 21, 47, 48 **Addr.:** 1758 West 49th Ave., Vancouver, BC V6M 2S5 Canada.

Kennemer, Phyllis K. (My. 18, 1940, Oak Creek, CO) Lib. Media Spec., Jefferson Cnty. Pub. Schs., 1975–; Tchr., Jefferson Cnty. Pub. Schs. 1969–70, 1972–75; Tchr., Denver Pub. Schs., 1966–67; Tchr., CO Springs Pub. Schs., 1962–66. **Educ.:** Univ. of North. CO, 1958–62, BA (Elem. Educ.), 1962–64, MA (Elem. Educ.), Univ. of CO, 1972–75, Educ. Spec. (Lib. Media), 1975–, 1980, EdD (Elem. Educ.). Intl. Graphoanalysis Socty., 1968–69, Cert. **Orgs.:** ALA: Notable Bks. Com. (1981–83); AASL; ALSC. CO Educ. Media Assn.: Wkshop Presenter (1977); Conf. Presenter (1980). Intl. Readg. Assn.: CO Cncl., Various coms. Natl. Cncl. of Tchrs. of Eng. CO Lang. Arts Socty.: Exec. Bd. (1978–) Intl. Graphoanalysis Socty.: CO Chap. (Ch., 1971–72). **Pubns.:** "From the Elementary School Bookshelf, Statement," *Jnl. of the CO Lang. Arts Socty.* (1975–). **Activities:** 10; 15, 21, 24; 63 **Addr.:** 1745 S. Queen Way, Lakewood, CO 80226.

Kenney, Brigitte L. (Ag. 14, 1927, Halberstadt, Germany) Pres., INFOCON, INC., 1980–; Sr. Anal., Solar Energy Resrch. Inst., Intl. Prog. Div., 1979–80; Branch Chief, Database Syst. Branch, Solar Energy Resrch. Inst., 1978–79; Assoc. Prof., Grad. Sch. of Lib. and Info. Sci., Drexel Univ., 1970–77; Resrch. Assoc., Dept. of Psyt., Univ. of MS Med. Ctr., 1968–70, Syst. Anal., Med. Lib., 1966–70; Dir., Info. Srvs. Div., MS Resrch. and Dev. Ctr., 1964–66; Libn., MS Indus. and Tech. Resrch. Comsn., 1962–64; various libn., consult. positions. **Educ.:** Univ. of Graz, Austria, 1945–46 (Msc., Eng.); Univ. of Chicago, 1957–59 MA (LS). **Orgs.:** ALA: Cncl. (1977–81), Legis. Com. (1978–80); LITA, Pres. Elect (1981–82); ALA Plng. Com. (1972–74). ASIS: Cncl. (Secty., 1972–74). SLA. AALS: Prog. Com. (Ch., 1975–77). AAUP: Drexel Chap. (Secty., 1971–73). ACLU. Philadelphia Cmnty. Cable Coal.: Steering Com. **Honors:** Beta Phi Mu, 1959; Fulbright Sr. Resrch. Fellow, 1974–75. **Pubns.:** "The Future of Cable Communications in Libraries," *Jnl. of Lib. Autom.* (D. 1976); "National and International Information Systems Planning," *Procs. Amer. Socty. Info. Sci.* (1975); jt. auth., "Library Use of Cable," *Reader on Media in Libraries* (1975); jt. auth., *Neighborhood Communication Centers: Planning Information and Referral Services in the Urban Library* (1974); "Ten Credos for Libraries and Cable TV," *Over the Cable* (1974). **Activities:** 11, 12; 17, 24, 26; 56, 75, 91 **Addr.:** 400 Plateau Pkwy., Golden, CO 80401.

Kenney, Donald J. (F. 24, 1945, Richlands, VA) Asst. Head, Gen. Ref. Div., VPI & SU, 1979–; Libn., Blacksburg Mid. Sch., 1974–79; Readers Srvs. Libn., Sweet Briar Coll., 1973–74. **Educ.:** Berea Coll., 1963–67, BA (Eng.); Univ. of VA, 1967–69, MEd (Eng. Educ.); Cath. Univ., 1973–74, MLS. **Orgs.:** ALA. Southeastern LA. VA LA: Treas. (1980–82); Ed., *Lifline,* Instr. Forum. VA Educ. Media Assn.: Const. Com.; Prog. Com. (1979). VA Assn. of Eng. Tchrs. Phi Delta Kappa: Pub. Com. **Pubns.:** "Universal Bibliographic Instruction: An Outdated Concept," *Southeastern Libn.* (1980); Jt. auth., "A Basic Library about the English Language," *Eng. Jrnl.* (Ja. 1979); "Great English Teaching Ideas," *VA Eng. Bltn.* (Win. 1978); *Activating the Passive Student* (1978); "Planning a Curriculum Library," *Kappa Delta Pi Record* (Ap. 1975). **Activities:** 1, 10; 31, 39, 48 **Addr.:** P. O. Box 747, Blacksburg, VA 24060.

Kenny, Robin Luana (Jy. 11, 1937, Honolulu, HI) Libn., Pacific Resrcs. Inc. 1977–; Resrch. Assoc. Bob Kenny & Assoc. 1972–77; Head, Acq., East-West Ctr. Lib., 1962–65. **Educ.:** Univ. of HI, 1964, BA (Eng., Soc. Sci.); 1968 MLS. **Orgs.:** SLA: HI Pac. Chap. (Secy., 1977–79, Pres., 1979–80). **Activities:** 12; 15, 17; 86 **Addr.:** Pacific Resources, Inc., P.O. Box 3379, Honolulu, HI 96842.

Kenny, William McKenzie (S. 19, 1953, Sarnia, ON) Lib. Dir., Fort McMurray Pub. Lib., 1978–. **Educ.:** Huron Coll., Hon BA (Hist.); Univ. of West. ON, MLS. **Orgs.:** LA of AB: Exec. Cnclr. North. AB Lib. Dev. Bd.: Bd. Mem. Fort McMurray Further Educ. Cncl.: Ch. **Activities:** 9; 15, 17, 20; 55, 73, 86 **Addr.:** Fort McMurray Public Library, 10012 Franklin Ave., Fort McMurray, AB T9H 2K6 Canada.

Kent, Allen (O. 24, 1921, New York City, NY) Disting. Srv. Prof., Dir., Ofc. of Comm. Prog., Assoc. Dean, Sch. of Lib. and Info. Sci., Ch., Interdisciplinary Dept. of Info. Sci., Univ. of Pittsburgh, 1963–; Assoc. Dir., Ctr. for Documtn. and Comm. Resrch., Prof., Lib. Sci., Case West. Rsv. Univ., 1955–63; Prin. Documtn. Engin., Battelle Meml. Inst., 1953–55; Resrch. Assoc., MA Inst. of Tech., 1951–53. **Educ.:** Coll. of City of NY, 1938–42, BS (Chem.); NY Univ., 1942, Cert. (Metallurgical Testing). **Orgs.:** ALA. PA LA. ASIS: Spec. Com. on Gifts and Contrib. (1978). Amer. Inst. of Chem. Amer. Assn. for the Advnc. of Sci. Assn. for Comp. Mach. **Honors:** ASIS, Best Info. Sci. Bk., 1980; ASIS, Awd. of Merit, 1977; Eastman Kodak Co., Awd. for significant contrib. to advnc. of sci. of info. tech., 1968. **Pubns.:** Co-ed., *The Structure & Governance of Library Networks* (1979); Jt. auth., *Use of Library Materials: The University of Pittsburgh Study* (1979); "The On-line Revolution in Libraries, 1969–," *Amer. Libs.* (Je. 1979); exec. ed., *Encyclopedia of Library and Information Science,* starting 1968. **Activities:** 11; 26, 41; 75 **Addr.:** Office of Communications Programs, 801 L.I.S. Bldg., University of Pittsburgh, Pittsburgh, PA 15260.

Kent, Carl Albert (Ja. 8, 1931, Kansas City, MO) Coord. of Libs., Kansas City (KS) Pub. Schs., 1963–, W. Jr. HS Libn., 1957–63. **Educ.:** Kansas City Jr. Coll.; Univ. of MO, Kansas City, 1956 (Hist.); Emporia State Univ., 1957–60, MS (LS). **Orgs.:** KS Assn. of Sch. Libs.: Cncl. KS LA. Untd. Sch. Admins. ALA: AASL. **Activities:** 10, 11; 17, 21, 46 **Addr.:** Kansas City (KS) Public Schools, 625 Minnesota Ave., Kansas City, KS 66101.

Kent, Eben Lee (Ap. 28, 1953, Philadelphia, PA) Asst. Head of Bus., Chicago Pub. Lib., 1979–, Asst. Med. Libn., 1977–79. **Educ.:** Bowdoin Coll., 1971–75, AB (Classics/Russ.); Univ. of Chicago, 1975–77, MALS. **Orgs.:** SLA. Med. LA. Chicago On Line User Grp.: Treas. (1979–80). Chicago TRS-80 Users Grp.: Nwsltr. Pub. (1979–). Chicago Area Comp. Hobbyist Exch. **Pubns.:** "Microcomputer Review Journals," *Serials Review* (Ja. 1980). **Activities:** 9; 15, 39; 56, 80, 93 **Addr.:** Business/Science/Technology Division, Chicago Public Library, 425 N. Michigan Ave., Chicago, IL 60614.

Kent, Frederick James (My. 21, 1928, Miami, FL) Head, Msc. Dept., The Free Lib. of Philadelphia, 1974–, Asst. Head, 1965–74, Libn. I, 1961–65. **Educ.:** DePauw Univ. 1946–50, BM (Organ); Univ. of IL, 1950–51, MM (Composition), 1960–61, MLS, 1954–60 (Msclgy.). **Orgs.:** Msc. LA: PA Chap. PA LA. Amer. Guild of Organists. **Honors:** Phi Mu Alpha. **Pubns.:** Ed., *Crescendo* (1978–). "Come, my way, my truth, my life," anthem (1974); reviews. **Activities:** 9; 16, 39, 45; 55 **Addr.:** The Free Library of Philadelphia, Logan Square, Philadelphia, PA 19130.

Kenyon, Carleton W. (O. 7, 1923, Lafayette, NY) Law Libn., Lib. of Congs., 1971–, Assoc. Law Libn., 1969–71; Law Libn., CA State Lib., 1960–69; Head Cat. Libn., Los Angeles Cnty. Law Lib., 1954–60, Asst. Ref. Libn., 1952–54. **Educ.:** Yankton Coll., 1940–47, AB (Soc. Sci.); Univ. of SD, 1947–50, MA (Hist.), JD; Univ. of MI, 1950–51, AMLS. **Orgs.:** AALL. Law Libns. Socty. of DC. Intl. Assn. of Law Libs. Amer. Bar Assn. Fed. Bar Assn. State Bar of SD. **Pubns.:** *California County Law Library Basic List* (1963–68); *Los Angeles County Law Library Classification Schedule, Class K Law* (1965); "Library of Congress Law Library," *Law Lib. Jnl.* (1974); "The Dimensions of Law Librarianship," *Spec. Libs.* (1971). **Activities:** 4, 13; 17; 77 **Addr.:** 11407 Grago Dr., Fort Washington, MD 20744.

Keogh, Judith L. (S. 22, 1937, Philadelphia, PA) Asst. Dir., Ext. Srvs., Chester Cnty Lib., 1979–, Coord., Chlds. Srvs., 1973–79, Chlds. Libn., 1972–73; Chld. Libn., Tredyffrin Pub. Lib., 1969–72. **Educ.:** Smith Coll. 1955–60, BA; Villanova Univ., 1967–69 MLS; Miami Univ., Cert. (Lib. Admin.), 1979. **Orgs.:** PA LA: Bd. (1978–80); SE Chap. (Ch., 1978–79); Nom. Com. (1979–80); Leg. Com. (1980–81) Interlib. Delivery Srv. of PA: Bd. (1980–83). ALA. AAUW. **Activities:** 9; 24, 25, 27; 72 **Addr.:** 464 St. Davids Ave., St. Davids, PA 19087.

Keough, Francis P. (Ap. 2, 1917, Brookline, MA) Lib. Bldg. Consult., 1964–; Dir., City Lib., Springfield, MA, 1964–78; Dir., Framingham, MA Pub. Lib., 1951–64; Ref. Libn., Harvard Coll. Lib., 1947–51; Lectr., Ref. Srvs., Sch. of Lib. Sci., Simmons Coll., 1954–56; Archvst., Radiation Lab., M.I.T., 1945–46. **Educ.:** Harvard Univ., 1936–40, AB (Hist.); Columbia Univ., 1946–47, MS (LS); Harvard Grad. Sch. of Arts and Sci., 1940–41, (Hist.). **Orgs.:** ALA. MA LA: Pres., VP, Ch., various coms. Springfield Adult Educ. Cncl.: Prog. Com. (1975–). Philips Lect. Com.: Secy. Treas. (1964–78). **Activities:** 9; 17, 19, 24 **Addr.:** 16 Oxford St., Springfield, MA 01108.

Kephart, John E. (Ja. 4, 1920, Wilkinsburg, PA) Interim Dean (LS), State Univ. Coll., Geneseo, 1980–, Prof. (LS), 1966–80; Asst. Prof. (LS), Univ. of South. CA, 1963–66; Libn., Westmont Coll., 1959–63; Educ. Resrch. Libn., Field Enterprises, 1957–58; Libn., Wheaton Coll., 1949–57. **Educ.:** Wheaton Coll., 1945–48, BA (Hist.) Univ. of IL, 1948–49, MA (Hist.), 1949–51, MS (LS); Univ. of MI, 1951–60, PhD (LS). **Orgs.:** ALA. AALS. **Honors:** Beta Phi Mu. **Addr.:** 13 Tuscarora Ave., Geneseo, NY 14454.

Kepper, Anna Dean Nohl (My. 12, 1938, Seattle, WA) Cur. of Spec. Coll., Univ. of NV, Las Vegas, 1976–, Lib. Asst., 1974–76; Pub. Asst., Reg. Conf. of Hist. Agencies, 1972–73. **Educ.:** Univ. of WA, 1956–60, AB (Hist.); SUNY, Oneonta, 1970–72, MA (Musm. Std./Amer. Folk Cult.); Univ. of Denver, 1978, Cert. (Arch. Admin.). **Orgs.:** NV LA. Western States Mtrls. Cons. Proj.: NV liaison (1979). Gov. Conf. on NV Lib. and Info. Needs: Delegate (1978). Nat. Trust for Hist. Prsrvn.: Bd. of Adv. (1976–). Admin. Com. (1978–). Prsrvn. Action: Dir. (1978–). Prsrvn. Assn. of Clark Cnty: Pres. (1974–78). **Activities:** 1; 45; 55, 85 **Addr.:** Special Collections Dept., James R. Dickinson Library, University of Nevada, Las Vegas, Las Vegas, NV 89154.

Kepple, Robert R. (Jl. 26, 1925, Altoona, PA) Libn., Applied Physics Lab, Johns Hopkins Univ., 1968–; Ofcr.-in-Charge, Lib., Intl. Atomic Energy Agency, 1963–68; Readers' Srvs. Libn., Argonne Natl. Lab, 1961–63; Libn., Pratt & Whitney Aircraft, 1957–61; Catlgr., E.J. duPont Savannah River Lab, 1952–57. **Educ.:** PA State Univ., 1945–49, BS (Math); Carnegie Mellon Univ., 1950–51, MLS. **Orgs.:** Interlib. Users Assn.: Treas. (1977–); Bd. of Dir. (1972–). SLA. **Pubns.:** "Missions for an international Library," *Spec. Libs.* (O. 1969); "Serving readers in a special international library," *Coll & Resrch. Lib.* (My. 1967). **Activities:** 12; 17, 39; 64, 88, 91 **Addr.:** 5443 Ring Dove Ln., Columbia, MD 21044.

Ker, Robert Harold (Ag. 6, 1920, San Francisco, CA) Ref. Libn., Univ. of Victoria, 1967–; Archvst., BC Arch., 1960–63; Dir. of Libs., US Air Force, England, 1955–60. **Educ.:** McGill Univ., 1938–40, 1944–45, BA (Arts); Univ. of CA, Berkeley, 1951–53, MA (Eng.), 1954–55, MLS; Sorbonne, Paris, 1946–47, Dip. (Fr.). **Orgs.:** Can. LA: Ch., Newspaper Index Com. (1967–68). Inst. of Victorian Libns.: Dir. (1978–80). **Honors:** Beta Phi Mu, 1955. **Activities:** 1; 34, 39; 55, 74 **Addr.:** 2991 Spring Bay Rd., Victoria, BC V8N 5S4 Canada.

Keresztesi, Michael (Ja. 24, 1929, Ratko, Hungary) Assoc. Prof., Wayne State Univ., 1973–; Lectr., Univ. of MI, 1969–73; Lib. Dir., Tusculum Coll., 1967–69; Head, Acq., Law Lib., Univ. of MI, 1962–67. **Educ.:** Univ. of MI, 1961, BA Equivalent, 1961–62, MALS; East. MI Univ., 1969–70, MA (Hist.); Univ. of MI, 1977, PhD (LS). **Orgs.:** ALA: ACRL; GODORT. Assn. for Bibl. of Hist.: Conf. Com. (Ch., 1980). **Honors:** Beta Phi Mu. **Pubns.:** Jt. auth., *German American History and Life* (1980); "Diffusion of Modern Library Thought and Practice by Means of UNESCO Fellowships for Travel and Study Abroad," *LIBRI* (1979); "Prolegomena to the History of International Librarianship," *Jnl. of Lib. Hist.* (1981); "Bibliographic Instruction in 1980s and Beyond," *Directions for the Decade; Library Instruction in the 1980's* (1981); *The Contribution of UNESCO to Library Education and Training; The First Twenty-five Years* (1977). **Activities:** 1, 11; 24, 26, 31; 59, 92, 95-Intl. libnshp. **Addr.:** Division of Library Science, Wayne State University, 315 Kresge, Detroit, MI 48202.

Kerker, Ann E. (My. 19, 1912, Butte, MT) Interim Exec. Dir., Med. LA, 1981–; Vetny. Med. Libn., Purdue University, 1959–77, Admin. Asst., Libs., 1956–59; Med. Technologist, ESSO Frgn. Afflts., 1945–55. **Educ.:** Purdue Univ., 1929–33, BS (Microbio.); Univ. of IL, 1957–59, MS (Libnshp.); Med. LA, 1960, Cert. Med. Libn. **Orgs.:** Med. LA: Pres.-Elect; Pres.; Immediate Past-Pres. (1976–78). SLA: IN Chap., Pres. (1972). ALA: ACRL/Agr. and Bib. Sci. Sect. (Ch., 1973). **Honors:** Beta Phi Mu, 1960; Phi Zeta, 1970. **Pubns.:** *Comparative and Veterinary Medicine; A Guide to the Resource Literature* (1973); "The Library - The Workshop," *Jnl. Vetny. Med. Educ.* (1978). **Activities:** 1, 3; 17, 24, 36; 58, 80 **Addr.:** 237 Sheetz St., West Lafayette, IN 47906.

Kern, Janet Linde (F. 4, 1952, Chicago, IL) Asst. Univ. Archvst., Univ. of VA Lib., 1981–; Tech. Srvcs. Archvst.,

Special Subjects/Services: 50. Adult educ.; 51. Advert./Mktg.; 52. Aerosp.; 53. Agric.; 54. Area std.; 55. Arts/Hum.; 56. Autom.; 57. Bibl./Prtg.; 58. Bio. sci.; 59. Bus./Fin.; 60. Chem.; 61. Copyrt.; 62. Documtn.; 63. Educ.; 64. Engin.; 65. Env.; 66. Eth. grps.; 67. Film; 68. Food/Nutr.; 69. Geneal.; 70. Geo.; 71. Geol.; 72. Handcpd.; 73. Hist.; 74. Int. frdm.; 75. Info. sci.; 76. Insr.; 77. Law; 78. Legis.; 79. Math./Comp. sci.; 80. Med.; 81. Metals; 82. Nat. resrcs.; 83. Newsp.; 84. Nuc. sci.; 85. Oral hist.; 86. Petr./Energy; 87. Pharm.; 88. Phys./Astr./Math.; 89. Readg.; 90. Relig.; 91. Sci./Tech.; 92. Soc. sci.; 93. Telecom.; 94. Transp.; 95. (other).

1979–81; Acq. Asst., 1976–77. **Educ.:** Knox Coll., 1969–73, BA (Amer. Std.); Univ. of London, England, 1974–75, MA (U. S. Std.); Inst. in Arch. Admin., Nat. Arch., 1978, Cert.; Adv. Inst. on Case Files, Nat. Arch., 1979, Cert. **Orgs.:** Mid-Atlantic Reg. Arch. Conf.: VA State Rep. (1979–80); Socty. of Amer. Archvsts.: Steering Com., Prof. Affinity Grp. on Mss. Col. (1978–80). **Activities:** 1, 2; 23, 45, 46; 62, 92 **Addr.:** Manuscripts Department, University of Virginia Library, Charlottesville, VA 22903.

Kernan, Mary Anne (Ap. 5, 1918, Louisville, KY) Ref. Libn., Vanderbilt Univ. Lib., 1978–; Head, Ref., 1972–78, Ref. Libn., 1966–72; Ref. Libn., Univ. of the S., 1965–66; Bibl. and Ref. Asst., Air Univ. Lib., 1954–65; Law Libn., Emory Univ., 1947–54; Army Libn., 1943–46; Libn., Atlanta Pub. Lib., 1939–43. **Educ.:** Agnes Scott Coll., 1934–38, AB (Eng.); Emory Univ., 1938–39, BALS, 1947–49, MA (Eng.). **Orgs.:** ALA. SELA. TN LA. **Honors:** Phi Beta Kappa; Beta Phi Mu. **Pubns.:** Various articles. **Activities:** 1; 15, 31, 39 **Addr.:** 602 Bowling Ave., Nashville, TN 37215.

Kerns, Ruth B. (S. 15, 1923, Brooklyn, NY) Hum. Libn., George Mason Univ., 1977–; Ref. Libn., IN Univ.-Purdue Univ., Fort Wayne, 1971–77; Site Libn., Polytech. of N. London, 1975–76. **Educ.:** Coll. of William and Mary, 1941–45, BA (Eng.); IN Univ., 1967–71, MLS; Cntrl. MI Univ., 1978–80, MA (Mgt.). **Orgs.:** ALA: RASD/Com. on Lib. Srvs. to an Aging Popltn. (1978–80). DC LA: Mgt. Interest Grp. (Treas., 1980–). Women's Natl. Bk. Club: Prog. Com. (1979–80). **Honors:** George Mason Univ. Ofc. of Intl. Progs. and Srvs. Seed Grant Awd., 1981; Beta Phi Mu, 1972. **Pubns.:** Jt. auth., "Mystery-Base Personalized Instruction in Pharmacology" (ERIC Docum. 151011); "Candles for the Bicentennial Cake," *Wilson Lib. Bltn.* (F. 1976); "Hoosier in England," *Focus on IN Libs.* (Fall 1975); "A Year in Britain – the Other Side of the Coin," *Educ. Exch. World* (Fall 1976); "Women's Issue in England 1975–76 as Reflected in the Mass Media: An Annotated Bibliography," *Can. Nsltr. of Resrch. on Women* (N. 1978); various sp. **Activities:** 1, 11; 26, 31, 39; 55, 85, 92 **Addr.:** Fenwick Library, George Mason University, 4400 University Dr., Fairfax, VA 22030.

Kerr, Audrey M. (D. 25, 1932, Winnipeg, MB) Assoc. Prof. & Med. Libn., Univ. of MB, 1963–; Resrch. Asst., Food and Drug Directorate, 1959–62; Resrch. Asst., Dept. Biochem., Univ. of MB, 1953–59. **Educ.:** Univ. of MB, 1949–53, BA (Gen. Arts); Univ. of BC, 1962–63, BLS. **Orgs.:** Med. LA. Assn. of Can. Med. Coll.: Assoc. Com. on Med. Sch. Libs. (Ch., 1979–80). Can. Hlth. Libs. Assn. MB Hlth. Libs. Assn.: Serials Holding Com. Assn. of Amer. Med. Coll.: Grp. on Med. Educ. Can. Assn. of Univ. Tchrs. Univ. of MB Press Bd. **Pubns.:** "Information needs of the community physician," *Can. Med. Assn. Jnl.* (1981); "The MLA certification examination," *CHLA/ABSC Nsltr.* (Win. 1978); "The Medical Library or the Problem of Solomon," *Univ. Of MB Med. Jnl.* (1970). **Addr.:** Medical Library, Faculty of Medicine, University of Manitoba, 770 Bannatyne Ave., Winnipeg, MB R3E 0W3 Canada.

Kerr, Elaine B. (Mr. 24, 1943, Philadelphia, PA) Consult., Electronic Info. Exchange Syst., 1976–; Assoc. Prof. (Soclgy.), OH State Univ., 1970–75. **Educ.:** Vassar Coll., 1960–64, BA (Soclgy.); Columbia Univ., 1964–71, PhD (Soclgy.). **Orgs.:** ASIS. WHCOLIS, Consult. (1979). Amer. Soclgy. Assn. **Pubns.:** Jt.-auth., *Computer-Mediated Communications: Status and Evaluation* (1982); Various resrch. rpts. and presented papers. **Activities:** 6; 17, 24, 41; 75, 92, 93 **Addr.:** 264 E. S. St., Worthington, OH 43085.

Kerr, Margaret Burdette (D. 8, 1920, Jesup, GA) Adjunct Asst. Prof., Div. of Libnshp., Emory Univ., 1979–; Media Coord., Decatur City Schs., 1964–79; Asst. Dir., Decatur-DeKalb Pub. Lib. Syst., 1949–64; Libn., LaGrange Mem. Lib., 1945–46; Ref. Libn., Sacramento City Lib, CA, 1944–45. **Educ.:** Furman Univ., 1937–41, BA (Eng.); Emory Univ., 1943–44, BALS, Emory Univ., 1966, MLn. **Orgs.:** GA LA: Pres. (1971–73); VP (1969–71); Ch., Budget Com. (1973–75); Chair, Ad Hoc Sup. Com. (1977–79). Southeastern LA: Ch., Nom. (1974–76); HQ Com. (1976–80). GA Lib. Media Dept., GA Assn. of Educ.: Const. & Bylaws Com. (1978). Delta Kappa Gamma: Pres. (1967–69); Ch.-Prog. (1974–76); Ch. Resrch. (1976–78); Ch., Initiation (1978–80). **Pubns.:** Jt. Auth., "Reading–a family affair" (1978). **Activities:** 9, 10; 17, 26, 32; 50, 63, 89 **Addr.:** 116 Garden Ln., Decatur, GA 30030.

Kerr, Robert Riggs (F. 15, 1921, New Alexandria, PA) Supvsr., Cat., The Pierpont Morgan Lib., 1967–; Libn., The Newark NJ Musm., 1951–67. **Educ.:** Hunter Coll., City of NY, 1947–50, AB (Eng. Lit.); Columbia Univ., 1950–51, MS (LS). **Orgs.:** Art Libs. Socty. of N. Amer. and NY. **Honors:** Phi Beta Kappa. **Pubns.:** Indxr., *Master Drawings;* various articles in *Grolier Encyc.* **Activities:** 12; 15, 20, 46; 55, 57, 95-Rare bks. **Addr.:** The Pierpont Morgan Library, 29 E. 36th St., New York, NY 10016.

Kerr, Virginia Margaret (Jl. 24, 1949, CT) Dir., Art, Archit. and Urban Sci. Resrc. Ctr., Univ. of IL at Chicago Circle, 1977–; Libn., Inst. for Comp. Resrch., Univ. of Chicago, 1976–77; Asst. Ref. Libn., Atkins Lib., Univ. of NC, Charlotte, 1972–75. **Educ.:** Mt. Holyoke Coll., 1967–71, AB (Eng. lit.); Drexel Univ., 1971–72, MSLS; Univ. of Chicago, 1975–77, MA (Art Hist.), 1977–, PhD Cand. (Art Hist.). **Orgs.:** ARLIS/NA: Constn. Rev. Com. (1978–79). Mid-America Coll. Art Assn.: Visual Resrcs. Grp. Socty. of Archit. Histns.: Chicago Chap. **Pubns.:** "Slide Libraries under Library Jurisdiction," *Intl. Bltn. for Photographic Documen. of the Visual Arts,* (Spr. 1980). **Activities:** 1, 12; 15, 17, 20; 55 **Addr.:** AAUS Resource Center, Box 4348 UICC, Chicago, IL 60680.

Kershner, Bruce S. (N. 18, 1931, Conneaut, OH) Dir., Fairfield (CT) Pub. Lib., 1972–, Asst. Dir., 1970–72; Fld. Dir., Amer. Red Cross, 1959–69. **Educ.:** Denison Univ., 1950–54, BA (Hist.); SUNY, Albany, 1969–70, MSL; Amer Inst. of Frgn. Trade, 1957–58, BFT. **Orgs.:** SW CT Lib. Cncl.: Treas. (1977–78). Coop. Lib. Srv. Unit Review Bd.: Secy. (1980–81). Fairfield Cnty. Lib. Admins. Grp.: Ch. (1974). ALA. Various other orgs. Fairfield Hist. Socty: Cncl. (1977–81). Rotary. **Activities:** 9; 17 **Addr.:** Fairfield Public Library, 1080 Old Post Rd., Fairfield, CT 06430.

Kershner, Lois M. (D. 9, 1941, Doylestown, PA) Dir., Lib. Srvs., Resrch. Libs. Grp., 1977–; Mgr., Cust. Support, C. L. Syst., Inc, 1974–77; User Srvs. Libn., Univ. of PA, 1967–74. **Educ.:** Ursinus Coll., 1959–63, BA (Hist.); Univ. of WI, 1963–64, MLS; Pepperdine Univ., 1978–79, MBA. **Orgs.:** ALA. ASIS. CA LA. Phi Nu Epsilon. **Honors:** Beta Phi Mu. **Pubns.:** "Research Libraries Information Network: The Computerized Bibliographic Network Supporting the Cooperative Programs of the Research Libraries Group, Inc.," *Bltn. of the Amer. Socty. for Info. Sci.* (Je. 1979); "User Services: 1973 Application Status" in *Library Automation: The State of the Art II* (1975); "Management Aspects of the Use of the IBM System/7 in Circulation Control" in *Procs. of the 1974 Clinic on Library Applications of Data Processing: Applications of Minicomputers to Library and Related Problems* (1975); reviews. **Activities:** 1; 17, 22, 34 **Addr.:** Research Libraries Group, Jordan Quadrangle, Stanford, CA 94305.

Kershner, Stephen A. (Ap. 15, 1949, Bluffton, IN) Dir., Geauga Cnty. (OH) Pub. Lib., 1979–; Branch Libn./Adult Srvs., Cuyahoga Cnty. Pub. Lib., 1976–79; Asst. Dir./Head, Adult Srvs., Hayner Pub. Lib. Dist., 1973–76; Instr., Lib. Tech., Lewis and Clark Cmnty. Coll., 1974. **Educ.:** IN Univ., Fort Wayne, 1967–71, BS (Educ.); IN Univ., Bloomington, 1972–73, MLS; South. IL Univ., 1976 (Bus.). **Orgs.:** ALA. OH LA: Org. Com. (1980–82). North. OH LA: Trustees (1981–84). Jaycees. Geauga Alliance. **Activities:** 9; 17, 47 **Addr.:** Geauga County Public Library, 110 E. Park St., Chardon, OH 44024.

Kersten, Dorothy Barbara (Jl. 15, 1912, Peoria, IL) Libn., Cherry Hill Untd. Presby. Church, 1964–; Ref. Asst., Tech. Dept., Detroit Pub. Lib., 1937–40; Ref. Asst., Bus. and Tech. Dept., Peoria Pub. Lib., 1932–36. **Educ.:** Bradley Univ., 1930–34, BS (Bus.); Univ. of IL, 1936–37, BS (LS). **Orgs.:** CS LA: Pubns. Com. AAUW: Bk. Sale Mktg. Com. (1958–70). **Honors:** AAUW, Dearborn Branch, Cent. Fund Awd., 1974. **Pubns.:** *Classifying Church or Synagogue Library Materials* (1977); *Subject Headings for Church or Synagogue Libraries* (1978). **Activities:** 12; 17, 39; 59, 64, 90 **Addr.:** 23656 Wilson Ave., Dearborn, MI 48128.

Kertland, Diana C. (Ap. 4, 1939, Montreal, PQ) Chief Libn., Lakehead Univ., 1980–; Chief Libn., Algoma Coll., 1977–80; Coord., Media Resrcs., Vanier Coll., 1970–77; Head, Acq., Sir George Williams Univ. 1966–70. **Educ.:** Bishop's Univ., 1957–61, BA (Hist.); McGill Univ., 1961–62, BLS; Sir George Williams Univ., 1968–73, MA (Hist.). **Orgs.:** Can. LA: Can. Assn. of Coll. and Univ. Libs. Div. (Secy., 1977–78). ON LA. ALA. ON Cncl. of Univ. Libs. **Activities:** 1; 17†

Kesarwani, Malti (Mr. 24, 1936, Kanpur, Uttar Pradesh, India) Head Cat. Libn., Nepean Pub. Lib., 1980–; Actg. Head, Tech. Srvs., Mnstry. of Solicitor Gen., 1978–80, Cat./Ref. Libn., 1977–78; Asst. Head, ILL Telephone Srvs., Natl. Lib. of Can., 1975–77, Ref. Libn., 1974–75; Asst. Libn., Gloucester HS, Ottawa, 1971–74, Catlgr., 1969–71. **Educ.:** Agra Univ., 1953–55, BSc, 1957–59, MA (Soclgy.); Univ. of Ottawa, 1968–69, BLS. **Orgs.:** Can. LA. ON LA. **Activities:** 4, 9; 20, 39, 46; 63, 92, 95-Crminology. **Addr.:** 1964 Camborne Cr., Ottawa, ON K1H 7B7 Canada.

Kesner, Richard Michael (My. 26, 1950, Streator, IL) Dir., Arch. of Appalachia, E. TN State Univ., 1978–; Rsrch. Assoc. and Archvst., Arch. of Labor and Urban Affairs, Wayne State University, 1977–78; History Bibliographer, Stanford University Libraries, 1976–77. **Educ.:** Oberlin Coll., 1968–73, AB (Hist.), MB (Msc.); Stanford Univ., 1973–77, MA, PhD, (Hist.); Wayne State Univ., 1977–78, Cert., (Arch.). **Orgs.:** SAA. Assn. of Recs. Mgrs. and Admins. TN Archvsts. Assn. Assn. of Can. Archvsts. Other orgs. Amer. Hist. Assn. Amer. Assn. for State and Lcl. Hist. Natl. Trust for Hist. Pres. Appalachian Stds. Conf. Other orgs. **Pubns.:** *A Primer on the Conservation of Books and Manuscripts* (1978); *Automation, Machine-Readable Records, and Archival Administration: An Annotated Bibliography* (1980); *Economic Control and Colonial Development: Crown Colony Financial Management in the Age of Joseph Chamberlain* (1981); "Harvesting the Hardwoods," "Long Steel Rail: Southern Appalachian Railroads," "Pat Alderman: The Making of a Local Historian," "Holston Country Houses: Preserving the Past," slides-tapes (1980); Various articles. **Activities:** 1, 2; 15, 17, 28; 55, 75, 85 **Addr.:** Archives of Appalachia, The Sherrod Library, East Tennessee State University, Johnson City, TN 37614.

Kessel, Shirley (Ag. 16, 1926, Waterbury, CT) Owner, Mgr., Bibliotechnics, 1979–; Catlgr., Acq., Amer. Petroleum Inst., 1977–78; Spec. Cat. Proj., Med. Lib., George Washington Univ., 1977. **Educ.:** Mt. Holyoke Coll., 1944–48, BA (Pol. Sci.); Univ. of Chicago, 1974–76, MA (LS), 1951–52 (Soc. Wk.). **Orgs.:** Info. Indus. Assn. SLA. ALA. AALL. Other orgs. Canoe Cruisers Assn. **Activities:** 6; 17, 20, 24; 77, 95-Econ. **Addr.:** Biblio Technics, 4615 N. Park Ave., Chevy Chase, MD 20015.

Kesselman, Martin Alan (Jl. 1, 1953, Brooklyn, NY) Life Sci. Libn., NY Univ., 1980–; Sci. Libn., Cuyahoga Cnty. Pub. Lib., 1978–80; Sci. Libn., SUNY Coll., Fredonia, 1976–78. **Educ.:** SUNY, Coll. of Env. Sci. and Forestry, 1971–74, BS (Zlgy.); Pratt Inst., 1975–76, MS (LS); Univ. of Akron, 1978–80, MS (Bot.). **Orgs.:** ALA: Ref. and Subscrpn. Bks. Review Com. (1980–); ACRL/Sci. and Tech. Sect., Plng. Com. (1981–). NY LA. NJ LA. AAAS. **Honors:** Beta Phi Mu. **Activities:** 1; 31, 39, 42; 58, 80, 91 **Addr.:** 8 Tulip Dr., Apt. 3J, Fords, NJ 08863.

Kessler, Carl Reed (F. 27, 1945, Winthrop, MA) Chief, Law Branch, Ctr. for Info. and Lib. Srvs., U.S. Dept. of the Interior, 1979–, Ref. Libn., Law Branch, 1976–79; Resrch. Libn., Proj. for Race and Soc. Policy, 1974–76; Pub. Srv. Libn., Antioch Sch. of Law, 1972–74. **Educ.:** Boston Univ., 1962–67, BA (Econ.); Univ. of MD, 1969–72, MLS; George Mason Univ., 1978– (Law). **Orgs.:** AALL. SLA. Law Libns. Socty. of DC. Assn. for Fed. Info. Resrcs. Mgt. **Activities:** 1, 4; 17, 39, 41; 59, 77, 78 **Addr.:** 3636 Alton Pl., N.W., Washington, DC 20008.

Kessler, Ridley R., Jr. (Mr. 20, 1941, Hendersonville, NC) Adjunct Instr., Sch. of Lib. Sci., Univ. of NC, 1978–, Fed. Docum. Libn. 1973–, Intl. Docum. Libn., 1971–73, Part-time Instr. Sch. of Lib. Sci., 1975–78, Asst. Docum. Libn., 1970–71; Tchr., Gastonia City Sch. Syst., 1964–69. **Educ.:** Univ. of NC, 1961–64, AB (Hist., Eng.), 1964–66, MAT (Educ.), 1968–70, MSLS. **Orgs.:** Docum. Libns. of NC: VP (1974–75); Pres. (1975–76); Exec. Bd. (1973–). SLA: NC Div., Archvst. (1978–); Exec. Bd. (1975–76). NC LA. NC OLUG. **Pubns.:** *Index to Readex Microprint Edition of JPRS Reports, 1974–76* (1978); "State Documents, an Expanding Resource," *Southeastern Libn.* (Fall 1971); Ed., *The Docket* nsltr. (1976–77). **Activities:** 1; 29, 33, 39 **Addr.:** BA/SS Division–Documents, Wilson Library, University of North Carolina, Chapel Hill, NC 27514.

Kessler, Selma P. (Ag. 31, 1922, Atlantic City, NJ) Asst. Coord., Pub. Libs., NJ State Lib., 1972–; Dir., Gloucester City Lib., 1965–72; Libn., Temple Sinai, 1963–72. **Educ.:** Univ. of PA, 1939–43, BA (Pol. Sci.); Drexel Univ., 1963–65, MLS. **Orgs.:** NJ LA: Rec. Secy. (1970); Treas. (1972–1976). AJL. ALA: PR Srvs. to Pub. Libs. Com.; Small Libs. Pubns. Com.; Stats. for State Agencies Com.; ALTA, Task Force on Persnl. Policies; Relshps. with State Assns. Com. **Honors:** ALA, John Cotton Dana Awd., 1967; Lib. PR Cncl., Outstan. Pubcty., 1971. **Pubns.:** *Industry Wide Collective Bargaining (An Annotated Bibliography)* (1948); The Moorestown Index of Historical articles," *Drexel Qtly.* 1966. **Activities:** 4, 9; 17, 24, 25; 77 **Addr.:** 10 Lambeth House, Moorestown, NJ 08057.

Ketchersid, Arthur L. (O. 16, 1932, Asbury Park, NJ) Asst. Dir., Tech. Srvs., Univ. of S. FL, 1973–; Asst. Dir., Tech. Srvs., Univ. of Ctrl. FL, 1967–70; 1st Asst. Catlgr., Univ. of GA, 1964–67, Catlgr., 1961–64. **Educ.:** FL State Univ., 1957–59, BS (Hist.), 1960–61, MLS; Univ. of IL, 1970–73, CAS (LS). **Orgs.:** ALA. FL LA. **Activities:** 1; 15, 17, 20 **Addr.:** 13801 Lazy Oak Dr., Lutz, FL 33549.

Ketchin, Jewell Marie W. (N. 11, 1923, Augusta, GA) Cmnty. Srvs., Dekalb Lib. Syst.; Audio Visual Coordinator, 1977; Media Specialist, Dekalb Cnty. Schs. **Educ.:** GA Coll.; GA State Univ.; Emory Univ. **Orgs.:** ALA: LITA RT; ASCLA. SELA. GA LA. Natl. Educ. Assn. GA Educ. Assn. GA Educ. Media Assn. Sch. Media Srvs. to Spec. Chld. Com. **Honors:** GA LA, 1st Place, PR, 1978; ALA, AASL, Sch. Media Srvs. Awd., 1976. **Pubns.:** *Integrating Communications Skills into Curricula for Elementary Schools* (1976); *Safety Education: Crime Prevention for Young Children* (1977); various sound synchronized multi-media programs (1978–79). **Activities:** 9, 10; 15, 24, 32; 66, 67, 72 **Addr.:** The Dekalb Library System, 3560 Kensington Rd., Decatur, GA 30032.

Key, Jack Dayton (Fb. 24, 1934, Enid, OK) Head Libn., Mayo Clinic, 1970–; Med. Libn., Lovelace Fndn. for Med. Educ. and Resrch., 1965–70; Pharm. Libn., Univ. of IA, 1962–64. **Educ.:** Phillips Univ., 1955–58, BA (Hist.); Univ. of NM, 1958–60, MA (Hist.); Univ. of IL, 1960–62, MS (LS). **Orgs.:** Med. LA. Amer. Med. Writers Assn. Amer. Inst. Hist. of Pharm. Amer. Assn. Hist. of Med. Amer. Osler Socty. Rotary. **Pubns.:** *The Origin of the Vaccine Inoculation by Edward Jenner* (1977); *Library Automation: The Orient and South Pacific* (1975); *Automated Activities in Health Sciences Libraries* (1975–78); *William A. Hammond (1828-1900)* (1979); various prof. articles. **Activities:** 12; 17, 24, 41; 80 **Addr.:** 624-23rd St. N.E., Rochester, MN 55901.

PROFESSIONAL ACTIVITIES: Institutions: 1. Acad. lib.; 2. Arch.; 3. Assn.; 4. Fed./Gvt. lib.; 5. Inst. lib.; 6. Mfr./Suppl.; 7. Milit. lib.; 8. Musm.; 9. Pub. lib.; 10. Sch. lib.; 11. Sch. of lib. sci.; 12. Spec. lib.; 13. State lib.; 14. (other). **Functions/Activities:** 15. Acq./Col. dev.; 16. Adult srvs.; 17. Admin.; 18. Apprais.; 19. Archit./Bldgs.; 20. Cat./Class.; 21. Chld. srvs.; 22. Circ.; 23. Cons./Pres.; 24. Consult.; 25. Cont. ed.; 26. Educ. lib. sci.; 27. Ext. srvs.; 28. Fund/Grants; 29. Gvt. pubs.; 30. Indx./Abs.; 31. Instr. lib. use; 32. Media srvs.; 33. Micro.; 34. Netwks./Coop.; 35. Persnl.; 36. PR; 37. Publshg.; 38. Recs. mgt.; 39. Ref. srvs.; 40. Repro.; 41. Resrch.; 42. Review.; 43. Secur.; 44. Serials; 45. Spec. col.; 46. Tech. srvs.; 47. Trustees/Bds.; 48. YA srvs.; 49. (other).

Keys, Marshall (Mr. 19, 1945, Ann Arbor, MI) Dir., Levin Meml. Lib., Curry Coll., 1980–, Reader Srvs. Libn., 1979–80; Sr. Ref. Libn., Univ. of MS, 1977–80; Asst. Ref. Libn., Hampden-Sydney Coll., 1975–76; Visit. Lectr., LS, Univ. of NC, Sum. 1979, 1980. **Educ.:** Rutgers Univ., 1962–66, AB, hons. (Eng.); Vanderbilt Univ., 1966–76, MA, PhD (Eng.); Univ. of NC, 1976–77, MS (LS). **Orgs.:** MS LA: Int. Frdm. Com. (1978–79); Legis. Com. (1978–89). ALA. **Pubns.:** "Faculty Status: An Heretical View," *MS Libs.* (Spr. 1979); "Burl Hunt: The Other Side of the Lens," *MS Libs.* (Sum. 1978). **Activities:** 1, 11; 24, 31, 35; 57, 65, 78 **Addr.:** Levin Memorial Library, Curry College, Milton, MA 02186.

Keys, Thomas Edward (D. 2, 1908, Greenville, MI) Med. Lib. Consult., Self-employed, 1973–; Libn. Emeritus, Mayo Clinic, 1973–, Sr. Lib. Consult., 1970–72, Libn., 1946–70; Rare Bks. Libn.; Army Med. Lib., (Cleveland, OH), 1942–46; Ref. Libn., Mayo Clinic, 1935–42, Asst. Libn., 1934–35. **Educ.:** Beloit Coll., 1926–31, AB (Econ.); Univ. of Chicago, 1932–34, MA (LS), Sc. D., L.C. Beloit College, 1972. **Orgs.:** Med. LA: Pres., 1957–58; Noyes Award, 1966; Editor of Med. LA Bull., 1942–45. Mayo Foundation for the History of Medicine: Pres., 1965–66. American Osler Society: Charter Member, 1970. **Honors:** Phi Beta Kappa; Med. LA, Flw., 1973; Univ. of MN, Cert. of Merit, 1973, Knight of the Order of the Falcon, Iceland, 1980. **Pubns.:** Comp., *Classics and Other Selected Papers in Medical Librarianship* (1980); Jt. auth., *Foundations of Anesthesiology* (1965); *Applied Medical Library Practice* (1958); *The History of Surgical Anesthesia* (1945); "The Mayo Clinic Library: An Introduction to Its Use," film (1953); various papers in libnshp. and hist. of med. **Activities:** 1, 12; 15, 17, 23; 57, 58, 80 **Addr.:** Pendleton Club Apt. 108, 1224 South Peninsula Dr., Daytona Beach, FL 32018.

Khan, Marta M. (Prague, Czech.) Asst. Dir., (Natl. Srvs.) Cat. Br., Nat. Lib. of Can., 1977–; Acting Asst. Dir. (Field Lib. Srvs.), Agriculture Can., 1976–77, Lib. Coord., 1973–76, Agriculture Can., Chief Libn., Water Mgt. Lib., Environment Can., 1972–73. **Educ.:** McGill Univ., 1961–66, BSc (Bio.), 1966–68, MLS. **Orgs.:** SLA: Nat. Resrcs. Div. (1972–76). Can. LA. **Activities:** 4, 12; 17, 20, 46; 57, 58, 91 **Addr.:** Cataloguing Branch, National Library of Canada, Ottawa, ON K1A 0N4 Canada.

Khan, Mohammed A. S. (Mr. 14, 1950, Hyderabad, Andhra Pradesh, India) Lib. Consult., US Pub. Hlth. Srvcs., 1979–; Libn., Univ. of Sulaimaniyah, Iraq, 1976–78; Libn., City Lib., Hyderabad, A. P. India, 1970–75. **Educ.:** Osmania Univ., Hyderabad, India, 1967–70, BS (Chem.); Long Island Univ., 1978–79, MLS; Institute of Human Study–Osmania University, 1972–73, Dip. (Educ.). **Orgs.:** ALA. ASIS. SLA. Intl. Assn., India: Gen. Secy. (1970–76). AU India Med. Prac. Academy: Gen. Secy. (1970–76). **Pubns.:** "History of Classification and Cataloging," *Univ. of Salaimauiyah Lib. Jnl.* (1977). **Activities:** 1, 12; 20, 24, 39; 77, 80, 91 **Addr.:** 918 E 14th St., Apt. C-10, Brooklyn, NY 11230.

Khan, Syed M. A. (O. 7, 1945, Hyderabad, India) Asst. Prof. of Lib. Sci., Asst. Life Sci. Libn., Purdue Univ., 1980–; Dryland Agr., Vetny. Med. Libn., OR State Univ., 1978–80; Sci. Libn., Univ. of AZ, 1976–78. **Educ.:** A. P. Agr. Univ., Hyderabad, India, 1966–70, BSc (Agr.); Univ. of IL, 1972–74, MS (Horticulture), 1974–75, MS (LS). **Orgs.:** ALA. AAUP. AAAS. **Pubns.:** Cmplr., *Bibliography of Dryland Agriculture Bibliography* 3rd Ed. (1980); "Influence of Nitrogen fertilization upon Protein and Nitrate Concentration in some Vegetable Crops," *Hortscience* (Ap. 1974); "Energy in Agriculture," *Serials Review* (O. 1981); various bibl., guides (1977–80). **Activities:** 1; 15, 39, 41; 57, 58, 91 **Addr.:** Life Sciences Library, Lilly Hall of Life Science, Purdue University, W. Lafayette, IN 47907.

Kheel, Susan T. (D. 6, 1945, Brooklyn, NY) Head, Ref. and Info. Srvs., The Lib., E. Brunswick, 1976–, Ref. Libn., 1973–75. **Educ.:** Rutgers Univ., 1963–67, BA (Fr., Educ.), 1970–72, MLS. **Orgs.:** ALA. NJ LA: Ref. Sect. (Secy., 1980–81). **Honors:** Beta Phi Mu. **Activities:** 9; 39 **Addr.:** The Library, 2 Jean Walling Civic Center, East Brunswick, NJ 08816.

Kibildis, Melba Lucille (F. 25, 1918, Litchfield, IL) Libn., Untd. Auto Workers, 1979–, Asst. Libn., 1974–79; Ed., Work Related Abs., Info. Coord., 1964–74; Libn., Untd. Auto Workers, 1948–57. **Educ.:** Univ. of MI, 1939–42, (Soc. Sci.); Wayne State Univ., 1950–57, (Lib. Courses). **Orgs.:** Com. of Indus. Rel. Libns. SLA. Women's Intl. Leag. for Peace and Frdm. **Activities:** 12; 15, 17, 20; 59, 92, 95-Indus. rel. **Addr.:** Research Library, United Automobile Workers, 8000 E. Jefferson, Detroit, MI 48214.

Kidd, Betty H. (Ja. 23, 1943, Russell, ON) Dir., Natl. Map Col., Pub. Arch. of Can., 1974–, Head, Can. Sect., Natl. Map Col., 1972–74, Catlgr., Head, Cat. Unit, 1966–72; Tchr., Ottawa Collegiate Bd. and N. Dundas Dist. Bd., 1963–66. **Educ.:** Carleton Univ., 1960–63, 1971, BA Honours (Hist.); Arch. Course, Pub. Arch. of Canada, 1966; Sec. Sch. Tchg. Cert., Prov. of ON; Sem. in Admin./Mgt. **Orgs.:** Assn. of Can. Archvsts. Assn. of Can. Map Libs.: Pres. (1973–74); Treas. (1972–73); Ch., Cons. Com. West. Assn. of Map Libs. New Zealand Mapkeeper's Circle. Other orgs. Can. Cartographic Assn.: Contrib. ed., *The Canadian Cartographer.* Can. Hist. Assn. Intl. Socty. for the Hist. of Cartography: Contrib. ed., *Imago Mundi.* Socty. for the Hist. of Discoveries. Other orgs. **Pubns.:** *County atlases of Canada: A descriptive catalogue* (1970); "National Map Collection: An Update," SLA, Geo. and Map Div., *Bltn.* (1979); "Maps in genealogical research," *Families* (1977); "The Map User in Libraries and Archives," Assn. of Can. Map Libs. *Bltn.* (1977); "Maps as sources of historical evidence," *Procs.* of Assn. of Can. Map Libs. (1970); other articles. **Activities:** 2; 17; 70 **Addr.:** Public Archives of Canada, 395 Wellington St., Ottawa, ON K1A 0N3 Canada.

Kidd, Claren M. (Mr. 14, 1944, Geary, OK) Geo. Libn., Univ. of OK, 1973–; ILL Libn., Univ. of OK, 1972–73. **Educ.:** Univ. of OK, 1962–66, BA (Geog.), 1966–67, MA (Geog.); Univ. of Pittsburgh, 1971–72, MLS. **Orgs.:** SLA. Geoscience Info. Socty.: Guidebook Com. (1975), Open-File Rpts. Com. (1978). **Honors:** Sigma Gamma Epilson, OK, Spec. Recog. Awd., 1978. **Pubns.:** "Coll. Dev. in Geoscience Libs: Guidebooks," Geoscience Info. Socty., *Prcs.* (1980). **Activities:** 1; 15, 17, 31; 70, 86, 91 **Addr.:** Geology Library, University of Oklahoma, Norman, OK 73019.

Kidd, Jerry S. (O. 29, 1928, Decatur, IL) Prof. (LS), Univ. of MD, 1967–; Prog. Dir., Natl. Sci. Fndn., 1964–67; Prin. Staff Sci., A.A.I. Corp., 1962–64; Assoc. Lab. Dir., OH State Univ., 1956–62. **Educ.:** IL Wesleyan Univ., 1946–50, BS (Biol.); Northwest. Univ., 1952–56, MA, Ph.D. (Psy.). **Orgs.:** ASIS. AAAS. **Honors:** US Govt., Fulbright Fellow, 1978; US Govt., USICA Fellow, 1979. **Pubns.:** *New Teachers for the Inner-City* (1972); "Redundancy, Relevance and Value to Users," *Jnl. of Docum.* (S. 1976); "On-Line Bibliographic Services," *Coll. & Resrch. Libs.* (Jl. 1977). **Activities:** 12; 17, 26, 41; 54, 75, 91 **Addr.:** College of Library and Information Science, University of Maryland, College Park, MD 20742.

Kidder, Charles Peter (Ag. 30, 1925, Staten Island, NY) Asst. Cat. Ed., Lib. of Congs., 1969–; Descr. Catlgr., 1968–69; Head Catlgr., Kenyon Coll., 1963–68; Head, Tech. Srvs., Denison Univ., 1960–63. **Educ.:** Ripon Coll., 1944–48; Univ. of WI, 1948–50, BA (Econ.), MA (LS). Yale Univ. (Army Spec. Trng. Prog.), 1945–46 (Japanese). **Orgs.:** ALA. DC LA. Potomac Tech. Prcs. Libns. Socty. of Fed. Linguists. Lib. of Congs. Prof. Assn. **Activities:** 1, 4; 15, 20; 94 **Addr.:** 3513 Dupont Ave., Kensington, MD 20795.

Kidder, Frederick Elwyn (S. 22, 1919, White Bear Lake, MN) Asst. Priest/Libn., St. Stephen's Episcopal Church, Guaynabo, PR, 1976–; Dir., Grad. Sch. of LS, Univ. of PR, Rio Piedras, 1969–76; Visit. Assoc. Prof., LS, Univ. of IL, 1968–69; Dir., Div. of Soc. Sci., Univ. of PR, Mayaguez, 1962–68. **Educ.:** Univ. of CA, Berkeley, 1936–40, AB (Intl. Rel.), 1949–50, BLS, 1950–52, MA (Pol. Sci.); Univ. of FL, 1956–65, PhD (Latin-Amer. Std.). **Orgs.:** CSLA. ALA. Socty. of Libns. of PR: Pres. (1967–68, 1973–74). Amer. Pol. Sci. Assn. Amer. Socty. for Pub. Admin. **Honors:** Phi Beta Kappa; Beta Phi Mu; Socty. of Libns. of PR, Libn. of the Yr., 1977. **Pubns.:** *Latin America and UNESCO: The First Five Years* (1960); "Puerto Rico's Libraries and Librarians," *FL Libs.* (Mr. 1958); "Puerto Rico al dia: A Brief Bibliography," *Doors to Latin Amer.* (O. 1956); "Survey of Investigations in Progress in the Field of Latin American Studies," *Pan American Union* (1956). **Activities:** 1, 11; 20, 26, 39; 54, 90, 92 **Addr.:** 103 Elemi St., Guaynabo, PR 00657.

Kidman, Roy L. (Jl. 25, 1925, Redondo Beach, CA) Libn., Univ. South. CA Lib., 1971–; Libn., Rutgers Univ., 1968–71; Biomed. Libn., Univ. CA, San Diego, 1963–68; Asst. Dir., Tulane Univ., 1960–62, Acting Dir., 1959–60; Sci. Libn., Univ. KS, 1954–59; Cat., Univ. CA, Los Angeles Law Sch., 1953–54. **Educ.:** Univ. CA, Los Angeles, 1945–51, BS (Chem.); Univ. South. CA, 1952–53, MS (LS). **Orgs.:** ALA. CA LA. Zamorano Club. **Honors:** Beta Phi Mu. **Activities:** 1; 17, 39; 80, 91 **Addr.:** University of Southern California Library, Los Angeles, CA 90007.*

Kidney, Sr. Mary Olivia (N. 4, 1931, Dover, NH) Lib. Dir., Regis Coll., 1979–; Acq./Serials Libn., Colby-Sawyer Coll., 1978–79; Coll. Libn., Mt. St. Mary Coll., 1973–78, Asst. Coll. Libn., 1968–73. **Educ.:** Mt. St. Mary Coll., 1963, BA (Eng.); Simmons Coll., 1969, MS (LS). **Orgs.:** ALA. New Eng. LA. MA LA. Cath. LA. **Activities:** 1; 15, 17 **Addr.:** Regis College Library, Weston, MA 02193.

Kienitz, LaDonna T. (S. 27, 1930, Bay City, MI) Lib. Dir., Lincolnwood Lib., 1978–, Proj. Dir., 1977–78; Head Libn., Woodlands Acad., Lake Forest, IL, 1973–77; Instr., Pirmasens Amer. Sch., Pirmasens, Germ., 1960–63; Instr., Waukegan Pub. Schs., 1956–57. **Educ.:** Westmar Coll., 1949–51, BA (Math); Rosary Coll., 1966–70, MALS, 1970–73 (Hist. of Libs.). **Orgs.:** ALA. IL LA. Reg. Lib. Adv. Cncl.: Exec. Com. (Secy., 1980). Glencoe League of Women Voters: League Obs. of Local Govt. (1979–). **Honors:** Beta Phi Mu, 1970. **Activities:** 9, 10; 17, 35, 47 **Addr.:** 361 Madison Ave., Glencoe, IL 60022.

Kies, Cosette N. (S. 2, 1936, Platteville, WI) Assoc. Prof., LS, Vanderbilt Univ., 1978–, Asst. Prof., 1975–78; Asst. Dir., Persnl. and PR, Ferguson Lib., Stanford (CT), 1971–74; Lib. Career Consult., IL State Lib., 1969–71; Prof. Asst., ALA, 1968–69; Sr. Asst. Libn/Asst. Prof., Univ. of NE, 1963–67; Chld. Libn., Fond du Lac Pub. Lib., 1962–63; Art Tchr., Grafton Pub. Schs., 1957–59. **Educ.:** WI State Coll., 1954–57, BS (Hist.); Univ. of WI, 1958–61, MA (Art Hist.), 1961–62, MA (LS); Columbia Univ., 1973–77, DLS. **Orgs.:** ALA: LAMA, Stats. for Lib. Educ. Com. (1979–80); PLA; RASD; SRRT; Ofc. of Lib. Persnl. Rel., Adv. Com. (1979–81); ALSC, Newbery-Caldecott Com. (1976); Lib. Educ. Div., Beta Phi Mu Awd. Com. (1975–76). AALS: Comm. Com. (1978–80); Nom. Com. (1977–78). Women's Natl. Bk. Assn.: PR Dir. (1980–). CLENE: Adv. Com. (1977–80). Various other orgs. Leag. of Women Voters. **Honors:** Beta Phi Mu; Halsey W. Wilson Rcrt. Awd., IL State Lib., 1970; Fulbright Hayes Awd., 1979. **Pubns.:** *Problems in Library Public Relations* (1974); *Projecting a Positive Image Through Public Relations* (1978); "Publishing and Censorship in Brazil," *The Bookwoman.* (F. 1981); "The Inside Story: School Media Specialists and Their Public Relations Effectiveness," *Excel. in Sch. Media Progs.* (1980); various articles, reviews, other pubns. **Activities:** 9, 14-Lib. educ.; 26, 35, 36; 50, 55, 93 **Addr.:** Box 501, Dept. of Library and Information Science, George Peabody College for Teachers, Vanderbilt University, Nashville, TN 37203.

Kiewitt, Eva L. (Ag. 12, 1927, Crothersville, IN) Assoc. Dir., CBN Univ. Lib., 1981–; Head, Branch Lib., Sch. of Lib. & Info. Sci., IN Univ., 1973–, Educ. Libn., 1967–73; Libn., Binford Jr. HS, 1962–67; Libn., Elementary/Jr. High, Ulm, Germany, 1960–62. **Educ.:** Ball State Univ., 1945–49, BS (Educ.); IN Univ., Bloomington, 1959–60, MLS, 1973, PhD (Lib. Sci.), 1967, Lib. Supvsr. Cert. **Orgs.:** ALA: ACRL: Ch. Educ. & Bhvl. Sci. Sect. (1980–81); Ch. of Libn. of Lib. Sci. Coll. Grp. (1979–80). Assn. of IN Media Educ.: Dist. 10 Dir. (1980–82). ASIS. Delta Kappa Gamma: State Nom. Com. Ch. (1979–81). **Honors:** Pi Lambda Theta, 1979. **Pubns.:** *Evaluating Information Retrieval Systems: The PROBE Program* (1979); "Reference Collections in Accredited Library Schools," *Jnl. of Educ. for Libnshp.* (Sum. 1978); "A User Study of a Computer Retrieval System," *Coll. and Resrch. Libs.* (N. 1975); (Microfiche) *Cost-Benefit Analysis of a Computer Retrieval System* (Ag. 1976). **Activities:** 1; 17, 26 **Addr.:** 4912 Admiration Dr., Virginia Beach, VA 23464.

Kigar, Lorraine Shirley (Ja. 4, 1936, Paris, MI) Dir. of Lib., Grand Rapids Bapt. Coll. and Semy., 1975–; Media Spec./Dir., North. Schs. (Portage, MI), 1968–75; Dir. of Libs., Hastings Pub. Schs., 1961–67. **Educ.:** Ctrl. MI Univ., 1954–58, BS (Sp., Bio.); West. MI Univ., 1962–68, MS (LS), 1970–75, Spec. (Admin.). **Orgs.:** MI LA. Christ. Libns. Assn. Grand Rapids Assn. of Univ. Libs. Kant Ottawa Acad. LA. Various other orgs. MI Educ. Assn. **Honors:** Beta Phi Mu; Delta Kappa Gamma, Outstan. Educ., 1975. **Pubns.:** "Managing Your Library by Objectives," *Christ. Libn.* (19–); twelve cable TV progs. on YA and readg. (1973–75). **Activities:** 1, 10; 17, 19, 24; 90 **Addr.:** 2701 Mayfield N.E., Grand Rapids, MI 49505.

Kiger, Anne Fox (Ap. 17, 1932, Cleveland, OH) Staff Spec., Indexing, Amer. Hosp. Assn., 1977–; Actg. Head Libn., Ctr. for Bioethics, Georgetown Univ., 1976–77, Asst. Libn., 1975–76; Catlgr., DC Chld. Hosp. Lib., 1974–75. **Educ.:** Rosemont Coll., 1952–56 (Math.), Amer. Univ., 1966–70, BA (Anthro.); Univ. of MD, 1972–75, MLS; Med. LA, 1976, Cert. **Orgs.:** Med. LA. ASIS. Montgomery Cnty. (MD) Chevy Chase Branch Adv. Bd. **Honors:** Beta Phi Mu. **Pubns.:** Jt. cmplr., *Hospital Literature Index* (1978–); jt. ed., *Hospital Literature Subject Headings Transition Guide to Medical Subject Headings* (1979); "Current Document Coverage in Health Planning and Administration Data Base," *Natl. Lib. Med. Tech. Bltn.* (Ag. 1980). **Activities:** 3, 4; 20, 30, 37; 56, 57, 80 **Addr.:** American Hospital Association/National Library of Medicine, Index Section, 8600 Rockville Pike, Bethesda, MD 20014.

Kijanka, Dorothy M. (S. 4, 1933, Mt. Olive, IL) Asst. Univ. Libn., Fairfield Univ., 1974–; Ref. Libn., Fairfield Univ., 1968–74; Greenwich, CT Pub. Lib., 1966–68. **Educ.:** Univ. of IL, 1951–55, AB (Hist.); Rutgers Univ., 1965–66, MLS. **Orgs.:** ALA. New England LA. CT LA: Ch., Ref. and Adult Srvcs. Sect. (1975). Natl. LA. Lib. Group of Southwestern CT: Pres. (1977–78). Women's Natl. Book Assn. Socty. of Creative Arts of Newtown. **Honors:** Phi Alpha Theta, 1955; Alpha Lambda Delta, 1952. **Pubns.:** "Faculty Library Privileges," *Jnl. of Acad. Libnshp.* (Mr. 1978). **Activities:** 1; 17, 22, 39; 54, 55 **Addr.:** Nyselius Library, Fairfield University, Fairfield, CT 06430.

Kile, Barbara G. (Jl. 6, 1945, Decatur, IL) Head, Gvt. Docum. and Micro. Dept., Rice Univ. Lib., 1972–, Gifts and Exch. Libn., 1971–72; Gifts and Exch. Libn., Purdue Univ. Libs., 1970–71; Ref. and Gvt. Docum. Libn., CT Coll. Lib., 1968–70. **Educ.:** Univ. of IL, 1964–67, BA (Pol. Sci.), 1967–68, MS (LS). **Orgs.:** ALA: GODORT, Clearinghse. (Ch., 1980–81), Fed. Docum. Task Frc. (1979–80); Secy. Pro-tem, 1978). TX LA: Dist. 8 Legis. Com. (1977–79); Docum. RT, Ch. (1976–77), Secy.-Treas. (1974–76); various other coms. **Honors:** Beta Phi Mu, 1968. **Pubns.:** Cmplr., ed., of "Proceedings of Federal Documents Workshop for Region VI," *TX Libs.* (Sum. 1976); "Highlights of Federal Documents Workshop," *Gvt. Docum. Review* (1977). **Activities:** 1; 29, 33; 95-Patents. **Addr.:** Fondren Library, Rice University, P.O. Box 1892, Houston, TX 77001.

Kilgour, Frederick G. (Ja. 6, 1914, Springfield, MA) Vice Ch., Bd. of Trustees, OCLC, Inc., 1981–; Pres., Exec. Dir., 1967–80; Assoc. Libn., Resrch. and Dev., Yale Univ., 1965–67, Lectr., Hist. of Sci. and Med., 1961–67, Lectr., Hist. of Sci.,

Special Subjects/Services: 50. Adult educ.; 51. Advert./Mktg.; 52. Aerosp.; 53. Agric.; 54. Area std.; 55. Arts/Hum.; 56. Autom.; 57. Bibl./Prtg.; 58. Bio. sci.; 59. Bus./Fin.; 60. Chem.; 61. Copyrt.; 62. Documtn.; 63. Educ.; 64. Engin.; 65. Env.; 66. Eth. grps.; 67. Film; 68. Food/Nutr.; 69. Geneal.; 70. Geo.; 71. Geol.; 72. Handcpd.; 73. Hist.; 74. Int. frdm.; 75. Info. sci.; 76. Insr.; 77. Law; 78. Legis.; 79. Math./Comp. sci.; 80. Med.; 81. Metals; 82. Nat. resrcs.; 83. Newsp.; 84. Nuc. sci.; 85. Oral hist.; 86. Petr./Energy; 87. Pharm.; 88. Phys./Astr./Math.; 89. Readg.; 90. Relig.; 91. Sci./Tech.; 92. Soc. sci.; 93. Telecom.; 94. Transp.; 95. (other).

1950–59; Managing Ed., *Yale Jnl. of Bio. and Med.*, 1949–65; Libn., Yale Med. Lib., 1948–65; Deputy Dir., Ofc. of Intelligence Coll. and Dssm., Dept. of State, 1946–48; other positions in libnshp., 1940–46. **Educ.:** Harvard Coll., AB, Harvard Univ., 1939–42; Columbia Univ., 1939–41. Marietta Coll., LLD, 1980; OH State Univ., DHL, 1980; Coll. of Wooster, LLD, 1981. **Orgs.:** ALA. ASIS. LA (UK). LA Australia. Other assns. **Honors:** Central Ohio Chapter of the American Society for Information Science, Recognition of Achievement, 1974; ASIS, Awd. of Merit, 1979; ACRL, Co-recipient, Acad./Resrch. Libn. of the Year, 1979. LITA, Lib. and Info. Tech. Awd., 1979. ALA, Melvil Dewey Awd., 1978. Other awds. **Pubns.:** *Library of the Medical Institution of Yale College and Its Catalogue of 1865* (1960); jt. auth., *Engineering in History* (1956); many articles; ed., *Jnl. of Lib. Autom.* (1968–72). **Activities:** 14-Comp. Lib. Ntwk.; 34 **Addr.:** OCLC, Inc., 6565 Frantz Rd., Dublin, OH 43017.

Kilpatrick, Sr. Barbara Anne (Mr. 12, 1932, Bessemer, AL) Tchr., Libn., St. Aloysius Sch., 1970–; Tchr., Libn., St. Mary's (AL), 1968–70; Tchr., Libn., St. Peter's (MD), 1967–68; Tchr., Prin., Immaculate Conception (GA), 1965–67; Tchr., Libn., Our Lady of the Assumption (GA), 1963–65; Tchr., Our Lady of the Assumption (AL), 1961–63; Tchr., Various other Cath. schs., 1953–61. **Educ.:** Mt. St. Agnes Coll., 1950–57, BS (Educ.); Emory Univ., 1966–70, MLS; Univ. of AL, 1978–80, Ed.S. (LS). **Orgs.:** Cath. LA: Chlds. Sect. (Secy., 1977–79); (Ch., 1981–); AL Unit. (Ch., 1968–). AL LA. SELA. Other orgs. Natl. Cath. Educ. Assn. **Activities:** 9, 10; 20, 21, 39; 63, 90 **Addr.:** St. Aloysius School, P. O. Box 664, Bessemer, AL 35020.

Kilpatrick, Thomas L. (N. 27, 1937, Henry Cnty., TN) Interlib. Loan Libn./Resrch. and Ref. Coord., Southern IL Univ., Carbondale, 1975–, Asst. Educ. Psych. Libn., Southern IL Univ., Carbondale, 1964–75; Libn., Herrin Com. HS, 1958–64. **Educ.:** Univ. of TN, Martin, 1955–56; Southern IL Univ., Carbondale, 1956–59, BS (Eng.); Univ. of IL, Urbana, 1960–63, MSLS; Vanderbilt/Peabody Coll., 1978, PhD (Educ. Admin.). **Orgs.:** ALA: ACRL. IL LA. IL Assn. of Coll. and Resrch. Libs. **Honors:** Phi Delta Kappa. Beta Phi Mu. **Pubns.:** "Illinois! Illinois! An Annotated Bibliography of Fiction" (1979). **Activities:** 1; 17, 34, 39; 61, 63 **Addr.:** 102 S. Hewitt, Carbondale, IL 62901.

Kilpela, Raymond Earl Oliver (Hancock, MI) Assoc. Prof., Sch. of Lib. and Info. Mgmt., Univ. of Soutn. CA, 1980–; Assoc. Dean & Assoc. Prof., Sch. of LS, 1963–80; Head Card Prep. Unit, Purdue Univ., 1960–63; Instr., LS, Univ. of MI, 1960; Asst. Dept. Mgr., MI Hosp. Srv.; insurance work; Asst. Prof. of Hist. & Pol. Sci., Hillsdale Coll. **Educ.:** Flint Jr. Coll., AA (Liberal Arts); Univ. of MI, BA (Pol. Sci.), MA (Pol. Sci.), MA in LS, PhD (LS). **Orgs.:** ALA: ACRL; RTSD. CA Assn. of Resrch. Libs. South. CA Tech. Prcs. Grp. CA LA: Grtr. Los Angeles Chap. Phi Beta Kappa. Phi Kappa Phi. **Honors:** Beta Phi Mu. **Pubns.:** "The administrative structure of the university library," *Coll. & Resrch. Libs.* (1968); "The university library committee," *Coll. & Resrch. Libs.* (1968). **Activities:** 1; 17, 20, 35, 46; 63, 92 **Addr.:** School of Library and Information Management, University of Southern California, Los Angeles, CA 90007.

Kim, Bang Ja (S. 2, 1940, Pusan, Korea) Docum. Libn., SD State Univ., 1978–; Asst. Ref. Libn., 1967–70, 1972–77; Instr., Univ. of OR, 1965–66. **Educ.:** Ewha Womens Univ., 1958–61, BA (Eng.); Univ. of OR, 1963–65, MA (LS); OR State Univ., 1966–67. **Orgs.:** ALA: GODORT. SD LA: Docum. Com. (1975–)/Acad. Sect. (Pres., 1978; Secy. Treas., 1977). Leag. of Women Voters. SD State Univ. Acad. Senate. **Pubns.:** Ed., *The Sioux Falls Argus Leader Index* (1979–). **Activities:** 1; 29, 30, 39; 63, 83 **Addr.:** Library, South Dakota State University, Brookings, SD 57007.

Kim, Chisu (O. 9, 1931, Seoul, Korea) Head, Docum. and Maps Dept., CA Polytech. State Univ., 1974–; Acq. Libn., Humboldt State Univ., 1969–74. **Educ.:** Dan Kook Univ., 1955–59, LLB; Univ. of OR, 1962–67, MA (Pub. Admin.), 1968–69, MLS. **Orgs.:** CA LA. West. Assn. Map Libs. CA Map Socty. **Activities:** 1; 15, 29; 54, 70, 92 **Addr.:** California Polytechnic State University Library, San Luis Obispo, CA 93407.

Kim, Choong H. (N. 25, 1923, Seoul, Korea) Prof. of Lib. Sci., IN State Univ., 1977–, Assoc. Prof. of Lib. Sci., 1968–77; Asst. Prof. of Lib. Sci., Eastern IL Univ., 1965–68; Cat. Libn., Hlth. Sci. Lib., Univ. of MD, 1964–65. **Educ.:** Honylk Univ., Seoul, Korea, 1954–59, BA (Eng. Lit.); IN Univ., Bloomington, 1959–60, MALS; Rutgers Univ., 1960–64, PhD (Lib. Sci.). **Orgs.:** ALA. IN LA. SLA. ASIS. **Honors:** Fulbright Resrch. Flwshp., 1977. **Pubns.:** *Books by Mail–A Handbook for Libraries* (1977); "Reading Public of Mini-Libraries in Rural Korea," *Libri* (Jl. 1978); "The Mini-Library Movement in Rural Korea," *Intl. Lib. Review* (1979). **Activities:** 11; 26; 75 **Addr.:** Dept. of Library Science, IN State Univ., Terre Haute, IN 47809.

Kim, Ik-Sam (D. 17, 1936, Seoul, Korea) Head, Oriental Lib., Univ. of CA, Los Angeles, 1979–, Actg. Head, Oriental Lib., 1976–78, Chief Ref. Libn. and Catlgr., Japanese & Korean Mtrls., 1970–76; Lect. in Chinese, Seoul Natl. Univ., 1967–68. **Educ.:** Seoul Natl. Univ., 1957–61, BA (Chinese), 1961–63, MA (Chinese); Harvard Univ., 1964–66, MA (Far East. Lang.); Univ. of CA, Berkeley, 1969–70, MLS; Univ. of CA, Los Angeles, 1974– (Oriental Lang.). **Orgs.:** ALA: ACRL. South. CA Tech. Prcs. Grp. Assn. for Korean Std.: Pres. (1979–); VP (1976–77). Assn. for Asian Std. Amer. Oriental Socty. South. CA China Colloquium. Other orgs. **Pubns.:** *Kongja ui chihye* (1971). **Activities:** 1, 12; 15, 17, 45; 54, 55, 92 **Addr.:** Oriental Library, Univ. of California at Los Angeles, Los Angeles, CA 90024.

Kim, Sanok P. (Ja. 10, 1933, Seoul, Korea) Sr. Catlgr., Washington Univ., 1978–, Catlgr., 1968–78. **Educ.:** Clark Univ., 1954–56, BA (Rom. Langs.); Univ. of WI, 1956–58, MA (Fr.); Univ. of IL, 1967–68, MS (LS). **Orgs.:** ALA. MO LA. **Honors:** Phi Beta Kappa; Beta Phi Mu. **Activities:** 1; 20 **Addr.:** Washington University Libraries, Sinclair & Lindell Blvds., St. Louis, MO 63130.

Kim, Sook-Hyun (N. 1, 1939, Seoul, Korea) Asst. Prof., Univ. of TN, 1980–; Asst. Prof., IA State Univ., 1979–80; Asst. Prof., Graceland Coll., 1969–79; Catlgr., KS Univ., 1967–69. **Educ.:** Ewha Women's Univ. (Seoul, Korea) 1958–62, BA (Eng.); IN Univ., 1963–65, MA (LS). **Orgs.:** ALA. IA LA. **Activities:** 1; 20, 26, 44; 75 **Addr.:** 103 Howell Cir., Maryville, TN 37801.

Kim, Theodore Ungchang (Ap. 2, 1936, Choon Chun, Korea) Chief, Bk. Div., Unvsl. Serials and Bk. Exch., Inc., 1965–, Asst. Chief, Serials Div., 1964–65. **Educ.:** Georgetown Univ., 1958–61, BSFS (Intl. Affairs); Cath. Univ. of Amer., 1962–64. **Orgs.:** Potomac Tech. Prcs. Libns. **Addr.:** 12402 Stonehaven Ln., Bowie, MD 20715.

Kimball, Jane A. (My. 6, 1939, Saginaw, MI) Asst. to the Univ. Libn., Univ. of CA, Davis, 1980–; Ref. Libn., 1976–80, Head, Ref. Dept., 1970–76, Asst. Head, Ref. 1969–70; Head, Spec. Col./Arch., Univ. of CA, Irvine, Asst. Head, Ref., 1966–67; Sr. Asst. Ref. Libn./Lcl. Hist. Libn., Northampton (Eng.) Pub. Lib., 1965–66; Gen. Ref. Libn., Univ. of CA, Berkeley, 1963–65. **Educ.:** Scripps Coll., 1957–61, BA (Phil.); Univ. of CA, Irvine, 1965–70, MA (Hist.); Univ. of South. CA, 1962–63 (LS). **Orgs.:** CA LA. ALA: Mem. Com. (1977). **Pubns.:** "Entomology," *Guide to Sources for Agricultural and Biological Research* (1981); *Honorary Freemen of the County Borough of Northampton* (1966). **Activities:** 1; 17, 19, 28 **Addr.:** Shields Library, University of California, Davis, CA 95616.

Kimball, Richard H. (Ja. 10, 1927, Cambridge, MA) Exec. Dir., N. Country 3R's Cncl., 1971–; Reg. Sales Mgr., Info. Dsgn., Inc., 1971; Sci. Biblgphr., SUNY, Albany, 1966–69; Ref. Libn., Skidmore Coll., 1965–66. **Educ.:** Univ. of NH, 1948–53, BS (Geo.); Simmons Coll., 1963–64, MLS; Auburn Univ., 1969–70, MPS (Pol. Sci.). **Orgs.:** ALA: ASCLA/Multitype Lib. Coop. Sect., Legis. Com. (1979–82), Nom. Com. (1980–82). NY LA. Antique Auto Club of Amer.: Andirondack-St. Lawrence Chap. (Secy., 1977–79). **Activities:** 1, 13; 15, 34, 39 **Addr.:** North Country 3R's Council, Box 568, Canton, NY 13617.

Kimbrough, J. Marion (Ja. 27, 1926, Wales, TN) Assoc. Prof., LS, Vanderbilt Univ., 1969–; Asst. Libn., Martin Coll., 1967–69; Asst. Prof., LA State Univ., New Orleans, 1964–67; Libn., Cumberland Coll., 1961–64; Libn., Giles Cnty. Pub. Schs., 1950–61. **Educ.:** George Peabody Coll., Vanderbilt Univ., 1947–49, BA (Soc. Sci.), 1949–50, MA (Hist.), 1959–61, MA (LS). **Orgs.:** ALA. AALS. SELA. TN LA. Various other orgs. **Activities:** 1; 17, 20, 46 **Addr.:** Route 5, Lawrenceburg, TN 38464.

Kimbrough, Joseph (Ap. 21, 1930, Bowling Green, KY) Dir., Minneapolis Pub. Lib. and Info. Ctr., 1975–; Asst. Libn., Dir. of Pub. Srvs., Denver Pub. Lib., 1970–75; Chief Libn., Lansing Pub. Lib., 1966–70. **Educ.:** West. KY Univ., 1948–52, AB (LS); IN Univ., 1955–56, MA (LS). **Orgs.:** ALA: LAMA, Cncl. (1980–81); MN LA: Midwest Fed. of Lib. Assns. (Liaison, 1979–). MI LA: Pres. (1968). MN Assn. for Cont. and Adult Educ.: Awds. Com. (Ch., 1980). **Activities:** 9; 17; 50 **Addr.:** Minneapolis Public Library and Information Center, 300 Nicollet Mall, Minneapolis, MN 55401.

Kimmage, Dennis A. (Ja. 23, 1943, Yonkers, NY) Sr. Asst. Libn./Coord., Bibl. Instr., SUNY Coll., Plattsburgh, 1976–; Asst. Prof., Russ., SUNY, Binghamton, 1970–76. **Educ.:** SUNY, Binghamton, 1961–65, BA, hons. (Hum.); Cornell Univ., 1965–70, MA, PhD. (Russ.); Syracuse Univ., 1975–76, MLS. **Orgs.:** ALA: ACRL/Slavic and E. European Sect. SUNY LA. Amer. Assn. for Advnc. of Slavic Std. **Activities:** 1; 31, 39; 54, 56, 57 **Addr.:** Feinberg Library, State University College, Plattsburgh, NY 12901.

Kimmel, Minna G. (F. 24, 1912, New Brunswick, NJ) Chld. Libn., Montclair (NJ) Pub. Lib., 1969–; Tech. Libn., CeLummus, 1967–68; Sr. Libn., Bloomfield Pub. Lib., 1963–67, Soc. Worker, NJ, 1935–40. **Educ.:** Douglass Coll., 1928–32, LittB (LS, Langs.); Rutgers Univ., 1960–63, MLS; NJ Prof. Libns. Cert. Untd. Fund. Hadassah. Temple Ner Tamid. **Honors:** Beta Phi Mu. **Activities:** 9; 20, 21, 39 **Addr.:** 488 Broad St., Bloomfield, NJ 07003.

Kimzey, Ann Combs (Ag. 26, 1940, Houston, TX) Instr., Lib. Sci./Lrng. Resrcs., Univ. Of Houston, Clear Lake City, 1976–; Libn., Tech. Srvs., Coll. of the Mainland, 1971–76; Instr., Lib. Sci. and Cat., Univ. of IL, 1967–68. **Educ.:** Rice Univ., 1958–62, BA (Romance Lang.); Univ. of IL, 1966–67, MSLS. **Orgs.:** ALA. Southwest LA. TX LA: Ch., Pub. Com. (1978–79); Plng. Com. (1979–81). TX Assn. for Educ. Tech.: Cert. Com. (1980). **Honors:** Univ. of IL Grad. Sch. of Lib. Sci., Shapiro Award, 1967; Beta Phi Mu. **Pubns.:** "Paperback Processing," *Unabashed Libn.* (Fall 1973); "An Automated Book Catalog for a Periodical Collection," *Serials Libn.* (Sum. 1978); "A Small Jewel for Children," *American Libraries* (Jan. 1981). **Activities:** 1, 11; 20, 26, 46 **Addr.:** 1882 Saxony Ln., Houston, TX 77058.

Kinchen, Robert P. (Mr. 12, 1933, New Orleans, LA) Dir., Onondaga Cnty. Pub. Lib., 1975–; Assoc. Dir., Rochester (NY) Pub. Lib., 1972–75; Admin. Asst. to Asst. Dir., Enoch Pratt Free Lib., Branch Head. **Educ.:** Northwest. of LA, 1952–56, BA (Hist.); LA State Univ., 1972–73, MA (LS); State Univ. Coll. of NY, Brockport, 1971–72, (Urban Admin.). **Orgs.:** ALA. NY LA: Persnl. Admin. Com., Ch. (1977–79); VP elect, Pub. Lib. Sect. (1980–81). Ctrl. NY Reg. Resrch. Cncl.: Bd. of Trustees (1976–). Univ. Club of Syracuse. **Activities:** 9; 28, 47; 77, 78 **Addr.:** Onondaga County Public Library, 327 Montgomery St., Syracuse, NY 13202.

King, Anne Ida (Ja. 2, 1925, Bronx, NY) Educ. Media Spec., Dorchester Sch., 1968–; Lang. arts tchr., Saddle Brook Schs., 1966–68. **Educ.:** Douglass Coll., 1942–44, (Chem.); William Paterson Coll., 1960–66, BA (Elem Educ.); Montclair State Coll., 1968–74 (Media); Rutgers Univ., 1975–76, MLS. **Orgs.:** NJ LA: Exhibits Ch. (1974–79). Bergen Cnty. Sch. Libns. Assn.: Pres. (1972–73). Educ. Media Assn. of NJ: Mem. ch. (1976–77); Treas. (1977–78); Jnl. Bus. Ed. (1978–79); Pres. (1980–81). Woodcliff Lake Educ. Assn.: Pres. (1972–74). **Activities:** 10; 21, 31, 32; 63 **Addr.:** 3-25 Dorothy St., Fair Lawn, NJ 07410.

King, Annie G. (Ja. 19, 1922, Trenton, NC) Lib. Dir., Tuskegee Inst., 1967–, Ref. Libn., 1952–66; Libn., FL Meml. Coll., 1948–50; Libn., NC Pub. Schs., 1948. **Educ.:** NC Ctrl. Univ., 1938–42, AB (Fr., Hist.), 1945, Tchr. Libn. Cert., 1945–47, BSLS; Univ. of IL, 1950–52, MSLS. **Orgs.:** ALA. SELA. AL LA. **Honors:** Delta Sigma Theta. **Pubns.:** "The Tuskegee Institute Libraries," *Encyc. of Lib. and Info. Sci.* (1981); "Civil Rights: Selected States/Alabama," *Encyc. of Black Amer.* (1981). **Activities:** 1; 17, 31, 35 **Addr.:** Hollis Burke Frissell Library, Tuskegee Institute, AL 36088.

King, Arline T. (Tampa, FL) Univ. Libn., Univ. of S. FL, 1980–; Assoc. Libn., Univ. of S. FL, 1978–; Asst. Libn., 1970–78, Lib. Asst., 1964–70. **Educ.:** Univ. of S. FL, 1961–64, BA (Art), 1964–68, MA (Educ.); FL State Univ., 1969–70, MSLS. **Orgs.:** ALA. FL LA. Hillsborough Cnty. LA. SELA. **Honors:** Beta Phi Mu. **Pubns.:** "Soap: Victorian Style," *Ex Libris* (Sum.-Fall, 1979); "The George Alfred Henty Collection," *Notes of the Friends* (S. 1974). **Activities:** 1; 20, 34, 45; 56 **Addr.:** University of South Florida Library, Fowler Ave., Tampa, FL 33617.

King, Bonnie Jean (Ag. 3, 1947, Wisner, LA) Bus., Econ. Bibl. Instr. Libn., Univ. of Toledo, 1979–, Ref. Libn., Oscar Rose Jr. Coll., 1978–79; Resrch. Libn., Anta Corp., 1975–78; Resrch. Libn., Doric Corp., 1974–76. **Educ.:** Ctrl. State Univ., 1965–69, BA (Eng.); Univ. of OK, 1969–71, MLS; Ctrl. State Univ., 1978–79, MBA. **Orgs.:** SLA: OK Chap. (Treas., 1977–79). ALA. **Activities:** 1, 12; 15, 31, 39; 51, 54, 59 **Addr.:** University of Toledo Library, 2801 W. Bancroft, Toledo, OH 43606.

King, Charles D. (D. 18, 1946, Norristown, PA) Libn. I, Louisville Free Pub. Lib., 1972–; Supervsr., Goodwill Indus. of KY, 1970–72. **Educ.:** Morehead State Univ., 1964–68, BA (Hist.); Univ. of KY, 1974–76, MSLS; Duke Univ. Dvnty. Sch., 1968–69. **Orgs.:** ALA: Staff Org. RT (Ch., 1980–81), Steering Com. (1979–); RASD/Hist. Sect., Geneal. Com. (1979–). KY LA. Louisville Free Pub. Lib. Staff Assn.: Pres. (1978–79). Louisville Free Pub. Lib. Cmnty. Plng. Com. for ALA/HEW Grant (1978–79). Louisville Pub. Lib. Credit Un.: Treas. (1974–). Third Century/Louisville Ctrl. Area: Secy. (1981–82); Arts Com. (1978–). Filson Club. Erie (PA) Socty. for Geneal. Resrch. **Activities:** 9; 16, 31, 39; 69, 70 **Addr.:** Box 682, Louisville, KY 40201.

King, Charles L. (O. 13, 1934, Fillmore, NY) Head, Pub. Srv., Downstate Med. Ctr., 1978–, Head, Ref., 1974–78; Asst. Libn., Harlem Hosp., 1972–74; Ref. Libn., Columbia Hlth. Sci., 1971–72. **Educ.:** Houghton Coll., 1951–55, BS (Chem.); Univ. of MO, 1956–62, PhD (Organic Chem.); Columbia Univ., 1970–71, MSLS (Libnshp.). **Orgs.:** Med. LA. NY Lib. Club. NY Reg. Grp./Med. LA: Prog. Com. (1972, 1976); Cont. Ed. Com. (1974); Mem. Com. (Ch., 1976–78); Pubcty. Com. (1980). AAAS. **Honors:** Sigma Xi. **Activities:** 1; 15, 17, 36; 60, 63, 80 **Addr.:** Medical Research Library of Brooklyn, Box 14, 450 Clarkson Ave., Brooklyn, NY 11203.

King, Cynthia (Ag. 20, 1921, Fresno, CA) Coord., Srvs. to Chld., Fresno Cnty. Pub. Lib., 1961–, Head, Chld. Rm., 1960–61, Branch Libn., W. Fresno Branch, 1959–60. **Educ.:** CA State Univ., Fresno, 1959, BA (Educ.); Univ. of Denver, 1961, MA (LS). **Orgs.:** ALA: ALSC, Newbery Com. (1981), Soc. Issues Discuss. Grp. (1980–81). CA LA: Chld. Srvs. Chap. (VP, Pres.-Elect, 1982), Governing Bd. (1977), Nom. Com. (Ch., 1978);

PROFESSIONAL ACTIVITIES: Institutions: 1. Acad. lib.; 2. Arch.; 3. Assn.; 4. Fed./Gvt. lib.; 5. Inst. lib.; 6. Mfr./Suppl.; 7. Milit. lib.; 8. Musm.; 9. Pub. lib.; 10. Sch. lib.; 11. Sch. of lib. sci.; 12. Spec. lib.; 13. State lib.; 14. (other). **Functions/Activities:** 15. Acq./Col. dev.; 16. Adult srvs.; 17. Admin.; 18. Apprais.; 19. Archit./Bldgs.; 20. Cat./Class.; 21. Chld. srvs.; 22. Circ.; 23. Cons./Pres.; 24. Consult.; 25. Cont. ed.; 26. Educ. lib. sci.; 27. Ext. srvs.; 28. Fund/Grants; 29. Gvt. pubs.; 30. Indx./Abs.; 31. Instr. lib. use; 32. Media srvs.; 33. Micro.; 34. Netwks./Coop.; 35. Persnl.; 36. PR; 37. Publshg.; 38. Recs. mgt.; 39. Ref. srvs.; 40. Repro.; 41. Resrch.; 42. Review.; 43. Secur.; 44. Serials; 45. Spec. col.; 46. Tech. srvs.; 47. Trustees/Bds.; 48. YA srvs.; 49. (other).

Cncl. (1979–81); various other coms. Assn. of Chld. Libns. of North. CA.: Pres. (1970, 1979); Nom. Com. (1971, 1981); various other coms. Ctrl. Sierra Lib. and Media Assn. Various other orgs. Fresno Storyland: Bd. of Dirs. (1961–80). Fresno Arts Ctr. Fresno Cnty.-City Hist. Socty. AAUW. Various other orgs. **Honors:** Assn. of Chld. Libns. of North. CA, Hon. Mem., 1980; Storyland Bd. of Fresno, Frnd. Plaque, 1980. **Activities:** 9; 21, 27, 42; 50, 63 **Addr.:** Fresno County Public Library, 2420 Mariposa St., Fresno, CA 93721.

King, Dan Madison (N. 7, 1914, Muncie, IN) Head Libn. and Ch., Dept. of Lib. Sci., KY Wesleyan Coll., 1954–; Head Libn., MN State Hist. Socty., 1949–54; Asst. Libn., Ref. Dept., NY Pub. Lib., 1948–49; Chief, Ref. Dept., Grand Rapids Pub. Lib., 1946–48; Libn.-in-Charge, Cooper Un. Libs. 1943–46; Asst. Libn., Art Sch. Lib., Cooper Un., 1942–43; Dist. Supvsr., WPA Lib. Srv. Proj., IN State Lib., 1940–42; Asst., Muncie Pub. Lib., 1938–39. **Educ.:** Hanover Coll., 1934–38, AB (Hist. and Eng.); Syracuse Univ., 1939–40, BS (LS); McGill Univ., 1937, Cert. (Fr. Lang.); Ball State Univ., Sum. 1935–39, (Eng., Soc. Sci. and LS); NY Univ., 1948–49, (Hist. of Archit.). **Orgs.:** ALA. SLA: Musm. Div. (Natl. Ch., 1953–54). Southeastern LA. KY LA: State Pres. (1964–65); Acad. Sect. (State Ch., 1975–76). Green River LA. Filson Club. Daviess Cnty. Hist. Socty.: Pres. (1975–76). Thea. Wkshp. of Owensboro. **Pubns.:** Ed., *NY Lib. Club Bltn.* (1944–45); various articles. **Activities:** 1; 17, 24, 26; 55, 63 **Addr.:** Library Learning Center, Kentucky Wesleyan College, 3000 Frederica St., Owensboro, KY 42301.

King, David Edgar (N. 25, 1936, Waterloo, IN) Libn., Ed. Lib., Standard Educ. Corp., 1969–; Visit. Lectr., Grad. Sch. of Lib. Sci., Univ. of IL, 1976–77; Libn., R. R. Donnelley & Sons Co., 1965–69; Coll. Rep., Amer. Book Co., 1963–65. **Educ.:** Ball State Univ., 1954–58, BS (Educ.); Rosary Coll., 1969–71, MALS; Hofstra Univ., 1959–60. **Orgs.:** SLA: Pres., IL Ch. (1979–80); Conf. Ch., SLA Anl. Conf. (1975); Ch., Pub. Div. (1974–75); Ch., SLA Pub. Rel. Com. (1969–71); Pubns. Com. (Ch., 1980–). IL LA: Ch., Con. Educ. Com. (1975). Del., WHOCLIS (1979). **Pubns.:** Co-ed., *Special Libraries: A Guide for Management*, 2nd ed. (1981). **Addr.:** Editorial Library, Standard Educational Corp., 200 W. Monroe St., Chicago, IL 60606.

King, Dennis W. (O. 20, 1939, Valley Stream, NY) Dir., Island Trees Pub. Lib., 1968–; Ref. Libn., Bryant (Roslyn) Pub. Lib., 1961–68. **Educ.:** C.W. Post Coll. 1958–62, BS (Bus.), 1962–67, MSLS. **Orgs.:** NY LA. Nassau Cnty. LA. **Activities:** 9; 17, 35, 36; 85 **Addr.:** Island Trees Public Library, 3601 Hempstead Turnpike, Levittown, NY 11756.

King, Donald Ross (N. 17, 1933, Camden, NJ) Assoc. Dean, Assoc. Prof. (LS), Rutgers Univ., 1971–, Assoc. Dir., Comp. Ctr., 1962–71, Syst. Anal., RCA Corp., 1957–62. **Educ.:** Rutgers Univ., 1951–55, BA (Math.), 1955–57, MS (Math.), 1965–68, MLS, 1968–71, PhD (LS). **Orgs.:** ALA. NJ LA. AALS. ASIS: NJ Chap. (Pres., 1975). Assn. for Comp. Mach. WHCOLIS, NJ Del. (Co-Ch.), 1978. **Pubns.:** "Improving Organizations and the Professions," *Information in the 80's* (in press); "Proposed Reorganization of the Rutgers GSLIS," *NJ Libs.* (F. 1981). **Activities:** 11; 17, 26; 56, 63, 75 **Addr.:** Graduate School of Library and Information Studies, Rutgers University, New Brunswick, NJ 08903.

King, Geraldine Beaty (My. 23, 1936, Omaha, NE) Assoc. Dir., Ramsey Cnty. Pub. Lib., 1978–, Head, Ref., 1973–77; Lectr., Asst. Prof. (LS), Univ. of MN, 1966–73; Assoc. Dir., Coll. of St. Thomas Lib., 1964–67. **Educ.:** Grinnell Coll., 1954–58, BA (Eng.); Univ. of MN, 1958–62, MA (LS), 1967–71, PhD (LS). **Orgs.:** ALA: RASD, *RQ*(Ed., 1976–79); LAMA/Persnl. Admin. Sect., Com. on Staff Dev. (1974–76). MN LA: Pres. (1973–74). Midwest Fed. of Lib. Assns.: Bd. of Dir. (1972–75). Sp. Comm. Assn. Ramsey Cnty. Humane Socty. **Pubns.:** "Try It–You'll Like It! A Comprehensive Management Information System for Reference Service," *Ref. Libn.* (1981); "Minnesota Library Association," *Ency. of Lib. and Info. Sci.* (1976); "Interlibrary Loan," *Ency. of Lib. and Info. Sci.* (1974); "Open and Closed Questions: the Reference Interview," *RQ* (Win. 1972). **Activities:** 9, 11; 25, 26, 39 **Addr.:** Ramsey County Public Library, 1910 W. City Rd. B, St. Paul, MN 55113.

King, Hannah M. (F. 1, 1944, Watertown, WI) Info. Spec., Frederick Cancer Resrch. Ctr., 1981–, Ref./Eppley Inst. Libn., Univ. NE Med. Ctr., 1978–81; Asst. Libn./Catlgr., WI Reg. Primate Resrch. Ctr., Univ. WI, Madison, 1974–78; Supvsr., Mono. Receipts, Acq. Dept., MA Inst. Tech. Libs., 1968–72. **Educ.:** Univ. of AZ, 1962–66, BA (Anthro.), West. MI Univ., 1972–73, MSL; Med. LA, 1976–81, Med. Libn. I. **Orgs.:** Med. LA. ALA. DC OLUG: Bylaws Com. (1981). **Honors:** Medline Users Grp. of the Midwest, Naming the *MUG'M* Nsltr., 1978. **Activities:** 12; 20, 31, 39; 56, 75, 80 **Addr.:** 807 Quince Orchard Blvd. #33, Gaithersburg, MD 20760.

King, Harold D. (Ja. 12, 1928, Plymouth, WI) Pub. Ed., Univ. of WI, 1967–, Resrc. Agent, Ext., 1962–67, Agr. Agent, 1960–62, Radio Farm Dir., 1959–60. **Educ.:** Univ. of WI, 1947–51, BS (Agr. Educ.), 1953–54, MS (Agr. Educ.). **Orgs.:** ASIS. Assn. for Com. in Educ.: Chap. Rep. **Activities:** 14-Information Service; 17, 27, 37; 82, 91 **Addr.:** 1545 Observatory Dr., Madison, WI 53711.

King, Jack Burge (S. 9, 1931, Minneapolis, MN) Univ. Libn., Hamline Univ., 1975–, 973–75, Head, Tech. Srvs., 1965–75; Cat. Libn., Univ. of MN, 1964–65. **Educ.:** Univ. of MN, 1950–53, BA Magna Cum Laude (Hist.), 1958–59, MA (Econ. Hist.), 1961–62, MA (LS). **Orgs.:** MN LA: Nom. Com. (Treas., Ch.). AECT. ALA: LAMA/Pub. Admin. Sect. (Ch., 1976). Econ. Hist. Assn. **Honors:** Beta Phi Mu. **Pubns.:** *A Feasibility Study for Establishing an Information Switching Center* (1970). "Put a Prussian Spy in Your Library," *RQ* (Fall 1978); "What Future, Reference Librarian," *RQ* (Spr. 1971); "Information Systems Management in the Small Liberal Arts College," *Coll. & Resrch. Libs.* (N. 1979); other articles. **Activities:** 1, 9; 17, 20, 39; 58, 75, 91 **Addr.:** Bush Memorial Library, Hamline University, St. Paul, MN 55104.

King, Judith D. (Ap. 9, 1948, Brockton, MA) Ref. Libn., Ann Arbor Pub. Lib., 1979–; Asst. Libn., Univ. of MI Eng./Trans. Lib., 1978; Ref. Libn., Grand Valley State Coll. Lib., 1972–78. **Educ.:** Wheaton College, (MA), 1966–70, AB (Eng. Lit.); Univ. of MI, 1971–72, AMLS. **Orgs.:** ALA. MI LA: Bibl. Instr. Com. (1975–78). Women Lib. Workers. **Pubns.:** *Women's Studies Sourcebook* (1976). **Activities:** 1, 9; 16, 31, 39; 54, 57, 92 **Addr.:** Reference Department, 343 South Fifth Ave., Ann Arbor, MI 48104.

King, Kenneth E. (Jl. 9, 1925, Brooklyn, NY) Dir., Mt. Clemens Pub. Lib., 1973–; Assoc. Dir., Branch Srvs., Detroit Pub. Lib., 1963–73, Coord., Cmnty. and Grp. Srvs., 1956–63. **Educ.:** Brown Univ., 1946–50, BA (Eng.); Simmons Coll., 1950–51, MSLS. **Orgs.:** ALA: Adult Srvs. Div. (VP, 1965–66). MI LA: (Sec. VP, 1967–68). Mt. Clemens Reg. Arts Cncl.: Pres. (1977–). Bright Future for Mt. Clemens Com.: Ch. (1977–). **Honors:** MI LA, Libn. of the Yr., 1976. Grt. Mt. Clemens Cham. of Cmrce.: Outstan. Cmnty. Srv., 1976. **Pubns.:** Jt. ed., *Centennial History of Mount Clemens, Michigan, 1879–1979* (1980); various articles in *Lib. Jnl., UNESCO Bltn. for Libs., ON Lib. Review, MI Libn., Adult Leadership, Top of the News.* **Activities:** 9; 16, 17, 25; 50, 72, 95-Srvs. to sr. citizens. **Addr.:** Mount Clemens Public Library, 150 Cass Ave., Mount Clemens, MI 48043.

King, Margot H. (Ja. 28, 1934, Winnipeg, MB) Libn., St. Thomas More Coll., 1972–, Ch., Dept. of Eng., 1974–75; Libn., Inst. of North. Std., 1967–72. **Educ.:** Univ. of SK, 1951–54, BA (Eng.); Univ. of Toronto, 1954–55, BLS, 1959–61, MA (Eng.); Univ. of CA, Berkeley, 1961–67, PhD (Comp. Lit.). **Orgs.:** Can. LA. SK LA. ALA. Prairie Reg. LA. Medvl. Acad. of Amer. Medvl. Assn. of the Pac. **Honors:** Woodrow Wilson Flwshp., 1965. **Pubns.:** *Saints, Scholars, and Heroes* (1979); *Commentarii et Glossae Remigii Autissiodorensis De Arte Metrica et De Schematibus et Tropis* (1975); *Latin Instruction in an Age of Illiteracy* (1979); *Grammatica Mystica; A Study of Bede's Grammatical Curriculum* (1979). **Activities:** 1 **Addr.:** St. Thomas More College, 1437 College Dr., Saskatoon, SK S7H 2Z9 Canada.

King, Patricia Miller (Jl. 26, 1937, New York, NY) Dir., Arthur and Elizabeth Schlesinger Lib. on the Hist. of Women in Amer., Radcliffe Coll., 1973–; Dir. of Resrch., Haney Assocs., Inc., 1971–73; Asst. Prof., Wellesley Coll., 1970–71; Tchg. Fellow, Harvard Coll., 1965–67, 1968–70. **Educ.:** Radcliffe Coll., 1955–59, AB (Hist.), 1959–61, AM (Hist.); Harvard Univ., 1963–70, PhD (Hist.). **Orgs.:** ALA. Amer. Antiq. Socty. New Eng. Archvsts. Amer. Hist. Assn. Berkshire Conf. of Women Histns. MA Hist. Socty. Org. of Amer. Histns. Various other orgs. **Honors:** Phi Beta Kappa. **Pubns.:** "Sonja Henie," *Notable American Women: The Modern Period* (1980); "The 'Maimie' Letters," *Women's Std. Nsltr.* (1975); reviews. **Activities:** 1; 15, 17, 28; 85, 95-Women's hist. **Addr.:** Schlesinger Library, Radcliffe College, 10 Garden St., Cambridge, MA 02138.

King, Richard Louis (My. 21, 1937, Portland, OR) Consult.; Ed./Publshr., Noise Pollution Publications Abstracts; Bus. Ref. Libn., CA State Univ., Long Beach, 1977–78, Head, Soc. Sci. Ref. Dept., 1976–77, Head, Bus./Econ. Ref. Dept., 1971–77; Head, Circ. Dept., Acting Cur., Gross Col. of Rare Books Mgt. Lib., UCLA, 1966–70. **Educ.:** CA State Univ., Sacramento, 1964, BA (Hist.); UCLA, 1970, MLS. **Orgs.:** ALA: RASD (Ch., Bus. Ref. Srvs. Com., 1973–75); Pub. Com. (1976–77). CA LA. **Pubns.:** *Business Serial Publications of the U.S. Government* (1978); *Airport Noise Pollution:* (1973); "Book Collections of the N.Y. & San Francisco Mercantile Libraries in the 19th Century," *Bus. Hist.* (Ja. 1978); "Corporation as History," SLA (Ap. 1969). "Cataloging the Small Law Library," *Los Angeles Bar Bltn.* (N. 1968). **Activities:** 1, 12; 24, 39, 41; 57, 59, 75 **Addr.:** 12614 E. Park St., Cerritos, CA 90701.

King, Ruth Sanborn (S. 20, 1909, Loudon, NH) Retired; Freelance Indxr., 1975–; Libn., NH Tech. Inst., 1972–75, Asst. Libn., 1971–72; Libn., Media Spec., Broad Meadows Jr. HS (Quincy MA), 1959–71; Sch. Libn., Marshfield, MA, 1957–59; Cur., Coll. on Bus. and Aviation, Grad. Sch. of Bus., Harvard Univ., 1944–53; Asst. Libn., Cortland State Tchrs. Coll., 1942–44; Other Prof. positions, 1931–41. **Educ.:** Boston Univ., 1927–31, AB (Eng.); Columbia Univ., 1938–39, BS (LS), 1940, MA (Eng.). **Orgs.:** ALA. NH LA. Henniker NH Pub. Lib. Friends. AAUW. UUWF. **Activities:** 1, 10; 17, 21, 41; 63, 92 **Addr.:** R.F.D. Bradford Rd., Henniker, NH 03242.

Kingma, Ruth M. (O. 24, 1942, Capetown, S. Africa) Asst. Head, Ctrl. Lib., N. York Pub. Lib., 1981–, Asst. Area Branch Head, 1980–81, Libn. Supvsr., 1976–80, Libn., 1973–76; Libn./Info. Ofcr., Indian Eskimo Assn. of Can., 1968–69; Libn., Toronto Pub. Lib., 1968; Sch. Libn., Inner London Educ. Athrty., 1967; Libn., Manchester (Eng.) Pub. Lib., 1966–67; Libn., S. Africa, 1963–65. **Educ.:** Univ. of Capetown, 1960–62, BA (Hist.), 1963, Dip. (LS); LA UK, 1968, Assoc.; Univ. of Toronto, 1968–72, MLS. **Orgs.:** Can. LA. ON LA. LA UK. ON Com. on the Status of Women. **Pubns.:** "Islam in South Africa," bibl. (1964). **Activities:** 9; 16, 17, 39 **Addr.:** North York Public Library, 5126 Yonge St., Willowdale, ON M2N 5N9 Canada.

Kingsbury, Mary Emily (Ja. 3, 1932, Sioux City, IA) Assoc. Prof., Lib. Sci., Univ. of NC, 1976–, Asst. Prof., Lib. Sci., 1973–76; Asst. Prof., Lib. Sci., Univ. of Portland, 1968–71, Instr. of Lib. Sci., 1967–68. **Educ.:** Briar Cliff, 1950–54, BA (Eng.); Rosary Coll., 1956–57, MALS; OR State, 1963–64, MEd (Couns.); Univ. of OR, 1971–73, PhD (Educ.). **Orgs.:** ALA: ALSC/Resrch. and Dev. Com. (Ch., 1976–77); Newbery-Caldecott Com. (1977). AAUP. **Pubns.:** "A Retort Courteous," *Sch. Lib. Jnl.* (My. 1979); "Educating Young Adult Librarians," *Drexel Lib. Qtly.* (Ja. 1978). **Addr.:** School of Library Science, Manning Hall 026–A, University of North Carolina, Chapel Hill, NC 27514.

Kingston, Jo Ann (O. 27, 1936, Fremont, NE) Branch Head, Flint Pub. Lib., 1959–, Tchr., Flint Pub. Schs., 1958–59. **Educ.:** NE State Tchrs. Coll., 1954–58, BA (Sp.); Univ. of MI, 1959–62, MLS. **Orgs.:** ALA: PLA, Educ. of Pub. Libns. Com. (1980–82); YASD, Org. and Bylaws Com (1980–81), Bylaws Com. (Ch., 1978–80), Bd. of Dirs. (1975–78) Mem. Promo. Com. (Ch., 1981–). ALTA (Ch., 1972–74). Frdm. to Read Fndn. MI LA: Int. Frdm. Com. (1980–). Grand Blanc Un. Meth. Church Choristers Gld. Girl Scouts of Amer. Grand Blanc Cmnty. HS. **Activities:** 9; 15, 17, 27 **Addr.:** 614 Bedford Pl., Grand Blanc, MI 48439.

Kinney, John Mark (Jn. 4, 1932, Syracuse, NY) State Archvst., AK State Arch., 1976–; State Archvst., TX State Arch., 1968–76; Resrch. Archvst., Church Hist. Socty., 1967–68. **Educ.:** Univ. of TX, 1951–56, BS (Educ.); Episcopal Theo. Semy. of the SW, 1955–58, MDiv (Theo.); Nashotah House, 1964–67, STM (Hist.); Univ. of TX, 1967–68, MLS, 1968–70, MA (Hist.). **Orgs.:** SAA: Nom. Com. (1979), Anl. Mtg. Prog. Com. (1974–75), Security Adv. Com. (1975–79), other coms. Natl. Assn. of State Arch. and Recs. Admins.: Exec. Bd. (1976–77). Socty. of SW Archvsts.: Pres. (1974–76), Exec. Bd. (1973–78). **Pubns.:** *Index to Texas Confederate Pension Applications* (1975, 1977); *Directory of State & Provincial Archives,* (1975); "Archives of the Episcopal Church," *Amer. Archvst.* (Jy. 1969); "Copper and the Settlement of South Central Alaska," *Jnl. of the West* (Ap. 1971); various other articles; mem. of several ed. bds. **Activities:** 2, 13; 17, 33, 38, 45; 54, 90 **Addr.:** Alaska State Archives, Pouch C, Juneau, AK 99811.

Kinney, Lisa F. (Mr. 13, 1951, Laramie, WY) Dir., Albany Cnty. Pub. Lib., 1977–, Actg. Dir., 1976–77, Asst. Dir., 1976–76. **Educ.:** Univ. of WY, 1969–73, BA (Span.); Univ. of OR, 1974–75, MLS. **Orgs.:** Action for Laramie Libs.: Founding Off. WY LA: Pres. (1981); Parlmt. (1975–76); Cont. Educ. Ch. (1977); Local Arrange. Ch. (1978). Mt. Plains LA: Secy., Junior Mem. RT (1978–79); ALA Aff. Cncl. Rep. 1980–81. ALA: Inst. Plng. Com., Ch.; John Dana Awds. Com. Zonta Intl. of Laramie. Quadra Dangle Club. Snowy Range Folk Dance Club. **Honors:** WY LA: Outstanding Libn. of the Year, 1977. **Pubns.:** Articles in *WY Lib. Roundup* (1975–80). **Activities:** 9; 19, 28, 36; 65, 72, 83 **Addr.:** c/o Albany Cnty. Pub. Lib., 310 South 8th, Laramie, WY 82070.

Kinney, Mary Jane (Ag. 19, 1924, Filer, ID) Trustee, Vice-Ch., ID State Lib., 1976–, Ch. of Trustees, 1978–79; Trustee, Twin Falls Pub. Lib., 1969–74, Ch. of Bd., 1971–72. **Educ.:** Stanford Univ., Whitman Coll., 1942–46, BA, magna cum laude (Eng.). **Orgs.:** ID LA: Trustee Div. (Ch., 1972–74); Legis. (Ch., 1971–75). ALA. Pac. NW LA. ID State Lib. Bd. of Trustees: Ch. (1981–82). Natl. Fed. Msc. Club. Magic Valley Cmnty. Concert Assn. **Honors:** ID LA, Trustee of the Yr., 1975; Phi Beta Kappa; Mu Phi Epsilon. **Activities:** 4, 9; 28, 36, 47 **Addr.:** 150 Los Lagos, Rte. 6, Twin Falls, ID 83301.

Kinzer, Sr. Ferdinelle (Jy. 21, 1914, Killam, AB) Archvst., N. Amer. Province, Srs. of the Divine Savior, 1978–; Head Libn., Divine Savior Holy Angels HS, 1962–78, Tchr., 1952–64. **Educ.:** Marquette Univ., 1948, BA (Eng.); Rosary Coll., 1961–62, MALS. Various workshops. **Orgs.:** Catholic LA.: WI Chap., Nom. Com. (1979), Bk. Wk. Ch. (1968–73), Mem. Ch. (1963–66). SAA. Midwest Arch. Conf. WI LA. State Hist. Socty. of WI Smithsonian Assoc. **Activities:** 2, 14-Religious Lib.; 15, 17, 20; 62, 69, 85 **Addr.:** Sisters of the Divine Savior Community House, 4311 N. 100th St., Milwaukee, WI 53222.

Kirby, Barbara Lynn (Ag. 3, 1933, Troy, NY) City Libn., El Segundo Pub. Lib., 1978–, Asst. City Libn., 1974–78, Ref.

Special Subjects/Services: 50. Adult educ.; 51. Advert./Mktg.; 52. Aerosp.; 53. Agric.; 54. Area std.; 55. Arts/Hum.; 56. Autom.; 57. Bibl./Prtg.; 58. Bio. sci.; 59. Bus./Fin.; 60. Chem.; 61. Copyrt.; 62. Documtn.; 63. Educ.; 64. Engin.; 65. Env.; 66. Eth. grps.; 67. Film; 68. Food/Nutr.; 69. Geneal.; 70. Geo.; 71. Geol.; 72. Handcpd.; 73. Hist.; 74. Int. frdm.; 75. Info. sci.; 76. Insr.; 77. Law; 78. Legis.; 79. Math./Comp. sci.; 80. Med.; 81. Metals; 82. Nat. resrcs.; 83. Newsp.; 84. Nuc. sci.; 85. Oral hist.; 86. Petr./Energy; 87. Pharm.; 88. Phys./Astr./Math.; 89. Readg.; 90. Relig.; 91. Sci./Tech.; 92. Soc. sci.; 93. Telecom.; 94. Transp.; 95. (other).

Libn., 1970–74; Sch. Libn., Schenectady NY, Pub. Sch., 1954–56. **Educ.:** Geneseo State Tchrs. Coll., 1950–54, BSLS; SUNY, Albany, 1956–63, MSLS. **Orgs.:** ALA. CA LA. Quota Intl.: VP (1977–78). Order Eastern Star. **Activities:** 9, 10; 16, 21, 39; 50, 69, 72 **Addr.:** 5133 Pickford Way, Culver City, CA 90230.

Kirby, Christine L. (Ag. 10, 1947, Troy, NY) Consult., MA Bd. of Lib. Comsns., 1981–; Pub. Lib. Consult., State Lib. of FL, 1978–81; Inst. Libn., Orlando Pub. Lib., 1975–78, YA Libn., 1973–75; YA Coord., Haverhill Pub. Lib., 1972–73. **Educ.:** SUNY Albany, 1965–69, BA (Eng.), 1969–71, MLS. **Orgs.:** ALA: ASCLA/Lib. Srv. to Prisoners Sect., Mem. Promo. (1978–80), Lcl. Jails Resol. Com. (1977–80), Survey on Srv. to Lcl. Insts. (1977–79), Nom. Com. (Ch., 1978–79). FL LA: Outreach Caucus (1979–80); Women in Libs. (Founding Com., 1979–80). Natl. Org. for Women: Orlando Chap. (Pres., 1976); Tallahassee Chap. (Prog. Coord., 1979). **Honors:** Orange Cnty. Criminal Justice Cncl., Awd. for Lib. Srv. to Jails, 1978. WMFE - TV (Pub. Broadcasting Srv.), Cert. (Auction Wk. Ch.), 1975–78. WFSU - TV (Pub. Broadcasting Srv.), Awd. (Auction Wk. Ch.), 1979. **Pubns.:** Jt.-ed., *Keystone*, (1979–81). **Activities:** 5, 13; 16, 24, 27; 65, 95-Jails, 95-Disadvantaged. **Addr.:** Massachusetts Board of Library Commissioners, 648 Beacon St., Boston, MA 02215.

Kirchner, Andras K. (Jl. 5, 1931, Budapest, Hungary) Med. Libn., Univ. of Calgary, 1971–; Med. Libn., Laval Univ., 1963–71, Med. Libn., Montreal Univ., 1961–63. **Educ.:** Eôtvôs Lorand Univ., Budapest, 1950–54, BA (Lit.), 1954–56, MA (Lit.); McGill Univ., 1960–61 (LS). Columbia Univ., 1963, Cert. (Med. LS). **Orgs.:** Med. LA. CHLA. **Pubns.:** *Guide à la Consultation de la Literature Médicale* (1969); *L'Informatique et la Documentation Médicale* (1970); "French Canadian Literature," *Encyc. of World Lit.* (1979). **Activities:** 1; 17; 80 **Addr.:** Medical Library, The University of Calgary, Calgary, AB T2N 1N4 Canada.

Kirchner, Elizabeth M. (O. 26, 1929, Budapest, Hungary) Chief Med. Libn., Calgary Gen. Hosp., 1977–; Head Libn., L'Hosp. Christ-Roi, 1967–71; Head, Per. Dept., Univ. Laval, 1964–66; Head, Med. Lib., Univ. de Montreal, 1961–64; Head, Med. Lib., L'Hsp. Ste. Justine, 1957–61. **Educ.:** Eotvos Lorand Univ. of Budapest, 1949–55, MA (Lit.), 1955–56, BLS; Columbia Univ., 1963, Cert. (Med. LS). **Orgs.:** Med. LA. CHLA. Can. LA. LA of AB. Various other orgs. Natl. Film Lib. of Can. **Pubns.:** "English Canadian Literature," *Encyc. of World Lit.* (1979). **Activities:** 12; 15, 17; 80 **Addr.:** Hospital Library, Calgary General Hospital, 841 Centre Ave. E., Calgary, AB T2E 0A1 Canada.

Kiresen, Evelyn-Margaret Marta (Ag. 13, 1932, Long Island, NY) Head, Interlib. Loan Srv., Univ. of CA, Berkeley, 1978–, Ref. Srvs. Libn., Pub. Hlth. Lib., 1968–77; U.S. Docu. Lib., 1964–68; Ref. Libn., Multnomah Cnty. Lib., Portland, OR, 1958–61. **Educ.:** Hunter Coll., 1950–54, BA (Fine Arts); Columbia Univ., 1954–56, MLS. **Orgs.:** MLA. SLA. ASIS. **Honors:** Phi Beta Kappa, 1953. NIH Fellowship, 1975–76. **Activities:** 1; 17, 31, 34 **Addr.:** Interlibrary Borrowing Service, University of California, Berkeley, CA 94520.

Kirk, Mary Lou (Ja. 4, 1929, Atlantic, IA) Media Spec., Valley HS, W. Des Moines, 1968–; Tchr. (Eng.), W. Des Moines Cmnty. Sch., 1960–68; Tchr. (Eng.), Denison Cmnty. Sch., 1955–60; Tchr. (Eng./Sp.), Mapleton Cmnty. Sch., 1950–55. **Educ.:** Simpson Coll., 1946–50, BA (Eng. Educ.); Univ. of IA, 1959–63, MA (Eng. Educ.), 1965–70, MA (LS). **Orgs.:** IA Educ. Media Assn.: Pres. (1974–75). IA LA: IALA/IEMA Coop. Com. (1981). ALA: AASL. IA Gvr.'s WHCOLIS (Strg. Com., 1979). Delta Kappa Gamma: State Mem. Ch. P.E.O. Various other orgs. **Activities:** 10; 15, 17, 20; 74 **Addr.:** 704 12th St., W. Des Moines, IA 50265.

Kirk, Sherwood (Jl. 12, 1924, Kermit, WV) Assoc. Dir., Lib. Opers., IL State Lib., 1971–; Dir., FL State Lib., 1969–71; Asst. State Libn., KY Dept. of Libs., 1957–69; Ref. Asst., Natl. Agr. Lib., 1956–57, Cat. Asst., 1955–56, Serials Liason, U.S. Dept. Agr./Lib. of Congs., 1955–56; Agr. Libn., Univ. of NE, 1953–54; Libn., various positions, 1949–52. **Educ.:** Univ. of KY, 1946–49, AB (Hist.); Univ. of IL, 1949–50, MSLS. **Orgs.:** ALA: Cncl. (1967–69); PLA, Com. for Functional Illitcy. (1967). IL LA: Pub. Lib. Stats. Com. (1978–80). Frnds. of Lincoln Lib: Bk. Sale (Ch., 1980–81). **Honors:** KY LA, Libn. of the Yr., 1968. **Activities:** 1, 13; 17, 20, 24; 55 **Addr.:** 1425 Whittier Ave., Springfield, IL 62704.

Kirk, Thomas G. Jr. (Ag. 2, 1943, Philadelphia, PA) Coll. Libn., Berea Coll., 1980–; Sci. Libn., Earlham Coll., 1965–80; Actg. Dir., Univ. of WI, Parkside, 1979–80. **Educ.:** Earlham Coll., 1961–65, BA (Bio.); IN Univ., 1965–69, MA (LS). **Orgs.:** IN LA. ALA: Instr. in the Use of Libs. Com. (1974–77, Ch., 1975–77); ACRL, Bibl. Instr. Task Force (Ch., 1971–77); Bibl. Instr. Sect., Policy and Plng. Com. (Ch., 1977–78); Nom. Com. (1979–80); ACRL Sci. and Tech. Sect. (Vice-ch., Ch.-elect, 1979–80 Ch., 1980–81); ACRL Bd. of Dir. (1979–81). IN Area 9 Reg. Lib. Plng. Comsn. Whitewater Valley Area Lib. Srvs. Athrty.: Pres. (1973–75). AAAS. **Pubns.:** *Library Research Guide to Biology* (1978); Jt. auth., "Structuring Services and Facilities for Library Instruction," *Lib. Trends* (Sum. 1980); "Course-related library and literature use instruction: an attempt to develop model programs" in *New Horizons for Academic Libraries* (1979); *Course-related Library and Literature Use Instruction: Working Models for Programs in Undergraduate Science Education* (1979); "Past, present, and future of library instruction," *The Southeast. Libn.* (1977); other articles. **Activities:** 1, 12; 17, 31, 39; 58, 70, 91 **Addr.:** Berea College, Berea, KY 40404.

Kirkby, Arthur M. (S. 22, 1911, Didsburg, AB) Retired, 1976–; Dir., Norfolk Pub. Lib., 1952–76; Admin. Asst., Enoch Pratt Free Lib., 1946–52; Branch Libn., Calgary Pub. Lib., 1940–42. **Educ.:** Mt. Royal Coll., 1940–42; Univ. of BC, 1942–44, BA (Hist.); Columbia Univ., 1945–46, BSLS. **Orgs.:** ALA: Cncl. SELA. VA LA: Pres. (1966–67). Intl. Assn. of Torch Clubs: Pres. (1960–61). Rotary. Mary Bell Washington Musm. and Lib.: Bd. (Vice-Ch., VP, 1979–80). **Activities:** 9; 17, 24 **Addr.:** Rte. 1, Box 669, White Stone, VA 22578.

Kirkendall, Carolyn A. (Jl. 6, 1938, Bedford, OH) Dir., Clearinghse.: LOEX Exch., East. MI Univ. Lib., 1975–; Libn., Marshall Jr. HS, 1971; Ref. Libn./Instr., East. MI Univ., 1966–69; Libn., Lib. Ext. Srv., Univ. of MI, 1962–63; YA Libn., Detroit Pub. Lib., 1961–62. **Educ.:** Univ. of MI, 1956–60, BA (Eng.); 1960–61, MA (LS). **Orgs.:** ALA. MI LA. MI Acad. of Sci., Arts, and Letters. **Pubns.:** Ed., *Directions for the Decade: Library Instruction in the 1980s* (1981); *Reform and Renewal in Higher Education: Implications for Library Instruction* (1980); "Information Exchanges for Library Instruction," *Drexel Lib. Qtly.* (Ja. 1981); "Library Use Education: Current Practices and Trends," *Lib. Trends* (Sum. 1980); ed., *LOEX News* (1976–); various other articles. **Activities:** 1; 24, 31, 49-Clearinghse. **Addr.:** LOEX Clearinghouse Exchange, Division of Educational Resources, Eastern Michigan University, Ypsilanti, MI 48197.

Kirkland, Janice J. (S. 2, 1935, San Diego, CA) Cat. and Serials Libn., CA State Coll., Bakersfield, 1970–; Ref. Libn., Contra Costa Cnty. Lib., 1967–69; Libn., Ctrl. Fndn. Sch., London, 1966–67. **Educ.:** Univ. of CA, Berkeley, 1965, BA (Comp lit), 1966, MLS; Univ. of CA, Los Angeles, 1976, MA (Eng.). **Orgs.:** NLA. CA LA: CSUC Chap. ALA: ACRL. Untd. Prof. of CA. Mod. Lang. Assn. **Honors:** Phi Beta Kappa. **Activities:** 1; 20, 44; 92 **Addr.:** Library, California State College, Bakersfield, 9001 Stockdale Hwy., Bakersfield, CA 93309.

Kirkland, Kenneth L. (D. 18, 1938, Fort Worth, TX) Serials Libn., De Paul Univ., 1977–, Per. Libn., 1972–77, Ref. and Circ. Libn., 1967–72. **Educ.:** Univ. of Houston, 1957–61, BA (Span.); Univ. of CA, Berkeley, 1966–67, MLS, 1961–65 (Slavic Lang.); Northeastern IL Univ., 1974–77 (Ling.). **Orgs.:** ALA: Cat. Com. (1970). IL LA: Reg. Com. (1973); Circ. Com. (1971–72); Secy. (1972). Chicago Lib. Club. AAUP: Treas., Chap. (1972–73); VP (1973–74, 1974–75). **Activities:** 1; 29, 38, 44; 54, 69 **Addr.:** 2948 N. Pine Grove Ave., Chicago, IL 60657.

Kirschenbaum, Arthur S. (O. 10, 1932, Bronx, NY) Eval. Spec. (Educ.), U.S. Dept. of Educ., 1966–. **Educ.:** City Coll. of NY, 1950–59, BBA (Persnl. Mgt.), 1960–61. **Orgs.:** Prince George Cnty. Meml. Lib. Syst.: Bd. of Trustees (1973–78; Ch., 1976). ALA: Ofc. of Lib. Srv. to the Disadv. (Adv. Com., 1979–81); ALTA, Int. Frdm. (Ch., 1976–77), Reg. VP (1979–80). Frdm. to Read Fndn.: Bd. (1976). MD State Gvrs. Conf.: Del. (1979). **Pubns.:** Ed. Bd., *Pub. Lib. Qtly.* (1979–81). **Activities:** 9, 11; 41, 47, 49-Eval.; 63, 66, 74 **Addr.:** 13000 Cheswood Ln., Bowie, MD 20715.

Kirshenbaum, Anna Schreiber (Ag. 27, 1912, Rochester, NY) Libn., Temple Beth El, 1962–; Libn., Jewish Young Men's and Women's Assn., 1950–53; Cat./Book Sel. Libn., Rochester Pub. Lib., 1941–45. **Educ.:** Univ. of Rochester, 1930–34, BA (Eng.), 1934–35; Columbia Univ., 1939–40, MLS. **Orgs.:** AJL: Anl. Mtg. (Ch., 1966, 1967); Synagogue, Sch., and Ctr. Div. (Pres., 1969–71); Pres. (1971–73); Chld. Bk. Awd. Com. (1969, 1978–81). **Honors:** Phi Sigma Iota; Phi Beta Kappa. **Activities:** 5, 12; 15, 16, 21; 50, 63, 90 **Addr.:** 165 Mayflower Dr., Rochester, NY 14618.

Kirsner, Mildred D. (N. 4, 1923, New York, NY) Libn., Assoc. Prof., Miami Dade Cmnty. Coll., 1972–; Asst. Libn., Inst. for Advanced Study, 1947–49. **Educ.:** Univ. of Cincinnati, 1943–46, BA (Fr.); Pratt Inst., 1946–47, BLS. **Orgs.:** ALA: ACRL/CJCLS Instr. and Use Com. (1978–80, Ch., 1979–80). FL LA: Lib. Orien. and Bibl. Instr. Com. (Secy. 1978); Ed. Com. (1979–); Cmnty. and Jr. Coll. Lib. Sect. (Ch., 1980–). Dade Cnty. LA. **Activities:** 1; 31, 39 **Addr.:** Miami Dade Community College, North Campus Library, 11380 N.W. 27 Ave., Miami, FL 33167.

Kirwan, William J. (Ap. 15, 1936, Buffalo, NY) Univ. Libn., West. Carolina Univ., 1977–; Dir., Lib. Srvs., WV Coll. of Grad. Std., 1974–77; Dir., Loyola-Notre Dame Lib., Inc., 1969–74; Dir., Lib. Srvs., Loyola Coll., 1966–69; Asst. Libn., Essex Cmnty. Coll., 1963–66; Jr. Libn., Buffalo and Erie Cnty. Pub. Lib., 1961–63. **Educ.:** St. Bonaventure Univ., 1955–59, BA (Hist.); Drexel Inst. of Tech., 1960–61, MSLS. **Orgs.:** ALA. NC LA. Southeastern LA. **Activities:** 1; 17, 19 **Addr.:** Hunter Library, Western Carolina University, Cullowhee, NC 28723.

Kirwin, Florence Margaret (O. 30, 1946, Morristown, NJ) PhD Std., LS, Univ. of Southern CA, 1979–; Dir., Pitkin Cnty. Lib., 1976–79. **Educ.:** Skidmore Coll., 1964–68, BA (Hist.); Simmons Coll., 1970–71, MLS. **Orgs.:** ALA. CO LA: Ch., Pub. Lib. Div.; Mem., Leg. Com. Three Rivers Reg. Lib. Srvc. Syst.: Plng. Com., Gov. Brd. Ch. Pitkin Cnty. Lib. Mt. Plains LA: Brd. **Pubns.:** *Community Analysis for the Pitkin County Library* (1979); "Library Shopping at Garage Sales," *Lib. Jrnl.* (O. 1978). "Four New Ways to Serve Nonresidents Without Losses," *Lib. Jnl.* (Mr. 1979). **Activities:** 9, 11; 17, 26, 47; 59, 63, 92 **Addr.:** School of Library Science, University of Southern California, Los Angeles, CA 90007.

Kishibe, Kaye (F. 18, 1938, Vancouver, BC) Head, Tech. Srvs., Toronto Pub. Lib., 1976–, Admin. Asst., Tech. Srvs., 1973–76, Coord., Cat., 1972–73, Branch Libn., 1970–72. **Educ.:** Univ. of West. ON, 1959–63, BA (Hist., Phil.), Univ. of Toronto, 1965–66, BLS, 1975, MLS. **Orgs.:** ALA. Can. LA. ON LA. **Pubns.:** "Cataloguing Books in Chinese," *Intl. Cat.* (Ja./Mr. 1974). **Activities:** 9; 15, 20, 46; 56, 75, 93 **Addr.:** 184 Degrassi St., Toronto, ON M4M 2K7 Canada.

Kislitzin, Elizabeth H. (D. 24, New York, NY) Asst. Head, Coll. Dev./Ref. Srvcs. Dept., Univ. of CA, Berkeley, 1978–, Ref. Libn., 1972–78, Head, Loan Dept., 1970–72, Head, Resrv., 1965–70. **Educ.:** Cornell Univ., 1949–53, AB (Eng.); Syracuse Univ., 1953–54, MLS. **Orgs.:** ALA. CA LA. **Honors:** Beta Phi Mu. **Activities:** 1; 15, 17, 39; 55 **Addr.:** Collection Development/Reference Services Dept., 208 Library, University of California, Berkeley, CA 94720.

Kissman, Henry M. (1922) Assoc. Dir., Spec. Info. Srvs., Natl. Lib. of Med., 1970–. **Educ.:** Sterling Coll., 1944, BS; Univ. of Cincinnati, 1948, MS; Univ. of Rochester, 1950, PhD. **Orgs.:** ASIS: Biomed. and Chem. Spec. Interest Grp. (Ch., 1969). Amer. Chem. Socty.: Chem. Lit. Div., Chem. Docum. Com. (Ch., 1965–68). Natl. Acad. of Sci.: Com. on Chem. Info. (1969–72). *Drug Info. Jnl.* Ed. Bd. **Honors:** Natl. Lib. of Med., Dir. Hon. Awd., 1975; Sterling Coll., Disting. Alum. Awd., 1974. **Activities:** 4; 17; 75, 80 **Addr.:** National Library of Medicine, 8600 Rockville Pike, Bethesda, MD 20209.

Kissner, Arthur J. (Jl. 27, 1927, New York City, NY) Chief Libn., Fitchburg Pub. Lib., 1961–; Asst. Chief Libn., Oak Park Pub. Lib., 1958–61; Asst. Branch Libn., Brooklyn Pub. Lib., 1954–58; Tchr., NY City Sch. Syst., 1948–52. **Educ.:** NY Univ., 1944–47, BS (Sci.), 1947–58, MA (Sci. Educ.); Pratt Inst., 1954–56 MLS; Univ. of MA, 1970–73, CAGS (Educ. Media). **Orgs.:** MA LA: Pres. (1967–68). ALA: Cnclr. (1977–81). MA Adv. Com. on Libs.: Secy. (1972–77). **Pubns.:** "Massachusetts" article, *ALA Yrbk.* (1978–81). **Activities:** 9; 16, 35, 36; 63, 66, 67 **Addr.:** Fitchburg Public Library, 610 Main St., Fitchburg, MA 01420.

Kister, Kenneth F. (N. 3, 1935, New Cumberland, PA) Ref. Bk. Reviewer, Freelnc., 1976–; Ref. Libn., W. Palm Beach Pub. Lib., 1975–76; Asst. Dir., Palm Beach Cnty. Pub. Lib. Syst., 1973–75; Co-ed., *Kirkus Reviews*, 1971–73; Ref. Libn., SUNY, Potsdam, 1970–71; Asst. Prof., Simmons Coll., Grad. Sch. of Lib. and Info. Sci., 1965–70; Overseas Libn., Nottingham, Eng. City Lib. and Nottinghamshire Cnty. Lib., 1964–65; Ref. Libn., Simmons Coll., 1962–64; various Eng. tchg. positions, 1957–60. **Educ.:** Shippensburg State Coll., 1953–57, BS (Educ., Eng.); Simmons Coll., 1961–62, MSLS. ACLU. Dictionary Socty. of N. Amer. **Pubns.:** *Encyclopedia Buying Guide* (1976, 1978); *Dictionary Buying Guide* (1977); *Social Issues and Library Problems* (1968); "Wanted: More Professionalsim in Reference Book Reviewing," *RQ* (Win. 1979); "Cheap Words: A Paperback Dictionary Roundup," *Lib. Jnl.* (N. 15, 1979). **Activities:** 14-Freelnc.; 37, 39, 42; 70, 74, 92 **Addr.:** 10508 Lakeway Cir. #2536, Tampa, FL 33612.

Kister, Suzon O. (Ja. 20, 1937, Danville, PA) Head Libn., Jefferson Cmnty. Coll., 1976–; Admin. Libn., Agr. and Tech. Coll. (Canton, NY) 1975–76, Ref. Libn., 1970–75; Head Libn., Chamberlayne Jr. Coll., 1969–70. **Educ.:** Wilson Coll., 1954–58, AB (Eng.); Simmons Coll. 1960–63 SM (LS), 1967–68, MA (Eng.). **Orgs.:** N. Country Ref. and Resrcs. Cncl.: Bd. of Trustees (1978–). NY LA. SUNY Chancellor's Adv. Com. on Awds. for Excel. in Libnshp. Family Couns Srv.: Bd. of Dir. (1979–). Jefferson Cnty. Cncl. of the Arts. **Activities:** 1; 15, 17, 36 **Addr.:** Melvil Dewey Library, Jefferson Community College, Watertown, NY 13601.

Kitchen, Paul H. (N. 14, 1937, Toronto, ON) Exec. Dir., Can. LA, 1975–; Gvt. Libs. Liaison Ofcr., Natl. Lib. of Can., 1973–75, Spec. Asst. to Natl. Libn., 1971–72. **Educ.:** Carleton Univ., 1960–63, BA (Eng.); Univ. of BC, 1963–64, BLS. **Orgs.:** Can. LA. ALA. Inst. of Assn. Exec. **Pubns.:** Ed., *Federal Government Library Survey Report* (1974); "Canadian Library Association," *ALA Yrbk.* (1976–); various articles. **Addr.:** Canadian Library Association, 151 Sparks St., Ottawa, ON K1P 5E3 Canada.

Kitchens, Philip H. (Mr. 16, 1945, Greenville, NC) Engin. Libn., Univ. of AL, 1976–; Chem. Engin., Ethyl Corp., 1974–75; Mech. Engin., U.S. Env. Protection Agency, 1973–74; Aerospace Engin., U.S. Natl. Aeronautics and Space Admin., 1967–72. **Educ.:** LA Tech. Univ., 1963–67, BS (Chem. Engin.); Univ. of

PROFESSIONAL ACTIVITIES: Institutions: 1. Acad. lib.; 2. Arch.; 3. Assn.; 4. Fed./Gvt. lib.; 5. Inst. lib.; 6. Mfr./Suppl.; 7. Milit. lib.; 8. Musm.; 9. Pub. lib.; 10. Sch. lib.; 11. Sch. of lib. sci.; 12. Spec. lib.; 13. State lib.; 14. (other). **Functions/Activities:** 15. Acq./Col. dev.; 16. Adult srvs.; 17. Admin.; 18. Apprais.; 19. Archit./Bldgs.; 20. Cat./Class.; 21. Chld. srvs.; 22. Circ.; 23. Cons./Pres.; 24. Consult.; 25. Cont. ed.; 26. Educ. lib. sci.; 27. Ext. srvs.; 28. Fund/Grants; 29. Gvt. pubs.; 30. Indx./Abs.; 31. Instr. lib. use; 32. Media srvs.; 33. Micro.; 34. Netwks./Coop.; 35. Persnl.; 36. PR; 37. Publshg.; 38. Recs. mgt.; 39. Ref. srvs.; 40. Repro.; 41. Resrch.; 42. Review.; 43. Secur.; 44. Serials; 45. Spec. col.; 46. Tech. srvs.; 47. Trustees/Bds.; 48. YA srvs.; 49. (other).

Who's Who in Library and Information Services

AL, 1970–71, MS (Mech. Engin.); LA State Univ., 1975–76, MLS. **Orgs.:** ALA. LA: Bibl. Com. (1978–80). ALA. SLA: AL Chap./Empl. and Career Guid. Com. (Ch., 1977–). Amer. Socty. Engin. Educ.: Engin. Libs. Dir. (1979–). Amer. Chem. Socty. Amer. Inst. of Aeronautics and Astronautics. Amer. Inst. of Chem. Engin. **Honors:** Tau Beta Pi. Beta Phi Mu. **Pubns.:** "Library-Use Instruction for Engineers at the University of Alabama," *AL Libn.* (N.-D. 1977); "Engineers Meet the Library," *Jnl. of Acad. Libnshp.* (N., 1979); "Combushau Technology Manual," *Chem. Engin.* (N. 1978); "Control of Air Pollution Sources," *Chem. Engin.* (Je. 1978); Reviews; Other articles. **Activities:** 1; 15, 31, 39; 64, 91 **Addr.:** 121 Fox Run, 22nd St. N., Tuscaloosa, AL 35406.

Kittrell, Winifred E. (S. 8, 1938, Tulsa, OK) Mgr., Tech. Info. and Comms. Srvs., Williams Brothers Engin. Co., 1981–, Dir., Tech. Info. Ctr., 1977–81, Supvsr., 1974–77. **Educ.:** Duke Univ., 1956–60, BA (Psy.); Univ. of OK, 1971–75, MLS. **Orgs.:** SLA: OK Chap., Dir. (1980–83), Pres. (1977–78), Bltn. Ed. (1975–76). OK Gvr.'s WHCOLIS: Prog. Plng. Com. (1977–78). Tulsa Area Lib. Coop.: Strg. Com. (1980–81). Psi Chi. Toastmaster's Intl. **Pubns.:** Jt. ed., *Directory of Special Libraries and Information Centers in Oklahoma* (1974, 1976, 1980). **Activities:** 12; 17; 64, 65, 86 **Addr.:** Technical Information Center, Williams Brothers Engineering Company, 6600 S. Yale Ave., Tulsa, OK 74177.

Kizlyk, Olga Margaret (N. 29, 1944, Edmonton, AB) Prov. Cts. Libn., Dept. of the AB Gvt. Attorney Gen., 1976–, Calgary Ct. Hse. Libn., 1970–75. **Educ.:** Univ. of AB, 1963–67, BA (Psy., Soclgy.), 1975–76, BLS, 1978– (LS). **Orgs.:** Can. ALL: Nsltr. Ed. (1979), Ed. Bd. (1977–79), various other coms. AALL. Edmonton Law Libns. Assn. Univ. of AB Alum. Exec. Cncl. **Pubns.:** Contrib., *Law Library Guide for Alberta Practitioners* (1979). **Activities:** 12, 13; 15, 17, 39; 77 **Addr.:** Provincial Courts Libraries, Century Pl., 9803–102 A Ave., Edmonton, AB T5J 3A3 Canada.

Klappersack, Dennis (D. 10, 1942, Wallingford, CT) Coord. of Tech. Srvcs., Houston Comnty. Coll. Syst., 1979–; Acq. Libn., Univ. of TN, Nashville, 1977–79, Cat. Libn., 1975–77, Asst. Cat. Libn., 1973–75. **Educ.:** Boston Univ., 1960–65, BA (Hist.); Univ. of TN, Knoxville, 1972–73, MLS. **Orgs.:** ALA. TN LA: Ch., JMRT (1977–78); Ch., Grievance Com. (1977–78). **Activities:** 1; 15, 20, 46; 55, 56 **Addr.:** Learning Resources Center, Houston Community College System, 1300 Holman, Houston, TX 77004.

Klasing, Jane P. (O. 24, 1940, S. Weymouth, MA) Dir., Lib. Media Srvs., Cooper City HS, 1971–; Lib. Media Spec., Lakeland Ctrl. Schs., 1962–71. **Educ.:** SUNY, Albany, 1958–61, BA (Eng.); Columbia Univ., 1971, MS (LS). **Orgs.:** ALA: AASL. AECT. FL Assn. Media in Educ.: Bd. of Dirs. (1977–80), Legis. Com. (1975–79), Resrch. Com. (Ch., 1980), Com. on Lib. Autom. (Ch., 1980–81). *FL Media Qtly.* (Ed., 1980–). Delta Kappa Gamma: Mu State Schol. Com. (Ch., 1980–81). **Honors:** Lakeland (NY) Ctrl. Sch., Cit., 1971. **Pubns.:** "So You're Considering a Security System," *Sch. Media Qtly.* (Win. 1979); "Security Systems Do Work," *Sch. Lib. Jnl.* (N. 1979). **Activities:** 10; 17, 26, 32; 55, 63, 92 **Addr.:** 2501 N.E. 26 Terr., Fort Lauderdale, FL 33305.

Klassen, Krysanne Cathryn (D. 5, 1950, Leamington, ON) Info. Srvs. Coord., Vinto Engineering Ltd., 1979–; Pub. Srvs. Libn., Alberta Dept. of Energy, 1978–79; Libn., Boundary Layer Wind Tunnel, 1975–78; Ref. Libn., Hum., London Pub. Lib., 1974–75. **Educ.:** Univ. of Guelph, 1969–72, BA (Eng.); Univ. of Western Ont., 1972–74, MLS. **Orgs.:** Can. Lib. Jrnl.: Ed. Brd. Can. Assn. of Spec. Lib. and Info. Srvs.: Ch., Edmonton Chap. SLA: Arch. Com. (1977). Can. LA. **Activities:** 12; 31, 39; 64, 82, 86 **Addr.:** P. O. Box 7972, Station A, Edmonton, AB T5J 3G7 Canada.

Klassen, Robert Leonard (N. 10, 1935, Patterson, CA) Chief, Program Coordination Staff, Office of Libraries and Learning Technologies, United States Dept. of Education, 1968–; Asst. Supvsr., CA State Lib., 1962–68; Head Libn., Fresno Pac. Coll., 1960–62; Ref. Libn., CA State Lib., 1959–60. **Educ.:** CA State Univ., Fresno, 1957, BA (Soc. Stds.); Univ. of CA, Berkeley, 1959, MLS; George Washington Univ., 1977–78. **Orgs.:** ASIS: Pub. Affairs Com. (Ch., 1977–79; 1980–). DC LA. ALA: Resrch. Com. (1975–77); ACRL, Leg. Com. (1978–); RASD, Mudge Citn. Com. (1976–77; Ch., 1977–79), Stans. Com. (1969, Ch., 1970–74). SLA: Exec. Bd. of Dir. (1973–76). River Crest Civic Assn. (Arlington, VA). Fourth Presbyterian Church, Bethesda, MD. Fed. Mgrs. Assn. **Honors:** Beta Phi Mu; Phi Kappa Phi; Pi Gamma Mu; N. CA Libn. of the Year, 1968. **Pubns.:** "The Council on Library Resources; an Interview with President Warren J. Haas," *Bltn. of ASIS* (Ap. 1979); "The National Need for Standards for Reference," *Prcs. of the Symp. on Measurement of Ref.* (1974); "Support for Libraries in the New Department of Education," *Educ. Libs.* (Fall 1980); "From Library to Information System," *Bltn. of ASIS* (Ag. 1978); Various other articles. **Activities:** 1, 14-Fed. agency; 17, 24, 39; 63, 78 **Addr.:** Office of Libraries and Learning Technologies, United States Department of Education, 7th and D Sts., S.W., Washington, DC 20202.

Klatt, Melvin J. (My. 19, 1929, Milwaukee, WI) Coll. Libn., Elmhurst Coll., 1974–; Asst. Dean, Rosary Coll., Grad. Sch. of Lib. Sci., 1972–74; Assoc. Dir. of Tech. Srvcs. Acting Dir. of Libs., Univ. of Denver, 1965–69; Head, Acq. Dept., Univ. of IL, Chicago Circle, 1961–65; Head, Branch Lib., Milwaukee Pub. Lib., 1958–61. **Educ.:** Univ. of WI, 1953–56, BS (Hist./Econ.); Univ. of Denver, 1957–58, MALS; IN Univ., 1969–72, PhD Cand. (Lib. Sci.). **Orgs.:** ALA. IL LA. Chicago Lib. Club: VP (1979–80). IL Arts Cncl.: Visual Arts Com. (1978–81). LIBRAS: VP/Pres. (1979–81). Southwest Denver Human Rel.: Ch., Educ. Com. (1968–69); VP (1969). AAUP: Exec. Com. (1964–65). IL OCLC Users' Group: Treas. (1977–78). Private Acad. Libs. in IL: VP/Pres. (1977–79). **Honors:** Beta Phi Mu, 1971. **Pubns.:** *Dictionary of Wisconsin Biography* (1960); Jt. ed., *Colorado Academic Libraries* (1968); Ed., *Dictionary of Human Resources* (1979). **Activities:** 1; 15, 17, 25; 57, 59, 63 **Addr.:** 1011 Arbor Ave., Wheaton, IL 60187.

Kleckner, Simone-Marie (Mr. 7, 1927, Bucharest, Romania) Legal Libn., Untd. Nations, 1975–; Catlgr./Asst. Cur., NY Univ. Law Lib., 1969–74; Libn. (Trainee) Per. Div., NY Pub. Lib., 1968; Asst. to Legal Couns., Judicial Ofc., Dept. of Construct., Bucharest, 1960–65. **Educ.:** Bucharest Univ., 1949–53, Dip. (Law); Columbia Univ., 1968–69, MLS; NY Univ., 1969–73, LLM (Intl. Law). **Orgs.:** AALL. Intl. Assn. of Law Libs. Law LA of Grt. NY. Amer. Socty. of Intl. Law. Amer. Frgn. Law Assn. **Pubns.:** transl., introduction, "Romanian Constitution," *Constitutions of the Communist World* (1980); *Penal Code of the Romanian Socialist Republic, Amer. Ser. of Foreign Penal Codes* (1976); "Foreign Trade Arbitration in Romania," *NY Univ. Jnl. of Intl. Law and Pol.* (1972); "NYU Classification Scheme on Economic Integation," *Law Lib. Jnl.* (1975); "Major Publications of the U.N. Office of Legal Affairs," *Law Lib. Jnl.* (1981). **Activities:** 1; 15, 39, 41; 57, 62, 77 **Addr.:** 110 W. 69th St., New York, NY 10023.

Kleiber, Michael C. (My. 6, 1943, San Francisco, CA) Head Libn., Inst. of Transp. Stds., Univ. of CA, Berkeley, 1981–; Tech. Srvs. Libn., 1966–80. **Educ.:** San Francisco State Univ., 1961–64, AB (Geo.), 1964–65 (Geo.); Univ. of CA, Berkeley, 1965–66, MLS. **Orgs.:** SLA: Transp. Div. (Ch., 1976–77). **Pubns.:** *Rapid Transit in the San Francisco Bay Area* (1979); *New and Novel Passenger Transportation Systems* (1971). **Activities:** 12; 46; 94 **Addr.:** University of California, Institute of Transportation Studies Library, 412 McLaughlin Hall, Berkeley, CA 94720.

Kleiman, Allan Martin (N. 1, 1951, Brooklyn, NY) Chief, Srv. to the Aging/SAGE, Brooklyn Pub. Lib., 1981–; Adj. Asst. Prof., LS, St. John's Univ., 1980–81; LS and Indus. Div., Brooklyn Pub. Lib., 1973–. **Educ.:** Brooklyn Coll., CUNY, 1969–73, BA, cum laude (Hist.); St. John's Univ., 1973–74, MLS; Columbia Univ., 1979–, DLS Cand. **Orgs.:** ALA: JMRT, *Cognotes Can.* (Sum. 1980); RASD, Lib. Srv. to an Aging Popltn. Discuss. Grp. (Ch., 1981–). Long Island Hist. Socty. NY LA. **Pubns.:** "Library Service to the Aging with a Brooklyn Accent," *Cath. Lib. World* (Ap. 1982); *Kings County Source Material, to 1775: A Bibliography* (1974); "When the Silents Were Made in Brooklyn," *New Brooklyn Qtly.* (Sum. 1981). **Activities:** 9, 11; 16, 26, 39; 67, 91, 95-Aging. **Addr.:** 1775 E. 13 St., Apt. 3E, Brooklyn, NY 11229.

Klein, Adaire J. (D. 1, 1931, Leavenworth, KS) Dir. of Lib. and Lib. Srvs., Yeshiva Univ. of LA, Wiesenthal Ctr. for Holocaust Std., 1978–; Libn., Catlgr., Sinai Temple, 1974–79; Instr., Lib. Cat. of Judaica, Hebrew Union Coll., 1978. **Educ.:** Brandeis Univ., 1949–53, BA (Hebrew Lit.), 1953–57, MA (Near East. and Judaic Std.); Libn.-Tchr. Cert., Bur. of Jewish Educ. **Orgs.:** Assn. of Jewish Libs. of Southern CA: Corresponding Secy. (1974–75); Pres. (1975–79). Assn. of Jewish Libs.: VP, Synagogue, Sch. Ctr. Beth Jacob Cong.: Adult Educ. Com. Amer. Mizrachi Women Bureau of Jew. Educ.: Pers. Com. **Pubns.:** *Bibliography on American Jewish History* (1976). **Activities:** 1, 12; 15, 17, 20; 90 **Addr.:** Yeshiva University of Los Angeles, 9760 W. Pico Blvd., Los Angeles, CA 90035.

Klein, Joanne S. (Jy. 16, 1942, Pittsburgh, PA) Tech. Libn., Jones & Laughlin Steel Corp., 1975–; SDI Spec., Calgon Corp., 1970–75; Libn., Pittsburgh Corning Corp., 1967–70; Eng. Tchr., Ambridge Area Sr. HS, 1964–67. **Educ.:** Clarion State Coll., 1960–64, BS (Eng., Soc. Sci.); Univ. of Pittsburgh, 1967–70, MLS. Various short courses and Trng. sessions. **Orgs.:** SLA: Pittsburgh Chap. (Pres., 1981–82), various coms. and ofcs. Pittsburg OLUG: Co-Organizer (1977), Mem. Com. (Ch., 1978–79). Amer. Iron and Steel Inst.: Subcom. on Libs. and Info. Ctrs., Prog. Com. (Ch., 1978), Nom. Com. (Ch., 1979). **Honors:** Pi Gamma Mu. Beta Phi Mu. **Activities:** 12; 17, 30, 39; 56, 81, 91 **Addr.:** Jones and Laughlin Steel Corporation, 900 Agnew Rd., Pittsburgh, PA 15227.

Klein, Michele Schutte (Mr. 14, 1951, Pittsburgh, PA) Dir., Lib. Srvs., Chlds. Hosp. of MI, 1978–, Ref. Libn., TX Med. Assn., 1978–; Prog. Policy Spec., Natl. Hlth. Insr. Co., Electronic Data Systs., 1977–78; Lib. Dir., Chlds. Hosp., Cincinnati Med. Ctr., 1973–76. **Educ.:** Univ. of Pittsburgh, 1969–72, BA (Comm.) Case West. Rsv. Univ., 1972–73, MSLS. Med. LA, 1976, Cert. **Orgs.:** Med. LA: Ed. Com., MLA NEWS (Ch., 1977). Metro Detroit Med. Lib. Grp.: Pres.-Elect (1980–81), Pres. (1981–82), Cont. Educ. Com. (Ch., 1979–80). SLA. **Honors:** Beta Phi Mu. **Pubns.:** "Report of the Editorial Committee for the *MLA News*," *Bltn. Med. LA* (1978); "Space Utilization in a Hospital Library With Space Shortages," *Bltn. Med. LA.* (1977); "Evolution of Children's Hospital," *Cincinnati Jnl. of Med.* (1976). **Activities:** 5, 12; 17, 39; 56, 80, 87 **Addr.:** Library, Children's Hospital of Michigan, 3901 Beaubien Blvd., Detroit, MI 48201.

Klein, Phyllis Ann (My. 31, 1939, Newark, NJ) Asst. Dir., Arch. Trng. Prog., NY Univ., 1979–; Instr., Hist., Minot State Coll., 1965–67; Asst. Ed., Doubleday and Co., 1962–65. **Educ.:** Smith Coll., 1957–61, BA (Hist.); Harvard Univ., 1961–62, MAT (Hist.); NY Univ., 1977–81, MA (Amer. Hist.), Cert. (Arch. Admin.). **Orgs.:** Mid-Atl. Reg. Arch. Conf. Archvsts. RT of Metro. NY. SAA. Org. of Amer. Histns. Amer. Hist. Assn. AAUW. **Activities:** 1, 2; 17, 26, 41; 55, 75 **Addr.:** 435 E. 70th St., New York, NY 10021.

Klein, Robert F. (Dubuque, IA) Dir., Lrng., Resrcs., 1974–, Loras Coll., Libn., 1969– Asst. Libn., Loras Coll., 1964–69; Reader's Adv., DC Pub. Lib., 1961–62. **Educ.:** Loras Coll., 1955–59, BA (Latin); Catholic Univ. of Amer., 1962–64, MSLS. **Orgs.:** IA OCLC Cncl. Exec. Com. (1977–78). Northeast IA Acad. Libs. Secy. (1968), Exec. Dir. (1969). IA Hist. Socty. Dubuque Cnty. Hist. Socty.: Bd. of Dir. (1974–), Pres. (1978–). **Activities:** 1; 15, 17, 19; 55, 69, 75 **Addr.:** Loras College, Dubuque, IA 52001.

Klein, Stephen C. (Je. 23, 1950, Passaic, NJ) Cnty. Libn., Sutter Cnty. Free Lib., 1979; Cnty. Libn., Lake Cnty. Lib., 1974–79; Bkmobile., Chld. Libn., Lake Cnty. Lib. Proj., 1973–74. **Educ.:** Cowell Coll., Univ., CA, Santa Cruz, 1968–72, AB (Relig. Std.); Sch. of Libnshp., Univ. of CA, Berkeley, 1972–73, MLS; CA Bd. of Lib. Examiners, 1978, Cert. (Cnty. Libn.). **Orgs.:** N. Bay Coop. Lib. Syst.: Ch. (1975–76). CA Cnty. Libn. Assn.: Pres. (1980). CA Inst. of Libs.: Secty. (1980). Cong. of CA Pub. Lib. Systs. (Ch., 1981). Lake Cnty. Jaycees. Peach Bowl Lions Club. N. Coast Reg. Ctr. for the Dev. Disabled: VP (1978–79). **Activities:** 9; 17, 47 **Addr.:** Sutter County Free Library, 750 Forbes Ave., Yuba City, CA 95991.

Kleiner, Janellyn Pickering (D. 9, 1936, Harrisburg, IL) Ref. Libn., LA State Lib., 1979–, Head, Interlib. Loan Dept., 1968–78, Asst. Docu. Libn., 1967–68, Info. Desk Libn., 1968, Chief Circ. Libn., 1966–67, Asst. Circ. Libn., 1965. **Educ.:** LA State Univ., 1954–58, BA (Jrnlsm.), 1963–65, MSLS, 1974, MA (Jrnlsm.); Wayne State Univ., 1968, (Interlib. Coop.). **Orgs.:** ALA. Southwestern LA: Ed., Joint SELA, SWLA. LA LA. **Honors:** Phi Kappa Phi. Beta Phi Mu. Theta Sigma Phi. **Pubns.:** Ed., *Southeastern LA-Southwestern LA Joint Papers and Proceedings* (1973); Ed., *Proceedings of the Inst. for Adv. Study in Libnshp. on the Concept of Systems of Libraries* (1969); Jt. auth., "The Role of the Academic Librarian in Library Governance," (1979); Jt. auth., "Louisiana Libraries 'Cope with Copyright' " (Win. 1978). **Activities:** 1; 34, 36, 39; 56, 83, 93 **Addr.:** Louisiana State University Library, Baton Rouge, LA 70803.

Klement, Susan Paula Lobel (Ag. 7, 1941, Leicester, Eng.) Prin., Info. Resrcs., 1969–; Docum. Libn., Educ. Ctr. Lib., Toronto Bd. of Educ., 1967–70. **Educ.:** Univ. of Toronto, 1959–63, BA (Soclgy.), 1966–67, BLS, 1971–74, MLS. **Orgs.:** Can. LA. Indx. and Abs. Socty. of Can.: Exec. Com. (1977–78). ON LA: Cncl. (1976–77). SLA: Toronto Chap., Pres. (1974–75). Other orgs. **Pubns.:** *Who Knows What; an Inventory of Expertise for Metropolitan Toronto Public Library* (1976); "Increasing Library Effectiveness," *Can. Lib. Jnl.* (O. 1977); Guest ed., "Alternatives in Librarianship," *Can. Lib. Jnl.* (Ap. 1977); "Feminism and Professionalism in Librarianship," *Can. Lib. Jnl.* (D. 1974). **Activities:** 11, 14-info. brokerage; 24, 26, 41; 92 **Addr.:** Information Resources, 45 Inglewood Dr., Toronto, ON M4T 1G9 Canada.

Klemm, Carol Bauman (My. 20, 1936, Hillsdale, NJ) Libn., Union Carbide Corp., 1978–; Lit. Chem., Self-employed, 1975–78; Chem. Libn., Intl. Flavors and Fragrances, 1964–66; Organic Chem., Union Carbide Resrch., Inst., 1958–64. **Educ.:** Douglass Coll., Rutgers Univ., 1953–57, BA (Chem.); Columbia Univ., 1957–58, MA (Chem.); Rutgers Univ., 1976–78, MLS. **Orgs.:** SLA: NJ Chap., Prog. Com. (1979–80), OLUG. Amer. Chem. Socty.: Div. of Chem. Info. **Honors:** Beta Phi Mu. Phi Beta Kappa. Sigma Xi. **Pubns.:** Articles on Organic Chem., 1961–64. **Activities:** 12; 39; 60, 64 **Addr.:** Technical Information Service, Union Carbide Corporation, P.O. Box 670, Bound Brook, NJ 08805.

Klempner, Irving M. (N. 28, 1924, Poland) Prof. (LS), SUNY Albany, 1967–; Mgr., Info. Srvs., Untd. Nuclear Corp., 1958–67; Supvsr. Libn., U.S. Navy Dept., 1956–58; Cat. Libn., U.S. Natl. Lib. Med., 1955–56 Lib. Intern, Lib. of Congs., 1953–54; Lib. Intern., U.S. Dept. of State Lib., 1952–53. **Educ.:** Brooklyn Coll., 1949–51, BA; Columbia Univ., 1951–52, MSLS, 1959–67, DLS. **Orgs.:** SLA: Com. on WHCOLIS (Ch., 1978–80). ASIS: Mem. Com. (1974–77), other ofcs. ALA. AALS. Other orgs. **Honors:** SLA, Prof. Awd., 1980. SLA, Best Paper Publ. in Spec. Libs. Awd., 1974. ASIS, Best Spec. Interest Grp Pubn., 1971. **Pubns.:** *Diffusion of Abstracting and Indexing Services for Government-Sponsored Research* (1968); *Audiovisual Materials*

Special Subjects/Services: 50. Adult educ.; 51. Advert./Mktg.; 52. Aerosp.; 53. Agric.; 54. Area std.; 55. Arts/Hum.; 56. Autom.; 57. Bibl./Prtg.; 58. Bio. sci.; 59. Bus./Fin.; 60. Chem.; 61. Copyrt.; 62. Documtn.; 63. Educ.; 64. Engin.; 65. Env.; 66. Eth. grps.; 67. Film; 68. Food/Nutr.; 69. Geneal.; 70. Geo.; 71. Geol.; 72. Handcpd.; 73. Hist.; 74. Int. frdm.; 75. Info. sci.; 76. Insr.; 77. Law; 78. Legis.; 79. Math./Comp. sci.; 80. Med.; 81. Metals; 82. Nat. resrcs.; 83. Newsp.; 84. Nuc. sci.; 85. Oral hist.; 86. Petr./Energy; 87. Pharm.; 88. Phys./Astr./Math.; 89. Readg.; 90. Relig.; 91. Sci./Tech.; 92. Soc. sci.; 93. Telecom.; 94. Transp.; 95. (other).

in Support of Information Science Curricula (1977); "The Concept of "National Security" and Its Effect on Information Transfer," *Spec. Libs.* (Jy. 1973); "The New Imperatives: Decisions for Library School Curricula," *Spec. Libs.* (S. 1976); other articles, reviews, and AV pubns. **Activities:** 11; 26, 29, 34; 56, 62, 75 **Addr.:** School of Library and Information Service, SUNY Albany, 1400 Washington Ave., Albany, NY 12222.

Klika, Demaris Benner (Ap. 5, 1917, Pittsburgh, PA) Admin. Libn., US Army/Giessen Lib. Syst., 1977–; Ref. Libn., US Army Transp. Sch. Lib., 1972–77. **Educ.:** Butler Univ., 1948–59, BS (Eng, Hist.), Butler Univ., 1969, MA (Eng.); Indiana Univ., Bloomington, 1970, MLS. **Orgs.:** SLA: VA Div. Assn. of the U. S. Army. Nat. Def. Tran. Assn. Butler Univ. Alum. Assn. IN Univ. Alum. Assn. AAUW. **Honors:** Phi Kappa Phi, 1959; Beta Phi Mu, 1970. **Activities:** 4; 17, 39; 74, 94 **Addr.:** US Army Library, Pendleton Barracks, Giessen Military Community, APO, NY 09169.

Klinck, Cynthia A. (N. 1, 1948, Salamanca, NY) Dir., Washington Twp. Pub. Lib., 1978–; Dir., Paul Sawyier Pub. Lib., 1974–77; Ref./YA Libn., Bartholomew Cnty. Lib., 1970–74. **Educ.:** Ball State Univ., 1966–70, BS (Gen. Arts); Univ. of KY, 1975–76, MSLS. **Orgs.:** ALA. OH LA. Miami Valley Lib. Org.: Vice-Ch. (1981). KY Gvr.'s WHCOLIS: Del. (1979). S. Cmnty. Mental Hlth. Ctr.: Bd. of Trustees. **Pubns.:** "Success with Volunteers, or How to Keep the Library Doors Open," *KY LA Bltn.* (Win. 1977). **Activities:** 9; 17, 35, 36; 50, 75 **Addr.:** Washington Township Public Library, 6060 Far Hills Ave., Dayton, OH 45459.

Klinck, Patricia E. (Ja. 13, 1940, Albany, NY) State Libn., VT Dept. of Libs., 1977–; Asst. State Libn., Dir. of Dev., 1972–77, Reg. Lib. Dir., 1970–72; Dir. of Libs., Simon's Rock Coll., 1967–70; Libn., Colonie Ctrl. HS (Albany), 1963–67; Ref. Libn., USA Pavilion, NY. **Educ.:** Smith Coll., 1957–61, AB (Hist.); Simmons Coll., 1961–63, MS (LS); SUNY Albany, 1964–67 (LS). **Orgs.:** COSLA: Bd. of Dir. (1979–80), Vice Ch. (1980–82). ALA: ASCLA/Multitype Lib. Coop. Sect., Nom. Com. (Ch., 1980). VT LA. CLENE: Bd. (1978–79). Other orgs. and ofcs. VT Hist. Assn.: Bd. of Dir. **Pubns.:** "Books by Mail," *Handbook on Books by Mail* (1977); "Staff Development: Inherent Roles Within the Organization," Prcs., *Third CLENE Asm.* (1977). **Activities:** 13; 17, 25; 50, 59, 78 **Addr.:** Vermont Dept of Libraries, State Office Building PO, Montpelier, VT 05602.

Kline, Nancy M. (O. 9, 1937, Providence, RI) Head, Lib. Orien. and Instr. Srvs. Dept., Univ. of CT Lib., 1979–, Head, Map Lib., 1973–79. **Educ.:** Univ. of CT, 1955–59, BS (Foods/Nutr.), 1959–61, MS (Home Econ.); Univ. of RI, 1970–73, MS (LS). **Orgs.:** ALA: ACRL/New Eng. Chap. New Eng. LA: Nom. Com. (1980–81). CT LA: Pres. (1980–81), Coll. and Univ. Sect., Exec. Bd. (1975–78). SLA: Geo. and Map. Div., *Bltn.* Assoc. Ed. (1973–77), CT Chap., *Bltn.* Ed. (1976–79), Chap. Educ. Com. (Ch., 1979–80). **Honors:** Mortar Bd.; Beta Phi Mu; Phi Kappa Phi. **Pubns.:** "Catalogs of State Geological Survey Publications," *SLA Geo. and Map Div. Bltn.* (D. 1974); "Official Highway Maps: A Source List," *SLA Geo. and Map Div. Bltn.* (D. 1974); "Research and Research-related Reports in Geography and Mapping," *SLA Geo. and Map Div. Bltn.* (S. 1976, Mr. 1976, Je. 1974, D. 1973, S. 1973, Mr. 1973); "Yonge, Ena Laura (1895–1971)," *Dictionary of American Library Biography* (1978). **Activities:** 1, 12; 17, 31, 39; 70 **Addr.:** Library, U-5H, University of Connecticut, Storrs, CT 06268.

Kline, Sims DuBose (Ag. 30, 1946, Orlando, FL) Ref. and Gvt. Pubns. Libn., Stetson Univ., 1976–; Adj. Fac. mem., Univ. of Ctrl. FL, Dept. of Eng., 1980–; Actg. Head, Tech. Srvs., Univ. of NC, Asheville, 1975–76. **Educ.:** Johns Hopkins Univ., 1964–65; Georgetown Univ., 1965–68, BS (Intl. Affairs); FL State Univ., 1974–75, MLS; Univ. of FL, 1972–73, 78, MA (Eng.); Stetson Univ., 1979–, (Bus. Admin.). **Orgs.:** ALA. SELA. FL LA. ASIS. Mod. Lang. Assn. **Pubns.:** Cont., "Instruction in Negotiating the Reference Inquiry" in *Ref. and Info. Srv.: A Reader* (1978); Contrib., "A Computer-Searched and Printed Index to Reference Queries" in *The Process of Answering Ref. Questions* (1977); "An Online Chic Index," *Nsltr. for FL Online Srchrs.* (F. 1981); "Dissent and Descent from the Ivory Tower," *Georgetown Courier* (Sum. 1966). **Activities:** 1; 15, 17, 31, 39; 56, 57, 59 **Addr.:** duPont-Ball Library, Stetson University, DeLand, FL 32720.

Kline, Sr. Theodore (Jy. 2, 1899, Hastings, NB) Archvst., Dominican Srs. of St. Catharine, KY, 1976–; Libn., St. Catharine Coll., 1973–75; VP, Congregation, Dominican Srs. of St. Catharine, KY, 1966–72; Prin., Ctrl. Catholic HS (Grand Island, NE), 1959–66. **Educ.:** Creighton Univ., 1922–27, AB (Eng.); Univ. of NE, 1931–34, MA (Latin). **Orgs.:** SAA. KY Cncl. on Arch.: Com. on Relig. Arch. **Honors:** Honorable Order of KY Colonels, KY Colonel, 1970–79. **Pubns.:** "Open Forum on High School Curriculum" *Phi Theta Kappa* (O. 29, 1947); "Meeting the Need for Remedial Reading in High School," *Phi Theta Kappa* (O. 12, 1961); "A Challenge to Latin Teachers," *Phi Theta Kappa* (1934). **Activities:** 2, 5; 38, 41; 90 **Addr.:** St. Catharine Motherhouse, St. Catharine, KY 40061.

Kling, Susan S. (My. 25, 1948, Lincoln, NE) Div. Chief, Ref. and ILL Srvs. Div., NE Lib. Comsn., 1978–, Supvsr., NE Pubn. Clearinghse., Docum. Div., 1974–78, Abstctr., *NE Pubn. Checklist*, 1973–74, ILL Loan Libn., 1970–72. **Educ.:** Univ. of NE, Lincoln, 1966–70, BS (Educ.); Emporia State Univ., 1975–78, MLS. **Orgs.:** Mt. Plains LA: State Lib. Sect., JM RT, Awds. Com. ALA: GODORT, Elec. Com. (1975–76). NE LA: Mem. Com. (1978–79); Natl. Lib. Week Com. (1980–81). Natl. Micro. Assn. First Grmn. Congregational Church. **Honors:** Beta Phi Mu. **Activities:** 12, 13; 17, 29, 39 **Addr.:** Nebraska Library Commission, 1420 P St., Lincoln, NE 68508.

Klingbiel, Paul H. (N. 3, 1919, Watertown, WI) Syst. Anal., PRC Govt. Info. Systs., 1981–; Sr. Consult., Aspen Syst. Corp., 1979–81; Resrch. Ling., Defense Documtn. Ctr., 1975–79, Actg. Dir., Directorate of Dev., 1973–75, Supervisory Ling. Resrch., 1972–73, various positions in phys. sci., 1965–67, Supervisory Libn., 1964–65, Phys. Sci. Admin., 1962–64; Supervisory Libn., Armed Srvs. Tech. Info. Agency, 1962; various libn. positions, 1958–60. **Educ.:** Univ. of Chicago, 1946–50, BS (Math.); Amer. Univ., 1962–66, MA (Ling.). **Orgs.:** ASIS. Assn. for Comp. Ling. Ling. Socty. of Amer. AAAS. **Honors:** Defense Logistics Agency, Disting. Career Awd., 1979; Defense Documtn. Ctr., Merit. Civilian Srv. Awd., 1974. **Pubns.:** "Evaluation of Machine-Aided Indexing," *Info. Pres. and Mgt.* (1976); "A Technique of Machine-Aided Indexing," *Info. Storage and Retrieval* (S. 1973). **Activities:** 4, 12; 24, 30, 41; 55, 56, 75 **Addr.:** 7480 Jayhawk St., Annandale, VA 22003.

Klingensmith, Patricia Jane (Mr. 29, 1922, Pittsburgh, PA) Info. Retrieval Spec., The Univ. of Pittsburgh, 1974; Tchr., Pittsburgh Sch. Syst., 1944–46. **Educ.:** Univ. of Pittsburgh, 1939–43, BA (Hist., Eng.), 1944–49, ML (Eng.), 1972–73, MLS (Ref.); 1977, Advnc. Cert. (Info. Sci.); Writers Wkshp., Sum. 1971–73, (Non-fiction). **Orgs.:** ASIS. Pittsburgh Reg. Lib. Ctr.: Data Base Srvs. Com. (1978–). Pittsburgh On-Line Users Forum. PLA. SLA. Chautauqua Inst.: Bd. of Trustees (1977–). Third Presbyterian Church: Trustee (1973–79). Coll. Club of Pittsburgh: Bd. of Dirs. (1970–72). **Honors:** Beta Phi Mu. **Pubns.:** Jt. auth., "On-Line Training Center" manuals (1978); jt. auth., "An Exercise in Utility; Training in Search and Seizure at the University of Pittsburgh," *Online* (Ja. 1980); "Melvil Dewey," *The Chautauqua Daily* (Ag. 23, 1976); "A New Chapter" *Themis* (Sum. 1972); various articles, sp. **Activities:** 11; 26, 34, 41; 56, 63, 75 **Addr.:** 197 Farmington Rd., Pittsburgh, PA 15215.

Klingerman, Ethel (Mr. 4, 1929, Muncy, PA) Lib. Dir., Moorestown (NJ) Lib., 1966–, Head Libn., East. Coll., 1956–66, Cat. Libn., Brown Pub. Lib., Williamsport, PA, 1954–56, Catlgr., and Clasfr. 1951–54. **Educ.:** Wilson Coll., 1946–50, AB (Math.); Drexel Univ., 1950–51, MS (LS). **Orgs.:** ALA. NJ LA: Adult Srvs. Sect. (1971–72); ACRL (Secy.-Treas., 1965–66). Leag. of Women Voters. AAUP. Lib. Srvs. Construct. Act. Adv. Cncl. on Libs. for NJ. **Honors:** ALA, John Cotton Dana PR Awd., 1971. **Pubns.:** Ed., 3rd ed., *Moorestown and Her Neighbors: Historical Sketches* (1973). **Activities:** 9; 15, 17, 19 **Addr.:** Moorestown Library, 111 W. Second St., Moorestown, NJ 08057.

Klingle, Philip A. (Jl. 24, 1950, Brooklyn, NY) Libn., Inst. of Judicial Admin., 1981–; Asst. Prof./Ref. Libn., John Jay Coll. of Criminal Justice, 1978–81; Libn., Brooklyn Pub. Lib., 1977–78; Asst. Ref. Libn., NY Hist. Socty., 1973–77. **Educ.:** Fordham Univ., 1968–71, BA (Hist.), NY Univ., 1972–73, MA (Hist.); Columbia Univ., 1974–76, MS (LS). **Orgs.:** LA CU NY: LA CUNY Exec. Cncl. (Del., 1978–81). ALA. Can. LA. Long Island Hist. Socty. Co. of Milit. Histns. **Honors:** Carleton Univ., Paterson Flwshp., Intl. Affairs, 1971. **Pubns.:** "Kings County During the American Revolution," *Brooklyn, U.S.A.: Fourth Largest City in America* (1979); "The Literature of Criminal Justice," *Law Enforcement News* (May 12, 1980); "Soldiers of Kings," *Jnl. of Long Island Hist.* (Spr. 1976). **Activities:** 1, 12; 17, 39, 41; 50, 77, 92 **Addr.:** 62 - 8th Ave., Brooklyn, NY 11217.

Klugman, Simone (Ja. 14, 1922, Grodno, Poland) Ref. and Col. Dev. Libn., Univ. of CA, Berkeley, 1963–; Ref. Libn., Oakland Pub. Lib., 1962. **Educ.:** Univ. of CA, Berkeley, 1959–61, BA (Slavic), 1961–62, MLS. **Orgs.:** ALA. **Honors:** Phi Beta Kappa. **Pubns.:** "Integrating Online Searching with Reference Services," paper presented at 3d Intl. Online Info. Mtg., London (1979); jt. auth., "History Online: A Sampler of the Use of Online Databases for Historical Research," paper presented at ALA Annual Conference, 1981. **Activities:** 1; 15, 31, 39; 56 **Addr.:** 6012 Margarido Dr., Oakland, CA 94618.

Knachel, Philip A. (Je. 23, 1926, Indianapolis, IN) Assoc. Dir., Folger Shakespeare Lib., 1959–; Ctr. Histn., Rome Air Dev. Ctr., 1957–59; Instr., Hist., Hunter Coll., 1954–57. **Educ.:** Northwest. Univ., 1944–48, BS (Hist.); Johns Hopkins Univ., 1948–50, MA: Univ. de Tours, France, 1950–52, Cert.; 1952–54, PhD (Hist.); Syracuse Univ., 1957–59, MSLS. **Orgs.:** ALA. Amer. Hist. Assn. Fr. Hist. Socty. Conf. for Brit. Std. Shakespeare Socty. **Honors:** Johns Hopkins Univ., John Vincent Fellow, 1952; Fulbright Fellow, 1950–52. **Pubns.:** *England and the Fronde* (1968); ed., *The Case of the Commonwealth* (1969); ed., *Eikon Basilike* (1966). **Activities:** 12; 17 **Addr.:** Folger Shakespeare Library, Washington, DC 20003.

Knapp, John F. (N. 25, 1935, Sacramento, CA) VP, Ringgold Mgt. Systs., 1980–; VP, Blackwell N. Amer., 1978–80; VP, Resrch. Libs. Grp., 1975–78; Mgr., Syst. Anal. and Programming, Richard Abel and Co., 1972–75; Head, Syst. Ofc., Univ. of CA, Berkeley, 1969–72; Lib. Syst. Anal., Lib. of Congs., 1966–69. **Educ.:** Univ. of CA, Berkeley, 1954–59, AB (Eng.), 1965–66, MLS; Univ. of CA, Los Angeles, 1959–61, MA (eng.); CA State Jr. Coll., 1961, Tchg. Cert. **Orgs.:** ALA. **Honors:** Lib. of Congs., Spec. Rcrt. Prog., 1967. **Pubns.:** Contrib., *The MARC II Format Papermaking: Art and Craft* (1968). **Activities:** 1, 6; 20, 24, 34; 93, 95-Syst. dev. **Addr.:** Box 368, Beaverton, OR 97075.

Knapp, Sara D. (Jn. 5, 1936, NY, NY) Coord. Info. Retrieval, SUNY Albany 1972–, Ref. Libn., 1971–72, Serials Libn., 1968–71, Catlgr., 1967–68; Asst. Libn., NY State Lib., 1964–67; Soc. Casework Aide, Albany (NY) Med. Ctr. **Educ.:** Coll. of William and Mary, 1955–58, AB (Soclgy.); SUNY Albany, 1963–64, MLS, 1968–72, MA (Soclgy.). **Orgs.:** ALA: RASD Mach. Assisted Ref. Srvs. (Ch., 1977–79); ACRL, *Coll. & Resrch. Libs.* (Ed. Bd., 1980–). ASIS: various grps. **Honors:** SUNY, Chancellor's Awd. for Excel. in Libnshp., 1977. **Pubns.:** "Instructing Library Patrons About Online Reference Services," *Bookmark* (Fall, 1979); "Online Searching in the Behavioral and Social Sciences," *Bhvl. and Soc. Sci. Libn.* (S. 1979); jt.-auth., "Budgeting to provide computer-based reference services, a case study," *Jnl. of Acad. Libnshp.* (Mr. 1979); "The Reference Interview in the Computer-based Setting," *RQ* (S. 1978); various other articles. **Activities:** 1; 17, 39, 49-Online srch.; 56, 72, 92 **Addr.:** Library, SUNY Albany, 1400 Washington St., Albany, NY 12222.

Knauff, Elisabeth Shepard (Ap. 11, 1935, Baltimore, MD) Mgr., Info. Srvs. Div., Ofc. of the Secy., Treas. Dept., 1979–; Chief, Resrcs. Mgmt. Branch, Info. Mgt., Srvs. Div., Exec. Ofc. of the Pres., Ofc. of Admin., 1978–79; Lib. Dir., Ofc. of Mgmt. and Budget, 1972–78, Asst. Lib. Dir., Head Ref., Circ., 1970–72; Various positions, Exec. Ofc. of the Pres., Ofc. of Mgmt. and Budget, 1964–70; Branch Libn., Prince George's Cnty. (MD) Meml. Lib., 1961–64. **Educ.:** Univ. of NC, Greensboro, 1953–56, AB (Hist.); Johns Hopkins Univ., 1956–58, MA (Intl. Affairs); Catholic Univ., 1961–67, MSLS. **Orgs.:** ALA: GODORT; FLRT (Dir., 1978–81). SLA: Washington DC Chap.: Various ofcs. AALL. ASIS. Other orgs. AAUW. Bus. and Prof. Women's Assn. **Honors:** Phi Beta Kappa; Beta Phi Mu. **Activities:** 4; 17; 59, 78, 92 **Addr.:** 2326 19th St. N.W., Washington, DC 20009.

Kneeland, Marjorie H. (S. 26, 1940, Danbury, CT) Dir., So. Burlington Cmnty. Lib., 1978–; Libn., Fairfax Cmnty. Lib., 1972–78. **Educ.:** Wellesley Coll., 1957–61, BA (Pol. Sci.) Univ. of VT, 1970–76, MEd (Sch. LS). **Orgs.:** VT Educ. Media Assn.: Pres. (1979–80), VP (1978–79), Reg. Rep. (1976–77). ALA. VT LA. New Eng. Educ. Media Assn. Fairfax News: Ed. Bd. AECT. **Activities:** 9, 10; 17, 21 **Addr.:** Fairfax, VT 05454.

Knepper, Edith G. (F. 24, 1927, Jeffersonville, IN) Head, Ref. Dept., Univ. of S. FL Lib., 1975–; Head, Ref. Dept., Univ. of Louisville Lib., 1968–75, Interim Head, Library, 1971–72; Head, Ref. Dept., Rollins Coll., 1965–68; Asst. Libn., KY Wesleyan Coll. Lib., 1960–64. **Educ.:** Murray State Coll., 1945–49, BA (Eng.); Univ. of KY, 1960, MS (LS). **Orgs.:** ALA. SELA. FL LA. KY LA: Coll. and Resrch. Lib. Sect. (Secty., Treas., 1963–64); Prog. Com.; Nom. Com. AAUP: Louisville Chap. (Secty., 1972–73). **Activities:** 1; 31, 39 **Addr.:** University of South Florida Library, Tampa, FL 33620.

Kniemeyer, Justin M. (Mr. 1, 1936, St. Louis, MO) Sr. Autom. Plng. Spec., Lib. of Congs., 1971–; Instr., Cath. Univ., 1978–; Dir., Autom., Tarrant Cnty. Jr. Coll., 1970–71; Info. Syst. Resrch. Anal., Lib. of Congs., 1969–70; Libn., St. Mary's Coll., 1967–69. **Educ.:** WI State Univ., LaCrosse, 1958–62, BS (Eng.); West. MI Univ., 1966–67, MSLS. **Pubns.:** "Computerized Production of Library Catalogs," *ISLIC Intl. Conf. on Info. Sci.* (1972). **Activities:** 4, 11; 26, 46; 56, 63 **Addr.:** Automation Planning and Liaison Office, Processing Services, Library of Congress, Washington, DC 20540.

Knier, Timothy E. (Ag. 23, 1945, Sheboygan, WI) Assoc. Law Libn., Law Sch., Marquette Univ., 1973–, Head, Circ. Dept., 1971–73, Asst. Reader Srvs. Lib., 1968–71. **Educ.:** Lakeland Coll., 1967, BA (Eng.); Rosary Coll., 1967–68, MALS; Marquette Univ. 1968–71, MA (Eng.); AALL, 1976, Cert. **Orgs.:** Knier Assocs./Lib. Mgt. Srvs.: Dir. (1978–). AALL. **Pubns.:** "A Guide to Buying and Managing Loose-Leaf Services," *Law Ofc. Econ. and Mgt.* (Spr. 1981); "Shopping the Second-Hand Legal Book Market," *Legal Econ.* (Jl.–Ag. 1981); *Filer's Guide: For Looseleaf Services in a Law Library* (1979); "A Guide to Select, Acquire and Manage Looseleaf Services," *WI Bar Bltn.* (Ag. 1980); "The Secondhand Market in Law Books," *AB Bookman's Wkly.* (F. 23, 1981). **Activities:** 12; 15, 17, 18; 57, 75, 77 **Addr.:** P.O. Box 13186, 7225 W. Garfield Ave., Milwaukee, WI 53213.

Knieriem, A. (S. 8, 1943, Brooklyn, NY) Serials Cat., Docum. Libn., City Coll. Lib., 1979–, Serials Cat., Docum., Per., Ref. Libn., 1977–79, Serials Libn., 1973–76, Acq. Libn., 1967–73. **Educ.:** City Coll. of NY, 1961–65, BA (Eng.); Columbia Univ., 1965–67, MS (LS); NY Univ., 1967–70 MA (Eng.). **Orgs.:** LA of

PROFESSIONAL ACTIVITIES: Institutions: 1. Acad. lib.; 2. Arch.; 3. Assn.; 4. Fed./Gvt. lib.; 5. Inst. lib.; 6. Mfr./Suppl.; 7. Milit. lib.; 8. Musm.; 9. Pub. lib.; 10. Sch. lib.; 11. Sch. of lib. sci.; 12. Spec. lib.; 13. State lib.; 14. (other). **Functions/Activities:** 15. Acq./Col. dev.; 16. Adult srvs.; 17. Admin.; 18. Apprais.; 19. Archit./Bldgs.; 20. Cat./Class.; 21. Chld. srvs.; 22. Circ.; 23. Cons./Pres.; 24. Consult.; 25. Cont. ed.; 26. Educ. lib. sci.; 27. Ext. srvs.; 28. Fund/Grants; 29. Gvt. pubs.; 30. Indx./Abs.; 31. Instr. lib. use; 32. Media srvs.; 33. Micro.; 34. Netwks./Coop.; 35. Persnl.; 36. PR; 37. Publshg.; 38. Recs. mgt.; 39. Ref. srvs.; 40. Repro.; 41. Resrch.; 42. Review.; 43. Secur.; 44. Serials; 45. Spec. col.; 46. Tech. srvs.; 47. Trustees/Bds.; 48. YA srvs.; 49. (other).

CUNY: Secty. (1974–75); Exec. Cncl. (1974–75, 1976–77); Del. (1976–77); Pubns. Com. Ed. Bd. (1977–79). NY Tech. Srvs. Libns. ALA: ACRL; RTSD. Intl. Maledicta Socty. US Handball Assn. **Pubns.:** "Tenure Survey," *LACUNY Jnl.* (Spr. 1974). **Activities:** 1; 15, 20, 44; 57 **Addr.:** City College Library, Convent Ave. at W. 135th St., New York, NY 10031.

Kniesner, John T. (D. 19, 1949, Berea, OH) Libn. III/Asst. Head, AV, Pub. Lib. of Columbus and Franklin Cnty., 1979–, Libn. II/Comp. Info. Srv., 1977–78, Libn. I/Ref., 1972–76. **Educ.:** Kent State Univ., 1967–71, BA (Pol. Sci.); Univ. of MI, 1971–72, AMLS; Univ. of Chicago, 1978 (LS). **Orgs.:** OH LA: State Fair (1974), Hosts and Monitors (1980). EF LA: Pre-Screening Juror (1980–81). Columbus Area Shared Use of Autom. Resrcs. **Honors:** Columbus Area Shared Use of Autom. Resrcs., Cmdn., 1977; Pi Sigma Alpha; Moreau Lib. Volun. Trophies, 1964–66. **Activities:** 9; 32; 56, 67 **Addr.:** Public Library of Columbus and Franklin County, 96 S. Grant Ave., Columbus, OH 43215.

Knight, Katherine Anne (My. 15, 1928, Sanford, NC) Head Libn., Waikiki-Kapahulu Lib., 1968–; Readrs. Adv., Lib. of HI, 1965–68, Ref. Asst., 1963–65, Asst. Art and Msc. 1961–63; Adult Educ. Asst., Queens Coll. (NC), 1957–59, Admis. Couns., 1955–57. **Educ.:** Queens Coll. (NC), 1945–49, BA (Fine Arts); Univ. of NC, 1959–61, MS (LS). Un. Theo. Semy. 1951 (Msc.). **Orgs.:** HI LA: Pres. (1976–77), Dir. (1974–75, 1981–83), Exhibits Ch. (1965–75). ALA: Isadore Gilbert Mudge Citn. Com. (1977–79). First Presby. Church. Waikiki Hlth. Ctr. **Honors:** State of HI Cert. of Merit, 1981. **Activities:** 9; 16, 17 **Addr.:** Waikiki-Kapahulu Library, 400 Kapahulu Ave., Honolulu, HI 96815.

Knight, Nancy Hoyt (S. 1, 1943, New York, NY) Freelance Writer, Ed., 1971; Head, Info. Srvcs., ALA, 1969–71, Asst. Ed. Lib. Tech. Reports, 1967–69. **Educ.:** Simmons Coll., 1961–65, BS (Soc Sci); Univ. of Chicago, 1965–67, MALS. **Orgs.:** ALA. Amer. Socty. of Indexers. **Pubns.:** Indexer, *American Libraries* (1976); *RQ* (1971); *History of Children's Literature* (1980); "Theft Detection Systems for Libraries Revisited: An Updated Survey," *Lib. Tech. Reports* (My-Je. 1979); "Security Systems," *ALA Yrbk.* (1976, 1977, 1978, 1979). **Activities:** 30, 41; 92 **Addr.:** 10608 Fiesta Rd., Fairfax, VA 22032.

Knightly, John J. (Jl. 28, 1936, Hutchinson, KS) Nuc. Recs. Admin., U.S. Clinch River Breeder Reactor, 1979–, Asst Prof., LS, Univ. of TN, 1973–79; Libn. II, Pub. Srvs., Univ. of NV, 1967–70; Libn. I, Pub. Srvs., Univ. of KS, 1964–67. **Educ.:** Univ. of KS, 1954–58, BA (Amer. Std.); KS State Univ., 1963–64, MLS; Univ. of TX, 1970–73, PhD. **Orgs.:** ALA: Natl. Lib. Week (NV Exec. Dir., 1969–70). AALS: Fac. Resrch. Presentations (1977–78). **Honors:** U.S. Ofc. of Educ., Doct. Flwshp., 1970; Nuc. Recs. Mgt. Assn., Case Std. Competition Awd., 1980. **Pubns.:** Ed., *Planning and Implementing a Nuclear Records System: Proceedings of the Nuclear Records Management Association.* (1979); "Overcoming the Criterion Problem in the Evaluation of Library Performance," *Spec. Libs.* (Ap. 1979); "Searching the Water Resources Literature by Computer," *Water Resrcs. Bltn.* (O. 1979); "Traditional Information Gathering vs The Computer," *TN Libn.* (Sum. 1979); various articles. **Activities:** 12; 17, 26, 37, 46; 75, 84 **Addr.:** U.S. Clinch River Breeder Reactor, P.O. Box U, Oak Ridge, TN 37830.

Knobbe, Mary L. (Ag. 26, 1918, Cherryvale, KS) Lib. Consult., Self-Employed, 1975–; Libn., Metro. WA Cncl. of Govts., 1967–79; Plng. Libn., Natl. Pk. and Plng. Libn., 1961–67; Ref. Libn., Steubenville (OH) Pub. Lib., 1950–51; Libn., Dept. of Resrch., City of Kansas City, 1944–46. **Educ.:** Washburn Univ., 1936–40, AB (Hist.); Univ. of MD, 1965–67 (LS). **Orgs.:** Cncl. of Plng. Libns.: Secy. (1967–71). Law Libns. Socty. of Washington, DC. SLA: Govt. Info. Srvs. Com. (1971–75; Ch., 1975–77); Urban Affairs Grp. (1975–76); Various Lcl. Ofcs. ILL Users Assn.: Bd. of Dir. (1972–79). Washburn Alum. **Honors:** Pi Gamma Mu. **Pubns.:** Ed., *Planning & Urban Affairs Library Manual* (1970, 1975); Ed., *Directory of Planning, Building and Housing Libraries, U.S. and Canada* (1969); "Pleasures and Problems in a Planning Library," *Spec. Libs.* (Mr. 1966); Various presented papers. **Activities:** 12; 24, 29, 38; 75, 92, 94 **Addr.:** 2300 Eccleston St., Silver Spring, MD 20902.

Knoblauch, Carol Jean (Ap. 21, 1949, Washington, DC) Syst. Libn., Pub. Lib. of Columbus and Franklin Cnty., 1980–, Branch Head, 1976–80, Media Spec., 1975–76; Branch Libn., Gloucester Cnty. (Eng.) Lib. Syst., 1979. **Educ.:** OH State Univ., 1968–72, BSSW; Kent State Univ., 1974–75, MLS. **Orgs.:** ALA. OH LA: Cont. Lcl. Arrange. Com. (1976, 1980, 1981). Franklin Cnty. LA: Pres. (1978). Natl. Assn. for the Pres. and Perpet. of Storytel. **Honors:** OH LA *Bltn.*, Best Article of Yr., 1980. **Pubns.:** "The England Experience/The Gloucestershire Connection," *OH LA Bltn.* (Spr. 1980). **Activities:** 9; 16, 17, 27; 50, 56, 92 **Addr.:** Public Library of Columbus & Franklin County, 28 S. Hamilton Rd., Columbus, OH 43213.

Knoblauch, Mark G. (O. 8, 1947, Fort Wayne, IN) Head, Acq. Div., Chicago Pub. Lib., 1978–, Head, Serials Dept., 1974–78, Catlgr., 1970–74. **Educ.:** Valparaiso Univ., 1965–69, BA (Hist.); Univ. of MI, 1969–70, AMLS. **Orgs.:** ALA. IL LA. Chicago Lib. Club. **Pubns.:** "Chicago: A Restaurant Roundup," *Lib. Jnl.* (Je. 1, 1978); various articles, *Chicago Tribune*. **Activities:** 9; 15, 46 **Addr.:** 2252 N. Orchard St., Chicago, IL 60614.

Knoblich, Paul L. (Ja. 12, 1950, Oakland, CA) Dir., Lassen Cnty. Lib., 1981–; Dir., George Amos Meml. Lib., Gillette, WY, 1978–81; Inst., Sheridan Coll., 1979–80; Branch Lib. Dir., Monterey Cnty. Lib., 1975–78; Dir., White Pine Cnty. Lib., 1973–75. **Educ.:** Chabot Jr. Coll., 1968–70, AA; Univ. of the Pac., 1970–72, BA (Hist., Phil.); Univ. of Denver, 1972–73, MA (LS); Golden Gate Univ., 1975–77, MPA. **Orgs.:** WY LA: Conv. Lcl. Arrange. (Ch., 1980); VP/Pres.-Elect. (1980–81). Mt. Plains LA: Prof. Dev. Grants Com. (1979–80). ALA. Rotary. Cham. of Cmrce. Gillette Branch Campus of Sheridan Coll.: Adv. Cncl. Planned Parenthood. **Honors:** Bristlecone Toastmaster of the Yr., 1975. **Activities:** 9; 17, 35, 36 **Addr.:** P.O. Box 814, Susanville, CA 96130.

Knoop, Gene Harrison (D. 22, 1925, Richmond, VA) Lib. Dir., Chesterfield Cnty. Lib. Syst., 1968–; Boys & Girls Libn., Richmond Pub. Lib., 1940–50, Head of Ref., 1964–66; Asst. Head of Ref., VA State Lib., 1966–68. **Educ.:** Longwood Coll., 1943–47, BS (Eng.); Univ. of NC, Chapel Hill, 1947–48, BSLS. **Orgs.:** VA LA. ALA. Southeastern LA. VA Musm. **Activities:** 9; 17 **Addr.:** Chesterfield County Library System, P. O. Box 29, 9501 Lori Rd., Chesterfield, VA 23832.

Knoppers, Jake V. Th. (Ap. 17, 1945, The Netherlands) Sr. VP, Infoman Inc., 1980–, Consult., Telidon Proj., Dept. of Comms., Can.; Sr. Consult. to Dominion Archvst., Pub. Arch. of Can., 1979–80; Consult., Treasury Bd., Can., 1979–81; Dir., Soc Scan (Soc. Sci. Info. Bank), Soc. Sci. Fed. of Can., 1977–79. **Educ.:** Calvin Coll., 1962–66, BA (Hist., Phil.); McGill Univ., 1966–69, MA (E. European Std.), 1970–75, PhD (Econ. Hist.), 1980–81, Dip. (Bus. Admin.). **Orgs.:** ALA. SLA. ASIS. Can. Assn. Info. Sci. Various other orgs. Intl. Congs. of Econ. Hist. Can. Futures Socty. Can. Oper. Resrch. Assn. Can. Hist. Assn. Various other orgs. **Pubns.:** "Freedom of Information and Privacy," *Recs. Mgt. Qtly.* (O. 1980, Ap. 1981); *Dutch Trade With Russia From the Time of Peter I to Alexander I, a Quantitative Study of Eighteenth Century Shipping* (1976); "The Future of Social Science Research and Freedom of Information Legislation," *Soc. Sci. in Can.* (F. 1980); "Les chercheurs en Sciences Social et le problème de la confidentialité," *Arch.* (Mr. 1980); "The Machine Readable Archives and the Research Community," *The Archvst.* (1973); various articles in econ. hist., LS. **Activities:** 6; 24; 56, 75, 93 **Addr.:** Information Management Service, P.O. Box 2231, Station D, Ottawa, ON K2P 1A4 Canada.

Knowles, Caroline Mary (Mr. 7, 1944, Kenilworth, Warwick, Eng.) Drummond Sci. Libn., Concordia Univ., 1979–81, Lect., Lib. Std., 1977–81; Docum. Ctr., Univ. of Guelph, 1972–75; Aeronautical Lib., Natl. Resrch. Cncl. of Can., 1966–71. **Educ.:** Univ. of Ottawa, 1962–65, BSc (Phys.); McGill Univ., 1968–69, MLS. **Orgs.:** SLA: Union List Com. (1979–80). Can. LA. **Pubns.:** Jt. auth., "Documentation Centre of the University of Guelph," *Gvt. Pubns. Review* (1973). **Activities:** 1; 17, 39; 88, 91 **Addr.:** Vegreville, AB Canada.

Knowles, Dorothy Aileen (Mr. 15, 1918, Toronto, ON) Retired, D. 1982; Chief Libn./Spec. Proj. Catlgr., Natl. Energy Bd., 1957–; Asst. Libn./Catlgr., Can. Dept. of Fisheries, 1956; Ref. Libn./Catlgr., Mann Lib., Cornell Univ., 1955–56; Ref. Asst., Univ. of BC Lib., 1953–55. **Educ.:** Macdonald Coll., McGill Univ., 1936–40, BS (Foods, Nutr.); McGill Univ., 1952–53, BA (LS). **Orgs.:** Can. LA: Com. on Class. of Lib. Clerks. ALA. **Activities:** 4; 20, 39; 86 **Addr.:** Library, National Energy Board, Ottawa, ON Canada.

Knowles, Em Claire (Je. 6, 1952, Sacramento, CA) Assoc. Libn., Hum./Soc. Sci. Ref. Dept., Shields Lib., Lectr., Eng. Dept., Univ. of CA, Davis, 1975–, Fac.–in–Residence, Fac.–in–Residence, 1976–78; Team Leader, Data Col., Spec. Proj. Ofc. Docum. Lib. Univ. of CA, Berkeley, 1975. **Educ.:** Univ. of CA, Davis, 1969–73, BA (Intl. Rel.); Univ. of CA, Berkeley, 1973–74, MLS (Libnshp.), 1974, Cert. CA Sec. Tchg. Cred., 1975, Cert. in Lib. Mgt. **Orgs.:** CA LA: Cnclr. (1977–80); Cncl. Rules Com. (Ch., 1980); Cmnty. Rel. Com. (1979). CA Black Libns. Caucus–N. ALA: Jr. Mem. RT. Delta Sigma Theta, Sorority, Inc.: Adv. to Undergrad. Chap. Lambda X (1977–1979). CA Gvr. Conf. on Lib. and Info. Srvs.: Steering Com.; Packet Dsgn. Com. (Co-Ch., 1979). **Honors:** Beta Phi Mu; Delta Sigma Theta Sorority, Recog. for outstan. srv. to eth. minority students, 1980; *Sacramento Observer*–news. educ. supplement, Outstan. Staff Mem. at Univ. of CA, Davis, 1979. **Pubns.:** *Dual Career Couple Relationships: an annotated bibliography* (1980); jt. auth., *Black Women in Science and Medicine: a bio-bibliography* (1977); jt. auth., various indx. and abs. (1978). **Activities:** 1; 31, 39; 55, 92 **Addr.:** Humanities/Social Sciences Reference Department, Shields Library, University of CA, Davis, CA 95616.

Knowles, Jane (N. 26, 1940, NY, NY) Med. Libn., St. Vincent Hosp., 1977–; Catlgr., Bexley Publ. Lib., 1974–76, Libn., Northland HS, 1966–70; **Educ.:** Ohio Univ., 1958–62, BA (Hist.), 1962–64, MA (Hist.); Univ. of Denver, 1970–71, MLA; OH Dominican Univ., 1967–68, Cert. (LS), DePaul Univ., 1965–66, Cert. (Educ.). **Orgs.:** Med. LA. **Activities:** 5, 9; 20, 39; 80 **Addr.:** Medical Library, St. Vincent Hospital, Santa Fe, NM 87501.

Knudsen, Lawrence R. (Ap. 20, 1920, Chicago, IL) Admin. Libn., Elmhurst Pub. Lib., 1965–; Instr., Rosary Coll., 1967–68; Tchr., East HS, Rockford, IL, 1953–55; Tchr., Malta Sch. Syst., 1952–53. **Educ.:** Grinnell Coll., 1946–50, BA (Hist.); Chicago Msc. Coll., 1950–52, MMsc; Rosary Coll., 1964–65, MALS; Northern IL Univ., 1952–53, (Tch. Cert.); Boston Univ., 1955–56. **Orgs.:** ALA: Recruiting Ntwk. (1965–68). IL LA: Secy., Pub. Lib. Div. (1966); Lib. Admin. Conf. of Northern IL: Lib. Survey. Chicago Lib. Club. Kiwanis Club: Pres., Elmhurst Chap. (1976–77). United Way: 1st VP (1979). Elmhurst Symphony Bd. of Dir.: Assoc. Dir. (1979). Elmhurst Chamber of Commerce. **Activities:** 9; 17, 26, 34; 95-Music. **Addr.:** Elmhurst Public Library, 211 Prospect, Elmhurst, IL 60126.

Knudsen, Patricia Catherine (Mr. 8, 1947, Brookings, SD) Deputy Dir., Hlth. Sci. Lib., Univ. of MD, Baltimore, 1979–; Head, Pub. Srvs., Med. Lib., Johns Hopkins Univ., 1974–79; Circ. Libn., Med. Coll. of GA Lib., 1973–74; Med. Ref. Libn., KS Reg. Med. Prog., 1972–73. **Educ.:** SD State Univ., 1965–70, BA (Eng.); KS State Tchrs. Coll., 1970–71, MLS. **Orgs.:** MD Assn. of Hlth. Sci. Libns.: Pres. (1976–77). Med. LA: Mid-Atl. Reg. Grp. (Pres., 1978–79), Prog. Com. (Ch., 1977–78). Mid-Atl. Reg. Med. Lib. Prog.: Exec. Bd. (1977–78); other coms. **Activities:** 12; 17; 80 **Addr.:** Health Sciences Library, University of Maryland, 111 S. Greene St., Baltimore, MD 21201.

Ko, Jean Sang Hooh (Je. 18, 1937, Seoul, Korea) Dir., Bib. Mncpl. de Montréal-est, 1970–. **Educ.:** Seoul Natl. Univ., 1957–61, BA (Fr. Lit.); Univ. de Montréal, 1967–69, BB (LS). **Orgs.:** PQ LA. ASTED. Corp. des Bibtcrs. Profs. du PQ. Conf. des Dirs. de Bibs. Pubs. de l'Ile de Montréal. **Pubns.:** *La Pratique de Catalographie* (1974). **Activities:** 9; 17 **Addr.:** Bibliothèque Municipale de Montréal-est, 3, place de l'église, Montréal-est, PQ H1B 4Z4 Canada.

Kobasa, Paul Anton (Ja. 30, 1952, Seymour, CT) Acq. Ed., Greenwood Press, 1980–; Mgr. Bibl. Info., 1979–80; Ref. Asst. Fairfield Univ. Lib., 1979–; Ed. Asst., *Index to Current Urban Docum.*, Greenwood Press, 1978–79. **Educ.:** Fairfield Univ., 1970–74, BA (Eng.); South. CT State Coll., 1975–77, MLS. **Honors:** Beta Phi Mu. **Activities:** 1, 12; 15, 38, 39; 55, 92 **Addr.:** 158 Ridgeview Ave., Fairfield, CT 06430.

Kobayashi, Hanako (My. 11, 1932, Makaweli, Kauai, HI) Resrch. Libn. Leg. Ref. Bureau, 1959–; Jr. Libn., Joint Ref. Lib., 1956–58. **Educ.:** Univ. of HI, 1950–54, BA (Pol. Sci.); Simmons Coll., 1955–56, MS (LS). **Orgs.:** SLA. Acad. of Pol. Sci. **Activities:** 12, 13; 15, 17, 24; 77, 78, 92 **Addr.:** Legislative Reference Bureau, Room 004, State Capitol, Honolulu, HI 96813.

Kobelski, Jane Ann Hudson (S. 2, 1945, Alexandria, LA) Proj. Dir., Portsmouth (VA) Pub. Lib., 1980–82; Writer, Instr. Mat. in Lib. skills, CTB/McGraw-Hill, 1979–80; Lib. Dir., Morgan Mem. Lib., 1976–78; Libn., Barry-Robinson HS, 1975–76; Lib. Dir., Lincoln Parish Lib., 1972–75; Ref. Libn., Trail Blazer Lib. Syst., 1970–72. **Educ.:** LA Tech Univ., 1963–67, BA (Eng.); LA State Univ., 1969–70, MSLS. **Orgs.:** LA LA: Secy., Pub. Lib. Sect. (1973–74). LA LA: V-Ch. (JMRT, 1973–74); Cont. Educ. Com. (1977). ALA. **Pubns.:** Instr. matls. for lib. skills, *Prescriptive Reading Inventory* (1978). **Activities:** 9; 17, 21, 39 **Addr.:** 1474 Poinsettia Arch, Virginia Beach, VA 23456.

Kobelski, Pamela G. (My. 15, 1946, Detroit, MI) Tech. Info. Chem., Spencer Kellogg, 1981–; Chem. Sci. Libn., SUNY, Buffalo, 1978–81; Agr. Libn., Univ. of DE, 1974–77; Chem., Physics Libn., Univ. of VT, 1973–74; Asst. Ed., Gale Research Co., 1972–73. **Educ.:** Northwest. Univ., IL., 1964–68, BA (Chem.); Wayne State Univ., 1968–71, MLS. **Orgs.:** ALA: ACRL; RASD; Lib. Instr. RT; Lib. Resrch. RT. **Pubns.:** Jt. auth., "Student Use of Online Bibliographic Services," *Jrnl. of Acad. Libnshp.* (Mr. 1978); Jt. auth., "Conceptual Frameworks for Bibliographic Instruction," *Jrnl. of Acad. Libnshp.* (My. 1981). **Activities:** 1; 15, 31, 39; 58, 60, 75 **Addr.:** Research Center Library, Spencer Kellogg, Division of Textron. Inc., P.O. Box 210, Buffalo, NY 14225.

Koch, Charles William (Mr. 12, 1926, Sikeston, MO) Prof., Dir., Libs. and Lrng. Resrcs., Northwest MO State Univ., 1972–; Dir., Lib. Srvs., Lyons Township HS, Jr. Coll. (LaGrange, IL), 1965–70; Consult., Lib. Srvs., K-Coll., St. Louis Bd. of Educ., 1962–65; Head, Lib. Srvs., Hinsdale (IL) Twp. HS Dist., 1961–62; Libn., Berwyn (IL) HS and Jr. Coll., 1958–61; Tchr., Libn., Nashville (IL) HS, 1954–57; Libn., Labor Rel. Clerk., 1949–54. **Educ.:** South. IL Univ., Carbondale, 1945–49 BSEduc., Univ. of IL, 1957–58, MSLS; South. IL. Univ., Carbondale, 1970–76, PhD (Educ.). Additional courses in Hist., LS, at various univs. **Orgs.:** ALA: ACRL; AASL; LITA; RASD; LRTS. AECT. Natl. Educ. Assn. MO Educ Assn. **Honors:** Phi Delta Kappa. Beta Phi Mu. Kappa Delta Pi. **Activities:** 1, 10; 15, 19, 34; 56, 78, 93 **Addr.:** 1257 E. Crestview Dr., Maryville, MO 64468.

Kochen, Manfred (Jl. 4, 1928, Vienna, Austria) Prof. of Info. Sci., Univ. of MI, 1970–, Assoc. Prof., 1965–70; Mgr., Info.

Special Subjects/Services: 50. Adult educ.; 51. Advert./Mktg.; 52. Aerosp.; 53. Agric.; 54. Area std.; 55. Arts/Hum.; 56. Autom.; 57. Bibl./Prtg.; 58. Bio. sci.; 59. Bus./Fin.; 60. Chem.; 61. Copyrt.; 62. Documtn.; 63. Educ.; 64. Engin.; 65. Env.; 66. Eth. grps.; 67. Film; 68. Food/Nutr.; 69. Geneal.; 70. Geo.; 71. Geol.; 72. Handcpd.; 73. Hist.; 74. Int. frdm.; 75. Info. sci.; 76. Insr.; 77. Law; 78. Legis.; 79. Math./Comp. sci.; 80. Med.; 81. Metals; 82. Nat. resrcs.; 83. Newsp.; 84. Nuc. sci.; 85. Oral hist.; 86. Petr./Energy; 87. Pharm.; 88. Phys./Astr./Math.; 89. Readg.; 90. Relig.; 91. Sci./Tech.; 92. Soc. sci.; 93. Telecom.; 94. Transp.; 95. (other).

Retrieval, IBM Th. J. Watson Resrch. Ctr., 1956–64; Prog.-Anal., Inst. for Adv. Study, Princeton, 1953–55. **Educ.:** MA Inst. of Tech., 1947–50, BS (Physics); Columbia Univ., 1950–55, PhD (Math.). **Orgs.:** ASIS: Cnclr. at large (1976–78); Ch., SIG/BSS, MI Chap., Com. on Future. Amer. Math. Society. Amer. Physics Socty. Resrch. Socty. of Amer. Assn. Comput. Mach. **Honors:** ASIS, First Distinguished Lectr., 1968; Ford Fndn. Fellow. **Pubns.:** Jt. auth., *Decentralization* (1980); *Information for Action* (1975); Jt. ed., *Information for the Community* (1976); *Principles of Informational Retrieval* (1974); *Integrative Mechanisms in Literature Growth* (1974). **Activities:** 12; 26, 37, 41 **Addr.:** MHRI, Univ. of Michigan, Ann Arbor, MI 48109.

Kocher, Evelyn M. (N. 21, 1925, Scranton, PA) Chief Cat. Libn., WV Univ., 1965–, Sr. Cat. Libn., 1958–65; Instr., LS, Univ. of NC, Sum. 1960; Asst. Libn., Huntingdon Coll., 1947–57. **Educ.:** Meredith Coll., 1943–46, BA (Fr.); Univ. of NC, 1946–47, BSLS, 1957–58, MSLS. **Orgs.:** ALA: ACRL/Tri-State Chap. WV LA. AAUW. Morgantown Woman's Msc. Club. **Honors:** Beta Phi Mu. **Activities:** 1; 20, 26 **Addr.:** 916 Garrison Ave., Morgantown, WV 26505.

Kochoff, Stephen Thomas (Ja. 9, 1951, Bridgeport, CT) Dev./Progs./PR Libn., Providence Pub. Lib., 1979–; Branch Head/Chief Methods Anal., Chicago Pub. Lib., 1979, Dir., Wrtg. in Chicago Prog., 1975–79, Coord., Task Frcs., 1975, Liaison, Writer in Residence Prog., 1974–75, Asst. Branch Libn., 1974. **Educ.:** Univ. of MA, Amherst, 1968–72, BA (Italian); Univ. of IL, 1972–73, MLS; Middlebury Coll., Sum. 1971, 1972 (Italian). **Orgs.:** ALA: RASD, Srvs. to Adults Com. (1977–81), Cont. Prog. Subcom. (1981); ASCLA/Srvs. to Blind and Phys. Handcpd. Sect., Cont. Prog. Com. (Ch., 1981); LAMA/PR Sect., Com. on Pubns. (1980–82). RI LA: Exec. Bd. (Secy., 1979–80); Conf. Plng. Com. (Co.-Ch., 1980–81); PR Com. Trinity Sq. Repertory Co., Volun. **Activities:** 9; 17, 28, 36; 55, 74, 78 **Addr.:** 230 Butler Ave., Apt. 5, Providence, RI 02906.

Kochtanek, Thomas R. (Ja. 21, 1951, Cleveland, OH) Asst. Prof., Info. Sci., Univ. of MO, Columbia, 1977–. **Educ.:** Case West. Rsv. Univ., 1969–73, BS (Opers. Resrch.), 1978, PhD (Info. Sci.). **Orgs.:** AALS: Stats. Com. (1981–82). ASIS. MO LA. SLA. **Honors:** AALS, Anl. Resrch. Awd., 1981. **Pubns.:** "A Model for Serials Acquisition," *Lib. Acq.: Prac. and Theory* (1980); "A Network Educational Study," *Jnl. of Lib. Admin.* (1981). **Activities:** 11; 24, 26; 56, 75 **Addr.:** Dept. of Information Science, 113 B Stewart Hall, Columbia, MO 65211.

Koda, Paul S. (Ja. 15, 1942, Hartford, CT) Cur., Rare Bks., Univ. of NC, Chapel Hill, 1975–; Libn., Rare Bks. and Spec. Cols., IN State Univ., 1972–75, Asst. to Dean of Lib., 1971–72. **Educ.:** Univ. of CT, 1959–63, BA (Lit., Hist.), Univ. of Chicago, 1963–65, MA (Lit.); IN Univ., 1969–76, CVS (Vict. Std.), PhD (Bibl., Lit.), MLS; various wkshps., insts. **Orgs.:** Bibl. Socty. Bibl. Socty. of Amer. ALA: ACRL/Rare Bks. and Mss. Sect., Nom. Com. (Ch., 1978–79), *Col. & Resrch. Libs.* Ed. Bd. (1980–); RTSD/Prsrvn. of Lib. Mtrls. Sect. Amer. Prtg. Hist. Assn. Dictionary Socty. of N. Amer. Caxton Club. Grolier Club. Various other orgs. **Honors:** Beta Phi Mu. **Pubns.:** *A Short-Title Catalogue of the Cordell Collection of Dictionaries* (1975); "Collecting Rare Books for a University Library," *Lib. Acq.* (1978); "The Analytical Bibliographer and the Conservator," *Lib. Jnl.* (1979); "Dictionaries and Glossaries: The Language of the Book Trade," *AB Bookman's Wkly.* (S. 8, 1980); reviews. **Activities:** 1; 15, 17, 45; 55, 57, 63 **Addr.:** Rare Book Collection, Wilson Library 024-A, University of North Carolina, Chapel Hill, NC 27514.

Koder, Sr. Alma K. (O. 13, 1914, Allentown, PA) Libn., Sch. of Nursing, Lankenau Hosp., 1953–; Libn., St. Paul's Luth. Church, 1962–; Libn., Luth. Deaconess Cmnty., Luth. Church in Amer., 1950–53. **Educ.:** Muhlenberg Coll., 1950, AB; Drexel Univ., 1956, MS (LS). **Orgs.:** ALA. CS LA. Muhlenberg Coll. Alum. Assn. Luth. Deaconess Cmnty. St. Paul's Luth. Church. **Addr.:** Lankenau Hospital Residence, City Ave. at 64th St., Philadelphia, PA 19151.

Koehler, Henry M. (O. 13, 1931, Offenbach, Hessen, Germ.) Principal, Henry M. Koehler & Assocs., 1975–; Ed., Oral Resrch. Abs., Amer. Dental Assn., 1965–79. **Educ.:** Roosevelt Univ., 1950–52, BS (Chem), 1954–57, MS (Biochem.), 1962, MBA. **Orgs.:** ASIS: Ch. (1970). Amer. Med. Writers Assn.: Ch., Chicago Sect. (1969). Amer. Translators Assn. Amer. Chem. Socty. **Pubns.:** *Gnathology* (Eng. translation) (1978). **Activities:** 24, 30, 44; 51, 57, 95-Dentistry. **Addr.:** 5000 East End Ave., Chicago, IL 60615.

Koel, Ike Ilmar (My. 20, 1920, Kuressaare, Estonia) Assoc. Libn. for Tech. Srvs., Yale Univ. Lib., 1974–, Head Libn., Cat. Dept., 1969–74; Head, Dutch-Scandinavian Sect., Shared Cat. Div., Lib. of Congs., 1966–69; Head, Tech. Srvs., Hamilton Coll. Lib., 1965–66; Head, Serials Div., Cat. Dept. Univ. of Toronto Lib., 1963–65, Cat., 1962; Costing Clerk, Salesman, Ctrl. Sci. Co. of Can., 1954–61; Libn., Doclmst., Resrch. Lib. of AB BAHCO, Sweden, 1944–54. **Educ.:** Univ. of Toronto, 1961, BA (Psy.), 1962, BLS, 1969, MLS; Swedish Socty. for Tech. Documtn., Sweden, 1953, Dip. (Documtn.). **Orgs.:** ALA: Descr. Cat. Com. (1970–74), Cat. Code Revision Com. (1975–79), Tech. Srvs. Dirs. of Large Resrch. Libs. Discuss. Grp. (1974–), various coms.; ARL, Task Force on Bibl. Cntrl. (1978–); RLG, Com. on Lib. Tech. Systs. and Bibl. Cntrl. ASIS. New Haven Colony Hist. Socty. Kiwanian. **Pubns.:** "Can the Problems of Corporate Authorship Be Solved?" *Lib. RTSD* (Fall 1974); "The Corporate Complex" in *The Making of a Code* (1980); various papers. **Activities:** 1; 17, 46; 56, 75 **Addr.:** Yale University Library, Box 1603A Yale Station, New Haven, CT 06520.

Koel, M. Ottilia (Ap. 3, 1923, Felsögalla, Hungary) Libn. and Cur. of Mss., New Haven Colony Hist. Socty., 1971–; Head Cat., South. CT State Coll., 1969–70; Asst. Head of Cat. Dept., Georgetown Univ. Lib., 1968–69. **Educ.:** Univ. of Toronto, 1966, BA (Phil. and Fine Arts); Cath. Univ. of Amer., 1968, MSLS; NARS/Amer. Univ., 1973, Dip. (Arch. Mgt.). **Orgs.:** ALA: Hist. Sect., Nom. Com. (1979–80); Gen. Com. (1973–77, Ch., 1974–75); Lcl. Hist. Com. (1979–83). SAA: Lib./Arch. Rel. Com. (1976–79). New Eng. Archvsts.: Nom. Com. (1976); Bd. mem. (1979–82). CT Com.: Com. for a New Eng. Bibl., CT Com. (1980–). CT Leag. of Hist. Socties.: Prog. Com. (1977–78); Pubns. Com. (1978–). CT LA: Lcl. Hist. and Gen. Com., By-laws Com. (1980). **Honors:** Beta Phi Mu, 1969. **Pubns.:** Chap. in *Jews In New Haven* (1978). **Activities:** 2, 12; 17, 45; 55, 69 **Addr.:** 89 Charlton Hill, Hamden, CT 06518.

Koenig, Michael E. D. (N. 1, 1941, Rochester, NY) Assoc. Prof. of Info. Sci., Sch. of Lib. Srv., Columbia Univ., 1980–; VP, Oper., Swets N. Amer., 1979–80; Info. Mgt. Consult., Mitre Corp., 1978–79; Dir., Lib. Oper., Inst. for Sci. Info., 1974–78; Mgr. of Info. Srvs., Pfizer Inc., 1970–74. **Educ.:** Yale Univ., 1959–63, BA (Psy.); 1964–65 (Bibl.); Univ. of Chicago, 1966–68, MA (LS), 1969, Cert. (LS), 1970, MBA; Drexel Univ., 1981, PhD (Info. Sci.). **Orgs.:** Assn. of Info. Ofcrs. of the Pharmaceutical Indus. SLA: CT Valley Chap. (Pres. Elect. 1973–74). ASIS: DE Valley Chap. (Pres., 1980–81); Comp. Retrieval Spec. Interest Group (Ch., 1976–77). Elizabethan Club. AAAS. **Honors:** Beta Phi Mu. SLA, Best Paper of 1977. **Pubns.:** "On-line Serials Collection Analysis," *Jnl. ASIS* (My. 1979); jt.-Auth., "Special Features of Knowledge as a Commodity," *Jnl. Informatics* (D. 1978); "Bradford Distribution of Data Elements," *Jnl. ASIS* (Mr. 1979); "Citation Analysis for the Arts and Humanities," *Col. Mgmt.* (O. 1978); other articles. **Activities:** 1, 12; 17, 24, 41, 44; 56, 75, 91 **Addr.:** Swets North America, P.O. Box 517, Berwyn, PA 19312.

Koepp, Donald W. (Ap. 27, 1929, Shell Lake, WI) Univ. Libn., Princeton Univ., 1978–; Univ. Libn., AZ State Univ., 1973–78; Univ. Libn., Humboldt State Univ., 1968–73; Asst. Univ. Libn. for Pub. Srvs., Lectr. (LS), Univ. of CA, Berkeley, 1965–68, Actg. Asst. Prof., 1964–65, Libn. II, Pub. Admin. Anal., Bureau of Pub. Admin., 1961–64; Circ. Libn., Chico State Coll., 1956–58. **Educ.:** Univ. of WI, 1946–51, BA (Eng.) 1954–56, MLS; Univ. of CA, Berkeley, 1958–65, DLS. **Orgs.:** AMIGOS Bibl. Cncl.: Exec. Bd. (1975–77). Ctr. for Resrch. Libs.: Bd. of Dir. (1975–78). Resrch. Libs. Grp.: Bd. of Gvrs. (1979, Ch. 1981–82). **Pubns.:** *Public Library Government,* (1968). **Activities:** 1; 17, 29, 39 **Addr.:** 128 FitzRandolph Rd., Princeton, NJ 08540.

Koff, Manuel J. (Ag. 9, 1949, Los Angeles, CA) Law Libn., Baker and McKenzie, 1979–, Law Libn., Lincoln Univ., 1977–79; Asst. Law Libn., San Francisco Cnty. Law Lib., 1976–77. **Educ.:** San Francisco State Coll., 1975, BA (Hist., Geo.); Univ. of CA, Berkeley, 1976–77, MLS. **Orgs.:** AALL: North. CA Chap., Nom. Com. (1980), Audit and Budget Com. (1980–81). SLA. **Activities:** 12; 15, 17, 20; 59, 77, 78 **Addr.:** Library, Baker & McKenzie, P.O. Box 7258, San Francisco, CA 94120.

Kogan, Jenny (My. 1, 1933, Pouso Alegre, Minas Gerais, Brazil) Resrch. Assoc. Libn., Soybean Insect Resrch. Info. Center, 1975–; Consult. for the Info. Ctr., Inst. Agr. Parana, Brazil, 1975. **Educ.:** Univ. of IL, 1970–72, BA (Port. & Brazilian Lit.), 1972–74, MLS. **Orgs.:** SLA. ALA. IL LA. **Honors:** Beta Phi Mu. **Pubns.:** *The Literature of Arthropods Associated with Soybean* (1978); "Soybean Entomology Information Systems," page 26 in *Abstracts World Soybean Resrch. Conf.-II* (1979); *Diretorio de Informacoes Agropecuarias no Estado do Parana* (1975). **Activities:** 12; 30, 39 **Addr.:** SIRIC, 172 Natural Resources Building, 607 East Peabody, Champaign, IL 61820.

Koh, Gertrude Soonja Lee (F. 22, 1943, Seoul, Korea) Assoc. Prof., Grad. Sch. of LS, Rosary Coll., 1978–, Instr., 1974–75, Asst. Prof., 1975–78; Tchg. Fellow, Grad. Sch. of Lib. & Info. Sci., Univ. of Pittsburgh, 1973–74; Instr., Sch. of Lib. & Info. Sci., Univ. of WI, Milwaukee, 1970–73. **Educ.:** Sogang Jesuit Univ., 1961–65, BA summa cum laude (English Lit. Phil.); Catherine Spalding Coll., 1965–66, MS; Univ. of Pittsburgh, 1968, MLS, 1969–77, PhD (LS), 1969–70, CAS (LS). **Orgs.:** ALA: RTSD. AALS. ASIS. Korean LA. Other orgs. **Honors:** Beta Phi Mu, 1968. **Pubns.:** Jt. auth., *Manuscripts and Microforms* (1980); *The Semantic Problems of Translated Subject Headings* (1979); "Libraries in the Republic of Korea," *Encyc. of Lib. and Info. Sci.,* (1975); Jt. auth., "Comparative Education: The International Student–An Asset to the Graduate Library School," *The Admin. Aspects of Educ. for Libnshp.: A Symp.* (1975); oral presentations. **Activities:** 1, 11; 20, 26, 44, 46; 75, 92 **Addr.:** Graduate School of Library Science, Rosary College, 7900 West Division St., River Forest, IL 60305.

Kohl, Barbara H. (Ap. 18, 1941, Buffalo, NY) Head, Adult Srvs., Brookline Pub. Lib., 1978–, Supvsr., Loan Dept., 1974–78; Libn., Proj. MAC, MA Inst. of Tech., 1970–74; Libn., Rsv. Ofc., Undergrad. Lib., Univ. of MI, 1968–69. **Educ.:** Univ. of VT, 1959–63, BA (Eng.); Univ. of MI, 1965–67, AMLS. **Orgs.:** MA LA: Educ. Com. (1979–). New Eng. LA. ALA. **Activities:** 9; 16, 36 **Addr.:** Brookline Public Library, 361 Washington St., Brookline, MA 02146.

Kohl, David F. (Jy. 31, 1942, Grand Island, NE) Asst. Dir. for Pub. Srvs. and Undergrad. Libn., Univ. of IL, Urbana, 1980–; Head, Ctrl. Circ., WA State Univ., 1977–80, Ref. Libn., Soc. Sci., 1972–77; Asst. Dir., Admissions and Aid, Univ. of Chicago, 1969–72. **Educ.:** Carleton Coll., 1961–65, BA (Hist.); Univ. of Chicago, 1965–69, MTh, DMn, 1970–73, MLS. **Orgs.:** ALA: RASD, Bd. (1980–82), Cat. Use Com. (1974–78; Ch., 1975–78), Facts on File Awd. Com. (1979–80); LAMA/Circ. Srvs. Sect., Oper. Resrch. Com. (Ch., 1978–), Com. on Sect. and Div. Dev. (Ch., 1978–); RTSD, Cat. Cod. Rev. Com. (1976–78), Anglo Amer. Filing Rules Com. (1976–). Koinonia House Board. **Pubns.:** Ed., *Commercial COM Catalogs: How to Choose, When to Buy* (1978); "Public Service & the Disappearing Card Catalog," *RQ* (Sum. 1978); "Examing the LC Subject Catalog," *LRTS* (Win. 1979); Ed., "Public Service & the On-line Catalog," (1977). **Activities:** 1; 15, 17, 22; 56, 59, 92 **Addr.:** Undergraduate Library, University of Illinois, Urbana, IL 61801.

Kohl, Michael Francis (Jn. 19, 1949, Marshfield, WI) Proj. Archvst., City of Milwaukee, 1980–; Proj. Archvst., Lib. Cncl. of Metro. Milwaukee, 1979–80; Archvst., State Hist. Socty. of WI, 1977–79; Spec. Coll. Libn., RI Coll., 1974–77. **Educ.:** Univ. of WI, 1967–69, BA (Hist.), 1969–73, MA (Hist.), 1973–74, MS (LS), 1977–79, MBA; Univ. of RI, 1975–77 (Bus.). **Orgs.:** SAA: Finding Aids Com. (1974–79). Assn. of Recs. Mgrs. and Admins. Assn. for State and Lcl. Hist. **Pubns.:** 'Trends in Funding Archival Programs,' *GA Arch.* (Spr. 1979); 'A Profile of a Professional Society in Transition,' *Midwest Arch. Conf. Nsltr.* (O. 1974); "The State Records Center and the State Archives," *RI Lib. Bltn.* (Mr. 1976); other presented papers. **Activities:** 1, 2; 23, 24, 38, 45 **Addr.:** 303 Praire Ave., Lake Mills, WI 53551.

Kohler, Carolyn W. (F. 18, 1944, Birmingham, AL) Head, Gvt. Pubn. Dept., Univ. of IA Libs., 1970–, Docum. Libn., 1968–70, Actg. Docum. Libn., North. IL Univ., 1967–68. **Educ.:** North. IL Univ., 1963–66, BA (Soclgy.), 1966–68, MALS. **Orgs.:** ALA: GODORT, Intl. Docum. Task Frc., Secy. (1973–74), Cocoord. (1974–75), Dir. (1975–76). IA LA: Exec. Bd. (Dir., 1976–79)/Gvt. Docum. Sect. (Fndn. Ch., 1973–75). **Pubns.:** Ed., "Documentation of Intergovernmental Organizations: Proceedings of a Workshop," *Gvt. Pubn. Review* (1979); "Acquisition and Organization of International Documents in the University of Iowa Libraries," *Gvt. Pubn. Review* (1975); "Distribution of Intergovernmental Depository Collections Among Libraries in the United States," *Gvt. Pubn. Review* (1976); exec. ed., "Intl. Orgs.," *Gvt. Pubn. Rev.* (1976–). **Activities:** 1; 15, 17, 29 **Addr.:** University of Iowa Libraries, Iowa City, IA 52242.

Kok, John (Jl. 19, 1941, Amsterdam, The Netherlands) VP, Dir. of the Info. Ctr., Foote, Cone & Belding, 1977–; Readers Srvcs. Libn., The Newberry Lib., 1974–77; Asst. Prof. of the Lib., Oakland Univ. (MI), 1973–74; Asst. Prof. of Eng., Purdue Univ., 1971–72. **Educ.:** Univ. of MI, 1959–64, BA (Eng. Lit.), 1972–73, MALS; MI State Univ., 1966–68, PhD (Eng. Lit.). **Orgs.:** SLA. AIM. ALA. **Pubns.:** "Now That I'm in Charge, What Do I Do?," *Spec. Libs.* (D. 1980); "Foote, Cone & Belding's Corporate Information Service," *The Info. Mgr.* (Sum. 1980); "Moving Up: A Study of Librarians Who Have Been Made Officers of their Organizations," *Spec. Libs.* (D. 1979). **Activities:** 12; 17, 38; 51 **Addr.:** The Information Center, Foote, Cone & Belding Communications, Inc., 401 North Michigan Ave., Chicago, IL 60611.

Kolarik, Ruth N. (D. 24, 1927, Norristown, PA) Libn., Sandy Run Middle Sch., 1979–, Libn., Ft. Washington Elem. Sch., 1969–79; Libn., Washington Elem Sch., 1967–68. **Educ.:** PA State Univ., 1945–49, BS (Elem. Educ.); Drexel Univ., 1966–70, MLS. **Orgs.:** PA Sch. Libns. Assn.: Secy. (1978–80), Conf. Com. (1974–78), Adv. Com. (1976–78). PA Lrng. Resrcs. Assn.: Lib./Media Interest Com. (1976–78). ALA: AASL, Lcl. Arrange. Com. (1980–81). AECT. Natl. Educ. Assn. **Honors:** Beta Phi Mu. **Pubns.:** "School Library Media Center Week," *027.8* (F. 1981); "Adapt a Children's Book Idea," *027.8* (F. 1981). **Activities:** 10; 21; 63 **Addr.:** 1314 Hoffman Rd., Ambler, PA 19002.

Kolb, Audrey P. (O. 3, 1927, Astoria, OR) North. Reg. Coord., AK State Lib., 1978–; Consult., WA State Lib., 1975–78; Ref. Libn., Univ. of WA, 1973–75; Lib. Dir., Wenatchee Valley Coll., 1968–73. **Educ.:** OR State Univ., 1945–50, BS (Sci.); Univ. of WA, 1960–63, MLS. **Orgs.:** ALA. Pac Northwest LA. AK LA. **Pubns.:** "Development and Potential of a Multitype Library Network," *Sch. Media Qtly.* (Fall 1977); "Initiating School Participation in Networking," *Sch. Media Qtly.* (Fall 1977); "Interpersonal Communication: A Workshop," slide/tape (1971); "Library-Media Center," slide/tape (1973); "Wood Stoves and Data Bases," *Sourdough* (Ja. 1980). **Activities:** 13; 24, 25, 34 **Addr.:** Alaska State Library, 1215 Cowles St., Fairbanks, AK 99701.

PROFESSIONAL ACTIVITIES: Institutions: 1. Acad. lib.; 2. Arch.; 3. Assn.; 4. Fed./Gvt. lib.; 5. Inst. lib.; 6. Mfr./Suppl.; 7. Milit. lib.; 8. Musm.; 9. Pub. lib.; 10. Sch. lib.; 11. Sch. of lib. sci.; 12. Spec. lib.; 13. State lib.; 14. (other). **Functions/Activities:** 15. Acq./Col. dev.; 16. Adult srvs.; 17. Admin.; 18. Apprais.; 19. Archit./Bldgs.; 20. Cat./Class.; 21. Chld. srvs.; 22. Circ.; 23. Cons./Pres.; 24. Consult.; 25. Cont. ed.; 26. Educ. lib. sci.; 27. Ext. srvs.; 28. Fund/Grants; 29. Gvt. pubs.; 30. Indx./Abs.; 31. Instr. lib. use; 32. Media srvs.; 33. Micro.; 34. Netwks./Coop.; 35. Persnl.; 36. PR; 37. Publshg.; 38. Recs. mgt.; 39. Ref. srvs.; 40. Repro.; 41. Resrch.; 42. Review.; 43. Secur.; 44. Serials; 45. Spec. col.; 46. Tech. srvs.; 47. Trustees/Bds.; 48. YA srvs.; 49. (other).

Kolb, Edward J. (Ag. 24, 1926, Calumet City, IL) Instr. (LS, part-time), Amer. Univ. and U.S. Dept. Agr. Grad. Sch.; Prin. Army Tech. Info. Ofcr., U.S. Army, 1975–; Asst. Dir., Adv. Systs. Plng., U. S. Navy, 1964–75, Phys., Plans and Prog. Mgr., 1962–64; Resrch. Phys., U. S. Army, 1955–62. **Educ.:** Univ. of IA, Northwest. Univ., 1959, BS (Phys.), 1957, PhB, (Psy.); Amer. Univ., 1971, MS (Resrch. and Tech. Info. Mgt.). WHCOLIS Staff (1979). **Pubns.:** Many guest lectrs. **Activities:** 4, 12; 17, 41; 56, 75, 93 **Addr.:** 906 Annmore Dr., Silver Spring, MD 20902.

Kolbe, Helen K. (O. 18, 1927, Bradford, PA) Co-Dir., Popltn. Info. Prog., Johns Hopkins Univ., 1978–; Assoc. Dir., Hlth. Sci. Lib., George Washington Univ., 1977–78, Dir., Popltn. Info. Prog., 1975–77, Deputy Dir., 1972–75; Consult. to World Hlth. Org., Ford Fndn., Indonesia, and UN Latin Amer. Demog. Ctr., 1974–77. **Educ.:** Houghton Coll., 1945–50, BA (Fr.); Catholic Univ., 1967–72 (LS). **Orgs.:** Med. LA: Leg. Com. (1979–80); Natl. Prog. Com. (1978–79). ASIS: Chesapeake Bay Chap. (Ch., 1970–71). Assn. for Popltn. Fam. Plng. Intl. Libs. and Info. Ctrs.: Pres. (1977–78); Intl. Actv. Com. (1973–74); Resrc. and Dev. Com. (Ch., 1979–80). Popltn. Assn. of Amer. World Popltn. Socty. AAAS. **Pubns.:** *Population/Fertility Control Thesaurus* (1976); "A Worldwide Population Information Network: Status and Goals," *Spec. Libs.* (Jl. 1978); "Networks," *Bltn. ASIS* (Mr. 1975); "POPINFORM - A Computerized Population Information Network," *Information in Support of Population Activities* (1974). **Activities:** 1, 12; 17, 24, 34; 56, 62, 93 **Addr.:** 10594 Twin Rivers Rd., Columbia, MD 21044.

Kolesar, Andrew (Je. 15, 1933, Homestead, PA) Gift and Exch. Libn., Asst. Prof., CO State Univ. Libs., 1975–; Head (Libn. II), FL Dept. of Agr. and Con. Srvs., 1970–75; Asst. Libn., Univ. of FL, 1970–75; Catlgr., Srv. Tech. Corp./LTV (Kennedy Space Ctr.), 1969–70; Cat. Instr., Alliance Coll. Lib., 1966–68, Actg. Dir., 1968–69; Asst. Acq. Libn., OH Univ., 1963–66. **Educ.:** St. Mary's Univ., TX, 1955–59, BA (Soclgy.); Univ. of Pittsburgh, 1962–63, MLS; Worden Sch. of Soc. Srv., 1960–61, Soc. Work. **Orgs.:** ALA: Dupl. Exch. Un. Com. (Ch., 1979–80). SLA: FL Chap., Treas. (1973–74); Mem. Ch. (1972–73). CO LA: Tech. Srvs. RT on Acq. (1977–); Mem. Rep. (1977–). Mt. Plains LA. AAUP. CO-WY Acad. of Sci. Natl. Retired Tchrs. Assn. **Honors:** Natl. Aeronautics and Space Admin., Cert. of Awd., 1970. **Pubns.:** *A Bibliography of Colorado State University Imprints in the Colorado State University Libraries* (1977–); *A Cost Effectiveness and Benefits Study of a Bibliography of Colorado State University Imprints in the Colorado State University Libraries* (1979). **Activities:** 1; 15, 34, 46; 52, 58, 82 **Addr.:** 1101 Emigh St., Apt. 9, Fort Collins, CO 80524.

Kolesar, Patricia Marie (S. 18, 1949, Natal, BC) Asst. Libn., Cat., David Thompson University Centre, 1981–; Libn., Reg. Nurses Assn. of BC, 1979–; Bibl. Stan. Libn., BC Union Cat. Off., 1978–79; Gen. Libn., Simon Fraser Univ., 1977–78; Proj. Off., Bibl. Stand., Nat. Lib. of Can., 1976–77; Marc Libn., Nat. Lib. of Can., 1975–76, Catlgr., 1973–75. **Educ.:** Univ. of BC, 1966–70, BA (Eng.), 1971–73, MLS, 1970–71, Cert. (Primary Educ.). **Orgs.:** ALA. **Pubns.:** *Sharaf Authorities Coding Manual for Use with the Utlas Authority System* (1979). **Activities:** 12; 38, 39, 46 **Addr.:** 509 Innes St., Nelson, BC V1L 5G1 Canada.

Kollegger, James G. (F. 16, 1942, Klagenfurt, Carinthia, Austria) Pres., Env. Info. Ctr. Inc., 1970–; Asst. to Pres., Heald/Hobson, Div. of MacMillan Info., 1968–70; Asst. Dir., Mktg. Div., Structural Clay Prods. Inst., 1966–68. **Educ.:** Boston Univ., 1960–64, BS (Jnlsm., Gvt.); NY Univ., 1968–70 (Mktg.). **Orgs.:** Indus. Info. Assn.: Bd. Assoc. Info. Mgrs.: Fndr.; Co-Ch. Natl. Info. Conf. and Exposition: Fndr.; 1st Ch. (1977). NY Env. Plng. Lobby. Merit Sel. Com. for Archvst. of the U.S., G.S.A. (1979–80). **Pubns.:** "Environment Summary," *Amer. Anl./Encyc. Yrbk.* (1976–78); "Socio Economic Information Services in the Environmental Sciences," *Procs., Natl. Env. Info. Symp.* (S. 1972); *Socio Economic Environment Information Resources in the Private Sector* (1972); "The Information Bomb," *New Engin.* (N. 1972). **Addr.:** Environment Information Center, Inc., 48 W. 38th St., New York, NY 10018.

Kollin, Richard (D. 20, 1935, New York, NY) VP, Pubns., Info. Access Corp., 1977–; Pres., Book Pub., Oliver Press, 1971–77; VP, Crowell Collier MacMillan, 1967–71; Pres., Pandex, Inc., 1967–71; Dir., World Data Ctr. A, Columbia Univ., 1965–67; Libn., Columbia Univ. Tech. Report Ctr., 1963–65; Libn., Cornell Med. Coll. Lib., 1961–63. **Educ.:** Univ. of FL, 1954–58, BS (Elec. Eng.); Columbia Univ., 1965, MLS. **Orgs.:** Amer. Booksellers Assn. ASIS. Info. Industry Assn. **Pubns.:** *The Magazine Index* (a COM & online index to over 370 periodicals) (1977–); *Consumer Complaint Guide; Kits and Plans; College Blue Book; Current Index to Journals in Education.* **Activities:** 14-Publisher; 20, 30, 37; 77, 83, 92 **Addr.:** Information Access Corporation, 404 Sixth Ave., Menlo Park, CA 94025.

Kolner, Stuart James (D. 24, 1951, Borger, TX) Branch Libn./Asst. Prof., Lib. of the Hlth Scis., Rockford, Univ. of IL Med. Ctr., 1979–, Ref. Libn., Lib. of the Hlth. Scis., Chicago, 1977–79. **Educ.:** Coll. of William and Mary, 1970–74, BS (Bio.); Emory Univ., 1975, (Bio.); Case West. Rsv. Univ., 1976–77, MS (LS); Med. LA, 1977, Cert. **Orgs.:** Med. LA: Med. Sch. Libs. Sect. (Ch., 1981–82). Biomed. Comm. Netwk.: Bd. of Dirs. (1980–). Bibl. Retrieval Srvs., Inc.: Tech. Subcom., Ch., User Adv. Bd. (1980–). Stateline OLUG: Fndn. Coord. (1980–). Various other orgs., ofcs. **Honors:** Beta Phi Mu. **Pubns.:** Ed., *MEDLINE Users Grp. of the Midwest Nsltr.* (1981); *Consumer Health Catalog* (1981); "Improving the MEDLARS Search Interview: A Checklist Approach," *Bltn. of the Med. LA* (Ja. 1981); "MeSH Explosions," *BCN Postings* (Ag. 1978). **Activities:** 1, 12; 17, 35, 36; 58, 80, 87 **Addr.:** Library of the Health Sciences, Rockford School of Medicine, 1601 Parkview Ave., Rockford, IL 61101.

Koltay, Emery I. (Cluj, Romania) Dir., Bibl. and Stan., Dir., ISBN/SAN Agency, R. R. Bowker Co., 1965–; Ed., Intl. Univ. Books, 1963–64; Mgr., Plng. Srv., Romanian Gvt., 1952–63. **Educ.:** Univ. Bolyay, Cluj, Romania, 1945–49, MS (Law, Econ.), 1949–51, PhD (Educ. Plng.); Pratt Inst., 1973–75, MLS. **Orgs.:** Amer. Natl. Stan. Inst. Com. Z39: Com. on ISBN, ISSN, SAN. ASIS: Pubn. Com. ALA: Serials and AV Com. AECT. **Honors** Cnsrtm. of Univ. Film Ctrs., Silver Reel Awd., 1979. **Pubns.:** "The International Standard Book Numbering System" in *Bowker Anl;* "The International Serial Numbering," *Pubs. Wkly.; Educ. Film Locator* (1978). **Activities:** 6; 32, 37, 44; 56, 57, 75 **Addr.:** 2 Stewart Ave., Eastchester, NY 10707.

Komidar, Joseph S. (Jl. 19, 1916, Chisholm, MN) Univ. Libn., Prof., Tufts Univ., 1956–; Chief, Dept. of Ref. and Spec. Col. and Srvs., Northwestern Univ., 1951–56; Ref. Libn., Northeastern Univ., 1948–51; Ref. and Loan Libn., Carleton Coll., 1941–43. **Educ.:** Hibbing Jr. Coll., 1934–36, AA; Univ. of MN, 1936–40, BLS, BA, (Hist.); Univ. of Chicago, 1946–48, MA (LS). **Orgs.:** ALA: Div. of Cat. and Class., Spec. Adv. Com. in Class. (1952–55); RTSD/By-Law Com. (Ch., 1967–68). MA LA: Educ. Com. (1960–62). New Eng. Lib. Bd.: Panel of Cnclrs. (1972–75). New Eng. Lib. Info. Netwk.: Exec. Com. (Vice-Ch., 1974); Com. on Policies and Proc. (Ch., 1974). AAUP. **Honors:** Beta Phi Mu. **Pubns.:** "Indefinite Time System of Book Loans in a College Library," *Coll. and Resrch. Libs.* (Je. 1943); "Tufts Steps Down a Slope," *Lib. Jnl.* (D. 1, 1965); reviews. **Activities:** 1; 15, 17, 39; 75 **Addr.:** 8 Wells Rd., Reading, MA 01867.

Kondayan, Betty Ruth (Jl. 9, 1930, Mobile, AL) Libn., Julia Rogers Lib., Goucher Coll., 1981–; Head of Ref. & Pub. Srvs., Washington & Lee Univ., 1971–81; Tchr., Eng. and Amer. Lit., Amer. Coll. for Girls, Istanbul, Turkey, 1955–70; Asst. Dir., Women's residence, Stanford Univ., 1954–55; Instr. in Eng., Berea Coll., 1952–54. **Educ.:** Univ. of IL, 1947–51, BA (Eng. Lit.), 1951–52, MA (Eng. Lit.); Univ. of WI, 1970–71, MALS. **Orgs.:** ALA. MD LA: Ch., Lib. Instr. Forum (1979–80). Mid. Atlantic Reg. Arch. Conf. **Honors:** Phi Beta Kappa, 1950. Phi Kappa Phi, 1950. Beta Phi Mu, 1972. **Pubns.:** *A Historical Sketch of the Library of Washington and Lee University* (1980); "The Library of Liberty Hall Academy," *VA Mag. of Hist. and Bio.* (O. 1978). **Activities:** 1, 2; 31, 39, 45 **Addr.:** Julia Rogers Library, Goucher College, Towson, MD 21204.

Kondelik, John P. (Ja. 28, 1942, Chicago, IL) Dir. of Libs., Olivet Coll., 1974–; Acting Libn., Eckerd Coll., 1972–73, Catlgr., 1968–74; Acq. Libn., FL Pres. Coll., 1966–68. **Educ.:** Univ. of FL, 1961–64, BA (Hist.); FL State Univ., 1965–66, MSLS. **Orgs.:** FL LA: Ch., Acad. Div. (1973). ALA. MI LA. Nat. Libns. Assn. **Activities:** 1; 17, 29, 46; 57, 63, 85 **Addr.:** 116 Yale St., P. O. Box 176, Olivet, MI 49076.

Konerding, Erhard F. (O. 7, 1947, Celle, Germany) Govt. Docum. Libn., Wesleyan Univ., 1972–; Adj. Instr. (LS), South. CT State Coll., 1977–80. **Educ.:** Long Island Univ., 1965–69, BA (Hist.); Columbia Univ., 1971–72, MS (LS). **Orgs.:** ALA: GODORT; ACRL. **Pubns.:** Reviews. **Activities:** 1; 29, 39 **Addr.:** Olin Library, Wesleyan University, Middletown, CT 06457.

Koo, Suen-Yan David (Ja. 17, 1934, Canton, China) Sr. Resrch. Libn., Firestone Tire and Rubber Co., 1968–; Libn. II/Catlgr., Columbus Pub. Lib., 1965–68; Asst. Libn., NM Highlands Univ., 1962–63; Dir., Readers' Srvs., Chung Chi Coll., Hong Kong, 1959–61. **Educ.:** Chung Chi Coll., 1955–59, BS (Chem.); Atlanta Univ., 1961–62, MSLS. **Orgs.:** SLA. **Activities:** 17; 39, 41; 60, 64, 91 **Addr.:** Central Research Library, Firestone Tire and Rubber Co., 1200 Firestone Pkwy., Akron, OH 44317.

Kopischke, John L. (F. 28, 1928, Marinette, WI) Dir., NE Lib. Comsn., 1976–; Dir., WI Ref. and Loan Lib., 1967–76, Dir., Scottsbluff Pub. Lib., 1963–67, Libn., U.S. Air Frc. Base, Lakenheath, Eng., 1962–63; Libn., U.S. Air Frc. Schs., Azores, Libya, and Chateauroux, France, 1958–62; Libn., St. Louis Cnty. Day Sch., 1956–58. **Educ.:** Univ. of WI, 1946–51, BA (Eng.), 1959, MA (LS). **Orgs.:** NE LA: Pres. (1966). WI LA: Secy. (1975). WI LA: Int. Frdm. Com. (1972). WHCOLIS: Del. (1979). Bibl. Ctr. for Resrch.: Bd. of Trustees, Pres. (1980–81), VP (1978–79). **Honors:** WI LA, Lib. of the Yr., 1975. **Activities:** 13; 17, 27, 34 **Addr.:** 1950 Sewell St., Lincoln, NE 68502.

Koppel, Theodore P. (N. 29, 1954, Cleveland, OH) Pub. Srv. Coord., Univ. of Denver Lib., 1981–; Ref. Libn., 1977–81. **Educ.:** Georgetown Univ., 1972–76, BS (Langs.); Case West. Rsv. Univ., 1976–77, MS (LS). **Orgs.:** Beta Phi Mu: Phi Chap. (Pres., 1980–81), Treas. (1978–79). Rocky Mt. OLUG: Treas. (1979–81). ALA. Assn. of Jewish Libns. **Activities:** 1; 15, 31, 39; 56, 59, 92 **Addr.:** 1696 S. Mobile St., Aurora, CO 80017.

Koppelman, Connie E. (D. 25, 1930, Astoria, NY) AV Ref. Libn., SUNY Stony Brook, 1969–77. **Educ.:** SUNY Stony Brook, 1968, BA (Art Hist.) Queens Coll., 1969, MLS; SUNY Stony Brook, 1970–76, MALS; 1976– (Hist.). **Orgs.:** ARLIS/NA: Acad. Libs. (Ch., 1973–76)/NY Chap. (Ch., 1978). **Pubns.:** "Dead Men/Women Do Tell Tales," *Long Island Forum* (Ja. 1981); "Researching a Burying Ground," *Musms. of Stony Brook Nsltr.* (Sum. 1980); "Art Orientation in Academic Libraries," *Spec. Libs.* (My.-Jn. 1976); "Metamorphosis of a Idea," *ARLIS/NA Nsltr.* (Fb. 1974); "More Impressions," ARLIS/NA Nsltr. (Jn. 1973). **Activities:** 1; 31, 32, 39; 55, 67, 95-Women's Stds. **Addr.:** 5 Cakewalk Terr., Smithtown, NY 11787.

Korda, Marion A. (Je. 14, 1922, Portland, ME) Prof. of Bibl., Msc. Libn., Univ. of Louisville, 1947–. **Educ.:** Westbrook Jr. Coll., 1940–42, Univ. of ME, 1942–43, BA (Eng., Hist.); Columbia Univ., 1953 MS (LS); Royal Danish Msc. Consvty., 1957–58 (Msc. Hist., Theory, Grmn.). **Orgs.:** Msc. LA: Bd. of Dirs. (1971–72); Midwest Chap., (Ch., 1977–79); (Prog. Ch., Panelist, 1975). KY LA. Intl. Assn. Msc. Libs. Musicians Un. Lcl. #11–637. AAUP. Amer. Viola Socty. **Pubns.:** "The New Music Law in Denmark," *FONTES* (1977); various reviews in *Notes.* **Activities:** 95-Music. **Addr.:** Dwight Anderson Memorial Music Library, Univ. Louisville School of Music, 2301 S. Third St., Louisville, KY 40292.

Kordish, Heike Christiane (Ja. 11, 1942, Zoppot, Danzig, Germany) Syst. Plng. Coord., Columbia Univ. Libs., 1974–, Head, Syst. Ofc., 1972–74, Lib. Syst. Anal., 1968–72; Asst. Acq. Libn., Yale Univ. Libs., 1967–68. **Educ.:** City Coll. of NY, 1964–65, BA (Comp. Lit.); Columbia Univ., 1965–67, MS (LS), 1979–80, MBA. **Orgs.:** ALA: LITA, Bylaws Com. (Ch., 1980–); ACRL; RTSD; various coms. **Activities:** 1; 24, 34, 41; 56, 62, 75 **Addr.:** 15 Claremont Ave., New York, NY 10027.

Korf, Harold Edward (O. 28, 1925, Osakis, MN) Dir., Lib. Srvs., Golden Gate Univ. Lib., 1960–; Assoc. Hum. Libn., Stanford Univ. Lib., 1957–60; Libn., Free Lib. of Philadelphia, 1953–57. **Educ.:** Univ. of CA, Berkeley, 1953, BA, BLS. **Orgs.:** Amer. Mktg. Assn. SLA. ALA. AAUP. **Activities:** 1; 17; 59, 75 **Addr.:** 1549 Beach St., San Francisco, CA 94123.

Kornblum, Lee F. (O. 1, 1947, St. Louis, MO) Computer Oper. Mgr., Houston Pub. Lib., 1979–, Adult Ref. Libn., 1975–79. **Educ.:** IN Univ., 1965–68, AB (Classics); Univ. of MI, 1968–71, MA (Classics, 1969); Columbia Univ., 1973–75, MSLS. **Orgs.:** TX LA. ALA: Standrds. for Lib. Srvc. to the Deaf (1979). **Honors:** Beta Phi Mu, 1975; Phi Beta Kappa, 1968. **Activities:** 9; 39, 46; 56 **Addr.:** Houston Public Library, 500 McKinney, Houston, TX 77002.

Kornfeld, Carol E. (Jl. 20, 1926, Newark, NJ) Libn., Thomas J. Lipton, Inc., 1975–; Asst. to Dir. of Resrch., H. W. Wilson, 1969–73; Instr. (Chem.), Barnard Coll., 1951–54. **Educ.:** PA State Univ., 1942–45, BS (Chem.); Columbia Univ., 1946–48, MA (Chem.), 1966–69, MLS. **Orgs.:** SLA: NJ Chap., *Bltn.* (Bus. Mgr., 1978–). ASIS. Bergen-Passaic Hlth. Sci. Lib. Cnsrtm.: Various ofcs. **Honors:** Beta Phi Mu. Sigma Xi. **Activities:** 12; 30, 41; 56, 60, 68 **Addr.:** 64 Creston Ave., Tenafly, NJ 07670.

Korty, Margaret Barton (Jl. 6, 1919, Lincoln Cnty., MO) Ed., Church Lib. Cncl., 1975–; Volun., ILL Dept., Prince George's Cnty. Lib., 1972–81. **Educ.:** Lindenwood Coll., 1937–41, BA (Hist.); Univ. of IL, 1941–42, MA (Hist.); Cath. Univ., 1959–64, MS (LS). **Orgs.:** Church Lib. Cncl.: Secy. (1967–69; 1974–75); Workshop Leader; Ed. (1975–). CSLA: AV columnist (1978–). Riverdale Presby. Church: AV Libn. **Honors:** MD Srv. Corps, Cert. of Merit, 1979; Beta Phi Mu. **Pubns.:** *Audio-Visual Materials in the Church Library* (1977); *Benjamin Franklin and Eighteenth Century American Libraries* (1965); "Franklin's World of Books," *Jnl. Of Lib. Hist.* (O. 1967). **Activities:** 9, 12; 32, 42; 90 **Addr.:** 5406 Quintana St., Riverdale, MD 20737.

Kosek, Reynold (F. 25, 1947, Wilkes-Barre, PA) Ref. Libn./Asst. Prof., George Sch. of Law, Mercer Univ., 1977–, Head Pub. Srvs. Libn., Law Ctr., Univ. of South. CA, 1975–76; Asst. Lib. Consult. to State Gvt. Agencies, NC State Lib., 1971–72. **Educ.:** WV Univ., 1964–68, AB (Hist.); SUNY, Albany, 1970–71, MLS; Univ. of NC, 1972–75, JD. **Orgs.:** AALL: Acad. Law Libs. Spec. Interest Sect. (Ch., 1980–81); Stans. Com. (1979–81)/Southeast. Chap. State Bar of CA. State Bar of PA. **Pubns.:** "Professional Responsibility of Lawyers and Accountants Before the Securities and Exchange Commission," *Law Lib. Jnl.* (Sum. 1979); "West Virginia Legislative Information," *Southeast. Law Libn.* (1980). **Activities:** 1; 39, 41; 77, 78 **Addr.:** Walter F. George School of Law, Mercer University, 1021 Georgia Ave., Macon, GA 31210.

Koshatka, Beverly V. (Ja. 9, 1928, New Haven, WY) Media Spec., Ctrl. Jr. HS, 1965–. **Educ.:** Univ. of IA, 1962–65, BA (Elem. Educ.); 1968–69, MALS. **Orgs.:** Friends of IA City Pub. Lib.: Steering Com. (1976–77). Natl. Educ. Assn. IA Educ.

Special Subjects/Services: 50. Adult educ.; 51. Advert./Mktg.; 52. Aerosp.; 53. Agric.; 54. Area std.; 55. Arts/Hum.; 56. Autom.; 57. Bibl./Prtg.; 58. Bio. sci.; 59. Bus./Fin.; 60. Chem.; 61. Copyrt.; 62. Documtn.; 63. Educ.; 64. Engin.; 65. Env.; 66. Eth. grps.; 67. Film; 68. Food/Nutr.; 69. Geneal.; 70. Geo.; 71. Geol.; 72. Handcpd.; 73. Hist.; 74. Int. frdm.; 75. Info. sci.; 76. Insr.; 77. Law; 78. Legis.; 79. Math./Comp. sci.; 80. Med.; 81. Metals; 82. Nat. resrcs.; 83. Newsp.; 84. Nuc. sci.; 85. Oral hist.; 86. Petr./Energy; 87. Pharm.; 88. Phys./Astr./Math.; 89. Readg.; 90. Relig.; 91. Sci./Tech.; 92. Soc. sci.; 93. Telecom.; 94. Transp.; 95. (other).

Who's Who in Library and Information Services

Assn. IA City Educ. Assn. Delta Kappa Gamma. **Activities:** 10; 15, 48 **Addr.:** 2508 Potomac Dr., Iowa City, IA 52240.

Kosher, Helene J. (O. 4, 1948, Portland, OR) Cur. of Slides & Photos., Univ. of CA, Riverside, 1978–; Coord. of Media Srvs., Contra Costa Cnty. Lib., 1975–78; Head, Art/Audiovisual Dept., Stanislaus Cnty. Free Lib., 1973–75. **Educ.:** San Jose State Coll., 1966–71, BA (Art Hist.); San Jose State Univ., 1971–72, MLS; Comnty. Coll. Instr. Cred. Inter-Personal Comm. Wkshp. Cert. 1972–77, (Lib. Sci. Comm.). **Orgs.:** Coll. Art Assn.: Prof. Stans. Sub-Com., Visual Resrcs. Com. (1977–). Art Libs. Socty. of N. Amer.: Adv. Com., Visual Resrcs. Spec. Interest Group (1977–). Ch., N. CA Chap. (1977–78). Riverside Art Ctr. and Musm.: Exhibits Com. (1979–). **Pubns.:** "Video Access in Modesto," *Patch Panel* (Dec. 1975); videotape shows, art. **Activities:** 1, 12; 17, 20, 45; 55, 63, 67 **Addr.:** Art History Department, University of California, Riverside, Riverside, CA 92521.

Koslov, Marcia J. (S. 8, 1949, St. Louis, MO) State Law Libn., WI State Law Lib., 1974–; Head Libn., Missouri Supreme Ct. Lib., 1972–74, Asst. Libn., 1971. **Educ.:** Univ. of MO, Columbia, 1967–71, BA (Pol. Sci.), 1971–72, MA (LS); AALL, Cert. **Orgs.:** AALL: Exec. Bd. (1980–83); Anl. Conv., Hotel Arrange. Ch. (1980); State, Ct., and Cnty. Law Libs.: Exec. Bd. (Ch., 1978–79); Educ. Com. (1976–78), Wkshp. Ch. (1978); other coms. WI LA: PR Com. (Ch., 1981). Madison Area Lib. Cncl. Frnds. of Channel 21 (PBS Afflt.). **Pubns.:** "The Legislative Process," *Law Lib. Jnl.* (N. 1977); "Federal Funds: Availability to Law Libraries," *Law Lib. Jnl.* (My. 1975); "Missouri Supreme Court Library," *Show-Me Libs.* (Jl. 1974). **Activities:** 4, 12; 17; 77 **Addr.:** Wisconsin State Law Library, P.O. Box 7881, Madison, WI 53707.

Kosman, George Oliver (Fb. 11, 1932, Catasauqua, PA) Adjunct Prof., Matthew A. Baxter Schl. of Info. and LS, 1980–; Govt. Docum. Libn., Case West. Resrv. Univ. 1967–, Acq. Libn., 1966–67. **Educ.:** OH State Univ., 1950–54, BA (Jnlsm.) West. Resrv. Univ., 1960–66, MSLS. **Orgs.:** ALA: Pub. Docum. Com. (1974–1976); GODORT, Const. Com. (1978–). Sigma Delta Chi. **Activities:** 1; 26, 29; 78 **Addr.:** Freiberger Library, Case Western Reserve University, 11161 East Blvd., Cleveland, OH 44106.

Koss, Helen G. (N. 25, 1926, Waterbury, CT) Ch., LS, South. CT State Coll., 1980–, Assoc. Prof., LS, 1975–81, Instr., LS, 1969–75; Co-Libn., LaSallette Semy. Lib., 1968–69. **Educ.:** Univ. of CT, 1944–48, BS (Mktg.); South. CT State Coll., 1964–69, MS (LS); Univ. of CT, 1973–79, PhD (Educ.). **Orgs.:** ALA. **Pubns.:** "Picture Book Sexism: Two Steps Forward and One Step Back," *Resrcs. in Educ.* (My. 1981); "An Analysis of Current Reference Problems," *The Ref. Libn.* (Spr. 1981); "Southern Connecticut State College Division of Library Science and Instructional Technology," *Encyc. of Lib. and Info. Sci.* (Fall 1979); "Total Media: Southern Connecticut State College's Contribution to Media Education," *CEMA Bltn.* (Fall 1976); jt. auth., "The Source-erer's Apprentice," *CT Eng. Jnl.* (Fall 1972). **Addr.:** Division of Library Science and Instructional Technology, Southern Connecticut State College, 501 Crescent St., New Haven, CT 06515.

Kossey, John Andrew (Jn. 23, 1945, Pittsburgh, PA) Dir. of Libs., W. Coast Univ., 1980–; Dir. of AV Srvs., Ambassador Coll., 1979–80, Lib. Dir., 1978–79, Asst. Libn., Pub. Srvs., 1974–78. **Educ.:** Univ. of Pittsburgh, 1963–66, BS (Phys.); Ambassador Coll., 1967–70, BS (Theo.), 1970–73, MA (Educ. Media); Univ. of South. CA, 1973–74, MSLS. **Orgs.:** ASIS: LA Chap., Educ. Com (Ch., 1976–77), Prog. Com. (Ch., 1978). Christian Libns. Assn.: South. CA Chap. (Pres., 1978–79). AECT. ALA. Other orgs. ATLA. Socty. for Tech. Comm. Assn. for Multi-Image. Natl. Socty. for Perf. and Instr. AECT. **Honors:** Beta Phi Mu. ASIS, Los Angeles Chap., Outstan. Mem., 1978. **Pubns.:** *The Hebrew Calendar: A Mathematical Introduction* (1971, 1973); "Collection Analysis Measures and Techniques for Academic Libraries," Summary of Prcs., 32d Anl. Conf., ATLA; 1978 (1980); various slide tape productions. **Activities:** 1; 15, 17, 24; 90 **Addr.:** 280 S. Euclid, 123, Pasadena, CA 91101.

Koster, Diana M. (N. 14, 1947, New York, NY) Tech./Bus. Libn., Yonkers Pub. Lib., 1971; YA Libn., Yonkers Pub. Lib., 1970–71. **Educ.:** Fordham Univ., 1965–69, BA (Math); Columbia Univ., 1969–70, MSLS. **Orgs.:** Westchester LA: Com. on Coop. (Secy., 1977–); Co-Ch. (1978–). SLA: Liaison, West. LA (1980–). NY LA. **Honors:** Beta Phi Mu, 1970. **Pubns.:** Jt. ed., *Westchester Union List of Serials* (1979). **Activities:** 9; 26, 29, 39; 51, 59, 91 **Addr.:** Technical & Business Dept., Yonkers Public Library, Yonkers, NY 10701.

Koster, Gregory Edward (Ag. 1, 1947, Glen Cove, NY) Asst. Law Libn., Pace Univ., 1977–, Head of Tech. Srvs., 1975–77; Serials Catlgr., Columbia Univ. Libs., 1970–75. **Educ.:** Stanford Univ., 1965–69, BA (Hist.); Columbia Univ., 1969–70, MS (LS), 1971–74, MIA (E. Ctrl. Europe); Pace Univ., Sch. of Law, 1977–81, JD. **Orgs.:** AALL: Cat. and Class. Com. (1976–77, 1977–78). Beta Phi Mu: Nu Chap. Pres. (1976–77); VP (1975–76). Columbia Univ. Sch. of Lib. Srv. Alum. Assn.: Secy./Treas. (1977–78, 1978–79). Law Lib. Assn. of Grt. NY. Other orgs. NY State Bar Assn. **Honors:** West Publishing Co., Hornbook Awd. For Scholastic Achvmt., 1977–79; Lawyers Coop. Publishing Co., Amer. Jurisprudence Awd. For Achvmt., 1977–78. **Pubns.:** Casenote ed., *Pace Law Review* (1980–81); "Application of New York Estates, Powers & Trusts Law Section 3-3.2 to Dispositions to Attesting Witnesses," *Pace Law Review* (1981); Jt. auth., "Starting a Law School Library," *Law Lib. Jnl.* (1977). **Activities:** 1; 15, 17, 46; 54, 77 **Addr.:** Pace University Law School Library, 78 North Broadway, White Plains, NY 10603.

Kostinko, Gail A. (Ag. 10, 1951, Pottsville, PA) Sr. Info. Spec., African Bibl. Ctr., 1981–; African Affairs Info. Spec., Consult., 1978–81; African Ref. Spec., Howard Univ., Moorland-Spingarn Res. Ctr, 1975–78; Adjunct Lectr., Univ. of MD Coll. of Lib. & Info Srv., 1975–. **Educ.:** PA State Univ., 1969–73, BA (Fr. Lit.); Univ. of MD, 1974, MLS. **Orgs.:** DC LA. ASIS. African Std. Assn. African Lit. Assn. **Honors:** Phi Beta Kappa, 1973. **Pubns.:** *African Refugees-A Guide to Contemporary Information Sources* (1981); *Rural Development in Senegal–An Annotated Bibliography* (1980); *A Selected Bibliography of Club du Sahel and CILSS Documents* (1979); Index, *A Current Bibliography on African Affairs* (1976). **Activities:** 4, 12; 24, 30, 49-Info. dissemination; 54, 62 **Addr.:** African Bibliographic Center, 1346 Connecticut Ave. N.W., Suite 901, Washington, DC 20036.

Kosuda, Kathleen L. (O. 25, 1938, Springfield, MA) Libn., Pasco-Hernando Cmnty. Coll., 1979–; Dir., Gloversville Free Lib., 1973–79; Libn., Fulton Montgomery Cmnty. Coll., 1971–73. **Educ.:** SUNY, Albany, 1969–71, BA (Anthro.); 1971–72, MLS. **Orgs.:** Hudson-Mohawk LA: VP (1973), Bd. (1975). Tryon Lib. Assocs.: Treas. (1974). Leag. of Women Voters. Fulton Cnty. Arts Cncl. **Honors** NY LA, Margaret E. Martignoni Awd., 1976, Std. Grant, 1978; State of NY, Dept. of Cvl. Srv., Spec. Examiner, 1974. **Activities:** 1, 9; 17, 35, 39; 59, 92 **Addr.:** 1416 Mill Creek Ln., New Port Richey, FL 33553.

Kotin, David B. (Mr. 31, 1947, San Luis Obispo, CA) Head, Can. Col., N. York Pub. Lib., 1978–, Can. Libn., 1974–77, Gen. Libn., 1974. **Educ.:** York Univ., 1970–72, BA (Eng.); Univ. of WI, 1965–68, (Comp. Lit.); Univ. of BC, 1972–74, MLS. **Orgs.:** Bibl. Socty. of Can.: Cncl. (1979–); Review Ed., *BSC Papers* (1981); Tremaine Medal Com. (1981). Bibl. Socty. of Amer. Toronto Area Archvst. Grp.: V-Ch. (1977–78); Treas. (1979–80). Assn. of Can. Archvsts. Amtmann Circle: Bd. of Dir. (1980–). Can. LA. **Pubns.:** Jt. auth., *Reader, Lover of Books: The Book Arts in Ontario* (1981); complr., *Reader, Lover of Books, Lover of Heaven...* (1978); complr., *Annual Bibliography of Ontario History: 1980* (1980); "Graphic Publishers and the Bibliographer: An Introduction and Checklist," *Papers of the Bibliographical Society of Canada*, 18 (1979); reviews. **Activities:** 9, 12; 15, 39, 41; 55, 57 **Addr.:** Canadiana Collection, North York Public Library, 35 Fairview Mall Dr., Willowdale, ON M2J 4S4 Canada.

Kotzin, Sheldon (S. 1, 1943, Baltimore, MD) Chief, Bibl. Srvs. Div., Natl. Lib. of Med., 1981–, Reg. Med. Lib. Coord., 1978–81, Head, Loan & Stack Sect., 1971–78, Spec. Asst. to the Assoc. Dir., Lib. Oper., 1970–71. **Educ.:** Univ. of MD, 1960–64, BA (Hist.); IN Univ., 1964–68, MLS. **Orgs.:** Med. LA: Eliot Prize Com. (1978–80); Ed. Panel (Thru 1981). MD LA. Montgomery Cnty. Pub. Lib. Bd.: Vice-Ch. (1979–). **Activities:** 4, 12; 34; 80, 93 **Addr.:** National Library of Medicine, Bethesda, MD 20209.

Kovacic, Ellen Siegel (S. 30, 1951, Pittsburgh, PA) Judaica Libn., Hebrew Un. Coll., Jewish Inst. of Relig., 1979–; Serials Cat., PA State Univ., 1975–79. **Educ.:** Univ. of Pittsburgh, 1969–73, BA (Soclgy.), 1973–75, MLS. **Orgs.:** ALA: RTSD/SS Com. to Std. Serials Cat. (1978–80; Ch., 1980–81); RTSD/SS Nom. Com. (1981–). Assoc. of Jewish Libs. (1980–). OH Valley Grp. of Tech. Srvs. Libns. (1981–). PA LA. PA State Univ. Fac. Women: Newcomers Club, Publicity Ch. (1976–77). Amer. Assn. of Univ. Women. **Honors:** Beta Phi Mu, 1975. **Activities:** 1; 20, 39, 44; 56, 90, 92 **Addr.:** Klau Library, Hebrew Union College–Jewish Institute of Religion, 3101 Clifton Ave., Cincinnati, OH 45220.

Kovacic, Mark E. (Je. 1, 1944, Bellefonte, PA) Asst. Head, Acq., Univ. of Cincinnati Libs., 1979–; Gifts and Exch. Libn., PA State Univ. Libs., 1971–79. **Educ.:** PA State Univ., 1962–66, BA (Sp., Jnlsm.); Univ. of Pittsburgh, 1969–71, MLS (Lib. and Info. Sci.). **Orgs.:** ALA. OH Valley Grp. of Tech. Srvs. Libns. (Ch., 1981–82); Cncl. of Reg. Grps. **Honors** Cncl. on Lib. Resrcs., Flwshp., 1977–78. **Pubns.:** "The Organization and Function of Gift and Exchange Programs in Eighteen Selected U.S. Academic Libraries," ERIC (Ja. 1980); "Gifts and Exchanges in U.S. Academic Libraries," *Lib. Resrcs. and Tech. Srvs.* (Spr. 1980). **Activities:** 1; 15, 44, 46; 51, 83 **Addr.:** Acquisitions Dept., Central Library, Univ. of Cincinnati, Cincinnati, OH 45221.

Kovacs, Gabor (Ap. 11, 1923, Sarkad, Hungary) Asst. Dir. for Pub. Srvs., Univ. of North. CO, 1974–, Circ. Libn., 1963–74. **Educ.:** Air Force Acad., Hungary, 1944, BA (Milit. Sci.); West. MI Univ., 1962–63, MA (LS). **Orgs.:** ALA. Mt. Plains LA. CO LA. Amer.-Hungarian Educ. Assn. **Pubns.:** Cmplr., *Annotated Bibliography of Bibliographies on Selected Government Publications and Supplementary Guides to the Superintendent of Documents Classification System* (1979, 1980). **Activities:** 1; 17 **Addr.:** 1945 24th Ave., Greeley, CO 80631.

Kovacs, Laszlo L. (Je. 2, 1935, Hodmezovasarhely, Hungary) Libn., Sch. of Human., Soc. Sci. and Educ.; Head of Gen. Lib.; Prof. of Lib. Sci., Purdue Univ. Libs., 1974–; Assoc. Prof. of Lib. Sci., Purdue Univ., 1974–80; Head, Dept. of Hist., Cleveland Pub. Lib., 1970–73; Lectr., IN Univ., 1966–70; Head, Microfilm Div., UN Secretariat, NY, 1958–60. **Educ.:** Reformed Theo. Acad., Debrecen, Hungary, 1956, BTh (Church Hist.); Colgate Rochester Div. Sch., 1964, MDiv (Church Hist.); IN Univ., 1966, MA (Lib. Sci.), 1968, MA (Hist., Pol. Sci.), 1970, Cert. in Hungarian Std. **Orgs.:** ALA: ACRL. Amer. Assn. for the Adv. of Slavic Std. **Pubns.:** Contrib., *East Central and Southeast Europe: A Handbook of Library and Archival Resources in North America* (1976); "Hungarian Collections in Academic and Research Libraries in North America," *Ural-Altaische Jahrbucher* (1980); "The Hungarian Collection in the Lilly Library of Indiana University Parts I and II," *Ural-Altaische Jahrbucher* (1978) (1979); "The Dragon in the Folktales of Lajos Ami" in *Std. in E. European Folk Narrative* (1978). Reviews. **Activities:** 1; 15, 41, 45; 55, 57 **Addr.:** 2051 Robinhood Ln., W. Lafayette, IN 47906.

Kovel-Jarboe, Patricia (D. 4, 1950, Bethesda, MD) Ext. Spec., Census Info., Univ. of MN, 1980–, Actg. Dir., Lib., Coll. of St. Thomas, 1979–80; Exec. Dir., MN LA, 1978–79; Tech. Srvs. Libn., Coll. of St. Thomas, 1975–78. **Educ.:** Univ. of MI, 1969–72, BGS (Liberal Arts); Simmons Coll., 1973–74, MSLS; Univ. of MN, 1977–80, MA (Comm.), 1980–, PhD (Comm.). **Orgs.:** ALA: ACRL. MN LA: Various coms. MN Women in Higher Educ. Leag. of Women Voters. Natl. Org. for Women. **Pubns.:** "Human Resource Development," *MN Libs.* (Sum. 1980); reviews. **Activities:** 1, 3; 15, 17, 24; 93 **Addr.:** 5144 Russell Ave. S., Minneapolis, MN 55410.

Kowitz, Aletha A. (S. 26, Chicago, IL) Dir., Bureau of Lib. Srvcs., Amer. Dental Assn., 1977–, Ref. Libn., 1970–76, Asst. Dir., 1976–77; Per. Libn., Med. Lib., Northwestern Univ., 1967–70; Asst. Circ./Ref. Libn., Med. Lib., Univ. of IL, 1959–67; Chem. Libn., Glidden Co., 1954–59. **Educ.:** Univ. of Chicago, 1945–51, SB (Chem.); Rosary Coll., 1954–59, MALS. **Orgs.:** SLA. Med LA. ASIS. ALA. Amer. Chem. Socty. Amer. Inst. of Chem. **Activities:** 1, 12; 17, 39, 46; 60, 80, 95-Dentistry. **Addr.:** 211 East Chicago Ave., Chicago IL 60611.

Kozlowski, Ronald S. (O. 18, 1937, Chicago, IL) Dir., Louisville Free Pub. Lib., 1977–; Dir., W. FL Reg. Lib., 1974–77; Asst. Dir., Evansville Pub. Lib., 1971–74; Head, Ref. and Acq., IN State Univ., 1970–71. **Educ.:** IL State Univ., 1959–61, BSEd (Eng.); Rosary Coll., 1966–68, MALS. **Orgs.:** ALA: PLA/Metro Lib. Sect., Pres. (1980–81); State Lib. Agency Sect., Secty., (1979–80). Southeastern LA: PR Com. KY LA: Legislative Com. (Ch. 1981). Jefferson Cnty. Cable TV Com.: Ch. (1978). Louisville Orch. Adv. Bd. **Honors** Pensacola Cham. of Cmrce., Bicent. Com., Outstan. Lib. Srvs., 1977. **Pubns.:** "Community Delivery Services," *ALA Yearbook* (1978); "Books-By-Mail in Evansville, IN.," mono. (1974). **Activities:** 9; 17 **Addr.:** Louisville Free Public Library, Louisville, KY 40203.

Kraehe, Mary Alice (O. 1, 1924, Minneapolis, MN) African Biblgphr./Out-of-Print Libn., Univ. of VA, 1970–, Out-of-Print Libn., Univ. of NC, 1964–68; Libn. in Acq., Univ. of KY, 1963–64. **Educ.:** Univ. of MN, 1942–45, BA (Eng., Phil.); Univ. of KY, 1962–63, MS (LS). **Orgs.:** ALA. VA LA. African Std. Assn. Arch.: Libs. Com. (Secy., 1981–). Leag. of Women Voters. **Honors:** Beta Phi Mu. **Pubns.:** *African Languages: A Guide to Materials in the Alderman Library of the University of Virginia* (1981). **Activities:** 1; 15 **Addr.:** 130 Bennington Rd., Charlottesville, VA 22901.

Kraemer, Linda Lee (My. 31, 1950, White Plains, NY) Mgr., Info. Srvcs., McKinsey and Co., Inc., 1981–; Libn., 1979–81; Resrch. Spec., Varian Assoc., 1979; Resrchr., Ref. Supvsr., BBDO Intl., 1975–78. **Educ.:** Syracuse Univ., 1968–70, Barnard Coll., 1970–72, AB (Hist.); Columbia Univ., 1973–74, MSLS. **Orgs.:** SLA: S.F. Bay Chap., Educ. Com. (1978–80). **Pubns.:** Ed., *What's New in Advertising and Marketing* (1976–78). **Activities:** 12; 17, 41; 51, 59 **Addr.:** McKinsey & Company, Inc., 555 California St., Suite 4800, San Francisco, CA 94104.

Kraemer, Mary Pat (Ja. 8, 1946, Kansas City, MO) Chief Libn., Kenya Tech. Tchrs. Coll., 1978–; Assoc. Libn., Inglewood (CA) Pub. Lib., 1977, Libn., 1974–76; Lib. Tech., Univ. of Liberia, W. Africa, 1971–72; Tchr./Libn., Konia Elem. Sch., W. Africa, 1968–70. **Educ.:** Univ. of Santa Clara, 1964–68, BA (Pol. Sci.), Univ. of CA, Los Angeles, 1972–73, MLS; CA State tch. cred., 1973–75. **Orgs.:** Kenya LA. ALA. CA LA. Southern CA Cncl. on Lit. for Chldrn and Young People. **Pubns.:** Contrib., *Library Materials Selection Policy* (1975); "Good News for the Cataloguing Community" (N. 1978). **Activities:** 9; 17, 20, 21; 63, 91 **Addr.:** c/o T. Kraemer, 1051 Waterbird Way, Santa Clara, CA 95051.

Kraft, Donald H. (D. 21, 1943, Omaha, NE) Assoc. Prof. (Comp. Sci.), LA State Univ., 1976–; Visit. Asst. Prof., Univ. of CA, Berkeley, 1975–76; Asst. Prof., Univ. of MD, 1970–75; Instr., Purdue Univ., 1968–70. **Educ.:** Purdue Univ., 1961–65, BSIE (Indus. Engin.); 1965–66, MSIE, 1966–71, PhD (Indus. Engin.). **Orgs.:** ASIS. Assn. for Comp. Mach.: Spec. Interest Grp.

PROFESSIONAL ACTIVITIES: Institutions: 1. Acad. lib.; 2. Arch.; 3. Assn.; 4. Fed./Gvt. lib.; 5. Inst. lib.; 6. Mfr./Suppl.; 7. Milit. lib.; 8. Musm.; 9. Pub. lib.; 10. Sch. lib.; 11. Sch. of lib. sci.; 12. Spec. lib.; 13. State lib.; 14. (other). **Functions/Activities:** 15. Acq./Col. dev.; 16. Adult srvs.; 17. Admin.; 18. Apprais.; 19. Archit./Bldgs.; 20. Cat./Class.; 21. Chld. srvs.; 22. Circ.; 23. Cons./Pres.; 24. Consult.; 25. Cont. ed.; 26. Educ. lib. sci.; 27. Ext. srvs.; 28. Fund/Grants; 29. Gvt. pubs.; 30. Indx./Abs.; 31. Instr. lib. use; 32. Media srvs.; 33. Micro.; 34. Netwks./Coop.; 35. Persnl.; 36. PR; 37. Publshg.; 38. Recs. mgt.; 39. Ref. srvs.; 40. Repro.; 41. Resrch.; 42. Review.; 43. Secur.; 44. Serials; 45. Spec. col.; 46. Tech. srvs.; 47. Trustees/Bds.; 48. YA srvs.; 49. (other).

on Info. Retrieval. Oper. Resrch. Socty. of Amer.: Tech. Sect., Comp. Sci. Inst. of Mgmt. Sci. Sigma Xi. Alpha Pi Mu. **Pubns.:** "Evaluation of Information Retrieval Systems," *Jnl. ASIS* (Ja. 1978); "Journal Selection Decisions," *Bltn. Med LA* (Jy. 1976); "A Journal Selection Model and its Implications for Librarians," *Info. Storage and Retrieval* (1973); Jt. auth., "Journal Deposition Decision Policies," *Jnl. ASIS* (Jy.-Aug. 1974); other articles, presented papers, Tech. Rpts. **Activities:** 11, 14-Comp. Sci. Dept.; 15, 17, 26; 56, 75, 95-Oper. Resrch. **Addr.:** Department of Computer Science, Louisiana State University, Baton Rouge, LA 70803.

Krahn, Frederic A. (O. 8, 1917, Milwaukee, WI) Asst. Dir., E. Meadow Pub. Lib., 1955–; Ed., Educ. Film Guide, The H. W. Wilson Co., 1949–55. **Educ.:** Univ. of WI, 1945–47, BS (Educ.); Columbia Univ. Sch. of Lib. Srv., 1947–48, BS (LS); Tchrs. Coll., Columbia Univ. 1948–51, MA (AV Educ.). **Orgs.:** NY LA. Nassau Cnty. LA: Cont. Ed. Com. Ch. Film Lib. Info. Cncl. Educ. Film LA: Pres. (1962–64). **Activities:** 9; 25, 32 **Addr.:** 67 Rim Ln., Hicksville, L.I., NY 11801.

Krakaner, Elizabeth Gottschalk (Ag. 2, 1911, Hanover, Germany) Freelnc. Libn., 1981–; Peace Corps Libn., Univ. of Los Andes and Centro Antropologico, Bogota, Colombia, 1975–80; Head Libn., Goddard Coll., 1972–74; Head Libn., Prescott Coll., 1969–72; Libn., Yale Univ., 1968; Libn., SUNY, Buffalo, 1962–68; Ofc. Mgr. and Lab. Asst., 1939–61. **Educ.:** SUNY, Buffalo, 1963, BA, 1965, MA (Anthro.); SUNY, Geneseo, 1966, MLS. **Orgs.:** ALA. **Pubns.:** *Incunables en Bibliotecas Columbianas* (forthcoming); various articles, exhibit cats. **Activities:** 1; 23, 24, 45; 63 **Addr.:** c/o School of Library and Information Science, SUNY, Geneseo, NY

Krakauer, Eleanor H. (Jn. 30, 1931, Corning, NY) Lib. Dir., AMC Cancer Resrch. Ctr. and Hosp., 1970–; Libn., N. St. Paul HS, 1969–70; Asst. Libn., Ramsey Cnty. Pub. Lib., 1962–69; Jr. Libn., Biomed. Lib., Univ. of MN, 1960–62; Bindery Libn., Syracuse Univ., Lib., 1956–58. **Educ.:** Roberts Wesleyan Coll., 1951–54, BA (Educ.) Syracuse Univ., 1954–56, MS (LS). **Orgs.:** Med. LA. CO Cncl. of Med. Libns.: Nom. Com. (1977–78); Un. List Com. (1978–81); Pres.–Elect (1980); Pres. (1981). **Pubns.:** Jt.-auth., *Abbreviations and Acronyms in Medicine and Nursing* (1976). **Activities:** 12; 17, 20, 39; 58, 60, 80 **Addr.:** 6401 West Colfax Ave., Lakewood, CO 80214.

Kramer, Cecile E. (Ja. 6, 1927, NY, NY) Dir., Med. Lib., Northwest. Univ., 1975–; Asst. Libn., Columbia Univ. Med. Lib., 1962–75, Asst. to the Libn., 1961–62. **Educ.:** Coll. of the City of NY, 1944–56, BS; Columbia Univ., 1956–60, MS (LS), 1962–(LS). **Orgs.:** Med. LA: Midwest Reg. Grp, Various coms. and ofcs. **Pubns.:** "Medical Library Collections," *ALA World Ency. of Lib. and Info. Srvs.* (1980). **Activities:** 1, 12; 15, 17, 34; 58, 75, 80 **Addr.:** Northwestern University Medical Library, 303 E. Chicago Ave, Chicago, IL 60611.

Kramer, Helen Tobaben (Walnut, KS) Head of Ref. Srvs., Pittsburgh State Univ., Lib., 1965–; Consult., Supvsr., Roux Distribution Corp., 1948–63. **Educ.:** KS State Coll., 1964, BS (Elem. Educ.); KS State Tchrs. Coll., 1965, MS (LS); Pittsburgh State Univ., 1977, MS (Elem. Educ.). **Orgs.:** ALA. KS LA: Coll. and Univ. Sect., Exec. Cncl. (1970–72). Altrusa. **Honors:** Phi Delta Kappa; Delta Kappa Gamma; Phi Alpha Theta; Pi Omega Pi; other hons. **Addr.:** Library, Pittsburgh State University, Pittsburgh, KS 66762.

Kramer, Lloyd A. (Ja. 21, 1924, Des Moines, IA) Assoc. Dir., CA State Univ., Long Beach, 1973–; VP for Admin., Coll. of St. Francis, 1972–73; Dir. of Libs., Lewis-St. Francis, 1971–72; Chief, Reader Srvs., CA State Polytech. Univ., 1963–70. **Educ.:** Univ. of CA, Berkeley, 1942–48, BA (Russ.), 1949–50, BLS; CA State Univ., Long Beach, 1974–79, MPA. **Orgs.:** CA LA. **Pubns.:** "The College Library and the Dropout," *Coll. and Resrch. Libs.* (Jl. 1968); "A Procedure for Dividing the Catalog," *Lib. Resrcs. and Tech. Srvcs.* (Spr. 1963). **Activities:** 1; 17, 35 **Addr.:** University Library, California State University, Long Beach, Long Beach, CA 90803.

Kranich, Nancy Carol (D. 26, 1950, York, PA) Dir., Admin. Srvs., NY Univ. Libs., 1980–, Resrch. & Dev. Libn., Asst. to the Dean, 1978–80, Head, Fine Arts Dept & Gen. Ref. Libn., Bridgeport (CT) Pub. Lib., 1974–76; Ref. & ILL Libn., Windsor (CT) Pub. Lib., 1974; Actg. Head and Asst. to the Libn., Madison (WI) Mncpl. Ref. Srvs. (1973–74); Head, Grad. Readg. Coll., Univ. of WI Memorial Lib., 1972–73. **Educ.:** Univ. of WI, 1968–72, BA (Anthro.), 1973–73, MA (LS); New York Univ., 1976–78, MPA (Pub. Admin.). **Orgs.:** ALA: Equal Access Com. (1978); ACRL Leg. Com. (1981–). NY LA: Ch., Coll. & Univ Lib. Sect. Legis. Com. (1978–); Coll. and Univ. Lib. Sect. Bd. (1978–). CT LA. New York Metro. Ref. and Resrch. Lib. Syst.: Legis. Com. Amer. Socty. for Pub. Admin. Leag. of Women Voters. **Honors:** Beta Phi Mu, 1974; U.S. Presidential Mgt. Intern finalist, 1978. **Pubns.:** "Fees for Library Service: They Are Not INEVITABLE!" *Lib. Jnl.* (May 1980); *Guide to Information Resources in Public Administration* (1977); Contrib., *Focus on Bridgeport* (1976); "Urban Libraries: A Strategy for Survival," *The Pub. Sector* (Spr. 1977); "Information Power... to the people" *Search:* Newsletter of the CT LA (Ag. 1975). **Activities:** 1, 9; 17, 28, 41; 59, 78, 92 **Addr.:** 320 W. 87th St., 1R, New York, NY 10024.

Krantz, Linda Law (Je. 19, 1943, Princeton, NJ) Dir., Rockbridge Reg. Lib., 1974–; Ref. Libn., Wright State Univ., 1969–73; Ref. Libn., Sci. and Tech., Cleveland Pub. Lib., 1968–69. **Educ.:** Univ. of Rochester, 1963–65, BA (Fr.); Rutgers Univ., 1965–67, MLS. **Orgs.:** ALA: Ref. and Subsrcpn. Bks. Review Com. (1977–81). VA LA. Rockbridge Cmnty. Orch. Rockbridge Cmnty. Chorus. Intl. Folk Dancers of Rockbridge Cnty. **Activities:** 9; 17; 55 **Addr.:** Rte. 4 Box 325, Lexington, VA 24450.

Krasean, Thomas K. (F. 21, 1940, South Bend, IN) Field Rep., IN Hist. Socty., 1977–; Dir., Byron R. Lewis Hist. Lib., Vincennes Univ., 1970–77; State Archvst., IN, IN State Lib., 1969–70, Field Rep., IN Div., 1965–69. **Educ.:** Kellogg Cmnty. Coll., 1958–60, AA (Hist.); East. MI Univ., 1962–63, BA (Hist.); West. MI Univ., 1964–65, MA (Hist.). **Orgs.:** IN State Lib. Staff Assn.: Pres. (1968–69). Socty. of IN Archvsts.: Sec/Treas. (1972–). Midwest Arch. Conf.: Past Cncl. Mem. (1972–). SAA: Com. on State and Local Records (1970). Oral Hist. Assn.: Educ. Com. (1969). Amer. Assn. for State and Local Hist. IN Oral Hist. Assn.: various coms. (1972–). IN Hist. Socty. Other orgs. **Pubns.:** *Guide to the Regional History Collection of the Byron R. Lewis Historical Library* (1974); Contrib., *The French, the Indians, and George Rogers Clark* (1977); Intro., *Local History Today* (1978); "Lewis Library Studies Great Depression," *The Recorder* (Mr. 1975); "Techniques of Oral History," *IN Military Hist. Jnl.* (July 1976); other articles. **Activities:** 2; 24, 39, 45; 55, 73, 85 **Addr.:** Indiana Historical Society, 315 West Ohio St., Indianapolis, IN 46202.

Krash, Ronald D. (Fb. 20, 1933, Akron, OH) Dir. of Libs., Univ. of MO, St. Louis, 1979– Dir. of Lib., State Lib. of PA, 1974–79; Assoc. Dir. St. Louis Univ. Lib. 1967–74. **Educ.:** Wayne State Univ., BS (Educ.), MLS. **Orgs.:** ALA. MO LA. Indep. Sch. Assn. **Pubns.:** *St. Louis Statistical Abstract* 1972–; *Black America: Research Bibliography* (1974); "Thomas Lynch Montgomery," *Lib. Biog.* (1979). **Activities:** 1; 15, 35, 39; 55, 92 **Addr.:** Thomas Jefferson Library, University of Missouri, 8001 Natural Bridge Rd., St. Louis, MO 63121.

Kraska, Daniel J. (O. 20, 1947, Buffalo, NY) Arch. Supvsr., FL State Arch., 1978–; Lcl. Rec. Spec., OH Hist. Socty., 1976–78; Instr., Cuyahoga Cmnty. Coll., 1973–76. **Educ.:** Canisius Coll., 1965–69, BA (Lang.); Purdue Univ., 1969–71, MA (Hist.); Case West. Rsv. Univ., 1972–78, PhD (Hist.). **Orgs.:** SAA. Amer. Assn. for State and Lcl. Hist. Assn. of Rec. Mgrs. and Admin. South. Hist. Assn. **Honors:** Phi Alpha Theta, Pubns. Awd., 1972. **Pubns.:** *Guide to Sources on the American Revolution Located in Ohio Libraries* (1976); "Government in the Sunshine: Freedom of Information in the US Congress," *Drexel Lib. Qtly.* (Win. 1979). **Activities:** 2; 15, 34, 38; 55, 59, 74 **Addr.:** Florida State Archives, Dept. of State, R. A. Gray Bldg., Tallahassee, FL 32304.

Kraske, Gary E. (Ja. 15, 1941, Billings, MT) Budget and Plng. Ofcr., Univ. of MD, 1980–; Asst. to Dean, Sr. Libn., IN State Univ., 1977–80; Spec. Ed., Resrch. Libn., Intl. Encyc. of Higher Educ., Northeastern Univ., 1974–76; Admin. Libn., US Army Spec. Srvs. Agency, Europe, 1967–72. **Educ.:** East. MT Coll., 1959–63, BS (Educ.); Univ. of WA, 1966–67, MLS; Northeastern Univ., 1975–76, MA (Hist.). **Orgs.:** ALA: LAMA/PR Sect. (1978–); LAMA Pubns. Com. (1980); Intl. Relat. RT, (Secy., Treas., 1979–); LHRT Nom. Com. (1980). **Honors** Beta Phi Mu. **Pubns.:** "Documentation and Information Centers on Higher Education," "International Directory of Documentation and Information Centers in Higher Education," *Intl. Encyc. of Higher Educ.* (1977); "International Organizations in Higher Education; A Survey of Their Library, Documentation, and Information Services," *Higher Educ.* (1979); "Pattern of Diversity: A Survey of Higher Education Information Resources in the United States," *World Higher Educ. Communique* (Je. 1980); "The British Council Libraries Abroad: A Modern Contribution to International Librarianship," *Libri* (1980). **Activities:** 1; 17, 37 **Addr.:** University of Maryland Libraries, College Park, MD 20742.

Kraus, Elizabeth W. (N. 12, 1918, Cornish, ME) Info. Assoc., Mgr. Libs., Eastman Kodak Co., 1958–; Libn., Natl. Resrch. Corp., 1952–58; Resrch. Asst., MA Inst. Tech., 1941–44. **Educ.:** Wellesley Coll., 1936–40, BA (Chem.); Simmons Coll., 1955–58, MS (LS). **Orgs.:** SLA: Chap. Pres.; Div. Ch. Assn. Info. Mgrs. Rochester Reg. Resrch. Lib. Cncl. Adv. Com.: (Ch., 1980–). Amer. Chem. Socty.: Asst. Ed., Lcl. pubn. (1961–63). Socty. Photographic Sci. and Engin.: Ed. Bd.; Abs. Srv. (1966–1971). **Pubns.:** *Guide to Metallurgical Information* (1961, 1965); *Bibliography on High-Speed Photography* (1965); *Guide to Photographic Information* (1973); *Current Bibliography on High-Speed Photography, 1964–1970* (1970); *Literature of Photographic Chemistry* (1968). ; 13, 29; 51, 55, 84. **Addr.:** Eastman Kodak Co., Research Laboratories, 1669 Lake Ave., Rochester, NY 14650.

Kraus, Joe W. (Ag. 31, 1917, Gorin, MO) Dir. of Libs., IL State Univ., 1966–; Dir. of Libs., KS State Univ., 1962–66; Libn., Head of Lib. Sci. Dept., Madison Coll., 1951–62; Asst. Libn., Tulane Univ., 1948–51; Libn., Westminster Coll., 1946–48; Instr. in Lib. Sci., Univ. of IL, 1946. **Educ.:** Culver-Stockton Coll., 1934–38, AB (Eng.); Univ. of IL, 1938–39, BSLS, 1939–41, MALS, 1957–60, PhD (Lib. Sci.). **Orgs.:** ALA: ACRL (Ch., Pub. in Libnshp. Bd., 1976–); Mono. Bd. (1972–76); Constn. and Bylaws Com. (1954–56, 1973–76); Lippincott Awd. Jury, (1972–73). IL LA: Pres. (1970–71). IL ACRL: Pres. (1979–80). **Pubns.:** *Messrs. Copeland & Day, 69 Cornhill, Boston, 1893–1899* (1979); "Comment" *Jrnl. of Lib. Hist.* (Fall 1978); "The Publication of William Allen White's *The Real Issue,*" *KS Hist. Qtly.* (Sum. 1977); "William Beer" and "Reuben Brooks Poole," *Dict. of Amer. Lib. Bio.* (1977); "The Publishing Activities of Way & Williams, Chicago, 1895–1898," *Papers of the Bibl. Socty. of Amer.* (1976). **Activities:** 1; 17, 42, 45 **Addr.:** 302 Mecherle Dr., Bloomington, IL 61701.

Krause, Mary Anna Sears (N. 20, 1921, Hutchins, TX) Selector for Anglo-Amer. Law, Harvard Law Sch. Lib., 1981–, Acq. Libn., 1970–81, Acq. Asst., 1966–70, Catlgr., 1961–65, Bibl. Asst., Widener Lib., Harvard Univ., 1945–51; Libn., U.S. Air Transport Cmnd., Dallas, 1943–45. **Educ.:** TX Womans Univ., 1938–41, BA (LS); AALL, 1976, Cert. **Orgs.:** New Eng. Law Libns. AALL. **Activities:** 1, 4; 15, 20, 46; 56, 77, 78 **Addr.:** 1 Stonehill Dr., Stoneham, MA 02180.

Kreger, Louise Parker (D. 20, 1945, Cartersville, GA) Dir., Darien Lib., 1979–; Head, Adult Srvs., Westport Pub. Lib., 1975–79; Sr. Libn., New York Pub. Lib., 1974–75, Libn., 1972–74; Circ. Supvsr., MI State Univ. Lib., 1969–71. **Educ.:** Univ. of NM, 1968–69, BA (Eng.); Columbia Univ., 1971–72, MS (LS); Cmnty. Analysis Inst., 1975–76, Cert.; Mktg. for Libs., 1979, Cert. **Orgs.:** ALA: RASD, Cat. Use Com. (1974–78), Stan. Com. (1979–83); LAMA, Stats. for Ref. Srvs. Com. (1977–81), Bylaws Com. (Ch., 1981–83); Mem. Com., (CT State Ch., 1979–81). CT LA. New Eng. LA. Fairfield Cnty. Lib. Admin. Grp. Columbia Univ. Lib. Sch. Alum. Assn.: Pres. (1978–79); VP (1977–78); Bd. of Dir. (1974–77). **Pubns.:** Jt. auth., *The Library in Transition: A Study of the Westport Public Library* (1976); Contrib., *Commercial Com Catalogs: How to Choose, When to Buy* (1978); Jt. auth., "Better Service Through Community Analysis," *CT Libs.* (Sum. 1979). **Activities:** 9; 16, 17, 24; 92 **Addr.:** Darien Library, Darien, CT 06820.

Kreider, Janice (D. 29, 1942, Wauseon, OH) Ref. Libn., Douglas Coll., 1977–; Ref. Libn., SUNY, Geneseo, 1972–75; Libn., Phys., Astr., Columbia Univ., 1968–71. **Educ.:** Goshen Coll., 1960–64, BA (Math.), IN Univ., 1965–68, MAT (Math.), MLS. **Orgs.:** SLA. Can. LA. Congregational LA of BC. **Pubns.:** "A Bibliography of Library Planning," *Plng. the Spec. Lib.* (1972). **Activities:** 1; 31, 39 **Addr.:** 4090 W. 31st Ave., Vancouver, BC V6S 1Y6 Canada.

Kreilick, Kristine R. (Ja. 21, 1951, Kalamazoo, MI) Assoc. Law Libn., St. Louis Univ. Law Lib., 1977–. **Educ.:** Valparaiso Univ., 1969–73, BA (Hist.), 1973–76, JD; Univ. of WA, 1976–77, MLL (Law Libnshp.). **Orgs.:** AALL: Com. on Rel. with Publshrs. (1979–81). Mid-Amer. Assn. of Law Libs: Prog. Com. (Ch., 1981 Mtg.). Amer. Bar Assn. MO Bar Assn. **Honors:** Mortar Bd. **Addr.:** St. Louis University Law Library, 3700 Lindell Blvd., St. Louis, MO 63108.

Kreilkamp, Hermes Donald (Ap. 8, 1923, Milwaukee, WI) Asst. Head Libn., St. Joseph's Coll., 1976–; Resrch. Asst., CLENE, Catholic Univ., 1975–76; Assoc. Prof. of Hist. and Phil., St. Joseph's Coll., 1967–78; Assoc. Prof. of Philo., Capuchin Sem. of St. Mary, 1959–69. **Educ.:** Pontifical Oriental Inst., Rome, 1949–51, SEOL (Theo.); Catholic Univ. of America, 1952–63, PhD (Hist.), Catholic Univ., 1966, MA (Eng. Lit), 1975–76, MLS. **Orgs.:** Cont. Lib. Educ. Ntwk. and Exch.: Rules Com. (1977–78). Northern IN Area Lib. Srvcs. Auth.: Cont. Educ. Com. (1977–79). ALA. Nat. Libn. Assn. IN LA. Amer. Hist. Assn. N. Amer. Acad. of Ecumenists. IN Phil. Assn. **Honors:** Beta Phi Mu, 1976. **Pubns.:** "National Agricultural Library's Data Base: AGRICOLA," *Coll. & Resrch. Libs.* (Jl. 1977); *Complete List of Citations/Annotated Bibliography of Recent Continuing Library Education Literature* (microfiche) (1976). **Activities:** 1; 17, 29, 39; 55, 90, 92 **Addr.:** 114 North College Ave., Rensselaer, IN 47978.

Kreissman, Bernard (Je. 17, 1919, New York, NY) Univ. Libn., Univ. of CA, Davis, 1974–; Chief Libn., City Coll. of NY, 1962–74; Asst. Dir. of Libs. for Hum., Univ. of NE-Lincoln, 1954–62. **Educ.:** City Coll. of New York, 1936–39, 1946–48, BSS (Eng. Lit.), 1948–49, MA (Eng. Lit); Columbia Univ., 1953–54, MLS (LS); Univ. of NE, 1960–62, PhD (Eng. Lit.). **Orgs.:** ALA: ACRL, Urban Univ. Libs. Com. (1962–69; Ch., 1967–69); LAD, Bldgs. for Coll. and Univ. Libs. (1964–68, 1974–78; Ch. 1967–68); LAMA/Building & Equip. Sect. (Exec. Com., 1978–80; Ch. 1980–81). CA Lib. Athrty. for Syst. & Srvs.: Plng. Com. (1974–76); Governance Com. (1974–76), Interim Plng. Com. (1976); Congs. of Mem. (Ch., 1977–). CA State Lib. Adv. Cncl. on Libs. Archons of Colophon: Conv. (1971–72). UNESCO Consult., Lib. of the Universidad de Oriente, Venez., Ap., My. 1980. Columbia Univ. Schl. of Lib. Srv., Alumni Pres., 1969–70. Sierra Club. **Honors:** Grolier Scholar, Rutgers Univ. Grad. Sch. of LS, 1956. **Pubns.:** Jt. auth., *The Naval War College Libraries - A Management Survey* (1967); Ed., *Sir Walter Scott's Life of*

Special Subjects/Services: 50. Adult educ.; 51. Advert./Mktg.; 52. Aerosp.; 53. Agric.; 54. Area std.; 55. Arts/Hum.; 56. Autom.; 57. Bibl./Prtg.; 58. Bio. sci.; 59. Bus./Fin.; 60. Chem.; 61. Copyrt.; 62. Documtn.; 63. Educ.; 64. Engin.; 65. Env.; 66. Eth. grps.; 67. Film; 68. Food/Nutr.; 69. Geneal.; 70. Geo.; 71. Geol.; 72. Handcpd.; 73. Hist.; 74. Int. frdm.; 75. Info. sci.; 76. Insr.; 77. Law; 78. Legis.; 79. Math./Comp. sci.; 80. Med.; 81. Metals; 82. Nat. resrcs.; 83. Newsp.; 84. Nuc. sci.; 85. Oral hist.; 86. Petr./Energy; 87. Pharm.; 88. Phys./Astr./Math.; 89. Readg.; 90. Relig.; 91. Sci./Tech.; 92. Soc. sci.; 93. Telecom.; 94. Transp.; 95. (other).

John Dryden (1963); *Pamela-Shamela: A Study of the Criticisms, Burlesques, Parodies and Adaptations of Richardson's "Pamela"* (1960); "Zero Growth," Symposium Respondent, *Jnl. of Acad. Libnshp.* (N. 1975); "Gems for Research," *The NE Alum.* (S. 1965); other articles. **Addr.:** 108 Shields Library, University of California, Davis, CA 95616.

Krelizer, Sr. Mary Rosella (Ja. 4, 1912, Spokane, WA) Media/Curric. Libn., Cath. Educ. Ctr., 1979–; Libn., Mt. Mary Coll., 1969–72, 1977–79; Head Libn. N. Amer. Coll. (Rome), 1972–77; Ref. Libn., Gonzaga Univ., 1964–69. **Educ.:** Holy Name Coll., Spokane, 1939–41, BA (Eng.); Univ. of Portland, 1961–65, MLS. **Orgs.:** ALA. Cath. LA. **Activities:** 10, 12; 20, 32, 39 **Addr.:** Catholic Education Center, 328 W. 6th St., St. Paul, MN 55102.

Kremer, Jill (My. 26, 1947, Lynchburg, VA) Dir., TF Jenkins Meml. Law Lib., 1974–; Adj. Prof., LS, Drexel Univ., 1977–; Chief Libn., U.S. Ct. of Appeals, 3rd Circuit, 1973–74; Asst. Libn., Morgan, Lewis and Bockius, 1970–72. **Educ.:** Univ. of NC, 1965–69, BFA (Art Educ.); Univ. of Denver, 1969–70, MA (LS); AALL, 1979, Cert. **Orgs.:** AALL: Various coms. Grt. Philadelphia Law LA: Pres. (1977–78), various coms. **Addr.:** 516 Conshohocken State Rd., Bala Cynwyd, PA 19004.

Krettek, J. Germaine (N. 18, 1907, Council Bluffs, IA) Retired; Assoc. Exec. Dir., ALA, 1962–72, Dir., ALA, WA Ofc., 1957–72; Head, Circ. Dept., Council Bluffs, IA, Pub. Lib., 1939–41, Head, Ref. Dept., 1941–48, Chief Libn., 1948–57. **Educ.:** Coll. of St. Elizabeth, Convent, NJ, 1925–29, AB; Univ. of Denver, 1942, BS (LS); Coll. of St. Elizabeth, 1969, Hon. Doctor of Laws. **Orgs.:** Cath. LA. IA LA. Frnds. of Cncl. Bluffs Pub. Lib.: Exec. Bd. (1976). ALA: Lib. Dev. Com.; Fed. Rel. Com.; Cncl. Rep. from IA; Staff Liaison, Legis. Com. Altrusa Intl.: WA, DC Treas. (1959–61); Cncl. Bluffs Adult Lit. Com. (1979–). PEO Sisterhood: Rec. Secty. (1942–). City Plng. Comsn. of Cncl. Bluffs, IA (1952–57). Task Grp. on Lib. Prog. of the Com. on Sci. and Tech. Info. (1969–). **Honors:** Univ. of Denver, Grad. Sch. of Libnshp., Outstan. Alum. Awd., 1964; Drexel Inst. of Tech., Disting. Achvmt. Awd., 1967; Joseph J. Lippincott Awd., Disting. Srv. in Prof. of Libnshp., 1969. **Pubns.:** "The Role of the Trustee in the Public Library System in the United States," *Frankfurt em Main Stadtsbibliothek* (My. 1970); "What you should know about library insurance," *Lib. Jnl.* (O. 1957); "The changing focus of libraries," *Cath. Lib. World* (S. 1969); jt. auth., "Government activities for library development," *Lib. Trends* (O. 1961); Contrib., *Encyc. of Lib. & Info. Sci.* (1975); various articles. **Activities:** 9, 12, 13; 17, 36, 39; 78 **Addr.:** 717 Fifth Ave., Council Bluffs, IA 51501.

Krieger, Clarence Robert (Ap. 9, 1917, Hastings, NE) Plans, Maps, Docum. and Hist. Photo. Resrch. Coord., CA Dept. of Transportation, 1944–, Supvsr. of Drafting Srvs., 1957–, Sr. Delineator, 1946–57, Delineator, 1944–46. **Educ.:** CA State Univ., Sacramento, 1946–60, (Hist. Sci.). **Orgs.:** Western Assn. of Map Libs. CA Remote Sensing Cncl. Socty. of CA Archvsts. Map Socty. of CA. Westerners Hist. Socty. Sacramento Cnty. Hist. Socty. **Pubns.:** "Maps in Our Everyday Life" (1972). **Activities:** 12; 15, 18, 24; 62, 70, 94 **Addr.:** Department of Transportation, 1120 N St., Room 2450, Sacramento, CA 95814.

Krieger, Tillie (Detroit, MI) Prof., Sch. of Lib. and Info. Sci., LA State Univ., 1981–; Actg. Dir., Lib. Srvs., Boys Town Ctr. for the Std. of Youth Dev., 1979–81; Dir., Law Class. Proj., Law Lib., Univ. of IL, 1976–79; Instr. (LS), 1975–76, Resr. Assoc., Lib. Resrch. Ctr., 1974–75; Libn., Progmr., MARC Dev. Ofc., Lib. of Congs., 1971–74; Resrch. Assoc., Natl. Serials Pilot Proj., ARL, 1970–71; Head, Acq., AZ State Univ. Lib., 1968–70; Various other positions in libnshp. **Educ.:** Univ. of CA, Los Angeles, 1962, AB (Hist.); Univ. of South. CA, 1964, MLS; Univ. of IL, 1981, PhD. **Orgs.:** ALA: ACRL/Law and Pol. Sci. Sect. (Ch., 1979–80). ASIS. SLA. **Pubns.:** *Subject Headings for Law and International Law and Index to the K Schedules of the Library of Congress* 3d. ed. (1981); *Interim Index to the Library of Congress, Class KF, Law of the United States* (1968); various articles in Prof. Jnls. **Activities:** 1, 5; 15, 17, 20; 56, 77, 90 **Addr.:** School of Library and Information Science, Louisiana State University, Baton Rouge, LA 70803.

Krikelas, James (D. 17, 1932, Cudahy, WI) Assoc. Prof. (LS), Univ. of WI, 1967–; Libn., Milwaukee-Downer Coll., 1959–63. **Educ.:** Univ. of WI, 1956–58, BS (Hist.), 1958–59, MS (LS); Univ. of IL, 1963–67, PhD (LS). **Orgs.:** ASIS. AALS. **Pubns.:** *Centralized Processing for Public Libraries in Wisconsin* (1970); *Library Statistics and State Agencies: A Comparative Study of Three States* (1968); Jt. auth., "General vs. Specialized Library Education" in *Targets for Resrch. in Lib. Educ.* (1973); "Catalog Use Studies and Their Implications" in *Adv. in Libnshp.*, Vol. 3 (1972). Other articles and rpts. **Activities:** 26; 56, 75 **Addr.:** Library School, University of Wisconsin, 600 N. Park St., Madison, WI 53706.

Kritzer, Hyman William (N. 9, 1918, New York, NY) Dir. of Libs., Kent State Univ., 1966–; Asst. Dir. of Libs., OH State Univ., 1962–66, Head, Acq. Dept., 1960–62; Univ. of MD, 1959–60; Univ. of Notre Dame, 1957–59. **Educ.:** American Univ., 1951–52, BS; Inst. des Etudes Pol., (Paris), 1952–53; Catholic Univ., 1954–58, MSLS. **Orgs.:** OH Coll. Lib. Ctr.: Brd. of Trustees (1969–73); Ch. (1970–72). ALA. OH LA. OH Coll. Assn. Rowfant. **Activities:** 1; 15 **Addr.:** Kent State Univ. Lib., Kent, OH 44242.

Kritzler, Charles A. (Ag. 13, 1932, Brooklyn, NY) Prin. AV Libn., Hennepin Cnty. Lib., 1977–, Asst. Prof./Asst. Dean, LS, SUNY, Geneseo, 1973–77; Asst. Prof./Dir., Instr. Media Ctr., C. W. Post Ctr., Long Island Univ., 1971–73; Assoc. Dir., Univ. Media Srvs., Boston Univ., 1968–71; Dir., AV Ctr., South. CT State Coll., 1964–68; Catlgr., West. Americana, Yale Univ. Lib., 1962–63; AV Coord./Dir./Tchr., Locust Valley HS, 1959–62. **Educ.:** SUNY, Albany, 1956–59, BS (Bus. Educ.); Long Island Univ., 1960–62, MS (LS); Univ. of CT, 1962–68, Cert. (Educ.). **Orgs.:** ALA: LITA, AV Util. Com. (1978–); LAMA, Stats. for Non-Print Media Com. (1980–). **Pubns.:** Jt. cmplr., *Catalogue of the Frederick W. and Carrie S. Beinecke Collection of Western Americana* (1965). **Activities:** 9; 32; 93 **Addr.:** Hennepin County Library, 7009 York Ave. S., Edina, MN 55435.

Krivatsy, Nati H. (Budapest, Hungary) Ref. Libn., The Folger Shakespeare Lib., 1973–, Sr. Catlgr., 1957–73; Libn., Lib. of Parlmt., Budapest, 1945–49. **Educ.:** Pazmany Univ. of Budapest, 1944–48, PhD (Art Hist.); Cath. Univ. of Amer., 1962–65, MSLS. **Orgs.:** Bibl. Socty. of Amer. ALA. **Honors:** Beta Phi Mu. **Pubns.:** "Two Unique STC Books at the Folger Shakespeare Library," *Gutenberg Jahrbuch* (1979); "Walsingham's Copy of Bailey's *Brief Discourse*," *The Library* (1979); "Herbert of Cherbury's *De Veritate* (1633) Given to Leiden Professor by English Pupil," *Quaerendo* (Spr. 1976); reviews. **Activities:** 12; 39, 41, 45; 55, 62 **Addr.:** The Folger Shakespeare Library, Washington, DC 20003.

Krober, Alfred C. (Ag. 31, 1941, McPherson, KS) Dir. of Lib. Srvs., Roberts Wesleyan Coll., 1971–; Ref. Libn., Greenville Coll., 1966–68, Catlgr., 1965–66. **Educ.:** Greenville Coll., 1959–63, BS (Chem.); Univ. of IL, 1963–65, MS (LS). **Orgs.:** ALA. Assn. of Christ. Libns: *Christ. Per. Index* Ed. Com. (1971–). NY LA. Pearce Meml. Free Meth. Church. Urban Leag. Rochester Reg. Resrch. Cncl.: Adv. Cncl. (1971–). **Activities:** 1; 15, 17 **Addr.:** Keating Library/Roberts Wesleyan College, 2301 Westside Dr., Rochester, NY 14624.

Kroeker, Renata (Ap. 11, 1923, Russia) Lib. Consult., Rena's Lib. Consult., 1977–; Lib. Consult., Man. Assn. of Reg. Nurses, 1971–77; Grace Gen. Hosp., 1974; Concordia Gen. Hosp., 1975–79; Manitoba Hlth. Org., 1978; Ref. Libn., Univ. of Manitoba, 1950–56. **Educ.:** Univ. of Saskatchewan, 1947–49, BA (Hist.); McGill Univ., 1949–50, BLS; Univ. of Saskatchewan, Tchg. Cert. **Orgs.:** MB Hlth. Libs. Assn.: Pres. (1976–78). Union List of Serials Com. (1978). **Pubns.:** "Birth & Growth of the Manitoba Health Libraries Association" (1979). **Addr.:** Rena's Library Consultant Services, 230 Yale Ave., Winnipeg, MB R3M 0L9 Canada.

Krogh, Elva Leonora (D. 9, 1898, Farwell, NE) Retired, Lib. of Congs., 1968–, Asst. Chief, Decimal Class. Ofc., 1964–68, Prin. Decimal Class., 1960–64, Decimal Class. Descr. Cat. Sect., Subj. Cat. Div., 1938–60; Libn., Works Proj. Admin. Lib., 1936–38; Catlgr., Univ. of IL Lib., 1930–36. **Educ.:** Univ. of NE, 1918–22, AB (Latin, Fr.); Univ. of IL, 1932–36, BS (LS), AM (Anglo-Saxon Philology). **Orgs.:** ALA: Can. on Cat. and Class. (Ch., 1950–52). DC LA. **Pubns.:** "Decimal Classification Offices in the Library of Congress," *DC Libs.* (1953); contrib., "Add to" concept adopted in *Dewey Decimal Classification* Ed. 18. **Addr.:** 200 Glenwood Cir. #523, Monterey, CA 93940.

Kroll, H. Rebecca (Ap. 30, 1948, Ottawa, ON) Head of Interlib. Loan, SUNY, Buffalo, 1974–, Asst. Interlib. Loan Libn., 1973–74. **Educ.:** Univ. of Toronto, 1970, BA (Mod. Lang.); SUNY, Buffalo, 1970–73, MLS, 1975–80, MBA (Mgt.). **Orgs.:** ALA: RASD/Interlib. Loan Com. (Ch., 1978–80). SUNY LA: Secy. (1978–80). **Activities:** 1; 17, 34 **Addr.:** Lockwood Memorial Library, Room 236, Interlibrary Loan Department, State University of New York at Buffalo, Buffalo, NY 14260.

Kroll, Susan M. (S. 13, 1951, New York, NY) Libn., Bendix Indus. Grp. Resrch. Div., 1980–; Sr. Asst. Libn., SUNY, Buffalo, 1976–80; Asst. Libn., Roswell Park Meml. Inst., 1975–76. **Educ.:** SUNY Coll., Buffalo, 1971–73, BS (Excep. Educ.); SUNY, Buffalo, 1974–75, MLS. **Orgs.:** ALA: JMRT, Anl. Conf. Com. (1978–80). SLA: Buffalo Area Cootd. (1976–7), Nom. Com. (1976–77), Netwk. Com. (Ch., 1979–80). NY LA. SLA. **Pubns.:** Ed., *NETLET* (SLA Networking Nsltr.) (1979–); ed., *Physics/Astronomy Mathematics Directory* **Activities:** 1, 12; 15, 32, 39; 58, 80, 88 **Addr.:** 2814 E. Overlook, Cleveland Heights, OH 44118.

Kromnick, Philip Joseph (D. 19, 1949, New York, NY) Info. Mgt. Consult., Nolan Info. Srvs., 1981–; Prog. Off., Nat. Info. Ctr. for Educ. Media, 1977–81; Media Spec., Dept. of Educ. Media and Tech., Montgomery Cnty., MD Pub. Schs., 1974–76. **Educ.:** American Univ., 1968–71, BA (Hist.); Univ. of MD, 1973–74, MLS. **Orgs.:** ASIS. **Honors:** Beta Phi Mu, 1974. **Pubns.:** *NICEM Indexes to Non-print Educational Media; NICSEM Special Education Indexes.* **Activities:** 12; 17, 24, 37; 51, 62, 63 **Addr.:** 6313 1/2 Ocean Front Walk, Playa del Rey, CA 90291.

Krompart, Janet A. (Ja. 30, 1927, Los Angeles, CA) Assoc. Prof.; various positions, including Actg. Dean, in Colleaquial syst., Oakland Univ., 1969–; Chief, Current Serials; Korean Biblgphr., Chinese Biblgphr., E. Asiatic Lib., Univ. of CA, Berkeley, 1956–68. **Educ.:** Univ. of CA, Berkeley, 1946–48, AB (Pol. Soc.), 1962–64, MLS; Univ. of MI, 1973–79, MA (Chinese). **Orgs.:** ALA: ACRL, Secy., Asian and African Sect. (1979–82). MI LA: Secy., Tech. Srvs. Div. (1975–76). NLA. Assn. for Asian Std. MI Acad. of Sci., Arts, and Letters. **Pubns.:** *A Personal Name Index to Biographical Dictionary of Republican China*, Vol. 5 of *Biographical Dictionary of Republican China* (1967–79). **Activities:** 1; 17, 20, 39 **Addr.:** 243 West Tienken Rd., Rochester, MI 48063.

Kronebusch, John Jacob (S. 28, 1943, Austin, MN) Recs. Mgt. Spec., Pub. Docum. Rm., U.S. Nuclear Regulatory Comsn., 1980–; Coord. of Autom. Prcs., Tech. Info. Srvs., Inst. for Defense Anal., 1974–80; Info. sci. assistant, Univ. of Pittsburgh, 1969–73; Math. instr., St. Procopius Coll., 1968–69; Northern IL Univ., 1967–68. **Educ.:** St. Mary's Coll., 1961–65, BA (Math.); Northern IL Univ., 1965–67, MS (Math.); Univ. of Pittsburgh, 1969–74, (Info. sci.). **Orgs.:** ALA. ASIS. SLA: Aerospace Div. Mem. Dir. Com. (1977–79). Math. Assn. of Amer. **Pubns.:** "Curricula in Information Science: Four Year Progress Report" (Ja. 1975); "Curricula in Information Science" (Fall 1974). **Activities:** 12; 17, 26, 38; 59, 75, 88 **Addr.:** 4526 Kingsley Rd., Woodbridge, VA 22193.

Kronenfeld, Michael R. (N. 15, 1949, Coral Gables, FL) Dir., Educ. Rsrc. Ctr., SC Dept. of Hlth. and Env. Control, 1981–; Pub. Hlth. Libn., Univ. of AL, Birmingham, 1978–; Prcs., Papers of Senator Lister Hill, Hlth. Sci. Lib., Univ. of AL, 1975–78. **Educ.:** Duke Univ., 1967–71, BA (Hist.); Univ. of RI, 1973–75, MLS; Univ. of AL, Birmingham, 1975–79, MBA; Med. LA, 1978–, Cert. **Orgs.:** Med. LA. AL LA: Int. Frdm. Com. Amer. Pub. Hlth. Assn. **Honors:** Beta Phi Mu. **Pubns.:** "The Effect of Inflation upon the Cost of Journals in the Brandon List," *Bltn. Med. LA* (Ja. 1980); "Evaluation of Xerox 6500 Color Photocopy Machine," *Bltn. Med. LA* (O. 1979); "Gutenberg Medical Institute," *AL Jnl. of Med. Sci.* (O. 1979); "Southern Medical College," *AL Jnl. of Med. Sci.* (Jl., 1979); "The Impact of Inflation on Journal Costs," *Lib. Jnl.* (Ap. 1, 1981); Other articles. **Activities:** 1, 12; 17, 39, 41; 59, 75, 80 **Addr.:** South Carolina Department of Health and Environmental Control–Library, 2600 Bull St., Columbia, SC 29201.

Kronick, David A. (O. 5, 1917, Connelsville, PA) Lib. Dir., Univ. of TX Hlth. Sci. Ctr., 1965–; Chief, Ref. Srvs., Nat. Lib. of Med., 1963–65; Dir., Cleveland Med. Lib., 1959–63; Med. Libn., Univ. of MI, 1955–59. **Educ.:** Western Reserve Univ., 1936–40, BSLS; Univ. of Chicago, 1950–53, PhD (Libnshp.). **Orgs.:** Med. LA: Jrnl. Bus. Mgr. (1959–62); Brd. (1961–63). ALA. ASIS. Amer. Assn. for the Hist. of Med. Hist. of Sci. Socty. **Honors:** Cncl. on Lib. Resrcs., Resrch. Flwshp., 1972. **Pubns.:** *History of the Scientific Technical Periodical* (1976); "Indexing of Early Scientific Periodicals," *Serials Libn.* (1979); "Authorship and Authority," *Lib. Qtly.* (1978). **Activities:** 1; 17, 31, 41; 58, 80, 91 **Addr.:** University of Texas Health Science Center, 7703 Floyd Curl Dr., San Antonio, TX 78284.

Krubeck, Ralph David (My. 13, 1929, Chicago, IL) Coord., Qual. Assurance Field Data Syst., Sears Roebuck and Co., 1969–, Oper. Anal., Nat. Field Oper., 1964–69. **Educ.:** Univ. of IL, Champaign, 1950–52, BS (Jrnlsm.). **Orgs.:** ASIS. Assn. for Syst. Mgt. Amer. Socty. for Qual. Cont. **Pubns.:** "Training the Business Information User," "Training the Business Information Specialist," 1971 Intl. Conf. on Training for Info. Work. (1972). Cons. Returns Anal. Sort of Hist. Data, Comp. Sci. Conf. OH State Univ. (1972). **Activities:** 12; 24, 41, 46; 56, 64, 75 **Addr.:** Route #2 Box 251, Mt. Carroll, IL 61053.

Krueger, Gerald J. (N. 11, 1935, Two Rivers, WI) Gvt. Docum. Libn., Univ. of WI, Oshkosh, 1965–. **Educ.:** Univ. of WI, Oshkosh, 1957, BS (Chem.); Univ. of Denver, 1964–65, MA (LS). **Orgs.:** ALA. WI LA: Docum. Srv. Sect. (Ch., 1982). Elks. Rotary. **Honors:** Univ. of WI, Undergrad. Tchg. Improvement Grant, 1977. **Activities:** 1; 17, 29, 39 **Addr.:** Polk Library, University of Wisconsin, Oshkosh, WI 54901.

Krueger, Mabre (S. 26, 1914, Potomac, IL) Head Libn., Jackson Cmnty. Coll., 1966–; Libn., Addison HS, 1961–66; Libn., Huron Valley Sch. Syst., 1955–60. **Educ.:** Univ. of IL, 1932–35, BA (Eng.), 1935–36, MA (Eng.); Univ. of MI, 1954–55, MALS. **Orgs.:** ALA. Natl. Educ. Assn. MI Educ. Assn. **Honors:** Phi Beta Kappa. **Addr.:** 31 Crystal Lake, Cement City, MI 49233.

Krug, Judith F. (Mr. 15, 1940, Pittsburgh, PA) Exec. Dir., Frdm. to Read Fndn., 1969–; Dir., Ofc. for Int. Frdm., ALA, 1967–, Resrch. Anal., 1965–67; Catlgr., Northwest. Univ., Dental Sch., 1963–65; Ref. Libn., John Crerar Lib., 1962–63. **Educ.:** Univ. of Pittsburgh, 1958–61, BA (Pol. Theory); Univ. of Chicago, 1961–64, MA (LS). Chicago Area Phi Beta Kappa: Exec. Com. (1970–73, 1980–). Amer. Cvl. Liberties Un.: IL Div., Bd. of Dirs. (1976–79). **Honors:** Amer. Booksellers Assn., Irita Van Doren Bk. Awd., 1976; Univ. of IL, Robert B. Downs Awd., 1978; Amer. Cvl. Liberties Un., Harry Kalven Frdm. of Expression Awd., 1976; Beta Phi Mu. **Pubns.:** "In Defense of Liberty:

PROFESSIONAL ACTIVITIES: Institutions: 1. Acad. lib.; 2. Arch.; 3. Assn.; 4. Fed./Gvt. lib.; 5. Inst. lib.; 6. Mfr./Suppl.; 7. Milit. lib.; 8. Musm.; 9. Pub. lib.; 10. Sch. lib.; 11. Sch. of lib. sci.; 12. Spec. lib.; 13. State lib.; 14. (other). **Functions/Activities:** 15. Acq./Col. dev.; 16. Adult srvs.; 17. Admin.; 18. Apprais.; 19. Archit./Bldgs.; 20. Cat./Class.; 21. Chld. srvs.; 22. Circ.; 23. Cons./Pres.; 24. Consult.; 25. Cont. ed.; 26. Educ. lib. sci.; 27. Ext. srvs.; 28. Fund/Grants; 29. Gvt. pubs.; 30. Indx./Abs.; 31. Instr. lib. use; 32. Media srvs.; 33. Micro.; 34. Netwks./Coop.; 35. Persnl.; 36. PR; 37. Publshg.; 38. Recs. mgt.; 39. Ref. srvs.; 40. Repro.; 41. Resrch.; 42. Review.; 43. Secur.; 44. Serials; 45. Spec. col.; 46. Tech. srvs.; 47. Trustees/Bds.; 48. YA srvs.; 49. (other).

Extremism and Other Vices," *Rep. Amer. Sps.* (1975–76); "Libraries and Censorship," *Update* (1981); "The Speaker . . . A Film About Freedom" 16 mm film (1977); "Freedom in America: The Two-Century Record" snd. filmstp. (1978); "Libraries and Censorship," *Update* (Spr. 1981); various articles, chaps. **Activities:** 1, 3; 20, 25, 41; 74 **Addr.:** 2770 Sheridan Rd., Evanston, IL 60201.

Kruger, Kathleen Joyce (Portland, OR) Asst. Cat. Libn., CO State Univ. Libs., 1974–; Night Supvsry. libn., Cmnty. Coll. of Denver, N. Campus, 1974; Cat. Libn., Lib. of Congs., 1968–72. **Educ.:** Portland State Univ., 1963–67, BA (Soc. Std., Arts and letters); Univ. of Denver, 1967–68, MA (Libnshp.). **Orgs.:** ALA. Msc. LA. CO LA. **Pubns.:** Jt. Cmplr., "Imaginary War Fiction in Colorado State University Libraries; bibliography," *Bltn. of Bibl.* (1978); "Subject Headings and Semantics," *Lib. Scene* (1977). **Activities:** 1; 20 **Addr.:** 1625 W. Elizabeth St., J-4, Fort Collins, CO 80521.

Kruger, Linda Markson (S. 11, 1936, Elmira, NY) Catlgr. of Rare Books, Columbia Univ., 1979–; Consult., Art and Rare Book Col., 1970–75; Reclass. Libn., Montclair State Coll., 1968–69; Libn., Carl F. Pforzheimer Rare Book Lib., 1965–67; Libn., Fndn. Ctr., 1964–65; Indxr., Art Indx., H. W. Wilson Co., 1964; Cur., Rose Art Musm., Brandeis Univ., 1959–62. **Educ.:** Univ. of VT, 1954–58, AB (Eng. Lit. & Eur. Hist.); Boston Univ., 1960–64, AM (Art Hist.); Columbia Univ., 1963–65, MSLS, 1970–80, DLS (18th c. Amer. Hist.). **Orgs.:** ALA: Rare Book and Mrss. Sect. Amer. Prtg. Hist. Assn. Lib. Co. of Philadelphia. New-York Hist. Socty. Victorian Socty. in Amer.: Pres., Northern NJ Chap. (1979–80). William Morris Socty. **Honors:** HEW, Title II-B Flwshp., 1969–72; NY Lib. Club, Schol., 1963. **Activities:** 1; 20, 45; 57 **Addr.:** Columbia University, Butler Library, Room 320, New York City, NY 10027.

Krull, Jeffrey R. (Ag. 29, 1948, North Tonawanda, NY) Dir., Mansfield-Richland Cnty. Pub. Lib., 1978–; Head Libn., OH Univ., Chillicothe, 1976–78; Ref. Libn., Buffalo and Erie Cnty. Pub. Lib., 1973–76. **Educ.:** Williams Coll., 1966–70, BA (Eng.); SUNY, Buffalo, 1972–73, MLS. **Orgs.:** ALA. OH LA: Org. Com. (1978–79); Ch. (1980). Rotary Intl.: Career Ed. Com. (1979–). **Honors:** Beta Phi Mu. **Activities:** 9; 17, 19, 23 **Addr.:** Mansfield-Richland County Public Library, 43 W. Third St., Mansfield, OH 44902.

Krumholz, Virginia E. (Je. 29, 1931, Evanston, IL) Dir., Arch., Roman Cath. Dio. of Cleveland, OH, 1979–; Asst. to the Archvst., Case West. Rsv. Univ., 1975–79. **Educ.:** Univ. of MO, 1950–52, BA (Jnlsm.); Case West. Rsv. Univ., 1973–75, MA (Hist., Arch. Admin.). **Orgs.:** SAA: Bus. Arch. (1975–77); Relig. Arch. (1979–). Assn. Recs. Mgrs. and Admins. Socty. OH Archvsts. **Activities:** 2; 15, 17, 24; 66, 90 **Addr.:** 3001 Chadbourne Rd., Shaker Heights, OH 44120.

Krumm, Carol Mae Rhodeback (Jn. 17, 1923, Pataskala, OH) Libn. for Tech. Srvs., Plng., Spec. Proj., OH State Univ. Libs., 1980–, Head, Serial Holdings Conversion, 1976–79, Head, Bibl. Recs., 1972–76, Head, Cat. Maintenance and Card Prod., 1971–72, Cat. Maintenance Libn., 1965–71, Catlgr., 1959–65; Serials Catlgr., Cleveland Pub. Lib., 1957–58; Other positions in Libnshp., 1946–1957. **Educ.:** Capital Univ., 1941–45, BA (Bible, Eng.); Case West. Rsv. Univ., 1945–46, BS (LS). **Orgs.:** ALA. OH LA: OH Lib. Dev. Com. (1976–77); Meals Ch., Anl. Conf. (1980). Franklin Cnty. LA. Other orgs. OH State Univ. Fac. Women's Club. Kiwanikwee. **Pubns.:** "Conversion of Serial Holdings to On-Line Automated Library Control System at the Ohio State University Libraries," Supplement to *Serials Libn.* (Sp. 1981); *Index to the Ohio State University Monthly (1909–1950)* microfilm (1974); ed., of *Acad. LA of OH Qtly. Nsltr.* (1976–78). **Activities:** 1, 12; 20, 30, 38; 50, 89, 90 **Addr.:** 5768-B Pine Tree N., Columbus, OH 43229.

Krummel, D. W. (Jl. 12, 1929, Sioux City, IA) Prof. of Lib. and Info. Sci. and of Msc., Univ. of IL, 1970–; Assoc. Libn., Newberry Lib., 1962–69; Ref. Libn., Msc. Div., Lib. of Congs., 1956–61; Instr. in Msc. Lit., Univ. of MI, 1952–56. **Educ.:** Univ. of MI, 1947–51, BMsc, 1951–58, MMsc, AMLS, PhD. **Orgs.:** Msc. LA: Pres. (1980–83). ALA: Cnclr. (1964–68). Intl. Assn. of Msc. Libs.: Ch., Comsn. for Bibl. Resrch. (1967–77). Amer. Msclg. Socty.: Cnclr. (1966–69, 1977–79). Bibl. Socty. (London). Bibl. Socty. of Amer. Caxton Club. **Honors:** Newberry Lib., Travelling Resrch. Flw., 1969–70; Amer. Philo. Socty., Resrch. Awd., 1970; Univ. Coll. (London), Hon. Resrch. Flw., 1974–75; Guggenheim Fellow, 1976–77. **Pubns.:** *Physiology of the Opera* (1981); *Resources of American Music History* (1981); *A Librarian's Collacon* (1971); *English Music Printing, 1553–1700* (1975); *Bibliographical Inventory to the Early Music in the Newberry Library* (1977). **Activities:** 1, 11; 15, 37, 45; 55, 57, 95-Library history. **Addr.:** 432 David Kinley Hall, University of Illinois, Urbana, IL 61801.

Kruse, Kathryn Warren (D. 9, 1940, Pittsburgh, PA) Libn. of Info. Retrieval Branch, Food and Drug Admin., Bur. of Drugs, Med. Lib., 1980–; Head, Ref. and Bibl., Duke Univ., Med. Ctr. Lib., 1975–80, Ref. Libn., 1968–74; Ref. Libn., Welch Med. Lib., Johns Hopkins Univ., 1965–68. **Educ.:** Mount Holyoke Coll., 1958–62, AB (Zlgy., Span.); Univ. of Pittsburgh, 1964–65, MLS (Med. Libnshp.); Med. LA, 1968, Grade I Cert. **Orgs.:** SLA: NC Chap., Secy. (1979); Nom. Com. (Ch., 1978). NC OLUG. Duke Univ. Libns. Asm.: Exec. Com. (1975–77); Nom. Com. (1974–75). Med. LA: Mid-Atl. Reg. Grp., Nom. Com. (1975–76); Cont. Ed. Com. (1967–68). PA Acad. of Sci. **Honors:** Beta Phi Mu, 1965. **Pubns.:** *CE II: Techniques of Interlibrary Loan* (1967, 1968); jt. auth., "A college course for nurses on the utilization of library resources," *Bltn. Med. LA* (Ap. 1977). **Activities:** 12; 31, 36, 39; 58, 80, 91 **Addr.:** Apt. 404, 118 Monroe St., Rockville, MD 20850.

Kruse, Theodore H. (D. 22, 1948, St. Paul, MN) Tech. Srvs. Libn., IIT Resrch. Inst., 1979–; Per. Libn., Old Dominion Univ., 1974–79; Pub. Srvcs. Libn., Univ. of ND, 1973–74, Ser. Libn., 1972–73. **Educ.:** Univ. of MN, 1966–70, BA (Amer. Std.), 1970–71, MALS; Old Dominion Univ., 1974–79, MBA. **Orgs.:** ALA. SLA. AAUP. **Pubns.:** Reviews. **Activities:** 1, 12; 15, 17, 44; 59, 64, 93 **Addr.:** Technical Library, IIT Research Institute, North Severn, Annapolis, MD 21402.

Kruzas, Anthony Thomas (Jl. 23, 1914, Brooklyn, NY) Publshr., Ed. Consult., 1974–; Prof., Univ. of MI Sch. of LS, 1956–74; Assoc. Libn., State Univ. of NY Coll. of Ceramics, 1952–56; Assoc. Libn., Univ. of KS Med. Ctr., 1951–52. **Educ.:** Polytech. Inst. of Brooklyn, 1931–36, (Chem. Engin.); City Coll. of NY, 1947–50, BBA (Bus.); Univ. of MI, 1950–51, AMLS; Alfred Univ., 1952–56, MA (Educ.); Univ. of MI, 1956–60, PhD (LS). **Orgs.:** SLA. Med. LA. ASIS. **Pubns.:** *Health Services Directory* (1981); *Encyclopedia of Information Systems and Services* (1981); *Medical and Health Information Directory* (1980); *Business Organization and Agencies* (1980); Contrib., *Government Research Centers Directory* (1980); other books. **Activities:** 11; 37; 56, 80, 91 **Addr.:** 1810 Longshore Dr., Ann Arbor, MI 48105.

Krynicki, J. Marguerite (Ag. 22, 1930, Warsaw, Poland) Head Libn., IL Bell Telephone Co. Lib., 1969–; Head Libn. and Tchr., VanderCook Coll. of Msc., 1965–69. **Educ.:** Univ. of Warsaw, 1948–53, MA (Comp. Lit.). **Orgs.:** Friends of the Chicago Pub. Lib. Bd.: Secy., Bd. (1970–). **Pubns.:** Ed., Critic, European Lit. (Poland). **Addr.:** IL Bell Telephone Co., Company Library, HDQ 20-D, 225 W. Randolph St., Chicago, IL 60606.

Kryszak, Wayne D. (N. 9, 1936, Canton, OH) Chief, Bus. Div., DC Pub. Lib., 1968–, Reader's Adv., 1961–68. **Educ.:** Kent State Univ., 1954–58, BS (Bus. Admin.), 1964–65, MLS. **Orgs.:** ALA. Cottage City Fire Co. **Pubns.:** *Small Business Index* (1978); Contrib., *Not Of One Mind* (1976). **Activities:** 9; 51, 59 **Addr.:** 3308 Mill Branch Pl., Mitchellville, MD 20716.

Krzys, Richard A. (Ap. 30, 1934, Cleveland, OH) Prof./Dir., Intl. Lib. Info. Ctr., Univ. of Pittsburgh, 1971–; Assoc. Prof./Asst. Dir., LS, Dalhousie Univ., 1969–71; Assoc. Prof., C. W. Post Coll., Long Island Univ., 1967–69; Asst. Prof., LS, FL State Univ., 1965–67. **Educ.:** John Carroll Univ., 1952–56, BSS, cum laude (Sp.); NM State Univ., 1956–58, MA (Sp); Univ. of Denver, 1956–58, MA (LS); Case West. Rsv. Univ., 1955–65, PhD (LS). **Orgs.:** ALA. **Honors:** Fulbright Schol., 1961. **Pubns.:** Jt. auth., *A History of Education for Librarianship in Colombia* (1969); various articles, *Encyc. of Lib. and Info. Sci.* various encycs., and jnls. **Activities:** 11, 12; 26, 39; 95-Intl. libnshp. **Addr.:** 5619 Kentucky Ave., Apt. G-1, Pittsburgh, PA 15232.

Krzys, Richard Andrew (Ap. 30, 1934, Cleveland, OH) Prof., Sch. of Lib. and Info. Sci. Univ. of Pittsburgh, 1971–; Consult., Long Branch Pub. Lib., 1974–; Dir., Intl. Lib. Info. Ctr., Univ. of Pittsburgh, 1971–; Asst. Dir. and Assoc. Prof., Schl. of Lib. Srv., Dalhousie Univ., 1969–71; Consult., Clarion Dist. Lib. Assn., 1971–1974; various assoc. prof., 1965–75; Ref. Libn., John Carroll Univ., 1962–1964; Consult., Sociedad Técnica Agrícola Colombo-Americana, Colombia, 1960. Ref. Libn., Cleveland Pub. Lib., 1958–1960. **Educ.:** John Carroll Univ., 1956, BSS cum laude; NM State Univ., 1958, MA (Span.); Univ. of CO, 1957, Grad. Std. (Span.); Univ. of Denver, 1958, MA (Libnshp.); El Instituto Caro y Cuervo, Bogotá, Colombia, 1960, Grad. Std. (Span.); La Universidad de los Andes, Bogotá, Colombia, 1961, Grad. Std. (Span.); Case West. Rsv. Univ., 1965 PhD (LS); Univ. of Pittsburgh, 1974–, Post-doct. Std. (Interdisciplinary). **Orgs.:** ALA. FL LA. **Honors:** Bogota, Colombia, Fulbright Schol., 1960–61. **Pubns.:** Jt. auth., "Cultural Antecedents of Library Education in Colombia," *Jnl. of Lib. Hist.* (Jl. 1966); jt. auth., "The International Student: An Asset to the Instructional Program of Graduate Library Education" in *A Reader in the Administrative Aspects of Library Education* (1975); jt. auth., "College and University Library Administration," *Intl. Ency. of Higher Educ.* (1977); jt. auth., "Reference Books," *Encyc. of Lib. and Info. Sci.* (1978); jt. auth., *A History of Education for Librarianship in Colombia* (1969). **Addr.:** School of Library and Information Science, University of Pittsburgh, Room 620, LIS Bldg., 135 North Bellefield Ave., Pittsburgh, PA 15260.

Kubiak, Janice Anne (Ja. 1, 1947, Philadelphia, PA) Reg. Libn., NW Reg. Lib., Free Lib. of Philadelphia, 1977–, Lib. Coord. 1, 1973–77, Libn. II, 1971–73, Libn. I, 1969–71. **Educ.:** Holy Fam. Coll., 1964–68, BA (Math.); Drexel Univ., 1968–69, MSLS. **Orgs.:** PA LA: Chld., Young People's and Sch. Libns. Mem. Com. (1976). ALA: RASD, Adult Mtrls. Com., AV Subcom. (Ch., 1980–81). **Activities:** 9; 16, 17 **Addr.:** Northwest Regional Library, Chelten Ave. & Greene St., Philadelphia, PA 19144.

Kubiak, Matthew C. (Ja. 4, 1947, London, England) Lit. Apprec. WV North. Cmnty. Coll., Instr., 1979–; Asst. Dir., Mary H. Weir Pub. Lib., 1977–; Head of Branches, Peoria Pub. Lib., 1976; Cat. Instr., IL Ctrl. Coll., 1975–76; Head of Tech. Srvs., 1973–76; Ref. Libn., MI State Univ. Lib., 1972–73. **Educ.:** Univ. of MI, 1967–69, BA (Econ.), 1971–73, AMLS; Heidelberg Coll., 1965–67. **Orgs.:** IL LA: R.T.S.S. Prog. Com. (1975–76); R.T.S.S. Mem.-at-Large (1976). IL Valley Libn. Assn.: Ofcr. (1973–74). WV LA: J.M.R.T. Ch. (1978–80). ALA: PLA, Mem. Com. (1979–81); Small and Medium-Sized Libs. Nom. Com. (1979–80). Kiwanis: VP (1979–80). Jaycees: Secty. (1977–78). Amer. Cancer Socty.: Hancock Co. Bd. (1979–). All WV Cities: Weirton (1979–). **Pubns.:** "Info Corner" weekly clmn. *Weirton Daily Times;* various articles in *WV Libs.* **Activities:** 9; 17 **Addr.:** 330 Ritchie #8, Weirton, WV 26062.

Kubinec, Janet Ann (Mr. 4, 1950, Greensburg, PA) Cur., Hist. Col., Falk Lib. of the Hlth. Profs., Univ. of Pittsburgh, 1974–. **Educ.:** Univ. of Pittsburgh, 1968–71, BA (Fr., Educ.), 1972–73, MLS; Univ. de Rouen, France, 1970, Cert. Scholaire. **Orgs.:** Med. LA: Hist. of Med. Sect., Bd. (1979–). Assn. Libns. Hist. of the Hlth. Scis.: Pres. (1980–). Beta Phi Mu: Pi Chap. (Secy., 1979–). Amer. Assn. Hist. of Med.: Lcl. Arrange. Com. (Treas., 1979). Assn. Prof. Transls., Pittsburgh. Assn. Univ. Pittsburgh Libns. **Activities:** 1, 12; 20, 23, 45; 73, 80 **Addr.:** Falk Library, 200 Scaife Hall, University of Pittsburgh, Pittsburgh, PA 15601.

Kuch, Terence D. C. (Je. 15, 1940, Leavenworth, WA) Grp. Leader, Sci. and Mgt. Info. Syst., MITRE Corp., 1978–; Chief, Sci. Info. Anal. Branch, Con. Product Safety Comsn., 1974–78; Chief Info. Tech. Spec., Natl. Inst. of Hlth., 1969–74; Mgr., Comp. Oper., Appld. Data Resrch., Inc., 1966–69. **Educ.:** Reed Coll., 1958–61, BA (phil.); Amer. Univ., 1975–77, MS (Info. Sci.). **Orgs.:** ASIS: SIG nsltr. ed. Assn. for Comp. Mach. Socty. for Soc. Std. of Sci. **Pubns.:** *Development and Uses of the Chemical Information Resources Directory* (1979); "Model of the Chemical Regulation Process" mono. (1978); "Relation of Title Length to Number of Authors in Journal Articles," *JASIS* (1978). **Activities:** 12; 17, 24, 41; 56, 60, 75 **Addr.:** 13339 Fones Pl., Herndon, VA 22070.

Kuczynski, Kathleen E. (S. 13, 1952, Amsterdam, NY) Lib. Dir., Helen Hayes Hosp. Lib., 1979–; Asst. Libn., NYS Dept. of Hlth. Resrch. Lib., 1978–79; Asst. Libn., SUNY, Albany, Lib., 1976–77; Libn., Rensselaer Cnty. Hist. Socty., 1976. **Educ.:** SUNY, Albany, 1970–74, BA (Fr.), 1975, MLS. **Orgs.:** Med. LA: NY Reg. Grp. Hlth. Info. Libs. of Westchester: Board and Prog. Com. Ch. (1980–81), VP (1981–82). **Honors:** Beta Phi Mu, 1975. Phi Beta Kappa, 1974. **Pubns.:** Editorial Staff, *Jrnl. of Clin. Pharmacology* (1980). **Addr.:** Helen Hayes Hospital Lib., Route 9W, West Haverstraw, NY 10993.

Kudej, Blanka (Kutna Hora, Czechoslovakia) Intl. and Frgn. Law Libn., Columbia Univ., 1976–; Resrchr., Law Libn., Gulf & West. Indus., Inc. 1972–75; Resrchr. Austrian Gallup Inst., (Vienna), 1967; Attorney, Prague, Czechoslovakia, 1950–67. **Educ.:** Charles Univ. (Prague, Czechoslovakia) 1946–50, JUDr (LLd Equiv.), 1951–52, MBA; Columbia Univ., 1971–72, MS (LS). **Orgs.:** AALL: Com. on Frgn., Comp., and Intl. Law (1976–). Law Lib. Assn. of Grtr. NY Intl. Assn. of Law Libs. SLA. **Activities:** 1, 12; 17, 39, 41; 62, 77, 78 **Addr.:** 48-15 195th St., Fresh Meadows, NY, NY 11365.

Kudrick, Linda W. (N. 26, 1951, New Milford, CT) Chief, Mtrls. Utilization Branch, Natl. Med. AV Ctr., Natl. Lib. of Med., 1980–; Asst. Head, Sel./Acq., 1979–80, AV Coord., 1976–79, Lib. Intern, 1975–76; Contract Libn., Tracor-Jitco, Inc., 1974–75. **Educ.:** Univ. of CT, 1971–72, BA summa cum laude (Fr.); Simmons Coll., 1973–73, MLS; Georgetown Univ., 1969–71. **Orgs.:** Med. LA: AV Stan. & Practices Com. (1979–); CE Fac. mem. (1978–). Hlth. Sci. Comm. Assn.: Bd. Dirs. (1981–83); HeSCA/NLM Liaison Com. (1978–); contrib. ed., nsltr. (1978–). **Pubns.:** "An Audiovisual Information Retrieval System: AVLINE," *Jnl. of Nursing Educ.* (1979); "AVLINE: a Search Resource for Audiovisual Instructional Materials," *Jnl. of Dental Educ.* (1979). **Activities:** 4, 12; 15, 32, 46; 56, 80 **Addr.:** 5200 Crossfield Ct., Rockville, MD 20852.

Kudryk, Oleg (D. 14, 1912, Rohatyn, Ukraine) Head Acq. Libn., IN Univ., 1971–, Head Ord. Libn., 1963–70, Cat. Libn., 1960–63; Rep./Consult., Prudential Insr. Co., 1955–60; Asst. Treas./Mgr., Self-Reliance Fed. Credit Un., Detroit, 1953–60; Admin., UNRRA and Intl. Refugee Org., Stuttgart, Germany, 1947–50; Mgr./Legal Adv., Import and Export Co., Cracov, Poland, 1940–44. **Educ.:** Queen Hedwig Gymnasium, Ukraine, 1932, Abitur; State Cnsvty. of Msc., Lviv, Ukraine, 1932, Dip. (Violin); Univ. of Lviv, Ukraine, 1933–37, LLM (Law), 1936–38, MA (Econ.); Univ. of Vienna, 1945–46 (Econ.); Univ. of MI, 1959–60, MALS; U.F.U., Munich, Germany, 1973–75, PhD (Pol. Sci.). **Orgs.:** ALA: ACRL, Nom. Com. (1973–74)/Slavic and E. European Sect., Nom. Com. (Ch., 1966, 1972–74, 1977), Bylaws Com. (Ch., 1979). Midwest Acad. Libns. Conf.: Prog.

Special Subjects/Services: 50. Adult educ.; 51. Advert./Mktg.; 52. Aerosp.; 53. Agric.; 54. Area std.; 55. Arts/Hum.; 56. Autom.; 57. Bibl./Prtg.; 58. Bio. sci.; 59. Bus./Fin.; 60. Chem.; 61. Copyrt.; 62. Documtn.; 63. Educ.; 64. Engin.; 65. Env.; 66. Eth. grps.; 67. Film; 68. Food/Nutr.; 69. Geneal.; 70. Geo.; 71. Geol.; 72. Handcpd.; 73. Hist.; 74. Int. frdm.; 75. Info. sci.; 76. Insr.; 77. Law; 78. Legis.; 79. Math./Comp. sci.; 80. Med.; 81. Metals; 82. Nat. resrcs.; 83. Newsp.; 84. Nuc. sci.; 85. Oral hist.; 86. Petr./Energy; 87. Pharm.; 88. Phys./Astr./Math.; 89. Readg.; 90. Relig.; 91. Sci./Tech.; 92. Soc. sci.; 93. Telecom.; 94. Transp.; 95. (other).

Com. (1971). Ukrainian LA of Amer.: VP (1972–75); Exec. Bd. (1975–). OH Valley Tech. Srvs. Libns.: Prog. Com (1978). Various other orgs. and coms. Amer. Econ. Assn. AAUP. Amer. Acad. of Pol. and Soc. Scis. Shevchenko Sci. Socty. Various other orgs. **Honors:** IN Univ., Std. Grant, 1972. **Activities:** 1; 15, 17, 26; 54, 66, 92 **Addr.:** 409 Clover Ln., Bloomington, IN 47401.

Kuehn, Melody A. (N. 4, 1947, Miller, SD) Libn., Ctrl. Campus, Minot Pub. Schls., 1981–; Asst. Dir., Minot Pub. Lib., 1970–81. **Educ.:** Dickinson State Coll., 1966–70, BS (Educ.); Univ. of Denver, 1973–74, MLS. **Orgs.:** ALA. Mt. Plains LA: Schol. Com. (Ch., 1974–76). ND LA: Pub. Lib. Sect. (Secy., 1975). Amer. Heart Assn., Dakota Affil.: Bd. (1979–). Bus. and Prof. Women. **Pubns.:** "Minot Serves the Aged," *Amer. Libs.* (D. 1971); "Library I&R, Volunteer Clearinghouse Meet Flood Emergency in N.D.," *Amer. Libs.* (Jy. 1976). **Activities:** 9; 16, 17, 39; 55, 69 **Addr.:** Central Campus, Minot Public Schools, Minot, ND 58701.

Kuehn, Phyllis R. (O. 29, 1931, Saginaw, MI) Media. Spec., Ctr. for the Arts and Scis., Saginaw, MI, 1981–; Media Spec., Webber Jr. HS, Saginaw, MI, 1971–81; Elem. Libn., Saginaw Pub. Schs., 1969–71. **Educ.:** Delta Coll., 1961–66, AA; Ctrl. MI Univ., 1966–69, AB (Fr.); Univ. of MI, 1970–72, AMLS. **Orgs.:** ALA: AASL. MI Assn. for Media in Educ.: Reg. 9. Saginaw Cnty. Chessplayers' Assn.: Pres. (1978–). Com. to compile *Michigan Authors.* U.S. Chess Fed. MI Chess Assn. **Pubns.:** "Microfiche for Research," *Media Spectrum* (Spr. 1979); "The Principal and the Media Center," *NASSP Bltn.* (S. 1975); reviews. **Activities:** 10; 15, 32, 48; 66, 74, 89 **Addr.:** 2927 Deindorfer St., Saginaw, MI 48602.

Kuhlman, Augustus Frederick (S. 3, 1889, Hubbard, IA) Consult., Acad. Libs., 1960–; Dir., Jt. Univ. Libs., Nashville, 1936–60; Assoc. Dir., Libs., Univ. of Chicago, 1929–36; Assoc. Prof., Soclgy., Univ. of MO, 1924–29, Asst. Prof., 1920–24; Dir., Srvys., Amer. Red Cross, 1919–20; various positions as consult., 1940–60. **Educ.:** Northwest. Coll., 1916, BS; Univ. of Chicago, 1922, AM (Soclgy.), 1929, PhD (Soclgy.). **Orgs.:** TN LA: Pres. (1954–55). Nashville Lib. Club: Pres. (1953–54). Assn. of Southeast. Resrch. Libs.: Ch. (1956–60). ALA: Cncl. (1932–36); Com. on Arch. and Libs. (Ch., 1936–40); Univ. and Ref. Libns. RT, Strg. Com. (Ch., 1938); ACRL, Pubns. Com. (Ch., 1939–41), *Coll. & Resrch. Libs.* (Ed., 1939–41). AAUP. Christ Episcopal Church. Rotary Intl. **Honors:** Phi Beta Kappa, 1912; Amer. Lib. Inst., Fellow. **Pubns.:** *A Guide to Material on Crime and Criminal Justice* (1929); *College and University Library Service: Trends, Standards, Appraisal, Problems* (1939); *Consumer Survey of New Serial Titles* (1967); *Story of the Joint University Libraries of Nashville, Tennessee* (1972); Jt. ed., *Report on Some Library Problems and Proposed Solutions for the Atlanta University Center* (1968); various monos. **Activities:** 1; 19, 24 **Addr.:** 1908 Blakemore Ave., Nashville, TN 37212.

Kuhn, Judy Carole (S. 12, 1941, Los Angeles, CA) Mem., Bd. of Lib. Com., Los Angeles Pub. Lib., 1977–, Pres., Los Angeles City Bd. of Lib. Com., 1978–79. **Educ.:** Immaculate Heart Coll., Los Angeles, 1973–77, BA (Hist.); Univ. of CA, Los Angeles (Bus. Admin.) (1977-Present). **Orgs.:** ALA. CA LA. LA LA. **Activities:** 9; 15, 16, 21; 59, 66, 92 **Addr.:** 835 South Wooster St., #316, Los Angeles, CA 90035.

Kuhn, Lydia J. (Je. 6, 1944, Brooklyn, NY) Acq. Libn., Fresno Cnty. Free Lib., 1971–. **Educ.:** Whittier Coll., 1962–66, BA (Pol. Sci.); LA State Univ., 1969–71, MLS; Univ. of Denver Publshg. Inst., Sum. 1980. **Orgs.:** ALA. CA LA: Libns. and Publshrs. Com. (1977, 1980–81, 1981–82); Tech. Srvs. Chap. (Secy., 1978). Sierra Lib. and Media Assn.: Pres. (1978). AAUW. Zonta. **Honors:** Beta Phi Mu. **Activities:** 9; 15 **Addr.:** 708–A W. Bullard, Fresno, CA 93707.

Kuhn, Warren Boehm (F. 12, 1924, Jersey City, NJ) Dean, Lib. Srvs., IA State Univ., 1971–; Dir., 1967–71; Asst. Dir., Univ. Libs., Libn., Meyer Meml. Lib., Stanford Univ., 1965–67; Asst. Univ. Lib., Princeton Univ., 1956–65; Asst. Head Libn., AZ State Univ., 1955–56; Head, Circ., Univ. of NM, 1950, 1952–52. **Educ.:** NY Univ., 1942–43, 1946–48, AB (Eng.); Columbia Univ., 1949–50, MS (LS). **Orgs.:** ARL: Bd. of Dir. (1972–75), Nom. Com. (1978). ALA: ACRL, various Coms.; Yrbk. Adv. Com. (Ch., 1975–); Publ. Bd. (1972–75; Ch., 1973–75); Ed. Com. (1969–75, Ch., 1972–73); Cncl. (1971–75). Universal Serials and Bk. Exch.: Pres. (1976). Ctr. for Resrch. Libs.: Bd. of Dir. (1970–72). Midwest Reg. Lib. Netwk. (Pres., 1981, 1982). Other ofcs. and orgs. Phi Kappa Phi. Rotary. **Pubns.:** "Ninety Years of Library Instruction at ISU," *ALA Yrbk.* (1981); "The Future is Not What It Used to Be," *NB LA Qtly.* (Win. 1971); "Service," *Serial Publications in Large Libraries* (1970); "Undergraduate Libraries in a University," *Lib. Trends* (O. 1969); "The Current Pattern of Resource Development at the Iowa State University Library," *MO LA Qtly.* (D. 1968); other articles. **Activities:** 1; 17, 19, 28; 56, 59, 67 **Addr.:** Iowa State University Library, Ames, IA 50011.

Kuhner, David (Mr. 20, 1921, Columbus, OH) Asst. Dir., Libs., Claremont Coll., 1970–; Chief Sci. Libn., John Crerar Lib., 1966–69; Head, Pub. Srvs., Grad. Sch. of Bus. Lib., Stanford Univ., 1962–66. **Educ.:** OH State Univ., 1939–43, BSc (Chem.); Univ. of Miami, 1950–51, MEd (Educ.); Univ. of CA, Berkeley, 1961–62, MLS. **Orgs.:** ALA. SAA. Socty. of CA Archvsts. Bibl. Socty. of Amer. **Pubns.:** Co-Ed., *Bibliotheca De Re Metallica: the Hoover Collection* (1980); "Galileo, the Library, and the Venus de Mudd," *CA Libn.* (Ja. 1974); "Florida's Cape Canaveral," *FL Handbook* (1961); Ed., "Map of Florida Industry and Science" (1961). **Activities:** 1; 17, 39, 45; 52, 64, 91 **Addr.:** Sprague Library, Harvey Mudd College, Claremont, CA 91711.

Kuhns, Helen Faustine (Je. 8, 1922, Decatur, IL) Ref. Libn., Union Carbide Corp., Oak Ridge Natl. Lab., 1962–; Libn., Haynes-Stellite Co., 1955–62; Spec. Srvs. Libn., U.S. Frcs. (Germ.), 1952–54; Home Demonstration Agent, U.S. Dept. of Agr., Clay Cnty., IL, 1950–52; Asst. and Actg. Libn., Agr. Lib., Univ. of IL, 1947–50. **Educ.:** James Millikin Univ., 1940–44, BS (Home Econ.); Univ. of IL, 1946–47, BS (LS). **Orgs.:** SLA: Various ofcs. Delta Delta Delta. Oak Ridge Cmnty. Playhouse. **Activities:** 1, 12; 15, 31, 39; 57, 81, 91 **Addr.:** 418 Villanova Rd., Oak Ridge, TN 37830.

Kuklinski, Joan L. (N. 28, 1950, Lynn, MA) Instr., TX A&M Univ. Lib., 1979–; Class. Libn., Univ. of RI, 1974–79. **Educ.:** Salem State Coll., 1968–72, BA (Hist., Educ.); Univ. of RI, 1972–76, MLS. **Orgs.:** ALA: JMRT; RTSD, Educ. Com. (1981–83); ACRL/Educ. and Bhvl. Scis. Sect., Problems of Access and Cntrl. of Educ. Mtrls. Com. (1981–83). TX LA. **Honors:** Delta Tau Kappa. **Pubns.:** "Staffing Patterns and Work Assignments," *Technicalities* (N. 1981). **Activities:** 1; 20, 39 **Addr.:** Texas A&M University Library, College Station, TX 77843.

Kula, Sam (O. 11, 1932, Montreal, PQ) Dir., Natl. Film, Television and Sound Arch., Pub. Arch. of Canada, 1973–; Archvst., Amer. Film Inst., 1968–73; Libn., Univ. of Southern CA, 1962–68; Deputy Cur., Natl. Film Arch. (London), 1959–62; Archvst., Pub. Arch. of Can., 1954–57. **Educ.:** Concordia Univ., Montreal, 1951–54, BA (Hist.); Univ. of Southern CA, 1962–66 (Comm.). **Orgs.:** Assn. of Can. Archvst. ASA. Socty. for Cinema Std. Socty. of Motion Picture and TV Eng. Assn. for the Study of Can. Radio and TV. **Activities:** 2, 4; 17, 23, 45; 67, 85, 93 **Addr.:** 395 Wellington St., Ottawa, ON K1A 0N3 Canada.

Kulberg, Gretchen S. (D. 1, 1928, Pittsburgh, PA) Dir., W. Bloomfield Twp. Pub. Lib., 1973–, Head Libn., 1972–73, Ref. Libn., 1970–72; Advert. Copywriter, H.P. Wosson Co., 1950–53. **Educ.:** Wilson Coll., Chatham Coll., 1945–50, BA (Eng.); Wayne State Univ., 1968–70, MSLS. **Orgs.:** ALA. MI LA: Awds. Com. (1978, 1980). NLA. Mensa. Leag. of Women Voters: Pubn. Ch. (1968–70); Fin. Com. (1978–80). **Honors:** State of MI, MI Minute Man Awd., 1979; Beta Phi Mu. **Activities:** 9; 16, 17, 35; 56, 74 **Addr.:** West Bloomfield Township Public Library, 5030 Orchard Lake Rd., West Bloomfield, MI 48033.

Kulp, Aimee K. (O. 28, 1924, Mercersburg, PA) Lib. Dir., Mercersburg Acad., 1949–; Serials Libn., Princeton Univ., 1948–49. **Educ.:** Wilson Coll., 1942–46, AB (Fine Arts); Drexel Univ., 1947–48, BS (LS). **Orgs.:** Cumberland Valley LA: VP (1971–72). PA LA. ALA: AASL PA Sch. Libns. Assn. Chambersburg (PA) Hosp. Aux. Avon Literary Socty. Order of the East. Star. Fac. Women's Club. **Pubns.:** *History of the libraries of Marshall College, 1820–1871* (1978); "Mercersburg's Authors," *Mercersburg* (D. 1974); "Growth Is the Keynote," *Mercersburg Acad. Alum. Qtly.* (Win. 1968); "Teen-Agers Won't Read!" Wilson Lib. Bltn. (Ap. 1955); other articles. **Activities:** 10; 15, 17, 48; 55, 89, 92 **Addr.:** 304 Johnston's Ln., Mercersburg, PA 17236.

Kulp, Arthur C. (Ap. 4, 1921, Ithaca, NY) Coord. of Facilities, Assoc. Persnl. Ofcr., Cornell Univ. Lib., 1975–, Interim Dir., S. Ctrl. Resrch. Lib. Cncl., 1976–; Circ. Libn., Cornell Univ. Lib., 1950–75, Actg. Circ. Lib., 1949–50, Asst. Circ. Libn., 1947–49. **Educ.:** Cornell Univ., 1938–42, AB (Hist.); Columbia Univ., 1946–47, BSLS; Univ. of IL, 1951–54, MLS. **Orgs.:** ALA. NY LA: Dir., Coll. & Univ. Sect. (1965–67). Five Assoc. Univ. Libs.: Access Com. **Activities:** 1; 17, 19, 35; 72, 75 **Addr.:** 235 Olin Library, Cornell University, Ithaca, NY 14853.

Kulpa, Lorraine A. (Jn. 4, 1939, Buffalo, NY) Legal Staff Libn., Gen. Motors Corp., 1971–; Head, Pub. Srvs., Cornell Univ. Law Sch. Lib., 1967–71; Ref. Libn., Los Angeles Cnty. Law Lib., 1965–67. **Educ.:** Univ. of Buffalo, 1961, BA; SUNY Buffalo, 1964 LLB; Syracuse Univ., 1965, MSLS. **Orgs.:** AALL: Exec. Bd. (1977–). SLA. ALA. Intl. Assn. of Law Libs. Other orgs. Amer. Bar Assn. Amer. Socty. of Intl. Law. State Bar of MI. Woman Lawyers of MI. Other orgs. **Pubns.:** "Corprate Law Libraries - A Profile," *Law Lib. Jnl.* (1974); "Ethical Problems of Law Librarianship," *Law Lib. Jnl.* (1974); ed., *Law Lib. Jnl.* (1977–). **Activities:** 12; 17; 77 **Addr.:** Legal Staff Library, 14-224 General Motors Building, Detroit, MI 48202.

Kumatz, Tad G. (Mr. 31, 1929, Honolulu, HI) Asst. Dir./Prof., Pratt Inst., 1968–, Circ. Libn., 1959–68; Head, Rsv. Lib., Hofstra Coll., 1958–59; Head, Hum. Lib., Hunter Coll., 1955–58. **Educ.:** Frnds. Univ., 1948–52, AB (Soclgy.); Syracuse Univ., 1952–54, MS (LS). **Orgs.:** NY Metro., Ref. and Resrch. Lib. Agency: Resrcs. and Dev. Com. (1979–); Liaison Ofcr. to Film Coop. (1980–). Acad. Libs. of Brooklyn: Pres. (1974–76). **Honors:** Beta Phi Mu. **Pubns.:** Ed., *The Black Experience* (1971); "Academic Libraries of Brooklyn," *LA CUNY Jnl.* (Spr. 1975). **Activities:** 17, 22 **Addr.:** 405 E. 54 St., New York, NY 10022.

Kuney, Joseph H. (D. 29, 1917, Chicago, IL) VP, Genl. Mgr., Informatics, Inc., 1974–; Mgr., Jnls. and Ency. Dept., John Wiley & Sons, Inc., 1973–74; Dir., Bus. Oper., Amer. Chem. Socty., 1946–73; Compositor, M & L Typesetting Co., 1935–46. **Educ.:** Univ. of Chicago, 1945, BS (Chem.); Amer. Univ., 1962, MA (Comm.). **Orgs.:** ASIS: Pubn. Com. (1977–); Jnl. of ASIS (Ed. Bd., 1977–). Amer. Chem. Socty.: Copyright Com. (1973–). AAAS: Com. T (Info. Sci.) (1975–). Sigma Xi: *Amer. Sci.* (Ed. Bd., 1971–). **Pubns.:** "Role of Microforms in Journal Publication," *Jnl. Chem. Docum.* (My. 1972); "A Publisher's Viewpoint–Not for Profit," *Copyright, Current Viewpoints on Hist., Law, Legis.* (1972); "An Experiment in Selective Dissemination–The ACS Single Article Service," *Jnl. Chem. Docum.* (F. 1971); "New Developments in Primary Journal Documentation," *Jnl. Chem. Docum.* (F. 1970); Other articles. **Activities:** 6, 12; 17, 34, 37; 61, 75, 95-publishing. **Addr.:** Informatics Inc., 6011 Executive Blvd., Rockville, MD 20852.

Kunitz, Donald (F. 7, 1929, Los Angeles, CA) Dept. Head, Spec. Col., Univ. of CA, Davis, 1963–. **Educ.:** Univ. of CA, Los Angeles, 1946–50, BA (Pol. Sci.), 1962–63, MLS; Carnegie-Mellon Univ., 1954–56, BA (Prtg. Mgt.). **Orgs.:** Socty. of CA Archvsts. CA Assn. of Thea. Spec.: Pres. (1979–81). **Activities:** 1, 2; 17, 39, 45 **Addr.:** Department of Special Collections, Shields Library, University of California, Davis, CA 95616.

Kunkle, Hannah Josephine (Cork, Ireland) Prof., TX Woman's Univ. Sch. of LS, 1970–; Coord. of Sec. Eval., Jr. HS and Sr. HS libn., Los Angeles Indp. Sch. Dist., 1961–70; Fac. Mem., Univ. of South. CA, Immaculate Heart Coll., and West. MI Univ., 1964–69; US Air Force Staff Libn. and Post Libn., 1953–58. **Educ.:** FL State Univ., 1952–54, BA (LS), 1957–58, MLS, 1955–56, MA (Educ.), 1965–69, PhD (Adult Educ.); Libnshp., Jr. Coll., Sec. Tchg., Gen. Supvsn. Cred., 1960–66. **Orgs.:** ALA: Cncl. (1972–76); AASL. AALS. Intl. Assn. of Sch. Libns. TX LA. AAUW. **Honors:** Phi Kappa Phi, 1955; Beta Phi Mu, 1977. **Pubns.:** "Bibliography of the History of Libraries in California," *Jnl. of Lib. Hist.* (1976); "Adult Reading Programs" in *Right to Read Worktext for Program Directors* (1975); "Librarians and Adult Basic Education: Old Philosophy and New Needs," *TX Lib. Jnl.* (1975); "A History of the Texas Library Association" in *Encyc. of Lib. and Info. Sci.;* "The California State Library School," *Jnl. of Educ. for Libnshp.* (Spr. 1972); reviews. **Activities:** 10, 11; 15, 26, 39; 50, 89, 92 **Addr.:** Texas Woman's University, School of Library Science, Denton, TX 76204.

Kunoff, Hugo (Ap. 1, 1929, Tiege, Russia) Libn. for Mod. Lang., IN Univ., 1965–; Ref. Asst., New York Pub. Lib., 1960–65. **Educ.:** Mexico City Coll., 1957–58, BA (Hist.); Columbia Univ., 1959–60, MSLS; IN Univ., 1966–72, PhD (Lib Sci). **Orgs.:** ALA. IN LA. Mod. Lang. Assn. **Honors:** Cncl. on Lib. Resrcs., Flwshp., 1978. **Pubns.:** "Emigres, Emigration Studies, and Libraries," (1975). "Literatur Betrieb in der Vertreibung," (1973). **Activities:** 1; 15; 54, 55 **Addr.:** 4313 Deckard Dr., Bloomington, IN 47401.

Kunselman, Joan D. (S. 19, 1946, Bastrop, TX) Ref. Libn. and ILL Libn., CA State Univ., 1981–; Ref. Libn., Coord. of Lib. Instr., Gen. Lib., Univ. of CA, Riverside, 1976–81, Cat. Libn., LA State Univ., 1974–76. **Educ.:** Vassar Coll., 1964–68, AB (Msc.); Univ. of MD, 1968–70, MM (Msclgy.); LA State Univ., 1971–76, MLS, PhD (LS and Msclgy.). **Orgs.:** ALA: ACRL. Msc. LA: Prog. ch. (1982 Conv.). Amer. Musicological Socty. **Honors:** Beta Phi Mu, 1974; Pi Kappa Lambda, 1971. **Pubns.:** Jt. auth., *Library Research Strategies* (1978); "The Oswald Jonas Memorial Collection," *Wilson Lib. Bltn.* (My. 1979); various reviews in *Notes.* **Activities:** 1, 12; 15, 39, 41; 55, 75, 92 **Addr.:** University Library, California State University, PO Box 4150, Fullerton, CA 92634.

Kupersmith, John J. (Jn. 13, 1948, Washington, DC) Ref. Libn., Univ. of PA, 1976–; Asst. Ref. Libn., Haverford Sch. (PA), 1975–76; **Educ.:** Univ. of WA, 1966–70, BA (Eng.); Brown Univ., 1972–74, MA (Eng.); Rutgers Univ., 1974–75, MLS. **Orgs.:** ALA: ACRL/Univ. Libs. Sect., Conf. Prog. Plng. Com. (1980–81). Philadelphia Area Ref. Libns. Info. Exch. Libns. Asm., Univ. of PA. **Honors:** Phi Beta Kappa. **Pubns.:** "The Role of the Design Consultant," *Sign Systems for Libs.* (1979); "Informational Graphics and Sign Systems as Library Instruction Media," *Drexel Lib. Qtly* (1980). **Activities:** 1; 31, 39, 49-sign systs.; 55, 92 **Addr.:** Van Pelt Library, University of Pennsylvania, Philadelphia, PA 19104.

Kurman, Judith F. (Mr. 27, 1949, East Orange, NJ) Ext. Srvs. Consult., OH Valley Area Libs., 1979–. **Educ.:** Univ. of FL, 1968–71, BA (Anthro.); Univ. of Pittsburgh, 1978–79, MLS. **Orgs.:** ALA: YASD, Int. Frdm. Com. (1979–; Ch., 1980–81). OH LA. Frdm. to Read Fndn. Amer. Cvl. Liberties Un. **Honors:** Beta Phi Mu. **Pubns.:** Jt.-auth., "Stump the Librarian–An Outreach Project," *Sch. Lib. Jnl.* (Mr. 1980); jt. auth., "How I Use Comicbooks Good at My Branch," *Unabashed Libn.* (Win. 1976); "Young Adult Programs at Reisterstown," *The Crab* (Ap.-Jn. 1978); "Public Libraries: Changing Needs and New Responses"

PROFESSIONAL ACTIVITIES: Institutions: 1. Acad. lib.; 2. Arch.; 3. Assn.; 4. Fed./Gvt. lib.; 5. Inst. lib.; 6. Mfr./Suppl.; 7. Milit. lib.; 8. Musm.; 9. Pub. lib.; 10. Sch. lib.; 11. Sch. of lib. sci.; 12. Spec. lib.; 13. State lib.; 14. (other). **Functions/Activities:** 15. Acq./Col. dev.; 16. Adult srvs.; 17. Admin.; 18. Apprais.; 19. Archit./Bldgs.; 20. Cat./Class.; 21. Chld. srvs.; 22. Circ.; 23. Cons./Pres.; 24. Consult.; 25. Cont. ed.; 26. Educ. lib. sci.; 27. Ext. srvs.; 28. Fund/Grants; 29. Gvt. pubs.; 30. Indx./Abs.; 31. Instr. lib. use; 32. Media srvs.; 33. Micro.; 34. Netwks./Coop.; 35. Persnl.; 36. PR; 37. Publshg.; 38. Recs. mgt.; 39. Ref. srvs.; 40. Repro.; 41. Resrch.; 42. Review.; 43. Secur.; 44. Serials; 45. Spec. col.; 46. Tech. srvs.; 47. Trustees/Bds.; 48. YA srvs.; 49. (other).

video (1979). **Activities:** 9; 24, 27, 48; 74 **Addr.:** Rte. 2, Box 326, Apt. D, Jackson, OH 45640.

Kurmey, William John (Mr. 7, 1940, Vancouver, BC) Dean, Fac. LS, Univ. of AB, 1980–; Assoc. Prof., Univ. of Toronto, Fac. of LS, 1965–79; various positions in data processing. **Educ.:** Univ. of BC, 1957–60, B.Sc. (Chem., math.); Univ. Chicago, 1960–61, AM (LS). **Orgs.:** C LA. ASIS. AALS. SLA. Assn. Comp. Mach. **Honors:** Beta Phi Mu. **Activities:** 11; 26 **Addr.:** University of Alberta, Faculty of Library Science, Edmonton, AB T6G 2J4 Canada.*

Kurzig, Carol M. (Je. 24, 1946, Teaneck, NJ) Dir., Pub. Srvs., Fndn. Ctr., 1975–; Ref. Supvsr., Batten Barton Durstine & Osborne, 1974–75; Ref. Libn., Campbell Ewald, 1972–74. **Educ.:** Georgetown Univ., 1964–66, (Frgn. Srv.); MI State Univ., 1966–68, BA (Hist.); Univ. of MI, 1971–72, MA (LS). **Orgs.:** SLA: Ch., NY Chap. SLA Directory–14th ed. Cnsrtm. of Fndn. Libs. Women & Fndns./Corp. Philanthropy. **Honors:** Phi Beta Kappa, 1968; Beta Phi Mu, 1972. **Pubns.:** Ed., *Foundation Grants to Individuals* (1978, 1979); Managing Ed., *Source Book Profiles* (1977–); *Foundation Fundamentals: A Guide for Grantseekers* (1980); "Private Foundation Grants: What You Need to Know" in *The Nonprofit Org. Handbook* (1980); "Analysis of Foundation Grants to Libraries" in *The Bowker Anl. of Lib. and Book Trade Info.* (1977). **Activities:** 12; 17, 28, 37; 50 **Addr.:** The Foundation Center, 888 Seventh Ave., New York, NY 10106.

Kusack, James M. (N. 19, 1946, Oelwein, IA) Inst., Univ. of IA, 1979–; Pub. Srv. libn., Wartburg Coll., 1975–77. **Educ.:** Univ. of IA, 1965–69, BA (Jrnlsm.), 1974, MALS; IN Univ., 1977–79, (Lib. Sci.). **Orgs.:** ALA. ASIS. AALS. **Pubns.:** "Online Reference Service in Public Libraries", *RQ* (Sum. 1979); "Integration of Online Reference Service," *RQ* (Fall 1979). **Activities:** 1; 26, 39; 75 **Addr.:** School of Library Science, 3070 Library, University of IA, Iowa City, IA 52242.

Kusnerz, Peggy Ann F. (Ja. 12, 1947, Detroit, MI) Art and Arch. Libn., Univ. of MI Lib., 1980–, Head, Lib. Ext. Srv., 1973–80, Musms. and Exhibits Libn., 1972–73, Photograph Libn., Bentley Lib., 1971–72. **Educ.:** Univ. of MI, 1971, BA (Hist. of Art), MLS. **Orgs.:** ALA: IF RT, Prog. Com. (1978–80). ARLIS/NA. MI LA: Com. on Intl. Frdm. (Ch., 1977–80). **Honors:** Beta Phi Mu; Natl. Univ. Press Awd. for *Images of Old Age*, 1979. **Pubns.:** Jt. auth. *Images of Old Age in America 1790 to the Present* (1978); "Oral History," *Drexel Lib. Qtly.* (forthcoming); press); "Selection and Acquisition of Slides and Photos in Special Libraries," *PICTURESCOPE* (1972); "Elsa Fuller: Perceptions of Another Era," *CHRONICLE* (1974); cur., Smithsonian Inst., traveling exhibition srv. exhibit, "Images of Old Age in America," (1977, 1980). **Activities:** 1; 17, 32, 35; 55, 73, 95 **Addr.:** P.O. Box 7585, Ann Arbor, MI 48107.

Kutteroff, Ethel C. (Ap. 1, 1928, Philadelphia, PA) Dir., Media Ctr., Lenape Valley Reg. HS, 1974–, Media Spec., Ironia Elem. Sch., 1963–74; Dir., Cherry Hill Free Pub. Lib., 1957–63; Chld. Libn., Free Lib. of Philadelphia, 1945–56. **Educ.:** Temple Univ., 1947–55, BA (Eng.); Drexel Inst. of Tech., 1957–61, MLS. **Orgs.:** NJ Educ. Media Assn.: Pres. (1981–82). Sussex Cnty Sch./Media Assn.: Pres. (1978–79). Morris Cnty. Sch./Media Assn.: Pres. (1965–66). Coll. Club of Dover: Pres. (1970). **Honors:** Beta Phi Mu. **Pubns.:** "A Time of Wonder," *Hornbk.* (S. 1961). **Activities:** 10; 17, 21; 57 **Addr.:** RR 3 M56 (16 Mile Dr.), Chester, NJ 07930.

Kwan, Julie Kuenzel (N. 17, 1945, Grand Rapids, MI) Head, Ref. Div., Biomed. Lib., Univ. of CA, Los Angeles, 1973–, Ref. Libn., 1968–72. **Educ.:** MI State Univ., 1963–67, BS (Biochem.); Univ. of IL, 1967–68, MS (LS); Med. LA, 1978, Cert. **Orgs.:** Med. LA. ASIS. **Activities:** 1; 39; 58, 80, 91 **Addr.:** University of California, Los Angeles, Biomedical Library, Los Angeles, CA 90024.

Kysely, Elizabeth Coxe (F. 21, 1933, Philadelphia, PA) Chief, Ref. Branch, U.S. Air Frc. Acad. Lib., 1977–, Ref. Libn., 1964–77. **Educ.:** CO Coll., 1951–55, BA (Hist.), Univ. of Denver, 1962–63, MA (LS). **Orgs.:** ALA. Mt. Plains LA. CO LA. CO Mt. Club. **Activities:** 1, 4; 39; 52 **Addr.:** 3011 E. Springlake Cir., Colorado Springs, CO 80906.

Kyvig, David E. (Mr. 8, 1944, Ames, IA) Assoc. Prof. (Hist.)/Consult. Archvst., Amer. Hist. Resrch. Ctr., Univ. of Akron, 1979–, Asst. Prof., 1971–79; Archvst., Ofc. of Pres. Libs., Natl. Arch. and Recs. Srv., 1970–71. **Educ.:** Kalamazoo Coll., 1966, BA (Hist.); Northwest. Univ., 1971, PhD (Amer. Hist.). **Orgs.:** OH Hist. Recs. Pres. Adv. Bd. SAA: Com. on Urban Arch. (1972–75); Com. on Col. Personal Papers and Mss. (1975–76); Com. on Ethics (1977–80). Socty. OH Archvsts: Exec. Cncl. (1973–75); SAA-OH Acad. of Hist. Jt. Arch.-Lib. Com. (Ch., 1977–78). Amer. Assn. for State and Lcl. Hist. Org. of Amer. Histns.: Com. on Bibl. and Resrch. Needs (1980–). OH Netwk. of Amer. Hist. Resrch. Ctrs.: Admin. Com. (1975–79). Socty. for Histns. of Amer. Frgn. Rel. **Pubns.:** *FDR's America* (1976); jt. auth., *Your Family History: A Handbook for Research and Writing* (1978); *Repealing National Prohibition* (1979); jt. auth., *Nearby History* (1982); "Pauline Morton Sabin," *Notable Amer. Women* (1980); various articles. **Activities:** 2; 15, 31, 45; 57, 62 **Addr.:** Department of History, University of Akron, Akron, OH 44325.

L

Laatz, Mary J. (Indianapolis, IN) Dir., Sch. of Med. Lib., IN Univ., 1957–, Ref. Libn., 1953–57, Actg. Dir., 1951–53, Catlgr., 1941–51; Libn., IN Univ. Ext. Div., 1939–41. **Educ.:** Butler Univ., 1934–38, AB (Soclgy.); West. Rsv. Univ., 1938–39, BSLS. **Orgs.:** Midwest Hlth. Sci. Lib. Netwk.: Asm. of Resrc. Libs. (Ch., 1975–76); ILL Com. (1977); Arch. Com. (1979–). Med. LA: Schol. Com. (Ch., 1973–74); SLA: IN Chap. (Pres., 1960–61). Delta Gamma. John Shaw Billings Hist. of Med. Socty.: Secy.—Treas. (1965–67). **Pubns.:** "The Indiana Biomedical Information Program," *Bltn. of the Med. LA* (1970). **Activities:** 12; 17 **Addr.:** School Medical Library, Indiana University, Indianapolis, IN 46202.

LaBorie, Tim (Je. 11, 1944, Rochester, NY) LS Libn., Drexel Univ. Lib., 1972–; Asst. Libn., NY State Lib., 1968–72; Admin. Anal., NY State Educ. Dept., 1967–68. **Educ.:** Siena Coll., 1962–66, BA (Eng.); SUNY, Albany, 1968–71, MS (LS); Drexel Univ., 1975–76, Sch. Libn. Cert. **Orgs.:** ALA: Libns. of LS Cols. Discuss. Grp. (Ch., 1978); Lib. and Info. Lit. Mem. Initiative Grp. (1980–). Philadelphia Area Ref. Libns. Info. Exch.: Strg. Com. (1979–). **Pubns.:** "Library Science Libraries, a Quantitative Survey," ERIC (1974); "Citation Characteristics of Library Science Dissertations," *Jnl. of Educ. for Libnshp.* (1976); "Graffiti on a Database," slide tape prog. (1980); reviews. **Activities:** 1, 11; 26, 32, 42; 75, 95-Online Databases. **Addr.:** Drexel University Library, 32nd and Chestnut Sts., Philadelphia, PA 19104.

LaBrake, Orlyn Barron (S. 2, 1930, Bridgeport, CT) Assoc. Dir. of Univ. Libs., Univ. of Ctrl. FL, 1977–; Asst. Dir. of Libs., Rensselaer Polytech. Inst., 1973–77, Head of Readers Srvs., 1974–77, Asst. to Dir., 1972–73, Libn.-in-Charge, Ch., Libns. Com., 1970–72, Head, Cat. Dept., 1968–71, Cat. Libn., 1967–68. **Educ.:** Skidmore Coll., 1948–51, 1954–55, BA (Psy.); SUNY, Albany, 1966–67, MLS. **Orgs.:** Cap. Dist. Lib. Cncl.: Treas. (1975–77); Bd. of Trustees (1974–77); Coord. Circ. Com. (1973–74). NY LA: Coll. and Univ. Sect. (Mem. Ch., 1976–77). FL Gvr.'s Conf. on Lib. and Info. Srvs.: Exhibit Com. (1978). 4–H. **Addr.:** University Libraries, University of Central Florida, P.O. Box 25000, Orlando, FL 32816.

LaBudde, Kenneth James (Ja. 20, 1920, Sheboygan Falls, WI) Dir. of Libs. and Prof. of Hist., Univ. of MO, Kansas City, 1950–; Grt. Univ. Fellow, Univ. of MN, 1949–50, Instr. in Hum., 1949–; Instr. in Eng., Milton Coll., 1946–47; Libn., Sheboygan Press, 1945–46. **Educ.:** Univ. of WI, 1941, BA (Compar. Lit.), 1942, BLS; Univ. of Chicago, 1943–44, Cert. (Army Spec. Trng. Prog.); Univ. of MN, 1948, MA (Amer. Std.), 1954, PhD (Amer. Std.). **Orgs.:** ALA: Com. on Accred.; ACRL. Bibl. Socty. of Amer. MO LA: Lib. Dev. Com. Amer. Std. Assn. Org. of Amer. Histns. Mid-Continent Amer. Std. Assn. Socty. of Archit. Histns. **Honors:** Beta Phi Mu. **Pubns.:** "A National Voice for University Librarians," *Personnel in Libraries* (1979); "Faculty Status of College Librarians in Missouri," *MLA Qtly.* (Win. 1950, D. 1952); various articles in hist. jnls. **Activities:** 1; 15, 17, 28 **Addr.:** 311 Brush Creek Blvd. #701, Kansas City, MO 64112.

Lacey, Samuel A. (Jl. 21, 1926, Arlington, TX) Chief, Ext. Srvs., Queens Borough Pub. Lib., 1969–; Asst. Chief, 1964–69, Adm. Asst., 1963–64, Asst. Reg. Lib., 1960–63. **Educ.:** Howard Payne Coll., 1943–47, BA (Eng.); N. TX State Univ., 1950–51, BSLS; Univ. of MI, 1952–54, MALS. **Orgs.:** ALA. NY LA. **Addr.:** 888 8th Ave., New York, NY 10019.

Lachance, Anne-Marie (Mr. 29, 1947, Montréal, PQ) Resonsable des Srvs. Tech., Bib. CEGEP de Bois-de-Boulogne, 1976–; Catlgr., Srvs. Tech., Univ. de Montréal, 1971–76; Bibtcr. de Réf. École des Hautes Études Cmrcs., 1969–71. **Educ.:** Univ. de Montréal, 1978, M. Bib. **Orgs.:** Corp. des Bibtcrs. Prof. du PQ: Bur. (1977–80); Treas. (1979–80). ASTED. Assn. Can. des Scis. de l'Info. **Activities:** 1; 20, 31, 46 **Addr.:** 140 DeNoirmoutier, Apt. 7, Laval, PQ H7N 5H2 Canada.

Lack, Clara Evelyn (Je. 18, 1925, Tecumseh, OK) Dir. Biblther. Srv. Projs., Santa Clara Cnty. Lib., 1972–; Libn., Biblther., Agnews State Hosp., San Jose, CA, 1970–72; Soc. Worker, Alameda Cnty. (CA) Soc. Welfare Dept., 1957–59; Prog. Dir., YWCA, Clinton, IA, 1953–56. **Educ.:** Anderson Coll., 1944–48, BS (Psy., Hist.); San Jose State Univ., 1968–70, MA (LS); Berkeley Baptist Div. Sch., 1951–53, MA (Relig. Educ.). **Orgs.:** ALA: ASCLA, Biblther. Com. (1974–80). CA LA: Inst. Libns. **Pubns.:** "Group Bibliotherapy," *Hlth. and Rehab. Lib. Srvs.* (O. 1975); "Bibliotherapy through a One-Way Mirror," *IL Libs.* (S. 1975); "Bibliotherapy in the Community," *News Notes of CA Libs.* (Fall 1973); "Adult Bibliotherapy Discussion Group Bibliography," *Using Biblther.* (1978); Various video cassettes. **Activities:** 9, 10; 24, 27, 72, 95-Bibliotherapy. **Addr.:** 1095 N. 7th St., San Jose, CA 95112.

Lackner, Irene V. (Montreal, PQ) Libn., Econ. Cncl. of Can., 1964–; Libn., Natl. Resrch. Cncl. of Can., 1956–64. **Educ.:** Carleton Univ., 1953, BA (Soc Sci.); McGill Univ., 1956, (LS). **Orgs.:** SLA. Can LA. ASIS. ASTD. Natl. Gallery (Can.) Assn. Natl. Arts Centre: Orchestra Assn., Bd. (1979–). Heritage Ottawa. Can. Inst. of Intl. Affairs. **Pubns.:** Jt.-ed., *Economic Libraries in Canada, 1977,* Sch. of Lib. and Info. Sci., Univ. of W. ON and IFLA, Soc. Sci. Libs. Sect. (1977). **Activities:** 4, 12; 17, 33; 59, 92, 95-Econ. **Addr.:** Economic Council of Canada, P.O. Box 527 - Station "B", Ottawa, ON K1P 5V6 Canada.

Lacroix, Eve-Marie (F. 21, 1945, Worcester, MA) Head, Hlth. Sci. Resrc. Ctr., Can. Inst. for Sci. and Tech. Info., 1978–, Resrch. & Plng., 1975–78; Proj. Mgr., New Products, Ames Div., Miles Labs., 1972–75; Info. Spec., Univ. Notre Dame, Radiation Lab., 1966–70. **Educ.:** Rivier Coll., 1962–66, BA (Chem.); IL Inst. of Tech., 1970–72, MS (Sci. Info.). **Orgs.:** Can. Hlth. Libs. Assn.: Bd. of Dir. (1979–); Ch., Mem. Com. (1979–); CHLA/MLA Liaison (1979–). Can. Hlth. Libs. Assn.: Ottawa Chap., Vice-Ch. (1978–79). Med. LA. ASIS. Assn. of Can. Med. Coll.: Spec. Resrc. Com. on Med. Sch. Lib. (1978–). **Pubns.:** Various articles. **Activities:** 4, 12; 17, 34, 39; 80 **Addr.:** Health Sciences Resources Centre, Canada Institute for Scientific Information, National Research Council, Ottawa, ON K1A 0S2 Canada.

Lacroix, Yvon-Andre (Je. 1, 1944, Montreal, PQ) Dir., Bib. Mncpl. de Brossard, 1976–; Ref. Libn., TV, Radio-PQ, 1974–76; Ref./Acq./Mss. Libn., Bib. Natl. du PQ, 1969–74; Tchr. (Lib. Technicians), Coll. de Maisonneuve, Tchr. (LS), Univ. de Montréal. **Educ.:** 1968, BA (Hum.); 1969, BLS; 1974, MA (Hist.). **Orgs.:** ASTED: Pub. Libs. Sect. (Pres., 1979–81). Corp. des Bibtcrs. Profs. du PQ. Com. Consult. du livre and lecture du PQ: Pres. Salon du livre de Montréal: Couns. **Pubns.:** *Les Ouvrages de Référence du Québec* Supp. 1967–74 (1974); *Catalogue Général des Manuscrits Conservés à la Bibliothèque Nationale du Québec* (1974); "Présent et futur des bibliothèques publiques au Québec," *Docum. et Bibs.* (D. 1979); various articles about pub. libs. in Fr. and Belgium. **Activities:** 9, 13; 17, 19, 39; 55 **Addr.:** Bibliotheque Municipale De Brossard, 3200, boul. Lapinière, Brossard, PQ J4Z 2L4 Canada.

Lacy, Dan Mabry (F. 28, 1914, Newport News, VA) Sr. VP, Exec. Asst. to Ch., McGraw-Hill, Inc., 1974–; Sr. VP, McGraw-Hill Bk. Co., 1966–74; Managing Dir., Amer. Bk. Publshrs. Cncl., 1953–66; Asst. Admin., Intl. Info. Admin., Dept. of State, 1951–53. **Educ.:** Univ. of NC, 1933, AB (U.S. Hist.), 1933–35, AM (U.S. Hist.), 1937–39. **Orgs.:** Pres. Natl. Adv. Comsn. on Libs. (1966–68). Natl. Comsn. on New Tech. Uses of Copyrighted Works. Natl. Hum. Ctr.: Exec. Com. Ch. **Honors:** Dept. of State, Superior Srv. Medal, 1952; Univ. of NC, LittD, 1968. **Pubns.:** *The Abolitionists* (1978); *The Birth of America* (1975); *Freedom and Communications* (1961; rev. ed, 1965); *The Meaning of the American Revolution* (1964); *The White Use of Blacks in America* (1972); various bks., articles. **Activities:** 2, 4, 6; 37; 61, 74, 93 **Addr.:** McGraw-Hill, Inc., 1221 Ave. of the Americas, New York, NY 10021.

Lada, Lynn M. (Jl. 15, 1951, Custer, MI) Chld. Libn., Ericson Pub. Lib., Boone, IA, 1975–. **Educ.:** West. MI Univ., 1969–73, BA (Soclgy.), 1973–75, MSL. **Orgs.:** ALA. IA LA: Secy./Treas., Chld. Young Peoples Sect. (1976–1977). Boone Cmnty. Thea.: VP (1979–80); Secy. (1978–79). **Activities:** 9; 21, 48 **Addr.:** Ericson Public Library, 702 Greene St., Boone, IA 50036.

Ladd, Dorothy Pierce (Ja. 16, 1917, Brooklyn, NY) Assoc. Dir., Boston Univ. Libs., 1979–; Assoc. Dir., Tech. Srvs., 1970–79, Head, Cat. Dept., 1955–69, Cat. Libn., 1949–55, Ref. Libn., 1948–49, Libn., Various positions, 1937–48. **Educ.:** Coll. of William and Mary, 1933–37, AB (Educ.); Columbia Univ., 1940–43, BS (LS). **Orgs.:** ALA: Cat. and Class. Sect. (Ch., 1967–68); RTSD, Pres. (1973–74); ACRL, Com. on Psnl., (1978–). New Eng. LA: Dir. (1973–75). MA LA: Various Coms. MA Govs. Conf on Libs. and Info. Srvs., (1976–). Other orgs. and ofcs. Delta Kappa Gamma. AAUW. **Pubns.:** *The Microform Revolution in libraries* (1980). **Activities:** 1; 17, 20, 46 **Addr.:** Boston University Libraries, 771 Commonwealth Ave., Boston, MA 02120.

Ladd, Frances Roberta (Ap. 28, 1917, Rochester, NY) Head, Cat. Dept., Univ. of Rochester, 1962–, Asst. Head, 1953–62, Catlgr., 1944–52; Sr. Asst. Libn., Rochester Pub. Lib., 1941–45. **Educ.:** Univ. of Rochester, 1936–39, BA (Eng.); Columbia Univ., 1940–41, BS (LS); Univ. of South. CA Lib. Inst., 1970. **Orgs.:** Five Assoc. Univ. Libs. ALA: RTSD/Cat. and Class. Sect., Descr. Cat. Com. (Ch., 1978–79), Subcom. on Descr. Cat. of Asian and African Mtrls. (Ch., 1976–78); Nom. Com.; ACRL; LITA. NY LA: Resrcs. and Tech. Srvs Sect., Dir. at Lg. (1969–71, 1979–82); other coms. Various other orgs. **Honors:** Delta Kappa Gamma. **Activities:** 1; 20 **Addr.:** 25F Colonial Pkwy., Pittsford, NY 14534.

Ladd, Jay Louis (Mr. 26, 1932, St. Louis, MO) Head, Dept. Libs., OH State Univ., 1968–, Head, Cmrce. Lib., 1965–68, Admin. Asst. to Dir., 1961–65, Circ. Desk Libn., 1960–61; Asst. Ref. Libn., Univ. of NM, 1957–60, Asst. Acq. Libn., 1956–57. **Educ.:** FL State Univ., 1949–53, BA (LS), 1953–54, MA (LS); ARL, Lib. Mgt. Skills Inst., 1978. **Orgs.:** ALA. Acad. LA of OH. OH LA: Bd. of Dirs. (1977–80); OH Dev. Com. (1977–78); Anl. Conf.

Special Subjects/Services: 50. Adult educ.; 51. Advert./Mktg.; 52. Aerosp.; 53. Agric.; 54. Area std.; 55. Arts/Hum.; 56. Autom.; 57. Bibl./Prtg.; 58. Bio. sci.; 59. Bus./Fin.; 60. Chem.; 61. Copyrt.; 62. Documtn.; 63. Educ.; 64. Engin.; 65. Env.; 66. Eth. grps.; 67. Film; 68. Food/Nutr.; 69. Geneal.; 70. Geo.; 71. Geol.; 72. Handcpd.; 73. Hist.; 74. Int. frdm.; 75. Info. sci.; 76. Insr.; 77. Law; 78. Legis.; 79. Math./Comp. sci.; 80. Med.; 81. Metals; 82. Nat. resrcs.; 83. Newsp.; 84. Nuc. sci.; 85. Oral hist.; 86. Petr./Energy; 87. Pharm.; 88. Phys./Astr./Math.; 89. Readg.; 90. Relig.; 91. Sci./Tech.; 92. Soc. sci.; 93. Telecom.; 94. Transp.; 95. (other).

Com. (1978–81); Com. on Lib. Educ. (Ch., 1980); Bltn. Com. (1981); ILL Com. (1980). State Lib. of OH, LSCA Title I and II Proj. (Reviewer, 1979–80). **Honors:** Beta Phi Mu. **Pubns.:** "Problems in the Use of the Library Circulation System," *An Automated Online Circulation System, Evaluation, Development, Use* (1973); "Metamorphosis— Professor into Librarian," *OH LA Bltn.* (Je. 1974); "Who Was Who or Test Your Ohio Library History Memory," *OH LA Bltn.* (Ap. 1976); "Cornerstones and Landmarks in Ohio Library History," *OH LA Bltn.* (O. 1976). **Activities:** 1; 17, 35, 39; 59 **Addr.:** 2111 Iuka Ave., Columbus, OH 43201.

Ladenson, Alex (S. 25, 1907, Kiev, Russia) Exec. Dir., Urban Libs. Cncl., 1980–; Exec. Asst., Bd. of Dir., Chicago Pub. Lib., 1975–77, Chief Libn., 1970–74, Actg. Chief Libn., 1967–70, Asst. Chief Libn., Acq. and Prep., 1944–67, Exec. Asst. to Chief Libn., 1943–44; Dir. WPA Lib. Omnibus Proj. sponsored by Chicago Pub. Lib., 1938–43. **Educ.:** Northwest. Univ., 1929, BS (Law), 1932, JD; Univ. of Chicago, 1935, MA (Hist.), 1938, Ph.D. (Hist.). **Orgs.:** ALA: Const. and Bylaws Com. (Ch., 1953, 1966–69); Cat. and Class. Div., Com. on Admin. (Ch., 1950–51). IL LA: Pres. (1959) Other orgs. and ofcs. Chicago Lit. Club. Rosary Coll., Grad. Lib. Sch., Adv. Bd. (1974–). Ctr. for the Std. of Ethics in the Prof, IL Inst. of Tech.: Lib. Policy Com. (1980–). **Honors:** IL Lib. Assn., Libn. Citn. of the Yr., 1965. Rosary Coll., D. Litt., 1968. **Pubns.:** Ed., American Library Laws (1964). Ed., American Library Laws (1975). Various articles in Lib. jnls. **Activities:** 9; 17, 46; 77, 78 **Addr.:** Chicago Public Library, 425 N. Michigan Ave., Chicago, IL 60611.

LaFogg, Mary C. (Mr. 21, 1948, New Haven, CT) Archvst., Yale Univ. Lib., 1973–. **Educ.:** Albertus Magnus Coll., 1966–71, BA (Hist.); South. CT State Coll., 1971–77, MA (Hist.). Various wkshps. **Orgs.:** SAA. NEA. AASHL. ASCH. Socty. for the Std. of CT Hist. **Activities:** 1, 2; 15, 17, 23; 55 **Addr.:** Yale University Library, Mss and Archs., Box 1603A, Yale Station, New Haven, CT 06520.

Laforest, Marthe (Je. 24, 1929, Rivière du Loup, PQ) Cons. Péd. en moyens d'enseignement, Com. Scol. de Châteauguay, 1975–, Bibtcr., 1968–75. **Educ.:** Univ. de Montréal, 1970–72, BA (Educ.), 1972–75, MBib. **Orgs.:** ASTED: Various coms. Corp. des Bibtcrs. Prof du PQ. **Pubns.:** "Litterature de Jeunesse au Canada Français," *Docum. et Bibls.* (S. 1975); reviews. **Addr.:** 7239 Ave. d'Outremont, Montréal, PQ H3N 2L5 Canada.

Lafranchi, William Emil (D. 6, 1926, Brookville, PA) Dir., Libs., Media Resrcs., IN Univ. of PA, 1953–; Libn., Clarion Sr. HS, 1949–53. **Educ.:** Clarion State Coll., 1944–49, BS (Educ.); Univ. of IL, 1949–52, MS (LS); Univ. of Pittsburgh, 1954–57 (Liberal Arts). **Orgs.:** ALA: ACRL/Tri-State Chap. Pittsburgh Reg. Lib. Ctr.: Pres. (1978–79). ILL Delivery Syst. of PA: Pres. (1978–80). PA LA. Rotary. IN Free Lib. Bd. Clarion Free Lib. Bd. **Activities:** 1, 9; 17, 18, 19; 56, 89, 92 **Addr.:** 351 S. 13th St., Indiana, PA 15701.

Lage, Alice Mary (D. 14, 1925, New York, NY) Lib. Ofcr., U.S. Intl. Comm. Agency, 1977–; Lib. Trng. Ofcr., U.S. Info. Agency, Washington, D.C., 1975–77; Reg. Lib. Consult., U.S. Info. Srv., West Africa, 1972–75; County. Lib. Ofcr., U.S. Info. Srv., Brazil, 1966–62; Asst. Dir., U.S. Info. Srv. Lib., Mexico City, 1965–66; Libn., Peace Corps., Malaysia, 1963–65; Asst. Libn., Carnegie Endow. for Intl. Peace, 1961–62; various other positions in libnshp., 1953–60. **Educ.:** Gettysburg Coll., 1943–47, BA (Hist.); NY Univ., 1947–50, MA (Hist.); Columbia Univ., 1960, MS (LS); various wkshps. **Orgs.:** ALA. ASIS. Common Cause. Smithsonian. **Pubns.:** "Government Publications as Information Sources (U.S.A.)," *BIBLOS* (D. 1979); "Recent Developments in Services & Activities Offered by Special Libraries in the U.S.," *Libn* (Kansai SLA) (Ap. 1979); "Recent Public Library Activities in the U.S.," *Hokkaido Lib. Std. Circ. Jnl.* (1980); lectrs. and presentations, 1966–. **Activities:** 4; 17, 24, 31; 75, 92 **Addr.:** ICA Tokyo, American Embassy, APO San Francisco, CA 96503.

LaGrutta, Charles J. (S. 27, 19–, Teaneck, NJ) Info. and Recs. Mgr., Urban Investment and Dev. Co., 1975–. **Educ.:** Gettysburg Coll., 1963–67, AB (Eng.), Fairleigh Dickinson Univ., MA (Eng.); Univ. of Chicago, 1977, MA (LS). **Orgs.:** SLA: IL Chap., Secy. ASIS. ALA. **Pubns.:** Jt. auth., *SLA, IL Chap., Consult. Docum.* (1980). **Activities:** 12; 17 **Addr.:** Information Center, Urban Investment and Development Co., 845 N. Michigan Ave., Chicago, IL 60611.

Lahiri, Amar Kumar (F. 1, 1931, Bettiah, India) Assoc. Prof., Catlgr., Bibl., Univ. of RI, 1970–; Catlgr., MA Inst. of Tech., 1969–70; Catlgr., London Sch. of Econ., Univ. of London, 1964–69; Libn., Dept. of Physiology, Univ. of Calcutta, 1960–64. **Educ.:** Univ. of Calcutta, India, 1952–54, B.Com. (Acct.), 1962–64, MA (Hist.); Univ. of RI, 1970–72, MA (Pol. Sci.); Univ. of Calcutta, 1955–58, Dipl. (Russ.), 1957–60, Dip. (Chinese), 1960–61, Dipl. (LS). **Orgs.:** ALA. N. Eng. LA. IASLIC. AAUP. **Pubns.:** Comp., "An Annotated Bibliography of the International Standard Bibliographic Description" (1977); "IFLA Working Group on Corporate Headings Meeting, London 26–28 April," *Intl. Cat.* (Jl.-S. 1977); "On Standardized Cataloging," Letter, *Lib. Jnl.* (Mr. 15, 1978); "Call for Precis Adoption," *Amer. Libs.* (O. 1978); "AACR2–Harbinger," *Lib. Jnl.* (O. 1, 1980); Various articles. **Activities:** 1; 20, 44, 46; 54, 77, 92 **Addr.:** 58 Greenwood Dr., Peace Dale, RI 02879.

Lai, John Yung-hsiang (S. 21, 1922, Taiwan, China) Assoc. Libn., Harvard-Yenching Lib., Harvard Univ., 1978–, Asst. Libn., Cat., 1973–77, Resrch. Assoc., 1972–73; Prof. (LS), Natl. Taiwan Univ., 1964–73, Head, LS Dept., 1965–73; Assoc. Prof. (LS), 1961–64, Head, Reader's Srvs., 1951–69. **Educ.:** Tokyo Univ., 1942–44, LL.B.; George Peabody Coll., 1958–59, MA (LS). **Orgs.:** ALA: ACRL and other Divs. Asian-Pac. Amer. Libns. Assn.: VP (1980–81). Chinese Amer. Libns. Assn.: Pres. (1979–80). Intl. Assn. of Orientalist Libns.: Adv. Cncl. (1967–70). Other orgs. Assn. for Asian Stds.: Com. on E. Asian Libs.; Natl. Un. Cat. Com. (Ch., 1978–80); Tsk. Frc. for Autom. and Un. Cat. (1980–81). **Honors:** Amer. Biog. Inst., Cmnty. Leaders and Noteworthy Amers. Awd., 1979–80. **Pubns.:** *New Classification scheme for Chinese Libraries: Tables & Indexes* (1961). *Historical Studies on Koxinga* (4 v.; 1954–56, 1968); jt. ed., *Old maps of North Taiwan,* (1957); ed., *Jnl. of Lib. & Info. Sci.* (1980–83); ed. *Catalog of Protestant Missionary Works in Chinese* (1980); other bibls., cats., articles, and monographs. **Activities:** 1, 12; 17, 20, 45; 54, 57, 66 **Addr.:** Harvard-Yenching Library, 2 Divinity Ave., Cambridge, MA 02138.

Laich, Katherine (W. S.) (Ja. 24, 1910, Bridgeton, NJ) Retired, 19–; Lectr., Coord., Progs., Sch. of LS, Univ. of South. CA, 1970–75; Asst. City Libn., Los Angeles Pub. Lib., 1961–70, Admin. Asst., 1947–60, Asst. Dept. Libn., 1946–47, Libn., 1944–46, Chld. Libn., 1942–44, Student Libn., 1941–42. **Educ.:** Wilson Coll., 1926–30, AB (Eng., Latin); Univ. of South. CA, 1940–42, BS (LS). **Orgs.:** ALA: Pres. (1972–73); Exec. Bd. (1964–68, 1971–74); Cncl. (1957–58, 1962–68, 1971–74); Nom. Com. (Ch., 1969–70); Actv. Com. on New Directions for ALA (Ch., 1969–71); various coms; Lib. Admin. Div., Bd. of Dirs. (1957–58, 1963–66); PLA, Metro. Area Lib. Srv. Com. (Ch., 1969–70). CA LA: Fed. Rel. Coord. (1957–58); various coms. SLA: South. CA Chap. (Pres., 1947). Amer. Cvl. Liberties Un. Amers. for Dem. Action. Common Cause. **Honors:** Sch. of LS, Univ. of South. CA, Disting. Alum. Awd., 1974. **Activities:** 9; 17, 35 **Addr.:** 5007 Cahuenga Blvd., N. Hollywood, CA 91601.

Laine, Edward W. (Mr. 31, 1940, Montreal, PQ) Archvst., North. European Grps., Pub. Arch. of Can., 1974–; Prof., Dawson Coll., 1971–72; Asst. Prof., St. Josheph's Tchrs. Coll., 1967–68. **Educ.:** Sir George Williams Univ., 1958–62, BA (Eng., hist.); McGill Univ., 1963–67, MA (Hist.), 1967–74, PhD (Hist.). **Orgs.:** Assn. of Can. Archvsts. East. ON Archvsts. Assn. Can. Hist. Assn. Can. Ethnic Std. Assn. Amer. Assn. for the Advnc. of Slavic Std. Can. Assn. of Slavists. **Pubns.:** "Finland's Military Significance for Nineteenth-Century Russia," *The New Review* (D. 1971); "The Expanding Opportunities for the Study of the Finnish Canadian Heritage at the Public Archives of Canada," *Siirtolaisuus-Migration* (1977); *Selections from the Finnish Organization of Canada Collection* (1979); "Archival Resources relating to the Finnish Canadians," *Archivaria* (Win. 1978); "Finnish Canadian Radicalism and Canadian Politics: The First Forty Years" in *Ethnicity, Power, and Politics in Canada.*; reviews. **Activities:** 2, 4; 15, 39, 45; 66 **Addr.:** Ethnic Archives, Public Archives of Canada, 395 Wellington St., Ottawa, ON K1A 0N3 Canada.

Laird, Nicola Renée (F. 14, 1947, The Dalles, OR) Dept. Head, Tchg. Resrc. Ctr., Lane Educ. Srv. Dist., 1977–; Resrch. Anal., Northwest Reg. Educ. Lab., 1976–77; Dssm. Spec., OR Dept. of Educ., 1974–75. **Educ.:** OR State Univ., 1966–69, BS (Recreation); Drexel Univ., 1972–73, MLS. **Orgs.:** ALA: LITA; ALSC; YASD; JMRT. OR LA: ILL Com. (1979). OR Educ. Media Assn.: PR Com. (1979); Div. Rep. (1980–82). **Pubns.:** Ed., Career Ed Resource Catalog, Oregon Dept. of Ed. (1974); jt. ed., "Aids to Integrating Career Education into the Educational Program," *Oregon ASCD Curric. Bltn.* (1975); "Career Ed Data Bases and Systems," *Sch. Media Qtly.* (Fall 1977); "Which Media Do Teachers Use Most?" *AV Instr.* (S. 1978). **Activities:** 12; 15, 17, 39; 63, 67, 75 **Addr.:** 2566 Elysium, Eugene, OR 97401.

Laird, W. David (Mr. 15, 1937, Kansas City, MO) Univ. Libn., Univ. of AZ, 1972–; Assoc. Dir., Libs., Univ. of UT, 1971–72, Asst. Dir. of Libs., Tech. Srvs., 1970–71, Acq. Libn., 1969–70, Mono. Order Libn., 1967–69; Ref. Libn., Univ. of CA, Davis, 1966–67. **Educ.:** Univ. of CA, Los Angeles, 1962–65, BA (Amer. Lit.), 1965–66, MLS. **Orgs.:** ALA: Cncl. (1974–75); ACRL, Nom. Com. (1970–71, 1974–75). AZ LA: Pres. (1978–79). **Pubns.:** *Hopi Bibliography* (1977); Jt. ed., *Voices from the Southwest* (1976); "Time Study of General Reference Work," *Resrch. in Libnshp.* (Ja. 1968); "A Truly Modest Proposal," *Wilson Lib. Bltn.* (Mr. 1969); Reviews; Other articles. **Activities:** 1; 15, 17, 19; 57, 95-American Southwest. **Addr.:** A349 Main Library, University of Arizona, Tucson, AZ 85721.

Lajeunesse, Marcel (Je. 28, 1942, Mont-Laurier, PQ) Assoc. Prof., Ecole de Bibliotheconomie, Univ. de Montréal, 1970–, Asst. Prof., 1972–78, Actg. Dir., 1972–73, Lectr., 1970–72. **Educ.:** Univ. de Montréal, 1963–64, BBibl (LS); Univ. of Ottawa, 1972–77, PhD (Hist.). **Orgs.:** ASTED: Com. of Intl. Rel.; Del. to IFLA (1977–81). AALS. Can. Assn. of Lib. Schs. Assn. Intl. des Écoles des Sci. de l'Info.: Exec. Secy. **Honors:** H.W. Wilson Lib. Per. Awd., 1977. **Pubns.:** *Répertoire des Écoles des Sciences de l'Information* (1979); *Les Sulpiciens et la Vie Culturelle Montréalaise au XIXe Siècle* (1980); *Le Role Social de l'Imprimé et de ses Agents au Québec* (1980); "Education and Training of Information Specialists in French Speaking Countries," *Unesco Jnl. of Info. Sci., Libnshp. and Arch. Admin.* (Ap.–Je 1979); Contrib., *Documentation et Bibliothèques* (Mr. 1977); various articles. **Activities:** 11; 26, 41 **Addr.:** Ecole de bibliothéconomie, Université de Montréal, C.P. 6128, Succ. "A", Montréal, PQ H3C 3J7 Canada.

Lakshmanan, Teresa Romanowska (Warsaw, Poland) Lib. Consult., 1965–; Head Lib., Metro. Washington Cncl. of Gvts., 1965–67; Resrch. Libn., Ling. Col., Ctr. for Applied Ling., 1964–65. **Educ.:** Univ. of Warsaw, Poland, 1952–57, MSc (Geo.); Cath. Univ., 1962–64, MS in LS; Univ. of Pittsburgh, 1975–80, PhD cand.; N. Atl. Treaty Org. Advnc. Std. Inst. in Info. Sci., 1972; Intl. Grad. Lib. Sum. Sch., Coll. of Libnshp., Aberystwyst, Wales, 1974. **Orgs.:** ALA: MARS Ch., Cost & Finance Com. (1976–78). ASIS. Doct. Gld., Univ. of Pittsburgh: Pres. (1975–76). **Honors:** Catherine Ofiesm Orner, Awd. for Excel. in Info. Sci., 1980. **Pubns.:** Editor, "Abstracts of Papers," 21st Intl. Geo. Congs., India (1968). **Activities:** 5, 12; 17, 24, 41, 46; 56, 57, 75 **Addr.:** 1328 Wightman St., Pittsburgh, PA 15217.

Laliberté, Madeleine Anne (St-Henri-de-Lévis, PQ) Libn., Laval Univ., 1977–; Ref. Libn., Cleveland Pub. Lib., 1972–75; Sch. Libn., École Sec., Beauceville, 1970–71. **Educ.:** Laval Univ., 1962–65, BA (Arts); Univ. of Ottawa, 1968–70, MLS; Case West. Rsrv. Univ., 1972–76, PhD (Info. Sci.). **Orgs.:** ALA. Can. LA. Corp. des Bibtcrs. Prof. du PQ. Assn. Can. des Sci. de l'Info.: Exec. Cnclr. (1979–). **Pubns.:** "Quelques Problèmes Rencontre's dans l'Application de Precis à la Langue Française," *Revue Can. des Sci. de l'Info.* (1977). **Activities:** 1; 20, 30; 75, 90 **Addr.:** 2047, Chemin Saint-Louis, Quèbec, PQ G1T 1P2 Canada.

LaLonde, Agathe (S. 4, 1928, Ottawa, ON) Asst. Prof., Ottawa Univ. Fac. of Educ., 1969–; Dept. of Educ., ON Mnstry. of Educ., 1966–69; Sch. Libn., Cornwall Collegiate, 1959–66; Tchr., Casselman HS, 1952–59. **Educ.:** Ottawa Univ., BA; Toronto Univ., BLS; Ottawa Univ., MEd. **Orgs.:** Can. LA: Cnclr. (1970–72). ON LA. Cncl. des Enseignants. ACBLF-ASTED. **Pubns.:** *La Bibliothèque Scolaire* (1968); *La Bibliothèque Professionnelle: Bibliographie* (1970); *Instruments de Choix* (1979); Manuel de Catalogage (1981). **Activities:** 1, 10; 15, 25, 32; 50, 63, 89 **Addr.:** Faculty of Education, Ottawa University, 651 Cumberland St., Ottawa, ON K1N 6N5 Canada.

Lamb, Gertrude (Jl. 30, 1918, Basin, MT) Dir., Hlth. Sci. Libs., Hartford Hosp., 1973–; Univ. Asst. Libn., Dir., Clinical Libn. Prog., Univ. of CT Hlth. Ctr., 1973–80; Med. Libn. and Assoc. Prof., Med., Univ. of MO-Kansas City Sch. of Med., 1971–73; Head, Acq. and Circ. Dept., Wilbur Cross Lib., Univ. of CT, 1956–62. **Educ.:** Radcliffe Coll 1936–40, AB (Econ.); Boston Univ., 1944–45, AM (Pub. Admin.); Case West. Rsv. Univ., 1967–68, MSLS, 1968–71, PhD (Info. Sci.). **Orgs.:** Med. LA: Pres. (1980–81). Cap. Area Hlth. Cnsrtm. Libs.: Pres. (1974–78). ALA. N. Atl. Hlth. Sci. Libs.: Ch. (1978). Various other orgs. Amer. Lung Assn. **Honors:** Case West. Rsv. Univ., Overseer, 1975–81; 3 Natl. Lib. of Med., Grants, 1972, 1974, 1977. **Pubns.:** "The Rediscovery of Librarianship," *Quantitative Methods in Librarianship* (1972); jt. auth., "The Librarian in Clinical Care," *The Hosp. Med. Staff* (D. 1977); jt. auth., "And Now Clinical Librarians on Rounds," *Hartford Hosp. Bltn.* (Je. 1975); slide-tape progs.: *Clinical Librarian, What do You Really Do?* (1975); *Clinical Librarian Sharing in Patient Care* (1978). **Activities:** 12, 14-Hospital; 17, 39, 41; 63, 75, 80 **Addr.:** Health Science Libraries, Hartford Hospital, 80 Seymour St., Hartford, CT 06115.

Lambert, Alloyd Patrick Jr. (F. 11, 1935, New Orleans, LA) Reg. Libn., William Carey Coll. Sch. of Nursing Lib., 1978–; Pub. Srvs. Libn., Dillard Univ., 1973–77; Head Libn., Circ. Dept., Tulane Univ., 1972–73; Ref. Libn., SUNY, Stony Brook, 1967–71. **Educ.:** Southeast. LA Univ., 1953–58, BA (Bus. Admin.); LA State Univ., 1962–64, MS (LS); Columbia Univ., 1967–68, Cert. Med. Libn. **Orgs.:** SELA: Jt. Conf., Regis. Com. (1973). Med. LA. William Carey Coll. Fac. Assn. Task Frc. For Lib. and Resrcs. Dev.: Ch. (1978–). **Honors:** LA LA, Pelican Publshg. Co. Awd., 1966. **Pubns.:** Various articles, bibls. **Activities:** 1, 12; 15, 17, 24; 80, 95-Nursing. **Addr.:** William Carey College School of Nursing Library, 2700 Napoleon Ave., New Orleans, LA 70115.

Lambert, Helene D. (Mr. 9, 1932, New York, NY) Hlth. Sci. Libn., New Rochelle Hosp., 1973–; Med. Libn., Rutland Hosp., 1969–73; Lib. Dir., Coll. of St. Joseph the Provider, 1968–69. **Educ.:** Brandeis Univ., 1949–52, AB cum laude (Eng. Lit.); Columbia Univ., 1952–53, MLS; Med. LA Cert., 1978–83. **Orgs.:** Hlth. Info. Libns. of Westchester: Pres. (1976–77); Bd. Mem. (1974–79). Med. LA: NY Reg. Grp., Nsltr. Com. (1976), Reg. Plan Subcom. (1978–80); Long Range Plng. Com. (Ch., 1980–81). SLA: Hudson Valley Chap. Hospice Plng. of Westchester. Dem. Soc. Org. Com. (Westchester). **Activities:** 12; 15, 17, 39; 58, 80 **Addr.:** Health Sciences Library, New Rochelle Hospital Medical Center, New Rochelle, NY 10802.

PROFESSIONAL ACTIVITIES: Institutions: 1. Acad. lib.; 2. Arch.; 3. Assn.; 4. Fed./Gvt. lib.; 5. Inst. lib.; 6. Mfr./Suppl.; 7. Milit. lib.; 8. Musm.; 9. Pub. lib.; 10. Sch. lib.; 11. Sch. of lib. sci.; 12. Spec. lib.; 13. State lib.; 14. (other). **Functions/Activities:** 15. Acq./Col. dev.; 16. Adult srvs.; 17. Admin.; 18. Apprais.; 19. Archit./Bldgs.; 20. Cat./Class.; 21. Chld. srvs.; 22. Circ.; 23. Cons./Pres.; 24. Consult.; 25. Cont. ed.; 26. Educ. lib. sci.; 27. Ext. srvs.; 28. Fund/Grants; 29. Gvt. pubs.; 30. Indx./Abs.; 31. Instr. lib. use; 32. Media srvs.; 33. Micro.; 34. Netwks./Coop.; 35. Persnl.; 36. PR; 37. Publshg.; 38. Recs. mgt.; 39. Ref. srvs.; 40. Repro.; 41. Resrch.; 42. Review.; 43. Secur.; 44. Serials; 45. Spec. col.; 46. Tech. srvs.; 47. Trustees/Bds.; 48. YA srvs.; 49. (other).

Lambert, James H. (F. 10, 1947, Guelph, ON) Redacteur-Histn., Les Presses De L'Univ. Laval 1978–; Archvst., (HR 2), Pub. Arch. of Can., 1973–75. **Educ.:** Univ. of Guelph, 1967–69, BA (Hist.); Carleton Univ. (Ottawa), 1969–70, MA (Hist.); Université Laval, 1970–81, PhD (Hist.). **Orgs.:** Assn. Can. Archvst. Assn. Archvst. PQ. **Pubns.:** "Toward A Religious Archives Programme for the Public Archives of Canada," *Archivaria* (Win. 1976–77); "Public Archives and Religious Records: Marriage Proposals," *Archivaria* (Win. 1975–76); "Pour un programme d'archives cultuelles aux Archives publiques du Canada," *Arch.* (PQ) (S./D. 1975). **Activities:** 2; 15, 20, 39; 90 **Addr.:** 1251 Ave Forget, Sillery, PQ G1S 3Y6 Canada.

Lambert, Robert Allen (S. 30, 1936, Hagerstown, MD) Asst. Libn. for Tech. Srv., US Naval Acad., 1969–, Spec. Proj. Libn., 1968–69, Head, Acq. Dept., 1967–68, Head, Sci-Tech Branch, 1967–67; Chief Libn., Tech. Info. Ctr., Fairchild Indus., 1966–67; Supvsr., Tech. Info. Srv., Electromagnetic Compatibility Anal. Ctr., 1963–66. **Educ.:** Univ. of MD, 1954–59, BA (Hist.); Catholic Univ. of Amer., 1959–63, MS (LS); Anne Arundel Cmnty. Coll., 1976–, (Fncl. Acct.). **Orgs.:** Fed. Lib. Com.: Fnc. Com. (1979–). **Pubns.:** "Notable Naval Books: The First 100 Years, 1873-1973," *US Naval Inst. Proc.* (O. 1973). **Activities:** 1, 4; 17, 24, 35, 46; 59 **Addr.:** RFD 4, 985 St. Margaret's Avenue, Annapolis, MD 21401.

Lambkin, Claire A. (N. 16, 1925, Brooklyn, NY) Chief Libn., Amer. Mgt. Assn., 1969–, Libn., 1961–69; Admn. Libn., US Army Europe, 1959–61; Tchr. of Lib., Bd. of Educ., City of New York, 1953–58. **Educ.:** Brooklyn Coll., 1953, BA (Hist.); St. John's Univ., 1957, MLS. **Orgs.:** SLA: Info. Tech. Grp. (Ch. 1980–81); Bus. Fnc. Grp. (Secy. 1978–79); NY Chapt. ASIS. Long Island Hist. Socty.: Couns. (1980–82). Brooklyn Coll. Alum. Assn.: Bd. of Dir. (1970–). Acad. of Intl. Bus. **Activities:** 12; 17; 51, 59, 95-Mgt. **Addr.:** American Management Association, 135 West 50th St., New York, NY 10020.

Lamers, Carl Fritz (Ag. 20, 1921, Malang, East Java, Indonesia) Frgn. and Intl. Law Libn., Yale Law Sch. Lib., 1972–; Soc. Sci. Bibl., Yale Univ. Lib., 1964–72, Head, Gifts and Exch., 1963–64. **Educ.:** Lyceum A. Zutphen (The Netherlands), 1942; Univ. of Leiden (The Netherlands), 1947–54, LLM; Univ. of TX, 1959–63, MLS. **Orgs.:** AALL: Com. Indx. to Frgn. Legal Per. (1973–). Intl. Assn. Law Libs. **Activities:** 1; 15, 22, 31, 39; 77 **Addr.:** Yale Law School Library, Box 401-A Yale Station, New Haven, CT 06520.

Lamirande, Armand (Ap. 30, 1925, PQ) Chief Libn., Coll. Milit. Royal, 1952–; Sch. Libn., St. Lawrence HS (ON), 1960–64; Head Cat., Can. Bur. of Stats. 1955–60; Head of Per., Can. Dept. of Agr., 1950–59. **Educ.:** Univ. Laval, 1947–49, BA (Arts); Univ. McGill, 1949–50, BLS; Univ. of Toronto, 1960–62, BPed (Tchg.). **Orgs.:** Can. LA. Assn. Can. Bibtcr. Lang. Fr. **Activities:** 1, 4; 15, 20 **Addr.:** College Militaire Royal de Saint-Jean Library, St. Jean, PQ J0J 1R0, Canada.

Lampe, Sister Mary Ellen, C.PP.S. (My. 23, 1941, Denver, CO) Lib. Dir., Alumni Memorial Lib., 1981–; Lib. Dir., Luke M. Power Cath. HS, 1973–81; Libn., Elem. Sch., Archdiocese of Cincinnati, 1971–73, Elem. Sch. Tchr., 1963–70. **Educ.:** Univ. of Dayton, 1959–66, BS (Educ.); Rosary Coll., 1969–71, MALS. **Orgs.:** MI LA. MI Cath. LA: Bd. (1975); VP (1977–79); Pres. (1979–81); Rep. to Jt. Com. for Media Ctr. Dev. (1975). Cath. LA: Adv. Cncl. (1979–81). MI Assn. for Media in Educ. Sisters of the Precious Blood (C.PP.S.): Asm. Rep. (1978–). Sisters Cncl., Diocese of Lansing: VP (1977–79); Pres. (1979). **Honors:** Beta Phi Mu, 1971. **Pubns.:** *Guidelines for Library/Media Skill Objectives, K-12* (1979); *Guidelines for Media Programs in Michigan Schools, 2nd. ed.* (1979). **Activities:** 10; 17, 31, 48; 63, 75, 90 **Addr.:** Alumni Memorial Library, Orchard Lake Schools, Orchard Lake, MI 48033.

Lamprecht, Sandra Jean (Ap. 18, 1947, Duluth, MN) Geo. and Map Libn., CA State Univ., Long Beach, 1971–. **Educ.:** Univ. of CA, Los Angeles, 1967–69, BA (Geo.); 1970–71, MLS; CA State Univ., Long Beach, 1973–78, MA (Geo.). **Orgs.:** SLA. Map Socty. of CA. West. Assn. Map Libns.: *Info. Bltn.* Rev. Ed. (1979–). ALA. **Pubns.:** *Of Atlases and Adventures* (1976). *California: A Bibliography of Theses and Dissertations in Geography* (1975); "Goals and Objectives for the University Library Map Room," SLA Geo. and Map Div. *Bltn.* (D. 1977); Other bibls., reviews, articles. **Activities:** 1; 29, 31, 39; 59, 70, 92 **Addr.:** California State University Library, 1250 Bellflower Blvd., Long Beach, CA 90840.

Lampson, Virginia E. (Je. 5, 1932, River Forest, IL) Libn., Temple Univ. Dental-Allied Hlth.-Pharm. Lib., 1963–; Asst. Libn., 1960–63. **Educ.:** Univ. of MN, Duluth, 1953–56, BA (Eng.); Drexel Univ., 1958–60, MSLS. **Orgs.:** Med. LA: Ch., Dent. Sch. Libs Grp. (1964–65); other coms., Phila Reg. Grp. SLA. Geneal. Socty. of PA. Hist. Socty. of PA. **Honors:** Chapel of Four Chaplains, Legion of Honor, 1980. **Activities:** 1, 12; 15, 17, 45; 58, 80, 87 **Addr.:** 2101 Chestnut St. #806, Philadelphia, PA 19103.

Lamson, Merle E. (Ag. 10, 1930, Yakima, WA) Rare Bks. Catlgr., Assoc. Libn., Brigham Young Univ., 1981–; Assoc. Prof. (LS), 1966–81, Sci. Tech. Catlgr., 1963–66, Serials Libn., 1961–63; YA Libn., S. Puget Sound Reg. Lib. (WA), 1960–61. **Educ.:** Yakima Valley Jr. Coll., 1949–50, 1952–53, AAS (Phys.); Brigham Young Univ., 1953–55, BS (Math); Columbia Univ., 1957–60, MS (LS); Univ. of UT, 1970–75, PhD (Educ. Admin.). **Orgs.:** ALA. AALS. UT LA. Socty. of Educs. and Schols. UT Acad. of Sci., Arts, Letters. **Honors:** Sigma Pi Sigma. **Pubns.:** *Classification: An Introduction* (1980); "Toward a Theory of Classification," *Schol. and Educ.* (Spr. 1978); Jt. auth., "Cataloging 1966 vs 1976," *Jnl. of Educ. for Libnshp.* (Fall 1979); **Activities:** 11; 20, 41 **Addr.:** P. O. Box 498, Woodland Hills, UT 84653.

Lamy-Rousseau, Francoise (Ja. 21, 1924, Trois-Rivières, PQ) Consult. Libn., 1980–; Org. and Chief of Cat. Dept., PQ Minstry. of Educ., 1973–79, Chief of Eval., AV Dept., Ctrl. des Bibs. 1970–72, Org. and Chief Libn., ENET, 1965–69. **Educ.:** Univ. de Montréal, 1952–56, BA 1957–58, BA (LS). (Ped.), **Orgs.:** IFLA Intl. Stan. Org. Can. LA. Assn. of Can. Publshrs. **Pubns.:** *Traitement Automatisé des Documents Multi-media avec les Systèmes ISBD Unifié* (1974); "Classification, Catalogage et Indexation des Documents Multi-media," *Les Cahiers de Cap Rouge* (Mr. 1974); *Easy Method for Inventory and Classification of Audio-Visual Materials* (1972). **Activities:** 12, 13; 20, 32, 41; 56, 62, 75 **Addr.:** 485, Brais Street, Longueuil, PQ J4H 1T7 Canada.

Lancaster, F. Wilfrid (S. 4, 1933, Stanley, Durham, Eng.) Prof. (LS), Univ. of IL, 1972–, Assoc. Prof. (LS), 1970–72; Dir., Info. Retrieval Srvs., Westat Resrch., Inc., 1969–70; Info. Systs. Spec., Natl. Lib. of Med., 1965–69; Consult. and Head, Syst. Eval. Grp., Hernyer and Co., 1964–65. **Educ.:** Flw. (by thesis), British LA, 1969. **Orgs.:** LA (UK). ASIS. **Honors:** ASIS, Best Info. Sci. Bk., 1970, 1975, 1979. ALA, Ralph Shaw Awd., 1978. Other awds. **Pubns.:** *Information Retrieval Systems,* 2d. ed. (1979); *Toward Paperless Information Systems* (1978); *The Measurement and Evaluation of Library Services* (1977); Jt.-auth., *Information Retrieval On-Line* (1973); Other articles, rpts., papers. **Activities:** 11; 24, 26, 30; 62, 75 **Addr.:** 1807 Cindy Lynn, Urbana, IL 61801.

Lancaster, Herman Burtram (Mr. 6, 1942, Chicago, IL) Dir., Prof. (Legal Resrch.), Glendale Law Sch., 1973–; Pres., The Legal Inst., 1976–; Dir. of Info., Univ. of Chicago, 1970–73; Asst. Dir., Law Lib., De Paul Univ., 1967–70. **Educ.:** Chicago State Univ., 1961–65, BS (Educ.); Rosary Coll., 1966–68, MA (LS); De Paul Univ., 1968–72, JD. **Orgs.:** AALL. S CA Assn. of Law Libs. Amer. Bar Assn. **Honors:** Student Bar Assn., Prof. of the Yr., 1979. **Pubns.:** *Legal Research Casebook* (1977); *Prisoner Legal Research Training* (1979); "The Organization and Bureaucracy of Drug Abuse Control," *Jnl. of Drug Issues* (1973); "Title Insurance–A Survey Inquiry," Glendale Law Rev. (1976); Other articles in law jnls. **Activities:** 1, 14-Law Sch.; 31, 37, 41; 77 **Addr.:** Suite E, Park Professional Bldg., 912 N. Hollywood Way, Burbank, CA 91505.

Lancaster, John (Jl. 20, 1943, New York, NY) Spec. Col. Libn. and Archvst., Amherst Coll., 1977–; Rare Bk. Cat., Houghton Lib., 1970–76. **Educ.:** Williams Coll., 1960–64, BA (Ger.); Cornell Univ., 1964–67, (Germ. Ling.); Simmons Coll., 1969–70, MS (LS). **Orgs.:** ALA: ACRL, Rare Bk. Mss. Sect., Stan. Com. (1980–). NELINET: Rare Bk. Mss. Users OCLC Grp. (Ch. 1979–80). SAA. Athenaeum Grp.: Ch. (1980–). New Eng. Archvst. Bibl. Socty. of Amer. Socty. Bibl. Nat. Hist. Amer. Prtg. Hist. Assn. **Pubns.:** Ed., *Modern Illustrated Books: The Selma Erving Collection* (1977); Ed., *Papers of the Bibliographical Society of America* (1982–); "Edward Hitchcock," *N. East. Geo.* (Fall 1980). **Activities:** 1, 2; 20, 45; 56, 57 **Addr.:** Amherst College Library, Amherst, MA 01002.

Lancaster, Richard F. (Ag. 10, 1937, Roanoke, VA) Coord. of Lib. and Media Srvs., John Tyler Cmnty. Coll., 1970–; Coord. of Lib. Srvs., VA West. Cmnty. Coll., 1966–70; Catlgr., VA Milit. Inst., 1965–66; Head, Tech. Srvs., Roanoke Pub. Lib., 1964–65. **Educ.:** Roanoke Coll., 1955–59, BA (Hist.); Univ. of NC, 1963–64, MSLS; Univ. of Richmond, 1970–74, MH (Hum.). **Orgs.:** VA LA. Capital Cnsrtm. for Cont. Higher Educ.: Lib. Com. (1976–). State Cncl. for Higher Educ.: Lib. Adv. Com. (1980–). Richmond Area Film Coop. **Activities:** 1; 15, 17, 32; 50 **Addr.:** John Tyler Community College, 13101 Jefferson Davis Hwy., Chester, VA 23831.

Land, Phyllis M. (Ag. 29, 1944, Winona, MS) Dir., Div. of Instr. Media, IN Dept. of Pub. Instr., 1974–, Sch. Lib. Consult., 1971–74; Matls. Spec., Fulton Cnty. Bd. of Educ. (GA), 1969–71; Head Libn., Natchez Adams HS (MS), 1967–68. **Educ.:** Univ. of South. MS, 1965–67, BS (Educ.); Univ. of TN 1968–69, MS (LS); Purdue Univ., 1972–74, Educ. Media; IN Univ., 1976–80, Pub. and Environ. Affairs. **Orgs.:** ALA: Int. Com. Frdm. (1974–76); AASL, Sch. Lib. Media Prog. Yr. (1977); Right to Read (1973–76). AECT: Nom. Com. (1978). Natl. Assn. State Educ. Media Prof.: Pres. (1976). IN Coop. Lib. Srv. Auth.: Exec. Com., Dir. Lg. (1978–79), VP (1979–80), Pres. (1980). **Honors:** Intl. Readg. Assn., Cit. of Excel., 1975. **Pubns.:** "Schools - the On-Line Connection," *In Excellence in School Media Programs* (1980); "Preface," *In Networks for Networkers* (1980); "A New Breed for the 80s," *Sch. Lib. Jnl.* (Ag. 1980); "The Eighties and the 30 Mile Per Gallon Concept," *IN Media Jnl.* (Fall 1979); Jt. Auth., "An Empirical Study of Media Services in Indiana Elementary Schools," *Sch. Media Qtly.* (Fall 1975); other pubns. **Activities:** 14-State Educ. Agency; 17, 24, 34; 63, 68 **Addr.:** Division of Instructional Media, Indiana Department of Public Instruction, Room 229 State House, Indianapolis, IN 46204.

Land, R. Brian (Jy. 29, 1927, Niagara Falls, ON) Dir, Leg. Lib. Resrch. and Info. Srvs., ON Leg Asm., 1978–, Prof. (LS), Univ. of Toronto, 1972–; Prof. and Dean (LS), 1964–72; Exec. Asst. to Mnstr. of Finance, Ottawa, 1963–64; Assoc. Libn., Univ. of Toronto, 1963, Asst. Libn., 1959–63; Assoc. Ed., *Canadian Business,* 1958–59, Asst. Ed., 1957–58; Head, Bus. and Indus. Div., Windsor (ON) Pub. Lib., 1956–57; Other positions. **Educ.:** Univ. of Toronto, 1945–49, BA (Pol. Sci., Econ.), 1952–53, BLS, 1955–56, MLS, 1960–63, MA (Pol. Sci.). **Orgs.:** Can. LA: Pres. (1975–76); Ed. and Pubn. Policy Com. (Ch., 1968–71). ALA: Com. on Accred. (Ch., 1973–74); ACRL. ON LA: VP (1962–63). Can. Assn. of Lib. Schs.: Pres. (1966–67). Other orgs. and ofcs. Can. Radio-TV and Telecom. Comsn.: Comsn. (1973–78). **Honors:** Beta Phi Mu. ON Lib. Trustees Assn., Disting. Achvmnt. Awd., 1968. Queen's Silver Jubilee Medal, 1977. **Pubns.:** *Directory of Associations in Canada* (1981); *Sources of Information for Canadian Business* (1978); "A Description and Guide to Canadian Government Publications," *Politics: Canada* (1981); "Canadian correspondent," *ALA Yrbk.* (1976–81); Other pubns. **Activities:** 13; 17; 77, 78 **Addr.:** Legislative Library, Research and Information Services, Legislative Building, Queen's Park, Toronto, ON M5S 1A1 Canada.

Landau, Herbert B. (O. 24, 1940, New York, NY) Info. Syst. Div. Mgr., Solar Energy Resrch. Inst., 1978–; Prin. Mgr., Info. Storage and Retrieval, Auerbach Assocs., Inc., 1967–78; Lib. Oper. Supvsr., Bell Telephone Labs., 1964–67. **Educ.:** Hunter Coll., 1958–63, AB (Chem.); Columbia Univ., 1963–64, MS (LS). **Orgs.:** ASIS: Pres. (1979–80); Cnclr. (1972–75). Amer. Socty. of Indxrs.: Treas. (1969–71). ALA. SLA. Engin. Index: Trustee. Assn. for Comp. Mach. Data Prcs. Mgmt. Assn. **Honors:** Beta Phi Mu, 1964. **Pubns.:** "Document Dissemination," *Anl. Rev. of Info. Sci. and Tech.* (1969); "Can the Librarian Become a Computer Data Base Manager?" *Spec. Libs.* (1971). **Activities:** 6, 12; 17, 34; 56, 75, 91 **Addr.:** Solar Energy Research Institute, 1617 Cole Blvd., Golden, CO 80401.

Lander, James H. (Je. 14, 1946, Freeport, IL) Mgr. of Lib. Srv., Mercy Hlth. Ctr., 1971–. **Educ.:** IL State Univ., 1964–68, BA (Math), 1970–71, (Math). **Orgs.:** Med. LA: Hlth. Sci. AV Sect. (Secy./Treas. 1979–80; Treas. 1978); Hosp. Lib. Sect.; Mental Hlth. Sect.; Midwest Reg. Chap. IA LA. Hlth. Sci. Libn. IA. **Pubns.:** "Mercy Is Love in Action," 3/4" video (1978). **Activities:** 5, 12; 17, 32, 34; 58, 59, 80 **Addr.:** A.C. Pfohl Health Science Library, Mercy Health Center: St. Joseph Unit, Dubuque, IA 52001.

Landers, John J. (Ap. 16, 1939, Fort Scott, KS) Asst. Archvst. Rec. Info. Mgt., US Natl. Arch., 1980–, Exec. Dir., 1976–80, Deputy Exec. Dir., 1972–76, Dir., Tech. Srv. Div., 1967–72. **Educ.:** Rockhurst Coll., 1957–61, AB (Econ.); Univ. PA, 1961–63, MGA (Pub. Admin.). **Orgs.:** SAA. Assoc. of Rec. Mgrs. and Admins. Amer. Socty. Pub. Admin. **Honors:** Natl. Arch. Rec. Srv., Comdn. Srv. Awd., 1975, 1980. **Activities:** 2, 4; 38 **Addr.:** Office of Records and Information Mgt., National Archives and Records Service, Washington, DC 20408.

Landers, Lora (Mr. 14, 1927, Maplewood, NJ) Deputy Dir., Hennepin Cnty. Lib., 1975–, Dir., Read. Srvs., 1970–75, Coord., Adult and YA Srvs., 1965–70, Libn., II and Coord., YA Srvs., Minneapolis Pub. Lib., 1957–65; Libn., U.S. Army (Europe), 1954–56; Clerk, Libn., NY Pub. Lib., 1949–54. **Educ.:** Mount Holyoke Coll., 1945–49, BA (Econ.); Columbia Univ., 1950–53, MS (LS). **Orgs.:** ALA: OLPR Adv. Com. (1981–82); Nom. Com. (1978); PLA, Actv. Com. (1973–75); RASD, Adult Mtrls. Com. (1974–77); YASD, Best Bks. for YA (Ch., 1966–67); Various other coms. MN LA: Various coms. and ofcs. **Pubns.:** "Young Adult Services in the Small Public Library" pamphlet (1961). **Activities:** 9; 17, 35, 39; 63, 74 **Addr.:** Hennepin County Library, 7001 York Ave. S., Edina, MN 55435.

Landesman, Betty J. (Je. 9, 1947, Bronx, NY) Serials Libn., Wellesley Coll., 1980–; Serials Cat., N. East. Univ., 1977–80, Cat., 1976–77, Serials Asst., 1976–76, Instr. Fr. and Latin, 1968–75. **Educ.:** Hunter Coll., 1963–67, BA (Fr.); Harvard Univ., 1967–68, MA (Fr.); Simmons Coll., 1975–76, MLS. **Orgs.:** ALA. New Eng. LA. Boston Lib. Consort.: Serials Com. (Secy., 1979–80; Ch., 1980–81). NELINET: Rep. to OCLC Serials Cntrl. Adv. Com. (1979–). **Honors:** Phi Beta Kappa, 1966; Pi Delta Phi, 1967; Woodrow Wilson Flwshp., 1967; Beta Phi Mu, 1976. **Activities:** 1; 20, 44 **Addr.:** Serials Department, Margaret Clapp Library, Wellesley College, Wellesley, MA 02181.

Landis, Martha (N. 22, 1935, Champaign, IL) Prin. Ref. Libn., Univ. of IL, 1981–, Sr. Ref. Libn., 1979–81, Ref. Libn., 1971–79, Assoc. Ref. Libn., 1968–71; Asst. Ref. Libn., Cornell Univ., 1963–68; Union Browsing Rm. Libn., Univ. of IL, 1959–63, Asst. Undergrad. Libn., 1959. **Educ.:** Univ. of IL, 1954–57, BA (Hist.), 1957–59, MS (LS). **Orgs.:** ALA: RASD, Ref. and Subscrpn. Bk. Com. (1971–74); Ad-Hoc Com. on Ref.

Special Subjects/Services: 50. Adult educ.; 51. Advert./Mktg.; 52. Aerosp.; 53. Agric.; 54. Area std.; 55. Arts/Hum.; 56. Autom.; 57. Bibl./Prtg.; 58. Bio. sci.; 59. Bus./Fin.; 60. Chem.; 61. Copyrt.; 62. Documtn.; 63. Educ.; 64. Engin.; 65. Env.; 66. Eth. grps.; 67. Film; 68. Food/Nutr.; 69. Geneal.; 70. Geo.; 71. Geol.; 72. Handcpd.; 73. Hist.; 74. Int. frdm.; 75. Info. sci.; 76. Insr.; 77. Law; 78. Legis.; 79. Math./Comp. sci.; 80. Med.; 81. Metals; 82. Nat. resrcs.; 83. Newsp.; 84. Nuc. sci.; 85. Oral hist.; 86. Petr./Energy; 87. Pharm.; 88. Phys./Astr./Math.; 89. Readg.; 90. Relig.; 91. Sci./Tech.; 92. Soc. sci.; 93. Telecom.; 94. Transp.; 95. (other).

Srv. in Lg. Resrch. Lib. (Ch., 1976). IL LA. **Honors:** Beta Phi Mu. **Addr.:** 609 W. Oregon St., Urbana, IL 61801.

Landon, Richard G. (D. 27, 1942, Armstrong, BC) Head, Thomas Fisher Rare Book Lib., Univ. of Toronto, 1976–, Asst. Head, 1969–76. **Educ.:** Univ. of BC, 1960–65, BA (Thea.); Leeds Univ., 1971–72, MA (Bibl.); Univ. of BC, 1966–67, BLS. **Honors:** Cncl. on Lib. Resrcs., Flwshp., 1975. **Pubns.:** Ed., *Book Selling and Book Buying: Aspects of the Nineteenth Century... Book Trades* (1978); *Species of Origin* (1971); "Rare Books and Special Collections Libraries" in *New Horizons for Academic Libraries* (1979); "The Bibliography of Canadian Literature in English" in *Procs. of the Natl. Conf. on the State of Can. Bibl.* (1977). **Activities:** 1; 15, 17, 41; 55, 57, 91 **Addr.:** Thomas Fisher Rare Book Library, University of Toronto, Toronto, ON M5S 1A5 Canada.

Landram, Christina L. (D. 10, 1922, Paragould, AR) Head, Cat. Dept., GA State Univ., 1963–; Coord., Shelby Cnty. Libs., Memphis Pub. Lib., 1961–63; Lib., Jacksonville (AR) HS, 1959–61; Lib., St. Mary's Hosp., West Palm Beach, 1957–59; Lib., Yokota (Japan) Air Frc. Base, 1954–55; Catlgr., U.S. Dept. of Agr. Lib., 1953–54; Catlgr., TX Tech. Univ., 1950–51. **Educ.:** TX Woman's Univ., 1945, BA (Hist.), 1946, BSLS, 1951, MLS. **Orgs.:** ALA: Cat. Norms Discuss. Grp. (Ch., 1979–80); Nom. Com.; Cat. Class. Sect. SELA: Gvtl. Rel. Com. (1975–78). GA LA: Constn. Com. (Ch., 1979–81). Metro-Atlanta LA.: Pres. (1967–68). **Pubns.:** "A Visit to Libraries in the People's Republic of China," *Southeast. Libn.* (Fall, 1978); "OCLC Terminal Plus Printer," *Lib. Resrcs. & Tech. Srvs.* (Spr. 1977); "Increasing Production in a Small University Catalog Department," *Lib. Resrcs. & Tech. Srvs.* (Sum. 1971). **Activities:** 1; 17, 20 **Addr.:** 1478 Leafmore Ridge, Decatur, GA 30033.

Landrum, Frank (F. 13, 1939, Philadelphia, PA) Asst. Supvsr. of Lib. Media Srvs., Prince George's Cnty. Pub. Schs., 1975–, Spec., Lib. Media Prog. Dev., 1966–75; Sch. Libn., Forest Hts. Elem. Sch. 1965–66; Persnl. Spec., U.S. Army, 1963–65; Sch. Libn., Susquenita HS, 1962–63. **Educ.:** Millersville 1958–62, BS (Educ.); Villanova Univ., 1967–70, MS (LS). **Orgs.:** MD Educ. Media Org. Treas. (1972–74), Nsltr. (Ch., 1975–76), Spring Conf. Plng. Com. (1978–79). Southeast. Reg. Media Leadership Conf.: Conv. Plng. Com. (1976). Natl. Educ. Assn. MD. Educ. Assn. Prince George's Cnty. Educ. Assn. **Pubns.:** "Closing schools means moving library materials," *Amer. Sch. and Univ.* (My. 1978). **Activities:** 10; 17, 28, 32; 63 **Addr.:** Palmer Park Services Center, 8437 Landover Rd., Landover, MD 20785.

Lane, Margaret T. (F. 6, 1919, St. Louis, MO) Libn., Lane & Clesi (L), 1976–; Recorder of Docum., LA Secy. of State Ofc., 1949–75; Law Libn., LA State Univ. Law Lib., 1946–48; Law Libn. and Asst. Prof., Univ. of CT Law Lib., 1944–46; Ref. and Circ. Libn., Columbia Univ. Law Lib., 1942–1944. **Educ.:** LA St. Univ., 1935–39, BA (Gvt.); Columbia Univ., 1940–41, BS (LS); LA St. Univ., 1939–42 JD. **Orgs.:** ALA: Pub. Docum. Com. (1959–62, 1967–74, Ch., 1967–70); GODORT, State Local Docum. Task Force (Coord., 1980–). AALL: Jt. Com. Union List Serials (Rep. 1967–73). LA LA: Parlmt.; various com. Depos. Lib. Cncl. Pub. Printer: (1973–77). **Honors:** LA LA, Culver Awd. for Disting. Lib. Srv., 1976; ALA GODORT, James Bennett Childs Awd., 1981. **Pubns.:** *State Publications and Depository Libraries* (1981); Ed. *Louisiana Union Catalog, Supplement 1959–1962* (1963); Cmplr. *State of Louisiana Official Publications* 1952–75); "Acquisition of State Documents," *Law Lib. Jnl.* (F. 1970); "List of Current State Documents Checklists," *Lib. Resrc. and Tech. Srv.* (Fall 1966); Various other pubns. **Activities:** 1, 12; 29; 77 **Addr.:** c/o Lane & Clesi, P.O. Box 3335, Baton Rouge, LA 70821.

Lane, Mary Seminara (Ag. 26, 1948, Quincy, MA) Dir. of libs. and Cur. of Spec. Col., Wentworth Inst. of Tech., Boston, MA., (1981–); Consult., 1979–; Dir., Canton (MA) Pub. Lib., 1973–79; Libn., Boston Mus. of Fine Arts, 1970–71; Visit. Lectr., Bridgewater State Coll., 1977–78. **Educ.:** Rosemont Coll., 1966–70, BA (Art Hist.); Simmons Coll., 1972–73, MS (LS). **Orgs.:** MA LA: Natl. Lib. Wk. (Dir., 1974, 1975), PR Com. (1974–), Schol. Com. (1974–75). New Eng. LA: PR Com. (1978–). ALA. AAUW: Prog. Com. (1978). Ray Meml. LA: Trustee (1978–). **Honors:** Beta Phi Mu; New Eng. LA, PR Cert., 1979; MA LA, Lib. of the Yr. Awd., 1979; Lib. PR Cncl., Spec. Mention, 1975, 1977, 1978. **Pubns.:** "Town of Canton" (Video-Oral Hist.) (1978). **Activities:** 9; 17, 19, 36; 55 **Addr.:** 95 Pine Ridge Dr., Franklin, MA 02038.

Lane, Robert B. (D. 6, 1930, San Francisco, CA) Dir., Air Univ. Lib., 1974–; Field Dir., Karachi Ofc., Lib. of Congs., 1971–73; Chief, Reader Srvs. Div., Air Univ. Lib., 1967–71; Staff Libn., Ankara, Turkey, U. S. Air Frc., 1965–67. **Educ.:** Univ. of CA, Berkeley, 1950–54, AB (Eng.), 1956–57, MLS. **Orgs.:** ALA: FLRT (Pres., 1975–76); Nom. Com. (Ch., 1978–79). SLA: Ntwkg. Com. (Ch., 1976–77); Conf. Prog. Com. (Ch., 1978). **Pubns.:** "Toward New Horizons: Impressions of the First National ACRL Conference," *Spec. Libs.* (F. 1979); "SOLINET Meets with State Librarians," *Southeast Libn.* (Spr. 1977); "The Conference on Interlibrary Communications and Information Networks," *Spec. Libs.* (N. 1970). **Activities:** 1, 4; 17, 24, 34; 52, 74, 92 **Addr.:** 2571 Churchill Dr., Montgomery, AL 36111.

Lane, Rosemary (Jl. 11, 1927, Little Rock, AR) City Libn., Chula Vista Pub. Lib., 1981–; Dir., Albuquerque Pub. Lib., 1979–81, Asst. Dir., 1972–79; Head of Adult Srv., Greenwich Lib. (CT), 1971–72; Chief of Pub. Srv., Fairfax Cnty. Pub. Lib. (VA), 1968–69; Asst. Chief, Div. Blind Phys. Handcpd., Lib. of Congs., 1967–68, Ref. Libn., Legis. Ref., 1967–68; Art, Archit. Libn., Univ. CO, 1964–66; Other lib. positions. **Educ.:** Univ. of CA, Riverside, 1954–56, AB (Hist.); Univ. of CA, Berkeley 1956–57, MLS. **Orgs.:** ALA: Com. Srv. Aging Popltn. (1969–71). SWLA: Jt. Conf. Mt. Plains LA, Local Arrange. (1976). Grt. Albuquerque LA: Pres. (1976); First VP (1975); Sec. VP (1974). NM LA: Cont. Educ. Com. (Ch., 1978). **Addr.:** Chula Vista Public Library, 365 "F" St., Chula Vista, CA 92010.

Lane, Sandra G. (Ap. 8, 1943, Memphis, TN) Libn., Nuc. Waste Mgt., Brookhaven Natl. Lab, 1976–. **Educ.:** Brooklyn Coll., 1959–63, BA (Eur. Lit.); C. W. Post, 1974–75, MLS. **Orgs.:** SLA: Nuc. Sci. Div., Treas. (1979–81), Ch. Elect (1981–82); Long Island Chap. (Treas., 1979–81); Dir. (1981–83). **Activities:** 4, 12; 39, 41, 46; 60, 84, 91 **Addr.:** Building 830, Nuclear Waste Management Division, Brookhaven National Laboratory, Upton, NY 11973.

Lanese, Lewis L. (F. 19, 1931, Cleveland, OH) Asst. City Libn., Bridgeport Pub. Lib., 1980–; Consult., Autom. Syst., Tech. Prcs., 1979–; Asst. Dir., Tech. Srv., Ferguson Lib., 1967–78; Head Libn., Sachem HS, 1966–67; Head Libn., Pembroke Coll. Lib., 1964–66; Asst. Chief Order Libn., Brown Univ. Lib., 1962–64; Libn., Lib. USA, World's Fair, Sum. 1965. **Educ.:** Univ. of CA at Los Angeles, 1949–50, 52–53, (Hist.); OH State Univ., 1953–55, BS (Educ.); Case West. Reserve Univ., 1961–62, MS (LS). **Orgs.:** ALA. New Eng. Lib. Info. Netwk.: Exec. Bd., Bd. Dir. (1974–80). CT LA: 2 VP (1976–77); Exec. Bd. (1972–74). New Eng. Tech. Srv. Libn.: Treas., VP, Pres. (1975–79). Other orgs. OCLC Users Cncl.: 1979–80, 1980–83. **Pubns.:** Speeches. **Activities:** 1, 9; 17, 24, 34; 56 **Addr.:** 296 Orchard St., Bridgeport, CT 06608.

Laney, Elizabeth J. (Je. 4, 1923, Winston-Salem, NC) Dir., Pettigrew Reg. Lib., 1981–; Dir., Tech. Info., NC Dept. of Transp., 1978–81; Dir., Prcs. Ctr., NC State Lib., 1973–78; Libn., Raleigh City Sch., 1968–73; Libn., Amer. Sch. of Lima, Peru, 1966–68. **Educ.:** Univ. of NC, Greensboro, 1940–44, BA (Soc. Std.); Univ. of NC, Chapel Hill, 1970–73, MS (LS). **Orgs.:** NC LA: Scholar. Com. (1977–83); State Cncl. Soc. Legis. (1979–81). Cap. City LA: Org. Strg. Com. (1980). ALA. SELA. Other orgs. AAUW: Raleigh Branch, Pres. (1979–81). Women's Club Raleigh: Bk. Carolina Art Gallery (Ch., 1970–81). Altrusa Club of Raleigh: VP (1981–82). NC Cncl. Women's Org.: Fall Forum, Ch. (1979–81). **Pubns.:** *Serials Received in the NC Department of Transportation* (1979, 80). **Activities:** 12; 17; 94 **Addr.:** N.C.D.O.T., Technical Information Center, Route 1, Box 281 F, Spring Hope, NC 27882.

Lang, Anita E. (O. 5, 1946, Cranston, RI) Libn., Our Lady of the Lake Univ., 1979–; Catlgr., St. Philip's Coll., 1977–79; Catlgr., Spec. Proj., Inst. of Texan Cult., 1977. **Educ.:** Mt. St. Mary Coll., 1964–69, AB (Amer. Hist.); Our Lady of the Lake Univ., 1975–77, MSLS. **Orgs.:** ALA. SWLA. TX LA: District 10, Treas. (1981–1982). Cath. LA: Local Chap. Secy. (1980–). San Antonio Women's Credit Un.: Bd. (1979–); Secy. (1980–). Natl. Women's Pol. Caucus: Bd. (1979–). Bexar Cnty. Women's Pol. Caucus: Treas. (1975–1976); Policy Cncl. (1976–1977). TX Bus. Prof. Women's Clubs Inc.; Dist 2 Legis. Ch. (1979–). **Honors:** Women's Equity Action Leag., Woman in Action, 1979. **Activities:** 1, 10; 15, 17, 21; 63, 66, 89 **Addr.:** 302 Kingsman Dr., Converse, TX 78109.

Lang, Sr. Franz, O. P. (S. 7, 1921, Highland Park, MI) Dir. of Lib. Srvs., Barry Coll., 1970–; Dir. of Lib., St. Dominic Coll., 1963–70; Asst. Libn., Siena Hts. Coll., 1962–63; Tchr./Libn., Bishop Quarter Milit. Acad., 1956–62; Tchr./Libn., St. Joseph Sch., 1952–56. **Educ.:** Siena Hts. Coll., 1952–59, BA (Eng.); Univ. of MI, 1960–64, AMLS; Marywood Coll., 1979, CEU (Arch.). **Orgs.:** Cath. LA: Pres. (1979–81); VP (1977–79); Nom. Com. (Ch., 1974); FL Chap. (VCh., 1973–75). ALA: ACRL/Coll. Sect., Nom. Com. (1975). WHCOLIS: FL. Del. FL LA. Adrian Dominican Congregation of Most Holy Rosary. Netwk. Common Cause. **Honors:** City of St. Charles, IL, Cert. of Merit for Outstan. Srv. to the Cmnty., 1970; Barry Coll., Prof. Achvmt., 1979, 1980. **Pubns.:** "Academic Libraries in the 80s: A Question of Priorities," *FL Libs.* (Mr.–Ap. 1980); various articles, *Cath. Lib. World.* **Activities:** 1; 17, 24, 26 **Addr.:** Barry College, 11300 N. E. 2nd Ave., Miami, FL 33161.

Lang, Jovian Peter (Je. 2, 1919, Sioux City, IA) Assoc. Prof., Div. of Lib. & Info. Sci., St. John's Univ., 1974–; Asst. Prof., Univ. of S. FL, 1971–74; Libn./Assoc. Prof., Quincy Coll., 1960–71; Archvst./Asst. Prov. Libn., Provincialate, St. Louis, MO, 1957–59; Asst. Prof. & Asst. Libn., St. Joseph Semy., 1955–57; Libn./Asst. Prof., Quincy Coll., 1947–55. **Educ.:** St. Joseph Semy./Our Lady of Angels Semy., 1937–43, A B (Phil. & Latin); St. Joseph Semy., 1943–47, (Theo.); Case-Western Reserve Univ., 1948–50, MS in LS, 1951–55, MA (Sp. Therapy). **Orgs.:** Cath. LA: Pres. (1967–69); Metro. Cath. Coll. Libns. Unit (Ch., 1981–83); Lib. Educ. Sect. (Ch., 1979–81). ALA: Cncl. (1972–76, 1964–68); RASD, Com. of Outstan. Ref. Srcs. (Ch., 1978–80); Mudge Cit. Com. (1977–79). NY LA: Coll. and Univ. Lib. Sect., Legis. Com. for Nassau Cnty; other coms. Liturgical Comsn. of Sacred Heart Province, OFM: Ch. (1964–69). N. Amer. Acad. of Liturgy. Teams of Our Lady. **Honors:** Beta Phi Mu, 1954; FL Cncl. on Stuttering, Cert. of Honor, 1973. **Pubns.:** *Your Search Key to LC* (1979); "Religion, Psychology, Philosophy, Games & Sports," *Ref. Bks. for Small & Medium-sized Libs.* (Je. 1979); "Reference Books of 1978," *Lib. Jnl.* (Ap. 15, 1979); Ed., "Discipline Resource packages in Psychology, Religion & Philosophy," *Ref. Srcs.* (1979); "Franciscan Librarianship in the New World," *Cath. Lib. World* (D. 1975); other books and articles. **Activities:** 1, 11; 26, 39, 42; 72, 90 **Addr.:** 37 South Ocean Ave., P.O. Box 8, Freeport, NY 11520.

Langdon, Bruce E. (Ja. 7, 1944, Milford, MA) Chief, Soc. Sci. Div., Columbia Univ. Libs., 1980–; Dir., Palos Verdes Lib. Dist., 1976–80; Asst. Exec. Ofcr., Congressional Resrch. Srv., 1974–76; Asst. Sect. Head, Lib. Srvs. Div., Lib. of Congs., 1972–74, Asst. to Deputy Dir., Congressional Resrch. Srv., 1971–72, Spec. Rcrt., 1970–71. **Educ.:** Brown Univ., 1961–65, AB (Pol. Sci.); Duke Univ., 1965–68, MA (Pol. Sci.); Univ. of NC, 1969–70, MLS. **Orgs.:** ALA. CA LA. Amer. Socty. for Pub. Admin. **Activities:** 1, 9; 17, 35, 41; 56, 78, 92 **Addr.:** Social Science Division, Columbia University Libraries, 219 M Butler Library, 535 West 114th St., New York, NY 10027.

Lange, Clifford E. (D. 29, 1935, Fond du Lac, WI) State Libn., NM State Lib., 1978–; Asst. Prof. (LS), Univ. of South. CA, 1975–78; Dir., Wauwatosa Pub. Lib., 1973–75; Asst. Prof. (LS), Univ. of IA, 1971–73; Asst. Dir., Lake Cnty. (IN) Pub. Lib., 1966–68; Dir., Eau Claire (WI) Pub. Lib., 1963–66; Head, Ref., Oshkosh (WI) Pub. Lib., 1962–63, Head, Ext. Srvs., 1960–62. **Educ.:** St. Norbert Coll., 1954–57; WI State Univ., 1958–59, BS; Univ. of WI, 1959–60, MSLS, 1968–72, PhD (LS). **Orgs.:** ALA. NM LA. **Pubns.:** "The Rural Public Library Trustee: A Preliminary Assessment," *Lib. Trends* (Spr. 1980). **Activities:** 9, 13; 17, 36, 47; 56, 93 **Addr.:** 1011 Calle Vianson, Santa Fe, NM 87501.

Lange, Elizabeth Ann (S. 20, 1938, Webster, SD) Asst. Dir. for Tech. Srv., Univ. of SC, 1979–; Head, Cat. Div., Univ. of MN, 1972–79; Head, Cat. Dept., IA State Univ., 1968–72, Catlgr., 1961–68. **Educ.:** North. State Coll., 1957–60, BS (Eng.); Univ. of MN, 1960–70, MA (LS). **Orgs.:** SC LA. SE LA. ALA: ACRL; RTSD, Cat. Class. Sect., Cat. Norms Discuss. Grp. (Ch. elect, 1976). **Activities:** 1; 17, 46; 75 **Addr.:** 1829 Senate St., Columbia, SC 29201.

Lange, R. Thomas (Ag. 30, 1936, Jackson, TN) Chief Med. Libn., Coord. of Educ. TV Actv., Coord. of Comp. Dev., Sch. of Med., Univ. of SC, 1975–; Adj. Fac., Coll. of Libnshp., 1977–; Biomed. Libn., Asst. Prof. of Med. Bibl., Coll. of Med., Univ. of S. AL, 1972–75; Libn. and Instr., South. Coll. of Optometry, 1968–72, Admis. Ofcr., 1967–68. **Educ.:** Memphis State Univ., 1957–61, BA (Eng.); George Peabody Coll., 1969–70, MLS; Univ. of SC, 1977–80, MMA (Media Arts). Med. LA, 1970, Cert. Med. Libn., Grade 1. **Orgs.:** Med. LA: Pubn. Com. (Ch., 1975–76); Exch. Com. (1979–81); South. Reg. Grp. (Vice–Ch., 1975–76), Nom. Com. (Ch., 1976–77). SC LA. Gvr.'s Conf. on Libs. and Info. Srvs. **Pubns.:** Proj. coord., *South Carolina Union List of Medical Periodicals* (1979); proj. dir., *Columbia Area Medical Libraries Union List of Periodicals* (1977); "Library Services to South Carolina Via the State's Two Medical Schools," *Jnl. SC Med. Assn.* (D. 1978); "Large Type Reading Materials and Their Sources," *Amer. Jnl. of Optometry* (N. 1972); proj. coord., "School of Medicine Cardiovascular Conference" TV broadcast (1978). **Activities:** 1, 12; 17, 19, 34; 56, 80, 93 **Addr.:** School of Medicine Library, University of South Carolina, Columbia, SC 29208.

Langer, Frank A. (Mr. 2, 1922, Elizabeth, NJ) Asst. Libn., Clarksburg Pub. Lib., 1976–; Head Bus. Libn., Coll. of Grad. Std., 1974–76; Head Libn., Salem Coll., 1969–74; Head Libn., Berry Coll., 1968–69. **Educ.:** Univ. of Miami, 1946–50, AB, cum laude (Eng.), 1952–53 MA (Eng.); FL State Univ., 1953–54, MA (LS). **Orgs.:** ALA: State Participation Com. WV LA: Conv. Plng. Com. Natl. Educ. Assn. **Honors** Beta Phi Mu. **Pubns.:** *Bibliography for the First Two Years of College* (1965); *The Philosophy of the Undergraduate Program in Library Science* (1970); "Rare, But Not Unavailable," *WV Libs.* (S. 1, 1972); various articles, sps., media progs. **Activities:** 1, 9; 20, 39, 46; 51, 63, 90 **Addr.:** 58 Front St., Salem, WV 26426.

Langevin, Ann Thompson (Ap. 18, 1944, Kansas City, MO) Ext. Admin., Clark Cnty. Lib. Dist., 1972–; st Asst., Lancaster–Kiest Branch, Dallas Pub. Lib., 1969–71. **Educ.:** Univ. of MO, 1962–66, BA (Pol. Sci.); Univ. of Denver, 1968–69, MLA (Libnshp.); Univ. of WI, Inst. in Lib. Soc. Action, 1971–72, Spec. **Orgs.:** NV LA: Pres. (1979); Bd. of Trustees (1975–79). ALA/ASCLA, Com. on Intl. Yr. of Disabled Persons (1981). WHCOLIS: NV Del. (1979). NV Legis. Comsn.: Subcom. on Lib. and Info. Needs (1979–80). **Honors:** Las Vegas *Review–Jnl.*, Woman of the Yr., 1979. **Activities:** 9; 17, 25, 27; 72 **Addr.:** Clark County Library District, 1401 E. Flamingo Rd., Las Vegas, NV 89109.

Langlands, Sandra A. (Jl. 30, 1951, Toronto, ON) Ref. Libn., Sci. and Med. Lib., Univ. Toronto, 1980–; Ext. Libn., Med. Lib., Univ. MB, 1976–80. **Educ.:** York Univ., 1970–74, BA with

PROFESSIONAL ACTIVITIES: Institutions: 1. Acad. lib.; 2. Arch.; 3. Assn.; 4. Fed./Gvt. lib.; 5. Inst. lib.; 6. Mfr./Suppl.; 7. Milit. lib.; 8. Musm.; 9. Pub. lib.; 10. Sch. lib.; 11. Sch. of lib. sci.; 12. Spec. lib.; 13. State lib.; 14. (other). **Functions/Activities:** 15. Acq./Col. dev.; 16. Adult srvs.; 17. Admin.; 18. Apprais.; 19. Archit./Bldgs.; 20. Cat./Class.; 21. Chld. srvs.; 22. Circ.; 23. Cons./Pres.; 24. Consult.; 25. Cont. ed.; 26. Educ. lib. sci.; 27. Ext. srvs.; 28. Fund/Grants; 29. Gvt. pubs.; 30. Indx./Abs.; 31. Instr. lib. use; 32. Media srvs.; 33. Micro.; 34. Netwks./Coop.; 35. Persnl.; 36. PR; 37. Publshg.; 38. Recs. mgt.; 39. Ref. srvs.; 40. Repro.; 41. Resrch.; 42. Review.; 43. Secur.; 44. Serials; 45. Spec. col.; 46. Tech. srvs.; 47. Trustees/Bds.; 48. YA srvs.; 49. (other).

honors (Eng.); Univ. of Toronto, 1974–76, MLS. **Orgs.:** MB Hlth. LA: Pres. (1978–79); Past Pres. (1979–80); Select. Bk. Jnls. (Ch., 1978–79); Conf. Plng. Com. (Ch., 1979); Un. List Com. (1977–80). Med. LA. Can. Hlth. LA. SLA. Other orgs. Can. Inst. of Mgt. **Honors:** Fac. of LS, Univ. of Toronto, Kathleen Meml. Prize in Spec. Librnshp., 1976. **Pubns.:** *Libraries for Hospitals in Rural Manitoba* (1979); Ed. *Selected Books & Journals for Manitoba Health Care Facilities* (1979); "Manitoba's Growing Information Resource," *Dimensions in Hlth. Srv.,* (O. 1980); "Manitoba Core List," *Bibliotheca Medica Canadiana* (Vol. 1, 1979). **Activities:** 1, 12; 25, 27, 39; 80, 91 **Addr.:** Reference Dept., Science & Medicine Library, University of Toronto, Toronto, ON Canada.

Langlois, Dianne Current (Ag. 16, 1946, Jersey City, NJ) Assoc. Dir., Choate Rosemary Hall, 1981–, Asst. Dir., 1978–81. **Educ.:** St. Lawrence Univ., 1964–68, BA (Phil.); S. CT State Coll., 1974–76, MS (LS). **Orgs.:** ALA: AASL; LIRT, Mem. Com. Bibl. Instr. Sec. Sch.: Coord. **Pubns.:** "Journal Usage Survey," *Spec. Lib.* (My. Je. 1973). **Activities:** 10, 12; 17, 20, 31; 63 **Addr.:** Choate Rosemary Hall, Wallingford, CT 06492.

Langlois, Janet L. (F. 25, Milwaukee, WI) Asst. Prof. Eng. and Dir. Folklore Arch., Wayne State Univ., 1977–; Archvst., IN Univ., Folklore Archive, 1972–74; Resrchr., Musm. of Intl. Folk Art, (Santa Fe, NM), 1972; Libn., NY Pub. Lib., 1969–71. **Educ.:** CO State Univ., 1964–68, BA (Eng.); Columbia Univ., 1968–69, MSLS; IN Univ., 1971–77, PhD (Folklore). **Orgs.:** SAA. Amer. Folklore Socty. Amer. Ethnological Socty. **Honors:** Beta Phi Mu, 1969. **Pubns.:** Jt. Auth., "Using a Folklore Archive" *Handbook of American Folklore* (forthcoming); Jt. Auth., "Highlights of a Lively First Twenty-Five Years," *El Palacio: Qtly. Jnl. of the Museum of NM* (Win. 1978); "Spotlight: Folklore Archive, Dept. of English, WSU," *Open Entry: MI Arch. Assn. Nsltr.* (Fall 1980). **Activities:** 1, 2; 16, 17, 37; 66, 85 **Addr.:** Folklore Archive, Dept. of English, 431 State, Wayne State University, Detroit, MI 48202.

Langmead, Lydstone Stephen (S. 16, 1933, Southborough, Kent, Eng.) Partner, Beckman Assoc. Inc., Lib. Consult., 1975–; Visit. Lectr., Sch. of Lib. and Info. Sci., Univ. of West. ON, 1970–. **Educ.:** Regent St. Polytech., London, Eng., 1950–56, Dipl. (Archit.). Royal Inst. of British Archit. Royal Archit. Inst. of Can. Toronto Socty. of Archit. **Pubns.:** Jt. auth., *New Library Design* (1970); "Critique John Robarts Library," *Can. Arch.* (Ag. 1974); "Special Report: UNESCO International Conference," *Wilson Lib. Bltn.* (Je. 1976). **Addr.:** 75 Metcalfe St., Toronto, ON M4X 1S1 Canada.

Langner, Mildred C. (Jl. 30, 1911, Chattanooga, TN) Prof., Libn. Emeritus, Univ. of Miami Sch. of Med., 1979–, Dir. and Prof. of Med. Bibl., 1968–79, Libn. and Assoc. Prof. of Med. Bibl., 1963–68; Chief of Ref., Srv. Div., Natl. Lib. of Med., 1961–62; Libn. and Asst. Prof. Med. Bibl., Univ. Miami Sch. Med. Lib., 1955–61; Libn. and Asst. Prof. Med. Bibl., Univ. AL Med. Ctr. Lib., 1945–55; Intern and Asst., Vanderbilt Med. Lib., 1944–45; **Educ.:** Univ. of Chattanooga, 1933, BA; Peabody Coll. for Tchrs., 1945, BS (LS); Vanderbilt Univ., 1945 (Med. Lib. Internship). **Orgs.:** Med. LA: Pres.; Ed., *Med. LA Bltn.;* Secy.; many com. SLA: AL Chap., Pres. elect, com. mem.; FL Chap., Dir. FL LA. Amer. Assn. Hist. Med. **Honors:** Med. LA, Ed. Awd.; Med. LA, Marcia C. Noyes Awd. **Pubns.:** "User and User Services in Health Science Libraries: 1945–1965," *Lib. Trends* (Jl. 1974); "The National Library of Medicine's Services: Initial Observations on Indexing, Interlibrary Loan and Reference," *Bltn. Med. LA* (Ja. 1967); "Eileen Roach Cunningham 1894–1965," *Bltn. Med. LA* (Ja. 1966); "The Bulletin's Anniversary," *Bltn. Med. LA* (O. 1962); "Medical Libraries in Florida," *FL Lib.* (S. 1958); Other articles. **Activities:** 1, 10; 15, 20, 39; 57, 75, 80 **Addr.:** 1408 S.E. Bayshore Dr., #505, Miami, FL 33131.

Lanier, Donald Lee (Ap. 11, 1939, Shawnee, OK) Asst. Dir., Tech. Srvs., North. IL Univ., 1979–; Asst. Dir., Tech. Srvs., Auburn Univ., 1978–79; Head, of Acq., 1975–78; Acq. Libn., OK State Univ., 1969–75; LS Libn., Univ. of IL, 1967–69; Missn., Hong Kong Bapt. Missn., 1966–67; Acq. Libn., Univ. of TX, Arlington, 1964–66. **Educ.:** OK Bapt. Univ., 1957–60, BS (Educ.); Univ. of IL, 1963–64, MS (LS). **Orgs.:** ALA: RTSD, Plng. Com., 1977–81. **Pubns.:** "The Library and Series Books," *Southeast. Libn.* (Fall, 1978); "Proposal for Reorganization of Technical Services," *Show-Me Libs.* (F., 1979); "Gift Books and Appraisals," *Coll. & Resrch. Libs.* (S. 1979); reviews. **Activities:** 1; 15, 18, 46 **Addr.:** Northern Illinois University Library, DeKalb, IL 60115.

Lanier, Gene D. (Mr. 13, 1934, Conway, NC) Ch., Dept. of LS, E. Carolina Univ., 1966–; Instr., Sch. of Educ., Univ. of NC, 1964–66; Assoc. Prof., E. Carolina Univ., 1963–64, Head, Acq. Joyner Lib., 1959–63; Counterintelligence Spec., West. Europe, 1957–59. **Educ.:** E. Carolina Univ., 1952–55, BS (Soc. Std.); Univ. of NC, 1955–57, MS (LS), 1964–66, PhD (Educ. & LS). **Orgs.:** ALA: White House Conf. State Contact (1973–75). SELA: Implementation Com., SE States Coop. Lib. Survey (1974–76). NC LA: Pres. (1973–75); Ch., Int. Frdm. Com. (1980–81); Ch., Nom. Com. (1978–80); Ed. Bd., NC Libs. (1975–78). NC Assn. of Sch. Libns.: Stans. Com. (1980–81); Dir. (1968–71). Other orgs. Phi Sigma Pi. Beta Phi Mu. Phi Delta Kappa. Kappa Alpha. **Pubns.:** "Curricular Aids and the Materials Center," "The Textbook–Major Curriculum Problem" in *Curriculum Principles And Social Trends* (1969); "The Present Status & Projected Plans for Library Education in North Carolina," *NC Libs.* (1971). **Activities:** 11; 17, 26, 36; 50, 63, 74 **Addr.:** Department of Library Science, East Carolina University, Greenville, NC 27834.

Lankford, Mary D. (D. 7, 1932, Denton, TX) Dir., Lib. & Media Srv., Irving Sch. Dist., 1966–; Libn., Walker Air Force Base, Roswell Pub. Sch., 1963–65; Elem. Libn., Delaware Pub. Sch., 1962–63. **Educ.:** N. TX State Univ., 1949–52, BA (LS); TX Woman's Univ., 1979–. **Orgs.:** TX LA: Pres. (1976). TX Assn. Sch. Libn.: Pres. (1973). TX AECT. AECT Phi Delta Kappa. **Activities:** 10; 15, 17, 24; 67, 74 **Addr.:** 820 O'Connor Rd., Irving, TX 75061.

Lansdale, Metta T., Jr. (Ag. 28, 1947, Cleveland, OH) Mgr. of Lib. Srv., St. Joseph Mercy Hosp., 1972–. **Educ.:** Transylvania Coll., 1965–69, BA (Eng.); Univ. of MI, 1970–71, AMLS. **Orgs.:** Med. LA: Cert. Exam. Review Com. (1980–). KY, OH, MI Reg. Med. Lib. Prog.: Exec. Com. SLA. MI Hlth. Sci. LA: Exec. Bd. (1977–80). Natl. Leag. for Nursing. **Pubns.:** "The Medical Librarian and Accountability," *Natl. Leag. for Nursing* (V. 16, 1976). **Activities:** 12; 17, 32, 34; 75, 80 **Addr.:** St. Joseph Mercy Hospital, Riecker Memorial Library, PO Box 995, Ann Arbor, MI 48106.

Lantz, Karen Stultz (F. 24, 1949, Harrisonburg, VA) Lib. Media Spec., Ashby-Lee Primary Sch., 1975–; Lib. Media Spec., New Market Elem. Sch., 1971–75. **Educ.:** Madison Coll., 1968–71, BS (Educ., LS), 1972–74, MS (Educ., LS). **Orgs.:** VA Educ. Media Assn.: Exec. Bd. (1975–76). VA LA. ALA. Dist. 5 Libns. Shenandoah Cnty. Educ. Assn. Natl. Educ. Assn. VA Educ. Assn.: Del. to Asm. (1978). **Activities:** 10; 15, 20, 31; 63 **Addr.:** 2043 E. Ct., Harrisonburg, VA 22801.

Lapides, Linda F. (Ja. 12, 1936, Baltimore, MD) Asst. YA Spec., Enoch Pratt Free Lib., 1979–; Reg. YA Libn., Enoch Pratt Free Lib., 1973–79. **Educ.:** Univ. of MD, 1954–57, BA (Eng.); Columbia Univ., 1957–58, MSLS. **Orgs.:** MD LA. ALA: YASD, Org. Com. (1979–81), Bd. (1970–73), Best Bks. Com. (1968–70); Survival Kit Com. (1975–77). Baltimore Bibliophiles. MD Cmsn. on Afro-Amer. Hist. & Culture. The Baltimore Cncl. on Adlsnt. Pregnancy, Parenting, and Pregnancy Prev.: Strg. Com. Mt. Royal Dem. Club. **Pubns.:** Preface, Reprint Ed., *The Cries of London, The Cries of New York* (1977). "Choosing with Courage: The Young Adult Best Books, 1965–1969" *Young Adult Literature in the Seventies, A Selection of Readings* (1978), "What's In It For You at YA Meetings?" *Sch. Lib. Jnl.* (Mr. 1976). "Unassigned Reading: A Decade of Teen-Age Reading in Baltimore, 1960–1970." *Top of the News* (Ap. 1971). Other articles. **Activities:** 9; 15, 42, 48 **Addr.:** Enoch Pratt Free Lib., 400 Cathedral St., Baltimore, MD 21201.

Lapierre, Maurice Edmond (My. 21, 1934, Woonsocket, RI) Asst. Dean of The Lib., Tech. Srvs., Univ. of AL, 1978–; Adult Srvs. Libn., Brooklyn Pub. Lib., 1977–78; Asst. Univ. Libn., New York Univ., 1973–76; Assoc. Univ. Libn., McGill Univ., 1968–69; Head, Acq. Dept., OH State Univ., 1966–68, Serials Catlgr., 1965–66; Admin. Asst. to Head, Acq. Dept., Univ. of CA, Los Angeles, 1963–65, Biblio. Srchr., 1962–63. **Educ.:** Boston Coll., 1955–59, AB (Rom. Lang., Phil.); Univ. of CA, Los Angeles, 1961–62, MLS; Case-Western Reserve Univ., 1969–72, PhD (Lib. & Info Sci). **Orgs.:** AL LA. ASIS. ALA: RTSD/Acq. Sect., Bookdealer Lib. Rel. Com. (1966–68); Bd. of Dir. (1970–71); Cat. and Class. Sect., Nom. Com. (1975–76); Policy and Resrch. Com. (1971–76, Ch., 1974–76); Cncl. of Reg. Grps. (Ch., 1970–71); *Library Resources and Technical Services* (Ed. Adv., 1970–71). AAUP. **Activities:** 1, 9; 17, 26, 46 **Addr.:** The University of Alabama Library, P.O. Box S, University, AL 35486.

LaPlante, Kathleen R. (Mr. 5, 1948, St. Peter, MN) Libn., NM Energy and Minerals Dept., 1978–; Lrng. Mtrls. Spec., Univ. of NM, 1977–78; Prog. Libn., Santa Clara Cnty. Lib., 1974–77, Libn. I, 1972–74. **Educ.:** Univ. of CA, Berkeley, 1966–69, BA (Hist.); CA State Univ., San Jose, 1971–72, MA (Librnshp.), 1974–76, MA (Educ., Instr. Tech.). **Orgs.:** SLA: Rio Grande Chap. (Treas., 1980–82), Mem. Com. (1979–80). West. Info. Netwk. on Energy: Secy. (1980–82). ALA. **Activities:** 12; 15, 38, 46; 82, 86, 91 **Addr.:** NM Energy & Minerals Dept., 525 Camino de los Marquey, Santa Fe, NM 87501.

La Plume, Sr. Mary Kathleen (Jn. 23, 1938, Chicago, IL) Libn., St. Hubert Elem. Sch., 1976–; Libn., St. Linus Sch., 1974–76; Libn., St. Joseph Day Care Ctr., 1973–74; Tchr., Libn., St. Stanislaus, 1968–73; Tchr., Libn., Our Lady of Ransom Sch., 1964–68. **Educ.:** Mundelein Coll., 1960–62, BA (Soclgy.); Chicago State Univ., 1969–72, MALS. **Orgs.:** Felician Lib. Srv.: Coord. (1974–). Cath. Lib. Assn.: N. IL Unit., Exhibits Ch. (1972–77), Secy. (1979–80). IL LA: PR Com. (1975–79). ALA. **Honors:** Grolier Educ. Srvs., Today's Cath. Tchr., Spec. Srv. Awd., 1979. **Pubns.:** "The Need for Consistency In Cataloging Audio-Visual Materials," *Cath. Lib. World* (F. 1979); Caption/article "Rub-a-dub,dub, three men in a tub," *Today's Cath. Tchr., Amer. Libs., Cath. Lib. World,* and various Newsp. (S. 1977). **Activities:** 10; 21, 32, 39; 63, 75, 90 **Addr.:** St. Hubert School Library, 255 Flagstaff Ln., Hoffman Estates, IL 60194.

Larason, Larry D. (N. 7, 1935, Shattuck, OK) Lib. Dir., N.E. LA Univ., 1977–, Actg. Lib. Dir., 1976–77, Coord. of Tech. Srv., 1974–76; Lib. Syst. Anal., Univ. of OK, 1973–74; Syst. Coord., AZ State Univ., 1968–71, Head, Serials Srv., 1965–68; Order Lib., Univ. of NE, 1963–65, Asst. Ref. Libn., 1961–63. **Educ.:** Univ. of OK, 1959, BA (Anthro.), 1961, MLS, 1975, PhD (Indus. Engin.). **Orgs.:** LA LA. SWLA. ALA: LAMA, Bldgs. Equip. Sect., Equip. Com. (1979–82). **Pubns.:** Jt. Auth., *A Survey of the Status of Academic Library Automation in Louisiana* (1980); Ed., *Intermountain Union List of Serials,* (1969), Second Ed., (1970). **Activities:** 1; 17, 19; 56 **Addr.:** Sandel Library, Northeast Louisiana University, Monroe, LA 71209.

Larimer, Hugh C. (O. 9, 1939, Ebensburg, PA) Map, Ref. Libn., Univ. MB, 1977–; Ref. Libn., Purdue Univ., 1969–77; Ref. Libn., Boston Univ., 1965–69. **Educ.:** West. KY State Univ., 1960–63, BS (Acct.); Univ. Pittsburgh, 1963–65, MLS. **Orgs.:** ALA. Assn. Can. Map Libns. MB LA: Treas. (1979–81). SLA. **Pubns.:** Reg. Ed., *Assn. Can. Map Lib. Bltn.;* Reviews. **Activities:** 1; 15, 33, 39; 59, 70 **Addr.:** 605 Kilkenny Dr., Winnipeg, MB R3T 3E2 Canada.

Larivière, Jules (Mr. 21, 1943, Ibervile, PQ) Dir., Law Lib., Univ. of Ottawa, 1981–; Chief, Official Pub. Div., Natl. Lib. of Can., 1980–81, Head, 1973–80, Head, Gvt. Docum. Cat. Sect., 1970–73. **Educ.:** Univ. de Montreal, 1965, BA, 1966, BBibl. **Orgs.:** ASTED: Com. du droit d'auteur (Pres., 1978–81). **Activities:** 4; 17, 29, 39; 61, 77, 78 **Addr.:** Law Library, University of Ottawa, 57 Copernicus, Ottawa, ON K1N 6N5 Canada.

Larsen, A. Dean (Ag. 23, 1930, Provo, UT) Asst. Dir., Col. Dev., Brigham Young Univ., 1971–, Acq. Libn., 1961–71, Serials Libn., 1958–61, Docum. Libn., 1956–58. **Educ.:** Brigham Young Univ., 1948–50, 1952–54, BS (Hist.); Univ. of MI, 1961, MLS. **Orgs.:** ALA. Mt. Plains LA. UT LA: Coll. and Univ. Sect. (Pres., 1963–64). UT Hist. Socty. MT Hist. Socty. West. Hist. Socty. **Pubns.:** "The Role of Retrospective Materials in Collection Development," *Collection Development in Libraries A Treatise* (1980). **Addr.:** Brigham Young University, 6210F Harold B. Lee Library, Provo, UT 84602.

Larsen, John Christian (Ag. 1, 1929, Menominee, MI) Assoc. Prof., North. IL Univ., 1977–; Asst. Prof., Columbia Univ., 1971–77; Asst. Prof., Univ. of KY, 1968–71; Instr., Univ. of MI, 1965–68; Assoc. Libn., Pub. Srv., Towson State Univ., 1961–64; Head, Art and Msc. Sect., State Lib. of MI, 1959–61; Ref. Libn., Detroit Pub. Lib., 1954–58. **Educ.:** Univ. of MI, 1945–50, B. Des. (Design), 1950–51, MA (Art Hist.), 1954–55, MALS, 1964–67, Ph.D. (LS). **Orgs.:** ALA: Cncl. (1970–73); ACRL, Art. Sect. (Actg. Ch., 1980–); Ref. Subscrpn. Bks. Rev. Com. (1975–79, 1981–). IL Assn. of Coll. and Resrch. Libs.: Comm. Com. (1980–81). ARLIS. AALS: Exec. Bd. (1970–73). Coll. Art Assn. IL WHCOLIS: Del. (1978). **Honors:** Phi Kappa Phi. Beta Phi Mu. **Pubns.:** "An evaluation of reference sources used by public libraries in three Illinois regional library systems," *IL Libs.* (Ap. 1980); "Information sources currently studied in general reference courses," *RQ* (Sum. 1979); "The Education of Fine Arts/Music Librarians," *Lib. Trends* (Ja. 1975). **Activities:** 11; 26, 39; 55 **Addr.:** Department of Library Science, Northern Illinois University, DeKalb, IL 60115.

Larsen, Mary Todd (My. 3, 1940, Knoxville, TN) Libn., Fernbank Sci. Ctr., 1980–; Asst. Libn., Dental Sch., Emory Univ., 1976–80, Asst. Libn. (LS), 1974–76. **Educ.:** Jacksonville Univ., 1967–70, BA (Eng.); Emory Univ., 1973–74, MLn. **Orgs.:** SLA: S. Atl. Chap. (Pres., 1976–77). Med. LA. **Honors:** Beta Phi Mu. **Pubns.:** "Technical Assistance for the Bureau of Outdoor Recreation," *Spec. Libs.* (Jl.-Ag., 1977). **Activities:** 12; 15, 20, 39; 65, 88, 91 **Addr.:** Library, Fernbank Science Center, 156 Heaton Park Dr., NE, Atlanta, GA 30307.

Larsen, Violet P. (Ja. 27, 1921, Mukwanago, WI) Ch., Trustees, Sweetwater Cnty. Lib. Bd., 1975–. **Educ.:** Univ. of WY, 1938–42. **Orgs.:** WY LA: Awds. Com. (Ch., 1980). ALA: ALTA. WY Gov. Conf. on Libs. (1979). Right-to-Read Acad.: Bd. of Dir., Mem. (Ch., 1977–80). **Activities:** 9; 47; 50, 89 **Addr.:** 210 Hay St., Rock Springs, WY 82901.

Larsgaard, Mary Lynette (Ag. 4, 1946, Dickinson, ND) Map Libn., CO Sch. of Mines Lib., 1978–; Govt. Docum., Maps Libn., Ctrl. WA Univ., 1969–78. **Educ.:** Macalester Coll., 1964–68, BA (Geol.); Univ. of MN, 1968–69, MA (LS); Univ. of OR, 1976–78, MA (Geo.). **Orgs.:** SLA: Geo. and Map Div. (Ch., 1979–80). West. Assn. Map. Libs.: Pres. (1975). Anglo-Amer. Cat. Com. for Cartographic Mtrls.: SLA Rep. (1979–). Assn. Can. Map Libs. Assn. of Amer. Geog. **Honors:** Phi Beta Kappa; Beta Phi Mu. **Pubns.:** *Map Librarianship: An Introduction* (1978); Ed., Issue on map libnshp., *Lib. Trends* (Win. 1980); "Beginner's Guide to Indexes in the 19th Century U.S. Serial Set," *Govt. Pubns. Rev.* (1975); "Map Classification," *Drexel Lib. Qtly.* (O. 1973). **Addr.:** Arthur Lakes Library, Colorado School of Mines, Golden, CO 80401.

Special Subjects/Services: 50. Adult educ.; 51. Advert./Mktg.; 52. Aerosp.; 53. Agric.; 54. Area std.; 55. Arts/Hum.; 56. Autom.; 57. Bibl./Prtg.; 58. Bio. sci.; 59. Bus./Fin.; 60. Chem.; 61. Copyrt.; 62. Documtn.; 63. Educ.; 64. Engin.; 65. Env.; 66. Eth. grps.; 67. Film; 68. Food/Nutr.; 69. Geneal.; 70. Geo.; 71. Geol.; 72. Handcpd.; 73. Hist.; 74. Int. frdm.; 75. Info. sci.; 76. Insr.; 77. Law; 78. Legis.; 79. Math./Comp. sci.; 80. Med.; 81. Metals; 82. Nat. resrcs.; 83. Newsp.; 84. Nuc. sci.; 85. Oral hist.; 86. Petr./Energy; 87. Pharm.; 88. Phys./Astr./Math.; 89. Readg.; 90. Relig.; 91. Sci./Tech.; 92. Soc. sci.; 93. Telecom.; 94. Transp.; 95. (other).

Who's Who in Library and Information Services

Larson, Evva L. (Ag. 11, 1923, St. Louis, MO) Asst. State Libn., ID State Lib., 1971–; Dir. of Libs., Mehlville Sch. Dist., 1967–70; Libn., Mehlville Sr. HS, 1961–67; Branch Libn., St. Louis Cnty. Lib., 1958–61. **Educ.:** WA Univ., 1941–47, AB (Hist., Eng.), 1947–48, BS Ed.; LA State Univ., 1952–53, MSLS. **Orgs.:** ALA. ID LA. Pac. Northwest LA. Chlds. Rdg. RT (Boise, ID). Other orgs. **Honors:** Beta Phi Mu. **Activities:** 9, 13; 21, 24, 27; 66, 67, 72 **Addr.:** 1919 No. Beach St., Boise, ID 83706.

Larson, Jean M. (F. 25, 1924, Plymouth, WI) Exec. VP, Roa Films, 1948–. **Educ.:** Univ. of WI, 1941–45. **Orgs.:** Natl. AV Assn.: Relig. Cncl.; Film Cncl. Educ. Film LA. Pilot Club Intl.: Intl. Pres. (1977–78). Milwaukee Advert Club. Amer. Camping Assn. Natl. Recreation & Park Assn. **Activities:** 6; 17, 32, 36; 67 **Addr.:** 1696 North Astor St., Milwaukee, WI 53202.

Larson, Joan Keilholz (Ag. 29, 1929, Champaign, IL) Pub. Srv. Coord., San Mateo Cnty. Lib., 1981–; Ref. Coord., Peninsula Lib. Syst., 1974–80; Ref. Libn., San Mateo Pub. Lib., 1972–74; Asst. Libn., Langley Porter Neuropsyt. Inst., 1972; Ref. Libn., Burlingame Pub. Lib., 1968–72; Ref. Libn., San Mateo Cnty. Lib., 1966–68; Dept. Head, Circ. and Reserve Bk., Radcliffe Coll. Lib., 1952–56. **Educ.:** Univ. of PA, 1947–51, BA (Fine Arts); Drexel Univ., 1951–52, MS (LS). **Orgs.:** CA LA. ALA. SLA. **Activities:** 9; 16, 17, 34 **Addr.:** 1216 Cortez Ave., Burlingame, CA 94010.

Larson, Julian R. (Aberdeen, SD) Consult., self-empl., 1981–; Consult., Drug & Alchl. Div., NSW, Australia 1980; Asst. to Lib. Mgr., Chem. Abs. Srv., 1971–80; Resrch. Libn., PPG Indus., 1961–71. **Educ.:** North. State Coll., BS (Sec. Educ.); Case West. Reserve Univ., MS (LS). **Orgs.:** SLA: Cleveland Chap., Pres. (1967–68) Ctrl. OH Chap., Pres. (1975–76). Akron Area LA: Pres. (1968–70). Franklin Cnty. Libn. Assn.: Pres. (1977–78). **Pubns.:** "Comparison of printed bibliographic descriptions distributed by BIOSIS, CAS, and Ei," *Jnl. of Amer. Socty. Info. Sci.* (1976); "Problems in Accessing Scientific and Technical Serials," *Spec. Lib.* (1977); "CASSI: File For Document Access," *Spec. Lib.* (1978). **Activities:** 12; 38, 44, 46; 60, 91 **Addr.:** 263 Weydon Rd., Worthington, OH 43085.

Larson, Richard Farrel (Ja. 26, 1923, Seattle, WA) Assoc. Libn., Univ. of CA, Berkeley, 1972–; Head, Biblgph. Div., 1956–72; Ref. Libn., Map Cur., Stanford Univ. Libs., 1952–56. **Educ.:** Harvard Coll., 1946–48, AB (Rom. Langs.); Harvard Univ., 1948–49, AM (Rom. Langs.); Univ. of Stockholm, 1949–50, Cert. (Swedish Lit.); Univ. of CA, Berkeley, 1951–52, BLS. **Orgs.:** ALA. American Scandinavian Fndn.: CA Chap. (Pres., 1964–67). King County Hist. Assn. House of Gordon. **Activities:** 1; 15, 17, 39; 57, 69, 70 **Addr.:** 14 Montezuma Ave., San Francisco, CA 94110.

Larson, William L. "Larry" (Jl. 18, 1940, El Dorado, AR) Libn., Dir., N. AR Reg. Lib., 1975–; Head Libn., Univ. of AR (Monticello), 1973–75; Asst. Libn., Hendrix Coll., 1967–73; Asst. Libn., AR Tech. Univ., 1965–67. **Educ.:** Ouachita Baptist Univ., 1958–62, BSE (Educ.); George Peabody Coll., 1967, MLS. **Orgs.:** AR LA: Sec. VP (1969); Pub. Lib. Div. (Ch. 1979–80). SWLA. ALA. Kiwanis Club: Educ. Com. **Activities:** 1, 9; 17, 32, 39; 63 **Addr.:** North Arkansas Regional Library, 123 Jaycee Ave., Harrison, AR 72601.

Lary, Marilyn Searson (S. 3, 1943, Walterboro, SC) Asst. Prof., Univ. of S. FL, 1978–; Asst. Prof., Univ. of MI, 1975–78; Ref. Libn., Clemson Univ., 1972–73; Asst. Prof., E. Carolina Univ., 1970–72. **Educ.:** Newberry Coll., 1961–64, AB (Eng.); Univ. of NC (Chapel Hill), 1964–65, MSLS; FL St. Univ., 1973–75, PhD (LS). **Orgs.:** ALA., FL LA., AALS. **Honors:** Beta Phi Mu. **Pubns.:** *Young Adult Services in Florida Public Libraries* (1980); "Literature for the Adolescent..." *Catholic Lib. World* (O. 1978). **Activities:** 1, 11; 17, 39, 48; 63, 75 **Addr.:** University of South Florida, Human Services Bldg. #448, Tampa, FL 33620.

Laseter, Ernest P. (S. 13, 1933, Montgomery, AL) Asst. Dir., AL Pub. Lib. Srv., 1981–; Fed. and State Progs. Ofcr., 1977–81; Dir., Ector Cnty. (TX) Pub. Lib., 1975–77; Head, Ref. Dept., Dir., Lubbock Christian Coll. Lib., 1972–75; Field Consult., TX State Lib., 1971–72. **Educ.:** Abilene Christian Coll., 1952–56, BS; Pittsburg State Univ. (KS), 1961–62, MA (Hist.); N. TX State Univ., 1970–71, MLS. **Orgs.:** ALA. SELA. AL LA. Phi Delta Kappa. Phi Alpha Theta. Lions Club. **Pubns.:** "Texas and the 'Right To Read': The Ector County Case," *TX Lib. Jnl.* (Ja. 1976). **Activities:** 9, 13; 17, 24, 28; 50, 74, 78 **Addr.:** 1104 Sycamore Ct., Prattville, AL 36067.

Laseter, Shirley Brooks (O. 4, 1947, Dallas, TX) Biblgphr, Air Univ. Lib., Maxwell AFB, AL, 1980–; Dir., Autauga-Prattville Pub. Lib., 1977–80; Branch Libn., Irving (TX) Pub. Lib. Syst., 1976–77; Chld., AV Libn., Ector Cnty. Lib., 1975–76. **Educ.:** Austin Coll., 1966–69, BA (Educ.); N. TX State Univ., 1974–75, MLS. **Orgs.:** AL LA: Pub. Lib. Div. (Pres., 1980–81). SELA. ALA. Kappa Kappa Gamma. AAUW. **Honors:** Beta Phi Mu. **Addr.:** 1104 Sycamore Ct., Prattville, AL 36067.

Lash, David Barry (Jl. 6, 1930, Pittsburgh, PA) Head Libn., SUNY Agr. & Tech. Coll., Alfred, 1977–; Head of Tech. Srvs., SUNY Coll. of Geneseo, 1968–77; Catlgr., Reed Coll., 1967. **Educ.:** Westminster Coll., 1948–52, BA (Grmn.); Pittsburgh Theo. Semy., 1952–55, MDiv (Biblical Lang.); Univ. of Portland, 1966–67, MLS. **Orgs.:** SUNY Cncl. of Head Libns.: Treas. Amer. Prtg. Hist. Assn. Hidden Spring Press: Ed. & Publshr. **Pubns.:** *By and About Aldous Huxley* (1973). **Activities:** 1, 2; 17, 23, 28; 55, 57, 90 **Addr.:** Walter C. Hinkle Memorial Library, State University of New York, Agricultural and Technical College, Alfred, NY 14802.

Lasslo, Andrew (Ag. 24, 1922, Mukacevo, Czechoslavakia) Prof. and Ch., Dept. of Med. Chem., Univ. of TN Ctr. for the Hlth. Sci., 1960–; Dir., Postgrad. Trng. Prog. Organic Med. Chem., Food and Drug Admin., 1971; Dir., Postgrad. Trng. Prog. Sci. Libns., U.S. Pub. Hlth. Srv., 1966–72; Asst. Prof., Pharmgy., Basic Hlth. Sci. Div., Emory Univ., 1954–60; Resrch. Chem., Organic Chem. Div., Monsanto Chem. Co., 1952–54. **Educ.:** Univ. of IL, 1948, MS; 1952, PhD; 1961, MLS. **Orgs.:** Med. LA: Com. on Reg. Med. Lib. Progs. (Ch., 1971–72). ALA. Drug Info. Assn.: Dir. (1968–69). Amer. Inst. Chems.: Natl. Cnclr. for TN (1969–70); Fellow. Amer. Socty. Pharmgy. and Exper. Therapy: Subcom. on Pre- and Post-doct. Trng. (Ch., 1974–78); Exec. Com. Educ. and Prof. Affairs (1974–78). **Honors:** Sigma Xi, Resrch. Prize, 1949; TN Chems., Scroll of Hon., 1976; Geschickter Fund, Med. Resrch. Grantee, 1959–65; U.S. Pub. Hlth. Srv., Resrch. and Trng. Grantee, 1958–64, 1966–72; other hons. **Pubns.:** "An Estimate of Comparative Serial Literature Resources Supporting Research in Medicinal and Pharmaceutical Chemistry in Major Libraries of the United States," *Bltn. of the Med. LA* (1962); "The Library," *Amer. Jnl. of Pharm. Educ.* (1966); "The Librarian and the Scientist," *Bltn. of the Med. LA* (1968); "The Librarian's Mission in Contemporary Health Care," *Bus. Hlth. and Educ. Disciplines* (1 supplement 1975); various articles, mono., media progs. in the scis. **Addr.:** Department of Medicinal Chemistry, College of Pharmacy, University of Tennessee Center for the Health Sciences, Memphis, TN 38163.

Laszlo, George A. (My. 8, 1949, Budapest, Hungary) Mgr., Info. Admin., Ayerst Lab., 1976–; Info. Sci., Hoechst-Roussel Pharm., 1975–76; Info. Sci., Schering-Plough Corp., 1973–75. **Educ.:** Wagner Coll., 1967–72, BA (Phil., Bio.); Rutgers Univ., 1972–73, MLS. **Orgs.:** SLA: NJ Chap.; Princeton Trenton Chap., Prog. Com. (1975). ASIS: Ctrl. NJ Chap. (Fndn. mem., 1973). Ctrl. NJ OLUG (Fndn. Mem., 1975). Bronx Manhatten Hlth. Sci. Lib. Grp. Assn. of Rec. Mgr. and Admin. Pharm. Mfr. Assn.: Info. Sect. Frnds. Glen Ridge Pub. Lib.: Fndn. Mem. (1978); VP (1978); Pres. (1979). **Pubns.:** Contrib. Ed., *New Serial Titles Cumulative* (1973); "Document Ordering Through Lockheed's Dialog and SDC's Orbit - A User's guide," *ONLINE* (O. 1980). **Activities:** 5; 17, 38, 49-On-Line Systems; 56, 80, 87 **Addr.:** 272 Ridgewood Ave., Glen Ridge, NJ 07028.

Latham, Dorothy M. (Jl. 12, 1928, Chehalis, WA) Asst. Prof., Coord. Sch. Lib. Prog., Univ. of OR, 1978–; Lib. Media Spec., Eugene Pub. Sch., 1971–77; Libn., Springfield Pub. Sch., 1952–54; Libn., Gates Pub. Sch., 1950–52. **Educ.:** Willamette Univ., 1946–50, BA (Drama); Univ. of OR, 1965–69, MS (LS), 1975–78, DEd (Educ.); Tchg. cert. lib. & Eng. 1950–85. **Orgs.:** OR LA. Pac. N.W. LA. OR Educ. Media Assn. Jr. Leag.: Secy. (1965). Alpha Chi Omega Alum.: Pres. (1960). **Activities:** 1; 26 **Addr.:** 140 E. 37th Ave., Eugene, OR 97405.

Lathem, Edward Connery (D. 15, 1926, Littleton, NH) Dean, Libs. and Libn. of Coll. Emeritus, Dartmouth Coll., 1978–, Lib. Staff, 1952–78. **Educ.:** Dartmouth Coll., 1951, AB; Columbia Univ., 1952, MS (Libnshp.); Univ. of Oxford, 1961, DPhil. **Orgs.:** ARL: Pres. (1976–77). **Pubns.:** Ed., cmplr., various bks. on lit., bibl., biog., hist. **Addr.:** Office of the Bezaleel Woodward Fellow, Dartmouth College, 213 Baker Library, Hanover, NH 03755.

Lathrop, Alan K. (Ja. 24, 1940, Dell Rapids, SD) Cur., Mss. Div., Univ. of MN Lib., 1970–; Mss. Libn., Univ. of IA, 1968–70; Head, Archit. Lib., AZ State Univ., 1967–68, Ref. Libn., 1966–67. **Educ.:** Augustana Coll., 1957–61, BA (Eng., Hist.); Univ. of MN, 1961–64, MA (Hist.), 1964–66, MALS; Univ. of Denver, 1970 Cert. (Arch. Admin.). **Orgs.:** SAA: Com. on Intl. Arch. Affairs, (1971–72); Com. on Mss. & Pvt. Papers, 1976–77); Com. on Bldgs. & Tech. Equip. (1978–79). Socty. of Archit. Hist.: Sel. Com. for Attingham (Eng.) Std. Prog. (1981). Natl. Cat. of Amer. Archit. Rec.: Adv. Bd. (1980–). **Pubns.:** "A French Architect in Minnesota," *MN Hist.* (Sum. 1980); "The Provenance & Preservation of Architectural Records," *The Amer. Archvst.* (Sum. 1980); "The Archivist & Architectural Records," *GA Arch.* (Sum. 1977); Jt. Auth., "Drafting a House History" (1979). **Activities:** 1, 2; 15, 17, 19; 55, 62 **Addr.:** Manuscripts Division, University of Minnesota Libraries, 826 Berry St., St. Paul, MN 55114.

Latour, Terry Stephen (S. 5, 1955, Brackenridge, PA) Cur. of Spec. Col., Univ. of South. MS, 1980–; Asst. Archvst., Univ. of Akron, 1980; Intern, Natl. Hist. Pubns. Rec. Com., Natl. Arch., 1979. **Educ.:** Allegheny Coll., 1974–78, BA (Hist.); Case West. Reserve Univ., 1978–79, MSLS, 1978–79, MA (Hist.). **Orgs.:** SAA: Strg. Com. of the Mss. Prof. Afnty. Grp. (1980–82). ALA. Socty. of MS Archvsts. Socty. of OH Archvsts.: State Accession Guide Proj. (1980). Amer. Assn. For State and Local Hist. Org. of Amer. Histn. **Activities:** 1, 2; 23, 45; 65, 73 **Addr.:** University of Southern Mississippi, Southern Station, Box 5148, Hattiesburg, MS 39406-5148.

Latzke, Henry Raymond (Jl. 3, 1931, Janesville, WI) Dir. of Lib. Srv., Concordia Coll., 1960–; Libn., Los Angeles Luth. HS, 1958–60; Tchr., Libn., AL Luth. Acad. and Coll., 1956–58. **Educ.:** Concordia Coll., 1954–56, BS (Educ.); Case West. Reserve Univ., 1956–59, MS (LS); IN Univ., 1962–71, EdD (Instr. Syst. Tech.) **Orgs.:** ALA: Libns.-at-Lg. Day Com. (1976). AECT: IL Chap., Constn. Com. (1968). IL LA: Int. Frdm. Com. (1977–78). IL Assn. Coll. Resrch. Lib.: Bd. Higher Educ. Liason Com. (1978–80). Lutheran Educ. Assn.: Treas. (1981–). Phi Delta Kappa. IL Higher Educ. Media Assn.: Treas. (1979–82). **Honors:** Phi Delta Kappa, 1970. **Activities:** 1; 17, 32; 63 **Addr.:** Concordia College, 7400 Augusta St., River Forest, IL 60305.

Laucus, John (D. 30, 1933, Cambridge, MA) Univ. Libn., Boston Univ., 1969–, Asst. Dir., 1967–69, Undergrad. Libn., 1965–66, Head, Gen. Educ./Fine & Appld. Arts Lib., 1963–65, Head, Bus. and Econ. Lib., 1960–63; Sel. Officer, Harvard Bus. Sch. Lib., 1959–60, Head, Collating and Binding Dept., 1958–59; Head, Transp. Coll., 1957–58. **Educ.:** Harvard Coll., 1951–55, AB (Eng.); Rutgers Univ., 1955–56, MLS. **Orgs.:** Boston Lib. Cnsrtm.: Pres. (1978–79); Treas. (1977–78, 1979–81). New Eng. Lib. Info. Netwk.: Exec. Bd. (1974–75). ALA: ACRL. MA State Adv. Cncl. on Libs. (1980–82). **Activities:** 1; 15, 17, 34; 57, 75, 93 **Addr.:** 70 Park St., Apt. 63, Brookline, MA 02146.

Lauerhass, Ludwig, Jr. (Ja. 6, 1935, Asheville, NC) Latin Amer. Biblgphr., Exec. Dir., Latin Amer. Ctr.; Lectr. (Hist.), Univ. of CA, Los Angeles, 1968–; Asst. Prof. (Hist.), Univ. of CA, Riverside, 1964–67. **Educ.:** Univ. of NC, 1955–57, BA (Poli. Sci.), MA (Latin Amer.); Univ. of CA, Los Angeles, 1957–75, PhD (Hist.), MLS. **Orgs.:** SALALM: Pres. (1979–80). Pac. Coast Cncl. on Latin Amer. Stds: Gov. Bd. (1976–78; 1980–). Latin Amer. Stds. Assn.: Nom. Com. (1977). S. CA Conf. on Intl. Stds.: Latin Amer. Com. (Ch., 1976–). **Honors:** Hubert Herring Meml. Prize, 1975. **Pubns.:** Jt. auth., *Education in Latin America: A Bibliography* (1981). **Activities:** 1; 15, 26, 37; 54 **Addr.:** Latin American Center, 10343 Bunche Hall, University of California, Los Angeles, CA 90024.

Laughlin, Jeannine Lackey (O. 31, 1931, Memphis, TN) Asst. Prof., Univ. of South. MS, 1978–; Supvsr., Lib. Media Srvs., Meridian Pub. Schs., 1971–77; Head Libn., Meridian HS, 1968–71. **Educ.:** Univ. of South. MS, 1965–68, BS (LS), 1968–70, MSLS, 1972–76, EdS (Media). **Orgs.:** ALA: Ref. and Subscrpn. Bks. Review Com. (1980–); AASL: Supvsn. Sect. MS LA: Autom. and Netwk. RT (1978–). MS Assn. of Sch. Libns. Citizens Adv. Bd. MS Educ. TV: Ch. (1981–). MS Assn. of Sch. Admins. **Honors:** MS Gvr.'s Conf. on Libs.: Del. (1979). **Pubns.:** *Manual for School Media Centers* (1974); "Impact of Educational Television," *Sch. Media Qtly.* (Spr. 1977); "Mississippi Libraries" slide-tape (1977). **Activities:** 11; 21, 32, 48; 72, 74, 75 **Addr.:** School of Library Service, University of Southern Mississippi, Box 5146 Southern Station, Hattiesburg, MS 39401.

Laughlin, Mildred Knight (Mr. 23, 1922, Glasco, KS) Prof. (LS), Univ. of OK, 1979–; Assoc. Prof. (LS), Univ. of IA, 1973–79; Asst. Prof. (LS), Univ. of S. MS, 1972–73; Resrc. Dir., Kennedy Elem. Sch., 1968–72. **Educ.:** Fort Hays Kansas State Coll., 1943–46, AB (Eng.); Wichita State Univ., 1950–52, MA (Educ.); Univ. of OK, 1968–70, MLS, 1970–72, PhD (Educ.). **Orgs.:** ALA: AASL, Awd. Com. (1976); Various ofcs. OK LA. IA LA. NEA. AECT. **Honors:** Beta Phi Mu. **Pubns.:** *Reading for Young People: The Great Plains* (1979). *Reading for Young People: The Rocky Mountains* (1980); "School Media Center Public Library Relationships," *MN Libs.* (Sum. 1976); "Action Activities," column, *Lrng. Today* (Fall 1972–). **Activities:** 10, 11; 21, 26, 32; 63 **Addr.:** 3432 Rambling Oaks, Norman, OK 73069.

Laughlin, Sara Gaar (Ap. 2, 1949, Richmond, IN) Admin., Stone Hills Area Lib. Srvs., 1980–; Dir., Admis., IN Univ. Sch. of Lib. and Info. Sci., 1979–80, Arch. Assoc., Arch., 1978–79; Proj. Resrch., Art Assn. of Richmond, IN, 1978; Art and Msc. Ref. Libn., Pub. Lib. of Cincinnati, 1973–76. **Educ.:** Univ. of Cincinnati, 1967–71, BA (Hist.); IN Univ. 1971–72, MLS, 1978– (Art Hist.). **Orgs.:** SLA: Cincinnati Chap. (Secy., 1976); IN Chap., Nom. Com. (Ch., 1980). ALA: JMRT; ASCLA. IN LA. Assn. of IN Media Educs. IN Hist. Socty. Amer. Assn. of State and Lcl. Hist. IN Univ. Libns. Assn.: Natl. Lib. Week Com. IN Univ. Sch. of Lib. and Info. Sci. Alum. Assn. **Pubns.:** *Art in Richmond, 1876–1976* (1978). **Activities:** 11, 14-Reg. Multi-type Netwk.; 17, 25, 34; 50, 55, 86 **Addr.:** P.O. Box 28, Solsberry, IN 47459.

Laughlin, Steven G. (S. 25, 1950, Oklahoma City, OK) Ref. Biblgphr. for Bus. and Spec. Std., Univ. of AL, Birmingham, 1977–. **Educ.:** Univ. of TX, 1974–76, BBA (Mktg.), 1976–77, MLS. **Orgs.:** AL LA: Mdrtr., ALIRT (1978–1980). **Pubns.:** "Review the Literature the Easy Way-Find out about Computer Based Information Services," *Decision Line* (N. 1978). **Addr.:** Mervyn H. Sterne Library, University Station, University of Alabama in Birmingham, Birmingham, AL 35294.

PROFESSIONAL ACTIVITIES: Institutions: 1. Acad. lib.; 2. Arch.; 3. Assn.; 4. Fed./Gvt. lib.; 5. Inst. lib.; 6. Mfr./Suppl.; 7. Milit. lib.; 8. Musm.; 9. Pub. lib.; 10. Sch. lib.; 11. Sch. of lib. sci.; 12. Spec. lib.; 13. State lib.; 14. (other). **Functions/Activities:** 15. Acq./Col. dev.; 16. Adult srvs.; 17. Admin.; 18. Apprais.; 19. Archit./Bldgs.; 20. Cat./Class.; 21. Chld. srvs.; 22. Circ.; 23. Cons./Pres.; 24. Consult.; 25. Cont. ed.; 26. Educ. lib. sci.; 27. Ext. srvs.; 28. Fund/Grants; 29. Gvt. pubs.; 30. Indx./Abs.; 31. Instr. lib. use; 32. Media srvs.; 33. Micro.; 34. Netwks./Coop.; 35. Persnl.; 36. PR; 37. Publshg.; 38. Recs. mgt.; 39. Ref. srvs.; 40. Repro.; 41. Resrch.; 42. Review.; 43. Secur.; 44. Serials; 45. Spec. col.; 46. Tech. srvs.; 47. Trustees/Bds.; 48. YA srvs.; 49. (other).

Laughrey, Edna C. (N. 29, 1940, Great Falls, MT) Purchasing & Bus. Oper. Head, Univ. of MI Lib., 1970–, Head Book Purchasing, 1969–70, Asst. Head, Serial Acq., 1967–69; Tchr., Manchester Pub. Sch., 1962–65. **Educ.:** Adrian Coll., 1958–61, BA (Eng.); Univ. of MI, 1965–67, AM (LS). **Orgs.:** ALA: RTSD, Prog. Eval. and Budget Com. (1969–70); Bookdealer - Lib. Rel. Com. (1970–74; Consult., 1974–75; Ch., 1975–77); Acq. Discuss. Grp. (Ch., 1973–74); Resrcs. Sect. Nom. Com. (1977–78); Acq. Preconf. (Co-ch., 1978–80). SLA. MI LA. Saline Pub. Lib.: Bd. of Trustees (1973–); Pres., VP Secy. Other orgs. **Pubns.:** "Dilemma of Prepaying Publishers," *Amer. Libs.* (N. 1977); Jt. Auth., *Guidelines for Handling Library Orders for Microfilms* (1977); *Guidelines for Handling Library Orders for Serials and Periodicals* (1974); *Guidelines for Handling Library Orders for In-Print Monographic Publications* (1973). **Activities:** 1, 9; 15, 17, 34 **Addr.:** 291 Tower Dr., Saline, MI 48176.

Laurin, Pushpamala (Bangalore, India) Dir., Info. Srvs., Gould Inc., 1976–; Lectr., Electronics, Harper Coll., 1971–76; Lectr., Electrical Engin., South. IL Univ., Edwardsville, 1969–71; Resrch. Sci., McDonnell-Douglas, St. Louis, 1968–69. **Educ.:** Gujarat Univ. (India), 1954–56, BSc (Phys.); Karnatak Univ., 1956–58, MSc (Phys.); Univ. of MI, 1960–62, M.E.E., (Electrical Engin.), 1963–67, PhD (Phys.). **Orgs.:** ASIS. Assn. Info. Mgrs.: Midwest Reg. Coord. (1979–). Socty. of Info. Display. Inst. of Electrical and Electronic Engins. **Pubns.:** Technical papers. **Activities:** 12; 17, 46 **Addr.:** Gould Information Center, 40 Gould Center, Rolling Meadows, IL 60008.

Lauritzen, Robert L. (Ag. 13, 1929, Rio Vista, CA) Tech. Srvs. Coord., San Jose State Univ., 1977–, Col. Coord., 1968–77, Head, Pub. Srvs., 1962–68, Head, Soc. Sci. Ref., 1958–62, Gvt. Docum. Libn., 1955–58, Ref. Asst., 1953–55. **Educ.:** Univ. of CA, 1947–51, BA (Fr.), 1951–52, BLS; San Jose State Univ., 1968–73, MA (Fr.). **Orgs.:** CA LA. SLA. **Addr.:** c/o San Jose State University Library, 250 S. Fourth St., San Jose, CA 95192.

Laux, Peter J. (Ja. 7, 1922, New London, WI) Dir., Canisius Coll. Lib., 1960–; Assoc. Libn., Georgetown Univ., 1954–60; Librarian I, II, Milwaukee Pub. Lib., 1951–54. **Educ.:** St. Norbert Coll., 1945–48, BA (Educ., Eng.); Marquette Univ., 1949–50, MA (Eng.); Univ. of WI, 1951–52, MS (LS). **Orgs.:** West. NY Lib. Resrcs. Cncl.: Various ofcs. Cath. LA: Pubn. Com. (Ch., 1965); Finance Com. (1967). **Pubns.:** *A Man's Home is His Hassle* (1969); Reviews; Contrib. Ed., *Cath. Lib. World* (1965–67). **Activities:** 1; 17 **Addr.:** Canisius College Library, 2001 Main St., Buffalo, NY 14208.

Lavendel, Giuliana A. (Milan, Italy) Mgr., Tech. Info. Ctr., Xerox Palo Alto Resrch. Ctr., 1975–, Cat., Ref. Libn., 1971–75; Other positions in libs. and comm. **Educ.:** CA State Univ. San Jose, MA (LS); Univ. Milan (Italy), Doctor of Classics. **Orgs.:** ASIS. SLA: San Andreas Chap., Consult. Ofcr. (1980–81). Assn. Comp. Mach. IEEE. **Pubns.:** Ed., *A Decade of Research, Xerox Palo Alto Research Center* (1980); Chap. in *Special Librarianship: A New Reader* (1980); "The Computer in Research," *IEEE Spectrum* (D. 1978); "Special Libraries," *Chem. Engin. News* (Ap. 1977); Other articles. **Addr.:** 1511 Hamilton Ave., Palo Alto, CA 94303.

La Verdi, Adelaide L. (F. 15, 1937, East Aurora, NY) Head of Cat., SUNY, Geneseo, 1968–, Docum. Libn. and Cat., 1965–68, Serials and Docum. Libn., 1963–65, Circ. Libn., 1959–63. **Educ.:** SUNY, Geneseo, 1954–58, BS (Educ.), 1959–64, MLS. **Orgs.:** ALA: RTSD; ACRL; LITA. SUNY Libn. Assn. **Activities:** 1; 20 **Addr.:** Milne Library, State University College, Geneseo, NY 14454.

Lavergne, Rodolphe C. (F. 25, 1926, Prince Albert, SK) Lib. Dir., Ecole des Hautes Études Commerciales de Montréal, 1977–; Assoc. Dir. (LS), McGill Univ., 1968–77, Assoc. Univ. Libn., Sci., 1966–68, Med. Libn., McGill Univ., 1963–66; Supvsr., Engin. Lib., Canadair Ltd., 1956–63; Libn., US Air Frc., 1953–56; Libn. Engin. Inst. of Can., 1949–53. **Educ.:** Univ. de Montréal, 1947, BA, 1949, BS; McGill Univ., 1959, MLS. **Orgs.:** PQ LA: Cncl. (1971–73); Coll. and Resrch. Libs. Sect. (VP. 1971–72). Corp. Prof. Libns. of PQ: Cncl. (1971–73), Disciplinary Com. (1975–76). Can. Assn. of Lib. Schs.: Nom Com. (1975–76, Ch., 1976). Can. Assn. for Info. Sci.: Exhibets Com. (1973). Various other orgs. and ofcs. Conf. of Rectors and Prins., PQ: Com. on Coord. of Univ. Libs. (1967–68). Nat. Resrch. Cncl.: Various coms. **Activities:** 1, 12; 17; 59 **Addr.:** Bibliothèque, École des Hautes Études Commerciales, 5255, ave. Decelles, Montreal, PQ H3T 1V6 Canada.

Lavine, Frank (Ap. 3, 1924, Boston, MA) Dir., Medford Pub. Lib., 1969–; Educ. Supvsr., MD State Lib., 1967–69; Reg. Libn., Lib. of Congs., 1966–67; Dir., Perkins Sch. Lib., 1964–66. **Educ.:** Boston Univ., Brandeis Univ., 1952–55, AB (Soclgy.); Simmons Coll., 1963–64, MLS. **Orgs.:** ALA. East. Reg. Adv. Bd.: Ch. (1973–75). **Activities:** 9; 24, 37; 51, 66 **Addr.:** Medford Public Library, 111 High St., Medford, MA 02155.

Law, Aileen Elizabeth (Libby) (Je. 14, 1944, Augusta, GA) Field Srv. Libn., SC State Lib., 1972–; Ext. Libn., Florence Cnty. Lib., 1967–72. **Educ.:** Columbia Coll., 1963–66, BA (LS); Univ. of MI, 1966–67, MLS. **Orgs.:** SC LA: Secy. (1972). SELA. ALA. SC State Empl. Assn. **Activities:** 9, 13; 27, 36, 47; 50, 74, 89 **Addr.:** South Carolina State Library, P.O. Box 11469, Columbia, SC 29211.

Law, Daniel T. (My. 13, 1941, Hong Kong) Info. Spec., Miles Labs. Inc., 1981–; Co-Dir., Reg. Info. Comm. Exch., Rice Univ., 1978–81, Asst. Dir., 1977–78, Coll. Dev. Libn. Sci. Tech., 1975–77; Other positions tchg. bio. **Educ.:** Univ. CA, Los Angeles, 1964–66, BA (Zlgy.); OR State Univ., 1966–68, MS (Zlgy.), 1972–75, PhD (Zlgy.); Rosary Coll., 1970–72, MALS. **Orgs.:** SLA. Houston OLUG: Pubns. Com.; Prog. Com. AAAS. Natl. Assn. Bio. Tchrs. Amer. Sci. Afflt. Malacological Socty. (Taiwan). **Honors:** Phi Sigma. **Pubns.:** "Science Periodicals Drain Budgets," *Fondren Lib. Bltn.* (V. 5, 1978); "Bibliometric Characteristics of Chemical Engineering Research at Rice Univ." *TX Chap. SLA BLtn.* (V. 28, 1977). **Activities:** 1, 12; 17, 39, 49-Info. Broker; 64, 86, 91 **Addr.:** Miles Laboratories, Inc., PPLS Section, P.O. Box 40, Elkhart, IN 46515.

Law, Gordon T. (O. 27, 1945, Norwood, MA) Ref. Libn., Martin P. Catherwood Lib., NY State Sch. of Indus. and Labor Rel., 1972–. **Educ.:** SUNY, Albany, 1963–67, BA (Hist.), 1967–68, MA (Soc. Sci.), 1971–72, MLS. **Orgs.:** Com. of Indus. Rel. Libns. Indus. Rel. Resrch. Assn. of Ctrl. NY. ACRL: East. NY Chap. **Pubns.:** "Recent Publications," *Indus. and Labor Relations Review* (1972–); "Cold Type Composition: Its Impact on Library and Information Science," *Jnl. of the Amer. Socty. For Info. Sci.* (1974). **Activities:** 1, 12; 31, 39; 59, 92 **Addr.:** Martin P. Catherwood Library, New York State School of Industrial and Labor Relations, Cornell University, Ithaca, NY 14850.

Lawless, Paul B. (S. 13, 1932, Tobyhanna, PA) Lib. Dir., Wesley Coll., 1969–; Serials Libn., Bethlehem Steel Corp., 1965–69. **Educ.:** Kutztown State Coll., 1957–61, BS (Soc. Std.); Rutgers Univ., 1963–65, MLS. **Orgs.:** DE LA: Bd. of Dir. (1972–73). **Activities:** 1; 15, 17, 22; 59, 65, 80 **Addr.:** Wesley College, College Sq., Dover, DE 19901.

Lawrence, Arthur P. (Jl. 15, 1937, Durham, NC) Ed. and Publshr., *The Diapason,* 1976–; Assoc. Prof., Dept. Ch., Msc. Libn., St. Mary's Coll., Notre Dame, IN, 1969–80; Instr., Ctr. Coll. of KY, 1968–69. **Educ.:** Davidson Coll., 1955–59, AB (Msc.); FL State Univ., 1959–61, MMsc (Theory); Amer. Gld. of Organists, 1966, AAGO, ChM; Stanford Univ., 1966–68, DMA (Performance Prac.); Univ. of MI, 1971–74, AMLS. **Orgs.:** Msc. LA: NUC Card Proj. Ed. (1972–74); *Notes* Reviewer (1975–). Intl. Msc. LA. Amer. Gld. of Organists: San Francisco, Treas. (1966–68); South Bend Dean (1971–73); Organ Hist. Socty.: Chicago Chap. (Fndn. Mem., 1979). **Pubns.:** Ed., *The Diapason* (S. 1976–); various articles in msc. Jnls. **Activities:** 2, 14-Prof. Jnl.; 24, 37, 42; 55, 63 **Addr.:** *The Diapason,* 380 Northwest Hwy., Des Plaines, IL 60016.

Lawrence, Barbara (D. 16, 1944, New York, NY) Head, Info. Srvs. Unit, Resrch. Env. Hlth. Div., Exxon Corp., 1979–; Data Base Mgt. Supvsr., Exxon Resrch. Engin. Corp., 1976–79, Staff Info. Chem., 1973–76, Info. Chem., 1969–73 Asst. Docum. Sci., Schering Corp., 1967–69; Jr. Organic Chem., Burroughs Wellcome & Co., 1966–67. **Educ.:** Univ. of VT, 1961–65, BA (Chem.); Yale Univ., 1965–66 (Chem.). **Orgs.:** ASIS: Ch., Spec. Int. Grp. on Bio. & Chem. Info. Syst. (1975–76); Org. Structure Task Force (1979–80); Educ. Com. (1980–1982). SLA: Chem. Div. (Ch., 1979–80; Ch-Elect, 1978–79). Natl. Micrographics Assn. Amer. Chem. Socty. **Pubns.:** "Information Retrieval," *Kirk-Othmer Encyc. of Chem. Tech.* (1981); Jt. cmplr., "OnLine Commands: A User's Quick Guide for Bibliographic Retrieval Systems" (1977); "Preparation of Desk-Top Literature Indexes for Ongoing Research Projects," *Jnl. Amer. Socty. for Info. Sci.* (1976); "Project Evaluation, Any Technologist Can Do It, A Guide to Sources of Business Information," *Chem. Tech.* (1975); "Making On-Line Search Services Available in an Industrial Research Environment," *Jnl. Amer. Socty. for Info. Sci.* (1974); other articles. **Activities:** 12; 17, 30; 56, 60, 80, 86 **Addr.:** Research & Environmental Health Division, Medical Department, Exxon Corporation, PO Box 235, East Millstone, NJ 08873.

Lawrence, Elizabeth W. (Ag. 17, 1925, Seattle, WA) Head, Circ. Dept., Ann Arbor Pub. Lib., 1974–; Ref. and Readers Adv. Libn., White Plains (NY) Pub. Lib., 1968–72. **Educ.:** Whitman Coll., 1943–47, AB (Pol. Sci.); Univ. of MD, 1966–68, MLS. **Orgs.:** ALA. MI LA: Spec. Srvs. RT, Litcy. Workshop Com. (1979–80; Ch. 1980–81). Westchester (NY) LA: Soc. Responsibilities Com. (1970–72), (Ch., 1970–71). Litcy. Cncl. of Washtenaw Cnty.: Bd. (1973–); Pres. (1975–77). MI Litcy., Inc.: Bd. (1977–79). Ann Arbor Right To Read: Strg. Com. (1975–76). Cont. Educ. Adv. Com., Ann Arbor Pub. Sch. **Pubns.:** *Adult Basic Reading Collection* (1978). **Activities:** 9; 17, 22; 89 **Addr.:** 1405 Beechwood Dr., Ann Arbor, MI 48103.

Lawrence, Frances Sayre Webster (My. 31, 1923, Los Angeles, CA) Retired, 1980; Elem. Libn., Tucson Unified Sch. Dist. # 1, 1966–80. **Educ.:** Univ. of NB, 1940–44, BS (Educ.); Univ. of AZ, 1966–69, M.Educ. (LS). **Orgs.:** Tucson AV Assn.: Secy. (1975–76; 1979–80); Pres. (1977–78). AZ State LA: Sch. Libs. Div., Various ofcs. ALA. Jr. Leag. of Tucson. P.E. O. **Activities:** 10; 15, 17, 21 **Addr.:** 944 S. Magnolia, Tucson, AZ 85711.

Lawrence, Gary S. (Ag. 31, 1946, Portland, OR) Assoc. Mgr. for Resrch. and Anal., Ofc. Asst. VP, Lib. Plans and Policies, Univ. CA, Berkeley, 1976–. **Educ.:** Claremont Men's Coll., 1964–68, BA (Eng.); Univ. CA, Berkeley, 1972–80, MLS, MPP (Pub. Policy), DLIS. **Orgs.:** ALA: ACRL, LAMA, LITA, LRRT. CA LA. ASIS: Bay Area Chap., Treas. (1978–79). **Pubns.:** "A Cost Model for Storage & Weeding Programs," *Coll. Resrch. Lib.* (Mr. 1981); *An Economic Criterion for Housing & Disposing of Lib. Material* (Resrch. Rpt. Univ. CA) (1979); *The Use of General Collections at the Univ. of Calif.* (Resrch. Rpt. Univ. CA) (1980). **Activities:** 1; 17, 34, 41; 56, 92 **Addr.:** Office of the Assistant Vice President-Library Plans and Policies, University of California Systemwide Administration, Berkeley, CA 94720.

Lawrence, Geraldine Givens (Jl. 30, 1954, Tallahassee, FL) Info. Anal., Hlth., Safety, Env., Shell Oil Co., 1979–; Clin. Med. Libn., Univ. of MO, Kansas City, 1978–79; Biomed. Info. Spec., Resrch. Med. Ctr., 1977–78; Coord., Supreme Ct. Proj., FL State Univ. Law Sch., 1975–77. **Educ.:** FL State Univ., 1971–75, BA (Anthro.), 1976–77, MS (Soc. Sci.), 1975–76, MLS. **Orgs.:** Natl. Online Circuit: Ch. (1978–79). Houston OLUG: Prog. Com. (1979). SLA. Zeta Tau Alpha Alum. Assn. **Pubns.:** "C.M.L." (Clin. Med. Libn.) *Online* (Jl. 1979); reviews. **Activities:** 1, 12; 30, 39, 41; 58, 65, 80 **Addr.:** Shell Oil Company Library, P.O. Box 4320, Houston, TX 77210.

Lawrence, Patricia A. (N. 3, 1946, Bowling Green, OH) Asst. Lib. Dir., Napa City Cnty. Lib., 1979–; Asst. Cnty. Libn., Marin Cnty. Lib., 1977–79; City Libn., Sausalito Pub. Lib., 1970–79; City Libn., Granville Pub. Lib., 1968–70. **Educ.:** Bowling Green State Univ., 1964–68, BA (Amer. Std.); Univ. of CA, Berkeley, 1975–76, MLS. **Orgs.:** ALA: LAMA, Circ. Srv. Conf. Local Arrange. (1981). CA LA. ASIS. Pac. Reg. CLSI Users Grp.: Pres. (1980–81). Univ. of CA Berkeley Lib. Sch. Alum. Assn.: Pres. Elect (1979); Pres. (1980). **Pubns.:** Various articles on energy. **Activities:** 9, 17 **Addr.:** Napa City County Library, 1150 Division, Napa, CA 94558.

Lawrence, Philip Drake, Jr. (Mr. 1, 1919, Burlington, VT) Supvsr., Info. Srv., W. Point Pepperell Resrch. Ctr., 1972–; Resrch. Info. Spec., Lockheed GA Co., 1963–72; Info. Ctr. Supvsr., The Chemstrand Resrch. Ctr., 1959–63. **Educ.:** Univ. of Richmond (VA), 1936–40, BS (Chem.); Univ. of PA, 1940–41; Case West. Reserve, 1958. **Orgs.:** SLA: S. Atl. Chap., Treas. (1966–68); AL Chap., Secy., Treas. (1980–81). ASIS. AL LA. Amer. Chem. Socty.: Chem. Info. Div. **Activities:** 5, 12; 17, 30, 39; 80, 91, 95-Textiles. **Addr.:** Westpoint Pepperell Research Center Library, P.O. Box 398, Shawmut, AL 36876.

Lawry, Martha P. (N. 5, 1925, Clyde, OH) Libs. Serial Catlgr., 1980–; Women's Catlgr., OH State Univ. Libs., 1979–, Catlgr., 1976–79; Instr. (Sp.), Milwaukee-Downer Coll., 1948–49. **Educ.:** Coll. of Wooster, 1943–47, BA (Sp.); Northwest. Univ., 1947–48, MA (Sp.); Case West. Resrv. Univ., 1974–75, MSLS. **Orgs.:** ALA. N. OH Tech. Srvs. Libns. Acad. Lib. Assn. of OH. OH LA. Other orgs. Natl. Women's Stds. Assn. Hayes Hist. Socty. OH State Univ. Senate: Prog. Com. (1978–80; Ch., 1979–80). **Honors** Phi Beta Kappa. Delta Sigma Rho. Beta Phi Mu. **Pubns.:** "Recordings of Brahms' *Rhapsodie* (Op. 53)," *Jnl. of the Assn. for Rec. Sound Coll.,* (1980); Ed., *Women's Stds. Rev.* (1979–80); Reviews. **Activities:** 1; 15, 20, 42; 55, 92, 95-Women's Studies. **Addr.:** Ohio State University Library, 1858 Neil Ave. Mall, Columbus, OH 43210.

Lawson, A(bram) Venable (Ja. 9, 1922, South Boston, VA) Dir., Div. of Libnshp., Emory Univ., 1965–; Asst. Prof. (LS), FL State Univ., 1960–65; Coord., Pub. Srvs., Atlanta Pub. Lib., 1956–60, Head, Ref., Atlanta Pub. Lib., 1953–56. **Educ.:** Univ. of AL, 1946, BA (Eng.); Emory Univ., 1950, MLn; Columbia Univ., 1969, DLS. **Orgs.:** ALA: Budget Asm. (1974); Com. on Appts. (1974); Lib. Educ. Div. (Pres., 1974–75). AALS: Dir. (1973–76); Cncl. of Deans and Dirs. (Ch., 1975–76). SELA: Manpower Com. (1976–81). CLENE: Nom. Com. (1975–76). Other orgs. and ofcs. GA Adult Educ. Assn. AAUP. **Pubns.:** "Library Education," *The ALA Yearbook* (1976–80). **Activities:** 11; 25, 26, 39 **Addr.:** Division of Library and Information Management, Emory University, Atlanta, GA 30322.

Lawson, Clinton D. (Ja. 14, 1928, Montreal, PQ) Dir., Midwest. Reg. Lib. Syst., 1974–; Head, Prcs., Midwest. Reg. Lib., 1967–73; Catlgr., Wilfrid Laurier Univ., 1966–67; Head, Bib. Srch., Univ. of Waterloo, 1964–66. **Educ.:** Univ. of Toronto, 1947–51, BA (Arts), 1951–54, BD (Theo.), 1963–64, BLS. **Orgs.:** Can. LA. ALA. ON LA. **Pubns.:** "Midwestern and Computers," *ON Lib. Rev.* (D. 1980); "Autom. Acq. at Midwestern," ON Lib. Rev. (S. 1977). **Activities:** 9, 14-Reg.; 17, 34, 46; 56 **Addr.:** Midwestern Regional Library System, 637 Victoria St. N., Kitchener, ON N2H 5G4 Canada.

Lawson, Michael Edwin (Je. 26, 1945, Spartanburg, SC) Media Libn., Seneca Valley HS, 1980–; Media Libn., Montgomery Cnty. Pub. Sch., 1977–80; Media Libn., Col. Zadok Magruder HS, 1970–77; Media Spec., Albert Einstein HS, 1969–70. **Educ.:** E. TN State Univ., 1967, BS (Sci.), 1968, MA (LS). **Orgs.:** ALA: AASL, Natl. Exhibit Mgr. (1980–1982). MD LA: YA Div., Prog. Com. (Ch. 1975). AECT: Reg. Rep. (1975). Montgomery Cnty. Sch. LA: Secy. (1974). Montgomery Cnty. Tchr. Assn. MD Tchr.

Special Subjects/Services: 50. Adult educ.; 51. Advert./Mktg.; 52. Aerosp.; 53. Agric.; 54. Area std.; 55. Arts/Hum.; 56. Autom.; 57. Bibl./Prtg.; 58. Bio. sci.; 59. Bus./Fin.; 60. Chem.; 61. Copyrt.; 62. Documtn.; 63. Educ.; 64. Engin.; 65. Env.; 66. Eth. grps.; 67. Film; 68. Food/Nutr.; 69. Geneal.; 70. Geo.; 71. Geol.; 72. Handcpd.; 73. Hist.; 74. Int. frdm.; 75. Info. sci.; 76. Insr.; 77. Law; 78. Legis.; 79. Math./Comp. sci.; 80. Med.; 81. Metals; 82. Nat. resrcs.; 83. Newsp.; 84. Nuc. sci.; 85. Oral hist.; 86. Petr./Energy; 87. Pharm.; 88. Phys./Astr./Math.; 89. Readg.; 90. Relig.; 91. Sci./Tech.; 92. Soc. sci.; 93. Telecom.; 94. Transp.; 95. (other).

Assn. Natl. Educ. Assn. **Pubns.:** Jt. ed., "Above and Beyond" (ERIC) 1979. **Activities:** 10; 24, 32, 46 **Addr.:** 7832 Briardale Terrace, Rockville, MD 20855.

Lawton, James (Ag. 6, 1939, Chicago, IL) Biblgphr. and Lib. Consult., self-empl., 1980–; Cur. of Mss., Boston Pub. Lib., 1968–80; Rare Book Biblgphr., Syracuse Univ., 1967–68. **Educ.:** St. Procopius Coll., 1957–61, AB (Lit.); Univ. of MI, 1963–66, MA (Eng.), 1966–67, MA (LS). **Honors:** Univ. of MI, Intercult. Awd., 1966. **Pubns.:** *The Four Seas Company: A Bibliography* (1981); Ed. *Shop Talk* (1975); "Caxton's Autograph," *Typophiles Chapbook* (1976). **Activities:** 1, 2; 17, 18, 45; 55, 57 **Addr.:** 16 Linden Pl., Brookline, MA 02146.

Laythe, Rosamond O. (Jy. 12, 1913, Carlyle, IL) Asst. Dir., Pub. Srvs., Lovejoy Lib., South. IL Univ., Edwardsville, 1975–, Asst. to the Dir., 1973–75, Head, Gen. Ref., 1971–73, Head, Alton Ctr., 1965–71, Chlds. Libn., Walla Walla (WA) Pub. Lib., 1962–65, Various other positions in bus. and educ., 1935–1962. **Educ.:** Shurtleff Coll., 1931–35, BA (Eng.); Univ. of WA, 1963–64, MLS. **Orgs.:** ALA. IL LA. AAUP. **Pubns.:** "Of Boxes and Birds," *PNLA Qtly.* (Jy. 1964); "More Frontlogs," *Lib. Jnl.* (Ja. 1970); "Who are We?" *Lrng. Today* (Win. 1973); "Heavy Apple Use at SIU" *Small Computers in Libraries* (A. 1981). **Addr.:** Rt. 2, Box 302, Godfrey, IL 62035.

Layton, Jeanne (F. 12, 1930, Kaysville, UT) Dir., Davis Cnty. Lib., 1970–, Asst. Libn., 1965–70, Head Circ., HS Libn., 1959–64. **Educ.:** Univ. of UT, 1948–52, BS (Mkt.), 1964–76, M.Ed. **Orgs.:** ALA. UT LA: Pub. Lib. Sect. (Ch. 1967–68); Job Opportunities Com. (Ch., 1967–68); Natl. Lib. Wk. (Exec. Dir. 1972). Urban Pub. Lib. Cncl. (Ch., 1978–). Kaysville Cham. of Cmrc. **Honors:** Univ. of IL, Robt. B. Downs Awd., 1980. **Activities:** 9, 10; 17, 32, 36; 55, 59, 74 **Addr.:** 95 S. 100 E., Kaysville, UT 84037.

Lazar, Jon H. (Ap. 4, 1945, Cleveland, OH) Supvsr., Tech. Srvs., Rochester Pub. Lib., 1982–; Head, Order Dept., Buffalo & Erie Cnty. Pub. Lib., 1976–82, Serials Libn., 1973–76, Cat., 1971–72, Ref. Libn., 1968–71. **Educ.:** Hobart Coll., 1963–67, BA (Pol. Sci.); Syracuse Univ., 1967–68, MS (LS). **Orgs.:** ALA. NY LA: Resrc. and Tech. Srv. Div., Resrc. Com. 1976–77; Treas. 1970–74. Libn. Assn. of the Buffalo & Erie Cnty. Pub. Lib.: VP (1976–77). **Activities:** 9; 15, 17 **Addr.:** Rochester Public Library, 115 South Ave., Rochester, NY 14604.

Lazarow, Jane Klein (Chicago, IL) Sr. Resrch. Anal., MN Dept. of Hlth.; Resrch. Assoc., Hlth. Comp. Sci. Univ. MN 1974–, Diabetes Lit. Indx., 1958–75; Trainee, Natl. Lib. Med., 1970. **Educ.:** Univ. of Chicago, 1935–39, BS (Physio.); Univ. of MN, 1967–70, MS (Info. Sci., LS). **Orgs.:** ASIS: Local Treas. (1975–76); Med. Info. Spec. Interest Grp. (Ch., 1978–80). Med. LA. Amer. Comp. Mach. Natl. Micro. Assn. **Honors** Beta Phi Mu, 1970; Signa Delta Epsilon, 1975. **Activities:** 12; 41; 75, 80 **Addr.:** 221 Woodlawn Ave., St. Paul, MN 55105.

Lazenby, Gail Rogers (My. 6, 1947, Charlotte, NC) Branch Coord., DeKalb (GA) Lib. Syst., 1977–; Head, Hapeville Branch, Atlanta Pub. Lib., 1972–77, Head, Peachtree Branch, 1971–72; YA Libn., Stewart-Lakewood Branch, Atlanta Pub. Lib., 1970–71. **Educ.:** Salem Coll., 1965–69, BA (Fr.); Univ. of NC., 1969–70, MSLS. **Orgs.:** ALA: PLA, Pub. Lib. Systs. Sect., Nom. Com. (Ch., 1979). GA LA: Pub. Com. (1977–79); Jr. Mems. RT, Ed., *News in the Round* (1977–79), Nom. Com. (1979), Lcl. Arrange. Com. (Ch., 1979–81). SELA: Pub. Lib. Sect. (Secy., 1978–80); Cont. ed. and Staff Dev. Com., 1980–82; Site Sel. Com., 1980–82. Metro Atlanta LA: Nom. Com. (Ch., 1979). **Activities:** 9; 16, 17, 27; 50 **Addr.:** DeKalb Library System, 3560 Kensington Rd., Decatur, GA 30032.

Lazer, Ellen A. (O. 22, 1950, New York, NY) Sr. Ed., Books & Monographs, Knowledge Indus. Pubns., Inc, 1979–; Ed., Praeger Publshrs., 1976–79; Writer/Ed., Catalyst, 1974–76. **Educ.:** Coll. of the City of NY, 1967–71, BA (Econ.); Case-Western Reserve Univ., 1971–73, MS (Soc. Admin.). **Orgs.:** ASIS: Pubns. Com. (1979–). Women's Natl. Book Assn. **Pubns.:** Reviews. **Activities:** 6; 37; 56, 75, 93 **Addr.:** Knowledge Industry Publications, Inc., 701 Westchester Ave., White Plains, NY 10604.

Lazerow, Samuel (Jy. 29, 1912, Baltimore, MD) Sr. VP, Inst. for Sci. Info., 1972–, Chief, Serial Rec. Div., Lib. of Congs., 1965–72; Chief, Tech. Srvs. Div., Natl. Lib. of Med., 1952–65; Chief, Acq. Div., Natl. Agr. Lib., 1947–52; Asst. Chief, Army Lib. Srv., 1946. **Educ.:** Johns Hopkins Univ., 1930–38, BS (Langs.); Columbia Univ., 1939–41, MLS. **Orgs.:** ALA. Med. LA. ASIS. Amer. Mgt. Assn. AAAS. **Honors:** Lib. of Congs., Superior Srv. Awd., 1967. **Pubns.:** "Institute for Scientific Information," *Ency. of Lib. and Info. Sci.* (1974); "National collaboration and the National Libraries Task Force," Proc. of the Stanford Conf. on Collaborative Lib. Systs. Dev. (1969); "The National Medical Library: Acquisitions Program," *Bltn. of the Med. LA* (1954). **Activities:** 14-Info. Co.; 17, 30, 37; 56, 62†

Leab, Katharine Kyes (Mr. 17, 1941, Cleveland, OH) Co-Mgr. Ed., *Amer. Bk. Prices Current,* and Syst. Chief, 1972–; Ref. Ed., Columbia Univ. Press, 1964–72; Permissions Ed., D. C. Heath, 1962–63. **Educ.:** Smith Coll., 1958–62, BA (Eng.); Columbia Univ. 1962–63, (Eng.); Yeats Summer Sch., Sum. 1962. **Orgs.:** ALA: ACRL. Bibl. Socty. of Amer.: Nom. Com. (1977). Cosmopolitan Club. Washington Club. First Congregational Church of Washington, CT. **Honors:** Phi Beta Kappa 1962. **Pubns.:** Jt. Auth., *The Auction Companion* (1981); Jt. Auth., "Appraisal," *Modern Bookcollecting* (1978); Reviews. **Activities:** 6; 24, 30, 38; 57, 62, 93 **Addr.:** c/o Bancroft Parkman Inc., 121 E. 78th St., New York, NY 10021.

Leach, Maurice Derby (Je. 23, 1923, Lexington, KY) Prof. and Univ. Libn., Washington and Lee Univ., 1968–; Prog. Adv., Near East-Beirut, Ford Fndn., 1967–68; Prof. & Head, Dept. of LS, Univ. of KY, 1959–68; Prog. Ofcr., Near East, US Info. Agency, 1958–59; Asst. Attache, US Frgn. Srv. and US Info. Srvs., 1950–58. **Educ.:** Univ. of KY, 1941–45, AB (Hist.); Univ. of Chicago, 1945–46, BLS; Mid-Career Prog., US Dept. of State, 1959. **Orgs.:** VA LA: Pres. (1975–76); Ch., Coll. Sect. (1973–74). SELA. Egyptian LA: Bd. (1953–58). AAUP. English-Speaking Un.: Pres. Lexington Branch (1970–73). Assn. for the Prsrvn. of VA Antiquities: Bd., Lexington Chap. (1974–76). Rockbridge Hist. Socty. **Pubns.:** Various articles. **Activities:** 1; 17, 19; 54 **Addr.:** The University Library, Washington and Lee University, Lexington, VA 24450.

Leach, Ronald G. (F. 22, 1938, Monroe, MI) Dean of libs., In State Univ., 1980–; Assoc. Dir., of Libs., Ctrl. MI Univ., 1976–; Actg. Dir., Lake Superior State Coll. Lib., 1975–76; Tchr. (LS), North. MI Univ., 1973–76; Asst. Dir., Lake Superior State Coll. Lib., 1970–75; Head Libn., OH State Univ., Mansfield, 1969–70; HS Libn., Rudyard Cmnty. Sch., 1967–68. **Educ.:** Ctrl. MI Univ., 1962–67, BS (Sec. Educ.); Univ. of MI, 1968–69, MA (LS); MI State Univ., 1975, PhD. (Higher Educ.). **Orgs.:** ALA: RASD, Info. Retrieval Com. (Ch., 1979–); LAMA, Middle Mgt. DG (Ch., 1979–); LITA; ACRL. ARL: Ofc. of Mgt. Consult. Trng. Prog. (1980–); Instr. in Mgt. Wkshps. (1981–). AECT. MI Lib. Cnsrtm.: Bd of Trustees (1973–), Exec. Cncl. (1978–). MI LA. Other orgs. and ofcs. **Pubns.:** "Finding Time You Never Knew You Had," *Jnl. of Acad. Libnshp.* (1980); "Budget Implications" paper for (1979); "Collection Development Strategies for Academic and Research Libraries" "Time Management," speech Ctrl. MI Univ. wkshp. (1979). **Activities:** 1; 17, 24, 34; 56, 63 **Addr.:** Rural Route #32, Box 199, Terre Haute, IN 47803.

Leahy, Lynda C. (Jl. 21, 1944, Oklahoma City, OK) Head of Ref., Brandeis Univ., 1979–; Ref. Libn., Bus., Boston Pub. Lib., 1977–79, Ref. Libn., Gvt. Docum., 1972–77. **Educ.:** Wellesley Coll., 1962–66, BA (Hist.); Univ. of CT, 1966–68, MA (Hist.); Simmons Coll., 1971–72, MSLS. **Orgs.:** SLA. MA LA. ALA. **Honors:** Beta Phi Mu, 1972. **Pubns.:** Reviews. **Activities:** 1; 17, 39; 55, 92 **Addr.:** Brandeis University Library, Waltham, MA 02254.

Leamon, David L. (Jy. 31, 1939, Kansas City, MO) Dir., Jackson Dist. Lib., 1978–; N. Reg. Admin., Seattle Pub. Lib., 1976–78; Head, Readers' Srvs., Tulsa City and Cnty. Lib., 1973–76; Dist. Supvsr., Educ. Media, Mid-Continent Pub. Lib., 1968–73. **Educ.:** Ctrl. MO State Univ., 1961–65, BA, BS (Educ.); Case West. Rsv. Univ., 1971–72, MSLS. **Orgs.:** ALA: PLA, AV Com. (1976–78), Mem. Com. (1978–80). MI LA. NLA. Detroit Suburban Libns. RT. **Activities:** 9; 17, 25, 36; 55, 63, 75 **Addr.:** Jackson District Library, 244 W. Michigan Ave., Jackson, MI 49201.

Learmont, Carol L. (S. 5, 1927, Meriden, CT) Assoc. Dean, Sch. of Lib. Srv., Columbia Univ., 1979–, Asst. Dean, 1971–79, Head-Circ., 1967–71, Asst. Libn., Bus., 1965–67. **Educ.:** Duke Univ., 1945–49, BA (Pol. Sci.); Wesleyan Univ., 1959–62, MS (Liberal Std.); Rutgers Univ., 1964–65, MS (LS). **Orgs.:** ALA: LAD-PAS Staff Dev. Com. (1972–76); ACRL Cont. Educ. Com. (1978–). AALS: Liaison (1975–). NY LA: Educ. Sect. (1976–78). **Honors:** Beta Phi Mu, 1965. **Pubns.:** "Placements and Salaries", *Lib. Jnl.* (annually, 1972–). **Activities:** 1; 25, 26, 35; 50 **Addr.:** School of Library Service, Columbia University, New York, NY 10027.

Leary, Margaret A. (Jy. 2, 1942, Oberlin, OH) Asst. Dir., Univ. of MI Law Lib., 1973; Catlgr., William Mitchell Coll. of Law, 1970–72; Catlgr., Law Sch., Univ. of MN, 1968–70, Catlgr., Walter Lib., Univ. of MN, 1965–68. **Educ.:** Cornell Univ., 1960–64, BA (Govt.); Univ. of MN, 1964–66, MA (LS); William Mitchell Coll. of Law, 1969–73, JD. **Orgs.:** ALA. AALL. MI Assn. of Law Libs. State Bar of MI: Libs., Legal Resrch., and Pubn. Com. (1974–; Ch., 1976–77, 1978–79). **Pubns.:** "International Executive Agreements," *Law Lib. Jnl.* (Win. 1979). **Activities:** 1, 12; 17, 19, 26; 61, 77, 78 **Addr.:** Legal Research Building, University of Michigan, Ann Arbor, MI 48109.

Leather, Victoria P. (Je. 12, 1947, Chattanooga, TN) Dir., Eastgate Branch, Chattanooga–Hamilton Cnty. Lib. 1977–; Chief Libn., Baroness Erlanger Hosp. (Chattanooga), 1975–77, Libn. and Media Coord., Sch. Nursing, 1971–75. **Educ.:** Univ. of Chattanooga, 1964–68, BA cum laude (Psy.); Univ. of TN, 1972–78, MSLS. **Orgs.:** TN LA: PR Com. (1979–80); Spec. Lib. Nom. Com. (Ch., 1978). Chattanooga Area LA: Pres. (1978–79); VP (1977–78); Secy. (1976–77). Hlth. Educ. Lib. Prog.: Pres. (1975–77). Alpha Hon. Socty. TN Lib. Legis. Netwk.: Reg. Coord. (1978–). **Honors:** Beta Phi Mu, 1978. **Activities:** 9, 12; 17, 34, 39; 50, 78, 80 **Addr.:** Eastgate Branch Library, 5900 Bldg., Chattanooga, TN 37411.

Leatherbury, Maurice C. (Ap. 19, 1944, Madisonville, LA) Pres., MetaMicro Lib. Syst. Inc., 1980–; Asst. Dir. for Syst. & Resrch., Houston Acad. of Med.-TX Med. Ctr. Lib., 1977–79; Acq. Libn., Stetson Univ., 1971–72. **Educ.:** Univ. of Southwest. LA, 1961–66, BA (Eng.); FL State Univ., 1970, MS (LS); Univ. of TX, 1972–79, PhD (Lib. & Info. Sci). **Orgs.:** ALA. Med. LA: Tchr., Cont. Educ. Course. ASIS: Ch.-Elect, TX Chap. **Honors:** Beta Phi Mu, 1970; Phi Kappa Phi, 1978. **Pubns.:** *Annual Statistics of Medical School Libraries in the U.S. and Canada* (1978, 1979); "Friends of the Library Groups for Health Sciences Libraries," *Bltn. of the Med. LA* (Jl. 1978). **Activities:** 24; 56 **Addr.:** MetaMicro Library Systems, Inc., 1818 San Pedro Ave., San Antonio, TX 78212.

Leatherdale, Donald (Ja. 18, 1920, Thornton Heath, Surrey, Eng.) Prog. Ofcr. (Info. Sci.), Intl. Dev. Resrch. Ctr., Ottawa, 1972–; Head, Info. Class., Resrch. Branch, Agr. Can., 1969–71; Sci. Info. Ofcr., Cmwlth. Inst. of Entomology (London), 1959–69; Sci. Info. Ofcr., Imperial Chem. Indus. Ltd, 1951–59. **Educ.:** City of London Freemen's Sch.; Univ. of London. **Orgs.:** ASIS. Intl. Assn. of Agr. Libn. and Docmlst. Royal Entomological Socty.: Ed. (1965–68). **Pubns.:** *AGROVOC: A Multilingual Agricultural Thesaurus* (1981); *Thesaurus on Tropical Grain and Forage Legumes* (1977); *Cassava Thesaurus* (1977); *Canadian Agricultural Thesaurus* (1971); "Use e Preparazione di Thesauri...," *Politica Della Documentazione* (V. 22, 1978); "International Frontiers in Agricultural Information Services," in *'International Agricultural Librarianship'* (1979). **Activities:** 4; 26, 34, 41; 58, 68, 75 **Addr.:** AGRIS Processing Unit, c/o International Atomic Energy Agency, Vienna International Centre, Wagramerstrasse 5, P.O. Box 100, A-1400 Vienna, Austria.

Leavens, Willis L. (O. 17, 1941, Kansas City, MO) Chief, Lib. Srv., Vetns. Med. Ctr. (Allen Park, MI), 1977–; Prog. Dev. Ofcr., Univ. of NB Med. Ctr., 1973–76; Libn., Trinity Lutheran Hosp., Kansas City, 1970–73; Asst. N. Area Coord., Mid-Continent Pub. Lib., 1968–70. **Educ.:** Ctrl. MO State Univ., 1963–65, BS (Educ.); Univ. of Denver, 1965–66, MA (LS). **Orgs.:** Med. LA: Various coms. Metro Detroit Med. Lib. Grp. **Pubns.:** Various slide tape sets on med. libs. **Activities:** 4; 22, 32, 39; 58, 68, 80 **Addr.:** Veterans Administration, VA Medical Center, Allen Park, MI 48101.

Le Butt, Katherine L. (Mr. 28, 1926, Cornwall, ON) Reg. Libn., York Reg. Lib., 1963–, Bk. mobile. Libn., 1962–63; Chld. Libn., Sault Ste Marie Pub. Lib., 1951–62. **Educ.:** McMaster Univ., 1946–49, BA (Gen.); Univ. of Toronto, 1950–51, BLS. **Orgs.:** Atl. Prov. LA: NB, V. Ch. Can. LA: Chld. Libn. Sect., Pres. (1966); Awd. Com. (Ch., 1973), YA Sect. Cnclr. **Activities:** 9, 10; 17, 35, 47 **Addr.:** York Regional Library, 4 Carleton St., Fredericton, NB E3B 5P4 Canada.

Lecavalier, Monique (Jl. 3, 1943, Quebec, PQ) Head of Serials Dept., Univ. de Montréal, 1974–, Head of the Interlib. Loans Dept., 1969–74, Head of Nursing-Hygiene Lib., 1967–69, Cat. Pub. Docum. Dept., 1965–67. **Educ.:** Coll. Jésus-Marie d'Outremont, 1960–64, BA (Arts); Univ. de Montréal, 1964–65, BBibl, 1975 MBibl. 1975–79, D.S.A. (Admin.). **Orgs.:** IFLA: 1982 Org. Com.; Pubns. Subcom. (Ch., 1980–82). Can. Assn. Info. Sci.: Bd. Treas. (1980–82). Corp. des bibtcrs. prof. du PQ: Com. d'Argus-Jnl. (Prés., 1979–81). Can LA. Concours intl. de Montréal (msc.): Com. fém. **Pubns.:** "L'Augmentation des coûts des publications en série, les budgets des collections et le développement," *Argus* (Ja.–F. 1980). **Activities:** 1; 15, 44 **Addr.:** Chef du Service des périodiques, Université de Montréal, C.P. 6128, Succ.a, Montréal, PQ H3C 3J7 Canada.

LeClaire, Ann Elnore (My. 3, 1917, Willimantic, CT) Dir. of Lib. Srv., Miriam Hosp. (Providence, RI), 1969–. **Educ.:** St. Joseph Coll. (CT), 1935–39, BS (Nutr., Chem.); Univ. of RI, 1970–73, MLS; Simmons Coll., 1976, Cert. (Med. LS). **Orgs.:** Med. LA: Mem. Com. (1981–82). RI Assn. Hlth. Sci. Libns.: Pres. (1976). RI LA. SLA. Various orgs. Amer. Contract Bridge Leag. The Fac. Club, Brown Univ. **Activities:** 17, 39, 49-Online; 68, 80 **Addr.:** 15 Starbrook Dr., Barrington, RI 02806.

LeClercq, Angie Whaley (Ja. 14, 1942, Charleston, SC) Head, Undergrad. Lib., Univ. of TN, 1977–, Head, Non-Print Dept., 1972–77, Head, Film Dept., Atlanta Pub. Lib., 1968–72. **Educ.:** Duke Univ., 1963, AB; Univ. of CA, Berkeley, 1965 (Hist.); Emory Univ., 1967, MLS. **Orgs.:** ALA. Educ. Film Lib. Assn. **Pubns.:** "One-half inch Videocassette Equipment for Library Use," *Lib. Tech. Rpts.* (S. 1978); "The Nontheatrical Film Industry," *Lib. Tech. Rpts.* (N. 1977); Ed. and comp., "Video Column," *Booklist.* **Activities:** 1; 15, 17, 32, 42; 67 **Addr.:** 2806 Kingston Pike, Knoxville, TN 37919.

Ledenbach, Thelma M. (Ag. 31, 1922, Dyersville, IA) Dir., Media Ctr., Kuemper HS, 1976–; Dir., Media Ctr., Kenton HS, 1972–75; Instr., Dept. of LS, Univ. of North. IA, 1971–72; Libn., IA Falls HS, 1969–71. **Educ.:** Clarke Coll., 1940–43, BA (Econ.); Univ. of IA, 1963–64, MA (LS), 1965–72, EdS (Educ. Media). **Orgs.:** ALA: AASL. IA Educ. Media Assn. AAUW. **Honors:** NDEA Institute, N. TX State Univ., Sum. 1969. **Pubns.:**

PROFESSIONAL ACTIVITIES: Institutions: 1. Acad. lib.; 2. Arch.; 3. Assn.; 4. Fed./Gvt. lib.; 5. Inst. lib.; 6. Mfr./Suppl.; 7. Milit. lib.; 8. Musm.; 9. Pub. lib.; 10. Sch. lib.; 11. Sch. of lib. sci.; 12. Spec. lib.; 13. State lib.; 14. (other). **Functions/Activities:** 15. Acq./Col. dev.; 16. Adult srvs.; 17. Admin.; 18. Apprais.; 19. Archit./Bldgs.; 20. Cat./Class.; 21. Chld. srvs.; 22. Circ.; 23. Cons./Pres.; 24. Consult.; 25. Cont. ed.; 26. Educ. lib. sci.; 27. Ext. srvs.; 28. Fund/Grants; 29. Gvt. pubs.; 30. Indx./Abs.; 31. Instr. lib. use; 32. Media srvs.; 33. Micro.; 34. Netwks./Coop.; 35. Persnl.; 36. PR; 37. Publshg.; 38. Recs. mgt.; 39. Ref. srvs.; 40. Repro.; 41. Resrch.; 42. Review.; 43. Secur.; 44. Serials; 45. Spec. col.; 46. Tech. srvs.; 47. Trustees/Bds.; 48. YA srvs.; 49. (other).

"Be an 'In' Librarian!," *Lib. Lines* (Win. 1970). **Activities:** 10; 17, 20, 39 **Addr.:** P.O. Box 396, 533 Southdale Dr., Carroll, IA 51401.

Lederer, Norman (Mr. 1, 1938, Milwaukee, WI) Dean of Instr., Washtenaw Cmnty. Coll., 1977–; Dean of Sci. Sci. Careers, Camden Cnty. Coll., 1974–77; Admin. Dir., Menard Jr. Coll., 1973–74; Dir., Ethnic and Minority Stds. Ctr., Univ. of WI, 1971–73. **Educ.:** Univ. of WI, Milwaukee, 1956–60, BS (Hist.); LA State Univ., 1961–63, MA (Hist.); Rice Univ., 1960–61; LA State Univ., 1968–70. **Orgs.:** ALA: Ref. and Subscrpn. Bks. Rev. Com. **Pubns.:** *Contrib. Ed., Polamerica Mag.* Adv. Ed., *Perspectives: A Polish Amer. Educ. and Cult. Mag.* Reviews. **Activities:** 1; 17, 25, 42; 63, 66, 92 **Addr.:** Washtenaw Community College, P.O. Box D-1, Ann Arbor, MI 48106.

Ledwidge, Jean F. (Ja. 6, 1923, Camden, AK) Dir., Tri-Lakes Reg. Lib., 1975–; Tech. Libn., Nicholson Meml. Lib., 1969–75; Head, Tech. Prcs., Richardson Pub. Lib., 1967–69. **Educ.:** LA State Univ., 1945, BA (Eng.); N. TX State Univ., 1965–67, MLS. **Orgs.:** AK LA: Secy. (1978). SWLA. ALA. Ouachita Cnty. Hist. Assn. AK Endow. for the Hum.: Exec. Bd. (1978–). **Activities:** 9 **Addr.:** Tri-Lakes Regional Library, 200 Woodbine St., Hot Springs, AR 71901.

Lee, Betsy Maureen (Ja. 23, 1937, Wilkie, SK) Head, Serials Dept., Univ. of Toronto Lib., 1975–, Asst. Head, Searching Dept., 1969–74. **Educ.:** Univ. of SK, 1955–59, BA (Hist. & Eng.); Univ. of MI, 1961–62, MA (Hist.); Univ. of Toronto, 1967–68, BLS. **Orgs.:** Can. LA. Cncl. of ON Univ., UNICAT/TELECAT Proj.: Members' Asm. Univ. of Toronto Rep. (1976–); Serials Task Force (1978–). **Activities:** 1; 15, 20, 44; 55, 63 **Addr.:** 1 Rosedale Rd., Toronto, ON M4W 2P1 Canada.

Lee, Chang C. (N. 18, 1935, Tainan Hsien, Taiwan, Repub. of China) Head Libn., Behrend Coll., PA State Univ., 1978–; Assoc. Libn., FL A. & M. Univ., 1974–78, Asst. Libn., 1969–74. **Educ.:** Natl. Chengchi Univ., 1955–59, LLB (Jnlsm.); FL State Univ., 1967–69, MS (LS), 1972–76, PhD (Educ.). **Orgs.:** ALA: Middle Mgt. Discuss. Grp. Com. (1978–80); Ch., Subcom. of Pubns. (1979–80). PA LA: Org. and Bylaws Com. (1979–80); Lib. Dev. Com. (1979–80). Chinese-Amer. Libns. Assn.: Bd. (1979–82); Pres., Mid-Atl. Chap. 1980–81. Kappa Delta Pi. Pi Delta Kappa. **Pubns.:** Exec. Ed., *Jnl. of Educ. Media* (1980–82). **Activities:** 1; 17; 55, 91, 92 **Addr.:** 4022 David Rd., Erie, PA 16510.

Lee, Charles Donald (F. 17, 1929, Benson, NC) Dir., Lrng. Resrcs. Ctr., Coll. of the Albemarle, 1971–; Asst. Ref. Libn., Fayetteville State Univ. Lib., 1970–71; HQ Libn., Cheasapeake Pub. Lib., 1969–70; Asst. Dir., Cumberland Cnty. Pub. Lib., 1966–69. **Educ.:** Univ. of Denver, 1958, BA (Eng.); LA State Univ., 1965–66, MS (LS); State of NC, 1967, Pub. Libns. Cert.; Cmwlth. of VA, 1968, Libns. Prof. Cert.; CA Cmnty. Colls., 1976, Life Cred. **Orgs.:** ALA. Lrng. Resrcs. Assn. **Pubns.:** Reviews. **Activities:** 1; 17, 31 **Addr.:** Learning Resources Center, College of the Albemarle, Elizabeth City, NC 27909.

Lee, Ethel M. (Ap. 11, 1926, Providence, RI) Head Docum. Libn., Brown Univ. Lib., 1968–, Catlgr., 1950–68. **Educ.:** Simmons Coll., 1943–47, BS (LS). **Orgs.:** ALA. RI LA: Corres. Secy. (1969–70). New Eng. LA. SLA. Nelinet Task Force on Gvt. Docum.: Secy. (1978–79). Consort. of RI Acad. and Resrch. Lib.: Gvt. Docum. Com. (Secy., 1978–81). **Activities:** 1; 29 **Addr.:** Pole Bridge Rd., R.D. 2, N. Scituate, RI 02857.

Lee, Hwa-Wei (D. 7, 1933, Canton, China) Dir. of Libs. and Prof., OH Univ., 1978–; Assoc. Dir. of Libs. & Prof., CO State Univ., 1975–78; Dir of Lib. & Info. Ctr., Asian Inst. of Tech., 1968–75; Chief Libn. and Assoc. Prof., Edinboro State Coll., 1965–68; Head of Tech. Srvs. & Acq., Duquesne Univ. Lib., 1962–65. **Educ.:** Natl. Taiwan Normal Univ., 1950–55, BEd (Educ.); Univ. of Pittsburgh, 1957–59, MEd (Educ.); Carnegie-Mellon Univ., 1959–61, MLS; Univ. of Pittsburgh, 1959–64, PhD (Educ. & LS); Intl. lib. sems. in Japan, Belgium, England, and US. **Orgs.:** ALA: ACRL, Tri-state Chap., Bd. of Dirs. (1967). Chinese-Amer. Libns. Assn.: Bd. of Dirs. (1975–); Mem. Ch. (1976–77); Pres. (1978–79); Nom. Ch. (1979–80). OH LA: SE Reg. Meeting Ch. (1979–80). Acad. LA of OH. Other orgs. Phi Delta Kappa Intl.: OH Univ. Chap., Resrch. Rep. (1979–80). **Honors:** Edinboro State Coll., Disting. Prof. Awd., 1967; Beta Phi Mu. **Pubns.:** *The Possibility of Establishing a Regional Centre for the International Serials Data System in Thailand* (1976); Jt. auth., *Library Automation at the Asian Institute of Technology—Bangkok* (1974); "Sharing information resources through computer-assisted systems and networks" in *Resources Sharing of Libraries in Developing Countries,* (1979); "Cooperative Regional Bibliographic Projects in Southeast Asia," *UNESCO Bltn. for Libs.* (N.-D. 1977); "Regional Cooperation for ISDS," *Procs. of the Third Conf. of SE Asian Libns.* (1977); other articles. **Activities:** 1; 17, 24; 54, 56 **Addr.:** 19 Mulligan Rd., Athens, OH 45701.

Lee, Joann H. (Ja. 18, 1928, Escanaba, MI) Head, Reader Srvs., Lake Forest Coll., 1961–; Libn., World Bk. Ency., 1951–52; Indxr., Amer. Med. Assn., 1951. **Educ.:** Univ. of MO, 1945–49, BA (Eng.); Univ. of MI, 1949–50, AMLS. **Orgs.:** ALA: ACRL/Coll. Lib. Sect., Mem. Com. (1980–81). Chicago OLUG: Plng. Com. (1979–). **Pubns.:** "Instruction Communication and the Faculty," *Improving Library Instruction* (1979). "Introducing Online Data Base Searching in the Small Academic Library," *Jnl. of Acad. Libnshp.* (Mr., 1981). **Activities:** 1; 15, 16, 29; 55, 75 **Addr.:** Donnelley Library, Lake Forest College, Lake Forest, IL 60045.

Lee, Joel M. (Ag. 13, 1949, San Antonio, TX) Headquarters Libn., ALA, 1977–; Head, Tech. Srvs., Lake Forest (IL) Coll., 1973–77; Catlgr., The Newberry Lib., 1971. **Educ.:** Oberlin Coll., 1967–71, AB (Eng.); Univ. of Chicago, 1971–72, MA (LS); 1974–76 (LS). **Orgs.:** ALA: ACRL/CLS (Secy., 1977). SLA. IL Reg. Lib. Cncl.: Resrcs. Com. (1973–78). Cinema Chicago. **Pubns.:** Ed. in Chief, *Who's Who in Library and Information Services* (1981); Assoc. ed., *ALA World Encyclopedia of Library and Information Services* (1980); ed., *As Much to Learn as to Teach* (1979); "Collections in Library and Information Science," *Drexel Lib. Qtly.,* (Spr. 1979); guest ed., *Serials Rev.* (Jy.-S. 1979); other articles and works edited. **Activities:** 3, 12; 17, 37, 39; 62, 95-Libnshp. **Addr.:** 50 E. Huron St., Chicago, IL 60611.

Lee, Joyce C. (N. 11, 1952, Chippewa Falls, WI) Head of Ref., NV State Lib., 1980–, Asst. Docum. Libn., 1979–80, Lib. Consult., 1978–79, Head of Circ. Dept., Marquette Univ., 1975–77. **Educ.:** Univ. of WI (Eau Claire), 1970–74, BA (Eng.); Univ. of WI (Madison), 1974–75, MA (LS). **Orgs.:** NV LA: Exec. Secy. (1980–81). ALA. **Activities:** 1, 13; 29, 35, 39; 59, 78 **Addr.:** 411 W Caroline St., Carson City, NV 89701.

Lee, June Ann (D. 31, 1946, Detroit, MI) Asst. Dir., Farmington Cmnty. Lib., 1978–, Coord., Adult Srvs., 1977–; Sr. Libn., Farmington Hills Branch, 1975–78; Adult Srvs. Libn., 1972–75. **Educ.:** Oakland Univ., 1965–69, BA (Hist.); Univ. of MI, 1969–70, AM (Hist.); 1970–71, AMLS. **Orgs.:** ALA. MI LA: Cont. Educ. Com. (1975–); Jr. Mems. RT (Ch., 1979; Bd., 1977). Farmington Area Arts Cncl. Leag. of Women Voters: Farmington Chap. **Honors:** Beta Phi Mu. **Activities:** 9; 15, 16, 17 **Addr.:** Farmington Community Library, 32737 W. Twelve Mile Rd., Farmington Hills, MI 48018.

Lee, Lynda M. (Mr. 3, 1944, Shreveport, LA) Dir., Calcasieu Parish Pub. Lib., 1978–; Dir., Bossier-Red River Par. Pub. Lib., 1972–78; Branch Libn., Quachita Par. Pub. Lib., 1971–72; Asst. Ref. Libn., E. TX State Univ. Lib., 1968–70. **Educ.:** Northwest. State Univ., 1963–66, BA (Eng.); LA State Univ., 1967–68, MSLS. **Orgs.:** ALA: ASCLA/Lib. Srvs. to the Deaf, Bylaws Com. (1979–), Strg. Com. (1978–). LA LA: Leg. Com. (Ch., 1976–78); Pres. (1978–79). SWLA: Projs. Cncl. (1977–78), Exec. Bd. (1978–79). Quota Club. Bus. and Prof. Women. **Honors:** LA LA Jr. Mems. RT, Mid-Career Awd., 1979. Bossier Par. Jaycees/Jaynes, Outstand. Young Woman, 1976. **Pubns.:** "Job Bank Service," *LA LA Bltn.* (Win. 1975). "The Walls were Bare," *LA LA Bltn.* (Sum. 1974). "Needed: One Strong Voice," *LA LA Bltn.* (Sum. 1975). "1977 Legislative Wrap-up," *LA LA Bltn.* (Fall 1977). Other articles. **Activities:** 9; 17, 27, 34; 72, 78 **Addr.:** Calcasieu Parish Public Library, 411 Pujo St., Lake Charles, LA 71101.

Lee, Margaret Liao (Jy. 12, 1942, Hong Kong) Mgr., Lib. Srvs., Genentech, Inc., 1981–; Dir., Lib. Resrcs. and Srvs., Miles Labs., 1979–81; Head Libn., Cetus Corp., 1979–79; Asst. Libn., Pub. Hlth. Lib., Univ. of CA, Berkeley, 1975–78. **Educ.:** Coll. of St. Elizabeth, 1964–68, BS (Chem.); Univ. of CA, Berkeley, 1972–73, MLS; Univ. of CA, Los Angeles, 1973–74, Cert. (Med. LS). **Orgs.:** Med. LA. SLA. N. CA Med. Lib. Grp.: Cont. Educ. Com. (Ch., 1978–79). **Honors:** Beta Phi Mu 1974. **Activities:** 12; 17, 39; 59, 60, 87 **Addr.:** Genentech, Inc., 460 Point San Bruno Blvd., South San Francisco, CA 94080.

Lee, Michael Minsong (D. 29, 1936, Canton, China) Dir. Lib. and Lrng. Resrcs., Assoc. Prof. (Educ.), Saginaw Valley State Coll., 1979–; Coord. Dev. and Plng., Assoc. Prof. (LS), Chicago State Univ., 1977–79, Head, Lib. Oper., 1975–77, Actg. Dir., Libs., 1974–, Head, Pub. Srvs., Douglas Lib., 1973–74, Head, W. Ctr. Lib., 1969–73, Catlgr., Texas A&I Univ., 1965–67. **Educ.:** Natl. Taiwan Univ., 1956–60, BA (Langs.); National Ankara Univ., 1961–63, (Hist.); West. MI Univ., 1964–65, MA (LS); Loyola Univ. of Chicago, 1976–78, PhD (Educ.). **Orgs.:** ALA: ACRL; LAMA; LITA. Chinese Amer. Libns. Assn. Asian Amer. Lib. Assn. Phi Delta Kappa. **Pubns.:** *Melvil Dewey (1851–1931): His Educational Contributions and Reforms* (1979). **Activities:** 1, 4; 17, 26, 34; 56, 62, 63 **Addr.:** 5411 Wallbridge Ln., Midland, MI 48640.

Lee, Minja P. (Seoul, Korea) Assoc. Prof./Chief, Tech. Srvs., Bernard M. Baruch Coll. Lib., 1980–, Actg. Chief, Tech. Srvs., 1979–80, Head, Cat. Div., 1970–78; Head, Cat. Div., William Paterson Coll., 1967–70; Catlgr./Ref. libn., Fordham Univ., 1966–67; Reader Srvs./Asst. Branch libn., New York Pub. Lib., 1965–66. **Educ.:** Ewha Women's Univ., 1954–58, BA (Eng. Lit); Columbia Univ., 1962–65, MLS; New York Univ., 1972–74, MA (Hist.). **Orgs.:** ALA/RTSD: Policy and Resrch. Com., 1981–83. LA of the City Univ. of NY: Vice-Ch., Inst. Com. (1975–76); Ch., Sem. Com. (1977); Ch., Budget Com. (1979–80). New York Tech. Srvs. Libns.: Bd. (1980–). **Pubns.:** Jt. auth., *Converting to a divided catalog: a practical approach* (1974); jt. cmplr., *Libraries on line* (1978). **Activities:** 1; 15, 17, 46 **Addr.:** Technical Services, Bernard M. Baruch College Library, 156 East 25th St., New York, NY 07470.

Lee, Pauline Willis (N. 6, 1933, Simsboro, LA) Dir. of the Lib., Grambling State Univ., 1978–, Asst. Prof. and Actg. Dir., 1977–78, Coord. of Pub. Srv., 1975–77, Educ. Div. Libn., 1962–76, Circ. Libn., 1958–62; Libn., St. Tammany HS, 1955–58. **Educ.:** South. Univ., 1951–55, BA (Soc. Sci.); Univ. of MI, 1957–61, MALS. **Orgs.:** Acad. Lib. Admn. of LA. ALA. SWLA. Lincoln Parish Democratic Exec. Com.: Task Force on Acad. Lib. Ruston-Grambling Leag. of Women Voters: Vice-Chair, Interdepartmental Cncl. (1980–81) South. Assn. of Coll. & Sch.: Team Leader, Anl. Fund Raising Campaign. **Honors:** LA Priorities of the Future, Cert. of Merit, 1978; Alpha Kappa Alpha Sorority, Awd. of Recog., 1976. **Activities:** 1; 15, 17, 22, 34 **Addr.:** A. C. Lewis Memorial Library, Grambling State University, Grambling, LA 71245.

Lee, Robert Andrew (D. 7, 1923, Washington, DC) Head, Resrch. Dept. Lib., Universal City Studios, 1969–, Libn., Resrch., 1960–69; Ref. Libn., Collier's Encyc., 1959–60. **Educ.:** Oberlin Coll., 1940–42, 46–47, BA (Eng. Lit.); Univ. of South. CA, 1961–66, MLS; Univ. of Zurich (Switzerland), 1950 (Cert.). **Orgs.:** SLA. Amer. Film Inst.: Lib. Sem. Acad. of TV Arts and Sci. **Honors:** Motion Picture Acad. Bd. of Gvr., 1973–75. **Pubns.:** "Role of the Motion Picture Library in 1963," *Spec. Lib.* (N. 1963); "The Research Department of Universal City Studios," *Spec. Lib. Assn. Bltn.* (Win. 1966); "Motion Picture Libraries Today," *Spec. Lib. Assn. Bltn.* (O. 1972). **Activities:** 5; 39, 41; 67 **Addr.:** Research Department Library, Universal City Studios, 100 Universal City Plaza, Universal City, CA 91608.

Lee, Robert E. (S. 7, 1924) Dir. of Libs., Univ. of West. ON, 1970–; Ch., Dept. of Libnshp., KS State Univ., Emporia, 1963–70; Resrch. Assoc., Univ. of Chicago Indus. Rel. Ctr., 1958–63; Field Worker, Consult., ALA, 1954–58; Head, Adult Educ. Dept., Greensboro Pub. Lib., 1952–54. **Educ.:** Guilford Coll., 1950, BA; Univ. of NC, 1951, BSLS, 1954, MFA; Univ. of Chicago, 1963, PhD. **Orgs.:** ALA: Lib. Educ. Div. (Pres., 1965–66); Cncl. (1968–71); Com. on Accred. (1971–72); Lib. Binding Inst. Schol. Awd. Jury (Ch., 1964–65). KS LA: Bkmanship Com. (Ch., 1966). Adult Educ. Assn. Natl. Assn. of Pub. Sch. Adult. Educ. **Pubns.:** *Continuing Education for Adults through the American Public Library* (1966); *Getting the Most Out of Discussion* (1956); *The Library-Sponsored Discussion Group* (1957). **Activities:** 1; 26 **Addr.:** AB Weldon Library, University of Western Ontario, 1151 Richmond St. N, London, ON N6A 3K7 Canada.*

Lee, Sang Chul (Seoul, Korea) Assoc. Prof. and Chief, Cat. Div., Herbert H. Lehman Coll. Dept. of Libr., 1969–; Visit. Assoc. Prof. of Lib. Srv., Columbia Univ., 1978–; Dir., Ctrl. Tech. Srvs., Standard Oil Co. of NJ, 1968–69; Tech. Srvs. Libn., Pace Univ., 1963–68. **Educ.:** Yonsei Univ., Seoul, Korea, 1955–60, BM (Msc.); Union Theo. Semy., 1960–62, SMM (Msc.); Columbia Univ., 1962–64, MSLS; Pace Univ., 1964–69, MBA; Columbia Univ., 1969–75, MA (Archit.), 1976–, DLS cand. **Orgs.:** ALA. LA CUNY: VP & Pres.-Elect (1976–77); Pres. (1977–78). Delta Mu Delta. **Pubns.:** "Converting to A Divided Catalog: A Practical Approach," *LACUNY Occasional Papers* (N. 1974); "CUNY Libraries: A Proposal for Self Study," *LACUNY Journal* (Spr. 1972). **Activities:** 1, 11; 17, 19, 46; 56, 59, 75 **Addr.:** Herbert H. Lehman College, Dept. of Library, Bedford Park Blvd. West, Bronx, NY 10468.

Lee, Soo Kyung (F. 6, 1939, Seoul, Korea) Assoc. Dir., Bowman Gray Sch. Med. Lib., 1976, Chief, Tech. Srv., 1972–76; Catlgr., VA Cmwlth. Univ. 1965–69; Per. Libn., State Univ. Coll. NY, Buffalo, 1964–65. **Educ.:** Yonsei Univ. (Korea), 1957–61, BA (Hist.); SUNY, Albany, 1962–64, MLS. **Orgs.:** Med. LA. ASIS: SIG/MED, Chair-elect (1979–80), Ch. (1980–81). **Pubns.:** "Reclassification and Documentation in a Medical Library," *Bltn. Med. LA* (Ja. 1971); "Computer Stored Faculty Publication File Using the MT/ST...," *Bltn. Med. LA* (Ja. 1976); "Planning and Management of a Regional Learning Resources Network," *Jnl. Bio. Comm.* (N. 1978). **Activities:** 1; 15, 17; 80 **Addr.:** 300 S. Hawthorne Rd., Winston-Salem, NC 27103.

Lee, Sul H. (Jl. 13, 1936, Taegu, Korea) Dean, Univ. Libs., Univ. of OK, 1978–; Dean, Lib. Srvs., IN State Univ., 1975–78; Assoc. Dir. of Libs., Univ. of Rochester, 1973–75; Actg. Dir., Lib., East. MI Univ., 1972–73, Assoc. Dir., Lib., 1970–72; Dir., Ctr. for Lib. and Info. Syst., Univ. of Toledo, 1968–70; Supvsr., Info. Anal. Corp. Tech. Plng., Owens-Illinois, Inc., 1967–68; Asst. Head, Sci. and Tech. Dept., Toledo Pub. Lib., 1961–67. **Educ.:** Bowling Green State Univ., 1959–61, BA (Pol. Sci.); Univ. of Toledo, 1962–64, MA (Pol. Sci.); Univ. of MI, 1965–66, MA (LS). **Orgs.:** Resrch. Libs. Grp.: Bd. of Gvrs. (1980–). ALA: Telecomm. Com. (1974–75); Mem. Com. (1972–76). OK LA. Ok Cncl. of State Univ. Lib. Dir.: Ch. (1978–). Other orgs. Frnds. of Libs. In OK: Bd. of Dir. (1978–80). Collegiate Cnsrtm. of West. IN: Ch. (1975–76). IN Higher Educ. Telecomm. Syst. **Pubns.:** Ed., *Emerging Trends in Library Organization* (1978); Ed., *Library Budgeting* (1977); Ed., *Planning-Programming-Budgeting System* (1973); Ed., *A Challenge for Academic Libraries* (1973);

Special Subjects/Services: 50. Adult educ.; 51. Advert./Mktg.; 52. Aerosp.; 53. Agric.; 54. Area std.; 55. Arts/Hum.; 56. Autom.; 57. Bibl./Prtg.; 58. Bio. sci.; 59. Bus./Fin.; 60. Chem.; 61. Copyrt.; 62. Documtn.; 63. Educ.; 64. Engin.; 65. Env.; 66. Eth. grps.; 67. Film; 68. Food/Nutr.; 69. Geneal.; 70. Geo.; 71. Geol.; 72. Handcpd.; 73. Hist.; 74. Int. frdm.; 75. Info. sci.; 76. Insr.; 77. Law; 78. Legis.; 79. Math./Comp. sci.; 80. Med.; 81. Metals; 82. Nat. resrcs.; 83. Newsp.; 84. Nuc. sci.; 85. Oral hist.; 86. Petr./Energy; 87. Pharm.; 88. Phys./Astr./Math.; 89. Readg.; 90. Relig.; 91. Sci./Tech.; 92. Soc. sci.; 93. Telecom.; 94. Transp.; 95. (other).

Ed., *Library Orientation* (1972). **Activities:** 1, 17 **Addr.:** University Libraries, University of Oklahoma, Norman, OK 73019.

Lee, Thomas H. (N. 2, 1930, Kaifeng, Honan, China) E. Asian Lang. Cat. Team Captain, Meml. Lib., Univ. of WI, 1965–76, 1978–; Head Cat. Libn., E. Asian Col., Yale Univ. Lib., 1977. **Educ.:** Natl. Taiwan Univ., 1953–57, BA (Eng.); Univ. of WI, 1963–65, MA (LS), 1969–72, MA (Comp. Lit.). **Orgs.:** ALA: Ch., Com. on Cat. Asian and African Mtrls. (1979–). Assn. for Asian Std.: Com. on E. Asian Libs., Subcom. on Tech. Prcs. (Ch., 1972–). **Pubns.:** Ed., *China Yearbook* (1961, 63); Transl., *Mei-Kuo ti nung ts'un sheng huo* (1959); "Romanized Titles on East Asian Catalog Cards," *Univ. of WI Lib. News* (Mr. 1971); Ed., "What's New in Technical Processing," *CEAL Bltn.* (Jl. 1974–). **Addr.:** 6610 Piping Rock Rd., Madison, WI 53711.

Lee, Young S. (Ag. 15, 1932, Chindo, Chollanamdo, Korea) Dir. of Lib., William Carey Coll., 1969–; Dir. of Lib., Mokpo Tchr. Coll., 1964–67; Other positions tchg. **Educ.:** Seoul Natl. Univ., 1951–55, BA (Ling.); George Peabody Coll., 1968–69, MLS; Univ. of South. MS, 1976–80, PhD (Educ. Admin.). **Orgs.:** ALA. SELA. MS LA. **Pubns.:** Articles and bks. about readg. and tchg. in Korean. **Activities:** 1; 15, 17, 20; 63, 89, 92 **Addr.:** 1412 Cherry St., Hattiesburg, MS 39401.

Leech, Sara H. (F. 4, 1923, Lexington, KY) Assoc. Dir., Med. Ctr. Lib., Univ. of KY, 1976–, Coord., Tech. Srvs., Med. Ctr. Lib., 1974–76, Head, Cat. Dept., 1973–74, Head, Circ. Dept., 1969–73, Catlgr., Main Lib., 1962–69. **Educ.:** Northwest. Univ., 1941–44, BS (Psy.); Univ. of KY, 1961–63, MSLS; various crs. **Orgs.:** SLA: Positive Action Com. (Ch., 1979–81). Med. LA: Midwest Reg. Grp. ALA. KY LA: Pres. (1980–81) VP, Pres.-Elect (1979–80); Spec. Libs. Sect. (Ch., 1977–78); Acad. Sect. Various other orgs. Univ. of KY Fac. Sen. **Honors:** KY LA, Spec. Libs. Sect., Outstan. Spec. Libn., 1981. **Activities:** 12; 17, 22, 46; 58, 80 **Addr.:** Medical Center Library, University of Kentucky, Lexington, KY 40536–0084.

Leeper, Dennis Patterson (N. 19, 1941, Charleroi, PA) Assoc. Dir., AV Ctr., Temple Univ., 1981–; Asst. Prof., Media Lab. Supvsr., Sch. LS, Drexel Univ., 1975–81; Instr. Sch. Educ., Univ. CO, 1972–75; Asst. Dir. Reader Srv., Asst. Prof., Edinboro State Coll., 1970–71, Reader Srv. Libn., Asst. Prof., 1968–70, Ref. Libn., 1967–68; Gift Libn., Univ. Pittsburgh, 1966–67. **Educ.:** Millersville State Coll., 1959–63, BS (Educ.); Univ. Pittsburgh, 1964–66, MLS, 1966–70, Adv. Cert. (LS); Univ. CO, 1971–75, PhD (LS). **Orgs.:** ALA: ACRL; LITA. PA LA: Bldgs. Equip. RT, VP (1980–81), Pres. elect (1981–82); Resrch. Mtrls. Com. (Ch., 1980–); Nom. Com. (1979–80); Various other com. AECT: Prof. Educ. Com. (1980–); Leadership Dev. Com. (1976–79); Various other com. AALS. Wayne Presby. Church: Christ. Educ. Com. (Ch., 1981–); Elder (1979–); Scholar. Com. (Ch., 1979–); AV Srv. Coord. (1980–). **Honors:** Beta Phi Mu, 1966. **Pubns.:** Jt. ed., "Mediated Approaches to Library Instruction," *Drexel Lib. Qtly* (Ja. 1980); Speeches and media demonstrations. **Activities:** 1; 17, 26, 32; 63, 93, 95-AV Prod. Technique. **Addr.:** Audiovisual Center, Temple University, 15 Annenberg Hall, Philadelphia, PA 19122.

Leesment, Helgi (S. 7, 1942, Tallinn, Estonia) Freelance Librn., Access Info. Srv., 1976–; Dir., SIRLS Proj., Univ. of Waterloo 1973–75; Ref. Libn., Brock Univ. Lib., 1970–72; Ref. Libn., Hum., Univ. of Calgary Lib., 1969–70. **Educ.:** Univ. of BC, 1961–64; McMaster Univ., 1964–65, BA (Span.); Univ. of AB, 1968–69, BLS; Tchg. Cert., 1966, 1968. **Orgs.:** Can. LA. Can. Assn. Spec. Lib. Info. Srv.: Natl. Dir. (1976–79); Calgary Chap., Local Nsltr. Ed. (1977–80). LA AB: Calgary Area News Ed. (1977–80). Assn. of Recs. Mgrs. and Admins. **Honors:** Beta Phi Mu, 1969. **Activities:** 1, 12; 24, 39, 41; 55, 59, 92 **Addr.:** Access Information Services, 539 Lessard Dr., Edmonton, AB T6M 1A9 Canada.

LeFevre, Geraldine (N. 18, 1925, Seminole, OK) Asst. Lib. Dir., San Antonio Pub. Lib., 1970–, Branch Supvsr., Chld. Coord., 1961–70; Asst. Supvsr. Branches, San Pedro Park Branch Lib., 1956–61; Asst. to the Head of Chld. Dept., San Antonio Pub. Lib., 1950; Asst. Cnty. Libn., Monroe Cnty. (MI), 1947. **Educ.:** Univ. of OK, 1947, BLS. **Orgs.:** TX LA: Chld. RT (Ch., 1964–65); Pub. Lib. Div. (Ch., 1979–80); Dist. 10. (Ch., 1971–72); Schol. Resrch. Com.; Various other com. Bexar LA: Pres. (1960–61). ALA. Frnds. TX Lib.: Corres. Secy. (1970–71). San Antonio Coll.: Lib. Tech. Prog., Adv. Bd. Our Lady of the Lake Coll.: Educ. Sch., Adv. Bd. Zonta Club San Antonio: Pres. (1979–80); Treas. (1976–78); Bd. Mem. (1974–76). Beautify San Antonio Com.: Bd. Mem. (1975–81). **Honors:** San Antonio Cncl. of Pres., Spec. Recog., 1979–80; San Antonio Youth Org., Awd. of Apprec., 1979–80; San Antonio Indp. Tchr. Cncl., Awd. of Apprec. **Activities:** 9; 17, 25, 36 **Addr.:** San Antonio Public Library, 203 S. St. Mary's Street, San Antonio, TX 78205.

Leff, Barbara Young (O. 27, 1932, Pittsburgh, PA) Head Libn., Stephen S. Wise Temple, Los Angeles 1968–, Instr., Hebrew Union College, Los Angeles, 1979–, Coord. for Creation of Natl. Jewish Database, 1979–. **Educ.:** Univ. of CA, Los Angeles, 1949–53, BS (Home Econ.); Univ. of South. CA, 1976–79, MS (LS). Univ. of Judaism, 1954–56 (Jewish Stds.); Hebrew Union Coll., 1968–74 (Judaica Libnshp.); Los Angeles Bureau of Jewish Educ., 1974, Cert., (Libn., Tchr.). **Orgs.:** AJL: (Pres., 1980–82). Com. on Coop. (Ch., 1979–), *AJL Bltn.* (Ed. Staff, 1976–). Assn. of Jewish Libs. of South. CA: Pres. (1973–75). Jewish Libns. Caucus. ALA. Other orgs. Coalition for Alternatives in Jewish Educ.: West. Reg. (Gov. Cncl., 1978–); Educ. Mtrls. Clearinghouse (1978–); Lib. Tchrs. Ctr., Biennial West. Conf. (Co-ch., 1978–). **Honors:** Beta Phi Mu. **Pubns.:** *I want to go on Living Even after my Death* (1979), *Research Puzzles for Judaica Resources* (1979). "Association of Jewish Libraries," *ALA Yrbk.* (1980), "Creative Use of Library," *The Jewish Tchrs. Handbk.* (1980). Other articles. **Activities:** 10, 12; 24, 32, 34; 63, 66, 90 **Addr.:** 3431 Castlewoods Pl., Sherman Oaks, CA 91403.

Leffall, Dolores C. (O. 23, –, Orlando, FL) Lib. Consult. and Info. Spec.; Libn., Howard Univ., 1974–75, Asst. Libn., 1955–60; Cat. Libn., Atlanta Univ., 1953–55; Ref. Libn., Lincoln Univ., 1952–53. **Educ.:** FL A & M Coll., 1947–51, AB (Soclgy.); IN Univ., 1951–52, MS (LS); DC Tchrs. Coll., 1960–69; Univ. of DC, 1971–72, MA (Media); Rutgers Univ., 1975–81, Phd. **Orgs.:** ALA. DC LA. DC Assn. of Sch. Libns. SLA. Natl. Educ. Assn. Assn. for the Std. of Afro-Amer. Life and Hist. Alpha Kappa Alpha. **Pubns.:** Jt.-auth., *Black English: Bibliography* (1973). *The Black Church: Bibliography* (1973). "The Black Experience in Africa...a Selected Bibliography...," *Jnl. of Negro Hist.* (O. 1974). Indxs.; Reviews. **Activities:** 1, 10; 24, 30, 41; 57, 63, 89 **Addr.:** 55 Hamilton St. N.W., Washington, DC 20011.

Legel, Dave (Jn. 8, 1938, Detroit, MI) Anthro. and Psych. Biblgphr., Univ. of Rochester Lib., 1971–; Ref. Libn., Lafayette Coll., 1969–71; Tchr., Utica (MI) Cmnty. Sch., 1964–65. **Educ.:** Univ. of Detroit, 1959–64, BA (Psy., Eng.); Wayne State Univ., 1964–69, MSLS. Tchr. Cert., 1963–64. **Orgs.:** ALA: ACRL/Bibl. Instr. Sect. (1975–). EBSS: Psy.-Psyt. Com. (Ch., 1980–82). West. NY-ON ACRL, Prog. Com. (1977), Mem. Com. (1978). NY LA: Leg. Com. (1978–80). **Activities:** 1; 15, 31, 39; 54, 63, 92 **Addr.:** Rhees Library, University of Rochester, Rochester, NY 14627.

Legere, Monique (My. 10, 1943, St-Eugène, ON) Dir., Data Admin., CIDA, 1981–; Chief Frgn. and Intl. Official Pubns. Sect., Natl. Lib. of Can., 1971–75; Dir., Dev. Info. Ctr., CIDA, 1976–81. **Educ.:** Univ. d'Ottawa 1961–65, BA (Soclgy.), 1966–67, BLS; Untd. Nations (UNITAR-Geneva), 1974, (Documtn.). **Orgs.:** Can LA. ASTED: VP; Com. Coor. des Coms. (1979–81). **Pubns.:** "Le rôle du bibliothécaike dans un système d'information de gestion," *Documtn. et Bibs.* (S. 1981); *Rapport de Mission sur la Constitution d'un Centre de documentation à l'intérieur du Pro PP* (1979). **Activities:** 4; 17, 24; 75 **Addr.:** 6 rue Ste-Marie, Hull, PQ J8Y 2A3 Canada.

Lehman, James O. (D. 22, 1932, Apple Creek, OH) Dir. of Lib., East. Mennonite Coll., 1973–, Asst. Libn., 1969–73; Libn., Ctrl. Christian HS, 1961–68; Other positions tchg. **Educ.:** East. Mennonite Coll., 1957–59, BA (Soc. Sci.); Kent State Univ., 1961–65, MLS, 1968–69, Cert. Adv. Std. (LS). **Orgs.:** SELA. VALA: Reg. VI (Ch. 1981). Sonnenberg Mennonite Sch. Bd. Hist. Com. Mennonite Church. VA Conf. Hist. Com. (Ch., 1975–). East. Mennonite Assoc. Lib. Arch. **Honors:** Beta Phi Mu. OH Assn. Hist. Socty., Cit., 1969. **Pubns.:** Many pubns. about church history, also Lib. Science pubns.; Reviews. **Activities:** 1; 15, 16, 17; 90, 92 **Addr.:** Library, Eastern Mennonite College, Harrisonburg, VA 22801.

Lehman, Lois J. (Ap. 25, 1932, Danville, PA) Libn., Hershey Med. Ctr., PA State Univ., 1968–, Actg. Libn., 1971–72, Asst. Libn., Head, Pub. Srvs., 1968–71; Ref. Libn., Univ. of PA, 1966–68. **Educ.:** PA State Univ., 1950–54, BA (Eng.); Columbia Univ., 1957–59, MS (LS). **Orgs.:** Med. LA: Philadelphia Reg. Grp. (Ch., 1964–65). Ctrl. PA Hlth. Sci Lib. Assn.: Prog. Com. (1976–77). Mid-East. Reg. Med. Lib. Srvs.: Com. on Ext. Srvs. (1977–); Com. on Resrc. sharing (1977–); Com. on Subreg. (1976–77). **Pubns.:** "Effect of Fees on an Information Service for Physicians," *Bltn. Med LA* (Ja. 1978); "Circulation," *Library Practice in Hospitals; A basic guide* (1972); Review. **Addr.:** Hershey Medical Center, Pennsylvania State University, 500 University Dr., Hershey, PA 17033.

Lehman, Sharon Ballard (Ap. 4, 1947, Monroe, MI) Supvsr., Lit. Srvs., Warner-Lambert Co., 1979–; Sr. Info. Spec., 1977–79; Info. Spec., Parke-Davis Co., 1972–77; Asst. Info. Spec., 1969–72. **Educ.:** East. MI Univ., 1965–69, BS (Bio. Sci.), 1969–70, MS (Bio. Sci.). **Orgs.:** ASIS. MIDBUG. **Activities:** 12; 17, 30, 49-Online Srch.; 60, 80, 87 **Addr.:** Warner-Lambert Pharmaceutical Research Division, 2800 Plymouth Rd., Ann Arbor, MI 48106.

Lehnus, Donald James (N. 7, 1934, Lyons, KS) Assoc. Prof., Grad. Sch. of Lib. and Info. Sci., Univ. of MS, 1979–; Assoc. Prof., Grad. Sch. of Libnshp., Univ. of PR, 1973–78; Asst. Prof., Sch. of Libnshp., West. MI Univ., 1967–70; Prof. of Cat. and Class., Univ. de Antioquia, 1964–66; Catlgr., Ref. Libn., San Leandro Cmnty. Lib. Ctr., 1962–63; Asst. Dir., Franklin Sq. Pub. Lib., 1958–62; Asst. to Branch Libn., Queens Boro. Pub. Lib., 1957–58. **Educ.:** Univ. of KS, 1952–56, BA (Span.); Univ. of CA, Berkeley, 1956–57, MLS; Case West. Rsv. Univ., 1967–70, PhD (Lib. and Info. Sci.). **Orgs.:** ALA: Ref. and Subscrpn. Bks. Review Com. (1978–81). AALS. AAUP. SELA. MS LA. **Pubns.:** *Sistema de clasificación decimal planeado originalmente por Melvil Dewey* (1980); *Book Numbers : Their History, Principles, and Application* (1980); *Léxico de -ologías* (1977); *Milestones in Cataloging: Famous Catalogers and Their Writings, 1835-1969* (1974); "AACR 2 : A Cataloging Instructor's viewpoint," *Southeast. Libn.* (Fall 1979); various bks., articles. **Activities:** 11; 20; 95-Latin Amer. **Addr.:** P. O. Box 6526, University, MS 38677.

Lehr, Robert M. (N. 15, 1922, Alexandria, SD) Serials Ref. Libn., Head Cat. Libn., McGoogan Lib. of Med., Univ. of NE Med. Ctr., 1970–; Ref., Cat., Sci. Div. Lib. and Cat., Tech. Srvs. Div., WA State Univ. Lib., 1963–70. **Educ.:** Sioux Falls Coll., 1954–56 (Bio.); Augustana Coll., Sioux Falls, SD, 1956–58, BA (Hist.); Univ. of Denver, 1962–63, MA (LS); State of SD, 1958, Sec. Tchg. Cert.; various crs. **Orgs.:** Med. LA ALA. NE LA: Persnl. Com. (1976–78). ASIS. **Activities:** 1, 12; 20, 44, 46; 56, 58, 80 **Addr.:** 2116 S. 43rd St., Omaha, NE 68105.

Leide, John E. (N. 1, 1943, Minneapolis, MN) Asst. Prof. (LS), Univ. of HI, 1976–; Coord., Syst. Dev. Sect., Columbia Univ. Libs., 1974–76, Lib. Syst. Anal., 1972–74; Asst. Circ. Libn., Univ. of Chicago, 1967–69. **Educ.:** MA Inst. of Tech., 1961–65, BS (Math); Univ. of WI, 1965–66, MS (LS); Rutgers Univ., 1970–74, PhD (LS). **Orgs.:** ASIS: Arts and Hum. Spec. Int. Grp. (Ch., 1977–79). ALA. HI LA: Int. frdm. Com. (Ch., 1977–79). Intl. Assn. of Orientalist Libns.: Secy.-Treas. (1978–). Various other orgs. AAUP. Amer. Cvl. Liberties Un. **Activities:** 1; 20, 26, 41; 55, 56, 75 **Addr.:** Graduate School of Library Studies, University of Hawaii, 2550 The Mall, Honolulu, HI 96822.

Leigh, (Mrs.) Carma Russell (N. 15, 1904, McLoud, OK) Retired. State Libn., CA, 1951–72; State Libn., WA State, 1945–51; Cnty. Libn., San Bernardino Cnty., CA, 1942–45; Cnty. Libn., Orange Cnty., CA, 1938–42. **Educ.:** OK Coll. for Women, AB (Hist.); Univ. of CA, Berkeley, MA (Libnshp.), 1929–32, MA (Hist.). **Orgs.:** ALA: VP (1970); Ch., Natl. Legis. Com. (1969–70). Pac. NW LA: Pres. (1950–51). CA LA: Pres. (1955). San Diego State Univ.: Treas. (1980–81); Bd. of Dirs., Friends of Malcolm A. Love Lib. (1976–82). **Honors:** Univ. of the Pacific, LhD, 1965. **Pubns.:** Various articles. **Activities:** 9, 13; 17 **Addr.:** 6927 Amherst St., #7, San Diego, CA 92115.

Leinbach, Philip Eaton (S. 17, 1935, Winston-Salem, NC) Asst. Univ. Libn. for Persnl., Harvard Univ., 1972–; Bk. Sel. Spec., 1967–71; Deputy Libn., Queen Mary Coll., Univ. of London, 1970–71; Asst. Libn., Acq., Harvard Univ. Lib., 1966–67; Admin. Asst., Acq., 1964–66. **Educ.:** Duke Univ., 1952–56, BA (Pol. Sci.); IN Univ., 1961–62, MA (Hist.), 1963–64, MA (LS); U.S. Army Lang. Sch., 1958–59, Cert. (Russ.). **Orgs.:** ALA: Tsk. Frc. on Place (Ch., 1979–80) ACRL, Persnl. Ofcrs. DG (Ch., 1978–79). **Pubns.:** Jt.-auth., *Afro-American Resources in the Harvard Univ. Library* (1970); *Handbook for Librarians* (1977). **Activities:** 1; 17, 35 **Addr.:** 198 Lexington Ave., Cambridge, MA 02138.

Leisinger, Albert H., Jr. (Mr. 15, 1915, NY, NY) Archives Consultant, 1981–; Dir., Sci. Tech. Arch. Div., Natl. Arch. and Recs. Srv., 1978–81; Deputy Asst. Arch., 1972–78, Spec. Asst., Acad. Liaison, 1968–72, Dir., Educ. Progs., 1963–68. **Educ.:** Cornell Univ., 1933–37, AB (Hist.), 1937–38, MA (Hist.), 1938–41, ABD. **Orgs.:** International Council on Archives Chairman, 1968–76 Secretary, Microfilm Committee, 1976–date National Micrographics Association Chairman, Joint National Micrographics Assn.-Society of American Archivists Committee on Standards for Public Records, 1977 to present Society of American Archivists Microfilm Committee, 1977–79. Amer. Hist. Assn. **Honors:** SAA, Flw., 1962. **Pubns.:** *Microphotography for Archives* (1968); *A Study of the Basic Standards for Equipping, Maintaining, and Operating a Reprographic Laboratory in Archives of Developing Countries* (UNESCO) (1973); "Physical Aspects of Archival Storage," *Proc.* of the Natl. Microfilm Assn. (1965); other pubns. **Addr.:** 5312 Wriley Rd., Bethesda, MD 20016.

Leisner, Tony B. (S. 13, 1941, Evanston, IL) VP, Mktg., Quality Bks., Inc., 1968–. **Educ.:** Northwestern Univ., 1960–62 (Bus.). **Orgs.:** ALTA: Leg. Com. (Ch., 1975). IL LA: Exhibits Com. (1975); Conf. Com. (1973). ALA: JMRT, Booth Com. (1974–78); YASD, Pubs. Liaison Com. (1980–). WHCOLIS, Be With a Book For A Day Fund Raising (Ch.). Lake Villa (IL) Pub. Lib.: Bd. of Trustees (Ch., 1972–78). N. IL Lib. Syst.: Trustee (1973–77). **Honors:** IL LA, Best Booth, 1978; Gerald L. Campbell Awd., 1980. **Pubns.:** *Official Guide To Country Dance Steps* (1980); "Secrets Of Selling Out Your Conference," *Amer. Libs.* (Jn. 1978); "Buying Remainders," *Emanations* (NJ LA) (Spr. 1980); PR kit for Sp.-speaking Lib. users (1978). **Activities:** 6, 9; 37, 47; 51, 78 **Addr.:** Quality Books, Inc., 400 Anthony Trail, Northbrook, IL 60062.

Leister, Jack (Ap. 7, 1933, Emmaus, PA) Head Libn., Inst. of Gvtl. Stds., Univ. of CA, Berkeley, 1973–; Ref. Libn., 1960–72; Bus. Credit Anal., Dun & Bradstreet, 1956–57; Interpreter, U.S. Army, 1953–56. **Educ.:** Univ. of CA, Berkeley, 1958–59, BA (Eng.), 1959–60, MLS. **Orgs.:** SLA: San Francisco Bay Reg. Chap. (Pres., 1977); Soc. Sci. Div. (Ch., 1975); Dir. (1979–82). CA LA. Cncl. of Plng. Libns. ALA. West. Gvtl. Resrch. Assn. **Pubns.:** *California Politics and Problems, 1964–1968* (1969);

PROFESSIONAL ACTIVITIES: Institutions: 1. Acad. lib.; 2. Arch.; 3. Assn.; 4. Fed./Gvt. lib.; 5. Inst. lib.; 6. Mfr./Suppl.; 7. Milit. lib.; 8. Musm.; 9. Pub. lib.; 10. Sch. lib.; 11. Sch. of lib. sci.; 12. Spec. lib.; 13. State lib.; 14. (other). **Functions/Activities:** 15. Acq./Col. dev.; 16. Adult srvs.; 17. Admin.; 18. Apprais.; 19. Archit./Bldgs.; 20. Cat./Class.; 21. Chld. srvs.; 22. Circ.; 23. Cons./Pres.; 24. Consult.; 25. Cont. ed.; 26. Educ. lib. sci.; 27. Ext. srvs.; 28. Fund/Grants; 29. Gvt. pubs.; 30. Indx./Abs.; 31. Instr. lib. use; 32. Media srvs.; 33. Micro.; 34. Netwks./Coop.; 35. Persnl.; 36. PR; 37. Publshg.; 38. Recs. mgt.; 39. Ref. srvs.; 40. Repro.; 41. Resrch.; 42. Review.; 43. Secur.; 44. Serials; 45. Spec. col.; 46. Tech. srvs.; 47. Trustees/Bds.; 48. YA srvs.; 49. (other).

Contrib., *Reapportionment in the 1970s* (1971); "Western Research News," column, *West. City* (1973–); "Local Publications," column, *Govt. Pubn. Rev.* (1979–). **Activities:** 1, 12; 15, 17, 29; 59, 78, 92 **Addr.:** Institute of Governmental Studies Library, University of California, Berkeley, CA 94720.

Leita, Carole (N. 30, 1944, Waco, TX) Ref. Libn., Berkeley Pub. Lib., 1980–, and Ref. Libn., Bay Area Lib. and Info. Syst., 1978–; Exec. Dir., Women Lib. Workers, 1975–78; Co-Ed., Booklegger Press, 1973–76; Ref. Libn., Univ. of MN, 1968–73. **Educ.:** Minot State Coll., 1963–67, BA (Eng.); Univ. of MN, 1969–70, MA (LS); Midwest Acad., 1976, Organizer. **Orgs.:** Women Lib. Workers: Natl. Coord. (1975–77). Bay Area Women Lib. Workers: Cncl. Rep. (1979–80). ALA: SRRT Task Force on Women (1974–). CA LA. People's Transl. Srv.: Ed. **Pubns.:** Ed., *SHARE: A Directory of Feminist Library Workers* (1975–80); Ed., *Second Class, Working Class: An International Women's Reader* (1979); Co-ed., *Booklegger Mag.* (1974–76); Ed., Women Lib. Workers Nsltr. (1975, 1979); "Beyond Awareness - Women in Libraries Organizing for Change," *Sch. Lib. Jnl.* (Ja. 1977). **Activities:** 3, 9; 17, 37, 39; 74, 92, 95-Women. **Addr.:** P.O. Box 9052, Berkeley, CA 94709.

Leiter, Joseph (My. 14, 1915, New York, NY) Assoc. Dir., Lib. Opers., Natl. Lib. of Med., 1965–; Chief Cancer Chemotherapy, Natl. Cancer Inst., 1963–65, Asst. Chief, 1955–63; Chief, Biochem. Sect. Lab. of Chem. Pharmgy., 1949–55. **Educ.:** Brooklyn Coll., 1934, BS (Biochem.); Georgetown Univ., 1949, PhD (Biochem.). **Orgs.:** ASIS. Med. LA. Amer. Chem. Socty. Amer. Assn. of Cancer Resrch. Fed. of the Amer. Socty. of Exper. Bio. AAAS. **Honors:** Dept. of Health, Educ. and Welfare, Superior Srv. Awd., 1972; Natl. Lib. of Med., Dir.'s Awd., 1980. **Pubns.:** Various articles in flds. of info. sci., cancer resrch. **Activities:** 4, 12; 17, 34; 56, 75, 80 **Addr.:** National Library of Medicine, 8600 Rockville Pike, Bethesda, MD 20209.

Leith, Anna R. (N. 22, 1923, Prince George, BC) Head, Biomed. Lib., Univ. of BC, 1967–, Lectr. (LS), 1962–, Head, Sci. Div. Lib., 1961–67, Jr. Libn., Biomed. Lib., 1960–61, Jr. Libn., Ref. Div., Bacteriologist, Various Insts., 1946–1958. **Educ.:** Univ. of BC, 1941–45, BA (Bacteriology and Preventive Med.); Univ. of WA, 1958–59, MA (LS). **Orgs.:** Can. LA. Assn. of Can. Med. Colls.: Com. on Med. Libs. (Ch., 1970–72). Assn. of Acad. Hlth. Srvs. Lib. Dirs. Med. LA: Status and Econ. Int. Grp. (1979–81); various other ofcs. Other orgs. and ofcs. **Pubns.:** "Use of caronamide in penicillin therapy". *Can. Jnl. of Med. Tech.* (Jn. 1949); "Glacier Park Conference Proceedings," *Pac. NW LA Qtly.* (O. 1964); Report of trip to China, *CHLA-ABSC Nsltr.* (Win. 1977). **Activities:** 1, 12; 17; 58, 80 **Addr.:** 4665 W. 10th Ave., Apt. 301, Vancouver, BC V6R 2J4 Canada.

Leitzke, Nowell D. (D. 23, 1928, Wausau, WI) Pub. Lib. Spec., Ofc. of Pub. Libs., MN Dept. of Educ., 1971–; Dir., Ramsey Cnty. Pub. Lib., 1970–71; Dir., Austin Pub. Lib., 1964–70; Dir., Faribault Pub. Lib., 1958–64. **Educ.:** Univ. of WI, 1953–57, BA (Eng.); Univ. of MN, 1957–58, MA (LS). **Orgs.:** MN LA: Media RT. ALA. **Activities:** 4 **Addr.:** Office of Public Libraries, 301 Hanover Bldg., 480 Cedar St., St. Paul, MN 55101.

Leja, Ilga (Je. 30, 1948, Höxter, W. Germany) Asst. Libn., NS Legis. Lib., 1977–; Libn., NS Dept. of Dev. Lib., 1977. **Educ.:** Dalhousie Univ., 1965–69, BA (Fr.), 1975–77, MLS; Meml. Univ. of NF, 1971–72, BEd (Educ.). **Orgs.:** Atl. Prov. LA: Conf. Prog. Com. (1979–80). Can. LA: Lib. Resrch. and Dev. Com. NS LA: Resrch. and Dev. Com. **Pubns.:** Various articles. **Activities:** 4; 20, 29, 39; 55, 78 **Addr.:** Nova Scotia Legislative Library, P.O. Box 396, Province House, Halifax, NS B3J 2P8 Canada.

Lem, Nancy E. (Oshkosh, WI) Libn. Supvsr., Lab. Lib., Hewlett-Packard Co., 1975–, Ref. Libn., Supvsr., Corp. Lib., 1974–79, Ref. Libn., 1967–73; Ref. Libn., Engin. Lib., Univ. WI, 1967–67. **Educ.:** Univ. WI, BS (Microbiology), 1965–66, MLS. **Orgs.:** SLA: Engin. Div. (Ch., 1979–80). Med. LA. Chinese Amer. Libns. Assn. Inst. of Electrical and Electronics Engins. Assn. for Comp. Mach. Chinese Cmnty. Ctr. of the Peninsula. Lim Women Benevolent Assn. **Activities:** 5, 12; 15, 17, 39; 56, 60, 64 **Addr.:** HP Laboratories Library, Hewlett-Packard Co., 3500 Deer Creek Rd., Palo Alto, CA 94304.

Le Master, Charles R. (Ap. 4, 1927, Sioux City, IA) Dir., Lib. Srvs., Ch., LS Dept., Morningside Coll., 1964–; Tchr., Sioux City Cmnty. Sch. Dist., 1962–64; Insurance Salesman, John Hancock Co., 1956–61; Electrician, San Diego and IA, 1947–55. **Educ.:** Morningside Coll., 1947–48, 1960–62, BA (Divisional Major); West MI Univ., 1968–69, MLS; Miami Univ., Oxford, OH, Exec. Dev. Prog. for Lib. Admin., 1975 Sum, Cert., Lib. Adm. **Orgs.:** IA LA: Int. Frdm. Com. (1979–). IA Private Acad. Lib. Cnsrtm.: Strg. Com. (1978–80). ALA: ACRL/IA Chap. (Pres., 1978–79). Siouxland Hlth. Sci. Lib. Cnsrtm. Other orgs. Masonic Lodge. Grace Un. Meth. Church. **Activities:** 1, 11; 17, 26, 35; 57, 63, 75 **Addr.:** Morningside College Library, 1501 Morningside Ave., Sioux City, IA 51106.

Le May, Denis (Mr. 8, 1947, Québec, PQ) Cnslr. à la Documtn. en Droit, Univ. Laval, 1975–. **Educ.:** Univ. Laval, 1965–68, BA, 1969–72, LLB (Law). **Orgs.:** Can. Assn. of Law Libs. Can. Assn. for Info. Sci. Can. Law Info. Cncl.: Com. on Substantive Legal Lit. Bar of PQ. Can. Bar Assn. Comsn. de Refonte des Lois et des Règlements du PQ. **Pubns.:** *LE Code Civil du Québec Tableaux Synoptiques* (1979); *Méthode de Recherche en Droit Québécois et Canadien* (1974); "L'Informatique au Québec," *Cahiers de Droit* (1978); "Pour un Dictionnaire Jurisdique...," *Revue du Barreau* (1979); reviews. **Activities:** 1; 24, 31, 39; 75, 77, 78 **Addr.:** Bibliotheque, Pavillon Bonenfant, Université Laval, Sainte-Foy, PQ G1K 7P4 Canada.

Le May, François R. (Mr. 13, 1945, Ottawa, ON) Asst. Dir., Info. and Ref. Branch, Lib. of Parlmt., 1976–; Sect. Head, Official Pubns., Natl. Lib. of Can., 1975–76; Sect. Head, Official Pubns., Lib. of Parlmt. 1971–75, Ref. Libn., 1968–71. **Educ.:** Univ. of Ottawa, 1964–67, BA (Psy.); Univ. of Toronto, 1967–68, BLS, 1978–80, MLS. **Orgs.:** ASTED: Copyrt. Com.; Rcrt. Com. Can. LA. Ottawa-Hull LA: Past Pres. Patro. **Activities:** 4; 17, 35, 39; 61 **Addr.:** Library of Parliament, Parliament Bldgs., Ottawa, ON K1A 0A9 Canada.

Lembke, Melody Jean (Je. 30, 1951, Batesville, IN) Catlgr. I, Los Angeles Cnty. Law Lib., 1979–, Catlgr. II, 1977–79, Catlgr. III, 1974–77. **Educ.:** Purdue Univ., 1969–73, BA (Radio & TV); IN Univ., 1973–74, MLS. **Orgs.:** AALL: Tech. Srvs. Spec. Int. Sect., Nsltr. Ed., South. CA Assn. of Law Libs., South. CA Tech. Prcs. Grp. **Honors** Phi Beta Kappa, 1973; Beta Phi Mu, 1974. **Pubns.:** "California Legislative History," slide show (1978). **Activities:** 9, 12; 20, 25, 26; 77 **Addr.:** Los Angeles County Law Library, 301 W. First St., Los Angeles, CA 90012.

Lemee, Loretta F. (Ja. 9, 1927, St. Louis, MO) Libn., Ralston Purina Co., 1970–; Asst. Libn., 1972–74. **Educ.:** WA Univ., 1971–74, BS (Bus. Admin.); Webster Coll., 1977–79, MA (Mgt.); Florissant Valley Cmnty. Coll., 1967–69, AA (Bus. Admin.). **Orgs.:** SLA: St. Louis Chap. (Treas., 1979–81); Postive Action (Ch., 1978–79). Assn. of Rec. Mgrs. and Admins.: Bd. of Dirs. (1972–74); Awds. Com. (Ch., 1977). MO Gvrs. Conf. on Lib. and Info. Srvs. (1978). St. Louis Lib. Club. **Honors:** Assn. of Rec. Mgrs. and Admins., Chap. Mem. of the Yr., 1975. **Activities:** 12; 17, 38; 68 **Addr.:** 102 Carmel Woods Dr., Ellisville, MO 63011.

Lemieux, Louise (N. 19, 1936, Victoriaville, PQ) Bibtcr. de Réf., Coll. Marguerite-Bourgeoys, 1970–; Prof., Ens Sec., Pens. Notre-Dame-de-la-Trinité, 1964–67; Prof., Coll. Marguerite-Bourgeoys, 1962–63; Prof., Villa Maria, 1961–62. **Educ.:** Coll. Marguerite-Bourgeoys, Univ. de Montréal, 1967, Bac. (Arts); Univ. d'Ottawa, 1968, BLS, 1972, MLS. **Orgs.:** Corp. des Bibtcrs. Prof. du PQ. Can. LA. ASTED: Com. Lit. de Jeunesse, Prix Alvine Bélisle. Comm.-Jeunesse: Cnsl. d'Admin. Com. (1970–78). Assn. Can. pour l'Advnc. de la Lit. de Jeunesse: Bur. de Dir., Com. de Rédaction de Revue *Des Livres et des Jeunes* (1978–). **Pubns.:** *Pleins Feux sur la Littérature de Jeunesse au Canada Français* (1972); "Le Livre Québécois pour la Jeunesse," *Livre, Bibliothèque et Culture Québécoise* (1977); "L'Humour dans la Littérature de Jeunesse," *Documtn. et Bibs.* (D. 1978). **Activities:** 1; 39; 95–Chld. Lit. **Addr.:** 393 de Lanaudière, Joliette PQ J6E 3L9 Canada.

Lemkau, Henry L., Jr. (O. 19, 1941, New York, NY) Dir. and Assoc. Prof., Louis Calder Meml. Lib., Univ. of Miami Sch. of Med., 1979–; Med. Libn., Asst. Prof. of Med. Bibl., Univ. of Rochester Sch. of Med., 1970–79; Asst. Prof., Dept. of Med. Lib. Srv., Mt. Sinai Sch. of Med., 1969–70; Branch Libn., 1968–70. **Educ.:** St. John's Univ., Jamaica, NY, 1963, BA (Hist.); Pratt Inst., 1967, MLS. **Orgs.:** Med. LA: Nom. Com. (1977); Hlth. Sci. Libs. Srvy. Coms. (Ch., 1975–77); Mem. Com. (1970). Amer. Assn. for the Hist. of Med. **Pubns.:** "Crossroads: The Story of the Medical Library," *To Each His Farthest Star* (1975); jt. auth., "The Design of the Automated Serials Accession System at the Library of the Mount Sinai School of Medicine of the City University of New York," *Bltn. of the Med. LA* (Ap. 1970); "Computerization of Serials Records in the Medical School Library," *Jnl. of the Mt. Sinai Hosp.* (N.–D. 1967). **Activities:** 1, 5; 17, 26, 34; 57, 75, 80 **Addr.:** Louis Calder Memorial Library, University of Miami School of Medicine, P.O. Box 016950, Miami, FL 33101.

Lemke, Antje Bultmann (Jl. 27, 1918, Breslan, Germany) Prof. (Info. Sci.), Syracuse Univ., 1974–; Assoc. Prof., 1966–73, Asst. Prof., Asst. Dean, 1961–66, Msc., Fine Art Libn., 1952–60; Dir., Srv. Bureau for Citizen Org., Wiesbaden, Germ., 1950–52; Asst. Libn., Instr., State Lib. of Thuvingia, Germ., 1945–47; Other libn. positions in Leipzig, Germ., 1942–45. **Educ.:** Leipzig Univ., 1941–44, BA equiv. (LS); Syracuse Univ., 1954–56, MS (LS); Bryn Mawr Coll., 1949–50 (Poli. Sci.). **Orgs.:** ALA: ACRL/Art. Sect. (Ch., 1977–78). ARLIS/NA: Educ. Com. (Ch., 1977–78). SAA. Other orgs. Albert Schweitzer Flwshp.: Trustee. Albert Schweitzer Flwshp. Hse.: Exec. Dir. Coll. Art. Assn. Amer. Adv. for the Adv. of the Hum. Other orgs. **Honors:** Guggenheim Fndn., Flw., 1959–60; Syracuse Post Standard, Woman of Achvmnt.; German Sci. Fndn., Flwshp., 1980. **Pubns.:** Jt. auth., *Museum Companion* (1974); Transl., *Aldus Manutius and His Thesaurus Conrucopiae* (1957); "William Caxton–The Beginning of Printing in England," *Conrier* (Spr. 1978); "Alternative Specialties in Library Education," *Jnl. of Educ. for Libnshp.* (Spr. 1978); other pubns. **Activities:** 2, 12; 24, 26, 41; 54, 55, 57 **Addr.:** School of Information Studies, Syracuse University, Syracuse, NY 13210.

Lemke, Darrell H. (N. 16, 1935, Oshkosh, WI) Coord., of Lib. Progs., Consort. of Univs. of the Washington Metro. Area, 1970–; Dir., Capital Consort. Ntwk. (CAPCON), 1975–; Head, Pub. Srvs., IN Univ. Reg. Campus Libs., 1966–67; Ref. Libn., Asst. to Dir., Univ. of IL, Chicago Circle, 1962–66; Libn., Branch Head, Milwaukee Pub. Lib. (1960–62). **Educ.:** Univ. of WI, 1953–57, BA (Hist.), 1959–60, MSLS; IN Univ., 1967–75, PhD. **Orgs.:** ALA: Cncl. (1973–77); Budget Asm. (1974–75); ACRL: Urban Libs. Com. (1978–80), various other coms. Assn. of Coop. Lib. Orgs.: Ch. (1973–74). Dist. of Columbia LA: Exec. Bd. (1973–77). OCLC, Inc.: Users Cncl. (1978–82). Other orgs. and ofcs. Amer. Film Inst. Amer. Prtg. Hist. Assn. Natl. Trust for Hist. Pres. Smithsonian Inst. Resident Assoc. **Honors:** Beta Phi Mu. **Pubns.:** "Library Activities in the District of Columbia," *ALA Yrbk.* (1976, 1977); "Library Networks and the Provision of Management Information," *Cath. Lib. World* (Ap. 1978). **Activities:** 14-Ntwk.; 17, 25, 34; 56 **Addr.:** Consortium of Universities, 1717 Massachusetts Ave. N.W., Washington, DC 20036.

LeMoyne, Beryl L. (My. 7, 1928, Montréal, PQ) Chef du Dept., Bib. de la Ville de Montréal, 1979–; Bibtcr. de Réf., 1976–79; Ref. Libn., McGill Univ., Redpath Lib., 1972–76; Libn., Wellesley Coll. Lib., 1950–51. **Educ.:** McGill Univ., 1945–49, BA (Lit.), 1949–50, BLS, 1970–72, MLS. **Orgs.:** Corp. des Bibtcrs. Prof. du PQ. Can. LA. PQ LA: Coll. and Resrch. Lib. Sect. (Pres., 1973–74). ASTED. **Activities:** 1, 9; 15, 26, 39 **Addr.:** 4141 Wilson Ave., Montreal, PQ H4A 2V1 Canada.

Lennon, Donald R. (O. 6, 1938, Brunswick Cnty., NC) Assoc. Prof. of Hist., Dir., E. Carolina Mss. Col., E. Carolina Univ., 1967–; Archvst., NC Div. of Arch. & Hist., 1964–67. **Educ.:** Univ. of NC, Wilmington, 1956–58; E. Carolina Univ., 1958–60, BS (Hist.), 1960–62, MA (Hist.); Amer. Univ. - Natl. Arch., 1965, (Arch. Admin.); NC State Univ., 1966, (Archives Admin). **Orgs.:** SAA. S. Atl. Arch. Conf. Hist. Socty. of NC. NC Literary & Hist. Assn.: Exec. Com. (1975–77). **Honors:** Lower Cape Fear Hist. Socty., Clarendon Cup, 1974. **Pubns.:** *Guide To Military History Resources in the East Carolina Manuscript Collection* (1979); Jt. auth., *Harnett, Hooper & Howe: Revolutionary Leaders of the Lower Cape Fear* (1979); Jt. ed., *Politics, Bar and Bench: A Memoir of John D. Larkins, Jr.* (1980); Jt. ed., *The Wilmington Town Book, 1743–1778* (1973). **Activities:** 1; 15, 17, 36; 62, 74, 85 **Addr.:** East Carolina Manuscript Collection, J. Y. Joyner Library, East Carolina University, Greenville, NC 27834.

Lennon, Robert H. (Mr. 23, 1931, Providence, RI) YA Libn., Los Angeles Pub. Lib., 1972–; Asst. Branch Libn., New York Pub. Lib., 1961–71; Mitchel Air Force Base Lib. (Long Island), 1957–60; Vets. Admin. Hosp. Libn., (Montrose, NY), 1953–57. **Educ.:** AZ State Univ., 1948–52, BA (Educ.); Univ. of Denver, 1952–53, MA (LS). **Orgs.:** ALA: PLA; YASD. CA LA. San Pedro Cmnty. Coord. Cncl.: VP. Angels Gate Cult. Ctr. (San Pedro): Bd. Mem. **Activities:** 9; 16, 39, 48; 80, 74, 93 **Addr.:** San Pedro Regional Public Library, 931 S. Gaffey St., San Pedro, CA 90731.

Lennox, Thomas George (D. 17, 1935, Easton, PA) VP, Herner and Co., 1980–; Mgr. Ed., WHCOLIS, 1979–80; Consult., Info. Syst. and Pubn. Plng., 1977–79; Owner/VP, Documtn. Assoc. Info. Srv., Inc., 1971–77; Assoc., Contemporary Resrch., 1972–74; Libn., Beverly Hills Pub. Lib., 1971–72; Libn., CA Inst. of the Arts, 1969–71; Pub. Info. Spec., Cooper Hewitt Musm., 1961–68. **Educ.:** PA St. Coll., 1958, BS (Educ.); Univ. CA, Los Angeles, 1970, MLS. **Orgs.:** ASIS. Socty. for Schol. Publshg. **Pubns.:** Ed., various WHCOLIS pubns.; "Slides Acquisitions," *Lib. Jnl.* (N. 1973); Other reports, films, filmstrips, indexes. **Activities:** 4, 6; 17, 24, 37; 62, 75, 92 **Addr.:** The Dorchester, 2480 16th St., N.W., #441, Washington, DC 20009.

Lenox, Mary F. (Jl. 19, 1944, Chicago, IL) Assoc. Prof., LS, Univ. of MO, Columbia, 1978–; Media Spec., Chicago Pub. Schs., 1975–78; Prof., Mgr. of Circ., Dept. Lrng. Resrc. Ctr., Gvr.'s State Univ., 1973–75; Dir., Educ. Mtrls. Ctr., Chicago State Univ., 1971–72; Tchr./Libn., Chicago Pub. Schs., 1967–71. **Educ.:** Chicago State Univ. 1963–66, BS (Elem. Educ.); Rosary Coll., 1966–67, MA (LS); Univ. of MA, 1972–75, EdD (Urban Ed.). **Orgs.:** ALA: YASD, Best Bks. Com. (1977–79); AASL, *Encyc. Britannica* Sch. Media Prog. of the Yr. Awd. Sel. Com. (1979–80); Grolier Awd. Jury (1979–80); Awds. Com. for Outstan. Work for Chld. and Young People (1979–); various other coms. MO LA: Outrch. RT (Ch., 1980–81); Lib. Educs. (Ch., 1978–). MO Assn. of Sch. Libns. Assn. for the Std. of Afro-Amer. Life and Hist. AAUW. MO Black Leadership Assn. Legal Inst.: Adv. Bd. **Honors:** Pi Lambda Theta, 1981; Kappa Delta Pi, 1968; Chicago Bd. of Educ., Outstan. Educ., 1977. **Pubns.:** Jt. auth., "How to Be a Winner: The School Library Media Program of the Year Award," *Sch. Media Qtly.* (Sum. 1980); "The Use of Non-Legal Data in the Decision Making Process of the Law," *Glendale Law Review* (1976); "Library Outreach: Getting the Program to Youth," *Sch. Lib. Jnl.* (Ap. 1980); "Dispelling the Hi-Low Blues: A Conceptual Model," *Show-Me Libs.* (Mr.–Ap. 1979); bk. reviews. **Activities:** 11; 26, 32, 48 **Addr.:** 103A Stewart Hall, University of Missouri, Columbia, MO 65211.

Lentz, Edward R. (S. 21, 1945, St. Petersburg, FL) Assoc. Archvst., AV Mtrls., OH Hist. Socty., 1974–, Mss. Spec., 1969–74. **Educ.:** Princeton Univ., 1963–67, AB (Hist.); OH State

Special Subjects/Services: 50. Adult educ.; 51. Advert./Mktg.; 52. Aerosp.; 53. Agric.; 54. Area std.; 55. Arts/Hum.; 56. Autom.; 57. Bibl./Prtg.; 58. Bio. sci.; 59. Bus./Fin.; 60. Chem.; 61. Copyrt.; 62. Documtn.; 63. Educ.; 64. Engin.; 65. Env.; 66. Eth. grps.; 67. Film; 68. Food/Nutr.; 69. Geneal.; 70. Geo.; 71. Geol.; 72. Handcpd.; 73. Hist.; 74. Int. frdm.; 75. Info. sci.; 76. Insr.; 77. Law; 78. Legis.; 79. Math./Comp. sci.; 80. Med.; 81. Metals; 82. Nat. resrcs.; 83. Newsp.; 84. Nuc. sci.; 85. Oral hist.; 86. Petr./Energy; 87. Pharm.; 88. Phys./Astr./Math.; 89. Readg.; 90. Relig.; 91. Sci./Tech.; 92. Soc. sci.; 93. Telecom.; 94. Transp.; 95. (other).

Who's Who in Library and Information Services

Univ., 1968–69, MA (Hist.). **Orgs.:** Socty. of OH Archvsts. OH Acad. of Hist. **Pubns.:** Jt. auth., *Columbus: America's Crossroads* (1980); *Ihna To Frary: An Inventory to His Audiovisual Collection at the Ohio Historical Society* (1976); *Oral History Manual* (1975); "The People Are The City," AV presentation (1970); "Columbus, Ohio History," AV presentation (1976–80). **Activities:** 2, 12; 17, 32, 49-Audiovisual Archives; 62, 73 **Addr.:** Ohio Historical Society, I-71 and 17th Ave., Columbus, OH 43211.

Lenz, Millicent A. (Ap. 17, 1936, Webster City, IA) Assoc. Prof., Dept. of LS, Memphis State Univ., 1975–; Cur., Belknap Col. for the Performing Arts, Univ. of FL, Gainesville, 1974–75, Asst. Prof., Eng., 1973–74. **Educ.:** Luther Coll., 1954–59, BA (Eng.); Univ. of KS, 1959–61, MA (Eng.); Univ. of WI, 1964–65, MA (LS); North. IL Univ., 1971–73, PhD (Eng.). **Orgs.:** ALA: AASL; YASD; ALSC. TN LA: Educ. Sect. (Ch. 1978–79). Chld. Lit. Assn.: Schol. Com. (1979–). **Honors:** Phi Beta Kappa, 1961. **Pubns.:** *Young Adult Literature: Backgrounds and Criticism* (1981); "Russell Hoban's *The Mouse and His Child* and the Search to Be Self-Winding," *Procs. of the 5th Anl. Conf. of the Chld.'s Lit. Assn.* (1979); "Robert Henryson's 'The Tale of the Country Mouse and the City Mouse,' Retold for Our Times," *Univ. of S. FL Lang. Qtly.* (Spr.–Sum. 1977); reviews. **Activities:** 11; 16, 21; 48 **Addr.:** Dept. of Library Science, Memphis State University, Memphis, TN 38152.

Leo, Karen Ann (Je. 5, 1945, Akron, OH) Head, Ctrl. Lib., Riverside City and Cnty. Pub. Lib., 1981–; Prin. Libn., Pomona Pub. Lib., 1977–81; Admin. Asst. to Cnty. Libn., Stanislaus Cnty. Free Lib., 1977, Head, Turlock Branch Lib., 1972–73, Head, Ref. Dept., 1971–72. **Educ.:** Baldwin-Wallace Coll., 1963–67, BA (Eng. and Psy.); Univ. of MI, 1967–68, AMLS. **Orgs.:** CA LA. ALA. Soroptimist Intl. of Pomona: 1st VP (1981–82). Pomona Mncpl. Mgt. Club: Pres. (1980–81). **Activities:** 9; 17 **Addr.:** P.O. Box 5112, Riverside, CA 92517.

León, Carmencita (Quebradillas, PR) State Dir. Sch. Lib. Syst., PR Dept. of Educ., 1972–, Asst. to the Under-Secy., 1971; Reg. Coord. of Educ. Sch. Lib. Syst., San Juan Educ. Reg., 1970–71; Coord., Remedial Readg. Ctr. Libs., PR Dept of Educ., 1967–69. **Educ.:** Univ. of PR, 1951–55, BA (Elem. Educ.), 1969–70, MLS, 1970–71, Cert. (Sch. Lib. Supvsr.). **Orgs.:** PR WHCOLIS: Coord. (1978). WHCOLIS: Del. (1979). PR Socty. of Libns.: Pres. (1978–80); Secy. (1973); Legis. Com. ALA: AASL, PR Sch. Lib. Awd. Liaison PR PR Assn. PR Tchrs. Assn.: Anl. Asm. (Del., 1967–69). **Honors** PR Sch. Libns., Plaques of Acknowledgement, 1971–80; PR Socty. of Libns., Plaque of Acknowledgement, 1980; Phi Delta Kappa. **Pubns.:** *Library Legislation in Puerto Rico* (1971); *El niñoy su expresión creadora* (1972); various articles. **Activities:** 10, 13; 15, 17, 26 **Addr.:** 880 Ruiseñor St., Country Club, Rio Piedras, PR 00924.

Leonard, Carolyn M. (S. 11, 1936, Lincoln, NE) Asst. Head, New Serial Titles, Lib. of Congs., 1979–; Coord., Media Prcs., North. VA Cmnty. Coll., 1978–79; Supvsg. Libn., Tech. Srvs., Santa Clara Cnty. Lib., 1974–78; Serials Catlgr., IL State Univ., 1969–73; Serials Catlgr., Univ. of IL, 1968–69; Head, Serials Dept., Univ. of CO, 1965–68, Serials Catlgr., 1964–65; Head Catlgr., Riverside City/Cnty. Lib., 1963–64; other prof. positions. **Educ.:** Hastings Coll., 1954–58, BA (Eng., Educ.); Univ. of Denver, 1958–59, MA (Libnshp.); Univ. of IL, 1971–72, CAS (LS). **Orgs.:** ALA: Cat./Class. Exec. Com. (1977–79). DC LA. **Honors:** BETA Phi Mu, Membership, 1960. **Activities:** 4; 20, 44, 46; 56, 57 **Addr.:** 5905 Sherborn Ln., Springfield, VA 22152.

Leonard, Charlotte C. (Mr. 16, 1922, Delaware, OH) Coord., Chld. Srvs., Dayton & Montgomery Cnty. Pub. Lib., 1963–, Head of Bkmobile Dept., 1958–62, Chld. Libn., 1950–57; Asst. Libn., Monsanto Resrch. Corp., 1948–49. **Educ.:** Heidelberg Coll., 1943, BA (Eng.); Case-Western Reserve Univ., 1949–50, MSLS. **Orgs.:** OH LA: Secy. (1974–1976); Pres. (1978). ALA: Newbery-Caldecott Com. (1972, 1981); Preschool & Parent Educ. Com. (1974–75); Ref. & Subscrpn. Books Review Com. (1975–76). OH Educ. Lib. Media Assn. Soroptimist Intl. of Dayton: Pres. (1969–71). AAUW: Dayton Chap., Pres. (1960–62). **Pubns.:** *Tied Together* (1980); *Start Early for an Early Start* (1976); "Poetry to Please Preschoolers," "Prescribed for Preschool Problems," weekly chld. book column, *Jnl. Herald* (1976–). **Activities:** 9, 10; 21; 74, 89 **Addr.:** Dayton & Montgomery Co. Public Library, 215 E. Third St., Dayton, OH 45402.

Leonard, David W. (F. 17, 1945, Fairview, AB) Territorial Archvst., Prince of Wales North. Heritage Ctr., 1979–; Archvst., City of Edmonton Arch., 1976–79; Archvst., Prov. Arch. of AB, 1969–71. **Educ.:** Univ. of AB, 1964–69, MA (Hist.); Univ. of Sheffield, Eng., 1971–75, PhD (Hist.). **Orgs.:** Assn. of Can. Archvsts. Hist. Socty. of AB. Can. Hist. Assn. **Activities:** 2; 15, 38, 41; 61, 62, 85 **Addr.:** Territorial Archives, Prince of Wales Northern Heritage Centre, Government of the Northwest Territories, Yellowknife, NT X1A 2L9 Canada.

Leonard, Harriet V. (N. 2, 1932, Lexington, NC) Ref. Libn., Duke Dvnty. Sch., 1960–. **Educ.:** Catawba Coll., 1950–54, AB; Yale Dvnty. Sch. 1954–58, MDvnty.; Univ. of NC, 1958–60, MS (LS). **Orgs.:** ATLA: Bd. of Dir. (1979–82). NC LA. **Activities:** 1, 12; 15, 39, 41; 90 **Addr.:** Duke Divinity School Library, Durham, NC 27706.

Leonard, James W. (Mr. 30, 1940, Berkeley, CA) Mgr. Resrch. Lib., IBM Resrch. Ctr., 1979–, Ref. Libn., 1978–79; Head Libn, Phys./Astr./Math. Lib., Univ. TX, 1975–78; Sci. Libn., Univ. Canterbury (Christchurch, NZ), 1972–75. **Educ.:** Univ. CA (Santa Barbara), 1962, AB (Phys.); Univ. OR, 1962–68, MA, PhD (Phys.); Univ. West. ON, 1971–72, MLS. **Orgs.:** SLA: Phys./Astro./Math. Div., Nom. Com. (Ch., 1977–78), Bltn. Ed. (1980–82). TX LA: Ref. RT, Secy./Treas. (1977–78). Amer. Phys. Socty. Socty. Sigma Xi: North. Westchester Chap., Treas. (1979–80), Secy. (1980–81). **Pubns.:** Various articles in phys. **Addr.:** Library 16-226, IBM Research Center, P.O. Box 218, Yorktown Heights, NY 10598.

Leonard, Lawrence Edwards (Ag. 15, 1934, Hartford, CT) Chief, Tech. Prcs. Branch, Lib. Srvs. Div., U. S. Dept. of Transp., 1980–; Lib. Srvs. Prog. Ofcr., U. S. Ofc. of Educ., Region IX (San Francisco), and Washington DC, 1976–80: Chief, Cat. Dept., Stanford Univ. Libs., 1973–76; Proj. Dir., CO Acad. Libs. Bk. Prcs. Ctr. Feasibility Std., 1967–68; Libn., Natl. Bureau of Stans., Boulder Resrch. Labs., 1964–67; Ref. Libn., U.S. Naval Ordnance Lab. (Corona, CA), 1963–64. Other positions 1959–63. **Educ.:** Univ. of CO, 1953–54, Univ. of IL, 1954–56, BA (Geol.); Univ. of Denver, 1958–59, MA (LS); Univ. of IL, 1968–75, Ph.D. (LS); San Jose Univ., 1975–76; various wkshps. **Orgs.:** ALA: Cncl. (1972–74); ASCLA, Grantsmanship Com. (1978–); RTSD (Cat. and Class Sect., Nom. Com. (1975–76); LRRT, Nom. Com. (1970), Secy.-Treas. (1972–74); Other Divs. and ofcs. SLA. DC LA. ASIS. Univ. of Denver Lib. Sch., Alum. Assn. AECT. **Pubns.:** Jt.-auth., *Centralized Book Processing* (1969); Jt.-auth., *Management and Costs of Technical Processes* (1970); "Colorado Academic Libraries Book Processing Center" *Coll. & Resrch. Libs.* (S. 1968); "The Colorado Academic Libraries Book Processing Center Project – Time Study Methodology," *Lib. Resrcs. and Tech. Srvs.* (Win. 1969); reviews, other articles and reports. **Activities:** 4; 17, 34, 46; 52, 77, 94 **Addr.:** 5905 Sherborn Ln., Springfield, VA 22152.

Leonard, Louise F. (Ja. 19, 1924, Easthampton, MA) Latin Amer. Catlgr., Univ. of FL, 1978–; Libn., FL Sch. for Boys, 1976–78; Libn., Ctr. Africain de Formation et de Recherche Admin. pour le Dev., 1973–74; Tchr./Libn., Amer. Sch. of Tangier, Morocco, 1972–73; various positions in other countries. **Educ.:** OH Univ., 1942–43, 1947–48, BA (Rom. Langs.); Univ. of Denver, 1959–60, MA (LS); Univ. of CA, Berkeley, 1964–69, ABD (Educ., Mid E. Std.); State of OH, 1955, Elem. and Sec. Tchg. Certs. **Orgs.:** FL LA. ALA. **Pubns.:** Jt. ed., *Caribbean Acquisitions* (1980); reviews. **Activities:** 1; 54 **Addr.:** 1314 N.W. 39 Dr., Gainesville, FL 32605.

Leonard, Lucinda E. (Winthrop, MA) FEDLINK Coord., Fed. Lib. Com., 1978–; Head, Users Support Proj., Autom. Systs. Ofc., Lib. of Congs., 1977–78, Progmr., Sr. Info. Systs. Anal., MDO/BSO, 1969–76, Catlgr., Rom. Langs., Descr. Cat., 1968–69. **Educ.:** Northeast. Univ., 1961–66, BA (Eng.); George Washington Univ., 1972–77, MBA (Persnl.); Drexel Univ., 1966–67, MSLS (Cat., Autom.). **Orgs.:** ALA: FLRT, Nom. Com. (Ch., 1981). SLA: Lib. Mgt. Div. (Treas., 1978–80). Data Prcs. Mgt. Assn. OCLC Users Cncl.: Syst. Priorities and Needs Task Frc. (Ch., 1980–81). Amer. Socty. for Trng. and Dev. Assn. of Comp. Mach. **Honors** Phi Kappa Phi, 1967. **Pubns.:** "FLC/FEDLINK and the Field Libraries—Management Aspects," *FLC Nsltr.* (D. 1980); "FLC/FEDLINK Services: On-line Cataloging, Retrieval, Interlibrary Loan and Acquisitions," *Lib. Mgt. Bltn.* (Spr. 1981). **Activities:** 4; 17, 26, 34; 56, 59, 93 **Addr.:** 1600 S. Eads St. 1004–N, Arlington, VA 22202.

Leonard, W. Patrick (N. 2, 1939, Beech Grove, IN) Dean, Lib. and Lrng. Resrcs., Chicago State Univ., 1972–, Dir. of Libs., 1974–77, Dir., Instr. Media, 1972–74; Dir., Instr. Mtrls. Ctr., Temple Univ., 1969–72; Lectr. (Educ. Comm.), Univ. of Pittsburgh, 1966–69. **Educ.:** IN Univ., 1957–61, BS (Educ.), MS (Educ.); Univ. of Pittsburgh, 1965–69, Ph.D. (Ed. Comm. and LS); various wkshps. **Orgs.:** ALA. IL LA. Other orgs. AECT. IL AV Assn. Other orgs. **Pubns.:** "A Survival Manual for Newly Appointed Chairpersons," *Phi Delta Kappau* (S. 1979); "Contemporary Instructional Design is Banal," *Educ. Comm. and Tech.* (Sum. 1979). "The Aftermath of Retrenchment," *Jnl. of Acad. Libnshp.* (Mr. 1979); "The New Reality of Higher Education Governance," *Phi Delta Kappau* (O. 1978); reviews, other articles. **Activities:** 1; 17; 59, 69 **Addr.:** Chicago State University, Chicago, IL 60628.

Leondar, Judith C. (F. 8, 1931, Boston, MA) Mgr., Tech. Info. Srvs., Amer. Cyanamid Co., 1973–; Mgr., Lib. Oper., Squibb Inst. for Med. Resrch., 1966–73; Resrch. Assoc., Asst. Prof., Rutgers Univ., 1965–66; Sci. Info. Ofcr., Inst. of Naval Stds., 1961–65; Resrch. Libn., Ethicon Inc., 1956–61; Tech. Libn., RCA Intl. Div., 1955–56; Tech. Resrch. Libn., Amer. Can. Co., 1952–55. **Educ.:** Alfred Univ., 1948–52, BA (Chem.); Rutgers Univ., MLS. **Orgs.:** ASIS: Ctrl. NJ Chap. (Secy. Treas. 1975–77); Liason to Amer. Chem. Socty. (1971–74); Educ. Com. (Ch., 1968–70); Other ofcs. SLA: Documtn. Div. (Secy. 1975–77); Prof. Consult. (1965–70); PR Com. (Ch., 1969–72); other ofcs. ALA. Med. LA. Amer. Chem. Socty. Drug Info. Assn. NJ State Lib.: Ad Hoc Com. on Cont. Lib. Educ. (1976–77). **Pubns.:** *Bibliography of Research Relating to the Communication of Scientific and Technical Information* (1967); Subject-Index Standards. *Proc. of the Amer. Documtn. Inst.* (O. 1967, v. 4); "Report Literature and Sources of Information," *Spec. Libs.* (F. 1968). **Activities:** 12; 17, 24; 56, 60, 87 **Addr.:** P.O. Box 306, Kingston, NJ 08528.

Leone, Donna R. C. (O. 13, 1947, St. Louis, MO) Assoc. Libn. & Dir., Univ. Media. Ctr., Univ. of S. FL, 1980–; Lib. Dir., Asst. Prof., Parks Coll., St. Louis Univ., 1976–79, Lib. Dir., Asst. Prof., Sch. of Soc. Srv. Lib., 1974–76; Asst. Libn., Quincy Coll., 1971–74. **Educ.:** Univ. of MO, St. Louis, 1969, BA (Eng.); Rosary Coll., 1971, MALS; St. Louis Univ., 1976, MA (Comm.), PhD in progress (Educ.). **Orgs.:** ALA. AECT. FL Assn. of Media Educ. FL LA. **Pubns.:** "On the Road to Find Out," a slide tape orientation to Parks College Library (1978). **Addr.:** University Media Center, EDU 113, University of South Florida, Tampa, FL 33620.

Lerman, Linda P. (My. 23, 1953, Detroit, MI) Tech. Srvs. Libn., Andover-Newton Theo. Sch., 1981–; Serials Cat., CONSER Proj., Boston Theo. Inst., 1979–81; Coord., Serials and Circ., Hebrew Union Coll., 1978–79, Judaica Libn., 1976–78. **Educ.:** Univ. of MI, 1970–74, AB (Judaic Std.), 1974–75, AMLS; N. East. Univ., 1980– (Bus. Admin.). **Orgs.:** Assn. of Jewish Lib.: Rec. Secy. (1980–82). ALA: LAMA; LITA. **Pubns.:** "Audio-Visual Materials for Judaic Libraries," *Assn. of Jewish Lib. Proc.* (1980); "The Freeze, AACR2 and AJL: a selective bibliography," *Assn. of Jewish Lib. Proc.* (1978); "The Freeze, AACR2 and GCLC: a selective bibliography," *GCLC Update* (Jl./Ag. 1978); Jt. Auth., *A Beginner's Guide to Jewish Genealogy* (1979); Reviews. **Activities:** 1, 12; 17, 39, 46; 50, 56, 90 **Addr.:** 151 North St., Apt. C, Newtonville, MA 02160.

Lerner, Adele Ann (N. 5, 1938, NY, NY) Archvst., NY Hosp., Cornell Med. Ctr., 1972–; Medlars/Medline Anal., NY Acad. of Med., 1971–72; Insurance Anal., 1969–70. **Educ.:** Univ. of Rochester, 1956–60, BA (Eng.); Columbia Univ., 1970–71, MLS. Various insts. and wkshps. **Orgs.:** SAA: Prog. Com. (1979); Arch. of Sci. Com. (1974–; Ch., 1980–). ALA SLA Jt. Com. on Arch. Lib. Rels. Mid. Atl. Reg. Arch. Conf.: Strg. com. (1976–78); Prog. Com. (1973–74; Co-Ch., 1975–76), Lcl. Arrange. Com. (1980–81), Com. on Future Sites (1978–79). Beta Phi Mu: Various ofcs. Other orgs. Amer. Assn. for the Hist. of Med. **Activities:** 2, 12; 15, 17, 38; 80, 91 **Addr.:** New York Hospital—Cornell Medical Center, 1300 York Ave., New York, NY 10021.

Lerner, Fred (D. 27, 1945, Mount Vernon, NY) Head, Tech. Info. Srvs., Creare Innovations, Inc., 1979–; Head, Ref. Srvs. Unit, VT Dept. of Libs., 1974–78; Info. Spec., Resrch. Fndn., City Univ. of NY, 1970–72; Ref. Libn., Hamilton Coll., 1969–70. **Educ.:** Columbia Univ., 1962–66, AB (Hist.), 1968–69, MS (LS), 1974, Cert. (Adv. LS), 1981, DLS. **Orgs.:** VT LA. SLA. ASIS. VT Pub. Radio: Bd. of Dir. (1976–). Kipling Socty. **Pubns.:** *An Annotated Checklist of Science Fiction Bibliographical Works* (1969); "A Classified Vertical File," *Unabashed Libn.* (1978); "The Science Fiction Library," *Spec. Libs.* (Ja. 1973); "2001: A Vermont Odyssey," VT Pub. Radio Prog. (1979). **Activities:** 12, 13; 26, 34, 39; 57, 64, 91 **Addr.:** 5 Worcester Ave., White River Junction, VT 05001

Lerner, Rita G. (My. 7, 1929, New York, NY) Mgr., Mktg. Srvs., Amer. Inst. of Phys., 1969–; Dir. of Labs., Bio. Sci. Dept., Columbia Univ., 1968; Mgr., Plng. and Dev., Amer. Inst. of Phys., 1964–67; Resrch. Assoc., Columbia Univ., 1956–64. **Educ.:** Radcliffe Coll., 1945–49, AB (Chem.); Columbia Univ., 1949–56, PhD (Chem. Phys.). **Orgs.:** ASIS: Com. on Intersocty. Coop. (1979–); NY Chap. (Ch., 1974). AAAS: Sect. T, Nom. Com. (1978–80). Assn. of Info. Dssm. Ctrs.: Prog. Com. (Ch., 1977–80), Exec. Com. (1975–77). Amer. Phys. Socty. Amer. Chem. Socty.: ASIS Liaison (1975–79). **Pubns.:** Jt. ed., *Encyclopedia of Physics* (1980); "SPIN," *Online* (O. 1979); "Access to Data in the Primary Literature," *CODATA Sourcebook for Data Handling* (1979); "Physics, American Institute of Physics," *Ency. of Lib. and Info. Sci.* (1977); Various articles and invited papers. **Activities:** 6, 14-Non-profit inst.; 37, 41; 51, 75, 88 **Addr.:** American Institute of Physics, 335 E. 45th St., New York, NY 10017.

Lesh, Nancy L. (My. 25, 1944, Anchorage, AK) Asst. Dir., Tech. Srvs., Univ. of AK, Anchorage, 1972–; Libn., Anchorage Cmnty. Coll. 1969–72, Asst. Libn., 1968–69. **Educ.:** Willamette Univ., 1962–66, BA (Eng.); Simmons Coll., 1966–67, MLS. **Orgs.:** ALA: AK Chap. (Cnclr., 1979–), various coms. AK LA: VP (1971); Pres. (1972–73); *Sourdough* Jt. Ed. (1976–79); Rep. to ALA (1977–81); Southetrl. Chap. (Ch., 1970–71); various coms. Pac. NW LA: Exec. Bd. (1974–76); various actv. Anchorage Concert Assn. Pioneers of AK. Anchorage Hist. and Fine Arts Musm. Assn. Cook Inlet Hist. Assn. **Honors:** ALA, Cit. for Excel. in Nsltr. Publshg. for *Sourdough*, 1978. **Pubns.:** "Alaska Library Association, 1975–1976," *PNLA Qtly.* (Spr. 1977); "Library Development in Alaska," *ALA Yrbk.* (1978, 1979, 1980); "The Anchorage Merger: Pros and Cons," *Sourdough* (Je. 1970); "Marketing Library Resources," *Sourdough* (Ap. 1971); ed., *Alaska Library Association Conference Planning Handbook* (1977); various articles, *ALA Yrbk.* (1978–80). **Activities:** 1; 15,

PROFESSIONAL ACTIVITIES: Institutions: 1. Acad. lib.; 2. Arch.; 3. Assn.; 4. Fed./Gvt. lib.; 5. Inst. lib.; 6. Mfr./Suppl.; 7. Milit. lib.; 8. Musm.; 9. Pub. lib.; 10. Sch. lib.; 11. Sch. of lib. sci.; 12. Spec. lib.; 13. State lib.; 14. (other). **Functions/Activities:** 15. Acq./Col. dev.; 16. Adult srvs.; 17. Admin.; 18. Apprais.; 19. Archit./Bldgs.; 20. Cat./Class.; 21. Chld. srvs.; 22. Circ.; 23. Cons./Pres.; 24. Consult.; 25. Cont. ed.; 26. Educ. lib. sci.; 27. Ext. srvs.; 28. Fund/Grants; 29. Gvt. pubs.; 30. Indx./Abs.; 31. Instr. lib. use; 32. Media srvs.; 33. Micro.; 34. Netwks./Coop.; 35. Persnl.; 36. PR; 37. Publshg.; 38. Recs. mgt.; 39. Ref. srvs.; 40. Repro.; 41. Resrch.; 42. Review.; 43. Secur.; 44. Serials; 45. Spec. col.; 46. Tech. srvs.; 47. Trustees/Bds.; 48. YA srvs.; 49. (other).

17, 20 **Addr.:** University of Alaska Anchorage Library, 3211 Providence Ave., Anchorage, AK 99504.

Lesieur, Denis J. (My. 28, 1950, Chicopee, MA) Supvsr., Lcl. Hist., Lit. Srvs., Berkshire Athen., 1975–; Libn., Canal Mus. (Syracuse, NY), 1973–75. **Educ.:** Univ. of MA, 1968–72, BA Hist.; Boston Coll., 1972–75, M.A. (Hist.); Syracuse Univ., 1973–75, MLS. **Orgs.:** MA LA: New Mems. RT (VP, Pres. 1977–80); Lcl. Hist. and Geneal. Sect. (Pres., 1978–80; Prog. Ch. 1980–). ALA. Bay State Hist. Leag.: Bd. of Dir. (1978–). Berkshire Family Hist. Assn.: VP (1977–78); Pres. (1978–). Amer. Hist. Assn. Natl. Fed. of Geneal. Soctys. (Del., 1978–). **Honors:** Beta Phi Mu. Berkshire Geneal. Socty., Srv. Awd., 1979. **Pubns.:** Columns, *Berkshire Eagle* (1976–78); "Roots," *Bay State Libn.* (F. 1978; Fall 1978); Ed., *Berkshire Geneal.* (1978–); bk. review ed., *Bay State Hist. Leag. Jnl.* and *Jnl. of MA Hist.*; other reviews. **Activities:** 9, 12; 17, 39, 45; 50, 69, 73 **Addr.:** Berkshire Athenaeum, 1 Wendell Av., Pittsfield, MA 01201.

Lesnak, Stephen R. (Je. 24, 1944, Bakersfield, CA) Asst. Dir., Rochester Pub. Lib., 1977–, Branch Mgr., 1973–77, Adult, YA Libn., 1969–73. **Educ.:** St. Vincent Coll., 1962–66, BA (Hist.); George Peabody Coll., 1968–69, MLS; Univ. WI (Madison), 1971–72, 6th Yr. Cert. (LS). **Orgs.:** ALA: RASD, Adult YA Com. Coop. (1971–73). NY LA: Mem. Com. (1969–71); Cont. Educ. (1973–81). Inst. Cult. Affairs: Guardian (1972–81). **Honors:** Beta Phi Mu, 1970. **Activities:** 9; 16, 17, 25; 50, 75, 89 **Addr.:** Rochester Public Library, 115 S. Ave., Rochester, NY 14610.

Lesser, Charles H. (Mr. 15, 1944, DuBois, PA) Asst. Dir. for Arch. and Pubns., SC Dept. of Arch. and Hist., 1975–; Resrch. Ed., Amer. Revolution Bicent. Proj., William L. Clements Lib., Univ. of MI, 1972–75. **Educ.:** PA State Univ., 1962–66, BA (Hist.), 1966–68, MA (Hist.); Univ. of MI, 1968–74, PhD (Hist.); Inst. of Mod. Arch. Admin., Natl. Arch. and Recs. Srv., 1976, Cert. **Orgs.:** SAA: Gvt. Recs. Prof. Afnty. Grp. (Vice-Ch., 1979–81). Org. of Amer. Histns. Amer. Hist. Assn. South. Hist. Assn. SC Hist. Assn. **Pubns.:** Jt. auth., *Fighters for Independence; A Guide to Sources of Biographical Information on Soldiers and Sailors of the American Revolution* (1977); various other pubns. in hist. **Activities:** 2; 17, 23, 37; 56, 57 **Addr.:** South Carolina Dept. of Archives and History, P.O. Box 11,669, Capitol Station, Columbia, SC 29211.

Lester, Daniel W. (F. 5, 1943, Long Beach, CA) Pres., Raindance Enterprises, 1981–; Asst. Dean for Tech. Srvs., Univ. of NM Gen. Lib., 1976–81; Asst. Dean for Tech. Srvs., Univ. of NE, 1973–76; Assoc. Dir. for Syst., Mankato State Univ., 1969–73; Syst. Libn., Bowling Green State Univ., 1968–69. **Educ.:** North. IL Univ., 1963–66, BA (Eng.), 1966–68, MA (LS). **Orgs.:** ALA: various coms. (1968–80). SLA: Pres., Rio Grande Chap. (1978–79). NM LA: Ch., Pubns. Com. (1979–80). Grt. Albuquerque Lhasa Apso Club. Rio Grande Kennel Club. Amer. Shih Tzu Club. **Pubns.:** *Cumulative Title Index to United States Public Documents, 1789–1976* (1979–81); *Checklist of U.S. Public Documents, 1789–1976* (1977); *Checklist of U.S. Public Documents, 1789–1970* (1973); "A Management Information System for Serials and Continuations," ASIS *Procs.*, (1973); *Development of an Automated Book Catalog*, ERIC (1974). **Activities:** 1; 17, 29, 46; 56, 70, 75 **Addr.:** 2809 Christine N.E., Albuquerque, NM 87112.

Lester, Linda L. (N. 4, 1941, Davenport, IA) Asst. Head, Ref., Univ. of VA, 1980–; Pub. Srvs. Libn., Findlay Coll., 1974–80. **Educ.:** OH State Univ., 1959–63, BS (Soc. Wk.); Univ. of MI, 1973–74, AMLS. **Orgs.:** ALA: ACRL/Bibl. Instr. Sect., Com. on Coop. (1977–79); ACRL/AV Com. (1981–82). Acad. Lib. Assn. of OH: Exec. Bd. (1976–78). **Honors:** Beta Phi Mu. **Pubns.:** *Library Instruction Programs in Ohio Academic Libraries* (1977). **Activities:** 1; 31, 39; 63, 92 **Addr.:** 944 Old Brook Rd., Charlottesville, VA 22901.

Lester, Marilyn Ann (Ja. 1, 1947, Chicago, IL) Assoc. Dir. for Lib., Natl. Coll. of Educ., 1978–; Dir., Lrng. Resrc. Ctr., S. E. Cmnty. Coll., 1974–78; Ref. Libn., Lincoln City Lib. (NE), 1974. **Educ.:** Mankato State Univ., 1969–72, BA (Eng., LS), 1972–73, MS (LS). **Orgs.:** N. Suburban (IL) Lib. Syst.: Cont. Educ. Com. (1981). ALA: GODORT, Treas. (1972–74). NE LA: Coll. and Univ. Sect. (Secy.-Treas., 1976–77). Post-Secondary Educ. Lib. Dir. of NE: Ch. (1978). Phi Delta Kappa: Natl. Coll. of Educ. Chap., Secy. .(1979–1981). **Pubns.:** *Checklist of U.S. Public Documents, 1789–1970 and 1970–1975* (1972, 1979); *Federal and State Government Publications of Professional Interest to the School Librarian: A Bibliographic Essay* (Univ. IL Occasional Paper 100). **Activities:** 1; 17, 27, 26; 50, 56, 63 **Addr.:** National College of Education, 2840 Sheridan Rd., Evanston, IL 60201.

LeSueur, Charles Robin (Jn. 8, 1923, Sarnia, ON) Libn., Countway Lib. of Med., Harvard Univ., 1977–; Libn., Rockefeller Univ., 1972–77; Libn., Stevens Inst. of Tech., 1968–72; Libn., Coll. of Engin. and Sci., NY Univ., 1961–68; Ref. Libn., Engin. Soctys. Lib. (NY), 1960, Admin., Gen. Electric Co. (Toronto), 1953–55; Soc. Worker, Toronto Chlds. Aid., 1951–53. **Educ.:** Univ. of Toronto, 1946–50, BA, 1950–51, BSW (Soc. Wk.); Columbia Univ., 1957–59, MLS. Various Bus. Trng. Progs., 1946–49. **Orgs.:** New Eng. Reg. Med. Lib.: Dir. (1977–). Columbia Univ. LS Alum. Assn.: Pres. (1967–72). Columbia Univ. Senate: Com. on Libs. (Ch., 1974–77). Med. LA. Various other orgs. **Activities:** 1; 17; 80 **Addr.:** Countway Library of Medicine, 10 Shattuck St., Boston, MA 02115.

Letson, Ruth S. (O. 21, 1944, Oak Ridge, TN) Libn., TN Dept. of Transp., 1978–; Serials Libn., TN State Univ., 1977; Tech. Srvs. Libn., Vanderbilt Univ. Libs., 1972–77. **Educ.:** E. TN State Univ., 1964–66, BS (Span. Educ.); George Peabody Coll., 1969–72, MLS. **Orgs.:** SLA: South. Appalachian Chap., Career Guid. Com. (1979–80). TN LA: *TN Libn.* Bus. Mgr. (1974–77). **Activities:** 4, 12; 15, 17, 20 **Addr.:** Tennessee Dept. of Transportation Library, Suite 900, James K. Polk Bldg., Nashville, TN 37219.

Leveillee, Louis Roger (D. 27, 1934, Woonsocket, RI) Coord., of Media Srvs., Woonsocket Educ. Dept., 1969–; Libn., Woonsocket Sr. HS, 1957–69. **Educ.:** Assumption Coll., 1953–57, AB (Fr.); Univ. of RI, 1966, MLS. **Orgs.:** New Eng. Educ. Media Assn.: PR (Ch., 1980). RI LA: Cont. Educ. Com. (1980). RI Educ. Media Assn.: Nom. Com. (Ch., 1979–81). ALA. Various other orgs. Woonsocket Sch. Admins. Assn. **Pubns.:** Jt.-auth., *Brief History of Crime & Delinquency* (1961). **Activities:** 10; 17, 24, 25; 63 **Addr.:** Cass Park Media Center, 350 Newland Ave., Woonsocket, RI 02895.

Level, June Saine (N. 1, 1933, Ft. Pierce, FL) Spec., Lib. Media, KS State Dept. of Educ., 1980–; Media Spec., Butterfield Trail Sch., 1973–80; Rsv. Bk. Rm. Libn., Purdue Univ., 1957–59. **Educ.:** Univ. of FL, 1951–55, BAEd (Sec. Educ.); Purdue Univ., 1956–59, MSEd (Lib. Media); Univ. of AR, 1973–79. **Orgs.:** ALA: AASL. AECT. AR Assn. of Sch. Libns.: VP (1978); Pres. (1979). KS LA. Various other orgs. Phi Mu Soc. Sorority. **Activities:** 10, 13; 24, 25; 63 **Addr.:** 3017 Quail Creek Dr., Topeka, KS 66614.

Levering, Mary Berghaus (Je. 1, 1940, West Palm Beach, FL) Chief, Netwk. Div., Natl. Lib. Srv. for the Blind and Phys. Handcpd., Lib. of Congs., (LC) 1978–; Asst. Coord. of Review, Congsnl. Resrch. Srv. Lib. of Congs., 1975–78; Spec. Asst. to the Asst. Dir. for Acq. and Overseas Oper., Prcs. Dep., Lib. of Congs., 1967–75. **Educ.:** Univ. of Portland, 1961–65, BA, maxima cum laude (Eng., Educ.); Univ. of WA, 1965–66, MLS, highest hons.; Georgetown Univ. Law Ctr., 1973–77, JDL. **Orgs.:** ALA: Stdg. Com. on Lib. Educ. (1981–83) ASCLA, Ed. Policy Com. (1979–81)/Lib. Srv. to the Blind and Phys. Handcpd. Sect., Interface Adv. Com. (1981–83). DC LA. DC Bar Assn. Women's Natl. Bk. Assn.: DC Chap. (VP, 1979–83). Fed. Bar Assn. **Honors:** Delta Epsilon Sigma, 1965; Beta Phi Mu, 1966. **Pubns.:** "Services Are 500 Percent Better," *Amer. Libs.* (Je. 1979); "Equalizing Information Access by Handicapped Persons," *ASIS Procs.* (O. 1979); "Input from Organized and Nonorganized Consumers," *Jnl. of Visual Impairment and Blindness* (Mr. 1981). **Activities:** 1, 4; 15, 17, 34; 72, 77, 78 **Addr.:** National Library Service for the Blind and Physically Handicapped, Library of Congress, Washington, DC 20542.

Levering, Philip C. (Ag. 1, 1936, Mt. Vernon, OH) Head of AV Srvs., Suffolk Coop. Lib. Syst., 1967–; Asst. Head, Films & Recordings Ctr., Pub. Lib. of Cincinnati, 1965–67; Asst. Dir., Clermont Cnty. (OH) Pub. Lib., 1962–65. **Educ.:** Kenyon Coll., 1955–60, AB (Eng.); Western Reserve Univ., 1961–62, MSLS. **Orgs.:** EFLA. Film Lib. Info. Cncl.: Ch. (1976–78). NY LA. Suffolk Cnty. LA: Ch., A-V Com. (1975–77). **Pubns.:** "Eight milimeter films in public libraries," *Lib. Trends* (Sum. 1978). **Activities:** 9; 32; 67, 93 **Addr.:** Suffolk Cooperative Library System, 627 N. Sunrise Serive Rd., Bellport, NY 11713.

Lévesque, Albert (Je. 3, 1933, Campbellton, NB) Head Libn., Univ. de Moncton, 1973–; Dir., Ctr. de Bibl. Rwandaise, Univ. Natl. du Rwanda, 1970–72, Fndr., Head-Libn., 1964–69. **Educ.:** Sem. St.-Francois, Cap Rouge (PQ), 1946–55, BA (Arts); Univ. de Montréal, 1961–62, BLS; Cath. Univ., 1969–70, (MLS). **Orgs.:** Can. LA. ASTED: Com. de Rel. Intl. (Ch.) ALA. Assn. of Coll. and Univ. of Can. Various other orgs. **Pubns.:** Contrib., *National Bibliography of Rwanda 1965–70* (1979). **Activities:** 1, 12; 30, 34, 42; 57 **Addr.:** Université de Moncton, Bibliothèque Champlain, Moncton, NB E1A 3E9 Canada.

Levesque, Janet A. (Je. 2, 1949, Taunton, MA) Lib. Dir., Greenville Pub. Lib., 1979–; AV Libn., Taunton Pub. Lib., 1971–79. **Educ.:** Regis Coll., 1967–71, AB (Fr.); Univ. of RI, 1976–78, MLS; "Mgt. of the Effective Lib." at Stonehill Coll., 1979, Cert.; other courses. **Orgs.:** ALA: PLA; LAMA. New Eng. LA. RI LA: Gvt. Rel. Com., Ch. (1979–); Persnl. Com., Salary Srvy. Subcom. (Ch., 1980–). RI JMRT. Citizens for RI Libs., Inc.: Exec. Bd. (1979–). **Honors:** Beta Phi Mu, 1978. **Pubns.:** Jt. auth., "RILA Personnel Committee Report of the First Annual Salary Survey," *RILA Bulletin* (Ap. 1981). **Activities:** 9; 15, 17, 35; 78 **Addr.:** Greenville Public Library, Putnam Pike, Greenville, RI 02828.

Levesque, Raymond (Mr. 9, 1946, Cap-De-La-Madeleine, PQ) Ref. Libn., Cegep-Trois-Rivieres, 1978–; Libn., Soc. Srv. Ctr., Trois-Rivieres, 1975–78. **Educ.:** Univ. du PQ, Trois-Rivieres, 1971–73, BAC (Theo.); Univ. de Montreal, 1973–75, MALS; Univ. du PQ, 1968–69 (Educ.). **Orgs.:** ASTED. Corp. des Bibtcrs. **Pubns.:** "Le cougrès du XÈ, Tel que Vècu," *ARGUS* (My. 1979). **Activities:** 1; 39 **Addr.:** 68 Rue Guillet, Cap-De-La-Madeleine, PQ G8T 1N1 Canada.

Levin, Amy Elizabeth (Evans) (Salt Lake City, UT) Asst. Chief, Ctrl. Resrch. Srv., Smithsonian Libs., 1974–; Ref. Libn., U.S. Geol. Srvy. Lib., 1972–74; Resrch. Asst. Harvard Med. Sch., Lab. of Cmnty. Psyt., 1971–72; Head Libn. & Instr., Geol. Lib., Univ. of MN, 1969–71; Med. Lib. Trainee, Vets. Hosp., Pittsburgh, PA, 1968–69. **Educ.:** Univ. of WI, 1961–65, BS (Nat. Sci.); Univ. of Pittsburgh, 1967–69, MLS; Cert. Med. Libn., 1977; Online Bibl. Info Syst. Cert., Univ. of Pittsburgh, 1978. **Orgs.:** ALA. SLA. ASIS. Geosci. Info. Socty.: Asst. Ed., Nsltr. (1973–74). DC Online Users Grp. AFJC Jewish Congregation Srhood. Hadassah. AAUW. Natl. Cncl. of Jewish Women. Other orgs. **Activities:** 1, 4; 17, 39; 56 **Addr.:** Smithsonian Institution Libraries, Room 25 NHB, Washington, DC 20560.

Levin, Irene Staub (S. 30, 1928, Brooklyn, NY) Ref. Libn., Prog. Coord., Henry Waldinger Lib., 1976–, Ref./YA Libn., 1969–76; Judaica Libn., Temple Bnai Israel-Elmont, NY, 1967–69. **Educ.:** Hunter Coll., 1945–49, BA (Pol. Sci.); Long Island Univ., 1967–69, MLS; ULPAN-YMHA Franklin Sq. NY, Cert., 1970–73; other courses. **Orgs.:** Nassau Cnty. LA: PR Ch. (1978–79). AJL: Ed., AJL Bltn. (1973–). Jewish Libns. Caucus. Sisterhood Temple Bnai Israel. Hadassah. Natl. Mizrachi Women. Natl. Assn. for Hist. Prsrvn. **Honors:** Lib. Resrch. Cncl., Best Flyer Awd., 1978. **Pubns.:** Reviews. **Activities:** 9, 12; 16, 24, 36; 50, 66, 90 **Addr.:** 48 Georgia St., Valley Stream, NY 11580.

Levin, Marc A. (Ap. 21, 1955, Baltimore, MD) Libn., Inst. of Gvtl. Std., Univ. of CA, Berkeley, 1979–; Asst. Libn., Docum. Dept., Univ. of HI, Manoa, 1978–79. **Educ.:** Gettysburg Coll., 1973–77, BA (Hist.); Univ. of HI, 1978–79, MLS. **Orgs.:** HI LA: Nsltr. Ed. (1978–79). SLA: San Francisco Bay Reg. Chap. Bltn. ed. (1980–). UC Berkeley Gen. Lib. Syst.: Staff Dev. Com., Non-Gen. Lib. del. **Pubns.:** *A Directory of Special Libraries in Hawaii* (1979); *A Descriptive Bibliography of the Holdings of Hamilton Library Rare Bookroom Concerning Travel, Discovery and Exploration Literature* (1980). **Activities:** 1, 12; 29, 39, 41, 42; 78, 92 **Addr.:** Institute of Governmental Studies Library, 109 Moses Hall, University of California, Berkeley, CA 94720.

Levin, Pauline Gilda (Ja. 16, 1931, Philadelphia, PA) Info. Mgr., US Env. Protection Agency, 1972–; Info. Anal., Franklin Inst., 1967–72; Libn., Free Lib. of Philadelphia, 1963–67. **Educ.:** Temple Univ., 1948–52, BA (Chem.); Drexel Univ., 1952–55, MSLS. **Orgs.:** SLA: Env. Com. (1974). **Activities:** 4; 17, 37, 49-Online; 60, 65, 91 **Addr.:** 1919 Chestnut St., #808, Philadelphia, PA 19103.

Levine, Amy M. (F. 22, 1946, Cambridge, MA) Dir., Info. Srvs., USV Pharm. Corp., 1977–, Mgr., Info. Srvs., 1975–76; Head Libn., Pfizer, Inc., 1974–75, Asst. Libn., 1971–74. **Educ.:** Boston Univ., 1963–65; Univ. of CA, Berkeley, 1965–67, AB (Eng.); Columbia Univ., 1972–75, MS (LS); Certificat d'études françaises, 1963; New York Univ., 1975–, MBA cand. **Orgs.:** Drug Info. Assn.: Finance Com. (1978–); Treas. (1978–); Ch., Audit Com. (1977). SLA: Bd. of Dir., Hudston Valley Chap. (1979–); Treas., Pharm. Div. (1977–79); Ch.-elect, Pharm. Div., (1979–80); Local Rep. and Prog. Planner, (1977–78). Med. LA. ASIS. AAAS. Pharm. Mfrs. Assn.: Sci. Info. Subsect. **Honors:** Beta Phi Mu, 1975. **Activities:** 12; 17; 59, 62, 87 **Addr.:** Department of Information Services, USV Pharmaceutical Corporation, 1 Scarsdale Rd., Tuckahoe, NY 10707.

Levine, Beryl (D. 10, 1931, Milwaukee, WI) Coord., Lib. Tech. Prog., Grossmont Coll., 1978–; Ref. Libn., and Instr., San Diego State Univ., 1976–79; Hum. Div. Libn., MI State Univ., 1959–64; Ref. Libn., Northwest. Univ. Lib., 1958–59, Libn., Carter Hosp., 1957; Branch Asst., Brooklyn Pub. Lib., 1955–57. **Educ.:** Univ. of WI, 1949–53, BA (Comp. Lit.); Columbia Univ., 1953–55, MS (LS). **Orgs.:** ALA. SLA: San Diego Chap. CA LA. **Activities:** 1, 14-Acad. Prog. for Lib. Tech. Assts.; 26, 31, 39 **Addr.:** Library Technology Program, Grossmont College, 8800 Grossmont College Dr., El Cajon, CA 92020.

Levine, David (Jy. 5, 1952, Detroit, MI) Asst. state Archvst., OH Hist. Socty., 1980–; Arch., Martin Luther King, Jr., Ctr. for Soc. Change, 1978–79; Regional Archvst., TX State Arch., 1976–77. **Educ.:** Oakland Univ., 1970–73, BA (Hist.); Wayne State Univ., 1974–75, MA (Hist.); GA State Univ., 1978–79 (Hist.). **Orgs.:** SAA: Com. on State and Lcl. Recs. (1975–77); Com. on Finding Aids (1978). Socty. GA Archvsts.: Anl. Wkshp. Com. (1978), Treas. (1979–80). Socty. of SW Archvsts.: Com. on Prof. Dev. (1977). Org. of Amer. Histns. **Honors:** Phi Alpha Theta. **Pubns.:** "Regional Depositories: Complications of Compromise," *GA Arch.* (Fall 1979); "Management and Preservation of Local Public Records," *Amer. Arch.* (Ap. 1977). **Activities:** 2; 17, 38 **Addr.:** Ohio Historical Society, I-71 and 17th Ave., Columbus, OH 43211.

Levine, Emil H. (N. 21, 1937, Oklahoma City, OK) Supervisory Comp. Spec., Drug Enforcement Admin., 1973–; Supervisory Intelligence Resrch. Spec., Ofc. of Natl. Narcotics Intelligence, 1972–73; Supervisory Intelligence Resrch. Spec., Ofc. of Nvl. Intelligence, 1966–72. **Educ.:** Univ. of OK, 1955–60,

Special Subjects/Services: 50. Adult educ.; 51. Advert./Mktg.; 52. Aerosp.; 53. Agric.; 54. Area std.; 55. Arts/Hum.; 56. Autom.; 57. Bibl./Prtg.; 58. Bio. sci.; 59. Bus./Fin.; 60. Chem.; 61. Copyrt.; 62. Documtn.; 63. Educ.; 64. Engin.; 65. Env.; 66. Eth. grps.; 67. Film; 68. Food/Nutr.; 69. Geneal.; 70. Geo.; 71. Geol.; 72. Handcpd.; 73. Hist.; 74. Int. frdm.; 75. Info. sci.; 76. Insr.; 77. Law; 78. Legis.; 79. Math./Comp. sci.; 80. Med.; 81. Metals; 82. Nat. resrcs.; 83. Newsp.; 84. Nuc. sci.; 85. Oral hist.; 86. Petr./Energy; 87. Pharm.; 88. Phys./Astr./Math.; 89. Readg.; 90. Relig.; 91. Sci./Tech.; 92. Soc. sci.; 93. Telecom.; 94. Transp.; 95. (other).

BA (Jnlsm.); Amer. Univ., 1964–71, MPA (Info. Sci.). **Orgs.:** ASIS: Law and Info. Tech. (Ch., 1979); SIG Cnclr. (1980–81); SIG Autom. Lang. Prcs. (Ch., 1980). Can. Assn. Info. Sci. Natl. Micro. Assn. **Honors:** Drug Enforcement Admin., Sustained Superior Performance, 1974; Drug Enforcement Admin., Excep. Performance, 1977. **Pubns.:** *Information Science: Law Enforcement Applications* (1979); jt. auth., "Use of Microfilm in Federal Narcotics Intelligence and Law Enforcement," *Jnl. of Micro.* (Mr. 1976); "Effect of Instantaneous Retrieval on Indexing Criteria," *Jnl. of the Amer. Socty. for Info. Sci.* (My.–Je. 1974); "National Security Council Directive Establishes Data Index System," *JASIS* (Ja.–F. 1973); "MIS Spinoff of a Conventional STINFO System," *JASIS* (Jl.–Ag. 1973); various sps., Other articles. **Activities:** 4, 12; 24, 33, 38; 75 **Addr.:** 8815 Churchfield Ln., Laurel, MD 20708.

Levine, Marilyn M. (Ap. 11, 1933, Brooklyn, NY) Consult., LIBSCI Consult. Grp., 1979–; Resrch. Libn., Milwaukee Urban Observatory, 1970–73. **Educ.:** Queens Coll. City of New York, 1950–54, BS (Math); Univ. of WI (Milwaukee), 1968–72, MS (LS), 1975–, PhD in progress, (Educ.). **Orgs.:** ASIS: WI Chap., Pres. (1974); SIG Fndn. Info. Sci. (Ch., 1980). Amer. Interprof. Inst. **Pubns.:** "The Circulation/Acquisition Ratio: An Input-Output Measure for Libraries," *Info. Prcs. and Mgt.* (V. 16 1980); "The Informative Act and Its Aftermath: Toward A Predictive Science of Information," *Jnl. Amer. Socty. Info. Sci.* (Mr. 1977). **Activities:** 12; 24, 41; 75, 92 **Addr.:** 4210 N. Farwell, Shorewood, WI 53211.

Levine, Marion Holena (F. 21, 1939, New York, NY) Head, Ref. Dept., Harvard Univ. Francis A. Countway Lib. of Med., 1979–, Coord., Docum. Delivery, Ext., 1976–79, Ref. Libn., 1972–76, Vision Info. Ctr., Info. Spec., 1969–70; Head, Bibl. Sect., Parkinson Info. Ctr., Columbia Univ. Med. Lib., 1965–67, Ref. Libn. and Trainee in Ref., 1962–65. **Educ.:** Hunter Coll., 1956–61, BA (Zlgy.); Columbia Univ., 1961–64, MLS. **Orgs.:** Med. LA: MLA Bltn. Ed. Com. (1979–); Secy./Treas. (1980–). N. Atl. Hlth. Sci. Lib.: Prog. Plng. Com. (1977). MA Hlth. Sci. Libn.: Prog. Plng. Com. (1978–79). Excerpta Medica: Adv. Bd. (1978–80). **Activities:** 1; 17, 39; 80 **Addr.:** Francis A. Countway Library of Medicine, 10 Shattuck St., Boston, MA 02115.

Levis, Joel (S. 13, 1944, Toronto, ON) Chief Libn., Wapiti Reg. Lib. (SK), 1980–; Reg. Libn., Ctrl. Reg. Libs. (NF), 1972–80; Docum. Libn., Meml. Univ., 1970–72; Ref. Libn., Atomic Energy of Can. Ltd., 1969–70. **Educ.:** Univ. of Toronto, 1963–67, BA (Hist., Anthro.); SUNY Albany, 1967–69, MLS. **Orgs.:** Can. LA. ALA. Atl. Prov. LA. SK LA. Toastmasters Intl. Mary March Reg. Mus. **Pubns.:** "Books-by-Mail in Newfoundland's Central Region," *APLA Bltn.* (Spr. 1976); "Canadian Publications in the English Language: CBI vs *Canadiana*," *Lib. Resrcs. and Tech. Srvs.* (Sum. 1971); Can. contrib., *Magazines for Libraries* (1979); Book Rev. Ed., *RQ* (1969–1974). **Activities:** 9, 14-Reg. Libs.; 17, 27, 36; 50, 74, 83 **Addr.:** Wapiti Regional Library, 145-12th St. E., Prince Albert, SK S6B 1B7 Canada.

Levitan, Karen B. (Mr. 6, 1942, Newark, NJ) Dir., Resrch., Procurement Info. Mgt. Srv., Intl. Data Corp., 1981–; Dir. Info. Mgt. and Srvs., Ofc. of Admin., Exec. Ofc. of the Pres., 1979–81; Tech. Staff Proj. Leader, Mitre Corp., 1977–79; Freelnc. Consult., 1976–77; Resrch. Asst., Univ. of MD, 1970–75. **Educ.:** Cornell Univ., 1960–64, BA (Hist.), 1964–65, MEd (Sec. Educ.); Univ. of MD, 1970–73, MLS, 1973–76, PhD (Info. Sci.); 1968, Cert. de Francaise. **Orgs.:** ASIS: Pub.–Pvt. Interface (Ch., 1979–1982); Pub. Affairs Com. (1979–81); Ad Hoc Com. for Future of Info. Sci. (1978–79). Assn. for Info. Mgrs. AAAS. Socty. for Soc. Std. of Sci. Policy Stds. Org. Socty. for Gen. Systs. Resrch. **Honors:** Pi Lambda Theta, 1965; Ford Fndn., Flwshp., 1964–65. **Pubns.:** "The Collapse of Traditional Distinctions," *Bltn. of ASIS* (Ap. 1981); "The New Information Hybrid," *Bltn. of ASIS* (Ap. 1981); Jt. auth., *A Process for Planning School Media Centers* (1972); *Chemical Information Resources Directory* (1979–); *A Holistic Approach for Integrating Information Science Research: A Formative Evaluation* (1979); "Opportunities and Risks in the Information Business: The Next Ten Years," *Bltn. of ASIS* (F. 1979); various articles. **Activities:** 4, 12; 17, 24, 34; 56, 75, 92 **Addr.:** 212 Dale Dr., Silver Spring, MD 20910.

Levstik, Frank R. (Mr. 3, 1943, Chicago, IL) State Archvst., OH Hist. Socty., 1976–, Asst. State Archvst., 1974–76, Arch. Spec., 1970–74, Arch. Prcs., 1969–70. **Educ.:** Pikeville Coll., 1963–66, BA (Hist.); VA Polytech. Inst., 1966–68, MA (Hist.); Oh. State Univ., 1981, PhD. (Hist.). **Orgs.:** SAA. Socty. of OH Archvsts.: Secy. Treas (1978–). Assn. of Recs. Mgrs. and Admins. Natl. Assn. of State Archvsts. and Recs. Admins. Soc. Welfare Hist. Grp. **Pubns.:** Jt. auth., *Union Bibliography of Ohio Printed State Documents 1803–1970* (1974); "Life among the Lowly," *OH Hist.* (1979); "The Network System and Administration of Local Government Records," *GA Arch.* (1980); "Record-Keeping," *The Ofc.* (Ap. 1979); "Researching Black Genealogy through Ohio Public Records," *Jnl. of Geneal.* (1979); Other articles. **Activities:** 2, 14-Hist. Socty.; 17, 38, 41; 55, 62, 69 **Addr.:** Ohio Historical Society, 1982 Velma Ave., Columbus, OH 43211.

Levy, Charlotte L. (Ag. 31, 1944, Cincinatti, OH) Law Libn. & Assoc. Prof. of Law, Brooklyn Law Sch., 1979– Bibl. Srv. Ed., Fred B. Rothman & Inc., 1977–79; Law Libn., Assoc. Prof. of Law, Pace Univ., 1975–77; Law Libn., Salmon P. Chase Coll. Of Law, 1971–75. **Educ.:** Univ. of KY, 1963–66, BA (Frgn. Lang.); Columbia Univ., 1968–69, MSLS; Salmon P. Chase Coll. of Law, 1971–75, JD. **Orgs.:** AALL: Mem. Com. (Ch., 1980–81); Autom. and Sci. Dev. Com. (1973–74). Natl. Ad Hoc Com. Law Lib. Netwks.: (1976–77). **Honors:** Salmon P. Chase Coll. of Law, Amer. Jurisprudence Bk. Awd. in Domestic Rel., 1974, Amer. Jurisprudence Bk. Awd. in Trusts, 1975. **Pubns.:** *The Human Body and the Law: Legal and Ethical Considerations in Human Experimentation.* (1975); "Starting a Law School Library," *Law Lib. Jnl.* (1977); "In Re Law Library Miscellany," *Law Lib. Jnl.* (1974); "An Experimental Concordance Program," *Comp. and the Hum.* (1970); Other articles in law. **Activities:** 1; 15, 17, 24; 77, 78, 92 **Addr.:** Brooklyn Law School Library, 250 Joralemon St., Brooklyn, NY 11201.

Levy, Judith B. (S. 12, 1926, Cleveland, OH) Dir., Hlth. Sci. Info. Srv., Univ. CA, Berkeley, 1980–; Lib. Dir., Hlth. Welfare Lib., San Mateo Cnty., 1979–80; Libn., Crocker Natl. Bank Lib., 1978–79; Per. Libn., San Mateo Cnty. 1976–78. **Educ.:** Case West. Reserve Univ., 1944–48, BS (Sci.); Univ. CA, Berkeley, 1973–74, MLS; Tchg. Cert., 1973–74. **Orgs.:** ALA. CA LA. Med. LA: North. CA Med. Lib. Grp. North. CA Jewish LA: Pres.; Secy. **Pubns.:** Pubn. in bacteriology. **Activities:** 1; 17, 31, 39; 58, 80 **Addr.:** Health Sciences Information Service, Univ. of California, Berkeley, T-7 Rm 226, Berkeley, CA 94720.

Levy, Suzanne Sheldon (Jl. 2, 1947, Chicago, IL) VA Rm. Libn., Fairfax Cnty. Pub. Lib., 1981–; Catlgr., NC Col., Univ. of NC, 1975–81; Asst. Docum. Libn., NC Div. of State Lib., 1973–75; Sr. Ref. Libn., Schomburg Ctr. for Resrch. in Black Culture, NY Pub. Lib., 1972–73, Libn., Bloomingdale Reg. Branch, 1971–72. **Educ.:** MI State Univ., 1965–69, BA (Hist.); Pratt Inst., 1970–71, MLS. **Orgs.:** ALA. NC LA: Vice-Ch., Docum. Sect. (1977–78); Ch. (1978–79); Exec. Bd. (1978–79); Intl. Frdm. Com. (1980–81). VA LA. Leag. of Women Voters of Durham, NC. Gamma Phi Beta. **Honors:** Beta Phi Mu. **Pubns.:** Contrib., *Municipal government documents reference sources: publications and collections* (1978); North Carolina Books section, *NC Libs.* (Spr. 1978–81); New North Carolina books section, *Tar Heel Libs.* (My./Je. 1979–81). **Activities:** 1, 13; 20, 29, 45; 66, 69, 70 **Addr.:** Virginia Room, Fairfax County Public Library, 3915 Chain Bridge Rd., Fairfax, VA 22030.

Lewallen, David Daniel (Wessington Springs, SD) Branch Mgr., Bus. and Gvt. Lib., Alameda Cnty., 1979–; Asst. Libn. for Ref. & Pub. Srv., Dewey Lib., MIT Libs., 1974–79. **Educ.:** IN Univ., 1965–69, AB (Eng. Lit.); Univ. of CA, Los Angeles, 1969–70, (Eng. Lit.); Simmons Coll., 1972–74, MLS. **Orgs.:** ALA: Local Arrange. 1981 Anl. Conf.; LAMA; ACRL. CA LA. SLA: Bay Area Chap., Hospitality Com. (1980–81); Prog. Com. (1981–82); Pubcty. Com., Ch. (1981–82). **Honors:** Phi Beta Kappa. **Addr.:** Business and Government Library, 2201 Broadway, Oakland, CA 94612.

Lewicky, George I. (My. 14, 1933) Dir. of Indexing Srvs., H. W. Wilson Co., 1974–, Dir. of Persnl., 1967–74, Asst. to the Dir. of Indexing Srvs., 1965–67; Asst. Proj. Dir., Lib. USA, New York World's Fair, 1963–65; Ref. Libn., New York Pub. Lib. Econ. Div., 1961–63. **Educ.:** St. John's Univ., 1952–55, BA (Econ.); Pratt Inst., 1960–61, MLS; New York Univ., 1963–65, MBA (Mgt.). **Orgs.:** Amer. Socty. of Indxrs.: Bd. of Dir. (1976–78); VP (1979–80); Pres. (1980–81). ASIS. ALA. SLA: New York Conf. Pubcty. (1978). Amer. Mgt. Assn. **Pubns.:** Reviews. **Activities:** 6; 20, 30, 37, 39, 42, 44; 59, 75 **Addr.:** The H. W. Wilson Co., 950 University Ave., Bronx, NY

Lewin, Martin (Jl. 24, 1925, Kassel, Germany) Asst. Deputy Dir., Buffalo & Erie Cnty. Pub. Lib., 1968–, Head, Book Care Dept., 1964–68, Head, E. Delavan Branch, 1961–64, Head, N. Jefferson Branch, 1958–61. **Educ.:** Syracuse Univ., 1946–50, AB, 1950–51, MS (LS). **Orgs.:** ALA. NY LA: Ch., Schol. Com.; Persnl. Admin. Com. Lib. PR Cncl.: Ch., Packet Com. (1974). PR Assn. of West. NY. Niagara Frontier Bus. Communicators. Scriptores. Buffalo Cncl. on World Affairs. **Honors:** John Cotton Dana Awds., 1972, 1975, 1977; "Pica" Awds., 1978, 1979, 1977, 1980. **Pubns.:** "Buffalo Slaughter," *Amer. Libs.* (Mr. 1977); Ed., Buffalo & Eric Cnty. Pub. Lib. *Bltn.* (1969–). **Activities:** 9; 17, 36 **Addr.:** 202 Abbington Ave., Kenmore, NY 14223.

Lewis, Aileen M. (Ft. McMurray, AB) Chief Libn., Dartmouth Reg. Lib., 1978–; Chief Libn., Halifax Cnty. Reg. Lib., 1973–78, Asst. Libn., 1971–73; Bkmobile. Libn., Cape Breton Reg. Lib., 1966–67. **Educ.:** Mt. Allison Univ., 1961–64, BA (Hist.); McGill Univ., 1964–65, BLS. **Orgs.:** Can LA: Ed. Bd., Can. Lib. Jnl. (1974–); Conv. (1976–78). Jt. Reg. Lib. Bd.: Dir. (1976). Jt. Reg. Assn. Bd.: Secy. (1979–81). Atl. Prov. LA: Bibl. Ctr. Com. (1976–80). **Activities:** 9; 17, 35, 47; 50, 67 **Addr.:** Dartmouth Regional Library, 100 Wyse Rd., Dartmouth, NS B3A 1M1 Canada.

Lewis, Alan D. (Mr. 25, 1935, Ottumwa, IA) Asst. Dir., and Supvsr. of Lib. Dev., Ofc. of Pub. Libs. and Interlibrary Coop., MN Dept. of Educ., 1975–; Consult., 1971–75; Consult., Admin., State Lib. Cmsn. of IA, 1967–71; Dir., Burlington (IA) Pub. Lib., 1969–70. **Educ.:** Parsons Coll., 1963, BA (Educ.); Univ. of IA, 1969, MA (LS). **Orgs.:** ALA: LAMA; ASCLA, Various coms. MN LA. Bald Eagle Sportsmans Assn. Boy Scouts of Amer. **Honors:** Iowa Jaycees, Outstan. IA Jaycee, 1965. Ottumwa Jaycees, Outstan. Ottumwa Jaycees, 1964, 65. **Activities:** 9, 13; 17, 24, 34 **Addr.:** Office of Public Libraries and Interlibrary Cooperation, 301 Hanover Bldg., 480 Cedar St., St. Paul, MN 55101.

Lewis, Alfred J. (Ja. 27, 1935, Philadelphia, PA) Asst. Law Libn., Univ. of CA, Davis, 1969–; Chief, Readers' Srvs., Law Lib., Univ. of MI, 1965–69. **Educ.:** Temple Univ., 1959–62, BA, 1963–65, JD; Univ. of MI, 1966–68, MLS. **Orgs.:** AALL: Stats. Com. (Ch., 1969–79). CA Hist. Socty. **Pubns.:** *Using Law Books* (1976); "1978 Statistical Survey of Law School Libraries and Librarians," *Law Lib. Jnl.* (Sp. 1979). **Activities:** 1, 12; 17; 77 **Addr.:** Law Library, University of California, Davis, CA 95616.

Lewis, Annie M. Alston (N. 26, 1917, Henning, TN) Libn., Harding Grad. Sch. of Relig., 1962–; Libn., Harding Coll., 1947–62, Asst. Prof. of Eng., 1944–47; Tchr./Libn., W. Memphis HS, 1941–44; Tchr./Libn., Gibson HS, 1939–41. **Educ.:** David Lipscomb Coll., 1935–37, Harding Coll., 1937–39, BA (Eng.); George Peabody Coll., 1943, BS (LS); Univ. of Chicago, 1952, AM (LS); Harding Grad. Sch. of Relig., 1967, MA (Relig.). **Orgs.:** TN LA: Coll. and Univ. Sect., Ch. (1966–67), Secy. (1969). TN Theo. LA: Ch. (1978–79). Memphis Libns. Com.: Ch. (1971–72). ATLA. **Honors:** Harding Coll., Disting. Alum., 1968; Harding Coll., Disting. Srv. Awd., 1979. Twentieth Century Christ., Christ. Lit. Awd., 1975. **Activities:** 1; 15, 39; 90 **Addr.:** 1132 S. Perkins, Memphis, TN 38117.

Lewis, Catherine Heniford (F. 24, 1924, Richmond, VA) Cnty. Libn., Horry Cnty. Meml. Lib., 1960–; Libn., Coastal Carolina Jr. Coll., 1958–60; Reviewer, Biblgphr., US Info. Agency, 1951–55; Asst. Libn., Sch. of Adv. Intl. Std., 1950–51. **Educ.:** Coker Coll., 1940–43, AB (Eng., Latin); Univ. of NC, 1944–45, MA (Eng.), 1946–48, BS (LS). **Orgs.:** SC LA: Pub. Lib. Stan. Com. (Ch., 1964–80). Assn. Pub. Lib. Admin. SC: Pres. (1980). WHCLIST: SC Prof. Del. (1980–). Waccamaw Econ. Opportunity Cncl.: Ch. (1969–73, 1978–79). Horry Cnty. Musm. Bd. Trustees: Ch. (1978–79). Horry Cnty. Hist. Socty.: Pres. (1977–79). **Honors:** Coastal Educ. Fndn., Merit. Srv., 1967; Conway Field & Herald, Woman of the Yr. 1973; Horry Cnty. Hist. Socty., E.E. Richardson Awd. for Disting. Srv., 1981. **Activities:** 9; 17 **Addr.:** 1409 8th Ave., Conway, SC 29526.

Lewis, Dale Elizabeth (O. 5, 1943, Providence, RI) Ref. Libn., Bell Telephone Lab., 1976–; Tech. Info. Spec., Engelhard Min. and Chem. Corp., 1974–76. **Educ.:** Univ. of RI, 1961–65, BA (Chem.), 1970–74, MLS. **Orgs.:** ASIS: SIG-CRS Nsltr. (Ed. 1980–81); Ctrl. NJ chpt. nsltr. (Ed. 1981–82). SLA: NJ Chap., 2nd VP, Prog. (1980–81). Leag. of Women Voters. Amer. Chem. Socty. **Activities:** 12; 39; 91, 93 **Addr.:** Room 6E-201, Bell Telephone Laboratories, Holmdel, NJ 07733.

Lewis, G. Gordon, Jr. (Ja. 1, 1945, Youngstown, OH) Dir., Farmington Cmnty. Lib., 1974–; Branch Head, Free Lib. of Philadelphia, 1969–74, Libn., Pub. Lib. of Youngstown & Mahoning Cnty., 1967–69. **Educ.:** Capital Univ., 1963–66, BA; Univ. of Pittsburgh, 1967–69, MLS; Temple Univ., 1972–74, MEduc.; Univ. of MI, 1980, doctoral std. **Orgs.:** ALA: Lib. Admin. Div., Arch. for Pub. Libs. Com. (1978–80); PR Srvs. to Libs. Com. (1972–76; Ch., 1975–76). ASIS. MI LA: Leg. Com. (1976–78); Conf. Exhibits Co.-Ch. (1980). AECT. Farmington Exch. Club. Econ. Club of Detroit. **Honors:** Beta Phi Mu. Delta Sigma Rho-Tau Kappa Alpha. **Activities:** 9; 17, 19, 24 **Addr.:** Farmington Community Library, 32737 W. 12 Mile Rd., Farmington Hills, MI 48018.

Lewis, George R. (Jl. 15, 1929, Eupora, MS) Dir. of Libs., MS State Univ., 1963–; Head Libn., KY South. Coll., 1962–63; Head, Circ. Dept., Lib., Auburn Univ., 1958–62; Pub. Srvs. Libn./Catlgr., Baylor Univ., 1956–58. **Educ.:** MS Coll., 1950–52, BA (Eng.); LA State Univ., 1954–56, MSLS; FL State Univ., 1972–75, PhD (LS). **Orgs.:** ALA: MS Chap. Cnclr.; Rcrt. Com.; MS Mem. Ch. MS LA: Treas. (1975). MS Lib. Comsn.: Bd. of Comsns. Univ. Lib. Dirs. Cncl.: Pres. (1978–). Rotary Intl. **Honors:** Phi Kappa Phi; MS LA, Peggy May Awd. for Outstan. Libnshp., 1978. **Pubns.:** "Introducing and Administering On-line Information Retrieval Services," *Agr. Libs. Info. Notes* (1977); contrib. ed. *ALA Yrbk.* **Activities:** 1; 17, 19, 25 **Addr.:** P. O. Drawer 5408, Mississippi State, MS 39762.

Lewis, Linda Kathryn (F. 21, 1947, Amarillo, TX) Ref. Libn., Univ. of NM, 1969–. **Educ.:** Univ. of OK, 1965–68, BA (Hist.), 1968–69, MLS. **Orgs.:** ALA. NM LA: Legis. and Int. Frdm. Com. (Ch., 1979–81); Fed. Rel. Coord. (1978–81). Amnesty Intl. Beta Sigma Phi: Epsilon Eta Chapter. **Honors:** Beta Phi Mu, 1969. **Pubns.:** "Women in Literature: A Selected Bibliography," *Bltn. of Bibl.* (V. 35, 1978). **Activities:** 1; 15, 33, 39; 55, 95-Women's Std. **Addr.:** University of New Mexico General Library, Albuquerque, NM 87131.

Lewis, Margaret S. (S. 27, 1925, Indianapolis, IN) Head Libn., SUNY, State Coll. of Optometry, 1971–. **Educ.:** Oberlin Coll., 1943–47, BA (Hist.); St. John's Univ., 1969–70, MLS; Inst.

PROFESSIONAL ACTIVITIES: Institutions: 1. Acad. lib.; 2. Arch.; 3. Assn.; 4. Fed./Gvt. lib.; 5. Inst. lib.; 6. Mfr./Suppl.; 7. Milit. lib.; 8. Musm.; 9. Pub. lib.; 10. Sch. lib.; 11. Sch. of lib. sci.; 12. Spec. lib.; 13. State lib.; 14. (other). **Functions/Activities:** 15. Acq./Col. dev.; 16. Adult srvs.; 17. Admin.; 18. Apprais.; 19. Archit./Bldgs.; 20. Cat./Class.; 21. Chld. srvs.; 22. Circ.; 23. Cons./Pres.; 24. Consult.; 25. Cont. ed.; 26. Educ. lib. sci.; 27. Ext. srvs.; 28. Fund/Grants; 29. Gvt. pubs.; 30. Indx./Abs.; 31. Instr. lib. use; 32. Media srvs.; 33. Micro.; 34. Netwks./Coop.; 35. Persnl.; 36. PR; 37. Publshg.; 38. Recs. mgt.; 39. Ref. srvs.; 40. Repro.; 41. Resrch.; 42. Review.; 43. Secur.; 44. Serials; 45. Spec. col.; 46. Tech. srvs.; 47. Trustees/Bds.; 48. YA srvs.; 49. (other).

on Mgt. of Libs. Cert., 1978. **Orgs.:** SUNY, Cncl. of Head Libns.: Exec. Com. (1978–80). Assn. of Vision Sci. Libns.: Ch. (1976–77). ALA. NY Reg. Med. LA. Other orgs. Amer. Acad. of Optometry. **Pubns.:** "Report from the Association of Vision Science Librarians," *Jnl. of Optometric Educ.* (Sum. 1978). **Activities:** 1; 15, 17, 22; 58, 88, 95-Optometry. **Addr.:** 100 East 24th St., New York, NY 10010.

Lewis, Merwin (Ap. 27, 1945, Cadillac, MI) Libn.-in-Charge, Msc. Lib., Univ. of West. ON, 1977–, Msc. Ref. Libn., 1971–77. **Educ.:** Kalamazoo Coll., 1963–67, BA (Msc.); 1968–71, MM (Msc. composition) MLS. **Orgs.:** Can. Assn. of Msc. Libs.: Ed. *CAML Nsltr.* (1974–). **Pubns.:** "The orientation of freshmen to an academic music library," *CAML Nsltr.* (N. 1973); "Notes on Canadian notes," *CAML Nsltr.* (N. 1979). **Activities:** 1; 17, 39, 45; 95-Music. **Addr.:** Music Library, The University of Western Ontario, London, ON N6A 2K7 Canada.

Lewis, Ollie H. (Je. 13, 1911, Monroe, LA) Lib. Trustee, Ouachita Parish Pub. Lib., 1977; Jr. HS Libn., Ouachita Parish Schs., 1960–76; HS Tchr., Libn., 1947–60. **Educ.:** South. & Grambling Univs., 1947, BS (Elem. Ed.); LA St. Univ., 1954–57, MS (LS); N.E. LA Univ., 1966–72. **Orgs.:** LA LA. Lib. Dept. of LA Educ. Assn.: Pres. (1964–66). ALA: ALTA, Com. on Eval. (1978–80). Nat. Assn. of Univ. Women, Monroe Branch, Pres. (1976–78). Ouachita Educ. Assn., Pres. (1968–70). **Honors:** NAACP, Woman of the Year, 1978. **Activities:** 9; 47 **Addr.:** 2025 Adams St., Monroe, LA 71201.

Lewis, Ralph W. (Ag. 31, 1929, Salt Lake City, UT) Chief, Lib. Branch, NASA Ames Resrch. Ctr., 1969–; Lib. Dir., Environ. Sci. Srv. Admin. Boulder Lab. Lib., 1966–69; Ref. Lib., Martin Co. (Denver, CO), 1965–66, Engin. Lit. Resrch. and Indxr., 1962–63. **Educ.:** Univ. of UT, 1954–57, BA (Sec. Educ.); Univ. of Denver, 1962–63, MA (LS); Golden Gate Univ., 1977–81, MBA. **Orgs.:** SLA: San Andreas Chap., Netwking. Com. (1980–81), Consult. Com. (1980–81). Coop. Inf. Netwk.: Bd. Dir. (1973–80). NASA Lib. Netwk.: Jnl. Com. (1976–79); Multi-Part Pubn. Com. (1971–72). ASIS: San Francisco Chap. (Ch., 1971). Untd. Way of Santa Clara (CA) Cnty.: Loaned Exec. (1976); Volun. Exec. (1977). **Pubns.:** "Miss Fibblesworth, Doctors, Bedpans and Such," *Spec. Lib.* (N. 1969); "User Reaction to Microfiche," *Coll. and Resrch. Lib.* (Jl. 1970); many speeches. **Activities:** 4; 17; 52, 58, 91 **Addr.:** NASA Ames Research Center, Library N 202-3, Moffett Field, CA 94035.

Lewis, Robert French (N. 26, 1918, Broken Arrow, OK) Biomed. Libn., Univ. of CA, San Diego, 1966–; Asst. Biomed. Libn., Univ. of CA, Los Angeles, 1961–65, Head, Pub. Srvs., 1950–60; Catlgr., Univ. of South. CA, 1949–50. **Educ.:** Univ. of OK, 1936–40, BA (Sci.); Univ. of South. CA, 1948–49, MSLS. **Orgs.:** Med. LA: Bd. of Dir. (1968–71). SLA: Chap. Pres. (1971–72). CA LA. ALA. **Activities:** 1, 12 **Addr.:** Biomedical Library, University of California, San Diego, La Jolla, CA 92093.

Lewis, Ronald Alan (S. 5, 1931, Cleveland, OH) Univ. Libn., Patrick Power Lib., St. Mary's Univ., 1976–; Head, Cat. Dept., SUNY, Binghamton, 1974–76; Libn. for Tech. Srvs., Colgate Rochester Dvnty. Sch., 1968–74; Asst. Libn. and Catlgr., Bexley Hall Dvnty. Sch. of Kenyon Coll., 1964–68. **Educ.:** London (ON) Coll. of Bible and Missions, 1953, Dipl. (Theo.); Wheaton Coll., 1956, BA (Phil.), 1961, MA (Dvnty.); Kent State Univ., 1970, MLS. **Orgs.:** Halifax LA: Pres. (1978–79). Bibl. Ctr. Com.: Conv. (1977–80). AALI/BNA User Grp. ALA. Other orgs. Senate Lib. Com.: Ch. (1978–79). Community Tape Resrc. Lib. User Grp.: Ch. **Honors:** Beta Phi Mu. **Activities:** 1, 12; 17, 34, 46; 56, 72, 90 **Addr.:** Patrick Power Library, Saint Mary's University, Halifax, NS B3H 3C3 Canada.

Lewis, Rosalyn (F. 24, 1940, Stamford, TX) Libn., Untd. Meth. Publshg. House, 1973–; Instr. in Eng., Hardin-Simmons Univ., 1966–69; Tchr./Libn., Jayton, TX, HS, 1965–66; Tchr., Stamford, TX, HS, 1961–64. **Educ.:** McMurry Coll., 1957–61, BA (Eng.); Univ. of Denver, 1964–65, MA (Libnshp.). **Orgs.:** ALA. SLA: South. Appalachian Chap. (Ch., 1976–77); Career Guid. (ch., 1978–79); Nom. Com. (1977, 1980). ATLA: Persnl. Exch. Com. (Ch., 1977–78); Nom. Com. (1979–82, Ch., 1981–82). Meth. Libns. Flwshp.: VP/Pres.-Elect (1979–81); Pres. (1981–). Other orgs. AAUW: Nashville Branch, 1st VP (1978–1980). Women's Natl. Book Assn.: Const. Rev. (Ch. 1977–79). **Pubns.:** Ed. Dir., *United Methodist Periodical Index* (1973–81). **Activities:** 12; 17; 57, 69, 90 **Addr.:** 201 Eighth Ave., South, Nashville, TN 37202.

Lewis, Shirley C. (My. 16, 1948, Dover, OH) Dir. of Lib. Srv., Providence Hosp., 1978–; Libn., Reg. Meml. Hosp., 1972–74. **Educ.:** OH Univ., 1966–69, BSJ (Jnlsm.); Univ. of HI, 1974–75, MLS. **Orgs.:** Med. LA: Pac. N. W. Grp., Legis. Com. (1980–). WA Med. LA: Legis. Com. (Ch., 1981); Pres. (1980). SLA. WA LA: Exec. Bd.; ILL Interest Grp. (1980–81). **Honors:** Beta Sigma Phi, 1975. **Activities:** 12; 17, 19, 24; 58, 59, 80 **Addr.:** Director of Library Services, Providence Hospital, P.O. Box 1067, Everett, WA 98206.

Lewis, Stanley T. (Ag. 14, 1926, NY, NY) Prof. (LS), Queens Coll., City Univ., 1967–, Head, Art Lib., 1956–67; Head, Dover (NJ) HS Lib., 1955–56; Lectr., Columbia Univ., 1959–64; Instr., Fine and Appld. Arts, OH State Univ., 1951–55. **Educ.:** NY Univ., 1946–49, BA (Fine Art), 1949–51, (Art Hist.); OH State Univ., 1951–55, MA, PhD (Art Hist.). **Orgs.:** ALA: ACRL/Art. Sect.; Subscpn. and Ref. Bks. Com. Amer. Prtg. Hist. Assn.: Educ. Com. (1978–). ARLIS/NA. SLA: NY Pic. Grp. (1963–64); Publshr. Rels. Com. (1974–77). Amer. Socty. of Pic. Profs. AALS. Belgian Amer. Educ. Fndn. Alum. Assn. Grolier Club. Typophiles. **Honors:** Beta Phi Mu. **Pubns.:** Jt. auth., *Reinhold Visuals, Aids for Art Teaching* (1968–81); "Experimentation with an Image Library," *Spec. Libs.* (Ja. 1965); "Classicism in New York Theatre Architecture: 1825–1850," *Thea. Survey; the Amer. Jnl. of Thea. Hist.* (My. 1965); "Periodicals in the Visual Arts," *Lib. Trends* (Ja. 1962). **Activities:** 11; 26; 55, 85, 93 **Addr.:** Graduate School of Library and Information Studies, Queens College, Flushing, NY 11367.

Leysack, Frances M. (Ag. 18, 1923, Albany, NY) Libn., Rosary HS, 1975–. **Educ.:** Siena Coll., 1942–46, BA (Soc. Eng.); CA State Univ., Fullerton, 1973–75, MS (LS). **Orgs.:** CA State Univ., Fullerton, LS Alum. Assn.: Pres. (1975–76). Cath. LA: Natl. Bd., Parish and Cmnty. Libs. Sect.; So. CA Chap., Ch., HS Libs. Sect.; Pres. (1976–79); Bd. (1979–). Phi Kappa Phi. **Activities:** 10; 15, 17, 20, 22, 31, 32, 39 **Addr.:** Rosary High School Library, 1340 N. Acacia, Fullerton, CA 92631.

Leyte-Vidal, Celia A. (O. 21, 1920, Havana, Cuba) Monograph cat., Mazzoni Col., Duke Univ., 1966–. **Educ.:** Inst. de la Habana, Cuba, 1936–38, Bachiller (Art and Sci.); Univ. de la Habana, 1938–44, Bachelor of Hlth. Sci.; Emporia State Univ., 1964–65, MS (Libnshp.). **Orgs.:** SALALM: Vice ch., Ad Hoc Subcom. on the Pubn. of Guides to the Libs. in Latin America (1979–); Ch., Subcom. on Lib. Oper. (1976–1979); Ch., Subcom. on Cuban Bibl. (1979–); Subcom. on Collaboration with the Org. of Amer. States (1976–1977). Durham Cnty. LA. Second Century Club, Emporia State Univ. Emporia State Univ. Alum. Assn. Asociación de Mujeres Profesionales Cubanas en el Exilio. Frnds. of the Lib., Duke Univ. **Pubns.:** Jt. ed., *Reunión de Expertos sobre los Proyectos LILIBU-CATACEN (REPLICA)* (1973); Lista de Trabajos que son Imprescindibles en la Compilación de LILIBU (1973); "Mazzoni's Library," Duke Univ. Lib. *Nsltr.* (F. 1978). **Activities:** 1; 20, 41, 45; 55, 57, 80 **Addr.:** 4168 Deepwood Cir., Durham, NC 27707.

Li, Dorothy In-lan Wang Head, Tech. Srvs. Dept., Oak Park Pub. Lib., 1972–; Catlgr., Chicago Pub. Lib., 1967–68; Ref. Libn., Oak Park Pub. Lib., 1968–70; Libn. U.S. Air Frc., Taipei, 1970–72. **Educ.:** Natl. Taiwan Univ., BA (Law); Rosary Coll., 1966–67, MA (LS), 1981, MBA. **Orgs.:** ALA. Chineae Amer. Libns. Assn. Chicago Lib. Club. Oak Park ZONTA. **Pubns.:** *Guide to Chinese Reference Works* (1972). **Activities:** 9; 17, 20, 46 **Addr.:** Oak Park Public Library, Oak Park, IL 60301.

Li, Hong-Chan (Ja. 9, 1934, Shanghang, Fukien, China) Asst. Libn., School of Soc. Wk., Univ. of CT, 1968–; Ref. Libn., St. Joseph Coll., 1965–67. **Educ.:** Natl. Taiwan Univ., 1953–57, BA (Hist.); Univ. of IL, 1959–63, MS (Acct.); West. MI Univ., 1963–65, MA (LS). **Orgs.:** ALA. SLA: CT Valley Chap., Positive Act. Com. (Ch., 1977–79). Chinese Amer. Libns. Assn.: Bd. (1977–83); Northeast Chap. (Pres., 1979–80). **Pubns.:** *Social Work Education: A Bibliography* (1978). **Activities:** 1, 12; 20, 22, 39; 92 **Addr.:** 51 St. James St., W. Hartford, CT 06119.

Li, Tze-chung Prof., Dir., Cont. Educ. (LS), Rosary Coll., 1973–; Dir., Natl. Ctrl. Lib. (Rep. of China), 1970–73; Assoc. Prof. (LS), Rosary Coll., 1969–70, Asst. Prof. (LS, Pol. Sci.), 1966–69; Asst. Libn., Asst. Prof. (LS), IL State Univ., 1965–66; VP, Atl. Fiscal Corp., 1961–64. **Educ.:** Soochow Univ., 1948, LL.B. Cum Laude; South. Meth. Univ., 1957, MCL (Law); Harvard Univ., 1958, LL.M. (Law); New Sch. for Soc. Resrch., 1963, Ph.D. (Pol. Sci.); Columbia Univ., 1965 (LS). **Orgs.:** ALA: IRRT (Secy. Treas., 1976–78); ACRL, Const. and Bylaws Com. (1976–79). Chinese Amer. Libns. Assn.: Pres. (1973–76); Exec. Dir. (1976–). Intl. Assn. of Orientalist Libns.: Area Rep. (1971–76). Other orgs. Chinese Amer. Educ. Fndn.: Pres. (1968–70). Phi Tau Phi. Assn. for Asian Stds. China Cncl. on Cult. Renaissance. **Pubns.:** *A manual for Basic DIALOG Searching* (1980); *Social Science Reference Sources* (1980); *A List of Doctoral Dissertations by Chinese Students in the United States* (1967); *American Librarianship* (in Chinese) (1972); Various articles in libnshp., law, poli. sci., and land econ. **Activities:** 11; 25, 26; 54, 59, 66, 77 **Addr.:** Rosary College Graduate School of Library Science, 7900 W. Division St., River Forest, IL 60305.

Liang, Diana F. (Je. 10, 19–, Shanghai, China) Univ. Libn., Univ. of S. FL, 1979–, Assoc. Univ. Libn., 1977–79, 1972–77; Asst. Ed., *Chem. Abs.*, 1967–69; Actg. Libn., Fairfield Cnty. Dist. Lib., 1964–67. **Educ.:** Natl. Taiwan Univ., 1956–60, BA (Lit.); George Peabody Coll., 1962–64, MA (LS). **Orgs.:** ALA. FL LA. Hillsborough Cnty. LA. Chinese-Amer. Libns. Assn. **Activities:** 1; 15, 46; 58, 60, 88 **Addr.:** University of South Florida, LIB 125, Tampa, FL 33620.

Liao, Helen Lin (Je. 28, 1937, Chia Yi, Taiwan) Head of Bethany Med. Lib., Bethany Med. Ctr., 1976–. **Educ.:** Natl. Univ. of Taiwan, 1956–60, BA (Law); Emporia State Univ., 1974–75, MA (LS); Univ. of MO, 1968–69, (Educ.). **Orgs.:** SLA: Heart of Amer. Chap., Positive Action Scholar. (Liason, 1977–). Med. LA: Kansas City Chap., Ed. Bltn. (1978–). Kansas City Lib. Netwk.: Bd. Dir. (1977–); Purchasing Com. (1979–). ALA. Formosan Club in Kansas City: Ch. (1970, 1973). Japan-Amer. Socty. in Kansas City: Ed. (1980). Indian Height Country Club. **Honors:** Sigma Sigma Sigma, 1974. **Activities:** 12; 17, 25, 39; 58, 80, 87 **Addr.:** Medical Library, Bethany Medical Center, 51 North 12th St., Kansas City, KS 66102.

Liao, Tien Ren (My. 28, 1916, Kienning, Fukien, China) Sci. Ref. Libn., Sci. Tech. Div., Lib. of Congs., 1968–; Oriental Sci. Spec., 1967–68, Resrch. Anal., Defense Research Div., 1960–67; Sr. Resrch. Anal., Air Info. Div., 1954–60. **Educ.:** Univ. of Nanking, China, 1936–41, BS (Agr. Econ.); Univ. of KY 1947–48, MS (Agr.). Cath. Univ., 1962–67, MSLS. Govt. Banking Inst., China 1944–44 Dipl. **Orgs.:** Assn. for Asian Stds. SLA. Univ. of Nanking Alum. Assn.: Washington, DC (Pres., 1978–79). **Pubns.:** "Energy Resources in China," (Lib. of Conas., Sci. Tracer Bullet. TB 79–2) (1979); "Dryland Agriculture," (TB 78–4) (1978); "Ginseng," (TB 77–10) (1977); "Hydroponics," (TB 76–9) (1976). **Activities:** 1, 4; 15, 39, 46; 68, 75, 91 **Addr.:** 6504 Westland Rd., Bethesda, MD 20034.

Libbey, David Carleton (Ag. 29, 1916, Detroit, ME) Assoc. Prof. (LS), South. CT State Coll., 1964–; Head, Ref., Rutgers Univ., Newark, 1954–63; Chief, Ref., WA State Univ., 1947–51; Cryptographer, US Army Air Frc., 1943–46; Ref. Asst., NY Pub. Lib., 1942–43; Asst. Libn., Washington Coll., 1940–42. **Educ.:** Colby Coll., 1935–39, AB (Hist.); Columbia Univ., 1939–40, BS (LS); Univ. of Chicago, 1946–47, MA (LS); Columbia Univ., 1951–54, MA (Hist.); Rutgers Univ., 1963–64 (LS). **Orgs.:** ALA. Bibl. Socty. of Amer. IFLA: Del. (1972). Com. for a New Eng. Bibl., Inc.: Bd. of Dir. (1979–). Other orgs. **Pubns.:** "Andrew Keogh," *Dict. of Amer. Lib. Bio.* (1978); reviews. **Activities:** 1; 40; 58, 73, 93 **Addr.:** 57 Austin St., New Haven, CT 06515.

Libbey, Miles A. (Mr. 21, 1917, Brooklyn, NY) Info. consult., Self-employed, 1979–; Asst. Prof. (LS), Columbia Univ., 1977–79; Asst. Prof. (LS), Queens Coll., City Univ. of NY, 1974–77; Asst. Prof. (LS), IN Univ., 1968–73; Dir., Info. Plng. Prog., Amer. Inst. of Phys., 1966–68; Sub-Dept. Head., The MITRE Corp., 1962–66; Resrch. Staff, Lockheed Electronics Co. (NJ), 1960–61; Ofcr. (Retired as Commander), U.S. Navy, 1940–60. **Educ.:** U.S. Naval Acad., 1936–40, BS (Naval Sci.), Mass. Inst. of Tech., 1943–45, SM (Naval Sci., Marine Engin.); Rutgers Univ., 1975– (PhD Cand.). **Orgs.:** ASIS: Cncl. (1968–70)/IN Chap. (Ch., 1967); Spec. Interest Grp. on Class. Resrch., 1967; various other coms. SLA. Assoc. Info. Mgrs. Assn. for Computational Ling. CLENE. AAAS. Socty. of Naval Archits. and Marine Engins. **Pubns.:** "Very High Level Programming Languages in the Special Librarian's Future," *Spec. Libs.* (Ag. 1975). "Research Programs in Technical Information Services," *Info. Storage and Retrieval* (Jy. 1973). "Development of a Research Design for a Comprehensive Study of Government Publications," *IL Libs.* (Jn. 1971). "The Use of Second Order Descriptors for Document Retrieval," *Amer. Docum.* (Ja. 1967). **Activities:** 11; 26, 41, 49-Syst. Design; 56, 62, 75 **Addr.:** 88-16 173rd St., Jamaica, Queens, NY 11432.

Libbey, Miriam H. Libn., A. W. Calhoun Med. Lib., Emory Univ., 1966–, Dir., Southeast. Reg. Med. Lib. Prog., Emory Univ., 1969–; Libn., Hlth. Scis. Lib., SUNY, Buffalo, 1963–66; Ref. Libn., Asst. Head, Ref. Div., Natl. Lib. of Med., 1955–63; Ref. Libn., Chief, Srvs. to the Pub., A. W. Calhoun Med. Lib., 1950–55. **Educ.:** Shorter Coll., 1938–42, BA; Emory Univ., 1949–50 MA (Libnshp.); Med. LA, Cert. **Orgs.:** Med. LA: *Bltn of the Med. LA* Consult. Ed. (1978–80); Nom. Com. (1980–81); Med. Lib. Educ. Grp. (Ch., 1975–76); South. Reg. Grp. (Conv. Ch., 1974); Med. Sch. Grp. (Ch., 1965–66). SLA: Adv. Cncl. (1971–73); S. Sch. Grp. (Ch., 1965–66). SLA: Adv. Cncl. (1971–73); S. Atl. Chap., Mem. Ch. (1970–71), Pres.-Elect (1971–72), Pres. (1972–73). ASIS. GA Hlth. Sci. LA. **Activities:** 17; 58, 80 **Addr.:** A. W. Calhoun Medical Library, Emory University, Atlanta, GA 30322.

LiBretto, Ellen V. (F. 7, 1947, New York, NY) YA Consult., Queens Borough Pub. Lib., 1978–; YA Spec., New York Pub. Lib., 1968–78. **Educ.:** Queens Coll., 1964–68, BA (Anthro.), 1968–70, MLS. **Orgs.:** ALA: YASD, High Interest Low Litcy. Eval. (Ch., 1976–80). NY LA. **Pubns.:** *High-Low Handbook* (1981); "Creative Programming for Young Adults," *Bookmark* (Win. 1978); "Polanski Inspires Singapore Teens," *Film Lib. Qtly.* (V. 8, 1975). **Activities:** 9; 48; 89 **Addr.:** 29-29 167th St., Flushing, NY 11358.

LiBrizzi, Rose Marie M. (Ap. 15, 1940, Newark, NJ) Supvsr. Chld. Srv., Jersey City Pub. Lib., 1973–; Dir., Matawan Jt. Free Pub. Lib., 1968–70; Adj. Fac., Kean Coll., 1968–72; Head Chld. Srv., Belleville Pub. Lib., 1966–68; Asst. Dir., Kearny Pub. Lib., 1968. **Educ.:** Bloomfield Coll., 1963–65, BA (Magna Cum Laude) (Hist.); Rutgers Univ., 1965–67, MLS; Tchg. Cert. and Libn. Cert. **Orgs.:** NJ LA: Admin. Sect., VP (1976), Pres. (1977); Persnl. Admn. Com. (1976–79); CLENE Rep. (1980); Nom. Com. (Ch., 1976–78); Exec. Bd. Corres. Secy. (1981–82); various other ofcs. AAUW: Livingston Chap., VP (1978–79); Treas. (1979–80). Rutgers Univ. LS Alum. Assn.: Pres. (1977). **Pubns.:** "Is Anybody There? Does Anybody Care?" *NJ Lib.* (D. 1980).

Special Subjects/Services: 50. Adult educ.; 51. Advert./Mktg.; 52. Aerosp.; 53. Agric.; 54. Area std.; 55. Arts/Hum.; 56. Autom.; 57. Bibl./Prtg.; 58. Bio. sci.; 59. Bus./Fin.; 60. Chem.; 61. Copyrt.; 62. Documtn.; 63. Educ.; 64. Engin.; 65. Env.; 66. Eth. grps.; 67. Film; 68. Food/Nutr.; 69. Geneal.; 70. Geo.; 71. Geol.; 72. Handcpd.; 73. Hist.; 74. Int. frdm.; 75. Info. sci.; 76. Insr.; 77. Law; 78. Legis.; 79. Math./Comp. sci.; 80. Med.; 81. Metals; 82. Nat. resrcs.; 83. Newsp.; 84. Nuc. sci.; 85. Oral hist.; 86. Petr./Energy; 87. Pharm.; 88. Phys./Astr./Math.; 89. Readg.; 90. Relig.; 91. Sci./Tech.; 92. Soc. sci.; 93. Telecom.; 94. Transp.; 95. (other).

Activities: 9; 21, 31, 42; 72 **Addr.:** 5 Squier Ct., Livingston, NJ 07039.

Licata, Salvatore J. (Ag. 31, 1939, Chicago, IL) Dir., Arch. of Homosexuality, San Francisco State Univ., 1978–81; Resrch., Assoc., San Francisco State Univ., 1978; Tchng. Asst., (Hist.), Univ. of South. CA, 1971–77; Tchr., Los Angeles City Schs., 1969–71. **Educ.:** Elmhurst Coll., 1957–61, BS (Bus. Admin.); North. IL Univ., 1961–67, MS (Educ.); CA State Univ., Los Angeles, 1969–71, MA (Hist.); Univ. of South. CA, Los Angeles, 1971–78, Ph.D. (Hist.). **Orgs.:** SAA. Socty. CA Archvsts. Gay Acad. Un.: Bd. Inst. for the Std. of Hum. Resrcs.: Adv. Bd. of Trustees. Org. of Amer. Histns. **Pubns.:** Jt. ed, *Perspectives on Homosexuality in History* (1981); jt.-auth., "The Collection & Analysis of Documents..." *Jnl. of Homosexuality* (Spr. 1979); "The Emerging Gay Presence," *The Advocate,* (Jy.-Ag. 1978); "The Period of Pioneers, 1948–1960", *An Annotated Bibl. of Homosexuality,* ed. Vern Bullough et al; reviews. **Activities:** 1, 2; 23, 28, 45; 85, 92, 95-Minorities. **Addr.:** 190 Bleeker St., #16, New York, NY 10012.

Lichtenberg, Elsa Russell (Ag. 22, 1929, New York, NY) Acq. Libn., Villanova Univ. Law Lib., 1972–; Acq. Libn., Cheyney State Coll., 1971–72; Catlgr., Bryn Mawr Coll., 1968–70; Catlgr., Johns Hopkins Bologna Ctr., 1967–68. **Educ.:** Western Reserve Univ., 1946–50, BA (Psy.); Drexel Univ., 1965–67, MSLS. **Orgs.:** AALL. Grt. Philadelphia Law Lib. Assn.: Pres. (1979–80); VP, Prog. Ch. (1978–79). **Activities:** 1, 4; 15, 29; 77 **Addr.:** Pulling Law Library, Villanova University, Villanova, PA 19085.

Lichtenfels, David Dean (Mr. 15, 1945, Pittsburgh, PA) Libn., St. Petersburg Jr. Coll., 1973–. **Educ.:** Univ. of S. FL, 1963–68, BA (Mgt.), 1971–73, MA (LS). **Orgs.:** FL LA. ALA. FL Assn. Media Educ. AECT. Univ. S. FL Lib. Sci. Alum. Assn.: Bd. of Dir. (1980–81). **Activities:** 1, 10; 15, 32, 39; 56, 59 **Addr.:** St. Petersburg Junior College, 2465 Drew St., Clearwater, FL 33515.

Lichtenwanger, William (F. 28, 1915, Asheville, NC) Archvst., The Sonneck Socty., 1977–; Head, Ref., Msc. Div., Lib. of Congs., 1960–74, Asst. Head, 1940–60; Head, Msc. Lib., Univ. of MI, 1938–40. **Educ.:** Univ. of MI, 1934–37, BM (Msc. Educ.), 1937–40, MM (Msclgy.); IN Univ., Army. Lang. Prog., Dipl. (Turkish). **Orgs.:** Msc. LA: *Notes* (Ed. in Chief, 1960–63); VP (1967–68). Amer. Msclgy. Socty.: Exec. Bd. (1955–56). Socty. for Ethnomsclgy.: Cnclr. (1958–68). **Honors:** Msc. LA, Citn., 1976. **Pubns.:** *Modern Music: An Analytical Index* (1976); *A Survey of Musical Instrument Collections in the U. S. and Canada* (1974); "The Music of "The Star-Spangled Banner" from Ludgate Hill to Capitol Hill," *Qtly. Jnl. of the Lib. of Congs.* (Jl. 1977); "94-553 and All That; Ruminations on Copyright," *Msc. LA Notes* (Je. 1979); Reviews; Other articles. **Activities:** 2, 4; 17, 39, 45; 55, 61 **Addr.:** Box 127, Berkeley Springs, WV 25411.

Liddle, Carol J. (Mr. 16, 1930, Fort Atkinson, WI) Pub. Srv. Coord., Janesville Pub. Lib., 1978–, Ref. and Adult Srv., 1967–78; Lib. Sci. Instr., Univ. WI (Platteville), 1965–67; Mid. Sch. Libn., Menomonee Falls Pub. Sch., 1962–65; Branch Libn., Kenosha Pub. Lib., 1958–62. **Educ.:** Univ. WI (Platteville), 1948–52, BS (Eng.); Univ. WI (Madison), 1957–58, MS (LS). **Orgs.:** WI Assn. Pub. Libn.: Dir. (1974–77). Janesville Libn. Assn.: Pres. (1970–71). WI LA: Various com. Cap. Dist. LA: Pres. (1973–74). AAUW: Janesville Chap., Secy. (1960–62). **Activities:** 9; 16, 17, 36; 50, 69 **Addr.:** 316 S. Main St., Janesville, WI 53545.

Liddle, Ernest V. (Je. 10, 1923, Enniskillen, N. Ireland) Dir. of Lib. Srvs., Prof. of LS, Liberty Bapt. Coll., 1979–; Dir., of the Lib., Palm Beach Atl. Coll., 1976–79; Acq. Libn., West. IL Univ., 1969–71; Head Libn., Seattle Pac. Univ., 1966–69; Undergrad. Libn., Univ. of PA, 1965–66; Circ. Libn., East. Bapt. Coll. and Semy., 1963–65; Assoc. Prof., Hist., Grand Rapids Bapt. Coll., 1960–63. **Educ.:** Univ. of Edinburgh, 1947–51, BA (Hist.); Bucknell Univ., 1959–60, MA (Hist.); Drexel Univ., 1964–66, MS (LS); Asbury Theo. Semy., 1951–54, BD & ThM (Church Hist.); North. Bapt. Theo. Semy., 1954–56, ThD (Church Hist.). **Orgs.:** ALA: ACRL. VA LA. **Pubns.:** "Library Performance Appraisal," *The Christ. Libn.* (Ag. 1981); "Individualism of Faith," *The Outlook* (S. 1969); "Revival Through the Bible," *Christianity Today* (Ja. 1958). **Activities:** 1; 15, 17, 35; 90, 92 **Addr.:** 311 Robin Dr., Lynchburg, VA 24502.

Lieberman, Irving (Ja. 6, 1914, Newark, NJ) Prof. & Dir. Emeritus, Sch. of Libnshp., Univ. of WA, 1979–; Lect., Dept. of Lib. Std., West. Australian Inst. of Tech., 1979–81; Prof., Sch. of Libnshp., Univ. of WA, 1973–79, Dir. & Prof., 1956–73; Advisory Dir., Inst. of Libnshp., Univ. of Ibadan (Nigeria), 1963–64; Assoc. in Lib. Srv., Sch. of Lib. Srv., Columbia Univ., 1954–56; Resrch. Assoc., AV Proj., Univ. of CA, Berkeley, 1952–54; Spec. Asst., Superintendent of Ctrl. Srv., Brooklyn Pub. Lib., 1949–52; Head, Ext. Div., MI State Lib., 1946–48; Lib. Ofcr., US Army, 1944–46. **Educ.:** New York Univ., 1929–35, BS (Bus. Admin.); Columbia Univ., 1938–39, BS (LS), 1949–50, MA (Adult Educ.), 1951–55, Ed.D. (Educ. Admin.). **Orgs.:** Pac. NW LA: Lib. Dev. Proj., Ch., Gen. Policy and Exec. Com. (1956–60). AECT: Info. Syst. Div., (Pres., 1974–75). ASIS: Spec. Int. Grp. on Non-print Media (Ch., 1975–76). ALA: Interdiv. Com. on Educ. for Hlth. and Rehab. Lib. Srvs. (Ch., 1976–77); Intl. Rel. Com. (1975–77); ALA Devastated Libs. Proj. (Ch.); LED, Com. on Equivalences and Reciprocity. **Honors:** Cncl. on Lib. Resrcs., Mid Career Flwshp., 1969; WA LA, Life Mem., 1979; Pac. NW LA, Life Mem., 1979. **Pubns.:** Ed., *Proceedings of an Invitational Conference on Education for Health Sciences Librarianship* (1968); "Audiovisual Services in Libraries" in *Advances in Librarianship* (1975); "Library Education: Changing Goals" in *As Much to Learn as to Teach* (1979); "Relating Instructional Methodology to Teaching in Library Schools" in *Targets for Research in Library Education,* (1973); "The Use of Non-Print Media in Library School Instruction" in *Library Education: An International Survey,* (1968); other books and articles. **Activities:** 9, 13; 16, 24, 26; 50, 54, 95-AV. **Addr.:** 19009 11th Ave N.W., Seattle, WA 98177.

Lieberman, Vilma M. (Ap. 1, 1948, Gloucester City, NJ) Head, Comp. Based Info. Ctr., Free Lib. of Philadelphia, 1972–; Refer. Libn., Montgomery Cnty. Norristown Pub. Lib. (PA), 1971–72. **Educ.:** Douglass Coll., 1966–70, BA (Amer. Stds.); Drexel Univ., 1970–71, MSLS. **Orgs.:** ALA: RASD/Machine-Assisted Ref. Sect. (Secy. (1981–82). SLA. Philadelphia Area Libns. Info. Exchange. **Activities:** 9; 16, 39, 49-On Line Srchg.; 56 **Addr.:** Free Library of Philadelphia, Logan Circle, Philadelphia, PA 19119.

Liebman, Roy S. (Ag. 4, 19–, Brooklyn, NY) Head, Bibl. Cntrl., Media Libn., CA State Univ., Los Angeles, 1978–, Head, Mtrls. Cntrl., Prep., 1971–78, Asst. Chief, Cat., 1970–71, Chief, Acq., 1969–70; Head, Acq., CA Inst. of Tech., 1964–69; Head, Ref., Buena Pk. Dist. Lib., 1962–64; Catlgr., Arcadia Pub. Lib., 1961–62; other positions as libn., 1958–61. **Educ.:** Brooklyn Coll., 1954–58, BA (Eng.); Pratt Inst., 1958–60, MLS; CA State Univ., Los Angeles, 1976–78, MA (Educ. Media). **Orgs.:** CA LA: State Univ. Libns. CA Media and Lib. Educs. Assn. S. CA Tech. Prcs. Grp. **Honors** Phi Kappa Phi. **Pubns.:** "The Media Index: Computer-Based Access to Nonprint Materials, *RQ* (Spr. 1981); "Make 'Em Laugh: A Different Approach to Library Orientation," *T.H.E. Jnl.* (May 1980); "A KWOC Index to Unpublished Education Theses," *Unabashed Libn.* (Win. 1976). "Media and the Resistant University Librarian," *T.H.E. Jnl.* (N. 1979); "The Use of Media in the Work of University Librarians" a videotape (1978); various other articles. **Activities:** 1; 20, 32, 46; 56, 67 **Addr.:** Kennedy Memorial Library, California State University, 5175 State University Dr., Los Angeles, CA 90032.

Liebrecht, Mrs. Doris F. (Ap. 18, 1917, Bethlehem, PA) Libn., Holy Fam. Sch., Hillcrest Hts., MD, 1966–; Libn., Geodetic Ref., U.S. Nvl. Hydrograph. Ofc., 1946–52. **Educ.:** San Diego State Coll., 1935–37; Coll. of St. Elizabeth, Convent Station, NJ, 1937–40, AB (Hist.); Univ. of CA, Berkeley, 1940–42, Cert. (LS). **Orgs.:** Cath. LA: DC Chap., Elem. Sect., Vice Ch., (1975–76), Treas. (1977–78). MD Educ. Media Assn. Gvr.'s Conf. on Lib. and Info. Srvs.: Del. (1978). Libns. Assn., Archdio. of DC.: Ch. (1977–78). **Activities:** 4, 10; 20, 21, 31; 63, 64, 70 **Addr.:** 2416 Gaither St., Hillcrest Heights, MD 20031.

Liggett, Suzanne L. (F. 28, 1939, Syracuse, NY) Coord. of Coop. Cat. Proj., Lib. of Congs., 1979–, Sr. Descr. Catlgr., 1972–79, Descr. Catlgr., 1970–72; Libn., Standard Oil Co., 1967–69. **Educ.:** Harpur Coll., 1957–61, AB (Econ.); Cornell Univ., 1961–63 (Econ.); Univ. of CA at Los Angeles, 1966–67, MLS; Adv. Mgt. Resrch., Inc., 1980, Cert (Proj. Mgt.). **Orgs.:** ALA: AACR 2 Reg. Inst. (Fac., 1980). Lib. of Congs. Prof. Assn. **Honors:** Beta Phi Mu, 1967; Lib. of Cong., Merit. Srv. Awd., 1978. **Activities:** 4; 20, 29, 34 **Addr.:** Descriptive Cataloging Division, Library of Congress, Washington, DC 20540.

Lightwood, Martha B. (Ja. 24, 1923, Natrona Heights, PA) Asst. Libn., Wharton Sch., Univ. PA, 1963–. **Educ.:** Univ. Pittsburgh, 1940–43, AB Summa Cum Laude (Econ.); Wharton Sch., Univ. PA, 1943–44 (Gvt. Admin.), 1965–69, MA (Pol. Sci.); Drexel Univ., 1962–63, MLS; Univ. PA, 1969–78, PhD (Pol. Econ.). **Orgs.:** SLA. ALA: ACRL, DE Valley Chap. PA LA. **Pubns.:** *Public and Business Planning in the US: A Bibliography* (1972); *A Selected Bibliography of Significant Works About Adam Smith* (1981). **Activities:** 1; 17, 35, 39 **Addr.:** Lippincott Library, Van Pelt West, University of Pennsylvania/CA, Philadelphia, PA 19104.

Liivak, Arno (O. 8, 1942, Tallinn, Estonia) Prof. Law, Dir. Lib., Rutgers Univ. Law Sch., 1969–. **Educ.:** Rutgers Univ., 1961–65, BA (Eng.), 1965–66, MLS, 1966–69, JD. **Orgs.:** Intl. Assn. Law Lib.: Secy./Treas. (1977–80); Treas. (1980–83). AALL. Assn. Amer. Law Sch. NJ Bar and Fed. Bar NJ. **Pubns.:** Mgr. Ed., *Intl. Jnl. Law Lib.* (1980); Ed. Chief, *Intl. Jnl. Law Lib.* (1981); Ed., *Rutgers Camden Law Jnl.* (1968–69). **Activities:** 1; 17; 77, 78 **Addr.:** Rutgers University Law School Library, Fifth and Penn St., Camden, NJ 08102.

Lilley, Dorothy B. (Mr. 30, 1914, Towanda, PA) Visit. Prof., Univ. AL, 1980–; Prof., Univ. E. TX State, 1969–79. **Educ.:** Univ. VT, 1954–58, BA (Eng.); Columbia Univ., 1960–69, MS, DLS (LS). **Orgs.:** TX LA. **Pubns.:** Library and Information Science: A Guide to Information Sources (1982); "Selecting and Promoting Information Networks Curriculum," *Intl. Forum on Info. and Docum.* (V. 5, 1980). **Activities:** 11; 25, 26; 63 **Addr.:** 2200 W. Neal #109, Commerce, TX 75428.

Lim, Josefina P. (Mr. 19, 1941, Floridablanca, Pampanga, Philippines) Tech. Srvs. Libn., Cornell Univ. Med. Coll. Lib., 1978–; Tech. Srvs. Libn., Georgetown Univ. Med. Ctr. Lib., 1976–78; Asst. Cat., Mount Sinai Sch. of Med. Lib., 1971–76. **Educ.:** Univ. of the E. (Philippines), 1959–63, BSE (LS); Pratt Inst., 1970–72, MLS. **Orgs.:** Med. LA: NY Reg. Grp., Hosp. Com. (1975); Cont. Educ. Com. (1980), Nsltr. Com. (1979). NY Tech. Srvs. Libns. NY Lib. Club. **Honors:** Beta Phi Mu. **Activities:** 1, 12; 15, 20, 46; 56, 58, 80 **Addr.:** Cornell University Medical College Library, 1300 York Ave., New York, NY 10021.

Lim, Lourdes P. (Mr. 19, 1941, Floridablanca, Pampanga, Philippines) Libn., Gen. Motors Corp. Econ. Staff Lib., 1980–, Libn., PR Lib., 1973–79. **Educ.:** Univ. of the E. (Manila, Philippines), 1959–63, BSE (Eng., Math); Pratt Inst., 1972–73, MLS. **Orgs.:** SLA. Asian Pac. Amer. Libn. Assn.: Rcrt., Mem. Com. (1980–81). NY Tech. Srvs. Libns. Philippine Assn. of Yorkville, NY. **Activities:** 5, 12; 15, 20, 41; 54, 59, 94 **Addr.:** General Motors Corporation, Economics Staff Library, 767 Fifth Ave., New York, NY 10153.

Limbacher, James L. (N. 30, 1926, St. Marys, OH) AV Libn., Dearborn Dept. of Lib., 1955–. **Educ.:** Bowling Green State Univ., 1945–49, BA (Jnlsm.), 1949–53, MA (Sp.); IN Univ., 1953–55, MS (Educ.); Wayne State Univ., 1969–72, MS (LS); Temple Univ., Sem. in Brit. Film, 1971. **Orgs.:** EFLA: Pres. (1966–70). Amer. Fed. of Film Socty.: Pres. (1962–65). Educ. Media Cncl.: MI Rep. (1980–). **Honors:** Grt. Detroit Motion Picture Cncl., 1971; Atlanta Film Fest., Gold Medallion 1972; MI LA, Libn. of the Yr., 1974. **Pubns.:** *A Reference Guide to AV Information* (1972); *Sexuality in World Cinema* (1982); *The Song List* (1974); *Film Music: From Violins to Video* (1974); Other bks. and articles. **Activities:** 9; 32; 50, 67 **Addr.:** 21800 Morley Ave., (Morley Manor), Dearborn, MI 48124.

Lincoln, Harry B. (Mr. 6, 1922, Fergus Falls, MN) Prof. of Msc., SUNY, Binghamton, 1951–. **Educ.:** Macalester Coll., 1940–46, BA (Msc.); Northwestern Univ., 1946–51, MMUS, PhD (Msc. Hist.); Univ. of Rome, Italy, 1950–51, Cert. (Msc. Hist.). **Orgs.:** Msc. LA. Intl. Msc. LA. Assn. for Comp. and Hum. Coll. Msc. Socty.: Natl. Pres. (1968–70). Amer. Musicological Socty.: Cncl. (1967–70). **Honors:** Natl. Endow. for the Hum., Grants, 1977–78; 79–80. **Pubns.:** Ed., *The Computer And Music* (1970); Ed., *Early Seventeenth-Century Keyboard Music in the Vatican Chigi Manuscripts* (1968); Ed., *The Madrigal Collection "L'Amorosa Ero"* (1968); "A Computer Application to Musicology; the thematic index," *Info. Prcs.* (1969); "Some criteria for preparation of thematic indexes by computer" in *Elektronische Datenverarbeitung in der Musikwissenschaft* (1967); other articles. **Activities:** 14-Univ. Prof.; 30, 39; 55 **Addr.:** Department of Music, State University of New York, Binghamton, NY 13901.

Lincoln, Robert S. (N. 10, 1944, Margarita, CZ) Actg. Asst. Dir. for Tech. Srvs., Dafoe Lib., Univ. of MB, 1981–, Head, Acq. Dept., 1974–80, Catlgr., Verification Libn., 1971–74. **Educ.:** CA State Univ., Chico, 1962–66, BA (Eng.); Univ. of West. ON, 1970, MLS. **Orgs.:** Can. LA. ALA. Amer. Prtg. Hist. Assn. **Pubns.:** "Vendors and Delivery, an Analysis," *Can. Lib. Jnl.* (F. 1978); "Controlling Duplicate Orders," *Lib. Acq. Prac. and Theory* (1978); reviews. **Activities:** 1; 15, 37, 46; 57 **Addr.:** Dafoe Library, University of Manitoba, Winnipeg, MB R3T 2N2 Canada.

Lindauer, Dinah (My. 25, 1926, Brooklyn, NY) Asst. Dir./Coord., Prog. and Srvs., Nassau Lib. Syst., NY, 1965–; Asst. Coord., YA Srvs., Brooklyn Pub. Lib., 1951–56; YA Libn., Enoch Pratt Lib., 1949–51; Visit. Instr., Pratt Inst. Lib. Sch., 1958. **Educ.:** Hunter Coll., 1943–47, BA (Soclgy./Phil.); Columbia Univ., 1948–49, MLS. **Orgs.:** NY LA: Pres. (1979); VP (1978); Ch., Gvrs. Conf. Plng. Com. (1976–78). ALA: Cnclr. (1972–74); Ed., *Top of the News* (1955). Nassau Cnty. LA: Exec. Bd (1968–78). Merrick Lib. Bd. of Trustees. Other orgs. Gvrs. Comsn. on Libs.: Exec. Com., Resol. Com., Del. Sel. Com. (1977–78). Commissioner's Com. on Lib. Dev. in NY (1967–70). State Adv. Com. on ESEA Title II (1968). **Activities:** 9; 17, 28, 48 **Addr.:** 81 Marion Ave., Merrick, NY 11566.

Lindeman, LeRoy R. (My. 3, 1928, Salt Lake City, UT) Admin., Curric. and Instr. Div., UT State Ofc. of Educ., 1979–, Admin., 1974–79, Admin., Instr. Media Div., 1965–74; Ch., Dept. of Educ. Media Srvs., Brigham Young Univ., 1959–64; Dir., AV Educ., Davis Dist., 1957–59, Elem. Sch. Tchr., 1951–57. **Educ.:** Univ. of UT, 1951, BS (Bio.), 1957, MS (AV Comm.); Brigham Young Univ., 1965, EdD (Educ. Admin.). **Orgs.:** UT Educ. Media Assn. UT LA. UT Media Bd. UT State Lib. Bd.: Ch. (1980–). State and Natl. Assns. for Supvsn. and Curric. Dev. **Honors:** Phi Kappa Phi. **Pubns.:** Ed., *Guidelines for Developing an Instructional Media System, Parts 1 through 4* (1971); *The Art of Communication* (1972); Contrib., "Media Services in State Departments of Education," *Media and Methods* (1972); Ed., *Guidelines for Developing an Instructional Media System, Part 5, District and Regional Centers* (1976); Ed., *Cataloging and Inventorying Instructional Materials in Utah*

PROFESSIONAL ACTIVITIES: Institutions: 1. Acad. lib.; 2. Arch.; 3. Assn.; 4. Fed./Gvt. lib.; 5. Inst. lib.; 6. Mfr./Suppl.; 7. Milit. lib.; 8. Musm.; 9. Pub. lib.; 10. Sch. lib.; 11. Sch. of lib. sci.; 12. Spec. lib.; 13. State lib.; 14. (other). **Functions/Activities:** 15. Acq./Col. dev.; 16. Adult srvs.; 17. Admin.; 18. Apprais.; 19. Archit./Bldgs.; 20. Cat./Class.; 21. Chld. srvs.; 22. Circ.; 23. Cons./Pres.; 24. Consult.; 25. Cont. ed.; 26. Educ. lib. sci.; 27. Ext. srvs.; 28. Fund/Grants; 29. Gvt. pubs.; 30. Indx./Abs.; 31. Instr. lib. use; 32. Media srvs.; 33. Micro.; 34. Netwks./Coop.; 35. Persnl.; 36. PR; 37. Publshg.; 38. Recs. mgt.; 39. Ref. srvs.; 40. Repro.; 41. Resrch.; 42. Review.; 43. Secur.; 44. Serials; 45. Spec. col.; 46. Tech. srvs.; 47. Trustees/Bds.; 48. YA srvs.; 49. (other).

Schools (1976); various filmstps., articles. **Activities:** 13; 17, 26 **Addr.:** 250 E. 5th St. S., Salt Lake City, UT 84111.

Lindeman, Leroy Russell (My. 3, 1928, Salt Lake City, UT) Admin., Curric. Div., State Bd. Educ. (UT), 1965–, Admin., Div. Instr. Media, 1965; Dir., Educ. Media Srv., Brigham Young Univ., 1964–65, Ch., Dept. AV Comm., 1959–64; Dir., AV Educ., Davis Cnty. Sch. Dist. (UT), 1957–59; Tchr. **Educ.:** Univ. UT, 1951, BS, 1957, MS; Brigham Young Univ., 1965, EDD. **Orgs.:** UT State Lib. Comsn. (1965–). UT LA. Natl. Educ. Assn. **Honors:** Phi Delta Kappa; Phi Eta Sigma; Phi Kappa Phi. **Pubns.:** Various articles. **Activities:** 10, 13; 32; 63 **Addr.:** Curriculum Division, State Board of Education, 250 E. 5th S., Salt Lake City, UT 84111.*

Lindenfeld, Joseph F. (My. 22, 1942, Syracuse NY) Dir. of Lib. Srvs., Shelby State Cmnty. Coll., 1972–; Head, Girard Ave. Branch, Free Lib. of Philadelphia, 1968–71, Ref. Libn., 1964–66. **Educ.:** Boston Univ., 1959–63, AB (Amer. Hist.); Columbia Univ., 1963–64, MS (LS); Univ. of PA, 1964–66, MA (Amer. Cvlztn.); Univ. of WI, 1971–72, Spec. Cert. (Libnshp.). **Orgs.:** ALA: AFL-CIO/ALA Jt. Com. on Lib. Srv. to Labor Grps. (1969–74); RASD, Srvs. to Adults Com. (1976–78); JMRT, Exec. Com. (1969–71); PLA; ACRL/Cmnty. and Jr. Coll. Lib. Sect. (Ch.–Elect, Vice–Ch., 1981–83). TN LA. SELA. TN State Bd. of Regents Libns. Cncl.: Ch. (1979). TN Adv. Cncl. on Libs. Cmnty. Coll. Assn. of Instr. Tech. Frdm. to Read Fndn. **Pubns.:** "International Understanding: A Booklist," *Amer. Libs.* (Ja. 1972); "Cooperation Can Work: A Public/Community College Library," *PLA Nsltr.* (Win. 1977); "Experiential Learning: A New/Old for Role for Libraries," *RQ* (Spr. 1979). **Activities:** 1, 9; 16, 17, 25; 50, 61, 74 **Addr.:** Library, Shelby State Community College, P.O. Box 40568, Memphis, TN 38104.

Linder, Evelyn B. (Brown) (Ag. 9, 1946, Orangeburg, SC) Dir., Jefferson Parish Lib., 1980–; Head of Branch Supvsn. Dept., Jefferson Parish Lib., 1977–80, Branch Supvsr., 1977, Head of Cat. Dept., 1975–77, Asst. Acq. Libn., 1971–75; Chem. tchr., Lafayette Parish Schools, 1970–71; Ref. Libn., Jacksonville Pub. Lib., 1969–70. **Educ.:** Columbia Coll., Columbia, SC, 1964–68, BA (LS, Chem.); FL State Univ., 1968–69, MSLS; Univ. of Denver Grad. Sch. of Libnshp., 1977, Cert.; LA State Univ., 1978, Cert. **Orgs.:** ALA. LA LA. SWLA. Grt. New Orleans Lib. Club. Chi Beta Phi. Beta Phi Mu. New Orleans Musm. of Art. **Activities:** 9, 12; 17, 35, 36; 60, 86, 89 **Addr.:** 2172 LaSalle Ave., Gretna, LA 70053.

Linder, LeRoy Harold (F. 6, 1917, Minneapolis, MN) Mgr., Tech. Info. Srvs., Ford Aerosp. and Comms. Corp., 1959–; Assoc. Prof. of LS, Univ. of South. CA, 1958–59; Asst. Prof. of LS, Univ. of TX, 1954–58; Libn., U.S. Atomic Energy Comsn. Natl. Reactor Test Station, 1952–54. **Educ.:** Univ. of MN, 1935–40, BA (Fine Arts), BS (LS), MS (Hist. of Sci.); Univ. of Chicago, 1946–58, PhD (LS). **Orgs.:** SLA: South. CA Chap. (Pres., 1966–67); Gvt. Info. Srv. Com. (Ch., 1962–64). ASIS. AAAS. **Honors:** Phi Alpha Theta; Croix de Guerre avec Palme (Belgium), 1945; SLA, John Cotton Dana Lectr., 1967; Beta Phi Mu; **Pubns.:** *Rise of Current Complete National Bibliography* (1959); various articles. **Activities:** 12; 17; 52, 56, 64 **Addr.:** Ford Aerospace and Communications Corp., Ford Rd., Newport Beach, CA 92663.

Linderman, Winifred B. (Harmony, MN) Prof. Emerita (LS), Columbia Univ., 1966–, Prof. (LS), Columbia Univ., 1947–66; Visit. Prof. (LS), Univ. of IL, 1968–71; Visit. Prof. (LS), Emory Univ., 1967–68; Consult., U.S. Ofc. of Educ., Lib. Srvs. Div., 1968; Libn. and Cult. Ofcr., U.S. Info. Srv., S. Africa, 1945–47; Ref. Libn., Vassar Coll., 1944–45. **Educ.:** Carleton Coll., 1915–19, BA (Hist.); Columbia Univ., 1933–35, BS (LS), 1936–40, MS (LS), 1945–50, PhD (Amer. Hist.). **Orgs.:** ALA: ACRL/Lib. Educ. Div.; RASD. AALS. AAUP. Amer. Hist. Assn. AAUW. **Honors:** Phi Beta Kappa; Beta Phi Mu. **Pubns.:** *The Present Status and Future Prospects of Reference/Information Service* (1968); "Melvil Dewey," *Ency. of Ref. and Info. Sci.*; "Columbia Univ. School of Library Service," *Ency. of Ref. and Info Sci.* **Activities:** 1, 11; 26, 39; 55, 75, 92 **Addr.:** Hotel Ansonia, Apt. 5-126, Broadway at 73rd. St., New York, NY 10023.

Lindgren, Jon (N. 29, 1938, Ft. Wayne, IN) Asst. Libn., St. Lawrence Univ., 1975–; Asst. Libn. for Readers' Srvs., Coll. of Wooster, 1971–75; Instr., Albion Coll., 1967–70. **Educ.:** Univ. of MI, 1956–61, AB (Eng.); IN Univ., 1965–66, AM (Eng.); West. MI Univ., 1970–71, MLS. **Orgs.:** ALA: LIRT, Exec. Bd. (1978–); Coord. (1979–80). **Honors:** Omicron Delta Kappa, 1979. **Pubns.:** "Seeking a Useful Tradition for Library User Instruction in the College Library" in *Progress in Educating The Library User* (1978); "Toward Library Literacy," *RQ* (Spr. 1981). **Activities:** 1; 15, 31, 39; 55 **Addr.:** St. Lawrence University Library, Canton, NY 13617.

Lindgren, William Dale (Mr. 8, 1936, Peoria, IL) Ch., Lrng. Rsrc. Ctr., IL Ctrl. Coll., 1968–; Libn., Limestone Cmnty. HS, 1960–68. **Educ.:** Bradley Univ., 1954–58, BA (Eng.), 1958–59, MA (Educ.); Univ. of IL, 1967, MSLS. **Orgs.:** ALA: ACRL/Cmnty. Col. Libs. Sect., Mem. Com. (1977–80). IL LA. IL Assn. Educ. and Comm. Tech. IL Valley Lib. Syst.: Bd. of Trustees (1975–78). **Activities:** 1, 10; 17, 26; 50 **Addr.:** Learning Resources Center, Illinois Central College, East Peoria, IL 61635.

Lindgren, William F. (F. 27, 1927, Wadena, MN) Head, Cat., Assoc. Prof., CO State Univ. Libs., 1960–; Cat. Libn., Univ. of AZ, 1955–60; Asst. Cat. Libn., Univ. of OR, 1948–54. **Educ.:** Univ. of MN, 1944–47, BS (Hist.), 1947–48, BS (LS), 1954–55, MA (Hist.). **Orgs.:** ALA: RTSD, Margaret Mann Citn. Com. (Ch., 1972–73); Mem. Promo. (CO Ch., 1963–65). **Pubns.:** Jt. auth., *A Guide to Theses at Colorado State University, 1970–72* (1973); *A Guide to Theses at Colorado State University,* 1920–69 (1970); jt. auth., A Guide to Theses at Colorado State University, 1920–61 (1962); jt. auth., "A Study of Discrepancies between CIP and Proof Slip Information," *CO Libs.* (D. 1977); "CSU Reorganizes Technical Services," *CO Acad. Libs.* (Spr. 1970). **Activities:** 1; 20, 44 **Addr.:** 1513 Independence Rd., Fort Collins, CO 80526.

Lindley, Margaret A. (S. 25, 1930, Mansfield, OH) Lib. and Media Supvsr., Mansfield Bd. of Educ., 1960–; Tchr., Mansfield City Schs., 1953–59. **Educ.:** Oberlin Coll., 1948–52, BA (Hist.); West. Resrv. Univ., 1952–54, MA (Educ.). **Orgs.:** OH Assn. of Sch. Libns.: Pres. (1974). OH Educ. Lib. Media Assn.: Stan. Com. (1979). WHCOLIS: Del. (1979). **Activities:** 10; 15, 32; 63 **Addr.:** 709 Coleman Rd., Mansfield, OH 44903.

Lindsay, Carol (Jl. 15, 1930, Toronto, ON) Chief Libn., Toronto Star Newspapers Ltd., 1967–; Chief of Resrch., CTV TV Network, Pub. Affairs, 1966–67; Asst. Libn., *Globe and Mail,* 1965–66; Resrchr., Writer, Star Weekly, 1959–64. **Educ.:** Univ. of Toronto, 1948–52, BA (Lang. Hist.), 1964–65, BLS. **Orgs.:** SLA: Newspaper Div. Sect; Ch. (1972–73); Toronto Chap., Pres. (1977–78). **Pubns.:** Contrib., *Guidelines for Newspaper Libraries* (1974). **Activities:** 12; 15, 17, 39; 83 **Addr.:** Toronto Star Newspapers Ltd., One Yonge St., Toronto, ON M5E 1E6 Canada.

Lindsey, Thomas K. (O. 5, 1947, Knoxville, TN) Libn., Elkem Metals Co., 1980–; Asst. Libn., Sci. and Engin. Lib., SUNY, Buffalo, 1975–; Inventory Mgt. Spec., US Navy Aviation Supply Ofc., 1971–74; Sales Spec., Liberty Mut. Insr. Co., 1969–70. **Educ.:** Brown Univ., 1965–69, BA (Soclgy.); Univ. of Pittsburgh, 1974–75, MLS. **Orgs.:** SLA: Upstate NY Chap., Chap. Boundaries Com. (Ch., 1978–79); Schol. and Minority Affairs (Ch., 1979–80). **Honors:** Beta Phi Mu, 1975. **Pubns.:** Reviews. **Activities:** 1; 15, 33, 39; 64, 84, 91 **Addr.:** 127 Margaret Rd., Amherst, NY 14226.

Lindvall, Karen J. (Santa Ana, El Salvador) Latin Amer. Biblgphr., Univ. of CA, San Diego, 1975–. **Educ.:** Univ. of CA, Santa Cruz, 1968–72, AB (Anthro., Latin Amer. Std.); Univ. of TX, Austin, 1973–74, MLS. **Orgs.:** SALALM: Lib. Opers. and Srvs. Com. (1980–); Policy, Resrch. and Investigation Com. (1980–). Latin Amer. Std. Assn. **Pubns.:** *Research in México City: A Guide to Selected Libraries and Research Centers* (1977); "México City Libraries, Research Centers, and Bookstores: Report on a Librarian Exchange," *SALALM Nsltr.* (D. 1977). **Activities:** 1; 15, 31, 39; 54 **Addr.:** Central University Library C-075R, University of California, La Jolla, CA 92093.

Lineback, Corrie A. Tomlin (O. 3, 1918, New Orleans, LA) Retired, 1981–; Libn., Sci. Atlanta, 1965–. **Educ.:** GA State Coll. for Women, Emory Univ., 1935–39, AB (Eng.–Jnlsm.); Emory Univ., 1965 (Libnshp.). **Orgs.:** SLA: S. Atl. Chap. (Pres., 1973); New Projs. Com., Pubn. of Dir. (1975). **Pubns.:** Jt. ed., *Directory of Special Libraries in Georgia-South Carolina Area* (1975). **Activities:** 12; 16, 20, 39 **Addr.:** Scientific Atlanta, 3845 Pleasantdale Rd., Atlanta, GA 30340.

Linehan, Janice E. (My. 14, 1943, Lowell, MA) Bus. Libn., Rochester Inst. of Tech., 1972–; Ref. Libn., Batten Barton, Durstine Osborn, 1968–72; Info. Anal., Dept. of Defense, 1964–67. **Educ.:** Merrimack Coll., 1960–64, BA (Hist.); Rutgers Univ., 1967–68, MLS; Rochester Inst. of Tech., 1973–79, MBA. **Orgs.:** SLA: Upstate NY Chap., PR Ch. (1978–79); Prog. Ch. (1977–78); Archvst. (1973–75). **Honors:** Beta Phi Mu. **Activities:** 1, 12; 17, 39, 41; 51, 59 **Addr.:** Rochester Institute of Technology, 1 Lomb Memorial Dr., Rochester, NY 14623.

Linford, A. John (Je. 13, 1936, Garland, UT) Exec. Dir., NELINET, Inc., 1977–; Asst. Dir. for Syst. Dev., SUNY at Albany, 1972–77; Pres., G.I.C. Technigraphics Corp., 1970–72; Info. Syst. Libn., OH State Univ., 1966–70; Info. Syst. Spec., Documentation, Inc., 1963–66; Co. Libn., Hercules Powder Co., 1961–63; Tech. Writer/Abs., Thiokol Chem. Corp., 1958–60. **Educ.:** UT State Univ., 1958, BS (Psy.); Western Reserve Univ., 1961, MS (LS). **Orgs.:** SLA. New Eng. LA. ALA: LITA/Info. Sci. & Autom. Sect., Bd. Mem.-at-Large (1978–79); ASCLA/Multitype Lib. Coop. Sect., Exec. Com. Mem.-at-Large (1980–81). ASIS. **Pubns.:** "To Charge or Not to Charge: A Rationale," *Lib. Jnl.* (O. 1, 1977). **Activities:** 1, 12, 14-library network; 17, 34; 56, 75 **Addr.:** NELINET, Inc., 385 Elliot St., Newton, MA 02164.

Ling, Evelyn R. (Mrs. Robert) (F. 9, 1931, Akron, OH) Church Libn. (Volun.), H. A. Valentine Meml. Lib., High St. Christ. Church, 1965–. **Orgs.:** CSLA: Pubcty. Ch. (1977–78); Northeast. OH Chap., (Treas., 1981). Luth. LA. Cokesbury Church LA. Ord. of East. Star. **Honors:** CSLA, Awd. for Outstan. Contrib. to Churches and Synagogues, 1980. **Pubns.:** "Akron Library Takes on New Life," *Church and Synagogue Libs.* (Mr./Ap. 1977); ""Holy Land" Reading Plan A Success," *Church and Synagogue Libs.* (S./O. 1979); "Use Your Church Archives Fruitfully!" *Disciplina* (Fall 1980); *Archives in the Church or Synagogue Library* (1980). **Activities:** 12; 15, 17, 20; 50, 90 **Addr.:** H. A. Valentine Memorial Library, High St. Christian Church, 131 S. High St., Akron, OH 44308.

Link, Margaret M. (N. 15, 1941, Hartford, CT) Dir., Owen Mgt. Lib., Vanderbilt Univ., 1977–; Prog. Coord., The Hartford Grad. Ctr., 1974–77, Assoc. Libn., 1971–74. **Educ.:** Univ. of CT, 1967–70, BA (Hist.); Univ. of HI, 1970–71, MLS, Rensselaer Polytech. Inst., 1975–77, MS (Mgt.). **Orgs.:** SLA: Bus. and Fin. Div. (1979); South. Appalachian Chap. (Pres. Elect, 1979). Assoc. Info. Mgrs. **Honors** Phi Beta Kappa, 1970. **Activities:** 1, 12; 17, 25; 51, 59 **Addr.:** Vanderbilt University, Management Library, 2505 W. End Ave., Nashville, TN 37203.

Linkhart, Edward G. (Jn. 26, 1922, Wilmington, OH) Lib. Dir., Nez Perce Cnty. Free Lib., 1963–, Reg. Dir., North-Central Idaho Reg. lib. Syst., 1975–; Lib. Dir., lewiston-Nez Perce Cnty. lib. Syst., 1971–77; Lib. Dir., New Castle-Henry Cnty. (IN) Pub. Lib., 1955–63; Lib. Dir., Logan Cnty. (OH) Dist. Lib., 1951–55; Biblgphr., Univ. of IL, 1949–51. **Educ.:** OH State Univ., 1941–47, BA (Eng.); Univ. of IL Lib. Sch., 1947–49, MSLS. **Orgs.:** ALA. Pac. NW LA: VP (1975–77). ID LA: Pres. (1967–68). Kiwanis. Assn. of the Arts: Various ofcs. **Honors:** Idaho's libn. of the Year, 1980. **Addr.:** Nez Perce County Library, 533 Thain Rd., Lewiston, ID 83501.

Linkins, Germaine C. (S. 10, 1939, Seattle, WA) Serials Libn., VA Polytech. Inst. and State Univ., 1977–, Serials Catlgr., 1975–77; Prin. Catlgr., Asst. Dept. Head, Univ. of CA, San Diego, 1973–74; Prin. Catlgr., Univ. of CA, Riverside, 1972–73, Hum. Biblgphr., Catlgr., 1969–73; Ref., Circ., Libn., Rosary Coll., 1967–69; Libn., Edmonds Branch, Seattle Univ., 1964–67. **Educ.:** Seattle Univ., 1957–62, BA (Soc. Studs.); Rosary Coll., 1962–64, MALS; Univ. of WA, grad. crs. (Fr. Lit.). **Orgs.:** ALA: RTSD/Serials Sect., Lib. Sch. Educ. Com. (1979–82; Ch. (1980–81) SELA: Resrcs. and Tech. Srvs. Sect. (1978–80). VA LA: Mem. Com. (1977). **Honors:** Beta Phi Mu. **Activities:** 1; 17, 20, 44 **Addr.:** Newman Library, Virginia Polytechnic Institute and State University, Blacksburg, VA 24061.

Linsley, Laurie S. (S. 22, 1945, Spokane, WA) Coord., ILL, Univ. of Ctrl. FL, 1971–. **Educ.:** FL Tech. Univ., 1969–71, BA (Eng.); FL State Univ., 1973–74, MSLS. **Orgs.:** FL LA: ILL Caucus (Ch., 1978–79); Lcl. Arrange. Com., Ch. (1978–79); Secy. (1979–80). **Pubns.:** "A Business of Your Own," *FL. Libs.* (Ja.–F. 1981); ed., *Florida Business Publications Index* (1977–); "FAME Interview with Judith Letsinger," *FL Media Qtly.* (Fall 1975); "FTU Orientation Exhibit," *FL Libs.* (N.–D. 1976); "University System Interlibrary Loan," *FL Libs.* (N.–D. 1979); various other articles. **Activities:** 1; 39 **Addr.:** University of Central Florida, Library Interlibrary Loan, P. O. Box 25000, Orlando, FL 32816.

Linsley, Priscilla M. (Mr. 20, 1934, Erie, PA) Consult., Gossage Regan Assocs., 1981–; Consult., Inst. Srvs., NJ State Lib., 1979–81; Coord. of Libs., Garden State Sch. Dist., 1975–78; Libn., Educ. Testing Srv., 1968–75, Assoc. Libn., 1966–68. **Educ.:** Univ. of NH, 1952–56, BA (Eng.); Univ. of North. IL, 1964–66, MA (LS). **Orgs.:** ALA: Lib. Srv. to Prisoners (Secy., 1979–). SLA: Princeton-Trenton Chap. (Pres., 1974–75); Educ. Div. (Ch., 1974–75). Litcy. Voluns. of NJ. Forum Proj. **Pubns.:** Various sps. **Addr.:** 2 Cleveland Rd. W., Princeton, NJ 08540.

Linville, Herbert (Je. 5, 1928, Paris, KY) Head, Gvt. Pubns. Dept., Univ. of CA, Santa Barbara Lib., 1953–; Catlgr., Army Med. Lib., Washington, DC, 1951. **Educ.:** Southwest. at Memphis, 1946–50, BA (Fr.); Columbia Univ., 1950–51 MS (LS). **Orgs.:** ALA: RTSD/Serials Sect. (Ch., 1972–74); various coms. (1969–76). South. CA Tech. Prcs. Grp.: Ch. (1968). **Activities:** 1; 29, 44, 46; 78 **Addr.:** 14 Alisal Rd., Santa Barbara, CA 93103.

Lipton, Howard (My. 25, 1919, Mt. Vernon, NY) Retired, 1981–; Ed., *New Technology,* Coord. of PR, Untd. Auto Workers, 1967–, Ed. and PR Rep., 1952–67; Rpt. and Labor Ed., *St. Louis Star-Times,* 1945–51; Area Chief of Info., War Manpower Comsn., 1943–45. **Educ.:** Univ. of MO, 1937–41, BA (Pub. Admin.). **Orgs.:** MI LA: Pres. (1980–); VP (1979–80); Legis. Com. (1981). St. Clair Shores Lib. Bd.: Pres. (1973–); Lib. Coop. of Macomb Cnty.: Trustee (1967–73). Macomb Cnty. Lib. Trustees Assn. Lakeview Sch. Bd., St. Clair Shores. **Honors:** ALTA, Lib. Trustee of Yr., 1981; MI LA, Walter H. Kaiser Awd., 1975; MI Legis., Resol. of Tribute, 1975, 1981. **Pubns.:** Various articles. **Activities:** 9; 36, 47; 83, 91, 93 **Addr.:** 22504 Statler, St. Clair Shores, MI 48081.

Lisbon, Peter Wallace (My. 26, 1933, NY, NY) Chief Subj. Catlgr., Harvard Coll. Lib., 1965–, Subj. Catlgr., 1961–65; Admin. Asst., Lamont Lib. (Harvard), 1960–61. **Educ.:** Brown Univ., 1951–55, AB (Phil.), 1956–57, (Psych.); Simmons Coll., 1958–60, MS (LS). **Orgs.:** ALA: RTSD, Subj. Anal. Com.

Special Subjects/Services: 50. Adult educ.; 51. Advert./Mktg.; 52. Aerosp.; 53. Agric.; 54. Area std.; 55. Arts/Hum.; 56. Autom.; 57. Bibl./Prtg.; 58. Bio. sci.; 59. Bus./Fin.; 60. Chem.; 61. Copyrt.; 62. Documtn.; 63. Educ.; 64. Engin.; 65. Env.; 66. Eth. grps.; 67. Film; 68. Food/Nutr.; 69. Geneal.; 70. Geo.; 71. Geol.; 72. Handcpd.; 73. Hist.; 74. Int. frdm.; 75. Info. sci.; 76. Insr.; 77. Law; 78. Legis.; 79. Math./Comp. sci.; 80. Med.; 81. Metals; 82. Nat. resrcs.; 83. Newsp.; 84. Nuc. sci.; 85. Oral hist.; 86. Petr./Energy; 87. Pharm.; 88. Phys./Astr./Math.; 89. Readg.; 90. Relig.; 91. Sci./Tech.; 92. Soc. sci.; 93. Telecom.; 94. Transp.; 95. (other).

(1974–78). **Honors:** Phi Beta Kappa. **Activities:** 1; 20, 39, 46; 54, 55, 92 **Addr.:** 24 Woodbridge St., Cambridge, MA 02140.

Liszewski, Edward H. (S. 19, 1934, Baltimore, MD) Asst. Chief Libn., U.S. Geol. Srvy., 1973–; Asst. to Univ. Libn., George Washington Univ., 1972–73; Libn., Ctr. for Nvl. Analyses, 1970–73; Dir., Third U.S. Army Lib. Srv. Ctr., HQ, Third U.S. Army, 1969–70; Asst. Libn. for Tech. Srvs., U.S. Nvl. Acad., 1967–69; Chief, Readers Srvs., U.S. Army Chem. Resrch. and Dev. Labs., Edgewood Arsenal, 1964–67; Chief Libn., Spec. Srvcs., Edgewood Arsenal, 1962–64; Ref. Libn., Enoch Pratt Lib., 1961–62, 1959–60. **Educ.:** Loyola Coll., 1952–56, BS (Bus. Admin.); Syracuse Univ., 1960–61, MSLS. **Orgs.:** SLA. **Activities:** 4, 12; 15, 17, 24; 75, 82, 86 **Addr.:** 9400 Union Pl., Gaithersburg, MD 20760.

Litchfield, Dorothy Hale (N. 14, 1902, Philadelphia, PA) Retired; Head, Print and Picture Dept., Free Lib. of Philadelphia, 1954–64, Head, Trng. Dept., 1944–54; Supvsr., Per. and Micro., and Resrch. Asst. to Dir. of Libs., Columbia Univ., 1938–44, Lectr. (LS), 1938–44; Head, Ref., Univ. of PA Lib., 1934–38, Libn., Botany Lib., 1930–34. **Educ.:** Bryn Mawr Coll., 1920–24, AB (Eng., Fr.); Drexel Univ., 1924–25, Dipl. (LS). **Orgs.:** ALA. **Pubns.:** *The Fabulous Decade; Prints of the Nineteen Fifties* (1964); jt.-Auth., "Microfilm Reading Machines," *Spec. Libs.* (Six issues, 1943); jt.-Auth., "Problems of Microphotography," *Bltn. Med. LA.* (1939); "Teaching Microphotography to Librarians," *Lib. Jnl.* (1945). **Activities:** 1, 9; 33, 39, 44; 55 **Addr.:** P.O. Box 142, Cape May Point, NJ 08212.

Litkowski, Sr. Mary Pelagia O.P. (N. 6, 1911, Saginaw, MI) Elem. Libn., St. Francis Elem. Sch., 1979–; Libn., St. Mary Cathedral HS, Saginaw, MI, 1971–79; Libn., St. Michael HS, New Lothrop, MI, 1964–71; Elem. Tchr. and Libn., St. Michael Elem. Sch., New Lothrop, MI, 1957–62. **Educ.:** Aquinas Coll., 1932–51, BA (Latin); West. MI Univ., 1953–61, MA (LS); MI State, 1960, Permanent Elem. Cert., 1974, Permanent Sec. Cert. **Orgs.:** MI Cath. LA: Com. on Natl. Mem. (1978–81). Assn. of Media in Educ.: Secy. (1977–79). **Activities:** 10; 15, 20, 25; 63, 66, 90 **Addr.:** St. Francis Convent, 120 E. Tenth St., Traverse City, MI 49684.

Litt, Dorothy E. (NY, NY) Sr. Libn., Queens Borough Pub. Lib., 1970–79. **Educ.:** Queens Coll. City Univ. of NY, 1959–66, BA (Eng.); SUNY Stony Brook, 1966–68, MA (Eng.); Queens Coll., City Univ. of NY, 1968–70, MLS. **Orgs.:** ALA: RASD, Bibl. Com. (1976–79). NY LA: Ref. Com. (1975–). Thea. LA: West. Eur. Lang. Specs. (1977–). Assn. for the Bibl. of Hist.: Bibl. as an Art Com. (1980–). Natl. Bk. Critics' Circle. Amer. Socty. of Indxrs. Queens Coll. Alum. Assn. **Pubns.:** "Unity of Theme in Volpone," *NY Pub. Lib. Bltn.* (Ap. 1969); "A Cygnet among Ducklings," *Spectrum*, (S. 1966); Reviews. **Activities:** 9; 16; 55 **Addr.:** 147-30 38th Ave., Flushing, NY 11354.

Little, Paul L. (Ap. 9, 1932, Oklahoma City, OK) Chief, Ext. Srvs., Metro. Lib. Syst., 1976–, Chief, Pub. Srvs., 1974–76, Head Libn., Main Lib., 1971–74, Head Libn., Bkmobiles, 1966–71. **Educ.:** Ctrl. State Univ., 1961–68, BA (Econ.); Univ. of OK, 1968–70, MLS; LA State Univ., HEA Title II B Inst., 1975; various other courses. **Orgs.:** OK LA: Ch., Pub. Libs. Div. (1981); Ch., Cont. Educ. Com. (1978–79); Ch., Resol. Com. (1974–75). ALA. SWLA: Lib. Dev. Com. (1977). CLENE: Adv. Com. (1976–77); Ch., Income Dev. Com. (1977–78). Cosmopolitan Intl.: OK City Chap., (Pres., 1974–76). **Pubns.:** *Task-Oriented Staff Allocation* (1978); "Library Cooperation and the Lifelong Learning Process," *Rural Libs.* (Spr. 1980); jt. auth., "OASES in Oklahoma," *Lib. Jnl.* (Jl. 1977); "The Effectiveness of Paperbacks," *Lib. Jnl.* (N. 15, 1979); "Converting Bookmobiles to Paperbacks," Lib. Jnl. (Ap. 1, 1976); other articles. **Activities:** 17, 24, 41; 50, 59, 92 **Addr.:** P.O. Box 12071, Oklahoma City, OK 73157.

Little, Robert David (Jl. 11, 1939, Milwaukee, WI) Ch. and Prof. of LS, IN State Univ. 1971–; Actg. Dir., Univ. of WI, Milwaukee, 1971, Asst. Prof., LS, 1970–71; Prog. Admin. for ESEA, Title II, WI Dept. of Pub. Instr., 1969–70, State Sch. Lib. Supvsr., 1965–67, Supvsr. of Instr. Mtrls., Gibraltar and Sevastopol Pub. Schs., 1963–65; Sch. Libn., Highland Pk. HS, IL, 1962–63; Tchr.–Libn., Sevastopol Pub. Schs., 1959–62. **Educ.:** Univ. of WI, Milwaukee, 1955–59, BA (Hist., Educ.); Univ. of WI, Madison, 1960–64, MA (LS), 1967–69, PhD (LS). **Orgs.:** ALA: Legis. Asm. (1975–79); YASD, Legis. Com. (Ch., 1978–79); Lib. Educ. Div., Media Resrch. Com. (Ch. 1974–78); LAMA, Stats. for Sch. Libs. (1979–83); AASL/AECT Guidelines Implementation Task Frc. (Ch. 1979–80), various other coms. AECT: *AV Instr.* Ed. Adv. Bd. (1979–80). IN Sch. Libns. Assn. **Pubns.:** Jt. auth., *The Library Aide's Guide to the Card Catalog and the Dewey Decimal System* (1979); "NCES Surveys of School Library Media Centers," *Bowker Anl.* (1979); "Adult Themes in Children's Literature," *IN Media Jnl.* (Spr. 1979); "Public School Library Media Centers: Analysis of NCES Survey," *Bowker Anl.* (1978); "Children's Books: A Reflection of Today's Society," *A Pageant of Reading* (1978); various other articles. **Activities:** 10, 11; 17, 32, 48; 74, 78 **Addr.:** 376 Keane Ln., Terre Haute, IN 47803.

Little, Rosemary Allen (Je. 14, 1938, Newark, NJ) Libn., Pub. Admin. Col., Princeton Univ. Lib. 1964–, Asst. Ref. Libn., 1961–64. **Educ.:** Douglass Coll., 1956–60, AB (Eng.); Rutgers Univ., 1958–61, MLS. **Orgs.:** AALL. ALA. Gvt. Docum. Assn. of NJ: Secy. (1974–76); VP and Pres.-Elect (1978–79); Pres. (1979–80). SLA: Princeton/Trenton Chap., Secy./Treas. (1968–69), VP, Pres.-Elect (1976–77), Pres. (1977–78). Metro. Musm. of Art. Frnds. of the Princeton Univ. Art Musm. Frnds. of the Princeton Univ. Lib. **Activities:** 1; 15, 29, 39; 77, 78, 92 **Addr.:** 1 Grandview Ave., Lawrenceville, NJ 08648.

Littleton, Isaac T. (Ja. 28, 1921, Hartsville, TN) Dir. of Libs., NC State Univ., 1964–, Asst. Dir., Tech. Srvs., 1959–64; Asst. Libn., Persnl./Asst. to Libn., Univ. of NC, 1953–59, Head, Circ., 1951–53. **Educ.:** Univ. Of NC, 1939–43, AB (Soclgy.); Univ. of TN, 1947–50, MA (Psy.); Univ. of IL, 1950–51, MS (LS), 1963–68, PhD (LS). **Orgs.:** ALA: ACRL, Strg. Com., Univ. Lib. Sect. (1968–71); Nom. & Appt. Com. (1972–73). SELA: Treas. (1958–60); Adv. Com. on Southeast. Lib. Survey, Exec. Bd. (1974–78). NC LA: Exec. Bd. (1974–78); 2nd VP (1969–71). Southeast. Lib. Network: Exec. Bd. (1973–74). Other orgs. **Honors:** Cncl. on Lib. Resrcs., Fellow, 1976–77; Beta Phi Mu. **Pubns.:** *State Systems of Higher Education and Libraries: A Report to the Council on Library Resources* (1977); *The Literature of Agricultural Economics: Its Bibliographic Organization and Use* (1969); "The Current Status of University Librarians in Association of Southeastern Research Libraries," *Southeast. Libn.*, (Spr. 1971); "The Literature of Agricultural Economics: Its Bibliographic Organization and Use," *Lib. Qtly.* (Ap. 1969). **Addr.:** 4813 Brookhaven Dr., Raleigh, NC 27612.

Litzenberg, Marcia H. (N. 16, 1944, Ann Arbor, MI) Dir., Santa Fe Pub. Lib., 1981–, Coord. of Chld. Srvs., 1978–81. **Educ.:** Univ. of MI, 1966, BA (Educ.), 1975, MA (LS), 1978, Educ. Spec. **Orgs.:** NM LA. **Honors:** Phi Beta Kappa, 1965; Beta Phi Mu, 1974. **Activities:** 9; 17, 36 **Addr.:** P.O. Box 2247, Santa Fe, NM 87501.

Liu, David Ta-Ching (D. 6, 1936, China) Lib. Dir., Pharr Meml. Lib., 1973–; Head Libn., Bay de Noc Cmnty. Coll., 1964–73; Chief, Adult Srvs., Joliet (IL) Pub. Lib., 1964–64; Catlgr., Chicago Pub. Lib., 1963–64. **Educ.:** Natl. Taiwan Univ., 1955–59, BA (Eng.); George Peabody Coll., 1962–63, MALS. Natl. Normal Univ., Taiwan, 1960–61; Univ. of WA, 1962. **Orgs.:** Chinese Amer. Libns. Assn.: Pres. 1981–. PR Ch. (1979–80); Mem. Com. (Ch., 1978–79). Hidalgo Cnty. Lib. Syst. Adv. Cncl.: Pres. (1980). Rotary. **Pubns.:** "Historical Study of Sino-American Mutual Tready," *Peimei New* (D. 15, 17, 18, 1979); "On the case of Wei Jingsheng," *Peimei New* (D. 20, 1979). **Activities:** 9; 15, 17, 20; 54, 66, 92 **Addr.:** 311 Cypress Circle, Pharr, TX 78577.

Liu, Helen Cheng (Mr. 29, 1934, Shanghai, Kiangsu, China) Head, Cat. Div., Univ. of MN Libs., 1979–; Head, Mono. Cat., 1976–79, Chief Soc. Sci. Catlgr., 1976–79, Head, Copy Cat. Sect., 1972–76, Soc. Sci. Catlgr., 1969–76; Head Libn., Concordia Acad. (St. Paul, MN), 1967–68. **Educ.:** Natl. Taiwan Univ., 1951–55, BA (Eng.); Univ. of MN, 1965–67, MA (LS); Various wkshps. **Orgs.:** ALA. MN LA: Tech. Srvs. Sect. (Ch., 1978–80). Univ. of MN Libs.: Lib. Cncl. (1976–78). **Pubns.:** "Faculty Citation and Quality of Graduate Engineering Departments," *Jnl. of Engin. Educ.* (Ap. 1978); jt. auth., "Literature Filing and Retrieving System of the Particle Technology Laboratory," Particle Tech. Lab., Dept. of Mech. Engin., Univ. of MN (Jl. 1968). **Activities:** 1; 17, 20, 46; 63, 70, 92 **Addr.:** 1 North Deep Lake Rd., North Oaks, MN 55110.

Liu, Leo Yueh-yun (Ap. 3, 1940, Canton, China) Ch., Lib. Com., Fac. of Arts, Ch., Dept. of Pol. Sci., Brandon Univ., 1979–; Dir. and Secy., Can.–Chin. Libns. Assn., 1980–; Dir., Chin.–Amer. Libns. Assn., 1979–; Ch., Lib. Com., Sen., Brandon Univ., 1972–73. **Educ.:** Natl. Taiwan Univ., 1958–62, BA (Law); Univ. of West. ON, 1967–68, MLS; Univ. of HI, 1963–65, MA (Pol. Sci.); Univ. of AB, 1970, PhD (Pol. Sci.). **Pubns.:** *China As a Nuclear Power in World Politics* (1972); "Modernization of China's Military," *Current Hist.* (S. 1980); "China as a Nuclear Power and Its Effects on the Asian Political System," *Tse Yeo Ren Monthly* (F. 1980); "The Chinese People's Liberation Army: Its Capability and Strategy in Asia," *Current Hist.* (S. 1978); "Comparative Nuclear Policies: China and Other Developing Countries," *Asian Profile* (F. 1978); various articles, reviews. **Activities:** 1; 17, 41, 46 **Addr.:** Brandon University, Brandon, MB R7A 6A9 Canada.

Livingston, Carolyn W. (Mr. 23, 1933, Akron, OH) Libn., Greenwood Lab. Sch., Southwest MO State Univ., 1977–; Resrch. Assoc., Indust. Rel. Ctr., Univ. of Chicago, 1957–62; Resrch. Asst., U.S. House of Rep., 1957. **Educ.:** Denison Univ., 1950–54, BA (Hon.) (Hist.); Stanford Univ., 1954–55, MA (Hist.); Univ. of MO, 1978–80, MA (LS); Fulbright Schol., Univs. of Goettingen and Freiburg, Germ., 1955–56. **Orgs.:** Springfield Area Libns.: Pres. (1980–81). MO LA. Leg. Com. MO Assn. of Sch. Libns.: Bd. (1978–); Educ. Com. (Ch., 1978–80); Leg. Com. (Ch., 1980–). ALA: AASL. Other orgs. Springfield (MO) City Cncl. (1977–81). Leag. of Women Voters: Various ofcs. MO Mncpl. Leag.: Bd. (1978–81). Other orgs. and ofcs. **Activities:** 10; 17, 26, 31; 78, 92 **Addr.:** 1002 East Portland Street, Springfield, MO 65807.

Livingston, Lynn Wellman (Mr. 23, 1933, Akron, OH) Libn., Greenwood Lab. Sch., S.W. MO State Univ., 1977–; Instr. (Hist.), Drury Coll., 1966–69; Resrch. Assoc., Indus. Rel. Ctr., Univ. of Chicago, 1957–62; Resrch. Asst., U.S. Hse. of Reps. (Congsnl. Staff), 1957. **Educ.:** Denison Univ., 1950–54, BA, hons. (Hist.); Stanford Univ., 1954–55, MA (Hist.); Univ. of MO, 1977–80, MA (LS). **Orgs.:** Springfield Area Libns. Assn.: Pres. (1980–81). MO Assn. of Sch. Libns.: State Bd. (1978–), Legis. Ch. (1980–); Educ. Ch. (1978–80). MO LA. ALA. Various other orgs. MO Mncpl. Leag. Leag. of Women Voters of MO. Leag. of Women Voters of Springfield. Springfield Park Bd. Various other orgs. **Honors:** Fulbright Schol., 1955; Phi Alpha Theta, 1955. **Activities:** 10; 17, 21, 26; 78, 92 **Addr.:** 1002 E. Portland St., Springfield, MO 65807.

Lloréns Ana Maria R. (Ap. 26, 1919, Guayanilla, PR) Head, Frgn. Langs. Grad. Lib., Assoc. Prof., OH State Univ., 1965–; Ref. Libn., FL State Univ., 1962–65; Sr. HS Libn., Mobile, AL, 1959–62; Catlgr., Miami (FL) Pub. Lib., 1958–59; Various lib. consult. positions in Ctrl. Amer. **Educ.:** LA State Univ., 1956–57, BA (Span.), 1957–58, MSLS; FL State Univ., 1963–70, MA (Span.). Univ. of PR, Rio Pedras, 1936–39, Normal Dipl. **Orgs.:** Acad. Libs. of OH. **Honors:** Ministry of Education, Nicaragua, C.A., Diploma of Recognition (while serving as School Library Consultant, Jul.-Oct.), 1975; Second Inter-American Meeting of Specialists on Educational Materials, held in Venezuela, March 26–30, 1973, Delegate Representing U.S.A. at Libraries Section, 1973; School Librarians, Colombia, S.A., Certificate of Recognition, 1971. **Pubns.:** "Bibliographic Indexes to Periodical Literature in the Romance Languages", *Mod. Lang. Jnl.* (Ja.-F. 1976); "Review of Garcia Lorca Review", *Serials Rev.* (1976); "Review of Diacritics," *Serials Rev.* (1979); "Bibliografía sobre Florencio Sánchez," *Helicon*, (Fall, 1979); Other articles. **Activities:** 1; 15, 24, 39; 54, 57 **Addr.:** 1858 Neil Ave., Ohio State University Libraries, Columbus, OH 43210.

Lloyd, James B. (Ja. 13, 1945, Columbus, OH) Cur., Spec. Cols., West. Carolina Univ., 1980–; Ed., MS Auths. Proj., Univ. of MS, 1977–80, Asst. Archvst., 1975–77. **Educ.:** AR State Univ., 1966–69, BA (Eng.); Univ. of MS, 1969–75, MA, PhD (Eng.); Natl. Arch. Inst., 1976, Cert.; George Peabody Univ., 1978–79, MLS. **Orgs.:** SAA. **Honors:** Natl. Endow. for the Hum. Resrch. Grant, 1977; Beta Phi Mu. **Pubns.:** *Lives of Mississippi Authors, 1817–1967* (1981); *The University of Mississippi: The Formative Years, 1848-1906* (1979); *The Oxford Eagle, 1900-1962: An Annotated Checklist of Material on William Faulkner and the History of Lafayette County* (1977); "Epsilon Sigma Omicron Reading List, 1976–78," *MS Clubwoman* (Ja.–F. 1977); "The Oxford *Eagle*, 1902-1962: A Census of Locations," *MS Qtly.* (Sum. 1976). **Activities:** 1, 2; 17, 41, 45; 55, 65, 95-Wilderness. **Addr.:** Special Collections, Hunter Library, Western Carolina University, Cullowhee, NC 28723.

Lo, Catherine Pascual (O. 26, 1937, Laoag City, Ilocos Norte, Philippines) Libn./Catlgr., Lrng. Resrc. Ctr., Kauai Cmnty. Coll., 1975–; Media Catlgr., 1974–75; Libn., Waimea Elem. Sch. (Kauai), 1973–74; Asst. Dir., Upper Peninsula Lib. Syst. (Soo, MI), 1964–66; Catlgr., Kauai Pub. Lib., 1963–64, Bkmobile. Libn., 1961–63; Cat. Libn., Lib. of HI, 1960–61. **Educ.:** Univ. of HI, 1958–59, BA (Eng.); Thiel Coll., 1955–58 (Eng.); Univ. of WA, 1959–60, MS (LS). **Orgs.:** ALA: RTSD. HI LA: Mem. Ch., Kauai (1963); Conf. Com. (1974). Kauai LA: Various ofcs. Kauai Hist. Socty. Lihue Lutheran Church. **Honors:** Beta Phi Mu. **Pubns.:** "Notes on Books" (weekly column) *Evening News*, Soo, MI (Ap.-Je. 1966); Ed., *The Garden Island Index* (1977–); *Lihue Lutheran Church: Centennial Album* (1981). **Activities:** 1, 9; 17, 20, 46 **Addr.:** P. O. Box 887, Koloa, HI 96756.

Lo, Karl K. (Ap. 28, 1935, Chungshan, Kwangtung, China) Head, E. Asia Lib., Univ. of WA, 1968–; Head, E. Asia Lib., Univ. of KS, 1964–68, Oriental Catlgr., 1961–64, Gifts and Exch. Libn., 1960–61, Biblgphr., 1959–60. **Educ.:** Chung Chi Coll., 1954–58, Dip. (Chem.); Atlanta Univ., 1958–59, MSLS. **Orgs.:** ALA: ACRL, Nom. Com. (Ch., 1976). E. Asia Lib. Cnsrtm.: Japan–U.S. Frndshp. Comsn. (1975–). Assn. of Asian Std.: Com. on E. Asian Libs./Autom. Task Frc. (Ch., 1980–); Autom. Subcom. (Ch., 1978–80); Natl. Un. Cat. Subcom. (1978–80); Exec. Mem. (1967–70). Chin. Lang. Comp. Socty. Chin. Hist. Socty. of Amer. Chin. Hist. Socty. of the Pac. N.W.: First VP/Prog. Ch. (1980–81). **Honors:** Cncl. on Lib. Resrcs., Resrch. Flwshp., 1972. **Pubns.:** Jt. cmplr., *Chinese Newspapers Published in North America, 1954-1975* (1975); "Publication Trends in the People's Republic of China," *CEAL Bltn.* (Je. 1979); "East Asian Scripts and Library Automation in North America: 'Print Chain Expansion' or 'File Enhancement'?" *CEAL Bltn.* (F. 1979); "Rationed Like Rice–Information Service in the People's Republic of China," *PNLA Qtly.* (Fall 1977); jt. auth., "Serials from the People's Republic of China, 1966–76: A Guide," *The Serials Libn.* (Fall 1977). **Activities:** 1; 17; 54, 74 **Addr.:** East Asia Library, DO-27, University of Washington, Seattle, WA 98195.

Lo, Lydia (Jy. 1, 1943, Manila, Philippines) Dir., Lrng. Resrcs. Ctr., Shasta Coll., 1977–; Actg. Libn., Gen. Theo. Semy., 1975–76, Asst. Libn., Catlgr., 1967–75; Libn., St. Andrew's Theo. Semy., 1964–66. **Educ.:** Univ. of the Philippines, 1960–64, BSLS; Columbia Univ., 1966–68, MSLS; NY Univ., 1973–75, MA (Hist.); Univ. of CA, Berkeley, 1976–77, Cert. (LS). **Orgs.:**

PROFESSIONAL ACTIVITIES: Institutions: 1. Acad. lib.; 2. Arch.; 3. Assn.; 4. Fed./Gvt. lib.; 5. Inst. lib.; 6. Mfr./Suppl.; 7. Milit. lib.; 8. Musm.; 9. Pub. lib.; 10. Sch. lib.; 11. Sch. of lib. sci.; 12. Spec. lib.; 13. State lib.; 14. (other). **Functions/Activities:** 15. Acq./Col. dev.; 16. Adult srvs.; 17. Admin.; 18. Apprais.; 19. Archit./Bldgs.; 20. Cat./Class.; 21. Chld. srvs.; 22. Circ.; 23. Cons./Pres.; 24. Consult.; 25. Cont. ed.; 26. Educ. lib. sci.; 27. Ext. srvs.; 28. Fund/Grants; 29. Gvt. pubs.; 30. Indx./Abs.; 31. Instr. lib. use; 32. Media srvs.; 33. Micro.; 34. Netwks./Coop.; 35. Persnl.; 36. PR; 37. Publshg.; 38. Recs. mgt.; 39. Ref. srvs.; 40. Repro.; 41. Resrch.; 42. Review.; 43. Secur.; 44. Serials; 45. Spec. col.; 46. Tech. srvs.; 47. Trustees/Bds.; 48. YA srvs.; 49. (other).

ATLA: Com. on Cat. and Class. (1973–75); ALA Cat. Code Rev. Com. Rep. (1975–77). ALA. CA LA: N. Chap. (Vice-Ch., 1979–80). AAUW. Friends of Shasta Cnty. Libs. **Pubns.:** Ed. Bd., *Serials for Libns.* (1979). **Activities:** 1; 17, 20; 90 **Addr.:** Shasta College Learning Resources Center, 1065 N. Old Oregon Trail, Redding, CA 96001.

Lobou, Robert (Jl. 14, 1935, New York, NY) Ref. Libn., Melville Lib., SUNY, Stony Brook, 1973–; Coord. of Voc. Rehab. Couns., St. Joseph's Hosp., Syracuse, NY, 1968–71; Clin. Psy., Columbia-Presby. Med. Ctr., 1960–65. **Educ.:** Queens Coll., 1952–56, BA (Psy.); Univ. of CT, 1957–58, MA (Clin. Psy.); Syracuse Univ., 1965–68, (Rehab. Couns.), 1971–73, MSLS. **Orgs.:** ALA. **Activities:** 1; 15, 31, 39; 72, 92 **Addr.:** Interlibrary Loans, Melville Library, SUNY at Stony Brook, Stony Brook, NY 11794.

LoBue, Benedict J. (Ja. 7, 1942, Colchester, VT) Head, Ref. Dept., Univ. of CO, 1979–, Ref./Biblgphr., 1974–79; Ref./Circ., Univ. of NE, Las Vegas, 1972–74. **Educ.:** SW TX State Univ., 1966–69, BA (Hist.); Univ. of TX, 1969–71, MA (Hist.), 1971–72, MLS. **Orgs.:** CO LA: Ch., Lib. Instr. RT Org. Com. (1979–). ALA: RASD/Hist. Sect., Bibl. And Index Com. (1975–79); Lib. Instr. RT, Org. Com. (1976–77); Nom. Com. (Ch., 1979–80). **Pubns.:** "Evaluating Faculty Involvement in Library Instruction" in *Library Instruction in the Seventies* (1977). **Activities:** 1; 31, 39; 56 **Addr.:** University Libraries, Campus Box 184, University of Colorado at Boulder, Boulder, CO 80309.

Locascio, John Francis (Ja. 16, 1945, Chicago, IL) City Libn., Freeport Pub. Lib., 1972–; Asst. Libn. and Head of Adult Srvs., Glenview Pub. Lib., 1968–72. **Educ.:** North Park Coll., 1965–67, BA (Eng.); Rosary Coll., 1967–68, MLS. **Orgs.:** ALA: Small Lib. Pubns. Com. (1973–75). IL LA: Conf. Com. (1972–73); Int. Frdm. Com. (1975–78); Pub. Lib. Sect. (Pres., 1981). Lib. Admins. Conf. of North. IL: Pres. (1980–81); VP (1979–80). North. IL Lib. Syst. **Activities:** 9; 16, 17 **Addr.:** Freeport Public Library, 314 W. Stephenson St., Freeport, IL 61032.

Locke, Jill L. (S. 22, 1948, Wyandotte, MI) Branch Head, The Farmington Cmnty. Lib., 1977–, Chlds. Coord., 1975–, Chlds. Libn., 1972–75. **Educ.:** Brigham Young Univ., 1966–70, BA (Hum.), 1970–71, MLS. **Orgs.:** ALA: ALSC, Caldecott Com. (1981), Presch. Srvs. and Parent Educ. Com. (Ch., 1980–); PLA, Srvs. to Chld. Com. (1978–81). MI LA: Chlds. Srvs. Caucus. Various ofcs. Wayne-Oakland Lib. Fed.: Chlds. Srvs. Com. (1979–). Natl. Assn. for the Educ. of the Young Chld. Farmington Musicale. **Honors:** Beta Phi Mu. MI LA, Loleta D. Fyan Awd., 1977. Brigham Young Univ. Outstan. Alumni Srvs. Awd., 1981–82. **Activities:** 9; 17, 21, 24; 55 **Addr.:** The Farmington Community Library, 32737 W. Twelve Mile Rd., Farmington Hills, MI 48018.

Lockhart, Helen Deloise (McVeigh, KY) Cmnty. Rel. Libn., Memphis/Shelby Cnty. Pub. Lib., 1969–; Dir., Shiloh Reg. Lib. Ctr., 1953–69; Libn., Belfry, 1966–68. **Educ.:** Un. Univ., 1945–46, BA (Eng.); George Peabody Coll., 1968–69, MA (LS). **Orgs.:** ALA: Cnclr. (1968–72). SELA: Pres. (1978–80). TN LA: Pres. (1967–68). Women in Comms.: Parlmt. (1976–79). Altrusa Club of Memphis. **Honors:** Delta Kappa Gamma. **Pubns.:** "The Shiloh Regional Library," *TN Libn.* (Ja. 1963); "From the President's Desk," *Southeast. Libn.* (N. 1978–N. 1980). **Activities:** 9; 16, 36; 50, 51 **Addr.:** 5286 Boswell, Memphis, TN 38117.

Lockwood, Deborah Lincoln (Ag. 23, 1951, Celina, OH) Mgmt. Asst., State of OR, 1981–; Dir. of Lib. Srvs., Univ. of MD, Univ. Coll., 1979–80; Govt. Docum. Libn., Georgetown Univ. Law Sch., 1979; Ref. Libn., George Washington Univ., 1978–79; Ref. and Instr. Libn., IN Univ. Libs., 1976–78. **Educ.:** MI State Univ., 1971–74, BA (Eng.); Univ. of MI, 1975–76, AMLS. **Orgs.:** ALA: ACRL/Bibl. Instr. Sect., Conf. Plng. Com. DC LA: Leg. Com. MD LA. **Pubns.:** Comp., *Library Instruction: A Bibliography* (1979). "Instructing Adult Students in Public Libraries," *The Crab* (Nsltr. of the MD LA) (1979). **Activities:** 1; 17, 27, 31; 50, 55, 63 **Addr.:** 2510 Skopil Ave. S., Salem, OR 97302.

Lockwood, James D. (S. 7, 1949, Santa Barbara, CA) Asst. to Ch., Higher Educ. lib. Council, OR State Univ., 1980–; Asst. Dir., Washington Ofc., ALA, 1978–80; Ref. Libn., IN Univ. Sch. of Law, 1976–78. **Educ.:** Los Angeles Valley Coll., 1968–69, AA (Arts); Univ. of CA, Santa Cruz, 1969–70, BA (Psy.); CA State Univ., Los Angeles, 1971, BA (Soc.); CA State Univ., Northridge, 1971–72, (Soclg.); Univ. of MI, 1972–76, MA (Soclg.), MALS. **Orgs.:** ALA: Lib. Admin. Div./Pers. Admin. Sect., Staff Dev. Com. (1977–78); ACRL Leg. Com. (1981–83); A SCLA Conf. Prog. Com. (1981–83). OR LA: OLA/WLA Jnt. Conf. Prog. Com. (1980–81); Mem. Com. (1981–82); Lib. Dev. Com. (1980–81). DC LA: Natl. Lib. Wk. Com. (1978–). **Pubns.:** "A Look at LEXIS," *Bill of Particulars* (Win. 1977–78); "Involving Consultants in Library Change," *Coll. & Resrch. Libs.* (N. 1977); "Employers' Expectations of Recent Library School Graduates; A Review of the Recent Literature," ERIC Docum. ED 114 078 (1975); "Information Sources on U.S. Radio Regulations in The Law Library," ERIC Document ED 114 079 (1975); various articles. **Activities:** 6; 28, 36, 49-Lobbying; 78 **Addr.:** Kerr Library, Oregon State University, Corvallis, OR 97331.

Loepprich, Joyce C. (S. 26, 1927, Upper Sandusky, OH) Serials Libn., Univ. of CA, Irvine, 1969–. **Educ.:** Cleveland State Univ., 1966–68, BA (Hist.); Case West. Rsv. Univ., 1968–69, MSLS; CA State Univ., Long Beach, 1971–75, MA (Hist.); OH State Univ., 1945–48, RN. **Orgs.:** ALA: ASCLA, Patient/Cons. Hlth. Educ. Com. (1980–). Med.-Tech. Libns. of Orange Cnty.: Pres. (1973–74). Med. Lib. Grp. of South. CA: Treas. (1978–80). Med. LA: Rep. to Z85 ANSI (1976–79). Info. for Task Frc. for Coop. Hlth. Info. for Orange Cnty. Nursing Info. Cnsrtm. of Orange Cnty. **Pubns.:** "Errata Control in Biomedical Journals," *Bltn. of the Med. LA* (1973). **Activities:** 1; 31, 44; 80 **Addr.:** Biomedical Library, P.O. Box 19556, University of California, Irvine, CA 92713.

Loewenstein, C. Jared (O. 25, 1944, Washington, DC) Ibero-Amer. Biblgphr., Univ. of VA Lib., 1972–, Approval Orders Libn., 1970–72. **Educ.:** Univ. of VA, 1962–66, BA (Span.), 1966–68, MA (Span.), 1968–79, (Span.). **Orgs.:** Sem. on the Acq. of Latin Amer. Lib. Mtrls.: Lib.-Bookdealer-Publ. Rel. Subcom. (1976–). **Pubns.:** *Jorge Luis Borges: A Checklist of Materials in the University of Virginia Library* (forthcoming); "Rare Iberian Imprints," *Chap. & Verse* (Jy. 1977); "A Bibliographer in Residence," *VA Lib. Assn. Nsltr.* (Ag. 1975); "Ibero-American Collection Development..." *Chap. & Verse* (F. 1975). **Activities:** 1; 15; 54 **Addr.:** University of Virginia Library, Charlottesville, VA 22901.

Logan, Darryl L. (Jl. 29, 1933, Stigler, OK) Med. Libn., St. Francis Hosp., Tulsa, OK, 1969–; Libn., Charles Page HS, 1966–69. **Educ.:** OK A and M, 1951–55, BS (Bus. Admin.). **Orgs.:** Med. LA. SLA: OK Chap., Bd. of Dirs. (1978–80); Pres.-Elect (1980–81); Pres. (1981–82). **Activities:** 5, 10; 15, 17, 34; 63, 80 **Addr.:** St. Francis Hospital, 6161 S. Yale Ave., Tulsa, OK 74177.

Logel, Annie Wheeler (Ann) (Mr. 2, 19–, Tuscumbia, AL) Serials Libn., Redstone Sci. Info. Ctr., 1971–; Tech. Libn., Rohm and Haas Co., Redstone Div., 1949–70. **Educ.:** Univ. of North. AL, 1954–55 (LS); Univ. of UT, 1956–57 (LS). **Orgs.:** SLA: Pres. (1963–64); Dir. (1964–65, 1969–70). AL LA: *AL Libn.* Bus. Mgr. (1959–63); Coll., Univ. and Spec. Libs. Div. (Secy., 1965–66). Huntsville Pub. Lib.: Trustee (1969–72). Frnds. of the Lib. Huntsville Cmnty. Concert Assn. First Bapt. Church (Huntsville). **Activities:** 22, 39, 44 **Addr.:** 4018 E. Crestview Dr. N.W., Huntsville, AL 35805.

Logsdon, Richard H. (Je. 24, 1912, Upper Sandusky, OH) Prof. Emeritus of LS, Queens Coll., 1980–, Prof. of LS, 1971–80; Univ. Dean for Libs., CUNY, 1969–71; Dir. of Univ. Libs., Columbia Univ., 1953–69, Asst. and Assoc. Dir. of Libs., 1947–53; Asst. Dir., Vets. Admin. Lib. Srv., 1947; Chief Libn., U.S. Ofc. of Educ., 1945–47; Prof. of LS and Ch. of Dept., Univ. of KY, 1943–45. **Educ.:** West. Rsv. Univ., 1929–33, AB (Econ.), 1933–34, BS (LS); Univ. of Chicago, 1937–42, PhD (LS). **Orgs.:** ALA: Bd. of Educ. for Libnshp. (1946–51); LED (Pres., 1948–49); ACRL/Univ. Sect. (Ch., 1954–55). ARL: Com. on Slavic and E. European Acq. (Ch., 1961–62). NY LA: Pres. (1965–66). Tufts Univ. Visit. Com. on the Libs. Mid. States Assn. of Coll. and Sec. Sch. **Honors:** Carnegie Flwshp., 1938–39. **Pubns.:** Jt. auth., *The Columbia University Libraries* (1958); jt. auth., *Library Careers* (1963); *Library Manpower and Education in Indiana* (1973). **Activities:** 1, 2; 17, 24, 26; 54, 63, 85 **Addr.:** 601 W. 113th-6A, New York, NY 10025.

Logsdon, Robert Lester (Ap. 13, 1947, Covington, KY) Libn. III, IN State Lib., 1977–; Branch Libn., Evansville (IN) Pub. Lib., 1974–77; Ref. Libn., Indianapolis-Marion Cnty. Pub. Lib., 1970–74. **Educ.:** East. KY Univ., 1966–70, AB (Soclgy.); IN Univ., 1971–76, MLS. **Orgs.:** IN LA: Secy. (1976–1978); Ch., Local Arrang. Com. (1972, 1974). SLA. IN Hist. Socty. **Pubns.:** Contrib., "Charles E. Rush," *Dict. of Amer. Lib. Biog.* (1978). **Activities:** 9, 13; 24, 39; 72 **Addr.:** 6632 Troon Way, Indianapolis, IN 46227.

Lohf, Kenneth A. (Ja. 14, 1925, Milwaukee, WI) Libn. for Rare Bks. and Mss., Columbia Univ. Libs., 1968–, Lectr. in Lib. Srv., 1970–; Asst. Libn., Spec. Cols., Columbia Univ. Libs., 1957–67, Ref. Libn., 1953–57, Asst. Libn., Sch. of Lib. Srv. Lib., 1952–53. **Educ.:** Northwest. Univ., 1947–49, AB (Eng. Lit.); Columbia Univ., 1949–50, MA (Eng. Lit.), 1950–51, MS (LS). **Orgs.:** Frnds. of the Columbia Libs.: Secy./Treas. (1973–). Bibl. Socty. of Amer. Grolier Club. Century Assn. **Pubns.:** *Joseph Conrad at Mid-Century: Editions and Studies* (1968); *Frank Norris: A Bibliography* (1968); *Sherwood Anderson: A Bibliography* (1968); *Index to Little Magazines* (1957–64); *The Literary Manuscripts of Hart Crane* (1967); various bks., articles. **Activities:** 1, 2; 18, 23, 45; 55, 57 **Addr.:** Rare Books and Manuscript Library, 800 Butler Library, Columbia University, New York, NY 10027.

Lohrentz, Kenneth P. (D. 3, 1940, Newton, KS) Asst. Prof., Hum./Soc. Sci. Div., Univ. of NE Libs., 1976–. **Educ.:** Bethel Coll., 1958–62, BA (Hist.); KS State Univ., 1966–68, MSEd (Sec. Educ.); Syracuse Univ., 1968–74, PhD (Hist.); IN Univ., 1975–76, MLS. **Orgs.:** ALA. NE LA. CSLA. African Std. Assn. **Pubns.:** Jt. auth., *Africana microfilms at the E.S. Bird Library, Syracuse University: an annotated guide* (1974); *A Bibliography of anthropology-related serial publications in the University of Nebraska Libraries* (1978); "Joseph Booth, Charles Domingo, and the Seventh-Day Baptists in northern Nyasaland, 1910–1912," *Jnl. of African Hist.* (1971); "The Campaign to depose Chief Mulama in Marama Location: a case study in the politics of kinship," *Kenya Hist. Review* (1976). **Activities:** 28, 31, 39; 54, 63, 92 **Addr.:** 210 Skyway Rd., Lincoln, NE 68505.

Lohrstorfer, John K. (Ap. 16, 1949, Toledo, OH) Inst. Lib. Coord., Dupage Lib. Syst., 1975–; Libn., Detroit Pub. Lib., 1974–75; Libn., Grosse Pointe Park Pub. Lib., 1973–74. **Educ.:** Wayne State Univ., 1970–72, BA (Hist.); 1973–74, MSLS. N. IL Univ. Coll. of Law, 1977–81 J.D. (Law). **Orgs.:** ALA: ASCLA/Lib. Srv. to Prisoners Sect. (Ch., 1978–79; Co-Ch., 1979–80). ALA and Amer. Correct. Assn. Jt Com. on Inst. Libs. (1978–80). Christian Legal Socty. IL WHCOLIS: Del. (1978). **Honors:** H.W. Wilson Co., H.W. Wilson Awd., 1974. **Pubns.:** Various sp. at wkshps. **Activities:** 5, 13 **Addr.:** Dupage Lib System, 127 S. 1st St., Geneva, IL 60134.

Loke, Lesley C. (Ja 18, 1950, Milwaukee, WI) Resrch. and Grants Coord., Detroit Pub. Lib., 1979–; LSCA Prog. Consult., MA Bd. of Lib. Cmsnrs. 1976–79, Chief, Bk. Srvs., 1976–76, Head Libn., Garland Jr. Coll. 1973–76. **Educ.:** Univ. of WI, 1968–72, BS (Engl. Phil.); 1972–73, MA (LS). Various Cont. Educ. Activities. **Orgs.:** ALA: PLA; ASCLA, Plng., Org., and By-Laws Com. (1982); LAMA, Plng. and Eval. of Lib. Srvs. Comm. Leag. of Women Voters of Southfield/ Lathrup Village. **Honors:** Beta Phi Mu. Phi Kappa Phi. **Addr.:** 16208 Carriage Lamp Ct., Apt. #713, Southfield, MI 48075.

Loken, Sarah F. (N. 12, 1938, Seattle, WA) Asst. Dir. for Ctrl. Srvs., Timberland Reg. Lib., 1978–, Supvsr. of Ctrl. Srvs., 1976–78; Ext. Libn., Kitsap Reg. Lib., 1974–76, Adult Srvs./Outrch. Libn., 1971–73. **Educ.:** Univ. of WA, 1959–71, BA (Eng.), 1972–74, MLS; Evergreen State Coll., 1980–81 (grad. mgt. crs.). **Orgs.:** ALA: Booklist. Adv. Com. (1981–83); Cncl. (1979–83); ASCLA, Lib. Srv. Shut-Ins Com. (1978–80); Mem. Com. (Consult., 1978–79); Hlth. and Rehab. Srvs. Div., Mem. Promo. Com. (Ch., 1976–77). Pac. NWLA. WA LA: Exec. Bd. (1979–83); Legis. Com. (Ch., 1976–77). WA Lib. Netwk.: Exec. Cncl. (1979–81). **Honors:** Phi Beta Kappa, 1971. **Activities:** 9; 17, 27, 34; 56, 78 **Addr.:** Timberland Regional Library, 415 Airdustrial Way, S.W., Olympia, WA 98501.

Lolley, John Louis (N. 24, 1937, Shreveport, LA) Dir. of Lib. Srvs., Tarrant Cnty. Jr. Coll., S. Campus, 1969–, Ref. Libn., 1968–69; Dir. of Lib., St. James Parish, LA, 1966–68; Catlgr., Tempe Pub. Lib., 1965–66. **Educ.:** LA Tech Univ., 1960, BA (Geo.); LA State Univ., 1965, MA (LS); N. TX State Univ., 1978, PhD (LS). **Orgs.:** TX LA. SWLA. Alpha Lambda Sigma. TX Jr. Coll. Tchrs. Assn. Phi Delta Kappa. **Pubns.:** *Your Library: What's In It For You?* (1974); "Recent Directions in Educating the Library User in Junior and Community Colleges" in *Progress in Educating the Library User* (1978); "Vocational-Technical Faculty and the Library; Why Some Use It and Some Don't!" *TX Lib. Jnl.* (Spr. 1979); "Educating the Library User," *TX Lib. Jnl.* (Spr. 1975); color video presentation. **Activities:** 1; 17, 31, 32; 75 **Addr.:** Tarrant County Junior College, 5301 Campus Dr., Fort Worth, TX 76119.

Lombardo, Rita Marie (Ag. 5, 1939, Brooklyn, NY) Exec. Dir., Assoc. Info. Mgrs., 1980–; Admin. Asst. to Pres., Congsnl. Info. Srv., 1973–80. **Educ.:** Univ. of Hartford, 1961–65 (Liberal Arts). **Addr.:** Associated Information Managers, 316 Pennsylvania Ave. S.E., Suite 400, Washington, DC 20003.

Lonergan, Lawrence Anthony (Ap. 21, 1917, Lindsey, ON) Dir. of Libs., St. John's Univ., 1976–, Media and Spec. Coll. Libn., 1971–76, Prof, Fine Arts Dept., 1968–71, Ch., Fine Arts Dept., 1948–68; Prof., St. Joseph's Coll., 1943–47. **Educ.:** St. Joseph's Coll., 1934–38, BA (Phil.); Mary Immaculate Semy., 1940–43 (Theol.); Catholic Univ., 1948, MFA; St. John's Univ., 1949, BLS. **Orgs.:** ALA. NY LA. Cath. LA. Knights of Columbus. **Honors:** St. John's Univ., Pres. Medal, 1977. **Pubns.:** Paintings and Sculptures in Permanent Colls. Filmstrips. **Activities:** 1; 17, 32, 45; 55 **Addr.:** St. John's University, Grand Central & Utopia Pkwys., Jamaica, NY 11439.

Long, Charles Robert (S. 20, 1936, Long Beach, CA) Asst. VP and Dir., Lib. and Plant Info Srvs., NY Botanical Garden, 1972–; Libn., Gray Herbarium and Arnold Arboretum, Harvard Univ., 1969–72; Asst. Dir., Nashua (NH) Pub. Lib., 1968–69. **Educ.:** Univ. of Toronto, 1954–59, BA; Univ. of MA, 1959–62, MA; Simmons Coll., 1967–68, SMLS. **Orgs.:** ALA: ACRL/Sci. and Tech. Sect., Ch. (1981–82). Cncl. on Botanical and Horticultural Libraries. NY LA: RTSD/Presentation Sect., Ch. (1981–82). SAA. ASIS. Other orgs. Intl. Assn. for Plant Taxonymy. **Pubns.:** "Natural History Manuscripts and Related Materials in the Archives of the New York Botanical Garden," *Jnl. Socty. Bibl. Natl. Hist.* (Vol. 8, no. 4). **Activities:** 5; 15, 17; 58, 65 **Addr.:** Library, The New York Botanical Garden, Bronx, NY 10458.

Long, Dorothy E. (O. 7, 1908, Pfafftown, NC) Assoc. Dir. Emeritus, Hlth. Sci. Lib., Univ. of NC, 1973–, Head of Ref. Dept., 1954–72, Catlgr., 1952–53; Ref. Libn., Univ. of KY, 1950–52; Ref. Libn., Winston-Salem Pub. Lib., 1950; Lib. Dir., Vets. Ad-

Special Subjects/Services: 50. Adult educ.; 51. Advert./Mktg.; 52. Aerosp.; 53. Agric.; 54. Area std.; 55. Arts/Hum.; 56. Autom.; 57. Bibl./Prtg.; 58. Bio. sci.; 59. Bus./Fin.; 60. Chem.; 61. Copyrt.; 62. Documtn.; 63. Educ.; 64. Engin.; 65. Env.; 66. Eth. grps.; 67. Film; 68. Food/Nutr.; 69. Geneal.; 70. Geo.; 71. Geol.; 72. Handcpd.; 73. Hist.; 74. Int. frdm.; 75. Info. sci.; 76. Insr.; 77. Law; 78. Legis.; 79. Math./Comp. sci.; 80. Med.; 81. Metals; 82. Nat. resrcs.; 83. Newsp.; 84. Nuc. sci.; 85. Oral hist.; 86. Petr./Energy; 87. Pharm.; 88. Phys./Astr./Math.; 89. Readg.; 90. Relig.; 91. Sci./Tech.; 92. Soc. sci.; 93. Telecom.; 94. Transp.; 95. (other).

min. Lib., Martinsburg, WV, 1948–49; Libn., Vets. Admin. Hosp., Uteen, NC, 1946–47. **Educ.:** Univ. of NC, Greensboro, 1924–29, AB (Eng. Lit.); Univ. of WI, 1939–42, MA (Eng.); Univ. of IL, 1946, BS (LS); courses in med. bibl., Columbia Univ., 1949. **Orgs.:** Med. LA. NC LA. **Honors:** Med. LA, Murray Gottlieb Prize Essay, 1956. **Pubns.:** Ed., *Medicine in North Carolina* (1972); Jt. auth., *One Hundred Year History of Board of Medical Examiners* (1959); various articles, poetry. **Activities:** 1, 12; 17, 20, 31; 57, 73, 80 **Addr.:** 4993 Vienna-Dozier Rd., Pfafftown, NC 27040.

Long, Jean F. (Je. 14, 1930, Saugus, MA) Med. Libn., Newington Chld. Hosp., 1977–; Ref. Libn., Kitsap Reg. Lib., 1973–75; Srch. Libn., Gen. Electric Co., 1972–73. **Educ.:** SUNY, Albany, 1968–71, BA (Eng.), 1971–73, MLS; Med. LA, 1973, Cert. **Orgs.:** Cap. Area Hlth. Cnsrtm. Libns.: Pres. (1979). CT Assn. Hlth. Sci. Libs.: Secy. (1978). Med. LA. SLA: SUNY, Albany Student Chap. (Pres., 1972). **Activities:** 12; 15, 39, 46; 72, 80 **Addr.:** 2 Monticello Dr., E. Lyme, CT 06333.

Long, Sara Ellen (D. 27, 1942, Los Angeles, CA) Coord. of Lib. and Media Srvs., Sch. Dist. U-46, 1979–, Libn., Abbott Jr. HS, 1969–78, Tchr., Coleman Sch., 1964–68. **Educ.:** IL Wesleyan Univ., 1960–64, BS (Elem. Educ.); Univ. of IL, 1968–69, MS (LS), 1978–79, MS.Ed (Educ. Admin). **Orgs.:** IL LA: JMRT (Bd. Mem. 1976–77). ALA: IL Mem. Ch. (1974–77). AAUW. Delta Kappa Gamma. Natl. Educ. Assn. IL Educ. Assn. **Honors:** Beta Phi Mu, City of Elgin, Outstan. Young Women of Elgin, 1977. **Activities:** 10; 17, 32, 35; 63, 95-AV. **Addr.:** 4 South Gifford St., Elgin, IL 60120.

Long, Susan D. (D. 12, 1948, Washington, DC) Med. Libn., Providence Hosp., Cincinnati, OH, 1978–; Ref. Libn., Xavier Univ., 1977–78; Resrch. Libn., Christ Hosp. Inst. of Med. Resrch., 1975–76. **Educ.:** Russell Sage Coll., 1966–70, BA (Hist. & Gvt.); Univ. of KY, 1974–75, MSLS. **Orgs.:** Cincinnati Area Hlth. Sci. Libs. Assn.: Pres. (1979–80); Secy. (1979); Participating Lib. Adv. Com. (1979–80); Area Plng. Com. (1979–80). **Activities:** 5, 12; 15, 24, 34; 80 **Addr.:** 230 Wilmuth Ave., Cincinnati, OH 45215.

Longland, Jean R. (Ja. 11, 1913, Boston, MA) Cur. of the Lib., Hispanic Socty. of America, 1953–, Cur. of Portuguese Books, 1946–53, First Catlgr., 1936–46. **Educ.:** Wheaton Coll., MA, 1930–35, AB (Fr.); Simmons Coll., 1935–36, SB (LS). **Orgs.:** SLA: Ch., Musm. Grp., NY Chap. PEN Amer. Ctr. Auth. Gld. Poetry Socty. of Amer. Amer. Transl. Assn. Other orgs. **Honors** Phi Lambda Beta; Intl. Poetry Assn. and Portuguese gvt., Portugal Prize, 1973; *Poet Lore* Transl. Awd., 2nd Prize, 1970, 74. **Pubns.:** Transls. of Portuguese poetry in *Jnl. of the Amer. Portuguese Socty.* (Sum. 1978); *Literary Review* (Win. 1978); *Prose Poem* (1976); *Latin Amer. Resrch. Review* (1977); *Chicago Review* (Aut. 1975); *Selections from Contemporary Portuguese Poetry* (1966); other books and journals. **Activities:** 12; 17, 20; 57 **Addr.:** The Hispanic Society of America, 613 West 155th St., New York, NY 10032.

Lonnberg, Charles Mitchell (N. 1, 1926, Jetmore, KS) Libn., Prof. of LS, IN State Univ., Evansville, 1969–; Dir., Educ. Resrch. and Resrc. Ctr., Anderson Pub. Schs., 1966–69; Prof. of Msc., Anderson Coll., 1955–66; Supvsr. of Msc., Copeland HS, 1949–50; Instr. in Band Trng. Sch., U.S. Army, Fort Riley, 1950–52. **Educ.:** Emporia State Univ., 1945–49, BS (Msc.), 1949–53, MS (Msc.); IN Univ., Bloomington, 1960–64, MALS. **Orgs.:** ALA. IN LA: Exec. Com. of Tech. Srv. (1979–). Frnds. of Willard Lib.: Treas. (1978–). Trinity Untd. Meth. Church. Evansville Philharmonic Chorus. **Honors:** Phi Mu Alpha Sinfonia; Sigma Tau Gamma. **Pubns.:** Reviews. **Activities:** 1; 20, 39, 46; 56 **Addr.:** RR 10, Box 436, Evansville, IN 47712.

Lonney, Janet P. (Mr. 4, 1938, Philadelphia, PA) Sect. Chief, Lib. and Admin. Srvs., West. Electric Corporate Educ. Ctr., 1979–, Sect. Chief, Tech. Lib., 1973–79, Ref. Libn., 1971–73; Ref. Libn., Amer. Cyanamid, 1963–71; Ed. Asst., Merck, Sharp and Dohme, 1959–63. **Educ.:** Chestnut Hill Coll., 1955–59, BS (Chem.); Rutgers Univ., 1967–70, MLS. **Orgs.:** SLA: Princeton-Trenton Chap.; NJ Chap., Bltn. Ed. (1973–74), Dir. (1979–80), Treas. (1972–73), PR Ch. (1976–77), Archvst. (1980–). World Future Socty. Assn. for Comp. Mach. Inst. of Mgt. Sci. **Honors:** Beta Phi Mu. **Activities:** 12; 15, 17, 39; 63, 75, 93 **Addr.:** Western Electric Company, Inc., Corporate Education Center, P.O. Box 1000, Hopewell, NJ 08525.

Lonning, Roger Dean (F. 12, 1927, Iowa City, IA) Media Supvsr., Sr. HS, Albert Lea, 1961–; Instr., Mankato State Univ., Spr. 1981, Sum. 1976; Libn., Lea Coll., Sum. 1969, 1968; Libn., Clarion Pub. Schs., 1954–56. **Educ.:** IA State Tchrs. Coll., 1951–54, BA (LS), 1956–57, MA (Admin.); Univ. of MN, Minneapolis, 1966–71, MA (LS). **Orgs.:** ALA: AASL. MN Assn. of Sch. Libns.: Pres. (1969–70); Secy. (1974–75). MN Educ. Media Org.: Secy. (1975–76). Freeborn Cnty. Hist. Socty. **Pubns.:** *History of Albert Lea Senior High School - 1880-1980* (forthcoming). **Activities:** 10; 17, 26, 32; 55, 69, 85 **Addr.:** 601 Cherry Ave., Albert Lea, MN 56007.

Loo, Shirley (My. 14, 1939, Honolulu, HI) Spec. in Info. Cntrl. and Autom. Systs., Congsnl. Resrch. Srv., Lib. of Congs., 1980–, Sect. Head of Sub. Spec. Sect., 1972–80, Asst. Sect. Head, 1970–72, Educ. and Pub. Welfare Biblgphr., 1967–70; Soc. Std. Tchr., New York City Bd. of Educ., 1964–66; Soc. Std., Jnlsm. and Math. Tchr., HI State Dept. of Educ., 1961–63. **Educ.:** Univ. of HI, 1957–61, BEd; Columbia Univ., 1963–64, MA (Tchg. of Amer. Hist.); Univ. of HI, 1961, Cert; 1966–67 MS (LS). **Orgs.:** SLA: Cont. Ed. (Ch., 1980–81); Jt. Spr. Wkshp. (1979–80). DC LA: Asst. Treas. (1981–83); Ref. Interest Grp. Com. (1979–81), Mgt. Interest Grp. Com. (1980–81). ALA. Lib. of Congs. Prof. Assn. Cap. Hill Restoration Socty: Lib. of Congs. Cooking Club: Pres. (1974); VP (1970–71). Eng.–Speaking Un. **Honors:** Lib. of Congs., Incentive Awd., 1971; Lib. of Congs., Merit. Srv. Awd., 1976; Beta Phi Mu, 1967. **Pubns.:** "Selective Dissemination of Information to Congress: The Congressional Research Service SDI Service," *Lib. Resrcs. & Tech. Srvs.* (Fall 1975); various bibls. **Activities:** 4; 17, 30, 39; 56, 57, 63 **Addr.:** Library Services Division, LM 221, Congressional Research Service, Library of Congress, Washington, DC 20540.

Lookout, Charles (D. 29, 1922, Pawhuska, OK) Ref., Pers. Dept., Tulsa City–Cnty. Lib. Syst., 1964–; **Educ.:** OK State Univ., 1947–52, BA (Lib. Arts); OK Univ., 1964–68, MLS. **Orgs.:** ALA. OK LA: Rcrt. Com. (Ch., 1978–79). Tulsa Lib. Staff Assn. Vets. of Frgn. Wars. Amer. Legion. Theta Chi. **Honors:** Vets. of Frgn. Wars, Captain (OK), All-State Team of Post Commanders, 1961; Vets. of Frgn. Wars, Natl. Champion, Poppy Sales, 1963; Kihekah-Steh Pow-Wow, Winner, Straight War Dance, 1978. **Activities:** 9; 16, 31, 39; 55, 83, 92 **Addr.:** 1120 South Winston, Tulsa, OK 74112.

Loomis, Barbara Lee (N. 1, 1931, Cleveland, OH) Air Command Libn. & Base Libn., Elmendorf AFB, AK, 1977–; Lib. Dir., MacKenzie Meml. Pub. Lib., 1972–76; Branch Libn., Willoughby-Eastlake Pub. Lib., 1971–72. **Educ.:** OH Univ., 1950–52, AA (Jnlsm.); OH State Univ., 1952–54, BS (Bus. Admin.); Case-Western Reserve Univ., 1970–71, MSLS. **Orgs.:** AK LA: Anchorage Chap. (Secy. 1978). Pac. NW LA. ALA. Anchorage Mncpl. Lib. Adv. Bd. AAUW. Amer. Mgt. Assn. **Honors:** Beta Phi Mu. **Activities:** 4, 9; 15, 17, 47; 50, 59, 74 **Addr.:** 3836 Telequana, Anchorage, AK 99503.

Looney, Robert Fain (Jy. 20, 1925, Rocky Mount, NC) Cur., Print and Pic. Dept., Free Lib. of Philadelphia, 1964–; Libn., Art Dept., 1960–64; Instr. (Eng.), Berry Coll., 1955–58. **Educ.:** Univ. of NC, 1949–53, AB (Eng.); 1953–55, MA (Eng.); 1958–60, MS (LS). **Orgs.:** SLA: Pic. Div. (Ch., 1972–73). Philadelphia Print Club. **Pubns.:** *Old Philadelphia in Early Photographs* (1976); *Philadelphia Printmaking; American Prints Before 1860* (1976); "Thomas Doughty, Printmaker," *Imprint*, (Ag. 1979); "Philadelphia Views, 1800–1830," Imprint (Ap. 1978). **Activities:** 9; 15, 17; 55 **Addr.:** Free Library of Philadelphia, Logan Square, Philadelphia, PA 19103.

Lopato, Esther W. (Ag. 29, 1920, New York, NY) Pres., Bd. of Trustees, Brooklyn Pub. Lib. Syst., 1978–, Trustee, 1972–. **Educ.:** City Coll. of NY, 1939–48, BS (Educ.); New York Univ., 1950–60, PhD (Psy.); NY State Cert. as Psy., 1961–. **Orgs.:** NY LA. NY State Assn. of Lib. Bds.: Bd. of Dir. (1973–); VP (1980). ALA: ALTA, Pubns. Com. (1978–); Educ. Com. (1980) Reading Is Fundamental in N.Y.C.: Ch. (1973–78); Bd. (1972–). Cmnty. Plng. Bd. 14: Vice Ch. (1978–). Midwood-Kings Highway Dev. Corp.: Bd. of Dir. (1977–). Cmnty. Sch. Bd. Dist. 22: Vice-Ch. (1970); Ch. (1971–72). **Activities:** 47 **Addr.:** 1231 E. 21 St., Brooklyn, NY 11210.

López, Heriberto (Jl. 16, 1940, Naguabo, PR) Lib. Dir., Humacao Univ. Coll., 1978–, Coord. of Tech. Srvs., 1976–78, Head, Cat. Dept., 1975–78, Catlgr., 1972–75; Asst. Dir. of Financial Aid Prog., PR Jr. Coll., 1970–71. **Educ.:** Spanish Amer. Bapt. Semy., 1960–63, BTh (Theo.); East. Bapt. Coll., 1964–67, BA (Educ., Phil.); Univ. of PR, 1970–72, MLS; Evang. Semy. of PR, 1973–76, M Div (Relig., Theo.). **Orgs.:** Asociación de Ex-Alumnos de la Escuela Graduada de Bibliotecología. SB PR. Concilio de Ministros Evangélicos de PR. TESOL. **Honors:** City of Philadelphia, Merit. Cit. for Outstan. Srvs., 1970. **Pubns.:** "Directores del Colegio Universitario de Humacao", *El Buho* (Ag. 1977). **Activities:** 1, 13; 17, 35, 46; 55, 63, 75 **Addr.:** Humacao, University College, Humacao, PR 00661.

López, Lillian (Je. 24, 1924, Salinas, PR) Coord., NY Pub. Lib. 1980–, Coord. of Spec. Srvs., 1972–79, Admin. of the S. Bronx Proj., 1967–72, Supvsg. Branch Libn., 1967, Sr. Libn., 1962–66. **Educ.:** Hunter Coll., 1953–59, BA (Span.); Columbia Univ., 1960–62, MLS; NY State, Pub. Libn. Cert. **Orgs.:** NY LA: Rass Litcy. Com. (1977–79). ALA: RASD, Subcom. on Affirmative Action (1975–78); Schol. Com. (1975–78). Oral Hist. Assn. Natl. Com. on Libs. and Info. Sci.-Cult. Minorities Task Frc. (1980–82). El Museo del Barrio. S. Bronx Cult. Ctr. **Honors:** Inst. de PR, Spec. Awd. for Valuable Contrib. to the Dev. of PR Cult. in U.S., 1977; Untd. Women of the Amers., Spec. Awd. for Exec. in Achvmt., 1980; Kings Cnty. PR Leadership Conf., Cmnty. Srv. Awd., 1978. **Pubns.:** "Reminiscences of Two Turned-On Librarians," *PR Perspective* (1974); "Puerto Ricans and the Public Library," *Oppts. For Minorities in Libnshp.* (1977); "South Bronx Project," *Wilson Lib. Bltn.* (Mr., My. 1970). **Activities:** 9; 15, 16, 17; 50, 66, 89 **Addr.:** 392 Central Park W., 10H, New York, NY 10025.

Lord, Harold G. (Ja. 25, 1935, Newark, NJ) Pres., Lord Brooks Enterprises, Inc.; Dir., of Media Srvs., Littleton (CO) Pub. Schs., 1962–; Math Tchr., Union (NJ) HS, 1959–61. **Educ.:** Lafayette Coll., 1953–57, AB (Hist); Syracuse Univ., 1957–58, MAT (Educ.). **Orgs.:** ALA: AASL, ASCLA, LITA, LAMA. AECT. Natl. Assn. of Educ. Broadcasters. NAVA. CO Educ. Media Assn. **Honors:** Kappa Phi Kappa; AASL/EBC National Award, 1976. **Pubns.:** Various articles and educ. wkbks. **Activities:** 10, 11; 17, 24, 34; 61, 75, 93 **Addr.:** Curtis Media Services, School Dist. #6 Arapahoe County, 5895 S. University Blvd., Littleton, CO 80121.

Lord, Milton Edward (Je. 12, 1898, Lynn, MA) Dir., Libn., Emeritus, Boston Pub. Lib., 1965–, Dir., Libn., 1932–65; Dir., Lib., Amer. Acad. in Rome, 1975–76, Libn.-in-Residence, 1971–74, Libn., 1926–30; Dir., Univ. Libs., Univ. of IA, 1930–31; Mem., Comsn. of 5 Amer. Libns. Aiding in Recat. Vatican Lib., Rome, 1928; various positions in lib., Harvard Univ., 1919–25. **Educ.:** Harvard Coll., 1919, AB; Harvard Univ., 1921–24; Ecole des Sci. Politiques, Paris, 1925–26; Middlebury Coll., Grad. Lang. Schs., 1966–68 (Fr., Italian, Grmn.). **Orgs.:** ALA: Pres. (1949–50). MA LA: Pres. (1955–56). CNLIA: Ch. (1944–45). IFLA: 1st VP (1947–54). Amer. Bk. Ctr. for War-Devastated Libs. Inc.: Bd. Ch. U.S. Bk. Exch. Inc.: Pres. (1948–52). Conseil Intl. des Monuments et des Sites (Paris): Consult. (1969–79); Com. Intl. pour la Documtn. (Pres., 1970–79); U.S. Natl. Com. (1970–79). Boxford Town Lib. Various other orgs. Simmons Coll.: Trustee (1947–). **Honors:** Phi Beta Kappa, 1968; Conseil Intl. des Monuments et des Sites (Paris), Mem. d'Hon., 1979, Disting. Srv. Medal, 1980; France, Chevalier de la Legion d'Hon., 1951; other hons. **Pubns.:** Jt. auth., *Shakespeare in Cambridge: A Centennial History of the Old Cambridge Shakespeare Association* (1980); various articles. **Activities:** 1, 9; 17, 47; 55, 62 **Addr.:** R.F.D. 85 Main St., Boxford, MA 01921.

Lorenz, John G. (S. 28, 1915, New York, NY) Consult., Fac., Cath. Univ., 1980; Exec. Dir., ARL, 1976–79; Deputy Libn., Lib. of Congs., 1965–76; Dir., Lib. Progs., U.S. Ofc. of Educ., 1956–65. **Educ.:** Coll. of City of NY, 1934–38, BS (Soc. Sci.); Columbia Univ., 1939–40, MLS; MI State Univ., 1949–52, MA (Pub. Admin.). **Orgs.:** ALA: Cncl; Exec. Bd.; various Coms. AALS. IFLA: Prof. Bd. Natl. Hist. Pubns. and Recs. Comsn.: Pres. Appt. (1978–81). Cosmos Club. **Honors:** Dept. of Hlth., Educ. and Welfare, Superior Achvmt., 1960. **Pubns.:** *Library Services Act* (1960); "Effective Use of Library Consultants," *Lib. Trends* (Win. 1980). **Activities:** 1, 4; 17, 24, 26; 50, 63, 78 **Addr.:** 5629 Newington Rd., Bethesda, MD 20816.

Lorenzi, Nancy M. (Indiana, PA) Dir., Med. Ctr. Libs., Univ. of Cincinnati, 1972–; Head of Reg. Ext. Srv., Univ. of Louisville, 1970–72, Head of Info. Srvs., 1968–70; Chief Libn., St. Elizabeth Hosp., Youngstown, OH, 1963–67. **Educ.:** Youngstown State Univ., 1962–66, AB (Bio. Sci., Soc. Sci.); Case West. Rsv. Univ., 1967–68, MS (Med. Lib.); Univ. of Louisville, 1969–72, MA (Soclgy.); Univ. of Cincinnati, 1974–80, PhD (Soclgy.). **Orgs.:** Med. LA: Pres.-Elect (1981–82); Pres. (1982–83). Cincinnati Area Hlth. Scis. Lib. Assn. N. Ctrl. Sociological Assn. **Honors:** Med. LA, Rittenhouse Awd., 1968; Natl. Lib. of Med., Resrch. Grant, 1975. **Pubns.:** Jt. auth., "Health Sciences Library: University of Cincinnati," *Bltn. of the Med. LA* (Jl. 1977); jt. auth., "Drug Information to Patient Care Areas via Television: Preliminary Evaluation of Two Years' Experience," *Spec. Libs.* (1978); jt. auth., "Information to Patient Care Areas via Television: An Update," *Hlth. Comm. and Informatics* (5, 1979); jt. auth., "Information via Television as an Aid to Patient Care," *T.H.E. Jnl.* (Ja. 1979); "Medical Libraries," *ALA Yrbk.* (1979, 1980). **Activities:** 1; 17; 80 **Addr.:** University of Cincinnati, Medical Center Libraries, 231 Bethesda Ave., Cincinnati, OH 45267.

Lothyan, Phillip E. (Ag. 29, 1938, Los Angeles, CA) Chief, Seattle Arch. Branch, Natl. Arch. of the U.S., 1970–, Archvst., 1970–71; Mgt. Intern, Reg. 10, Gen. Srvs. Admin., 1969–70. **Educ.:** Brigham Young Univ., 1962–65, BA (Hist.), 1965–68, MA (Hist.); Inst. for Admin. of Mod. Arch., Amer. Univ., 1971, Cert. **Orgs.:** SAA: Prog. Com. (1975); Ad Hoc Com. (1976); Actv. Com. (1977–79). WA State Hist. Recs. Adv. Bd. Church of Jesus Christ of Latter-day Saints. **Honors:** State of WA, Outstan. Citizen Awd., 1975; Gen. Srvs. Admin., Outstan. Performance Awd., 1974. **Pubns.:** "Operation of a Regional Branch:Seattle," *IL Libs.* (Mr. 1975); various other pubns. **Activities:** 2; 23, 36, 39; 54, 66, 69 **Addr.:** Federal Archives and Records Center, GSA, 6125 Sand Point Way, N.E., Seattle, WA 98115.

Lotz, James Wendell (D. 18, 1944, Yonkers, NY) Mgr., Intl. Mktg., Baker & Taylor Co., 1981–, Mgr., Approval Prog. Srvs., 1974–81, Mgr., Approval Prog. Book Sel., 1972–74; Head, Purchase Div., Acq. Dept., OH St Univ Libs., 1970–72, Soc. Sci. Biblgphr., 1968–72. **Educ.:** Heidelberg Coll., 1962–66, BA (Hist.); Univ. of Cincinnati, 1966–67, MA (Amer Hist.); West. MI Univ., 1967–68, MLS. **Orgs.:** ALA. **Honors:** Beta Phi Mu, Phi Alpha Theta. **Pubns.:** Contrib., *What Else You Can Do with a Library Degree* (1980). **Activities:** 1; 15, 46 **Addr.:** c/o Baker & Taylor, 6 Kirby Ave., Somerville, NJ 08876.

PROFESSIONAL ACTIVITIES: Institutions: 1. Acad. lib.; 2. Arch.; 3. Assn.; 4. Fed./Gvt. lib.; 5. Inst. lib.; 6. Mfr./Suppl.; 7. Milit. lib.; 8. Musm.; 9. Pub. lib.; 10. Sch. lib.; 11. Sch. of lib. sci.; 12. Spec. lib.; 13. State lib.; 14. (other). **Functions/Activities:** 15. Acq./Col. dev.; 16. Adult srvs.; 17. Admin.; 18. Apprais.; 19. Archit./Bldgs.; 20. Cat./Class.; 21. Chld. srvs.; 22. Circ.; 23. Cons./Pres.; 24. Consult.; 25. Cont. ed.; 26. Educ. lib. sci.; 27. Ext. srvs.; 28. Fund/Grants; 29. Gvt. pubs.; 30. Indx./Abs.; 31. Instr. lib. use; 32. Media srvs.; 33. Micro.; 34. Netwks./Coop.; 35. Persnl.; 36. PR; 37. Publshg.; 38. Recs. mgt.; 39. Ref. srvs.; 40. Repro.; 41. Resrch.; 42. Review.; 43. Secur.; 44. Serials; 45. Spec. col.; 46. Tech. srvs.; 47. Trustees/Bds.; 48. YA srvs.; 49. (other).

Who's Who in Library and Information Services

Loucks, Cami L. (Jl. 7, 1947, Kansas City, MO) Dir. of Med. Lib. Srvs., Trinity Luth. Hosp., 1977–; Consult., Freelnc., 1978–; Med. Info. Retrieval Spec., Resrch. Med. Ctr., 1973–77. **Educ.:** Longview Cmnty. Coll., 1968–71, AA (Arts and Sci.); Ctrl. MO State Univ., 1971–72, BS (Eng., Lib. Educ.); MO Univ., Columbia, 1974–77, MA (LS). **Orgs.:** Med. LA: Instr. (1980–). SLA: SLA–Med. LA Liaison. OLUG of Grt. Kansas City. Kansas City Lib. Netwk., Inc.: Co–fndr., Bd. **Pubns.:** *Basic Budgeting for Health Sciences Libraries* (1981). **Activities:** 12; 17, 24, 32 **Addr.:** Medical Library and Media, Trinity Lutheran Hospital, Kansas City, MO 64108.

Louie, Ruby Ling (Ap. 11, 1931, Chicago, IL) Fac., CA State Univ., Los Angeles, 1979–; Elem. Sch. Libn., Long Beach Unfd. Sch. Dist., 1963–70; Reg. Chld. Libn., Los Angeles Cnty. Pub. Lib., 1961–62; Sr. Chld. Libn., New York Pub. Lib., 1959–60; Elem. Pub. Libn., Greenwich Pub. Lib., 1957–59; Chld. Bk. Reviewer, *Lib. Jnl.*, 1957–60. **Educ.:** Long Beach City Coll., 1952, AA; Univ. of CA, Los Angeles, 1952–56, BA (Gen. Elem.); Carnegie Inst. of Tech., 1956–57, MLS; Univ. of South. CA, 1970–76, PhD (LS). **Orgs.:** WHCOLIS: CA Del. (1979). CA LA. Frnds. of the Chinatown Lib., Los Angeles: Pres. (1977–). ALA: Com. for the Treatment of Minority Grps. in Lib. Bks. and Other Instr. Mtrls. (1971–78); Aurianne Bk. Awd. Com. (1960–63). Cncl. for Peace and Equality. Frnds. of Chld. and Lit.: Los Angeles Pub. Lib., Bd. (1978–81). **Honors:** Los Angeles Cnty. Human Rel. Comsn., Salute to Voluns. 1976; Phi Kappa Phi, 1957; Beta Phi Mu, 1957; South. CA Volun. Activist, 1981. **Pubns.:** *A Community Profile Approach for Expanding Public Library Services* (1976); various presentations, wkshps. **Activities:** 9, 10; 21, 24, 25; 63, 89, 95-Frnds. Grps. **Addr.:** 636 Alpine St., Los Angeles, CA 90012.

Loup, Jean L. (Ap. 18, 1941, Council Bluffs, IA) LS, Ref. Libn., Univ. of MI, 1978–; Ref. Libn., 1974–78, Head, Prcs. Sect., 1971–74; Vetny. Med. Libn., IA State Univ. Lib., 1970–71, Cat. Libn., 1967–70; Order Libn., 1966–67; Ref. Libn. and Consult., IA State Travelling Lib., 1965–66. **Educ.:** IA State Univ., 1959–63, BS (Hist.); Univ. of OK, 1963–66, MA (Hist.), 1963–65 MLS. **Orgs.:** ALA: ACRL; RASD. AAUP: Univ. of MI Chap. (Pres., 1979–80). **Pubns.:** Jt.-Auth., "Position Classification at Michigan: Another Look," *Coll. & Resrch. Libs.* (My. 1979); "Colonel Ranald S. Mackenzie at Fort Sill," *Chronicles of OK* (Spr. 1966). **Activities:** 1; 15, 39; 75, 92 **Addr.:** 3354 Bluett, Ann Arbor, MI 48105.

Louzin, Brenna Ann (O. 7, 1950, Pittsfield, MA) Dir. of Lib., Battelle Human Affairs Resrch. Ctr., 1977–; Cat. Asst., Univ. of WA, 1976–77, Serials Asst., 1976; City Bkmobile. Libn., The Berkshire Athen., 1973–74. **Educ.:** Univ. of MA, Amherst, 1968–72, BA (Eng.); Drexel Univ., 1972–73, MLS. **Orgs.:** SLA: Pac. NW Chap., Secy. Treas; Educ. Com. (Ch., 1979–80). Citizens for WA Libs. Fndn. King Cnty. Lib. Srvs. Area Grp. WHCOLIS: Spec. Libs. Liason to WA Dels. (1979–80). **Activities:** 12; 17, 36, 39; 78, 86, 92 **Addr.:** 1136 N. 83rd St., Seattle, WA 98103.

Lovas, Irene Mary (N. 13, 1945, Perth Amboy, NJ) AV Libn., Vets. Admin. Med. Ctr., Long Beach, CA, 1980–; Med. libn., Vets. Admin. Med. Ctr., NY, 1974–80; Per. libn., Cornell Univ. Med. Coll. Lib., 1973–74. **Educ.:** Douglass Coll., 1963–67, BA (Span.); Pratt Inst., 1972–74, MLS. **Orgs.:** Med. LA. NY Reg. Grp./Med. LA: Ch., Nom. Com. (1980); Small Hlth. Sci. Libs. Com. (1979–80). Manhattan/Bronx Hlth. Sci. Libs. Grp.: Treas. (1979–80); Ch.-elect (1980). **Honors:** Beta Phi Mu, Sigma Delta Pi. **Activities:** 4, 12; 15, 34, 39; 63, 75, 80 **Addr.:** Veterans Administration Medical Center, Medical Library, 5901 E. 7th St., Long Beach, CA 90822.

Lovas, Paula-Marie (Mr. 15, 1941, DC) Head, Natl. Grntlgy. Resrc. Ctr., Natl. Retired Tchrs. Assn., 1978–, Ref. Libn., 1975–77; Asst. Serials Libn., Georgetown Univ., 1971–74; Admin. Libn., U.S. Army Spec. Srvs., 1968–70. **Educ.:** Gonzaga Univ., 1961–63, BA (Fr.); Univ. of CA, Berkeley, 1966–68, MLS. **Orgs.:** SLA: Prof. and Trade Assns. RT (1980–). ASIS. Gerontological Socty.: (Co–Org., 1976); Libns. Com. (1976); Prog. Ch. (1977). **Pubns.:** "The National Gerontology Resource Center: The Public Perspective," *Spec. Cols.* (forthcoming). **Activities:** 12; 17, 34, 49-Autom.; 92 **Addr.:** 5703 Namakagan Rd., Bethesda, MD 20816.

Love, Erika (Berlin, Germany) Prof., Dir., Med. Ctr. Lib., Univ. of NM, 1977–; Deputy Assoc. Dir., Lib. Oper., Natl. Lib. of Med., 1971–77; Libn., Bowman Gray Sch. of Med., 1967–71; Chief Libn., Larue D. Carter Meml. Hosp., IN Dept. of Mental Hlth., 1958–67. **Educ.:** Heidelbert (Germ.), 1946–47; IN Univ., 1949–60, AB, 1951–53, MA (LS); Various wkshps., sems., insts. **Orgs.:** Med. LA: Pres. (1978–79); Bd. of Dir. (1974–80); Finance Com. (1974–80); Com. on Coms. (1974–79); Other Ofcs. Netwk. Adv. Com. to Libn. of Congs. (1978–). NM Perinatal Com.: Hlth. and Educ. Subcom. (1979–). Other orgs. **Pubns.:** "Research: The Third Dimension of Librarianship," *Bltn. Med. LA* (Ja. 1980); "Our Coming of Age (Innaugural Address)," *Bltn. Med. LA* (Apr. 1979); "Electing the President," *Bltn. Med. LA* (Ja. 1979); "The Medical Library Association," *ALA Yrbk.* (1979). **Activities:** 1, 12; 17, 25, 41; 80 **Addr.:** Medical Center Library, University of New Mexico, Albuquerque, NM 87131.

Love, Jane Hazelton (S. 24, 1931, New York, NY) Adj. Prof., Lib./Media Srvs., West. MD Coll., 1981–; Media Spec., Anne Arundel Cnty., 1972–; Libn., MacArthur Jr. HS, 1967–68; Libn., Elem. Sch., Anne Arundel Cnty., 1964–67; Classrm. Tchr., Anne Arundel Cnty., 1959–64. **Educ.:** Univ. of MD, 1971, BA (Hist.); WV Univ., 1973–74, MEd, 1975–77, EdD; Supvsr. of Sch. Libs., Cert.; various other certs. **Orgs.:** ALA: AASL, Legis. Com. (Ch., 1980–82); ALA–Amer. Vocational Assn. Jt. Com. (1977–79) MD Educ. Media Org.: Pres. (1979–80); Prog. Ch. (1978–80). Educ. Media Assn. of Anne Arundel Cnty: Pres. (1979–81). AECT: Cncl. (1979–82); Strg. Com. (Secy., 1981–82). Amer. Assn. of Sch. Admins. **Pubns.:** Reviews. **Activities:** 1, 10; 26, 32, 41; 50, 74, 78 **Addr.:** 11253 Crystal Run, Columbia, MD 21044.

Love, Wayne (S. 14, 1936, Dothan, AL) Dir., Houston Meml. Lib., 1964–; Admin., Southeast AL Coop. Lib. Syst., 1977–80; Adult Srvs. Libn., Houston Meml. Lib., 1961–64, Bkmobile Libn., 1956–61. **Educ.:** Troy State Univ., 1954–58, BS (Eng.); Vanderbilt Univ., 1961–63, MALS; Coursework at various univs., 1956–76. **Orgs.:** AL LA: Pres. (1968–69); Lib. Dev. Com. (1965–66, 1970–71, 1973–75); Pub. Lib. Div. (Ch., 1966–67); Various other Coms. and Ofcs. SELA: Exec. Bd. (1974–78). ALA: Com. on Lib. Stnds. (1976–78). Rotary. AECT. Houston Arts and Hum. Cncl.: VP (1977–79). Houston Acad.: Bd. of Dir. Other orgs. **Honors:** Lib. and Media Profs., Srv. Awd., 1979. AL Pub. Lib. Srv., Srv. Awd., 1961. **Activities:** 9; 17, 19, 47; 50, 89 **Addr.:** Route 1, Box 313, Ashford, AL 36312.

Lovejoy, Eunice G. (Ap. 18, 1924, Harrisonburg, VA) Lib. Dev. Consult., Srvs. to Handcpd. and Aging, State Lib. of OH, 1972–; Libn., Srvs. to State Govt., 1969–72, Abs. and Ind. Ed., ERIC Clearinghouse for Vocational and Tech. Educ., OH State Univ., 1966–68, Head, Dept. Libs., 1965–66, Asst. to Supvsr., Dept. Libs., 1963–65, Libn., Soc. Wk. Lib., 1960–63; Ref. Libn., Educ. Lib., 1959–60; Various other positions. **Educ.:** Marion Coll., 1939–41; Madison Coll., 1941–43, BA (Eng.); Univ. of NC, 1943–44, BS (LS). **Orgs.:** ALA: ASCLA, Bd. of Dir. (1977–79), Com. on Stans. for Lib. Srvs. to the Blind and Phys. Handcpd. (1977–78), Std. of State Admin. of Lib. Srvs. to the Blind and Phys. Handcpd. Com. (Ch., 1976–78); Hlth. and Rehab. Lib. Srvs. Dir., Pubn. Com. (Ch., 1976–77), Lib. Srvs. for the Blind and Phys. Handcpd. Sect. (Mem. at Large, 1975–76). Pres. Com. on Employment of the Handcpd.: Lib. Com. (1974–). Amer. Assn. of Workers with the Blind: Oh Chap., Readg. Mtrls. and Resrcs. Int. Grp. (Ch., 1976–79). **Pubns.:** "Change Isn't Easy," *Dikta* (Spr. 1979); "The Disabled Student on American Campuses," *Coll. & Resrch. Libs. News* (F. 1978); guest ed., "Library Services for the Blind and Physically Handicapped" *HRLSD Jnl.* (Fall 1976); "School Librarians and Children with Handicaps," *OH Assn. of Sch. Libns. Bltn.* (Ja. 1975); other articles. **Activities:** 13; 24, 27; 72, 95-Aging people. **Addr.:** 172 West Main St., Westerville, OH 43081.

Lovett, Robert W. (S. 18, 1913, Beverly, MA) Retd. Cur. of Mss. and Arch., Baker Lib., Harvard Bus. Sch., 1948–79; Asst. in Arch., Harvard Univ., 1937–48. **Educ.:** Harvard Univ., 1931–35, BA (Eng. Hist., Lit.), 1935–36, MA (Hist.); Columbia Univ., 1941–47, BS (LS). Amer. Univ., 1948, Cert. (Arch.). **Orgs.:** SAA: Bus. Arch. Com. (1955–). Essex Inst.: Cncl., Lib. Com. (1968–). Merrimack Valley Textile Mus: Incorporator, Lib. Com. (1960–). **Honors:** SAA, Flw., 1958. Phi Beta Kappa. **Pubns.:** Jt. comp., *Business Manuscripts in Baker Library,* (1978); Ed., *Documents from the Harvard University Archives, 1638–1750* (1975); *American Economic and Business History Information Sources* (1971); Other articles on Lcl. Hist., Lib. Hist., and Bus. Arch. **Activities:** 1, 2; 15, 39, 45; 57, 59, 92 **Addr.:** 27 Conant St., Beverly, MA 01915.

Low, Edmon (Ja. 4, 1902, Kiowa, OK) Libn., New Coll., 1972–; Prof. of LS, Univ. of MI, 1967–72; Libn., OK State Univ., 1940–67; Libn., Bowling Green State Univ., 1938–40; Asst. Libn., E. Ctrl. State Coll., 1927–37. **Educ.:** E. Ctrl. State Coll., 1922–26, BS (Math.); Univ. of IL, 1929–30, BS (LS); Univ. of MI, 1937–38, MALS. **Orgs.:** ALA: VP (1961–62, 1964–65); ACRL (Pres. 1960–61); Com. on Legis. (Ch., 1967–68); Subcom. on Copyrt. (Ch., 1968). SWLA: Pres. (1949–51). OK LA: Pres. (1950–52). **Honors:** ALA, Hon. Mem., 1976; OK LA, Disting. Srv. Awd., 1958; ALA, Lippincott Awd., 1967; East. MI Univ., DLitt, 1967; other awds. **Activities:** 1; 17, 20 **Addr.:** 4611 18th Ave. W., Bradenton, FL 33529.*

Lowance, Alma V. (F. 13, 1909, Clifton Forge, VA) Ch., Lib. Com., Reveille Meml. Lib., 1972–; HS Eng. Tchr. **Educ.:** Concord Coll., 1923–33, BA; Univ. of TN, 1941–43, MEd. **Orgs.:** CSLA: Pres. (1979–80); Exec. Bd. (1977–81). VA LA. Delta Kappa Gamma Socty.: First VP. **Pubns.:** "Who Uses the Church Library," *VA Advocate* (Ja. 1981); reviews. **Activities:** 10, 12; 15, 17, 25; 90 **Addr.:** 1717 Bellevue Ave., A–826, Richmond, VA 23227.

Lowe, Joy Lambert (O. 23, 1939, Minden, LA) Assoc. Prof., LS, LA Tech Univ., 1977–; Dir., Opelousas–Eunice Pub. Lib., 1967–70; Admin. Libn., Ascension Par. Lib., 1964–66; Asst. Par. Libn., Bossier Par. Lib., 1962–64. **Educ.:** Centenary Coll., 1957–61, BA (Drama); LA Tech Univ., 1972–73, BA (Educ.); LA State Univ., 1961–62, MSLS. **Orgs.:** ALA: LA Mem. Ch. (1971). SELA. LA LA: Parlmt. (1968); Manual Bylaws Com.; LA Lit. Awd. Com.; Rcrt. Com. Phi Delta Kappa: Treas. (1980–). Intl. Readg. Assn. LA Assn. of Educs. **Honors:** Assn. of Childhood Educ., Outstan. Tchr. of Childhood Educ., 1980; Phi Beta; Beta Phi Mu; Alpha Beta Alpha. **Activities:** 25, 26; 63 **Addr.:** Teacher Education, Louisiana Tech University, Ruston, LA 71272.

Lowe, Lorna Dallas (F. 15, 1948, Vancouver, BC) Ref. Libn. (III), Erindale Coll. Lib., Univ. of Toronto, 1973–. **Educ.:** Univ. of Toronto, 1966–70, BA (Anthro., Hist.); Univ. of Toronto, 1971–73, MLS; **Orgs.:** Can. LA: Nom. Com. (1981). Libns. Assn. of the Univ. of Toronto: Acad. Status Com. (1976–77); Part-time Libns. Com. (1980). Delta Gamma Fraternity: Erindale Coll. Cncl.: Exec. Cncl. and Com. of Coll. Affairs. Mississauga Choral Socty. **Pubns.:** "Collegial Management Works at Erindale," *Feliciter* (F. 1977); "Minority Groups and the Professional Librarian," *Inst. of Prof. Libns. of ON News* (Ap. 1974); "Collective Bargaining Options for Librarians," *Inst. of Prof. Libns. of ON News* (Mr. 1975). **Activities:** 1; 15, 39, 46; 51, 57, 95-Orien. **Addr.:** 798 Edgehill Rd., Mississauga, ON L5H 3Y3 Canada.

Lowe, Mildred (Ap. 4, 1927, New York City, NY) Actg. Dir., St. John's Univ., Div. of Lib. and Info. Sci., 1979–, Assoc. Prof., 1978–, Asst. Prof., 1973–78; Gvt. Docum., Serials Libn., SUNY, Farmingdale, 1965–68. **Educ.:** Brooklyn Coll., 1960, BA (Soclgy.); Pratt Inst., 1964–65, MLS; Columbia Univ., 1968–72, DLS. **Orgs.:** ALA: LRRT; GODORT; ACRL/Educ. and Bhvl. Sci. Sect., Nom. Com. (1980–81); various sects. NY Lib. Club: Exec. Cncl. (1966–68). NY LA: GODORT, Fndr., 1st Pres. (1978–80); Exec. Cncl. (1976–78), Pubns. Com. (Co-Ch., 1979–); various coms. Nassau Cnty. LA: Exec. Bd. (1975–76); Coll. and Univ. Libs. Div. (VP, 1977); Pres. (1978); various coms. Amer. Prtg. Hist. Assn.: Educ. Com. (1976–). NY State Gvrs. Docum. Task Frc. SUNY Farmingdale LA. YIVO Inst. for Jewish Resrch. Various other orgs. **Honors:** Beta Phi Mu, 1965. **Pubns.:** Jt. ed., *Procs., 2nd Anl. Mtg., NY LA GODORT, O. 1980, Occasional Paper, #2* (1981); jt. ed., *Procs. of Inaugural Mtg., NY LA GODORT, O. 1979, Occasional Paper #1* (1980); jt. ed., "New York State Government Documents Task Force," *Procs. of the 4th Anl. Gvt. Docum. Wkshp. Mncpl. and Lcl. Docum.* (1977). **Activities:** 11; 17, 26; 63, 92, 95-Gvt. docum. **Addr.:** St. John's University, Div. of Library and Information Science, Jamaica, NY 11439.

Lowe, William C. (S. 18, 1930, Brooklyn, NY) Asst. Dir. For Ref. Srvs., D.H. Hill Lib., NC State Univ., 1971–, Head, Tech. Info. Ctr., 1966–71; Sr. Tech. Libn., Xerox Corp., 1957–66, Physicist, 1953–57. **Educ.:** Colgate Univ., 1948–52, BA (Amer. Cvlztn.); Suny, Geneseo, 1957–60, MS (LS). **Orgs.:** SLA: Pres., West. NY Chap. (1961–62); Pres. NC Chap. (1970–71). NC LA: Ed. Bd., *NC Libs.* (1971–76). SELA: Ch., Spec. Libs. Sect. (1974–76). NC State Univ.: Fac. Senate (1976–78). Univ. of NC: Del., Fac. Asm. (1978–80). **Pubns.:** "The Literature of Quality Control," *Rochester Soc. For Quality Control Yrbk.* (1962); "Special Libraries," *NC Libs.;* (Win. 1970–71); Ed., *Rochester (NY) Area Union List of Serials* (1966); Cmplr., *The Furniture Industry Information Guide* (1971). **Activities:** 1; 17, 39; 59, 91 **Addr.:** D.H. Hill Library, North Carolina State University, P.O. Box 5007, Raleigh, NC 27650.

Lowell, Howard P. (My. 10, 1945, Rockland, ME) Consult., Self-employed, 1976–; Dir., Revere (MA) Pub. Lib., 1975–76; Educ. Spec., MA Bureau of Lib. Ext., 1974–75; Admin. Srvs. Ofcr., ME State Arch., 1968–73. **Educ.:** Univ. of ME, 1963–67, BA (Hist.); Simmons Coll., 1973, MS (LS); Amer. Univ., 1971, Cert. (Arch.). **Orgs.:** SAA: Cons. Prof. Afnty. Grp. ALA. **Pubns.:** "Conserving Library Collections," *Pac. Northwest LA Qtly.* (Fall 1977); "Preserving Recorded Information–The Physical Deterioration of Paper," *Recs. Mgmt. Qtly.* (Ap. 1979); "Preparing for Your Library Disaster," *Pac Northwest LA Qtly.* (Fall 1979); "Conservation Planning in the West," *The Library Scene* (S. 1980). **Activities:** 2, 13; 17, 23, 24 **Addr.:** 1310 Franklin St., #202, Denver, CO 80218.

Lowell, Marcia (Ag. 4, 1940, Lewiston, ME) State Libn., OR State Lib., 1976–; Dir., Wayland Pub. Lib., 1973–76; Exec. Secy., ME Lib. Adv. Com., 1972–73; Dir., Lithgow Pub. Lib., 1969–72. **Educ.:** Univ. of ME, 1965, BS (Eng.); Simmons Coll., 1967, MS (LS). Boston Univ. (Adult Educ.). **Orgs.:** West. Cncl. of State Lib. Agencies: Pres. (1980–81). Pac. Northwest Bibl. Ctr. CLENE. COSLA: Leg. Com. (Secy. 1981). OR LA. Pac. Northwest LA. State Mgmt. Assn.: Secy./Treas. (1978–79). Amer. Assn. of Pub. Admins. **Activities:** 13 **Addr.:** Oregon State Library, Salem, OR 97310.

Lowell, Virginia (N. 21, 1940, San Jose, CA) Dir., Tech. Srvs., Cuyahoga Cnty. Pub. Lib., 1979–, Head Cat. Dept., 1976–79; Consult., Cuyahoga Cmnty. Coll., 1972–74, Head, Cat. Dept., 1968–70. **Educ.:** Reed Coll., 1958–61; Univ. of CA, Berkeley, 1961–63, BA (Eng.); Wes. Rsrv. Univ., 1964–65, MSLS. **Orgs.:** ALA. North. OH Tech. Srvs. Libns. Acad. Libns. Assn. of OH. **Activities:** 9; 17, 24, 46; 56 **Addr.:** Cuyahoga County Public Library, 4510 Memphis Ave., Cleveland, OH 44144.

Lowenthal, Jane Elizabeth (O. 10, 1916, Los Angeles, CA) Libn.–in–Charge, Carnegie Endow. for Intl. Peace, 1979–, Asst. Libn., 1970–79; Libn., Resrch. Inst. for the Std. of Man,

Special Subjects/Services: 50. Adult educ.; 51. Advert./Mktg.; 52. Aerosp.; 53. Agric.; 54. Area std.; 55. Arts/Hum.; 56. Autom.; 57. Bibl./Prtg.; 58. Bio. sci.; 59. Bus./Fin.; 60. Chem.; 61. Copyrt.; 62. Documtn.; 63. Educ.; 64. Engin.; 65. Env.; 66. Eth. grps.; 67. Film; 68. Food/Nutr.; 69. Geneal.; 70. Geo.; 71. Geol.; 72. Handcpd.; 73. Hist.; 74. Int. frdm.; 75. Info. sci.; 76. Insr.; 77. Law; 78. Legis.; 79. Math./Comp. sci.; 80. Med.; 81. Metals; 82. Nat. resrcs.; 83. Newsp.; 84. Nuc. sci.; 85. Oral hist.; 86. Petr./Energy; 87. Pharm.; 88. Phys./Astr./Math.; 89. Readg.; 90. Relig.; 91. Sci./Tech.; 92. Soc. sci.; 93. Telecom.; 94. Transp.; 95. (other).

1966–69; Asst. Libn., Carnegie Endow. for Intl. Peace, 1964–66; Libn., NY Pub. Lib., 1963–64; Instr., Child Std. Dept., Vassar Coll., 1950–55. **Educ.:** Barnard Coll., 1934–38, BA (Zlgy.); Bank St. Coll. of Educ., 1955, MA (Educ.); Columbia Univ., 1962–64, MS (LS); CUNY, 1976, Cert. (Prof. Dev. in Lib.–Info. Sci.). **Orgs.:** SLA. Bibl. Socty. of Amer. Amer. Prtg. Hist. Assn. ALA. **Activities:** 5, 12; 54 **Addr.:** Apt. 306, 3100 Connecticut Ave., N.W., Washington, DC 20008.

Lowndes, Ann Stewart (Jl. 23, 1937, N. Wilkesboro, NC) Assoc., Bur. of Sch. Libs., NY State Educ. Dept., 1970–; Lib. Media Spec., Atkinson Sch., Freeport, NY, 1966–70; Indxr., Book Review Digest, H W Wilson, 1965–66; Asst. Prof., Eng. Dept., Winston-Salem State Univ., 1959–63. **Educ.:** Bennett Coll., NC, 1953–57, BA (Fr.); Case-Western Reserve, 1957–58, MSLS; SUNY, Albany, 1972–74, Cert. (Sch. Supvsn.). **Orgs.:** ALA. NY LA. Delta Kappa Gamma. Delta Sigma Theta. **Honors:** Beta Phi Mu. **Pubns.:** Contrib., *What Black Librarians Are Saying* (1975); Contrib., *Handbook of Black Librarianship* (1978); Coord., *Elementary Library Media Skills Curriculum.* **Activities:** 10; 26, 31; 55, 85 **Addr.:** 57 Eileen St., Albany, NY 12203.

Lowrey, Anna Mary S. (Jy. 27, 1918, Lancaster, PA) Assoc. Prof. (LS), SUNY Buffalo, 1974–; Assoc. Dir., Sch. Lib. Manpower Proj., ALA/AASL, 1969–74; Prog. Spec., Lib. Srvs., Sacramento Sch. Dist., 1967–69; Supvsr. of Libs., San Leandro Sch. Dist., 1959–67; Lectr. (LS), Univ. of San Francisco, 1963–67. **Educ.:** Millersville State Coll., 1935–39, BS (Educ.); Univ. of Denver, 1958, MA (LS); Univ. of San Francisco, 1966, Adv. Cert., (Admin.). **Orgs.:** ALA: Conf. Plng. Com. (1980); AASL, Pres. (1978–79), Pubn. Com. (1977–80), Secy. (1975–76), Cert. Com. (1973–76). Univ. of Denver LS Alumni Assn.: Pres. (1980–81). NY LA: Leg. Tsk. Frc. on Elem. Libns. (Ch., 1975–76). Natl. Educ. Assn. AECT. AALS: Conf Com. (1980). **Honors:** Beta Phi Mu. CA Assn. of Sch. Libns. and CA AV Assn., Cmdn., 1969. AASL, Cmdn., 1974. NY Regents Adv. Cncl. on Libs., 1974–79. Other honors. **Pubns.:** Jt.-auth., *Behavioral Requirements Analysis Checklist* (1973); jt.-auth., *Evaluation of Alternative Curricula: Approaches to School Library Media Education* (1975); "Measuring Program Effectiveness," Drexel Lib. Qtly. (Jy. 1978); "Further Thoughts on Needs Assessment and Program Evaluation," *Issues in Media Mgt.* (1979); other articles. **Activities:** 10, 11; 21, 24, 26; 63 **Addr.:** 803 Charlesgate Circle, E. Amherst, NY 14051.

Lowrie, Jean E. (O. 11, 1918, Northville, NY) Prof., Sch. of Libnshp., West. MI Univ., 1958–, Campus Sch. Libn., 1951–56; Elem. Sch. Libn., Oak Ridge (TN) Pub. Sch., 1944–51; Tchr. libn., Nottingham, Eng., 1948–49; Chld. Libn., Toledo Pub. Lib., 1941–44. **Educ.:** Keuka Coll., 1936–40, BA (Eng. & Hist.); West. Reserve Univ., 1940–41, BSLS; West. MI Univ., 1956, MA; West. Reserve Univ., 1959, PhD. **Orgs.:** ALA: VP (1972–73); Pres. (1973–74); Exec. Bd. (1969–75); Cncl. (1967–71); Intl. Ref. Com.; AASL, Pres. (1963–64). IFLA: Dir. (1979–83). Intl. Assn. of Sch. Libnshp.: Pres. (1971–77); Exec. Secy. (1978–). MI LA. AAUP. **Honors:** AASL, 1st Presidents Awd.; MI Libn. of the Yr., 1969; Beta Phi Mu; Disting. Women of MI, 1978; Hon. Litt D, Keuka Coll., 1973. **Pubns.:** Ed., *School Libraries: International Developments* (1972); *Elementary School Libraries* (1970). **Activities:** 10, 11; 17, 26, 32; 54, 63, 89 **Addr.:** 1006 Westmorland, Kalamazoo, MI

Lowry, Andree F. (My. 21, 1938, Marianna, FL) Libn., Env. Resrch. Lab., 1978–; Head, of Loan Dept. McKeldin Lib., Univ. of MD, 1975–77; Inst. Lib. Consult., State Lib. of FL, 1970–75; Head, of Bibl. Srch., FL State Univ. Lib., 1969–70. **Educ.:** FL State Univ., 1958–59, BS (Eng.), 1967–68, MS (LS). **Orgs.:** ALA: Hlth. and Rehab. Srvs. Div. (Bd. of Dir., 1976–77), various other ofcs.; Lib. Srv. to the Blind and Phys. Handcpd., Nom Com. (1976–77), various other ofcs.; Assn. of State Lib. Agencies, Various ofcs. SELA. FL LA: Secy. (1974–75); Cit. and Awds. Com. (Ch., 1973–74); Outreach Caucus (1974–75). Amer. Correct. Assn.: Com. on Inst. Libs. (Ch., 1975–76); Prog. Plng. Com. (1972–75); Com. on Afflt. Bodies (1972–74). Amer. Correct. Assn. and ALA Jt. Com. on Inst. Libs. (Ch., 1972–75). **Pubns.:** Comp., *Library Standards for Juvenile Correctional Institutions* (1975); "Standards for Library Service In Institutions," *Lib. Trends,* (O. 1972); "The Role of the Consultant for Specialized Library Services," *IL Libs.* (S. 1975). **Activities:** 5, 12; 17, 22, 24; 56, 65, 72 **Addr.:** Library, U. S. Environmental Protection Agency, Environmental Research Laboratory Sabine Island, Gulf Breeze, FL 32561.

Lowry, Charles Bryan (N. 9, 1942, Pensacola, FL) Head Libn. & Dir. of Lrng. Resrcs., Elon Coll., 1978–; Asst. Prof., Soc. Sci. Ref. Biblgphr., Univ. of NC, Charlotte, 1974–78; Instr., Faulkner State Cmnty. Coll., 1965–69. **Educ.:** Spring Hill Coll., 1960–64, BS (Hist.); Univ. of AL, 1964–65, MA (Hist.); Univ. of FL, 1969–79, PhD (Hist.); Univ. of NC, 1973–74, MLS. **Orgs.:** ALA: ACRL/Coll. Lib. Sect., Com. on Mem. (Ch., 1979–81); Bibl. Instr. Sect., Bylaws Com. (1977–78); Ref. and Subscrpn. Books Com. (1978–80). ARL: Consult. Trainee (1979–). Amer. Hist. Assn. Amer. Assn. for State and Lcl. Hist. Phi Alpha Theta: Pres., Gamma Eta Chap. (1971–72). **Pubns.:** Biographical sketches of Fred Jones (1670–1722) and William Maule (1680–1726) in *Dict. of NC Biog.* (1977–); "Holdings of the North Carolina Collection," *NC Libs.* (Fall 1976); "The ACRL Standards and Library Governance, a Comparison of the Personnel Systems of Five Major Academic Libraries," ERIC (N. 1975); "'The City on a Hill' and Kibbutzim, Seventeenth-Century Utopias as Ideal Types," *Amer. Jewish Hist. Qtly.* (Je. 1974); "The PWA in Tampa: A Case Study," *FL Hist. Qtly.* (Ap. 1974). **Activities:** 1; 15, 17, 39; 57, 92 **Addr.:** Iris Holt McEwen Library, Box 187, Elon College, NC 27224.

Lowry, Harold Maynard (Ag. 14, 1946, Windsor, ON) Dir. of Univ. Libs., Loma Linda Univ., 1981–, Assoc. Dir., 1976–81, Asst. to the Dir., 1974–76; Admin. Asst., State Lib. of OH, 1972–74. **Educ.:** Andrews Univ., 1964–68, BA (Hist.); Kent State Univ., 1968–70, MAT (Hist.); West. MI Univ., 1971–72, MSL (LS). **Orgs.:** ALA: ACRL. Med. LA. Assn. for the Std. of Higher Educ. **Honors:** Beta Phi Mu, 1971. **Addr.:** University Library, Loma Linda University, Loma Linda, CA 92350.

Lowry, William H. (Ag. 27, 1921, Cleveland, OH) Dir., Pioneer Multi–Cnty. Lib., 1958–; Visit. Asst. Prof., Univ. of OK Sch. of LS, 1958–77; Dir. of Prcs., OK City Lib., 1953–58; Catlgr., Univ. of NM, 1950–53. **Educ.:** Univ. of MI, 1940–48, BA (Soclgy.); Case West. Rsv. Univ., 1949–50, MS (LS). **Orgs.:** OK LA: Pres. (1959–60). SWLA. ALA. Lions Intl. **Honors:** Beta Phi Mu; OK LA, Disting. Srv. Awd., 1973. **Activities:** 9; 17, 34, 46; 78 **Addr.:** Pioneer Multi-County Library, 225 N. Webster, Norman, OK 73069.

Lowy, George (My. 17, 1924, Budapest, Hungary) Dir. of Lib., Pratt Inst., 1979–; Chief, Soc. Sci. Div., Columbia Univ. Libs., 1974–79, Lehman Lib., Sch. of Intl. Affairs, 1971–74, Asst. Head, Acq. Dept., 1968–71. **Educ.:** Univ. of Econ. Sci., Budapest, 1948–52, BA (Econ.); Columbia Univ., 1959–61, MLS, 1969, PhD (Ling.). **Orgs.:** ALA: RTSD/Resrcs. Sect., Policy and Resrch. Com. (Ch., 1964). SLA. **Pubns.:** *A Searcher's Manual* (1965); *Guide to Russian Reprints and Microforms* (1973). **Activities:** 1; 15, 17; 54, 92 **Addr.:** 110-26 68th Rd., Forest Hills, New York, NY 11375.

Lubans, John, Jr. (Jn. 15, 1941, Riga, Latvia) Campus Libn., Houston Cmnty. Coll., 1980–; Asst. Libn., Pub. Srvs., Univ. of Houston, Downtown Campus, 1978–80; Asst. Dir., Pub. Srvs., Univ. of CO Libs., 1970–78; Head, Reader Srvs. Div., Rensselaer Polytech. Inst., 1968–70, Head, Circ., 1966–68. **Educ.:** Lebanon Valley Coll., 1960–64, BA (Eng.); Univ. of MI, 1964–66, MALS; Univ. of Houston, 1978–80, MA (Pub. Admin.). **Orgs.:** ALA: ACRL/Univ. Libs. Sect. (Secy., 1976–79); *Amer. Libs.* Ed. Adv. Com. (1976–80; Ch., 1977–80); LIRT; other coms. and ofcs. CO LA: Pres., 1976. Houston Area Pub. Srvs. Libns. Lions Club. **Honors:** IFLA, T.P. Sevensma Prz., 1967–68. **Pubns.:** Jt.-auth., *Library Systems Analysis Guidelines* (1970); Ed., *Educating the Library User* (1974); Ed., *Progress in Educating the Library User* (1978); "Evaluating Sign Systems in Libraries," *Sign Systems for Libs.* (1979); Ed., *Public Library User Education* (1981); other articles. **Activities:** 1, 9; 17, 31, 39; 92 **Addr.:** 2604 Quenby, Houston, TX 77005.

Lubetski, Edith E. (Jl. 16, 1940, NY) Head Libn., Stern Coll., Yeshiva Univ., 1969–, Asst. Libn., 1965–69. **Educ.:** Brooklyn Coll., 1962, BA; Columbia Univ., 1965, MS (LS); Yeshiva Univ., 1968, MA (Jewish Hist.). **Orgs.:** AJL: Corres. Secy. (1980–82). ALA. NY LA. **Pubns.:** *Writings on Jewish History.* (1971, 2nd ed. 1974); "Recent Acquisitions in the Jewish Field", *Lib. Resrcs. & Tech. Srvs.* (Fall 1974). **Activities:** 1; 15, 17, 39 **Addr.:** Hedi Steinberg Library, Stern College For Women, 245 Lexington Ave., New York, NY 10016.

Lucas, Linda Sue (N. 5, 1939, Creston, IA) Asst. Prof., Coll. of Libnshp., Univ. of SC, 1977–; Asst. Prof., IA State Univ. Lib., 1966–73; Asst. Libn., Minot HS, 1962–65; Lib., Sidney HS, 1961–62. **Educ.:** Univ. of North. IA, 1958–61, BA (LS); Univ. of WA, 1965–66, ML (LS); Univ. of IL, 1974–80, PhD (LS). **Orgs.:** ALA. SELA. SC LA. Amer. Coal. of Citizens with Disabilities. Amer. Cvl. Liberties Un. **Pubns.:** "Library Service to Institutionalized and Disabled Adults," *RQ* (Spr. 1979); "Life Style, Reading, and Library Use," *Pub. Libs.* (Spr. 1979); "Volunteers: Altruists or Prima Donnas?" *Pub. Libs.* (Fall 1980); "Information Needs of the Aging," *Southeast. Libn.* (Win. 1980). **Activities:** 5, 9; 16, 39, 46; 55, 72, 89 **Addr.:** 28D Woodmere Apts., Columbia, SC 29210.

Luce, Richard E. (Ag. 21, 1951, Santa Monica, CA) Asst. Dir., Boulder Pub. Lib., 1980–81, Asst. to the Lib. Dir., 1978–79, Admin. Asst., 1978, Statewide Coord., Mncpl. Gvt., Ref. Ctr., 1976–77; Dir., Pub. Admin. Ctr., San Diego State Univ., 1974–76. **Educ.:** Univ. of San Diego, 1969–73, BA (Pol. Sci.); San Diego State Univ., 1974–75, MPA (Pub. Admin.). **Orgs.:** ALA. CO LA. CO Mncpl. Leag.: Lib. Sect. (Ch. Elect, 1980–81). CO Mncpl. Mgt. Assts. Assn. Amer. Socty. of Pub. Admin. CA Pub. Interest Resrch. Grp. **Honors:** Pi Alpha Alpha, 1980. **Pubns.:** Contrib., *Municipal Government Reference Sources* (1978); jt. auth., "A Prospective Regional Planning and Development Agency for Southwest Michigan," *Metro-Urban Nsltr.* (Ap. 1975). **Activities:** 9, 12; 17, 34, 41; 56, 75, 93 **Addr.:** Boulder Public Library, Drawer H, Boulder, CO 80027.

Lucker, Jay K. (F. 23, 1930, NY, NY) Dir. of Libs., MA Inst. of Tech., 1975–; Assoc. Univ. Libn., Princeton Univ., 1968–75, Asst. Univ. Libn., Sci. and Tech., 1959–68; First Asst., Sci. Tech. Div., NY Pub. Lib., 1957–59, Chief, Procurement, Acq. Div., 1954–57. **Educ.:** Brooklyn Coll., 1948–51, AB (Psy., Eng.); Columbia Univ., 1951–52, MS (LS); New York Univ., 1955–57 (Pub. Admin.). **Orgs.:** ARL: Pres. (1980–81), Bd. of Dir. (1978–), ILL Com. (Ch., 1976–80), ALA: Cncl. (1979–); ACRL, Stans. and Accred. Com. (1976–), Ed. Bd., *C&RL News* (Ch., 1979–). NELINET: Bd. (1978–; Ch., 1980–81). SLA. Middle States Assn. of Colls. and Secy. Schs.: Accred. Teams (Ch., 1973–78). Mass. Inst. of Tech. Press: Ed. Bd. (1975–). Boston Lib. Cnsrtm.: Bd. of Dir. (1975–). Unvsl. Serials and Bk Exch.: Bd. of Dir. (1979–). **Honors:** Coll. and Univ. Sect., NJ LA, Disting. Srv. Awd., 1975. Cncl. on Lib. Resrcs., Flwshp., 1970. Phi Beta Kappa. **Pubns.:** Assoc. Ed., *Bibliographic Index* (1957–68); Assoc. Ed., *Ulrich's Periodical Directory* (1959–61); "Phonograph Now Perfect; the Edison-Mayer Letters," *Princeton Univ. Lib. Chronicle* (Spr. 1964); "Library Resources and Bibliographic Control," *Coll. & Resrch. Libs.* (Mr. 1979); Various other pubns. **Activities:** 1; 17, 24, 34; 91 **Addr.:** Room 14S-216, Massachusetts Institute of Technology, Cambridge, MA 02139.

Lucy, Mary Lou (Jl. 5, 1922, Lebanon, KY) Chief, Hum. and Hist. Div., Columbia Univ. Libs., 1974–, Butler Libn., 1967–74, Circ. Libn., 1961–67; Circ. Libn., Univ. of NC, 1952–61; Ref. Libn., Columbia Univ. Libs., 1950–52, other positions at Columbia, 1946–50. **Educ.:** East. KY, 1939–43, AB (Eng.); Peabody Lib. Sch., 1943–44, BS/LS; Columbia Univ., 1953, MS in LS. **Orgs.:** ALA: RTSD/RLMS Rep. to ILL Com., Secy. ILL Com. (1970–1973); ALA rep. to Natl. Micrographics Assn., PH5 Com. (1975–76); Ch., ACRL Com. on Comm. Use of Acad. Libs. (1973–1974). **Activities:** 1; 17, 31, 43; 75 **Addr.:** Butler Library, 535 W. 114th St., New York, NY 10027.

Ludlow, Virginia Felicy (Ag. 27, 1919, Toronto, ON) Libn. in charge, Travelling Branch, Toronto Pub. Lib., 1956–, Circulating Staff, 1943–56. **Educ.:** Univ. of Toronto, 1937–42, BA (Eng.), 1942–43, BLS, 1969, MLS, 1972, MA (Eng.). **Orgs.:** ALA. Can. LA. ON LA. The LA. **Pubns.:** "Libraries and the Older Adult," *Can. Lib. Jnl.* (F. 1975); jt. auth., "A Survey of National Organizations for the Handicapped, Based in Toronto," *Can. Lib. Jnl.* (Jl.–Ag. 1972); "The Toronto Public Library's Service to Shut-ins," *Can. Lib. Jnl.* (My.–Je. 1972); "Library Service to Hospitals and the Handicapped," *ON Lib. Review* (Je. 1969). **Activities:** 9; 16, 22; 72 **Addr.:** Travelling Branch, Toronto Public Library, 40 Orchard View Blvd., Toronto, ON M4R 1B9 Canada.

Lueb, Sr. Miriam Dorothy (D. 23, 1921, Lindsay, TX) Dir. of Libs., Our Lady of the Lake Univ., 1974–; Head, Media Lrng. Ctr., 1971–74, Asst. Prof. (LS), 1965–71; Libn. and Tchr., Prompt Succor (LA) Sec. Schs., 1962–65, Prin., 1957–62; Elem. Sch. Tchr., 1943–57. **Educ.:** Our Lady of the Lake Univ., 1948, BA (Eng.); 1955, MS (LS). IN Univ., 1964–65. **Orgs.:** ALA. Cath. LA. AECT. TX LA. Other orgs. Congregational Reg. Cnclrs.: Ctrl. Reg. (Ch., 1977–79). **Pubns.:** Reviews. **Activities:** 1; 17, 35; 50, 63, 92 **Addr.:** 411 S. W. 24th St., San Antonio, TX 78285.

Lueder, Dianne Bertelsen (Ag. 5, 1944, Racine, WI) Lib. Dir., Bartlett Pub. Lib. Dist., 1980–; Outrch., Ref. Libn., Elk Grove Vlg. Pub. Lib., 1979–80; Libn., Un. Grove Mid. Sch., 1970–72. **Educ.:** Univ. of WI, 1969–72, BA (Hist.), 1978–79, MLS; Roosevelt Univ., 1981–, MPA. **Orgs.:** ALA: PLA (1979–81); LITA, AV Mem. Com. (1980–81). Lib. Admin. Cncl. of North. IL: Outrch. Sect., Strg. Com. (1980–81). IL LA: Dist. Lib. RT (1980–81). Univ. of WI, Milwaukee Sch. of LS: Adv. Com. (1978–79); Accred. Com., Fac. (1981). **Honors:** Beta Phi Mu, 1980. **Activities:** 9; 17, 27, 47; 50, 72 **Addr.:** 27798 N. Forest Garden, Wauconda, IL 60084.

Lufkin, Beatrice A. (Ag. 3, 1947, Los Angeles, CA) Coord., Reg. Lib. Systs., MA Bd. of Lib. Comsns., 1979–; Supvsr., Adult Srvs., RI Dept. of State Lib. Srv., 1975–79; Ref., ILL, Libn., Corn Belt (IL) Lib. Syst., 1972–75. **Educ.:** Northwestern Univ., 1964–67; Univ. of IL, 1967–68, AB (Pol. Sci.), 1971–73, MS (LS). **Orgs.:** New Eng. LA/Coop. Lib. Agencies Sect. (Ch., 1979–81). ALA: ASCLA/Multitype Lib. Coop. Sect., Leg. Com. (1980–82), Plng. Com. (1980–82). **Activities:** 13; 17, 24, 34; 59, 78 **Addr.:** Massachusetts Board of Library Commissioners, 648 Beacon St., Boston, MA 02215.

Lukác, Jenko (Mr. 17, 1947, Prague, Czechoslovakia) Head, Tech. and Comp. Srvs., Lewis & Clark Coll., 1979–; Head, Tech. Srvs., Pac. Univ., 1978–79, Sci. Libn., 1977–78. **Educ.:** Lowell Tech. Inst., 1964–68, BS (Phys.); Univ. of CT, 1968–70, MS (Phys.); Univ. of BC, 1970–75, PhD (Phys.), 1975–77, MLS. **Orgs.:** ALA: ACRL/OR Chap. (Ch., 1978–79). ASIS. **Pubns.:** "A No-Cost On-Line Acquisitions System for a Medium Sized Library," *Lib. Jnl.* (Mr. 15, 1980); "Is the Nuclear Strength Function Lorentzian?" *Can. Jnl. of Phys.* (1976); "Architecture for Resource Sharing in a Multi-Utility Environment," *Technicalities* (Ap. 1981); "The Evolution of an Online Acquisitions System," *Jnl. of Lib. Auto.* (Je. 1981). **Activities:** 1; 20, 39, 46; 56, 91 **Addr.:** 4076 S.E. Hemlock St., Hillsboro, OR 97123.

PROFESSIONAL ACTIVITIES: Institutions: 1. Acad. lib.; 2. Arch.; 3. Assn.; 4. Fed./Gvt. lib.; 5. Inst. lib.; 6. Mfr./Suppl.; 7. Milit. lib.; 8. Musm.; 9. Pub. lib.; 10. Sch. lib.; 11. Sch. of lib. sci.; 12. Spec. lib.; 13. State lib.; 14. (other). **Functions/Activities:** 15. Acq./Col. dev.; 16. Adult srvs.; 17. Admin.; 18. Apprais.; 19. Archit./Bldgs.; 20. Cat./Class.; 21. Chld. srvs.; 22. Circ.; 23. Cons./Pres.; 24. Consult.; 25. Cont. ed.; 26. Educ. lib. sci.; 27. Ext. srvs.; 28. Fund/Grants; 29. Gvt. pubs.; 30. Indx./Abs.; 31. Instr. lib. use; 32. Media srvs.; 33. Micro.; 34. Netwks./Coop.; 35. Persnl.; 36. PR; 37. Publshg.; 38. Recs. mgt.; 39. Ref. srvs.; 40. Repro.; 41. Resrch.; 42. Review.; 43. Secur.; 44. Serials; 45. Spec. col.; 46. Tech. srvs.; 47. Trustees/Bds.; 48. YA srvs.; 49. (other).

Luke, Ann W. (F. 15, 1936, Los Angeles, CA) Instr., Bus. Comm., UCLA Ext., 1981–, and Mgr. of Pubns., Xerox Comp. Srvs., 1978–; Admin. Mgr., Pubns., Rand Corp., 1975–78; Sr. Syst. Anal., System Dev. Corp., 1960–72, 1974–75. **Educ.:** Pomona Coll., 1953–57, BA (Liberal Arts). **Orgs.:** ASIS. Socty. for Scholly. Publshg. Women in Bus.: Los Angeles Chap., Dir. (1979–80); Treas. (1981). Org. of Women Execs. **Honors:** ASIS, Spec. Recog. Awd., 1975. **Pubns.:** Asst. Ed., *Annual Review of Information Science & Technology* (1965–75); various research reports. **Activities:** 6; 17, 37, 46; 51, 56, 93 **Addr.:** 864 Brooktree Rd., Pacific Palisades, CA 90272.

Lukenbill, Shirley Hébert (Ja. 29, 1940, Mamou, LA) Lectr., Univ. of TX, 1975–; Ref. Libn., NE. LA State Univ., 1968–69; Asst. Prof., Libn., Univ. of Southwest. LA, 1964–68; Libn., N. Shore Sr. HS, 1962–64. **Educ.:** Univ. of Southwest. LA, 1957–61, BS (Eng. Educ.); LA State Univ., 1961–62, MS (LS). **Orgs.:** ALA. SWLA: Youth Srvs. Interest Grp., Com. on "A Selective Guide to In-Print Children's Books About the Southwest, 1974–77," "Texas in Children's Bks." (Ch.). Ctrl. TX Puppetry Gld. **Pubns.:** Jt. auth., *In Search of Texas Treasures: A Librarian's Planning Handbook* (1979); Jt. auth., "Come to Chimera!," *A Librarian's Planning Handbook* (1978). **Activities:** 10, 11; 21, 26, 39; 50, 63, 89 **Addr.:** P.O. Box 7576, Univ. Station, University of TX at Austin, Austin, TX 78712.

Lukenbill, Willis Bernard (Mr. 27, 1939, Mt. Sylvan, TX) Assoc. Prof. (LS), Univ. of TX, 1981–; Asst. Prof. (LS), 1975–81; Asst. Prof., Univ. of MD, 1972–74; Instr., LA Tech. Univ., 1964–69; Ref. Libn., Austin Coll., 1963–64; Libn., Seguin HS, 1961–63. **Educ.:** Tyler Jr. Coll., 1955–59, AA (Hist.); N State Univ., 1959–61, BS (Educ.); OK Univ., 1963–64, MLS; IN. Univ, 1969–72; 1973, Ph.D. (LS). **Orgs.:** ALA: Resrch. Com. (1978–); YASD, Resrch. Com. (Ch., 1974–77), Subcom. on *Media and the YA Supplement* (Co-Ch., 1977–); AASL; PLA, Resrch. Com. (1977–81, Ch., 1978–80); Pub. Lib. Rpt. Com. (1981–). AALS. AECT. TX LA. Various other orgs. **Honors:** Beta Phi Mu. **Pubns.:** Ed., *Media and the Young Adult, 1950–72* (1977); "Doctoral Dissertations in Children's and Adolescents' Literature: A Working Bibliography," (ED 071 725) (1972); "Research in Children's Literature," *Children and Books* (1972); "Research in Young Adult Literature Services," *Libraries and Young Adults* (1979); "Homosexual conflicts . . . in five adolescent novels"; "Fathers in adolescent novels . . ." *Young Adult Literature: Background and Criticism* (1980) various other articles. **Activities:** 10, 11; 26, 32, 48 **Addr.:** Box 7576, University Station, University of Texas, Austin, TX 78712.

Lukens, Beatrice L. (F. 8, 1918, Milnor, ND) Earth Sci. Libn., Univ. of CA, Berkeley, 1963–; Astronomy, Math., Stats. Libn., 1962–63. **Educ.:** Coll. of St. Catherine, 1935–39, BA (Chem., Math); Univ. of Berkeley, 1956–62, MLS. **Orgs.:** Geoscience Info. Socty. Guidebook and Ephemeral Pubns. Com. (1975–1977); Guidebooks Com. (Ch., 1977–). West. Assn. of Map Libs.: Pres. (1973–74); Nominating Com. (Ch., 1971); Exec. Bd. (1974–75); Mem. Com. (Ch., 1978–). SLA. CA LA. Alum. Assn. of the Univ. of CA. Alumni Assn. of the Univ. of CA Lib. Schs. **Honors:** Beta Phi Mu. **Pubns.:** Arrangement and organization of Geologic Maps in the Library," West. Assn. of Map. Libns. Nsltr. (Mr. 1970). **Activities:** 1; 15, 17, 39; 65, 70, 91 **Addr.:** Earth Sciences Library, Dept. of Geology and Geophysics, University of California, Berkeley, Berkeley, CA 94720.

Lundahl, Margaret A. (N. 26, 1948, Chicago, IL) Libn., Isham, Lincoln & Beale, 1976–; Catlgr., Univ. of Chicago Law Lib., 1971–76. **Educ.:** Univ. of Chicago, 1966–68, (Eng.), 1968–69, MBA, 1969–76, MA (LS). Chicago Kent Coll. of Law, 1976–80, JD. **Orgs.:** ASIS. AALL: Dupl. Exch. Com. (1978–). Chicago Assn. of Law Libs.: Exec. Bd. (1980–). SLA. Other orgs. Amer. Bar Assn. IL State Bar Assn. Chicago Cncl. on Frgn. Rel. Chicago Bar Assn. **Activities:** 1, 12; 29, 39, 46; 59, 77, 78 **Addr.:** 10128 Ave. "J", Chicago, IL 60617.

Lundberg, Susan Ona (Mr. 15, 1947, Mandan, ND) Coord. of Chld. Srvs., Orange Cnty. Pub. Lib., 1972–75; Ref. Libn., Arcadia Pub. Lib., 1972; Ref. Libn., Univ. of TN, Knoxville, 1971–72; Ref. and Chld. Libn., Bismarck Pub. Lib., 1970–71. **Educ.:** Stephens Coll., 1966–69, BA (Soc. Std.); West. MI Univ., 1969–70, MLS; CA State Univ., Fullerton, 1973–80, MPA. **Orgs.:** CA LA: Chld. Srvs. Div. (Ch., 1973–74); Cncl. (1974); Bd. of Dirs. (1974). ALA: Mem. Promo. for CA (1973–74); Lib. Admin. Coms. (1973–75); Newbery-Caldecott Com. (1973, 1975). **Pubns.:** "A Delphi Study of Public Library Goals, Innovations and Performance Measurements," *Lib. Resrch.* (1981). **Activities:** 1, 9; 16, 17, 25 **Addr.:** 112 Ave. E W., Bismarck, ND 58501.

Lundeen, Gerald Wayne (Je. 5, 1937, Moose Lake, MN) Assoc. Prof., Univ. of HI, 1981–, Asst. Prof., 1974–; Asst. Sci. and Tech. Libn., East. MI Univ., 1972–74; Adj. Lectr., Univ. of MI, Sch. of LS, 1974; Sr. Resrch. Chem., Battelle Meml. Inst., 1966–71. **Educ.:** Univ. of WI, Madison, 1955–59, BS (Chem.); Univ. of MN, Minneapolis, 1959–64, PhD (Phys. Chem.); Univ. of MI, Ann Arbor, 1971–72, AMLS. **Orgs.:** SLA. ASIS. Assoc. Info. Mgrs.: *Jnl. of Educ. for Libnshp.* Ed. Bd.; *Resrch. Rec.* Ed. **Honors:** Woodrow Wilson Flwshp. Fndn., Flwshp., 1959; Natl. Sci. Fndn., Postdoct. Flwshp., 1965. **Pubns.:** Jt. auth., *Illustrative Computer Programming for Libraries* (1981); "Microcomputers in Personal Information Systems," *Spec. Libs.* (Ap. 1981); "The Role of Microcomputers in Libraries," *Wilson Lib. Bltn.* (N. 1980). **Activities:** 11; 24, 26, 41; 56, 75, 91 **Addr.:** Graduate School of Library Studies, 2550 The Mall, Honolulu, HI 96822.

Lundquist, David A. (S. 2, 1943, Medford, OR) Assoc. Libn., Shields Lib., Univ. of CA, Davis, 1966–. **Educ.:** South. OR Coll., 1961–65, BA (Soc. Stds.); Univ. of CA, Berkeley, 1965–66, MLS. **Orgs.:** West. Assn. of Map Libs.: Pres. (1980–81). CA LA. SLA. AALL. Socty. of Philatelic Amers. Germ. Philatelic Socty. Amer. Topical Assn. **Activities:** 29; 70 **Addr.:** Shields Library, University of California, Davis, CA 95616.

Lundy, Kathryn Renfro (Ag. 15, 1918, Horse Cave, KY) Prof., Plng. and Resrch., Univ. Libs., Univ. of NE, 1974–; Actg. Dir., Libs. (Sum. 1973), Assoc. Dir., Gen. Srvs., 1968–74, Assoc. Dir., Tech. Srvs., 1964–68, Asst. Dir., Tech. Srvs., 1953–64, Tech. Srvs. Libn., 1950–53, Cat. Libn., 1949–50, Sr. Asst. Libn., Cat., 1946–49; Other libn. positions, various libs., 1939–45. **Educ.:** Colorado Coll., 1935–38; Univ. of Denver, 1939, ABLS. **Orgs.:** ALA: Cncl. (1957–61, 1965–69); ACRL, Bd. of Dir. (1965–69); RTSD, Bd. of Dir. (1957–61). NE LA: Pres. (1963–64). Mountain Plains LA: Coll. and Univ. Sect. (Ch., 1954–55). **Honors:** Beta Phi Mu: Exec. Cncl. (Dir., 1968–71); NE LA 1980 Meritorious Srv. Awd. **Pubns.:** "Sarah Rebecca Reed: 1914–1978," *Amer. Libs.* (S. 1978); "Raters and Rating," *Mountain Plains Lib. Qtly.* (Fall 1971); "Nebraska Centralized Processing," *Mountain Plains Lib. Qtly.* (Win. 1969); "The 'Services' in Technical Services," *Southeastern Libn.* (Spr. 1967); *Women View Librarianship: Nine Perspectives,* 1980; Other articles. **Activities:** 1; 41, 49-Systems Anal. **Addr.:** 1913 Monterey Dr., Lincoln, NE 68506.

Lunin, Lois F. (Schenectady, NY) VP, Herner and Co., 1978–; Dir., Info. Sci., Env. Prog., Inc., 1977–78; Co-dir., Prog. Dir., Info. Ctr. for Hearing, Sp. and Disorders of Human Comm., Johns Hopkins Med. Inst., 1965–76; Resrch. Assoc., Univ. of TX, 1959–64; various positions in med. resrch. **Educ.:** Radcliffe Coll., 1942–45, AB (Psy.); Drexel Univ., 1962–66, MS (Info. Sci.). **Orgs.:** Med. LA. ASIS: Ed., Bltn. (1974–78); Ed. Bd., *JASIS* (1978–80); Assoc. Ed., *Perspectives* (1981–); Spec. Int. Grp. on Info. Anal. Ctr., Secy. (1968); Vice-Ch. (1969); Awd. of Spec. Merit Com. (1969, 1970); Secy. (1971, 1972); Ch., Liaison Com. (1971, 1972); Ch., SIG/Info. Generation and Publshg. (1978–79); SIG/IGP Cabinet Rep. (1980). AAAS. Assn. for Comp. Mach. Cncl. of Bio. Eds.: Com. on Arms and Goals (1978–). Drug Info. Assn. Other orgs. **Honors:** Phi Kappa Phi; Beta Phi Mu, 1966; Inst. of Info. Sci., Flw., 1967; ASIS, Watson Davis Awd., 1976; AAAS, Flw., 1981. **Pubns.:** *Health Sciences and Services: A Guide to Sources of Information* (1979); jt. auth., *Index-Handbook of Ototoxic Agents, 1966–71* (1973); "Teaching Information and Communication in a Medical Center," *Jnl. of Med. Educ.* (1972); "The Biblio-Profile–A Two-in-One Package of Information," *Jnl. of the Amer. Socty. for Info. Sci.* (1976); "A Multifaceted Medical Data Information System and One Product," *JASIS* (1976); other articles and various book chapters. **Activities:** 14-Consult.; 17; 75, 93 **Addr.:** Herner and Company, 1700 N. Moore St., Arlington, VA 22209.

Lunn, Alice Jean Elizabeth (Je. 30, 1910, Montreal, PQ) Retired, 1975–; Dir., Ofc. of Lib. Stans., Natl. Lib. of Can., 1973–75, Dir., Cat. Branch and "Canadiana," 1950–73; Chief Libn., Fraser Inst. Lib., 1946–50. **Educ.:** McGill Univ., 1928–32, BA (Hist.), 1932–34, MA (Hist.), 1934–42, PhD (Hist.), 1939–40, BLS. **Orgs.:** Can. LA. Bibl. Socty. of Can. Stans. Cncl. of Can.: Adv. Com. on a Stans. Info. Srv. **Pubns.:** Various articles in hist. and lib. jnls. **Activities:** 1, 4; 17, 20, 49-Stans.; 57, 92 **Addr.:** Rural Route 3, Carp, ON K0A 1L0 Canada.

Lupp, Denise Marie (S. 19, 1952, Frederick, MD) Hosp. Libn., WA Cnty. Hosp., 1978–; Rom. Lang. Libn., Natl. Agr. Lib., 1977–78; Ref. Libn., Hagerstown Jr. Coll., 1976–77; Branch Libn., Carroll Cnty. Pub. Lib., 1975–77. **Educ.:** Mount Saint Mary's Coll., 1973, BA (Fr.); Univ. of MD, 1974, MLS. **Orgs.:** Med. LA. ALA. MD Assn. Hlth. Sci. Libns. **Honors** Beta Phi Mu. **Activities:** 12; 17, 20, 39; 55, 80 **Addr.:** 318 South Seton Ave., Emmitsburg, MD 21727.

Lupton, David Walker (O. 12, 1934, Madison, WI) Head, Serials Dept., CO State Univ., 1968–; Asst. Serials Libn., Purdue Univ., 1967–68; Asst. Life Sci. Libn., Purdue Univ., 1963–66. **Educ.:** Univ. of WI, 1952–56, BS (Zlgy.), 1958–60, MS (Entomology); 1961–63, MS (LS). **Orgs.:** ALA. CO LA. CO Hist. Socty. CO Geneal. Socty. Westerners Intl. Museum of the Fur Trade. **Honors:** Beta Phi Mu. **Pubns.:** "Zoo and Aquarium Design," *Cncl. of Plng. Libns. Exch. Bibl. #1484* (1978); ed., *CO Field Ornithologist* (1969–74); ed., *Ptarmigan,* (1969–74); ed., *The Luptonian,* (1974–); ed., "Serials Digest" column, *Serials Review* (1978–79); other articles in various fields. **Activities:** 1; 15, 44 **Addr.:** Serials Department, Colorado State University Libraries, Fort Collins, CO 80523.

Lushington, Nolan (F. 15, 1929, Cross Roads, Jamaica, West Indies) Dir., Greenwich Lib., 1966–, Asst. Dir., 1962–66; Libn., Free Lib. of Philadelphia, 1960–61; Libn., St. Andrews Sch., 1953–60. **Educ.:** Columbia Univ., 1946–50, AB, 1952–53, MA (Hist.), 1953–58, MS (LS). **Orgs.:** ALA: LAMA/BES (Ch., 1979); (NE Region Ch., 1974). CT LA: (Pres., 1970). DE LA: (Pres., 1960). US Marine Corps Reserve: Colonel. Rotary Intl. **Honors:** Cncl. on Lib. Res., Fellow, 1972. **Pubns.:** *Libraries Designed for Users* (1979); "Information Center Library," *Lib. Jnl.* (1976); "The Flow of Function," *Amer. Libs.* (1976). **Activities:** 9; 16, 17, 19, 24; 55, 56, 67 **Addr.:** 50 Sound View Dr., Greenwich, CT 06830.

Luskay, Jack R. (Ap. 29, 1942, North Charleroi, PA) Asst. Prof. of LS, Clarion State Coll., 1972–; Lib. Media Spec., Ligonier Valley Sch. Dist., 1964–72; Tchr., Butler Area Sch. Dist., 1963–64. **Educ.:** Clarion State Coll., 1960–63, BS/ED (Eng., LS); Univ. of Pittsburgh, 1964–66, MLS. **Orgs.:** PA Sch. Libns. Assn.: Pres. (1974–76). ALA: AASL, *Sch. Media Qtly.* Ed. (1979–); Louisville Conf. (Ch., 1980). **Honors** Beta Phi Mu, 1966. **Activities:** 10, 11; 16, 32, 48; 55, 89, 90 **Addr.:** School of Library Science, Clarion State College, Clarion, PA 16214.

Lussky, Warren A. (Ap. 16, 1919, Chicago, IL) Lib. Dir., TX Luth. Coll., 1956–; Head Libn., NE Wesleyan Univ., 1955–56; Head Libn., Rocky Mt. Coll., 1950–55; Libn., Hopkins Transp. Lib., Stanford Univ., 1949–50; Asst. Libn., Pac. Luth. Coll., 1948–49. **Educ.:** Univ. of CO, 1940–46, BA (Sci.); Univ. of Denver, 1947–48, MA (LS), 1947–48, Dipl. (LS). **Orgs.:** TX LA: Dist. Ch. (1965–1966). Cncl. of Resrch. and Acad. Libs.: Secy.-Treas (1972–74); Pres. (1976–78). ALA. SWLA. TX Educ. Agency: Accred. team, coll. (1961). South. Assn. of Coll. and Sch.: Accred. team roster (1974–). **Pubns.:** "Blumberg Memorial Library, Texas Lutheran College," *TX Lib. Jnl.* (Sum. 1971). **Activities:** 1; 17, 49-Lib. Consortium. **Addr.:** 357 Irvington Dr., San Antonio, TX 78209.

Luster, Arlene Leong (Ja. 11, 1936, Honolulu, HI) Dir., Command Libs., U.S. Air Frc., Pacific, 1959–; Naval Reg. Libn., Pearl Harbor, HI, 1973–79; Base Libn., Wheeler Air Frc. Base, 1968–73. **Educ.:** TX Woman's Univ., 1956–57, BA (LS); West. Resrv. Univ., 1957–58, MS (LS); Univ. of South. CA, 1974–77, ED.D. **Orgs.:** ALA: PLA/Armed Frcs. Libns. Sect. (Pres., 1976–); Reg. Mem. (Ch., 1978–81). HI LA: Pres. (1973–74); Ed. (1974–76); Other Ofcs. Delta Kappa Gamma: Various ofcs. Fed. Employed Women: Various ofcs. Delta Epsilon. **Honors:** H. W. Wilson Co./ALA, John Cotton Dana Awd., 1970, 1971, 1972, 1973. Other hons. **Pubns.:** Jt. auth., *Military Reference Sources: An Annotated Bibliography* (1979); Jt. auth., *Stress–Selected Readings* (1980); *Pearl Harbor Attack: An Annotated Bibliography* (1979); "Tribute to John and Mary," *HI LA Jnl.* (1964); Various other pubns. **Activities:** 9; 17, 25, 36; 50, 74, 85 **Addr.:** HQ PACAF/DPSRL, Hickam AFB, HI 96853.

Lyders, Richard A. (Jn. 16, 1934, Minot, ND) Exec. Dir., Houston Acad. of Med.–TX Med. Ctr. Lib., 1976, Assoc. Dir., 1972–76; Asst. Dir., Tech. Srvs., Univ. of ND Lib., 1970–72; Dir., Assoc. Colls. of the Midwest Per. Bank, 1968–70; Serials Libn., Univ. of MD Biomed. Lib., 1966–68. **Educ.:** Univ. of MN, 1961–63, BA (Psych., English); Univ. of South. CA, 1965–66, MLS. **Orgs.:** Med LA: Schol. Com. (Ch., 1975–77); Status and Econ. Interest Com. (Ch., 1979–80); S. Ctrl. Reg. Grp. (Pres., 1979). Reg. Med. Lib. Prog.: Reg. IV, Adv. Com. (Ch., 1980). ALA: Com. on Org. (1980–83). Assn. of Acad. Hlth. Sci. Lib. Dirs.: Bylaws Com. (1979–80). Houston Area Resrch. Lib. Cnstrtm.: Bd. of Dir. (1978–). **Pubns.:** "Results-oriented Management through MBO," *Bltn. Med LA* (Jl. 1979); Jt.-auth., "Classification of Support Staff in a Consortium Medical Library," *Bltn. Med. LA* (Ap. 1979); jt.-auth., "Friends of the library groups in health sciences libraries," *Bltn. Med. LA* (Jl. 1978); "New Library Buildings, the Houston Academy of Medicine—Texas Medical Center Library," *Bltn. Med. LA* (Ap. 1977); other papers and articles; one Med. LA Cont. Educ. syllabus. **Activities:** 1, 12; 17; 80 **Addr.:** Jesse H. Jones Library Building, Houston Academy of Medicine, Texas Medical Center Library, Houston, TX 77030.

Lyerla, Gloria R. (F. 15, 1929, TX) Ref. Libn./ILL, TX Tech. Univ., 1967–; Base Libn., Wheelus Air Frc. Base, 1963–64; Serials Libn., TX Tech. Univ., 1952–62; Catlgr., Howard Payne Coll., 1950–51. **Educ.:** N. TX State Univ., 1946–50 (Soc. Sci.), 1950–51 (Educ.). **Orgs.:** ALA. TX LA: ILL RT/Org. Com. (1975–76), Cnclr. (1980–81), Nom. Com. (1979); Ref. RT/Nom. Com. (1978); S.W. Acad. Lib. Cnsrtm.: Coord. ILL Mtgs. and Wkshp. (1975, 1977). AMIGOS: Users Adv. Com., ILL. Natl. Bus. and Prof. Women. **Pubns.:** *Texas Reference Sources; A Selective Guide* (1975, 1978). **Activities:** 1; 29, 34, 39 **Addr.:** 3215 64th St., Lubbock, TX 79413.

Lyman, Helen Huguenor (Mr. 16, 1910, Hornell, NY) Prof. Emeritus, Univ. of WI-Madison, Consult., 1978–; Lectr., SUNY, Buffalo, 1977–. Prof., Assoc. Prof., Asst. Prof., Lib. Sch., Univ. of WI, 1967–78; Pub. Lib. Spec. for Adult Srvs., Lib. Srvs. Branch, Ofc. of Educ., HEW, 1965–67; Dir., Ref. Dept., Assoc. Prof., SUNY, Buffalo, 1964–65; Pub. Lib. Consult., Spec. in Adult Srvs., WI Free Lib. Comsn., 1959–63; Chicago Pub. Lib., 1954–59; Dir., ALA Adult Educ. Srvy., 1952–53; various positions, Buffalo Pub. Lib., 1932–52. **Educ.:** Univ. of Buffalo, 1929–32, BA (Hist. & LS), 1940, BS in LS; Univ. of Chicago, 1955–56; Cert. in NY, WI. **Orgs.:** ALA: Cncl. (1962–65, 1968–70); Adult Srvs. Div. (Pres. 1969–70); PLA Nom. Com.

Special Subjects/Services: 50. Adult educ.; 51. Advert./Mktg.; 52. Aerosp.; 53. Agric.; 54. Area std.; 55. Arts/Hum.; 56. Autom.; 57. Bibl./Prtg.; 58. Bio. sci.; 59. Bus./Fin.; 60. Chem.; 61. Copyrt.; 62. Documtn.; 63. Educ.; 64. Engin.; 65. Env.; 66. Eth. grps.; 67. Film; 68. Food/Nutr.; 69. Geneal.; 70. Geo.; 71. Geol.; 72. Handcpd.; 73. Hist.; 74. Int. frdm.; 75. Info. sci.; 76. Insr.; 77. Law; 78. Legis.; 79. Math./Comp. sci.; 80. Med.; 81. Metals; 82. Nat. resrcs.; 83. Newsp.; 84. Nuc. sci.; 85. Oral hist.; 86. Petr./Energy; 87. Pharm.; 88. Phys./Astr./Math.; 89. Readg.; 90. Relig.; 91. Sci./Tech.; 92. Soc. sci.; 93. Telecom.; 94. Transp.; 95. (other).

(1977–78); Ofc. for Lib. Srv. to Disadv. (Adv. Bd. 1974–78). NY LA. Ctr. for the Book in the Lib. of Congs.: Natl. Adv. Bd. (1978–82). WI LA. AAUP. Adult Educ. Assn. WI Arts Fndn. and Cncl.: Dir. (1961–63). **Honors:** Joseph W. Lippincott Awd., Notable Achvmt. in Libnshp., 1979. **Pubns.:** *Literacy and the Nation's Libraries* (1977); *Reading and the Adult New Reader* (1976); *Library Materials in Service to the Adult New Reader* (1973); "Literacy Education as Library Community Service," *Lib. Trends* (Fall 1979); "Literacy, Library Programs," *ALA Yrbk.* (1977–80); other books and articles. **Activities:** 9, 11; 16, 26, 41; 50, 89 **Addr.:** S4528 Freeman Rd., Orchard Park, NY 14127.

Lynch, Beverly P. (D. 27, 1935, Moorhead, MN) Univ. Libn., Univ. of IL, Chicago Circle, 1977–; Exec. Secy., ACRL, 1972–76; Head, Serials Div., Yale Univ. Libs., 1965–68, Asst. Head, 1963–65; Asst. Cat. Libn., Marquette Univ., 1962–63; Asst. Ref. Libn., Plymouth (Eng.) Pub. Lib., 1961–62; Libn., Marquette Univ., 1959–61. **Educ.:** ND State Univ., 1953–57, BS; Univ. of IL, 1957–59, MS; Univ. of WI, 1968–72, PhD. **Orgs.:** ALA: Cncl. (1979–), Com. on Prog. Eval. and Support (1979–); ACRL, *Coll. & Resrch.* Libs. (Ed. Bd., 1977–). Ctr. for Resrch. Libs.: Bd. of Dir. (1977–; Ch., 1980). Ctr. for the Bk. in the Lib. of Congs.: Exec. Com., Adv. Bd. (1978–). Midwest Reg. Lib. Ntwk.: Bd. of Dir. (1981–). Caxton Club. Grolier Club. Lib. of Intl. Rel.: Gov. Bd. (1977–). Bibl. Socty. of Amer. Amer. Soclgy. Assn. **Honors:** ACRL and Baker & Tayler Co., Resrch. Libn. of the Yr., 1981. ND State Univ., D.Litt., 1980. Phi Kappa Phi. **Pubns.:** "An Empirical Assessment of Perrow's Technology Construct," *Admin. Sci. Qtly.* (S. 1974). Various articles in the Lib. press. **Activities:** 1; 17, 24, 41 **Addr.:** 1859 N. 68 St., Milwaukee, WI 53213.

Lynch, Frances H. (Jl. 1, 1949, Huntington, WV) Asst. Dir. for Tech. Srvs., Vanderbilt Med. Ctr. Lib., 1979–, Serials Libn., 1977–79, Mono. Libn., 1976–77, VLEF Libn., 1974–76. **Educ.:** Marshall Univ., 1967–71, BS, summa cum laude (Bio. Sci.); George Peabody Coll., 1973–74, MLS. **Orgs.:** Med. LA. TN LA. TN Hlth. Sci. LA: Interim Pres. (1976–77). Mid-TN Hlth. Sci. Libns.: Pres. (1976–77). Nashville Lib. Club. **Honors:** Beta Phi Mu, 1976; Peabody Coll. Sch. of LS, A. Stan Rescoe Cat. Awd., 1974. **Activities:** 1, 12; 15, 17, 46; 68, 80, 95-Nursing. **Addr.:** Vanderbilt University, Medical Center Library, Nashville, TN 37232.

Lynch, Margie Ruth (Je. 8, 1925, CA) Dir., Hattiesburg Pub. Lib. Syst., 1974–; Par. Libn., Calcasieu Par. Pub. Lib., 1961–74; Par. Libn., Vernon Par. Lib., 1957–61; Demonstration Libn., LA State Lib., 1956–57; Par. Libn., Vermilion Par. Lib., 1955–56; Asst. Libn. (Circ.), Lake Charles Pub. Lib., 1951–54; Asst. Libn., Avoyelles Par. Lib., 1950–51; Branch Libn., Ouachita Par. Pub. Lib., 1949–50. **Educ.:** LA State Univ., 1946–48, BA (Eng.), 1948–49, BS (LS). **Orgs.:** ALA: ALTA. LA LA: Lib. Dev. Com., Exec. Secy. (1965–67), Secy. (1958–59); Com. on Org. and Structure of Pub. Libs. (Ch. 1962–63). MS LA: Pub. Lib. Sect. (Ch., 1980); Ad Hoc Com. on Persnl. Grants (Ch., 1979–80); Com. to Standardize Circ. Stats. (Co-Ch., 1978–79). Various other orgs. Bus. and Prof. Women's Club of Hattiesburg. Hattiesburg Leag. of Women Voters. Delta Kappa Gamma: VP (1972–74); 2nd VP (1970–72). **Honors:** LA LA, Modisette Awd. for Pub. Libs., 1959, 1960, 1966. **Pubns.:** "Welcome to Southwest Louisiana," *LA LA Bltn.* (Ja. 1974). **Activities:** 9; 17, 34, 36; 50, 75 **Addr.:** 723 Main St., Hattiesburg, MS 39401.

Lynch, Sr. Mary Dennis (Ap. 23, 1920, Philadelphia, PA) Dir., Lib. Srvs., Rosemont Coll., 1962–; Libn., Tchr., Sch. of the Holy Child (Sharon Hill, PA), 1953–62; Tchr. (Soc. Stds.), W. Philadelphia Cath. HS for Girls, 1947–53; Libn., Tchr., Sch. of the Holy Child (Oak Knoll, PA), 1945–47; Libn., Tchr., Sch. of the Holy Child (Sharon, PA), 1942–45. **Educ.:** Temple Univ., 1937–41, BA (Soclgy); Drexel Inst. of Tech., 1941–42, BSLS; Cath. Univ., 1951–56, MSLS; Villanova Univ., 1966–70, MA (Pol. Sci.); St. Charles Semy., 1974–80, MA (Relig. Educ.). **Orgs.:** OCLC: Users Cncl. (1978–). PALINET: Bd. of Trustees (1979–). ALA. Cath. LA.: VP/Pres. Elect (1981–). Other orgs. St. Charles Semy.: Educ. Adv. Bd. (1968–76; 1978–). Women for Greater Philadelphia. **Honors:** Beta Phi Mu. **Pubns.:** "Bibliographic Instructor," series, *Cath. Lib. World* (O. 1977–My. 1978); Column Ed., *Cath. Lib. World* (1973–75). **Activities:** 1; 15, 17, 34; 90, 92 **Addr.:** Rosemont College Library, Rosemont, PA 19010.

Lynch, Mary Jo (Jn. 3, 1939, Detroit, MI) Dir., Ofc. for Resrch., ALA, 1978–, Assoc. Exec. Secy., ALA: PLA; RASD, 1976–78; Asst. Prof. (LS), Univ. of MI, 1971–73; Sr. Ref. Libn., Univ. of MA, 1969–71; Head, Ref., Univ. of Detroit Lib., 1966–69, Ref. Libn., 1962–66. **Educ.:** Marygrove Coll., 1957–61, BA (Eng.); Univ. of MI, 1961–62, AMLS; Univ. of Detroit, 1962–66, MA (Eng.); Rutgers Univ., 1973–77, PhD (LS). **Orgs.:** ALA: JMRT, Exec. Bd. (1969–71); RASD, Bd. of Dir. (1972–74). ASIS. AALS. **Honors:** Univ. of MI, Dept. of LS, Disting. Alum. Awd., 1971. **Pubns.:** "Educational, Cultural and Recreational Services for Adults in the Public Library," *Lib. Qtly.* (O. 1978); "Reference Interviews in Public Libraries," *Lib. Qtly.* (Ap., 1978); Jt.-auth., "Design for Diversity: Alternatives to Standards for Public Libraries," *PLA Nsltr.* (Jn. 1974); "Trials, Tactics, and Timing: Some Thoughts on Library Instruction Programs" in *A Challenge for Academic Libraries* (1973); pamphlet: *Community Colleges, Public Libraries, and the Humanities: A Study.* **Activities:** 1, 9; 26, 39, 41; 61, 92, 95-Resrch. **Addr.:** 2728 N. Hampden Ct., Chicago, IL 60614.

Lynch, Michael Patrick (N. 10, 1937, San Rafael, CA) Dir., N. Ctrl. Reg. Lib., 1967–, Asst. Dir., 1965–67; Ref. Libn., S. Puget Snd. Reg. Lib., 1963–65. **Educ.:** Univ. of San Francisco, 1955–59, BS (Eng.); Univ. of Denver, 1962–63, MA (LS). **Orgs.:** ALA. Pac. NW LA. WA LA: Exec. Bd. (1966–67); Statewide Lib. Dev. Com. (Ch., 1970); 2nd VP (1971–72); WA State Adv. Cncl. on Libs. (Ch., 1975); Pub. Lib. Funding Com. (Ch., 1979–80). WA Lib. Netwk.: Exec. Bd. (1977); Comp. Srvs. Cncl. (1981–). Leavenworth Rotary. WA State Hist. Socty. **Pubns.:** Ed., *On the Upper Columbia and How I Saw It* (1980); "Mail Order Library Service," *Bk. Cats.* (1971); "A Library in your Mailbox...," *Bks. By Mail: A Hand Book For Libraries.* **Activities:** 9; 17, 27; 55, 78, 95-Mail ord. lib. **Addr.:** 11654 Riverbend, Leavenworth, WA 98826.

Lynch, Minnie-Lou Chittick (F. 28, 1916, Cutler, IN) Trustee, Allen Par. Lib., 1957–; Exec. Dir., Gvr.'s Conf. on Libs. and Info. Srvs., LA, 1977–78. **Orgs.:** ALA: ALTA (Pres., 1961–63), various coms. (1964–); Cncl. (1961–63). LA LA: Trustee Sect., Ch. (1962); 2nd VP (1970); Lib. Dev. Com. (Ch., 1965–68). SWLA. Intl. Platform Assn. LA Cncl. for the Performing Arts. **Honors:** LA LA, Modisette Awd. to Trustees, 1961; ALA, Awd. to Trustees, 1964; Pi Kappa Delta. **Pubns.:** *Guidelines for Holding a Governor's Conference on Libraries* (1963, 1976); ed., *Handbook for Library Trustees of Louisiana* (1980); "Libraries in the Political Environment," *Bltn. LA LA* (Spr. 1965); jt. auth., "Board Organization," "Planning," *The Library Trustee* (1964, 1968, 1978). **Activities:** 9; 24, 36, 47; 50 **Addr.:** 404 E. 6th Ave., Oakdale, LA 71463.

Lynden, Frederick C. (Ja. 20, 1939, San Jose, CA) Asst. Univ. Libn. for Tech. Srvs., Brown Univ. Lib., 1977–; Asst. Chief, Acq. Dept., Stanford Univ. Libs., 1967–77, Ref. Libn., Meyer Undergrad. Lib., 1966–67; Ref. Libn., Bancroft Lib., Univ. of CA, Berkeley, 1964–66. **Educ.:** Stanford Univ., 1956–60, BA (Intl. Rel.), 1960–61, MA (Amer. Hist.). Univ. of MN, 1962–63, MA (LS). **Orgs.:** ALA: RTSD/Resrcs. Sect. (Ch., 1978–79), Lib. Mtrls. Price Index Com. (1974–78; Ch., 1976–78). Amer. Natl. Standards Com. Z39: Committee I to Rev. ANSI Z39.20 (Ch., 1979–). **Honors:** Cncl. on Lib. Resrcs., Flwshp. Awd., 1977–78. **Pubns.:** "Library Materials Budgeting in the Private University library: Austerity and Action," *Advances in Libnshp.* (1980); "The Library Materials Price Situation in the United States", *LIBER Bulletin* 9/10, 1978; "Collection Development," *ALA Yrbk.* (1978); "Sources of Information on the Costs of Library Materials," *Lib. Acq.: Practice and Theory* (Ap. 1977); Other articles and surveys. **Activities:** 1; 15, 17, 46 **Addr.:** Rockefeller Library, Brown University, Providence, RI 02912.

Lynn, Kenneth C. (My. 22, 1924, Bellefontaine, OH) Dental Resrch., Data Ofcr., Natl. Inst. of Dental Resrch., Natl. Inst. of Hlth., 1968–; Spec. Asst. to Chief of Ref. Srvs., Natl. Lib. of Med., 1967–68; Coord., Dental Affairs, 1965–68; Dental Ofcr., U.S. Pub. Hlth. Srvc. 1956. **Educ.:** OH State Univ., 1942–51, 1952–56, DDS; Univ. of MD, 1966–67, MLS. **Orgs.:** Med. LA: Dental Spec. Int. Grp. (Ch., 1980). Amer. Dental Assn. Amer. Pub. Hlth. Assn. Cmsn. Ofcrs. Assn. of the U.S. Pub. Hlth. Srv. **Honors:** Omicron Kappa Upsilon. Beta Phi Mu. **Pubns.:** "Bibliographic Reference Study of a Dental Journal," *Jnl. Amer. Coll.* Dents (1967); "The National Library of Medicine serves dentistry," *Jnl. Amer. Soc. Geriat.* Dent (1969); "A Quantitative Comparison of Conventional Compression Techniques in Dental Literature," *Amer. Docum.* (1969); "Directory of Medical Libraries for Dentists in the State of Maryland," *Jnl. MD State Dent. Assn.* 1969. **Activities:** 12; 17; 58, 80 **Addr.:** National Institute of Dental Research, National Institutes of Health, Bethesda, MD 20205.

Lynn, Ruth Nadelman (S. 26, 1948, Kalamazoo, MI) Head of Chld. Srvs., Waltham Pub. Lib., 1977–80; Chld. Libn., Skokie Pub. Lib., 1974–77. **Educ.:** Univ. of MI, 1966–70, BA (Educ.); Rosary Coll., 1973–74, MLS. **Orgs.:** ALA: Ref. and Subscrpn. Bks. Review Com. (1976–80); Laura Ingalls Wilder Awd. Com. (1977–80). New Eng. LA: RT of Chld. Libns. (Corres. Secy., 1980–81). MA LA. **Honors:** Beta Phi Mu, 1974. **Pubns.:** *Fantasy for Children; An Annotated Checklist* (1979); various reviews, (1976–80). **Activities:** 9; 21 **Addr.:** 33 Maple St., Lexington, MA 02173.

Lyons, Albert S. (My. 28, 1912, New York, NY) Archvst. and Coord., Hist. of Med., Mt. Sinai Sch. of Med., 1967–, Clinical Prof. of Surgery. **Educ.:** New York Univ., 1928–32, BS; Columbia Univ., 1932–36, MD. **Orgs.:** Med. Archvsts. of NY: Pres. (1977–79). SAA. Middle Atl. Reg. Arch. Conf. Oral Hist. Assn.: Founding Mem., Nom. Com. (Ch. 1966). Med. Socty. of the Cnty. of NY: Secy. (1973–78). Hist. of Sci. Socty. Frnds. of the Rare Book Room, NY Acad. of Med.: Pres. (1970–72). Amer. Assn. for the Hist. of Med. **Honors:** Coll. of Physicians of Philadelphia, Kate Hurd Mead Lect., 1972. **Pubns.:** Jt. auth., *Medicine, An Illustrated History* (1978); "Teaching The History of Medicine–New Approaches," *Trans. Coll. Phys. Phila.* (1972); "A Stitch in Time," *The Sciences* (O. 1979); "The History of Medicine and Medical Education," *Medical Tribune* (S. 19, 1979); other articles. **Activities:** 2, 14-Med. Sch.; 25, 42, 45; 73, 80, 85 **Addr.:** Mount Sinai School of Medicine, One Gustave Levy Pl., New York, NY 10029.

Lyons, Donald W. (D. 11, 1945, Lexington, KY) Dir., Libs., KY State Univ., 1976–; Assoc. Dir., Libs., 1975–76, Asst. Libn., 1971–75; Tchr., MI and KY, 1968–75. **Educ.:** KY State Univ., 1964–68, AB (Hist. and Pol. Sci.); Univ. of KY, 1969–71, MSLS. **Orgs.:** ALA. KY LA. Alpha Phi Alpha. Lexington Northside Lions Club. **Honors:** Alpha Phi Alpha, Man of the Yr., 1980. Beta Phi Mu. **Activities:** 1; 15, 17, 26 **Addr.:** Blazer Library, Kentucky State University, Frankfort, KY 40601.

Lyons, Grace J. (Jn. 22, 1932, NY, NY) Chief, DC Reg. Lib. Blind Phys. Handcpd., Homebound and Inst. Srvs., 1973–; Sr. Libn. Kings Pk. Sr HS, 1960–72, Bibl., Med. Lib., Amer. Cancer Socty., NY, 1957–60. **Educ.:** St. John's Univ., 1950–54, BS (Chem.); Columbia Univ., 1956–60, MLS; Univ. of MD, 1977– (Bus.). **Orgs.:** ALA: ASCLA, various ofcs.; Hlth. and Rehab. Lib. Srv. Dir., Bd. (1974–76)/Lib. Srv. to the Blind and Phys. Handcpd. Sect. (Ch., 1977–78). Pres.'s Com. on Empl. of the Handcpd.: Lib. Com. (1975–). **Honors:** ALA, Excep. Srv. Awd., 1977. **Pubns.:** Various pubns. **Activities:** 5, 9; 27; 72 **Addr.:** 11615 Vantage Hill Rd., Reston, VA 22090.

Lytle, Richard H. (Jl. 16, 1937, Topeka, KS) Archvst., Smithsonian Inst., 1970–; Univ. Archvst., Rice Univ., 1968–70; Univ. Archvst., WA Univ., 1964–68; Asst. Lcl. Recs. Archvst., State of IL, 1963–64. **Educ.:** Rice Univ., 1955–59, BA (Hist.); WA Univ., 1959–61, AM (Hist.); Univ. of MD, 1974–78, MLS, PhD (LS). **Orgs.:** SAA: Cncl. (1978–). Amer. Assn. of Musms. ASIS. **Pubns.:** "Intellectual Access To Archives," *Amer. Archvst.* (Ja.–Ap. 1980); ed., *Management of Archives and Manuscript Collections for Librarians* (Ja. 1975); jt. auth., "Intellectual Control of Historical Records," *The Amer. Archvst.* (Jl. 1977); various articles, reviews. **Activities:** 2, 4; 17, 38, 41; 56, 75 **Addr.:** Smithsonian Institution Archives, 900 Jefferson Dr. S.W., Washington, DC 20560.

Lytle, Susan Steele (S. 18, 1951, Kansas City, MO) Map and Multi-Media Libn., TX A & M Univ., 1978–, Resrch. Assoc., 1976–78. **Educ.:** IN Univ., 1969–73, AB (Thea.); Univ. of TN, 1975–76, MSLS. TX A & M Univ., 1977–80 Med. (Educ. Tech.). **Orgs.:** SLA: Geog. and Map Div., Mem. Com. (1979–80), Standards Com. (1980–); TX LA: AV Interest Grp., Mem. Com. (1978–). ALA. AECT. TX Assn. Educ. Tech. **Honors:** Phi Kappa Phi. Phi Beta Kappa. Beta Phi Mu. **Pubns.:** Jt. comp. *Energy Bibliography & Index* (1978–79–80); jt. auth., "The Systematic Study of the Literature on Terrorism," *Military Police Law Enforcement Jnl.* (Sum. 1979); *Energy Bibliography & Index* (1978, 79, 80). **Activities:** 1; 15, 32, 39; 63, 67, 70 **Addr.:** Sterling C. Evans Library, Texas A&M University, College Station, TX 77843.

Lyvers, Sr. Mary Eulema (D. 5, 1916, Rome, KY) Libn., Our Lady of Mount Carmel Elem. Sch., 1975–; Libn., St. Mary of the Pines, (MS), 1974–75; Libn., Tchr., St. Joseph Elem. and HS (AR), 1969–70; Libn., Tchr., Redemptorist Jr. and Sr. HS (LA), 1968–69; Prin. and Libn., Holy Rosary Sch. (TX), 1962–68); Prin. and Libn., St. Mary Sch., Gainesville, TX, 1955–61. **Educ.:** LeClerc Coll., 1945–49, BA (Hist.); St. Louis Univ., 1950–54, M.Ed.; LA State Univ., 1970–73, MS (LS). **Orgs.:** Cath. LA: Various lcl. ofcs. (1965–). TX LA. **Pubns.:** "Pebbles from the Ark," Nsltr., CLA: AK Chap. (1971–73). **Activities:** 10; 15, 21, 23 **Addr.:** Our Lady of Mount Carmel Library, 6703 Whitefriars, Houston, TX 77087.

M

Maack, Dr. Mary Niles (D. 14, 1945, Paris, IL) Assoc. Prof., Univ. of MN Lib. Sch., 1975–; Visit. Instr., Univ. of OR Sch. of Libnshp., 1973; Libn., NY Pub. Lib., 1969–72. **Educ.:** Univ. of IL, 1964–68, BA (Hist.); Columbia Univ., 1969–70, MLS, 1972–78, DLS. **Orgs.:** ALA: IRRT; Exec. Com. (1977–79). MN LA: Cont. Educ. Com. (1976–78). AALS. AAUW. **Honors:** Phi Beta Kappa, 1967; Beta Phi Mu, 1970. **Pubns.:** *Libraries in Senegal: Continuity and Change in an Emerging Nation* (1981); "Museum of the Mind: Rare Books and the Public Library," *Wilson Lib. Bltn.* (Ja. 1980); "The A.O.F. Archives and the Study of African History," *Bltn. de l'Inst. Fondamental d'Afrique Noire* (1980); "Libraries for the General Public in French Speaking Africa: Their Cultural Role, 1803–1975," *Jnl. of Lib. Hist., Phil. and Compar. Libnshp.* (Win. 1981). **Addr.:** University of Minnesota, Library School, 117 Pleasant St. S.E., Minneapolis, MN 55455.

Maag, Albert F. (Ja. 24, 1941, Newark, NJ) Univ. Libn., Capital Univ., 1971–; Lib. Dir., Harcum Jr. Coll., 1969–71; Asst. Libn., Actg. Dir. of Lib. Srvs., Luzerne Cnty. Cmnty. Coll., 1967–69; Tchr./Libn., Newark Pub. Schs., 1962–67. **Educ.:** Seton Hall Univ., 1959–62, BS in Educ. (Eng.); Rutgers Univ., 1964–67, MLS; OH State Univ., 1971–75, PhD (Educ.); Other courses. **Orgs.:** ALA. NLA. Acad. Libns.' Assn. of OH. **Pubns.:** "So You Want to Be a Director," *Jnl. of Acad. Libnshp.* (1981); "Design of the Library Director Interview: The Candidate's Perspective," *Coll. & Resrch. Libs.* (Mr. 1980); reviews. **Activities:** 1; 17, 31, 42 **Addr.:** Capital University Library, 2199 East Main St., Columbus, OH 43209.

Maass, Eleanor A. (S. 17, 1919, Champaign, IL) Spec. Proj. Libn., Univ. of PA, 1981–, Actg. Libn., Biomed. Lib., 1980–81; Sci. Libn., SUNY, Binghamton, 1977–78; Sci. Libn., Swarthmore Coll., 1963–77. **Educ.:** Univ. of IL, 1937–41, BS (Chem.), 1941–42, MA (Chem.); Univ. of WI, 1942–47, PhD (Biochem.). **Orgs.:** SLA. Socty. for the Hist. of Tech. **Pubns.:** "Greville Bathe's Theater of Machines: Evolution of a Scholar and His Library," *Tech. and Culture* (O. 1978); "Low Cost Automation of Periodicals in a College Library," *Cost Reduction for Special Libraries and Information Centers* (1973); transl., *Genesis and Evolutionary Development of Life* (1968); "Photosynthesis," "Nitrogen Cycle," *A.W. Library Pathfinders* (1973); "A Public Watchdog: Thomas Pym Cope and the Philadelphia Waterworks," *Procs. of the Amer. Phil. Socty.* (Ap. 1981); articles in bacteriology, reviews. **Activities:** 1; 17; 58, 80 **Addr.:** 415 Cornell Ave., Swarthmore, PA 19081.

Mabry, Raymond Edward (J. 23, 1938, Little River, KS) Libn., Art & Msc. Dept., Richmond Pub. Lib., 1975–; Asst. Head, Fine Arts Dept., Atlanta Pub. Lib., (GA) 1971–73; Dir. of Msc., Second Presby. Church (VA) 1962–67. **Educ.:** Curtis Inst. of Msc., 1958–62, BM (Msc.); Indiana Univ., 1967–71, MM (Msc.), MLS; KS State Tchrs. Coll. 1955–58. **Orgs.:** Msc LA. **Honors:** Phi Mu Alpha Sinfonia, 1957; Pi Kappa Lambda, 1969; Beta Phi Mu, 1973. **Pubns.:** "A Chronological Survey of Organ Compositions from the 14th Century to J. S. Bach," *Amer. Guild of Organists Qtly.* (Jl. 1965); "When All Else Fails, Read the Instructions," *Diapason* (My. 1972); Complr. "Immanuel, God With Us," (1974); "Requiem for the Living," (1977); Transl. "The Renaissance of the French School," *Msc.* (Je 1974); Transl. *The Milieu, Work and Art of Cesar Franck* **Activities:** 9, 12; 15, 20, 39; 55 **Addr.:** Art & Music Department, Richmond Public Library, 101 E. Franklin St., Richmond, VA 23219.

MacArthur, William Joseph, Jr. (Ap. 19, 1938, Gaffney, SC) Head, McClung Hist. Coll., Knoxville-Knox Cnty. Pub. Lib., 1970–; Instr., Hist., Presbyterian Coll. SC, 1965–67; Univ. of SC, 1964–65. **Educ.:** Limestone Coll., 1959–63, BA (Hist.); Univ. of SC, 1963–65, MA (Hist.); Univ. of TN, 1967–75, PhD (Hist.). **Orgs.:** E. TN Hist. Socty.: Man. Ed. (1975–). TN Archvst.: VP (1979–81). TN LA. SAA. **Pubns.:** *Knoxville's History: An Interpretation* (1978); "The Clinch", Rolling Rivers: *The Ency. of Amer. Rivers* (1980); "The Early Life of Charles McClung McGhee," *E. TN Hist. Socty. Pub.* (1972). **Activities:** 2, 9; 17, 36, 45; 55, 69, 92 **Addr.:** Lawson McGhee Library, 500 W. Church Ave., Knoxville, TN 37919.

Macauley, C. Cameron (O. 20, 1923, Grand Rapids, MI) Systemwide Media Rep., Univ. of CA, 1980–; Dir., Ext. Media Ctr., Univ. of CA, 1969–, Head, Media Distribution, 1964–68, Asst. Head, Film Prod., 1958–63; Film producer, Univ. of WI, 1951–58. **Educ.:** Kenyon Coll., 1945–49, AB (Eng., Art); CA Sch. of Fine Arts, 1949–51, (Photography, Film); Univ. of WI, 1957–58, MS (Art). **Orgs.:** EFLA: Pres. (1973–74); VP (1972–73); Bd. (1971–74). Cnsrtm. of Univ. Film Ctrs.: Bd. (1971–72, 1974–75). Univ. Film Assn.: Ch., Distribution Com. (1968–78). AECT. Amer. Fed. of Film Societies: Bd. (1971–76). **Honors:** Various film awds. **Pubns.:** "Oceans–Our Continuing Frontier", *Filmography Sourcebook* (1976); "University Film Distribution," *Jnl. of the Univ. Film Assn.* (Vol 25., No. 2); "Cinema Canada," *Sightlines* (N./D. 71); Produced 50 films (1951–1965). **Activities:** 10, 14-Intl. Media Distributor; 15, 27, 32; 50, 67, 92 **Addr.:** 731 Sea View Dr., El Cerrito, CA 94530.

Macbeth, Eileen M. (Ag. 27, 1930, Chinook, MT) Pres., Lib. Mgt. Srvs. Ltd., 1981–; Law Libn., Chester Cnty. Law LA, 1975–81; Tredyffrin Twp. Pub. Lib., Bd. of Trustees, Pres., 1969–74. **Educ.:** Whitman Coll., 1948–52, BA (Pol. Sci.); Drexel Univ., 1971–74, MLS. **Orgs.:** AALL: Stan. Com. (1976). State Court and Cnty. Law Libs.: Stan. Com. (1978, 1979). Grt. Philadelphia Law LA: Exec. Com. (1978); PR Com. (Ch., 1979). Tredyffrin Easttown Bd. of Sch. Dir. **Honors** Beta Phi Mu, 1974. **Activities:** 4; 17, 41, 47; 72, 77, 78 **Addr.:** 766 Hickory Ln., Berwyn, PA 19132.

MacCallum, Alice A. (My. 24, 1921, Highland Park, MI) Chief of Dept., Detroit Pub. Lib., 1978–, Libn. III, 1969–78, Libn. II, 1966–69, Libn. I, 1965–66. **Educ.:** Hillsdale Coll., 1938–42, BA (Soclgy.); Univ. of MI, 1962–65, MA (LS). **Orgs.:** ALA. MI LA. **Activities:** 9; 15, 16, 39 **Addr.:** Jefferson Branch, Detroit Public Library, 12350 E. Outer Dr., Detroit, MI 48224.

MacClaren, Robert H. (Ag. 24, 1913, Scranton, PA) Chief Chemist, U.S. Natl. Arch., 1976–; Mgr., Paper Div., Xerox Corp., 1965–72; Dir., Wood Cellulose, Eastman Kodak, 1935–65. **Educ.:** Wayne State Univ., 1930–34, BS (Chem. Engin.); Univ. of MI, 1934–35, MS (Engin.). **Orgs.:** SAA: Tech. Com. (1977–). Amer. Socty. for Testing and Mtrls.: D–6 Paper (1946–). Tech. Assn. Pulp and Paper Indus.: 1966 Amer. Natl. Stans. Inst. NY Acad. of Sci. Amer. Inst. of Chems. **Activities:** 2, 4; 24, 40, 41; 60, 64, 91 **Addr.:** 7120 Sea Cliff Rd., McLean, VA 22101.

MacDermaid, M. Anne (Je. 4, 1942, Napanee, ON) Univ. Archvst., Archvst. of the City of Kingston, Queen's Univ., 1977–, Actg. Univ. Archvst., 1976–77, Asst. Archvst., 1969–76. **Educ.:** McGill Univ., 1961–65, BA hons (Hist.); Carleton Univ., 1966–67, MA (Can. Std.); Carleton Univ. and Pub. Arch. of Canada, 1968, Dipl. (Arch. Prin. and Admin.). **Orgs.:** Assn. of Can. Archvsts.: Jt. Ed., *Can. Archvst.* (1973); Com. on Ref. Syst. (1973–76); Educ. Com. (Ch., 1978–). Prof. Libns. Assn. at Queen's: Pres. (1976); Salary brief com. (1973–4). Kingston Hist. Socty. **Pubns.:** "A Select List of Publications by A.R.M. Lower," and "The A.R.M. Lower Papers: An Inventory," in *His Own Man: Essays in Honour of Arthur Reginald Marsden Lower* (1974); "Kingston in the Eighteen-Nineties," *Historic Kingston* (F. 1972); "The Visit of the Prince of Wales to Kingston in 1860," *Historic Kingston* (Mr. 1973); "A General Listing of Sources Relating to Women's History in the Queen's University Archives," *Lib. News and Notes* (1975); "The City of Kingston Archives," *Urban Hist. Review* (Je. 1978); Reviews. **Activities:** 2; 17, 26, 41 **Addr.:** Queen's University Archives, Queen's University, Kingston, ON K7L 5C4 Canada.

MacDonald, Alan H. (Mr. 3, 1943, Halifax, NS) Dir. of Libs., Univ. of Calgary, 1979–; Hlth. Sci. Libn., Dalhousie Univ., 1972–78, Asst. Univ. Libn., 1970–72, Law Libn., 1969–71, Asst. to Dir. of Libs. for Plng. and Dev., 1966–69, Law Libn., 1965–67, Gvt. Docum. Libn., 1965–66, Asst. Soc. Sci. Libn., 1964–65. **Educ.:** Dalhousie Univ., 1960–63, BA (Hist.); Univ. of Toronto, 1963–64, BLS. **Orgs.:** Can. LA: Pres. (1980–81). Atl. Provinces LA: Pres. (1977–78). Can. Assn. for Info. Sci.: Pres. (1979–80). LA of Australia. **Pubns.:** "Planning for the second century: an approach to library planning in theory and practice." *APLA Bltn.* (Mr. 1968); "Management problems encountered by the Librarian" *CACUL Nsltr.* (Ja. 1973); "The constraints of restraint - Doing more with less." *APLA Bltn.* (1978); "The constraints of restraint - Deeds not words." *APLA Bltn.* (1978); **Activities:** 1; 17; 75, 77, 80 **Addr.:** University of Calgary Library, 2500 University Dr. N.W., Calgary, AB T2N 1N4 Canada.

MacDonald, Barbara Birmingham (Ja. 18, 1948, Denver, CO) Head, Ref. Srvs., CO Sch. of Mines, 1977–; Resrch. Libn., Great West. Sugar Co., 1972–77, Info. Spec., 1970–72. **Educ.:** Univ. of IA, 1967–69, BA (Soclgy.); Denver Univ., 1969–70, MA (LS). **Orgs.:** SLA: Pres., CO Chap. (1975–76); Pres. Elect/Prog. Ch. (1974–75); Mem. Ch. (1972–74); Directory Com. (1980). CO LA. Geosci. Info. Socty. Rocky Mt. OLUG. Denver Univ. Grad. Sch. of Lib. and Info. Sci. Alum. Assn.: Rocky Mtn. Chap., Rec. Secy. (1980–81). **Pubns.:** Specialized Library Resources of Colorado (1979, 1974). **Activities:** 1; 39; 71, 82 **Addr.:** 28855 Little Big Horn, Evergreen, CO 80439.

MacDonald, Christine (N. 13, 1950, Montreal, PQ) Libn., Citadel Assurance Co., 1976–. **Educ.:** Univ. of Waterloo, 1970–74, BA (Geo., Hist.); Univ. of Toronto, 1974–76, MLS. **Orgs.:** SLA: Toronto Chap., Secy. (1979), Bus. Mgr. (1980), Networking Ch. (1981–82) Can. LA. Can. Assn. Info. Sci. **Activities:** 12; 15, 17, 39, 41; 59, 76, 77 **Addr.:** Citadel Assurance Co., Information Centre, 1075 Bay St., Toronto, ON M5S 2W5 Canada.

Macdonald, Lorna J. (Montreal, PQ) Psyt. Libn., Metro. Hosp., 1968–; Ref. Libn., Brooklyn Pub. Lib., 1949–62. **Educ.:** McGill Univ., 1944–48, BA, 1948–49, BLS. **Orgs.:** Med. LA. **Activities:** 12; 16, 39, 41; 95-Psyt. **Addr.:** Psychiatry Library, Rm. 10 M 13, Metropolitan Hospital Center, 1901 First Ave., New York, NY 10029.

MacDonald, Margaret Read (Ja. 21, 1940, Seymour, IN) Chld.'s Spec., King Cnty. Lib. Sys., 1977–; Visiting Lectr., Univ. of WA Sch. of Libnshp., 1977–80; Chld.'s Libn., II, Montgomery Cnty. Lib. Sys., 1970–72; Chld.'s Consult., Mountain-Valley Reg. Lib. Sys., 1969–70. **Educ.:** IN Univ., 1959–62, AB (Anthro.); Univ. of WA, 1963–64, MLS; Univ. of HI, 1966-68, MS (Educ. Comm.); IN Univ., 1972–79, PhD (LS and Folklore). **Orgs.:** ALA: ALSC (Film Eval. Com. 1978–81). WA LA: Chld.'s and YA Srvs., Film Com. (1978–81). Amer. Folklore Socty. **Pubns.:** *The Storyteller's Sourcebook:* (1981). **Activities:** 9, 11; 21, 26; 85 **Addr.:** 11507 N.E. 104th, Kirkland, WA 98033.

MacDonald, Margot B. (Ap. 19, 1919, New York, NY) Rare bk. catlgr., Huntington Lib., 1971–; Serials and Docum. Libn., Honnold Lib., Claremont Coll., 1957–70, Asst. Libn. Pub. Srvs., 1952–57; Serials and Docum. Libn., Pomona Coll. Lib., 1946–51; Chief, Travelers Censorship Div., U.S. Ofc. of Censorship, Los Angeles, 1941–45. **Educ.:** Pomona Coll., 1936–40, BA (Hist.); Univ. of CA at Los Angeles, 1970–71, MLS. **Orgs.:** ALA: Dupl. Exch. Union Com. (1952–56; Ch. 1953–54); ACRL. NLA. CA LA: State Docum. Com. (1955); Reg. Resrcs. Coord. Com. (1953–55). AAUW. **Honors:** Phi Beta Kappa; Beta Phi Mu. **Pubns.:** "Processing U.S. Govt. Publications", *U.S. Government Publications: Acquisition, Processing and Use* (1966). **Activities:** 1, 14-Indp. Rsrch. Lib.; 20, 29, 45; 55, 57, 92 **Addr.:** 1070 Cascade Pl., Claremont, CA 91711.

MacDonald, Mary Jane (Ag. 11, 1925, Springfield, IL) Assoc. Prof., Lib. Instr. Srvs., Sangamon State Univ. Lib., 1970–; Head, Docum. Unit, IL State Lib., 1968–70, Chief, Resrch. and Ref. Sect., 1966–68, Head, Docum. Unit, 1963–66. Libn., Cmrce. and Soclgy. Lib., Univ. of IL, 1956–1962; Resrch. Libn., Fed. Rsv. Bank of Kansas City, 1952–1956; Ref. Libn., Yakima Valley Reg. Lib., 1950–1952. **Educ.:** Univ. of IL, 1943–46, BA (Pol. Sci.), 1947–48, BS (Lib. Sci.), 1967–74, MA (Pol. Sci.). **Orgs.:** ALA. IL LA. Amer. Socty. for Pub. Admin. **Activities:** 1, 12; 29, 31, 39; 59, 78, 92 **Addr.:** 45 Glen Aire Dr., Springfield, IL 62703.

Mac Donald, Roderick (Mr. 13, 1931, Minneapolis, MN) Dir., Dakota Cnty. Lib. Syst., 1978–; Dir., Pub. Lib. of Des Moines, 1969–78; Dir., Anoka Cnty. Lib., 1966–69; Ref. Libn., Macalester Coll. Lib., 1961–66; Dir., Kaukauna Pub. Lib., 1959–61. **Educ.:** Macalester Coll., 1949–53, BA (Pol. Sci.); Univ. of MN, 1958–59, MA (LS). **Orgs.:** ALA. MN LA: Pres. (1968); Legis. Com. (Ch., 1967, 1969); Fed. Rel. Coord. (1966); Ref. Sect. (Ch., 1965); Exhibits Ch. (1966); Dist. Mtg. (Ch., 1967). **Pubns.:** "Involvement-People," *IA Lib. Qtly.* (Ja. 1973). **Activities:** 9; 17, 39 **Addr.:** 2712 Teton Ct., Burnsville, MN 55337.

Macdonald, Russell H. (S. 29, 1915, Prince Albert, SK) Writer, Consult. Jnlst., 1977–; Exec. Ed., Western Producer, 1949–77; Ch., Prairie Books, 1953–77. **Educ.:** Univ. of SK, 1936–39, BA (Eng/Hist.). **Orgs.:** SK LA. SK Lib. Trustees Assn. 1968–73, 1979– (Hon. Life Member). Can. LA. 1968–73 1979–. SK Lib. Inquiry Com. Saskatoon Press Club: Ch. (1954). Can. Club. Univ. of SK Alum. Assn. **Pubns.:** *Saskatchewan Landscapes* (1979); *Grant MacEwan: No Ordinary Man* (1979); *Four Seasons West* (1975). *In A Manner of Speaking* (1981). **Activities:** 9, 13; 47 **Addr.:** 1048 Spadina Cresc. E., Saskatoon, SK S7K 3H7 Canada.

MacDonald, W. James (D. 9, 1942, Buffalo, NY) Ref. Libn., CT Coll. Lib., 1974–; Instr., Dept. of Classics, Hobart and William Smith Colls., 1968–72. **Educ.:** Canisius Coll., 1960–64, AB (Classical Langs.); Univ. of MN, 1964–66 (Classics); Univ. of TX, 1966–68 (Classics); SUNY, Albany, 1973–74, MLS. **Orgs.:** ALA: ACRL/New Eng. Chap., Bibl. Instr. Com. (1980–). New Eng. Lib. Netwk. Gvt. Docum. Task Grp. Archlg. Inst. of Amer. Classical Assn. of New Eng. AAUP. **Activities:** 1; 29, 39; 55, 67 **Addr.:** Reference Department, Connecticut College Library, New London, CT 06320.

MacEllven, Douglass T. (Jl. 15, 1945, Buffalo, NY) Dir. of Libs., Law Socty. of SK, 1977–; Asst. Law Libn., Adj. Prof. of Law, Univ. of SD, 1976–77. **Educ.:** Univ. of CA, Santa Barbara, 1963–67, BA (Econ.); Univ. of the Pacific, 1972–75, JD (Law); Univ. of WA, 1975–76, MLL (Law Libnshp.). **Orgs.:** Can. Assn. of Law Libs. AALL. SK LA. SLA. **Pubns.:** "Saskatchewan Legal Research," *The Legal Support Staff Desk Reference: Saskatchewan Edition* (1980). **Activities:** 12; 15, 16, 17; 27, 41; 77 **Addr.:** Law Society of Saskatchewan Libraries, Court House, Regina, SK S4P 3E4 Canada.

Machovec, George Machovec (Je. 10, 1952, Columbus, OH) Sci. Ref. & Solar Energy Libn., AZ State Univ. Lib., 1977–. **Educ.:** Univ. of AZ, 1970–74, BS (Phys., Astr.), 1975–77, MLS. **Orgs.:** AZ OLUG: Ch. (1979–80); Prog. Ch. (1978–79). ASIS. SLA. ALA. AZ Solar Energy Assn. BRS User Adv. Bd.: Amigos Rep. (1979). **Pubns.:** Ed., *Solar Energy Index* (1980); ed., *Inf. Intelligence Online Nsltr.* (Ja. 1981–). **Activities:** 1; 30, 39; 75, 91 **Addr.:** Solar Energy Collection, Arizona State University Library, Tempe, AZ 85287.

Maciuszko, Jerzy (George) J. (Jl. 15, 1913, Warsaw, Poland) Prof. and Lib. Dir. (retired), Baldwin-Wallace Coll., 1974–; Ch., Dept. of Slavic Std., Alliance Coll., 1969–74; Head, John G. White Dept., Cleveland Pub. Lib., 1963–69, Asst. Head, Frgn. Lit. Dept., 1953–63. **Educ.:** Univ. of Warsaw, 1932–36, MA (Eng.); West. Rsv. Univ., 1952–53, MS (LS), 1954–62, PhD (LS). **Orgs.:** ALA: ACRL/Slavic Subsect. (Ch., 1968–69). Cleveland Pub. Lib. Staff Assn.: Pres. (1964–65). Case West. Rsv. Univ. Lib. Sch. Alum. Assn.: Pres. (1970–71). Amer. Assn. of Tchrs. of Slavic and E. European Langs. Mod. Lang. Assn. Amer. Assn. for the Advnc. of Slavic Std. Assn. for the Advnc. of Polish Std. Various other orgs. **Honors:** The Kosciuszko Foundation, Doctoral Dissertation Awd., 1967; Baldwin-Wallace Coll., The Hilbert T. Ficken Awd., 1973. **Pubns.:** *The Polish Short Story in English* (1968); *Catalog of Folklore and Folk Songs, John G. White Department Cleveland Public Library* (1964); "Polish Letters in America," *Poles in America; Bicentennial Essays* (1978); contrib., *Encyclopedia of World Literature in the 20th Century* (1975); *Catalog of the Chess Collection (including Checkers), John G. White Department, Cleveland Public Library* (1964); reviews. **Activities:** 1, 9; 17, 24, 45; 54, 57, 66 **Addr.:** 133 Sunset Dr., Berea, OH 44017.

Maciuszko, Kathleen Lynn (Ap. 8, 1947, Nogales, AZ) Dir., Ferne Patterson Jones Meml. Msc. Lib., Baldwin-Wallace Coll., 1977–, Ref. Libn., 1974–76; Catlgr., Kent State Univ., 1970–74. **Educ.:** East. MI Univ., 1965–69, BA (Fr.); Kent State Univ., 1970–74, MLS. **Orgs.:** SLA. Msc. LA. OH Acad. Libns. Assn. Msc. OCLC Users Grp. Baldwin-Wallace Coll.: Fac. Women's Clb.; Cnsvty. of Msc., Women's Com. **Activities:** 1, 12; 17; 55 **Addr.:** 133 Sunset Dr., Berea, OH 44017.

Mack, Marilyn J. (Je. 24, 1950, Chicago, IL) Supvsr., Info. Srvs. Needham, Harper and Steers Advert., 1978–; Libn., Clinton E. Frank, Inc., Advert., 1975–78. **Educ.:** Univ. of IL, 1969–71,

Special Subjects/Services: 50. Adult educ.; 51. Advert./Mktg.; 52. Aerosp.; 53. Agric.; 54. Area std.; 55. Arts/Hum.; 56. Autom.; 57. Bibl./Prtg.; 58. Bio. sci.; 59. Bus./Fin.; 60. Chem.; 61. Copyrt.; 62. Documtn.; 63. Educ.; 64. Engin.; 65. Env.; 66. Eth. grps.; 67. Film; 68. Food/Nutr.; 69. Geneal.; 70. Geo.; 71. Geol.; 72. Handcpd.; 73. Hist.; 74. Int. frdm.; 75. Info. sci.; 76. Insr.; 77. Law; 78. Legis.; 79. Math./Comp. sci.; 80. Med.; 81. Metals; 82. Nat. resrcs.; 83. Newsp.; 84. Nuc. sci.; 85. Oral hist.; 86. Petr./Energy; 87. Pharm.; 88. Phys./Astr./Math.; 89. Readg.; 90. Relig.; 91. Sci./Tech.; 92. Soc. sci.; 93. Telecom.; 94. Transp.; 95. (other).

BA (Eng.); Simmons Coll., 1973–74, MS (Lib. Sci.). **Orgs.:** SLA: Advert. and Mktg. Div. (Secty., 1980). **Activities:** 12; 39, 41; 51, 59, 92 **Addr.:** Needham, Harper and Steers Advertising, 303 E. Wacker Dr., Chicago, IL 60601.

Mack, Sara R. (N. 20, 1921, Topton, PA) Ch., Dept. of LS, Kutztown State Coll., 1958–; Libn., Mt. Penn-Lower Alsace Jr.-Sr. HS, 1949–58; Tchr., Chalfont (PA) Elem. Sch., 1943–45. **Educ.:** Kutztown State Coll., 1939–43, BS (LS & Eng.); Columbia Univ., 1950–55, MS (LS); Courses at Temple Univ., Univ. of PA, 1955–72. **Orgs.:** ALA: AASL, Improvement of Sch. Lib. (1969–72); Minority Groups in Lib. Books (1972–77). PA LA: Awds. Com. (1970–71); Lib. Dev. Com. (1978–). PA Sch. Libns. Assn.: Pres. (1963–65); Exec. Bd. (1977–80). PA Lrng. Resrcs. Assn. Other orgs. Assn. of Kutztown State Coll. Alum.: Pres. (1978–80). Delta Kappa Gamma Socty. AAUW. PA German Socty. **Honors:** PA Sch. Libns. Assn., Outstanding Contrib. to Sch. Lib. Media Progs., 1981; Kutztown State Coll., Pres. Awd. for Superior Tchg., 1962; Kappa Delta Pi; PA LA, Awd. of Merit, 1969. **Pubns.:** Cmplr., *Inspirational Readings for Elementary Grades* (1964); "Inner London's Multimedia Resource Centers" *Sch. Libs.* (Spr. 1972); "Promoting Librarianship: a Forward Look" *AACTE* (1971); Issue ed. *Drexel Lib. Qtly.* (Jl. 1969); "Print Materials in the Sciences" *Drexel Lib. Q.* (Jl. 1969); Other articles, Reviews. **Activities:** 10, 11; 21, 26, 32; 55, 63, 89 **Addr.:** Department of Library Science, Kutztown State College, Kutztown, PA 19530.

Mackaman, Frank H. (Mr. 28, 1950, Mason City, IA) Exec. Dir., Everett McKinley Dirksen Congsnl. Leadership Resrch. Ctr., 1979–, Archvst., 1976–; Mss. Spec., West. Hist. Mss. Col., Univ. of MO, Columbia, 1971–76. **Educ.:** Drake Univ., 1968–71, BA (Hist.); Univ. of MO, Columbia, 1971–72, MA (Hist.), 1972–77, PhD (Hist.); OH Hist. Socty. Lib. Arch. Inst., 1974, Dip. **Orgs.:** Midwest Arch. Conf.: Prog. Com. (Ch., 1980–81). SAA. Org. of Amer. Histns. Amer. Pol. Sci. Assn. **Honors:** Phi Beta Kappa, 1970; Phi Kappa Phi, 1970; Omicron Delta Kappa, 1970. **Pubns.:** Ed., *Understanding Congressional Leadership* (1982); *Understanding Congressional Leadership: A Conference Report* (1981); "Managing Case Files in Congressional Collections: The Hazards of Prophecy," *The Midwest. Archvst.* (1979); jt. auth., *How a Bill Becomes Law: A Study of the Legislative Process and the 1964 Civil Rights Act* (1979). **Activities:** 2, 12; 17, 41, 47; 78, 92, 95-U.S. congs. **Addr.:** The Dirksen Center, Broadway and Fourth, Pekin, IL 61554.

Mackesy, Eileen M. (Mr. 3, 1949, Brooklyn, NY) Dir., Ctr. for Bibl. Srvs., Mod. Lang. Assn. of Amer., 1979–, Managing Ed., Intl. Bibl., 1976–, Coord., Resrch. Data Bank, 1975–76, Asst. Ed., *Abs.*, 1971–75. **Educ.:** Richmond Coll., 1971, BA (Eng. Lit.); St. John's Univ., 1978–80, MLS. **Orgs.:** ALA. ASIS: Metro. NY Chap. (Secy., 1980–81); Janus Sem. Prog. Com. (1980). Mod. Lang. Assn. of Amer. Socty. for Schol. Publshg.: Mem. Com. (1980–82); Prog. Com. (1980). St. John's Univ. Div. of Lib. and Info. Sci.: Adv. Bd. (1981–). **Honors:** Phi Beta Mu, 1980. **Pubns.:** Cmplr., *MLA Directory of Periodicals* (1979); cmplr., *MLA Abstracts of Articles in Scholarly Journals* (1970–75); ed., *MLA International Bibliography* (1975–); "The MLA International Bibliography: Enumerative Classification in an Online Data Base," *Data Bases in the Humanities and Social Sciences* (1980); "Searching Problems in the MLA Bibliography Online," *Procs. of the 1981 Natl. Online Mtg.* (1981); "MLA Thesaurus of Literary, Linguistic, and Folkloric Terms: A Work in Progress," *Procs. of the ASIS O. 1981 Mtg.* **Activities:** 6, 12; 17, 30; 55, 56, 57 **Addr.:** Center for Bibliographical Services, Modern Language Association of America, 62 Fifth Ave., New York, NY 10011.

Mackey, Neosha A. (Ap. 5, 1947, San Francisco, CA) Home Ec. Libn., OH State Univ., 1980–, Persnl. Libn., 1978–80; Asst. to the Dean, Univ. of NM, 1975–77, Bus. Libn., 1970–75. **Educ.:** Univ. of OK, 1965–69, BA (Econ.), 1969–70, MLS; Univ. of NM, 1972–77, MBA. **Orgs.:** ALA: Ofc. of Lib. Persnl. Resrcs., Minority Rcrt. Com. (1979–80); LAMA, Budgeting, Acct. and Costs Com. (1978–80); Women Admin. Discuss. Grp. (Co-ch., 1978–79); Ad Hoc Com. on Persnl. Dynamics for Supvsrs. (Ch., 1979–80). OH LA. Acad. LA of OH. NM LA: Coll., Univ. and Spec. Libs. Div. (Ch., 1975). **Honors:** ARL, Acad. Lib. Consult. Trng. Prog., 1979. **Pubns.:** "More staff for no money," *NM LA Nsltr.* (F. 1976); "AMIGOS bibliographic Council Workshop," *NM LA Nsltr.* (N. 1975). **Activities:** 1; 17, 24, 35; 59, 95-Home Econ. **Addr.:** The Ohio State University Libraries, 1787 Neil Ave., Columbus, OH 43210.

Mackler, Leona T. (Ja. 17, 1925, New York, NY) Dir., Lib. and Info. Srvs., Postgrad. Ctr. for Mental Hlth., 1970–; Libn., Mental Hlth. Mtrls. Ctr., 1964–69. **Educ.:** Univ. of CA, Los Angeles, 1942–45, BA (Intl. Rel.); Pratt Inst., 1961–64, MLS. **Orgs.:** Med. LA: Mental Hlth. Libns. Sect. (Ch., 1977–78); NY Reg. Chap. (Treas., 1977–78). Assn. of Mental Hlth. Libns. **Honors:** Pi Sigma Alpha, 1945; Beta Phi Mu, 1964. **Pubns.:** "H. Peter Laqueur, M.D. 1909-1979 Bibliography," *Group and Family Therapy 1980* (1980); "Donald de Avila Jackson, 1920-1968: Bibliography," *Group Therapy, 1977: An Overview* (1977); "The Mental Health Librarian," *Lib. Trends* (Ap. 1982). **Activities:** 5, 12; 17, 25, 41; 63, 95-Psyt./Psy. **Addr.:** Emil A. Gutheil Library, Postgraduate Center for Mental Health, 124 E. 28th St., New York, NY 10016.

MacLaury, Keith D. (Ja. 18, 1948, Ames, IA) Progmr./Anal., Resrch. Lib. Grp., 1978–; Progmr./Anal., Info. Retrieval Resrch. Lab, Univ. of IL, 1976–78; Catlgr., Univ. of IL Lib., 1971–76. **Educ.:** Univ. of IL, 1966–70, BA (Math), 1970–71, MLS, 1975–78, MS (Comp. Sci.). **Orgs.:** ALA. ASIS. Assn. for Comp. Mach. **Pubns.:** Jt. auth., "Automatic Merging of Monographic Data Bases," *Jnl. of Lib. Autom.* (Je. 1979). **Activities:** 1; 34; 56 **Addr.:** Research Library Group, Stanford, CA 94305.

MacLean, Eleanor A. (Jl. 31, 1947, Winnipeg, MB) Blacker-Wood Libn., McGill Univ., 1972–; Ref. Libn., Engin., Math., Sci. Lib., Univ. of Waterloo, 1969–72. **Educ.:** McGill Univ., 1963–67, BSc (Bio.), 1967–69, MLS. **Orgs.:** Can. LA: Com. Int. Frdm. (1977–). SLA: East. Can. Chap., Chap. Bltn. Ed. (1974–75); Ed., Dir. Spec. Lib. Montreal (1975–77); Secy. (1977–79); Archvst. (1979–). ALA. Corp. Prof. Libn. PQ. Raptor Resrch. Fndn. **Activities:** 1, 12; 15, 17, 39, 45; 58 **Addr.:** Blacker-Wood Library of Zoology and Ornithology, Redpath Library Building, McGill University, 3459 McTavish St., Montreal, PQ H3A 1Y1 Canada.

MacLowick, Frederick (Rick) Bryan (D. 23, 1948, Edmonton, AB) Head, Info. Srvs., Legis. Lib. of MB, 1981–; Asst. Head, City Ctr. Fort Rouge Area, Winnipeg Pub. Lib., 1974–81; Catlgr., Natl. Defence HQ Lib., 1971–74. **Educ.:** Univ. of AB, 1967–70, BA (Soclgy.), 1970–71, BLS. **Orgs.:** Can. LA. MB LA: Dir. (1976–77, 1978–79); Treas. (1977–78). Winnipeg Philharmonic Choir. **Activities:** 9; 15, 16, 39 **Addr.:** 911–240 Stradbrook Ave., Winnipeg, MB R3L 2P7 Canada.

MacMorran, Thomas J. (D. 17, 1943, Houston, TX) Network Consult., TX State Lib., 1981–; Cur. of Spec. Col., Transylvania Univ., 1978–80; Asst. to Cur. of Spec. Col., Univ. of Houston, 1972–77. **Educ.:** Univ. of Houston, 1967–70, BA Cum Laude (Eng.), 1971–73, MA (Eng.); Fulbright Schol., Eberhard Karls Univ., Tübingen, W. Germany, 1970–71, (Lit.); Univ. of TX, 1977–78, MLS. **Orgs.:** ALA. NLA. KY LA: Secy./Treas., Lib. Instr. Subsect., Acad. Libs. Sect. **Honors:** Phi Kappa Phi, 1970. **Pubns.:** "The Information Manager," *Bltn. of ASIS* (Ag. 1978); "The Small Press Scene in Texas: A Representative Sample," *Aldus* (Ap. 1976); reviews. **Activities:** 1, 2; 17, 23, 45; 55, 56 **Addr.:** Library Development Division, Texas State Library, P.O. Box 12927, Austin, TX 78736.

MacNeil, Kathrine Jean (O. 2, 1943, Geary, OK) Assoc. Prof., Vetny. Med. Libn., OK State Univ., 1968–; Eng. Tchr., Glencoe Pub. Schs., 1966–67; Eng. Tchr., Alice Pub. Schs., 1965–66; Eng. Tchr., Denver Pub. Schs., 1964–65. **Educ.:** OK Univ., 1961–64, BA (Lang. Arts.), 1967–68, MLS; OK State Univ., 1968–75, MA (Hist.); Med. LA, Cert., Grade I. **Orgs.:** Med. LA: Vetny. Med. Libns. Grp. (Ch., 1978–79); Com. to Compile Un. List of Sel. Vetny. Serials (Ch., 1977–); Com. to Compile Basic List of Vetny. Serials (1977–). OK LA: Gvrs. Mansion Lib. Com. (1970); Cont. Ed. Com. (1977–80). OK Hlth. Scis. LA. AAUP. **Pubns.:** Jt. ed., *Veterinary Serials: A Union List of Selected Titles* (forthcoming); jt. auth., "Sources of Published Information on the Science and Technology of Hides and Leather," *Jnl. of the Amer. Leather Chem. Assn.* (O. 1979). **Activities:** 1; 15, 31, 39; 58, 80 **Addr.:** Veterinary Medicine Library, Oklahoma State University, Stillwater, OK 74078.

Macon, Myra Faye (S. 29, 1937, Slate Springs, MS) Assoc. Prof., Sch. of Lib. and Info. Sci., Univ. of MS, 1979–, Asst. Prof., 1971–79, Actg. Ch., Dept. of LS, 1972–73; Lib. Supvsr., Cuyahoga Falls (OH) City Schs., 1965–71, Asst. Libn., 1964–65; Libn., various MS schs., 1959–64. **Educ.:** Delta State Univ., 1959, BSE (Bus. Educ.); LA State Univ., 1965, MA (LS); MS State Univ., 1977, EdD (Admin.); various courses. **Orgs.:** ALA: AASL, Srv. Awd. for Sch. Admin. Com. (1979–80); LITA, AV Util. Com. (1979–81). MS LA: Natl. Lib. Week Com. (1977); Const. and Bylaws Com. (1979). MS Assn. of Media Educ.: VP (1975); N. Delta Reg. of Legis. Com. (Ch., 1978–80). AALS. Other orgs. **Honors:** Beta Phi Mu; Kappa Delta Phi; Phi Delta Kappa; Delta Kappa Gamma. **Pubns.:** Jt. auth., "The Newberys: A Diversionary Approach," *Top of the News* (Sum. 1980); "A School Library for the Mentally Retarded," *AR Libs.* (D. 1980); *School Library Services to the Handicapped* (1982); Ed., *ANRT Newsletter* (1979–); jt. auth., *A Guide to the Contents of the Mississippi United Methodist Advodate, 1947–74* (1975); "The Principal, the School Library Media Specialist, and PL 94-142" *MS Libs.* (Ag. 1979). **Activities:** 10, 11; 17, 32, 34; 63, 72 **Addr.:** 3006 Hillmont Dr., Oxford, MS 38655.

MacPherson, Lillian V. (Ag. 30, 1940, Winnipeg, MB) Law Libn., Univ. of AB, 1979–, Asst. Law Libn., 1970–79; Ref. Libn., Govt. Docum. Libn., Bibl., Univ. of WA Law Lib., 1965–68. **Educ.:** Univ. of SK, 1957–61, BA (Eng. & Hist.); Univ. of WA, 1963–65, MLibs. **Orgs.:** Can. ALL: Pres. (1979–81); VP (1977–79); Ed., *Newsletter* (1978–79). AALL. LA of AB: Exec. Bd. (1978–79); Cont. Educ. Can. Assn. of Prof. Libns, Univ. of AB: Pres. (1971–72). Can. Assn. of Univ. Tchrs.: Com. on Prof. Libns. (1976–79). Can. Assn. of Law Tchrs. Assn. of Acad. Staff, Univ. of AB: Libn. Rep. on Cncl. (1974–77). **Pubns.:** "How to Update a Statute in Alberta", *Clic's legal materials letter* (D. 1979); "Rank or classification for librarians?" *CAUT Bltn.* (S. 1977); "Certification of library employees, pt. 1", *LAA Bltn.* (Ja. 1974). **Activities:** 1, 12; 17, 39; 77, 78 **Addr.:** Law Library, Law Centre, University of Alberta, Edmonton, AB T6G 2H5 Canada.

MacRae, Lorne G. (F. 22, 1943, Calgary, AB) Coord., Media Srvs., Calgary Bd. of Educ., 1974–, Asst. Prof., Lib. Sci., Univ. of SK, 1975–77; Tchr.-libn., Calgary Bd. of Educ., 1963–73. **Educ.:** Univ. of AB, 1960–64, BEd (Eng.); Univ. of MI, 1967–69, AMLS. **Orgs.:** Can. Sch. LA: Role of Sch. Libs. in Networking. AB Lrng. Resrcs. Cncl.: Pres.-elect. (1975), Pres. (1976). AB Heritage Lrng. Resrcs. Proj. AB Tchrs. Assn. **Honors:** Beta Phi Mu, 1968; AB Gvt. Lib. Awd., 1966. **Pubns.:** "Too Many Chickens–Too Few Hogs," *Emergency Libn.* (My.–Ag., 1979); "Idealia," multi-media kit, (1977); "Cryogenics, Cybernetics, the Geodesic Dome–Resources for All," *The Medium* (Ja., 1974). **Activities:** 10; 15, 17, 20; 56, 63, 67 **Addr.:** Calgary Board of Education, Media Services Group, Program Development Dept., 3610 9th St. S.E., Calgary, AB T2G 3C5 Canada.

MacVean, Donald S. (O. 25, 1919, Kalamazoo, MI) Head Ref. Libn., West. IL Univ., 1975–, Dir. of Libs., 1965–75; Asst. Libn. for Rdr. Srvs., Ball State Univ., 1958–65, Curric. Lab. Libn., 1953–58. **Educ.:** West. MI Univ., 1938–42, AB (Hist.); Univ. of MI, 1946–47, AM (Educ.), 1952–53 AMLS, 1953–58, EdD (LS). **Orgs.:** ALA: Lib. Srvs. Com. (1967–69). IL LA: Int. Frdm. Com. (1971–73). US Trotting Assn. **Honors:** Beta Phi Mu. **Pubns.:** "Parasite Control in Horse Pastures," *Hoof Beats* (D. 1979); *An NCATE Evaluation of a University Library: A Case History* (1979); *Faculty Use of a University Library Circulating Book Collection* (1978); "A New Library–Second Time Around," *The Westerner* (N. 1972); "Collection Development at Western Illinois University," *MO Lib. Qtly.*, (D. 1968); various articles. **Activities:** 1; 31, 35, 39 **Addr.:** R.R. 1, Macomb, IL 61455.

Madaj, Menceslaus J. (Je. 15, 1912, Chicago, IL) Archvst., Archdiocese of Chicago, 1968–; Asst. Prof., St. Mary of the Lake Semy., 1968–73; Asst. Prof., St. Joseph Coll., 1965–67; Asst. Prof., Hist., St. Norbert Coll., 1963–65. **Educ.:** St. Mary of the Lake Semy., 1931–33, BA (Phil.); De Paul Univ., 1943–45, MA (Hist.); Loyola Univ., 1946–56, PhD (Hist.); Vatican Sch. of LS, 1952–53; Vatican School of Arch., 1952–53. **Orgs.:** SAA: Awds. Com. (1979–80); Local arrange. Com. (1979). Midwest Arch. Conf. Polish Amer. Hist. Assn.: Exec. Secy. Assn. of Recs. Mgrs. and Admin.: Chicago Chap., Exec. VP. **Honors:** Polish Amer. Hist. Assn., Haiman Awd., 1973; PUSH Fndn., 1977. Contrib., *The New Catholic Encyclopedia* (1967); "Polish Catholic Missions in the Crimea, 1475–1624.", *Sacrum Poloniae Millenium*, (1957). **Activities:** 2; 15, 17; 55, 66, 90 **Addr.:** Archdiocesan Archives, St. Mary of the Lake Seminary, Mundelein, IL 60060.

Madan, Raj (F. 22, 1936, Sitpur, Punjab, India) Head, Acq., SUNY, Brockport, 1966–; Resrv. and Circ. Libn., Rutgers Univ., 1962–64; Biblgphr., Univ. of MO, Columbia, 1959–62. **Educ.:** Punjab Univ., India, 1951–55, BA (Hist.), 1955–56, B. Tch. (Educ.); Univ. of MO, Columbia, 1957–60, MA (Soc.); Rutgers Univ., 1962–64, MLS. **Orgs.:** ALA: ACRL. NY/ON ACRL Chap. SUNY LA. Brockport Coll. Fac. Sen.: Sen. (1970–72, 1978–); Ch., Nom. Com.; Exec. Com. **Pubns.:** *Colored Minorities in Great Britain; a comprehensive bibliography, 1970–1977* (1979); "Status of Librarians in Four-year State Colleges and Universities," *Coll. and Resrch. Libs.* (S. 1968). **Activities:** 1; 15, 17; 63, 66, 92 **Addr.:** 82 Valley View Dr., Brockport, NY 14420.

Madaus, J. Richard (O. 23, 1944, Joplin, MO) Dir., Lib./Lrng. Resrcs., Northeastern State Univ. (OK); Assoc. Dir. for Lib. Srvs and Dev., AR State Lib., 1978–81; Lib. Dir., Henderson State Univ., 1974–78; Head, Non-Print Lib. Resrcs., LBJ Sch., Univ. of TX, Austin, 1971–74. **Educ.:** LA State Univ., New Orleans, 1962–67, BA (Educ. & Lib. Sci.); Univ. of TX, Austin, 1969–74, MLS, PhD (Educ. Tech.). **Orgs.:** ALA. NLA. SW LA. AR LA. **Pubns.:** Jt. auth., *Long Range Program for Library Development in Arkansas 1979–84* (1979); *Arkansas Funds Its Libraries* (1978); "Aggressive Reference Service," *AR Libs.* **Activities:** 1, 13; 17, 24, 34; 56, 63, 93 **Addr.:** John Vaughan Library/Learning Resources Center, Northeastern State University, Tahlequah, OK 74464.

Madden, Doreitha R. (Baltimore, MD) Coord., Outrch. Srvs., NJ State Lib., Lib. Dev. Bur. (1969–, Coord., Lending Srvs., 1957–69, Ref. Libn., 1954–57; Chld. Libn., Enoch Pratt Free Lib., Baltimore, 1949–50. **Educ.:** Hampton Inst., 1943–47, BS (Soc. Std.); Atlanta Univ., 1948–49, BS in LS; Various insts. **Orgs.:** ALA: Hlth. Rehab Lib. Srv. Div., Nom. Com. (1979–80); Bd. of Dir. (1976–78); Ofc. for Lib. Srv. to Disadv., Adv. Com. (1977–79, Ch. 1980); PLA, Ed. Com, *Pub. Libs.*. NJ LA: Outrch. Com. (1976–1980); Exec. Bd. Plng. for Action (1976–77). Ewing Twp. Bd. Educ. NJ Sch. Bd. Assn. Natl. Sch. Bds. Assn. NJ Educ. Assn. **Honors:** Litcy. Volun. of America, NJ Chap., Litcy. Awd., 1979; Robert M. Worthington Cmnty. Srvs. Awd., 1974; OMEGA Psi Phi, Citizen of the Yr. Awd., 1979. **Pubns.:** "Thinking Out Loud," *What Black Librarians are Saying* (1972); "Lib 21-A Provocative Experience," *NJ LA Bltn.* (1963). **Addr.:** 97 Browning Ave., Trenton, NJ 08638.

Madden, John Michael (F. 7, 1939, Ottumwa, IA) Intelligence Resrch. Spec., Soviet Navy, Defense Intelligence Agency, 1981–, Mid. E. Ref. Libn., 1979–81; Persian/Arabic Catlgr.,

PROFESSIONAL ACTIVITIES: Institutions: 1. Acad. lib.; 2. Arch.; 3. Assn.; 4. Fed./Gvt. lib.; 5. Inst. lib.; 6. Mfr./Suppl.; 7. Milit. lib.; 8. Musm.; 9. Pub. lib.; 10. Sch. lib.; 11. Sch. of lib. sci.; 12. Spec. lib.; 13. State lib.; 14. (other). **Functions/Activities:** 15. Acq./Col. dev.; 16. Adult srvs.; 17. Admin.; 18. Apprais.; 19. Archit./Bldgs.; 20. Cat./Class.; 21. Chld. srvs.; 22. Circ.; 23. Cons./Pres.; 24. Consult.; 25. Cont. ed.; 26. Educ. lib. sci.; 27. Ext. srvs.; 28. Fund/Grants; 29. Gvt. pubs.; 30. Indx./Abs.; 31. Instr. lib. use; 32. Media srvs.; 33. Micro.; 34. Netwks./Coop.; 35. Persnl.; 36. PR; 37. Publshg.; 38. Recs. mgt.; 39. Ref. srvs.; 40. Repro.; 41. Resrch.; 42. Review.; 43. Secur.; 44. Serials; 45. Spec. col.; 46. Tech. srvs.; 47. Trustees/Bds.; 48. YA srvs.; 49. (other).

Princeton Univ., 1976–79. **Educ.:** Princeton Univ., 1957–61, AB (Oriental Std.); Univ. of WA, Seattle, 1971–74, MA (Near East. Lang. and Lit.), 1975–76, MLibnshp. **Orgs.:** Mid. E. Libns. Assn. Air Frc. Intelligence Srv. Rsvs. **Pubns.:** "The Defense Intelligence Agency Library," *Mid. E. Libns. Assn. Notes* (F. 1980). **Activities:** 4; 15, 39, 41; 54, 74 **Addr.:** Defense Intelligence Agency, DIA/DB–1C1, Washington, DC 20301.

Madden, Mary A. (Chicago, IL) Pres., Madden Consult., Inc., 1979–; VP, Comp. Syst., Blackwell N. America, 1977–79, Exec. Mgr., Tech. Srvs., 1975–77; Bus. & Oper. Mgr., Intl. Scholarly Books Inc, 1973–75. **Educ.:** Vassar Coll., 1963–67, AB (Math.); Columbia Univ., 1967–68, MLS. **Orgs.:** ALA: LITA/ Ch., Info. Sci. and Autom. Sect. (1979–80); Comm. Ed., *Jnl. of Lib. Autom.* (1978–81); Intl. Mechanization Com. (1980). ASIS: Secy., Lib. Autom. and Networks Sect. (1976–78); Ed., *Points Northwest,* nsltr. of the Pac. NW Chap. City Club of OR. Women Entrepreneurs of OR. **Pubns.:** "The Network Role in Acquisitions," *Jnl. of Lib. Auto.* (S. 1980). **Activities:** 1, 9; 17, 24; 56, 75, 93 **Addr.:** Madden Consultants, Inc., 956 Myrtle St., NE, Atlanta, GA 30309.

Madden, Susan B. (Ag. 7, 1944, Portland, OR) Coord., YA Srvs., King Cnty. Lib. Syst., 1979–; Staff and Resident's Libn., King Cnty. Juvenile Ct., 1972–79; Ref., Bkmobile., and Acq. Libn., Clackamas Cnty. Pub. Lib., 1967–71. **Educ.:** Univ. of Portland, 1962–66, BA (Eng.); Univ. of Denver, 1966–67, MALS, WA State Cert., 1972–. **Orgs.:** ALA. WA Lib. Media Assn. Pac. NW LA. WA State YA Review Grp. WA LA. Amer. Correct. Assn.: Amer. Correct. Assn./ALA Jt. Com. on Insts. (1976–80). Piranhas': Seattle Chap. **Pubns.:** "The Rights of Young Adults in Correctional Institutions," *Top of the News* (Spr. 1979); "Button Up," *Sch. Lib. Jnl.* (N. 1977); "Reflections on Corrections," *Wilson Lib. Bltn.* (F. 1977); jt. auth., "Hidden People" slide/tape (1973, 1979). **Activities:** 5, 12; 24, 48; 89, 92 **Addr.:** King County Library System, 300 8th Ave. N., Seattle, WA 98109.

Maddock, Jerome T. (F. 7, 1940, Darby, PA) Chief, Solar Energy Info. Ctr., Solar Energy Resrch. Inst., 1979–; Sr. Consult., CALCULON Corp., 1971–79; Mgr., Resrch. Info., Merck and Co., Inc., 1963–71; Ed. Assoc., *Bio. Abs.,* 1962–63. **Educ.:** Muhlenberg Coll., 1957–61, BS (Bio.); Drexel Univ., 1963–68, MS (Info. Sci.). **Orgs.:** ASIS: Awds. and Hons. Com. (Ch., 1980); DE Valley Chap. (Ch., 1978). AAAS. **Honors:** Beta Phi Mu, 1965; Pi Delta Epsilon, 1960. **Pubns.:** Jt. auth., "PICS: The Pharmaceutical Information Control System of Merck Sharp and Dohme Research Laboratories," *Amer. Documtn.* (O., 1966); various papers. **Activities:** 5, 12; 17, 24, 34; 58, 87, 91 **Addr.:** 545 W. Laurel Ct., Louisville, CO 80027.

Maddox, W. Jane (Je. 3, 1943, McDonough, GA) N. Amer. Rep., Otto Harrassowitz, 1978–; Mgr., Coutts Lib. Srvs., Inc., 1976–77; Mono. Ord. Libn., Univ. of TN, Knoxville Lib., 1974–76; Mgr., Richard Abel Co., 1973–74. **Educ.:** Emory Univ., GA State Univ., 1960–70, BA (Soclgy.); Emory Univ., 1971–72, MLS. **Orgs.:** ALA: RTSD/Resrcs. Sect., Nom. Com. (1976–77), Discuss. Grp. on Acq. of Lib. Mrtls. (Ch., 1975–76). **Pubns.:** "Approval Plans-Viable?" *Jnl. Acad. Libnshp.* (Ja. 1976); "Serials Management at Otto Harrassowitz," *Serials Review* (Jl./S. 1981). **Activities:** 1, 12; 15, 44, 46; 56, 58 **Addr.:** P.O. Box 340, Cassville, MO 65625.

Madinger, Elsbeth K. (Je. 11, 1927, Indianapolis, IN) Coord. Media Resrcs., Punahou Sch., 1974–; Libn., St. Andrew's Priory, 1970–74; Libn., Moanalua Intermediate Sch., 1969. **Educ.:** Univ. of HI, 1963–67, B Ed (Elem. educ.), 1967–68, MLS. **Orgs.:** HI LA: Ed., Nsltr. (1973–1974); Ch., Int. Frdm. Com. (1972); Secy., (1977–78); Dir. (1974–76). Beta Phi Mu: Secy. (1979–80). HI Assn. of Sch. Libns.: Ed. "Golden Key" (1976–77). Private Sch. Film Pool: Secy. (1974–80). Lyon Arboretum Assn. **Activities:** 10; 15, 20, 32; 67 **Addr.:** Punahou School, 1601 Punahou St., Honolulu, HI 96822.

Mador, Harriet S. (Je. 5, 1948, Springfield, MA) Lib. Mgr., Dallas Pub. Lib., 1978–; Libn. II, Buffalo and Erie Cnty. Pub. Lib., 1974–78, Libn. I, 1971–74. **Educ.:** SUNY, Buffalo, 1966–70, BA (Eng.); SUNY, Albany, 1970–71, MLS; NY State, 1973, Permanent Cert. (Libn.). **Orgs.:** ALA: Lcl. Arrange. (1979); PLA, Plng. Com. (1979–80). Staff Assn.–Dallas Pub. Lib. TX LA. **Activities:** 9; 49-Branch mgr. **Addr.:** Casa View Library, 10355 Ferguson, Dallas, TX 75228.

Madson, Judy I. (Je. 14, 1941, Miller, IA) Dir., Med. Lib., St. Joseph Mercy Hosp., 1973–. **Educ.:** Waldorf Coll., 1959–61, AA (Bus.); Upper IA Univ., 1972, BGS (LS). **Orgs.:** Med. LA: Hosp. Lib. Sect.; Midwest Reg. Grp. IA LA: Hlth. Sci. Sect. (VP, 1979; Pres., 1980). CORE Book Com. for IA Hlth. Sci. Libs. AAUW. **Activities:** 12, 14; 15, 17, 41; 80 **Addr.:** Medical Library, St. Joseph Mercy Hospital, Mason City, IA 50401.

Mafit, Randy B. (S. 4, 1946, Cincinnati, OH) Sr. Mgt. Anal., Ln. Cnty., 1977–; Dir., Recs. Mgt., Arch., Ln. Cmnty. Coll., 1974–77. **Educ.:** OR State Univ., 1968–69, BA (Eng.); Univ. of OR, 1973–74, MLS; Univ. of WA, 1976, Cert., (Arch. Mgt.). **Orgs.:** ALA. SAA: State and Lcl. Recs. Com. (1977–78). OR LA: *OR Jobline* Job Place. Com. (1975–76). NW Archvsts. Univ. of OR, Frnds. of the Lib. Assn. of Recs. Mgrs. and Admins. **Honors:** Beta Phi Mu, 1974; Natl. Assn. of Cntys., Achvmt. Awd., 1978, 1979. **Pubns.:** *Oregon County Law Library Survey 1978: A Status Report* (1979); jt. auth., *Toward an Automated Multipurpose Land Data System for Lane County, Eugene, Oregon* (1978); jt. auth., "The Collection of Rare Books at the University of Oregon," *Imprint: OR* (Sum. 1978); "Lane County's Geographic Data System" snd. slide (1979). **Activities:** 2, 14-Recs. Ctr.; 17, 33, 38; 56, 62, 75 **Addr.:** Lane County Dept. of General Services, Courthouse/PSB-Plz. 125 E. 8th St., Eugene, OR 97401.

Magaro, John D. (Ja. 14, 1940, Natrona Heights, PA) Prof./Ch., Lib. Sci. Dept., Shippensburg State Coll., 1973–; Coord. of Libs., Highlands Sch. Dist., 1964–68; Jr. HS Libn. and A-V Coord., Prince Georges Cnty. Schs., 1963–64; HS Libn., Kiski Area Sch. Dist., 1962–63. **Educ.:** Clarion State Col., 1962, BS, (Educ.); Univ. of Pittsburgh, 1966, MLS, 1973, PhD (Educ. Comm.), 1970, (Lib. Sci.). **Orgs.:** ALA. PA LA: Bylaws Com. (Ch., 1975–76); Eval. Com. (1976); Nom. Com. (1975). PA Sch. LA: Bd. of Dir. (1979); Conf. Mod. (1979); Conf. Com. (Ch., 1978); VP (1977). PA Cncl. of Lib. Educ. Shippensburg Pub. Lib. Bd. of Trustees (1979–80). **Pubns.:** "Library Media Program Evaluation," *Learning and Media* (Win. 1979); "Comments on Library Comparisons," *Learning and Media* (N. 1977); "Teacher Librarian Cooperation in Learning and Media," *Learning and Media* (F. 1977); "PPBS–A Means Toward Accountability," *AV Instr.* (D. 1975). **Activities:** 10, 11; 26, 32, 48; 61, 63, 78 **Addr.:** Library Science Department, Shippensburg State College, Shippensburg, PA 17257.

Maggs, Margaret L. (Ag. 31, 1938, Glasgow, Scotland) Assoc. Libn. for Reader Srvs., McMaster Univ., 1979–, Asst. Libn. for Reader Srvs., 1977–79, Coord. of Circ. Srvs., 1973–77, Circ. Libn., 1971–73, Ref. Libn., 1970, Cat. Cur., 1969–70, Catlgr., 1968–69; Libn., Univ. of St. Andrews, 1963–68. **Educ.:** Glasgow Univ., 1956–60, MA, hons. (Hist.); McMaster Univ., 1975– (Anthro.); LA of Grt. Brit., 1961–65, ALA. **Orgs.:** Can. LA. ON LA. LA of Grt. Brit. **Pubns.:** *Guide To Research In History* (1970). **Activities:** 1; 17, 36; 50, 61 **Addr.:** Mills Memorial Library, McMaster University, Hamilton, ON L8S 4L6 Canada.

Magnuson, Norris A. (Je. 15, 1932, Midale, SK) Resrc. Ctr. Dir. and Prof. of Hist., Bethel Theo. Semy., 1972–, Assoc. Prof. of Hist. and Assoc. Libn., 1965–72, Asst. Prof. and Asst. Libn., 1959–65. **Educ.:** Bethel Coll., 1950–54, BA (Phil.); Bethel Theo. Semy., 1954–58, BD; Univ. of MN, Minneapolis, 1959–61, MA (LS), 1961–68, PhD (Hist.). **Orgs.:** ATLA. MN Theo. LA: Pres. (1974–75, 1979–80). Conf. on Faith and Hist. Bapt. Gen. Conf. of Amer.: Hist. Com. (Ch., 1974–). MN Bapt. Conf. **Pubns.:** *Salvation in the Slums; Evangelical Social Service, 1865-1920* (1977); *How We Grew: A Brief History of Swedish Baptists in America* (1976); "The Church in Practical Responsibility; The Evangelical Church and Social Concern," *Bethel Semy. Jnl.* (Spr. 1966); jt. auth., "Current Trends in Evangelism," *Jnl. of Pastoral Care* (Spr. 1956); "A Tradition Continues; (Bethel Seminary and the Churches)," *The Stan.* (Ja. 1981). **Activities:** 1; 15, 17, 34; 66, 90, 92 **Addr.:** 3949 Bethel Dr., St. Paul, MN 55112.

Magrill, Rose Mary (Je. 8, 1939, Marshall, TX) Prof. of Lib. and Info. Sci., N. TX State Univ., 1981–; Prof. of LS, Univ. of MI, 1976–81, Assoc. Prof., 1972–76, Asst. Prof., 1970–72; Asst. Prof. of LS, Ball State Univ., 1969–70; Instr., Asst. Prof., E. TX State Univ., 1964–67, Libn. II, 1961–63, Asst. to the Dean of Women, 1960–61. **Educ.:** E. TX State Univ., 1957–60, BS, 1960–61, MA; Univ. of IL, 1962–64, MS (LS), 1967–69, PhD. **Orgs.:** ALA: RASD Com. on Srv. to Adults (1974–78); RTSD Nom. Com. (1978). ASIS. AALS: Task Force on Accred. Issues (1976–78); Bd. of Dir. (1977–80); Com. on Lib. Educ. Stat. (1979–80). Beta Phi Mu: Schol. Com. (1975–76); Nom. Com. (1979). **Honors:** ALA, RTSD, Resrcs. Sect., Pubn. Awd., 1979. **Pubns.:** Jt. auth., *Building Library Collections* (1979); Jt. auth., *Library Technical Services* (1977); Jt. auth., "Collection Development in Large Univ. Libs," *Advances in Libnship* (1978); "Collection Development and Preservation in 1979," *Lib. Resrcs. and Tech. Srvs.* (Sum. 1980) "Collection Development and Preservation in 1980," *Lib. Resrcs. and Tech. Srvs.* (Sum. 1981). **Activities:** 1, 11; 15, 41 **Addr.:** 804 Caddo St., Marshall, TX 75670.

Magruder, Mary Magruder (Jl. 25, 1940, Houston, TX) Dean of Libs., KS State Univ., 1981–; Assoc. Univ. Libn., Univ. SK Libs., 1975–81; Head, Lockwood Meml. Lib., SUNY, Buffalo, 1974–75; Chief, Soc. Sci. Biblgphr., 1971–74; Ref. Biblgphr., 1967–71; Lat. Amer. Catlgr., Univ. TX, 1966–67. **Educ.:** Univ. TX 1958–62, AB (Hist.); 1963–64 (Lat. Amer. Hist.); Univ. Nacional, Buenos Aires, Arg., 1962–63, Fulbright Flwshp. (Hist. and Lit.); 1964–70, MLS (Lat. Amer. Bibl.); SUNY, Buffalo, 1972–74, MS in progress, (Soc. Sci.). **Orgs.:** SALALM: Pres. (1976–77). ALA: LAMA/PAS, Un. Rels. for Mgrs. *ad hoc* Com. (1979–). Can. LA: Status of Women Com. (1975–77). SK LA: Ed. Bd. (1978–79). Lat. Amer. Std. Assn. Saskatoon LA. **Pubns.:** "Review of Life in Brazil; or a Journal of a Visit ...," *Amer.* (May 1972). **Activities:** 1; 15, 17, 35; 54, 95-Col. bargaining, 92 **Addr.:** Libraries, Kansas State University, Manhattan, KS 66506.

Mahalingam, Vaithilingam (Jl. 8th, 1931, Telok Anson, Perak, Malaysia) Coord., Branch Libs., Queen's Univ., 1979; Asst. Chief Libn., Pub. Srvs., 1975–79, Acting Law Libn., 1974–75, Asst. Head, Cat. Dept., 1968–74. **Educ.:** Calcutta Univ., 1952–56, BA (Eng.); McGill Univ., 1957–58, BLS; Columbia Univ., 1965–68, Adv. Std. (Libnshp.). **Orgs.:** Ceylon LA: Educ. offcr. (1962–65); Secy. (1960–62). Can. LA. ALA. Vedanta Socty. of Toronto. Hindu Temple Socty. of Canada. **Honors:** Fulbright Schol., Columbia Univ., 1965–68. **Pubns.:** "Education for Librarianship in Ceylon," *Jnl. of Educ. for Libnshp.* (Spr. 1966). **Activities:** 1, 12; 17, 20, 46; 62, 75, 91 **Addr.:** 848 Danbury Rd., Kingston, ON K7M 6E4 Canada.

Mahan, Ruth E. (S. 2, 1943, Mexico, MO) ND State Libn., ND State Lib., 1981–, Fld. Libn., 1977–81; Coord., Med. Lib., Univ. of ND, 1975–77; Ref. Libn., Huron Pub. Lib., 1974–75; Coord., Lewis and Clark Lib. Syst., 1972–74. **Educ.:** Univ. of MO, 1961, BA (Eng.), 1972, MA (LS). **Orgs.:** ALA. ND LA. Leag. of Women Voters. ND Pub. Radio Msc. Com. ND Hist. Socty. Adv. Bd. **Addr.:** North Dakota State Library, Bismarck, ND 58505.

Mahaney, Denise R. (D. 9, 1949, Chicago, IL) Libn., Vedder, Price, Kaufman & Kammholz, 1972–. **Educ.:** Rosary Coll., 1967–71, BA (Eng.), 1971–72, MALS. **Orgs.:** Chicago Assn. of Law Libs.: Pres. (1979–80); Pres.-Elect (1978–79); Secy. (1976–1978). AALL. SLA. **Activities:** 12; 17, 39, 41; 77 **Addr.:** Vedder, Price, Kaufman & Kammholz, 115 S. La Salle St., Chicago, IL 60603.

Mahar, Ellen P. (Ja. 15, 1938, Washington, DC) Libn., Covington and Burling, 1978–; Libn., Shea and Gardner, 1974–78; Asst. Libn., Covington and Burling, 1971–74; Libn., Intl. Sugar Resrch. Fd., 1969–70; Chief, Class. Lib., Inst. for Defense Anal., 1965–67, Chief, Cat. Sect., 1963–64, Catlgr., Class. Lib., 1962–63; Asst. to Libn., Navy Department, Bureau of Ships, Nuclear Propulsion Br., 1959–62. **Educ.:** St. Joseph Coll., 1955–59, BA (Bio.); Univ. of MD, 1967–69, MLS. **Orgs.:** ALA. DC LA. SLA: Washington DC Chap., Docu. Group, Treas. (1968–69); Secy. (1969–70). AALL: Ch., Private Law Libs. Spec. Interest Sec. (1977–78). **Honors:** Beta Phi Mu, 1969. **Pubns.:** Jt. ed., *Legislative History of the Securities Act of 1933 and Securities Exchange Act of 1934* (1973). **Activities:** 12; 17; 77, 78 **Addr.:** Covington & Burling, 1201 Pennsylvania Ave., N.W., Washington, DC 20044.

Mahar, Mary Helen (F. 12, 1913, Schenectady, NY) Ref. Libn., Hotchkiss Sch. Lib., 1981–; Chief, Sch. Media Resrcs. Branch, U.S. Ofc. of Educ., 1972–78, various admin. lib. positions, 1957–72; Prof., Div. of Lib. Educ., State Univ. Tchrs. Coll., Geneseo, 1956–57; Exec. Secy., AASL, ALA, 1954–56; Libn., Garden City HS, 1944–54; Libn., Scotia HS, 1942–44; Asst. Libn., Meml. HS, 1940–42; Tchr., Libn., Pierson HS, 1935–40; various positions as visit. instr., Univ. of DE, SUNY-Geneseo, Columbia Univ., 1965, 1952–53, 1948–50. **Educ.:** NY State Coll. for Tchrs., Albany, 1935, AB, 1944, BS (LS); Columbia Univ., Sch. of Lib. Srv., 1950, MS. **Orgs.:** AECT. Chld. Bk. Gld. **Honors:** AASL, Pres. Awd., 1981; Untd. Kingdom, Std. of Lib. Srvs. to Chld. and Young People, Fulbright Flwshp., 1951–52. **Pubns.:** *Public School Library Statistics, 1958–1959* (1960); *The School Library as a Materials Center: Educational Needs of Librarians and Teachers in Its Administration and Use, Proceedings of a Conference* (1963); *Statistics of Public School Libraries, 1960–1961, Part I, Basic Tables* (1964); *School Library Supervision in Large Cities* (1966); "Evaluation of Media Services to Children and Young People in Schools," *Lib. Trends* (Ja. 1974); various articles in prof. jnls. **Activities:** 10; 63 **Addr.:** P.O. Box 1733, Lakeville, CT 06039.

Maher, Deborah B. (D. 4, 1937, Akron, OH) Asst. Univ. Libn., FL State Univ., 1979–; Catlgr., Suffolk Coop. Lib. Syst., 1977–79; Asst. Prof., Catlgr., NY City Cmnty. Coll., 1964–69; Adult Srvs. Libn., Brooklyn Pub. Lib., 1961–64. **Educ.:** Kent State Univ., 1958–60, BA (Hist.), 1960–61, MA (LS). **Orgs.:** ALA. FL LA. SELA. **Activities:** 1, 9; 16, 20, 46; 68, 85, 89 **Addr.:** Robert Manning Strozier Library, Florida State University, Tallahassee, FL 32306.

Mahmoodi, Suzanne H. (Ag. 5, 1935, Chariton, IA) Cont. Educ. and Lib. Resrch. Spec., MN Ofc. of Pub. Libs. & Interlib. Coop., 1977–; Visit. Lectr., Univ. of MN, 1974–77, 80; Asst. Prof./Instr., Coll. of St. Catherine, 1967–72, Readers Srvs. Libn., 1962–67; Jr. Libn., Circ. & Ref. Dept., Univ. of MN, 1958–60. **Educ.:** Ottumwa Heights Coll., 1953–55, AA; Coll. of St. Catherine, 1955–57, BA (Amer. Std.); Univ. of MI, 1957–58, MALS; Univ. of MN, 1972–78, PhD (LS). **Orgs.:** CLENE: Bd. (1977–82); Pres. (1980–81). ALA: ASCLA Cont. Educ. Com. (1979–); *Lib. Resrcs. & Tech. Srvs.* Asst. Ed. (1975–77); PLA Educ. for Pub. Libs. Com. (Ch., 1981–82). ASIS: Secy., MN Chap. (1971–76). MN LA: Cont. Educ. Com. (Ch., 1975–77). Other orgs. AAUP. Amer. Socty. for Trng. and Dev. **Honors:** Phi Beta Kappa, 1957; Beta Phi Mu, 1958. **Pubns.:** Jt. auth., "Educational Needs Assessment Group Interview Technique: A Manual," ERIC (1979); Jt. auth., "Assessing Educational Needs of Minnesota Library Personnel; A Proposed Technique," *MN Libs.* (Sum. 1976); "Continuing Education For Librarians in Minnesota," *MN Libs.* (Aut. 1976). **Activities:** 11, 13; 24, 25, 41; 50,

Special Subjects/Services: 50. Adult educ.; 51. Advert./Mktg.; 52. Aerosp.; 53. Agric.; 54. Area std.; 55. Arts/Hum.; 56. Autom.; 57. Bibl./Prtg.; 58. Bio. sci.; 59. Bus./Fin.; 60. Chem.; 61. Copyrt.; 62. Documtn.; 63. Educ.; 64. Engin.; 65. Env.; 66. Eth. grps.; 67. Film; 68. Food/Nutr.; 69. Geneal.; 70. Geo.; 71. Geol.; 72. Handcpd.; 73. Hist.; 74. Int. frdm.; 75. Info. sci.; 76. Insr.; 77. Law; 78. Legis.; 79. Math./Comp. sci.; 80. Med.; 81. Metals; 82. Nat. resrcs.; 83. Newsp.; 84. Nuc. sci.; 85. Oral hist.; 86. Petr./Energy; 87. Pharm.; 88. Phys./Astr./Math.; 89. Readg.; 90. Relig.; 91. Sci./Tech.; 92. Soc. sci.; 93. Telecom.; 94. Transp.; 95. (other).

59, 63 **Addr.:** OPLIC, 301 Hanover Bldg., 480 Cedar St., St. Paul, MN 55101.

Mahony, Doris Dinova (Je. 13, 1930, Waterbury, CT) Assoc. Libn., Ref., Info., Alfred Taubman Med. Lib., Univ. of MI, 1975–; Libn., Med. Lib., Chelsea Cmnty. Hosp., 1976–79. **Educ.:** East. MI Univ., 1968, BS (Soc. Std., Bio.); Univ. of MI, 1975, AMLS; Med. LA, 1975, Cert. (Med. Libnshp.). **Orgs.:** Med. LA. SLA. ALA. MI LA. **Activities:** 1, 5; 24, 39, 47; 58, 80, 87 **Addr.:** Alfred Taubman Medical Library, University of Michigan, Box 038, Ann Arbor, MI 48109.

Mahood, Ramona M. (Je. 7, 1933, Brigham City, UT) Asst. prof., Memphis State Univ., 1964–; Ref. Libn., Weber State Coll., 1955–62. **Educ.:** UT State Univ., 1951–55, BS (Retail.); Univ. of IL, 1959, MSLS, 1971, CAS. **Orgs.:** ALA: ALSC (Tchrs. of Chld.'s Lit., Disc. Grp. Conv. 1978–79; Co-Cov. 1979–81). ASIS: Southern Chap. Secy/Treas.(1976–77). TN LA: Educ. Sect. (Ch. 1973–74); Resrcs. and Tech. Srvs. Div. (Ch. 1981–82); Gvt. Docum. Org. (Ch. 1978–79). Southeastern LA: Educ. Sect., Secy., (1974–76); 1976–78; 1978–80). Phi Kappa Phi: Memphis State Univ. chap. (Secy. 1969–71; 1972–73); Pres.-elect, (1973–74); Pres. (1974–75). **Honors:** Delta Kappa Gamma. Beta Phi Mu. **Pubns.:** Jt. ed., *Young Adult Literature* (1980); jt. auth., Manual for Cataloging with Sample Cards (1968); 2nd ed. (1972); jt. auth., "Some Psychological Aspects of a computer-oriented Society," Proceedings *ASIS Proc.* (1977); "Book Catalogs–Present and Future," *Southeastern Libn.* (Sum. 1970). **Activities:** 1, 11; 20, 26, 46; 56, 89, 92 **Addr.:** Memphis State University, Dept. of Library Science, Memphis, TN 38152.

Mahrer, Judith K. (Jl. 6, 1929, Pittsfield, MA) Dir., Lib. Srvs., 1977–; Law Libn., Holme, Roberts and Owen, 1975–76; Ref. Libn., Jefferson Cnty. Pub. Lib., 1970–74. **Educ.:** Pembroke Coll., 1947–51, BA, cum laude (Hist.); Univ. of Denver, 1968–70, MA (LS). **Orgs.:** AALL. CO LA. Southwest. Assn. of Law Libs. CO Cnsrtm. of Law Libs. Amer. Cvl. Liberties Un. Natl. Org. of Women. Common Cause. **Honors:** Phi Beta Kappa, 1951. **Pubns.:** Jt. auth., "The Law Library Consultant, Help When You Need It," *Legal Econ.* (My./Je. 1981); "Law Library Services," *What Else You Can Do With a Library Degree* (1980). **Activities:** 12; 24 **Addr.:** Library Services, 1600 Broadway, No. 1510, Denver, CO 80202.

Maier, Robert C. (F. 6, 1949, Mineola, NY) Dir., Bedford Pub. Lib., 1976–; Branch Libn., Cranston Pub. Lib. Syst., 1973–76. **Educ.:** Un. Coll., 1967–71, BA (Eng.); Univ. of RI, 1971–73, MLS. **Orgs.:** MA LA: Pres. (1981–83); Legis. Com. (Ch., 1978–). New Eng. LA. ALA. **Activities:** 9; 17, 34; 78 **Addr.:** Bedford Public Library, Bedford, MA 01730.

Maillet, Lucienne G. (Ap. 16, 1932, Lewiston, ME) Asst. Prof. of LS, Palmer Grad. Lib. Sch., Long Island Univ., 1975–; York Coll., CUNY, 1970–75; Ctrl. Sch. Dist. #2, Syosset, NY, 1969–70; Montgomery Cnty. Sch. Syst., 1963–69; Punahou Acad., Honolulu, HI, 1959–60. **Educ.:** Bates Coll., 1952–56, BS (Chem.); George Washington Univ., 1960–63, MA (Educ.); Cath. Univ., 1965–69, MS (LS); Columbia Univ., 1970–, DLS; Cert., 1973–75 (Info. Sci.). **Orgs.:** ASIS. ALA. Med. LA: Reg. Grp., Educ. Ad Hoc Com. (1980–81). Beta Phi Mu: Beta Mu Chap. (Dir., 1978–79); Awds. Com. (Ch., 1979–81). **Pubns.:** "Media for Consumer Health Care," *Previews* (O. 1979). **Activities:** 12; 20, 26, 30; 75, 80 **Addr.:** Palmer Graduate Library School, C.W. Post Center, Long Island University, Greenvale, NY 11548.

Mailloux, Elizabeth N. Mgr., Engin. Info. Ctr., Mobil Resrch. and Dev. Corp., 1978–; Info. Anal., Mobil Chem. Co., Plastics Div., 1976–78, Div. Libn., 1975–76. **Educ.:** Nazareth Coll., Rochester, NY, 1974, BA; SUNY, Geneseo, 1975, MS (LS). **Orgs.:** ASIS. SLA. Assoc. Info. Mgrs. Natl. Micro. Assn. Inquire Petr./Energy Users Grp: Ch. **Activities:** 12; 17, 30, 38; 64, 86 **Addr.:** Mobil Research and Development Corp., P.O. Box 1026, Princeton, NJ 08540.

Maina, William Edward (O. 2, 1948, Oak Park, IL) Asst. Dir. for Pub. Srvs., Lib., Univ. of TX Hlth. Sci. Ctr. at Dallas, 1979–; CLR/NLM Hlth. Sci. Lib. Mgt. Intern, Hlth. Sci. Lib., Univ. of NC, Chapel Hill, 1978–79; Coord., Comp. Lit. Srch., Univ. Lib., Univ. of CA, San Diego, 1975–78, Ref. Libn., Biomed. Lib., 1972–75. **Educ.:** Univ. of CA, Berkeley, 1968–70, AB (Eng.); 1970–71, MLS. **Orgs.:** Med. LA: Mem. Com. (1975–76). ALA. **Honors:** Beta Phi Mu. **Pubns.:** "The CLR/NLM Health Sciences Library Management Intern Program: First Year," *Bltn. of the Med. LA* (Ja. 1980); jt. auth., "Health Information in San Diego," *CA Libn.* (Ja. 1978); jt. auth., "Health Info for All: San Diego Meet," *Lib. Jnl.* (Ag. 1977); "Undergraduate Use of Online Bibliographic Retrieval Services: Experiences at the University of California, San Diego," *Online* (Ap. 1977); jt. auth., "Medical Reference Works for the Public Library," *News Notes of CA Libs.* (1975). **Activities:** 1; 17; 80 **Addr.:** University of Texas Health Science Center, Library, 5323 Harry Hines Blvd., Dallas, TX 75235.

Maizen, Arnold (N. 2, 1948, Montreal, PQ) Chief Libn., N. Bay Pub. Lib., 1979–, Libn.-in-charge, Adult Fr. and AV Depts., 1976–79; Fr. Lib. Srvs. Coord., Algonquin Reg. Lib., 1973–76. **Educ.:** Sir George Williams Univ., 1968–71, BA (Soclgy.); McGill Univ., 1971–73, MLS. **Orgs.:** ON LA. **Pubns.:** "Le développement des services de langue français par la Bibliothèque Régionale Algonquin," *ON Lib. Review* (Je. 1974). **Activities:** 9; 15, 17, 36 **Addr.:** North Bay Public Library, 271 Worthington St. E., North Bay, ON P1B 1H1 Canada.

Majcher, Michael Dinn (Ag. 30, 1947, Pittsburgh, PA) Mgr., Tech. Info. Ctr., Xerox Corp., 1975–; Micro. Supvsr., Calspan Corp., 1973–75; Libn., Calspan Corp., 1970–73. **Educ.:** SUNY, Buffalo, 1971–73, BA (Psych.), 1974–75, MLS. **Orgs.:** Assn. Info. Mgrs.: Exec. Com. (1978–). SLA. ASIS. Nat. Micro. Assn.: Past Pres., West. NY Chap. (1979–80). **Activities:** 12; 17; 59, 91 **Addr.:** Xerox Corporation, 800 Phillips Rd., Building 105, Webster, NY 14580.

Major, Jean Armour (Ag. 28, 1939, Dixon, IL) Dir., Univ. Libs., North. IL Univ., 1978–; Head, Undergrad. Libs., OH State Univ., 1974–76; Ref. Libn., Univ. of IL, 1968–74, Asst. Ref. Libn., 1968–71; Asst. Cat. Libn., Univ. of IL, Chicago Circle, 1965–68; Catlgr., SD State Univ., 1964–65. **Educ.:** North. IL Univ., 1957–59; Lake Forest Coll., 1959–61, BA; Rosary Coll., 1962–64, MALS; IN Univ., 1977–81, PhD (LS). **Orgs.:** ALA: ACRL Chap. Cncl., IL rep. (1980); Com. on Instr. in the Use of Libs. (1975–77); Ralph R. Shaw Awd. Jury (1980); Ref. and Subscrpn. Books Review Com. (1975–78). Cncl. of Dir. of State Univ. Libs.: Treas. (1978–). IL ACRL: Pres. (1980–). IL State Lib. Com. on Educ. and Trng. **Honors:** Beta Phi Mu. **Pubns.:** *Collections Acquired by the University of Illinois Library at Urbana-Champaign, 1897–1974, A Catalog.* (1974); "The Visually Impaired Reader in the Academic Library" *Coll. and Resrch. Libs.* (My. 1978); Jt. auth., "Funding Support for Research in Librarianship" *Advances in Libnshp.* (1979); Reviews. **Activities:** 1; 17, 34, 39; 56, 72 **Addr.:** University Libraries, Northern Illinois University, DeKalb, IL 60115.

Mak, Loretta (Ag. 20, 1946, China) Libn., Heller, Ehrman, White and McAuliffe, 1970–. **Educ.:** Boston Univ., 1966–68, BA (Soclgy.); Univ. of CA, Berkeley, 1969–70, MLS; Armstrong Coll., 1975–79, JD. **Orgs.:** AALL. SLA. CA LA. CA Bar Assn. Amer. Bar Assn. **Honors:** Beta Phi Mu, 1970. **Activities:** 12; 15, 17; 77 **Addr.:** Heller, Ehrman, White and McAuliffe, 44 Montgomery St., 30th Floor, San Francisco, CA 94104.

Makar, Ragai N. (Ja. 1, 1928, Minia, Egypt) Visit. Head of Middle East Lib., Univ. of UT, 1981–82; Sabbatic-leave-of-absence, Adelphi Univ., 1980–81; Head, Soc. Work Lib., 1977–80, Head, Soc. Work Desk, 1972–77; Head, Saidia Sr. HS Lib., Cairo, Egypt, 1963–69; HS Tchr., Egypt and the Sudan, 1950–63. **Educ.:** Cairo Univ., 1946–50, BA (Soclgy.); Pratt Inst., 1970–72, MLS; Adelphi Univ., 1974–79, MA (Soclgy.). **Orgs.:** ALA. Middle E. Libns. Assn. AAUP. Amer. Resrch. Ctr. in Egypt. **Pubns.:** Transl. into Arabic bibls.; reviews. **Activities:** 1; 15, 17; 57, 63, 92 **Addr.:** Middle East Library, University of Utah, Salt Lake City, UT 84112.

Malamud, Judie (D. 25, 1940, Detroit, MI) Asst. Libn. for Pub. Srvs., Univ. of PA, Biomed. Lib., 1981–; Vetny. Libn., Univ. of PA, 1977–81; Biomed. Libn., Lawrence Meml. Hosp., 1972–77; Chem. Libn., Ventron Corp., 1971–72. **Educ.:** West. MI Univ., 1961–62, BS (Bio.). **Orgs.:** Med. LA. **Pubns.:** "Preselected Literature for Routine Delivery to Physicians in Community Hospital Based Patient Care Related Reading Program," *Bltn. of the Med. LA* (Ap. 1981). **Activities:** 1; 17, 22, 39; 58, 80 **Addr.:** University of Pennsylvania, Biomedical Library, Philadelphia, PA 19104.

Malamud, Sylvia (Ag. 8, 1927, New York, NY) Coord. of Bibl. Instr., B. Davis Schwarz Meml. Lib., C W Post Ctr., Long Island Univ., 1979–, Docum. Libn., 1971–79, Acq. Libn., 1969–71. **Educ.:** New York Univ., 1944–48, BS (Psy.); Long Island Univ., 1963–69, MLS, 1970–74 (Crim Just). **Orgs.:** ALA: LIRT, Natl. Progs. Study Task Force Com. (1981–); GODORT, Treas. (1979–); Fed. Doc. Task Force (1979–); ACRL. Nassau Cnty. LA: Coll. and Univ. Div. Pres. (1979). Treas. (1972–73). C. W. Post Collegial Fed.: Exec. Bd. (1971–); Treas. (1974–76, 1978–80). **Pubns.:** *Reviews of the Newberry Award Winners, 1955–1965: A Statistical Analysis* (1972); "An Analysis of Federal Depository Library Claims," *Docum. to the People* (S. 1979). **Activities:** 1; 15, 20, 29, 31 **Addr.:** 30 Wedgewood Dr., Westbury, NY 11590.

Malanchuk, Iona R. (Je. 17, 1944, Brooklyn, NY) Acq. Libn., Univ. of FL, Gainesville, 1980–; Bus. Libn., Assoc. Prof., Libs., Western MI Univ., 1978–80; Educ. Libn., Asst. Prof. Libs., 1970–78; Asst. Ser. Libn., IN Univ., 1970, Engl. and Fr. Lit. Catlgr. (Rare Books), J. K. Lilly Rare Books Lib., 1969–70; Libn. Intern, Math, Physics, Astronomy Lib., IN Univ., 1967–69. **Educ.:** SUNY-, Oneonta, 1962–1964, (Eng.); Adelphi Univ., 1964–66, BA (Eng.); IN Univ., 1967–69, MLS; Western MI Univ., 1973, MA (AV Media). **Orgs.:** ALA. MI LA. Assn. for Educ. Comm. and Tech. AAUP. Midwest Adv. Bd., MI Rep., Exper. in Intl. Living. **Pubns.:** Instr. Media Progs., "How to Use the ERIC Information System" and "How to Use Periodical Indexes." **Activities:** 1; 15, 31, 39; 59, 63, 72 **Addr.:** 2510 NW 90th Terr., Gainesville, FL 32601.

Malanchuk, Peter P. (S. 2, 1943, Rockville Ctr., NY) Ch., Ref. and Bibl. Dept., Univ. of FL, Gainesville, 1980–; Soc. Sci. Libn./Assoc. Prof., Libs., Western MI Univ., 1970–80. **Educ.:** Cornell Univ., 1961–64, (Bus. Admin.); Adelphi Univ., 1964–66, BA (Hist.); IN Univ., 1966–1968, MA (Hist.), 1970, MLS; Western MI Univ., 1977–79, MA (AV Media). **Orgs.:** ALA: ACRL: BIS Post-Conf. Plng. Com. (1983); RASD: Ref. Srvs. in Large Resrch. Libs. Discuss. Grp. (Ch., 1981–82); LAMA. MI LA: Bibl. Instr. Com. (1975–); Acad. Div., Bd. Mem. (1979). Mid-MI Socty. for Instr. Tech. (1979–). AAUP (1975–). Phi Alpha Theta (Natl. Hist. Hon.) 1965–. **Honors:** Natl. Endow. for the Hum., J. K. Lilly Flwshp., 1975. **Pubns.:** *The Institute of International and Area Studies Library: A Bibliography* (1978); *Library Instruction: A Guide to Programs in Michigan;* reviews; "Social Sciences Index," slide/tape prog. (1980); "Essay and General Literature Index," slide/tape prog. (1980). **Activities:** 1, 11; 15, 31, 39; 54, 92, 93 **Addr.:** 2510 NW 90th Terr., Gainesville, FL 32601.

Malchman, Marian C. (D. 10, 1931, Philadelphia, PA) Asst. Head Tech. Prcs./Serials Libn., Montgomery Cnty. Norristown Pub. Lib., 1979–; Admin. Asst./WIC Prog., Visit. Nurse Assn. of Norristown, 1978–79, Libn., 1976–78; Libn., Insr. Socty. of Philadelphia, 1968–74; Libn., Fairchild Corp., 1958–60; Docum. Libn., Gen. Electric, Philadelphia, 1956–58; Asst. Libn., RCA, Camden, NJ, 1953–56. **Educ.:** Douglas Coll., 1949–53, BA (Hist., Pol. Sci.); Drexel Univ., 1955–58, MSLS. **Orgs.:** SLA. PA LA. **Activities:** 9; 20, 33, 44 **Addr.:** 232 Redwood Rd., King of Prussia, PA 19406.

Malchow, Beatrice Noble (Jl. 14, 1920, Longmont, CO) Lib. Dir., Longmont Pub. Lib., 1967–, Ref. Libn., 1965–67; Educ. Asst., Loveland Meth. Church, 1963–65; Catlgr., Dayton & Montgomery Cnty. Pub. Lib., 1944–45; Catlgr., Denver Pub. Lib., 1942–43. **Educ.:** Univ. of Denver, 1938–42, AB (Libnshp.). **Orgs.:** CO LA: Secy., Pub. Lib. Div. (1969, 1977–78); Int. Frdm. Com. (1980–). Ctrl. CO Lib. Syst.: Governing Bd. (1978–). ALA. AAUW. Longmont Symph. Bd. **Activities:** 9; 17, 20 **Addr.:** Longmont Public Library, 409 Fourth Ave., Longmont, CO 80501.

Maleady, Antoinette O. (D. 9, 1918, Powell, WY) Head, Acq. Dept, Lib., Sonoma State Univ., 1972–, Sound Rec. Libn., 1968–72. **Educ.:** WV Wesleyan Coll., 1936–39, BS (Bus. Admin.); Univ. of CA, Berkeley, 1967–68, MLS; Eastman Sch. of Msc., 1971. **Orgs.:** Msc. LA: Secy.-Treas. (1972–73); Place. Ofcr. (1975–). CA LA: Campus Rep. (1970–71). Pvt. Libs. Assn. New York and San Francisco Opera Assns. Amer. Recorder Socty. Amer. Choral Socty. **Pubns.:** *Record and Tape Reviews Index,* (1971, 1972, 1973, 1974); *Index to Record and Tape Reviews: A Classicial Music Buying Guide,* (1975, 1976, 1977, 1978, 1979, 1980). **Activities:** 1; 15, 30, 37 **Addr.:** 1040 Butterfield Rd., San Anselmo, CA 94960.

Malgeri, Dina G. (Ag. 19, 1929, Chicago, IL) Dir., Malden (MA) Pub. Lib., 1972–; Inst. Consult., MA Bureau of Lib. Ext., 1970–72; Admin. Libn., U.S. Army Spec. Srvs. Libs., Germany, 1967–70; Admin. Asst., MA Bureau of Lib. Ext., 1965–67. **Educ.:** Harvard Univ., 1956–63, BA (Hum.); Simmons Coll., 1964–65, MLS; MA Prof. Libn. Cert., 1965. **Orgs.:** ALA. MA LA: PR Com. (1975–77). Grt. Boston Pub. Lib. Admin.: VP (1976). **Pubns.:** "A Century of Service," *Harvard Ext. Alum. Bltn.* (My. 1979); "Mass. Prison Libraries: A Case for Reform," *Bay State Libn.* (O. 1971). **Activities:** 9; 17, 28, 36; 55 **Addr.:** Malden Public Library, 36 Salem St., Malden, MA 02148.

Malin, Ethel Rita (Jl. 8, 1948, St. Louis, MO) Chld. Libn., Santa Barbara Pub. Lib., 1974–; Chld. Libn., Stanislaus Cnty. Free Pub. Lib., 1972–74; Chld. Libn., Seattle Pub. Lib., 1971–72. **Educ.:** Purdue Univ., 1966–70, BA (Elem. Educ.); Univ. of Denver, 1970–71, MLS. **Orgs.:** CA LA. ALA. **Activities:** 9; 15, 21, 36 **Addr.:** Goleta Branch Public Library, Goleta, CA 93117.

Malin, Morton V. (Ja. 21, 1922, New York, NY) VP, Prof. Rel., Inst. for Sci. Info., 1966–; Staff Assoc., Natl. Sci. Fndn., 1961–66; Resrch. Assoc., Univ. of Pittsburgh, 1959–61; Field Correspondent, MA Inst. of Tech., 1958–59; Sr. Resrch. Anal., Univ. of Pittsburgh, 1954–56; Histn., Nat. Park Srv., 1947–49. **Educ.:** Univ. of Chattanooga, 1943, AB (Hist., Econ.); Vanderbilt Univ., 1947, MA (Hist.); Univ. of MD, 1954, PhD (Hist.). **Orgs.:** AAAS. AAAH. ASIS. Franklin Inst., Com. for Sci. and the Arts. U.S. Natl. Com. for ICSU/AB. **Pubns.:** "Training of Information Specialists in Western Europe," *Proc. of GA Inst. of Tech. Conf. on Training of Sci. Info. Spec.* (Ap. 1962); "Faculty Consulting in Colleges and Universities. Policies, Practices, and Problems," *Reviews of Data on Sci. Resrcs.* (Ap. 1966); "The Science Citation Index," *Lib. Trends* (1968); Jt. Auth., "Can Nobel Prize Winners be Predicted," *AAAS* (1968); Jt. Auth., "A System for Automatic Classication of Scientific Literature," *J. Indian Inst. of Sci.* (1975). **Activities:** 28, 41; 75, 91, 92 **Addr.:** Institute for Scientific Information, 3501 Market St., University City Science Center, Philadelphia, PA 19104.

Malinconico, S. Michael (Mr. 12, 1941, Brooklyn, New York, NY) Assoc. Dir., Tech. & Comp. Srvs., NY Pub. Lib., 1978–, Asst. Chief, Syst. Anal., Data Prcs. Off., 1973–78, Mgr., Syst. Anal., 1971–73. Syst. Anal., 1969–71; Data/Syst. Anal., Nat. Aeronautics and Space Admin., 1967–69; Lectr, Brooklyn Coll. Dept. of Physics, 1965–67. **Educ.:** Brooklyn Coll., 1958–62,

PROFESSIONAL ACTIVITIES: Institutions: 1. Acad. lib.; 2. Arch.; 3. Assn.; 4. Fed./Gvt. lib.; 5. Inst. lib.; 6. Mfr./Suppl.; 7. Milit. lib.; 8. Musm.; 9. Pub. lib.; 10. Sch. lib.; 11. Sch. of lib. sci.; 12. Spec. lib.; 13. State lib.; 14. (other). **Functions/Activities:** 15. Acq./Col. dev.; 16. Adult srvs.; 17. Admin.; 18. Apprais.; 19. Archit./Bldgs.; 20. Cat./Class.; 21. Chld. srvs.; 22. Circ.; 23. Cons./Pres.; 24. Consult.; 25. Cont. ed.; 26. Educ. lib. sci.; 27. Ext. srvs.; 28. Fund/Grants; 29. Gvt. pubs.; 30. Indx./Abs.; 31. Instr. lib. use; 32. Media srvs.; 33. Micro.; 34. Netwks./Coop.; 35. Persnl.; 36. PR; 37. Publshg.; 38. Recs. mgt.; 39. Ref. srvs.; 40. Repro.; 41. Resrch.; 42. Review.; 43. Secur.; 44. Serials; 45. Spec. col.; 46. Tech. srvs.; 47. Trustees/Bds.; 48. YA srvs.; 49. (other).

BS (Physics); Columbia Univ., 1962–64, MA (Physics), 1964–67 (Physics), 1976– (Lib. Sci.). **Orgs.:** ALA: LITA (Pres., 1980–81); RTSD (Dir. 1977–78). ASIS: Ch., Spec. Int. Grp. Lib. Autom. and Networking. NY Tech. Srvs. Libns. Assn. NY Book Pub. League. **Honors:** Sigma Xi, 1962. NSF Fellow, 1963–66. ALA, Esther Piercy Awd., 1978. **Pubns.:** *The Future of The Catalog: The Library's Choice* (1979); *The Nature and Future of the Catalog* (1979); various articles on cat., bibliographic autom., and the application of tech. to lib. activities. **Activities:** 9; 46; 56, 75 **Addr.:** Technical Services, The New York Public Library, 8 E. 40th St., New York, NY 10016.

Malinowsky, H. Robert (D. 7, 1933, Wakeeney, KS) Assoc. Dean of Libs., Univ. of KS, 1975–, Asst. Dir. of Libs., 1970–75, Sci. Libn., 1967–70; Sci. Libn., Univ. of Denver, 1964–67. Univ. of KS, Lawrence, 1952–55, BS (Geol.); Univ. of Denver, 1961–62, MS (LS). **Orgs.:** SLA: Fin. Com. (1979–80); Bd. of Dirs. (1972–77). ALA: Ref. and Subscrpn. Bks. Review Com. (1979–). **Honors:** Tau Beta Pi. **Pubns.:** *Science and Engineering Literature* (1976, 1980). **Activities:** 1; 17; 55, 56, 91 **Addr.:** 3105 Creekwood, Lawrence, KS 66044.

Malinski, Richard M. (F. 23, 1944, Brotty Ferry, Angus, Scotland) Head, Lib. Loans Div., Simon Fraser Univ., 1981–, Ofc. Syst. Anal., 1980–81, Head, Lib. Loans Div., 1978–80, Soc. Sci. Libn., 1974–78; Geo. and Map Libn., York Univ., 1972–74. **Educ.:** York Univ., 1963–67, BA (Geo.); Univ. of Toronto, 1967–68, BLS; Univ. of AB, Edmonton, 1971–73, MA (Geo.); Simon Fraser Univ., 1977–80, MBA. **Orgs.:** Can. LA. Can. Assn. Info. Sci. W. Coast Comp. Socty. **Activities:** 1, 12; 17, 22, 24; 56, 70, 75 **Addr.:** 2696 Burnside Pl., Coquitlam, BC V3E 1A2 Canada.

Mallette, Mildred Hazel (Ag. 6, 1934, Maxton, NC) Instr., Eng., St. Augustine's Coll., 1981–; Asst. to Dir., Spec. Cols., Shaw Univ., 1980–, Lib. Dir., 1972–80; Catlgr., Meredith Coll., 1971–72; Catlgr., Shaw Univ., 1969–71; Asst. to the Dir., Acq. Libn., Bowie State Coll., 1968; Asst. to the Lib. Dir., Ref. Libn., Winston-Salem State Coll., 1962–68; Asst. Libn., Instr. of LS, Albany State Coll., 1960–62. **Educ.:** Bennett Coll., 1952–55, BA (Eng., LS); NC Ctrl. Coll., 1959–60, MSLS. **Orgs.:** ALA: Black Caucus. NC LA. AAUW. Bennett Coll. Alum. **Activities:** 1, 10; 17, 26, 39 **Addr.:** 1105 Carlisle St., Raleigh, NC 27610.

Mallinson, Gwyneth Heynes (Ap. 24, 1935, Rotherham, Yorkshire, Eng.) Mgr., Tech. Info. Srvs., Ampex Corp., 1969–; Chief Libn., Singer Bus. Machines, 1964–69, Libn., Newton Free Lib., 1960–63. **Educ.:** Univ. of Bristol, 1953–56, BA (Eng.); San Jose State Univ., 1973–77, MA (LS). **Orgs.:** SLA: Misc. Chap. ofcs. ASIS. Coop. Info. Ntwk.: Bd. (1975–6, 1979–). Inst. of Electrical and Electronics Engins. **Pubns.:** "Digital Television: a Glossary and Bibliography," *Socty. of Motion Pict. and TV Engin. Jnl.* (Ja. 1979). **Activities:** 12; 17, 39; 59, 64, 91 **Addr.:** Ampex Corp., 401 Broadway, Redwood City, CA 94063.

Malone, Alton H. Bill (Ap. 4, 1934, Plant City, FL) Asst. Libn., Asst. Prof., Morehead State Univ., 1976–; Lib. Dir., Gardner Webb Coll., 1969–76; Ref. Libn. Mars Hill Coll., 1968–69; Circ. Ref. Libn. Undergrad. Lib., Univ. of SC, 1965–68; Bkmobile. Libn., Nolichucky Reg. Lib., 1962–64. **Educ.:** Carson Newman Coll., 1953–56, 1960–61, BA (Hist., Pol. Sci.); Univ. of IL., 1964–65, MSLS. **Orgs.:** ALA. SELA. NC LA. KY LA. Civitan. Lions. Morehead Mens Clb. **Activities:** 1; 17, 19, 39; 75, 90, 92 **Addr.:** 711 Sherwood Forest, Morehead, KY 40351.

Maloney, James John (Jl. 20, 1949, Chicago, IL) Head, Info. Retrieval Srvs. Dept., Bibl. Ctr. for Resrch., 1981–; Asst. Ref. Libn., Univ. of IL, Chicago, 1979–, Asst. Cat. Libn., 1979–80; Consult., Lincoln Trails Lib. Syst., 1979; Consult., Larson and Darby, Inc., 1979. **Educ.:** Bradley Univ., 1967–71, BA (Hist.); North. IL Univ., 1972–76, MA (Russ. Hist.); Univ. of IL, 1977–78, MSLS. **Orgs.:** ALA: RASD/Machine–Assisted Ref. Sect., Prog. Com. (Ch., 1981–82); ACRL/Slavic and E. European Sect., Prog. Com. (1980–81). Chicago OLUG: Wkshp. Coord. (1980–81). Amer. Assn. for the Advnc. of Slavic Std.: Bibl. and Docum. Com. (1979–81). **Honors:** Phi Alpha Theta, 1974. **Pubns.:** "Problem Patrons: The Other Kind of Library Security," *IL Libs.* (Ap. 1981); "Public Service Use of OCLC" media presentation (1981). **Activities:** 1; 17, 31, 39; 54, 56 **Addr.:** 1320 Detroit, Denver, CO 80206.

Maloney, Margaret Crawford (S. 27, 1942, Toronto, Ont.) Head, Osborne Coll. Early Chld. Books (and Lillian H. Smith and Canadiana Collections), Toronto Pub. Lib., 1979–; Libn., 1971–79; Libn., Chld. Srvs., 1964–65. **Educ.:** Univ. of Toronto, 1959–63, BA (Hist./Fr.); 1963–64, BLS; 1971, MLS. **Orgs.:** Can. LA. ALA. **Pubns.:** Cont., *Penguin Companion to Children's Literature;* Preface to *Dear Ivy, Dear June: Letters from Beatrix Potter* (1977); Intro. to *The Fantastic Kingdom* (1974); "Letters from Beatrix Potter," *Can. Coll.* (N./D. 1976); Reviews. **Activities:** 9, 12; 15, 23, 45; 57 **Addr.:** Osborne Collection, Boys and Girls House, 40 St. George St., Toronto, ON M5S 2E4 Canada.

Maloy, Robert M. (Jl. 12, 1935, Cleveland, OH) Dir. of Libs., Smithsonian Inst., 1979–; Dir. of Lib., Union Theo. Semy., New York, 1975–79; Dir. of Lib., Sch. of Theo., Claremont, CA, 1972–75; Prof., Grad. Lib. Sch., Rosary Coll., 1971–72. **Educ.:** Univ. of Dayton, 1952–56, BA (Phil.); Univ. of Chicago, 1959–60, AM (LS); Univ. Freiburg, Switzerland, 1960–66, STD (Hist.); St. Benet Hall, Oxford Univ., 1966; Ludwig-Maximilians Univ., Munich, 1966–67; Harvard Univ., 1972. **Orgs.:** ALA. Archons of Colophon. Bibl. Socty. of Amer. Medvl. Acad. of Amer. Intl. Cncl. of Musmns. Amer. Assn. of Musms. **Honors:** Beta Phi Mu; Medvl. Acad. of Amer. Flw., 1972; U.S. Ofc. of Educ., Lib. Mgt. Sem. Flw., 1978. **Pubns.:** *The Sermonary of Ildephonsus of Toledo: Scholarship and Manuscripts "Classical Folia"* (1971); "A Correction in Text of a Recent Edition of Paschasius Radbertus' De partu," *Marianum* (1971); "The *Speculum historiale* of Vincent of Beauvais and Works Attributed to Ildephonsus," *Ephemerides Mariologicae* (1972); "A Carolingian and an Eleventh Century Monastic Sermon on Luke 10:38–42," *Marianum* (1978). **Activities:** 1; 17 **Addr.:** Smithsonian Institution Libraries, Washington, DC 20560.

Maltais, Louis Adhémar (Ag. 25, 1935, Ottawa, ON) Tchr., Documtn. Tech., John-Abbott Coll., 1977–; Tchr., Documtn. Tech., Lionel-Groulx Coll., 1974–77; Libn., Plantagenet HS, 1968–74; Catlgr., Hull Pub. Lib., 1965–68; Asst. Libn., Econ. Cncl. of Can., 1964–65; Libn., Oblate Fathers' Sem., 1962–63. **Educ.:** Univ. of Ottawa, 1953–57, BA (Pol. Sci.), 1961–62, BLS, 1963–71, MA (LS), 1972–75, MEd (Sch. Admin.); McArthur Coll. of Educ., 1968–69, HSA (Tchg.); ON gvt., Spec. Cert. in Sch. Libnshp., 1970. **Orgs.:** PQ Corp. of Prof. Libns. ASTED: Rep. (1977–). Prov. Coord. Com. for the Documtn. Tech. Courses: Rep. (1978–). Plantagenet Cham. of Cmrc.: Secy. (1969–74). ON Sec. Sch. Tchrs. Fed.: Dist. 38, Secy. (1973–74). **Honors:** Plantagenet Cham. of Cmrce., Hon. Plate and Diploma, 1974. **Activities:** 14-Coll. Tchr.; 26, 31; 62, 75 **Addr.:** John Abbott College, P.O. Box 2000, Ste-Anne-de-Bellevue, PQ H9X 3L9 Canada.

Maltese, Susan Miller (F. 2, 1941, Decatur, IL) Coord. of Lib. Srvs., Oakton Cmnty. Coll., 1977–, Ref., Circ. Libn., 1971–77. **Educ.:** Univ. of IL, 1959–63, BA (Eng.), 1965–67, MA (Soc. Std.), 1970–71, MS (LS). **Orgs.:** ALA: ACRL/Cmnty. and Jr. Coll. Sect., Bibl. Stans. for Non-Print Media (1975–77); Srv. to Disadv. (1977–80). IL LA: ACRL, Exec. Bd. (1981–82); IL Cmnty. Coll. Guidelines Com. (1973–76); Hist. and Arch. Com. (1976–77); Cont. Educ. Com. (Ch., 1980–81). **Activities:** 1; 17, 31, 39; 85 **Addr.:** 123 Columbia, Elmhurst, IL 60126.

Malumphy, Sharon M. (S. 11, 1950, Akron, OH) Corp. Libn., OH Edison Co., 1981–, Recs. Anal., 1978–81; Libn., Cleveland Electric Illuminating Co., 1976–78; Libn., Sci. and Tech. Div., Cleveland Pub. Lib., 1974–76. **Educ.:** Univ. of Akron, 1968–72, BA (Eng., Geol.); Univ. of Pittsburgh, 1972–73, MLS. **Orgs.:** SLA: Cleveland Chap., Bltn. Ed. (1978–79). ALA. Geoscience Info. Socty. OH Acad. of Sci.: Info. and LS Div. **Honors:** Univ. of Pittsburgh Grad. Sch. of LS, Class Rep. at Graduation, 1974. **Activities:** 12; 15, 17, 39; 59, 64, 91 **Addr.:** 1950 Larchmont Rd., Akron, OH 44313.

Maman, Marie (D. 27, 1931, Amli, Norway) Info. Spec., Ctr. of Alchl. Std., Rutgers Univ., 1978–; Info. Spec., Mobil Resrch. and Dev. Corp., 1976–78. **Educ.:** Rutgers Univ., 1974–75, BA (Eng.), 1975–76, MLS; Stockholm Tekniska Inst., Sweden, 1954–56 (Chem.). **Orgs.:** SLA. Amer. Socty. of Indxrs. Libns. and Info. Spec. in Addictions. **Activities:** 12; 30; 75 **Addr.:** 40 Hawthorne Ave., Princeton, NJ 08540.

Mancall, Jacqueline Cooper (Mr. 31, 1932, Philadelphia, PA) Asst. Prof. of Lib. and Info. Sci., Drexel Univ., 1979–, Resrch. Assoc., 1978–79, Coord., Cont. Educ., 1976–78; Libn., Miquon Sch., 1968–75. **Educ.:** Univ. of PA, 1949–54, BA (Hist.); Drexel Univ., 1966–70, MS (LS), 1975–78, PhD (Lib. & Inf. Sci.). **Orgs.:** ALA: AASL, Resrch. Com. (1979–81); ALSC. PA Sch. LA: Media review com. (1977–79); Conf. Com. (1979–80). ASIS. Intl. Reading Assn. **Honors:** Beta Phi Mu, 1970; Phi Delta Kappa, 1977. **Pubns.:** Jt. auth., "Materials Used by High School Students in Preparing Independent Study Projects: A Bibliometric Approach," *Lib. Resrch.* (1979); Jt. auth., "Management by Objectives as a Process to Facilitate Supervision and Staff Development," *Drexel Lib. Qtly.* (Ap. 1978); Jt. auth., "Bradford's Law and Libraries: Present Applications-Potential Promise," *Aslib Proceedings* (Je. 1979); Jt. auth., "Jobs and Applicants: An Analysis of Placement Records from Three AALS Annual Meetings," *Jnl. of Educ. for Libnshp.* (Summer 1979); Jt. auth., "The Application of Bibliometric Techniques to the Analysis of Materials for Young Adults," *Col. Mgt.* (Fall 1978); Other articles. **Activities:** 10, 11; 15, 21, 26, 41; 95-Resrcs. for Chld. **Addr.:** Drexel University/School of Library and Information Science, Philadelphia, PA 19452.

Mancevice, Mark F. (Ap. 11, 1949, Worcester, MA) Libn., New Eng. Telephone, 1978–; Tech. Libn., New Eng. Electric, 1972–78. **Educ.:** Clark Univ., 1967–71, AB (Hist.); Simmons Coll., 1971–72, MLS. **Orgs.:** SLA: Consult. Ofc. (1977, 1980–). New Eng. OLUG. ASIS. MA Archlg. Socty. Amer. Numismatic Socty. **Pubns.:** Ed., *SLA Pub. Util. Div. Bltn.* (1976–77). **Activities:** 12; 17, 24, 30; 50, 59, 62 **Addr.:** Resource Center, New England Telephone, Marlboro, MA 01752.

Mancuyas, Natividad Descartin (Ja. 26, 1930, Manila, Philippines) Docum. Libn., Asst. Prof., Chicago State Univ. Lib., 1978–, Instr., 1972–78, Lib. Tech. Asst. III, 1968–1972; Libn., 1955–68; Instr., Philippine Coll. of Cmrce., Manila, Philippines, 1966–1968; Lib. consult., Philippine Cham. of Indus., 1966. **Educ.:** The Nat. Tchrs. Coll., Manila, Philippines, 1950–53, BSEd (Lib. Sci.); Rosary Coll., River Forest, IL, 1969–71, MALS; Univ. of IL, Chicago, 1975–77, (Soclgy.). **Orgs.:** ALA: Gvt. Docum. RT (1978–1979); IL LA: IL Docum. Libn. Grp. (1978–1979). Asian-Amer. Libn. Caucus. Chicago State Univ. Lib.: Accession List Com. (Ch., 1978–), Col. Dev. Com. (1979–), Univ. Curric. Com. (1979–). The Chicago Temple First Untd. Methodist Church. Chicago State Univ. Woman's Clb. **Honors:** Philippine Coll. of Cmrce., Manila, Philippines, Most Outstan. Libn., Sch. Year 1966–1967, 1967; Chicago State Univ., Merit Awd. Recipient, 1979. **Pubns.:** Jt. Auth., "A Survey Report on Public Library Services to Asian Americans," *Jnl. of Lib. & Info. Sci.* (O. 1977). **Activities:** 1, 12; 15, 17, 29; 59, 63, 92 **Addr.:** Documents Center–Rm. 334E, Chicago State University Library, Chicago, IL 60628.

Mandel, Carol Ann (D. 18, 1946, Brooklyn, NY) Assoc. Exec. Dir., ARL, 1979–; Head, Orig. Mono. Cat., Columbia Univ. Libs., 1977–79, Asst. to Head, Orig. Mono. Cat. Dept., 1975–77, Avery Catlgr., 1971–75. **Educ.:** Univ. of MA, 1964–68, BA (Art); Columbia Univ. 1969–70, MSLS, 1973–1975, MA (Art Hist.). **Orgs.:** ALA: Stats. Coord. Com.; Com. on Cat., Descr. and Access. DC LA: Prog. Com. (1980). Art Libs. Socty./N. Amer.: Cat. Adv. Com. (1974–79); Ch. (1975–77). **Honors:** Phi Kappa Phi, Alpha Lamba Delta; Phi Beta Mu. **Activities:** 1; 17, 41, 46; 55, 78 **Addr.:** Association of Research Libraries, 1527 New Hampshire Ave., Washington, DC 20036.

Mandel, George (F. 11, 1921, Cleveland, OH) Chief, Mgt. Srvs. Div., NASA Lewis Resrch. Ctr., 1979–, Asst. to Chief, 1976–79, Chief, Info. & Pubns. Branch, Aero/Space Safety Inst., 1968–76, Asst. Chief, Tech Info. Div., 1961–68, Chief, Lib. Branch, 1953–61. **Educ.:** West. Resrv. Univ., 1939–42, BA (Soclgy./Psy.), 1946–47, BSLS, 1950–53, MA (Soclgy.). **Orgs.:** SLA: Pres., Cleveland Chap. (1958–59); Ch., Engin. Div. (1961–62); Natl. Tech. Transl. Activities Com. (1961–63); Aerospace Div. (Treas., 1974–75; Ch., 1977–78). Intl. Word Prcs. Assn. Socty. for Schol. Publshg. Natl. Bureau of Stan.: Fire Info. Users Working Grp. (1971–73). Western Resrv. Univ. Lib. Sch.: Visit. Com. (1964–65; 1966–67); Alum. Adv. Com. on Rcrt. (1979–80). **Honors:** SLA, John Cotton Data Lect., 1966; NASA, Spec. Achvmt. Awd., 1978. **Pubns.:** NASA Tech. Briefs; various speeches. **Activities:** 4, 12; 17, 34, 37; 52, 62, 91 **Addr.:** NASA Lewis Research Center, M.S. 5-5, 21000 Brookpark Rd., Cleveland, OH 44135.

Mandour, Cecile A. (D. 4, 1926, Port-Said, Egypt) Prin. Cat. Libn., Yale Univ., 1979–, Sr. Cat. Libn., 1974–79, Cat. Libn. I, 1972–74; Biblgphr., Univ. of OK, 1972. **Educ.:** Univ. of OK, 1963–69, BA (Fr., Grmn.), 1969–71, MLS. **Orgs.:** ALA: RTSD/ACRL. NY Tech. Srvs. Libns. Yale Lib. Assocs. **Honors:** Beta Phi Mu. **Activities:** 1; 20; 66, 70, 92 **Addr.:** Yale University Library, Catalogue Dept., Social Sciences Unit, 120 High St., New Haven, CT 06520.

Maness, L. George (D. 13, 1915, Gretna, LA) Asst. Admin., Libn. IV, Jefferson Parish Lib. Syst., 1976–, Asst. Supvsr. of Branches, Libn. II, 1970–76, Order Libn./Circ. Libn. (Lib. II) 1967–69, Br. Libn., Libn. I, 1963–67. **Educ.:** Tulane Univ., 1936–41, BA (Educ.); LA State Univ., 1969–70, MSLS, Hanson Normal Sch., 1934–36, Tchrs. Cert. (Educ.). **Orgs.:** LA LA: Pres. (1974–75); VP (1973–74); Lib. Dev. Com. of LA (1973–75). ALA. Greater New Orleans Lib. Club. **Honors:** Beta Phi Mu, 1970. **Pubns.:** "LA LA President's Report," *LA LA Bltn.* (Sum. 1975). **Activities:** 9; 17, 19; 50, 75 **Addr.:** 1024 Flanders Dr., Metairie, LA 70001.

Maney, James (N. 24, 1945, Oklahoma City, OK) Lib. Dir., Oblate Sch. of Theo., 1981–; Asst. Libn., St. Vincent Semy., Boynton Beach, FL, 1974–80; Asst. Prof. of Hist., Biscayne Coll., 1971–74, Instr. of Hist., 1968–71. **Educ.:** Univ. of Dallas, 1962–65, BA (Hist.); Univ. of Notre Dame, 1965–67, MA (Hist.); FL State Univ., 1979–80, MS (LS). **Orgs.:** ALA. SLA. ATLA. Amer. Hist. Assn. **Honors:** Phi Alpha Theta, 1965; Beta Phi Mu, 1981. **Activities:** 1; 15, 20, 34; 90, 92 **Addr.:** P.O. Box 13583, San Antonio, TX 78213.

Mangan, Elizabeth Unger (Mr. 18, 1945, Cleveland, OH) Head, Data Prep. and Files Maintenance Unit, Geo. and Map Div., Lib. of Congs., 1976–, Map Cat., 1969–76, Spec. Rcrt., 1968–69. **Educ.:** Coll. of Wooster, 1963–67, BA (Math.); Univ. of Pittsburgh, 1967–68, MLS (Info. Sci.). **Orgs.:** ALA: LITA. MAGERT MOUG: Pres. (1980–). Amer. Contract Bridge Leag. **Honors:** Lib. of Congs., Merit. Srv., 1975. **Pubns.:** *Maps: A MARC Format* (1976); *Data Preparation Manual for the Conversion of Map Cataloging Records to Machine-Readable Form* (1971). **Activities:** 4, 12; 17, 20, 24; 56, 70 **Addr.:** Geography and Map Division, Library of Congress, Washington, DC 20540.

Mangion, Marion Blair (My. 25, 1918, Buffalo, NY) Ref. & Bus. Libn., head of dept., Richland Cnty. Pub. Lib., Columbia, SC, 1973–; Dir., Westbrook Coll. Lib., 1971–72; Dir., Deering HS Lib., 1961–71; Asst. Ref. Libn., Portland (ME) Pub. Lib.,

Special Subjects/Services: 50. Adult educ.; 51. Advert./Mktg.; 52. Aerosp.; 53. Agric.; 54. Area std.; 55. Arts/Hum.; 56. Autom.; 57. Bibl./Prtg.; 58. Bio. sci.; 59. Bus./Fin.; 60. Chem.; 61. Copyrt.; 62. Documtn.; 63. Educ.; 64. Engin.; 65. Env.; 66. Eth. grps.; 67. Film; 68. Food/Nutr.; 69. Geneal.; 70. Geo.; 71. Geol.; 72. Handcpd.; 73. Hist.; 74. Int. frdm.; 75. Info. sci.; 76. Insr.; 77. Law; 78. Legis.; 79. Math./Comp. sci.; 80. Med.; 81. Metals; 82. Nat. resrcs.; 83. Newsp.; 84. Nuc. sci.; 85. Oral hist.; 86. Petr./Energy; 87. Pharm.; 88. Phys./Astr./Math.; 89. Readg.; 90. Relig.; 91. Sci./Tech.; 92. Soc. sci.; 93. Telecom.; 94. Transp.; 95. (other).

1956–61; Resrch. Histn., Admin. Hist. Div., US Navy Dept., 1943–50; Instr., Lib. Tech., South. ME Tech. Inst., 1968–72. **Educ.:** Coll. of William & Mary, 1937–41, BA (Europ. Hist.); George Washington Univ., 1943–47 (Hist.); Simmons Coll., 1959–62, MLS; Univ. of South. ME, 1967, 1968 (Medieval Lit.). **Orgs.:** ALA. ME Sch. Lib. Assn.: Exec. Bd. (1968–72). ME LA: Legis. Com. (1968–70). SC LA: Parlmt. (1975–79); Ref. Stat. Com. (1974); Cont. Educ. Com. (1980–82). Other orgs. Leag. of Women Voters. ME Hist. Socty.: Lib. Com. (1967–72). Columbia Musm. of Art. Frnds. of the Lib. **Honors:** Pi Gamma Mu, 1947. **Pubns.:** Ed., *South Portland, Maine, An All America City* (1971); "Westbrook Initiates a Career Program in Library Technology" *Alumnae News,* Westbrook Coll. (Winter 1971); "Library Education in Maine," *Bltn. ME LA* (1969); "Reply and Report to the Governor's Task Force Committee on Libraries," *Bltn. of ME LA* (Ag. 1970). **Activities:** 9, 10; 25, 32, 39; 50, 59, 75 **Addr.:** 2713 Eastlawn Dr., Columbia, SC 29210.

Mangum, Sheila A. (Mr. 21, 1946, Burlington, VT) Head, Acq. Dept., Univ. of N. FL Lib., 1974–; Catlgr., Univ. of FL, 1970–74. **Educ.:** Univ. of VT, 1965–69, BA (Hist.); LA State Univ., 1969–70, MS (Lib. Sci.) **Orgs.:** ALA. SELA. FL Lib. Assn.: Tech. Srvs. Caucus (Ch., 1978–79); Tech. Srvs. Caucus (Vice-Ch., 1977–78, Secty., 1973–75). Duval Cnty. Lib. Assn. Univ. of N. FL Press: Ed. Bd. (1979–). **Activities:** 1; 15, 25, 37; 50, 59 **Addr.:** University of North Florida Library, P.O. Box 17605, Pottsburg Station, Jacksonville, FL 32216.

Manheim, Theodore (Jl. 21, 1921, Detroit, MI) Head, Educ. Lib., Wayne State Univ., 1949–, Asst. Libn., Soc. Sci., 1948–49, Asst. Libn., Circ., 1947. **Educ.:** Wayne State Univ., 1939–43, BA (Educ., LS); Univ. of MI, 1946–47, AB (LS), 1947–48, AM (LS). **Orgs.:** ALA. **Honors:** Wayne State Univ., G. Flint Purdy Meml. Awd., 1976, Pres. Cit. Outstan. Achvmt. and Srv., 1977. **Pubns.:** *Sources in Educational Research* (1969); *Culturally Disadvantaged: A Bibliography and Keyword-out-of-Context Index* (1966); "Curriculum Laboratory Materials," *Choice* (Ja. 1965). **Activities:** 1; 15, 31, 39; 63, 75 **Addr.:** 20230 Annchester Rd., Detroit, MI 48219.

Manheimer, Martha Lose (O. 9, 1921, Fairmont, WV) Prof., SLIS, Univ. of Pittsburgh, 1969–, Resrch. Assoc., KASC, 1967–69, Biblgphr., Eng. Dept., 1966–67. **Educ.:** Carnegie Inst. of Tech., 1939–41; Univ. of IA, 1941–43, BFA (Drama); Univ. of Pittsburgh, 1963, MLS, 1963–69, PhD (LS). **Orgs.:** AALS. ALA. AAUP. **Pubns.:** *OCLC: An Introduction to Searching and Input* (Revised ed., 1981). *Style manual: a guide for the preparation of reports and dissertations* (1973); *Cataloging and Classification: A workbook* (1975, 1980); jt. auth., *Classified Library of Congress Subject Headings* (1972); In *Encyclopedia of Library and Information Science:* "Didot Family," "The Dolphin," "The Estiennes," "The Fleuron," "The Colophon", "Inventories of Books", "The Lamont Classification", "Main Entry". **Activities:** 11; 20 **Addr.:** 650 LIS Bldg., School of Library and Information Sciences, University of Pittsburgh, Pittsburgh, PA 15260.

Maniece, Olivia S. (N. 9, 1929, Gainesville, AL) Chief Lib. Srv., VA Med. Ctr., 1966–; Libn., Druid HS, Tuscaloosa, AL, 1953–66; HS Tchr., West End HS, York, AL, 1950–53. **Educ.:** AL State Univ., Montgomery, 1950–54, BS (Eng.); Univ. of MI, Ann Arbor, 1956–62 (Summ.), AMLS. **Orgs.:** Med. LA: Mem. Com. Hosp. Lib. Sect., (1978–80); Prog. Com. Mem. (1979). AAUP: Ch., Women's Com. (1975–76); Ed. of Nwsltr. (1975–76); Treas. (1977–79). **Activities:** 4; 17, 34; 56, 80 **Addr.:** VA Medical Center, Tuscaloosa, AL 35404.

Manion, Elizabeth Stapleton (N. 3, 1935, Clifton Springs, NY) Pres., Bd. of Trustees, Mid-Hudson Lib. Syst., 1979, 1980, Trustee, 1974–; Pres., Bd. of Trustees and Trustee, Marlboro Free Lib., 1968–79; Tchr. and Libn., Haviland Jr. HS, 1957–60. **Educ.:** SUNY, Albany, 1953–57, BA (Eng.), 1965, MSLS. **Orgs.:** NY State Assn. of Lib. Bds., Adv. Cncl. (1980–). ALA. NY LA. Dutchess Cnty. Med. Socty. Auxiliary. Women in Srv. to Educ., Ulster Cnty. Cmnty. Coll. Vassar Brothers Hosp. Auxiliary. NY State Sch. Bds. Assn. **Addr.:** Western Ave., Marlboro, NY 12542.

Mankin, Carole J. (Je. 24, 1931, Boston, MA) Resrch. Proj. Libn., Treadwell Lib., MA Gen. Hosp., 1975–. **Educ.:** Boston Univ., 1948–52, BA (Psy.); Simmons Coll., 1973–75, MS (LS). Med. LA, 1976, Cert., 1981, Recert. **Orgs.:** Med. LA. New Eng. Reg. Med. Lib. Adv. Cncl.: Funding Srcs. Com. (Ch., 1980–). **Honors:** Phi Beta Kappa, Epsilon MA, 1952. **Pubns.:** Jt. auth., "A Simple Objective Method For Determining a Dynamic Journal Collection," *Bltn. Med. LA* (O. 1980); jt. auth., "An Analysis of the Differences Between Density of Use Ranking and Raw Use Ranking of Library Journal Use," *Jnl. of ASIS* (Ja.–F. 1981). **Activities:** 5, 12; 39, 41; 58, 80 **Addr.:** Treadwell Library, Massachusetts General Hospital, Boston, MA 02114.

Manley, Irwin G. (Ja. 5, 1920, De Smet, SD) Admin., Info. Srvs., Gibson, Dunn & Crutcher, 1979–, Dir. of Libs., 1974–79, Libn., 1968–74; Assoc. Prof. of Law, Law Libn., Sch. of Law, Univ. SD, 1965–68; Fac., Sch. of Paralegal Std., Univ. of W. Los Angeles, 1974–. **Educ.:** SD State Univ., 1938–41; Duke Univ., 1946–48, LLB (Law); AALL 1969 (Cert. Law Libn.). **Orgs.:** Assoc. Info. Mgrs. AALL: Exhibits Com. (1966–69); Mem. Com. (1969–72); Rcrt. Com. (1970–71); Conv. Plng. Com. (1974–76). South. CA. Assn. of Law Libs. (Pres. 1971–72). **Pubns.:** "How to Set Up an On-Line Legal Memorandum Retrieval System," *Manual for Mgt. Law Ofc. Srvs.* (S. 1979). **Activities:** 1, 12; 17, 30; 63, 75, 77 **Addr.:** Gibson, Dunn & Crutcher, 515 South Flower St., Los Angeles, CA 90071.

Manley, Robert Joseph (Ap. 27, 1942, New York, NY) Trustee, W. Islip Pub. Lib., 1978–. **Educ.:** Iona Coll., 1959–63, BA (Span.); St. John's Univ., 1974–78, PhD (Admin.). **Orgs.:** ALA. NY LA. Long Island Task Force on Reg. Resrch. Lib. Srvs. Phi Delta Kappa. W. Islip Cham. Cmrc.: Pres. **Honors:** Phi Delta Kappa, Chap. Young Educ. Awd., 1980. **Pubns.:** "Multilateral Bargaining and Its Outcomes," *SAAYNS Jnl.* (Mr. 1978); "The Impact of the Leadership Behavior of the Principal," *The Principal* (F. 1980); poetry. **Addr.:** National Education Leadership Services, Inc., 816 Union Blvd., West Islip, NY 11795.

Mann, Elizabeth B. (Yale, OK) Asst. Prof., Sch. of Lib. Sci., FL State Univ., 1968–; Adj. Asst. Prof., Coll. of Educ., Univ. of FL, 1975–78; Assoc. Dir. of Lrng. Resrcs., FL Mental Hlth. Inst., 1973–74; Coord. of Lib. Srvs., Polk Cnty. (FL) Sch. Sys., 1962–67. **Educ.:** FL State Univ., 1941–45, AB (Hist.); Carnegie Tech Inst., 1945–46, BSLS; FL State Univ., 1968–69, AMD (Lib. Sci.), 1969–72, PhD (Lib. Sci.). **Orgs.:** ALA: Cncl. Mem. (1967–73); Intl. Frdm. Com. (1971–73); Com. on Chap. Rel. (1967–69); AASL (Sch. Lib. Awards Com., 1970; Stan. Com., 1971–73). (Mem. of the Bd. (1980–). SLA: FL Chap. FL Assn. of Sch. Libns.: Secy. (1956–57); Vice Ch. and Ch. Elect (1959–60); Ch. (1960–61); Merger Com. (1971–73). FL Assn. of Media in Educ.: Leg. Com. Ch. (1973–75). Zonta. Florida Women's Ntwk. PEO Sisterhood. **Honors:** Beta Phi Mu; Kappa Delta Pi; Delta Kappa Gamma. **Pubns.:** "Freedom to Know and Florida's Libraries," FL Conf. Lib. and Info. Srvs. (1978); "The Florida School Library Media Program," *Innovations in Sch. Libnshp.* (Jl/Ag 1972); jt. auth., "The Media Supervisor as an Agent of Change," *Drexel Lib. Qtly.* (Ap. 1977). **Activities:** 10, 12; 17, 26, 45; 63, 78 **Addr.:** School of Library Science, Florida State University, Tallahassee, FL 32306.

Mann, Kathleen A. (S. 15, 1953, Bartow, FL) Info. Srvs. Supvsr., Leon Cnty. Pub. Lib., 1980–; Dir., Bartow Pub. Lib., 1976–80. **Educ.:** Univ. of S. FL, 1972–75, BA (Pol. Sci.); FL State Univ., 1975–76, MLS. **Orgs.:** ALA. FL LA: *FL Libs.* Asst. Ed. (1981–). SELA. **Activities:** 9; 15, 39, 44 **Addr.:** 418 W. 4th Ave., A–8, Tallahassee, FL 32303.

Mann, Ruth J. (N. 2, 1920, Rochester, MN) Hist. of Med. Libn., Mayo Fndn., 1946–; Circ. Asst., Army Med. Lib., 1944–45; Biol. Sci. Div. Libn., Brown Univ., 1941–44. **Educ.:** Univ. of MN, 1938–40, BA (Hist.), Univ. of MN, 1940–41, BS (LS). **Orgs.:** Med. LA: Secy. (1961–62); Ch., Hist. of Med. Grp. (1973–74). Amer. Assn. Hist. of Med. Mayo Fndn. Hist. Med. Socty.: Secy. Treas. (1964–). **Pubns.:** "Cataloging and Classification" in *Handbook of Medical Library Practice* (1970); other articles in hist. of med. **Activities:** 1, 12; 39, 41, 45; 58, 73, 80 **Addr.:** 605 - 11th St. S.W., Rochester, MN 55901.

Mann, Thomas W., Jr. (Ag. 6, 1949, Waukegan, IL) Asst. Lib. Dir., CA State Univ., Long Beach, 1977–; Head, Col. Org. Dept., FL Atl. Univ., 1974–77. **Educ.:** Univ. of IL, Urbana, 1967–71, BA (Hist.), 1971–72, MA (Hist.), 1973–74, MLS. **Orgs.:** ALA: ACRL. CA LA: Acad. Lib. Chap. Amer. Hist. Assn. **Pubns.:** *Planning College and University Library Buildings* (1981); *Shaping Library Collections for the 1980s* (1980); Ed., *Goals & Objectives of the University Library* (1978); "Florida Imprints, 1784," *SLA* (1976). **Activities:** 1; 17, 36, 46; 56 **Addr.:** California State University Library, 1250 Bellflower Blvd., Long Beach, CA 90840.

Manning, Beverley J. (S. 20, 1942, Ticonderoga, NY) Univ. Libn. III, Univ. of CT, Hartford, 1968–; HS Libn., Carmel HS, 1967–68; Elem. Sch. Libn., Bd. of Coop. Educ. Srvs., 1965–67. **Educ.:** SUNY, Albany, 1960–64, BA (Soc. Std.), 1964–66, MLS. **Orgs.:** ALA. CT LA. **Pubns.:** *Index to American Women Speakers, 1828 to 1978* (1980). **Activities:** 1; 15, 20, 29 **Addr.:** University of Connecticut at Hartford, Regional Campus Library, Greater Hartford Campus, West Hartford, CT 06111.

Manning, Josephine Asaro (Jl. 24, 1940, New York, NY) Sr. Libn., Reader's Digest Genl. Bks., 1976–; Sr. Ref. Libn., Fin. Lib., Citibank, 1973–76; Asst. Prof., Lib. Sch., Ctrl. MI Univ., 1972; Libn. and Indexer, Arch., MSS Div., WA State Univ. Lib., 1969–70; Circ. Libn., St. Lawrence Univ., 1966–69; Libn., Park Hill Sch. (E. Syracuse), 1965–66. **Educ.:** Queens College, City Univ. of NY, 1958–63, BA (Eng. Lit.); Syracuse Univ., 1963–65, MSLS; Univ. of CA, Berkeley, 1967 (Lib. Srvcs.). **Orgs.:** SLA: Ed., Pub. Div., *Bulletin* (1981–); V-Ch., NY Chap., Comm. Grp. (1981–). Lib. Party of NY State: Com. Women (1972–). **Honors:** Beta Phi Mu, 1965. **Pubns.:** "Doordarshan Knows Best," *TV Guide* (O. 1979); "Facsimile Transmission," *Lib. Jrnl.,* (O. 1969); "The Mary Martin Rebow Letters, Parts I and II," *The Record* (1971 and 1972). **Activities:** 15, 17, 24, 37, 39; 57, 89, 90, 91 **Addr.:** Reader's Digest, 750 Third Ave., New York, NY 10017.

Manning, Leslie Ann (Ag. 9, 1947, Waltham, MA) Head, Tech. Srvs., Univ. of CO, Colorado Springs, 1976–; Head, Serials Recs., Univ. of NE 1974–76, Ref. Libn., UGL, 1972–74. **Educ.:** Univ. of CO, 1967–69, BA (Eng.); Univ. of Denver, 1970–72, MA (Libnshp.). **Orgs.:** CO LA: Tech. Srvs. RT (Ch., 1978–79). ALA. OCLC, Inc. User Cncl.: BCR Rep. (1979–). **Honors:** Beta Phi Mu, 1972. **Activities:** 1; 17, 44, 46; 56, 75, 93 **Addr.:** University of CO at Colorado Springs Library, Austin Bluffs Pkwy., Colorado Springs, CO 80907.

Manning, Ralph W. (Mr. 1, 1949, Toronto, ON) Asst. Libn., Tech. Srvs., Univ. of Ottawa, 1978–; Chief, Serials and Spec. Material Cat. Div., Natl. Lib. of Canada, 1977–78, Chief, Descrip. Cat. Div., 1976–77, Head, Gvt. Docum. Cat. Sect., 1974–76. **Educ.:** Univ. of Toronto, 1967–71, BA (Mod. Lang.); Univ. of West. ON, 1971–72, MLS; Carleton Univ., 1974–80, MA (Fr.). **Orgs.:** Can. LA: Conv., Tech. Srvs. Coord. Grp. (1978–80). ALA. **Pubns.:** "AACR2 from two viewpoints", *Can. Lib. Jnl.* (D. 1979). **Activities:** 1; 17, 44, 46; 55 **Addr.:** Morisset Library, University of Ottawa, Ottawa, ON K1N 9A5 Canada.

Manning, Robert Lawrence (Je. 4, 1941, Atlanta, GA) Libn., LaFayette Talking Bk. Ctr., 1977–; Libn., GA Reg. Lib. for the Blind and Phys. Handcpd., 1969–71. **Educ.:** Emory Univ., Oglethorpe Univ., 1959–64, AB, cum laude (Hist.); Emory Univ., 1965–66, MLS, 1964–72, MA (Hist.). **Orgs.:** GA LA: RT for the Blind and Phys. Handcpd. (Ch., 1977–79); Pubcty. Com. (1980–81). ALA: ASCLA. Walker Cnty. Interagency Cncl. **Honors:** ALA, John Cotton Dana Awd. for Spec. Libs., 1970, 1978. **Pubns.:** "Chairman's Report: Round Table for the Blind and Physically Handicapped," *The GA Libn.* (N. 1979). **Activities:** 12; 17, 36; 72 **Addr.:** Cherokee Regional Library Talking Book Center, LaFayette, GA 30728.

Manning, S. Patricia (Ag. 30, 1933, Bronx, NY) Chld. Libn., Eastchester Pub. Lib., 1970–; Libn., Hackley Sch., 1969–70. **Educ.:** SUNY, Albany, 1950–54, BA (Eng., Bio.); Pratt Inst., 1965–69, MLS. **Orgs.:** ALA. Westchester LA. Westchester Storytel. Gld. **Activities:** 9; 21, 42 **Addr.:** c/o Eastchester Public Library, 11 Oak Ridge Pl., Eastchester, NY 10709.

Mansbach, Carolyn E. (S. 5, 1938, New York, NY) Dir., Med. Lib., Jamaica Hosp., 1963–; Asst Me. Libn., Mem. Sloan Kettering Cancer Ctr., 1961–62. **Educ.:** City Coll. of NY, 1956–60, BS (Bio.); Columbia Univ., 1960–61, MLS; LSe Med. LA Cert., 1962. **Orgs.:** Brooklyn, Queens, & Staten Is. Hlth Sci. Libns.: Prog. Ch. (1979–); Pres. (1977–79). Med. Libs. of Long Island. Member Med. LA: NY Reg. Gp; Hosp. Lib. Gp., Com. on Small Hlth. Sci. Libns. Reg. Med. Lib.: Subcom. on Educ. **Honors:** Me. LA; Schol., 1961. **Pubns.:** "Making the Most of Library Space," audio-cassette (1976). **Activities:** 12; 15, 17, 39; 58, 80 **Addr.:** Jamaica Hospital, Medical Library, 89th Avenue & Van Wyck Expy., Jamaica, NY 11418.

Mansbridge, John (N. 13, 1935, Essex, Eng.) Coll. Libn., Selkirk Coll., 1966–, Asst. Coll. Libn., 1965–66; Ref. Libn., Moose Jaw Pub. Lib., 1964–65. **Educ.:** Univ. of Ottawa, 1952–55, BA; McGill Univ., 1963–64, BLS, 1970–71, MLS; Case West. Resrv. Univ., 1977–78. **Orgs.:** Can. LA. BC LA: Dir. (1976–77). ASIS. **Pubns.:** "Selkirk College: A Photo Essay," *BC Lib. Qtly.* (Jl. 1970). **Activities:** 1; 17, 34, 39; 75 **Addr.:** Selkirk College, Box 1200, Castlesar, BC V1N 3J1 Canada.

Mansfield, Jerry W. (Ja. 26, 1952, Garrett, IN) Asst. Eng. Libn./Asst. Prof. of Lib. Sci., Purdue Univ., 1978–; Ref. Lib./Instr., GA State Univ., 1975–78. **Educ.:** Hanover Coll., 1970–74, BA (Fr.); Univ. of KY, 1974–75, MSLS. **Orgs.:** ALA. IN. Jr. Mem. RT. (Pres., 1980–81). SLA. IN LA. Amer. Socty. for Eng. Educ. Festival Singers of Lafayette, Inc: Pres. (1979–80). **Pubns.:** "A Queueing Model for Library Circulation Desk" *Amer. Inst. for Decision Scis.* (March 1981); "G.I. Joe, Raggedy Ann and Friends," *GA Libn.* (1976); "Supervisory Training," *Jnl. of Educ. for Libnshp.* (Win. 1977); "Human Factors of Queuing" *Jrnl. of Acad. Libnshp.* (Ja. 1981). Review. **Activities:** 1, 12; 22, 39, 46; 64, 91 **Addr.:** Potter Center/Purdue University, West Lafayette, IN 47907.

Manson, Bill B. (D. 30, 1945, Orange, CA) Asst. Dir., Comnty. Srvs., Calgary Pub. Lib., 1977–, Head, Ext. Srvs. 1975–77; Instr. Sr., Lib. Arts, S. AB Inst. of Tech., 1971–75; Libn. 2, Univ. of Calgary, 1968–71. **Educ.:** Rockford Coll., 1963–67, BA (Eng.); Drexel Inst. of Tech., 1967–68, MSLS. **Orgs.:** Lib. Assn. of AB: Pres. (1976–77), Int. Frdm. Com. (Ch., 1975–77), *Bulletin* ed. (1971–72). Can. LA: Int. Frdm. Com. (1973–75, 1977–). **Activities:** 9; 17, 19, 27; 72, 74, 78 **Addr.:** 616 Macleod Trail S.E., Calgary, AB T2G 2M2 Canada.

Mansur, Ovad M. (N. 14, 1937, Jerusalem, Israel) Asst. Prof., Comp. and Info. Sci., Cleveland State Univ., 1978–; Dir. of Econ. Resrch. Stats. and Long Range Plng., Israel Ports Athrty., 1972–74; Dir., Syst. Anal. and Prog., Natl. Insr. Inst., 1970–72, Syst. Anal., Proj. Mgr., 1966–70. **Educ.:** Hebrew Univ., 1961–65, BA (Econ. Stats.), 1965–69, MBA; Case West. Rsv. Univ., 1974–77, PhD (Info. Sci.). **Orgs.:** ASIS. Assn. for Comp. Mach.: Cleveland Chap., Educ. Com. (1979–80). Data Prcs. Mgt. Assn. Fncl. Mgt. Assn. **Honors:** Israel Gvt. Efficiency Com., Highest Com. Awd., 1969. **Pubns.:** "An Associative Search Strategy for

PROFESSIONAL ACTIVITIES: Institutions: 1. Acad. lib.; 2. Arch.; 3. Assn.; 4. Fed./Gvt. lib.; 5. Inst. lib.; 6. Mfr./Suppl.; 7. Milit. lib.; 8. Musm.; 9. Pub. lib.; 10. Sch. lib.; 11. Sch. of lib. sci.; 12. Spec. lib.; 13. State lib.; 14. (other). **Functions/Activities:** 15. Acq./Col. dev.; 16. Adult srvs.; 17. Admin.; 18. Apprais.; 19. Archit./Bldgs.; 20. Cat./Class.; 21. Chld. srvs.; 22. Circ.; 23. Cons./Pres.; 24. Consult.; 25. Cont. ed.; 26. Educ. lib. sci.; 27. Ext. srvs.; 28. Fund/Grants; 29. Gvt. pubs.; 30. Indx./Abs.; 31. Instr. lib. use; 32. Media srvs.; 33. Micro.; 34. Netwks./Coop.; 35. Persnl.; 36. PR; 37. Publshg.; 38. Recs. mgt.; 39. Ref. srvs.; 40. Repro.; 41. Resrch.; 42. Review.; 43. Secur.; 44. Serials; 45. Spec. col.; 46. Tech. srvs.; 47. Trustees/Bds.; 48. YA srvs.; 49. (other).

Information Retrieval," *Info. Prcs. and Mgt.* (1980); "On Selection and Combining of Relevance Indicators," *Info. Prcs. and Mgt.* (1980). **Activities:** 11; 24, 41; 56, 63, 75 **Addr.:** Computer and Information Science Dept., Cleveland State University, Cleveland, OH 44115.

Manzer, Bruce Monroe (Ap. 8, 1936, Ballston Spa, NY) Head Libn., Univ. Coll., Bahrain, 1981–; Sci. Libn., IL State Univ., 1979–81, Serials Catlgr., IL State Univ., 1974–79; Ed., Access, Chem. Abs. Srv., 1967–70; Asst. Libn., Tech. Proc. Lawrence Radiation Lab. Univ. of CA, 1966–67; Libn., Inorganic Chem. Div., The Glidden Co., (1964–66); Acq. Libn., Battelle Meml. Inst., (1962–64); various tchg. positions. **Educ.:** Union Coll., 1955–59, BS (Chem.); Univ. of MI, 1959–60, AMLS; Univ. of Chicago, 1970–73, PhD (LS). **Orgs.:** ALA. Fulbright Alum. Assn. **Honors:** Beta Phi Mu, 1960; Fulbright tchg. grant, Cairo Univ., Cairo, Egypt, 1978–79. **Pubns.:** Ed., *Chemical Abstracts Service Source Index (CASSI)* (1969); *The Abstract Journal, 1790–1920: Origin, Development, and Diffusion* (1977). **Activities:** 1, 12; 15, 39, 46; 54, 62, 91 **Addr.:** P.O. Box 1082, Bahrain, Arabian Gulf.

Mapp, Erwin E. (S. 13, 1923, La Grange, GA) Lib. & Geneal. Consult., 1978–; Consult., Pub. Lib. Div., TN State Lib. & Arch., 1972–77; Dir., Jackson Mncpl. Lib., 1966–72; Tech. Lib. Dir., Research Division West Point-Pepperell Co., 1965–66; Chief Libn., SUNY Ag. & Tech. Coll., Alfred, 1962–65; Dir., Lanier Lake Reg. Lib., 1954–62; Branch Asst., Brooklyn Pub. Lib., 1953–54; Asst., B&I Div., Atlanta Pub. Lib., 1951–53. **Educ.:** LA State Univ., 1947–50, BA (Eng.), 1950–51, BS (LS); George Peabody Coll., 1977–78, MLIS. **Orgs.:** ALA. SELA. MS LA: Ch., Int. Frdm. Com. (1968). SLA: LA Chap., Pres. (1970). **Honors:** MS Natl. Lib. Week, Spec. Awd., 1970. **Pubns.:** "Jackson, Miss.", *Encyclopedia Americana* (1970). **Activities:** 9; 17 **Addr.:** PO Box 1315, Smyrna, GA 30081.

Marble, Beatrice N. (Syracuse, NY) Head, Art and Msc. Dept., Onondaga Cnty. Pub. Lib., 1972–, Asst. Ref. Libn., 1969–71, Libn., 1966–68; Med. Photographer, Rochester Gen. Hosp., 1952–54; Optical Lens Comp., Bausch and Lomb Optical Co., 1944–51. **Educ.:** Syracuse Univ., 1940–43, AB (Phys.), 1965–66, MLS. **Orgs.:** ALA. NY LA. ARLIS/NA. **Honors:** Beta Phi Mu. **Activities:** 9; 16, 22; 55 **Addr.:** Art and Music Dept., Onondaga County Public Library, 335 Montgomery St., Syracuse, NY 13205.

Marble, Lawrence W. (O. 10, 1938, Fitchburg, MA) Educ. Ref. Libn. and Biblgphr., Temple Univ., 1975–; Dir. of Libs., Lesley Coll., 1968–75. **Educ.:** Tufts Univ., 1956–60, AB (Soc.); Keene State Coll., 1962–63, MEd (Educ.); Simmons Coll., 1966–67, MS LS; Inst. in Indian Hist. and Cult., 1965. **Orgs.:** ALA: ACRL/Educ. and Bhvl. Sci. Sect. (1977–79). AAUP. **Activities:** 1; 15, 31, 39; 63 **Addr.:** 4825 Germantown Ave., Philadelphia, PA 19144.

Marchant, Maurice P. (Ap. 20, 1927, Peoa, UT) Dir., Sch. of Lib. & Info. Sci., Brigham Young Univ., 1969–; Branch Libn., Ann Arbor Pub. Lib., 1966–69; City Libn., Carnegie Free Lib., Ogden, UT, 1958–66; Head Libn., Tech. Lib., Dugway Proving Ground, UT, 1953–58. **Educ.:** Univ. of UT, 1944–49, BA (Eng.), 1950–53, MS (LS); Univ. of MI, 1965–66, AMLS, 1968, MA (Higher Ed), 1970, PhD (Higher Ed). **Orgs.:** ALA: LED Resrch. Com. (Ch., 1977–78); Chap. Rel. Com. (1981–82); LRRT Forums Com. (Ch., 1980–81). AALS: Cont. Educ. Com. (1972–79). UT LA: Pres. (1964–65); Exec. Bd. (1963–66). CLENE. Other orgs. AAUP. Sigma Xi. Phi Kappa Phi. **Honors:** UT LA, Acad. Sect., Disting. Srv. Awd., 1977; ALA, LRRT, Best Resrch. Paper Awd., 1975. **Pubns.:** *SPSS as a Library Research Tool* (1978); *Participative Management in Academic Libraries* (1977); "University Libraries as Economic Systems," *Coll. & Resrch. Libs.* (N. 1975); "Participative Management as Related to Personnel Development," *Library Trends* (Jl. 1971); "Library School Instruction in Discrimination Awareness," *Amer. Libs.* (Ja. 1979); other articles. **Activities:** 11; 17, 26, 41; 74 **Addr.:** 2877 North 220 East, Provo, UT 84601.

Marchese, Marie-Ann (D. 5, 1945, New York, NY) Head Libn., Lexington Sch. for the Deaf, 1968–. **Educ.:** St. John's Univ., 1961–65, BS (Educ.), 1965–67, MLS; Queens Coll., 1977–79, Prof. Dip. (LS, Educ. Admin., Supvsn.). **Orgs.:** NY LA. ALA. Queens Boro. Pub. Lib. Hearing Impaired Prog. Adv. Bd. **Activities:** 10, 12; 17, 20, 21 **Addr.:** Lexington School for the Deaf, 30th Ave. and 75th St., Jackson Heights, NY 11370.

Marchiafava, Louis J. (Jl. 24, 1940, New Orleans, LA) Head, Archs. and Ms. Dept., Houston Pub. Lib., 1976–; Coord., Oral Hist. Prog., Houston Metro. Archs. and Resrch. Ctr., 1974–76; Tchg. Asst., Rice Univ., 1972–73; Case Worker and Supvsr., LA State Welfare Dept., 1967–69. **Educ.:** LA State Univ., 1958–64, BA (Hist.); Rice Univ., 1965–69, MA (Hist.), 1976, PhD (Hist.). **Orgs.:** Socty. of SW Archvsts. Oral Hist. Assn. TX State Hist. Assn. S. Hist. Assn. Harris Cnty. Hist. Socty.: VP. **Pubns.:** *The Houston Police, 1878–1948* (1977); "The Police Reform Movement in Houston, 1945–48," *E. TX Hist. Jnl.*, (Sp. 1975). **Activities:** 2, 9; 15, 23, 41; 73, 85, 92 **Addr.:** 4130 Levonshire Dr., Houston, TX 77025.

Marchman, Watt P. (S. 1, 1911, Eatonton, GA) Dir. Emeritus, The Rutherford B. Hayes Lib. and Musm., 1980–, Dir., 1946–80; Dir. of Resrch., The Rutherford B. Hayes and Lucy Webb Hayes Fndn., 1946–80; Libn., Exec. Secy., The FL Hist. Socty., 1939–42; Archvst., Rollins Coll., 1935–40; Dir., Alum. Place. Srv., Rollins Coll., 1937–40. **Educ.:** Rollins Coll., 1929–33, AB (Amer. Lit.), 1935–37, MA (Amer. Hist.). **Orgs.:** FL LA: Treas. (1942). Martha Kinney Cooper Ohioana LA: Trustee (1970–80). Birchard Pub. Lib.: Trustee (1968–), Secy. (1968–). Ms. Socty.: VP (1950–64). Rotary Club. **Honors:** OH Acad. of Hist., Merit Awd., 1969; Martha Kinney Cooper Ohioana LA, Merit Cit., 1971; Findlay Coll., Doctor of Humane Letters, 1980. **Pubns.:** Ed., *Hayes Hist. Jnl.* (1976–80); "Rutherford B. Hayes," *World Bk. Encyc.* (1962–); various mono., articles on hist. **Activities:** 2, 14-Pres. ctr. **Addr.:** 534 Crestwood Ave., Fremont, OH 43420.

Marco, Guy Anthony (O. 4, 1927, New York, NY) Dir., Prof. Div. of Lib. Sci., San Jose State Univ., 1981–; Partner, Dir. for N. Amer., Lib. Devel. Consult., 1979–81; Chief, Gen. Ref. and Bibl. Div., Lib. of Congs., 1977–78; Dean, Prof., Sch. of Lib. Sci., Kent State Univ., 1960–77; Libn., Instr. in Human. and Msc., Amundsen Jr. Coll., 1957–60; Asst. Libn., Circ. and Serials, Wright Jr. Coll., 1954–56; Asst., Classics Lib., Univ. of Chicago, 1952. **Educ.:** Amer. Cons. of Msc., 1947–51, B.Msc.; DePaul Univ., 1947–50; Univ. of Chicago, 1952, MA Msc.; 1955, MA LS; 1956, PhD (Msc.). **Orgs.:** ALA: Cncl (1968–71); Com. on Intl Lib. Sch. (Ch., 1968–71); Intl Lib. Educ. Com. (Ch., 1973–74, 1976–77); Com. on Accred. (1977–79). Intl. Assn. of Msc Libs. Msc LA: Ch., Midwest Chap. (1966–68); Coord. of Inter-Assn. Rel. (1968–71); Cont. Educ. Com.; various Other Orgs. **Honors:** OH LA, Merit Cit., 1970. **Pubns.:** Jt. auth., *Information on Music* (1975, 1977); Trans., *The Art of Counterpoint; Part Three of Le Istitutioni harmoniche, 1558* (1968); (Paperback ed., NY: Norton, 1976). **Activities:** 4, 11; 17, 24, 26; 55, 57 **Addr.:** 998 Meridian Ave., San Jose, CA 95126.

Marcotte, Joan M. (Ap. 6, 1953, Providence, RI) Educ. Srvs. Libn., Univ. of TN Ctr. for the Hlth. Sci. Lib., 1976–. **Educ.:** Brown Univ., 1971–75, AB (Math.); Univ. of RI, 1975–76, MLS; Med. LA, 1980, (Cert.). **Orgs.:** Med. LA: Mem. Com. (1979–80); Ch., Southern Reg. Grp. Mem. Com. (1979–80). TN LA: Staff Dev./Recruit. Com. (1978–80); JMRT (1979–80); Pres., JMRT (1978–80). AAUP: Ch. Univ. of TN Ctr. for the Hlth. Sci. Chap. Nom. Com. (1979–80). **Honors:** Beta Phi Mu, 1979. **Pubns.:** Cont., *The expected role of beginning librarians* (1979). Computer-Asst. Instr. Lesson. **Activities:** 1, 11; 25, 31, 35; 58, 60, 80 **Addr.:** 978 Buford Ellington Dr. W., Memphis, TN 38111.

Marcum, Deanna B. (Ag. 5, 1946, Salem, IN) Prog. Assoc., Cncl. on Lib. Resrcs., 1981–; Sr. Consult., Info. Syst. Consult. Inc., 1980–81; Trng. Prog. Spec., ARL, 1977–80; Asst. Dir., Jt. Univ. Libs., 1976–77, Dir. of Resrch. & Dev., 1974–76; Acq. Libn., Univ. of KY, 1972–74, Cat. Libn., 1970–72. **Educ.:** Univ. of IL, 1964–66, BA (Eng.); South. IL Univ., 1968–69, MA; Univ. of KY, 1969–70, MLS. **Orgs.:** ALA: RTSD RS Policy & Resrch. (1972–75); Instr. in use of Lib. (1976–77); ACRL Nom. Com. (1977–78); RTSD By-laws Com. (1978–79). DC LA. SELA. Amer. Socty. for Trng. & Dev. **Honors:** ALA, Students to Dallas, 1971. **Pubns.:** *Resource Note book on Staff Development* (1979); "Staff Development," *ALA Yearbook* (1978, 1979, 1980); "Guinea Pigs & Goals," *Lib. Jnl.* (Ag. 1971). **Activities:** 1; 24, 26, 35 **Addr.:** 622 Ellsworth Dr., Silver Spring, MD 20910.

Marcus, Joan E. (D. 16, 1948, St. Louis, MO) Libn., Corporate Dev. Spec., Human Dev. Corp. of Metro. St. Louis, 1976–; Head Catlgr., MO Botanical Garden, 1973–75. **Educ.:** Univ. of MO, St. Louis, 1967–71, BA (Soclgy.); Univ. of MO, Columbia, 1971–72, MA (LS). **Orgs.:** MO LA. Jewish Cmnty. Ctrs. Assn. **Activities:** 12, 14-Non profit anti-poverty agency; 17, 28, 41; 92, 95-Poverty urban issues. **Addr.:** 18 Country Squire Ct., Creve Coeur, MO 63141.

Marcus, Richard S. (Jl. 26, 1933, Atlantic City, NJ) Prtn. Resrch. Sci., MA Inst. of Tech., 1967–; Syst. Engin., Itek Corp., 1962–67. **Educ.:** Univ. of PA, 1951–55, BS (Engin.); MA Inst. of Tech., 1955–58, MS (Engin.). **Orgs.:** ASIS. Assn. Computational Ling. Assn. Comp. Mach. MA Gov. Conf. Lib. Info. Syst. **Pubns.:** "Catalog Information and Text as Indicators of Relevance", *Jnl. of the Amer. Socty. for Info. Sci.* (Ja. 1978); "Retrieval Parameters in Growing Data Bases," *Jasis* (S. 1972); "Experiments and Analysis on a Computer Interface to an Information Retrieval Network", *M.I.T. LIDS Report* (1979); "A Translating Computer Interface for End-User Operation of Heterogeneous Retrieval Systems," *Jnl. of the Amer. Socty. for Info. Sci.* (Jl. 1981). **Activities:** 14-Univ.; 41; 64, 75, 93 **Addr.:** Massachusetts Institute of Technology, Laboratory for Information and Decision Systems, Room 35-414, Cambridge, MA 02319.

Marcus, Richard W. (Jl. 3, 1950, New York, NY) Dir. and Head Libn., Norman and Helen Asher Lib., Spertus Coll. of Judaica, 1975–; Asst. Archvst., Zionist Arch. and Lib., 1972–75. **Educ.:** Brooklyn Coll., 1967–71, BA (Hist.); Columbia Univ., 1971–74, MA (Jewish Hist.); 1974–75, (MSLS). **Orgs.:** SAA: Audit. Com. (Ch., 1977–). ALA. AJL. Cncl. on Arch. and Resrch. Libs. in Jewish Std.: Arch. Com. (Treas., Ch., 1980–). **Pubns.:** Review. **Activities:** 1, 2; 15, 17, 23; 66, 90, 95-Judaica. **Addr.:** Asher Library, Spertus College of Judaica, 618 S. Michigan Ave., Chicago, IL 60605.

Marcy, Henry Orlando 4th (Ag. 27, 1938, Boston, MA) Comsn. of Finance, State of VT, 1981–, Comsn. of Budget and Mgt., 1981, Dir. of Budget & Mgt. Oper., 1977–81, Budget & Mgt. Anal., 1976–77, Dir. of Lib. Users Srvs., Dept. of Libs., 1971–76; Dir. VT State Bibl. Ctr., 1969–71; Instr., Simmons Coll. Sch. of LS, 1966–69. **Educ.:** Harvard Coll., 1956–60, AB (Hist.); Columbia Univ., 1960–62, MA (Tchg. & Hist.); Simmons Coll., 1963–66, SM (LS). **Orgs.:** ALA. New Eng. LA: Cncl. (1973–75); Schol. Com. (1971–75, Ch., 1973–75). VT LA: Treas. (1973–1974), Grievance Com. (Ch., 1973–77) co-ch., conf. (1981). Amer. Socty. for Pub. Admin.: Pres., VT Chap. (1979–80). **Honors:** New Eng. LA: Merit. Srv. Awd., 1975. **Pubns.:** "Would You Believe One Reference Instructor," *Ref. Qtly.* (Sum. 1967); Ed., *VT Libs.* (1972–76); "Interlibrary Cooperation and Coordination in Vermont," *Cath. Lib. World* (Mr. 75). **Activities:** 13; 17, 20, 34; 59, 63, 75 **Addr.:** 14 Summer St., Apt. 17, St. Johnsbury, VT 05819.

Marcy, Jean F. (Madden) (Ja. 3, 1944, Boston, MA) Libn., St. Johnsbury Athenaeum, 1973–; Asst. Libn., Reading (MA) Pub. Lib., 1970–73; Lib. Sci. Libn., Simmons Coll., 1966–70, Instr., Sch. of LS, 1968–70. **Educ.:** Simmons Coll., 1961–65, SB (Psy./Soclgy.), 1965–66, SM (LS). **Orgs.:** VT LA: Co-ch., conf. (1981); Treas. (1977, 1978); Nom. Com. (Ch., 1975); Int. Frdm. Com. (1973–1976); Secy.-Treas., Pub. Lib. Sect. (1975, 1976). New Eng. LA: Ch., Bylaws Com. (1975/76 & 1976/77), PR Com. (1981). ALA. New England Lib. Bd. Panel of Counsellors: Exec. Com. (1979–80). **Activities:** 9; 16, 17 **Addr.:** St. Johnsbury Athenaeum, 30 Main St., St. Johnsbury, VT 05819.

Margeton, Stephen G. (Mr. 22, 1945, Elizabeth, NJ) Head Law Libn., Steptoe and Johnson, 1972–; Asst. Ref. Libn., Amer. Brit. Law Div., Lib. of Congs., 1970–72. **Educ.:** Mt. St. Mary's Coll., 1963–67, AB (Eng.), George Washington Univ., 1967–70, JD, Cath. Univ., 1971–73, MSLS. **Orgs.:** AALL. ASIS. SLA. Law Libn. Socty. of DC. Various other orgs. **Pubns.:** "Documents of the Federal Trade Commission," *Law Lib. Jnl.* (1976); "Continuing Education for Law Librarianship," *Law Lib. Jnl.* (1977). **Addr.:** Library Steptoe and Johnson, 1250 Connecticut Ave., N.W., Washington, DC 20036.

Margolis, Bernard A. (O. 2, 1948, Greenwich, CT) Dir., SE MI Reg. Film Lib., 1976–; Dir., Monroe Cnty. Lib. Syst., 1976–, Deputy Dir., 1973–75; Dir., Raisin Valley Lib. Syst., 1976–1978, Asst. Dir., 1974–75; Branch Head, VA Village Lib, Denver Pub. Lib., 1972–73. **Educ.:** Univ. of Denver, 1966–70, BA (Pol. Sci.), 1971–73, MA(LS); Univ. of MI, Masters in Pub. Admin. in progress. **Orgs.:** Alliance of Info. & Referral Srvs.: Natl. Memb. Coord. ALA: PLA, Info. & Referral Srvs. Com.; Hlth. & Rehab. Lib. Srvs. Div., Mem. Promotion Com. MI LA: Second VP (1978–79); Ch., AV Div. (1976–77). MI Lib. Cnsrtm.: Exec. Cncl. (1977–80); Treas. (1980). Other orgs. Natl. Assn. of Educ. Broadcasters. Urban & Reg. Info. Syst. Assn. MI Leag. for Human Srvs. **Pubns.:** "Graphic Services Center", *Lib. Jnl. Spec. Reports* (1979); "A Public Library: Serving the Developmentally Disabled", *Amer. Rehab.* (O. 1979); "Symbiosis in the Provision of Information & Referral Services", *Proc. of the Alliance of Information & Referral Services* (1976); "Those New Fangled Machines", *MI Libn.* (Sum. 1976); "Obscenity Legislation - A Review", *MI Libn.* (Fall 1975). **Activities:** 9, 14-Film Library; 17, 28, 35; 56, 67, 95-Developmentally Disabled. **Addr.:** Monroe County Library System, 3700 S. Custer Rd., Monroe, MI 48161.

Marik, Margaret Jane (Ap. 28, 1943, Philadelphia, PA) Assoc. Dir., Dev., Marquette Univ., 1981–; State Prog. Coord., LS, Univ. of WI, Ext., 1980–81; Dir., Midwest Reg. Fndn. Coll., Marquette Univ., 1977–80; Dir., Med. Lib., Elmbrook Meml. Hosp., 1973–77. **Educ.:** Old Dominion Univ., 1965–69, BA (Hist.); San Jose State Univ., 1971–77, MLS. **Orgs.:** Med. LA: Ch. Patient Educ (1978). WI LA. WI Hlth. Sci. LA: Area rep. (1979). Lib. Cncl. of Metro. WI: Ch., Cont. Educ. Com. (1978–79). WI Women's Network. Amer. Angus Assn. Natl. Org. for Women. Amer. Assn. of Univ. Admin. Chap. Secy.-Treas. (1979). **Pubns.:** *Foundations in Wisconsin; a Directory* (1977, 1978); "The Foundation Collection of Marquette Univ.," *WI Lib. Bltn.* (Mr. 1980); "Ready Reference in Health Science Libraries" in *Basic Library Management for Health Science Librarians* (1978). **Activities:** 1, 12; 25, 28, 39; 50, 80, 95-Fndns. **Addr.:** Marquette University, 1217 W. Wisconsin Ave., Milwaukee, WI 53233.

Marín, Christine (D. 28, 1943, Globe, AZ) Coord., Chicano Std. Coll., Hayden Lib. AZ State Univ., 1970–, Bibl., 1968–70, Clerk, 1967–68. **Educ.:** AZ State Univ., Tempe, 1961–74, BA (Eng.), (His.), 1981, MA. **Orgs.:** REFORMA: AZ Chap. (1978–80). AZ State LA: Srvcs. to the Spanish-Speaking Roundtable (1979–80). AZ Hist. Socty.(1977–80). AZ State Univ.: Chicano Fac. and Staff Assn. (1970–80). AZ State Univ. Latin Amer.: Ctr. for Latin Amer. Std. (1972–80). AZ Chicano Mobile Inst.: Adv. Bd. (1972–76). **Pubns.:** *A Spokesman of the Mexican-American Movement:* (1977); "The Mexican-American War Heroes of Silvis, Illinois," *Jnl. of Mex.-Amer. Hist.* (1980); Reviews. "Go Home, Chicanos," *An Awakened Minority:* (1974).

Special Subjects/Services: 50. Adult educ.; 51. Advert./Mktg.; 52. Aerosp.; 53. Agric.; 54. Area std.; 55. Arts/Hum.; 56. Autom.; 57. Bibl./Prtg.; 58. Bio. sci.; 59. Bus./Fin.; 60. Chem.; 61. Copyrt.; 62. Documtn.; 63. Educ.; 64. Engin.; 65. Env.; 66. Eth. grps.; 67. Film; 68. Food/Nutr.; 69. Geneal.; 70. Geo.; 71. Geol.; 72. Handcpd.; 73. Hist.; 74. Int. frdm.; 75. Info. sci.; 76. Insr.; 77. Law; 78. Legis.; 79. Math./Comp. sci.; 80. Med.; 81. Metals; 82. Nat. resrcs.; 83. Newsp.; 84. Nuc. sci.; 85. Oral hist.; 86. Petr./Energy; 87. Pharm.; 88. Phys./Astr./Math.; 89. Readg.; 90. Relig.; 91. Sci./Tech.; 92. Soc. sci.; 93. Telecom.; 94. Transp.; 95. (other).

Activities: 1, 2; 15, 39, 41; 66, 83, 85 **Addr.:** 1614 West Belfast St., Mesa, AZ 85201.

Marin, Federico Emilio (F. 4, 1922, Havana, Cuba) Ref. Libn. III, Univ. of PR, Mayagüez, 1980–, Circ. Libn., Chief, 1976–80, Spec. Proj. Libn., 1974–76, Serials Libn., Chief, 1970–74; Asst. Serials Libn., TX A&M Univ., 1968–70. **Educ.:** Inst. of Havana, 1937–41, BS (Sci.); Univ. of Havana, 1943–48, DL; KS State Tchrs. Coll., 1967–68, MLS. **Orgs.:** SBPR. **Pubns.:** "La Biblioteca del Futuro," *Boletin de la SBPR* (1974); "Juan Rius Rivera," *El Reg.* (O. 9, 1974); "Conozca su Biblioteca" videotape (1980). **Activities:** 1; 39, 44; 75 **Addr.:** P.O. Box 5195, College Station, Mayagüez, PR 00709.

Marinelli, Anne V. (Hibbing, MN) Retired, 1973–; Head Libn., Hibbing Jr. Coll., 1960–73; Assoc. Prof., Grad. Sch. Lib. Sci., TX Woman's Univ., 1956–60; Asst. Prof., Grad. Sch. Lib. Sci., FL State Univ., 1953–55; Biblgphr., Univ. of IL, 1945–52; Head, Libs., Chishom Pub. Schs., 1944–45; Head, Cat. Dept., Scoville Lib., Carleton Coll., 1938–44; various positions as libn., Coll. of St. Teresa, New York Pub. Lib., 1930–38. **Educ.:** Hibbing Jr. Coll., 1925–27, Dip.; Univ. of WI, 1927–29, BA (Hist., Soc. Sci., Fr.); Columbia Univ., 1930–31, BS (LS); Univ. of IL, 1948, MA (LS, Italian); Univ. of Perugia, Italy, 1951, Dip.; Gen. Srvs. Admin., Natl. Arch. and Rec. Srv., 1959 (Arch. Mgt.); various grad. crs. **Orgs.:** AALS. ALA: RT on Lib. Srv. Abroad; various com. Associazione per le Biblioteche Italiane. Various orgs. Italian—Amer. Fndn. Amer.—Italian Hist. Assn. Univ. of IL Alum. Assn. Metro. Musm. of Art. Various orgs. **Honors:** Univ. of Roma, Italy, Fulbright Lectr., 1951–52; Italian Repub., Knighthood in Ord. of the Star of Solidarita, 1975; Beta Phi Mu; other hons. **Pubns.:** *Seminari di Biblioteconomia* (1952); "The State Public Libraries of Italy," *Lib. Qtly.* (Ap. 1955); "La imprenta en las Colonias angloamericanas," *Biblioteconomia* Spain (Ja. 1957); Cmplr., *A Bibliography of U S Literature Dated 1901–1952 Concerning Italian Libraries, Books and Related Phases* (1954); Cmplr., *Don Luigi Sturzo; a Bibliographical Contribution of United States published Works* (1954); various bk. reviews, articles. **Activities:** 1; 17, 20, 24; 57, 63, 75 **Addr.:** 909 Minnesota St., Hibbing, MN 55746.

Marion, Donald James (My. 5, 1939, Youngstown, OH) Phys. Libn., Univ. of MN, Minneapolis, 1970–. **Educ.:** PA Tech. Inst., 1956–58, AS (Electrical Engin.); OH State Univ., 1963–67, BA (Pol. Sci.); Univ. of Chicago, 1967–70, MA (LS). **Orgs.:** SLA. CSLA. AAAS: Info. and Comm. Sect. **Activities:** 1; 15, 31, 39; 52, 88, 73 **Addr.:** Physics Library, University of Minnesota, 116 Church St., S.E., Minneapolis, MN 55455.

Marion, Phyllis Castle (Ap. 28, 1944, Jackson, MI) Asst. Libn., Univ. of MN Law Lib., 1981–; Head Catlgr., 1970–; Catlgr., Univ. of Chicago Law Lib., 1967–70. **Educ.:** MI State Univ., 1962–66, BA (Eng.); Univ. of Chicago, 1966–68, MA (LS). **Orgs.:** AALL: Cat. and Class. Com. (Ch., 1977–80); Tech. Srvs. Spec. Int. Sect. (Ch., 1978–); Com. on Indexing of Per. Lit. (1979–). ALA. MN Assn. of Law Libs.: Pres. (1971–73). **Honors:** Beta Phi Mu, 1969. **Pubns.:** "Sources for Determining Citation Practice for Court Reports Throughout the World," *Lib. Resrcs. and Tech. Srvs.* (Ap.-Je. 1981); "Planning for change: AACR2," *Law Lib. Jnl.* (N. 1978). **Activities:** 1, 12; 20, 44, 46; 77, 78, 92 **Addr.:** University of Minnesota, Law Library, 229 19th Ave., S., Minneapolis, MN 55455.

Marke, Julius J. (Ja. 12, 1913, New York, NY) Law Libn., Prof. of Law, New York Univ., 1942–, Interim Dean of Libs., 1975–77. **Educ.:** Coll. of The City of New York, 1930–34, BSS (Soc. Sci.); New York Univ., 1939–37, JD (Law); Columbia Univ., 1940–42, MS in LS. **Orgs.:** AALL: Pres. (1962–3). Columbia Univ. Sch. of Lib. Srv. Alum. Assn.: Pres. (1973–75). CNLA: Exec. Bd., VP (1959–60). Jt. Com. on Lib. Educ.: Ch., (1950–52, 60–61). Order of The Coif: Pres., New York Univ. Chap. Amer. Bar Assn. Assn. of Amer. Law Schs. **Pubns.:** *Vignettes of Legal History* (1977); Jt. ed., *Coordinated Law Research* (1977); Ed., *National Conference on New Directions in Law Libraries* (1977); Jt. ed., *Expanding Use of Microform in Law Libraries: Conference Proceedings* (1973); Jt. auth., *Commercial Law Information Services* (1971); other books and articles. **Activities:** 1; 17, 26; 61, 77 **Addr.:** New York University School of Law, 40 Washington Sq. South, New York, NY 10012.

Markee, Katherine Madigan (F. 24, 1931, Cleveland, OH) Asst. Prof., Lib. Sci., Data Bases Libn., Purdue Univ. Lib., 1968–. **Educ.:** Trinity Coll., 1949–53, AB (Pol. Sci.); Columbia Univ., 1960–62, MA (Guid., Student Persnl. Admin.); Case West. Rsv. Univ., 1967–68, MSLS. **Orgs.:** ALA. ASIS. Med. LA: Hon. and Awds., Ida and George Eliot Subcom. (Ch., 1979–80). SLA: Rcrt. Com. (1970–75); IN Chap., Exec. Bd., Secy. (1970–71); *SLANT* Assoc. Ed. (1969–70, 1974–75), Bus. Mgr. (1969–70, 1972–74). AAUP. **Pubns.:** Jt. Auth., "A Bibliography For Horticultural Therapy (1970–1978)"; "Comparison of Literature Search Techniques in an Interdisciplinary Field," *Hortscience* (D. 1979); "Online User Training—A "Team" Approach," *Sci. and Tech. Libs.* (Sp. 1981); "Sports Medicine—Health Care Information—Supply—Demand," *Proc. Fourth Intl. Congs. on Med. Libnshp.*, (1980); "The Price of Online Information," *Collected Abstracts 1st Online Meeting* (1980). **Activities:** 1; 39, 49-Online Bibl. Retrieval Srvs.; 56, 58, 91 **Addr.:** Purdue University Library, W. Lafayette, IN 47907.

Markel, J. Louise (My. 12, 1924, Somerset, PA) Libn., Oak Ridge Assoc. Univs. Inst. for Energy Analysis, 1974–, Lib. Supvsr., 1962–74, Assoc. Lib. Supvsr., 1956–62, Libn., 1949–55, Libn., U.S. Army, Germany, 1947–49. **Educ.:** Cedar Crest Coll., 1942–46, BA (Hist.); Drexel Inst. of Tech., 1946–47, BS (LS). **Orgs.:** E. TN LA. TN LA. ALA. SLA. **Activities:** 12; 17, 39; 80, 84, 91 **Addr.:** Library, Institute for Energy Analysis, Oak Ridge Associated Universities, Oak Ridge, TN 37830.

Markham, Robert Paul (Je. 4, 1926, Denver, CO) Coord. of Micro., Univ. of North. CO, 1975–; Coord. of Ref. Srvs., 1973–75; Prof. of Relig. and Phil., Messiah Coll., 1970–72; Prof. of Relig. and Phil., Salem Coll., 1967–70; Resrch. Assoc., Amer. Bible Socty., 1959–67; Meth. Mnstr., Untd. Meth. Church, 1954–59. **Educ.:** Univ. of Denver, 1946–49, BA (Grk.); Drew Univ., 1949–52, BD (Bible); Univ. of Denver, 1972–73, MLS; Drew Univ., 1958, PhD (Bible). **Orgs.:** ASIS. ALA: Micro. Subcom. (1977–80). CO LA. Natl. Micro. Assn.: Chap. Secy. (1979–80). Amer. Acad. of Relig. Amer. Schs. of Oriental Resrch. Socty. of Biblical Lit. **Honors:** Phi Beta Kappa, 1949; Drew Univ., Fulbright Fellow, 1953. **Pubns.:** *National Lands Index* (1980); "Topographic Maps on Microfiche," *Jnl. of Micro.* (My.–Je. 1978); "Current Trends in Academic Use of Microforms," *CO Libs.* (Mr. 1979); ed., *Colorado Union List of Major Microform Holdings* (1978). **Activities:** 1; 30, 33; 57, 70, 75 **Addr.:** University of Northern Colorado, James A. Michener Library, Micrographics Laboratory, Greeley, CO 80639.

Markowetz, Marianna C. (Jl. 6, 1925, Milwaukee, WI) Asst. Dir. for Pub. Srvs., Univ. of WI, Milwaukee, 1977–, Coord., Media Resrc. Ctr., 1974–77, Curric. Libn., 1964–74; Sch. Libn., W. Allis Sch. Syst. **Educ.:** Marquette Univ., 1954–58, BS (Educ.); Univ. of WI, Madison, 1965, MLS; Univ. of WI, Milwaukee, 1971, MED (Educ.). **Orgs.:** WI LA: Pres. (1977), Treas. (1974–75). ALA: Cnclr. (1980–83); ACRL/ Educ. & Bhvl. Sci. Sect., Curric. Mtrls. Com. (1976–79). Univ. of WI, Milwaukee Fac. Senate: Senator (1979–82). Kappa Delta Pi, Co-Cnclr. (1974–). Beta Omicron Chap. **Pubns.:** "Audiovisuals in the Curriculum Library," *Cath. Lib. World* (Mr. 1978); "Films on Wis.," *WI Lib. Bltn.* (S. 1970). **Activities:** 1; 17, 32, 33; 63, 67 **Addr.:** Golda Meier Library, University of Wis-Milwaukee, Milwaukee, WI 53201.

Marks, Barbara S. (F. 7, 1918, New York NY) Retired, 1979; Head of Ref., NY Univ., 1972–79, Head, Educ. Lib., 1966–72; various consult. positions, 1963–77. **Educ.:** Radcliffe Coll., 1934–38, BA (Fine Arts); Columbia Univ., Sch. of Soc. Work, 1940–41, MS, Sch. of Lib. Srv., 1959–1960, MS. **Orgs.:** ALA:ACRL/Educ. and Bhvl. Sci. Sect., (Ch., 1968–69), Subj. Spec. Sect., Nom. Com. (Ch., 1973–74); RTSD. SLA: Soc. Sci. Div. (Ch., 1972–73). Amer. Socty. of Indxr.: Exec. Bd. (1970–73). ASIS: Metro. NY Chap. (Secty. 1971–73, Ch. 1973–74). **Honors:** Phi Beta Kappa, 1938; Beta Phi Mu, 1960. **Pubns.:** *New York University List of Books in Education* (1968); "The Language of Signs," *Sign Syst. for Libs.* (1979); Contrib., *Books for College Libraries Core Collections Serials for Libraries* (1979). **Activities:** 1; 39 **Addr.:** General Delivery, c/o C.R. Wright, Amston, CT 06231.

Marks, Cicely P. (My. 24, 1947, Boston, MA) Tech. Srvs. Spec., Vet. Admin., 1970–. **Educ.:** Trinity Coll., 1965–69, BA (Math.); Univ. of MD, 1969–70, MLS. **Orgs.:** Med. LA Mid-Atl. Reg. Gp.: Pres. (1979); VP/Prog. Ch. (1978–79). SLA: Biol. Sci. Grp.: Pres., DC Chap. (1974–75). ASIS. Hlth. Sci. OCLC Users Grp. Fed. Lib. and Info. Ntwk.: Vice-Ch., Exec. Adv. Cncl. (1981); Secy. (1980). Reg. Med. Lib. **Pubns.:** *Spinal Cord Injury Bibliography Supplement 1971–75* (1976); *Problem-oriented medical record - Bibliography* (1972). **Activities:** 4; 20, 34, 46; 80 **Addr.:** Central Office Library (142D1), Veterans Administration, 810 Vermont Ave., N.W., Washington, DC 20420.

Marks, Estelle (N. 28, 1924, New York, NY) Supvsr., Libs. and Media, Woodbrodge Twp. Pub. Schs., 1964–; Colonia Jr. HS, 1960–64; Morris Hills Reg. HS, 1957–60; Brooklyn Pub. Lib., 1951–53. **Educ.:** NY Univ., 1943–50, BS (Educ.); Columbia Univ., 1950–51, MS (Lib. Srvs.), 1965–70, Spec. Dip. (Curric.). **Orgs.:** ALA: AASL. Assn. for Supvsn. and Curric. Dev. Educ. Media Assn. of NJ. **Honors:** AAUW, Woman of the Year, 1964. **Pubns.:** Jt. Auth., "Project Moppet" fed. prog., Title III and IVC ESEA. **Activities:** 1, 10; 28, 32; 55, 63, 67 **Addr.:** Woodbridge Board of Education, Administration Bldg., School St., Woodbridge, NJ 07095.

Marks, Juanell S. (My. 11, 1945, Oakdale, LA) Rsrc. Ctr. Supvsr., Litwin Engs. and Constructors, Inc., 1980–; Lrng. Resrcs. Spec., Spr. Woods HS, 1976–80; Media Resrc. Tchr., Bunker Hill Elem., 1971–76; Eng. Tchr., Meml. Sr. HS, 1968–69; Asst. Libn., Baker HS, 1967–68; Libn., Eng. Tchr., S. P. Arnett Jr. High, 1967–68. **Educ.:** Northwestern State Univ., 1963–66, BA (Eng.); Sam Houston State Univ., 1974–75, MLS, 1975–76, MEd (Educ. Admin.); TX, Prof. Mid-Mgt. Admin., 1978, Prof. Supvsr., 1977, Prof. All-Level Lrng. Resrcs. Spec., 1977, Prov. HS Eng., 1971. **Orgs.:** ALA. TX LA. TX Assn. of Sch. Libns.: Ch.-Elect (1980–81); State Secty. (1977–78); (Ch., Admin. Awd. Com. (1978–79); Reg. IV Spr. Branch Cncl. of Lrng. Resrcs. Spec.: Secty. (1978–79, 1980–81); Sr. High Rep. (1978–79); various com. Spr. Branch Educ. Assn.: Fac. Rep. (1978–79). Natl. Educ. Assn. TX State Tchrs. Assn. Parent Tchrs. Assn. **Honors:** TX Assn. of Sch. Libns., First Place, Anl. AV Prod. Awds. Contest (Slide-tape presentation), 1979; TX Assn. of Sec. Sch. Prin., Awd. Plaque for "furthering Lrng. Resrcs. Ctrs. in the state of TX," 1979; Spr. Branch Sch. Dist. Bd. of Trustees, Three Cert. of Merit for Oustan. Educ. in Dist. **Pubns.:** "Extending School Programs via Community Resource Files," *Sch. Lib. Jnl.* (Ja. 1976); "Orientation in the High School LRC," *TX Lib. Jnl.* (Fall 1978); "All Around Texas on the LRC Trail," slide-tape presentation (1978); "Swapshop Article on Bicentennial," *TX Outlook* (O. 1973). **Activities:** 10, 11; 17, 26, 39; 63, 93 **Addr.:** 3023 Kevin Ln., Houston, TX 77043.

Markuson, Carolyn A. (S. 14, 19–, Evanston, IL) Supvsr., Libs., Brookline Pub. Schs., 1980–; Co-Adj. Instr., Rutgers Univ., 1974–; Dir., Instr. Media, Un. Cnty. Reg. HS Dist. #1, 1974–80; Dir., Media Srvs., Watchung Hills Reg. HS Dist. #1, 1970–74; Chld. Libn., Chatham Pub. Lib., 1962–69; Chemical Libn., Allied Chemical Corp., 1958–62. **Educ.:** Un. Coll., 1952–53, AA (Sci.); OH Univ., 1953–55, BS (Chem.); Rutgers Univ., 1969–70, MLS, 1975–78, 6th Year Cert. (NJ Educ. Media Spec.); Cert. (Sch. Admin.); MA, Cert. (Sch. Libn.); Cert. (AV Spec.); Cert. (Unfd. Media Spec.); Boston Univ., EdD cand. **Orgs.:** AECT. ALA: Com. on Accred. (1979–); AASL, Vid. Comm. (Ch., 1979–81), Bd. of Dir., (1980–81), Prog. San Francisco (Co-ch., 1981). Educ. Media Assn. of NJ: Bd. (1972, 1974–80); Pres. (1979–80). Beta Phi Mu: Pres. (1972–73). NJ Assn. for Supvsn. and Curric. Natl. Educ. Assn. Leag. of Women Voters. **Honors:** Watchung Hills Reg. HS, Outstan. Tchr., 1974; Outstan. Sec. Educ. of Amer., Cert. of Cmdn., 1974. **Activities:** 9, 10; 12; 17, 19, 32; 63, 79, 91 **Addr.:** 30 Gardner Rd., Apt. 4H, Brookline, MA 02146.

Marquardt, Steve Robert (S. 7, 1943, St. Paul, MN) Dir. of Libs., Univ. of WI-Eau Claire, 1981–; Asst. Dir. for Resrcs. and Tech. Srvcs., OH Univ. Lib., 1979–81; Head Cat. Libn., Western IL Univ., 1978–79, OCLC Coord., 1977–78, Acq. Libn., 1976–77, Asst. Cat. Libn., NM State Univ., 1974–75, Acting Univ. Archvst., 1973–74. **Educ.:** Macalester Coll., 1961–66, BA (Hist.); Univ. of MN, 1966–70, MA (Hist.), 1972–73, MA (Lib. Sci.); 1970–78, PhD (Hist.). **Orgs.:** ALA: RTSD (Coll. Dev.). OHIONET Ch., Acq. Cncl. ASIS. Acad. WI LA. Amer. Assn. of Univ. Admin. **Pubns.:** "In the Dark with Chapter 6," (O. 1975); Ed., *Rio Grande Hist.* (Sum. 1974). **Activities:** 1; 15, 20, 46 **Addr.:** 1004 E. Tyler Ave., Eau Claire, WI 54701.

Marquart, Margaret (Markle) (Mr. 5, 1922, State College, PA) Head, Cat. Dept., Enoch Pratt Free Lib., 1967–, Asst. Head, 1962–66, Sr. Catlgr., 1953–62, Catlgr., 1947–53. **Educ.:** PA State Univ., 1937–41, BS (Msc. Educ.); Univ. of IL, 1944–46, BS (LS). **Orgs.:** ALA. MD LA. Potomac Tech. Prcs. Libns.: Ch. (1966–68). **Activities:** 9; 17, 20 **Addr.:** Catalog Dept., Enoch Pratt Free Library, 400 Cathedral St., Baltimore, MD 21201.

Marquis, Julien (O. 6, 1943, St. Louis, PQ) Head, Tech. Srvs., Coll. de Rimouski, 1968–. **Educ.:** Univ. de Montreal, 1966–68, BACC (LS), 1979–, MS (LS). **Orgs.:** ASTED. Corp. des Bibtcrs. Prof. du PQ. **Activities:** 1; 5; 63 **Addr.:** 469 Terrasse Bon Air, Pointe Au Pere, Rimouski, PQ G0K 1G0 Canada.

Marquis, Rollin Park (N. 29, 1925, Badin, NC) City Libn., Dearborn (MI) Dept. of Libs., 1964–; Cnty. Libn., Allegany Cnty. (MD), 1963–64; Dir., River Edge (NJ) Free Pub. Lib., 1959–63; Dir., Citizens Lib., Washington, (PA), 1958–59. **Educ.:** Columbia Univ., 1942–48, AB (Art/Ling.); Carnegie Inst. of Tech., 1957–58, MLS; Art Students League of NY, 1950–52 (Painting); Oxford Univ., 1948–50 (Ling.). **Orgs.:** ALA. MI LA. Detroit-Suburban Libns. RT. Rotary Club. Dearborn (MI) Cmnty. Arts Cncl. Torch Club of Detroit. Dearborn (MI) Choral Art Socty. **Activities:** 9; 17, 19; 50 **Addr.:** Dearborn Department of Libraries, 16301 Michigan Ave., Dearborn, MI 48126.

Marriott, Lois I. (Je. 4, 1931, Burlington, VT) Dean, Instr. Resrcs., Southwest. Coll., 1981–, Dir., Lib. Srvs., 1976–81; Coord., Circ. Srvs., San Diego State Univ., 1972–76, Head, Lower Div. Lib., 1966–72; Readrs. Srvs. Libn., Salinas Pub. Lib., 1961–65; Bkmobile. Libn., Monterey Cnty. Lib., 1958–59. **Educ.:** Univ. of IA, 1954–56, BA (Hist.); Univ. of WI, 1957–58, MA (LS); San Diego State Univ., 1972–78, MA (Educ. Tech.). **Orgs.:** ALA. CA LA. Photographic Socty. of Amer. San Diego Hist. Socty. **Activities:** 1; 17, 25, 32; 50, 85 **Addr.:** Library Services, Southwestern College Library, 900 Otay Lakes Rd., Chula Vista, CA 92010.

Marsh, John S. (F. 12, 1932, High Point, NC) Libn., Simpson Thacher and Bartlett, 1970–; Admin. Dir., LA State Univ. Law Sch. Lib., 1969–70; Libn., Cadwalader Wickersham and Taft, 1967–69; Libn., Cleary Gottlieb Steen and Hamilton, 1964–66. **Educ.:** Berea Coll., 1950–54, AB (Eng.); NY Univ., 1962–66, LLB (Law); Pratt Inst., 1970–72, MLS. **Orgs.:** AALL. SLA. **Activities:** 12; 17, 39; 77 **Addr.:** Simpson Thacher & Bartlett, 1 Battery Park Plz., New York, NY 10004.

Marsh, Sharon Lee (O. 25, 1941, Waseca, MN) Docum. Sect. Chief, East. KY Univ., 1972–; Asst. Docum. Libn., Map

PROFESSIONAL ACTIVITIES: Institutions: 1. Acad. lib.; 2. Arch.; 3. Assn.; 4. Fed./Gvt. lib.; 5. Inst. lib.; 6. Mfr./Suppl.; 7. Milit. lib.; 8. Musm.; 9. Pub. lib.; 10. Sch. lib.; 11. Sch. of lib. sci.; 12. Spec. lib.; 13. State lib.; 14. (other). **Functions/Activities:** 15. Acq./Col. dev.; 16. Adult srvs.; 17. Admin.; 18. Apprais.; 19. Archit./Bldgs.; 20. Cat./Class.; 21. Chld. srvs.; 22. Circ.; 23. Cons./Pres.; 24. Consult.; 25. Cont. ed.; 26. Educ. lib. sci.; 27. Ext. srvs.; 28. Fund/Grants; 29. Gvt. pubs.; 30. Indx./Abs.; 31. Instr. lib. use; 32. Media srvs.; 33. Micro.; 34. Netwks./Coop.; 35. Persnl.; 36. PR; 37. Publshg.; 38. Recs. mgt.; 39. Ref. srvs.; 40. Repro.; 41. Resrch.; 42. Review.; 43. Secur.; 44. Serials; 45. Spec. col.; 46. Tech. srvs.; 47. Trustees/Bds.; 48. YA srvs.; 49. (other).

Libn., Univ. of WI, Parkside, 1970–72. **Educ.:** Univ. of WI, Milwaukee, 1967–69, BS (Geo.), 1969–70, MS (LS); East. KY Univ., 1976–79, MA (Geo.). **Orgs.:** ALA: GODORT, Secy., Admin. & Org. Task Force (1973–75); Clearinghouse Ch. (1975–77); Liaison to State & Local Affiliates (1977–79). KY LA: GODORT Ch. (1978–79). **Pubns.:** Reviews. **Activities:** 1; 29 **Addr.:** Documents Section, John Grant Crabbe Library, Eastern Kentucky University, Richmond, KY 40475.

Marshall, David C. (My. 21, 1938, Grove City, PA) Chief, Pub. Srvs., Anne Arundel Cnty. Pub. Lib., 1980–, Branch Libn., 1973–80. **Educ.:** Harvard Univ., 1956–61, AB (Soclgy.); Univ. of Pittsburgh, 1967–68, MLS; Univ. of Baltimore, 1974–78, JD (Law). **Orgs.:** ALA. MD LA. MD State Bar Assn. **Activities:** 9; 17 **Addr.:** Library HQ, 5 Harry S. Truman Pkwy., Annapolis, MD 21401.

Marshall, Doris B. (Je. 27, 1918, Troy, OH) Retired. Info. Sci., Ralston Purina Co., 1972–81, Libn., 1966–72; Tech. Sales Corres., Mallinckrodt Chem. Co., 1966; Libn., Amer. Zinc, Lead & Smelting Co., 1956–60; Libn., Monsanto Chem. Co., 1941–44; Asst. Libn., Universal Oil Products Co., 1940–41. **Educ.:** OH State Univ., 1936–40, BA (Chem.); Univ. of MO, 1973–75, MA (LS); other courses, online trng. **Orgs.:** SLA: Adv. Cncl. (1971–73); Nom. Com. (1974–75); Div. Cab. (1976–78); Stan. Com. (1978–79, 1979–82); Food and Nutrition Div., Ch., Prog. Planner for Anl. Conf. (1977–78); Chap. Dir. (1970–71); Pres. (1972–73). ASIS. Inst. of Info. Sci. ALA. Other orgs. Socty. of Mayflower Descendants in the State of MO. Luth. Church Women. Natl. Geneal. Socty. Church Women Untd. **Honors:** First Hon. Mem., St. Louis' Online Users Grp., 1981. **Pubns.:** "To Improve Searching, Check Results," *ONLINE* (Jl. 1981); "I Learned about searching from That . . .," *ONLINE* (Ja. 1981); "User Criteria for Selection of Commercial On-Line Computer-Based Bibliographic Services," *Spec. Libs.* (1975); "The Commonwealth Scientific Industrial Research Organization in Australia," *Spec. Libs.* (Ap., 1975); various speeches. **Activities:** 12; 17, 39, 41; 60, 68, 75 **Addr.:** 477 Burns Ave., Kirkwood, MO 63122.

Marshall, James C. (Mr. 18, 1948, Toledo, OH) Branch Mgr., Sylvania Branch, Toledo-Lucas Cnty. Public Lib., 1977–; Branch Mgr., Kent Branch, 1975–77, Adult Asst., 1974–75, Libn., Fiction and Lit. Dept., 1971–72. **Educ.:** OH State Univ., 1969–71, BS; Univ. of MI, 1972–73, MA (LS). **Orgs.:** OH LA. Sylvania Exch. Club. **Honors:** Beta Phi Mu, 1973. **Activities:** 1, 9; 15, 16, 39; 75 **Addr.:** 3753 Grantley Rd., Toledo, OH 43613.

Marshall, Joan K. (O. 29, 1929, Brooklyn, NY) Assoc. Libn., Tech. Srvs., Brooklyn Coll., 1966–. **Educ.:** NY Univ., 1960–64, BA (Eng.); Columbia Univ., 1965–66, MS (LS); NY Univ., 1965–67, MA (Eng.). **Orgs.:** ALA: Com. on the Status of Women (1978–); RTSD, Cat. Code Rev. Com. (1975–78), Subj. Analysis Com., Subcom. on Racism and Sexism in Subj. Analysis (1976–81). NY LA: Int. Frdm. and Due Procs. Com. (Ch., 1976–78). NY Tech. Srvs. Libns.: Pres. (1980–81). FTRF: Trustee (1969–72). NY Lib. Club: Bd. (1979–). Columbia Univ. Sch. of Lib. Srv. Alum. Assn. Leroy C. Merritt Hum. Fund: Trustee (1977–80). **Honors:** ALA, Ralph R. Shaw Awd., 1979; CLR, Fellow, 1975–76; Phi Beta Kappa, 1964. **Pubns.:** *Serials for Libraries* (1979); *On Equal Terms* (1977). **Addr.:** Brooklyn College Library, Brooklyn, NY 11210.

Marshall, Joanne Gard (D. 19, 1945, Paulton, Somerset, Eng.) Info. Srvs. Libn., Ref. and Clinical Srvs., Hlth. Sci. Lib., McMaster Univ., 1977–, Pub. Srvs. Libn., 1972–77; Actg. Coord., Hosp. Libs., Hamilton Wentworth Dist. Hlth. Cncl., 1977, 1974; Serials Libn., Hlth. Sci. Lib., McMaster Univ., 1970–71; Ref., Orien. Libn., Univ. of Calgary, 1968–69; Catlgr., Macdonald Coll., McGill Univ., 1967–68; Catlgr., Ref. Asst., Head Ofc., Bank of Montreal, 1965–66; various positions as instr., 1976–77. **Educ.:** Univ. of Calgary, 1966, BA; McGill Univ., 1968, MLS; 1972, Cert. (Med. Libnshp.); McMaster Univ., 1978, MS (Hlth. Sci., Hlth. Care Prac.); various crs. **Orgs.:** Med. LA: Mem. Com. (Can. Rep., 1975–76); Relevance Grp. (Ch., 1978–79); Nom. Com. (Cand., 1980); Upstate NY and ON Reg. Chap. Can. Assn. on Grntlgy.: Adv. Com. on the Running Can. Bibl. on Grntlgy. (1979–). CHLA. Toronto Med. Libs. Grp. McMaster Univ. Prof. Libns. Assn. Can. Assn. of Univ. Tchrs. Sheridan Coll. of Appld. Arts and Tech. **Pubns.:** Jt. Auth., "The treatment of death in children's literature," *Omega; Jnl. of Death and Dying* (1971); "A selected list of children's books relating to death," *Omega: Jnl. of Death and Dying* (1971); Jt. Auth., "The clinical librarian and the patient; Report of a project at McMaster University Medical Centre," *Bltn. of the Med. LA* (O. 1978); "A bibliography of clinical librarianship," *Bibliotheca Med. Can.* (1979); Jt. Auth., "A Randomized Trial of Librarian Educational Participation in Clinical Settings," *Jnl. of Med. Educ.* (My. 1981); various articles. **Activities:** 1, 12; 26, 39, 41; 80 **Addr.:** Health Sciences Library, McMaster University, Hamilton, ON L8N 3Z5 Canada.

Marshall, John David (S. 7, 1928, McKenzie, TN) Univ. Bibl., Mid. TN State Univ., 1976–, Prof., 1980–, Univ. Libn., 1967–76; Head, Acq. Div., Univ. of GA Lib., 1957–67; Head, Ref. Dept., Auburn Univ. Lib., 1955–57; Ref. Libn., Clemson Univ. Lib., 1952–55. **Educ.:** Bethel Coll., 1947–50, BA (Hist./Eng.); FL State Univ., 1950–51, MALS; FL State Univ., 1950–51 (Hist./Lib. Sci.). **Orgs.:** ALA: LHRT (Secy. 1968–70); ACRL (Pub. Com. 1957–62). Southeastern LA: Ch., Resrcs./Tech. Srvs. Sect. (1968–70); Ch., Univ. and Coll. Libs. Sect. (1972–74); Ch., Nom. Com. (1976–78); Ch., Hon. Mem. Com. (1978–80). TN LA: Ch., Int. Frdm. Com. (1968–70); Constitution Rev. Com. (1971–72); By-Laws and Proc. Com. (1973–75). Manus. Socty. TN Hist. Socty. **Honors:** Beta Phi Mu; Phi Kappa Phi. **Pubns.:** *The Southern Books Competition at Twenty-Five* (1980); *Louis Shores, Author-Librarian: A Bibliography* (1979); "Crusading for Calmness", *Learning Today* (Spr. 1976); "The Book Remains Alive and Well," *Educ. Catlyst* (Fall 1975); "As I Remember Wayne Shirley," *Jnl. of Lib. Hist.* (O. 1974); Review. **Activities:** 1; 15, 39, 42; 57, 63, 92 **Addr.:** 802 E. Main St., Riviera Apts. 38, Murfreesboro, TN 37130.

Marshall, Joseph W. (N. 16, 1922, Boston, MA) Sup. Libn., Franklin D. Roosevelt Lib., 1959–; Libn., U.S. Naval Ord. Sta., Indian Head (MD), 1957–59; Readers' Adv., Public Lib. of DC, 1951–57. **Educ.:** Northeastern Univ., 1941–43; Tufts Univ., 1947–49, BA (Hist.), Syracuse Univ., 1950–51, MSLS. **Orgs.:** Southeast. NY Lib. Resrcs. Cncl.: Secy/Treas., (1971); Trustee (1977–81). Dutchess Cnty. LA: VP (1970). Hyde Park Free Lib.: Trustee (1961–65). Hyde Park Hist. Assn.: Trustee (1974–78). **Honors:** Beta Phi Mu, 1951. **Pubns.:** "The Franklin D. Roosevelt Library," *Encyc. of Lib. and Info. Sci.* (1973). **Activities:** 4; 39, 45 **Addr.:** 23 Caywood Pl., Hyde Park, NY 12538.

Marshall, Kenneth Eric (O. 25, 1930, Kings Lynn, Norfolk, Eng.) Head Scientific Info. Srvs. and Lib., Freshwater Inst., 1967–; Sci. Libn., Univ. of London, 1964–67; Libn., Freshwater Bio. Assn., 1955–64. **Educ.:** Univ. of London, 1949–52, BSc (Zlgy.). **Orgs.:** Can. Assn. Info. Sci.: Pres. (1975–76). ASIS: West. Can. Chap. (Ch., 1972–73). SLA: Nat. Resrcs. Div. (Ch., 1978–79). Inst. of Info. Sci. Falcon Yacht Clb.: Commodore. **Pubns.:** *Advances in Ephemeroptera Biology* (1980); "Online Retrieval of Information," tech. rpt. (1979). "Library Services at the National Inland Fisheries Institute Bangkok" (O., 1978); *Journal of Ecology, Index to Vol. 21-50, 1933-62* (1966). **Activities:** 4, 12; 18, 40, 45; 59, 66, 83 **Addr.:** Freshwater Institute Library, 501 University Crescent, Winnipeg, MB R3T 2N6 Canada.

Marshall, Margaret E. (Ja. 23, 1955, Gainesville, GA) Dir., Pelham Pub. Lib., 1976–. **Educ.:** SUNY, Binghamton, 1972–75, BA (Eng.); Univ. of RI, 1975–76, MLS. **Orgs.:** ALA. New Eng. LA. NH LA. NH Lib. Cncl.: Conf. Com. (Ch., 1981). NH PR Adv. Cncl. for Libs. **Activities:** 9; 17, 34, 36; 56 **Addr.:** Pelham Public Library, Gage Hill Rd., Pelham, NH 03076.

Marshall, Nancy H. (N. 3, 1932, Stamford, CT) Assoc. Dir., Libs./Pub. Srvs., Univ. of WI, 1979–; Dir., WILS/WLC Netwk., Madison, WI, 1972–79; Ref. Libn., Univ. of WI, 1971–72. **Educ.:** OH Wesleyan Univ., 1949–53, BA (Eng.); Univ. of WI, 1970–72, MLS. **Orgs.:** ALA: Copyrt. Subcom./ALA Legis. Com; (Ch., 1978–); RASD, (Pres., (1979–80); ILL (Co-Ch., 1977–78); Cncl.: (1980–84). ASIS Lib. Autom. & Networking Interest Grp. WI LA. OCLC Users Cncl. AAUP: Copyrt. Com. (1979–1983). Madison Acad. Staff Assn. Steering Com. (1975–76). **Honors:** Beta Phi Mu. **Pubns.:** "Copyright," *ALA Yrbk.* (1980); "Reference & Adult Services Division," *ALA Yrbk.* (1980, 1981); "Programs Underway to Evaluate the Impact of the Copyright Law," *The Bookmark* (Sum. 1979); "From Public Law to Practice: The Copyright Revision Act of 1976," *WI Lib. Bltn.* Mr.-Ap. 1978); "What Price Oral History?" *GA Arch.* (Win. 1975). **Activities:** 1, 14-Network; 17, 34, 39; 56, 61, 93 **Addr.:** 372D Memorial Library, 728 State St., Madison, WI 53706.

Marshall, Peter W. (S. 6, 1946, Halifax, Nova Scotia) Coord. of Tech. Srvs., Greater Victoria Pub. Lib., 1979–; Systems Coord., Univ. of MB, 1977–79; Info. Srvs, Calgary, AB, 1974–77; Libn., AB Resrch. Cncl., 1972–74. **Educ.:** Univ. of Victoria, 1965–69, BA (Geo.); Univ. of AB, 1969–71, MSc (Geo.); 1971–72 BLS. **Orgs.:** Can. LA: Lib. Resrch. and Dev. (1978–80). BC LA. **Honors:** Nat. Resrch. Cncl., Lib. Schol., 1971–72. **Pubns.:** Jt. Auth., "Ice in Coulthard Cave," *Proc. of the Intl. Speleological Cong., Abstr.*, Vol. 6, (1973); *Athabasca Oil Sands Index 1789–1974*, (Ja. 1974); "How much, How often," *Coll. and Resrch. Libs.* (N. 1974); "Ice-blocked Tubes in the Aiyansh Flow," *Arctic and Alpine Resrch.* (Fall 1975); "Automation in Manitoba Libraries," *Am. Socty. for Info. Sci.* (S. 1978); reviews. **Activities:** 1, 9; 17, 39, 46; 56, 59, 91 **Addr.:** Greater Victoria Public Library, 735 Broughton St., Victoria, BC V8W 3H2 Canada.

Marshall, Ruth Ann (D. 8, 1919, Hazleton, PA) Head, Tech. Prcs., Carnegie—Mellon Univ., 1956–; Head Catlgr., Carnegie—Inst. of Tech., 1951–56, Catlgr., 1947–51, Engin. Libn., 1946–47. **Educ.:** PA State Univ., 1938–42, BA (Educ.); Carnegie Inst. of Tech., 1945–46, BS (LS). **Orgs.:** ALA: Decimal Class. Adv. Com. (1954–57). PA LA: Mem. Com. **Pubns.:** Jt. Ed., *PA LA Bltn.* (1948–51). **Addr.:** 5540 5th Ave., Pittsburgh, PA 15232.

Martel, Anne S. (D. 4, 1926, Montreal, PQ) Asst. Prof., Lib. Admin., Illini Un. Browsing Rm. Undergrad. Lib., Univ. of IL, 1978–, Head Libn., 1967–78; Elem. Tchr., Ithaca, NY, 1951–52. **Educ.:** Univ. of IL, 1945–49, BA (Hist.); Univ. of Miami, 1950–51, Tchg. Cert.; Univ. of IL, 1965–67, MSLS. **Orgs.:** ALA: IFRT, Exec. Com.; Immroth Awd. Com. (1981–82); Mem. Ch. (1980–); ACRL. IL LA. Amer. Cvl. Liberties Un.: Secy.-Treas. (1978–). Audubon Socty. Beta Phi Mu: Alpha Chap. (Treas., 1970–71). **Activities:** 1; 15, 22, 39; 74, 92 **Addr.:** Undergraduate Library, University of IL, 1402 W. Gregory Dr., Urbana, IL 61801.

Martell, Charles R., Jr. (S. 18, 1939, Cambridge, MA) Ref. Libn., Educ., Psy Lib., Univ. of CA, Berkeley, 1980–; Asst. to the Univ. Libn., Univ. of CA, Berkeley, 1976–80; Proj. Leader, Swedish Natl. Bd. for Tech. Dev., 1975–76; Resrch. Asst., Inst. of Lib. Resrch., Univ. of CA, Berkeley, 1973–75, Lectr., 1977–79. **Educ.:** Brown Univ., 1960–64, AB (Russ.); Syracuse Univ., 1970–72, MSLS; Univ. of CA, Berkeley, 1972–79, DLS. **Orgs.:** ALA: ACRL, Local Arrange. Com. (Ch., 1975). Libns. Assn. of the Univ. of CA, Berkeley: Vice Ch./Ch.-Elect (1979–80). **Honors:** ALA, Student Goals Awd., 1971. **Pubns.:** "War of AACR2: Victor, or Victims?" *Jnl. of Acad. Libnshp.* (Mr. 1981); "Copyright: One Year Later–A Symposium", *Jnl. of Acad. Libnshp.* (Jl. 1979); Jt. auth., "Role of Continuing Education and Training in Human Resource Development: An Administrator's Viewpoint," *Jnl. of Acad. Libnshp.* (Jl. 1978); "Erasing the Past: Technological Shift and Organizational Renewal" in *New Horizons for Academic Libraries* (1979); "Copyright Law and Reserve Operations: An Interpretation," *Coll. & Resrch. Libs. News.* (1978); other articles. **Activities:** 1; 15, 17, 41; 59, 61, 63 **Addr.:** General Library, University of California, Berkeley, CA 94720.

Marthaler, Sr. Margaret K. (O. 12, 1919, Meire Grove, MN) Libn., Scotus Ctrl. Cath. HS, 1978–; Libn., Paul VI HS, Omaha, NE, 1974–78; Head of Pub. Srvs., Acq., Coll. of St. Thomas, St. Paul, MN, 1970–74; Sch. Lib. Consult., St. Cloud (MN) Diocese, 1965–70; Sch. Lib. Consult., Schools of Sisterhood, 1958–65. **Educ.:** Coll. of St. Catherine, St. Paul, MN, 1958–62, BS (LS); Rosary Coll., 1967–70, MALS. **Orgs.:** ALA: AASL. AECT. NE LA. Cath. LA: NE Chap., Pres. (1979–81); Vice-Ch., (1977–79); MN-Dakota Unit, Ch. (1968–70); HS Sect., Awds. Com. (1971–72); Parish and Lending Libs. Sect., Mem. Com. (1971–72). Natl. Cncl. of Tchrs. of Eng. **Honors:** Beta Phi Mu, 1970. **Activities:** 10; 21, 48 **Addr.:** 1472-27th Ave., Columbus, NE 68601.

Martin, Anthony A. (Ag. 18, 1920, Pittsburgh, PA) Dir., Carnegie Lib. of Pittsburgh, 1969–, Asst. Dir., 1964–69, Chief Libn., N. Side Branches, 1956–64; Libn., US Bur. of Mines, Pittsburgh, 1955–56; Admin. Asst., Carnegie Lib. of Pittsburgh, 1954–55, Asst. Head, Ref. Dept., 1949–52, Asst., Ref. Dept., 1946–48. **Educ.:** Duquesne Univ., 1938–42, BEd (Eng., Hist.); Carnegie Lib. Sch., 1945–46, BSLS; Univ. of Pittsburgh, 1946–49 (Pol. Sci.). **Orgs.:** PA LA: Treas. (1961–64); 2nd VP (1965–66). ALA: PLA. Pittsburgh Reg. Lib. Ctr. Cncl. for Comp. Lib. Netwks. Other orgs. YMCA. Rotary. WQED TV: Dir. Univ. of Pittsburgh: Bd. of Visitors. **Honors:** Univ. of Pittsburgh, Disting. Alum. Awd., 1975. **Pubns.:** Ed., *Technical Book Review Index* (1956–69). **Activities:** 9 **Addr.:** Carnegie Library of Pittsburgh, 4400 Forbes Ave., Pittsburgh, PA 15213.*

Martin, Daniel William (Ag. 22, 1950, Crawfordsville, IN) Libn., Mgt. and Phys. Oper., Tarlton Law Lib., Univ. of TX, Austin, 1980–, Cat. Dept. Admin., 1978–80, Catlgr., 1976–78. **Educ.:** Cedarville Coll., 1968–72, BA (Soc. Sci.); IN Univ., 1975–76, MLS. **Orgs.:** AALL: Indexing of Per. Lit. Com. (1980–). Southwestern Assn. of Law Libs. **Pubns.:** Jt. Ed., Jt. Cmplr., *Index to Periodical Articles Related to Law, 1974–1978 Cumulation* (1980); Jt. Cmplr., "Current Literature on Aerospace Law: Bibliography," *Jnl. of Air Law and Cmrce.* (qtly. 1977–). **Activities:** 1; 17; 77 **Addr.:** Tarlton Law Library, University of TX, Austin, School of Law, Austin, TX 78705.

Martin, Elizabeth Ann (Je. 30, 1931, Waverly, IA) Assoc. Prof., Dept. Head, Univ. of North. IA, 1962–; Asst. Libn., Wartburg Coll., 1960–62; HS Libn., Dubuque, IA, 1957–60; Tchr., HS, Oelwein, IA, 1956–57. **Educ.:** Wartburg Coll., 1949–56, BA (Eng.); Univ. of MN, 1958–61, MA (LS); various grad. crs. in LS. **Orgs.:** ALA: AASL, Legis. Com. (1979–81). IA Educ. Media Assn.: Treas. (1977–79). AECT. IA LA: Pres. (1982). **Honors:** Phi Delta Kappa. **Pubns.:** Cmplr., *The Small Town Stage: a Historical Celebration* (1980). **Activities:** 10, 11; 20, 26, 31; 63, 74, 78 **Addr.:** Dept. of Library Science, University of Northern IA, Cedar Falls, IA 50613.

Martin, Elizabeth DuVernet (Betty) (Ja. 12, 1910, Greenville, SC) Retired, 1975–; Media Srvs. Consult., Freelnc., 1970–; Instr., LS, Furman Univ., 1967–70; Instr., LS, Univ. of SC, 1964–65; Dir. of Media Srvs., Sch. Dist., Greenville Cnty., 1958–75, Libn., 1931–44; Instr. of LS, Fisk Univ., 1939. **Educ.:** Univ. of NC, 1929–31, AB (LS); Furman Univ., 1964, MA (Educ.). **Orgs.:** ALA: Supvsr. Sect. (Ch., 1968–69). SC LA: Pres. (1964). SELA: Pres. (1974–76). AASL: Reg. Rep.; Exec. Bd. of Dirs. (1963–66). Natl. Educ. Assn. SC Educ. Assn. Assn. for Supvsn. and Curric. Dev. **Pubns.:** Jt. auth., *Principal's Handbook on the School Library Media Center* (1978); jt. auth., *Teacher's Handbook on the School Library Media Center* (1980); jt. auth., *The District Director of Media Servies* (1981); *The Shape of Things to Come: The School Library Media Center in 2050*

Special Subjects/Services: 50. Adult educ.; 51. Advert./Mktg.; 52. Aerosp.; 53. Agric.; 54. Area std.; 55. Arts/Hum.; 56. Autom.; 57. Bibl./Prtg.; 58. Bio. sci.; 59. Bus./Fin.; 60. Chem.; 61. Copyrt.; 62. Documtn.; 63. Educ.; 64. Engin.; 65. Env.; 66. Eth. grps.; 67. Film; 68. Food/Nutr.; 69. Geneal.; 70. Geo.; 71. Geol.; 72. Handcpd.; 73. Hist.; 74. Int. frdm.; 75. Info. sci.; 76. Insr.; 77. Law; 78. Legis.; 79. Math./Comp. sci.; 80. Med.; 81. Metals; 82. Nat. resrcs.; 83. Newsp.; 84. Nuc. sci.; 85. Oral hist.; 86. Petr./Energy; 87. Pharm.; 88. Phys./Astr./Math.; 89. Readg.; 90. Relig.; 91. Sci./Tech.; 92. Soc. sci.; 93. Telecom.; 94. Transp.; 95. (other).

(forthcoming); various articles. **Activities:** 10, 11; 17, 21, 24; 63, 75 **Addr.:** 48 Coventry Ln., Greenville, SC 29609.

Martin, Eva M. (Ap. 24, 1939, Woodstock, ON) Coord., Srvs. for Chld. and YA, Scarborough Pub. Lib., 1977–; Lectr., Univ. of Toronto Fac. of Lib. Sci., 1975–76; Head, Cmnty. Branch, Toronto Pub. Lib., 1971–77, Head, Chld. Dept., 1963–71, Chld. Libn., 1961–63. **Educ.:** Univ. of Toronto, 1957–60, BA (Arts), 1960–61, BLS, 1967–72, MLS. **Orgs.:** Can. LA. ALA. Can. Assn. of Chld. Libns. ON LA: Chld. Srvs. Gld. (Ch., 1979–80); sec. VP (1981–83). ON Puppetry Assn. ON Assn. for Chld. With Lrng. Disabilities. **Pubns.:** "Services for Children and Young Adults in the Eighties," *In Review* (O. 1980); "Folksongs: A Living Tradition in Urban Canada," *In Review* (Spr. 1974); various storytel. progs. for lcl. educ. TV. **Activities:** 9; 15, 21 **Addr.:** Scarborough Public Library, 1076 Ellesmere Rd., Scarborough, ON M1P 4P4 Canada.

Martin, Fenton S. (N. 3, 1943, Topeka, KS) Libn., Pol. Sci. Resrch. Col., IN Univ., 1971–. **Educ.:** FL State Univ., 1961–64, BS (Eng. Educ.); IN Univ., 1968–70, MLS. **Orgs.:** ALA. IN LA. IN Univ. Libns. Assn. **Honors:** Beta Phi Mu. **Activities:** 1; 17, 20, 39; 92 **Addr.:** Political Science Research Collection, Woodburn 200, Indiana University, Bloomington, IN 47401.

Martin, Jean K. (N. 25, 1938, San Angelo, TX) Lib. Mgr., Molycorp, Inc., 1980–; Chief, Lib. Srv., V A Med. Ctr., 1978–79; Head, Lib., Russell Resrch. Ctr., 1975–78; Ref. Libn., Univ. of GA Sci. Lib., 1974–75; Head, Physics-Math-Astronomy Lib., Univ. of TX, Austin, 1970–74; Syst. Anal./Ref. Libn., Southwestern Med. Sch., Dallas, TX, 1969–70. **Educ.:** Univ. of TX, Austin, 1964–66, BA (Soc.); Univ. of AL, Huntsville, 1963–64; TX Luth. Coll., 1957–58; Univ. of GA, Athens, 1975–78, MA (Bus. Admin.); Univ. of TX, Austin, 1968–69, MLS. **Orgs.:** ASIS: Secy./Treas., Mgt. SIG (1979–81). SLA: Ch., Sci-Tech Div. (1979–81); Treas., S. Atl. Chap. (1976–78); Pres. and VP., TX Chap. (1973–75); Secy., Physics-Math-Astron. Div. (1972–75). Geosci. Info. Socty. **Honors:** Beta Gamma Sigma, 1978; Sigma Iota Epsilon, 1977. **Pubns.:** "Preparation of Proposals for Online Bibliographic Services in Academic, Government, and Industrial Libraries," *Sci. and Tech. Libs.* (Fall 1980); "Academic Library Management," *Lib. Mgt. Bltn.* (Spr. 1979); "Zero-Base Budgeting," *Lib. Mgt. Bltn.* (Win. 1979); "Computer-Based Literature Searching Impact on Interlibrary Loan Service," *Spec. Lib.* (Ja. 1978); Ed. *Lib. Mgt. Bltn.* (1978–80). **Activities:** 12; 17, 36, 39; 51, 81 **Addr.:** Molycorp, Inc. Library, Union Oil Center, 461 S. Boylston, P.O. Box 54945, Los Angeles, CA 90054.

Martin, Jess A. (My 2, 1926, Picher, OK) Dir. of Lib., Univ. of TN, Ctr. For Hlth. Sci., 1971–; Dir. of Lib., Temple Univ. Med. Ctr., 1968–71; Chief, Lib. Br., Nat. Inst. of Hlth., 1963–68; Dir. of Lib., OH State Univ. Med. Ctr., 1960–63. **Educ.:** San Diego State Coll., 1948–53, AB (Hist.); Univ. of Southern CA, 1954–55; MSLS. **Orgs.:** Med. LA: Ch. Mem. Com. (1962–63); Ch. Cont. Educ. Com. (1970–71). SLA: Pres., Mid-S. Chap. (1979–80). TN LA: Pres. (1975–76). AAUP: Pres., UTCHS Chap. (1979–80). **Honors:** Med. LA: Schol., 1954. **Pubns.:** "Staff Evaluation of Supervisors," *Spec. Libs.* (Ja. 1979); jt. Auth., "Tennessee State Plan for Libraries," *TN State Lib.* (1978); "Booz, Allen, Hamilton Report. Public Hearings," *TN Libn.* (Spr. 1977); Jt. Auth., "Circulation: Professional or Clerical?" (Sum. 1976); Jt. Auth., "Library Staff Orientation," (Fall 1975). **Activities:** 1, 12; 17, 26, 35; 80, 91, 92 **Addr.:** Univ. of Tenn. Ctr. for Health Sci. Lib., 800 Madison Ave., Memphis, TN 38163.

Martin, John H., Jr. (Ap. 24, 1944, Huntington, WV) Head, Lit. and Fine Arts Dept., Orlando Pub. Lib., 1980–, Head, Spec. Srvs. Dept., 1976–80, Admin. Asst., 1975–76, Catlgr., 1974–75. **Educ.:** Univ. of FL, 1970–73, BA (Anthro.); Columbia Univ., 1973–74, MSLS. **Orgs.:** ALA: *Booklist* Ed. Adv. Bd. (Ch., 1981–82); RASD, Srvs. to Adults Com. (1978–82). FL LA. **Pubns.:** "The Public Library's Role in Providing Library Services to Inmates," *Keystone* (Ap.–My. 1980). **Activities:** 9; 16, 17, 39 **Addr.:** Literature and Fine Arts Dept., Orlando Public Library, 10 N. Rosalind, Orlando, FL 32801.

Martin, June Robertson (O. 9, 1922, Charleston, WV) Chief Ref. Libn., Kanawha Cnty. Pub. Lib., 1979–, Ref. Libn., 1963–79; Exec. Secy., Kanawha Cnty. Socty. for Crippled Chld., 1951–61; Tchr., Sarah Dix Hamlin Sch., 1947–49. **Educ.:** WV Univ., 1939–43, BA (Hist.); Univ. of WI, 1943–44, MA (Hist.), 1962–63, MA (LS). **Orgs.:** ALA: JMRT (Secy., 1967). WV LA: Secy. (1965–66); State Natl. Lib. Week (Dir., 1966). SELA. AAUW. Eng.–Speaking Un. Kanawha Valley Hist. Prsrvn. Socty. WV Hist. Assn. **Activities:** 9; 16, 29, 39; 50, 74, 85 **Addr.:** 1627 Quarrier St., Charleston, WV 25311.

Martin, La Quita Vernell (Ap. 12, 1955, Lebanon, TN) Libn., Dearborn and Ewing, 1979–; Lib. Consult., LaQuita Martin Lib. Mgt. Inc., 1978–; Libn., Boult, Cummings, Conners and Berry, 1977–; various positions as consult. Libn. **Educ.:** George Peabody Coll., 1973–76, BA (Soc. Sci.), 1977, MLS; Vanderbilt Univ., 1979–, EdS in progress; various crs. **Orgs.:** AALL. **Activities:** 1, 12; 17, 19, 24; 56, 77, 92 **Addr.:** P.O. Box 3204, Nashville, TN 37219.

Martin, Lillian M. (F. 14, 1926, Lewiston, ID) Lib. Admin., Lewis–Clark State Coll., 1976–; Ref. Libn., OR State Univ., 1960–61; Ref. Libn., Univ. of MN Law Sch. Lib., 1958–60. **Educ.:** Univ. of Puget Snd., 1951–52, BA (Eng. Lit.); Univ. of MN, 1957–59, MA (LS). **Orgs.:** ALA. ID Educ. Media Assn. Pac. Northwest LA. ID LA. **Activities:** 1, 9; 17, 39; 77 **Addr.:** Library, Lewis—Clark State College, Lewiston, ID 83501.

Martin, Louis E. (S. 16, 1928, Detroit, MI) Univ. Libn., Cornell Univ., 1979–; Libn. of Harvard Coll., 1972–79; **Educ.:** Univ. of Detroit, 1951, PHB (Eng.), 1954, MA (Eng.); Univ. of MI, 1960, AMLS. **Orgs.:** ALA. Grolier Club. **Activities:** 1; 17, 23, 34; 54, 56, 57 **Addr.:** Cornell University, 201 Olin Library, Ithaca, NY 14853.

Martin, Lowell A. (Mr. 12, 1912, Chicago, IL) Visit. Prof., SUNY, Albany, 1977–; Prof., Sch. of Lib. Srv., Columbia Univ., 1970–77; VP, Grolier Inc., 1960–70; Dean, Sch. of Lib. and Info. Sci., Rutgers Univ., 1954–59. **Educ.:** IL Inst. of Tech., 1932–38, BS (Soc.); Univ. of Chicago, 1938–43, PhD (Lib. Sci.). **Orgs.:** ALA. NJ LA. NY LA. Amer. Mgt. Assn. **Honors:** Scarecrow Press Awd., 1971. **Pubns.:** *Library Response to Urban Change* (1969); *Public Administration and the Library* (1941); "Demographic Trends and Social Structure," *Lib. Trends* (Win. 1979); "User Studies and Library Planning," *Lib. Trends* (J. 1976); Series Ed., Scarecrow Press Series on Lib. Admin. (1980). **Activities:** 9, 13; 17, 24, 26; 50, 92 **Addr.:** R.D. 1, Ticonderoga, NY 12883.

Martin, Margaret B. (Ap. 10, 1951, Little Falls, NY) Head Libn., Hawkins, Delafield and Wood, 1976–; Asst. Libn., Cadwalader, Wickersham and Taft, 1975–76; Ref. Libn., Price Waterhouse, 1974–75. **Educ.:** CT Coll., 1969–73, BA (Hist., Fr.); Columbia Univ., 1973–74, MS (LS); NY Univ., 1976–80, MBA (Finance). **Orgs.:** AALL: SIS—PLL (Treas., 1978–79). Law LA of Grt. NY: Bd. (1976–77). SLA. **Pubns.:** Asst. Ed., *NY State* (1975–76). **Activities:** 12; 15, 17, 39; 77 **Addr.:** 157 Wyckoff St., Brooklyn, NY 11217.

Martin, Margaret Duckworth (O. 12, 1953, Cambden, AR) Law Libn., Fulton Cnty. Law Lib., 1979–; Acq. Libn., Duke Univ. Law Lib., 1978–79; Ref. Libn., 1978–78; Sch. Libn., St. Mary's Country Day Sch., 1977–78; Libn., Belton—Honea Path HS, 1976–77. **Educ.:** Univ. of SC, 1971–75, BA (Eng.), 1975–76, ML (Libnshp.). **Orgs.:** Atlanta Law Libs. Assn.: Secy.–Treas. (1981); Cont. Educ. Com. (Ch., 1982). AALL: Rel. with Pubshrs. and Dlrs. (1980–81); Exch. of Dupl. (1979–80); Constn. and Bylaws Com. (1981–82); Southeast. Chap., Resol. Com. (1979–80), Cnty. and Ct. Lib. Com. (Ch., 1980–81). **Honors:** South East. Chap., AALL, Lucile Elliot Schol., 1980–; AALL, Schol. for Natl. Con., 1978. **Activities:** 4, 12; 15, 17, 39; 77, 78 **Addr.:** Fulton County Law Library, Rm. 709, Fulton Superior Court, 136 Pryor St., S.W., Atlanta, GA 30303.

Martin, (Irma) Margareta (Ag. 6, 1930, Helsinki, Finland) Info. Sci., Tech. Info. Srvs., The Coca-Cola Co., 1975–; Ref. Libn., Emory Univ., 1973–74; Prin. Investigator, US Ofc. of Educ. Grant, George Peabody Coll., 1970. **Educ.:** Svenska Handelshögskolan, Helsinki, Finland, 1949–52, BA (Lang., Econ.); IN Univ., 1953–54, MA (Compar. Lit., Pol Sci.); George Peabody Coll., 1968–69, MLS. **Orgs.:** SLA: S. Atl. Chap., Exec. Bd. (1975–). AAUW. Atlanta Suomi–Finland Socty. **Honors:** Beta Phi Mu, 1969; Pi Sigma Alpha, 1954. **Pubns.:** Jt. Auth., "An Investigation of More Effective Means of Organization and Utilization of the Nashville Union Catalog," ERIC (1971); Jt. Auth., "Alcoholic and Non-Alcoholic Beverages," *Food Science and Technology: A Bibliography of Recommended Materials* (1978); Jt. Auth., "The Nashville Union Catalog," *TN Libn.* (1971); *Guide to the Use of Foreign Libraries* (1974); *Locating Book Reviews and Critiques* (1974). **Activities:** 1, 12; 20, 34, 39; 68, 91, 92 **Addr.:** 222 Woodview Dr., Decatur, GA 30030.

Martin, Margy E. (S. 28, 1924, Mill Valley, CA) Dir., Lib. Srvs., NE West. Coll., 1965–; Chld. Libn., Oakland Pub. Lib., 1946–48. **Educ.:** NE West. Coll., 1942–44, AA; Univ. of Denver, 1944–46, BA (LS), 1967–69, MA (LS). **Orgs.:** ALA. NE LA. Panhandle Lib. Adv. Cncl.: Pres. NE State Lib. Adv. Cncl.: Pres. AAUW. P.E.O. **Honors:** Delta Kappa Gamma. **Activities:** 1; 17, 20, 31 **Addr.:** Nebraska Western College Library, 1601 E. 27th N.E., Scottsbluff, NE 69361.

Martin, Marilyn J. (Ja. 17, 1940, Golden Meadow, LA) Asst. Ref. Libn., Pac. Luth. Univ., 1979–; Cat., Ref. Libn., St. Martin's Coll., 1976–79. **Educ.:** Univ. of WA, 1974–75, BA (Hist.), 1975–76, ML (Libnshp.). **Orgs.:** WA LA. Pac. NW LA. Untd. Meth. Church. **Honors:** Phi Beta Kappa, 1976; Beta Phi Mu, 1976. **Pubns.:** Asst. Ed., *A Catalogue of Materials Found in the Archives of the Pacific Northwest Annual Conference of the United Methodist Church* (1981). **Activities:** 1, 2; 31, 34, 39; 59, 92, 95-On-line srch. **Addr.:** Mortvedt Library, Pacific Lutheran University, Tacoma, WA 98447.

Martin, Mary H. (Ap. 12, 1924, Flint, MI) Pub. Srvs. Libn., Gen. Motors Inst., 1968–, Ref. Libn., 1965–68, Libn., Dsgn. Staff, 1965; Elem. Tchr., Flint Syst., 1962–64. **Educ.:** Mott Cmnty. Coll., 1956–58, AA (Liberal Arts); Univ. of MI, 1958–60, AB (Liberal Arts, Sci.), 1964–65, AMLS. **Orgs.:** SLA: Bylaws Com. (1975–76); Mem. Com. (1974). **Activities:** 1; 22, 39, 45; 64, 81, 91 **Addr.:** 5238 Briar Crest Dr., Flint, MI 48504.

Martin, Murray S. (Jl. 21, 1928, Lower Hutt, New Zealand) Univ. Libn., Tufts Univ., 1981–; Assoc. Dean of Libs., PA State Univ., 1973–81; Assoc. Dir. for Col. Dev., 1970–72, Chief Acq. Libn., 1967–70; Head, Serials Dept., Univ. of SK, 1965–66, Branch Lib. Coord., 1963–65; Order Libn., New Zealand Natl. Lib. Srv., 1957–63; First Asst., Palmerston N., Country Lib. Srv., 1954–57. **Educ.:** Univ. of New Zealand, 1946–48, BA (Eng./Fr.), 1949, MA (Eng.), 1953–58, B. Comm. (Acctg.); New Zealand Lib. Sch., 1950, Dip. **Orgs.:** ALA: RTSD Ch., Bookdealer-Lib. Rel. Com. (1967–73); Ch., Resrcs. Sect.; Mem. Com. (1978–, Ch., 1979–); LAMA, By-Laws Com. (1979–80). Pittsburgh Reg. Lib. Ctr.: Ch., Resrch Dev. Com. (1977–79); VP (1979–80) Pres. (1980–81). PA LA. Universal Serials and Book Exch. Sierra Club. Amer. Philatelic Socty. Mensa. Amer. Assoc. of Univ. Admin. **Honors:** New Zealand LA, Assoc., 1956. **Pubns.:** *Budgetary Control in Academic Libraries* (1978); "Buying, Borrowing, and Bibliographers", *Library Acquisitions: Theory and Practice* (1979); "Promoting Microforms to Students and Faculty," *Microform Review* (Spr. 1979); "The Allocation of Money Within the Book Budget", *Collection Development in Libraries* (1980); "Faculty and Other Resources," IN *The College of Liberal Arts in the 1980's* (1978); Other articles. **Activities:** 1; 17, 24, 35; 54, 70, 94 **Addr.:** Tufts University Library, Medford, MA 02155.

Martin, Nina Nix (F. 12, 1932, Laurel, MS) Assoc. Prof., Grad. Sch. of lib. Srv., Univ. of AL, 1973–; Coord., ESEA Title II, AL State Dept. Educ., 1966–73; Libn., Rain HS, Mobile, 1961–66; Tchr./Libn., Mobile Pub. Sch., 1951–61. **Educ.:** Univ. South. BS, 1949–55; LA State Univ., 1963–65, MS (LS); Auburn Univ., 1969–73, Ed.D. (Educ. Admin). **Orgs.:** AECT: Bd. of Dir. (1972–75). AL Instr. Media Assn.: Legis. Ch. AL LA: VP (1973); Ch., Rcrt. Com. (1978). ALA. **Honors:** Beta Phi Mu. **Pubns.:** Jt. auth., "Instructional Development at the K-12 level" *Southeastern Libn.* (Spr. 1979); "Media for Moppets" (1969); "The Media Center" (1969); other articles; reviews. **Activities:** 10, 11; 17, 28, 32; 50, 63, 89 **Addr.:** Box 6242, University, AL 35486.

Martin, Noelene P. (D. 14, 1929, Palmerston N., New Zealand) Chief, ILL Dept., PA State Univ., 1973–, ILL Libn., 1969–73, Asst. Agri. and Bio. Sci. Libn., 1967–69; Vetny. Med. Libn., Univ. of SK, 1965–67; Sr. Asst., Sch. Lib. Srv., Wellington, New Zealand, 1957–64. **Educ.:** Univ. of New Zealand, 1948–51, BA (Fr.), 1951–53, MA (Fr.); New Zealand LA, 1954–56, Cert. **Orgs.:** Pittsburgh Reg. Lib. Ctr.: Clearinghouse Com. (Ch., 1978–). ALA: RASD, ILL Com. (1978–82; Ch. 1980–82). OCLC Inc.: ILL Adv. Com. (1979–). **Honors:** New Zealand LA, Assoc., 1960. **Activities:** 1, 14; 27, 34, 40; 54, 55, 58 **Addr.:** Pattee Library, The Pennsylvania State University, University Park, PA 16802.

Martin, R. Lawrence (Ja. 31, 1936, Palo, MI) Coord., Ferris Arch., Ferris State Coll. Lib., 1975–, Head, Indp. Std. Dept., 1972–75, Asst. Libn., 1960–72. **Educ.:** Univ. of MI, 1954–58, AB (Art Hist.); 1958–60, AM (LS). **Orgs.:** SAA. MI Arch. Assn.: Exec. Bd. (1978–81). Amer. Assn. for State and Lcl. Hist. Hist. Socty. of MI. **Pubns.:** "Mr. Ferris' Clock," *Ferris Heritage* (Fall 1979); "1950 Fire Stuns Community," *Ferris Heritage* (Spr. 1980). **Addr.:** Ferris State College Library, 901 S. State, Big Rapids, MI 49307.

Martin, Rachel S. (Ag. 18, 1918, Mount Olive, NC) Dir., Furman Univ. Lib., 1978–, Assoc. Libn., 1972–78, Ref., Serials Libn., 1957–72; Head, Hum. Div., FL State Univ., 1956–57; Libn., Mary Baldwin Coll., 1951–56; Asst. Ref. Libn., Auburn Univ., 1949–51; Libn., Lindley Jr. HS, 1946–49; Tchr., NC Pub. Sch., 1939–46. **Educ.:** Brenau Coll., 1936–39, BA (Hist., Eng.); Univ. of NC, 1947–49, BSLS; State Univ. of IA, 1954–55, MA (Hist., Gvt.). **Orgs.:** ALA: Ref. and Subscrpn. Bks. Review Com. (1968–74). SELA: Nom. Com. (Ch., 1960); Ref. Srvc. Div. (Ch., 1964–66). SC LA: Sec. (1959); Mem. Com. (Ch., 1961). AAUP. Altrusa Clb.: Pres. (1969–71). Zeta Tau Alpha. **Honors:** Beta Phi Mu. **Pubns.:** "Index to Furman Studies", *Furman Std.* (1959). **Activities:** 1; 39 **Addr.:** 220 Covington Rd., Greenville, SC 29609.

Martin, Roger M. (Jl. 8, 1928, Stamford, TX) Dept. Head, Readr. Srvs. Div., Nvl. Postgrad. Sch., 1974–; Mgr., Info. Ctr., Amer. Express Investment Mgt. Co., 1968–74; Chief Libn., Shell Dev. Co., 1961–68; various positions, John Crerar Lib., 1954–60. **Educ.:** Univ. of TX, 1947–49, BS (Chem., Chemical Engin.), 1950–53, MS (Chem.), 1953–58, MLS. **Orgs.:** SLA: Bd. of Dir. (1973–75). ALA: Subscrpn. Bks. Bltn. Com. (1958–61). **Activities:** 1, 12; 15, 16, 17; 59, 60, 62 **Addr.:** P.O. Box 8724 NPS, Monterey, CA 93940.

Martin, Rosary Anne Henry (N. 6, 1946, New Orleans, LA) Med. Libn., Luth. Med. Ctr., 1975–; Ref. Libn., Cleveland State Univ., 1970–71; Bio. Libn., Case West. Rsv. Univ., 1968–70. **Educ.:** Xavier Univ. of LA, 1963–67, BS (Bio.); Case West. Rsv. Univ., 1967–68, MSLS. **Orgs.:** Med. LA. OH Hosp. Assn.: Lib. Srvs. Com. (1978–80). Natl. Assn. Negro Bus. and Prof. Women: Cleveland Chap., Parlmt. Eta Phi Beta Sorority. NAACP. Cleveland Bus. Leag. **Activities:** 5; 15, 17, 39; 80 **Addr.:** 2609 Franklin Blvd., Cleveland, OH 44113.

PROFESSIONAL ACTIVITIES: Institutions: 1. Acad. lib.; 2. Arch.; 3. Assn.; 4. Fed./Gvt. lib.; 5. Inst. lib.; 6. Mfr./Suppl.; 7. Milit. lib.; 8. Musm.; 9. Pub. lib.; 10. Sch. lib.; 11. Sch. of lib. sci.; 12. Spec. lib.; 13. State lib.; 14. (other). **Functions/Activities:** 15. Acq./Col. dev.; 16. Adult srvs.; 17. Admin.; 18. Apprais.; 19. Archit./Bldgs.; 20. Cat./Class.; 21. Chld. srvs.; 22. Circ.; 23. Cons./Pres.; 24. Consult.; 25. Cont. ed.; 26. Educ. lib. sci.; 27. Ext. srvs.; 28. Fund/Grants; 29. Gvt. pubs.; 30. Indx./Abs.; 31. Instr. lib. use; 32. Media srvs.; 33. Micro.; 34. Netwks./Coop.; 35. Persnl.; 36. PR; 37. Publshg.; 38. Recs. mgt.; 39. Ref. srvs.; 40. Repro.; 41. Resrch.; 42. Review.; 43. Secur.; 44. Serials; 45. Spec. col.; 46. Tech. srvs.; 47. Trustees/Bds.; 48. YA srvs.; 49. (other).

Martin, Rosemary S. (F. 12, 1935, Cumberland, MS) Dir., Ctrl. AR Lib. Syst., 1978–; Mgr., N. Zone, Branch Srvs., Dallas Pub. Lib., 1977–78; Coord., Chld. Srvs., Memphis Pub. Lib., 1974–76, Asst. Coord., Chld. Srvs., 1973–73, Head, Student Ctr., 1971–72; Head Libn., Memphis Acad. of Arts, 1968–70; Catlgr., Austin Pub. Lib., 1967–68; Asst. Branch Head, Memphis Pub. Lib., 1967; Various other lib. positions, 1965–66. **Educ.:** MS Women's Univ., 1953–56, 1961, BSLS; Univ. of WI, 1972–73, MLS. **Orgs.:** ALA: PLA (Educ. for Pub. Libns., 1978–79; Mem. Com. 1979–81; Prog. Com. Ch., 1982; other Coms.); YASD, Task Force on Personal Crisis (1976–79); LAMA, Ad Hoc Com. on Prog. Actv. (1977–78); AR LA: Legis. Com. (1980–81). **Honors:** Beta Phi Mu. **Addr.:** Central Arkansas Library System, 700 Louisiana, Little Rock, AR 72201.

Martin, Sally E. (My. 2, 1942, Janesville, WI) Supvsr. of Chld. Srvs., Pasadena Pub. Lib., 1974–, Supvsg. Libn. Branch, Prog. Libn., Ctrl. Chld. Room, Libn., Ctrl. Chld. Room, 1965–74. **Educ.:** Univ. of WI, 1960–64, BA (Eng.); Univ. of South. CA, 1964–65, MSLS. **Orgs.:** ALA. CA LA: Chld. Srvs. Chap. (Secy. 1980–81). South. CA Cncl. on Lit. for Chld. and Young People: Bd. (1979–81). Chld. Liter. Assn. **Activities:** 9; 17, 21 **Addr.:** Pasadena Public Library, 285 E. Walnut St., Pasadena, CA 91101.

Martin, Sarah S. (S. 1, 1945, Charleston, SC) Libn., Natl. Radio Astr. Observatory, 1975–; Head Catlgr., Univ. of VA Law Lib., 1974–75, Admin. Asst. to Law Libn., 1973–74; Chief, Tech. Order Lib., Edwards AFB, CA, 1972, Base Libn., 1970–72. **Educ.:** College of Charleston, 1963–67, BA (Grmn.); Univ. of MD, 1968–70, MLS. **Orgs.:** SLA: Phys.-Astr. Math. Div. (Ch., 1980–81); VA Chap., Mem. (Ch., 1979–80); Phys.-Astr.-Math. Div. (Proj. Ch., 1976–77). **Pubns.:** Jt. auth. *Bibliographic Guide to Astronomy and Astrophysics for the 70s* forthcoming; "Managing Reprints and Preprints in an Observatory Library," *Spec. Libs.* (N., 1979); "Bibliography of IAU Colloquia," *PAM Bltn.* (D. 1975, D. 1976). **Activities:** 12; 17, 20, 39; 56, 64, 88 **Addr.:** Library, National Radio Astronomy Observatory, Edgemont Rd., Charlottesville, VA 22901.

Martin, Shelby Ann (Ap. 22, 1943, South Boston, VA) Head Cat. Libn., Montgomery Cnty. Cmnty. Coll., 1975–; Catlgr., SUNY, New Paltz, 1969–75. **Educ.:** Radford Coll., 1961–65, BSLS; Rutgers Univ., 1968–69, MLS; GA Dept. of Arch. and Hist. Arch. Inst., 1973, Cert. (Arch.). **Orgs.:** ALA. SAA. Mid-Atl. Reg. Arch. Conf. Natl. Trust for Hist. Prsrvn. **Pubns.:** "Winifred Bryher," *Bltn. of the NY Pub. Lib.* (Sum. 1976). **Activities:** 1, 2; 20, 39; 55, 56 **Addr.:** 52 Shannon Rd., North Wales, PA 19454.

Martin, Susan K. (N. 14, 1942, Cambridge, Eng.) Dir., Milton S. Eisenhower Lib., Johns Hopkins Univ., 1979–; Head, Lib. Sys. Off., Univ. of CA, Berkeley, 1973–79; Syst. Libn., Harvard Univ. Lib., 1965–73. **Educ.:** Tufts Univ., 1959–63, BA (Romance Lang.); Simmons Coll., 1964–65, MLS; Univ. of CA, Berkeley, 1976. **Orgs.:** ALA: LITA (Pres., 1978–79). ASIS: Ch. Tech. Prog., 1976. **Honors:** Simmons Coll., Disting. Alum. Awd., 1977; Cncl. on Lib. Resrcs., Flwshp., 1973; Phi Beta Kappa, 1963. **Pubns.:** *Library Networks, 1981–82* (1981); *Library Automation:* (1975); Ed., *Jrnl. of Lib. Auto.* (1973–77); Cont. Ed., Adv. Tech./Libs. (1973–). **Activities:** 1; 17, 24, 34; 56 **Addr.:** Milton S. Eisenhower Library, Johns Hopkins University, 34th and Charles St., Baltimore, MD 21218.

Martin, Thomas H. (S. 2, 1941, Portland, OR) Assoc. Prof., Sch. of Info. Std., Syracuse Univ., 1980–; Asst. Prof., Annenberg Sch. of Comm., Univ. of Southern CA, 1974–80; Lectr., Resrch. Assoc., Stanford Univ., Inst. for Comm. Resrch., 1972–74, Syst. Prog., 1969–71. **Educ.:** Dartmouth Coll., 1959–63, BA (Math.); Univ. of CA, Berkeley, 1963–66, LLB (Law); Stanford Univ., 1969–74, PhD (Comm.). **Orgs.:** ASIS: SIG/VOI Ch. (1971–72, 74–75); SIG/LAW Ch. (1976–77); Future of Info. Sci. Com. (1978–80); Mktg. Com. (1978–80). Assn. for Comp. Mach. Intl. Comm. Assn. Amer. Assn. for the Adv. Sci. CA Bar Assn. **Pubns.:** *The Emerging Network Marketplace* (1980); *A Feature Analysis of Interactive Retrieval Systems* (1974); "Network Information Services," *Jrnl. of Telecomm. Pol.* (S. 1979); "Balance: An Aspect of the Right to Communicate," *Jrnl. of Comm.* (Spr. 1977); "Information Retrieval," *Human Interaction with Computers* (1980). **Activities:** 12; 26, 37, 41; 56, 75, 93 **Addr.:** Annenberg School of Communications, University of Southern California, Los Angeles, CA 90272.

Martin, Vernon E. (D. 15, 1929, Guthrie, OK) Head, Art and Msc. Dept., Hartford Pub. Lib., 1974–; Dir. of Lib. Srvs., Morningside Coll., 1970–74; Msc. Libn., N. TX State Univ., 1966–70; Msc. Libn., Lib. of Performing Arts, NY Pub. Lib., 1964–66. **Educ.:** Univ. of OK, 1956, BM; Columbia Univ., 1959, MM, 1965, MS. **Orgs.:** EFLA. Amer. Socty. of Composers, Auths. and Publshrs. **Honors:** Amer. Socty. of Composers, Auths. and Publshrs., Stan. Awd., 1968, 72. **Pubns.:** *Bibliography of Writings on Electronic Music* (1964); "Ladies Voices," cham. opera (1981). **Activities:** 9; 17; 55, 67 **Addr.:** Hartford Public Library, 500 Main St., Hartford, CT 06103.

Martin, William Terry (S. 5, 1948, Tuscaloosa, AL) Tech. Srvcs. Libn., Southeastern Baptist Theol. Sem., 1979–; Head, Tech. Srvcs./Asst. Prof., Lib., Samford Univ., 1977–79; Cat. Libn., Asst. Prof., Lib., 1974–77; Microfilm Libn., Instr. Lib., 1973–74. **Educ.:** Samford Univ., 1967–69, AB (Hist./Rel.); Univ. of AL, 1971–73, MLS, Samford Univ., 1974–76, MA (Rel.). **Orgs.:** Amer. Theo. LA. Southeastern LA. NC LA. AL LA: Nom. Com., JMRT (1977–78). AL Baptist Hist. Socty. Ed. Nwsltr. (1979); Dist. VP (1977–78). Southern Baptist Hist. Socty. **Activities:** 1; 15, 20; 46; 61, 69, 90 **Addr.:** Rt. 4, Box 197A, Wake Forest, NC 27587.

Martinelli, James A. (Ap. 24, 1951, Paterson, NJ) Serials / Hlth. Sci. Catlgr., VA Commonwealth Univ., 1976–. **Educ.:** William Paterson Coll., 1969–73, BA (Hist.); Rutgers Univ., 1974–75, MLS; Med. Libn. Cert. 1980. **Orgs.:** ALA. Med. LA. Hlth. Sci. OCLC Users Grp. VA LA. **Honors:** Beta Phi Mu. **Pubns.:** "Descriptive Cataloging of Serials," *Bltn. of the Med. LA* (Ja. 1980); Jt. auth., "Recruitment of Academic Librarians," *Behvl. and Soc. Sci. Libn.* (Win. 1979); "Bilingual Slide-tape Library Orientation," *AV Instr.* (Ja. 1976); Ed., *Terminal Talk,* nsltr. of the VA LA SOLINET Users Forum (1979–). **Addr.:** Virginia Commonwealth Univ. Library Cataloging Dept., 901 Park Ave., Richmond, VA 23284.

Martinez, Angelina (Ag. 27, 1920, Ponce, PR) Asst. Dir., Univ. Lib., CA Polytech. State Univ., 1966–, Actg. Dir., Lib., 1979–80; Dir., Readr. Srvs. Div., NV State Lib., 1964–66; Head, Ref. Dept., Subj. Spec. in Bio. Sci. and Agr., Univ. of CA, Davis, 1962–64, Gvt. Docum. Libn., 1959–62; Head Libn., Inter-Amer. Inst. of Agr. Sci., Org. of Amer. States, Turrialba, Costa Rica, 1946–59; Jr. Catlgr., Org. of Amer. States, Washington, DC, 1946; Asst. Libn., Inter-Amer. Univ., 1945–46. **Educ.:** Inter-Amer. Univ., 1939–43, AB (Eng., Psy., Educ.); LA State Univ., 1944–45, BS LS; Univ. of IL, 1956–57, MS (LS). **Orgs.:** ALA. CA LA. Lib. and Media People, San Luis Obispo. Lib. Assoc., Univ. Lib. CA Polytech. State Univ. **Honors:** Beta Phi Mu, 1957. **Pubns.:** *Coffee Bibliography* (1953); *Cacao Bibliography* (1954); "Problems of Latin American Agricultural Libraries," *Intl. Assn. of Agr. Libns. and Documlsts.* (Ja.–Ap. 1957); *Corn Bibliography* (1960); "Service to Special Clienteles," *A Century of Service, Librarianship in the United States and Canada* (1976). **Activities:** 1; 17, 35, 36; 56, 57, 61 **Addr.:** 1148 Atascadero St., San Luis Obispo, CA 93401.

Martinez, Eloise F. (Havana, Cuba) Lib. Supvsr., Amoco Intl. Oil Co., 1980–; Info. Technologist, Shell Oil Co., 1972–80; Sr. Libn., LA State Univ., 1968–72; Supvsr., Ctrl. Amer. Bank for Economic Integration, Tegucigalpa, Honduras, 1963–68. **Educ.:** Univ. of Miami, BA (Liberal Arts); LA State Univ., MS (Lib. Sci.); Univ. of Honduras, LB (Lib. Sci.); Hollywood Prof. Coll. CB (Bus.). **Orgs.:** ASIS. SLA: Cont. Ed. Com. Houston Online Users Grp. Geoscience Info. Socty. **Honors:** UNESCO Awd. for Prof. Merit, 1968. **Activities:** 12; 17, 34, 39; 64, 86, 91 **Addr.:** P.O. Box 4381, Houston, TX 77210.

Martinez, Joan S. (O. 7, 1932, Casa Grande, AZ) Coord. of Ref. Srvs., Riverside City and Cnty. Pub. Lib., 1977–; Ref. Libn., Libn. in Charge, Los Angeles Cnty. Pub. Lib., 1970–77, Ref. Libn., Los Angeles Pub. Lib. 1970. **Educ.:** OH State Univ., 1950–53, BA (Psy.); Immaculate Heart Coll., 1968–69, MLS; CA State Univ, Fullerton, 1976–79, MPA (Pub Admin.). **Orgs.:** CA LA: Cncl. (1977–80); Ch., South. Col. Dev. Chap. (1979); CA Socty. of Libns. nom. com. (1979). ALA. **Activities:** 9; 15, 17, 39 **Addr.:** 10961 Marian Dr., Garden Grove, CA 92640.

Martinez, Julio Antonio (O. 4, 1931, Santiago, Oriente, Cuba) Assoc. Libn., San Diego State Univ., 1973–; Ref. Libn., St. Clair Shores Pub. Lib., 1966–68. **Educ.:** South. IL Univ., 1958–63, BA (Rom. Lang.); Univ. of MI, 1966–67, MALS; Univ. of MN, 1969–71, MA (Phil.); Univ. of CA, Riverside, 1975–80, PhD (Phil.). **Orgs.:** NLA: Prof. Welfare Com. (Ch., 1975–80), Exec. Bd. (1978–80). CA LA: Coll. Univ. Chap. REFORMA. Socty. Interdisciplinary Std. Mind: Edit. Bd. (1977–). Mensa. **Pubns.:** *Estudio Español* (1961); *A Bibliography of Writings on Plato* (1978); *Chicano Scholars and Writers* (1979); Ed., *Cyclopedia of Chicano Literature* (Forthcoming); "The Comparable Worth Study", *LJ Special Report* (#10); various articles. **Activities:** 1; 55, 66 **Addr.:** Malcolm A. Love Library, San Diego State University, San Diego, CA 92182-0511.

Martinez, Katharine (Ja. 17, 1950, Baltimore, MD) Head of Access and Support Servs., Avery Lib., Columbia Univ., 1981–. Chief Libn., Lib. of the Natl. Col. of Fine Arts and the Natl. Portrait Gallery, Smithsonian Inst., 1974–. 1980–81, Asst. Libn., 1974–80. **Educ.:** Univ. of DE, 1968–72, BA (Art Hist.); IN Univ., 1972–74, MLS, George Washington Univ., 1977, PhD (Amer. Std.). **Orgs.:** ARLIS/NA: Natl. Ch. (1978); Nom. Com. (1977); Art Publshg. Awd. Com. (1977). **Activities:** 1, 17, 39; 41, 55 **Addr.:** Avery Library, Columbia University, Broadway at 116th St., New York, NY 10027.

Martinez, Nancy Carol (N. 18, 1948, Utica, NY) Head Branch Libn., Weber Cnty. Lib., 1979–, YA Libn., 1977–79, Satellite Branch Lib., 1976–77; Elem. Media Spec., Hillcrest Elem., 1975–76. **Educ.:** Univ. of CA, Davis, 1968–70, BA (Eng.); Univ. of MI, 1971–72, AMLS. **Orgs.:** ALA. UT LA: Pub. Lib. Strg. Com. (1979–81). Planned Parenthood, Ogden. UT State Univ. Ext. Srv. **Activities:** 9, 10; 16, 39, 48; 66, 89 **Addr.:** Weber County Library, Southwest Branch, 1950 W. 4800 S., Roy, UT 84067.

Martini (Queirolo-Martini), Sarah V. (Je. 10, 1934, Philadelphia, PA) Libn., Consult., Lib. Dev., Freelnc., 1977–; Head, Tech. Srvs., Lib. Dev., IL Inst. of Tech., Kent Coll. of Law, 1974–77; Head., Cat., Cat. Dev., IL Lib. Mtrls. Prcs. Ctr., 1971–73; Libn., Dev. Proj., Cook Cnty. Law Lib., 1969–70; Head Catlgr., Loyola Univ. Law Sch., Chicago, 1965–67; Libn., Dev. Proj., IN Univ., Kokomo Campus, 1964–65; Catlgr., Mss. Proj., Pius XII Meml. Lib., St. Louis Univ., 1960–64; various positions in lib. sci. **Educ.:** Chestnut Hill Coll., 1952–56, AB (Phil., Eng. Lit.); Univ. of Chicago, 1968, MA (LS). **Orgs.:** Chicago Assn. of Law Libns. AALL. AAUP. **Addr.:** 4940 S. East End Ave., Chicago, IL 60615.

Martyn, Dorian E. (S. 25, 1951, Detroit, MI) Catlgr., Univ. Miami Med. Lib., 1981–; AV Srvs. Libn., Med. Coll. of GA, 1978–80, Interpretive Srvs. Libn., 1976–78. **Educ.:** MI State Univ., 1969–73, BA (Hum.); Case-Western Reserve Univ., 1975–76, MSLS; Med. Lib. Assn. cert., 1976. **Orgs.:** Med. LA: Ad Hoc Com. to Study MLA's Role in Lib.-Related Resrch., (1978–80); South. Reg. Grp., Bylaws Rev. Com. (1979). GA LA: Exec. Com. (1977–79); Spec. Libs. Sect., (Ch., 1977–79); Gvt. Rel. Com. (1979–81). Augusta Area Com. for Hlth. Info. Resrcs.: Bd. (1979–80). GA Hlth. Sci. LA. Other orgs. **Honors:** Phi Beta Kappa, 1973; Beta Phi Mu, 1976. **Pubns.:** *Source List for Patient Education Materials* (1978); Ed., *UPDATE. GA Hlth. Sci. LA Nsltr.* (1977–79). **Activities:** 1, 12; 20, 32, 39; 58, 80, 95-Allied Hlth. Sci. **Addr.:** Louis Calder Memorial Library, University of Miami, School of Medicine, P.O. Box 16950, Miami, FL 33101.

Martz, David J. Jr. (Je. 2, 1946, Williamsport, PA) Dir., Ward M. Canaday Ctr. for Spec. Cols., Univ. of Toledo, 1980–; Coord. of Resrch. Col., Colonial Williamsburg Fndn., 1977–80; Cur. of Mss., Brown Univ. Lib., 1975–77. **Educ.:** Duke Univ., 1964–68, BA (Hist.), 1970–78, PhD (Hist.); Univ. of NC, Chapel Hill, 1974–75, MSLS. **Orgs.:** ALA: Ofc. of Lib. Persnl. Resrcs. Adv. Com. (1977–79). SAA: Com. on Arch./Lib. Rel. (1976–78). SLA. **Orgs.:** Amer. Hist. Assn. **Honors:** Beta Phi Mu, 1975. **Pubns.:** "Manuscripts as Literary Property," *Mss.* (Win. 1977); "Beyond Innovation," *Learning Today* (Spr. 1979); "Peter Force," *ALA Encyc.* (1980). **Activities:** 1, 2; 15, 45; 55 **Addr.:** The Ward M. Canaday Center, William S. Carlson Library, The University of Toledo, Toledo, OH 43606.

Marulli-Koenig, Luciana (F. 29, 1948, Genova, Italy) Biblgphr., UN Lib., 1980–; Docum. Ref. Libn., 1977–80, Docum. and Syst. Anal., 1973–77; Supervsr., Cat. Sect., Fine Arts Lib., Harvard Univ., 1971–73; Tech. Srvs. Libn., Dept. of Human Physio. Lib., Univ. of Rome, Italy, 1966–69. **Educ.:** Univ. of Rome, Italy, 1964–68, (Econ.); Kent State Univ., 1969–71, MLS; Columbia Univ., 1975–79, PhD (LS); Scuola Vaticana Di Biblioteconomia, Vatican City, 1968–69, Dip. (LS) Columbia Univ., 1973–75, Cert. (LS). **Orgs.:** Italian LA. Art Libs. Socty. of N. Amer.: Intl. Rel. Com. (1973). ASIS. **Honors:** Fulbright-Hayes, Travel grant; 1969–71; Columbia Univ., George Virgil Fuller Awd., 1977. **Pubns.:** *Documentation of the United Nations System: Coordination of its Bibiographic Control* (1979); *The Coordination of Bibliographic Control in the Organizations of the United Nations System* (1979); "International Documents Round-Up," (bimonthly clmn. *Documents to the People* (Ja. 1980–); "Bibliographic Products and Services of the Dag Hammarskjold Library," *Docum. to the People* (Je. 1979); "Bradford Distribution of Data Elements," *Jnl. of the Amer. Socty. for Info. Sci.* (Mr. 1979); "The Dag Hammarskjold Library and United Nations Documentation," *UNESCO Bltn. for Libs.,* (Ja.–F. 1978); various reviews and articles. **Activities:** 1, 4; 29, 31, 39; 54, 56, 62 **Addr.:** 320 E. 42nd St., New York, NY 10017.

Maruskin, Albert F. (Ja. 8, 1933, Harmarville, PA) Coord., Tech. Srvs., Manderino Lib., CA (PA) State Coll., 1966–; Acad. Adv., Univ. of Pittsburgh, 1964–66. **Educ.:** PA State Univ., 1954–58, BA (Gen. Arts and Letters); Univ. of Pittsburgh, 1964–65, MLS, 1975–79, PhD (Higher Educ. Admin.). **Orgs.:** ALA. PA LA: Bd. of Dir. (1975–76); State Legis. Com. (1979–80); Tech. Srvs. RT Div. (Ch., 1975–76); Southwest Chap., Mem. Com. (Ch., 1975–76), Exec. Bd. (1975–76, 1980–81); various com., ofcs. AAUP. Natl. Educ. Assn. **Honors:** Beta Phi Mu, 1966; Phi Delta Kappa, 1980. **Pubns.:** *OCLC: Its Governance, Function, Financing and Technology* (1980). **Activities:** 1; 15, 34, 46; 56, 63, 75 **Addr.:** Manderino Library, CA State College, California, PA 15062.

Marvin, James C. (Ag., 1927, Warroad, MN) Adjunct Fac., Emporia State Univ. Grad. Sch. of Lib. Sci., 1970–; Consult., Northeast KS Lib. Syst., 1970–; Dir., Topeka Pub. Lib., 1967–; ALA/Rockefeller Fndn. Visit. Prof., Univ. of the Philippines Grad. Lib. Sch. Proj., 1964–65; Dir., Cedar Rapids Pub. Lib., 1956–57; Dir., Eau Claire Pub. Lib., 1954–56. **Educ.:** Univ. of MN, 1946–50, BA (Econ.), 1950–52, MALS. **Orgs.:** WHCOLIS: KS Del. (Ch., 1979). KS LA: Legis. Com. (1978–). ALA: Cnclr., (1964–68); IRRT (Ch., 1969–70). IA LA: Pres. (1961–62). Various org. **Activities:** 9; 24, 26; 78 **Addr.:** 40 Pepper Tree Ln., Topeka, KS 66611.

Special Subjects/Services: 50. Adult educ.; 51. Advert./Mktg.; 52. Aerosp.; 53. Agric.; 54. Area std.; 55. Arts/Hum.; 56. Autom.; 57. Bibl./Prtg.; 58. Bio. sci.; 59. Bus./Fin.; 60. Chem.; 61. Copyrt.; 62. Documtn.; 63. Educ.; 64. Engin.; 65. Env.; 66. Eth. grps.; 67. Film; 68. Food/Nutr.; 69. Geneal.; 70. Geo.; 71. Geol.; 72. Handcpd.; 73. Hist.; 74. Int. frdm.; 75. Info. sci.; 76. Insr.; 77. Law; 78. Legis.; 79. Math./Comp. sci.; 80. Med.; 81. Metals; 82. Nat. resrcs.; 83. Newsp.; 84. Nuc. sci.; 85. Oral hist.; 86. Petr./Energy; 87. Pharm.; 88. Phys./Astr./Math.; 89. Readg.; 90. Relig.; 91. Sci./Tech.; 92. Soc. sci.; 93. Telecom.; 94. Transp.; 95. (other).

Marvin, Kathleen A. Parsons (S. 29, 1953, Bohemia, NY) Syst. Anal., Burroughs Corp., 1980–; Comp. Syst. Libn., Univ. of PA, 1979–80; Autom. Syst. Libn., Univ. of PR, 1978–79; Indxr., Abs., ERIC/IR, Syracuse Univ., 1977–78; Mktg. Resrchr., W. R. Simmons, Inc., 1974–76. **Educ.:** Elmira Coll., 1971–75, BA (Programming, Psy.); Syracuse Univ., 1976–78, MLS. **Orgs.:** ASIS. SLA. Socty. de Bibtcrs. de PR: Com. on PRILINET. **Honors:** Beta Phi Mu, 1979; Phi Beta Kappa, 1975. **Pubns.:** "Role of Facilitators in a Learning Resources Center," *Converging Trends* (1978); *Directory of Federal Grant Sources and Sources of Private Funds Given to New York State Public Libraries,* NY docum. **Activities:** 1; 30, 41, 46; 56, 62, 80 **Addr.:** 1407 Dodd Dr., Downington, PA 19335.

Marvin, Stephen G. (Mr. 2, 1952, Syracuse, NY) Gvt. and Bus. Libn., Chester Cnty. (PA) Lib., 1981–; Bus. Srvs. Consult., Ridley Twp. (PA) Pub. Lib., 1980–81; Dir., Lrng. Resrcs. Ctr., Intl. Inst. of the Americas of World Univ., 1978–79. **Educ.:** SUNY, Albany, 1972–74, BA (Span., Educ.); New York Univ., 1975–76, MA (Span.); Syracuse Univ., 1976–78, MLS. **Orgs.:** ALA. SBPR: Com. on PRILINET (1978–79). SALALM. AECT: Com. on Terms and Definitions (1979–81). **Pubns.:** "Role of Facilitators in a Learning Resources Center", *Converging Trends* (1978). **Activities:** 1, 9; 24, 25, 41; 59, 63, 66 **Addr.:** 1407 Dodd Dr., Downingtown, PA 19335.

Marwick, Lawrence (S. 16, 1909, Sopockinie, Poland) Head, Hebraic Sect., Lib. of Congs., 1948–; Adjunct Prof., Arabic and Islamic Std. Dropsie Coll.; Hebrew Lang. and Lit., NY Univ., 1954–70. **Educ.:** Univ. of Chicago, 1930–31, PhB (Ancient Hist.), 1931–32, MA (Ancient Hist.); Dropsie Coll., 1933–1937 PhD (Arabic Std.). Amer. Oriental Socty. Amer. Acad. for Jewish Resrch. **Honors:** Dropsie Coll. Distinguished Alum. Awd. **Pubns.:** *Diplomatic Hebrew* (1980); *A Century of American Yiddish Plays,* bibl. (1980); *American Yiddish Folksongs,* bibl. (1980); *Biblical and Judaic Acronyms* (1979); Co-ed., *Bloch Memorial Volume* (1960); various articles in *Jewish Qtly. Review* and *Std. in Bibl.* **Activities:** 1; 15, 17, 24; 54†

Marx, Victor F. (Ja. 18, 1934, Szentbekkalla, Hungary) Assoc. Prof. of Libnshp., Head Ref. Libn., Ctrl. WA Univ., 1969–; Libn., Libs. of Arnold Arboretum and Gray Herbarium, Harvard Univ., 1967–69; Instr. of Libnshp., Head Acq. Libn., Ctrl. WA State Coll., 1965–67. **Educ.:** Coll. of Horticulture and Viticulture, Budapest, Hungary, 1952–56; Univ. of BC, 1959–61, BSA (Agr.), 1961–64, MSA (Agr.); Univ. of WA, 1964–65, MLibr. **Orgs.:** WA LA. ALA: ACRL/Agr. and Bio. Sci. Subsect. (Secy., 1969–70), Ad Hoc Com. on Bot. Lit. (1969–71); RTSD/Resrc. Sect., Micropublshg. Com. (Ch., 1975–76)/Reprodct. of Lib. Mtrls. Sect., Policy and Resrch. Com. (1975–77). AAUP: WA State Conf. (Secy., 1976–78); Chap. Pres. (1978–79). **Honors:** Beta Phi Mu, 1966. **Pubns.:** Ed. bd., *Micro. Review* (1971–). **Activities:** 1; 31, 33, 39; 56, 63, 91 **Addr.:** Central Washington University Library, Ellensburg, WA 98926.

Marzone, Jean A. (S. 9, 1945, Jersey City, NJ) Assoc. Dir., Women's Educ. Equity Comm. Network, Far West Lab. for Educ. Resrch. and Dev., 1977–; Asst. Dir., ERIC Clearinghouse on Urban Educ., Tchrs. Coll., Columbia Univ., 1974–77, Acq. and User Srvs. Coord., 1969–74; Tchr., Petersburg (VA) Pub. Schs., 1968. **Educ.:** Douglass Coll., 1963–67, BA (Eng.); Tchrs. Coll., Columbia Univ., 1968–71, MA (Educ. Psy.). **Orgs.:** ASIS: Secy., Spec. Int. Grp./Info. Srvs. to Educ. (1979–80). ALA. SLA. Amer. Educ. Resrch. Assn. **Pubns.:** *The Assessment of Minority Groups: An Annotated Bibliography* (1973); *Women: Their Educational and Career Roles.* (1972); *Directory of Information Sources on the Disadvantaged* (1972); "Early Childhood: Implications for Sex Role Socialization Programming," *Network News and Notes* (Fall 1979). **Activities:** 12; 17, 39, 49-database building/maintenance; 63, 75 **Addr.:** Women's Educational Equity Communications Network, Far West Laboratory for Educational Research and Development, 1855 Folsom St., San Francisco, CA 94103.

Maseda, Maria M. (Ja. 23, 1930, Havana, Cuba) Libn., Cardinal Gibbons HS, Ft. Lauderdale, FL, 1972–; Asst. Prof., Span., Univ. of CT, 1964–70; Instr., Span., Univ. of Hartford, 1963–64; Tchr., Apostolado HS, 1955–61. **Educ.:** Univ. de la Habana, 1947–54, Doctor en Filosofia y Letras; Middlebury Coll., 1969–76, MA (Span.); State of FL, Tchrs. Cert. (Span., Media Spec., FL State Univ., 1979–81, MLS. **Orgs.:** ALA. Cath. LA. Amer. Assn. of Tchrs. of Span. and Portuguese. **Honors:** Beta Phi Mu. **Activities:** 10; 17, 48; 63 **Addr.:** 445 Alhambra Cir., Coral Gables, FL 33134.

Masek, Doris Bettie (Jl. 8, 1928, Chicago, IL) Elem. Sch. Libn./Media Spec., Jane Stenson Sch., 1964–; Sec. Grade Tchr., Devonshire Sch., 1957–64; Sec. Grade Tchr., Amer. Dependent Sch., Kaiserslautern, Germany, 1955–57; Sec. Grade Tchr., Lombard, IL, 1951–55; Sec. Grade Tchr., Des Plaines, IL, 1950–51. **Educ.:** North. IL Univ., 1946–50, BS (Educ.); Natl. Coll. of Educ., 1972–75, MA (Educ.). **Orgs.:** ALA: AASL. IL Assn. for Media in Educ.: Secy. (1979–80). Delta Kappa Gamma Socty. Intl.: Chap. Pres. (1976–78). **Honors:** Phi Delta Kappa; IL Congs. of Parents and Tchrs., Hon. Life Mem., 1978. **Pubns.:** "PR Through PETAL," *Sch. Lib. Jnl.* (D. 1977). **Activities:** 10; 17, 21, 31, 32 **Addr.:** 6815 N. Algonquin Ave., Chicago, IL 60646.

Masiello, Dennis R. (D. 31, 1946, Montebello, CA) Lib. Dir., Tempe Pub. Lib., 1979–; Lib. Dir., Porterville Pub. Lib., 1974–79; Reg. Ref. Libn., Los Angeles Cnty. Lib. Syst., Huntington Park, 1972–74, Libn. In-Charge, City of Bell, 1971–72. **Educ.:** CA State Coll., Los Angeles, 1969, BA (Amer. Std.); Univ. of South. CA, 1972, MSLS; CA State Coll., Cnsrtm., Fresno, 1976, MPA. (Pub. Admin.). **Orgs.:** ALA. AZ LA. **Activities:** 9; 17, 35, 36 **Addr.:** Tempe Public Library, 3500 S. Rural Rd., Tempe, AZ 85282.

Maslansky, Hannah V. (My. 15, 1943, Newport, S. Wales, Untd. Kingdom) Asst. Libn., Un. Carbide Corp., 1976–; Info. Sci., Amer. Cyanamid Co., 1975–76. **Educ.:** SUNY, Binghamton, 1961–65, BA (Chem.); Rutgers Univ., 1973–75, MLS. **Orgs.:** SLA. **Activities:** 12; 15, 20, 39; 60, 75, 91 **Addr.:** 5 Overhill Rd., Monsey, NY 10952.

Masling, Charles R. (Jl. 28, 1949, Monroe, LA) Head Libn., Neighborhood Info. Ctr., Houston Pub. Lib., 1979–, various positions as Branch Head, 1975–79; Head Ref. Libn., Austin Campus, Houston Cmnty. Coll., 1974–75. **Educ.:** Miltonvale Wesleyan Coll., 1969–70, AA (Eng.); Sam Houston State Univ., 1970–72, BA (Eng.); N. TX State Univ., 1973–74, MLS. **Orgs.:** ALA. TX LA. Alliance of Info. and Ref. Srvs. TX Alliance of Info. and Ref. Srvs.: Exec. Bd., Secy. **Pubns.:** *Directory of Community Resources for the Handicapped Child* (1980); "Community Analysis in a Fast Growth Situation," *Lib. Jnl. Spec. Rpt.* (Mr. 15, 1981). **Activities:** 75 **Addr.:** Houston Public Library, 500 McKinney Ave., Houston, TX 77002.

Maslyn, David C. (Ag. 11, 1936, Geneva, NY) Head, Spec. Col., Univ. Archvst., Univ. of RI, 1974–, Tchg., Grad. Lib. Sch., 1975–; Asst. Libn. for Mss. & Arch., Yale Univ., 1968–74; Assoc. Admin. of Mss., Syracuse Univ., 1965–67, Asst. Archvst., 1964–65. **Educ.:** St. Bonaventure Univ., 1956–60, BA (Hist.); Syracuse Univ., 1961–63, MA (Hist.), 1967, MSLS. **Orgs.:** SAA: Com. on Autom. Tech., Educ., Control & Descr., Terminology. New Eng. Archvst.: Treas. (1976–78). RI State Recs. Adv. Bd. **Pubns.:** Reviews. **Activities:** 1, 2; 17, 24, 26, 45; 57, 86 **Addr.:** University Library, Special Collections, Univ. of Rhode Island, Kingston, RI 02881.

Mason, Alexandra (Mr. 17, 1931, Greenfield, MA) Spencer Libn., Univ. of KS, 1975–, Asst. Dean of Libs., 1971–78, Head, Dept. of Spec. Col., 1963–74, Rare Bks. Catlgr., 1957–63; Asst. Rare Bks., Durham Univ., (Eng.), 1961–62. **Educ.:** Mt. Holyoke Coll., 1948–52, AB (Grk.); Carnegie Inst. of Tech., 1953–55, MLS. **Orgs.:** ALA: ACRL/Rare Bks. Mss. Sect. (Secy. 1970; Exec. Bd. 1976; Ch., 1981–82), Trng. Rare Bk. Libns. Com. (1972), Stan. Com. (1980–83); RTSD. Bibl. Socty. Amer. Indp. Rsrch. Libs. Grp./Rare Bks. Libs. Grp.: Com. on Mach. Readable Cat. of Rare Bks. (1979). Medvl. Acad. Amer. Renaissance Socty. Amer. **Honors:** Phi Beta Kappa, 1952. **Pubns.:** "Catesby, Corll, and Cook", *Eighteenth Century English Books* (1976). **Activities:** 1; 15, 20, 45; 55, 57, 95-Palaeography. **Addr.:** Kenneth Spencer Research Library, University of Kansas, Lawrence, KS 66045.

Mason, Charlene Kay (Jl. 19, 1942, Ames, IA) Dir., Ctrl. Admin. Srvs., Univ. of MN Libs., 1980–, Actg. Dir., Interim Coord., St. Paul Campus Libs., 1978–80, Asst. Dir., 1977–78, Head, Col. Prcs., 1976–77; Ref. Libn., Tech. Lib. and Bus. Info. Srv., MN Mining and Mfr., 1976; Asst. Libn., Tech. Lib., Cargill, Inc., 1975; Resrch. Fellow, Instr., Lib. Sch., Docum. Anal., Educ. Resrcs. Info. Ctr. Clearinghouse for Lib. and Info. Sci., Univ. of MN, 1966–69; Instr., Math. Dept., St. Cloud Univ., 1965. **Educ.:** IA State Univ., 1960–63, BS (Math.); Univ. of MN, 1964–76, MA (LS). **Orgs.:** ALA: ACRL, Legis. Com. (1980–82). MN LA. SLA: MN Chap. (Pres., 1977–78), Bd. (1979), Consolation Ofcr. (1976–78). ASIS: MI Chap. (Secy., 1971–72), Natl. Asm. (Rep., 1968–69). Untd. Church of Christ. **Honors:** Beta Phi Mu, 1965. **Pubns.:** Jr. Ed., *Information Retrieval with Special Reference to the Biomedical Sciences* (1964); "Bibliography of Library Automation," *ALA Bltn.* (S. 1969). **Activities:** 1, 12; 17, 35; 56, 75, 91 **Addr.:** 2140 Pennsylvania Ave. N., Golden Valley, MN 55427.

Mason, Elizabeth Branch (Ja. 1, 1919, Washington, DC) Actg. Dir., Oral Hist. Resrch. Ofc., Columbia Univ., 1980–, Assoc. Dir., 1968–80, Asst. Dir., 1964–68, Lectr., Sch. of Lib. Srv., 1973–. **Educ.:** Mt. Holyoke Coll., 1936–40, BA (Hist.); Columbia Univ., 1940–41, MA (Hist.). **Orgs.:** Oral Hist. Assn.: Prog. Ch. (1967); Nom. Com. (1968–69); Archvst. (1969–76); Exec. Cncl. (1978–81); Prog. Com. (1979–80); VP–Pres. elect (1981). **Pubns.:** Jt. Ed., *The Oral History Collection* (1960, 1964, 1973, 1979); Ed. Bd., *Oral Hist. Assn. Review* (1972–78). **Activities:** 1; 15, 24, 26; 85 **Addr.:** Box 20, Butler Library, Columbia University, New York, NY 10027.

Mason, Ellsworth G. (Ag. 25, 1917, Waterbury, CT) Head, Spec. Col. Dept., Univ. of CO Lib., 1976–, Dir., 1972–76; Dir., Hofstra Univ. Lib., 1963–72; Libn., CO Coll. Lib., 1958–63. **Educ.:** Yale Univ., 1934–38, BA (Econ.), 1939–48, MA, PhD (Eng. Lit.). **Orgs.:** ALA: Cncl. (1961–65); ACRL Stan. Com. (1962–66); ACRL Goals Com. (1961–65) other coms. Library Association (London). Colorado Book Collectors: Pres. (1972–). Bibl. Socty. of Amer.: Mem. Com. (1958–63). Pvt. Libs. Assn. Alcuin Socty. James Joyce Fndn.: Ch., Transl. of Joyce sect. (1972). Mod. Lang. Assn.: Ch., Robert Graves Sem. (1972). **Honors:** NY State Assn. of Archit./Amer. Inst. of Archit. Design Awd., 1974; Progressive Archit. Awd., 1975; Assn. of Coll. of the Midwest, Harry Bailly Speaker's Awd., 1975; Hofstra Univ., LHD, 1973. **Pubns.:** *Mason on Library Buildings* (1980); Ed. *The Critical Writings of James Joyce* (1959, 1964, 1966, 1973); "The Great Gas Bubble Prick't; or Computers Revealed," *Coll. & Resrch. Libs.* (My. 1971); "The Impact of Technology on the Library Building," *Can. Archit.* (Jl. 1968); *James Joyce's Ulysses and Vico's Cycle* Yale Library Microforms Editions (1973); Other books and articles. **Activities:** 1; 17, 19, 45; 55, 57, 95-Book Collecting. **Addr.:** Special Collections Department, University of Colorado Libraries, Boulder, CO 80309.

Mason, Florence Yoshioka (F. 21, 1928, Honolulu, HI) Head Libn., Barr Meml. Lib., Fort Knox, KY, 1968–, Ref. Libn., Post Lib., 1963–68; Libn., Army Lib. Srvs., Europe, 1954–56; Branch Libn., Honolulu, HI, 1951–54. **Educ.:** Univ. of HI, 1946–50, BA (Hist.); Univ. of MN, 1950–51, BSLS; various sem., crs. **Orgs.:** KY LA. KY 4th Dist. LA. GFWC, KFWC Radcliff Woman's Club. St. Christopher Altar Socty. Fort Knox Fed. Empl. Women. **Honors:** Fort Knox Equal Oppt. Ofc., Letters of Apprec., 1979, 1980; Fort Knox Jewish Chaplain's Sect., Letter of Apprec., 1980; Alpha Kappa Alpha, Mu Delta Omega Chap., work towards providing better lib. srv. for chld., 1980. **Activities:** 4, 9; 16, 17, 21; 50, 74 **Addr.:** 376 Park Ave., Radcliff, KY 40160.

Mason, Frank O. (Je. 25, 1941, Santa Rita, NM) Head Libn., Univ. of South. CA Dental Lib., 1971–, Circ. Libn., Med. Lib., 1970–71. **Educ.:** Los Angeles State Coll., 1959–64, BA (Eng.); Univ. of South. CA, 1968–70, MSLS. **Orgs.:** Med. LA: Dental Libs. Spec. Interest Grp. (Ch., 1978–79); Rittenhouse Awd. Com. (Ch., 1973–75); Dental Libs. Grp. (Secy., 1973–74). Med. Lib. Grp. of South. CA. Amer. Assn. of Dental Schs.: Lrng. Resrcs. Grp. **Pubns.:** Contrib., *McGill's Bibliography of Literary Criticism* (1979); "A Dental Library Current Awareness Service," *Jnl. of Dental Educ.* (Ap. 1978). **Activities:** 1; 15, 17, 31; 80 **Addr.:** University of South. CA, Dental Library, DEN 201, P.O. Box 77951, Los Angeles, CA 90007.

Mason, Hayden (Ag. 1, 1918, Westfield, NJ) Libn., Chas. T. Main, Inc., 1974–; Libn., Nutter, McLennan & Fish, 1972–73; Libn., Natl. Fire Protection Assn., 1963–72. **Educ.:** Haverford Coll., 1936–40, BA (Fr.); Harvard Univ., 1940–41, MA (Fr.), 1947–48, 1952–54 (Fr.); Univ. de Poitiers, L'Inst. de Touraine, 1949, Dipl. (Fr.); Strategic War Coll., 1950, Dipl., U.S. Army Comnd. & General Staff Coll., 1964, Dipl. **Orgs.:** SLA: Boston Chap., (Pres.-Elect, 1979–80); Advert. Mgr. (1971–73); Pubns. Com., Engin. Div. (Ch., 1977–79). Reserve Officers Assn., U.S. Army. Eastern Dog Club. **Pubns.:** *NFPA Library Classification System for Fire Protection* (1964); "The NFPA Technical Reference Library," *Qtly. of the Natl. Fire Protection Assn.* (O. 1964); "Information Retrieval - Three Practical Methods," *Fire Tech.* (F. 1965); Contrib., *Thesaurus of Engineering and Scientific Terms* (1967). **Activities:** 12; 17, 24, 46; 64, 91 **Addr.:** Greengate Farm, 881 Congress St., Duxbury, MA 02332.

Mason, Laura Lea (Krog) (My. 2, 1953, Versailles, MO) Freelnc. libn., 1981–; Coord., Northeast MO Lib. Netwk., 1980–81; Pub. Srv. Libn., Archvst., Lib. Sci. Instr., Southwest Bapt. Univ., 1976–80; Libn., Env. Educ. Org., Univ. of MO, 1973. **Educ.:** Univ. of MO, 1971–74, BA cum laude (LS, Phil.); 1975–76, MA (LS); various grad. crs.; Northeast MO State Univ., 1980–, Sch. Lib. Cert., MA (Eng. Educ.). **Orgs.:** ALA: JMRT, Arch. Com. (1980–); ASCLA, Multitype Lib. Coops. Div., Mem. Com. (1980–); Ref. and Subscrpn. Bks. Review Com. (1980–). Springfield Area Libns. Assn.: Secy. (1979–80). MO ACRL: VP., Pres. elect (1979–80); Pres. (1980–81). MO LA: IFC (Ch., 1979–81); Lib. Educ. and Manpower Com. (1978–); Lib. Educs. Com. (1979–80); various coms. Various orgs. Univ. of MO Alum. Assn. MO State Hist. Socty. Beta Phi Mu: Psi Chap., VP, Pres. elect (1979–80), Pres. (1980–81); Awds. Com. (Ch., 1979). Polk Cnty. Hist. Socty. Various orgs. **Honors:** Chi Omega, 1977; Delta Psi Omega, 1979. **Pubns.:** Jt. Auth., *Ozark Per. Inx.* (1979–80). **Activities:** 14-netwk.; 24, 25, 34; 63, 69 67. **Addr.:** Rte. 1, Box 81, Shelbyville, MO 63469.

Mason, Martha Dinwiddie (Jl. 28, 1947, Charlottesville, VA) Catlgr., Univ. of SC, 1975–; Catlgr., Clemson Univ., 1973–75. **Educ.:** Clemson Univ., 1967–69, BA (Fr.); Univ. of SC, 1970–73, MA (Frgn. Langs.), 1972–73, ML. **Orgs.:** SC LA. SELA. ALA. **Activities:** 1; 20 **Addr.:** Catalog Dept., Cooper Library, University of South Carolina, Columbia, SC 29208.

Mason, Mary Stuart (Je. 25, 1925, Washington, DC) Supvsr.-Sch. Libs. and Text Bks., VA Dept. of Educ., 1967–, Asst. Supvsr., 1961–67; Libn., Westhampton Sch., 1948–61. **Educ.:** Coll. of William and Mary, 1942–46, BA (LS), 1961–63, MED (Sec. Educ.). **Orgs.:** ALA: AASL/Supvsrs. Sect., Early Childhood Educ. Com., Nom. Com., Ch. SELA: Com. on South. Bks. Competition (1978). VA LA: VP (1972); Pres. (1973); Nom. Com. (Ch., 1974). VA Educ. Media Assn.: Awds. Com. (1978–79, 1981); Futures Com. (1975). Assn. for Prsrvn. of VA Antiquities. VA Musm. Natl. Assn. of State Educ. Media Profs. Natl. Assn. of State Textbk. Admins.: Secy., Treas. (1980–81). **Pubns.:** Reviews. **Activities:** 10, 14-State Educ. Agency; 17, 21,

PROFESSIONAL ACTIVITIES: Institutions: 1. Acad. lib.; 2. Arch.; 3. Assn.; 4. Fed./Gvt. lib.; 5. Inst. lib.; 6. Mfr./Suppl.; 7. Milit. lib.; 8. Musm.; 9. Pub. lib.; 10. Sch. lib.; 11. Sch. of lib. sci.; 12. Spec. lib.; 13. State lib.; 14. (other). **Functions/Activities:** 15. Acq./Col. dev.; 16. Adult srvs.; 17. Admin.; 18. Apprais.; 19. Archit./Bldgs.; 20. Cat./Class.; 21. Chld. srvs.; 22. Circ.; 23. Cons./Pres.; 24. Consult.; 25. Cont. ed.; 26. Educ. lib. sci.; 27. Ext. srvs.; 28. Fund/Grants; 29. Gvt. pubs.; 30. Indx./Abs.; 31. Instr. lib. use; 32. Media srvs.; 33. Micro.; 34. Netwks./Coop.; 35. Persnl.; 36. PR; 37. Publshg.; 38. Recs. mgt.; 39. Ref. srvs.; 40. Repro.; 41. Resrch.; 42. Review.; 43. Secur.; 44. Serials; 45. Spec. col.; 46. Tech. srvs.; 47. Trustees/Bds.; 48. YA srvs.; 49. (other).

48; 63, 89 **Addr.:** Virginia Department of Education, Richmond, VA 23216.

Mason, Philip P. (Ap. 28, 1927, Salem, MA) Dir., Prof. of Hist., Wayne State Univ., 1958–; Dir., State of MI Arch., 1953–58; Asst. Mss. Cur., Univ. of MI Hist. Col., 1951–53. **Educ.:** Boston Univ., 1947–50, BA (Hist.); Univ. of MI, 1950–51, MA (Hist.), 1951–56, PhD (Hist.). **Orgs.:** SAA: Exec. Secy. (1963–68); VP (1969); Pres. (1970). Amer. Assn. for State and Local Hist.: Cncl. (1967–70). Hist. Socty. of MI: Secy./Treas., (1965–70); Pres. (1965–66). Can. Arch. Assn. Midwest Arch. Conf. Org. of Amer. Hist. Amer. Hist. Assn. Detroit Hist. Socty. Trustee, 1962–75). **Pubns.:** *Schoolcraft's Expedition to Lake Itasca* (1958). *From Bull Run to Appomattox* (1961). *Schoolcraft, the Literary Voyager or Muzzeniegun* (1962). Jt. Auth., *Harper of Detroit, The Origin and Growth of a Great Metropolitan Hospital* (1964). *A History of American Roads* (1967). **Activities:** 2, 12; 17, 26, 45 **Addr.:** Reuther Library of Labor and Urban Affairs, Wayne State University, 5401 Cass Ave., Detroit, MI 48202.

Mason, Robert M. (Ja. 16, 1941, Sweetwater, TN) Pres., Metrics Resrch. Corp. Inc., 1980–, Ch., VP, 1973–80; Sr. Resrch. Sci., Engin. Exp. Station, GA 1975 Instr. of Tech., 1975–76, Resrch. Sci., 1971–75; Tech. Staff Member, Sandia Labs., 1965–68. **Educ.:** MA Inst. of Tech., 1959–65, SB and SM (Elec. Engin.); GA Inst. of Tech., 1968–73, PhD (Indus. & Syst. Engin.). **Orgs.:** ASIS. AAAS. Inst. for Mgt. Sci. **Pubns.:** Jt. ed., *Information Services: Economics, Management, and Technology* (1981); "A Lower Bound Cost Benefit Model for Information Services," *Inf. Proc. & Mgt.* (1978); "The Marketing Ideal vs Actual Cases: A Synthesis," *ASIS Procs.* (1978); "The Economics and Cost Benefit of Analysis Services - The Case of Information Analysis Centers" in *Evaluating New Telecommunications Services* (1978); various speeches. **Activities:** 14-Research Consult.; 24, 25, 41; 91, 93, 95-Econ. of Info. **Addr.:** Metrics Research Corporation, 180 Allen Rd., Suite 200 South, Atlanta, GA 30328.

Mason, Sharon L. (Ag. 7, 1940, Keaney, NE) Head, Cat. Dept., Kearney State Coll., 1981–; Head, Cat. Dept., Wichita State University, 1977–80, Head, Circ. Dept., 1974–76, Catlgr., 1971–73; Head, QUE Prcs. Div., OH State Univ., 1971, Head, Serial Div., 1970–71, Serial Biblgphr., 1968–70; Asst. Libn., Homewood–Flossmoor HS, 1966–68; various libn. positions, 1963–66. **Educ.:** Kearney State Coll., 1958–62, BA (Eng.); Univ. of Denver, 1962–63, MA (LS); Wichita State Univ., 1972–78, MA (Eng.). **Orgs.:** ALA: ACRL; RTSD. AMIGOS Bibl. Netwk.: OCLC Serials Cntrl. Sybsyst. Adv. Com. (Recorder, 1979). **Activities:** 1; 20, 44, 46; 55, 56 **Addr.:** 3507 17th Ave., Kearney, NE 68847.

Masoni, Daniel (Mr. 12, 1948, Marysville, CA) Dir., Emporia Pub. Lib., 1975–; Dir., Pottawatomie-Wabaunsee Reg. Lib. Syst., 1972–75. **Educ.:** Linfield Coll., 1966–70, BS (Bus. Admin.); Portland State Univ., 1970–71, Cert. (Fr.); Univ. of Denver, 1971–72, MA (Libnshp.). **Orgs.:** KS LA: Pres. (1980–81); VP (1979–80); Legis. Com. (1979–82). Lib. Srv. and Construct. Act Adv. Cncl. for the State of KS. ALA. Mt. Plains LA. KS Cncl. for Info. Sci. **Activities:** 9, 11; 17, 19, 39; 56, 67, 74 **Addr.:** Emporia Public Library, 110 E. 6th, Emporia, KS 66801.

Massey, Katha D. (S. 1, 1942, Roanoke Rapids, NC) Head, Cat. Dept., Univ. of GA, 1981–; Head, Nonbk. Prcs. Dept., 1974–81, Head, Nonbk. Cat. Sect., 1968–74; Catlgr., West. Carolina Univ., 1967–68; Class. Rec. Asst., LC, 1964–66. **Educ.:** Univ. of Richmond, 1960–64, BA (Eng. Lit.); Rutgers Univ., 1966–67, MLS; various grad. crs. **Orgs.:** ALA. SELA. GA LA: Com. Libnshp. as a Career (1980–). NLA. Natl. Micro. Assn. On-Line AV Catlgrs. **Honors:** Phi Beta Kappa, 1964; Phi Alpha Theta, 1964. **Activities:** 1; 17, 33, 46 **Addr.:** University of Georgia Libraries, Cataloging Dept., Athens, GA 30602.

Massey, Pamela Grace (N. 14, 1948, Los Angeles, CA) Msc. Catlgr., Univ. of CO, 1977–; Msc./Media Catlgr., SUNY, Fredonia, 1975–76. **Educ.:** Northwest. Univ., 1967–71, BME; Univ. of MI, 1974–75, AMLS; Northwest. Univ., 1972–74, MM (Msc. Hist.). **Orgs.:** Msc. LA: Mt.–Plains Chap. (Secy./Treas., 1978–80); Nom. Com. (1979); Prog. Com. (1978). CO LA. Msc. Users OCLC Grp. Socty. for Ethnomsclgy. **Pubns.:** "Julia Ettie Crane," *Biog. Dictionary of Amer. Educ.* (1978). **Activities:** 1; 20, 31, 39; 55 **Addr.:** 1410-19th St., Apt. 9, Boulder, CO 80302.

Massman, Virgil Frank (Jl. 19, 1929, New Munich, MN) Exec. Dir., James Jerome Hill Ref. Lib. 1971–; Dir. of Libs. Univ. of SD 1966–71, Assoc. Prof. of Eng. 1965–66; Head Ref. Libn. Bemidji State Coll. 1960–65. **Educ.:** St. John's Univ., Collegeville, MN, 1957, BA (Eng.); Univ. of MN, 1960, MA (Eng., Lib. Sci.); Univ. of MI, 1970, PhD (Lib. Sci.). **Orgs.:** ALA: ACRL/Natl. Conf. Plng. Com. (Ch., 1981). MINITEX OCLC Users Grp.: Ch. (1979–). MN LA: Acad. and Resrch. Libns. Div. (Ch., 1974–75). SD LA: Pres. (1970–71). Various com. AAUP. MN Educ. Comp. Cnsrtm.: Lib. Com. Ch., (1973–75). **Pubns.:** *Faculty Status for Academic Librarians* (1972); "ENWACBUCL–A Librarian's Dream," *Amer. Libs.* (Mr. 1972); various articles. **Activities:** 12; 17 **Addr.:** 3411 Vivian Ave., St. Paul, MN 55112.

Masson, Debra L. (Jl. 20, 1953, Detroit, MI) Chld. Libn., Farmington Cmnty. Lib., 1979–; Chld. Libn., Wayne-Westland Lib., 1978–79; Co. Libn., K. J. Law, Engin. Inc., 1977–78. **Educ.:** Alma Coll., 1971–75, BA (Eng.); 1975, MI Sec. Provisional Tchg. Cert.; Univ. of MI, 1976–77, AMLS. **Orgs.:** MI LA: Mem. Com. (1980). ALA. MI Assn. for Media in Educ. **Activities:** 9; 21, 31, 32; 63, 89, 95-Pers. **Addr.:** Farmington Community Library, 23500 Liberty St., Farmington Hills, MI 48024.

Masson, Sandra K. (My. 3, 1945, Chicago, IL) Mgr., Lib., CNA, 1978–; Staff Spec., Inf. Anal., Amer. Hos. Assn., 1974–78; Chld. Libn., Dept. Head, Oak Lawn Pub. Lib., 1971–74; Head Libn., Emerson Jr. HS, 1969–70. **Educ.:** West. IL Univ., 1963–67, BS (Bus. Educ.); Univ. of WI, 1970–71, MS (LS). **Orgs.:** Med. LA: Reception Com., 1978 Anl. Conv. SLA: Conv. Plng. Com. (1975). IL LA: Secy., Chld. Div. (1973). ALA. Oak Lawn Safety Cncl. **Honors:** Kappa Delta Phi, 1967; Sigma Phi Epsilon, 1967. **Pubns.:** Ed., *Administrator's Collection* (1977). **Activities:** 12; 15, 17, 39; 59, 76 **Addr.:** CNA Library, CNA Plaza - 3 S., Chicago, IL 60685.

Massonneau, Suzanne (F. 24, 1926, New York, NY) Asst. Dir., Tech. Srvs., Univ. of VT, 1976–; Asst. Dir., Tech. Srvs., TX A & M Univ., 1975–75; Head, Cat. Dept., Ctrl. MI Univ., 1973–75; Asst. Prof., Sch. of LS, FL State Univ., 1967–73, Head, Cat. Dept., 1960–67, Sr. Catlgr., 1957–60; Sci. Catlgr., Purdue Univ., 1955–57; Catlgr., FL State Univ., 1953–55. **Educ.:** George Washington Univ., 1943–46, BA (Psy.); FL State Univ., 1951–52, MA (LS). **Orgs.:** ALA: RTSD, Bd. of Dir. (1979–82); AV Com. (Ch., 1974–77). VT LA. ACRL: New Eng. Chap., Bd. of Dir. (1978–80). NELINET, Inc.: Bd. of Dir. (1980–83). Other orgs. **Honors:** Beta Phi Mu, 1958. **Pubns.:** "Technical Services and Technology: The Bibliographical Imperative" in *A Century of Service,* (1976); "Which Code for the Multimedia Catalog?" *Sch. Media Qtly.* (Win. 1974); also in *Reader in Children's Librarianship,* (1979); "Developments in the Organization of Audiovisual Materials," *Lib. Trends* (Ja. 1977). **Activities:** 1; 17, 20, 46 **Addr.:** Bailey/Howe Library, University of Vermont, Burlington, VT 05405.

Mast, Lois Ann (Zook) (Je. 6, 1951, Belleville, PA) Libn., Genealogist, Lancaster Mennonite Hist. Socty., 1977–; Libn., AV Coord., Lancaster Mennonite HS, 1972–77. **Educ.:** Millersville State Coll., 1969–72, BS (Elem. Educ., Educ. Media); George Peabody Coll., 1973–75, MLS; Natl. Arch., Inst. for Genealogical Resrch., 1977. **Pubns.:** *Annotated Bibliography of Lancaster Mennonite Conference Publications, 1850–1975* (1975); *Who Begot Thee? Descendants of Jacob Brubaker of Snyder County, PA* (1976); *Only a Twig—A Branch of the Zooks/Zugs From PA* (1979); Indxr., *1875 Lancaster County Atlas* (1980); "Bishop John N. Durr and His Times," *PA Mennonite Heritage* (Ja. 1978); various articles. **Activities:** 12; 17, 37, 45; 63, 69, 73 **Addr.:** P.O. Box 171, Elverson, PA 19520.

Masters, Deborah C. (Ap. 6, 1950, Philadelphia, PA) Ref. & Lib. Instr. Libn., SUNY, Albany, 1979–; Ref. Libn., PA State Univ., 1976–79, Per. Asst., 1973–76. **Educ.:** PA State Univ., 1968–71, BA (Hist.), BS (Sec. Educ); Univ. of Pittsburgh, 1975–76, MLS. **Orgs.:** ALA: RASD, Outstan. Ref. Srcs. Com. (1978–82, Ch., 1980–82); *RQ* Ed. Bd. (1980–82); ACRL/Conf. Prog. Plng. Com. (1981). Bibl. Instr. Sect., NY LA. ACRL: East. NY Chap. **Pubns.:** Ed., "Reference Sources of 1980," *Lib. Jnl.* (My. 15, 1981); *A Guide to Sources in Black Studies in the Pennsylvania State University Libraries.* (1978). **Activities:** 1; 31, 39, 49-comp. lit. srchg.; 92 **Addr.:** B16 University Library, State University of New York at Albany, 1400 Washington Ave., Albany, NY 12222.

Masters, Fred N., Jr. (Ap. 21, 1934, Webster City, IA) Mgr., Tech. Info. Resrcs., C.H. Dexter Div., Dexter Corp., 1965–; Tech. Libn., Amer. Machine and Foundry Co., 1962–65; Ref. Libn., OH State Univ., 1961–62; Engin. Libn., Univ. of TN, 1958–60. **Educ.:** Univ. of TN, 1958, BA (Hist.); Case West. Rsv. Univ., 1961, MSLS. **Orgs.:** Assn. of Rec. Mgrs. and Admins.: Dir. (1976–78); Treas. (1979–80); VP, (1980–81). Tech. Assn. Pulp and Paper Indus.: Info. Mgt. Com. (Ch., 1981–); Cont. Educ. Com. SLA: CT Autom. Coord. Com. (Liaison, 1980–81). Inst. of Paper Chem. Info. Srvs.: Adv. Com. (1980–). Assoc. Info. Mgrs. **Pubns.:** "Why-A Company Library," *Indus. Resrch.* (Ja. 1973); "The Company Library in the Paper Industry," *TAPPI* (Ja. 1974). **Activities:** 12; 17; 59, 82 **Addr.:** C.H. Dexter Div. Dexter Corp., 2 Elm St., Windsor Locks, CT 06096.

Masumoto, Lynn A. (Jl. 2, 1953, Honolulu, HI) Libn. III, YA Libn., Kauai Reg. Lib., 1979–; Lib. Asst. IV, Univ. of HI, Hamilton Lib., 1978–79; Milit. Occupational Specialty Libn., Army Educ. Ctr., Fort Shafter, 1976–77. **Educ.:** Univ. of HI, 1971–74, BA (Fr.), 1975–76, MLS. **Orgs.:** ALA. HI LA. Pac. Assn. for Comm. and Tech. **Honors:** Phi Kappa Phi. **Activities:** 9; 39, 48 **Addr.:** Kauai Regional Library, 4344 Hardy St., Lihue, HI 96766.

Matarazzo, James Michael (Ja. 4, 1941, Stoneham, MA) Assoc. Dean, Prof., Simmons Coll. Grad. Sch. of Lib. and Info. Sci. 1969–; Serials Libn., Docum. Libn. Head, Tech. Rpts., MA Inst. Tech., 1968–69, Docum. Libn. 1967–68, Asst. Sci. Libn., 1965–67. **Educ.:** Boston Coll., 1959–63, BS (Hist.); Simmons Coll. 1963–65, MSLS; Boston Coll. 1965–1972, MA (Pol. Sci.); Univ. of Pittsburgh, 1976–79, PhD (Lib. and Info. Sci.). **Orgs.:** ALA: Com. on Wilson Indxs. (1974–76); Ch., (1976–78); Com. on Accred. (1979–82); Cncl. (1979–83). SLA: Boston Chap. (Dir., 1973–75; Pres., 1979–81). MA LA. New Eng. Chap. ACRL. **Honors:** Marian and Jasper Whiting Fndn., Flwshp., 1976; Univ. of Pittsburgh Grad. Sch. of Lib. and Info. Sci., Tchg. Flwshp., 1976. **Pubns.:** Jt. ed., *Scientific, Medical and Engineering Societies Publications in Print* (1974, 1976, 1979, 1981); "Guides to the Scientific Literature: A Review Article," *The Lib. Qtly.* (O. 1977); "The Condition of the Law Librarian in 1976: Career Development," *Law Lib. Jnl.* (S. 1976); Ed., *The Serials Librarian: Acquisitions Case Studies* (1975); *Library Problems in Science and Technology* (1971). **Activities:** 1, 12; 18, 27, 30; 76, 92 **Addr.:** Simmons College Graduate School of Library and Information Science, 300 The Fenway, Boston, MA 02115.

Matcher, Rita H. (My. 9, 1943, Baltimore, MD) Dir., Lib. Srvs., Eisenberg Med. Staff Lib., Sinai Hosp. of Baltimore, 1979–; Lib. Assoc. I, Enoch Pratt Free Lib., 1971–79; Dsgn., Co-owner, Boutique Unique, 1968–73; Dsgn., The Leather People, 1968–73; Asst. to Dsgn., Ctr. Stage, 1966. **Educ.:** MD Inst. Coll. of Art, 1962–65, BFA (Fashion Dsgn.); MD State Dept. of Educ., Div. of Lib. Dev. and Srvs., 1974–75, Bachelor Libn. Trng. Prog.; Cath. Univ. of Amer., 1977–80, MS (LS). **Orgs.:** Med. LA. SLA. MD Assn. of Hlth. Sci. Libns.: Un. List Com. (1980–81). Baltimore Cnsrtm. for Resrc. Sharing: Prog. Com. (Ch., 1981). Enoch Pratt Free Lib.: Various coms. **Honors:** Beta Phi Mu, 1980. **Activities:** 12; 15, 17, 39; 58, 80 **Addr.:** Eisenberg Medical Staff Library, Sinai Hospital of Baltimore, Belvedere and Greenspring Aves., Baltimore, MD 21215.

Mate, Albert Valentine (Ja. 1, 1931, Walkerville, ON) Univ. Libn., Univ. of Windsor, Leddy Lib., 1980–, Assoc. Libn., Info. Srvs., 1973–80, Asst. Libn., Pub. Srvs., 1966–73, Head, Hum. and Soc. Sci. Div., 1961–66. **Educ.:** Assumption Coll., 1949–52, BA (Eng.); Univ. of MI, 1952–54, MA (Eng.), 1957–58, AMLS. **Orgs.:** ALA. Can. LA. ON LA: Exec. (1974–77). **Honors:** Beta Phi Mu, 1959. **Addr.:** 1406–111 Riverside Dr. E., Windsor, ON N9A 2S6 Canada.

Mateer, Carolyn S. (Baltimore, MD) Head, Ref. Div., Suzzallo Lib., Univ. of WA, 1979–; Head of Ref., Cleveland State Univ., 1978–79, Hum. Biblgphr., 1970–78; Asst. Libn., PA State Univ., Cap., 1968–70. **Educ.:** PA State Univ., 1941–45, AB (Econ.); Drexel Univ., 1967, MSLS. **Orgs.:** ALA: RASD; ACRL. **Pubns.:** *Research Guide to Women's Studies* (1978). **Activities:** 1; 33, 39 **Addr.:** Reference Division, Suzzallo Library, University of Washington, Seattle, WA 98195.

Matejka, Marcella M. (Ja. 15, 1921, Cleveland, OH) Head, Bus., Econ., Labor Dept., Cleveland Pub. Lib., 1976–, Head, Gen. Ref., 1972–76; Head Ref. Libn., Head, various branches, Cleveland Hts., Univ. Hts. Pub. Lib. Syst., 1963–72. **Educ.:** Case West. Rsv. Univ., 1945–48, BA (Span. Hist.), 1949–50, MLA (Coll., Univ. Resrch.), Cleveland State Univ., 1957–60, JD. **Orgs.:** OH LA. ALA. OH Bar. Grt. Cleveland Bar Assn. **Activities:** 9; 17, 31, 39; 51, 59, 92 **Addr.:** Business, Economics & Labor Dept., Cleveland Public Library, 325 Superior Ave., Cleveland, OH 44113.

Materi, Gloria M. (S. 29, 1942, Wakaw, SK) Libn., Catlgr., SK Prov. Lib., 1971–; Branch Libn., Regina Pub. Lib., 1966–71. **Educ.:** Univ. of SK, 1961–64, BA (Chem.); Univ. of BC, 1965–66, BLS. **Orgs.:** SK LA. Can. LA. **Activities:** 9, 13; 20, 21 **Addr.:** 3412 Parliament Ave., Regina, SK S4S 2M3 Canada.

Matesic, Kathleen (Jl. 24, 1949, Wilkinsburg, PA) Asst. Dir. Media Srvs., Univ. of Pittsburgh, 1975–; Eng. Tchr., Pittsburgh Pub. Sch., 1971–74. **Educ.:** Univ. of Pittsburgh, 1967–71, BA (Eng. Lit.; teaching cert.); IN Univ. of PA, 1974–75, MEd (Media Spec.); Univ. of Pittsburgh, 1976–78, MLS. **Orgs.:** PA Learning Resrcs. Assn. Southwestern PA Learning Resrcs. Assn.: Pres. (1979–80); Secy./Treas. (1978–79). **Pubns.:** *Univ. of Pittsburg 1978 Film Cat.* (1978); "Burrell Township Community Center" 16mm film (1975). **Activities:** 1; 15, 32, 39; 63, 67, 93 **Addr.:** 424 Lloyd St., Pittsburgh, PA 15208.

Matheson, J. William (Je. 14, 1927, Montreal, PQ) Chief, Rare Bk. and Spec. Col. Div., Lib. of Congs., 1972–, Prin. Acq. Ofcr., Ref. Dept., 1972, Asst. to Chief, Rare Bk. Div., 1971; Anglo–Amer. Biblgphr., WA Univ., St. Louis, 1967–71, Chief, Rare Bk. Dept., 1962–71; various positions at Lib. of Congs., 1958–61; various positions as consult., 1966–77. **Educ.:** Univ. of WA, 1950, BA (Eng.), 1955, MA (Eng.); 1958, MLS; various grad. crs. **Orgs.:** ALA: ACRL/RBMS (Ch., 1977). IFLA: Rare and Precious Bks. Sect., Stan. Com. Ms. Socty.: VP. Bibl. of Amer. Lit.: Supervisory Com. 18th Century Short Title Cat.: Adv. Com.; N. Amer. Com. Various orgs. Bibl. Socty. of Univ. of VA. Grolier Club. Assn. Intl. de Bibliophilie. Bibl. Socty. of London. **Honors:** Univ. of WA Sch. of Lib. Srv., Disting. Alum. Awd., 1978; Phi Beta Kappa; IN Univ., Lilly Lib., Lilly Flwshp., 1961–62. **Pubns.:** "George Watterston, Advocate of the National Library," *Librarians of Congress 1802–1974* (1977); "Microcosm of the Library: The Rare Book and Special Collections Division," *Qtly. Jnl.* (Jl. 1977); "What Book Collecting Is All About," *Book Collecting: A Modern Guide* (1977); Introduction, *Collectible Books: Some New Paths* (1979); "Lessing J. Rosenwald: A Splendidly Generous Man," *Qtly. Jnl.* (Win. 1980); various exhibit

Special Subjects/Services: 50. Adult educ.; 51. Advert./Mktg.; 52. Aerosp.; 53. Agric.; 54. Area std.; 55. Arts/Hum.; 56. Autom.; 57. Bibl./Prtg.; 58. Bio. sci.; 59. Bus./Fin.; 60. Chem.; 61. Copyrt.; 62. Documtn.; 63. Educ.; 64. Engin.; 65. Env.; 66. Eth. grps.; 67. Film; 68. Food/Nutr.; 69. Geneal.; 70. Geo.; 71. Geol.; 72. Handcpd.; 73. Hist.; 74. Int. frdm.; 75. Info. sci.; 76. Insr.; 77. Law; 78. Legis.; 79. Math./Comp. sci.; 80. Med.; 81. Metals; 82. Nat. resrcs.; 83. Newsp.; 84. Nuc. sci.; 85. Oral hist.; 86. Petr./Energy; 87. Pharm.; 88. Phys./Astr./Math.; 89. Readg.; 90. Relig.; 91. Sci./Tech.; 92. Soc. sci.; 93. Telecom.; 94. Transp.; 95. (other).

cats., articles. **Activities:** 4; 15, 17, 45; 55, 57 **Addr.:** 338 M St., S.W., Washington, DC 20024.

Matheson, Nina W. (Je. 25, 1933, Seattle, WA) Asst. Dir., Hlth. Info. Mgt. Std., Assn. of Amer. Med. Colls., 1980–; Dir., Himmelfarb Hlth. Sci. Lib., The George Washington Univ. Med. Ctr., 1974–80; Chief, Ofc. of Prog. Plng. and Eval. Natl. Lib. of Med. Extramural Progs., 1973–74, Spec. Asst., 1972–73, Prog. Ofcr., 1971–1972; Libn., MO Inst. of Psyt., 1962–71; Libn. Acq. Sect., Natl. Lib. of Med., 1959–61. **Educ.:** Univ. of WA, 1951–56, (Eng.), 1957–58, ML (Libnshp.). **Orgs.:** ASIS. ALA. SLA. Med. LA: Bd. of Dirs. (1977–80); Legis. Com. (1975–77). Gld. of BookWorkers. Prog. Ch. (1980). **Honors:** Univ. of WA, Sch. of Libnshp., Disting. Alum., 1978; Phi Beta Kappa; Beta Phi Mu. **Pubns.:** Jt. auth., *Some principles of good writing and the library search: Pt. 11. The library search in the social sciences* (1980); "The clouded crystal ball and the library profession," *Mod. Lang. Assn.* (Ja. 1977); "NLM Medical Library Resource Improvement Grant Program: An Evaluation," *Bltn.* (Jl. 1976); "User reactions to Current Contents: Behavioral, Social and Management Sciences," *Mod. Lang. Assn. Bltn.* (Ap. 1971). **Activities:** 1, 4; 17, 24, 41; 80, 93 **Addr.:** 338 M St. S.W., Washington, DC 20024.

Matheson, Wallace A. (Jl. 29, 1931, Montreal, PQ) Pres., Prentice-Hall of Canada, Ltd., 1965–, VP, 1961–65, Can. Dist. Mgr., 1958–61, Can. Field Rep., 1953–58. **Educ.:** Acadia Univ., 1953, BA (Hist.). **Orgs.:** Can. Lib. Exhibitors' Assn.: Pres. (1966–68). Can. Book Publshrs. Cncl.: Pres. (1972–73); VP (1970–71). Assn. For The Export of Can. Books: Dir. (1973). Can. Copyright Inst.: Govr. (1973–74). Montreal Intl. Book Fair: Dir. (1974–75). **Activities:** 6; 17, 37 **Addr.:** Prentice-Hall of Canada, Ltd., 1870 Birchmount Rd., Scarborough, ON M1P 2J7 Canada.

Mathews, Anne J. (F. 5, 1928, Philadelphia, PA) Assoc. Prof. Grad. Sch. of Libnshp. and Info. Mgt., Univ. of Denver, 1970–; Prog. Dir., Ctrl. CO Lib. Syst., 1968–70, Consult., 1967–68; Ref. Libn., OR State Univ., 1965–67. **Educ.:** Wheaton Coll., 1946–49, AB (Speech); Univ. of Denver, 1963–65, MA (LS), 1974–77, PhD (Comm.). **Orgs.:** ALA: Cncl. (1979–83). CO LA: Bd. (1973–76); Pres. (1974). CLENE: Bd. of Dir., Secy. (1979–80); Voluntary Recog. Srvs. Bd. (1981–). Mt. Plains LA: Prof. Dev. Com. (1979). Frnds. of Libs. USA: Bd. (1980–82). Rocky Mt. Workshops, Inc.: Bd. (1977–80). **Pubns.:** *You Cannot Not Communicate* (in press); "Your Public Image", In *Friends of Libraries Sourcebook* (1981); "Now It Can Be Told/Taught" *LIPP* (Jl. 1980); "Networks of Friends of Libraries", *Allerton Proc.* (S. 1980); Training for Library Change, Audiotape (1980); other articles. **Activities:** 11; 25, 26, 36, 39 **Addr.:** Graduate School of Librarianship and Information Management, University of Denver, Denver, CO 80208.

Mathews, Eleanor (Ja. 7, 1937, Melrose, MA) Asst. Prof., Ref. Libn., IA State Univ., 1977–; Gvt. Docum. Libn., Drake Univ. Law Lib., 1975–77. **Educ.:** Wheaton Coll., Norton, MA, 1954–58, BA (Bio.); Univ. of IA, 1974–75, MA (LS). **Orgs.:** ALA: RASD; ACRL/Agr. and Bio. Sci. Sect., By-laws Com. (1978–79); ACRL/Sci. and Tech. Secy. (1981–82). IA LA: Vice-Ch. Gvt. Docum. Sect. (1976–77). Intl. Assn. of Agri. Libns. and Documlst. AAUP. IA State Univ. World Food Inst.: Lib. and Info. Task Force Com. **Honors:** Beta Phi Mu. **Pubns.:** "Iowa, General Publications" and "Des Moines" in *Municipal Government Reference Sources: Publications and Collections,* (1978); "The Bibliography of Agriculture," *Ref. Srvs. Review* (Ap./Je. 1979). **Activities:** 1; 31, 39; 53, 58, 91 **Addr.:** Reference Dept., Iowa State University Library, Ames, IA 50011.

Mathews, Mary P. (F. 1, 1932, Baltimore, MD) Media Spec., Prince George's Cnty. Pub. Schs., 1968–. **Educ.:** Univ. of Zurich, 1951–54; Univ. of MI, 1954–55, BA (Hist.), 1955–57, MA (Hist.); Univ. of MD, 1967–68, MLS. **Orgs.:** ALA: AASL, IFC. MD Educ. Media Org. Prince George's Cnty. Educ. Media Assn.: Pres. (1975–76). AAUW: Treas. (1966–68); Corres. Secy. (1975–77). **Activities:** 10; 21, 31, 32; 63, 74 **Addr.:** 12425 Sarah Ln., Bowie, MD 20715.

Mathews, Virginia Hopper (Mr. 9, 1925, New York, NY) VP, Lib. Prof. Pubns., Shoe String Press, 1980–; Dir., Lib. Prof. Pubns., Gaylord Brothers, 1975–79; Lib., Litcy. Consult., 1973–75; Dir., Natl. Bk. Com., Natl. Lib. Week, 1957–73; Dir., Readg. Dev. Srvs., Amer. Bk. Pubshrs. Cncl., 1957–72; Educ. and Lib. Consult., Ed., David McKay Co., 1950–57; Indp. Consult., 1950; Buyer, Head, Chld. Bk. Dept., 1944–49. **Educ.:** Goucher Coll., 1941–44, BA (Hist.); Univ. of Geneva, Switzerland, 1949–50 (Fr., Pol. Sci., Grmn.). **Orgs.:** ALA: Broadcasting Com. (Ch., 1962–68); Amer. Indian Libs. (Ch., 1976–); AASL, Official Liaison with Intl. Readg. Assn. (1980–82). Natl. Comsn. on Lib. and Info. Srvs.: Cult. Minorities Task Force (1980–). Lib. of Congs. Ctr. for the Bk.: Adv. Com., Readg. Dev. Subcom. (1979–). Intl. Readg. Assn.: Stimulating Litcy. Com. (Ch., 1980–). Natl. Cncl. for Soc. Std.: World Hist. Bibl. Com. NCTE: IFC. **Honors:** SWLA, Cit., Exemplary Srvs. to libns. and libs., 1970; AASL, Outstan. contribs. to the natl. dev. of sch. libs., 1967; Women's Natl. Bk. Assn., Constance Lindsay Skinner Awd., 1965. **Pubns.:** *Libraries: Aids to Life Satisfaction for Older Women* (1981); *Libraries for Today and Tomorrow* (1976); Jt. Auth., *Response to Change: Libraries for the Seventies* (1970); *Guidelines for Vistas for Use with Vista Book Kits* (1967); "Adult Reading Studies and Their Implications," *Lib. Trends* (1973); various articles, chld. bks., multi-media kits. **Activities:** 1, 2, 4; 24, 25, 36; 78, 89 **Addr.:** Vice President, Shoe String Press, 995 Sherman Ave., P.O. Box 4327, Hamden, CT 06514.

Matiisen, Tina (F. 21, 1946, Eckville, AB) Head, Info. Srvs., Defence Resrch. Estab., Ottawa, 1980–; Head, Readrs. Srvs., Natl. Musms. of Can., 1973–80; Asst. Libn., Inst. of Sedimentary & Petr. Geol., 1971–73; Libn., Chevron Stan., 1970–71. **Educ.:** Univ. of AB, 1964–67, BA (Hist.); McGill Univ., 1968–70, MLS. **Orgs.:** Can. Assn. Info. Sci. SLA. Can. LA: Mem. Com. (1974–76); Lcl. Arrange. Com. (Conf. Conv., 1979); Elec. Com. (1975–76); Can. Assn. of Spec. Libs. and Info. Srvs. (Dir., 1972–74). **Honors:** Beta Phi Mu, 1970. **Activities:** 4, 12; 17, 37; 91 **Addr.:** 66 5th Ave. Apt. #1, Ottawa, ON K1S 2M6 Canada.

Matlack, Robert K. (O. 11, 1924, Pittsburgh, PA) Libn., Carnegie Lib. of Pittsburgh, 1968–; Libn., Free Lib. of Philadelphia, 1962–68. **Educ.:** Univ. of Pittsburgh, 1943–46, BS (Psy.); Carnegie—Mellon Univ., 1960–62, MLS. **Orgs.:** PA LA. **Pubns.:** Ed., *Science and Technology; A Purchase Guide for Branch and Public Libraries* (1978–). **Activities:** 9; 37, 39, 42; 91 **Addr.:** Science and Technology Dept., Carnegie Library of Pittsburgh, 4400 Forbes Ave., Pittsburgh, PA 15213.

Matos, Antonio (O. 23, 1923, Rio Piedras, PR) Dir. of Libs., Cath. Univ. of PR, 1971–; Lib. Dir., Arecibo Reg. Coll., Univ. PR, 1967–70, Actg. Dir. of the Coll., 1969–70; Lib. Dir., Humacao Univ. Coll., Univ. of PR, 1966–67. **Educ.:** Univ. of PR, 1940–44, BA (Hist.); Syracuse Univ., 1949–50, MSLS Univ. of MI, 1958–59; Univ. of MD, Cert. in Admin., 1972. **Orgs.:** ALA. Cath. LA. SBPR: Pres. (1961–63). AECT. Ateneo de Ponce, PR. **Honors:** Mobil Premium, 1977. **Pubns.:** *Guide to the Reviews of Books About Hispanic America* (1965, 1972–78); *Intereses de lectura de los estudiantes del programa de maestro bibliotecario* (1971). **Activities:** 1; 17 **Addr.:** Encarnación Valdés Library, Catholic University of Puerto Rico, Ponce, PR 00731.

Matson, Madeline (Mr. 4, 1947, Kansas City, KS) Coord. of Pubns., MO State Lib., 1974–. **Educ.:** KS Univ., 1965–71, BS (Jnlsm.); Emporia State Univ., 1973–74, ML (LS). **Orgs.:** MO LA: PR Cncl. (1978–; ch., 1978–79). ALA. MO Assn. for Soc. Welfare. **Pubns.:** Ed., *Show-Me Libs.* (1974–); "Missouri Library News," *ALA Yrbk.* (1977, 1978, 1979, 1980). **Activities:** 13; 36, 37; 55 **Addr.:** 413 East Capitol Ave., Jefferson City, MO 65101.

Matta, Seoud M. (O. 28, 1937, Cairo, Egypt) Prof., Pratt Inst., Grad. Sch. of Lib. and Info. Sci., 1976–, Assoc. Prof., 1972–76; Dir., Tech. Srvs. Div., NY Univ. Libs., 1968–72; Dir., Tng., Documtn. Ctr. for Educ., Cairo, Egypt, 1966–68. **Educ.:** Cairo Univ., 1953–57, BA (LS); Columbia Univ., 1960–61, MLS, 1961–65, DLS. **Orgs.:** ALA: LITA, Prog. Com. (1974–76). AALS. METRO: Tech. Srvs. Com. (Ch., 1978–79). **Pubns.:** *The Card Catalogue in a Large Research Library* (1965); *MILCS: Metropolitan Inter-Library Cataloging System* (1975); various articles. **Activities:** 1, 9; 24, 26, 46; 56, 62, 75 **Addr.:** 319 E. 24th St., New York, NY 10010.

Matte, Pierre (Jl. 31, 1918, Shawinigan, PQ) Dir., PQ Pub. Lib. Srv., 1975–, Asst. Dir., 1960–75; Chief Libn., Shawinigan Pub. Lib., 1957–60; Ed., Shawinigan Chemicals Limited, 1950–57. **Educ.:** Trois-Rivières Coll., 1935–42, BA; Laval Univ., 1942–43, BPh (Phil.); Univ. of Montreal, 1947–48, BLS. **Orgs.:** Assn. Can. Des Bibtcrs. de Lang. Fr.: Pres. (1960). Can. LA: VP (1964). ALA: Cncl. (1965–69). Can. Lib. Week: VP (1965). **Pubns.:** Collaborator, *Livre, Bibliothèque et Culture québecoise* (1977); "Droits des bibliothecaires," *7th Anl. Conf. Assn. Can. des Bibtcrs. de Lang. Fr.* (1951); "Un service difficile et important; le choix," *10th Anl. Conf. ACBLF* (1954); "L'auxilliaire de bibliothèque," *17th Anl. Conf. ACBLF* (1961); "Le bibliothecaire et les pouvoirs publiques," *17th Anl. Conf. ACBLF* (1961); various conf. papers, articles. **Activities:** 9; 13; 17, 19, 28; 50, 78, 93 **Addr.:** 225, est, Grande Allée, Bloc C, Rez-de-chaussée, PQ G1R 5G5 Canada.

Mattern, Penny G. (Ag. 24, 1943, Jersey City, NJ) Instr. Coord., Cat., OCLC, Inc., 1981–; Mem. Srvs. Libn., NELINET, Inc., 1979–81; Head Catlgr., Worcester Pub. Lib., 1977–79; Libn., Worcester Art Musm., 1970–77; Catlgr., Simmons Coll. Lib., 1969–70. **Educ.:** Clark Univ., 1961–65, AB (Eng.); Simmons Coll., 1968–69, SMLS. **Orgs.:** Worcester Area Coop. Libs.: Mem. Bd. (1972–77); Treas. (1976–77). Art Libs. Socty. of N. Amer.: Treas., New Eng. Chap. (1975–76). **Activities:** 9, 12; 34, 46; 55, 56 **Addr.:** 2215 Country Corners Dr., Columbus, OH 43220.

Matteucig, Iole L. (Mr. 1, 1926, San Francisco, CA) Asst. Dean, Lib. Srvs., City Coll. of San Francisco, 1973–, Actg. Dir. of Lib. Srvs., 1972–73, Head Cat. Dept., Adv. Coord. Lib. Tech. Prog. 1968–72; Instr., Lib. Srvs. Univ. of San Francisco, 1968–69; Lib. Consult., George Wilson Meyer Lib., Lowell HS, 1966–67; Day-to-Day Substitute Libn., San Francisco Unified Sch. Dist., 1958–68. Long-term substitute Libn., Jefferson Union HS, 1957–58; Head, Cat. Dept., Univ. of San Francisco, 1948–50; various tchg. and consult. positions. **Educ.:** Univ. of CA, Berkeley, 1943–47, BA (Fr.), 1947–48, BLS; Univ. of San Francisco and San Francisco State Univ., 1956, (Libnshp. Cred.); Cmnty. Coll. Supvsr. Cred., 1972. **Orgs.:** ALA: Cmnty. Coll. Actv. (Ch., 1975 Anl. Conf.). CA LA. Assn. of CA Cmnty. Coll. Admin. Univ. of CA Alum. Assn. CA Schol. Fed. Univ. of CA Lib. Sch. Alum. Assn. **Pubns.:** "Broad New Horizons–Computer Usage in The Learning Resource Center," *The Tattler* (Ag. 1975). **Activities:** 1, 10; 17; 63, 75 **Addr.:** 55 Aerial Way, San Francisco, CA 94116.

Matthew, Jeannette M. (Mr. 6, 1922, St. Louis, MO) Archvst. and Spec. Col. Libn., IN Univ., Purdue Univ. at Indianapolis, 1975–, Head Libn., IN Univ., Indianapolis, 1956–75; Libn., Adjutant Generals Sch. Lib., 1951–56; Libn., Columbia Univ., 1949–51; Libn., Denver Pub. Lib., 1946–49. **Educ.:** Park Coll., 1942–46, BA (Psy.). **Orgs.:** SLA: Natl. Mem. Com. (Ch., 1957–1961), Pres. IN Chap. (1956–1957) Natl. Persnl. Com. (1961–62), ALA: Natl. Lib. Wk. (IN Dir., 1963–64) IN LA: Liason Com. (1965–67) SAA: Coll. and Univ. Arch. Com. (1975–1977), Cons. Com. (1978–1979). Midwest Arch. Conf. Prsrvn. Com. (1976–1977), Coll. and Univ. Arch. (1975–). Amer. Assn. of Univ. Prof.: Lcl. Chap. (various ofcs., 1973–1977). **Pubns.:** *Smack Dab in the Middle of a Swamp: The Evolution of INPUT* forthcoming; "Indianapolis First Town Square," *Indianapolis Star* (Jl. 1980). **Activities:** 1, 2; 15, 17, 36; 86 **Addr.:** Indiana University- Purdue University at Indianapolis, 815 W. Michigan, University Library, Indianapolis, IN 46202.

Matthews, Christine A. (Ja. 4, 1952, Muskegon, MI) Syst. Libn., MAXIMA Corp., 1980–; Resrcs. Dev. & Utilization Libn., Med. Lib., George Washington Univ., 1978–79; Asst. Ref. Libn., VA Commonwealth Univ., 1975–78. **Educ.:** West. MI Univ., 1970–73, BS (Dietetics), 1974–75, MLA (Libnshp.). **Orgs.:** SLA. DC LA. VA LA: JMRT (Secy., 1977–78). Youth for Understanding. **Pubns.:** International Affairs Section Membership Directory, SLA (1980); "Recruitment of Academic Librarians," *Bhvl. and Soc. Sci. Libn.* (Win. 1979). **Activities:** 1, 4; 17, 39, 46; 58, 68, 91 **Addr.:** The MAXIMA Corporation, 962 Wayne Ave., Silver Spring, MD 20910.

Matthews, Donald N. (Ag. 20, 1930, Allentown, PA) Libn., Luth. Theo. Semy., Gettysburg, 1966–; Asst. Libn., Lafayette Coll., 1961–66; Catlgr., Prof. Asst., Luth. Theo. Semy., 1959–61. **Educ.:** Lafayette Coll., 1949–53, AB (Phil.); Princeton Theo. Semy., 1953–56, MDiv; Rutger Univ., 1957–59, MLS, 1973 (Natl. Arch. Inst.). **Orgs.:** ATLA. AAUP. **Pubns.:** *Union List of Periodicals, Washington Theological Consortium* (1976, 1979); *Union List of Periodicals, Southeast PA Theo. LA* (1977, 1981); "That Your Sons and Daughters May Prophesy" filmstp. (1980). **Activities:** 1; 17; 90 **Addr.:** Lutheran Theological Seminary, 66 W. Confederate Ave., Gettysburg, PA 17325.

Matthews, Elizabeth Woodfin (Jl. 30, 1927, Ashland, VA) Assoc. Prof., Lib. Affairs, South. IL Univ. Sch. of Law, 1974–; Asst. Prof. and Med. Catlgr., South. IL Univ., Morris Lib. 1972–74; Cat. Instr., South. IL Univ. Coll. of Educ., 1967–70; Instr. and Catlgr., South. IL Univ., Morris Lib., 1964–67; Catlgr., VA Milit. Inst., 1963–64; Catlgr., Instr., Univ. of IL, 1962–63; Catlgr., OH State Univ., 1952–59. **Educ.:** Randolph Macon Coll., 1944–48, BA (Eng.); Univ. of IL, 1951–52, MS LS; South. IL Univ., 1971–72, PhD (Higher Educ.); 1963, Cert. Med. Libn. I, 1975, Cert. Med. Libn. III; 1978, Cert. Law Libn. **Orgs.:** ALA. AALL. Med. LA. IL LA. Amer. Assn. of Univ. Women: Branch Pres. (1976–78). Post-Doct. Acad. of Higher Educ. Mid Amer. Assn. of Law Libs. **Honors:** Beta Phi Mu, 1952; Phi Kappa Phi, 1972. **Pubns.:** "Questionnaire Construction for Maximum Survey Response," ERIC (1979); "Characteristics and Academic Preparation of Directors of Library-Learning Resource Centers in Selected Community Junior Colleges: Summary," ERIC (1975); "Effect of OCLC on Workflow in Law Libraries," *Law Lib. Jnl.* (N. 1978); "Update in Education for Community College Library Administrations," *Jnl. of Educ. for Libns.* (Spr. 1979); "Describing the Descriptive Survey," *IL Libs.* (Mr. 1978); various articles. **Activities:** 1; 20, 26; 63, 77, 80 **Addr.:** 811 Skyline Dr., Carbondale, IL 62901.

Matthews, Fred W. (N. 27, 1915, Carbonear, NF) Prof., Sch. of Lib. Srv., Dalhousie Univ., 1972–; Mgr., Ctrl. Info. Srvs., Imperial Chem. Indus., London, Eng., 1969–72; Mgr., Info. Srvs., Can. Indus. Ltd, 1958–69. **Educ.:** Mt. Allison Univ., 1932–36, BSc (Chem.); McGill Univ., 1939–41, PhD (Chem.); West. Rsv., 1957. **Orgs.:** ASIS. Can. Assn. for Info. Sci.: Pres. (1980–81). Intl. Union of Crystallography: Data Comsn. (Ch., 1948–70). Chem. Inst. Canada: Dir. (1958–62). **Honors:** Amer. Socty. for Testing and Mtrls., Awd. of Merit, 1968. **Pubns.:** "Library Catalogue Automation: Cost Benefit Factors," *Proceedings, Can. Assn. for Info. Sci.* (1979); "Weighted Term Search: A Computer Program for an Inverted Coordinate Index," *Jnl. Chem. Docum.* (1967). **Activities:** 11, 12; 23, 24, 41; 60, 75, 91 **Addr.:** School of Library Service, Dalhousie University, Halifax, NS B3H 4H8 Canada.

Matthews, Gertrude Ann Urch (Jl. 16, 1921, Jackson, MI) Retired. Asst. dir., Franklin Sylvester Lib., 1963–81; Adult Srvs., Jackson (MI) Pub. Lib., 1956–58, Ref. Srvs., 1958–63. **Educ.:** Jackson Jr. Coll., 1939–41, AA; Univ. of MI, 1956–58, BA (Pol. Sci.), 1958–59, LSCA (LS). **Orgs.:** ALA: Mem. com. (1963). OH LA: PR (1963–). Leag. of Women Voters. AAUW. Hist. Socty. Medina. St. Paul's Episcopal Church. **Pubns.:** "Bibliotherapy for long-term patient in short-term hospital"

PROFESSIONAL ACTIVITIES: Institutions: 1. Acad. lib.; 2. Arch.; 3. Assn.; 4. Fed./Gvt. lib.; 5. Inst. lib.; 6. Mfr./Suppl.; 7. Milit. lib.; 8. Musm.; 9. Pub. lib.; 10. Sch. lib.; 11. Sch. of lib. sci.; 12. Spec. lib.; 13. State lib.; 14. (other). **Functions/Activities:** 15. Acq./Col. dev.; 16. Adult srvs.; 17. Admin.; 18. Apprais.; 19. Archit./Bldgs.; 20. Cat./Class.; 21. Chld. srvs.; 22. Circ.; 23. Cons./Pres.; 24. Consult.; 25. Cont. ed.; 26. Educ. lib. sci.; 27. Ext. srvs.; 28. Fund/Grants; 29. Gvt. pubs.; 30. Indx./Abs.; 31. Instr. lib. use; 32. Media srvs.; 33. Micro.; 34. Netwks./Coop.; 35. Persnl.; 36. PR; 37. Publshg.; 38. Recs. mgt.; 39. Ref. srvs.; 40. Repro.; 41. Resrch.; 42. Review.; 43. Secur.; 44. Serials; 45. Spec. col.; 46. Tech. srvs.; 47. Trustees/Bds.; 48. YA srvs.; 49. (other).

Amer. Libs. (1969); other articles. **Activities:** 9; 17, 36, 39; 69, 83, 86 **Addr.:** 750 Weymouth, Medina, OH 44256.

Matthews, Islwyn Lynn (Ap. 12, 1929, Dowlais, Glamorganshire, Wales) Chief Libn., Kitchener Pub. Lib., 1973–; Team Leader, N. York Pub. Lib., 1972–73; Asst. Reg. Libn., Parkland Reg. Lib., 1968–69. **Educ.:** Univ. of Toronto, 1965–70, BA (Hist.), 1970–72, MLS. **Orgs.:** Can. Assn. of Pub. Libs.: Vice-Ch. (1976–77); Ch. (1977–78). ON Pub. Libns. Adv. Com.: Ch. (1977–78). Can. LA: Nom. Com. (1979–80). ON LA. Cham. of Cmrce. Waterloo Hist. Socty. **Pubns.:** "Reconciling the Individual with the Organization," *O.L.A. Nsltr.* (Ja., 1973); "Public Library - University Collaboration in Kitchener," *ON Lib. Review* (S., 1974). **Addr.:** Kitchener Public Library, 85 Queen St. North, Kitchener, ON N2H 2H1 Canada.

Matthews, Joseph R. (Ap. 15, 1942, Los Angeles, CA) Pres., J. Matthews & Assoc., Inc., 1976–; Resrch. Assoc., Pub. Policy Resrch. Org., 1972–76. **Educ.:** CA State Univ., Long Beach, 1970, BS (Bus. Admin.; Univ. of CA, Irvine, 1972–74, MS, (Admin.). **Orgs.:** ALA. Socty. for Mgt. Info. ASIS. Urban and Reg. Info. Syst. Assn. **Pubns.:** *Choosing an Automated Library System* (1980); "Gauging the Impact of Change," *Datamation* (S. 1978); "A Survey of EDP Performance Measure," *Gvt. Data Systs.* (Jl./Ag. 1978). **Activities:** 22, 24; 56 **Addr.:** J. Matthews & Associates, Inc., 213 Hill St., Grass Valley, CA 95945.

Matthews, Sidney E. (F. 28, 1920, Staunton, VA) Dir., Lib. Srvs., Southern IL Univ., Carbondale, 1976–, Asst. Dir., Morris Lib., 1964–76; Dir. of Libs., VA Mil. Inst., Lexington, 1960–64; Acq. Libn., OH State Univ. Lib., 1956–59, Asst. Acq. Libn., 1953–55, Head, Serial Div., 1952–53. **Educ.:** Randolph-Macon Coll., 1941–43, 1946–48, BA (Soc. Sci.); Univ. of NC, 1949–50, BSLS; Univ. of IL, 1951–52, MSLS. **Orgs.:** ALA: RTSD/Prsrvn. of Lib. Mtrls. (1977–). IL LA: Resrcs. and Tech. Srvs., Secy. (1979–80). IL State Hist. Socty.: Dir. (1979–); VP (1978–79); Dir. (1970–75). Rotary Intl., Carbondale: Pres. (1973–74); VP (1972–73). Congs. of IL Hist. Socty.: VP (1978–). United Way, Carbondale; Dir., (1978–80). **Honors:** Phi Beta Mu. **Pubns.:** Contrib. *Teaching for Better Use of Libraries* (1970); "Operation and Cost of Running Library Circulation On-Line with IBM System/7-2790," *IL Libs.* (Ja. 1979); "From a 357 to a System/7," *Lib. Jnl. Spec. Report 4* (1978); "The Not-So-Retiring Ralph E. McCoy," *I CarbS* (Spr./Sum. 1976); "The Marshall Library, A New Concept," *The News-Gazette* (1964). **Activities:** 1; 17 **Addr.:** Morris Library, Southern Illinois University at Carbondale, Carbondale, IL 62901.

Matthews, Stephen L. (Ja. 12, 1948, Martinsburg, WV) Libn., Currier Lib., Foxcroft Sch., 1977–; Dir. Lib. Srv., Loudoun Cnty. Pub. Lib., 1976–77; Ref., Outrch. Libn., YA Spec., Fairfax Cnty. Pub. Lib., 1974–75; YA Libn., James V. Brown Lib., 1973–74. **Educ.:** Hiram Coll., 1967–71, BA (Eng., Amer. Std.); Univ. of MI, 1972–73, MLS; CT Coll., 1975–76, MAT (Eng.). **Orgs.:** ALA: YASD; AASL, Bylaws Com. VA LA: IFC; Oral Hist. Forum, Ch. Oral Hist. in the Mid–Atl. Reg. **Pubns.:** Reviews. **Activities:** 9, 10; 32, 39, 48; 74, 85 **Addr.:** Box 1233, Middleburg, VA 22117.

Mattison, Helen S. (S. 2, 1917, Cloyds Landing, KY) Educ. Spec., Media, Sch. Bd. of Broward Cnty., 1968–; Dir. of Lrng. Resrcs., Nova HS, 1963–68; Media Spec., McArthur HS, 1957–63; Libn., Lakeland Jr. HS, 1953–57; Libn., Crawfordville HS, 1951–53; Libn., Blountstown HS, 1949–51; Tchr., Millville Elem. Sch., 1947–49; Comm. Tchr., Tompkinsville HS, 1941–47. **Educ.:** Western KY State Tchrs. Coll., 1934–38, AB (Eng.); FL State Univ., 1950–52, MLS. **Orgs.:** AECT. ALA. FL Assn. for Media and Educ.: Secy. (1969–70). Broward Cnty. Assn. of Media Spec.; Pres. (1959–60). Broward LA. Delta Kappa Gamma: Second VP (1978–80). Soroptomist. Women of the Moose. **Pubns.:** "Nova Resource Centers", *FL Assn. Sch. Libns.* (Ap. 1964); "Author Speaks", *Wilson Lib. Bltn.* (Ap. 1959); "Literary Dolls," *Wilson Lib. Bltn.* (O. 1951). **Activities:** 10; 32; 63, 67 **Addr.:** 3641 S. W. 21 Ct., Fort Lauderdale, FL 33312.

Matz, Ruth G. (Boston, MA) Chief Libn., MA Dept. of Attorney Gen., 1975–; Law Libn., Mintz, Levin, Cohn, Glovsky and Popeo, 1970–75. **Educ.:** Radcliffe Coll., 1943–47, (Amer. Gvt.); Simmons Coll., 1966–70. **Orgs.:** AALL. New Eng. Law Libs. Assn: Dir. (1981–). Assn. of Boston Law Libns.: Pres. (1973–74); Un. List, (Ch., 1977–). Boston Org. of Gvt. Libns.: Bylaws Com.; Nom. Com. **Pubns.:** "Lawyers and Shays' Rebellion," *Boston Bar Jnl.* (F. 1977). **Activities:** 4; 15, 20, 39; 77 **Addr.:** Law Library, Dept. of Attorney General, One Ashburton Pl., Boston, MA 02108.

Matzek, Richard A. (N. 18, 1937, Milwaukee, WI) Dir. of the Lorette Wilmot Lib., Nazareth Coll. of Rochester, 1977–; Dir. of the Lib., Sacred Heart Univ., 1966–77, Asst. Dir., 1963–66; Libn. I, Marquette Univ., 1962–63. **Educ.:** Marquette Univ., 1955–59, BA (Eng./Latin); Univ. of WI, 1959–60, MA (LS). **Orgs.:** ALA. New Eng. LA. Rochester Reg. Resrch. Lib. Cncl.: Adv. Com. (1977–). New Eng. Lib. Bd.: Panel of Couns. (1971–77). **Honors:** Rotary Intl., Exch. Fellow, 1975. **Pubns.:** *Academic Library Cooperation in Fairfield County.* (1973); "Current Index to Religious Books" *Religious Book Review;* Reviews; RRRLC Sound-slide show, Co-Producer (1979). **Activities:** 1; 17, 19, 32; 61, 90 **Addr.:** Lorette Wilmot Library, Nazareth College of Rochester, P.O. Box 3908, Rochester, NY 14610.

Maudslien, Clifton N. (My. 6, 1943, Seattle, WA) Libn., Mt. Rainier HS, 1980–; Libn., Glacier HS, 1978–80; Tchr., Puget Snd. Jr. High, 1977–78; Libn., Highline HS, 1976–77. **Educ.:** Univ. of WA, 1964–66, BA (Hist.), 1966–67, MLS. **Orgs.:** WA Lib. Media Assn. WA LA. ALA. Natl. Educ. Assn. WA HS Coaches Assn. **Activities:** 10; 48 **Addr.:** 16923—32nd S.W., Seattle, WA 98166.

Mauerhoff, Georg R. (Ap. 23, 1947, Lüneburg, W. Germany) Dir., Data Base Publshg., INFOMART, 1980–, Mktg. Mgr., 1975–79; Prod. Dev. Ofcr., Southam Press Ltd., 1974–75; Head, Tape Srvs., Canada Inst. for Sci. and Tech. Info., 1971–74. **Educ.:** Univ. of SK, 1965–68, BA (Math.); Case West. Resrv. Univ., 1968–69, MSLS. **Orgs.:** Info. Indus. Assn. Can. Assn. for Info. Sci. Can. LA. ASIS. **Pubns.:** "Selective Dissemination of Information", *Advances for Libnshp.* (1973); "An Information Industry for Canada", *Bus. Qtly.* (1977); "CAN/SDI: A National SDI System for Canada", *LIBRI* (D. 1973); "Distribution of SDC Search Service in Canada by INFOMART," *ONLINE REVIEW* (1977); "A MARC II-Based Program for Retrieval and Dissemination", *Jnl. of Lib. Autom.* (S. 1971). **Activities:** 6; 17, 37, 49-Info. Retrieval; 51, 56, 93 **Addr.:** INFOMART, Village by the Grange, 122 St. Patrick St., Toronto, ON M5T 2X8 Canada.

Mauerhoff, Jocelyn R. (Ap. 18, 1942, Preston, Lancashire, Eng.) Head, Coll. Dev. Ont. Leg. Lib., 1979–; Head, Docum., Intergovtal. Com. on Urban and Reg. Resrch., 1977–79; Exec. Dir., Can. Comm. Resrch. Info. Ctr., 1974–76; Head, Lib. Srvs., Dept. of Comm., 1972–74; Head, Sci. and Eng. Lib., Sir George Williams Univ., 1970–72, Head, Ref. Dept., 1969–70, Ref. Libn., 1966–68, Ref. Libn., London Pub. Lib. and Art Mus., 1965–66. **Educ.:** Univ. of MB, BA (Eng.); McGill Univ., BLS; Lib. Univ. of MD, 1970 (Lib. Admin.). **Orgs.:** Can. Assn. for Info. Sci. Can. Comm. Assn. **Pubns.:** Ed., *Communications: Research in Canada - Recherche au Canada* (1975); asst. ed., *The Chld. Broadcast Inst. Nwsltr.* (1979); "Can. Comm. Research Information Centre," *Edu. Broadcasting Intl.* (D. 1975); "Canadian Comn. Resrch. Info. Ctr" *Educ. Broadcasting Intl.* (1975). **Activities:** 4; 15, 29, 39; 62, 75, 78 **Addr.:** Legislative Library, Research and Information Services, Legislative Building, Queen's Park, Toronto, ON M7A 1A2 Canada.

Mauldin, E. Eugenia (N. 4, 1916, Baldwyn, MS) Prof. Grad. Sch. of Lib. and Info. Sci., Univ. of TN, Knoxville, 1957–; HS Libn., Corinth, MS, 1956–57. **Educ.:** Millsaps Coll., 1934–38, BA (Eng.); Univ. of MS, 1950, MEd; Univ. of IL, Champaign-Urbana, 1954–56, MS LS. **Orgs.:** TN LA: Ch., Library Educ. Sec. (1979–80). Southeastern LA: Ch., Lib. Educ. Sect. (1978–80). Pi Lambda Theta: Fac. Adv. (1970–78); Delta Kappa Gamma: Recording Sec. (1978–80). **Activities:** 10, 11; 21, 26, 48; 63, 89, 93 **Addr.:** 1631 Laurel, Apt. 109, Knoxville, TN 37916.

Maurer, Bradley Gerald (My. 31, 1951, Long Beach, CA) Head Libn., S. Branch Lib., Davis Cnty. Lib., 1977–. **Educ.:** Brigham Young Univ., 1969–75, BA (Asian Std. & Chinese), 1975–76, MLS. **Orgs.:** ALA. UT LA: Ch., Int. Frdm. Com. (1977); Ch., Resrch. Com. (1979); Nom. Com. (1978). **Pubns.:** "The Influence of Hindu Epistemology on Ranganathan's Colon Classification," *ERIC* (1977). **Activities:** 9, 14-Cnty. Lib. Syst.; 15, 17, 39; 54, 55, 74 **Addr.:** Davis County Library, South Branch, 725 S. Main, Bountiful, UT 84010.

Maurer, Charles B. (Ja. 17, 1933, Oak Park, IL) Dir., Denison Univ. Libs., 1971–; Asst. Prof. of Grmn., Univ. of MI, 1965–71; Instr. of Grmn., Lawrence Univ., 1962–65. **Educ.:** Univ. of ID, MI, 1950–54, BA (Grmn.); Northwestern Univ., 1957–60, MA,PhD (Grmn.); Univ. of Munich, 1970–71; Univ. of MI, 1967–70, AMLS. **Orgs.:** ALA. Acad. LA OH: various coms. (1975–78). OHIONET: Inst. Rep. (1977–). OCLC Users Cncl.: OHIONET Del. (1978–). **Honors:** Beta Phi Mu, 1970. **Pubns.:** *Call to Revolution* (1971). **Activities:** 1; 15, 16, 17; 55, 70 **Addr.:** Denison University, Granville, OH 43023.

Maurice, Leatrice (Jl. 4, 1932, Montreal, PQ) Libn., Ville Marie Soc. Srv. Ctr., 1976–; Instr., Concordia Univ., Loyola Campus; various positions in bus. **Educ.:** Sir George Williams Univ., 1968–72, BA (Hist.); McGill Univ., 1973–75, MLS; various crs. **Orgs.:** Can. Hlth. LA. Can. LA. Corp. des bibtcrs. profs. du PQ. Med. LA. various orgs. McGill Med. and Hosp. Libns. Assn. Indexing and Abs. Socty. of Can. **Activities:** 4, 12; 15, 29, 39; 75, 78, 95-Soc. Srvs. **Addr.:** 250 Kensington Ave. Apt. 304, Montreal, PQ H3Z 2G8 Canada.

Maurin, Mrs. Raissa B. (Mr. 10, 1909, St. Petersburg, Russia) Chief, Lib. Srv., Admin. Libn., Miami Vets. Admin. Med. Ctr., 1974–; Deputy Libn., Univ. of Miami Sch. of Med., 1971–74; Ref. Libn., Univ. of CT Sch. of Med., 1969–71; Libn., US Dept. of Cmrce. Bur. of Fisheries, 1966–69. **Educ.:** Coll. of the City of New York, BS (Educ.); Cath. Univ. of Amer., 1955, MS (LS). **Orgs.:** SLA. Med. LA. FL LA. **Activities:** 4; 17, 39; 80 **Addr.:** Miami Veterans Administration Medical Center, 1201 N. W. 16th St., Miami, FL 33125.

Maurstad, Betty Louise (F. 3, 1922, Spokane, WA) Assoc. Prof., Div. of LS, Wayne State Univ., 1972–; Libn., Musm. Asst., Cur., Univ. Gallery, Univ. of MN, 1946–66. **Educ.:** Univ. of MN, 1942–47, BA (Art Hist.), 1966–67, MA (LS), 1967–69, MA (Art Hist.); Case West. Resrv. Univ., 1968–72, PhD (Lib. and Info. Sci.). **Orgs.:** ALA. SLA. ARLIS/NA: Ch., MI Chap. (1976–77). Msc. LA. Other orgs. Coll. Art Assn. Amer. Assn. for the Advnc. of the Hum. AAUP. **Honors:** U S Fulbright Grant, Paris, 1954–55. **Pubns.:** Ed., *The Library and the Contemporary Arts* (1977); "Women and Book Collecting" *Among Friends* (1980); jt. auth., "Wayne State University, Division of Library Science," *Encyclopedia of Library and Information Science* (1980). **Activities:** 11; 26, 39; 55, 57 **Addr.:** Division of Library Science, 315 Kresge Library, Wayne State University, Detroit, MI 48202.

Mautino, Patricia (N. 3, 1942, West Chester, PA) Dir., Curric. Resrc. Ctr., Oswego Bd. of Coop. Educ. Srvcs., 1972–; Assoc. for Info. Srvcs., Educ. and Cul. Ctr., Syracuse, NY, 1969–72; Asst. Prof., Libs., Onondaga Comnty. Coll., 1966–69. **Educ.:** Syracuse Univ., 1960–64, BA (Span./Educ.), 1965–66, MSLS, (Educ. Admin.). **Orgs.:** ALA: AASL (Conf. Plng. Com, Dallas, 1978–79); Fac. Plng. Com. (1976–78); Legis. Com., 1978–80); Dist. Sch. Admin. Awd. Com. (1978–79). NY LA (Annual Conf. Plng Com. (1974–75); Mem. of Cncl. (1975–76); Ch. Legis. Com. (1976–79). Sch. Lib. Media Sect. (Nom. Com., 1973; Awds. Com., 1973–74; 1st VP, 1974–75; Pres. 1975–76). NY State Reading Assn. ERIC Clearinghouse for Info. Resrcs.: Nat. Adv. Bd.; Nat. Comsn. on Libs. and Info. Sci.: Task Force on the Role of Sch. Libs. in Netwks. NY State Gov.'s Conf. on Libs.: Del. **Honors:** Encyc. Brit. Educ. Corp., "First Fifty" Anniv. Awd., 1979. Beta Phi Mu. **Pubns.:** *Mini-Pac: Differentiated Staffing* (1970); *Differentiated Staffing Compendium, Compiler* (1971); "These Animals Go To School," *Instr.* (O. 1974); "BOCES Support School Library Media Centers," *Bookmark* (Fall 1976); "Support of Library Services in New York," *Libs. in the Pol. Prcs.* **Activities:** 10; 17, 32, 34; 63, 67, 78 **Addr.:** 4505 S. Salina St., Apt. 22, Syracuse, NY 13205.

Mautner, Robert William (S. 24, 1925, Los Angeles, CA) Sci. Libn., Univ. of AZ, 1965–; Head, Sci.-Tech. Ref. Room, CA State Univ. Coll., Sacramento, 1960–64; Head, Bus. Libn., CA State Univ. Coll., Los Angeles, 1956–60; Eng. Libn., Rocketdyne, 1956. **Educ.:** Univ. of CA, Berkeley, 1947–49, BS (Psych.), 1951–52, BLS. **Orgs.:** AZ State LA: Pres., Coll. and Univ. Div. 1966–67); Treas., ASLA (1973–75); Ch., Intell. Freedom Com. (1973–74). ALA. AAUP. Pres. Univ. of AZ Chap. (1978); Treas. (1968–70); Univ. of Arizona, Faculty Senate Sen. (1969–71). **Pubns.:** "Higher education in Arizona," *AZ Blue Book* (1971). "Special libraries (in Arizona)," (1971). reviews. **Activities:** 1; 17, 39; 56, 74, 91 **Addr.:** Science-Engineering Library, University of Arizona, Tucson, AZ 85721.

Mavor, Anne Schumacher (My. 7, 1938, Albany, NY) VP, W/V Assoc. Inc., 1969–, Resrch. Sci., 1966–69; Resrch. Assoc., Human Sci. Resrch. Inc., 1964–66; Resrch. Assoc., Army Persnl. Resrch. Ofc., 1962–64. **Educ.:** OH Wesleyan Univ., 1956–60, BA (Psy.); Purdue Univ., 1960–62, MS (Exper. Psy.). **Orgs.:** ASIS. Human Factors Socty. **Pubns.:** Jt. Auth., "An assessment of mechanisms for international exchange of science information," rpt. for Natl. Sci. Fndn. (1980); "Identification and preparation of derivative information products required by selected users of science information," (1977); Jt. auth., "An overview of the national adult independent learning project," *Resrch. Qtly.* (1976); Jt. auth., "The role of the public libraries in adult independent learning. Final Report," Coll. Entrance Examination Bd. (1976); "A system for evaluating services to the adult independent learner through the public library," Coll. Entrance Examination Bd. (May 1975); various tech. rpts. **Activities:** 1, 9; 16, 24; 50, 75 **Addr.:** W/V Associates, 422 6th St., Annapolis, MD 21403.

Mawdsley, Katherine F. (S. 16, 1940, Wilmington, DE) Head, Gvt. Docum. Dept., Shields Lib., Univ. of CA, Davis, 1973–, Asst. Head, 1972–73, U.S. Docum. Libn., 1965–69. **Educ.:** Univ. of DE, 1958–61, BA (Eng.), 1961–64, MA (Eng.); Univ. of MN, 1964–65, MALS. **Orgs.:** CA LA. ALA: GODORT Microforms TF (Coord., 1979–80); RTSD Repro. Lib. Mtls. Sect., Nom. Com. (1980); Guidelines for Lib. Microform Facility Com. (1980–). Depository Lib. Cncl. to the Pub. Printer: Ch. (1979–80). Phi Beta Kappa: Kappa Chap. (Secy., 1974–). **Activities:** 1; 29, 33 **Addr.:** Government Documents Dept., Shields Library, University of California, Davis, Davis, CA 95616.

Max, Elizabeth Assoc. Prof., Coord., LS, Coll. of Educ., OK State Univ., 1974–, Asst. Prof., Coord. LS Dept., 1972–74, Head, Fine Arts Div., Lib., 1970–72, Instr., Dept. of LS, Media Libn., West. IL Univ., 1969–70; Libn., Breckenridge (TX) HS, 1963–69; Tchr., Breckenridge (TX) Schs., 1950–60. **Educ.:** TX Woman's Univ., 1940–44, BA (Thea.); N. TX State Univ., 1964–66, MLS; OK State Univ., 1971–74, EdD. **Orgs.:** ALA. OK LA. Natl. Educ. Assn. OK Educ. Assn. OK AECT. **Honors:** Beta Phi Mu; Phi Delta Kappa. **Pubns.:** Journal articles, book and film reviews. **Addr.:** 2203 W. 4th Ave., Stillwater, OK 74074.

Maxfield, David Kempton (My. 12, 1913, Waterville, ME) Retired, 1977–; Head, Med. Ctr. Lib., Univ. of MI, 1959–77,

Special Subjects/Services: 50. Adult educ.; 51. Advert./Mktg.; 52. Aerosp.; 53. Agric.; 54. Area std.; 55. Arts/Hum.; 56. Autom.; 57. Bibl./Prtg.; 58. Bio. sci.; 59. Bus./Fin.; 60. Chem.; 61. Copyrt.; 62. Documtn.; 63. Educ.; 64. Engin.; 65. Env.; 66. Eth. grps.; 67. Film; 68. Food/Nutr.; 69. Geneal.; 70. Geo.; 71. Geol.; 72. Handcpd.; 73. Hist.; 74. Int. frdm.; 75. Info. sci.; 76. Insr.; 77. Law; 78. Legis.; 79. Math./Comp. sci.; 80. Med.; 81. Metals; 82. Nat. resrcs.; 83. Newsp.; 84. Nuc. sci.; 85. Oral hist.; 86. Petr./Energy; 87. Pharm.; 88. Phys./Astr./Math.; 89. Readg.; 90. Relig.; 91. Sci./Tech.; 92. Soc. sci.; 93. Telecom.; 94. Transp.; 95. (other).

Who's Who in Library and Information Services

Asst. to Dir. of Libs., 1956–59; Libn., Chicago Undergrad. Div., Univ. of IL, 1946–55; Asst. Libn., Cooper Un., 1939–46; Asst. Jnlsm. Libn., Columbia Univ., 1937–39; **Educ.:** Haverford Coll., 1932–36, BS (Hist.); Columbia Univ., 1936–37, BSLS, 1939–46, MSLS. **Orgs.:** ALA. N. Amer. Shortwave Assn. Amer. Philatelic Socty. Baker St. Irregulars. **Honors:** Beta Phi Mu. **Pubns.:** "Counselor Librarianship: A New Departure," Univ. of IL Lib. Sch., Occasional Papers, No. 38; Ed., *ACRL Monographs, 1952–1956;* "Library Punched Card Procedures," *Lib. Jnl.* (Je. 15, 1946); "Watson: Medical Author," *Bltn. of the Med. LA* (Jl. 1975). **Activities:** 1; 17; 80 **Addr.:** 2217 Manchester Rd., Ann Arbor, MI 48104.

Maxin, Jacqueline A. (Ap. 13, 1950, Potsdam, NY) Supvsr./Info. Srvcs., PPG Fiber Glass Resrch. Ctr., 1979–; Ser. and Acq. Libn., Clarkson Coll. of Tech., 1973–78; Consult., Norfolk Hepburn Pub. Lib., 1975. **Educ.:** SUNY, Potsdam, 1968–71, BA (Soc. Sci.); SUNY, Albany, 1972–73, MLS; Univ. of Pittsburgh, 1978–81, PhD (Lib. Sci.); Clarkson Coll. of Tech., 1974–77, postgrad. (Account.). **Orgs.:** ALA: ACRL (Coll. Libs. Sect., Com. on Cont. Educ., 1978–81). Univ. of Pittsburgh, Sch. of Lib. and Info. Sci. (Doct. Guild, Secy/Treas. 1978–79). NY LA: RTSD (Mem. Com. 1976–77). ACRL: Eastern NY Chap., (Comms. Com., 1977; Interim Plng. Com. 1975). **Honors:** Beta Phi Mu, 1973. **Pubns.:** Contrib. *Job Descriptions* (1981); Contrib. *Performance Appraisals* (1980); Contrib. *Continuing Education Survey. Part I.* (1978); "Periodical Use and Collection Development," *Coll. and Resrch. Libs.* (My. 1979); "Cooperative Purchasing by a New York 3R's Council," *Ser. Libn.* (Spr. 1978). **Activities:** 1, 12; 17, 41, 44; 59, 60; 91 **Addr.:** 4310 Sample Court, Allison Park, PA 15101.

Maxon, William N. (Ja. 16, 1920, New York, NY) Head of Ref. Dept., Georgetown Univ. Law Sch., 1979–, Ref. Libn., 1974–78; Frgn. Affairs Anal., US Gvt., 1951–73; Attorney, 1950–51; Newspaper Reporter, 1946–47. **Educ.:** Columbia Univ., 1938–42, BA (Gvt.); Univ. of VA Law Sch., 1947–50, LLB (Law); Cath. Univ., 1973–74, MSLS. **Orgs.:** AALL. Law Libns. Socty. of Washington, DC. NY Bar. **Pubns.:** "Tax Law Research – Easy Does It", *Legal Times of Washington* (My. 21, 1979). **Activities:** 1, 12; 39; 77 **Addr.:** 8527 Betterton Ct., Vienna, VA 22180.

Maxson, Wayne C. (My. 26, 1935, Stoughton, WI) Ref. Libn., Temple Univ. Lib., 1970–. **Educ.:** Salem Coll., 1953–57, BA (Eng.); Hartford Semy. Fndn., 1962–63, STM; Rutgers Univ., 1968–70, MLS. **Orgs.:** ALA. Assn. for the Dev. of Relig. Info. Systs. **Activities:** 1; 39; 90 **Addr.:** Temple University Library, Philadelphia, PA 19122.

Maxton, L. Pauline (Mr. 15, 1920, Birdsboro, PA) Asst. Dir., Reading Pub. Lib., 1966–, Asst. Dir., Head, Ref. Dept., 1961–66, Acting Dir., 1965–66, Head, Ref. Dept., 1949–61, Asst. Ref. Libn., 1947–49; Tchr., Libn, Oley HS, 1945–47; Tchr., Spring City HS, 1943–45. **Educ.:** Kutztown State Coll., 1938–42, BS (Educ.); Drexel Univ., 1949–50, MLS; Columbia Univ., 1944; Albright Coll., 1945 (Sci., Hist.). **Orgs.:** ALA. PA LA.: Lehigh Valley Chap. (Ch., 1968–69). Altrusa Club of Reading. **Activities:** 9; 17, 24, 27 **Addr.:** 815 Main St., Birdsboro, PA 19508.

Maxwell, Barbara (O. 1941, Greeley, CO) Chief Ref. Libn., George Washington Univ. Lib., 1975–; Msc. Catlgr., Lib. of Congs., 1973–75; Msc. Libn., SUNY, Binghamton, 1970–73, Ref. Libn., 1969–70; Ref. Libn., Univ. of CA, Berkeley, 1966–69. **Educ.:** Pomona Coll., 1958–62, BA (Msc.); Univ. of CA, Berkeley, 1965, MA (Msc.), 1967, MLS. **Orgs.:** Msc. LA: Chesapeake Chap., Nom. Com., Ch. (1975). DC LA. Medul. Acad. of Amer. Amer. Assn. for the Adv. of Sci. **Honors:** Phi Beta Kappa. **Pubns.:** "Art Songs," *Antiphony* (1974). **Activities:** 1; 17, 20, 39; 55, 92 **Addr.:** 7859 Coddle Harbor Ln., Potomac, MD 20854.

Maxwell, Barbara A. (Je. 9, 1937, Pittsburgh, PA) Head, Chld. Dept., Northwest Reg. Lib., Free Lib. of Philadelphia, 1978–, Head of Spec. Col., 1975–78, Spec. for Chld. Spec. Col., 1974–75; Asst. Libn., Haverford Sch., 1971–74; Ref. Libn., Univ. of DE, 1966–71; Head, Ref. Srvs., Duquesne Univ., 1963–66, Asst. Ref. Libn., 1961–63; Ref./Catlgr. Libn., Tech. Lib., E. I. du Pont de Nemours & Co., 1960–61. **Educ.:** Wilson Coll., 1955–59, AB (Fr.); Drexel Univ., 1959–60, MSLS. **Orgs.:** ALA: Nat. Plng. of Spec. Col. Com. (Ch., 1979–81). PA LA. SLA. **Honors:** Beta Phi Mu. **Pubns.:** Jt. auth., *Checklist of Children's Books, 1837–1876* (1975); jt. auth., *Bibliography of Reference Books for Freshmen Class of 1973* (1969); "Research Collections on Public Libraries," *Lib. Trends* (Spr. 1979). **Activities:** 1, 9; 21, 39 **Addr.:** Apt. 809 A Alden Park Manor, Wissahickon and Chelten Aves., Philadelphia, PA 19144.

Maxwell, Barbara Ann (N. 4, 1944, Martinsburg, WV) Tech. Srvs. Libn., Shepherd Coll., 1979–, Chief Catlgr., 1971–79, Asst. Catlgr., 1968–71. **Educ.:** Shepherd Coll., 1962–66, BA (Educ., Eng.); Drexel Univ., 1967–68, MSLS; Johns Hopkins Univ., 1971–73, MLA (Liberal Arts). **Orgs.:** Cumberland Valley LA: Pres. (1979–80), VP (1978–79). Potomac Tech. Prcs. Libns. SELA. ALA: ACRL. AAUW. Alpha Sigma Tau: Various lcl. ofcs. **Honors:** Beta Phi Mu; Kappa Delta Pi. **Pubns.:** "Library at Shepherd College Proves Servicable," *WV Libs.* (S. 1968). **Activities:** 1; 46 **Addr.:** Ruth Scarborough Library, Shepherd College, Shepherdstown, WV 25443.

Maxwell, Littleton M. (O. 24, 1940, Lynchburg, VA) Sch. of Bus. Admin. Libn., Univ. of Richmond, VA, 1971–; Ref. Libn., Acting Br. Libn., Henrico Cnty., VA, Pub. Lib., 1969–71. **Educ.:** Randolph-Macon Coll., 1958–62, AB (Hist.); Univ. of KY, Lexington, 1967–68, MSLS; Univ. of VA, 1962–63, (Law); Univ. of Richmond, 1972–, (bus. crs.). **Orgs.:** SLA. VA Spec. LA: VP (1975–76); Pres. (1976–77); Dir. (1977–79). SELA: Conf. Local Arrange. Com. (1974). AAUP. Old Dominion Chap. Cystic Fibrosis Fndn.: State Bd. of Dir. (1977–). **Honors:** Beta Phi Mu, 1968; Beta Gamma Sigma, 1975. **Pubns.:** Ed., *Guide to the Libraries in the Richmond Area* (1970, 1974); "A Library's Social Responsibility," *VA Libn.* (Fall, 1969); "Be Concerned and Involved - Join ALA, SELA, VLA," *VA Libn.* (Sum. 1970). **Activities:** 1, 12; 24, 31, 39; 51, 59, 76 **Addr.:** 8610 Oakcroft Dr., Richmond, VA 23229.

Maxwell, Margaret Finlayson (S. 9, 1927, Schenectady, NY) Prof. of LS, Grad. Lib. Sch., Univ. of AZ, 1971–; Lect. in LS, Univ. of MI, 1970–71; Instr. in Eng. & LS, Upper IA Univ., 1966–68, Assoc. Libn., 1956–66; Intern & Descr. Catlgr., Lib. of Congs., 1950–56. **Educ.:** Pomona Coll., 1944–48, BA (Eng. lit.); Univ. of CA, Berkeley, 1949–50, BLS; George Washington Univ., 1950–53, MA (Eng. lit.); Univ. of MI, 1968–71, PhD (LS). **Orgs.:** ALA: LHRT, Nom. Com. (1973–74); Ch. elect, (1975–76); Ch. (1976–77); RTSD, Ad-hoc Com. to Introduce the Anglo-American Cat. Rules (1978–79); Cat., Descr. and Access Com. (1980–). AZ LA. AALS. SW LA. AZ Hist. Socty. Sharlot Hall Hist. Socty. **Honors:** Phi Beta Kappa, 1947; ALA, writing competition prize winner, 1978. **Pubns.:** *Handbook for AACR2* (1980); Jt. ed., *Voices from the Southwest: a Gathering in Honor of Lawrence Clark Powell* (1976); *Shaping a Library: William L. Clements as Collector* (1973); "The Lion and the Lady; the Firing of Mary Jones," *Amer. Libs.* (My. 1978); "The Genesis of the Anglo-American Cataloging Rules," *LIBRI* (1977). **Activities:** 11; 20, 26, 45; 57 **Addr.:** Graduate Library School, University of Arizona, 1515 E. First St., Tucson, AZ 85719.

Maxwell, Mary M. (Mr. 16, 1944, Danville, VA) Coord. of Resrch., Univ. Rel. Dept., Univ. of Richmond, 1981–; Libn., Smithdeal Massey Bus. Coll., 1978–81; Branch Libn., Henrico Cnty. Pub. Lib., 1969–72, Ref. Libn., 1969; Head Libn., Woodford Cnty. Pub. Lib., 1967–68. **Educ.:** Emory and Henry Coll., 1962–66, BA (Eng.); Univ. of NC, 1966–67, MS (LS). **Orgs.:** ALA. VA LA: JMRT (Treas., 1971–72). CSLA. Episcopal Church of the Holy Comforter. Episcopal Bk. Store of Diocese of VA. **Honors:** Beta Phi Mu, 1968. **Activities:** 9, 10; 17, 32, 39; 50, 55, 59 **Addr.:** 8610 Oakcroft Dr., Richmond, VA 23229.

Maxwell, Rodney J. (D. 19, 1942, Catskill, NY) Owner, Maxwell Lib. Systs., 1980–; Sales Dir., Warner—Eddison Assoc., 1979–80; Dir., Sioux City Pub. Lib., 1975–79, Head, Prcs. Div., 1973–75. **Educ.:** SUNY, Albany, 1970–72, BA (Eng.), 1972–73, MLS. **Orgs.:** New Eng. LA. ALA: LAMA/BES, Archit. for Pub. Libs. Com. (Ch., 1977–79); RASD, Srv. to Adults Com. (1976–77); various coms. IA LA: Fed. Rel. Coord. (1976); various ofcs. IA Pub. Libs. Com.: Comp. Circ. (Ch., 1978); Stan. (1978). IA Gvrs. Conf.: Del. Sel. Com. (Ch., 1978–79); Strg. Com. (1978–79); Prog. Plng. Subcom. (1978–79). Rotary Intl. Siouxland Arts Cncl. Films for IA Lib. and Media Srvs., Inc. Plng. Com. for Bicent. Observance. various orgs. **Pubns.:** "The Futurist," *Aardvark* (S. 1976); various sp. **Activities:** 9, 12; 17, 24, 38; 56, 93 **Addr.:** Suite 206, 186 Alewife Brock Pwky., Cambridge, MA 02138.

May, Cynthia L. (Ja. 10, 1950, Shawano, WI) Cat., Micro. Libn., Univ. of WI Law Lib., 1979–, Cat. Libn., Criminal Justice Ref. and Info., Ctr., 1973–79. **Educ.:** Univ. of WI, 1968–72, BA (Compar. Lit.), 1972–73, MLS. **Orgs.:** WI LA. AALL. Madison Area Lib. Cncl.: Pubns. Com. (Ch., 1976–77); Plng. and Eval. Com. (1980–); Policy and Plng. Bd. (1979–); VP (1979–). Amer. Cvl. Liberties Un. Univ. of WI Prof. Schs. Libns. Grp. **Activities:** 1; 20, 33, 39; 77, 78 **Addr.:** University of WI Law Library, Madison, WI 53706.

May, F. Curtis (Ap. 28, 1930, Santa Maria, CA) Dir. of Lib. Srvs., San Mateo Cnty. Sch., 1970–; Libn., Sequoia HS, 1960–70; Libn., North Highlands, 1958–60; Tchr., Delano HS, 1955–57. **Educ.:** Univ. of CA, Berkeley, 1950–53, BA (Pol. Sci.); Univ. of Denver, 1957–58, MA (Libnshp.), 1971, PhD (Higher Educ., Libnshp.). **Orgs.:** ALA: Cncl. (1981–84); AASL, Ch., Distin. Lib. Srv. Awd. for Sch. Admin. Com. (1973–74); Nom. Com. (1974–75); Eval. of Sch. Lib. Media Prog. (1978–81). CA AECT: North. Sect., Pres. (1976–77). CA Lib. Athrty. for Syst. and Srvs.: Adv. Cncl. (1977–80). CA Media and Lib. Educ. Assn.: Pres. (1980–81); Past Pres. (1981–82). **Pubns.:** "Information Retrieval for Teachers." *CA Sch. Libn.* (N. 1968); Reprinted in: *Learning Resource Centers: Selected Readings.* (1973); "Plastic Covers Lengthen the Life of Paperbounds." *Lib. Jnl.* (Ja. 15, 1960). **Activities:** 10, 12; 63 **Addr.:** 216 Swett Rd., Woodside, CA 94062.

May, James D. (Mr. 9, 1948, Sandusky, OH) Head, Ctr. for Lib. and AV Educ., St. Cloud State Univ., 1979–; Dir., Media Srvs., IN State Univ., 1971–77. **Educ.:** Bowling Green State Univ., 1966–70, BS (Educ.); Univ. of Toledo, 1970–71, MEd (Educ. Media); IN Univ., 1977–79, MLS, 1977–79, PhD (Instr. Syst. Tech.–Media). **Orgs.:** AECT. MN Educ. Media Org.: Licensure Com. (Ch.). **Honors:** AECT, Okoboji Leadership Fellow, 1979. **Pubns.:** "Should your Staff Help Make Decisions?" *AV Instr.* (O. 1978). **Addr.:** Center for Library and Audiovisual Education, St. Cloud State University, St. Cloud, MN 56301.

May, James H. (Ag. 30, 1937, Trenton, MO) Assoc. Lib. Dir., Sonoma State Univ., 1974–; Dir., Ctr. for Comm. and Info. Resrch., Assoc. Prof., Grad. Sch. of Libnshp., Univ. of Denver, 1972–74; Treas., VP, co-fndr., Pandex, Inc., Macmillan Pubshg. Co., 1966–72; Intl. Econ. Engin., Gilbert Assoc., Inc., 1964–67. **Educ.:** Stanford Univ., 1956–58, BS (Cvl. Engin.); Harvard Univ., 1962–64, MBA (Admin.); Columbia Univ., 1971–77, Cert. (Advnc. Libnshp), 1971–78, DLS. **Orgs.:** Amer. Indian LA: VP (1980–). ASIS: Bay Area Chap. (Ch., 1977). ALA: LITA, Tech. Stans. for Lib. Autom. Com. (1981–); Ofc. of Lib. Srv. to the Disadv., Adv. Com. (1978–80). Ch., Mems. of the Cherokee Nation of OK Living in CA. Santa Rosa Indian Ctr. **Pubns.:** *Identification of Design Principals for Efficient Computerized Data Input* (1978); *Bibliography of the Cherokees* (forthcoming). **Activities:** 1; 17, 24, 30; 56, 66, 75 **Addr.:** 7179 Circle Dr., Rohnert Park, CA 94928.

May, Jill P. (Ag. 23, 1943, Rocky Ford, CO) Asst. Prof., Purdue Univ., 1970–; Coord., Bkmobile. Experiences, Madison Pub. Lib., 1967–69, Chld. Libn., 1966–67. **Educ.:** WI State Univ., 1961–65, BA (Eng.); Univ. of WI, 1966, MSLS. **Orgs.:** Assn. of IN Media Educ. IN LA: Pubn. Ch. (1980–82); Cont. Lib. Instr. Media Ch. (1980). ALA. Chld. Lit. Assn.: Bd. of Dir. (1979–81); Elec. Ch. (1980–81). Natl. Cncl. of Tchrs. of Eng. **Honors:** IN LA, Humanist in Residence, 1979; Delta Kappa Gamma, Gertrude Krueger Schol., 1980. **Pubns.:** "Copyright Clearance Problems in Educational Television", *Jnl. of Educ. for Libnshp.* (Win. 1977); "Butchering Children's Literature: Walt Disney's Cuts in the Classics," *Film Lib. Qtly.* (V. 11 1978); "The American Literary Fairy Tale and Its Classroom Uses," *The Jnl. of Reading* (N. 1978); "Media Bibliography: The Arts," *Art Tchr.* (Win. 1980); "Using Folklore in the Classroom," *Eng. Educ.* (F. 1980); various other articles. **Activities:** 11; 21, 26, 32; 55, 63, 67 **Addr.:** 118 Matthews Hall, Purdue Univ., W. Lafayette, IN 47907.

May, Ruby S. (D 22, 1934, Seattle, WA) Assoc. Reg. Med. Lib. Dir., Univ. of IL, Med. Ctr., 1980–; Coord. of Reg. Dev., John Crerar Lib., 1978–79; Hlth. Sci. Lib. Coord., IN Univ. Sch. of Med.; 1976–78; Asst. Coord., Reg. Lib. Srvs., Univ. of OK, 1972–74. **Educ.:** Univ. of WA, 1952–57, BA (Bus. Ed.); Univ. of OK, 1971–72, MALS. **Orgs.:** Med. LA. SLA. **Honors:** Beta Phi Mu. **Pubns.:** Contrib., *ALA World Encyclopedia of Library and Information Services* (1980); ed., *Union List of Serials for Oklahoma Medical Libraries* (1974); "Books in Clinical Practice 1971–1975," *Postgrad. Med.* (D. 1974); "Procedural Guide to Cataloging and Indexing Historical Pamphlet Collections," *Spec. Lib.* (Ap. 1975). **Activities:** 1, 12; 34; 80 **Addr.:** Library of the Health Sciences, University of Illinois at the Medical Center, 1750 W. Polk St., Chicago, IL 60612.

Mayden, Priscilla M. (S. 2, 1918, Boston, MA) Dir., Spencer S. Eccles Hlth. Sci. Lib., Univ. of UT, 1966–; Chief Libn., Vets. Admin. Hosp., Salt Lake City, UT, 1952–66; Chief Libn., Vets. Admin. Hosp., Bedford, MA, 1946–52; Libn., Women's Army Corps, Hosp. Lib., 1944–46. **Educ.:** Simmons Coll., 1941, BSLS; Columbia Univ., 1967, MSLS. **Orgs.:** Natl. Lib. of Med.: Biomed. Review Com. (1975–79). Med. LA: Bd. of Dir. (1975–78). Midcontl. Reg. Med. Lib. Adv. Com.: Vice-Ch. (1972–73). UT LA: Pres. (1961–62). Other orgs. **Honors:** UT LA, Coll. & Univ. Sect., Distin. Srv. Awd., 1979–1980; Beta Phi Mu, 1967. **Pubns.:** "RMP Phase-out," *Med. LA Bltn.* (Jl. 1973); "Problems of Entering a Computerized Serials Network," *LARC Assn.* (My. 1973); "Planning Hospital Library Facilities," Syllabus Med. LA (1975). **Activities:** 1, 12; 17, 25, 34; 58, 80 **Addr.:** Spencer S. Eccles Health Sciences Library, University of Utah, Salt Lake City, UT 84112.

Mayer, Albert I. (Je. 9, 1906, Cincinnati, OH) Ch., Lib. Comsn., Ocean Cnty. NJ Area Lib., 1964–. **Educ.:** Univ. of Cincinnati, 1924–28, AB (Hist.). **Orgs.:** NJ Lib. Cnty. Comsnr. Assn.: Pres. (1967–68). NJ Lib. Trustees' Assn.: Pres. (1975–77). Amer. Lib. Trustees' Assn.: Action Dev. Con. **Honors:** NJ LA Trustee of the Year, 1977; Amer. Lib. Trustee Assn. Lib. Trustee of the Year, 1978. **Pubns.:** "Nouns? We Need Verbs," *Wilson Lib. Bltn.* (N. 1978). "Unions? Plus or Minus," (D. 1979). **Addr.:** Apt. #8, 100 E. Water St., Toms River, NJ 08753.

Mayer, Dale C. (D. 12, 1938, Indianapolis, IN) Archvst., Hoover Presidential Lib., 1970–; Archvst., Natl. Arch., 1969–70; Tchr., Concordia HS, Ft. Wayne, IN, 1963–69. **Educ.:** Concordia Tchrs. Coll., 1956–61, BS (Educ.); Univ. of MI, 1962–63, MA (Hist.); Arch. trng. course, Natl. Arch. and Records Srv., 1969–71, Cert. **Orgs.:** SAA. Midwest Arch. Conf. IA Hist. Mtrls. Prsrvn. Socty.: Cncl. (1976–79); Prog. Ch. (1977–79); VP (1979–). Lions Club: Dir.; Pres. (1980–81). **Pubns.:** Various speeches. **Activities:** 2; 23, 39, 45; 92 **Addr.:** Herbert Hoover Presidential Library, West Branch, IA 52358.

Mayer, June Cason (Jl. 19, 1933, Atlanta, GA) Sr. Info. Chemist, FMC Corp., 1976–, Tech. Libn., 1972–76, Sup., Tech.

PROFESSIONAL ACTIVITIES: Institutions: 1. Acad. lib.; 2. Arch.; 3. Assn.; 4. Fed./Gvt. lib.; 5. Inst. lib.; 6. Mfr./Suppl.; 7. Milit. lib.; 8. Musm.; 9. Pub. lib.; 10. Sch. lib.; 11. Sch. of lib. sci.; 12. Spec. lib.; 13. State lib.; 14. (other). **Functions/Activities:** 15. Acq./Col. dev.; 16. Adult srvs.; 17. Admin.; 18. Apprais.; 19. Archit./Bldgs.; 20. Cat./Class.; 21. Chld. srvs.; 22. Circ.; 23. Cons./Pres.; 24. Consult.; 25. Cont. ed.; 26. Educ. lib. sci.; 27. Ext. srvs.; 28. Fund/Grants; 29. Gvt. pubs.; 30. Indx./Abs.; 31. Instr. lib. use; 32. Media srvs.; 33. Micro.; 34. Netwks./Coop.; 35. Persnl.; 36. PR; 37. Publshg.; 38. Recs. mgt.; 39. Ref. srvs.; 40. Repro.; 41. Resrch.; 42. Review.; 43. Secur.; 44. Serials; 45. Spec. col.; 46. Tech. srvs.; 47. Trustees/Bds.; 48. YA srvs.; 49. (other).

Info. Srvs., 1968–72, Tech. Libn., 1962–68. **Educ.:** Wesleyan Coll., 1951–54, AB (Chem.). **Orgs.:** Amer. Chem. Socty.: Ch. Educ. Com., Trenton Sect. (1975–). SLA: Baltimore Chap. Pres. Elect & Prog., Ch. (1968–69); Pres. (1969–70). **Activities:** 12; 39, 46; 60 **Addr.:** FMC Corporation, P. O. Box 8, Princeton, NJ 08540.

Mayer, Marcel W. (Mr. 14, 1947, Vienna, Austria) Ref. Libn., Natl. Air and Space Musm., Smithsonian Inst., 1980–; Mgt. Info. Syst. Coord., Lib. of Congs., Natl. Lib. Srv. for the Blind and Physically Handcpd., 1977–80; US Air Force, 1971–77. **Educ.:** US Air Force Acad., 1966–70, BS (Gen Std.); Cath. Univ., 1975–77, MLS. **Orgs.:** Lib. of Congs. Prof. Assn. **Honors:** Beta Phi Mu, 1978; Air Force, Merit. Srv. Medal, 1978. **Pubns.:** Science: A Bibliography of Science Titles for the Blind and Physically Handicapped (1979); "Participative Management: Not a Four-Letter Word," *Cath. Lib. World* (My. 1980); "The Air Force Base Library Program," *Wilson Lib. Bltn.* (F. 1978); "The Role of Paperbacks in Libraries," *Cath. Lib. World* (My./Je. 1978). **Activities:** 4, 12; 17, 38; 56, 72 **Addr.:** 6570 Yadkin Ct., Alexandria, VA 22310.

Mayer, Marilyn Wiedemann (Mr. 27, 1942, Elmhurst, IL) AV Dir./Libn., Richard J. Daley Coll., 1970–; Libn., Archit. Lib., Univ. of IL, 1969–70; Head Libn., Urbana HS, 1968–69; Eng. Tchr, Evanston, Flossmoor HS, 1964–67. **Educ.:** Univ. of IL, 1960–64, BA (Eng.), 1967–68, MLS. **Orgs.:** ALA. AECT. AAUW: VP. IL Gvr.'s Adv. Cncl. **Honors:** Phi Beta Kappa, 1963; Beta Phi Mu, 1968; Phi Kappa Phi, 1964. **Pubns.:** "Women Administrators in Higher Education," *Jnl. of N. Ctrl. Assn.* (Ag. 1980); "I'm OK, You're OK," *AV Instr.* (Je/Jl. 1974); "The Culturally Deprived Reader," *Lib. Jnl.* (Ap. 1969). **Activities:** 1; 15, 17, 32; 55, 63, 67 **Addr.:** 373 Oak St, Glen Ellyn, IL 60137.

Mayer, Mary Bride (Ag. 6, 1953, Boston, MA) Branch Libn., Virginia Beach Pub. Lib., 1980–; Branch Libn., Portsmouth Pub. Lib., 1977–80. **Educ.:** Univ. of MA, 1971–75, BA (Hist.); McGill Univ., 1975–77, MLS. **Orgs.:** VA LA: JMRT, VP (1980), Pres. (1981–). SELA. ALA: JMRT, Prof. Dev. Grant Com. (1980). **Honors:** ALA, JMRT, 3M Prof. Dev. Grant, 1979. **Pubns.:** Ed., *Cognotes* (1981). **Activities:** 9; 17, 36 **Addr.:** Bayside Branch Library, 936 Independence Blvd., Virginia Beach, VA 23455.

Mayer, Sr. Mary Charles (Ap. 21, 1910, Brooklyn, NY) Acq. Libn., Molloy Coll., 1955–; Tchr., Libn., Dominican Cmrcl. HS, 1936–55; Tchr., Villa Maria HS, 1934–36; Tchr., Elem. Sch., 1927–34. **Educ.:** St. John's Univ., 1927–34, BA (Educ., Eng.), 1937–40, BLS; Fordham Univ., 1956–58, MS (Educ., Phil.). **Orgs.:** Cath. LA: Brooklyn-Long Island Unit (Secy., 1948–54). Metro. Cath. Coll. Libns. Nassau Cnty. LA. ALA. **Honors:** Molloy Coll., Spec. Srv. Medal, 20 years, 1975; Molloy Coll., Pres. Medal, 25 years, 1980. **Pubns.:** "Molloy College," *New Cath. Encyc.* (1958); "Molloy's Library," *Remington Rand* (1959); "Molloy's Library," *Nassau Cnty. Acad. Libs.* **Activities:** 1; 15, 20, 39; 90 **Addr.:** Molloy College, Rockville Centre, NY 11570.

Mayer, William J. (S. 30, 1939, Springfield, OH) Mgr., Tech. Info. Srvs., Gen. Mills, Inc., 1974–; Info. Sci., Olin Corp., 1971–74; Patent Liaison Chem., Parke-Davis & Co., 1965–71. **Educ.:** Xavier Univ., Cincinnati, OH, 1957–61, BS (Chem.); Univ. of MI, 1961–63, MS (Med. Chem.), 1963–65, PhD (Med. Chem.). **Orgs.:** Inst. of Food Technologists. ASIS. Amer. Chem. Socty. **Pubns.:** "Management of Technical Information Activities and Resources," (1981–82 IFT short course); "A Technologist's Guide to Food Regulatory Information," *Food Tech.* (O. 1978); "Advancing Your Company Technologically," *Food For Thought* (My. 1978); "Food Information File" General Mills Online Database (1979). **Activities:** 12; 17, 38, 39; 68, 80, 87 **Addr.:** General Mills, Inc., James Ford Bell Technical Center, 9000 Plymouth Ave. N., Minneapolis, MN 55427.

Mayeski, John K. (Ja. 12, 1941, St. Louis, MO) Dir., Kearney State Coll. Lib., 1980–; Lib. Persnl. Ofcr., Univ. of WA, 1973–80, Plng. Asst., Lib., 1971–73; Exec. Ofcr., Lib., US Air Force Acad., 1969–71. **Educ.:** St. Louis Univ., 1958–62, BS (Eng.); Univ. of MI, 1965–66, MALS; Seattle Univ., 1974–79, MBA. **Orgs.:** ALA: LAMA/PAS, Exec. Bd. (1980–82). Mt. Plains LA. NE LA. **Activities:** 1; 17, 35 **Addr.:** Calvin T. Ryan Library, Kearney State College, Kearney, NE 68847.

Mayles, William F. (Ap. 2, 1924, Flint, MI) Sci., Eng. and Tech. Libn., IN Univ., Purdue Univ., Indianapolis, 1976–, Head Libn., 38th St. Campus, 1971–76, Head Libn., Purdue Univ., Indianapolis, 1966–71; Acting Eng. Libn., Purdue Univ., West Lafayette, IN, 1965–66; Sci. and Eng. Libn., Tufts Univ., 1960–65; Asst. Ref. Libn., Union Coll., Schenectady, NY, 1959–60. **Educ.:** Case Western Resrv. Univ., 1946–49, AB (Soc.), 1956–59, MSLS. **Orgs.:** ALA. SLA: IN Chap. Consult. Off. (1970–75). Nat. LA. ASIS: Ch., IN Chap., Nom. Com. (1971–72, 1978). IN LA: Ch., Coll. and Univ. Rd. Table Sect. (1970–71). AAUP. **Honors:** Beta Phi Mu. **Pubns.:** "The Chapter Consultation Service," *IN Slant* (Mr. 1975). **Activities:** 1; 15, 39; 91 **Addr.:** 833 Park Central Ct., Indianapolis, IN 46260.

Maylie, Sr. Mary Hubert (Je. 22, 1909, Philadelphia, PA) Libn., Xavier Prep., 1967–; various positions as tchr.–libn., 1929–67. **Educ.:** Loyola Univ., Villanova, PA, 1930–39, BS (Educ.); LA State Univ., 1940–43, BS (LS). **Orgs.:** Cath. LA. SWLA. Grt. New Orleans Cath. LA: HS Div. (Ch., 1978–80). LA LA. **Activities:** 10; 15, 17, 48 **Addr.:** Xavier Prep., 5116 Magazine St., New Orleans, LA 70115.

Maylone, R. Russell (Ja. 16, 1940, Brockton, MA) Cur., Spec. Col. Dept., Northwestern Univ. Lib., 1969–; Ref. Libn., Rare Book Dept., Free Lib. of Philadelphia, 1965–69. **Educ.:** Syracuse Univ., 1957–61, BA (Intl. Rel.); Univ. of WA, 1964–65, MLS. **Orgs.:** Bibl. Socty. of America. Caxton Club of Chicago: Cncl. (1978–). Chicago Area Cons. Grp. ALA: ACRL/Rare Books and Mss. Sect. **Pubns.:** Reviews. **Activities:** 1, 2; 15, 23, 45; 55, 57 **Addr.:** Northwestern University Library, Evanston, IL 60201.

Maynard, Marilyn Kay (F. 20, 1941, Sullivan, IN) Lrng. Ctr. Dir., Fairfield Cmnty. HS, 1972–; Tchr., Palestine HS, 1966–72; Tchr., Paoli Jr. HS, 1963–66. **Educ.:** IN State Univ., 1959–63, BS (Soc. Std.), 1963–68, MS (U.S. Hist.), 1968–72 MLS. **Orgs.:** ALA: AASL. IL LA. IL Assn. for Media in Educ.: Dir. Reg. VII (1980, 1981). Natl. Educ. Assn. IL Educ. Assn. Frontier Comnty. Coll.: Lrng. Resrc. Cncl. (1979–). **Pubns.:** "Book Mobile," *Media Memo* (Ap. 1979); "Filmstrip Tape Measure," *Media Memo* (Ja. 1979). **Activities:** 10; 17, 31, 32 **Addr.:** Fairfield Community High School, 300 W. King St., Fairfield, IL 62837.

Mayo, Diane Marie (N. 15, 1950, Burbank, CA) Head, Ctrl. Lib., Anaheim Pub. Lib., 1980–; VP, Cibbarelli and Assoc., 1978–80; Account Rep., CL Systems, Inc., 1976–78; Head Libn., Tech. Srvs., Huntington Beach Pub. Lib., 1972–76. **Educ.:** Univ. of CA, Irvine, 1968–72, BA (Hist.); CA State Univ., Fullerton, 1972–73, MS (LS). **Orgs.:** ALA. CA LA: Cmnty. Rel. Com. (1980); Cont. Educ. Com. (1979). **Pubns.:** "Automation: How to Work with the Vendors," *News Notes of CA Libs.* (1979); various speeches. **Activities:** 9, 12; 24, 38, 46; 56 **Addr.:** Central Library, Anaheim Public Library, 500 W. Broadway, Anaheim, CA 92805.

Mayo, Kathleen O. (My. 23, 1948, Miami Beach, FL) Inst. Consult., State Lib. of FL, 1978–; Pat. Libn., FL State Hosp., 1973–78; Sch. Libn., Funston and Hamilton Elem. Sch., GA, 1971–72. **Educ.:** Baylor Univ., FL State Univ., 1966–70, BS (Art Educ.); FL State Univ., 1970–71, MSLS. **Orgs.:** ALA: ASCLA (Bd. of Dir., 1979–81; Lib. Srvs. to the Impaired Eld. Sect., Exec. Com., 1979–80; Lib. Srvs. to the Deaf Sect., Prog. Com. (Ch., 1981–82). Nat. Org. for Women. Unitarian Univ. Assn. **Pubns.:** Ed., *Keystone* (1979–); Ed., *Bibli-therapy Disc. Grp. Nwsltr.* (F. 1978); "Patient library in action," *IL Libs.* (S. 1975); "Library Services to Emotionally Disabled Persons," *FL Libs.* (My./Je. 1980). **Activities:** 5, 13; 16, 24, 48; 50, 72 **Addr.:** State Library of Florida, R.A. Gray Building, Tallahassee, FL 32301.

Mayol, Josefina (Ja. 28, 1918, Havana, Cuba) Acq. Libn., St. Petersburg Jr. Coll., Clearwater Campus, 1964–; Ref. libn., Miami Pub. Lib., 1962–64; Cat., instr., Univ. of PR, 1962; Instr., LS, Univ. de Antioquia, Colombia, 1961–62; Libn., instr., Unesco's Centro Reg. de Educ., Mexico, 1955–61; Head Prcs. Dept., Sociedad Econ. Amigos del Pais, Habana, 1945–53; Libn., Agri. Exper., Havana, 1941–45. **Educ.:** Univ. of Tampa, 1937–40, AB (Hist.); George Peabody Coll., 1940–41, BS in LS; Univ. of S. FL, 1970–74, (Educ. & LS); Appalachian State Univ. Lib. Sch., Inst. for Jr. Coll. Libns., 1970. **Orgs.:** ALA: Spec. Com. on Coop. with Latin America (1955–56). FL LA. FL Assn. of Cmnty. Coll. World Circle Lang. Club. **Pubns.:** Transl., "Clasificación Decimal de Dewey para Pequeñas Bibliotecas Públicas Escolares". (1967); "Innovations in the junior college library: new concept within the instructional program". *The Link* (Ja. 1971); jt. auth., "Cuban Libraries" *Library Quarterly* (Ap. 1952). **Activities:** 1; 15, 31, 39; 92 **Addr.:** 1112 Live Oak Ct., Clearwater, FL 33516.

Mayover, Steven Joseph (Ag. 27, 1942, Philadelphia, PA) Lib. Film Opers. Supvsr., Free Lib. of Philadelphia, 1975–, Head, Spec. Srvs. Dept., NERL, 1973–75; Tech. Libn., Philadelphia Nvl. Shipyard, 1971–73; YA Libn., Free Library of Philadelphia, 1969–71, Ref. Libn., 1968–69, Catlgr., 1968. **Educ.:** Rider Coll., 1963–67, BA (Span.); Univ. of Pittsburgh, 1967–68, MLS; Temple Univ., 1971–73, MEd (Educ. Media); PA State Univ., 1978–80, MPA (Pub. Admin.). **Orgs.:** ALA: PLA, AV Com. (1981–82). PA LA. Amer. Socty. for Pub. Admin. **Honors:** Beta Phi Mu, 1969. **Activities:** 9; 32; 67 **Addr.:** 223 Nauldo Rd., Philadelphia, PA 19154.

Mayrand, Florian A.A. (Ag. 1, 1943, Guérin, Témiscamingue, PQ) Asst. Head Libn., Tech. Srvs., Can. Dept. of Energy, Mines and Resrcs., 1980–; Catlgr. Head, Lib., Can. Secret. of State Transl. Bur., 1977–80; Head Catlgr., Head, Fr. Srvs., Can. Dept. of Finance, Treas. Bd., 1971–77; Catlgr., Reg. Sch. Bd., Hull, 1970–71; Tchr., Sudbury Bd. of Educ., 1969–70; Tchr.–Libn., Comsn. Scolaire Reg. Du Cuivre, Rouyn-Noranda, PQ, 1968–69, Tchr., 1966–67. **Educ.:** Univ. of Montreal, 1958–66, BA (Arts); Univ. of Ottawa, 1968, BLS; Univ. of West. ON, 1981, MLS; PQ Dept. of Educ., 1971, HS Tchg. Cert. (LS); various crs. **Orgs.:** Can. Assn. Info. Sci. SLA. Ottawa–Hull LA. **Activities:** 1, 12; 15, 20, 39; 59, 86, 92 **Addr.:** Resource Economics Library, Dept. of Energy, Mines and Resources, 580 Booth St., 16th Floor, Ottawa, ON K1A 0E4 Canada.

Mayton, Regina A. (F. 25, 1937, Montgomery, AL) Chief, Systs. Div., Air Univ. Lib., 1981–, Biblgphr., 1976–81, Docum. Catlgr., 1971–76; Admin. Libn., Maxwell AFB, AL, 1971; Admin. Libn., Gunter AFB, AL, 1970–71. **Educ.:** Huntingdon Coll., 1965–68, BA (Eng.); Univ. of Denver, 1968–69, MA (Libnshp.). **Orgs.:** ALA. SLA: Pres., AL Chap. (1979–80). AL LA: Schol. Com. (1979–80). Montgomery LA. **Activities:** 1, 4; 30, 39; 52, 54, 57, 74 **Addr.:** 1713 Radcliffe Rd., Montgomery, AL 36106.

Mazur, Marjorie A. (Ja. 5, 1927, Glasgow, KY) Dir., Tech. Srvs., SC State Lib., 1978–; Head, Cat. Dept., Cleveland Public Library, 1970–78, Asst. Head, Cat. Dept., 1966–70, Catlgr., 1960–66; Tech. Srv. Libn., Cleveland Hts. Pub. Lib., 1958–59; 1st Asst., Tech. Srv., WV Univ., 1955–58; Catlgr., Univ. of KY, 1951–54. **Educ.:** Sullins Coll., 1944–46, Dip.; Univ. of KY, 1946–48, BA (Soc. Sci.); Univ. of NC, 1950–51, BS (LS). **Orgs.:** ALA. SELA. SC LA. Alpha Xi Delta. **Activities:** 9, 13; 15, 20, 46 **Addr.:** SC State Library, P.O. Box 11469, Columbia, SC 29211.

Mazzola, Agnes L. (My. 10, 1913, Rochester, NY) Adj. Instr., Sch. of Lib. and Info. Sci., SUNY, Geneseo, 1975–; Lib. Media Spec., Dansville HS, Dansville Ctrl. Sch., 1965–; Lib. Media Spec., Rush Henrietta Ctrl. Sch., 1963–65. **Educ.:** SUNY, Geneseo, 1962–64, BS (LS), 1971–76, MLS. **Orgs.:** NY LA. **Pubns.:** "Developing Collections in School Library Media Centers: A Joint Partnership Between Teachers and Library Media Specialist," *The Bookmark* (Fall 1976). **Activities:** 10, 11 **Addr.:** 6919 Bald Hill Rd., Springwater, NY 14560.

McAdams, Cecilia Daniels (Mr. 18, 1944, Greenville, SC) Branch Mgr., Northside Lib., Pub. Lib. of Columbus and Franklin Cnty., 1981–; Sch. Lib. Media Coord., Diocese of Columbus, 1977–81; Libn., Wherle HS, 1975–77; HS Libn., Sacred Heart Acad., Buffalo, NY, 1974–75; Ref. Libn., Daemen Coll., 1973–74. **Educ.:** Rosary Hill Coll., Buffalo, NY, 1962–67, BA (Eng.); SUNY, Buffalo, 1972–73, MLS; 1975–76, OH Cert. Media Spec.; various grad. crs. **Orgs.:** OH Educ. Lib. Media Assn.: Supervisory Div. (Ch., 1979–80). AECT. ALA. Cath. LA. Socty. for Hist. Prsrvn. OH Cath. Educs. Assn.: Conv. Plng. Com. (1979, 1981). **Honors:** Beta Phi Mu, 1973. **Activities:** 10; 17, 24, 35; 74, 75, 89 **Addr.:** 1260 N. High St., Columbus, OH 43201.

McAdams, Nancy R. (Jl. 28, 1929, Kansas City, MO) Assoc. Dir., Ofc. of Plng. Srvs., Univ. of TX, Austin, 1980–; Asst. Dir., Facilities and Plng., Gen. Libs., 1978–80, Facilities Planner, 1974–78, Actg. Assoc. Dir., 1972–74, Archit. Libn., 1965–72. **Educ.:** Univ. of TX, Austin, 1946–51, BArch, 1962–65, MLS. **Orgs.:** ALA: LAMA/Com. on Org. (Ch., 1980–82); Bldgs. and Equip. Sect. (Ch., 1979–80); Com. on Bldgs. for Coll. and Univ. Libs. (Ch., 1977–78). Amer. Inst. of Archits. Practice Mgt. Com. (Ch., 1978, 1979). TX Socty. of Archits., VP (1981), Treas. (1979, 1980). **Activities:** 1, 12; 17, 19, 24 **Addr.:** 2607 Great Oaks Pkwy., Austin, TX 78756.

McAfee, Robert (Skip), Jr. (D. 5, 1937, New York, NY) Asst. Exec. Dir., ASIS, 1970–; Managing Ed., *Glossary of Geol.*, Amer. Geol. Inst., 1966–70; Sci. Anal., Smithsonian Sci. Info. Exch., 1965–66; Geol. Libn., Columbia Univ., 1962–65. **Educ.:** Wesleyan Univ., 1955–59 AB (Geol.); Stanford Univ., 1959–61, MS (Geol.); Columbia Univ., 1962, MS (Lib. Srv.). **Orgs.:** ASIS. SLA. Geoscience Info. Socty. Assn. of Earth Sci. Eds. **Honors:** Beta Phi Mu; Sigma XI. **Pubns.:** Co-ed., *Glossary of Geology* (1972); Mgt. Ed. *Bltn. of ASIS* (1975–80); Ed., *ASIS News* (1981–). **Activities:** 3; 17, 25, 37; 75 **Addr.:** American Society for Information Science, 1010 16th St., N.W., Washington, DC 20036.

McAlister, George Lawrence (D. 16, 1950, Spokane, WA) Assoc. Dir., Del E. Webb Meml. Lib., Loma Linda Univ., 1979–; Dir., Jorgensen Meml. Lib., 1978–79. **Educ.:** Pac. Un. Coll., 1969–73, BA (Hist.); Univ. of South. CA, 1976–77, MSLS; Med. LA, 1977, Cert. **Orgs.:** Med. LA. ALA. Assn. of Acad. Hlth. Sci. Lib. Dirs. **Honors:** Beta Phi Mu, 1977. **Pubns.:** Ed., *Bibliography for the Control of Anxiety, Fear and Pain in Dentistry* (1978–). **Activities:** 1; 17, 19, 24; 56, 80 **Addr.:** Del. E. Webb Memorial Library, Loma Linda University, Loma Linda, CA 92350.

McAllister, Desretta V. (S. 17, 1940, Kinston, NC) Assoc. Prof., Sch. of LS, NC Cntrl. Univ., 1973–; Dir., Curric. Mtrls. Cntr., Morgan State Coll., 1972–73; Cat. Libn., Hampton Inst., 1971–72; School Libn., J. H. Sampson Sch., 1962–70. **Educ.:** Bennett Coll., 1958–62, BA (Fr.-Span.); Atlanta Univ., 1970–71, MSLS; Univ. of Pittsburgh, 1976–81, PhD. **Orgs.:** Durham Cnty. LA. NC LA. ALA. **Pubns.:** "Telefacsimile in Libraries and Information Centers," *NC Libs.* (Sum. 1979); "The New Role of Librarians as Professionals: A Literature Review," *The Information Society: Issues and Answers.* **Addr.:** North Carolina Central University, Durham, NC 27707.

McAninch, Lillian L. (Ag. 16, 1932, Chicago, IL) Ref. Supvsr., Oak Lawn Pub. Lib., 1973–; Lib. Mgr., CPC Intl. Inc., 1963–71; Libn., Dearborn Chemical Co., 1952–63. **Educ.:** Coll. of

Special Subjects/Services: 50. Adult educ.; 51. Advert./Mktg.; 52. Aerosp.; 53. Agric.; 54. Area std.; 55. Arts/Hum.; 56. Autom.; 57. Bibl./Prtg.; 58. Bio. sci.; 59. Bus./Fin.; 60. Chem.; 61. Copyrt.; 62. Documtn.; 63. Educ.; 64. Engin.; 65. Env.; 66. Eth. grps.; 67. Film; 68. Food/Nutr.; 69. Geneal.; 70. Geo.; 71. Geol.; 72. Handcpd.; 73. Hist.; 74. Int. frdm.; 75. Info. sci.; 76. Insr.; 77. Law; 78. Legis.; 79. Math./Comp. sci.; 80. Med.; 81. Metals; 82. Nat. resrcs.; 83. Newsp.; 84. Nuc. sci.; 85. Oral hist.; 86. Petr./Energy; 87. Pharm.; 88. Phys./Astr./Math.; 89. Readg.; 90. Relig.; 91. Sci./Tech.; 92. Soc. sci.; 93. Telecom.; 94. Transp.; 95. (other).

St. Teresa; Univ. of Chicago, Grad. Lib. Sch. **Orgs.:** SLA. **Activities:** 9; 16, 39; 59, 91 **Addr.:** Adult Services Dept., Oak Lawn Public Library, 9427 S. Raymond Ave., Oak Lawn, IL 60453.

McArthur, Wenda Jean (Ag. 24, 1942, Moose Jaw, SK) Pvt. Consult., Chld. Lit., Lib. Srvs., 1981–; Chld. Consult., SK Prov. Lib., 1977–81; Sessional Lectr., Univ. of Regina, 1973–74. **Educ.:** Univ. of SK, 1960–63, BA (Eng., Psy.); 1964–65, Dip. (Educ.); Univ. of Toronto, 1968–69, BLS. **Orgs.:** Can. LA. SK LA: Chld. Lib. Srvs. Sect.; Exec. Secy.; Exec. VP. **Activities:** 4, 13; 21, 24, 42; 63, 89 **Addr.:** 3034 Rae St., Regina, SK S4S 1R7 Canada.

McAuley, Lynn C. (Mr. 23, 1947, Charlotte, NC) Asst. Ref. Libn., Cabell Lib., VA Cmwlth. Univ., 1980–. **Educ.:** Univ. of NC, 1965–69, BA (Hist.); Univ. of WI, 1974–77; Cath. Univ. of Amer., 1978–80, MSLS, hons. **Orgs.:** ALA. VA LA: Conf. Lcl. Arrange. Com. (1980); Mem. Com. (1981); JMRT (Vice-Ch., Ch.-Elect, 1981). **Honors:** ALA, JMRT Shirley Olofson Awd., 1981. **Pubns.:** *Belgian-American Research Materials: A Selected Bibliography*; *The Development of the Labor Movement in Wisconsin*; *Germans in Wisconsin: A Guide to Sources for Potential Projects*; *Research Sources on Wisconsin Geography: A Selected Bibliography*; *Retirement and Pre-Retirement Planning Resource Materials Available in Brown County, Wisconsin: A Selected Bibliography*. **Activities:** 1, 2; 16, 31, 39; 85, 92 **Addr.:** James Branch Cabell Library Reference Dept., VA Commonwealth University, 901 Park Ave., Richmond, VA 23284.

McBride, Donna J. (Jl. 3, 1940, Kansas City, KS) Dir., Support Srvs., Leon Cnty. Pub. Lib., 1980–; Lib. Consult., C.L. Syst. Inc., 1977–80; Syst. Coord., Kansas City Pub. Lib., 1967–77. **Educ.:** Ctrl. Meth. Coll., 1958–61, AB (Eng.); Univ. of MO, 1968–69, MLS. **Orgs.:** ALA. FL LA. Natl. Women's Std. Assn. **Activities:** 9; 17, 22, 46; 56, 74, 75 **Addr.:** Rte. 1, Box 3319, Havana, FL 32333.

McBride, Ruth B. (Charleston, IL) Libn., Autom. Rec. Dept., Univ. of IL, 1979–, Serials Catlgr., 1972–78; Asst. Dir. of Non-Acad. Persnl., Purdue Univ., 1949–51. **Educ.:** Univ. of IL, 1945–48, BS (Psy.), 1970–72, MS (LS). **Orgs.:** Lincoln Trail Lib. Syst.: Bd. of Trustees, Pres. (1966–68). ALA: ALTA (Secy., 1967); IFRT (1965); ACRL; RTSD. IL LA: IL LTA (Secy., 1966–68); Trustee Cit. Com. (1965). Beta Phi Mu: Alpha Chap. (Pres., 1980). Various other orgs. Junior Leag. Pi Beta Phi. **Pubns.:** "Psychology Journal Usage," *Bhvl. & Soc. Sci. Libn.* (Fall 1980); "Serials Usage by Social Scientists," *Coll. & Rsrch. Libs.* (S. 1979); "Community Support and the Library," *IL Libs.* (N. 1970); "What I Expect of My Librarian," *IL Libs.* (S. 1967); "Foreign Language Serial Use by Social Scientists," *Serials Libn.* (Vol. 5, no. 4); various other articles. **Activities:** 1; 20, 41, 46; 75, 85, 92 **Addr.:** Automated Records Department, University of Illinois, 220 B - Main Library, 1408 West Gregory Ave., Urbana, IL 61801.

McBurney, Margot B. (Lethbridge AB) Chief Libn., Queen's Univ., 1977–; Head, Acq., Univ. of AB 1974–77, Serials Catlgr. 1973–74, Ed., Serials List, 1972–73; Undergrad. Ref., Univ. of AB, 1971–72, Ref. Libn., Principia Coll., 1969–70; Lib. Syst. Analt., Univ. of AB, 1970–71. **Educ.:** Principia Coll., 1949–53, BA (Math.); Univ. of IL 1968–69, MSc (Lib. Sci.). **Orgs.:** ALA. ASIS: Cncl. (1976–79); - West. Can. Chap. (Cnclr., 1976–79, Ch., 1976–77) ARL: Bd. (1978–81), Task Force on Lib. Educ. (Ch., 1980–82). CARL. Can. LA. **Activities:** 1; 17, 23, 34; 56, 75 **Addr.:** Queen's University at Kingston, Douglas Library, Administration Office, Kingston, ON K7L 5C4 Canada.

McCabe, James Patrick (My. 24, 1937, Philadelphia, PA) Libn., Allentown Coll., St. Francis de Sales, 1968–. **Educ.:** Univ. of Niagara, 1960–63, AB (Eng. Lit.); Univ. of MI, 1965–68, PhD (LS), MA (Eng. Lit.). **Orgs.:** Cath. LA. PA LA. ALA. **Honors:** Beta Phi Mu, 1968. **Pubns.:** *Critical Guide to Catholic Reference Books* (1971, 1980). **Activities:** 1; 17; 55, 90 **Addr.:** Allentown College Library, Center Valley, PA 18034.

McCain, Ella Byrd (Mr. 8, 1925, Dothan, AL) Libn., Geo. M. Rogers Area Vocational Ctr., 1967–; Visit. Instr., Atlanta Univ. Sch. of Lib. and Info. Std., 1955–; Libn., Wenonah HS, 1947–67; Instr., SC State Coll., LS Sept., 1954; Tchr., East St. HS, 1945–47. **Educ.:** AL A. and M. Univ., 1941–45, BS (H.E.); Univ. of MI, 1950–53, AMLS. **Orgs.:** AL Instr. Media Assn.: Pres. (1979–). Southeast. Reg. Media Leadership Cncl.: Exec. Bd. (1976–77). AECT. ALA: AASL. SELA. AL LA: Chld.'s & Young People Div. (Secy. 1969). Other orgs. Jefferson Cnty. Mental Hlth. Bd. Jefferson Cnty. Day Care Srv. Bd. St. Anne's Home Exec. Bd. Progressive Action Civic Club. **Addr.:** One Greensprings Ave., S. W., Birmingham, AL 35211.

McCall, John Dean (F. 24, 1934, Dallas, TX) Consult., Comm. Tech., 1981–; Writer, Ed., Census Bur., 1972–; Writer, freelnc., 1966–72; Biblgphr., Natl. Agr. Lib., 1964–66; Ref. Libn., Liaison, Lib. of Congs., 1961–64; Basic Ref. Tchr., US Dept. of Agr., 1961; Biblgphr., Duke Univ. Lib., 1958–60; various sems. **Educ.:** Univ. of NC, 1954–57, BA (Hist.); Univ. of IL, 1960–61, MSLS; Advanced Trng. in Comp. fields, 1973–78. **Orgs.:** ALA. WA Writers' Grp. **Honors:** ALA, Outstan. Ref. Bk., 1979. **Pubns.:** Jt. ed., *1980 Census of Population and Housing: User's Guide* (1982); Sr. ed., *Directory of Federal Statistics for Local Areas, 1977–78* (1979); Jt. ed., *Directory of Federal Statistics for Local Areas, 1976* (1978); Sr. ed., *Guide to Programs and Publications, 1973* (1974); "A Visual Aid for Quick Reference," chart (1976); various articles and stories. **Activities:** 1, 4; 30, 37, 39; 57, 91, 92 **Addr.:** Apt. 402, 2227 20th St. N.W., Washington, DC 20009.

McCall, Margaret Ruth (N. 7, 1915, Maryville, TN) Retired, 1980; Libn., Lake Highland Prep. Sch., 1977–80; Lib. Supvsr., Orange Cnty. Schs., 1962–74; Libn., Boone HS, 1955–62; Libn., Howard Jr. High, 1954–55; Libn., Lakeview High, 1948–54; Tchr., Friendsville High, 1942–48; Tchr., Walland HS, 1939–42. **Educ.:** Maryville Coll., 1935–39, BA (Eng.); George Peabody Coll., 1947–49, BS (Lib. AV); Rollins Coll., FL State Univ., Univ. of FL, Univ. of S. FL, Univ. of WA, Cert. (Admin. Supvsn.). **Orgs.:** FL Assn. of Sch. Libs.: Treas. (1955–56); Exhibits Ch. (1963–70). FL AV Assn.: Secy. (1965–66). ALA: Com. for Sel. Admin. for Oustan. Srv. to Schs. (1971). SELA. FL Assn. for Supvsn. and Curric. Dev. Assn. for Supvsn. and Curric. Dev. **Activities:** 10, 13; 21, 32, 48 **Addr.:** 1418 Georgia Blvd., Orlando, FL 32803.

McCallum, Elizabeth Ilene (S. 19, 1919, Tring, AB) Libn., Freelnc. Writer, Consult., 1979–; Sch. Libn., Edmonton Pub. Sch. Bd., 1974–79; Catlgr., Univ. of AB, 1968–73; Sch. Libn., Edmonton Pub. Sch., 1963–67; Sessional Instr., Sch. Libs., Univ. of AB, 1965–66; Branch Libn., Edmonton Pub. Lib., 1949–56. **Educ.:** Univ. of AB, 1942–45, BA (Eng.); Univ. of Toronto, 1948–49, BLS. **Orgs.:** Can. LA. AB LA: Secy. (1952–53). Edmonton LA: Secy. (1951–52). Lrng. Resrcs. Cncl. AB Hist. Socty. Can. Auths. Assn. AB Tchrs. Assn. Can. Cons. Assn. **Honors** Delta Kappa Gamma. **Pubns.:** "Library Displays," *AB Sch. Lib. Review;* bk. reviews; various scripts. **Activities:** 1, 9; 15, 16, 17; 50, 89 **Addr.:** 11917—90 St., Edmonton, AB T5B 3Y8 Canada.

McCallum, Heather (Ap. 11, 1927, Toronto, Ont.) Head, Theatre Dept., Met. Toronto Lib., 1961–. **Educ.:** Univ. of Toronto, 1945–49, BA, 1956–57, BLS. **Orgs.:** Assn. for Can. Theatre Hist.: VP (1977–79); Off.-at-large (1979–80). Amer. Socty. for Theatre Resrch.: Exec. Com. (1978–81). Can. Theatre Hist. Resrch. Prog.: Coord. and Sr. Resrch. Assoc. (1975–76). **Honors:** Univ. of Toronto, Fac. of LS Alum. Assn., Jubilee Awd., 1981. **Pubns.:** *Theatre resources in Canadian collections* (1973). Bibl., *The awkward stage;* (1969). **Activities:** 2, 9; 15, 17, 45; 55 **Addr.:** Theatre Department, Metropolitan Toronto Library, 789 Yonge St., Toronto, ON M4W 2G8 Canada.

McCann, Gary L. (Mr. 28, 1948, Cincinnati, OH) Assoc. Dir. for Readrs. Srvs., Amer. Univ., 1979–; Asst. Law Libn., Seton Hall Univ., 1978–79; Indxr., OR Legis. Couns., 1975–77. **Educ.:** CA State Univ., Fullerton, 1966–70, BA (Psy.); Willamette Univ., 1973–76, JD; Univ. of TX, Austin, 1977–78, MLS. **Orgs.:** Socty. of Law Libns. of Washington DC: Place. Com. (1979–); Nsltr. Com. (1979–); Loc. Arrange. Com. (1981–); Memb. Com. (1981–). **Pubns.:** Jt. Indxr., *Oregon Criminal and Juvenile Codes Pamphlet Index* (1976); Jt. Indxr., *Cumulative Index to Legislative Measures* (1977); Jt. Indxr., *Oregon Revised Statutes Index* (1975, 1977); Jt. Indxr., *Oregon Session Laws Index* (1975, 1977). **Activities:** 1, 12; 17, 30, 39; 56, 77, 78 **Addr.:** American University Law Library, Massachusetts and Nebraska Aves. N.W., Washington, DC 20016.

McCann, Katharine Talbott (Ap. 22, 1944, Dayton, OH) Head, Acq., Cleveland Pub. Lib., 1978–, Asst. Head, Acq., 1975–78, Gifts and Exchs. Libn., 1974–75. **Educ.:** Duquesne Univ., 1968–72, BA (Eng.); Univ. of Pittsburgh, 1972–74, MLS. **Orgs.:** ALA. OH LA. North. OH Tech. Srvs. Libns. Assn.: VP (1978–80); Pres. (1980–82). **Activities:** 9; 15, 44, 46 **Addr.:** Cleveland Public Library, 325 Superior Ave., Cleveland, OH 44112.

McCanon, Marilyn J. (Jl. 4, 1923, Quincy, IL) Assoc. Dir., Ext. Srvs., Indianapolis-Marion Cnty. Pub. Lib., 1973–, Supvsr., Ext. Srvs., 1960–73, Bkmobile. Libn., 1957–60. **Educ.:** Culver-Stockton Coll., 1942–44, BS (Educ.); IN Univ., 1957, MAT (LS). **Orgs.:** IN LA. ALA. **Honors:** Beta Phi Mu. **Activities:** 9; 17, 19, 27 **Addr.:** Indianapolis-Marion County Public Library, 40 E. St. Clair, Indianapolis, IN 46204.

McCarn, Davis B. (O. 15, 1928, Chicago, IL) Dir., Computerized Bibl. Srvs., H.W. Wilson Co., 1980–; Pres., Online Info. Intl., Inc., 1978–80; Assoc. Dir., Plng., Nat. Lib. of Med., 1976–78, Assoc. Dir., Comp. and Comm. Syst., 1972–76, Dep. Dir., Lister Hill Nat. Ctr. for Biomed. Comm., 1968–72. **Educ.:** Haverford Coll., 1947–51, BA (Math.). **Orgs.:** Med. LA. ASIS: Mem. Com. (1976). Amer. Assn. for Adv. of Sci. **Honors:** Phi Beta Kappa, 1951; Dept. of Hlth., Educ., and Welfare, Sup. Perf. Award, 1975. **Pubns.:** Jt. auth., *The Information Resources and Services of the United States:* (1979); "Online Systems-Techniques and Services" *Ann. Review of Info. Sci. and Tech.* (1978); "MEDLINE Users, Usage and Economics" *Med. Info.* (S. 1978); "MEDLINE," *JASIS Reviews* (Mr. 1980). **Activities:** 4, 12; 26, 34, 41; 56, 75, 80 **Addr.:** 9 Wyndham Rd., Scarsdale, NY 10583.

McCarter, Bobbye L. (Ag. 9, 1936, Fort Worth, TX) Head Libn., Bethel Coll., 1978–; Soclgy., Anthro., Geog. Subj. Spec., North. IL Univ., 1976–78; Asst. Acq. Libn., GA South. Coll., 1974–76. **Educ.:** TX Woman's Univ., 1954–58, BS, BA, (Soclgy.); LA State Univ., 1958–59, MA (Soclgy.); Univ. of MO, 1974, MALS. **Orgs.:** ALA. SELA. TN LA. Amer. Soclgy. Assn. **Activities:** 1; 15, 17, 20 **Addr.:** Burroughs Learning Center, Bethel College, McKenzie, TN 38201.

McCarthy, Ellen B. (Ag. 26, 1946, Winston—Salem, NC) Libn., MI Dept. of Cvl. Rights, 1976–. **Educ.:** Wayne State Univ., 1966–72, BA (Classical Grk.), 1972–74, MSLS. **Orgs.:** MI Assn. of Law Libs.: Pub. Access to Law Com. (Ch., 1978–). Cncl. of State Agency Libs.: Exec. Com. (1980); Exec. Bd. (1982); Projs. Com. (Ch., 1981–). Detroit Assoc. Libs. Reg. of Coop.: Exec. Bd. (1981–). **Honors:** Beta Phi Mu, 1977. **Activities:** 4; 17, 39, 41; 77 **Addr.:** MI Dept. of Civil Rights, 1200 6th St., 7th Floor, Detroit, MI 48226.

McCarthy, Mrs. Jane C. (F. 3, 1919, New York, NY) Libn., Muhlenberg Hosp., 1965–. Consult., Runnells Hosp. **Educ.:** Douglass Coll., 1936–40, AB (Hist., Pol. Sci.); Rutgers Univ., 1963–65, MLS. **Orgs.:** Med. LA: NY Reg. Grp. (Ch., 1980–81), AV Stan. and Prac. Com. (1979–81). Hlth. Sci. LA of NJ: Pres. (1974–76). Hlth. Sci. Comm. Assn. **Activities:** 12; 15, 17, 20; 80 **Addr.:** Muhlenberg Hospital, Plainfield, NJ 07061.

McCarthy, Mary Constance (My. 7, 1928, Potsdam, NY) Asst. Head, Ref. Dept., Northwestern Univ. Lib., 1972–; Asst Ref. Libn., Univ. of IL, Chicago Circle, 1970–72; Circ. Libn., SUNY, Buffalo, 1962–68. **Educ.:** State Univ. Coll. of NY, Potsdam, 1944–48, BE (Educ.); Univ. of Denver, 1950–51, MA (LS); SUNY, Buffalo, 1963–67, MS (Soc. Sci.); Univ. of Chicago, 1968–70, CAS (LS). **Orgs.:** ALA. **Activities:** 1; 31, 39, 49-comp. assisted ref. srv.; 55, 92 **Addr.:** Reference Department, Northwestern University Library, Evanston, IL 60201.

McCarthy, Paul H. (O. 16, 1939, Rochester, NY) Archvst., Cur., of Mss., Univ. of AK, 1964–. **Educ.:** St. John Fisher, BA (Hist.); Syracuse Univ., MSLS; Amer. Univ., Cert. (Arch. Adim.). **Orgs.:** SAA: Coll. and Univ. Arch. Com. (1968–74); Sub-com. on Bibl. (Ch. 1973); Personal Papers Com. (1974–). Intl. Cncl. on Arch. ALA. AK LA: Pres. (1970); Bd. of Dir. (1969–71). Various other orgs. AK Hist. Socty.: Bd. of Dir. (1967–); Secy. (1969); Pres. (1973). Tanana Yukon Hist. Socty. Fairbanks Fac. Assn. Untd. Campus Ministry. Various other orgs. **Pubns.:** "Vapor Phase Deacidification: a new preservation method," *Amer. Archvst.* (O. 1969); "Medicine and Medical History," *AK Med.* (Jl. 1971); jt. cmplr., "College and University Archives: a Select Bibliography," *Amer. Archvst.* (Ja. 1974); "Alaska's Historic Records," in *Writing AK Hist.* (Vol. 1 1974); "Overview: Essentials of an Archives and Manuscript Program," *Drexel Lib. Qtly.* (Ja. 1975). **Addr.:** University of Alaska, Elmer E. Rasmuson Library, Fairbanks, AK 99701.

McCartney, Julia Helen (N. 18, 1953, Charles City, IA) Resrch. Consult., Rockefeller Fndn., 1978–; Consult., Catalyst, 1979; Ref. Libn., Columbia Univ., 1979; Resrchr., Popltn. Cncl., 1978–79. **Educ.:** Univ. of IA, 1972–76, BA (Psy.); Rutgers Univ., 1977–78, MLS; Univ. de Valencia, Spain, 1976–77, (Hist.). **Orgs.:** ALA: SRRT, Clearinghouse Ofcr.; Ed., SRRT Nsltr.; 1980 Anl. Conf. Plng. Com. SLA: NY Chap., Women's Caucus Com. (1979). **Activities:** 12; 30, 37, 41; 55, 92 **Addr.:** 6 Jones, # 2A, New York, NY 10014.

McCaughtry, Dorothy Hamel (Ag. 12, 1948, Cleveland, OH) Freelnc. Resrch., 1981–; Corp. Libn., Co. Histn., Travelers Insurance Co., 1980–81, Libn., 1974–79, Asst. Libn., 1973–74; Elem. Sch. Tchr., Windham Pub. Sch., 1970–72. **Educ.:** Capital Univ., 1966–69, BS (Educ.); Univ. of RI, 1971–73, MLS. **Orgs.:** SLA: CT Valley Chap., Pres. (1978–79); Pres.-Elect (1977–78); Rec. Secy. (1975–77). State Adv. Cncl. on Libs.: Budget Com. (1980), Eval. Com. (1981–). Willington Pub. Lib. Bd.: Treas. (1980–). Gvrs. Conf. on Libs. and Info. Sci.: Del. (1979). **Activities:** 12; 17, 23, 41; 59, 76, 77 **Addr.:** Rte. 44, Box 262, W. Willington, CT 06279.

McCauley, Elfrieda B. (Ag. 11, 1925, Milwaukee, WI) Coord., Media Srvs., Greenwich Pub. Sch., 1971–; Libn., Greenwich HS, 1964–71; Pubcty. and Copyrt., Edward L. Wertheim Agency; various part time fac. positions, 1973–. **Educ.:** Univ. of WI, Milwaukee, 1942–48, BS (Educ.); Columbia Univ., 1965–67, MS (LS), 1968–71, DLS. **Orgs.:** CT Educ. Media Assn.: *Newsletter* Ed. (1974–76). Assn. for Educ. Data Systs. WHOLIS: Del. (1979). ALA: AASL. Natl. Educ. Assn. Greenwich Assn. of Sch. Admins. **Honors** John Cotton Dana Awd., 1971, 1976; Britannica/AASL, Sch. Lib. Media Prog. of The Yr., 1979; CT Educ. Media Assn., Disting. Srvc. Awd., 1980; Phi Delta Kappa. **Pubns.:** *New England Mill Girls: Feminine Influence in Library Movement* (1971); "Some Early Women Librarians in New England," *Wilson Lib. Bltn.* (Ap. 1977); "Budgeting For School Libraries," *Sch. Media Qtly.* (Win. 1976); contrib., *World Encyclopedia of Librarianship* (1980); contrib., *Frontiers of Library Service For Youth* (1979). **Activities:** 10; 17, 21, 32; 63, 67, 93 **Addr.:** 32 Long Meadow Rd., Riverside, CT 06878.

McCauley, Hannah V. (S. 14, 1929, Houston, TX) Dir. of Lib. Srvs., OH Univ., Lancaster, 1968–; Coord., Lib. Dept., Lancaster (OH) City Sch., 1953–68; Tchr.-Libn., Judson Schs., Long-

PROFESSIONAL ACTIVITIES: Institutions: 1. Acad. lib.; 2. Arch.; 3. Assn.; 4. Fed./Gvt. lib.; 5. Inst. lib.; 6. Mfr./Suppl.; 7. Milit. lib.; 8. Musm.; 9. Pub. lib.; 10. Sch. lib.; 11. Sch. of lib. sci.; 12. Spec. lib.; 13. State lib.; 14. (other). **Functions/Activities:** 15. Acq./Col. dev.; 16. Adult srvs.; 17. Admin.; 18. Apprais.; 19. Archit./Bldgs.; 20. Cat./Class.; 21. Chld. srvs.; 22. Circ.; 23. Cons./Pres.; 24. Consult.; 25. Cont. ed.; 26. Educ. lib. sci.; 27. Ext. srvs.; 28. Fund/Grants; 29. Gvt. pubs.; 30. Indx./Abs.; 31. Instr. lib. use; 32. Media srvs.; 33. Micro.; 34. Netwks./Coop.; 35. Persnl.; 36. PR; 37. Publshg.; 38. Recs. mgt.; 39. Ref. srvs.; 40. Repro.; 41. Resrch.; 42. Review.; 43. Secur.; 44. Serials; 45. Spec. col.; 46. Tech. srvs.; 47. Trustees/Bds.; 48. YA srvs.; 49. (other).

view, TX, 1949–51. **Educ.:** Univ. of TX, 1946–50, BS (Educ.); George Peabody Grad. Sch. of LS, 1952. **Orgs.:** OHIONET: Ch. (1977–). OH LA: Pres. (1978–79). ALA: AASL (2nd V.P. 1974–75). OH Assn. Sch. Libns.: Pres. (1973–74). Hist. Assn. of Fairfield Cnty.: Bd. of Trustees (1978). Frnds. of Fairfield Cnty. Dist. Lib.: VP (1978). **Honors:** OH Educ. Lib. Media Assn., Awd. of Merit, 1977; Ohio Lib. Assn. Lib. of Year Awd., 1980; Ohio Univ., Outstanding Admin. Awd., 1981. **Pubns.:** "The Media Way," *OH Media Spectrum* (Win. 1979); "OLDP: A Serious Cooperation Game," *OH LA Bltn.* (Jl. 1977); sound/slide program, "Bicentennial History of Fairfield County" (1976). **Activities:** 1; 17, 26, 34; 50, 56 **Addr.:** Ohio University-Lancaster, 1570 Granville Pike, Lancaster, OH 43130.

McCauley, Julianne R. (N. 18, 1927, Easton, MD) Libn., Media Spec., St. Mary's HS, 1980–; Head, Ref., Info. and Ref., Volun. Progs., Outrch., Info. Spec., Caroline Cnty. Pub. Lib., 1976–79; Ext. Libn., Dorchester Cnty. Free Lib., 1975–76; Asst. HQ Libn., Caroline Cnty. Pub. Lib., 1969–74; Home Econ. Tchr., Ridgely Spec. Sch., 1968–69; Tchrs. Aide, Denton Sch., 1966–68; Sub. Tchr., Caroline Cnty. Pub. Schs., Burlington Cnty. Schs., 1958–66. **Educ.:** Univ. of MD; Univ. of DE, 1944–48, BS (Foods and Nutr.); Univ. of MD, 1974–75, MLS; MD Pub. Lib., 1975, Advnc. Prof. Libn.; 1975, Advnc. Prof. Cert. (LS Grades 7–12). **Orgs.:** MD LA. ALA. Bd. of Dirs., Upper Shore Aging. Denton Armory Com. Bus. and Prof. Women's Club. Parents-Tchrs. Assn. **Activities:** 9, 10; 15, 32, 48; 75 **Addr.:** 110 Sunset Dr., Denton, MD 21629.

McCauley, Margery Jean (Ja. 7, 1926, Sharon, PA) Chief, Info. Branch, Natl. AV Ctr., 1975–; Branch Info. Ctr. Mgr., Battelle Meml. Inst., 1972–75; Asst. Med. Libn., Berkshire Med. Ctr., 1970–72; Systs. Anal., Systs. Dev. Corp., 1968–69; Proj. Leader, Battelle Meml. Inst., 1964–68; Tech. Info. Spec., Gen. Electric Co., 1960–64; Chem., Oil Well Resrch., 1957–60. **Educ.:** Grove City Coll., 1943–47, BS (Chem.). **Orgs.:** Amer. Documtn. Inst.: Chap. Secy. and Coord. (1962–63). ASIS: Nonprint Media Grp. Ch. (1981), Vice-Ch. (1980), Secy. (1977–79). Systs. Mgt. Assn. **Pubns.:** "Information Policy and the National AV Center," *Gvt. Pubns. Review* (Jl. 1981); "The National Audiovisual Center," *Information Hotline, Info. Ctr. Profile* (Ja. 1979); contrib., *Educational Media Yearbook* (1977); various speeches to ASIS and SLA (1961–80). **Activities:** 12; 17, 29; 50, 51, 75 **Addr.:** 15225 Barnesville Rd., Boyds, MD 20841.

McCauley, Nancy P. (Ap. 6, 1931, San Mateo, CA) Slide Cur., Slide Libn., Stanford Univ., 1980–; Prof., Hist. of Art, Stephens Coll., 1974–80; Asst. Prof., Hist. of Art, Portland State Univ., 1967–72; Instr., Hist. of Art, CA Coll. of Arts and Crafts, 1963–67. **Educ.:** Univ. of CA, Berkeley, 1952–56, BA (Art), 1956–60, MA (Art Hist.); Univ. of MO, 1972–74, MLS. **Orgs.:** ARLIS/NA: Natl. Chap.; Reg. Chap. Coll. Art Assn. **Honors:** Natl. Hum. Inst., Yale Univ., Fellow, 1977–78; NEH, Sum. Sem., Fellow, 1975. **Activities:** 1; 15, 17, 20; 55 **Addr.:** Slide Library, Dept. of Art, Cummings Bldg., Stanford University, Stanford, CA 94305.

McCauley, Philip F. (My. 28, 1931, New York, NY) Cur. of Spec. Col., Archvst., SD Sch. of Mines and Tech., 1979–, Dir. of Lib., 1968–79; Tech. Libn., Phillips Petroleum Co., Bartlesville, OK, 1966–68. **Educ.:** Univ. of Denver, 1962–64, BA (Hist.), 1964–66, MA (LS). **Orgs.:** SLA. Mt. Plains LA: Parlmt. (1973–78). SD LA: Parlmt. (1972–78); Ch., Acad. Sect. (1969). Rocky Mt. Biblgphcl. Ctr. for Resrch.: Bd. (1970–1974); VP (1971); Pres. (1972). **Honors:** Phi Alpha Theta. **Pubns.:** Reviews. **Activities:** 1, 12; 17, 23, 39; 56, 74, 85 **Addr.:** P. O. Box 2124, Rapid City, SD 57709.

McChesney, Kathryn M. (Ja. 14, 1936, Curwensville, PA) Asst. Prof., Sch. of LS, Kent State Univ., 1969–, Asst. Dean, 1969–77, Asst. to Dean & Instr., 1968–69; Head Libn., Springfield HS, Akron, OH, 1962–68. **Educ.:** Univ. of Akron, 1958–62, B.Ed. (Hist.); Kent State Univ., 1964–65, MLS, 1971–, (Hist.). **Orgs.:** ALA. OH LA: Ch., Lib. Educ. RT (1971–72). OH Educ. Lib./Media Assn. AALS. AAUP. **Pubns.:** "Student Involvement in Education," *Jnl. of Educ. for Libnshp.* (Spr. 1971); "Kent State University, School of Lib. Sc.," *Encyc. of Lib. and Info. Sci.* **Activities:** 10; 20, 48; 72 **Addr.:** 3611 Edison St. N.W., P.O. Box 57, Uniontown, OH 44685.

McClain, David C. (Ja. 13, 1940, Warren, OH) Head Libn., Bapt. Bible Coll. of PA, 1974–, Asst. Libn., 1968–74. **Educ.:** Bapt. Bible Coll., 1957–62, ThB (Bible Theo.); Drexel Univ., 1968–71, MS (LS). **Orgs.:** Assn. of Christ. Libns.: VP (1971–72); Pres. (1972–73); Bd. of Dirs. (1971–76). ATLA. **Pubns.:** "Bible College Library Standards: A Reappraisal," *Christ. Libn.* (O. 1971). **Activities:** 1; 15, 17; 63, 90, 92 **Addr.:** Murphy Memorial Library, Baptist Bible College, 538 Venard Rd., Clarks Summit, PA 18411.

McClain, Harriet V. (My. 23, 1950, Columbus, OH) Libn., Blatchley Jr. High, 1971–. **Educ.:** Bowling Green State Univ., 1968–71, BS (Educ.); Univ. of HI, 1975–76, MLS; Simmons Coll., 1979–80, MA (Chld. Lit.). **Orgs.:** ALA: State Mem. Ch. (1980–82). Pac. Northwest LA. AK LA: Treas. (1978–79). Sitka LA: Pres. (1980–82). Natl. Educ. Assn. Intl. Readg. Assn. **Honors:** ALA, Chld. Srvs. Div., Charles Scribner's Sons Awd., 1977. **Pubns.:** Reviews. **Activities:** 10; 48; 63 **Addr.:** Box 66, Sitka, AK 99835.

McClarren, Robert Royce (Mr. 15, 1921, Delta, OH) Syst. Dir., N. Suburban Lib. Syst., 1967–; Dir., IN State Lib., 1962–67; Dir., Huntington (WV), Pub. Lib. & Western Counties Reg. Lib., 1958–62; Head Libn., Crawfordsville (IN) Pub. Lib., 1955–58; Head, Circ. Dept., Oak Park (IL) Pub. Lib., 1954–55; Lect., Dept. of LS, Rosary Coll., 1968–. **Educ.:** Antioch Coll., 1938–40; Muskingum Coll., 1940–42, BA (Econ., bio.); OH State Univ., 1950–51, MA (Eng.); Columbia, Univ., 1953–54, MS (LS). **Orgs.:** ALA: Treas. (1968–72); Cnclr.-at-large (1966–68, 1974–78); Pubshg. Bd. (1972–75); RASD, Pres. (1975–76); Amer. Assn. of State Libs. Pres. (1978–79); ALTA, Libn. VP (1976–77). IL LA: Pres. (1981). WHCOLIS: Del. (1979). Other orgs. and coms. Adult Educ. Assn. of IN: Pres. (1965–66). Indianapolis Lit. Club. Railway and Locomotive Hist. Socty. OH Hist. Socty. Other orgs. **Honors:** Joseph Towne Wheeler Awd., Columbia Univ., 1954; IL Libn. of the Yr., 1978; IN LA, Cit., 1967; Beta Phi Mu, 1954. **Activities:** 9, 14-Syst.; 17, 24, 34; 50, 78 **Addr.:** 1560 Oakwood Pl., Deerfield, IL 60015.

McClaskey, Harris Clark (Ap. 4, 1931, Trenton, NJ) Assoc. Prof., Lib. Sch., Univ. of MN, 1972–, Asst. Prof., 1970–72; Dir., Inst. Lib. Srvs., WA State Lib., 1965–70, Lib. Consult., 1962–65; Dir., Renton Pub. Lib., 1957–61, Asst. Libn., 1956–57; Dir., WA Lib. Film Circuit, 1962–65; various positions in tchg., consult. **Educ.:** Coll. of Wooster, 1953, BA; Univ. of WA, 1956, MLS, 1970, PhD; various crs. **Orgs.:** ALA: Cnclr.–at–Large (1972–76); Hlth. and Rehab. Lib. Srvs. Div., Pres. (1975–76), Nom. Com. (Ch., 1977–78), various com. ch.; LAMA, Rcrt. Netwk., WA State Rep. (1959–61), Pac. Northwest Rep. (1961–67). MN LA: Chld. and Young People's Sect., Loan Fund Com. (Ch., 1973–74); Cont. Educ. Com. (1975–76); various coms. Med. LA: Midwest Reg. Grp., Anl. Conf., 1979, Panel on Hlth. Educ., Ch. WA LA: Exec. Bd. (Dir.–at–Large, 1959–61); various com. Various orgs. Univ. of MN Lib. Sch.: Various coms., ofcs. Natl. Assn. for Retarded Citizens. WA Assn. for Retarded Citizens. Natl. Educ. Assn.: Cncl. for Excep. Chld. (1966–). Various orgs. **Honors:** Beta Phi Mu, 1956; Phi Delta Kappa, 1968. **Pubns.:** Consult., *The Librarian and the Patient; An Introduction to Library Services to Patients in Health Care Institutions* (1977); Jt. auth., *Project Media Evaluation, Fiscal 1974* (1974); Jt. auth., *The Library Technician and the American Junior College: An Annotated Bibliography* occasional paper, Univ. of WA (1968, 1969); *Demonstration of Library Services to Exceptional Children at the Public Library of Cincinnati and Hamilton County, Ohio: A Proposal for a Demonstration Project* (1966); various articles. **Addr.:** Library School, University of MN, 409 Walter Library, 117 Pleasant St. S.E., Minneapolis, MN 55455.

McClatchey, Sally-Bruce B. (Je. 28, 1922, Seattle, WA) Church-Sch. Libn., Mt. Paran Church of God, 1978–; Libn., Cherokee Garden Lib., 1979–81; Lib. Consult., St. Luke's Episcopal Church, 1978–81; Lib. Consult., N. Ave. Presby. Church, 1977–78. **Educ.:** Univ. of WA, 1938–42, BS (Chem., Bot.); Emory Univ., 1969–72, MLn, MAT (Elem. Educ.). **Orgs.:** CSLA: Metro. Atlanta Chap. (Pres., 1979–81). Cncl. Botanical and Horticult. Libns. ALA. **Activities:** 10, 12; 15, 21, 24; 90, 91 **Addr.:** 3355 Ridgewood Rd. NW., Atlanta, GA 30327.

McClear, Mary-Eileen (Mickie) (D. 30, 1948, Owosso, MI) Head of Chld. Srvs., Midwest. Reg. Lib. Syst., 1977–; Head of Chld. Srvs., St. Catharines Pub. Lib., 1975–77, Chld. Libn., 1971–75. **Educ.:** Nazareth Coll., 1966–70, BA (Eng.); West. MI Univ., 1970–71, MLS. **Orgs.:** Can. LA: Can. Assn. of Chld. Libns. (Vice ch., ch. elect, 1980–81). ON LA: Chld. Srvs. Com. (Ch., 1978–79). Chld. Book Ctr. Natl. Assn. for Prsrvn. and Perpetuation of Storytelling. Frnd. of Intl. Bd. of Books for Young People. Chld. Lit. Assn. **Honors:** Beta Phi Mu. **Pubns.:** "Bubblegum Gumshoes: Canada's Young Detectives," *Canadian Children's Literature* (1981); "Profile: Shizuye Takashima," *In Review* (Ap. 1980); *You Can Come, Too* (1978); "Children's Services in the Ontario Library Association," *ON Lib. Review* (1979); ed. MERLIN., nsltr. (1981). reviews. **Activities:** 9, 14-Reg. Lib.; 24, 25, 42; 57, 85, 89 **Addr.:** Midwestern Regional Library System, 637 Victoria St. N., Kitchener, ON N2H 5G4 Canada.

McCleary, William Ernest Hearte (My. 29, 1927, Alexandria, LA) Asst. Libn., Docum. Dept., LA State Univ. Library (Shreveport), 1976–, Sr. Libn., Ref. Dept., 1967–76; Libn., Union Producing Co., 1961–67; Cat. and Acq. Libn., Shreve Mem. Lib., 1958–61; Tchr., Caddo Parish Sch., 1951–58. **Educ.:** Centenary College of LA, 1944–48, BA (Hum.); LA State Univ., 1948–50, MA (Jrnlsm); 1957–58, MSLS; Univ. of IL, 1966–71, CAS (Lib. Sci.); LA State Univ., 1978 (Hlth. Sci. Libnshp. Cert.). **Orgs.:** LA LA: Treas. (1964–65); Bltn. Ed. (1965–66); Ch., Subj. Spec. Sect. (1971–72); Ch., Intell. Freedom Com. (1972–73). SLA: LA Chap. (Pres. 1966–67); Musms, Arts and Hum. Div. (Vice Ch. 1981–82). AAUP: Secy./Treas., LA State Univ. Chap. (1977–78). Shreveport Bicycle Club: Pres. (1976–77). **Pubns.:** "Index" *LA LA Bltn* (1967–70); "Index" *N. LA Hist. Bltn.* (1967–71); Reviews. **Activities:** 1, 12; 29, 39; 55, 92 **Addr.:** 6147 Creswell Ave., Shreveport, LA 71106.

McClellan, William Monson (Ja. 7, 1934, Groton, MA) Dir., Msc. Lib., Prof. Lib. Admin., Univ. of IL, 1965–; Msc. Libn., Instr. in Msc., Univ. of CO, 1959–65. **Educ.:** CO Coll., 1952–56, BA (Msc.); Univ. of MI, 1958–59, AMLS, CO Coll., 1961, MA (Msc. Hist.). **Orgs.:** Msc. LA: Prog. Ch. (1967). VP (1970–71). Pres./Past Pres. (1971–74). Assn. for Recorded Sound Col.: Const. and Legal Com. (1966–69). **Honors:** Cncl. on Lib. Resrcs., Flwshp., 1976–77. **Pubns.:** "Judging Music Libraries," *Coll. & Resrch. Libs.* (Jl. 1978); "Guidelines for Surveying Music Library Resources and Services," *Procs. Anl. Mtg. of the Natl. Assn. of Schs. of Msc.* (1977); Ed., *Notes* (1977–). **Activities:** 1, 14; 15, 17, 24; 55 **Addr.:** University of Illinois at Urbana - Champaign, Music Library, Music Building, Urbana, IL 61801.

McCloskey, Elinor Florence (Je. 18, 1933, New York, NY) Dist. Coord., Lib. Srvs., Albuquerque Pub. Schs., 1968–; Asst. Prof., Lib. Sci., Univ. of NM, 1966–68, 1961–63; Sch. Libn., Amer. Depy. Schs., Baumholder, Germany, 1960–61; Sch. Libn., Bellevue Pub. Schs., 1958–60. **Educ.:** WA State Univ., 1951–55, BA (Educ.); Univ. of Denver, 1956–58, MLS; Columbia Univ., 1963–66, EdD (Curric.). **Orgs.:** MN LA: Pres. (1975–76); Secy. (1969–70); Constn. and Bylaws Com. (Ch., 1976–78). ALA: LAMA/SS, Secy. (1979–81), Stats. for Sch. Lib. Media Ctrs. (Ch., 1977–79), Stats. for Nonprint Media (1979–81); AASL, Afflt. Asm. Del. (1976, 1980–81). NM Media Assn.: Bd. of Dir. (1976–79). AECT. various orgs. Leag. of Women Voters. Frnds. of the Albuquerque Pub. Lib. NM State Dept. of Educ.: Lib. Media Adv. Com. (1976–79). NM State Dept. of Educ., Elem. and Sec. Educ. Act: Title IV Adv. Com. (1975–78, 1979–82). **Activities:** 10; 17 **Addr.:** 3304 Morris N.E., Apt. 10, Albuquerque, NM 87111.

McClure, Charles R. (My. 24, 1949, Syracuse, NY) Prof., Univ. of OK, Sch. of LS, 1977–; Instr., Grad. Sch. of Lib. and Info. Std., Rutgers Univ., 1975–77, Dir., AV Lab., 1974–77; Head, Hist.-Gvt. Dept., Univ. of TX at El Paso, Lib., 1972–73; Stack Supvsr., OK State Univ. Lib., 1969–71. **Educ.:** OK State Univ., 1967–70, BA (Span.), 1970–71, MA (Hist.); Univ. of OK, 1971–72, MLS; Rutgers Univ., 1974–77, PhD (Lib., Info. Sci.). **Orgs.:** ASIS. AALS: Resrch. Com. (Ch., 1981–82). OK LA: Bd. of Dirs. (1980–81). ALA: ACRL; Info. Sci. and Lib. Autom. Div.; GODORT; LAMA. Gvt. Pubns. Review: Ed. Bd.; Asst. Ed. Info./Mgt. Consult. Srvs., Inc.: Pres. West. Hist. Assn. **Honors:** LRRT, Resrch. Awd., 1979; Beta Phi Mu, 1973. **Pubns.:** *Information for Academic Library Decision Making* (1980); jt. ed., *Approaches to Library Administration* (1981); "A Planning Primer for ONLINE Reference Services in a Public Library," *ONLINE* (Ap. 1980); "From Public Library Standards to Statewide Levels of Adequacy," *Lib. Resrch.* (1980); "The Planning Process: Strategies for Action," *Coll. & Resrch. Libs.* (N. 1978); various articles, sps. **Activities:** 9, 11; 17, 24, 26; 75, 92, 95-Gvt. Pubns. **Addr.:** School of Library Science, University of Oklahoma, Norman, OK 73019.

McClure, Frances L. (O. 10, 1942, Montgomery, AL) Supvsr., Ext. Srvs., Montgomery Cnty., MD, Pub. Libs., 1979–, Reader's Adv. Silver Spring Lib., 1978–79, Chld. Libn., 1971–77, Asst. Comnty. Libn., Aspen Hill Lib., 1969–70; Ref. Libn., Bus., Columbia Univ., 1968–69; Br. Libn.,Chld., Miami Pub. Lib., 1968; Chief, Chld. Srvs., Jacksonville, FL Pub. Lib., 1966–68; Br. Libn., Chesapeake, VA, Pub. Lib., 1965. **Educ.:** Western KY Univ., 1960–63, AB (Eng.); Univ. of KY, 1963–64, MSLS; Columbia Univ., 1968–69. **Orgs.:** ALA. DC LA. Modern Lang. Assn. **Honors:** Beta Phi Mu. **Activities:** 9; 17, 27, 36; 50, 74, 89 **Addr.:** Extension Services, Montgomery County Public Libraries, 99 Maryland Ave, Rockville, MD 20902.

McClure, Jean M. (S. 21, 1948, Rochester, NY) Asst. to Assoc. Dir., Branches, Rochester Pub. Lib., 1981–, Chld. Libn., 1974–81, YA Libn., 1971–74. **Educ.:** Coll. of Mt. St. Vincent, 1966-70, BA (Hist., Pol. Sci.); Pratt Inst., 1970–71, MLS. **Orgs.:** NY LA. ALA. Untd. Protestant Expression Marriage Encounter. **Honors:** City of Rochester, Pub. Srv. Awd., 1980. **Activities:** 9; 15, 21, 42 **Addr.:** 105 Rossiter Rd., Rochester, NY 14620.

McClure, Lucretia W. (Ja. 2, 1925, Denver, CO) Med. Lib., Assoc. Prof. of Med. Bibl., Univ. of Rochester Sch. of Med. & Dentistry, 1979–, Assoc. Libn., Readers Srvs. Libn., Serials Libn., Cat. Libn., Edward G. Miner Library 1964–78. **Educ.:** Univ. of MO, 1945, BJ (Jnlsm.); Univ. of Denver, 1964, MA (Libnshp.); Med. LA Cert., 1972. **Orgs.:** Med. LA: Bd. of Dir. (1980–83); Upstate NY and ON Chap., Ch. (1969). Amer. Assn. for the Hist. of Med. CLENE. Biomed. Comm. Network: Secy. Treas. (1976–79). **Pubns.:** "Reference Services: Policies and Practices," *Handbook of Med. Lib. Prac.* (in press); *Fifty Years of Medicine at Rochester* (1975); *Management of Reference Services* (1976). **Activities:** 1; 17; 80 **Addr.:** University of Rochester, School of Medicine, 601 Elmwood Ave., Rochester, NY 14642.

McClurg, Roger A. (Ag. 10, 1946, Albany, OR) Dir., Oregon City Pub. Lib., 1978–; Cnty. Libn., Lake Cnty. Lib., 1975–78. **Educ.:** South. OR State Coll., 1970–74, BS; Univ. of OR, 1974–75, MLS. **Orgs.:** ALA. OR LA. **Activities:** 9; 17 **Addr.:** Oregon City Public Library, 606 John Adams St., Oregon City, OR 97045.

McConnell, Anne Young (S. 17, 1917, Paris, KY) Assoc. Prof., Coll. of Lib. Sci., Univ. of KY, 1973–; Libn., Ctrl. Elem. Sch., 1967–73; Libn., Arlington Elem. Sch., Maxwell St. Sch.,

Special Subjects/Services: 50. Adult educ.; 51. Advert./Mktg.; 52. Aerosp.; 53. Agric.; 54. Area std.; 55. Arts/Hum.; 56. Autom.; 57. Bibl./Prtg.; 58. Bio. sci.; 59. Bus./Fin.; 60. Chem.; 61. Copyrt.; 62. Documtn.; 63. Educ.; 64. Engin.; 65. Env.; 66. Eth. grps.; 67. Film; 68. Food/Nutr.; 69. Geneal.; 70. Geo.; 71. Geol.; 72. Handcpd.; 73. Hist.; 74. Int. frdm.; 75. Info. sci.; 76. Insr.; 77. Law; 78. Legis.; 79. Math./Comp. sci.; 80. Med.; 81. Metals; 82. Nat. resrcs.; 83. Newsp.; 84. Nuc. sci.; 85. Oral hist.; 86. Petr./Energy; 87. Pharm.; 88. Phys./Astr./Math.; 89. Readg.; 90. Relig.; 91. Sci./Tech.; 92. Soc. sci.; 93. Telecom.; 94. Transp.; 95. (other).

1960–61. **Educ.:** Randolph–Macon Women's Coll., 1935–37; Univ. of KY, 1958–60, BA (LS, Eng.), 1960–67, MLS; Univ. of IL, 1974–78, Cert. of Advnc. Std. (LS). **Orgs.:** ALA: Grolier Fndn. Awds. Com. (1975–76); Hammond Awd. Com. (1976–77); AASL, Plng. Com. for 1980 Conf. in NY; ALSC, Natl. Plng. of Spec. Col. Com. (1979–81), Newberry–Caldecott Com. (1977). KY LA: Lcl. Arrange. Ch. (1979). KY Sch. Media Assn.: Treas. (1971–72); Bd. of Dir. (1970–77). AALS. Gvrs. Com. on Stan. for KY Sch. Libns. Media Cadre Dept. of Educ., Cmwlth. of KY (1978–). Univ. of South. MS Medallion Com. (1980–). **Honors:** Phi Beta Kappa, 1960; Kappa Delta Pi, 1960; Beta Phi Mu, 1967. **Pubns.:** Cmplr., *Books from Other Countries, 1972–1976* (1978); "To a Young Author," *Cath. Lib. World* (S. 1976); "Promote Picture Books," *Sch. Lib. Jnl.* (Mr. 1976); "Now and Then: Thoughts on Children's Literature Past and Present," *CA Sch. Libs.* (Fall 1976). **Activities:** 11; 21, 25, 26 **Addr.:** 433 Patterson Office Tower, College of Library Science, University of KY, Lexington, KY 40506.

McConnell, Elaine H. (D. 25, 1948, Pittsburgh, Pa) Dir., Lib. Srvs., Piscataway Twp. Pub. Lib., 1975–, Comnty. Srvs. Libn., 1974–75. **Educ.:** Lake Erie Coll., 1966–70, BA (Span.); Rutgers Univ., 1973–74, MLS. **Orgs.:** ALA: PLA (AV Com. 1979). NJ LA: Exec. Bd. (1979–); Pers. Admin. Com. (1976–); Secy. (1976–79); Ch. Sal. Guide Subcom. (1978–). Piscataway Cable Adv. Com.: Vice Ch. (1977–). Piscataway Human Resrcs. Cncl. League of Women Voters. **Activities:** 9; 17 **Addr.:** Piscataway Public Library, 500 Hoes Ln., Piscataway, NJ 08854.

McConnell, Fraiser (Ja. 18, 1951, Tampa, FL) Asst. Libn., CA Coll. of Arts & Crafts, 1975–; Lectr., Dept. of Anthro., San Francisco State Univ., 1979–80; Indxr., *Artweek,* 1977–78; Chief Libn., Aircraft Tech. Publshrs., 1974–75. **Educ.:** Univ. of TX, Arlington, 1968–71, BM (Msc.); N. TX State Univ., 1972–73, MLS; San Francisco State Univ., 1976–, MA in progress (Anthro.). **Orgs.:** SLA: San Francisco Chap., Adv. Cncl. (1976–79). ALA: ACRL. ARLIS/NA. Amer. Anthro. Assn. Southwest. Anthro. Assn. Amer. Socty. for Ethnohist. **Pubns.:** "Jazz and Education; a selection bibliography," *Natl. Assn. of Jazz Educators* (1975); reviews. **Activities:** 92 **Addr.:** 3882 23d St., San Francisco, CA 94114.

McConnell, Karen S. (Ap. 1, 1949, Port Arthur, TX) Libn., Gulf States Utilities Co., 1979–; Coord. of Spec. Coll., Lamar Univ., 1978–79, Gvt. Docum. Libn., 1976–78, Soc. Sci. Libn., 1973–76. **Educ.:** N. TX State Univ., 1969–71, BA (LS), 1972–73, MLS; Lamar Univ., 1973–79, MBA (Mgt.). **Orgs.:** SLA. ALA: JMRT Anl. Conf. Soc. Com. (1979); JMRT Liason to LAMA (1979); JMRT Ch. of Cont. Educ. Com., Liason to CLENE (1979/80). TX LA: JMRT Dist. Rep. (1977–1978); Cont. Educ. Com., Ch. (1978–1979); Conf. Prog. Ch. (1981). TX Assn. of Coll. Tchrs.: State Exec. Bd. (1977–79). Kappa Delta Sorority. **Activities:** 1, 12; 17, 29, 39; 59, 64, 86 **Addr.:** Gulf States Utilities Company, P.O. Box 2951 or 285 Liberty St., Beaumont, TX 77704.

McConnell, Pamela Jean (O. 2, 1953, Dearborn, MI) Resrch. Park Libn., Univ. of MO, Columbia, 1977–. **Educ.:** Univ. of MI, Dearborn, 1971–76, AB (Art Hist.), BS (Exper. Bio.); Columbia Univ., 1976–77, MS (LS). **Orgs.:** ALA: ACRL. SLA: Mid–MO Chap., Secy.–Treas. (1978–79), Pres.–Elect. (1979–); Bio. Sci. Div.; Nuc. Sci. Div. **Honors:** Beta Phi Mu. **Pubns.:** "The Research Park Library at the University of Missouri-Columbia," *Show-Me Libs.* (My. 1979); "The New Copyright Law," *Engin. in Med. and Bio. Socty. Nsltr.* (Mr. 1978). **Activities:** 1, 12; 17, 39; 58, 84, 91 **Addr.:** Research Park Library, University of Missouri, Columbia, MO 65211.

McConomy, Sr. Eileen Elizabeth, SNJM (Ja. 19, 1928, Montreal, PQ) Lib. Consult., Comsn. Des Ecoles Cath. De Montréal, 1971–; HS Libn., Marymount Comprehensive HS, 1970–71; HS Libn., Marylrose Acad., Albany, NY, 1969–70; HS Libn., S. Shore Cath. HS, Ville Jacques Cartier, PQ, 1965–68. **Educ.:** Outremont Normal, 1948–49, Superior Normal Tchrs. Dip.; Villanova Univ., 1953–57, BA (Eng.); Cath. Univ. of Amer., 1966–69, MSLS; Univ. of Ottawa, 1960–65, BLS. **Orgs.:** Can. Sch. LA: Secy.–Treas. (1976). PQ LA: Youth Sect. (Secy., 1976). PQ Assn. of Sch. Libns. Corp. of Prof. Libns. PQ: Sch. Libs. Com. (1977–78). Educ. Consults. Assn. of Montreal. Saint Lawrence Choir. **Honors:** Beta Phi Mu, 1970. **Activities:** 10, 14-sch. bd. syst.; 15, 17, 24 **Addr.:** Bureau Des Média D'Enseignement, 4590 Orleans Ave., Montreal, PQ H1X 2K4 Canada.

McCool, Donna L. (Ja. 25, 1942, Oklahoma City, OK) Asst. Dir. for Admin. Srvs., WA State Univ. Libs., 1978–, Sci. Ref. Libn., 1972–78; Head, Bus. & Tech. Dept., Tulsa City-Cnty. Lib. Syst., 1965–72; Spec. Instr., Sch. of LS, Univ. of OK, 1970–71. **Educ.:** OK State Univ., 1960–64, BA (Geol.); Columbia Univ., 1964–65, MS (LS). **Orgs.:** ALA. SLA. **Honors:** Phi Kappa Phi, 1963; Beta Phi Mu, 1965. **Activities:** 1; 17, 39; 59, 86, 91 **Addr.:** Library Administrative Office, Washington State University Libraries, Pullman, WA 99164.

McCorison, Marcus Allen (Jl. 17, 1926, Lancaster, WI) Dir., Libn., Amer. Antiq. Socty., 1967–, Libn., 1960–67; Head, Spec. Col., State Univ. of IA, 1959–60; Chief, Rare Books Dept., Dartmouth Coll., 1955–59; Lecturer, Amer. Col. Hist., Clark Univ., 1967–; Libn., Kellogg-Hubbard Lib., 1954–55. **Educ.:** Ripon Coll., 1946–50, AB (Eng.); Univ. of VT, 1950–51, MA (Amer. Hist.); Columbia Univ., 1953–54, MSLS. **Orgs.:** ALA: ACLR (Ch., Rare Book Sect., 1965–6). Short-Title Cat. of Eighteenth-Cent. Eng. Books: N. Amer. Strg. Com. Com. for a New Eng. Bib.: Treas. (1970–7); Bd. mem. (1970–). Ind. Resrch. LA: Ch. (1972–3; 1978–80). Amer. Antiq. Socty. MA Hist. Socty. Bibl. Socty. of Amer.: Pres. (1980–81). VT Hist. Socty.: Trustee (1956–9 1960–6). **Honors:** Beta Phi Mu, 1957. **Pubns.:** Ed., *The History of Printing in America* (1970); *The 1764 Catalogue of the Redwood Library Company in Newport, R.I.* (1965); *Vermont Imprints, 1778–1820* (1963); "The Nature of Humanistic Societies in Early America" in *The Pursuit of Knowledge in the Early American Republic* (1976). **Activities:** 12; 15, 17, 45; 55, 57 **Addr.:** 185 Salisbury St., Worcester, MA 01609.

McCorkle, Barbara Backus (S. 9, 1920, New York City, NY) Map and Ref. Libn., Yale Univ., 1979–; Ref. Libn., Purdue Univ. 1975–78, Head, Ref. Dept., 1978–79; Ref. Libn., Yale Univ., 1974–75; Rare Bk. and Map Libn., Univ. of KS, 1968–74. **Educ.:** Hunter Coll., 1938–42, BS (Eng.), Emporia State Univ., 1967–68, MLS. **Orgs.:** ALA. SLA. Socty. for the Hist. of Discoveries: Secy.-Treas. (1978–). Intl. Socty. for the Hist. of Cartography. **Pubns.:** "Recent Literature in Discovery History," *Terrae Incognitae* (1979–81). **Activities:** 1; 15, 39, 45; 70 **Addr.:** Map Collection, Yale University, 1603A Yale Station, New Haven, CT 06520.

McCormick, Edith Joan (Ag. 18, 1934, Chicago, IL) Asst. Managing Ed., *Amer. Libs.,* ALA, 1981–, Asst. Ed., 1969–81, Admin. Asst., Knapp Sch. Libs. Proj., AASL, 1965–69; Tchr., Eng., Berlitz Sch., Darmstadt, Germany, 1960–61. **Educ.:** Univ. of Chicago, 1956–59, AB (Grm., Lang., Lit.). **Orgs.:** ALA: SRRT (1974–80). Nat. Wildlife Assn. **Honors:** Educ. Press Assn. of Amer., Disting. Achvmt. Awd. for Excel. in Educ. Jnlsm., 1981. **Pubns.:** *Mystery of the Roman Ransom* transl. (1972); *A Bridge of Children's Books* transl. (1969); *Tobias, the Magic Mouse* transl. (1968); "Minding the Miniatures," *Amer. Libs.* (Mr. 1980); various clmns., *Amer. Libs.* **Activities:** 3 **Addr.:** 3155 N. Pine Grove Ave., Chicago IL 60657.

McCormick, Mona (Cleveland, OH) Assoc. Libn., Ref., Univ. of CA, Los Angeles, 1979–; Ref. Libn., Univ. of CA, San Diego, 1977–79; Ed., Salk Inst., 1975–77; Resrch. Assoc., Western Bhvl. Scis. Inst., 1971–75; Ed. Ref. Libn., NY Times 1967–71. **Educ.:** Univ. of IA, 1948–52, BA (Eng.); Pratt Inst., 1964–65, MLS. **Orgs.:** ALA. CA ARL. CA LA. **Pubns.:** Jt. Auth., *Too Dangerous to be at Large* (1975); Contrib., *Educating the Library User* (1974); *Who-What-Where-How-Why Made Easy* (1971). Contrib., *New York Times Encyclopedic Almanac* (1970). **Activities:** 1; 15, 31, 39; 83 **Addr.:** University Research Library - Reference Dept., 405 Hilgard Ave., Westwood, CA 90024.

McCown, Leonard Joe (S. 9, 1942, Port Lavaca, TX) Libn., Irving (TX) HS, 1980–; Interim Lib. Dir., Dallas Baptist Coll., 1979–80, Coord. of Pub. Srvs. 1969–79, Ref. and Acq. Libn., 1968–69; Adult Libn., Dallas Pub. Lib., 1967, YA Libn., 1964–1967. **Educ.:** Victoria Coll., 1960–1962, AA; N. TX State Univ., 1962–64, BA (Lib. Srv.), 1967–68, MLS. **Orgs.:** ALA. TX LA: Dist. V/Ch. (1974–75), Cont. Ed. Com. (1977–1978), Lib. Dev. Com. (1971–1972), Nom. Com. (Ch., 1978), ALA Mem. Com. (1975–1976) Arch. RT/various ofcs. (1971–1973); YA RT/various ofcs. (1966–1970). Dallas Cnty. LA: various ofcs. (1970–1978). SAA. TX State Geneal. Socty.: Contrib. ed., *Stirpes.* Sons of the Amer. Revolution. **Honors:** Vasa Ord. of Amer. Alpha Lambda Sigma; Alpha Beta Alpha. **Pubns.:** Mono. on 7th–10th census of the U.S., 1850, 1860, 1870, 1880 (1980); *Cemeteries of Seadrift, Texas* (1980); *Cemeteries of Indianola, Texas* (1979); "Index to Naturalization Records: Calhoun Co., Texas," *Stirpes* (Je. 1979–S. 1979). **Activities:** 1, 9; 15, 22, 39; 63, 69, 92 **Addr.:** 217 W. 14th St., Irving, TX 75060.

McCoy, Lynda Louise (Ja. 23, 1943, Picton, ON) Head, Lib. Dept., S. Carleton HS, Richmond (ON), 1968–, Tchr., 1964–68. **Educ.:** Univ. of Toronto, 1961–64, BA (Geo.), 1975–76, MLS; ON Tchg. Cert., 1970; ON Spec. Cert. in Sch. Libnshp., 1970. **Orgs.:** ON Sch. Lib. Assn.: Resrch. (1976–). Can. Sch. Lib. Assn. Goulbourn Twp. Lib. Bd.: Trustee (1972–73). ON Mnstry. of Educ. ON Sec. Sch. Tchrs. Fed. Carlton Bd. of Educ. **Pubns.:** "Resource Centres in the Curriculum: Guidelines for Library Use," *ON Mnstry. of Educ.* (S. 1980); *Stuff: Outreach Materials for Teacher-Librarians* (1977); "School Librarians on Keyes and Brunet," *Council Communique: Canadian Book Publishers Council* (Mr. 1978); various articles. **Activities:** 10; 25, 31, 48, 89 **Addr.:** 33 St. Remy Dr., Nepean, ON K2J 1H5 Canada.

McCoy, Ralph E(dward) (O. 1, 1915, St. Louis, MO) Interim Exec. Dir., ARL, 1980–81; Interim Dir. of Libs., Univ. of GA, 1978–79; Dean, Lib. Affairs, South. IL Univ., 1970–76, Spec. Asst. to VP for Plng. 1963–64, Dir. of Libs., 1955–70; Libn., Asst. Prof., Inst. of Labor and Indus. Rel., Univ. of IL, 1948–55; Libn., Quartermaster Tech. Lib., 1946–48; Ed., Pubns. and Admin. Asst., IL State Lib., 1943–46. **Educ.:** IL Wesleyan Univ., 1934–37, AB (Hist.); Univ. of IL, 1938–39, BSLS, 1950, MS (LS), 1956, PhD (LS). **Orgs.:** ALA: Cncl. (1966), Plng. Com. (1967), Jt. Com. with AFL/CIO (1953), Com. on the Support of the Depos. Lib. Syst., (Ch., 1972–74); ACRL, Pres. (1966). Ctr. for Rsrch. Libs. IL LA: Pres. (1960). Bibl. Socty. of Amer. Amer. Cvl. Liberties Union IL State Hist. Socty.: VP (1974–75). AAUP. **Honors:** IL LA, Outstan. Contrib. to Lib. Prof., 1961; IL LA, Int. Frdm. Awd., 1969; ALA, Scarecrow Press Awd. for Lib. Lit., 1969. AALL, Joseph L. Andrews Bibl. Awd., 1969. **Pubns.:** *Freedom of the Press; A Bibliocyclopedia* (1979); *Freedom of the Press; An Annotated Bibliography* (1968); *Theodore Schroeder, A Cold Enthusiast* (1973); *Personnel Administration for Libraries* (1953); "Libraries in the Emerging Institutions," *Lib. Trends* (O. 1966); various articles and bibl. **Activities:** 1, 2; 15, 17, 24; 57, 74, 83 **Addr.:** 1902 Chautauqua St., Carbondale, IL 62901.

McCoy, W. Keith (Ja. 17, 1954, Cambridge, MA) Prin. Libn., Ref., Plainfield Pub. Lib., 1981–; Ref. Libn., E. Brunswick Pub. Lib., 1978–81. **Educ.:** Harvard Univ., 1972–76, AB (Hist.); Drexel Univ., 1976–78, MSLS. **Orgs.:** PA LA: SE Chap., Bd. (1977–78). Frnds. of the New Brunswick Pub. Lib.: VP (1979–). Frnds. of Plainfield Pub. Lib. ALA. **Pubns.:** *A Mission at Harvard Lawn: A History of St. Andrew's Episcopal Church* (1980); *Run It Right! A Selective Bibliography on Municipal Management* (1979); *VOTE: A Guide to Voting in Cambridge* (1975); "Landmarks of Reference: National Cyclopedia of American Biography," *Ref. Srvs. Review* (Volume 9, No. 4). **Activities:** 9; 39, 42, 44; 69, 85, 86 **Addr.:** 730 Park Ave. #3, Plainfield, NJ 07060.

McCracken, Barbara L. (Ag. 20, 1927, Seattle, WA) Dir., Lib./Lrng. Ctr., AZ West. Coll., 1977–; Libn., Tucson Sch. Dist. #1, 1965–77. **Educ.:** Univ. of CO, 1945–48, BA (Eng./Educ.); Univ. of AZ, 1965, MA (Educ./LS); Univ. of OK, 1975, MLS; Univ. of AZ, 1976, Educ. Spec. (Educ. Admin.). **Orgs.:** AZ LA: Pres. Sch. Lib. Div. (1978). ALA. Yumohave Reg. Adv. Lib. Bd.: Secy. (1979). Natl. Educ. Assn. AZ Educ. Assn. **Activities:** 1, 10; 17 **Addr.:** 1509 S. 8th Ave., Yuma, AZ 85364.

McCracken, John R. (Ja. 4, 1941, Victoria, TX) Proj. Dir., Coll. of Bus. and Pub. Admin., Univ. of AZ, Dir., Dept. of Mgt. Srvs., City of Yuma, AZ, 1977–78, Dir., Yuma City-Cnty. Lib., 1975–77; Dir., Main Lib., Tucson Pub. Lib., City of Tucson, 1970–74; Coord., Lib. Srvs., Lincoln-Sudbury Reg. HS Dist., 1968–70. **Educ.:** Univ. of CA, Berkeley, 1964–67, BA (Scan.); Univ. of Denver, 1967–68, MLS; Univ. of AZ, 1979–80, MPA. **Orgs.:** ALA: Com. on Accred., visiting team mem. (1973–77); JMRT (Ch., Western States Aff. Com. (1971–73); AASL (Pub. LA Lib. Educ. Div. 1975–78). Southwestern LA: Bibl. Network Resrc. Sharing Int. Grp., Ch. (1976–78). AZ State LA: Jr. AZ Mem., Ch. (1971–72); Conf. Com., Exh. Ch. (1971–74); Pol. and By-Laws Com., Mem. (1972–73). Tucson Area Lib. Cncl.: Subcom. Ch. for Com. Needs (1971–73). Amer. Socty. for Pub. Admin. AZ Educ. Media Assn. Intl. City Mgrs. Assn. Mun. Fin. Off. Assn. **Pubns.:** "Information & Referral in the Public Library," *Roadrunner: AZ State Lib. Ext. Srv.* (Ap. 1976); "Information & Referral in the Public Library Setting," *Ideas for AZ Comnts.* (My. 1976); "Contemporary United States Parole Board Practices." *GPO-(1979) and Univ. of AZ. Press* (1979); reviews. **Activities:** 9; 15, 17, 24; 92 **Addr.:** 1509 S. 8th Ave., Yuma, AZ 85364.

McCrank, Lawrence Joseph (Ap. 17, 1945, Fargo, ND) Asst. Prof., Coll. of Lib. & Info. Srv., Univ. of MD, 1976–; Visit. Prof., Sch. of Lib. Srvs., Univ. of West. ON, 1979; Visit. Lect., Dept. of Hist., Univ. of CA, Berkeley, 1976; Instr., Whitman Coll., 1971–72. **Educ.:** Moorhead State Univ., 1963–67, BA (Hist.); Univ. of KS, 1967–69, MA (Hist.); Univ. of VA, 1969–74, PhD (Hist.); Univ. of OR, 1975–76, MLS; Natl. Arch. & Recs. Srv. Inst. Arch. Admin. **Orgs.:** Assn. for the Bibl. of Hist.: Prog. ch. (1980–81). SAA: Cons. Arch. Lib. Relat. ALA: ACRL, Manpower Task Force; Prsrvn.; Rare books and Mss. Amer. Hist. Assn. Amer. Acad. of Resrch. Histns. on Medieval Spain. **Honors:** ALA, Essay Awd., *American Libraries* 1977. **Pubns.:** Ed., *Automating the Archives: Current Issues and Future Problems* (1981); *Education for Rare book Librarianship: A Re-examination of Trends and Problems* (1980); "Conservation Education....," *Jnl. of Educ. for Libnshp.* (1981); "Archival Education: Prospects for Integrating Historical & Information Studies," *Amer. Archvst.* (1980); Other articles; videotapes. **Activities:** 1, 2, 11; 17, 23, 26, 45; 55, 57 **Addr.:** College of Library & Information Services, University of Maryland, College Park, MD 20742.

McCray, Jeanette Conover (Ja. 5, 1949, Miami, FL) Assoc. Libn./Head of Pub. Srvs., Univ. of AZ Hlth. Sci. Ctr. Lib., 1981–, Asst. Libn., 1976–81, Ref. Libn., 1974–76; Chief Libn., St. Louis Med. Socty., 1972–74. **Educ.:** Emory Univ., 1967–71, BA (Phys.); Case West. Reserve Univ., 1971–72, MS (LS). **Orgs.:** Med. LA: Murray Gottlieb Prize Subcom. (1979–83). Med. Lib. Grp. of South. CA and AZ. ALA: ACRL. AZ LA. Health Sciences OCLC Users Group. **Honors:** Natl. Lib. of Med., Natl. Inst. of Hlth., Med. Libnshp. Training Awd., 1971–72. **Pubns.:** Cmplr. *Union list of Serials in the St. Louis Metropolitan Area,* (1974); "Laennec's Stethoscope," *Bltn. of the Cleveland Med. Lib.* (O. 1979). **Addr.:** University of Arizona Health Sciences Center Library, 1501 N. Campbell Ave., Tucson, AZ 85724.

McCray, Maceo Edward (F. 10, 1935, Bucksport, SC) Assoc. Libn., Hlth. Sci. Libs., Howard Univ., 1975–, Serials Libn., Med.-Den. Lib., 1965–75. Circ. Asst., Founders Lib., Howard Univ. 1962–64. **Educ.:** SC State Coll., Orangeburg, 1952–56, BS

PROFESSIONAL ACTIVITIES: Institutions: 1. Acad. lib.; 2. Arch.; 3. Assn.; 4. Fed./Gvt. lib.; 5. Inst. lib.; 6. Mfr./Suppl.; 7. Milit. lib.; 8. Musm.; 9. Pub. lib.; 10. Sch. lib.; 11. Sch. of lib. sci.; 12. Spec. lib.; 13. State lib.; 14. (other). **Functions/Activities:** 15. Acq./Col. dev.; 16. Adult srvs.; 17. Admin.; 18. Apprais.; 19. Archit./Bldgs.; 20. Cat./Class.; 21. Chld. srvs.; 22. Circ.; 23. Cons./Pres.; 24. Consult.; 25. Cont. ed.; 26. Educ. lib. sci.; 27. Ext. srvs.; 28. Fund/Grants; 29. Gvt. pubs.; 30. Indx./Abs.; 31. Instr. lib. use; 32. Media srvs.; 33. Micro.; 34. Netwks./Coop.; 35. Persnl.; 36. PR; 37. Publshg.; 38. Recs. mgt.; 39. Ref. srvs.; 40. Repro.; 41. Resrch.; 42. Review.; 43. Secur.; 44. Serials; 45. Spec. col.; 46. Tech. srvs.; 47. Trustees/Bds.; 48. YA srvs.; 49. (other).

(Ind. Educ.); Howard Univ., 1959–62, BD (Theo.); Univ. of MD, College Park, 1969, MLS; Univ. of Southern CA, Los Angeles, 1970 (Info. Sci.), Drexel Inst. of Tech., Philadelphia, 1964–65 (Lib. Sci.); DC Tchrs. Coll., 1968–69. **Orgs.:** Med. LA: Ad Hoc Com., Goals and Struc. (1970–72). ALA. MLA Mid-Atl. Reg. Grp. Urban League. Big Brothers of Amer. **Activities:** 1, 12; 15, 39; 56, 57, 80 **Addr.:** 3818 - 5th St., N.W., Washington, DC 20011.

McCrea, Katherine L. (O. 4, 1926, Egg Harbor City, NJ) Med. Libn., Nesbitt Meml. Hosp., 1970–; Libn., Hackensack Hosp. Assn., 1965–70; Ref. Libn., Lancaster Free Lib., 1948–50. **Educ.:** Douglass Coll., Rutgers Univ., 1944–48, BA (LS); Med. LA, 1975, Cert. **Orgs.:** Med. LA. Hlth. Info. Lib. Netwk. of N. East. PA: Secy.-Treas. (1975–76), Ch. (1977–80). **Activities:** 12; 17, 20, 39; 80 **Addr.:** Nesbitt Memorial Hospital, 562 Wyoming Ave., Kingston, PA 18704.

McCready, R. R. (F. 21, 1925, OR) Head, Archit. and Arts Lib., Univ. of OR, 1976–, Head, Gen. Ref. Div., 1970–76, Gen. Ref. Div. Libn., 1961–70. **Educ.:** John Brown Univ., 1950, BA (Relig. Educ.); Univ. of Denver, 1960–61, MA (LS). **Orgs.:** OR LA. ARLIS/NA. Assn. of Archit. Sch. Libn.: West. Reg., Dir. (1980–81). **Activities:** 1, 12; 17, 19; 55 **Addr.:** University of Oregon Library, Eugene, OR 97403.

McCree, Mary Lynn (Mr. 25, 1937, Effingham, IL) Ms. Libn., Cur., Jane Addams Hull-House, Univ. of IL, Chicago, 1966–; Ed., Papers of Jane Addams, 1975–; Dir., Chicago Sch. of Archit. Fndn., 1975–76; Dir. Resrch., Civil War Centennial Comsn., IL, 1964–65; Arch. Asst. IV, Asst. to Prog. Dir., IL State Arch., 1960–64. **Educ.:** Auburn Univ., 1955–59, BA (Hist.); Univ. of IL, Urbana, 1959–60, MA (Soc. Sci.); Univ. of IL Ext., Springfield, 1960–63 (Pub. Admin.); Univ. of Chicago Grad. Sch. of Bus., 1973–75, MBA (Exec. Prog.). **Orgs.:** Midwest Arch. Conf.: Steering Com. (1971–72); Cncl. (1972–73). Ms. Socty. Newberry Lib. Assoc. SAA: Exec. Com. (1973–1974, 1977–) Com. on Ref., Access, and Photoduplication Policies (Ch., 1970–73); Treas., (1977–81). Natl. Hist. Pubns. and Records Comsn. IL State Hist. Records Adv. Bd. IL State Arch. Adv. Bd. Natl. Endow. for Human.: Internal Review Panel Resrch. Div. (1975–78). **Honors:** SAA, Fellow; Frnds. of Lit., Disting. Book Awd., 1970. **Pubns.:** Jt. auth., *Eighty Years at Hull-House* (1969); jt. auth. *Prairie State, Impression of Illinois, 1673–1967* (1968); "The First Year of Hull-House, 1889–1890, in Letters by Jane Addams and Ellen Gates Starr," *Chicago Hist.* (1970); *Guide to Records Holdings, Illinois State Archives*, guide (1964); jt. auth., *Archival and Manuscript Resources for the Study of Women's History: A Beginning*, guide (Ap. 1972); various speeches. **Activities:** 2, 5; 17, 23, 24; 55, 63, 86 **Addr.:** University of Illinois at Chicago Circle Campus, Box 4348, Chicago, IL 60680.

McCrimmon, Barbara S. (My. 3, 1918, Anoka, MN) Self-empl., 1978–; Adj. Asst. Prof., FL State Univ., Sch. LS, 1976–77; Actg. Managing Ed., *Jnl. Lib. Hist.*, 1973–74, Ed. Asst., 1967–69; Libn., Amer. Meteorological Socty., 1965–67; Libn., IL State Water Srvy., 1964–65. **Educ.:** Univ. of MN, 1935–39, BA (Fine Art); Univ. of IL, 1959–61, MS (LS); FL State Univ., 1969–73, PhD. **Orgs.:** ALA. Beta Phi Mu: Gamma Chap., Nom. Com. (1980–81); VP (1978–79), Pres. (1979–80). Mss. Socty.: Dir. (1974–75); VP (1975–78); Pres. (1978–80). Bibl. Socty. Amer. Bibl. Socty. Private LA. Ephemera Socty. **Pubns.:** *Power, Politics & Print: The Publication of the British Museum Catalogue 1881–1900* (1981); *American Library History: An Anthology* (1975); "Victoria Woodhull Sues the British Museum for Libel," *Lib. Qtly.* (O. 1975); "Nineteenth Century'Swingers': The Movable Press at the British Museum," *Lib. Review* (Aut. Win. 1975–76); other pubns. Reviews. **Activities:** 1; 45, 47; 57 **Addr.:** 1330 West Indian Head Dr., Tallahassee, FL 32301.

McCrosky, Janet Ellen (Mr. 2, 1933, Springfield, OH) Order Libn. and Asst. Catlgr., Warder Pub. Lib., 1957–; Ref. Asst., Warder Pub. Lib., 1955–57. **Educ.:** Wittenberg Univ., 1950–54, BA (Eng.) BS in Educ.; Univ. of Pittsburgh, 1954–55, MLS. **Orgs.:** ALA: RTSD; RASD. OH LA: Secy., Div. 3 (1977); Action Cncl., Div. 7 (1979–81). OH Gen. Socty.: Clark Cnty. Chap. Treas. of Atlas sales (1974); Chap. Treas. (1975); Recording Secy. (1976, 1977); VP (1978). Friends of the Lib. Gen. Resrch. Gp. (Secy./Treas. (1974–). **Honors:** Beta Phi Mu. **Pubns.:** *Index to The Trumbo family* (1978); short stories, poems, etc. **Activities:** 9; 20, 38, 46; 69 **Addr.:** 480 Forest Dr., Springfield, OH 45505.

McCrossan, John A. (D. 20, 1930, Duluth, MN) Ch., Grad. Dept. of Lib., Media, and Info. Std., Univ. of S. FL, 1979–, Assoc. Prof., 1977–79; State Libn., VT State Dept. of Libs., 1973–77; Coord., Interlib. Coop. and Pub. Lib. Consult., PA State Lib., 1970–73; Asst. Prof., Sch. of Lib. Sci., Univ. of MI, 1968–70. **Educ.:** Univ. of MN, 1956–59, BA, 1959–60, MALS; Univ. of IL, 1963–66, PhD (Lib. Sci.). **Orgs.:** ALA: Cncl. (1979–83); Ch., Resrch. Com. (1979–81). **Honors:** Phi Beta Kappa, 1959; Beta Phi Mu, 1960; Lambda Alpha Psi, 1959. **Pubns.:** Ed. *Lib. Trends* (1978); "Public Library Systems and Networks," in *Ency. of Lib and Info. Sci.* (1981); "The Role of Library Systems and Networks in Local Library Services," in *Local Pub. Lib. Admin., ALA* (1980). **Activities:** 9, 12; 16, 26, 39; 50, 78, 89 **Addr.:** Graduate Dept. of Library, Media, and Information Studies HMS301, University of South Florida, Tampa, FL 33620.

McCuaig, Helen E. (D. 21, 1922, Apple Hill, Ont.) Data Base Srvs. Libn., Dept. of the Environment, 1972–; Info. Retr. Spec., Dept. of Ext. Aff., 1971–72. **Educ.:** Carleton Univ., ONT., 1966–68, BA (Eng.); Univ. of Western Ont., 1969–70, MLS. **Orgs.:** ASIS. Can. Socty. for Info. Sci. Can. Assn. of Spec. Libs. and Info. Srvs. Can. Fed. of Univ. Women. **Pubns.:** "Navigating Your Way through Oceanic Abstracts," Database. (S. 1978); "Merging Environment Canada's Library Mosaic," *Natl. Lib. News,* (Ja.-F. 1975); "Use of a thesaurus," (In Proc. ASIS) (1973); Proc. ASIS 36th Ann. Mt. (1973). **Activities:** 4, 12; 65, 75, 82 **Addr.:** 195 Clearview Ave., Apt. 1121, Ottawa, ON K1Z 6S1 Canada.

McCully, William C., Jr. (S. 15, 1947, Richmond Heights, MO) Dir., Pekin Pub. Lib., 1975–; Dir., Everett M. Dirksen Congsnl. Leadership Resrch. Ctr., 1976–78. **Educ.:** Univ. of Notre Dame, Notre Dame, IN, 1965–69, BA (Hist.), 1969–73, MA (Mod. European Hist.); PhD (Mod. European Hist.); Univ. of IL, 1974–75, MSLS. **Orgs.:** IL Valley Lib. Syst.: Bd. Mem. (1980–). ALA. IL LA. Amer. Hist. Assn. Socty. for Fr. Hist. Std. Kiwanis Clb. **Activities:** 9; 17, 35, 42; 55, 56 **Addr.:** Pekin Public Library, 301 S. 4th St., Pekin, IL 61554.

McCune, Lois Maughan (S. 12, 1941, Morris, MN) Cat. Consult., Autom. Prcs. Dept., IN Univ. Lib., 1977–, Sr. Catlgr., 1964–77. **Educ.:** Wilmington Coll., 1959–63, BA (Eng./Art); IN Univ., 1963–64, MALS. **Orgs.:** ALA. IN LA. **Honors:** IN Univ. Flwshp. 1963. **Pubns.:** Ed. *West of the Pomme de Terre,* (1974). **Activities:** 1; 20, 34, 46; 56 **Addr.:** 5771 E. King Rd., Bloomington, IN 47401.

McCusker, Sr. M. Lauretta, OP (Ja. 18, 1919, Sillery, PQ) Dean, Grad. Sch. of LS, Rosary Coll., 1971–, Dir., Prof., 1967–70; Visit. Prof., Univ. of MN, 1958–59; Asst. Prof., IA State Tchrs. Coll., 1948–59; Libn., McDonogh Milit. Sch., 1944–47; Libn., Annapolis HS, 1942–44. **Educ.:** West. MD Coll., 1942, BA; Columbia Univ., 1963, DLS. **Orgs.:** ALA: Cncl. (1979–1983); Scarecrow Press Awd. Jury (1973); Ch., Coll. Lib. Assn. (1972–1974); Legis. Com., Lib. Educ. Div. (1968–1969, Ch., 1970–73). Cath. LA: Ch., elect, Lib. Educ. Com. (1979–); Adv. Cncl. (1967–). IL LA. ASIS. Other orgs. Bus. & Prof. Women's Club. Zonta Intl. AAUP. **Honors:** Beta Phi Mu. **Pubns.:** Jt. auth., "Rosary College Grad. School of Lib. Sc.", *Cath. Lib. World* (O. 1976); "Rosary College Grad. School of Lib. Sci.", *Lib. Scene* (Sum. 1973); "Rosary College Graduate School of Library Science," *Encyclopedia of Library and Information Science.* Ed., *Seminar on Library Automation* (1966); "Implications of Automation for School Libraries," *School Libraries* (Fall, 1967); Other articles. **Activities:** 11; 26 **Addr.:** Rosary College, Graduate School of Library Science, 7900 W. Division St., River Forest, IL 60305.

McCutcheon, Dianne E. (Mr. 8, 1952, Cleveland, OH) Dir., Med. Lib., Kaiser Fndn. Hosps., 1982–; Syst. Libn., Natl. AV Ctr., Natl. Lib. Med., 1981–82; Libn., Natl. Lib. Med., 1979–80, Lib. Assoc., 1978–79; Libn., Bazzell-Phillips and Assoc., 1978. **Educ.:** Cleveland State Univ., 1974–77, BA (Psy.); Univ. IL, 1977–78, MS (LS). **Orgs.:** Med. LA. ASIS. World Future Socty. **Honors:** Dept. Hlth. Educ. Welfare, Spec. Achvmt., 1980. **Pubns.:** Jt. Auth., "Some Achievements and Limitations of Quantitative Procedures Applied to the Evaluation of Library Services," in *Quantitative Measurement and Dynamic Library Services* (1978). **Activities:** 4, 12; 34, 56; 80 **Addr.:** Medical Library, Kaiser Foundation Hospital, 12301 Snow Rd., Parma, OH 44130.

McDavid, Michael W. (Mr. 31, 1946, Greenville, SC) Corp. Libn., Equifax, Inc, 1978–; Ref. Libn., GA State Univ., 1975–78; Archvst., GA Dept. of Arch., 1973–75. **Educ.:** Furman Univ., 1964–68, BA (Hist.); Emory Univ., 1968–73, MA (Hist.), MLn (Libnshp.). **Orgs.:** SLA: Pres.-elect, S. Atl. chap. (1979–). SELA: Interstate Coop. com. (1978–). GA LA: vice-ch., Ref. Srvs. Sect. (1979–). **Pubns.:** "Beyond Faculty Status: Creating a Library Constitution," *Southeast. Libn.* (1979); Ed., Index to the *Atlanta Constitution* (1976–78). **Activities:** 1, 12; 15, 17, 39; 51, 59, 76 **Addr.:** Equifax Inc, Library, P.O. Box 4081, Atlanta, GA 30302.

McDavid, Sara June (D. 21, 1945, Atlanta, GA) Mgr., Mem. Srvs., SOLINET, 1981–; Head Libn., Fed. Rsv. Bank of Atlanta, 1977–81; Head Libn., Fernbank Sci. Ctr., 1969–77; Asst. Libn., GA Power Co. 1968–69. **Educ.:** Mercer Univ., 1963–67, BA (Eng.); Emory Univ., 1968–69, M Libn. (LS), 1976, Med. Lib. Cert. **Orgs.:** SLA: S. Atl. Chap. (Pres., 1975–76), VP (1974–75), Bio. Sci. Div., Bltn. Ed. (1977–1978); Phys. Astr. Math. Div., Proj. Ch. (1973–1974), Nom. Com. (1974–75, Ch., 1975). GA LA. SELA. Southeast. Lib. Netwk.: Bd. of Dirs. (1977–1980); Bd. Vice-Ch. (1979–1980). Women's Auxiliary, Atlanta Humane Socty. Pub. Rel. Ch. (1976–1978); Bd. of Dirs. (1976–1980); First VP (1981–82). **Pubns.:** "Research Skills Take the Pain Out of Science Projects," *Sci. Actv.* (N./D. 1976); "Astronomy Materials Available for Display," *SLA Phys. Ast., Math. Div. Bltn.* (S., D. 1974); *Prescription for Painless Science Projects,* pamphlet 1974; *Steps to a Successful Science Project,* kit (1976). **Activities:** 4, 12; 15, 17, 39; 58, 59, 88 **Addr.:** SOLINET, 400 Colony Sq., 1201 Peachtree St., NE, Atlanta, GA 30361.

McDermand, Robert V. (F. 18, 1941, Davenport, IA) Assoc. Prof./Coord., Pub. Srvs., Plymouth State Coll., 1968–; Head Tchr., Hist. Dept., Keota HS, 1964–67. **Educ.:** Cornell Coll., 1959–63, BA (Hist.); Univ. of IA, 1967–68, MA (LS). **Orgs.:** Acad. Libns. of NH: Ch. (1972–73). NH LA: State Dir., Natl. Lib. Week (1971–72). New Eng. OLUG: Admin./Mgt. Com. Kappa Delta Pi. **Pubns.:** "Marketing, Publicity And Other Public Service Aspects of On-Line Searching" in *Aspects of Information Service Management* (1979). **Activities:** 1; 22, 31, 39; 67 **Addr.:** Lamson Library, Plymouth State College, Plymouth, NH 03264.

McDermott, Margaret Helen (F. 27, 1947, Forest City, IA) Ref.-Readers Srvs. Libn., Washington Univ. Law Lib., 1981–; Ref. Libn., Washington Univ., 1971–81. **Educ.:** Barat Coll., 1965–69, BA (Pol. Sci.); Univ. of IL, 1969–71, MLS; Univ. MO (St. Louis), 1980– (Pol. Sci.). **Orgs.:** ALA. MO LA. St. Louis OLUG. St. Louis Reg. Lib. Netwk.: Info. Srv. Com. (Ch.). **Activities:** 1, 4; 29, 31, 39; 56, 75, 78 **Addr.:** Washington University Law Library, Washington University, St. Louis, MO 63130.

McDiarmid, Errett Weir (Jl. 13, 1909, Beckley, WV) Prof. Emeritus, Univ. of MN Lib. Sch., 1963–, Dean, Coll. of Sci., Lit. and the Arts, 1951–63, Univ. Libn., Dir., Div. of Lib. Instr., 1943–51; Assoc., Asst. Prof., Asst. Dir., Univ. of IL Lib. Sch., 1937–43; Libn., Baylor Univ., 1934–37. **Educ.:** TX Christ. Univ., 1925–29, AB (Hist.), 1929–30, AM (Hist.); Emory Univ., 1930–31, AB (LS); Univ. of Chicago, 1931–34, PhD. **Orgs.:** ALA: Pres. (1948–49); ACRL (Pres., 1947–48). Assn. of MN Colls.: Pres. (1962–63). MN Com. for UNESCO. AAUP: Cncl. (1941–44). **Pubns.:** *The Library Survey* (1939); Jt. auth., *The Administration of the American Public Library* (1941); publshr., *Cultivating Sherlock Holmes* (1979); various articles. **Addr.:** 1473 Fulham St., St. Paul, MN 55108.

McDonald, Ann M. (Jersey City, NJ). Libn., Metro. Transp. Athty., 1967–80; Lectr., Pratt Inst. Grad. Lib. Sch., 1967; Libn., Tatham Laird and Kudner, 1965–67; Libn., Un. Carbide Corp., Chemicals Div., 1957–65; Methods Anal., Reuben H. Donnelly Corp., 1953–57; Consult., WHO, Geneva, Switzerland, 1950; Libn., Ballard Sch., Young Women's Christ. Assn., Lib. Trng. Prog., 1949. **Educ.:** Columbia Univ., 1947; NY Univ., 1949; City Coll. of NY, 1959; Pratt Inst., 1963. **Orgs.:** Assn. of Recs. Mgrs. and Admins.: Pres. (1948–50). SLA. **Activities:** 12, 13; 17, 20, 24; 51, 60, 94 **Addr.:** 119 Washington Pl., New York, NY 10014.

McDonald, Arlys L. (Ja. 6, 1932, Edison, NE) Assoc. Libn. and Msc. Lib. Head, AZ State Univ., 1968–; Asst. Prof. of Msc., St. Mary of the Plains, 1965–68; Instr., Sacred Heart, Dodge City, KS, 1962–63; Tchr., Various Elem. Sch., 1951–61. **Educ.:** St. Mary of the Plains Coll., 1952–63, BMus (Msc.); Univ. of IL, 1963–65, MMus (Msc.); N. TX State Univ., Msc. Lib. Workshop, 1969. **Orgs.:** Msc. LA. Intl. Assn. of Msc. Libs. AZ LA. **Activities:** 1; 15, 17, 39; 55 **Addr.:** 2700 E. Allred D-47, Mesa, AZ 85204.

McDonald, Dana M. (Ag. 3, 1931, Pontiac, MI) Ch., Dept. of Info. and Comm. Scis., S. IL Univ. Sch. of Med., 1979–; Dir. and Prof., Med. Lib., S. IL Univ. Sch. of Med., 1978–79; Branch Libn. and Prof. of Lib. Admin., Rockford Sch. of Med., Univ. of IL, 1973–78; Med. Libn. S. IL Univ., 1970–73. **Educ.:** Purdue Univ., 1949–52, BS summa cum laude, (Chem.); IN Univ., 1968–69, MLS. Univ. of TN, 1970–71, Sci. Libnshp. Cert.; Univ. of IL, 1970–71, Mgt. Cert.; Med. Lib. Assn., 1975, Cert. **Orgs.:** Med. LA: Honors and Awds. Com. (Ch., 1980–81); Rittenhouse Awd. Subcom. (1978–81, Ch., 1981). Midwest Hlth. Sci. Lib. Netwk.: Asm. Ch. 1981–82; ILL Com. (Ch., 1977–). Med. LA: Midwest Reg. Grp. Pres. (1976), Exec. Com. (1974–78), Cncl. Rep. (1981–82). Tri-State Hosp. Asm.: Lib. Conf. (Ch., 1978). Univ. of IL Med. Ctr.: Sen. Com. on Budgetary Matters (1978–79). **Honors:** Univ. of IL, Rockford Sch. of Med., Exec. Com. Cmdn., 1976; Univ. of TN, Cert. of Excel., 1970. **Activities:** 1, 12; 15, 17, 19; 80, 87, 91 **Addr.:** Southern Illinois University, School of Medicine Library, 801 N. Rutledge St., Springfield, IL 62702.

McDonald, David R. (Mr. 9, 1950, Los Angeles, CA) Syst. Libn., Stanford Univ. Libs., 1979–, Cubberley Ref. Libn., 1978–79; Soc. Sci. Biblgphr., KS State Univ. Lib., 1976–78. **Educ.:** CA State Univ., Long Beach, 1970–73, BA (Anthro.); WA State Univ., 1973–74, MA (Anthro); Univ. of OR, 1974–75, MLS. **Orgs.:** ALA: Resol. Com. (1979–1981); ACRL, Appt. & Nom. Com. (1978–1980); RASD, Ch., Amer. Indian Matls. & Srv. Com. (1977–79); Nom. Com. (1978–1979); ACRL, Ch., Anthr. Sect. Nom. Com. (1978–79); Bibl. Instr. Sect., Educ. for Bibl. Instr. Com. (1977–78). **Pubns.:** *Masters' Theses in Anthropology: A Bibliography of Theses from U.S. Colleges and Universities* (1977); "Food Taboos a Primitive Environmental Protection Agency," *Anthropos* (72:734–748); "Native American Fishing/Hunting Rights: an Annotated Bibliography," *Indian Histn.* (1978); jt. auth., "The Reference Library: Resource for the Small Business", *Journal of Small Business Management* (1979);

Special Subjects/Services: 50. Adult educ.; 51. Advert./Mktg.; 52. Aerosp.; 53. Agric.; 54. Area std.; 55. Arts/Hum.; 56. Autom.; 57. Bibl./Prtg.; 58. Bio. sci.; 59. Bus./Fin.; 60. Chem.; 61. Copyrt.; 62. Documtn.; 63. Educ.; 64. Engin.; 65. Env.; 66. Eth. grps.; 67. Film; 68. Food/Nutr.; 69. Geneal.; 70. Geo.; 71. Geol.; 72. Handcpd.; 73. Hist.; 74. Int. frdm.; 75. Info. sci.; 76. Insr.; 77. Law; 78. Legis.; 79. Math./Comp. sci.; 80. Med.; 81. Metals; 82. Nat. resrcs.; 83. Newsp.; 84. Nuc. sci.; 85. Oral hist.; 86. Petr./Energy; 87. Pharm.; 88. Phys./Astr./Math.; 89. Readg.; 90. Relig.; 91. Sci./Tech.; 92. Soc. sci.; 93. Telecom.; 94. Transp.; 95. (other).

jt. auth., "Sequential Sampling: Methodology for Monitoring Approval Plans", *Coll. & Resrch. Libs.* (1979); other articles. **Activities:** 1; 17, 39, 41; 56, 92, 95 **Addr.:** Systems Office, Stanford University Libraries, Stanford, CA 94305.

McDonald, Dennis Damian (My. 1, 1949, Columbus, OH) VP, King Resrch., Inc., 1979–, Resrch. Assoc., 1975–79; Resrch. Assoc., Market Facts, Inc., 1974–75; Lib. Consult., Westat, Inc., 1974. **Educ.:** OH State Univ., 1967–71, BA (Psy.); Univ. of MD, 1971–73, MLS, 1973–79, PhD (Lib. and Info. Sci.). **Orgs.:** ASIS: SIG/IGP Nsltr. Ed. (1978–79); Pub. Affairs Com. (Ch. 1981–82). Socty. for Scholarly Publshg. Assn. Info. Mngrs. AAAS. **Activities:** 14-Resrch./Consult. Firm; 24, 41; 61, 75, 95-Scholarly Jnls. **Addr.:** 3908 Valley Dr., Alexandria, VA 22302.

McDonald, Eloise E. (Ag. 19, 1948, Little Rock, AR) Head, Fine Arts Lib., Univ. of AR, 1976–; Msc. Libn., Univ. of WI, Milwaukee, 1974–76. **Educ.:** Henderson State Univ., 1966–70, BM (Piano); LA State Univ., 1970–74, MA (Msc. Hist.), MLS. **Orgs.:** AR LA. ALA. SWLA. Msc. LA. **Honors:** Beta Phi Mu. **Pubns.:** "Program Notes" *North Arkansas Symphony* (1977–); Photographs *Arkansas Libraries,* (D. 1978). **Activities:** 1, 12; 17, 22, 39; 55, 65 **Addr.:** Fine Arts Library, FA-104, U of A, Fayetteville, AR 72701.

McDonald, John F. (O. 31, 1949, Toronto, Ont.) Data Archvst., Mach. Readable Arch. Pub. Arch. of Can., 1975–; Info. Retrieval, Environment Can., 1975. **Educ.:** Carleton Univ., Ottawa, 1976–80, MA (Hist. Geo.). **Orgs.:** Intl. Assn. for Soc. Sci. Info. Srv. and Tech.: Educ. Com. Records Mgt. Inst. Data Prcs. Inst.: Data Base Sub-Grp. Assn. of Can. Archvsts. Assn. for Comps. and Hum. **Activities:** 2; 15, 23, 38; 56, 75, 92 **Addr.:** Machine Readable Archives, Public Archives Canada, 395 Wellington St., Ottawa, ON K1A 0N3 Canada.

McDonald, John P. (O. 17, 1922, Philadelphia, PA) Dir. of Univ. Lib., Univ. of CT, 1963–; Exec. Dir., ARL, 1974–76; Assoc. Dir. of Lib., Washington Univ. (St. Louis), 1959–63, Various positions, 1954–59; various positions, Univ. of PA Libs., 1949–54. **Educ.:** Univ. of VA, 1940–46, AB (Eng.); Drexel Univ., 1950–51, MSLS; Rutgers Univ., Carnegie Flw., Metcalf Prog., 1958. **Orgs.:** ALA: Nom. Com. (1967–68); Cncl., (1962–66); LAD, Bd. of Dir. (1962–66); ACRL, various positions. ARL: Bd. of Dir. (1969–72); Pres. (1971). New England LA: Various ofc. and Com. CT LA: various ofc. and com. Pub. Affairs Info. Srv.: Bd. of Dir. (1976–). H. W. Wilson Co.: Bd. of Dir. (1978–). **Honors:** Phi Kappa Phi, 1951; Drexel Univ., Sch. of Lib. and Info. Sci., Disting. Alumnus Awd., 1975; WHCOLIS, Del., 1979. **Pubns.:** Contrib., *Scholarly Communication: The Report of the National Enquiry,* (1979); Contrib., *American Libraries as Centers of Scholarship* (1978); Contrib., *Research Universities in the National Interest: A Report from Fifteen University Presidents* (1977); "Problems Needing Attention," in *Library Resource Sharing* (1976); "Interlibrary Cooperation in the United States," in *Issues in Library Administration* (1974); various other articles. **Activities:** 1, 3; 17, 19, 24; 61 **Addr.:** 18 Westwood Rd., Storrs, CT 06268.

McDonald, Joseph (Jl. 10, 1942, Buenos Aires, Argentina) Dir. of the Lib., Long Island Univ./Brooklyn Ctr., 1981–; Asst. Dir. of Libs. for Access Srvs., SUNY, Albany, 1978–80; Dir., Lib. Srvs., Triton Coll., 1975–77; Asst. Dir. of Lib. Srvs. for Pub. Srvs., Stockton State Coll., 1972–75; Head Libn., Asst. Prof. of LS, NCA Cmnty. Coll., 1970–72; Docum. Libn., Asst. Prof., West Chester State Coll., 1968–70; Head, Bus. and Tech. Dept., Wilmington Inst. Free Lib., 1967–68. **Educ.:** Eastern Coll., 1959–63, AB (Eng/Phil.); Drexel Univ., 1963–66, MSLS. **Orgs.:** ALA: LAMA, Bldgs. for Coll. & Univ. Libs. Com. (1979–); ACRL. **Pubns.:** *Public Library Architecture* (1967); "Kingdom of God and Library Science," *Reformed Jnl.* (D. 1979); "How I Got My Library Job Good," *Lib. Jnl.* (F. 1, 1973); "This is Kim..." sound-on-slide program (1971); "Rights in Conflict and Rights in Conflict," *RQ,* (Win., 1969). **Addr.:** P.O. Box 402, Pineville, PA 18946.

McDonald, Judith L. (Ja. 17, 1939, Rockville, NE) Dean, Lib. and Lib. Srv., Bemidji State Univ., 1977–; Admin. Asst., Univ. of NE, 1975–77; Assoc. Libn., Chadron State Coll., 1968–74; Lrng. Ctr. Coord., State Univ. of NE, 1974–75. **Educ.:** Univ. of NE, 1961–65, BA (Eng./Hist.); Denver Univ., 1969–72, MA (LS); Univ. of NE, 1975–80, PhD (Cmnty. & Human Resrc.). **Orgs.:** ALA. MN LA. MN Educ. Media Org. West. Hist. Assn. **Pubns.:** "Song of the Plains," TV Documentary (1979). **Activities:** 1; 17, 26, 32; 50, 63, 93 **Addr.:** Library, Bemidji State University, Bemidji, MN 56601.

McDonald, Marilyn M. (My. 24, 1935, Scranton, PA) Sr. Libn., SRI Intl. Lib., 1980–; Ofc. Mgr., Stanford Alum. Assn., 1979–80; Libn., Palo Alto Unfd. Sch. Dist., 1976–79; Libn., San Jose Unfd. Sch. Dist., 1975–76. **Educ.:** Stanford Univ., 1953–57, BA (Econ.), 1958–62, MA (Econ.); San Jose State Univ., 1972–75, MLS. **Orgs.:** ALA. CA Media and Lib. Educs. Assn. SLA. Leag. of Women Voters. **Honors:** Beta Phi Mu, 1975. **Activities:** 10, 12; 20, 39, 44; 59, 63, 92 **Addr.:** SRI International Library, 333 Ravenswood Ave., Menlo Park, CA 94025.

McDonald, Mary Lucy (RSM) (Ap. 9, 1911, Grand Rapids, MI) Prov. Archvst., Srs. of Mercy, Prov. of Detroit, 1969–; Tchr.–Libn., Mount Mercy, Grand Rapids, MI, 1968–74; Tchr.–Libn., St. John HS, Independence, IA, 1965–68; Tchr.–Libn., St. Michael, Pinconning, MI, 1962–65. **Educ.:** Mercy Coll., Detroit, MI, 1941–45, AB (Latin, Eng.); Univ. of MI, 1945–48, ABLS, 1962–64, AMLS, 1965–68 MA (Eng.); Wayne State Univ. 1976–77 (Arch. Prog.). **Orgs.:** SAA: Relig. Arch. Com. MI Arch. Assn.: Exec. Bd. (1980–83). Midwest Arch. Conf.: Relig. Arch. Panel (1980). Cath. LA: Nsltr. Ed. (1971–75); Secy.–Treas. (1979–). **Pubns.:** Ed., Prov. Nsltr., *Mercy Detroiter* (1969–74); *By Her Fruits: S.M. Joseph Lynch, Sister of Mercy* (1981); various articles and reviews, 1969–. **Activities:** 2; 17, 24, 41; 63, 86, 90 **Addr.:** 29000 Eleven Mile, Farmington Hills, MI 48018.

McDonald, Patricia Eileen (My. 6, 1941, Mitchell, SD) Lib. Dir., Yankton Coll., 1971–, Catlgr., 1970–71; Eng. Tchr., Denver Pub. Sch., 1963–66 & '69–'70; Eng. Tchr., Sacramento Pub. Sch., 1966–68. **Educ.:** SD State Univ., 1959–63, BS (Eng.); Univ. of Denver, 1968–69, MA (LS). **Orgs.:** SD LA. Yankton LA: Pres. (1973) Secy.-Treas. (1971–72). Colls. of Mid America, Lib. Sect.: Indian Std. Com. (1977). Delta Kappa Gamma. Leag. of Women Voters. **Activities:** 1; 17 **Addr.:** Yankton College Library, 1016 Douglas, Yankton, SD 57078.

McDonald, Stanley Montrose, Jr. (Ag. 28, 1935, Boston, MA) Lib. Dir., Framingham State Coll., 1971–; Asst. Dir., Wellesley Free Lib. (MA), 1967–71, Ref. Libn., 1962–67; Ref. Libn., Concord Free Pub. Lib. (MA), 1960–61. **Educ.:** Univ. of MA, 1953–58, BA (Eng. Lit.); Univ. of RI, 1966, MLS; Sorbonne Univ., 1958 (Cert. Fr.); Breadloaf Writers Conf., 1962. **Orgs.:** New Eng. LA: Bibl. Com. (1968). MA LA: Exec. Bd. (1969); Nom. Com. (1974–75); Schol. Com. (1972, 1975–77). ALA: ACRL. MA Cncl. Chief Libn. Pub. Higher Educ. Inst.: Prog. Com. (1978–79); Stan. Com. (1971–81); various other com. MA Tchr. Assn. Trout Unlimited. MA Audubon Socty. Cons. Law Fndn. **Honors:** MA LA, Exec. Dir., Natl. Lib. Wk. (MA), 1970. **Activities:** 1; 17, 31, 39; 58, 63, 92 **Addr.:** Henry Whittemore Library, Framingham State College, Framingham Centre, MA 01701.

McDonald, Susan M. (My. 24, 1946, London, Eng.) Supvsr., Info. Srv., Bus. Info. Ctr., Imperial Oil Ltd., 1978–; Head, Tech. Srv., ON Mnstry. Labor, 1977–78; Head, Bibl. Searching, ON Inst. Std. Educ., 1975–77; Libn., Peat, Marwick, Mitchell (London), 1973–75; Head Catlgr., Toronto Bd. Educ., 1969–73. **Educ.:** Univ. Toronto, 1964–68, BA (Eng.), 1968–69, BLS, 1980, MLS. **Orgs.:** SLA: Toronto Chap., OLUG (Treas.). Can. Assn. Info. Sci.: Toronto Chap., Secy./Treas. **Activities:** 12; 39; 59, 86 **Addr.:** Business Information Centre, Imperial Oil Ltd., 111 St. Clair Ave., W., Toronto, ON M5W 1K3 Canada.

McDonell, W. Ellen (N. 18, 1952, Jackson, MS) Inst., Serials Libn., Univ. of TN, Ctr. for the Hlth. Sci., 1978–; Head, Jnl./Serials/Per. Dept. Med. Lib., Univ. of MS Med. Sch., 1976–78; Learning Resrcs. Coord., Hlth. Educ. Cons., Sardis, MS, 1975–76; Libn., Flomaton HS, 1974. **Educ.:** Univ. of MS, 1970–73, BAE (Eng., Lib. Sci.); Univ. of TN, Knoxville, 1974–75, MSLS. Med. LA 1979–84 Cert. **Orgs.:** TN LA: Coord., W. TN Leg. Ntwk. Memphis, Shelby Co. Coord. (1978–79); Coll. and Univ. Sect., Nom. Com. (1979–80); Leg. Com. (1980–83). Med. LA. SLA. Mid-S. Chap. SLA. (Pres.-elect 1981–82). **Honors:** Beta Phi Mu, 1970; Kappa Delta Pi, 1973. **Pubns.:** Jt. Auth. "Time Lag in the 1972 Monthly Catalog of United States Government Publications," *Govt. Pub. Review* (Sum. 1976). **Activities:** 1, 12; 15, 44, 46; 80 **Addr.:** Univ. of Tenn. Center for the Health Sciences Library, 800 Madison Ave., Memphis, TN 38163.

McDonnell, Christine (Jl. 3, 1949, Westhampton, NY) Dir., Cmnty. Prog., Simmons Coll. Ctr., for Study of Chld. Lit., 1979–; Sch. Libn., Arlington (MA) Pub. Schs. 1976–79; Chld. Libn., NY Pub. Lib. 1972–75. **Educ.:** Barnard Coll., 1967–72, BA (Eng.); Columbia Univ., 1972–73, MLS. **Orgs.:** ALA: Caldecott Awd. Comm. (1980). **Pubns.:** Reviews. **Activities:** 1, 12; 21, 25, 27; 50, 63, 89 **Addr.:** Simmons College, Center for the Study of Children's Literature, 300 The Fenway, Boston, MA 02115.

Mc Donnell, Janice M. (Ag. 8, 1945, Philadelphia, PA) Head of Cat. Dept., Temple Univ. Law Lib., 1972–; Part-time Ref. Libn., Cmnty. Coll. of Philadelphia, 1971–72; Libn., Mgt. Concepts, Inc., 1969–70. **Educ.:** W. Chester State Coll., 1963–67, BA (Liberal Arts); Drexel Univ., 1968, MSLS. **Orgs.:** AALL. **Activities:** 1; 20; 77 **Addr.:** Temple University Law Library, 1715 N. Broad St., Philadelphia, PA 19122.

McDonnell, Jeremiah (Jerry) Patrick (My. 22, 1945, Stratford, ON) Tchr. Libn., S. Huron Dist. HS, 1973–; Tchr. Libn., Clarke Rd. Sec. Sch., 1971–73; Tchg. **Educ.:** Univ. West. ON, 1964–67, BA (Hist.), 1967–69, MA (Hist.), 1975–80, MLS, 1970–71, Dip. (Educ.). **Orgs.:** ON Sch. LA: Pubns. Ed. (1974–75); Bd. Educ. Contact (1975–). Can. Sch. LA. ON Sec. Sch. Tchr. Fed., Dist. 45: Col. Bargaining Com. (1980–). **Pubns.:** Reviews. **Activities:** 10; 17, 20, 31, 33; 92 **Addr.:** Resource Centre, South Huron District High School, Exeter, ON N0M 1S0 Canada.

McDonough, Irma K. (N. 19, 1924, Sault Ste Marie, ON) Co-ord., Chld. and Young Peoples' Lib. Srvs., Libs. and Cmnty. Info., Mnstry. of Culture and Recreation, 1965–; Young Peoples' Libn., Toronto Pub. Lib. 1954–64. **Educ.:** Univ. of Toronto, 1946–65, BA, 1965–66 BLS. **Orgs.:** Can. LA: Young Peoples Sect. (Ch., 1965–66). ON LA: Pres. (1970–71); Bd. (1969–1973). Chld. Bk. Ctr.: Bd. Ch. (1977–). **Pubns.:** Ed. and initiator of *In Review: Can. Bks. for Young People* (1967–); Can. ed. of *Twentieth Century Children's Writers* (1978). Ed., *Canadian Books for Children/Livres Canadiens pour enfants* (bibl.) (1976); Ed., *Canadian Books for Young People/Livres canadiens pour la jeunesse* (1976 and 1980 eds.); Ed., *Profiles* (1971 and 1975 eds.). **Activities:** 4, 9; 21, 42, 48 **Addr.:** Ministry of Culture & Recreation, 77 Bloor St. W., Toronto, ON M7A 2R9 Canada.

McDonough, Jean R. (Roberts) (Ap. 24, 1920, Jerome, ID) Lib. Coord., Princeton Reg. Schs., 1966–; Instr., Ext. Div., Trenton State Coll., 1965–68; Instr. (Sum.), Lib. Ext., Univ. of VT, 1964–65; Libn., Princeton HS, 1955–65; Libn., Miss Fine's Sch. (Princeton), 1953–55; Lib. Dir., W. Orange Pub. Lib. (NJ), 1948–51; Asst. Libn., Lib., Fortune Mag., 1946–48; Catlgr., Baker Lib., Harvard Univ., 1944–46. **Educ.:** Wilson Coll., 1938–42, BA (Eng.); Columbia Univ., 1942–43, BS (LS); Rutgers Univ., 1954–57, MS (LS). **Orgs.:** ALA. NJ LA: Legis. Com., Sch. Pub. Lib. Coop. Educ. Media Assn. NJ: Exec. Bd. (1968–73), Sch. Pub. Lib. Coop. Natl. Educ. Assn. NJ Educ. Assn. Princeton Reg. Educ. Assn.: Secy. (1977–79); Pres. (1979–80). Princeton Pub. Lib.: Bd. Trustees, Ch. (1957–60). **Activities:** 10; 17, 21, 32; 63, 89 **Addr.:** 43 Bainbridge St., Princeton, NJ 08540.

McDonough, Roger H. (F. 24, 1909, Trenton, NJ) Consult., Lib./Gvt. Rel., 1975–; Dir., State Libn., NJ State Lib., 1947–75; Dir., New Brunswick Pub. Lib., 1937–47; Ref. Libn., Rutgers Univ. Lib., 1934–37. **Educ.:** Rutgers Univ., 1930–34, AB (Hist); Columbia Univ., 1934–36, BSLS. **Orgs.:** ALA: Pres. (1968–69); Fed. Rel. Com. (Ch., 1956–60); Exec. Bd. (1958–62). Natl. Assn State Libs.: Pres. (1951–52). Westminster Choir Coll.: Trustee (1966–78). NJ Hist. Socty.: Trustee (1958–). **Activities:** 2, 13; 17, 38, 39; 78 **Addr.:** 43 Bainbridge St., Princeton, NJ 08540.

McDougall, Donald Blake (Mr. 6, 1938, Moose-Jaw, SK) Libn., Legis. Lib., 1974–; Head of Pub. Srvs., Edmonton Pub. Lib., 1973–74, Supvsr. of Info. Srvs., 1972–73; Chief Libn., Stratford Pub. Lib., 1970–72, Asst. Chief Libn., 1969. **Educ.:** Univ. of SK, 1956–66, BA (Hist.), 1956–66, BEd; Univ. of Toronto, 1968–69, BLS. **Orgs.:** AB Gvt. Libs. Cncl.: Ch. (1975); Cnclr. (1976). Assn. of Parlmt. Libs. in Canada: VP (1978–1980; Pres. (1980–1982). Edmonton LA. LA AB. Other orgs. Edmonton Antique Car Club. Edmonton Art Gallery. Edmonton Opera Socty. Edmonton Scottish Socty. Other orgs. **Honors:** Gvt. of Canada, Queen's Silver Jubilee Medal, 1977. **Pubns.:** Ed., *A History of the Legislature Library* (1980); Ed., *Alberta Scrapbook Hansard, 1906–1964 (Microfilm version)* (1976). **Activities:** 9, 12; 17, 29, 37; 61, 62, 78 **Addr.:** Legislature Library, 216 Legislature Building, Edmonton, AB T5K 2B6 Canada.

McDougall, Maria Sophie Laddy (D. 25, 1928, St. Paul, AB) Consult. Libn., 1968–; Head, Sci. and Tech. Div., Libn. I, Vancouver Pub. Lib., 1961–66, 1960–61; Jr. Libn., Biomed. Lib., Univ. of BC, 1959–60; Lib. Asst., Sci. and Tech. Dept., Seattle Pub. Lib., 1952–57; Jr. Libn., Fac. of Agr., PA State Univ., 1951. **Educ.:** Univ. of BC, 1946–50, BSA; Univ. of WA, 1950–51, BSL. **Orgs.:** Can. LA. Richmond Pub. Lib.: Trustee (1979–80). Frnds. of the Richmond Libs.: Ch. (1975–76). Polish Can. LA: Secy.-Treas. (1979–80). Univ. Women's Club of Richmond. Grt. Vancouver Mining Women's Assn. **Addr.:** 7720 Sunnydene Rd., Richmond, BC V6Y 1H1 Canada.

Mc Dowell, Judith May Hudson (Ja. 24, 1941, Moline, IL) Educ. Libn., US Dept. Educ., 1974–; Libn., Indus. Comsn. OH, 1974; Ref. Libn., Columbus (OH) Pub. Lib., 1971–74; Ref. Libn., Pub. Lib. DC, 1969–70. **Educ.:** OH Wesleyan Univ., 1958–62, BA (Eng.); Simmons Coll., MS (LS); Harvard Coll., MEd OH State Univ., (Educ.); various tchg. certs. **Orgs.:** SLA: Educ. Sect. ALA: ACRL. World Future Socty. Garrett Park Citizen Assn.: Secy. (1981). Parents Without Partners, Inc.: DC Chap., VP (1978); Columbus Chap., Bd. Mem. (1973). Toastmaster's Intl.: VP (1980); Secy. (1978). **Activities:** 4, 12; 17, 18, 24, 25; 93, 95-Future std. **Addr.:** Box 92, Garrett Park, MD 20896.

McDowell, William Lewis, Jr. (S. 3, 1926, Chester, SC) Deputy Dir., SC Dept. of Arch. & Hist., 1968–, Asst. Dir., 1961–68, Archvst., 1953–60. **Educ.:** Clemson Coll., 1946–49, BS (Hist., Govt.); Univ. of SC, 1952–53, MA (Hist.); Natl. Arch. Mod. Arch. Admin. Inst., 1962; Natl. Arch. Recs. Mgt. Inst., 1964. **Orgs.:** SAA: Prsrvn. Com. (1969–74); Basic Arch. Cons. Wkshp. Prog. Adv. Com. (1980–81). Natl. Assn. State Archvsts. and Recs. Admin. Natl. Micro. Assn. SC Hist. Assn. **Honors:** SAA, Fellow, 1971; Amer. Assn. State & Local Hist., Awd. of Merit, 1971. **Pubns.:** Ed., *Documents Relating to Indian Affairs, 1754–65* (1970); *Documents Relating to Indian Affairs, 1750–54* (1958); *Journal of Commissioners of Indian Trade, 1710–1718* (1955). **Activities:** 2, 14-Recs. Ctr.; 17, 18, 38; 73, 75 **Addr.:** SC Dept. of Archives & History, 1430 Senate St., Columbia, SC 29201.

PROFESSIONAL ACTIVITIES: Institutions: 1. Acad. lib.; 2. Arch.; 3. Assn.; 4. Fed./Gvt. lib.; 5. Inst. lib.; 6. Mfr./Suppl.; 7. Milit. lib.; 8. Musm.; 9. Pub. lib.; 10. Sch. lib.; 11. Sch. of lib. sci.; 12. Spec. lib.; 13. State lib.; 14. (other). **Functions/Activities:** 15. Acq./Col. dev.; 16. Adult srvs.; 17. Admin.; 18. Apprais.; 19. Archit./Bldgs.; 20. Cat./Class.; 21. Chld. srvs.; 22. Circ.; 23. Cons./Pres.; 24. Consult.; 25. Cont. ed.; 26. Educ. lib. sci.; 27. Ext. srvs.; 28. Fund/Grants; 29. Gvt. pubs.; 30. Indx./Abs.; 31. Instr. lib. use; 32. Media srvs.; 33. Micro.; 34. Netwks./Coop.; 35. Persnl.; 36. PR; 37. Publshg.; 38. Recs. mgt.; 39. Ref. srvs.; 40. Repro.; 41. Resrch.; 42. Review.; 43. Secur.; 44. Serials; 45. Spec. col.; 46. Tech. srvs.; 47. Trustees/Bds.; 48. YA srvs.; 49. (other).

McElderry, Margaret K. (Pittsburgh, PA) Dir., Margaret K. McElderry Books/Atheneum Pub., 1971–; Ed., Books for Chld.; Harcourt Brace Jovanovich, 1945–71; Libn. and Chief of Spec. Proj., Off. of War Info., 1943–45; Chld.'s Libn., N.Y. Pub. Lib., 1934–43. **Educ.:** Mt. Holyoke Coll., 1929–33, BA (Eng. Lit.); Carnegie Lib. Sch., 1933–34, BSLS. **Orgs.:** ALA. Chld.'s Book Cncl. **Honors:** Women's Nat. Book Assn. Constance Lindsay Skinner Awd. Doctor of Humane Letters, Mt. Holyoke Coll., 1978. **Activities:** 9, 10; 21, 37 **Addr.:** c/o Atheneum Publishers, 597 Fifth Ave., New York, NY 10017.

McElroy, Elizabeth Warner (Dixon, IL) Head, Chem. Lib., Univ. of MD, 1980–, Chief, HQ Lib., U.S. Env. Pro. Agency, 1977–78; Chief, Silver Spring Lib. Ctr., U.S. Nat. Oceanic and Atmos. Admin., 1969–77; Asst. Libn., J.Walter Thompson Co., 1967–68. **Educ.:** Carleton Coll., BA (Chem.); Univ. of Chicago, 1964–67, MALS. **Orgs.:** SLA: DC Chap. (Dir., 1980–82), Info. Tech. Grp. (Ch., 1979–); Interlib. Loan Com. (1971–76). **Pubns.:** "Subject Variety in Adult Reading," *Lib. Qtly.* (Ap./Je. 1968). **Activities:** 1, 4; 17, 39; 60, 65, 91 **Addr.:** 3016 Tilden St., N.W., Washington, DC 20008.

McElroy, F. Clifford (S. 14, 1923, MA) Sci. Libn., Boston Coll., 1954–. **Educ.:** Boston Coll., 1941–44, AB (Eng.); Simmons Coll., 1954–58, MLS. **Orgs.:** SLA: Boston Chap., Sci. Tech. Div. (Ch., 1969), Manual Rev. Com. (1979). ALA: ACRL. Men's Lib. Assn. Cath. Alum. Sodality. **Activities:** 1, 12; 15, 16, 17; 57, 58, 91 **Addr.:** Boston College Science Library, Devlin Hall, Chestnut Hill, MA 02167.

McElroy, Mary Johns (Pittsburgh, PA) Head, Engin. Lib., Cornell Univ., 1973–; Ref. Libn., Sci-Tech, Dept. Carnegie Lib. of Pittsburgh, 1972–73; Cat. Libn., Monessen Pub. Lib., 1971–72; Lit. Srchr., Westinghouse Nuclear Energy Syst., 1970–71; Grad. Asst., Univ. of Pittsburgh, 1968–70, 1964–66; Consult., Westinghouse Nuclear Energy Syst., 1967; Head, West. PA Conservancy Lib., 1966; Cat. Libn., Westinghouse Resrch. & Dev. Ctr., 1961–64. **Educ.:** Mount Mercy Coll., 1945–49, BA (Bio., Chem.); Carnegie Inst. of Tech., 1959–60, MLS. **Orgs.:** SLA: Upstate NY Chap., Pres. (1978–79); Ch., Policy Manual Com. (1979–80); Ch., Empl. Com. (1977–78). S. Ctrl. Resrch. Lib. Cncl.: Plng. and Adv. Com. (1979–80, 1980–81). ALA. Assoc. Info. Mgrs. Other orgs. Finger Lakes Kennel Club. Amer. Socty. for Engin. Educ.: Ch., Info. Syst. Com. (1978–79); Secy. (1975–76). **Honors:** Beta Phi Mu, 1979. **Pubns.:** Cmplr., *Directory of Members and Resources, Engineering Libraries Division, American Society for Engineering Education,* (1976). **Activities:** 1; 17 **Addr.:** Engineering Library, Carpenter Hall, Cornell University, Ithaca, NY 14853.

McEwen, Barney R. (S. 16, 1944, Tylertown, MS) Div. Head, IN State Lib.-Div. for the Blind and Phys. Handcpd., 1975; Branch Libn., Indianapolis-Marion Cnty. Pub. Lib., 1974–75, Ref. Libn., 1972–74; Tax Libn., Internal Revenue Srvs., 1971–72; Ref. Libn., Indianapolis-Marion Cnty. Pub. Lib., 1969–71. **Educ.:** MS Coll., 1962–66, BS (Hist.); Ball State Univ., 1969–71, MLS. **Orgs.:** IN LA: Spec. Srvs. Div., (1977–). Amer. Assn. of Workers for the Blind (IN). Amer. Cncl. of the Blind (IN). Natl. Fed. of the Blind (IN): Lib. Com. (1975–). IN Hist. Socty. **Honors:** Natl. Fed. of the Blind, Dinsmore, 1977. **Activities:** 13; 17, 36; 72 **Addr.:** Division for the Blind and Physically Handicapped, Indiana State Library, 140 North Senate Ave., Indianapolis, IN 46204.

McFadyen, Jolynn K. (Ja. 19, 1951, Chicago, IL) Libn., Patterson, Belknap, Webb and Tyler, 1978–; Libn., Day, Berry, and Howard, 1975–78; Asst. Libn., Morgan, Lewis, and Bockius, 1973–75. **Educ.:** Wheaton Coll. 1968–72, MA, BA (Art Hist.); Drexel Univ., 1972–73, MS (LS). **Orgs.:** AALL: Pvt. Law Libs. Sect. (1977–); Constn. and Bylaws Com. (1978–). SLA: Bus. and Fin. Div. (1975–). South. New Eng. Law Libns. Assn.: Pres. (1977–78). Law LA of Grt. NY. **Activities:** 12; 17; 56, 77, 78 **Addr.:** Patterson, Belknap, Webb and Tyler - Library, 30 Rockefeller Plz., New York, NY 10112.

McFadyen, Margaret Elizabeth (Je. 8, 1941, Macclesfield, Cheshire, Eng.) Chief Libn., Whitney Pub. Lib., 1981–; Coord. of Info. Srvs., Ctrl. ON Reg. Lib., 1975–81; Ref. Libn., Oshawa Pub. Lib., 1970–75; Intermed. Clerical, Hamilton Pub. Lib., 1960–65. **Educ.:** McMaster Univ., 1966–69, BA (Hist.); Univ. of Western ON, 1969–70, MLS. **Orgs.:** ON LA. Can. LA: Info. Srvs. Coord. Grp. (1977–79). Persnl. Assn. of Toronto. Creativity Can. Assn.: Secy. (1977–80). **Activities:** 9, 12; 17, 35, 39; 50, 89 **Addr.:** 235 Bay Thorn Dr. Apt. 310, Thornhill, ON L3T 3V6 Canada.

McFarland, Jane E. (Je. 22, 1937, Athens, TN) Head, Ref. and Info., Chattanooga-Hamilton Cnty. Bicent. Lib., 1980–; Ref. Libn., Asst. Prof., Univ. TN (Chattanooga), 1977–80; Head Libn., Bradford Coll., 1972–77; Head, Ref. and Circ., Yale Dvnty. Lib., 1963–71. **Educ.:** Smith Coll., 1955–59, AB (Relig.); Yale Univ., 1959–63, MA (Theo.); Univ. of NC (Chapel Hill), 1971, MS (LS). **Orgs.:** Chattanooga Area LA. TN LA. SELA. **Pubns.:** "Bibliography of the writings of H. Richard Niebuhr," *The Theology of H. Richard Niebuhr* (1970); Jt. Cmplr., "A Select Bibliography of Robert Lowry Calhoun's Writings," *The Heritage of Christian Thought; Essays in Honor of Robert Lowry Calhoun* (1965); Jt. Complr., "A bibliography of H. Richard Niebuhr's writings," *Faith and Ethics: The Theology of H. Richard Niebuhr* (1965). **Activities:** 1, 9; 17, 39; 90 **Addr.:** Chattanooga-Hamilton County Bicentennial Library, 1001 Broad St., Chattanooga, TN 37402.

McFarland, Sarah C. (My. 7, 1938, Anderson, IN) Ref. Libn., Williams Coll., 1971–; Circ., Ref. Libn., Univ. of Botswana and Swaziland, 1978–79; Asst. Ref., Docums. Libn., Williams Coll., 1970–71, Circ. Libn., 1969–70. **Educ.:** Purdue Univ., 1956–60, BS (Pol. Sci); Columbia Univ., 1966–68, MLS. **Orgs.:** ALA: ACRL, East. NY Chap. Botswana LA. **Activities:** 1; 22, 31, 39; 54, 59, 92 **Addr.:** 380 Syndicate Rd., Williamstown, MA 01267.

McFarland, Sharon Duncan (Ag. 30, 1939, Corpus Christi, TX) Head, Lib. Srvs., Natl. Rehab. Info. Ctr., 1981–, Head, Tech. Srvs., 1979–81, Sr. Info. Spec., 1977–79; Abstctr., Indxr., Congsnl. Info. Srv., 1976–77. **Educ.:** Univ. of TX, 1970–74, BA (Eng.), 1974–76, MLS. **Orgs.:** SLA: DC LA. ALA: ASCLA Gvt. Docum. RT., Rehab. Info. RT (1979–); LAMA. TX Ex-Students Assn. **Honors:** Phi Kappa Phi, 1976; Beta Phi Mu, 1976. **Pubns.:** *Thesaurus of NARIC Descriptors* (1980); *Texas Constitutional Revision, 1973–1974,* bibl. (1976); *CIS Indx.* monthly abs. (1976–1977); contrib., "Information Exchange," clmn. *The Pathfinder.* **Activities:** 12; 15, 17, 46; 72 **Addr.:** National Rehabilitation Information Center, Catholic University of America, 4407 Eighth St. N.E., Washington, DC 20017.

McFerrin, James Blakely (Jl. 2, 1920, Fayetteville, TN) Head Libn., Un. Coll., 1958–; Docum. Libn., Emory Univ., 1951–58; Circ. Asst., DePauw Univ., 1948–50. **Educ.:** Erskine Coll., 1938–42, AB (Math.); Univ. of IL, 1947–48, BS (LS), 1950–51, MS (LS). **Orgs.:** KY LA: Lib. Educ. Com. (1966–71). ALA. SELA: Mem. Com. (1976–78). AAUP. **Honors:** KY Colonel, 1973. **Activities:** 1; 29, 44; 63 **Addr.:** 110 College Park Dr., Barbourville, KY 40906.

McGarity, Mary Sue (Mr. 25, 1924, Kingsport, TN) Assoc. Prof., (Lib. Media), Univ. of AL (Birmingham), 1972–; Libn., Our Lady of Sorrows Sch., 1970–72; Libn., Brooke Hill Sch. for Girls, 1964–70; Asst. Prof., Cat., LA State Univ., 1967; Asst. Prof., Ref., Univ. of AL (Tuscaloosa), 1966; Catlgr., Birmingham Pub. Lib., 1964; Catlgr., Univ. of AL (Tuscaloosa), 1961–62; Ref. Lib., LA State Univ., 1960–61; various positions. **Educ.:** Univ. of AL (Tuscaloosa), 1941–45, BS (LS); LA State Univ., 1960, MS (LS); Univ. of AL (Tuscaloosa), 1975–77, EdD (Curric. Dev.). **Orgs.:** ALA: State Cnclr. (1979). AL LA: Pres. (1974–75); Bylaws; Handbook; Nom. Com. SELA: PR Com. AECT. Delta Kappa Gamma. Phi Delta Kappa. **Pubns.:** "The Use of Simulation Techniques in Education for Librarianship," *AL Libn.,* (S., O. 1978). **Activities:** 1, 10; 20, 26, 32 **Addr.:** 1416 Sutherland Pl., Birmingham, AL 35209.

McGarr, Sheila M. (S. 25, 1949, Beverly, MA) Depos. Lib. Inspector, Gvt. Prtg. Ofc., 1981–; Circ. Libn., Mary Washington Coll., 1976–81; Spec. Srv. Libn., N. Shore Cmnty. Coll., 1973–76; Asst. Ref. Libn., Memorial Hall Lib. (Andover, MA), 1973. **Educ.:** Merrimack Coll., 1967–71, BA (Hist.); Catholic Univ., 1971–73, MLS; 27th Inst. Intro. to Arch. Admin., 1972 (Cert.). **Orgs.:** ALA: ACRL; RASD. VA LA: ACRL Chap., By Law Com. (1978). AAUW: Fredericksburg Branch, Cult. Interest Rep. Branch; Exec. Bd. (1979–). Beverly (MA) Pub. Lib.: Bd. Trustees; Secy. Bd. (1975–76); Pres. (1976). **Honors:** Phi Alpha Theta; Beta Phi Mu. **Activities:** 1; 22, 34, 39; 55, 92 **Addr.:** 4323 Raleigh Ave., Apt. 204, Alexandria, VA 22304.

McGarty, John F. (O. 30, 1947, Amityville, NY) Media Srvcs. Spec., Anne Arundel Cnty., Pub. Lib., 1978–; Libn., Cardinal Gibbons HS, 1970–78. **Educ.:** Univ. of Dayton, 1966–70, BA (Eng.); Univ. of MD, 1972–75, MLS. **Orgs.:** ALA. MD LA: Anl. Conf. Com. (1980); AV Div. (VP, 1981). **Activities:** 9; 16, 21, 32; 56, 67 **Addr.:** 5 Truman Pkwy., Annapolis, MD 21401.

McGarvey, Alan R. (My. 11, 1914, Philadelphia, PA) Mgr., Tech. Info. Srvs., Armstrong Cork Co., 1963–, Mgr., Indus. Insulation Resrch., 1955-63, Chem. Engin., 1936–54. **Educ.:** Univ. of PA, 1931–36, BS (Chem.); 1943 (Chem. Engin.). **Orgs.:** ASIS. Amer. Chem. Socty.: Div. of Chem. Info. Amer. Inst. of Chem. Engins. **Pubns.:** "A Reverse Coordinate Concept System for Retrieving Engineering Site and Building Drawings," *Jnl. of Chem. Documtn.* (My. 1969); "Uniterm Index to U.S. Chemical Patents–User Evaluation," *Jnl. of Chem. Documtn.* (F. 1968); "Information Retrieval (IR) for an Outdoor Exposure Evaluation Facility," *Appld. Polymer Symposia* (1967); "Wrap Your Cold Storage Room in a Vapor Barrier," *ASHRAE Jnl.* (D. 1964). **Activities:** 12; 17, 46 **Addr.:** Armstrong Cork Co., Research and Development, Box 3511 Lancaster PA 17604.

McGavern, John Howard (D. 23, 1926, Cambridge, MA) Univ. Libn., Univ. of Hartford, 1960–, Ref. Libn., 1959–60; Acq. Libn., Harvard Bus. Sch., 1955–59; various positions, Harvard Univ., 1952–54. **Educ.:** Harvard Univ., 1945–49, BA (Phil.); Simmons Coll., 1952–54, MLS. **Orgs.:** Capitol Region Lib. Cncl.: Bd., Exec. Com. (1977–). CT LA. New Eng. Lib. Info. Netwk. **Activities:** 1; 17 **Addr.:** Mortensen Library, University of Hartford, 200 Bloomfield Ave., Hartford, CT 06117.

McGaw, Howard F. (O. 5, 1911, Nashville, TN) Retired, 1978–; Treas., Frnds. of the Bellingham Pub. Lib., 1979–; Prof. of LS, West. WA Univ., 1967–78, Dir., Lib., 1963–67; Actg. Dir., Lib., TX South. Univ., 1962–63; Dir., Lib., Univ. of Houston, 1950–61; Dir., Lib., OH Wesleyan Univ., 1946–49; Dir., Lib., Memphis State Univ., 1940–42. **Educ.:** Vanderbilt Univ., 1928–29, 1930–33, BA (Eng.); George Peabody Coll., 1937–39, MA (Soc. Sci.), 1939–41, BS (LS); Grad. Lib. Sch., Univ. of Chicago, 1942–43; Columbia Univ., 1947–50, EdD (Admin. of Higher Educ.). **Orgs.:** TX LA: Int. Frdm. Com. (Ch., 1952–53, 1955–56); Exec. Bd. (1956–57); Coll. and Univ. Div. (Ch., 1957–58). WA LA: Treas. (1966–67). ALA: Constn. and Bylaws Com. (1954–55); Stats. (1955–56). AAUP: West. WA Chap. (Pres., 1969–70). Natl. Educ. Assn. Amer. Cvl. Liberties Un. **Honors:** Phi Delta Kappa, 1939; Kappa Delta Pi, 1949; Beta Phi Mu, 1954; WA LA, Emeritus Life Mem., 1979. **Pubns.:** *Marginal Punched Cards in College and Research Libraries* (1952); "Policies and Practices in Discarding," *Lib. Trends* (Ja. 1956); "Theft in the Library," *PNLA Qtly.* (Ap. 1965); "Reclassification: A Bibliography," *Lib. Resrcs. & Tech. Srvs.* (Fall 1965); "Academic Libraries Using the LC Classification System," *Coll. & Resrch. Libs.* (Ja. 1966). **Activities:** 1, 11; 17, 20, 22, 74 **Addr.:** 120 Underhill Rd., Bellingham, WA 98225.

McGeachy, John A. (S. 27, 1948, Statesville, NC) Lib. Coord. for Docum. Srvs., AR State Lib., 1980–; Ref. Docum. Libn., AR State Univ., 1978–79, Cat. Libn., 1976–78; Cat. Libn., Hampden-Sydney Coll., 1974–76. **Educ.:** Davidson Coll., 1966–70, AB (Classics); Univ. of Chicago, 1970–73, MA (LS). **Orgs.:** ALA: ACRL; RTSD; GODORT. AR LA. Ozark States Folklore Socty. AR Archeological Socty. **Pubns.:** "The *Monthly catalog's* first response to its 1947 Congressional charge," *Library resources and technical services,* (Win. 1976); "Student nicknames for college faculty," *Western folklore,* (O. 1978); "Shipping list notes," *Documents to the People* (S. 1980). **Activities:** 1, 13; 20, 29, 39 **Addr.:** Arkansas State Library, One Capitol Mall, Little Rock, AR 72201.

McGee, Rob (N. 29, 1941, Washington, DC) Lib. Autom. Consult., RMG Consult. Inc., 1980–; Deputy Syst. Libn., Univ. Chicago, 1967–; Asst. Ref. Libn., Univ. IL Chicago Circle, 1965–66. **Educ.:** Univ. NC (Chapel Hill), 1961–63, AB (Liberal Arts), 1963–65, MLS; Glasgow Univ., 1966–67, Dip. (Comp. Sci.); Univ. Chicago, 1965–71 (LS). **Orgs.:** ALA: LITA. Adv. Grp. Natl. Bibl. Control: Plng. Com. Auto. Ident. Syst. (1976–). Bk. Indus. Syst. Adv. Com.: Aut. Ident. Bibl. Subcom. (1977–). **Honors:** Rotary Fndn., Flwshp. Int. Understan., 1966. **Pubns.:** Ed., *MIDLNET Technical Plan for Automation of Libraries of a Region* (1978); Ed., *Proposal for Joint Development of a Network Library System by The University of Chicago; The University of Wisconsin-Madison; IBM* (1978); "An Analysis of Manual Circulation Systems for Academic Libraries," *Jnl. of the Amer. Socty. for Info. Sci.* (My.-Je. 1973), "Key Factors of Circulation System Analysis and Design," *Coll. and Resrch. Lib.* (Mr. 1972); "Two Types of Designs for On-Line Circulation Systems," *Jnl. of Lib. Autom.* (S. 1972); other pubns. **Activities:** 1, 9; 22, 24, 34; 56 **Addr.:** RMG Consultants, Inc., Chicago, IL 60680.

McGeehan, Thomas Joseph (Jl. 25, 1941, Hazleton, PA) Mgr., Proj. Coord., Wyeth Labs., 1978–; Sr. Consult., Auerbach Assoc. Inc., 1972–78; Mgr., Info. Ctr., Smith Kline & French Labs., 1968–72; Libn., Lib. for the Blind & Phys. Handcpd., 1966–68; Libn., Free Lib. of Philadelphia, 1964–66. **Educ.:** King's Coll., 1959–63, BS (Bio.); Drexel Univ., 1963–64, MS (Info. Sci.); Rutgers Univ., 1971–78, PhD (Mgt. Sci.). **Orgs.:** ASIS. Proj. Mgt. Inst. Gov. Adv. Cncl. for Lib. (Commonwealth of PA). **Pubns.:** "Programming to Goals", *ASIS* (Mr. 1977); *Decision Analysis Technique for Program Evaluation* (Mr. 1977); Jt. Auth., *DDC 10 Year Requirements and Planning Study. Final Report* (Je. 1976); *DDC 10 Year Requirements and Planning Study* (D. 1975); *Systems Analysis of Langley Research Center Technical Library Operations* (Je. 1975). **Activities:** 12; 24, 46; 59, 87 **Addr.:** Wyeth Laboratories, P.O. Box 8299, Philadelphia, PA 19101.

McGill, Michael J. (O. 16, 1942, Detroit, MI) Assoc. Prog. Dir., Info. Sci. Prog., Div. of Info. Sci. and Tech., Natl. Sci. Fndn., 1981–; Sr. Info. Comp. Sci., US Environ. Protection Agency, 1980–81; Assoc. Prof., Sch. Info. Std., Syracuse Univ., 1974–80; Asst. Prof., Comp. Sci., SUNY, Oswego, 1972–74; Resrch. Assoc., Comp. Sci., Syracuse Univ., 1971–72. **Educ.:** MI State Univ., 1963–65, BA (Comm.); Syracuse Univ., 1973, PhD (Comp. Sci.). **Orgs.:** Assn. Comp. Mach.: SIG, Info. Retrieval; 5th Intl. Retrieval Conf. Ch. ASIS: SIG, Ch.; User OL Mtg. Natl. Conf. (Ch., 1976). **Pubns.:** Jt. Auth., *Introduction to Modern Information Retrieval* (1981); "Knowledge and Information Spaces: The Implication for Information Storage and Retrieval Systems," *Jnl. Amer. Socty. Info. Sci.* (Jl./Ag. 1976); "Automatic Ranked Output from Boolean Searches in SIRE," *Jnl. Amer. Socty. Info. Sci.* (N. 1977); speeches and resrch. rpt. **Addr.:** 5715 Aberdeen Rd., Bethesda, MD 20014.

McGill, Theodora (Orlando, FL) Libn., Export-Import Bank of U.S., 1968–; Ref. Libn., US Dept. Hlth., Educ., Welfare, 1967–68; Area Libn., Dept. of the Army, Korea, 1955–67; Libn., Natl. Cath. Sch. Soc. Srv., Cath. Univ., 1952–55. **Educ.:** Miner Tchr. Coll., 1937–41, BS (Educ.); Cath. Univ. of Amer., 1950–52,

Special Subjects/Services: 50. Adult educ.; 51. Advert./Mktg.; 52. Aerosp.; 53. Agric.; 54. Area std.; 55. Arts/Hum.; 56. Autom.; 57. Bibl./Prtg.; 58. Bio. sci.; 59. Bus./Fin.; 60. Chem.; 61. Copyrt.; 62. Documtn.; 63. Educ.; 64. Engin.; 65. Env.; 66. Eth. grps.; 67. Film; 68. Food/Nutr.; 69. Geneal.; 70. Geo.; 71. Geol.; 72. Handcpd.; 73. Hist.; 74. Int. frdm.; 75. Info. sci.; 76. Insr.; 77. Law; 78. Legis.; 79. Math./Comp. sci.; 80. Med.; 81. Metals; 82. Nat. resrcs.; 83. Newsp.; 84. Nuc. sci.; 85. Oral hist.; 86. Petr./Energy; 87. Pharm.; 88. Phys./Astr./Math.; 89. Readg.; 90. Relig.; 91. Sci./Tech.; 92. Soc. sci.; 93. Telecom.; 94. Transp.; 95. (other).

MS (LS); SLA, 1979, 1980, Cont. Educ. Cert. **Orgs.:** SLA: Bus. Fin. Div., Nom. Com. (Ch.); Secy.; Soc. Sci. Grp. (Ch.); Washington, DC Chap., Nom. Com., 2nd VP. Law Libn. Socty. Washington, DC: Com. Elections (Ch.). AAUW: Washington, DC Branch, Intl. Rel. Com. (Ch.), Bd. Mem. US China Peoples Frndshp. Assn.: Mem. Com. Frnds. Lib. Cath. Univ.: Exec. Cncl.; Treas. **Honors:** U.S. Army (Korea), Cert. of Achvmt., 1960; Dept. of the Army, Merit. Civilian Awd., 1966. **Activities:** 4; 17, 39; 59 **Addr.:** Library, Export-Import Bank of the US, 811 Vermont Ave., N.W., Washington, DC 20571.

McGinn, Howard F., Jr., (S. 14, 1943, Pittsburgh, PA) Managing Ed., Microfilming Corp. of Amer., 1978–; Mgr., AV Sales, J. B. Lippincott Pub. Co., 1973–78, Eng. Prof., Ursuline Acad., 1972–73; Dir. of Lib., Chestnut Hill Coll., 1969–72; Asst. Dir. of Libs., St. Charles Sem., 1968–69; Ed./Indexr., Cath. LA, 1966–68. **Educ.:** Villanova Univ., 1962–66, BA (Phil.); Drexel Univ., 1968–70, MSLS; Temple Univ.; Univ. of PA; Ctrl. Carolina Tech. Coll. **Orgs.:** ALA. SLA: Educ. Com. NC Chap. (1979; Ch. 1980); Consultation Com. (Ch. 1981). PA Lrng. Resrcs. Assn.: Copyright Task Force Com. (1977–78). MLA. Lee Cnty., NC: Lee Cnty. Pers. Brd. (1979–). Rotary Club, Sanford NC. Boy Scouts of Amer., Asst. Scoutmaster (1979–). **Activities:** 1; 17, 33, 37; 51, 55, 93 **Addr.:** Microfilming Corporation of America, A New York Times Co., 1620 Hawkins Ave., P.O. Box 10, Sanford, NC 27330.

McGinnis, Callie Bergen (Mr. 10, 1944, New Orleans, LA) Assoc. Prof. / Assoc. Libn., Columbus Coll., 1974–; Instr./Asst. Libn., Macon Jr. Coll., 1969–70. **Educ.:** Southwest. at Memphis, 1962–66, BA (Eng.); LA State Univ., 1966–69, MS (LS). **Orgs.:** SELA. GA LA. Phi Kappa Phi: Chap. Secy. (1976–); Triennial Conv. Del. (1977). **Pubns.:** Contrib., *Georgia Women; A Celebration.* (1976); bk. reviews. **Activities:** 1; 20, 31, 36; 55, 95 **Addr.:** Columbus College Library, Columbus College, Columbus, GA 31907.

McGinnis, Joan M. (Ap. 2, 1936, Philadelphia, PA) Med. Libn., Vets. Admin. Med. Ctr., 1973–; Tchg. positions. **Educ.:** Bob Jones Univ., 1955–59, BA (Relig.); Simmons Coll., 1971–73, MLS; Plymouth State Coll., 1963–70, MEd (Educ.); **Orgs.:** Med. LA. MA Hlth. Sci. Libn. N. Atl. Hlth. Sci. Libn. New Eng. LA: Hosp. Libn. Sect., Nom. Com. (1978–79). **Activities:** 4, 15, 31, 39; 80, 92 **Addr.:** 66 Litchfield Rd., Londonderry, NH 03053.

McGinniss, Dorothy A. (Ap. 11, 1911, Schenectady, NY) Prof. Emeritus, Syracuse Univ., 1974–; Libn., Chilmark Pub. Lib. (MA), 1974–; Prof., Sch. LS, Syracuse Univ., 1966–74; Exec. Secy., AASL, ALA, 1962–66; Supvsr., Sec. Sch. Lib., Baltimore Cnty., 1959–62; Asst. Prof., Dept. LS, South. IL Univ., 1951–59; various positions tchg. and in lib. **Educ.:** NY State Coll. Tchr. (Albany), 1928–32, AB (Latin, Eng.), 1934–39, BLS; Columbia Univ., 1941–51, MS (LS). **Orgs.:** ALA. MA LA. New Eng. LA. Martha's Vineyard LA: Pres. (1977–79). **Honors:** NY State Univ., Disting. Alum., 1972. **Pubns.:** Numerous pubns. **Activities:** 9, 10; 21, 26; 63 **Addr.:** RFD State Rd., Vineyard Haven, MA 02568.

McGinty, John W. (N. 5, 1947, New Brunswick, NJ) Circ., ILL Libn., Univ. CT Hlth. Ctr., 1977–; Ref. Libn., SUNY Med. Ctr. Downst., 1975–77. **Educ.:** Columbia Univ., 1968–72, BA (Anthro.); Rutgers Univ., 1973–75, MLS; Univ. CT, 1978–81, MBA. **Orgs.:** New Eng. Reg. Med. Lib. Adv. Cncl.: Docum. Delivery Stan. Com. (Ch.). Cap. Reg. Lib. Cncl. (Hartford, CT): Comp. Circ. Com. CT Assn. Hlth. Sci. Lib.: Shared Srv. Com. **Pubns.:** "Marketing For Libraries," *SLA/CT Valley Bltn.* (Ja. 1981). **Activities:** 1, 17, 22, 34; 51, 56, 80 **Addr.:** University of Connecticut Health Center Library, Farmington, CT 06032.

McGonagill, JoAnn P. (Ap. 10, 1953, Bethesda, MD) Geneal. and Asst. Ref. Libn., State Lib. of FL, 1978–, US Docum. Asst. (LTA II), 1975–78. **Educ.:** FL State Univ., 1972–74, BA (lib. sci.), 1976–78, MLS. **Orgs.:** FL LA: Docum. Caucus (Secty., 1978–79). FL State Geneal. Socty., Inc.: Mem. Ch. (1979–). **Pubns.:** Cmplr., *First Supplement to Genealogy and Local History: A Bibliography* (1979). **Activities:** 13; 30, 39, 42; 57, 69 **Addr.:** 1906 Fairlane Rd., Tallahassee, FL 32303.

McGowan, John Patrick (My. 11, 1926, New York, NY) Univ. Libn., Northwestern Univ., 1971–, Assoc. Univ. Libn., 1966–71; Dir. of the Lib., The Franklin Inst. (Philadelphia, PA), 1959–66; Libn. of the Tech. Inst., Northwestern Univ., 1956–59; Libn., New York Univ., 1951–56. **Educ.:** Hunter Coll., 1950, AB (Eng.); Columbia Univ., 1951, AMLS; New York Univ., 1966, BE (Indus. Engin.). **Orgs.:** ALA: RASD, Pres. (1967–69); LITA, Ed. Jnl. Lib. Autom. Tech. Comm. MIDLNET: Pres. (1977–78). EDUCOM: Bd. Trustees (1967–73). Chem. Abstracts: Adv. Com. (1971–72). **Honors:** Cncl. of Lib. Resrc., Flwshp., 1970. **Pubns.:** "Private University Libraries and a National Information Policy," *Coll. and Resrch. Lib.* (Ja. 1979); "Telecommunications: A Micro and Macro View," *IL Lib.* (Ap. 1978); "The Venezuela Project," *Final Report and Working Papers* SALALM (Jl., 1978); Ed., *A Guide to a Selection of Computer-Based Science and Technology Reference Services in the U.S.A.,* (1969); "The Library and the Technical Information Center," in *Conference on Technical Information Center Administration* (1965); other pubns. **Addr.:** Northwestern University Library, 1935 Sheridan Rd., Evanston, IL 60201.

McGowan, Owen T. P. (Ap. 9, 1922, Fall River, MA) Dir. Lib. Srvs., Bridgewater State Coll., 1964–; Libn., Durfee HS, 1962–64; Libn., Morton Jr. HS, 1956–62; Owner, Mgr. Book Store, Fall River, MA, 1949–56. **Educ.:** Maryknoll Coll., 1941–45, BA (Phil.); Cath. Univ. of Amer. 1959–64, MSLS, 1973–76, PhD (Intl. Educ.). **Orgs.:** ALA. Cath. LA: HS Sect., Past Ch. Southeastern MA Coop. Libs.: Ch. and Coord. MA Conf. Chief Libns. Pub. Insts. of Higher Educ.: Past Pres. Natl. Educ. Assn. MA Tchrs. Assn. **Honors:** World Book Childcraft Awd., 1974; Gulbenkian Fndn. Awd., 1978. **Pubns.:** *Library Research Tools: How To Use Them,* ten captioned filmstps (1964); *Library Materials: The Preparation, Organization and Circulation,* four filmstps., two cassettes (1978); "Eighteen Nineties Society," *Cath. Lib. World* (My.–Je. 1978); "SMCL–A Working Cooperative," *Bay State Libn.* (Je. 1977); "Library Instruction Needed," *Cath. Lib. World* (N. 1976); various bk. reviews. **Activities:** 1; 17, 19, 24; 90 **Addr.:** 96 French St., Fall River, MA 02720.

McGowan, Sarah M. (Ag. 4, 1945, Chicago, IL) Dir. of Lib., Ripon Coll., 1980–; Head Ref. Libn., AR State Univ., 1978–80; Asst. Libn., Admin., Lake Forest Coll., 1973–78; Asst. Libn., Exch., Nuffield Coll., Oxford, Eng., 1973–74; Asst. Libn., Ref., Lake Forest Coll., 1970–73. **Educ.:** Wilmington Coll., 1963–67, AB (Eng.); Univ. of Denver, 1969–70, MA (Libnshp.). **Orgs.:** ALA: ACRL. WI LA. AR LA: JMRT (Ch., 1979–80); On-line Users Grp., (1979–80). NE AR LA: Nsltr. ed. (1979–80); Nom. Com. (Ch., 1979–80). **Activities:** 1; 17, 39 **Addr.:** Ripon College, Ripon, WI 45971.

McGrath, Margaret M. (Mr. 29, 1918, Syracuse, NY) Head, Ref., Univ. of St. Michael's Coll., Univ. of Toronto, 1972–, Asst. Libn., 1966–72, Pub. Srv. Libn., 1962–65. **Educ.:** Syracuse Univ., 1935–39, BA (Soc. Sci.); Univ. of Toronto, 1977–80, MA (Hist.). **Orgs.:** Can. LA. Libn. Assn., Univ. of Toronto. Bibl. of Phil. in Can.: Resrch. Univ. of Toronto Fac. Assn. **Pubns.:** *Reference Bibliography in Medieval Studies* (1976), *Etienne Gilson: A Bibliography* (1981). **Activities:** 1; 15, 39, 41; 55, 90, 95-Medieval Std. **Addr.:** 64 Unsworth Ave., Toronto, ON M5M 3C5 Canada.

McGrath, Patricia J. (Ja. 20, 19–, Providence, RI) Chief, Lib. Srv., Vets. Admin. Med. Ctr., Boston, 1977–; Dir., Hlth. Sci. Info. Ctr., Women & Infants Hosp. of RI, 1973–77; Persnl. Dir., St. Joseph's Hosp., 1967–70; Asst. Persnl. Dir., New Eng. Deaconess Hosp., 1966–67. **Educ.:** Bryant Coll., 1963, BS (Bus. Admin.); Univ. of HI, 1972, MLS; Northeastern Univ., 1978–, MPA Cand.; Med. LA, 1975, Cert.; Various inst., sems., Online trng. **Orgs.:** Assn. of RI Hlth. Sci. Libs.: Secy. (1975–77). MA Hlth. Sci. Libns.: Ch., Hosp. Stan. Com. Med. LA: Hosp. Lib. Sect., (Pres., 1981–82); Ed., HLS Nsltr.(1979–80). New Eng. LA: Hosp. Lib. Sect., (VP/Prog. Ch., 1977–78; Pres., 1978–79). Other orgs. Natl. Socty.–D.A.R. MA Hosp. Assn. **Honors:** Beta Phi Mu, 1972. **Pubns.:** "The Medical Library Exchange: A Hospital Vantage Point," *Hosp. Libs.* (Sum. 1980); "Hospital Library Resources in Massachusetts," *Bltn. of the Med. LA* (O. 1980); "Informal Learning Experiences - Less than Continuing Education, More than Scanning the Literature," *Hosp. Libs.* (O. 1977); "Improving Job Performance through Journal Clubs," *HLS Nsltr.* (1981). **Activities:** 4, 5; 24 **Addr.:** Veterans Administration Medical Center, 150 South Huntington Ave., Boston, MA 02130.

McGrath, William E. (N. 27, 1926, Somerville, MA) Visit. Disting. Scholar, OCLC, Inc., 1979–80; Dean of Lib. Srvs., Univ. of Lowell, 1977–; Dir. of Libs., Univ. of Southwestern LA, 1968–77; Head Libn., SD Sch. of Mines and Tech., 1964–68; Sci. Libn., Univ. of NH, 1956–64. **Educ.:** Univ. of MA, 1948–52, AB (Eng.); Univ. of MI, 1954–56, MALS; Syracuse Univ., 1971–75, PhD (Info. Transf.). **Orgs.:** ALA. ASIS. **Pubns.:** Various articles. **Activities:** 1; 15, 22, 41; 75, 88, 91 **Addr.:** Univ. of Lowell, 1 Wilder St., Lowell, MA 01854.

McGregor, James Wilson (Ag. 21, 1935, Bartlesville, OK) Asst. Univ. Libn. for Tech. Srvs., Northeastern IL Univ., 1971–, Cat., 1966–71; Sr. Cat., SUNY, Stony Brook, 1964–66; Law Cat., Univ. of Chicago, 1962–64. **Educ.:** Univ. of Chicago, 1960–63, AM (Libnshp.). **Orgs.:** ALA. Chicago Acad. Libns. Cncl.: Serials Subcom.; Tech. Srvs. Subcom. IL LA: Exec. Bd. (1970–71); Exhibits Com. (Ch., 1978); IL IACRL, Cont. Ed. Com. (Ch., 1979–80); Resrcs. and Tech. Srvs. Sect. (Ch., 1970–71). ACLU. Univ. of Chicago Grad. Lib. Sch. Alum. Assn.: Secty.-Treas. (1977–79). **Honors:** Cncl. on Lib. Resrcs. Flwshp. Grant, 1975. **Pubns.:** "In Defense of the Dictionary Catalog," *Lib. Resrcs. and Tech. Srvs.* (Win. 1971); "Serials Staffing in Academic Libraries," *Serials Libn.* (Spr. 1977). **Activities:** 1; 46 **Addr.:** Northeastern Illinois University Library, 5500 N. St. Louis Ave., Chicago, IL 60625.

McGrogan, Marcella C. (Mrs. Daniel J. Jr.) (Jl. 20, 1924, Pittsburgh, PA) Asst., Microfilm Col., Hillman Lib., Univ. of Pittsburgh, 1981–; Ed. Southwest PA Chap., CSLA nwsltr. 1981 Pres. Southwest. PA Chap., 1977–79; CSLA Nat. Mem. Ch., 1977–78. **Educ.:** Seton Hill Coll., Greensburg, 1942–44; Univ. of Pittsburgh, 1969. **Orgs.:** Cath. LA. CSLA, Southwest PA Chap. PA LA. ALA. St. Luke Parent Teacher Guild: Pres. (1962). Diocesan Cncl. of Cath. Women. **Honors:** Life Trustee, Andrew Carnegie Free Lib., 1981. CSLA Southwest PA Chap., Outstanding Cont. to Libs., 1978. **Addr.:** 430 Center Ave., Carnegie, PA 15106.

McGuire, Laura H. (F. 14, 1919, Ludell, KS) Docum. Libn., Golden Lib., East. NM Univ., 1969–. **Educ.:** Univ. of KS, 1937–41, AB (Eng.); TX Woman's Univ., 1967–69, MLS. **Orgs.:** ALA: Mem. ch., NM (1969–71); GODORT. NM LA: Docum. Com. (1970–79, ch. 1971–76); Velle Galle Resrch. Com. (1969–73); Legis. and Int. Frdm. Com. (1977–78). SWLA. Luth. Church LA. AAUW. AAUP. Delta Kappa Gamma. **Honors:** Phi Beta Kappa, 1940; Beta Phi Mu, 1969. **Pubns.:** "Pioneer Years of the New Mexico Library Association," *Greater Llano Estacado Southwest Heritage* (Spr. 1973); "National Depository Librarian Workshop," *NM Libs. Nsltr.* (O. 1979); "Upcoming State Publications Legislation," *NM Libs. Nsltr.* (Ja. 1975); Reviews. **Activities:** 1, 14-church lib.; 29, 39, 42; 61, 78, 92 **Addr.:** Golden Library, Eastern New Mexico University, Portales, NM 88130.

McIlvaine, Betsy (Ja. 26, 1945, Lafayette, IN) Head Libn., Philips Labs., 1979–; Intl. Docum. Libn., Univ. of CT Lib., 1973–79. **Educ.:** Univ. of IL, 1963–67, BA (Eng.); Univ. of RI, 1971–73, MLS. **Orgs.:** ALA: ACRL; GODORT, Intl. Docum. Task Frc. (Secy., 1978–80). SLA. CT LA. **Pubns.:** *Aging: A Guide to Reference Sources, Journals and Government Publications* (1978); gvt. docum. clmn., *Wilson Lib. Bltn.* (1979–); gvt. docum. clmn., *Serials Review* (1978–); assoc. ed., *Serials Review* (1981–). **Activities:** 1, 12; 17, 39; 64, 77, 88 **Addr.:** 218 Southern Blvd., Danbury, CT 06810.

McIntosh, Fred H. (My. 19, 1936, Flin Flon, MB) Dir., Sch. of Lib. Tech., Lakehead Univ., 1980–; Assoc. Prof., 1973–80; Tchr. Libn., Westgate, 1966–73. **Educ.:** Univ. of MB, 1960, BA; Toronto Univ., 1970, BLS; Dalhousie Univ., 1979, MLS; Ont Dept. of Edu., 1967, Spec. Cert. in Sch. Libnshp. **Orgs.:** ON LA. Can. LA: Com. on Educ. for Lib. Persnl. Thunder Bay Pub. Lib. Bd. Mem. (1971–71); Ch. (1976). **Pubns.:** "The Library Technician in Ontario," *Expression* (S./O. 1979). **Activities:** 9, 11; 26, 31 **Addr.:** Lakehead University, School of Library Technology, Thunder Bay, ON P7B 5E1 Canada.

McIntosh, Geraldine Flynn (D., 1926, Flint, MI) Asst. Ed., Gale Resrch. Co., 1977–; Libn., Detroit Pub. Lib., Model Cities Bkmobile., 1970–71; Ms. Ed., Amer. Med. Assn., Chicago, 1960–61; Eng. Transl., *Migration Digest,* Intl. Cath. Migration Comsn., Switzerland, 1955–58. **Educ.:** Univ. of Detroit, 1946–48, 1966–68, BA (Eng., Phil.); Univ. of Geneva, Switzerland, 1953–55, Transl. Dip. (Fr., Eng., Span.); Wayne State Univ., 1969–71, MSLS. **Orgs.:** ALA. Bk. Club of Detroit. **Pubns.:** Eng. Transl., *Our Children and the Lord* (1965); Eng. Transl., *Ecumenism and the Future of the Church* (1967); Asst. Ed., *National Directory of Newsletters and Reporting Services* (1977–81); Eng. Transl., Chap. in *Ecumenism and the Future of the Church* (1967); Ed., other bks. **Activities:** 6; 30, 37, 49-ed. work; 57, 90, 95-Fr. Trans. **Addr.:** 120 Glynn Ct. Apt. 408, Detroit, MI 48202.

McIntosh, John D. L. (S. 19, 1940, Whitewood, SK) Slavic Biblgphr., Univ. of BC, 1975–, Sci. Biblgphr., 1972–75, Math. and Sci. Ref. Libn., 1970–72. **Educ.:** Univ. of BC, 1958–62, BA (Math, Phy.), 1965–68, MA (Slavonic Std.), 1969–70, BLS. **Orgs.:** Can. LA. Can. Assn. Slavists. Amer. Assn. Adv. Slavic Std. **Activities:** 1; 15; 54, 66 **Addr.:** 6248 Tiffany Blvd., Richmond, BC V7C 5B1 Canada.

McIver, Vivian (Downes) (Jl. 14, 1921, Needham, MA) Dir., Needham Free Pub. Lib., 1960–, Asst. Libn., 1957–59, Catlgr., 1943–44, 1946–57. **Educ.:** Simmons Coll., 1939–43, BS (LS). **Orgs.:** ALA. MA LA: Study Com. on Org. & Control (Ch.); Adult Educ. Com. (Ch., 1965–69). Grt. Boston Lib. Admins. Grp.: Pres. (1962–63). East. Reg. Lib. Adv. Cncl.: Ch. (1976–78). Monday Club of Needham. New Century Club of Needham. Charles River Simmons Club. Vestry, Christ Church, Needham. **Activities:** 9; 17, 20, 39; 50 **Addr.:** Needham Free Public Library, 1139 Highland Ave., Needham, MA 02194.

McKann, Michael R. (N. 2, 1941, Franklin, VA) Asso. State Libn., LA State Lib., 1978–; Ch., Acq. Dept., Univ. of FL Libs., 1970–77; Spec. Rep., Dept. of Def., Saigon, Vietnam, 1968–69; Org., Presl. Files, Intl. Situation Room, White House, Washington, DC, 1967–68; Resrch. Anal., Nat. Secur. Agency, 1966–70. **Educ.:** Coll. of William and Mary, 1960–64, AB (Eng.); Univ. of MI, 1965–66, AMLS. **Orgs.:** ALA: ASCLA, LAMA. Southwest LA. LA LA: Ch., Exhibits (1979). Sierra Club, Baton Rouge Grp. (Pres. 1980). Gainesville FL Cit. Adv. Com.: Ch. (1974–75). **Honors:** Beta Phi Mu; Univ. of MI, Margaret Mann Schol., 1966. **Pubns.:** "Library Cooperation in Louisiana: an Overview," *LA Lib. Assn. Bltn.* (Sum. 1981); "Flextime at Florida," *Lib. Jnl.* (N. 1973); reviews. **Activities:** 13; 17, 43; 54, 65, 67 **Addr.:** Louisiana State Library, P.O. Box 131, Baton Rouge, LA 70821.

McKannan, Ann Elaine Lindberg (F. 6, 1950, Chippewa Falls, WI) Recs. Libn., Arthur Young and Co., 1978–; Archvst., Ft. Sill Artly. Musm., 1974–77; Young People's Libn., Camp Kuwae, Okinowa, 1973–74. **Educ.:** Univ. of MI, 1969–71, BA (Anthro.); Our Lady of the Lake, San Antonio, TX, 1971–72,

PROFESSIONAL ACTIVITIES: Institutions: 1. Acad. lib.; 2. Arch.; 3. Assn.; 4. Fed./Gvt. lib.; 5. Inst. lib.; 6. Mfr./Suppl.; 7. Milit. lib.; 8. Musm.; 9. Pub. lib.; 10. Sch. lib.; 11. Sch. of lib. sci.; 12. Spec. lib.; 13. State lib.; 14. (other). **Functions/Activities:** 15. Acq./Col. dev.; 16. Adult srvs.; 17. Admin.; 18. Apprais.; 19. Archit./Bldgs.; 20. Cat./Class.; 21. Chld. srvs.; 22. Circ.; 23. Cons./Pres.; 24. Consult.; 25. Cont. ed.; 26. Educ. lib. sci.; 27. Ext. srvs.; 28. Fund/Grants; 29. Gvt. pubs.; 30. Indx./Abs.; 31. Instr. lib. use; 32. Media srvs.; 33. Micro.; 34. Netwks./Coop.; 35. Persnl.; 36. PR; 37. Publshg.; 38. Recs. mgt.; 39. Ref. srvs.; 40. Repro.; 41. Resrch.; 42. Review.; 43. Secur.; 44. Serials; 45. Spec. col.; 46. Tech. srvs.; 47. Trustees/Bds.; 48. YA srvs.; 49. (other).

MLS. **Orgs.:** SLA. Amer. Recs. Mgrs. Assn. **Honors:** Ft. Sill Artly. Musm., Letter of Comdn., 1977. **Activities:** 2, 9; 17, 38; 55, 59 **Addr.:** 8323 Cinnamon Ln. #707, Houston, TX 77072.

McKay, David N. (Ag. 31, 1929, San Diego CA) Dir./State Libn., NC State Lib., 1976–; Gen. Mgr., Richard Abel do. Brasil, 1975–76; Dir., Met. Lib. Srvc., 1969–75; Cul. Affairs Off., USIS Brazil, 1963–69; Dir., Palos Verdes Dist. Lib., 1958–63. **Educ.:** San Diego State Univ., 1949–53, AB (Phil.); Univ. of Southern CA, 1957–58, MSLS; Govt. Exec. Inst., 1979–, (cert); For. Srv. Inst., 1963. **Orgs.:** ALA: ASCLA/SLAS (Exec. Bd.). Exec. Bd. NC LA: Leg. Com. Southeastern LA. **Activities:** 13; 17 **Addr.:** 109 E. Jones St., Raleigh, NC 27611.

McKay, Eleanor (F. 19, 1946, Washington, DC) Cur., MS Valley Coll., Memphis State Univ., 1976–; Mss. Cur., State Hist. Socty. of WI, 1972–76, Asst. Mss. Cur., 1969–72. **Educ.:** Univ. of MD, 1963–67, BA (Hist.); Univ. of WI, 1967–69, MA (Hist.), Univ. of WI, 1972–75, MALS. Miami Univ., 1974 (Cert. Lib. Mgt.). **Orgs.:** SAA: Ch., Desc. Com. (1979–81); Ch., Status of Women Com. (1976–79). TN Archvst. Assn.: Steering Com. (1978); Midwest Arch. Conf.: Prog. Com. (1973–74); Rev. Cont. (1975–); Nwsltr., accessions ed. (1975–76). Amer. Assn. for State & Local Hist. W. TN Hist. Socty.: Cur. (1976–). Memphis Heritage, Inc. **Honors:** Phi Kappa Phi, 1978. **Pubns.:** *Guide to the Collections of the West Tennessee Historical Society* (1979); *Women's History: Resources at the State Historical Society of Wisconsin* (1975); 4th ed, 1979; "Random Sampling Techniques," *Amer. Archvst.* (Jl. 1978); Cont., "Bibliographic Resources of the Mid-South," *Memphis, the Mid-South, and the Mississippi Valley* (1980); "Randon Sampling Techniques," *Amer. Archvst.* (Jl. 1978). **Activities:** 1, 2; 20, 28, 45; 85 **Addr.:** Mississippi Valley Collection, Memphis State University, Memphis, TN 38152.

McKay, Kate W. (Fairmount, GA) Copyrt. Libn., NY Univ., Sch. of Law, 1978–; Libn., Inst. of Judicial Admin., 1975–78. **Educ.:** Univ. of GA, BS (Bus.); Columbia Univ., MLS; New York Univ., MBE. **Orgs.:** AALL. Law LA of Grt. NY. Metro. Resrch. and Ref. Org. **Addr.:** New York University School of Law Library, 40 Washington Sq. S., New York, NY 10012.

McKee, Christopher (Je. 14, 1935, Brooklyn, NY) Libn. of the Coll., Grinnell Coll., 1972–; Asst. Dir., Lovejoy Lib., South. IL Univ., 1969–72, Bk. Sel. Ofcr., 1967–69, Soc. Sci. Libn., 1962–66; Cat. Libn., Washington and Lee Univ., 1958–62. **Educ.:** Univ. of St. Thomas, 1957, AB (Eng., Phil.); Univ. of MI, 1960, AMLS. **Orgs.:** IA State Lib. Adv. Cncl.: Acad. Lib. Rep. (1976–77). IA OCLC Cncl.: Exec. Com. (1976–77). IA LA: Nom. Com. (1976–77). IA Pvt. Acad. Libns.: Ch. (1977–78). Amer. Milit. Inst. Org. of Amer. Histns. Socty. for Nautical Resrch. U.S. Nvl. Inst. **Honors:** Univ. of MI, H.W. Wilson Flwshp., 1957–58; Univ. of St. Thomas, Anl. Alum. Awd., 1973. **Pubns.:** "The Navy in the Nineteenth Century, 1789–1889," *A Guide to the Sources of United States Military History: Supplement I* (1981); various pubns. on milit. hist. **Addr.:** Burling Library, Grinnell College, Grinnell, IA 50112.

McKee, Eugenia V. (My. 22, 1951, St. Louis, MO) Head of Tech. Srv., Maryville Coll. Lib., 1977–, OCLC Libn., 1976–77, Asst. Prof., Tech. Srv. Classes, 1977–; Instr. of Cat., Washington Univ., 1980. **Educ.:** Kenyon Coll., 1969–73, AB (Relig.); Univ. of MO (Columbia), 1974–75, MA (LS). **Orgs.:** St. Louis Tech. Srv. Assn.: Prog. Com. (1980–). Midwest Reg. Lib. Netwk.: OCLC Qual. Control Grp. (1978–79); OCLC Users Adv. Com. (1980–). ALA: LITA; RTSD. **Activities:** 1; 20, 29, 46 **Addr.:** Maryville College Library, 13550 Conway Rd., St. Louis, MO 63141.

McKell, Linda J. (Je. 23, 1949, Palo Alto, CA) Lib. Mgr., Four-Phase Systs., 1978–; Ref. Libn., Stanford Univ. 1981–82; Lib. Mgr., Systs. Cntrl. Inc., 1974–78. **Educ.:** Brigham Young Univ., 1969–71, BA (Hum.), 1972–74, MLS. **Orgs.:** SLA: San Andreas Chap. (Treas., 1980–82). Midpenninsula Open Space Dist. Los Altos Hills Horseman Assn. **Activities:** 12; 17, 32; 56 **Addr.:** 938—23 Clark, Mountain View, CA 94040.

McKelvey, Josephine Faulkner (S. 3, 1918, Gallipolis, OH) YA Libn., 1971–; Comp. Proj. Coord., Chappaqua Lib., 1978–; Sub. Tchr., Chappaqua Ctrl. Sch. Dist., No. 4, 1960–64; Tchr., Plymouth (OH) HS, 1939–41. **Educ.:** Oberlin Coll., 1935–39, AB (Latin); Columbia Univ., 1967–71, MS hons. (LS). **Orgs.:** ALA. NY LA. Westchester LA. **Honors:** Phi Beta Kappa, 1939; Beta Phi Mu, 1971. **Activities:** 9; 15, 39, 48; 55, 63 **Addr.:** Chappaqua Library, 195 S. Greeley Ave., Chappaqua, NY 10514.

McKelvey, Sr. Mary Joanne (Jl. 11, 1919, Holtwood, PA) Libn., O'Connell HS (Arlington, VA), 1961–; Libn., Villa Maria Acad. (Malvern, PA), 1955–61; Asst. Libn., Immaculata Coll., 1952–55; various sch. libn. positions, 1941–47. **Educ.:** Millersville State Coll., 1937–41, BS (LS); Drexel Univ., 1954, MS (LS); Franklin & Marshall Coll., 1941; MI State Univ., 1966 (Educ. Media). **Orgs.:** Cath. LA: Unit Ch. (1969–73). Natl. Cath. Educ. Assn. **Honors:** Beta Phi Mu, 1954. **Activities:** 1, 10; 15, 17, 20 **Addr.:** Immaculate Heart Convent, 27th & Trinidad St., Arlington, PA 22213.

McKelvey, Sandra Spitzer (O. 20, 1940, Scranton, PA) Sci. Info. Mgt. Coord., Merck, Sharp and Dohme Resrch. Labs., 1977–, Sr. Lit. Chem., 1968–77, Chem., 1962–68. **Educ.:** PA State Univ., 1958–62, BS (Chem.); Villanova Univ., 1966–69, MS (LS); Drexel Univ., 1977, (LS). **Orgs.:** SLA. PA Lib. Netwk.: Users Cncl. Nom. Com. (1981). Digital Equip. Comp. Users Socty. Amer. Chem. Socty. Intl. Info. and Word Prcs. Assn.: Mtgs. Regis. Com. (1981). **Pubns.:** Various pubns. chem. and pharm. **Activities:** 12; 17, 35; 56, 60, 87, 91 **Addr.:** Merck Sharp & Dohme Research Laboratories, Scientific Literature Resource Center, Bldg. 26-276, West Point, PA 19486.

McKenna, Florence M. (My. 5, 1930, Homestead, PA) Asst. Dir. for Tech. Srvs., Univ. of Pittsburgh, 1981–; Coord., Prcs. Dept., 1972–80, Nat. Sci. Biblgphr., 1967–72; Supvsr., Tech. Lib., Westinghouse Electric Corp. Astronuclear Lab., 1961–67; Libn., Hagan Chem. & Controls, Inc., 1954–61; Asst., Sci. and Tech. Dept., Carnegie Lib. of Pittsburgh, 1953–54. **Educ.:** Duquesne Univ., 1948–52, BEd (Bio.); Carnegie Inst. of Tech., 1952–53, MLS. **Orgs.:** ALA. SLA: Tech. Book Review Index Com. (1967–70); Ch., Place. Policy Com., (1970–72); Deputy Conf. Ch., (1973); Pittsburgh Chap., Pres. (1959–60); Dir. (1960–61; 1966–68; 1978–79). Pittsburgh Reg. Lib. Ctr.: OCLC Com. (1976–). Bus. and Prof. Women's Club of Pittsburgh. Univ. of Pittsburgh: Senate Cncl. (1977–). **Activities:** 1, 12; 17, 46; 91 **Addr.:** 4517 Parade St., Pittsburgh, PA 15207.

McKenzie, Donald Ross (Ap. 10, 1951, Bowmanville, ONT) Chief Libn. and Secy./-Treas., Town of Caledon Pub. Libs., 1978–; Libn. 1, Toronto Pub. Libs., 1975–78. **Educ.:** Univ. of Toronto, 1970–73, BA (Drama), 1973–75, MLS. **Orgs.:** Admin. of Medium-sized Pub. Libs. of ON: Ch. (1979–). Can. LA. Corp. des Bibl. Prof. du Quebec. Ont. LA. ON Pub. Libns. Adv. Cncl. **Activities:** 9; 17, 47; 74, 89 **Addr.:** Town of Caledon Public Libraries, Box 788, Bolton, ON L0P 1A0 Canada.

McKenzie, Dorothy Clayton (N. 2, 1910, Garden City, KS) Prof. of Chld. and YA Lit., CA State Univ., Los Angeles, 1960–; Visit. Prof., Univ. of UT Grad. Sch. of LS, 1969–70; Tchr., Pasadena City Schs., 1942–59; Libn., Windsor Consolidated Schs., 1931–34. **Educ.:** Univ. of North. CO, 1931, BA; Claremont Grad. Sch., 1945–50; Univ. of South. CA, 1959, BSLS. **Orgs.:** ALA: YASD; ALSC. CA Cncl. on Lit. for Chld. and Young People: Pres. South. CA Readg. is Fundamental: VP. CA Writer's Gld. PTA. **Honors:** Grolier Awd., 1978; Univ. of North. CO Alum. Assn., Outstand. Women Educ., 1973; CA State Univ., Los Angeles, Prof. of the Yr., 1966; South. CA Cncl. on Lit. for Chld. and Young People, Outstand. Srv. Awd., 1964. **Pubns.:** Various articles, reviews. **Activities:** 14-Eng. Dept.; 21, 48 **Addr.:** 1260 Brookmere Rd., Pasadena, CA 91105.*

McKenzie, Duncan John (D. 31, 1950, Port Huron, MI) Head, Admin. Srvs., Hammond Pub. Lib., 1978–; Head, Adult Srvs., St. Clair Cnty. Lib., 1977–78, Admin. Asst., 1974–77. **Educ.:** Western MI Univ., 1970–73, BA (Eng/Sec. Educ.), 1973–74, MSL. Miami Univ., Oxford, OH, 1975, (Cert. Lib. Admin.). **Orgs.:** ALA. IN LA. MI LA: Secy./Treas., Pub. Lib. Div. (1976–77); Ed. Bd., *MI Libn.* (1977–78). **Pubns.:** "Library Schools Are Preparing Librarians, Not Library Adminstrators," *MI Libn.* (Spr. 1977); "Performance Measurement," *Lib. Occurrent* (Ag. 1979). **Activities:** 9; 17 **Addr.:** Hammond Public Library, 564 State St., Hammond, IN 46320.

McKenzie, Mary A. (Ag. 6, 1928, Olton, TX) Head, Pub. Srvs., U.S. Coast Guard Acad. Lib., 1980–; Exec. Dir., New Eng. Lib. Bd., 1974–78; Coll. Libn., CT Coll. Lib., 1968–74, Asst. Libn., 1967–68; Asst. Info. Ofcr., Lib. of Congs., 1965–67, Info. & Ed. Spec., 1964–65, Head, Monthly Checklist Sect., 1962–64, Asst. Head, Amer.-British Exch. Sect., 1961–62, Other positions, 1948–61. **Educ.:** N. TX State Univ., 1945–48, 60, BA (Eng.); Cath. Univ., 1960–61, 70, MSLS; Mgt. Cert., Lib. of Congs., 1963. **Orgs.:** CT State Lib. Adv. Cncl.: Vice Ch. (1972–74). CT LA: Strg. Com., Target '76 (1971–73); Secy., Coll. and Univ. Sect. (1968–69). New Eng. LA: Pres. (1972–73) ALA: Cncl. (1972–73); ACRL, Ch., Pubns. Com. (1975–77). Other orgs. **Honors:** Beta Phi Mu, Iota Chap., Outstan. Scholar Awd., 1970. **Pubns.:** Ed., *Proceedings of the 3d Assembly on the Library Functions of the States* (1964); "Challenges and Prospects: The Library in the '70's," *CT Coll. Alumn. News* (Spr. 1971); "New England Library Association," *Encyclopedia of Lib. & Information Science* (1977); Ed., *Lib. of Congs. Info. Bltn.* (1965–67); Ed., NELB LINK: (1976–78). **Activities:** 1, 4; 17, 37, 39; 55 **Addr.:** Heritage Cove, River Rd., Essex, CT 06426.

McKevitt, Gerald (Jl. 3, 1939, Longview, WA) Univ. Archvst., Asst. Prof. of Hist., Univ. of Santa Clara, 1974–. **Educ.:** Univ. of San Francisco, 1957–61, AB (Hist.); Univ. of South. CA, 1961–64, MA (Hist.); Univ. of CA, Los Angeles, 1975, PhD (Hist.); Pontifical Gregorian Univ., Rome, 1977, BST (Theo.). **Orgs.:** SAA. CA Hist. Socty. West. Hist. Assn. Org. of Amer. Histns. Amer. Cath. Hist. Assn. **Pubns.:** *The University of Santa Clara, a History, 1851-1977* (1979); "Franciscan Mission to Jesuit College," *South. CA Qtly.* (Sum. 1976); "Jesuit Arrival in California," *Recs. of the Amer. Cath. Hist. Socty.* (S.–D. 1974); "Gold Lake Rush," *Jnl. of the West* (Jl. 1965); various articles. **Activities:** 2; 17 **Addr.:** University of Santa Clara, Santa Clara, CA 95053.

McKiernan, Lester I. (F. 13, 1943, Keokuk, IA) Dir., Choctaw Nation Multi-Cnty. Lib. Syst., 1979–; Dir., Cahaba Reg. Lib., 1977–79. **Educ.:** Culver-Stockton Coll., 1969–73, BS (Bus. Admin.); Univ. of AL, 1976–77, MS (LS). **Orgs.:** ALA. AL LA. OK LA. SWLA. Lion's Intl. Work Proj., Inc. **Activities:** 9, 14-Reg. Lib. Syst.; 17, 35; 59 **Addr.:** 1012 S. Strong, McAlester, OK 74501.

McKinney, Barbara Jean (N. 6, 1944, Temple, TX) Lib. Media Spec., Oak Grove HS (N. Little Rock, AR), 1975–; Elem. Libn., Libertyville (IL) Pub. Sch., 1972–73; Mid. Sch. Libn., Spaudling Pub. Sch. (Waukegan, IL), 1970–72. **Educ.:** Ouachita Bapt. Univ., 1962–66, BSE (Eng.); TX Woman's Univ., 1975–79, MLS. **Orgs.:** AR Assn. of Sch. Libn. & Media Educ.: Secy. (1981). Ctrl. AR Media Educ. Org.: Secy. (1980–81). AR AV Assn., Bd. (1980–83). **Honors:** AR AV Assn., Heloise Griffon Media Scholar., 1980. **Activities:** 10; 31, 32, 48; 63 **Addr.:** 10607 Breckenridge Dr., Little Rock, AR 72211.

McKinney, Eleanor Ruth (Ag. 6, 1918, Comstock, NE) Assoc. Prof., West. MI Univ., 1967–; Head Libn., Hanover Park Reg. HS Dist., 1956–66; Libn., Montclair HS 1954–56; Libn., Columbia HS, 1949–54; Libn., Elmwood and Nassau Schs., 1946–48; Libn., Neptune HS, 1941–46; Tchr.–Libn., Oaklyn Jr. HS, 1939–41. **Educ.:** Trenton State Coll., 1934–39, BS (Hist., Eng.); Columbia Univ. 1939–49, BLS; West. MI Univ., 1967–68, EDS (Libnshp.). **Orgs.:** NJ Sch. LA: Pres. (1952–54). ALA: MI Mem. Ch. (1970–76); AASL, Reg. Ch. (1972–75). Assn. for Supvsn. and Curric. Dev. MI LA. MI Assn. for Media in Educ. Delta Kappa Gamma: Local Chap. (Treas., 1976–78). **Honors:** Beta Phi Mu, 1969. **Pubns.:** *The Good Seed: Library Planning for the Disadvantaged Child Three to Seven* (1970); Jt. auth., *Library Service to Families* (1981); "Another degree? What For?" *Sch. Libs.* (Spr. 1969). **Activities:** 10, 11; 21, 32, 48; 63, 66 **Addr.:** 3226 Tamsin Ave., Kalamazoo, MI 49008.

McKinney, Norma Gayle (S. 7, 1939, Troy, AL) Ref. Libn. and Comp. Srch. Coord., Pullen Lib., GA State Univ., 1979–, Asst. Head, Ref. Dept., 1970–79; Gen. Srvs. Libn., Price Gilbert Meml. Lib. GA Inst. of Tech., 1966–70; Ref. Libn., ILL, Emory Univ. Lib., 1964–66, Ref. Libn. and Russ. Cat., 1962–64; Head Ref. Libn., Montgomery Pub. Lib. 1961. **Educ.:** Auburn Univ., 1957–60, BS (Educ.); FL State Univ., 1960–62, MS (Libnshp.); Emory Univ., 1962–64 (Russ.). **Orgs.:** Metro-Atlanta LA: Secty. (1974–75). GA LA: Pubcty. Com. (1970–71); Coll. and Univ. Sect., (Secy., 1979–); Handbook Com. (1971–81), Ch., 1975–79). Southeast. LA: Ch., Handbook Com. (1980–82). AAUP: Exec. Com., GSU chap. (1978–79). **Honors:** Phi Kappa Phi; Beta Phi Mu; Sigma Tau Delta. **Activities:** 1, 12; 17, 31, 39; 56, 59, 63 **Addr.:** 5108 Falconwood Ct., Norcross, GA 30071.

McKinnie, William George (My. 31, 1942, Strathroy, ON) Head, Lib. Srv., Guelph Collegiate and Vocational Inst., 1977–; Tchr., Libn., Hagersville Secondary Sch., 1967–77; Tchr., Libn., Lahr Senior Sch., Lahr, Ger., 1969–71. **Educ.:** Univ. of West. ON, 1964, BA (Eng.), 1976, MLS; Spec. Cert., Sch. Libnshp., 1969. **Orgs.:** Wellington Cnty. Libn. Assn.: Prog. Com. (1977–78, Ch., 1979–80); Staffing Com. (1980–81). Can. Sch. LA: Secy., Treas. (1980–81). ON Sch. LA. Univ. West. ON Assoc. Tchr. Assn. ON Sec. Sch. Tchr. Fed.: Dist. Comm. Ofcr. (1975–76). Mocha Shrine Club. **Pubns.:** "Woodland Indian Cultural Education Centre Library: Its Development and Holdings ...," *Moccasin Telegraph* (Sum. 1976); various local pubns.; Reviews. **Activities:** 10; 63, 72, 89 **Addr.:** Library, Guelph Collegiate Vocational Institute, Guelph, ON Canada.

McKinnon, Linda M. (Ag. 27, 1940, Manchester, NH) Mgr., Lib. Srvs., Sanders Assoc. Inc., 1977–; Supvsr., Tech. Lit. Resrch., 1972–77, Info. Spec., Mtrls. Sci., 1967–71; Chemical Libn., Monsanto Resrch. Corp., 1963–67. **Educ.:** Boston Univ., 1963, BS (Chem.); Rivier Coll., 1979, MBA (Bus. Admin.); Boston Univ., grad. prog. in comp. sci. **Orgs.:** NH State Lib. Adv. Cncl.: Autom. Com. (Ch., 1980–83). SLA. NH Legis. Acad. Sci. and Engin.: Exec. Cncl. (1980–83). Inst. Electrical and Electronics Engins. Assn. for Comp. Mach. Amer. Chemical Socty. Amer. Socty. for Metals: Secy. (1970–73). **Honors:** Amer. Socty. for Metals, Outstan. Young Mem., 1975. **Pubns.:** "Technology Transfer from the Corporate Library," *Mgt. Review* (My. 1979); "The Corporate Library as a Source for New Technology," *Long Range Plng.* (Ap. 1980); "Sanders Assoc. Solar Energy Data Base," (1975). **Activities:** 12; 17, 24, 30; 56, 60 **Addr.:** Courtland Ave. RFD #3, Manchester, NH 03103.

McKirdy, Pamela Reekes (Ag. 8, 1949, Woodbury, NJ) Syst. Libn., Harvard Univ. Lib., 1976–; Visit. Lectr., Simmons Coll., Sch. of LS, 1977–; Head, LC Cat., OCLC Coord., MA Inst. of Tech. Lib., 1975–76, Cat., OCLC Coord., 1973–75. **Educ.:** MA Inst. of Tech., 1967–71, SB (Hum.); Simmons Coll., 1973–76, MLS. **Orgs.:** ALA: ACRL, New Eng. Prog. Plng. Com. (1978). MIT Alum. Assn.: Tech. Day Plng. Com. (1977–79, Ch., 1980). MIT Alum. Cncl. **Honors:** MA Inst. Tech., Harold E. Lobdell Disting. Srv. Awd., 1980. **Activities:** 1, 11; 26; 56, 75 **Addr.:** 60 Rounsevell Rd., Tewksbury, MA 01876.

McKissick, Mabel F. Rice (Je. 12, 1922, Union, SC) Libn./Media Spec., New London HS, 1979–, Libn./Media Spec., New London Jr. HS, 1968–79; Libn., Sims HS, 1948–68, Tchr.,

Special Subjects/Services: 50. Adult educ.; 51. Advert./Mktg.; 52. Aerosp.; 53. Agric.; 54. Area std.; 55. Arts/Hum.; 56. Autom.; 57. Bibl./Prtg.; 58. Bio. sci.; 59. Bus./Fin.; 60. Chem.; 61. Copyrt.; 62. Documtn.; 63. Educ.; 64. Engin.; 65. Env.; 66. Eth. grps.; 67. Film; 68. Food/Nutr.; 69. Geneal.; 70. Geo.; 71. Geol.; 72. Handcpd.; 73. Hist.; 74. Int. frdm.; 75. Info. sci.; 76. Insr.; 77. Law; 78. Legis.; 79. Math./Comp. sci.; 80. Med.; 81. Metals; 82. Nat. resrcs.; 83. Newsp.; 84. Nuc. sci.; 85. Oral hist.; 86. Petr./Energy; 87. Pharm.; 88. Phys./Astr./Math.; 89. Readg.; 90. Relig.; 91. Sci./Tech.; 92. Soc. sci.; 93. Telecom.; 94. Transp.; 95. (other).

1943–48. **Educ.:** Knoxville Coll., 1939–43, AB (Soclgy.); Teachers Coll., Columbia Univ., 1952–54, MA (Curric., Tchg.), 1960–66, MSLS. **Orgs.:** ALA: AASL (1970–73) Treatment of Minority Grps. in lib. materials com. CT Educ. Media Assn.: Bd. of Dir. (1978–81). CT Sch. LA: Pres. (1973–74). New Eng. Educ. Media Assn.: Bd. of Dir. (1974–75). AAUW. Delta Kappa Gamma Socty. For Women Educ. Delta Sigma Theta Sorority, Inc. Zonta Intl. **Honors:** ALA, Coretta Scott King Awd. Com., Distin. Srv. in Promoting Black writing, 1974. CT Educ. Media Assn. Rheta Clark Award, 1980. **Activities:** 10; 15, 17, 20, 22, 32 **Addr.:** P.O. Box 1122, 201 Hempstead St., New London, CT 06320.

McKown, Cornelius J. (My. 25, 1931, Pittsburgh, PA) Phys. Sci. Libn., PA State Univ., 1973–, Asst. Head, Agri. & Biol. Sci. Lib., 1971–73. **Educ.:** Univ. of Pittsburgh, 1949–53, 1956–57, BS (Zlgy.); PA State Univ., 1958–60, MS (Entomology); Univ. of Pittsburgh, 1969–70, MLS. **Orgs.:** SLA: Ctrl. PA Chap., Secy., Mem. Bd. of Dir. ALA. PA LA. CSLA. Hist. of Sci. Socty. Dictionary Socty. of N. Amer. Intl. Sci. Assn. of Esperantists. **Pubns.:** "Use of Chem. Abstracts On-line," *Proc. PA Acad. of Sci.* (1980). **Activities:** 1, 12; 17; 60, 88 **Addr.:** Physical Sciences Library, 230 Davey Lab., University Park, PA 16802.

McLaren, Duncan (O. 29, 1939, Toronto, ON) Pres., McLaren Micropublshg. Ltd., 1973–; Proj. Mgr., ON Ethnic Newspaper Microfilming Proj., Cncl. of ON Univ., 1971–73; Ref. Libn., Ryerson Polytech. Inst., 1968–70; Head, Coll. Dept., Pergamon of Canada Ltd., 1965–68. **Educ.:** Univ. of Toronto, 1957–60, BA (Eng.), 1967–68, BLS, 1970–71, MLS. **Orgs.:** Can. LA. ALA. Bibl. Socty. of Can. Can. Assn. of Archvsts. Can. Ethnic Std. Assn. Can. Hist. Assn. **Pubns.:** *Ontario Ethno-Cultural Newspapers* (1973). **Activities:** 6; 17, 33, 37; 55, 66, 83 **Addr.:** McLaren Micropublishing Limited, P.O. Box 972, Station F, Toronto, M4Y 2N9 Canada.

Mc Laren, M. Bruce (N. 17, 1940, Detroit, MI) Dir., Lrng. Resrc. Ctr. and Instr. TV, NM Milit. Inst., 1976–; Dir., Media Srv., Wayne-Westland Sch., 1971–76; Asst. Prof., LS, Long Island Univ., 1968–71; Lib. Syst. Design, Oakland (MI) Sch., 1967–68; HS Libn., Holly Sch., 1963–65. **Educ.:** West. MI Univ., 1959–63, BA (Hist., LS); Wayne State Univ., 1963–68, MEd (Instr. Tech.). **Orgs.:** AECT: Media Mgt. Div. (Pres., 1975–76); Reg. 8 Coord. (1979–). NM Media Assn.: Pres. (1978–79). NM LA. Phi Delta Kappa. **Pubns.:** *Media Accountability: Keystone of the Freedom to Learn* (1980); "Management of Media Resources for Special Education," *T. H. E. Jnl.* (S. 1979); "Making Media Accountability Work," *Educ. and Indus. TV* (O. 1979); "Educated Americans Today or Functional Illiterates Tomorrow," *DEMM (AECT) Nsltr.* (Fall 1979); "Media Managers Are Evaluators and Facilitators," *Educ. and Indus. TV* (De. 1979); other pubns. **Activities:** 1 **Addr.:** Learning Resource Center & Instructional Television, New Mexico Military Institute, Roswell, NM 88201.

McLaughlin, Douglas F. (N. 4, 1942, Long Beach, CA) Ref. Libn., Oxnard Pub. Lib., 1974–; Ref. Libn., Oxnard Cmnty. Coll. Lib., 1976–. **Educ.:** Univ. of Redlands, 1961–64, BA (Econ.); Univ. of Denver, 1969–70, MSBA (Mktg.), 1972–73, MALS. **Orgs.:** CA LA. Reforma. **Activities:** 1, 9; 15, 16, 39; 59, 69 **Addr.:** Oxnard Public Library, 214 S. "C" St., Oxnard, CA 93030.

McLellan, Mary Theresa (F. 25, 1927, Quincy, MA) Legis. Ref. Libn., MA State Lib., 1973–, Ref. Libn., 1969–73; Ref. Libn., Thomas Crane Pub. Lib., Quincy, MA, 1962–69. **Educ.:** Suffolk Univ., 1977–78, (Gvt.); Cert., Prof. Libn., 1965. **Orgs.:** Assn. of Boston Law Libns. AALL. Law Libns. of New Eng. **Pubns.:** Jt. auth., *Guide to Massachusetts Legislative and Government Research* (1981); jt. auth., *Interns Guide to Legislative Research* (1973). **Activities:** 4, 13; 30, 39, 41; 77, 78, 83 **Addr.:** Massachusetts State Library, Rm. 341, State House, Boston, MA 02133.

McLemore, Andrew J. (F. 6, 1932, Memphis, TN) Dir. Lib., Savannah State Coll., 1966–; Libn., Miles Coll., 1962–66; Libn., Spec. Srv., Atlanta Univ., 1958–62. **Educ.:** Morehouse College, 1950–54, AB (Econ.); Atlanta Univ., 1958–60, MLS; GA South., 1970–75, MBA; John Marshall, 1972–76, LLB (Law). **Orgs.:** ALA. SELA. GA LA. Alpha Phi Alpha Fraternity. F. and A. M. Prince Hall Masons. GA Bar Assn. **Addr.:** 1412 Stillwood Dr., Savannah, GA 31406.

McLeod, Emilie Warren (Boston, MA) Dir., Ed., Unicorn Books, 1978–; Ed., Chld. Book, 1956–78; Assoc. Dir., Atlantic Monthly Press, 1976–78; Asst. Ed., Chld. Bks, Houghton, 1950–52. **Educ.:** Mt. Holyoke Coll., 1944–48, BA (Eng.). **Orgs.:** ALA. New Eng. LA. Socty. Chld. Book Writers. IBBY. **Pubns.:** Several chlds. books. **Activities:** 6, 14; 21, 37, 48 **Addr.:** Unicorn Books, 90 Commonwealth Ave., Boston, MA 02116.

McLeod, Herbert Eugene (Ag. 27, 1930, Rembert, SC) Libn. and Prof. of Bibl., Southeastern Baptist Theol. Sem., 1967–; Prof., Agri. Eng., OH State Univ., 1962–64; Assoc. Prof. of Agri. Eng., Clemson Univ., 1960–62, Asst. Prof., 1958–60, Instr., 1953–55. **Educ.:** Clemson Univ., 1947–51, BS (Agri. Eng.); IA State Univ., 1955–57, MS (Agri. Eng.), 1957–59, PhD (Agri. Eng.); Southeastern Sem., 1964–67, BD; Univ. of NC, Chapel Hill, 1967–72, MSLS. **Orgs.:** Amer. Theo. Lib. Assn.: Per. Exch. Com. (1970–73); Ch. (1972–73). ALA. NC LA. Southeastern LA. Assn. of Bapt. Profs. of Rel. Southern Bapt. Hist. Socty. Rotary Intl. Wake Forest Bapt. Ch. **Honors:** Gamma Sigma Delta. **Pubns.:** "Characteristics of Biblical Research Journal Literature," Amer. Theo. LA *Nwsltr. Supp.*, (F. 1973); "The Seminary Library and the Pursuit of Excellence", *The Outlook.* (Mr/Ap. 1969). **Activities:** 1; 17; 90 **Addr.:** Southeastern Seminary Library, P. O. Box 752, Wake Forest, NC 27587.

McLeod, Norman C. (N. 11, 1943, Sackville, NB) Chief Libn., Guelph Pub. Lib., 1977–; Chief Libn., Sources Pub. Lib., 1973–77; Head of Pub. Srv., Bishop's Univ., 1970–73. **Educ.:** Mt. Allison Univ., 1961–65, BA (Eng.); Univ. of Toronto, 1966–67, BLS; McGill Univ., 1973–75, MLS. **Orgs.:** Can. LA: Local Arrange. Com. Conf. (1977). ON LA. **Activities:** 9; 17 **Addr.:** Guelph Public Library, Guelph, ON N1H 4J6 Canada.

McMahon, Nathalie Gibbens (D. 29, 1933, Baton Rouge, LA) Asst. Dir., Air Force Lib., HQ/AFMPC, 1977–; Base Libn., Fairchild Air Force Base, 1972–77; Base Libn., NAHA Air Base Okinawa, 1971–72. **Educ.:** LA State Univ., 1951–55, BA (Eng.), 1968–69, MSLS. **Orgs.:** ALA: PLA, Armed Forces Libn. Sect., PR Com. (Ch., 1974–76), Mem. (1979–80), Secy. (1976–77), VP/Pres. Elect (1980), Pres. (1981). **Honors:** Strategic Air Command Pubcty. Awd., 1973, 1974, 1975, 1976; Strategic Air Command First Fed. Women's Prog. Awd., 1976; Outstand. Support Human Rel. Prog. Awd., 1976; various other honors. **Pubns.:** *PACAF Basic Bibl.: Okinawa* (1971); "Armed Forces Libraries," *ALA Yrbk.* (1976 and 1977). **Activities:** 4, 10; 17 **Addr.:** HQ AFMPC/MPCSOA, Randolph Air Force Base, TX 78148.

McManus, Margaret Patricia (Ag. 23, 1934, Windsor, ON) Libn. Consult., Windsor Separate Sch. Bd., 1966–; Tchr., various places. **Educ.:** Univ. of Windsor, 1952–57, BA (Hist.); London Tchr. Coll., 1958–59 (Tchr. Cert.). **Orgs.:** ON LA: Treas. (1969–71); Awd. Com. (1979–81). Can. LA. Beta Sigma Phi: Xi Delta Chap., Pres. (1980–81). ON Eng. Cath. Tchr. Assn.: Secy./Treas. (1964–65). **Activities:** 10, 14-Tchr. ctr.; 20, 24, 32; 63 **Addr.:** Windsor Separate School Board, 1485 Janette Ave., Windsor, ON Canada.

McMartin, Ruth C. (Je. 12, 1915, Lansing, MI) Retired. Dir. of Instr. Resrcs., Fargo Pub. Sch., 1966–80; HS libn., Celina (OH) Pub. Sch., 1955–66; Tchr., Coldwater (OH) Pub. Sch., 1954–55; Catlgr., Univ. of TX, 1940–43. **Educ.:** MI State Univ., 1932–36, BA (Frgn. Lang.); Univ. of IL, 1936–40, MS LS; other courses. **Orgs.:** ALA: Cncl. (1972–76); Com. on Educ. for Libnshp. (1973–75); AASL, Media Ctr. Facilities Com. (1977–1980, Ch., 1978–80). ND Dept. of Pub. Instr.: Lib. Media Support Persnl. (Ch., 1979); Handbook Com. (1973–74); State Cred. (1968–69). Delta Kappa Gamma. Girl Scouts of America. **Pubns.:** "Standards for School Libraries," *Delta Kappa Gamma Bltn.* (Sum. 1972); "Encouraging Interest in Local Art," *School Media Qtly.* (Fall, 1977). **Activities:** 10; 17, 32 **Addr.:** 1103 26th Ave., South, Fargo, ND 58103.

McMaster, Deborah L. (D. 4, 1949, Davenport, IA) Coord., Pub. Srvs., Bowman Gray Sch. of Med., 1978–; Ref. Libn., Libn., Univ. of NE Med. Ctr., Eppley Inst. for Cancer Resrch., 1972–78. **Educ.:** IL State Univ., 1967–71, BS (Bio.); Univ. of MO, 1971–72, MALS; 1975, Med. LA, Cert. **Orgs.:** Med. LA: Mid-Atl. Reg. Grp., RML IV On-Line Srvs. Com. (1980–81). NC OLUG. **Activities:** 1, 12; 22, 31, 39; 58, 80 **Addr.:** Bowman Gray School of Medicine, Winston-Salem, NC 27103.

McMichael, Betty J. (F. 15, 1921, Stoughton, WI) Church Libn., Calvary Bible Church, Boulder, CO, 1960–; Resrch. Anal., Univ. of CO, 1961–; Freelnc. Writer and Ed., 1972–. **Educ.:** Univ. of North. IA, 1938–41, BA (Math.); Univ. of CO, 1963–65, MEd. **Orgs.:** CSLA. Evangelical Church Lib. Assn. **Honors:** *Christianity Today* Outstan. Evang. Bk. for 1977. **Pubns.:** *The Library and Resource Center in Christian Education* (1977); "Making the Most of Your Church Library," *Profile* (Spr. 1978); "How to Finance a Church or Synagogue Library," *Church and Synagogue Libs.* (N. 1977); "The Church Library and the Christian Bookstore," *Bookstore Jnl.* (O. 1974); "How Does Your Church Library Compare with Others?" *The Evang. Beacon* (Ag. 20, 1974); various articles. **Activities:** 12; 90 **Addr.:** 3150 18th St., Boulder, CO 80302.

McMillan, Barclay F. H. (Je. 25, 1932, Belfast, Northern Ireland, UK) Head, Msc. Cat., Natl. Lib. of Can., 1979–, Srch. Spec., Comp.-Based Ref., 1978–79, Serials Catlgr., 1977–78; Mgr., Radio Can. Army Europe (Germany), Can. Broadcasting Corp., 1967–71. **Educ.:** Carleton Univ., 1971–73, BA (Msc.), 1973–74, BMus (Hons.); Univ. of Toronto, 1975–77, MLS. **Orgs.:** Msc. LA. Can. LA. Can. Assn. of Msc. Libs.: Jt. Com. on Can. Msc. Bibl. (1979–). Bibl. Socty. of Can. **Honors:** Beta Phi Mu, 1977. **Pubns.:** "Tune-book Imprints in Canada to 1867: A Descriptive Bibliography" *Papers of the Bibl. Socty. of Canada* (1977). **Activities:** 4; 17, 20, 39; 55, 56, 57 **Addr.:** 1210 Prince of Wales Dr., Ottawa, ON K2C 1M9 Canada.

McMillan, Jacqulyn S. (S. 4, 1947, Lubbock, TX) Legal Libn., J.C. Penney Co., 1976–80; Acq. Libn., Washington & Lee Univ. Law Sch., 1974–76; Indexer-Minutes of Board of Reg., Univ. of TX, Austin, 1974. **Educ.:** TX Tech Univ., 1965–69, BA (Hist.); Univ. of TX, Austin, 1973–74, MLS. TX, 1969, (Sec. Tchrs. Cert.). **Orgs.:** AALL: Rel., Pub. and Dealers Com. (1975–79). Law Libn. Assn. of Greater NY: Pres. (1979–80); VP (1978–79). SLA. Oral Hist. Assn. Gamma Phi Beta. Pres., Alumni 1971–72. **Honors:** Beta Phi Mu, 1974. **Pubns.:** "Subject Heading Lists for Legal Memoranda," *Legal Econ.* (ABA) (Mr., Ap. 1980). **Activities:** 12; 15, 17, 39; 59, 77, 78 **Addr.:** 29 Cambridge Ave., Garden City, NY 11530.

McMillan, Patricia Ann (Ja. 1, 1940, Kendallville, IN) Educ. Libn., North. IL Univ. Lib., 1968–; Head - Readers' Adv. Dept., St. Paul Pub. Lib., 1967–68; Asst. Ref. Libn., WI State Univ., Eau Claire, 1966–67; Soc. Sci. Libn., Univ. of Notre Dame Lib., 1963–66. **Educ.:** IN Univ., 1960–62, BS (Elem. Educ.); Univ. of Denver, 1963–65, MA (LS); North. IL Univ., 1969–72, MS (Educ.). **Orgs.:** ALA. IL LA. Natl. Educ. Assn. IL Assn. of Higher Educ. **Pubns.:** *Library Research Guide to Sociology* (1981). "In Depth Analysis of a Term Paper Clinic," *IL Libs.* (Mr. 1978). **Activities:** 1; 31, 39; 63 **Addr.:** Founders Library, Northern Illinois University, DeKalb, IL 60115.

McMillen, Carolyn J. (Ag. 16, 1927, Newark, OH) Asst. Dir., Tech. Srvs., MI State Univ., 1972–, Head, Cat. Div., 1968–72, Serials Libn., 1965–68; Serials Cat. Libn. CO State Univ., 1962–65; Head of Srch., Univ. of MI, 1960–1962, Cat. Libn., 1957–1960. **Educ.:** West. Coll. for Women, 1945–49, BA (Lang.); Univ. of MI, 1955–57, MALS. **Orgs.:** MI LA: Pres. (1979–80); 1st VP (1978–79); Acad. Div. (Ch., 1977–78). ALA: Cncl. of Reg. Grps. (Ch., 1971–72), Descr. Cat. Com. Cat. and Class. Sect. (Ch., 1975–77). Univ. of MI Lib. Sci. Alum. Socty.: Pres. (1978–79). Zonta Clb. of E. Lansing Area: 1st VP (1979–81). AAUP. **Honors:** MI State Univ., Distinguished Fac. Awd., 1975. **Pubns.:** "Michael Gorman and Paul Winkler," *Lib. Resrcs. & Tech. Srvs.* (Fall 1979). **Activities:** 1; 17, 46 **Addr.:** P.O. Box 1495, E. Lansing, MI 48823.

McMillen, Sophia A. (Je. 11, 1941, Amarillo, TX) Serials Catlgr., Cat. Div., Univ. of HI, 1975–; Catlgr., Univ. of Denver, 1972–75; Catlgr., Univ. of FL, 1971–72. **Educ.:** Stanford Univ., 1961–64, BA (Fr.); Univ. of HI, 1969–70, MLS. **Orgs.:** ALA. HI LA. **Activities:** 1; 20, 44, 46 **Addr.:** 2444 Hihiwai St., Apt. 1206, Honolulu, HI 96826.

McMorrow, Kathleen (Ag. 22, 1944, Edinburgh, Scotland) Head Libn., Fac. of Msc., Univ. of Toronto, 1973–, Asst. Libn., 1967–73. **Educ.:** Univ. Toronto, 1962–66, BA with Hon. (Phil.), 1966–67, BLS. **Orgs.:** Can. Assn. Msc. Lib.: Pres. (1980–81); VP (1976–77); RILM Abs. Natl. Com. (Ch., 1973–); Constn. Com. (1977–78); Proc. Com. (1978–79); Elec. Com. (1974, 1978); various other positions. Libn. Assn. Univ. Toronto: various positions. Msc. LA: NY/ON Chap.; various com. and ofc. **Pubns.:** "Current Canadian Music Periodicals," *MLA Notes* (Je. 1980); "The Music Library and Automation," *CAML Nsltr.* (v. 5, 1976); "IAML Questionnaire on Libraries of Musical Performance and Pedagogy," *CAML Nstlr.* (v. 2, 1973). **Activities:** 1; 17, 20, 31; 55 **Addr.:** Edward Johnson Music Library, Faculty of Music, University of Toronto, Toronto, ON M5S 1A1 Canada.

McMullen, (Charles) Haynes (Mr. 3, 1915, Tarkio, MO) Prof., Lib. Sci., Univ. of NC, Chapel Hill, 1972–; Prof., Lib. Sci., IN Univ., 1958–72; Assoc. Prof., Lib. Sci., 1951–58; Libn., Prof. of Lib. Sci., Madison Coll., 1945–51; Libn., Western State Coll., 1941–43; Ref. Asst. Univ. of IL, Urbana, 1936–41. **Educ.:** Centre Coll. of KY, 1931–35, AB (Fr.); Univ. of IL, Urbana, 1935–36, BSLS; 1936–40, MSLS; Univ. of Chicago, 1943–45, 1949, PhD (Lib. Sci.). **Orgs.:** ALA: Bd. of Dir., Lib. Educ. Div. (1965–68). AALS. IN LA. NC LA. Popular Cult. Assn. **Honors** Beta Phi Mu. **Pubns.:** Various articles. **Activities:** 11; 16, 26; 55, 67 **Addr.:** 1306 Willow Dr., Chapel Hill, NC 27514.

McNally, Peter F. (Tillsonburg, ON) Asst. Prof., Grad. Sch., Lib. Sci., McGill Univ., 1972–, Lande Canadiana Libn., 1970–72, Acq. Dept., 1968–69, Ref. Dept., 1966–68. **Educ.:** Univ. of West. ON, 1960–64, BA (Hist.); McGill Univ., 1965, BLS, 1966, MLS, 1977, MA (Hist.). **Orgs.:** Can. LA: Cont. Ed. Coord. Grp. (1978–1980); Use of Prof. Staff Sub-Com. (1972–1973). Bibl. Socty. of Can. CALS. ALA. Royal Socty. of Arts, London. **Honors:** Ctr. for Resrch. in Libnshp., Univ. of Toronto, Resrch. Fellow, 1979. **Pubns.:** "Teaching and learning the Reference Interview" in *Symposium on the Reference Interview* (1979); "A preliminary guide to materials relating to the history of the McGill University Libraries," *Lib. News* (S. 1978); "Recent developments in reference work: an update on new reference sources, 1970–76," PQ Lib. Assn. *Bulletin* (Ja.–Je., 1977). "The McGill University Libraries," *Encyc. of Lib. and Info. Sci.* (1976). **Activities:** 1, 11; 26, 39, 45; 55, 57, 92 **Addr.:** Graduate School of Library Science, McGill University, 3459 McTavish St., Montreal, PQ H3A 1Y1 Canada.

McNamara, Brooks (F. 1, 1937, Peoria, IL) Prof. of Drama, New York Univ., 1971–, Assoc. Prof., 1968–71; Asst. Prof., Univ. of DE, 1965–68; Instr., Monmouth Coll., 1961–63. **Educ.:** Knox Coll., 1959, BA; Univ. of IA, 1961, MA; Tulane Univ.,

PROFESSIONAL ACTIVITIES: Institutions: 1. Acad. lib.; 2. Arch.; 3. Assn.; 4. Fed./Gvt. lib.; 5. Inst. lib.; 6. Mfr./Suppl.; 7. Milit. lib.; 8. Musm.; 9. Pub. lib.; 10. Sch. lib.; 11. Sch. of lib. sci.; 12. Spec. lib.; 13. State lib.; 14. (other). **Functions/Activities:** 15. Acq./Col. dev.; 16. Adult srvs.; 17. Admin.; 18. Apprais.; 19. Archit./Bldgs.; 20. Cat./Class.; 21. Chld. srvs.; 22. Circ.; 23. Cons./Pres.; 24. Consult.; 25. Cont. ed.; 26. Educ. lib. sci.; 27. Ext. srvs.; 28. Fund/Grants; 29. Gvt. pubs.; 30. Indx./Abs.; 31. Instr. lib. use; 32. Media srvs.; 33. Micro.; 34. Netwks./Coop.; 35. Persnl.; 36. PR; 37. Publshg.; 38. Recs. mgt.; 39. Ref. srvs.; 40. Repro.; 41. Resrch.; 42. Review.; 43. Secur.; 44. Serials; 45. Spec. col.; 46. Tech. srvs.; 47. Trustees/Bds.; 48. YA srvs.; 49. (other).

1965, PhD (Drama). **Orgs.:** Thea. LA: Pres. (1981). Amer. Thea. Assn. Amer. Socty. for Thea. Resrch. Univ. and Coll. Thea. Assn.: Secy. Treas. (1971–72). **Pubns.:** *The American Playhouse in the Eighteenth Century* (1969); "David Douglass and the Beginnings of American Theatre Architecture," *Winterthur Portfolio* (1967); "The Indian Medicine Show," *Educ. Thea. Jnl.* (D. 1971); Contrib. ed., *Drama Review.* **Activities:** 14-Dept. of Drama; 55 **Addr.:** Department of Drama, Press Bldg., New York University, New York, NY 10003.*

McNamara, Martha E. (Jl. 17, 1947, New York, NY) Ref. Libn., Boston Coll., 1978–; Comp. Resrch., Foley, Hoag and Eliot, Boston (Law), 1977–78; Couns., Equal Oppt. Prog., San Bernardino, CA State Coll., 1975–77; Law Libn., Rifkin, Wharton and Pierce, 1973–75. **Educ.:** WA Coll., 1965–69, BA (Soclgy.); Drexel Univ., 1970–71, MLS. **Pubns.:** *An Orientation Course and Tutorial Curriculum for Reading and Study Skills Programs* (1976). **Activities:** 1; 33, 34, 39; 55, 56, 92 **Addr.:** Boston College, Bapst Library, Chestnut Hill, MA 02167.

McNamee, Gilbert W. (Ag. 6, 1918, Harrisonburg, VA) Prin. Libn., SFPL Bus. Lib., 1978–; Dir., Bay Area Ref. Ctr., 1973–78, Asst. Dir., 1967–73; Sci. & Tech. Dept., San Francisco Pub. Lib., 1959–67. **Educ.:** George Washington Univ., 1948–54, AB (Hist.); Univ. of CA, Berkeley, 1964, MLS. **Orgs.:** ALA: Cncl. (1974–1977): Com. on Org. (1977); Local Arrang. Ch. of Anl. Conf. (1975); Ch., Interlib. Coop. Com. (1972–73). SLA. CA LA: Pres. (1976). CA Socty. of Libns.: Pres. (1972). Other orgs. **Honors:** Phi Beta Kappa, 1954. **Pubns.:** Various articles. **Activities:** 9; 16, 25, 39; 59, 69 **Addr.:** 1767 Green St., San Francisco, CA 94123.

McNeal, Archie Liddell (S. 3, 1912, Ruleville, MS) Dir. of Libs. Emeritus, Univ. of Miami, Dir. of Libs., 1952–79; Chief of Readrs. Srvs., Univ. of TN, 1948–52; Libn., E. TN State Univ., 1936–48; various positions as univ. prof. at FL State Univ., Univ. of NC and Columbia Univ., 1954–69. **Educ.:** Memphis State Univ., 1928–32 BS (Math.); Peabody Lib. Sch., 1934–36, BS (Lib. Sci.); Univ. of Chicago, 1948, 1951, PhD (Lib. Admin.). **Orgs.:** ALA: 2nd VP (1968–69), Exec. Bd. (1961–65, 1968–69), Cncl. (1940, 1955–65); Lib. Admin. Div. (Pres., 1960–61), ACRL (Pres., 1964–65). Southeastern Lib. Assn. FL LA. Assn. of Caribbean Univ. and Resrch. Libs. **Honors:** Univ. of Miami, Ord. of Merit, 1979. **Pubns.:** "Libraries look to the agency: the academic library," *Amer. Lib.* (Jl. 1971); "William H. Jesse–a memorial," *Southeast. Libn.* (Spr. 1971); "What is obscene?" *Rub-Off* (S. 1969); "Librarians as enemies of books: or, how to succeed in censorship without really trying," *Southeast. Libn.* (Spr. 1969); "John Hall Jacobs: in memoriam," *Southeast. Libn.* (Fall 1967); various articles. **Addr.:** 8445 S.W. 108 St., Miami, FL 33156.

McNeer, Elizabeth Jane (D. 27, 1946, Radford, VA) Coord., Columbus Ext. Prog., Sch. of LS, Kent State Univ., 1980–; Head of Undergrad. Lib., OH State Univ. Lib., 1972–78; Asst. Cur., Spec. Coll., Univ. of Houston, 1969–71. **Educ.:** Randolph-Macon Woman's Coll., 1964–68, BA (Hist.); Emory Univ., 1968–69, MLn (LS); OH State Univ., 1978–81, PhD (Higher Educ. Admin.). **Orgs.:** ALA. OH LA. Women Lib. Workers. Phi Delta Kappa. **Honors:** OH State Univ., Ruth Weimer Mount Awd., 1974, 1977; Beta Phi Mu. **Pubns.:** "The Organizing of a Women's Studies Library," *Coll. and Resrch. Lib. News* (Mr. 1978); "Women in Libraries, Index to Volumes 1-6, 1970-1977," (1978). **Activities:** 1, 11; 17, 26 **Addr.:** 226 Main Library, O.S.U., 1858 Neil Ave. Mall, Columbus, OH 43210.

McNiff, Philip James (F. 10, 1912, Cambridge, MA) Dir. and Libn., Boston Pub. Lib., 1965–; Assoc. Libn., Harvard Coll. Lib., 1956–65, Archibald Cary Coolidge Biblgphr., 1962–65, Libn. of Lamont Lib., 1948–56, Ref. and Supvsr. of Readg. Rm., 1942–48; Asst. Head, Cat. Dept., Newton Free Lib., 1933–42. **Educ.:** Boston Coll., 1929–33, AB (Phil.); Columbia Univ., 1940, BSLS. **Orgs.:** ALA: ACRL, Pres. MA Hist. Socty.: Cncl.; Lib. Com. MA LA. New Eng. LA. many other orgs. Grolier Club. Bostonian Socty. Pan Amer. Socty. New Eng. Club of Odd Volumes. **Honors:** Boston Coll., DHL, 1969; Tufts Univ., Litt.D., 1977; Univ. of MA, DHL, 1980; Gvt. of Spain, Order of Alfonso X el Sabio. **Pubns.:** Ed., *Catalogue of the Lamont Library, Harvard College* (1953); *List of Book Dealers in Underdeveloped Countries* (1963); *Freedom & Responsibility* (1966). **Activities:** 1, 9; 15, 19, 24; 54, 57, 61 **Addr.:** 101 Waban Hill Rd., Chestnut Hill, MA 02167.

McNinch, Allison J. (O. 24, 1945, Pembroke, Ont.) Head Tchr./Libn., Colonel By Sec. Sch., 1977–; Asst. Tchr., Libn., S. Carleton HS, 1974–77; Tchr. Laurentian HS, 1969–72; Tchr., Chatham-Kent Sec. Sch., 1968–69; Tchr., Sir Wilfrid Laurier Sec. Sch. (1967–68). **Educ.:** Carleton Univ., 1963–66, BSc. (Bio.); Univ. of Western ON, 1967–, (Microbio.); Univ. of Western ON, 1966–67, HSA (Sci./Math); Queens Univ., 1969, 1974, 1975, Spec. Cert. (Sch. Libnshp.). **Orgs.:** ON LA: Fin. Com. (1977–78). ON Sch. LA: Treas. (1977–78); Conf. Com. 1977–80). ON Sec. Sch. Tchrs. Fed.: Branch Pres. (1979–80), Dist. Exec. Ofcr. (1980–). Prof. Dev. Com. (1975–76). Carleton Condo. Corp. #7 Pres. (1974–76); Secy. (1973–74). Kanata Condo. Cncl.; Township Liaison Com. (1975–76). **Pubns.:** Ed., *Who's Where In Ontario School Libraries* (1979); Jt. auth. *Teacher Utilization of Secondary School Libraries* (1979); reviews. **Activities:** 10, 13; 17, 31, 48; 63 **Addr.:** Colonel By Secondary School, 2381 Ogilvie Rd., Ottawa, ON K1J 7N4 Canada.

McNiven, Jean W. (Shawinigan, PQ) Head, Client Srvs., Dept. of Indian Affairs and North. Dev., 1974–; Libn. and Consult., Prot. Sch. Bd. Grt. Montreal, 1962–70; Catlgr., Natl. Lib. Can., 1961–62. **Educ.:** McGill Univ., 1939–43, BA (Fr. and Latin); Simmons Coll., 1960–61, MS (LS). **Orgs.:** Can. LA. **Activities:** 4, 12; 15, 31, 39 **Addr.:** Dept. of Indian Affairs and Northern Development Library, Ottawa, ON K1A 0H4 Canada.

McNulty, Francine H. (D. 28, 1954, Buffalo, NY) Middle East. Catlgr., Harvard Coll. Lib., 1977–. **Educ.:** Georgetown Univ., 1972–76, BS (Fr., Arabic); Columbia Univ., 1976–77, MS (LS). **Orgs.:** ALA. Middle East. Libns. Assn. **Pubns.:** "Harvard's Middle Eastern CONSER Project," *Frgn. Acq. Nsltr.* (Fall 1978); "The Conversion of Middle Eastern Serials at LC," *MELA Notes* (F. 1979). **Activities:** 39, 44, 46; 54 **Addr.:** Middle Eastern Department, Harvard College Library, Room S, Cambridge, MA 02138.

McOuat, Donald F. (Ap. 12, 1915, Ottawa, ON) Retired, 1978–; Prov. Archvst. of ON, Arch. of ON, 1963–78; Dir. Hist. and Musm. Branch, ON Dept. of Travel and PR, 1957–63; Archvst. I and II, Arch. of ON, 1950–57. **Educ.:** Bishops Univ. (Lennoxville, PQ), 1936–39, BA with hon. (Hist.); McGill Univ., 1946–50, MA (Hist.); Amer. Univ., 1951, Cert. (Arch. Admin.). **Orgs.:** Assn. of Can. Archvsts. Amer. Rec. Mgt. Assn. Can. Hist. Assn. Champlain Socty.: Exec. Cncl. (1977–). ON Hist. Std. Series: Bd. of Trustees (1977–). ON Geo. Names Bd.: VCh. (1976–). **Honors:** Gvt. of Can., Centennial Medal, 1967; Gvt. of Can., Queens Silver Jubilee Medal, 1977. **Activities:** 2, 13; 18, 23, 30; 54, 55, 56 **Addr.:** 140 Carlton, Suite 1111, Toronto, ON M5A 3W7 Canada.

McPherson, Flora M. (F. 18, 1922, West Lorne, ON) Chief Libn., Middlesex Cnty. Lib., 1976–, Deputy Libn., 1967–75; Catlgr., London Pub. Lib., 1960–63; Asst. Libn., Cambridge Pub. Lib., 1956–58; Adult Srv. Libn., London Pub. Lib., 1948–55. **Educ.:** Univ. of West. ON, 1938–42, BA (Eng.); McGill Univ., 1947–48, BLS. **Orgs.:** Can. LA. ON LA. **Pubns.:** Jt. ed., *Christmas in Canada* (1959); *Watchman Against the World* (1962). **Addr.:** Middlesex County Library, St. John's Dr., Arva, ON N0M 1C0 Canada.

McPherson, Myrna M (O. 11, 1928, Lefroy, ON) Msc. Libn., Catlgr., McMaster Univ., 1974–. **Educ.:** Univ. of Toronto, 1961–68, BA (Arts), 1972–74, MLS. **Orgs.:** Can. Assn. of Msc. Lib.: Conv.; Local Arrange. Msc. LA: (NY/ON Chap.) Intl. Assn. of Msc. Lib. ON Musm. Assn. Oakville Arts Com. **Activities:** 1; 18, 20, 24; 55, 75 **Addr.:** McMaster University, Library Technical Services, 1280 Main St. West, Hamilton, ON L8S 4P5 Canada.

McQueen, Judith D. (Jl. 31, 1946, Maffra, Victoria, Australia) Sr. Consult., Information Systems Consultants, Inc., 1982–; Liaison Libn. (N. Amer.), Natl. Lib. of Australia, 1981–82, Prin. Libn., Bibl., 1979–80, Chief Libn., Sub. & Serials Bibl., 1976–78, Secy., Australian Adv. Cncl. on Bibl. Srv., 1973–75. **Educ.:** Monash Univ., 1965–67, BA; Canberra Coll. of Adv. Educ., 1971, Dip. (LS). **Orgs.:** Lib. Assn. of Australia: Gen. Secy. (1977). ALA. **Activities:** 1, 4; 30, 34, 46; 56, 75, 93 **Addr.:** Information Systems Consultants, Inc., P.O. Box 34504, Bethesda, MD 20817.

McQuillan, David C. (S. 30, 1949, Amsterdam, NY) Map Libn., Univ. of SC, 1974–. **Educ.:** Univ. of South. MS, 1969–71, BS (Geo.); Univ. of SC, 1971–75, MA (Geo.), 1973–74, ML (LS). **Orgs.:** SLA: Geo. Map Div., Educ. Com. (1979–), Awd. Com. (1978–79, Ch., 1979). West. Assn. Map Lib. SC LA. Assn. Can. Map Lib. Assn. Amer. Geo. Amer. Geo. Socty. SC Acad. Sci.: Cur. (1976–). **Honors:** Gamma Theta Upsilon. **Pubns.:** "History of the Map Collection at the University of South Carolina," *SLA Geo. and Map Div. Bltn.* (Mr. 1977). **Activities:** 1, 12; 15, 17, 20; 70 **Addr.:** Map Library, University of South Carolina, Columbia, SC 29208.

McReynolds, Joe Elston (S. 15, 1948, Lockwood, MO) Resrch. Libn. and Asst. Prof. LS, Harding Univ., 1976–; other positions in tchg., 1966–75. **Educ.:** MO South. State Coll., 1966–68, AA (Lit.); Harding Coll., 1968–71, BA (Eng.); Memphis State Univ., 1974–76, MEd (LS); Oxford Univ. (Eng.), 1974, (Sem. in Elizabethan Lit.). **Orgs.:** AR LA: Mem. Com. (1980–). ALA: Lib. Instr. RT, Reg. Rpt. (1980–). Phi Theta Kappa. Alpha Chi: Eta Chap. (Pres., 1970–71). Kappa Phi Kappa. Alpha Phi Gamma. **Pubns.:** *Research Reverie* (1976); Poetry. **Activities:** 1; 15, 31, 39; 55, 89, 90 **Addr.:** Route 4, Box 358, Honeyhill Rd., Searcy, AR 72143.

McReynolds, R. Michael (Ja. 16, 1940, Los Angeles, CA) Asst. Chief, Ref., Judicial and Fiscal Branch, Natl. Arch., 1978–, Deputy Asst. to Archvst., 1975–78, Archvst., 1969–75; Instr., SUNY, Fredonia, 1967–69. **Educ.:** Univ. of MI, 1958–61, AB (Hist.); Univ. of Chicago, 1961–68, AM (Hist.). **Orgs.:** SAA: Intl. Com. (Ch., 1977–80). Amer. Legal Hist. Socty. Mid. Atl. Archvsts. Conf. Org. of Amer. Histns. **Pubns.:** "Documentary Sources for the Study of U.S. Supreme Court Litigation," *Law Lib. Jnl.* (N. 1976). **Activities:** 2; 17, 39 **Addr.:** Judicial and Fiscal Branch, National Archives, Washington, DC 20408.

McSweeney, Josephine (My. 5, 1931, New York, NY) Prof. and Ref. Libn., Pratt Inst. Lib., 1960–; Tchr., Dependent School Sys., Italy, 1958–59, Germ., 1956–58, Philippines, 1955–56, Japan, 1954–55, Tchr., Board of Educ., Huntington Station, 1951–54. **Educ.:** SUNY, Plattsburgh, 1948–51, BA (Soc. Sci.), Columbia Univ., 1951–52, MA (Educ.); Pratt Inst., 1959–60, MLS. **Orgs.:** ALA: Cncl. (1980–)); Ref. and Subscrpn. Books Review Com. (1976–); Ch., Omnibus Reviews Subcom. (1978–). NY Ref. and Resrch. Lib. Agency: Ch., Ref. Libns. Group (1975–79). Acad. Libs. of Brooklyn: Ch., Union List of Serials Com., (1975–). Beta Phi Mu: Dir. (1975–78). Metro. Coll. Inter-LA Secy./Treas. (1964–66). Middle States Assn. of Coll. and Secondary Sch.: Eval. Team. AAUP: Chap. Secy./-Treas. (1965–67). United Federation of College Teachers, local 1460 Treasurer 1974–79 Pratt Inst. Alum. Socty.: Exec. Cncl. (1970–75); VP 1972–74). **Pubns.:** Jt. auth., *Cuba from Columbus to Castro* (1981); ed., "Periodicals in the Libraries of Pratt Institute, St. Joseph's College" (1979). **Activities:** 1; 29, 39, 44; 92 **Addr.:** Pratt Institute Library, 200 Willoughby Ave., Brooklyn, NY 11205.

McSweeney, Maria Jones (Ap. 20, 1948, Wolverhampton, Staffordshire, Eng.) Mgr., Tech. Info. Srvs., SCM Corp., 1980–, Supvsr., Tech. Info. Srvs., 1977–80, Tech. Libn., 1977; Tech. Staff Asst., Univ. of TX at Dallas, 1974–75; Quality Control Chem., Dr Pepper Bottling Co., 1972–74. **Educ.:** Univ. of Manchester, Eng., 1966–70, B.Sc Hons (Chem.); N. TX State Univ., 1975–76, MLS. **Orgs.:** SLA: Cleveland Chap., Program Com. (1977–78); Betty Burrows Com. (Ch., 1978–79); Treas. (1979–80). Assn. for Info. Mgrs. ASIS. Amer. Chem. Socty. Cleveland Socty. for Coatings Tech. **Activities:** 12; 17, 36, 39; 60, 68, 91 **Addr.:** 16799 Woodleaf, Strongsville, OH 44136.

McTaggart, John B. (My. 9, 1918, Dayton, OH) Dir., Lib. Srv., Meth. Theo. Sch. (OH), 1960–; Libn., Berkeley Bapt. Dvnty. Sch., 1956–60; Asst. Libn., Un. Theo. Semy., 1955–56. **Educ.:** Eastern Coll., 1947–51, BA (Theo.); Drexel Univ., 1953–55, MS (LS). **Orgs.:** ATLA: Exec. Com. (1958–60). **Honors:** Cncl. on Lib. Resrc., Flwshp., 1972–73. **Activities:** 1; 17 **Addr.:** 149 Grandview Ave., Delaware, OH 43015.

McVey, Susan C. (Mr. 28, 1951, Chickasa, OK) Dir. of the Lib., Oklahoma City Univ. Lib., 1979–, Ref. Libn., 1976–79; Libn., Coord. for Srv. to the Aged, San Patricio Cnty. Lib. Syst., 1975–76. **Educ.:** Univ. of OK, 1970–73, BA (Soc. Wk.); Univ. of TX (Austin), 1973–75, MA (LS). **Orgs.:** TX LA. OK LA: Ref. Div., Secy. (1979–80), Vice-Ch., Chair-Elect (1980–81). AAUW. Women's Pol. Caucus of Oklahoma City. **Activities:** 1; 17, 31, 35 **Addr.:** Library, Oklahoma City University, Oklahoma City, OK 73106.

McWilliams-Woerner, Elizabeth M. (My. 23, 1947, Cheverly, MD) ILL Libn., Univ. of WA, 1976–; Spec. Libn., Univ. of MT, Bur. of Bus. and Econ. Resrch., 1975–76; Ref. Libn., Msc. Catlgr., South. IL Univ., 1972–73; Msc. Ref. Libn., Univ. of IA, 1971–72. **Educ.:** Univ. of MD, 1965–69, BMus; Univ. of IA, 1970–71, MALS; Univ. of MD, 1969–74, MMus. **Orgs.:** NLA: Prof. Welfare Com. (1977–). Msc. LA. Intl. Assn. of Msc. Libs. **Pubns.:** *Music Manuscripts in the Folger Shakespeare Library: an Inventory and Thematic Catalogue* (1980). **Activities:** 1, 2; 34, 39, 45; 55 **Addr.:** 2912 SW Arnold, Portland, OR 97219.

Meacham, Mary (Ag. 17, 1946, Leon, IA) Writer; Instr., Sch. of LS, Univ. of OK, 1974–78, Libn., Lab. Sch., 1971–73. **Educ.:** Columbia Coll., 1964–66, AA (Fine Arts); Univ. of OK, 1966–69, BA (Lang. Arts), 1970–71, MLS. **Honors:** Beta Phi Mu. **Pubns.:** *Information Sources in Children's Literature* (1978); "Development of School Libraries Around the World," *Intl. Lib. Rev.,* (O. 1976); "What's Going On Down the Hall?," *Lrng. Today,* (Win. 1979); *Reading for Young People: The Northwest* (1980); "Further Development of School Libraries Worldwide," *Unesco Bltn.* (1980); various articles. **Activities:** 10, 11; 21, 26; 89 **Addr.:** 419 Park Dr., Norman, OK 73069.

Mead, Kenneth D. (S. 14, 1946, Garden City, MI) Dir., Med. Lib., Halifax Hosp. Med. Ctr., 1974–; Drug Abuse Info. Libn., Daytona Beach Comnty. Coll., 1971–74, 1977. **Educ.:** Univ. of MI, 1966–69, BA (Eng.), 1969–71, MALS. **Orgs.:** Med. LA: Hosp. Lib. Consult. (1979–80); Southern Reg. Grp. (By-Laws Com. 1979). Volusia Cnty LA: Pres. (1979). FL Socty. for Hlthcare Educ. and Training: Secy. (1978); Pres. (1980). **Activities:** 12; 17, 25, 34; 80 **Addr.:** P.O. Box 9064, Daytona Beach, FL 32020.

Meador, Joan S. (D. 23, 1931, Stroudsburg, PA) Head, Ref. Dept., Tulsa City-Cnty. Lib., 1975–, Exec. Asst., 1974–75. **Educ.:** Skidmore Coll., 1949–53, BA (Eng.); Univ. of OK, 1971–74, MLS. **Orgs.:** ALA: PLA, Adult Litcy. Lrng. Com. (1975–76); RASD, Outstan. Ref. Bk. Com. (1977–79). SWLA. OK LA: Ref. Div., VP (1976–77), Pres. (1977–78). Leadership Tulsa. **Activities:** 9; 15, 39 **Addr.:** Reference Department, Tulsa City-County Library, 400 Civic Center, Tulsa, OK 74103.

Meador, John Milward, Jr. (N. 4, 1946, Louisville, KY) Assoc. Libn., Asst. Dir. for Pub. Srvs., Marriott Lib., Univ. of UT,

Special Subjects/Services: 50. Adult educ.; 51. Advert./Mktg.; 52. Aerosp.; 53. Agric.; 54. Area std.; 55. Arts/Hum.; 56. Autom.; 57. Bibl./Prtg.; 58. Bio. sci.; 59. Bus./Fin.; 60. Chem.; 61. Copyrt.; 62. Documtn.; 63. Educ.; 64. Engin.; 65. Env.; 66. Eth. grps.; 67. Film; 68. Food/Nutr.; 69. Geneal.; 70. Geo.; 71. Geol.; 72. Handcpd.; 73. Hist.; 74. Int. frdm.; 75. Info. sci.; 76. Insr.; 77. Law; 78. Legis.; 79. Math./Comp. sci.; 80. Med.; 81. Metals; 82. Nat. resrcs.; 83. Newsp.; 84. Nuc. sci.; 85. Oral hist.; 86. Petr./Energy; 87. Pharm.; 88. Phys./Astr./Math.; 89. Readg.; 90. Relig.; 91. Sci./Tech.; 92. Soc. sci.; 93. Telecom.; 94. Transp.; 95. (other).

1980–; Assoc. Prof. and Head, Gen. Ref. Dept. Univ. of Houston, 1977–80, Asst. Prof. and Head, Soc. Sci. and Hum. Ref., 1974–77, Inst. and Eng. Bibl., 1973–74; Stacks Supvsr., Univ. of Louisville, 1965–68. **Educ.:** Univ. of Louisville, 1964–68, BA (Eng.); Univ. of TX, Austin, 1968–72, MA (Eng.), 1972–73, MLS; KY State Tchg. Cert., grades 7–12; TX State Tchg. Cert., grades 7–12; Univ. of UT, 1980–, Phd (in progress). **Orgs.:** ALA: ACRL/Acad. Status Com. (1979–81); RASD/Ref. Srvs. in Medium-sized Resrch. Libs. Discuss. Grp. (Ch., 1979–80); RTSD/Chief Col. Dev. Ofcrs. of Medium-Sized Resrch. Libs. (1977–); LAMA. Southwestern LA: Biennial Conf. Prog. Com. (1974). TX LA. UT LA. Bibl. Socty. of Amer. Mod. Lang. Assn. of Amer. S. Ctrl. Mod. Lang. Assn. **Pubns.:** Jt. Auth., *The Robinson Jeffers Collection at the University of Houston: A Bibliographical Catalogue* (1975); "Addendum to Hanneman: Hemingway's *The Old Man and the Sea," The Papers of the Bibl. Socty. of Amer.* (1973). **Activities:** 1; 15, 17, 39; 55, 57, 63 **Addr.:** 6341 S. 725 East, Murray, UT 84107.

Meador, Patricia Lane (Mr. 19, 1943, Memphis, TN) Archvst., LA State Univ., Shreveport, 1975–; Hist. Instr., Baptist Christ. Coll., 1973–75; Hist. Inst., Coll. of Emporia, KS, 1971–73; Dean of Women, Hist. Inst., WA Coll. Acad., TN., 1970–71; Eng. Instr., Seinan Jo Gakuin, Kitakyushu, Japan. **Educ.:** Memphis State Univ., 1962–66, BS (Hist./Pol. Sci.); Univ. of OK, 1968–70, MA (Hist.); LA State Univ., 1976–78, MLS. **Orgs.:** SAA: Exec. Bd. (1974–76); VP (1977–79); Pres. (1979–80). Friends of LA Arch. LA LA. LA Hist. Assn.: Ad Hoc Arch. Com. (1978–79). N. LA Hist. Assn. Amer. Assn. of State and Local Hist. Pres. Socty. of Shreveport. **Honors:** Beta Phi Mu. NEH, Grant, 1979. **Pubns.:** "Sources for Northwest Louisiana History", in *Research Guide to Louisiana History* (1981). **Activities:** 1, 2; 17, 41, 45; 54, 55, 92 **Addr.:** Library-Archives Department, LSU-Shreveport, 8515 Youree Dr., Shreveport, LA 71115.

Meadow, Charles T. (D. 16, 1929, Paterson, NJ) Prof., Info. Sci., Drexel Univ., 1974–; Asst. Dir., MIT Div., US Atomic Energy Comsn., 1971–74; Chief, Systs. Dev. Div., Natl. Bureau of Stans., 1968–71; Sr. Systs. Anal., IBM Corp., 1960–68. **Educ.:** Univ. of Rochester, 1947–51, BA (Math.); Rutgers Univ., 1953–54, MS (Math.). **Orgs.:** ASIS: Ed., JASIS (1977–). Assn. for Computing Mach. Inst. of Info. Sci. (UK). Benjamin Franklin Colloquium on Info. Sci.: Pres. (1977–78); Exec. Com. (1979–80). **Honors:** Fellow, Inst. of Info. Sci., 1979. **Pubns.:** Jt. auth., *Basics of Online Searching* (1981); *Applied Data Management* (1976); *Sounds and Signals: How We Communicate* (1975); *The Analysis of Information Systems* (1973); *The Story of Computers* (1970). **Activities:** 11; 26, 41; 75, 93 **Addr.:** School of Library and Information Science, Drexel University, Philadelphia, PA 19104.

Meadow, Mary Louise (O. 16, 1939, Buffalo, NY) Libn., Cecilian Acad., 1979–; Free lance biblgphr., tech. writer, 1974–79; Staff Libn., Natl. Educ. Assn., 1973–74; Head of Pub. Srvs., Univ. of MD, Baltimore Cnty, 1968–73. **Educ.:** Coll. of New Rochelle, 1957–61, AB (Hist.); Univ. of MD, 1965–66, MLS. **Orgs.:** ASIS: Chesapeake Bay Chap., Prog. Ch. (1972); Mem. Com. (1974); DE Valley Chap., Ch. (1976). **Pubns.:** "Prestel, Pixel, and Prediction," *Bltn. of the Amer. Socty. for Info. Sci.* (Ag. 1979). Review. **Activities:** 5, 10; 21, 31, 39; 63, 92 **Addr.:** 8407 Ardleigh St., Philadelphia, PA 19118.

Meadows, Judith Adams (Spartanburg, SC) Law Libn., Aspen Syst. Corp., 1979–; Lib. Asst., Baker & Hostetler, Attys, 1978–79; Consult. for Inf. Syst. Desgn., U.S. Dept. of Labor, 1978–79. **Educ.:** American Univ., 1964–67, BA (Poli. Sci.); Univ. of MD, 1977–79, MLS; Cert., Legal Std., Univ. of MD, 1976–77. **Orgs.:** DC Law Libns Soc. AALL: Com. on Govt. Docums; Autom. & Sci. Dev. Assoc. Info. Mgrs.: Com. on Qualifica. Stans. Metro. Washington Lib. Cncl. **Honors:** Pi Sigma Alpha, 1967. **Pubns.:** Ed. "Information Sources" *Hazardous Waste Report* (Ag. 1979–); Bibliography *Toxic Substances Reporter* (1981). **Activities:** 12; 17, 29, 39; 77, 78 **Addr.:** Aspen Systems Corporation, 1600 Research Blvd., Rockville, MD 20850.

Meakin, Faith Anne (O. 15, 1943, Philadelphia, PA) Assoc. Dir. and Head, Pub. Srvs., Biomed. Lib, Univ. of CA, San Diego, 1979–, Head, Ref. Dept., 1967–79; Intern, CLR/NLM Hlth. Sci. Lib. Mgt. Trng. Prog., Bio-Med. Lib., Univ. of MN, 1978–79; Internship in Med. Libnshp., Biomed. Lib., Univ. of CA, Los Angeles, 1966–67. **Educ.:** Coe Coll., 1961–63; Syracuse Univ., 1963–65, BA (Eng.), 1965–66, MLS; Univ. of CA, Los Angeles, Cert. Med. Libn., 1966–67. **Orgs.:** Med. LA: Ch., Honors & Awds. Com. (1979–80); Ch., Rittenhouse Awd. Subcom. (1979–80); Ch., Curric. Com. (1973–74). Med. Lib. Grp. of South. CA & AZ: Ch., Bylaws Com. (1974); Cont. Educ. Com. (1977–78). Libns. Assn., Univ. of CA: Statewide Pres. (1974). ALA: ACRL. **Honors:** Beta Phi Mu, 1966. **Pubns.:** Jt. auth. "Bibliographical fugitives; Papers presented at meetings", IN: *Proc. 3rd Int Congress on Med. Libnshp.* (1970); Jt. auth., "CLR/NLM Health Sciences Library Management Intern Program: First Year," *Bltn. Med. LA* (1980). **Activities:** 1, 12; 17, 35, 39; 80 **Addr.:** Biomedical Library C-075B, University of California, San Diego, La Jolla, CA 92093.

Mealey, Catherine E. (Ap. 4, 1928, Ames, IA) Law Libn., Univ. of WY, 1962–; Private Practice of Law, 1958–60. **Educ.:** Univ. of IA, 1944–50, BA (Psy.), 1950–51, MA (Spec Educ), 1954–57, SD (Law); Univ. of WA, 1961–62, MLL (Law Libnshp.). **Orgs.:** AALL. WY Bar Assn. **Addr.:** 121 Ivinson, Laramie, WY 82071.

Means, Raymond B. (Ja. 4, 1930, Des Moines, IA) Lib. Dir., Creighton Univ., 1977–; Actg. Dir., Univ. of NE, Omaha, 1977, Assoc. Dir., 1967–77, Head of Pub. Srvs., 1961–67. **Educ.:** Univ. of Omaha, 1953–56, BS (Educ.); Univ. of Denver, 1958–61, MA (LS). **Orgs.:** ALA: Cncl. (1971–75); Com. on Lib. Educ. NELA: Exec. Secy.; Pres. (1967–68). **Honors:** NE LA, Merit. Srv. Awd., 1979. **Activities:** 1; 17, 19, 26; 63 **Addr.:** Alumni Memorial Library, Creighton University, 2500 California St., Omaha, NE 68178.

Mechanic, Sylvia G. (Ag. 4, 1920, New York, NY) Bus. Libn., Brooklyn Pub. Lib. Bus. Lib., 1962–; Instr., Columbia Univ. Sch. of Lib. Srv., 1967–76; Chief Sci. and Indus. Div., Brooklyn Pub. Lib., 1953–61, Chief, Soc. Sci. Div., 1946–53, Libn., Hist. Div., 1943–45. **Educ.:** Hofstra Coll., 1938–42, BA; Columbia Univ., 1942–43, BSLS. **Orgs.:** SLA: Ch., Bus. & Fin. Grp. (1964–66). NY Lib. Club. NY LA. **Pubns.:** *Annotated List of Selected Government Publications Available to Depository Libraries* (1971); Contrib., *Financial Analyst's Handbook* (1975). **Activities:** 9; 17, 26, 39; 59 **Addr.:** Brooklyn Public Library, Business Library, 280 Cadman Plz. West, Brooklyn, NY 11201.

Mechtenberg, Paul (Mr. 1, 1935, Parkston, SD) Head Libn., Dundee Twp. Lib., 1971–; Syst. Resrc. Libn., DuPage Lib. Syst., 1969–71; Ref. Libn., Flint Pub. Lib., 1966–68. **Educ.:** SD State Univ., 1956–60, BS (Eng.); Univ. of IL, 1964–65, MS (LS). **Orgs.:** ALA: PLA, Mem. Com. (1976–78). IL LA. Lib. Admin. Conf. North. IL. Dundee Bus. and Prof. Assn.: Secy. (1980–81). Dundee Twp. Pub. Empl. Credit Un. **Activities:** 9; 16, 17, 39; 68, 89 **Addr.:** 107 N. Van Buren, Dundee, IL 60118.

Mecinski, Adam M. (N. 25, 1928, Baltimore, MD) Head, Ref. Branch, Nimitz Lib., US Naval Acad., 1973–, Sr. Ref. Libn., 1969–73; Branch Head, Enoch Pratt Free Lib., 1968–69, Admin. Asst., Branch, 1963–68. **Educ.:** Loyola Coll., 1954–56, BS (Hist.); Rutgers Univ., 1956–58, MLS. **Orgs.:** MD LA. **Activities:** 1, 7; 31, 39 **Addr.:** 2101 Echodale Ave., Baltimore, MD 21214.

Meckler, Alan Marshall (Jl. 25, 1945, New York, NY) Publshr., *Micro. Review*, 1971–. **Educ.:** Columbia Coll., 1967, BA (Amer. Hist.); Columbia Univ., 1968, MA (Amer. Hist.), 1980, PhD (Amer. Hist.). **Orgs.:** ALA. SLA. Natl. Micro. Assn. Amer. Hist. Assn. **Pubns.:** *Micropublishing: A History of Scholarly Micropublishing in America, 1938–1980* (1981); "The Early Years of Scholarly Micropublishing," *Scholarly Publishing,* (Vol. 12, No. 4); *The Draft and Its Enemies* (1974); "Smaller and Smaller," *Times Lit. Supplement* (S. 22, 1978); *Oral History Collections* (1975). **Activities:** 6; 33; 57 **Addr.:** 520 Riverside Ave., Westport, CT 06880.

Meckstroth, Edward Stephen (Ag. 11, 1942, Cincinnati, OH) Fine Arts Libn., Hum. Coord., Milner Lib., IL State Univ., 1974–; Instr., Chicago State Univ., 1968–69; Instr., Luther Coll., 1967–68. **Educ.:** Univ. of Chicago, 1960–64, BA (Eng.), 1964–65, MA (Eng.); Art Inst. of Chicago, 1968–71; Univ. of Chicago, 1971–74, MA (LS). **Orgs.:** ARLIS/NA. Coll. Art Assn. **Pubns.:** "Ylem", exper. film (1979); other films. **Activities:** 1; 15, 17, 39; 55, 67 **Addr.:** Milner Library, Illinois State University, Normal, IL 61761.

Medeiros, Rosemary (Ap. 9, 1949, Dorchester, MA) Dir., Dartmouth Pub. Lib., 1979–; Branch Libn., Howland-Green Branch, New Bedford Pub. Lib., 1973–79. **Educ.:** Southeast. MA Univ., 1967–71, BA (Eng.); Simmons Coll., 1972–74, MLS. **Orgs.:** MA LA. New Bedford Young Womens Christ. Assn.: Bd. Dir. (1975–81); VP (1979–80); Pres. (1980–81). **Activities:** 9 **Addr.:** 711 Belleville Ave., New Bedford, MA 02745.

Meder, Marylouise Dunham (Danbury, CT) Prof., Sch. of LS, Emporia State Univ., 1971–; Prof., Sch. of LS, TX Woman's Univ., 1967–71; Prof., Soc. Sci. Libn., CA State Coll., 1966–67; Asst. Prof., Grad. Sch. of Lib. and Info. Std., Rutgers Univ., 1964–66; Asst. Prof., Asst. Libn., Ctrl. CT State Coll., 1953–62; Catlgr., OH State Univ., 1949–53. **Educ.:** Mary Washington Coll., 1945–47, BA (Hist.); Carnegie Mellon Univ., 1948–49, MLS; Trinity Coll., 1959–62, MA (Hist.); Univ. of MI, 1960–64, PhD (LS). **Orgs.:** ALA: LAMA/Stat. Sect. (1978–80). AALS. KS LA: Coll. and Univ. Sect, Nom. Com. (1979–). Beta Phi Mu: Handbook Com. (1974–75). Other orgs. Mediaeval Acad. CT Hist. Socty. KS Hist. Socty. AAUW: Pres. (1979–). Other orgs. **Pubns.:** "Student Concerns in Choice of Library School" *Jnl. of Educ. for Libnshp.* (Sum. 1980); "Adventure in Miniature Book Publishing" *The Microbibliophile* (F./Mr. 1980); "Sarah Rebecca Reed; Teacher-Librarian-Administrator" *Lib. Sch. Review* (1979); "Khensu Press - Its Story", *Lib. Sch. Review* (1980); "People in Our Past and Present; the Story of the School of Library Science," *Lib. Sch. Review* (1978). **Activities:** 1, 11; 20, 26, 39; 57, 75, 92 **Addr.:** School of Library Science, Emporia State University, Emporia, KS 66801.

Medina, Sue O'Neal (N. 18, 1945, Knoxville, TN) Consult. for Plng. and Resrch., AL Pub. Lib. Srv., 1977–; Lib. Consult., ALA-TOM Reg. Plng. Comsn., 1975–76; Branch Libn., Mobile Pub. Lib., 1972–74; Ref. Libn., Univ. of GA Libs., 1971–72; Libn., Dept. of Defense/US Army, 1968–69. **Educ.:** FL State Univ., 1963–67, BA (Hist.), 1970–71, MS (LS), 1977, Adv. Master's Degree (LS), 1977–, Doct. Cand. (LS). **Orgs.:** ALA. SELA. AL LA: Ch., Handbook Com. (1979–80). AAUW. **Honors:** Beta Phi Mu. **Pubns.:** Jt. auth., *A Study of the Combined School-Public Library, Phase 1* (1977). **Activities:** 9, 13; 17, 24, 28, 34 **Addr.:** 6030 Monticello Dr., Montgomery, AL 36130.

Meglio, Delores D. (Mr. 27, 1946, New York, NY) VP Editorial, New York Times Info. Bank, 1979–, Managing Ed., 1978–; Deputy Ed., NY Times Index, 1977–78, Assoc. Ed., 1976–77, Copy Ed., 1973–76, Indxr., 1971–73. **Educ.:** City Coll. of New York, 1963–70, BA (Psy.); St. Johns Univ., 1975–77, MLS. **Orgs.:** ASIS. **Honors:** Harlem YMCA Black Achvmt. Awd., 1977. **Activities:** 12; 30, 33; 83 **Addr.:** New York Times, Corporate Records Library, 229 W. 43 St., New York, NY 10036.

Mehler, Gloria (O. 1, 1931, Brooklyn, NY) Libn. in Charge, Julia Richman HS, 1963–; Libn., Midwood HS, 1955–62. **Educ.:** Brooklyn Coll., 1949–53, BA (Eng. Lit.), 1954–56, MA (Eng. Lit.); Columbia Univ., 1956–58, MS (LS). **Orgs.:** AJL. New York City, Bd. Educ., Libns. in Charge. Columbia Univ., Sch. LS, Alum. Assn. **Activities:** 10; 17, 32, 48; 63, 66 **Addr.:** Julia Richman High School, 317 East 67 St., New York, NY 10021.

Mehr, Joseph O. (Ap. 3, 1925, Louisville, KY) Libn., Providence Jnl. Co., 1968–; Asst. Libn., Louisville Courier-Jnl., 1953–68. **Educ.:** Univ. of Louisville, 1947–50, (Liberal Arts). **Orgs.:** SLA: Newspaper Div., Pres. (1976–77); RI Chap., Pres. (1979–80). RI LA. **Pubns.:** Ed., *Journal-Bulletin Almanac* (1968–); "Filing Supplies", *Guidelines for Newpaper Libraries* (1974, 1976). **Activities:** 12; 15, 17; 83 **Addr.:** Providence Journal Co., 75 Fountain St., Providence, RI 02902.

Meichelbeck, Sr. Mary Joseph (Watertown, NY) Lib. Dir., Mater Dei Coll., 1963–; Tchr., various positions. **Educ.:** St. Univ. of NY at Potsdam, 1930–33, BE (Educ.); Syracuse Univ., 1944–50, MS (LS). **Orgs.:** ALA. NY LA. Cath. LA: Diocesan Unit, Co-Fndn. **Honors** Beta Phi Mu, 1949. **Activities:** 1; 15, 17 **Addr.:** Mater Dei College, Ogdensburg, NY 13669.

Meier, Marjorie Ann (F. 6, 1931, Alva, OK) Assoc. Prof. of Msc., Msc. Catlgr., Concordia Tchr. Coll., Seward, NE, 1954–78; Tchr. **Educ.:** Concordia Tchr. Coll., River Forest, IL, 1948–52, BS (Educ.); Northwestern Univ., 1953–57, MMsc. (Educ.); Univ. of MI, 1976–78, AMLS. **Orgs.:** Msc. LA. Msc. OCLC Users Grp. Msc. Tchr. Natl. Assn. **Activities:** 1; 15, 20, 39; 55 **Addr.:** 309 S. Fifth, Apt. 5, Seward, NE 68434.

Meier, Patricia Lynn (Ag. 14, 1944, Davenport, IA) Elem. libn., Bettendorf Cmnty. Sch. Dist., 1968–; Libn., Gladbrook (IA) Cmnty. Sch. Dist., 1966–67. **Educ.:** Univ. of IA, 1962–66, BA (Hist.), 1973–75, MLS. **Orgs.:** ALA: Cncl. (1981–85); AASL. IA Educ. Media Assn.: Bd. (1971–73, 1974–77); Cert. and Stan. Com. (Ch., 1975–80); K-12 Survey Com. (Ch., 1976–80); IA Chld.'s Choice Book Awd. Com. (1977–78). AAUW. Pi Lambda Theta. Natl. Educ. Assn. IA State Educ. Assn. Other orgs. **Activities:** 10; 21, 31, 32 **Addr.:** 2230 1/2 Ripley, Davenport, IA 52803.

Meinel, Nancy Reno Thomas (Jl. 7, 1938, Oshkosh, WI) Libn., Mangham HS, 1978–; Dir. of Lrng. Ctr., Conrad Elvehjem Sch., (McFarland, WI), 1968–70; Libn., Evangelical Tchr. Trng. Sch. (Ethiopia), 1965–66; Elem. Libn., Ctrl. Lib. Dist. (Columbus, OH), 1960–62; Tchg. **Educ.:** Ripon Coll., 1956–60, BA (Bio. and Hist.); Univ. of WI (Madison), 1967–68, MA (LS); Coop. Lang. Inst. (Addis Ababa, Ethiopia), 1964–65 (Dip.). **Orgs.:** ALA. LA LA. SWLA. Daughters of the Amer. Revolution. **Honors:** Phi Beta Kappa, 1960; Beta Phi Mu, 1970; Ouachita Parish Cncl. on Aging, Srv. Awd., 1979, 80. **Pubns.:** Reviews. **Activities:** 10; 22, 39, 48; 58, 89, 92 **Addr.:** Mangham High School Library, P.O. Box 248, Mangham, LA 71259.

Meining, Olive A. (Jl. 2, 1925, Pelkie, MI) Ref. Libn., Mountain-Valley Lib. Syst., 1981–; Area Ref. Libn., Mt. Valley Lib. Syst., 1976–81; Gvt. Docum. Libn., North. AZ Univ., 1973–75, Ref. Libn., 1970–73; Career Offcr., US Navy, 1948–69. **Educ.:** Wayne State Univ., 1944–46; Univ. of IA, 1946–48, BA (Educ.); Roosevelt Univ., 1960–62, MA (Educ. Admin.); Univ. of MI, 1969–70, AMLS. **Orgs.:** ALA. CA LA. AAUW: Corres. Secy. (1980–81). **Pubns.:** Reviews. **Activities:** 9; 16, 25, 39; 50, 92 **Addr.:** Mountain-Valley Library System, 828 I St., Sacramento, CA 95814.

Meinke, Darrel M. (Je. 19, 1929, Plymouth, NE) Dean of Instr. Resrc., Moorhead State Univ., 1973–; Dean, Assoc. Acad. Affairs, Concordia Coll., 1970–72, Dir. of Lib., 1960–70; Sch. Libn., Concordia Coll. HS, 1954–60; other positions in educ. **Educ.:** Univ. of NE, 1947–51, BSEd (Eng.), 1951–55, MEd (Educ.); Denver Univ., 1955–59, MA (LS); Univ. of NE, 1966, DEd (Sec. Educ.). **Orgs.:** ALA. **Pubns.:** *From Box to Bookshelf* (1962). **Activities:** 1; 17, 32, 34 **Addr.:** Moorhead State University, Moorhead, MN 56560.

PROFESSIONAL ACTIVITIES: Institutions: 1. Acad. lib.; 2. Arch.; 3. Assn.; 4. Fed./Gvt. lib.; 5. Inst. lib.; 6. Mfr./Suppl.; 7. Milit. lib.; 8. Musm.; 9. Pub. lib.; 10. Sch. lib.; 11. Sch. of lib. sci.; 12. Spec. lib.; 13. State lib.; 14. (other). **Functions/Activities:** 15. Acq./Col. dev.; 16. Adult srvs.; 17. Admin.; 18. Apprais.; 19. Archit./Bldgs.; 20. Cat./Class.; 21. Chld. srvs.; 22. Circ.; 23. Cons./Pres.; 24. Consult.; 25. Cont. ed.; 26. Educ. lib. sci.; 27. Ext. srvs.; 28. Fund/Grants; 29. Gvt. pubs.; 30. Indx./Abs.; 31. Instr. lib. use; 32. Media srvs.; 33. Micro.; 34. Netwks./Coop.; 35. Persnl.; 36. PR; 37. Publshg.; 38. Recs. mgt.; 39. Ref. srvs.; 40. Repro.; 41. Resrch.; 42. Review.; 43. Secur.; 44. Serials; 45. Spec. col.; 46. Tech. srvs.; 47. Trustees/Bds.; 48. YA srvs.; 49. (other).

Meirose, Leo H. (O. 25, 1922, Cincinnati, OH) Dir., Tampa-Hillsborough Cnty. Pub. Lib. Syst., 1972–; Dir., Ft. Lauderdale Pub. Lib., 1964–72; Asst. Libn., Xavier Univ., 1947–52; Head, Branches and various other positions, Cincinnati Pub. Lib., 1952–64. **Educ.:** Xavier Univ., 1942–45, AB; Case West. Reserve, 1948–51, MSLS. **Orgs.:** FL LA: Pres. (1971); Legis. and Plng. Com. (Ch., 1966–71, 1980–81); Pub. Lib. Div. (Ch., 1969). ALA. SELA: Legis. Com. (1979). **Activities:** 9; 17, 19; 74, 78 **Addr.:** 1412 Moss Laden Ct., Brandon, FL 33511.

Meisels, Henry R. (Mr. 26, 1920, Vienna, Austria) Dir., Corn Belt Lib. Syst., 1967; Dir., Bethpage Pub. Lib., 1958–66; Libn., Goethe House, 1957–58; Libn. II, Brooklyn Pub. Lib., 1955–56. **Educ.:** Hochschule fuer Welthandel, Vienna, Austria, 1945–48, BBA (Econ.); Columbia Univ. 1954–56, MS (LS); NY State Dept. of Educ., Pub. Libn. Prof. Cert. 1956. **Orgs.:** ALA. IL LA: Ch., Pub. Lib. Sect., (Ch., 1970–71). McLean Cnty. LA: Pres. (1979–80). Libns. Assn.: Tech. Prcs., (Ch., 1961–63). Nassau Cnty. Lib. Syst.: Sub-Com. **Honors:** *Jnl. of Lib. Hist.,* Awd. for Ms. Excel., 1967; Untd. Way of McLean Cnty., Awd. of Merit, 1978. **Pubns.:** "Gustav Langenscheidt: Printer, Publisher, Businessman - Pathbreaker for International Understanding," *Bibls.* (1973); *Josef Stummvoll: Lebenslauf und Bibliographie* (1970); "Corn Belt Library System," *IL Libs.* (D. 1968–79); *Mail Order Library Service in the Illinois Corn Belt: Books by Mail a Conference Report* (1974); "The Illinois Library Network," *Bibls.* (1974); various articles. **Activities:** 9, 13; 35, 39, 47 **Addr.:** 1809 W. Hovey Ave., Normal, IL 61761.

Melanson, Robert George (D. 7, 1948, Schenectady, NY) Head, Ref./Docums. Dept., Chesapeake Pub. Lib., 1979–; Ref. Libn., Old Dominion Univ. Lib., 1975–79. **Educ.:** Rider Coll., 1966–70, BS (Cmrce.); SUNY, Albany, 1974–75, MLS; Old Dominion Univ., 1982, MA (Hum.). **Orgs.:** VA LA. SELA. **Pubns.:** "Using the SIC in Business Reference," *RQ* (Fall 1978); "The Subject Specialist and Professional Development," *Southeast. Libn.* (Sum. 1980). **Activities:** 1, 9; 29, 39; 59, 77 **Addr.:** Chesapeake Public Library, Civic Center, 300 Cedar Rd., Chesapeake, VA 23320.

Melcher, Daniel (Jl. 10, 1912, Newton Center, MA) Publshg. Consult., 1969; Ch., RR Bowker Co., 1968–69, Pres., 1963–68, VP, 1959–63; other positions in publshg., 1934–42, 1946–59. **Educ.:** Harvard Coll., 1930–34, AB (Econ.). **Orgs.:** ALA: Cncl. (1972–74). Montclair Pub. Lib.: Trustee (1972–73). Inst. for Achvmt. of Human Potential: Bd. (1969–). **Pubns.:** *Melcher on Acquisition* (1971); *Printing & Promotion Handbook* (1949, 1956, 1967). **Activities:** 24, 26, 37; 51, 57, 89 **Addr.:** Glen Echo Farm, RFD 4, Charlottesville, VA 22901.

Melin, Nancy Jean (F. 15, 1941, Cleveland, OH) Chief Serials Libn., CUNY/Grad. Sch., 1980–; Lib. Syst. Anal., OCLC, Inc., 1979–80; Lib. Syst. Anal., RLG/RLIN, 1979; Head, Serials/Microforms Dept., Ctrl. MI Univ., 1975–78; Serials Libn., Univ. of VT, 1972–75. **Educ.:** Mt. Union Coll., 1958–62, AB (Eng./Psy.); Wayne State Univ., 1967, MA (Eng. Lit.); Simmons Coll., 1972, MS (LS). **Orgs.:** ALA: RTSD/Serials Sect., Med. Size Resrch. Libs. Disc. Grp. (Ch., 1978–79); Resrcs. Section, Resrch. and Policy Com. (1978–). New York Lib. Club. New York Tech. Srvs. Libns. **Honors:** Beta Phi Mu, 1972. **Pubns.:** Ed., *International Subscription Agents* (1978); Ed.-in-chief, *Serials Review*; *Reference Services Review*; Series Ed., Current Issues in Serials Management "Professional Without Portfolio," *Wilson Lib. Bltn.* (1979–80); "The Specialization of Library Literature," *Drexel Lib. Qtly.* (1980); other articles. **Addr.:** 215 West 75th St., #10E, New York, NY 10023.

Melius, Charlotte B. (N. 12, 1944, Baton Rouge, LA) Circ. Libn., Law Lib., LA State Univ., 1968–; Asst. Ref. Libn., New York Pub. Lib., 1966–68. **Educ.:** LA State Univ., 1962–65, BS (Educ.), 1965–66, MS (LS). **Orgs.:** AALL. LA LA. **Activities:** 1, 12; 16, 17, 22; 77 **Addr.:** Law Library, Paul M. Hebert Law Center, L.S.U., Baton Rouge, LA 70803.

Mellinger, Sydney S. (Ag. 14, 1931, White Plains, NY) Lib. Admin., Lake Forest Lib., 1978–, Asst. Libn., 1968–78; Catlgr., Picatinny Arsenal (Dover, NJ), 1954–55; Legal Libn., Hawkins, Delafield & Wood (NY), 1952–53. **Educ.:** Bucknell Univ., 1949–52, BA (Pol. Sci.); Rosary Coll., 1967–68, MALS with honors. **Orgs.:** ALA. IL LA: Hosplty. Com. (1976–77). Coop. Computerized Circ. Syst.: Pres., Governing Bd. (1980–81). Reg. Libn. Adv. Cncl.: Exec. Com. (1979–81). **Honors:** Beta Phi Mu, 1968. **Pubns.:** "InterLibrary Cooperation In Lake County," *IL Lib.* (My. 1972). **Activities:** 9; 17, 28, 34; 77, 92 **Addr.:** Lake Forest Library, 360 E. Deerpath, Lake Forest, IL 60045.

Mellott, Constance M. (O. 6, 1930, Washington, DC) Asst. Prof., Sch. of Lib. Sci., Kent State Univ., 1976–; Asst. Libn., Tech. Srv., Springfield (MA) Tech. Cmnty. Coll., 1973–76; Assoc. Libn., Bettis Atomic Power Lab., Westinghouse, 1970–72; Assoc. Info. Anal., K.A.S. Ctr., Univ. of Pittsburgh, 1965–67; Tech. Srv. Libn., Oak Ridge Gaseous Diffusion Plant, Union Carbide Corp., 1962–65. **Educ.:** Pfeiffer Jr. Coll., 1948–50, AA (Math.); Mt. Union Coll., 1950–52, BS (Phy.); Case West. Reserve Univ., 1961–62, MSLS; Univ. of Pittsburgh, 1965–77, PhD (LS), 1968, MA (Ling.). **Orgs.:** ALA. ASIS. OH LA. SLA. AALS. AAUP. AAUW. **Honors:** Beta Phi Mu. **Activities:** 11, 12; 56, 75, 91 **Addr.:** School of Library Science, Kent State University, Kent, OH 44240.

Melnick, Ralph (S. 14, 1946, New York, NY) Head of Spec. Col., Coll. of Charleston, 1977–; Archvst./Libn., Zionist Arch. and Lib., 1975–77; Archvst./Libn., Amer. Jewish Hist. Socty., 1971–72. **Educ.:** New York Univ., 1964–68, BA (Relig.); Columbia Univ., 1969–70, MLS, 1972–77, PhD (Relig.). **Orgs.:** SAA: Univ. Arch. Grp. (1979). Socty. of GA Archvsts.: Ed. Bd. (1978–79). ALA. Assn. for Jewish Std. Amer. Assn. for State and Local Hist. **Honors:** Phi Beta Kappa, 1968. **Pubns.:** "Billy Simmons: The Black Jew of Charleston," *Amer. Jewish Arch.* (1981); "Rediscovering the Past: The Old Slave Mart of Charleston, South Carolina," *Civil War Hist.* (1981); *From Polemics to Apologetics: Jewish-Christian Rapprochment in 17th-Century Amsterdam"* (1980); "The Ubiquitous Archivist," *GA Arch.* (1979); "The Philonic Conception of the Whole Man," *Jnl. for the Study of Judaism* (1979); other articles. **Activities:** 1, 2; 31, 41, 45; 55, 66, 92 **Addr.:** 3 Charlestowne Rd., Charleston, SC 29407.

Melton, Marie F., Sr. (Bay Shore, NY) Asst. Dir. of Libs., St. John's Univ., 1976–, Lib. & Info. Sci. Libn., 1972–76; Dir. of Media Ctr., Mater Christi HS, 1961–72; Asst. Libn., Bishop McDonnell HS, 1957–60. **Educ.:** St. John's Univ., 1960, BS (Educ.); Pratt Inst., 1961, MLS; St. John's Univ., 1974, MSEd. (Admin.), St. John's Univ., 1981, EdD (Admin. & Sup.). **Orgs.:** ALA. Cath. LA: Bklyn. L. I. Unit Ch. (1966–68); Natl. Finance Com. (1975–77); Ch., Ed. Bd., *Cath. Lib. World* (1979–). NY LA. Metro. Cath. Coll. Lib. Assn.: Vice-Ch., Ch.-Elect (1980–). Mercy Higher Educ. Colloquim. **Honors:** Cath. LA, Outstan. Libn. of the Year, 1974; Brooklyn-Long Island Unit, Beta Phi Mu. **Pubns.:** Clmn. Ed., "Professional Books," *Cath. Lib. World* . **Activities:** 1, 11; 22, 26, 42; 63 **Addr.:** St. John's University, Grand Central & Utopia Pkwys., Jamaica, NY 11439.

Meltzer, Ellen J. (Mr. 25, 1948, Los Angeles, CA) Assoc. Libn., Univ. of CA (Berkeley), 1975–. **Educ.:** Univ. of CA (Los Angeles), 1972, BA (Hist.), 1973–75, MLS; Univ. de Paris, 1969–70, Cert. (Fr.). **Orgs.:** CA LA: N. CA Chap., Clearhouse on Lib. Instr., Strg. Com. (1978–), Secy. (1978–79). CA Acad. and Resrch. Libn. ALA: ACRL, Bibl. Instr. Sect., Preconf. Plng. Com. (1981); RASD; SRRT; LIRT. Libn. Assn. of the Univ. of CA Berkeley: Secy. (1979–80); *LAUC Nsltr.* Ed. (1980–81). **Honors:** Beta Phi Mu. **Pubns.:** Jt. Auth., "Moffitt Library: A Commitment to Participation," *UgLi* (Undergraduate Library) *Nsltr.* (My. 1977). **Activities:** 1; 31, 39; 92 **Addr.:** Moffitt Undergraduate Library, University of California, Berkeley, CA 94720.

Meltzer, Morton Franklin (Ap. 15, 1930, New Bedford, MA) Info. Mgr., Martin Marietta Corp., 1959–. **Educ.:** Boston Univ., 1955–57, BS (Jrnlsm.); Rollins Coll., 1962–64, MBA; Nova Univ., 1974–77, MPA, DPA. **Orgs.:** Assoc. Info. Mgrs.: 1980 Adv. Bd.; 1981 Exec. Bd. SLA. Intl. Socty. for Gen. Sem. Intl. Comm. Assn. Amer. Bus. Comm. Assn. **Honors:** Kappa Tau Alpha. **Pubns.:** *The Information Imperative* (1971); *The Information Center:* (1967); *Information: The Ultimate Management Resource* (1981); "Information Managers Must Set Policy," *The Info. Mgr.* (Jl./Ag. 1979). **Activities:** 12; 17, 24; 52, 59, 91 **Addr.:** 301 Glenridge Way, Winter Park, FL 32789.

Melun, Margaret E., (S. 15, 1942, Fort Worth, TX) Sr. Ref. Spec., Congsnl. Resrch. Srv., Lib. of Congs., 1974–; Ref. Libn., Georgetown Univ. Lib. 1970–74; Ref. Libn., Natl. Jnl., 1969–70. **Educ.:** Rosary Coll., River Forest, IL, 1960–64, BA (Hist); Cath. Univ., Washington, DC, 1967–69, MSLS. **Orgs.:** ALA. DC LA. **Pubns.:** Complr., "The Reference Book Collection of the Conference Information Center," WHCOLIS (1979). **Activities:** 4, 12; 29, 31, 39; 54, 78, 92 **Addr.:** CRS/C Rm. LM 219, Library of Congress, Washington, DC 20540.

Melvin, Sister M. Constance (O. 28, 1918, Pittston, PA) Ex. Dir., Lrng. Resrcs. Ctr., Marywood Coll., 1981–; Dean, Grad. Sch. of Arts and Sci., 1976–81, Ch., Grad. Dept. of Libnshp., 1960–76; Sch. Libn./Eng. tchr., Scranton Diocesan Schs., 1950–60; Asst. Libn., Marywood Coll., 1946–48; Sch. Libn., Mt. Kisco HS, 1943–46; Sch. Libn., Eastport HS, 1941–43. **Educ.:** Marywood Coll., 1936–40, AB (Soc. Sci.); Columbia Univ., 1940–41, BS in LS; Univ. of Chicago, 1951–62, PhD. **Orgs.:** ALA: Cnclr. (1979). Cath. LA. PA LA: VP, Pres. (1975–76); Exec. Bd. (1975–77); Bd. of Dir. (1965–66, 1969–70, 1974–77, 1978–). WHCOLIS: Del. (1979). Northeast. Assn. of Grad. Schs. PA Assn. of Grad. Schs. **Honors:** Kappa Gamma Pi, 1940; Delta Kappa Gamma, 1978; Beta Phi Mu. 1963. **Pubns.:** "Pennsylvania" in *ALA Yearbook* (1981). **Activities:** 1; 17, 32, 34; 57, 63, 93 **Addr.:** Marywood College, Scranton, PA 18509.

Menack, Marilyn (D. 26, 1935, New York, NY) Assoc. Dean, Westchester Cmnty. Coll., 1980–, Head of Lib. Instr. Srv., 1973–80, Dir. of Lrng. Ctr., 1971–73. **Educ.:** Brooklyn Coll., 1953–57, BA (Speech Pathology); Pratt Inst., 1969–71, MLS. **Orgs.:** Westchester LA: Pres. (1980–81); VP (1979–80); Cont. Educ. Com. (Ch., 1977–79). ALA. **Honors:** Beta Phi Mu, 1971. **Pubns.:** "The Case of Pringle's Potato Chips: From Library Warehouse to Learning Resource Center," *Cmnty. Coll. Frontiers* (Fall, 1977). **Activities:** 1; 17, 25, 31; 50, 59 **Addr.:** 44 Mayhew Ave., Larchmont, NY 10538.

Mendel, Roger (Mr. 30, 1943, Buffalo, NY) Dir., Alpena Cnty. Lib. and Northland Lib. Coop., 1970–; ILL Libn., Buffalo and Erie Cnty. Lib., 1966–68. **Educ.:** NY State Univ. Coll. at Buffalo, 1960–64, BS (Educ.); West. MI Univ., 1966, MLS. **Orgs.:** ALA. MI LA: Coop. Caucus (Secy.). MI Lib. Film Circuit. Mitten Bay Girl Scout Cncl.: Bd. Mem. **Activities:** 9; 17 **Addr.:** Alpena County Library, 211 North First, Alpena, MI 49707.

Mendelsohn, John (O. 19, 1928, Berlin, Ger.) Asst. Chief, Proj. Branch, Natl. Arch. and Rec. Srv., Gen. Arch. Div., 1978–, Supvsr. Archvst., 1977–78, Archvst., 1971–77. **Educ.:** Univ. of MD, 1953–61, BA (Hist.), 1962–67, MA (Hist.), 1968–74, PhD (Hist.). **Orgs.:** SAA. Amer. Hist. Assn. Amer. Com. for the Hist. of the Sec. World War. **Honors:** B'nai B'rith Argo Lodge, Haym Solomon Frdm. Medal, 1980. **Pubns.:** "Trial By Document," *Prologue* (Win. 1975); "The OMGUS Records Project," *Prologue* (Win. 1978); "The Holocaust," *Annals of the Amer. Acad. of Pol. and Soc. Sci.* (Jl. 1980). **Activities:** 2, 4; 15, 17, 18, 33; 62, 75, 74 **Addr.:** 10404 Hayes Ave., Silver Spring, MD 20902.

Mendenhall, Bethany R. (Je. 2, 1940, New Haven, CT) Assoc. Libn., Resrch. Lib., J. Paul Getty Musm., 1977–; Asst. Libn., Fine Arts Lib., Harvard Univ., 1967–77, Fine Arts Catlgr., 1965–77; Asst. in Cat. and City Plng., Art Lib., Yale Univ., 1964–65. **Educ.:** Bryn Mawr Coll., 1958–62, AB (Hist.); Columbia Univ., 1962–63, MLS. **Orgs.:** Art Libs. Socty. of N. Amer.: Cat. Adv. Com. (Ch., 1978–). ALA. Circolo Italiano di Boston: Mem. Secy. (1975–77). **Activities:** 1, 12; 20, 35, 46; 55 **Addr.:** Research Library, J. Paul Getty Museum, 17985 Pacific Coast Hwy., Malibu, CA 90265.

Mendenhall, Donna June MacMillan (Ag. 2, 1925, Bakersfield, CA) Sr. Info. Sci., Oxirane Intl., 1980–; Mgr., Info. Ctr.-Lib., Uniroyal Chemical Co., 1967–80. **Educ.:** South. CT State Coll., 1968–71, BA (Chem.), 1972–75, BS (LS); MLA Med. Libn. Cert., 1975; Various sems. and wkshps. **Orgs.:** SLA. ASIS. Fed. of Info. Users. Indus. Tech. Info. Mgrs. Grp.: Treas. (1979–80). Amer. Chemical Socty.: Div. Chem. Lit., Position Referral Coord. (1976–77). W. Hill Condominium Assn. Chemical Notation Assn. Chem. Club: Lib. Com. **Pubns.:** "I Learned About Searching from That....No. 2, Trademark Clearance," *Online* (Ja. 1980); "Indexing Laboratory Notebooks in a Chemical R&D Environment," *Spec. Libs.* (1978); "Cost Comparison of Four Data Input Methods," *Jnl. of Chemical Docum.* (1974). **Activities:** 12; 15, 17, 39; 60, 64, 91 **Addr.:** Oxirane International, Library, 120 Alexander St., P.O. Box 2155, Princeton, NJ 08540.

Menechian, Ludovic M. (O. 15, 1916, Adana, Turkey) Head, Acq. and Cat. Depts., Law Lib., Univ. of Ottawa, 1967–; Asst. Law Libn., 1967–73. **Educ.:** Cairo Coll., 1930–33, BSc (MAT); Univ. of Paris, 1935–39, BLL (Law); Univ. of Ottawa, 1968–74, BLS, MLS. **Orgs.:** AALL: Educ. Com. Can. ALL: Reception Com. **Activities:** 1; 77 **Addr.:** 912–B Elmsmere Rd., Ottawa, ON K1J 7T6 Canada.

Menewitch, Myron E. (Ap. 18, 1949, Brooklyn, NY) Tech. Libn., Malcolm Pirnie, Inc., 1977–; Resrch. Libn., Cons. Un. of US, Inc., 1972–77. **Educ.:** Queens Coll., CUNY, 1967–71, BA (Eng. Lit.); SUNY, Geneseo, 1971–72, MLS. **Orgs.:** SLA. Westchester LA.: Spec. Libs. Sect. (Co.-Ch., 1976–78). **Activities:** 12; 15, 17, 20; 59, 64, 65 **Addr.:** Library, Malcolm Pirnie, Inc., 2 Corporate Park Dr., White Plains, NY 10602.

Menges, Gary L. (S. 11, 1937, Garrison, IA) Assoc. Dir. of Libs., Pub. Srvs., Univ. of WA, 1979–; Asst. Dir. for Pub. Srvs., Univ. of TX, Austin, 1973–79; Asst. Head, Ref. Dept., Univ. of MA, 1970–71, Coord. of Branch Libs., 1969–73; City Plng. Libn., Fine Arts Lib., Cornell Univ., 1966–69, Rsv. Bk. Libn., Undergrad. Lib., 1965–66, Circ. Libn., 1962–65. **Educ.:** Cornell Coll., 1955–59, BA (Hist., Pol. Sci.); Univ. of MI, 1959–61, AMLS. **Orgs.:** ALA: ACRL, Chaps. Com. (Ch., 1980–81), TX Info. Exch. (Ch., 1975–79); LAMA; RASD; RTSD. ASIS. Natl. Micro. Assn. TX LA: Nom. Com. (1977–78); Coll. and Univ. Libs. Div. (Ch., 1978–79). Socty. of Archit. Histns. Amer. Cvl. Liberties Un. Sierra Club. **Pubns.:** "Perry-Castaneda Library," *TX Libs.* (Spr. 1978); "Historic Preservation Programs," (1969); "Model Cities: A Bibliography," (1968). **Activities:** 1; 17, 39, 45; 75, 92 **Addr.:** Suzzallo Library, FM-25, University of Washington, Seattle, WA 98195.

Mennella, Dona M. (Mr. 6, 1932, New York, NY) Mgr., Resrc. Ctr., Booz, Allen and Hamilton, Inc., 1979–; Prog. Asst., Ref. Srvs., Smithsonian Inst., Peace Corps Env. Prog., 1977–78; Assoc. Dir., Partner, Info. and Lib. Srvs., 1975–78. **Educ.:** George Mason Univ., 1971–72, BA (Hist.); Univ. of MD, 1973–74, MLS. **Orgs.:** SLA. ALA. Frnds. of Kings Park Lib.: Bd. (1978–80). **Honors:** Beta Phi Mu; Phi Kappa Phi. **Activities:** 12; 24, 39, 41; 65, 86 **Addr.:** Booz, Allen & Hamilton, Energy & Environment Resource Center, 4330 East-West Hwy., Bethesda, MD 20814.

Mensch, Harold L. (Je. 10, 1933, Brooklyn, NY) Assoc. Dir., Tech./Info. Srvs., Inst. of Gas Tech., 1964–; Tech. Ed., Chemetron Corp., 1962–63; Tech. Writer, Sherwin-Williams Co., 1959–62. **Educ.:** Brooklyn Coll., 1950–54, BS (Geol.); IL Inst. of Tech., 1964–67, MS (Sci. Info.). **Orgs.:** ASIS. Assoc. of Earth Sci. Eds. **Honors:** Socty. of Tech. Comm., Awd. of Merit, 1974. **Pubns.:** "Cost Analysis of an Information System for the

Special Subjects/Services: 50. Adult educ.; 51. Advert./Mktg.; 52. Aerosp.; 53. Agric.; 54. Area std.; 55. Arts/Hum.; 56. Autom.; 57. Bibl./Prtg.; 58. Bio. sci.; 59. Bus./Fin.; 60. Chem.; 61. Copyrt.; 62. Documtn.; 63. Educ.; 64. Engin.; 65. Env.; 66. Eth. grps.; 67. Film; 68. Food/Nutr.; 69. Geneal.; 70. Geo.; 71. Geol.; 72. Handcpd.; 73. Hist.; 74. Int. frdm.; 75. Info. sci.; 76. Insr.; 77. Law; 78. Legis.; 79. Math./Comp. sci.; 80. Med.; 81. Metals; 82. Nat. resrcs.; 83. Newsp.; 84. Nuc. sci.; 85. Oral hist.; 86. Petr./Energy; 87. Pharm.; 88. Phys./Astr./Math.; 89. Readg.; 90. Relig.; 91. Sci./Tech.; 92. Soc. sci.; 93. Telecom.; 94. Transp.; 95. (other).

Gas Utility Industry," *Proc. Am. Soc. Inf. Sci.* (1973); Ed., *Proceedings of the 14th International Technical Communications Conference,* (1967); Various articles and speeches. **Activities:** 5, 12; 30, 33, 39; 64, 86, 91 **Addr.:** Institute of Gas Technology, 3424 S. State St., Chicago, IL 60616.

Menthe, Melissa (Je. 16, 1948, Hackensack, NJ) Ref. Libn., Rutgers Univ., 1976–; Ref. Libn., Art Dept., Newark Pub. Lib., 1971–76. **Educ.:** Montclair State Coll., 1970, BA (Eng.); Rutgers Univ., 1971, MLS. **Orgs.:** ARLIS/NA. SLA. ALA: ACRL. Gvt. Docum. Assn. NJ. Coll. Art Assn. **Activities:** 1; 15, 39; 55, 67 **Addr.:** E65 Prospect St., Paramus, NJ 07652.

Menzenska, Sister Mary Jane, CSFN (F. 20, 1914, Worcester, MA) Archvst., Holy Family Coll., Philadelphia, PA, 1973–, Libn., 1954–73; Tchr./Libn., Nazareth Acad., 1946–54; Elem. sch. tchr., St. Stanislaus Kostka Sch., 1943–46; HS tchr., Little Flower Catholic Girls HS, 1939–43; Tchr., Nazareth Academy HS, 1938–39. **Educ.:** Marywood Coll., 1935–38, AB (Math.); St. John's Univ., 1944–46 BS LS; Drexel Univ., 1955–58 MS LS; 1977 (Arch. Cert.). **Orgs.:** ALA: ACRL DE Valley Reg., Dir.-at-Large, 1969–70). Cath. LA: Small Lib. Workshop, (1965); Resol. Com.; Advnc. Pubcty. Com. **Honors:** Beta Phi Mu, 1958. **Pubns.:** *Archives and Other Special Collections: A Library Staff Handbook* (1973); *Guide to Nazareth Literature, 1873–1973* (1975); "Cataloging Archival Material," *Cath. Lib. World;* "Cataloging and Classification: a Bibliography," *Cath. LA* (1965). **Activities:** 2; 23, 38, 45; 57, 62 **Addr.:** Holy Family College, Philadelphia, PA 19114.

Menzies, Annelie (N. 9, 1945, Berlin, Germany) Exec. Asst., Salt Lake City Pub. Lib., 1977–, Dir. of PR, 1971–76. **Educ.:** N. TX State Univ., 1963–67, BA (Soclgy./Eng); Univ. of TX, 1968–69, MA (Eng.), 1976–77, MLS. **Orgs.:** ALA. UT LA. Chld. Lit. Assn.; UT Chap., Ed. *Book Flight* (1979–). Intermt. Bus. Comm. Assn.: Secy. (1975–76). **Honors:** ALA, John Cotton Dana Spec. Awd., 1977. **Activities:** 9; 17, 25, 36; 95-Chld. lit. **Addr.:** Salt Lake City Public Library, 209 East 500 South, Salt Lake City, UT 84111.

Mercer, John Herbert (F. 6, 1932, Fredericton, NB) Head Ref. Libn., Gvt. Docum. Libn., Acadia Univ., Wolfville, NS, 1970–, Catlgr., 1967–70; Catlgr., Ref. Libn., Halifax City Reg. Lib., 1964–67; Catlgr., Law Lib., Dalhousie Univ., 1963–64; HS Tchr., Pub. Sch. of NS, 1957–62. **Educ.:** Dalhousie Univ., 1950–54, BA (Hist., Pol. Sci.), 1954–56 (Hist.), 1956–57, BEd; Univ. of Toronto, 1962–63, BLS, 1967–69, MLS. **Orgs.:** Atl. Provs. LA. Can. LA. NS Sch. LA. **Honors:** Beta Phi Mu, 1963. **Activities:** 1; 29, 39 **Addr.:** P.O. Box 614, Wolfville, NS B0P 1X0 Canada.

Mercure, Gerard (Ap. 17, 1935, St-Alban, PQ) Chief Libn., Univ. du PQ, Rimouski, 1969–; Libn. (Catlgr.), Ctrl. des Bibs., 1968–69; Chief Libn., CEGEP de Hull, 1965–68; Chief Libn., Coll. St-Alexandre, 1964–65; Libn., Bib. du Parlmt., Ottawa, 1963–64. **Educ.:** Univ. de Montréal, 1957, BA, 1962–63, BBibl. **Orgs.:** ASTED: VP (1977–79); Com. de Réd. de *Documtn. et Bibs.* (1979–). Natl. Micro. Assn. Corp. des Bibtcrs. Prof. du Can. Can. Cncl.: Com. en Matière de Promo. du Livre et Pér. Can. (1976–79). **Pubns.:** Contrib., "La Télécopie et le Pret entre Bibliothèques," *Documtn. et Bibs.* (1979); *Method and Apparatus for Photographing Pages of a Book* (1979); *Binding for Microfiches and the Like* (1974); *Copying Instrument for Filed Documents.* (1970); "La Place de l'Audiovisuel dans les Programmes d'Enseignement des Écoles de Bibliothéconomie," *Documtn. et bibs.* (1976); Various articles. **Activities:** 1; 17, 33 **Addr.:** Universite du Quebec A Rimouski, 300 Des Ursulines, Rimouski, PQ G5L 3A1 Canada.

Mercure, Rosemary P. (Ap. 24, 1928, Bostic, NC) Head, Pub. Srvs., Asst. Prof., Clinch Valley Coll., 1966–; Asst. Libn., Unicoi Cnty. Pub. Lib., 1964–66; Tchr., Unicoi Cnty. HS, 1950–51. **Educ.:** Lincoln Meml. Univ., 1946–50, BA (Fr.); Univ. of KY, 1967–68, MLS; Arch. Inst. (Atlanta), 1976, Cert. (Arch.); Intl. Traveling Sum. Sch., 1978, Cert. (LS). **Orgs.:** VA LA: Reg. I Rep. (1978–79). SELA. Mt. Empire Older Citizens (Ch.). Knights of Okra. **Honors:** Altrusa Schol., 1965; Beta Phi Mu, 1968. **Pubns.:** Various bibls. **Activities:** 1, 2; 31, 39, 45 **Addr.:** Clinch Valley College, Wise, VA 24293.

Meredith, Don L. (S. 11, 1941, Batesville, MS) Assoc. Libn., Harding Grad. Sch. of Rel., 1968–. **Educ.:** Harding Univ., 1959–63, BA (Bibl. Lang.), 1963–67, MTh (Bib. Stud.); Univ. of NC, 1967–68, MSLS. **Orgs.:** Amer. Theo. LA: Mem. Com. (1977–80); Ch. (1979–80). TN LA. TN Theo. LA (V.Pres. 1980–81, Pres. 1981–82). Memphis Lib. Cncl.: Com. on Coop. (1978–80); Ch. (1978–80). **Activities:** 1; 20, 30, 44; 90 **Addr.:** 3859 Danny Ave., Memphis, TN 38111.

Meriam, Philip W. (N. 26, 1929, Lincoln, MA) Dir., Wilmington (MA) Meml. Lib., 1971–; Dir., Dedham (MA) Pub. Lib., 1965–70; Asst. Dir., Wellesley (MA) Free Lib., 1962–64. **Educ.:** Alfred Univ., 1958, BA (Pol. Sci.); Rutgers Univ., 1958–59, MLS. **Orgs.:** ALA. MA LA. Grt. Boston Lib. Admin. MA Men's Libn. Club. St. Anne's Episcopal Church. **Activities:** 9; 16, 17, 39 **Addr.:** Wilmington Memorial Library, Wilmington, MA 01887.

Merikangas, Robert J. (My. 20, 1934, Washington, DC) Asst. Head, Ref. Srvs., Hornbake Lib., Univ. of MD, 1973–, Libn., Serials Dept., 1970–72; Asst. Prof. of Hist., Belmont Abbey Coll., 1967–69; Asst. Prof., Coll. of the Holy Names, 1966–67. **Educ.:** Tulane Univ., 1951–55, BA (Math.); Cath. Univ., 1959–66, PhD (Hist.); Univ. of MD, 1969–70, MLS. **Orgs.:** ALA: ACRL. MD LA: Ch., Lib. Orien. Exch. Com. (1977–78); Acad. & Resrch. Libs. Div., Prog. Com. (1978–79, 1980–81); Ed. Com. (1979–81). **Honors:** Phi Beta Kappa, 1955; Phi Alpha Theta, 1960; Beta Phi Mu, 1970. **Pubns.:** "The Academic Reference Librarian: Roles and Development," *New Horizons for Academic Libraries* (1979); "Library Instruction as Consulting" *The Crab* (D. 1979). **Activities:** 1; 31, 39; 92 **Addr.:** 204 Mowbray Rd., Silver Spring, MD 20904.

Merk, P. Evelyn (D. 8, 1943, Macon, GA) Head Libn., Nola Brantley Meml. Lib., 1977–; Ref. Libn., 1976–77, Tech. Srvs. Libn., 1975–76; Sch. Libn., Mary Persons Jr. High, 1973–75. **Educ.:** Mercer Univ., 1962–66, AB (Eng.); Univ. of GA, 1972–73, MEd (Lib. Educ.). **Orgs.:** ALA. SELA. GA LA. AAUW. **Activities:** 9, 10; 15, 17, 39; 63, 74 **Addr.:** 293 Peachtree Cir., Warner Robins, GA 31093.

Merrell, Sheila J. (D. 4, 1949, Ft. Dodge, IA) Netwk. Admin., St. Louis Reg. Lib. Netwk., 1979–; Dir., Div. for the Blind & Phys. Handcpd., KS State Lib., 1976–78; Dir., IA Lib. Teletype Exch., State Lib. Comsn. of IA, 1972–74. **Educ.:** Luther Coll., 1968–72, BA (Eng.); Univ. of MO, 1975–76, MA (LS). **Orgs.:** ALA: ASCLA, Multitype Lib. Coop. Sect., Pubns. Com. (1981–83), Interlib. Coop. Discuss. Grp. (Ch., 1980–82); JMRT, Afflt. Cncl. Rep. (1977–78), Afflt. Cncl. Pres. (1979–80). MO LA: Outreach RT (Ch. elect., 1980–81); Treas. (1981–82). Greater St. Louis Lib. Club. First Congregational Church: Bd. of Christ. Educ. (1981–83). **Pubns.:** Jt. Ed., *I-LITE Interlibrary Loan Procedures Manual* (ERIC 1973). **Activities:** 12, 14-Network; 24, 25, 34; 56, 63, 93 **Addr.:** St. Louis Regional Library Network, 13550 Conway Rd., St. Louis, MO 63141.

Merrick, Olga Srepel (Mr. 24, 1949, Santiago, Chile) Dir., Palmer (MA) Pub. Lib., 1981–; Film Libn., West. MA Pub. Lib. Syst., 1978–81; various positions in tchg., other flds. **Educ.:** Smith Coll., 1966–70, BA (Slavic Std., Russ.); IN Univ., 1977–78, MLS; grad. work in Russ. **Orgs.:** ALA. New Eng. LA: Coop. Lib. Agencies Sect. (1980–); Media Sect. (1981–). MA LA. EFLA. **Activities:** 13; 24, 32, 34; 57, 67 **Addr.:** Village Park Apts., #126, Amherst, MA 01002.

Merritt, Gertrude E. (Jl. 23, 1909, Goldsboro, NC) Retired; Assoc. Univ. Libn., Col. Dev., Duke Univ., 1975–79, Asst. Univ. Libn., Tech. Srv., 1966–75, Head, Tech. Prc., 1942–65, Head, Serials Dept., 1940–42, Serials Catlgr., 1938–39, Searcher, Order Dept., 1931–39. **Educ.:** Duke Univ., 1927–31, BA (Hist.). **Orgs.:** ALA. Durham Cnty. LA. SELA. NC LA. Altrusa Club Durham: Treas. (1968–71); Corres. Secy. (1974–76); Finance Ways and Means (Ch., 1972–73, 1975–76). **Pubns.:** Jt. Auth., "Costs of Expanding the Card Catalog of a Large Library," *Coll. Resrch. Lib.* (Ja., 1954). **Addr.:** 621 Swift Ave., Durham, NC 27701.

Merritt, Sylvia Stern (Mr. 24, 1924, Chicago, IL) Ref. Libn., Univ. of CA, Los Angeles, Law Lib., 1965–; Admin. Policy Coord., Los Angeles City Schs., 1949–56; Ed., Trade Regulation Rpt., Commerce Clearing Hse., 1947–49. **Educ.:** Univ. of IL, 1945, BSL, 1946, LLB (Law); Immaculate Heart Coll., 1965, MALS. **Orgs.:** AALL: Com. on Contemporary Soc. Problems (1974–78); Com. on Index to Legal Pers. (1978–79). South. CA Assn. of Law Libs. Amer. Lung Assn.: Los Angeles Coastal Reg. Cncl. (1978–). ACLU. Common Cause. Public Citizen. **Pubns.:** *The Rights of Nonsmokers: A Selected Bibliography* (1978). **Activities:** 1, 12; 39; 77 **Addr.:** UCLA Law Library, 405 Hilgard, Los Angeles, CA 90024.

Merskey, Marie G. (Mrs.) (O. 10, 1914, Kimberley, S. Africa) Lib. Dir., Harrison Pub. Lib. and W. Harrison Branch, 1969–; Adult Srvs. & Ref. Libn., Westchester Lib. Syst., 1966–69; Resrch. Libn., Consumers Union, 1963–66; Ref. Libn., New Rochelle Pub. Lib., 1960–63. **Educ.:** Univ. of Cape Town, 1956–58, BA (Hist.), 1959, Dip. (Libnshp.). **Orgs.:** ALA. NY LA: Cont. Educ. Com. (1973–76). Westchester LA. Pub. Lib. Dirs. Assn: Exec. Bd. (1981–82). Coast Guard Auxiliary: Pubns. Ofcr. Founder, Charles Dawson History Ctr., 1981. Harrison Hist. Socty. Hadassah. Leag. of Women Voters'. **Honors:** B'nai B'rith Brotherhood Awd., 1975. **Pubns.:** "Where is Harrison's History?" *Spotlight Mag.* (1979); Ed., Bicentennial cookbook, *On Harrison's Table* (1976); various articles. **Activities:** 9; 17, 36, 42, 47; 78, 83 **Addr.:** 316, South Barry Ave., Mamaroneck, NY 10543.

Mersky, Roy Martin (S. 1, 1925, New York City, NY) Prof. of Law and Dir. of Resrch., Univ. of TX Law Lib., (1965); Interim–Dir., Jewish Natl. and Univ. Lib., Hebrew Univ., 1962–73; Exec. Secty., Judicial Cncl. and Comsn. WA Court Rpt., State of WA, 1959–63; Dir., WA State Law Lib., 1959–63. Chief, Rdrs. and Ref. Srv., Yale Law Lib., 1954–59; Rdrs. Adv., Ref. and Cat. Libn., City Hall Mncpl. Ref. Libn., Milwaukee Pub. Lib., 1953–54; WI Law Prac., 1952–54; various law tchg. positions. **Educ.:** Univ. of WI, 1944–48, BS, 1952, JD (Law), MALS. **Orgs.:** ALA. AALL. NLA: VP, Pres.–Elect (1980–81). TX LA. TX Com. for the Human.: Bd. of Dirs. SCRIBES Socty. of Amer. Law Tchrs.: Bd. of Gvrs.; Amer. Bar Assn.: Gavel Awds. Com. **Pubns.:** Jt. auth., *Fundamentals of Legal Research* (1981); jt. auth., *The First One-Hundred Justices: Statistical Studies on the Supreme Court of the United States* (1978); jt. auth., *Index to Periodicals Articles Related to Law* (1981); jt. auth., "A Decade of Academic Law Library Construction," *Lib. Jnl.* (D. 1, 1979); jt. auth., "Computer-Assisted Legal Research Instruction–Texas Law Schools," *Law Lib. Jnl.* (Win. 1980). **Activities:** 1, 12; 15, 17, 19; 75, 77 **Addr.:** The University of TX Tarlton Law Library, 2500 Red River, Austin, TX 78705.

Merubia, Sonia M. (S. 18, 1947, La Paz, Bolivia) Serial Rec. and Acq. Libn., Benson Latin Amer. Coll., Univ. TX, 1976–, Serials Libn., 1973–76. **Educ.:** Univ. of TX, 1966–69, BA (Hist.), 1970–73, MLS, 1977–, (Latin Amer. Std.). **Orgs.:** SALALM: Rapporteur Gen. (1979); Nom. Com. (Ch., 1980–81). TX LA. S.W. Conf. on Latin Amer. Std. Jane Austen Socty. of N. Amer. TX Meth. Hist. Socty. **Honors:** Phi Beta Kappa, 1969. **Pubns.:** Cmplr., "Argentine History," *Biblio Noticias* (Ja. 1981); "The Acquisition of Serials at the Benson Latin American Collection," *Serials Libn.* (N. 1980); Cmplr., "Current Newspapers in the Benson Collection," *Biblio Noticias* (O. 1979); Indxr., *Hispanic Amer. Per. Indx.* (1975, 1976). **Activities:** 1; 44, 45; 54, 90 **Addr.:** 2204 Southern Oaks, Austin, TX 78754.

Mesa, Rosa Q. (O. 14, 1923, Havana, Cuba) Head, Latin Amer. Coll. and Univ. Libn., Univ. of FL, 1977–, Latin Amer. Docum., Assoc. Libn., 1973–77, Latin American Docum., Asst. Libn., 1961–73; Asst. Libn., Bib. Natl. (Havana), 1959–61; Asst. Libn., Ruston Acad. (Marianao, Cuba), 1960–61. **Educ.:** Inst. de Marianao, 1937–41, BA (Liberal Arts); Univ. de la Habana, 1941–45, DR (Pharm.), 1959–61, MS (LS); Escuela Superior de Marianao, 1947–49, Cert. (Eng.). **Orgs.:** SALALM: Pres. (1973–74); Local Arrange. Com. (Ch., 1977); Cuban Bibl. Com. (Ch., 1975–76); Com. Official Pubns. (Ch., 1969–74, 1976–79); Com. Gift Exch. (Consult.). Assn. Caribbean Univ. Resrch. Inst. Lib.: Secy. (1977–80). FL LA. Alachua Cnty. LA. Latin Amer. Std. Assn. Caribbean Std. Assn. **Pubns.:** Ed., *Latin American Serial Documents: a Holdings List* (1968–1978); *Sources of Information of the Governmental Organizations of the Countries of Latin America* (1965); *Bibliography of Organization Manuals and Other Sources of Information on the Governmental Organization of the Countries of Latin America* (1970); *The Publications of the Interamerican Development Bank* (1974); *The Central Banks of Latin America and Their Libraries* (1976); various other pubns. Reviews. **Activities:** 1; 45; 54, 57, 92 **Addr.:** Latin American Collection, University of Florida Libraries, Gainesville, FL 32611.

Messer, Nancy C. (Mr. 29, 1947, Portland, OR) Continuations Libn., Baker & Taylor Co., 1977–; Asst. Prof., Intro. to Bibl. and Resrch. Methods, Coll. of Charleston Lib., 1976–77; Admin. Per. Div., Washburn Univ. of Topeka, 1972–76. **Educ.:** Univ. of OK, 1965–69, BA (Geo.); Univ. of Denver, 1969–70, MA (LS); Seton Hall Univ., 1980–, (Bus. Admin.). **Orgs.:** ASIS. Assoc. Info. Mgr. ALA. **Honors:** Beta Phi Mu. **Activities:** 1, 6; 15, 17, 46; 56, 75, 93 **Addr.:** P.O. Box 46, Somerville, NJ 08876.

Messerle, Judith R. (Ja. 16, 1943, Litchfield, IL) Dir., Educ. Resrcs., Cmnty. Rel., St. Joseph Hosp., 1972–; Dir., Lib., St. Joseph's Sch. of Nursing, 1967–72. **Educ.:** South. IL Univ., 1961–66, BA (Zlgy.); Univ. of IL, 1966–67, MLS. **Orgs.:** Med. LA: Bd. of Dirs. (1981–84); Legis. Com. (1977–80); Ad Hoc Com. to Std. Feasibility of Accred. Prog. for Hosp. Libs. (1975–77; Hosp. Lib. Sect. (Pres., 1977–78). St. Louis Med. Libns.: Pres. (1975–76, 1976–77). Cncl. of Hlth. Sci. Libs.: Bd. of Dirs. (1975–78). IL State Lib. Adv. Com.: (1979–81). Fam. Srvs. and Visit. Nurse Assn.: Bd. of Dirs. (1976–78); Nom. Com. (Ch., 1977–78). Alton Sr. HS: Hlth. Sci. Occupations Adv. Com. (1974–). Gt. St. Louis Hlth. Syst. Agency: Task Force on Long Term Care (1975–76); Pediatric Tech. Adv. Grp. (1978–79). Hosp. PR Socty. of St. Louis. **Honors:** Beta Phi Mu, 1967; Med. LA Cert., Grade I. **Pubns.:** Co-ed., *Hospital Library Management* (forthcoming); "Hospital Librarianship" in *Special Librarianship: A New Reader* (forthcoming); "Hospital Library Consortia," *Cath. Lib. World* (Jl.–Ag. 1978). **Activities:** 12; 17, 27, 36; 59, 78, 80 **Addr.:** St. Joseph Hospital, 915 E. 5th, Alton, IL 62002.

Messier, Réal (O. 21, 1945, Drummondville, PQ) Dir. gén., BCP - Région de PQ, 1978–; Asst. Prof., Univ. of Montréal, 1975–78; Docmlst., Mnstry. of Cult. Affairs, 1972–75. **Educ.:** Univ. Laval, 1967–70, L.èsL.; Univ. de Montréal, 1970–72, MLS; Univ. Laval, 1969–70, CES (Arch.). **Orgs.:** ASTED. ALA. **Honors:** Students to Dallas, J. Morris-World Book, 1971; PQ Mnstry. of Cult. Affairs, Coop. with Fgrn. Affairs, 1972. **Pubns.:** "La bibliothèque publique n'est pas un privilège, mais un droit ...," *La Parole* (Ja. 1972); "Traitement du personnel professionnel dans les bibliothèques publiques du Québec", *Biblio-contact* (Automne 1975); "Les bibliothèques à double allégeance: évolution du concept", *Documentation et bibliothèques* (D. 1977); "Mémoire et évolution des bibliothèques publiques", *Biblio-contact* (Été 1977); "Bibliothècaires professionnels dans les bibliothèques publiques au Québec en 1979", *Biblio-contact* (Été 1979); other articles, reviews. **Activities:** 9; 15, 17 **Addr.:** 412, rue de l'Escale, Bernières, PQ G0S 1C0 Canada.

PROFESSIONAL ACTIVITIES: Institutions: 1. Acad. lib.; 2. Arch.; 3. Assn.; 4. Fed./Gvt. lib.; 5. Inst. lib.; 6. Mfr./Suppl.; 7. Milit. lib.; 8. Musm.; 9. Pub. lib.; 10. Sch. lib.; 11. Sch. of lib. sci.; 12. Spec. lib.; 13. State lib.; 14. (other). **Functions/Activities:** 15. Acq./Col. dev.; 16. Adult srvs.; 17. Admin.; 18. Apprais.; 19. Archit./Bldgs.; 20. Cat./Class.; 21. Chld. srvs.; 22. Circ.; 23. Cons./Pres.; 24. Consult.; 25. Cont. ed.; 26. Educ. lib. sci.; 27. Ext. srvs.; 28. Fund/Grants; 29. Gvt. pubs.; 30. Indx./Abs.; 31. Instr. lib. use; 32. Media srvs.; 33. Micro.; 34. Netwks./Coop.; 35. Persnl.; 36. PR; 37. Publshg.; 38. Recs. mgt.; 39. Ref. srvs.; 40. Repro.; 41. Resrch.; 42. Review.; 43. Secur.; 44. Serials; 45. Spec. col.; 46. Tech. srvs.; 47. Trustees/Bds.; 48. YA srvs.; 49. (other).

Messineo, Anthony (D. 15, 1933, Rochester, NY) Dir., Greenville Cnty. Lib., 1980–; Dir., Mohawk Valley LA, 1977–, Deputy Dir., 1973–77; Bldg. Consult., N. Tonawanda Pub. Lib., 1973–74; Visit. Lectr., SUNY, Buffalo, 1972; Dir., N. Tonawanda (NY) Pub. Lib., 1968–73; Head, Adult Srvs., Ferguson Lib., Stamford, CT, 1966–68; Branch Head, Rochester (NY) Pub. Lib., 1964–66, YA Srvs. Libn., 1962–64. **Educ.:** Univ. of Miami, 1956–60, BA; Syracuse Univ., 1961–62, MSLS. **Orgs.:** ALA: Lib. PR Cncl. (1972–); Awds. Com. (1973). NY LA: Schol. and Grants Com. (1978–80; Ch., 1978–79); Com. for a Gvrs.'s Conf. on Libs. (1975–78); Bldg. Com., Pub. Lib. Sect., (1974–), Dir., Adult Srvs. Sect., (1974–75). Adv. Cncl. to the NY State Senate Subcomm. on Libs. (1978–80). Phillis Wheatley Center: Bd. of Dir. (1980–). Schenectady Freedom Forum: Bd. of Dir. (1975–); Ch. (1978–79). WMHT. Schenectady Access Cable Cncl.: Treas., (1974–75). **Pubns.:** "Adequate Facilities for Optimum Utilization of Film in Libraries," *The Bookmark* (Fall 1977); "Meredith Willson's Legacy," *Amer. Libs.* (F., 1971). **Activities:** 9; 17; 50, 67, 78 **Addr.:** Greenville County Library, 300 College St., Greenville, SC 29601.

Meszaros, Imre (Jl. 2, 1934, Budapest, Hungary) Head of Hum. Srvs., Washington Univ., 1981–; Art & Archit. Libn., 1976–80; Lect., Coll. of Lib. and Info. Srvs., Univ. of MD, 1972–76, Assoc. Libn., Fine Arts, McKeldin Lib., 1969–75. **Educ.:** Johns Hopkins Univ., 1960–64, BS (Eng.); Univ. of MD, 1964–66, MA (Eng.); Cath. Univ., 1968–69, MS in LS; Cert. in Intl. Libnshp., Univ. of MD, 1972. **Orgs.:** ALA. Socty. of Archit. Histns. **Honors:** Beta Phi Mu, 1969. **Activities:** 1; 15, 39, 45; 55, 64 **Addr.:** Art and Architecture Library, Washington University, St. Louis, MO 63130.

Metcalf, Keyes D (Ap. 13, 1889, Elyria OH) Consult., 1955–; Adj. Prof., Rutgers Univ., 1955–58; Dir. of Libs., Harvard Univ., 1937–55; Jr. Asst. to Chief, Ref. Dept., New York Pub. Lib., 1913–37; Student Asst. to Actg. Libn., Oberlin Coll. Lib., 1905–17. **Educ.:** Oberlin Coll., 1907–11, BA (Hist.); New York Pub. Lib. Sch., 1911–14, Dipl. **Orgs.:** ALA: Pres. (1942–43); ACRL. Amer. Antiq. Socty.: 1st VP. Belmont Pub. Lib.: Trustee. Boston Athenaeum: Trustee (1952–80). Radcliffe Coll.: Trustee. MA Hist. Socty. **Honors:** ACRL Awd. for Disting. Srv., 1978; New York Pub. Lib., 50th Anniversary Awd., 1961; 12 hon. doctorates. **Pubns.:** *Random Recollections of an Anachronism* (1980); *Planning Academic and Research Library Buildings* (1965); over 200 articles. **Activities:** 1; 17, 19, 24 **Addr.:** 68 Fairmont St., Belmont, MA 02178.

Metcalf, Linda M. (Jl. 22, 1945, Kansas City, MO) Branch Mgr. I, Denver Pub. Lib., 1981–, Chld. Libn., II, 1972–81, Chld. Lib. II (Main Lib.), 1969–72, Chld. Libn. I, 1968–69. **Educ.:** NE Wesleyan, 1964–65; Univ. of Denver, 1966–67, BA (Eng.), 1968, MLS. **Orgs.:** ALA. CO Chld. Bk. Awd. Com.: Nom. Com. (1980). CO Intl. Readg. Assn. (1981). Park Hill Toy and Game Lib.: Dir. (1979–81). Various other orgs. Denver Cncl. Intl. Readg. Assn. Org. **Honors:** Denver Pub. Lib., Empl. of the Yr., 1979; Denver Pub. Lib. Frnds. Org., Neil Scott Awd. for Cmnty. Srv., 1980. **Pubns.:** "From 'Star Wars' to King Arthur," *The CO Comm.* (1979). Reviews. **Activities:** 9; 17, 21, 26; 63, 89, 95-Storytelling. **Addr.:** 4458 East Eastman Ave., Denver, CO 80222.

Metoyer-Durán, Cheryl (F. 18, 1947, Los Angeles, CA) Asst. Prof., Univ. of CA, Los Angeles, 1977–; Dir., Indian Lib. Proj., Natl. Indian Educ. Assn., 1976–77; Branch Lib. Dir., Inglewood Pub. Lib., 1971–73, Ref. Libn., 1971. **Educ.:** Immaculate Heart Coll., 1965–68, BA (Eng.), 1968–69, MLS; IN Univ., 1973–76, PhD (LS). **Orgs.:** ALA: Indian Srvs. Subcom. Natl. Indian Educ. Assn. **Pubns.:** "The Native American Woman" in *The Study of Women* (1979); "American Indian People and Children's Resources" in AASL Research Monograph, *Cultural Pluralism and Children's Media* (1979); "Library Service to Native Americans," *ALA Yrbk.* (1977); "Library Service to American Indian People," *Bowker Annual* (1978); Ed., *Amer. Indian Libs. Nsltr.* (1976–); other articles, reviews. **Activities:** 9, 12; 17, 24, 41; 50, 66, 78 **Addr.:** Graduate School of Library & Information Science, University of California at Los Angeles, Los Angeles, CA 90024.

Metros, Mary Teresa (Teri) (N. 10, 1951, Denver, CO) Lib. Syst. Consult., Data Phase Syst., 1981–; Admin. Asst., Englewood Pub. Lib., 1981; Adult Srvs. Libn., 1975–80. **Educ.:** CO Womens Coll., 1969–73, BA (Eng.); Univ. of Denver, 1973–74, MA (Libnshp.). **Orgs.:** ALA. CO LA. **Activities:** 9; 17, 20, 39 **Addr.:** Data Phase Systems, 3770 Broadway, Kansas City, MO 64111.

Metsker, Marie Anne (Ja. 26, 1949, Portland, OR) Libn., Traveling Lib. Ctr., King Cnty. Lib. Syst., 1980–; Info. Spec., Oceanograph. Inst. of WA, 1978–80; Libn., Vashon Island Sch. Dist., 1974–78; Libn., Ocosta Consolidated Schs., 1971–74. **Educ.:** OR Coll. of Educ., 1967–71, BS (Lit.); Univ. of WA, 1971–76, MLib. **Orgs.:** SLA. WA Assn. of Sch. Libns. ALA: PLA. WA LA. **Pubns.:** Ed., *Compendium of Current Marine Studies in the Pacific Northwest 1978* (1978, 1979); ed., *NW Currents* (1978–89). **Activities:** 12; 30, 37, 39 **Addr.:** 4415 Holgate S.W., Seattle WA 98116.

Metts, Daniel L. Jr. (Je. 9, 1925, Pulaski, TN) Univ. Libn., Mercer Univ., 1963–; Asst. Head, Acq., Univ. MN, 1956–63; Head, Serials and Acq., FL State Univ., 1954–56, Asst. Acq., 1950–54. **Educ.:** Emory Univ., 1942–44, BA (Eng.), 1946–48, MA (Eng.); Univ. of NC, 1948–49, (Eng.); Emory Univ., 1949–50, MLn (LS). **Orgs.:** GA LA. SELA. **Activities:** 1; 17, 33, 34 **Addr.:** 3020 Clairmont Ave., Macon, GA 31204.

Metz, Betty A. (Jl. 2, 1946, Humboldt, TN) Libn., Cohen, Shapiro, Polisher, Shiekman and Cohen Law Firm, 1978–; Adj. Fac., Drexel Univ., Sch. of Lib. & Info. Sci., 1975–; Actg. Dir. and Ref. Libn, Theo. Jenkins Law Lib., 1975–78; Ref. Asst., Univ. of PA Law Lib., 1972–78; Ref. Staff, Yale Univ. Sterling Lib., 1970–72. **Educ.:** Purdue Univ., 1969, BA (Eng.); Drexel Univ., 1974, MS LS; AALL, 1981, (Cert.); Inst. on Tchg. Legal Resrch., 1978, (Cert.). **Orgs.:** AALL. Greater Philadelphia Law LA: Pres. (1980–81); Exec. Bd., and various ofcs. Drexel Lib. Sch. Alum. Assn.: Nom. Com. (1979). Drexel Univ., Alum. Travel Com. **Activities:** 1, 12; 17, 26; 77 **Addr.:** Law Offices, Cohen, Shapiro, Polisher, Shiekman & Cohen, Philadelphia Saving Fund Building, Philadelphia, PA 19107.

Metz, Carolyn J. (Ja. 17, 1943, Mt. Vernon, IN) Dir., Visual Resrcs. and Srvs., Indianapolis Musm. of Art, 1979–; Slide Libn., 1973–79; Tchr., Highland Jr. and Sr. HS, 1970–71; Tchr., Tipton Jr. High, Goshen HS, Elkhart Cmnty. Schs., 1965–70. **Educ.:** Anderson Coll., 1961–65, BA (Art); Ball State Univ., 1965–71, MA (Art); State of IN, 1971, Tchg. Licn./Sec. Cert., Prof.; IN Univ., 1979–80, MLS. **Orgs.:** ARLIS/NA: Visual Resrcs. Assn. for IN Media Educs. SLA. Socty. of IN Archvsts. Women's Caucus for Art. IN Hist. Socty. Hist. Landmarks Fndn. of IN. **Activities:** 8; 15, 22, 32; 55 **Addr.:** Visual Resources and Services, Indianapolis Museum of Art, 1200 W. 38th St., Indianapolis, IN 46208.

Metz, Karen S. (Ag. 10, 1949, Gary, IN) AV Consult., Univ. of MI, 1976–, Asst. Libn., 1974–76. **Educ.:** IN Univ.; Univ. of MI, 1967–72, AB (Eng., Germn.), 1973–74, AMLS; Med. LA, 1974–, (cert.). **Orgs.:** MI Hlth. Sci. LA: Ch., Educ. Com. (1979–81); Nom. Com. (1979); Conf. Com. (1979). S. Ctrl. MI Hlth. Sci. LA: Constn. Com. (1976); VP (1977–79). Med. LA. **Pubns.:** *Information Sources in Power Engineering* (1975); "A Computerized Cataloging Management System for Health Science Audiovisuals," *Bltn. of the Med. LA* (O. 1981); "Audiovisual Producers and Services," *Med. and Hlth. Inf. Dir.* (1977); "A Computerized Approach to Management of Utilization Data in a Media Center," *T.H.E. Jrnl.* (N. 1979). **Activities:** 1, 12; 32; 57, 80 **Addr.:** 14 Auburn St., Plaistow, NH 03865.

Metz, Paul (D. 4, 1948, White Plains, NY) User Srv. Libn., VA Tech., 1981–, Asst. Plng. and Resrch. Libn., 1979–81; Spec. in Autom. Info. Resrc., Cong. Resrch. Srv., Lib. of Cong., 1978; Intern, Lib. of Cong., 1977–78. **Educ.:** Univ. of NC, 1966–70, BA (Eng.); Univ. of MI, 1972–77, PhD (Soclgy.), MLS. **Orgs.:** ALA. VA LA. **Honors:** Phi Beta Kappa, 1970. **Pubns.:** Jt. Auth., "A Proposed Staffing Formula for Virginia's Academic Libraries," *Coll. & Resrch. Lib.* (Mr. 1981); Jt. Auth., "The Availability of Cataloging Copy on the OCLC Data Base," *CRL* (S. 1980); "The Use of the General Collection in the Library of Congress," *Lib. Qtly.* (1979); "Administrative Succession in the Academic Library," *CRL* (S. 1978). **Activities:** 1; 17, 22, 49-ILL. **Addr.:** 712 Barringer Dr., Blacksburg, VA 24060.

Metzger, Eva C. (F. 23, 1924, Chicago, IL) Owner, Dir., Carolina Lib. Srvs., 1977–; Lib. Opers. Supvsr., US Env. Protection Agency, 1976–79; Indxr., Charles Scribners Son, 1974–76; Admin. Ofc., Dept. Biostats., Univ. of NC, 1973–74. **Educ.:** Univ. of Chicago, 1942–46, PhB (Phil.); Tulane Univ., 1946–48, MA (Phil.); Univ. of NC, 1963–67, (Russ. Hist.), 1976–77, MSLS. **Orgs.:** SLA. NC SLA. SELA. **Activities:** 12; 17; 56, 58, 60 **Addr.:** Carolina Library Services, 137 E. Rosemary St., Chapel Hill, NC 27514.

Mevers, Frank C. (O. 10, 1942, New Orleans, LA) State Archvst. & Dir., NH State Arch., 1979–, Dir., NHPRC Arch. Recs. Proj., 1977–79; ed., Papers of William Plumer, NH Hist. Socty., 1977–79; ed., Papers of Josiah Bartlett, 1974–77. **Educ.:** LA State Univ., 1960–65, BA (Hist.), 1965–67, MA (Hist.); Univ. of NC, 1969–72, PhD (Hist.). **Orgs.:** SAA. New Eng. Archvsts. Org. of Amer. Histns. **Pubns.** *The Papers of Josiah Bartlett* (1979). **Addr.:** N. H. Division of Records & Archives, Department of State, 71 South Fruit St., Concord, NH 03301.

Meyer, Barbara Jean (Jl. 10, 1942, New Orleans, LA) Libn., Univ. of WI Law Sch., 1975–. **Educ.:** Univ. of WI, 1964–66, BA (Eng.), 1973–75, MS (LS). **Orgs.:** WI LA: Hlth. Rehab. Sect., Pres. (1979–80). AALL: Nom. Com. (1977). Univ. WI Spec. Campus Lib. Grp.: Strg. Com. (1980–81). Univ. WI Prof. Lib. Libn. Grp.: Nom. Com. (1980–81). Midvale Heights Cmnty. Assn.: Pres. (1980–81). **Pubns.:** Abstracts. **Activities:** 1, 12; 20, 22, 39; 77 **Addr.:** Criminal Justice Reference Center, Law School L140, University of Wisconsin, Madison, WI 53706.

Meyer, Diane S. (D. 19, 1930, New York, NY) Sch. Lib. Media Spec., E. Syracuse-Minoa Sch. Dist., 1972–. **Educ.:** Syracuse Univ., 1948–52, BA (Eng. Lit.), 1972–73, MLS. **Orgs.:** ALA. NY LA. Ctrl. NY Media Specs. Assn. **Honors:** Natl. Cncl. of Jewish Women, Volun. Sch. Lib. Prog., 1970; Syracuse Fed. of Women's Clubs, Volun. Sch. Lib. Prog., 1970; Beta Phi Mu. **Pubns.:** Reviews. **Activities:** 10 **Addr.:** 137 Oak Hollow Rd., Dewitt, NY 13214.

Meyer, Elaine Edna (My. 3, 1915, Wolsey, SD) Prof. Emeritus, Univ. of SD, 1978–, Asst. Prof. of Lib. Media, Ref. Libn., 1960–78; HS Libn., Lead, SD, 1955–60; Field Worker, SD State Lib., Sum. 1955; HS Libn., Los Alamos, NM, 1954–55; various other positions in tchg. **Educ.:** Huron Coll., 1934–38, BA Magna Cum Laude (Math., Bio.); Univ. of Denver, 1953–54, MA (LS). **Orgs.:** ALA: Recruit. Com. Mt. Plains LA. Delta Kappa Gamma: Secy. (1964–66); Scholar. Com. (Ch., 1976); PR (Ch.). **Honors:** SD Press Assn., Cert. Outstan. Achvmt. in HS Jnlsm., 1953. **Pubns.:** Jt. Auth., "Characteristics of School Libraries in SD and Qualifications of Personnel Who Staff Them," *SDEA Jnl.* (Mr., 1968). **Activities:** 1, 10; 26, 32, 39 **Addr.:** 854 Eastgate Dr., Vermillion, SD 57069.

Meyer, Janet Ann (O. 1, 1918, Punxatawney, PA) Lrng. Resrc. Ctr. Dir., Maine Township HS E., 1943–. **Educ.:** IL State Univ., 1936–37; Univ. of IL, 1937–40, BS, 1940–41, MLS. **Orgs.:** IL Assn. Media Educ. Delta Kappa Gamma. **Activities:** 10; 15, 17, 48; 55, 92 **Addr.:** Maine Township High School East, 2601 W. Dempster St., Park Ridge, IL 60068.

Meyer, Laura McIntyre (N. 22, 1946, Yosemite Natl. Park, CA) Chld. Libn. II, Seattle Pub. Lib., 1969–. **Educ.:** Univ. of WA, 1964–68, BA (Hist.), 1968–69, MLS. **Orgs.:** WA LA: Chld. and YA Srvs. Div., Exec. Bd. (1972–73, 1980–82). ALA. Pac. NW LA: Pac. NW Young Readrs. Choice Awd. Com. (1979). Puget Snd. Cncl. for Review of Chld. Media: Corres. Secy. (1975–76, 1979–80). Pac. NW Assn. of Church Libns. Pac. NW Writers Conf. **Activities:** 9; 16, 21, 42 **Addr.:** 10702 Evanston Ave. N., Seattle, WA 98133.

Meyer, Richard W. (Ja. 22, 1943, St. Louis, MO) Assoc. Dir., Clemson Univ., 1979–; Dir., Lib. Tech. Srvs., IN State Univ., 1976–79; Asst. Dir. for Tech. Srvs., Univ. of TX, 1970–76; Info. Spec., E. I. DuPont de Nemours, 1967–69. **Educ.:** Univ. of MO, 1961–67, BS, BA (Chem., LS); Univ. of IL, 1969–70, MS (LS). **Orgs.:** ALA: LITA/Nom. Com. (Ch., 1979–80). Christ. Libns. Flwshp. **Honors:** Beta Phi Mu. **Pubns.:** "COM Catalog Based on OCLC Records," *Jnl. of Lib. Autom.* (D. 1975); "Two Shared Cataloging Data Bases: A Comparison," *Coll. & Resrch. Libs.* (Ja. 1977); "Computer Output Microfiche Catalogs: Some Practical Considerations," *Jnl. of Micro.* (N. 1977); "Library Professionalism and the Democratic Way," *Jnl. of Acad. Libnshp.* (N. 1980). **Activities:** 1; 17, 33, 46; 56, 60 **Addr.:** Robert Muldrow Cooper Library, Clemson, SC 29631.

Meyer, Roger L. (Mr. 24, 1926, Soultz, Haut-Rhin, France) Mgr., Tech. Info. Ctr., Engelhard Minerals & Chemicals, 1970–; Mgr., Info. Srvs., Celanese Corp., 1960–70; Head, Documtn. Sect., Heurtey SA, Paris, 1957–59; Info. Spec., Vsines Diélectriques Delle, 1957. **Educ.:** Univ. of Paris, 1945–48, Dipl. (LS); Univ. of Strasbourg, (Ling.). **Orgs.:** SLA. ASIS. Assoc. of Info. Mgrs. **Pubns.:** Various articles. **Activities:** 60, 64, 81, 86, 88, 91 **Addr.:** Regency Village 12F, North Plainfield, NJ 07060.

Meyer, Sandra K. (Ag. 23, 1940, Pittsburgh, PA) Free-Lance Lib. Resrch., Meyer Research, Inc. 1976–1980; Cent. Islip Sch. of Nur. Libn., Psych. Ctr., 1970–76; Ref. Asst., Hofstra Univ., 1969–70. **Educ.:** IN State Univ., 1958–62, BS (Child.); C.W. Post, 1969–71, MSLS; Univ. of Pittsburgh, 1964–65. **Orgs.:** Beta Phi Mu: Guest Speaker Com. (1978). ALA. Med. LA. NY LA. **Pubns.:** *The Suffolk Academy of Medicine Library, Hauppauge, New York (1966–1970): A Study* (1970). "Hospital Learning Resource Centers," *SCLA Bltn.* Vol. 29 #1 (1973). **Activities:** 5; 16, 17, 20; 58, 72, 80 **Addr.:** 2 Mayflower Drive, Port Jefferson, NY 11777.

Meyer, Ursula (N. 6, 1927, Free City of Danzig) Dir. of Lib. Srv., Stockton-San Joaquin Cnty. Pub. Lib., 1974–; Coord., Mt. Valley Coop. Lib. Syst. (Sacramento, CA), 1972–73; Asst., Div. of Lib. Dev., NY State Lib., 1969–72; Cnty. Libn., Butte Cnty. Lib. (CA), 1961–68; Branch Libn., Contra Costa Cnty. Lib. (CA), 1959–60; Bookmobile Libn., Yakima Reg. Lib. (WA), 1954–59; Ref., Circ. Libn., Olympia Pub. Lib. (WA), 1953–54. **Educ.:** Univ. of CA at Los Angeles, 1945–49, BA (Intl. Rel.); Univ. of South. CA, 1952–53, MLS; Univ. of WI, 1968–69, (Pub. Lib. Admin.). **Orgs.:** CA LA: Pres. (1978); Legis. Com. (1976–79); Int. Frdm. Com. (1960); Cnclr. (1974–79). ALA: Cncl. (1979–82). AAUW. Leag. of Women Voters. Soroptimist Intl. NOW. **Activities:** 9; 17, 34, 35; 50, 74, 78 **Addr.:** Stockton-San Joaquin County Public Library, 605 North El Dorado St., Stockton, CA 95202.

Meyerhoff, Erich (N. 24, 1919, Braunschweig, Germany) Libn., Asst. Dean, Info. Resrcs., Cornell Univ. Med. Coll., 1970–; Libn., Hlth. Sci. Lib., SUNY, Buffalo, 1967–70; Dir., Med. Lib. Ctr. of NY, 1961–67; Libn., Asst. Prof., Down State Med. Ctr., SUNY, 1957–61; various tchg. positions, Columbia Univ. 1961–. **Educ.:** Coll. of the City of NY, 1937–43, BS (Soc. Sci.); Columbia Univ., 1950–51, MSLS, 1974, Cert. of Advnc. Libnshp. **Orgs.:** Med. LA: Dir. (1972–76). SLA. Cncl. of Natl. LA: Dir. (1975–78). **Pubns.:** "Foundations of Medical Librarinship," *Bltn. Med. LA* (1977); Jt. auth., "Regional Plans for Medical Library

Special Subjects/Services: 50. Adult educ.; 51. Advert./Mktg.; 52. Aerosp.; 53. Agric.; 54. Area std.; 55. Arts/Hum.; 56. Autom.; 57. Bibl./Prtg.; 58. Bio. sci.; 59. Bus./Fin.; 60. Chem.; 61. Copyrt.; 62. Documtn.; 63. Educ.; 64. Engin.; 65. Env.; 66. Eth. grps.; 67. Film; 68. Food/Nutr.; 69. Geneal.; 70. Geo.; 71. Geol.; 72. Handcpd.; 73. Hist.; 74. Int. frdm.; 75. Info. sci.; 76. Insr.; 77. Law; 78. Legis.; 79. Math./Comp. sci.; 80. Med.; 81. Metals; 82. Nat. resrcs.; 83. Newsp.; 84. Nuc. sci.; 85. Oral hist.; 86. Petr./Energy; 87. Pharm.; 88. Phys./Astr./Math.; 89. Readg.; 90. Relig.; 91. Sci./Tech.; 92. Soc. sci.; 93. Telecom.; 94. Transp.; 95. (other).

Service New York State and the New York Metropolitan Area," *Bltn. Med. LA* (1964); Jt. auth., "Library Participation in a Biomedical Communication and Information Network," *Bltn. Med. LA* (1970); Jt. auth., "Ilse Bry–A Tribute," *Bltn. Med. LA* (1976). **Activities:** 1, 12; 17, 31; 80 **Addr.:** 1161 York Ave., New York, NY 10021.

Meyers, Arthur Solomon (D. 14, 1937, New York, NY) Dir., Muncie Pub. Lib., 1980–; Mgr., Branches and Cmnty. Srvs., St. Louis Pub. Lib., 1973–80; Adult and YA Field Worker, Enoch Pratt Free Lib. 1967–73; Asst. Branch Libn., Detroit Pub. Lib., 1963–67; YA Libn., NY Pub. Lib., 1961. **Educ.:** Univ. of Miami, 1955–59, AB (Hist.); Columbia Univ., 1959–61, MLS; Univ. of MO, St. Louis, 1975–80, MA (Eng.). **Orgs.:** ALA: Ref. and Subscrpn. Bks. Review Com. (1975–79). Frdm. to Read Fndn. IN LA. MO LA. Retired Sr. Volun. Prog.: Adv. Cncl. (1980–). Advocates for Handcpd. Rights.: Adv. Cncl. (1981–). WA Univ. Eth. Heritage Std. Cncl. Untd. Way of Grt. St. Louis: Cmnty. Srvs. and Info. and Ref. Srvs. Coms. **Pubns.:** "Communication and Cooperation in Public Libraries," *Cath. Lib. World* (Jl. 1978); "Responding to Change," *Show-Me Libs.* (Ja. 1978); "Keeping Up: A Checklist," *American Libraries* (F. 1977); "Action Summer in Baltimore," *Top of the News,* (Ap. 1970). "The Unseen and Unheard Elderly," *Amer. Libs.* (S. 1971). **Activities:** 9; 16, 17, 27; 50, 66, 67 **Addr.:** Muncie Public Library, 301 E. Jackson, Muncie, IN 47305.

Meyers, Barbara E. (Jl. 28, 1953, Passaic, NJ) User Std. Prog./Pubn. Assessment, Amer. Chem. Socty., Resrch. & Dev. Dept., 1978–; Assoc. Ed./Proj. Mgr., Capital Syst. Grp., Inc., 1976–78; Writer/Consult., Natl. Acad. of Sci., 1976. **Educ.:** George Washington Univ., 1971–75, BA (Jnlsm., Nat. Sci), 1975–76, MA (Sci., Tech. & Pub. Policy). **Orgs.:** Socty. for Schol. Pubshg.: Bd. of Dir. (1978–84); Ch., Mem. Com. (1981–); Vice-Ch., 1980 Prog. Com. (1979–80). ASIS: Treas., Potomac Valley Chap. (1979–80) Secy. (1980–81); Mktg. Com. (1980). CISCO, 1981. Smithsonian Inst. Sigma Delta Chi. Early Amer. Socty. **Pubns.:** Jt. ed., *Proceedings of the First National Energy Youth Conference* (1974); Ed., *Federal Environmental Data: A Directory of Selected Sources* (1978); "New Scholarly Society Builds on Communication & Interaction", *ASIS Bltn.* (Ap. 1979); "The Society for Scholarly Publishing", *Schol. Publshg.* (Ap. 1979); jt. auth., "Evaluation of an Alternative Journal Format" *Proceedings, ASIS 1979 Anl. Mtg.* **Activities:** 3; 37, 41; 60, 91, 93 **Addr.:** 1836 Metzerott Rd., #1003, Adelphi, MD 20783.

Meyers, Donna Rae (Jl. 22, 1951, Pittsburgh, PA) Reg. Head of YA Srv., Cuyahoga Cnty. Pub. Lib., 1979–, YA Libn., 1976–79. **Educ.:** PA State Univ., 1969–73, BA (Psy.); Univ. of Pittsburgh, 1975–76, MLS. **Orgs.:** ALA: YASD, Select. Film YA Com. (1978–82, Ch., 1980–82); LAMA. OH LA. Berea Little Thea.: Bd. Mem. (1978–82). **Honors:** Beta Phi Mu, 1976; Phi Beta Kappa, 1973; Phi Kappa Phi, 1973. **Pubns.:** Jt. Auth., "A Programming Roundup II," *Top of the News* (Fall 1978). **Activities:** 9; 15, 24, 48; 67, 89 **Addr.:** Cuyahoga County Public Library, Fairview Park Regional, 4449 West 213, Fairview Park, OH 44126.

Meyers, Judith K. (Ap. 18, 1934, Columbus, OH) Coord., Media Srvs., Admin. Asst. to Supt., Lakewood Bd. of Educ., 1971–; Dir., Curric. Resrcs., AV Ctr., IN Univ., 1969–71; Asst. Dir., Grad. Sch. of LS, Univ. of IL, 1968–69; Coord., Media Srvs., Tuscarawas Valley Educ. Srv. Ctr., 1966–67. **Educ.:** OH Wesleyan Univ., 1952–56, BA (Hist.); Kent State Univ., 1963, MA (LS); FL State Univ., 1976, AdM (Lib. Educ.); IN Univ., 1976, ED (Instr. Syst.). **Orgs.:** ALA. AECT. Lakewood Org. of Sch. Admin. Women's Natl. Book Assn., Natl. Sch. PR Assn. **Honors** OH Assn. of Sch. Libns., Outstand. Srv. Awd., 1974. **Pubns.:** *Ohio Audiovisual Survey* (1977); "How to Run a Successful School Levy Campaign" Info. Syst. Div., AECT (1979); "Research Responsibilities of School Supervisor," *Drexel Lib. Qtly.* (Jl. 1979). **Activities:** 10; 24, 32, 36; 63, 67, 93 **Addr.:** Media Services, Lakewood Board of Education, 1470 Warren Rd., Lakewood, OH 44107.

Meyers, Rosa Mae Miller (Ag. 18, 1918, Torras, LA) Head, Centroplex Br., E. Baton Rouge Parish Lib., 1980–, Head, Downtown Br., 1975–80, Head, Circ. Dept., 1974–75, YA Libn., 1971–74, Spec. lectr. LSU Lib. Sch., 1972–73, Ref. Libn., 1963–71, Asst., 1961–63. **Educ.:** LA State Univ., 1957–61, BS (Educ.), 1961–63, MSLS, 1966–71, MA (Hist.), 1966. **Orgs.:** ALA. LA LA: Reg. (1979); Gov. Docum. (1966–67); LA Lit. Awd. (1963–65); YA Sect.-Prog. (1971–73). Southwestern LA. Baton Rouge Lib. Club. **Honors:** Phi Kappa Phi, 1962; Beta Phi Mu, 1963; Phi Alpha Theta, 1961, Alpha Beta Alpha, 1962; Flwshp. in Lib. Sci., 1966. **Pubns.:** "Just like having two stores" *LA LA Bltn.* (1974); *A History of Baton Rouge, 1699–1812* (1976). **Activities:** 9; 17, 39, 48; 55 **Addr.:** 944 Magnolia Wood Ave., Baton Rouge, LA 70808.

Meyerson, Sara (Ja. 20, 1933, New York, NY) Mgr., Lib. Info. Srv., ABC Broadcasting, 1973–; Head Libn., Amer. Fndn. for the Blind, 1956–65. **Educ.:** Long Island Univ., 1950–54, BA (Eng.); Columbia Univ., 1954–56, MSLS. **Orgs.:** SLA: Ch., By-Laws Co. (1960–61); Ch., Soc. Sci. Grp. (1959–60); Adv. Cncl. (1978–79); Ch., Networking (1979–80). **Activities:** 2; 17, 23, 24 **Addr.:** American Broadcasting Company News, 2040 Broadway, New York, NY 10023.

Micciche, Pauline F. (F. 5, 1939, Scranton, PA) Dept. Mgr., Resrc. Mgt. Srv., OCLC, Inc., 1979–, User Adv., 1979, Lib. Syst. Anal., 1978; Autom. Assoc., SUNY, Stony Brook, 1972–78. **Educ.:** Univ. Buffalo, 1957–61, BA (Eng.); Canisius Coll., 1961–63, MS (Educ.); Case West. Reserve Univ., 1962–63, MLS. **Orgs.:** ALA: LAMA, Persnl. Dynamic Supvsr. (1980–81). ASIS. Assn. Comp. Mach. **Pubns.:** "The Future Conjunction: How to Manage the Psychological Impact of Change" *LASIE* (Mr./Ap. 1979); *Staff Training for On-line Processing Systems.* (ERIC ED 167 174, 1980); "The OCLC Serials Control Subsystem," *Serials Libn.* (Supplement Jl. 1981). **Activities:** 1, 6; 24, 34, 46; 56, 75 **Addr.:** OCLC, Inc., 6565 Frantz Rd., Dublin, OH 43017.

Michael, Ann B. (D. 27, 1945, Greencastle, IN) Chief Libn., Corp. Info. Ctr., Manville Corp, 1976–; Syst. Libn., Sr. Ref. Libn. & Biblgphr., Cat., Lib., US Civil Srv. Comsn., 1972–76; Assoc. Libn., Bus. Lib., Eli Lilly & Co., 1968–71. **Educ.:** Monmouth Coll., 1963–67, AB (Bus. admin); Butler Univ., 1967–69, MBA (Gen. mgt.); Univ. of Denver, 1971–72, MA (LS). **Orgs.:** SLA: Rocky Mt. Chap., Cont. Educ. Com. (1977–79); Pres.-Elect (1977–78); Pres. (1978–79); Exec. Bd. (1979–80). ASIS: CO Centennial Chap., Secy.-Treas. (1979–80). ALA. Rocky Mt. OLUG: Ch., Nom. Com. (1979, Vice ch. 1981). Other orgs. **Honors:** Beta Phi Mu, 1972. **Activities:** 12; 17, 39; 51, 59, 77 **Addr.:** 4332 W. Pond View Dr., Littleton, CO 80123.

Michael, Douglas O. (F. 8, 1947, Cumberland, MD) Dir. of Lib., Lrng. Resrc., Cayuga Cmnty. Coll., 1979–; Dir. of Lrng. Resrc., Allegany Cmnty. Coll., 1977–79, Dir. of the Lib., 1973–77, Assoc. Dir. of the Lib., 1972–73; Asst. Libn., Waynesburg Coll., 1970–72. **Educ.:** WV Wesleyan Coll., 1967–69, BS (LS); Syracuse Univ., 1969–70, MSLS. Allegany Cmnty. Coll., 1965–67, AA (Liberal Arts). **Orgs.:** ALA. SUNY Cncl. of Head Libn. Jr. Coll. Cncl. of the Mid. Atl. States: Exec. Bd. (1978). **Honors:** Beta Phi Mu, 1970. **Pubns.:** *Western Maryland Materials in Allegany & Garrett County Libraries* (1977); "Local History Preservation & Promotion: a new role for the Community College," *Cmnty. Coll. Frontiers* (Sum. 1978). **Activities:** 1; 17, 23, 36; 85 **Addr.:** Cayuga Community College, Franklin St., Auburn, NY 13021.

Michael, James Dietrich (Ap. 8, 1947, Murphysboro, IL) Assoc. Univ. Libn., Univ. of S. FL, 1974–. **Educ.:** South. IL Univ., Carbondale, 1965–69, BS (Zlgy.); FL State Univ., 1973–74, MSLS. **Orgs.:** ALA. FL LA: caucus ch. (1977–78). SELA. Hillsborough Cnty. LA: Treas. (1979–80). **Activities:** 1; 20, 44 **Addr.:** 2413 East Linebaugh Ave., Tampa, FL 33612.

Michalak, Thomas J. (My. 18, 1940, Chicago, IL) Dir. of Libs. Carnegie Mellon Univ., 1980–; Chief, Sci. and Engin. Div., Columbia Univ. Libs., 1975–80; Libn., Econ. and Pol. Sci., IN Univ. Libs., 1967–75; Serials Biblgphr., Univ. of IL Lib., 1966–67. **Educ.:** Loyola Univ., 1963, BS (Pol. Sci.); Univ. of IL, 1966, MS (LS), 1967, MA (Pol. Sci.). **Orgs.:** ALA. ASIS. SLA. **Honors:** Beta Phi Mu, 1966; Cncl. on Lib. Resrcs., Acad. Lib. Mgt. Intern, 1974–75. **Pubns.:** *Reform of Local Structures in the United States: 1945–1971* bibl./index (1976); "Presidential Elections: Returns, Surveys, Voter Characteristics, Campaigns, Conventions, Information Sources and Services," *DEA News* (Fall 1976); "Library Services to the Graduate Community: The Role of the Subject Specialist Librarian," *Coll. & Resrch. Libs.* (My. 1976). **Activities:** 1; 15, 17, 44; 56, 91, 92 **Addr.:** Hunt Library, Carnegie-Mellon University, Schenley Park, Pittsburgh, PA 15213.

Michaud, Guy R. (D. 16, 1920, St-Jacques, NB) Sch. Libn., A.M. Sormany Sch. (Edmundston, NB), 1972–; Various positions in tchg., 1946–72. **Educ.:** Sacred Heart Coll., Bathurst, NB, 1936–43, BA (Classics); Univ. of Ottawa, MEd; Laval Univ., 1968–70, MAdmin.; Cath. Univ. of Amer., 1973–74, MLS; Tchg. cert. V1, Dept. of Educ., NB, 1952–53. **Orgs.:** Atl. Prov. LA. Can. LA. Assn. des Bibtcrs. Scolaires du NB: Pres. (1980–81). La Société Hist. du Madawaska: VP. **Honors:** Société des poètes du PQ, 2ème prix, 1960. **Pubns.:** *La paroisse de l'Immaculée-Conception, Edmundston, NB 1880–1980* (1980); *Entre-deux...* (1959); "Les bibliothèques scolaires au Nouv. Brunswick," *Nouvelles de l'AEFNB* (15 My. 1977); "School Libraries in New Brunswick," *Sch. Lib.-Media News* (S. 1977); other articles. **Activities:** 10; 20, 22, 32 **Addr.:** 253 St. Francois, Edmundston, NB E3V 1G2 Canada.

Michell, B. Gillian (Ag. 20, 1943, Montreal, PQ) Assoc. Prof., Sch. LS, Univ. West. ON, 1980–, Asst. Prof., 1975–80, Lect., 1974–75. **Educ.:** McGill Univ., 1961–64, BA (Classics), 1964–65, BLS, 1969–70, MLS; Univ. South. CA, 1970–75, PhD (Ling.). **Orgs.:** Intl. Fed. Documtn.: Ling. Doc. Com. (Can. Rep., 1976–). ASIS: SIG Class. Resrch., Secy./Treas. (1980–81). Ling. Socty. Amer. Assn. Comp. Ling. **Pubns.:** "Does PRECIS Have Clay Feet?," *7th Can. Conf. Info. Sci.* (1979); "Natural Language Foundation of Indexing Language Relations," *Can. Jnl. Info. Sci.* (1979); Reviews. **Activities:** 11; 17, 30, 41 **Addr.:** School of Library and Information Science, University of Western Ontario, London, ON N6A 5B9 Canada.

Michener, David H. (D. 15, 1942, Englewood, NJ) Head, Cat. Dept., Univ. of Louisville Lib., 1980–; Assoc. Prin. Investigator, Northwestern Univ. Africana Proj., 1977–79, Sr. Africana Catlgr., 1976–79, Africana Catlgr., 1969–76. **Educ.:** Univ. of KS, 1960–64, BA (Hist.); Univ. of CA (Los Angeles), 1966–68, MA (African Hist.); Univ. of Denver, 1968–69, MA (LS). **Orgs.:** ALA. KY SOLINET Users Grp. African Std. Assn.: Cat. and Class. Subcom. (1975–). **Activities:** 1; 20; 54 **Addr.:** Cataloging Dept., University of Louisville Library, Louisville, KY 40292.

Michie, Jean H. (Ag. 12, 1944, Mt. Vernon, MO) Head Libn., Richards Free Lib. (Newport, NH), 1971–; Asst. Ref. Libn., MO State Lib., 1970–71; Info. and Math. Sci. Libn., Univ. of MO, 1968–70; Sr. Chld. Libn., St. Louis Pub. Lib., 1966–67. **Educ.:** Univ. of MO, 1964–66, BA (LS), 1968–69, MA (LS, Eng.). **Orgs.:** NH Lib. Cncl.: VCh. (1978); Ch. (1979). NH LA: VP (1976); Pres. (1977). ALA. New Eng. LA. **Honors:** ALA, JMRT, Shirley Olofson Awd., 1976; Newport Bus. and Prof. Women's, Woman of Achvmt. Awd., 1976; NH "Libn. of the Yr." Awd., 1981. **Activities:** 9; 17, 36, 47 **Addr.:** P.O. Box 534, Newport, NH 03773.

Mick, Colin K. (Ja. 17, 1941, Lansing, MI) Dir. of Resrch., Decision Info. Srv., 1979–; Pres., Appld. Comm. Resrch., 1974–; Pres., Decision Info. Srv., 1977–79; Resrch. Assoc., Lectr., Stanford Univ., 1971–75. **Educ.:** Univ. of AK, 1958–63, BA (Anthro.); Stanford Univ., 1967–69, MA (Comm.), 1969–72, PhD (Comm. Resrch.). **Orgs.:** ASIS. Socty. for Schol. Publshg. IEEE Comp. Socty. Citizens Tech. and Empl. Prog.: Adv. Bd. (1981). Coll. Terrace Residents Assn.: Coord. (1979–). **Pubns.:** Jt. Auth., *Evaluation of the Minority Services Information Program* (1981); Jt. Auth., *Barriers to the Development of VLSI Technology* (1980); Jt. Auth., "Toward Usable User Studies," *Jnl. of the Amer. Socty. for Info. Sci.* (S. 1980); Jt. Auth., "Planning for On-Line Search in the Public Library," *Spec. Lib.* (Jl. 1978); "Potential STI Innovations: A Behavioral Perspective," in *Technology, Management and Economics of Information Centers* (1981); other pubns. **Activities:** 5, 6; 24, 41; 75, 91, 93 **Addr.:** Decision Information Services, Ltd., P.O. Box 5849, Stanford, CA 94305.

Mickey, Melissa Brisley (Ap. 10, 1944, Santa Monica, CA) Corp. Libn., Kraft, Inc., 1977–; Ref. Libn., Indus. Rel. Ctr., Univ. of Chicago, 1974–77, Lect., Grad. Lib. Sch., 1970–74; Asst. Ref. Libn., Main Lib. IN Univ., 1967–69. **Educ.:** Reed Coll., 1962–66, BA (Amer. Std.); Univ. of Chicago, 1966–67, MA (LS), 1969–71, Cert. of Adv. Std. **Orgs.:** SLA. ALA. Assoc. Info. Mgrs. SAA. **Pubns.:** "Cornelia Marvin Pierce" *Dictionary of American Library Biography;* "Cornelia Marvin Pierce: Pioneer in Library Extension," *Lib. Qtly.* (Ap. 1968). **Activities:** 1, 12; 17, 39; 59, 68 **Addr.:** Corporate Library, Kraft Inc., Kraft Ct., Glenview, IL 60025.

Micuda, Vladimir (Ja. 26, 1926, Sv. I. Zabno, Croatia) Chief, Sci. and Tech. Dept., Univ. Libs. PA State Univ., 1977–, Head, Life Scis. Lib., 1974–77, Head, Agr. and Bio. Sci. Lib., 1966–74; Assoc. Libn., A. R. Mann Lib., Cornell Univ., 1961–66. **Educ.:** Univ. of Zagreb, 1946–52, BS (Forestry); Agr. Univ. of Wageningen, 1955–56 (Forestry); IN Univ., 1960–61, MALS; Amer. Mgt. Assn., 1971, Cert. **Orgs.:** ALA. PA LA. Natl. Agr. LA. PA Acad. of Sci. **Honors:** Beta Phi Mu, 1962. **Pubns.:** "Agricultural and Biological Sciences Library Celebrates 80th Year," *Lib. Lion* (D. (1968); "From Old Main to Pattee, the Agricultural Library," *Sci. in Agr.* (1974); jt. auth., "CAIN On-Line Testing and Assistance 1974–75," (Ag. 1975); jt. auth., "Library Computers Used in Literature Searches to Speed Up Retrieval," *Sci. in Agr.* **Addr.:** E309 Pattee Library, The Pennsylvania State University, University Park, PA 16802.

Middendorf, Jack L. (D. 13, 1925, St. Louis, MO) Dir., Info. Srvs., Wayne State Coll., 1978–; Instr. Dev. Spec., Aid Assn. for Luth., 1974–78; Prof. of Educ., Concordia Tchrs. Coll., 1958–73. **Educ.:** Concordia Tchrs. Coll., 1943–49, BSEd (Theo/Educ); Univ. of Houston, 1949–52, MEd (Reading); IN Univ., 1961–64, EdD (Comm.). **Orgs.:** ALA. NE LA: Ch., Coll. & Univ. (1979–80). AECT: Bd. of Dir. (1966–69). Comsn. on Church Lit., Luth. Church, MO Synod. **Pubns.:** *Notable Books for Children* (1960); "Media Primer," *Interaction* (1973); "From Ball Point to Camera", *AV Guide* (1971). **Activities:** 1, 11; 17, 25, 26; 50, 63, 75 **Addr.:** Wayne State College, Wayne, NE 68787.

Middleton, Bernice Bryant (N. 11, 1922, Orangeburg, SC) Ch., Dept. of LS, SC State Coll., 1958–, Asst. Prof., 1953–58, Circ. Libn., 1949–52; Asst. Catlgr., Atlanta Univ., 1944–46; Tchr., Libn., Granard HS (Gaffney, SC), 1942–43. **Educ.:** Claflin Coll., 1938–42, AB Summa Cum Laude (Eng.); Atlanta Univ., 1957–58, MSLS; Univ. of Pittsburgh, 1967–68, Adv. Cert. (LS). **Orgs.:** SELA. SC LA. SC Assn. Sch. Libn.: Pres. (1972–73). AAUP: SC Conf., Secy., Treas. (1973–79). AAUW. Untd. Meth. Women. Palmetto Cabinet. **Honors:** SC State Coll., Quarter Century Club, 1976; Beta Phi Mu, 1958; SC State Coll., Thirty Year Srv. Awd., 1981. **Activities:** 10, 11; 17, 26, 32 **Addr.:** Box 1868, South Carolina State College, Orangeburg, SC 29117.

Middleton, Dorothy J. (Ja. 3, 1938, Lincoln, NE) Libn., E. HS, 1969–; Eng. tchr., North Platte, NE, 1960. **Educ.:** Univ.

PROFESSIONAL ACTIVITIES: Institutions: 1. Acad. lib.; 2. Arch.; 3. Assn.; 4. Fed./Gvt. lib.; 5. Inst. lib.; 6. Mfr./Suppl.; 7. Milit. lib.; 8. Musm.; 9. Pub. lib.; 10. Sch. lib.; 11. Sch. of lib. sci.; 12. Spec. lib.; 13. State lib.; 14. (other). **Functions/Activities:** 15. Acq./Col. dev.; 16. Adult srvs.; 17. Admin.; 18. Apprais.; 19. Archit./Bldgs.; 20. Cat./Class.; 21. Chld. srvs.; 22. Circ.; 23. Cons./Pres.; 24. Consult.; 25. Cont. ed.; 26. Educ. lib. sci.; 27. Ext. srvs.; 28. Fund/Grants; 29. Gvt. pubs.; 30. Indx./Abs.; 31. Instr. lib. use; 32. Media srvs.; 33. Micro.; 34. Netwks./Coop.; 35. Persnl.; 36. PR; 37. Publshg.; 38. Recs. mgt.; 39. Ref. srvs.; 40. Repro.; 41. Resrch.; 42. Review.; 43. Secur.; 44. Serials; 45. Spec. col.; 46. Tech. srvs.; 47. Trustees/Bds.; 48. YA srvs.; 49. (other).

of NE, 1956–60, BSc (Educ.); Univ. of Denver, 1970–72, MALS. **Orgs.:** WY LA: Secy., (1975); Vice Ch., (1976); Ch., Sch. Sect. (1977). Mt. Plains LA: VP/Pres.-Elect (1980–82); Sch. Sect. Ch. (1979–80), Vice-ch. (1978), Secy. (1974). ALA. AAUW. Natl. Educ. Assn. **Activities:** 10; 15, 20, 48 **Addr.:** East High School Library, 2800 E. Pershing Blvd., Cheyenne, WY 82001.

Middleton, Robert Kent (My. 3, 1946, Dallas, TX) Info. Srvs. Supvsr., Austin Pub. Lib., 1978–, Admin. Asst., 1977–78, Libn. I, 1975–77; Libn. I Austin Cmnty. Coll., 1974–75. **Educ.:** Austin Coll., 1964–68, BA (Soclgy.); Univ. of TX, Austin, 1973–74, MLS. **Orgs.:** ALA. TX Lib. Assn. Austin Lib. Clb.: VP. (1975–76). **Honors:** Beta Phi Mu, 1974; Phi Kappa Phi, 1974. **Activities:** 9; 15, 19, 39; 56, 63, 92 **Addr.:** 3200 McElroy, Austin, TX 78757.

Miele, Anthony W. (F. 12, 1926, Williamsport, PA) Dir., AL Pub. Lib. Srv., 1975–; Asst. Dir., Tech. Srvs., IL State Lib., 1970–75; Asst. Dir., Oak Park (IL) Pub. Lib., 1968–70; Dir., Elmwood Park (IL) Pub. Lib., 1967–68. **Educ.:** Marquette Univ., 1951, BS (Bus. Admin.); Univ. of Pittsburgh, 1966, MLS. **Orgs.:** ALA: Ch., GODORT (1974–76); Natl. Lib. Week (1971–74). Chief Ofcrs. of State Lib. Agencies: Secy. (1978). AL LA. SLA. Other orgs. Rotary. Amer. Socty. for Pub. Admin. **Honors:** Beta Phi Mu. **Pubns.:** Assoc. Ed., *Government Publication Review* (1973–); jt. Auth., "Illiterary," *Pub. Lib. Qtly.* (Mr. 1981); other articles. **Activities:** 9, 13; 29, 33, 46; 50, 56, 72 **Addr.:** Alabama Public Library Service, 6030 Monticello Dr., Montgomery, AL 36130.

Mielke, Linda J. (Mr. 10, 1947, Detroit, MI) Dir, Clearwater Pub. Lib., 1981–; Spec. Comnty. Srvs., MD State Dept. of Educ., 1976–81; Head, Spec. Srvs., Tampa-Hillsborough Cnty. Pub. Lib., 1974–76; Film Libn., Detroit Pub. Lib., Branch Libn., 1972–74. **Educ.:** Wayne State Univ., 1965–70, BA (Bus. Admin.), 1970–72, MSLS, Wayne State, Univ. of MI, 1972, (Geron.). **Orgs.:** ALA. **Honors:** Beta Phi Mu, 1977. **Pubns.:** *Interface ASCLA Nwsltr* (1979). **Activities:** 9, 13; 24, 27; 89 **Addr.:** Clearwater Public Library, 100 N. Osceola Ave., Clearwater, FL 33515.

Mielke, Thelma J. (D. 14, 1916, Rochester, NY) Head, Ref. Srvs., Long Island Univ., The Brooklyn Ctr., 1978–; Ref. Libn., 1963–78; Asst. Ref. Libn., NY Univ., 1954–63. **Educ.:** Elmhurst Coll., 1933–37, AB (Soclgy.); Univ. of Rochester, 1937–39, MA (Phil.); Columbia Univ., 1941–45 (Phil.); NY Univ., 1954–60 (Politics); 1959–60, MS (Lib. Srv.). **Orgs.:** ALA: ACRL. Long Island Univ. Fac. Fed. Untd. Fed. of Coll. Tchrs. **Activities:** 1; 31, 39, 41; 54, 74, 92 **Addr.:** 175 W. 12th St., Apt. 14G, New York, NY 10011.

Migneault, Robert L. (Ja. 7, 1937, Nashua, NH) Asst. Dir. for Coll. and Tech. Srvs., San Francisco State Univ., 1979–; Asst. Dir., Tech. Srvs., Univ. of SK, 1975–79; Head, Ctrl. Serials Dept., SUNY, Buffalo, 1973–75; Chief, Serials Div., Asst. Acq. Libn., U.S. Air Force Acad., 1969–73; Catlgr., Lib. of Congs., 1968–69. **Educ.:** Univ. of NH, 1958–66, BA (Eng. Lit.); Univ. of Denver, 1966–68, MALS. **Orgs.:** ALA. ACRL: Persnl. Com. (1975). LAMA: Ch., Union Rel. for Mgrs. Com. (1979). LITA; RTSD. CA LA. **Honors:** Beta Phi Mu, 1966. **Addr.:** 31-A Red Hill Cir., Tiburon, CA 94920.

Mika, Joseph J. (Mr. 1, 1948, Pittsburgh, PA) Asst. Prof./Asst. Dean, Sch. of Lib. Srv., Univ. of South. MS, 1977–; Tchg. Fellow, Univ. of Pittsburgh, 1976–77; Asst. Libn./Asst. Prof., Johnson State Coll., 1973–75; Asst. Libn./Instr., OH State Univ., 1971–73. **Educ.:** Univ. of Pittsburgh, 1966–69, BA (Eng.), 1970–71, MLS, 1980–, PhD (LS). **Orgs.:** ALA: Stdg. Com. On Lib. Educ. (1979–); Lib. Educ. Asm. (1979); David H. Clift Sel. Jury (1979–). AALS. CLENE: Mem. Com. (Ch., 1980–). MS LA: Int. Frdm. Com. (1979–); Pubns. Com. (Ch., 1980–). Other orgs. **Honors:** Beta Phi Mu, 1971; Phi Delta Kappa, 1979. **Pubns.:** Contrib., *Multi-Media Reviews Index* and *Media Review Digest* (1973–75); Library Education in Mississippi: State of the Art, *MS Libs.* (Sum. 1979); "Staff Associations," *Encyc. of Lib. and Info. Sci.* (1980). **Activities:** 1, 11; 17, 25, 46; 56, 63, 95-Collective Bargaining. **Addr.:** University of Southern Mississippi, School of Library Service, Southern Station, Box 5146, Hattiesburg, MS 39401.

Mikel, Hazel R. (N. 12, 1923, Yorktown, TX) Dir., Kendall Young Lib., 1978–; Chld. Libn., Victoria (TX) Pub. Lib., 1977–78; Elem. Sch. Libn., NM Cmnty. Sch., 1975–77. **Educ.:** IA State Univ., 1971–73, BA (Eng., Pol. Sci.); Univ. of IA, 1974, MA (LS). **Orgs.:** IA LA: Dist. Prog. Ch. (1981). ALA. N. IA Lib. Coop.: Rec. Grant Coord. Hamilton Cnty. Lib.: Ch. **Activities:** 9; 15, 17, 36 **Addr.:** Kendall Young Library, 1201 Willson Ave., Webster City, IA 50595.

Mikel, Sarah A. (Ag. 29, 1947, Brooklyn, NY) Chief, Tech. Info. Div., US Army Corps of Engin., 1976–, Dist. Libn., 1975–76; Serials Catlgr., Purdue Univ., 1973–74; Ed. Resrchr., Field Educ. Enterprises, 1971–72. **Educ.:** Univ. of Miami, 1965–69, BA (Eng.); Univ. of FL, 1969–71, MA (Eng.); Rosary Coll., 1972–73, MALS. **Orgs.:** ALA: GODORT, Cat. Manual Com. (1977–). SLA: DC Chap., Rec. Secy. (1979–); Milit. Libns. (Ch., 1977–78). **Activities:** 4; 17, 20; 64, 74 **Addr.:** 1101 S. Arlington Ridge Rd., No. 917, Arlington, VA 22202.

Miklosvary, Jozsef (Je. 19, 1938, Budapest, Hungary) Assoc. libn., catlgr., Univ. of CA, Davis, Law Lib., 1978–; Asst. libn., Catlgr., Univ. of CA, Berkeley, Law Lib., 1975–78; Visit. Instr., Catlgr., Univ. of OR, 1974–75; Head of Distribution, Catlgr., Budapest Univ. Lib., 1966–70. **Educ.:** Eötvös Univ., Budapest, Hungary, 1958–64, MA (Hungarian & Latin); Univ. of CA, Berkeley, 1973–74, MLS. **Orgs.:** Hungarian Libns. Assn.: Bd. (1965–1968). AALL: Frgn. Compar. and Intl. Law Com. (1977–78). **Activities:** 1, 12; 20, 46; 77, 92 **Addr.:** 555 Guava Ln. Apt. # 7D, Davis, CA 95616.

Miksa, Francis L. (S. 24, 1938, Aurora, IL) Assoc. Prof., Sch. of Lib. and Info. Sci., LA State Univ., 1972–; Libn., North. Bapt. Theo. Semy., 1968–70; Libn., Bethel Coll., St. Paul, MN, 1964–66. **Educ.:** Wheaton Coll., 1956–60, AB; Bethel Theo. Semy., St. Paul, MN, 1961–65, DB; Univ. of Chicago, 1968–70, AM (LS), 1970–74, PhD (LS). **Orgs.:** ALA: Publshg. Com. (1978–82); RTSD/Cat. and Class. Sect., CC:DA (1979–). LA LA. **Pubns.:** Ed., *Charles Ammi Cutter: Library Systematizer* (1977); "The Making of the 1876 Report on Public Libraries," *Jnl. of Lib. Hist.* (Ja. 1973); jt. auth., "Suggested Author Headings for the Official Publication of the State of Louisiana Established in Accordance with the Anglo-American Cataloging Rules," *State of Louisiana, Public Documents* (Ja.–Je. 1976). **Activities:** 11; 20, 46; 73 **Addr.:** School of Library & Information Science, Louisiana State University, Baton Rouge, LA 70813.

Milac, Metod M. (O. 2, 1924, Prevalje, Slovenia, Yugoslavia) Assoc. Dir. of Libs., Col. Dev. & Pub. Srvs., Syracuse Univ., 1980–, Asst. Dir., 1974–80, Actg. Dir. of Libs., 1973–74, Asst. Dir. of Libs., 1968–73, Head, Ref. Dept., 1965–68, Msc. Libn., 1962–63. **Educ.:** Cleveland Inst. of Msc., 1953–57, BM (Msc.), 1957–60, MM (Msclgy.); West. Resrv. Univ., 1960–62, MSLS; Lib. Autom. Sem., Univ. of IL, 1969; Exec. Dev. Prog. for Lib. Admin., Miami Univ., 1970. **Orgs.:** ALA: ACRL; Ch., Chief Col. Dev. Ofcrs., Medium size Resrch. Libs. (1977–78). Five Assoc. Univ. Libs.: Access Com. (1968–70, Ch. 1969–70); User Srvs. Com. (1970–); Col. Dev. Com. (1973–); Bd. of Dir. (1973–74). Intl. Musicological Socty. Socty. for Slovene Std.: Prog. Coord. (1978–). **Activities:** 1, 2; 15, 17, 45; 55 **Addr.:** 100 Bird Library, Syracuse University, Syracuse, NY 13210.

Milam, Margaret Mitchell (New Orleans, LA) Assoc. Dir., Law Lib., Amer. Univ., 1973–, Co-Dir., Legal Method Prog., 1980–, Actg. Law Libn., 1972–73, Asst. Law Libn., 1971–72; Head, Acq. Dept. and Jr. Instr., Univ. of VA Law Lib., 1970–71, Head Cat. Dept. and Jr. Instr., 1968–70, Catlgr., 1968; Catlgr., Alderman Lib., Univ. VA, 1968. **Educ.:** Tulane Univ., 1957–59 (Liberal Arts); Univ. MD, 1963–66, BA with Hon. (Pol. Sci.), 1966–68, MLS; Amer. Univ., 1971–75, JD; AALL, 1974, Cert.; State VA, 1971, Cert. **Orgs.:** AALL: Com. Rel. with Publshr. (1977–78; Com. Exch. Persnl. Brit. Irish Law Libs. (1977–, Ch., 1981–); Hotel Search Com. (1986). Law Libn. Socty. Washington DC.: Com. Un. List Per. (1975–77); Arrange. Com. (1973–75); Constn. Rev. Com. (1979–); various com. Assn. of Amer. Law Sch.: Sect. on Women in Legal Educ.; Sect. on Law and the Arts. Amer. Mensa. **Honors:** Pi Sigma Alpha, 1965; AALL, Scholar. Awd., 1970, 1973. **Pubns.:** Assoc. Ed., *Who's Who in Consulting* (1968); Contrib., *Checklist of Current State, Federal, and Canadian Publications,* (1971–). **Activities:** 1, 12; 15, 17, 46; 63, 77, 80 **Addr.:** Washington College of Law Library, American University, Massachusetts & Nebraska Aves., N.W., Washington, DC 20016.

Milanich, Melanie (N. 17, 1945, Cleveland, OH) Soc. Sci. Ref. Libn., Metro Toronto Lib., 1977–; Head, Tech. Srvs., Niagara Reg. Lib. Syst., 1973–77. **Educ.:** Univ. of Toronto, 1969–71, BA (Soc.); Univ. of West. ON, 1971–73, MLS. **Orgs.:** ON LA. Can. LA. **Activities:** 9, 13; 34, 39, 46; 56, 78, 92 **Addr.:** Social Sciences Dept., Metro Toronto Library, 789 Yonge St., Toronto, ON M4W 2G8 Canada.

Milczewski, Marion A. (F. 12, 1912, Saginaw, MI) Prof. Emeritus, Univ. of WA Sch. of Libnshp., 1977–81; Dir., Univ. of WA Libs., 1960–77; Lib. Consult., Univ. del Valle, Cali, Columbia, Sum. 1962, 1968, 1969; Asst. Univ. Libn., Univ. of CA, Berkeley, 1949–60; Dir., Southeast. States Coop. Lib. Srvy., 1947–49; Dir., Intl. Rel. Ofc., ALA, 1946–47; Asst. to Dir., 1944–46. **Educ.:** Univ. of MI, 1930–36, AB (Eng.); Univ. of IL, 1937–38, BSLS, 1939–40, MS (LS). **Orgs.:** ALA. Pac. NW LA. WA LA. Bks. for the People Fund: Bd. of Dirs. **Honors:** Fulbright, Resrch. Grant, 1954–55. **Pubns.:** *Estructura de la Biblioteca Universitaria en la America Latina* (1967); jt. auth., *Libraries of the Southeast* (1949); *British and American University Libraries* (1955); various lib. srvy. rpts. **Activities:** 1, 11; 17, 24, 26; 54†

Miles, Donald D. (Ap. 10, 1940, Fillmore, IN) Resrch. Libn., Milliken Resrch. Corp., 1978–; Sci. Ref. Libn., Clemson Univ., 1976–78. **Educ.:** IN Univ., 1962–65, AB (Chem.), 1974–76, MLS, 1968–72, MS (Biochem.). **Orgs.:** SLA. Textile Info. Users Cncl. SC LA. SELA. Piedmont LA: Secy. (1979–). **Activities:** 1, 12; 17, 34, 39; 58, 60, 91 **Addr.:** Milliken Research Corporation Library, P.O. Box 1927, Spartanburg, SC 29304.

Miles, Herman Wilbur (D. 10, 1924, Vandergrift, PA) Deputy Admin., Defense Tech. Info. Ctr., 1958–; Tech. Info. Spec., Defense Documtn. Ctr., 1973, Digital Comp. Syst. Admin., 1966–73. **Educ.:** Amer. Univ., 1947–55, BS (Bus. Admin.); George Washington Univ., 1971–72, MSA; various crs. **Orgs.:** ASIS. SLA. Natl. Acad. of Scis.: Maritime Info. Com.; Com. of Transp. Resrch. Info. Syst. Natl. Insts. of Hlth.: Com. on Neurological and Communicative Disords. and Stroke. **Honors:** H.W. Wilson Co., Best Paper Published in *Spec. Libs.,* 1977. DSA, Excep. Civilian Srv. Awd. for the Period 1967–75, 1975; DSA, One of the Ten Outstan. Persnl., 1968. Other Hons. **Pubns.:** "What Information Does Management Need?" *Defense Mgt. Jnl.* (Fall, 1969); "Dialog with Defense Documentation Center," *Spec. Libs.* (N. 1976); various bibls., sps. **Activities:** 4, 12; 17, 29, 41; 62, 75, 74 **Addr.:** Defense Logistics Agency, DTIC-AD, Rm. 5D121, Defense Technical Information Center, Cameron Station, Alexandria, VA 22314.

Miles, Sally Jeanne (Jl. 10, 1947, Baltimore, MD) Head Libn., Ropes and Gray Law Firm, 1979–; Law Libn., Bucks Cnty. Ct. of Common Pleas, 1970–79. **Educ.:** Kent State Univ., 1965–69, BA (Eng.); Drexel Univ., 1969–70, MSLS. **Orgs.:** AALL. Law Libns. of New Eng. Assn. of Boston Law Libns. SLA. Grt. Philadelphia Law LA. **Honors:** Beta Phi Mu, 1970. **Activities:** 12; 15, 17, 41; 77, 78 **Addr.:** 123 Elm St., C-10, Quincy, MA 02169.

Miletich, Ivo (Ap. 18, 1936, Pucisca, Split, Croatia, Yugoslavia) Head, Acq. Dept., Asst. Prof. of Lib. Sci., Chicago State Univ. Lib., 1979–, Bibl., Asst. Prof., 1974–79; Bibl., Asst. Acq., Libn. and Instr., Old Dominion Univ., 1971–74; Asst. to Bibl. for Slavic Lang. and Lit., Joseph Regenstein Lib., Univ. Chicago, 1967–71. **Educ.:** Acad. of Educ., Split, Yugoslavia, 1956–60, BA (Lang., Lit.); Univ. of Skopje, Macedonia, Yugoslavia, 1960–63, MA (Hist.); Cert. for Prof. Tchrs., Yugoslavia, 1966; Cmwlth. of VA, 1971, Cert. of Prof. Libnshp. Inst. of Eng. Lang., Chicago, 1967–69 (Cert.); Rosary Coll., Grad. Sch. of Lib. Sci., River Forest, IL, 1970–71. **Orgs.:** Amer Transl. Assn. Amer. Fed. of Tchrs. Chicago Acad. Lib. Cncl. ILLINET: Acq. Amer. Assn. for Advnc. of Slavic Std. AAUP. Amer. Assn. for the Contrl. of Tension. **Honors:** Beta Phi Mu, 1971; Ctrl. YMCA Coll., Frgn. Lang. Tchr., Co-ed Div., Cert. of Recog., 1974. **Pubns.:** Various bibl., rpts., reviews, articles. **Activities:** 1; 15, 41; 57 **Addr.:** Room E-203F, Chicago State University, 95th St. at King Dr., Chicago, IL 60628.

Milkovic, Milan (Mr. 20, 1924, Gospic, Croatia, Yugoslavia) Campus Libn., Cuyahoga Cmnty. Coll., 1965–; Per. Libn., Cleveland State Univ., 1961–65; Lit. Srchr., Univ. of MI, 1960–61. **Educ.:** Univ. of Salzburg (Austria), 1947–50, BA (Phil.); Case West. Reserve Univ., 1959–60, MS (LS); Univ. of Detroit, 1955–58, (Math, Phys.). **Orgs.:** Natl. Micro. Assn. AAUP. **Pubns.:** "Binding records for periodicals," *Spec. Lib.* (Ag. 1974); "Continuation publication: Some fundamental acquisition concepts and procedures," *The Serials Libn.* (Spr. 1981). **Activities:** 1; 33, 44; 91 **Addr.:** Cuyahoga Community College, 4250 Richmond Rd., Eastern Campus Library, Warrensville Township, OH 44122.

Millar, Barbara P. (My. 14, 1927, Montreal, PQ) Assoc. Univ. Libn. for Tech. Srvs., Lib. of the Hlth. Scis., Univ. of IL Med. Ctr., Chicago, 1980–, Head, Cat. Dept., 1968–80; Catlgr., 1964–68; Coord., Lab. Supvsr., Papanicolaou Cancer Resrch. Inst., 1951–63; Resrch. Asst., Cytotechnologist, McGill Univ., 1948–51. **Educ.:** McGill Univ. 1944–48, BSc (Bio.); Univ. of IL, Champaigne, 1963–64, MSLS. **Orgs.:** Hlth Sci. OCLUG.: Com. on Cont. Ed. (1978–80); Nom. Com. (1981). IL OLUG.: Com. on Stans. for Mono. Cat. (1975–77). ALA: RTSD.; LITA; ACRL. Med. LA. **Honors:** Beta Phi Mu, 1964. **Pubns.:** "OCLC Profile: Production in a Multi-Purpose Setting," *Network* (1977). **Activities:** 1; 20; 56, 58, 80 **Addr.:** 2851 So. King Dr. Apt. 1317, Chicago, IL 60616.

Millar, Louise Oldebrook Littleton (O. 30, 1921, Muncie, IN) Deputy/Assoc. Dir., Grand Rapids Pub. Lib., 1974–; Assoc. State Libn., NM State Lib., 1972–74; Dir., Oil City Pub. Lib., 1969–70; Actg. Dir., Altoona Area Pub. Lib., 1969, Asst. Dir., 1968, Head of Ref., 1967. **Educ.:** West. Coll. for Women, 1941–44, BA (Eng.); Central MI Univ., 1955, Tchg. Cert.; Univ. of Pittsburgh, 1967, MA/MLS (Eng.). **Orgs.:** MI Lib. Cnsrtm.: Exec. Cncl. (1978–). Lakeland Lib. Coop.: Pres., Exec. Bd. (1980–81). Lakeland Lib. Fed.: Pres. of Bd. (1977–81). ALA: Circ. Com. Various other orgs. and coms. Zonta Internatl.: Bd. (1978–80). **Pubns.:** *The Tree That Never Dies* (Native American Oral History) (1978). **Activities:** 9, 13; 17, 34, 35; 56, 85 **Addr.:** Grand Rapids Public Library, 60 Library Plaza, N.E., Grand Rapids, MI 49503.

Millenson, Roy H. (O. 1, 1921, Washington, DC) Dir., Educ. and Lib. Affairs, Assn. of Amer. Publshrs., 1974–; Minority Staff Dir., Com. on Labor and Pub. Welfare, US Senate, 1965–74; Washington Natl. Rep., Amer. Jewish Com., 1959–65; Exec. Asst., Hon. J. K. Javits, US Sen., 1957–59. **Educ.:** George Washington Univ., 1947, AB (Gvt.). **Orgs.:** ALA. MD LA. WHCOLIS: Del. MD Gvr.'s Conf. on Lib. and Info. Serv.: Plng. Com.; Del. Atlant Congs.: Alternate U.S. Del. (1959). Intl. Congs. on Educ. of the Deaf: Del. (1970). Natl. Civil Liberties Clearing-

Special Subjects/Services: 50. Adult educ.; 51. Advert./Mktg.; 52. Aerosp.; 53. Agric.; 54. Area std.; 55. Arts/Hum.; 56. Autom.; 57. Bibl./Prtg.; 58. Bio. sci.; 59. Bus./Fin.; 60. Chem.; 61. Copyrt.; 62. Documtn.; 63. Educ.; 64. Engin.; 65. Env.; 66. Eth. grps.; 67. Film; 68. Food/Nutr.; 69. Geneal.; 70. Geo.; 71. Geol.; 72. Handcpd.; 73. Hist.; 74. Int. frdm.; 75. Info. sci.; 76. Insr.; 77. Law; 78. Legis.; 79. Math./Comp. sci.; 80. Med.; 81. Metals; 82. Nat. resrcs.; 83. Newsp.; 84. Nuc. sci.; 85. Oral hist.; 86. Petr./Energy; 87. Pharm.; 88. Phys./Astr./Math.; 89. Readg.; 90. Relig.; 91. Sci./Tech.; 92. Soc. sci.; 93. Telecom.; 94. Transp.; 95. (other).

house: Ch. (1961–63). **Honors:** Assn. for Chld. with Lrng. Disabilities, John Fogarty Awd., 1968; Goodwill Industries, Cit. for Exceptional Srvs. to the Nation's Handcpd., 1971; Cncl. for Exceptional Chld., Cit. for Legis. Statesmanship, 1977. **Pubns.:** *Selected Federal and State Book Program Information* (1980); "The New Faces of the Congressional Budget Act," *Educ. Times* (S. 15, 1980). **Activities:** 14-Trade assn.; 37; 63, 78 **Addr.:** Association of American Publishers, 1707 L Street, N.W.–Rm. 480, Washington, DC 20036.

Miller, Anthony G. (Ap. 10, 1944, Richford, VT) Asst. Head, Fine Arts Dept., Atlanta Pub. Lib., 1978–; Rec. Libn., Msc. Lib., SUNY, Buffalo, 1976–78; Libn. (Msc. Spec.), Gen. Lib. of the Performing Arts, Lincoln Ctr., New York Pub. Lib., 1973–76; Bibl. Asst., Avery Archit. Lib., Columbia Univ., 1973. **Educ.:** Harvard Univ., 1962–72, AB (Msc.); Columbia Univ., 1972–73, MSLS. **Orgs.:** Msc. LA: Pub. Lib. Com. (1980–); SE. Chap., Exec. Com. (1980–). **Activities:** 9; 16, 32, 39; 55 **Addr.:** Fine Arts Department, Atlanta Public Library, 1 Margaret Mitchell Sq., N.W., Atlanta, GA 30303.

Miller, Arthur H., Jr. (Mr. 15, 1943, Kalamazoo, MI) Coll. Libn., Lake Forest Coll., 1972–; Asst. Libn. for Pub. Srvs., Newberry Lib., 1970–72, Ref. Libn., 1966–70. **Educ.:** Kalamazoo Coll., 1961–65, BA (Eng.); AM (Eng.), Univ. of Chicago, 1965–68, AM (LS); Northwestern Univ., 1967–73, PhD (Eng.); Univ. of Caen, France, 1963–64. **Orgs.:** ALA: *Choice* Ed. Bd. (1978–80); RASD: Hist. Sect. (Vice-ch./Ch.-Elect, 1981–82). ARL/OMS Consult. Trng. Prog. (1980). LIBRAS: Pres. (1979–80). OCLC Strg. Com. Caxton Club: Pres. (1978–80). **Pubns.:** "Trains and Railroading," *Handbook of Amer. Pop. Culture* (1981); "Collection Development," *ALA Encyc.* (1980); jt. auth., "Introducing Online Data Base Searching in the Small Academic Library," *Jnl. of Acad. Libnshp.* (Mr. 1981). Jt. auth., *Melville Dissertations: An Annotated Directory,* (1972). **Activities:** 1; 17, 34, 45; 55, 66 **Addr.:** Donnelley Library, Lake Forest College, Lake Forest, IL 60045.

Miller, Barbara S. (Ag. 19, 1912, Chattanooga, TN) Retired; Coord. of Chld. Srvs., Louisville Free Pub. Lib., 1970–78, Head of the Chld. Dept., Main Lib., 1960–70, Asst. Head of Chld. Dept., 1957–60, Chld. Libn., West. Branch, 1951–57; Instr., Chld. Lit., Spalding Coll., 1958–64, Instr., Chld. Lit. and YA Lit., Univ. of KY, 1964–75; Msc. Tchr., Madison Jr. HS, 1935–37. **Educ.:** Univ. of MI, 1932–35, Msc B (Msc.); Spalding Coll., 1950–51, BS (LS); Spalding Coll., 1954, MA (Educ.). **Orgs.:** KY LA: Pres. (1978–79). ALA: Cncl. (1974–77; 1978–79); ALSC (Pres., 1977–78), Newbery–Caldecott Awds. Com. (1962–63; 1967–68; 1978–79), Bd. of Dirs. (1973–75), Org. and Bylaws Com. (1973–74). SELA: Pub. Lib. Sect., Mem. Com. (1979–81). WHCOLIS: Official Observer (1979). Various other orgs. Norton Chld. Hosp.: Bd. of Dirs. Cmnty. Coord. Child Care: Bd. of Dirs. Arts Forum: Bd. of Dirs. Sr. House W.: Bd. of Dirs. Various other orgs. **Honors:** KY LA, Outstan. Pub. Libn., 1969; Spalding Coll., Caritas Medal, Disting. Alum., 1971; Women's Clubs of Louisville, Woman of Achvmt., 1973. **Pubns.:** "Association for Library Services to Children," *ALA Yrbk.* (1978); "Children's Library Services," *ALA Yrbk.* (1980). **Activities:** 9; 21 **Addr.:** 215 North 46th St., Louisville, KY 40212.

Miller, Betty Davis (D. 17, 1926, Jarratt, VA) Youth Srvs. Consult., State Lib. of FL, 1972–, Recruitment Spec., 1969–71; Instr., FL State Univ., 1966–67; Libn. I (Chld. Mtrls.), State Lib. of FL, 1965–66. **Educ.:** Coll. of William and Mary, 1946–49, AB (Eng.); FL State Univ., 1958–63, MLS. **Orgs.:** FL LA: Chld. Caucus; YA Caucus; Int. Frdm. Cncl. ALA: State Consults. Disc. Grp. (Ch., 1975); ALSC, Prog. Support Pubns. Com. (1980); CSD Legis. Com. (Ch., 1976). **Pubns.:** *Florida Intern Program: An Experiment in Recruitment to Public Librarianship* (1969); "Who We Are," *Amer. Libs.* (1976); Youth Notes Page, *Orange Seed.* **Activities:** 9, 13; 21, 24, 48 **Addr.:** State Library of Florida, R. A. Gray Bldg., Tallahassee, FL 32301.

Miller, Beverly B. (F. 8, 1933, Champaign, IL) Asst. Prof., East. IL Univ., 1967–; Head Libn., Rantoul HS, 1965–67; Tchr., Libn., Oakland HS, 1963–64; Tchr. Assumption Jr. HS. **Educ.:** East. IL Univ., 1951–55, BS (Eng.); Univ. of IL, 1955–67, MS (LS). **Orgs.:** ALA. IL LA: Comm. Com. (1979). **Honors:** East. IL Univ., Spec. Merit Awd., 1974; **Pubns.:** "New Media Center Completes Successful First Year–Right to Read Project Winner," *IL AV Assn. Jnl.* (S. 1972); *IL Libs.* (O. 1970); *Illinois Literary Reflections of the Bicentennial Year* mono. (1977); various reviews. **Addr.:** 1129 Woodlawn Dr., Charleston, IL 61920.

Miller, Bonnie Ray (Ja. 29, 1921, Lasca, AL) Libn., Physical, Soc. Sci. & Engin., US Army Missile Cmnd., Missile Intelligence Agency, 1968–; Libn., US Army, Redstone Sci. Info. Ctr., 1966–68; Tech. Data Resrch. Spec., Brookley Air Force Base, 1943–56; Tchr., Baldwin Cnty. Bd. of Educ., 1941–43. **Educ.:** Livingston Univ., 1938–41, Cert., (Educ.); Univ. of AL, 1964–65, BS (LS); George Peabody Coll., 1968–69, MS (LS); Natl. Security Mgt. Course, 1970–72; other courses. **Orgs.:** SLA: Past Pres. and Secy./Treas., AL Chap. AL LA: Ch. Elect, Coll. Univ. and Spec. Lib. Div. SELA. Alpha Beta Alpha Fraternity. Federally Employed Women, Inc. Assn. of the US Army. Intl. Toastmistress Org. Dept. of Defense Sci. and Tech. Intelligence Info. Support Prog. Review Grp. **Honors:** U.S. Army Missile Cmnd., Outstan. Performance Rating, 1968. **Activities:** 4, 12; 34, 39, 46; 52, 62, 91 **Addr.:** 6418 Deramus Ave., Huntsville, AL 35806.

Miller, Charles Edmond (Ag. 3, 1938, Bridgeport, CT) Dir. Of Univ. Libs., FL State Univ., 1973–; Assoc. Dir., Lib., Tulane Univ., 1971–73, Asst. Dir. 1970–71, Libn., Assoc., Med. Lib., 1969–70; Head, Order & Acq., Lib., LA State Univ., 1967–69. **Educ.:** McNeese State Univ., 1959–64, BA (Eng. Educ.); LA State Univ., 1965–66, MS (LS). **Orgs.:** ALA: ACRL, Com. on Budget and Finance (1978–82), Univ. Lib. Stan. Com., Upper Div. Univ. Libs. Subcom. (1975–). SELA: Gvt. Rel. Com. (Ch., 1979–80). FL LA: Bd. of Dir. (1979–81); White House Conf. Plng. Com. (1976–); ACRL Chap., Org. Ch. (1978–79). Assn. of Southeast. Resrch. Libs.: Mem. Com. (Ch., 1978–79). Other orgs. South. Assn. of Coll. and Schs.: Comsn. on Coll. Visit. Com. (1974–). **Honors:** Sigma Tau Delta; Phi Kappa Phi; Beta Phi Mu. **Pubns.:** Asst. Ed., *LLA Bltn.* (1967); "White House and Governor's Conferences," *FL Libs.* (Ja.-F. 1977); "FSU Library: An Opportunity to Help," *FSU Alum. Mag.* (Spr., 1977); "The Role of the Private Sector in the Governor's Conference," *FL Libs.* (N.-D., 1977); "The Role of the Private Sector in the Governor's Conference," *Cornerstones* (D., 1977). **Activities:** 1; 17, 34; 63, 74, 93 **Addr.:** 2911 Shamrock South, Tallahassee, FL 32308.

Miller, Charles G. (Mr. 10, 1942, Bridgeport, CT) Libn., Mullen HS, 1978–; Media Libn., De La Salle HS, 1967–78; Libn., Cathedral Sch., 1966–67. **Educ.:** Coll. of Santa Fe, 1961–65, BA (Soc. Std.); E. TX State Univ., 1965–70, MSLS. **Orgs.:** Cath. LA. **Activities:** 10; 15, 17, 20; 54, 92 **Addr.:** 3601 S. Lowell Blvd., Denver, CO 80236.

Miller, Claire G. (Ap. 29, New York, NY) AV Consult. Exec. VP., Miller-Brody Prods., Inc., 1964–79; Pres., Newbery Awd. Records, Inc. 1968–79. **Educ.:** Hunter Coll., 1933–37, BA (Eng.); Columbia Univ., 1937–39, MA (Eng.). **Orgs.:** ALA: ALSC, Legis. Com. (1980–). Natl. Citizens for Pub. Libs.: Steering Com. (1980–). WHCOLIS: Alternate Del. Town Hall Fndn.: Bd. of Trustees (1979–). Hunter Coll. Alum. Assn.: Bd. of Dirs. (1981–). Westport Weston Arts Cncl.: Thea. Com. (1980–). **Honors:** Phi Beta Kappa, 1937. Hunter Coll., Hall of Fame, 1979; **Pubns.:** "The Medium Behind the Media," *Hoosier Libs.* (1973). "Childrens Books as Sidelines," *Pubshrs. Wkly.* (Jl. 17, 1978); **Activities:** 51, 89, 95-Prog. Dev. **Addr.:** 18 Hockanum Rd., Westport, CT 06880.

Miller, Clayton Martin (Ja. 12, 1941, Danville, IL) Head, Soc. Sci. Dept., Miami Univ. Lib., 1970–, Admin. Asst. to Dir. of Libs., 1969–70, Head, Circ. Dept., 1968–69; Head, Circ. Dept., Univ. of VT Lib., 1965–68; Bookstacks Libn., Univ. of IA Lib., 1964–65. **Educ.:** Univ of IL, 1958–62, BA (Hist.), 1962–64, MS (LS); Miami Univ., 1971–76, MA (Educ. Leadership). **Orgs.:** ALA. Acad. LA of OH. **Honors:** Beta Phi Mu, 1964. **Activities:** 1; 17, 35, 39; 51, 59, 92 **Addr.:** 602 Glenview Dr., Oxford, OH 45056.

Miller, David Alan (Je. 3, 1944, Princeton, IN) Latin Amer. Biblgphr., 1980–, and Asst. Southeast Asian Libn., OH Univ., 1979–, Asst., Interlib. Loan Dept., 1974–78, Asst., Southeast Asia, 1968–74. **Educ.:** Cornell Univ., 1962–66, BA (Hist.), Ohio Univ., 1967–72, MA (Hist.); Kent State Univ., 1978–79, MLS. **Orgs.:** SALALM. OH LA. Acad. LA of OH. Amer. Fed. of State, Cnty., and Mun. Employees. **Honors:** Beta Phi Mu. **Pubns.:** *A Checklist of the Works of Tom Harrisson (1911–1976).* (1978); "Bornean Materials at Ohio University Library," *Borneo Resrch. Bltn.* (Ap. 1974). **Activities:** 1; 20, 39; 54, 92 **Addr.:** P. O. Box 609, Athens, OH 45701.

Miller, Deborah (Mr. 3, 1938, Chicago, IL) Dir., Gvtl. Srvs., IL LA, 1980–; Bd. of Dirs. Pres., Secty., Treas.; Schaumburg Twp. Pub. Lib., 1971–, Bd. of Dirs., Pres., VP, N. Suburban Lib. Syst., 1974–80. **Educ.:** Univ. of IL, Chicago, 1971–75, BA (Eng.). **Orgs.:** ALA: ALTA/Legis. Com. (Ch., 1979–), Speaker's Bur. (1981–). IL LA: Treas. (1977) Chair, Legis. Com. (Ch., 1978–80). IL Lib. Trustees Assn.: Pres. (1981). Schaumburg-Hoffman Estates Leag. of Women Voters: Bd. of Dirs. **Honors:** IL LA, Outstan. Trustee of the Year, 1979; Crescent Newsp., Woman of the Year, Hoffman Estates, 1974. **Pubns.:** "Blue Sky," videotape, (1979); *A Very Special Trust,* slide-tape, (1976). **Activities:** 9, 13; 24, 36, 47; 78 **Addr.:** 840 Rosedale Ln., Hoffman Estates, IL 60195.

Miller, Deborah Elizabeth (O. 26, 1941, Hartford, CT) Circ. Libn., US Dept. of Cmrce., 1974–. **Educ.:** Gallaudet Coll., 1969–74, BSLS. **Orgs.:** Law Lib. Socty. of Washington, DC. **Honors:** US Dept. of Cmrce., Unit Cit., 1978; US Dept. of Cmrce., Outstan. Performance, 1975–79. **Activities:** 4; 22; 72, 77 **Addr.:** US Dept. of Commerce Library, Law Branch, Rm. 1894, 14th & Constitution Ave. NW, Washington, DC 20230.

Miller, Dick R. (Ja. 2, 1948, Coffeyville, KS) Assoc. Libn., NE OH Univ. Coll. of Med., 1980–; Coord. of Tech. Srvs., 1977–80; Visit. Asst. Prof., Kent State Univ. Sch. of LS, 1977–80; Biomed. Info. Spec. Univ. of S. AL Med. Lib., 1972–77. **Educ.:** Univ. of OK, 1966–70, BS (Zlgy.), 1970–71, MLSc; Univ. of TN Med. Units, 1971–72, Cert. (Med. Libnshp.). **Orgs.:** Med. LA: Bibl. and Info. Srvs. Assessment Com. (Ch., 1979–80). Northeast. OH Major Acad. Libs. Cnsrtm.: Tech. Com. #1 (Serials) (Secy. 1977–78). Hlth. Sci. OCLC Users Grp. (Secy./Treas., 1980–81). Med. LA of Northeast. OH: Secy. (1979). **Pubns.:** "Dual pricing of health science periodicals, *Bltn. of the Med. LA* (O. 1980); The Physician and MEDLINE *South. Med. Jnl.* (Ap. 1973); (reprinted) *South. Med.* (Je. 1973). **Activities:** 11, 12, 14; 26, 46, 49-Online srchg.; 58, 75, 80 **Addr.:** Basic Medical Sciences Library, Northeastern Ohio Universities College of Medicine, Rootstown, OH 44272.

Miller, Donald William (Jl. 19, 1933, Cornwall, ON) Dir. of Lib. Srvs., Grt. Victoria Pub. Lib., 1971–; Asst. Dir., London (ON) Pub. Lib., 1966–71; Head, Ref. Dept., Calgary Pub. Lib., 1964–66. **Educ.:** Univ. of Toronto, 1954–57, BA (Eng.); Univ. of BC, 1963–64, BLS. **Orgs.:** BC LA: Pres. (1974–75). Can. LA: Adult Srvs. Sect. (Ch., 1970–71); Fed. Aid Com. (Conv., 1976–78). Inst. of Victoria Libns. Art Gallery of Grt. Victoria: Pres. (1976–78). **Activities:** 9; 17 **Addr.:** Greater Victoria Public Library, 735 Broughton St., Victoria, BC Y8W 3H2, Canada.

Miller, Edward P. (My. 10, 1924, St. Catharines, ON) Dean, Sch. of Lib. & Info. Sci., Univ. of MO, 1975–, Asst. Prof. of Lib. & Info. Sci., 1972–75; Adult Srvs. Coord., Tulsa City-Cnty. Lib., 1965–70. **Educ.:** Univ. of Toronto, 1942–46, BASc (Aero. Engin.); Kenyon Coll., 1950–53, BD (Theo.); Univ. of OK, 1964–65, MLS, 1969–72, PhD (Ind. Engin.). **Orgs.:** ALA. ASIS. SLA: By Laws Com. (Ch., 1970–72); Resrch Com. (1972–74); Mgt. Div., Nom. Com. (1976–77). AAAS. World Futures Socty. **Honors:** SLA, John Cotton Dana Lect., 1973. **Pubns.:** Jt. auth., "Acquisitions and Records Management: Help Where It Is Needed," *Lib. Acq.* (1977); *Spec. Libs.* (1981); "Library Education in Missouri," *Show-Me Libs.* (Jl. 1980); "Curriculum Changes at the University of Missouri-Columbia, School of Library and Informational Science," *Nsltr.,* MO Assn. of Sch. Libns. (May 1980); jt. auth., "A Method for Assessing Continuing Education Needs in a Metropolitan Library Network," *Jnl. of Lib. Admin.* (Spr. 1981); other articles. **Activities:** 9, 11, 12; 17, 26, 49-Eval. of Oper.; 56, 75 **Addr.:** School of Library & Informational Science, 104 Stewart Hall, UMC, Columbia, MO 65211.

Miller, Elizabeth Kubota (A. 9, 1931, Dairen City, U.S.S.R.) Sr. Tech. Adv., UN Energy Conf., 1980–; Chief, Info. Sys. Unit UN Dept. of Econ. and Soc. Affairs, 1976–80; Visiting Prof., St. John's Univ., 1979–80; Visiting Lectr., Drexel Univ., 1974–75; Asst. Univ. Libn., NY Univ., 1973–74; Chief Libn., Port Authority-World Trade Ctr., NY 1972–73; Dir. of Lib., Urban Inst., 1968–72. **Educ.:** Wheaton Coll., 1951–54, BA (Lit.); Univ. of Minnesota, 1955–57, MA LS; NY Univ., 1974–75, MA (Art Educ.); Drexel Univ., 1975–76; Univ. of PA, 1975–76 (Mgt. Sci.). **Orgs.:** Cncl. of Plng. Libns.: Secy. (1970) Pres. (1972–73). SLA: Ch., Soc. Sci. Div. (1969). ASIS: Nom. Com. (1968, 1970). Urban and Reg. Info. Sys. Assn. Founding mem.; Nom. Com. (1968–70). AAUP. Data for Dev. Assn. **Honors:** Colonial Dames of American Flwshp. 1955. **Activities:** 24, 41, 49; 54, 91, 92 **Addr.:** 40 Central Park South, New York NY 10019.

Miller, Ellen G. Wasby (Je. 14, 1939, Kansas City, MO) Dir., Lib. Systs. Devel., Univ. of Cincinnati, 1981–, Actg. Dir., Contracts Div., Comp. Ctr., 1979–80, Asst. Dir., 1976–79, Systs. Anal., 1975–76, Sr. Resrch. Anal., 1973–74; Exec. Asst. for Plng. and Budgets, Shawnee Mission Pub. Schs., 1970–72, Systs. Anal., 1969–70; Info. Systs. Resrch. Anal., Lib. of Congs., 1966–69, Catlgr., 1965. **Educ.:** Univ. of OR, 1959–63, BS (Soclgy.); Univ. of IL, 1963–65, MS (LS). **Orgs.:** ASIS: SOASIS Bd. (1976–). Assn. for Comp. Mach.: SIG on Comp. Persnl. Resrch. **Honors:** Beta Phi Mu, 1965; ALA/LITA, Spec. Cit. for ISAD/LC MARC Inst. Lectures, 1969. **Pubns.:** "Managing a Training Project for a Complex Software System," *Proceedings of the 16th Anl. Comp. Persnl. Resrch. Conf.* (1979); "The Case for Replacing Your District's 'Hierarchies' with Teams," *Amer. Sch. Bd. Jnl.* (Jl. 1975); "Shawnee Mission's On-line Cataloging System: The First Two Years," *Proceedings of the 1972 Clinic on Lib. Applications of Data Prcs.* (1972); "Sensible Steps Towards Library Automation," *Lib. Jnl.* (F. 1972); "Shawnee Mission's On-line Cataloging System," *Jnl. of Lib. Autom.* (Ja. 1971). **Activities:** 4, 14-Comp. Ctr.; 17, 28, 49-Syst. Dsgn.; 56, 75 **Addr.:** 797 Danvers Dr., Cincinnati, OH 45240.

Miller, Ellen L. (F. 26, 1947, Newark, NJ) Mgr. Resrch. Srv., Booz-Allen & Hamilton, Inc., 1978–; Head Libn., White, Weld & Co. Inc., 1974–78; Asst. Libn., The First Boston Corp., 1968–74. **Educ.:** Chestnut Hill Coll., 1964–68, AB (Psy.); Columbia Uni., 1970–72, MSLS. **Orgs.:** SLA: Pres., NY Chap. (1980–81); Ch. Tellers Com. (1979–80). Assoc. Info. Mgrs. Assn. of Recs. Mgrs. and Admin. **Activities:** 12; 17, 24, 41; 51, 59 **Addr.:** 40 East End Ave., 3C, New York, NY 10028.

Miller, Elsa Alma (My. 8, 1926, Canal Zone, Panama) Acq. and Circ. Libn., South. Bapt. Theo. Semy. Lib., 1974–. **Educ.:** Univ. of Louisville, 1961, BS (Cmrce.); Spalding Coll., 1968–71, MA (LS). **Orgs.:** ALA. ATLA. KY LA. CSLA. Amer. Bus. Women's Assn. **Honors:** Univ. Coll., Univ. of Louisville, Outstan. Woman, 1961. **Activities:** 1, 12; 15, 16, 22; 55, 90, 92 **Addr.:** Southern Baptist Theological Seminary Library, 2825 Lexington Rd., Louisville, KY 40280.

Miller, F. Gordon (N. 17, 1946, Edmonton, AB) Supvsr., Lib. Srvs., Pacific Biological Stat., 1979–; Reg. Libn., Can. Wild-

PROFESSIONAL ACTIVITIES: Institutions: 1. Acad. lib.; 2. Arch.; 3. Assn.; 4. Fed./Gvt. lib.; 5. Inst. lib.; 6. Mfr./Suppl.; 7. Milit. lib.; 8. Musm.; 9. Pub. lib.; 10. Sch. lib.; 11. Sch. of lib. sci.; 12. Spec. lib.; 13. State lib.; 14. (other). **Functions/Activities:** 15. Acq./Col. dev.; 16. Adult srvs.; 17. Admin.; 18. Apprais.; 19. Archit./Bldgs.; 20. Cat./Class.; 21. Chld. srvs.; 22. Circ.; 23. Cons./Pres.; 24. Consult.; 25. Cont. ed.; 26. Educ. lib. sci.; 27. Ext. srvs.; 28. Fund/Grants; 29. Gvt. pubs.; 30. Indx./Abs.; 31. Instr. lib. use; 32. Media srvs.; 33. Micro.; 34. Netwks./Coop.; 35. Persnl.; 36. PR; 37. Publshg.; 38. Recs. mgt.; 39. Ref. srvs.; 40. Repro.; 41. Resrch.; 42. Review.; 43. Secur.; 44. Serials; 45. Spec. col.; 46. Tech. srvs.; 47. Trustees/Bds.; 48. YA srvs.; 49. (other).

life Srv., 1974–79; Ref. Libn., Univ. of AB, 1970–74; Catlgr., 1969–70. **Educ.:** Univ. of Calgary, 1964–68, BA (Hist.); Univ. BC, 1968–69, BLS. **Orgs.:** Can. Assn. of Spec. Libs. & Info. Srvcs.: Dir. (1979–81). Intl. Assn. of Marine Sci. Libs. & Info. Ctrs. Can. LA. SLA. **Honors:** Beta Phi Mu. **Pubns.:** *The American bison* (1977); jt. auth., "Bibliography of Fisheries & Environment," *Arctic Islands Pipeline Routes* (1978); *Canadian Wildlife Service studies in Canada's national parks* (1978). **Activities:** 4, 12; 15, 16, 17; 58, 65, 82 **Addr.:** Pacific Biological Station Nanaimo, BC V9R 5K6 Canada.

Miller, Frances (Ashton) (F. 25, 1918, Shannon City, IA) Sr. Libn., Dir. NY Dept. of Motor Vehicles Resrch. Lib., 1974–; Asst. Law Libn., NY State Dept. of Law, 1973–74; Lib. Media Dir., Media Ctr. HS, Ballston Spa, NY, 1971–73; Educ. Biblgphr., SUNY, Albany, 1965–71; Cat. Libn., Coe Coll., 1964–65; Curric. Ctr. Libn., Cmnty. Pub. Sch., Cedar Rapids, IA, 1962–64; Asst. Resrch. Libn., Info. Srv., Field Enterprises, Inc., 1961–62; Tchr. and Libn., various schs., 1941–61. **Educ.:** Drake Univ., 1937–41, AB (Eng., Soc. Sci.); Columbia Univ., 1946–47, BS LS, other courses. **Orgs.:** ALA: ACRL. SLA. NY LA. Hudson-Mohawk LA. Amer. Fed. Tchr. Assn. Untd. Tchrs. Assn. Natl. Educ. Assn. NY State Interagency Info. Grp. **Activities:** 13; 15, 17, 20, 29; 91, 94 **Addr.:** New York (State) Dept. of Motor Vehicles, Research Library, Empire State Plz., Albany, NY 12228.

Miller, Harold W. (F. 25, 1941, Ohio City, OH) Chief Libn., Touche Ross & Co., 1967–. **Educ.:** Bowling Green State Univ., 1959–63, BA (Hist.); Univ. of KY, 1963–64, MA (Intl. Affairs); Columbia Univ., 1965–67, MLS. **Orgs.:** SLA: Copyrt. Com. (1978–82); Tellers Com. (1976–79, Ch., 1979); Alt. Rep. to CNLIA Copyrt. Com. (1979–82); Bus./Fin. Div., Ch.-Elect (1980–81). **Activities:** 12; 17, 38 **Addr.:** Touche Ross & Co., 1633 Broadway, New York, NY 10019.

Miller, Helen M. (S. 13, 1918, Conway, MO) Retired. State Libn., ID State Lib., 1962–80; Pub. Lib. Consult., WV Lib. Comsn., 1959–61; US Air Force Libn., Air bases in Germany, Eng., 1955–58; City/Cnty. Libn., Jefferson City/Cole Cnty., MO, 1947–55. **Educ.:** Drury Coll., 1936–40, AB (Eng.); Univ. of Denver, 1940–41, BS in LS. **Orgs.:** ALA. Pac. NW LA. ID LA: Exec. Bd. (1962–80). **Honors:** Pac. NW LA, Hon. Life Mem., 1978; ID LA, Hon. Life Mem., 1979. **Activities:** 13; 17 **Addr.:** 4023 Whitehead St., Boise, ID 83703.

Miller, Helen R. (Ja. 6, 1934, Westminster, SC) Order Sect. Head, Acq. Dept., Univ. of NC, 1972–; Circ. Libn., GA State Univ., 1961–66; Media Spec., Bellaire HS, 1958–61; Libn., Columbia (SC) HS, 1954–58. **Educ.:** Winthrop Coll., 1951–55, BS (LS); George Peabody Coll., 1956–58, MA (LS). **Orgs.:** ALA. SELA. Piedmont Lib. Acq. Info. Netwk. AAUW: Pres. (1979–81). **Activities:** 1, 10; 15, 22 **Addr.:** 1507 Murray Ln., Chapel Hill, NC 27514.

Miller, Hester Marcia (N. 3, 1920, Morenci, MI) Arts Spec., Albuquerque Pub. Lib., 1977–, Head, Fine & Performing Arts Dept., 1967–77, Coord., Main Lib., 1973–75, Ref. Asst., 1958–67; First Asst., Fine Arts Dept., Detroit Pub. Lib., 1956–57; Ref. Asst., Gen. Ref. Dept., MI State Univ. Lib., 1955–56; Ref. Asst., New York Pub. Lib., 1952–54; Asst. and First Asst., Music & Drama Dept., Detroit Pub. Lib., 1943–51. **Educ.:** MI State Univ., 1937–41, BA (Eng. Lit.); Univ. of MI, 1941–42, MA (Eng. Lit.), 1942–43, BLS. **Orgs.:** NM LA: VP (1964–65); Pres. (1965–66); Bd. (1966–67). Albuquerque LA: VP (1963–64). ARLIS/NA. Msc. LA. Thea. LA. Other orgs. Albuquerque Opera Gld. Albuquerque Arts Cncl. **Honors:** Phi Beta Kappa, 1942. **Pubns.:** Jt. auth., "Building a nonspecialized collection," *Lib. Trends* (Ja. 1975). **Activities:** 9; 39; 55 **Addr.:** 3607 Calle del Ranchero N.E., Albuquerque, NM 87110.

Miller, Howard Ernest (Ag. 12, 1939, Elmira, NY) Lib. Dir., Westwood Pub. Lib., 1971–; Reg. Ext. Libn., East. MA Reg. Lib. Syst., 1968–71; Ref. Libn., Morrill Meml. Lib., 1966–68; Ref. Libn., N. Country Lib. Syst., 1963–66. **Educ.:** Alfred Univ., 1957–61, BA (Liberal Arts); Syracuse Univ., 1961–63, MS (LS). **Orgs.:** MA LA: Int. Frdm. Com. (1976–79); PR Com. (1973–76, 1979–). Grt. Boston Pub. Lib. Admin.: Pres. (1972). **Pubns.:** "Body Building," *Lib. Jnl.* (Je. 15, 1979). **Activities:** 5, 9; 17, 36, 42; 55, 67, 74 **Addr.:** 97 Pond St, Westwood, MA 02090.

Miller, J. Gormly (Ja. 5, 1914, Rochester, NY) Prof. Emeritus, Cornell Univ., 1979–, Dir. of Libs., 1974–79; Deputy Chief, Ctrl. Lib. and Docum. Branch, Intl. Labor Ofc., Geneva, 1970–74; Asst. Dir. of Libs., Prof., Indus. and Labor Rel., Cornell Univ., 1962–70; Libn. and Prof., New York State Sch. of Indus. and Labor Rel., 1946–62. **Educ.:** Univ. of Rochester, 1932–36, AB (Eng.); Columbia Univ., 1937–38, BS in LS. **Orgs.:** ALA. ASIS. Indus. Rel. Resrch. Assn. **Activities:** 1; 17, 24; 59, 75, 92 **Addr.:** 7-D Wildflower Dr., Eastwood Commons, Ithaca, NY 14850.

Miller, Jacqueline E. (Ap. 15, 1935, New York, NY) Lib. Dir., Yonkers Pub. Lib., 1975–; Br. Admin., Grinton I. Will Lib., Branch of Yonkers Pub. Lib., 1970–75; Head of Ext. Srvs., New Rochelle Pub. Lib., 1969–70; Dir. Young Teen Srvs., Brooklyn Pub. Lib. 1964–68, Br. Libn., 1963–64, Young Teen Spec., 1960–63, Reading Improvement Instr., 1959–60. **Educ.:** Morgan State Coll., 1954–57, BA (Eng.), Pratt Inst., 1958–60, MLS. **Orgs.:** ALA: Pub. LA: Plng. Com. (1980–82); Nom. Com. (1980–81); Brd. of Dir. (1976); YA Srvs. Div.-Publishers Relations Comm. 1969–70 NY LA: VP (1980); Chldn. and YA Srvs Brd Mem. (1967–68); Leg. Com. (1978). Pub. Lib. Dir. Assn: Exec. Brd. (1976–80). Westchester LA: VP (1978); Pres. (1979). NAACP: Labor & Industry Com. (1981). Leag. of Women Voters, Yonkers Chapter. Chamber of Commerce, Yonkers, N.Y. Colonial Heights Assn. of Taxpayers. **Activities:** 9; 17 **Addr.:** Yonkers Public Library, 7 Main St., Yonkers, NY 10701.

Miller, Janet W. (Je. 1, 1948, Memphis, TN) Libn. II, Shelby State Cmnty. Coll., 1979–; Libn. I, Memphis/Shelby Cnty. Pub. Lib., 1976–79. **Educ.:** Univ. of TN, 1966–71, BA (Eng.); Univ. of WI, 1974–76, MSLS. **Orgs.:** TN LA. ALA: PLA, Lib. Srvs. to Chld. (1978–80); Pub. Lib. Supt. Sect., Com. on Coms. (Ch., 1979–80); ALSC, Lib. Srvs. to Disadv. Chld. Com. (1977–79); RASD; SRRT. **Honors:** Beta Phi Mu. **Activities:** 1, 9; 15, 39, 44; 55, 66, 92 **Addr.:** 3733 Charleswood, Memphis, TN 38122.

Miller, Jean K. (F. 5, 1925, Buffalo, NY) Dir. of the Lib., Univ. of TX Hlth. Sci. Ctr. at Dallas, 1978–; Dir., Med. Lib. Ctr. of New York, 1974–78; Assoc. Hlth. Sci. Libn., SUNY Buffalo, 1971–74; Proj. Dir. for Info. Dssm. Srv., Lakes Area Reg. Med. Prog., 1970–73. Head of Circ., Hlth. Sci. Lib., SUNY, Buffalo, 1969–71; Asst./Assoc. Dir. of Nursing, Chld. Hosp., Buffalo, 1959–67, Asst. Dir. of Educa., 1958–59; various positions in nursing educ., supvsn. and clinical nursing. **Educ.:** Univ. of Buffalo, 1950, BS (Nursing); West. Rsv. Univ., 1958, MS (Nursing Educ.); Syracuse Univ., 1968, MSLS; WA Univ. Sch. of Med. Lib., 1968–69, (Comp. Libnshp.); various courses. **Orgs.:** Med. LA: Bd. of Dir. (1978–81); S. Ctrl. Reg. Grp. Natl. Lib. of Med.: Biomed. Lib. Review Com. (1977–81). SLA. Syracuse Univ. Sch. of Lib. Sci. Alum. Assn. **Pubns.:** *Union List of Serials: Information Dissemination Service* (1973); "Study of the Information Dissemination Service–Health Sciences Library, State University of New York at Buffalo," *Bltn. of the Med. LA* (Jl. 1975); "Computer Assisted Circulation Control at Health Sciences Library SUNYAB," *Jnl. of Lib. Autom.* (Je. 1972); "Mechanization of Library Procedures in the Medium-sized Medical Library: XI. Two Methods of Providing Selective Dissemination of Information to Medical Scientists," *Bltn. Med. LA* (Jl. 1970). **Activities:** 1, 12; 17, 26, 27; 56, 80, 91 **Addr.:** The University of Texas Health Science Center at Dallas Library, 5323 Harry Hines Blvd., Dallas, TX 75235.

Miller, Jean R. (Ag. 4, 1927, St. Helena, CA) Chief Libn., Beckman Instruments, 1966–; Data Systs. Libn., Auronetics, 1963–65; Post Libn., U.S. Marine Corps Air Station, 1955–63; Base Libn., U.S. Air Force, Wethersfield, Eng., 1952–55. **Educ.:** Occidental Coll., 1948–50, BA (Psy.); Univ. of South. CA, 1951–52, MS (LS). **Orgs.:** Orange Cnty. LA: Pres. (1971). ASIS: Los Angeles Chap., Prog. Ch. (1973), Secy. (1972). SLA: South. CA Chap. (Pres., 1975–76; Secy., 1973–74); Sci./Tech. Div. (Treas., 1980–82). South. CA Assn. of Law Libs. Inst. of Electrical and Electronic Engin. Med–Tech Libns. of Orange Cnty. South. CA Tech. Prcs. Grp.: Nom. Com. (Ch., 1980). **Addr.:** Research Library, Beckman Instruments, Inc., 2500 Harbor Blvd., Fullerton, CA 92634.

Miller, Jerome K. (Ap. 18, 1931, Great Bend, KS) Asst. Prof., Univ. of IL Grad. Sch. of Lib. & Info. Sci., 1975–; Coord. of AV Lib. Srvs., Ctrl. WA Univ., Cat., Bibl. Srchr. **Educ.:** Emporia KS State Univ., 1963–65, BA (Hist.); Univ. of MI, 1965–66, AMLS: Univ. of KS, 1966–67, MA (Hist.); Univ. of CO, 1974–76, EdD (Educ. Media). **Orgs.:** ALA: LITA/Bd. of Dirs. (1977–80)/AV Sect., Nominating Com. (1977)/Vid. and Cable Comms. Sect., Tech. Stans. Com. (1976–77). AECT: Com. to Eval. Instr. Mtrls. (1978–). AALS. Consrtm. of Univ. Films Ctrs.: Archvst. (1971–78), Ch. (1974–76). AAUP. WA Assn. for Educ. Comms. and Tech. Ch. (1972–74). Ctr. for (Ecumenical) Campus Mnstry. Adv. Bd. (1971–73), Ch. (1972–73). Ellensburg, WA Kiwanis Clb.: Bd. of Dirs., (1970–74), VP. **Honors:** AECT, Okoboji Flwshp., 1975; Educ. Press Assn. of Amer., Disting. Achvmt. Awd. for Excel. in Educ. Jnlsm., 1976. **Pubns.:** "The Duplication of Audiovisual Materials in Libraries" in *Fair Use and Free Inquiry: Copyright Law and the New Media* (forthcoming); *Applying the New Copyright Law: A Guide for Educators & Librarians* (1979); "Applying the New Copyright Law to Nonbroadcast Telecommunications," *Video Systems* (Ja. 1978), "Four Copyright Infringment Court Cases Involving Educators," *Intl. Jnl. of Instr. Media* (1977–78); Ed., *Copyright and the Teaching/Learning Process: Issues Analyzed at the Critical Issues Conference 4, Washington, DC, March 21–23, 1977* (1977); various reviews and speeches. **Activities:** 1, 11; 26, 32; 61, 67 **Addr.:** Graduate School of Library & Information Science, 1407 W. Gregory Dr., 410 David Kinley Hall, University of Illinois, Urbana, IL 61801.

Miller, Jewell J. (Ag. 3, 1948, Cedar Rapids, IA) Asst. Libn., Cordell Hull Law Lib., Samford Univ., 1981–; Actg. Law Libn., Univ. of SD, 1980–81, Asst. Law Libn., 1979–80. **Educ.:** Cornell Coll., 1967–70, BA (Eng.); Univ. of IA, 1971–72, MA (LS); Valparaiso Law Sch., 1975–78, JD. **Orgs.:** AALL. MN Assn. of Law Libs. Amer. Bar Assn. IA State Bar Assn. **Activities:** 1, 12; 17, 31, 36; 77 **Addr.:** Cordell Hull Law Library, Cumberland School of Law, Samford University, 800 Lakeshore Dr., Birmingham, AL 35209.

Miller, John (Ap. 12, 1922, Trenton, NJ) Asst. to the Andrew W. Mellon Dir. of the Resrch. Libs., New York Pub. Lib., 1981–, Actg. Chief, Schomburg Ctr. for Resrch. in Black Cult., 1980–81, Chief, Amer. Hist. Div., 1969–80, Exec. Asst., Resrch. Libs., 1967–69, First Asst., Bk. Delivery Div., 1962–67, Supvsr., Bk. Delivery Div., 1957–61, Ref. Asst., Econ. Div., 1957, Head, Pers. Posting Sect., Acq. Branch, Prep. Div., 1955–56; Various prof. tchg. positions (1951–53). **Educ.:** Rutgers Univ., 1946–47, BA (Hist., Pol. Sci.); Columbia Univ., 1950–51, MA (Pol. Sci.), 1957–58, MS (LS). **Orgs.:** ALA. **Pubns.:** *The American Idea: Discovery and Settlement, Revolution and Independence* (1976); "The New York Public Library and the Bicentennial," *The Bkmark.* (My.–Je. 1974); Various reviews. **Activities:** 1, 12; 17, 45; 54, 55, 92 **Addr.:** The Research Libraries, New York Public Library, 5th Avenue and 42d St., New York, NY 10018.

Miller, Julia E. (Ap. 9, 1951, Bellefonte, PA) Ref. libn., VanPelt Lib., Univ. of PA, 1976–; Actg. Libn., Pine Manor Coll., 1975–76; Lib. Consult., Boston Univ. Grntlgy. Ctr., 1975–76. **Educ.:** Kenyon Coll., 1969–73, AB (Classics); Simmons Coll., 1974–75, MS (LS); Univ. of PA, 1978–, MA in progress (Folklore). **Orgs.:** ALA: RASD, Cat. Use Com. (1980–82); LIRT, Mem. Com.; Plng. Taskforce (1979–80). Mod. Greek Std. Assn. **Pubns.:** "RLIN at The Reference Desk" *Resrch. Libs. Grp. News;* "Wealth of Information" *Ref. Srvs. Review* (1979); Contrib., *Magazines for Libraries* (1978); Ed., "Reference Serials" in *Ref. Srvs. Review* (1979–). **Activities:** 1; 31, 39, 49-Online Searching; 92 **Addr.:** Van Pelt Library/CH, Univ. of Pennsylvania, Philadelphia, PA 19146.

Miller, Kenneth B., Jr. (S. 22, 1947, Detroit, MI) Libn. II, Detroit Pub. Lib., 1973–. **Educ.:** Wayne State Univ., 1972, BA (Liberal Arts), 1976, MSLS. **Orgs.:** ALA: Sort; SRRT/LUTF. MI LA. Prof. Org. of Libns.: Treas. (1974–77); VP (1978); Negotiating Team (Ch., 1980–81). **Activities:** 9; 16; 72 **Addr.:** Service to Shut-Ins and Retirees, Detroit Public Library, 8726 Woodward Ave., Detroit, MI 48202.

Miller, Larry A. (Ag. 12, 1950, Hammond IN) Asst. Libn., Pub. Srvs., Moraine Valley Cmnty. Coll., 1973–. **Educ.:** East. IL Univ., 1968–72, BA (Eng.); Univ. of IL, 1972–73, MSLS. **Orgs.:** ALA: ACRL/Cmnty. and Jr. Coll. Sect., Bibl. Com. (Ch. 1976–1981), ACRL Nom. Com. (1980–81). IL LA: Dir.-at-Large (1979–); Bibl. Instr. Com. (Ch., 1977–80). **Honors:** Phi Delta Kappa, 1976. **Pubns.:** Jt. auth., *Library Skills Test* (1980); *Library Instruction Programs in Illinois Community College LRC'S* (1979). **Activities:** 1; 17, 39, 44; 86 **Addr.:** 4422 Blanchan Ave., Brookfield, IL 60513.

Miller, Laurence A. (Ja. 19, 1940, Bloomsburg, PA) Dir. of Libs., FL Intl. Univ., 1981–; Dir., Univ. Lib., E. TX State Univ., 1974–; Dir. of Lib. Srvs., California (PA) State Coll., 1971–74; Area Dir. of Libs., Inter Amer. Univ. of PR, 1966–69; Acq. Libn., Bucknell Univ., 1963–65. **Educ.:** Kutztown State Coll., 1958–62, BS (Educ.); FL State Univ., 1962–63, MS (LS), 1969–71, PhD (LS). **Orgs.:** TX Cncl. of State Univ. Libns.: Vice-Ch., Ch.-Elect, (1979–). Interuniv. Cncl. of the N. TX Area: (1977–79). Ch., Lib. Com. TX LA: Ch., Int. Frdm. Com. (1978–79); Ch., Bylaws Com. (1975–77). ALA: LAMA/Circ. Srvs. Sect., Ch., Conf. Prog. Com. (1979–80); Ch., Plng. and Action Com. (1974–75). Common Cause of TX: Vice Ch. (1979–80). **Pubns.:** "The Smith Decision vs. the Marketplace of Ideas," *TX Lib. Jnl.* (Win., 1978); "Liaison Work in the Academic Library," *Ref. Qtly.* (Spr. 1977); "The Role of Circulation Services in the Major University Library," *Coll. and Resrch. Libs.* (N. 1973). **Addr.:** Florida International University, Miami, FL 33199.

Miller, Lewis R. (Jl. 24, 1942, Bonifay, FL) Dir., Lib. Srvs., Mars Hill Coll., 1978–; Media Spec., Media Coord., Gainesville City Schs., 1974–78. **Educ.:** Piedmont Coll., 1960–63, BA (Hist.); Univ. of GA, 1972–74, MEd, EdS (Lib. Media). **Orgs.:** ALA. West. NC LA. **Pubns.:** "Reading Habits of the Behaviorally Disordered Male," *Jnl. of Readg.* (O. 1975). **Activities:** 1; 17; 65, 82, 85 **Addr.:** Box 745, Mars Hill, NC 28754.

Miller, Lois Blake (McGirt) S. 4, 1919, Richmond, VA) Asst. Libn., Myrtle Beach HS, 1975–; Asst. Prof., Dept. of Educ. Media, Appalachian State Univ., 1970–74; Instr., Lib. Educ. Prog., Univ. of NC, Greensboro, 1967–70; Coord. of Instr. Mtrls., Winston-Salem/Forsyth Cnty. Schs., 1966–67; Libn., Pub. Schs., Forsyth Cnty., 1949–66; Libn., Bethany HS, Rockingham Cnty., 1948–49; Descr. Catlgr., Duke Univ., 1946–48. various other lib. positions. **Educ.:** Univ. of Richmond, 1936–40, BA (Eng.); Univ. of NC, 1941–42, BS (LS), 1962–66, MS (LS); Appalachian State Univ., 1971–73, EdS. (Educ. Leadership and Media). **Orgs.:** ALA. SELA. SC LA. Natl. Educ. Assn. SC Assn. of Educ. **Honors:** Beta Phi Mu. **Activities:** 10, 11; 26, 39, 48; 63 **Addr.:** Rte. 1, Box 26-C, Murrells Inlet, SC 29576.

Miller, Marilyn D. (My. 25, 1927, Pittsburgh, PA) Assoc. Prof. of Med. Bibl., Assoc. Libn., Ref. Srvs., LA. State Univ. Med. Ctr., Shreveport, 1975–, Asst. Prof. of Med. Bibl., Asst. Libn. Ref. Srvs., 1972–75; MEDLARS Indxr./Srchr., Asst. Prof., Med. & Dent. Bibl., MEDLARS Ctr., Univ. of AL, Sch. of Med., Bir-

Special Subjects/Services: 50. Adult educ.; 51. Advert./Mktg.; 52. Aerosp.; 53. Agric.; 54. Area std.; 55. Arts/Hum.; 56. Autom.; 57. Bibl./Prtg.; 58. Bio. sci.; 59. Bus./Fin.; 60. Chem.; 61. Copyrt.; 62. Documtn.; 63. Educ.; 64. Engin.; 65. Env.; 66. Eth. grps.; 67. Film; 68. Food/Nutr.; 69. Geneal.; 70. Geo.; 71. Geol.; 72. Handcpd.; 73. Hist.; 74. Int. frdm.; 75. Info. sci.; 76. Insr.; 77. Law; 78. Legis.; 79. Math./Comp. sci.; 80. Med.; 81. Metals; 82. Nat. resrcs.; 83. Newsp.; 84. Nuc. sci.; 85. Oral hist.; 86. Petr./Energy; 87. Pharm.; 88. Phys./Astr./Math.; 89. Readg.; 90. Relig.; 91. Sci./Tech.; 92. Soc. sci.; 93. Telecom.; 94. Transp.; 95. (other).

mingham, 1970–72; Admin. Libn., Prof. Asst. for Med. Lib. Resrc. Grants, Nat. Lib. of Med., Bethesda, 1966–70. **Educ.:** Univ. of Pittsburgh, 1952–64, BA (Geog.); 1965–66, MLS. Med. LA Cert., 1967–; MEDLARS Cert. - Nat. Lib. of Med., 1970. **Orgs.:** Med. LA: Com. on Surveys and Stat., (1966–70); Com. on Bibl. Proj. and Prob. (1971–74). Caddo-Bossier Lib. Club: Secy./Treas. (1973–74). S. Ctrl. Reg. Med. Lib. Prog.: Training and Cont. Educ. Com. (1978–82). LA State Univ. Med. Ctr. Fac.: Secy. to the Fac. (1977–78); Retirement & Fringe Benefits Com. (1975–78); Basc. Sci. Fac. Rep. (1976–77). **Activities:** 1; 25, 31, 39; 56, 57, 80 **Addr.:** LSU Med Center Library, PO Box 33932, Shreveport, LA 71130.

Miller, Marilyn L. (O. 9, 1930, St. Joseph, MO) Assoc. Prof., Sch. of Lib. Sci. Univ. of NC, Chapel Hill, 1977–; Asso. Prof., Western MI Univ., 1973–77; Asst. Prof., 1966–73; Sch. Lib. Consult., KS Dept. of Pub. Instr., 1962–66; Head Libn., Topeka KS. HS, 1956–66; Libn., Arthur Capper Jr. HS, 1954–56, Tchr./Libn., Wellsville KS. HS, 1952–54. **Educ.:** Graceland Coll., 1948–50, AA; Univ. of KS, 1950–52, BS (Eng.); Univ. of MI, 1956–59, AMLS; 1972–76, PhD (Lib. Sci.). **Orgs.:** ALA: Cncl. (1976–80); Awds. Com. (1971–72); Ch. (1973–75); ALA Schol. Jury (1972–74); Ch. ALA Grolier Ad. (1975). AASL: Reg. Dir. (1959–61); Rec. Secy. (1969–70); Encyc. Brit. Elem. Sch. Lib. Ad. (1969); Ch. (1970). Assn. for Lib. Srv.: Bd. of Dir. (1976–78); VP (1978–79); Pres. (1979–80). NC LA: Ch., Educ. for Libnshp. Com. (1977–79). **Honors:** Beta Phi Mu. Delta Kappa Gamma. **Pubns.:** Jt. Ed., "Proc. of the Higher Educ. Inst." *Futurism and Sch. Media Dev.* (1975). **Addr.:** School of Library Science, The University of North Carolina, Chapel Hill, NC 27514.

Miller, Marjorie Miller (Ja. 7, 1925, Pittsburgh, PA) Head Libn., Fox Chapel Area Sch. Dist., 1966–. **Educ.:** Univ. of Pittsburgh, 1943–46, BS (Educ.), 1965–66, MLS. **Orgs.:** Cncl. of Sch. Libns. PA Sch. Libns. Assn. ALA. **Activities:** 10; 17, 21, 31; 63 **Addr.:** 725 Field Club Rd., Pittsburgh, PA 15238.

Miller, Marjorie Mithoff (My. 28, 1922, La Porte, IN) Docum. Libn., Prince George's Cnty. Meml. Lib. Syst., 1977–; Libn., Adult Srvs., 1970–76; Tchr., Prince George's Cnty. Pub. Schs., 1967–68. **Educ.:** Cottey Jr. Coll., TX Coll. of Mines; Univ. of TX, 1939–43, BA (Eng.); Univ. of MD, 1968–69, MA (Amer. Std.); Cath. Univ. of Amer., 1971–73, MSLS. **Orgs.:** ALA. MD LA: Gvt. Docum. Sect. Sci. Fiction Resrch. Assn. Prince George's Cnty. Geneal. Assn. **Honors:** Phi Beta Kappa, 1943; Phi Kappa Phi, 1969. **Pubns.:** *Isaac Asimov: a checklist of works published in the U S* (1972); "The Social Science Fiction of Isaac Asimov," *Isaac Asimov* (1976). **Activities:** 9, 13; 17, 20, 29 **Addr.:** Prince George's County Documents Library, County Administration Bldg., Upper Marlboro, MD 20772.

Miller, Mary Celine (Ap. 20, 19—, O'Hara Twp., PA) Dir. of Libs., Robert Morris Coll., 1966–; Head Libn., LaRoche Coll., 1959–66; Tchr., St. Anne Sch., 1956–59; Tchr., St. Joseph Sch., 1952–56. **Educ.:** Duquesne Univ., 1950–59, BEd (Sec. Educ.), 1959–63, MEd (LS); Univ. of Pittsburgh, 1972–73, MLS. **Orgs.:** ALA. PA LA: Anl. Conf., Hosplty. Com. (Ch., 1980); SW. Chap. (Ch., 1976–77). Pittsburgh Reg. Lib. Ctr.: Trustee (1967–81). Cath. LA. Various other orgs. **Pubns.:** "Library Handbooks, College and University," *Ency. of Lib. and Info. Sci.* (1975). **Activities:** 1; 17, 32, 35; 56, 93 **Addr.:** Robert Morris College Library, Narrows Run Rd., Coraopolis, PA 15108.

Miller, Mary Elizabeth (Ag. 11, 1935, Fort Madison, IA) Info./Docum. Libn., Univ. of Pittsburgh, 1966–; Readg. Tchr., Jr. High Level, St. Pius Sch., 1961–63; Elem. Tchr., St. Austins Sch., 1955–59. **Educ.:** Webster Coll., 1960–61, BA (Soc. Sci.); Univ. of Pittsburgh, 1964–66, MLS. **Orgs.:** ALA. PALA: Coll./Resrch. Lib. Div. (Treas., 1980–); Gvt. Docum. RT (1974–77). Pittsburgh Reg. Lib. Ctr.: AV Instr. Com. (1975–). AAUP. **Activities:** 1; 15, 29, 39; 54, 78, 92 **Addr.:** Hillman Library, Documents Office, G-8, University of Pittsburgh, Pittsburgh, PA 15260.

Miller, Mary Jane (Ja. 22, 1938, Salisbury, MD) Lib. Grp. Supvsr., Bell Labs., Whippany, NJ, 1977–; Lib. Grp. Supvsr., Bell Labs., Norcross, GA, 1971–77; Ref. Libn., West. Electric, Greensboro, NC, 1969–71. **Educ.:** Berea Coll., 1956–60, BA (Eng.); Univ. of NC, 1968–69, MSLS. **Orgs.:** SLA: North. NJ Chap.; S. Atl. Chap. (Treas., 1974–76). **Honors:** Phi Kappa Phi, 1959. **Activities:** 12; 17; 56, 64, 93 **Addr.:** Bell Laboratories, Whippany Rd., Whippany, NJ 07981.

Miller, Michael D. (S. 3, 1948, Flushing, NY) Dept. Head, AV Srvs., Mid-Hudson Lib. Syst., 1974–; Adj. Asst. Prof., Palmer Grad. Lib. Sch., Long Island Univ., 1979–; Ref. and AV Libn., Comsewogue Pub. Lib., 1972–74. **Educ.:** C.W. Post Coll., Long Island Univ., 1966–70, BA (Bus. Mgt.), Palmer Grad. Lib. Sch., 1970–72, MS (LS); SUNY, 1974, Prof. Cert. (Pub. Lib.). **Orgs.:** NY LA: Film/Vid. RT (Member-at-Large, 1978; VP, 1979; Pres., 1980), State Liaison Com. (1981). Film Lib. Info. Cncl.: Bd. of Dir. (1981–82). ALA: LITA/AV (Member-at-Large, 1981–82). Pre-Screening Ch., 1980–81). EFLA. NY State Cncl. on the Arts: Film Panelist (1979–81); Ch. (1980). **Pubns.:** "Video Centers Enrich Rural Libraries," *Amer. Libs.* (F. 1981); "Have You Checked Your Enthusiasm Level Lately," *Natl. Film Bd. of Can. Nsltr.* (Fall 1978); *MHLS: A Library for Libraries* vid. (1978). **Activities:** 11, 13; 17, 24, 32; 56, 67, 93 **Addr.:** c/oMid-Hudson Library System, 103 Market Street, Poughkeepsie, NY 12601.

Miller, Nancy Elizabeth (S. 17, 1916, Campbellsville, KY) Asst. Dir., Coll. of Law Lib., OH State Univ., 1957–; Head, Ext. Dept., Akron Pub. Lib., 1956–57, Head, Chamberlain Branch Lib., 1955–56; Assoc. Prof., LS, Kent State Univ., 1949–55. **Educ.:** SD State Coll., 1934–36; Univ. of KY, 1936–38, AB (LS); Univ. of IL, 1939–42, BS in LS, 1946–47, MS (LS); Western Reserve Univ., 1951–52, MA (Amer. Cult.). **Orgs.:** OH Reg. Assn. of Law Libs.: Secy. (1960–64); Pres. (1964–65). AALL: Ch., Cat. & Class. Com. (1962–64; 1967–68); Instr. in Catlg. AALL Inst., (1955, 1974). Pilot Intl. Kappa Delta Pi. **Honors:** Beta Phi Mu. 1947. **Activities:** 1, 9; 20, 39, 46; 77 **Addr.:** 1995 Tewksbury Rd., Columbus, OH 43221.

Miller, Paul F. (S. 13, 1949, Chicago, IL) Dir., Verona Pub. Lib., 1979–; Head, Outrch. Dept., Plainfield Pub. Lib., 1978–79. **Educ.:** Univ. of IL, 1967–71, AB (Pol. Sci.); Rutgers Univ., 1977–78, MLS. **Orgs.:** ALA: SRRT, Clearinghouse Com. (1978–80). NJ LA: Admin. Sect. (Secy., 1980–81). **Honors:** Beta Phi Mu, 1978. **Activities:** 9; 17; 66 **Addr.:** Verona Public Library, 17 Gould St., Verona, NJ 07044.

Miller, Pauline Monz (Ap. 2, 1931, Harrisburg, PA) Head, Sci. and Tech. Libs., Syracuse Univ., 1978–, Life Sci. Biblgphr., 1976–78, Resrch. Assoc. in Bio., 1963–74. **Educ.:** PA State Univ., 1949–52, BS (Botany); Univ. of PA, 1952–56, PhD (Botany); Syracuse Univ., 1975–76, MLS. **Orgs.:** ALA. SLA. Sigma Xi National Audubon Socty. **Honors:** AAUW, Flwshp. 1955–56. Phi Beta Mu, 1976. Sigma Xi. **Activities:** 1; 15, 17, 31; 58, 68, 91 **Addr.:** Engineering and Life Sciences Library, Syracuse University, Syracuse, NY 13210.

Miller, Pearl Ann (Je. 11, 1932, Cedar Rapids, IA) Libn., State of MI, Dept. of Mgt. and Budget, Ofc. of Hlth. and Med. Affairs, 1978–. **Educ.:** MI State Univ., 1970–74, BA (Soc. Sci., Educ.); West. MI Univ., 1976–78, MLS; Lansing Cmnty. Coll., 1977–78, Assoc. (Bus.). **Orgs.:** MI LA: PR Com. (1978–81); Ch.-elect, Docum. Caucus, 1981. Med. LA. MI Hlth. Sci. LA: Ch., Legis. Com. (1982). Mid-MI Hlth. Sci. LA: Ch. (1981–82). Various other orgs. E. Lansing Pub. Lib. Bd.: Comsn. (1980–85). **Pubns.:** "PR Clipboard," *MI Libn.* (S. 1980). **Activities:** 13; 15, 20, 39 **Addr.:** Office of Health & Medical Affairs, 1st Floor, Lewis Cass Bldg., Box 30026, Lansing, MI 48909.

Miller, Philip E. (F. 18, 1945, Providence, RI) Libn., Hebrew Un. Coll., Jewish Inst. of Relig., 1978–, Actg. Libn., 1976–78, Asst. Libn., 1974–76. **Educ.:** Georgetown Univ., 1963–67, BS (Ling.); Univ. of MI, 1967–70, MA (Near East), 1973, AMLS. **Orgs.:** AJL: VP/Pres. Elect (1980–84). NY Area Theo. LA: Netwk. Com. (1979–); Mem. Com. (1981–). **Pubns.:** "Jewish Religious Children's Literature in America," *Phaedrus* (Volume 7, No. 1); "Judaic Theological Journals," *Serials Review* (Volume 7, No. 1); various bk. reviews, *AJL Bltn.* **Activities:** 1, 12; 15, 17, 45; 90 **Addr.:** Klau Library, Hebrew Union College - Jewish Institute of Religion, 1 W. 4th St., New York, NY 10012.

Miller, Richard Anderson (O. 31, 1941, Bowling Green, VA) Lib. Dir., Handley Lib., 1973–; Med. Lib. Dir., Tompkins-McCaw Lib., 1970–73, Asst. Libn., 1965–70. **Educ.:** FL State Univ., 1962–63, BA (Eng, LS), 1964–65, MS (LS); Emory Univ., 1968, Cert. (Med. Libnshp.). **Orgs.:** ALA. VA LA: Legis. Com. (1979–); Int. Frdm. Com. (1977–79). SLA: VA Chap. (Pres., 1971–72). **Activities:** 9; 17; 74, 78, 80 **Addr.:** Handley Library, P.O. Box 58, Winchester, VA 22601.

Miller, Richard E. (Mr. 26, 1943, Hartford, CT) Assoc. Libn., Carleton Coll. Lib., 1971–. **Educ.:** IN Univ., 1967, BA (Hist.), 1967–69, MA (Hist.), 1969–71, MLS; Univ. of MN, 1978–, (LS). **Orgs.:** ALA: LITA; ACRL. **Pubns.:** "Planning Information Services in the Liberal Arts College Library," *ERIC doc.* **Activities:** 1; 33, 34, 39; 56, 61, 93 **Addr.:** Carleton College Library, Northfield, MN 55057.

Miller, Richard T., Jr. (F. 4, 1947, Emmaus, PA) Coord. for Dev. of Spec. Lib. Srvs., MO State Lib., 1974–. **Educ.:** Grove City Coll., 1965–69, BA (Eng./Educ.); Drexel Univ., 1973–74, MLS. **Orgs.:** ALA: ASCLA Lib. Srv. to Prisoners Sect.,-Srv. to Local Jails Resol. Com. (Ch., 1979–); Lib. Srv. to Fed. Correct. Inst. Com.; Excep. Srv. Awd. (Ch., 1979–80); Lib. Srv. to the Impaired Elderly Nom. Com. (Ch., 1979–80); YASD, Lib. Srvs. to YA in Inst. MO LA: JMRT (Ch., 1979–80). Lib. Outreach Coop. **Honors:** Drexel Univ., Grad. Sch. of Lib. and Info. Sci., Outstan. Grad., 1974. **Pubns.:** Jt. auth., *Interim Standards for Libraries in Residential Institutions for the Mentally Retarded in Missouri and Iowa* (1977); Jt. Cmplr., *Directory: Groups Concerned with Adult Corrections*, ERIC (1976); "in SIGHT out" "Show-Me Libraries" (1974–); "Libraries Limited: Library Services to the Imprisoned," *Cath. Lib. World* (N. 1980). **Activities:** 13; 49; 66, 72, 89 **Addr.:** Missouri State Library, P.O. Box 387, Jefferson City, MO 65102.

Miller, Robert (F. 27, 1947, New York, NY) First Asst., Memphis/Shelby Cnty. Pub. Lib. and Info. Ctr., 1979–; Libn., Natl. Coll. of Educ., 1975–79; Libn., New York Pub. Lib., 1974–75. **Educ.:** Wagner Coll., 1969–71, BA (Hist.); Columbia Univ., 1973–74, MLS. **Orgs.:** TN Archvst. IL LA. SELA. ALA: LITA/Vid. Cable Comm. Sect. (Ch., 1979–80). Phi Delta Kappa. **Pubns.:** "Memphis: Old and New," *TN Libn.* (Win. 1981); Various reviews (1980). **Activities:** 9; 32; 69, 85 **Addr.:** 4146 Tarry Wood Dr., Memphis, TN 38118.

Miller, Robert Bruce (O. 22, 1946, Dallas, TX) Spec. Asst., Autom. and Systs. Ofc., Univ. of TX, Gen. Libs., 1976–, Asst. Head, Automated Cat. Dept., 1976–78. **Educ.:** Univ. of TX, Arlington, 1964–68 BA (Psy.); Univ. of TX, Austin, 1973–75, MLS. **Orgs.:** ALA: RTSD; LITA. Beta Phi Mu: Beta Eta Chap. (Pres., 1978–79). **Pubns.:** *Name Authority Control for Card Catalogs in the General Libraries* (1981); "Planning, Creating, and Maintaining the Bibliographic Data Base," TX Lib. Assn. Conf.: Online Pub. Cats. (forthcoming); "Authority Control in the Network Environment," *Lib. and Info. Tech. Inst.: Athrty. Contrl.-The Key to Tomorrow's Cat.* (forthcoming). **Activities:** 1; 24, 41, 46; 56, 75 **Addr.:** 4408 Ave. D, Austin, TX 78751.

Miller, Robert C. (My. 9, 1936, Evanston, IL) Dir. of Libs., Univ. of Notre Dame, 1978–; Dir. of Libs., Univ. of MO, St. Louis, 1975–78; Assoc. Dir., Gen. Srvs., Univ. of Chicago Lib., 1973–75, Assoc. Dir., Reader Srvs., 1971–73, Head, Acq. Dept., 1968–71. **Educ.:** Marquette Univ., 1958, BS (Hist./Phil); Univ. of WI, Madison, 1962, MS (Amer. Hist.); Univ. of Chicago, 1966, MALS. **Orgs.:** ALA: ACRL. ARL: Com. on Nonacad. Libs. (1981–82). IN LA. **Pubns.:** "Approval Plans," *Shaping Lib. Coll. for 1980s* (1980); jt. auth., "MARC Utilization in the Univ. of Chicago (1971); "Inter. Publishers' Assoc., the History of a Trade Organization, 1896–1962" *Lib. Hist. Sem. Prcdgs.* (1968); "Practical Applications of MARC II" *Law Lib. Jnl.* (N. 1970). **Activities:** 1; 15, 17 **Addr.:** 857 Forest Ave., South Bend, IN 46616.

Miller, Robert Harvey (F. 4, 1922, St. Petersburg, FL) Supvsr., Educ. Media, MN Dept. of Educ., 1975–; Dir. of Lrng. Resrcs., Sch. Bd. of Broward Cnty., 1960–75, Tchr. and Elem. Prin., 1954–60; Elem. Prin., Hernando Cnty., 1951–54; Eng. Tchr., Escambia Cnty., 1949–51. **Educ.:** Univ. of FL, 1941–48, BAJ (Jnlsm.), 1948–49, MED (Sch. Admin.), 1951–54, EdS (Elem. Educ.); IN Univ., 1962–64, EdD (Educ. Tech.). **Orgs.:** ALA: AASL. AECT. Natl. Assn. of State Educ. Media Profs.: Pres. (1979). Various other orgs. Phi Delta Kappa. Sigma Delta Chi. Natl. Educ. Assn. Natl. Assn. of Educ. Broadcasters. **Pubns.:** "Capitol Comments," *MN Media* (Four times yrly.); "Production in Action" *Sch. Mgt.* (My. 1973); "The Media Specialists," *AV Instr.* (F. 1967); "The Portable Sch.," *FEA Jnl.* (My. 1956); Various articles. **Activities:** 13; 25, 26, 32; 61, 74, 93 **Addr.:** Department of Education, Capitol Square, 550 Cedar St., St. Paul, MN 55101.

Miller, Rosalind (Je. 18, 1929, Neosho, MO) Assoc. Prof., GA State Univ., 1972–; Libn., Clayton HS, 1968–72; Lectr., Sums., Univ. of IL, 1968–70. **Educ.:** Drury Coll., 1941–51, BA (Eng.); Univ. of IL, 1966–67, MLS; St. Louis Univ., 1969–72, PhD (Educ.). **Orgs.:** ALA. GA LA: Ed. Bd. (1976–77); Bd. Mem. (1979–80). SELA. **Pubns.:** "Stop Counting the Books," *The Clearing House* (Ja. 1976); "Why I Can't Create a Learning Center," *Sch. Media Qtly.* (Spr. 1979). **Activities:** 14-Sch. of Educ.; 26, 32 **Addr.:** 404 Urban Life, Georgia St. Univ., University Plz., Atlanta, GA 30303.

Miller, Rosanna (Au. 19, 1940, Success, MO) Head, Map Coll., AZ State Univ. Lib., 1975–, Libn., Acq. Dept., 1974–75. **Educ.:** AZ State Univ., 1968–70, BA (Hum.); Univ. of AZ, 1972–73, MLS; AZ State Univ., 1974–79, MA (Art Hist.). **Orgs.:** West. Assn. of Map Libs.: Mem. & Hosplty. Com. (1979–80); Secy. (1980–81). SLA: AZ Chap., Empl. Ch. (1979–81). ARLIS/NA: AZ Chap., Secy./Treas. (1980). **Pubns.:** "The Paraprofessional," *Lib. Jnl.* (Mrch. 15, 1975); "KWOC Index for Maps," *West. Assn. of Map Libs. Info. Bltn.* (N. 1978). **Activities:** 1; 30, 39; 70 **Addr.:** Map Collection, Arizona State University Library, Tempe, AZ 85287.

Miller, Roy Daniel, Jr. (F. 12, 1929, Sharon, PA) Coord. of Adult Srvs., Brooklyn Pub. Lib., 1971–, Chief, Hist.-Travel-Biography Div., 1967–71, Various branch assignments, 1960–67. **Educ.:** Gettysburg Coll., 1954–58, AB (Soclgy.); Columbia Univ., 1960–62, MS (LS); Univ. of MD, 1974, Cert. (Lib. Admin. Dev. Prog.). **Orgs.:** ALA: PLA, Conf. Plng. (1979–); Consumer Info. (1979–); YASD Srvs. Statement Dev. Com. (1975–76). NY LA: Ref. & Ad. Srv. Sect., VP/Pres. Elec. (1980–81), Pres. (1981–2), Ch.,-Litcy. Com. (1977–79). New York Lib. Club. Lib. PR Cncl.: VP/Pres. elect (1974–75); Pres. (1975–76). NY Adult Educ. Cncl.: VP (1978). Litcy. Volun. of New York City: Bd. (1979–). Learning-For-Living, Inc. **Pubns.:** "Public libraries" in *BUT NOT TO LOSE* (1968). **Activities:** 9; 16, 25, 48; 50, 89 **Addr.:** Adult Services Office, Brooklyn Public Library, Grand Army Plaza, Brooklyn, NY 11238.

Miller, Rush Glenn, Jr. (Mr. 13, 1947, Atlanta, GA) Dir., Lib. Srvs., Delta State Univ., 1975–; Asst. Prof., LS, Univ. of MS, 1974–75. **Educ.:** Delta State Univ., 1966–69, BA (Hist.); MS State Univ., 1970–73, MA PhD (Hist.); FL State Univ., 1973–74, MS (LS). **Orgs.:** ALA: SE Reg. Mem. Ch. (1978–82). SELA: Exec. Bd. (1976–82). MS LA: Treas. (1978); Ch., Legis. Com. (1980, 1977); Ch., Autom. and Networking RT (1979); Ch., Long Range Plng. Com. (1979). Socty. of MS Archvsts. Bolivar Cnty.

PROFESSIONAL ACTIVITIES: Institutions: 1. Acad. lib.; 2. Arch.; 3. Assn.; 4. Fed./Gvt. lib.; 5. Inst. lib.; 6. Mfr./Suppl.; 7. Milit. lib.; 8. Musm.; 9. Pub. lib.; 10. Sch. lib.; 11. Sch. of lib. sci.; 12. Spec. lib.; 13. State lib.; 14. (other). **Functions/Activities:** 15. Acq./Col. dev.; 16. Adult srvs.; 17. Admin.; 18. Apprais.; 19. Archit./Bldgs.; 20. Cat./Class.; 21. Chld. srvs.; 22. Circ.; 23. Cons./Pres.; 24. Consult.; 25. Cont. ed.; 26. Educ. lib. sci.; 27. Ext. srvs.; 28. Fund/Grants; 29. Gvt. pubs.; 30. Indx./Abs.; 31. Instr. lib. use; 32. Media srvs.; 33. Micro.; 34. Netwks./Coop.; 35. Persnl.; 36. PR; 37. Publshg.; 38. Recs. mgt.; 39. Ref. srvs.; 40. Repro.; 41. Resrch.; 42. Review.; 43. Secur.; 44. Serials; 45. Spec. col.; 46. Tech. srvs.; 47. Trustees/Bds.; 48. YA srvs.; 49. (other).

Hist. Socty.: Pres. (1979–1980). MS Hist. Socty. Cleveland Noon Lions Club, Pres. (1980–81). N. MS Conf., Untd. Meth. Church: Archvst. (1975–80). **Honors:** MS LA, Past Pres.'s Awd., 1976. **Pubns.:** Ed., *MS Libs.* (1981–); "The Influx of Ph.D.'s into Librarianship, Intrusion or Transfusion?" *Coll. and Resrch. Libs.* (Mr. 1976); "John G. Jones: Pioneer Circuit Rider and Historian," *Jnl. of MS Hist.* (F. 1977); "Religion in Rosedale" in *History of Rosedale, Mississippi 1876–1976* (1976); "Special Collections in Libraries in Mississippi" in *Special Collections in Libraries of the Southeast* (1978). **Activities:** 1, 2; 17, 34, 41 **Addr.:** Box 3282, Delta State University, Cleveland, MS 38733.

Miller, Sally (D. 6, 1925, New York, NY) Dir. of Mktg. and Promo., Lib. Dir. Assocs., 1981–; Pub. Rel. Dir. (Half Hollow Hills Comnty. Lib., 1969–81; Copy Writer, Asst. to Gen. Mgr., Radio Station WGSM & WCTO, 1966–68; Ed. Secy. Supt. of Sch., School Dist. # 3 Huntington, NY, 1965–66; Tchr., Huntington and Farmingdale, 1951–64. **Educ.:** SUNY, Stonybrook, 1977–, (Comm.). **Orgs.:** ALA: LAMA (John Cotton Dana Com., 1975–79, Ch., 1978); Exec. Com. (1979–81). Suffolk Cnty. LA: Pres. (1981); Ed., *DATA* Mag. (1976–77). Nassau Cnty LA. Nassau-Suffolk Inst. Com.: Pub., 1974–79. N.Y. Women in Communication. **Honors:** ALA, John Cotton Dana Award, 1972. **Activities:** 9; 36, 37; 55, 67, 92, 93 **Addr.:** 157 E. Pulaski Rd., Huntington Station, NY 11746.

Miller, Sarah Jordan (Pittsburgh, PA) Asst. Prof., Rutgers Univ., Grad. Sch. of Lib. and Info. Stds., 1979–, Adj. Instr., 1978–79; Lectr., Columbia Univ., Sch. of Lib. Srvs., 1968–77; Head, Serials and Docums. Acq., Columbia Univ. Libs., 1961–67, Asst. Libn., Sch. of Lib. Srv. Lib., 1960–61, Head, Serials and Docums. Acq., 1955–58; Libn. and Head, Frederick St. Branch, Houston Pub. Lib., 1953; Instr., Pol. Sci., South. Univ., 1948–49. **Educ.:** Univ. of Pittsburgh, 1946, BA (Soc. Scis.); Columbia Univ., 1951, MA (Pol. Sci.), 1955, MS (LS), 1980, DLS. **Orgs.:** ALA: ACRL, Grt. New York Metro. Area Chap. NY Tech. Srvs. Libns. AALS. ASIS. Various other orgs. **Honors:** Beta Phi Mu, 1955. **Activities:** 1, 11; 26, 29, 46; 54, 57, 92 **Addr.:** Rutgers University, Graduate School of Library and Information Studies, 4 Huntington St., New Brunswick, NJ 08903.

Miller, Stephen Arnold (Ap. 4, 1942, St. Louis, MO) Ref. Libn., OR State Univ., 1974–; Prog. Coord., IA State Arts Cncl. 1974; Acq. Libn., Asst. to the Dir., Rockford Coll., 1969–72; Serials Libn. and Catlgr., IA State Univ., 1967–69. **Educ.:** Cornell Coll., 1960–62; Westminster Coll. (MO), 1962–65, BA (Econ.); Western Reserve Univ., 1965–67, MSLS; Univ. of WI, 1972–74, MA (Arts Admin.). **Orgs.:** SLA. Assn. of Master of Bus. Admin. Exec. Assn. for Evolutionary Econ. Mid Valley Lions Club. **Activities:** 1; 16, 31, 39; 55, 59, 92 **Addr.:** P. O. Box 1360, Corvallis, OR 97330.

Miller, Stuart W. (F. 20, 1950, Champaign, IL) Info. Spec., Intl. Assn. of Assess. Ofcrs., 1976–; Tchr., Barrington (IL) Mid. Sch., 1972–74. **Educ.:** Wabash Coll., 1967–71, BA (Hist.); Univ. of Chicago, 1971–72, MAT (Hist.), 1974–76, MA (LS). **Orgs.:** ALA: ACRL. **Honors:** Beta Phi Mu, 1977. **Pubns.:** "Library Use Instruction in Selected American Colleges," Occasional Paper, Univ. of IL, Grad. Sch. of LS, (1978); reviews. **Activities:** 12; 39, 41, 46; 59, 78, 92 **Addr.:** 5050 S. Lake Shore Dr., #3615, Chicago, IL 60615.

Miller, Susan E. (F. 11, 1947, Harrisburg, PA) Ref. Libn., Xavier Univ., New Orleans, 1979–; Docmlst., Purdue Univ., W. African Proj., 1977–78; Bibl. Libn., Credit Resrch. Ctr., 1976–77. **Educ.:** IN Univ., 1965–70, BA (Eng.); Univ. of WA, 1973–75, MLS. **Orgs.:** SLA. **Pubns.:** *A Bibliography of Consumer Financial Services and Regulation* (1977); *Thesaurus of Terms in Mortgage and Consumer Credit* (1977). **Activities:** 1, 12; 29, 30, 39; 54, 59, 91 **Addr.:** 4452 Maple Leaf Dr., New Orleans, LA 70114.

Miller, Tamara J. (Ag. 26, 1946, Ross, CA) Head of Machine-Readable Cat., Univ. of WI - Madison Libs., 1981–; Network Coord., WI Lib. Cnsrtm., 1976–80; Head, Bibl. Srchg. Sect., MI State Univ., 1973–76, Cat. Libn., 1971–72. **Educ.:** Univ. of UT, 1968–69, BA (Econ.); Univ. of KY, 1970–71, MLS. **Orgs.:** ALA: LITA WI LA: Tech. Srvs. Sect. (Ch.) WI Assn. of Acad. Libns. **Pubns.:** "Study of Collection Overlap in the UW System Libraries," *Coll. & Resrch. Libs.* (in press). **Activities:** 13, 14-Library Network; 17, 25, 34; 56 **Addr.:** University of Wisconsin-Madison, 324 Memorial Library, 728 State St., Madison, WI 53706.

Miller, Terry Joy (N. 19, 1940, Detroit, MI) Head Libn., Encyc. Britannica Ed. Lib., 1972. **Educ.:** Univ. of MI, 1958–61, BA (Hist.); Rosary Coll., 1969–71, MLS; Univ. of Chicago, 1979, CAS. **Orgs.:** ALA. SLA. NLA. Chicago Lib. Club. Friends of the Lincolnwood Lib.: Treas. (1979–). **Honors:** Beta Phi Mu, 1971. **Activities:** 5, 12; 17, 39, 45 **Addr.:** Editorial Library, Encyclopaedia Britannica Inc, 425 N. Michigan Ave., Chicago, IL 60611.

Miller, William (Ja. 9, 1947, Philadelphia, PA) Actg. Head of Ref., MI State Univ., 1981–, Asst. Head of Ref., 1980–81; Ref. Libn., Albion Coll., 1976–80. **Educ.:** Temple Univ., 1964–68, BA (Eng.); Univ. of Rochester, 1968–74, MA, PhD (Eng.); Univ. of Toronto, 1974–76, MLS. **Orgs.:** ALA: Choice Mag., Ch., Ed. Bd. (1980–82); RASD/Mach. Asst. Ref. Srvs. Sect., Cost and Fnc. Com. (1981–83); ACRL/Bibl. Instr. Com., Ch. (1981–82). MI LA: Ch., Acad. Div. (1981–82); Ed., Acad. Div., *MI Libn.* (1979–81). MI Lib. Cnsrtm.: Mem., Exec. Cncl. (1978–80); Data Base Task Force, Interlib. Docum. Delivery Task Force. NLA: Pres., MI Chap. (1979–80). **Honors:** ON LA, Ad., 1976; Univ. of Toronto, Rare Bks. and Mss. Ad., 1976; Blackwell N. Amer., Prize Essay Contest, 1976. **Pubns.:** Ed., *College Librarianship* (1981); *Citation Analysis of Humanities Literature* (1977); "Some Very Practical Suggestions for Term Paper Assignments," *Lit. Resrch. Nwsltr.* (1981); "MLA and NLA: On Library Associations and Librarians' Associations," *MI Libn.* (Jan. 1980); Jt. Auth., "Collection Development from a College Perspective," *Coll. and Resrch Libs.* (1979). **Activities:** 1, 11; 15, 24, 31; 55, 56, 57 **Addr.:** Reference Department, Michigan State University Libraries, East Lansing, MI 48824.

Miller, William Bayard (Mr. 17, 1924, Latrobe, PA) Mgr., Presby. Hist. Socty., 1961–, Asst. Secy., 1960–61, Asst. Resrch. Hist., 1957–60. **Educ.:** Allegheny Coll., 1942–47, AB (Hist.); Univ. of PA, 1947–50, MA (Hist.). **Orgs.:** ALA. SAA. Amer. Socty. of Church Hist.: Secy.–Treas. (1972–). Amer. Assn. of State and Lcl. Hist. Assn. of Recs. Mgrs. and Admin. **Honors:** SAA, Sr. M. Claude Lane Awd., 1978. **Pubns.:** Assoc. ed., *Jnl. of Presby. Hist.* (1961–). **Activities:** 2, 12; 37, 41, 45; 55, 90 **Addr.:** Presbyterian Historical Society (Department of History), 425 Lombard St., Philadelphia, PA 19147.

Miller, William Charles (O. 26, 1947, Minneapolis, MN) Libn., Nazarene Theo. Semy., 1978–; Acq. & cat. libn., Mt. Vernon Nazarene Coll., 1974–78; Ref. Staff, Kent State Univ., 1972–74. **Educ.:** Marion Coll., 1965–68, AB (Relig.); Kent State Univ., 1972–74, MLS, 1976–, PhD cand. (Educ. Admin). **Orgs.:** Kansas City Theo. LA: Pres. (1979–80). MO LA. Christian Libns. Flwshp.: Finance Com. (1975–76). ATLA. ALA: ACRL. Assn for the Std. of Higher Educ. **Honors:** Beta Phi Mu. **Activities:** 1; 15, 17, 31; 57, 63, 90 **Addr.:** William Broadhurst Library, Nazarene Theological Seminary, 1700 East Meyer Blvd., Kansas City, MO 64131.

Miller, William F. (Ag. 8, 1933, Sterling, OH) Dir., Instr. Mtrls. Ctr., Goshen Coll., 1975–; Assoc. Prof., Phys. Sci., 1967–75, Dir. Std. Srv. Prog., Haiti, 1972–73, Regis., Asst. Prof., Educ., 1963–67. **Educ.:** Goshen Coll., 1951–55, BA (Phys.); OH State Univ., 1961–62, MA (Sci. Educ.); IN Univ., 1977–78, EdS (Instr. Systs. Tech.). **Orgs.:** Assn. of IN Media Educs.: Equip. Com. (1979–). AECT. Natl. Sci. Tchrs. Assn. Astronomical Socty. of the Pac. **Activities:** 1, 10; 17, 32, 46; 67, 93 **Addr.:** Instructional Materials Center, Goshen College, Goshen, IN 46526.

Millich, Eugene Joseph (Jl. 26, 1924, S. St. Paul, MN) Assoc. Prof., LS, Univ. of WI, La Crosse, 1961–, Asst. Prof. (Ref. and Pers.), 1957–61; Med. Lib. Consult., Luth. Hosp./Gundersen Clinic, 1958–60; Ref. Libn., Minneapolis Pub. Lib., 1954–57; Asst. Ref. Libn., Ann Arbor Pub. Lib., 1951–54. **Educ.:** Coll. of St. Thomas, 1946–50, BA (Soc. Sci.); Univ. of MN, 1950–51, BSLS; Univ. of MI 1952–54, AMLS. **Orgs.:** ALA. WI LA. Assn. of Univ. of WI Facs. La Crosse Rifle Club. AAUP. **Pubns.:** Various Reviews. **Activities:** 1; 31, 39, 42; 63, 80, 92 **Addr.:** 2003 S. 29th St., La Crosse, WI 54601.

Milligan, Stuart C. (Ag. 8, 1940, Rochester, NY) Circ. Libn. & Micro. Spec., Sibley Msc. Lib., Eastman Sch. of Msc., Univ. of Rochester, 1970–; Asst. Prof. Of Msc., Milligan Coll., 1966–70. **Educ.:** Univ. of Rochester, 1961–64, BM (Msc. Theory), 1964–66, MA (Msc. Theory); State Univ. Coll. at Geneseo, 1973–79, MLS. **Orgs.:** Msc. LA: Ch., Micro. Com. (1980–); AV and Micro. Com. (1976–80). Natl. Micrographics Assn. **Pubns.:** Jt. auth., *Index to audio equipment reviews* (1979, 1980); "Music and other performing arts serials available in microform and reprint editions" *Notes;* (D. 1980). **Activities:** 1; 22, 33, 40; 55, 56, 61 **Addr.:** Sibley Music Library, Eastman School of Music, Rochester, NY 14604.

Milliken, Ruth Longhenry (Ja. 19, 1920, Brooklyn, NY) Dir., Cocoa Beach Pub. Lib., 1975–; Dir., U.S. Army War Coll. Lib., 1969–74, Chief, Bibgphr., Prcs., Srv. Br., 1951–68; Catlgr., U.S. Armed Forces Staff Coll., 1948–51; Lib., First Army Gov. Island, 1945–48, Chief, Records Sect., 1941–45. **Educ.:** SUNY, New Paltz, 1937–40, (Educ.); SUNY, Geneseo, 1940–41, BSLS; Columbia Univ., 1945–50; (Human.); State Univ., Shippensburg, PA, 1969–72, MSLS. **Orgs.:** ALA. SLA: Secy/Treas, Mil. Libns. Div. (1962–68). FL LA: Ch. Outreach Caucus (1976). US Army War Coll.: ADP Steering Com. (1970). Mil. Libns. Workshops: Org. Com. (1968). **Pubns.:** *Guide to Student Research Elements* (1960–69); *Subject Index to Periodicals Currently Received* (1960–69); video cassettes (1967). **Activities:** 9, 12; 17, 20, 31; 56, 74 **Addr.:** 1605 Minutemen Causeway, Apt 217, Cocoa Beach, FL 32931.

Milliron, Annette M. (Ap. 21, 1947, Tarentum, PA) Dir., Basalt Reg. Lib., 1978–; Dir., Douglas Cnty. Pub. Lib., 1974–76; Dir., Vail Pub. Lib., 1972–73. **Educ.:** Univ. of CO, 1965–69, BA (Eng. Lit); Univ. of Denver, 1970–71, MA (LS). **Orgs.:** CO LA: Ch., Pub. Lib. Div. (1979–81). Mt. Plains LA: Ch., JMRT (1975–77); JMRT Affilates Cncl. at ALA (1975–77); Mt. Plains/CO LA Jt. Conv. com. (1975). **Activities:** 9; 17, 19, 28, 42 **Addr.:** 805 Red Mountain Dr., Glenwood Springs, CO 81601.

Mills, David L. (Mr. 30, 1947, Brooklyn, NY) Asst. Branch Libn., Brooklyn Pub. Lib., 1981–, Adult Srvs. Libn., 1979–81; Adult Srvs. Libn., Paterson Free Pub. Lib., 1977–79; Dir., Bedford Hills Free Lib., 1974–76; Adult Srvs. Libn., John C. Hart Mem. Lib., 1972–74. **Educ.:** St. Andrews Presbyterian Coll., 1965–69, BA (Hist.); Hunter Coll., 1969–70 MA (Soc. Stds.); Rutgers Univ., 1971–72; MLS. **Orgs.:** Westchester LA: Treas. (1976–78). ALA. NY LA. Ridgeview Cong. Church: Deacon (1976–79). Bedford Hills Chamber of Comm.: Secy. (1975–76). **Honors:** Beta Phi Mu, 1972. **Pubns.:** "Running a YA Film Series: the Elation and Frustration of It All," *YA Alt. Nwsltr.* (S. 1976); reviews. **Activities:** 9; 16; 67 **Addr.:** 515 Woodland Hills Rd., White Plains, NY 10603.

Mills, Donald M. (F. 25, 1946, Virden, MB) Chief Libn., West Vancouver Mem. Lib., 1980–; Coord. of Chld. Srvs., Cariboo-Thompson Nicola Lib. Syst., 1975–78; Chief Libn., St. Albert Pub. Lib., 1972–75. **Educ.:** Univ. of Winnipeg, 1964–68; BA (Eng.); Univ. of BC, 1971–72, MLS. **Orgs.:** Can. LA. LA of AB. BC LA. Pac. Northwest LA. Puppeteers of Amer. Union Intl. De La Marionnette. **Activities:** 9; 17, 21, 36; 67 **Addr.:** 2135 Nelson Ave., West Vancouver, BC Canada.

Mills, Douglas E. (Mr. 3, 1922, Portland, OR) Dir., Tech. Srvs., Univ. of MT Lib., 1960–; Ed., Union Cat., CA State Lib., 1956–60; Gifts and Exch. Libn., Agri. Econ. Libn., Univ. of CA, Davis, 1951–56. **Educ.:** San Jose State Coll., 1939–41; Univ. of CA, Berkeley, 1941–43, BA (Hist.), 1945–51, MA (U.S. Hist.), 1950–51, BLS. **Orgs.:** ALA. Pac. NW LA: Ch., Tech. Srvs. Div. (1973–75); PNLA Rep. for MT (1978–80). MT LA: Pres. (1971–72). Exch. Club of Missoula. **Pubns.:** "A new look at recruitment," *CA Libn.* (Jl. 1955) "A photographic recruitment exhibition," *CA Libn.* (Ja. 1956) "Library catalogs: changing dimensions," *MT Libs.* (O. 1963). **Activities:** 1; 15, 17, 46; 57 **Addr.:** 604 E. Central, Missoula, MT 59801.

Mills, Emma Joyce White (F. 17, 1944, Marianna, FL) Asst. Prof., Atlanta Univ., 1973–; Libn., Amer. Sch. in London, Eng., 1971–72; Libn., WI Resrch. and Dev. Ctr., 1969–70; Libn., Plantation HS, Fort Lauderdale, FL, 1966–68; Tchr., Lanier Jr. High, 1964–66. **Educ.:** Spelman Coll., 1960–64, BA (Eng.); Univ. of WI, 1968–69, MA (LS); Emory Univ., 1980–81, Dip. Advnc. Sta. Libnshp. **Orgs.:** ALA: AASL. AALS. GA Assn. of Educ.: Lib./Media Dept., Ex-Officio Bd. Mem. (1975–76); Media Fest. Eval. Com. (1978–79). African Amer. Family Hist. Assn.: Docum. Com. AAUW. **Honors:** Beta Phi Mu, 1969. **Pubns.:** *The Black World in Literature for Children: A Bibliography of Print and Non-Print Materials* (1975, 1976, 1977); "Trends in Using Children's Literature in the Curriculum," GA Assn. of Elem. Sch. Prin. *Qtly.* (Win., 1975). **Activities:** 10, 11; 21, 26; 66 **Addr.:** 3378 Ardley Rd., S.W., Atlanta, GA 30311.

Mills, Jeanne M. (O. 18, 1942, Portland, OR) Cur. of Mss. and Bks., Pilgrim Socty., 1978–; Town Archvst., Scituate (MA), 1974–77; Resrch. Asst., Publicist, Doris Duke Amer. Indian Oral Hist., 1968. **Educ.:** Bucknell Univ., 1960–64, AB (Psy.); Columbia Univ., 1964–65, MA (Educ.); Inst. of Arch. Admin., Natl. Arch., 1974, Cert. **Orgs.:** SAA. New Eng. Archvsts. N. and S. Rivers Watershed Assn. Scituate Env. Effort, Inc. **Pubns.:** "History of Scituate's Libraries," *South Shore News* (1974). **Addr.:** Pilgrim Society, Pilgrim Hall, 75 Court St., Plymouth, MA 02360.

Mills, Jesse Cobb (F. 13, 1921, Morristown, TN) Chief Libn. and Hist., TN Valley Auth., 1969–; Lectr., Grad. Sch. of Lib. and Info. Sci., Univ. of TN, Knoxville, 1972–75, Undergrad. Libn., 1966–69; Asst. Dir. of Libs., Univ. of PA, 1962–66, Dir. of Pub. Srvs., 1959–62. **Educ.:** Harvard Univ., 1938–42, BS (Intl. Law); Univ. of TN, 1946–49, MA (Eng.); Rutgers Univ., 1956–59, MLS; Univ. of PA, 1951–54. **Orgs.:** E. TN LA. SLA: Appalachian Chap., Past Pres. Past Pres. E. TN Hist. Socty: Past Adv. Com. Mem. TN Adv. Cncl. on Libs.: Ch.; Southeastern States Coop. Lib. Survey: Bd. Mem. **Honors:** TN LA Awd., 1981. **Activities:** 1, 4; 15, 17, 19; 65, 69, 82 **Addr.:** 2001 Emoriland Blvd., Knoxville, TN 37917.

Mills, Mary Alice (Je. 29, 1930, Columbia, SC) Dir., Library, Ctrs. for Disease Control, 1966–; Dir., Lib., Walter Reed Army Inst. of Resrch., 1961–66; Chief Libn., Ofc. of the Surgeon Gen., 1956–61; Ref. Libn., Natl. Lib. of Med., 1953. **Educ.:** Univ. of SC, 1947–51, BA (Eng.); Columbia Univ., 1952–53, BSLS. **Orgs.:** Med. LA: Vital Notes Com. (1978–). SLA: Reg. Pres.; Bltn. Ed. (1968–70). GA Hlth. Sci. LA. Atlanta Assn. of Fed. Exec. Exec. Bd. (1980). **Honors:** Phi Beta Kappa, 1951; US Army Med. Dept., Cert. of Achvmt., 1966. **Pubns.:** "The Index Medicus: Why it Works and When It Doesn't," *Bltn. Med. LA* (1966); *Union List of Biomedical Periodicals in the Libraries of WRAIR, WRGH and AFIP* (1965). **Activities:** 4; 17, 24, 25 **Addr.:** CDC Library, Centers for Disease Control, Building 1, Room 4007A, Atlanta, GA 30333.

Mills, Robin K. (Ja. 10, 1947, Chicago, IL) Law Libn., Assoc. Prof. of Law, Univ. of SC, 1976–, Asst. Law Libn., 1973–76; Ref. Libn., IN Univ. Sch. of Law, 1971–73, Circ. Libn., 1970–71. **Educ.:** IN Univ., 1965–69, AB (Comp. Lit.), 1969–70, MLS; Univ. of SC, 1973–76, JD (Law). **Orgs.:** AALL: Rcrt. Com. (Ch., 1978, 1979); Southeast. Chapt., VP/Pres.-Elect (1978–80). SC

Special Subjects/Services: 50. Adult educ.; 51. Advert./Mktg.; 52. Aerosp.; 53. Agric.; 54. Area std.; 55. Arts/Hum.; 56. Autom.; 57. Bibl./Prtg.; 58. Bio. sci.; 59. Bus./Fin.; 60. Chem.; 61. Copyrt.; 62. Documtn.; 63. Educ.; 64. Engin.; 65. Env.; 66. Eth. grps.; 67. Film; 68. Food/Nutr.; 69. Geneal.; 70. Geo.; 71. Geol.; 72. Handcpd.; 73. Hist.; 74. Int. frdm.; 75. Info. sci.; 76. Insr.; 77. Law; 78. Legis.; 79. Math./Comp. sci.; 80. Med.; 81. Metals; 82. Nat. resrcs.; 83. Newsp.; 84. Nuc. sci.; 85. Oral hist.; 86. Petr./Energy; 87. Pharm.; 88. Phys./Astr./Math.; 89. Readg.; 90. Relig.; 91. Sci./Tech.; 92. Soc. sci.; 93. Telecom.; 94. Transp.; 95. (other).

LA: Lib. Admin. Sect. (Ch., 1979). Assn. of Amer. Law Schs.: Sect. on Legal Resrch. & Writing (Secy., 1978. SC Bar Assn. Amer. Bar Assn. **Honors:** Phi Beta Kappa, 1969; Beta Phi Mu, 1970. **Pubns.:** Jt. auth., *South Carolina Legal Research Handbook* , (1976); "Legal Research Instruction in Law Schools," *Law Lib. Jnl.* (Ag. 1977); jt. auth., "Minorities Employed in Law Libraries," *Law Lib. Jnl.* (My. 1978); "Reference Service vs. Legal Advice," *Law Lib. Jnl.* (Spr. 1979). **Activities:** 1, 12; 17, 26; 77 **Addr.:** Coleman Karesh Law Library, University of South Carolina, Law Center, Columbia, SC 29208.

Mills, William R. (Je. 4, 1950, Brooklyn, NY) Tech. Srvs. Libn., Paul, Weiss, Rifkind, Wharton and Garrison, 1980–81; Head Libn., Willkie Farr and Gallagher, 1975–79, Asst. Libn., 1971–75. **Educ.:** SUNY, Stony Brook, 1967–71, BS (Math.); Columbia Univ., 1975–78, MSLS hons; Fordham Univ., Sch. of Law, 1979–82, JD. **Orgs.:** Law LA of Grt. NY: Bd. of Dirs. (1977–78). AALL. **Honors:** Beta Phi Mu. **Activities:** 5, 12; 17, 39, 41; 59, 77, 78 **Addr.:** 161 Warren St., Brooklyn, NY 11201.

Mills-Fischer, Shirley C. (Ja. 19, 1936 Shelbyville, TX) Exec. Dir., PLA, ALA, 1978–; Dir., Miracle Valley Reg. Lib. Syst., Moundsville, WV, 1974–78; Asst. Libn., Raleigh Cnty. Pub. Lib., Beckley, WV, 1973–74; Lib. Asst., Colburn Lib., Dvnty. Sch. of Kenyon Coll., Gambier, OH, 1964–66. **Educ.:** LA State Univ., 1971, BS (Soc. Sci.), 1971–72, MSLS. **Orgs.:** ALA: Mem. Com. (1975–77); Dallas Conf. Prog. Com. (1978); ASLA, Mem. Promo. Com. (Ch., 1976–78); JMRT, Com. on Governance (Ch., 1974–76). SELA: *Southeast. Libs.* Ed. Staff (1975–77). *WV Libraries* - Ed. (1975–77). WV Gvr.'s Conf. on Lib. and Info. Srvs. Adv. Com. (1978). Various other orgs. **Honors:** Beta Phi Mu. **Pubns.:** Managing Ed., *Pub. Libs.* **Activities:** 3, 9; 17, 24, 49-Assn. mgt. **Addr.:** Public Library Association, 50 East Huron St., Chicago, IL 60611.

Milner, Linda D. (O. 8, 1948, Kosciusko, MS) Head of Ext. Srvs., Mid–MS Reg. Lib. Syst., 1977–, Head of Col. Devel., 1977, Attala Cnty. Libn., 1975–76, Bkmobile. Libn., 1974. **Educ.:** MS State Univ., 1971–74, BS (LS); Univ. of AL, 1976, MA (LS). **Orgs.:** ALA. MS LA: Lib. Instr. RT (1980–); Nat'l. Lib. Week (Strg. Com., 1982). Kosciusko Bus. and Prof. Womens Club. **Honors:** MS LA, Best Reg. Effort, Natl. Lib. Week Awd., 1978 and 1980. **Activities:** 9; 17, 27, 31; 63, 72 **Addr.:** 201 South Huntington St., Kosciusko, MS 39090.

Milo, Albert J. (S. 9, 1951, San Jose, CA) Chicano Resrc. Ctr. Coord., CA State Univ., Fullerton, 1980–; Book Sel. Coord., Adult Srvs. Dept., Anaheim Pub. Lib., 1977–79; Ref. Libn., Info. Ctr., Chicago Pub. Lib., 1975–77. **Educ.:** Stanford Univ., 1969–73, AB (Latin Amer. Std.); Univ. of MI, 1974–75, AMLS. **Orgs.:** ALA: RASD, Ch., Com. on Lib. Srv. to the Spanish-Speaking (1979). CA LA. REFORMA: Pres., Orange Cnty. Chap. (1980–81). CA Master Plan for Libs.: Steering Com. (1980–82). Concilio of Orange Cnty.: Brd. (1980–81). **Activities:** 1; 39; 66, 92 **Addr.:** 2900 Madison Ave., B-37, Fullerton, CA 92631.

Milstead, Agnes (McDow) (Jl. 23, 1915, Covington, TN) Asst. Prof. Emeritus, 1981–; Asst. Prof. of LS, Univ. of WY, 1966–81; Sch. Libn., Ouachita Parish, LA, 1960–66; Tchr., WY schs., 1953–60. **Educ.:** Univ. of WY, 1950–54, BA (Elem. Educ.); NE LA State Univ., 1963, (Educ.); LA State Univ., 1962–66, MSLS; Other courses. **Orgs.:** LA Assn. of Sch. Libns.: Pres. (1965). WY Assn. of Sch. Libns.: Pres. (1970). ALA: AASL, Reg. Dir. (1976–79); Awds. Com. (1979–81). Mt. Plains LA: Sch. & Chld. Sect. (Pres. 1971–72). Phi Kappa Phi. Delta Kappa Gamma: Pres. (1975–77). Kappa Delta Pi. **Honors:** Repub. of the Philippines, Hon. Cit., 1979; Beta Phi Mu. **Pubns.:** Various articles. **Activities:** 11; 26, 31 **Addr.:** 321 S. 13th St., Laramie, WY 82070.

Milstead, Jessica L. (Je. 4, 1939, Bryans Road, MD) Mgr., Indexing Dept., Resrch. Pubns., Inc., 1979–; Assoc. Prof., Div. of Lib. and Info. Sci., St. John's Univ., 1974–79; Visit. Assoc. Prof., Grad. Sch. of Lib. and Info. Sci., Univ. of CA, Los Angeles, 1978; Asst. Prof., LS Dept., Queens Coll., 1972–74; Asst. Prof., Sch. of Lib. Srv., Columbia Univ., 1969–72. **Educ.:** East. Nazarene Coll., 1956–60, AB (Soc. Sci.); Columbia Univ., 1964–65, MS (Lib. Srv.), 1966–69, DLS. **Orgs.:** ALA: Subj. Analysis Com. (1977–81). ASIS: Liaison Rep. (1975–79); Educ. Com. (1978–80); Intl. Rel. Com. (1978–80). Amer. Socty. of Indxrs.: Secy. (1979–81). SLA. **Pubns.:** Ed., *Cumulative Index to the Annual Review of Information Science and Technology* Volumes 1–10 (1976); jt. ed., *Annual Review of Information Science and Technology* Volumes 9 and 10 (1974–75); *Subject Analysis* (1969); jt. auth., *Computer Filing of Index, Bibliographic and Catalog Entries* (1967); "Treatment of People and Peoples in Subject Analysis," *Lib. Resrcs. & Tech. Srvs.* (1979). **Activities:** 6; 17, 30, 37; 56, 83 **Addr.:** 875 Marion Rd., Cheshire, CT 06410.

Mimnaugh, Ellen Nulty (Jl. 31, 1940, Montclair, NJ) Consult. and Fndr., Info. Consult., Inc., 1975–; Supvsr., User Srvs., Douglas Aircraft Co., 1968–70; Info. Chem., Natl. Lead Co., Titanium Div., 1967; Lit. Chem., Shell Chem. Co., 1962–67. **Educ.:** Rosemont Coll., 1958–62, BA (Chem.); Columbia Univ., 1963–66, MS (LS). **Orgs.:** SLA: Ctrl. OH Mem. Ch. (1980–81); NJ Bltn. Ed. (1977–78). ASIS: Columbus Chap. Amer. Chem. Socty.: Div. of Chem. Info. **Pubns.:** *Thesaurus of Air Pollution Terms* (1976). **Activities:** 4, 12; 24, 49-Info. Retrieval; 52, 60, 64, 81 **Addr.:** Information Consulting, Inc., 2584 Coventry Rd., Upper Arlington, OH 43221.

Mims, Dorothy H. (Mr. 19, 1922, Memphis, TN) Libn. for Spec. Coll., Med. Coll. of GA Lib., 1976–; Ref. Libn., Med. Coll. of GA, 1963–76; Asst. Circ. Libn., McKissick Lib., U. of SC, 1946. **Educ.:** Winthrop Coll., 1940–44, BA (Eng.); Univ. of NC, 1945–46, BS LS; Med. LA Cert. 1975. **Orgs.:** Med. LA. SC LA. GA Hlth. Sci. LA. Aiken-Bamberg-Barnwell-Edgefield Reg. Lib. Bd.: Vice-Ch. (1980–). Edgefield Cnty Lib. Bd.: Ch. (1978–). Amer. Assn. for the Hist. of Med. **Pubns.:** "MLA Certification by Examination; Survey of Participants," *Bltn. Med. LA* (Ap. 1979); "The Sydenstricker Wing- Tribute to a Giant," *MCG Today* (Win. 1976); "Dr. Richard Torpin Remembered," (Spr. 1976). **Activities:** 1, 12; 23, 39, 45; 80 **Addr.:** Library, Medical College of Georgia, Augusta, GA 30912.

Mims, Julian L. (Jl. 20, 1941, Edgefield, SC) Info. Mgt. Consult., Data Mgt., 1977–; Asst. Dir. for Lcl. Recs., SC Dept. of Arch. and Hist., 1968–79; Adj. Prof., Univ. of SC, 1973–. **Educ.:** Univ. of SC, 1969, MA (Hist.); Amer. Univ./Natl. Arch., 1970, Cert. in Arch. Admin. **Orgs.:** Assn. of Rec. Mgrs. and Admins.: VP (1975–79). SAA: State and Lcl. Rec. Com.; Rec. Mgt. Com.; Micro. Com.; Prog. Com. Natl. Assn. of State Arch. and Recs. Admin. **Honors:** Assn. of Rec. Mgrs. and Admins., Cert. of Apprec., 1977, 1979; Assn. of Recs. Mgrs. and Admins., Awd. of Merit, 1980; Assn. of Recs. Mgrs. and Admins., SC Chap., Mem. of The Yr., 1975. **Activities:** 2, 12; 24, 33, 38; 56, 62, 75 **Addr.:** Data Management, Box 11,212, Columbia, SC 29211.

Mims, Katherine A. (Ja. 16, 1934, Charleston, SC) Libn., Springdale Elem. Sch., 1967–; Lib. Supvsr., Brookland Cayce Schs., 1968; Libn., Dreher HS, 1965–67; Libn., Richland Cnty. Pub. Lib., 1961; Libn., Alcorn Mid. Sch., 1961–62; Libn., Anderson Coll., 1958–60; Libn., Watkins Elem. Sch., 1956–58. **Educ.:** Columbia Coll., 1952–56, BA (LS); Univ. of NC, 1958, (LS); Clemson Univ., 1959, (Couns.); Univ. of SC, 1966–79, (Educ., LS). **Orgs.:** ALA:AASL. SC LA. SC Assn. of Sch. Libns.: Conv. Local Arrange. (Ch. 1980); Guidelines Com. for Disting. Lib. Srvs. Awd. (Ch. 1979); Spr. Conf. Com. (1971). Assn. Educ. Comm. Tech. of SC. Other orgs. Natl. Educ. Assn. PTA. Daughters of Amer. Revolution: Univ. SC Chap., First Vice-Regent (1979–82). Delta Kappa Gamma: Rsrch. Com. (Ch. 1978–80). Other orgs. **Honors:** Springdale Elem. Sch. PTA, Hon. Life Mem., 1979. **Activities:** 10; 15, 17, 21 **Addr.:** 1148 Baywater Dr., West Columbia, SC 29169.

Mims, Susan (Ag. 14, 1951, Laredo, TX) Law Libn., Bracewell and Patterson, 1978–; Law Libn., Hutcheson and Grundy, 1976–78. **Educ.:** Univ. of Houston, 1969–73, BA (Eng.); Univ. of TX, 1975–76, MLS. **Orgs.:** AALL. Southwest. Assn. of Law Libs.: Pvt. Law Libs. Com. (Ch., 1979–80). Houston Area Law Libs. AAUW. **Addr.:** Bracewell and Patterson, 2900 South Tower, Pennzoil Pl., Houston, TX 77002.

Minadakis, Nicholas J. (Ja. 22, 1924, Chios, Greece) Lib. Dir., Chelsea Pub. Lib., 1968–; Lib. Dir., Hellenic Coll., 1964–67. **Educ.:** Boston Univ., 1958–62, BA (Econ.); Simmons Coll., 1962–64, MS (LS). **Orgs.:** ALA. New Eng. LA. MA LA. Grt. Boston Pub. Lib. Admin. Assn. Rotary Club of Chelsea, MA.: Pres. (1979–80). Atlantic Bank of Chelsea and Revere: Trustee. The Helicon Socty. Pan Creatan Assn. of Amer. **Pubns.:** Reviews. **Activities:** 2, 9; 17, 36, 45; 55, 66, 85 **Addr.:** 8 St. Paul St., Cambridge, MA 02139.

Minckler, Jane T. (D. 23, 1930, St. Louis, MO) Resrch. Libn., Ethicon, Inc., 1980–; Asst. Resrch. Libn., 1978–80; Resrch. Asst., Northwest. Univ., Chem. Dept., 1954–55; Chem., G.D. Searle, Inc., 1952–53. **Educ.:** South. IL Univ., 1948–51, BA (Chem.); Rutgers Univ., 1975–77, MLS. **Orgs.:** SLA: NJ Chap., Prog. Com. (1978–79). ALA. ASIS. **Honors:** Beta Phi Mu, 1978. **Activities:** 12; 17; 58, 60, 80 **Addr.:** Scientific Information Services—Ethicon, Inc., Somerville, NJ 08876.

Mindeman, George Andrew (Ap. 26, 1954, Iowa City, IA) Cat. Libn., Reformed Theological Semy.; 1981–; Tech. Srvs. Libn., Hist. Fndn. of the Presby. and Reformed Churches, 1978–81. **Educ.:** Wheaton Coll., 1972–76, BA (Hist.); Univ. of Chicago, 1976–77, MA (US Hist.); Univ. of WA, 1977–78, MLS. **Orgs.:** ATLA. SAA. N. Amer. Socty. for Sport Hist. **Honors:** Beta Phi Mu. **Activities:** 2, 12; 15, 20, 46; 90 **Addr.:** Library, Reformed Theological Seminary, 5422 Clinton Blvd., Jackson, MS 39209.

Minett, E. Everet (F. 23, 1918, Toronto, ON) Dir., UTLAS, 1971–; Mgr., Resrch. and Dev., Xerox Corp., 1962–71; Chief Engin., Cmrcl. Comp., Univac Div., 1958–62; Mgr., AWS Prog. Ofc., RCA, 1948–58; Asst. to Dir. Resrch., Oak Ridge Natl. Lab., 1946–48. **Educ.:** Univ. Toronto, 1934–38, BA with Honors (Math, Chem.); MA Inst. of Tech., 1938–41, (Chem.); Harvard Bus. Sch., Short Course, 1969. **Orgs.:** ALA. IEEE: Philadelphia Sect., Ch. (1960–62). AFIPS: Natl. Comp. Conf., 1962, (V. Ch.). Xerox Ctr. Hlth. Care Resrch.: Secy., Treas. (1969–74). Einstein Com. Atomic Sci.: Actg. Exec. Dir. (1947–48). **Honors:** U.S. Army, Corp. Engin., Manhattan Proj., Silver Medal, 1946. **Pubns.:** Jt. Auth. "The RCA Bizmac Computer System," *Proc. West. Jt. Comp. Conf* (1956). **Activities:** 6; 34; 56, 57, 93 **Addr.:** UTLAS, Rm. 8003, 130 St. George St., Toronto, ON M5S 1A5 Canada.

Miniter, John Joseph (Je. 9, 1924, Hamden, CT) Assoc. Prof. LS, TX Woman's Univ., 1964–; Engin. Libn., Collins Radio Co., 1962–64; Mgr., Info. Srvs., Alpha Corp., 1960–62; Assoc. Libn., U.S.N. Underwater Sound Lab., 1956–60. **Educ.:** Univ. of CT, 1946–50, BA (Lang.); Univ. of MA, 1951–52, MA (Lang.); Columbia Univ., 1955–56, MLS; North TX State Univ., 1972–75, PhD (Educ.); Alliance Francaise (Paris), 1953–54, Cert. **Orgs.:** AALS. ALA. TX LA. SLA. **Honors:** Beta Phi Mu, Awd. for Good Tchg., 1972. **Pubns.:** Jt. Ed., *Music Therapy Index* (1976); Jt. Ed., *Music Psychology Index* (1978). **Activities:** 11, 12; 17, 24, 25, 26; 56 **Addr.:** 525 Mimosa Dr., Denton, TX 76201.

Mink, James Vantine (Je. 3, 1923, Wisconsin Rapids, WI) Lectr., Grad. Sch., Lib. and Info. Sci., Univ. Archvst., Head, Dept. of Spec. Cols., Univ. Resrch Lib., Univ. of CA, Los Angeles, 1972–, Dir., Oral Hist. Prog., Univ. Archvst., 1965–72, Asst. Head and Univ. Archvst., Dept. of Spec. Cols., 1952–65; Asst. to Head Catlgr., Mss. Div., Univ. of CA, Berkeley, 1950–51. **Educ.:** Occidental Coll., 1941–43 (Chem.); Univ. of CA, Los Angeles, 1945–46, BA (Hist.), 1946–49, MA (Hist.); Univ. of CA, Berkeley, 1951–52, BLS; American Univ., 1953 (Cert. Arch. Admin.). **Orgs.:** SAA: Coll. and Univ. Arch. Com. (1967–68); Com. on Oral Hist. (1970–79); Secur. Consult. (1976–). Libns. Assn. of Univ. of CA: Univ. of CA, Los Angeles Div. (Pres., 1968–69). Hist. Socty. of South. CA: Bd. of Dir. (1978–82). Oceanic Navigation Resrch. Socty. Oral Hist. Assn: Fndn. Ch. (1960–67); Cncl. (1968–69); Ed, OHA Nwsltr., (1970–72). **Honors:** Pi Gamma Mu, 1946; Phi Alpha Theta, 1950. **Pubns.:** Jt. Ed., *Oral Hist at Arrowhead* (1967); jt. auth., *Papers of Gen. William Starke Roseceans* (1961); *Guide to the Dept. of Spec. Cols.* (1958); "The UCLA Story," *UCLA Alum. Mag.* (S. 1961); "Making of A Southwestern Novel," *Mss.* (Sum. 1957). **Activities:** 1, 11; 17, 26, 45; 63, 85, 92 **Addr.:** Dept. of Special Collections, University Research Library, University of California, Los Angeles, CA 90024.

Minkel, Vera (Prague, Czechoslovakia) Mgr., Lib. Srvs., Honeywell Info. Systs., 1970–; Tech. Libn., Gen. Electric Co., 1959–69. **Educ.:** Charles Univ., BA (Frgn. Langs.). **Orgs.:** ASIS. SLA. Assn. for Comp. Mach. Phoenix Pub. Lib. **Pubns.:** *Data Terminal and Your Library* (1972). **Activities:** 12; 17, 20, 22; 56, 93 **Addr.:** Honeywell Information System, Library B–120, P.O. Box 6000, Phoenix, AZ 85005.

Minnich, Nancy P. (F. 5, 1927, Norristown, PA) Lib. Dir., Tower Hill Sch., 1969–; Elem. Libn., Haverford Sch., 1966–69; Tchr., Upper Darby, PA, 1949–52. **Educ.:** Ursinus Coll., 1945–49, BA (Liberal Arts); Drexel Univ., 1962–65, MS (LS); Temple Univ., 1968–71, MS (Educ. Media). **Orgs.:** DE Sch. Lib. Media Assn.: Pres. (1978–79). YASD, TV Com. (1980–82). ALA: AASL, Sch. Lib. Media Srvs. to Chld. with Special Needs Com.; By-laws Com. AECT: Nom. & Plng. Com. (1979–80). DE LA. Other orgs. Leag. of Women Voters. AAUW. **Pubns.:** "Microforms & Secondary Schools," *Sch. Lib. Jnl.* (Ap. 1972). **Activities:** 10; 17, 32, 48; 63, 67, 89 **Addr.:** Tower Hill School, 2813 W. 17th St., Wilmington, DE 19806.

Minnick, Nelle F(rances) (S. 24, 1920, Spokane, WA) Asst. Cnty. Libn., Fresno Cnty. Free Lib., 1969–, Coord. of Branch Oper., 1961–69, Dir. of Branch Srvs., 1959–61, Adult Srvs. Libn., Ext. Dept., 1950–59; Jr. Libn, CA Sect., CA State Lib., 1948–50; First Asst., West. Hist. Dept., Denver Pub. Lib., 1946–48, Asst., 1943–45, Asst., Circ. Dept., 1942–1943. **Educ.:** Univ. of NM, 1937–41, BA (Hist.); Univ. of Denver, 1941–42, BS in LS; Univ. of Chicago, 1945–46, MA (LS). **Orgs.:** ALA: Mem. Promotion Taskforce (1971–73). CA LA: Pres., Yosemite Dist. (1968). Ctrl. Sierra Lib. & Media Assn. Fresno Cnty. Hist. Socty. Amer. Socty. for Pub. Admin. AAUW. CA Hist. Socty. **Activities:** 9; 16, 17, 19, 27; 50 **Addr.:** 2420 Mariposa St., Fresno, CA 92721.

Minor, Barbara B. (Ja. 24, 1927, Hampton, VA) Pubns. Coord., ERIC Clearinghouse on Info. Resrcs., 1977–; Resrch. Anal., Chase Archit. Assoc., 1976; Admin. Asst., - Sch. of Info. Std., Syracuse Univ., 1975–76; Tchr. of Fr., Canandaigua Jr. Acad., 1968–74. **Educ.:** Birmingham-South. Coll., 1943–47, BA (Eng.); Middlebury Coll., 1946–50, MA (Fr.); Syracuse Univ., 1973–75, MLS; Certs., Sorbonne 1947–48, (Fr.). **Orgs.:** ALA. **Honors:** Phi Beta Kappa, Phi Sigma Iota, 1946–47. **Pubns.:** Ed., "Alternative Careers in Information/Library Services: Summary of Proceedings of a Workshop," ERIC (1977); Ed., "Proceedings of the Information Broker/Free Lance Librarian–New Careers–New Library Services Workshop," ERIC (1976); Jt. auth., "Development and coordination of library services to state government", *Lib. Trends* (Fall 1978); Jt. auth., "Information: How to cope with the deluge," *Educ. Broadcasting Intl.* (1979); "Wie en wat is ERIC," *Registratie* (Mr. 1979); Other ERIC pubns. **Activities:** 12; 30, 37, 39; 56, 75, 95-Educ. Tech. **Addr.:** 1 Centennial Dr., #2-B, Syracuse, NY 13207.

Minsker, Eliot A. Pres. & Pub., Knowledge Indus. Pubns., Inc., 1967–. **Educ.:** Cornell Univ., BS (Mech. Eng.); Harvard Univ., MBA. **Orgs.:** ASIS. **Activities:** 14-Pub; 17 **Addr.:** Knowledge Industry, Publications, Inc., 2 Corporate Park Dr., White Plains, NY 10604.

Minster, Bernadette F. (Ag. 24, 1922, Pontiac, MI) Head Libn., Ext. Dept., Waukegan Pub. Lib., 1975–; Branch Libn., Shegoygan Pub. Lib., 1948–49; Ref. Libn., Waukegan Pub. Lib., 1945–48. **Educ.:** Lake Forest Coll., 1941–45, BA (Eng.); Univ. of WI, 1946–47, BLS. **Orgs.:** ALA. IL LA. **Activities:** 9; 27 **Addr.:** Waukegan Public Library, 128 N. County St., Waukegan, IL 60085.

Minster, Johanna Willemina (Ag. 6, 1923, Gendringen, The Netherlands) Slide Cur., Instr. Resrc. Ctr., LA State Univ., 1966–; Asst. Mgr. of Craft Shop, LA State Univ., 1964–66. **Educ.:** LA State Univ., 1975, BA (Paint.), 1979, MA (Educ. Media). **Orgs.:** Art Lib. Socty. of N. Amer.: Stan. Com. Mid Amer. Coll. Art Assn. LA Assn. for Educ. Comm. & Tech.: Srvs. Com. Nat. Conv. Alpha Sigma Lambda: Pres. (1968). **Pubns.:** Slide Classification System (1976). **Activities:** 1, 10; 20, 32; 55, 63 **Addr.:** Route I, Box 110, Gonzales, LA 70737.

Minton, James O. (S. 2, 1942, Knoxville, TN) Map Libn., Univ. of Mi., 1974–; Univ. of KY, 1972–74; Asst. Map Libn., Geo. Dept, Univ. of TN, 1970–72; Topographic Computing Spec., U.S. Air Force, 1961–65. **Educ.:** Univ. of TN, Knoxville, 1965–68, BS (Geo.), 1969–71, MS (Geo.), 1971–72, MSLS; Ft. Belvoir, VA, 1961, Dipl. Mapping. **Orgs.:** SLA: Geo. and Map. Div. Western Assn. of Map Libs. Map Online Users Grp. ALA. Assn. of Amer. Geo. Amer. Cong. on Surveying & Map. **Pubns.:** "Mill Map Cataloging: Past & Present," *The Libn.* (1977); "OCLC Map Cataloging: An Emerging Standard Practice," *SLA* (S. 1978). **Activities:** 1, 12; 29, 39, 45; 70, 82, 92 **Addr.:** Map Room, 825 Hatcher Graduate Library, The University of Michigan, Ann Arbor, MI 48109.

Mintz, Anne P. (O. 11, 1948, New York, NY) Libn., Lazard Freres and Co., 1972–; Asst. Libn., Postgrad. Ctr. for Mental Hlth., 1971–72. **Educ.:** Univ. of MA, 1966–70, BA (Eng.); Rutgers Univ., 1970–71, MLS. **Orgs.:** Med. LA. SLA: NY Chap., Cont. Educ. (Ch., 1979–80), Bus. and Fin. Div., Prog. Com. (1977–78); Pubn. Com., 1981–82. Jewish Women's Resrc. Ctr.: Adv. Bd. (1978–80). **Pubns.:** Fellow, *Sh'ma Magazine* (1978–79); Various Reviews. **Activities:** 12; 15, 17, 39; 59, 62 **Addr.:** Library, Lazard Freres & Co., One Rockefeller Plz., New York, NY 10020.

Mintz, Edith Bornstein (Je. 22, 1926, Pittsfield, MA) Head Libn., Mgt. Lib., Arthur D. Little, Inc, 1975–, Catlgr., 1968–75; Ref. Libn., Belmont Meml. Lib., 1965–68; Asst. Ref. Libn., Boston Univ. Sch. of Educ., 1964–65. **Educ.:** Boston Univ., 1943–47, BS (Educ.), 1965–70, MEd (Sch. Lib.); Simons Coll., 1973–75, MLS, Babson Coll. Mgt. Prog. for Women, 1979, Cert. **Orgs.:** SLA: Boston Chap., Ed., News Bltn. (1978–79). New Eng. LA. MA LA. **Activities:** 12; 17, 24; 51, 56, 59 **Addr.:** 58 Lincoln St., Belmont, MA 02178.

Mintz, Elaine P. (N. 22, 1927, Pittsfield, MA) Law Libn., Bergson, Borkland, Margolis & Adler, 1973–. **Educ.:** Montgomery Coll., 1971, AA; Univ. of MD, 1973, BA (Eng.), 1974, MLS. **Orgs.:** Law Libns. Socty. of Washington, DC: Arrange. Com. (1976–80); Elec. Com. (1980). AALL. **Honors:** Phi Beta Kappa, 1973; Phi Kappa Phi, 1974. **Activities:** 12; 15, 17, 20; 59, 77 **Addr.:** Bergson, Borkland, Margolis & Adler, 11 Dupont Cir., N.W., Washington, DC 20036.

Minudri, Regina U. (My. 9, 1937, San Francisco, CA) Dir. of Lib. Srvs., Berkeley Pub. Lib., 1977–; Asst. Cnty. Libn., Alameda Cnty. Lib., 1972–77; Proj. Coord., Fed. YA Proj., 1968–71; Reg. Libn., Santa Clara Cnty. Lib., 1962–68; Ref. Libn., Menlo Park (CA) Pub. Lib., 1959–62; Lect., Grad. Sch. of Lib. and Info. Sci., Univ. of CA, Berkeley, 1978–. **Educ.:** San Francisco Coll. for Women, 1954–58, BA (Eng.); Univ. of CA, Berkeley, 1958–59, MLS. **Orgs.:** ALA: Exec. Bd. (1981–85); Cncl. (1980–85); Com. on Accred. (1980–81); YASD, Bd. of Dir. (1971–74). CA LA: Pres. (1981); Cncl. (1969–72; 1975–79, 1980–82). Bay Area YA Libns. Leag. of Women Voters of Berkeley. Soroptomist Int. of Berkeley. Berkeley Hospice: Bd. of Dir. (1981–). **Honors:** ALA, Grolier Awd., 1974. **Pubns.:** Jt. Auth., *Getting It Together* (1970); "Irresistible Forces & Immovable Objects," *Sch. Lib. Jnl.* (D. 1979); "Objective Management," *Sch. Lib. Jnl.* (Mr. 1978); Ed., Adult Books for Young Adults Column, *Sch. Lib. Jnl.* (1967–75); jt. auth., "Hip Pocket Books," *Library Journal* (N. 15, 1973); other articles. **Activities:** 9; 17, 24, 48; 74 **Addr.:** Berkeley Public Library, 2090 Kittredge St., Berkeley, CA 94705.

Miranda, Altagracia (N. 23, 19—, San Pedro de Macoris, Dominican Republic) Head, Ref. and Bibl., Law Lib., Univ. of PR, 1980–, Head, Tech. Srvs., 1971–80, Actg. Libn., 1972–73, Head, Cat. Dept., 1967–71, Catlgr., 1966–67; Libn., Payne Whitney Clinic, NY Hosp. Conell Med. Ctr., 1951–66; Libn., Sch. of Med., Univ. of PR, 1950–51. **Educ.:** Univ. of PR, 1946, BS (Bio.); Syracuse Univ., 1950, MSLS. **Orgs.:** AALL. SALALM. Assn. de Bibliotecas de Derecho de PR: Treas. (1980); Pres. (1981–82). SBPR: Schol. Com. (Ch., 1978–80); VP (1974); Mem. Com. (Ch., 1968); Various Coms. **Pubns.:** *Fuentes Puertorriqueñas en el Área de las Ciencias Sociales* (1975); "Bibliografía de Tesis Sometidas para el Grado de Bachiller en Derecho...," *Revista Juridica* (1975); Bibl. Ed., *Jnl. of the Hist. of the Behavioral Scis.* (1966). **Activities:** 1; 39, 46; 77 **Addr.:** University of Puerto Rico, Law Library–School of Law, San Juan, PR 00931.

Miranda, Robert N. (Jl. 1, 1934, Brooklyn, NY) Sr. VP, Pergamon Press Inc, 1965–. **Educ.:** SUNY, Farmingdale, 1959–67, AA (Bus. Mgt., Acctg.). **Orgs.:** Med. LA. Natl. Micro. Assn. SLA. ALA. Fulfillment Mgt. Assn. Socty. of Schol. Publshg. **Activities:** 6; 24, 33, 44; 61 **Addr.:** Pergamon Press Inc, Fairview Park, Elmsford, NY 10523.

Miranda, Salvador (O. 18, 1939, Havana, Cuba) Latin Amer. Biblgphr., Univ. of FL Libs., 1976–. **Educ.:** Biscayne Coll., 1970–72, BA (Amer. Hist., Phil.); Villanova Univ., 1972–74, MA (Hist.); FL State Univ., 1974–76, MLS. **Orgs.:** SALALM: Coop. with the Org. of Amer. States (1977–); Acq. (1979–); Policy, Resrch. and Investigation Com. (1980). FL LA. Alachua Lib. Leag.: Treas. (1977–78). **Honors:** Beta Phi Mu. **Activities:** 1; 15, 17, 46; 54, 57, 92 **Addr.:** P.O. Box 14211, University Station, Gainesville, FL 32604.

Mirsky, Phyllis Simon (D. 18, 1940, Petach Tikva, Israel) Head, Ref. Sect., Natl. Lib. of Med., 1979–; Assoc. Dir., Pac. SW Reg. Med. Lib. Srv., Biomedical Lib., UCLA, 1973–79, Asst. Dir., 1971–73, Head, Consult. Trng. (PSR MLS), 1969–71, Ref. Libn., 1965–69; Hosp. Libn., Hosp. and Inst. Div., Cleveland Pub. Lib., 1963–64. **Educ.:** OH State Univ., 1959–62, BS (Soc. Welfare); Univ. of MI, 1964–65, AMLS; Columbia Univ. 1962–63, (Soc. Work). **Orgs.:** Med. LA: Bd. of Dirs. (1977–80); Cont. Ed. Com. (Ch. 1976–77); 1982 Prog. Com. (Co-ch., 1979–82); Ad Hoc Com. on WHCOLIS (1978–79); Consult. Ed. *MLA Bltn.* (1974–77). MD Assn. of Hlth. Sci. Libns. Med. Lib. Grp. of South. CA and AZ: Pres. (1972–73). UCLA - Assn. of Fac./Acad. Women: Exec. Cncl. (1977–79); Hosplty. Ch. (1976–77); Mem. Ch. (1973–75). Libns. Assn. of the Univ. of CA: Nom. Com. (Ch., 1978), Del., Statewide Asm. (1975, 1978); LA Div., Pres. (1973). **Pubns.:** *Directory of Health Science Libraries: Arizona, California, Hawaii, Nevada,* 3rd ed. (1979); "Looking at and Beyond the Looking Glass; A Guest Editorial," *Bltn., Med. LA* (Jl. 1979); Jt. auth., "Evaluation of a Library Program in A Carnegie - Model Area Health Education Center," *Bltn., Med. LA* (AP. 1978); "The Pacific Southwest Regional Medical Library Service," *Natl. Lib. of Med. News* (Je. 1979); Jt. Auth., *Manual for Librarians in Small Hospitals,* 4th ed. (1978). **Activities:** 4, 12; 17, 25, 39; 58, 80, 91 **Addr.:** Reference Section, National Library of Medicine, 8600 Rockville Pike, Bethesda, MD 20209.

Mirth, Karlo J. (Jl. 15, 1917, Otocac, Croatia, Yugoslavia) Mgr., Foster Wheeler Devel. Corp., 1967–, Libn., 1964–67, Dsgn., Engin. Dept., 1956–64; Dsgn., Engin. Dept., Babcock and Wilcox Co., 1952–56. **Educ.:** Univ. of Zagreb, 1936–42, MS (Civil Engin.); Columbia Univ., 1961–62, MS (LS). **Orgs.:** ASIS. SLA: NY Chap., Docum. Grp. Com. (1968–69). Croatian Acad. of Amer.: Pres. (1958–68); Exec. Cncl. (1968–). **Pubns.:** Fndr., publshr. and ed.–in–chief, *Croatia Press* (1947–); Managing ed., *Jnl. of Croatian Stds.,* (1960–). **Activities:** 12; 17; 62, 64, 91 **Addr.:** Research Information Center & Library, Foster Wheeler Development Corporation, 9 Peach Tree Hill Rd., Livingston, NJ 07039.

Mishkoff, Adina (Ag. 13, 1950, Brooklyn, NY) Resrch. Libn., Moran, Stahl & Boyer, 1981–; Corp. Libn., FIND/SVP, 1974–80. **Educ.:** Brooklyn Coll., 1968–72, BA (Eng.); Pratt Inst., 1972–74, MLS. **Orgs.:** SLA: Union list of Serials Com. (1979–81). Assoc. Info. Mgrs. Nation Micro. Assn. NY Jewish Hist. Socty. **Honors:** Beta Phi Mu. **Pubns.:** *Subject Index to Bureau of Census Population Reports* (1979); *Pratt Student Handbook* (Spr. 1973); "Picture Collection at Zionist Archives, NY," *Picturescope* (Fall 1974). **Activities:** 12; 15, 17, 20; 51, 59 **Addr.:** 200 W. 86 St., Apt. 8M, New York, NY 10024.

Miska, John Paul (Ja. 20, 1932, Nyirbéltek, Hungary) Chief Libn. and Area Coord., Alberta Agr. Can., 1972–, Chief Coll. Dev., 1968–72; Catlgr., Forestry and Rural Dev. Ottawa, 1966–67; Head, Engin. Lib., Univ. of MB, 1962–66. **Educ.:** Univ. of Budapest, 1953–56, McMaster Univ., 1957–61; BA (Hist.); Univ. of Toronto, 1961–62; BLS. **Orgs.:** Univ. MB. Lib. Staff Assn.: Pres. (1965–66). Can. LA. Bibl. Soc. Can. Hungarian-Can. Authors' Assn.: Founding Pres. (1968–75). Hungarian Lit. Socty. of Winnipeg: Pres. (1965–66). **Honors:** Gov. Gen. of Can., Queen's Jubilee Medal, 1977; Premier of AB Achievement Awd. for Excellence in Lit., 1978. **Pubns.:** *A magunk portáján/Mending Our Fences: Selected Writings 1963-1973* (1974); *Egy bögre tej/A Mug of Milk: Short Stories* (1968); "Research Station Library," *Feliciter* (F. 1977); "Special Collections in the LRS Library," *Qtly. Bltn.* (1978); "A User's Manual for the Lethbridge Research Station Library" (1979). **Addr.:** Agriculture Canada Research Station, Lethbridge, AB T1J 4B1 Canada.

Missar, Charles Donald (Jl. 16, 1925, Cleveland, OH) Supvsr. Libn., Nat. Inst. of Educ., Educ. Resrch. Lib., 1978–; Head, Educ. Ref. Ctr., Nat. Inst. of Educ., 1973–78, ERIC, Info. Spec., U.S. Off. of Educ., 1966–72; Ref. Spec., Lib. of Congs., 1963–66; Abst., Indexer, Ref. Spec., Def. Docu. Ctr., 1961–63; Supvsr., Ref. Lib., U.S. Navy Bureau of Aeronautics, 1957–61; Serials, Circ., and Ref. Libn., U.S. Weather Bureau Lib., 1956–57. **Educ.:** Sacred Heart Coll., 1943–45; St. Mary Sem., 1945–49; John Carroll Univ., 1950–51, AB (Phil.); Cath. Univ. of Amer., 1954–60, MS LS. **Orgs.:** SLA: Educ. Div. Secy./Treas. (1977–79), Ch.-Elect (1979–80), Ch. (1980–81). ASIS. DC LA: Treas. (1972–74). Cath. Univ. of Amer.: Lib. Sci. Alumni, Pres. (1976–77). Online Mag.: Ed. Adv. Bd. (1976–). **Pubns.:** "Historical Collections of North American Textbooks Identified," *Educ. Libs.* (Win. 1978). **Activities:** 4; 17, 38, 39; 56, 63, 75 **Addr.:** 5617 - 32nd St., N.W., Washington, DC 20015.

Missonis, George Edward (Mr. 11, 1943, Pottsville, PA) Asst. Libn., Gingrich Lib., Albright Coll., 1973–; Asst. Libn., Reading Area Cmnty. Coll., 1971–73. **Educ.:** PA State Univ., 1961–65, BS (Sec. Educ.); Drexel Univ., 1969–71, MS (LS). **Orgs.:** PA LA. ASIS. **Pubns.:** "Electronic Calculators Popular at Albright College Library," *PLA Bltn.* (Mr. 1974); *Art as Autobiography* vid. (1981). **Activities:** 1; 32 **Addr.:** 1429 Mulberry St., Reading, PA 19604.

Mistrik, Marion G. (S. 3, 1936, Montreal, PQ) Libn., Air Transport Assn. of Amer., 1975; Asst. Libn., Amer. Inst. of Archit., 1973–75; Chld. Libn., DC Pub. Lib., 1960–63; Asst. Libn., Bank of Montreal, 1958–59. **Educ.:** Marianopolis Coll., 1954–57, BA (Eng.); McGill Univ., 1957–58, BLS. **Orgs.:** SLA: Transp. Resrch. Info. Systs. Netwk. Coord. Com. (1979–81). Law Libns. Socty. of Washington, DC: Arrange. Com. (1979–82). **Pubns.:** Contrib., *Current Techniques in Architectural Practice* (1976). **Activities:** 12; 17, 20, 39; 77, 94 **Addr.:** Air Transport Association of America Library, 1709 New York Ave., NW, Washington, DC 20006.

Mitchell, Betty Jo (My. 2, 1931, Coin, IA) Assoc. Dir. of Libs., CA State Univ., Northridge, 1972–, Actg. Assoc. Dir. of Libs., 1971–72, Asst. Coll. Libn., 1969–71, Asst. Acq. Libn., 1967–69. **Educ.:** SW MO State, 1949–52, AB (Geog. Sci & Soclgy.); Univ. of South. CA, 1966–67, MSLS, Amer. Mgt. Assn., 1981, Cert. in Bus. Mgt. **Orgs.:** ALA: Mem. Com., Reg. II Ch., (1976–78); Lib. Admin. Div./Persnl. Admin. Sect., Econ. Status, Welfare and Fringe Benefits Com., Subcom. on Cert., Ch., 1977); Exec. Com. (1975–77); Staff Dev. Com., Subcom. on Current Lit. Review (Ch., 1975–76). CA LA: PR Com. (Co-Ch., 1976–77). NLA: Legis. Com. (1976–78). South. CA Tech. Prcs. Grp. Assn. of CA State Univ. Prof.: Exec. Com. (1971–72); Secy. (1971–72). CA Women in Higher Educ. **Honors:** Pi Beta Chi; Alpha Mu Gamma. **Pubns.:** Jt. Auth., *Cost Analysis of Library Functions; A Total System Approach,* (1978); "In-House Training of Supervisory Library Assistants in a Large Academic Library," *Coll. and Resrch. Libs.,* (Mr. 1973); "Methods Used in Out-of-Print Acquisition; A Survey of Out-of-Print Book Dealers," *Lib. Resrcs. and Tech. Srvs.* (Spr. 1973); Ed., "Staff Development" column, *Spec. Libs.* (1975–76); "Professional Judgment & Cost Analysis: an Essential Evaluative Duality," in *Library Effectiveness: a State of the Art,* (1980). **Activities:** 1; 17, 35 **Addr.:** Library, California State University, Northridge, 18111 Nordhoff St., Northridge, CA 91330.

Mitchell, Eleanor (Ap. 4, 1907, Orange, NJ) Retired; Proj. Ofcr., Intl. Rel. Ofc., ALA, 1969–72; Lib. Consult., Univ. Católica, Quito, Ecuador, 1963–68; Spec., Books for the People Fund, Inc., Pan American Union, 1961–62; Exec. Dir., Fine Arts Com., People-to-People Prog., 1957–61; US Spec., Dept. of State, Colombia, 1955–57; Dir., Lib. Srv., US Info. Srv., Italy, 1951–54; Chief, Art Div., New York Pub. Lib., 1943–51; Other lib. positions. **Educ.:** Douglass Coll., 1924–28, BA; Columbia Univ., 1928–29, BS (LS); Smith Coll., 1936, MA (Fine Arts); Univ. de Paris, 1932, (Fine Arts). **Orgs.:** ALA. Socty. of Woman Geographers: Libn./Arch., Mem. Ch. **Honors:** Intl. Rescue Com., Medal, 1962; Douglass Coll., Litt. D, 1968. **Pubns.:** Various articles. **Activities:** 1, 9; 17, 24, 39; 55, 85 **Addr.:** Potomac Plaza Terraces, 415, 730–24th St., N.W., Washington, DC 20037.

Mitchell, Elizabeth P. (Liz) (N. 6, 1946, Quantico, VA) Pres., Proj. Comms., Inc., 1980–; Acct. Exec., The PR Bd., 1978–80; Sr. Ed., Mktg. Pubns., CNA Ins., 1977–78; Asst. Ed., *Amer. Libs.,* 1975–77; Ed. Libn., Harvard Univ. Lib., 1974–75. **Educ.:** Boston Univ., 1968–70, BA (Eng.); Smith Coll., 1964–68 (Relig.); Simmons Coll., 1971–74, MS (LS). **Orgs.:** ALA: ACRL/New Eng. Chap. (Secy., 1974–75), Wkshp. on Lib. Pubns., Leader; Plng. Com. for Session on Staff Nsltrs. (1975). Intl. Assn. of Bus. Communicators. Chicago Assn. of Bus. Communicators. **Honors:** EDPRESS, Awd. for Excel. in Educ. Jnlsm., 1977. **Pubns.:** Auth./ed., *Winning the Money Game* (1979); jt. auth., *What Else You Can Do with a Library Degree* (1980); "The Library Press," *ALA Yrbk.* (1977–80); various articles, reviews. **Activities:** 14-Consult.; 28, 36, 37 **Addr.:** Project Communications, Inc., 1555 N. Sandburg Terr., #304, Chicago, IL 60610.

Mitchell, Joan M. (O. 8, 1941, Long Branch, NJ) Dir. of Lib. Srvs., Carlow Coll., 1980–; Ref. and Media Srvs. Libn., Butler Cnty. Cmnty. Coll., 1971–80; Instr., Dept. of Mod. Langs., Carnegie–Mellon Univ., 1966–69; Instr., Dept. of Mod. Langs., Duquesne Univ., 1965–66; Instr., Berlitz Sch. of Langs., 1965–66; Tchr., West Genesee Sr. HS, 1964–65. **Educ.:** Wilson Coll.,

Special Subjects/Services: 50. Adult educ.; 51. Advert./Mktg.; 52. Aerosp.; 53. Agric.; 54. Area std.; 55. Arts/Hum.; 56. Autom.; 57. Bibl./Prtg.; 58. Bio. sci.; 59. Bus./Fin.; 60. Chem.; 61. Copyrt.; 62. Documtn.; 63. Educ.; 64. Engin.; 65. Env.; 66. Eth. grps.; 67. Film; 68. Food/Nutr.; 69. Geneal.; 70. Geo.; 71. Geol.; 72. Handcpd.; 73. Hist.; 74. Int. frdm.; 75. Info. sci.; 76. Insr.; 77. Law; 78. Legis.; 79. Math./Comp. sci.; 80. Med.; 81. Metals; 82. Nat. resrcs.; 83. Newsp.; 84. Nuc. sci.; 85. Oral hist.; 86. Petr./Energy; 87. Pharm.; 88. Phys./Astr./Math.; 89. Readg.; 90. Relig.; 91. Sci./Tech.; 92. Soc. sci.; 93. Telecom.; 94. Transp.; 95. (other).

1959–63, AB (Fr.); Harvard Univ., 1963–64, MAT (Fr.); Univ. of Pittsburgh, 1970–71, MLS. **Orgs.:** ALA. PA LA: Chap. Ch. (1976–77); Coll. and Resrch. Libs. Prog. Com. (1980–81). **Activities:** 1; 17, 31, 39; 56 **Addr.:** Grace Library, Carlow College, 3333 Fifth Ave., Pittsburgh, PA 15213.

Mitchell, Patrick C. (My. 4, 1944, Seattle, WA) Sr. Software Consult., Intel Corp., 1976–; Asst. Chief, Legal Info. Retrieval Software, U.S. Dept. of Justice, 1973–76; On-Line Tactical Info. Systs. Devel., U.S. Army, Comp. Systs. Command, 1971–73. **Educ.:** WA State Univ., 1962–66, BA (Math.), 1966–68, MS (Info. Sci.), 1968–71, PhD (Comp. Sci.). **Orgs.:** ASIS. Assn. for Comp. Mach. Inst. of Electrical and Electronics Engin. Acacia Frat. **Pubns.:** "A Note about the Proximity Operators in Info. Retrieval," *SIGIR FORUM, ACM* (Win. 1974); "TCCS: A Telecommunications Conversational Control System," *Proceedings of 13th Annual Technical Symposium, ACM/National Bureau of Standards* (Je. 1974); "SOLAR: A Storage and On-Line Automatic Retrieval System," *Jnl. of ASIS* (S.–O. 1973); "Methods of Randomization of Large Files with High Volatility," *Jnl. of Lib. Autom.* (Mr. 1970); "LOLA: Library On-Line Acquisitions Subsystem at Washington State University," *Proceedings of the 14th Annual College and University Machine Records Conference* (Ap. 1969). **Activities:** 4, 12; 15, 22, 41; 77 **Addr.:** Intel Corporation, P.O. Box 9968, Austin, TX 78766.

Mitlin, Laurance Robert (F. 8, 1947, Brooklyn, NY) Asst. Dean for Lib. Srvs., Winthrop Coll., 1981–, Asst. Coll. Libn. for Pub. Srvs., 1976–81, Docum. Libn., 1971–76. **Educ.:** MS State Univ., 1965–69, BA (Econ.); Univ. of NC, 1969–71, MSLS. **Orgs.:** SC LA: *SC Libn.* (Ed., 1977–). SELA: Resols. Com. (1979–80). ALA. AAUP: Chap. Vice-Pres. (1976–77). **Pubns.:** Jt. auth., "The ISSN as a Retriever of OCLC Records," *Serials Libn.* (forthcoming). **Activities:** 1; 17, 22, 39; 56, 59, 92 **Addr.:** Dacus Library, Winthrop College, Rock Hill, SC 29733.

Mitra, Himansu Bhusan (F. 6, 1928, Calcutta, W. Bengal, India) Assoc. Libn., Mt. Allison Univ., 1969–; Deputy Libn., Indian Inst. of Tech., 1961–67. **Educ.:** Calcutta Univ., 1952–56, BA; The Lib. Assn., 1958–60, ALA. **Orgs.:** Lib. Assn., London. Can. LA. Atl. Prov. LA: Bltn. (1970–72); Bib.–Cap. (1978–80). **Addr.:** Box 1088, Sackville, NB E0A 3C0 Canada.

Mittermeyer, Diane (My. 15, 1945, Malartic, PQ) Ph.D. Cand., Fac. of LS, Univ. of Toronto, 1977–; Biling. Libn., Can. Forces Cmnd. and Staff Coll., Toronto, 1973–76; Catlgr., Univ. du PQ à Montréal, 1972–73, Ref. Libn., 1971–72. **Educ.:** Univ. de Montréal, 1964–68, Bacc. (Ès-Arts), Univ. of Toronto, 1968–71, Bacc. (LS); 1974–77, MLS, 1977–. **Orgs.:** ALA. Can. LA. ON LA. ASTED. **Honors:** Howard V-Phalin World Book Awd., 1977. **Pubns.:** "The Knowledge Base for the Administration of Libraries," *Lib. Resrch.* (1979); "Ontario Public Library "System": Channels of Communication and Flow of Funds." *Argus* (1978). **Activities:** 9, 13; 26, 41, 47; 51, 62, 89 **Addr.:** Faculty of Library Science, University of Toronto, 140 St. George St., Toronto, ON M5S 1A1 Canada.

Miu, Anna L. (Ap. 18, 1949, Taipei, Taiwan, Rep. of China) Head, Cat. Dept., TX South. Univ., 1978–; Slavic Catlgr., Univ. of KS, 1976–77. **Educ.:** Natl. Cheng-chi Univ., 1967–71, BA (Russ.); SUNY, Buffalo, 1973–75, MLS. **Orgs.:** Houston Area Resrch. Libs. Cnsrtm.: Tech. Srvs. Com. (1978–). SLA. Chin. Amer. LA. **Activities:** 1; 17, 20, 39; 63, 91, 92 **Addr.:** Texas Southern University Library, Cataloging Department, Houston, TX 77004.

Mixter, Keith Eugene (My. 22, 1922, Lansing, MI) Prof. of Msc., OH State Univ., 1974–; 1961–65; Assoc. Prof. of Msc., 1965–74, Asst. Prof. of Msc., 1961–65; Msc. Libn., Univ. of NC, 1954–61, Msc. Ref. Libn., 1953–54. **Educ.:** MI State Univ., 1940–47, BM (Msc.); Univ. of Chicago, 1951–52, MA (Msc.); Univ. of NC 1953–61, PhD (Msc.). **Orgs.:** Msc. LA: Prog. Com. (1958–60); Exec. Bd. (1961–63). Intl. Assn. of Msc. Libs.: Intl. Com. of Msc. Resrch. Libs. (Secy., 1964–65). Amer. Musicological Socty.: Natl. Cncl. (1978–81). Intl. Musicological Socty. Pi Kappa Lambda. Phi Mu Alpha Sinfonia. **Honors:** Harriet Cohen Internatl. Msc. Awds., Prize for Msclgy., 1962. **Pubns.:** *General Bibliography for Music Research* (1975); *An Introduction to Library Resources for Music Research* (1963); "A Visit to Some Music Libraries in Eastern Europe," *Coll. and Resrch. Libs.* (1967); "Music in the National Libraries of Europe," *Coll. Msc. Symp.* (1968); Various articles and reviews. **Activities:** 14-Univ. Tchg.; 49-Tchg.; 55, 57 **Addr.:** 4455 Shields Pl., Columbus, OH 43214.

Mize, Patricia J. (N. 10, 1941, Beech Grove, KY) Head of Pub. Srvs. and Asst. Prof. of LS, KY Wesleyan Coll., 1978–; Adj. Fac. Mem., West. KY Univ., 1977–78; Media Spec., McLean Cnty. Sch. Syst., 1970–78; Libn., Daviess Cnty. Sch. Syst., 1963–70. **Educ.:** KY Wesleyan Coll., 1960–62, BA (Bus. Educ.); West. KY Univ., 1974, MA (Educ.); Univ. of KY, 1978–, (LS). **Orgs.:** ALA: AASL. SELA. KY LA: Bd. of Dirs. (1980–81); Bibl. Instr. RT, Pres.-elect (1981–82). KY Sch. Media Assn.: Pres. (1980–81); Bd. of Dirs. (1973–82). Various other orgs. AAUP. AAUW. Girl Scouts of the U.S.: Cmnty. Resrc. Dir. (1979–80). **Honors:** Girl Scouts of the U.S., Silver Cardinal, 1979. **Pubns.:** "British Libraries," ERIC (1981); Various reviews. **Activities:** 1, 10; 22, 26, 39; 63, 74 **Addr.:** Route 1, Calhoun, KY 42327.

Mizener, Warren Earl (My. 17, 1943, Sweetsburg, PQ) Treas., Chief of Admin., Nepean Pub. Lib., 1974–; Head, Auxiliary Srvs. Sect., Pub. Arch. of Can., 1970–72, Archvst./Hist. Resrch. Ofcr., 1964–70. **Educ.:** Univ. of NB, 1960–64, BA (Hist.); Algonquin Coll. of Applied Arts and Tech., 1972–74 Dipl. (Bus. Admin.). **Orgs.:** Assn. of Can. Archvsts. SAA. Assn. of Records Mgrs. and Admin. ON Persnl. Assn. ON Mncpl. Persnl. Assn. **Pubns.:** Contrib., *Archives: Mirror of Canada Past* (1972). **Activities:** 2, 9; 17, 35; 55, 59, 90 **Addr.:** 1465 Baseline Rd., Apt. 611, Ottawa, ON K2C 3L9 Canada.

Moberg, F. Alden (D. 28, 1932, Harris, MN) Inst. Lib. Consult., OR State Lib., 1973–, Consult., Lib. for the Blind & Phys. Handcpd. 1972–73, Ref. Consult., Hist. & Oregoniana, 1962–72. **Educ.:** Bethel Coll., 1953–57, BA (Lit.); Univ. of South. CA, 1960–61, MS LS. **Orgs.:** ALA: ASCLA/Lib. Srv. to Prisoners Sect. (1975–). Pac. NW LA. OR LA. OR Hist. Socty. **Activities:** 5, 13; 24, 25; 50, 72 **Addr.:** 236 25th St. N.E., Salem, OR 97301.

Mobley, Emily R. (O. 1, 1942, Valdosta, GA) Staff Libn., Gen. Motors Resrch. Labs. Lib., 1976–; Libn. Wayne State Univ., 1969–75; Engin. Libn., Chrysler Corp., 1965–69. **Educ.:** Univ. of MI 1960–64, AB, 1967, AMLS, PhD cand., 1975. **Orgs.:** ALA. AALS. SLA: Resrch. Com. (1977–80); Engin. Div./Mem. Com. (Ch., 1971–73); MI Chap.: Pres. (1980–81), Prog. Com. (1976–79), Educ. Com. (1974–76), Bltn. Ed. (1972–73). **Pubns.:** "Frisbees, Turbines, and Ice," *MI Libs.* (Fall 1977). **Activities:** 12; 17, 39; 64, 91, 94 **Addr.:** General Motors Research Laboratories, Library, GM Technical Center, Warren, MI 48090.

Mobley, Richard L. (O. 29, 1946, Marshall, TX) Branch Libn., Monte L. Moorer Br., Mobile Pub. Lib., 1980–, YA Coord., 1978–79; Tech. Srvs. Libn., FL Reg. Lib. for the Blind and Phys. Handcpd., 1977–78; Libn., Glades Correctional Inst., 1972–77. **Educ.:** Univ. of S. AL, 1965–69, BS (Sec. Educ.); FL State Univ., 1974–75, MSLS. **Orgs.:** Fla. Dept. of Corrections, Chairman, Lib. Services Committee (1975–77) ALA: Srv. to Prisoners Sect., Fed. Prisons Com. (1978–81); Srv. to Impaired Elderly Sec., By-Laws Com. (1979–80). AL LA: conv. ch. (1980–81). **Pubns.:** Complr., *Florida Directory of Special Transportation Services* (1978); Ed., *Florida Division of Corrections Library Handbook* (1974); Index, *DIKTA* (Fall-Win. 1978). **Activities:** 5, 9; 16, 48; 72 **Addr.:** 1809 Shelton Beach Rd., Mobile, AL 36618.

Mobley, Sara M. (N. 11, 1948, Normal, IL) Asst. Libn. for Pub. Srvs., Pitts Theo. Lib., Emory Univ., 1977–, Ref. Libn., 1976–77, Catlgr., 1974–76; Catlgr., Duke Univ., 1972–74. **Educ.:** Univ. of FL, 1966–70, BA (Hist.); Univ. of NC, 1971–72, MSLS. **Orgs.:** ATLA: Reader Srvs. Com. (1978–, Ch., 1980–); Resol. Com. (1978). Meth. Libns.' Flwshp.: Pres. (1980–); VP (1977–79). **Pubns.:** "Interpretative Services of Theological Libraries," *Proc. of the 34th Anl. Conf. of the ATLA* (1980). **Activities:** 1, 12; 17, 31, 39; 90 **Addr.:** Pitts Theology Library, Emory University, Atlanta, GA 30322.

Mochedlover, Helene Genevieve (Boston, MA) Prin. Libn., Lit./Fiction, Los Angeles Pub. Lib., 1975–, Sr. Libn., Lit., 1969–75, Libn. I, Lit., 1966–69, Catlgr., Rand Corp., 1964–66; Libn.-in-Charge, Eastern Gas & Fuel Co., 1961–64; Libn., Allied Resrch. Corp., 1959–61. **Educ.:** Boston Univ., 1949–53, BA (Psych./Phil); Simmons Coll., 1956–61, MLS. **Orgs.:** Libns. Guild: Ed., Comm. (1978–). **Pubns.:** *Ottemiller's Index to Plays in Collections* (1980–81). **Activities:** 9; 15, 39; 55, 57, 75 **Addr.:** Los Angeles Public Library, Literature Dept., 630 West 5th St., Los Angeles, CA 90071.

Modesti de Maurás, Smyrna (D. 3, 1924, Maunabo, PR) Libn., Univ. of PR, 1972–, Ref. Srvs. to Adults, Colección Puertorriqueña, Bib. José M. Lázaro, 1980–, Catlgr., Tech. Srvs. Div., 1972–79; Elem. Sch. Libn., Dept. of Educ., Río Piedras, PR, 1963–72, Elem. Sch. Tchr., 1958–61. **Educ.:** Univ. of PR, 1961–63, BA (Educ.), 1969–70, MLS. **Orgs.:** SB PR: Vocal (1970–72); Mem. Com. (1974–75, 1980). Assn. Ex-Alum. Escuela Graduada de Bibliotecología. Lions Club. **Honors:** Parents–Tchrs. Assn. of Villa Nevárez Elem. Sch., Plaque for Wk. with Chld. and Org. of Sch. Lib., 1972. **Activities:** 1, 10; 16, 20, 21; 62, 75, 93 **Addr.:** Yale C4, Urb. Sta. Ana, Río Piedras, PR 00927.

Moeller, Kathleen A. (F. 2, 1943, Long Beach, CA) Dir., Lib. Srvs., Overlook Hosp., 1978–; Asst. Libn., 1976–78. **Educ.:** Mt. St. Mary's Coll., 1960–64, BA (Bio.); Rutgers Univ., 1977–80. **Orgs.:** Med. LA. ALA. SLA. Hlth. Sci. LA of NJ: Secy. (1980–82). NJ Hosp. Assn. **Activities:** 12; 15, 17, 39; 80 **Addr.:** Health Sciences Library, Overlook Hospital, 193 Morris Ave., Summit, NJ 07901.

Moeller-Peiffer, Kathleen Ann (N. 9, 1955, Bound Brook, NJ) Cnty. Libn., Orange Cnty. Pub. Lib., 1979–; Cat. and Acq. Asst., Univ. of NC Law Lib., 1978–79; Asst. Cnty. Libn., Columbia Cnty. Pub. Lib., 1977–78. **Educ.:** Univ. of SC, 1973–76, BA (Eng.); FL State Univ., 1976–77, MS (LS). **Orgs.:** SELA. NC LA. ALA: JMRT, 3M Prof. Devel. Grant Com. (1980–81). Orange Cnty. Mental Hlth. Assn. Educ. Oppt. Ctr.: Adv. Cncl. (1980–81). **Activities:** 1, 9; 15, 20, 39 **Addr.:** 201 N. Churton St., Hillsborough, NC 27278.

Moen, Arthur J., Jr. (My. 22, 1947, Madison, WI) Asst. Inst. Srvs. Libn., Corn Belt Lib. Syst., 1977–; Correct. Libn., Bur Oak Lib. Syst., 1974–76; Dir.–Pub. Libn., Monroe Pub. Sch. Dist. #1, 1972–74. **Educ.:** Univ. of WI-Oshkosh, 1965–69, BA (Psy.), 1970–71, MLS. **Orgs.:** ALA: ASCLA/Lib. Srvs. to Prisoners Sect., Access and Censorship Problems in Inst. Com. (Ch., 1979–82), 1981 Prog. Com. (Co.-Ch., 1979–81); Jail Adv. Grp. (1979–80); Jail Resol. Com. (1977–79); Prog. Com. (1977–79). IL LA. **Pubns.:** *Public Library Service to Business* (1974). **Activities:** 5, 9 **Addr.:** 416 W. Livingston, Pontiac, IL 61764.

Moffat, Riley Moore (Mr. 22, 1947, Ogden, UT) Map Libn., Brigham Young Univ., 1976–; Dir. of Lib. Srvs., LDS Church Schs., Tonga, 1973–76. **Educ.:** Brigham Young Univ., 1968–72, BS (Bus.); Univ. of HI, 1972–73, MLS; Brigham Young Univ., 1977–80, MS (Geo.). **Orgs.:** UT LA: Gvt. Docums. RT (Secy., 1978). West. Assn. Map Libns.: Pres.–Elect (1981–82). Phi Alpha Theta. Alpha Chi: Natl. Del. (1972). **Pubns.:** *Printed Maps of Utah to 1900: An Annotated Cartobibliography* (1981); "Genealogy and Maps: Some Reference Resources," *WAML Info. Bltn.* (N. 1980). **Activities:** 1; 15, 20, 39; 69, 70 **Addr.:** 1354 HBLL, Brigham Young University, Provo, UT 84602.

Moffeit, Tony A. (Mr. 14, 1942, Claremore, OK) Head, Tech. Srvs. Dept., Univ. of S. CO Lib., 1976–; Head, Soc. Scis. Area, West. KY Univ. Lib., 1974–76; Archvst. and Ref. Libn., OK State Univ. Lib., 1972–74; Ref. Libn., Ctrl. State Univ. Lib., 1968–72. **Educ.:** OK State Univ., 1970–74, BS (Psy.); Univ. of OK, 1974–75, MLS. **Orgs.:** CO Lib. Assn.: Educ. Com. (1979–80). OK Lib. Assn.: Pubns. Com. (1968–72). KY Lib. Assn. **Pubns.:** "Literary Notes," clmn. in *OK Libn.* (1967–1971). **Activities:** 1; 15, 17 **Addr.:** 1701 Constitution, No. 2001, Pueblo, CO 81001.

Moffett, William Andrew (Ja. 25, 1933, Charlotte, NC) Azariah Smith Root Dir. of Libs., Oberlin Coll., 1979–; Dir. of Libs., State Univ. Coll., Potsdam, 1974–79; Asst. Prof. of Hist., Univ. of MA, Boston, 1968–74; Asst. Prof. of Hist., Alma Coll., 1964–68. **Educ.:** Davidson Coll., 1950–54, AB (Hist.); Duke Univ., 1955–63, MA, PhD (Hist.); Simmons Coll., 1972–73, MLS. **Orgs.:** ALA: ACRL. MA Lib. Trustees Assn.: Exec. Com. (1973–74). SUNY Cncl. of Head Libns.: Ch. (1976–78). **Honors:** Natl. Endow. for the Hum., Flwshp., 1968; NY Cncl. on the Humanities, Awd., 1976. **Pubns.:** "College Libraries in a National Information Policy: Whistling in the Graveyard," *Coll. and Resrch. Libs.*, (Ja. 1979); reports. **Activities:** 1; 15, 17, 28; 56, 92 **Addr.:** Oberlin College Library, Oberlin, OH 44074.

Mogavero, I. Frank (Jl. 12, 1913, Buffalo, NY) Archvst., Niagara Univ., 1957–, Prof., 1946–79. **Educ.:** Canisius Coll., 1936–44, BSSS, 1944–46, MA (Hist.); Univ. of Ottawa, 1947–50, PhD (Hist.). **Orgs.:** West. NY Lib. Resrcs. Cncl.: Bd. Dir. (1963–64). SAA. Judges & Police Exec. Conf. of Erie County, NY: Bd. Dir. (1975–); Archvst. (1976–). Buffalo & Erie Cnty. Hist. Socty. Bd. Mgrs. (1957–). **Honors:** Medaille Coll., Doct. of Pedagogy, 1973; D'Youville Coll., Cmnty. Srv., 1977. **Pubns.:** *Centennial History of Niagara University, 1856–1956* (1956); *Brief History of the Diocese of Buffalo* (1956); *Guide to Historic Buffalo* (1961); Contrib., *Catholic Encyclopedia* (1961 & 1963). **Activities:** 2; 15, 39, 41 **Addr.:** 3091 Second Ave., Grand Island, NY 14072.

Moger, Elizabeth (Haas) (Ag. 14, 1921, Minneapolis, MN) Keeper of the Recs. (Archvst.), Haviland Recs. Rm., NY Yearly Mtg., Rel. Socty. of Frnds., 1978–; Ext. Libn. (Bkmobile.), Mount Vernon Pub. Lib., 1972–77; Chld. Libn. and Branch Libn., Elmont Pub. Lib., 1964–72; Head of Chld. Dept., Branch Libn., Bkmobile. Libn., Great Neck Lib., 1950–64; Jr. Asst., Civics and Soclgy. Dept., Enoch Pratt Free Lib., 1947–50. **Educ.:** Carleton Coll., 1939–43, BA (Classical Langs.); Columbia Univ., 1946–47, BS (LS). **Orgs.:** Mid. Atl. Reg. Arch. Conf. SAA. **Honors:** Phi Beta Kappa, 1943. **Activities:** 2, 9; 21, 45; 90 **Addr.:** 91 Remsen Ave., Roslyn, Long Island, NY 11576.

Mohajerin, Kathryn Sherlock (Ja. 21, 1943, Fort Sill, OK) Asst. Prof., Dept. of Educ. Media, Auburn Univ., 1975–; Instr., LS, Shepherd Coll., 1970–73; Ref. Libn., Washington Cnty. (MD) Free Lib., 1968–70. **Educ.:** LA State Univ., 1960–63, BA (Span.); FL State Univ., 1967–68, MS (LS), 1973–77, Ph.D. (Educ. Admin.). **Orgs.:** AL LA. AL Instr. Media Assn. Action for Chld. TV. Phi Delta Kappa. **Pubns.:** Contrib., *The Yellow Brick Road: Guide to Elementary Career Ed.* (1975); "Perceptions of The Role of The School Media Specialist," *Sch. Lib. Qtly.* (Sp. 1981); Slide-tape program: "Elementary Career Education" (1974). **Activities:** 14-School of Educ.; 24, 26, 41; 63, 67, 93 **Addr.:** Dept. of Educational Media, Room 3408 Haley Center, Auburn University, Auburn, AL 36830.

Mohn, Kari (O. 19, 1942, Riverside, CA) Dist. Media Libn., Kenai Penisula Boro. Sch. Dist., 1979–; Law Libn., Kenai, 1978–79. **Educ.:** Univ. of Redlands, 1960–64, BA (Eng.); Univ. of OR, 1975–79, MLS. **Orgs.:** ALA: AASL. AECT. AK LA: Exec. Bd. (1977–80). Kenai Peninsula LA: Pres. (1977–80). **Ac-**

PROFESSIONAL ACTIVITIES: Institutions: 1. Acad. lib.; 2. Arch.; 3. Assn.; 4. Fed./Gvt. lib.; 5. Inst. lib.; 6. Mfr./Suppl.; 7. Milit. lib.; 8. Musm.; 9. Pub. lib.; 10. Sch. lib.; 11. Sch. of lib. sci.; 12. Spec. lib.; 13. State lib.; 14. (other). **Functions/Activities:** 15. Acq./Col. dev.; 16. Adult srvs.; 17. Admin.; 18. Apprais.; 19. Archit./Bldgs.; 20. Cat./Class.; 21. Chld. srvs.; 22. Circ.; 23. Cons./Pres.; 24. Consult.; 25. Cont. ed.; 26. Educ. lib. sci.; 27. Ext. srvs.; 28. Fund/Grants; 29. Gvt. pubs.; 30. Indx./Abs.; 31. Instr. lib. use; 32. Media srvs.; 33. Micro.; 34. Netwks./Coop.; 35. Persnl.; 36. PR; 37. Publshg.; 38. Recs. mgt.; 39. Ref. srvs.; 40. Repro.; 41. Resrch.; 42. Review.; 43. Secur.; 44. Serials; 45. Spec. col.; 46. Tech. srvs.; 47. Trustees/Bds.; 48. YA srvs.; 49. (other).

tivities: 10; 32 **Addr.:** Special Services IMC, Box 1200, Soldotna, AK 99669.

Mohr, Elizabeth B. (Ag. 8, 1943, Danville, KY) Chief, Tech. Support, U.S. Dept. of Energy, Bartlesville Energy Tech. Ctr., 1979–, Admin. Libn., 1976–79, Asst. Libn., 1975–76; Libn., Coll. HS, Bartlesville (OK), 1972–75. **Educ.:** Univ. of Tulsa, 1961–65, BA (Eng.); Univ. of OK, 1969–72, MLS. **Orgs.:** SLA: OK Chap. (Pres., 1980–81). ALA. **Honors:** Beta Phi Mu, 1972. **Pubns.:** "Bibliographic Data Bases: Key to EOR Information," *Proc. of 5th Anl. DOE Symposium on Enhanced Oil Recovery and Improved Drilling Technology* (1979). **Activities:** 4, 12; 17, 49-Online Srchg.; 56, 75, 91 **Addr.:** Bartlesville Energy Technology Center, P.O. Box 1398, Bartlesville, OK 74003.

Mohrhardt, Foster E. (Mr. 7, 1907, Lansing, MI) Consult., Concl. on Lib. Resrcs., 1975–, Sr. Prog. Ofcr., 1968–75; Dir., Natl. Agr. Lib., 1954–68; Dir., Lib. Srvs., Vet. Admin., 1948–54. **Educ.:** MI State Univ., 1926–29, AB (Lib. Arts); Columbia Univ., 1929–30, BS LS; Univ. of MI, 1930–33, MALS. **Orgs.:** ALA: Pres. (1967–68); ACRL (Pres., 1966). Intl. Assn. of Agr. Libns.: Pres. (1955–68). Natl. Fed. of Abs. and Indexing Srvcs.: Pres. (1964–65). U.S. Bk. Exch.: Pres. (1958–60). Amer. Lib. in Paris: Bd. Mem. (1966–73). Bio. Abs.: Bd. (1966–67). U.S. Exec. Ofc. of the Pres.: Com. on Sci. and Tech. Info. (1962–68). U.S. Natl. Comsn. for Intl. Fed. for Documtn.: Ch. (1965–67). **Pubns.:** Jt. Auth., *Guide to Information Sources in Space Science* (1963); *Personnel administration in libraries* (1966); numerous articles. **Activities:** 1, 4; 17, 19, 24; 50, 91 **Addr.:** 2601 South Joyce St., Arlington, VA 22202.

Molholt, Pat A. (O. 19, 1943, Fond du Lac, WI) Assoc. Dir. of Libs., Rensselaer Polytech. Inst., 1978–; Adjunct Fac., SUNY, Albany, Sch. of Lib. and Info. Sci., 1979–; Asst. Prof. and Dir. Sci. and Tech. Lib., Univ. of WY, 1977–78; Physics Libn., Univ. of WI, 1973–77, Astronomy Libn., 1970–73. **Educ.:** Univ. of WI, 1964–66, BS (Eng, Phil.), 1969–70, MLS, 1976–78, Spec. Cert. (Lib. Autom.). **Orgs.:** ALA. SLA: Bd. of Dir. (1978–80). Intl. Fed. of Lib. Assn. and Inst.: Secy., Sci. and Tech. Sect. (1979–81); Fin. Off., Spec. Libs. Div. (1979–81). **Pubns.:** "*Library Automation,*" *ERIC* (1978); Jt. auth., *Bibl. of Aquatic Ecosystem Effects* (1980). **Activities:** 1, 10; 17, 26; 56 **Addr.:** Folsom Library, Rensselaer Polytechnic Institute, Troy, NY 12181.

Moline, Gloria (Jl. 1, 1931, Chicago, IL) Mgr., Bibl. Div., Engin. Info., Inc., 1975–; Serials Libn., NASA Ames Resrch. Ctr. Libs., 1973–74. **Educ.:** Univ. of Chicago, 1946–50, BA (Lib. Arts), 1950–52, (Educ.); San Jose State Univ., 1972–73, MA (LS). **Orgs.:** SLA. ASIS: Mgt. SIG, Nom. Com. (Ch., 1980). Natl. Fed. of Abs. and Indexing Srvs.: Serials and Access Com. (1977–78); Common Practices and Stans. Com. (Ch., 1978–80); ASIDIC/NFAIS Task Force on Interchange Specifications (Alt., 1977–78). **Honors:** Beta Phi Mu, 1973. **Pubns.:** *An Evaluation of Approval Plan Performance: The Acquisition of Titles in Political Science* (1975); "Engineering Index, Inc.: An Abstracting and Indexing Service in Perspective," *Special Librarianship: A New Reader* (1980). **Activities:** 5; 17, 44, 46; 56, 62 **Addr.:** Engineering Information, Inc., Bibliographic Division, 345 East 47th St., New York, NY 10017.

Moline, Sandra R. (D. 13, 1938, San Antonio, TX) Phys. Libn., Univ. of WI, 1977–. **Educ.:** Austin Coll., 1954–60, BA (Chem.); Univ. of WI, 1973–75, MA (Hist. of Sci.), 1975–76, MA (LS). **Orgs.:** WI LA. SLA. **Activities:** 1; 15, 39; 88 **Addr.:** Physics Library, 1150 University Ave., Madison, WI 53706.

Moll, Joy Kaiser (Ag. 14, 1930, Trenton, NJ) Assoc. Prof., Stockton State Coll., 1981–, Asst. Prof., 1980–81; Assoc. Dir., Resrch. Bureau, Rutgers Univ., 1978–80; Staff Anal., Computer Horizons, Inc., 1974–78; Media Spec., Moorestown NJ Pub. Sch., 1967–73. **Educ.:** Douglass Coll., 1947–51, BA (Span.); Drexel Univ., 1963–67, MLS; Rutgers Univ., 1971–74, PhD (Info. Sci.); Univ. de San Marcos, Lima, Peru, 1951–52, (Peruvian Cult.). **Orgs.:** Med. LA. NY and NJ Reg. Med. LA (Tech. Srvs. Subcom., 1978); (State Netwks. Com., 1974); Ad Hoc Com. for Intl. Exch. (1980–). SLA. ASIS. NJ LA. State of NJ: Dept. of Higher Educ., Jt. Adv. Com. on Biling. Educ. (1979–). Cncl. for Intl. Visitors of Philadelphia (1973–). AAUW: Rancocas Valley Br. (1954–67). **Honors:** Beta Phi Mu, 1967; NJ LA, Rust Schol. 1965; Sigma Delta Pi, 1951. **Pubns.:** Jt. auth., *Bibliometrics Anl. Review of Info. Sci. and Tech* (1977); "Bibliometrics in Library Collection Management", *Col. Mgt.* (Fall 1978); "A Bibliographic Brew from Alcoholism Research", *Jnl. of Irreproducible Results* (1978). **Activities:** 10, 12; 26, 34, 41; 56, 75, 80 **Addr.:** 9 E. Harris Ave., Moorestown, NJ 08057.

Mollberg, Amy Ann (Ap. 30, 1944, Port Arthur, TX) Coord., Houston Area Lib. Syst., 1977–, Asst. to the Coord., 1976–77; Head, Chld. Carousel, Houston Pub. Lib., 1975–76, Branch Head, Lakewood Branch, 1973–75; Libn., Mad River Twp. Schs., 1967–70. **Educ.:** Univ. of N. AL, 1962–65, BS (Elem. Educ.); LA State Univ., 1966–67, MS (LS). **Orgs.:** ALA. TX LA: Pub. Lib. Div. (Secy. 1981–82). SWLA. Neartown Civic Assn. Houston Area Women's Ctr. **Honors:** Beta Phi Mu, 1968; Educ. Prof. Devel. Act, Flwshp., 1971. **Activities:** 9, 10; 21, 24, 25 **Addr.:** 3601 Allen Pkwy., #1133, Houston, TX 77019.

Möller, Hans (N. 10, 1918, Copenhagen, Denmark) Dir. & Assoc. Prof., GSLS, McGill Univ., 1981–; Undergrad. Area Libn., McGill Univ., 1977–81, Sessional Lectr., Grad. Sch. of Lib. Sci., McGill Univ., 1979–80; Sessional Lectr., Sch. of Lib. and Info. Sci., Univ. of West. ON, 1978; Dir. of Libs., Univ. of Ottawa, 1974–77; Dir. of Lrng. Media, VP, Visual Educ. Ctr. Toronto, 1969–74; Exec. Producer, Natl. Film Bd. of Can., Montreal, 1956–69; Asst. Dir., Royal Lib., Copenhagen, Denmark, 1952–55. **Educ.:** Univ. of Copenhagen, Denmark, 1937–45, PhD (Danish Lit.); Royal Lib., Natl. Lib. of Denmark, 1948–50, (LS). **Orgs.:** CARL: Pres. (1976-78). Can. Assn. of Coll. and Univ. Libs.: Pres. (1979–80). Can. Cncl. Consult. Grp. on Resrch. Libs. Grants: Ch. (1977). Can. Inst. for Hist. Microreproduction: Bd. of Dirs. (1978–). **Honors:** UNESCO, Flwshp. for lib. sci. and AV media, 1954; Fed. Repub. of Germany, Std. Tour of German resrch. libs., 1976. **Pubns.:** "Media for Discovery, a Handbook for Teachers," (1970); "Specialization may be Confronting You," *Can. Lib. Jnl.* (O. 1979); various educ. filmstps., multi-media kits, and films, (1956–74). **Activities:** 1, 11; 17, 26, 32; 55, 63, 67 **Addr.:** Graduate School of Library Science, McGill University, 3459 McTavish St., Montreal, PQ H3A 1Y1 Canada.

Molod, Samuel E. (Ag. 27, 1921, Trenton, NJ) Deputy State Libn., CT State Lib., 1979–, Assoc. State Libn., Div. of Lib. Dev., 1966–79; Dir. James V. Brown Lib., Williamsport & Lycoming Cnty., 1962–66; Dir. Upper Peninsula Branch, MI State Lib., 1953–62; Tchr. LS, various inst., 1955–79. **Educ.:** Long Island Univ., 1939–43, BS (Hist.); Clark Univ., 1945–46, MA (Intl. Rel.); Univ. of MI, 1952–53, MALS. **Orgs.:** New Eng. LA: State Lib. Srvc. (Ch. 1977–79). ALA: ASLA, Plng. Com. (1979), Aging Com. (1981), Intl. Rel. Com. (1981), Deaf Com. (1981). CT LA. **Pubns.:** Various articles. **Activities:** 13; 17, 24, 25; 50, 56, 75 **Addr.:** 47 Huntington Dr., West Hartford, CT 06117.

Molz, R. Kathleen (Mr. 5, 1928, Baltimore, MD) Melvil Dewey Prof. of Lib. Srv., Sch. of Lib. Srv., Columbia Univ., 1980–, Prof. of Lib. Srv., 1976–80; Chief, Plng. Staff, Bur. of Libs. and Lrng. Resrcs., U.S. Ofc. of Educ., 1971–73, Chief, Lib. Plng. and Devel. Branch, Div. of Lib. Progs., Bur. of Adult, Vocational, Lib. Progs., 1968–71; Ed., *Wilson Lib. Bltn.,* H.W. Wilson Co., 1962–68; PR Ofcr., Free Lib. of Philadelphia, 1958–62, TV Spec., 1957–58; Libn. I and Libn. II, Enoch Pratt Free Lib., 1953–56. **Educ.:** Johns Hopkins Univ., 1945–49, BS (Eng.), 1949–50, MA (Eng.); Univ. of MI, 1952–53, MA (LS); Columbia Univ., 1974–76, DLS. **Orgs.:** ALA: Exec. Bd. (1976–80); Cncl. (1972–74; 1976–80); IFC (Ch., 1973–75); Nom. Com. (1969), Amer. Bk. Publshrs. Cncl. and ALA Jt. Com. on Readg. Devel. (1966–70). Frdm. to Read Fndn.: Various ofcs. (1972–79). Lib. PR Cncl. of New York. Alum. Assn., Sch. of LS, Univ. of MI: Pres. (1967–68). **Honors:** ALA, Ralph R. Shaw Awd., 1977; Pres. Com. on Employ. of the Handcpd., Cmdn., 1966; Sch. of LS, Univ. of MI, Disting. Alum. Awd., 1969; Beta Phi Mu, 1953; various other hons. **Pubns.:** *Federal Policy and Library Support* (1976); Jt. ed., *The Metropolitan Library* (1972); *National Planning for Library Service, 1935 to 1975: From the National Plan to the National Program* (forthcoming); "National Information Policy," *Networks for Networkers* (1980); "The American Public Library: Its Historic Concern for the Humanities," *The Role of the Humanities in the Public Library* (1979); Various articles, repts. **Activities:** 9, 11; 17, 34; 74, 78 **Addr.:** School of Library Service, Columbia University, New York, NY 10027.

Monaco, Marcia Eglof (My. 17, 1929, Niagara Falls, NY) Tech. Srvs. Coord., Charles Cnty. Cmnty. Coll., 1972–; Sch. Libn., Valley View Elem. Sch., 1969–72; Cat. Libn., Arlington Cnty. (VA) Pub. Lib., 1966–67; Serials Catlgr., Univ. of MD Mckeldin Lib., 1965–66; Catlgr., Arlington Cnty. Pub. Lib., 1963–64; Head Libn., Upper Marlboro Branch, Prince Georges Cnty. Meml. Lib., 1964–65. **Educ.:** Mary Washington Coll., Univ. of VA, 1946–50, BS (Psy.); Cath. Univ. of Amer., 1960–64, MSLS; Various courses (1967–80). **Orgs.:** ALA: Dallas Preconf. on AACR-2 (MD Del.). Prince George's Cnty. Media Assn.: Charter mem. and first Pres. MD LA: Tech. Srvs. Div. (Pres., 1979–80; VP/Prog. Ch., 1978–79). Alpha Phi Sigma. Chi Beta Phi. **Honors:** Beta Phi Mu. **Activities:** 1, 2; 20, 46; 49-Arch. Mgt.; 58, 92, 73 **Addr.:** 2314 Pinefield Rd., Waldorf, MD 20601.

Monahon, Ruth C. (Jl. 3, 1919, E. Liverpool, OH) Ref. Libn., Med. Biblgphr., Univ. Southern CA, Sch. of Med., 1955–; Med. Biblgphr.; Univ. Southern CA; Sch. of Med.; Norris Med. Lib. 1972–, Head Ref. Libn., III, 1968–72, Serials and Ref. Libn., II, 1967–68, Serials and Pub. Srvs. Libn., I, II, 1955–67. **Educ.:** Greenville Coll., 1937–41, AB (Bio., Modrn. Lang.); Univ. of Pittsburgh, 1943–45; Univ. Southern CA, 1946–53, MSLS; Biomed. Work. **Orgs.:** Med. LA: Reg. Com., Subcom. on Educ. Exhibits, San Diego. Med. Lib. Grp. of South. CA & AZ: Treas. 1966–68; Univ. Southern Calif. Sch. Lib. Sci. Alumni Assoc. Univ. Southern CA: Fac. Senate (1968–69). Nat. Trust for Hist. Pres. Met. Musm. of Art, NY. **Honors:** Alpha Kappa Sigma, 1939–41; Beta Phi Mu, Beta ch., 1956. **Activities:** 1, 14-Medical School library; 31, 39, 44; 57, 80, 87 **Addr.:** University of Southern California, Health Sciences Campus, Norris Medical Library, Los Angeles, CA 90033.

Mondolfo, Vittoria I. (F. 14, 1916, Ancona, Italy) Asst. Libn., Hamilton Coll., 1967–; Chemistry Libn., Univ. of Chicago, 1958–66, Classics Libn., Univ. of Chicago, 1951–58. **Educ.:** Univ. of Rome, 1932, BS (Chem.), 1938, PhD (Chem.). **Orgs.:** OCLC, Inc.: Users Cncl., SUNY: OCLC, Adv. Com. Cte. NY LA: Resrcs and Tech. Srvcs. Sect., Bd. (1980–). NYLA. Cons. of Lib. Mat. Ch. (1980–). **Pubns.:** Ed., *Letters to Ibbotson, 1935-1952 / Ezra Pound* (1979); "Annotated bibliography of criticism of Ezra Pound, 1918-1924," *Paideuma* (1976); Jt. auth., "Annotated checklist of criticism of Ezra Pound, 1930-35," *Paideuma* (Sum. 1976). "Bibliography of Carl Darling Buck," *Lang.* (1956). **Activities:** 1; 15, 17, 46 **Addr.:** Hamilton College Library, Clinton, NY 13323.

Mongan, Janet (Jl. 14, 1931, New York, NY) Asst. Dir. For Col. Dev., Cleveland State Univ., 1976–, Head, Ref. Srv. Div., 1973–76; Environ. Lit. Spec., Case Westrn Reserve Univ., 1972–73; Asst. Head, Bus. Info. Dept., Cleveland Pub. Lib., 1969–70; Libn., U.S. Nvl. Ord. Test Station, 1963–66; Adult Srvs. Libn., Cuyahoga Cnty. Pub. Lib., 1961–62; Libn., Gen. Ref. Dept., Cleveland Pub. Lib., 1957–58. **Educ.:** Cornell Univ., 1949–53, BA (Eng.); Univ. of TX, 1955–57, MLS; Case-Western Reserve Univ., 1966–70, PhD (Inf. Sci.). **Orgs.:** ALA. SLA. Acad. LA of OH. **Pubns.:** "Coping with Environmental Information Resources" in *Information Resources in the Environmental Sciences,* (1973); "Clinician Search for Information," *Jnl. of the ASIS,* (1973); "Environ. Chem.," *Jnl. of Chem. Doc.* (1973). **Activities:** 1; 15 **Addr.:** Cleveland State University Libraries, 1860 E. 22 St., Cleveland, OH 44115.

Monkhouse, R. Edward (Ja. 11, 1939, Guelph, ON) Educ. Media Consult., Wellington Cnty. Bd. of Educ., 1978–; Lib. Head, Centennial C.V.I., 1973–78; Tchr.–Libn., College Ave. Pub. Sch., 1971–73; Vice Prin., Ottawa Cresc. Pub. Sch., 1968–69. **Educ.:** Waterloo Luth. Univ., 1971, BA (Eng.); Univ. West. ON, 1972–73, MLS. **Orgs.:** Can. Sch. LA: Pres.; Secy./Treas.; Cnclr. ON LA: Mem. Com. (Sch. Lib. Rep.). ON Sec. Sch. Tchrs. Fed.: Branch Pres. **Honors:** ON Sec. Sch. Tchr. Fed., Silver Jubilee Awd. of Merit, 1980. **Pubns.:** "What Are You Doing About Periodicals?," *Reviewing Libn.* (S. 1979); "Promotion Programming for School Libraries," *Revolting Libn.* (S. 1979); "President's Memo," *Sch. Libs. in Can.* (1980–81); Ch., Ed. Bd., *CM: Canadian Materials for Schools and Libraries* (1981–84). **Activities:** 10, 12; 15, 18, 24; 63 **Addr.:** Wellington County Board of Education, 500 Victoria Rd. N., Guelph, ON N1E 6K2 Canada.

Monokoski, Patricia Felch, (Mr. 14, 1947, Boston, MA) Law Libn., Coffield Ungaretti Harris & Slavin, 1981–; Asst. Libn. for Pub. Srvs., Northwestern Univ. Msc. Lib., 1975–81; Asst. Head, Fine Arts Dept., Atlanta Pub. Lib., 1974–75; Reader Srvs. Libn., 1973–74. **Educ.:** Pine Manor Jr. Coll., 1965–1967, AA; Univ. of Denver, 1967–69, BA (Msc.); 1971–73, MA (Msc. Hist.); 1972–73, MA (Libnshp.). **Orgs.:** AALL. Msc. LA: Secy./Treas. SE Chap. (1974–75). Intl. Assn. of Msc. Libs. Coll. Msc. Socty. **Honors:** Beta Phi Mu, 1973. **Pubns.:** "Recordings: How to Arrange Them," *Clavier* (D. 1976); reviews. **Activities:** 1, 14-Law Library; 15, 31, 39; 55, 95 **Addr.:** 145 Chandler Ave., Elmhurst, IL 60126.

Monroe, Dawn E. (O. 27, 1945, Toronto, ON) Chief, Col. Devel. Srvs., Pub. Arch. Lib., 1978–, Head, Hist. Docum. Ctr., 1976–77, Head, External Srvs., 1974–76; Srch. Anal., Natl. Lib., Can., 1971–74. **Educ.:** Univ. of Guelph, 1966–70, BA (Can. Hist.); Univ. of West. ON, 1970–71, MLS. **Orgs.:** ON Assn. of Archvsts. Assn. Can. Archvsts.: *Archivaria* Indexing Team (1979). Can. LA. Fed. of Can. Archers: Pubcty. Dir. (1977–78). ON Assn. of Archers: Pubcty. Dir. (1975–77). **Pubns.:** Various articles, *Can. Archer.* **Activities:** 2, 4; 15, 17, 45; 73 **Addr.:** 395 Wellington St., Ottawa, ON K1A 0N3 Canada.

Monroe, Margaret Ellen (My. 21, 1914, New York, NY) Prof. Emeritus, Univ. of WI, Madison, 1981–; Prof. of LS, 1963–81; Assoc. Prof. of LS, Rutgers Univ., 1954–63; Dir. and Mtrls. Spec., Amer. Heritage Proj., ALA, 1951–54; Various positions, New York Pub. Lib., 1939–51. **Educ.:** Adelphi Coll. 1931–35, BA (Eng.); NY State Coll. for Tchrs., 1933–37, BSLS, 1939, MA (Eng.); Columbia Univ., 1954–62, DLS. **Orgs.:** ALA: Cncl. (two terms); Adult Srvs. Div. (Pres., 1960–61). AALS: Pres. (1971–72). WI LA: Assn. of Pub. Libs. (Pres.). Adult Educ. Assn.: Exec. Bd. (1962–64). **Honors:** Fund for Adult Educ., Leadership Grant, 1954–55; NJ LA, Awd. of Honor, 1963; Beta Phi Mu, Awd. for Disting. Contrib. to Educ. for Libnshp., 1972. **Pubns.:** *Library Adult Education* (1963); *Seminar in Bibliotherapy: Proceedings* (1978); "Community Development as a Mode of Community Analysis," *Lib. Trends* (Ja. 1976); "The Cultural Role of the Public Library," *Advnc. in Libnshp.* (1981); Various monos. and articles. **Activities:** 9; 16, 25, 26; 50, 89, 95-Comm. Dev. **Addr.:** 1219 Rutledge St., Madison, WI 53703.

Montana, Edward J., Jr. (Boston, MA) Asst. to the Reg. Admin., East. MA Reg. Lib. Syst., 1969–; Lib. Pubns. Ofcr., Boston Pub. Lib., 1964–68, Ref. Asst., 1957–64. **Educ.:** Boston Coll., 1951–55, BS (Hist., Gvt.), 1955–57, MA (Hist.); Simmons Coll., 1958–62, MS (LS). **Orgs.:** MA LA: PR Com. (Ch., 1970–71); Exec. Dir., Natl. Lib. Week, (1969). Lib. PR Cncl: Bd. of Dir. (1971–73); (Treas., 1973–74). Simmons Coll. Sch. of LS Alum. Assn.: Bd. of Dir. (1971–73). ALA: LAMA/PR Sect., John Cotton Dana PR Awards Com. (1977–79). Natl. Trust for Hist. Prsrvn. Royal Oak Socty. Prsrvn. Socty. of Newport (RI)

Special Subjects/Services: 50. Adult educ.; 51. Advert./Mktg.; 52. Aerosp.; 53. Agric.; 54. Area std.; 55. Arts/Hum.; 56. Autom.; 57. Bibl./Prtg.; 58. Bio. sci.; 59. Bus./Fin.; 60. Chem.; 61. Copyrt.; 62. Documtn.; 63. Educ.; 64. Engin.; 65. Env.; 66. Eth. grps.; 67. Film; 68. Food/Nutr.; 69. Geneal.; 70. Geo.; 71. Geol.; 72. Handcpd.; 73. Hist.; 74. Int. frdm.; 75. Info. sci.; 76. Insr.; 77. Law; 78. Legis.; 79. Math./Comp. sci.; 80. Med.; 81. Metals; 82. Nat. resrcs.; 83. Newsp.; 84. Nuc. sci.; 85. Oral hist.; 86. Petr./Energy; 87. Pharm.; 88. Phys./Astr./Math.; 89. Readg.; 90. Relig.; 91. Sci./Tech.; 92. Soc. sci.; 93. Telecom.; 94. Transp.; 95. (other).

Cnty. **Pubns.:** "Public Relations for the Metropolitan Library," *Public Relations for Libraries* (1973); "Literary Boston," *Cath. Lib. World* (Mr. 1970); "Boston: A Great Place for Librarians," *Cath. Lib. World* (F. 1970); "Candid Look at National Library Week," *Bay State Libn.* (Ap. 1969); "Boston Public Library," *Hl LA Jnl.* (Je. 1966); Other articles. **Activities:** 9; 17, 24, 36 **Addr.:** 11 Stearns St., Newton Center, MA 02159.

Montanelli, Dale S. (F. 17, 1945, Bayshore, NY) Lib. Budget Plng. Dir., Univ. of IL, 1978–, Staff Assoc., Ofc. of Resrc. Plng., 1975–78, Resrch. Asst., Prof. of Educ., Inst. for Resrch. on Exceptional Chld., 1972–74, Asst. Prof. of Psy., 1970–72. **Educ.:** MI State Univ., 1962–65, BA (Psy.); Univ. of IL, 1966–70, MA, PhD (Psy.). **Orgs.:** ALA: LAMA, Women Admins. Disc. Grp. Strg. Com. (1979–80)/Lib. Org. and Mgt. Sect., Budgeting, Acct., and Cost Com. (1979–80; Ch., 1980–81). Natl. Assn. of Coll. and Univ. Bus. Ofcrs.: Ed. Bd. (1978–). **Pubns.:** Jt. auth., "Conjoined Structures in the Written Language of Deaf Students," *Jnl. of Speech and Hearing Resrch.* (1975); Jt. auth., "Pronominalization in the Language of Deaf Children," *Jnl. of Speech and Hearing Resrch.* (1976); Jt. auth., "Some Aspects of the Verb System in the Language of Deaf Children," *Jnl. of Speech and Hearing Resrch.* (1976); Jt. auth., "Complementation in the Language of Deaf Children," *Jnl. of Speech and Hearing Resrch.* (1976); Jt. auth., "Space Management In College and University Business Administration," *Admin. Srv.* (1978); Various articles and papers in psy. **Activities:** 1; 17, 19, 35; 63, 89, 92 **Addr.:** University of Illinois at Urbana–Champaign, 230 University Library, 1408 West Gregory Dr., Urbana, IL 61801.

Montgomery, Ann Hess (S. 23, 1953, Springfield, MA) Admin., Lib. Systs. Support Srvs., Cincinnati Electronics, 1980–; Rec. Libn., Univ. of Cincinnati, 1978–80; Rec. Catlgr., Ferguson Lib., 1976–78; AV Libn., New Canaan Lib., 1977–78. **Educ.:** Trinity Coll., 1973–75, BA (Msc.); South. CT State Coll., 1975–76, MS (LS); Univ. of Cincinnati, 1978–82, MBA (Info. Syst.). **Orgs.:** Msc. LA: Midwest Cat. Com. (1979–80). Msc. OCLC Users Grp.: Treas. (1978–80). ASIS: South. OH Chap., Long–range Plng. (1980–81). **Pubns.:** Various workshops. **Activities:** 6; 49-Sales Support, Trng., Documentation, Analysis; 55 **Addr.:** Cincinnati Electronics, 2630 Glendale–Milford Rd., Cincinnati, OH 45241.

Montgomery, Beatrice (Ja. 4, 1919, Knoxville, TN) Head, Cat. Dept., Univ. of Akron, 1972–; Head, Cat. Dept., Univ. of NC, 1967–72, Hd. of Srchg. Sec., Acq., 1963–67; Catlgr., Univ. of CA, Davis, 1961–63; Head, Cat. Dept., GA St. Univ., 1959–60. **Educ.:** Randolph-Macon Woman's Coll., 1936–39, AB (Eng.); Emory Univ., 1943–44, ABLS; Univ. of NC, 1953–57, MSLS. **Orgs.:** ALA. OH LA. Acad. LA of OH: Treas. (1977–78). Alpha Omicron Pi. Daughters of the American Revolution. Untd. Daughters of the Confederacy. **Activities:** 1; 20 **Addr.:** Apt. 9-C-9 77 Fir Hill, Akron, OH 44304.

Montgomery, James Houston (O. 22, 1930, Greensboro, NC) Head, Tech. Srvs., VC/UHVC Lib., 1979–; Head, Cat. Dept., OK State Univ. 1972–79; Prin. Cat., Univ. of GA, 1970–72; Sr. Latin Amer. Cat., Univ. of FL, 1968–70; Head, Tech. Srvs., Rutgers Univ., 1967–68; Asst. Head, Tech. Srvs., Univ. of CA, 1966–67; Latin Amer. Bibl., Jt. Univ. Lib., 1963–66. **Educ.:** Guilford Coll., 1949–53, BA (Span.); Univ. of NC, 1955–57, MA (Rom. Lang.); Univ. of CA, LA, 1957–59, (Span., Portuguese); George Peabody Coll., 1962–63, MLS. **Orgs.:** ALA. LA. **Honors:** Beta Phi Mu, 1963; Ford Fndn. Consult., Bogotá, 1970. **Pubns.:** *Cataloging Service: an Index to Bulletins 79–121* (1977); *Index to LC's Cataloging Service, Bulletins 79–125* (1978); "Latin Americana in the Joint Universities Library," *TN Libn.* (Fall 1964); *Cumulative Index to Cataloging Service Bulletin, no. 1–6* (1980); "Index to Record Reviews, #1–#20," *Old Time Msc.* (Jubilee issue 1977). **Activities:** 1, 12; 20, 46; 54, 55, 57 **Addr.:** VC/UHVC Library, 2602 N. Ben Jordan, Victoria, TX 77901.

Montgomery, Kathleen L. (F. 24, 1933, Benton, AR) Ref. Libn., Arnold and Porter Law Lib., 1978–; Attorney-at-law, Dukes and Troese Law Firm, 1975–78; Ref. Libn., Prince Georges Cnty. Lib. Syst., 1968–73; Asst. Head of Circ., Univ. of MD, Undergrad. Lib., 1958–60. **Educ.:** Cornell Coll., 1950–55, BA (Eng.); Cath. Univ., 1956–58, MSLS; Univ. of MD, 1973–76, JD. **Orgs.:** AALL. Amer. Bar Assn. AAUW: Area Branch Pres., VP (1966–73). **Honors:** AAUW, Anl. Achvmt. Awd., 1977. **Pubns.:** *Women and the Law - Maryland* (1976). **Activities:** 39; 77 **Addr.:** 13400 Forest Dr., Bowie, MD 20716.

Montgomery, Margaret (Ja. 9, 1940, Yorkton, SK) Tchr.–Libn., West Vernon Elem. Sch., 1981–; Tchr.–Libn., Coldstream Elem. Sch., 1978–81; Tchr.–Libn., Quadra Elem. Sch., 1974–78; Chld. Libn., Richmond Branch, Fraser Valley Reg. Lib., 1971–74; Part-time Instr. Univ. of BC, 1981; Part–time Instr., Univ. of Lethbridge, 1979; Part–time Instr., Univ. of Victoria, 1978–80. **Educ.:** Univ. of BC, 1961, BA (Eng.); Univ. of OR, 1968–70, MLS. **Orgs.:** BC Sch. Libns. Assn.: Corr. Secy. (1979–81); BCSLA Reviews (Ed., 1980–). Victoria Sch. Libns. Assn.: Pres. Can. LA. BC Tchrs. Fed. **Activities:** 10; 21, 26, 42 **Addr.:** Site 6, Box 9, R.R. #7, Vernon, BC V1T 7Z3 Canada.

Montgomery, Mary E. (D. 6, 1925, Detroit, MI) Resrch. Libn., Eaton Corp., 1966–; Corp. Libn., Burroughs Corp., 1962–66; Ref. Libn., Gen. Motors Resrch. Labs., 1956–62; Bkmobile. Libn., Dearborn Pub. Lib., 1952–55. **Educ.:** Wayne Univ., 1944–48, BA (Pol. Sci.); Univ. of MI, 1950–51, MA (LS). **Orgs.:** SLA: MI Chap. (Pres., 1961–62); various coms. and ofcs. **Activities:** 12; 17, 20, 39; 81, 91, 94 **Addr.:** Eaton Corp., Engineering & Research Library, 26201 Northwestern, P.O. Box 766, Southfield, MI 48037.

Montgomery, Paula Kay (S. 23, 1946, Omaha, NE) Chief, Sch. Media Srvs., MD State Dept. of Educ., 1979–; Tchr. Spec., Eval. & Sel., Div. of Educ. Media and Tech., Montgomery Cnty. Pub. Sch., 1977–79, Tchr. Spec., Field Srvs., 1973–77, Sch. Lib. Media Spec., 1969–73. **Educ.:** FL State Univ., 1964–67, BA (Eng./LS), 1967–68, MLS. **Orgs.:** ALA: AASL. AECT. Assn. for Early Childhood Educ. Intl. Reading Assn. Natl. Educ. Assn. **Honors:** Scribner Awd., 1973. **Pubns.:** *Teaching Media Skills* (1977); Contrib., *Reading For Young People; The Middle Atlantic* (1980); "Dragons, Dragons, Dragons and More," *Good Apple Nsltr.* (Ap., 1977); Filmstrip Column *Instructor Mag.* (1979–81); Film Review Column *Childhood Educ.* (1979–81). **Activities:** 10, 11; 17, 21, 24, 31, 32; 63 **Addr.:** Division of Library Development and Services, Maryland State Department of Education, 200 W. Baltimore St., Baltimore, MD 21201.

Montour, Lillian G. (S. 6, 1930, Six Nation's Rsrv., ON) Libn., Woodland Indian Cult. Educ. Ctr.; Libn., Six Nation's Pub. Lib. **Orgs.:** Can LA: Ch., Lib. & Info. Needs of Native People Com. ON LA. **Activities:** 12; 15, 16, 17 **Addr.:** Woodland Indian Cultural Educational Centre, 184 Mohawk St., Box 1506, Brantford, ON N3T 5V6 Canada.

Monty, Vivienne I. F. (Mr. 20, 1948, Budapest, Hungary) Asst. Head, Docum. Srvs., York Univ., 1973–. **Educ.:** Univ. of Toronto, 1967–71, BA (Hist.), 1971–73, MLS. **Orgs.:** SLA: Local arrange. com. (1973/74). Can. Assn. for Info. Sci. Can. Assn. of Spec. Libs. and Info. Srvs.: Pres. (1978–79). Can. LA: Treas. (1981–83); Cncl. (1979–80); Coll. and Univ. Sect., Acad. Status Com. (1979–81). Can. Assn. of Univ. Tchrs.: Acad. Libns. Com. (1978–81). York Univ. Fac. Assn.: Treas. (1977–78). **Pubns.:** *Bibliography of Canadian Tax Reform* (1973); "War of the WORDS," *CAUT Bltn.* (S. 1980). **Activities:** 1; 15, 17, 29; 59, 62, 66 **Addr.:** 223 Lonsdale Rd., Toronto, ON M4V 1W7 Canada.

Moody, Eleanor Louise (S. 9, 1914, St. Paul, MN) Dir. of Lib. Resrcs., Umpqud Cmnty. Coll., 1967–; Libn., John C. Fremont Jr. High, 1954–67; Libn., Instr., Camas Valley HS, 1944–54; Libn., Instr., Plaza HS, 1943–44; Instr., Carlton HS, 1941–42; Instr., Osakis HS, 1939–41; Instr., Souris HS, 1937–39; Instr., Streeter HS, 1936–37; Various prof. tchg. positions (1935–36). **Educ.:** St. Olaf Coll., 1931–35, BA (Eng., Hist.); Univ. South. CA, 1955–57, MA (LS). **Orgs.:** OR LA: Strg. Com. (1971–72); Conf. (Co–Ch., 1972). OR Cmnty. Coll. LA. Lane/Douglas Lib. Cnsrtm.: Strg. Com. (1979–81). South. OR Lib. Fed. Natl. Fed. of Garden Clubs: Riverbend Club. AAUW. **Activities:** 1, 10; 15, 17, 35 **Addr.:** 5013 Melgua Rd., Roseburg, OR 97470.

Moody, Jeanne Christensen (O. 25, 1942, Winchester, MA) Libn., CACI, Inc., 1980–; Consult., 1980–; Tech. Info. Spec., Natl. Injury Info. Clearinghouse, 1977–80; Lib. Dir., U.S. Consumer Product Safety Comsn., 1975–77, Deputy Dir. Lib., 1974–75; Sr. Anal. and Indxr., Herner and Co., 1969–73. **Educ.:** Temple Univ., 1967, BA (Psy.); Drexel Univ., 1967–69, MS (Info. Sci.). **Orgs.:** ASIS. Assoc. Info. Mgrs. Natl. Micro. Assn. SLA. World Future Socty. **Honors:** Beta Phi Mu, 1969; U.S. Consumer Product Safety Comsn., Superior Performance Awd., 1975. **Pubns.:** Jt. Cmplr., *Exhibit of Sources of Scientific and Technical Information* (1971). **Activities:** 4, 14-Consult. Firm; 17, 29, 30; 75, 82, 95-Consumer Affairs. **Addr.:** 11585 Links Dr., Reston, VA 22090.

Moody, Marilyn D. (Ag. 28, 1937, Little Rock, AR) Dist. Lib. Ctr. Ofc. Sr. Consult., Coord., Free Lib. of Philadelphia, 1976–, Consult. Libn., 1971–76, Libn. I, II, Gvt. Pubns., 1964–70. **Educ.:** Hendrix Coll., 1954–59, BA (Eng.); Univ. of AR, 1959–60, (Eng.); Drexel Univ., 1963–64, MS (LS). **Orgs.:** ALA. PA LA: Legis. Com. (1980, Ch. 1981–82); Ref. Mtrls. (1976–79); Nom. (1978); Chap. (1979). Cardinal Key. **Activities:** 9; 14-Reg. Lib.; 24, 25, 29; 77, 78 **Addr.:** 3310 W. Coulter St., Philadelphia, PA 19129.

Moody, Roland H. (Jl. 17, 1916, Manchester, NH) Dean of Libs. & Lrng. Resrcs., Northeastern Univ., 1975–, Dir. of Libs., 1953–75; Circ. Libn., Lamont Lib., Harvard Univ., 1948–53, Gen. Asst., Widener Lib., 1941–48. **Educ.:** Dartmouth Coll., 1934–38, AB (Econ.); Columbia Univ., 1940–41, BLS. **Orgs.:** Boston Lib. Cnsrtm.: Pres. (1979–80); Exec. Com. (1980–81). ALA. **Activities:** 1; 17 **Addr.:** Northeastern Univ. Library, 360 Huntington Ave., Boston, MA 02115.

Moon, Eric (Mr. 6, 1923, Yeovil, Eng.) Ed. and Prof. Rel. Spec., Grolier, Inc., 1979–; Pres., Scarecrow Pr., Inc., 1971–78; Exec. Off., 1969–71; Dir. of Ed. Dev., R. R. Bowker Co., 1968–69; Ed.-in-Chief, Lib. Jnl., 1959–68; Dir., Lib. Srvs. and Secy./Treas., Newfoundland Pub. Libs. Bd., Can., 1958–59; Head, Bibl. Prcs., Kensington Pub. Lib., Eng., 1956–58; Deputy Libn. and Cur., Brentford and Chiswick Pub. Libs. and Musm., Eng., 1954–56. **Educ.:** Loughborough Coll., Eng., 1947–49, (Flw. of Lib. Assn.). **Orgs.:** ALA: Pres. (1977–78); Com. on Org. (1971–73; Ch., 1972–73); Cncl (1965–72); Exec. Bd. (1976–79); Nom. Com. (1980–81); H.W. Wilson Lib. Per. Awd. Jury (1961); Lib. Admin. Div., Pub. Rel. Sect.; Publ. Com. (1964–65). NJ LA: Exec. Bd. (1971–73); Grievance Com. (1972–73). Lib. Pub. Rel. Cncl.: VP (1964–65). CAN. LA: Fed. Aid Com. (1958–59); Comp. Lib. Educ. Com. (1958–59). The Lib. Assn. (UK): (Cncl., 1955–58). Assn. of Asst. Libns. (UK) VP, 1958; Natl. Secy., 1955–58). Amer. Arts All.: Bd. (1977–81); Exec. Com. (1977–79). Ctr. for the Book, Lib. of Cong.: Nat. Adv. Bd. (1978–81). Nat. Assn. of Local Govt. Off. (U.K.): Pres., Brentford and Chiswick Br., (1955–56); Exec. Mem., Kensington Br., (1957–58) Cncl. for FL. Libs: Bd. of Dir. (1980–). The Maurice F. Tauber Foundation: Bd. of Advs. (1981–). **Honors:** Savannah State Coll., GA, Lib. Awd. for Dist. Srv., 1966. AIA, Joseph W. Lippincott Awd. for Notable Achievement in Librarianship, 1981. **Pubns.:** *Book Selection and Censorship in the Sixties* (1969); *Library Issues: The Sixties* (1970); reviews; various articles; "I Want to Be a Librarian," (1955). **Activities:** 9; 17, 24, 37; 57, 74 **Addr.:** 2811 Palm Aire Dr., Sarasota FL 33580.

Moon, Ilse B. (O. 7, 1932, Nürnberg, Germany) Consult., 1979–; Dir., Prof. Dev. Std., Rutgers Grad. Sch. of Lib. & Info. Std., 1976–78; Head, Info. Resrcs. & other positions, Montclair Pub. Lib., 1971–76; Ref. Libn., Drew Univ. Lib., 1970–71; Cat. Libn., Coll. of William & Mary, 1966–70; Libn., Univ. of GA Marine Inst., 1960–65. **Educ.:** Antioch Coll., 1948–52, AB (Soclgy.); Columbia Univ., 1965–66, MSLS. **Orgs.:** ALA: Stdg. Com. on Lib. Educ. (1978–80). CLENE: Bd. of Dir. (1977). NJ LA: Asst. ed., *NJ Libs.* (1971–74); Schol. Com. (1975–78); Exec. Bd. (1973–74); Lib. Dev. Com. (1971–78). VA LA: Asst. Ed., *Virginia Librarian,* (1969). FL LA. Women's Political Caucus **Honors:** Beta Phi Mu, 1966. **Pubns.:** "Libraries" *New Book of Knowledge* (1980); Contrib., *Current Biog.* (1980–); "Essex County Core Collection" *Unabashed Librarian* (1976); Reviews; Ed. bd., *Collection Building* (1978–). **Activities:** 1, 9, 11; 17, 25, 39 **Addr.:** 2811 Palm Aire Dr., Sarasota, FL 33580.

Moon, Martha Louise (M.) (N. 23, 1930, Omaha, GA) Assoc. Libn., Geo. C. Wallace State Cmnty. Coll., 1973–; Dir. of Media Ctr., Dothan City Schs., 1968–71; Assoc. Libn., Columbus (GA) HS, 1967–68; Head Libn., Enterprise State Jr. Coll., 1965–67; Head Libn., Louisville (AL) HS, 1961–65; Head Libn., Luverne HS, 1958–61. **Educ.:** Troy State Univ., 1955–60, BS (Eng., Soc. Stds.); Auburn Univ., 1960–64, MED (LS), 1973–77, AA (Sup., Admin.). **Orgs.:** AL Jr. Coll. LA. AL LA. ALA. Various other orgs. Natl. Educ. Assn. AAUW. Phil Delta Kappa. Alpha Delta Kappa: Pres. (1964). **Activities:** 1; 15, 31, 39; 63 **Addr.:** 2003 Hardwick Dr., Dothan, AL 36303.

Moon, Myra Jo (D. 26, 1931, Emporia, KS) Prep. Libn., CO State Univ. Libs., 1969–, Asst. Cat. Libn., Serials, 1967–69, Asst. Cat. Libn., Monograph, 1965–67; Head Clinical Chem., St. Francis Hosp., Tulsa, OK, 1960–63; Med. Tech., St. John's Hosp., Tulsa, OK, 1954–60. **Educ.:** Univ. of OK, 1950–53, BS (Med. Tech.), 1963–65, MLS. **Orgs.:** ALA. CO LA. AAUP: CO State Univ. Chap., Secy. (1974–80). **Honors:** CO State Univ. Libs., Distin. Libnshp. Awd., 1975; Beta Phi Mu. **Pubns.:** "Use of Automation in Bindery Procedures at Colorado State University" *Lib. Scene* (S. 1974); "Bibliography of Mari Sandoz", *Bltn. of Bibl.* (1981); reviews. **Activities:** 1; 17, 23, 46 **Addr.:** 1412 Constitution, Fort Collins, CO 80521.

Mooney, James E. (My. 13, 1932, Manchester, NH) Dir., Hist. Socty. of PA, 1974–, Asst. Dir., 1973–74; Adj. Prof., Temple Univ., 1975–76; Asst. Dir., Ed., Amer. Antiq. Socty., 1971–73, Ed. of Pubns., 1967–71; Instr., Asst. Prof., Worcester Polytech. Inst., 1963–67. **Educ.:** Harvard Coll., 1960, AB (Hist.); Clark Univ., 1962, AM, 1971, PhD (Hist.). **Orgs.:** New Eng. Hist. and Geneal. Socty.: Ed. Com. Geneal. Socty. of PA: Bd. PA Hist. Recs. Adv. Bd. NH Hist. Socty.: Pubns. Com. Indian Rights Assn. Cons. Ctr. for Art and Hist. Artifacts. Grt. Philadelphia Cult. Alliance. Univ. of PA Press: Trustee. Various other orgs. **Pubns.:** Jt. auth., *A Rising People: The Founding of the United States, 1765–1789* (1976); jt. auth., *The National Index of American Imprints through 1800* (1969); "A Bibliography of Loyalist Source Material in the U.S., Part I, II, III," *Procs.* (1975, 1976); *City Chronicles: Philadelphia—The City Politic* (1976); various edshps. **Activities:** 2, 12; 17, 45, 47; 55, 57, 70 **Addr.:** Historical Society of Pennsylvania, 1300 Locust St., Philadelphia, PA 19107.

Mooney, Martha T. (S. 15, 1935, New York, NY) Ed., *Bk. Review Digest,* H. W. Wilson Co., 1977–, Asst. Ed., 1973–77, Catlgr., 1966–73. **Educ.:** Fordham Univ., 1956–60, MS (Eng. Lit.); Queens Coll., 1965–70, MLS. **Orgs.:** New York Lib. Club. ALA. NY Tech. Srvs. Libns.: Secy.–Treas. (1976–77); Bd. Mem. (1980–81). Westside Workshop Cable TV Prog. **Activities:** 6; 20, 42; 95-Editing. **Addr.:** 392 Central Park West, 9A, New York, NY 10025.

Mooney, Philip F. (D. 14, 1944, Lowell, MA) Mgr., Arch./Bus. Info. Srvs., Coca-Cola Co., 1977–; Lib. Dir., Balch Inst., 1972–77; Asst. Dir., George Arents Resrch. Lib., Syracuse Univ., 1968–72. **Educ.:** Boston Coll., 1962–66, BS (Hist.); Syracuse

PROFESSIONAL ACTIVITIES: Institutions: 1. Acad. lib.; 2. Arch.; 3. Assn.; 4. Fed./Gvt. lib.; 5. Inst. lib.; 6. Mfr./Suppl.; 7. Milit. lib.; 8. Musm.; 9. Pub. lib.; 10. Sch. lib.; 11. Sch. of lib. sci.; 12. Spec. lib.; 13. State lib.; 14. (other). **Functions/Activities:** 15. Acq./Col. dev.; 16. Adult srvs.; 17. Admin.; 18. Apprais.; 19. Archit./Bldgs.; 20. Cat./Class.; 21. Chld. srvs.; 22. Circ.; 23. Cons./Pres.; 24. Consult.; 25. Cont. ed.; 26. Educ. lib. sci.; 27. Ext. srvs.; 28. Fund/Grants; 29. Gvt. pubs.; 30. Indx./Abs.; 31. Instr. lib. use; 32. Media srvs.; 33. Micro.; 34. Netwks./Coop.; 35. Persnl.; 36. PR; 37. Publshg.; 38. Recs. mgt.; 39. Ref. srvs.; 40. Repro.; 41. Resrch.; 42. Review.; 43. Secur.; 44. Serials; 45. Spec. col.; 46. Tech. srvs.; 47. Trustees/Bds.; 48. YA srvs.; 49. (other).

Univ., 1966–69, MA (Hist.). **Orgs.:** SAA: Nom. Com. (1979–80); Prog. Com. Assn. of Rec. Mgrs. and Admins. Socty. of GA Archvsts. **Pubns.:** "Philadelphia's Ethnic Press 1876–1976", *Drexel Lib. Qtly.* (Jl. 1976). **Activities:** 2; 15, 36, 41; 51, 59 **Addr.:** Archives Dept., The Coca-Cola Company, P. O. Box 1734, Atlanta, GA 30301.

Mooney, Sandra Taylor (Je. 20, 1943, Wichita, KS) Ref. Libn. (Asst. Lib.), Troy H. Middleton Lib., LA State Univ., 1977–, Actg. Head, Hum. Div., 1976–77, Ref. Libn., Hum. Div., 1972–76. **Educ.:** AR State Univ., 1961–65, BSE (Eng.); LA State Univ., 1965–71, MLS. **Orgs.:** ALA: ACRL; RASD. SWLA. LA LA. AAUW. **Activities:** 1; 15, 39; 55 **Addr.:** Central Reference Department, Troy H. Middleton Library, Louisiana State University, Baton Rouge, LA 70803.

Mooney, Shirley E. (Regina, SK.) Lib. Mgr., Pac. Press Ltd., Vancouver, 1968–; Libn., SK Resrch. Cncl., 1967–68; Resrch. Libn., Imperial Oil Ltd., 1963–66; Ref. Libn., Univ. of Alberta, 1960–63. **Educ.:** Univ. of SK, 1953–56, BA (Eng.); Univ. of Toronto, 1959–60, BLS. **Orgs.:** SLA: Newspaper Div. **Pubns.:** Contrib., *Guidelines To Newspaper Libraries* (1974); "A House Divided," *Shorttakes* (1979). **Activities:** 12; 15, 17, 18; 83 **Addr.:** 2250 Granville Street Vancouver, BC V6H 3G2 Canada.

Moore, Adam Gillespie Nichol (O. 21, 1931, Boston, MA) Secy., Boston Med. Lib., 1979–; Trustee, 1975–79. **Educ.:** Harvard Coll. 1950–55, AB (Phys. Anthro.); Univ. of Aberdeen, 1956–64, MD equivalent. **Orgs.:** Boston Med. Lib. Countway Assocs., Boston, MA. Carney Hosp. Lib. Com. Boston Athen. Lib.: Proprietor. various other orgs. AAAS. Assn. of Milit. Surgeons. Brit. Med. Assn. MA Med. Socty. various other orgs. **Pubns.:** various med., hist., lib. articles. **Activities:** 5, 12; 15, 34, 47; 50, 58, 80 **Addr.:** 10 Crabtree Rd., Squantum, Boston, MA 02171.

Moore, Barbara Niewoehner (D. 4, 1948, St. Louis, MO) Cat. Libn., Mankato State Univ. Lib., 1981–; Cat. Coord., 1977–81; Head Catlgr., Loyola (LA) Univ. Lib., 1973–77, Sci. Libn., 1971–73. **Educ.:** Lake Erie Coll., 1966–70, BA (Chem.); Rutgers Univ., 1970–71, MLS; Mankato State Univ., 1978– (Mgt., Admin.). **Orgs.:** ALA. MN LA. MN AACR2 Trainers. **Pubns.:** *A Manual of AACR2 Examples for Cartographic Materials* (1981); Contrib., *A Manual of AACR2 Examples* (1980); *Mankato State University's Online Catalog* (1981). **Activities:** 1; 20, 35, 46 **Addr.:** P.O. Box 19, Mankato State University, Mankato, MN 56001.

Moore, Bessie Boehm (Ag. 2, 1902, Owensboro, KY) Retired. Exec. Dir., AR Cncl. on Econ. Educ., 1962–79; Dir., Elem. Educ., AR Depart. of Educ., 1959–62. **Educ.:** Univ. of Ctrl. AR, BSE (Educ.); Univ. of CT, MA (Educ.). **Orgs.:** Natl. Comsn. on Libs. and Info. Sci.: Vice Ch. (1970–). Natl. Adv. Comsn. on Libs. ALA: ALTA, Pres. (1957–59); Legis. Com. (1960–66). AR LA: Ch. Soroptimist Intl. **Honors:** Univ. of AR, LLD, 1959, Distin. Alum., 1974; Univ. of MI, LLD, 1959; Hon. Mem. Lib. Sch. Alum., 1977; WHCOLIS Cit.; Univ. of AZ, LLD, 1977. **Pubns.:** Various articles. **Addr.:** 712 Legato Dr., Little Rock, AR 72205.

Moore, Beverly Ann (Mr. 17, 1934, Evanston, WY) Lib. Dir., Univ. of South. CO, 1976–, Head Catlgr., 1974–76, Ref./Docum. Libn., 1970–74; Branch Libn., Pueblo Reg. Lib., 1966–70. **Educ.:** Univ. of North. CO, 1954–57, BA (Eng., Soc. Sci.); Univ. of Denver, 1967–70, MA (LS); Hutchinson Jr. Coll., 1952–54, AA. **Orgs.:** ALA. CO LA: Coll. and Univ. Div. (Ch., 1978–79). AR Valley Reg. Lib. Srv. Syst.: Governing Bd. Ch. (1978–79); Treas. (1979–). CO Netwk. Adv. Com. Leag. of Women Voters of Pueblo. Admin. Mgt. Socty. **Honors:** Beta Phi Mu. **Activities:** 1, 9; 17, 20, 39 **Addr.:** LRC/Library Division, University of Southern Colorado, Pueblo, CO 81001.

Moore, Curtis P. (Mr. 14, 1935, Philipsburg, PA) Admin., Lebanon Cnty. Lib. Syst., 1970–; Dir., Centre Cnty. Lib., 1964–70. **Educ.:** Lock Haven State Coll., 1960–63, BS (Educ.); Drexel Inst. of Tech., 1965–66, MSLS. **Orgs.:** ALA: Various coms. PA LA: Treas. (1981–83); Various coms. Kiwanis Club of Lebanon: Pres., 1980–81. **Activities:** 9; 17 **Addr.:** 624 Chestnut St., Lebanon, PA 17042.

Moore, Edythe (Coxton, KY) Mgr., Lib. Srvs., Charles C. Lauritsen Lib., Aerosp. Corp., 1964–; Lit. Resrch. Anal., 1962–64; Head, Tech. Info. Ctr., American Potash and Chemical Corp., 1956–62; Resrch. Libn., Behr-Manning Corp., 1953–55; Resrch. Libn., Hydrocarbon Resrch., Inc., 1948–53; Admin., Tech. Info. Ctr., Philips Labs., Inc., 1946–48; Patent Resrchr., L. P. Graner, Inc., 1944–45; Engin., Brewster Aeronautical Corp., 1943–44; Various LS tchg. positions (1965–77). **Educ.:** PA State Univ., 1943, BS (Phys.); Univ. of South. CA, 1965, MS (LS). **Orgs.:** SLA: Depository Lib. Cncl. to the Pub. Printer (1979–82); Awds. Com. (1973–74; 1976–78; Ch., 1977–78); Past Pres. (1975–76); Pres. (1974–75); Pres.-elect (1973–74); Dir. (1969–72); Various coms. and ofcs. CA LA: Various coms. and ofcs. ASIS. South. CA Tech. Prcs. Grp. Various other orgs. and ofcs. West. Info. Netwk. on Energy. Frnds. of Torrance Lib. **Pubns.:** "A New Role for Divisions?" *Sci-Tech News* (1975); "Systems Analysis: An Overview," *Spec. Libs.* (1967); "Literature Research for a Space Materials Research Program," *Jnl. of Chem. Docum.* (1963). **Activities:** 12; 17 **Addr.:** Charles C. Lauritsen Library, The Aerospace Corporation, P.O. Box 92957, Los Angeles, CA 90009.

Moore, Erdeal A. (D. 1, 1924, Marion, AL) Serials Libn., Univ. of AL, Birmingham, 1954–; Catlgr., Coll. of Educ., Univ. of AL, Tuscaloosa, 1950–53; Libn., W. Blocton HS, 1947–49. **Educ.:** Univ. of AL, Tuscaloosa, 1943–47, BS (Educ., LS), 1952, MA (Educ., LS). **Orgs.:** Med. LA. AL LA: Tech. Srvs. RT, Mem. Com. (1980). Southeast. Reg. Med. Lib. Prog.: Un. List Com. (1979–80). **Pubns.:** Ed., "Selected Periodicals for the Medical Library" (1974–79); oral presentations. **Activities:** 20, 44, 46; 58, 80, 95-Dentistry. **Addr.:** Lister Hill Library of the Health Sciences, University of Alabama in Birmingham, University Station, Birmingham, AL 35294.

Moore, Evelyn Alice (S. 15, 1936, Houston, TX) Dir. of Info. Srvs., Edgehill Newport Inc., 1980–; Assoc. Prof., Sch. of LS, Univ. of NC, 1975–80; Asst. Prof, Grad. Sch. of Bus., DePaul Univ., 1973–75; Resrch. Assoc., Northwestern Univ., 1969–72; Sci. Engin. Libn., Univ. of IL, Chicago Circle, 1965–69; Resrch. Assoc., Washington Univ. Sch. of Med., 1964–65; Lib. Ref. Asst., Battelle Meml. Inst., 1963–64; Intern, Ref. Libn., Lib. of Congs., 1961–63. **Educ.:** Univ. of Denver, 1954–58, BS (Chem.); Western Reserve Univ., 1959–61, MS (LS); Northwestern Univ., 1969–73, PhD. **Orgs.:** ASIS: Nom. Com. (1978); Educ. Com. (1978–80); Awd. of Merit Nom. Com. (1978–80); Ch., Carolinas Chap. (1976–78); Ed., *Nsltr.* of Spec. Int. Grp. on Educ. (1977–); Ch., Chap. Review Com. (1977–78). ALA. Sigma Xi. Amer. Chem. Socty. AAAS. Acad. of Mgt. **Pubns.:** *Directories in Science & Technology*. (1963); jt. auth., "Mechanization of Library Procedures in the Medium-sized Medical Library," *Bltn. of the Med. LA,* (Jl. 1965); "Data Processing in the Washington University School of Medicine Library," *in Information Retrieval with Special Reference to the Biomedical Sciences* (1966); jt. auth., "Explorations on the Information-Seeking Style of Researchers," *Communication Among Scientists and Engineers,* (1970); jt. auth., "Behavioral Factors Influencing the Adoption of an Experimental Information System," *Hosp. Admin.* (1973). **Activities:** 14-Hospital; 17 **Addr.:** Edgehill Newport Inc., Harrison Ave., Newport, RI 02840.

Moore, Everett L. (My. 24, 1918, Eugene, OR) Dir. of Lib. Srvs., Woodbury Univ., Los Angeles, 1976–; Dir., Lib. Srvs., Prof. of Libnshp., Coll. of the Desert, 1962–75; Dir., Univ. Lib., Cairo, Egypt, 1970–72; Head, Soc. Sci. and Bus. Lib., CA State Univ., Chico, 1960–62; Head, Tech. Prcs., N. Ctrl. Reg. Lib., Tillamook, OR, 1958–60; Head Libn., Evangel Coll., Springfield, Missouri, 1955-57. **Educ.:** Wheaton Coll., 1946–49, AB (Bible); Point Loma Coll., 1950–54, MA (Rel.); Vanderbilt Univ., 1956–60, MA LS; Univ. of Southern CA, 1962–73, PhD (Lib. Sci.). **Orgs.:** ALA: ACRT; Jr. Coll. Lib. Sect., Stan. and Crit. Com. (1966–68). CA LA: JCRT (1965–66). CA Comnty. Coll. Lib. Coop.: Ch., Tech. Prcs. Sec. (1968–70). CA Tchrs. Assn. AAUP. **Pubns.:** *The Library in the Administrative and Organizational Structure of the American Public Community College* (1973); Ed., *Junior College Libraries:* (1969); "Processing Center for California Junior College Libraries", (Sum., 1965); "Merit Pay: Bane or Blessing," *Jr. Coll. Jnl.* (Oct. 1965); "North Coastal Regional Library Cooperative Ordering & Cataloging Project," *OR State Lib. Letter to Libs.* (Ap. 1959). **Activities:** 1, 9; 15, 17, 41; 56, 59, 90 **Addr.:** 3719 Trinity Ct., Chino, CA 91710.

Moore, Florence A. (S. 30, 1922, Cobalt, ON) Dir., Tech. Srvs. Branch, Lib. of Parlmt., 1970–; Chief, Cat. Branch, 1963–70, Head, Eng. Cat., 1949–53, Catlgr., 1947–49. **Educ.:** Univ. of Ottawa, 1940–43, BA (Eng.), 1947–49, BLS. **Orgs.:** Can. LA. Can. ALL. Can. Task Grp. on Cat. Stans.: Subgrp. on the Class. of Can. Law (Ch.). Zonta Club of Ottawa. **Activities:** 4; 17, 45, 46; 56, 77 **Addr.:** Library of Parliament, Ottawa, ON K1A 0A9 Canada.

Moore, Gale (Jl. 26, 1944, Ottawa, ON) Info. Consult., Prog. in Grntlgy., 1979–; Assoc. Instr., Fac. of LS, Univ. of Toronto, 1978–, Hlth. Scis. Bk. Selector, 1975–; Ref. Libn., Gen. Ref. Dept., 1974–75, Head of Circ., Sci. and Med. Lib., 1970–72, ILL Libr., 1968–70. **Educ.:** Dalhousie Univ., 1961–65, BSc, Hon (Zlgy.); Univ. of Toronto, 1967–68, BLS, 1976–79, MLS. **Orgs.:** CHLA. Med. LA. Can. Assn. Info. Sci. Libns. Assn., Univ. of Toronto. Educ. Cncl. for Hlth. and the Env. Univ. of Toronto Fac. Assn. **Pubns.:** *A Guide to the Literature of the History of Medicine* (1978); Jt. auth., "Canadian Information Resources and Services in Gerontology and Geriatrics," *Spec. Col.* (1981); "Communications and Health," *Outside In: Health and the Environment* (1980); "Interdisciplinarity and Information Needs; Towards the Concept of an Academic Library Information Centre," *Argus* (1979). **Activities:** 1, 11; 15, 26, 41; 58, 75, 80 **Addr.:** Book Selection Dept., University of Toronto Library, 130 St. George St., Toronto, ON M5S 1A5 Canada.

Moore, Grace G. (Jl. 6, 1930, Atlanta, GA) Recorder of Docum., LA State Lib., 1979–; Serials Libn., 1971–79, Serials/Ref. Libn., 1973–76, Catlgr./Tech. Srvs., 1969–71. **Educ.:** Univ. of AR, 1948–52, BA (Hist.); LA State Univ., 1968–69, MSLS. **Orgs.:** ALA: GODORT, State and Lcl. Docums. Task Force, Docums. on Docums. Col. (Coord., 1980). LA LA: Subj. Spec., Nom. Com. (1977). SELA. Beta Phi Mu: BZ Chap. (Treas., 1980–81). Baton Rouge Lib. Club. LA State Lib. Staff Assn. Mortar Board Alum.: Secy. (1969–70). **Honors:** Phi Beta Kappa. **Pubns.:** Ed., *Public Documents* (1979–); Complr., *Louisiana State Library List of Serials* (1977); Jt. ed. and contrib., *Proceedings of LA LA Docums. Com. Wkshp. and Legislative Revision* (1981). **Activities:** 13; 17, 20, 29; 57, 62 **Addr.:** 4554 Whitehaven St., Baton Rouge, LA 70808.

Moore, Heather (Je. 11, 1948, ON) Chief Libn., Lib. and Ref. Ctr., Ministry of the Solicitor Gen., 1981–; Head, Tech. Srvs., Dept. of Justice Lib., 1977–81; Head of Cat., Dept. of the Secy. of State Lib., 1976–77. **Educ.:** Univ. of Toronto, 1969–73, BA (Hist.), 1973–75, MLS. **Orgs.:** Can. LA. Can. ALL: Gvt. Docum. Com. Assn. Can. Map Libns. Cncl. of Fed. Libs.: Com. on Cons./Presrvn. of Lib. Mtrls.; Col. Rationalization Com., Sub-Com. on the Soc. Scis. and the Hum.; Cont. Educ. Com., Sub-Com. on Trng. for AACR2 (Ch.). Bibl. Socty. of Can. **Addr.:** 39 Mark Ave., Apt. 6, Vanier, ON K1L 6A6 Canada.

Moore, Ivy P. (Ja. 13, 1932, Quail, TX) Pub. Info. Spec., Fed. AV. Admin. AK. Reg., 1981–, Chief, Lib. Staff, Fed. Aviation Adm., AK Reg., 1965–81; Libn., Cat., San Diego Pub. Lib., 1962–65; Asst. Cat. Libn., N. TX State Univ., 1958–62; Catlgr., Ser. Libn., Hardin-Simmons Univ., 1957–58. **Educ.:** Wayland Baptist Coll., 1949–53; W. TX State Coll., 1954–55, BS (Speech); TX Woman's Univ., 1955–57, MLS. **Orgs.:** AK LA: Secy. (1967); Treas. (1968); Secy., Anchorage Chap. (1980). **Honors:** Alpha Beta Alpha. **Activities:** 1, 4; 17, 33, 46; 52, 64, 67 **Addr.:** FAA Public Affairs Office, 701 C Street, Box 14, Anchorage, AK 99513.

Moore, James D. (D. 16, 1940, Cheyenne, WY) Reg. Archvst., WA State Arch., 1975–; Dir., Univ. Recs. Ctr., West. WA Univ., 1974–75. **Educ.:** West. WA Univ., 1969–71, BA (Hist.); Grad. Prog., 1974–75, Cert. (Arch. Admin.). **Orgs.:** Assn. of Recs. Mgrs. and Admins.: Seattle Chap., Bd. of Dirs. (1977–78). SAA. Gvr.'s WA State Hist. Recs.: Adv. Bd. **Activities:** 2; 17, 24, 38; 69, 75, 95-Reg. Stds. **Addr.:** State Archives Regional Center, Western Washington University, Bellingham, WA 98225.

Moore, Jane Ross (Ap. 24, 1929, Philadelphia, PA) Prof. and Chief Libn., Grad. Sch. and Univ. Ctr., City Univ. of New York, 1976–; Assoc. Libn. for Admin. Srvs., Brooklyn Coll., 1973–76, Chief, Cat. Div., 1965–73, Chief, Serials Cat. Libn., 1958–64; Chief, Tech. Srvs. Grp., Lib., Lederle Labs., Amer. Cyanamid Co., 1954–58; Catlgr., Sterling Meml. Lib., Yale Univ., 1952–54; Adj. Prof., Grad. Sch. of Lib. and Info. Stds., Queens Coll., 1977–, Adj. Assoc. Prof., 1974–76. **Educ.:** Smith Coll., 1947–51, AB (Zlgy.); Drexel Univ., 1951–52, MS (LS); New York Univ., 1960–65, MBA; Case West. Rsrv. Univ., 1970–74, PhD (LS). **Orgs.:** ALA: RTSD (Dir., 1968–70, 1975–76), Ch., Cncl. of Reg. Grps. (1968–69), Cat. and Class. Sect. (Ch., 1975–76), Exec. Com. (1974–77), Margaret Mann Awd. Com. (Ch., 1977–78), Various coms.; IRRT (Exec. Com., 1976–77). ASIS: Metro. New York Chap., various coms. NY LA: Pres., 1979–80; Various ofcs. New York Lib. Club: Pres., 1980–81; Various ofcs. Various other orgs. and ofcs. AAUP. AAUW. **Honors:** NY Tech. Srvs. Libns., Cit., 1976; Higher Educ. Act, Title IIB Flwshp., 1970–72. **Pubns.:** *Information and the Urban Dweller: A Study of an Information Delivery System* (1974); "Cataloging and Classification," *ALA Yearbook* (1976); "On Interrelationships of the Sciences and Technology as Expressed by a Categorized List of Journals and Modified by a Classification System," *Jnl. of ASIS* (1973); Various reviews. **Activities:** 1, 11; 17, 26, 46 **Addr.:** Library, Graduate School and University Center, City University of New York, 33 West 42nd St., New York, NY 10036.

Moore, John R. (N. 12, 1921, Birmingham, AL) Head, Engin. Sect., Bus. Sci. Tech. Div., Chicago Pub. Lib., 1976–, Head, Adult Bk. Sel., 1973–75, Asst., Adult Srvs., 1970–73; various positions in engin., 1957–69; various positions in tchg., 1948–57. **Educ.:** Maryville Coll., 1940–47, AB (Bio.); Rosary Coll., 1969–1970, MALS; Cert. Med. Libn., 1976; various crs. in bot. **Orgs.:** SLA: Engin. Div. (Ch., 1981–82). IL Reg. Lib. Cncl.: Sci. Tech. Engin. Stans. Srvy. Com. (Ch., 1978–80). West. Socty. of Engins.: Pubns. Com. (Ch., 1978–80). **Honors:** West. Socty. of Engin., Anl. Srv. Awd., 1980; Theta Alpha Phi, 1946. **Pubns.:** Jt. Auth. *Standards, Specifications and Codes Available in the Chicago Area* (1980); "A Bicentennial Look at Engineering in the Midwest (1850–1875 segment)," *Midwest Engin.* (O. 1976); Anl. Indx. and various articles in *Midwest Engin.* **Activities:** 9; 15, 16, 45; 64, 65, 91 **Addr.:** Business/Science/Technology Division, Chicago Public Library, 425 N. Michigan Ave., Chicago, IL 60611.

Moore, Julie L. (S. 11, 1941, Sioux City, IA) Owner, Mgr., Biol. Info. Srv., 1969–; Coord., Lib. and Info. Srvs., Ger. Ctr., Univ. of Southern CA, 1969–74; Head Indxr., Fed. Aid to Wildlife Rest. Prog., Denver Pub. Lib., 1965–68; Asst. Libn., NY Bot. Gardens, 1964; Sci. Libn., Univ. of NE, 1963–64. **Educ.:** llniv. of Denver, 1959–62, BA (Bio./Anthro.); Post graduate: Univ. of Southern CA 1962–63, MA LS; 1968–69, (Lib. Sci.). **Orgs.:** SLA. Wildlife Socty. Amer. Socty. of Mammalogists. **Pubns.:** *Bibliography of Wildlife Theses, 1900–1968* (1970); "Wildlife Manage-

Special Subjects/Services: 50. Adult educ.; 51. Advert./Mktg.; 52. Aerosp.; 53. Agric.; 54. Area std.; 55. Arts/Hum.; 56. Autom.; 57. Bibl./Prtg.; 58. Bio. sci.; 59. Bus./Fin.; 60. Chem.; 61. Copyrt.; 62. Documtn.; 63. Educ.; 64. Engin.; 65. Env.; 66. Eth. grps.; 67. Film; 68. Food/Nutr.; 69. Geneal.; 70. Geo.; 71. Geol.; 72. Handcpd.; 73. Hist.; 74. Int. frdm.; 75. Info. sci.; 76. Insr.; 77. Law; 78. Legis.; 79. Math./Comp. sci.; 80. Med.; 81. Metals; 82. Nat. resrcs.; 83. Newsp.; 84. Nuc. sci.; 85. Oral hist.; 86. Petr./Energy; 87. Pharm.; 88. Phys./Astr./Math.; 89. Readg.; 90. Relig.; 91. Sci./Tech.; 92. Soc. sci.; 93. Telecom.; 94. Transp.; 95. (other).

ment Literature," in *Wildlife Tech. Man.* (1980). "Microfilm Information System." *JOLA Tech. Comm.* (Ap. 1971); "A History of Bibliographic Control of American Doctoral Dissertations," *Spec. Libs.* (My/Je 1972); Reviews. **Activities:** 1; 24, 30; 58, 82, 95-Gerontology. **Addr.:** 3319 Avalon St. #14, Riverside, CA 92509.

Moore, (Mr.) Kay K. (N. 26, 1910, Pembina, ND) Chief Cat. Libn., Emeritus, Brown Univ., 1976–, Chief Catalog Libn., 1945–76; Libn., Norwich Univ., 1934–45; Catlgr., Mt. Union Coll., 1933; Educ. docum. catlgr., desk Asst., Tchrs. Coll. Libn., Columbia Univ., 1933–34. **Educ.:** Mt. Union Coll., 1928–32, AB (Eng.); Columbia Univ., 1932–33, BS(LS). **Orgs.:** ALA. RI LA: Past Pres.; Ch., Com. on Gvt. Rel. (1947–1963). New Eng. Tech. Srvs. Libns.: Past Pres. VT LA: Exec. Com. (1938–45); Pres. (1939–40). Greenville Pub. Lib. Trustee (1950–79). Other orgs. Amer. Gld. of Organists. **Honors:** Brown Univ., MS (Hon.), 1967. **Pubns.:** Ed. *Report of the Legislative Commission on Libraries to the General Assembly of the State of Rhode Island and Providence Plantations* (1964); Ed., *Contribution to a Union Catalog of Sixteenth Century Imprints in Certain New England Libraries* (1953); Ed., *List of Latin American Imprints before 1800 Selected from Bibliographies of Jose Toribio Medina* (1952); *Checklist and Index of the University of the State of New York Bulletins, nos. 255-1094* (1938). **Activities:** 1, 9; 20, 46, 47; 69, 78 **Addr.:** 73 Austin Ave., Greenville, RI 02828.

Moore, M. Elizabeth (Boston MA) Human Resrcs. Supvsr., Lib., MI Bell, 1979–; Mgr. Corp. Info. & Ref. Ctr., Burroughs Corp., 1967–79; Supvsr. Ref. Srvcs. Cat., Detroit Pub. Lib., 1955–67, Ref. Libn., 1953–54, Catlgr., 1949–53; Catlgr., Ref. Libn., Instr. of Lib. Sci., Fisk Univ., 1945–48; Asst. Libn., NC A&T State Univ., 1943–44. **Educ.:** NC A & T State Univ., 1937–40, BS (Fr./Hist.), 1940–41. Univ. of Chicago, 1944/45, BLS; Wayne State Univ. **Orgs.:** ALA: Ch. Subj. Headings Com., Div. of Cat. & Class. (1955–58). Women's Nat. Book Assn.: VP, Detroit Chap. (1972–77). SLA: MI Chap.: Prog. Com. (1968–69); Ch. Election Com. (1968–69, 1969–70); Ch., Mem. Com. (1971–72); VP and Ch., Prog. Com. (1972–73). Women's Econ. Club of Detroit: Bd. of Dir. (1972–73); Archvst. (1971–72); Hosp. and Mem. Com: (1976–77); Nom. Com. (1974). NAACP. Friends of the Detroit Pub. Lib.: Bd. of Dir., (1970–76; 1980–). Nom. Com., (1974–75); Acq. Com. (1974–). Your Heritage House: Ch. Founding Com. (1969–72); Bd. of Dir. (1970–date. **Honors:** Delta Sigma Theta. **Activities:** 12; 17; 59, 93 **Addr.:** Michigan Bell - Corporate Reference Center, 1365 Cass Ave., Room 1200, Detroit, MI 48226.

Moore, Mary Grace (Ag. 24, 1947, Morgantown, WV) Serials Catlgr., Univ. of OK, 1979–; Serials Cat. Libn., Frostburg State Coll., 1974–79; Serials Catlgr., U.S. Geol. Srvy., 1973–74, Asst. Exch. and Gift Libn., 1971–74. **Educ.:** Allegheny Coll., 1965–69, BS (Math); Univ. of NC, 1969–71, MSLS; Frostburg State Coll., 1977–79, MSM (Mgt.); various crs. in langs. and comps. **Orgs.:** ALA. OK LA. Frostburg State Coll. Campus Women. AAUW. **Honors:** Beta Phi Mu, 1971. **Pubns.:** Indxr., *Allegany County–A History* (1976). **Activities:** 1, 4; 15, 20, 44; 59, 71 **Addr.:** 901 24th Ave., S.W., Apt. 110, Norman, OK 73069.

Moore, Mary L. (Ap. 11, 1927, Oklahoma City, OK) Libn., Gen. Srvs. Lib., Exxon Co., 1963–. **Educ.:** TX Women's Univ., 1944–48, BA, BS (Art). **Orgs.:** SLA: Petr. Div. (Ch., 1971–72; Ch.-elect, 1970–71; Treas., 1968–70); TX Chap. (Treas., 1966–67), Mem. Com. (1962–63; 1965–66). **Activities:** 12; 15, 34, 39; 59, 86 **Addr.:** General Services Library, Exxon Company, U.S.A., P.O. Box 1280, Houston, TX 77001.

Moore, Mattie Ruth (F. 2, 1903, Marlin, TX) Retired; Dir., Media Srvs., Dallas Indp. Sch. Dist., 1952–72; Consult., Lib. Srvs., TX Educ. Agency, 1946–52; Libn., Dallas Schs., Dallas Indp. Sch. Dist., 1926–46. **Educ.:** South. Meth. Univ., 1925, BA (Speech); Peabody Coll., 1939–42, BS (LS); Univ. of TX, 1950–54, MEdA. **Orgs.:** TX LA: Pres. (1950). SWLA: Pres. (1962; 1964). ALA: State Sch. Lib. Sup. (Pres., 1947); Newbery Com. (1944; 1948; 1954); Auraine Awd. Com. (Ch., 1959). AAUW. Altrusa. Zeta Phi Eta. Delta Kappa Gamma. **Honors:** TX LA, Libn. of the Yr.; South. Meth. Univ. Alum., Woman of Achvmt., 1973. **Activities:** 11, 13; 27, 31, 32 **Addr.:** 3883 Turtle Creek, Dallas, TX 75219.

Moore, Maureen McCann (S. 26, 1944, Detroit, MI) Libn., World Bank/Intl. Monetary Fund, 1981–; Lib. Dir., Dept. of Justice, 1979–81; Lib. Dir., Fed. Trade Comsn., 1972–79; Libn., DC Bar Assn., 1970–72; Chief Circ. Libn., Univ. of MI Law Lib., 1967–70. **Educ.:** Univ. of MI, 1962–66, BA (Pol. Sci.); 1966–67, MALS. **Orgs.:** Law Libn. Socty. of Washington DC: Pres. (1977–79). AALL: Local Arrange., Ch. (1981). Fed. Lib. Com.: Exec. Adv. Com. (1979–81). **Pubns.:** Review. Indexer, *Law Lib. Jnl.* (1971). **Activities:** 5; 17; 54, 59 **Addr.:** Joint Bank-Fund Library, International Monetary Fund, 700 19th St., N.W., Washington, DC 20431.

Moore, Maxwell J. (Je. 23, 1931, Mercer, PA) Asst. Mgr. Acq., Chem. Abs. Srvs., 1973–; Coord., Info. Dssm., MI State Univ., 1970–73; Pub. Health Srvs. Intern, Washington Univ., 1969–70. **Educ.:** Univ. of MD, 1961–63, BA (Russ.); IN Univ., 1963–65, MA (Russ.), 1968–69, MLS. **Orgs.:** SLA. ASIS. **Pubns.:** *Operations of a Small Computer-Assisted Information Center* (1972); *Prescriptive Instructional Materials Manual Information Retrieval System* (1973). **Activities:** 12; 15, 30, 44; 60, 63, 72 **Addr.:** 864 Ivy Brush Ct., Columbus, OH 43228.

Moore, Phyllis C. (Ja. 31, 1927, Binghamton, NY) Dir. of Libs., City of Alameda (CA), 1978–; Lib. Dir., Falls Church (VA) Pub. Lib., 1972–77; Consult. for AV Srvs., Westchester (NY) Cnty. Lib. Syst., 1968–72; Dir., Hastings-on-Hudson (NY) Pub. Lib., 1967–68; Dept. Head, Yonkers (NY) Pub. Lib., 1962–67; Libn.-Admin. Spec. Srvs., Lib. Div./Europe, 1957–62; Libn. I, Free Lib. of Philadelphia, 1954–57. **Educ.:** Hartwick Coll., 1945–49, BA (Eng. Lit.); Syracuse Univ., 1953–54, MS (LS); Univ. of WI, 1970–73, PhD (Lit. & Comm. Arts). **Orgs.:** ALA: Coop. Resrcs. Com. (1961–62); Exec. Cncl. (1975–79). VA LA: Natl. Lib. Week (Ch., 1973). CA LA. Mask and Lute: Pres. (1978–). Defenders of Wildlife: Adv. Bd. (1972–). **Honors:** CO State Univ., Hon. Litt. D, 1971. **Pubns.:** "Getting Involved in the Community," *Natl. Sch. Bd. Jnl.* (S. 1980); "The Endangered Species List, Expanded," *Natl. Wildlife Bltn.* (D. 1980); Several plays; Recording/Tape/Cassette of musical comedy, "Blues in the Bibliotheque," (1979). **Activities:** 9; 17; 95-AV Srvs. **Addr.:** Alameda Free Library, Oak Street & Santa Clara Ave., Alameda, CA 94501.

Moore, Richard E. (My. 21, 1932, Abilene, KS) Lib. Dir., South. OR State Coll., 1976–, Tech. Srvs. Libn., 1968–76; Acq. Libn., Univ. of CA, Santa Cruz, 1965–68; Acq. Libn., Portland State Univ., 1964–65; Asst. Acq. Libn., Univ. of IA, 1962–64. **Educ.:** Ft. Hays State Univ., 1955–58, BA (Hist., Eng.); Univ. of OK, 1960–61, MLS; Univ. of KS, 1958–60, MA (Latin Amer. Hist.). **Orgs.:** OR LA: Parlmt. (1972–73, 1979–80); Pres., (1977–78). Pac. NW LA: Parlmt. (1978–79); *PNLA Qtly.* Ed. (1972–76); Conf. Ch. (1970). OR Bk. Socty.: Bd. of Dirs., (1972–78). South. OR LA: Pres. (1971–73). OR State Syst. of Higher Educ.: Lib. Cncl. (Ch., 1979–80). **Honors:** ALA/H.W. Wilson, Per. Awd., 1975. **Pubns.:** *Pacific Northwest Americana, a Supplement, 1949–1974* (1980); *Asturias, a Checklist of Works and Criticism* (1979); *Historical Dictionary of Guatemala* (1973); *SOLF Union List of Serials* (1973); "Care and Retrieval of Local Documents," *PNLA Qtly.* (Win. 1979); various articles. **Activities:** 1, 10; 15, 17, 32; 57, 59 **Addr.:** Southern Oregon State College Library, 1250 Siskiyou Blvd., Ashland, OR 97520.

Moore, Virginia B. (My. 13, 1932, Laurens, SC) Libn., Anacostia Sr. HS, 1975–; Libn., Kramer Jr. HS, 1978–80; Libn., Ballou Sr. HS, 1972–75; Libn., Davis Elem. Sch., 1965–69; Libn., Miner Elem. Sch., 1970–72; Tchr., Elem. Schs., DC, 1958–65; Tchr. (Msc.), Happy Plains HS, 1955–58; Tchr., John R. Hawkins HS, 1954–55. **Educ.:** Winston-Salem Tchrs. Coll., 1950–54, BS (Educ.); Univ. of MD, 1965–68, Cert. (Lib. Sch. Educ.), 1969–70, MLS. **Orgs.:** ALA: AASL, Com. of Consults.-Exhibit, Anl. Conf. of Natl. Sci. Tchrs. Assn. (1971), Legis. Netwk. (1973–76), Amer. Cancer Socty. (Ad Hoc) Com. (1975–78), Com. on Treatment of Minor. in Lit. (1977–78), Student Involvement in the Media Ctr. Com. (1977–80). DC LA: Mem. Com. (1968). DC Assn. of Sch. Libns.: Various coms. and ofcs. Natl. Educ. Assn.: DC Area Rep. (1964–67). DC Educ. Assn.: Rep. (1978–79). Amer. Fed. of Tchrs. Frdm. to Read Fndn. Various other orgs. **Honors:** DC Assn. of Sch. Libns., Outstan. Srv., 1973; DC Pub. Libs., Outstan. Black Hist. Month Progs., 1980. **Pubns.:** "Idea Exchange," *Libs. A-Go-Go* (O. 1967–My. 1969); "The President Speaks," *Libs. A-Go-Go* (1971–73); *Church Libraries Bicentennial Celebration* tape–slide (1976). **Activities:** 10; 15, 17, 31; 63, 66, 89 **Addr.:** Anacostia Senior High School, 16th & R Sts., SE, Washington, DC 20020.

Moorman, John A. (S. 15, 1947, Humboldt, NE) Lib. Dir., Elbert Ivey Mem. Lib., 1975–; Pub. Srvc. Libn., Guilford Coll., 1972–75. **Educ.:** Guilford Coll., 1965–69, AB (Pol. Sci.); Univ. of NC, Chapel Hill, 1971–72, MSLS; Univ. of NC, Greensboro, 1974–75, (Hist.). **Orgs.:** ALA: JMRT (Ch., Const. and Bylaws Com., 1979); PLA (Small, Med-Sized Libs. Sect., Dir. 1979–80; Ch., By-laws Com., 1979). NC LA: Pub. Lib. Sect. (Ch., Stan. Com., 1979). Kiwanis Club of Western Catawba Cnty (Dir. 1977–78; Treas. 1978–). **Pubns.:** Jt. auth., "The Classification of Fiction into The Library of Congress Literature Schedule," *NC Libs.* (Win. 1974); reviews. **Activities:** 9; 17 **Addr.:** 1166 11th St. Cir. N.W., Hickory, NC 28601.

Morahan, Marie Joseph, Sr. (Ag. 19, 1926, New York, NY) Di. of Lib. Comm. Srvs., St. Thomas Aquinas Coll., 1964–, Lib. Dir., 1970–, Lib. Asst. 1964–70; Libn./Tchr., Albertus Magnus HS, 1960–64. **Educ.:** Manhattan Coll., 1947–55, BA (Eng.); St. John's Univ., 1955–57, MLS; Columbia Univ. & City Univ. of NY; Cert. of Info. Sci. 1975. **Orgs.:** LA of Rockland Conty: Secy (1974–79); Pres. (1979–). Rockland Co. Coll. LA: V. Ch. (1980–). Met. Cath. Coll. Libn.: Exec. Cncl. (1979–). Nat. Cath. LA: Coll., Univ. and Sem. Sect. (V-Ch., 1980). Ancient Order of Hibernians (Ladies Auxiliary): Hist. & Pub. Rel. Ch. **Pubns.:** "Touching Bottom in a Bottomless Pitt," *Cath. Lib. World* (S. 1975); "Cooperation between Academic & Public Libraries," (Jl./Ag. 1978). **Activities:** 1; 15, 17, 24 **Addr.:** St. Thomas Aquinas College Library, Rt. 340, Sparkill, NY 10976.

Morales, Catherine P. (N. 20, 1949, Grand Junction, CO) Head, Netwk. Srvs. Sect., Natl. Lib. Srv. for the Blind and Phys. Handcpd., Lib. of Congs., 1979–; Labor-Mgt. Rel. Spec., 1979, Persnl. Spec., 1977–79, Intern, 1976–77. **Educ.:** Univ. of MO, 1968–71, BA (Eng.); TX Tech. Univ., 1972–74, MA (Eng.); Univ. of CA, Los Angeles, 1974–76, MLS; George Washington Univ., 1977– (Bus. Admin.). **Orgs.:** ALA: ASCLA, Intl. Yr. of Disabled Persons Com. (1980–). Mod. Lang. Assn. **Honors:** Beta Phi Mu. **Activities:** 1, 4; 17, 34, 35; 54, 72 **Addr.:** Library of Congress, NLS/BPH, Washington, DC 20542.

Moran, Ann Elizabeth (Jl. 13, 1919, Franklin, TN) Superior of Lib. and Instr. Mtrls., Williamson Cnty. Sch. Syst., 1964–; Tchr., Franklin City Sch., 1959–64; Libn., McMinnville City Sch., 1956–59; Libn., Warren Cnty. Sch., 1951–56; Libn., Coffee Cnty. Sch., 1943–51. **Educ.:** Middle TN State Univ., 1936–40, BS (Soc. Sci., Math.); George Peabody Coll., 1941–43, BS (LS), 1961–63, MS (LS). **Orgs.:** ALA. TN LA: Sch. Sect. (Ch., 1977–80). Mid. TN LA. Women's Natl. Bk. Assn. Delta Kappa Gamma: Phi chap., Secy. (1972–74), Treas. (1976). **Honors:** McMinnville Bus. and Prof. Clb., Woman of the Year, 1958; Franklin Bus. and Prof. Clb., Woman of the Year, 1980. **Pubns.:** Various Historical articles. **Activities:** 10; 21, 32; 59, 63 **Addr.:** Route 11, Franklin, TN 37064.

Moran, Barbara Burns (Jl. 8, 1944, Columbus, MS) Asst. Prof., Sch. of Lib. Sci., Univ. of NC, 1981–; Head, Lib., The Park Sch. of Buffalo, 1974–78. **Educ.:** Mt. Holyoke Coll., 1962–66, AB (Eng. Lit.); Emory Univ., 1972–73, MLn (Libnshp.); SUNY, Buffalo, 1978–81, PhD. **Orgs.:** ALA. Assn. for the Study of Higher Educ. **Activities:** 1, 11; 17, 26, 41; 55 **Addr.:** School of Library Science, University of North Carolina, Chapel Hill, NC 27514.

Moran, Marguerite Katherine (Pringle, PA) Dir., Tech. & Bus. Info., M & T Chemicals Inc., 1949–; Chem., Reichhold Chemicals Inc., 1943–49. **Educ.:** Coll. Misericordia, 1939–43, BS (Chem.); Rutgers Univ., Columbia Univ., 1960, MLS; MS (Chem.). **Orgs.:** SLA: NJ Chap., (Pres., 1965–66); Metals/Mtrls. Div. (Ch., 1973–74). ASIS. Amer. Chem. Socty. Amer. Socty. for Testing and Mtrls. AAUW. **Pubns.:** "The Technical Information Center of Metal and Thermit Corporation," *Bltn., NJ Chap. of SLA* (Ap. 1960); Ed., *Putting Knowledge to Work - the Profession of the Special Librarian* (1960); "The Transition - Metals to Materials," *Spec. Libs.* (Mr. 1965); Contrib., *McGraw-Hill's Chemical and Process Technology Encyclopedia* (1974); Jt. auth., *Industrial Chemicals* (1975). **Activities:** 12; 17, 38, 41; 59, 60, 91 **Addr.:** 13 Longfellow Dr., Colonia, NJ 07067.

Moran, Sr. Regina Miriam (Je. 27, 1912, Brooklyn, NY) Asst. Archvst., St. Joseph's Convent, 1980–; Head Libn., Semy. of the Immaculate Conception, 1970–80; Head Libn., Brentwood Coll., 1955–70; Tchr.–Libn. (HS), Juniorate of Srs. of St. Joseph, 1940–55. **Educ.:** St. Joseph's Coll., 1930–40, BA (Eng.); St. John's Univ., 1941–45, BLS. **Orgs.:** ALA. NY LA. ATLA. Cath. LA: Exec. Bd. (1951–57); Coll., Univ., Semy. Bd., Bd. Arch. (1979–83). **Activities:** 1, 2; 17, 38; 90 **Addr.:** St. Joseph's Convent, Brentwood, NY 11717.

Moran, Robert F., Jr. (My. 3, 1938, Cleveland, OH) Dir. of Lib. Srvs., IN Univ. NW, 1980–; Acq. Libn., Univ. of IL at Chicago Circle, 1977–80, Serials Libn., 1973–77; Ref. Libn., Univ. of Chicago, 1970–73; Head Libn., St. Patrick's Coll., Menlo Park, CA, 1965–69. **Educ.:** Cath. Univ., 1959–61, BA (Phil.), 1963–65, MSLS; Univ. of Chicago, 1972–76, MBA. **Orgs.:** ALA: LAMA, LOMS, Comp. Lib. Org.: Ch. (1981); RTSD, Resrcs., Policy and Resrch. (1980–81). ASIS. Chicago OLUG. **Pubns.:** "Moving a Large Library," *Spec. Libs.* (Ap. 1972); "Library Cooperation and Change," *Coll. and Resrch. Libs.* (Jl. 1978); "Improving the Organization of an Academic Library," *Jnl. of Acad. Libnshp.* (Jl. 1980). **Activities:** 1; 15, 17, 39; 59 **Addr.:** The Library, Indiana University Northwest, 3400 Broadway Ave., Gary, IN 46408.

Morehouse, Harold G. (Jl. 27, 1928, Covina, CA) Dir. of Libs., Univ. of NV, Reno, 1969–, Asst. Dir. of Libs., 1963–69; Resrch. Assoc. III, Inst. of Lib. Resrch., Univ. of CA, Berkeley, 1966; Sci. Libn., Univ. of NV, Reno, 1961–63; Asst. Libn., Aerojet-Gen. Corp., 1959–61; Ref. Libn., CA State Lib., 1958–59, Catlgr., 1956–58. **Educ.:** Santa Rosa Jr. Coll., 1945–47, AA; San Francisco State Coll., 1947–48; Univ. of CA, Berkeley, 1953–55, AB, 1955–56, MLS. **Orgs.:** ALA: Ch., Reprodct. of Lib. Mtrls. Sect. NV LA: Pres. (1967, 1968, 1969). Mt. Plains LA: Pres. (1970–71). CA LA. **Honors:** Mt. Plains LA, Spec. Awd., 1971. **Pubns.:** "Telefacsimile Services Between Libraries with the Xerox Magnavox Telecopier" (1966); "Equipment for Facsimile Transmission Between Libraries; a Description and Comparative Evaluation of Three Systems" (1967); "The Future of Telefacsimile in Libraries: Problems and Prospects," *Lib. Resrcs. and Tech. Srvs.* (Win. 1969); "Document Transmission Systems," *Encyc. of Lib. and Info. Sci.* (1972). **Activities:** 1, 12; 17, 26; 93 **Addr.:** P. O. Box 8937, Reno, NV 89507.

Morehouse, Valerie J. (Ja. 30, 1947, Taft, CA) Asst. Lib. Dir., Plymouth Pub. Lib., 1977–; Sr. Asst. for Tech. Srvs., Sandwich Pub. Lib., 1974–77, Tech. Srvs. Asst., 1971–73. **Educ.:** Univ. of CA, Berkeley, 1964–68, AB (Eng.); Simmons Coll., 1976–77, MS (LS). **Orgs.:** MA LA: Int. Frdm. Com. (1979–). New Eng. Small Press Assn. **Honors:** Com. Small Mag. Eds. and Publshrs., Cit., 1977; Beta Phi Mu, 1977; MA Cncl. on The Arts and Hum.,

PROFESSIONAL ACTIVITIES: Institutions: 1. Acad. lib.; 2. Arch.; 3. Assn.; 4. Fed./Gvt. lib.; 5. Inst. lib.; 6. Mfr./Suppl.; 7. Milit. lib.; 8. Musm.; 9. Pub. lib.; 10. Sch. lib.; 11. Sch. of lib. sci.; 12. Spec. lib.; 13. State lib.; 14. (other). **Functions/Activities:** 15. Acq./Col. dev.; 16. Adult srvs.; 17. Admin.; 18. Apprais.; 19. Archit./Bldgs.; 20. Cat./Class.; 21. Chld. srvs.; 22. Circ.; 23. Cons./Pres.; 24. Consult.; 25. Cont. ed.; 26. Educ. lib. sci.; 27. Ext. srvs.; 28. Fund/Grants; 29. Gvt. pubs.; 30. Indx./Abs.; 31. Instr. lib. use; 32. Media srvs.; 33. Micro.; 34. Netwks./Coop.; 35. Persnl.; 36. PR; 37. Publshg.; 38. Recs. mgt.; 39. Ref. srvs.; 40. Repro.; 41. Resrch.; 42. Review.; 43. Secur.; 44. Serials; 45. Spec. col.; 46. Tech. srvs.; 47. Trustees/Bds.; 48. YA srvs.; 49. (other).

Lit., Adv. Panel, 1980–82. **Pubns.:** Contrib., *Anthology: A Collection of Cape Cod poets* (1974); "Bum Steer: for all–one meat cut, one name," *Hennepin Cnty. Lib. Cat. Bltn.* (S./O. 1977); Column, "Small Press Scene," *Booklist* (1977–79, 1980–); Ed., *Second Sight: Visual Resources Newsletter* (1977–78); Reviews. **Activities:** 9; 17, 42, 45; 55, 74, 95-Small and Alternative Presses. **Addr.:** P.O. Box 1172, Plymouth, MA 02360.

Morein, Pierre Grady (Je. 16, 1939, Ville Platte, LA) Univ. Libn., Univ. of Evansville (IN), 1980–; Assoc., Off. of Mgt. Stud., Assn. of Resrch. Libs., 1978–80; Dir., Acad. Lib. Dev. Prog., Cncl. on Lib. Resrcs., NC Ctrl. Univ., 1976–78, Proj. Coord., 1975–76; Asso. Prof., Sch. of Lib. Sci., NC Ctrl. Univ., 1973–75; Instr., Grad. Sch. of Lib. Sci., LA State Univ. (1973–73); Asst. Libn., Nicholls State Univ., (1965–71). **Educ.:** Univ. of Southwestern LA, 1958–61, BS (Bus.); LA State Univ., 1964–66, MSLS; Nicholls State Univ., 1968–70, MBA; LA State Univ., 1971–75, PhD (Mgt.). **Orgs.:** ALA: ACRL. Assn. of Amer. Lib. Sch. Acad. of Mgt. **Pubns.:** Jt. auth., *Planning Program for Small Academic Libraries* (1980); jt. auth., *The Academic Library Development Program* (1977); "Assisted Self-Study," *Cath. Lib. World* (My/Je 1979); "The Academic Library Development Program," *College & Research Libraries* (Ja. 1977). **Activities:** 1, 11; 17, 24, 26; 59, 75, 92 **Addr.:** Clifford Library, University of Evansville, Evansville, IN 47702.

Moreland, Carroll Collier (D. 20, 1903, Edgewood, PA) Co–Dir., Law Libnshp. Prog., CA West. Sch. of Law, 1979–; Prof. of Law and Law Libn., 1975–78; Libn., Cromwell Lib., Amer. Bar Fndn., 1964–72; Visit Prof. of LS, Univ. of Dacca, 1962–64; Lib. Adv. for Pakistan and Korea, Asia Fndn., 1962–64; Biddle Law Libn., Univ. of PA, 1946–62; Asst. Libn., Assn. of the Bar of the City of New York, 1943–46; Libn., MI State Law Lib., 1938–43; Various prof. positions (1935–38). **Educ.:** Princeton Univ., 1920–24, AB; Univ. of Pittsburgh, 1924–27, JD; Carnegie Lib. Sch., 1936–37, BSLS. **Orgs.:** AALL: Exec. Com. (1947–48; 1954–57); Pres. (1955–56). Cncl. of Natl. LAs.: Pres. (1958–59). **Honors:** CA West. Sch. of Law, Dr. of Laws Honoris Causa, 1980. **Pubns.:** *Professional Education of the Bar: Growth and Perspectives* (1972); *Equal Justice under Law; the American Legal System* (1957); "Bibliography of Reports Published or Adopted by the Survey of the Legal Profession," *Law Lib. Jnl.* (My. 1970); "Checklist of State Bar Proceedings," *Law Lib. Jnl.* (F. 1970); Jt. auth., *Research in Pennsylvania Law* (1953); Various articles. **Addr.:** 12286 Lomica Dr., San Diego, CA 92128.

Moren, Anthony J. (Ap. 20, 1951, West Bromwich, Eng.) Head, Tech. Srvs., Stats. Can. Lib., 1981–; Sr. Catlgr., 1977–80, Catlgr., 1976–77. **Educ.:** Queen's Univ., 1969–73, BA (Hist.); McGill Univ., 1974–76, MLS. **Orgs.:** Can. LA: Can. Assn. of Spec. Libs. and Info. Srvs. **Activities:** 4, 12; 17, 46; 56, 59, 92 **Addr.:** 20 Dante Ave., Nepean, ON K2H 5Z8 Canada.

Moreno, Esperanza A. (D. 23, 1932, El Paso, TX) Head Libn., Nursing/Med. Lib., Univ. of TX at El Paso, 1976–; Chief Libn., Univ. of TX Systs. Sch. of Nursing, 1972–76; Libn., Hotel Dieu Sch. of Nursing, 1964–72; Libn., Human Resrcs. Resrch. Ofc., 1958–64; General Asst. Libn., Pub. Lib. Youngstown and Mahoning Cnty., 1955–58. **Educ.:** Univ. of TX (El Paso), 1951–54, BA (Span.); Univ. of IL, 1954–56, MSLS; Cont. Ed. Crs., 1954–. **Orgs.:** Med. LA. ALA. SLA. Border Reg. Lib. Assn.: Libn. of the Year Com. (1979). Various other orgs. AAUW. Leag. of Women Voters: Bd. of Dirs. (1972–74). Crockett Sch. PTA. **Honors:** Border Reg. Lib. Assn., Libn. of the Year, 1967. **Pubns.:** "Library Orientation for Graduate Students," *Proc. of the S. Ctrl. Reg. Grp. of the Med. LA* (1979). **Activities:** 1, 12; 15, 17, 20; 63, 80, 95-Nursing. **Addr.:** Box 3823, El Paso, TX 79923.

Moreo, Stanley D. (F. 5, 1947, Ft. Wayne, IN) Head, Resrcs./Info. Srvs., Lewis and Clark Lib. Syst., 1980–81; Tech. Srvs. Libn., Parkland Coll., 1972–79. **Educ.:** Wabash Coll., 1964–68, AB (Chem.); Univ. of IL, 1968–69, MLS; U.S. Pub. Hlth. Srv. Traineeship, Sch. of Med., Washington Univ., 1971–72, Cert. (Autom., LS). **Orgs.:** Beta Phi Mu: Alpha Chap. (VP, 1975–76; Pres., 1976–77; Past Pres., 1977–78). IL OCLC Users' Grp.: Grp. Organizer; Pres. (1976–77); Exec. Com. (1977–79). IL LA: Treas. (1981); Resrcs. Tech. Srvs. Sect. (Various ofcs., 1977–80). **Activities:** 9, 14-Lib. Network; 17, 39, 46 **Addr.:** 803 1/2 Hollycrest Dr., Champaign, IL 61820.

Morey, Thomas J. (D. 10, 1920, Hornell, NY) Mgr., Xerox Lib. Srvs., Xerox Corp., 1965–; Head, Info. Srvs., Continental Oil Co., 1958–65; Chief Libn., Hooker Chem. Co., 1956–58; Asst. Libn., Cornell Aeronautical Corp., 1951–56. **Educ.:** Univ. of Buffalo, Canisius Coll., 1946–51, BS (Bio-Chem); Data Prcs. Trng., 1964–65 Cert. **Orgs.:** ALA. ASIS: Chap. Pres. (1973); Asm. Rep. (1974–79). SLA: Prog. Plng. (1968); Nom. Com. (1974). Amer. Chem. Socty.: Chem. Lit. Assn. for Info. Mgrs. **Pubns.:** "This Work For Us-" *Spec. Libs.* (My./Je. 1972). **Activities:** 12; 17, 33, 46; 56, 75, 91 **Addr.:** 646 Cumberland Way, Webster, NY 14580.

Morgan, Betty J. (S. 4, 1931, Humnoke, AR) Spec., Lib. Srvs., Educ. Admin. Supvsr., AR Dept. of Educ., 1976–; Jr. High Libn., Lakewood Jr. HS, 1971–76; Tchr., McRae Elem. Sch., 1968–71; Elem. Tchr., Humnoke-Carlisle, AR, 1959–68. **Educ.:** Little Rock Univ., 1957–63, BA (Elem. Educ.); Univ. of Ctrl. AR, 1966–68, MSE (Elem. Educ.); Univ. of AR, 1977–80, Lib. Cert. (Elem. Prin.). **Orgs.:** ALA. Natl. Assn. of State Educ. Media Profs. AR LA. AR AV Assn. **Honors:** Alpha Delta Kappa; Kappa Kappa Iota. **Addr.:** Arkansas Dept. of Education, Arch Ford Education Bldg., Little Rock, AR 72209.

Morgan, Carolee Elizabeth (N. 10, 1954, New Hyde Park, NY) Adult Srvs. Libn., Elmont Pub. Lib., 1980–; Ref. Libn., Bellmore Meml. Lib., 1978–80; Asst. Libn., C.W. Post Suffolk Branch Campus, 1978–80. **Educ.:** SUNY, Farmingdale, 1972–74, AA (Liberal Arts); C.W. Post Ctr., 1974–76, BA (Mod. Langs.), 1976–78, MS (LS). **Orgs.:** ALA. NY LA: JMRT. Nassau Cnty. LA. Suffolk Cnty. LA. **Activities:** 1, 9; 16, 20, 39 **Addr.:** 559 Kirkman Ave., Elmont, NY 11003.

Morgan, Erma Jean (S. 23, 1939, Columbus, OH) Deputy Libn. for Tech. Srvs., King Cnty. Lib. Syst., 1972–; Bibl. Systs. Libn., Sangamon State Univ., 1970–72; Actg. Head Catlgr., North. IL Univ., 1967–70; Catlgr., Bowling Green State Univ., 1962–67. **Educ.:** Bowling Green State Univ., 1957–61, BA (Eng.); Univ. of MI, 1961–62, AMLS. **Orgs.:** ALA: RTSD; ACRL; LITA. WA Lib. Netwk: King Cnty. Lib. Srv. Area (Ch., 1977–78). Bus. and Prof. Women: Totem Chap. **Activities:** 1, 9; 17, 34, 46 **Addr.:** King County Library System, 300 Eighth Ave. North, Seattle, WA 98109.

Morgan, Ina K. (S. 11, 1932, Hawthorne, FL) Media Dir., Palatka (FL) HS Res. Ctr., 1977–; Media Spec., Madison Sch. Media Ctr., 1968–76; Elem. Lib. Supvsr., Marietta (GA) Sch. Syst., 1966–67; Librn./Media Spec., Winter Garden (FL) Elem. Schs., 1959–66. **Educ.:** Univ. of FL, 1950–54, BAE (Educ.); FL State Univ., 1962, MSLS; various grad. crs. **Orgs.:** ALA. FL Assn. Media in Educ. CSLA. AECT. AAUW. Phi Delta Kappa. Alpha Delta Kappa. Untd. Tchrs. of FL. Other orgs. **Activities:** 10; 17, 20 **Addr.:** P.O. Box 65, Hawthorne, FL 32640.

Morgan, James E. (Je. 30, 1941, Whelling, WV) Dir. of Libs., OR Hlth. Scis. Univ., 1976–; Dir. of Libs., Univ. of CT Hlth. Ctr., 1973–76; Dir. of Pub. Srvs., Univ. of TX Med. Branch, 1969–73; Head of Pub. Srvs., GA Coll., 1967–69. **Educ.:** Otterbein Coll., 1959–61; AZ State Coll., 1962–65, BS (Educ.); FL State Univ., 1965–66, MSLS. **Orgs.:** Med. LA: Legis. Com.; Exch. Com. (1974–76; Ch. 1975–76); Pac. NW Grp., Ch. ALA. SLA. OR LA. Other orgs. Univ. of OR Hlth. Sci. Ctr.: Educ. Support Srvs. Task Force (1978–). **Pubns.:** Jt. auth., "Journal Evaluation Study at the University of Connecticut Health Center," *Bltn. of the Med. LA* (Ap. 1977); "Library Service Tailored to Dental Needs," *Jnl. of the CT Dental Assn.* (Jl. 1974); "The Lyman Maynard Stowe Library, alias the Health Center Library," *CT Libs.* (Ja. 1975). **Activities:** 1; 17; 80 **Addr.:** Oregon Health Sciences University Library, 3181 S.W. Sam Jackson Park Rd., P. O. Box 573, Portland, OR 97207.

Morgan, James Edward (Jl. 1, 1941, Seattle, WA) Inst. Consult., Lib. Ext. Srv., Dept. of Lib., Arch., & Pub. Recs., 1972–; Per. Acq. Libn., Univ. of South. CA, 1966–69; Acq. Libn., Pasadena Pub. Lib., 1969–70; YA Libn., Los Angeles Pub. Lib., 1970–71. **Educ.:** Univ. of OR, 1959–63, BA (Pol. Sci.); Syracuse Univ., 1964–66, MLS. **Orgs.:** SWLA. ALA: Ch. Inst. Consult. Discuss Grp. (1977–78); ASCLA, Conf. Prog. Plng. Com., Lib. Srvs. to Prisoners Sect. (1979–1981); Com. to Write Lib. Srv. Stan. to Residents of Inst. Serving the Mentally Retarded (1977–79). AZ LA: Pres., Spec. Libs. Div. (1977–78). West. Cncl. of State Libs. Inc. Natl. Cncl. on Crime and Delinquency. Amer. Correctional Assn. **Pubns.:** Various articles, *The Roadrunner* (1974–); *"Out of the Dust;* Library Services to Arizona's Correctional Institutions," *IL Libs.* (S. 1974). **Activities:** 5, 13; 24, 25, 28; 72 **Addr.:** 2219 S. 48th St., Suite D., Tempe, AZ 85282.

Morgan, Jane Hale (My. 11, 1926, Dines, WY) Dir., Detroit Pub. Lib., 1978–; Deputy Dir., 1975–78, Exec. Asst. Dir., 1973–75, Staff Mem., 1954–73. **Educ.:** Howard Univ., 1945–47, BA (Eng. Lit.); Univ. of Denver, 1953–54, MA (LS). **Orgs.:** ALA: Com. on Accred. (1977–80). MI Lib. Cnsrtm.: Bd. of Trustees (1978–). SE MI Reg. Film Lib.: Exec. Bd. (1976–). Various other orgs. New Detroit, Inc. Rehabilitation Inst. Univ.–Cultural Ctr. Assn. Untd. Fndn. **Activities:** 9; 17; 63, 75 **Addr.:** Detroit Public Library, 5201 Woodward Ave., Detroit, MI 48202.

Morgan, Linda Meredith (Ap. 8, 1947, Berkeley, CA) Sci. Ref. Libn., Univ. of Houston, 1976–; Head of Info. Dissm. Srv., SUNY, Buffalo, 1974–76, Hist. of Med. Col. Libn., 1972–74; Libn., MA Coll. of Optometry, 1970–72. **Educ.:** Raymond Coll., Univ. of the Pac., 1965–68, BA (Liberal Arts); Univ. of CA, Berkeley, 1968–69, MLS; 1978, Cert. of Hlth. Scis. Libnshp. **Orgs.:** Assn. of Visual Sci. Libns. CA LA. Med. LA: Intl. Coop. Com. (1979–). Amer. Acad. of Optometry. **Honors:** Lakes Area Reg. Med. Prog., Recog. for Outstan. Contrib. to Cont. Ed., 1975. **Pubns.:** "Patron Preference in Reference Service Points," *Ref. Qtly.* (Sum. 1980); "Overlooked Resources: The Place of the Library in Visual Science Research," *Amer. Jnl. of Optometry and Physio. Optics* (Mr. 1979); "Pre-Nineteenth Century Imprints in the Health Sciences Library," (1976). **Activities:** 1; 15, 31, 39; 68, 80, 88 **Addr.:** 11707 Meadow Joy Ct., Houston, TX 77089.

Morgan, Madel Jacobs (Mrs. Adlia) (Ap. 26, 1918, Rosedale, MS) Dir., Arch. & Lib. Div., MS Dept. of Arch. & Hist., 1979–; Spec. Prog. Consult., MS Lib. Comsn., 1968–79; Libn., St. Andrew's Episcopal Sch., 1955–68. **Educ.:** MS Univ. for Women, 1935–39, BA (Eng.); MS Coll., 1968–71, (Eng.), Lib. Cert., 1963–65. **Orgs.:** MS LA: Pres. (1979). ALA: Cncl. (1971–75). SELA: Const. & Bylaws (1979–80); Author Awd., Criteria Com. (1977–1978). SAA. MS Hist. Socty. Geneal. Ed., *Jnl. of MS Hist.* **Pubns.:** "A History of the Mississippi Library Commission" in *A History of Mississippi Libraries* (1975). **Activities:** 2, 4; 17, 45; 69, 83, 85 **Addr.:** Department of Archives and History, Box 571, Jackson, MS 39205.

Morgan, Mendell D., Jr. (N. 29, 1940, Alice, TX) Lib. Dir., Incarnate Word Coll., 1975–; Pub. Srv. Libn., Lib. Dir., Mtview. Cmnty. Coll., 1970–75; Field Consult., Asst. Field Srvs. Dir., TX State Lib., 1965–70; Asst. Adult Srvs. Libn., Catonsville Branch, Baltimore Cnty. Pub. Lib., 1964–65. **Educ.:** Univ. of TX, 1960–63, BA (Soclgy.); LA State Univ., 1964–65, MS (LS). **Orgs.:** TX LA: Vice-Ch., Ch. Dist. X (1976–77); Various coms. Bexar LA: Pubcty. Ch. (1976); Directory Ch. (1977); Nom. Com. (1978). Cncl. of Resrch. and Acad. Libs., Inc.: Secy. (1979); Pres. (1980–82). Frnds. of the San Antonio Pub. Lib.: Bd. of Dirs. (1981). Boy Scouts of Amer.: Adult Com. Lcl. Troops (1974–81). St. Matthews Episcopal Church. **Activities:** 1; 17, 32, 34 **Addr.:** 574 Shin Oak Dr., San Antonio, TX 78233.

Morgan, Patricia L. (Ap. 6, 1934, Wayne, OH) ILL Libn., Wayne Oakland Reg. of Interlib. Coop., 1981–; Asst. Libn., Detroitbank Corp., 1981; Adult Ref. Libn., W. Bloomfield Pub. Lib., 1977–80; Libn., Inst. for Advnc. Pastoral Stds., 1974–80. **Educ.:** MI State Univ., 1952–56, BS (Educ.); Wayne State Univ., 1973–77, MSLS. **Orgs.:** MI LA: Cont. Educ. Com. (1978–81; Ch. 1980–81); Pol. Netwk. (Area coord., 1977–78). WHCOLIS: Reg. Grp. Leader; State Elected Del. Pub. Lib. Trustees Assn. of Oakland Cnty. (MI): Bd. (1978–81); Ch. (1979–80). SLA. Church of Our Saviour. **Honors:** Beta Phi Mu, 1977. **Activities:** 9, 12; 20, 39, 47; 59, 90 **Addr.:** 26177 W. Thirteen Mile Rd., Franklin, MI 48025.

Moriarty, Sister Dolores Ann (Ag. 8, 1936, Syracuse, NY) Libn., Holy Trinity Sch., 1975–; Staff, St. Ann's Home, Villanova Univ., 1972–75; House Parent/Libn., Catholic Home for Girls, 1969–72; Tchr./Libn., St. Rose School, 1968–69; Tchr. 1957–68. **Educ.:** Chestnut Hill Coll., 1954–69, AB (Fr.); Villanova Univ., 1972–75, MSLS. **Orgs.:** Cath. LA: Washington, MD Unit (Treas. 1979–80; Vice-Ch., Ch.-elect, 1981–83); Sch. Sect., Ch., (1977–78); Vice-Ch. (1976–77). DC Assn. of Sch. Libns. Cncl. of Women Rel./Archdi. of Washington, Life Plng. Com. (1979–). **Activities:** 10; 22, 31, 48; 89, 90 **Addr.:** 3513 "N" St., N.W., Washington, DC 20007.

Moriarty, Judith E. (F. 23, 1944, Madison, WI) Head of Cat. and Serial Dept., Karrmann Lib., Univ. of WI, Platteville, 1978–; Actg. Head of Cat., 1977–78, Catlgr./Serial Libn., 1974–77, Catlgr., 1967–74. **Educ.:** Univ. of WI, Platteville, 1963–66, BS (Eng.); Univ. of WI, Madison, 1967–68, MS (LS). **Orgs.:** ALA: ACRL; RTSD. WI LA. WI Assn. of Acad. Libns. Univ. of WI Lib. Sch. Alum Assn. Univ. of WI, Platteville, Fndn. Assn. of WI Facs. **Activities:** 1, 11; 20 **Addr.:** 615 Ridge Ave., Platteville, WI 53818.

Moriarty, Paul V. (Mr. 22, 1940, Jacksonville, IL) Asst. Dir., Univ. of WI, Platteville, 1981–; Actg. Tech. Srvs. Coord., 1976–78, Acq. Libn., 1968–. **Educ.:** Pepperdine Univ., 1962–65, BA (Hist.); Univ. of WI, 1966, MA (LS). **Orgs.:** ALA: ACRL; IFRT; LAMA; RTSD. WI LA. WI Assn. of Acad. Libns. WI Int. Frdm. Coal. Univ. of WI Syst. Task Force on Lib. Plng. Std. Com. Various other orgs. Univ. of WI, Platteville, Fndn. **Activities:** 1, 11; 15, 17, 31; 52, 74, 78 **Addr.:** 615 Ridge Ave., Platteville, WI 53818.

Morisset, Auguste-M., O.M.I., C.M. (O. 27, 1900, Fall River, MA) Retired–Prof. emeritus, Univ. of Ottawa, 1971–; Dir.–Fndr., Lib. Sch., 1938–71, Chief Libn., 1934–58; Curate, Sacré–Coeur Parish, 1930–34. **Educ.:** Univ. of Ottawa, 1929–30, LJC, 1930–35, BA (Arts); Columbia Univ., 1936–38, BLS, 1948, MLS. **Orgs.:** ALA. ASTED. Can. LA. Bibl. Socty. of Can.: Fndr. Mem.; Pres. (1950–52). Various other orgs. Alliance Francaise. Can. Writers Fndn. Socty. des Ecrivains Can. Socty. Hist. et de Geneal. d'Ottawa. **Honors:** Centennial Medal; 1967; Order of Can. Mem., 1976; Silver Jubilee Medal, 1977. **Pubns.:** Various articles in *Ency. Can., Ency. Intl. de Orientation Bibl.,* and prof. jnls. **Addr.:** 305 Nelson St., Ottawa, ON K1N 7S5 Canada.

Morita, Ichiko T. (N. 17, 1931, Osaka, Japan) Asst. Prof., Head, Autom. Prcs. Div., OH State Univ. Libs., 1977–, Instr., Asst. Head, Autom. Prcs. Div., 1975–77, Instr., Catlgr., 1972–75; Instr., Dept. of Classics and of Chinese and Japanese, Univ. of OR, 1969–72; Instr. in Japanese, Frgn. Lang. Dept, Chicago Loop Coll., 1968–69; Serial Catlgr., Univ. of Chicago Lib., 1963–68. **Educ.:** Okayama Univ., Okayama, Japan, 1950–54, BA (Eng. Lit.); Univ. of Chicago, 1962–63, MA (LS). **Orgs.:** ALA. ASIS. Acad. LA OH. OH Valley Grp. of Tech. Srvs. Libns.: Secy. (1974–75). OHIONET Trng. and Instr. Cncl.: Cncl. mem. (1979–). Intl. Cncl. of Mid-OH. Japanese Am. Club of Columbus. **Honors:** Japan Fndn. Professional Flwshp., 1979; Univ. Resrch. Grant, OH State Univ., 1974. **Pubns.:** "OCLC - Ohio College Library Center," *Documtn. Kenkyu* (My. 1974); "A cost analysis

Special Subjects/Services: 50. Adult educ.; 51. Advert./Mktg.; 52. Aerosp.; 53. Agric.; 54. Area std.; 55. Arts/Hum.; 56. Autom.; 57. Bibl./Prtg.; 58. Bio. sci.; 59. Bus./Fin.; 60. Chem.; 61. Copyrt.; 62. Documtn.; 63. Educ.; 64. Engin.; 65. Env.; 66. Eth. grps.; 67. Film; 68. Food/Nutr.; 69. Geneal.; 70. Geo.; 71. Geol.; 72. Handcpd.; 73. Hist.; 74. Int. frdm.; 75. Info. sci.; 76. Insr.; 77. Law; 78. Legis.; 79. Math./Comp. sci.; 80. Med.; 81. Metals; 82. Nat. resrcs.; 83. Newsp.; 84. Nuc. sci.; 85. Oral hist.; 86. Petr./Energy; 87. Pharm.; 88. Phys./Astr./Math.; 89. Readg.; 90. Relig.; 91. Sci./Tech.; 92. Soc. sci.; 93. Telecom.; 94. Transp.; 95. (other).

of the Ohio College Library Center On-line Shared Cataloging System in the Ohio State University Libraries," *Lib. Resrcs. and Tech. Srvs.* (Sum. 1977); "Processing unit cost calculation and its problems," *Documtn. Kenkyu.* (S. 1977); "Production, personnel, and unit cost: OCLC processing viewed from OSUL statistics," *Jnl. of Coll. and Univ. Libs.* (1977); "OCLC at OSU: The effect of the adoption of OCLC on the management of Technical Services at a large academic library," *Lib. Resrcs. and Tech. Srvs.* (Win. 1978); reviews. **Addr.:** 2120 Haverford Rd., Columbus, OH 43220.

Moritz, Charles Fredric (Ja. 23, 1917, Cleveland, OH) Ed., *Current Biog.,* H.W. Wilson Co., 1958–; Asst. Prof., Rutgers Univ., 1955–58; Ed. Staff, *Booklist,* ALA, 1952–55; Libn., NY Pub. Lib., 1950–52; Asst. Libn., Rare Book Room, Yale Univ., 1948–50. **Educ.:** OH State Univ., 1936–42, BA (Eng.); Harvard Univ., 1946–47, (Eng.); Columbia Univ., 1947–48, BSLS; Middlebury Coll., 1947–50, MA (Eng.). **Orgs.:** ALA. Bibl. Socty. of Amer. NY Lib. Club. **Honors:** Joseph Towne Wheeler Awd., Columbia Univ. Sch. of Lib. Srvc., 1948. **Pubns.:** Ed., *Current Biography* (1958–79); Ed., *Book of Knowledge* (1961). **Activities:** 37; 50, 78 **Addr.:** 518 West 232d St., New York, NY 10463.

Moritz, William Dean (S. 21, 1935, Tyler, MN) Assoc. Prof., Assoc. Lib. Dir., Univ. of WI, 1971–; Actg. Lib. Dir., 1970–71, Asst. Prof., Asst. to Dir., 1968–70, Instr., Admin. Asst., 1966–68. **Educ.:** Mankato State Univ., 1954–57, BS (Eng.); Denver Univ., 1963–65, MLS, 1974, Mgt. Sem. **Orgs.:** ALA. WI LA: Exec. Bd. (1969–71). WI Assn. of Acad. Libns.: Ch. (1969–71). Midwest Fed. of Lib. Assn.: Conf. Plng. Com. (1966–67, 1978–79). WI State Hist. Socty. AAUP. SE WI Reg. Plng. Comsn. Tech. Adv. Com. Lib. Cncl. of Metro. Milwaukee. various orgs. **Activities:** 1; 17, 19, 24; 56, 70, 91 **Addr.:** 1934 Cedar Dr., Grafton, WI 53024.

Morner, Claudia Jane (My. 17, 1946, Ladysmith, WI) Libn., Cape Cod Cmnty. Coll. Lib., 1980–; Dir., Osterville Free Lib., 1972–80, Asst. Libn., 1971–72; Resrch. and Eval. Spec., Cambridge Model Cities, 1970–71. **Educ.:** Univ. of MN, 1966–68, BA (Eng.); Simmons Coll., 1975–78, MSLS. **Orgs.:** MA LA: Treas. (1981–83). East. MA Reg. Lib. Syst., Adv. Com. (1978–1981), Plan of Srv. Com. (Ch., 1974). Cape Cod Lib. Clb. Pubcty. Com. (Co-ch., 1978), Nom. Com. (Ch., 1979). Town of Barnstable, MA Town Mtg. Mem. (1975–). **Honors:** Beta Phi Mu, 1978; ALA, John Cotton Dana Lib. Spec. Awd., 1973. **Pubns.:** Contrib., "Adult books for young adults" (clmn.) *Sch. Lib. Jnl* (1977–). **Activities:** 9; 15, 17, 42; 50, 67, 95-Science Fiction. **Addr.:** 18 Parker Rd., W. Barnstable, MA 02668.

Morphet, Norman D. (O. 14, 1930, Marcus Hook, PA) Chief, Lib. and Info. Srv., Sun Co., 1978–, Resrch. Libn., 1965–78. **Educ.:** Widener Univ., 1954–58, BA (Eng.); Drexel Univ., 1964–67, MLS. **Orgs.:** SLA: Philadelphia Chap., Treas. (1965–70); Empl. Ch. (1978–79). **Activities:** 12; 17, 29, 33; 86, 91 **Addr.:** Sun Co. Library & Information Service, P.O. Box 1135, Marcus Hook, PA 19061.

Morris, Effie Lee (Ap. 20, Richmond, VA) Lib. Consult., Freelance Author/Ed., 1977–; Lectr., Mills Coll., 1979; Lectr., Univ. of San Francisco, Dept. of Libnshp., 1975–76; Coord., Chld. Srvs., San Francisco Lib., 1963–78; Chld. Spec., Lib. for the Blind, New York Pub. Lib., 1958–63, Chld. Libn., 1955–58; Chld. Libn., Cleveland Pub. Lib., 1946–55; Lectr., Atlanta Univ., Sch. of Lib. Sci., 1954. **Educ.:** Univ. of Chicago, 1941–1943, (Soc. Sci.); Case Western Reserve Univ., 1944–45, BA, 1945–46, BLS, 1956, MSLS; Univ. of San Francisco, 1977– PhD in progress (Educ.). **Orgs.:** Lib. of Congs., Ctr. for The Book, Adv. Bd. (1983). ALA: Cncl. (1967–1971; 1975–1979); Com. on Org. (1979–1982); PLA, Pres. (1970–1972); ALSC, Newbery-Caldecott Com. (1950–56, 1966, 1967); Bd. of Dir. (1963–1966). CA LA: Cncl. (1971–1972; 1976–1979); Libns. and Publshrs. Com. (Ch. 1978–81); Chld. Srvs. Div., Pres. (1969–1970; 1970–1971). Women's Natl. Book Assn.: Natl. Secy. (1974–76), Founding Pres., SF Chap., 1968. Natl. Braille Assn.: Pres. (1960–62). Mills Coll.: Assoc. Cncl. (1972–). Educ. Cable TV Corp.: Pres. (1976). NAACP. Other orgs. **Honors:** Sch. of Lib. Sci., Case Western Reserve Univ., Distin. Alum. Awd., 1979; ALA Black Caucus, Distin. Srv. Awd., 1978; CA Black Libns. Assn., Distin. Srv. Awd., 1978; E. P. Dutton-John McRae Awd., Advnc. in Lib. Srv. to Chld. and Young People, 1975; Other awds. **Pubns.:** "And Everywhere Children" (1979); "Told Under the City Umbrella" (1972); "Reading Ladders for Human Relations" (1973); "Adventures With Books" (1973); "We Build Together" (1970). **Activities:** 9, 14-Coll. Dept. of Educ.; 21, 24, 42; 63, 66, 89 **Addr.:** 66 Cleary Ct. #1009, San Francisco, CA 94109.

Morris, Joan Lee (Mr. 11, 1935, Burlington, MA) Assoc. Libn., Cur., Photo Arch., Strozier Lib., FL State Univ., 1970–. **Educ.:** St. Petersburg Jr. Coll., 1952–54, AA; FL State Univ., 1964–67, BA (LS), 1967–70, MS (LS). **Orgs.:** FL LA. SLA. SAA. Frnds. of FL State Univ. Lib. FL State Hist. Recs. Adv. Bd. Hist. Prsrvn. Proj. Review Cncl. Amer. Assn. for State and Lcl. Hist. **Honors:** Beta Phi Mu, 1970. **Pubns.:** "FSU-25 Years," photographic exhibit (1972); "We The People," travelling photographic exhibit (1976). **Activities:** 1, 2; 15, 20, 23; 67, 73 **Addr.:** Rm. 66, Strozier Library, Florida State University, Tallahassee, FL 32306.

Morris, Leslie R. (D. 18, 1935, Sewickley, PA) Dir. of Libs., Xavier Univ., 1976–; Visit. Prof., Univ. of SC, Coll. of Libnshp., 1981–; Head, Tech. Srvs., SUNY, Fredonia, 1970–76; Head Catlgr., E. Stroudsburg State Coll., 1964–70; Catlgr., St. Francis Coll., 1964. **Educ.:** Geneva Coll., 1953–57, BS (Educ.); Duquesne Univ., 1959–61, MLS. **Orgs.:** ALA. LA LA: Ch., Audit. Com. (1980–81). Met. Educ. Media Org.: Pres. (1979–80). Greater New Orleans Lib. Club: Pres. (1980–81). Southwest LA. **Pubns.:** "AACR, COM and all that jazz," *Proc. of the Cath. LA.* (1980); "Serials listing on the Hewlett-Packard 3000," *Que Pasa.* (Ap. 1980); "A comparison of cost factors used by OCLC service centers," *ERIC.* (1979); "A union catalog of books relating to Chautaqua Co., N.Y.," (1974); "A bibliography of Chautauqua County, N.Y. Newspapers, 1810–1975," (1976). **Activities:** 1, 11; 17, 20, 41; 56, 87 **Addr.:** 4709 Senac Dr., Metairie, LA 70003.

Morris, Margaret J. (O. 10, 1951, Bronx, NY) Asst. Mgr., Amer. Assn. of Advert. Agencies, Mem. Info. Srvs., 1976–. **Educ.:** State Univ. Coll., Oneonta, 1969–73, BA (Lit.); Queens Coll., 1973–76, MLS. **Orgs.:** SLA. **Activities:** 3; 51 **Addr.:** 82–74 166th St., Jamaica, NY 11432.

Morris, Miriam Lynn (Jl. 11, 1951, Indianapolis, IN) Branch Libn., Madisonville Branch, Pub. Lib. of Cincinnati and Hamilton Cnty., Chld. Libn., Roselawn Branch; Chld. Libn., Cheviot Branch, Adult Asst. Libn., Hyde Park Branch. **Educ.:** IN Univ., 1969–73, AB (Grmn., Hebrew), 1973–74, MLS. **Orgs.:** ALA: JMRT, OH Statewide Coord. (1981–82), Exhibit Com. (1980 Conf.). OH LA. IN Univ. Alum. Assn. of Cincinnati. **Activities:** 9; 16, 17, 22; 66 **Addr.:** 6306 Kincaid Rd., Cincinnati, OH 45213.

Morris, R. Philip (D. 4, 1942, New Haven, CT) Asst. Dir., High Point Pub. Lib., 1976–; Dir., Ctrl. Meth. Coll., 1968–75. **Educ.:** Ctrl. Meth. Coll., 1960–64, BA (Eng. Lit.); Pratt Inst., 1964–65, MLS. **Orgs.:** ALA. SELA: Int. Frdm. Com. (1979–81). Guilford Cnty. Lib. Club. NC LA: Int. Frdm. Com. (Ch., 1978–80); Pub. Lib. Sect., Frnds./Trustee Liaison Com. (1980–), Stans. Com. (1980–). Rotary Intl. **Pubns.:** "1979 Study on Censorship in North Carolina," *NC Libs.* (Spr. 1981). **Activities:** 1, 9; 17, 35; 74 **Addr.:** High Point Public Library, P.O. Box 2530, High Point, NC 27261.

Morris, Raymond Philip (Mr. 16, 1904, Garnett, KS) Prof. Emeritus, Yale Univ. Dvnty. Sch., 1972–; Prof., Rel. Lit., 1951–72, Assoc. Prof., 1949–51, Asst. Prof., 1941–72, Libn., 1934–72, Asst. Libn., 1932–34; Libn., Garrett Sch. of Theo., 1931–32. **Educ.:** Baker Univ., 1923–26, BA (Hist.); Garrett Sch. of Theo., 1926–29, BD (Dvnty.); Columbia Univ., 1930, BS (LS), 1932, MS (LS). **Orgs.:** ALA: Relig. Bks. RT (Ch., 1932–48). ATLA: Pres. (1951–53); Bd. of Microtext; Lib. Dev. Prog. (Ch.). Amer. Socty. of Church Hist. SAA. Amer. Assn. of Theo. Seminaries: Bd. of Dirs. (1962–70). Inst. for Ecumenical and Cult. Resrch.: Ch. of Bd. (1971–77). Consult., various rel. orgs. **Honors:** Baker Univ., Litt D, 1952; Drake Univ., DD, 1965; Yale Univ., MA (hon.), 1951. **Pubns.:** *Libraries of Theological Seminaries* (1934); *A Theological Book List* (1960); *Aids to Theological Libraries* (1970); *Yale's Selective Book Retirement Program: Concluding Statement* (1963); Various articles and bk. reviews. **Activities:** 1, 2; 17, 33, 41 **Addr.:** 159 Westwood Rd., New Haven, CT 06515.

Morris, Rollyn Charles (Je. 28, 1938, Sioux City, IA) Dir., Lrng. Resrc. Ctr., Keyano Coll., 1981–; Coll. Libn., 1980–; Musical Dir., Touchstone Dance Band, 1977–80; Freelance Musician, 1974–77; Msc. Libn. and Asst. Prof., Univ. of Victoria, 1968–74; Acq. Libn., Alameda Pub. Lib., 1967–68; Ref. Libn., Los Angeles Cnty. Pub. Lib., 1967; Msc. Libn., CA State Univ. Lib., 1965–66; Asst. Prof., Univ. of AK, 1963–65. **Educ.:** CA State Univ., Long Beach, 1958–61, BA, cum laude (Msc.); Univ. of IA, 1961–63, MA (Msclgy.); Univ. of South. CA, 1966–67, MSLS. **Orgs.:** Msc. LA: Rec. Analytics Com. (1968–71); Admin. Plng. Com. (1970–74); Pac. NW Chap., Cnstn. Com. (1970–73). AB Cncl. of Coll. Libs.: Networking Com. (1980–). CAML. Can. LA. Can. Assn. of Univ. Tchrs. Broadcast Music Inc. (Can.). Amer. Socty. of Composers, Authors and Publshrs. **Pubns.:** "The Canadian Composer," *BC Lib. Qtly.* (Ap. 1970); Various pieces of msc. **Activities:** 1, 12; 15, 17, 39; 55, 56 **Addr.:** Keyano College, Learning Resource Center, 8115 Franklin Ave., Fort McMurray, AB T9H 2H7 Canada.

Morris, Stephanie A. (Je. 28, 1950, Philadelphia, PA) Archvst., Temple Univ., Natl. Immigration Arch., 1978–; Archvst., Coll. of Physicians of Philadelphia, 1977–78; Arch. Assoc., Dept. of Hist. Progs., Franklin Inst., 1973–77. **Educ.:** Stonehill Coll., 1972, BS, high hons. (Bio.); Univ. of PA, 1972–75, MA (Hist. of Sci. and Tech.); Amer. Univ., 1973, Cert. (Arch. Admin.). **Orgs.:** Mid–Atl. Reg. Arch. Conf.: Strg. Com. (PA Rep., 1976–78). SAA: Arch. of Sci. Com. (1976–78); Eth. Arch. Grp. (1979–). Socty. for Hist. of Tech.: Musm. Com. (1975–77). **Pubns.:** Jt. auth., *Technology in Industrial America: The Committee on Science and the Art of the Franklin Institute 1824–1900* (1977); "The Franklin Institute Archives," *City Arch. Nsltr.* (O. 1977); "The Franklin Institute: Women and Technology," *Signs* (Fall 1978); Asst. Ed., *The Records of the Committee on Science and the Arts of the Franklin Institute, 1824–1900* (micro.) (1977); Consult., "Work, Work, Work," NJ Pub. Broadcasting (1974). **Activities:** 2; 17, 45, 49-Comp. Indexing Proj.; 55, 56, 91 **Addr.:** National Immigration Archives, Temple University, Paley Library, Philadelphia, PA 19122.

Morris, William Eugene (D. 23, 1944, Rocksprings, TX) IMC Dir., Maryvale HS, Phoenix, AZ, 1979–; AV Coord., Camelback HS, 1977–79; Libn., S. Mountain HS, 1974–77; Libn., Ogontz Jr. HS, 1973–74; Head Libn., Amer. Sch. of Kuwait, 1971–73. **Educ.:** AZ State Univ., 1968–70, BA in Ed (Hist.); Villanova Univ., 1973–75, MSLS; AZ State Univ., 1975–78, MA in Ed (Instr. Media). **Orgs.:** AZ LA: Pres. Elect (1979–80); Pres. (1980–81); Sch. Lib. Div., Pres. (1978); Lib. Dev. & Legis. Com. (Ch., 1975–77). **Honors:** Villanova Univ., Phi Kappa Phi, 1975. **Activities:** 10; 17, 32, 48; 63, 67, 78 **Addr.:** 1336 E. Lawrence Ln., Phoenix, AZ 85020.

Morrison, Carol J. (Ap. 11, 1931, Cleveland, OH) Netwk. Coord., DuPage Lib. Syst., 1978–; Ref. Libn., IL Valley Cmnty. Coll., 1977–78; Resrc. Libn., Starved Rock Lib Syst., 1967–78; Libn., Linwood Sch., 1965–66. **Educ.:** Vassar Coll., 1948–52, BA (Soclgy.); North. IL Univ., 1973–76, MLS. **Orgs.:** DuPage LA. IL LA. ALA. SLA. Wheaton–Area Bus. and Prof. Women's Club. **Honors:** Phi Beta Kappa, 1952. **Activities:** 14-Lib. Syst.; 24, 34, 36; 63, 89 **Addr.:** 4N602 Brookside Ct., St. Charles, IL 60174.

Morrison, H. Frances (S. 28, 1918, Saskatoon, SK) Chief Libn., Saskatoon Pub. Lib., 1961–, Asst. Chief Libn., 1951–61, Head of Ref. Dept., 1948–51, Chld.'s Libn., 1947–48. **Educ.:** Univ. of SK, 1936–39, B.H.Sc.; Univ. of Toronto, 1946–47, BLS. **Orgs.:** LA of Saskatoon: Pres. (1949). SK LA: Pres. (1951–52). CAN LA: 2nd VP (1969–70, 1972). Saskatoon Bus. and Prof. Women's Club: Pres. (1955–57). Univ. Women's Club. Nat. Lib. Adv. Bd. SK Arts Bd.: V-Ch. (1978–). **Honors:** Queen's Jubilee Medal, 1977. **Pubns.:** Ed. *SK Lib. Bltn.* (1947–50). **Activities:** 9; 16, 17, 21; 50, 63, 72 **Addr.:** 318 Cumberland Ave. South, Saskatoon, SK S7N 1M1 Canada.

Morrison, Lillian (O. 27, 1917, Jersey City, NJ) Coor., YA Srvs., NY Pub. Lib., 1968–, Asst. Coord., 1952–68, Vocational HS Spec., 1947–52. **Educ.:** Rutgers Univ., 1934–38, BS (Math.); Columbia Univ., 1939–42, BSLS. **Orgs.:** ALA: various committees over the years, including Grolier Awd., Local Arrange., Stans. Com. NY LA. Author's League. **Honors:** Phi BeTa Kappa, 1937; **Pubns.:** *The Ghosts of Jersey City* (1967); jt. auth., *Miranda's Music* (1968); *The Sidewalk Racer and Other Poems of Sports and Motion* (1978); *Who Would Marry A Mineral?* (1979); *Overheard in a Bubble Chamber* (1981). **Activities:** 9; 32, 37, 42 **Addr.:** Office of Young Adult Services, 455 Fifth Ave., New York NY 10016.

Morrison, Mildred W. (Je. 20, 1918, Barboursville, VA) Asst. Dir. in Charge of Pub. Srvs., Ctrl. Piedmont Cmnty. Coll., 1972–, Head of Ref., 1968–72; Libn., Garinger HS, 1959–68; Libn., Ctrl. HS (Charlotte), 1954–59; Libn., Charlotte City Schs., 1952–54; Catlgr. and Head of Circ., Charlotte Pub. Lib., 1940–43; Catlgr., Durham Pub. Lib., 1939–40. **Educ.:** Hollins Coll., 1934–38, AB (Latin); Pratt Inst., 1938–39, BLS; Appalachian State Univ., 1969–70, ME. **Orgs.:** Mecklenburg LA: Pres. (1959–60). Metrolina LA: Pres. (1979–81); VP (1978–79). NC Lrng. Resrcs. Assn.: Nsltr. Ed. (1975–77). NC LA. Various other orgs. NC Assn. of Educs.: Cmnty. Coll. Div. (Pres., 1975–76; VP, 1974–75); CPCC Chap. (Pres., 1973–74). **Pubns.:** "Central Piedmont Tries Walk-ins and Likes Them," *NC Libs.* (Fall 1974). **Activities:** 1, 9; 20, 22, 39 **Addr.:** 1817 Maryland Ave., Charlotte, NC 28209.

Morrison, Perry D. (N. 30, 1919, Minneapolis, MN) Asst. Univ. Libn. (Actg.) and Prof. of Libnshp., Univ. of OR, 1979–, Coord. of Lib. Resrch., 1978–79, Prof. of Libnshp., 1967–78; Assoc. Prof. of Libnshp., Univ. of WA, 1965–67; Coll. Libn. and Dir. of LS Prog., Sacramento State Coll., 1963–65; Asst. Libn., Head Soc. Libn. and Prof. of Libnshp., Univ. of OR, 1949–63. **Educ.:** Pasadena City Coll., 1938–40, AA (Eng.); Whittier Coll., 1940–42, AB (Eng., Soc. Sci.), 1946–47, MA (Hist.); Univ. of CA, 1948–49, BLS, 1956–58, DLS. **Orgs.:** ALA: Lib. Binding Inst. Schol. Jury. OR LA: Pres. (1961–62); ILL Com. Pac. N.W. Lib. Assoc.: Conv. Ch. (1961) Ed., *PNLA Quarterly* (1967–71). SLA: OR Provisional Chap., Pres. (1974–75). Eugene Kiwanis Clb.: Bd. of Dirs. (1977–79). Univ. of OR Fac. Clb.: Bd. of Dirs. First Congregational Church of Eugene. AAUP. **Honors:** Sch. LA of Australia, 7th Anl. C.A. Housden Lect., 1975. **Pubns.:** "Since Bath: A Review of Published Information Transfer Studies in the Social and Behavioral Sciences, 1975 through 1978," *Bhvl. and Soc. Sci. Libn.* (Fall 1979); "Cooperative Use of Serials in Australian Libraries," *Serials Libn.* (Spr. 1977); jt. auth., "The Edward S. Burgess Collection," *Imprint: OR* (Spr. 1978); ed., *PNLA Qtly.* (1967–71); *The Career of the Academic Librarian* (1969); various articles, reviews. **Activities:** 1; 17, 26, 41 **Addr.:** Library, University of Oregon, Eugene, OR 97403.

Morrison, Ray Leon (S. 17, 1952, Boise, ID) Bibl. Instr. Libn., Pittsburg State Univ., 1981–; Asst. Prof., LS, Olivet Nazarene Coll., 1975–81. **Educ.:** San Jose State Univ., 1971–74, BA (Jnlsm.), 1974–75, MA (LS); CA Cmnty. Coll., 1974–75, (Media

PROFESSIONAL ACTIVITIES: Institutions: 1. Acad. lib.; 2. Arch.; 3. Assn.; 4. Fed./Gvt. lib.; 5. Inst. lib.; 6. Mfr./Suppl.; 7. Milit. lib.; 8. Musm.; 9. Pub. lib.; 10. Sch. lib.; 11. Sch. of lib. sci.; 12. Spec. lib.; 13. State lib.; 14. (other). **Functions/Activities:** 15. Acq./Col. dev.; 16. Adult srvs.; 17. Admin.; 18. Apprais.; 19. Archit./Bldgs.; 20. Cat./Class.; 21. Chld. srvs.; 22. Circ.; 23. Cons./Pres.; 24. Consult.; 25. Cont. ed.; 26. Educ. lib. sci.; 27. Ext. srvs.; 28. Fund/Grants; 29. Gvt. pubs.; 30. Indx./Abs.; 31. Instr. lib. use; 32. Media srvs.; 33. Micro.; 34. Netwks./Coop.; 35. Persnl.; 36. PR; 37. Publshg.; 38. Recs. mgt.; 39. Ref. srvs.; 40. Repro.; 41. Resrch.; 42. Review.; 43. Secur.; 44. Serials; 45. Spec. col.; 46. Tech. srvs.; 47. Trustees/Bds.; 48. YA srvs.; 49. (other).

Spec.); Univ. IL, Cert. of Advnc. Std. in Progress (LS). **Orgs.:** ALA. Nazarene Lib. Flwshp. IL Clearinghouse on Acad. Lib. Instr. Socty. of Prof. Jnlst.: VP (1972–73); Treas. (1972–75). N.A.I.A. Coaches Assn. N.C.C.A.A. Coaches Assn. Various other orgs. **Pubns.:** *An Annotated Bibliography of Track and Field Literature Published in the United States Between 1960-74* (1978); "A Father, A Son, and a Three Mile Run," *Christ. Libn.* (O. 1976). **Activities:** 1; 22, 31, 39; 61, 90, 92 **Addr.:** Pittsburg State University Library, Pittsburg, KS 66762.

Morrison, Samuel (D. 19, 1936) Asst. Dir., Broward Cnty. Libs., 1976–, Admin. Asst., 1974–76; Dir., Frostproof Living Lrng. Ctr., 1972–74. **Educ.:** Compton Jr. Coll., 1959, AA; CA State Univ., 1971, BA (Eng.); Univ. of IL, 1972, MSLS. **Orgs.:** SELA. ALA: Cncl. (1975–78); JMRT; SRRT; LAMA. FL LA: Pres. (1980); VP (1979). Broward Cnty. LA. **Honors:** Broward Cnty. LA, Outstan. Empl. of the Yr., 1978, 1979. **Pubns.:** "The Frostproof Living Learning Library Center," *The Lib. Scene* (Win. 1979). **Activities:** 9; 17 **Addr.:** Broward County Libraries, 1301 W. Copans Rd., Bldg. "D", Pompano Beach, FL 33064.

Morrison, Sylvia E. (Jl. 15, 1929, Vancouver, BC) Ed., Can. Per. Index, Can. LA, 1968–; Cape Breton Reg. Lib., Libn. (Chld.'s, Cat., Bkmobile), Lib., Sydney, NS, 1952–64. **Educ.:** Queen's Univ., Kingston, ON, 1948–51, BA; Univ. of Toronto, 1951–52, BLSc. **Orgs.:** Can. LA. Indexing and Abstr. Socty. of Can.: Secy. (1977–78). **Pubns.:** *"CPI Surveys-A Service to Subscribers," Can. Lit. Jnl.* (Jn. 1981); "A Subscription Rate Survey at the *Canadian Periodical Index," IASC/SCAD Nsltr.* (Ap. 1980). **Activities:** 12; 17, 30, 37; 57 **Addr.:** Canadian Periodical Index, Canadian Library Association, 151 Sparks St, Ottawa, ON K1P 5E3 Canada.

Morrissett, Elizabeth (Akron, OH) Dir., Lib., MT Coll. of Mineral Sci. and Tech., 1980–; Head of Acq. and Serials, Auraria Lib., Univ. of CO at Denver, 1976–80, Ref. and ILL Libn., Bromley Lib., 1974–76. **Educ.:** Univ. of Akron, 1937–41, AB; Univ. of MI, 1941–44, ABLS, AMLS. **Orgs.:** CO LA: Int. Frdm. (Ch., 1973–74, 1979–80); CO Libns. in Transition, (Ch., 1974–75). ALA: SRRT (Ch., 1977–78); Action Cncl. (1976–78); Task Force on Peace Info. Exch. (Ch., 1978–). Mt. Plains LA: (1977–78). IFLA: Soc. Sci. Libs. Sect./Working Party on Conflict Mgt. and Peace Info. (Ch.). Other Orgs. Boulder Cnty. Volun. and Info. Ctr. Women's Intl. Leag. for Peace and Freedom. AAAS. Other orgs. **Activities:** 1; 34, 86 **Addr.:** Montana College of Mineral Sciences and Technology, Library, Butte, MT 59701.

Morroni, June Rose (Ja. 8, 1938, Smithmill, PA) Ext. Srvs. Libn., Centre Cnty. Lib., 1977–; Microform Libn., PA State Univ., 1970–76, Ref. Libn., 1969–70; Libn., Elmira (NY) City Sch. Dist., 1967–69. **Educ.:** Lebanon Valley Coll., 1955–56, (Msc.); PA State Univ., 1956–59, BS (Educ.); Univ. of Chicago, 1959–68, AM (Libnshp.). **Orgs.:** ALA. PA LA: Juniata Conemaugh Chap., Int. Frdm. Com. (1978–79). Mu Phi Epsilon. Smithsonian Assoc. **Pubns.:** "Music Librarians," *Encyclopedia of Library and Information Science* (1976); "The Music Library Association," *Fontes Artis Musicae* (1971); "Yale Collection of German Baroque Literature," *Microform Review* (1973); "The Library of American Civilization," *Microform Review* (1972); *Samuel Gompers Letterbooks Index, Vols. 1-20* (1970–76). **Activities:** 1, 9; 27, 33, 39; 63, 74, 89 **Addr.:** 742 Holmes St., State College, PA 16801.

Morrow, Carolyn Clark (Ap. 13, 1952, Oak Park, IL) Cons. Lib./Asst. Prof., Morris Lib., South. IL Univ., 1978–; Resrch. Asst., ALA Arch., Univ. of IL, 1976–78. **Educ.:** South. IL Univ., 1971–74, BA (Food and Nutr.); Univ. of IL, 1976–77, MLS, 1977–79 (Cert. of Advnc. Study). **Orgs.:** ALA. SAA. Midwest Archs. Assn. Amer. Inst. for Cons. of Hist. and Artistic Works. Guild of Bk. Workers. **Pubns.:** *A Conservation Bibliography for Librarians, Archivists, and Administrators* (1979); "The Status of Research and Techniques in Archival Conservation," *Midwest Archvst.* (1978). **Addr.:** Morris Library, Southern Illinois University, Carbondale, IL 62901.

Morse, A(rthur) Louis (Je. 29, 1917, Peekskill, NY) Dir. of Lib. Media Srvs., E. Meadow Union Free Sch. Dist., 1954–; Adj. Assoc. Prof., C W Post Ctr., Long Island Univ., 1960–80; Asst. Libn., Head Tech. Srvs., Iona Coll., 1947–54; Tchr., New York City, 1939–47. **Educ.:** Cath. Univ., 1936–39, AB (Eng.); Manhattan Coll., 1939–45, MA (Eng.); St. John's Univ., 1945–49, BLS; Columbia Univ., 1951–54, MS (LS). **Orgs.:** NY LA: Exhibits Com. (Ch., 1977–80); Awds. Com. (1977–80). Long Island Sch. Media Assn.: Pres. (1959–60); Exec. Bd. (1960–61). Nassau Cnty. LA: Bd. of Dir. (1978–80); Grants Com. (Ch., 1979–80). Cath. LA. NY State Educ. Dept.: Adv. Com., ESEA Title II (1965–77). Nassau Bd. of Coop. Srvs.: Adv. Com. on Sch. Lib. Media Srvs. (1978–80). Phi Delta Kappa. **Honors:** Cath. LA, Bklyn-L.I. Unit, Outstan. Contrib. to Libnshp., 1972; Long Island Sch. Media Assn., Merit. Srv. to Sch. Libs., 1976; St. John's Univ., Disting. Alum. Awd., 1979. **Pubns.:** "How to Get Going With Federal Funds" *Grade Tchr.* (N. 1965). **Activities:** 10, 11; 17, 26, 32; 63, 75 **Addr.:** 3778 Lincoln St., Seaford, NY 11783.

Morse, Anita L. (Ag. 28, 1941, South Bend, IN) Prof. of Law and Dir. of Law Lib., Cleveland Marshall Coll. of Law, Cleveland State Univ., 1978–; Dir. of Lib., Assoc. Prof., Univ. of Detroit Sch. of Law, 1975–78; Law Libn., Asst. Prof., Albany Law Sch., Union Univ., 1974–75; Asst. Prof., Univ. of KY Coll. of Law, 1972–74; Asst. Prof. of Law, Univ. of FL, 1969–71; Attorney, Fed. Trade Cmsn., 1968–69. **Educ.:** Purdue Univ., 1958–62, BS (Prelaw); IN Univ., 1964–68, JD; George Washington Univ., Natl. Law Ctr., 1968–70, LLM (Intl. Law); Univ. of KY, 1973–74, MSLS; Cleveland State Univ., 1978–80, MPA (Admin.). **Orgs.:** MI Assn. of Law Libns.: VP (1977–78). AALL: Co–Ch. and Wkshp. Coord. (1978–80). OH Reg. Assn. of Law Libns.: Educ. Com. (Ch., 1980–). Amer. Bar Assn.: Legal Educ. and Admission to the Bar. Amer. Assn. of Law Schs. IN State Bar Assn. **Honors:** Beta Phi Mu, 1974. **Pubns.:** Jt. auth., *Powers of the State of Kentucky in Implementing an Effluent Tax as a Part of an Interstate Ohio River Basin Water Pollution Control Program* (1974); *FDA: National Consumer Awareness and Access Project Handbook* (1980); Jt. auth., "Air Pollution Control in Lindiana in 1968," *VA Univ. Law Review* (1968); "The Cost of Purity: The Use of the Effluent Charge in Water Pollution Control," *VA Univ. Law Review* (1972); "New Directions in Education for Law Librarians," *Law Lib. Jnl.* (1977); Various articles and reviews. **Activities:** 1; 29; 77, 78 **Addr.:** Cleveland Marshall College of Law Library, Cleveland, OH 44115.

Morse, David H. (S. 27, 1953, Bryn Mawr, PA) Tech. Srvs. Libn., USC Norris Med. Lib., 1979–; Head of Tech. Srvs., Philadelphia Coll. of Pharm. and Sci., 1977–79, Ref. Libn., 1976–77. **Educ.:** Wesleyan Univ., 1971–75, BA (Comp. Lit.); Columbia Univ., 1975–76, MS (LS). **Orgs.:** Med. LA: Ad Hoc Com. to Prepare a Cnstn. (1978–80); Contrib. Papers Referee (1979–80); Pharm. Sect. (Ch., 1980–), Rep. to Cncl. of Sects. (1980–). **Honors:** Phi Beta Kappa, 1975; Beta Phi Mu, 1976. **Activities:** 1; 15, 20, 46; 80, 87, 91 **Addr.:** Norris Medical Library, 2025 Zonal Ave., Los Angeles, CA 90033.

Morse, Elliott H. (N. 9, 1916, New Haven, CT) Libn., Coll. of Physicians of Philadelphia, 1949–81, Admin. Assoc. Libn., 1949–53; Ref. Libn., Univ. of PA, 1944–49; Acting Ref. Libn., Temple Univ., 1942–44; Pers. Asst., 1941–42; Ref. Asst., Univ. of PA, 1939–41. **Educ.:** Haverford Coll., 1934–38, BS (Grmn.); Drexel Univ., 1938–39, BS LS; Univ. of PA, 1941–43, MA (Grmn.); Med. LA, Grade I Cert., 1962. **Orgs.:** Drexel Lib. Sch. Alum. Assn: Pres. (1939–41). Spec. Libs. Cncl. Philadelphia: Pres. (1949–50). Med. LA: Philadelphia Reg. Grp. (Ch., 1952–53); Convention Ch. (1965); Pres. (1969). Union Lib. Cat. of PA PALINET: Pres. (1973–74). **Honors:** Drexel Univ. Lib. Sch., Dist. Alum. Awd., 1965. **Pubns.:** "After the flood: recovery of water-damaged books at the College of Physicians of Philadelphia," *Lib. and Arch. Secur. News* (Fall 1980); "Supply and Demand in Medical Literature," *Einstein Med. Ctr.* (O. 1960); "Management Methods in Libraries," *Bltn. Med. LA* (Ap. 1962); "Regional Plans for Medical Library Service, Medical Library Cooperation in the Philadelphia Area," *Bltn. Med. LA.* (Jl. 1964). **Activities:** 5, 12; 17, 24, 39; 75, 80, 87 **Addr.:** College of Physicians of Philadelphia, 19 South 22nd St., Philadelphia, PA 19103.

Morse, Kenneth Thompson (Jl. 15, 1926, Winchester, MA) Chief Libn. (Assoc. Prof.), Pell Marine Sci. Lib., Univ. of RI, 1973–; Mgr. of Lib. Srvs., Inst. for Space Stds., NASA, 1971–73; Tech. Info. Ofcr., Hudson Labs., Columbia Univ., 1952–69; Biblgrphr., New York Socty. of Electron Microscopists, 1952–64. **Educ.:** Boston Univ., 1946–50, BA (Psy.); Columbia Univ., 1951–52, MS (LS). **Orgs.:** SLA. ASIS. AAAS. **Pubns.:** Jt. auth., *The International Bibliography of Electron Microscopy* (1959–62). **Activities:** 1, 12; 15, 17; 58, 65, 91 **Addr.:** Pell Marine Science Library, University of Rhode Island, Narragansett Bay Campus, Narragansett, RI 02882.

Morse, Mark P. (N. 24, 1945, Chester, PA) Dir., L. E. Phillips Meml. Pub. Lib., Eau Claire, WI, 1979–; Dir., Mifflin Cnty. Lib., Lewistown, PA, 1974–79. **Educ.:** Villanova Univ., 1964–68, BA (Mod. Lang.); Univ. of IA, 1970–72, MA (Phil.); Univ. of Pittsburgh, 1973–74, MLS. **Orgs.:** ALA: PLA, Legis. Com. (1980–82). PA LA: Ch., Legis. Com. (1977–78). WI LA: Ch., Multitype Coop. Sect. (1981–82). **Activities:** 9; 17, 34; 78 **Addr.:** 400 Eau Claire St., Eau Claire, WI 54701.

Mortenson, Jayne B. (F. 28, 1940, Pittsburgh, PA) Head, Pub. Srv., Edmonton Pub. Lib., 1978–; Supvsr., Pub. Libs., Province of NS, 1975–78; Pub. Srv. Libn., Kellogg Med. Lib., Dalhousie Univ., 1970–75; Libn., Nat. Sci. - Nat. Resrcs. Lib., Univ. of MI, 1967–69. **Educ.:** Coll. of Wooster, 1958–62, BA (Chem.); Univ. of MI, 1963–66, MALS. **Orgs.:** Can. LA. AB LA. Atl. Prov. LA: Treas. (1976–78). Can. Hlth. LA. **Activities:** 1, 9; 16, 17, 39; 58, 60, 80 **Addr.:** Edmonton Public Library, 7 Sir Winston Churchill Sq., Edmonton, AB T5J 2V4 Canada.

Mortimer, Louis R. (My. 24, 1941, Philadelphia, PA) Dir. of Persnl., Lib. of Congs., 1980–; Exec. Off., Resrch. Srvs. Dept., 1978–80, Admin. Coord., Cong. Ref., 1975–78, Pers. Placement and Class. Spec., 1972–75, Econ. Anal., Cong. Res. Srv., 1971–72. **Educ.:** Temple Univ., 1959–63, BA (Hist/Econ.); Penn State Univ., 1963–65, MA (Econ. Hist.); Univ. of IL, 1969–70, MSLS; George Washington Univ., 1971–77, MPhil (Amer. Std.). **Orgs.:** ALA. D.C. LA. Lib. of Congs. Credit Union: VP, Bd. of Dir. **Honors:** Phi Alpha Theta, 1963. **Activities:** 1, 4; 17, 35, 41; 59, 85, 92 **Addr.:** 1321 East Capitol St., Washington, DC 20003.

Mortimer, William J. (Mr. 30, 1925, Randolph, VT) Mgr., Lib. and Ref. Srv., Life Insur. Mktg. and Resrch. Assn., 1951–. **Educ.:** Amherst Coll., 1947, AB (Hist.); Cornell Univ., 1948, MA (Soc. Stds.); Columbia Univ., 1950, MS (LS). **Orgs.:** SLA: CT Valley Chap. (Pres., 1955–56); Insur. Div. (Ch., 1957–58; Treas., 1970–75). **Activities:** 12; 17, 39; 76 **Addr.:** LIMRA, P.O. Box 208, Hartford, CT 06141.

Morton, Ann W. (S. 27, 1939, Atlanta, GA) Exec. Secy., GA LA, 1970–; Asst. Rsv. Libn. Part time, Emory Univ., 1968–70; Asst. to the Libn., Agnes Scott Coll., 1965–66. **Educ.:** Tift Coll., 1957–61, AB (Eng.); Emory Univ., 1962–65, MSLS. **Orgs.:** Metro Atlanta Lib. Club. Friends of Atlanta Pub. Lib.: Exec. Secty. (1978–79). Southeast. LA: Exec. Secy. (1970–77, 1979–). Div. of Libnshp., Emory Univ.: Adv. Cncl. (1980). Atlanta Boy Choir: Bd. of Ofcrs. (1978–). Tift Coll. Alum. Assn.: Exec. Cncl. (1978–). **Activities:** 1, 9; 26, 36, 47; 55, 63, 75 **Addr.:** P.O. Box 833, Tucker, GA 30084.

Morton, Bruce (S. 14, 1947, New York, NY) Info. Srvs., Docum. Libn., Carleton Coll., 1977–; Cat., Dickinson Coll., 1976–77; Educ. Planner, South. Tier W. Plng. Bd., 1975–76; Info. Spec., NY Ctr. for Migrant Std., 1974–75; Russ. Ling., US Army Secur. Agency, 1969–72. **Educ.:** PA State Univ., 1965–69, BA (Eng.); SUNY, Geneseo, 1974, MLS; PA State Univ., 1972–73, MA (Eng.). **Orgs.:** ALA: ACRL. GODORT (1976–); Asst. Coord. for Machine Readable Data Files Task Force (1981–82). Bibl. Socty. of Amer. (1978–). Mod. Lang. Assn. (1974–). **Pubns.:** "An Items Record Management System: First Step in Automation of Collection Development in Selective U.S. Depository Libraries," *Gvt. Pubns. Review* (forthcoming); "Toward a Comprehensive Collection Development Policy for Partial U.S. Depositories," *Gvt. Pubns. Review* (1980); *John Gould Fletcher: A Bibliography* (1979); "An Interview with Philip Young," *Hemingway Notes* (Fall 1980); "Twelve New H. L. Mencken Letters," *Manuscripts* (Sum. 1979); various articles and poems. **Activities:** 1, 4; 15, 29, 39; 55, 57, 92 **Addr.:** The Library, Carleton College, Northfield, MN 55057.

Morton, Donald J. (Ja. 11, 1931, Brooklyn, NY) Lib. Dir., Univ. of MA Med. Sch., 1970–; Sci. Libn., Neast. Univ., 1968–70; Assoc. Prof., Univ. of DE, 1965–68; Plant Pathologist, U.S. Dept. of Agr., 1961–68; Asst. Prof., ND State Univ., 1959–61; Asst. Prof., NM State Univ., 1957–58. **Educ.:** Univ. of DE, 1948–52, BS (Bio.); LA State Univ., 1952–54, MS (Bio.); Univ. of CA, Berkeley, 1954–57, PhD (Bio.); Simmons Coll., 1968–69, MS (LS), 1973–76, D Arts (LS). **Orgs.:** N. Atl. Hlth. Scis. Libs.: Pres. (1975). Simmons Coll. Lib. Sch. Alum. Assn.: Pres. (1976). Worcester Area Coop. Libs.: Pres. (1974). ALA: ACRL. Various other orgs. and ofcs. Phi Kappa Phi. Sigma Xi. Univ. of MA Press. **Pubns.:** "Use of a Subscription Agent's Computer Facilities," *Lib. Resrcs. and Tech. Srvs.* (1978); "Analysis of Requests by Hospital Libraries," *Bltn. Med. LA* (1977); "President's Message," *Simmons Libn.* (1976); "SDC and Dialog; User's Point of View," *Bltn. of the Med. LA* (1976); "Theory Y is Not Participative Management," *Human Resrcs. Mgt.* (1975); Various articles. **Activities:** 1, 5; 17; 58, 80, 91 **Addr.:** Univ. of Massachusetts Medical School, 55 Lake Avenue N., Worcester, MA 01605.

Morton, Dorothy Jean (My. 14, 1939, Madisonville, KY) Resrch. Libn., DuPont Tech. Lib., 1962–. **Educ.:** Univ. of KY, 1958–61, AB (Chem.), 1961–62, MS (LS). **Orgs.:** SLA. **Activities:** 12; 30, 39; 59, 60 **Addr.:** 608 Lea Blvd., Apt. C–6, Wilmington, DE 19802.

Morton, Florrinell (Francis) (D. 20, 1905, Pollock, TX) Retired, 1971–; Dir., LA State Univ. Lib. Sch., 1944–71, Actg. Dir., Asst. Dir., Asst. to Dir., 1940–44, Prof., 1947–71, Assoc. Prof., 1942–47, Asst. Prof., Instr., 1933–42; Catlgr., N. TX State Coll., 1927–30. **Educ.:** W. TX State Coll., 1921–23; Univ. of CA, Berkeley, 1923–25, BA (Eng.), 1926–27, Cert. (LS), 1930–31, MA (LS). **Orgs.:** ALA: Pres. (1961–62); Exec. Bd. (1959–62); Lib. Educ. Div. (Pres., 1956–58). AALS: Pres. (1946–47). SWLA: Pres. (1960–62). LA LA: Pres. (1941–42). AAUP. AAUW. **Honors:** Beta Phi Mu, Awd. for Contrib. to Educ. for Libnshp.; Essae M. Culver Awd. for Contrib. to LA Lib. Dev. **Activities:** 11; 20, 26 **Addr.:** 402 Stanford Ave., Baton Rouge, LA 70808.*

Morton, Katharine D. (Ag. 2, 1945, Shenandoah, PA) Actg. Head, Mss. and Arch., Yale Univ. Lib., 1980–; Asst. Head, 1976–80, Sr. Arch. Spec., 1974–76, Arch. Spec., 1971–73. **Educ.:** Dickinson Coll., 1963–67, BA (Fr.); Univ. of WI, 1967–68, MA (Fr.); South. CT State Coll., 1977–80, MLS. **Orgs.:** SAA. New Eng. Archvsts. Amer. Assn. for State and Lcl. Hist. **Activities:** 1, 2; 15, 17, 45; 55, 92 **Addr.:** 64 Christian Hill Rd., Waterbury, CT 06706.

Morton, Margaret L. (Mr. 3, 1932, South Cove, NS) Dir., Libs. Div., Agr. Can., 1979–; Exec. Secy., Natl. Lib. of Can., 1978–79, Asst. Dir., Cat. Branch, Pub. Srvs. Branch, 1976–78; Head, Tech. Srvs., Lib., Transp. Can. **Educ.:** St. Francis Xavier Univ., 1947–51, BSc (Chem.); Univ. of Ottawa, 1969–70, BLS. **Orgs.:** Can. LA. Can. Assn. Info. Sci. Inst. for Gen. Mgt. **Activities:** 4, 12; 17; 58, 91 **Addr.:** Libraries Division, Sir John Carling Building, Ottawa, ON K1A 0C5 Canada.

Special Subjects/Services: 50. Adult educ.; 51. Advert./Mktg.; 52. Aerosp.; 53. Agric.; 54. Area std.; 55. Arts/Hum.; 56. Autom.; 57. Bibl./Prtg.; 58. Bio. sci.; 59. Bus./Fin.; 60. Chem.; 61. Copyrt.; 62. Documtn.; 63. Educ.; 64. Engin.; 65. Env.; 66. Eth. grps.; 67. Film; 68. Food/Nutr.; 69. Geneal.; 70. Geo.; 71. Geol.; 72. Handcpd.; 73. Hist.; 74. Int. frdm.; 75. Info. sci.; 76. Insr.; 77. Law; 78. Legis.; 79. Math./Comp. sci.; 80. Med.; 81. Metals; 82. Nat. resrcs.; 83. Newsp.; 84. Nuc. sci.; 85. Oral hist.; 86. Petr./Energy; 87. Pharm.; 88. Phys./Astr./Math.; 89. Readg.; 90. Relig.; 91. Sci./Tech.; 92. Soc. sci.; 93. Telecom.; 94. Transp.; 95. (other).

Who's Who in Library and Information Services

Mosby, Margaret A. (F. 8, 1947, Paterson, NJ) Info. Anal., Philip Morris USA, 1981–; Head, Ref. Dept., Med. Coll. of VA, 1977–81; Head, Tech. Srvs., Sci./Tech. Ctr., Univ. of VA, 1974–77; Chem. Libn., Cath. Univ. of Amer., 1972–73. **Educ.:** Caldwell Coll., 1964–68, BA (Chem.); Cath. Univ. of Amer., 1972–73, MSLS. **Orgs.:** Med. LA: Cert. Exam. Com. (1979–81); Mid-Atl. Reg. Grp., Nom. Com. (Ch., 1979). ASIS. **Pubns.:** "Method for Generating a Chemical Reaction Index for Storage and Retrieval of Information," *Jnl. of Chem. Info. and Comp. Scis.* (N. 1980); Med. LA Cont. Ed. Course #68, *Clinical Librarianship* (1981). **Activities:** 1, 12; 25; 60, 80 **Addr.:** 1425 Avondale Ave., Richmond, VA 23298.

Moscatt, Angeline A. (N. 9, 1926, Brooklyn, NY) Supvsg. Libn., Central Chld. Room, Donnell Lib. Ctr., NY Pub. Lib., 1967–, Sr. Chld.'s Libn., 1961–67; Chld.'s Libn., 1957–61. **Educ.:** Hunter Coll., 1944–46, BA (Eng.); Pratt Inst., 1957–59, MLS. **Orgs.:** Chld. Srvs. Div. ALA: Sel. of Frgn. Chld.'s Books Ch. (1967–72); Com. on Nat. Plng. of Spec. Coll. (1969–77); Discuss. Grp. for Resrch. in Chld.'s Coll. (1974–77). Woman's Natl. Book Assn.: NY Chap.: Bd. of Mgrs. (1978–80). NY Pub. Lib. Guild: VP, Prof. (1968–80). **Pubns.:** "A Historical Account of the New York Public Library Central Children's Room Research Collections," *Phaedrus* (Fall 1976). **Activities:** 9; 21, 39, 45 **Addr.:** Central Children's Room, Donnell Library Center, 20 West 53 St., New York, NY 10019.

Mosel, Arlene, E. (Ag. 27, 1921, Cleveland, OH) Prof. Emeritus, Case West. Resrv. Univ., 1981–, Assoc. Prof., Sch. of LS, 1971–, Asst. Prof., 1967–71; Asst. Coord., Chld. Srvs., Cuyahoga Cnty. Pub. Lib., 1965–67, Reg. Chld. Libn., 1961–65; Chld. Libn., Shaker Hts. Pub. Lib., 1960–61; Sch. Libn., Pinellas Cnty. Schls., 1959–60; Chld. Libn., Cleveland Hts. Pub. Lib., 1951–58; Asst. Chld. Libn., Enoch Pratt Lib., 1943–45. **Educ.:** OH Wesleyan Univ., 1939–43, BA (Eng., Hist.); West. Resrv. Univ., 1956–59, MSLS. **Orgs.:** ALA: ALSC, Melcher Schol. Com. (Ch., 1973–76), Hist. Col. (Ch., 1971–75), Tchrs. of Chld. Lit. (Ch., 1972–76), Lib. Educ. Com. (1972–76), Newbery–Caldecott Com. (1970–71). OH LA. Intl. Readg. Assn. **Honors:** Boston Globe–Horn Book Awd. for *Tikki Tikki Tembo*, 1968; ALA Notable Bk. Awd. for *Tikki Tikki Tembo*, 1968; "Best of the Best" Intl. List of Outstan. Classics for Chld., for *Tikki Tikki Tembo*, 1978; Caldecott Awd. for *The Funny Little Woman*, 1973; Various bk. awds. (1973–76). **Pubns.:** *The Funny Little Woman* (1972); *Tikki Tikki Tembo* (1968); "Storytelling Pamphlet," *Wilson Lib. Bltn.* (D. 1960). **Activities:** 21, 26 **Addr.:** 76 E. Pioneer Trail, Aurora, OH 44202.

Moseley, Eva Steiner (D. 25, 1931, Vienna, Austria) Cur. of Mss., Schlesinger Lib., Radcliffe Coll., 1971–; Lib. asst., Bodleian Law Lib., Oxford, 1965–66; Asst. libn., Asia Fndn., 1955–56. **Educ.:** Mt. Holyoke Coll., 1949–53, AB (Phil.); Radcliffe Coll., 1953–55, MA (Indian Std.). **Orgs.:** SAA: Prog. Com. (Ch. 1975, 1979); Mss. Repositories Prof. Afnty. Grp. (Ch., 1979–80); Nom. Com. (1980–81). New Eng. Archvsts.: Ed. Bd. (1980–); Nsltr. Ed. (1975–78); Prog. Com. (Ch., 1975, 1979). Boston Archvsts. Grp. Medford Hist. Socty. Civil Liberties Union of MA. **Honors:** Phi Beta Kappa, 1953. **Pubns.:** "Documenting the History of Women in America," *Amer. Archvst.* (Ap. 1973); "Sources for the 'New Women's History,'" *Amer. Archvst.* (Spr. 1980); "One-Half Our History," slide-tape (1976). **Activities:** 1, 12; 15, 17, 45; 86, 95-Women. **Addr.:** Schlesinger Library, Radcliffe College, 10 Garden St., Cambridge, MA 02138.

Moser, Marilyn Elaine (Mr. 19, 1941, Salisbury, NC) Sch. Lib. Media Spec., Amidon Elem. Sch., 1964–; Asst. to the Libn., Smithsonian Inst., 1964; Richman Cnty. Sch. Libn., Montross Elem. Sch., 1963–64. **Educ.:** NC Ctrl. Univ., 1959–63, BS (LS); grad. courses, 1976–79. **Orgs.:** WHCOLIS: Del. DC Assn. of Sch. Libns.: Pres. (1977–79). DC LA: Leg. Com. (1978–81). ALA: AASL, Gen. Com. for Louisville Conf. (1978–80). Natl. Cncl. of Women in Admin. Natl. Cncl. of Negro Women. **Honors:** DC Assn. of Sch. Libns., Pres. of the Yr. Awd., 1979; Richmond Cnty. Sch. Syst., Tch. of the Yr. Awd., 1963. **Pubns.:** "School Librarians: Stepping into the Third Centry," *DCASL Nsltr.* (Fall 1976). **Activities:** 10; 21, 31, 36; 63, 89 **Addr.:** 800 4th St. SW, Washington, DC 20024.

Moses, Richard Bradley (Jl. 1, 1933, Rochester, NY) Dir., Oakville Pub. Lib., 1971–; Dir. of Libs., Roger Williams Coll., 1970–71; Reg. Coord., Pawtucket Pub. Lib., 1969; Field Dir./Instr., "High John," Univ. of MD, 1967–69; Sr. Youth Libn., Cmnty. Action Prog., Enoch Pratt Free Lib., YA Asst.; YA Asst., Rochester Pub. Lib. **Educ.:** Harpur Coll., SUNY, 1960, BA (Soc. Sci.); Rutgers Univ., 1963, MLS. **Orgs.:** ON LA: Int. Frdm. Com. (Ch., 1979–80). **Pubns.:** "For Teens Interest Comes First," *What Is Reading Doing to the Child?* (1967); "Pome," *Revolting Libns.* (1972); "Taking Stock of the Library's Armory," *Quill and Quire* (Ag. 1976); "Exploding Library Myths," *Quill and Quire* (Jl. 1973); "Hindsight on High John," *Lib. Jnl.* (My. 1, 1972); Various articles. **Activities:** 9; 17 **Addr.:** 13 East St., Oakville, ON L6L 3K3 Canada.

Moses, Stefan B. (O. 31, 1930, Cologne, Germany) Exec. Dir., CA LA, 1969–; Mgt. Consult., Arthur D. Little, Inc., 1968–69; Pub.-Inst. Lib. Consult., NY State Lib., 1962–68; Tchg./Resrch. Asst., Columbia Univ., Sch. of Lib. Srv., 1958–62. **Educ.:** Univ. of CA, Berkeley, 1948–52, AB (Eng.); Columbia Univ., 1952–53, MA (Eng.), 1957–58, MS (LS); Golden Gate Univ., 1979, MBA (Mgt.); Amer. Socty. of Assn. Exec., 1979, Cert. Assn. Exec. **Orgs.:** ALA: Nom. Com. (1980–81); Conf. Streamlining Com. (1978–); Future Structures Com. (1978–80). Cncl. of Lib. Assn. Execs.: Pres. (1980–81). Amer. Correctional Assn.: Adv. Com. on Libs. (1973–). Amer. Socty. of Assn. Execs. Sacramento Socty. of Assn. Execs. **Honors:** Columbia Univ., Helen Vogelson Awd. **Pubns.:** "Library Legislation in California," *Libraries in the Political Process* (1979); "Continuing Education," *Coll. and Resrch. Libs. News* (Je. 1979). **Activities:** 3 **Addr.:** 717 K St., Suite 300, Sacramento, CA 95814.

Mosey, Jeanette Gail (Je. 24, 1948, Salem, AR) Asst. Prof., Sch. of LS, Univ. of MI., 1981–; Sr. Coord., OCLC Western/San Francisco, CA, 1979–81; Asst. Coord., OCLC Western/Claremont, CA, 1977–79; Asst. Catlgr., TX Woman's Univ., 1973–76; Inst. of Lib. Sci., Asst. Libn., Southern AR Univ., Magnolia, 1971–73. **Educ.:** Univ. of AR, Fayetteville, 1966–70, BSE (Eng. Educ.); George Peabody Coll. for Tchrs., Nashville, TN, 1970–71, MLS; Univ. of Southern CA, 1976–80, PhD. **Orgs.:** ALA: RTSD; LITA; ACRL. CA LA: Tech. Srvs. Chap. Acad. and Resrch. Libns.: CA Chap. Northern CA Tech. Prcs. Grp. **Honors:** Beta Phi Mu; Kappa Delta Pi. **Activities:** 12; 24, 34, 46; 56, 75 **Addr.:** School of Library Science, University of Michigan, Ann Arbor, MI 48104.

Mosher, Fredric John (F. 19, 1914, Oakes, ND) Prof., Univ. of CA, Berkeley, Sch. of Lib. and Info. Std., 1950–; Head, Ref. Dept., Newberry Lib., 1946–50. **Educ.:** Univ. of ND, 1931–34, AB (Eng.), 1934–35, AM (Eng.); Univ. of IL, 1936–50, PhD (Eng.); Univ. of Chicago, 1946–48, BLS. **Orgs.:** AALS. Prtg. Hist. Socty. Amer. Prtg. Hist. Assn. Wolfenbütteler Arbeitskreis für Geschichte des Buchwesens. Phi Eta Sigma. **Honors:** US State Dept., Fulbright Lect., Royal Danish Lib. Sch., 1963–64; Phi Beta Kappa. **Pubns.:** Jt. auth., *The Bibliographical History of Anonyma and Pseudonyma* (1951); Jt. auth., *A Guide to Danish Bibliography* (1965); Ed., *Freedom of Book Selection* (1954); "A New Estienne Catalogue", *The Lib.* (D. 1979); "The Fourth Catalogue of the Aldine Press," *La Bibliofilia* (Fall, 1978). **Activities:** 11; 26, 39, 41; 57 **Addr.:** School of Library and Information Studies, University of California, Berkeley, CA 94720.

Mosher, Paul H. (Ja. 3, 1936, Portland, OR) Assoc. Dir. for Col. Dev., Libs., Stanford Univ., 1979–, Lectr., Rel. Stds. Dept., 1976–; Asst. Dir. for Col. Dev., 1975–79; Instr., Sch. of Lib. and Info. Scis., Univ. of CA, Berkeley, 1980; Asst. Prof. of Hist., Univ. of WA, 1966–75. **Educ.:** Portland State Univ., 1961, BA (Hist.); Univ. of CA, Berkeley, 1961–62, MA (Hist.), 1969, PhD (Hist.). **Orgs.:** ALA: RTSD/Resrcs. Sect. (Vice–Ch./Ch.–Elect, 1979–80; Ch., 1980–81), Chief Col. Dev. Ofcrs. of Large Resrch. Libs. Discuss. Grp. (Ch., 1978–79; Secy./Ch.–Elect, 1977–78), Col. Mgt. and Dev. Com. (1978–; Consult., 1976–78), Col. Mgt. and Dev. Inst. Plng. Com. (Ch., 1979), ACRL, Stans. and Accred. Com. (1981)/West. European Specs. Sect., Plng. Com. (1980–). RLG: Col. Mgt. and Dev. Com. (Vice–Ch., 1979–). **Honors:** Fulbright-Hays, Sr. Resrch. Schol., 1971. **Pubns.:** "Friends Groups and Academic Libraries," *Organizing the Library's Support* (1980); "Managing Library Collections: The Process of Review and Pruning," and "Collection Evaluation or Analysis," *Collection Development in Libraries: A Treatise* (1980); "Guidelines for the Review of Library Collections," *ALA Guidelines for Col. Devel.* (1979); "Collection Evaluation in Research Libraries," *Lib. Resrcs. and Tech. Srvs.* (Win. 1979); "Waiting for Godot: Rating Approval Service Vendors," *Shaping Library Collections for the 1980's* (1980). **Activities:** 1; 15, 17, 45 **Addr.:** Stanford University Libraries/Green Library, Stanford, CA 94305.

Moshman, Annette G. (Ap. 23, 1926, Yonkers, NY) Asst. Libn., Fairfax Cnty. Pub. Lib., 1969–; Libn., Jt. Comsn. on Mental Hlth. of Chld., 1967–68. **Educ.:** NY Univ., 1947, BA (Hist.); Cath. Univ. of Amer., 1967, MS (LS). **Orgs.:** ALA. DC LA. VA LA. **Honors:** Beta Phi Mu, 1966. **Activities:** 9; 16, 39, 48 **Addr.:** 1244 Oak Ridge Ave., McLean, VA 22101.

Mosimann, Elizabeth A. (Ap. 24, 1944, Auburn, NY) Asst. Libn., Hunt Inst. for Bot. Docu., Carnegie-Mellon Univ., 1975–. **Educ.:** St. Michael's Coll., Univ. of Toronto, 1965, BA (Eng. Lit.); Univ. of Pittsburgh, 1972–74, MLS. **Orgs.:** ALA. **Honors:** Beta Phi Mu. **Pubns.:** Jt. complr., *Kate Greenaway; catalogue of an exhibition* (1980); Jt. Complr., *The Tradition of Fine Bookbinding in the Twentieth Century* (1979); "Leaves and flowers in Victorian Title Pages," *Nineteenth Century* (Spr. 1981). **Activities:** 1, 12; 20, 39, 45; 57, 91 **Addr.:** 215 Vernon Dr., Pittsburgh, PA 15228.

Mosley, Mary Mac (N. 11, 1926, Rome, GA) Head Libn., Shorter Coll., 1968–; Ext. Libn., Tri-Cnty. Reg. Lib., 1966–67; Tchr., Rome City Schs., 1964–66. **Educ.:** Auburn Univ., 1945–47, BS (Lab. Tech.); Athens Coll., 1963–64, Tchrs. Cert.; Emory Univ., 1967–68, MLn (Libnshp.). **Orgs.:** ALA. GA LA. SELA. Coosa Valley LA. AAUW. **Honors:** Delta Kappa Gamma. **Activities:** 1; 17, 20, 26 **Addr.:** Box 346, Shorter College, Rome, GA 30161.

Moss, William Warner, III (My. 11, 1935, New York, NY) Chief Archvst., John F. Kennedy Lib., 1975–; Sr. Archvst., 1973–75, Chief, Oral Hist. Prog., 1971–73, Interviewer, Oral Hist. Prog., 1969–71. **Educ.:** Haverford Coll., 1953–57, BA (Pol. Sci.); Columbia Univ., 1963–64, MA (Pub. law, Gvt.). **Orgs.:** SAA. Oral Hist. Assn.: Cncl. Mem. (1975–80); Pres. (1978–79). New Eng. Archvsts. New Eng. Assn. for Oral Hist. **Honors:** New Eng. Assn. for Oral Hist., Harvey Kantor Meml. Awd., 1978. **Pubns.:** *Oral History Program Manual* (1974); "Oral History: An Appreciation," *Amer. Archvst.* (O. 1977); "In Search of Values," *Oral Hist. Review* (1979); "The Future of Oral History," *Oral Hist. Review* (1974). **Activities:** 4; 15, 17, 45; 85, 92 **Addr.:** John F. Kennedy Library, Columbia Point, Boston, MA 02125.

Mossman, Jennifer Ann (S. 8, 1944, Melksham, Wiltshire, Eng.) Ed., Gale Resrch. Co., 1973–; Serials Libn., East. MI Univ., 1970–72; Ref. Libn., San Francisco Pub. Lib., 1968–69. **Educ.:** Univ. of MI, 1962–66, BA (Hist.), 1967–68, MLS. **Pubns.:** Ed., *Pseudonyms and Nicknames Dictionary* (1980); Assoc. Ed., *Eponyms Dictionaries Index* (1977). **Activities:** 37, 41 **Addr.:** Gale Research Co., Book Tower, Detroit, MI 48226.

Mostecky, Vaclav (Je. 29, 1919, J. Hradec, Bohemia, Czechoslovakia) Prof. of Law and Law Libn., Univ. of CA, Berkeley, 1971–; Prof. of Law & Law Libn., SUNY, Buffalo, 1969–71; Head of Pub. Srvs., Harvard Law Lib., 1958–69. **Educ.:** Lycee Carnot, Dijon, France, 1935–38, BA (Hum.); Charles Univ., Prague, Czechoslovakia, 1938–46, JD (Law); Cath. Univ., 1951–53, MSLS. **Orgs.:** AALL. Intl. Law Lib. Assn. Computer Law Assn. Amer. Assn. of Law Schs. AAUP. **Pubns.:** "How to Find the Law" (1977); Jt. auth., *Russian Publications in U.S. Libraries* (1960). **Activities:** 1, 12; 17, 30, 35; 56, 61, 77 **Addr.:** School of Law Library, Room 230 Boalt Hall, University of California, Berkeley, CA 94720.

Mosteller, Bette Vaughan (F. 1, 1937, Amelia Cnty., VA) Lib. Dir., Christopher Newport Coll., 1962–; Catlgr., VA State Lib., 1959–62. **Educ.:** Longwood Coll., 1954–58, BA; George Peabody Coll., 1958–59, MALS; Coll. of William and Mary, 1973–75 (Hist.). **Orgs.:** VA LA: Exec. Asst. Natl. Lib. Week Com. (1969–71). SELA. ALA: LAMA, BES Equipment Com. (1981–). State Cncl. of Higher Educ.: Lib. Adv. Com. (1971–). Tidewater Lib. Dir. Com: Vice Ch. (1978–). East. VA Hist. Assn. (1970–). **Honors:** VA State Lib., Flwshp. (1958). **Activities:** 1; 15, 17, 19; 55 **Addr.:** Captain John Smith Library, 50 Shoe Ln., Newport News, VA 23606.

Mosteller, Jean Snow (Jl. 23, 19–, South Gate, CA) Libn., San Diego Pub. Lib., 1979–; Lib. Consult., Woodward-Clyde Engin. Consults., 1978–80; Lib. Consult., Hawaiian Electric Co., 1965–70; Instr., E.-W. Ctr., Inst. for Tech. Interchange, Univ. of HI, 1967. **Educ.:** San Diego State Univ., BA (Bus. Admin.); Univ. of WA, Mstr. (Libnshp.). **Orgs.:** ALA: Stats. Com. San Diego Pub. Lib. Staff Assn. **Activities:** 9, 12; 21, 24; 64 **Addr.:** 1141 Albion St., San Diego, CA 92106.

Motley, Archie (D. 2, 1934, Chicago, IL) Cur. of Mss., Chicago Hist. Socty., 1960–, Broadside Libn., 1955–57. **Educ.:** DePaul Univ., Chicago, 1960, BA (Phil.); Loyola Univ., Chicago, 1961–65, MA (Phil.). **Orgs.:** Socty. of Amer. Archvsts.: Com. on the Wider Use of Archs., (Ch., 1975–78). Midwest Archs. Conf.: Pres. (1972–75). IL State Archvsts. Adv. Bd. Advisory Board of the North. IL Reg. Hist. Ctr.: Adv. Bd. NEH Italians in Chicago Proj.: Exec. Com. (1977–). **Addr.:** Curator of Manuscripts, Chicago Historical Society, Clark St. at North Ave., Chicago, IL 60614.

Motomatsu, Nancy Reiko (Je. 31, 1930, Woodinville, WA) Supvsr., Lrng. Resrc. Srv., Superindent Pub. Instr., Assoc. Supvsr., 1966; Jr. HS Libn., DuPont Ft. Lewis Sch. Dist. (WA), 1962–66; Tchr. **Orgs.:** ALA: AASL. WA LA: Sch. Libn., various com. Natl. Educ. Assn.: various com. WA Educ. Assn. Japanese Amer. Cit. Leag. Delta Kappa Gamma. **Activities:** 10, 13; 66 **Addr.:** Supervisor, Learning Resources Services, Old Capitol Building, Olympia, WA 98504.*

Mott, Thomas H., Jr. (Ja. 24, 1924, Houston, TX) Dean, Grad. Sch. of Lib. and Info. Std., Rutgers Univ., 1969–; Ch., Dept. of Comp. Sci., 1967–69, Dir., Ctr. for Comp. and Info. Srvs., 1966–69, Assoc. Prof., 1962, Prof., 1963–; Cofounder, Dir. and Treas., Applied Logic Corporation, 1962–71; Sr. Mem. Resrch. Staff, Lockheed Electronics Co., 1961–62; Tech. Staff, RCA Labs., 1958–61. **Educ.:** Rice Univ., 1948, BA; Yale Univ., 1956, PhD (Phil.). **Orgs.:** ALA. NJ LA. ASIS. Sigma Xi. Amer. Phil. Assn. Inst. of Electrical and Electronic Engin. AAAS. **Honors:** Phi Beta Kappa. **Pubns.:** Jt. auth., *Introduction to PL/I Programming for Library and Information Science* (1972); Jt. auth., *Introduction to FORTRAN IV Programming* (1966); Jt. auth., "A Goal Programming Model for Information Service Planning," *Proc. of 1978 ASIS Mid-Year Meeting* (May, 1978); Jt. auth., "Operations Research and the Academic Library" in *Academic Libraries by the Year 2000: Essays Honoring Jerrold Orne,* (1977); Jt. auth., "Tomorrow and Beyond: Future Prospects for Library Education," *Cath. Lib. World* (Ap. 1976); Jt. auth., "A Logical Description of the Deduction of Instances from Concepts" in *JSAS Catalog of Selected Documents in Psychology* (1975); other articles, reviews, oral presentations. **Activities:**

PROFESSIONAL ACTIVITIES: Institutions: 1. Acad. lib.; 2. Arch.; 3. Assn.; 4. Fed./Gvt. lib.; 5. Inst. lib.; 6. Mfr./Suppl.; 7. Milit. lib.; 8. Musm.; 9. Pub. lib.; 10. Sch. lib.; 11. Sch. of lib. sci.; 12. Spec. lib.; 13. State lib.; 14. (other). **Functions/Activities:** 15. Acq./Col. dev.; 16. Adult srvs.; 17. Admin.; 18. Apprais.; 19. Archit./Bldgs.; 20. Cat./Class.; 21. Chld. srvs.; 22. Circ.; 23. Cons./Pres.; 24. Consult.; 25. Cont. ed.; 26. Educ. lib. sci.; 27. Ext. srvs.; 28. Fund/Grants; 29. Gvt. pubs.; 30. Indx./Abs.; 31. Instr. lib. use; 32. Media srvs.; 33. Micro.; 34. Netwks./Coop.; 35. Persnl.; 36. PR; 37. Publshg.; 38. Recs. mgt.; 39. Ref. srvs.; 40. Repro.; 41. Resrch.; 42. Review.; 43. Secur.; 44. Serials; 45. Spec. col.; 46. Tech. srvs.; 47. Trustees/Bds.; 48. YA srvs.; 49. (other).

11; 17, 26, 41; 56, 63, 75 **Addr.:** 20 Merritt Ln., Rocky Hill, NJ 08553.

Mott, William R. (S. 15, 1953, Knoxville, TN) Lib. Dir., Martin Coll., 1980–. **Educ.:** Univ. of MS, 1972–76, BA (Hist.); George Peabody Coll. for Tchrs., 1977–78, MLS, 1979–80, PhD (Educ. Admin.). **Orgs.:** ALA. SELA: Lib. Orien.-Bibl. Instr. TN LA. Mid-State LA (TN). **Pubns.:** "The Academic Librarian as Educator," *Frnds. of the Lib. Nsltr. of King Coll.* (Fall 1980); "Higher Education: Challenge in the '80's," *Frnds. of the Lib. Nsltr. of King Coll.* (Spr. 1981). **Activities:** 1; 17, 31; 90, 92 **Addr.:** Warden Memorial Library, Martin College, Pulaski, TN 38478.

Motz, Minne R. (F. 3, 1915, New York, NY) Lib. Consult., Freelnc., 1977–; Head, Sch. Lib. Srvs., New York City Bd. of Educ., 1973–76, Asst. Dir., Sch. Lib. Srvs., 1963–73, Supvsr., Sch. Lib. Srvs., 1960–63. **Educ.:** Brooklyn Coll., 1932–36, BA (Lit.); Columbia Univ., 1956, MS (LS). **Orgs.:** ALA: Int. Frdm. Com. (1973–75); AASL/Networking Com. (1976–) NY LA: Int. Frdm. and Due Prcs. Com. (1976–78). Women's Natl. Bk. Assn.: Bd. of Mgrs. (1976–78). NY Pub. Lib.: Com. to Support Teenage Srvs. (Secy., 1977–). Child Std. Bk. Com., Bank St. Coll.: Bk. Review Com. (1977–). NY Acad. of Scis.: Educ. Adv. Com. (1973–77). **Honors:** Phi Beta Mu, 1968. **Activities:** 10; 42, 48; 63, 74 **Addr.:** 815 W. 181st St., New York, NY 10033.

Moulds, Michael J. (Je. 3, 1947, Wichita, KS) Spec. Srvs. Libn., Cumberland Trail Lib. Syst., 1976–; Tchr., Platte City, MO, 1970–72. **Educ.:** Wichita State Univ., 1965–70, BME, BM (Msc. Educ., Msc. Composition); West. State Coll. of CO, 1972–74, MA (Msc.); Emporia State Coll., 1974–75, MLS. **Orgs.:** IL LA. Msc. LA. Natl. Gay Task Force. **Honors:** Phi Mu Alpha Sinfonia; Kappa Kappa Psi; Omicron Delta Kappa. **Pubns.:** "Fore-Edge Painting," *Lib. Sch. Review* (1976). **Activities:** 5, 13; 15, 39; 72 **Addr.:** 4703 Turner St., Apt. 8, Rockford, IL 61107.

Moulton, Priscilla L. (O. 12, 1923, Brooklyn, NY) retired; Dir. of Lib. Srvs., Pub. Sch. of Brookline, MA, 1966–79; Coord. of Elem. Sch. Libs., Swampscott MA Pub. Sch., 1961–66; Libn., Shaw Jr. HS, Swampscott MA, 1959–61; Head Libn., Mentor OH Pub. Sch., 1957–59; Libn., Mentor OH Jr. HS, 1955–57. **Orgs.:** ALA: Intell. Freed. Com. (1976–78); Chld.'s Srvs. Div. (Pres. 1974; Exec. Bd., 1973–75; Bd. of Dir. 1965–68); RTSD. New Eng. LA: Round Table of Chld.'s Lbns. MA LA. Boston Pub. Lib. Lib. of Congs. Action for Chld.'s TV: Dir. (1978–). Horn Book, Inc.: Adv. Cncl. (1971–76). Parents' Choice: Adv. Bd. Phaedrus (Ed.). **Honors:** Beta Phi Mu, 1960; ALA, Dutton-Macrae Award, 1965; New Eng. LA, Hewins- Melcher Lectr., 1967. **Pubns.:** Ed., *African Encounter,* (1970); Ed., *Books for Elementary School Children.* (1969); "Children's Book Reviews and Reviewing," in *Encyc. of Lib. and Info. Sci.* (1978); reviews. **Activities:** 10; 21, 24, 45 **Addr.:** 10 Pinecliff Dr., Marblehead, MA 01945.†

Mounce, Marvin W. (Ag. 24, 1934, Lufkin, TX) Fed. Proj. Coord., State of FL, 1978–; Adj. Fac., Univ. of S. FL, 1978; Dir., Harborfields Pub. Lib., Greenlawn, NY, 1974–77; Dir., Bureau of Dev., State Lib. of PA, Harrisburg, 1970–74; Dir., Cnty. Lib. and Coop. Syst., Ingham Cnty. Lib. and Ctrl MI Lib., Mason, MI, 1968–70; Head, Tech. Srvs., New Orleans Pub. Lib., 1966–67; Coord., Tech. Srvs., Fresno Cnty. Free Lib., 1963–66; Stat. and Resrch. Libn., CA State Lib., Sacramento, 1962–63; Catlgr., 1960–62. **Educ.:** Lamar State Coll. of Tech., 1952–55, BS (Hist.); Univ. of Pittsburgh, 1967–68, MLS; FL State Univ., 1977–78, Adv. MA, 1978–, PhD, 1981. **Orgs.:** ALA: PLA: (Pub. Lib. Syst. Sect. Publ. Com. 1979–); Cont. Educ. Com. (1979–); Mem. Task Force (1979–). **Activities:** 9, 13; 24, 25, 46 **Addr.:** State Library of Florida, R. A. Gray Building, Tallahassee, FL 32301.

Mounce, Virginia Ann Newton (O. 5, 1938, Walters, OK) PhD Cand., The Univ. of TX at Austin, 1979–; Spec. Col. and Ref. Libn., Pan Amer. Univ., 1974–77; Archvst., Latin Amer. Libn., Trinity Univ., TX, 1969–73; Libn., Art Lib., Univ. of TX, Austin, 1965–67; Libn., Inst. of Pub. Affairs, Univ. of TX, Austin, 1964–65; various consult. positions. **Educ.:** Stephens Coll., 1956–58, AA (Bus.); OK State Univ., 1958–60, BA (Hist.); Amer. Univ. and Natl. Arch. and Records Srv. Inst., 1975, (Cert.); Univ. of WA, 1961–62, Mstr. (Libnshp.); University of TX, Austin, 1968, Cert. (LS), 1975, MA (Latin Amer. Std.: LS, Hist., Arch.). **Orgs.:** ALA. Southwest. LA: Mexico Proj. Com. (Ch., 1976–) Official Liaison to Mex. LA. Mex. LA. Amer. Archvst. Assn. Latin Amer. Std. Assn. Southwest Cncl. for Latin Amer. Std. ACLU. **Honors:** Fulbright-Hays Schol., 1979–80; Phi Kappa Phi, Phi Alpha Theta. **Pubns.:** *An Archivist's Guide to the Catholic Church in Mexico* (1979); "Honorary Deputy Sheriffs, A New Role for Librarians," *TX Lib. Jnl.* (Mr. 1972); "General List of Holdings from Municipal and Church Archives from Nuevo Leon, Mexico, Available at Trinity University, December 1969," rpt. SALAM (1970); "Report on Trinity University's Microfilming Activities," rpt. SALAM (1970); "The Texas Consortium for Microfilming Mexican Archival Resources; 4th Annual Report, 1972–73," rpt. SALAM (1975). **Activities:** 1, 2; 15, 39, 45; 54, 74, 89 **Addr.:** 206 Laurel Heights Pl., San Antonio, TX

Mount, Ellis (S. 25, 1921, Connersville, IN) Asst. Prof., Sch. of Lib. Srv., Columbia Univ., 1977–, Sci. Bibl., 1974–77, Sci. & Engin. Libn., 1964–74; Chief Libn., ITT Fed. Labs., 1955–64; Resrch. Assoc., John Crerar Lib., 1950–51, 1953–55; Tech. Libn., Gen. Electric Co., Aircraft Nuclear Propulsion Proj., 1951–53. **Educ.:** IN Univ., 1939–41; Principia Coll., 1946–48, BS (Phys.); Northwestern Univ., 1948–49, MS (Phys.); Univ. of IL, 1949–50, MS (LS); Columbia Univ., 1975–79, DLS. **Orgs.:** SLA: Treas. (1976–79); Ch., Sci/Tech Div. (1974–75); Pres., NJ Chap. (1963–64). ASIS. AALS. Amer. Natl. Stan. Inst.: Ch., Z39 Subcom. on Bibl. Ref. (1972–76). **Honors:** Beta Phi Mu; Cncl. for Lib. Resrcs., Flwshp., 1972. **Pubns.:** *Guide to basic information sources in engineering* (1976); *University science and engineering libraries: their operation collections and facilities* (1975); "Science-Technology Division, SLA" IN: *Encyclopedia of Library and Information Science;* jt. auth., "Sci-tech books of 1978" *Library Journal* (Mr. 1, 1979); Ed., *Sci. and Tech. Libs.* (1980–); other articles. **Activities:** 1, 12; 26, 29, 39; 63, 64, 91 **Addr.:** School of Library Service, Columbia University, New York, NY 10027.

Mount, Joan E. (Ja. 12, 1941, Montreal, QB) Head, Ref. and Circ. Dept., Laurentian Univ., 1974–, Head, Pub. Docum. Dept., 1971–74, Catlgr., 1969–71; Head, Circ. and AV Dept., Coll. of Educ., Univ. of Toronto, 1967–69. **Educ.:** McGill Univ., 1956–61, BA (Eng., Phil.); Univ. of Toronto, 1966–67, BLS; McGill Univ., 1961–62 (Educ.). **Orgs.:** Can. LA ON Univ. Lib. Coop. Sys. Inter-Univ. Borrowers' Proj.: Ch. (1979–80). Caraibbean Std. Assn. **Pubns.:** Jt. auth., "University Library Services for Live Off-campus, Television, and Correspondence Courses: A Challenge," *Can. Lib. Jnl.* (F. 1980); "Demise of a classified catalogue: victim of progress," *Lib. Resrcs. and Tech. Srvs.* (Fall 1979); "Faculty status at Laurentian - two years later," *Can. Lib. Jnl.* (D. 1978); jt. auth., "The classified catalogue, LU style" *Lib. Resrcs. and Tech. Srvs.* (Sum. 1971). **Activities:** 1; 17, 39; 56 **Addr.:** Laurentian University Library, Sudbury, ON P3E 2C6 Canada.

Mountain, Mary W. (D. 26, 1920, Philadelphia, PA) Libn., LaSalle Coll. H.S., 1967–; Philadelphia Sch. Dist., Lib. Asst., FitzPatrick Sch., 1965–67; Elem. Tchr., St. Bernard Sch., 1963–65; Elem. Tchr., St. Cecilia Sch., 1961–63. **Educ.:** St. Joseph Univ., 1961–67, BS (Soc. Std.); Villanova Univ., 1967–70, MSLS, 1971–73, (Lib. Sci.). **Orgs.:** PA Sch. LA: Arch. Com. (Ch., 1977–). Cath. LA: Election Com. (Ch., 1980–). PA LA. Independent Sch. Tchrs. Assn. **Activities:** 10, 11; 15, 17, 20 **Addr.:** 6662 Algard St., Philadelphia, PA 19135.

Mountford, Charles H. (Ap. 1, 1939, Thunder Bay, ON) Chief Libn., F.E. Madill Sec. Sch., 1967–. **Educ.:** Univ. of West. ON, BA (Eng.), MA (Eng.); Univ. of London, Eng., MA (Libnshp.). **Orgs.:** ON Sch. LA: Cnclr. (1979–82). **Activities:** 10; 48 **Addr.:** FE Madill Secondary School, Wingham, ON N0G 2W0 Canada.

Moushey, Eugene W. (D. 28, 1922, Fort Wayne, IN) Ref. Libn., West. IL Univ., 1970–; Consult., Libn., Univ. Catolica Madre y Maestra, Santiago, Dom. Repub., 1968–70; Head, Ref. Dept., MI State Lib., 1966–68; Ref. and Cat., Tchr., WI State Univ. 1951–57, Head, Ref. Dept., 1964–66, Ref. and Cat., 1958–62; Lib. Consult., Tchr., Nat. Univ. of El Salvador, 1957–58. **Educ.:** Univ. of MI, 1946–48, BA (Span.), 1948–49, MA (Span.), Univ. of MI 1949–50 BS (Span.), 1950–51 AMLS. **Orgs.:** SALALM: Jt. Com. on Lib. Mtrls. for Span. and Portuguese Speaking (Ch., 1977–). Leag. of Latin Americanists: Exec. Com. (1979–80). **Pubns.:** *Bibliography of the Spanish Bilingual, Bicultural Monographs and Government Publications in the Western Illinois University Library* (1977); "Dominican Republic Libraries," *Encyc. of Lib. and Info. Sci.* (1972); Jt. Indxr., *Hispanic American Periodical Index* (1976–). **Activities:** 1; 30, 39; 54, 66 **Addr.:** Library, Western Illinois University, Macomb, IL 61455.

Moutseous, Margaret L. (O. 15, 1953, Cleveland, OH) Lib. Dir., Chld. Hosp. Resrch. Fndn., 1979–; Branch Libn., Fels Resrch. Lib./Wright State Univ., 1978–79; Ref. Libn., AZ Hlth. Sci. Ctr. Lib., 1976–78. **Educ.:** Washington Univ., 1971–75, BA (Bio., Anthro.); Case Western Reserve Univ., 1975–76, MSLS; Med. LA, 1976, Cert. **Orgs.:** Med. LA: Midwest Reg. Grp., Spr. 1980 Mtg.; Co-ch., Cont. Educ. (1979–80). SLA. Miami Valley Assn. of Hlth. Sci. Libs. Cincinnati Hlth. Sci. LA: Pres. (1981–82); Prog. Com. (1979). **Pubns.:** Various speeches. **Activities:** 12; 17, 31, 46; 75, 80 **Addr.:** Children's Hospital Research Foundation, Research Library, Cincinnati, OH 45229.

Mowery, Bob Lee (Je. 22, 1920, Charlotte, NC) Dir. of Univ. Libs., Wittenberg Univ., 1964–; Dir. of the Lib., Stetson Univ., 1958–64; Head Libn., McNeese State Coll., 1953–58; Head Libn. and Head, Dept. of LS, Murray State Coll., 1951–53; Cat. Libn., Dickinson Coll., 1947–51. **Educ.:** Catawba Coll., 1937–41, AB (Hist.); Univ. of Chicago, 1946–51, BLS, MA (LS). **Orgs.:** Acad. LA of OH: Pres. (1975–76). ALA: ACRL, Tri-State Chap. (Pres., 1974–75). OH Coll. Lib. Ctr.: Bd. of Dirs. and Treas. (1967–71). Ohionet: Bd. of Dirs. (1977–81). Arthur Machen Socty.: Pres. (1968–). Reg. Cncl. on Intl. Educ.: Lib. Div. (Ch., 1966–68). Dayton-Miami Valley Cnsrtm.: Lib. Div. (Ch., 1968–70). Newberry Coll.: Trustee, Ch., Com. on Instr. (1962–64). **Activities:** 1, 2; 15, 23, 34, 45; 74 **Addr.:** The Library, Wittenberg University, Springfield, OH 45501.

Mowery, Robert L. (Mr. 22, 1934, Rochester, PA) Hum. Libn., IL Wesleyan Univ., 1968–; Pastor, United Meth. Church, 1963–68. **Educ.:** Purdue Univ., 1952–56, BS (Mech. Engin.); Garrett-Evang. Theo. Semy., 1956–60, BD (Theo.); Northwestern Univ., 1960–67, MA (Relig.), PhD (Relig.); Univ. of IL, 1967–68, MSLS. **Orgs.:** ALA: Com. on Problems of Access and Cntrl. of Educ. Mtrls., Educ. and Bhvl. Scis. Sect., (1980–). IL LA: Comm. Com. (1978–80). Western PA Conf. of The United Meth. Church. Socty. of Biblical Lit. **Honors:** Cncl. on Lib. Resrcs., Fellow, 1976–77. **Pubns.:** "The Cutter Classification: Still at Work," *Lib. Resrcs. and Tech. Srvs.* (Spr. 1976); "The 'Trend to LC' in College and University Libraries," *Lib. Resrcs. and Tech. Srvs.* (Fall 1975); Contrib. *Cataloging and Classification of Non-Western Material* (1980); Reviews. **Activities:** 1; 15, 31, 39; 55, 90 **Addr.:** Sheean Library, Illinois Wesleyan University, Bloomington, IL 61701.

Moy, Clarence Theodore (F. 10, 1930, NY, NY) Chief Catlgr., Half Hollow Hills Comnty. Lib., 1978–, Tech. Srvcs. Coord., 1974–78, Adult Srvs. Libn., 1969–74, Sch. Libn., Unqua Road Elem. Sch., 1966–69; Head Libn., Parks AFB Job Corps Ctr., 1965–66; Sr. HS Libn., Newfield HS, 1963–65; HS Libn., Stillwater Ctrl. Sch., 1962–63; Sch. Libn., Onondaga Cnty, 1960–62. **Educ.:** New Paltz State Tchrs. Coll., 1949–53, BS (Elem Educ); Pratt Inst., 1959–60, MLS; Potsdam State Univ. Coll., 1956–61, MS (Educ.); Scot. Lib. Assn. summer school, 1981; SUNY, Albany, 1962–63 (Lib. Sci.); Pratt Inst., 1962–62 (Lib. Sci.). **Orgs.:** ALA. NY LA. Suffolk Cnty. Sch. LA. Civil Srv. Employees Assn.: VP and Chief Neg. (1973). **Pubns.:** "Small H. S. Research Collection," *Saratoga Cnty Tchr.* (1963). **Activities:** 9, 10; 16, 31, 46 **Addr.:** Domus Dulcis Estate, 20 Richbourne Ln., Melville, NY 11747.

Moyers, Joyce C. (D. 21, 1927, Broadway, VA) Libn., Rockingham Pub. Lib., 1960–, Asst. Libn., 1959–60; Circ. Libn., Olivia Raney Lib., 1954–58. **Educ.:** James Madison Univ, 1948–50, BS (LS); Univ. of NC, 1958–59, MS (LS). **Orgs.:** ALA. VA LA: Reg. VI (Secy., 1980). Quota Club of Harrisonburg. **Activities:** 9; 15, 17, 22 **Addr.:** R. 1, P.O. Box 214, Broadway, VA 22801.

Mrozewski, Andrzej H. (F. 25, 1930, Paris, France) Chief Libn., Prof., Laurentian Univ. of Sudbury, 1972–; Actg. Dir. of Libs., Univ. de Sherbrooke, 1970–71, Asst. Dir. of Libs., 1965–71, Head, Tech. Srv., 1965–68, Head of Acq., 1964–65; Med. Libn., Hôpital d'Youville, 1962–64; Chief Libn., Coll. de Rouyn, 1960–64. **Educ.:** Univ. de Montréal, 1954, MA (Slavic Stds.); Univ. of Ottawa, 1960, BLS; McGill Univ., 1972, MLS. **Orgs.:** Can. LA: Tech. Srvs. Sect., Cncl. (1967–68). Can. Assn. of Coll. and Univ. Libn.: Nom. Com. (1969, 1970, 1976); Small Univ. Libs. Sect. (Ch., 1975–76). PQ LA: Pres. (1967–68). Polish Inst. of Arts and Scis. in Can. Polish Combattants Assn. Sudbury Reg. Minor Soccer Assn. **Honors:** Krzyz Armii Krajowej, Commemorative Cross for Srv. in the Polish Underground during WWII; Médaille d'argent de l'Univ. de Sherbrooke. **Pubns.:** "Communication, problème-clé dans la direction du personnel," *Bltn. de l'Assn. Can. des Bibltcrs. de Lang. Fr.* (S. 1969); Ed., *Bltn. des Nouvelles de l'ABQ/QLA Nsltr.* (1967–71). **Activities:** 1, 2; 17, 24, 41, 45; 55, 57 **Addr.:** Laurentian University, Ramsey Lake Rd., Sudbury, ON P3E 2C6 Canada.

Mudd, Sr. Hilda (New Haven, KY) Archvst., Brescea Coll., 1981–; Dir. of Lib., 1949–81; Tchr.-Libn., Fredrickstown HS, 1945–49; Tchr.-Libn., St. Charles HS, 1939–45. **Educ.:** St. Mary-of-the-Woods, 1938, AB (Hist.); Cath. Univ., 1952, BSLS; Creighton Univ., 1972, MA (Russ. Hist.). **Orgs.:** ALA. Cath. LA. KY LA: Treas. (1980). KY Cncl. on Arch. **Activities:** 1; 17, 20 **Addr.:** Brescia College Library, 102 West 7th St., Owensboro, KY 42301.

Mudd, Isabelle Van Tassel (S. 02, 1925, Watertown, NY) Admin. Libn., Dept. of the Army, Post Lib., Fort Wainwright, AK, 1976–; Educ. Spec., Bur. of Indian Affairs, Bethel, AK, 1969–76; Head, Cat. Dept., Univ. of AK Lib., 1964–69; Serials Catlgr., Syracuse Univ. Lib., 1962–64. **Educ.:** Geneseo State Tchrs. Coll., 1941–45, BS (Educ.); Syracuse Univ., 1958–61, MLS. **Orgs.:** ALA: Mem. com. (1968–71). Pac. NW LA. AK LA: Pres. (1974). WHCOLIS: Del. (1979). **Honors:** Beta Phi Mu, 1961. **Activities:** 1, 10; 17, 20, 32; 63, 74 **Addr.:** P.O. Box 1061, Fairbanks, AK 99707.

Mudge, Charlotte Regula (O. 6, 1944, Zurich, Switzerland) Ph.D. student, Fac. of LS, Univ. of Toronto, 1977–, Chief Libn., Law Lib., 1976–77, Head, Ctr. of Criminology Lib., 1973–76; Catlgr., Hlth. Sci. Lib., Univ. of West. ON, 1971–73. **Educ.:** Univ. of West. ON, 1966–69, BA (Hist.), 1969–71, MLS. **Orgs.:** Can. ALL.: Prog. Com. (1974); Strg. Com. (1976–77). Can. LA. ON LA. Elizabeth Fry Socty.: Ch., Lib. Com. (1978–79). Royal Can. Inst. Women's Can. Club. **Pubns.:** *Subject Headings for Criminology, Criminal Justice & Police Science Collection.* (1976). **Activities:** 1; 17, 20, 38; 77, 80, 92 **Addr.:** Faculty of Library Science, University of Toronto, 140 St. George St., Toronto, ON M5S 1A1 Canada.

Mueller, Dorothy A. (F. 10, 1938, Birmingham, AL) Asst. to the VP, Univ. of AL, Birmingham, 1976–; Assoc. Dir., Lister Hill Lib., 1970–76; Chief Schr., AL Medlars Ctr., 1967–70; Ref.

Special Subjects/Services: 50. Adult educ.; 51. Advert./Mktg.; 52. Aerosp.; 53. Agric.; 54. Area std.; 55. Arts/Hum.; 56. Autom.; 57. Bibl./Prtg.; 58. Bio. sci.; 59. Bus./Fin.; 60. Chem.; 61. Copyrt.; 62. Documtn.; 63. Educ.; 64. Engin.; 65. Env.; 66. Eth. grps.; 67. Film; 68. Food/Nutr.; 69. Geneal.; 70. Geo.; 71. Geol.; 72. Handcpd.; 73. Hist.; 74. Int. frdm.; 75. Info. sci.; 76. Insr.; 77. Law; 78. Legis.; 79. Math./Comp. sci.; 80. Med.; 81. Metals; 82. Nat. resrcs.; 83. Newsp.; 84. Nuc. sci.; 85. Oral hist.; 86. Petr./Energy; 87. Pharm.; 88. Phys./Astr./Math.; 89. Readg.; 90. Relig.; 91. Sci./Tech.; 92. Soc. sci.; 93. Telecom.; 94. Transp.; 95. (other).

Libn., Duke Univ. Med. Ctr. Lib., 1962–65. **Educ.:** Birmingham Southern Coll., 1955–59, BA (Educ.); George Peabody Coll., 1960–61, MA(LS); Univ. of CA, Los Angeles, 1961–62 (Cert.); Natl. Lib. of Med., 1966–67 (Cert.). **Orgs.:** Med. LA: Com. on Med. Lib. Tech. Training, (1970–74); Ch. (1973–74); Ann. Meeting Prog. Com. (1975–78); Cancer Libn., Spec. Int. Grp. Ch. (1977–78). AL LA: By-Laws Com. (1970–79); Ch. (1973–79); Res. Com. (1972); Ch. (1972). AAUW. Am. Assn. of Univ. Admins. Birmingham Zool. Socty. Zonta Intl. St. John's Evan. Ch.: Bd. of Trust: (1977). **Honors:** Kappa Delta Epsilon. Beta Phi Mu. **Pubns.:** Jt. Auth. "Survey of Health Professionals' Information Habits and Needs," *Jnl. of the Amer. Med. Assn.* (Ja. 1980): jt. auth., "Cataloging Audiovisual Materials," *Bltn. of the Med. LA* (Jl. 1975); review, "The Alabama MEDLARS Center," *Lib. Network/MEDLARS Tech. Bltn.*, No. 9, (Ja. 1970). **Activities:** 1, 12; 17, 39, 46; 58, 80 **Addr.:** Assistant to the Vice President, University of Alabama in Birmingham, Birmingham, AL 35294.

Mueller, Heinz Peter (D. 17, 1943, Naumburg/Saale, Weissenfels, Germany) Assoc. Law Libn., Brigham Young Univ., 1971–, Catlgr., 1970–71. **Educ.:** Brigham Young Univ., 1967–70, BA (Grmn.), 1970, MLS; AALL Cert., 1977. **Orgs.:** AALL: Mem. Com. (1979–80). UT LA: Const. and Bylaws Com. (1979–80). **Pubns.:** *Foreign Law Classification Schedule* (1972, 1975). **Activities:** 1; 17, 35; 77 **Addr.:** 358 A JRCB, Brigham Young University Law Library, Provo, UT 84602.

Mueller, Jeanne G. (Jl. 31, 1926, Louisville, KY) Tech. Srvs. Libn., IN Univ. Sch. of Med., 1958–; Chld. Libn., Indianapolis - Marion Cnty. Pub. Lib., 1954–58; Catlgr., Univ. of Louisville, 1953–54. **Educ.:** Spalding Coll., 1944–48, AB magna cum laude (Eng.); Univ. of KY, 1952–53, MA(LS). **Orgs.:** Med. LA: Midwest Reg. Chap. Med. LA: Ed. Com., *Bltn of the Med. LA*, (1976–78); Ch. (1977–78); Prog. and Convention Com. (1980–82); Ch. (1981–82). Hlth. Sci. OCLC Users Grp.: VP/ Prog. Ch. (1978–79); Pres. (1979–80). Indianapolis Horticult. Socty.: Lib. Com. (1979). IN State Symphony Socty. N. Grp. Women's Com. **Honors:** Beta Phi Mu; Kappa Gamma Pi. **Pubns.:** IN Univ. Serials Holdings (1978). **Activities:** 1, 12; 20, 44, 46; 80 **Addr.:** Indiana University School of Medicine Library, 1100 West Michigan St., Indianapolis, IN 46223.

Mueller, Martha Ann (Kansas City, MO) Assoc. Libn., NY State Coll. of Ceramics, Alfred Univ., 1969–; Head, Serials Dept., Oakland Univ. (Rochester, MI), 1967–69, Head, Cat. Dept., 1966–67; Ed., Un. List of Serials, Natl. Lib. of Australia, 1964–65, Serials Catlgr., 1964; Serials Catlgr., Univ. of KS, 1962–64, Mono. Catlgr., 1960–62; Asst. Circ. Libn., Univ. of MO, 1958–59; Various prof. positions (1954–57). **Educ.:** Univ. of KS, 1951–54, BS (Educ., Eng.); Carnegie Inst. of Tech., 1957–58, MS (LS); Various grad. courses (1959–78). **Orgs.:** ALA. **Pubns.:** Jt. auth., "Literature Search Guide for Ceramic Engineering and Science," *Scholes Lib. Pubn.* No. 29 (1978); "A Comparison of Library Co-operation at Two Universities in New York and England," *Scholes Lib. Pubn. No. 31* (1978); Ed., *Scholes Lib. Notes* (1980–). **Activities:** 1; 39 **Addr.:** 58 1/2 South Main, Alfred, NY 14802.

Mueller, Mary G. H. (F. 22, 1937, Litchfield, MN) Asst. Prof. and Ref. Biblgrphr., Bio–Med. Lib., Univ. of MN, 1979–, Instr. and Ref. Biblgrphr., 1974–79, Libn., 1966–74. **Educ.:** Univ. of MN, 1955–60, BS (Nursing), 1978, MA (LS). **Orgs.:** Med. LA. MN LA. MN Hlth. Sci. LA: Consult. Com. (1977–); Cont. Educ. Com. (1975–77; Ch., 1976–77). Midw. Hlth. Sci. Lib. Netwk.: Educ. Com. (1977–80). **Pubns.:** Jt. auth., "An Examination of Characteristics Related to Success of Friends Groups in Medical Rare Book Libraries," *Bltn. of the Med. LA* (forthcoming). **Activities:** 1; 15, 31, 39; 80 **Addr.:** Bio–Medical Library, University of Minnesota, Diehl Hall, 505 Essex St. S.E., Minneapolis, MN 55455.

Muellner, John Phillip (Je. 20, 1936, Chicago, IL) Head Libn., Schiller Park Pub. Lib., 1964–; Head Libn., Chicago Pub. Schs., 1956–. **Educ.:** Chicago Tchrs. Coll., 1955–56, BE (Educ.); Chicago State Univ., 1957–61, ME (LS); Loyola Univ., 1959–60, Cert. (Eng. Lit.). **Orgs.:** ALA: Natl. Lib. Week in IL. IL LA: Natl. Conf. Com. Chicagoland Assn. for Media in High Schs. Chicago Lib. Club. Chicago Tchrs. Un. **Activities:** 9, 10; 15, 17, 21; 50, 63 **Addr.:** 405 N. Lincoln Ave., Park Ridge, IL 60068.

Muir, Rodney Anne (N. 20, 1942, Calgary, AB) Chief Libn., Home Oil Co. Ltd., 1978–; Head Ref. Dept., S. AB Inst. of Tech., 1969–78. **Educ.:** Univ. of MT, 1963–66, BA (Eng.); Univ. of BC, 1972–74, MLS. **Orgs.:** ASIS-West. Can.: Ch. (1980–81). SLA. Can. Assn. Info. Sci. Can. LA. **Activities:** 12; 18, 37, 39; 60, 76, 87 **Addr.:** Home Oil Co. Ltd. Library, 2300–324–8 Ave. S.W., Calgary, AB T2P 2Z5 Canada.

Mulcahy, Margaret Milligan (N. 8, 1918, Syracuse, NY) Libn., Washington–Lee HS, 1978–; Libn., Stratford Jr. HS, 1968–78; Libn., Elem. Schs., Arlington (VA), 1962–78; Libn., Springfield (MI) HS, 1961–62; Libn., Lakeview (MI) HS, 1959–60; Chief Fiction Div., DC Pub. Lib., 1950–56, various prof. positions, 1948–50. **Educ.:** Syracuse Univ., 1936–40, AB (Latin), 1940–42, MA, cum laude (Latin), 1947–48, BLS, magna cum laude. **Orgs.:** ALA. VA LA. VA Educ. Media Assn. Arlington Educ. Assn. VA Educ. Assn.: Del., convs. (1975–78). Natl. Educ. Assn.: Del., Natl. Conv. (1974, 1976). Arlington Pol. Action Com. **Activities:** 10; 15, 32, 39 **Addr.:** 5211 N. Washington Blvd., Arlington, VA 22205.

Muldrey, Sr. Mary Hermenia, R.S.M. (F. 21, 1920, New Orleans, LA) Archvst., Srs. of Mercy, 1949–; Libn., Mercy Acad., 1966–; Libn., St. Joseph Sch., 1961–65; Libn.–Tchr., Redemptorist Girls, 1955–60; Libn.–Tchr., St. Alphonsus, 1940–54. **Educ.:** Loyola Univ. of the S., 1940–46, BA (Eng.); Our Lady of the Lake, 1947–49, Cert. (LS, Media). **Orgs.:** ALA. Cath. LA. LALA. Grt. New Orleans Cath. LA: Com. for Natl. Conv. 1980 (Art Ch.). SAA. Cath. Diocesan Archvsts. **Pubns.:** *This Is the Day: History of the Sisters of Mercy in Louisiana, 1869–1969* (1969); "Mother Austin Carroll," *Mercy U.S.–Mercy Union Scope* (1980); "Belize in Central America," *Mercy U.S.–Mercy Union Scope* (1978). **Activities:** 2, 10; 17, 31, 41 **Addr.:** 6220 La Salle Pl., New Orleans, LA 70118.

Mulinix, Martha G. (Je. 30, 1949, West Point, GA) Lib., Recs. Mgr., Long, Aldridge, Heiner, Stevens and Sumner, 1977–; Libn., Consult., Stokes and Shapiro, 1976; Libn., Smith, Currie and Hancock, 1972–75. **Educ.:** Berry Coll., 1967–71, BS (Bio., Chem.); GA State Univ., 1974–76, MLM (Lib.); AALL, Cert. **Orgs.:** Atlanta Law Libs. Assn.: Parlmt. (1981); Secy. (1977–78); Bylaws Com. (1979–80). AALL: Southeast. Chap. Assn. of Rec. Mgrs. and Admins.: Atlanta Chap.; Mem. Ch. (1981–82). **Activities:** 12; 17, 38, 39; 77 **Addr.:** 1900 Rhodes, Haverty Bldg., 134 Peachtree St., Atlanta, GA 30043.

Mulkey, Jack Clarendon (O. 31, 1939, Shreveport, LA) Dir., Jackson Metro. Lib. Syst., 1978–; Adj. Fac., Sch. of Lib. Srv., Univ. of South. MS, 1979–; Dir., MS State Lib. Cmsn., 1976–78, Asst. Dir., 1974–76, Mgt. Consult., 1973–74; Dir., Green Gold Lib. Syst., 1970–73. **Educ.:** Centenary Coll. of LA, 1957–61, BA (Fr., Eng.); Univ. of Dijon, 1961–62, Dip. (European Cvlztn.); LA State Univ., 1968–69, MS (LS). **Orgs.:** MS LA: VP–Pres. Elect (1980–82). SELA: Interstate Coop. (Ch., 1976–78). White House Conf. Com. on Implementation: Natl. Strg. Com. (Del., 1981–83). WHCOLIS: Del. (1978). Various other orgs. **Honors:** Beta Phi Mu, 1969. **Activities:** 9, 13; 17, 24, 26; 54, 78, 85 **Addr.:** 6467 Richwood Dr., Jackson, MS 39213.

Mullane, William H. (O. 6, 1935, San Angelo, TX) Spec. Col. Libn., North. AZ Univ., 1979–, Dir., Tech. Srvs., 1975–79; Lib. Dir., Prescott Coll., 1970–75; Asst. Undergrad. Libn., Univ. of NE, 1969–70, Admin. Asst. to the Dir., 1968–69, Asst. Librn., Hum. Div., 1967–68. **Educ.:** Univ. of NM, 1953–59, BA (Eng.); KS State Tchrs. Coll., 1966–67, MLS. **Orgs.:** AZ LA: Treas. (1975–79). NE LA: Ch., JMRT (1967–70). **Honors:** Beta Phi Mu, 1969. **Pubns.:** "Can Computers Help Select Books?", *Lib. Jnl.* Special Report No. 11 (Jl. 1979); "A Case in Point for Government Documents", *Mt. Plains Lib. Qtly.* (Win., 1967); "A Beginner Looks at Recruitment", *Mt. Plains Lib. Qtly.* (Sum., 1968). **Activities:** 1; 17, 35; .**Addr.:** 404 N. Beaver, Flagstaff, AZ 86001.

Mullen, Gail C. (Je. 2, 1949, Toronto, ON) Chief Libn., Valley E. Pub. Lib., 1978–; Ref. Libn., Etobicoke Pub. Lib., 1973–78. **Educ.:** York Univ., 1968–71, BA (Soclgy., Geo.); Univ. of Toronto, 1971–73, MLS; Various cont. educ. courses (1979–80). **Orgs.:** ONLA: ON Pub. LA (Secy., 1980); Mem. Com. (1981). Pub. Lib. Admins. of the Reg. Municipality of Sudbury: Secy. (1980–81). **Activities:** 9; 15, 16, 17 **Addr.:** Valley East Public Library, Box 700, Val Caron, ON P0M 3A0 Canada.

Mullen, Helen M. (Ja. 2, 1927, Hastings, NE) Asst. Coord., Work with Chld., Free Lib. of Philadelphia, 1953–, Head, Insrv. Trng. and Cmnty. Srv., OWC, 1966–68, Branch Libn., 1961–66, Chld. Libn., 1953–61. **Educ.:** Hastings Coll., 1947–51, BS (Eng., Hist.); Syracuse Univ., 1952–53, MSLS. **Orgs.:** PA LA: Nom. Com. (1972–73); Chld., Young Peoples and Sch. Lib. Sect. (Secy.-Treas., 1969–70). 2nd Pres. (1977–78). ALA: ALSC, VP, Pres.-Elect (1980–81), Pres. (1981–82). Bookseller's Assn. of Grt. Philadelphia. World Bk. Encyc. Lib. Com. **Honors:** Free Lib. of Philadelphia, Empl. of the Yr., 1965. **Activities:** 9; 17, 21 **Addr.:** Office of Work with Children, Free Library of Philadelphia, Logan Sq., Philadelphia, PA 19103.

Mullen, Jess S. (Ap. 26, 1940, St. Louis, MO) Head, Hum./ Info. Dept., Tampa Pub. Lib., 1974–; Adj. Instr., Univ. S. FL, 1977–79; Undergrad. Libn., Univ. of MO, 1970–74; Instr., Fine Arts Libn., IL State Univ., 1967–70, Instr., Asst. Ref. Libn., 1964–67. **Educ.:** Univ. of MO, 1959–63, BA (LS); Univ. of IL, 1963–64, MS (LS). **Orgs.:** FL LA: Cont. Educ. (1979–80). Lions Intl. **Activities:** 1, 9; 15, 25, 39; 50, 55 **Addr.:** Tampa Public Library, 900 N. Ashley, Tampa, FL 33602.

Mullen, Marion Louise (S. 4, 1927, Syracuse, NY) Head, Ref. Dept., Syracuse Univ., 1973–, Head, ILL Ref. Dept. & Ref. work, 1957–73, Various positions, 1947–57. **Educ.:** Syracuse Univ., 1946–49, AB (Psy., Hist.), 1949–52, (Guid. & Couns.), 1961–64, MS (LS). **Orgs.:** ALA: Ref. & Subscrpn. Books Review Com. (1974–78). Libns. Unlimited: Treas. (1978–79). NY LA. Beta Phi Mu: Natl. Asm. (1977–79); Bd. of Dir. (1979–82). AAUP: Rep., Fac. Asm. of Syracuse Chap. (1978–80). Syracuse Univ. Alum. Club: Pres. (1978–79). Univ. Senate. Canal Musm. Assoc. **Pubns.:** Reviews. **Activities:** 1; 39 **Addr.:** 124 Pattison St., Syracuse, NY 13203.

Muller, Claudya Burkett (S. 14, 1946, Fürth, Bavaria, Germ.) Dir., Worcester Cnty. Lib. (1978); Dir., Jackson Cnty. Pub. Lib., 1976–78; Bookmobile coord., Gallia Cnty. Pub. Lib., 1976; Catlgr., Tech. Lib., US Army Corps of Eng., Savannah, 1975; Assoc. Dir., Ottumwa Heights Coll. Lib., 1973; Asst. Dir., War Woman Reg. Lib., 1970–72; Asst. Circ. Libn., GA State Univ. Lib., 1968–69. **Educ.:** GA Southern Coll., 1964–68, BA (Hist.); Emory Univ., 1968–69, MLn. **Orgs.:** ALA: LAMA, Archit. for Pub. Libs. Com. (1980–82); Univ. Press Books for Pub. Libs. Com. (Ch., 1979–80); PLA/SMLS: Nom. Com. (1981–82), San Francisco Prog. Com. (1980–81). MD LA: Prog. Com. (1979–80). WV LA: Ch. Nat. Lib. Week. Com. (1978). Worcester Cnty. Arts Cncl.: Bd. of Dir. (1979–82) Lib. Pub. Rel. Cncl. **Honors:** Emory Univ., Barker Flwshp., 1968. **Pubns.:** "Dear LIPP," *Lib. Insights, Prom. and Prog.* (N. 1979). "PRemiere in a new place," *Lib. Imagination Paper* (Sum. 1979). **Activities:** 9; 17, 25, 36; 51, 55, 89 **Addr.:** Worcester County Library, 307 N. Washington St., Snow Hill, MD 21863.

Muller, Karen (Jl. 4, 1948, Cobleskill, NY) Head of Tech. Srvs., Ryerson and Burnham Libs., Art Inst. of Chicago, 1977–; Catlgr., Northwestern Univ., 1977; Cat. Libn., Yale Ctr. for British Art, 1973–76. **Educ.:** Mt. Holyoke Coll., 1966–70, AB (Art Hist.); Univ. of MI, 1971–73, AMLS; Univ. of Chicago, 1981– (Grad. Sch. of Bus.) **Orgs.:** IL LA: Resrcs. and Tech. Srvs. Sect. (Secy., 1978–81). ALA: ACRL; LITA; RTSD/Cat. and Class. Sect., Subj. Anal. Com., Subcom. on Sub. Headings for Individual Works of Art, (1979–81). ARLIS/NA: Vice-Ch., Ch.-Elect (1980) Ch. (1981); Ad hoc Const. rev. Com. (Ch., 1978–79); Cat. and Indexing Syst. Spec. Int. Grp. (Mdrtr., 1976–78). Coll. Art Assn. **Honors:** Beta Phi Mu, 1972. **Activities:** 1, 12; 20, 23, 46; 55 **Addr.:** Ryerson and Burnham Libraries, Art Institute of Chicago, Michigan at Adams, Chicago, IL 60603.

Muller, William A. (Ja. 1, 1943, Savannah, GA) Pub. Rel. Spec., Eastern Shore Reg. Lib., 1979–; Dir., Mason Cnty. Pub. Lib., 1976–79; Resrch. Libn., City of Savannah, GA, 1973–75; Right to Read Coord., Prairie Hills Reg. Lib., 1972–73; Dir., War Woman Reg. Lib., 1969–72. **Educ.:** GA Southern Coll., 1963–66, BA (Pol. Sci.); Emory Univ., 1968–69, MLN. **Orgs.:** ALA: LAMA, Pub. Rel. Srvs. to Libs. Com. (Ch., 1979–80), White House Conf. Pub. Com. (1977–80), Long Range Plng. Com. (1979–81), Nom. Com. (1978–79), Mem. Com. (1982–84); JMRT. SLA (Adver. and Mktg. Sect., Baltimore Chap.). Rotary Intl.: Pres., Snow Hill, MD Club (1980–81); Celebrations Com. Ch. (1979–80). **Pubns.:** Ed., *Prepare! The Library Public Relations Recipe Book* (1978). **Activities:** 9, 12; 24, 28, 36; 51, 57, 89 **Addr.:** Eastern Shore Regional Library, P.O. Box 951, Salisbury, MD 21801.

Mullikin, Angela G. (D. 27, 1919, Caltanissetta, Italy) Catlgr., Memphis State Univ., 1967–; Spec. Projs. and Ref., MT State Univ., 1964–66; Head Libn., Pace Coll., 1943–61. **Educ.:** SUNY, Geneseo, 1937–41, BS (LS, Educ.); Columbia Univ., 1951–54, MS (LS); Memphis State Univ., 1976–79, MA (Russ. Stds.). **Orgs.:** ALA. TNLA: Mem. Com.; Coll. and Univ. Sect. (Secy.); Grievance Com. AAUW. **Pubns.:** "The King Research Project: Design for a Library Catalog Cost Model," *Lib. Resrcs. and Tech. Srvs.* (Ap.-Je. 1981). **Activities:** 1; 20, 46; 54 **Addr.:** 137 Wallace Rd., Memphis, TN 38117.

Mullin, Viola Day (Jl. 24, 1945, New York, NY) Head of Tech. Srvs., Yale Dvnty. Sch. Lib., 1980–, Head Cat. Libn., 1974–80, Acq. Libn., 1968–74. **Educ.:** Univ. of Bridgeport, 1963–67, BA (Eng. Lit.); Rutgers Univ., 1967–68, MLS. **Orgs.:** ALA. ATLA. Episcopal Church. CT Audubon Socty. Royal Scottish Country Dance Socty. Amer. Musm. of Nat. Hist. **Activities:** 1; 20, 46; 90 **Addr.:** 52 Hillside Pl., New Haven, CT 06511.

Mullins, James L. (N. 29, 1949, Perry, IA) Dir. of Lib. Srvs., IN Univ., South Bend, 1978–; Assoc. Law Libn., IN Univ., Bloomington, 1974–78; Cat. Libn./Instr., GA Southern Coll., 1973–74. **Educ.:** Univ. of IA, 1968–72, BA (Rel./Hist.), 1972–73, MALS; IN Univ., 1975–, PhD in progress (Lib. Sci.). **Orgs.:** ALA: ACRL; LAMA (Bldgs. and Equip. Com., 1980–82). AALL (Com. of Law Lib. Jnl., 1977–78); (Ch., Tech. Srvs. Sect.). IN Univ. LA. Area Lib. Srvs. Auth. for Reg. 2: Dir. at Large (1978–80). **Pubns.:** "The Heart of the University" *IN Univ. LA Qtly* (Spr. 1979); "The Rehabilitation Act of 1973," (N. 1978); "Title IIa - A Bargain at the Price," *Jnl. of Acad. Libnshp.* (S. 79). **Activities:** 1; 15, 17, 24 **Addr.:** Indiana University at South Bend Library, 1700 Mishawaka Ave., South Bend, IN 46615.

Mulloy, Betty (S. 23, 1924, Laurel, MS) Libn., Lauren Rogers Lib. and Musm. of Art, 1976–; Libn., Jefferson Par. Pub. Lib., 1971–76; Resrch. Libn., various advert. agencies, 1948–70. **Educ.:** MS Univ. for Women, 1941–44, BA (Eng.); LA State Univ., 1970–71, BS (LS). **Orgs.:** SLA. **Activities:** 12; 15, 16, 45; 55, 69, 73 **Addr.:** 1209-6th Ave., Laurel, MS 39440.

Mulraney, Sr. Mary Luke (Ja. 31, 1926, Central Falls, RI) Libn., Holy Fam. Sch., Fitchburg, MA, 1977–; Libn., St. Bernard's HS, 1974–76; Elem. Sch. Prin., Holy Trinity Sch., Central Falls, RI, 1970–74, Tchr., 1948–70. **Educ.:** Cath. Tchrs. Coll., Providence, RI, 1948–60, BS (Educ.); 1964, MA Tchrs. Cert.; Regis Coll., 1968–70, Cert. (LS); 1970, MA Cert. Sch. Libn.;

PROFESSIONAL ACTIVITIES: Institutions: 1. Acad. lib.; 2. Arch.; 3. Assn.; 4. Fed./Gvt. lib.; 5. Inst. lib.; 6. Mfr./Suppl.; 7. Milit. lib.; 8. Musm.; 9. Pub. lib.; 10. Sch. lib.; 11. Sch. of lib. sci.; 12. Spec. lib.; 13. State lib.; 14. (other). **Functions/Activities:** 15. Acq./Col. dev.; 16. Adult srvs.; 17. Admin.; 18. Apprais.; 19. Archit./Bldgs.; 20. Cat./Class.; 21. Chld. srvs.; 22. Circ.; 23. Cons./Pres.; 24. Consult.; 25. Cont. ed.; 26. Educ. lib. sci.; 27. Ext. srvs.; 28. Fund/Grants; 29. Gvt. pubs.; 30. Indx./Abs.; 31. Instr. lib. use; 32. Media srvs.; 33. Micro.; 34. Netwks./Coop.; 35. Persnl.; 36. PR; 37. Publshg.; 38. Recs. mgt.; 39. Ref. srvs.; 40. Repro.; 41. Resrch.; 42. Review.; 43. Secur.; 44. Serials; 45. Spec. col.; 46. Tech. srvs.; 47. Trustees/Bds.; 48. YA srvs.; 49. (other).

various wkshps. **Orgs.:** ALA. New Eng. Educ. Media Assn. Cath. LA. Frnds. of Fitchburg Pub. Lib. Natl. Cath. Educ. Assn. **Activities:** 10; 21, 31, 48 **Addr.:** Sisters of the Presentation, B.V.M., 366 South St., Fitchburg, MA 01420.

Mulvaney, Carol E. (F. 1, 1925, Peoria, IL) Info. Ctr. Supvsr., Caterpillar Tractor Co., 1964–, Asst. Resrch. Libn., 1958–64. **Educ.:** Bradley Univ., 1944–47, BA (Hist.). **Orgs.:** SLA: Metals/Mtrls. Div. (Ch., 1974–76). IL LA. IL Valley Lib. Syst.: Afflt. Bd. Mem. WHCOLIS: IL Valley Lib. Syst. Ch. (1978); State Del. (1978). Amer. Socty. for Metals: Metals Info. Com. (1977–80). Peoria Art Guild. **Honors:** Amer. Bus. Women's Assn., Boss of the Yr., 1970. **Pubns.:** "Metallurgical Libraries and Literature," *Encyclopedia of Library and Information Sciences* (1976); "Technical Information Center: Caterpillar Tractor Co.," *IL Libs.* (Mr. 1980); "Planning the New Library, Caterpillar Tractor Co.," *Spec. Libs.* (Mr. 1965). **Activities:** 12; 17, 36, 38; 64, 81, 91 **Addr.:** Technical Information Center, Caterpillar Tractor Co., Peoria, IL 61629.

Mulvihill, John G. (Mr. 3, 1933, Minneapolis, MN) Dir., GeoRef Info. Syst., Amer. Geol. Inst., 1974–; Asst. to the Mgr., Ctrl. Abs. and Indx. Srvs., Amer. Petroleum Inst., 1966–74, Absctr. and Indxr., 1964–66; Libn., Astra Pharm. Prods., 1962–64; Assoc. Libn., St. Benedict's Coll., (Atchison) 1960–62. **Educ.:** Univ. of St. Thomas, TX, 1952–55, BA (Eng.); Rice Univ., 1955–58, MA (Eng.); Univ. of TX, Austin, 1958–60, MLS; Case Western Rsv. Univ., 1960–60 (Info. Sci). **Orgs.:** Geosci. Info. Socty: Pres., (1977). ASIS: Ch., NY Chap. (1973). SLA. ALA. Natl. Fed. of Abs. and Indx. Srvs.: Bd. Mem. (1979–81). Intl. Cncl. of Sci. Unions: Abs. Bd. (1974–80). Amer. Natl. Stans. Inst.: Subcom. on Thesaurus, Indx. and Src. File Ident. **Honors:** UNISIST International Centre for Bibliographic Descriptions/British Library Research and Development Department: Advisory Committee 1980–. **Pubns.:** (Amer. Petr. Inst.) *Subject Authority List* (1961–73); "GeoRef Coverage and Improvements in Bibliography and Index of Geology," *Geosci. Info. Socty* (1981); *Role of the UNISIST/ICSU-AB Reference Manual in Database Processing, Intl. Conf. on Geol. Info.* (1979); "Faceted Organization of a Thesaurus Vocabulary," *ASIS* 1966. **Activities:** 12; 17, 30; 56, 57, 62 **Addr.:** American Geological Institute, One Skyline Place, 5205 Leesburg Pike, Falls Church, VA 22041.

Mumford, L. Quincy (D. 11, 1903, Ayden, NC) Retired, 1974–; Libn. of Congs., 1954–74; Lectr., Sch. of LS, West. Rsv. Univ., 1946–54; Dir., Cleveland Pub. Lib., 1950–54, Asst. Dir., 1945–50; Exec. Asst., Coord., Gen. Srvs. Div., New York Pub. Lib., 1943–45, Staff, 1929–43. **Educ.:** Duke Univ., 1925, AB magna cum laude, 1928, AM; Columbia Univ., 1929, BS (LS). **Orgs.:** ALA: Pres. (1954–55). Mss. Socty.: Bd. dirs.; Pres. (1968–70). FLC: Ch. Amer. Antiq. Socty.: Natl. Adv. Com. Other orgs. MA Hist. Socty. Natl. Trust for Hist. Prsrvn. Natl. Bk. Com. Woodrow Wilson Intl. Ctr. for Schols.: Trustee. **Honors:** Beta Phi Mu; Duke Univ., Litt D, 1957; Univ. of Pittsburgh, LLD, 1964; Univ. of MI, LLD, 1970; other hon. degrees. **Pubns.:** Various articles. **Activities:** 4, 9 **Addr.:** 3721 49th St. NW, Washington, DC 20016.

Munch, Janet Butler (D. 1, 1950, New York, NY) Bronx Ext. Ctr. Libn., Mercy Coll., 1977–; Libn., Bronx Cnty. Hist. Socty., 1974–77. **Educ.:** Mercy Coll., 1968–72, BA (Hist.); Pratt Inst., 1972–74, MLS; Columbia Univ., 1979–, DLS Cand. **Orgs.:** The Bronx LA: Fndr., Pres. (1975–78). SLA: Secy., Bicent. Com. (1975–76); Ed., Soc. & Behvl. Sci. Sect., "*Special Libraries Directory of Greater New York*". Metro: Newspaper Union Task Force for NYC (1976–77). **Honors:** The Bronx LA, Plaque for Srv. as Fndr., 1979; Beta Phi Mu, 1974. **Pubns.:** *Genealogy in The Bronx: An Annotated Resource Guide to Sources...* (1977); *The Bronx Library Directory* (1976); *The Bronx County Historical Society Bibliog. of The Bronx* (1974, 1976). **Activities:** 1, 12; 17, 27, 31; 69, 85, 92 **Addr.:** Mercy College, 2250 Williamsbridge Rd., Bronx, NY 10469.

Mundstock, Aileen Mae (Krueger) (O. 16, 1926, Milwaukee, WI) Tech. Info. Spec., Universal Foods Corp., 1976–, Reporter, New Berlin Cit., 1970–71; Missionary - Tchr., Luth. Synodical Conf., Nigeria, 1950–56. **Educ.:** Valparaiso Univ., 1945–50, BA (Bio.); Univ. of WI, Milwaukee, 1973–76, MA (LS). **Orgs.:** SLA: Food and Nutrition Div., Secy. (1981); Treas. (1976–78); WI Chap., Affirmative Action Com. (Ch. 1981), Career Guid. (Ch. 1981), Mem. Ch. (1978–). Assn. of Info. Mgrs. WI Gvrs. Conf. on Lib. and Info. Srvs.: Del. (1978). **Activities:** 12; 17, 39, 46; 58, 68, 91 **Addr.:** Universal Foods Corp., 6143 N. 60 St., Milwaukee, WI 53218.

Mundt, Jeannie L. (Ap. 8, 1946, Rahway, NJ) Trng. Dev., Intl. Harvester, 1980–; Educ. Prog. Planner, Hlth. Hosp. Governing Comsn., 1977–79, Info. Spec./Resrch., 1974–77, Libn. II, 1971–74. **Educ.:** Northwestern Univ., 1964–68, BS (Jnlsm.); Univ. of Chicago, 1970–73, MA (LS), 1974–, PhD Cand. (Educ.). **Orgs.:** Med. LA. Oak Park Pub. Lib.: Ad hoc Com. Adult Educ. Assn. ASTD. ITDA. CODA. **Pubns.:** "Hospital Libraries' Consortium Blunts Impact of Budget Cuts," *Hosp.* (Je. 19, 1978). **Activities:** 12; 17, 25, 31; 50, 63, 80 **Addr.:** 1043 S. Harvey, Oak Park, IL 60304.

Munger, Nancy Terry (S. 22, 1928, Waterbury, CT) VP, Mgr. of Info. Srvs., J. Walter Thompson Co., 1975–, Dir. of Info. Ctr., 1961–75, Ref. Libn., 1958–61; Libn., Compton Advert., Inc., 1954–58. **Educ.:** CT Coll., 1946–50, BA (Psy.); Univ. of CA, Los Angeles, 1964–65, MLS. **Orgs.:** SLA: Finance Com. (1978–82); Info. Com. (Ch., 1977); NY Chap. (Pres., 1968–69); Advert. and Mktg. Div. (Ch., 1966–67). Advert. Women of New York: Coll. Career Conf. Com. (1977–78). CT Coll. Alum. Assn.: Bd. of Dirs. (1978–80). **Pubns.:** "Library Research," *A Handbook for Advertising Agency Account Executives* (1969; 1982). **Activities:** 12; 17; 51 **Addr.:** 404 East 66th St., New York, NY 10021.

Muñiz-de-Olmos, Sylvia (O. 28, 1932, Añasco, PR) Dir., Archit. Lib., Univ. of PR, 1967–, Head Catlgr. Srv., Humacao Reg. Coll., 1963–67; Catlgr., Rutgers Univ., 1962–63; Catlgr., Univ. of PR, Río Piedras, 1962; Head Catlgr., Univ. of PR, Mayaguez, 1960–62. **Educ.:** Polytech. Inst., San Germán, PR, 1953–57, BS (Pre-Med.); TX Women's Univ., 1959–60, MLS. **Orgs.:** ALA. SBPR: Mem. Com. (Secy., 1979–80). **Activities:** 1, 12; 17, 19, 22; 55, 65 **Addr.:** 2073 Hércules, Reparto Apolo, Guaynabo, PR 00657.

Munn, David C. (S. 11, 1941, Camden, NJ) Dir., Cherry Hill Free Pub. Lib., 1980–; Archvst., NJ State Lib., 1967–80. **Educ.:** Rutgers Univ., 1961–65, BA (Hist.); Drexel Univ., 1965–67, MS, MLS; Univ. of MD, 1972, Cert. (Lib. Admin.). **Orgs.:** ALA. NJ LA. Camden Cnty. Hist. Socty.: Trustee (1969–); Pres. (1974–77); 1st VP, (1980–). **Pubns.:** Ed., *History of Runnemede* (1981); Ed., NJ Arch., *Minutes of the Governor's Privy Council 1777–1789* (1974); Ed., NJ Arch., *Laws of the Royal Colony of New Jersey 1703–1745* (1978); Ed., NJ Arch., *Laws of the Royal Colony of New Jersey 1746–1760* (1980); Ed., *History of Lindenwold* (1979); Various articles and editorships in geneal. and hist. (1968–79). **Activities:** 2, 9; 17, 18, 23; 55, 62, 69 **Addr.:** Cherry Hill Free Public Library, 1100 Kings Hwy., N., Cherry Hill, NJ 08034.

Munn, Robert F. (Jl. 17, 1923, Seattle, WA) Dean, Lib. Srvs., WV Univ., 1957–, Provost, 1968–71, Asst. Provost, 1965–68. **Educ.:** Oberlin Coll., 1946–49, AB (Hist.); Univ. of Chicago, 1950, MA (LS); Univ. of MI, 1961, PhD (LS). **Pubns.:** *Coal Industry in America* (1977); "Appropriate Technology in Developing Countries," *Intl. Lib. Review* (1978); "East African Literature Service," *UNESCO Bltn. Lib.* (1973); Various other articles. **Activities:** 1; 17 **Addr.:** West Virginia University Library, Morgantown, WV 26506.

Munro, June E. (Je. 20, 1921, Echo Bay, Ont.) Dir. of Lib. Srvs., St. Catharines Pub. Lib., 1973–; Chief, Pub. Rel. Div., Natl. Lib. of Can., 1972–73; Book Acq. Adv., Coll. Biblioctr., 1970–72; Supvsr., Extension Srv., Ont. Prov. Lib. Srv., 1961–70. Asst. to the Exec. Dir., Can. LA, 1956–61; Chld. Libn., Leaside Pub. Lib. (Ont.), 1953–56; Chief Libn., Ajax Pub. Lib. (Ont.), 1952–53; Chld.'s Libn., London Pub. Lib. (ON), 1951–52. **Educ.:** Carleton Univ., Ottawa, 1961, BJ; Univ. of Toronto, 1962, BLS, 1972, MLS. **Orgs.:** Can. LA. ALA. ON LA. Cncl. of Admin. of Large Urban Pub. Libs. Carousel Players: Ch. of the Bd. Univ. Women's Club: Prog. Com. (1981–82). **Honors:** ON Lib. Trustees Assn., Libn. Award, 1971. **Pubns.:** *Role of the Lib. Trustee* (1962); "The Wind Has Wings," *In Review* (Aut. 1969); "Library Technicians," *ON Lib. Review* (Je. 1969). **Activities:** 9; 17, 36, 47 **Addr.:** St. Catharines Public Library, 54 Church St., St. Catharines, ON L2R 7K2 Canada.

Munro, Robert John (Jl. 4, 1948, Coral Gables, FL) Assoc. Law Libn., Univ. of FL, 1975–; Legal Ref. Libn., LA State Univ., 1974–75. **Educ.:** Lynchburg Coll., 1966–70, BA (Phil.); Univ. of IA, 1970–73, JD (Law); LA State Univ., 1972–73, MA (Polit. Sci.), 1974–75, MLS. **Orgs.:** AALL. Intl. Assn. of Law Libs. SLA. ALA. **Pubns.:** "Lexis vs. Westlow: On Analysis of Automated Education," *Law Lib. Jnl.* (Ag., 1978); reprinted in *Amer. Bar Assn. Jnl.*; "Plots, Educom, and Legal Education," *Comp./Law Jnl.* (Win., 1979). **Activities:** 1; 17, 24, 39; 63, 77, 92 **Addr.:** 3733 N.W. 49th Ln., Gainesville, FL 32611.

Murdoch, Faith Townsend (Ap. 28, 1909, Sault St. Marie, MI) Retired; Dir. of Sch. Libs., Detroit Pub. Schs., 1963–72, Supvsr. of Sch. Libs., 1958–62, Visit. Libn., 1953–61. **Educ.:** Wayne State Univ., 1927–34, BS (Educ.), 1936–38, MA (Educ.); Univ. of MI, 1962–64, MALS. **Orgs.:** ALA: AASL (VP, 1965–66). MI Assn. of Sch. Libns.: Various coms. (1950–62). **Honors:** Univ. of MI, Sch. of LS, Disting. Alum., 1971. **Pubns.:** "Relationship of the School Library to the Young Adult in the Public Library," *Lib. Trends* (O. 1968); "A Commitment To Achievement," *Amer. Libs.* (S. 1970); "Standard Bearers for School Libraries," *Women in the Library Profession* (1971). **Addr.:** 2908 Mayflower, Sarasota, FL 33581.

Murdock, Everlyne Kahn (F. 14, 1922, Birmingham, AL) Chief, Lib. Info. Srvs. Branch, Dir., Con. Prod. Safety Comsn. Lib., 1981–; Acting Dir., Consumer Prod. Safety Comsn. Lib., 1980–; Head Libn., Ref. Srvs., 1973–79; Div. of Resrch. Grants, Ref. Lib., 1965–73; Lib. Tech., NIH Lib., 1961–65. **Educ.:** Univ. of MD, 1971–72, MLS. **Orgs.:** ALA. Metro. Washington Cncl. of Gvt. Libs. FEDLINK. **Honors:** CPSC, Merit. Awd. as Ref. Lib., 1981. **Activities:** 4, 12; 24, 31, 39; 58, 77 **Addr.:** 3003 Van Ness St., N.W., Washington, DC 20008.

Murdock, J. Larry (D. 20, 1939, Provo, UT) Head, Pub. Srvs., Sam Houston State Univ. Lib., 1980–, Soc. Sci. Libn., 1978–80; Gvt. Docum. Libn., Johns Hopkins Univ. Lib., 1976–78; Gvt. Docum. and Maps Libn., Brigham Young Univ. Lib., 1969–76, Cat., 1968–1969; various positions, Univ. of UT Lib., 1967–1968; Ref. Libn., Univ. of WA Lib. 1965–1967. **Educ.:** Brigham Young Univ., 1957–59, 1962–64, BS (Anthro.); Univ. of MI, 1964–65, AMLS; Brigham Young Univ., 1970–75, MS (Geo.); Tech. Cert., 1962–64, (Geneal. Tech.). **Orgs.:** ALA. NLA. SLA. TX LA. **Pubns.:** "Documents Await *Your* Discovery," *UT Libs.* (Fall 1973). **Activities:** 1; 17, 29, 39; 70, 92 **Addr.:** 2104 Ave. "S", Huntsville, TX 77340.

Muro, Ernest A. (Ag. 18, 1944, Baltimore, MD) VP Tech. Srvs., The Baker & Taylor Co., 1980–, Dir., 1975–80; Syst. Libn., Univ. of DE, 1973–75, Circ. Libn., 1969–72, Lib. Sci. Instr., 1971–75; Lib. Sci. Prof., Queens Coll., 1979; DE Tech. and Comnty. Coll., 1968–75; Media Libn., Newark Spec. Sch. Dist. (1966–69); Curr. Adv. Com., DE Tech. and Comnty. Coll. (1969–75). **Educ.:** Clarion State Coll., 1962–66, BS LS; Villanova Univ., 1967–68, MS LS; Pratt Inst., 1972, Post MA Cert. (Lib. Sci.). **Orgs.:** ALA: ACRL; AASL; RTSD. NJ LA: Adv. Brd. (1968). Lib. of Cong.: CIP Div. Lib. Adv. Com. (1979–). State of DE: Gov. Peterson's "Com. for Lib. Reorg." (1970–72). DE LA: Pres. (1970–71); VP (1969–70). **Honors:** Beta Phi Mu, Nomination 1977; NEH grant, 1972. Phi Delta Kappa. **Pubns.:** "Turnkey Systems for Cataloging and Acquisition," *Microform Review* (1980); Contrib., *What Else You Can Do With A Library Degree,* (1980); Presentations: "PERT/CPM" *ASIS* (1975). **Activities:** 11; 24, 46; 56 **Addr.:** 26 Dorchester Dr., Oak Knoll, Annandale, NJ 08801.

Murphey, John A. (Pat), Jr. (Ag. 6, 1931, Oklahoma City, OK) State Libn., AR State Lib., 1981–; Tech. Consult., Lib. Insts., Traineeshps., Flwshps., U.S. Ofc. of Educ., 1978–79; Asst. Dir., Assoc. Dir., Univ. of TX Hlth. Sci. Ctr., Dallas, 1973–81. **Educ.:** Univ. of Corpus Christi, 1968–72, BS (Bus. Admin.); Univ. of TX, Austin, 1972–73, MLS; N. TX State Univ., 1974 (Postgrad work). **Orgs.:** TX LA. Med. LA: SCRG. SWLA. ALA. TX Cncl. of Lib. and Info. Netwks.: Pres. (1980–81). TX Lib. LSCA Adv. Cncl. (1978–81). Various other orgs. **Activities:** 13 **Addr.:** Arkansas State Library, One Capitol Mall, Little Rock, AR 72201.*

Murphree, Janie E. (N. 8, 1942, Buffalo, TN) Dir., Lib. Lrng. Resrcs. Ctr., Motlow State Cmnty. Coll., 1980–; Serials Libn., Univ. of TN, Nashville, 1977–79, Acq. Libn., 1975–77, Cat. Libn., 1972–75, Asst. Cat. Libn., 1971–72; Book Cat. Staff, Jt. Univ. Libs., 1968–71; Staff, Wyandotte Chem. Corp., 1966–67; Chem. tchr., Glynn Academy, 1965–66. **Educ.:** Martin Jr. Coll., 1960–62, AA; Vanderbilt Univ., 1962–64, BA (Chem.); George Peabody Coll., 1966–68, MLS. **Orgs.:** ALA: RTSD, Book Cat. Com. (1978–79). TN LA: Tech. Srvs. Div., Secy. Treas. (1976–77); *TN Libn.,* Bus. Mgr. (1977–80). **Honors:** Phi Theta Kappa; Beta Phi Mu. **Activities:** 1; 15, 17, 39 **Addr.:** 1110 E. Grundy St., Tullahomu, TN 37388.

Murphy, Anna Marie (Jl. 24, 1926, New York, NY) Dir. of Libs., Fordham Univ., 1970–; Assoc. Libn., Fordham Univ., 1956–70, Asst. Libn. for Pub. Srvs., 1954–56; Asst. Branch Libn., NY Pub. Lib., 1951–54, Prof. Asst., 1950–51. **Educ.:** Coll. of Mt. St. Vincent, 1944–48, AB (Fr.); Pratt Inst., 1949–50, BLS. **Orgs.:** ALA. Cath. LA. **Activities:** 1; 17 **Addr.:** Fordham University Library, Bronx, NY 10458.

Murphy, Charles G. (My. 17, 1942, Salem, MA) Libn., Appld. Resrch. Lab. PA State Univ., 1979–, Ref. Libn., Univ. Libs., 1974–79; Ref. Libn., St. Francis College, Biddeford, ME, 1972–74. **Educ.:** Univ. of Notre Dame, 1959–63, BA (Pol. Sci.); Columbia Univ., 1971–72, MSLS. **Orgs.:** ALA: RASD; ACRL, LITA, Mach. Asst. Ref. Sect. ASIS. SLA. Philadelphia Area Ref. Libns. Info. Exchange. **Activities:** 1, 12; 17, 39; 56, 91 **Addr.:** Applied Research Laboratory, The Pennsylvania State University, P.O. Box 30, State College, PA 16801.

Murphy, Harriet P. (My. 10, 1921, Santa Barbara, CA) VP, Suburban Lib. Syst. Bd. of Trustees, 1979–81; Trustee, Oak Lawn Pub. Lib., 1975–, Pres., 1977–79, VP, 1975–77. **Educ.:** Univ. of CA, Los Angeles, 1938–42, BA (Drama). **Orgs.:** ALA. IL LA: Trustees RT Div. **Activities:** 9, 14-Library System Bd.; 47; 56 **Addr.:** 4923 W. 99th St., Oak Lawn, IL 60453.

Murphy, Henry T. (D. 9, 1923, Lynn, MA) Libn., Albert R. Mann Lib., Cornell Univ., 1969–; Life Sci. Libn., Purdue Univ., 1957–69; Agr. Libn., OH State Univ., 1956–57; Agr. Exper. Sta. Libn., W. Lafayette, IN, 1954–56; Ref. Libn., U.S. Dept. of Agr., 1951–54. **Educ.:** Boston Univ., 1945–48, AB (Bio.); Univ. of MI, 1949–51, MALS; Univ. of NH, 1948 (Bio. Sci.). **Orgs.:** SLA. ALA: ACRL. **Honors:** ALA, Oberly Award, 1973. **Pubns.:** Jt. auth., *Comparative & Veterinary Medicine* (1973); Jt. auth, *Biological and Biomedical Resource Literature* (1968). **Activities:** 1; 15, 17; 58 **Addr.:** Albert R. Mann Library, Cornell University, Ithaca, NY 14853.

Special Subjects/Services: 50. Adult educ.; 51. Advert./Mktg.; 52. Aerosp.; 53. Agric.; 54. Area std.; 55. Arts/Hum.; 56. Autom.; 57. Bibl./Prtg.; 58. Bio. sci.; 59. Bus./Fin.; 60. Chem.; 61. Copyrt.; 62. Documtn.; 63. Educ.; 64. Engin.; 65. Env.; 66. Eth. grps.; 67. Film; 68. Food/Nutr.; 69. Geneal.; 70. Geo.; 71. Geol.; 72. Handcpd.; 73. Hist.; 74. Int. frdm.; 75. Info. sci.; 76. Insr.; 77. Law; 78. Legis.; 79. Math./Comp. sci.; 80. Med.; 81. Metals; 82. Nat. resrcs.; 83. Newsp.; 84. Nuc. sci.; 85. Oral hist.; 86. Petr./Energy; 87. Pharm.; 88. Phys./Astr./Math.; 89. Readg.; 90. Relig.; 91. Sci./Tech.; 92. Soc. sci.; 93. Telecom.; 94. Transp.; 95. (other).

Murphy, Sr. Jean Timothy (Ag. 10, 1923, Springfield, MA) Ch., Lib. Dept., Bishop Kearney HS, 1970–; Libn., St. Agnes HS, 1964–70; Libn., St. Francis Xavier Acad., 1956–64; Grade Tchr., Various Elem. Schs., 1942–56. **Educ.:** Manhattan Coll., 1948–52, BA (Hist.); St. John's Univ., 1952–55, MLS. **Orgs.:** ALA. NY LA. Cath. LA: Brooklyn Unit (Exec. Cncl., Treas., 1976–79). **Activities:** 1, 10; 15, 20, 48; 54, 58, 92 **Addr.:** Bishop Kearney High School, Brooklyn, NY 11204.

Murphy, (Margaret) Jims (Ap. 3, 1928, Boston, MA) Chief, Tech. Lib., U.S. Army Mtrls. & Mechanics Resrch. Ctr., 1969–; Head Resrch. Libn., Gillette Safety Razor Co., 1956–69, Chem., 1949–56. **Educ.:** Regis Coll., 1945–49, AB (Chem.), Simmons Coll., 1956–61, MLS; Indus. Coll. of the Armed Forces, 1972–73, Cert. (Natl. Security). **Orgs.:** SLA: Boston Chap., Pres. (1973–74); Milit. Libns. Div., (Ch., 1976–78); Student Rel. Ofcr. (1976–78); Nom. Com., (Ch., 1979); Bylaws Com. (Ch. 1981). ASIS: Nom. Com., (Ch., 1974); Prog. Com. (1973). Amer. Chem. Socty. AAAS. **Pubns.:** "Silicon Nitride for Structural Applications - An Annotated Bibliography," (1973); "Uranium Alloy Metallurgy - An Annotated Bibliography," (1974); "Stress Analysis of Structural Joints and Interfaces - A Selective Annotated Bibliography," (1974); "Silicon Nitride for Structural Applications - An Annotated Bibliography," (1975); "Design Analysis, Testing, and Reliability of Joints - An Annotated Bibliography," (1975); Other bibls. **Activities:** 4; 17; 81, 74, 91 **Addr.:** Technical Library, Army Materials and Mechanics Research Center, Watertown, MA 02172.

Murphy, Lawrence Parke (O. 18, 1924, Columbia, MO) Keeper of Rare Books, New York Pub. Lib., 1978–, Spec. Asst. to the Dir., 1971–78, Asst. to the Dir., 1967–71, Asst. to the Deputy Dir., 1966–67; Asst. to the Exec. Dir., New York Metro. Ref. and Resrch. Lib. Agency 1966–67; Libn., Gen. Resrch. and Hum. Div., New York Pub. Lib., 1962–66; Bibl. Libn., E.I. du Pont de Nemours & Co., 1953–57; Libn., Univ. of WA, 1949–53. **Educ.:** Whitman Coll., 1942–47, AB cum laude (Chem.); Univ. of WA, 1947–48, MA (Eng. lit.), 1948–49, BA (Libnshp.); Columbia Univ., 1957–62, (Eng. & Comp. lit.). **Orgs.:** SLA: Pres., Pac. NW Chap. (1952–53); Vice-Ch., Documen. Div., NY Chap. (1967–68). ALA. NY LA. New York Lib. Club. Other orgs. Sigma Chi New York Alum.: Secy. (1971–74); Exec. Com. (1974–). Phi Beta Kappa New York Alum. Goudy Socty. Typophiles. **Pubns.:** *Writing and the Scientist.* (1957); "Altemus & Co." and "Beadle & Co." in *Publishers for Mass Entertainment in the Nineteenth Century.* (1980); "Published for Book Lovers:" A Short History of American Book Collecting Magazines." *Book Collector's Market,* (S./O. 1979); "Franklin Ferguson Hopper" in *Dictionary of American Library Biography* (1979); "Introduction" *The Imprint Catalog in the Rare Book Division, NYPL.* (1979); Other articles. **Activities:** 1; 17, 26, 45; 55, 57 **Addr.:** The Rare Book Division, The New York Public Library, Fifth Avenue at 42nd St., New York, NY 10018.

Murphy, Mary (Ag. 14, 1917, Hibbing, MN) Retired, 1980–; Chief, Indexing Br., Defense Map. Agency, HTC, 1970–80; Chief, Info. Sect., Army Topographic Command, 1968–70; Chief, Docu. Br., Army Map Srv., 1965–68, Asst. Chief, Book Br., 1956–65, Chief, Ref. Sect., 1952–56, Book Catlgr., Reviser, 1946–52, Acq. and Interlib. Loan Asst., 1945–46. **Educ.:** St. Lawrence Univ., 1938–40, BA (Fr.); Univ. of IL, Urbana, 1940–43, BSLS. **Orgs.:** SLA: Rep. Int. Fed. of LA Geog. & Map Sec. (1978–); Geog. & Map Div., Ed. Div. Bltn. (1975–); Ch., Nom. Com. (1974–75). Assn. of Amer. Geographers. **Honors:** SLA, Geog. & Map Div., Honors Awd., 1976; Phi Beta Kappa; Beta Phi Mu. **Pubns.:** "DMATC and the Map & Chart Depository Program," *SLA Geog. & Map Div. Bltn.* (D. 1976); "Atlases of the Eastern Hemisphere," *Geog. Review* (Ja. 1974); "Aerial Photo.," *West. Assn. of Map Libs. Info. Bltn.* (Ag. 1971); "Map Collection Prepares to Automate," *Spec. Libs.* (Ap. 1970). **Activities:** 4, 12; 20, 31, 39; 56, 70, 74 **Addr.:** 8102 Birnam Wood Dr., McLean, VA 22102.

Murphy, Mary Dalton (D. 31, 1917, Lawrence, KS) Head, Ref., Lawrence Pub. Lib., 1968–; Consult., NE KS Lib. Syst., 1968; Head, In-Srvs. Trng., Johnson Cnty. Lib., 1966–68, HQ Libn., 1961–66; Per. Libn., Univ. of KS, 1941–66, Asst. Acquisitions, 1940–41. **Educ.:** Univ. of KS, 1935–39, AB (Span.); Columbia Univ., 1939–40, BS (LS). **Orgs.:** KS LA. Mt. Plains LA. ALA. **Activities:** 9, 12; 24, 27, 39; 69, 75, 89 **Addr.:** Lake Dabinawa, McLouth, KS 66054.

Murphy, Patricia Marie (O. 1, 1947, Toledo, OH) Asst. Prof., Dept. of Lib. Admin. Libn., Kent State Univ. (Stark), 1978–; Libn., Kent State Univ. (Tuscarawas), 1972–78; Verifier/Srch., Case West. Rsv. Univ., 1970–72. **Educ.:** St. Catharine Coll. (KY), 1965–66; Cleveland State Univ., 1966–69, BA (Hist.); Case West. Rsv. Univ., 1970–71, MS (LS). **Orgs.:** ALA. NLA. Acad. Lib. Assn. of OH: Asst. Treas. (1979); Treas. (1980). **Honors:** Beta Phi Mu. **Activities:** 1; 29, 31, 39; 65 **Addr.:** 4834 Cranberry N.W., Canton, OH 44709.

Murphy, Paul T. (Ja. 28, 1947, Windsor, ON) Law Libn. & Assoc. Prof., Fac. of Law Lib., Univ. of Windsor, 1975–, Head, Reader Srvs. Dept., 1971–75. **Educ.:** Univ. of Windsor, 1964–68, BA (Eng.), 1968–71, LLB (Law); Wayne State Univ., 1971–74, MSLS, 1974–80, Master of Urban Plng. **Orgs.:** Can. ALL: VP (1979–81). AALL. Mem. of the ON Bar. **Pubns.:** *A Short Guide to Legal Research in Ontario and Canadian Federal Law* (1976; 1977); "Colonial Subjects' Rights under British Law: Dutch N.Y. and French Acadia" *Can. Jnl. of Netherlandic Studies* (1980); "Canadian Legal Materials: An Introduction", in *Canadian Government Publications: A Reader* (1981). **Activities:** 15, 17, 39; 77 **Addr.:** Faculty of Law Library, University of Windsor, Windsor, ON N9B 3P4 Canada.

Murphy, Paula Christine (D. 15, 1950, Oberlin, OH) AV Libn., Columbia Coll. Lib., 1980–; Media Libn., Gvrs. State Univ. Lib., 1976–80; AV Libn., Chicago Pub. Lib., 1975–76, Admin. Asst. to Head of Spec. Ext. Srvs., 1974–75. **Educ.:** Rosary Coll., 1969–73, BA (Hist.), 1973–75, MALS. **Orgs.:** IL LA. ALA: JMRT (Treas., 1980–82). **Honors:** 3M/JMRT Prof. Devel. Grant; Beta Phi Mu. **Activities:** 1, 9; 17, 32; 55, 67, 89 **Addr.:** Columbia College Library, Chicago, IL 60605.

Murphy, Robert Lawrence (Jl. 12, 1926, Moundsville, WV) Dir., Med. Ctr. Lrng. Resrcs., WV Univ. Med. Ctr., 1979–, Dir., Med. Ctr. Lib., 1971–79, Dir., Agr./Engin. Lib., 1968–71; Tech. Info. Spec., NASA, DC, 1963–68. **Educ.:** WV Univ., 1948–50; George Washington Univ., 1950–56, AB (Jnlsm.); Cath. Univ. of Amer., 1959–69, MS (LS). **Orgs.:** WV LA: Pres. (1971–72). Med. LA: Parlmt. (1973–75). Amer. Assn. of Hlth. Sci. Lib. Dirs. Amer. Assn. of Dental Schs.: Lrng. Resrcs. Strg. Com. Amer. Assn. of Colls. of Pharm. **Pubns.:** "Father of Oral Surgery," *WV Univ. Mag.* (Spr. 1978); "History of Oral Surgery" videotape. **Activities:** 1, 12; 17, 24; 80 **Addr.:** West Virginia University, Medical Center Learning Resources Center, Morgantown, WV 26505.

Murrah, David J. (S. 13, 1941, Shattuck, OK) Univ. Archvst., SW Col., TX Tech. Univ., 1977–, Asst. Dir., 1976–77, Asst. Archvst., 1971–76; Tchr., Morton Pub. Schs., 1967–71. **Educ.:** Hardin-Simmons Univ., 1960–64, BA (Hist.); TX Tech. Univ., 1969–79, MA (Hist), PhD (Hist.). **Orgs.:** SAA. Socty. of Southwest Archvsts.: Exec. Bd. (1978–80). TX State Hist. Assn. W. TX Hist. Assn. **Honors** West TX Hist. Assn., Best Article Awd., 1977. **Pubns.:** *C.C. Slaughter, Rancher, Banker, Baptist* (1981); "W. C. Holden," *Gr. Plains Jnl.* (1979); "Muleshoe Ranch," *WTHA Yrbk.* (1976). **Activities:** 2, 12; 15, 17; 85 **Addr.:** Southwest Collection, TX Tech. University, Box 4090, Lubbock, TX 79416.

Murray, Carol Ann (Jl. 1, 1948, St. Louis, MO) Supvsr., Info. Srvs., Celanese Plastics and Specialties, 1977–; Supvsr., ILL Dept., VA Polytech. Inst., 1974–76. **Educ.:** St. Louis Univ., 1966–70, BA (Eng., Soc. Sci.); Univ. of MO, 1970–73, MA (LS). **Orgs.:** SLA. **Activities:** 12; 17, 39, 49-On-line Retrieval; 60, 91, 95-Patents. **Addr.:** Celanese Research Library, P.O. Box 99038, Jeffersontown, KY 40299.

Murray, Diane E. (O. 15, 1942, Detroit, MI) Tech. Srvs. Libn., Hope Coll., 1977–; Asst. Head, Receiving Sect., Acq., MI State Univ., 1972–77, Cat. Libn., Cat. Div., 1968–72. **Educ.:** Hope Coll., 1960–64, AB (Psy., Msc.); West. MI Univ., 1967–68, MLS; Aquinas Coll., 1978–, (Mgt.). **Orgs.:** Msc. LA. MI LA: Chair - Tech. Srvs. Caucus, (Ch., 1979–80), Acad. Div. (Sect. Treas., 1976–77). ALA. MI Serials Interest Grp.: (Ch., 1975, 1977–78). **Pubns.:** Ed., *Grand Rapids Area Union List of Serials* (1979–); Ed., *Directory of Michigan Academic Librarians* (1977). **Activities:** 1; 17, 44, 46 **Addr.:** Van Zoeren Library, Hope College, Holland, MI 49423.

Murray, James Michael (N. 8, 1944, Seattle, WA) Assoc. Law Libn., Washington Univ. Law Lib., 1981–; Bk. Apprais. Ed., *TX Bar Jnl.,* 1979–81; Rsv. Libn., Univ. of TX, Austin, 1978–81. **Educ.:** Gonzaga Univ., 1963–67, BA (Eng.), 1967–71, JD (Law); Univ. of WA, 1977–78, Mstr. (Law Libnshp.). **Orgs.:** AALL: *Law Lib. Jnl.* Com. (1980–82). Southwest. Assn. of Law Libs. WA State Bar Assn. WA Volun. Lawyers for the Arts. Amer. Bar Assn. Amer. Cvl. Liberties Un. **Honors:** Alpha Sigma Nu, 1967. **Pubns.:** "Selected, Annoted Bibliography on Treason," *Notes From the Tarlton Law Lib.* (N.–D. 1978); "Selected, Annotated Bibliography on Sports Law," *Notes From the Tarlton Law Lib.* (S.–O. 1979); various bk. reviews. **Activities:** 1, 12; 22, 39, 49-Rsv.; 77 **Addr.:** Freund Law Library, Washington University, Campus Box 1120, St. Louis, MO 63130.

Murray, Kathleen R. (Jl. 17, 1943, Texarkana, AR) Assoc. Dir. of Tech. Srvs., Lamar Univ., 1980–; Head, Cat. Dept., 1973–80; Catlgr., South. Methodist Univ., 1970–73. **Educ.:** Bryn Mawr Coll., 1961–65, BA (Geo.); Univ. of TX, Austin, 1968–70, MLS. **Orgs.:** ALA. Southwestern LA. TX LA: Booth Com. (Ch., 1974–75); Jr. Mem. RT (Ch., Secty., 1974–75); Schol. and Resrch. Com. (1976–77); Cont. Educ. Com. (1977–78); Coll. and Univ. Div. Cont. Ed. Com. (1979–80). **Pubns.:** Ed., *Current Studies in Librarianship* (1978). **Activities:** 1; 20, 44, 46 **Addr.:** 2630 Ashley, Beaumont, TX 77702.

Murray, Kay (S. 25, 1932, Connersville, IN) Assoc. Prof., Sch. of Lib. Sci., Univ. of NC, Chapel Hill, 1977–; Asst. Prof., Grad. Sch. of Lib. Srvs. Rutgers, the State Univ., 1972–77; Asst. Prof., Doct. Stud. in Educ. Lead. Fairleigh Dickinson Univ., 1971–72. **Educ.:** IN Univ., 1950–53, BA (Fr.); Rutgers Univ., 1965–68, MLS; Rutgers Univ., 1968–72, PhD (Lib. Sci.). **Orgs.:** AALS: Conf. Prog. Com. (1977–79); Ch. (1978–79). ALA Ref. and Subs. Books Com. (1974–78); NC LA. **Honors:** HEW, Flwshp, 1969. Phi Beta Kappa; Beta Phi Mu; Phi Sigma Iota; Alpha Lambda Delta. **Pubns.:** Ed., *Personnel Development in Libraries* (1977); "The Structure of M.L.S. Programs in American Library Schools," *Jrnl. of Educ. for Libnshp.* (Spr. 1978); "Passing Through the Turnstile," *ALA Yrbk.* (1978). **Activities:** 9, 11; 16, 26, 39; 57, 75 **Addr.:** School of Library Science, Manning Hall 026A, Chapel Hill, NC 27514.

Murray, Marilyn R. (D. 14, 1949, San Antonio, TX) Libn., Arthur Andersen & Co., 1978–; Asst. Libn., 1974–78; Libn., MI Mncpl. Leag., 1973–74. **Educ.:** Univ. of MI, 1967–72, AB (Eng.), 1972–73, AMLS. **Orgs.:** SLA. **Activities:** 12; 15, 17, 24; 59 **Addr.:** Arthur Andersen & Co., 33 W. Monroe St., Chicago, IL 60603.

Murray, Olin B. (Jl. 12, 1930, Bedford, VA) Coord., Col. Dev., Univ. of AB Lib., 1969–; Biblgphr. of Africana, Northwestern Univ., 1966–69; Soc. Sci. Biblgphr., Yale Univ., 1964–66, Acq. Asst., 1963–64. **Educ.:** Univ. of VA, 1951–53, BA (Grmn.); Univ. of NC, 1954–57, (Ling.); Rutgers Univ., 1961–62, MLS. **Orgs.:** Can. LA. LA of AB. Socty. for Schol. Pubshg. **Honors:** Phi Beta Kappa, 1953; Beta Phi Mu, 1962. **Pubns.:** "Urban Growth and Population Shifts in the Prairie Region", *Can. Lib. Jnl.* (S./O. 1971); "A National-International Approach to Library - Archive Resources for Historical Research," *Can. Lib. Jnl.* (My./Je. 1971); "Knowledge, Universities, and Libraries," (1970). **Activities:** 1; 15, 34, 37; 56, 92, 95 **Addr.:** University of Alberta Libraries, 5-12C Cameron Library, Edmonton, AB T6G 2J8 Canada.

Murray, R. R. B. (Ag. 27, 1921, Shediac Cape, NB) Lib. Dir., NY State Coll. of Ceramics, Alfred Univ., 1959–; Resrch. Libn., Ctrl. Resrch. Lab., Crucible Steel Co., 1955–59; Chief Libn., Saint John (NB) Free Pub. Lib., 1953–55; Branch Libn., Applied Chem. Div., NRC of Canada, 1950–53; Ref. Libn., Brooklyn Pub. Lib., 1949–50. **Educ.:** Univ. of Toronto, 1945–48, BA (General); McGill Univ., 1948–49, BLS; Libns. Cert., NY State Univ., 1950. **Orgs.:** NB LA: Pres. (1954–55). SUNY Head Libns. Grp.: Ch. (1963). SLA: Ch., Metals/Mtrls. Division (1979–80); Upstate NY Chap. (Pres., 1966–67). **Activities:** 1, 12; 17, 39, 44; 64, 81, 91 **Addr.:** 113 S. Main St., Almond, NY 14804.

Murray, Robin Mark (S. 12, 1953, Lima, OH) Progmr., Sears & Roebuck & Co., 1980–; Ref. Libn. Chicago Pub. Lib., 1979–80, Asst. Soc. Sci. Libn., 1977–79; Pub. Srvs. Mgr., Univ. of Chicago Lib. 1976–77. **Educ.:** Bob Jones Univ., 1972–75, BA (Hum.); Univ. of Chicago, 1975–77, MA (LS); Cult. Std. Acad. Salzburg, Austria Cert. in Advnc. Grmn. 1971. **Orgs.:** ALA (1975–80). Chicago Pub. Lib. Staff Assn.: Rep. (1978–1979). William Frederick Poole Socty.: Coord. (1978–80). Sunday Speakeasy. Chicago Lrng. Exch. **Pubns.:** "An Audition for Orchestra-80," *soft side.* **Activities:** 1, 9; 16, 31, 39; 59, 63, 92 **Addr.:** 640 W. Wrightwood #311, Chicago, IL 60614.

Murray, Rochelle Ann (D. 14, 1936, Davenport, IA) Head, Chld. Dept., Davenport Pub. Lib., 1965–, Head, Adult Srvs., 1964–65, Young People's Libn., 1960–65, A-V Libn., 1959–65. **Educ.:** Marycrest Coll., 1955–59, BA (Speech, Eng.); Univ. of WI, Madison, 1963–67, MA (LS). **Orgs.:** ALA: YASD, Mag. Eval. Com. (1965–69). IA LA: Rcrt. Ch. (1965–66); Secy. for Dist. (1967). Quad-City Libns. Assn.: Co-Ch. (1964–1966). Natl. Cncl. of Christians and Jews. Boy Scouts of America. AAUW. Chld. Lit. Fest.: Mem. Ch. (1979–). **Honors:** Beta Phi Mu, 1968; Alpha Delta Kappa, 1974. **Pubns.:** "8mm Films in Libraries," *IL Libs.* (1962); "Film, Art and Music Services Expand at Davenport Public Library," *Film News* (1964). **Activities:** 9, 10; 16, 21, 48; 63, 67, 72 **Addr.:** 407 East 30th St., Davenport, IA 52803.

Murray, Suzanne H. (F. 19, 1932, Syracuse, NY) Libn. and Assoc. Dir., SUNY Upstate Med. Ctr. Lib., 1980–, Assoc. Libn. and Assoc. Dir., 1973–80; Lib. Consult., Ctrl. NY Reg. Med. Prog., 1969–73; Asst. Libn., SUNY Upstate Med. Ctr., 1960–67. **Educ.:** LeMoyne Coll., 1950–54, BS (Chem.); Syracuse Univ., 1959–60, MS (LS). **Orgs.:** Ctrl. NY Lib. Resrcs. Cncl.: Nom. Com. (Ch., 1980); Bd. of Trustees (Secy., 1979–81). Med. LA: Copyrt. Com. (1981–84); Upstate NY and ON Reg. Grp./Coord. for Copyrt. (1979–81). NY and NJ Reg. Med. Lib. SUNY Libns. Assn.: Treas. (1975–79); Nom. Com. (Ch., 1977). AAUW. Prof. Women's Leag. of Syracuse. LeMoyne Coll. Alumn. Assn.: Natl. Bd. of Gvrs. (1980–83). **Honors:** Beta Phi Mu, 1960; Theta Chi Beta, 1968. **Pubns.:** *Health Science Librarianship, Libraries and Resources; A Selected Bibliography* (1979); *A Library Guide and Selectively Annotated Guide to the Literature* (1979); *A Library Guide and Guide to the Literature* (1978); *Literature Searching for the Clinical Laboratory* (1970); *Reading for Renewal; A Bibliography* (1965); various articles. **Activities:** 1, 12; 15, 17, 34; 61 **Addr.:** State University of New York, Upstate Medical Center Library, 766 Irving Ave., Syracuse, NY 13210.

Murray, Timothy Daniel (Je. 23, 1950, Buffalo, NY) Cur., Mss., WA Univ., St.Louis, MO, 1980–; Asst. Libn., SUNY, Buffalo, 1978–79. **Educ.:** SUNY, Buffalo, 1968–72, BA (Eng.); Univ. of ME, 1974–76, MA (Eng.); SUNY, Buffalo, 1976–77, MLS. **Orgs.:** Midwest Arch. Conf. **Activities:** 1, 2; 45 **Addr.:**

PROFESSIONAL ACTIVITIES: Institutions: 1. Acad. lib.; 2. Arch.; 3. Assn.; 4. Fed./Gvt. lib.; 5. Inst. lib.; 6. Mfr./Suppl.; 7. Milit. lib.; 8. Musm.; 9. Pub. lib.; 10. Sch. lib.; 11. Sch. of lib. sci.; 12. Spec. lib.; 13. State lib.; 14. (other). **Functions/Activities:** 15. Acq./Col. dev.; 16. Adult srvs.; 17. Admin.; 18. Apprais.; 19. Archit./Bldgs.; 20. Cat./Class.; 21. Chld. srvs.; 22. Circ.; 23. Cons./Pres.; 24. Consult.; 25. Cont. ed.; 26. Educ. lib. sci.; 27. Ext. srvs.; 28. Fund/Grants; 29. Gvt. pubs.; 30. Indx./Abs.; 31. Instr. lib. use; 32. Media srvs.; 33. Micro.; 34. Netwks./Coop.; 35. Persnl.; 36. PR; 37. Publshg.; 38. Recs. mgt.; 39. Ref. srvs.; 40. Repro.; 41. Resrch.; 42. Review.; 43. Secur.; 44. Serials; 45. Spec. col.; 46. Tech. srvs.; 47. Trustees/Bds.; 48. YA srvs.; 49. (other).

Special Collections, Washington University Libraries, St. Louis, MO 63130.

Murray, William A. (Bill) (Je. 29, 1927, Woodhaven, NY) Dir., Media Srvs., Aurora (CO) Pub. Schs., 1976–, Asst. Dir., AV/Info. Srv., 1970–75, Dir. Pub. Info. and Pubn., 1966–70, Dir. Info. Srvs./AV, 1958–66. **Educ.:** CO Coll., 1947–50, AB (Pol. Sci.), 1964, MA (Pol. Sci.); Univ. of Denver, 1972, Type B Spec., 1974, Type D Admin. **Orgs.:** ALA: ALTA, Legis. Com. (1978–); ASCLA Rep. to Frdm. to Read Fndn. (1981–83). CO Lib. Trustees: Ch. (1977). Ctrl. CO Lib. Syst. Bd.: Treas. (1967–70), Pres. (1977). EFLA: Bd. (1976–81) Pres., (1980–81); Secy. (1979). Other orgs. Phi Delta Kappa: Univ. of Denver Chap., Bd. (1973–79, 1981); Ed. (1973–76, 1981); Pres. (1979); Del. (1980). **Honors:** JACS, Volun. Srv. Awd., 1970; Camp Fire, Srv. Awd., 1974; DU Chap., Phi Delta Kappa, Srv. to Educ., 1976; U.S. Dept. of Labor, Youth Empl. Prog., Sum. Excel. Awd., 1979. **Pubns.:** Ed., *Union List of Periodicals* (1977); ed., *Media Curriculum for Teachers and Media Specialists* (1979–80); "Intellectual Freedom," *CO Trustees Handbook* (1980). **Activities:** 10; 17, 24, 32; 63, 67, 74 **Addr.:** Aurora Public Schools, Media-Peoria Center, 875 Peoria St., Aurora, CO 80011.

Murray-Lachapelle, Rosemary F. (F. 11, 1947, Ottawa, ON) Docum. Anal., Lib. of Parliament, 1978–; Asst. Prof., Inst. for Intl. Coop., Univ. of Ottawa, 1975–78; Asst. Libn., Royal ON Musm., 1971–73. **Educ.:** Univ. of Toronto, 1963–67, BA (Hons.) (Near Eastern Std.), 1968–70, MLS; Univ. de Strasburg, France, 1975, Dipl.; Goethe Inst., West Germany, 1974. **Orgs.:** Can. LA: Intl. Rel. Com. (1975–76). ASTED: Com. des rel. intl. (1978–81). Can. Assn. of Spec. Libs. and Info. Sci.: Cont. Educ. Ch. (1976–79). SLA. Socty. for Intl. Dev.: NS RT (1977–79). **Pubns.:** *Rural development in the third world; selective bibliography.* (1977); *Scientific and technical innovation;* self-reliance and cooperation: a selective bibliography. (1976); "Coopération canadienne avec l'Afrique francophone dans le domaine: de bibliothèque et documentation," *In Documentation et bibliothèques* (Vol. 25, No. 2). **Activities:** 12; 17, 29, 41, 46; 54, 56, 92 **Addr.:** Library of Parliament, Ottawa, ON Canada.

Musmann, Klaus (Je. 27, 1935, Magdeburg, Germany) Head Acq. Libn., Los Angeles Cnty. Law Lib., 1968–; Asst. Order Libn., San Luis Obispo, 1967–68; Asst. Serials Lib., Biblgphr., MI State Univ., 1965–67; Libn. II, Detroit Pub. Lib., 1962–65. **Educ.:** Wayne State Univ., 1959–62, BA (Geo.); Univ. of MI, 1962–63, MALS; Univ. of South CA, 1975–81, PhD. **Orgs.:** ALA. AALL. Amer. Assn. of Tchrs. of Germn. Amer. Transl. Assn. **Pubns.:** "Will There Be a Role for Librarians and Libraries in the Post-Industrial Society?" *Libri* (S. 1978); "The Southern California Experience with OCLC and BALLOTS," *CA Libn.* (Ap. 1978); "Socio-technical Systems Theory and Job Design in Libraries," *Coll. and Resrch. Libs.* (Ja. 1978); jt. auth., "Internship: A University of California and Los Angeles County Law Library Joint Venture," *Law Lib. Jnl.* (Ag. 1974); "Acquisitions: Some Functions and Problems," *Law Lib. Jnl.* (F. 1970). **Activities:** 4, 12; 15, 17, 26; 77 **Addr.:** Los Angeles County Law Library, 301 West First St., Los Angeles, CA 90012.

Musser, Necia A. (N. 25, 1928, Grand Rapids, MI) Head, Acq. and Col. Devel., West. MI Univ., 1968–, Catlgr., 1962–67; Catlgr., MI Tech. Univ., 1961–62; Ref. Libn., Univ. of MI, 1953–61. **Educ.:** Univ. of MI, 1948–50, BA (Hist.), 1951–52, MA (Hist.), 1952–53, MALS, 1964–67, PhD (LS). **Orgs.:** ALA. AAUP. **Honors:** Phi Beta Kappa, 1950. **Activities:** 1; 15, 18, 46 **Addr.:** D. B. Waldo Library, Western Michigan University, Kalamazoo, MI 49008.

Muth, Tom J. (N. 6, 1942, Lyons, KS) Asst. Libn., Topeka Pub. Lib., 1973–, Head, Adult Srvs. Dept., 1969–73, Reader's Adv., Adult Srvs. Dept., 1967–69. **Educ.:** KS State Tchrs. Coll., 1962–65, BA (Soc. Sci.), 1967–68, MLS. **Orgs.:** ALA: RASD/Hist. Sect. (Vice-Ch., Ch.-Elect, 1980–82), Lcl. Hist. Com. (1975–79; Ch., 1978–79); Geneal. Com. (1972–75; Ch., 1973–74), Nom. Com. (1972). KS LA: Int. Frdm. Com. (1968–; Ch. 1971–77); Nom. Com. (Ch., 1977–78). **Activities:** 9; 17, 23, 45; 69, 74, 73 **Addr.:** Topeka Public Library, 1515 W. 10, Topeka, KS 66604.

Mycue, David John (O. 4, 1935, Niagara Falls, NY) Sr. Archvst., IL State Arch., 1976–; Hist. Instr., Univ. of IL, 1972–75; Histn., U.S. Air Frc., 1968–71; HS Tchr., San Antonio, 1967–68. **Educ.:** N. TX State Univ., 1962–64, BA (Hist.); Univ. of IL, 1971–73, MA (Hist.), 1975–76, MS (LS); U.S. Army Secur. Agency, 1958–59, Dip. (Electronics). **Orgs.:** SAA: Intl. Arch. (1978–). ALA. Assn. of Gvt. Hstns. and Arch.: Secy. (1969–71). Amer. Hist. Assn. **Honors:** Scarecrow Press Jury, Best of Lib. Lit. Awd., 1978; Beta Phi Mu, 1977; Univ. of IL Sch. of LS, Donald G. Wing Awd., 1976. **Pubns.:** Jt. auth., *Descriptive Inventory of the Illinois State Archives* (1978); "Information Retrieval in Archives," *Annals of Schol.* (1980); "Archival Scholarship," *GA Arch.* (1980); "Founder of the Vatican Library: Nicholas Von Sixtus IV?" *Jnl. of Lib. Hist.* (Win. 1980); "Walker Papers Ready for Researchers," *For the Record: IL State Arch.* (Sum. 1973); various articles. **Activities:** 2, 4; 17, 37, 41; 55, 56, 75 **Addr.:** 1110 S. Walnut, Springfield, IL 62704.

Myers, Carolyn Wade (N. 29, 1942, Bristol, VA) Serials Libn., James Madison Univ., 1979–; Serials Libn. (Dept. Head), VA Cmwlth. Univ., 1970–77; Serials Libn. (Dept. Head), Univ. of AL, Huntsville, 1968–69; Circ. Head, Undergrad. Lib., Univ. of FL, 1967–68. **Educ.:** Univ. of FL, 1964–66, AB (Eng.); Peabody Grad. Lib. Sch., 1966–67, MLS. **Orgs.:** ALA. VA LA. AAUP: Vice-Ch. (1980–81), Ch. (1981–82). Lib. Fac. Sen. (1981–82). **Activities:** 1; 15, 17, 44; 56, 74, 75 **Addr.:** Serials Unit, Madison Memorial Library, James Madison University, Harrisonburg, VA 22807.

Myers, Charles John (N. 5, 1949, Philadelphia, PA) Ref./Col. Dev. Libn. for Engin., Rice Univ., 1979–; Ref. Libn., Univ. of MO (Rolla), 1978–79. **Educ.:** Trenton State Coll., 1968–72, BA (Eng.); East. MI Univ., 1972–74, MA (Eng.); Rutgers Univ., 1976–77, MLS. **Orgs.:** SLA: TX Chap., Local Plng. Com. **Pubns.:** Various reviews. **Activities:** 1; 15, 31, 39; 64, 65, 91 **Addr.:** Fondren Library, Rice University, Houston, TX 77001.

Myers, Elizabeth L. (S. 20, 1923, Evanston, IL) Head, Govt. Docum. Dept., Univ. of CA, Berkeley, 1979–; Deputy Chief, Tech. Srvs. Div., Nat. Lib. of Med., 1979, Head, Serial Rec. Sect., 1975–79; Asst. Dir. for Pub. Srvs., Ctrl. MI Univ., 1972–75; Head, Serial Rec. Dept., SUNY, Buffalo, 1970–72; Head, Ridge Lea Lib., 1968–70; Asst. Libn. in Circ. and Per., 1967–68. **Educ.:** Northwestern Univ., 1942–45, BS (Hist.); Univ. of WI, 1945–47, MA (Hist.); SUNY Coll. of NY, Geneseo and Buffalo, 1965–68, MLS. **Orgs.:** ALA. Med. LA: Vital Notes on Med. Per. Com. (1975–79); SLA. Ctrl. MI Univ.: Fac. Senate Com. on Comm. (1973–75); Admin. & Prof. Cncl. Salary & Fringe Benefits Comm. (1973–75). AAUP. **Activities:** 1, 4; 17, 29, 44; 56, 78, 92 **Addr.:** 109 Holly Oak Ln., Alameda, CA 94501.

Myers, Elizabeth M. (D. 5, 1926, Binghamton, NY) Ref. Law Libn., Temple Univ. Law Lib., 1980, Asst. Circ.–Ref. Libn., 1978–80. **Educ.:** Swarthmore Coll., 1944–48, AB (Pol. Sci.); Drexel Univ., 1976–77, MLS; Villanova Univ., 1973–76, JD. **Orgs.:** AALL. Grt. Philadelphia Law LA: Bd. Mem.–at–Large (1979–80); Legal Resrch. Com. (1978–). Amer. Bar Assn. PA Bar Assn. **Honors:** Beta Phi Mu, 1978. **Activities:** 1; 22, 31, 39; 56, 77, 78 **Addr.:** 90 Yale Ave., Swarthmore, PA 19081.

Myers, Frances Irene (D. 21, 1942, Plainfield, NJ) Prin. Libn., Trenton Free Pub. Lib., 1971–; Serials Catlgr., Princeton Univ., 1968–71; Chld. Libn., Summit Pub. Lib., 1966–68. **Educ.:** Univ. of PA, 1961–65, BA (Hist.); Rutgers Univ., 1965–66, MLS. **Orgs.:** Frnds. of the Cadwalader Branch Lib. Trenton Leag. of Women Voters. Natl. Org. for Women. Cadwalader Branch Lib. Adult Bk. Discuss. Club. **Honors:** Citizens of West. Trenton, Spec. Srv. Plaque, 1977; Women of Trenton, Top Lady of Distinction, 1980. **Pubns.:** "May The Stars Shine Upon Your Face, Veronica," *Trentonian* (D. 24, 1978). **Addr.:** Trenton Free Public Library, 120 Academy St., Trenton, NJ 08608.

Myers, Joe I. (Mr. 10, 1922, Edmond, OK) Dir. of Lib., Stetson Univ., 1974–; Dir. of Lib., Harcum Jr. Coll., 1972–74; Dir. Admis., Park Coll., 1965–71. **Educ.:** OK Univ., 1943–47, BA (Psych); Emporia State Univ., 1971–72, MLS; George Peabody Coll., 1950–52, MA (Educ. Admin.). **Orgs.:** S.E. LA. FL LA. Volusia Cnty. LA: Treas. Deland Pub. Lib.: Pres. (1979–80). Assoc. Mid- FL Coll.: Bd. of Dir., Libs. (1974–80). **Pubns.:** "Building a "Career Corner" in the Library," *Lib. Scene* (Mr. 1975). **Activities:** 1; 17, 35, 39 **Addr.:** DuPont-Ball Library, Stetson University, 421 N. Woodland, DeLand, FL 32720.

Myers, Judith Darlene (D. 18, 1944, Somerset, PA) Mgr., Comp. Info. Ctr., Univ. of WA, 1970–. **Educ.:** Univ. of CA, Riverside, 1965–69, AB (Eng.); Univ. of WA, 1969–70, MLibr (Libnshp.). **Orgs.:** Medial LA. SLA. ASIS: Natl. Mem. Com. (1975); Awds. Com. (1979); Chap. of the Yr. (1979); Leadership Dev. (1979–81); Nom. Com. (1979); Pac. NW Chap. (Nsltr. Ed., 1973–75). Univ. of CA, Los Angeles, Comp. Sci. Alum. Assn. Socty. for Info. Display. Inst. of Electrical and Electronics Engins. **Honors:** ASIS, Elaine D. Kaskela Awd. for Best Chap. or SIG Nsltr., 1973, 1975; ASIS, Awd. for Best Chap. or SIG Pubn., 1974; ASIS Chap. of the Yr. Awd., 1978. **Pubns.:** *Computer Science Resources: A Guide to Professional Literature* (1981); *Developing a Computer Science Collection* (Spr.–Sum. 1980); "How Can Educators Become Computer Literates?" *The Comp. Tchr.* (1980–81); "Computing Information Center," *Short Circuits* (1979). **Activities:** 1, 12; 15, 17, 30; 56, 93 **Addr.:** 8025 Earl Ave. N.W., Seattle, WA 98117.

Myers, Judith E. (Jl. 29, 1940, Baton Rouge, LA) Head, Docum. Dept., Univ. of Houston, 1973–, Head, Serials Dept., 1969–73. **Educ.:** LA State Univ., 1958–62, BS (Art, Fr.), 1969, MLS. **Orgs.:** ALA: GODORT, Fed. Docum. Task Force, Secy. (1976–78); Asst. Coord. (1978–79). TX LA: Ch., Docum. RT (1976–77). SLA. TX Assn. of Coll. Tchrs. **Pubns.:** "Designing an open-stack library for user success", in *Sign Systems for libraries, solving the wayfinding problem,* (1979); "A Subject fund accounting system for serials", *Serials Libn.* (Sum. 1979); "Government documents in the library card catalog: the iceberg surfaces", *Gvt. Pubns. Review,* (Fall 1978). **Activities:** 1; 29, 39, 40; 56; 75, 78 **Addr.:** Documents Department, University of Houston Library, Houston, TX 77004.

Myers, Judith L. (Ag. 15, 1929, New York, NY) Asst. Dir., New York Med. Coll., 1979–, Head Libn., L.M. Hetrick Lib., 1972–79, Ref. Libn., 1966–72. **Educ.:** Univ. of Richmond, 1946–50, BA (Pol. Sci.); Columbia Univ., 1966, MS (LS). **Orgs.:** Med. LA. NY Reg. Grp./Med. LA. **Activities:** 1, 12; 15, 17, 20; 80 **Addr.:** 47-30 61st St., Woodside, NY 11377.

Myers, Kurtz (F. 16, 1913, Columbus Grove, OH) Retired; Consult., Polley Msc. Lib., Lincoln City Libs., 1980–81; Head, Arts and Recreation Dept., Denver Pub. Lib., 1971–76; Head, Msc. Dept., Buffalo and Erie Cnty. Lib., 1969–71 Chief, Msc. and Performing Arts Dept., Detroit Pub. Lib., 1954–69, Chief, AV Dept., 1946–54; In charge, S. Pac. Lib. Bk. Supply, Espiritu Santo, New Hebrides, 1943–45; Lib. Asst., Detroit Pub. Lib., 1936–43; Lib. Asst., Thea. Col., New York Pub. Lib., 1937–39 (Sums.). **Educ.:** Hillsdale Coll., 1930–34, BA (Eng. Lit.); Univ. of MI, 1934–36, MA (Eng. Lit.), 1935–36, ABLS. **Orgs.:** ALA. Msc. LA: VP (1957–59); Bd. (1973–75). Thea. LA. Intl. Assn. of Msc. Libs. Assn. for Recorded Snd. Cols. Intl. Assn. of Snd. Arch. **Honors:** Msc. LA, Notes 33 1/3 Awd., 1981, Cit. for Disting. Srv., 1970; Detroit Chamber Msc. Socty., Awd. for Dedicated Srv., 1969; MI Arts Cncl., Cit., 1969; Detroit Common Cncl., 1969; Various other hons., 1958–69. **Pubns.:** *Index to Record Reviews* (1978–80); "Index to Record Reviews," (Qtly.) *Msc. LA Notes* (1948–); "The Public Library and the Musical Community," *Fontes Artis Musicae* (Jl.–D. 1969); "Man Who Played the Palace: The Professional Library of Will Aubry," *Among Frnds.* (Win. 1963–64); Jt. auth., "Building a Nonspecialized Collection," *Lib. Trends* (Ja. 1975); Various articles and reviews. **Activities:** 9; 30; 55, 67 **Addr.:** 789 Clarkson, Apt. 1101, Denver, CO 80218.

Myers, Marcia J. (Je. 6, 1941, Corry, PA) Assoc. Dir. of Libs. for Admin. Srvs., Univ. of TN, 1981–; Ch., Lib. Prog. Dept., Miami-Dade Comnty. Coll., 1977–81, Asst. Libn., 1967–75; Head, Circ. and Readers' Adv., Warren LA, 1964–67. **Educ.:** Thiel Coll., 1962–63, AB (Econ.); Univ. of Pittsburgh, 1963–64, MLS; FL State Univ., 1975–79, PhD (Lib. Sci.). **Orgs.:** ALA: ACRL; JMRT; LAMA; RASD. FL LA: ACRL Chap. Nom. Com. (1978–79); Prog. Com. for Mini-Conf. on Lib. Instr. (Spr. 1976); Local Arrange. Reg. Com. (1968); Plng. Com. and Prog. mod., Conf. on On-Line Srch. (My. 1979); Ref. Caucus (Ch. 1978–79). Southeastern LA: Univ. and Coll. Lib. Sect. Prog. Com., Ch. (1981–82). So. FL On-Line Srchr., Edit. Com. 1980–); various other Orgs. **Honors:** Beta Phi Mu, 1964. **Pubns.:** "The Accuracy of Telephone Reference Services in the Southeast," *Lib. Effect.* (1980); Jt. auth., "The Use of an On-Line Bibliographic Search Service in Chemistry," *Spec. Libs.* (My./Je. 1980); "The Guidelines and Performance in Academic Libraries," in *Is Reference Progressing?* (1979); *Lib. Resrcs. in Greater Miami* (1977). **Activities:** 1; 17, 22, 39; 63, 92 **Addr.:** University of Tennessee Library, 1401 Cumberland Ave., Knoxville, TN 37916.

Myers, Margaret (Ag. 9, 1933, Rockford, IL) Dir., Ofc. for Lib. Persnl. Resrcs., ALA, 1974–; Exec. Secy., Lib. Educ. Div., 1974–78; Assoc. Prof., Place. Dir., Rutgers Grad. Sch. of Lib. and Info. Std., 1970–74; Instr., 1969–70. **Educ.:** Augustana Coll., 1951–55, BA (Psy.); Univ. of IL, 1956–58, MSW (Soc. Work); Rutgers Univ., 1967–69, MLS. **Orgs.:** ALA: Ofc. for Lib. Persnl. Resrcs. Adv. Com. (1973–74). AALS. CLENE: Bd. of Dirs. (1975–77, 1979–); Cncl. on Qual. Cont. Ed. (1979–81); ALA Rep. (1976–). NJ LA. Amer. Socty. for Trng. and Dev. Amer. Socty. for Persnl. Admin. Natl. Com. on Pay Equity. **Honors:** Rutgers Grad. Sch. of Lib. and Info. Std., Alum. Assn., Disting. Srv. Awd., 1979. **Pubns.:** Jt. Ed., *Women in Librarianship: Melvil's Rib Symposium* (1975); Jt. Auth., "The American Library Association and Affirmative Action," *Affirmative Action and Libraries* (forthcoming); "Staffing Patterns in Libraries," *Personnel Administration in Libraries* (1981); "Employee Selection Practices," *Library Management Without Bias* (1980); Jt. Auth., "Affirmative Action and American Librarianship," *Advances in Librarianship* (1978); various articles. **Activities:** 3; 25, 26, 35 **Addr.:** American Library Association, 50 E. Huron, Chicago, IL 60611.

Myers, Milner Howard, Jr. (Je. 16, 1941, Hattiesburg, MS) Dir., Instr. Resrc. Prog., Sch. of Nursing, Libn. III, Univ. of South. MS, 1976–, Asst. Dir. for Inst. Dev., 1975–77, Lrng. Ctr. Coord., Sch. of Nursing, 1975–76; Asst. Media Dir., Hinds Jr. Coll., 1974–75; Sci. and Tech. Libn., Univ. of South. MS, 1970–74. **Educ.:** Univ. of South. MS, 1969–70, BS (LS), 1970–72, MS (LS), 1974–77, EdS (Educ. Media & Tech.); Univ. of MS, 1977–, EdD in progress (Higher Educ.). **Orgs.:** MS LA: Exhibits Ch., Awds. Com., Coll. and Univ. Sect., Vice-Ch. ALA. Med. LA. SELA. AECT: Med. & Hlth. Sci. Liaison Comm. MS Assn. of Media Educ. **Pubns.:** Slide/tape and videotape orientation progs. **Activities:** 17, 28, 41; 61, 63, 80 **Addr.:** Southern Station, Box 8248, Hattiesburg, MS 39401.

Myers, Patricia H. (Jl. 9, 1933, Chicago, IL) Libn. I, San Mateo Cnty. Pub. Lib., 1979–; Libn. I, San Jose Pub. Lib., 1980–81; Libn. I, Sunnyvale Pub. Lib., 1978; Ed., *Blacksburg Sun,* 1966–67. **Educ.:** Goucher Coll., 1952–55, BA (Eng.); San Jose State Univ., 1976–77, MLS. **Orgs.:** ALA. CA LA: Tech. Srvs. Chap. **Pubns.:** Bk. Reviews. **Activities:** 9; 20, 42, 46; 55 **Addr.:** 17475 Skyline Blvd., Los Gatos, CA 95030.

Special Subjects/Services: 50. Adult educ.; 51. Advert./Mktg.; 52. Aerosp.; 53. Agric.; 54. Area std.; 55. Arts/Hum.; 56. Autom.; 57. Bibl./Prtg.; 58. Bio. sci.; 59. Bus./Fin.; 60. Chem.; 61. Copyrt.; 62. Documtn.; 63. Educ.; 64. Engin.; 65. Env.; 66. Eth. grps.; 67. Film; 68. Food/Nutr.; 69. Geneal.; 70. Geo.; 71. Geol.; 72. Handcpd.; 73. Hist.; 74. Int. frdm.; 75. Info. sci.; 76. Insr.; 77. Law; 78. Legis.; 79. Math./Comp. sci.; 80. Med.; 81. Metals; 82. Nat. resrcs.; 83. Newsp.; 84. Nuc. sci.; 85. Oral hist.; 86. Petr./Energy; 87. Pharm.; 88. Phys./Astr./Math.; 89. Readg.; 90. Relig.; 91. Sci./Tech.; 92. Soc. sci.; 93. Telecom.; 94. Transp.; 95. (other).

Who's Who in Library and Information Services

Myers, Paul H. (Mr. 5, 1917, New York, NY) Cur., Billy Rose Theatre Coll., NY Pub. Lib., 1967–. **Educ.:** NY Univ., 1934–38, BFA (Thea.); Pratt Inst., 1954–60, MLS. **Orgs.:** The Players, NY: Lib. Com. Theatre LA. Nat. Thea. Conf.: Secy. Amer. Socty. for Thea. Resrch.: New Drama Forum. **Pubns.:** Jt. auth., *A Guide To Theatre Reading* (1949); Ed., *Theatre Colleges in Libraries and Museums* (1960); reviewer, *Library Journal*. **Activities:** 41, 42; 55 **Addr.:** Billy Rose Theatre Collection, 111 Amsterdam Ave., New York, NY 10023.

Myers, Rose E. (D., 16, 1928, Oakland, CA) Dir., W. Oahu Coll. Lib., 1976–: Autom. Spec., Univ. of HI Lib., 1972–76, Head, Acq., 1970–72. **Educ.:** Univ. of WA, 1960–64, BA (Art Hist.); Univ. of HI, 1964–66, MLS. **Orgs.:** HI LA: Secy. (1968). ALA: Cncl. (1973–77). Phi Kappa Phi. **Honors:** Beta Phi Mu. **Pubns.:** "Library Self Evaluation," *Measuring the Quality of Library Service* (1975); "Availability of Census Data in Hawaii," *HLA Jnl.* (D. 1971); "The Use of Library of Congress Proof Slips for Current Imprint Book Selection," *HLA Jnl.* (D. 1969). **Activities:** 1; 46 **Addr.:** West Oahu College Library, 96-045 Ala Ike, Pearl City, HI 96782.

Mylin, Dorothy J. (My. 23, 1916, Graceville, MN) Libn., Med. Scis., Fitzsimons Army Med. Ctr., 1969–. **Educ.:** Univ. of North. IA, 1933–37, BA (Liberal Arts); Univ. of Denver, 1968–70, MLS. **Orgs.:** Med. LA. CO Cncl. of Med. Libns.: Secy. (1980–81). Milit. Med. Libns. Midcontl. Reg. Med. Lib. Grp. **Activities:** 4, 12; 15, 20, 39; 80 **Addr.:** Medical Technical Library, Fitzsimons Army Medical Center, Aurora, CO 80045.

Myong, Jae Hwi (Korea) Head, Cat. Dept., Biomed. Lib., Univ. of CA, Irvine, 1969–; Cat. Libn., NY Acad. of Med. Lib., 1967–69; Asst. Prof., Dept. of Lib. Sci., Yonsei Univ., Seoul, Korea, 1961–65. **Educ.:** George Peabody Coll., 1961, BA; Columbia Univ., 1965–67, MS. **Orgs.:** Med. LA. **Activities:** 1; 20 **Addr.:** 5841 Hacienda Dr., Huntington Beach, CA 92647.

N

Naber, Faith (S. 27, 1920, Miltonvale, KS) Media Spec., H.H. Conrady Jr. HS, 1971–; Head Libn., Bluffton-Richland Pub. Lib., 1970–71; Sch. Libn., Middletown HS, 1967–70; Sch. Libn., Wayne Sch., 1965–67. **Educ.:** Kendall Coll., 1939–42, AA; Otterbein Coll., 1942–44, AB (Eng.); Ball State Univ., 1963–70, MLS. **Orgs.:** ALA. Sch. OH LA: Legis. Com. (1969–71). AAUW: Legis. Com. (1966–69, 1974–76). Leag. of Women Voters. Natl. Org. of Women. **Pubns.:** *MABIDBIDKU* (1954); *AAPO NA PUNLIYAKAN* (1954); "A Library Happening," *OH Sch. Lib. Jnl.* (O. 1970). **Activities:** 9, 10; 17, 32, 39; 57, 89, 95-Storytel. **Addr.:** 14924 Riverside Dr., Harvey, IL 60426.

Nabors, Eugene (Ag. 29, 1931, Talladega, AL) Ref. Spec., Law Lib., Lib. of Congs., 1976–, Tech. Info. Spec., 1971–73, Ref. Libn. 1967–71. **Educ.:** Howard Univ., 1954–57, (Soclgy.); Univ. of DC, 1974–76, MLS; Cert. Law Libn., 1976. **Orgs.:** Law Libns. Socty. of DC: Secty., (1969); Bd. of Dirs. (1971). AALL: Gvt. Docum. (1972, 1974–75). Educ. Fndn. of Micronesia: Bd. of Dirs. (1971–). Boy Scouts of Amer.: Pack Leader, Inst. Rep. **Pubns.:** "The Environment, Race Relations, and Poverty," *Gvt. Pubn. Review* (1976); "Legal History and Government Documents–Another Step in Legal Research," *Gvt. Pubn. Review* (1976); "Legal Bibliography of Current Social Problems," *Law Lib. Jnl.* (1971). **Activities:** 4; 20, 23, 24; 78 **Addr.:** 6413 9th St. N.W., Washington, DC 20012.

Nadeau, Johan (N. 23, 1951, Quebec, PQ) Admin. Delegue, Bib. Ctrl. de Pret de la Cote N., 1980–; Bibtcr. en Chef, Bib. Mncpl., Saint-Jean-Sur-Richelieu, PQ, 1979; Adj. a l'Admin. Delegue, Bib. Ctrl. de Pret de l'Outaouais et des Laurentides Inc., 1978–79. **Educ.:** Univ. de Montreal, 1973–76, BSc (Chem.), 1976–78, M Bibl (Bibl.). **Orgs.:** Corp. des Bibtcrs. Prof. du PQ. ASTED. **Honors:** Cnsl. Natl. de Recherches du Can., Bourse En Bibl. et Documtn. Sci., 1977; SLA/East. Can. Chap., Prix Anl. 1978. **Pubns.:** "La Documentation Informatisée," *Eau du PQ* (F. 1978). **Activities:** 9; 15, 17, 20; 60, 65, 91 **Addr.:** 733, Rivière-Aux-Pins, Boucherville, PQ J4B 3A8 Canada.

Nadeau, Léonard (My. 24, 1930, Lac Mégantic, PQ) Dir., Bib. mncpl. de Ste-Thérèse, 1975–; Catlgr., Univ. de Montréal, 1973–75; Chef de dép. Bibliotechnique, Cégep de Rouyn, 1971–73; Chef de dép. Bibliotechnique, Cégep de Jonquière, 1967–71. **Educ.:** Marist Coll., Framingham MA, 1951, BA, 1952–56, MA (Theo.); Cath. Univ., WA, DC, 1963–64, MSLS. **Orgs.:** ASTED. Corp. des bibltcrs. profs. du Québec: (VP., 1977), various coms. **Pubns.:** "Un programme d'accueil," *Bibliovision* (1973). "Problèmes auxquels les bibliotechniciens auront à faire face," *Nouvelles A.C.B.L.F.* (1969). *Votre bibliothèque et ses services* (1967); *Développement des plans et spécifications pour la construction de la bibl* (1966). **Activities:** 9; 17, 35 **Addr.:** 931, carré Valois, Ste-Thérèse, PQ J7E 4L8 Canada.

Nadler, Myra (N. 10, 1945, New York, NY) Assoc. Dir., Long Beach Pub. Lib., 1979–; Dir., Main Lib., Torrance Pub. Lib. (CA), 1977–79; Supvsr., AV Dept., Palos Verdes Lib. Dist. (CA), 1970–77, Asst. Supvsr., Ref. Dept., 1970–70; Branch Libn., 1969–70; Area Ref. Libn., Clifton (NJ) Pub. Lib. 1968–70; Asst. Coord. Adult Srv., Free Pub. Lib. (Woodbridge, NJ), 1966–68. **Educ.:** City University, New York, 1962–66, BA (Eng. lit.); Rutgers Univ., 1966–67, MLS; CA Cnty. Libn. Cert., 1973. **Orgs.:** ALA: PLA, Publshg. Com. (1977–78); Com. Org. (1980–); AV Com. (Ch., 1974–76); Goals, Guidelines, Stan. (1976–80). CA LA: Publshg. Com.; AV Com.; Cncl.; Other com. EF LA. Other orgs. Intl. Toastmasters Assn. Peninsula Symp. Assn.: Bd. of Dir. (1976–78). Long Beach Area Cham. of Cmrce. **Honors:** Beta Phi Mu, 1967. **Pubns.:** *How to Start an Audio Visual Collection* (1978); *Guidelines for Audiovisual Materials and Services for Large Public Libraries* (1975); "Cine Opsis" Column, *Wilson Lib. Bltn.* (1974–75); Asst. Ed. *NJ Lib.* (1966–68); *Recommendations for Audiovisual Materials and Services for Small and Medium-sized Public Libraries* (1975). **Activities:** 9; 17, 28, 35; 56, 74, 78 **Addr.:** Long Beach Public Library, 101 Pacific Ave., Long Beach, CA 90802.

Naeseth, Gerhard Brandt (Ap. 14, 1913, Valley City, ND) Retired, 19–; Assoc. Dir., Univ. of WI Lib., 1948–78; Assoc. Libn., OK State Univ. Lib., 1940–48; Sr. Catlgr., Univ. of MI Law Lib., 1937–40; Jr. Libn., Univ. of MI Lib., 1934–37. **Educ.:** Luther Coll., 1930–34, BA (Hist.); Univ. of MI, 1934–40, BALS, MALS. **Orgs.:** ALA: Cncl. WI LA: Int. Frdm. Com., Ch. State Hist. Socty. of WI. Norwegian-Amer. Hist. Assn. Norwegian-Amer. Musm.: Exec. Com. (1964–). Amer.-Scandinavian Fndn.: Madison Chap., Pres. **Honors:** Norwegian Gvt., Knight's Cross, First Class, Ord. of St. Olav, 1978–; Luth Coll., Disting. Srv. Awd., 1969; Norwegian Gvt., Emigration Fund of 1975 Schol., 1977. **Activities:** 1; 17, 20; 66, 69, 90 **Addr.:** 4909 Sherwood Rd., Madison, WI 53711.

Naftalin, Frances Healy (Mr. 20, 1919, Minneapolis, MN) Pres., Minneapolis Pub. Lib. Bd., 1978–, Mem., 1971–77. **Educ.:** Univ. of MN, 1939, BA (Psy.); Univ. of IA, 1939–40. **Orgs.:** NCLIS: Comsn. (1978–82). MN State Lib. Adv. Comsn.: Mem. (1971–). ALA: PLA; ALTA. **Activities:** 9; 47 **Addr.:** 39 Greenway Gables, Minneapolis, MN 55403.*

Naftalin, Mortimer L. (N. 13, 1921, Fargo, ND) Retired, 1982–; Asst. Law Libn., U.S. Dept. of Agr., Tech. Info. Syst., 1970–82; Hist. Prog. Libn., Natl. Agricultural Lib., 1966–70, Biblgphr., 1964–66, Chief, Agency Field Libs. Sect., 1962–64, Asst., Ofc. of the Dir., 1961–62, Prin. Sel. Ofcr., 1960–61, Sel. Ofcr., 1959–60; Asst. Chief, Resrch. Files, Arch. Div., Intl. Bank for Reconstruction and Dev., 1956–58; various other lib. positions. **Educ.:** Univ. of MN, 1939–46, BA (Fr.), 1946–47, BS (LS), 1947–50, MA (Fr.). **Orgs.:** AALL. DC Law Libns. Socty. **Pubns.:** *Historic Books and Manuscripts Concerning General Agriculture in the Collection of the National Agricultural Library* (1967); *Historic Books and Manuscripts Concerning Horticulture in the Collection of the National Agricultural Library* (1968); *Linneana in the Collection of the National Agricultural Library* (1968). **Activities:** 4; 15, 39; 77 **Addr.:** Apartment 548, 2800 Quebec St. N.W., Washington, DC 20008.

Nagle, Helen M. (Pitcairn, PA) Dir. of Lib., Mt. Aloysius Jr. Coll., 1979–; Catlgr., St. Francis Semy., 1977–79; Lib. Supvsr., IN Cnty., 1975–77; Acq. Libn., St. Francis Coll., 1974–75; Head Libn., Coll. Misericordia, 1963–67. **Educ.:** Coll. Misericordia, BA (Eng.); St. John's Univ., MLS. **Orgs.:** ALA. PA LA. **Honors:** Adult Educ. Assn., Cit., 1972. **Pubns.:** "Pope Paul And the Spirit," *St. Francis Chronicle* (1979). **Activities:** 1; 15, 17, 25; 63, 90 **Addr.:** Mt. Aloysius Junior College, Cresson, PA 16630.

Nagy, Karen N. (S. 15, 1950, Ft. Knox, KY) Asst. Msc. Libn. for Pub. Srvs., Northwestern Univ., 1981–; Msc. Catlgr./Head of Recorded Snd. Srvs., 1980–81, Acq. Asst., Msc. Lib., 1975–80; Reader's Asst./Ref. Libn., Evanston Pub. Lib., 1977–78. **Educ.:** Univ. of IL, 1968–72, BS (Msc. Educ.), BMus (Appld. Flute); Northwestern Univ., 1973–76, MMus (Msclgy.); Rosary Coll., 1976–77, MALS. **Orgs.:** Msc. LA: Midw. Chap. (Secy.-Treas., 1981–83). Intl. Assn. of Msc. Libs. Assn. of Recorded Snd. Arch. Amer. Musicological Socty.: Midw. Chap. **Pubns.:** "The Pleasures of Baroque Music," *Accent Mag.* (Ja.–F. 1978); Reviews, Ed., Necrology Column *Msc. LA Notes* (1977–). **Activities:** 1, 12; 15, 20, 39; 55 **Addr.:** Music Library–Deering 212, University Library, Northwestern University, Evanston, IL 60201.

Nagy, Thomas L. (My. 5, 1948, Hungary) Ref. Ofcr., Natl. Map Col., Pub. Arch. of Can, 1972–. **Educ.:** Carleton Univ., 1967–71, BA, hons. (Pol. Sci.); 1979– (Can. Std.); Arch. Admin. **Orgs.:** Assn. Can. Map Libs.: Pres. (1978–80). Assn. Can. Archvsts. **Pubns.:** *Ottawa in Maps 1825-1973* (1974); "Map Libraries and the Map User," *Assn. of Can. Map Libs. Bltn.* (F. 1975). **Activities:** 2; 36, 39, 41; 70 **Addr.:** National Map Collection, Public Archives of Canada, 395 Wellington St., Ottawa, ON K1A 0N3 Canada.

Nairn, Charles E. (Ag. 26, 1926, Columbus, OH) Ref. and Spec. Cols. Libn., Lake Superior State Coll., 1974–, Assoc. Prof., LS, Phil., Relig., 1974–, Lib. Dir., Assoc. Prof., 1968–74; Head Libn., Findlay Coll., 1964–68; Head Libn., Upper IA Univ., 1960–64; Ref., Branch Libn., Lorain Pub. Lib., 1955–60; Ref. Asst., Cleveland Pub. Lib., 1951–53. **Educ.:** Kent State Univ., 1946–50, BA (Phil., Relig.), 1950–51, MA (LS); Oberlin Coll., 1953–58, BD (Bible); Vanderbilt Univ., 1972, MA (Bible); MI State Univ., 1974– (Adult Educ.). **Orgs.:** Northwest. OH Acad. Libns.: Organizing Mem. (1964–68). N. MI Lib. Srv. Assn.: Organizing Mem. (1970–). Sault Area Intl. LA: Co-Ch. (1968–). ALA. Various other orgs. Natl. Educ. Assn. Amer. Acad. Relig. Flwshp. Relig. Hum. ATLA. **Pubns.:** "Scholarship Begins with SOS at LSSC," *MI Libn.* (Sum. 1976); "'(My) Ethics of Service'–A Statement of Personal Aspects of Librarianship," *Ref. Qtly.* (Spr. 1979); various sps. pubns. in phil., relig. **Activities:** 1, 14-Sem., Phil. of Relig.; 17, 34, 39; 50, 55, 90 **Addr.:** 903 Prospect St., Sault Ste. Marie, MI 49783.

Naismith, Patricia Ann (D. 29, 1948, Centralia, WA) Branch Libn., Free Lib. of Philadelphia, 1979–, Chld. Libn., 1976–79. **Educ.:** Univ. of WA, 1967–71, BA (Hist.); Drexel Univ., 1973–76, MSLS. **Orgs.:** PA LA. ALA: ALSC, Mem. Com. (1979–); JMRT, Booth Com. (1977–78), Mem. Com. (1978–79), Orien. (1980–81), Local Arrange./Soc. (Ch., 1981–82). **Honors:** Pi Lambda Theta. **Activities:** 9; 17, 21; 95-Folklore Chld. Lit. **Addr.:** 753 Marlyn Rd., Philadelphia, PA 19151.

Naiz - González, Pilar (O. 12, 1929, Santurce, PR) Retired, 1981–; Dir., Pub. Srv. Dept., Bayamón Univ. Tech. Coll., Univ. of PR, 1979–; Dir., Ofc. of Attorney Gen. Lib., PR Dept. of Justice, 1970–79; Asst. Libn., Supreme Ct. Lib., PR, 1957–70. **Educ.:** Univ. of PR, 1946–51, BA (Hum.), 1969–71, MLS; AALL, 1968–71, 1976, Insts. **Orgs.:** SBPR: Bd. of Dirs. (1977–80). Mujeres Grad. Univ. de PR. Assn. Exalum. Univ. de PR. **Activities:** 1, 12; 31, 36, 39; 55, 62, 77 **Addr.:** 6 Alameda St., Muñoz Rivera, Guaynabo, PR 00657.

Nalty, James Newsome (Ag. 18, 1919, Beloeil, PQ) Chief, Pub. Srv. Div., Lib. of Parliament, 1973–; Ref. Libn., Carleton Univ., 1968–73; Ref. Libn., Bus. Ref., Toronto Pub. Lib., 1967–68. **Educ.:** Carleton Univ., 1960–65, B. Com (Econ.); Univ. of Toronto, 1966–67, BLS; Univ. of Ottawa, 1969–1973, MLS; Edmonton Normal Sch., 1939–40, (Cert Tchr.). **Orgs.:** Can. LA. **Honors:** Univ. of Toronto Lib. Sch., William L. Graff Mem. Awd., 1967. **Addr.:** 896 Aaron Ave., Ottawa, ON K2A 3P3 Canada.

Narin, Francis (My. 10, 1934, Philadelphia, PA) Pres., Comp. Horizons, Inc., 1968–; Sr. Staff Assoc., IIT Resrch. Inst., 1963–68; Staff Mem., Los Alamos Sci. Lab., 1959–63. **Educ.:** Franklin & Marshall Coll., 1952–55, BS (Chem.); NC State, 1955–57, MS (Nuc. Engin.); Walden Univ., 1981, PhD (Bibl.). **Orgs.:** ASIS. Scientometrics: Ed. Adv. Bd. World Future Socty. **Honors:** AAAS, Fellow. **Pubns.:** *Evaluative Bibliometrics: The Use of Publication and Citation Analysis in the Evaluation of Scientific Activity* (1976); "Objectivity vs. Relevance in Studies of Scientific Advance", *Scientometrics* (1978); "Structure of the Psychological Literature", *Jnl. of the Amer. Socty. for Infor. Sci.* (1979); Jt. Auth., "Structure of the Psychological Literature," *Jnl. of the Amer. Socty. for Info. Sci.* (My. 1979); "Objectivity vs. Relevance in Studies of Scientific Advance," *Scientometrics* (1978). Other pubns. **Activities:** 14-Private Resrch. Co.; 24, 41; 91 **Addr.:** Computer Horizons, Inc., 1050 Kings Highway N., Cherry Hill, NJ 08034.

Nartker, Raymond H. (Ap. 11, 1920, Dayton, OH) Dir., Univ. Lib., Univ. of Dayton, 1962–; Tchr–Libn., St. Joseph HS, Cleveland, OH, 1960–62; Chaminade HS, Mineola, NY, 1952–60; N. Cath. HS, Pittsburgh, PA 1950–52. **Educ.:** Univ. of Dayton, 1939–42, BA (Soc. Std.); Case-West. Rsv. Univ., 1954–55, MSLS; Univ. of IL, Univ. of MD, Lib. Certs. from FL State Univ., Univ. of HI, 1964–70. **Orgs.:** ALA. Acad. LA of OH. Cath. LA: HS Sect., (Ch., 1961–62). Dayton Miami Valley Cnsrtm.: Lib. Dir./Exec. Com. (Ch., 1976–78). **Activities:** 1; 15, 17, 45; 56, 89, 90 **Addr.:** University of Dayton Library, 300 College Park, Dayton, OH 45469.

Nash, Mary Margaret (S. 5, 1947, Amsterdam, The Netherlands) Freelance Info. Spec., 1981–; Mgr., Info. Srvs., I, Bell–North. Resrch., 1979–81; Online Srvs., Transport Can. Lib., 1976–78; Ref. Libn., Can. Inst. for Sci. and Tech. Info., 1973–75. **Educ.:** Univ. of Calgary, 1966–69, BSc (Chem.); Univ. of AB, 1969–70, BLS; Univ. of Wales, 1975–76, MA (LS). **Orgs.:** Can. LA. LA (UK). Can. Micro. Socty. Can. Assn. Info. Sci. Amnesty Intl.: Pubcty. Secy. (1976–80); Grp. Co-ch. (1980–). **Pubns.:** *Books on Demand* (1976); "Justifying an Automated Library System–A Case Study," *ASIS Proceedings* (1980); "Globe and Mail Database," *Online Review* (1979); "Microforms in Libraries," *Micro Notes* (F. 1978); "The Publishers' Dilemma," *Asst. Libn.* (S. 1978); Various articles (1970–77). **Activities:** 4, 12; 17, 37, 39; 60, 91, 93 **Addr.:** 188 Dagmar Ave., Vanier, ON K1L 5T2, Canada.

Nasri, William Z. (Ap. 19, 1925, Tanta, Egypt) Assoc. Prof., Sch. of Lib. and Info. Sci., Univ. of Pittsburgh, 1979–, Asst. Prof., 1974–79, Lectr., 1970–73; Resrch. Assoc., KAS Ctr., Univ. of Pittsburgh, 1965–70. **Educ.:** Univ. of Alexandria, Egypt, 1949–53, BA (Soc. Sci.), 1953–57, JD (Law); Univ. of Pittsburgh, 1964–65, MLS, 1966–67, Adv. Cert. (Lib. Admn.), 1968–75, PhD (LS, Info., Law). **Orgs.:** ALA: Copyrt. Com. (1979), Liaison (1980–). AALS: Mem. Com. (Ch. 1981); Cont. Ed. Com. (1979–80). ASIS. Natl. Assn. of Coll. and Univ. Attorneys. AAUP. **Honors:** Beta Phi Mu, 1965. **Pubns.:** *Crisis in Copyright* (1976); asst. ed., *Encyclopedia of Library and Information*

PROFESSIONAL ACTIVITIES: Institutions: 1. Acad. lib.; 2. Arch.; 3. Assn.; 4. Fed./Gvt. lib.; 5. Inst. lib.; 6. Mfr./Suppl.; 7. Milit. lib.; 8. Musm.; 9. Pub. lib.; 10. Sch. lib.; 11. Sch. of lib. sci.; 12. Spec. lib.; 13. State lib.; 14. (other). **Functions/Activities:** 15. Acq./Col. dev.; 16. Adult srvs.; 17. Admin.; 18. Apprais.; 19. Archit./Bldgs.; 20. Cat./Class.; 21. Chld. srvs.; 22. Circ.; 23. Cons./Pres.; 24. Consult.; 25. Cont. ed.; 26. Educ. lib. sci.; 27. Ext. srvs.; 28. Fund/Grants; 29. Gvt. pubs.; 30. Indx./Abs.; 31. Instr. lib. use; 32. Media srvs.; 33. Micro.; 34. Netwks./Coop.; 35. Persnl.; 36. PR; 37. Publshg.; 38. Recs. mgt.; 39. Ref. srvs.; 40. Repro.; 41. Resrch.; 42. Review.; 43. Secur.; 44. Serials; 45. Spec. col.; 46. Tech. srvs.; 47. Trustees/Bds.; 48. YA srvs.; 49. (other).

Science (1968–); "Malpractice Liability: Myth or Reality," *Jnl. of Lib. Admin.* (1981); "Continuing Education," *Jnl. of Educ. for Libnshp.* (Spr. 1981); "Libraries Beware: The Copyright Five Year Review Is Coming," *PA LA Bltn.* (F. 1980); various other pubns. **Activities:** 11; 24, 25, 26; 61, 75, 77 **Addr.:** 179 Parkedge Rd., Pittsburgh, PA 15220.

Natale, S. Fred (Ag. 17, 1938, Connellsville, PA) Lib. Dir., Mary H. Weir Pub. Lib. (Weirton, WV), 1972–; Asst. Area Branch Libn., Baltimore Cnty. Pub. Lib., 1970–71; Asst. Head Libn., Monessen Pub. Lib., 1965–70. **Educ.:** St. Vincent Coll., 1955–58, (Phil.); St. Mary's Semy. (Baltimore), 1958–59, AB (Phil.), 1959–60, (Theo.); Univ. Pittsburgh, 1964–65, MLS. **Orgs.:** PA LA. WV LA: Legis. Com. (Ch., 1980, 1978–81); 2nd VP (1980–). SELA. ALA. Mid. Atl. Reg. Lib. Fed. Weirton Kiwanis Club: Secy. (1974–78). Frnds. WV North. Cmnty. Coll.: Secy. (1981–). Weirtonian Lodge, Italian Sons and Daughters of Amer. Loyal Ord. of Moose. **Honors:** Weirtonian Lodge ISDA, Srv. Awd., 1978; Beta Phi Mu. **Activities:** 9; 16, 17, 19 **Addr.:** P.O. Box 2191, Weirton, WV 26062.

Natzke, Hannah V. (O. 22, 1943, San Antonio, TX) Head, Ref. Dept., Alum. Meml. Lib., Univ., of Scranton, 1980–; Head, Ref. Dept., Scranton Pub. Lib., 1977–80, Frgn. Trade Libn., 1976–77, Spec. Info. Srvs. Libn., 1973–77; Ref. Libn., Kalamazoo Lib. Syst., 1968–73. **Educ.:** Syracuse Univ., 1962–65, BA (Amer. Lit.); West. MI Univ., 1966–68, MSLS. **Orgs.:** PA LA: Bd. of Trustees (1980–82); Lib. Instr. Com. (1980–81); Arch. Com. (1979–80); NE Chap. (Ch., 1980–81; Vice–Ch.–Ch. Elect, 1979–80); Mem. Com. (Ch., 1981–82); Archvst. (1976–77). ALA: Various coms. (1977–). Beta Phi Mu: Kappa Chap. (VP–Pres. Elect., 1972–73). Frnds. of the Scranton Pub. Lib. YWCA. Grt. Scranton Cham. of Cmrc. **Addr.:** 1720 Adams Ave., Scranton, PA 18509.

Nauman, Ann Keith (Ag. 2, 1931, Greensboro, NC) Assoc. Prof., Southeastern LA Univ., 1976–, Assoc. Prof., St. Joseph Semy. College, 1980–; Consult., Capital Area Readg. Consrtm., 1979–80; Asst. Prof., Southeastern LA Univ., 1976–80; Sch. Libn., E. Baton Rouge Parish Pub. Schs., 1965–76. **Educ.:** LA State Univ. 1961, BA (Span.), 1965, BS (Educ., LS), 1963, MA (Hist., Anthro., Span.), 1969, MS (LS) 1974, PhD (Latin Amer. Hist., LS). **Orgs.:** ALA: AASL. LA LA. LA Assn. of Sch. Libns.: Exec. Bd. (1968–72). AAUP. AAUW. Natl. Assn. of Biling. Educ. Amer. Cncl. of Tchrs. of Frgn. Langs. Latin Amer. Std. Assn. **Honors:** Beta Phi Mu; Phi Sigma Iota; Org. of Amer. States, Santiago de Chile, Fellow, 1974; Southeastern LA Univ., Alum. Tchr. of the Year, 1979. **Pubns.:** "Bilingual Education, SLU; A Model Training Program for Teachers," *Jnl. of the Latin Amer. Std. Inst.,* (1976); "A Handbook for Foreign Students," handbook (1977); "Church and State in Chile," *Church and State* (Ja. 1981). **Activities:** 10, 11; 24, 26, 31; 63, 89 **Addr.:** P.O. Box 659, University Station, Hammond, LA 70402.

Naumer, Janet Noll (My. 26, 1933, Philadelphia, PA) Asst. Prof., Sch. LS, Univ. Denver, 1977–; Libn., Kubasaki HS (Okinawa, Japan), 1974–75; Instr., Coll. Educ., Univ. of NM, 1973–74; Educ. Spec., Inst. of Amer. Indian Arts (Santa Fe, NM), 1969–73. **Educ.:** PA State Univ., 1951–55, BA (Jnlsm.); Univ. of Denver, 1968, MA (LS); Univ. of CO, 1976–78, PhD (Educ.). **Orgs.:** Beta Phi Mu: Phi Chap. (Secy., 1978–79). ALA. CO LA: *CO Lib.* Ed. (1978–). AECT. Intl. Assn. Sch. Libns. **Honors:** Phi Delta Kappa; Theta Sigma Phi, 1954; Phi Delta Kappa, 1977. **Pubns.:** "Native Americans in School Libraries and Media Centers," *Opportunities for Minorities in Librarianship* (1977); "Library Services to American Indians," *Library and Information Services for Special Groups* (1974); jt. ed., "Frequently Cited Materials for Teaching Instructional Development," *Jnl. of Instr. Dev.* (Win. 1980); "American Indians: A Bibliography of Sources," *Amer. Libs.* (O. 1970). **Activities:** 11; 26, 32; 63, 66 **Addr.:** Graduate School of Librarianship and Information Management, Denver, CO 80208.

Navratil-Ciccone, Amy (S. 19, 1950, Detroit, MI) Libn., Chrysler Musm., 1981–; Libn., Norton Simon Musm., 1974–81. **Educ.:** Wayne State Univ., 1968–72, BA (Art Hist.); Univ. of MI, 1972–73, AMLS. **Orgs.:** ARLIS/NA: Mem. Campaign Coord. (1979–); Mem. Ch. (1975–77). **Pubns.:** Bk. review ed., *Umbrella* (1979–80). **Activities:** 12, 14-Mus.; 15, 20, 41; 55 **Addr.:** Chrysler Museum Library, Olney Rd. and Mowbray Arch, Norfolk, VA 23510.

Naylor, Alice P. (Jl. 17, 1928, Madison, WI) Ch., Dept. of Lib. and Media Std., Appalachian State Univ., 1979–, Prof., 1977–; Assoc. Prof., Univ. of Toledo, 1970–77; Deputy Dir., Cuyahoga Cnty. Pub. Lib., 1965–70. **Educ.:** Univ. of WI, 1945–50, BA (Jnlsm.), 1950–51, MA (LS); Univ. of Toledo, 1974–77, PhD (Educ. Admin.). **Pubns.:** *Measuring the Effectiveness of Library Service: A Handbook.* **Activities:** 10, 11; 21, 26, 48; 63, 66, 74 **Addr.:** Appalachian State University, Department of Educational Media, Boone, NC 28608.

Naylor, Lewis C. (Ag. 18, 1914, Osbornes Mills, WV) Pub. Lib. Consult. (1977–); Dir., Toledo-Lucas Cnty. Lib., 1970–77; Dir., Cuyahoga Cnty. Lib., 1955–70; Dir., Muncie Pub. Lib., 1951–55. **Educ.:** Kent State Univ., 1938–46, AB (Soc. Sci.); Case-West. Rsv. Univ., 1946–47, BS/LS. **Orgs.:** OH LA: Pres. (1963–64). ALA: PLA, Pres. (1974–5). OH Coll. Lib. Ctr.: (Bd. of Trustees, 1975–7). Amer. Socty. for Pub. Admin.: Pres., Toledo Chap., (1975). **Honors:** OH Lib. Assn., Libn. of the Year, 1974. **Pubns.:** *To The County Line* (1953); *Alternative Methods of Centralizing Library Services* (1963); various articles. **Activities:** 9, 11; 17, 19, 27; 56, 74, 78 **Addr.:** Rt. 1, Box 36A, Zionville, NC 28697.

Neal, Robert Louis (F. 5, 1926, Stewartstown, PA) Dir., Allegany Cnty. Lib. Syst., 1968–; Exec. Dir., Kingston Area Lib., 1966–68; Various positions in engin. **Educ.:** Gettysburg Coll., 1946–49, AB (Chem.); Drexel Inst. of Tech., 1964–66, MS (LS). **Orgs.:** ALA. MD LA: Legis. Plng. Com. (Ch. 1973); Fed. Rel. Com. (1977–); Pubcty. Com. (1974); Trustees Div. (Consult., 1970). MD Assn. Pub. Lib. Admin.: Secy. (1972); VP (1973); Pres. (1974). West. MD Pub. Lib.: Various coms. Various other orgs. Bd. Cnty. Comsn.: Various coms. **Pubns.:** "Film Cooperatives," *Drexel Lib. Qtly* (Ap. 1966). **Activities:** 9; 17, 24; 64, 78, 91 **Addr.:** Allegany County Library System, 31 Washington St., Cumberland, MD 21502.

Neale, Marilee (D. 30, 1944, Ft. Worth, TX) Head, Ext. Srvs. Dept., Rosenberg Lib., 1971–, Ref. Libn., 1970. **Educ.:** Univ. of KS, 1966, BA (Span., Fr.); N. TX State Univ., 1970–71, MLS. **Orgs.:** TX LA. SW LA. ALA: RASD, Lib. Srvs. to an Aging Popltn. (1977–80); Ch., (1980–1981). Galveston Mayor's Adv. Com. on Sr. Citizens and Handcpd. Persons. Galveston Cnty. Sr. Citizens Proj. Adv. Cncl. Houston-Galveston Area Cncl. Aging Prog. Adv. Com. **Activities:** 9, 16, 24, 27; 72, 92, 95-Aging. **Addr.:** 4610 Ave. Q, Galveston, TX 77550.

Neavill, Gordon B. (Ja. 27, 1945, Cleveland, OH) Asst. Prof., Sch. LS, Univ. of AL, 1978–; Ed. Asst., *Lib. Qtly.,* Univ. of Chicago Press, 1975–77; Lectr., Univ. of Chicago, 1974–77; Peace Corps Libn., Royal Univ. of Malta, 1971–72. **Educ.:** Oberlin Coll., 1962–66, AB (Hist.); Univ. Coll. London, 1966–67 (Hist., LS); Univ. of Chicago, 1967–69, MA (LS), 1973–, PhD (LS). **Orgs.:** ALA. Amer. Prtg. Hist. Assn. Malta LA. **Pubns.:** "The Modern Library Series: Format and Design 1917-1977," *Prtg. Hist.* (1979); "Role of the Publisher in the Dissemination of Knowledge," *Annals of the American Academy of Political and Social Science* (1975); "Victor Gollancz and the Left Book Club," *Lib. Qtly.* (1971). **Activities:** 11; 20, 26, 37; 57 **Addr.:** Graduate School of Library Service, P.O. Box 6242, University of Alabama, University, AL 35486.

Needham, William L. (Ja. 6, 1940, Baltimore, MD) Dir. of Admin., Homes and Land Publshg. Corp., 1979–; Info. Mgt. Consult., 1977–; Mgr., Resrch. and Info. and Assoc. Dir., Missions Advnc. Resrch. and Comm. Ctr., World Vision Intl., 1969–76. **Educ.:** Univ. of MD, 1963, BA honors (Pol. Sci.); FL State Univ., 1976–77, MS (LS). **Honors:** Beta Phi Mu, 1977. **Pubns.:** Jt. auth., *The Current State of Public Library Service to Physically Handicapped Persons* (1980); Jt. auth., *The Effect of On-Line Search Services on Chemists' Information Style* (1979); *Florida State Agency Libraries and Resource Centers in Tallahassee* (1976); Jt. auth., *MARC Data Bank, Parts I & II* (1970); "Vocational Aids Resource File for the Visually Impaired," *Jnl. of Visual Impairment and Blindness* (S. 1979); Various articles in LS and other fields. **Activities:** 6; 17, 24, 37; 72, 75 **Addr.:** P.O. Box 3236, Tallahassee, FL 32303.

Neely, Eugene Trahin (Ag. 20, 1940, Greenwood, MS) Head Libn., John Cotton Dana Lib., Rutgers Univ., Newark, 1980–; Coord. of Pub. Srvs., Univ. of MO, Kansas City, 1974–80; HQ Libn., Untd. Presbyterian Church in the USA 1974; Libn., Pogan Prods., Inc. 1971–74; Head, Ref. and Asst. Head, Pub. Srvs., Pub. Lib. of Charlotte and Mecklenburg Cnty., 1965–69, Ref. Libn., 1964–65. **Educ.:** Davidson Coll., 1958–62, AB (Eng.); Univ. of NC, 1963–64, MS (LS); Columbia Univ., 1969–72, (Cert., Advnc. Libnshp.). **Orgs.:** ALA: LAMA/Stats. Sect., Com. on Stats. for Ref. Srvs. (Ch., 1978–79), Bylaws Com. (Ch., 1978–80), Sect. Ch. (1979–80); ACRL/Bibl. Instr. Sect., Com. on Educ., (1977–78); RASD. SLA; NJ LA. Heart of Amer. Chap. (Secy., 1978–79; Pres. (1980). MO LA: Nom. Com. (Ch., 1979–80). **Pubns.:** *Bibliography on Alcoholic Beverage Control Systems* (1965); "Recent Library Statistical Activities," *The Bowker Anl.* (1980); "The MACRL Meeting," *Show-Me Libs.* (N. 1977). **Activities:** 1; 15, 16, 17; 55, 56, 92 **Addr.:** John Cotton Dana Library, Rutgers University, Newark, NJ 07102.

Neely, Glenda S. (N. 4, 1946, Chattanooga, TN) Assoc. Prof., Ref. Libn., Univ. of Louisville, 1971–; Ext. Instr., Sch. LS, Univ. of KY, 1974–; Instr., Asst. Ref. Libn., VA Cmwlth. Univ., 1970–71; Asst. Archvst., Spec. Cols., Vanderbilt Univ., 1968–69; Reader Srv. Libn., Atlanta Pub. Lib., 1969–70, 1968. **Educ.:** Univ. of GA, 1964–68, BS (Fr.); George Peabody Coll., 1968–70, MLS. **Orgs.:** ALA: ACRL/Bibl. Instr. Sect., Com. Coop. (1978–80); RASD, Cncl. of State and Reg. Grps. (Ch., 1981–82)/SELA: RASS, Secy. (1978–80), Ch. (1980–82), Lib. Orien. Bibl. Instr. Com. (1976–80). KY LA: Educ. RT (Secy., Treas., 1979–80). AAUP: Univ. Louisville Chap. (Secy., 1976–77). **Honors:** Alpha Chi Omega; Beta Phi Mu, 1970. **Pubns.:** "Online Databases: Effects on Reference Acquisitions," *Lib. Acq.: Prac. & Theory* (1981); "We Can't Go on Meeting this Way," *Jnl. of Acad. Libnshp.* (Ja. 1980). **Activities:** 1; 31, 39; 56, 63 **Addr.:** University of Louisville Library, Louisville, KY 40292.

Neenan, Peter A. (D. 12, 1946, Sioux City, IA) Asst. Prof., Simmons Coll. Grad. Sch. of Lib. & Info. Sci., 1978; Visit. Lect., Univ. of WA, 1978; Asst. Prof., North. IL Univ., 1977–78; Tchg. Asst., Lectr., Univ. of WI, 1974–77; Ref., Info. and Ref. Libn., Jackson Metro. Lib. Syst., 1972–74; Asst. Law Libn., Creighton Univ. Sch. of Law, 1972. **Educ.:** Creighton Univ., 1965–69, BA (Theo.); Univ. of IA, 1970–72, MA (LS); Univ. of WI, 1974–, (LS). **Orgs.:** ALA. AALS. MA LA. NELA. **Pubns.:** Jt. Auth., *Citizen Information Seeking Patterns* (1980); "Development of Library Education in the Two Germanies Since 1945," *A Search for New Insights in Librarianship: A Day of Comparative Studies* (1976). **Activities:** 9, 11; 16, 26, 39; 50, 89 **Addr.:** Graduate School of Library and Information Science, Simmons College, 300 The Fenway, Boston, MA 02115.

Neff, Mary Jane (Fowler) (Ag. 16, 1929, Emporia, KS) Soc. Sci., Educ. Libn., Emporia State Univ., 1972–, Asst. Cat. Libn., 1968–72, Sch. Libn., 1966–68, Cnclr. Asst., 1964–66; various other positions as couns., tchr. **Educ.:** Emporia State Univ., 1946–50, BSE (Soc. Sci.), 1959, MSE (Guid.), 1965, EDS (Educ. Guid.), 1966, MS (LS). **Orgs.:** ALA. Mt. Plains LA. KS LA: Coll. and Univ. Sect. Emporia LA: Pres. (1967–68). Beta Phi Mu: Beta Epsilon Chap. (Treas., 1978–81); Schol. Com. (1977–). AAUP. AAUW.: KS Div., Educ. Fndn. Com. (Ch., 1977–81).; Emporia Branch (Pres., 1975–77). **Honors:** Pi Lambda Theta. **Pubns.:** Reviews. **Activities:** 1; 15, 17, 39; 59, 63, 92 **Addr.:** 2020 W. 15th, Emporia, KS 66801.

Neff, William B. (Jl. 25, 1947, Pittsburgh, PA) Ord. Libn., Smithsonian Inst., 1974–; Libn., Queens Boro. Pub. Lib., 1970–74. **Educ.:** IN Univ. of PA, 1965–69, BS (Eng.); Univ. of Pittsburgh, 1969–70, MLS. **Orgs.:** SLA. **Honors:** Beta Phi Mu. **Pubns.:** Ed., *Musm., Arts and Hum. Div. Bltn., SLA* (1978–). **Activities:** 4, 8; 15, 46; 55 **Addr.:** Smithsonian Institution, Library - Acquisitions, Washington, DC 20560.

Neher, Jack (F. 1, 1918, New York, NY) VP, Mental Hlth. Mtrls. Ctr., 1955–; PR Writer, Natl. Assn. for Mental Hlth., 1950–55. **Educ.:** Wagner Coll., 1935–39, BA (Eng. Lit.); Columbia Univ., 1939–40, MA (Eng. Lit.). **Orgs.:** EFLA: Amer. Film Fest. Com. New York Film Cncl.: Bd. Mem. Natl. Com. for Mental Hlth. Educ. **Pubns.:** *The Selective Guide to Audiovisuals for Mental Health and Family Life Education* (1979); "Audiovisual Reviews," *Hosp. and Cmnty. Psyt.* (1956–); Various reviews, film jnls. **Activities:** 2, 12; 24, 32, 42; 50, 67, 95-Mental Hlth. **Addr.:** Mental Health Materials Center, 30 East 29th St., New York, NY 10016.

Neikirk, Harold D. (Mr. 25, 1940, Cleveland, OH) Libn., Acq., Univ. of DE Lib. 1974–; Coord. of Acq., Worcester State Coll., 1973–74, Asst. Prof. of Grmn., 1970–73; Instr., Grmn., Holy Cross Coll., 1967–70. **Educ.:** Rockhurst Coll., 1958–62, AB (Eng.); Univ. of OK, 1962–64, MA (Grmn.); Univ. of WI, 1964–67 (Grmn.); Univ. of RI, 1972–74, MLS. **Orgs.:** DE LA: Nom. Com. (1980). Philadelphia Acq. Info. Netwk. ALA: RTSD, Pre-order and Pre-cat. Discuss. Grp. (Vice–Ch./Ch.–Elect., 1980–82); LAMA; ACRL, DE Valley Chap. **Honors:** Beta Phi Mu, 1974. **Activities:** 1; 15, 46; 54, 55, 95-German & other foreign languages. **Addr.:** Acquisitions Department, University of Delaware Library, Newark, DE 19711.

Neill, Gretchen Haslbauer (N. 2, 1946, Knoxville, TN) Dir. of Lrng. Resrcs., DeKalb Cmnty. Coll., N. Campus, 1979–, Dir. of Lrng. Resrcs., S. Campus, 1972–79, Ref. Libn., Ctrl. Campus, 1971–72; Asst. Libn., Atlanta Pub. Lib., 1969–69. **Educ.:** Univ. of TN, 1963–67, BA (Eng., Sp.); Emory Univ., 1970, MLN (LS), 1976, DASL (Media). **Orgs.:** SELA. GA LA. NC Lrng. Resrcs. Assn. **Activities:** 1; 17, 32, 36 **Addr.:** DeKalb Community College - North Campus, 2101 Womack Rd., Dunwoody, GA 30338.

Neill, S.D. (My. 17, 1928, Port Arthur, ON) Prof., Sch. of Lib. and Info. Sci., Univ. of West. ON, 1967–; Libn., Thornlea Sec. Sch., 1966–67; Libn., Kirkland Lake Pub. Lib., 1956–62; Branch Supvsr., Cape Breton Reg. Lib., 1954–56. **Educ.:** Univ. of Toronto, 1946–50, BA (Hist.), 1951, BLS, 1968–70, MEd (Educ.). **Orgs.:** ON LA. Can. LA. **Pubns.:** *Canadian Libraries in 2010* (1980); "Annual Review of Canadian Libraries," *Jnl. of the Can. LS Socty.* (1980–). **Activities:** 9; 21, 39 **Addr.:** School of Library and Information Science, University of Western Ontario, London, ON N6G 1H1 Canada.

Nekritz, Leah K. (Ap. 6, 1932, New York, NY) Assoc. Dean, Lrng. Resrcs., Prince George's Cmnty. Coll., 1977–, Dir., Lrng. Resrcs., 1971–77, Dir., Lib. Srvs., 1967–71, Libn., 1962–67. **Educ.:** Brooklyn Coll., 1949–53, AB (Eng.); Cath. Univ. of Amer., 1960–63, MS (LS), 1969, (Educ. Tech.). **Orgs.:** ALA: ACRL/Quantitative Stan. for 2 year colls. (1975–78); Cmnty. and Jr. Coll. Libs. Sect. (Secy., 1974). MD LA Noms. (Ch., 1978). MD State Lib. Resrc. Ctr. Adv. Com. Assn. of Educ. and Comm. Tech.: Coll. and Univ. Plng. (1977–79); Cmnty. Coll. Assn. Instr. Tech. (Treas., 1974). WA Metro. Cncl. of Gvts.: Libns. Tech. Com. (Cmnty. Coll. Rep., 1976–77, 1979–). **Addr.:** Prince George's Community College, 301 Largo Rd., Largo, MD 20870.

Special Subjects/Services: 50. Adult educ.; 51. Advert./Mktg.; 52. Aerosp.; 53. Agric.; 54. Area std.; 55. Arts/Hum.; 56. Autom.; 57. Bibl./Prtg.; 58. Bio. sci.; 59. Bus./Fin.; 60. Chem.; 61. Copyrt.; 62. Documtn.; 63. Educ.; 64. Engin.; 65. Env.; 66. Eth. grps.; 67. Film; 68. Food/Nutr.; 69. Geneal.; 70. Geo.; 71. Geol.; 72. Handcpd.; 73. Hist.; 74. Int. frdm.; 75. Info. sci.; 76. Insr.; 77. Law; 78. Legis.; 79. Math./Comp. sci.; 80. Med.; 81. Metals; 82. Nat. resrcs.; 83. Newsp.; 84. Nuc. sci.; 85. Oral hist.; 86. Petr./Energy; 87. Pharm.; 88. Phys./Astr./Math.; 89. Readg.; 90. Relig.; 91. Sci./Tech.; 92. Soc. sci.; 93. Telecom.; 94. Transp.; 95. (other).

Nelsen, Alice R. (Ap. 14, 1923, Milwaukee, WI) Lib. Media Spec., Bowie HS, 1975–; Lib. Media Spec., Samuel Ogle Jr. HS, 1968–75; Soc. Stds. Tchr., Bowie Sr. HS, 1965–67; Soc. Stds. Tchr., Belair Jr. HS, 1963–65. **Educ.:** Univ. of WI, 1944–45, BS (Educ.), 1947–48, MS (Amer. Frgn. Policy); Univ. of MD, 1967–69, MLS. **Orgs.:** ALA. Educ. Media Assn. of Prince Georges Cnty.: Pres. (1978–79); First VP (1977–78). Intl. Assn. of Sch. Libnshp.: Media Adv. Com. (Soc. Ch., 1980–82). DC LA. **Activities:** 10 **Addr.:** 2404 Belair Dr., Bowie, MD 20715.

Nelson, Abigail (D. 13, 1944, Lynn, MA) Freelnc. Consult., 1980–; Sr. Info. Assoc., The Amer. Film Inst., 1978–80; Film Info. Dir., Univ. Film Std. Ctr., 1974–78; Ref. Spec., Branch Libs., NY Pub. Lib., 1967–73. **Educ.:** Tufts Univ., 1962–66, BA (Eng.); Simmons Coll., 1966–67, MS (LS); various crs. **Orgs.:** The Info. Ctr. For Soc. Issue Media: Natl. Adv. Com. (1978–). ALA. WHCOLIS: Official Observer (1979). **Pubns.:** *Independent Film and Video* (1979); Ed., *Women and Film/Television* (1979); "The Museum of Broadcasting Profile," *The Amer. Film Inst. Educ. Nsltr.* (Ja.–F. 1980); "International Museum of Photography at George Eastman House Profile," *The Amer. Film Inst. Nsltr.* (N.–D. 1979); Ed., *Film and Television Periodicals in English* (1979); various articles, monos. **Activities:** 12; 24, 28, 39; 55, 57, 67 **Addr.:** 812 Boston St., West Lynn, MA 01905.

Nelson, Bonnie R. (D. 31, 1951, New York, NY) Asst. Prof., Lib., John Jay Coll. of Criminal Justice, City Univ. of New York, 1980–; Anthro. Subj. Spec., New York Univ., Bobst Lib., 1978–80, Circ. Libn., 1974–78, Asst. Circ. Libn., 1973–74. **Educ.:** City Coll., City Univ. of New York, 1968–72, BA (Anthro.); Columbia Univ., 1972–73, MS (LS); New York Univ., 1973–76, MA (Anthro.). **Orgs.:** NY LA. ALA: ACRL/Anthro. and Soclgy. Sect. (Mem.–at–Large, 1980–82), Bibl. Com. (1981–). **Honors:** Phi Beta Kappa, 1972; Beta Phi Mu, 1973. **Pubns.:** *A Guide to Published Library Catalogs* (1981); Jt. ed., *Directory of Anthropological Resources in New York City Libraries* (1979); "The Chimera of Professionalism," *Lib. Jnl.* (O. 1, 1980); "Anthropological Research and Printed Library Catalogs," *RQ* (Win. 1979); "Implementation of On-line Circulation at New York University," *Jnl. of Lib. Autom.* (S. 1979). **Activities:** 1; 39, 49-Computerized Biblio. Searching; 56, 92 **Addr.:** Library, John Jay College of Criminal Justice, 445 West 59th St., New York, NY 10019.

Nelson, Carol B. A. (Ag. 24, 1949, Bridgeport, CT) Freelance Libn., 1980–; Tech. Srvs. Libn., NH Coll., 1977–80; Bus. and Mncpl. Libn., Nashua Pub. Lib., 1972–77. **Educ.:** Univ. of NH, 1967–71, BA (Eng.); Simmons Coll., 1973, MS (LS). **Orgs.:** SLA. NH LA: VP (1980–81); Pres. (1981–82). ALA. New Eng. LA. NH LA: Legis. and Int. Frdm. (Ch., 1976–79); Lobbyist, 1981. New Eng. Lib. Bd.: Task Force on Legis. Netwks. (1977–78). NH Mncpl. Assn.: Lib. Subcom. (Ch., 1978–79). Young Men's Christ. Assn. **Honors:** Lib. Pub. Rel. Cncl., Best Coord. Pubcty., 1976; NH Coll., Merit Awd., 1979. **Pubns.:** Indxr., *The Nashua Experience: History in the Making* (1978). **Activities:** 1; 24, 39, 46; 59, 91 **Addr.:** 43 Lyndon St., Concord, NH 03301.

Nelson, Charles E. (Je. 14, 1926, Jacksonville, TX) Media Dir., Reg. One Educ. Srv. Ctr., 1967–; Natl. Sales Mgr., Macmillan Films Inc., 1969–72; South. Reg. Mgr., McGraw Hill Inc., 1967–69; Admin., Round Rock Indep. Sch. Dist., 1960–67. **Educ.:** Rice Univ., 1946–51, BS (Educ., Bus.); Pan Amer. Univ., 1973–75, ME (Admin.). **Orgs.:** AECT: TX Chap. Natl. Assn. of Reg. Media Ctrs.: Mem. Com. (Ch.); Bd. of Dir. Rio Grande Valley Media Assn.: Pres. Phi Delta Kappa. Racquet Club of McAllen (TX). **Activities:** 14-Reg. Media Ctr.; 17, 22, 24; 67, 93 **Addr.:** Region One E.S.C., 1900 Schunion, Edinburg, TX 78539.

Nelson, Helen Martha (D. 20, 1929, Anaconda, MT) Lib. Dir., Oceanside Pub. Lib., 1969–; Librarian (Admin.), U.S. Army, Europe, 1960–68; Tchr. (Eng., Jnlsm.), Anaconda Sr. HS, 1956–59; Libn. and Tchr. (Eng.), Beaverhead Cnty. HS, 1954–56; Libn. and Tchr. (Eng.–Hist.), Laurel HS, 1952–54; Asst. Docum. and Serials Libn., Univ. of MT, 1951–52. **Educ.:** Univ. of MT, 1947–51, BA, hons. (Eng., Hist.); Univ. of WA, 1960, MA (LS); CA Cnty. Libn. Cert., 1969–80. **Orgs.:** CA LA: Cncl. (1978–80); Palomar Chap. (VP, 1978). CA Inst. of Libns.: Bd. (1978–80). Serra Coop. Lib. Syst.: Admin. Cncl. (1969–); Secy. (1971); Ch. (1973–74). ALA. Various other orgs. King of Kings Luth. Church. Oceanside–Carlsbad Branch, Amer. Red Cross. Christ. Sponsors: Ch. (1975). AAUW. **Addr.:** P.O. Box 238, Oceanside, CA 92054.

Nelson, James A. (Je. 13, 1941, Grand Junction, CO) Appointed State Libn. of KY, 1980–; Asst. Prof. of LS, Univ. of WI, 1977–80; Dir. of Cont. Educ., Univ. of KY, 1973–77; Coll. of LS, Staff Asst. to Comsn., KY Dept. Pub. Instr., 1972–73; Dir. of Interlib. Coop., KY Dept. of Libs., KY Dept. Lib., 1970–72; Head Libn., Hardin Cnty. Pub. Lib., 1969–70. **Educ.:** Univ. of CO, 1960–65, BS (Eng.); Univ. of KY, 1968–69, MS (LS). **Orgs.:** ALA: ASCLA, Cont. Educ. Com. (Ch., 1977–79); Mem. Promo. Task Frc. (State Ch., 1975–77); Lib. Educ. Div., Cont. Educ. Com. (Ch., 1976–78). CLENE: Pres. (1979–80). AALS: Cont. Educ. Com. (1976–79). WI LA: Various coms. Increase Lapham Proj. (Cmnty. Educ.): Pres. (1979–80). KY Assn. for Cont. Educ.: VP (1976–78). **Pubns.:** *Recognition for Your Continuing Education Accomplishments* (1979); *Conditions for Development: Continuing Education at Six Accredited Library Schools with Selected Additions Resourse* (1977); ed., *Cont. Educ. in Libnshp. Nsltr.* (1973–77); clmn. ed., "Continuing Education," *Jnl. of Educ. for Libnshp.* (1976–). **Activities:** 13; 17, 25, 34; 50 **Addr.:** Kentucky Department of Library & Archives, P.O. Box 537, Frankfort, KY 40602.

Nelson, James B. (O. 3, 1932, Hankow, Hupei, China) Dir., West. Cnties. Reg. Lib. and Cabell Cnty. Pub. Lib., 1966–; Dir., Cattermole Meml. Lib., 1963–66; Asst. to the Dir., Mayo Clinic Lib., 1962–63; Libn., Hastings (MN) State Hosp., 1959–62; YA Libn., Brooklyn Pub. Lib., 1956. **Educ.:** Univ. of MN, 1950–54, BS (Eng.), 1954–56, MS (LS). **Orgs.:** WV LA: Pres. (1970). ALA: PLA/Pub. Lib. Systs. Sect. (Pres., 1979–80); Ofc. of Lib. Outrch. Srvs. (Ch., 1975–77). **Activities:** 9, 14-Reg. Syst.; 17, 19, 24; 89 **Addr.:** Cabell County Public Library, 455 Ninth St. Plz., Huntington, WV 28701.

Nelson, Jean E. (F. 9, Los Angeles, CA) City Libn. Consult., City of Fullerton, 1974–81; City Libn., City of San Bruno, 1972–74; Branch Libn., City of Whittier Lib., 1968–72, Ref. Libn. **Educ.:** CA State Univ., Los Angeles, 1963–65, BA (Amer. Std.); Univ. of South. CA, 1965–66, MSLS; 1965–68, MPA. **Orgs.:** CA LA: CA Inst. Lib. (Secy., 1979). ALA. Pub. Lib. Execs. Assn. South. CA: Pres. (1977–78). CA Lib. Athrty. for Systs. and Srv.: Athrty. Adv. Cncl. (1979–81). **Pubns.:** *Ballroom Dancer's Guide to Southern California* (1981). **Addr.:** 1403 S. Klinedale, Downey, CA 90240.

Nelson, Jerold A. (Jl. 31, 1937, Minneapolis, MN) Asst. Prof. of LS, Univ. of WA, 1971; Asst. Prof. of LS, San Jose State Univ., 1970–71; Hum. Libn., AZ State Univ., 1964–66. **Educ.:** Univ. of MN, 1955–59, BA (Eng.), 1962–64, MA (LS); Univ. of CA, 1967–71, PhD (LS). **Orgs.:** Pac. NW LA. WA LA: Bd. of Dirs. (1975–79). **Honors:** Cncl. on Lib. Resrcs., Fellow, 1974; Phi Beta Kappa, 1959. **Pubns.:** Contrib., "Cutting Collection Space Needs; A Biological Model," *Library Space Planning* (1976); "Erotic Magazines and the Law," mono. supplement to *Serials Libn.* (Spr. 1980); "Professional Development Studies at the University of Washington," *PNLA Qtly.* (Win. 1977); ed., *Pac. NW Qtly.* (1977–79). **Addr.:** School of Librarianship FM-30, University of Washington, Seattle, WA 98195.

Nelson, Louise H. (D. 3, 1931, New York, NY) Dir., Wyckoff Pub. Lib., 1979–; Actg. Dir., 1979, Ref. Libn., 1969–79, Trustee, 1965. **Educ.:** Cornell Univ., 1949–53, AB (Eng.); Pratt Inst., 1965–69, MLS. **Orgs.:** ALA. NJ LA. Ridgewood Area Lib. Coord. Cncl.: Secy. (1972–75). **Honors:** Beta Phi Mu, 1969. **Pubns.:** "Library Shelf" clmn. *Wyckoff News.* **Activities:** 9; 17, 39 **Addr.:** 622 Lawlins Rd., Wyckoff, NJ 07481.

Nelson, Mary Lois (Ag. 2, 1927, Hampton, IA) Head, Adult Srvs., Cncl. Bluffs Pub. Lib., 1967–; Asst. Dir., Anoka Cnty. Lib., 1958–67; Tech. Prcs. Libn., IA State Traveling Lib., 1957–58; Catlgr., Scott Cnty. Lib., 1951–55. **Educ.:** IA State Tchrs. Coll., 1945–51, BA (Educ.); Univ. of TX, 1955–57, (LS). **Orgs.:** ALA. IA LA. **Addr.:** Free Public Library, 200 Pearl St., Council Bluffs, IA 51501.

Nelson, Milo Gabriel (Ja. 13, 1938, Clinton, IA) Ed., *Wilson Lib. Bltn.* (1978–); Hum. Libn., Univ. of ID, 1970–78. **Educ.:** Drake Univ., 1956–60, BA (Hist.); Univ. of WI, 1966–68, MA (Eng.), 1969–70, MLS. **Orgs.:** ALA: Ref. and Subscrpn. Bks. Review Com. (1977–); LED, Cont. Educ. Com. (1975–77). ID LA: Pres. (1977–78); Lib. Instr. RT (1980–). Pac. NW. LA: Secy. (1977–78). SLA. Various other orgs. **Pubns.:** *Idaho Local History* (1976); Ed. bd., *Ref. Srvs. Review* (1980–); Contrib. ed., *Serials Review* (1980–). **Activities:** 1; 31, 39, 41; 56, 57, 75 **Addr.:** Wilson Library Bulletin, 950 University Ave., Bronx, NY 10452.

Nelson, Norman L. (Je. 23, 1938, Battle Creek, MI) Asst. Univ. Libn., OK State Univ. Lib., 1981–, Asst. Libn. for Admin. Srvs., 1976–80, Asst. to the Dir., 1973–76; Dean of Men, Willamette Univ., 1968–72. **Educ.:** Olivet Coll., 1957–61, AB (Hist.); Univ. of VA, 1964–66, MA (Medvl. Hist.); Univ. of OR, 1972–73, MLS. **Orgs.:** OK Dept. of Libs.: Netwk. Adv. Cncl. (1978–; Ch., 1979–80; Vice–Ch., 1978–79); LSCA Adv. Cncl. (1979–80). OK LA: Treas. (1979–81); Exec. Bd. (1979–81); Budget Com. (1979–81); various coms. and ofcs. OK Gvr.'s Conf. on Libs.: Resrc. Person/Facilitator, Discuss. Sessions on Lib. Resrcs. and Tech. (1978). ALA: ACRL; LAMA; LITA. Various other orgs. and ofcs. **Pubns.:** "The Network Advisory Council at Work," *OK Libn.* (Jl. 1978); "The Proposed Oklahoma Library Network," *OK Libn.* (Ja. 1980); "Union List of Serials Project Under Way," *OK Libn.* (O. 1980); Supervising Ed., *Oklahoma Union List of Serials* (1975; 1977); Various rpts. **Activities:** 1; 17, 28, 34 **Addr.:** Oklahoma State University Library, Stillwater, OK 74078.

Nelson, Rachel Wayne (Mr. 13, 1925, Cleveland, OH) Dir., Cleveland Hts.-Univ. Hts. Pub. Lib., 1978–; Asst. Dir., 1963–78, Libn., 1960–63, Branch Libn., 1958–60, Asst. Libn., 1954–58, Asst. Branch Libn., Cleveland Pub. Lib., 1953–54, YA Libn., 1948–53. **Educ.:** Cleveland Coll., West. Rsv. Univ., 1943–47, BA; Sch. of Lib. Sci., Case West. Rsv. Univ., 1947–48, BSLS; Lib. Admin. Mgt. Dev. Inst., 1969. **Orgs.:** ALA: Reg. Mem. Ch. (1969–71); PLA: Human Srvs. Com. (1979–). Jewish LA: Pres. (1972–73). OH LA: Staff Dev. Com. (1969–70); Reg. Mtgs. Com. (1971–72); Ad Hoc Com. to Study Reorganization (1970–72); Lib. Dev. Com. (1972–73). Adult Educ. Cncl. of Grt. Cleveland: Bd. mem. (1967–70); Secy. (1970–71); VP (1971–72); Pres. (1972–73). Women's Natl. Bk. Assn.: Pres. (1969–70). Univ. Hts. Citizens Leag.: Bd. of Trustees (1970–71). PR Task Force, Fed. for Cmnty. Plng. **Pubns.:** Ed., *OH LA Bltn.* (1976–78). **Activities:** 9; 15, 16, 36; 50, 74 **Addr.:** 2359 Ashurst Rd., University Heights, OH 44118.

Nelson, Serena S. (N. 1, 1922, Fond du Lac, WI) Dir., SW WI Lib. Syst., 1972–. **Educ.:** Northwest. Univ., 1942–44, BS (Soclgy.); Univ. of WI, Madison, 1971–72, MA (LS); Miami Univ., 1975, Exec. Dev. Prog. for Lib. Admin. **Orgs.:** ALA. Cncl. of WI Libns.: Ch. (1980–81). WI LA: Treas. (1978, 1979); WI Assn. of Pub. Libns.: Ch. (1976); Admn. RT; SW WI Assn. of Libs.: Secy., Treas. (1974–76); Resrc. Adv. Com. (Ch., 1980–81). State Adv. Cncl. for Cmnty. Educ.: Educ. Com. (1981). **Honors:** Phi Beta Kappa, 1944; Beta Phi Mu, 1973. **Activities:** 9, 14-Reg. Lib. Syst.; 17, 24, 34; 50, 69 **Addr.:** Southwest Wisconsin Library System, P.O. Box 10 1775 4th St., Fennimore, WI 53809.

Nemeyer, Carol Anmuth (Ja. 29, 1929, New York, NY) Assoc. Libn., Natl. Progs., Lib. Congs., 1977–; Sr. Assoc., Assn. Amer. Publshrs., 1971–77; Resrch. Dir., Natl. Bk. Com., 1971–75; Asst. Libn., McGraw-Hill, Inc., 1962–66. **Educ.:** Berea Coll., 1946–47; Long Island Univ., 1949, BA (Eng), BS (Psy.); Columbia Univ., 1961–62, MLS, 1968–71, DLS. **Orgs.:** ALA: Cncl. (Pres.-Elect, 1981); Publshg. Div. (Ch., 1978–79); RTSD, Bd. Dirs. (1976–). SLA: Publshg. Div. (Ch., 1976–77); Doc. Grp., Exec. Com. (1967–68). Mercantile LA NY: Bd. (1974–77). NY Tech. Srvs. Libns.: Pres. (1974–75). Various other orgs., coms. Lib. Congs. Cat. Pubn. Adv. Com.: Exec. Com. (1971–). Beta Phi Mu: Nu Chap. (Pres., 1960). Grolier Club. Princeton Univ. Lib. Adv. Cncl.: Mem. (1978–82). Women's Natl. Bk. Assn.: Washington/Baltimore Chap. (Pres., 1978–). **Honors:** SLA, Fannie Simon Awd., 1981; ALA, Esther J. Piercy Awd., 1972; ALA, RTSD, Resrc. Schol. Awd., 1976. **Pubns.:** *Scholarly Reprint Publishing in the United States* (1972); *Guide to the Development of Educational Media Selection Centers* (1972). **Activities:** 4, 12; 18, 38, 42; 58, 76, 89-Publshg. **Addr.:** National Programs, Library of Congress, Washington, DC 20540.

Nerboso, Donna L. (Jl. 18, 1952, New York, NY) Ext. Libn., Cornell Univ. NYSSILR, 1979–; Ref. Libn., Paterson Pub. Lib., 1977–79; Resrchr., Rockefeller Univ., 1975–77. **Educ.:** Univ. of Rochester, 1970–74, BA (Eng.); Columbia Univ., 1974–75, MS (LS). **Orgs.:** ALA: ALA/AFL–CIO Jt. Com. on Lib. Srv. to Labor (1980–). NY LA: Un. and Staff Org. Task Force (Secy., 1980–). SLA: NY Chap., Women's Caucus (Strg. Com., 1981–). Women Lib. Workers. New York City Labor Film Club. **Pubns.:** "The Institute's Collection on Women and Work," *Women and Work in the 1980's* (1980); "Pay Equity: A Selected Annotated Bibliography," *Pay Equity: Issue for the 1980's* (1981); reviews. **Activities:** 1, 12; 17, 27, 39; 92, 95-Labor Rel. **Addr.:** Metropolitan District Library, Cornell University–New York State School of Industrial and Labor Relations, 3 East 43rd St., New York, NY 10017.

Nesbit, Eva Marie (Ap. 4, 1932, Norfolk, VA) Media Spec., 74th St. Elem. Sch., 1965–; Tchr., North Shore Elem., 1962–64, 1955–56; Tchr., John F. Cox Elem., 1956–59. **Educ.:** St. Petersburg Jr. Coll., 1950–52, AA (Gen. Educ.); FL State, 1952–54, BA (Elem. Educ.); Univ. of S. FL, 1964–68, MA (Lib. Educ.). **Orgs.:** ALA. SELA. FL Assn. of Media in Educ. Pinellas Assn. of Lib./Media Specs. Delta Kappa Gamma: Chap. (Pres., 1980–82). Alpha Delta Kappa: Gamma Chap. (Pres.-Elect, 1980–82). **Pubns.:** "Media Center Volunteer Program," *FL Media Qtly.* (Sum.–Fall 1977). **Activities:** 10; 21, 26, 31; 63, 89 **Addr.:** 9061 St. Andrews Dr., Seminole, FL 33543.

Ness, Charles H. (My. 7, 1924, York, PA) Asst. Dean of Libs., PA State Univ., 1970–, Asst. Dir. for Admin. and Plng., 1967–70; Dir., Gen. Lib. Bur., State Lib. of PA, 1961–67; Head, Lib. for Blind and Phys. Handcpd., Free Lib. of Philadelphia, 1957–61, Ref. Asst., 1953–57. **Educ.:** PA State Univ., 1946–49, BA (Eng.); Univ. of PA, 1949–51, AM (Eng. Lit.); Drexel Inst. of Tech., 1952–53, MS (LS). **Orgs.:** PA LA: Pres. (1974–75); Exec. Com. (1973–76); Coll. and Resrch. Div. (Ch., 1972–73); various other coms. ALA: LAMA/Bldg. and Equip. Sect., Facilities for Spec. Lib. Srvs. Com. (Ch., 1981–82). Lib. Srvs. for the Handcpd. RT (Ch., 1958–59); Stats. Com. for State Libs. (1966–68); Ref. and Subscrpn. Bk. Review Com. (1972–74). Mid-Atl. Resrch. Lib. Info. Netwk.: Secy. (1970–). Interlib. Delivery Srv. of PA: Secy. (1979). Pres. Com. on Empl. of the Handcpd. Amer. Assn. for State and Lcl. Hist. PA Citizens for Better Libs. Lib. Co. of Philadelphia. **Honors:** PA LA, Cert. of Merit, 1978. **Pubns.:** Ed., *Early Pennsylvania Imprints in Pennsylvania State Library 1689-1750* (1966); ed., *Pennsylvania State University Libraries Bibliographical Series* (1969–); "Andrew Carnegie in Centre County," *Jnl. of the Alleghenies* (1974); "Home to Franklin: Excerpts from the Civil War Diary of George Randolph Snowden," *Mag. of West. PA Hist.* (Ap. 1971); "New Resources for Blind Readers," *Lib. Jnl.* (O. 1959); various other articles. **Activities:** 1, 13; 17, 34, 36; 57, 72, 78 **Addr.:** 1238 Park Hills Ave., State College, PA 16801.

PROFESSIONAL ACTIVITIES: Institutions: 1. Acad. lib.; 2. Arch.; 3. Assn.; 4. Fed./Gvt. lib.; 5. Inst. lib.; 6. Mfr./Suppl.; 7. Milit. lib.; 8. Musm.; 9. Pub. lib.; 10. Sch. lib.; 11. Sch. of lib. sci.; 12. Spec. lib.; 13. State lib.; 14. (other). **Functions/Activities:** 15. Acq./Col. dev.; 16. Adult srvs.; 17. Admin.; 18. Apprais.; 19. Archit./Bldgs.; 20. Cat./Class.; 21. Chld. srvs.; 22. Circ.; 23. Cons./Pres.; 24. Consult.; 25. Cont. ed.; 26. Educ. lib. sci.; 27. Ext. srvs.; 28. Fund/Grants; 29. Gvt. pubs.; 30. Indx./Abs.; 31. Instr. lib. use; 32. Media srvs.; 33. Micro.; 34. Netwks./Coop.; 35. Persnl.; 36. PR; 37. Publshg.; 38. Recs. mgt.; 39. Ref. srvs.; 40. Repro.; 41. Resrch.; 42. Review.; 43. Secur.; 44. Serials; 45. Spec. col.; 46. Tech. srvs.; 47. Trustees/Bds.; 48. YA srvs.; 49. (other).

Who's Who in Library and Information Services

Ness, Mary F. (N. 11, 1916, Minneapolis, MN) Coord., Srvs. to Chld. and Young Teens, Akron–Summit Cnty. Pub. Lib., 1975–, Asst. Coord., Chld. Srvs., 1970–75; Head of Chld. Rm., Euclid Pub. Lib., 1968–70; Chld. Libn., Euclid–Richmond Branch, Cuyahoga Cnty. Pub. Lib., 1966–68; Chld. Libn., Maple Valley Branch, Akron–Summit Cnty. Lib. **Educ.:** Univ. of MN, 1934–39, BS (Home Econ.); Case–Western Resrv. Univ., 1967–69, MLS. **Orgs.:** OH LA: Chld. RT (Asst. Coord., 1973); Srvs. to Chld. and Young Teens Div. (Coord., 1974). ALA: ALSC, Newbery–Caldecott Com. (1979), Rec. Eval. Com. (1979–81). Chld. Lit. Assn. Intl. Bd. on Bks. for Young People. **Honors:** Beta Phi Mu. **Activities:** 9; 21, 32, 48 **Addr.:** 2550 Chamberlain Rd. #4A, Akron, OH 44313.

Neufeld, Irving H. (F. 4, 1925, New York, NY) Chief, UTC Lib. Syst., Untd. Techs. Corp., 1965–, Head Libn., 1962–65, Head, Ref. Sect., 1959–62, Ref. Libn., 1957–59; Biblgphr.-Indxr., U.S. Dept. of Agr. Lib., 1952–57; Intern, Catlgr., Lib. of Congs., 1950–52. **Educ.:** Brooklyn Coll., 1947, BA (Psy.); Escuela Univ. De Bellas Artes, Mex., 1948–49, MS (Fine Arts); Columbia Univ., 1949–50, MS (LS). **Orgs.:** NLA. SLA: CT Valley Chap. (Pres., 1968–69). **Pubns.:** "The Second Kind of Knowledge; Corporate Libraries," *Mgt. Review* (D. 1978); "Computer Applications in the UAC Library System," *Spec. Libs.* (My.–Je. 1973). **Activities:** 12; 17; 52, 59, 91 **Addr.:** UTC Library System, United Technologies Research Center, East Hartford, CT 06108.

Neufeld, Judith Ginsberg (N. 7, 1935, Brooklyn, NY) Asst. to Dir., Long Island Lib. Resrcs. Cncl., 1974–; Admin. Libn., Jewish Theo. Semy., 1957–68; Libn., Ramaz Sch., 1956–57. **Educ.:** Queens Coll., 1952–56, BA (Eng. lit.); Jewish Theo. Semy., 1951–56, BHL (Judaics); Columbia Univ., 1956–58, MLS, 1966, (Cert., Advnc. Libnshp.). **Orgs.:** ALA. Suffolk Cnty. LA: VP. (1980). NY LA. AJL. Amer. Mizrachi Women. Mensa. Emunah. Hadassah. **Activities:** 15, 34, 44; 55, 75, 90 **Addr.:** 203 Bay Ave., Patchogue, NY 11772.

Neufeld, M. Lynne (S. 3, 1939, Edmonton, AB) Exec. Dir., Natl. Fed. of Abs. and Indexing Srvs., 1979–; Consult., Auerbach Assoc., 1974–79; Dir., Lib. Oper., Inst. for Sci. Info., 1971–74; Info. Sci., Franklin Inst., 1969–71. **Educ.:** Univ. of AB, 1956–59, BSc, magna cum laude (Chem.); Drexel Univ., 1970–72, MS (IS). **Orgs.:** SLA. ASIS: Awds. Com.; Educ. Com.; Mktg. Com.; DE Valley Chap., Lcl. Nsltr. (Ed., 1973–76), Secy. (1976–78). AAAS: Info. Sect. Amer. Chem. Socty.: Chem. Info. Div. **Honors:** U.S. Consumer Prod. Safety Cmsn., Spec. Cit., 1976. **Pubns.:** Jt. auth., "Building a Chemical Ingredient Data Base for Industrial and Consumer Products," *Jnl. Chem. Info. and Comp. Scis.* (1976); jt. auth., "Machine Aided Title Word Indexing for a Current Awareness Publication," *Info. Storage and Retrieval* (1974); jt. auth., "Unitedness of Articles in Jnl. of Amer. Chem. Socty.," *Info. Storage and Retrieval* (1974); jt. auth., "Automatic Title Word Indexing for a Weekly Current Awareness Service," *Proceedings ASIS* (1973); "Linguistic Approaches to the Construction and Use of Thesauri," *Drexel Lib. Qtly.* (1972); various articles and rpts. **Activities:** 17; 26, 30; 56, 60, 75 **Addr.:** National Federation of Abstracting and Indexing Services, 112 South 16th St., Suite 1130, Philadelphia, PA 19102.

Neuhofer, Sr. M. Dorothy, OSB (Je. 19, 1931, St. Joseph, FL) Lib. Dir., Saint Leo Coll., 1975–, Readr. Srvs. Libn., 1967–75; Ref. Libn., 1965–67. **Educ.:** Barry Coll., 1954–64, BS (Educ.); Rosary Coll., River Forest, IL, 1964–65, MALS; Catholic Univ. of Amer., WA, DC., 1976, MCHA (Church Admin.). **Orgs.:** ALA. Cath. LA: Cath. Bk. Week Com. (Ch. local unit, 1968). FL LA: Local Dist. NLW (Ch., 1969). Amer. Benedictine Acad.: Bd. Mem. (1972–); Exec. Secty. (1979–). Fed. of St. Scholastica: Cncl. Mem. (1978–80). Canon Law Socty. of Amer. **Pubns.:** Ed., *Un. List of Cath. Pers.* (1968); Ed., *Nsltr., Amer. Benedictine Acad.* (1979–). **Activities:** 1, 2; 17, 25, 36; 74, 90 **Addr.:** Holy Name Priory, San Antonio, FL 33576.

Neumann, Joan (N. 6, 1935, New York City, NY) Proj. Coord., Intershare Coop. Lib. Netwk., 1979–; Spec. Proj. Asst. to Dir., Brooklyn Pub. Lib., 1977–79, Branch Libn., 1975–77, Cmnty. Coord., 1972–74. **Educ.:** Brooklyn Coll., 1963–67, BA (Eng.); Columbia Univ., 1967–68, MSLS; NY Univ., 1977–81, MPA. **Orgs.:** ALA: SRRT Eth. Mtrls. Info. Exch. Task Force (Fndr., Coord., 1970–73); PLA/Metro. Libs. Sect. (Secty., 1978–); Bylaws Com. (Ch., 1978–80); RASD, Adult Lib. Mtrls. Com. (Ch., 1976–78). Beta Phi Mu: Nu Chap. (Pres., 1972–73). Lib. PR Cncl. NY LA: Sect. Pres. (1974–75). **Honors:** Phi Beta Kappa, 1967. **Pubns.:** *Whole Library Book Catalog* (1974); *Directory of Minority/Third World Publishers and Dealers* (1972, 1973, 1974); various articles. **Activities:** 14-Regional Network; 17, 24, 34; 56, 78, 93 **Addr.:** 1118 E. 38 St., Brooklyn, NY 11210.

Nevai, Maria I. (My. 21, 1934, Budapest, Hungary) Tech. Srvs. Libn., Cooley Law Sch. Lib., 1975–; Ref. Libn., MI State Univ. Lib., 1969–70, Serials Libn., 1967–69. **Educ.:** Eötvös Lóránd Univ. (Budapest, Hungary), 1953–56, (Lang., Lit., Jnlsm.); West. MI Univ., 1964–67, MA (LS). **Orgs.:** ALA. MI LA. AALL. MI Assn. Law Libs. Various other orgs. Amer. Assn. Law Schs. **Activities:** 15, 20, 46; 77, 78 **Addr.:** Thomas Hackney Braswell Memorial Library, 344 Falls Rd., Rocky Mount, NC 27801.

Neville, Janet Sylvia Chapman (O. 3, 1934, Chicago, IL) Elem. Libn./Media Prof., Arapahoe Cnty. Sch. Dist. 6, Peabody Elem., 1972–; Pub. Libn., Arapahoe Reg. Lib., 1970–72; Kindergarten Tchr., Denver Pub. Schs., 1959–69; Eng. Tchr. and Tech. Dir. for Dramas, W. Niles Twp. HS, 1958–59; Eng. and Drama Tchr., Shafter HS, 1956–57. **Educ.:** Univ. of Denver, 1952–55, BA (Eng., Thea.), 1963–66, MA (LS), 1977– (Sp. Comm.). **Orgs.:** ALA: AASL, Com. for Ency. Britannica/AASL Awd. (1977). CO LA. CO Educ. Media Assn. Thea. LA. Various other orgs. League of Hist. Amer. Theas. Bonfils Players Club. Zeta Phi Eta. Sp. Comm. Assn. **Honors:** Univ. of Denver Grad. Sp. Assn., Best Speaker Awd., 1979. **Pubns.:** *Elizabeth Palmer Peabody* (play) (1975); various sps. **Activities:** 2, 10; 15, 35, 36; 55 **Addr.:** Theatre Library–Museum, 6676 South Kit Carson St., Littleton, CO 80121.

Neville, Sandra H. (Ap. 5, 1938, Ft. Benning, GA) Assoc. Libn., Univ. of TX Hlth. Sci. Ctr. Lib. at San Antonio, 1981–; Asst. Dir., Interpretive Srv., Univ. of GA, 1977–81; Head, Tech. Prcs., Univ. of CA, Los Alamos Sci. Lab. Lib., 1975–77; Systs. Libn., Actg. Chief of Admin. Srv., Univ. of NM, 1973–75; Head, Col. Prcs., Univ. of NM Lib. of Hlth. Sci., 1969–73; Catlgr., Sch. of Aerosp. Med., Aeromed. Lib., 1965–69; Ref., Univ. of TX, Austin, 1963–65. **Educ.:** Univ. of TX, Austin, 1955–59, BA (Hist.), 1961–66, MLS; Univ. of NM, 1976–78, MAPA; Emory Univ., 1967, Med. LA Cert. **Orgs.:** ALA. GA LA: Task Frc. to Std. ACRL Chap. Status (Ch., 1979–80). ASIS. GA State Data Ctr.: Lib. Adv. Cncl. (1979–). **Pubns.:** "Job Stress and Burnout," *Coll. & Resrch. Libs.* (My. 1981); "Academic Libraries at the Mid-Life Transition," *Jnl. of Acad. Libnshp.* (Spr. 1980); "Integrating Data Resources," *Mgt. of Info. Syst. Procs. of the 7th ASIS Mid-Yr. Mtg.* (1978); "How Can a University Library Support Educational Needs in a Period of Educational Change," *Educ. Tech.* (S. 1975); "A Look at Our Libraries," *San Antonio Arts Review*, (1966); "A Regional Survey of Technical Processing Costs," *SW Acad. Lib. Cnsrtm. Nsltr.* (S. 1975); various other pubns., **Activities:** 1, 12; 17, 22, 49-Online Srvs. **Addr.:** The University of Texas Health Science Center Library at San Antonio, 7703 Floyd Curl Dr., San Antonio, TX 78284.

Nevin, Barbara Bedsworth (Ja. 10, 1944, Charleroi, PA) Libn., Rogovin, Huge & Lenzner, 1979–; Legis. Libn., Howrey and Simon, 1978; Acq. Ed., Congressional Info. Srv., 1975–78; Ref. Libn., WV Univ., 1970–75. **Educ.:** Waynesburg Coll., 1961–65, BA (Hist., Gvt.); Univ. of Pittsburgh, 1966–68, MLS. **Orgs.:** DC Law Libns. Socty. AALL. **Pubns.:** Acq. Ed., *Amer. Stats. Index* (1975–78). **Activities:** 1, 12; 39; 77, 78 **Addr.:** 12610 English Orchard Ct., Silver Spring, MD 20906.

New, Doris E. (Mr. 7, 1922, McPherson, KS) Head, Serials Dept., Univ. of CA, Irvine, 1975–, Gift and Exch. Libn., 1974–75. **Educ.:** Bethany Coll., Lindsborg, KS, 1939–41; Chapman Coll., 1970–72, BA (Hist.); CA State Univ., Fullerton, 1972–73, MSLS; Univ. of CA, Irvine, 1977– (Admn.). **Orgs.:** ALA. SLA. CA LA. South. CA Tech. Prcs. Grp.: Secy/Treas. (1979–80). **Pubns.:** "Interlibrary Loan Analysis as a Collection Development Tool," *Lib. Resrcs. & Tech. Srvs.* (Sum. 1974); "Serials Agency Conversion in an Academic Library," *Serials Libn.* (Spr. 1978). **Addr.:** University of California, Irvine, University Library, P. O. Box 19557, Irvine, CA 92713.

Newberg, Ellen J. (S. 29, 1941, Wellman, IA) Head, Tech. Srvs., Parmly Billings Lib., 1973–; Catlgr., Dowling Coll., 1978–79; Asst. Dir., Rocky Mt. Coll. Lib. 1969–73; Catlgr., Univ. of OR, 1967–69; Catlgr., Univ. of WY, 1966–67; Asst. Dir., Sioux Falls Coll. Lib., 1963–66. **Educ.:** Sioux Falls Coll., 1958–62, BA (Eng.); Univ. of IL, 1962–63, MLS. **Orgs.:** MT LA: Pac. NW LA Rep. for MT LA (1981–83). Pac. NW LA. ALA. **Pubns.:** "Libraries and Art," *PNLA Qtly.* (Win. 1969). **Activities:** 9; 20, 22, 46; 55, 56, 75 **Addr.:** 925 Burlington Ave., Billings, MT 59102.

Newberry, William F. (N. 17, 1949, San Diego, CA) Info. & Ref. Spec., Alachua Cnty. Info. & Ref. (Gainesville), 1981–; Autom. Planner, J. Hillis Miller Hlth. Ctr. Lib., Univ. of FL, 1979–81; Tech. Srv. Libn., FL Reg. Lib. for the Blind and Phys. Handcpd., 1978–79; LSCA Proj. Libn., Sunland Trng. Ctr. (Marianna, FL), 1977–78. **Educ.:** Univ. of Ctrl. FL, 1970–73, BA Magna Cum laude (Pol Sci); FL State Univ., 1976–77, MLS; US Army Admin. Sch., 1967–68 (Honor Grad.) **Orgs.:** NLA. FL State Univ.: Lib. Com. (1977). **Honors:** *Amer. Lib.* Prize Article Competition, 2d Prize, Round V, 1979. **Pubns.:** "Subject Perspective of Library Science Dissertations," *Jnl. of Educ. for Libnshp.* (Win. 1978); "The Institutionalized Mentally Retarded and Their Public Library," *Amer. Lib.* (Apr. 1980); "Materials Selection Policies in Regional Libraries for the Blind and Physically Handicapped," *Dikta* (Sum. 1979); Jt. Auth., "Subject Bibliographies: A Modest Proposal," *Dikta*, (Spr. 1979); "Edge–Notched Cards: Prematurely Buried," *Lib. Jnl.* (Mr. 1981). **Activities:** 5, 12; 17, 22, 46; 56, 72, 77 **Addr.:** 2521 SE 11th Ave., Gainesville, FL 32601.

Newman, Ann (IN) AV Libn., Vigo Cnty. Pub. Lib., Ref. Libn., 1961–66; Asst. Libn. Vincennes Pub. Lib., 1958–61; Statistician, Med., Hlth Div. Lib. 1956–58. **Orgs.:** ALA: SORT (Pres., Secy.). EFLA: Ed. Com. IN LA: IN Lib. Film Srv. (Bd. of Dir., 1962–) Pres.; Media Tech. Com. (Ch.); Natl. Lib. Week (Exec. Dir., 1973–74); Dist. V Prog. Ch. (1960, 1965). AECT. NAACP. Amer. Film Inst. Cham. of Cmrce.: Recreation and Tourism Com. (1972–); Comm. Com. (1972–); Anl. Dinner Steering Com. (1978–); PR Cncl. (1978–). Banks of the Wabash Fest. Assn., Inc.: Secy. (1973–78); Bd. of Dirs. (1973–). **Activities:** 9; 32; 67, 75 **Addr.:** Audiovisual Librarian, Vigo County Public Library, One Library Sq., Terre Haute, IN 47807.

Newman, John James (N. 12, 1942, Morehead City, NC) Spec. Cols. Libn., CO State Univ. Lib., 1974–; Assoc. Libn., Kirkwood Cmnty. Coll. Lib., 1970–73; Asst. Mss. and Serials Libn., Univ. of IA Lib., 1968–70. **Educ.:** Univ. of WA, 1960–67, BA (Hist.), 1967–68, M Libr (LS); CO State Univ., 1974–75, MA (Hist.). **Orgs.:** CO LA: Coll. and Univ. Div. (Ch., 1977–78). SAA. Conf. of Intermt. Archvsts. AAUP. Sci. Fiction Resrch. Assn. **Honors:** Phi Alpha Theta; Phi Kappa Phi. **Pubns.:** *Fundamentals of Shorin-Ryu Karate* (1975); "Novels of Post-Holocaust America," *Alternative Futures* (Fall 1978); "Imaginary War Fiction in CSU Libraries," *Bltn. of Bibl.* (O./D. 1978); jt. auth., "Indexing Local Newspapers," *Hist. News* (Ag. 1978); "The Germans from Russia Collection," *Germans from Russia in Colorado* (1978); various other pubns. **Activities:** 1, 2; 28, 33, 45; 70, 85 **Addr.:** Special Collections Department, Colorado State University Libraries, Fort Collins, CO 80523.

Newman, Linda P. (D. 6, 1943, Sumter, SC) Actg. mines Libn., Univ. of NV, 1981–, Instr. Srvs. Libn., 1972–, Asst. Gvt. Pubns. Libn., 1969–72. **Educ.:** Univ. of SC, 1961–64, BA (Intl. Std.); IN Univ., 1965–69, MLS. **Orgs.:** ALA: MAGERT. NV LA: State Mem. Ch. (1974–76); Anl. Conv. Prog. Ch. (1977). West. Assn. of Map Libs. **Pubns.:** *Use of the Library* (1976, 1980); "The Mines Library," *Mackay Miner* (1981). **Activities:** 1; 31, 39; 54, 70 **Addr.:** Mines Library, University of NV, Reno, NV 89557.

Newman, Rhoda Safran (Mr. 17, 1928, New York, NY) Team Leader, Congsnl. Ref. Div., Congsnl. Resrch. Srv., Lib. of Congs., 1976–, Ref. Spec., 1971–75, Catlgr., Shared Cat. Div., 1970–71. **Educ.:** Brooklyn Coll., 1944–48, BA (Fr.); Columbia Univ., 1948–49, MA (Fr.); Rutgers Univ., 1968–70, MLS. **Orgs.:** ALA. DC LA. **Activities:** 4; 17, 28, 36, 39; 55, 63, 92 **Addr.:** Congressional Reference Division, Congressional Research Service, Library of Congress, Washington, DC 20540.

Newman, Susan T. (My. 26, 1934, Washington, DC) Libn., Ford Fndn., 1977–, Asst. Libn., 1973–77, Ref. Libn., 1971–73; Docum. Biblgphr., Columbia Univ., 1970–71; Assoc. Ed., Frgn. Policy Assn., 1960–64. **Educ.:** Mt. Holyoke Coll., 1956, AB (Fr.); NY Univ., 1967, AM (Intl. Affairs); Columbia Univ., 1970, MLS; Inst. Std. Pol., Paris, France, 1956–57, Cert. of Std. **Orgs.:** SLA. ALA. Cnsrtm. of Fndn. Libs.: New York City Ch. (1977–78). NY Metro. Ref. and Resrch. Lib. Agency: Ref. Libn. RT (Ch., 1979–80); Mgt. Subcom. **Activities:** 12; 17, 39; 75, 92 **Addr.:** Ford Foundation Library, 320 E. 43 St., New York, NY 10017.

Newman, William (F. 18, 1937, Czechoslovakia) Univ. Libn., Tulane Univ., 1978–; Assoc. Dir., York Univ. 1971–77, Asst. Dir., 1969–71, Libn., Fac. of Admin. Std. 1967–69; Head, Ref. Dept., Univ. of MT, 1965–67; Serials Cat., Cornell Univ., 1963–65; Adult Srvs. Libn., Brooklyn Pub. Lib., 1959–63. **Educ.:** Brooklyn Coll. 1955–59, BA (Math.); Columbia Univ., 1959–60, MSLS. **Orgs.:** ALA. ASIS. **Activities:** 1; 17 **Addr.:** Howard-Tilton Memorial Library, Tulane University, New Orleans, LA 70118.

Newmark, Barbara L. (N. 12, 1946, Cleveland, OH) Reg. Head of YA Srv., Cuyahoga Cnty. Pub. Lib., 1970–; various other positions in tchging. **Educ.:** OH St. Univ., 1964–68, BS (Educ.); Case West. Reserve Univ., 1971–72, MSLS. **Orgs.:** ALA: Mem. Promo. Com. (1978–80); YASD, Bd. Dir. (1980–83), Mem. Promo. Com. (Ch., 1978–80), Act. Com. (1976–78). OH LA: YA Task Force (Ch. (1976–79); Div. I Coord., Defining Cmnty. Needs. Reach Out Drug Abuse Ctr.: Pres., Bd. of Dir. (1977–80). **Honors:** OH LA, Diana Vescelius Meml. Awd., 1977. **Pubns.:** "Doing A Young Adult Readers Survey: Results and Benefits," *Top of the News* (Sum. 1979); "Concerned Citizens Groups Working with Young Adults," *Sch. Lib. Jnl.* (O. 1978); "Survey of Young Adult Services," *OH LA Bltn.* (Jl. 1976) and *Lib. Jnl.* (D. 1976); Review Ed., *Voice of Youth Advocates* (1978–); YA Ed., OH LA Pubns. (1977). **Activities:** 9; 48 **Addr.:** Mayfield Regional Library, 6080 Wilson Mills Rd., Mayfield Village, OH 44143.

Newnan, Marjorie E. (O. 7, 19—, Spokane, WA) Libn., Los Altos HS, 1973–; Libn., Awalt HS, 1961–73; Libn., Los Altos HS, 1959–60. **Educ.:** Univ. of WA, 1938–41, BA (Gen. Stds.); San Jose State Univ., 1958–60, MA (LS). **Orgs.:** ALA. CA LA. CA Media and Lib. Educs. Assn. CA Assn. of Sch. Libns.: *CA Sch. Libs.* (Assoc. Ed., Bus. Mgr., Subscrpn. Mgr., 1967–70). Various other orgs. CA Fed. of Tchrs. CA Tchrs. Assn. AAUW. **Activities:** 10; 17, 31, 39; 63 **Addr.:** Los Altos High School Library, 201 Almond Ave., Los Altos, CA 94022.

Newton, William Rhese (S. 12, 1953, Louisville, KY) Mgr., Resrch. Srvs., Coca-Cola Co., 1978–; Asst. Dir., W. GA Reg. Lib., 1976–78. **Educ.:** Emory Univ., 1971–75, BA (Hist.), 1976, MLS. **Orgs.:** SLA: S. Atl. Chap. (Treas., 1980–). **Pubns.:**

Special Subjects/Services: 50. Adult educ.; 51. Advert./Mktg.; 52. Aerosp.; 53. Agric.; 54. Area std.; 55. Arts/Hum.; 56. Autom.; 57. Bibl./Prtg.; 58. Bio. sci.; 59. Bus./Fin.; 60. Chem.; 61. Copyrt.; 62. Documtn.; 63. Educ.; 64. Engin.; 65. Env.; 66. Eth. grps.; 67. Film; 68. Food/Nutr.; 69. Geneal.; 70. Geo.; 71. Geol.; 72. Handcpd.; 73. Hist.; 74. Int. frdm.; 75. Info. sci.; 76. Insr.; 77. Law; 78. Legis.; 79. Math./Comp. sci.; 80. Med.; 81. Metals; 82. Nat. resrcs.; 83. Newsp.; 84. Nuc. sci.; 85. Oral hist.; 86. Petr./Energy; 87. Pharm.; 88. Phys./Astr./Math.; 89. Readg.; 90. Relig.; 91. Sci./Tech.; 92. Soc. sci.; 93. Telecom.; 94. Transp.; 95. (other).

Reviews. **Activities:** 12; 17, 39, 41; 59, 68 **Addr.:** 632 Darlington Rd., N.E., Atlanta, GA 30305.

Ney, Neal J. (Ja. 8, 1947, Dubuque, IA) Dir., Kankakee Pub. Lib., 1979–; Adult Mtrls. Sel. Spec., Chicago Pub. Lib., 1978–79, Branch Libn., 1976–78; Asst. Ref. Libn., Chicago Hist. Socty., 1971–76. **Educ.:** George Williams Coll., 1965–70, BA (Soc. Sci.); Rosary Coll., 1971–74, MALS. **Orgs.:** ALA: JMRT, Pres. (1978), VP (1977), *JMRT Nsltr.* Ed. (1976). IL LA. **Honors:** Beta Phi Mu, 1975; Kappa Delta Pi, 1971. **Activities:** 9; 15, 17, 39, 89 **Addr.:** Kankakee Public Library, 304 S. Indiana, Kankakee, IL 60901.

Nicely, Marilyn K. (F. 18, 1945, Dayton, OH) Tech. Srvs. Libn., Univ. of OK Law Lib., 1976–; Actg. Educ. Srvs. Libn., Mesa Cmnty. Coll., 1976; Ref., Serials Libn., Pan Amer. Univ., 1974–75. **Educ.:** OH Univ., 1963–67, BA (Span.); AZ State Univ., 1969–73, MA (Eng.); Univ. of OK, 1973–74, MLS. **Orgs.:** AALL. OK LA. West. Cons. Congs.: OK Chap. **Honors:** Phi Beta Kappa, 1967; Beta Phi Mu, 1976. **Pubns.:** "Oklahoma Legal Documents," *Procs.; 21st Anl. Mtg. AALL Southwest. Chap.* (1978). **Activities:** 1, 12; 15, 29, 44; 77 **Addr.:** University of OK Law Library, 300 Timberdell, Norman, OK 73109.

Nicholaou, Mary P. (F. 14, 1938, Agiassos, Mytilene, Greece) Dir., Mohawk Valley LA, 1980–, Asst. Dir., 1977–80, Chld. Consult., 1967–77; Libn., U.S. Army Lib., 1963–66; Chld. and YA Libn., Delmar Pub. Lib., 1962–63. **Educ.:** Keuka Coll., 1957–58, (Eng.); SUNY, Albany, 1958–61, BA (LS), 1961–62, MLS; SUNY, Buffalo, 1977–79, CE Cert. **Orgs.:** NY LA: CYASS (Dir., 1968–71), Recs. for Chld. Com. (1968–72), Films Chld. Com. (1970–72), Nom. Com. (1971), Bylaws Com. (1971). Hudson Mohawk LA: Various coms. Coop. Lib. Srvs. Albany, Schenectady Schoharie Lib. Syst.: Bd.; various coms. ALA: Chld. Srvs. Div., Sel. Frgn. Chld. Bks. Com. (1972–75). Natl. Org. for Women: Schenectady Chap. (Treas., 1974–76). Common Cause. **Pubns.:** *Directory of Day Care Centers and Nursery Schools - Fulton, Montgomery, Schenectady and Schoharie Counties* (1973, 1978); reviews. **Activities:** 4, 9; 17, 21, 24; 61, 67, 72 **Addr.:** 50 Brookline Ave., Albany, NY 12203.

Nicholas, Martha Ann (Williams) (Ap. 15, 1936, Memphis, TN) Libn., South. Bapt. Coll., 1966–; Tchr., Hyatt Elem. Sch., Riverside, CA, 1965–66; Libn., Lewisville (TX) Pub. Sch., 1964–65; Tchr., Aubrey (TX) Pub. Sch., 1961–64; Tchr., Ft. Worth (TX) Pub. Sch., 1958–61; Tchr., Gideon (MO) Pub. Sch., 1955–58. **Educ.:** AR State Univ., 1955–58, BSE (Educ.); N. TX State Univ., 1961–65, MEd (LS). **Orgs.:** ALA. AR LA: Mem. com. (1970–71). AR Fndn. of Assn. Coll. Com. of Libns.: Pres. (1970–72); Secy. (1967–68). **Honors:** South. Bapt. Coll., Disting. SBC Alum. of the Year, 1973. **Activities:** 1; 15, 17, 28, 31, 39; 90, 92 **Addr.:** Box 457, Southern Baptist College, Walnut Ridge, AR 72476.

Nicholls, Pat (S. 18, 1951, Ituna, SK) Coord., Acad. Support Srvs., Univ. of West. ON, 1980–, Asst. Librn., Instr., Sch. of Lib. and Info. Sci., 1978–80, Tch. Srv. Libn. 1977–78, Cat. Dev. Libn., 1974–77. **Educ.:** Waterloo Luth. Univ., 1969–73, BA (Hist.); Univ. of West. ON, 1973–74, MLS, 1974–78, MA (Hist.). **Orgs.:** Univ. of West. ON Librn. Assn.: Treas. (1978–82). Can. Micro. Socty. Can. LA. **Activities:** 1, 12; 20, 33, 46 **Addr.:** School of Library and Information Science, Elborn College, University of Western Ontario, London, ON N6G 1H1 Canada.

Nichols, Barbara Best (Jl. 25, 1942, Durham, NC) Libn., Monsanto Triangle Park Dev. Ctr. Inc., 1979–. **Educ.:** NC Ctrl. Univ., 1973–76, BS (Home Econ.), 1977–78, MLS. **Orgs.:** Durham Cnty. LA: Pres. (1980–81). NC SLA: Positive Action Com. (Ch., 1980–81). Med. LA. NC OLUG. Other orgs. Durham Cnty. Cmnty. Educ. Adv. Bd. Durham Cnty. Schs. Adv. Bd. **Activities:** 12; 15, 17, 46; 60, 91 **Addr.:** Monsanto Triangle Park Development Center, Inc., P.O. Box 12081, Research Triangle Park, NC 27709.

Nichols, Betty Mitchell (Jl. 17, 1916, Topeka, KS) Persnl. Ofcr., KS City (MO) Pub. Lib., 1979–, Supvsr., Cont. Educ., 1974–79, YA Coord., 1968–74; Libn., Ctrl. Reg., Fed. Aviation Admin., 1966–67; Branch Libn., Johnson Cnty. (KS) Lib., 1958–65. **Educ.:** Washburn Univ., 1934–37, BA (Eng.); Emporia State Univ., 1967–68, MLS. **Orgs.:** CLENE: Adv. Bd. (1976–78). MO LA: Various coms. and ofcs. (1972–80). ALA: YASD (Sec. VP, 1974–75), Best Bks. for YAs Com. (1975–76), Educ. Com. (Ch., 1979), Nom. Com. (Ch., 1978); LAMA; Stand. Com. on Lib. Educ. (1979). KS City (MO) Pub. Lib. Staff Assn.: Pres. (1974–75). AAUW: KS City Branch. **Honors:** Beta Phi Mu, 1968. **Pubns.:** "Capital Recovery through Continuing Education," *Lib. Jnl.* (Jl. 1977); "Enrich Your Library with Volunteers," *Show-Me Libs.* (Ag. 1980); "Young Adult Services in Public Libraries," *Show-Me Libs.* (O.–N. 1979); "Choosing the Best Books for Young Adults," *Show-Me Libs.* (My. 1977); "Reaching Young Adults in Kansas City," *Show-Me Libs.* (My. 1974); Various articles. **Activities:** 9; 25, 35, 48; 50 **Addr.:** 4910 State Line, Shawnee Mission, KS 66205.

Nichols, Diane Pendleton (Jl. 27, 1941, Louisville, KY) Assoc. Prof., Circ. Libn., Univ. of Louisville, 1978–, Actg. Head, Pub. Srvs. Dept., 1977–78, Circ., Ref., Media Libn., 1971–77; Asst. Libn., Univ. Louisville, Sch. of Dentistry, 1968–71. **Educ.:** Univ. KY, 1959–61; IN Univ., 1961–62; Univ. Louisville, 1962–66, BA (Eng.); Catherine Spalding Coll., 1967–69, MS (LS); Univ. of Louisville, 1979– (Hist.). **Orgs.:** Med. LA. KY LA. AECT. **Activities:** 1; 22, 32, 39; 80 **Addr.:** University of Louisville, Kornhauser Health Sciences Library, P.O. Box 35260, Louisville, KY 40232.

Nichols, Gail Marian (Ja. 24, 1946, Rochester, NY) Gvt. Docum. Libn., Univ. of CA, Berkeley, 1974–; Gvt. Pubn. Libn., Univ. of CA, Riverside, 1969–74. **Educ.:** Smith Coll., 1964–68, AB (Hist.); Univ. of South. CA, 1968–69, MSLS. **Orgs.:** ALA: GODORT, various ofcs.; RTSD. SLA. West. Assn. of Map Libs.: Pres. (1974–75). Assn. of Intl. Libs. **Honors:** Beta Phi Mu, 1969. **Pubns.:** "Foreign and International Documents in Microform," *Micro. Review* (S.–O. 1978); jt. auth., "Map Cataloging-An Introduction," *Drexel Lib. Qtly.* (O. 1973); reviews. **Activities:** 1; 29, 39; 54, 59, 78 **Addr.:** Government Documents Dept., General Library, University of California, Berkeley, CA 94720.

Nichols, J. Gary (O. 10, 1940, Blakley, PA) State Libn., ME State Lib., 1969–, Dir. of Lib. Dev., 1971–73, Consult., Srvs. to Visually & Phys. Handcpd., 1969–71, Consult. Srvs. to the Institutionalized, 1969–71; YA Srvs. Libn., Free Lib. of Philadelphia, 1967–69, Chld. Libn., 1967–69; HS Libn., Plainfield HS, 1965–66; Asst. Supvsg. Libn., Scoth Plains Pub. Lib. 1964–65. **Educ.:** Concord Coll., 1960–64, BS ED (Educ.); Drexel Univ., 1966–67, MLS. **Orgs.:** New Eng. LA. ALA. COSLA: Vice-Ch. (1975–77). ME LA: Exec. Com. (1973–). New Eng. Lib. Bd.: Ch. (1977–79); Secy.-Treas. (1979–). N.E. Docum. Cons. Ctr.: Corp. Pres., Bd. of Dirs. (Ch., 1977–). **Activities:** 9, 13; 17, 23, 24; 78 **Addr.:** Maine State Library, Station #64, Augusta, ME 04333.

Nichols, Julia B. (Ag. 25, 1951, Louisville, KY) Coord. of Lrng. Resrcs., Med. Univ. of SC, 1976–; AV Libn., Educ. Oppt. Ctr., 1973–76. **Educ.:** Univ. of Louisville, 1971–73, BA (Hist.); Syracuse Univ., 1973–76, MLS. **Orgs.:** Med. LA: AV Exch. Com. SC LA. **Pubns.:** *Cataloging Health Science Materials* (1981). **Activities:** 1; 15, 20, 32; 80 **Addr.:** Medical University of South Carolina Library, 171 Ashley Ave., Charleston, SC 29425.

Nichols, Lucy (Je. 24, 1912, Everett, MA) Trustee, Carver Meml. Lib., 1978–; Media-spec., Libn., Pub. Sch., Lakewood, OH, 1943–77; Libn., Pub. Sch., Oswego, NY, 1936–43; Gen. Asst., Univ. of ME Lib., 1935–36. **Educ.:** Mt. Holyoke Coll., 1930–34, AB (Eng. Drama); Simmons Coll., 1934–35, BS (LS). **Orgs.:** ALA. AECT. OH Assn. of Sch. Libns.: Elem. Sch. Com. (Ch., 1959). Natl. Educ. Assn. **Pubns.:** "Facts and Fun in Lakewood," *Sch. Libs.* **Activities:** 9, 10; 21, 32, 47; 55, 63, 89 **Addr.:** Box 263, Searsport, ME 04974.

Nichols, Margaret Irby (Jl. 9, 1924, Maud, TX) Asst. Prof., Sch. of LS, N. TX State Univ., 1968–, Instr., 1956–67; Jr. HS Libn., S. Jr. HS, Roswell, NM, 1954–55; Ref. Libn., NM Milit. Inst., 1951–53; Biblgphr., LA State Univ., 1953; Ref. Libn., El Paso Pub. Lib., 1949–51; Ref. Libn., TX Tech. Univ., 1946–48; Catlgr., Bethany Coll., 1946. **Educ.:** N. TX State Univ., 1941–45, BA (Eng.); Univ. of TX, Austin, 1948–49, MLS. **Orgs.:** ALA. TX LA: Rcrt. (1976–1978), Pubns. (1979–), Cont. Ed. (1981–). SWLA: Nom. (1979–). AALS. **Honors:** Alpha Lambda Sigma, 1944; Student Gvt. Assn., N. TX. State Univ., Disting. Prof. Awd., 1974. **Pubns.:** "Lillian Gunter and Texas County Library Legislation," *Jnl. of Lib. Hist.* (Ja. 1973); "Lillian Gunter, Pioneer Texas County Librarian," *TX Libs.* (D. 1977); *Handbook of Reference Sources* (1977, 1979, 1981). **Activities:** 1, 11; 29, 39, 44 **Addr.:** 2514 Royal Ln., Denton, TX 76201.

Nichols, Nowlan K. (My. 4, 1921, Craigsville, VA) Art Libn., Univ. Archvst., LA Tech Univ., 1968. **Educ.:** LA Coll., 1956–64, BA (Eng., Educ.); LA Tech Univ., 1966–67, MA (Eng.), 1968–74, (Art, LS). **Orgs.:** LA LA. SAA. Natl. Archs. Socty. of SW Archvsts. AAUW. Fac. Clb., Fac. Women's Clb., LA Tech Univ. Leag. of Women Voters. **Pubns.:** *A Guide to Rome* (1973, 1977). **Activities:** 1, 2; 23, 39, 45; 55, 69 **Addr.:** 1400 St. John, Ruston, LA 71270.

Nicholson, Myreen Moore (Je. 2, 1940, Norfolk, VA) Ref. Libn., Norfolk Pub. Lib., 1975–, Art Libn., 1972–75, Actg. Model City Dir., 1970–72; Libn., Bonds-Wilson HS, 1968–69; Prof., Art, Lit., Palmer Jr. Coll., 1968; various tchg. and other positions. **Educ.:** Coll. of William and Mary, 1958–62, BA (Eng. Art); Old Dominion Univ., 1964– (Lit.); Univ. NC, 1969–70, MS (LS); Citadel, 1968–69; **Orgs.:** SELA. ARLIS/NA. VA LA. W. Ghent Arts Alliance: Dir. (1977–). Tidewater Artists Assn. VA Poetry Socty. Tidewater Writers Gld. Various Other orgs. **Honors:** Princess Anne Womens' Club, Most Progressive Artist Awd., 1958. **Pubns.:** Ed., *Acquisitions in Black Materials* (1974–); reviews, paintings, lithographs. **Activities:** 9, 12; 15, 16, 37; 55, 89 **Addr.:** 1404 Gates Ave., Norfolk, VA 23507.

Nickel, Edgar B. (F. 20, 1951, Chilliwack, BC) Dir., NW. KS Lib. Syst., 1977–; Consult., N. Ctrl. KS Lib. Syst., 1975–77; Adult Srvs. Libn., Manhattan Pub. Lib., 1974–75. **Educ.:** KS State Univ., 1971–73, BA (Hist.); Emporia State Univ., 1974, MLS. **Orgs.:** Mt. Plains LA. ALA. KS LA: Pub. Lib. Sect. (Pres., 1979–80). KS Lib. Netwk: Athrty. Cncl.; Task Force on Sch. Libs. in Netwks. Various other orgs. Norton Cnty. Cmnty. Educ. Assn.: VP (1980–). **Pubns.:** "Library Services by Mail and Toll–Free Telephone," *Books By Mail* (1977). **Activities:** 9, 14-Multitype Lib. Network; 17, 24, 34; 72, 53 **Addr.:** P.O. Box 4, Norton, KS 67654.

Nickerson, Susan Leslie (My. 26, 1944, Greenwood, MS) Branch Supvsr., Sylvan Oaks Cmnty. Lib., Sacramento Pub. Lib., 1978–; Msc. Cat. Libn., Univ. of IL, 1974–77, Catlgr., Cat. Dept., 1968–74. **Educ.:** Antioch Coll., 1962–67, BA (Drama); Univ. IL, 1967–68, MS (LS); CA State Univ., 1977–, MPA. **Orgs.:** ALA.: LAMA; PLA. CA LA. SLA. **Honors:** Beta Phi Mu, 1968. **Pubns.:** Reviews. **Activities:** 1, 9; 16, 17, 20; 55, 75, 92 **Addr.:** Sylvan Oaks Community Library, 6700 Auburn Blvd., Citrus Heights, CA 95610.

Nicoles, Richard H. (My. 3, 1938, Berkeley, CA) Sr. Libn., Gvt. Pubns., CA State Lib., 1974–, Libn., Cat., 1973; Asst. Acq. Libn., Univ. of San Francisco, 1972–73; Asst. Cat. Libn., 1971–72. **Educ.:** San Francisco State Univ., 1957–60, BA (Hist.); Univ. of CA, Berkeley, 1962–63 (Educ.), 1971, MLS. **Orgs.:** ALA: GODORT. CA LA: Gvt. Pubns. Chap. (Ch., 1981). **Pubns.:** *California Legislative Publications Charts* (1976). **Activities:** 1, 13; 20, 29, 39 **Addr.:** Government Publications Section, California State Library, P.O. Box 2037, Sacramento, CA 95809.

Nicoll, Heather Lynn (Ag. 13, 1949, West Bend, WI) Coord., Systs. and Pubns., WHCOLIS, (1977–); Netwks. Srvs. Libn., WA Lib. Netwks., (1975–77). **Educ.:** Univ. of WA, 1970–74, BA (Msc.), 1974–75, MA (Libnshp.). **Orgs.:** ALA: Lib. and Info. Tech. Legis. Com. (Vice-ch., 1978–). ASIS. WA State Adv. Cncl. on Libs.: Specialized Resrc. Ctrs. Task Frc. (1975). **Honors:** Univ. of WA Sch. of Libnshp., Ruth Worden Medal Awd., 1975. **Activities:** 4; 24, 34; 56 **Addr.:** National Commission on Libraries and Information Science, Suite 601, 1717 K St. N.W., Washington, DC 20036.

Nicula, Janet Gail (O. 31, 1946, Poughkeepsie, NY) Assoc. Head, Ref., Old Dominion Univ., 1978–; Sci. Libn., 1975–78; Orig. Cat. Libn., MI State Univ., 1973–75; Branch Libn., Virginia Beach Pub. Libs., 1969–73. **Educ.:** Univ. of MI, 1964–68, AB (Geo.); 1968–69, AMLS; Old Dominion Univ., grad. work for MBA. **Orgs.:** VA LA. SELA. SLA: VA Chap., Mem. Ch. Old Dominion Univ. Fac. Sen. **Honors:** Beta Phi Mu. **Activities:** 1; 17, 39, 49-Comp.-Assisted Lit. Srch.; 60, 64, 91 **Addr.:** Old Dominion University Library, Reference Dept., Norfolk, VA 23508.

Nida, Jane Bolster (Jl. 19, 1918, Chicago, IL) Retired 1980–; Info. Srv. Adv., U.S. Agency for Intl. Dev., 1979–80; Dir., Arlington Cnty. Lib. (VA) 1957–80, Asst. Dir., 1954–57; Dir., Falls Church (VA) Pub. Lib., 1951–54; Resrch. Libn., Info. Resrch. Srv., 1951; Order Libn., OH Univ., 1947; Ref. Libn., Aurora Pub. Lib., 1946; Various other lib. positions. **Educ.:** Aurora Coll., 1936–42, BA (Eng.); Univ. of IL, 1942–43, BS (LS). **Orgs.:** ALA: Women's Jt. Cong. Com. (Rep. 1969–80); Publi-Cable (Rep. 1971–78). VA LA: Pub. Lib. Sect. (Ch., 1960–61); 1st VP (1968–69); Pres. (1969–70); Other ofcs. DC LA: 1st VP (1959–60). Washington Cncl. Gvt.: Libn. Tech. Com. (1971–80, Ch. 1975). Reading is Fundamental: Arlington Cnty. Bd. (1977–79). Cult. Laureate Fndn.: Founder, VP, Dir., (1973–80). VA Adv. Legis. Cncl.: Com. Revise Lib. Laws (1968–70). Other orgs. **Honors:** American Red Cross Merit. Srv. Awd., 1946; Aurora Coll., Alum. Assn. Outstan. Alum. Awd., 1979. **Pubns.:** "Arlington County Libraries," *D. C. Lib.* (My. 1956). **Activities:** 4, 9; 17, 19, 29; 56, 78 **Addr.:** 4907 29th Street, North, Arlington, VA 22207.

Nieball, Mary L. (F. 27, 1929, Odessa, TX) Dir., Lrng. Resrcs. Srvs., San Jacinto Coll. Dist., 1979–; Assoc. Dir. of Libs., Univ. of TX at El Paso, 1976–79; Libn., Prof., Odessa Coll. Lib., 1964–76; Libn., Odessa Pub. Sch., 1959–64. **Educ.:** Sul Ross State Univ., 1956–59, BS (Eng.); U.S. Intl. Univ., 1969–71, MA (Educ.); TX Woman's Univ., 1959–63, MLS, 1971–75, PhD (LS). **Orgs.:** ALA: Equal Oppt. Subcom. (1976–79); Lib. Srv. for Amer. Indian People (1979–). SLA: Minority Rcrt. Com. (1977–78). WHCOLIS: Del. (1979). TX LA: Dist. Ch.; Cncl., Schol. Com., Rcrt. Com. Frdm. to Read Fndn. AAUW: Legis. Com. TX Conf. on Lib. and Info. Srvs.: Del. (1978). **Honors:** Odessa Coll., Woman Tchr. of The Yr., 1967. **Activities:** 1; 17, 35; 50, 63, 74 **Addr.:** 8060 Spencer Hwy., Pasadena, TX 77505.

Niehaus, Thomas (Ag. 3, 1939, Cincinnati, OH) Dir., Latin Amer. Lib., Tulane Univ., 1977–; Ref. Libn., Asst. Prof. of Hist., Southwestern Univ. 1976–77; Instr. in Span. and Hist., Grinnell Coll., 1972–74; Asst. Instr. in Span., Univ. of TX, 1968–71, Span. Biblgphr., 1965–69. **Educ.:** Xavier Univ., 1959–63, AB (Span.); Univ. of Cincinnati, 1963–64, MA (Span.); Univ. of TX, 1964–76, PhD (Hist.), MLS. **Orgs.:** SALALM: Com. on Acquisitions, (Ch., 1979–), Exec. Cncl. (1979–81). Ctr. for Resrch. Libs.: Latin Amer. Micro. Proj. (Bd., 1979–). Latin Amer. Std. Assn. **Honors:** Fulbright schol. in Spain 1967; Natl. Endow. for Hum., Resrch. Grant, 1979–81. **Pubns.:** "Tulane University Library: the Latin American Library," *Encyc. of Lib. and Info. Scis.* (1981); Jt. Auth. "The Catholic Right in Contemporary Brazil: The Case of the Society for the Defense of Tradition, Family, and Property (TFP)," *Religion in Latin American Life and Literature* (1980); "Two Studies on Lorenzo Hervás y Panduro, S.J. (1735–1809).

PROFESSIONAL ACTIVITIES: Institutions: 1. Acad. lib.; 2. Arch.; 3. Assn.; 4. Fed./Gvt. lib.; 5. Inst. lib.; 6. Mfr./Suppl.; 7. Milit. lib.; 8. Musm.; 9. Pub. lib.; 10. Sch. lib.; 11. Sch. of lib. sci.; 12. Spec. lib.; 13. State lib.; 14. (other). **Functions/Activities:** 15. Acq./Col. dev.; 16. Adult srvs.; 17. Admin.; 18. Apprais.; 19. Archit./Bldgs.; 20. Cat./Class.; 21. Chld. srvs.; 22. Circ.; 23. Cons./Pres.; 24. Consult.; 25. Cont. ed.; 26. Educ. lib. sci.; 27. Ext. srvs.; 28. Fund/Grants; 29. Gvt. pubs.; 30. Indx./Abs.; 31. Instr. lib. use; 32. Media srvs.; 33. Micro.; 34. Netwks./Coop.; 35. Persnl.; 36. PR; 37. Publshg.; 38. Recs. mgt.; 39. Ref. srvs.; 40. Repro.; 41. Resrch.; 42. Review.; 43. Secur.; 44. Serials; 45. Spec. col.; 46. Tech. srvs.; 47. Trustees/Bds.; 48. YA srvs.; 49. (other).

I. As Newtonian Popularizer. II. As Anthropoligist," *Archivum Historicum Societatis Iesu* (1975). **Activities:** 1, 2; 15, 17, 39; 54 **Addr.:** Latin American Library, Tulane University, New Orleans, LA 70118.

Niehoff, Robert T. (O. 29, 1938, Cincinnati, OH) Grp. Leader, Info. Sci.–Lib. Stds., Battelle–Columbus Labs., 1980–, Resrch. Sci., 1964–80. **Educ.:** Xavier Univ., 1956–60, BS (Chem.); American Univ., 1972–74, Cert. (Tech. of Mgt.). **Orgs.:** ASIS: Ctrl. OH Chap., Educ. Com. (Ch., 1980–81). **Pubns.:** Jt. auth., "Search Activity of Users of Online Bibliographic Data Bases," *Online Review* (forthcoming); Jt. auth., "Overcoming the Database Vocabulary Barrier: A Solution," *Online* (O. 1979); Jt. auth., "The Role of Automated Subject Switching in a Distributed Information Network," *Online Review* (1979); "Development of an Integrated Energy Vocabulary and the Possibilities for On-line Subject Switching," *Jnl. of ASIS* (1976); Various papers and rpts. **Activities:** 14-Resrch. Inst.; 38, 41, 49-Info. Syst. Design; 56, 62, 75 **Addr.:** Battelle-Columbus Labs, Applied Information and Data Management Systems Section, Columbus, OH 43201.

Nielsen, Brian (F. 12, 1948, Norman, OK) Head, Ref. Dept., Northwestern Univ. Lib., 1980–; Inter-dept. Srvs. Coord., Univ. of NC Media Ctr., 1977–78, Asst. Undergrad. Libn. for Ref. and Instr., 1974–78, Ref. Libn., Undergrad. Lib., 1973–74. **Educ.:** Bard Coll., 1966–70, BA (Hist.); Sch. of Lib. and Info. Sci., SUNY, Albany, 1971–71, MLS; Sch. of LS, Univ. of NC, 1977–80, doct. cand. **Orgs.:** ALA: ACRL/Bibl. Instr. Sect., Resrch. Com. (Ch., 1977–79). NC LA: Ref. and Adult Srvs. Sect. (Ch., 1975–77); AV Com. Univ. of NC-Chapel Hill Libns. Assn.: Pres. (1972–73). **Honors:** Natl. Online Info. Mtg., Best Paper Awd., 1980; Beta Phi Mu, 1980; ALA Student to Dallas Awd., 1971. **Pubns.:** "Change in Public Services: Perspectives of Three North Carolina Librarians," *NC Libs.* (Fall 1979); "Online Bibliographic Searching and the Deprofessionalization of Librarianship," *Online Review* (S. 1980). **Addr.:** Reference Department, Northwestern University Library, 1935 Sheridan Rd., Evanston, IL 60201.

Nielsen, Carol S. (My. 21, 1949, New York, NY) Freelnc. Ed. Wk., 1981–; LS Libn., Sch. LS, Univ. of NC, 1972–80. **Educ.:** Hartwick Coll., 1967–71, BA (Span., Comp. Lit.); SUNY, Albany, 1971–72, MLS. **Orgs.:** ALA: ACRL, LS Libns. Discuss. Grp. (Ch., 1977–78), Nsltr. Ed. (1976–77). NC LA: Cont. Educ. Lib. User (Coord., 1977); Conf. AV Media Acad. Lib. (Jt. coord., 1974). Unitarian Church of Evanston. IL Quilters Inc. **Pubns.:** Ed., *Directory of Library Science Librarians* (1975); Ed., *Directory of Library Science Collections* (1977); "The Librarian's Bookshelf," *Bowker Annual* (1978, 1979, 1980); Ed. Bd., *NC Lib.* (1979–80); reviews. **Activities:** 1, 11; 17, 26, 36; 62, 74, 75 **Addr.:** 2100 Noyes St., Evanston, IL 60201.

Nielsen, Katherine Anderson (Ap. 26, 1947, Berkeley, CA) Libn., Afternon Acad., 1981–; Head Libn., The Head-Royce Sch., 1979–81; Head Libn., The Hamlin Sch., 1975–79, Tchr., 1971–75; Tchr., Marymount HS, 1970–71. **Educ.:** Univ. of CA, Berkeley, 1964–68, AB (Hist.); Hunter Coll., 1968–72, MA (Hist.); Univ. of CA, Berkeley, 1975–77, MLS. **Orgs.:** ALA: ALSC. Assn. Chld. Libns.: Bd. (1979–1980); Disting. Bk. Com. (Ch., 1980–81). **Activities:** 10; 15, 21, 48; 63, 89 **Addr.:** 6942 Colton Blvd., Oakland, CA 94611.

Nielsen, Ralph (Ja. 10, 1930, Invermere, BC) Head, Cat. Dept., Univ. of ID, 1972–, Cat. Libn., 1964–72; Cat. Libn., Univ. AB Lib., Edmonton, 1959–64; Gen. Ref. Libn., Enoch Pratt Free Lib., 1958–59. **Educ.:** Univ. of AB, Edmonton, 1951–54, BA (Fr., Grmn.); Univ. of Toronto, 1957–58, BLS. **Orgs.:** ID LA. Pac. NW LA. AB LA. Palouse Hills Pony Club. Amer. Fed. of Tchrs. **Pubns.:** "Of *fiche* and *fiches*," *Amer. Lib.* (S. 1978); "KX Temporary Law Classification," *The Law Catlgr.* (Ja. 1977). **Activities:** 1; 20, 34, 44; 90, 95-European Langs. **Addr.:** University of Idaho Library, Moscow, ID 83843.

Nielsen, Roy J. M. (O. 26, 1916, San Francisco, CA) Libn., Serials Sect., Lawrence Berkeley Lab., 1980–, Head, Lib. Dept., 1968–80; Fld. Rep., Armed Srv. Tech. Info. Agency, 1957–61; Head, Lib. Dept., U.S. Nvl. Radiol. Defense Lab., 1951–57; Libn., State Div. of Mines, CA State, 1946–51. **Educ.:** Univ. of CA, Berkeley, 1935–39, AB (Geol.); 1940–41, Cert. (LS). **Orgs.:** ASIS. SLA: Doc. Div., Secy. (1971–72); San Francisco Chap., Educ. Com. (1966–69); Advert. Com. (1974–76). **Pubns.:** "Introduction," *Acquisition of Special Materials* (1966). **Activities:** 5, 12; 15, 17, 33; 56, 84, 91 **Addr.:** 638 Viona Ave., Oakland, CA 94610.

Niemi, Taisto John (D. 3, 1914, Aurora, MN) Dir. of the Lib., Le Moyne Coll., 1963–; Libn., NY State Univ. Coll. (Buffalo), 1960–63; Lectr., NY State Univ. (Geneseo), 1960–63; Libn., N. MI Univ., 1953–60; Ext. Lectr., Univ. MI, 1958–60. **Educ.:** VA Jr. Coll., 1936, AA; Univ. of MN, 1946, BS; Univ. MI, 1951, AM (LS), 1960, PhD. **Orgs.:** Cath. LA: Ctrl. NY Unit, Exec. Bd. NY LA. Ctrl. NY Lib. Resrc. Cncl.: Past Pres., Bd. of Trustees. Salt Springs Neighborhood Assn. **Pubns.:** Chapter in *The Faith of the Finns* (1972). **Activities:** 1; 15, 17, 19; 66, 90, 92 **Addr.:** Library, Le Moyne College Library, Le Moyne Heights, Syracuse, NY 13214.

Nilsen, Alleen Pace (O. 10, 1936, Phoenix, AZ) Assoc. Prof., Dept. of Educ. Tech. LS, AZ State Univ., 1975–; Asst. Prof., Univ. of North. IA, 1971–73; Instr., East. MI Univ., 1969–71; Tchr., Amer. Intl. Sch. of Kabul, Afghanistan, 1967–69. **Educ.:** Brigham Young Univ., 1954–58, BA (Eng.); Amer. Univ., 1960–61, MEd (Educ.); Univ. of IA, 1971–73, PhD (YA, Chld. Lit.). **Orgs.:** AZ LA: Exec. Bd. (1978–79). ALA. Natl. Cncl. of Tchrs. of Eng.: *The Eng. Jnl.* Co-ed. (1980–84); Women's Com. (1973–80). Mod. Lang. Assn. **Pubns.:** Jt. auth., *Literature for Today's Young Adults* (1980); ed. and jt. auth., *Sexism and Language* (1978); "The House that Alice Built: An Interview with the Author Who Brought You *Go Ask Alice*," *Sch. Lib. Jnl.* (O. 1980); "Five Factors Contributing to the Unequal Treatment of Females in Picture Books," *Top of the News* (Spr. 1978); "Children's Literature and the Mass Media," *Sch. Lib. Jnl.* (N. 1977); review ed., YA bks., *Eng. Jnl.* (1973–80). **Activities:** 11; 25, 26, 42 **Addr.:** 1884 E. Alameda, Tempe, AZ 85282.

Nisenoff, Sylvia (S. 15, 1928, Perth Amboy, NJ) Prof. Info. Spec., Amer. Persnl. and Guid. Assn., 1979–; Ref. Libn., Dayton and Montgomery Cnty. Pub. Lib. Syst., 1958–61; Tchr., NJ Sch., 1951–54. **Educ.:** Douglass Coll., 1947–51, BA (Eng.); Univ. of South. CA, 1957–58, MS (LS); George Washington Univ., 1976–77, Cert. (Edit., Publshg.). **Orgs.:** SLA. **Honors:** Beta Phi Mu, 1958. **Pubns.:** "Learning Disability: One Mother's View," *The Montgomery Jnl.* (Ap. 15, 1976); "One mother's experience with learning disability," *The Pointer* (Spr. 1978); *Bibliography of The School Counselor's Involvement in Career Education* (1980). **Activities:** 12; 15, 17, 20; 50, 92, 95-counsel. and guid. **Addr.:** 3707 Woodbine St., Chevy Chase, MD 20015.

Nisonger, Thomas E. (D. 14, 1943, Ashtabula, OH) Col. Dev. Libn., Univ. of TX, Dallas, 1981–; Biblgrphr., Univ. of MB, 1977–81, Catlgr. (Slavic), 1974–77. **Educ.:** Coll. of Wooster, 1962–66, BA (Pol. Sci., Hist.); Univ. of Pittsburgh, 1973–74, MLS; Columbia Univ., 1966–76, PhD (Compar. Pol.). **Orgs.:** MB LA. Cncl. of Acad. Libns. of MB: Exec. Bd. (1977–78). ALA: ACRL. **Honors:** Beta Phi Mu, 1974; Phi Beta Kappa, 1966. **Pubns.:** "Collection Evaluation: Nine Techniques Discussed in the Literature," *MB LA Bltn.* (D. 1980); "An In-Depth Collection Evaluation at the University of Manitoba Library...," *Lib. Resrcs. and Tech. Srvs.* (Fall, 1980); "Jack Kerouac: a Bibliography of Biographical and Critical Material, 1950-1979," *Bltn. of Bibl.* (Ja.–Mr. 1980); "The Sources of Canadian History," *MB LA Bltn.* (Je. 1981); various papers. **Activities:** 1; 15; 54, 92 **Addr.:** McDermott Library, University of Texas at Dallas, Richardson, TX 75080.

Nissler, Pamela L. (O. 9, 1945, Youngstown, OH) Lib. Dir., Edwin A. Bemis Pub. Lib., 1975–; Asst. Dir., 1973–75, Ref. Libn., 1970–72. **Educ.:** Bowling Green State Univ., 1963–67, BS (Educ.); Univ. of Denver, 1969–70, MA (LS). **Orgs.:** ALA. Mt. Plains LA: PR Com. (1978); Pres. (1979–80). CO LA: Legis. Com. (1978–); Educ. Com. (1974–78). Ctrl. CO Lib. Syst.: Bd. of Dirs. (Pres., 1979). Various other orgs. Littleton Cult. Arts Fndn. Frnds. of the Littleton Lib.: Bd. (1975–). **Honors:** Alpha Gamma Delta. **Activities:** 9, 10; 15, 17, 35; 55, 63, 68 **Addr.:** 1579 W. Briarwood Ave., Littleton, CO 80120.

Nist, Joan Stidham (Ap. 24, 1926, Chicago, IL) Asst. Prof., Dept. of Educ. Media, Auburn Univ., 1972–; Instr., Austin Coll., 1964–66; Instr., East. MI Univ., 1953–61. **Educ.:** Lawrence Univ., 1943–47, AB (Eng.); IN Univ., 1949–52, MA (Eng.); Auburn Univ., 1971–77, EdD. **Orgs.:** AL Instr. Media Assn.: Assoc. Ed. Nsltr. (1978–). Natl. Cncl. of Tchrs. of Eng. Adlsnt. Lit. Assn. Chld. Lit. Assn. Chld. Lit. Asm. Phi Delta Kappa: Auburn Chap., Pres., Natl. Del., 1st VP, 3rd VP (1975–). Pop. Culture Assn.: Chld. Lit. (Ch. 1976–78). **Honors:** Danforth Fndn., Danforth Assoc., 1978; Phi Beta Kappa, 1946; Phi Kappa Phi, 1976. **Pubns.:** "Cultural Constellations in Translated Children's Literature," *Bookbird* (F. 1979); "Aspects of Inservice Education in England," *Procs., Assn. Tchr. Educ.* (1977); "The Mildred L. Batchelder Award," *Lang. Arts* (Ap. 1979). **Activities:** 11; 26, 32, 41; 63, 74, 89 **Addr.:** Department of Educational Media, Auburn University, Auburn, AL 36830.

Nitecki, Andre (Ap. 30, 1925, Sosnowiec, Poland) Prof., Univ. of AB, 1975–; Assoc. Cur., Ethnography, Glenbow Musm., 1979–; Assoc. Prof. and Head, Dept. of Lib. Stds., Univ. of Ghana, 1968–74; Adj. Assoc. Prof., Dept. of Fine Arts, Syracuse Univ., 1968–, Asst. Prof., 1966–68, Cur., African Art, 1966–; Sr. Lectr., Univ. of Ibadan, 1964–66; Various prof. positions (1959–64). **Educ.:** Oxford Univ., 1946–48 (Law); Univ. of Chicago, 1956–63, MA (LS). **Orgs.:** ALA: Intl. Educ. Com. (1979–). Can. LA. LA (UK). Intl. and Compar. Libnshp. Grp. Can. Assn. of African Stds. **Pubns.:** Various bks. and articles. **Activities:** 11; 20, 26, 30; 54, 55 **Addr.:** Faculty of Library Science, The University of Alberta, Edmonton, AB T6G 2J4 Canada.

Nitecki, Danuta (D. 2, 1950, London, Eng.) Coord., IL Resrch. Ref. Act., Univ. IL, 1978–; Head, ILL and Auto. Info Srv., Univ. TN (Knoxville) 1972–78. **Educ.:** Univ. WI, Milwaukee, 1967–70, BA (Art Hist.); Drexel Univ., 1971–72, MLS; Univ. TN, 1973–76, MA (Comm.). **Orgs.:** ALA: RASD, Info. Retrieval Com. (1975–78, Ch. 1977–78), MARS, Org. Com. (1977–78), VCh. (1978–79), Ch. (1979–80); Various other com. TN LA: State ILL Code Com. (Ch. 1973–74); Treas. (1976–77); Legis. Com. (Ntwk. Coord. (1977–78). IL LA. Sierra Club: TN Chap. Ed. (1975). **Honors:** Beta Phi Mu: Beta Omicron Chap., Pres. (1977–78); Phi Beta Phi, 1970; Kappa Tau Alpha, 1977. **Pubns.:** "Effects of Sponsorship and Nonmonetary Incentive on Response Rate," *Jnlsm. Qtly.* (Aut. 1978); Jt. Auth. "A New Breed of Online Speciality: The Remote Profiler," *ONLINE* (Jl. 1978); "Some Questions Concerning the Proposed Tennessee Numerical Register (TENR)," *TN Libn.* (Spr. 1977); Complr. *Some Reprographic Concerns Related to Interlibrary Loan*, (Apr. 1977); "Integration of On-Line With Existing Reference Service," *in On-Line Bibl. Srvs.* (Apr. 1977); Various other Pubns. and Speeches. **Activities:** 1; 22, 34, 39; 56, 93, 95 **Addr.:** 804 S. Lincoln Ave., Urbana, IL 61801.

Nitecki, Joseph Zbigniew (Ja. 31, 1922, Dabrowa Gornicza, Poland) Dir. of Libs., SUNY, Albany, 1980–; Prof. and Exec. Dir. of Lib. and Lrng. Resrc., Univ. of WI (Oshkosh), 1978–80; Assoc. Dir. of Lib., Temple Univ., 1970–78; Assoc. Dir., Tech. Srv., Univ. of WI (Milwaukee), 1967–70; Branch Libn., Chicago City Coll., 1962–66; Law Catlgr., Univ. Chicago Law Sch. Lib., 1961–62. **Educ.:** Wayne Univ., 1950–55, BA (Phil.); Roosevelt Univ., 1956–59, MA (Phil.); Univ. of Chicago, 1960–62, MA (LS); Nvl. Coll., Eng., 1943–44, Comsn. **Orgs.:** ALA: ACRL, Elec. Com. (Ch., 1964–66); RTSD, Reprodct. Lib. Matls. Sect. (Ch., 1971, Mem. 1971–74); RTSD/LED, Com. Educ. Resrc. Tech. Srv. (Ch., 1973–75), Piercy Awd. Jury (Ch., 1978); Various other coms. ASIS. Various other orgs. Socty. for Gen. Systs. Resrch. **Honors:** Beta Phi Mu; *Jnl. of Lib. Hist.*, Awd. Outstan. Mss., 1969. **Pubns.:** *Directory of Library Reprographic Services: 5th, 6th & 7th ed.* (1973–78); "National Network of Information in Poland," *Jnl. of the Amer. Socty. for Info. Sci.* (1979); "Metaphors of Librarianship: A Suggestion for a Metaphysical Model," *Jnl. of Lib. Hist.* (1979). "Reprographic Services in American Libraries," *Lib. Resrcs. & Tech. Srvs.* (Fall 1979); "An Idea of Librarianship; An Outline for a Root-Metaphor Theory in Library Science," *Jnl. of Lib. Hist.* (1981); Various other pubns. **Activities:** 1; 17; 75, 92 **Addr.:** State University of New York at Albany, Libraries, 1400 Washington Ave., Albany, NY 12222.

Nix, James R. (Je. 22, 1947, Bakersfield, CA) Ch., Dept. of Arch. and Spec. Col., Loma Linda Univ. Lib. 1974–; VP, Adventist Hist. Prop., Inc., 1981–; Dir., Ellen G. White Resrch. Ctr., 1976–, Managing Ed., ADVENTIST HERITAGE, 1975–80, Assoc. Univ. Archvst., 1972–, Ed., E.G. White Resrch. Ctr. News Notes, 1979–. **Educ.:** Loma Linda Univ., 1964–69, BA (Theo., Hist.); Andrews Univ., 1969–72, MDiv; Univ. of South. CA, 1973–75, MSLS. **Orgs.:** SAA. Assn. of Seventh-Day Adventist Hist. Assn. of West. Adventist Hist. Amer. Hist. Socty. Phi Kappa Phi. **Honors:** Beta Phi Mu. **Pubns.:** "Cogitations of an Adventist Bibliophile," *Proceedings* 7th Day Adventist Conf. Coll. and Univ. Tchrs. (1976); "The American Centennial, An Adventist Perspective," *Adventist Heritage*, (Sum. 1976). **Activities:** 1, 2; 23, 39, 45; 80, 85, 90 **Addr.:** Loma Linda University Library, Loma Linda, CA 92350.

Nix, Larry T. (N. 7, 1943, Mt. Pleasant, TN) Lib. Consult., WI Div. for Lib. Srvs., 1980–; Dir., Greenville Cnty. Lib., 1974–80; Assoc. Dir., Pub. Lib. of Charlotte and Mecklenburg Cnty., 1971–74; Dir., Clinch-Powell Reg. Lib. Ctr., 1969–71; Libn. II, Pub. Lib. of Charlotte and Mecklenburg Cnty., 1967. **Educ.:** George Peabody Coll., 1961–65, BA (Eng.); Univ. of IL, 1965–67, MS (LS). **Orgs.:** ALA: PLA, Bd. of Dirs. (1977–78); Lib. Admin. Sect., Persnl. Admn. Sect., Secy. (1975–77), PR Sect. Pubn. Com. (1973–77). SELA: Exec. Bd. (Secy., 1976–78); Pub. Lib. Sect., Nom. Com. (Ch., 1978). SC LA: Comm. on Actv. of SC LA (Vice-Ch., 1976–77); Int. Frdm. Com. (1975–77). Various other coms., orgs. Rotary Club of Greenville: Nsltr. Com. (1979–80); World Srv. Com. (Ch., 1978–79); Cmnty. Srv. Com. (Ch., 1977–78). Greenville Litcy. Assn.: Exec. Bd. (1977–80); Pres. (1979–80). Metro. Arts Cncl.: Treas. (1976–79). Various other orgs. **Pubns.:** "The Disadvantaged and Discipline in the Public Library: A Case Study," *NC Lib.* (Sum. 1974); "PLSS: A Big Question Mark," *PLA Nsltr.* (Fall 1977). **Activities:** 9; 17, 35, 47; 78, 89 **Addr.:** 3605 Niebler Ln., Middleton, WI 53562.

Nobari, Nuchine (Ja. 10, 1946, Teheran, Iran) Chief Libn., Davis, Polk and Wardwell, 1977–; Asst. Libn., Paul Weiss Rifkind, 1971–76. **Educ.:** East. MI Univ., 1967–69, BA (Soc. Sci.); Wayne State Univ., 1970, MLS; Pace Univ., 1977–80, MBA. **Orgs.:** SLA. AALL. **Pubns.:** "Problems of Generating an In-house Database of Legal Memoranda," *Natl. Online Mtg. Proceedings* (1981). **Activities:** 59, 77 **Addr.:** Davis Polk & Wardwell, One Chase Manhattan Plz., New York, NY 10005.

Nobbs, Peter M. (My. 21, 1930, Mauritius) Dir., Info. Srvs. Div., Pulp and Paper Resrch. Inst. of Can., 1980–, Mgr., Tech. Info. Sect., 1968–80, Assoc. Tech. Spec., 1962–68; Resrch. Asst., McGill Univ., 1960–62; Asst. Conservator of Forests, Brit. Guiana Gvt., 1954–60. **Educ.:** Univ. of Wales, 1949–52, BSc (Forestry, Bot.); Univ. of Oxford, 1953–54, (Tropical Forestry). **Orgs.:** Can. Assn. Info. Sci. ASIS. Socty. Tech. Comm. Sci. and Tech. Std. Grp.: Rpt. on Sci. Tech. Info. in Can. (1967–68). Can. Pulp Paper Assn.: Tech. Sect., CPPA/TAPPI Jt. Textbk. Com. Tech. Assn. of the Pulp Paper Indus. **Pubns.:** Ed., *Thesaurus of Pulp and Paper Terms, 2nd Ed.* (1971); "Coordinate Indexing and the Pulp and Paper Thesaurus as Tools in Information Retrieval," *TAPPI*

Special Subjects/Services: 50. Adult educ.; 51. Advert./Mktg.; 52. Aerosp.; 53. Agric.; 54. Area std.; 55. Arts/Hum.; 56. Autom.; 57. Bibl./Prtg.; 58. Bio. sci.; 59. Bus./Fin.; 60. Chem.; 61. Copyrt.; 62. Documtn.; 63. Educ.; 64. Engin.; 65. Env.; 66. Eth. grps.; 67. Film; 68. Food/Nutr.; 69. Geneal.; 70. Geo.; 71. Geol.; 72. Handcpd.; 73. Hist.; 74. Int. frdm.; 75. Info. sci.; 76. Insr.; 77. Law; 78. Legis.; 79. Math./Comp. sci.; 80. Med.; 81. Metals; 82. Nat. resrcs.; 83. Newsp.; 84. Nuc. sci.; 85. Oral hist.; 86. Petr./Energy; 87. Pharm.; 88. Phys./Astr./Math.; 89. Readg.; 90. Relig.; 91. Sci./Tech.; 92. Soc. sci.; 93. Telecom.; 94. Transp.; 95. (other).

(1965); ed., *"Trend" Mag.* (1970–). **Activities:** 12, 14-Indus. Resrch. Inst.; 17, 37, 39; 75, 91 **Addr.:** Pulp and Paper Research Institute of Canada, 570 St. John's Blvd., Pointe Claire, PQ H9R 3J9 Canada.

Noble, Barbara Norwood (S. 22, 1936, Ocala, FL) Coord., Lib./AV Srvs., Parkway Sch. Dist., 1979–; Instr.–Media Spec., Harris-Stowe State Coll., 1973–78; Libn.–Media Spec., Winston-Salem Pub. Schs., 1970–72; Head Libn., Amer. Consulate, Dhahran, Saudi Arabia, 1966–69; Chld. Libn., New York Pub. Lib., 1960–62; Instr.–Libn., FL A & M Univ., 1959–60; Circ. Libn., Albany State Coll., 1958–59. **Educ.:** Talledega Coll., 1953–57, BA (Eng., Fr.); Syracuse Univ., 1957–58, MSLS. **Orgs.:** St. Louis Reg. Lib. Netwk.: Finance Com. (1980–82); Sch. Rep. Cncl. (1980–82). ALA: AASL, Critical Issues Discuss. Grp. (1981–82); Networking Com. (1981–82); Org. and Bylaws Com. (1979–81); LITA, various coms. (1980–); LAMA; Black Caucus. MO LA: Various coms. (1980–). MO Sch. LA: Various coms. Various orgs. and ofcs. MO Tchrs. Assn. Amer. Assn. Coll. Profs. Forest Park Adv. Bd. Intl. Yr. of the Child: St. Louis Task Force (1979–80). Various other orgs. **Honors:** N. Ctrl. Accred. Assn., Recog. of Outstan. Achvmt., 1979; Harris State Coll., Cert. of Recog., 1978; Untd. Way, Outstan. Achvmt., 1980–81; Black Resrcs. Info. Coord. Srvs., Inc., Outstan. Achvmt. of Minority Stds., 1979. **Pubns.:** "The Source," *Amer. Libs.* (Ja. 1980). **Activities:** 10, 11; 20, 21, 32; 56, 75 **Addr.:** 49 Kingsbury Pl., St. Louis, MO 63112.

Noble, David (Je. 20, 1940, Vancouver, BC) Libn., Cancer Control Agency of BC, 1976–; Ref. Libn., Kellogg Hlth. Scis. Lib., Dalhousie Univ., 1973–76, Ref. Libn., Sci. Lib., 1969–73. **Educ.:** Univ. of BC, 1961–65, BSc (Biochem.), 1968–69, BLS. **Orgs.:** Med. LA. Can. Hlth. LA. BC Hlth. LA: Exec. (1978–80); Pres. (1981–82); Un. List Com. (Ch.). **Activities:** 5, 12; 17; 80 **Addr.:** Cancer Control Agency of BC Library, 2656 Heather St., Vancouver, BC V5Z 3J3 Canada.

Noble, Hadley W. (Mr. 14, Rochester, NY) Head, Serials and Binding Dept., Univ. of Rochester, 1975–, Asst. Head, Serials and Binding Dept., 1970–75, Acting Head, Serials and Binding Sect., Acq. Dept., 1969–70, Serials Catlgr., 1961–69; Eng. Tchr. Rochester area HS, 1954–61. **Educ.:** Univ. of Rochester, 1949–53, BA (Eng.); SUNY at Albany, 1953–54, MA (Eng., Educ.); Syracuse Univ., 1961–64, MSLS. **Orgs.:** ALA: ACRL. NY LA. Monroe Cnty. Lib. Clb. **Honors:** Beta Phi Mu, 1964. **Activities:** 1; 15, 20, 44, 46; 95-Binding. **Addr.:** 1973 Five Mile Line Rd., Penfield, NY 14526.

Noble, Valerie (O. 28, 1931, Bakersfield, CA) Head, Bus. Biomed. Lib., The Upjohn Co., 1970–; Resrch. Libn., Wm. John Upjohn Assoc., 1963–68; Other positions in PR and comm. **Educ.:** Pomona Coll., 1951–53, BA (Art); West. MI Univ., 1963–65, MA (LS). **Orgs.:** SLA: Lib. Mgt. Div., Ch. Elect (1979), Ch. (1980–81), Ch. Elect Div. Cabinet (1981), Spec. Proj. Com. (Ch., 1978–79), Nom. Com. (Ch. 1977–78); Pharm. Div., Prog. Com. (Ch., 1978–79); Advert. Mktg. Div., Bltn. Ed., Ch. (1972–73). Pharm. Mfr. Assn.: Bus. Inf. Com. (Ch., 1978). PR. Women of HI: Secy. (1960). HI Restaurant Assn.: Exec. Secy. (1959–60). **Pubns.:** *Hawaiian Prophet: Alexander Hume Ford, A Biography* (1980); Ed. Com., *Special Delivery: A Collection of Papers* (1978); *The Effective Echo: A Dictionary of Advertising Slogans* (1970); Ed., *Perspectives: A Library School's First Quarter Century* (1970); Jt. Ed., "Information Sources in Pharmacy and Pharmacology," (1980); "A Librarians Guide to Personal Development," (1980); Other pubns. **Activities:** 12; 15, 17, 23; 59, 80, 87 **Addr.:** The Upjohn Co., Business Library 88-0, Kalamazoo, MI 49001.

Noel, Karen Anne (Mr. 17, 1947, Altoona, PA) Libn., Wilson Cnty. Tech. Inst., 1977–; Asst. Libn., Dutchess Cmnty. Coll., 1974–77; Ref. Libn., Univ. of OR, 1973–74, Serials Asst., 1972–73; Libn. III (Ref.), Salem Pub. Lib., 1972; Pub. Srvs. Libn., US Army Spec. Srvs. Thailand, 1971–72; Sr. Lib. Asst., Monmouth Cnty. Lib., 1968–70. **Educ.:** PA State Univ., 1964–68, BS (Bot.); Rutgers Grad. Sch. of Lib. Srv., 1969–71, MLS. **Orgs.:** ALA: ACRL. Dutchess Cnty. LA: VP (1976–77); Secty. (1975–76). Beta Phi Mu: Univ. of OR Chap. (Pres. 1973–74; Secty.-Treas., 1973). NC LA. Univ. of OR Lib. Staff Assn.: Secty. (1973–74). Wilson Cnty. Tech. Inst.: Persnl. Dev. Com. (Ch., 1977–78). **Honors:** Phi Epsilon Phi, 1968; Phi Sigma, 1968; **Pubns.:** Ed., *LRA Newsletter* (1978–79); "A Buying Guide to Reference Books in Women's Studies," *Southeast. Occasional Notes* (1976); Jt. ed., "Ask a Librarian," (1974); "A Municipal Reference Library for Salem, Oregon; Summary Report" (1972). **Activities:** 1, 10; 16, 17, 39; 50, 91 **Addr.:** 101 Boland Way, Knightdale, NC 27545.

Nokes, Jane E. (Je. 1, 1949, Toronto, ON) Archvst., Asst. Supvsr., Recs. Srv., The Bank of NS, 1971–. **Educ.:** Victoria Coll., Univ. of Toronto, 1967–71, BA, hons. (Hist.); Pub. Arch. of Can., 1972, Dip. (Arch. Admn.). **Orgs.:** Assn. Can. Archvsts.: Bus. Arch. Com. (Ch., 1977–). SAA: Lcl. Arrange. Com. (1975). Toronto Area Archvsts. Grp.: Fndn. Ch. (1974–75); Exec. Com. (1975–76); Adv. Com. (Ch., 1974); Constn. Com. (1974); various other coms. Assn. Recs. Mgrs. and Admins. Can Micro. Socty. Corporate Art Collectors Grp. **Pubns.:** "William Lawson," *Dictionary Can. Biog.* (1980); "Business Archives for Canadian Companies," *Can Jnl. Life Insr.* (Jl. 1979); "Aspects of Canadian Printmaking," *Cat. Miragodard Gallery* (1979). **Activities:** 2; 17, 24, 26; 55, 59, 75 **Addr.:** The Bank of Nova Scotia Archives, 44 King St. W., 3rd Floor, E. Mezzanine, Toronto, ON M5H 1H1 Canada.

Nolan, Charles E. (Ap. 6, 1935, Chicago, IL) Archvst.-Recs. Mgr., Archdio. of New Orleans, 1980–; Professorial Lectr., Loyola Univ., New Orleans, 1980–; Pres., Acad. Enterprises of New Orleans, 1978–; Dir., Bicent. Arch. Proj., Archdio. of New Orleans, 1975–80; VP, Gables Acad., 1978–80, Dir., 1971–78. **Educ.:** St. Bonaventure Univ., 1953–58, BA (Phil.); Lateran Univ., Rome, 1958–62, STB (Theo.); Gregorian Univ., Rome, 1962–70, HED (Hist.); Loyola Univ., New Orleans, 1973–80, MEd (Educ.). **Orgs.:** Assn. of Recs. Mgrs. and Admins.: New Orleans Chap., Bd. of Dirs. (1980–). SAA. Assn. for Chld. and Adults with Lrng. Disabilities. Jefferson Hist. Socty. of LA. Amer. Philatelic Socty. **Honors:** Natl. Secy. Assn., New Orleans Chap., Boss of the Yr., 1976. **Pubns.:** *A Southern Catholic Heritage, Volume I, Colonial Period (1704–1813)* (1976); *Bayou Carmel* (1977); Jt. auth., *A Blessed Gift of Gab by Sister Consuela Caillouet* (1980); various articles. **Activities:** 2; 38, 41; 63, 72, 90 **Addr.:** P.O. Box 73354, Metairie, LA 70033.

Nolan, Edward W. (S. 21, 1939, Seattle, WA) Archvst., Libn., Lane Cnty. Musm., 1977–; Archvst., Libn., Seattle Hist. Socty., 1975–77. **Educ.:** Ctrl. WA State Coll., 1961–63, BA (Hist.); Univ. of OR, 1969–71, MA (Hist.), 1974–75, MLS. **Orgs.:** SAA. NW Archvsts. West. Assn. Map Libns. Amer. Hist. Assn. Org. Amer. Histns. **Pubns:** *Catalogue of Manuscripts in the Lane County Museum Library* (1980). **Activities:** 2, 4; 15, 23, 45; 55, 70, 92 **Addr.:** 740 West 13th., Eugene, OR 97402.

Nolan, Joan P. (S. 16, 1934, Olean, NY) Supvsr. Lib. Srv., N. PA Sch. Dist., 1968–; Instr., Drexel Inst. Tech., 1965–69; Libn., Jr. HS, Wissahickon Sch. Dist., 1962–65; Libn., Sr. HS, Cameron Cnty. Sch. Dist., 1959–62; Sr. HS Libn., Linesville Sch. Dist., 1956–57; Cat., Emporium Pub. Lib., 1959. **Educ.:** Clarion State Coll., 1952–56, BS (Educ.); Case West. Rsv. Univ., 1957–59, MS (LS); Westminster Coll., 1957–59, Grad.; Temple Univ., 1971–75, Cert. (Educ. Media). **Orgs.:** PA Sch. LA: Supvsr. Com. (1979–80). Montgomery Cnty. Sch. LA: Secy. (1977–79). ALA. PA LA. Assn. Supvsn. Curric. Dev. PA Lrng. Resrc. Assn. **Honors:** Delta Kappa Gamma; Beta Phi Mu, 1959; Pi Gamma Mu, 1956; ALA, E. P. Dutton/John Macrae Awd., 1965. **Activities:** 10; 17, 32; 85 **Addr.:** 843 Lombardy Dr., Lansdale, PA 19446.

Nolan, Patrick B. (F. 4, 1942, Minneapolis, MN) Head of Arch. and Spec. Col., Wright State Univ., 1973–; Archvst. and Asst. Prof., Hist., Univ. of WI, River Falls, 1971–73. **Educ.:** Carleton Coll., 1960–64, BA (Hist.); Univ. of MN, 1964–71, PhD (Hist.). **Orgs.:** SAA: Nom. Com. (1979); Wkshops. Adv. Com. (Ch., 1978–); Educ. and Prof. Dev. Com. (1975–). Socty. of OH Archvsts.: Pres. (1977–78). Midw. Arch. Conf. Amer. Hist. Assn. Org. of Amer. Hists. **Pubns.:** *The Wright Brothers Collections* (1977); *First Stop for Local History Research* (1976); "Historical and Archival Administration at Wright State," *Grand River* (Win. 1980); "Archivists vs. Disaster," *Midw. Arch. Conf. Nsltr.* (Ap. 1975); Various papers. **Activities:** 1, 2; 17, 26, 45; 52, 55, 69 **Addr.:** Department of Archives and Special Collections, University Library, Wright State University, Dayton, OH 45435.

Noland, Jon (Mr. 17, 1945, Chicago, IL) Head, Circ. Dept., IA State Univ. Lib., 1979–; Asst. Dir., Lib., AYRA-MEHR Univ. of Tech., Isfahan, Iran, 1977–78; Asst. Branch Head, Team Leader, N. York Pub. Lib., ON, 1973–77; Chief Libn., Fort Erie Pub. Lib., 1970–73. **Educ.:** Univ. of KY, 1963–67, BA (Latin Amer. Culture), 1967–68, MSLS. **Orgs.:** ALA. CAN. LA. Inst. Prof. Libns. of ON: Pres. (1973–74). **Pubns.:** "Reactions to Accreditation–There Are Choices," *Can. Lib. Jnl.* (Ap. 1974). **Activities:** 1, 9; 17, 35, 36 **Addr.:** Iowa State University Library, Ames, IA 50011.

Nolin, Carolyn J. (F. 24, 1944, Booneville, MS) Asst. State Libn., ME State Lib., 1974–, Dir., Lib. Dev., 1973–74, Consult. to Handcpd., 1971–73; Dir., Bkmobile. Srvs., Brunswick Pub. Lib., 1969–71. **Educ.:** Blue Mt. Coll., 1966, BS (Educ.); Univ. of OR, 1967–69, MLS. **Orgs.:** ALA: Natl. Lib. Week (1980–82); PR for State Lib. and Assn. (1979–81). ME LA: VP (1978–80). New Eng. LA: State Lib. Srv. Sect. (Ch., 1972–73). ME Lib. Comsn. **Activities:** 13; 17 **Addr.:** 10 Lots Rd., Fairfield, ME 04937.

Noonan, Patricia Kwinn (F. 25, 1949, Chicago, IL) Catlgr., TN Valley Athrty. Tech. Lib., 1981–; Head, Tech. Srvs., Knoxville Coll., 1975–80; Asst. Hum. Libn., Miami Univ., 1972–74. **Educ.:** Univ. of IL, 1967–71, BA (Eng.), 1971–72, MS (LS); Univ. of TN, 1974–76, MA (Soclgy.). **Orgs.:** ALA. ASIS. TN LA: Mem. Com. (1976–77); Mem. Com. (Ch., 1977–79). E. TN LA. **Honors:** Beta Phi Mu; Phi Beta Kappa; Phi Kappa Phi. **Activities:** 1; 15, 17, 20; 66 **Addr.:** 5704 Pinellas Dr., Knoxville, TN 37919.

Norden, David James (Ja. 10, 1947, Bozeman, MT) Asst. Head, Circ. Dept., OH State Univ., 1976–81; Head, Russ. Div., Mod. Lang. Dept. and Assoc. Dir., Russ. Stds., Ctr. for Sec. Schs., Choate Sch., 1970–74. Libn., Boettcher Fndn. Lib., Kent-Denver Country Day Sch., 1974–76; **Educ.:** Dartmouth Coll., 1965–69, AB (Russ.); Yale Univ., 1969–70, (Slavic Lang.); Long Island Univ., 1972–74, MSLS. **Orgs.:** ASIS: Ctrl. OH Chap. (Secy., 1979). OH LA. Acad. LA of OH. ALA: LAMA/Circ. Srvs. Sect. (Secy., 1980), Nom. Com. (1981),/Persnl. Admin. Sect., Ad Hoc Com. on Un. Rels. for Mgrs. (1980–81). Frnds. of the Grove City Pub. Lib. AAUP. **Honors:** Beta Phi Mu, 1975; ASIS, Cert. of Recog. for Srv. as Secy. of Chap. of Yr., 1979. **Pubns.:** "User Response to an Online Catalog: Some Preliminary Results," *Coll. and Resrch. Libs.* (Jl. 1981); "Alexander Blok's City Cycle," *Paroles* (Spr. 1969); "Translations from the City Cycle," *Paroles* (Spr. 1969). **Activities:** 1; 17, 22; 56 **Addr.:** 1453 Wisteria, Ann Arbor, MI 48104.

Norden, Margaret K. (Jl. 23, 1937, Brooklyn, NY) Libn., Univ. of Pittsburgh, 1972–; Ref. Asst., Chatham Coll., 1972; Ref. Libn., Univ. of Rochester, 1968–71; Docum. Libn., Ref. Libn., Brandeis Univ., 1966–68. **Educ.:** Wellesley Coll., 1954–58, BA; Simmons Coll., 1958–59, MLS; West. Reserve Univ., 1964–66, (LS); Univ. of Pittsburgh, 1972– (LS). **Orgs.:** ALA: ACRL, Univ. Lib. Sect., Secy. (1973–76). Med. LA: Exch. Com. (1978–80). Pittsburgh Reg. Med. LA: Exch. Com. (1974–). Pittsburgh Reg. Lib. Ctr.: Coop. Acq. Com. (1977–79). Univ. of Pittsburgh: Various Lib. Com. and Univ. Com. Amer. Jewish Hist. Socty.: Various com. **Pubns.:** "First Supplement: The money's here," *RQ* (Win. 1971); "The money is here: financial assistance for study and research," *RQ* (Fall 1970); "From a sidestep to a goosestep, American editorial awareness of Hitlerism," *Amer. Jew. Hist. Qtly.* (Mr. 1970); "KWIC index to government publications," Jnl. Lib. Ant. (S. 1969); "Necrology, Fanny Goldstein (1888–1961)," *Ibid* (S. 1962); Reviews. **Addr.:** 5466 Fair Oaks St., Pittsburgh, PA 15217.

Nordmann, Terrance J. (O. 26, 1945, Monticello, IA) Assoc. Prof., AL A & M Univ., 1977–; Asst. Prof., North. IL Univ., 1974–77; Instr., IL Valley Cmnty. Coll., 1972–74; various positions in TV. **Educ.:** Loras Coll., 1963–67, BA (Hist.); North. IL Univ., 1970–71, MA (Radio, TV), 1974–76, EdD (Instr. Tech.). **Orgs.:** AECT. AL Instr. Media Assn. North. IL Media Assn.: Nsltr. Com. (Ch., 1975–76); Natl. Conv. Com. (Ch., 1976–77). Smithsonian Assn. **Honors:** N. AL Educ. Oppt. Ctr., Cert. of Apprec., 1978. **Activities:** 10, 11; 26, 32, 33; 57, 62, 94 **Addr.:** School of Library Media, P.O. Box 283, Alabama A & M University, Normal, AL 35762.

Nordquest, Corrine M. (S. 10, 1922, Ashtabula, OH) Sr. Cat. Libn., Yale Dvnty. Lib., 1971–81; Head Catlgr., Pittsburgh Theo. Semy., 1967–71; Libn., Congregational Lib., Boston, 1963–67, Asst. Libn., Catlgr., 1958–63. **Educ.:** Schauffler Coll., 1940–44; Simmons Coll., 1958–61; Natl. Arch., 1966, Arch. Admin. Cert. **Orgs.:** ATLA. SAA: Relig. Arch. Com. **Activities:** 1; 20, 39; 90 **Addr.:** 138 Hancock St., Auburndale, MA 02166.

Norell, Angela (Angie) Sara (Ag. 28, 1942, Appleton, MN) Libn., Info. Spec., Dir., MN Zoological Garden Lib., 1979–; Assoc. Libn., Hennepin Cnty. Lib., 1978–79; Prin. Libn., Prince George's Cnty. Lib., 1974–77, Sr. Libn., 1971–73, Libn., 1969–71. **Educ.:** Concordia Coll., St. Paul, MN, 1960–62; Concordia Coll., River Forest, IL, 1963–64, BS (Educ.); Univ. of MD, 1968–69, MLS. **Orgs.:** SLA. MN LA. Cap. Area Libs. in Cnsrtm. **Honors:** Beta Phi Mu, 1969; Phi Kappa Phi, 1969. **Pubns.:** "Dear Zoo Library...," *Animal Kingdom*, (Ag.–S. 1980). **Activities:** 12, 13; 15, 34, 39; 58, 65, 80 **Addr.:** Library, Minnesota Zoological Garden, 12101 Johnny Cake Ridge Rd., Apple Valley, MN 55124.

Norell, Irene Louise Palmer (Springfield, NH) Assoc. Prof., Div. of LS, San José State Univ., 1959–; Asst. Prof., North. IL Univ., 1958–59; Libn., Grand Forks Pub. Lib., 1950–56. **Educ.:** Univ. of MN, BS (Eng.), 1956–58, MA (LS); San José State Univ., 1977, MA (Hist.). **Orgs.:** ALA: Rcrt. Com. (1960–65). CA LA: Cncl. (1975–76). Amer. Prtg. Hist. Assn. San Jose City Lib. Comsn. Intl. Assn. Retired Libns.: Fndr., Secy. (1980–). Assn. Bibl. Hist. Amer. Std. Assn. Frnds. San Jose Pub. Lib.: Dir. (1969–78). **Honors:** Beta Phi Mu; Phi Kappa Phi; Phi Alpha Theta. **Pubns.:** "Hannah Logasa," in *Dict. of Amer. Lib. Biog.* (1977); "Lovell, Coryell and Company," *Publishers for Mass Entertainment in Nineteenth-Century America* (1980); *Literature of the Filipino American in the United States* (1976); *Maxfield Parrish, New Hampshire Artist, 1870–1966* (1971), addenda (1974). **Activities:** 9, 11; 26 **Addr.:** 522 S. 5, San Jose, CA 95112.

Norman, Anita L. (Je. 15, 1934, Baraboo, WI) Head, Ref. Dept., Kearney State Coll., 1980–, Ref. Libn., 1975–80, Circ. Libn., 1971–75; Supvsr., Branch Lib., Austin Pub. Lib., 1970–71. **Educ.:** Peru State Coll., 1967–69, BA (Eng.); Univ. of Denver, 1969–70, MA (LS). **Orgs.:** NE LA: Ed. Bd., *NE LA Qtly.* (1975–78). Alpha Delta Kappa: Treas. (1980–). **Pubns.:** Chapter in *How to Help a Friend* (1978). **Activities:** 1; 31, 39; 95-Bibliotherapy. **Addr.:** Calvin T. Ryan Library, Kearney State College, Kearney, NE 68847.

Norman, Carol G. (N. 8, 1945, Baltimore, MD) Tech. Srvs. Supvsr., Beverly Hills Pub. Lib., 1979–; Tech. Srvs. Libn., Azusa Pub. Lib., 1970–79, Gen. Assignment Libn., 1968–70. **Educ.:** Univ. of SK, 1963–66, BA (Fr.); McGill Univ., Sch. of Lib. Sci.,

PROFESSIONAL ACTIVITIES: Institutions: 1. Acad. lib.; 2. Arch.; 3. Assn.; 4. Fed./Gvt. lib.; 5. Inst. lib.; 6. Mfr./Suppl.; 7. Milit. lib.; 8. Musm.; 9. Pub. lib.; 10. Sch. lib.; 11. Sch. of lib. sci.; 12. Spec. lib.; 13. State lib.; 14. (other). **Functions/Activities:** 15. Acq./Col. dev.; 16. Adult srvs.; 17. Admin.; 18. Apprais.; 19. Archit./Bldgs.; 20. Cat./Class.; 21. Chld. srvs.; 22. Circ.; 23. Cons./Pres.; 24. Consult.; 25. Cont. ed.; 26. Educ. lib. sci.; 27. Ext. srvs.; 28. Fund/Grants; 29. Gvt. pubs.; 30. Indx./Abs.; 31. Instr. lib. use; 32. Media srvs.; 33. Micro.; 34. Netwks./Coop.; 35. Persnl.; 36. PR; 37. Publshg.; 38. Recs. mgt.; 39. Ref. srvs.; 40. Repro.; 41. Resrch.; 42. Review.; 43. Secur.; 44. Serials; 45. Spec. col.; 46. Tech. srvs.; 47. Trustees/Bds.; 48. YA srvs.; 49. (other).

1966–68; Univ. of South. CA, Los Angeles, 1971–76, MLS. **Orgs.:** South. CA Tech. Prcs. Grp. CA LA. ALA. Metro. Coop. Lib. Syst.: Tech. Prcs. Com. (Ch., 1981–). **Activities:** 9; 15, 20, 46 **Addr.:** Beverly Hills Public Library, 444 N. Rexford Dr., Beverly Hills, CA 90210.

Norman, (Orval) Gene (N. 2, 1937, Norman, IN) Head, Ref. Dept., IN State Univ., 1966–, Actg. Head, Ref. Dept., 1965–66, Asst. Ref. Libn., 1961–65; Docum., Asst. Ref. Libn., DePauw Univ., 1960–61; Assoc. Prof., Dept. df Lib. Sci., IN State Univ., 1974–, Asst. Prof., 1968–69. **Educ.:** IN State Tchrs. Coll., 1955–59, BA (Sp.); IN Univ., 1959–60, MA (LS). **Orgs.:** ALA: ACRL/Mem. Com. (1979–81). IN LA: Natl. Lib. Week Com. (1971–72); Dist. V Mtg. (Vice-Ch., 1973). AAUP: Local Chap. Secty. (1977–79). **Honors:** Alpha Beta Alpha. **Pubns.:** *Bibliographies By Campus Mail* ERIC (1977); "The Reference Interview: An Annotated Bibliography," *Ref. Srvs. Review* (Ja.–Mr. 1979); Contrib. *Dictionary of Anonymous and Pseudonymous English Literature* (1980–); various book reviews in *Lib. Jnl., RQ,* and *Contemporary Educ.* (1970–79). **Activities:** 1; 17, 31, 39; 61, 63, 77 **Addr.:** 2417 Morton St., Terre Haute, IN 47802.

Norman, Margaret Clarke (Je. 27, 1946, Nashua, NH) Dir., Lib. and Info. Srv., Inc., 1979–; Dir., Chld. Hosp. Resrch. Fndn. Lib., 1976–79; Ref. Libn., Georgetown Univ. Med. Lib., 1975–76; Hist. of Med. Libn., Univ. of TX Med. Branch, 1969–72; Instr. of Grmn. Lang. and Custs., U.S. Army Educ. Ctr., Germany, 1972–75. **Educ.:** Univ. of NH, 1964–68, BA (Grmn.); Simmons Coll., 1969–70, MLS. **Orgs.:** Cincinnati Area Hlth. Sci. LA: Pres. (1977–78); Nom. Com. (1978–79). Med. LA: Pres. (1969). SLA. **Pubns.:** "Continuing Education within a Hospital Medline Consortium," *Bltn. Med. LA* (1979); "Ohio Report from the Basic Unit Representatives," *KOMRML Kommentary* (1978); various std. from the Chld. Hosp. Resrch. Fndn., (1975–78). **Addr.:** 255 Colony Rd., New Haven, CT 06511.

Norman, Ronald V. (Jl. 10, 1929, Venice, CA) Lib. Dir., Kearney Pub. Lib., 1971–; Netwk. Coord., TX State Lib., 1970–71; Ref. Libn., Iliff Sch. of Theo., 1969–70. **Educ.:** Univ. of NM, 1949–53, BA (Eng.); Univ. of Denver, 1969–70, MALS; Luth. Sch. of Theo., 1956–60, MA (Dvnty.). **Orgs.:** ALA. NE LA: Pres. (1974–75). ASIS. Kearney Cham. of Cmrce. Kearney Area Arts Cncl.: Pres. (1979). **Pubns.:** "Science Fiction: Back to Basics," *Lib. Jnl. Spec. Rpt. #6* (1978); "The Golden Decade: Nebraskas Public Library Renaissance," *Spotlighting NE* (Fall 1977). **Activities:** 9; 17 **Addr.:** 2020 1st Ave., Kearney, NE 68847.

Norris, Loretta Wentz (Ag. 6, 1935, Long Branch, NJ) Chief, Law Srv., Lib. Srv. Div., U.S. Dept. of Transp., 1976–; Chief, Law and Resrch. Srv., U.S. Dept. of Hlth., Educ. and Welfare, 1967–73; Supvsr. Libn., Law, Lib. of Congs., 1973–76; Admn. Libn., 8th Army, Korea, 1965–66. **Educ.:** Bucknell Univ., 1953–57, BA (Pol. Sci.); Cath. Univ. of Amer., 1964–65, MS (LS); Ecole Pratique, Alliance Francaise, 1962, Cert. (Fr.). **Orgs.:** ALA: FLIRT (1980–81). AALL: Un. List of Legal Pers. (1976). SLA: Milit. Libns. Grp. (1967–81). Natl. Aviation Club. Soldiers, Sailors and Airmen Relief Assn. **Honors:** U.S. Army Phys. Disability Agency, Achvmt. Awd., 1980. **Pubns.:** "Colonial Courts and Lawyers," *LC Law Lib. Std.* (1977); "The 25th Amendment, A Bibliography," *LC Law Lib. Std.* (1976); *A Checklist of New Jersey Imprints, 1861-1865* (1964); reviews. **Activities:** 4; 17, 24; 77 **Addr.:** 2802 Linden Ln., Silver Spring, MD 20910.

Norstedt, Marilyn L. (Evers) (F. 22, 1936, Quincy, IL) Serials Autom. Coord., VA Polytech. Inst. and State Univ., 1979–, Serials Catlgr., 1976–79, Asst. Serials Catlgr., 1975–76; Ed., Irish Univ. Press, 1968–72; Ed., Garrard Publshg. Co., 1961–65; Ed., Spencer Press, 1960–61. **Educ.:** Valparaiso Univ., 1953–57, BA (Hist.); Univ. of PA, 1957–60, AM (Amer. Cvlztn.); Univ. of IL, 1974–75, MS (LS). **Orgs.:** ALA: RTSD, Assn. Amer. Publshrs. Jt. Com. (1979–)/Serials Sect., Lib. Sch. Educ. Com. (1981–); LITA. VA LA: *VA Libn.* Ed. (1976–77); Int. Frdm. Com. (1976–77). Women's Natl. Bk. Assn. Potomac Tech. Prcs. Libns. Amer. Com. for Irish Std. **Honors:** Beta Phi Mu. **Pubns.:** "A Checklist of the Works of Constance Lindsay Skinner and a Bibliography of the Rivers of America Series," *Constance Lindsay Skinner: Author and Editor* (1980). **Activities:** 1; 20, 34, 44; 56 **Addr.:** Carol M. Newman Library, Virginia Polytechnic Institute and State University, Blacksburg, VA 24061.

Norsworthy, James A. Jr. (S. 19, 1941, Richmond, KY) Libn./Media Spec., Dunn Elem. Sch., 1972–; Adj.–Asst. Prof., Spalding Coll., 1967–; Selecting Libn., Jefferson Cnty. Pub. Schs., 1971–72; Libn., Greathouse Elem. Sch., 1962–71. **Educ.:** Morehead State Univ., 1959–62, AB (Hist., Eng., LS); Univ. of KY, 1962–67, MS (LS); Spalding Coll., 1969–73, Rank I Cert. **Orgs.:** KY LA: ALA Cnclr. (1976–81). KY Sch. Media Assn.: Pres. (1974); Secy. (1971); Various coms. Cath. LA: Chld. Bk. Ed. (1974–). ALA: ALSC, Newbery–Caldecott, Various coms. Kappa Delta Phi. Phi Delta Kappa. **Honors:** KY LA, Outstan. Sch. Libn., 1972. **Pubns.:** "In Search Of An Image: The Adult Male Role In Picture Books," *Cath. Lib. World* (D. 1973). **Activities:** 10, 11; 21, 26, 32 **Addr.:** 3203 Goose Creek Rd., Louisville, KY 40222.

Norten, Melanie Nietmann (D. 26, 1951, Dallas, TX) Serials Libn., Dartmouth Coll., 1981–; Head Cat. Libn., Univ. of IA Law Lib., 1979–81, Cat. Libn., 1976–79. **Educ.:** Univ. of TX, 1970–73, BA (Fr.); Univ. of IA, 1975–76, MA (LS). **Orgs.:** ALA: RTSD. AALL: Tech. Srvs. Spec. Interest Sect. (1977–81); On-line Bibl. Spec. Interest Sect. (1979–81); Cat. and Class. Com. (1979–80); AV Com. (1978–79). **Pubns.:** "Computerized Cataloging in Law Libraries: OCLC and RLIN Compared," *Law Lib. Jnl.* (Win. 1980); "An Update on RLIN," *Proceedings of Anl. Mtg. of the Mid–Amer. Assn. of Law Libs.* (1980). **Activities:** 1; 44 **Addr.:** Serials Section, Baker Library, Dartmouth College, Hanover, NH 03755.

North, John Andrew (Mr. 13, 1942, St. Albans, Eng.) Dir., Lrng. Resrc. Ctr., Ryerson Polytech. Inst., 1974–; Coll. Libn., Mt. Royal Coll., Calgary, AB, 1972–74; Coll. Libn., Cent. Coll., Scarborough, ON, 1967–72; Mgr. and Ed., Co-op. Bk. Ctr., Toronto, ON, 1964–67; Libn., Morgan Brothers Ltd., 1961–64; Asst. Libn., Nat. Rubber Producers Resrch. Assn., 1959–61. **Educ.:** NW London Polytech., Eng., 1959–63, ALA (LS). **Orgs.:** Can. LA: Cnclr. (1974–76); Can. Assn. of Coll. and Univ. Libs. (Secy., 1972–73). ON LA: Various coms. (1974–). ALA. LA UK. **Pubns.:** "Card Catalog to CoM," *Lib. Jnl.* (O. 1977); "Librarianship: A Profession?" *Can. Lib. Jnl.* (Ag. 1977); reviews. **Activities:** 1; 17, 33, 42 **Addr.:** Learning Resources Centre, Ryerson Polytechnical Institute, 50 Gould St., Toronto, ON M5B 1E8 Canada.

Northcutt, Jane B. (Guthrie, OK) Dir., Ponca City Lib., 1963–; Libn., North. OK Coll., 1960–63. **Educ.:** Univ. of OK, 1959, BA (Hist.), 1960, MLS. **Orgs.:** OK LA: Pres. (1966–67). ALA: Cnclr. (1967–68). SWLA. Soroptimist Intl. of Ponca City: Pres. (1974–75). **Honors:** Kappa Alpha Theta. **Pubns.:** *A Study of the Community of Ponca City, Oklahoma and an Analysis of Library Services with Recommendations* (1979). **Addr.:** 1605 Meadowbrook, Ponca City, OK 74601.

Northup, Diana E. (S. 9, 1948, Morgantown, WV) Chief, Educ. and Instr. Progs., Med. Ctr. Lib., Univ. of NM, 1977–; Branch Libn., Lib. of the Hlth. Scis.–UC, Univ. of IL, 1974–77, Asst. Bio. Libn., 1972–74, Med. Bibl. Instr., 1975–77. **Educ.:** WV Univ., 1966–69, BA (Pol. Sci.); Univ. of IL, 1971–72, MSLS. **Orgs.:** Med. LA: Cont. Educ. Instr. Cave Resrch. Fndn.: Log Keeper, CRF-W. **Honors:** Beta Phi Mu, 1972, Grant, Natl. Lib. of Med., 1980. **Pubns.:** "Education for Health Sciences Librarianship: The Master's Curriculum Component," *Proceedings of the Allerton Invitational Conference on Education for Health Sciences Librarianship* (1979); Jt. auth., "A Two-Phased Model for Library Instruction," *Bltn. of the Med. LA* (1977). **Activities:** 1; 31, 39, 41; 80 **Addr.:** Medical Center Library, University of New Mexico, Albuquerque, NM 87131.

Norton, Alice (Ap. 20, 1926, Columbus, OH) Owner, Oper., Alice Norton PR, 1968–; PR Dir., Westchester Lib. Syst., 1962–66; PR Ofcr., Denver Pub. Lib., 1955–61; Various other positions in PR. **Educ.:** Wellesley Coll., 1943–47, BA (Hist.); Univ. of IL, 1961–62, MS (LS). **Orgs.:** ALA: 1959 Conf., Pubcty. Dir.; PR Sect. (Ch., 1963–64); Natl. Lib. Week (Ch., 1975–77). Lib. PR Cncl.: Pres. (1969–70). NY Lib. Club: Cncl. (1971–75). NY LA. NJ LA. PR Socty. Amer. Women Exec. PR: Bd. Dirs. (1978–80). Leag. Women Voters. AAUW. **Honors:** ALA, Wilson Co., John Cotton Dana Awds., 1957, 1976; NY Pub. Lib., Lib. PR Cncl. Awd. 1971. **Pubns.:** "Public Relations," *Local Public Library* (1980); *Public Relations: A Guide to Information Sources* (1971); "Public Relations," *ALA Yrbk.* (1978). **Activities:** 6; 24, 25, 36; 51 **Addr.:** Alice Norton Public Relations, Box 516, Ridgefield, CT 06877.

Norton, Eloise Speed (Ag. 14, 1928, West Point, MS) Lrng. Resrc. Spec., Houston Indp. Dist., 1979–; Adjunct Assoc. Prof., Sam Houston Univ., Sch. of LS. Asst. Prof., MS Univ. for Women, 1972–78; Libn., Lib. Consult., Spring Branch Sch. (Houston, TX), 1956–72; Libn., Harlengen HS (TX), 1952–53; Various tchg. positions, Sum. Sch., 1966–71. **Educ.:** MS Univ. for Women, 1952, BS (LS); MS State Univ., 1960, MEd, (Guid. Educ.); LA State Univ., 1968, MS (LS); MS State Univ., 1978, EdD. **Orgs.:** ALA: AASL, NEA Com. (1960), Elem. Sch. Lib. Com. (1960). TX LA: Sch. Lib. Sect. (Ch.), Chld. RT. MS LA. AALS. AAUW. **Pubns.:** *Folk Literature of the British Isles* (1978); "Home of C. Robin and Friends," *Top of News* (Ja. 1973); "Change, the Name of the Game," *MS Lib. News,* (Ap. 1970); "Paperback Cornicopia" *Lib. Jnl.* (My. 1968); "Time for a Special Lesson" *Lib. Jnl.* (Ap. 1965); "Spring Branch Processing Center," *TX Lib. Jnl.* (Win. 1965); Various other pubns. **Activities:** 10, 11; 21, 25, 32, 48; 54, 63, 67 **Addr.:** 4335 Queens Retreat, Houston, TX 77066.

Norton, Linda N. (Ag. 27, 1944, Kerrville, TX) Head Libn., Edgartown Free Pub. Lib., 1979–; Catlgr., Falmouth Pub. Lib., 1970–79; Asst. Libn. (Catlgr.), Pensacola Pub. Lib., 1965–69. **Educ.:** TX Woman's Univ., 1962–65, BA (LS); Univ. of RI, 1975–79, MLS. **Orgs.:** MA LA. ALA. **Pubns.:** "The Boston Public Library Automated System," *Current Stds. in Libnshp.* (Spr.–Fall 1978); "Information about Unions For Library Employees," *Current Stds. in Libnshp.* (Spr.–Fall 1979); "An Introduction to the Educational Resources Information Center," *Current Stds. in Libnshp.* (Spr.–Fall 1980). **Activities:** 9; 17, 20 **Addr.:** P.O. Box 1004, Vineyard Haven, MA 02568.

Norton, Marie Allison (Ap. 30, 1930, Philadelphia, PA) Dir., Med. Recs., Lankenau Hosp., 1976–; Lectr., Villanova Univ., 1967–; Proj. Coord., Div. Resrch., Lankenau Hosp., 1973–76, Med. Libn., 1966–73. **Educ.:** St. Joseph's Univ., 1963, BS (Soc. Sci.); Villanova Univ., 1966, MS (LS); Various courses (1971–78). **Orgs.:** ASIS. Amer. Med. Rec. Assn. Med. LA: Philadelphia Reg. (Ch., 1972–73); Cont. Educ. Com. (1972–74); MLA/NLM Liaison Com. (1974–77). **Pubns.:** Contrib. ed., MLA Cont. Ed. Manuals (1972–74); "Grant Upgrades Library Service," *Hosp. Progress* (1969). **Activities:** 1, 12; 17, 26, 38; 50, 80, 91 **Addr.:** Lankenau Hospital, Lancaster and City Line Aves., Philadelphia, PA 19151.

Norton, Patsy Gilliam (N. 21, 1938, Edinburg, TX) Dir. of Lrng. Ctr., Wharton Cnty. Jr. Coll., 1977–, Head of Tech. Srvs., 1965–71, Assoc. Dir., 1971–77. **Educ.:** Pan Amer. Univ., 1957–60, BA (Eng., Math); TX Woman's Univ., 1964–65, MLS. **Orgs.:** ALA: ACRL. TX LA. TX Jr. Coll. Tchrs. Assn. AECT. AAUW: Pres. (1972–74). **Honors:** Beta Phi Mu. **Activities:** 14-Cmnty. Coll.; 17, 32, 35; 69, 75 **Addr.:** P.O. Box 422, Wharton, TX 77488.

Notheisen, Margaret A (Chicago, IL) Head, Acq. Dept., Univ. IL, Med. Ctr. Lib., 1971–; Tech. Libn., Metro Sanitary Dist. Chicago, 1966–70; Tech. Libn., Argonne Natl. Lab. Lib., 1959–66; Ref. Libn., Field Enterprises Educ. Corp. 1958–59; Libn., Armour Pharm. Co., 1955–57; Libn., Michael Reese Hosp. Sch. of Nursing Lib., 1951–55; Ref. and Circ. Libn., Rush Med. Lib., Presby. Hosp., 1949–51; Ord. Libn., IL Inst. of Tech., 1948–49. **Educ.:** Rosary Coll., 1945–48, AB (Chem.); Univ. of Chicago, 1957–58, AM (LS), 1970–71, (Cert. of Adv. Study LS). **Orgs.:** ALA. ASIS: Chicago Chap., Secy., Treas. (1975–77); Strg. Com. (1976–77). Med. LA. SLA. Univ. of Chicago Grad. Lib. Sch. Alum. Assn.: Secy., Treas. (1965–66). **Honors:** Natl. Lib. of Med. Flwshp., 1970. **Pubns.:** "The Use of CATLINE by the Acquisitions Department," *Network* (1977). **Activities:** 1, 12; 15, 17, 24; 58, 80, 91 **Addr.:** Library of the Health Sciences, University of Illinois at the Medical Center, 1750 W. Polk St., Chicago, IL 60612.

Novak, Gloria J. (Ag. 31, 1934, Detroit, MI) Head of Engin. Lib., Univ. of CA, Berkeley, 1979–, Lib. Space Planner, 1972–, Lib. Bldg. Consult., Freelnc., 1974–; Admn. Intern, 1971–72, Head of Current Serials, Asst. Ref. Libn., E. Asiatic Lib., 1968–71. **Educ.:** Univ. of CA, Berkeley, 1956–58, (E. Asiatic Std.), 1966–68 (LS). **Orgs.:** ALA: Bldg. Com. for Coll. Univ. Libs. (Ch., 1973–76); Preconf., Renovation, Budget Crisis ... (Ch., 1973–74); Lib. Admin. Div.; Preconf., Running Out of Space (Ch., 1974–75); Preconf. Energy and Lib. Bldg. (Ch., 1977–78). **Pubns.:** Ed., *Running out of Space - What are the Alternatives?* (1978) cassette of preconf. procs. "Energy and Library Buildings," (1976). **Activities:** 1; 17, 19, 24; 64, 65, 72 **Addr.:** Librarian's Office, Main Library, University of California, Berkeley, CA 94720.

Novak, Margo J. (F. 29, 1952, Guelph, ON) Syst. Libn., Env. Can., 1980–; Bibl. Syst. Libn., Hlth. and Welfare Can., 1978–79; Cat., Acq. Libn., Intl. Dev. Resrch. Ctr., 1976–78; Catlgr., Bank of Can, 1975–76. **Educ.:** Carleton Univ., Ottawa, 1970–74, Hons. BA (Ger. Fr.); Univ. of West. ON, 1974–75, MLS. **Orgs.:** Can. Assn. Spec. Lib. Info. Srv.: Cont. Educ. Com. (Ch. 1979–); Ottawa Chap. Can. Assn. Info. Sci. SLA. Cncl. Fed. Lib.: Wking. Grp. Changing Lib. Srv. (1977–). Lib. Assn. Ottawa. **Activities:** 4, 12; 20, 49-Systems; 54, 65, 75 **Addr.:** RR #5, Kemptville, ON K0G 1J0 Canada.

Novak, Vickie (Lynn) (F. 17, 1952, Chicago, IL) Admin. Libn., Acorn Pub. Lib. Dist., 1974–. **Educ.:** Quincy Coll., 1969–73, BA (Span.); Univ. of KY, 1973–74, MSLS. **Orgs.:** ALA: PLA, Conf. Com. Dallas (1979). IL LA: Conf. Regis. Com. (1975); Conf. Job Exch. Com. (1976). S. Suburban LA: Prog. Com. (1977–78); VP (1978–79); Pres. (1979–80). Univ. KY Alum. Club. Abu Arabian Horse Club. Oak Forest Cham. Comrce. **Honors:** IL WHOCOLIS, Del., 1978; Beta Phi Mu. **Pubns.:** "Literature & The Spanish Child," *Catholic Lib. World* (D. 1974); Various articles on horses. **Activities:** 9; 17, 19, 35; 55, 63 **Addr.:** Acorn Public Library District, 15624 S. Central Ave., Oak Forest, IL 60452.

Novak, Victor (Je. 7, 1923, Vel. Poljane, Yugoslavia) Univ. Libn., Univ. of Santa Clara, CA, 1968–, Serials Libn., 1964–68, Loan and Serials Libn., 1958–64, Circ. Libn., 1957–58; Ref. Libn., Cuyahoga Cnty. Lib. Syst., 1955–57. **Educ.:** Univ. of Ljubljana, Slovenia, 1944; Univ. of Graz, Austria, 1945–49, PhD (Pol. Sci.); West. Rsv. Univ., 1954–55, MSLS; 1970–79, various certs. **Orgs.:** Cath. LA: North. CA Chap. (Ch., 1959–63). CA LA. ALA: ACRL; LITA. Amer. Inst. of Mgt.: Exec. Cncl. (1979–). West. Assn. of Schs. Colls. **Pubns.:** "The Librarian in Catholic Institutions," *Coll. & Resrch. Libs.* (1968); "Exchanges," *Cath. Lib. World* (Ap. 1966); "Let's Exchange Profitably," *Lib. Resrcs. & Tech. Srvs.* (Sum. 1965); "Permanent Binding Records for Periodicals," *Cath. Lib. World* (My. 1964); reviews. **Activities:** 1; 17, 35 **Addr.:** University of Santa Clara, Santa Clara, CA 95053.

Special Subjects/Services: 50. Adult educ.; 51. Advert./Mktg.; 52. Aerosp.; 53. Agric.; 54. Area std.; 55. Arts/Hum.; 56. Autom.; 57. Bibl./Prtg.; 58. Bio. sci.; 59. Bus./Fin.; 60. Chem.; 61. Copyrt.; 62. Documtn.; 63. Educ.; 64. Engin.; 65. Env.; 66. Eth. grps.; 67. Film; 68. Food/Nutr.; 69. Geneal.; 70. Geo.; 71. Geol.; 72. Handcpd.; 73. Hist.; 74. Int. frdm.; 75. Info. sci.; 76. Insr.; 77. Law; 78. Legis.; 79. Math./Comp. sci.; 80. Med.; 81. Metals; 82. Nat. resrcs.; 83. Newsp.; 84. Nuc. sci.; 85. Oral hist.; 86. Petr./Energy; 87. Pharm.; 88. Phys./Astr./Math.; 89. Readg.; 90. Relig.; 91. Sci./Tech.; 92. Soc. sci.; 93. Telecom.; 94. Transp.; 95. (other).

Novik, Sandra Platt (Jl. 23, 1940, New York, NY) Media Coord., Rocky Run Intermediate Sch., 1979–; Libn., Media Coord., Fairfax Cnty. Pub. Schs., 1979–; Head Libn., Model Sec. Sch. for Deaf, Gallaudet Coll., 1977–79; Media Spec., Montgomery Cnty. Pub. Schs., 1971–77. **Educ.:** Univ. of MD, 1958–61, BA (Hist.), 1962–69, MA (Amer. Std.); Pratt Inst., 1970–71, MLS; Univ. of MD, 1974–81, Doct. (Educ. Admin.); State of MD, Cert. (Sch., Cnty., State Level Admin., Tchr. of LS, Soc. Std.); State of VA, Prof. Cert. (LS, Hist.); various crs., sems. **Orgs.:** Fairfax Cnty. Sch. LA. ALA. Montgomery Cnty. Sch. LA. Fairfax Educ. Assn. **Pubns.:** *A History of the Printed Cookbook; Bibliography of Females in History; Museum Resource Utilization for the Deaf High School Student; The Russian Immigrant and The New York Shirtwaist Strike of 1909; George Washington Cable and Thomas Nelson Page;* various rpts., std. guides, films. **Activities:** 10; 15, 31, 32 **Addr.:** 7820 Carteret Rd., Bethesda, MD 20034.

Novosal, Paul Peter (O. 5, 1918, St. Louis, MO) Archvst., Socty. of Mary, 1973–, Dir. of Libs., 1958–73, Lib. Dir., 1947–58, Asst. Prof. of Eng., 1958–73. **Educ.:** Univ. Dayton, 1937–40, BS (Eng.); Our Lady of the Lake Coll., San Antonio, TX, 1940–41, BSLS; St. Mary's Univ., San Antonio, TX, 1964–65, MA (Eng.). **Orgs.:** SAA. Natl. Trust for Hist. Prsrvn. Socty. for SW Archvsts. Natl. Hist. Socty. Smithsonian Assoc. Amer. Assn. Retired Persons. Natl. Arch. Assoc. **Honors:** Alpha Sigma Tau, 1941. **Pubns.:** *125 Years of the Society of Mary in Texas* (1977); *Union Catalog of Marian Books in San Antonio* (1956); *Union List of Periodicals in the Larger Libraries of the San Antonio Area* (1952). **Activities:** 2, 14-Relig. Ord.; 15, 41, 45 **Addr.:** Marianist Archives, St. Mary's University, San Antonio, TX 78284.

Nowell, Mary Ann (Ap. 17, 1941, Wilkes-Barre, PA) Chief, Lib. Srv., VA Med. Ctr., Leavenworth, KS, 1975–; Med. Libn., VA Med. Ctr., Kansas City, MO, 1973–75; Catlgr., U.S. Army Cmnd. and Gen. Staff Coll., Fort Leavenworth, KS, 1972–73; Chief, Ref. Srv., MO West. State Coll. 1970–72; Gvt. Docum. Libn., KS State Coll. of Pittsburg, 1968–70; U.S. Army Lib., Germany, 1965–68. **Educ.:** Coll. of New Rochelle, 1959–63, AB (Phys.); Drexel Univ., 1963–65, MS (LS). **Orgs.:** Med. LA. SLA: Heart Amer. Chap., Bd. of Dirs. (1978–79), Pres. (1977–78), Treas. (1976–77). Vets. Admin. Lib. Netwk. (VALNET): Vets. Admin. Med. Dist. 22, Lib. Srv. Com. (Ch., 1975–79). **Activities:** 4; 17; 80, 91 **Addr.:** Library Service (142D), VA Medical Center, Leavenworth, KS 66048.

Noyes, Margaret Elizabeth (Ag. 29, 1950, Atlanta, GA) Circ. Libn., Waco-McLennan Cnty. Lib., 1980–, Assoc. Dir., 1978–80, Bkmobile. Libn., 1976–78; Asst. Libn., Cleburne Pub. Lib., 1973–76. **Educ.:** Univ. of The S., 1968–72, BA (Eng.); N. TX State Univ., 1972–73, MLS. **Orgs.:** ALA. TX LA: Dist. III (Secy., Treas., 1980). SWLA. Profs. For Cmnty. Volunteerism: Pubcty. Com. (Ch., 1978–79). Cmnty. Artists and Students Assn. **Pubns.:** Illustrator, *Fun and Fundamentals: Activities for the Classroom* (1977). **Activities:** 9; 17, 27, 35 **Addr.:** 1717 Austin Ave., Waco, TX 76701.

Noyes, Suzanne N. (D. 15, 19—, Marshfield, WI) Chief, Lib. Srv., Vets. Admin. Med. Ctr., Brockton (MA), 1980–, Med. Libn., 1975–80; Chief Libn., Vets. Admin. Hosp., Madison (WI), 1959–71. **Educ.:** Univ. of WI, 1952–55, BS (Eng. Lit.), 1956–57, MLS, Univ. of IL, 1960, Cert. (Med. Libnshp.). **Orgs.:** New Eng. LA: Mem. Ch. (1979–80); Hosp. Sect. (Pres., 1977–78). N. Atl. Hlth. Scis. Libs.: Pubcty. Ch. (1977). New Eng. Reg. Med. Lib. Srv.: Liaison Com., Guide (1980–), ILL (1979–). **Activities:** 4, 5; 17, 34, 35; 80 **Addr.:** Veterans Administration, Medical Center Library Service, 940 Belmont St., Brockton, MA 02401.

Nugent, Lynn L. (S. 20, 1954, Spirit River, AB) Libn., I. N. McKinnon Meml. Lib., 1979–; Libn. I, Univ. of Calgary, Sci. Div., 1978–79; Resrch., Libn., Info. Spec., 1977. **Educ.:** Cleveland State Univ., 1975–76, BA (Anthro.); Case West. Rsv. Univ., 1976–77, MSLS. **Orgs.:** Can. LA. Can. Assn. Info. Sci.: Secy., Treas. (1979–80). SLA. ASIS. **Activities:** 5, 12; 15, 17, 20; 64, 86 **Addr.:** I. N. McKinnon Memorial Library, 3512–33 St. N. W., Calgary, AB T2L 2A6 Canada.

Nugent, William R. (Ja. 29, 1931, Stamford, CT) Asst. Dir., Autom. Systs. Ofc., Lib. of Congs., 1973–; Consult., Ofc. of Telecom., Various others, 1972–73; Asst. Comsn., U.S. Patent Ofc., 1971–72; VP, Inforonics, Inc., 1962–71. **Educ.:** Polytech. Inst. of Brooklyn, 1950–54, BEE (Electronic Engin.); MA Inst. of Tech., 1957–61 (Comp., Autom.). **Orgs.:** ASIS: N.E. Chap. (Ch., 1970); SIG Autom. Lang. Prcs. (Ch., 1973). Assn. for Comp. Mach. Brit. Comp. Socty. Inst. of Electrical and Electronics Engins. IEEE Comp. Socty. Various other orgs. **Honors:** ALA/ISAD, Spec. Cit. ISAD/LC MARC Inst., 1969. **Pubns.:** "Configuration Analysis of Computer-Telecommunications Systems," *Advances in Data Communications Management* (1980); "The Information Intensive Community," *Proceedings* Indo-Amer. Wkshp. on Modelling Natl. Sci. and Tech. Info. Systs. (1979); "A Fast Incomplete Gamma Function for Improved Measures of Response Time Quality," *Proceedings* IEEE COMPCON (1978); Jt. auth., "A Page Image Transmission and Display System for Congressional Information Retrieval," *Proceedings* ASIS Anl. Mtg. (1978); *Information Systems at the Library of Congress* (Vid.) (1976). **Activities:** 4; 17; 56, 95-Info. Systs. **Addr.:** Automated Systems Office, Library of Congress, 10 First St. SE, Washington, DC 20540.

Nunez, Ana Rosa (Jl. 11, 1926, Havana, Cuba) Prof., Univ. Miami, Otto G. Richter Lib., 1966–; Various other positions teaching, poetry reading; Head Libn., Tribunal de Cuentas dela Republica de Cuba, 1950–61. **Educ.:** Academia Baldor (Havana, Cuba), 1940–45, BA; Univ. Bibtcr. de la Habana, Cuba, 1945–54, PhD, 1950–54, MLS. **Orgs.:** FL LA. SALALM. Dade Cnty. LA. Artistic Cult. Socty. Amer.: Pres. (1974–76). Inst. Cult. Hispanica: Hon. Libn., Exec. Cncl. (1973–). Socty. Writers, Painters, Artists: Miami Chap., Hon. mem. **Honors:** Sigma Delta Pi; Phi Alpha Theta. **Pubns.:** Poems, poetry books, anthologies. **Activities:** 1; 39 **Addr.:** 2142 S.W. 14 Terrace Apt. 4, Miami, FL 33145.

Nutter, Daniel Lyon (Ja. 16, 1932, Alcester, SD) Lib. Dir., Southwest. Coll., 1968–; Lib. Dir., E. TX Bapt. Coll., 1967–68; Libn., Hampshire-Fannett (TX) ISC, 1966–67; Lib. Dir., Clarendon Coll., 1961–66; Libn., Buna Indp. Sch. Dist., 1956–61. **Educ.:** Southeast. OK Univ., 1952–56, BA (Hist.); N. TX State Univ., 1967, MLS. **Orgs.:** ALA. KS LA: Trustees Cncl., Ch. Mt. Plains LA. Lions Intl.: Trustee. **Activities:** 1; 17, 39; 75 **Addr.:** Rte. 1, Box 179, Winfield, KS 67156.

Nutty, David J. (Jl. 26, 1951, Batesville, IN) AV Libn., Widener Univ., 1981–; AV Libn., Atlantic Cnty. Lib., 1979–81. **Educ.:** Univ. of Cincinnati, 1969–73, BFA (Broadcasting); Drexel Univ., 1977–79, MLS. various wkshps. **Orgs.:** ALA. NJ LA: AV Sect. (Secy., 1980–81). EFLA: Pre-screening Com., Amer. Film Fest., Juror. AECT. Garden State Lib. Film Circuit. S. Jersey Reg. Film Lib. **Honors:** Beta Phi Mu, 1980. **Pubns.:** "Wilmington's Grand Opera House," (1978). **Activities:** 9; 15, 22, 32; 67, 95-Recordings. **Addr.:** Wolfgram Memorial Library, Widener University, Chester, PA 19013.

Nye, James H. (O. 20, 1946, MN) Acq. and Ref. Libn., Gustavus Adolphus Coll., 1974–; VP and Ed., Musicdata, Inc., 1973–74; Libn., Cmnty. Legal Srvs., Philadelphia, 1971–73. **Educ.:** Augsburg Coll., 1964–68, BA (Phil.); Yale Univ., 1968–70, MAR (Relig.); Univ. of PA, 1970–71, (S. Asian Std.); Drexel Univ., 1972–74, MS (LS). **Orgs.:** ALA. Assn. for Asian Std. **Honors:** Phi Beta Mu, 1974; Amer. Luth. Church Future Fac. Flwshp., 1968–69. **Pubns.:** *Sacred Choral Music in Print* (1974); *Secular Choral Music in Print* (1974); *Library Automation in the Small College Environment* ERIC (1976). **Activities:** 1; 15, 31, 39; 54, 56, 90 **Addr.:** Folke Bernadotte Memorial Library, Gustavus Adolphus College, St. Peter, MN 56082.

Nyholm, Jens (Jl. 24, 1900, Hjörring, Denmark) Consult., Spec. Cols., Univ. of CA, Santa Barbara, Lib., 1969–; Univ. Libn., Northwestern Univ., 1944–68; Asst. Libn., Univ. of CA, Berkeley, 1939–44; Head, Cat. Dept., Univ. of CA, Los Angeles, 1938–39; Catlgr., Lib. of Congs., 1928–37. **Educ.:** Univ. of Copenhagen, 1919–21, "Filosofikum" (Phil., Compar. Lit.); Danish State Lib. Sch., 1922–23, Dip. (LS); Columbia Univ., 1927–28, BS (LS); George Washington Univ., 1932–34, MA (Eng. and Amer. Lit.). **Orgs.:** ALA: Dir. of Cat. and Class. (Ch., 1938–39); ACRL. Farmington Plan: Jt. Com. on African Resrcs. (Ch., 1959–64). Ctr. for Resrch. Libs.: Bd. of Dirs. (1949–65; Ch., 1955–56). Bibl. Socty. of Amer. Amer. Scan. Fndn. Caxton Club. Grolier Club. Rebild Natl. Park Socty. Various other orgs. **Pubns.:** *Portal til Amerika* (1953); *Amerikanske Stemmer* (1968); Article on Danish and Norwegian Lit., *Funk and Wagnalls New Encyclopedia* (1971–72); Various articles, reviews. **Activities:** 1, 4; 15, 17, 24; 55, 57 **Addr.:** 215 Canon Dr., Santa Barbara, CA 93105.

Nyland, Anne M. (F. 17, 1919, Lyn, ON, Dir., Chief Libn., Seaway Valley Lib., 1964–; Reg. Libn., Halifax Cnty. Reg. Lib., 1960–64; Asst. Dir., NS Prov. Lib., 1958–60; Cnty. Libn., Essex Cnty. Lib., 1950–58. **Educ.:** Queen's Univ., 1937–40, BA (Eng.); Univ. of Toronto, 1940–41, BLS. **Orgs.:** Can LA. ON LA. Cnty. Reg. Mncpl. LA Admins. of Medium Pub. Libs. Can. Fed. of Univ. Women. Cornwall Arts Dev. Com.: PR; Fin. Com. **Pubns.:** Jt. ed., *Golden Triangle* (1965–68). **Activities:** 9, 13; 15, 17, 20 **Addr.:** Seaway Valley Libraries, P.O. Box 939, Cornwall, ON K6H 5VI Canada.

Nyquist, Corinne Elaine (N. 1, 1935, Minnesota Falls Twp., MN) Dir., World Study Ctr., New Paltz, SUNY, 1971–, Cat. Libn., 1968–71; Actg. Acq. Libn., Rhodes Univ. Lib., S. Africa, 1967; Asst. Libn., Branch Lib., Skokie Pub. Lib., 1965–66. **Educ.:** Macalester Coll., 1953–57, BA (Intl. Rel.); Univ. of MN, 1958–69, MA (LS). **Orgs.:** ALA: ACRL, African/Asian Sect.,. Nom. Com. (Ch., 1981). African Std. Assn.: Arch. and Libs. Com. (Ch., 1975–77). NY African Std. Assn.: Treas. (1977–79); Secy. (1976–77). **Pubns.:** "Recent Books for South African Children," *Childrens Literature and Audio-Visual Materials* (1977); jt. ed., *NYASA Nsltr.* (1974–). **Activities:** 1; 54 **Addr.:** 62 S. Chestnut St., New Paltz, NY 12561.

Nyquist, Norma G. (S. 13, 1923, McPherson, KS) Lib. Dir., Santa Monica Coll., 1967–, Cat./Gen. Libn., 1954–67; Eng. Instr., Shawnee Mission HS, 1951–53. **Educ.:** Bethany Coll., 1941–45, AB (Eng.); Univ. of KS, 1947–50, MA (Eng.); Univ. of CA, Berkeley, 1953–54, BLS. **Orgs.:** CA LA. Lrng. Resrcs. Assn. of CA Cmnty. Colls: Ad Hoc Com. on Guidelines Concerning Staff and Mtrls. (1979) Assn. of Cmnty. Coll. Admins. **Honors:** Beta Phi Mu, 1954. **Pubns.:** Reviews. **Activities:** 1; 20, 35, 39; 65, 68, 90 **Addr.:** 16565 Chattanooga Pl., Pacific Palisades, CA 90272.

Nyren, Dorothy Elizabeth (S. 29, 1927, Portland, ME) Chief, Pub. Srvs., Brooklyn Pub. Lib., 1977–, Chief, Ctrl. Lib., 1971–77, Chief, Adult Srvs., 1968–71; Dir., Northbrook Pub. Lib. 1965–68. **Educ.:** Boston Univ., 1947–52, BA (Rom., lit.), 1953–54, MA (Amer. Lit.); Simmons Coll., 1957–60, MLS Lib. Sci. **Orgs.:** ALA: Cnclr., (1972–75); PLA, Exec. Bd., (1973–75); RASD, Exec. Bd. (1977–). Victorian Socty. **Honors:** Phi Beta Kappa, 1952. **Pubns.:** *Modern American Literature* (1978 and earlier eds.); *Modern Romance Literature* (1968); "Community Service," *Pub. Lib. Rpt.* (16); reviews, *Lib. Jnl.* (1956–75). **Activities:** 9; 17, 28, 37; 50, 66, 89 **Addr.:** Brooklyn Public Library, Grand Army Plz., Brooklyn, NY 11238.

Nyren, Karl (N. 25, 1921, Boston, MA) Sr. Ed., *Lib. Jnl.*, 1966–; Dir., Cary Meml. Lib., 1961–66; Dir., Peabody Inst. Lib., 1960–61; Ref. Asst., Boston Pub. Lib., Fine Arts Dept., 1956–60. **Educ.:** Boston Univ., 1939–49, AB (Eng.); 1949–50, MA (Eng. Lit.). **Orgs.:** ALA: Cncl. **Activities:** 14-Jnlsm. **Addr.:** 80 Jessen Pl., Beacon, NY 12508.

O

Oakley, Adeline Dupuy (S. 14, 1914, Cleveland, OH) Assoc. Prof., Dept. of Media and Libnshp., Bridgewater State Coll., 1967–; Libn. and Team Tchr., Catherine Labouré Sch. of Nursing, 1963–67; LS Instr., Cmnwlth. of MA Ext., 1966–67; Libn., Bridgewater–Raynham Reg. HS, 1962–63; Circ. Libn., Canton (MA) Pub. Lib., 1962; Various consults. and lectureships. **Educ.:** Bridgewater State Coll., 1958–62, BS (Sec. Sch. Eng.); Simmons Coll., 1962–64, MLS; Boston Univ., 1967–77, EdD (Eng.). **Orgs.:** ALA: Hlth. and Rehab. Srvs., Lib. Educ. (1971–73), Nom. Com. (1972–73); YASL, Publshrs. Liaison Com. (1976–80); ACRL/Bibl. Instr. Sect., Com. on Educ. for Bibl. Instr.; New Eng. Chap., Bibl. Instr. Com.; various other coms. AALS: Liaison for Bridgewater State Coll. (1974–79). Cath. LA: Various coms. and ofcs. MA LA: Various coms. Various other orgs. Women's Natl. Bk. Assn.: Secy. (1976–78); Skinner Awd. (Ch., 1973, 1976); Boston Chap., Pres. (1974–). Parent Tchr. Assn. Cncl.: Poughkeepsie. Great Bks. Discuss. Grp. Brockton. **Pubns.:** Hlth. Sci. Libs. Clmns., *Cath. Lib. World* (D. 1970; Mr. 1972); "Report to the Profession," *Bkwoman* (1976, 1980; forthcoming). **Activities:** 11; 24, 26, 31; 55, 63, 95-Chld. Lit. **Addr.:** 24 Reynolds Ave., Randolph, MA 02368.

Oakley, Robert L. (N. 6, 1945, New York, NY) Dir. of the Law Lib., Boston Univ., 1979–; Assoc. Dir., Cornell Law Lib., 1976–79, Asst. Ref. Libn., 1973–76, Circ. Libn., 1972–73. **Educ.:** Cornell Univ., 1964–68, BA (Gvt.); Syracuse Univ., 1970–72, MSLS, Cornell Univ., 1973–76, JD (Law). **Orgs.:** AALL: Resrch. Lib. Grp., Law Prog. Com., Ch.; Com. on Const. and Bylaws, Ch.; Com. Autom., Nsltr. Ed.; Liaison to ANSC Z-39. **Pubns.:** *Organized Crime: A Bibliography* (1976). **Activities:** 1, 12, 14; 15, 17, 34; 61, 74, 77 **Addr.:** Pappas Law Library, Boston University School of Law, 765 Commonwealth Ave., Boston, MA 02215.

Oaksford, Margaret J. (Gloversville, NY) Libn., Sch. of Hotel Admin., Cornell Univ., 1978–, Asst. Proj. Dir., Annex Lib., 1977, Ref. Libn., Uris Lib., 1976–77, Libn., Interlib. Lending, 1970–76; Chief Libn., Coll. Ctr. of the Finger Lakes, 1968–69; Ref. Libn., part-time, Tompkins Cnty. Pub. Lib., 1970–73. **Educ.:** Hartwick Coll., 1943–47, BA (Eng. Bus.); Cath. Univ., 1963–65, MLS; Cert., Arch. Admin., American Univ.; NY State Pub. Libns. Cert. **Orgs.:** ALA: Coop. Ref. Srvs. Com. (1976–78). S. Central Resrch. Lib. Cncl.: ILL Com. (1970–76). **Pubns.:** *Bibliography of Hotel and Restaurant Administration and Related Subjects* (1978, 1979, 1980). **Activities:** 1, 12; 15, 17, 39; 51, 59, 68 **Addr.:** Benn Conger Inn, 206 W. Cortland St., Groton, NY 13073.

O'Bar, Jack (D. 15, 1926, Cowlington, OK) Dir. of the Lib., Univ. of AK, Anchorage, 1972–; Head Libn., Mankato State Univ., 1962–72; Head Libn., Southwest. OK State Univ., 1957–62; Asst. Gvt. Docum. Libn., OK State Univ., 1955–57. **Educ.:** Univ. of OK, 1951–54, BA (Eng.), 1954–55, MLS; IN Univ., 1972, PhD (LS). **Orgs.:** ALA: Com. for Eval. AECT/NECS Educ. Tech. Handbook, (1974); Archit. for Coll. and Univ. Libs. Com. (1976–80). AK LA: Task Force on Long-Range Lib. Plng. (1973); Nom. Com. (1974, 1979). Amer. Fed. of Avi. Amer. Waterfowl and Pheasant Socty. Amer. Bantam Assn. Parrot Socty. (England). **Honors:** Phi Beta Kappa. **Activities:** 1; 17 **Addr.:** Star Route A, Box 191A, Anchorage, AK 99502.

Oberg, Larry R. (Je. 20, 1933, Midvale, ID) Ref. Libn., Database Srch., Cubberley Educ. Lib., Stanford Univ., 1979–; Head, Circ. Srv., Educ. Psy. Lib., Univ. of CA, Berkeley, 1965–79. **Educ.:** Univ. of CA, Berkeley, 1978, AB (Anthro.), 1978–79, MLS. **Orgs.:** ALA: ACRL. SLA. **Honors:** Phi Beta Kappa, 1978; Beta Phi Mu, 1980. **Pubns.:** "Death and Dying; a Guide to Bibliographical Sources," *Bhvl. and Soc. Sci. Libn.*

PROFESSIONAL ACTIVITIES: Institutions: 1. Acad. lib.; 2. Arch.; 3. Assn.; 4. Fed./Gvt. lib.; 5. Inst. lib.; 6. Mfr./Suppl.; 7. Milit. lib.; 8. Musm.; 9. Pub. lib.; 10. Sch. lib.; 11. Sch. of lib. sci.; 12. Spec. lib.; 13. State lib.; 14. (other). **Functions/Activities:** 15. Acq./Col. dev.; 16. Adult srvs.; 17. Admin.; 18. Apprais.; 19. Archit./Bldgs.; 20. Cat./Class.; 21. Chld. srvs.; 22. Circ.; 23. Cons./Pres.; 24. Consult.; 25. Cont. ed.; 26. Educ. lib. sci.; 27. Ext. srvs.; 28. Fund/Grants; 29. Gvt. pubs.; 30. Indx./Abs.; 31. Instr. lib. use; 32. Media srvs.; 33. Micro.; 34. Netwks./Coop.; 35. Persnl.; 36. PR; 37. Publshg.; 38. Recs. mgt.; 39. Ref. srvs.; 40. Repro.; 41. Resrch.; 42. Review.; 43. Secur.; 44. Serials; 45. Spec. col.; 46. Tech. srvs.; 47. Trustees/Bds.; 48. YA srvs.; 49. (other).

(Sum. 1980). **Activities:** 1, 12; 22, 39; 63, 92 **Addr.:** 5346 Broadway, Oakland, CA 94618.

Oberman-Soroka, Cerise G. (S. 7, 1952, Utica, NY) Head, Ref. Dept., Coll. of Charleston, 1978–, Asst. Ref. Libn., 1976–78. **Educ.:** SUNY, New Paltz, 1972–73, BA (Hist.); Emory Univ., 1975–76, MLn (LS), 1973–74, (Hist.). **Orgs.:** ALA: ACRL Bibl. Instr. Nom. Com. (Ch., 1980–81); Bibl. Instr. Int. Grp. (Ch., 1980–81); Educ. for Bibl. Instr.; LIRT, PR/mem. com. (Ch., 1979–80). SC LA: Bibl. Instr. Int. Grp. (Ch., 1979–80); Coll. Libs. Sect. Nom. Com. (1979). **Honors:** SC LA, Cont. Educ. Grant, 1979; ALA, Shirley Olofson Meml. Awd., 1977. **Pubns.:** Ed., *Procs. of the Southeastern Conference on Approaches to Bibliographic Instruction* (1980, 1978); "The Reference Librarian as Educator," *The Ref. Libn.* (Fall 1981); "F.A.R.: A New Beginning," *Lifeline* (D. 1980). **Activities:** 1; 31, 39 **Addr.:** College of Charleston Library, College of Charleston, Charleston, SC 29401.

Obloy, Elaine Cecilia (O. 21, 1947, Cleveland, OH) Bus. Libn., Meldrum & Fewsmith, Inc., 1979–; Instr., Asst. Ref. Libn., Baldwin-Wallace Col., 1977–79; Ref. Libn., Cleveland Pub. Lib., 1970–77. **Educ.:** Cleveland State Univ., 1965–69, BA (Soclgy.); Case-Western Reserve Univ., 1969–70, MSLS; various workshops. **Orgs.:** SLA: Advert. Mktg. Div., Bus. & Finance Div. Acad. LA of OH: Resrch. Bibl. Instr. Div. Amer. Mgt. Assn.: Info. Syst. Tech. Div.; Finance Div. Cousteau Socty. 1979. **Activities:** 1, 12; 17, 25, 31; 51, 59, 75 **Addr.:** 9108 Evergreen Dr., Parma, OH 44129.

Oboler, Eli Martin (S. 26, 1915, Chicago, IL) Univ. Libn. Emeritus, ID State Univ., 1981–, Univ. Libn., 1949–80; Head Resrv. Book Room, Univ. of Chicago Lib., 1946–49, Head, Univ. Coll. Lib., 1947–49; Bibl. Consult., Great Books Fndn., 1947–49. **Educ.:** Univ. of Chicago, 1931–41, BA (Eng.); Columbia Univ., 1941–42, BS (LS); Univ. of Chicago, 1941–49, (LS). **Orgs.:** ALA: Cnclr. (1951–59, 1977–81); Ch., IFRT (1980–81). Pac. NW LA: Pres. (1955–56); Ed. *PNLA Qtly.* (1958–67). ID LA: Pres. (1950–53). Frdm. To Read Fndn.: Bd. of Trustees (1971–80); VP (1979–80). Other orgs. Natl. Adv. Com. on Lib. Trng. and Resrch. Proj.: Ch. (1968–69). **Honors:** Univ. of IL Grad. Sch. of Lib. Sci., Robert B. Downs Awd. for Int. Frdm., 1976; ID LA, Libn. of the Yr., 1974; Pac. NW LA Honorary Life Mem., 1967; ALA/H.W. Wilson Co., Lib. Per. Awd., 1964. **Pubns.:** *Education and Censorship* (1981); *Defending Intellectual Freedom: The Library and the Censor* (1980); *Ideas and the University Librarian: Essays of an Unorthodox Academic Librarian* (1977); *The Fear of the Word: Censorship and Sex* (1974); Ed., *College and University Library Accreditation Standards* (1958); various articles. **Activities:** 1; 15, 17, 42; 61, 74, 92 **Addr.:** 1397 Jane St., Pocatello, ID 83201.

O'Brien, Betty Alice (Je. 12, 1932, Kingsburg, CA) Libn., St. Leonard Coll., 1974–, Catlgr., 1971–74; Asst. Libn., N. Park Theo. Semy., 1957–69. **Educ.:** N. Park Coll., 1950–52, AA; Northwestern Univ., 1954–56, BA (Hist.); Univ. of CA, Berkeley, 1956–57, MLS; N. Park Theo. Semy., 1952–54, dip. (Theo., Relig. Educ.). **Orgs.:** ATLA. OH Theo. Libns.: Ch. (1977–79); Secy. (1972–77). **Pubns.:** Jt. ed., *Religion Index Two: Festschriften, 1960–1969* (1980); Jt. ed., *Bibliography of Festschriften in Religion Published since 1960* (1972, 1973). **Activities:** 1, 2; 20, 30, 39; 90 **Addr.:** 7818 Lockport Blvd., Centerville, OH 45459.

O'Brien, Elmer J. (Ap. 8, 1932, Kemmerer, WY) Libn., Prof., Untd. Theo. Semy., 1969–; Asst. Libn., Garrett Evang. Theo. Semy., 1965–69; Circ.-Ref. Libn., Boston Univ. Sch. of Theo., 1961–65. **Educ.:** Birmingham South. Coll., 1950–54, AB (Hist.); Iliff Sch. of Theo., 1954–57, ThM (Church Hist.); Univ. of Denver, 1960–61, MA (LS). **Orgs.:** ATLA: Head, Bur. of Persnl. and Placement, (1969–73); Bd. of Dir., (1973–76); VP (1977–78); Pres. (1978–79). OH Area Theo. Libns.: Ch. (1970–73). OHIONET: Ch., Trng. and Instr. Cncl., (1979–81). **Honors:** Lib. Staff Dev. Grant, Assn. of Theo. Schs. in the US and Canada, 1977. **Pubns.:** *A Bibliography of Festschriften Published in Religion Since 1960* (1975); *Religion Index Two: Festschriften* 1960–69) (1980); "The Methodist Collections at Garrett Theological Seminary," *Meth. Hist.* (Ap. 1970); "OCLC: Challenges and Difficulties for the Independent Seminary Library," *ATLA Procs.*, (1975). **Addr.:** United Theological Seminary, 1810 Harvard Blvd., Dayton, OH 45406.

O'Brien, James M. (Jl. 1, 1934, Schenectady, NY) Head Libn., Oak Lawn Pub. Lib., 1976–; Dir. of Cust. Support, C. L. Syst., Inc., 1973–76; Dir. of Tech. Srvs., Cleveland Pub. Lib., 1971–73; Lib. Dir., Half Hollow Hills Lib., 1965–70; Lib. Dir., N. Babylon Pub. Lib., 1962–65; Asst. Dir., Huntington Pub. Lib., 1960–62; Gen. Asst., Great Neck Lib., 1958–59. **Educ.:** Manhattan Coll., 1952–56, BA (Hist.); Syracuse Univ., 1956–58, MS (LS); various courses. **Orgs.:** ALA: LAD Lib. Org. and Mgt. Sect., Ins. for Libs.: Com., Ch. (1965–68); JMRT, Ch. (1967–68); LAMA/Bldg. and Equip. Sect., Equipment Com. (1977–); ERT Bd. (1973–78). **Activities:** 9; 17; 56, 76 **Addr.:** Oak Lawn Public Library, 9427 S. Raymond Ave., Oak Lawn, IL 60453.

O'Brien, Marlys Carol Howe (D. 10, 1937, St. Paul, MN) Dir., Kitchigami Reg. Lib., 1969–; Dir., Cass Cnty. Lib., 1965–69; Consult., State of MN Dept. of Educ., 1963–65. **Educ.:** Univ. of MN, 1955–60, BA (Scan. Lang. and Lit.), 1960–63, MA (LS). **Orgs.:** Can. LA. MN LA: VP, Pres.-Elect (1981–82); ALA Cnclr. MN Educ. Media Org. ALA: PLA/Metro. Lib. Srv. Sect.; LAMA/Persnl. Admin. Sect., Econ. Status, Welfare, and Fringe Benefits Com.; Small Libs. Pubns. Com. Various other orgs. Nordmanns–Forbundet. Norwegian–Amer. Musm. **Honors:** MN LA, Cert. of Merit. **Activities:** 9; 17, 35, 47; 51, 66, 76 **Addr.:** Star Rte. 78, Pine River, MN 56474.

O'Brien, Nancy Patricia (Mr. 17, 1955, Galesburg, IL) Soc. Sci. Bibl., Asst. Prof. of Lib. Admin., Univ. of IL, 1979–, Serials Bibl., Visit. Instr., 1977–78. **Educ.:** Univ. of IL, 1973–76, AB (Eng.), 1976–77, MS (LS). **Orgs.:** ALA. Cousteau Socty. Smithsonian Assoc. **Pubns.:** Jt. ed., "Media/microforms," *Serials Review* (1979–). **Activities:** 1; 15, 44, 46; 92 **Addr.:** 802 S. Urbana, Urbana, IL 61801.

O'Brien, Patrick M. (Mr. 17, 1943, Newport, RI) Dir., Cuyahoga Cnty. Pub. Lib. 1979–; Asst. Commissioner for Ctrl. Lib. and Cult. Ctr., Chicago Pub. Lib., 1975–79, Chief, Bus. and Indus. Div., 1975; Asst. Dir. of Resrch., FIND/SVP, Info. Clearing House, 1973–74; Head of Ref., Newsweek Ed. Lib., 1965–72. **Educ.:** Merrimack Coll., 1960–64, BA (Eng. Lit.); Univ. of RI, 1964–65, MLS; Exec. Dev. Prog. for Lib. Admin., 1976. **Orgs.:** Depository Lib. OH LA. Cncl. to the Pub. Printer. Cleveland Area Metro. Lib. Syst.: Pres., Bd. of Dir. (1980–81). ALA: RASD, Com. on Stan. (Ch., 1978–79); Bd. (1978–81); Plng. Com. (1978); PLA Pub. Lib. Syst. Sect. (VP, Pres.-Elect, 1981); Prof. Ethics Com. (1978–82). Other orgs. Leadership Cleveland. Fed. For Comnty. Plng.: Human Resrcs. Educ. Adv. Com. (1980). Amer. Mgt. **Addr.:** Cuyahoga County Public Library, 4510 Memphis Ave., Cleveland, OH 44144.

O'Brien, Philip Michael (Ja. 5, 1940, Albion, NE) Coll. Libn., Whittier Coll., 1974–, Spec. Cols. Libn., 1970–74; Cmnd. Libn., Berlin Brigade, U.S. Army Europe, 1967–70; Libn., Soc. Sci and Bus. Div., Chico State Coll., 1966–67. **Educ.:** Whittier Coll., 1957–61, BA (Soclgy.); Univ. of South. CA, 1961–62, MSLS, 1970–74, PhD (LS). **Orgs.:** ALA. Christ. Libns. Assn.: Prog. Ch. (1980–81). Intl. Wizard of Oz Club. Los Compadres. **Pubns.:** *T.E. Lawrence and Fine Printing* (1980). **Activities:** 1; 17, 31, 45; 57 **Addr.:** Wardman Library, Whittier College, Whittier, CA 90608.

O'Brien, Roberta Luther (Mr. 15, 1946, Oak Park, IL) Instr., Kent State Univ., 1981–; Lib. Srvs. Proj. Libn., Proj. LEARN, 1979–81; Instr., Chicago City-Wide Coll., 1978–79; Chicago Pub. Lib. Dist. Chief, NE Branches, Dist. Chief - SW Branches, 1974–78, Chld. Libn., 1969–74. **Educ.:** New Coll., 1964–67, BA (Eng/Am Lit); Univ. of Chicago, 1967–71, MA (LS). **Orgs.:** ALA: YASD, Hi/Lo Bk. Eval. Com. (1980–82); ALSC, Publshrs. Liason Com. (1976–79); Alt. Educ. Prog. Sect. Pub. Liason Com. (1979–81); Secy. (1981–82). OH LA. Chld. Reading RT: Pres. (1975–76). Jane Addams Peace Assn. Chld. Book Awd. Sel. Com. (1972–74). Chicago Women in Publshg. Chld. Book Awd. Sel. Com. (1974). New College Alum. Assn.: VP (1974–78). **Activities:** 9, 14-litcy. org.; 15, 17, 21; 89 **Addr.:** 2904 Scarborough, Cleveland Heights, OH 44118.

O'Bryant, Fred (F. 28, 1949, Memphis, TN) Asst. Prof. & Head, AV Ctr., Claude Moore Hlth. Sci. Lib., Univ. VA Med. Ctr., 1975–; Ref. Libn., Carl A. Rudisill Lib., Lenoir Rhyne Coll., 1973–75. **Educ.:** Southwest. at Memphis, 1967–71, BA (Eng.); Univ. of NC, 1971–72, MS in LS; Med. Libnshp., 1976, Cert. **Orgs.:** Med. LA: Ch., AV Grp. By-Laws Revision Com. (1977–78). Mid-Atlantic Reg. Med. Lib. Grp.: AV Com. (1976–79, Ch., 1978–79). Hlth. Sci. Comm. Assn. **Pubns.:** Various speeches. **Activities:** 1; 17, 32, 39; 56, 80, 93 **Addr.:** Audiovisual Center, The Claude Moore Health Science Library, Box 234, Univ. of Virginia Medical Center, Charlottesville, VA 22908.

O'Bryant, Mathilda B. (Ap. 2, 1918, Logan, WV) Head Cat. Dept., Univ. of Notre Dame Libs., 1976–; Asst. Prof., Head Catlgr., Queens Coll. of CUNY, 1973–76; Assoc. Prof., Head of Acq., Univ. of Louisville Libs., 1967–73; Head, Cat. Dept., Princeton Univ., 1962–67; Head Catlgr., Union Coll., 1961–62; Head Catlgr., SUNY, Oneonta, 1957–61; Head Catlgr., Brandeis Univ., 1955–56; Catlgr., Montgomery Cnty. (MD) Pub. Lib., 1952–53; Other cat. positions, 1940–52. **Pubns.:** "Uncataloged Books at Brandeis," *Lib. Resrcs. & Tech. Srvs.* (Win. 1957); "Some Random Thoughts on the Cost of Cataloging," *Lib. Resrcs. & Tech. Srvs.* (Sum. 1965); "Acquisition Section Report," *Lib. Resrcs. & Tech. Srvs.* (Fall 1973). **Activities:** 1; 15, 20; 57, 69, 89 **Addr.:** 1659 S. Turtle Creek Dr., South Bend, IN 46637.

Ochal, Bethany J. (D. 2, 1917, Flint, MI) Dir., Orange Cnty. Law Lib., 1972–; Law Libn., Wayne State Univ., 1961–72; Law Libn., Detroit Bar Assn., 1952–61; Private Practice, 1945–52. **Educ.:** Wayne State Univ., 1944, AB; 1945, JD (Law). **Orgs.:** AALL. Intl. Assn. of Law Libs. State Court & Cnty. Law Libs. of US & Can. Cncl. of CA Cnty. Law Libns. State Bar of MI. Amer. Judicature Socty. **Honors:** John Cotton Dana Lib. PR Awd., 1975; CLA/PR Chap. of So. CA, PR Awd. of Merit, 1975. **Pubns.:** "A Bicentennial History of Public Law Libraries," *Law Lib. Jnl.* (1976); "Microform Brief," *Law Lib. Jnl.* (1975); "County Law Libraries," *Law Lib. Jnl.* (1974). **Activities:** 9, 14-Law; 17, 33; 77 **Addr.:** Orange County Law Library, 515 N. Flower, Santa Ana, CA 92703.

Ochs, Michael (F. 1, 1937, Cologne, Germany) Libn. of the Eda Kuhn Loeb Msc. Lib., Sr. Lect. on Msc., Harvard Univ., 1978–; Asst. Prof. of LS, Simmons Coll., 1974–78; Msc. Catlgr., Msc. Libn., Creative Arts Libn., Brandeis Univ., 1965–74; Catlgr., City Coll. of New York, 1963–65. **Educ.:** City Coll. of New York, 1958, BA (Msc.); Columbia Univ., 1963, MS (LS); New York Univ., 1964, AM (Msclgy.); Simmons Coll., 1975, DA (Lib. Admin.). **Orgs.:** Msc. LA: Ch., New Eng. Chap. (1968–69); Ch., Com. on Bib. Descr. (1971–73); Ch., Msc. Lib. Admin. Com. (1975–76); Bd. of Dir. (1976–78). Intl. Assn. of Msc. Libs.: Strg. Com., Comsn. on Bibl. Descr. (1978–); Ch., Prog. Com. (1979–). Assn. of Recorded Sound Col. Sonneck Socty. Boston Camerata: Bd. of Dir. (1979–). **Pubns.:** *An Alphabetical Index to Robert Schumann: Werke* (1967); *An Index to 'Das Chorwerk' Vol. 1–110* (1970); *Truth, Beauty, Love, and Music Librarianship* (1980); Ed., *Music in Harvard Libraries* (1980–); "Qualifications for Music Librarianship in the USA, *Fontes Artis Musicae* (No. 1, 1978); other articles. **Activities:** 1, 11; 26; 55, 57 **Addr.:** Music Library, Harvard University, Cambridge, MA 02138.

O'Clair, Robert M. (F. 28, 1923, Nashua, NH) Prof. of Eng., Dir. of the Lib., Manhattanville Coll., 1961–; Instr./Lect. in Eng., Harvard Univ., 1954–61, Allston-Burr Sr. Tutor, 1956–61. **Educ.:** Harvard Univ., 1945–49, BA (Eng.), 1949–50, MA (Eng. Philology), 1954, PhD (Eng. Philology). SIGNET Socty. **Honors:** Phi Beta Kappa. **Pubns.:** Jt. cmplr., *The Norton Anthology of Modern Poetry* (1973); *Reading Poems: An Introduction to Poetry.* **Activities:** 1; 17 **Addr.:** Manhattanville College, Purchase, NY 10577.

O'Connell, Catherine Ann (Ap. 8, 1946, Baltimore, MD) Asst. Dir., Washington Cnty. Free Lib., 1972–; Branch Libn., 1971–72, Various positions Pub. Lib. of Annapolis & Anne Arundel Cnty. 1962–70. **Educ.:** Univ. MD, 1964–68, BA (Eng.); Univ. IL, 1970–71, MLS. **Orgs.:** MD LA: Adult and YA Srvs. Div. (Ch. 1973–74). ALA: JMRT (Secy. 1971–72). Hagerstown Girls Club: Pres., Bd. Dir. (1978–80). AAUW. **Activities:** 9; 17, 27, 36; 51 **Addr.:** Washington County Free Library, 100 S. Potomac St., Hagerstown, MD 21740.

O'Connell, Thomas Francis (Ap. 5, 1921, Boston, MA) Univ. Libn., Boston Coll., 1976–; Dir. of Libs., York Univ., Toronto, 1963–76; Asst. Libn., Widener Lib., Harvard Univ., 1961–63, Actg. Libn., Lamont Lib., 1960–61, Circ. & Stacks Chief, Widener Lib., 1955–61, Circ. Dept. Head, 1952–55, Asst. Circ. Libn., 1951–52. **Educ.:** Boston Coll., 1946–50, AB (Econ.); Columbia Univ., 1950–51, MSLS. **Orgs.:** ALA: ACRL. Inter-Univ. Transit Srv.: Dir. (1970–75). Boston Lib. Cnsrtm.: Dir. (1976–). Peace Corps Nigeria Tchrs. Proj.: Consult. (1961). Atkinson Coll., York Univ.: Fellow (1966). **Honors:** Bishops Univ., PQ, Doctor of Civil Law, 1974. **Pubns.:** Various articles. **Activities:** 1; 17 **Addr.:** 3 High Rock Rd., Dover, MA 02030.

O'Connor, Anthony J. (S. 18, 1949, Albany, NY) Asst. Prof. Sci. Lib., Univ. of OR, 1975–. **Educ.:** Siena Coll., 1967–71, BS (Bio.); SUNY, Geneseo, 1973–75, MLS, 1974–81, MA (Bio.). **Orgs.:** ALA. ASIS: Mem. Coord. (1978–79). AAAS. Armor Assn. Mensa. **Pubns.:** "Air Cushion Vehicles," *Armor* (Ja.-F. 1979). **Activities:** 1, 12; 31, 39, 46; 91, 95-On Line Srchg. **Addr.:** 320 East 13th St., Eugene, OR 97401.

O'Connor, Daniel O. (Ag. 11, 1945, Niagara Falls, NY) Asst. Prof., Grad. Sch. of Lib. & Info. Std., Rutgers Univ., 1974–; Head, Tech. Srvs., Corning Cmnty. Coll., 1971–72; Asst. to Dean, Sch. of LS, Syracuse Univ., 1968–69. **Educ.:** Niagara Univ., 1963–67, BA (Eng.); Syracuse Univ., 1967–68, MSLS, 1972–78, PhD (Info. Transfer). **Orgs.:** ALA: Bibl. (1973–76); LRRT (1976–78). ASIS: Non-Print Media (1975–76). NJ LA Lib. Dev. (1978–80). **Pubns.:** *Access to Monographic Resources* (1976); *A Tutorial Introduction to Canonical Variate Analysis* (1974); Jt. auth., "Getting into Print," *Coll. & Resrch. Libs.* (S. 78); Jt. auth., "Toward a N.J. Numerical Register," *NJ Libs.* (N. 77). **Activities:** 1, 11; 41, 46; 95-Stats. **Addr.:** Graduate School of Library & Information Studies, 4 Huntington St., Rutgers University, New Brunswick, NJ 08903.

O'Connor, Dorothy M. (My. 24, 1919, Paterson, NJ) Circ. Libn., Montclair State Coll., 1970–; Libn. II, Thea. Col., LMPA, New York Pub. Lib., 1966–70. **Educ.:** Fordham Univ., 1955–64, BS (Sec. Educ.); Columbia Univ., 1965–66, MS (LS). **Orgs.:** ALA: LAMA/Circ. Srvs. Sect. (Exec. Com., 1976–77). SLA. Thea. LA. Cath. LA. Amer. Socty. for Thea. Resrch. **Pubns.:** Jt. auth., "A Checklist of Current Performing Arts Periodicals," *Thea. Docum.* (Spr. 1969); Contrib., Bibl. Vol., *F and W Encyclopedia* (1972); Various articles, *Grolier's Encyclopedia International* (1972). **Addr.:** Harry A. Sprague Library, Montclair State College, Upper Montclair, NJ 07043.

O'Connor, Elizabeth Wright (Ag. 25, 1927, Newton, NJ) Med. Libn., Burlington Cnty. Meml. Hosp., 1974–. **Educ.:** Douglass Coll., 1945–49, BA (Soclgy.); Rutgers Univ., 1979–81. (LS). **Orgs.:** Hlth. Sci. LA of NJ: Pres. (1979–80). South. NJ Hlth. Lib. Grp.: Ch. (1977–78). NY/NJ Reg. Med. Lib. Adv. and Plng. Exec. Com. Pinelands Hlth. Info. Cnsrtm. (1981). **Ac-**

Special Subjects/Services: 50. Adult educ.; 51. Advert./Mktg.; 52. Aerosp.; 53. Agric.; 54. Area std.; 55. Arts/Hum.; 56. Autom.; 57. Bibl./Prtg.; 58. Bio. sci.; 59. Bus./Fin.; 60. Chem.; 61. Copyrt.; 62. Documtn.; 63. Educ.; 64. Engin.; 65. Env.; 66. Eth. grps.; 67. Film; 68. Food/Nutr.; 69. Geneal.; 70. Geo.; 71. Geol.; 72. Handcpd.; 73. Hist.; 74. Int. frdm.; 75. Info. sci.; 76. Insr.; 77. Law; 78. Legis.; 79. Math./Comp. sci.; 80. Med.; 81. Metals; 82. Nat. resrcs.; 83. Newsp.; 84. Nuc. sci.; 85. Oral hist.; 86. Petr./Energy; 87. Pharm.; 88. Phys./Astr./Math.; 89. Readg.; 90. Relig.; 91. Sci./Tech.; 92. Soc. sci.; 93. Telecom.; 94. Transp.; 95. (other).

tivities: 12; 15, 17, 39; 80 **Addr.:** Burlington County Memorial Hospital, Health Science Library, 175 Madison Ave., Mount Holly, NJ 08060.

O'Connor, Joseph E. (Ap. 13, 1919, Stamford, CT) Head, Ref. Dept., Wahlstrom Lib., Univ. of Bridgeport, 1976–, Educ. Libn., 1975–76. **Educ.:** Yale Coll., 1946–49, BA (Eng., Drama); South. CT State Coll., 1974–75, MLS; Univ. of Bridgeport, 1975–76, MS (Educ. Media). **Orgs.:** CT LA: Coll. and Univ. Sect. (Bd., 1980). ALA. AECT. Phi Delta Kappa. **Pubns.:** "Index–In–Dice," *AV Instr.* (N. 1976); Various rpts. **Activities:** 1; 15, 39; 51, 63, 67 **Addr.:** Reference Dept., Magnus Wahlstrom Library, Univ. of Bridgeport, 126 Park Ave., Bridgeport, CT 06602.

Oddan, Linda A. (S. 24, 1947, Montevideo, MN) Assoc. Dir., Info. Srv., Med. Coll. of WI, 1980–; Ref. Libn., 1975–80, Circ. Libn., 1970–75. **Educ.:** Univ. of MN, 1964–68, BA (Math.), 1968–70, MA (LS). **Orgs.:** Med. LA. ASIS: WI Chap. (Ch.-Elect, 1981). WI Hlth. Sci. LA. Chicago Area OLUG. Milwaukee OLUG. **Activities:** 1; 17, 22, 39; 80 **Addr.:** Information Service, Medical College of Wisconsin, Todd Wehr Library, P.O. Box 26509, Milwaukee, WI 53226.

O'Dette, Ralph E. (Jl. 14, 1922, Norfolk, VA) Dir., Plng., Chem. Abs. Srv., 1981–, Sr. Staff Adv., 1963–; Prog. Dir., Natl. Sci. Fndn., 1955–63; Asst. to Dir. of Dev., Westinghouse Atomic Power Div., 1954–55; Dir., Econ. Reports Sect., UN Korean Reconstruction Agency, 1953; Asst. Dir., Ofc. of Sci. Pubns., Natl. Bur. of Stan., 1951–52; PR Dept., Stan. Oil Co. (NJ), 1945–50. **Educ.:** Univ. of VA, 1941–45, BhE (Chem. Eng.). **Orgs.:** ASIS. Socty. for Schol. Pubshg. Amer. Chem. Socty. N. Amer. Socty. for Corp. Plng. **Activities:** 6, 14; 17, 36, 49-Plng.; 60, 91 **Addr.:** Chemical Abstracts Service, P.O. Box 3012, Columbus, OH 43210.

O'Donnell, Holly D.S. (Je. 5, 1947, Itzaho, Germany) Coord. of User Srvs., ERIC Clearinghouse on Readg. and Comm. Skills, 1969–, Resrch. Assoc., 1973–75. **Educ.:** Univ. of IL, 1968–72, BS (Anthro.), 1972–73, MS (Eng. as Sec. Lang.). **Orgs.:** ASIS: Spec. Interest Grp. on Info. in Educ. (1975–76). Natl. Cncl. of Tchrs. of Eng.: Ex-Officio Liaison with Com. on Tchrs. of Eng. to Speakers of Other Langs. (1974–); Com. on Role and Image of Women (1975–78); Com. on Careers (1978–). **Pubns.:** "What Do We Know About Preschool Reading?," *Readg. Tchr.* (N. 1979); "Children Writing: Process and Development," *Lang. Arts* (O. 1979); "Language Can Be Fun: An Annotated Bibliography," *Lang. Arts* (F. 1979); "Balance Your Information Budget," *Jnl. of Readg.* (F. 1979); "Instructional Time as Related to Reading Achievement," *Readg. Tchr.* (N. 1978); Various articles. **Activities:** 6; 30, 39; 63 **Addr.:** 121 W. Franklin Ave., Urbana, IL 61801.

O'Donnell, Peggy (S. 20, 1933, Los Angeles, CA) Lib. Consult., 1981–; Proj. Dir., ALA/NEH/CBR Proj., 1979–80; Cont. Educ. for Lib. Staffs Coord., SWLA, 1974–79; Asst. Dir./Dir., Wkshp. Bay Area Ref. Ctr., San Francisco Pub. Lib., 1967–74; Ref. Libn., Santa Monica Pub. Lib., 1965–66; Head, Ref. and Circ., Fashion Inst. of Tech., 1962–64; YA Libn., Los Angeles Pub. Lib., 1960–62; various positions as consult., 1977–80. **Educ.:** Cornell Univ., 1951–55 BS; Columbia Univ., 1956–58, MLS. **Orgs.:** ALA: Cncl. (1978–82); Ofc. for Lib. Persnl. Resrcs., Adv. Com. (Ch., 1977–79); Stdg. Com. on Lib. Educ. (1978–79); various other divs., coms. CLENE: Bd. of Dirs. (1977–79); Pres. (1978–79); various coms., ofcs. CA LA: Cncl. (1973–74); CSL Bd. of Dirs. (1973–74); CLS Educ. Com. (Co-Ch., 1973); various other coms. AALS: Cont. Educ. Interest Grp. (Conv., 1976–77). Various other orgs. **Pubns.:** Jt. auth., "Audio for Current Awareness," *Lib. Jnl. Spec. Rpt. #4* (1978); "Continuing Education for Library Personnel," *Bowker Anl.* (1975); *Planning Library Programs* (1976); jt. auth., *SWLA Current Awareness Audio Cassette Jnl.* (1975–79); "Viewing, Using and Making Films," *Film Lib. Qtly.* (Fall 1970); various trng. mtrls. **Activities:** 3, 9; 24, 25, 26; 50, 55, 95-Eval. **Addr.:** 1135 W. Webster, Chicago, IL 60614.

O'Donnell, Rosemary F. (Ja. 18, 1948, Timmins, ON) Chem. Info. Spec., Polysar Ltd., 1980–, Tech. Writer/Ed., 1979–80; Info. Sci., Info. Retrieval Resrch. Lab, Univ. of IL, 1977–79; Libn., Sci. and Tech., Edmonton Pub. Lib., 1976–77. **Educ.:** Univ. of Montreal, 1966–70, BSc (Chem.), 1970–73 (Chem.); Univ. of Toronto, 1973–76, MLS. Amer. Chem. Socty.: Div. of Chem. Info. ASIS. **Pubns.:** Jt. auth., *Computer Readable Data Bases: A Directory and Data Sourcebook* (1979). **Activities:** 12; 15, 30, 39; 56, 60 **Addr.:** Technical Information Centre, Polysar Limited, Sarnia, ON N7T 7M2 Canada.

Oehler, Eileen L. (Je. 28, 19–, Lansing, MI) Head Libn., Hastings Pub. Lib., 1974–; Jr. coll. tchg. & sch. lib. positions, MI, 1969–74; Cnty. libn., Van Buren Cnty., MI, 1971; Asst. Prof. and Libn., Concordia Luth. Jr. Coll., 1962–69; Ref. Libn. and Head, Ref. Sect., MI State Lib., 1955–62; Ref. Libn. I, Enoch Pratt Free Lib., 1954–55; Tchr. Libn., Lake Odessa (MI) HS, 1950–51; Tchr., Alma (MI) HS, 1947–50. **Educ.:** MI State Univ., 1943–47, AB (Eng.); Univ. of MI, 1951, 1953–54, MALS, 1965–70, MA (Eng.); other courses; Sec. Tchg. Cert., MI; Cert. Libn. I, MI. **Orgs.:** Ch., SE MI Reg. (1968). MI LA: Int. Frdm.; PLA: Ed. Com. (1975–78); Starter List for Branch Libs. (1981–). ALA: ACRL; LAMA: Bldgs. and Equipment Com. (1980–). Lakeland Lib. Coop.: Ch., Centralized Prcs. Com. (1977–79). Various other orgs. AAUW. Delta Kappa Gamma. Luth. Human Rel. Assn., Concordia Hist. Inst., Natl. Trust for Hist. Prsrvn. **Activities:** 1, 9, 13; 16, 17, 39 **Addr.:** 1710 Center Rd., Hastings, MI 49058.

Oehlerts, Donald E. (Ag. 3, 1927, Waterloo, IA) Dir. of Libs., Miami Univ., 1972–; Asst. Dir. of Libs. for Ref. Srvs., Univ. of Houston, 1970–72; Life Sci. & Soc. Sci. Libn., CO State Univ., 1960–67; Per. Libn., SD State Coll., 1958–60; Newsp. Libn., State Hist. Socty. of WI, 1953–58. **Educ.:** Amherst Coll., Univ. of WI, 1949–53, BS (Amer. Std.), 1955–58, MLS; IN Univ., 1967–75, PhD (LS). **Orgs.:** ALA: ACRL/Univ. Libs. Sect., Nom. Com. (1979–80); Ch., LHRT (1979–80). **Pubns.:** *Guide to Colorado Newspapers, 1859–1963* (1964); *Guide to Wisconsin Newspapers, 1833–1957* (1958); "American Library Architecture and the World's Columbian Exposition" in *Milestones to the Present* (1978); Contrib., *Dict. of Amer. Lib. Biog.* (1978); "Sources for the Study of American Library Architecture," *Jnl. of Lib. Hist.* (Ja. 1976); other articles. **Activities:** 1; 17, 19 **Addr.:** Director of Libraries, Miami University, Oxford, OH 45056.

Oermann, Robert K. (Je. 6, 1947, Pittsburgh, PA) Head of Tech. Srvs., Country Msc. Fndn. Lib., 1978–, Ref. Libn., 1978–79. **Educ.:** Univ. of Pittsburgh, 1965–69, BA (Fine Arts); Syracuse Univ., 1977–78, MLS. **Orgs.:** Msc LA. Assn. for Recorded Sound Col. TN LA. SELA. Pop. Cult. Assn. **Pubns.:** "Rockabilly Women," *Jnl. of Country Msc.* (May, 1979); "Women In Country Music," *Cult. Correspondance* (Fall, 1978; *Soc. Practice* (Spr. 1979); "The Quick Way Out" educational film (1978); other articles. **Activities:** 2, 12; 20, 39, 46; 55, 74 **Addr.:** Country Music Foundation Library & Media Center, 4 Music Sq. East, Nashville, TN 37203.

Offerman, Sr. Mary Columba, PBVM (Je. 11, 1919, Delhi, IA) Lib. Coord., Elem. Schs. of Srs. of the Presentation of Dubuque, 1968–; Tchr.-Libn., Resurrection Sch., Dubuque, 1967–68; Tchr.-Libn., St. Joseph's Sch., 1964–67; Tchr.-Libn., St. Cecilia's Sch., 1960–64; Tchr., IA Cath. Schs., 1949–53. **Educ.:** Loras Coll., 1943–58, BA cum laude (Educ.); Rosary Coll., 1966–71, MA (LS); Prof. Cert. State of IA, 1971. **Orgs.:** ALA: Book Sel. Com. for ESEA, Area 8, (1968–69). Cath. LA: Dakota-MN Unit, Book Sel. Com. for ESEA, Area 12, (1969–70). **Honors:** Beta Phi Mu, 1972. **Pubns.:** "Free Magazines: Report by an Elementary Librarian," *Amer. Libs.* (F. 1977); "Metric System: A Bibliography," *Cath. Lib. World* (Apr. 1977); "To Make Good Again: Selected Bibliography On Reconciliation," *Review For Religious* (Ja. 1978); "Let's Make Better Use of Our Libraries," *Clearing House* (O. 1978); "Captive Captions," *Cath. Lib. World* (Mr. 1979); other articles, reviews. **Activities:** 10; 15, 20, 21 **Addr.:** 2360 Carter Rd., Dubuque, IA 52001.

Offermann, Glenn W. (My. 20, 1936, Waterloo, IL) Head Libn., Concordia Coll., 1967–; Libn., Luther HS S., Chicago, IL, 1960–67; Prin./Tchr., St. Stephen's Luth. Sch., Atkins, IA, 1958–60. **Educ.:** Concordia Tchrs. Coll., 1954–58, BS (Educ.); Univ. of Chicago, 1960–65, MA (LS); South. IL Univ., Carbondale, 1971–77, PhD (Educ./Instr. Mtrls.). **Orgs.:** MN LA: Plng. & Dev. Com. (Ch., 1978–). ALA: ACRL, Natl. Conf. Exec. Com. (1979–). J. J. Hill Ref. Lib.: Bd. of Trustees (1976–); Exec. Com. (1979–). Coop. Libs. in Cnsrtm.: Bd. of Dir. (1969–); Pres. (1975–76). Cncl. of lMN Acad. Lih. Dir.: Scy. (1975–77); Co-Ch. (1978–79). Concordia Hist. Inst.: Com. on Hist. Std. & Resrcs. (1979–). Luth. Educ. Assn. MN S. Dist., Luth. Church–MO Synod: Archvst. (1975). **Pubns.:** "Participants' View of an Academic Library Consortium" in *New Horizons for Academic Libraries* (1979); "The Present is Crucial: Contemporary Activities in College Archives" in *Archives and History, Minutes and Reports of the 14th Archivists' & Historians Conference* (1977). **Activities:** 1, 2; 15, 17, 34; 63, 85, 90 **Addr.:** Concordia College, St. Paul, MN 55104.

Ofstad, Odessa (Lang) (Jl. 28, 1938, LeMars, IA) Spec. Col. Libn., Archvst., Pickler Lib., NE MO State Univ., 1977–, Msc.-Curr. Libn., 1974–76, Head Catlgr., 1970–74, Catlgr., 1967–70; Tchr., Argo Cmnty. HS, 1964–65; Instr., North. IL Univ., 1963–64; Instr., Univ. of KY, 1961–63. **Educ.:** Swarthmore Coll., 1956–57; Univ. of SD, 1957–60, BA (Classics); Univ. of KY, 1960–61, MA (Classics); Univ. of MO, 1976–77, MA (LS). **Orgs.:** MO LA. ALA. Midwest Arch. Conf. Eta Sigma Phi. Audubon Socty. Pi Beta Phi. **Honors:** Phi Beta Kappa; Beta Phi Mu. **Activities:** 1, 2; 23, 39, 45; 55, 92 **Addr.:** Pickler Memorial Library, Northeast Missouri State University, Kirksville, MO 63501.

Ogden, Alan W. (N. 30, 1946, Ft. Wayne, IN) Law Lib. Dir., Univ. of Tulsa Coll. of Law, 1978–; Law Lib. Dir., Univ. of SD Sch. of Law, 1976–78; Law Libn., IN Supreme Court, 1974–76, Asst. Law Libn., 1972–74. **Educ.:** IN Univ., 1966–70, BA (Pol. Sci.); IN Univ., Indianapolis, 1971–75, JD; Univ. of WA, 1975–76, MLS. **Orgs.** AALL: Ad Hoc Com. on Long Range Plng., Stat. Sect. (Co–Ch., 1980–81); Place. Com. (1980–81). Southwest. Assn. of Law Libs.: Finance Com. (Ch., 1980–81). Mid–Amer. Assn. of Law Libs.: Mid–Amer. Cncl. of Law Libns. (1980–81). Assn. of Amer. Law Schs.: Legal Resrch., Wrtg. and Reasoning Sect., Accred. Inspection Team (1980–81). Amer. Bar Assn. **Activities:** 12; 17, 31, 77 **Addr.:** Univ. of Tulsa, College of Law, 3120 E. 4th Pl., Tulsa, OK 74104.

Ogden, Howard A. (O. 20, 1928, New York, NY) Dir., Hampton Pub. Lib., 1973–; Commander, U.S. Navy, 1952–72. **Educ.:** Univ. of PA, 1948–52, AB (Art Hist.); Univ. of NC, 1972–73, MSLS; Golden Gate Univ., 1978–79, MPA (Admin.). **Orgs.:** ALA: Satellite Sem. on Copyrt. (Site Coord., 1978). VA LA: Lib. Dev. Com. (1975–78); Legis. Com. (1976–77; 1979–); VA State Lib. LSCA Title III Adv. Com. (1977–80); VA State Lib. LSCA Title I Adv. Com. (1980–). City of Hampton Trng. Bd. Hampton Rotary Club. Hampton Rds. Horticultural Socty. VA Masters Swim Club. **Activities:** 9; 17, 35, 47 **Addr.:** 2 Kanawha Ct., Hampton, VA 23669.

Ogden, Nina M. (Mae) (S. 5, 1915, Orofino, ID) Libn., Pierce Free Pub. Lib., 1968–. **Educ.:** Univ. of ID, 1934–. **Orgs.:** Pac. NW. LA. ID LA: PR (Ch., 1974–77); Pub. Libs. Div. (Ch., 1977–78). Orofino Bus. and Prof. Women's Club. **Honors:** Xi Alpha Mu, Beta Sigma Phi, Woman of the Yr., 1976. **Pubns.:** ID State Ed., *Reading for Young People: The Northwest* (1980); Spec. features writer, *Clearwater Tribune* (1950–). **Activities:** 9; 15, 17, 20; 50 **Addr.:** Pierce Free Public Library, P.O. Box 386, Pierce, ID 83546.

Ogilvie, Martha M. C. (F. 16, 1918, Oakland, CA) Educ. Consult., World Book–Childcraft Intl., Inc. 1966–; Dir., Instr. Mtrls. Ctr., Evanston Elem. Sch., 1959–66; Libn., Dept. of Geo., Univ. of WA, 1957–59; Acq. Libn., Chico State Coll., 1950–57. **Educ.:** Northwestern Univ., 1936–40, BS (Geo.); Univ. of WA, 1954–58, MLibr (Libnshp.). **Orgs.:** ALA. Can. LA. Cath. LA. **Activities:** 10; 15, 26; 63, 70 **Addr.:** Educational Services Dept. Station 8, World Book-Childcraft Intl. Inc., Merchandise Mart Plaza, Chicago, IL 60654.

Ogle, Oren O. (Ag. 1, 1942, Vancouver, WA) Catlgr., Asst. Prof., Portland State Univ., 1969–. **Educ.:** OR State Univ., 1960–65, BS (Bus. Admin.); Univ. of WA, 1968–69, MLibr. **Orgs.:** ALA. Pac. NW. LA: Bibl. Com. (Ch., 1979–). Portland Area Spec. Libns. Assn.: Treas. (1972–74); Pres. (1980–81). AAUP: Portland State Univ. Chap. (Secy., 1978–81). **Honors:** Beta Phi Mu, 1970. **Activities:** 1; 20 **Addr.:** 1805 S.W. Moss, Portland, OR 97219.

Oglesbee, Harriet Barkley (S. 27, 1939, Statesville, NC) ILL Libn., Univ. of SC, 1977–; Head libn., asst. prof., Limestone Coll., 1970–76; Asst. Ref. Libn., Savannah (GA) Pub. Lib., 1968–70; Elem. Sch. Tchr., NC Schs., 1961–66. **Educ.:** Erskine Coll., 1957–61, AB (Elem. Educ.); FL State Univ., 1966–67, MS (LS). **Orgs.:** ALA. SELA. SC LA. Cherokee Cnty. (SC) LA: Ch. (1976). **Honors:** Beta Phi Mu, 1967. **Activities:** 1; 31, 39, 49-ILL. **Addr.:** Thomas Cooper Library, University of SC, Columbia, SC 29208.

O'Halloran, Charles (D. 7, 1926, Denver, CO) State Libn., MO State Lib., 1964–; Dir., Rosenberg Lib., Galveston, TX, 1959–64; Ref. Asst., Readers' Adv., Kansas City Pub. Lib., 1954–59; Tchr., Fort Morgan Pub. Schs., 1950–53. **Educ.:** Univ. of CO, 1947–50, BA (Eng.); Univ. of Denver, 1953–54, MA (LS). **Orgs.:** ALA. MO LA. MO Com. for the Hum.: Ch. (1978–79). **Pubns.:** Column, *Show-Me Libs.* **Activities:** 13; 17, 36; 74, 78 **Addr.:** Missouri State Library, 308 East High St., Jefferson City, MO 65101.

O'Halloran, Frances M. (D. 22, 1907, Newton, MA) Resrch. Afflt., Univ. of HI, 1975–; Visit. Prof., Univ. of WA, 1974–75; Asst. Prof., Univ. HI, 1971–74, Dir., USARPAC Lib. Prog., HQs Pac., 1967–71. **Educ.:** Wellesley Coll., 1927–31, BA (Eng., Educ.); Boston Coll., 1931–35, MA (Eng., Educ.); Simmons Coll., 1944–45, BLS; Univ. of HI, 1968–70, MLS. **Orgs.:** HI LA: Jnl. (Ed.). Beta Phi Mu: Nom. Com. (Ch.). Assocs. of Univ. of HI Lib.: Prog. Com. (Ch.). AAUW. Bishop Musm. **Honors:** U.S. Army, Merit. Civilian Awd., 1971; ALA, Disting. Libn. Awd., 1971. **Activities:** 4, 11; 17, 35, 39; 55, 57, 74 **Addr.:** Graduate School of Library Studies, University of Hawaii, Honolulu, HI 96814.

O'Hara, Edward J. (N. 22, 1941, New York, NY) Dir. of Lib., Sacred Heart Univ., 1978–; Head, Col. Dev., Univ. of KY, 1975–78; Biblgrphr., Boston Univ., 1972–75. **Educ.:** American Univ., 1959–63, BA (Intl. Rel.); New York Univ., 1966–68, MA (Hist.); Rutgers Univ., 1970–72, MLS. **Orgs.:** SW. CT Lib. Cncl.: Bd. of Trustees (1980–). Fairfield Lib. Admins. Grp.: Pres. (1979–80). CT Interagency Lib. Plng. Com. **Honors:** Beta Phi Mu, 1972. **Activities:** 1; 15, 17 **Addr.:** Sacred Heart University Library, P.O. Box 6460, Bridgeport, CT 06606.

O'Hara, Frederic J. (Je. 22, 1917, Watertown, MA) Prof. of LS, Long Island Univ., 1963–; Assoc. Prof. of LS, Pratt Inst., 1961–63; Assoc. Prof. of LS, West. MI Univ., 1956–61; Asst. Prof. of LS, TX Womens Univ., 1955–56. **Educ.:** Boston Coll., 1936–40, AB (Eng., Wrtg.); Columbia Univ., 1947, BS (LS), 1950, MS (LS), 1950–54, EdD (Comm.). **Orgs.:** ALA: Schol. Com. (Ch., 1965–68); SLA: Stats. Com. (Ch., 1973–74). **Pubns.:** *A Guide to Publications of the Executive Branch* (1979); *The Library in the Community: A Book of Readings and References* (1978); *Guidance for the Adult Learner: A Book of Readings and*

PROFESSIONAL ACTIVITIES: Institutions: 1. Acad. lib.; 2. Arch.; 3. Assn.; 4. Fed./Gvt. lib.; 5. Inst. lib.; 6. Mfr./Suppl.; 7. Milit. lib.; 8. Musm.; 9. Pub. lib.; 10. Sch. lib.; 11. Sch. of lib. sci.; 12. Spec. lib.; 13. State lib.; 14. (other). **Functions/Activities:** 15. Acq./Col. dev.; 16. Adult srvs.; 17. Admin.; 18. Apprais.; 19. Archit./Bldgs.; 20. Cat./Class.; 21. Chld. srvs.; 22. Circ.; 23. Cons./Pres.; 24. Consult.; 25. Cont. ed.; 26. Educ. lib. sci.; 27. Ext. srvs.; 28. Fund/Grants; 29. Gvt. pubs.; 30. Indx./Abs.; 31. Instr. lib. use; 32. Media srvs.; 33. Micro.; 34. Netwks./Coop.; 35. Persnl.; 36. PR; 37. Publshg.; 38. Recs. mgt.; 39. Ref. srvs.; 40. Repro.; 41. Resrch.; 42. Review.; 43. Secur.; 44. Serials; 45. Spec. col.; 46. Tech. srvs.; 47. Trustees/Bds.; 48. YA srvs.; 49. (other).

References (1977); *Reader in Government Documents* (1973); Ed., "Views and Overviews of Government Publications," Gvt. Pubns. Review (1974–); Various monos., articles and columns. **Activities:** 9; 16, 29; 50, 72, 89 **Addr.:** Graduate Library School, Long Island University, Greenvale, NY 11548.

O'Hare, James L. (My. 15, 1945, Sharon, PA) Dir., Library Srvs., Ministry of Atty. Genl., BC Govt., 1978–, Reg. Dir., Lib. Srvs. Branch, 1973–78. **Educ.:** Univ. of Pittsburgh, 1963–67, BA (Eng.); Univ. of BC, 1971–73, MLS. **Orgs.:** Can. Assn. of Law Libs. Can. Law Info. Cncl. BC Law Lib. Fndn. Various Ofcs. **Activities:** 4, 12; 15, 17, 20; 77 **Addr.:** BC Ministry of Attorney General Library Services, 609 Broughton St., Victoria, BC V8V 1X4 Canada.

O'Hearon, Doris M. (F. 28, 1928, Duluth, MN) Libn., Aquinas Cath. HS, 1979–; Dist. Libn., Yorkville Sch. Dist. #115, 1973–78; Dir., Lib. Srvs., Natl. Safety Cncl., 1971–73; Ref. Libn., Instr., Aurora Coll., 1967–71. **Educ.:** Aquinas Coll., Grand Rapids, MI, 1964, BA (Eng., Educ.); Rosary Coll., 1967, MA (LS); various crs. **Orgs.:** ALA. Cath. LA. **Pubns.:** Various reviews; Ed., *Lib. Scene;* Ed., *Natl. Safety News.* **Activities:** 10; 17, 48; 63 **Addr.:** Aquinas Catholic H.S. Library, 2100 E. 72nd St., Chicago, IL 60649.

Ohm, Elizabeth (Jl. 23, 1929, Henderson, KY) Admin. Libn., Park Forest Pub. Lib., 1975–; Assoc. Dir., Lincoln Lib., Springfield, IL, 1974–75; Head of Cat., Interim Dir., Tucson Pub. Lib., 1972–74; Asst. Dir., Lincoln Lib., 1968–72; Asst. Head Cat., IL State Lib., 1963–67. **Educ.:** IL Coll., 1959–60, AB (Eng.); Univ. of IL, 1967–68, MS (LS). **Orgs.:** ALA: Cncl. (1976–80); LAMA, Ed., Small Libs. Pubns. (1977–80); PLA, Bd. of Dir. (1973–77). IL Reg. Lib. Cncl.: Cont. Educ. Com. Park Forest Orch.: Bd. of Dir. (1977–80). Park Forest Cmnty. Arts Cncl. Creative Woman (Mag.): Adv. Cncl. (1979–). **Pubns.:** Ed., *The Right to Read and the Nation's Libraries* (1974); Ed., *Directory of Human Resources* (1979). **Activities:** 9; 17 **Addr.:** Park Forest Public Library, 400 Lakewood Blvd., Park Forest, IL 60466.

Ohr, Grace Marion (N. 29, 1917, New York, NY) Catlgr., Univ. of UT, 1960–; Catlgr., Univ. of DE, 1958–60; Libn., US Army, Europe, 1955–57; Catlgr., State Hist. Socty. of MO, 1953–54; Catlgr., West. Coll. for Women, 1949–52; Catlgr., Royal Oak (MI) Pub. Lib., 1947–49. **Educ.:** Wagner Coll., 1940, AB (Latin); Pratt Inst., 1946–47, BLS; Univ. of MI, 1951–52, AMLS. **Orgs.:** ALA. Msc. LA. UT LA. AAUP. **Activities:** 1; 20; 55 **Addr.:** 73 Elizabeth St., Apt. 4, Salt Lake City, UT 84102.

Ohta, Miwako T. (F. 25, 1926, Tokyo, Japan) Asst. Mgr., Chem. Abs. Srv. Lib., 1977–; Grp. Leader, 1973–76; Asst. Libn., 1972–73; Head, SDI Srv., Washington Univ. Sch. of Med. Lib., 1968–71; Head, Pub. Srvs., 1966–68; Ref. Libn., 1964–66; Ref. Libn., St. Louis Univ. Med. Ctr. Lib., 1961–64; Ref. Asst., Dayton & Montgomery Cnty. Pub. Lib., 1960–61. **Educ.:** Univ. of Akron, 1956–58, BS (Chem.); Case-Western Reserve Univ., 1958–60, MSLS; Columbia Univ., 1963, Cert. **Orgs.:** Med. LA: Com. on Bibl. Proj. & Problems. (1968–72, Ch., 1972–73). ASIS: Prog. Com. (1977). **Pubns.:** "Mechanization of library procedures in the medium sized medical library XII," *Bltn. Med. LA* (1970); "A comparision of some demand subject searches; machine vs. human," *Bltn. Med. LA* (1967); Jt. auth., "Medicine," *Lib. Trends* (1967). **Activities:** 12; 17, 39; 60, 75, 91 **Addr.:** Chemical Abstracts Service Library, P.O. Box 3012, Columbus, OH 43210.

O'Keeffe, Richard Bennett, Sr. (Ag. 11, 1930, Washington, DC) Libn., Asst. Prof., Fenwick Lib., George Mason Univ., 1977–, Asst. Dir. of Libs., 1969–77; Libn., Resrch. Assoc., Amer. Legion, Natl. Hqs., 1961–69; Asst. Ed., Bus. Mgr., Cath. Per. Index, 1958–61. **Educ.:** Washington & Lee Univ., Cath. Univ., 1948–55, AB (Eng. Lit.), 1955–58, MSLS. **Orgs.:** Socty. of Indxrs. Fairfax Cnty. Reg. Lib. Bd. ALA. VA LA. **Pubns.:** Ed., *Catholic Periodical Index, vol. 2 1934–1938* (1960); "Amid the alien corn," *Amer. Spectator* (O. 1979); reviews. **Activities:** 1, 12; 15, 30, 39; 55, 57, 74 **Addr.:** 3704 University Dr., Fairfax, VA 22030.

Okuizumi, Eizaburo (N. 5, 1940, Shibukawa, Gumma, Japan) Japanese Catlgr., Biblgphr., Univ. of MD, 1974–; Chief, Acq. Sect., Keio Univ. (Tokyo), 1965–74. **Educ.:** Keio Univ., 1961–65, BA (LS), 1965–68, BA (Law, Pol.), 1971–73, MS (LS). **Orgs.:** ASIS. CLENE. DC LA. Assn. for Asian Std. **Pubns.:** Ed., *Report of Library Mission to the U.S. & Canada* (1979); "The Organization and Intelligence Gathering Activities of the Far East Command in Occupied Japan," *Jnl. of the Tokyo Coll. of Econ.* (D. 1978); other publications. **Activities:** 1; 39, 44, 45; 54, 62 **Addr.:** East Asia Collection, University of Maryland Libraries, College Park, MD 20740.

O'Leary, Francis Bernard (O. 6, 1926, New York City, NY) Libn., Med. Ctr., St. Louis Univ., 1960–; Libn., Inst. of Tech., Univ. of MN, 1957–60; Asst. Libn., Nat. Sci., Columbia Univ., 1953–57, Zlgy. and Bot. Libn., 1949–53. **Educ.:** Manhattan Coll., 1944–49, BS (Sci.); Columbia Univ., 1949–51, MS (LS); Med. LA, Cert., Grade I. **Orgs.:** SLA: Grt. St. Louis Chap. (Pres., 1963–64). Med. LA: Med. Sch. Libs. Grp. (Ch., 1967–68). AAAS. **Honors:** Sigma Xi. **Pubns.:** Indxr., "Crust of the Earth," (1955); "Gregor Mendel's 'Lost' Work," *Med. Circle Bltn.* (Mr. 1961). **Activities:** 1; 17; 60, 80 **Addr.:** 1402 S. Grand Blvd., St. Louis, MO 63104.

O'Leary, Timothy J. (Ap. 23, 1928, New York, NY) Dir. of File Resrch. and Libn., Human Rel. Area Files, 1969–, Dir. of File Resrch., 1963–69, Assoc. in Resrch., 1957–63; Asst. Archeologist, Glenbow Fndn., 1957. **Educ.:** Manhattan Coll., 1946–50, BS (Hist.); Columbia Univ., 1953–57, MPhil (Anthro.); South. CT State Coll., 1973–77, MS (LS). **Orgs.:** ALA: ACRL. Class. Socty.: N. Amer. Branch. Amer. Anthro. Assn. Socty. for Amer. Archlgy. **Honors:** Beta Phi Mu. **Pubns.:** Jt. auth., *Ethnographic Bibliography of North America* (1975); jt. auth., *Circum-Mediterranean Peasantry: Introductory Bibliographies* (1969); *Ethnographic Bibliography of South America* (1963); "A Preliminary Bibliography of Cross-Cultural Studies," *Behavior Sci. Notes* (1969); Ethnographic bibls., *A Handbook of Method in Cultural Anthropology* (1973); articles. **Activities:** 1, 14-Interuniv. Corp.; 17, 20, 24; 54, 66, 92 **Addr.:** Human Relations Area Files, P.O. Box 2054, Yale Station, New Haven, CT 06520.

Olechno, Gillian (Mr. 1, 1930, Stockport, Cheshire, Eng.) Chief, Lib. Srvs., Los Angeles Cnty., Univ. of S. CA Med. Ctr., 1973–, Med. Libn., 1969–73, Head, Tech. Prcs., 1967–69; Tech. Srv. Libn., City of Inglewood Pub. Lib., 1961–66. **Educ.:** Leeds Univ., Leeds, Eng., 1948–51, BA (Soclgy.); Univ. of South. CA, Los Angeles, 1960–64, MSLS. **Orgs.:** Med. LA: Empl. Com. (Ch., 1977–79); Task Force on Cert. Examinations (1978). Med. Lib. Grp. of S. CA and AZ: Secty. (1971); Archvst. (1972–73); PR Com. (1974–75). Amer. Transl. Assn. S. CA Chap. (Secty., 1974–). Polish-Amer. Hist. Assn.: CA Chap. (Secty., 1975–79); VP (1980). **Pubns.:** "Sienkiewicz in California," *Polish-Americans in California* (1978); "From Poor Farm to Medical Center," *Bltn. Med. LA* (1975). **Activities:** 4, 12; 16, 17, 24; 63, 80 **Addr.:** Los Angeles County/University of Southern CA Medical Center, 1200 N. State St., Rm. 2050, Los Angeles, CA 90033.

Olin, Charlotte Dinsmoor (Ag. 12, 1924, St. Marys, WV) Assoc. Libn., Kimbell Art Musm., 1976–82; Sub. Libn., Ft. Worth Pub. Schs., 1974–75; Indp. Catlgr., 1974–. **Educ.:** Wellesley Coll., 1944–46, BA (Geo.); TX Woman's Univ., 1969–72, MLS. **Orgs.:** ARLIS/NA. SLA: TX Chap., Ft. Worth Lcl. Plng. Com. (1980). TX LA: Arch. RT (Secy., 1975–76; Vice–Ch., 1976–77; Ch., 1977–78). Eng.-Speaking Un.: Ft. Worth Chap. Frnds. of the TX Christ. Univ. Libs. **Honors** Beta Phi Mu. **Activities:** 2, 12; 20, 34, 39; 55 **Addr.:** 2909 Alton Rd., Fort Worth, TX 76109.

Olinger, Elizabeth B. (O. 17, 1932, Roda, VA) Head Libn., Greenville Tech. Coll., 1971–; Serials Libn., Oak Ridge Natl. Lab., 1970–71. **Educ.:** George Peabody, 1967–69, BS (Geo., Bus. Admin.); Case West. Resrv. Univ., 1969–70, MSLS. **Orgs.:** ALA. ASIS. SELA. SC LA. Natl. Org. for Women. Women in Cmnty. Colls. AAUW. League of Women Voters. **Activities:** 1; 15, 39, 44 **Addr.:** Greenville Technical College, P.O. Box 5539, Greenville, SC 29606.

Olive, Betsy Ann (Je. 9, 1923, Fuquay Springs, NC) Libn., Grad. Sch. of Bus. & Pub. Admin., Cornell Univ., 1965–, Assoc. Libn., 1957–65, Ref. Libn., 1955–57; Various bus. positions, 1945–53. **Educ.:** Duke Univ., 1941–45, AB (Bus. Admin.); Univ. of NC, 1953–55, MS (LS). **Orgs.:** SLA: Prof. Rcrt. Com. (1963–66); Case Std. Com., Ch. (1965–67); Chap. Prog. Ch. ALA. ASIS. **Honors** Beta Phi Mu, 1955. **Pubns.:** Cmplr., *Management: A Subject Listing of Recommended Books, Pamphlets and Journals* (1965); Cmplr., *Executives Guide to Information Sources* (1965); assoc. ed., *Encyclopedia of Business Information Sources* (1970, 1976); "Administration of Higher Education, a Bibliographic Survey," *Admin. Sci. Qtly.* (1967); reviews. **Activities:** 1, 12; 15, 17, 24; 51, 59, 80, 95 **Addr.:** Library, Graduate School of Business and Public Administration, Malott Hall, Cornell University, NY 14853.

Oliver, Joan A. (Je. 1, 1926, Montreal, PQ) Trustee, Ottawa Pub. Lib., 1974–; Ch. of Bd., 1976–78, Ch. of Finance, 1975–76. **Educ.:** McGill Univ., 1943–47, BSc (Biochem.); Carleton Univ., 1974–81, MA (Psy.). **Orgs.:** ON LA. Can. LA. East. ON Reg. Lib. Syst.: Trustee (1978–). **Activities:** 9; 19, 35, 47; 56 **Addr.:** 116 Buell St., Ottawa, ON K1Z 7E8 Canada.

Oliver, John A. (S. 14, 1926, Athol, MA) Dir., Flint Pub. Lib., 1980–, Actg. Dir., 1978–80, Asst. Dir., 1967–78; Dir., Oak Park Pub. Lib., 1962–67; Branch Lib., Detroit Pub. Lib., 1955–62; Bus. & Tech. Dept., Fort Wayne Pub. Lib., 1952–55. **Educ.:** Univ. of MA, 1946–50, BA (Eng.); Univ. of Denver, 1951–52, MA (LS). **Orgs.:** ALA: Frnds. of Libs. (1970–73, Ch., 1971–72); PR Sect. Bd. (1973); Metro. Lib. Com. (1970); Lib. Admin. Div., Fringe Benefits & Econ. Com. (1971–72). MI LA: VP (1969–70). Amer. Contract Bridge Leag. Genesee Valley Tennis Club. **Activities:** 9; 17, 35 **Addr.:** G-6024 W. Court St., Flint, MI 48504.

Oliver, Mary Wilhelmina (My. 4, 1919, Cumberland, MD) Prof. of Law and LS, Law Libn., Univ. of NC, 1955–, Asst. Law Libn., 1952–55; Asst. Soc. Sci and Ref. Libn., Drake Univ., 1947–49; Asst. in Law Lib., Univ. of VA, 1945–47; Asst. in Lib., Douglas Coll., 1943–45. **Educ.:** West. MD Coll., 1940, AB (Hist., Eng.); Drexel Univ., 1943, BS in LS; Univ. of NC, 1949–51, JD (Law). **Orgs.:** AALL: Exec. Com. (1971/72–1973/74) Pres. (1972/73). SLA. Intl. Assn. of Law Libs. Assn. of Amer. Law Schs.: Exec. Com. (1979–81). **Activities:** 1; 17 **Addr.:** P.O. Box 733, Chapel Hill, NC 27514.

Oliver, Patricia Ann (Ag. 25, 1948, Troy, NY) Mgr., Tech. Info. Exch., Gen. Electric, 1977–, Libn., 1973–, Lib. Trainee, Mechonicville Dist. Pub. Lib., 1972–73; Sci. Tchr., Whitehall Ctrl. Schs., 1970–71. **Educ.:** SUNY, Albany 1966–70, BS (Bio.), 1971–72, MLS; Med. Libnshp. Cert., 1975–80. **Orgs.:** SLA: Upstate NY Chap. (Secy., 1977–79). **Pubns.:** Jt. auth., "Costs of On-Line Bibliographic Searches in Industry," *Proceedings Sixth Mid-Yr. Mtg. ASIS* (1977). **Activities:** 12; 17, 33; 91 **Addr.:** General Electric Technical Information Exchange, 1 River Rd., Bldg. 81 A133, Schenectady, NY 12345.

Oliver, Valerie Burnham (F. 28, 1938, Nashua, NH) Ref. Libn., Univ. of CT Lib., 1968–; Sci. Biblgphr., SUNY, Albany, 1964–65; Ref. Libn., Untd. Techs. Corp., Lib., 1961–64. **Educ.:** St. Lawrence Univ., 1956–60, BS (Math.); McGill Univ., 1960–61, BLS. **Orgs.:** New Eng. OLUG. Costume Socty. of Amer. **Pubns.:** *Textile Reference Sources, a Selective Bibliography* (1973); *Water Resources, a Bibliographic Guide to Reference Sources* (1975); Ed., *Education, Guide to Selected Sources* (1977). **Activities:** 1; 31, 39, 49-On-line Srch.; 58, 91 **Addr.:** University of Connecticut Library, Reference Dept. U-5R, Storrs, CT 06268.

Olm, Jane G. (N. 5, 1925, Van Horn, TX) Law Libn., TX Tech. Univ. Sch. of Law, 1978–, Asst. Law Libn., 1975–78; Assoc. Libn., TX State Law Lib., 1971–75; Asst. Law Libn., Univ. of TX Sch. of Law, 1967–71; Ref. Libn., Univ. of NM Lib., 1966–67. **Educ.:** Univ. of NM, 1944–48, BBA (Bus., Econ.); Univ. of TX, Austin, 1965–66, MLS. **Orgs.:** Southwestern Assn. of Law Libs.: VP (1978–79); Pres. (1979–80). AALL. **Addr.:** School of Law Library, TX Tech. University, Box 4030, Lubbock, TX 79409.

Olmsted, Elizabeth Hiatt (O. 9, 1919, Topeka, KS) Msc. Catlgr., Univ. of Louisville, 1975–; Conservatory Libn., Oberlin Coll., 1958–74; Msc. Libn., OH State Univ., 1954–58; Prof. Asst., Msc. Dept., Minneapolis Pub. Lib., 1946–51. **Educ.:** Eastman Sch. of Msc., 1939–40, BMus (Theory); Univ. of MN, 1943–46, MA (Msc. Composition); 1948–50 BS in LS Lib. SC.; Univ. of MD, 1968–69, Postmaster's cert. **Orgs.:** Msc. LA: VP (1969); Midwest Chap. Ch. (1957–59). **Honors:** Msc. LA, Distin. Srv., 1974. **Pubns.:** *Music Library Association Catalog of Cards for Printed Music 1953–1972* (1974); *Music Library Association Midwest Chapter: A Brief History* (1978); reviews. **Activities:** 1, 9; 15, 17, 20; 55 **Addr.:** 8801 Perry Rd., Louisville, KY 40222.

Olsen, Charles O. (O. 18, 1921, Greenville, SC) Libn., Eagle Eds., 1981– Libn., Jt. Bank-Fund Lib., 1975–80, Asst. Libn., 1962–74; Chief, Resrch. Files, World Bank, 1958–62; Various positions, Lib. of Congs., 1954–58. **Educ.:** Stanford Univ., 1943–48, BA (Intl. Rel.); Columbia Univ., 1953–54, MLS. **Orgs.:** SLA: Gvt. Info. Srvs. Com. (1978–81); Intl. Affairs Sect., Pres. (1980–81). ALA. **Pubns.:** *Developing Areas: A Classed Bibliography of the Joint Bank-Fund Library* (1976). **Activities:** 12; 17, 29, 39; 54, 56, 59 **Addr.:** 2119 Bancroft Pl. N.W., Washington, DC 20008.

Olsen, David Louis (Ap. 20, 1939, Denver, CO) Acq. Libn., Lafayette Coll. Lib., 1968–; Libn. I, Detroit Pub. Lib., 1967–68; Jr. Libn., Milwaukee Pub. Lib., 1964–66. **Educ.:** Univ. of CO, 1958–61, BA (Hist.); Univ. of WI, 1961–63, MS (Hist.); Univ. of Denver, 1966–67, MA (LS); Rutgers Univ., 1975–78, 6th yr. Cert. (LS). **Orgs.:** ALA. PA LA. Phi Alpha Theta. **Activities:** 1; 15, 44 **Addr.:** 825 Porter St., Easton, PA 18042.

Olsen, Janus F. (Ja. 4, 1942, Portland, OR) Dir., Alexander Mitchell Pub. Lib., Aberdeen (SD), 1980–; Dir., Mitchell (SD) Pub. Lib., 1973–80; Actg. Dir., Actg. Asst. Dir., SD State Lib., 1972–73, Consult./Coord., 1972, Head of Cat. & Prcs., 1972, Ref. Libn., 1971. **Educ.:** Univ. of SD, 1960–64, BFA (Art Educ.); Luther Theo. Semy., 1964–65; Univ. of West. ON, 1970–71, MLS. **Orgs.:** ALA. Corn Palace Reading Cncl.: Pres. (1975). Mt. Plains LA: Co-Prog. Ch., Jt. MPLA/SDLA Conv. (1977). SD LA: Pres.-Elect 1976, Pres. (1977); Ch., Centennial Proj. Com. (1981–89); Ch., PR Com. (1973–75); Ch., Pub. Lib. Sect. (1975). Other orgs. Mitchell Jaycees: Secy. (1974–75). Mitchell Area Arts Cncl.: Pres. (1976). Mitchell Area Cham. of Cmrc. Mitchell Prehist. Indian Village Com. Other orgs. **Honors** SD LA, Cert. of Appreciation, 1976, 1978. **Pubns.:** "SD State Library Five-Year Plan of Service 1973–77," *SD Lib. Bltn.* (1973); "This Is Mitchell, S.D.," *On line data base* (1979); TV progs. **Activities:** 9, 13; 17, 25, 36; 56, 89, 95-TV. **Addr.:** Alexander Mitchell Public Library, 519 S. Kline, Aberdeen, SD 57401.

Olsen, Patricia L. (F. 27, 1948, Detroit, MI) Dir., Avon Twp. Pub. Lib., 1978–; Dir., Van Buren Cnty. (MI) Lib., 1974–78; Head Libn., Decatur (MI) Pub. Schs., 1970–74. **Educ.:** West. MI Univ., 1966–70, BA (Hist/LS), 1971–73, MSL (LS); Women in Lib. Mgt. Inst., SUNY, Buffalo, 1977; Dale Carnegie Course, 1976. **Orgs.:** ALA: PLA., Mem. Com. (1977–); LAMA; Women Lib. Admin. Discuss. Grp. (Co-ch., 1980–81). MI LA: Pub. Lib. Div., Ch. (1977–78); Exec. Bd. (1977–78 and 1980); Legis. Com. (1978–80); Pres. (1981–82). Women Lib. Workers. Rochester-

Special Subjects/Services: 50. Adult educ.; 51. Advert./Mktg.; 52. Aerosp.; 53. Agric.; 54. Area std.; 55. Arts/Hum.; 56. Autom.; 57. Bibl./Prtg.; 58. Bio. sci.; 59. Bus./Fin.; 60. Chem.; 61. Copyrt.; 62. Documtn.; 63. Educ.; 64. Engin.; 65. Env.; 66. Eth. grps.; 67. Film; 68. Food/Nutr.; 69. Geneal.; 70. Geo.; 71. Geol.; 72. Handcpd.; 73. Hist.; 74. Int. frdm.; 75. Info. sci.; 76. Insr.; 77. Law; 78. Legis.; 79. Math./Comp. sci.; 80. Med.; 81. Metals; 82. Nat. resrcs.; 83. Newsp.; 84. Nuc. sci.; 85. Oral hist.; 86. Petr./Energy; 87. Pharm.; 88. Phys./Astr./Math.; 89. Readg.; 90. Relig.; 91. Sci./Tech.; 92. Soc. sci.; 93. Telecom.; 94. Transp.; 95. (other).

Avon Hist. Socty. Human Resources Comsn.: Bd. (1977–78). West. MI Univ. Alum. Assn. **Honors:** Beta Phi Mu. **Addr.:** Avon Township Public Library, 210 W. University Dr., Rochester, MI 48063.

Olsen, Robert A. Jr. (Ap. 16, 1924, Detroit, MI) Theo. Libn., Brite Div. Sch., TX Christ. Univ., 1965–; Assoc. Libn., Coll. of Emporia, 1964–65; Pastor, Untd. Presby. Churches, 1953–63. **Educ.:** Coll. of Wooster, 1947–49, BA (Hist.); McCormick Theo. Semy., Chicago, 1949–52, MDiv (Theo.); Emporia State Univ., 1963–64, MLS. **Orgs.:** ATLA: Treas. (1974–). TX LA. Intl. Socty. of Theta Phi: Secy.-Treas. (1972–74). **Honors:** Assn. of Theo. Schs., Lib. Staff Dev. Awd., 1976. **Pubns.:** *Directory of Information Networks in Texas* (1971); *Bibliography of Theses Accepted by Brite Divinity School, 1929–1971* (1971). **Activities:** 1, 12; 15, 25; 90 **Addr.:** Brite Divinity School, Texas Christian University, Fort Worth, TX 76129.

Olsen, Rowena June (Jl. 29, 1937, Marion, KS) Libn., McPherson Coll., 1975–, Asst. Libn., 1970–75; Head, Circ. Dept., KS State Tchrs. Coll., 1967–70, Asst. Libn., Cat. & Ref. Depts., 1966–67; Head, Hilltonia Branch, Columbus (OH) Pub. Lib., 1965–66, Asst. Libn., Whitehall Br., 1964–65. **Educ.:** KS Wesleyan, 1955–59, BA (Eng.); Univ. of Denver, 1959–61, MA (LS); KS State Tchrs. Coll., 1967–71, (Eng., LS); South. IL Univ., Carbondale, 1979–, doct. std. **Orgs.:** ALA. Mt. Plains LA. KS LA: Coll. and Univ. Libs. Sect. (Secy.-Treas., 1977–78). Assoc. Coll. of Ctrl. KS: Libns. Com. (Secy. 1975–6, Ch. 1976–). Soroptimist Intl. **Activities:** 1; 15, 17, 34 **Addr.:** McPherson College, McPherson, KS 67460.

Olsgaard, Jane Kinch (F. 10, 1952, Brookings, SD) Serials Dept., Univ. Lib., Univ. of IL, 1981–; Acq./Pub. Srvs., Lommen Lib., School of Med., Univ. of SD, 1980–81, Ref./Ext. Srvs., 1978–80; Acq. Libn., Ellis Lib., Univ. of MO, 1977–78. **Educ.:** SD State Univ., 1970–74, BS (Hist.); Univ. of IA, 1976–77, MA (LS); Univ. of SD, 1980, MA (Higher and Adult Educ.). **Orgs.:** Med. LA. Midcontl. Reg. Med. Lib. Grp. SD LA: Issues Com. (1979–81); Constn. Rev. (1981). **Pubns.:** "Keyword Indexing of a Faculty Reprint Collection," *Bltn. of the Med. Lib. Assn.* (O. 1981); *Index to University of South Dakota School of Medicine Faculty Reprints* (1981); "Post-MLS Educational Requirements for Academic Librarians," *Coll. and Resrch. Libs.* (My. 1981); *South Dakota Agricultural Experiment Station and Extension Service Publications: A Keyword Index* (1976); "Authorship in Five Library Periodicals," *Coll. and Resrch. Libs.* (Ja. 1980). **Activities:** 1, 12; 25, 34, 44; 56, 83, 93 **Addr.:** Serials Department, University Library, University of Illinois, Urbana, IL 61801.

Olsgaard, John N. (D. 29, 1953, Jamestown, ND) Docum. Libn., Archvst., I.D. Weeks Lib., Univ. of SD, 1977–81. **Educ.:** Jamestown Coll., 1971–74, BA (Hist.); Univ. of ND, 1974–76, MA (Hist.); Univ. of IA, 1976–77, MLS; Univ. of IL, doct. sta., 1981. **Orgs.:** SD LA: Ch., Docum. Com. (1977–80); Ch., Acad. Sect. (1980). Mt. Plains LA. **Honors:** Mt. Plains LA: Beginning Prof., 1978. **Pubns.:** "Post-MLS Educational Requirements for Academic Librarians," *Coll. and Resrch. Libs.* (My. 1981); *Cumulative Index to S.D. State Government Publications: 1975–79* (1980); *Union list of Items received by S.D. Federal Document Depositories* (1980); "Authorship in Five Library Periodicals," *Coll. and Resrch. Libs.*, (1980); "Improving Keyword Indexing," *Jnl. of ASIS* (1981); other articles. **Activities:** 1, 2; 29, 41, 45; 56, 75, 92 **Addr.:** 410 David Kinley Hall, 1407 W. Gregory Dr., Urbana, IL 61801.

Olson, Eugene George (S. 22, 1940, Regina, SK) Ref. Libn., Univ. of AB Lib., 1974–, Head, Per. Dept., 1965–74, Gen. Libn., Educ. Lib., 1964–65. **Educ.:** Univ. of SK, 1959–62, BA (Eng.); McGill Univ., 1963–64, BLS. **Orgs.:** Can. LA. ALA. Assn. of Prof. Libns. of the Univ. of AB; Pres. (1977–78). Edmonton LA: Pres. (1965–66). **Activities:** 1; 29, 31, 39; 59, 70, 92 **Addr.:** 4716 105 B St., Edmonton, AB T6H 2R8 Canada.

Olson, Evelyn Naomi (Mansfield) (O. 17, 1923, Highland Twp., OH) Dir., Roselle Free Pub. Lib., 1970–; Asst. Prof. of LS, Head, Acq. Dept., Baptist Coll., 1967–70; Chld. Libn., Chicago Pub. Lib., 1965–67, Actg. Chld. Libn., 1964–65. **Educ.:** Defiance Coll., 1941–45, BA (Eng.); Rosary Coll. 1963–65, MALS. **Orgs.:** ALA. NJ LA: Schol. Com. (1972–77, Ch. 1976–77); PR Com. (1978–); Hon. and Awds. Com. (1979–). AAUW. Com. Roselle-Up. Roselle Town Meeting. Union Cnty. Cult.-Heritage: Adv. Bd. (1978–); Secy.-Treas. (1980–). **Activities:** 1, 9; 15, 17, 39; 63, 68, 75 **Addr.:** 104 W. Fourth Ave., Roselle, NJ 07203.

Olson, Gordon L. (Ap. 5, 1943, Frederic, WI) City Histn., Archvst., Grand Rapids Pub. Lib., 1979–; Asst. Dir., Grand Rapids Pub. Musm., 1973–79; Histn., WY State Hist. Dept. **Educ.:** Univ. of WI, River Falls, 1961–66, BS (Soc. Std.), 1966–68, MS (Hist.). Amer. Assn. for State and Local Hist. Hist. Socty. of MI: Bd. of Trustees. Org. of Amer. Hist. **Honors:** Ford Fndn., Flwshp., 1971. **Pubns.:** *The Calkins Law Office: Its History and Restoration* (1976); "The Grand River," *Rolling Rivers* (1982); "I Felt Like I was Entering Another World," *Annals of WY* (1975). **Activities:** 2, 9; 37, 41, 45; 55, 66, 85 **Addr.:** Grand Rapids Public Library, 60 Library Plz. N.W., Grand Rapids, MI 49503.

Olson, Jill D. (Je. 15, 1954, Spokane, WA) Libn. I, Young People's Srvs., Spokane Pub. Lib., 1978–; Ref. Libn., Pub. Srv., Whitworth Coll., 1976–77. **Educ.:** Whitworth Coll., 1971–75, BA (Eng.); Univ. of WA, 1975–76, MLS. **Orgs.:** WA LA: Bd., Chld. YA Srvs. Int. Grp. Pac. NW LA. ALA: ALSC. WA Lib. Media Assn. **Activities:** 9; 21 **Addr.:** N. 6405 Catherine, Spokane, WA 99208.

Olson, Linda M. (Mr. 19, 1951, Rice Lake, WI) Ref., Univ. of WI, Stout, 1976–. **Educ.:** Univ. of WI, 1969–75, BA (Scan. Stds.), 1975–76, MA (LS). **Orgs.:** ALA: ACRL, Ad Hoc Com. on Non-print Media and the Coll. Lib. WI LA. WI Assn. of Acad. Libns.: 1979 Conf. Plng. Com. (Ch.); Secy.–Treas. (1981). **Activities:** 1; 15, 31, 39; 63 **Addr.:** Library, University of Wisconsin–Stout, Menomonie, WI 54751.

Olson, Lowell Ellis (Maywood, IL) Assoc. Prof., Lib. Sch., Univ. of MN, 1964–; Libn., Tchr., Minneapolis Pub. Schs., 1953–64. **Educ.:** Univ. of IL, BS (Eng.); Univ. of Chicago, MA (Couns.); Univ. of MN, MS & PhD (LS). **Orgs.:** ALA. AALS. MN Educ. Media Assn. **Honors:** Fulbright Prof. in LS, Turkey, 1974–75. **Pubns.:** "Fiction of Fiction Collection Development," *Top of the News* (Fall, 1979); "Research: a Bibliographic Summary," *MN Media* (Ja., 1979). **Activities:** 10, 11; 21, 26, 32; 50, 63, 74 **Addr.:** Library School, Univ. of Minnesota, 429 Walter Library, Minneapolis, MN 55455.

Olson, Nancy B. (Ap. 10, 1936, Estherville, IA) Assoc. Prof., Mankato State Univ., 1970–. **Educ.:** IA State Univ., 1952–57, BS (Chem.); Mankato State Univ., 1969–70, MS (LS), 1978, Spec. (Media). **Orgs.:** MN LA: Pres. (1978–79). MN AACR2 Trainers: Ch. (1979/81). On-Line AV Catlgrs.: Natl. ch. (1980/82). ALA: ACRL, AV Com. (1972/74); RTSD, AV Com. (1979–); Ch. (1981–). **Honors:** ALA, RTSD, Esther J. Piercy Awd., 1980. **Pubns.:** *Cataloging of Audiovisual Materials* (1980); *Index to the Library of Congress Cataloging Service Bulletin* (1978); *Cumulative Subject Index to the MARC Database, 1968–1978* (1978); *Combined Indexes to the Library of Congress Classification Schedules* (1975). **Activities:** 1; 20, 49-AV Mtrls. **Addr.:** Memorial Library, Mankato State University, Mankato, MN 56001.

Olson, Rue E. (N. 1, 1928, Chicago, IL) Libn., IL Agr. Assn., 1966–, Asst. Libn., 1960–66; Acct., IL Farm Supply Co., 1948–59. **Educ.:** Northwestern Univ., 1948–50; IL State Univ., 1960–64. **Orgs.:** SLA: IL Chap. (Secy., 1970–72; Pres., 1977–78); Insur. Div. (Ch., 1973–74); Food and Nutrition Div. (Ch. Elect and Mem., 1980–81; Ch., 1981–82); Stats. Com. (1980–83). IL LA. ALA. IL White House Conf. on Libs. and Info. Srvs.: Del. (1978). Amer. Mgt. Assn. Admin. Mgt. Socty. **Pubns.:** "Serving in the Heartland of Illinois," *IL Libs.* (Mr. 1980). **Activities:** 12; 17; 59, 76, 53 **Addr.:** Illinois Agricultural Association, IAA & Affiliated Companies Library, 1701 Towanda Ave., P.O. Box 2901, Bloomington, IL 61701.

Olson, Thomas R. (Je. 26, 1949, Vermillion, SD) Ref. Libn., Lib. Assn. of Portland, 1975–; Asst. Soc. Sci. Libn., West. MI Univ., 1974–75. **Educ.:** Univ. of SD, 1967–72, BSE (Hist.), 1973–74, AM (Hist.); West. MI Univ., 1974–75, MSL. **Orgs.:** Amer. Socty. of Indxrs. OR LA. West. Area Map Libs. Clay Cnty. Hist. Socty. Phi Alpha Theta. **Pubns.:** Jt. Auth., *Register of Clay County Historic Sites* (1972); Jt. Auth., *Clay County Place Names* (1976). **Activities:** 1, 9; 30, 39; 69, 70, 92 **Addr.:** Box 19057, Portland, OR 97219.

Olsrud, Lois Christine (S. 21, 1930, Havre, MT) Ctrl. Ref. Libn., Univ. of AZ, 1977–, Hum. Libn., 1974–76, Ref. Libn., 1966–74; Libn., WJHS, Great Falls, MT, 1957–65; Libn., Havre HS, 1954–57; Libn., Eng. Tchr., Princeton HS, 1952–54. **Educ.:** Concordia Coll., 1948–52, BA (Eng.); Univ. of MN, 1954–64; IN Univ., 1965–66, MA (LS). **Orgs.:** ALA. AZ LA: Secy. (1970–71); Com. on Goals (1971–72); Awds. Com. (1973–74, 1975–76). SW LA. Tucson Area Lib. Cncl.: Treas. (1973–74). AAUP. Delta Kappa Gamma: Chap. pres. (1976–78); VP (1974–76); Tucson Coord. Cncl. Treas. (1977–79); State Schol. Com. (1979–80). **Activities:** 1; 31, 39; 55 **Addr.:** 969 N. Jones Blvd., No. 8, Tucson, AZ 85716.

Oltman, Florine A. (N. 13, 1915, Flatonia, TX) Retired; Chief, Reader Srvs. Div., U.S. Air Force Air Univ. Lib., Maxwell AFB, 1972–73, Chief, Ref. Branch, 1971–72, Chief, Bibl. Branch, 1958–71, Libn., Air War Coll., 1955–58, Ref. Libn. and Bibl. Asst., 1950–55, Libn., Spec. Staff Sch., 1947–50, Catlgr., 1946–47; Various prof. positions, 1937–46. **Educ.:** SW. TX State Univ., 1934–37, BA (Eng.); Univ. of Denver, 1941–43, BS (LS). **Orgs.:** SLA: Pres. (1970–71); Adv. Cncl. (Ch., 1960–61); Milit. Libns. Div. (Ch., 1959–60); AL Chap. (Pres., 1956–57). **Pubns.:** "Corporals and Colonels Get Briefings," *Lib. Jnl.* (Ap. 1, 1952); "Significant Military Literature," *Spec. Libs.* (F. 1959); "Tools for the Military Librarian," *Spec. Libs.* (Mr. 1960). **Activities:** 1, 4; 17, 31, 39; 52, 74, 85 **Addr.:** 8904B Trone Cir., Austin, TX 78758.

O'Malley, Kenneth Gerald (O. 30, 1936, Detroit, MI) Lib. Dir., Cath. Theo. Un., 1969–; Libn.–Tchr., Good Counsel Prep., 1965–69. **Educ.:** Holy Cross Acad. Inst., Chicago, 1954–59, BA (Phil.); Holy Cross Acad. Inst., Louisville, 1960–64, MA Th (Theo.); Univ. of MI, 1965–68, AMLS; Univ. of IL, 1974–79, PhD (LS). **Orgs.:** Cath. LA. ALA. ATLA. Chicago Area Theo. LA: Cncl. Various other orgs. **Pubns.:** *The Use of Corporate Headings With Form Subheadings...in Theological Libraries* (1979); "Corporate Headings With Form Subheadings in Theological Libraries," *Essays on Theological Librarianship* (1980); "New in the Field or Teletype in the Library," *Nsltr. of the North. IL Unit of the Cath. LA* (My. 1971); "Post Convention News," *Coll., Univ., and Semy. Libs.* (Spr.–Sum. 1970–71); "Pre-Convention Communique," *Coll., Univ., and Semy. Libs.* (Fall–Win. 1970–71); Various articles. **Addr.:** Library, Catholic Theological Union, 5401 S. Cornell St., Chicago, IL 60615.

O'Neal, Ellis Eldridge, Jr. (D. 18, 1923, Norfolk, VA) Libn., Andover Newton Theo. Sch., 1960–; Head, Transp. Col., Harvard Univ., Grad. Sch. of Bus. Admin., 1960; Pastor, Chamberlayne Bapt. Church, 1956–60; Pastor, Hillsboro Bapt. Church, 1949–56. **Educ.:** Univ. of Richmond, 1943–46, BA (Rel.); Andover Newton Theo. Sch., 1947–49, MDiv (Relig.); Simmons Coll., 1960–62, MS (LS). **Orgs.:** Amer. Bapt. Hist. Socty.: Bd. of Mgrs. (1961–); Budget Com. (Ch., 1967–70, 1973–74); Exec. Com. (1973–); Treas. (1975–); Nom. Com. (Ch., 1981). ATLA (1961–): Nom. Com. (1977–80, Ch., 1979–80); Various other coms. and ofcs. Boston Theo. Inst.: Library Com. (1968–); various ofcs. New Eng. Theo. Libns. (1960–): Various ofcs. Various other orgs. AAUP. **Pubns.:** "Thine Is the Glory," *Relig. Herald* (Ap. 3, 1958); "A Bible, A Commentary and a Concordance," *Andover Newton Qtly.* (N. 1966); Indexes, *Andover Newton Qtly.* (1970–); Various reviews. **Activities:** 1; 15, 17, 30; 55, 90 **Addr.:** 97 Herrick Cir., Newton Centre, MA 02159.

O'Neil, B. Joseph (Jl. 20, 1914, Boston, MA) Supvsr. of Readers Srvs., Boston Pub. Lib., 1967–, Coord. of Gen. Ref. Srvs., 1960–67, Deputy Supvsr. of Ref. and Resrch. Srvs., 1957–60, Cur. of Per. and Newsp., 1957–60. **Educ.:** Boston Coll., 1933–35, 1941–43, AB; Simmons Coll., 1946–48, BS (LS); MA Inst. of Tech., 1943–44, Cert. (Meteorology); Boston Univ., 1954–57, (Bus. Admin.). **Orgs.:** SLA: Boston Chap., Treas. (1963–64); Dir. (1974–76), Ch., Auditing Com. (1968–75, 1978–80). ALA: Ref. Subscrpn. Books Com. (1972–74); Ch., SORT. MA LA. **Activities:** 2, 9; 17, 33, 39; 83, 91 **Addr.:** Research Library Services, Boston Public Library, Boston, MA 02117.

O'Neil, Margaret M. (My. 25, 1948, Rochester, NY) Libn. II, Lit. & Recreation Div., Rochester Pub. Lib., 1979–, Libn. II, Educ. & Relig. Div., 1971–78. **Educ.:** Coll. of New Rochelle, 1966–70, BA (Classics); State Univ. Coll. at Geneseo, 1970–71, MLS; various courses. **Orgs.:** ALA: PLA, Mem. Com. (1980–); ASCLA (1979–). NY LA: RASD, Outreach Com. (1977–79). Monroe Cnty. Lib. Club: Pres. (1979–80); VP (1978–79). Coll. Rochester Pub. Lib. Staff Assn.: Secy. (1976–78). Coll. of New Rochelle Alum. Assn.: Treas. (1981). **Activities:** 9; 16, 39, 48; 50, 55, 72 **Addr.:** Literature and Recreation Division, Rochester Public Library, 115 South Ave., Rochester, NY 14604.

O'Neill, Edward T. (Jl. 20, 1940, Charlevoix, MI) Assoc. Prof., SUNY, Buffalo, 1968–; Visit. Disting. Scholar, OCLC Inc., 1978–79. **Educ.:** Albion Coll., 1958–61, BA (Sci.); Purdue Univ., 1961–70, PhD (Oper. Resrch.). **Orgs.:** ALA. ASIS: Vice-Ch., Ch.-Elect - Spec. int. grp. for Info. Sci. educ. NY LA. Oper. Resrch. Socty. of Amer. Assn. for Comp. Mach. **Pubns.:** *Subject Headings Patterns on OCLC Monographic Records* (1979); "Developing Corporate Author Search Keys," *Jnl. of Lib. Autom.* (Je. 1978); "The Effect of Demand Level on the Optional Size of Journal Collections," *Col. Mgt.* (Fall 78). **Activities:** 11; 26, 41; 56, 75 **Addr.:** School of Information and Library Studies, 213 Lawernce D. Bell Hall, State University of New York at Buffalo, Amherst, NY 14260.

O'Neill, James E. (F. 2, 1929, Renovo, PA) Deputy Archvst. US, Natl. Arch. and Rec. Srv., 1972–; Asst. to the Archvst., 1971–72, Dir., Franklin D. Roosevelt Lib., 1969–71; Assoc. Prof. of Hist., Loyola Univ., Chicago, 1965–69; Biblio. and Ed., *Guide to the Study of the United States of America,* Lib. of Congs., 1964–65, European Mss. Spec., 1963–64; Instr., Asst. Prof. of Hist., Univ. of Notre Dame, 1957–63. **Educ.:** Univ. of Detroit, 1948–52, AB (Hist.), 1952–54, MA (Hist.); Univ. of Chicago, 1954–56, PhD (Hist.); Fed. Exec. Inst., 1971, Cert., (Gvt.). **Orgs.:** SAA: Bicent. Com. (Ch. 1974–76); Com. on Ref. & Access Policies (Ch., 1976–79). Intl. Cncl. on Arch.: Exec. Com. (1979–); Pubns. Com. (1977–); Com. on Arch. Dev. (1977–). Sen. Hist. Ofc.: Adv. Com. (1977–). Dept. of the Army: Hist. Adv. Com. (1978–). **Honors:** St. Edward's Univ., Hon. degree, LHD, 1975; SAA, Flw., 1977. **Pubns.:** Jt. Ed., *World War II: An Account of Its Documents* (1976); Jt. Auth., *Episodes in American History* (1973); "Recent Records Management Legislation in the United States," *ARMA Rec. Mgt. Qtly.* (Ja. 1979); "Replevin: A Public Archivist's Perspective," *Coll. & Resrch. Libs.* (Ja. 1979); "Will Success Spoil the Presidential Libraries?," *Amer. Archvst.* (Jl. 1973); Various other pubns. **Activities:** 2; 17, 38, 45; 55, 74, 75 **Addr.:** 8500 Varsity Court, Annandale, VA 22003.

O'Neill, Luis (O. 12, 1888, Aguadilla, PR) Retired. Libn., Manuel Alonso Lib., Sociedad de Escritores of PR, 1955–71; Dir., Carnegie Lib. of PR, 1919–55 Asst. Libn., 1912–16. **Educ.:** Univ. of PR, 1916, Pratt Inst. (LS). **Orgs.:** PR LA: Pres., SBPR:

PROFESSIONAL ACTIVITIES: Institutions: 1. Acad. lib.; 2. Arch.; 3. Assn.; 4. Fed./Gvt. lib.; 5. Inst. lib.; 6. Mfr./Suppl.; 7. Milit. lib.; 8. Musm.; 9. Pub. lib.; 10. Sch. lib.; 11. Sch. of lib. sci.; 12. Spec. lib.; 13. State lib.; 14. (other). **Functions/Activities:** 15. Acq./Col. dev.; 16. Adult srvs.; 17. Admin.; 18. Apprais.; 19. Archit./Bldgs.; 20. Cat./Class.; 21. Chld. srvs.; 22. Circ.; 23. Cons./Pres.; 24. Consult.; 25. Cont. ed.; 26. Educ. lib. sci.; 27. Ext. srvs.; 28. Fund/Grants; 29. Gvt. pubs.; 30. Indx./Abs.; 31. Instr. lib. use; 32. Media srvs.; 33. Micro.; 34. Netwks./Coop.; 35. Persnl.; 36. PR; 37. Publshg.; 38. Recs. mgt.; 39. Ref. srvs.; 40. Repro.; 41. Resrch.; 42. Review.; 43. Secur.; 44. Serials; 45. Spec. col.; 46. Tech. srvs.; 47. Trustees/Bds.; 48. YA srvs.; 49. (other).

Who's Who in Library and Information Services

Hon. mem., Sociedad de Escritores: Lib. Com. (Pres.). **Honors:** Laureated by Ateneo Puertorriqueño, 1951; Rep. for PR in the First Intl. Congs. of Libn. and Biblgphrs., Rome, Italy, 1929. **Pubns.:** *Biography of Eugenio Maria de Hostos* (1950); poems: "Arca de Recuerdos" (1955); "Voces del Ayer" (in preparation); various articles. **Activities:** 9; 17 **Addr.:** 123 O'Neill St., Hato Rey, PR 00918.

O'Neill, Marta G. (Ag. 27, 1954, Goshen, IN) Asst. Cur., Spec. Cols., Chicago Pub. Lib., 1978–; Intern, IN State Lib., 1977. **Educ.:** Purdue Univ., 1972–76, BA (Ancient Hist.); Univ. of Chicago, 1976–78, MA (LS); Univ. of Denver, 1980, Cert. (Out-of-Print and Antiq. Bk. Trade Sem.). **Orgs.:** SAA. ALA: ACRL/Rare Bks. and Mss. Sect. Natl. Trust for Hist. Prsrvn. **Activities:** 9, 12; 15, 23, 45; 55, 57 **Addr.:** Special Collections Division, 78 E. Washington St., Chicago, IL 60602.

Onesto, Serene F. (Ag. 28, Chicago, IL) Coord., Div. of Lrng. Resrc., Chicago State Univ., 1975–; Head, Instr. Mtrls. Ctr., 1967–75; Tchr., Libn., Chicago Pub. Sch., 1965–67, Tchr., 1960–65. **Educ.:** DePauw Univ., 1944–48, BA (Art); IL Tchr. Coll. S., 1961–66, MS (Educ.); North. IL Univ., 1971–75, EdD (Instr. Tech.). **Orgs.:** North. IL Media Assn.: Pres. (1978–79); Exec. Com. (1977–78). AECT. IL AECT. IL Assn. Media Educ. Natl. Cncl. for Admin. Women in Educ. Delta Kappa Gamma. Phi Delta Kappa. Judge, Amer. Film Festival (1979–81). **Honors:** Chicago State Univ. Alum. Assn., Srv. Awd. 1979; IL Curric. Cncl., Srv. Awd., 1975. **Pubns.:** "Hello, Hello Can You Hear Us?" *AV Instr.* (Mr. 1977); "Multi-media Materials on Ethnic Studies," *IL Sch. Jnl.* (Fall 1975). **Activities:** 1; 17, 31, 32; 63, 66, 67 **Addr.:** 1055 D Peterson, Park Ridge, IL 60068.

Onsager, Lawrence W. (My. 30, 1944, Lindina, WI) Ch., Dept. of Per., Loma Linda Univ., 1977–, Extramural Srvs. Libn., 1975–76, Ref. Libn., 1972–75. **Educ.:** Univ. of WI, 1962–67, BS (Geog.); Univ. of WA, 1971–72, ML (LS). **Orgs.:** ALA. Med. LA. **Honors:** Beta Phi Mu. **Pubns.:** Jt. Auth., "Fees for information services to hospitals: the California experience," *Bltn. Med. LA* (O. 1978); "Bibliography of recommended lists of books and journals for health sciences libraries," *Bltn. Med. LA* (Jl. 1978). **Activities:** 1; 24, 39, 44; 80 **Addr.:** 12735 10th, Yucaipa, CA 92399.

Opas, Margaret Muller (O. 23, 1943, Chicago, IL) Asst. Libn., J. Walter Thompson Co., 1968–; Asst. to Dir., Ofc. of Rcrt., ALA, 1967–68. **Educ.:** Rosary Coll., 1961–65, BA (Grmn.), 1966–67, MALS; Northwestern Univ., Inst. for Advnc. Advert. Std., 1971–72, Cert. **Orgs.:** SLA. COLUG. **Honors:** Beta Phi Mu. **Pubns.:** "Commercial and Professional Sources of data for Advertising Research" in *Information Sources in Advertising History* (1979). **Activities:** 12; 39, 49-Online Srchg.; 51, 59, 68 **Addr.:** Information Center, J. Walter Thompson Co., 875 N. Michigan Ave., Chicago, IL 60611.

Opem, John D. (F. 23, 1933, Rochester, MN) Mgr., Resrch. Info. Ctr., Abbott Labs., 1978–, Head Libn., 1965–78; Lit. Chem., Swift & Co., 1962–65, Dev. Chem., 1958–62, Anal. Chem., 1955–56. **Educ.:** St. Olaf Coll., 1951–55, BA (Chem.); Univ. of Chicago, 1962–64, (LS). **Orgs.:** Assoc. Info. Mgrs. SLA: Ch., Pharm. Div. Prog., 1975 Anl. Mtg. Amer. Chem. Socty.: Ch., Chicago Sect., Chem. Lit. Grp. (1968–69). ALA. ASIS. **Pubns.:** "A reflection of society," *Lib. Jnl.* (1963); U.S. Patent (1962). **Activities:** 2, 12; 17, 38, 41; 60, 80, 87 **Addr.:** D-421, Research Information Center, Abbott Laboratories, AP9, Abbott Park, North Chicago, IL 60064.

Oplinger, Mary P. (Hickory, NC) Dir. of Lib. Srvs., Ctrl. Piedmont Cmnty. Coll., 1965–; Head Libn., Queens Coll., Charlotte, NC, 1961–65; Chief Engin. Libn., Douglas Aircraft Co., 1959–61. **Educ.:** Maryville Coll., 1944–46, AB (Eng.); Drexel Univ., 1958–59, MSLS. **Orgs.:** ALA. SELA. NC LA. **Honors:** Phi Kappa Phi, 1959; Beta Phi Mu, 1959. **Activities:** 1; 17, 24 **Addr.:** Central Piedmont Community College, P.O. Box 4009, Charlotte, NC 28204.

Oppenheim, Micha Falk (Ap. 7, 1937, Hamburg, Germany) Sr. Catlgr., Jewish Theo. Semy., 1966–; Branch Libn., NYC Cmnty. Coll., 1965–66; Libn., Natl. Conf. of Christ. & Jews, 1963–65; Cat. Libn., Brooklyn Coll., 1961–63. **Educ.:** Yeshiva Coll., 1954–58, BA (Soclgy.); Columbia Univ., 1959–61, MS (LS); Yeshiva Univ., 1973–77, MS (Jewish Educ.). **Orgs.:** AJL. Assn. for Jewish Std. Coalition for Alternatives in Jewish Educ. **Pubns.:** *Jewish Life Index* (1968); *Tradition Index* (1970); *The study and practice of Judaism; a selected, annotated list* (1979); "Research tools in Jewish education" in *Handbook for the Jewish Teacher* (1980). **Activities:** 1, 10; 20, 30; 57, 63, 90 **Addr.:** 951 56th St., Brooklyn, NY 11219.

Oppenheim, Stephen L. (Mr. 1, 1933, New York, NY) Attorney, 1956–; VP, Ramapo Catskill Lib. Syst., 1974, Dir., 1966–74, 1979–80. **Educ.:** Cornell Univ., 1950–54, BA, dist., 1953–56, LLB, dist. **Orgs.:** ALA: Int. Frdm. Com. (1976–80); ALTA, Grp. V Admin. (1976), Litcy. Task Force (1976–80), Bd. of Dirs. (1976); IFRT. NY Assn. of Lib. Bds.: Adv. Cncl. (1968–73); Pres. (1974–76). NY LA: Int. Frdm. Com. (1969–80). Amer. Bar Assn. NY Bar Assn. Amer. Trial Lawyers Assn. NY Trial Lawyers Assn. Various other orgs. **Honors:** Phi Beta Kappa; NY State Assn. of Lib. Bds., Velma K. Moore Awd., 1980. **Pubns.:** "Miller vs. California Comes to New York," *NYLA Bltn.* (O. 1974). **Activities:** 9, 14-Reg. Lib. Syst.; 47; 74, 77, 89 **Addr.:** P.O. Box 29, Monticello, NY 12701.

Oppenheimer, Gerald J. (My. 8, 1922, Frankfurt a. M., Germany) Dir., Hlth. Sci. Lib., Univ. of WA, 1963–, Asst. Dir. of Libs., 1963–, Dir., Pac. NW Reg. Hlth. Sci. Lib., 1968–; Mgr., Info. Srvs., Boeing Sci. Resrch. Labs., 1960–63; Fisheries-Oceanography Libn., Univ. of WA, 1955–60; Ref. Libn., Seattle Pub. Lib., 1953–55. **Educ.:** Univ. of WA, 1945–46, BA (Frgn. Lang.), 1946–47, MA (Phil.); Columbia Univ., 1952–53, MS (LS). **Orgs.:** Assn. of Acad. Hlth. Sci. Lib. Dir.: Pres. (1978–79). Med. LA: Dir., Exec. Com., (1974–77); Ch., Finance Com. (1974–77); Ch., MLA/NLM Liaison Com. (1976–77). AAUP: Secy., Univ. of WA Chap., (1973/75). Assn. for Symbolic Logic. **Honors:** Phi Beta Kappa, 1946; Delta Phi Alpha, 1946. **Pubns.:** Ed., *Regional Medical Library Service in the Pacific Northwest* (1967); "The Pacific Northwest Regional Health Sciences Library: A Centralized Operation," *Bltn. of the Med. LA* (Apr. 1971); "Coordination through Cooperation - The Boeing Approach," *Spec. Libs.* (O. 1962). **Activities:** 1; 17; 80 **Addr.:** Health Sciences Library, University of Washington, SB-55, Seattle, WA 98195.

Oppenneer, Bernard Lee (D. 5, 1928, Grand Rapids, MI) Admin., Des Plaines Pub. Lib., 1977–; Lib. Dir., Saginaw Pub. Lib. & Saginaw Area Lib. Syst., 1970–77; Admin., Grand Traverse Area Lib. Fed. & Traverse City Pub. Lib., 1966–70; Admin., Reddick's Lib., Ottawa, IL, 1958–66. **Educ.:** W. MI Univ., 1948–52, BA (Eng.); Univ. of MI, 1957, 60, MALS. **Orgs.:** ALA: Instr. in the Use of Libs. Com. (1976–77). IL LA: Pub. Lib. Sect. Bd. (1979–80); Conf. Treas. (1978). Reg. Libns. Adv. Com.: Ch. (1980). MI LA: Pres. (1974–75); Exec. Bd. (1975–76). Kiwanis: Pres. (1966–81). Cham. of Cmrce. Red Cross. Cmnty. Concerts: Bd. **Honors:** Distin. Srv. to the Cmnty. Awd., Jr. Cham. of Cmrce., 1965. **Pubns.:** Ed., IL LA Nsltr. *ILA Reporter* (1964–65). **Activities:** 9; 17 **Addr.:** 940 Beau Dr. #112, Des Plaines, IL 60016.

Oppman, Mary (Je. 6, 1923, Brooklyn, NY) Dir. of Lib. Media, Portage (IN) Twp. Schs., 1975–; Libn., Horace Mann HS, 1971–75; Libn., Beveridge Sch., 1967–71; Libn., Wirt HS, 1957–66. **Educ.:** IN Univ., 1940–43, BS (Educ.); Rosary Coll., 1966–67, MS (LS). **Orgs.:** ALA: AASL, Supvsrs. Task Force for Pubcty. (1980–81); Amer. Un. Press Support Com. (1966–67). Assn. of IN Media Educs.: Supvsr. Sect. (Ch.) Natl. Educ. Assn. Natl. Cncl. of the Soc. Stds. **Pubns.:** "Career Centers in the Library," *Hoosier Sch. Libn.* (Spr. 1975); "Operating A Media Center from a Closet," *IN Media Jnl.* (Win. 1981). **Activities:** 15, 17, 21; 67, 74, 85 **Addr.:** Department of Library Media, Portage Township Schools, 5894 Central Ave., Portage, IN 46368.

Opremcak, Jenny Lou (F. 1, 1929, Columbus, OH) Sch. Media Spec., Woodside Elem. Sch., 1967–. **Educ.:** OH State Univ., 1946–50, BSci (Educ.); Rutgers Univ., 1963–67, MLS, 1975–, PhD in progress (Educ.). **Orgs.:** ALA. Educ. Media Assn. of NJ: Pubcty. Ch. (1980–81). Bergen Cnty. Educ. Media Assn.: Pres. AECT. Natl. Educ. Assn. NJ Educ. Assn. **Addr.:** 820 Phelps Rd., Franklin Lakes, NJ 07417.

Oram, Robert W. (Je. 11, 1922, Warsaw, IN) Dir., Ctrl. Univ. Libs., South. Meth. Univ., 1979–; Assoc. Univ. Libn., Univ. of IL, 1971–79, Act. Univ. Libn., 1975–76, Dir., Pub. Srvs., 1968–71, Circ. Libn., Assoc. & Asst. Dir. Pub. Srvs., 1956–68; Asst. to Libn., Univ. of MO, 1953–56, Head, Circ., 1952–53, Acq. Libn., 1950–51. **Educ.:** Univ. of Toledo, 1946–49, BA (Eng.); Univ. of IL, 1949–50, MSLS. **Orgs.:** ALA: Publshg. Com. (1975–79); Ed. Adv. Bd., *Booklist* (1974–79). IL LA: Treas. (1973); Exec. Bd. (1969–72). TX LA. Colophon, Frnds. of SMU Libs.: Exec. Secy. (1980–). Urbana Free Lib. Frnds.: Pres. (1978–79). Frnds. of the Lib., USA: Bd. of Dir. (1980–). Urbana Free Lib.: Bd. of Dir. (1965–77). **Pubns.:** "Circulation Systems," *ALA Encyc.* (1980) "Circulation," *Encyc. of Lib. & Info. Scis.* (1971); "Observations of a Research Library Administrator," *Lib. Trends* (Ap. 1977); Jt. auth., "University Library Orientation by Television," *Coll. & Resrch. Libs.* (N. 1962). **Activities:** 1, 9; 15, 17, 22; 61, 74 **Addr.:** 7222 Colgate, Dallas, TX 75225.

Orcutt, Roberta Kiefer (Jl. 29, 1929, Los Angeles, CA) Desert Resrch./Physical Sci. Libn., Univ. of NV, 1970–, Ref. Libn., 1968–70; Asst. Order Libn., Univ. of FL, 1967–68; Asst. Head, Physical Sci. Libs., Univ. of CA, Berkeley, 1953–55; Asst. Ref. Libn., US Dept. of Agri. Lib., 1952–53; Jr. Libn., CA State Dept. of Pub. Hlth. Lib., 1951–52. **Educ.:** Univ. of CA, Los Angeles, 1947–50, AB (Pre-Libn.); Univ. of CA, Berkeley, 1950–51, BLS. **Orgs.:** SLA. ALA. NV LA. **Activities:** 1, 12; 17; 88 **Addr.:** Desert Research Institute Library, P.O. Box 60220, Reno, NV 89506.

Ordóñez, María E. (F. 1, 1940, Santurce, PR) Libn., Biblioteca Gen. Univ. PR, 1980–; Archvst., Archivo Gen. PR, 1972–80; Archvst., Archivo Secreto del Vaticano, 1972; Adj. & Guide, Museo Fam. Puertorriqueña Siglo XIX, 1966–67; Cat., Inst. Cult. Puertorriqueña, 1966–67; Art Tchr., PR schs., 1963–65. **Educ.:** Univ. de PR, 1959–63, BA (Hum.), 1971–71, MLS; Curso Documentalista, Biblioteca Nacionel, Madrid, 1967–69; Curso de Capacitación Archivistica, Escuela de Archiveros, Univ. de Córdova, Argentina, 1978. **Orgs.:** SBPR. Asociación Nacionel Archiveros, Bibliotecarios, Arqueólogos de España. Asociacion de Archiveros de PR. **Pubns.:** "Documentos eclesiástico en el Puerto Rico del Siglo XIX," *Caribean Studies.* (Ja. 1975). **Activities:** 1; 20, 39, 41 **Addr.:** Box 3821, Old San Juan Statio, San Juan, PR 00904.

Orgren, Carl F. (Mr. 5, 1937, Saginaw, MI) Dir., Sch. of Lib. Sci., Univ. of IA, 1981–; Assoc. Prof., 1970–, 1981. Asst. Prof., Dept. of Lib. Sci., Wayne State Univ., 1966–67; Head of Ref., Univ. of Detroit Lib., 1962–66, Head of Circ., Ref. Libn., 1960–62. **Educ.:** Univ. of Detroit, 1955–59, PhB (Eng.); Univ. of MI, 1959–62, AMLS; Univ. of Detroit, 1961–66, MA (Eng.); Univ. of MI, 1967–71, PhD (LS). **Orgs.:** ALA. AALS: Nom. Com. (1978). IA LA: Pres. (1975). **Pubns.:** "Education Aspects of a Teletype Reference Service Staffed by Students," *Jnl. of Educ. for Libnshp.* (Sum. 1976); "Statewide Teletype Reference Service," *RQ* (Spr., 1976); Ed., "Book Review Section," *RQ* (1973–76). **Activities:** 11, 12; 26, 34, 39; 57, 92, 93 **Addr.:** 3087 Main Library, School of Library Science, University of Iowa, Iowa City, IA 52242.

Orloske, Margaret Q. (Ag. 16, 1951, Bridgeport, CT) Libn., Timex Corp., 1979–; Ref. Coord., East. CT LA, 1976–79; Libn., Fncl. Acct. Stans. Bd., 1974–76. **Educ.:** Univ. of CT, 1969–73, BA (Hist.); Univ. of Pittsburgh, 1973–74, MLS. **Orgs.:** SLA: CT Valley Chap. (Pres., 1980–81). **Activities:** 12; 17, 38, 39; 59, 77 **Addr.:** 5 Glenwood Dr., East Hampton, CT 06424.

Ormsby, William G. (Mr. 29, 1921, Toronto, ON) Archvst. of ON, Arch. of ON, 1978–; Prof. of Hist., Brock Univ., 1964–78; Head, MSS Div., Pub. Arch. of Can., 1960–64, Sr. Archvst., 1948–60. **Educ.:** Univ. of Toronto, 1945–48, BA (Hist.); Carleton Univ., 1958–60, MA (Hist.); Amer. Univ., 1950, Cert. (Arch. Mgt.). **Orgs.:** SAA. Assn. of Can. Archvsts. Can. Hist. Assn.: Cncl. (1965–69). Champlain Socty.: Ed., ON Series (1972–78). ON Hist. Socty.: Pres. (1975). **Pubns.:** *Crisis in the Canadas* (1964); *The Emergence of the Federal Concept in Canada* (1968); "The Civil List Question in Canada," *Can. Hist. Review* (1951); "Francis Hincks," *Pre Confederation Premiers* (1980). **Activities:** 2; 17 **Addr.:** Archives of Ontario, 77 Grenville St., Toronto, ON M7A 2R9 Canada.

Orndoff, Crystel Lynn (Ja. 19, 1953, Middleburg, VA) Asst. Libn., IBM Syst. Resrch. Inst., 1979–; Info. Proc., InterAmer. Resrch., 1978–79; Ref. Resrch. Asst., Aspen Syst., 1977–78. **Educ.:** William and Mary Coll., 1971–75, BA (Span.); Univ. of NC, 1975–76, MSLS. **Orgs.:** NLA. SLA. **Pubns.:** "Coverage of Bilingual Education in On-Line Data Bases," *Educ. Libs.* (Vol. 4 1979). **Activities:** 12; 20, 30, 39; 56, 63, 75 **Addr.:** Box 20, Blaunet, NY 10913.

Orne, Jerrold (Mr. 25, 1911, St. Paul, MN) Prof. Emeritus, Sch. of LS, Univ. of NC, 1976–, Prof., 1973–76, Univ. Libn., 1957–72; Dir. of Libs., Air Univ., Maxwell AFB, AL, 1951–57; Dir. of Libs., Washington Univ., 1946–51; Libn., Prof. Mod. Langs., Knox Coll., 1941–43. **Educ.:** Univ. of MN, 1928–32, BA (Rom. Lang.), 1932–33, MA (Fr.); Univ. of Chicago, 1936–39, PhD (Ling.); Univ. of MN, 1939–40, BS (LS); Univ. of Paris, Sorbonne, 1934–35, Dipl. (Fr. Lang.). **Orgs.:** ALA: various coms. (1940–). Assn. South East. Resrch. Libs.: Ch. (1959–61); various coms. Am. Natl. Standards Inst.: Com. Z39 (Ch. 1965–78). SLA: Bd. (1953–55); Div. Ch. (1954–57). Other orgs. **Honors:** ALA, Melvil Dewey Medal, 1972; ALA, Joseph Lippingott Awd., 1974; ASIS, Awd. of Merit, 1971. **Pubns.:** *Language of the Foreign Book Trade* (1976); *Research Librarianship* (1971); various articles. **Activities:** 1, 11; 17, 19, 24; 56, 75, 74 **Addr.:** 516 Dogwood Dr., Chapel Hill, NC 27514.

Orosz, Barbara J. (Ag. 5, 1939, Glendale, CA) Head Libn., Union Oil Co of CA, 1964–, Info. Chem., 1961–64. **Educ.:** Immaculate Heart Coll., 1957–61, BA (Chem.); Univ. of South. CA, 1967, MLS. **Orgs.:** Geosci. Info. Socty. ASIS. SLA: Petr. Div. Mem. Ch. (1969–70); Treas. (1972–74); South. CA Chap., Mem. Dir. (1975–76); Pubns. Ch. (1976–78). Cmnty. Coll. Dist., No. Orange Cnty.: Lib Tech. Adv. Com. (1979–81). Univ. of South. CA Sch. of LS: Adv. Bd. (1970–73). Iota Sigma Pi. **Pubns.:** "UNISRCH: An Information Retrieval System," *Procs. Geosci. Info. Socty.* (1974). **Activities:** 12; 17, 38, 41; 60, 91 **Addr.:** Union Oil Co of Calif, Technical Information Center, P.O. Box 76, Brea, CA 92621.

O'Rourke, Dolores E. (My. 29, 1952, Providence, RI) Law Libn., Adler Pollock and Sheehan Inc., 1978–; Chld. Libn., Providence Pub. Lib., 1975–78. **Educ.:** Boston Univ., 1970–74, BA, magna cum laude, (Eng. Lang. and Lit.); Univ. of MI, 1974–75, MLS. **Orgs.:** SLA: Mem. (Ch., 1978–). AALL. ALA. RI Gvr.'s Conf. on Lib. and Info. Srvs. (1978). Providence Pub. Lib.: Corp. Mem. (1979–). St. Bartholomew's Sch., Providence: Adv. Com. (1979–). **Pubns.:** *The History of St. Bartholomew's Church* (forthcoming); Dsgn. and broadcast a series on prominent Italian-Americans for an Italian radio station. **Activities:** 12, 14-Law; 29, 39, 41; 77, 78 **Addr.:** Adler, Pollock & Sheehan Inc., One Hospital Trust Plz., Providence, RI 02903.

Orr, Cynthia (Mr. 19, 1949, Quinter, KS) Asst. to Dir., Lakewood Pub. Lib., 1979–; Head, Adult Dept., 1977–78, 1st

Special Subjects/Services: 50. Adult educ.; 51. Advert./Mktg.; 52. Aerosp.; 53. Agric.; 54. Area std.; 55. Arts/Hum.; 56. Autom.; 57. Bibl./Prtg.; 58. Bio. sci.; 59. Bus./Fin.; 60. Chem.; 61. Copyrt.; 62. Documtn.; 63. Educ.; 64. Engin.; 65. Env.; 66. Eth. grps.; 67. Film; 68. Food/Nutr.; 69. Geneal.; 70. Geo.; 71. Geol.; 72. Handcpd.; 73. Hist.; 74. Int. frdm.; 75. Info. sci.; 76. Insr.; 77. Law; 78. Legis.; 79. Math./Comp. sci.; 80. Med.; 81. Metals; 82. Nat. resrcs.; 83. Newsp.; 84. Nuc. sci.; 85. Oral hist.; 86. Petr./Energy; 87. Pharm.; 88. Phys./Astr./Math.; 89. Readg.; 90. Relig.; 91. Sci./Tech.; 92. Soc. sci.; 93. Telecom.; 94. Transp.; 95. (other).

Asst., 1972–77. **Educ.:** Marymount Coll., KS, 1967–71, AB (Eng.); Case West. Rsv. Univ., 1971–72, MSLS. **Orgs.:** OH LA: N. Chap. (Secy., 1981). ALA. Cleveland Area Metro. Lib. Syst.: Com. on Resrcs. (1975–79); Adv. Com. for Adult Litcy. Grantwriting Proj. (1978–79). Lakewood Little Thea. **Activities:** 9; 16, 17; 56, 69, 89 **Addr.:** Lakewood Public Library, 15425 Detroit Ave., Lakewood, OH 44107.

Orr, Joella Allen (S. 6, 1927, Justin, TX) Lib. Dir., Denton Pub. Lib., 1968–; Coord., NE Lib. Syst., 1974–75; Cat., TX Woman's Univ., 1967–68; Lib. Coord., Lewisville Indp. Sch. Dist., 1960–67. **Educ.:** TX Woman's Univ., 1960, BS, 1964, MLS, All Level Sch. Libn., Permanent Cnty. Libn. **Orgs.:** TX Mncpl. Libns. Assn.: Pres. (1975–76); VP (1974–75). TX LA: Dist. 7 (Ch., 1972–74). Pub. Lib. Admin. of N. TX: Pres. (1970–74). Denton Cnty. Hlth. Plng. Cncl. Daughters of Amer. Revolution: Libn. (1970–79). **Activities:** 9; 17, 35, 36; 50 **Addr.:** 1509 Kendolph, Denton, TX 76201.

Orr, Oliver H., Jr. (O. 6, 1921, Brevard, NC) Mss. Histn., Lib. of Congs., 1969–, Spec. in Amer. Hist., 1965–69; Instr., Asst. Prof. of Hist., NC State Univ., 1959–65; Lib. Asst., Circ. Dept., Univ. of NC Lib., 1940–56. **Educ.:** Brevard Jr. Coll., 1938–40, Dipl.; Univ. of NC, 1940–42, AB (Pol. Sci.), 1945–58, PhD (Hist.). **Orgs.:** SAA. Assn. for the Bib. of Hist.: Ch., Nom. Com. (1979, 1981). Org. of Amer. Histns.: Ch., Bibl. Resrch. Needs Com. (1978). South. Hist. Assn. Mem. Com.; Prog. Com. (1975). Forest Hist. Socty.: Lib. and Spec. Col. Com. (1977); Judge, Theodore C. Blegen Awd. (1977). NC Lit. and Hist. Assn. Other orgs. **Pubns.:** Ed., *A Guide to the Study of the United States of America, Supplement, 1956–1965* (1976); *Charles Brantley Aycock* (1961); "The Trials of Minor Biography," *Qtly. Jnl. of Lib. of Congs.* (O. 1967); "Charles Brantley Aycock," *Dict. of NC Biog.* (1979); "North Carolina: History" in *Merit Students Ency.* (1967); reviews. **Activities:** 1, 4; 15, 39, 45; 57 **Addr.:** 129 6th St., N.E., Washington, DC 20002.

Orr, Richard H. (Jl. 8, 1920, Topeka, KS) Adj. Prof., Sch. of Lib. and Info. Sci., Drexel Univ., 1976–; Dir., Inst. for Advnc. of Med. Comm., 1958–. **Educ.:** Univ. of Chicago, 1938–42, AA, 1945–48, BS (Bio. Sci.); Univ. of South. CA, 1948–50, MD. **Orgs.:** ASIS: *Anl. Review* Adv. Com. (1967–72). ASLIB: Sr. Visit. Resrch. Sci. (1971–72). Natl. Lib. of Med.: Consult. (1968–70). AAAS: Fellow. Amer. Physiological Socty. Amer. Sci. Film Assn.: Bd. of Dir. (1963–65). **Honors:** Phi Beta Kappa; Alpha Omega Alpha. **Pubns.:** "Development of Methodologic Tools for Planning and Managing Library Services," *Bltn. of the Med. LA* (Jl. 1970); jt. auth., "User Services Offered by Medical School Libraries in 1968: Results of a National Survey Employing New Methodology," *Bltn. of the Med. LA* (O. 1970); "The Scientist as an Information Processor: A Conceptual Model Illustrated with Data on Variables Related to Library Utilization" in *Communication Among Scientists and Technologists* (1970); jt. auth., "Document Delivery Capabilities of Major Biomedical Libraries in 1968: Results of a National Survey Employing Standardized Tests," *Bltn. of the Med. LA* (Jl. 1972); "Measuring the Goodness of Library Services: A General Framework for Considering Quantitative Measures," *Jnl. of Docum.* (S. 1973); other articles. **Activities:** 11, 14-Resrch. Inst.; 17, 24, 41; 75, 80, 93 **Addr.:** 916 Spruce St., Philadelphia, PA 19107.

Orser, Frank William (O. 3, 1940, Charlottesville, VA) Assoc. Libn., Asst. Ch., Acq. Dept., Univ. of FL, 1971–, Asst. to Dir., 1969–71; Cat. Libn., Yale Univ., 1968–69, Ref. Libn., 1965–68. **Educ.:** Univ. of VA, 1959–63, BA (Eng.); Simmons Coll., 1963–66, MS (LS). **Orgs.:** ALA. FL LA. SELA. Bib. Socty. of the Univ. of VA. Untd. Fac. of FL: Univ. of FL Chap., Treas., Exec. Com. (1975–79). **Pubns.:** "Florida Periodicals: A Reader's View," *Serials Review* (Jl.-S., 1979). **Activities:** 1; 15, 33, 44; 57 **Addr.:** Serials Section, University of Florida Libraries, Gainesville, FL 32611.

Ortiz, Barbara H. (F. 10, 1941, KY) Asst. Mncpl. Libn., Anchorage Mncpl. Lib., 1980–; Head, AV Sect., State Lib. of FL, 1977–80; Visit. Prof., NC Ctrl. Univ., 1977. **Educ.:** FL State Univ., 1959–64, BS (MS-LS); 1975–77, AMD (LS); 1976–, Doct. Cand. (LS). **Orgs.:** ALA: LITA, Mem. Com. Ch. AK LA. SELA: LITA, Prog. Com.; Media Caucus Util. Com. FL LA: YA Caucus Consult. FL Assn. for Media Educ. Natl. Film Market: Bd. of Dirs.; Prog. Ch. **Pubns.:** "Selected Films for YA'S," *Sunshine* (Je. 1979); "Know Them as People," *YA'S in the Sunshine* (Je., 1979); "Ethnic Films," *Keystone,* (O., 1979); Cath. Lib. World Multi-Media Kits, "Put It All Together in Church" (1978). **Activities:** 9, 13; 24, 32; 67 **Addr.:** 2910 Leighton, Anchorage, AK 99503.

Ortiz, Cynthia (Jl. 22, 1945, Minneapolis, MN) Libn., US Dept. of Energy, NV Oper. Ofc., 1979–; Mgr., Resrch. and Admin. Srvs., Util. Component Pedestal Corp., 1977–78; Asst. Libn., Amer. Gas Assn., 1974–75; Head Catlgr., AV Catlgr., Xerox Bibliographics, 1971–74, Catlgr., 1970–71. **Educ.:** Univ. of NV, Las Vegas, 1963–67, BA (Pol. Sci.); San Jose State Univ., 1968–70, MA (Libnshp.); Univ. of NV, Las Vegas, 1976–77, MPA (Pub. Admin.). **Orgs.:** ALA: Const. and Bylaws Com. (1976–78). SLA. Law Libns. Socty. of Washington, DC: Pubns. Com. (Co-Ch., 1973). NV LA. Amer. Socty. for Pub. Admin. West. Gvt. Resrch. Assn. **Honors:** Beta Phi Mu, 1970; Pi Sigma Alpha, 1978. **Pubns.:** Reviews. **Activities:** 4, 12; 17, 39, 46; 75, 84, 86 **Addr.:** 3968 Calle Mirador, Las Vegas, NV 89103.

Ortiz, Diane (Jl. 22, 1945, Minneapolis, MN) Mgt. Anal., Recs. Mgt. Coord., City of Las Vegas, 1978–; Proj. Mgr., Automated Typographics, Inc., 1974–75; Head Catlgr., AV Catlgr., Xerox BiblioGraphics, 1971–74; Asst. Law Libn., Georgetown Univ. Law Ctr. Lib., 1970–71. **Educ.:** Univ. of NV, Las Vegas, 1963–67, BA (Pol. Sci.); San Jose State Univ., 1968–70, MAL (Libnshp.); Univ. of NV, Las Vegas, 1976–77, MPA (Pub. Admin.). **Orgs.:** ALA: Ref. and Subscrpn. Books Review Com. (1976–78). Assn. of Recs. Mgrs. and Admin. Law Libns. Socty. of Washington, DC: Pubns. Com. (Co-Ch., 1973). NV LA. Amer. Socty. for Pub. Admin. West. Gvtl. Resrch. Assn. **Honors:** Beta Phi Mu, 1970; Pi Sigma Alpha, 1978. **Activities:** 12; 17, 39, 46; 75, 77, 92, 95 **Addr.:** 3968 Calle Mirador, Las Vegas, NV 89103.

Ortiz, Oneida (Rivera) de (S. 12, 1926, Santurce, PR) Lib. Dir., Humacao Univ. Coll., 1980–; Dir., Lrng. Resrcs. Ctr., Bayamón Univ. Coll., 1970–80; Assoc. Dean of Students, PR Jr. Coll., 1969–70; Chief Libn., Per. Room, Univ. of PR, Mayagüez Campus, 1966–69; Dir., Contact Srvs., Actg. Lib. Dir., 1959–66; Libn. & Tchr., Dept. of Educ., 1949–52, 1956–61; Dir. of Libs.,-Ext., Div., Univ. of PR, 1954–55. **Educ.:** Univ. of PR, 1945–49, BA; Drexel Univ., 1963–66, MSLS; New York Univ., Doct. prog., (Soc. Work); various workshops. **Orgs.:** ALA: Cncl. (1972–74); Bibl. Com. (1974–76). SBPR: Pres. (1972–74); Cont. Educ. (1971–72). ACURIL: Gen. Secy. (1977); Exec. Cncl. (1975–76). SALALM. Other orgs. Phi Delta Kappa: P.D.K. Fndn. (1979–80). Delta Kappa Gamma: Secy. (1979–80). **Honors:** "Honor al Mérito", Ciudad de Bayamón, 1976; Disting. Srvs. Awd., Rotary Club Bayamón, 1977–79; Colegio Reg. de Bayamón, Disting. Lib. Srv., 1977; PDK Disting. Educ., 1980. **Pubns.:** *La integración de los recursos en las Bibliotecas de Puerto Rico: estado actual* (1976); "The use of computers in Academy Libraries in Puerto Rico," *ACURIL Nsltr.* (1979); various articles. **Activities:** 1; 17, 24, 31; 63, 75 **Addr.:** 39 Humacao St., Villa Avila, Guaynabo, PR 00657.

Ortiz-de Matos, Maria C. (My. 3, 1932, Aibonito, PR) Dir., Lrng. Resrcs. Ctr., Interamer. Univ. of PR, San German Campus, 1979–; Dir., Tech. Srvs., Univ. of PR, Ponce, 1974–78; Dir., Tech. Srvs., Cath. Univ. of PR, 1971–74; Dir., Tech. Srvs., Univ. of PR, Arecibo, 1967–71; Instr., LS, 1965–71. **Educ.:** Univ. of PR, 1951–55, BSED (Home Econ.); Univ. of MI, 1958–59, MALS; Inst. for Lib. Admin., Miami Univ., 1979. **Orgs.:** SBPR: Pres. (1964–65). Assn. of Caribbean Univ. and Resrch. Libs.: VP, PR Com. (1979–80). ALA. Altrusa Intl. Bus. and Prof. Women's Clubs, PR Fed. **Honors:** Bus. & Prof. Women's Clubs, Plaque Outstan. Srvs., 1976; SBPR, Cert., 1976. **Activities:** 1; 20, 44, 46 **Addr.:** Inter-American University of Puerto Rico - San Germán Campus, San Germán, PR 00753.

Ortopan, LeRoy Donald (O. 1, 1925, Akron, OH) Libn., Cat. Dept., Univ. of CA, Berkeley, 1970–; Asst. Dir., Lib. Tech. Prog., ALA, 1970; Chief of Cat., Univ. of WI (Madison), 1965–70; Head, Cat. Dept., Northwestern Univ., 1957–65; Cat. Libn., Pontiac City Lib., 1956–1957; Cat. Libn., Grace A. Dow Memorial Lib. (Midland, MI), 1952–56. **Educ.:** Univ. of Akron, 1943–49, BA (Hum.); Case West. Reserve Univ., 1949–50, MA (Eng.), 1951–52, MS (LS). **Orgs.:** ALA: Serials Sect. Com. to Study Serials Rec. (Ch. 1973–78); ACRL, Rep. Cat. Code Rev. Com. (1974–78); Com. Cat. Descrp. and Access (1980–82); Graphics Subcom., AACR2 Intro. Prog. Com. (Ch. 1978–79); RTSD, Org. and Bylaws Com. (1981–83). CA LA. **Pubns.:** Ed., *Title Classified by the Library of Congress Classification: National Shelflist Count* 1973, 1975, 1977, 1979.; Ed., *Manually Maintained Serials Records: report of Ad Hoc Committee to Study Serials* (1976); "Support for Conversion to LC," *Lib. and Info. Std.* (no. 1 1968); "Catalog Card Reproduction at the University," *Current State of Catalog Card Reproduction* (1975); Ed., "Examples for Applying the Anglo-American Cataloguing Rules, 2d edition: a three-part slide program," (Graphics Subcommittee, AACR-2) (1980). **Activities:** 1; 15, 20, 46; 54, 55, 56 **Addr.:** Catalog Department, General Library, University of California, Berkeley, CA 94720.

Osborn, (Velva) Jeanne (Ap. 25, 1918, Revere, MO) Prof., Sch. of LS, Univ. of IA, 1971–; Assoc. Prof., Dept. of LS, North. IL Univ., 1967–71; Head, Cat. Dept., West. IL Univ., 1954–67; Ref. Libn., Chicago Undergrad. Div., Univ. of IL, 1953–54. **Educ.:** KS State Tchrs. Coll., Emporia, 1935–39, BS (Eng.); Univ. of Chicago, 1942–44, MA (LS); Univ. of IL, 1962–65, PhD (Phil.). **Orgs.:** ALA: ACRL, Ch., Const. and Bylaws Com. (1976–79); various Com. SLA: IA LA. AALS. ACLU. IA State Hist. Socty. AAUP. Natl. Educ. Assn. **Honors:** L. B. Johnson Presidential Lib., Resrch. Flwshp., 1974. **Pubns.:** *Early Developments in Storage Library Processing Univ. of IL Grad. Lib. Sch. Occasional Papers* (1957); *Classification: an Introductory Manual* (1978); Jt. auth., "The Effect of Literary Awards on Children's Book Recommendations," *Top of the News* (Ap. 1974); reprinted in: *Library Lit. 5–The Best of 1974.* **Activities:** 1, 11; 20, 26, 46; 62, 91 **Addr.:** School of Library Science, The University of Iowa, Iowa City, IA 52242.

Osborne, Nancy Seale (Mr. 5, 1936, San Angelo, TX) Ref. Libn., Curric. Mtrls. Ctr., Penfield Lib., State Univ. Coll., Oswego, NY, 1980–; Pub. Srvs. Libn., State Univ. Coll., Cortland, NY, 1979–80; Archvst., Ref. Libn., SUNY, Coll. of Env. Sci. and Forestry, Syracuse, 1978–79; Info. Spec., Grntlgy., Metro. Comsn. on Aging, Syracuse, NY, 1977–78. **Educ.:** State Univ. Coll., Oswego, NY, 1968–70, BS (Educ.), 1970–71, MS (Educ.); Syracuse Univ., 1976–77, MLS. **Orgs.:** ALA. SAA. NY LA. SUNY LA. Penfield Lib. Assocs. Oswego Varsity Sports Fndn. Inc. Natl. Women's Std. Assn. Amer. Socty. for Curric. Dev. **Honors:** Beta Phi Mu, 1977; Phi Delta Kappa. **Pubns.:** "From Scandinavian Traditional to "Happy Birthday, America: An Interview with Karen Bakke," *Open Chain* (1976); "National Women's Studies Association Conference," *Sipapu* (1977); "Upstate Oriental," *The Grapevine* (1980). **Activities:** 1, 14-Curric. Mtrls. Ctr.; 15, 31, 39 **Addr.:** Curriculum Materials Center, Penfield Library, State University College, Oswego, NY 13126.

Osborne, Reed E. (Ap. 3, 1948, Toronto, ON) Chief Libn., Markham Pub. Libs., 1980–; Chief Libn., St. Thomas Pub. Lib., 1976–80; Chief Libn., Parry Sound Pub. Lib., 1975–76; Ref. Libn., Woodstock Pub. Lib., 1973–75. **Educ.:** York Univ., 1967–71, BA (Eng.); Univ. of West. ON, 1972–73, MLS, 1978, Dipl. (Mncpl. Admin.). **Orgs.:** ON Pub. LA: Pres. (1978). Rotary Club. **Pubns.:** Jt. auth., *District of Parry Sound Bibliography* (1976). **Addr.:** St. Thomas Public Library, 153 Curtis St., St. Thomas, ON N5P 3Z7 Canada.

Osborne, Ruth Wright (Jl. 30, 1914, Avon, NY) Head, Bus./Sci./Tech. Ref., Pub. Lib. Charlotte & Mecklenburg Cnty., 1969–, Head, Main Ref. Srvs., 1965–69, Ref. Staff, US Govt. Pubns., 1964–65; Libn., Pub. Lib. Bethel Park, PA, 1956–61; Asst. Ref. Bus./Tech. Dept., Yonkers Pub. Lib., 1936–41. **Educ.:** Univ. of VT, 1932–35 (Pol. Sci.); Simmons Coll., 1935–36, BS (LS); various courses. **Orgs.:** SLA: NC Chap. Dir. (1979–81). NC LA: Governors Conf. SLA Com. (1978). Metrolina LA: Treas., (1977–79). Mecklenburg LA. **Activities:** 9; 16, 29, 39; 59, 91, 92 **Addr.:** 434 Blairmore Dr., Charlotte, NC 28211.

Osburn, Charles B. (My. 25, 1939, Pittsburgh, PA) Vice-Provost for Univ. Libs., Univ. of Cincinnati, 1980–; Asst. Univ. Libn. for Col. Mgt., Northwestern Univ., 1976–80; Asst. Dir. of Univ. Libs. for Col. Dev., SUNY, Buffalo, 1974–76; Hum. Biblgphr., Univ. of NC, 1969–74; Asst. Prof. of Fr., Univ. of WI - Whitewater, 1966–69; Instr. in Fr., PA State Univ., 1963–66. **Educ.:** Grove City Coll., 1957–61, BA (Fr.); PA State Univ., 1961–63, MA (Fr.); Univ. of NC, 1969–71, MS (LS); Univ. of MI, 1972–78, PhD (LS). **Orgs.:** ALA. Mod. Lang. Assn. of Amer.: Bibl. Com. (1972–80). Amer. Assn. of Tchrs. of Fr.: Natl. Comsn. on Resrch. Tools in Fr. Lang. and Lit. (1978–81). AAUP. **Honors:** Phi Sigma Iota; Beta Phi Mu. **Pubns.:** *Academic Research and Library Resources: Changing Patterns in America* (1979); Ed., *The Present State of French Studies: A Collection of Research Reviews* (1971); *Research and Reference Guide to French Studies* (1968, 1972; 1981, 2nd ed.); "Education for Collection Development" in *Foundations in Library and Information Science, Vol. 10: Collection Development in Libraries* (1980); "Some Practical Observations on the Writing, Implementation, and Revision of Collection Development Policy," *Lib. Resrcs. and Tech. Srvs.* (1979); other articles; reviews. **Activities:** 1; 15, 17, 24; 55 **Addr.:** University of Cincinnati Libraries, University & Woodside, Cincinnati, OH 45221.

Osburn, Linda M. (Ja. 22, 1952, Selma, AL) Sch. Libn., Glen Oaks Elem. Sch., 1978–; Cmnty. Educ. Coord., Fairfield, AL, 1979–80; Sch. Libn., Dunbar Middle Sch., 1975–78; Tchr., Hard Elem., 1974–75; Asst. Libn., Ctrl. Park Branch, Birmingham Pub. Lib., 1973–74. **Educ.:** Judson Coll., 1970–73, BS (Elem. Educ.); Univ. of AL, 1975–77, MLS. **Orgs.:** AL Instr. Media Assn.: Secy. (1979–80). AL LA: Chld. and Sch. Div.; ALA: AASL. Int. Frdm. **Pubns.:** "Lots a Work, Good Food, No Sleep," *AIMA Newsletter* (Ag. 1979); "Teacher Prepare Classroom Visuals," *AL Educ.* (Ap. 1979); "English Teachers, Librarians, Join in Poetry Workshop," *AL Educ.* (Mr. 1978). **Activities:** 10 **Addr.:** 713 Greenbriar Rd., Fairfield, AL 35064.

Oser, Anita K. (Ja. 21, 1937, New York, NY) Ref. Libn., West. Carolina Univ., 1973–. **Educ.:** Univ. of Miami, 1955–58, BA (Span.); FL State Univ., 1958–59, MA (LS); FL Atl. Univ., 1970–72, MA (Grmn.). **Orgs.:** SLA: Educ. Com. (1979–). SELA. NC LA. Amer. Assn. of Tchrs. of Grmn. **Pubns.:** Contrib., *Historical Abstracts* (1975–). **Activities:** 1; 15, 31, 39; 70 **Addr.:** Hunter Library, Western Carolina University, Cullowhee, NC 28723.

Osgood, James B. (Ap. 6, 1932, New Castle, PA) Asst. Dir., Cat. Libn., Kennedy-King Coll. Lib., 1969–; Head Libn./Asst. Head Libn., SE Coll., 1966–69; Law Circ. Libn., Univ. of Chicago Law Lib., 1964–66. **Educ.:** Univ. of Chicago, 1949–52, BA (Liberal Arts); New York Univ., 1955–57 (Fr., Span.); Carnegie Inst. of Tech., 1962–64, MLS; Univ. of Chicago, 1972–73, Cert. of Advnc. Std. (LS). **Orgs.:** ALA. IL LA. Cncl. on Lib. Tech. Assts.: Ch., Educ. & Resrch. Com. (1975–76). Buddhist Pubn. Socty. NY Com. to Abolish Capital Punishment. **Pubns.:** "The Library Technical Assistant," *Cath. Lib. World* (Je. 1973); also in: *Reader in Library Technology* (1975); "Gilmore Case Countdown," *Friends Jnl.* (Mr. 15, 1977). **Activities:** 1; 17, 20, 22; 55, 66, 90 **Addr.:** Kennedy-King College Library, 6800 S. Wentworth Ave., Chicago, IL 60621.

PROFESSIONAL ACTIVITIES: Institutions: 1. Acad. lib.; 2. Arch.; 3. Assn.; 4. Fed./Gvt. lib.; 5. Inst. lib.; 6. Mfr./Suppl.; 7. Milit. lib.; 8. Musm.; 9. Pub. lib.; 10. Sch. lib.; 11. Sch. of lib. sci.; 12. Spec. lib.; 13. State lib.; 14. (other). **Functions/Activities:** 15. Acq./Col. dev.; 16. Adult srvs.; 17. Admin.; 18. Apprais.; 19. Archit./Bldgs.; 20. Cat./Class.; 21. Chld. srvs.; 22. Circ.; 23. Cons./Pres.; 24. Consult.; 25. Cont. ed.; 26. Educ. lib. sci.; 27. Ext. srvs.; 28. Fund/Grants; 29. Gvt. pubs.; 30. Indx./Abs.; 31. Instr. lib. use; 32. Media srvs.; 33. Micro.; 34. Netwks./Coop.; 35. Persnl.; 36. PR; 37. Publshg.; 38. Recs. mgt.; 39. Ref. srvs.; 40. Repro.; 41. Resrch.; 42. Review.; 43. Secur.; 44. Serials; 45. Spec. col.; 46. Tech. srvs.; 47. Trustees/Bds.; 48. YA srvs.; 49. (other).

Osheroff, Shiela Keil (N. 13, 1946, Omaha, NE) Cat. Libn., OR Hlth. Scis. Univ., 1973–; Acq. Libn., Univ. of OR Med. Sch., 1971–73. **Educ.:** Univ. of Puget Sound, 1964–68, BA (Grmn.); Univ. of WA, 1968–69, ML (LS); Med. LA Cert., 1976–87. **Orgs.:** Med. LA. ALA: RTSD. Pac. NW Reg. Med. Lib. Grp. AACRZ Trainer for Natl. Lib. of Med. AAUP: Hlth. Sci. Chap., Secy.-Treas.; Pres. (1981–82). **Pubns.:** *Videocassette, Audiovisual Cataloging* (1980). **Activities:** 1, 12; 20, 26, 34; 58, 80 **Addr.:** Catalog Department, OHSU Library, P.O. Box 573, Portland, OR 97207.

Ossenkop, David Charles (Ja. 2, 1937, Pasadena, CA) Assoc. Libn., Crane Msc. Lib., State Univ. Coll., Potsdam, 1970–. **Educ.:** Drew Univ., 1954–58, BA (Grmn. Lit.); Columbia Univ., 1958–68, MA, PhD (Msclgy.), 1968–70, MS (LS). **Orgs.:** Msc. LA. SUNY Libns. Assn. Amer. Musicological Socty.: Treas., Grt. New York Chap. (1966–67). Intl. Musicological Socty. **Honors:** Beta Phi Mu. **Pubns.:** "Editions of Beethoven's Easy Piano Pieces," *Piano Qtly.* (Win. 1961–62); 6 articles for *New Grove Dictionary of Music and Musicians* (1981). **Activities:** 1; 15, 20, 39; 55 **Addr.:** 23 Pierrepont Ave., Potsdam, NY 13676.

Ostrander, Dona Jeanne (Ja. 25, 1935, Pontiac, MI) Curric. Lab. Libn., Ctrl. CT State Coll. 1971–; Ref., YA Libn., New Britain, Pub. Lib., 1966–70; Chld. Libn., Detroit Pub. Lib., 1962–64. **Educ.:** Univ. of MI, 1954–56, BA (Bio.), 1956–61, MSLS; Jackson Cmnty. Coll., 1952–54, AA. **Orgs.:** ALA. CT LA: Chld. Env. Com.; Dev. Com. CT Educ. Media Assn.: Pubns. Ch. New Eng. LA. **Honors:** Phi Delta Kappa. **Pubns.:** Jt. Auth., "Toys To Go," (1975); jt. Auth., "Considerations before Writing A Public Library Building Program," (1978); jt. Auth., "Beyond Complacency...," *Top of the News* (Je. 1972). **Activities:** 1, 10; 15, 31, 32; 66 **Addr.:** Elihu Burritt Library, Central CT State College, New Britain, CT 06050.

Ostrander, Gloria J. (F. 23, 1944, Caldwell, ID) Head, Mono. Div., Boise State Univ., 1980–, Cat. Libn., 1971–79; Ref. Libn., ID State Hist. Socty., 1970–71. **Educ.:** Boise State Coll., 1964–68, BA (Hist.); Univ. of WA, 1968–69, MLS. **Orgs.:** Pac. NW LA. ID LA. ALA. **Activities:** 1; 15 **Addr.:** 1910 University Dr., Boise State University Library, Boise, ID 83725.

Ostroff, Harriet (Ja. 14, 1930, New York, NY) Head, Mss. Sect., Ed., Natl. Un. Cat. of Mss. Col., Lib. of Congs., 1976–, Index ed., Natl. Un. Cat. of Mss. Col., 1967–76, Mss. Cat., 1959–67, Catlgr., 1952–59; Catlgr., City Coll. of New York NY, 1951–52. **Educ.:** City Coll. of New York, 1947–50, BBA (Frgn. trade); Columbia Univ., 1950–51, MS (LS). **Orgs.:** ALA: Rare Books and Mss. Sect. SAA. Mid-Atl. Reg. Arch. Conf. Org. of Amer. Histns. Assn. for State and Local Hist. Amer. Socty. of Indxr. Oral Hist. in the MidAtl. Reg. **Pubns.:** "Oral History Collections and NUCMC," *Jnl. of the Richmond Oral Hist. Assn.* (Win. 1978). **Addr.:** 6804 Sulky Ln., Rockville, MD 20852.

Ostrom, Kriss Taya (Mr. 23, 1948, Seattle, WA) Head, Circ. Dept., MI State Univ., 1978–, Asst. Head, Circ. Dept., 1977–78, ILL Libn., 1976–77, Sci. Ref. Libn., 1975–76. **Educ.:** Univ. of WA, 1966–70, BS (Eng/Hist); IN Univ., 1974–74, MLS. **Orgs.:** ALA: SRRT. MI LA. Lansing Area LA. **Pubns.:** "Community Information Centers," *RQ* (Fall 1975). **Activities:** 1; 17, 22, 49; 56 **Addr.:** 230 N. Fairview Ave., Lansing, MI 48912.

Ostrove, Geraldine E. Dir. of Libs., New Eng. Cnsvty. of Msc., 1976–; Lectr. in LS, Simmons Coll., 1980–; Head Libn., Peabody Cnsvty., 1965–76. **Educ.:** Goucher Coll., 1955–59, AB (Msc.); Peabody Cnsvty., 1964–65, MMus (Hist. & Lit.); Univ. of MD, 1965–67, MLS. **Orgs.:** Msc. LA: Rec. Secy. (1972–78); Ch., Const. Rev. com. (1978–); New Eng. Chap. (ch.). Intl. Assn. of Msc. Libs.: Bibl. Resrch. Comsn.; Cnsvty. and Schs. of Msc. libs. Comsn. (Ch., U.S. Branch, 1981–84). ALA: ACRL. Amer. Musicological Socty. Sonneck Socty. **Honors:** Beta Phi Mu. **Pubns.:** "Music Publishing Today - A Symposium," *Notes* (D. 1975); "Conservatory Libraries in the United States," *Fontes Artis Musicae* (1969); reviews. **Activities:** 1; 15, 17, 26; 55 **Addr.:** Harriet M. Spaulding Library, New England Conservatory, 33 Gainsborough St., Boston, MA 02115.

Otness, Harold M. (Ag. 20, 1938, St. Louis, MO) Asst. Lib. Dir., South. OR State Coll., 1979–, Tech. Srvs. Libn., 1976–79, Readers Srvs. Libn., 1974–76, Ref. Libn., 1966–74. **Educ.:** Portland State Univ., 1956–60, BS (Geo.); Univ. of Portland, 1964–66, MLS. **Orgs.:** West. Assn. of Map Libs.: Pres. (1977–78). OR LA. Prntg. Hist. Socty. Private Libs. Assn. **Pubns.:** *Index to Early Twentieth Century City Plans* (1978); *Lewis Osborne, Book Artist 1918–1978* (1979); "Baedekers One-Star American Libraries," *Jnl. of Lib. Hist.* (Sum. 1977), in *Library Lit - The Best of 1977* (1978); "Passenger Ship Libraries," *Jnl. of Lib. Hist.* (Win. 1979); other articles, reviews. **Activities:** 1; 17, 39, 45; 57, 70 **Addr.:** Southern Oregon State College, Ashland, OR 97520.

O'Toole, James M. (F. 25, 1950, Worcester, MA) Archvst., Roman Cath. Archdiocese of Boston, 1978–; Deputy Archvst., Commonwealth of MA, 1974–77, Actg. State Archvst., 1976–76; Asst. Cur., Mss. & Rare Books, New Eng. Hist. Geneal. Socty., 1974. **Educ.:** Boston Coll., 1968–72, AB (Hist.); Coll. of William and Mary, 1972–73, AM (Hist.); Simmons Coll., 1974–75, MS (LS). **Orgs.:** New Eng. Archvsts.: Pres. (1981–82), Exec. Bd. (1979–80); Educ. Com. (1979). SAA: Relig. Arch. Com. (1974–). Amer. Cath. Hist. Assn. Org. of Amer. Histns. **Pubns.:** Jt. auth., "Up from the Basement: Archives, History, and Public Administration," *GA Arch.* (Fall 1978); "Catholic Church Records: A Genealogical and Historical Resource," *New Eng. Hist. and Geneal. Register* (O. 1978); jt. auth., "Archives and the Flow of Records: Massachusetts as a Case Study," *GA Arc.* (Sum. 1976); "The Historical Interpretations of Samuel Adams," *New Eng. Qtly.* (Mr. 1976); "Catholic Diocesan Archives: A Renaissance in Progress," *Amer. Archvst.* (Sum. 1980); Ed., *Cath. Arch. Nsltr.* (J. 1979–). **Activities:** 2; 17, 28, 45; 55, 90, 92 **Addr.:** Archdiocese of Boston, 2121 Commonwealth Ave., Brighton, MA 02135.

Ott, Kathleen Galiher (O. 21, 1949, Washington, DC) Mgr., Info. Srvs., TRW Inc., 1976–; Persnl. Asst., World Hlth. Org., 1974–76; Instr., Cath. Univ., 1972–73. **Educ.:** Regis Coll., 1967–71, BA (Fr.); Univ. of Fribourg, Switzerland, 1969–70, Cert. (Fr.); Georgetown Univ., 1971–73, MS (Ling.); George Washington Univ., 1976–79, MPA (Bus./Gvt. Rel.). **Orgs.:** SLA. Women in Gvt. Rel., Inc.: Prog. Com. (Co-Ch., 1980–81). Women's Equity Action Leag.: Bd. of Dir. (1981–). Jr. Leag. of Washington. **Honors:** Pi Alpha Alpha, 1979. **Activities:** 12; 17, 41; 78 **Addr.:** TRW Inc. Suite 2700, 1000 Wilson Blvd., Arlington, VA 22209.

Otterson, Harry Sylvester (My. 6, 1936, Pittsburgh, PA) Sr. Libn., Sch. Lib., Attica Correctional Facility, 1980–; Instr., Sch. of Info. and Lib. Std., SUNY, Buffalo, 1978–80; Asst. Prof., Dept. of Info. Sci., IL State Univ., 1974–77; Asst. Prof., Sch. of Lib. and Info. Sci., SUNY, Geneseo, 1969–74; Instr., D'Youville Coll., 1968–69. **Educ.:** St. Bonaventure Univ., 1955–60, BA (Phil.); Whitefriars Hall, 1959–63, MA (Relig.); Cath. Univ. 1963–64, STL (Theo.), 1964–65, MSLS; SUNY, Buffalo, 1971–, PhD in progress (Comm.). **Orgs.:** ALA: ACRL. Cath. LA: Ed., *CULS* (1967–69). AALS. Natl. Educ. Assn. **Pubns.:** "Analytical, Cumulative Author and Subject Index to The Sword Vol. 21–28" *The Sword* (F. 1971); reviews. **Activities:** 11; 15, 20, 26; 55, 90, 93 **Addr.:** School Library, Attica Correctional Facility, Attica, NY 14011.

Otto, Margaret Amelia (O. 22, 1937, Boston, MA) Libn., Dartmouth Coll., 1979–; Assoc. Dir., MA Inst. of Tech., 1976–79, Assoc. Dir., Lib. Srvs., 1974–76, Staff, 1963–74. **Educ.:** Boston Univ., 1960, AB; Simmons Coll., 1963, MS (LS), 1970, MA. **Orgs.:** ALA: ACRL, Plng. Com. (1980–83); LAMA, Budget and Fin. Com. (1980–83); Exec. Com. (1980–82). MA Cert. of Libns.: Adv. Com. (1973–76). New Eng. Lib. Info. Netwk.: Exec. Com. (1975–). Unvsl. Serials and Bks. Exch.: Bd. Dir. (1976–). **Honors:** Cncl. on Lib. Resrcs., Fellow, 1972–73. **Activities:** 1; 17 **Addr.:** Dartmouth College Libraries, Hanover, NH 03755.*

Otto, Theophil M. (S. 8, 1940, Milwaukee, WI) Asst. Hum. Libn., Asst. Prof., South. IL Univ., 1972–; Asst. Msc. Cat., IN Univ., 1971–72. **Educ.:** Univ. of WI (Madison), 1959–63, BM (Msc.); South. IL Univ., 1974–79, PhD (Educ. Media); IN Univ., 1971–72, MLS; Union Theol. Semy., Sch. of Sacred Msc., 1964–1966, MSM (Msc.). **Orgs.:** ALA. Msc. LA. IL LA. Intl. Assn. for Exper. Resrch. in Singing. **Honors:** US Gov., Fulbright Grant for foreign study, 1966–67; Beta Phi Mu, 1972. **Pubns.:** "Messiaen and the Baroque Organ," *MUSIC* (D. 1978); "Utilization Strategies," in *Use of Radio Broadcast for Formal and Non-Formal Education in Developing Nations* (1978); "Computerized Register of Voice Research," (online register of resrch. 1975–). **Activities:** 1; 15, 30, 39; 55, 63, 75 **Addr.:** Morris Library - Humanities Division, Southern Illinois University, Carbondale, IL 62901.

Overbeck, James A. (S. 11, 1940, Eau Claire, WI) Dir., Columbia Theo. Semy., 1980–; Dir., Sch. of Theo. at Claremont, 1975–80; Ref. Asst., Univ. of IL, Circle, 1975; Ref. libn., City Coll. of Chicago, SW, 1974–75. **Educ.:** Carthage Coll., 1959–63, BA (Hist.); Univ. of Chicago, 1963–69, PhD (Rel. Hist.), 1973–74, MA (LS). **Orgs.:** ALA: ACRL. GA LA. ATLA: Mtrls. Exch. Ch. (1980). Univ. Cntr. in GA Libs. Grp., Pres.-Elect (1981). Amer. Socty. of Church Hist. Amer. Acad. of Relig. **Pubns.:** "Cover design and short article," *Lib. Qtly.* (Ap. 1975). **Activities:** 1, 12; 15, 17, 41; 55, 90, 92 **Addr.:** John B. Campbell Library, Columbia Theological Seminary, 701 Columbia Dr., Decatur, GA 30031.

Overby-Dean, Talulah Earle (My. 30, 1913, Lumpkin, GA) Lib. Consult., Freedom Univ., 1973–; Head Libn., Miccosukee Cmnty. Lib., 1976–80; Head Libn., Shelton Coll., 1972–74; Head Libn., Vineland Elem. Sch., Dade Cnty. FL Pub. Sch., 1966–69; Head Libn., Clay Cnty., FL, HQ, Clay Cnty. Pub. Lib., 1971–72; various tchg. and libn. positions. **Educ.:** Univ. of FL, 1944–50, BA (Elem. Educ., Soclgy.); Appalachian State Univ., 1965–70, MA (LS). **Orgs.:** FL LA. LA. Frnds. of the Lib.: Ch. Dade Cnty. Sch. Libns. Intl. Assn. for Christ. Educ. The Delta Kappa Gamma Socty. Intl.: Pi Chap. of FL (Pres., 1966–68); Soc. Ch.; Corres. Secty. **Pubns.:** "The Miccosukees Have a Media Center, too," *Jnl. of the Dade Cnty. Media Spec. Assn.* (Win. 1979); Creator, Ed., *The Sawgrass Breeze* (1977). **Activities:** 9; 13; 17, 20, 22; 63, 66 **Addr.:** 2106 E. Anderson Pl., Orlando, FL 32803.

Overholt, Maria B. (Ja. 15, 1918, Blairstown Twp., NJ) Dir., Miami Valley Lib. Org., 1976–; Admin., Whitewater Valley Area Lib. Srvs. Athrty., 1974–76; Media Ctr. Dir., (OH) Sr. HS, Greenville 1973–74; Dir., Appalachia Improved Ref. Srv., 1972–73. **Educ.:** OH Univ., 1935–39, BS (Educ., Bio.), 1940, (Botany); Kent State Univ., 1954–59, MA (LS); Miami Univ., 1956–68, Spec. (Educ.), various courses. **Orgs.:** OH Educ. Lib. Media Assn.: Legis. Com. ALA. OH LA: Legis. Com. (1978–). Piqua Area Amer. Natl. Red Cross. Natl. Educ. Assn. OH Educ. Assn. **Honors:** Phi Beta Kappa, 1939; Kappa Delta Pi, 1938. **Pubns.:** Ed., *Milo Matters* (1976–); "Solar Heating Installation" *Troy* (OH) *Daily News* (Ja. 13, 1980); "Library Services for Rural Ohioans," *OH Farmer* (Ap. 15, 1978); series of slide-tape presentations (1973). **Activities:** 10, 14-Multicounty coop.; 17, 34, 36; 58, 63, 89 **Addr.:** 212 Harrison St., Piqua, OH 45356.

Overley, Linda Jane (Mr. 21, 1949, Logansport, IN) Chld. Libn., Flesh Pub. Lib., 1977–; Chld. Coord., Troy-Miami Cnty. Pub. Lib., 1972–77. **Educ.:** Hanover Coll., 1967–71, BS (El. Educ.); IN Univ., 1971–72, MSLS. **Orgs.:** OH LA: Ch., Prog. Peddler Com. (1977, 1980); Asst. Coord., Div. VIII (1978); Coord., Div. VIII (1979). Piqua Altrusa. **Activities:** 9; 21, 32, 48; 67 **Addr.:** Flesh Public Library, 124 West Greene St., Piqua, OH 45356.

Overman, Dorothy M.P.S. (N. 17, 1917, Paterson, NJ) Head, Ref., Asst. Prof., St Louis Univ. Med. Ctr. Lib., 1976–; AV Libn., Jefferson Barracks VA Hosp., St. Louis, 1974–75; Field Libn., Bi-State Reg. Med. Prog., Washington Univ. Sch. of Med., 1971–73; Sr. Catlgr., Bryn Mawr Coll., 1970–71; Head Libn., Ellen Cushing Jr. Coll., 1967–70; Head Libn., Sioux Valley Hosp. Med. Lib., 1964–67; Head Libn., Sioux Falls Coll., 1956–58. **Educ.:** Montclair State Coll., 1935–39, AB (Eng.); Drexel Univ., 1967–71, MS (LS); Cert., Grade I, Med. LA, 1973. **Orgs.:** Med. LA: Ch., Nursing Libns.; Co-ch. RML/RMP (1972–73); Secy. RML/RMP Consult. (1971–72). St. Louis Med. Libns.: Exec. Com. (1972–73). Zonta Intl., Inst. for Intl. Understanding. **Honors:** Beta Phi Mu, 1971. **Pubns.:** Cmplr., *Audiovisual Clearinghouse Health Sciences Union List* (1975). **Activities:** 1, 14; 17, 39; 75, 80, 95-On-line srchs. **Addr.:** Saint Louis University Medical Center Library, 1402 S. Grand Blvd., St. Louis, MO 63104.

Overmier, Judith A. (Ag. 1, 1939, Columbus, OH) Cur., Wangensteen Hist. Lib. of Bio. and Med., Univ. of MN, 1967–; Libn., Bio-Med. Lib., 1965–67. **Educ.:** Bowling Green State Univ., 1957–62, BA (Eng.), BS (Educ.); Drexel Univ., 1963–65, MS (LS); Univ. of MN, 1978–, in progress (LS); Med. LA, Cert., Level I, 1966. **Orgs.:** Med. LA: Murray Gottlieb Prize Essay Com. (1972–77, Ch. 1976–77); Hist. of Med. Grp. (Ch., 1976/78); Oral Hist. Com. (Ch., 1977/79). Assn. of Libns. in the Hist. of the Hlth. Sci.: Strg. Com. (1975/80). MN LA: Acad. & Resrch. Libs. Div. (Secy., 1978/80). ALA: ACRL, Natl. Conf., Exec. Com., (Secy., 1978–81). Other orgs. Amer. Assn. for the Hist. of Med. Amer. Inst. for Cons. of Hist. and Artistic Works. **Pubns.:** *Preservation of Library Materials* (1973); "Bibliographical Notes on Mattioli's Dioscoridean Commentaries," *Bio-Med. Lib. Bltn.*, (Jl. 1969); "Dissemination of Medical Information in General Magazines from 1741–1776." *MnU Bltn.*, (O. 1971); "Notes from Abroad," *Bio-Med. Lib. Bltn.*, (1971–72); "Library Conservation at the University of Minnesota," *Conservation Admin.* (1975). **Activities:** 1; 15, 23, 45; 73, 95 **Addr.:** Wangensteen Historical Library, Bio-Medical Library, Diehl Hall, 505 Essex St. S.E., Minneapolis, MN 55455.

Overwein, Martha A. (Mrs. Joseph) (Mr. 21, 1921, Dayton, OH) Head, Indus. & Sci. Div., Dayton & Montgomery Cnty. Pub. Lib., 1963–; Libn., Sch. of Nursing, Good Samaritan Hosp., 1956–60. **Educ.:** Univ. of Dayton, 1939–43, BA (Soclgy.); Columbia Univ., 1960–61, MSLS. **Orgs.:** ALA. OH LA. **Pubns.:** Reviews. **Activities:** 9; 15, 31, 39; 51, 59, 91 **Addr.:** Dayton & Montgomery Co. Public Library, 215 E. Third St., Dayton, OH 45402.

Owen, Amy (Je. 26, 1944, Brigham City, UT) Deputy Dir., UT State Lib., 1981–, Dir., Tech. Srvs., 1974–81, Dir., Ref. Srvs., 1972–74, Syst. Libn., 1968–72. **Educ.:** Brigham Young Univ., 1962–66, BA (Hum.), 1966–68, MLS. **Orgs.:** UT LA: Bd. (1976–80); Pres. (1978–79). Mt. Plains LA: Secy. (1979–80). UT Educ. Media Assn. ALA. UT Coll. Lib. Cncl.: Exec. Secy (1978–). **Activities:** 13; 17, 24, 46 **Addr.:** Utah State Library, 2150 South 300 W., Suite 16, Salt Lake City, UT 84115.

Owen, Berniece M. (S. 14, 1941, Parker, SD) Acq. Libn., Gonzaga Univ., 1975–; Serials Catlgr., Asst. Head, Cat. Dept., AZ State Univ., 1965–70; Ref. Libn., Phoenix Pub. Lib., 1964–65. **Educ.:** Univ. of SD, 1959–63, BS (LS); Univ. of South. CA, 1963–64, MS (LS). **Orgs.:** NLA: Prof. Educ. Com. (1979–); WA State Chap., VP, Pres-Elect. (1979–80). **Honors:** Phi Beta Kappa, 1963. **Activities:** 1; 15, 20, 44 **Addr.:** Crosby Library, Gonzaga Univ., E. 502 Boone Ave., Spokane, WA 99258.

Owen, Dolores B. (Leesville, LA) Head Docum. Libn., Univ. of Southwest. LA Lib., 1972–; Sci. Ref. Libn., LA State Univ., 1968–71. **Educ.:** LA State Univ., 1950–54, BA (Msc.), 1962–68, MS (LS). **Orgs.:** LA LA: Docum. Com. (1976–, Ch., 1979–80); Ch., of Subj. Spec. Sect. (1980–81); Conf. Ch. (1980). ALA:ACRL/Sci. & Tech. Sect. (Secy., 1978, 79); Goals & Struc-

Special Subjects/Services: 50. Adult educ.; 51. Advert./Mktg.; 52. Aerosp.; 53. Agric.; 54. Area std.; 55. Arts/Hum.; 56. Autom.; 57. Bibl./Prtg.; 58. Bio. sci.; 59. Bus./Fin.; 60. Chem.; 61. Copyrt.; 62. Documtn.; 63. Educ.; 64. Engin.; 65. Env.; 66. Eth. grps.; 67. Film; 68. Food/Nutr.; 69. Geneal.; 70. Geo.; 71. Geol.; 72. Handcpd.; 73. Hist.; 74. Int. frdm.; 75. Info. sci.; 76. Insr.; 77. Law; 78. Legis.; 79. Math./Comp. sci.; 80. Med.; 81. Metals; 82. Nat. resrcs.; 83. Newsp.; 84. Nuc. sci.; 85. Oral hist.; 86. Petr./Energy; 87. Pharm.; 88. Phys./Astr./Math.; 89. Readg.; 90. Relig.; 91. Sci./Tech.; 92. Soc. sci.; 93. Telecom.; 94. Transp.; 95. (other).

tures Com. (1977–); Oberly Awd. Com. (1979–81). SWLA. Socty. of SW Archvsts. LA Hist. Assn. Atakapas Hist. Assn. AAUP. **Pubns.:** Jt. auth., *Abstracts and Indexes in Science & Technology; A Descriptive Guide* (1974); Jt. auth., *American guide to British Social Science Resources* (1976); "Revision of Documents Distribution Law," *LLA Bulletin* Win. 1976); "A study of coverage overlap among 14 major science and technology abstracting & indexing services," *Coll. & Resrch. Libs.* (Nov. 1977); "Report of STS/ACRL Meeting," *Agri. Libs. Info. Notes* (S. 1979). **Activities:** 1; 29, 39, 41; 77, 78, 92 **Addr.:** 218 Antigua Dr., Lafayette, LA 70503.

Owens, Calvin L. (O. 28, 1939, Council Bluffs, IA) Dir., Univ. of IL Film Ctr., 1978–; Dir., St. Louis Cnty. AV Ctr., 1966–78; Resrch. Asst., N. Circle Proj., 1965–66; Tchr., Mehlville Sch. Dist., 1961–65. **Educ.:** Ctrl. MO State Univ., 1957–62, BS (Chem.); IN Univ., 1967, MS (Comm.); St. Louis Univ., 1979, PhD (Admin.). **Orgs.:** ALA. AECT: Int. Frdm. (1976–78); Conv. Strg. Com. EFLA: Bd. of Dir. (1969–75). IL AV Assn. Various other orgs. Cnsrtm. of Univ. Film Ctrs.: Promo. (1978). Rotary Club: Hosplty. (1980). Phi Delta Kappa: Legis. Com.; Prog. Com. Natl. Univ. Ext. Assn. **Honors:** Media Assn., St. Louis, V.C. McCluer Awd., 1973. **Pubns.:** "Can You Get Films When You Need Them?" *AV Instr.* (S. 1978); "An Extension of the Friedman Test to Multi-Group Designs When the Original Data are Ranks," *Jnl. of Educ. Stats.* (1979); Various speeches and media productions. **Activities:** 1, 10; 17, 25, 32; 63, 67, 93 **Addr.:** University of Illinois Film Center - 1325 S. Oak, Champaign, IL 61820.

Owens, H. Jean (Ag. 3, 1944, Grand Rapids, MI) Dir., Lrng. Resrcs. Cntr., Inst. of Grntlgy., Wayne St. Univ., 1976–; Libn., Detroit Pub. Schs., 1969–75. **Educ.:** West. MI Univ., 1965–68, BS (Soclgy.); Wayne State Univ., 1975, MSLS; Med. Libn., Cert. **Orgs.:** SLA. Grntlgy. Libns. for Org. Recs. Mgt. Assn. Natl. Cncl. on Aging. **Pubns.:** *Directory of Gerontological Libraries in the United States* (1980); *An Analytical Survey of Libraries in Gerontological Centers* (1977). **Activities:** 1, 12; 15, 17, 39; 95-Grntlgy. **Addr.:** 9000 E. Jefferson, Apt. 7-5, Detroit, MI 48214.

Owens, Lessie V. (Ag. 9, 1945, Bucksport, SC) Branch Libn., DC Pub. Lib., 1975–; Asst. Branch Libn., 1971–75, Adult Readrs. Adv., 1969–71, Asst. Chld. Libn., 1967–69. **Educ.:** Howard Univ., 1963–67, BS (Bot., Allied Sci.); Univ. of MD, 1969–72, MLS 1972, Cert. (Lib. Srvs. to Disadv.); DC Dept. of Human Resrcs., 1974, Cert. (Mgt. Trng.); Metro. WA Cncl. of Gvts., 1977, Cert. Simmons Coll., 1979, Cert. (Lib. Mgt.). **Orgs.:** ALA: JMRT (1980); LIRT (1980). Friendship Cmnty. Settlement Hse. Bd. Adv. Bd. Juvenile Justice Proj., Near NE and SE DC. SW Fest. of The Arts Com. SW Schol. Com. **Pubns.:** Ed., *Young Voices, New Drums* (1980). **Activities:** 9; 16, 17, 21; 75 **Addr.:** 804 Geranium St. N.W., Washington, DC 20012.

Owens, Martha Armistead (Mrs. Joseph J. Jr.) (Ja. 12, 1930, Washington, DC) Head Libn., Lynnhaven Jr. HS, 1974–; Head Libn., Kellam HS, 1969–74; Asst. Libn., First Colonial HS, 1966–69; Tchr., Virginia Beach Schs., 1956–61; Tchr., Ingleside Elem., 1954–55; Broad Creek Jr. High, 1951–53. **Educ.:** James Madison Univ., 1947–51, BMEd (Msc.); Coll. of William and Mary, 1960–66, LS Cert.; Old Dominion Univ., 1969–74, MSEd (Sec. Admin., Supvsn.); Cath. Univ. of Amer., 1979–81, MSLS; various crs. **Orgs.:** ALA: AASL. VA LA. VA Educ. Media Assn. Virginia Beach LA: Pres. (1974–75); Exec. Bd. (1980–81); Nsltr. Ed. (1974–76, 1979–81). Norfolk Panhellenic Assn. AAUW. Natl. Educ. Assn. VA Educ. Assn. various orgs. **Honors** Kappa Delta Pi; Beta Phi Mu, 1981. **Activities:** 10; 17, 31, 39; 63, 95-PR. **Addr.:** Lynnhaven Junior High School Library, 1250 Bayne Dr., Virginia Beach, VA 23454.

Owens, Noel A.S. (D. 31, 1918, Vancouver, BC) Libn., Soc. Sci., Univ. of Calgary, 1971–; Soc. Sci. Biblgphr., Northwest. Univ., 1969–71, Chief, Ref. and Spec. Srvs., 1963–69, Head, Gvt. Pubns., 1959–63; Ref. Libn., Univ. of BC, 1951–57. **Educ.:** Univ. of BC, 1935–37, 1946–48, BA (Hist.); Univ. of Toronto, 1950–51, BLS; Univ. of BC, 1948–49, 1956–57, MA (Hist.). **Orgs.:** ALA. Can. LA. Foothills LA. LA of AB. **Pubns.:** "The F.W. Howay and R.L. Reid Collection of Canadiana at the University of British Columbia," *BC Lib. Qtly.* (O. 1959). **Activities:** 1; 15, 29, 39; 54, 92 **Addr.:** 5127 Carney Rd., N.W., Calgary, AB T2L 1G1 Canada.

Owens, Virginia L. (Jl. 11, 1918, Columbus, GA) Head, OK Resrcs. Branch, OK Dept. of Libs., 1976–, Assoc. Dir. for Plng. & Resrch., 1968–76, Grants-in-Aid Coord., 1966–67, Pub. Lib. Consult., 1957–66; Adult Srvs. Coord., OK City Libs., 1956–57; Asst. to Dir., 1948–55. **Educ.:** OK City Univ., 1936–39, BA (Eng. Lit.); Univ. of IL, 1956, MLS; Eng. Tchg. Cert., OK City Univ., 1939–40. **Orgs.:** ALA: Cncl. (1962–66); RASD, Exec. Bd. (1972–74). Amer. Assn. of State Libns.: Exec. Bd. (1967–70). OK LA: Pres. (1968–69); Stan. for Pub. Libs. Com. (1979–); Ed., *OK Libn.* (1958–60). SWLA. OK Women's Posse of the Westerners. White House Conf. on Aging: Del. (1961). **Pubns.:** "Community Delivery Services," *ALA Yearbook* (1977); "Bookmobiles," *ALA Yearbook* (1976). **Activities:** 2, 13; 17, 29; 73 **Addr.:** 5304 N. Hudson, Oklahoma City, OK 73118.

Owens, Warren Spencer (D. 28, 1921, Massena, NY) Dean of Instr. Srvs., Dir. of Libs., Univ. of ID, 1968–; Dir. of Libs., Temple Univ., 1961–68; Asst. to Dir. for Budget & Persnsl., Supvsr., Div. Libs., Univ. of MI, 1952–61; Instr., Univ. of ND, 1950–52. **Educ.:** Kalamazoo Coll., 1939–43, BA (Eng.); Univ. of Chicago, 1946–49, MA (Eng.); Univ. of MI, 1952–53, AMLS. **Orgs.:** Pac. NW LA: 1st VP (1971–73); Pres. (1973–75). ID LA: Ch., Lib. Dev. Com. (1971–72). ALA. Ballet Folk of Moscow: Bd. of Dir. (Secy. 1975–77, Ch. 1977–78). Friends of KUID: Bd. of Dir. (Secy., 1979–). Moscow United Way: Bd. of Dir. (Ch., 1972). **Honors:** Phi Kappa Phi: Pres., ID Chap. (1980). **Activities:** 1; 17 **Addr.:** University of Idaho Library, Moscow, ID 83843.

Owings, Loren C. (S. 29, 1928, San Fernando, CA) Col. Dev. Libn., Shields Lib., Univ. CA, Davis, 1969–, Head, Loan Dept., Gen. Lib., 1964–69, Asst. Head, Loan Dept., Gen. Lib., 1963–64; Soc. Sci. Tchr., Lompoc Jr. HS (CA), 1961–62. **Educ.:** Univ. of CA, Berkeley, 1948–53, AB (Hist.), 1953–57, MA (Hist.), 1962–63, MLS. **Orgs.:** Assn. for the Bibl. of Hist.: Mem. Com. (Ch., 1979). Org. of Amer. Hist. Agr. Hist. Socty.: *Agri. Hist.* (Consult. Ed.). **Pubns.:** *Environmental Values, 1860–1972* (1976); *The American Communitarian Tradition, 1683–1940* (1971). **Activities:** 1; 15, 37, 41; 55, 65, 92 **Addr.:** Collection Development Dept., Shields Library, University of California, Davis, Davis, CA 95616.

Ownby, Margaret H. (N. 8, 1940, Maryville, TN) Libn., North. VA Trng. Ctr. for the Mentally Retarded, 1978–; Sr. Ed., Natl. Un. Cat. Pubn. Proj., Lib. of Congs., 1969–78, Catlgr., Descr. Cat. Div., 1964–69. **Educ.:** TN Temple Univ., 1959–63, BA (Eng.); George Peabody Coll., 1963–64, MLS. **Orgs.:** ALA: ASCLA, Mem. Actv. Grp. on Lib. Srvs. to Developmentally Disabled Persons (Vice-Ch., Ch. Elect, 1980–81). VA LA. North. VA Assn. for Retarded Citizens. Epilepsy Fndn. of America. Epilepsy Assn. of VA. **Pubns.:** Jt. auth., "A Demonstration Project of Model Library Programs for Institutionalized Mentally Retarded and Multiply Handicapped Persons, Final Report" (1979). **Activities:** 5; 15, 36, 48; 63, 72 **Addr.:** 6419 Joyce Rd., Alexandria, VA 22310.

Owsley, Lucile C. (Ag. 3, 1934, Austin, TX) Chief, Lib. Srvs., Vets. Admin. Med. Cntr., Salisbury, NC, 1975; Chief, Lib. Srvs., Vets. Admin. Hosp., Boston, 1972–75; Persnl. Spec., Vets. Admin. Hosp., WY, 1969–72; Chief, Lib. Srvs., Vets. Admin. Hosp., MO, 1964–69; Recreation Spec., Vets. Admin. Hosp., TX, 1957–62. **Educ.:** TX Tech. Coll., 1953–57, BA (Gvt.); TX Woman's Univ., 1962–63, MLS; Simmons Coll., 1974, (Med. Lib.); Med. LA, 1975, Cert. **Orgs.:** Med. LA: Hosp. Lib. Sect., Prog. Com.; Mid–Atl. Reg. Grp. SLA. Altrusa Clb. of Amer. Daughters of Amer. AAUW. **Activities:** 4; 17, 32 **Addr.:** Veterans Administration, Medical Center Library, 1601 Brenner Ave., Salisbury, NC 28144.

Oxley, Anna Ruth (Ja. 12, 1947, Summerville Centre, Nova Scotia) Scotia-Fundy Reg. Libn., Fisheries and Oceans, Can., 1977–. Asst. Univ. Libn., Tech. Srvs., Dalhousie Univ., 1971–77. **Educ.:** Dalhousie Univ., 1964–68, (Eng. Lit.), 1969–71, (LS). **Orgs.:** Can. LA. Can. Assn. of Spec. Libs. Atl. Prov. LA: Nova Scotia VP (1972–73). **Pubns.:** *AAU/BNA Project: Systems Description* (1977); "Libraries in Atlantic Canada," *Can. Jnl. of Info. Sci.* (My. 1978); various papers. **Activities:** 4, 14-lib. netwk.; 17, 24, 34; 56, 58, 65 **Addr.:** 920 Belleville Ave., Halifax, NS B3H 3L7 Canada.

Oxley, Philip C. (N. 18, 1926, Lincoln, NE) Ref. Libn., Law, Columbia Univ. Law Sch. Lib., 1971–; Head Libn., Hughes, Hubbard and Reed, 1970–71; Ref. Libn., Bard Coll., 1967–70; Ref. Libn., Baruch Coll. of Bus. and Pub. Admin., 1963–67. **Educ.:** Univ. of CO, 1956–60, AB (Hist.); Rutgers Univ., 1962–63, MLS. **Orgs.:** AALL. Amer. Socty. of Indxrs. **Pubns.:** Cmplr., various subj. indxs. **Activities:** 1, 12; 30, 31, 39; 61, 77, 78 **Addr.:** Columbia University Law School Library, Box 22, 435 W. 116th St., New York, NY 10027.

Oxtoby, Fred B. (Mr. 13, 1918, Huron, SD) Retired. Sr. Descr. Catlgr., Lib. of Congs., 1967–81; Chief, Cat. Dept., John Crerar Lib., 1964–66; Chief, Acq. Dept., 1962–63; Head Catlgr., Lib., IL Inst. of Tech., 1948–62. **Educ.:** IL Coll., 1935–39, BA (Eng.); Univ. of IL, 1939–40, BS (LS), 1941–42, 1946–47, MA (LS). **Orgs.:** SLA: various coms. (1960–70). **Honors:** Phi Beta Kappa; Beta Phi Mu. **Activities:** 4; 20 **Addr.:** 801 A Street, S.E., Washington, DC 20003.

Oxton, John G. (S. 14, 1939, New York, NY) Mgr. Pubn., Lib. Srvs., IBM Corp., 1979–; Mgr., Resrch. Lib., 1975–79, Mgr., Lib. Prcs. Ctr., 1970–75. **Educ.:** Fordham Univ., 1964, BS; Pratt Inst., 1966, MLS. **Orgs.:** SLA. **Pubns.:** "Copyright Compliance Program," *Jnl. of Lib. Autom.* (Mr. 1980). **Activities:** 12; 17, 33, 40 **Addr.:** Publication & Library Services, P.O. Box 218, Yorktown Heights, NY 10598.

Oyler, David K. (Jl. 17, 1938, Chicago, IL) Dir., Lib. Humboldt State Univ., 1976–; Dir., Steenbock Meml. Lib., 1972–76; Asst. Dir., Lib., Univ. of WA, 1968–72; Forestry and Agr. Sci. Libn., CO State Univ. Lib., 1966–68; Circ. libn. and Asst. Ref. Libn., OR State Univ., 1962–1966. **Educ.:** Univ. of CA, Los Angeles, 1959–61, BA (Soclgy.); Univ. of South. CA, 1961–62, MSLS; Univ. of MD, 1972 (Cert., Lib. Admin.). **Orgs.:** SLA. ASIS. CA LA. ALA: ACRL, Bd. Dir. (1977–79), Cont. Educ. Com. (1979–81), Sci. Tech. Sect. (Ch., 1979), Agr. Bio. Sci. Sect., Various com.; LAD, Com. Econ. Status, Welfare (1976–78). **Pubns.:** *The Impact of the Forest and Forest Industry on The Environment: A Study of Bibliographic Coverage* (1975); *CAIN on-line at the University of Wisconsin* (1975); "Indexes to Forestry Literature - a bibliographic appraisal," *Jnl. of Forestry* (1977); "Specialized Data Base Utilization," *Agr. Lib. Info.* (1976). **Activities:** 1; 17 **Addr.:** 103 Jensen Dr., McKinleyville, CA 95521.

Oyler, Patricia Gail (N. 11, 1943, New York, NY) Assoc. Prof., Simmons Coll. Grad. Sch. of Lib. & Info. Sci., 1974–; Visit. Lectr., Univ. of Denver Grad. Sch. of Libnshp., 1978; Head, Tech. Srvs. Dept., Erie Metro. Lib., 1973–74; Lectr., Univ. of Pittsburgh Grad. Sch. of Lib. & Info. Sci., 1972–74; Libn., Tech. Docum. Dept., Alfa-Laval, Tumba, Sweden, 1969–70; Catlgr., Royal Lib. of Stockholm, 1969; Ref. Libn., Carnegie Lib. of Pittsburgh, 1966–68. **Educ.:** Chestnut Hill Coll., 1961–65, AB (Eng.); Univ. of Stockholm, 1968–69, (LS, Soclgy.); Univ. of Pittsburgh, 1978, PhD (LS); Simmons Coll., 1975–77, MA (Mgt.). **Orgs.:** ALA: RTSD/CCS Exec. Bd. (1980–82); Beta Phi Mu Awd. Jury (1979–1980); RTSD/LED Com. on Educ. for Resrcs. & Tech. Srvs. (Ch., 1977–1978). AALS: *Jnl. of Educ. for Libnshp.* Ed. Bd. (1979–1983). MA LA: Tech. Srvs. Sect., Ch., (1977–79); Exec. Bd. (1978–79). New Eng. LA. Other orgs. AAUP: Exec. Bd., Simmons Chap., (1977–79). **Honors:** Simmons Coll., Oper. Mgt. Awd., 1976; Univ. of Pittsburgh, August Alpers Awd., 1967. **Pubns.:** "Public Libraries, Scandinavia," *Encyc. of Lib. and Info. Sci.* (1978); "Interlibrary Loan, International" *Encyc. of Lib. and Info. Sci.* (1974). **Activities:** 9, 11; 17, 20, 25, 26; 56, 59, 75 **Addr.:** Simmons College, Graduate School of Library and Information Science, 300 The Fenway, Boston, MA 02115.

Ozaki, Hiroko (Ap. 25, 1939, Tokyo, Japan) Ref. Libn., Lib. Documtn. Ctr., Natl. Lib. of Can., 1981–, Subj. Anal., Cat. Branch, 1980, Head, NL Cols. Unit, Serials Cat., 1977–80; Docum. Libn., Transport Can. Ctrl. Lib., 1972–77; Catlgr., MNI, McGill Univ., Serials Libn., Natl. Lib. of Can.; Head, Lib. for Staff, Resrch. Sect., Kitosato Meml. Med. Lib., Keio Univ., Tokyo, Japan: various positions, 1962–70. **Educ.:** Keio Univ., 1958–62, BA (Arts, LS); Univ. of Ottawa, 1970–71, BLS, 1971–72, MLS. **Orgs.:** Can. LA. LA of Ottawa-Hull. Univ. Women's Club. Women's Can. Club. **Pubns.:** "Library and Information Science Abstracts," "Library Literature," *Lib. Syst.* (Tokyo) (1970); "The National Science Library Services in Canada," *Lib. Syst.* (Toyko) (1967); various bibls. **Activities:** 4, 12; 20, 30, 39; 62, 75, 92 **Addr.:** 77 Cartier St., Apt. 1208, Ottawa, ON K2P 1J7 Canada.

Ozolins, Karl L. (Mr. 11, 1923, Riga, Latvia) Dir., O'Shaughnessy Lib., Coll. of St. Thomas, 1980–; Dir., Lrng. Resrcs., Gustavus Adolphus Coll., 1973–80; Ch. and Prof., Lib. Sci., IL State Univ., 1970–73; Dir. of Lib., Augsburg Coll., 1960–70. **Educ.:** Augsburg Coll., 1949–51, BA (Liberal Arts); Univ. of MN, 1959–61, MA (LS), 1957–66, MA (Curric. and Instr.); Luther Theo. Semy., 1952–70, MDiv (Theo.); Univ. of MI, 1967–72, PhD (LS). **Orgs.:** ALA. MN LA. MN Educ. Media Org. Assn. for the Advnc. of Baltic Std.: Com. on Bibl., (Ch., 1974–80); Assoc. Ed., *Jnl. of Baltic Std.* (1974–). Lutheran Hist. Conf. **Honors:** Fulbright Lectureship in Taiwan, Visit. Prof., 1963–64; Beta Phi Mu, 1961. **Pubns.:** "An History of Augsburg Publishing House" microfilm (1961); *Book Publishing Trends in the American Lutheran Church and Its Antecedent Bodies* (1971); various reviews, articles in *Jnl. of Baltic Std.* (1976–). **Activities:** 1; 15, 17, 24; 57, 66, 90 **Addr.:** 1905 N. Fairview Ave., St. Paul, MN 55113.

P

Pabst, Kathleen T. (Yorkshire, Eng.) Dir., Mechanics' Inst. Lib., 1975–; Corp. Libn., Utah Intl., Inc., 1972–75; Ref. Libn., Standard Oil Co., 1971–72; Tech. Libn., U.S. Bur. of Mines, 1966–68. **Educ.:** Univ. of CA, Berkeley, BA (Eng. Lit.), MLS; Durham Univ., Eng., Cert. (Educ.). **Orgs.:** SLA: Mgt. Div. (Treas., 1980–82); Consult. Chap. (1978–80); Pubcty. Ch. (1975–76); Nom. Com. Chap. (1972). ALA. CA LA. Cmwlth. Clb. of CA. Tamalpais Cons. Clb. The Woodhouse Socty. **Activities:** 4, 12; 15, 17, 24; 55, 64, 67 **Addr.:** Mechanics' Institute Library, 57 Post St., San Francisco, CA 94104.

Pace, Julian H., Sr. (D. 11, 1938, Abilene, TX) Asst. to Libn., Instr. of Lib. Sci., Southwest MO State Univ., 1972–; Admin. Libn., Southwest Baptist Coll., 1963–72. **Educ.:** Baylor Univ., 1957–61, BA (Hist.); Univ. of OK, 1962–63, MLS. **Orgs.:** MO LA: Lib. Dev. Com. (1971–74); Exec. Bd. (1970–71, 1977–78). MO ACRL: Ch. (1970–71); Secy. (1968–69). Springfield Area Libns. Assn.: Treas. (1972–73); Ch. (1974–75). ALA. **Activities:** 1; 17, 19, 35; 92 **Addr.:** 535 E. Lindon, Bolivar, MO 65613.

Pachman, Barbara Margret (S. 19, 1922, Bergen, auf Rugen, Germany) Supvsr., Tech. Srvs., Paterson Pub. Lib., 1973–, Jr. Libn., 1948–73; Libn. U.S. Info. Ctr., Stuttgart, Germany, 1947. **Educ.:** Lib. Sch., Leipzig and Stuttgart, Germany, 1942–45. **Orgs.:** NJ LA: Tech. Srvs. Sect. (VP, Pres., 1979–81).

PROFESSIONAL ACTIVITIES: Institutions: 1. Acad. lib.; 2. Arch.; 3. Assn.; 4. Fed./Gvt. lib.; 5. Inst. lib.; 6. Mfr./Suppl.; 7. Milit. lib.; 8. Musm.; 9. Pub. lib.; 10. Sch. lib.; 11. Sch. of lib. sci.; 12. Spec. lib.; 13. State lib.; 14. (other). **Functions/Activities:** 15. Acq./Col. dev.; 16. Adult srvs.; 17. Admin.; 18. Apprais.; 19. Archit./Bldgs.; 20. Cat./Class.; 21. Chld. srvs.; 22. Circ.; 23. Cons./Pres.; 24. Consult.; 25. Cont. ed.; 26. Educ. lib. sci.; 27. Ext. srvs.; 28. Fund/Grants; 29. Gvt. pubs.; 30. Indx./Abs.; 31. Instr. lib. use; 32. Media srvs.; 33. Micro.; 34. Netwks./Coop.; 35. Persnl.; 36. PR; 37. Publshg.; 38. Recs. mgt.; 39. Ref. srvs.; 40. Repro.; 41. Resrch.; 42. Review.; 43. Secur.; 44. Serials; 45. Spec. col.; 46. Tech. srvs.; 47. Trustees/Bds.; 48. YA srvs.; 49. (other).

ALA. **Activities:** 9, 10; 20, 34, 46 **Addr.:** Technical Services, Paterson Free Public Library, 726 Market St., Paterson, NJ 07513.

Pachuta, June E. (Ag. 2, 1947, Lorain, OH) Slavic Biblgphr., Univ. of IL Lib., 1973–. **Educ.:** Case West. Rsv. Univ., 1966–69, BA (Russ., Fr.); OH State Univ., 1969–71, MA (Russ.); Univ. of Denver, 1972–73, MA (LS). Amer. Assn. for the Advnc. of Slavic Std. **Honors:** Phi Beta Kappa, 1969; Beta Phi Mu, 1981; Dobro Slovo, 1970. **Pubns.:** "Dostoevsky: Publications in East European Languages," *Bltn. of the Intl. Dostoevsky Socty.* (1975–79); "Resources for Southeastern European Studies at the University of Illinois Library," *Nsltr. of the Amer. Assn. for SE European Std.* (1978); "Annotated Bibliography," *The Family in Imperial Russia: New Lines of Historical Research* (1978). **Activities:** 1; 15, 39; 54, 55, 66 **Addr.:** Rm. 225 University Library, University of IL, 1408 W. Gregory Dr., Urbana, IL 61801.

Packard, Agnes K. (Je. 29, 1922, Brooklyn, NY) Libn., Huntington Hist. Socty., 1972–. **Educ.:** C. W. Post Coll., Long Island Univ., 1963–72, BA (Amer. Hist.), 1963–75, MLS; NY State, 1977, Pub. Libn. Prof. Cert. **Orgs.:** SLA: Long Island Chap. (Dir., 1977–78). SAA: Reg. Rep. (1979–80). ALA: NY Lib. Long Island Arch. Conf. (Secy., Treas., 1973–). Suffolk Cnty. LA. Guild of Bookworkers. Amer. Inst. for Cons. **Pubns.:** *Survey of Photograph Collection of Suffolk County (NY)* (1979). **Activities:** 2, 12; 15, 17, 45; 55, 69 **Addr.:** 18 Homestead Path, Huntington, NY 11743.

Packer, Joan Garrett (Je. 20, 1947, Houston, TX) Head Ref. Libn., Ctrl. CT State Coll., 1981–, Asst. Curric. Libn., 1971–81; Co. Libn., Houston Lighting and Power, 1969–70. **Educ.:** Univ. of TX, 1965–68, BA (Gvt.), 1968–69, MS (LS); Ctrl. CT State Coll., 1975–80, MA (Hist.). **Orgs.:** SLA: Rcrt. Ch. (1974–75); Hosplty. Ch. (1975–76); Asst. Ed., *SLA Bltn.* (1980–81). Reading is Fundamental Comsn. **Honors:** Phi Delta Kappa, 1978; Phi Alpha Theta, 1978. **Pubns.:** Abs., *Historical Abstracts, America History and Life* (1981–). **Activities:** 1; 15, 20, 39; 63, 72, 89 **Addr.:** Elihu Burritt Library, Central Connecticut State College, New Britain, CT 06032.

Packer, Katherine H. (Mr. 20, 1918, Toronto, ON) Prof. and Dean, Univ. of Toronto Fac. of LS, 1979–, Assoc. Prof., 1975–78, Asst. Prof., 1967–75; Chief Libn., ON Coll. of Educ., 1964–67; Head Catlgr., York Univ. Lib., 1963–64; Catlgr., Univ. of Toronto Lib., 1959–63. **Educ.:** Univ. of Toronto, 1937–41, BA; Univ. of MI, 1950–53, AMLS; Univ. of MD, 1970–75, PhD. **Orgs.:** ALA. Can. LA. Can. Assn. of Lib. Schs. AALS. Other orgs. **Honors:** Soc. Sci. and Hum. Resrch. Cncl. of Can., Grant, 1979–80; Phi Kappa Phi, 1973; Univ. of MI Sch. of LS, Disting. Alum. Awd., 1981. **Pubns.:** "Educational Implications of the Two-Year Program in Library Science" in *Extended Library Education Programs* (1980); Jt. auth., "The Importance of SDI for Current Awareness in Fields with Severe Scatter of Information," *Jnl. of the ASIS* (My. 1979); Jt. auth., "The Imprint Date in the Anglo-American Cataloging Rules", *Lib. Resrcs. & Tech. Srvs.* (Spr. 1976). **Activities:** 1, 11; 17, 26, 30; 56 **Addr.:** Faculty of Library Science, University of Toronto, 140 St. George St., Toronto, ON M5S 1A1 Canada.

Padgett, Frances (Buchanan) (Jl. 20, 1922, Fordwick, VA) Retired, 1981–; Libn., Baker Cnty. Sch. Syst., NE FL State Hosp., 1980–81; Media Spec., Baker Cnty. Sch. Bd., Baker Cnty. HS, 1959–80; Libn., Gilchrist Cnty. Sch. Bd., Trenton and Bell Schs., 1958–59; Libn., Collier Cnty. Sch. Bd., Immokalee Sch., 1955–58; Libn., Fluvanna Cnty. HS, 1951–55; Libn., Pasco Cnty. HS, 1946–51. **Educ.:** James Madison Univ., 1941–45, BS (Educ., LS); various grad. crs. **Orgs.:** ALA. FL LA. FL Assn. Sch. Libns. SELA. FL Educ. Assn. Christ. Libns. Flwshp. Baker Cnty. Educ. Assn. First Bapt. Church. **Activities:** 10, 12; 17, 21, 48; 63, 72, 90 **Addr.:** 505 S. 7th St., Macclenny, FL 32063.

Padua, Noelia (S. 3, 1943, San Sebastián, PR) Law Lib. Dir., Cath. Univ., PR, 1976–, Asst. Prof., Educ. Dept., 1975–76, Ref. Libn., 1962–74. **Educ.:** Cath. Univ. of PR, 1963–67, BSSE (Comm. Educ.); Univ. of PR, 1969–70, MLS; Cath. Univ. of PR, 1971–74, JD. **Orgs.:** AALL: By-Laws Com. Assn. de Bib. de Derecho: VP. Socty. de Bibtcr. de PR. Coll. de Abogados de PR. Amer. Bar Assn. **Activities:** 17; 57, 77 **Addr.:** Catholic University of PR, Law Library, Ponce, PR 00731.

Pady, Donald Stuart (Ag. 17, 1937, Kansas City, MO) Assoc. Prof., Ref. Libn., Bibl. IA State Univ. Lib., 1968–; Head, Hum. Ref. Div. KS State Univ. Lib., 1966–68; Cat., Hum. Ref. Libn., AZ State Univ. Lib., 1962–66. **Educ.:** Univ. of KS, 1955–59, BA (Eng., Hist.); Emporia State Univ., 1961–62 MLS (Libnshp.); IA State Univ., 1971–77, MA (Eng.). **Orgs.:** SLA: Musms., Arts and Hum. Sect. Socty. for the Std. of Midwestern Lit.: Bibl. Ed. (1973–). Masonic Lodge: Arcadia Lodge #249, Educ. Com. (1978–). **Honors:** Phi Alpha Theta. **Pubns.:** *Scientific, Agricultural, and Technological Artifacts in Iowa* (1979); *Horses and Horsemanship; a Bibliography of Books in the Iowa State University Library* (1973); "Matthew Arnold to Thomas Brower Peacock," *Notes and Queries* (D. 1974); "Scientific and Technological Artifacts among Iowa's Libraries, Museums, and Private Collections: a Computer-Produced, Annotated and Illustrated Index," *Gas Engine Mag.* (S.–O. 1977); "A London Medical Satire of 1607," *Jnl. of the Hist. of Med.* (Jl. 1978); various poems, articles, reviews, indxs. **Activities:** 1, 12; 15, 39, 41; 54, 55, 69 **Addr.:** 212 N. Riverside Dr., Ames, IA 50010.

Page, Benjamin Frederick (Ap. 16, 1927, Green Lake, WI) Assoc. Prof., Assoc. Dir., Sch. of Libnshp., Univ. of WA, 1966–; Asst. Prof., Univ. of RI, 1964–65; Doct. Cand., Resrch. Asst., Univ. of IL, 1959–64; Asst. Libn., NM West. Coll., 1956–59; Libn., Escanaba HS, 1954–56. **Educ.:** Ripon Coll., 1945–49, BA (Eng.); Univ. of WI, 1953–54, MALS (Libnshp.); Univ. of IL, 1959–64, (Libnshp.). **Orgs.:** ALA. SLA. **Honors:** Beta Phi Mu, 1954; Phi Kappa Phi, 1962. **Pubns.:** Jt. Ed., "Trends in Bibliographic Control: International Issues," *Lib. Trends* (Ja. 1977).†

Page, Betty Burke (Je. 29, 1935, Durham, CT) Lib. Media Prog. Ch., K-12, Guilford Pub. Schs., 1966–; Libn., Guilford HS, 1958–; Tchr., Guilford Lakes Sch., 1957–58. **Educ.:** South. CT State Coll., 1953–57, BS (Elem. Educ./LS), 1957–60, MS (Educ.), 1968–70, 6th Yr. (Educ. Supvsn. Admin.). **Orgs.:** ALA: Disting. Srv. Awd. for Sch. Admin. Com. (1970). CT Educ. Media Assn.: Elem. Sch. Lib. Dev. Proj. (1972); Schol. Com. (1974–75). Middlesex Lib. Srv. Ctr.: Adv. Bd. (1979–). South. CT Lib. Cncl.: Exec. Bd. (1979–80). CT Educ. Assn. Natl. Educ. Assn. **Pubns.:** Reviews. **Activities:** 10; 32; 63 **Addr.:** Guilford High School Library, New England Rd., Guilford, CT 06437.

Page, Kathryn (S. 30, 1949, Keokuk, IA) Ref. Coord., Bay Area Lib. and Info. Syst., 1981–; Ref. Coord., 49–99 Coop. Lib. Syst., 1976–81; AV Libn., Stockton-San Joaquin Cnty. Pub. Lib., 1974–76; Ref. Libn., Sacramento City-Cnty. Lib., 1972–74. **Educ.:** Stanford Univ., 1967–71, BA (Art Hist.); Univ. of CA, Berkeley, 1971–72, MLS. **Orgs.:** ALA. CA LA. **Activities:** 13; 34, 39 **Addr.:** BALIS Reference Center, c/o Oakland Public Library, 125-14th St., Oakland, CA 94612.

Page, Melda Jeanne W. (Ja. 10, 1941, Morristown, NJ) Chief Libn., Vets. Admin. Med. & Reg. Ofc. Ctr., Togus, ME, 1972–, Libn., 1971–72; Chld. Libn., Lewiston (ME) Pub. Lib., 1969–70; Catlgr. & Instr. FL State Univ. Lib., 1968–69; Elem. Sch. Libn., Lewiston (ME) Sch. Syst., 1965–67. **Educ.:** Emory Univ., 1959–63, BA (Pol. Sci.); FL State Univ., 1967–68, MLS. **Orgs.:** New Eng. LA: Hosp. Lib. Sect. (Ch., 1980–81). Hlth. Sci. Lib & Info. Coop. of ME: Co-ch. (1974–75). Med. LA. N. Atl. Hlth. Sci. Libs.: Conf. Plng. Com. (1979). Other orgs. Sch. Admin. Dist. #47, Oakland, ME: Dir. (1978–). Robertson Hlth. Ctr., Belgrade, ME: Dir. (1978–81). **Honors:** Phi Beta Kappa, 1963; Beta Phi Mu, 1968; Vets. Admin., Chief Med. Dir. Cmdn., 1980. **Pubns.:** The Reference Interview, Videocassette (1976, 1978). **Activities:** 4, 12; 15, 17; 80, 92 **Addr.:** RFD #1, Belgrade, ME 04917.

Page, Vera Nadia (N. 14, 1953, Chicago, IL) Frgn. Law Libn., Univ. of WI, 1978–; Libn., Dewitt, Sundby, Huggett & Schumacher, 1978–; Actg. Phys. Libn., Univ. of WI, 1977, Ref. Libn., 1976–77. **Educ.:** Univ. of WI, Baraboo, 1971–73; Univ. of WI, Madison, 1973–75, BA (Span.), 1975–76, MLS. **Orgs.:** AALL. Madison Area Lib. Cncl.: Pubns. Com. (Ch., 1980); Lib. Expo Com. (1978); Educ. and Prog. Com. (1978). **Activities:** 1, 12; 20, 46; 77 **Addr.:** Law Library, University of Wisconsin—Madison, Madison, WI 53706.

Pagel, Doris Bertha (F. 19, 1928, St. Charles, MN) Prof., Lib. Media Educ. Dept., Mankato State Univ., 1965–, Campus Sch. Libn., 1959–64; Chld. Libn., Rochester (MN) Public Lib., 1955–58; Catlgr.-Biblgphr., Law Lib., Univ. of MN, 1953–55; Ref.-Circ. Libn., Sioux City (IA) Pub. Lib., 1950–53. **Educ.:** Univ. of MN, 1947–50, BA (LS), 1958–59, BS (Elem. Educ.), 1958, MA (LS); Univ. of IL, 1964–66, Cert. of Advnc. Std. (LS); Univ. of NE, 1977, PhD (Adult Educ.). **Orgs.:** MN Assn. of Sch. Libns.: Pres. (1975–76). MN Educ. Media Org.: Ch., Lib. Coop. and Networking Com. (1977–79). Frnds. of the MN Valley Reg. Lib. Org.: Fndr., First Pres. (1977–78). ALA. MN Adult Educ. Assn.: Secy. (1972–74). MN Assn. for Cont. Adult Educ.: VP, Ch., Lib. and Info. Resrcs. Sect. (1978–79). **Honors:** Beta Phi Mu, 1965; MN LA, MN Libn. of the Yr., 1979. **Pubns.:** "Teaching the Principles of Intellectual Freedom," *MN Libs.* (Aut. 1979). **Activities:** 10, 11; 21, 31, 34; 50, 74 **Addr.:** 405 N. Fifth St., Mankato, MN 56001.

Pagés, José R. (Mr. 30, 1929, Matanzas, Cuba) Head, Acq. Dept., Univ. of GA Law Lib., 1968–; Frgn. and Intl. Law Libn., Univ. of IL, 1967–68, Asst. Law Libn., Recs. Prcs., 1965–67. **Educ.:** Inst. De Matanzas, 1943–48, BA; Univ. of Havana, 1948–54, Doctor of Laws; KS State Tchrs. Coll., 1964–65, MS (LS). **Orgs.:** AALL: Frgn. and Intl. Law Com. **Activities:** 1; 15, 17, 29; 77, 78, 92 **Addr.:** University of GA School of Law Library, Athens, GA 30602.

Pagonis, Stella (Mr. 31, 1950, Charleroi, PA) Info. Consult., Control Data Corp., Tech. and Info. Srvs., 1981–; Lib. Supvsr., Gulf Oil, Bus. Resrch. Lib., 1978–80; Head Libn., Bus. Info. Ctr., Gulf Oil, Corporate Plng., 1976–78, Info. Anal., 1973–76. **Educ.:** Univ. of Pittsburgh, 1967–71, BA (Eng.), 1972–73, MLS (Resrcs.), 1979–80, Advnc. Cert. (Info. Sci.). **Orgs.:** SLA: Pittsburgh Chap. (Pres. Elect, 1979–80); Treas. (1976–78); Finance Com. (Ch., 1974–76). ASIS. OLUG. Alum. Assn.: Place. Wkshp. (Ch., 1978–79). Exec. Women's Cncl.: Grt. Pittsburgh. **Honors:** Beta Phi Mu. **Addr.:** Control Data Corp., P.O. Box O, HQV001, Minneapolis, MN 55440.

Pai, Herman Hsung (F. 18, 1929, Peking, China) Assoc. Libn., Stanford Univ., 1970–; Admin. Ofcr., Chin. Info. Srvs., 1967–70; Instr., Taipei Normal Coll. 1958–65. **Educ.:** Taiwan Normal Univ., 1952–56, BEd (Educ.); Univ. of HI, 1965–67, MEd (Educ. Admin.); CA State Univ., 1972–73, MLS. **Orgs.:** ALA. Med. LA. North. CA Med. Lib. Grp. Amer. Chin. Libns. Assn. **Activities:** 1; 20, 39; 80 **Addr.:** Lane Medical Library, Stanford University Medical Center, Stanford, CA 94305.

Painter, Shirley Roe (Je. 12, 1930, Auburn, WA) Lib., Media Spec., Richland Sch. Dist., 1970–; Lib., Media Spec., Othello Sch. Dist., 1965–70, Elem. Sch. Tchr., 1956–65; Elem. Sch. Tchr., Enumclaw Sch. Dist., 1955–56. **Educ.:** WA State Univ., 1948–51; Univ. of Puget Sound, 1953–55, BA (Educ.); Ctrl. WA Univ., 1969–70, MEd (AV); various crs. **Orgs.:** WA Lib. Media Assn.: Jnl. *The Medium* (Ed., Elem. Levels, 1977–80). WA LA: Bd. of Dir. (1977–79). WA State Assn. of Sch. Libns.: Elem. Levels (State Ch., 1973); State Mem. Ch., (1974). WA Assn. for Educ. Comm. and Tech.: State Bd. of Dir. (1973–76). First Untd. Methodist Church: Pac. Northwest Anl. Conf. (1974–80). Housing and Urban Dev. Block Grant Com.: City of Kennewick. Richland Educ. Assn. Nsltr. Ed. (1971–72); Bd. (1971–73). Natl. Educ. Assn. Dem. Party: Ctrl. Com. (1978–80). **Pubns.:** "K–12 Resource Center," *Resrcs. for Tchg. and Lrng.* (Spr. 1975); various articles in *Lib. Leads*, 1973–76. **Activities:** 10; 21, 31, 32; 50, 63 **Addr.:** 118 W. 23rd Pl., Kennewick, WA 99336.

Palacios, Augusta Eliane (Jl. 1, 1927, Paris, France) Sr. Libn., Span.-Speaking, Los Angeles Cnty. Pub. Lib. Syst., 1972–; Libn. II, Univ. of South. CA, 1969–72; Sec. Sch. Tchr., ON, 1958–67. **Educ.:** Univ. of Vienna, Austria, 1946–55, PhD (Fr., Span.); LA State Univ., 1968–69, MLS, 1967, Spec. (Fr., Grmn., Span. Lang. Instr.). **Pubns.:** *Die spanischen Habsburger im spanischen Drama* (1955). **Activities:** 1, 9; 18, 20; 66 **Addr.:** 24711 Avalon Blvd., Wilmington, CA 90744.

Palais, Elliot S. (S. 12, 1933, Portland, ME) Ref. Libn., AZ State Univ., 1966–; Asst. Head, Ref. Dept., Washington Univ., 1962–66. **Educ.:** Bowdoin Coll., 1951–55, BA (Hist.); Univ. of MI, 1955–57, AMLS. **Pubns.:** "A Guide for Political Science Students," *Readrs. Adv. Srv.* (1978); "Significance of Subject Dispersion," *Jnl. of Acad. Libnshp.* (1976); "References to Indexes and Abstracts in Ulrich's International Periodicals Directory," *RQ* (1974); "Publications of the Royal Commission on Historical Manuscripts," *Col. and Resrch. Libs.* (1972); Abstctr., *America: History and Life;* various bk. reviews. **Activities:** 1; 15, 39, 42; 92 **Addr.:** AZ State University, Tempe, AZ 85281.

Palandri, Guido A. (N. 9, 1924, Portland, OR) Asst. Head, Cat. Dept., Univ. of OR, 1960–; Cat. Libn., Wayne State Univ., 1959–60; Cat. Libn., Univ. of Detroit, 1957–59. **Educ.:** Univ. of OR, 1946–49, BA (Frgn. Lang.); Univ. of CA, Berkeley, 1952–54, BLS; Univ. de Grenoble, 1951–52, dip. d'aptitude. **Honors:** Fulbright Grant, Grad. Std. in Italy, 1949–50. **Pubns.:** Ed., *Italian Images of Ezra Pound* (1979); "Waldport: an Interview with William Everson," *Imprint: OR* (Fall–Spr. 1978–79); "Beyond Vuturism: Back to Academic Librarianship," *Wilson Lib. Bltn.* (Mr. 1978). **Activities:** 1; 20, 39 **Addr.:** The Library, University of Oregon, Eugene, OR 97403.

Palerm, Catalina (Ja. 19, 1926, San Juan, PR) Asst. Prof., Dir. of Pubns., Fac. of Hum., Univ. of PR, 1976–; Assoc. Resrchr., Hist. Resrch. Ctr., Univ. of PR, 1969–72, Asst. Prof., Assoc. Dir., 1973–76; Asst. Prof., Fac. of Hum., Univ. of PR, 1972–. **Educ.:** Univ. of PR, BA (Pol. Sci., Econ., Hist.), MA (Pub. Admin.); Natl. Sch. for Archvsts., Libns. and Archaeologists, Madrid, Spain, Dipl. **Orgs.:** SAA. Amer. Rec. Mgt. Assn. Cncl. Intl. des Arch. Intl. Rec. Mgt. Fed. AAUP. Assn. of Caribbean Hist. Inst. of Hisp. Culture. Amer. Hist. Assn. **Honors:** Phi Alpha Theta. **Pubns.:** "Pequeño diccionario de paleografía," *Boletín de la Academia Puertorriqueña de la Historia;* "Los archivos en P.R. y la investigación histórica," *Revista Escuela Internacional de Archiveros;* "El municipio puertorriqueño," *Revista de Administración Pública;* "El municipio dentro de la planificación integral y sus proyecciones en el desarrollo nacional," *Revista de la Secretaría General de Municipios Iberoamericanos;* Jt. Auth., *Proceso abolicionista en Puerto Rico.* **Activities:** 1, 10; 37, 63 **Addr.:** Box 13254, Santiago, PR 00908.

Paliani, Mary Ann (Ja. 31, 1935, Rochester, NY) Mgr., Tech. Lib., Rockwell Intl. Energy Syst. Grp., 1975–; Mgr., Tech. Lib., Dow Chem., 1968–75, Info. Srvs. Supvsr., 1974–75; Ref. Libn., New York Pub. Lib., Sci. & Tech. Div., 1965–68; Lib. Supvsr., US Army Spec. Srvs., Giessen, Germany, 1962–64; Ref. Libn., Rochester Pub. Lib., 1960–62. **Educ.:** Univ. of Rochester, 1952–56, BA (Bio.); Syracuse Univ., 1959–60, MLS; Justus Liebig Univ., 1964–65. **Orgs.:** SLA: Chap. Pres (1970–71); Vice-ch., Ch., Nuclear Sci. Div. (1973–75). ASIS: Chap. Secy.-Treas. (1972). Socty. for Tech. Comm.: Chapt. Secy. (1973–74). CO Cncl. on Lib. Dev.: Rep. of Spec. Libs. (1973–76). Untd. Way. **Honors:** Beta Phi Mu, 1960. **Activities:** 12; 17; 56, 84, 91 **Addr.:** 3630 Iris Ave. B2, Boulder, CO 80301.

Special Subjects/Services: 50. Adult educ.; 51. Advert./Mktg.; 52. Aerosp.; 53. Agric.; 54. Area std.; 55. Arts/Hum.; 56. Autom.; 57. Bibl./Prtg.; 58. Bio. sci.; 59. Bus./Fin.; 60. Chem.; 61. Copyrt.; 62. Documtn.; 63. Educ.; 64. Engin.; 65. Env.; 66. Eth. grps.; 67. Film; 68. Food/Nutr.; 69. Geneal.; 70. Geo.; 71. Geol.; 72. Handcpd.; 73. Hist.; 74. Int. frdm.; 75. Info. sci.; 76. Insr.; 77. Law; 78. Legis.; 79. Math./Comp. sci.; 80. Med.; 81. Metals; 82. Nat. resrcs.; 83. Newsp.; 84. Nuc. sci.; 85. Oral hist.; 86. Petr./Energy; 87. Pharm.; 88. Phys./Astr./Math.; 89. Readg.; 90. Relig.; 91. Sci./Tech.; 92. Soc. sci.; 93. Telecom.; 94. Transp.; 95. (other).

Who's Who in Library and Information Services

Palko, Joanne D. (Ag. 14, 1941, Orange, NJ) Head, Cat. Dept., Univ. of CT, 1979–, Cat., Univ. of CT, 1975–79; Rare Bks., Spec. Col. Cat., North. IL Univ., 1967–75; Libn., Hum. Sect., Univ. of Notre Dame, 1964–67. **Educ.:** Ladycliff Coll., 1959–63, BA (Eng., Hist.); Univ. of MI, 1963–64, AMLS. **Orgs.:** ALA. New Eng. LA. New Eng. Tech. Srvs. Libns. **Activities:** 1; 20, 44, 46; 55, 75, 90 **Addr.:** 11 Brookside Ln., Coventry, CT 06238.

Palkovic, Mark A. (S. 22, 1954, Oberlin, OH) Record Libn., CCM Lib., Univ. of Cincinnati, 1981–; Hum., Msc. Cat., Libn. II, Auburn Univ., 1979–81; Asst. Cat. Libn., Instr., GA South. Coll., 1978–79. **Educ.:** OH Univ., 1972–76, BMus (Msc. Hist.), 1972–78, BA (Msc.); Kent State Univ., 1976–77, MLS. **Orgs.:** ALA. Msc. LA. Amer. Harp Socty.: Consult. and Reviewer. Phi Mu Alpha Sinfonia Prof. Msc. Fraternity. **Pubns.:** "Miniature Books at Auburn University," *Microbibliophile* (Jl. 1980). **Activities:** 1; 20, 24; 55 **Addr.:** College-Conservatory of Music, Gorno Library, University of Cincinnati, Cincinnati, OH 45221.

Palmer, David Cheetham (Ag. 26, 1925, Washington, DC) Asst. State Libn., NJ State Lib., 1969–, Actg. State Libn., 1975–78, Head, Readr. Srvs., 1965–69; Dir., Lib. Dev. Div., PA State Lib., 1964–65, Fld. Consult., Lib. Dev., 1961–64, Exec. Dir., Gvr. Comsn. on Pub. Lib. Dev. in PA, 1959–61, Exec. Secy., PA Lib. Srvy., 1957–59; various consult. **Educ.:** Peabody Cnsvty. of Msc., Johns Hopkins Univ., 1953, BS (Msc.); Rutgers Univ., 1955–56, MLS (Lbnship.). **Orgs.:** ALA: various coms. (1960–75). NJ LA: Lib. Dev. Com. (1968–75). State House Hist. Dist. Assn.: Pres. NJ Hist. Socty. Trent House Comsn.: Comsn. Frnds. of Trenton Pub. Lib.: Trustee. various orgs. **Honors:** State Lib. of PA, Adv. Cncl. on Lib. Dev., Cit. of Achvmt., 1965–; NJ LA, Disting. Srv. Awd., 1979–. Rutgers Grad. Sch., Lib. & Info. Std., Disting. Alumnus Awd., 1981. **Pubns.:** *Planning for a Nationwide System of Library Statistics* (1970); jt. auth., *Library Service in Pennsylvania, Present and Proposed* (1958); jt. auth., "Current Concepts in State Aid to Public Libraries," *Lib. Trends* (Jl. 1960); jt. auth., "Standards for State Libraries," *Lib. Trends* (O. 1972). **Activities:** 13; 17, 24, 25; 50, 59 **Addr.:** 336 W. State St., Trenton, NJ 08618.

Palmer, David Walter (N. 24, 1928, Detroit, MI) Lib. Dir., Univ. of MI, Flint, 1974–; Lib. Dir., Baldwin-Wallace Coll., 1968–74; Lib. Dir., Rockford Coll., 1964–68; Ref. Libn., CA State Univ., Humboldt, 1961–64; Pub. Info. Writer, Univ. of CA Press, 1959–60; Claims Rep., Royal Globe Insr. Grp., 1956–59; various tchg. positions. **Educ.:** Univ. of CA, Los Angeles, 1951, BA (Eng.), Univ. of CA, Los Angeles, Grad. Sch., 1951–52, (Eng.); Univ. of CA, 1961, MLS. **Orgs.:** ALA: ACRL. MI LA. Cncl. of State Coll. and Univ. Lib. Dirs. of MI. Univ. CA Lib. Sch. Alum. Assn. **Honors:** Dictionary of Intl. Biog., Cert. of Merit. **Pubns.:** *Quickly, Over the Wall* (1966); Ed., *Beloit Poetry Jnl.* (1964–67); "After Reading About the Latest Fascist Revival," *Quixote* (Ap. 1967); "After the Rain," *The Creat. Review* (Sum. 1962); "Afternoon," *The Creat. Review* (Sum. 1962); various articles, reviews, poems. **Activities:** 1, 2; 17, 37, 39; 55, 57, 89 **Addr.:** 919 Kensington Ave., Flint, MI 48503.

Palmer, Forrest Charles (O. 17, 1924, Burlington, WI) Prof. of Lib. Sci., Docum. Libn., James Madison Univ., 1974–; Head Libn., Head, Dept. of Lib. Sci., Madison Coll., 1962–74; Dir. of Libs., MS State Univ., 1955–62; Serials Libn., NC State Univ., 1950–55; Cat. Libn., Janesville Pub. Lib., 1949–50. **Educ.:** Valparaiso Univ., 1942–43, 1946–48, BA (Gvt.); George Peabody Coll. for Tchrs., 1948–49, BS (LS), 1951–53, MS (LS). **Orgs.:** ALA: ACRL (State Rep., 1957–60); Lib. Instr. RT Liaison Com. (1978–); various coms. Southeastern LA: Coll. and Univ. Sect. (Ch., 1960–62); Treas. (1974–76); various coms. VA LA: Ed., *VA Libn.* (1963–65); Pres. (1969–70); various ofcs. Republican Party: Harrisonburg City Com. (Vice-Ch., 1979–81). Presbyterian Church: Ruling Elder. **Honors:** Pi Gamma Mu, 1949; Beta Phi Mu, 1956; YMCA, Golden Triangle Awd., 1959; Alpha Beta Alpha, 1962. **Pubns.:** "Project REVAMP," *Wilson Lib. Bltn.* (Ap. 1978); "Simmons vs. Schwarzkopf," *Southeastern Libn.* (Fall 1977); Ed., *VA Libn.* (1963–65); Ed., *MS State Univ. Lib. Pubns.* (1955–62); various articles, reviews. **Activities:** 1, 11; 29, 39, 49-Law Library; 63, 75, 77 **Addr.:** Madison Memorial Library, James Madison University, Harrisonburg, VA 22807.

Palmer, Julia Reed (My. 4, 1915, New York, NY) Dir., Amer. Readg. Cncl., 1975–; Dir., Bkmobile. Srv. Trust, 1967–70. **Educ.:** Vassar Coll., 1933–35. **Orgs.:** NYLA: RASD, Lit. Com. ALA: YASD, Hi-Lo Com. Ctr. for the Bk. of the Lib. of Congs.: Adv. Com.; Radio and TV Com.; Readg. Improvement Com. **Honors:** ALA, ALA Notable Ref. Bk. Awd., 1974. **Pubns.:** *Read For Your Life* (1974); "An Open Letter to Librarians," *Top of the News* (Fall 1977); "Let's Get Them Reading," *The Bookmark* (Win. 1978); "Of Libraries and Literacy" ERIC; "Memo on the American Reading Council's Educational Program For Families" ERIC. **Activities:** 14; 49; 95 **Addr.:** American Reading Council, 20 W. 40th St., New York, NY 10018.

Palmer, Margaret Alison (D. 30, 1946, Birmingham, Eng.) Ministerial Libn., BC Mnstry. of Env., 1978–; Admin. Libn., BC Mnstry. of Recreation and Cons., 1977–78; Ref. Libn. Etobicoke Pub. Lib., 1970–77; Bus. Ref. Libn., Metro. Toronto Pub. Lib., 1970. **Educ.:** Carleton Univ., Ottawa, ON, 1965–69, BA (Soclgy.); Univ. of Toronto, 1969–70, BLS, 1972–76, MLS. **Orgs.:** BC LA. Gvt. Libs. Assn. of BC: Exec. Com. Inst. of Victoria Libns.: Exec. Com. Can. LA. SLA. Can. Assn. Info. Sci. **Activities:** 4, 9; 15, 17, 20 **Addr.:** BC Library, Ministry of Environment, Parliament Buildings, Victoria, BC V8V 1X4 Canada.

Palmer, Pamela R. (Ja. 21, 1949, Amory, MS) Head, Engin. Lib., Memphis State Univ., 1979–, Ref. Libn., 1973–79. **Educ.:** Univ. of MS, 1967–70, BAE (Eng. and LS); LA State Univ., 1971–72, MS (LS); Memphis State Univ., 1974–78, MA (Eng.). **Orgs.:** ALA. SELA. TN LA. AAUP. **Pubns.:** Ed., *The Robert R. Church Family of Memphis: A Guide to the Collection* (1979); Ed., *Subject Guide to Memphis State University Periodicals* (1977); Jt. Auth., "Subject Master's Degrees Among Academic Librarians in the Southeast," *Southeastern Libn.* (Fall 1978). **Activities:** 1, 12; 17, 31, 39; 55, 64 **Addr.:** 5957 Poplar Pike Ext. #4, Memphis, TN 38119.

Palmer, Paul Richard (Ja. 21, 1917, Cincinnati, OH) Libn., Columbiana Lib., Columbia Univ., 1974–, Libn., Thea. Arts Lib., 1967–74, Libn., Burgess-Carpenter-Classics Lib., 1951–67; Asst. Libn., Brooklyn Pub. Lib., 1950–51. **Educ.:** Univ. of Cincinnati, 1944–49, BA (Lit.); Columbia Univ., 1950–55 MA (Cont. Lit.), 1949–50 MS (LS). **Orgs.:** Thea. LA: Exec. Bd. of Dir., Rec. Secty. (1974–80). Bibl. Socty. of Amer. **Honors:** Phi Beta Kappa, 1949. **Pubns.:** Contrib., *The Hollywood Reliables* (1981); "D.H. Lawrence and the Q.B. in Sardinia," *Columbia Lib. Clmns.* (N. 1968); *Virginia Woolf, A Study of Her Novels* (1949); *D.H. Lawrence and His Travel Literature* (1955). **Activities:** 1, 2; 15, 17, 45; 55, 69 **Addr.:** Columbiana Library, 210 Low Memorial Library, Columbia University, New York, NY 10027.

Palmer, Raymond A. (My. 3, 1939, Louisville, KY) Exec. Dir., Med. LA, 1982–; Hlth. Sci. Libn., Wright State Univ., 1974–82; Asst. Libn., Francis A. Countway Lib. of Med., Harvard Med. Sch., 1969–74; Admin. Asst. to Dir., Welch Med. Lib., Johns Hopkins Med. Inst., 1966–69. **Educ.:** Univ. of Louisville, 1957–61, BA (Bio.); Univ. of KY, 1965–66, MS (LS). **Orgs.:** Med. LA Com. on Cont. Ed. (Ch., 1971–72); Bibl. and Info. Srvs. Assess. Com. (Ch., 1977–78); various coms. Miami Valley Assn. of Hlth. Sci. Libs.: various ofcs. Ch. (1977–79). Biomed. Comm. Netwk.: Bd. of Dir. (1978–). Dayton-Miami Valley Consrtm.: Lib. Div., Exec. Com. (1976–). various orgs. **Pubns.:** Jt. auth., "Interlibrary Loans for Hospital Libraries," *Library Practice in Hospitals: A Basic Guide* (1972); "Utopian Cataloging," *KOMRML Kommentary* (S. 1978); "The Operation of a Rational Acquisitions Committee," *Bltn. of the Med. LA* (Ja. 1977). **Activities:** 1, 12; 17, 32, 34; 80 **Addr.:** Medical Library Association 919 N. Michigan, Chicago IL 60611.

Palmer, Richard J. (N. 4, 1932, Madison, SD) Head Libn., Beal Lib., Macomb Intermediate Schs., 1974–; Instr., Lake MI Coll., 1965–73; Instr., IA Lakes Cmnty. Coll., 1962–65. **Educ.:** Dakota State Coll., 1950–54, BS (Hist.); St. Cloud State Univ., 1959–62, MS (Hist); West. MI Univ., 1973–74, MLS. **Orgs.:** ALA. MI LA. ASIS. **Activities:** 1, 12; 17, 24; 63 **Addr.:** Beal Library, Macomb Intermediate Schools, 44001 Garfield Rd., Mt. Clemens, MI 48044.

Palmer, Richard Phillips (Mr. 10, 1921, Milwaukee, WI) Assoc. Prof., Grad. Sch. of Lib. and Info. Sci., Simmons Coll., 1974–, Asst. Prof., 1970–74; Lectr., East. MI Univ., 1970; Resrch. Assoc., Cmnty. Syst. Fndn., 1968–69. **Educ.:** Bus. Inst. of Milwaukee, 1939–40, Cert.; Principia Coll., 1946–49, BA (Eng.); Univ. of WI, 1962–64, MA (Eng.), 1964–65, MA (LS); Univ. of MI, 1966–70, PhD (LS). **Orgs.:** ASIS: Natl. Educ. Com. (1976-78). AALL. ALA. Intl. Lib. Educ.: Resrc. Panel for Saudi Arabia. Wayland Pub. Lib.: Bd. of Trustees (Vice-Ch., 1974). Fulbright Alum. Assn. **Honors:** Phi Alpha Eta, 1949; Sigma Tau Delta, 1963; Beta Phi Mu, 1967; Fulbright-Hays Awd., Sr. Lectrshp., Univ. of Cairo, 1977–78. **Pubns.:** *Computerizing the Card Catalog in the University Library* (1970); *Case Studies in Library Computer Systems* (1973); "Impressions of Egyptians, Egyptian Libraries, and Egyptian Library Education," *Simmons Libn.* (Fall 1979); "Rewards for U. S. Professionals in Saudi Arabia," *SLA Boston Chap. News Bltn.* (S., O. 1979); *Toward Improving Librarianship in Greece: Needs Assessment and Recommendations* (Mr. 1978). **Activities:** 11; 24, 25, 26; 56, 75, 93 **Addr.:** Graduate School of Library and Information Science, Simmons College, 300 The Fenway, Boston, MA 02115.

Palmer, Robert B. (Ap. 5, 1938, Rockville Centre, NY) Dir., Barnard Coll. Lib., 1967–81, various positions as lib. adv. and consult. in Thailand and Pakistan, 1976; Asst. to Dir. of Libs., Columbia Univ., 1965–67; Tchr. of Eng., Latin and Greek, Brooks Sch., 1960–65, Libn., 1961–65. **Educ.:** Kenyon Coll., 1955–60, AB (Classics); Simmons Coll., 1962–65, MS (LS); Middlebury Coll., 1962–65, MA (Eng.). **Orgs.:** ALA. **Honors:** Sr. lectr., Fulbright-Hays, Kathmandu, Nepal, 1972–73, 1980, and Kabul, Afghanistan, 1972–73. **Pubns.:** "The Librarian as International Man," *Wilson Lib. Bltn.* (Je. 1973); "Scenes from a Southeast Asian Sabbatical," *Wilson Lib. Bltn.* (Je. 1977). **Activities:** 1; 17, 24, 31 **Addr.:** 190 Riverside Dr., New York, NY 10024.

Palmer, Roger Cain (O. 14, 1943, Corning, NY) Asst. Prof., Univ. of CA, Los Angeles, 1978–; Lectr., Univ. of MI, 1976–78; Deputy Head, Grad. Lib., SUNY, Buffalo, 1974–75, Ref. Libn., SUNY, Buffalo, 1972–74. **Educ.:** Hartwick Coll., 1964–66, BA (Eng.); SUNY, Albany, 1971–72, MLS (Libnshp.); The Univ. of MI, 1975–78, PhD (Libnshp.). **Orgs.:** ASIS: Plng. Com. for Anaheim '80 Conf. (1979–80). NY LA: Coll. and Univ. Libs. Sect., Bd. of Dir. (1973–74). ALA: Lib. Admin. Div./Lib. Org. Mgt. Sect., Com. for Non-Print Media (1973–74). **Honors:** Beta Phi Mu, 1972; Pi Delta Epsilon. **Pubns.:** Jt. auth., *Reader in Library Communication* (1976); jt. auth., *Selected References in Communication* (1975); "Internships and Practicums" in *A Reader in the Administrative Aspects of Education for Librarianship* (1975); "Charles Francis Dorr Belden," *Dict. of Amer. Lib. Biog.* (1978). **Activities:** 11; 56, 75, 93 **Addr.:** UCLA, GSLIS, 120 Powell, Los Angeles, CA 90024.

Palmieri, Lucien Eugene (N. 8, 1921, Cambridge, MA) Head, Ofc. for Col. Dev., State Univ. Coll., 1974–, Coll. Libn., 1967–74; Consult. to Mnstry. of Educ., Repub. of Tanzania (E. Africa), 1962–66; Head, Lib., Northeastern IL Univ., 1956–61. **Educ.:** Univ. of WI, 1945–47, BS (Phil.), 1948–49, MS (Phil.), 1950–53, PhD (Phil.), 1955–56, MSLS (Lib. Admin.). **Orgs.:** ALA. E. African LA. Amer. Phil. Assn. Mind Assn. (Oxford). **Pubns.:** "Bare Particulars, Names and Elementary Propositions," *Synthese*, (Mr. 1960); "Pragamatism and the Ideal Language," *Phil. of Sci.* (Jl. 1960); "Prof. Popper's Refutation of Historicism," *Theoria*, (1961); "To Sleep, Perchance to Dream," *Phil. and Phenomenological Resrch.*, (Je. 1962); "Comments on Pseudo-Paradoxes and the Truth Table," *Methodos*, (1962); various articles, indxs. **Activities:** 1; 15, 17, 24 **Addr.:** State University College, 1300 Elmwood Ave., Buffalo, NY 14222.

Palmiter, Sharron Snyder (N. 11, 1949, Endicott, NY) Admin. Anal., Unvsl. serials and Bk. Exch., 1980–; Head, Acq., Rice Univ. Lib., 1979–80; Mono. Ord. Libn., Cornell Univ. Libs., 1977–79, Gift & Exch. Libn., 1976–77. **Educ.:** Syracuse Univ., 1967–71, AB (Eng.); Univ. of MD, 1973–74, MLS; Univ. of Uppsala, Sweden, 1974–75 (Scan. Lit.). **Orgs.:** ALA. SLA. DC LA. **Addr.:** Universal Serials & Book Exchange, 3335 V St. N.E., Washington, DC 20018.

Palmore, Sandra Norris (Je. 3, 1939, Dayton, OH) Cmnty. Srvs. Libn., Skokie Pub. Lib., 1973–; Ref. Libn., 1972–73; Instr., Grad. Lib. Sch., Univ. of HI, 1971; Biblgphr., Fac. of Spec. Educ., East. MI Univ., 1968–70; Sch. of Nursing Lib., Assunta Hosp., Petaling Jaya, Selangor, Malaysia, 1967; Storyteller, Univ. of Chicago, Readg. Readiness Nursery Proj., 1965; Asst. Chld. Libn., Skokie Pub. Lib., 1963–65. **Educ.:** Antioch Coll., BA (Eng. Lit.); Univ. of Chicago, MA (LS); Univ. of HI, MA Cand. (Geo.). **Orgs.:** Amer. Socty. of Indxrs.: Natl. Indxr.-PRCom. (1981). West. World Haiku Socty. **Honors:** Beta Phi Mu. **Pubns.:** "Departmental Bibliographer: Information Retrieval in Special Education," *Elan* (Spr. 1970); "Nursing Home Services: Skokie Public Library," *IL Libs.* (Je. 1976); jt. auth. "Bibliography on Mathematics for the Blind" ERIC (1970); indxr., consult., *Mgt. Contents* (1978–); various poems *Dragonfly* (Jl. 1981). **Activities:** 9; 16, 25, 39; 59 **Addr.:** 200 S. Blvd. C-1, Evanston, IL 60202.

Palmquist, David W. (Ap. 23, 1947, Cleveland, OH) Head, Hist. Col., Bridgeport Pub. Lib., 1973–; Arch. Asst., Case West. Rsv. Univ., 1972; Cur. of Hist., Massillon Musm., 1971–72. **Educ.:** Syracuse Univ., 1965–69, AB (Hist.); Case West. Rsv. Univ., 1972–73, MSLS; Univ. of CT, 1975–80, MA (Hist.). **Orgs.:** SAA: Urban Arch. Com. (1974–77). New Eng. Archvsts. Fairfield CT Hist. Socty.: Lib. Com. (Ch., 1977–). CT LA: Newsp. Indexing Com. (Ch., 1974–76). Various orgs. Bridgeport Archit. Conservancy: VP (1975–78). Org. of Amer. Hist. Assn. for the Std. of CT Hist. **Honors:** CT Leag. of Hist. Socties., Awd. of Merit, 1971. **Pubns.:** *Bridgeport: A Pictorial History* (1981); jt. ed., *Directory of Historical and Genealogical Resources of Fairfield County, Connecticut* (forthcoming); "Documenting the Smaller City: The Public Library's Role," *Drexel Lib. Qtly.* (O. 1977); Ed., "Connecticut Newspaper Indexing Subject Heading List" (1981); *Bibliography on Connecticut Labor History* mono. (1978). **Activities:** 2, 9; 39, 45; 85, 92 **Addr.:** 140 Ellsworth St., Bridgeport, CT 06605.

Palsson, Mary Dale (N. 23, 1943, El Paso, TX) Asst. Univ. Libn. for Pub. Srvs., Univ. of AZ, 1975–, Head Docum. Libn., 1971–75; Docum. Ref. Libn., Univ. of BC, 1966–69. **Educ.:** Univ. of NM, 1962–65, BA (Hist.); Univ. of Denver, 1965–66, MA (LS); Univ. of AZ, 1969–71, MA (Hist.). **Orgs.:** AZ LA: Coll. and Univ. Libs. Div. (Pres., 1977–78); Pres.-Elect (1976/77); GODORT, Ch. (1973–74), Secy. (1972–73). ALA. SLA. **Pubns.:** Jt. ed., *Jews in the South* (1973); "Jews in the South," *Encyclopedia of Southern History* (1979); "The Arizona Constitutional Convention of 1910," *AZ and the W.* (Sum. 1974). **Activities:** 1; 17, 35, 39; 56, 73, 83 **Addr.:** Main Library Office, University of Arizona, Tucson, AZ 85721.

Paluka, Frank (Francis J.) (D. 2, 1927, Council Bluffs, IA) Head, Spec. Col. Dept., The Univ. of IA Libs., 1962–; Resrch. Asst., Univ. of IL, 1960–61; Instr., Univ. of IA, 1955–57; Instr., Univ. of CT, 1950–52. **Educ.:** Creighton Univ., 1947–50, AB (Eng.); Univ. of CT, 1950–52, MA (Eng.); Univ. of IL, 1960–61, MS (LS); E. M. Cryptographic Tech. Sch., 1946, Cert. (Cryptography). **Orgs.:** IA LA: Johnson-Brigham Com. (Ch., 1962–64). Mod. Lang. Assn. Univ. of IA Credit Un.: Bd. of Dir. (1970–76). **Honors:** Phi Kappa Phi, 1952; Alpha Sigma Nu. **Pubns.:** *The*

PROFESSIONAL ACTIVITIES: Institutions: 1. Acad. lib.; 2. Arch.; 3. Assn.; 4. Fed./Gvt. lib.; 5. Inst. lib.; 6. Mfr./Suppl.; 7. Milit. lib.; 8. Musm.; 9. Pub. lib.; 10. Sch. lib.; 11. Sch. of lib. sci.; 12. Spec. lib.; 13. State lib.; 14. (other). **Functions/Activities:** 15. Acq./Col. dev.; 16. Adult srvs.; 17. Admin.; 18. Apprais.; 19. Archit./Bldgs.; 20. Cat./Class.; 21. Chld. srvs.; 22. Circ.; 23. Cons./Pres.; 24. Consult.; 25. Cont. ed.; 26. Educ. lib. sci.; 27. Ext. srvs.; 28. Fund/Grants; 29. Gvt. pubs.; 30. Indx./Abs.; 31. Instr. lib. use; 32. Media srvs.; 33. Micro.; 34. Netwks./Coop.; 35. Persnl.; 36. PR; 37. Publshg.; 38. Recs. mgt.; 39. Ref. srvs.; 40. Repro.; 41. Resrch.; 42. Review.; 43. Secur.; 44. Serials; 45. Spec. col.; 46. Tech. srvs.; 47. Trustees/Bds.; 48. YA srvs.; 49. (other).

Three Voyages of Captain Cook (1974); *Iowa Authors: A Bio-Bibliography of Sixty Native Writers* (1967); "American Literary Manuscript in University of Iowa Libraries," *Resrcs. for Amer. Lit. Std.* (Spr. 1973); "Technique in Four Stevenson Stories," *FL State Univ. Std.* (1953); "Ruth Suckow," *Dictionary of Literary Biography* (1981). **Activities:** 1; 45; 55, 57 **Addr.:** Special Collections Dept., University of IA Libraries, Iowa City, IA 52242.

Pan, Elizabeth (D. 6, 1941, Manila, Philippines) Pres., Coadj. Fac., Inst. for Info. Std., Cath. Univ., 1978–; Chief Libn., U.S. Patent & Trademark Ofc., 1976–78; Prin. Investigator, U.S. Dept. of Hlth. Educ. & Welfare, 1976–77; Proj. Dir., George Washington Univ., 1974–76; Coadj. Fac., Rutgers Univ., 1972–74; Proj. Coord., Five Assoc. Univ. Libs., 1970–72; Lib. Systs. Anal., Systs. Archits., Inc., 1969–70; Mgr., Tech. Info. Ctr., Collins Radio Co., 1967–69. **Educ.:** Univ. of IL, 1961–63, BA (Eng.), 1964–66, MS (LS); Rutgers Univ., 1971–74, PhD (Info. Sci.). **Orgs.:** ALA: RTSD/Serials Sect. (Ch., 1974–75). ASIS: Spec. Interest on Mgt. (Ch., 1977–78). **Pubns.:** "Network-Building Conference in Support of Industry-wide Innovations," *Jnl. of Tech. Transfer* "Definition and Explanation of Network," *Rehab. Info. Netwk. Conf.* (Je. 1978); "Journal Citation as Predictor of Journal Usage in Libraries," *Coll. Mgt.* (Spr. 1977); *Library Serials Control Systems: A Literature Review and Bibliography* (1970); jt. ed., *Col. Mgt.* (1977–). **Activities:** 14-Consult. firm; 17, 28, 41; 50, 51, 72 **Addr.:** Institute for Information Studies, 400 N. Washington St., Suite 202, Falls Church, VA 22046.

Pancake, Edwina Howard (N. 10, 1942, Butte, MT) Dir., Sci., Tech. Info. Ctr., Univ. of VA, 1974–, Actg. Dir., 1973–74, Sci. Info. Spec., 1969–73. **Educ.:** Baylor Univ., 1966–67, BS (Bio.); Univ. of TX, Austin, 1967–69, MLS. **Orgs.:** VA LA: Nom. Com. (Ch., 1976–77). VA Microfilm Assn.: Secy./Treas. (1970–71); Exec. Bd. (1971–73). SLA: VA Chap., PR Com. (Ch., 1970–71), Pres. (1974–75); Sci.-Tech. Div., Ch. (1978–79); Bd. of Dirs. (1979–81); various coms. Cmnty. Chld. Thea., Inc.: Bd. of Dir. (1976–79). Charlottesville Light Opera Co.: Strg. Com. (1976–77); Sec. Vice-Pres. for Mem. (1977–79). **Pubns.:** "Intra-Library Science Information Service," *Spec. Libs.* (My. 1973). **Activities:** 1, 12; 17; 91 **Addr.:** Science/Technology Information Center, Clark Hall, University of VA, Charlottesville, VA 22901.

Pancero, Claire J. (Je. 12, 1937, Cincinnati, OH) Coll. Libn., Athen. of OH, 1968–. **Educ.:** Edgecliff Coll., 1955–64, BS (Educ.); Cath. Univ., 1969, MSLS; Xavier Univ., Cincinnati, 1972, MEd (Hist.). **Orgs.:** ALA. Acad. LA of OH. OH LA. Grt. Cincinnati Lib. Cnsrtm. Natl. Cncl. of Tchrs. of Eng. **Activities:** 1; 15, 17, 44 **Addr.:** Athenaeum of Ohio, St. Gregory Seminary Library, 6616 Beechmont Ave., Cincinnati, OH 45230.

Pankake, Marcia Jean (N. 1, 1940, Minneapolis, MN) Asst. Prof., Bibl., Wilson Lib., Univ. of MN, 1979–, Ch., Ref., Resrcs., 1977–79, Soc. Sci. Bibl., 1975–77, Lectr., Lib. Sch., 1971–73, Acq. Libn., 1967–69, Libn., Circ., 1965–67. **Educ.:** Univ. of MN, 1958–62, BA (Intl. Rels.), 1962–65, MA (LS), 1969–71, MA (Amer. Std.), 1971–75, PhD (Amer. Std.). **Orgs.:** ALA: Resrcs. Sect., Natl. Lib. Srvs. Schol. Awd. Jury (Ch., 1979–80); RTSD, Chief Col. Dev. Ofcrs., Nom. Com. (1979); ACRL, Ad Hoc Com. on Copyrt. (1978–). MNLA: Acad. and Resrch. Libs. Div. (Info. Coord., 1978–80); Exec. Bd. (1978–80); various coms. Amer. Std. Assn. Mod. Lang. Assn. of Amer. Socty. for the Hist. of Discoveries. AAUP: Twin Cities Chap., Exec. Bd. (1978–79). **Honors:** Amer. Antiq. Socty., Resrch. Flwshp., 1974; Newberry Lib., Flwshp. in the Hum., 1974; Phi Beta Mu, 1967. **Activities:** 1; 15, 26, 37; 55, 57, 61 **Addr.:** 180 Wilson Library, 309 19th Ave. S., University of MN, Minneapolis, MN 55455.

Panofsky, Hans E. (Ja. 30, 1926, Berlin, Germany) Cur. of Africana, Northwest. Univ., 1959–; Ref. Libn., Oak Park Pub. Lib., 1958–59; Asst. Ref. Libn., NY State Sch. of Indus. and Labor Rel., 1952–58. **Educ.:** London Sch. of Econ., Columbia Univ., 1943–44, 1949–51, BS (Soclgy.), 1951–52, MS (LS); Cornell Univ., 1952–58, (Econ.). **Orgs.:** ALA: IRRT, Com. on Africa (Ch., 1976–), Asian and African Sect. (Ch., 1977–79). ARL: Com. on Africa (Ch., 1970–). African Std. Assn.: Bd. of Dirs. (1976–79). Intl. Congs. of African Std.: Permanent Cncl. (1978–). **Pubns.:** *A Bibliography of Africana* (1975); "African Studies in American Libraries," *Lib. Qtly.* (O. 1965). **Activities:** 1; 15, 39; 54 **Addr.:** Northwestern University Library, Evanston, IL 60201.

Pantano, Richard (S. 23, 1937, New York City, NY) Lib. Dir., NH Coll., 1979–, Ref. Libn., NH Coll., 1977–79; Ref. Libn., Univ. of NH, 1976–77; Asst. Dir., Dover Pub. Lib., 1975–76. **Educ.:** St. Anselm's Coll., Manchester, NH, 1966–69, BA (Eng.); Univ. of RI, 1974–76, MLS; Army Lang. Sch., 1957–58, (Grmn.). **Orgs.:** Acad. Libns. of NH: Ch. (1980–). New Eng. ACRL: Bibl. Instr. Com. (1977–). ALA. NH Lib. Cncl.: Conf. Com. (1978–80). **Activities:** 1; 17, 31 **Addr.:** Shapiro Library, NH College, 2500 N. River Rd., Manchester, NH 03104.

Pantelidis, Veronica Sexauer (F. 3, 1935, Ft. Pierce, FL) Asst. Prof., E. Carolina Univ., 1976–; Dir., Resrch. Lib., FL Dept. of Cmrce., 1970–76; Ref. Libn., St. Lucie-Okeechobee Reg. Lib., 1968–69; Comp. Progmr., Litton Indus., 1958–60. **Educ.:** Univ. of FL, 1953–55, AA (Span.); Univ. of Miami, 1955–57, BA (Latin Amer. Affairs); FL State Univ., 1969–70, MS (LS), 1972–73, MS (Adult Educ.), 1971–75, PhD (Instr. Dev.) **Orgs.:** NC LA. Mid. E. Libns. Assn. Mensa. **Honors:** Phi Kappa Phi; Beta Phi Mu; Sigma Delta Pi. **Pubns.:** *Arab Education, 1956–1978* (1981); *The Arab World: Libraries and Librarianship, 1960–1976* (1979); jt. auth., *SIBE: A Sequential In-Basket Exercise Technique* (1971); jt. auth., "Experiential Methods of Teaching Special Librarianship," *Spec. Libs.* (1972); "A Computer-Assisted Sequential In-Basket Technique," *Educ. Tech.* (1971); various other articles, reviews. **Activities:** 11, 12; 15, 39, 41; 54, 56 **Addr.:** Department of Library Science, East Carolina University, Greenville, NC 27834.

Panum, Philip James (Ag. 9, 1942, Oakland, CA) Subj. Spec., Hist., Denver Pub. Lib., 1981–, Libn. III, Hist. Dept., 1980–81, Libn. II, Hist. Dept., 1971–80, Libn. I, Hist. Dept., 1969–71; Hist. Instr., Southwestern Cmnty. Coll., 1966–68; Hist. Instr., Dana Coll., 1967; Archeological dig foreman, Smithsonian Inst. and ND Hist. Socty., 1964. **Educ.:** Dana Coll., 1960–64, BA (Hist.); Bowling Green State Univ., 1964–65, MA (Hist.); Univ. of Denver, 1968–69, MA (Libnshp.). **Orgs.:** West. Assn. of Map Libs. SLA. Amer. Hist. Assn. Hist. Socty. of CO. **Activities:** 9, 12; 15, 16, 39; 55, 70, 92 **Addr.:** History and Travel Dept., Denver Public Library, 1357 Broadway, Denver, CO 80203.

Panz, Richard (S. 14, 1947, Buffalo, NY) Dir., Finger Lakes Lib. Syst., 1979–; Asst. Dir., Willard Lib., Battle Creek, MI, 1977–79; Libn., Buffalo and Erie Cnty. Pub. Lib., 1970–77. **Educ.:** Canisius Coll., 1965–69, BS (Soclgy.); Syracuse Univ., 1969–70, MSLS. **Orgs.:** NY LA: Lcl. Support Com. (1979); Legis. Com. (1981–). ALA. S. Ctrl. Reg. Lib. Cncl.: Trustee (1982–). NY State LSCA Adv. Com. **Activities:** 9, 14-Reg. syst.; 17, 28, 34; 50, 56, 78 **Addr.:** 216 Eastern Heights Dr., Ithaca, NY 14850.

Pao, Miranda Lee (F. 14, 1936, Shanghai, Kiangsu, China) Assoc. Prof., Sch. of Lib. Sci., Case West. Rsv. Univ., 1979–, Asst. Prof., 1973–79. **Educ.:** Juilliard Sch. of Msc., 1958–60, BS (piano), 1960–61, MS (piano); Case West. Rsv. Univ., 1967–70, MSLS (info. sci.), 1970–72, PhD (info. sci.). **Orgs.:** Msc. LA. ASIS. AALS. Sigma Alpha Iota. **Honors:** Beta Phi Mu. **Pubns.:** "Bibliometrics and Computational Musicology," *Col. Mgt.* (1979); "Automatic Text Analysis Based on Transition Phenomena of Word Occurrences," *Jnl. of the Amer. Socty. for Info. Sci.* (1978); "Training of Music Librarian: A Double Degree Program," *Fontes Artis Musicae* (1977); various articles. **Activities:** 12; 15, 30, 39; 55, 75 **Addr.:** School of Library Science, Case Western Reserve University, Cleveland, OH 44106.

Pape, Marion L. (O. 25, 1944, Malton, ON) YA Libn., Saskatoon Pub. Lib., 1979–; HS Libn., AB, YT, 1971–77. **Educ.:** Univ. of Toronto, 1962–65, BA (Eng., Hist.); Univ. of AB, 1977–79, MLS; ON Coll. of Educ., 1966–67, Cert. (Educ.). **Orgs.:** Can. LA. LA of AB. SK LA. Can. Sch. LA. various other orgs. Yukon Tchrs. Assn.: Prof. Dev. Ch. **Pubns.:** Reviews. **Activities:** 9, 10; 30, 32, 48; 74, 89 **Addr.:** 1314 Osler St., Saskatoon, SK S1N 0V2 Canada.

Papenfuse, Edward C. (O. 15, 1943, Toledo, OH) State Archvst. of MD, Comsn. of Land Patents, MD Hall of Rec., State Arch., 1975–, Asst. State Archvst., 1973–75; Assoc. Ed., Bibl., *The Amer. Hist. Review,* 1970–73. **Educ.:** Amer. Univ., 1965, BA (Pol. Sci.); Univ. of CO, 1967, MA (Hist.); Johns Hopkins Univ., 1973, PhD (Early Amer. Hist.). **Orgs.:** SAA. MD Hist. Socty. Amer. Assn. for State and Local Hist. **Pubns.:** *In Pursuit of Profit: The Annapolis Merchants in the Era of the American Revolution* (1975); "Planter Behavior and Economic Opportunity in a Staple Economy," *Agr. Hist.* (Ap. 1972); "The Public Records of the American Revolutionary Era: Some Suggestions for the Development of Bibliographic Guides," *Hist. Methods Nsltr* (S. 1971); jt. auth., *Directory of Maryland Legislators, 1635–1789* (1974); jt. auth., *Maryland: A New Guide to the Old Line State* (1976); various articles, bks., reviews. **Activities:** 2, 5; 29, 33, 39; 55, 57, 69 **Addr.:** Maryland Hall of Records, PO Box 828, Annapolis, MD 21404.

Papermaster, Cynthia Lynn (Jl. 28, 1946, Hollywood, CA) Law Libn., Orrick, Herrington and Sutcliffe, 1974–; Lib. Consult., Pac. Film Arch. and other positions; Lib. Consult./Libn., Crocker Natl. Bank, 1974; Libn., Francis Ford Coppola, 1974–76. **Educ.:** Univ. of CA, Berkeley, 1965–70, AB (Pol. Sci.), 1973–74, MLS. **Orgs.:** SLA. AALL. Pvt. Law LA of San Francisco. Natl. Org. of Women. Amnesty Intl. Univ. Art Musm., Berkeley, CA. Amer. Frnds. Srv. Com. Various other orgs. **Activities:** 12; 15, 17, 20; 59, 77 **Addr.:** 1907 McGee St., Berkeley, CA 94703.

Paplinski, William Elliott (Ag. 29, 1944, New Kensington, PA) Dir., Troy-Miami Cnty. Pub. Lib., 1977–; Dir., Willard Meml. Lib., 1974–77. **Educ.:** Kent State Univ., 1967–70, BA (Pol. Sci.); Univ. of RI, 1972–74, MLS; Miami Univ., 1978, Exec. Dev. Prog. for Lib. Admin. **Orgs.:** OH LA: Legis. Com., Fed. Rel. Coord. ASIS. Kiwanis Club, Troy, OH: VP. First Presbyterian Church, Troy, OH: Deacon; Bd. of Deacons; Treas. **Activities:** 9; 17 **Addr.:** 419 W. Main St., Troy, OH 45373.

Paquette, Diane (My. 19, 1946, Ste-Thérèse-de-Bl, PQ) Coord. de bib., Cegep de St-Jeérôme, 1975–; Telecat-Unicat, Univ. de Montréal, 1974–75; Prof. en tech. de documtn., Cegep Lionel-Groulx, 1970–74; Catlgr. Classificateur, Univ. de Montréal, 1968–70. **Educ.:** Sémy. de Ste-Thérèse, 1963–67, BA; Ottawa Univ., 1967–68, BLS; Univ. de Montréal, 1972–74, MA (Biblio.). **Orgs.:** ASTED. Corp. des bibtcrs. prof. du PQ. **Pubns.:** "Ensuite en revue... un complot à l'Horizon," *Ensuite* (F. 1981); "Les besoins documentaires et la pédagogie," *Ensuite* (D. 1977); "Des stages en bibliotechnique," *Documtn. et bibs.* (Je. 1979). **Activities:** 1; 15, 17 **Addr.:** Cegep de St-Jérôme, 455 Fournier, St-Jérôme, PQ J7Z 4V2 Canada.

Paradis, Gilles (My. 13, 1943, Québec, PQ) Cslr. à la Documtn. en Psy. et Phil., Bib. de l'Univ. Laval, 1966–. **Educ.:** Univ. McGill, 1973–75, MA (Bibl.); Univ. Laval, 1968–71, Doc. (Phil.). **Orgs.:** Corp. des Bibtcrs. Prof. du PQ. Assn. Can. des Sci. de l'Info. **Pubns.:** "L'Activité Professionnelle et les Bibliothécaires," *Argus* (My./Ag. 1979); "La Documentation en Philosophie: Bibliographies Courantes," *Philosophiques* (Ap. 1979); "Le Choix des Documents dans les Bibliothèques Universitaires ou de rEcherche," *Documtn. et Bibs.* (1977); *Introduction aux Ouvrages de Référence en Philosophie* (1969); Jt. auth., "Le Bibtcr. a l.Univ.: Bibtcr. on Univ.," *Argus* (Mr.-Ap. 1981); Other articles. **Activities:** 1; 15, 31, 39 **Addr.:** Bibliothèque-Pavillon Bonenfant, Université Laval, Ste-Foy, PQ G1K 7P4 Canada.

Paradis, Jacques R. (Je. 16, 1943, Montréal, PQ) Tchr., Lib. Tech., Coll. Lionel-Groulx, 1969–; Cat., Univ. de Montréal, 1968–69, Libn., Ecole de Bibl., 1965–67. **Educ.:** Coll. de l'Assomption, 1958–63, BA; Univ. de Montréal, 1963–65, BLS, 1970–74, MLS. **Orgs.:** Corp. des Bibtcrs. Prof. du PQ. ASTED. **Pubns.:** *Le Manuscrit* (1972). **Activities:** 20, 26, 46; 62 **Addr.:** College Lionel-Groulx, 100, rue Duquet, Ste-Thérèse, PQ J7E 3G6 Canada.

Paradise, Don M. (D. 27, 1947, Charleroi, PA) Lib. Supvsr., Title IV-B Prog. Dir., Belle Vernon Area Sch. Dist., 1979–, Ref. Libn., Westmoreland Cnty. Cmnty. Coll., Belle Vernon Educ. Ctr., 1978– HS Libn., 1969–. **Educ.:** Clarion State Coll., 1965–69, BS (LS), 1973–75, MSLS. **Orgs.:** ALA: AASL. PA Sch. Libns. Assn.: Supvsr.; Legis. Com. (1976–). Natl. Educ. Assn. PA State Educ. Assn. **Activities:** 10; 21, 39, 48; 50, 63, 78 **Addr.:** Box 122, 7th St., Apt. 2–G, W. Elizabeth, PA 15088.

Parch, Grace D. (My. 15, 19–, Cleveland, OH) Lib. Dir., Plain Dlr. Newsp., 1970–; Lib. Dir., Twinsburg Pub. Lib., 1965–70; Asst. Head, Ref. and Circ., VA State Lib., 1964; Consult., CA LA, 1960–64; Branch Lib. Dir., Cleveland Hts.-Univ. Hts. Pub. Lib. Syst., 1954–63; Post Libn., U.S. Army Spec. Srv., Italy, Germany, 1951–53. **Educ.:** Case-West. Rsv. Univ., 1943–46, BA (Hist.), 1947–50 (Post-grad. Work in Span.); McGill Univ., 1950–51 (LS); Cooper Sch. of Art, 1971–72 (Art); API News Lib. Sem., 1971; 1982–, Doct. Std. **Orgs.:** SLA: News Div., Hist. Com. (1981–), Natl. Dir. Com. (Ch., 1974–76); Pubcty. Com. (1973–). ALA: ACRL. Cath. LA: North. OH Co-Ch. (1960–63). OH LA. Cleveland Women's City Club. Woman's Natl. Bk. Com. Cleveland Musm. of Art. West. Rsv. Hist. Socty. **Honors:** ALA, Lib. PR Cncl. Awd., 1972; ALA, John Cotton Dana Awd., 1967. **Pubns.:** Adv. com., *Guide to Ohio Newspapers 1793–1973;* ed., *Directory of Newspaper Libraries in the U.S. and Canada* (1976); "Where in the World but in the Plain Dealer Library!" *Plain Dlr.* (1972); various articles, bk. reviews, news articles. **Activities:** 12; 17, 24, 39; 56, 83, 92 **Addr.:** 1801 Superior Ave., Cleveland, OH 44114.

Pardo, Thomas Clay (Jl. 20, 1952, Cincinnati, OH) Prog. Ofcr., SAA, 1979–; Assoc. Ed., Microfilming Corp. of Amer., 1976–79; Mss. Prcs., West. Rsv. Hist. Socty., 1974–75. **Educ.:** Miami Univ., 1970–74, BA (Amer. Std.); Case West. Rsv. Univ., 1974–76, MA (Amer. Std.). **Orgs.:** SAA: Micro. Com. 1977–79); Educ. Com. Liaison (1979–); Descr. Prof. Afnty. Grp. (1979–); Coll. and Univ. Prof. Afnty. Grp. (1979–); Prog. Com. Liaison (1979–). Org. of Amer. Histns. **Pubns.:** *Conducting Basic Archival Workshops* (1981); "Archives Classics and Classicists: An Overview," *Primary Src. of Socty. of MS Archvsts.* (Ag. 1980); *The National Woman's Party Papers, 1913–1974: A Guide to the Microfilm Edition* (1979); *Socialist Collections in the Tamiment Library, 1872–1956: A Guide to the Microfilm Edition* (1979). **Activities:** 2, 3; 25, 33, 41 **Addr.:** 930 S. McKinley Ave., Apt. 2B, Arlington Heights, IL 60005.

Pare, Richard (Mr. 29, 1938, Québec, PQ) Bibtcr. Parlementaire Associé., Bib. du Parlmt., Ottawa, 1980–; Asst. Dir., Legis. Lib., Natl. Asm., 1979–80; Dir., Srvs. of Documtn., Dept. of Comms., 1976–79; Dir., Admin. Lib., Dept. of Comms., 1973–76; Coord. of Coll. Libs., Srv. of Libs., Dept. of Educ., 1971–73; Chief of Pub. Srvs., Cmnty. Coll. Lib., CEGEP GARNEAU, 1970–71; Asst. Dir. to the Lib., Jesuit Coll. (PQ), 1964–69. **Educ.:** Laval Univ., 1961–68, BA; Ottawa Univ., 1969–70, BLS; Laval Univ., 1959–60, Dip. (LS). **Orgs.:** ASTED: Com. of Career Plng. for Lib. Techs. Assn. Can. des Scis. de l'info. Can. LA. **Pubns.:** *Le Service du Prêt dans la Bibliothèque* (1971). **Activities:** 12, 13; 17, 18, 34; 56, 62, 75 **Addr.:** Bibliothécaire Parlementaire Associé, Bibliothèque du Parlement, Ottawa, ON K1A 0A9 Canada.

Parent, Roger H. (Ap. 21, 1943, Holyoke, MA) Exec. Dir., ALA, LAMA, 1979–; Staff Dev. Libn., Princeton Univ.,

Special Subjects/Services: 50. Adult educ.; 51. Advert./Mktg.; 52. Aerosp.; 53. Agric.; 54. Area std.; 55. Arts/Hum.; 56. Autom.; 57. Bibl./Prtg.; 58. Bio. sci.; 59. Bus./Fin.; 60. Chem.; 61. Copyrt.; 62. Documtn.; 63. Educ.; 64. Engin.; 65. Env.; 66. Eth. grps.; 67. Film; 68. Food/Nutr.; 69. Geneal.; 70. Geo.; 71. Geol.; 72. Handcpd.; 73. Hist.; 74. Int. frdm.; 75. Info. sci.; 76. Insr.; 77. Law; 78. Legis.; 79. Math./Comp. sci.; 80. Med.; 81. Metals; 82. Nat. resrcs.; 83. Newsp.; 84. Nuc. sci.; 85. Oral hist.; 86. Petr./Energy; 87. Pharm.; 88. Phys./Astr./Math.; 89. Readg.; 90. Relig.; 91. Sci./Tech.; 92. Soc. sci.; 93. Telecom.; 94. Transp.; 95. (other).

1977–79; Dir., Mercantile LA, NY, 1975–77; Ref. Libn., Baruch Coll., 1974–75; Dept. Head, Springfield (MA) Pub. Lib., 1970–74. **Educ.:** Univ. of MA, 1966–68, BA (Fine Art); Simmons Coll., 1968–70, MLS. **Orgs.:** ARL: Ofc. of Mgt. Std., Consult. Trng. Prog. ALA: LAMA. Chicago Lib. Club. CLENE. Caxton Club. **Activities:** 1, 9; 17, 24, 35; 50, 55 **Addr.:** American Library Association, Library Administration and Management Association, 50 E. Huron St., Chicago, IL 60611.

Parham, M. Ann (My. 7, 1944, Columbus, GA) Admin. Libn., U.S. Army Lib., USMCA, Wiesbaden, 1979–; Ext. Libn., U.S. Army Lib., Nuernberg Milit. Cnfy., 1978–79; Fld. Libn., Rec. Srvs. Agency, Korea, 1976–77; Ext. Libn., Rowan Pub. Lib., 1974–76. **Educ.:** Columbus Coll., 1962–65, AA (Liberal Arts); FL State Univ., 1965–67, BS (Soc. Work), 1973–74, MS (LS). **Orgs.:** ALA. Frdm. to Read Fndn. **Honors:** Beta Phi Mu. **Activities:** 4, 9; 16, 17; 74 **Addr.:** USMCA Wiesbaden, Box 607, APO, New York, NY 09457.

Parham, Robert Bruce (Je. 4, 1948, Denver, CO) Archvst., Boulder Hist. Socty., 1979–; Film Archvst., Denver Musm. of Nat. Hist., 1979–80; Mss. Cur., Univ. of AR Lib., 1974–77. **Educ.:** West. State Coll. of CO, 1966–70, BA (Hist.); Univ. of WI, 1973–74, MA (LS); Univ. of CO, 1978–81, MA (U.S. Hist.). **Orgs.:** SAA: Ad Hoc Com. On Wider Use of Arch. (1976–77); Prof. Afnty. Grp. on Descr. of Recs. and Mss. (1979–80). Socty. of SW Archvsts.: Awds. Com. (1976–78). Conf. of Intermt. Archvsts. Socty. of GA Archvsts. Phi Alpha Theta. **Pubns.:** "Arkansas County and Local Histories: A Bibliography," *AR Hist. Qtly.* (Spr. 1977); "Emergency Procedures For Nitrate Film," *CO Libs.* (Ap. 1981). **Activities:** 1, 2; 17, 23, 45; 55, 67, 92 **Addr.:** Boulder Historical Society, 1655 Broadway, Boulder, CO 80302.

Paris, Janelle A. (O. 10, 1926, Houston, TX) Assoc. Prof., Sam Houston State Univ., 1974–; Elem. Sch. Libn., Stewart Elem. Sch., 1970–72; HS Libn., Clear Creek HS, 1950–70; HS Libn., Pearland HS, 1946–50. **Educ.:** Sam Houston State Univ., 1943–46, BS (LS); TX Woman's Univ., 1948–50, BS (LS); Univ. of Houston, 1949–56, MEd (Educ.); TX Woman's Univ., 1972–77, PhD (LS). **Orgs.:** ALA. SWLA: Nom. Com. (1981–82). TX LA: Natl. Lib. Week Com. (1975–76); Dist. VIII Nom. Com. (Ch., 1979–80); TX Bluebonnet Awd. Com. (Ch., 1979–81). AALS. Various other orgs. AAUW. Natl. Educ. Assn. TX Assn. of Coll. Tchrs.: Sam Houston Chap., Secy., VP. TX State Tchrs. Assn. **Honors:** Beta Phi Mu, 1977. **Pubns.:** "School Library Theft," *Lib. and Arch. Secur.* (Spr. 1980); "Announcing: The Texas Bluebonnet Award," *Eng. in TX* (Win. 1979); "The Proposed Texas Children's Book Award," *TX Lib. Jnl.* (Fall 1978); "Occupations in Children's Realistic Fiction," *Eng. in TX* (Win. 1978). **Activities:** 11; 26; 95-Chld. Lit., Sch. Lib. Media Ctrs. **Addr.:** 253 Normal Park Rd., Huntsville, TX 77340.

Paris, Terrence L. (N. 25, 1948, Winnipeg, MB) Head, Pub. Srvs., Mt. St. Vincent Univ. Lib., 1972–, Ref. Libn., 1972. **Educ.:** Univ. of MB, 1966–70, BA, hons. (Hist.); Univ. of West. ON, 1971–72, MLS. **Orgs.:** Can. LA: Gvt. Pubns. Com. (1978–). Atl. Provs. LA: Conf. (Regis./Treas., 1978); Resols. Com. NS Online Cnsrtm. Dalhousie Sch. of Lib. Srvs: Cont. Ed. Com. (1976–). **Pubns.:** Various articles on gvt. pubns. srvs. (1978–). **Activities:** 1; 31, 39, 41; 63, 68, 92 **Addr.:** Mount Saint Vincent University, Halifax, NS B3M 2J6 Canada.

Parish, Nancy Langdon (Ja. 25, 1944, Monroe, MI) Dir., Lib. and Media Srvs., St. Stephen's Episcopal Sch., 1973–; Head Libn., Bradenton Pub. Lib., 1972–73; Libn., Episcopal Day Sch., Augusta, GA, 1971–72; Libn., John Milledge Sch., 1970–71. **Educ.:** FL South. Coll., 1962–66, BA (Sp., Drama); Univ. of ME, 1969–71, MLS; Wesleyan Univ., 1980. **Orgs.:** ALA. FL Assn. for Media in Educ. Manatee Cnty. Assn. for Media in Educ. **Honors:** Edward Ford Fndn., Flwshp., 1980; Natl. Endow. for the Hum., 1980. **Activities:** 10; 15, 17, 31 **Addr.:** 309 Springdale Dr., Wildewood Springs, Bradenton, FL 33507.

Park, Leland Madison (O. 21, 1941, Alexandria, LA) Lib. Dir., Davidson Coll., 1975–, Asst. Dir. Lib., 1970–75, Head, Ref., Student Persnl., 1967–70; Ref. Libn., Pub. Lib., Charlotte and Mecklenburg Cnty.; Visit. Instr., Sch. of Lib. Sci. FL State Univ., 1973; Div. of Libnshp., Emory Univ., 1972. **Educ.:** Davidson Coll., 1959–63, AB (Pol. Sci.); Emory Univ., 1963–64, MLn (LS); Simmons Coll., 1968, (LS); FL State Univ., 1972–74, Adv M (LS), PhD. **Orgs.:** Southeastern LA: Ed., *The Southeastern Libn.* (1976–78); Univ. of Coll. Sect. (Ch., 1976–78); Exec. Bd. (1976–78). NC LA: Sec. VP (1975–77); VP, Pres.-Elect (1981–83). various coms. Metrolina LA: Pres. (1969–71). Mecklenburg LA: Treas. (1969–70). Various Orgs. Charlotte Rotary Club W.: Bd. of Dir. (1979–82). Sigma Nu Fraternity. Omicron Delta Kappa. Socty. of the Cincinnati. Various orgs. **Honors:** ALA, H. W. Wilson Lib. Per. Awd., 1979. Beta Phi Mu. **Pubns.:** Sect. Ed., Acad. Libs. Sect., *NC Libs.* (1972–77); "Audiovisual and Library Services–A Separatist View," *Library-Media: Marriage or Divorce* (1977); Jt. cmplr., *Bibliography on Alcoholic Beverage Control Systems,* (1965); *Directory of Librarians and Library Staff Members in Mecklenburg County* (1969); "Editor's Page," clmn. in *Southeastern Libn.* (1976–78); various articles. **Activities:** 1; 17, 19, 24 **Addr.:** E. H. Little Library, Davidson College, Davidson, NC 28036.

Park, Robert M. A. (S. 26, 1928, Winnipeg, MB, Libn. and Head Tchr., Pembina Crest Sch., 1973–; Libn., Fort Richmond Collegiate, 1972–73; Consult.-Srvy. Dir., Prov. of MB, 1971–72; Libn., Vincent Massey Collegiate, 1962–70. **Educ.:** St. John's Coll., Univ. of Winnipeg, 1945–50, BA (Latin, Eng.); Univ. of MB, 1950–58, BEd; Univ. of AB, 1970–71, BLS. **Orgs.:** MB LA: Pres. (1967–69); Constn. Prog. (1969, 1979). MB Sch. Lib. AV Assn.: Exec. Mem. (1976–79); Nom. Com. (Ch. 1976–78). Can. LA: Nom. Com. (1971). Can. Sch. LA: Pres. (1973). MB Tchrs. Socty.: Cnclr. **Pubns.:** Various articles. **Activities:** 10, 14-Fac. of Educ.; 26, 31, 32; 63 **Addr.:** 736 Townsend Ave., Winnipeg, MB R3T 2V4 Canada.

Park, Yong H. (Jl. 24, 1932, Puyo, Choong Nam, Korea) Ref. Libn., Tempe Pub. Lib., 1980–, Coord., Tech. Srvs., 1976–80; Head, Acq., Gary Pub. Lib., 1974–76; Head, Cat., MS Valley State Univ. Lib., 1970–73; Asst. Prof., Soong Jon Univ., Taejon, Korea, 1964–68. **Educ.:** Korea Univ., 1952–56, BA (Eng. Lit.), 1956–58, MA (Eng. Lit.); Atlanta Univ., 1969–70, MSLS. **Orgs.:** ALA. AZ State Lib. **Pubns.:** "Prose Epic of Henry Fielding" (1964). **Activities:** 9; 20, 46 **Addr.:** 2166 E. La Jolla, Tempe, AZ 85282.

Parke, Carol R. (D. 23, 1935, Bridgeport, CT) Head, Ref. Dept., James Branch Cabell Lib., VA Cmwlth. Univ., 1977–; Visit. Lectr., Sch. of LS, Univ. of NC, 1977–; Docum. Libn., Yale Univ. Lib., 1970–76, Ref. Libn., 1968–70; Chld. Libn., Bloomingdale Branch, NY Pub. Lib., 1966–68. **Educ.:** CT Coll., 1954–58, BA (Eng.); Columbia Univ., 1966, MS (Libnshp.). **Orgs.:** ALA. VA LA. **Addr.:** James Branch Cabell Library, Virginia Commonwealth University, 901 Park Ave., Richmond, VA 23284.

Parker, Barbara Coy (O. 4, 1950, St. Joseph, MO) Serials Acq. Libn., Smithsonian Inst., 1979–; Serials Cat., Natl. Gallery of Art, 1976–79; Head, Tech. Srvs., Ctrl. AR Lib. Syst., 1974–76; Asst. Libn., AR Arts Ctr., 1973–74. **Educ.:** CO Womens Coll., 1968–72, BA (Eng.); Univ. of MO, 1972–73, MA (LS). **Orgs.:** ALA. ARLIS/NA. **Honors:** Beta Phi Mu, 1973. **Pubns.:** Jt. auth., *Catalog of the John D. Reid Collection of Early American Jazz* (1975); "Marriage on the Boards," *Bk. Col. Market* (S.–O. 1979); various bk. reviews in *Lib. Jnl.* (1974–). **Activities:** 4, 12; 15, 44; 55 **Addr.:** Library–Acquisitions, Smithsonian Institution, 10th and Constitution, N.W., Washington, DC 20560.

Parker, Charles (Paul) Gerald (Je. 4, 1943, Bell, CA) Head, Rec. Sound Col., Msc. Div., Natl. Lib. of Can., 1979–, Head, Msc. Sect., Cat. Branch, 1978–79; Sr. Msc. Scores Cat., Lib., Fac. of Msc., Univ. of West. ON, 1976–78; Msc. Cat., Boston Pub. Lib., 1973–76; Tech. Srvs. Libn., New Eng. Cnsvty. of Msc., 1972–73. **Educ.:** Long Beach City Coll., 1965–67, AA (Eng.); Univ. of MA, 1969–71, BA (Msc.); Kent State Univ., 1971–72, MLS. **Orgs.:** Corporation des bibliothécaires professionels du Québec. CAML: Cat. Com. (Ch., 1978–); Pubns. Com. (1977–). Intl. Assn. of Msc. Libs. Assn. for Rec. Sound Col.: Bibl. Access to Sound Rec. Com. (1979–); Mem. Com. (1979–). Msc. LA: New Eng. Chap.; NY State/ON Chap. Jazz Ottawa. Amat. Cham. Msc. Players. Montreal Vintage Msc. Socty. **Honors:** Phi Beta Kappa. **Pubns.:** Consult., "Cherubini Series" rec. proj.; various articles, rec. and bk. reviews, abs. **Activities:** 1, 4; 15, 20, 39; 55 **Addr.:** 34 boul. Brunet, app. 8, Val Tétreau, PQ J9A 1N8 Canada.

Parker, Diane Cecile (D. 22, 1942, San Francisco, CA) Head, Ref., Lockwood Lib., SUNY, Buffalo 1975–, Actg. Head, Lockwood Lib., 1978–79, Ref., Geol. Libn., Sci. Lib., 1972–74, Head, Branch Lib., Seattle Pub, Lib., 1972–72, Ref., Map Libn., Hist. Dept., 1967–71. **Educ.:** City Coll., San Francisco, 1960–62, AA (Liberal Arts); Univ. of CA, Berkeley, 1962–64, BA (Compar. Lit.); Univ. of WA, 1966–67, MLS. **Orgs.:** ALA: ACRL/Univ. Libs. Sect., Strg. Com. (1977–1980); Mudge Cit. Com. (Ch., 1980–81). SUNY Libns. Assn.: Pres. (1976–77). Geoscience Info. Socty. **Pubns.:** Jt. ed., *Directory of Geoscience Libraries in the U.S. and Canada,* (1974); "Teaching Library and Literature Search Strategy to Geology Students," *Procs. of the Geoscience Info. Socty.* (1976); "Status of Information Education for Geoscientists in the United States and Canada" in *Geoscience Info.; a State-of-the Art Review* (1979); jt. auth., "A Zero-base Budget Approach to Staff Justification for a Combined Reference and Collection Development Department" in *New Horizons for Academic Libraries* (1979); various sp. **Activities:** 1; 15, 17, 39; 59, 63, 75 **Addr.:** Lockwood Memorial Library, SUNY, Buffalo, Amherst, NY 14260.

Parker, Edwin B. (Ja. 19, 1932, Berwyn, AB) VP, Equatorial Comms. Co., 1979–; Prof. of Comms., Stanford Univ., 1962–79; Asst. Prof. of Comms., Univ. of IL, 1960–62. **Educ.:** Univ. of BC, 1952–54, BA (Phil.); Stanford Univ., 1957–60, PhD (Comms.). **Orgs.:** ASIS. Intl. Comm. Assn. WHCLIS; Adv. Com. **Pubns.:** Jt. auth., *Television in the Lives of Our Children* (1961); jt. ed., *The Kennedy Assassination and the American Public: Social Communication in Crisis* (1965); jt. ed., *Handbook of Communication* (1973); "Communication Satellites for Rural Development," *Telecom. Policy* (F. 1978); "An Information-based Hypothesis," *Jnl. of Comm.* (1978); various bks., articles. **Addr.:** Equatorial Communications Company, 1294 Lawrence Station Rd., Sunnyvale, CA 94086.

Parker, Elizabeth Reid (Ap. 5, 1935, Roanoke, VA) Lib., Media Spec., Ruffner Jr. HS, Roanoke City Schs., 1970–; Lib., Media Spec., Stewartsville Elem. Sch., 1964–70; Lib., Media Spec., Bedford Cnty. Pub. Schs., Big Island HS, 1963–64; Asst. to Head Libn., Vets. Admin. Hosp., Salisbury, NC, 1959–61. **Educ.:** Mars Hill Jr. Coll., 1953–55, AA (Lib. Arts); Wake Forest Univ., 1955–57, BA (Soclgy., Psy.); Radford Univ., 1975–77, MS (Educ. Media); Univ. of NC, 1970–72, (LS), 1971, NDEA Inst.; various crs. LS, educ. **Orgs.:** ALA: Sch. Libns. Div. VALA: Ad Hoc Dist. 5 Org. Com. VA Educ. Media Assn.: Libn. Cert. Com. (1978–); Pubns. Com. (1979). AAUW. Roanoke Prof. Educ. Assn. **Honors:** Phi Kappa Phi; Alpha Delta Kappa. **Activities:** 10, 11; 20, 31, 32; 61, 75, 89 **Addr.:** 2609 Wycliffe Ave., S.W., Roanoke, VA 24014.

Parker, J. Carlyle (O. 14, 1931, Ogden, UT) Head of Pub. Srvs., Asst. Lib. Dir., CA State Coll., Stanislaus, 1963–; Asst. Libn., Actg. Libn., Church Coll. of HI, 1960–63; Libn. II, Humboldt State Coll., 1958–60. **Educ.:** Brigham Young Univ., 1955–57, BA (Hist.); Univ. of CA, Berkeley, 1957–58, MLS. **Orgs.:** ALA. CA LA: Cncl. (1980); CA Socty. of Libns., Nom. Com. (Ch., 1971); State Coll. Libns.' Div. (Pres., 1969). AAUP: Campus Chap. (VP, 1975/76). Congs. of Fac. Assns. CA Coll. and Univ. Fac. Assns. **Honors:** ALA, Lib./U.S.A., 1965. **Pubns.:** *Library Service for Genealogists* (1981); *City, County, Town, and Township Index to the 1850 Federal Census Schedules* (1979); "Resources in the Field–Genealogy," *Wilson Lib. Bltn.* (N., 1972); "Faculty Status and the Academic Work Year," *CA Libn.* (Jl., 1972); jt. auth., "Accessibility of Local History and Genealogy Materials" cassette (1976). **Activities:** 1; 17, 31, 39; 57, 69, 90 **Addr.:** Library, California State College, Stanislaus, 800 Monte Vista Ave., Turlock, CA 95380.

Parker, John A. (Ja. 25, 1944, Norfolk, VA) Head, Gen. Ref., Norfolk Pub. Lib., 1974–; ILL Libn., 1972–74, Libn., 1968–72. **Educ.:** Old Dominion Coll., 1961–65, BA (Eng.); Univ. of NC, 1965–66, MS (LS), 1968, (Span.). **Orgs.:** NLA: Bibl. on Professionalism (1978–79). Amer. Assn. of Span. and Portuguese Tchrs. **Pubns.:** "Literature of the Comics," *VA Libn.* (Sum. 1971); "Reference Work," *Ref. Libn.* (1981). **Activities:** 2, 9; 16, 39, 45; 55, 69, 83 **Addr.:** 539 Warren Crescent, Norfolk, VA 23507.

Parker, Malcolm G. (Ag. 23, 1930, Purvis, MS) Dir. of Lib., LA State Univ., Shreveport, 1966–; Asst. Libn., LA State Univ., Baton Rouge, 1958–66; Libn., E. Jr. HS, 1954–56. **Educ.:** Univ. of South. MS, 1952–54, BS; LA State Univ., 1956–58, MS (LS), 1962–64, MEd (Educ. Admin.). **Orgs.:** ALA. SWLA. LA LA. Socty. of Southwest Archvsts. Prsrvn. Socty. of Shreveport. N. LA Hist. Assn. **Addr.:** 306 Yolanda Ln., Shreveport, LA 71105.

Parker, Martha Anna (Ap. 6, 1917, Kokomo, IN) Cat. libn., TN State Univ., 1972–; Ref. Libn., Ball State Univ., 1970–71; Secty., Glass Mgr. and Mfr. Staff, Ball Corp., 1966–68; Exec. Secy., Boarding Unit, Amer. HS Boys and Girls, Amer. Intl. Sch., New Delhi, India, 1963–64; Tchr., Kodaikanal Sch., Kodaikanal, S. India, 1961–1962; Various secty. and bookkeeping positions, 1938–65. **Educ.:** Butler Univ., 1943–47, BA (Relig. Educ.); Ball State Univ., 1968–70, MLS; IN Bus. Coll., 1937–38, Cert. **Orgs.:** ALA. SELA. Mid-State LA: Adv. Cncl. (1977–80). TN LA: TN Tech. Srvs. Libns., Secy., Treas. (1975–76). **Pubns.:** "Tennessee Library Association Section and Chapter Minutes: Minutes of the Resources and Technical Services Librarians, April 16, 1976," *TN Libn.* (Sum. 1976). **Activities:** 1; 20, 29, 39 **Addr.:** 1002 E. Northfield Blvd., Murfreesboro, TN 37130.

Parker, Mary Alma Cole (S. 4, 1932, Memphis, TN) Head Libn., Media Spec., Dougherty HS, 1972–; Libn., Memphis Pub. Schs., 1970–72; Libn., Chicago Pub. Lib., 1969–70. **Educ.:** MS Women's Univ., 1950–54, BA (Hist., Eng.); Rosary Coll., 1968–69, MALS; VA, IL, TN, GA, Tchng. Certs. **Orgs.:** ALA. GA LA. GA Lib. Media Dept. Daughters of Amer. Revolution. GA Assn. of Educ. Natl. Educ. Assn. **Activities:** 10; 17, 31, 32; 63 **Addr.:** 207 Oleander Rd., Albany, GA 31705.

Parker, Nancy Boothe (D. 5, 1930, Austin, TX) Head, Spec. Cols., Dir., Woodson Resrch. Ctr., Rice Univ., 1972–; Asst. Head, Acq. Dept., 1972, Acq. Libn., 1965–72. **Educ.:** Rice Inst., 1948–52, BA, hons. (Fr.); Cath. Univ., 1963–65, MS (LS); Rice Univ., 1974–79, MA (Amer. Hist.); Case-West. Rsv. Univ. Wkshp. in Coll. and Univ. Arch., 1973, Cert.; Natl. Hist. Pubns. and Recs. Comsn. Inst. on the Ed. of Hist. Docum., 1977, Cert. **Orgs.:** SAA: Arch./Lib. Rel. Com. (1974–78); ALA/SAA Com. (1977–80). ALA: Rare Bks. and Mss. Sect. Socty. of SW Archvsts.: Bd. (1977–79); VP (1980/81); Pres. (1981–82). Houston Area Resrch. Libs. Cnsrtm.: (Ch., 1979–). Spec. Cols. Com. TX State Hist. Assn. TX State Hist. Recs. Adv. Bd. **Honors:** Phi Beta Kappa, 1952; Beta Phi Mu, 1965. **Pubns.:** "Mirabeau B. Lamar's Texas Journal," *Southwest. Hist. Qtly.* (O. 1980, Ja. 1981); "Huxley Papers Acquired by Rice University," *TX Libs.* (Sum. 1980); *A Bibliography of Cataloged Archival Publications in the Fondren Library* (1980). **Activities:** 1, 2; 15, 17, 45 **Addr.:** Woodson Research Center, Rice University Library, Houston, TX 77001.

PROFESSIONAL ACTIVITIES: Institutions: 1. Acad. lib.; 2. Arch.; 3. Assn.; 4. Fed./Gvt. lib.; 5. Inst. lib.; 6. Mfr./Suppl.; 7. Milit. lib.; 8. Musm.; 9. Pub. lib.; 10. Sch. lib.; 11. Sch. of lib. sci.; 12. Spec. lib.; 13. State lib.; 14. (other). **Functions/Activities:** 15. Acq./Col. dev.; 16. Adult srvs.; 17. Admin.; 18. Apprais.; 19. Archit./Bldgs.; 20. Cat./Class.; 21. Chld. srvs.; 22. Circ.; 23. Cons./Pres.; 24. Consult.; 25. Cont. ed.; 26. Educ. lib. sci.; 27. Ext. srvs.; 28. Fund/Grants; 29. Gvt. pubs.; 30. Indx./Abs.; 31. Instr. lib. use; 32. Media srvs.; 33. Micro.; 34. Netwks./Coop.; 35. Persnl.; 36. PR; 37. Publshg.; 38. Recs. mgt.; 39. Ref. srvs.; 40. Repro.; 41. Resrch.; 42. Review.; 43. Secur.; 44. Serials; 45. Spec. col.; 46. Tech. srvs.; 47. Trustees/Bds.; 48. YA srvs.; 49. (other).

Parker, Peter J. (Ja. 11, 1936, White Plains, NY) Chief, Mss. Div., Hist. Socty. of PA, 1970–; Instr., Hist. Dept., Skidmore Coll., 1966–69. **Educ.:** Harvard Coll., 1952–56, AB (Hist.); Univ. of PA, 1962–65, PhD (Hist.). **Orgs.:** SAA: Ad-hoc Replevin (1979–80); Lib. Arch. Rel. Mid-Atl. Reg. Arch. Conf.: Treas. (1977–). PA Abolition Socty. Ebenezer Maxwell Mansion, Inc. **Honors:** Richard Allen Awd., Mother Bethel A.M.E. Church, 1981. **Pubns.:** *Pennsylvania on Paper* (1977); Various other bks., articles. **Activities:** 2; 15, 17, 45; 55, 70, 73, 95 **Addr.:** Historical Society of Pennsylvania, 1300 Locust St., Philadelphia, PA 19107.

Parker, Ralph H. (Ap. 21, 1909, Bertram, TX) Prof. Emeritus, Univ. of MO, 1977–, Dean, LS, 1966–74, Libn., 1947–66; Dir. of Libs., Univ. of GA, 1940–47. **Educ.:** Univ. of TX, 1925–29, BA (Hist.), 1929–35, PhD (Hist.); Univ. of Chicago, 1936–37, (LS). **Orgs.:** ALA. ASIS. Sigma Delta Chi. **Honors:** SLA, Hon. Mem., 1980; Med. LA, Hon. Mem., 1982. **Pubns.:** *Library Applications of Punched Cards* (1952); various articles. **Addr.:** 1104 S Glenwood, Columbia, MO 65201.

Parker, Richard M. (My. 17, 1942, Red Oak, IA) Asst. Dir., Pub. Srvs., Tulsa City-Cnty. Lib., 1977–; Dir., Boonslick Reg. Lib., 1968–77; Sch. Libn., Linn HS, 1964–67. **Educ.:** Southwest MO State Univ., 1960–64, BS (Educ., Fr.); MO Univ., 1967–68, MA (LS). **Orgs.:** ALA: Eval. Com. for Autom. Circ. Syst. (1978–79); Metro., Syst. Sect.: Com. on Org. and Plng. (1980–). OK LA: Lib. Dev. Com. (1977–); Reorg. Com. (1979–80). MO LA: Reorg. Com. (1979); Treas. (1970); Legis. Com. (1972–74). Southwestern LA: Pub. Lib. Interest Grp. (Vice-Ch., 1978–80). **Activities:** 9; 17, 22, 35; 78 **Addr.:** Tulsa City-County Library, 400 Civic Center, Tulsa, OK 74103.

Parker, Robert Lawrence (F. 19, 1946, Mobile, AL) Dir., Lib. Srvs., Bishop State Jr. Coll., 1975–; Libn./Archvst., A & M Univ., 1971–74. **Educ.:** AL State Coll., 1967–68, BS (Eng.); Rutger's Univ., 1971–72, MLS. **Orgs.:** AL Jr. Coll. LA: Parlmt. ALA: ACRL, Comm. Com. Bay Area LA. **Activities:** 1; 17; 63, 75, 80 **Addr.:** SD Bishop State Junior College Library, 351 N. Broad St., Mobile, AL 36603.

Parker, Sandra A. (Mr. 12, 1943, Kingston, ON, Can.) Sr. Syst. Anal., Cida (Can.), 1981; Sr. Syst. Libn., Natl. Lib. of Can., 1977–80; Info. and Mgt. Syst., Hlth. and Welfare, Can., 1976–77; Lib. Syst. Anal., Carleton Univ. Lib., 1974–76, Catlgr., 1970–74. **Educ.:** Queen's Univ., 1962–65, BA (Bio.); Simmons Coll., 1974–77, MSc (LS); 1972, Cert. (Syst. Mgt.); 1974, Cert. (Comp. and Mgt. Info. Srvs.). **Orgs.:** Can. LA: Can. Assn. of Spec. Lib. and Info. Srvs., PR (1975–78); Ottawa Chap., Vice Ch. (1978), Ch. (1979–80). **Honors:** Beta Phi Mu, 1978. **Pubns.:** "The Use of English Language Cataloguing in Publication Data in a University Library," *ON Lib. Review* (S. 1976); "A Comparative Bibliometric Study of Two Professional Library Journals: Special Libraries and the Journal of the American Society for Information Science," *Current Awareness-Lib. Lit.* (Ja.–F. and S.–O. 1978); "A Conceptual Framework for the Performance Measurement of a Canadian Federal Government Health Sciences Library Network," *Quantitative Measure. and Dynamic Lib. Srvs.* (1979). **Activities:** 1, 4; 17, 20, 34; 51, 56, 59 **Addr.:** 61 Pine Ridge Rd., Carp, ON K0A 1L0 Canada.

Parker, Sara A. (F. 19, 1939, Cassville, MO) Supvsr., Reg. Systs. Coord., CO State Lib., 1978–; Netwk. Coord., SW MO Lib. Netwk., 1976–78; Bkmobile. Supvsr., Springfield-Greene Cnty. Lib., 1974–76, Adult Srvs. Libn., 1972–74, Ref. Libn., 1966–72. **Educ.:** OK State Univ., 1957–61, BA (Pol. Sci.); Univ. of NC, 1961–62, (Pol. Sci.); Emporia State Tchrs. Coll., 1967–68, ML (LS). **Orgs.:** ALA: ASCLA/Multitype Coop. Sect., Legis. Com. (Ch., 1978–); Netwks. Are People Com. (1979); State Agency Sect. (Secy., 1980–). Mt. Plains LA: State Agencies Ch. (1980). West. Cncl. of State Libs.: Consult. Task Frc. (1979–). MO LA: Lib. Dev. Com. (Ch., 1977). Various other orgs., coms. **Honors** Beta Phi Mu. **Activities:** 13, 14-Coop. lib. agencies; 24, 34, 35; 56, 78, 93 **Addr.:** Colorado State Library, 1362 Lincoln, Denver, CO 80203.

Parker, Stephen C. (Je. 13, 1944, Pipestone, MN) Proj. Dir., Natl. Diabetes Info. Clearinghse., CSR, Inc. 1980–; Proj. Supvsr., Natl. Hlth. Plng. Info. Ctr., Franklin Resrch. Ctr., 1978–80; Resrch. Asst., Univ. of MD, 1976–77; Ref. Libn., Univ. of AR, Little Rock, 1973–76. **Educ.:** Macalester Coll., 1962–66, BA (Eng.); Univ. of SD, 1970–72, MA (Eng.); Univ. of MO, 1972–73, MA (LS). **Orgs.:** AR LA: Treas. (1975–76); Int. Frdm. Com. (1976). SWLA: Awds. Com. (1975–76). ASIS. AAUP. **Honors:** Donaghey Fndn., Innovative Tchg. Grant, 1974; Beta Phi Mu, 1973. **Pubns.:** "Information Services for School Speech-Language Pathologists and Educational Audiologists," *Lang., Sp., and Hearing Srvs. in Schs.* (Ap. 1978); "A Manual SDI System for Academic Libraries," *RQ* (Fall 1975). **Activities:** 1, 12; 15, 17, 24; 58, 75, 91 **Addr.:** CSR, Inc., 805 15th St., N.W., Suite 500, Washington, DC 20005.

Parker, Velma Dorothy (D. 27, 1941, Sioux Lookout, ON) Documtn. Ofcr., Class. and Subj. Anal., Natl. Map Col., Pub. Arch. of Can., 1979–; Cat., Map Lib., Univ. of Ottawa, 1973–79; Sch. Libn., Tchr., Timmins High and Vocational Sch., 1967–72. **Educ.:** Univ. of West. ON, 1962–66, Hon. BA (Geo.), 1972–73, MLS, 1966–67, HS Type A (Geo.), Cert. (Sch. Libnshp.). **Orgs.:** Assn. of Can. Map Libs.: Natl. Un. Cat. Com. (1974–). Anglo-Amer. Cat. Com. for Cartographic Mtrls.: Secretariat and Ed. Com. (1979–). **Activities:** 1, 2; 20, 24; 70 **Addr.:** National Map Collection, Public Archives of Canada, 395 Wellington St., Ottawa, ON K1A 0N3 Canada.

Parker, Virginia (O. 10, 1916, Brookhaven, MS) Retired, 1981; Libn., Bracken Lib., Queen's Univ., ON, 1967–81; Libn., TX Med. Ctr. Lib., 1957–67; Assoc. Libn., Univ. of TX Med. Branch, 1956–57. **Educ.:** Tulane Univ., 1933–37, BA (Fr.); LA State Univ., 1941–42, BS (LS). **Orgs.:** Med. LA: Bylaws Com. (Ch., 1970–71). SLA: Los Angeles Chap. (Pres., 1949). Assn. of Can. Med. Colls.: Spec. Resrc. Com. on Med. Sch. Libs. (Secy., 1970–71); Stats. (1969–70, 1977–78, 1978–79). Can. Hlth. Libs. Assn. Natl. Audubon Socty. Toastmstrs. **Honors:** Phi Beta Kappa, 1937; Beta Phi Mu, 1942. **Pubns.:** Assoc. ed., *Bltn. of the Med. LA* (1971–74); "Antony van Leeuwenhoek," *Bltn. of the Med. LA* (Jl. 1965). **Activities:** 17; 80 **Addr.:** Bracken Library, Botterell Hall, Queen's University, Kingston, ON K7L 3N6 Canada.

Parker, Wyman W. (O. 31, 1912, Woburn, MA) Appraiser of Lit. Property, 1979– Asst. Prof., Div. of Lib. Sci., S. CT State Coll., 1976–81; Head Libn., Wesleyan Univ., 1956–77; Head Libn., Univ. of Cincinnati, 1951–56; Head Libn., Kenyon Coll., 1946–51. **Educ.:** Middlebury Coll., 1932–34, BS (Amer. Lit.), 1932–39, MA; Columbia Univ., 1934–35, BLS. **Orgs.:** ALA: ACRL, Pres. (1960). CT LA. Appraisers Assn. of Amer. Grolier Club. Columbiad Club. Acorn Club. **Pubns.:** *Henry Stevens of Vermont; American Rare Book Dealer in London 1845–1886* (1963); *Connecticut's Colonial and Continental Money* (1976); various articles. **Activities:** 1, 11; 18, 24, 45; 57 **Addr.:** Literary Appraisals, 330 Pine St., Middletown, CT 06457.

Parkes, Darla Vaughn (O. 31, 1940, Cuba, MO) Ref. and ILL Libn., MO State Lib., 1972–; Chld. Libn., Baden Branch, St. Louis Pub. Lib., 1969–71; Adv. Mgr., Bethany Press, Christ. Bd. of Pubns., 1963–68. **Educ.:** Univ. of MO, 1963, BJ (Jnlsm.), 1972, MA (LS); Harris Jr. Coll., 1959–61, (Assoc. in arts). **Orgs.:** ALA. SLA. MO LA. Beta Phi Mu: Secy., Treas. (1978–79). **Honors:** Sigma Tau Delta. **Pubns.:** *Index to Missouri Highways* (1980); various articles, poems. **Activities:** 13; 15, 34, 39 **Addr.:** Interlibrary Loans, Missouri State Library, P.O. Box 387, 308 High, Jefferson City, MO 65102.

Parkes, Katherine P. (Lakewood, OH) Libn., Natl. Housing Law Proj., Natl. Econ. Dev. and Law Ctr., 1977–; Libn., Inst. of Judicial Admin., 1963–75. **Educ.:** Oberlin Coll. and NY Univ., 1941–47, BA (Eng.); Columbia Univ., 1965–68, MSLS. **Orgs.:** AALL: Ethics Com. (1973–75). SLA. Assn. of Legal Srvs. Libns.: Nsltr. Ed. (1978–). Leag. of Women Voters. Inst. of Judicial Admin. **Honors:** Beta Phi Mu, 1968. **Pubns.:** Co-Auth., *Law Books Recommended for Libraries: Judicial Administration* (1970); Ed., *Judicial Administration in the Courts* (1976); "Judicial Administration," *Anl. Srvy. Amer. Law* (1974–75); bk. review clmn. in *Judges' Jnl.* (1970–73). **Activities:** 12; 15, 17, 39; 59, 65, 77 **Addr.:** 2150 Shattuck Ave. Ste 300, Berkeley, CA 94704.

Parkin, Margaret L. (Mr. 31, 1921, Toronto, ON) Indxr. *Can. Per. Indx.*, Can. LA, 1979–; Chief Libn., Archvst., Can. Nurses Assn., 1964–79; Libn., Unempl. Insr. Comsn., 1962–64; Libn., Econ. and Resrch. Branch, Dept. of Labour, 1961–62; Royal Can. Air Force, 1951–59; Resrch. Ofcr., Natl. Resrch. Cncl. of Can., 1946–50. **Educ.:** Univ. of Toronto, 1939–42, BA (Gen. Arts); Ottawa Univ., 1959–60, BLS. **Orgs.:** Can. LA. Indx. Abs. Socty. Can. ON LA. LA of Ottawa. Womens Can. Club. Can. Nature Fed. Can. Wildlife Fed. **Pubns.:** *Index of Canadian Nursing Studies* (1965–79); Indxr., Eng. and Fr. Ed., *Nursing Unit Administration* (1980); "Information Resources for Nursing Research," *Can. Nurse* (Mr. 1972); "Library Service and the Nursing Profession in Canada," *Intl. Nursing Review* (Ja. 1969); "Ten Years of Operation," *Agora* (Ja. 1975); various articles, indxs. **Activities:** 12; 17, 30, 38; 63, 80, 92 **Addr.:** 301–10 Driveway, Ottawa, ON K2P 1C7 Canada.

Parkkari, John (Je. 24, 1930, Meyronne, SK) Head, Acq. Dept., Can. Inst. for S.T.I., 1972–, Asst. Head, Acq. Dept., 1971–72; Lectr., Sch. of Lib. and Info. Sci., Univ. of West. ON, 1971. **Educ.:** Univ. of AB, 1951–56, BSc (Chem.); Univ. of West. ON, 1969–70, MLS. **Orgs.:** ALA. Can. LA. **Pubns.:** Ed., *Science and Technology Collections in Canadian Libraries* (1977). **Activities:** 4, 12; 15, 44; 91 **Addr.:** National Research Council, Canada Institute for S.T.I., Ottawa, ON K1A 0S2 Canada.

Parks, Dorothy Ruth (My. 20, 1928, Chattanooga, TN) Dir., Dvnty. Lib., Vanderbilt Univ. Lib., 1979–, Actg. Dir., 1979, Ref. Libn., 1970–78, Circ. Supvsr., 1967–70. **Educ.:** TN Tech. Univ., 1948–50, BS (Math.); Vanderbilt Univ., 1959–67, BD (Relig.); Peabody Coll., 1968–70, MLS; TN Tech. Univ., 1948–50, Tchrs. Cert. **Orgs.:** ATLA: Bd. Dir. (1981–84). Amer. Acad. of Relig. **Honors:** Lilly Fndn., 1968. **Pubns.:** "Tennessee Theological Library Association Union List of Current Subscriptions and Standing Orders" (1978). **Activities:** 1; 39, 41, 44; 90 **Addr.:** Divinity Library, Vanderbilt University Library, Nashville, TN 37203.

Parks, George Richard (Ap. 11, 1935, Boston, MA) Univ. Libn., Colgate Univ., 1980–; various positions as lib. bldg. consult.; Dean, Univ. Libs., Univ. of RI, 1969–80; Asst. Libn. for Admin., Actg. Dir., Univ. of Rochester, 1966–69; Asst. to Asst. Dir., Enoch Pratt Free Lib., 1965–66. **Educ.:** Univ. of NH, 1955–59, AB (Eng.); Univ. of MI, 1961–62, MALS; Univ. of IL, 1966, Sem. in Comp. Applications in Libs. **Orgs.:** Five Assoc. Libs.: Exec. Com. (1967–69). New Eng. Lib. Info. Netwk.: Exec. Bd. (1969–75); Ch. (1972–73). Univ. of MI LS Alum. Socty.: Ch. (1971–72). ALA: ACRL, 1978 Natl. Conf. Ch.; New Eng. Chap. (Pres., 1975). Various other orgs. and coms. Episcopal Cursillo of NY: Rector (1979). Dio. of RI: Lay Mnstry. Com. (1979–80). **Honors:** Phi Beta Kappa; Phi Kappa Phi; Beta Phi Mu. **Pubns.:** Various sps. **Activities:** 1; 17, 19, 24 **Addr.:** Everett Needham Case Library, Colgate University, Hamilton, NY 13346.

Parks, Hilda A. (Ag. 24, 1943, Mankato, MN) Sr. High Libn., Glencoe Pub. Schs., 1972–; Sec. Libn., Elmu Pub. Schs., 1970–72; Libn., Crandon Inst., 1967–69. **Educ.:** Univ. of MN, 1961–65, BS (Eng.), 1965–70, MA (LS); 1974, Media Generalist Cert. **Orgs.:** ALA. MN Media Org. Dem. Farmer Labor Party. **Activities:** 10; 15, 20, 39 **Addr.:** Glencoe Senior High School, Glencoe, MN 55336.

Parks, James F., Jr. (O. 14, 1942, Louisville, MS) Head Libn., Millsaps Coll., 1969–; Head, Circ. Dept., Univ. of AL Lib., 1968–69; Circ., Ref. Libn., MS Coll. Lib., 1964–68; various tchg. positions. **Educ.:** MS Coll., 1960–64, BA (Eng.); George Peabody Coll., 1965–67, MLS; various crs. **Orgs.:** MSLA: Pres. (1978); VP (1977); Treas. (1971); various coms.; Ed. *MS Libs.* (1979–80). Southeastern LA: Lib. Dev. Com. (1978–82). ALA: Chap. Cnclr. (1979–83); ACRL. AAUP. Frdm. to Read Fndn. **Activities:** 1; 25, 31, 37; 63, 74, 89 **Addr.:** Millsaps-Wilson Library, Millsaps College, Jackson, MS 39210.

Parks, (The Rev.) Ralph W., Jr. (Ap. 4, 1916, Nelsonville, OH) Historiographer, Archvst., The Diocese of MI, 19–; The Rector, All Saints Episcopal Church, Detroit, 1958–81; Archdeacon, the Diocese of MI, 1955–58; Prin., Instr., The Diocesan Sch. of Theo., 1954–74. **Educ.:** OH Univ., 1937–48, BS, MA (Phil.); Yale Univ., 1939–41, MDiv (Theo.); Wayne State Univ., 1968–72 MSLS; Diocesan Sch. of Theo., 1965–68, Dipl. (Theo.). **Orgs.:** ALA. ATLA. Adult Psyt. Clinic: Bd. Mem.; Pres. (1957–81). Diocesan Sch. of Theo.: Bd. Mem.; Pres. (1954–). **Honors:** Lambeth Coll., Doctor of Sacred Theo., 1948; Testimonial Scroll, St. Stephen's Church, Wyandotte, MI, 1955; Dipl. of Cmdn., Diocesan Sch. of Theo., Detroit, MI, 1979; Beta Phi Mu, 1977. **Pubns.:** *The Social Philosophy of William Temple* (1948); Chaplain's Clmn., *Wolverine Minute Man* (1976–); various articles. **Activities:** 2; 15, 23, 24; 90 **Addr.:** 19450 Lucerne Dr., Detroit, MI 48203.

Parlato, Salvatore J., Jr. (F. 26, 1936, Buffalo, NY) Natl. Eval. Coord., Captioned Films for the Deaf, 1973–; Media Coord., Asst. Prof., Rochester Inst. of Tech., 1969–73; NY State Dist. Mgr., Encyc. Britannica Films, 1961–69. **Educ.:** Holy Cross Coll., Worcester, MA, 1954–58, AB (Hum.); Syracuse Univ., 1959–61, MS (Media); various crs. **Orgs.:** AECT: Div. of Media Mgt. ALA: Tech. & Handcpd. Rochester Resrcs. Inc.: Pres. (1972–73). **Honors:** NY State AV Assn., Performance Cmdn., 1968. **Pubns.:** *Films Ex Libris* (1980); *Superfilms....Award Winners* (1976); *Films...Too Good for Words* (1973); Prod. Consult., "Immunize Your Child" film (1975); "Good Losers...Films the Festivals Missed," *Lifelong Lrng.* (Ja. 1980); "Movies for Mainstreaming," *Young Learners* (Ja. 1980); various articles. **Activities:** 4, 12; 24, 32, 37; 63, 67, 72 **Addr.:** 2328 Glenmont Cir., Apt. T6, Silver Spring, MD 20902.

Parming, Marju Rink (Ja. 28, 1948, Geislingen, W. Germany) Deputy Dir., Ofc. of Info. Systs. and Srvs., U.S. Gen. Acct. Ofc., 1981–, Mgr., Tech. Info. Srcs. and Srvs., 1980–81, Deputy Dir., Ofc. of Libn., 1979–80, Chief, Ref. Sect., Ofc. of Libn., 1977–79, Libn., Ref. Sect., 1974–77; Libn., Ref. and Readrs. Srvs., New Haven Free Pub. Lib., 1971–74. **Educ.:** Univ. of PA, 1965–69, BA (Eng.); Columbia Univ., 1970–71, MS (LS); Univ. of Helsinki, Finland, 1969–70, Cert. (Estonian lang. and lit.); various crs. **Orgs.:** ASIS. SLA: DC Chap. Ofc. of Persnl. Mgt. Task Force on Lib. Productivity. Assn. for the Advnc. of Baltic Std.: Bibl. Com. (Secy., 1974–). Estonian Learned Socty. in Amer. **Honors:** US Gen. Acct. Ofc., Ofc. Dir. Awd., 1978; US Gen. Acct. Ofc., Outstan. Performance, 1975. **Pubns.:** "English-Language Sources on Estonian Poetry," *The Poetry of Estonia* (1981); *Bibliography of English-Language Sources on Estonia* (1974); "Baltic Materials in On-Line Data Bases," *Jnl. of Baltic Std.* (Fall 1978); "Bibliographies on Estonia," *Jnl. of Baltic Std.* (Fall 1976); various sp. **Activities:** 4, 12; 17, 35, 39; 56, 59, 92 **Addr.:** Office of Information Systems and Services, Rm. 4131, US General Accounting Office, 441 G St., N.W., Washington, DC 20548.

Parr, Mary Anne (Ap. 10, 1925, Dardanelle, AR) Med. Libn., St. Francis Hosp.-Med. Ctr., 1969–; Bus., Sci. and Tech. Libn., Peoria Pub. Lib., 1962–64; Asst. Bus. Libn., Caterpillar Tractor Co., 1954–56. **Educ.:** OK Bapt. Univ., 1943–47, AB (Hist.); Univ. of IL, 1951–53, MS (LS); 1974–81, Med. Libnshp. Cert. **Orgs.:** Hlth. Sci. Libns. of IL: Treas. (1980–82). Med. LA: Midwest Reg. Grp. IL LA. **Activities:** 5, 12; 15, 20, 24; 80, 91

Special Subjects/Services: 50. Adult educ.; 51. Advert./Mktg.; 52. Aerosp.; 53. Agric.; 54. Area std.; 55. Arts/Hum.; 56. Autom.; 57. Bibl./Prtg.; 58. Bio. sci.; 59. Bus./Fin.; 60. Chem.; 61. Copyrt.; 62. Documtn.; 63. Educ.; 64. Engin.; 65. Env.; 66. Eth. grps.; 67. Film; 68. Food/Nutr.; 69. Geneal.; 70. Geo.; 71. Geol.; 72. Handcpd.; 73. Hist.; 74. Int. frdm.; 75. Info. sci.; 76. Insr.; 77. Law; 78. Legis.; 79. Math./Comp. sci.; 80. Med.; 81. Metals; 82. Nat. resrcs.; 83. Newsp.; 84. Nuc. sci.; 85. Oral hist.; 86. Petr./Energy; 87. Pharm.; 88. Phys./Astr./Math.; 89. Readg.; 90. Relig.; 91. Sci./Tech.; 92. Soc. sci.; 93. Telecom.; 94. Transp.; 95. (other).

Addr.: Medical Library, St. Francis Hospital-Medical Center, 530 N.E. Glen Oak Ave., Peoria, IL 61637.

Parr, Mary Y. (Je. 21, 1927, Cleveland, OH) Head, Pers. Dept., Hofstra Univ., 1975–; Head, Prog. Dev., Dist. of Columbia, Pub. Lib., 1973–74; Assoc. Prof., St. John's Univ., 1969–73; Assoc. Prof., Pratt Inst., 1962–69. **Educ.:** Coll. of Wooster, 1945–48, AB (Eng., Soclgy.); West. Rsv. Univ., 1948–49, MLS; Tchrs. Coll., 1957–60. **Orgs.:** ALA: John Cotton Dana Awd. Com. (1976–80). NY LA: Lib. Educ. Sect. (Pres., 1976–78). AAUP. **Pubns.:** Jt. auth., "University Library Search and Screen Committees," *Coll. and Resrch. Libs.* (Jl. 1976); "Library Technicians at Drexel," *Coll. and Resrch. Libs.* (My. 1966). **Activities:** 1, 11; 24, 26, 44 **Addr.:** Hofstra University, Hempstead, NY 11550.

Parr, Virginia H. (My. 23, 1937, Mansfield, OH) Asst. Univ. Libn. for Pub. Srvs., Univ. of OR, 1980–, Head, Educ.-Psy. Sect., 1979–80, Libn., 1973–79; Tchr., Livonia, MI, 1961–64. **Educ.:** Oberlin Coll., 1955–59, Univ. of Vienna, Austria, 1958; BA (Psy.); Univ. of MI, 1959–61, MA (Educ. Psy.); Univ. of OR, 1972–73, MLS. **Orgs.:** ALA: LAMA (1981–); LIRT (1977–78); ACRL/Educ. and Bhvl. Sci. Sect. (1977), Psy.-Psyt. Com. (Ch., 1978–), Bibl. Instr. for Educ. Com. (1980–), Exec. Com. (1977–80) Bibl. Instr. Sect., Nom. Com. (Ch., 1979–80), Educ. for Bibl. Instr. Com. (1977–79). OR LA. ASIS. **Honors:** Beta Phi Mu, 1973; Pi Lambda Theta, 1961. **Pubns.:** "Online Information Retrieval and the Undergraduate," *Tchg. of Psy.* (1979); "Course-Related Library Instruction for Psychology Students," *Tchg. of Psy.* (1978); ed., *Bhvl. and Soc. Sci. Libn.* (1978–). **Activities:** 1; 17, 39, 49-Pub. Srvs.; 63, 92 **Addr.:** 630 W. 30th, Eugene, OR 97405.

Parris, Lou B. (Ap. 26, 1935, Beaumont, TX) Supvsr., Info. Ctr., Exxon Prod. Resrch. Co., 1979–, Sr. Info. Spec., 1978–79, Info. Spec., 1970–78; Resrch. Libn., Collins Radio Co., 1969–70. **Educ.:** Southwest. Univ., 1953–54, BA, magna cum laude (Eng.); Univ. of TX, 1966–68, MLS. **Orgs.:** SLA: TX Chap., Pres. (1972–73); 1st VP (1971–72); 2nd VP, Bltn. Ed. (1970–71); Petr. and Energy Resrcs. Div. (Ch., 1977–78). ASIS. **Activities:** 12; 17, 24, 49-Lit. Srch.; 86 **Addr.:** Exxon Production Research Co., P.O. Box 2189, Houston, TX 77001.

Parrish, James Hilliard (My. 23, 1926, Nashville, TN) Prof., Coord. for Extramural Prog., Lib. of the Hlth. Sci., Univ. of IL at the Med. Ctr., Chicago, 1971–; Libn., HI Med. Lib., 1969–71; Actg. Dir., Asst. Libn., Falk Lib. of the Hlth. Profs., Univ. Pittsburgh., 1966–69; Asst. Med. Libn., Univ. of KY, 1964–66; Head Lib. Srvs., Manned Space Craft Ctr., NASA Tech. Lib., 1963–64; Ref. Libn., Sch. of Aerosp. Med., San Antonio, TX, 1960–63; Ref. Libn., Air Univ., Maxwell AFB, 1957–60; Circ. Ref. Libn., Univ. of TN Martin Branch, 1955–57. **Educ.:** Mid. TN State Univ., 1950–53, BS (Sci.); George Peabody Coll., 1953–55, MALS; Med. LA, 1960, Cert. **Orgs.:** Med. LA: Midwest Reg. Grp. Hlth. Sci. Libns. of IL. AAUP. **Pubns.:** "Consortia Development in Regions VII's RML Program of the National Library of Medicine," *Procs. of the Fourth Intl. Congs. on Med. Libnshp.* (1980); "Medical Libraries in the 50th State," *HI LA Jnl.* (Je. 1969); ed., *Illinois Health Science Libraries Serial Holdings List* (1973–). **Activities:** 1; 17, 24, 27; 58, 80 **Addr.:** Library of the Health Sciences, University of Illinois at the Medical Center, P.O. Box 7509, Chicago, IL 60680.

Parrott, Margaret Sangster (D. 31, 1922, Throckmorton, TX) Assoc. Prof. of LS, Univ. of NC, Greensboro, 1970–; Head, Pub. Srvs., NC State Lib., 1969–70, Head, Tech. Srvs., 1963–69, Docum. Libn., 1957–63; Asst. Circ. Libn., N. TX State Univ., 1947–57. **Educ.:** N. TX State Univ., 1943–47, AB (LS); Univ. of NC, 1954–57, MSLS. **Orgs.:** SLA: NC Chap. (VP/Pres., 1971–73); Mem. Com. (1974–79). ALA: Descr. Cat. Com. (1968–70). SELA: SE Reg. Grp. of Res. and Tech. Srvs. (Secy.–Treas., 1965–69); NC LA: Resrcs.-Tech. Srvs., Vice Ch./Ch.; various coms. (1958–). **Honors:** Delta Kappa Gamma; Sigma Tau Delta; Beta Phi Mu. **Pubns.:** *Classification Scheme for North Carolina State Documents* (1975); *Directory of Special Libraries in North Carolina* (1979). **Activities:** 12, 13; 15, 29, 39; 55, 63, 92 **Addr.:** Library Science/Educational Technology Department, School of Education, University of North Carolina at Greensboro, Greensboro, NC 27412.

Parry, Eleanor E. (Je. 25, 1916, Washington, DC) Retired, 1981–; Ref., Per. Libn., Evangel Coll., 1977–81; Dir. of Lib., Assm. of God Grad. Sch., 1974–77; Ref. Per. Libn., Evangel Coll., 1968–74; Dir. of Lib., Ctrl. Bible Coll., 1955–68. **Educ.:** Taylor Univ., 1938–41, BA (Soclgy., Psy.); George Washington Univ., 1948–50, MS (Psy.); Cath. Univ. of Amer., Washington, DC, 1955–59, MSLS; Ctrl. Bible Inst., Springfield, MO, 1935–38, Dip. (Bible). **Orgs.:** Amer. Socty. of Indxrs. Christian Libns. Flwshp. Springfield Area Libns. Assn. Socty. for Pentecostal Std. AAUW: Springfield Branch (Treas., 1970–72). **Honors:** Beta Phi Mu. **Activities:** 1; 30, 39, 44; 55, 90, 92 **Addr.:** 608 W. Kerr St., Springfield, MO 65803.

Parry, Pamela Jeffcott (Mr. 6, 1948, New York, NY) Exec. Secy., ARLIS/NA, 1980–; Libn., Data Arch. and Resrch. Ctr., Univ. of IA, 1979–81; Ed., The Art Ref. Col., Greenwood Press, 1979–; Ed., ARLIS/NA Nsltr., ARLIS/NA 1978–; Ed. Asst., *Arch. of Neurology*, Amer. Med. Assn., 1976–78; Asst. Fine Arts Libn., Columbia Univ., 1972–76; Asst. Slide Cur., Dept. of Art Hist. & Archlg., Columbia Univ. 1970–72. **Educ.:** Univ. of AZ, 1967–69, BA (Art Hist.); Columbia Univ., 1969–71, MA (Art Hist.), 1971–73, MS (LS). Coll. Art Assn. Amer. Socty. of Assn. Execs. Women's Caucus for Art. **Honors:** Phi Kappa Phi, 1968. **Pubns.:** *Photography Index* (1979); *Contemporary Art & Artists* (1978); "Joseph Christian Leyendecker, 1874–1951," *Dict. of American Bio.* (1971); Contrib., *From Realism to Symbolism: Whistler and this World* (1971). **Activities:** 1, 2; 15, 30, 37; 55 **Addr.:** 3775 Bear Creek Cir., Tucson, AZ 85715.

Parsley, Brantley H. (O. 15, 1927, Baltimore, MD) Lib. Dir., Campbellsville Coll., 1965–; Supt., Night Circ. and Stack, Theo. Sch., Emory Univ., 1961–65; Lib. Asst., New Orleans Pub. Lib., 1958–61; Pastor, Calvary Baptist Church, 1955–57. **Educ.:** A.A. Baltimore Jr. Coll., 1950; Univ. of MD, 1950–52, BA (Soclgy.); New Orleans Baptist Theo. Semy., 1955, BD, 1958, MRE (Theo., Relig. Educ.); Emory Univ., 1961–65, (LS). **Orgs.:** KY LA: Nom. Com. (1978); Educ. Com. (1967–70); Coll. and Resrch. Sect. Nom. Com. (Ch., 1970–71). Cncl. of Indp. KY Coll. and Univ.: Ch. (1970–75); Solinet Com. (1975–). ALA: ACRL. Southeastern LA. Campbellsville Coll. Geneal. Wkshps.: Dir. (1978–79). Sch. Merger Wkshp.: Dir. (1976). Ctrl. KY Arts Series: Bd. of Dir. (1970–79); Pres. (1975–77). Taylor Cnty. Hist. Socty.: Bd. of Dir. (1969). **Pubns.:** "Book Selection by Challenge," *Coll. Mgt.* (D. 1968); "Activism: Opiate of the People," *West. Recorder* (Ag. 1969); "Confrontation–Library Style," *KY LA Bltn.* (O. 1969). **Activities:** 1; 15, 17, 24; 63, 69, 90 **Addr.:** 114 Longview Dr., Campbellsville, KY 42718.

Parson, Lethiel C. (Ag. 11, 1946, Tela, Repub. of Honduras) Assoc. Libn., Atl. Un. Coll., 1977–; Libn. and Eng. Tchr., Chisholm Trail Acad., 1974–76; Libn., Eng. Tchr., Valley Grande Acad., 1971–74. **Educ.:** Atl. Un. Coll., 1965–69, BA (Span., Eng.); Loma Linda Univ., 1969–74, MA (Eng.); TX Woman's Univ., 1975–76, MLS; 1976–77 (LS). **Orgs.:** ALA. ACRL. **Honors:** Beta Phi Mu, 1977. **Activities:** 1; 22, 39, 45; 50 **Addr.:** P.O. Box 663, South Lancaster, MA 01561.

Parsons, A. Chapman (Ap. 30, 1922, Ripley, WV) Exec. Dir., OH LA, OH Lib. Trustees Assn., 1964–; Dir., Rodman Pub. Lib., 1956–64; Dir., Gallia Cnty. Dist. Lib., 1952–56; Cnty. Libn., Martins Ferry Pub. Lib., 1950–52. **Educ.:** WV Univ., 1946–49, BS (Educ.); West. Rsv. Univ., 1949–50, MS (LS); Inst. for Org. Mgt., Syracuse Univ., 1965–68, Cert. **Orgs.:** ALA: Chap. Cnclr. (1961–64), Cnclr. at Large (1968–72); PLA, Com. on Stan. (Ch., 1966–68), Nom. Com. Ch. Cncl. of LA Exec.: Pres. (1975–78). OH Lib. Fndn.: Exec. VP (1965–). **Honors:** Disting. Alum., Sch. of Lib. Sci., Case West. Rsv. Univ., 1979. **Pubns.:** Managing Ed., *OH LA Bltn.* (1964–); Ed., *OH Lib. Trustee* (1964–). **Activities:** 9, 12; 17, 37; 78 **Addr.:** 1139 Firth Ave., Worthington, OH 43085.

Parsons, George A. (Jl. 5, 1921, Buffalo, NY) Info. Systs. Spec., Cncl. on Lib. Resrcs., Inc., 1969–. **Educ.:** Cornell Univ., 1939–43, BS (Agr. Econ.). **Orgs.:** ALA: RTSD/Serials Sect.; LITA. ASIS: Lib. Autom. and Netwks.; User On-Line Interaction. **Activities:** 3; 24, 34, 44; 56 **Addr.:** Council on Library Resources Inc., One DuPont Circle N.W., Suite 620, Washington, DC 20036.

Parsons, Jane A. (O. 31, 1927, Montgomery, AL) Serials Libn., Towson State Univ., 1969–; Catlgr., Med. and Chirurgical Fac. of the State of MD, 1967–69; Elem. Sch. Libn., Bd. of Educ., Baltimore Cnty., MD, 1966–67; Asst. to the Supt. of Branches and Ref. Libn., Adult Srv. Libn., Asst. Branch Libn., Brooklyn. Pub. Lib., 1949–59. **Educ.:** Univ. of NC, Greensboro, 1944–48, AB (Hist.); Univ. of NC, Chapel Hill, 1948–49, BS (LS). **Orgs.:** ALA. MD LA: Acad. and Resrch. Lib. Div., Vice Ch./Prog. Ch. (1973–74), Ch. (1974–75); Nom. and Elec. Com. (1975–76); Ed. Bd. (1976–77). **Addr.:** 412 Woodbine Ave., Towson, MD 21204.

Parsons, Jerry L. (Mr. 1, 1942, Niagara Falls, NY) Asst. Univ. Libn. for Admin., CA State Univ., Sacramento, 1976–; Lib. Admin. Asst., Univ. of IL, 1971–76; Asst. Coord., Info. and Lib. Resrcs., SUNY, Buffalo, 1968–71. **Educ.:** SUNY, Buffalo, 1963–65, BA (Eng.), 1965–70, PhD (Higher Educ.); Univ. of IL, 1972–75, MSLS. **Orgs.:** ALA: ACRL. CA LA: Cncl. (1979–81). SLA. **Honors:** Phi Delta Kappa, 1970; Beta Phi Mu, 1975. **Pubns.:** "Characteristics of Research Library Directors, 1958 and 1973," *Wilson Lib. Bltn.* (Ap. 1976); "Accreditation in Legal Education and in Education for Librarianship, 1878–1961," *Law Lib. Jnl.* (My. 1975); "Setting the Capstone: the Special Collections Library," *Non Solus* (1977). **Activities:** 1; 17, 25; 56, 63 **Addr.:** 601A Library, California State University, 2000 Jed Smith Dr., Sacramento, CA 95819.

Parsons, Nancy E. (Mr. 16, 1946, New Haven, CT) Cmnty. Libn., Silver Spring Lib. Montgomery Cnty. Pub. Lib., 1981–; Asst. Cmnty. Libn., Montgomery Cnty. Dept. Pub. Libs., 1979–81, Readrs. Adv., 1976–79, Chld. Libn., 1973–76. **Educ.:** Clark Univ., 1963–65; Univ. of Hartford, 1965–67, BA (Eng., Psy.); Univ. of MD, 1971–73, MLA (LS). **Orgs.:** MD LA: AYASD Prog. Plng. Com. (1980–81); Nom. Com. (1981–82). ALA. **Honors:** Beta Phi Mu, 1973. **Activities:** 9; 16, 17 **Addr.:** Silver Spring Library, 8901 Colesville Rd., Silver Spring, MD 20910.

Parsons, Richard William (N. 6, 1926, Victoria, BC) Admin. Asst. to Dir., Baltimore Cnty. Pub. Lib., 1979–, Coord., Interorg. Dev., 1970–79, Coord., Adult Srvs., 1962–70; Asst. Coord. of Cat., Brooklyn Pub. Lib., 1961–62, Adult Srvs. Libn., Asst. Branch Libn., 1958–61, New Bk. Sect., Bk. Ord. Dept., 1954–58; Bkmobile Libn., Edmonton Pub. Lib., 1951–53. **Educ.:** Univ. of BC, 1951, BA (Slavonic Std.); McGill Univ., 1953–54, BLS; Prov. Normal Sch., 1946–47, BC Tchrs. Cert. **Orgs.:** ALA: Cncl. (1970–72); RASD (Dir., 1968–74); PLA (Dir., 1970–72); Dartmouth Medal Awd. Com. (Ch. 1974–75). MD LA: Int. Frdm. Com. (1963–65); Rec. Secy. (1967–68); Adult/YA Srvs. Div. (Ch. 1974–75); Ed., *MD Libraries*, 1968–70. Mid. Atl. Reg. Lib. Fed.: Secy., Treas. (1975–). Potomac Tech. Prcs. Libns. Baltimore Cnty. Heritage Pubns., Ch. Ed. Bd. (1980–). MD Cncl. on Educ.: Secy. (1969–75); Ch. (1976–78). MD Cncl. for Educ. TV. Musm. Lib. Partnership: NEH Grant Proposal (Proj. Dir., 1977–78). Baltimore Env. Ctr.: Secy. (1974–79). **Honors:** Lib. Binding Inst., Silver Bk. Awd., 1966. **Pubns.:** Introduction, *Historical View of the Government of Maryland* (1968); Introduction, *History of Maryland* (1968); *HELP!* (1972, 1974, Ed.); "Tours for families or groups in Metropolitan Baltimore," *MD Hist. Mag.* (Spr., 1977). Baltimore Cnty. Publications (1972, 74, 76 eds.). **Activities:** 9; 17, 34, 45; 56 **Addr.:** Baltimore County Public Library, 320 York Rd., Towson, MD 21204.

Partridge, William George (Jl. 13, 1941, Toronto, ON) Chief Libn., Huron Cnty. Pub. Lib., 1974–; Asst. Cnty. Libn., Essex Cnty. Pub. Lib., 1972–74; Chief Libn., Pine Hill Dvnty. Hall, Halifax, 1969–72. **Educ.:** Univ. of BC, 1960–64, BA (Hist., Soclgy.); Univ. of BC, 1964–69, BA; Univ. of Toronto, 1968–69, BLS. **Orgs.:** Can. LA: Can. Assn. of Pub. Libs. (Secy.-Treas., 1976–78). ON LA: Cnclr. (1979–81). Atl. Prov. LA: Treas. (1972). **Pubns.:** *History of the United Church in Vanderhoof, Fort St. James and Fort Fraser* (1976). **Activities:** 1, 9; 15, 16, 17; 74, 89 **Addr.:** Box 353, Goderich, ON N7A 4C6 Canada.

Pascarelli, Anne M. (Ja. 15, 1947, Boston, MA) Asst. Libn., NY Acad. of Med. Lib., 1979–; Med. Libn./Staff Assoc., Univ. of IL at the Med. Ctr., Drug Info. Ctr., 1979; Med. Libn., E. Jefferson Gen. Hosp., 1977–79; Med. Libn., Xavier Univ., Coll. of Pharm., 1973–77. **Educ.:** Univ. of ME, 1964–69, BA (Eng. Lit.); Emory Univ., 1972, MLn (Libnshp.); Med. LA, 1972, Cert. **Orgs.:** Med. LA: *MLA News* Ed. Com. (1980–); NY Reg. Grp., *NYRG/MLA News* Edit. Com. Reg. Med. Lib. Netwk., Reg. II: Subcom. for Ref. Srvs. (Ch., 1980–). **Honors:** Beta Phi Mu. **Pubns.:** Reviews. **Activities:** 12; 15, 17, 35; 58, 73, 80 **Addr.:** New York Academy of Medicine, 2 E. 103rd St., New York, NY 10029.

Pask, Judith Marie (N. 26, 1946, Marion, IN) Asst. Mgt. and Econ. Libn., Purdue Univ., 1975–; Asst. Cmrce. Libn., Univ. of IL, 1971–72; Sci. Ref. Libn., Rochester Inst. of Tech., 1969–71. **Educ.:** Allegheny Coll., 1964–68, BS (Bio.); Columbia Univ., 1968–69, MS (LS). **Orgs.:** ALA: Lib. Instr. RT Liaison Com. (1979–80), Elections Com. (1980–81). ASIS: Pathfinder Com., Spec. Interest Grp. Mgt. (1978). AAUP. **Honors:** Beta Phi Mu, 1969. **Pubns.:** Jt. auth., "Working Papers in Academic Business Libraries," *Coll. and Resrch. Libs.* (N. 1980); "Business Faculty Involvement in Library Instruction," *Collegiate News and Views* (Fall 1979); *Bibliographic Instruction in Business Libraries* (1979); *Women and the Economy: A Selected Bibliography* (1977); *The Emerging Role of Women in Management: A Bibliography* (1976). **Activities:** 1; 15, 31, 39; 59 **Addr.:** Krannert Library, Purdue University, W. Lafayette, IN 47907.

Pasmik, Eleonor E. (F. 6, 1925, New York City, NY) Assoc. Libn., NY Univ. Med. Ctr., 1962–; Med. Resrch. Libn., Metro. Life Insr. Co., 1951–62. **Educ.:** Queens Coll., 1942–46, BS (Chem.); Columbia Univ., 1949–51, MS (LS). **Orgs.:** Med. LA: Legis. Com. (1979, 82); Prog. Com. (1975–77); Facilities and Srvs. Com. (1970–71); NY Reg. Grp. Vice-Ch. (1963–64, 1970–71); Ch. (1964–65, 1971–72); Exec. Com. 1965–66, 1972–73); various coms. NY Univ. Libs.: Tenure Com. (1970–71); Promo. Tenure Panel (1971–74); Lib. Cncl. (Ch., 1973–75); Promo. and Tenure Com. (1974–75). **Pubns.:** "The Librarian as Lobbyist," *Med. LA News* (Mr. 1980); "Bellevue in the Arts," *NY Univ. Med. Qtly.* (Win. 1979). **Activities:** 1; 17, 35, 39; 58, 60, 80 **Addr.:** New York University Medical Center Library, 550 1st Ave., New York, NY 10016.

Pastine, Maureen Diane (N. 21, 1944, Hays, KS) Univ. Libn., San Jose State Univ., 1980–; Ref. Libn./Assoc. Prof. of Lib. Admin., Univ. of IL, 1979–80, Undergrad. Libn./Assoc. Prof., 1977–79; Ch.,/Asst. Prof., Ref. Dept., Univ. of NE, 1975–77, Asst. Ch./Asst. Prof., 1971–75, Ref. Libn/Instr., 1971. **Educ.:** Fort Hays State Univ., 1962–67, AB (Eng.); Emporia State Univ., 1969–70, MLS. **Orgs.:** ALA: ACRL, Copyrt. Com. (1977–79) Bibl. Instr. Sect., Educ. for Bibl. Instr. (Ch., 1980–81); Machine-Assisted Ref. Sect., Educ. and Trng. Com. (1980–81); LAMA/Serials Sect., Dev., Org., Plng. and Prog. Com. (1980–81). IL LA. Women Lib. Workers. AAUP. Natl. Org. of Women. **Honors:** Beta Phi Mu. **Pubns.:** Jt. auth., *Library and Library Related Publications: A Directory of Publishing Opportunities in Journals, Series, and Annals* (1973); contrib., *Women's Work and Women's Studies 1973–74* (1975); "Women's Studies Research Resources," *Women's Std. Intl. Qtly.* (O., 1979); jt. auth., "Student Perceptions of Libraries and Librarians," *Coll. & Resrch. Libs.*

PROFESSIONAL ACTIVITIES: Institutions: 1. Acad. lib.; 2. Arch.; 3. Assn.; 4. Fed./Gvt. lib.; 5. Inst. lib.; 6. Mfr./Suppl.; 7. Milit. lib.; 8. Musm.; 9. Pub. lib.; 10. Sch. lib.; 11. Sch. of lib. sci.; 12. Spec. lib.; 13. State lib.; 14. (other). **Functions/Activities:** 15. Acq./Col. dev.; 16. Adult srvs.; 17. Admin.; 18. Apprais.; 19. Archit./Bldgs.; 20. Cat./Class.; 21. Chld. srvs.; 22. Circ.; 23. Cons./Pres.; 24. Consult.; 25. Cont. ed.; 26. Educ. lib. sci.; 27. Ext. srvs.; 28. Fund/Grants; 29. Gvt. pubs.; 30. Indx./Abs.; 31. Instr. lib. use; 32. Media srvs.; 33. Micro.; 34. Netwks./Coop.; 35. Persnl.; 36. PR; 37. Publshg.; 38. Recs. mgt.; 39. Ref. srvs.; 40. Repro.; 41. Resrch.; 42. Review.; 43. Secur.; 44. Serials; 45. Spec. col.; 46. Tech. srvs.; 47. Trustees/Bds.; 48. YA srvs.; 49. (other).

(N., 1976). **Activities:** 1; 17, 31, 39 **Addr.:** San Jose State University Library, San Jose, CA 95192.

Patane, John Ross (My. 3, 1944, Canastota, NY) Head, Tech. Srvs., Racine Pub. Lib., 1979–; Head, Tech. Srvs., Onondaga Cnty. Pub. Lib., 1971–79; Head, Prcs. Div., Syracuse Univ. Libs., 1966–71. **Educ.:** Villanova Univ., 1962–66, BS (Pol. Sci.); Syracuse Univ., 1966–73, MLS. **Orgs.:** ALA. ASIS. WI LA. **Activities:** 9; 46; 56 **Addr.:** 5010 Biscayne Ave., Apt. #16, Racine, WI 53406.

Patch, William Henry (S. 28, 1919, Abington, PA) Col. Maintenance Ofcr., Univ. of WI, 1978–, Chief, Circ. Dept., 1965–78, Docum. Libn., 1953–65; Cat., Flint Pub. Lib., 1951–53; Cat., Univ. of SC, 1947–50. **Educ.:** Amherst Coll., 1938–42, AB (Hist.); Drexel Inst., 1946–47, BS (LS); Univ. of MI, 1950–51, AMLS. **Orgs.:** ALA. WI LA. **Activities:** 1; 23, 33 **Addr.:** 5817 Dorsett Dr., Madison, WI 53711.

Pate, Carolyn J. Admin. libn., U.S. Army Nye Lib., Fort Sill, OK, 1981–, Supervisory Libn., 1973–80, Ext. Libn., 1967–73, Branch Libn., 1964–67. **Educ.:** Univ. of Ctrl. AR, BSE (Lang.); Univ. of OK, 1968–70, MLS. **Orgs.:** ALA: Armed Frcs. Libns. Cit. Com. (1977–78, 1979–80); Resols. Com. (1975–76). OK LA: Tech. Div. (Secy., 1976–77). Frnds. of Libs. in OK: Bd. (1979–80). Lawton-Fort Sill Art Gld. Altrusa Intl. AAUW. **Honors:** Dept. of the Army, Patriotic Civilian Srv., 1980, Outstan. Performance Awd., 1980, Sustained Superior Performance, 1980; Beta Phi Mu. **Activities:** 4, 10; 16, 17, 39; 74, 92 **Addr.:** Nye Library, 1640 Randolph Rd., Fort Sill, OK 73503.

Pater, Thomas G. (N. 5, 1916, Hamilton, OH) Head Resrch. Catlgr., Cath. Univ. of Amer., 1959–; Prof., Theo., Mt. St. Mary's Semy., Cincinnati, 1949–59. **Educ.:** St. Gregory Semy., 1934–38, BA (Phil.); Mt. St. Mary's Semy., 1938–42; Cath. Univ. of Amer., 1944–46, STD; Angelicum Univ., Rome, 1946–48, PhD (Phil.). **Orgs.:** ALA. ATLA. Cath. LA. **Activities:** 1; 20; 90 **Addr.:** Mullen Library, Catholic University, Washington, DC 20064.

Paterson, Gail A. (Ag. 25, 1949, Buffalo, NY) Theo. Catlgr., Drew Univ., 1975–. **Educ.:** SUNY, Buffalo, 1967–71, BA (Classics), 1971–73, MA (Classics), 1973–75, MLS; Drew Univ., 1977–, MPhil, PhD Cand. **Orgs.:** ALA: ACRL. AAUP. **Honors:** Beta Phi Mu, 1975; Phi Beta Kappa, 1973. **Pubns.:** Jt. transl., "Giordano Bruno's View of Earth Without a Morn," *Pensée* (1971). **Activities:** 1; 20; 55, 90 **Addr.:** 40 Main St., Madison, NJ 07940.

Patmon, Marian G. (Mr. 1, 1933, Sapulpa, OK) Head, Lib. Resrcs. Branch, OK Dept. of Libs., 1969–, Assoc. Dir. for Spec. Srvs., 1967–69, Libn. for the Blind, 1965–67; Med. Libn., St. Anthony Hosp., 1964–65. **Educ.:** Langston Univ., 1950–54, BS (Elem. Educ.); OK Univ., 1960–63, MLS. **Orgs.:** Assn. of Hosp. and Inst. Libs.: Mem.-at-large (1969–73); Conf. Prog. Dallas (1971); Francis Joseph Campbell Awd. Com. (1976). ALA: LAMA/Econ. Status, Welfare and Fringe Benefits (1979–81); Stats. for State Lib. Agencies (1980–81). OK LA: Tech. Srvs. Div. (Ch., 1977–78). **Activities:** 5, 13; 15, 34, 35; 63, 66 **Addr.:** Oklahoma Department of Libraries, 200 N. E. 18th St., Oklahoma City, OK 73105.

Patrick, Carolyn M. (F. 2, 1927, Eastland, TX) Assoc. Prof. and Assoc. Dir., TX Tech Univ. Hlth. Sci. Ctr. Lib., Amarillo, 1975–; Acq. Libn., Univ. of TX Hlth. Sci. Ctr., San Antonio, 1968–75; Ref. Libn., Sandia Labs., 1965–68. **Educ.:** Univ. of TX, 1943–47, BS (Textiles), 1962–66, MLS, 1974 (LS); 1975, Cert. Med. Libn. **Orgs.:** Med. LA: Exhibits (1974); Vital Notes (1976). SLA: TX Chap., Secy., Nom., Assn. Liaison Com. (1973–77); Med. LA/SLA Liaison Com. (1981–82). Pilot Club of Amarillo. Leag. of Women Voters. **Activities:** 1, 12; 15, 17, 39; 80, 95-Online srch. **Addr.:** TTU-RAHC Library, 1400 Wallace Blvd., Amarillo, TX 79106.

Patrick, Lucia (O. 18, 1946, Tampa, FL) Head, Readers and Tech. Srvs., Div. of Pub. Lib. Srvs., GA Dept. of Educ., 1977–, Docum. & Sci. Libn., 1976–77, Ref. Libn., 1974–76, 1970–72. **Educ.:** Emory Univ., 1964–68, BA (Relig.), 1969–70, MLn (Libnshp.); GA State Univ., 1972–74, (Art, Chinese Lang.). **Orgs.:** ALA. SELA. GA LA: Audit Com. (1980); Interlib. Coop. RT (Secy., 1980–81). SLA. ASIS. Amer. Craft Cncl. **Pubns.:** "Is There a Videodisc in the House?" *GA Libn.* (Ag. 1979); "Georgia Library Information Network, 1969-1979: A Decade of Service," *GA Libn.* (My. 1980). **Activities:** 13; 17, 24, 34 **Addr.:** Readers Services, Division of Public Library Services, Georgia Dept. of Education, 156 Trinity Ave., S.W., Atlanta, GA 30303.

Patrick, Patricia M. (N. 25, 1937, Amsterdam, NY) Head, Chld. Srvs., Albany Pub. Lib., 1973–; Chld. Consult., Upper Hudson Lib. Fed., 1973–; Adj. Fac., SUNY, Albany Sch. of Lib. and Info. Sci., 1979–; Dir. Libn., Guilderland Free Lib., 1971–73; Tchr., Westmere Nursery Sch., 1969–71; Asst. Libn., SUNY/Albany Grad. Sch. of Pub. Affairs, 1964–66; Tchr., 1959–64. **Educ.:** Syracuse Univ., 1955–59, BS (Elem. Educ.); SUNY, Albany, 1962–66, MSLS, 1975–76, (Bus. Admin.). **Orgs.:** NY LA: Liaison with NY State Div. for Lib. Dev. (1980). ALA: Print and Poster Com. (Ch., 1979–80); Resrch. and Dev. Com. (1981–83). Readg. is Fundamental: Bd. Upstate Storytel. Inst. Albany Leag. of Arts. Hist. Albany Fndn. Empire State Youth Thea. Puppeteers of Amer. **Pubns.:** "I Thought It Was Obvious - A Look at Programming for Children," *Bookmark* (Fall 1980); "Youth in the Public Library," *Cath. Lib. World* (D. 1978). **Activities:** 9, 14-Reg. syst.; 17, 21, 24; 63, 72, 89 **Addr.:** 14 Ruth Terr., Albany, NY 12203.

Patrick, Ruth J. (Jl. 6, 1939, Saskatoon, SK) Asst. Dir., Lib. Opers., Wayne State Univ. Libs., 1978–; Sr. Proj. Anal., Appld. Mgt. Sci., 1976–78; Coord., Cont. Educ. Sch. of Info. Std., Syracuse Univ., 1974–76; Assoc. Proj. Dir., Grad. Dept. of LS, Cath. Univ., 1973–74; Resrch. Anal., Syst. Dev. Corp., 1969–73. **Educ.:** Univ. of SK, 1957–61, BA (Eng.); Univ. of CA, Berkeley, 1966–67, MLS, 1968–72, PhD (LS). **Orgs.:** Natl. Cncl. on Qual. Cont. Educ. for Lib., Info., and Media Persnl. (Secy., 1980–). CLENE: Recog. Syst. Implementation Task Frc. (Ch., 1978–); Pres. (1976–77); Past-Pres. (1977–78); Ad Hoc Adv. Com. (Ch., 1975–76); various adv. bds.; *Jnl. of Lib. Autom.* Ed. Bd. (1975–77). **Pubns.:** Jt. auth., *A Study of Library Cooperatives, Networks and Demonstration Projects* (1980); *An Annotated Bibliography of Recent Continuing Education Literature* ERIC (1976); "Career Planning and Continuing Education," *Procs. First Natl. Asm. of CLENE* (1976); jt. auth., *The Public Library and Federal Policy* (1974); jt. auth., "Survey of Academic Library Consortia in the U.S.," *Coll. & Resrch. Libs.* (Jl. 1972); Various other bks., articles, sps. **Activities:** 1; 17, 25, 34 **Addr.:** Purdy Library, Wayne State University, Detroit, MI 48202.

Patrick, Stephen Allan (F. 20, 1951, Memphis, TN) Gvt. Docum., Ref. Libn., Art Docum. Spec., Greenville Cnty. Lib., 1978–, Ref. Libn., Arts and AV Ref. Sect., 1976–78. **Educ.:** Southwestern at Memphis, 1969–73, BA (Art, Art Hist.); Univ. of TN, 1975–76, MSLS (Acad. and Sch. Libnshp.). **Orgs.:** ARLIS/NA: Ad Hoc Com. on Prof. Stan. for Fine Arts Slide Col. (1980); Southeast Chap., (Secy., Treas., 1978–79; Vice-Ch., 1980; Ch., 1981). Greenville Cnty. Lib. Staff Assn.: Nom. Com. (1980). Southeastern LA. SC LA: GODORT Nom. Com. (Ch., 1980). Southeastern Coll. Art Conf. Greenville Civic Chorale: Pubcty. Ch. (1978–). Greenville Savoyards: Gilbert and Sullivan Light Opera Socty. **Pubns.:** "Government Documents and the Art Librarian: a Selected Annotated Bibliography ...," *ARLIS/NA Nsltr.* (D. 1980). Ed., "New Docs in SuDocs – Artistiscally Speaking," *ARLIS/NA* (1981–); various articles, art bk. reviews in *Lib. Jnl., The Docum., Serials Review.* **Activities:** 9; 29, 36, 39; 55, 67 **Addr.:** 110 Hallcox St., Greenville, SC 29609.

Patrie, Milton I. (Jl. 5, 1926, Albany, NY) Head, Media and Micro. Dept., Univ. of Louisville, Ekstrom Lib., 1981–, Asst. to Dean, Univ. Coll., 1974–80, Dir., AV/TV Ctr., 1967–74; Lectr./Resrch. Assoc., Syracuse Univ., 1965–67. **Educ.:** SUNY Coll. at Buffalo, 1947–51, BS (Educ.); IN Univ., 1951–52, MS (AV Educ.); Syracuse Univ., 1965–67, EdD (Instr. Comm.). **Orgs.:** AECT: Eval. Instr. Mtrls. Com. (Ch., 1972–74); Int. Frdm. Com. (1975–). KY AECT: Pres. (1972). ALA. Various other orgs. Kentuckiana Radio Info. Srv., Inc.: Ch. (1978–). **Honors:** AECT, Edgar Dale Awd., 1978. **Pubns.:** "Radio for the Tuned-In Learner," *AV Instr.* (N., 1979); "How Does it Look From Where You Sit?" *AV Instr.* (Mr. 1966); ed., *Hearrsay* (1980–); "Your State Trooper" 16mm film (1954); Various other films. **Activities:** 1, 14-Univ. media ctr.; 32, 33; 72, 74, 95-Instr. tech. **Addr.:** University of Louisville Ekstrom Library, Media & Microforms Department, Louisville, KY 40292.

Pattela, Rao R. (Jl. 17, 1936, Nandivelugu, A.P. State, India) Asst. Law Libn., Temple Univ. Sch. of Law, 1973–, Ref. Libn., 1971–73; Ref. Libn., Pub. Lib. of Fort Wayne and Allen Cnty., 1963–70. **Educ.:** Andhra Univ., Waltair, India, 1955–58, BA, hons. (Phil.), 1958–59, MA (Phil.); IN Univ., 1962–63, MA (LS); AALL, 1975, Cert. (Law Lib. Admin.); Univ. of PA, 1979–, PhD Cand. (Intl. Rel.). **Orgs.:** AALL: Com. on Intl. Law (1975–76). PA Law LA. Natl. Assn. of Asian Amers. of Indian Descent: Bd. (1979–80, 1980–81). **Activities:** 1; 17, 35, 39; 77, 92 **Addr.:** Temple University School of Law Library, Broad & Montgomery Sts., Philadelphia, PA 19122.

Patten, David J. (My. 14, 1938, Bancroft, IA) Ed., *Art Index*, H. W. Wilson Co., 1970–; Art, Archit. Libn., WA Univ., 1968–70; Dsgn., Art and Archit. Libn., Univ. of Cincinnati, 1966–68; Lib. Asst., Univ. of MI, 1964–66. **Educ.:** Univ. of NE, 1956–60, BFA (Art); Univ. of IA, 1960–63, MA (Art Hist.); Univ. of MI, 1966, AMLS (LS). **Orgs.:** ARLIS/NA: Secty. (1973–74); NY Chap. (Ch., 1973–74). SLA: NY Musms., Arts and Hum. Grp. (Ch., 1976–77). ALA: NY Pic. Grp. (Ch., 1971–72). Amer. Socty. of Indxrs. NY Lib. Club. **Honors:** Beta Phi Mu. **Pubns.:** Ed., *Art Index* (1969–79); Ed. *The ARLIS/New York News* (1978–); Ed., *Classification Systems and the Visual Arts* (1976); Ed., cmplr., *ARLIS/NA Directory of Members* (1973–74); various articles. **Activities:** 1; 30, 37; 55 **Addr.:** 410 E. 81st St., Apt. 5A, New York, NY 10028.

Patterson, Charles Darold (Ag. 8, 1928, Wahpeton, ND) Prof., Grad. Sch. of Lib. Sci., LA State Univ., 1978–, Assoc. Prof., 1972–78; Asst. Prof., Grad. Sch. of Lib. Sci., Univ. of Pittsburgh, 1971–72, Instr., 1966–71; Asst. Prof., WV Univ., 1962–66; Dir. of Libs., Asst. Prof., Glenville State Coll., 1958–62; Head Libn., Bemidji State Univ., 1955–58; Msc. Tchr., Fargo Pub. Schs., 1950. **Educ.:** Bemidji State Univ., 1946–50 BS (Hist., Msc., Sp.); Univ. of MN, 1956, MA (LS, Msc., Educ.); WV Univ., 1964, M(Msc.); Univ. of Pittsburgh, 1968, Advnc. Cert. (Lib. and Info. Sci.), 1971, PhD (LS). **Orgs.:** ALA: Schol. Jury (Ch., 1972–73), Ref. and Subscrpn. Bks. Review Com. (1975–77); ACRL, Tri-State Chap. (Pres., 1972). AALS: Exec. Bd. (1980–), *Jnl. of Educ. for Libnshp.* (Ed., 1980–). WV LA: Exec. Bd. (1960–61, 1964–66). SWLA. AAUP: Mem. Com. (Ch., 1973–74). Pittsburgh Bibliophiles. Univ. Cham. Msc. Socty.: Bd. of Dir. (Pres., 1978–80). Amer. Gld. of Organists: Hist. (1975–). **Honors:** Beta Phi Mu, 1971. **Pubns.:** *Journal of Education for Librarianship, Cumulative Index, 1960–1975* (1979); "Analysis of the Library of Congress Music Subject Headings" (1971); various articles, bk. reviews. **Activities:** 1, 11; 17, 26, 39; 55 **Addr.:** Graduate School of Library Science, 126 Middleton Library, LA State University, Baton Rouge, LA 70803.

Patterson, Flora E. (D. 28, 1930, Moosomin, SK) Dir., Pub. Srvs. Branch, Natl. Lib. of Can., 1973–, Coord. for Pub. Srvs., 1973, Chief, Ref. and Circ. Div., 1971–73, Chief, Serials Div., 1965–71. **Educ.:** McMaster Univ., 1950–53, BA (Lang. Std.); Univ. of Toronto, 1956–57, BLS. **Orgs.:** Can. LA: Cnclr. (1973–76); 2nd VP (1977–78). Bibl. Socty. of Can. Can. Nature Fed. Ottawa Fld. Naturalists. **Honors:** Beta Phi Mu, 1957. **Activities:** 4; 17, 39 **Addr.:** #602-70 McEwen Ave., Ottawa, ON K2B 5M3 Canada.

Patterson, Jeanne M. (N. 22, 1927, Chariton, IA) Adult Educ. Spec., Cuyahoga Cnty. Pub. Lib., 1976–; Head, Pub. Lib. Adult Career and Ed., 1976–; Coord. and Couns., Cleveland Ofc. of Extended Lrng. Prog., OH Univ. External Degree Proj., 1973–74. **Educ.:** IA State Univ., 1945–49, BS (Home Econ.); Case West. Rsv. Univ., 1971–73, MA (Educ.), 1975–76, MSLS; Univ. of Pittsburgh, Grad. Sch. of Lib. and Info. Sci., 1978, Cert.; various crs. **Orgs.:** ALA: PLA/Alternative Educ. Prog. Sect., Pres. (1980–81); RASD/Staff Dev. Com. (1978–80). OH LA: Div. VI, Staff Dev. Task Force (1979–81). CLENE. OH Bd. of Regents: Educ. Info. Ctrs. Adv. Com. (1978–80). Adult Educ. Cncl. of Grt. Cleveland: Trustee (1977–). Displaced Homemaker Proj. of Cuyahoga Com. Coll.: Adv. Com. Merrick House Inst.: Adv. Com. **Honors:** Beta Phi Mu, 1976. **Pubns.:** "Update: Continuing Education, The Adult Student as Consumer," *Cleveland Mag.* (Ag. 1979). **Activities:** 9; 16, 24, 25; 50, 63 **Addr.:** Cuyahoga County Public Library, South Euclid Branch, 4645 Mayfield Rd., South Euclid, OH 44121.

Patterson, Myron Brett (My. 27, 1948, Ashton-Under-Lyne, Eng.) Libn., BC Telephone Co., 1979–; Ref. Libn., BC Inst. of Tech., 1978–79; Libn., Richmond Sch. Bd., 1974–75. **Educ.:** Univ. of BC, 1968–72, BMus; Trinity Coll. (Eng.), 1973–74, (Msc.); Royal Can. Coll. of Organists, 1975, (Msc.); Univ. of BC, 1976–78, MLS; Prof. Tchg. Cert., 1972; Prof. Libnshp. Cert., 1978. **Orgs.:** Can. LA. Vancouver OLUG. Royal Can. Coll. of Organists. **Activities:** 12; 17, 20, 39, 49-Online Srch.; 56, 59, 93 **Addr.:** B.C. Telephone Company, Business Library, 5-3777 Kingsway Ave., Burnaby, BC V5H 3Z7 Canada.

Patterson, Robert D. (O. 6, 1925, Flint, MI) Head, Pub. Srv. Div., Lib., MI Tech. Univ., 1962–; st. Asst., Gen. Ref., Flint Pub. Lib., 1958–62, Ref. Libn., 1955–58, Branch Libn., 1951–55. **Educ.:** Univ. of MI, 1946–50, BA (Educ.), 1950–52, MA (LS). **Orgs.:** ALA. MI LA. MI Arch. Assn.: Exec. Bd. (1977–80). Amer. Socty. for Engin. Educ.: Engin. Lib. Sect., N. Midwest (Co-Ch., 1968–69). Nat. Hist. Pubns. and Rec. Com.: MI Adv. Bd. (1975–). **Activities:** 1, 2; 31, 39, 45 **Addr.:** 1106 College Ave., Houghton, MI 49931.

Patterson, Robert H. (Hudson) (D. 11, 1936, Alexandria, LA) Dir. of Libs., Univ. of Tulsa, 1981–; Dir., of Libs., Univ. of WY, 1976–81; Asst. Dir., Col. Dev., Tulane Univ. Libs., 1973–76; Head, Spec. Col. Cat., Hum. Resrch. Ctr., Univ. of TX, Austin, 1970–73; Assoc. Hum. Libn., Fine Arts and Sci. Libn., Chief Catlgr., Latin Amer. Lib., Rare Bks. Libn., Tulane Univ., 1965–70. **Educ.:** Millsaps Coll., 1954–58, BA (Hist.); Tulane Univ., 1958–63, MA (Hist.); Univ. of CA, Berkeley, 1964–65, MLS. **Orgs.:** ALA: Prsrvn. of Lib. Mtrls. Sect. (1979–); Educ. Com., PLMS (Ch., 1980–). Mt. Plains LA: PR Com. (1978). WY LA: Int. Frdm. Com. (Ch., 1976–78). Bibl. Ctr. for Resrch.: Adv. Cncl. (1978–81); WLS Adv. Cncl. (Ch., 1978–81). **Pubns.:** Fndr., Ed., *Conservation Administration News* (Je. 1979); "Preservation of Library Materials," *1980 and 1981 ALA Yrbk.* "Organizing for conservation: a model charge to a conservation committee," *Lib. Jnl.* (My. 15, 1979); various articles, bk. reviews. ; 13, 19, 41. **Addr.:** McFarlin Library, University of Tulsa, 600 South College Ave., Tulsa, OK 74104.

Patterson, Susan S. (Ja. 23, 1948, Woodstock, ON) Pub. Srv. Libn., Gvt. Pubns. Sect., Robarts Lib., Univ. of Toronto, 1978–, Ref. Libn., Ref. Dept., 1977; Resrch. Libn., Jt. Prog. in Transp., Univ. of Toronto, York Univ., 1976; Cat. Libn., Transp. Dev. Ctr., Fed. Mnstry. of Transport, 1974–76. **Educ.:** Univ. of Toronto, 1967–71, BA (Fr., Span.); McGill Univ., 1972–74, MLS. **Orgs.:** Can. LA: Gvt. Pubns. Com. (1980–81). ON LA: Gvt. Pubns. Com. (1980–81). SLA: Montreal Chap., Asst. Bltn. Ed. (1975–76). **Pubns.:** *Canadian Great Lakes Shipping: An Annotated Bibliography* (1976); "Motor Carrier Industry: An Annotated Bibliography," *Public Policy Direction for the Highway*

Special Subjects/Services: 50. Adult educ.; 51. Advert./Mktg.; 52. Aerosp.; 53. Agric.; 54. Area std.; 55. Arts/Hum.; 56. Autom.; 57. Bibl./Prtg.; 58. Bio. sci.; 59. Bus./Fin.; 60. Chem.; 61. Copyrt.; 62. Documtn.; 63. Educ.; 64. Engin.; 65. Env.; 66. Eth. grps.; 67. Film; 68. Food/Nutr.; 69. Geneal.; 70. Geo.; 71. Geol.; 72. Handcpd.; 73. Hist.; 74. Int. frdm.; 75. Info. sci.; 76. Insr.; 77. Law; 78. Legis.; 79. Math./Comp. sci.; 80. Med.; 81. Metals; 82. Nat. resrcs.; 83. Newsp.; 84. Nuc. sci.; 85. Oral hist.; 86. Petr./Energy; 87. Pharm.; 88. Phys./Astr./Math.; 89. Readg.; 90. Relig.; 91. Sci./Tech.; 92. Soc. sci.; 93. Telecom.; 94. Transp.; 95. (other).

Transportation of Goods (1977). **Activities:** 1, 4; 29, 39, 41; 59, 92, 94 **Addr.:** 22 Rolph Rd., Toronto, ON M4G 3M6 Canada.

Patterson, Thomas H. (Mr. 7, 1944, Washington, NC) Head, Ref. Dept., Univ. of ME, 1977–; Instr. Srvs. Libn., Sangamon State Univ., 1976–77; Head, Pub. Srvs., Coll. of Charleston, 1973–75, Ref. Libn., 1972–73; Asst. Soc. Sci. Libn., Miami Univ., 1971–72. **Educ.:** St. Andrews Presby. Coll., 1962–66, BA (Hist.); Univ. of Pittsburgh, 1969–70, MLS, 1966–69, MA (Hist.). **Orgs.:** ME LA. Assn. for Can. Std. in the U.S. **Honors:** Beta Phi Mu. **Pubns.:** "Library Skills Workshops for Support Personnel," *RQ* (Sum. 1980); "Interchange Between Atlantic and Northern New England Librarians," *APLA Bltn.* (S. 1980); "Political Studies Library Skills Test" ERIC (1979). **Activities:** 1, 2; 17, 31, 39; 54, 92 **Addr.:** Raymond H. Fogler Library, University of Maine, Orono, ME 04469.

Pattillo, John W. (Ag. 16, 1930, Atlanta, GA) Dir., South. Tech. Inst., 1966–; Tech. proc., Archvst., GA Inst. of Tech., 1955–65. **Educ.:** Emory Univ., 1947–51, BA (Hist.), 1954–55, MLS. **Orgs.:** ALA. SELA. GA LA. South. Tech. Lions Clb. Cobb Cnty. Lions Clb. Atlanta Civil War Round Table. **Honors:** South. Tech. Fndn., Outstan. fac., 1978. **Pubns.:** Various hist. articles. **Activities:** 1; 17; 55, 64 **Addr.:** Southern Technical Institute Library, 534 Clay St., Marietta, GA 30060.

Pattison, Frederick Woodworth (Ja. 31, 1930, Cleveland, OH) Indxr., Intl. Nursing Indx., 1966–; Indxr., Asst. Libn., Amer. Jnl. of Nursing Co., 1963–; Asst. to Libn., Queens Coll., 1961–63; Asst. Libn., NYC Cmnty. Coll., 1957–61; Libn., Sch. of Soc. Work, Univ. of Pittsburgh, 1954–56. **Educ.:** Trinity Coll., 1949–53, A B (Art Hist.); Case-West. Rsv. Univ., 1953–54, MSLS; Med. LA, 1966, Cert. Grade 1; various crs. **Orgs.:** Med. LA: Adv. Com. on Med. Lib. Problems (1968–69); NY Reg. Grp. (Prog. Ch., 1966–67; Treas., 1967–69); Exec. Com. (1967–69). ALA: Hlth. and Rehab. Lib. Srvs. Div., Com. on Org. (1974–75); Assn. of Hosp. and Inst. Libs., Bylaws Com. (Ch., 1972–74); Spec. Bylaws Com. (1973). Manhattan/Bronx Hlth. Sci. Libs. Grp. Grolier Club: Admis. Com. (1977–). NY Lib. Club. Eng. Sp. Un. (London). Sons of the Amer. Revolution. **Pubns.:** Jt. auth., "Hot to Get an A on Your Term Paper; or Using the Library to Succeed," *Imprint* (S. 1980); Contrib., "Reference Sources for Nursing," *Nursing Outlook* (1974–80). **Activities:** 12; 30, 39, 40; 80 **Addr.:** Sophia F. Palmer Library, American Journal of Nursing Co., 555 W. 57 St., New York, NY 10019.

Patton, Elizabeth H. (Ag. 6, 1917, Charleston, SC) Libn. in Charge, Ctrl. Lib., New Haven Free Pub. Lib., 1969–; Supvsr., Sch. Lib. Srv., New Haven Lib. and Dept. of Educ. Jt. Prog., 1966–69; Head Libn., Univ. of New Haven, 1958–66; Cat., Washington, DC Pub. Lib., 1942–44. **Educ.:** Coll. of Charleston, 1934–38, BS; Columbia Univ., 1939–61, MS (LS). **Orgs.:** NLA. CT LA: Int. Frdm. Com. (1979–81); Ref. Sect. (Ch., 1972–73); Prog. Ch. (1965–66). Film Coop. of CT, Inc.: Ch. (1974); various com. (1969–79). Amer. Cvl. Liberties Un. Common Cause. CT Col. Liberties Un. **Honors:** Beta Phi Mu, 1969. **Activities:** 1, 9; 16, 17, 39; 56, 74, 89 **Addr.:** New Haven Free Public Library, 133 Elm St., New Haven, CT 06510.

Patton, Johnn I., Jr. (D. 18, 1927, El Dorado, KS) Ref. Coord., SuffolFK Coop. Lib. Syst., 1980–; Acct. Rep., EBSCO Subscr. Srvs., 1978–80; Consult., C. W. Post Ctr., Long Island Univ., 1977–78; Dir., Nassau Cnty. Resrch. Lib., 1976–77, Asst. Lib. Dir., Col. Srvs., 1972–76; Consult. Libn., Univ. of Saigon Fac. of Med., 1969–72; Libn., Stan. Educ. Corp., 1968–69; Libn., WBBM-TV (CBS) Ref. Lib., 1963–68; Asst. Libn., Univ. of Chicago Bus. and Econ. Lib., 1962–63; various libn. positions, 1952–62. **Educ.:** Univ. of NM, 1945–46, (Span.); Univ. of OK, 1949–52, BS (LS); Univ. of Chicago, 1955–57, (LS). **Orgs.:** SLA: Advert. and Mktg. Div. (Ch., 1976–77); *What's New in Advertising and Marketing* (Ed., 1968–69). Archons of Colophon: Secy. (1975–79). NY LA. **Activities:** 12; 15, 17, 34 **Addr.:** 28 Station Plz. S., Apt. 3K, Great Neck, NY 11021.

Paugh, Minnie Ellen (Ap. 7, 1919, Virginia City, MT) Spec. Col. Libn., MT State Univ. Lib., 1961–; HS Hist., Eng. Tchr., MT, 1941–60. **Educ.:** MT State Univ., 1937–39; Univ. of MT, 1939–41, BA (Hist.), 1946–52, ME (Educ.); Univ. of Denver, 1959–61, MA (LS). **Orgs.:** MT LA: Lcl. Hist. Com. (Secy., 1971; Ch., 1980–81). Pac. Northwest LA: Bibl. Com. (1965–80). Frnds. of the Gallatin Libs.: Secy. (1979–80). Amer. Assn. of State and Lcl. Hist. MT Archlg. Socty. MT Ghost Town Presrvn. Socty. **Pubns.:** Jt. Rsrchr., "Montana Bibliography," *Pac. Northwest Qtly.* (1965–80); Jt. Auth., *Bibliography of Montana Local Histories.* **Activities:** 1; 45 **Addr.:** 510 W. Story, Bozeman, MT 59715.

Paul, A. Curtis (S. 4, 1935, Monessen, PA) Dir., Lrng. Resrcs., Lenoir-Rhyne Coll., 1976–; Dir. of Lib., Asst. to Pres., Northwestern Lutheran Theo. Semy., 1963–76; Pastor, Redeemer Lutheran Church, 1961–63. **Educ.:** CA State Coll., 1953–57, BS (Educ.); Northwestern Theo. Semy., 1957–60, MDiv (Theo.); Univ. of MN, 1963–67, MSLS. **Orgs.:** ALA. NC LA. Southeastern LA. Metrolina LA. Various Orgs. Kiwanis (St. Stephen's): Pres. elect. **Activities:** 1; 17; 56, 63, 90 **Addr.:** Carl A. Rudisill Library, Lenoir-Rhyne College, Hickory, NC 28601.

Paul, André (N. 28, 1945, Montréal, PQ) Asst. Dir. (Cat.), Cat. Branch, Natl. Lib. of Can., 1979–, Chief, Serials and Spec. Mtrls. Cat. Div., 1978–79, Head, Fr. Subt. Anal. Sect., 1974–78, Sub. Anal., 1970–74. **Educ.:** Séminaire St. Jean, 1958–66, BA; Univ. de Montréal, 1967–69, BA (LS). **Orgs.:** ASTED: Com. des Srvs. Tech. Corp. des biblcr. prof. du PQ. **Pubns.:** "RCAA2; changements et implications," *RCAA2 pout tous.* **Activities:** 4; 17, 20, 29 **Addr.:** Cataloguing Branch, National Library of Canada, 395 Wellington St., Ottawa, ON K1A 0N4 Canada.

Paul, Donald Charles (Jl. 17, 1925, Newton, IA) Head Libn., Hughes Aircraft Co., Missile Syst. Grp., 1977–; Sr. Libn., Anaheim Pub. Lib., 1976–77; Tech. Lib. Consult., Hughes Aircraft Syst. Intl., Tehran, Iran, 1974–76; Head, Tech. Srvs., Anaheim Pub. Lib., 1968–74, Head, Ctrl. Div., 1967–68; Head Libn., Hughes Aircraft Co., Solid State Prod. Div., 1958–67; Oper. Asst. to Chief Libn., TRW Incorp., 1955–58. **Educ.:** Univ. of CA, Los Angeles, 1945–49, BA (Phil.); Univ. of South. CA, 1947–59, MS (LS). **Orgs.:** SLA: S. CA Chap. (Consult. Srv. Ofrc., 1965–67). ALA. CA LA. **Activities:** 9, 12; 17, 46; 52, 64, 91 **Addr.:** 6602 Berquist Ave., Canoga Park, CA 91307.

Paul, Huibert (Mr. 1, 1928, Rotterdam, Netherlands) Head Serials Libn., Univ. of OR Lib., 1966–, Asst. Serials Libn., 1965–66. **Educ.:** Sophia Univ., Tokyo, Japan, 1958–63, BA (Hist., Econ.); Univ. of CA, Berkeley, 1964–65, MLS. **Orgs.:** OR LA. Frnds. of the Lib., Univ. of OR. **Pubns.:** Ed. bd., *The Serials Libn.;* "Serials: Chaos and Standardization," *Lib. Resrcs. & Tech. Srvs.* (Win. 1970); "The Serials Librarian and the Journals Publisher," *Schol. Publshg.* (Ja. 1972); "Education for Librarianship in the Netherlands," *Jnl. of Educ. for Libnshp.* (Fall 1974); "Library Statistics, Questionnaires, and the Machlup Study," *Lib. Acq.: Prac. and Theory* (Ap. 1977); "Serials Processing: Manual Control vs. Automation," *Lib. Resrcs. & Tech. Srvs.* (Fall 1977). **Activities:** 1; 44 **Addr.:** Serials Section, University of Oregon Library, Eugene, OR 97403.

Paul, Jacqueline C. (F. 2, 1937, Hornell, NY) Dir., DE Lib. Cnsrtm., 1978–; Asst. libn., Tech. Srvs., DE Law Sch. Lib., 1977–; Ref. libn., DE Tech. & Cmnty. Coll., 1972–77; Med. libn., Riverside Hosp., Wilmington, DE, 1968–72; Libn., Temple Beth Sholom, Wilmington, DE, 1963–65; Med. Libn., Alfred I duPont Inst., 1960–62. **Educ.:** Boston Univ., 1958, BA (Fine arts); Columbia Univ., 1958–59, MS (LS), 1959–60, (Art & Archlg.). **Orgs.:** ALA: Ch., Heads of Cat. Dept. Discuss. Grp. (1979–81). AALL: Long range plng. com., cat. policy subcom. (1980–81); Tech. Srvs. Spec. Int. Sect., Ch., Nom. Com. (1980–81); Bd. of Dirs. (1979–80). DELA: Coll. & Resrch. Div., Ch., Nom. Com. (1980–81); Secy., Bd. of Dirs. (1979–80). AAUW. Greater Wilmington Dev. Cncl. Jewish Hist. Socty. Natl. Cncl. of Jewish Women: Bd. of Dir. (1961–65). **Pubns.:** "Small Library Participation in a Bibliographic Utility: The Consortium Experience," *Law Lib. Jnl.* (Fall 1980). **Activities:** 1; 20, 44, 46; 55, 77, 80 **Addr.:** Delaware Law School Library, Box 7475 Concord Pike, Wilmington, DE 19803.

Paul, Jeff H. (Mr. 15, 1952, Woodland, CA) Head, Media Srvs., San Jose State Univ. Lib., 1978–, Ref. Libn., 1978–79; Ref. Libn., CA State Univ., Chico Lib., 1976–78. **Educ.:** CA State Univ., Chico, 1972–75, BA (Span., Psy.); San Jose State Univ., 1976–77, MA (LS), 1977–78, MA (Educ.). **Orgs.:** ALA. AECT. CA LA: State Univ. and Coll. Libns. Chap. (Secy.-Treas., 1979–80). Untd. Profs. of CA. **Pubns.:** "Library Service to the Spanish-Speaking in The Public Libraries of the San Francisco Bay Area" ERIC (1976); "Promotion and Publicity for Online Services in Academic Libraries" ERIC (1978). **Activities:** 1, 10; 17, 32, 39; 63, 92 **Addr.:** Media Dept., Library, San Jose State University, San Jose, CA 95192.

Paul, Nancy A. (Ja. 25, 1946, Madison, WI) Head, Tech. Srvs., Univ. of WI Law Lib., 1974–, Catlgr., 1973–74; Catlgr., WI State Lib., 1970–73. **Educ.:** Univ. of WI, Platteville, 1964–68, BA (Eng., Fr.); Univ. of WI, Madison, 1968–70, MA (LS); AALL., 1980, Cert. **Orgs.:** AALL. WI LA. WI Assn. of Acad. Libns. WI Lib. Cnsrtm.: Peer Cncl. (1978–). **Activities:** 1; 20, 46; 56, 77, 78 **Addr.:** L487A Law Library, University of Wisconsin, Madison, WI 53706.

Paul, Rameshwar N. (O. 5, 1932, Batala, Punjab, India) Info. Mgt. Consult., 1976–; Head Libn., Gen. Electric Co., 1969–76; Resrch. Assoc. and Asst. Dir., ERIC Clearinghse., Univ. of MN, 1968–69; Resrch. Assoc., Univ. of MI, 1966–68; Asst. Prof., Head, Docum. Serials Unit, East. IL Univ., 1962–66; Math. Libn., Univ. of MI, 1959–62. **Educ.:** Univ. of Punjab, 1946–50, BA (Math); Univ. of MI, 1957–61, AMLS, AM (Educ.). **Orgs.:** ASIS: MN Chap., Bltn. Ed. (1968–69); SIG/CR Nsltr. Jt. Ed. (1972–75). **Honors:** Beta Phi Mu, 1960. **Pubns.:** Jt. auth., "Acquisition of Library Materials: A Quantitative Approach," *Procs. of ASIS* (1969). **Activities:** 4, 12; 24, 30, 38; 57, 62, 75 **Addr.:** 20817 Apollo Ln., Gaithersburg, MD 20760.

Paulin, Mary Ann (F. 27, 1943, Bay Port, MI) Lib., Media Spec., Negaunee Jr.-Sr. HS, 1973–, Adjunct Instr., Creat. Dramatics, North. MI Univ., Sp., 1976–79; Media Spec., 1973. Dir., Instr. Mtrls. Ctr., Beach Mid. Sch., 1970–73; Elem. Media Spec., Miller Elem. Sch., Lafayette, IN Sch. Corp., 1967–70; Sch. Libn., Warren Cmnty. Schs., 1965–67. **Educ.:** West. MI Univ., 1960–64, BA (Eng. Lib.), 1964–65, MSLS, 1968–71, EdS (Lib.). **Orgs.:** MI Assn. for Media in Educ.: Secy. (1977–78); VP (1979); Bd. of Dir. (1973–79). MI Assn. Sch. Libns.: Hist. (1972–73); Rcrt. Com. (Ch., 1971–72). ALA: Ref. and Subscrpn. Bks. Com. (1978); Charles Scribner's Sons Awds. Com. (1979–), Ch. (1981–82); AASL; ALSC. Various orgs. Intl. Readg. Assn.: Int. Frdm. Com. (1977–). Delta Kappa Gamma: Mem. Ch. (1978–). Marquette-Alger Readg. Cncl.: Exec. Bd. (1975–80); Pres. (1977–79); VP. (1976–77). MI Readg. Assn.: Int. Frdm. Conf. (Del., 1978). Various orgs. **Honors:** Beta Phi Mu, 1965; Kappa Kappa Iota, 1968–70; Phi Delta Kappa, 1981–. **Pubns.:** *Creative Uses of Children's Literature* (1981); Eds. in *MI Libn.* (1974); "Media Services at Negaunee Jr.-Sr. High School" Slide-tape set (1978); "Careers in the Mining Industry" Sound filmstp., std. guides (1979); various articles. **Activities:** 10; 21, 32, 48 **Addr.:** 1205 Joliet, Marquette, MI 49855.

Paulson, Peter J. (Ja. 30, 1928, New York City, NY) Dir., NY State Lib., 1972–, Prin. Libn., Tech. Srv., 1966–71, Assoc. Libn., Cat., 1965–66, Sr. Libn., Gift and Exch., 1955–65, Asst. Prof., Adjunct, SUNY, Albany, 1960–71; Lib. Asst., NY State Lib., 1952–55. **Educ.:** Coll. of the City of New York, 1946–49, BSS (Hist.); Columbia Univ., 1950, MA (Hist.); SUNY, Coll. of Educ., Albany, 1955, MA (LS). **Orgs.:** ALA: Legis. Com. (Ch., 1980–81). NY LA: Pres. (1975). ASIS. NY State Hist. Assn. **Honors:** Phi Beta Kappa. **Pubns.:** "Development and Coordination of Library Services to State Government," *Lib. Trends* (Fall 1978); jt. ed., *Meeting the Information Needs of State Government in New York* (1977); "Government Documents and Other Non-Trade Publications," *Lib. Trends* (Ja. 1970); "Networks, Automation and Technical Services: Experience and Experiments in New York State," *Lib. Trends and Tech. Srvs.* (Fall 1969); "Federal Depository Library Service in New York State," *Bookmark* (N. 1964); various articles. **Activities:** 13; 17, 29, 34; 56, 61, 78 **Addr.:** New York State Library, Cultural Education Center, Albany, NY 12230.

Pausch, Lois M. (O. 31, 1934, Chicago, IL) Coord., Sci. Sect., Orig. Cat. and Asst. Prof., Lib., Univ. of IL, 1978–, Catlgr., Asst. Prof., 1975–78, Catlgr., Instr., 1972–75; Libn., Jamaica Consolidated HS, Sidell, IL, 1971–72. **Educ.:** Univ. of IL, 1954–58, BS (Bio. Educ.), 1968–71, MSLS. **Orgs.:** ALA: RTSD, Esther J. Piercy Awd. Jury (1979–80); LIRT, Treas. (1979–80); Coord. (1980–81), Past Coord. (1981–82). IL LA: Resrcs. and Tech. Srvs. Sect., Exec. Bd. (1979–80); Vice-Pres./Pres.-Elect (1981); Cont. Educ. Com. (Ch., 1981); Various other coms. St. Joseph Twp. (IL) Lib. Bd. of Dir. Chicago Cncl. on Frgn. Affairs. **Pubns.:** Jt. auth., *Library Instruction Programs in Illinois Academic Libraries* (1978); jt. auth., *Guide to the Papers in the John Hunter Walker Collection, 1911–1953* (1980); "Observations on the Biology of the Slender Seedcorn Beetle," *Grt. Lakes Entomologist* (O. 1980). **Addr.:** 246 Library, University of Illinois at Urbana-Champaign, 1408 W. Gregory Dr., Urbana, IL 61801.

Paustian, P. Robert (Jl. 29, 1949, Kansas City, MO) Col. Libn., Univ. of MO Libs., 1979–; Pub. Srvs. Libn., Asst. Dir., Kansas City, KS Pub. Lib., 1979. **Educ.:** Univ. of MO, 1967–71, BA (Frgn. Lang.); Univ. of Heidelberg, 1969–70, (Phil.); Univ. of KS, 1973–75, MA (Ling.); Univ. of Toronto, 1977–78, (LS); Univ. of MO, 1978–79, MA (Lib. and Info. Sci.). **Orgs.:** MO LA: Awds. Com. (Ch., 1981). ALA. ASIS. Ling. Socty. of Amer. Mod. Lang. Assn. **Honors:** Beta Phi Mu. **Pubns.:** "Dante's Conception of the Genetic Relationship of European Languages," *Neophilologus* (1979); "The Evolution of Personal Naming Practices among American Blacks," *Names* (1978); "Bopp and 19th Century Distrust of the Indian Grammatical Tradition," *Indogermanische Forschungen* (1977). **Activities:** 1, 9; 15, 23, 41; 75, 88, 91 **Addr.:** General Library, University of MO, Kansas City, MO 64110.

Pautz, Martin R. (Wisconsin Rapids, WI) Dean, Lrng. Resrcs., Greenville Tech. Coll., 1972–; Dir., Lrng. Resrcs., Clayton Jr. Coll., 1971–72; Libn., Greenville Tech. Coll., 1968–71. **Educ.:** Concordia Coll., Univ. of WI, BS; Univ. of NC, 1967–68, MSLS; Air Cmnd. and Staff Coll. **Orgs.:** SC LA: Pres. (1979); Spec. Libs. Sect. (Ch., 1974–78). Southeastern LA: Constn. and By-Laws Com. (1978–). Piedmont LA: Pres. (1971). SC Gvr. and WHCOLIS: Adv. Com. (1977–79). **Pubns.:** "Library Support for Business and Industry," *Southeastern Libn.* (Spr. 1972); "TEC Libraries: Resource for Industry," *Impact* (O. 1972). **Activities:** 1, 12; 17, 24; 55, 64, 80 **Addr.:** Greenville Technical College, P. O. Box 5616, Greenville, SC 29606.

Pautzsch, Richard Oscar (Ag. 30, 1919, Boston, MA) Retired, 1975–; Asst. Chief Libn., Tech. Srvs., Chicago Pub. Lib., 1971–75; Coord. of Cat., Brooklyn Pub. Lib., 1956–71, Head, Cat. Unit, 1951–55, Catlgr., 1950; Supvsr., Circ. Dept., Lamont Undergrad. Lib., Harvard Univ., 1949, Cat. Supvsr., Harvard Undergrad. Lib. Proj., 1947–48, Catlgr., Harvard Coll. Lib., 1946–47. **Educ.:** Boston Univ., 1937–41, BS (Eng. Lit.); Columbia Univ., 1949–50, MS (LS), 1950–51, various crs. **Orgs.:** IL LA. Chicago Lib. Club. ALA: RTSD, Resrcs. Com. (1971–73), Nom. Com. (1960–61), Melvil Dewey Awd. Jury (Ch., 1962); cat. and Class. Sect., Policy and Resrch. Com. (Ch., 1968–69); Lib. Admin. Div./Lib. Org. and Mgt. Sect., Stats. Com. for Tech. Srvs. (Ch., 1965–66); Heads of Tech. Srvs. of Lg. Pub. Libs. Discuss. Grp., Ch.; various coms. NY Tech. Srvs. Libns.: Secy.-Treas.

PROFESSIONAL ACTIVITIES: Institutions: 1. Acad. lib.; 2. Arch.; 3. Assn.; 4. Fed./Gvt. lib.; 5. Inst. lib.; 6. Mfr./Suppl.; 7. Milit. lib.; 8. Musm.; 9. Pub. lib.; 10. Sch. lib.; 11. Sch. of lib. sci.; 12. Spec. lib.; 13. State lib.; 14. (other). **Functions/Activities:** 15. Acq./Col. dev.; 16. Adult srvs.; 17. Admin.; 18. Apprais.; 19. Archit./Bldgs.; 20. Cat./Class.; 21. Chld. srvs.; 22. Circ.; 23. Cons./Pres.; 24. Consult.; 25. Cont. ed.; 26. Educ. lib. sci.; 27. Ext. srvs.; 28. Fund/Grants; 29. Gvt. pubs.; 30. Indx./Abs.; 31. Instr. lib. use; 32. Media srvs.; 33. Micro.; 34. Netwks./Coop.; 35. Persnl.; 36. PR; 37. Publshg.; 38. Recs. mgt.; 39. Ref. srvs.; 40. Repro.; 41. Resrch.; 42. Review.; 43. Secur.; 44. Serials; 45. Spec. col.; 46. Tech. srvs.; 47. Trustees/Bds.; 48. YA srvs.; 49. (other).

(1966–67). Various other orgs. Amer. Gld. of Organists. **Pubns.:** "Classification," *Technical Services in Libraries* (1954). **Activities:** 1, 9; 20, 46 **Addr.:** 5465 Curry Ford Rd., Apt. B-102, Orlando, FL 32806.

Pauwels, Colleen Kristl (Ja. 25, 1946, Chicago, IL) Dir., IN Univ. Sch. of Law Lib., 1980–, Actg. Dir., 1978–79, Pub. Srvs. Libn., 1975–78. **Educ.:** Barat Coll., 1964–68, BA (Soclgy.); IN Univ., 1974–75, MLS. **Orgs.:** AALL: Gvt. Docum. Com. (Ch., 1981–82); Spec. Proj. Com. (Ch., 1978–79); Gvt. Docum. SIS (1977–); Law Lib. Jnl. Com. (1979–80); Readr. Srvs. SIS (1978–). IN Univ. LA: IN Univ. LA Qtly. Com. (1977–78). **Activities:** 1, 12; 17, 29, 39; 62, 77 **Addr.:** Law Library, IN University School of Law, Bloomington, IN 47405.

Pavlin, Stefanie A. (Ja. 13, 1929, Slovenia, Yugoslavia) Head, Lib. Srvs., Mnstry. of Transp. and Comm., ON, 1958–; Libn., Toronto Pub. Lib., 1953–56. **Educ.:** Mt. St. Vincent Univ., 1949–52, BA (Phil.); Univ. of Toronto, 1953–54, MLS. **Orgs.:** SLA: Transp. Div. (Ch., 1978–79); Toronto Chap. (Dir., 1980–81), Pres. Elect (1981–82). **Activities:** 13; 17, 34, 41; 64, 93, 94 **Addr.:** Ministry of Transportation and Communications, 1201 Wilson Ave., Central Bldg., Downsview, ON M3M 1J8 Canada.

Pawl, Patricia T. (Ja. 27, 1950, Beaver Dam, WI) Dir., Williams Free Lib., 1979–; Instr., Univ. of WI Ext., 1980–82; Dir., Park Falls Pub. Lib., 1974–79. **Educ.:** Carroll Coll., 1968–72, BA (Grmn., Pol. Sci.); West. MI Univ., 1972–73, MLS. **Orgs.:** WI LA: WI Assn. of Pub. Libns., Bd. of Dirs. (1980–82); Small Lib. Com. (Ch., 1978). ALA. **Honors:** Beta Phi Mu. **Pubns.:** Jt. auth., "When You Are the Staff," *WI Lib. Bltn.* (N.-D. 1979). **Activities:** 9; 17, 27 **Addr.:** Williams Free Library, 105 Park Ave., Beaver Dam, WI 53916.

Pay, Martha Gill (Mr. 11, 1932, San Augustine, TX) Libn., Clear Lake HS, 1971–; Libn., Dobie HS, 1968–71; Libn., Jackson Intermediate Sch., 1968. **Educ.:** San Jacinto Jr. Coll., 1961–66, AA; Univ. of Houston, 1965–68, BS (Educ.), 1968–71, MEd (C and I); Sam Houston State Univ., 1965–76, MLS; various crs. **Orgs.:** TX LA. CSLA. TX Sch. LA. Evang. Church LA. First Presby. Church, Pasadena, TX. Clear Creek Tchrs. Assn. TX State Tchrs. Assn. **Activities:** 10 **Addr.:** 4911 Ivy, Pasadena, TX 77505.

Paymer, Natalie S. (S. 2, 1951, Baltimore, MD) Law Libn., Ofc. of Attorney Gen., MD, 1975–. **Educ.:** Univ. of MD, 1969–73, BA (Eng.), 1973–75, MLS. **Orgs.:** Baltimore Legal Info. Sci. Socty.: Nsltr. Ed. (1980–81). State Agency LA of MD: Secty. (1977–79). AALL: Pubcty. Com. (1978–). SLA: Washington DC Chap. Ed. Bd. (1978–79). Unicon, Inc.: Dir. (1975–). **Honors:** Beta Phi Mu; Phi Kappa Phi. **Pubns.:** "The Problem Patron–The Attorney and the Law Library," *The Crab* (Jn. 1981); "Pollution and the Arts: A Bibliography" (1974). **Activities:** 13; 17, 39; 77 **Addr.:** Office of the Attorney General of Maryland, 1 S. Calvert St., 13th Floor, Baltimore, MD 21202.

Payne, Benjamin C. (Jl. 30, 1936, Wilmington, DE) Libn., Penn VA Corp., 1978–, Libn., 1978–; Med. Libn., VA Hosp., Elsmere, DE, 1969–75. **Educ.:** Univ. of DE, 1954–58, BA (Eng.); Brown Univ., 1958–59, (Amer. Cvlztn.); Univ. of PA, 1959–60 (Amer. Cvlzn.); Villanova Univ., 1967–69, MLS. **Orgs.:** SLA. ALA. **Activities:** 5, 12; 15, 29, 39; 59, 65, 86 **Addr.:** Library, Penn VA Corp., 2500 Fidelity Bldg., Philadelphia, PA 19109.

Payne, David L. (My. 9, 1927, Gulfport, MS) Dir., Prof., Lib. Srvs., MS Univ. for Women, 1969–; Asst. Prof., Elem. Educ., Northwestern State Coll. of LA, 1968–69; Asst. Prof., Soc. Sci., MS State Coll. for Women, 1967–68; Grad. Fellow, Educ. Admin., Univ. of South. MS, 1965–67. **Educ.:** MS State Univ., 1949–50, BS (Soc. Sci.), 1950–52, MS (Soclgy.); Univ. of South. MS, 1965–67, EdD (Educ. Admin.); Univ. of AL, 1970–72, MLS. **Orgs.:** Southeastern LA. ALA. MS LA: Coll. and Univ. Sect. (Ch., 1979); Pubns. Com. (Ch., 1979). MS Univ. for Women: Pres. (1979). Empl. Fed. Credit Un. Columbus Shrine Club: Pres. (1979). **Honors:** Outstan. Educs. of Amer., Outstan. Educ. of Amer., 1972. **Pubns.:** "How To Take Tests: Needed Library Holdings," *Southeastern Libn.* (Spr. 1979). **Activities:** 1; 17; 56, 69, 92 **Addr.:** 131 Juanita St., Columbus, MS 39701.

Payne, Eleanor R. (N. 28, 1920, E. Chicago, IN) Col. Dev. Libn., Univ. of CA, Davis, 1979–, Head, Cat. Dept., 1972–79, Cat. Libn., 1964–72; Ed., *CA State Pubns.*, CA State Lib., 1963–64. **Educ.:** Univ. of CO, 1946–50, BA (Soclgy.); Univ. of CA, Berkeley, 1950–52, (Slavic Lang.), 1952–53, MLS. **Orgs.:** ALA: ACRL/Educ. and Bhvl. Sci. Sect., Psy./Psyt. Com. (1980–); Slavic and E. European Sect., Prog. Com. San Francisco (1981); RTSD/Resrch. Conf. Plng. Com. (1982); Cat. and Class. Sect., Pol. and Res. Com. (1976–80), Nom. Com. (Ch., 1981). CA LA: Tech. Srvs. Chap. (Pres., 1978); Chap. of Acad. and Resrch. Libns., Mem. Com. (1981). **Honors:** Natl. Slavic Hon. Socty., Mem. in Perpetuity, 1970. **Pubns.:** "Catalogs and Catalogers: Evolution Through Revolution," *Jnl. of Acad. Libnshp.* (S. 1976); "Standardizing the Reporting of Cataloging in the University of California System," *Lib. Resrcs. & Tech. Srvs.* (Win. 1978); "NUC: Location or Cataloging Information–A Conflict of Role," ERIC (1978); "Cataloging Productivity Quotas," ERIC (1978). **Activities:** 1; 15, 20, 25; 92 **Addr.:** University Library, University of California, Davis, CA 95616.

Payne, Florence Haas (O. 11, 1934, Cleveland, OH) Libn., Supvsr. of Cat. and Pers. Depts., Mt. View Pub. Lib., 1968–; Libn., Syntex Resrch., 1967–68; Libn., Indus. and Sci. Div., Dayton and Montgomery Cnty. Pub. Lib., 1966–67; Libn., Cat., Frgn. Tech. Div., Wright-Patterson Air Frc. Base, 1965–66. **Educ.:** Maryville Coll., 1953–57, BS (Chem.); Univ. of CA, Berkeley, 1964–65, MLS (Libnshp.). **Orgs.:** SLA. CA LA: Org. Com. to Form the Bay Area Chap. (1978–79). Mt. View City Fed. Credit Un.: Pres. (1976); Treas. (1975). **Honors:** Beta Phi Mu; Pi Mu Epsilon. **Pubns.:** "Developing Your Dermatological Library; A Practical Guide" booklet (1967). **Activities:** 9, 12; 15, 39, 46; 52, 60, 91 **Addr.:** 1321 Byron St., Palo Alto, CA 94301.

Peabody, Brewster Earl (O. 18, 1934, Plymouth, MI) Asst. Head, Gift Sect., Lib. of Congs., 1977–; Lib. Dir., Old Dominion Univ., 1966–76; Asst. Libn., South. IL Univ., 1962–66; Serials Libn., Univ. of DE, 1959–62. **Educ.:** Univ. of MI, 1952–56, AM (Hist.), 1956–57, AMLS. **Orgs.:** ALA. Amer. Philatelic Socty. Light Railway Transport Assn. **Activities:** 1, 4; 15, 17, 46 **Addr.:** 5800 Quantrell Ave., Apt. 1518, Alexandria, VA 22312.

Peace, Nancy E. (F. 18, 1945, Providence, RI) Asst. Prof., Simmons Coll., Sch. of Lib. and Info. Sci., 1977–; Lib. Dir., RI Hist. Socty., 1971–76; Cur. of Printed Mtrls., MI Hist. Col., Univ. of MI, 1969–71. **Educ.:** OH Wesleyan Univ., 1963–68, BA (Hist.); Univ. of MI, 1968–69, AMLS (Libnshp.); Columbia Univ., 1976–80, DLS (Libnshp.). **Orgs.:** ALA: ACRL, Legis. Com. (1978–); ISAD Tech. Stan. for Lib. Autom. (1976–78). AALL: Ad Hoc Com. on Arch. Educ. (1980–). SAA: Com. on Educ. and Prof. Dev. (1977–); Lib. Arch. Rel. Com., (1972–75); Com. for a New Eng. Bibl. (MA VP., 1977–). Amer. Cvl. Liberties Un. Appalachian Mt. Club. Assoc. of the John Carter Brown Lib. RI Hist. Socty. **Pubns.:** *Rhode Island Records and the Rhode Island Documents Depository System: Study and Recommendations.* (1975); "Library Grievance Procedure: A Proposal," *RI LA Bltn.* (O. 1979); jt. auth., "Archivists and Librarians: A Common Mission, a Common Education," *Amer. Archvst.* (O. 1979); "Special Libraries in Rhode Island: Now and Ten Years from Now," *RI LA Bltn.* (D. 1976); "Consortium on a Shoestring: the Consortium of Rhode Island Academic and Research libraries." *Urban Acad. Libn.* (Je. 1981). **Activities:** 1, 2; 17, 24, 26; 78, 92 **Addr.:** Graduate School of Library and Information Science, Simmons College, 300 The Fenway, Boston, MA 02115.

Peach, Joan Brailey Turner (My. 2, 1926, Boston, MA) Dir., Westport Pub. Lib., 1974–; Assoc. Dir., Pub. Srvs., Ferguson Lib., 1970–74; Asst. Dir., Huntington Pub. Lib., 1969–70. **Educ.:** Wellesley Coll., 1943–47, BA (Pol. Sci.); Columbia Univ., 1962–66, MS (Lib. Srv.). **Orgs.:** Southwestern CT Lib. Cncl.: Bd. (1978–); Secy. (1979–). ALA: CT (Mem. Ch., 1976–79). CT LA: Ref. and Adult Srvs. Sect. (Ch., 1972–74). **Activities:** 9, 13; 17, 19, 35; 50, 55, 56 **Addr.:** Westport Public Library, 19 Post Rd. E., Westport, CT 06880.

Peacock, Daniel J. (IN) Dir., Lib. Srvs. Instr. Mtls., Dept. Educ., Trust Territory Pac. Islands, 1964–; Tchr., Libn., Trust Territory (Ponape); US Civil Srv. Post, Educ. and Admin., Palau Dist., 1953–58. **Educ.:** Drexel Univ., MLS. **Activities:** 4, 10; 55, 89 **Addr.:** Library Services and Instructional Materials, Department of Education, Trust Territory of Pacific Islands, Saipan, Mariana Islands 96950.*

Pean, Marie-Jose (Ag. 17, 1952, Port-au-Prince, Haiti) VP, Infoges, Inc., 1981–; Ref. Libn., Can. Broadcasting Corp., 1980–; Chief Libn., Banque Natl., 1977–80. **Educ.:** Ottawa Univ., 1970–73, BA (Hist.), 1973–75, MA (Archlg.); Univ. de Montreal, 1975–77, MLS. **Orgs.:** SLA: Dir. Com. (1978–79). Assn. Can. des Sci. del'Info: Rcrt. Ofcr. (1979–80). **Activities:** 12; 24, 39; 93 **Addr.:** 3825 Dupuis #19, Montreal, PQ H3T 7E5 Canada.

Pearce, (M.) Jean Kudo (F. 25, 1932, Champaign, IL) Head, Circ., Cushing-Martin Lib., Stonehill Coll., 1973–; Libn., Norton Pub. Lib., 1973; Ref. Libn., Bryant Coll. Lib., 1972–73. **Educ.:** Swarthmore Coll., 1949–53, BA (Grmn. Lit.); Simmons Coll., 1968–72, MLS; various sems. **Orgs.:** ALA. New England Chap. ACRL. New Eng. LA. Norton Hist. Socty. Norton Land Prsrvn. Socty. **Honors:** Beta Phi Mu, 1972. **Activities:** 1; 17, 22, 31; 55 **Addr.:** P.O. Box 445, Norton, MA 02766.

Pearce, Stanley K. (Je. 13, 1928, Sprague, WA) Dir. of Info. Srvs., O'Melveny and Myers, 1979–, Law Libn., 1959–79; Ref. Libn., Los Angeles Cnty. Law Lib., 1958–59, Acq. Libn., 1957–58. **Educ.:** Univ. of WA, 1952, BS (Psy.), 1956, JD (Law), 1957, MLL (Libnshp.). **Orgs.:** AALL: Exec. Bd. (1977–80). ASIS. Assoc. Info. Mgrs. South. CA Assn. of Law Libs.: Pres. (1969). **Activities:** 12; 17, 24; 75, 77, 78 **Addr.:** 4312 Babcock Ave. #4, Studio City, CA 91604.

Pearman, Sara Jane (S. 6, 1940, Dallas, TX) Slide Libn., Cleveland Musm. of Art, 1972–; Cur. of Slides, Univ. of KS, 1962–64; Lectr., Art Hist., Kearney State Coll., 1964–66; Catlgr., Slide Lib., Cleveland Musm. of Art, 1967–72. **Educ.:** Univ. of Wichita, 1958–62, BA (Art Educ.); Univ. of KS, 1962–64, MA (Art Hist.); Case-West. Rsv. Univ., 1966–74, PhD (Art Hist.). **Orgs.:** ARLIS/NA. ARLIS/OH: State Ch. Mid-Amer. Coll. Art. Cleveland Medvl. Socty. Midwest Art Hist. Socty. **Pubns.:** Various reviews and presentations. **Activities:** 12; 15, 17, 20; 55, 57 **Addr.:** Cleveland Museum of Art, 11150 East Blvd., Cleveland, OH 44106.

Pearson, Ellen M. (S. 25, 1937, Amherst, NS) Asst. Libn., Info. Srvs., Univ. of Guelph, 1979–, Asst. Libn., Srvs. and Staffing, 1978–79, Div. Head, Circ., Docum. Ctr., 1969–78; Chief Srch. Ed., Can. Inst. for Scientifica and Tech. Info., 1966–69. **Educ.:** Dalhousie Univ., 1954–57, BSc (Chem., Math.); McGill Univ., 1961–62, BLS. **Orgs.:** Can. Assn. Info. Sci. ASIS. SLA. Can. LA. **Pubns.:** Jt. auth., "The Document Centre of the University of Guelph Library," *Gvt. Pubns. Review* (1974); "CODOC - A Cooperative Approach to Managing Government Publications," *Expression* (Fall 1977); jt. auth., "CODOC - Bibliographic Control of Official Publications," *Bibl. Cntrl. of Official Pubns.* (1980); various papers. **Activities:** 1; 17, 24, 39; 75 **Addr.:** Information Services, University of Guelph Library, Guelph, ON N1G 2W1 Canada.

Pearson, Karl M., Jr. (Mr. 28, 1933, Haverhill, MA) Assoc. Dir., CA Lib. Athrty. for Systs. and Srvs., 1977–; Dir., West. Interstate Lib. Coop. Org., West. Interstate Comsn. for Higher Educ., 1975–77; Lib. Syst. Spec., Syst. Dev. Corp., 1968–75. **Educ.:** Bowdoin Coll., 1951–54, BA (Eng.); Univ. of CA, Los Angeles, 1966–68, MSIS (Documtn.). **Orgs.:** ALA. ASIS. CA LA. **Activities:** 14-Netwk.; 17, 24, 34; 56 **Addr.:** CLASS, 1415 Koll Cir., Suite 101, San Jose, CA 95112.

Pearson, Lois R. (S. 27, 1923, Chicago, IL) Assoc. Ed., *Amer. Libs.*, 1976–; Ref. Libn., NY Univ., 1971–76; Assoc. Ed., *Newsweek Mag.*, 1961–69, Asst. Ed., 1946–61. **Educ.:** Augustana Coll., Rock Island, IL, 1941–45, BA (Hist.); Univ. of TX, 1969–71, MLS. **Orgs.:** ALA. SLA. Chicago Lib. Club: Treas. (1979–80). **Activities:** 3; 36, 37; 93 **Addr.:** American Library Association, 50 E. Huron St., Chicago, IL 60611.

Pearson, Norman R. (D. 9, 1939, Johnsonburg, PA) Head, Serials Dept., Univ. of DE, 1981–; Asst. Univ. Libn. for Tech. Srvs., Wright State Univ., 1977–81; Assoc. Dir. of Libs., IN Univ. of PA, 1976–77; Ed., *UN List of Serials*, NW OH Cnsrtm., 1975–76; Actg. Dir., Assoc. Libn. for Tech. Srvs., Findlay Coll., 1969–75; Eng. Tchr., Bradford Area Sch. Dist., 1962–69. **Educ.:** Waynesburg Coll., 1957–62, BA (Eng.); St. Bonaventure Univ., 1963–66; Univ. of Pittsburgh, 1963–69, MLS; Bowling Green State Univ., 1975–76, EdS (Educ. Admin. and Supvsn.). **Orgs.:** ALA. Acad. LA of OH. Ohio Valley Grp. of Tech. Srv. Libns. ACRL: DE Valley Chap. DE LA. **Honors:** Beta Phi Mu, 1969. **Pubns.:** Ed., *Union List of Serials, Miami Valley Coop. Libs.* **Activities:** 1; 17, 33, 44; 56, 63 **Addr.:** University of Delaware, University Library, Newark, DE 19711.

Pearson, Robert H. (S. 7, 1928, Gainesville, TX) Staff Asst. for Tech. Info. Dept., Ofc. of the Secy. of Defense, 1980–; Dir. of Tech. Info., Nvl. Weapons Ctr., 1977–80; Prof., Ch., Dept. of LS, Ctrl. MI Univ., 1974–77; Dir. of Media Srvs., Univ. of WI, 1970–74. **Educ.:** N. TX State Univ., 1946–51, BS (Art), 1961–62, MEd (Admin.); Syracuse Univ., 1968–70, PhD (Inst. Tech.); Univ. of WI, 1973–74, MA (LS); Univ. of MI Lib. Sch., 1976–77. **Orgs.:** ALA: Com. on Resrch. (1980–82). AECT: Tchr. Educ. Com. (1974–77). AALS. ASIS. Socty. for Tech. Comm. **Honors:** Phi Delta Kappa; Univ. of MI, Sch. of Grad. Std., Visit. Schol. Appt., 1975. **Pubns.:** *Cost-Effectiveness Analysis: The Selection of a Decision Assisting Tool for Instructional Development* (1973); *An Instructional Management Guide to Cost-Effective Decision Making* (1974). **Activities:** 4, 12; 26, 32, 41; 75, 74, 91 **Addr.:** 205 Yoakum Parkway, Watergate/Landmark Suite 706, Alexandria, VA 22304.

Pease, Elaine Kelly (F. 4, 1943, Buffalo, NY) Fine Arts and AV Catlgr., Millersville State Coll., 1977–; Cat. Libn., Franklin & Marshall Coll., 1971–77; Sch. Libn., Grt. Amsterdam (NY) Sch. Dist., 1969–70; Chld. Libn., Schnectady Pub. Lib., 1968–69; Chld. Libn., Woodbridge (NJ) Pub. Lib., 1967–68. **Educ.:** SUNY, Buffalo, 1962–65, BA (Hist.); Rutgers Univ., 1966–67, MLS. **Orgs.:** ALA. PA LA. Assoc. Coll. Libs. of Ctrl. PA: Strg. Com. (1976–78); Tech. Srvs. Com. (Ch., 1972–74). Middlesex (NJ) LA: Corres. Secy. **Pubns.:** "Lancaster County Imprints from the German American Imprint Collection in the Franklin and Marshall College Library," *Lancaster Cnty. Hist. Socty. Jnl.* (1975); "Literary Predetermination," *UNABASHED Libn.* (N. 27, 1978). **Activities:** 1; 20, 21, 45; 55 **Addr.:** 17 Fresh Meadow Dr., Lancaster, PA 17603.

Pease, Mina Beth (F. 3, 1935, Marwayne, AB) Resrch. Dir., Mina Pease Consult. Ed. Srvs., 1979–; Sr. Ed., UNIFO Publshrs. Ltd., 1974–79; Ed., Docum. Resrch., Intl. Univ. Publns. Ltd., London, 1972–74; Acq., Sr. Asst. Libn., PA State Univ. Libs., 1971–72, Docum. Libn., Sr. Asst. Libn., Head, Docum. Sect., PA State Univ. Libs., 1969–71; Docum. Libn., Sr. II, Utica Pub. Lib., 1968–69; Docum. Libn., Sr. II Libn., Chief, Docum. Dept., Univ. of MA Libs., 1967–68; UN Docum. Libn., Libn. II, Univ. of WA Libs., 1960–67. **Educ.:** Univ. of WA, 1953–57, BA (Hist.), 1958–60, MLS. **Orgs.:** ALA: GODORT, Intl. Docum. Task Force (Coord., 1972–74). Assn. of Intl. Libs.: N. Amer. VP

Special Subjects/Services: 50. Adult educ.; 51. Advert./Mktg.; 52. Aerosp.; 53. Agric.; 54. Area std.; 55. Arts/Hum.; 56. Autom.; 57. Bibl./Prtg.; 58. Bio. sci.; 59. Bus./Fin.; 60. Chem.; 61. Copyrt.; 62. Documtn.; 63. Educ.; 64. Engin.; 65. Env.; 66. Eth. grps.; 67. Film; 68. Food/Nutr.; 69. Geneal.; 70. Geo.; 71. Geol.; 72. Handcpd.; 73. Hist.; 74. Int. frdm.; 75. Info. sci.; 76. Insr.; 77. Law; 78. Legis.; 79. Math./Comp. sci.; 80. Med.; 81. Metals; 82. Nat. resrcs.; 83. Newsp.; 84. Nuc. sci.; 85. Oral hist.; 86. Petr./Energy; 87. Pharm.; 88. Phys./Astr./Math.; 89. Readg.; 90. Relig.; 91. Sci./Tech.; 92. Soc. sci.; 93. Telecom.; 94. Transp.; 95. (other).

(1976–80). UN Assn.: USA, WA State Cncl. (1962–67). **Pubns.:** "A Reason for Being, A National Document Center and the Exchange of Official Publications," *Gvt. Publns. Review* (1975); Ed., *UNDEX SERIES "C" Cumulative Ed., 1974–77* (1979); "The Plain J, a Documents Classfication System", *Lib. Resrcs. and Tech. Srvs.* (Sum. 1972); "For Tormorrow is a Yesterday that will Never Come Again, A Paper on International Library Cooperation," *PNLA Qtly.*, (vol. 31, no. 3); *Basic Reference Publications for the Study of the United Nations* bibl. (1966); various papers. **Activities:** 1; 29, 30, 37; 56, 62, 92 **Addr.:** 7 Carhart Ave., White Plains, NY 10605.

Pease, William J. (My. 22, 1929, Long Beach, CA) Ch., Cat. Dept., San Diego State Univ., 1973–; Lib. Dir., Univ. of Portland, 1970–73; Cat. Libn., Reed Coll., 1964–70; Acq. Libn., Portland State Univ., 1958–64. **Educ.:** Pomona Coll., 1948–50, BA (Psy.); Fordham Univ., 1950–52, MA (Psy.); Univ. of CA, Berkeley, 1954–55, MLS. **Orgs.:** CA LA: Cnclr. (1977–80); Lcl. Chap. Secy. (1976); ALA: ACRL, Affirmative Action Com. (1975). San Diego State: Acad. Sen., Secy. (1979–81). Untd. Profs. of CA. **Pubns.:** "Black Subjects, White Subjectivity," *CA Libn.* (Ap. 1978). **Activities:** 1; 17, 20; 92 **Addr.:** 5750 Amaya Dr. #54, La Mesa, CA 92041.

Peat, W. Leslie (Ja. 13, 1941, Norwalk, CT) Libn., Prof. of Law, VT Law Sch., 1980–, Prof. of Law, 1974–80; Asst. to the VP, Dartmouth Coll., 1969–74; Asst. to Pres., Hamilton Coll., 1967–69. **Educ.:** Hamilton Coll., 1958–62, AB (Phil.); Yale Univ., 1962–66, LLB (Law), 1965–66, MA (Amer. Std.); Simmons Coll., 1979–80, MS (LS). **Orgs.:** AALL: Pubns. Com. (1980–). **Pubns.:** "The Constitutionality of New Section 2035: Is There Any Room for Doubt?" *Tax Law Review* (1978); "Administration of Endowment Funds, Quasi-Endowment Funds, and Other Similar Funds," *College and University Business Administration* (1974); "Non-Legal Reference Books for Law Libraries," *Legal Ref. Srvs. Qtly.* (1981); "The Use of Research Libraries: A Comment About the Pittsburgh Study and Its Critics," *Jnl. of Acad. Libnshp.* (1980–81); "On Being a Client: What Every Library Director Should Know About Lawyers," *Lib. Jnl.* (1981); Various bks., reviews. **Activities:** 1; 17, 31; 77 **Addr.:** Vermont Law School, Law Library, South Royalton, VT 05068.

Peattie, Noel R. (N. 28, 1932, Menton, Alpes-Maritimes, France) Col. Dev. Libn., Univ. of CA, Davis, 1966–; Cat. Libn., CA State Univ., 1961–66. **Educ.:** Pomona Coll., 1950–54, BA (Phil.); Yale Univ., 1954–55, MA (Phil.); Univ. of CA, Berkeley, 1960–61, MLS (Libnshp.). **Orgs.:** ALA. CA LA: Col. Dev. Chap. (Ch., 1977). Com. of Small Mag. Ed. and Publshrs. Bd. (1973–75). West. Indp. Publshrs.: Pres. (1978–79). **Honors:** Beta Phi Mu. **Pubns.:** "The Living Z" (1976). Ed., Publshr., *Sipapu* (1970–) Publshr., Konocti Bks.; Owner, Cannonade Press. **Activities:** 1; 15, 37; 57, 66, 90 **Addr.:** Route 1, Box 216, Winters, CA 95694.

Peck, Ann Day (Ag. 6, 1945, Ft. Lauderdale, FL) Educ. Couns., U.S. Interests Sect., Embassy of Belgium, Baghdad, Iraq, 1978–79; Ref. Libn., Amer. Univ., Cairo, 1974–77; Law Libn., U.S. Tariff Comsn., 1973–74; Sr. Ref. Libn., Dept. of State, 1971–73; Ref. Libn., Princeton Univ., 1968–70. **Educ.:** OH Wesleyan Univ., 1963–65, 1966–67, BA (Pol. Sci.); Amer. Coll. in Paris, 1965–66; Univ. of MI, 1967–68, MALS; George Washington Univ., 1972–74, 1978, MPA. **Orgs.:** ALA: Nom. Com. Hist. Sect. (Ch. 1970). Univ. MI LS Alum. Amer. Assn. of Frgn. Srvs. Women. **Addr.:** 106 Grafton St., Chevy Chase, MD 20815.

Peck, Jean M. (Buffalo, NY) Head, Cat. Dept., Univ. of CA, Berkeley, 1976–, Head, Mono. Cat. Div., Catlgr., 1966–76; Head, Lib. of Congs. Sect. Cat. Dept., MI State Univ., 1961–66; Nursing Srv. Supvsr., Buffalo Gen. Hosp., 1956–60. **Educ.:** Univ. of Buffalo, 1956, BS (Nursing Admin.); Syracuse Univ., 1961, MS (LS). **Orgs.:** ALA: RTSD, Bk. Cat. Com. (1972–76); Lib. Admin. Div./PAS, Supervisory Skills Com. (1981–83), Persnl. Dynamics for Supvsn. (1980). CA LA. North. CA Tech. Prcs. Grp. CA Acad. and Resrch. Libns. Natl. Audubon Socty. Sierra Club. Point Reyes Bird Observatory. **Honors:** Beta Phi Mu, 1961. **Activities:** 1; 17, 20, 46 **Addr.:** 212 Doe Library, University of California, Berkeley, CA 94720.

Peck, John G., Jr. (S. 19, 1930, Lynchburg, VA) Dir. of Lib. and Media Srvs., Westminster Choir Coll., 1959–; Asst. Msc. Libn., Catlgr., Vassar Coll., 1956–59. **Educ.:** Mars Hill Coll., 1948–50, AA (Msc.); Baylor Univ., 1953–55, BM (Organ); Univ. of NC, 1955–57, MS (LS). **Orgs.:** Msc. LA: Lcl. Arrange. Com., Sum. Mtg., Atlantic City (1969). NJ LA. ALA. Amer. Gld. of Organists.: Princeton Chap. (Sub-Dean, 1979–81; Dean, 1981–82). AAUP: Coll. Chap. (Pres., 1970–71). **Honors:** Beta Phi Mu, 1958. **Activities:** 1; 15, 17; 55 **Addr.:** 124 Main St., P. O. Box 164, Kingston, NJ 08528.

Peck, Kathleen Cifra (Je. 9, 1945, Sharon, PA) Asst. Dept. Head, Spec. Cols., Univ. of CA, Davis, 1969–. **Educ.:** Univ. of CA, Berkeley, 1963–67, BA (Fr.), 1968–69, MLS. **Orgs.:** Socty. of CA Archvsts.: Cncl. (1977–79). CA Assn. of Thea. Specs.: Treas. (1977–). Medvl. Assn. of the Pac.: Cncl. (1981–83). **Activities:** 1, 2; 17, 39, 45; 55, 57, 85 **Addr.:** Dept. of Special Collections, Shields Library, University of California, Davis, CA 95616.

Peck, Marian B. (Je. 28, 1920, Sauk Centre, MN) Head, Chld. Srvs., Montgomery Cnty., Norristown Pub. Lib., 1965–; Coord., Sch. Libs., Plymouth Twp., 1962–65. **Educ.:** IN State Univ., 1939–41; Drexel Lib. Sch., 1961. **Orgs.:** ALA: Chld. Srvs. Div., Com. on Liaison with Org. Serving the Child (1971); PA Dev. Com. (1979–81); PLA, Ad Hoc Com. on Gvr.'s Conf. (Chld. Srvs. Rep., 1976–77). Philadelphia Chld. Readg. RT. Booksellers Assn. Lib. PR Assn.: VP (1978–79). Various other orgs. Norristown Bus. and Prof. Women's Club.: Individual Dev. Com. (1978–79). **Activities:** 9, 13; 21; 55 **Addr.:** Swede & Elm Sts., Norristown, PA 19401.

Peck, Mary Rose (My. 22, 1924, Scranton, PA) Pub. Srvs. Libn., Essex Cmnty. Coll., 1967–; Branch Libn., Baltimore Cnty. Pub. Lib., 1965–67; Admin. Asst., Baltimore Cnty. Pub. Lib., 1962–65; Libn., Catlgr., U S Army War Coll., 1951–53; Asst. Libn., Loyola Coll., 1947–51; Libn., Bel Air Jr.–Sr. HS, 1946–47; Asst. Libn., Univ. of Scranton, 1945–46. **Educ.:** Marywood Coll., 1941–45, AB (LS) Cath. Univ. of Amer., 1965–69, MS (LS). **Orgs.:** SLA: Baltimore Chap., Dir. 1975–76; Exec. Bd. (1971–76). MD Assn. of Cmnty. and Jr. Coll.: Lrng. Resrcs. Div. Ch. (1969–70); Vice-Ch., Prog. Ch. (1968–69). Baltimore Cnty. Cmnty. Coll.: Staff Dev. Com. of Lrng. Resrcs. Com. (Ch., 1978–79). ALA: RSD. Montford Glen Cmnty. Assn.: Treas. (1975–) Hosp. Com. (Ch., 1974). **Honors:** Beta Phi Mu, 1969; U S Army War Coll., Cmdn. for Outstan. Work, 1953; Marywood Semy., Hoban Medal, 1941. **Activities:** 1, 10; 31, 34, 39; 55, 57, 92 **Addr.:** 1738 Pleasantville Rd., Forest Hill, MD 21050.

Pederson, Ann Elizabeth (O. 11, 1943, Johnson City, TN) Lectr., Arch. and Rec. Mgt., Sch. of Libnshp., Univ. of New S. Wales, Kensington (Sydney), Australia, 1981–; Dir., Arch. Div., GA Dept. of Arch. and Hist., 1974–81, Coord., Bicent. Proj., 1973–74, State Rec. Anal., 1972–73, Head, Microfilm Lib., 1972, Asst. to Dir., 1971–72. **Educ.:** OH Wesleyan Univ., 1962–66, BA (Hist., Educ.); GA State Univ., 1972–76, MA (Hist.); Dept. of Educ., State of New S. Wales, Australia, 1968, Sec. Tchg. Cert. **Orgs.:** SAA: Prog. Com. (1976), Nom. Com. (Ch. 1977). Socty. of GA Archvsts.: Pres. (1976); *GA Arch.* (Ed., 1977–79). Women's Rec. Proj. of GA, Inc.: Co-Fndr. and Dir. for Arch. (1975–). S. Atl. Arch. and Rec. Conf.: Conf. Ch. (1974). Amer. Assn. of State and Lcl. Hist. NEH: Consult., Grant Review Panelist (1978–79). **Honors:** Socty. of GA Archvsts., Outstan. Srv., 1980. **Pubns.:** Co-Auth., *Archives and Manuscripts: Public Programs Manual* (1981); Co-ed., *Documents of Georgia History 1730–1790* (1973); "The 1976 SAA Survey on Outreach," *The Amer. Archvst.* (Ap. 1978); "The State of the Art: Moscow, 1972," *GA Arch.* (1972); "A Very Fragile Resource: Our Documentary Heritage" multi- media/slide presentation (1977); various multi-media/slide presentations. **Activities:** 2, 11, 13; 17, 26, 38; 62, 75, 92 **Addr.:** c/o School of Librarianship, The University of New South Wales, P.O. Box 1, Kensington, New S. Wales, 2033, Australia.

Peduzzi, Roberta E. (Ag. 13, 1947, Munich, Germany) Acq. Libn., Belleville Area Coll., 1970–. **Educ.:** Belleville Jr. Coll., 1965–67, AA; South. IL Univ., 1967–69, BS (Educ.); Univ. of IL, 1969–70, MS (LS). **Orgs.:** ALA. IL LA. AAUP. South. IL Lrng. Resrcs. Co-op. Leag. of Women Voters: Lcl. Chap. (Bltn. Ed., 1981). **Activities:** 1; 15 **Addr.:** Belleville Area College Library, 2500 Carlyle Rd., Belleville, IL 62221.

Peel, Annette (N. 22, 1942, Ogden, UT) Southwest Libn., Mesa Pub. Lib., 1979–; Latin Amer. Subj. Spec., AZ State Univ., 1973–78; Oral Hist. Spec., Archvst., Weber State Coll., 1965–73. **Educ.:** Weber State Coll., 1960–65, BSc (Hist.); Univ. of WA, 1967–69, MA (LS); various crs. **Orgs.:** SALALM. SAA: Com. on Ref. and Access (1979–). Latin Amer. Std. Assn. AZ State LA. West. Hist. Assn. **Pubns.:** Jt. Auth., "Mission Life in America," *World Bk. Encyc.* (1979–); "Guide to Latin American Publications in Hayden Library," (1978). **Activities:** 1, 9; 39, 41, 45; 54, 85 **Addr.:** Box 535, Tempe, AZ 85281.

Peel, Bruce Braden (N. 11, 1916, Ferland, SK) Libn. to the Univ., Univ. of AB, 1955–, Asst. Libn., 1954–55, Chief Catlgr., 1951–54; Canadiana Libn., Univ. of SK, 1946–51. **Educ.:** Univ. of SK, 1940–43, BA (Hist.), 1943–44, MA (Hist.); Univ. of Toronto, 1945–46, BLS. **Orgs.:** Can. LA: Can. Assn. of Coll. and Univ. Libs. ALA. IFLA. Various other orgs. Alcuin Socty. Bibl. Socty. of Can. Assn. for Can. Std. Hist. Socty. of AB. **Honors:** Hist. Socty. of AB, Scroll of Merit, 1969; Edmonton Hist. Adv. Bd., Scroll of Merit, 1976; Bibl. Socty. of Can., Marie Tremaine Medal, 1975; Gvt. of Can., Queen Elizabeth Silver Jubilee Medal, 1978. **Pubns.:** *Bibliography of the Prairie Provinces to 1953* (1973); *Early Printing in the Red River Settlement, 1859–1870* (1974); *Rossville Mission Press* (1974); *Steamboats on the Saskatchewan* (1972); ed., *Librarianship in Canada, 1946–67* (1968); various articles. **Activities:** 1; 17 **Addr.:** University of Alberta Library, Edmonton, AB T6G 2J8 Canada.

Peele, David A. (Mr. 24, 1929, New York, NY) Deputy Chief libn., Coll. of Staten Island Lib.. 1978–, Ref. Libn., 1976–, Head, Tech. Srvs., Staten Island Cmnty. Coll., 1973–76, Head, Pub. Srvs., 1962–73, Deputy Chief Libn., 1962–76; Serials Acq. Libn., City Coll. of NY, 1958–62, Asst. Serials Libn., 1955–58; Circ. and Rsv. Asst., Swarthmore Coll., 1951–55. **Educ.:** Swarthmore Coll., 1946–50, BA (Hist.); West. Rsv. Univ., 1950–51, MS (LS); Swarthmore Coll., 1951–54, MA (Hist.). **Orgs.:** ALA: LAMA/Persnl. Admin. Sect., Com. on Econ. Status, Welfare, and Fringe Benefits (1978–82); RASD, Cat. Use Com. (1979–81). LA CUNY: Com. on Coms. (1979–81). U.S. Tennis Assn. **Pubns.:** Ed., *Racket and Paddle Games: A Guide to Information Sources* (1980); "Performance Ratings and Librarian's Rights," *Amer. Libs.* (Je. 1970); "The Cataloging on the Wall," *Wilson Lib. Bltn.* (Ap. 1971); "A Legend in His Own Time," *Wilson Lib. Bltn.* (Ap. 1975) "Staffing the Reference Desk," *Lib. Jnl.* (S. 1, 1980); Various other articles. **Activities:** 1; 17, 31, 39 **Addr.:** College of Staten Island Library, 130 Stuyvesant Pl., Staten Island, NY 10301.

Peeler, Elizabeth Hastings (Ap. 5, 1914, Nashville, TN) Retired, 1977–; Intl. Affairs Libn., FL Intl. Univ., 1971–77; Assoc. Dir., Tech. Srvs., Univ. of W. FL, 1967–71; Head, Cat. Dept., SUNY, Stony Brook, 1965–67; Chief, Cat. Sect., Untd. Nations Dag Hammarskjold Lib., 1964–65; Cat. libn., Lectr., Univ. of Ibadan, Ibadan, Nigeria, 1961–64; Head, Cat. Dept., Univ. of Miami, 1946–60; Cat. libn., Agnes Scott Coll., 1944–46; various libn., tchg. positions. **Educ.:** Vanderbilt, 1935, BA, 1936, MA; Emory, 1939, BS (LS); Columbia Univ., 1951, MS (LS). **Orgs.:** FL LA: Pres. (1956–57); *FL Libs.* (Ed., 1959–60). SELA: Reg. Grp. of Cat. (Ch., 1958–60). Dade Cnty. LA: Pres. (1958–59). W. FL LA: Pres. (1969–70). Zonta. AAUW. Natl. Socty. of South. Dames. Hist. Assn. of South. FL. Concerned Srs. of Dade Inc.: Resrch. Com. Ch. **Activities:** 1; 20, 26, 49-Special library; 65, 92 **Addr.:** 110 Mendoza, Apt. 7, Coral Gables, FL 33134.

Peer, Robert H. (Ap. 10, 1923, Denville, NJ) ILLs, Niagara Falls Pub. Lib., 1970–, Jr. Libn., 1967–70. **Educ.:** Bloomfield Coll., 1946–50, BA (Lit.); Biblical Semy., NY, 1951–53; SUNY, Geneseo, 1962–66, MLS. **Orgs.:** SLA. NY LA. The Nature Conservancy. Appalachian Trail Conf. **Activities:** 9; 34, 39 **Addr.:** 546 7th St., Niagara Falls, NY 14301.

Peffer, Margery E., (Ag. 19, 1928, Pittsburgh, PA) Asst. Head, Sci. and Tech. Dept., Carnegie Lib. of Pittsburgh, 1978–, Libn., 1966–78, Libn., 1950–52. **Educ.:** Allegheny Coll., 1945–49, BS (Chem.); Carnegie Inst. of Tech., 1949–50, MLS. **Orgs.:** SLA. **Activities:** 9; 17, 39, 44; 60, 91 **Addr.:** Science & Technology Dept., Carnegie Library of Pittsburgh, 4400 Forbes Ave., Pittsburgh, PA 15213.

Pegram, Joseph Wallerstein (Wally) (Ap. 17, 19–, Carson, VA) Head, Phys. Lib., Univ. of CA, Los Angeles, 1971–; Dept. Head and Ref. Libn., Hughes Aircraft Co., 1962–71; Head of Tech. Prcs., TRW Corp., 1959–62; Asst. Catlgr., Ramo-Wooldrige Corp., 1957–59; Resrch. Catlgr., Unvsl. Studios, 1955–56. **Educ.:** VA State Coll., 1947–51, BSLS; Univ. of South. CA, 1954–55, MSLS. **Orgs.:** ALA. SLA. CA LA. South. CA Tech. Prcs. Grp. **Pubns.:** "The Physics Library," *Univ. of CA, Los Angeles Libn.* (Jl.–Ag. 1978); "An Einstein Centennial Exhibit," *UCLA Libn.* (S. 1979). **Activities:** 1, 12; 17, 22, 39; 75, 88, 91 **Addr.:** 1813 - 17th St. #C, Santa Monica, CA 90404.

Peguese, Charles R. (Ag. 3, 1938, Philadelphia, PA) Coord., LSCA Title I, State Lib. of PA, 1974–; Dir., Action Lib., Sch. Dist. of Philadelphia, 1971–74, Coord., Non-Pub. Sch., AV Ctr., 1968–71; YA Coord., Free Lib. of Philadelphia, 1959–68. **Educ.:** La Salle Coll., 1956–60, BS (Bus. Admin.); Drexel Univ., 1962–65, MS (LS). **Orgs.:** ALA: LSCA Coord. Discuss. Grp. (Ch., 1979–80). PA LA: Long Range Plng. Com. **Activities:** 13; 17, 24 **Addr.:** State Library of Pennsylvania, Harrisburg, PA 17120.

Peischl, Thomas M. (Mr. 8, 1943, Easton, PA) Dir. of Coll. Libs. and Comp. Srvs., SUNY Coll. at Potsdam, 1979–; Admin. Libn., Acq., Multi-Media Libn., Circ. and Data Systs. Libn., Univ. of North. CO, 1974–79. **Educ.:** Susquehanna Univ., 1961–65, AB (Hist., Psy.); Temple Univ., 1965–68, MEd (Spec. Educ.); U.S. Air Frc. Secur. Srv. Inst., 1968–72, Dip.; Univ. of Denver, 1972–74, MA (LS); Univ. of North. CO, 1975–79, DED (Educ. Admin., Higher Educ.). **Orgs.:** ALA: ACRL; LAMA. SLA. SUNY LA. ASIS. Various other orgs. AAUP. Ctr. for Spec. and Adv. Progs. **Honors:** Mt. Plains LA, Cont. Educ. Awd., 1979. **Pubns.:** Jt. auth., "Management Data Generated by Automated Circulation Systems: Uses and Limitations," *The Information Age in Perspective* (1978); "Patron I.D. Cards Made Cheap and Easy," *Spec. Libs.* (Ap. 1978); "The Colorado Information and Communication Network," *Online Review* (D. 1977); "Common Myths of Library Management," *CO Libs.* (D. 1977); "Reciprocal Borrowing Reconsidered," *CO Libs.* (D. 1976); various other articles. **Activities:** 1, 12; 17, 22, 34; 56, 75, 95 **Addr.:** Frederick W. Crumb Memorial Library, SUNY College at Potsdam, Potsdam, NY 13676.

Pelchat, P. Eugene (N. 29, 1930, Ponteix, SK) Head, Acq. and Cat., Hlth. Sci. Lib., Dalhousie Univ., 1974–; Head, Tech. Srvs., Mt. Royal Coll., 1973–74, Head, Cat., 1971–73; Asst. Catlgr., NM State Univ. Lib., 1970–71. **Educ.:** Univ. of AB, 1963–65; NM State Univ., 1965–67, BS (Agr.); Univ. of TX, 1968–70, MLS. **Orgs.:** Can. LA. Can. Hlth. LA. Atl. Prov. LA. **Activities:** 1, 12; 15, 20, 32; 72, 80, 87 **Addr.:** Kellogg Health Sciences Library, Dalhousie University, Halifax, NS B3H 4H7 Canada.

PROFESSIONAL ACTIVITIES: Institutions: 1. Acad. lib.; 2. Arch.; 3. Assn.; 4. Fed./Gvt. lib.; 5. Inst. lib.; 6. Mfr./Suppl.; 7. Milit. lib.; 8. Musm.; 9. Pub. lib.; 10. Sch. lib.; 11. Sch. of lib. sci.; 12. Spec. lib.; 13. State lib.; 14. (other). **Functions/Activities:** 15. Acq./Col. dev.; 16. Adult srvs.; 17. Admin.; 18. Apprais.; 19. Archit./Bldgs.; 20. Cat./Class.; 21. Chld. srvs.; 22. Circ.; 23. Cons./Pres.; 24. Consult.; 25. Cont. ed.; 26. Educ. lib. sci.; 27. Ext. srvs.; 28. Fund/Grants; 29. Gvt. pubs.; 30. Indx./Abs.; 31. Instr. lib. use; 32. Media srvs.; 33. Micro.; 34. Netwks./Coop.; 35. Persnl.; 36. PR; 37. Publshg.; 38. Recs. mgt.; 39. Ref. srvs.; 40. Repro.; 41. Resrch.; 42. Review.; 43. Secur.; 44. Serials; 45. Spec. col.; 46. Tech. srvs.; 47. Trustees/Bds.; 48. YA srvs.; 49. (other).

Pellen, Rita M. (Ja. 18, 1950, Philadelphia, PA) Info. Spec., Perry Oceanographics, Inc. 1977–; Libn., Comex Seal, Marseille France, 1976–77; Tech. Libn., US Dept. Army, Army Mtrls. and Mechanics Res Ctr., 1972–75. **Educ.:** PA State Univ., 1967–71, BA (Hist.); Univ. of Pittsburgh, 1971–72, MLS; Med. LA, 1975, Cert. I. **Orgs.:** SLA: FL Chap. (Secy. 1978–79), Empl. Ch. (1979–80). Palm Beach Cnty. LA: VP (1980–81). Intl. Assn. of Marine Sci. Libs. and Info. Ctrs. FL Searchers. Natl. Assn. of Female Exec. **Honors:** Beta Phi Mu, 1972. **Activities:** 12; 15, 39, 41; 64, 86, 91 **Addr.:** Perry Oceanographics, Inc., 275 W. 10th St., P.O. Box 10297, Riviera Beach, FL 33404.

Pelletier, Rosaire (Jl. 25, 1931, St-Hyacinthe, PQ) Bibl., Anal. et Éval. de Docum., Ctrl. des Bibs., Ministry de l'Educ., PQ, 1972–; Prof. Coll. des Jésuites, PQ, 1969–70; Prof., Coll. Jésus-Marie et Coll. Notre-Dame de Bellevue, 1967–69; Dir. des Études, Sémy. St-Vincent, 1966–67, Prof., 1957–66. **Educ.:** Univ. Laval, 1952, BAé, 1952–57, Bac. (Théo.), 1958–60, Bac. (Péd.), 1964–66, Lic.-ès-lettres Classiques; Univ. de Montréal, 1970–72, MA (Bibl); Univ. Laval, 1967–69, Cert. (Grmn.). **Orgs.:** Corp. des Bibtcrs. Prof. du PQ: Bd. (1976–78). ASTED: Com. des Bourses (1977–). Can LA. Socty. des Études Grk. et Latin du PQ. Socty. Géneal. Can. Fr. Les Amis de l'Orgue. **Pubns.:** Contrib., *Current Words in Library Science* (1979); *Les Bibliothécaires Professionnels du Québec* (1979); *Education sexuelle* (1975); *Education Spécialisée* (1976); *Périodiques pour les Collèges* (1974); various articles and bibls. **Activities:** 4, 11; 26, 42; 55, 57, 63 **Addr.:** Centrale des bibliothèques (Ministère de l'Education), 1685 est, Fleury, Montréal, PQ H2C 1T1 Canada.

Pelletière, Jean Clarridge (Rochester, NY) Dir., Libs., Un. Coll., 1978–; Exec. Dir., Univ. of WI, Oshkosh, 1977–78, Assoc. Dir., Pub. Srvs., 1976–77; Dir., Spec. Proj., San Bruno Pub. Lib., 1974–76; Instr., Coord. Bibl., Univ. of CA, Berkeley, 1974–76, Libn. I, Mid. E. Sect., 1973–74. **Educ.:** Syracuse Univ., 1952–56, BA (Anthro., Jnlsm.); University of CA, Berkeley, 1966–74, MA (Near E. Lang., Lit.), 1972–73 MLS (Near E. Lang., Lit.), 1973–74 Cert. (Bibl.). **Orgs.:** ALA: Mem. Com. (1977–); ACRL/Mem. Com. (1977–); Cont. Ed. Com.; LAMA/Econ. Status, Welfare, Fringe Benefits Com. (1977–). NY LA: Persnl. Action Com. (1980–); Coll. and Univ. Libs. Sect., (Nsltr. ed., 1979). NEH: Div. of Resrch. Grants (Reviewer, 1978). OCLC: Circ. Control Adv. Com. (1981–). SUNY/OCLC Netwk. Adv. Cncl. (1981–). **Honors:** Ofc. of Mgt. Std., Consult. Prog., 1979. **Pubns.:** Jt. auth., *Surveys of Librarians' Benefits: An Annotated Bibliography* (1979); Jt. auth., *The Arabs in American Textbooks* (1975); Jt. auth., *Supplement to How to Use the U.C. Berkeley Library: Handbook for Bibliography I* (1975); "The American Peace Movement", *Al-Ahram* (1970); various articles, reviews in *Wkshp. in Nonviolence Mag.* (1966–76); various other articles, photographs. **Activities:** 1, 11; 17, 24 **Addr.:** 2167 Stuyvesant St., Schenectady, NY 12309.

Pelley, Janet D. (O. 8, 1951, Montréal, PQ) Tech. Srvs. Libn., Colchester-E. Hants Reg. Lib., 1976–. **Educ.:** McGill Univ., 1969–71, Dip. (Collegial Stds.), 1971–74, BA hons. (Classics); Univ. of Toronto, 1974–76, MLS. **Orgs.:** Can. LA. Atl. Prov. LA. NS LA: Nsltr. Com. (1977–78); Secy. (1978–79); Nom. Com. (Conv., 1979–80). Overseas Bk. Ctr. Belleek Collectors' Socty. Franklin Mint Collectors' Socty. **Activities:** 9; 17, 20, 46 **Addr.:** Colchester-East Hants Regional Library, 754 Prince St., Truro, NS B2N 1G9 Canada.

Pellowski, Anne (Je. 28, 1933, Pine Creek, WI) Lib. consult. and writer; Dir., Info. Cntr. on Chld. Cult., U.S. Com. for UNICEF, 1967–81; Storytel. and Grp. Work Spec., New York Pub. Lib., 1957–66. **Educ.:** Coll. of St. Teresa, 1951–55, BA (Comp. Lit.); Columbia Univ., 1957–59, MSLS. **Orgs.:** ALA: Intl. Rel. Com. (1975–79). Intl. Bd. on Bks. for Young People: Hans Christian Andersen Awd. Com. **Honors:** Coll. of St. Teresa, Alumnae Awd., 1970; ALA, Grolier Fndn. Awd., 1979; Women's Natl. Bk. Com., Constance Lindsay Skinner Awd., 1980. **Pubns.:** *The World of Children's Literature* (1968); *The World of Storytelling* (1977); "Beyond the Colonial Bias," in *Lib. Jnl.* (N. 1967); "Children's Cinema: International Dilemma or Delight?," *Film Lib. Qtly.* (Fall 1969); "Internationalism in Children's Literature," *Children and Books* (1977); various articles. **Addr.:** 639 West End Ave., New York, NY 10025.

Peloquin, Margaret I. (Jl. 6, 1943, Welsh, LA) Med. Libn., Hlth. Scis. Lib., 1981–; Data Base Coord., TX Med. Ctr., Houston Acad. of Med. Lib., 1980–81; Libn., Main Lib., Calcasieu Par. Lib. Syst., 1978–79. **Educ.:** McNeese State Univ., 1962–66, BA (Liberal Std.); Univ. of TX, 1977–78 (LS). **Orgs.:** ALA. Med. LA. ASIS. **Pubns.:** "Telemedicine; A Look at Telemedicine as a Solution to Health Care Delivery," *TX Nursing* (Ap. 1979). **Activities:** 12; 24, 39, 41; 80 **Addr.:** Health Sciences Library, 707 E. 14th St., Austin, TX 78701.

Pelz, Craig L. (Ap. 15, 1945, Detroit, MI) Ch., Tech. Lib. Branch, U.S. Army Corps of Engins., 1973–; Libn., USAED, Walla Walla, WA, 1973–76. **Educ.:** CA State Univ., Fullerton, 1970–72, BA (Hist.); Univ. of South. CA, 1972–73, MSLS. **Orgs.:** SLA: Fort Worth Chap., Lcl. Plng. Grp. (Ch.). **Activities:** 4, 12; 15, 17, 20; 64, 65, 91 **Addr.:** 3216 Fargo Ct., Ft. Worth, TX 76133.

Pemberton, J. Michael (D. 15, 1942, Nashville, TN) Asst. Prof., Univ. of TN, 1977–; Asst. Prof., Univ. of AL, Huntsville, 1975–77. **Educ.:** Univ. of the S., 1960–64, BA (Eng.); Univ. of TN, 1964–66, MA (Eng.), 1967–73, PhD (Eng.), 1974–75, MSLS. **Orgs.:** ALA. SELA. Assn. of Recs. Mgrs. and Admin. **Honors:** Beta Phi Mu, 1975. **Pubns.:** Jt. auth., "Measurement of Public Library Reference Effectiveness: A State Library Approach," *Pub. Lib. Qtly.* (1979). **Activities:** 1, 2; 19, 33, 38; 55, 67, 72 **Addr.:** Graduate School of Library and Information Science, University of Tennessee, 804 Volunteer Blvd., Knoxville, TN 37916.

Penchansky, Mimi Black (O. 7, 1925, New York, NY) Head, Gen. Ref. Dept., Queens Coll. Lib., 1977–, ILL Libn., 1964–77; Instr., Eng., Joseph Pulitzer Jr. HS, 1962–64. **Educ.:** Queens Coll., 1957–62, BA (Eng.); Columbia Univ., 1962–64, MS (LS); NY Univ., 1973–75, MA (Media Ecol.). **Orgs.:** ALA: SRRT, Feminist Task Frc., Task Frc. on Alternatives in Print, Coord.; RASD/Machine-Assisted Ref. Sect., Eval. of Srvs. Com.; ACRL. Women Lib. Workers, Com. on Non–Bibl. Databases. METRO: Ref. Libns. Discuss. Grp. Strg. Com. Prof. Staff Congs. B'nai B'rith Women. Intl. Comm. Assn. Intl. Socty. for Gen. Semantics. **Honors:** Phi Beta Kappa, 1961. **Pubns.:** *Alternatives in Print; A Catalog of Social Change Publications* (1972–80); "Alternatives in Print," *Lib. Jnl.* 1972; ed. bd., *Serials for Libraries: An Annotated Guide to Annuals, Directories, Yearbooks and Other Non-Periodical Serials* (1978); cmplr., *Libraries and Librarians in the 80's: Challenge and Change* (1980); cmplr., *The Information Industry and the Library–Competition or Cooperation?* (1979); Various other bibls. **Activities:** 1; 34, 39; 55, 56, 93 **Addr.:** 172-90 Highland Ave., Jamaica, NY 11432.

Pendergrass, Margaret Elizabeth (Ag. 9, 1912, Springfield, IL) Libn. II Catlgr., IL State Lib., 1973–, Head, Chld. Bk. Reviewing Ctr., 1970–73, Head, Juvenile Unit, 1957–70, Catlgr., 1950–57; Army Libn., various camps, 1941–49; Branch Libn., Phyllis Wheatley Branch, 1934–41. **Educ.:** Hampton Inst., 1934, BS; Univ. of IL, 1967–68 (LS); LaSalle Univ. 1972, Cert. (Comp. Prog.). **Orgs.:** ALA. IL LA: Chld. Sect., Vice-Ch. (1956–57), Ch. (1957–58). Cath. LA. Springfield Lib. Club: Past Pres., Secy. Springfield Urban Leag. World Federalists. NAACP. James Weldon Johnson Std. Gld. **Honors:** Chld. Sect., IL LA, Davis Cup Awd., 1976; NAACP, Cmnty. Srv. Awd., 1974. **Pubns.:** "Selected List of Books by and About the Negro," *IL Libs.* (Ja. 1969); "Illinois Authors and Illustrators," *IL Libs.* (N. 1970). **Activities:** 13; 20, 21, 48 **Addr.:** Illinois State Library, Centennial Bldg., Springfield, IL 62756.

Pengelly, Kenneth Clifford (S. 5, 1943, Akron, OH) Assoc. Prof., Mankato State Univ., 1968–; Instr., Chaminade Coll. of Honolulu, 1965–68. **Educ.:** OH North. Univ., 1961–63, BA (Pol. Sci., Hist.); Univ. of HI, 1966–68, MLS; Mankato State Univ., 1972, (AV); various crs. **Orgs.:** ALA. AECT: Eval. Com. MN Educ. Media Org.: Media Educ. Conf. (1980); Plng. Com. (1977). MN Assn. for Cont. and Adult Educ.: Prog. Plng. Com. *MN Assn. for Educ. Data Systs.* Frnds. of the Lib.: PR Co-ord. (1979–). **Pubns.:** "Computerized Data Bases," *MACAE Qtly.* (Spr. 1979); "Selection Sources" slide-tape series (1972). **Activities:** 25, 26, 31; 50, 63, 74 **Addr.:** #20, Mankato State University, Mankato, MN 56001.

Penich, Sofya Sonia (S. 10, 1917, Belgrade, Yugoslavia) Actg. Law Libn., NY State Supreme Ct., Criminal Branch Law Lib., 1978–; MidManhattan Lib., Ref. Libn., Soc. Sci. Dept., 1977–78; Ref. libn., NY State Supreme Ct., Buffalo, 1974–76; Asst. Cat. Libn., Columbia Univ. Lib., 1971–74. **Educ.:** Fac. of Law, Belgrade, Yugoslavia, 1935–39, Licenciee en Droít; Econ. Fac., Belgrade, Yugoslavia, 1939–52, Dip. (Econ.); Univ. of Paris, 1953–57, Doctorat (Intl. Law); Columbia Univ., 1969–71, MS (LS). **Orgs.:** AALL. Intl. Assn. Law Libs. **Activities:** 13; 15, 17, 23; 77, 78 **Addr.:** NY State Supreme Court–Criminal Branch Law Library, 100 Centre St., 17th floor, New York, NY 10013.

Penka, Carol Bates (Mr. 27, 1942, Kilgore, TX) Asst. Ref. Libn., Univ. of IL Lib., 1974–, Asst. Cat. Libn., 1968–74; Asst. Cat. Libn., E. TX State Univ. Lib., 1965–66. **Educ.:** Kilgore Coll., 1960–62, AS; E. TX State Univ., 1964–65, BA (Eng.); Univ. of IL, 1966–68, MS (LS). **Orgs.:** ALA: LIRT, Pubns. Com. IL LA: Resrcs. and Tech. Srvs. Sect., Mem. Com. Beta Phi Mu: Bd. of Dirs. **Activities:** 1; 31, 39 **Addr.:** Reference Department, 300 Main Library, University of Illinois, 1408 W. Gregory Dr., Urbana, IL 61801.

Penland, Mary C. (O. 1, 1923, San Antonio, TX) Lib. Media Spec., Los Alamos Pub. Schs., 1959–; Tchr., 1954–59; **Educ.:** Baylor Univ., 1941–45, BA (Educ., Lib., Msc., Fr.); West. MI Univ., (Media, NDEA Inst.); Univ. of HI, Cert. (Couns., Guid.). **Orgs.:** NM LA: Pres. (1979–80). NM Media Assn.: Pres. (1977–78); Secy., Nsltr. Ed. (1975–77). ALA: AASL. Natl. Educ. Assn.: NM Statewide Wkshp. (Instr., 1977–79); Lib. Sect. Ch. Delta Kappa Gamma: Rho Chap. (Pres., 1974–76). **Activities:** 10; 17, 31, 32; 63, 89 **Addr.:** 1968 40th St., Los Alamos, NM 87544.

Penland, Patrick R. (D. 27, 1928, Vancouver, BC) Prof., Sch. of Lib. and Info. Sci., Univ. of Pittsburgh, 1968–; Prof., Dir., South. CT State Div., Lib. and Media Sci., 1962–68. **Educ.:** Univ. of MI, 1956–60, PhD (Lib. and Comm.). **Orgs.:** ALA. AECT. **Pubns.:** "Self-Planned Learning in America" mono. (1977); "Library as a Learning Service Center" mono. (1978); various mono., articles. **Activities:** 11, 14-Netwks.; 17, 36, 41; 50, 92, 93 **Addr.:** SLIS, University of Pittsburgh, Pittsburgh, PA 15260.

Penne, Carol Blake (D. 5, 1949, Marietta, OH) Asst. Dir., Head of Pub. Srvs., Amer. Bankers Assn., 1978–; Libn., Natl. Econ. Rsrch. Assocs., 1974–78. **Educ.:** Earlham Coll., 1967–71, BA (Econ.); Univ. of MD, 1973–74, MLS. **Orgs.:** SLA. AALL. **Activities:** 12; 39, 41; 59 **Addr.:** American Bankers Association, 1120 Connecticut Ave., Washington, DC 20036.

Penner, Rudolf J. (O. 16, 1930, Hague, SK) Asst. Syst. Dir., Pub. Srvs. Branch, Natl. Lib. of Can., 1973–; Oper. Coord., Defence Sci. Info. Srvs., Defence Resrch. Bd., 1972–73, Head, Documtn. Sect., 1968–72, Sci. Info. Ofcr., 1959–67. **Educ.:** Univ. of Toronto, 1951–56, BASc (Electrical Engin.); Drexel Univ., 1967–68, MS (Info. Sci.). **Orgs.:** Can. Assn. Info. Sci.: Anl. Conf. (Eng. Co-Prog. Ch., 1974). ASIS. Assn. of Prof. Engin. of ON. Prof. Inst. of the Pub. Srv. of Can. **Pubns.:** "Measuring A Library's Capability," *Jnl. of Educ. for Libnshp.* (Sum. 1972); "The Practice of Charging Users for Information Services: A State of The Art Report," *JASIS* (Ja.–F. 1970). **Activities:** 4; 17, 30, 39; 52, 56, 88 **Addr.:** 2193 Lambeth Walk, Ottawa, ON K2C 1E9 Canada.

Penney, Pearce J. (Mr. 10, 1928, St. Anthony, NF) Chief Prov. Libn., NF Pub. Lib. Srvs., 1972–; Acq. Libn., Univ. of Guelph Lib., 1971–72; Acq. Libn., Meml. Univ. of NF, 1968–70. **Educ.:** Mt. Allison Univ., 1953–57, BA; Pine Hill Dvnty. Hall, 1957–59, MDiv. (Theo.); Syracuse Univ., 1967–68, MSLS. **Orgs.:** Can. LA. Atl. Provs. LA: Pres. (1974). NF LA: Pres. (1973–74). ALA. **Pubns.:** *School/Public Libraries; The Canadian School Houses Public Library* (1979). **Activities:** 9, 13; 17, 36, 47 **Addr.:** New Foundland Public Library Services, Arts & Culture Centre, St. John's, NF A1B 3A3 Canada.

Penniman, Blanche L. (N. 15, 1918, Beverly, MA) Sch. Libn., Bergenfield HS, 1960–; various positions in other flds. **Educ.:** Tufts Univ., 1935–39, AB (Hist.), 1939–40, MA (Hist.); Simmons Coll., 1961–64, MS (LS). **Orgs.:** Bergen Cnty. Educ. Media Assn.: Mem. Com. (1978). Educ. Media Assn. of NJ. ALA. Cncl. for the Arts, Bergenfield. Natl. Educ. Assn. NJ Educ. Assn. **Honors:** Phi Beta Kappa, 1940. **Activities:** 10; 15, 20, 48 **Addr.:** 12 Dick St., Bergenfield, NJ 07621.

Penniman, W. David (D. 19, 1937, St. Louis, MO) Mgr., Resrch. Dept., OCLC, Inc., 1978–; Resrch. Schol., Intl. Inst. for Appld. Syst. Analysis, 1977; Assoc. Mgr., Info. Syst. Sect., Battelle-Columbus Labs., 1966–77; Assoc. Dir., Engin. Pubns., Univ. of IL, 1965–66. **Educ.:** Univ. of IL, 1956–60, BS (Mech. Engin.), 1960–62, MS (Jnlsm. and Comm.); OH State Univ., 1972–75, PhD (Comm.); Regis. Prof. Engin., OH, 1968. **Orgs.:** ASIS: Spec. Interest Grp. User On-Line Interaction (Ch., 1978); Ch. Elect (1977); Chap. Ch. Elect (1979–80). Assn. for Comp. Mach. Intl. Comm. Assn. **Honors:** US Rep., Intl. Inst. for Appld. Syst. Analysis, 1977; Phi Eta Sigma, 1957; Pi Tau Sigma, 1959. **Pubns.:** Jt. Auth., "Initiation to Automation," *Spec. Libs.* (D. 1966); Jt. Auth., "A Framework for the Study of Emerging Network Technology," Jnl. of the Amer. Socty. for Info. Sci. (N.–D. 1974); Jt. Auth., "Cross Section of Information Activities," *Theory Into Practice* (Je. 1973); "This Issue," *Theory Into Practice* (Je. 1973); various papers, sps. **Activities:** 12, 14-Info. Netwk.; 17, 24, 41; 56, 75, 93 **Addr.:** Research Department, OCLC, Inc., Columbus, OH 43214.

Pennington, Rev. Jasper Green (Mr. 20, 1939, Clio, MI) Rector, St. Alban's Episcopal Church, 1981–; Dir. of Lib., Sheen Arch., St. Bernard's Semy., 1973–81; Ref. Libn., Sch. of Theo., Univ. of the South, 1970–73, Asst. Libn., DuPont Lib., 1968–70; Ref. Asst., Kalamazoo Coll., 1966–68. **Educ.:** Univ. of MI, 1960–64 (sc.); West. MI Univ., 1965–67, BA (Hist.), Univ. of the South, 1970–73, MDiv; Gvt. Docum. Inst., Emory Univ., 1968. **Orgs.:** ALA. ATLA. SAA. Assn. of Anglican Musicians. Amer. Guild of Organists. Royal Sch. of Church Msc. **Pubns.:** *Fulton John Sheen: a chronology and bibliography* (1976); *AN ADDRESS: Fulton John Sheen* (1978). **Activities:** 1, 2; 19, 23, 45; 57, 90, 93 **Addr.:** St. Alban's Rectory, 885 Shore Rd., Cape Elizabeth, ME 04107.

Pennington, Walter W. (N. 12, 1942, Mobile, AL) Circ. Supvsr./Info. Anal., Univ. of AL, Birmingham, 1979–; Head Media Spec., Dev. Resrch. Sch., FL State Univ., 1968–79; Head Libn., Hamilton Cnty. (FL) HS, 1965–67. **Educ.:** N. FL Jr. Coll., 1960–62, AA FL State Univ., 1962–65, BA (Eng./Educ.), 1967–68, MS (LS), 1977– (LS). **Orgs.:** FL Assn. for Media in Educ.: Pres. (1975-76); Bd. of Dir. (1973-77); Ch., Pubns. Com. (1977-79). FL LA: Ch., Pubns. Com. (1978-79). ALA: School Lib. Media Facilities Com. (1977–). AECT: State Conv. Com.-Miami Beach (Ch., 1976). SELA: Nom. Com. (1980–); Dev. Com. (1978–). **Pubns.:** Ed., *FL Media Qtly.* (1973–1975, 1976–80). **Activities:** 1, 10; 22, 32, 48; 56, 63 **Addr.:** 397 Cambo Ln., Birmingham, AL 35226.

Penrose, Anna Mae (My. 22, 1927, Baltimore, MD) Dir., Campbell Lib., Dept. of Food Mktg., St. Joseph's Univ., 1978–,

Special Subjects/Services: 50. Adult educ.; 51. Advert./Mktg.; 52. Aerosp.; 53. Agric.; 54. Area std.; 55. Arts/Hum.; 56. Autom.; 57. Bibl./Prtg.; 58. Bio. sci.; 59. Bus./Fin.; 60. Chem.; 61. Copyrt.; 62. Documtn.; 63. Educ.; 64. Engin.; 65. Env.; 66. Eth. grps.; 67. Film; 68. Food/Nutr.; 69. Geneal.; 70. Geo.; 71. Geol.; 72. Handcpd.; 73. Hist.; 74. Int. frdm.; 75. Info. sci.; 76. Insr.; 77. Law; 78. Legis.; 79. Math./Comp. sci.; 80. Med.; 81. Metals; 82. Nat. resrcs.; 83. Newsp.; 84. Nuc. sci.; 85. Oral hist.; 86. Petr./Energy; 87. Pharm.; 88. Phys./Astr./Math.; 89. Readg.; 90. Relig.; 91. Sci./Tech.; 92. Soc. sci.; 93. Telecom.; 94. Transp.; 95. (other).

Catlgr., 1977–78; Libn., Natl. Bd. of Med. Examiners, 1975–78. **Educ.:** Radcliffe Coll., 1945–49, AB (Eng.); Drexel Univ., 1972–75, MLS. **Orgs.:** SLA. Philadelphia Area Ref. Libns. Info. Exch. **Honors:** Beta Phi Mu. **Activities:** 1, 12; 15, 17, 39; 51, 59, 68 **Addr.:** Campbell Library, St. Joseph's University, Philadelphia, PA 19131.

Penski, Elizabeth W. (Ag. 12, 1940, Baltimore, MD) AV Libn., Essex Cmnty. Coll., 1973–; Out of Print Biblgphr., Univ. of MD, College Park, 1972–73; Head of Cat., Univ. of MD, Baltimore Cnty., 1968–72; Sr. Catlgr., Johns Hopkins Univ., 1965–68. **Educ.:** Swarthmore Coll., 1958–62, BA (Art); Drexel Univ., 1964–65, MSLS. **Orgs.:** MD LA. ALA. Potomac Area Tech. Proc. Libns. AAUP. **Pubns.:** Jt. Auth., "Pottery and Ceramics," *Serials Review* (Ap.–Je., 1979). **Activities:** 1; 20, 32; 55 **Addr.:** 2515 Jerusalem Rd., Joppa, MD 21085.

Pensyl, Mary E. (F. 15, 1941, Sunbury, PA) Head, Computerized Lit. Srch. Srv., MA Inst. of Tech., 1975, Northeast Acad. Sci. Info. Ctr. Coord., 1973–75; User Srvs. Libn., 1970–73. **Educ.:** Chatham Coll., 1959–63, BA (Eng.); Simmons Coll., 1967–68, MLS; various crs. **Orgs.:** ALA: RASD/Machine-Asst. Ref. Srvs., Measur. of Srv. Com. New Eng. OLUG. **Honors:** Cncl. on Lib. Resrcs., Flwshp., 1979–80. **Pubns.:** Various papers. **Activities:** 1; 20, 38, 39; 56, 75, 91 **Addr.:** Computerized Literature Search Service, M.I.T. Libraries, Room 14–SM–48, Cambridge, MA 02139.

Pensyl, Ornella L. (D. 15, 1954, Ft. Belvoir, VA) Chief, Lib./Lrng. Ctr., U.S. Army Intelligence Sch., 1981–; Libn., Ft. Dix Post Lib., 1979–81; Libn., Geophys. Fluid Dynamics Lab., 1978–79. **Educ.:** Rutgers Univ., 1972–76, BA (Eng., Educ.), 1976–78, MLS. **Orgs.:** ALA. SLA. **Activities:** 4; 17; 74 **Addr.:** 284 Codman Hill Rd., Boxborough, MA 01719.

Peplowski, Celia C. (Je. 4, 1918, Montreal, PQ) Supvsr. of Main Lib., Mobile Pub. Lib., 1970–, Intl. Trade Ctr. Libn., 1969–70, Admin. Asst. and Persnl. Ofcr., 1968–69, Asst., to Supvsr. of Ext., 1967–68; Catlgr., Ref. Libn., Actg. City Libn., Sterling Mncpl. Pub. Lib., 1964–67; Head of Tech. Srvs., Milwaukee Downer Coll., 1961–63; Sub. Tchr. Libn., Milwaukee Sch. Bd., 1959–61; Base Libn., Sioux City Air Base, 1957–59; various other prof. positions, 1955–57. **Educ.:** TX State Coll. for Women, 1952–53, BA, BS, hons. (LS); Univ. of WI, 1954–55, MA (LS) various crs. **Orgs.:** ALA: Ref. and Subscrpn. Bks. Review Com. (1973–75). SELA. AL LA. Bay Area LA: Secy.-Treas. (1976). AAUW. Univ. of WI Alum. Assn. TX Woman's Univ. Alum Assn. **Honors:** Pi Lambda Theta; Beta Phi Mu. **Activities:** 9; 15, 16, 17 **Addr.:** C-21, 351 Azalea Rd., Mobile, AL 36609.

Pepper, David A. (F. 6, 1946, Ipswich, Suffolk, Eng.) Chief Libn., Cominco Ltd., Vancouver, BC, 1979–; Info. Anal., 1978–79; Ref. Libn., Woodward Biomed. Lib., Univ. of BC, Vancouver, 1976–78. **Educ.:** Univ. of Victoria, 1972, BA (Eng.); Univ. of BC, 1976, M.L.S. **Orgs.:** Can. LA. SLA. Vancouver OLUG. Ctrl. Vancouver Libns. Grp.: Pres. **Honors:** Beta Phi Mu, 1976. **Activities:** 12; 15, 17, 41 **Addr.:** Cominco Ltd., 200 Granville Sq., Vancouver, BC V6C 2R2 Canada.

Pepper, Ruth M. (Ap. 25, 1913, Marianna, AR) Retired, 1981–; Lib. Media Spec., Scottsboro Jr. HS, 1962–81; Tchr., Pisgah HS, 1961–62; Org., Libn., Cumberland Presbyterian Church Lib. 1960; Lib. Asst., Memphis Pub. Lib., 1959–60; Org., Libn., E. Side Cumberland Presbyterian Church, 1952–60. **Educ.:** Bethel Coll., 1930–34, AB (Eng., Math.); Univ. of AL, 1967–69, (LS); various crs. (LS). **Orgs.:** ALA: Sch. Div., Chld. Srvs. (1962–81). AL Educ. Assn. AL Instr. Media Assn. (1962–81). AL LA: Sch. Div., Chld. Srvs. (Ch., 1970). AAUW: Secy. (1981–82), Scrap Bk. Ch. (1979–81). Natl. Educ. Assn. Scottsboro Educ. Assn. **Pubns.:** "Church Libraries," *Cumberland Presbyterian* (1959); "Programs for Women," *Missn. Messenger* (1958); "Public vs. School Libraries," *The Alabamian* (1970); various articles in *LAMP Wkshp., The Alabamian* (1978). **Activities:** 10, 12; 15, 17, 21; 63, 75, 90 **Addr.:** P.O. Box 666, Scottsboro, AL 35768.

Peppler, James Christopher (Jl. 4, 1947, Hanover, ON) Cnty. Libn., Frontenac Cnty. Lib., 1972–; Asst. Libn., Bruce Cnty. Lib., 1970–72. **Educ.:** Univ. of West. ON, 1965–69, BA, 1969–70, MLS. **Orgs.:** ON Pub. Libns. Adv. Com. Cnty and Reg. Mncpl. Libns.: Ch. (1977–78). ON LA: Legis. Action Grp. (Ch., 1973–75). **Pubns.:** Ed., *Directory of Community Services and Information: Central and North Frontenac County* (1977). **Activities:** 9; 15, 17, 35 **Addr.:** Frontenac County Library, 130 Days Rd., Kingston, ON K7M 3P8 Canada.

Peraza, Elena Vérez (Jl. 22, 1919, Havana, Cuba) Prof., Cat., Richter Lib., Univ. of Miami, 1967–; Asst. Libn., Univ. of FL Lib., 1962–67; Prof., Escuela Interamericana de Bibliotecologia, Univ. de Antioquia, Medellín, Colombia, 1961; Instr., Escuela de Bibtcr., Univ. de la Habana, Havana, Cuba, 1959–60; Libn., Archivo Natl. de Cuba, 1959–60; Head, Dept. de Bib., Consejo Natl. de Econ., Havana, Cuba, 1950–58; various tchg. positions, 1948–52; Dir., Bib. Púb. Panamericana of the Socty. Colombista Panamericana, Havana, Cuba, 1943–59. **Educ.:** Inst. de Segunda Enseñanza de la Habana, Havana, 1933–37, Bachiller en Letras y Ciencias; Univ. de la Habana, Havana, Cuba, 1946–49, Técnica Bib., 1941–56, PhD (Lit.). **Orgs.:** ALA. SALALM: Subcom. on Cuban Bibl. Assn. of Caribbean Univ. and Resrch. Lib. FL LA. Cuban Women's Club: Treas. (1976–78). YMCA Intl. José Martí: Bd. of Dir. (1980–). **Honors:** YMCA Intl. José Martí, Miami, FL, Dip. de Reconocimiento, 1970; Dept. of HEW, Dip. of Hon. Lincoln-Martí, 1973; Cruzada Educ. Cubana, Miami, FL, Dip. de Hon. Juan J. Remos, 1977; Metro. Dade Cnty., FL, Cert. of Apprec., 1980. **Pubns.:** *Bibliografía colombiana, 1969–1972* (1971–80); *Anuario bibliográfico cubano, 1969–1970* (1977–79); "El griego en Cuba," *Jnl. of Inter-Amer. Std.* (Ja. 1959); Jt. Cmplr., "Directorio de revistas y periódicos de Cuba" dir. (1968). **Activities:** 1; 20; 57 **Addr.:** 1550 Miller Rd., Coral Gables, FL 33146.

Percival, Mary C. (Je. 18, 1947, Toronto, ON) Law Libn., McCarthy and McCarthy, Barristers and Solicitors, 1981–; Law Libn., Borden and Elliot, Barristers and Solicitors, 1973–80; Ref. Libn., Univ. of Toronto Lib., 1970–73. **Educ.:** Queen's Univ., 1966–69, BA; Univ. of Toronto, 1969–70, BLS, 1975–76, MLS. **Orgs.:** Can. ALL. AALL. SLA. Toronto Assn. of Law Libns. **Addr.:** McCarthy & McCarthy, Barristers & Solicitors, P.O. Box 48, Toronto Dominion Bank Tower, Toronto Dominion Centre, Toronto, ON M5K 1E6 Canada.

Perelmuter, Susan A. (O. 21, 1949, Louisville, KY) Ref./ILL Libn., Lib. Ext. Srvs., 1980–; Substance Abuse Libn., AZ State Hosp., 1979–80; Acq. Libn., Spalding Coll., 1976–78. **Educ.:** Univ. of Cincinnati, 1967–71, BA (Fr.), 1971–72, (Acct.); Spalding Coll., 1976–78, MA (LS). **Orgs.:** ALA. AZ LA. Maricopa Biomed. Libns. Assn.: Coord. (1979–80). Med. Lib. Grp. of S. CA and AZ. KY Colonels. **Pubns.:** "Vendor Performance Evaluation," *Jnl. of Acad. Libnshp.* (N. 1978). **Activities:** 1, 13; 24, 27, 39; 57, 92, 95-ILL. **Addr.:** Library Extension Service, 2219 S. 48th St., Suite D, Tempe, AZ 85282.

Perez, Ernest R. (My. 10, 1943, San Marcos, TX) Chief Libn., Chicago *Sun-Times* Ed. Lib., 1979–; Lib. Dir., Houston *Chronicle* Ed. Lib., 1971–78; Acq. Libn., SW TX State Univ., 1969–70. **Educ.:** Univ. of TX, El Paso, 1961–64, BA (Jnlsm.); Univ. of TX, Austin, 1967–69, MLS, 1971, 6th yr. cert. (LS). **Orgs.:** SLA: Newsp. Div., Secy./Treas. (1975–76), Dir., (1974–75), Autom. Com. (1975–81), Awds. Com., (1979–80), Nom. Com. (1981). ALA. TX LA: Int. Frdm. Com. (1971–72); Awds. Com. (1971). **Pubns.:** "Newspaper Libraries: Automated and Non-automated Systems: Electronic Approaches" *Ed. and Publshr.* (Ja. 12, 1980); "Newspaper Library Automation," *Guidelines for Newsp. Libs.* (1976); "Filing Systems," "Newspaper Library Equipment," "Acquisitions of Out-of-print Material, " *Lib. Resrcs. & Tech. Srvs.* (Win. 1973). **Activities:** 12; 33, 39; 56, 83 **Addr.:** Chicago Sun-Times, 401 N. Wabash Ave., Chicago, IL 60611.

Perez-Lopez, Rene (My. 12, 1945, Santa Clara, Cuba) Branch and ext. coord., Norfolk Pub. Lib., 1971–; Dir., Cohoes Pub. and Tool Lib., 1970–71. **Educ.:** SUNY, Albany, 1965–67, BA (Inter-Amer. Std.); Case West. Rsv. Univ., 1967–69, MA (Pol. Sci.); SUNY, Albany, 1970–71, MLS; various crs. **Orgs.:** NLA. ALA. Natl. Assn. Hisp. Libns. VA LA: Int. Frdm. Com. Amer. Cvl. Liberties Un. Lib. Bd., City of Chesapeake. NAACP. Tidewater Amer. Red Cross: Intl. Srvs. Com., Bd. Mem. Norfolk Com. for Improvement of Educ.: Bd. Mem. **Honors:** Phi Theta Kappa, 1965; Del., Gvr.'s Conf. on Lib. and Inform Srvs., VA, 1978. **Pubns.:** "A Calendar of Cuban Bilateral Agreements 1959–75: Description and Uses," *Cuban Std./Estudios Cubanos* , (Jl. 1977); Transl. to Span., (D. "The Republican Flag Mastered the Sea," *Historia 16* (D. 1977); *Cuban International Relations: A Bilateral Agreements Perspective* (1978); *A Calendar of Cuban Bilateral Agreements 1959–1976* (1979); "Free Speech in the Public Workplace: Guidelines and Caveats," *Jnl. of Lib. Admin.* (Spr. 1981); various sp., papers. **Activities:** 9, 11; 17, 27; 66 **Addr.:** 1510 Wood Ave., Chesapeake, VA 23325.

Perica, Esther (Ap. 7, 1946, San Francisco, CA) Lib. Resrcs. Adv., Roosevelt Univ., NW Campus, 1980–; Libn., Rolling Meadows HS, 1973–; Libn., Rolling Meadows Pub. Lib., 1975–80; Volun., Asst. Spec. Cols., Univ. of MO Libs., 1974; Libn., St. Viator HS Lib., 1971–73; Grad. Instr. in Libs., Purdue Univ., 1970. **Educ.:** San Francisco Coll. for Women, 1964–68, BA (Amer. Std.); Rosary Coll., 1968–69, MA (LS); Northeast. IL Univ., 1970–71, MA (Amer. Std.); Univ. of MO, 1973–75, various crs. **Orgs.:** IL LA: Ch. (1976–77); Rcrt. and Schol. Com.; Conf. Com. (1978). ALA: PR Srvs. to Libs. Com.; LAMA/PR Sect., White Hse. Conf. Com. Task Frc., Natl. Lib. Week Com. (1978–80), various ofcs. Phi Alpha Theta: Pi Gamma Chap. (Pres., 1979–80). Girl Scout Cncl. of NW Cook: Bd. of Trustees (1979–82). **Pubns.:** *The American Woman: Her Role During the Revolution* (1981); *They Took the Challenge: The Story of Rolling Meadows* (1979); *Newspaper Indexing for Historical Societies, Colleges and Schools* (1975); "A Newspaper Index, Good Sense–Sound Journalism," *Sch. Press Review* (My. 1976); jt. auth., "Burglary: Securing Your Library," *Lib. Trustee Nsltr.* (My.–Je. 1979); "Collecting Local History," *Sch. Lib. Jnl.* (Ap. 1976); various articles. **Activities:** 9, 10; 30, 36, 41; 55, 83, 85 **Addr.:** 1 S. Ridge, Arlington Heights, IL 60005.

Perk, Lawrence J. (Ap. 12, 1932, Cleveland, OH) Head, Spec. Mtrls., OH State Univ., 1980–; Info. Spec., OH State Univ. Libs., 1975–80; Ref. Libn., Educ. Lib., OH State Univ., 1972–75. **Educ.:** Kent State Univ., 1950–54, BS (Archit.); Case West. Rsv. Univ., 1968–71, MSLS. **Orgs.:** ASIS. ALA. Acad. LA of OH. **Pubns.:** "Periodical Usage in an Education-Psychology Library," *Coll. and Resrch. Libs.* (Jl. 1977); "Secondary Publications in Education: A Study in Duplication," *Coll. and Resrch. Libs.* (My. 1977); jt. auth., "Ascertaining Activities in a Subject Area Through Bibliometric Analysis," *JASIS* (Mr.–Ap. 1973). **Activities:** 1; 31, 38, 39; 63, 91, 92 **Addr.:** 2032 N. 4th St., Columbus, OH 43201.

Perkins, David L. (Ja. 11, 1939, Wheeling, WV) Head Bibl. Libn., CA State Univ., Northridge, 1969–. **Educ.:** Univ. of CA, Los Angeles, 1960–61, BA (Anthro.); Univ. of South. CA, 1968–69, MS (LS); CA State Univ., Northridge, 1970–73, MA (Anthro.). **Orgs.:** NLA: Cert. Stans. Com. (Ch., 1979–). CA LA: Col. Dev. Chap. (Statewide Coord., 1975, 1979). ALA: RTSD, Micropublshg. Com. (1980–); Col. Dev. Com. (Ch., 1978–79); ACRL, Ad Hoc Com. on Coll. Lib. Stans. Rev. (1979–); Anthro. Sect. (Vice-ch., Ch., 1977–79). Sierra Club. **Honors:** Beta Phi Mu, 1969. **Pubns.:** *India and Its People: A Bibliography.* (1980); jt. auth., *China in Books* (1979); "Periodicals Weeding," *CA Libn.* (Ap. 1977); "Standards for College Libraries," *Coll. and Resrch. Libs. News* (O. 1975); *Native Americans of North America: a Bibliography...* (1975); various other bks. **Activities:** 1; 15; 55 **Addr.:** 20006 Superior St., Chatsworth, CA 91311.

Perkins, John W. (O. 30, 1917, Toledo, OH) Lib. Dir., Inglewood Pub. Lib., 1962–; City libn., Redondo Beach Pub. Lib., 1955–62; Area Libn., U.S. Air Frc. AMC, San Bernardino, 1953–55; Asst. City Libn., San Bernardino Pub. Lib., 1953; Cult. Ofcr., U.S. Dept. of State, Naples, Italy, 1952–53; Libn., Univ. of CA, Berkeley, 1947–52. **Educ.:** Univ. of Toledo, 1936–42; Univ. of CA, 1946–47, BA (Hist.), 1947–48, BLS, 1948–52, MA (Fine Arts). **Orgs.:** CA LA. SLA. Pac. NW LA. ALA. Various other orgs. South. CA Persnl. Mgrs. Assn. **Pubns.:** *Branch Library Service* (1977); *Library of Congress Classification Adapted for Children's Library Materials* (1976); "An Adapted Library of Congress Classification for Children's Materials," *Lib Resrcs. & Tech. Srvs.* (Spr. 1978). **Activities:** 9; 15, 17 **Addr.:** Inglewood Public Library, 101 W. Manchester Blvd., Inglewood, CA 90301.

Perkins, Marcia W. (Ag. 19, 1917, Taylorville, IL) Pub. Lib. Consult., LA State Lib., 1970–; Libn., Darlington Cnty. Lib., 1968–70; Libn., Audubon Reg. Lib., 1962–65, Demonstration Libn., 1960–62; Circ. Libn., Asst. Ref. Libn., E. Baton Rouge Par. Lib., 1958–60; Acq. Libn., LA State Lib., 1955–58; Par. Libn., Livingston (LA) Par. Lib., 1952–55; Ref. Libn., Springfield (MO) Pub. Lib., 1950–52; Various other prof. positions, NM, LA, TX, NY, 1941–50. **Educ.:** LA State Univ., 1936–40, AB (Eng.), 1940–44, BSLS; LA, 1970, Admin. Libn. Cert.; LA State Univ., 1974–76, MLS. **Orgs.:** ALA. SWLA. LA LA: Modisette Awds., Trustee. Baton Rouge Lib. Club. **Pubns.:** *Goals, Guidelines and Gauges for Public Library Service in Louisiana* (1975); ed., *Public Libraries in Louisiana* (1970–). **Activities:** 9, 13; 24, 35, 36; 50, 74, 89 **Addr.:** 301 Stanford Ave., Baton Rouge, LA 70808.

Perks, Ruth Elizabeth (Wills) (Ag. 29, 1936, Siloam Springs, AR) Chief, Info. Resrcs. and Syst. Branch, U.S. Ofc. of Admin., Exec. Ofc. of the Pres., 1980–; Chief, Lib. Branch, U.S. Dept. of Energy Libs., 1978–80, Systs. Libn., 1977–78; Ref. Libn., U.S. AEC Lib., 1972–77; Acq. Libn., Biomed. Lib. Univ. of MN, 1969–71. **Educ.:** John Brown Univ., 1953–56, BA (Sci.); Univ. of IL, 1957–58, MS (LS). **Orgs.:** SLA: DC Chap., Pres. (1979–80), 1st VP (1978–79). ASIS. Med. LA. Potomac Pedlars. **Activities:** 4; 17, 38; 56, 84, 91 **Addr.:** Information Resources and System Branch, G-102-LISD-U.S. Office of Administration, 706 Jackson Pl., Washington, DC 20545.

Perlongo, Suzanne T. (Mr. 2, 1942, Detroit, MI) Msc. Libn., Assoc. Prof., IN Univ. of PA, 1969–; Msc. Libn., Amer. Acad. in Rome (Italy), 1979–80. **Educ.:** North Park Coll., 1959–63, BM (Msc. Educ.); Univ. of MI, 1968–69, MM, AMLS (Msc. Hist.); Univ. of Pittsburgh, 1979– (LS). **Orgs.:** Msc. LA: Pubns. Cncl.; Nsltr. Ed. (1978–). Intl. Assn. of Msc. Libs. **Honors:** Pi Kappa Lambda, 1964; Beta Phi Mu, 1969. **Pubns.:** Jt. Auth., *A glossary of terms used in the cataloging of music and sound recordings* (1980); jt. auth., "Music Library Association meets in New Orleans," *Lib. Jnl.* (My. 15, 1979); Ed., *Msc. LA Nsltr.* (1978–). **Activities:** 1; 15, 17, 20; 55 **Addr.:** IN University of PA, Cogswell Music Library, Indiana, PA 15705.

Perlov, Dadie (Je. 8, 1929, New York, NY) Exec. Dir., NY LA, 1974–; Dir., Fld. Srvs., Natl. Cncl. of Jewish Women, 1971–74, Reg. Dir., 1969–71; Exec. Dir., Northeast Queens Fair Housing, 1962–64; various consult. **Educ.:** NY Univ., 1946–50, BA (Bio.); Adelphi Univ., 1964–65, (Educ. Psy.); Cert. Assn. Exec., 1979, (Assn. Mgt.). **Orgs.:** ALA: Chap. Rel. Com. (Ch., 1978–80). Cncl. of LA Exec.: Bd. Mem. (1979–80). NY Lib. Club. Lib. PR Cncl.: Awds. Jury (1978). Amer. Socty. of Assn. Exec. NY Socty. of Assn. Exec.: Educ. Com. (Ch., 1978–80); Bd. Mem. (1980–83). Intl. Platform Assn. New York City Bd. of Educ.: Sch. Bd. Sel. Panel (1967). **Honors:** NY LA, Spec. Srv. Awd., 1978; Pratt Inst., Grad. Sch. of Lib. and Info. Sci., Bd. of Visitors, 1980. **Pubns.:** Exec. Ed., *NYLA Bltn.* (1974–80); "White House Conference Coverage," *NYLA Bltn.* (D. 1979); *From Ad-Hocracy to Bureaucracy and Back: Toward the Year 2001* (1977); "Libraries in New York State" videotape (1979);

PROFESSIONAL ACTIVITIES: Institutions: 1. Acad. lib.; 2. Arch.; 3. Assn.; 4. Fed./Gvt. lib.; 5. Inst. lib.; 6. Mfr./Suppl.; 7. Milit. lib.; 8. Musm.; 9. Pub. lib.; 10. Sch. lib.; 11. Sch. of lib. sci.; 12. Spec. lib.; 13. State lib.; 14. (other). **Functions/Activities:** 15. Acq./Col. dev.; 16. Adult srvs.; 17. Admin.; 18. Apprais.; 19. Archit./Bldgs.; 20. Cat./Class.; 21. Chld. srvs.; 22. Circ.; 23. Cons./Pres.; 24. Consult.; 25. Cont. ed.; 26. Educ. lib. sci.; 27. Ext. srvs.; 28. Fund/Grants; 29. Gvt. pubs.; 30. Indx./Abs.; 31. Instr. lib. use; 32. Media srvs.; 33. Micro.; 34. Netwks./Coop.; 35. Persnl.; 36. PR; 37. Publshg.; 38. Recs. mgt.; 39. Ref. srvs.; 40. Repro.; 41. Resrch.; 42. Review.; 43. Secur.; 44. Serials; 45. Spec. col.; 46. Tech. srvs.; 47. Trustees/Bds.; 48. YA srvs.; 49. (other).

"Intellectual Freedom in Libraries" videotape (1977); Guest Ed., on lib. funding videotape (1976). **Activities:** 13; 17, 24, 25, 47; 74, 78 **Addr.:** NY Library Association, 15 Park Row, Suite 434, New York, NY 10038.

Perlungher, Jane R. (Jl. 2, 1946, Glen Cove, NY) Dir., Cold Spring Harbor Lib., 1978–, Chld. Libn., 1972–78; Chld. Libn., Half Hollow Hills Cmnty. Lib., 1969–71. **Educ.:** Barnard Coll., 1965–68, BA (Soclgy.); Columbia Univ., 1968–69, MLS. **Orgs.:** ALA. NY LA. Suffolk Cnty. LA: Secy. (1981–82); Cont. Educ. Com. (Ch., 1980). Barnard Coll. Club of Long Island. **Activities:** 9; 15, 16, 17 **Addr.:** Cold Spring Harbor Library, Cold Spring Harbor, NY 11768.

Permut, Steven L. (Mr. 25, 1945, Cleveland, OH) Msc. Catlgr., Lib. of Congs., 1980–, Ed., Msc., Bks. on Msc. and Snd. Recs., 1978–79; Libn., Msc. Catlgr., Ref. Libn., Univ. of MD, 1974–78. **Educ.:** Univ. of S. FL, 1964–67, BA, 1968–69, MM (Msc.); Univ. of MD, 1969–74, MLS. **Orgs.:** Msc. LA: Chesapeake Chap. Pubns. (Ch., 1978–79). Assn. for Rec. Snd. Cols. **Honors:** Beta Phi Mu. **Activities:** 4; 20; 55 **Addr.:** Music Section, Special Materials Cataloging Division, Library of Congress, Washington, DC 20540.

Perrault, Anna Hemer (S. 28, 1944, Biloxi, MS) Hum. Bibl., LA State Univ., 1976–, Asst. Libn., LA and Rare Bk. Rms., 1972–75, Cat., Reclass. Proj., 1970–71, Info. Desk Libn., 1969–70. **Educ.:** Univ. of MS, 1962–65, BA (Eng.); LA State Univ., 1965–67, MA (Eng.), 1967–69, MS (LS). **Orgs.:** ALA: ACRL/Rare Bks. and Mss. Sect.; Coll. and Resrch. Libs. Sect.; West. European Spec. Sect., Nom. Com. (1980–81); RTSD/Chief Col. Dev. Ofcrs. of Medium-sized Resrch. Libs. Discuss. Grp. (Ch., 1980–81). LALA: Subj. Spec. Sect. (Ch., 1979–80). Mod. Lang. Assn. **Honors:** Phi Kappa Phi. **Pubns.:** "The Role of the Academic Librarian in Library Governance" in *New Horizons for Academic Libraries* (1979); "Share the Wealth; a collection development column for Louisiana libraries," *LA LA Bltn.* (Sum. 1979). **Activities:** 15, 44, 45; 55, 57 **Addr.:** LA State University Library, Baton Rouge, LA 70803.

Perrin, Elizabeth A. (Mr. 29, 1941, Hartford, CT) Chld. Libn., Wethersfield Pub. Lib., 1969–; Chld. Libn., Queensborough Pub. Lib., 1965–69. **Educ.:** Emmanuel Coll., 1959–63, BA (Fr.); Pratt Inst., 1964–65, MLS. **Orgs.:** ALA. CT LA. CT Reg. Lib. Cncl.: Chld. Libns. RT. **Activities:** 9; 15, 21, 39 **Addr.:** Wethersfield Public Library, 515 Silas Deane Hwy., Wethersfield, CT 06109.

Perrine, Susan L. (Mr. 11, 1946, St. Louis, MO) Head Libn., Shea and Gardner, 1978–; Libn., Baker, Hostetler, 1977–78; Acq. Ed., Amer. Stats. Index, Congsnl. Info Srvs., Inc., 1977, Abstctr. and Indxr., 1976–77. **Educ.:** Univ. of MO, 1967–69, BA (Soclgy.); Wayne State Univ., 1970–71, MSLS. **Orgs.:** AALL. SLA. DC Law Libns. Socty.: Corres. Secy. (1980–81); Arch. Com. (Ch., 1977–80). **Activities:** 12; 15, 17, 39; 77 **Addr.:** Shea & Gardner Library, 1800 Massachusetts Ave., N.W., Washington, DC 20036.

Perrins, Barbara C. (My. 23, 1927, New Havan, CT) Asst. Prof., South. CT State Coll.; Sch. Libn., Cheshire Pub. Schs., 1968–69; Sch. Libn., LaSallette Semy., 1967–68. **Educ.:** CT Coll., 1941–45, BA (Econ.); South. CT State Coll., 1963–67, BS (LS), 1971–74, 6th Yr. Cert. **Orgs.:** ALA: Com. on Cat. Chld. Mtrls. (1979–81). CT Educ. Media Assn.: Bd. (1972–75). New Eng. Educ. Media Assn.: Bd. (1972–74). **Pubns.:** "Reference Service Commentary," *CT Libs.* (Spr. 1979); "Current Trends in Teenage Literature," *Cath. Lib. World* (N. 1971); "Source-erers' Apprentice," *CT Eng. Jnl.* (1972). **Addr.:** Division of Library Science & Instructional Technology, Southern Connecticut State College, 501 Crescent St., New Haven, CT 06515.

Perry, Beth I. (Jl. 6, 1948, Great Falls, MT) Asst. Dir., Head of Reader Srvs., RI Coll., 1978, Ref. Libn., 1972–78. **Educ.:** Univ. of WA, 1968–70, BA (Anthro.), 1970–71, MLS. **Orgs.:** ALA: ACRL, Bibl. Instr. Sect., Educ. for BI Subcom. (1977–79). RI LA: VP/Pres.-Elect (1979–80); Pres. (1980–81); Conf. Com. (Ch., 1974–79). Assn. of RI Hlth. Sci. Libns. New Eng. LA. Amer. Fed. of Tchrs. **Activities:** 1; 17, 39; 72 **Addr.:** James P. Adams Library, Rhode Island College, 600 Mt. Pleasant Ave., Providence, RI 02908.

Perry, Douglas F. (Ja. 6, 1950, Winchester, VA) Dir., Cleveland Cnty. Meml. Lib., 1980–; Cnty. Libn., Blue Ridge Reg. Lib., 1977–80; Libn., Consult., el Semy. Presby. en Mex., 1976–77. **Educ.:** Hampden-Sydney Coll., 1968–72, BA (Phil.); Univ. of NC, 1974–76, MSLS. **Orgs.:** ALA. SELA. NC LA. NC Pub. Lib. Dirs. Assn. Rotary Intl. **Activities:** 9, 12; 17, 24; 58, 90, 91 **Addr.:** Cleveland County Memorial Library, 104 Howie Dr., Shelby, NC 28150.

Perry, Emma Bradford (D. 25, 1943, Hodge, LA) Asst. Prof. and Head, Circ. Div., TX A&M Univ. Lib., 1977–; Head, W. Branch Lib., Evanston Pub. Lib., 1974–76, Coord., W. Evanston Lib. Proj., 1972–74; Coord., Instr., Lib. Educ. Prog., Grambling State Univ., 1967–70. **Educ.:** Grambling State Univ., 1961–65, BS (Sp., Drama); Atlanta Univ., 1966–67, MSLS; West. MI Univ., 1970–71, EdS (LS). **Orgs.:** ALA: LAMA/Circ. Srvs. Sect., Nom. Com.; Exec. Com.; Circ. Syst. Eval. Com.; Ad Hoc Com. on Prog. Needs. TX LA: Dist. III, Pres. South. Conf. on Afro-Amer. Std. **Honors:** Evanston, IL, Woman of the Yr., 1975; Beta Phi Mu. **Pubns.:** *Energy and Minorities: Women and the Poor* (1980); "Handle Carrel Books at Own Risk," *UNA-BASHED Libn.* (1979); "Action Exchange," *Amer. Libs.* (D. 1980). **Activities:** 1; 17, 22 **Addr.:** 2315 Devonshire, Bryan, TX 77801.

Perry, George Eleutherios (Ag. 27, 1929, New York, NY) Pres., Eth. Empl., of the Lib. of Congs., 1973–; Gen. Couns., Black Empl. of the Lib. of Congs., 1974–; Grk. Area Spec., 1971–77, Head, Slavic Rm., 1968–74, Cur., 1964–68; Staff, Acq. Libn., Columbia Univ. Libs., 1956–61. **Educ.:** Cornell Univ., 1950–52, BA, hons. (Eng. Lit.); Columbia Univ., 1954–56, MIA (Intl. Affairs), 1956–58, Russ. Inst. 1954–56, 1975, M Phil (Gvt.). **Orgs.:** ALA: Exec. Com., Slavic and E. European Subsect. (Secy., 1966–69). Lib. of Congs. Empl. Un.: Com. of Eth. Affairs (Ch., 1973). Gvt. Accountability Proj.: Whistleblower Rev. Panel (1979–). Ord. Ahepa. Amer. Revolution Bicent. Com. Natl. Ctr. Soc. Resrch., Greece. Ctr. Neo-Hellenic Std., Austin, TX. **Honors:** Lib. of Congs. Merit. Srv. Awd., 1965; Phi Beta Kappa, 1952. **Pubns.:** Cmplr., "Greece: General Reference Aids and Bibliographies," *Southeastern Europe: A Guide to Basic Publications* (1969); "The Modern Greek Collection in the Library of Congress: A Survey," *Grk. Review of Soc. Resrch.* (Ja./Je. 1973); ed., *Ethnic Racial Brotherhood* (1980–) and *Ethnic Racial Review* (1975); jt. per. pubns. of *Black Empl. of Lib. of Congs.* and *Eth. Empl. of Lib. of Congs.* **Activities:** 4; 17, 39, 49; 54, 66, 95 **Addr.:** 6100 E. View, Kenwood Pk., Washington, DC 20034.

Perry, Glenda L. (Mr. 21, 1940, Booneville, AR) Acq. Libn., Univ. of TN, Ctr. for the Hlth. Sci. Lib., 1978–, Serials Libn., 1975–78; Sch. Libn., Hughes Jr. High, 1971–74; Sch. Libn., Tuckerman HS, 1966–70; Sch. Libn., Pulaski Cnty. Dist., 1965–66; Bkmobile. Libn., Southeast AR Reg. Lib., 1964–65; Tchr., N. Little Rock Pub. Schs., 1963–64; Tchr., Pulaski Cnty. Sch. Dist. 1962–63. **Educ.:** AR Polytech. Coll., 1958–62, BS (Elem. Educ.); LA State Univ., 1968–72, MS (LS). **Orgs.:** Med. LA. TN LA: Spec. Libs. Sect. (Secty., Rpt., 1980). Delta Kappa Gamma Socty. **Activities:** 1, 12; 15, 44, 45; 58, 80 **Addr.:** University of TN, Center for the Health Sciences Library, 800 Madison Ave., Memphis, TN 38163.

Perry, Guest (New York City, NY) Libn., Houghton Mifflin, 1966–; Ref. Dept., Harvard Grad. Sch. Bus. Admin., 1952–54; Cat. Dept., 1950–51. **Educ.:** Keuka Coll., 1946–50, BA (Eng. Lit., Hist.); Simmons Coll., 1951–52, BS (LS); various crs. in mgt. **Orgs.:** ALA. SLA: Boston Chap.; Pres., Dir. ASIS. Libns. in Educ. and Resrch. in the Northeast: Fndr., Ofcr. (1970–). Watertow Free Pub. Lib.: Trustee. **Pubns.:** Ed., *Educ. Libs.* (1975–80); "Signs in Special Libraries," *Sign Systems in Libraries* (1976); various articles, bk. reviews. **Activities:** 12; 17, 26, 37 **Addr.:** The Library, Houghton Mifflin Co., One Beacon St., Boston, MA 02107.

Perry, Irene (O. 20, 1953, Long Beach, NY) Asst. Libn., Sci. and Engin., Cooper Un. for the Advnc. of Sci. and Art, 1980–; Recs. Libn., Shearman and Sterling, 1979–80; Info. Srvs. Coord., Inst. of Electrical and Electronics Engins., 1977–79. **Educ.:** SUNY, Old Westbury, 1972–76, BA (Eng.); Long Island Univ., 1977–78, MLS; Columbia Univ., 1980– (Libnshp.). **Orgs.:** ALA. **Activities:** 1; 15, 20, 22; 65 **Addr.:** 237 E. 88th St., New York, NY 10028.

Perry, Joanne M. (Ag. 20, 1949, Winchester, MA) Map Libn., OR State Univ., 1979–; Map Ref. Libn., Univ. of AZ, 1978–79; Ref. Libn., City Coll. of San Francisco, 1977–78. **Educ.:** Univ. of AZ, 1967–71, BA (Anthro.); Univ. of KY, 1971–72, MSLS; Univ. of AZ, 1975–76, MA (Geo.); Newberry Lib., Sem. in Hist. Cartography, 1980. **Orgs.:** West. Assn. Map Libs. SLA. Assn. of Amer. Geographers. Chicago Map Socty. **Activities:** 1; 15, 20, 39; 70, 91 **Addr.:** Map Rm. W. J. Kerr Library, Oregon State University, Corvallis, OR 97331.

Perry, Margaret (N. 15, 1933, Cincinnati, OH) Asst. Dir., Libs. for Reader Srvs., Univ. of Rochester, 1975–, Actg. Dir., Univ. Libs., 1980, 1976–77, Educ. Libn., 1970–75; Ref. Libn., Circ. Libn., US Milit. Acad., W. Point, 1967–70 Army Libn., US Army, Europe, 1959–67; YA Adult and Ref. Libn., NY Pub. Lib., 1954–58. **Educ.:** West. MI Univ., 1950–54, AB (LS); Cath. Univ. of Amer., 1958–59, MSLS; Univ. of Paris, 1956, Cert. d'Etudes Françaises; various crs. **Orgs.:** ALA: Prog. Ch. (1969); ACRL/Educ. and Bhvl. Sci. Sect., Stan. Com. Armed Forces LA: Prog. Ch. (1969). Mod. Lang. Assn. Coll. Lang. Assn. Natl. Socty. of Lit. and the Arts. ACLU. **Honors:** Armed Forces Writers Leag., 1st for Short Story, 1966; Panache Mag., 2nd: Frances Steloff Fiction Prize 1968. **Pubns.:** *The Harlem Renaissance: An Annotated Bibliography and Commentary* (1981); *A Bio-Bibliography of Countee P. Cullen, 1903–46* (1971); *Silence to the Drums; a Survey of the Harlem Renaissance* (1976); "Race and Education," *Amer. Libs.* (N. 1971); "Pinhead Libraries and Librarians, in Praise of," *What Black Librarians are Saying* (1973); various bks., articles, short stories. **Activities:** 1; 17 **Addr.:** Rush Rhees Library, University of Rochester, Rochester, NY 14627.

Pershing, Laura M. (N. 30, 1932, Chicago, IL) State Law Libn., ID State Law Lib., 1964–; Visit. Law Libn., Univ. of ID, Coll. of Law, 1963; Circ. Libn., IN Univ. Sch. of Law, 1961–62; Libn., Indianapolis Bar Assn., 1958–61. **Educ.:** Purdue Univ., 1950–54, BS (Home Econ.); IN Univ. Sch. of Law, Indianapolis, 1957–60, JD (Law); 1961, admitted to law prac. in Supreme Ct. and Fed. Ct. **Orgs.:** AALL: Sect. on Srv. to Inst. Residents (Treas., 1979–80); Sect. on State and Ct. Libs. (Secy., 1978–79); Assn. Nom. Com. (1972, 1979). IN State Bar Assn. **Honors:** ID Women's Yr., 100 Outstan. Women of ID, 1979. **Pubns.:** "Survey of State and Supreme Court Libraries," *Law Lib. Jnl.* (1974). **Activities:** 12, 13; 16, 17, 24; 77, 78 **Addr.:** Idaho State Law Library, Supreme Court Bldg., 451 W. State St., Boise, ID 83720.

Persky, Gail M. (N. 19, 1941, New York, NY) RLG Transition and Spec. Autom. Proj. Coord., NY Pub. Lib., 1980–; Head, Cat. with Copy Dept., Columbia Univ. Libs., 1975–80, Catlgr., 1972–75, Slavic Catlgr., 1970–72. **Educ.:** Hunter Coll., 1958–62, BA (Russ. Lang., Lit.); Columbia Univ., 1968–70, MLS, 1970–74, MIA (Soviet Un.). **Orgs.:** ALA: ACRL. NY Tech. Srvs. Libns. **Activities:** 1, 9; 20, 33, 34; 54, 56, 75 **Addr.:** 5836 Liebig Ave., Bronx, NY 10471.

Person, Ruth Janssen (Ag. 27, 1945, Washington, DC) Asst. Prof., Cath. Univ. of Amer., 1979–; Proj. Dir., Univ. of MI Ext. Srv., 1978–79, Coord. of Cont. Ed., 1977–79, Lectr., 1975–79, Univ. of MI, SLS; Head, Ref., Thomas Nelson Cmnty. Coll., 1971–74; Ref. Libn., Detroit Pub. Lib., Burton Hist. Col., 1969–71. **Educ.:** Gettysburg Coll., 1963–67, BA (Hist., Psy.); Univ. of MI, 1968–69, AMLS; Univ. of MI, 1974–80, PhD (LS); George Washington Univ., 1971–74, MSA (Indus. Persnl. Mgt.). **Orgs.:** ALA: ACRL/Cmnty. and Jr. Coll. Libs. Sect. (Secy., 1980–81), Nom. Com. (Ch., 1981–82), Comm. Com. (1976–81), Mem. Promo. Task Force (1978–79); LAMA/PAS Staff Dev. Com. (1981–82). CLENE: Adv. Bd. (1980–81); various coms. MI LA: Mem. Com. (Ch., 1977–78; 1976–79); various coms. Various other orgs. MI Adult Educ. Assn.: Exec. Bd. (1979). **Honors:** Beta Phi Mu, 1980; Pi Lambda Theta, 1976; Psi Chi, 1966. **Pubns.:** *Energy Resources for Public Libraries* (1979); *Personnel Management* Indp. Std. Modules 1980. **Activities:** 1, 11; 17, 25, 26; 59, 86, 92 **Addr.:** 10515 Deneane Rd., Silver Spring, MD 20903.

Perusse, Lyle Francis (O. 6, 1916, Lincoln, NE) Resrch., Writer, 1978–; Dir., Corona Pub. Lib., 1964–77; Supvsg. Libn., Pasadena Pub. Lib., 1957–64; Ref. Asst., Univ. of CA, Los Angeles, 1955–57; Libn., Sch. of Archit., Univ. of MN, 1952–54. **Educ.:** Oberlin Coll., 1946–50, AB (Art Hist.); Harvard Univ., 1950–51, MA (Art Hist.); Univ. of CA, Berkeley, 1951–52, BLS (Libnshp.). **Orgs.:** ALA: Bldg. and Equip. Com. (1959). CA LA: Hosplty. and Decor. Com. (Conf. Ch., 1960); Conf. Sites Com. (1965–67). Pasadena Pub. Lib. Club: Pres. (1961–62). Inland Lib. Syst. Exec. Cncl.: Secy. (1967–68); Pres. (1969–70, 1972–73). Various other orgs. Amer. Legion. Socty. of Archit. Histns. Alliance Fr. de la Riviera Californienne. Amer. Gld. of Organists: Los Angeles Chap. **Honors:** Phi Beta Kappa, 1950; U.S. Gvt., Older Residents Involved from Lib. Actv. in Mass Media Exper., 1973–75. **Pubns.:** Contrib. to various pers. **Activities:** 9; 17, 19, 28; 55, 72 **Addr.:** 974 W. Rancho Rd., Corona, CA 91720.

Petcoff, Phyllis Poole (D. 18, 1942, Cairo, IL) AV Coord., Hinsdale Ctrl. HS, 1977–; Media Dir., Hanover Ctrl. HS, 1972–77. **Educ.:** Purdue Univ., 1966–72, BA (Media); Rosary Coll., 1972–75, MALS. **Orgs.:** ALA: AASL. Assn. of IN Media Educs. Natl. Educ. Assn. IL Educ. Assn. **Activities:** 10; 15, 17, 32; 63 **Addr.:** 7885 Columbia, Dyer, IN 46311.

Peterdy, Kathleen Anne (Ag. 19, 1942, Rochester, NY) Tech. Info. Anal. Hlth., Safety, and Human Factors Lab., Eastman Kodak Co., 1978–, 1966–69, Libn., 1972–78; Bibl., Asst. Tech. Srvs. Libn., Edward G. Miner Med. Lib., Univ. of Rochester, 1969–72; Libn., Eastman Kodak Co., 1966–69; Libn., Detroit Pub. Lib., 1964–66. **Educ.:** Marygrove Coll., 1960–64, BA (Chem.); Univ. of MI, 1964–65, MALS. **Orgs.:** SLA. Med. LA. AAUW: Rochester Branch (Treas., 1979–81). **Activities:** 1, 12; 17, 39, 46; 60, 80, 91 **Addr.:** 4 Belmont Rd., Rochester, NY 14612.

Peters, Frances Elizabeth (N. 25, 1915, Philadelphia, PA) Libn., PA Coll. of Podiatric Med., 1968–; Asst. Libn., Holy Fam. Coll., 1967; Cmnty. Coll., Temple Univ., 1966–67; Libn., Cheltenham HS, 1963–66; Asst. Libn., Pedagogical Lib., Sch. Dist. Philadelphia, 1962–63; Libn., Curtis Publshg. Co., 1948–51; Libn., Free Lib. of Philadelphia, 1951–62, 1941–48. **Educ.:** Univ. of PA, 1936, BS (Educ.), 1938, MA (Latin); Drexel Inst., 1940, BSLS, 1966, MLS. **Orgs.:** SLA. ASIS. AAUW. Eng. Speaking Un. Hist. Socty. of PA. PA Classical Assn. Various other orgs. **Honors:** Beta Phi Mu. **Activities:** 1; 80 **Addr.:** Charles E. Krausz Library, Pennsylvania College of Podiatric Medicine, 8th St. at Race St., Philadelphia, PA 19107.

Peters, James L. (F. 21, 1943, Hanford, CA) Asst. Dir., Maurice Pine Pub. Lib., 1978–; Asst. Dir., Leonia Pub. Lib., 1973–78. **Educ.:** Univ. of CA, Berkeley, 1961–65, AB (Hist.); Rutgers Univ., 1972–73, MLS. **Orgs.:** Lib. PR Cncl.: Exec. Bd. (1980–82); Pubcty. Ch. (1980–82). NJ LA: Exec. Bd. (Mem.-at-large, 1979–82); NJ Libs. Adv. Bd.: Ch. (1979–81); PR Com. (Bd.

Special Subjects/Services: 50. Adult educ.; 51. Advert./Mktg.; 52. Aerosp.; 53. Agric.; 54. Area std.; 55. Arts/Hum.; 56. Autom.; 57. Bibl./Prtg.; 58. Bio. sci.; 59. Bus./Fin.; 60. Chem.; 61. Copyrt.; 62. Documtn.; 63. Educ.; 64. Engin.; 65. Env.; 66. Eth. grps.; 67. Film; 68. Food/Nutr.; 69. Geneal.; 70. Geo.; 71. Geol.; 72. Handcpd.; 73. Hist.; 74. Int. frdm.; 75. Info. sci.; 76. Insr.; 77. Law; 78. Legis.; 79. Math./Comp. sci.; 80. Med.; 81. Metals; 82. Nat. resrcs.; 83. Newsp.; 84. Nuc. sci.; 85. Oral hist.; 86. Petr./Energy; 87. Pharm.; 88. Phys./Astr./Math.; 89. Readg.; 90. Relig.; 91. Sci./Tech.; 92. Soc. sci.; 93. Telecom.; 94. Transp.; 95. (other).

Liaison, 1979–82); Exec. Bd. Plng. for Action Com. (1980–82); Conf. Com. (Pubn. Ed., 1979–82); various coms. Bergen-Passaic LA: Exec. Bd. (Treas., 1979–80). **Honors:** Beta Phi Mu, 1973. **Activities:** 9; 16, 17, 36 **Addr.:** 2 Tudor City Pl., New York, NY 10017.

Peters, Jean R. (Jl. 17, 1935, Belleville, IL) Libn., R. R. Bowker Co., 1964–; Ref. Libn., McGraw-Hill, Inc., 1961–64; Ref. Libn., Cat., Morgan Guaranty Trust Co., 1957–61. **Educ.:** Northwestern Univ., 1955–57, BA (Eng. lit., Composition); Columbia Univ., 1958–61, MS (LS). **Orgs.:** SLA: NY Publshg. Grp. (Ch., 1971–); NY Chap. (Secy., 1972–73); Publshg. Div. Ch. (1973–74); Arch. (1975–78). ALA. Amer. Prtg. Hist. Assn.: Trustee (1974–78); Secty. (1978–82). Pvt. LA Typophiles. **Pubns.:** Ed., *Collectible Books: Some New Paths* (1979); Ed., *Book Collecting: A Modern Guide* (1977); Ed., *Bookman's Glossary* (1975). **Activities:** 12; 15, 37, 39, 41; 57 **Addr.:** R.R. Bowker Co., 1180 Ave. of the Americas, New York, NY 10036.

Peters, Mary E. (Ap. 30, 1911, Cincinnati, OH) Retired, 1978–; Branch Libn., Cleveland Pub. Lib., 1966–78; Head, Chld. Dept., Lima Pub. Lib., 1958–66; Chld. Libn. in Branches & Ofc. of Supvsr., Pub. Lib. of Cincinnati and Hamilton Cnty., 1937–58. **Educ.:** Coll. of Sacred Heart, 1929–33, BA; Sch. of Lib. Sci., Columbia Univ., 1936–37, BS, 1949, Mstrs. Recog. **Orgs.:** OH LA: RT on Srv. to Chld. and YA (Ch., 1960). Cath. LA: Chld. Lib. Sect., Nom. Com. (Co-Ch., 1974). ALA: Chld. Srvs. Div., Chld. LA (Pubcty. Ch., 1950–52), Nom. Com. (Ch., 1971); Newbery-Caldecott Awds. Com. (1958, 1962); Ed., *Top of the News* (1954–55). Woman's Natl. Bk. Assn.: Constance Lindsay Skinner Awd. (Ch., 1968); various coms. Delta Kappa Gamma: Tau Chap., Chap. Arrange. (Ch., 1972–74). **Activities:** 9; 16, 21 **Addr.:** 2130 Surrey Rd. #12, Cleveland Heights, OH 44106.

Peters, Mary Nelson (My. 29, 1952, Galveston, TX) Med. Libn., Scottish Rite Crippled Chld. Hosp., Dallas, TX, 1980–; Tech. Libn., TX Area 5 Hlth. Syst. Agency, Irving, TX, 1977–80; Serials Libn., TX Coll. of Osteopathic Med., 1976–77. **Educ.:** Baylor Univ., 1970–74, BS (Bio.); Univ. of TX, 1974–76, MLS; 1976, Cert. Med. Libn. **Orgs.:** SLA: Dallas Lcl. Plng. Grp. (1978–80); TX Chap., Networking Com. Univ. of TX Student Grp.: (Pres., 1976). Med. LA: S. Ctrl. Reg. Grp., Mem. Com. (1979–80). Metroplex Cncl. of Hlth. Sci. Libns.: Ch. (1978–79). **Honors:** SLA, Sci. Tech Div., Travel Stipend, 1976; Beta Phi Mu. **Activities:** 12; 29, 39, 44; 80, 95 **Addr.:** 2104 Shady Brook Dr., Bedford, TX 76021.

Peters, P. Elizabeth (O. 6, 1942, London, Eng.) Dir., Comm./Info., Young Women's Christ. Assn. of Can., 1980–; Ref./Tech. Libn. Cons'. Gas Co., 1978–80; Comsn. Libn., Royal Comsn. on the North. Env., 1977–78; Resrch. Libn., ON Mnstry. of Energy, 1974–77; Libn./Trans., Rio Algom Mines Ltd. 1967–72. **Educ.:** Univ. of Toronto, 1964–67, BA (Fr.), MLS. **Orgs.:** Can. LA: Div. of Can. Spec. Libs. and Info. Sci. SLA: Toronto Chap., Mem. Com. (Ch., 1974–75); Secy. (1975–77); Prog. Com. (Ch., 1978–79); Info. Desk, 1974 Conf. Can. Assn. of Info. Sci. **Honors:** Fac. of LS, Univ. of Toronto, Kathleen Reeves Awd. for Spec. Libnshp., 1974. **Pubns.:** *Council of Planning Librarians. Exchange Bibliographies* "The Energy - Environment Dilemma," (1976); *The Central Business District of Canadian Cities* (1974); *The Toronto Waterfront* (1974). **Activities:** 4, 12; 30, 36, 41; 57, 86, 92 **Addr.:** Young Womens Christian Association of Canada, 571 Jarvis St., Toronto, ON M4Y 2J1 Canada.

Petersen, Carolyn Jean (Je. 10, 1953, Yakima, WA) Chld. Libn., Tenzler Branch, 1981–; Actg. Coord., Chld. Dept., Pierce Cnty. Lib., 1980–81, Chld. Libn., 1978–81. **Educ.:** Pac. Luth. Univ., 1971–75, BA (Eng., Hist.); Univ. of WA, 1975–76, MLS. **Orgs.:** ALA: ALSC. WA LA: Chld. and YA Srvs., Bd.; Nsltr. Ed. (1980–82). Puget Snd. Cncl. for the Review of Chld. Media. **Addr.:** Pierce County Rural Library District, 2356 Tacoma Ave. South Tacoma, WA 98402.

Petersen, Karla Diane (N. 16, 1945, Minneapolis, MN) Head, Cat. Dept., Ctr. for Resrch. Libs., 1976–; Catlgr., Hennepin Cnty. Lib., 1971–76; Span. Tchr., Indp. Sch. Dist. 197, 1967–69. **Educ.:** Macalester Coll., 1963–64; Univ. of MN, 1964–67, BS (Span.); Univ. Natl. de Méx., 1965; Univ. of MN, 1969–70, MA (LS). **Orgs.:** ASIS: MN Chap. (Secy., 1972–74); MN Chap. (Chap. Asm. Rep., 1974–76); 1977 Natl. Conf. Strg. Com. (1976–77); Chicago Chap., Vice-Ch./Ch.-Elect (1978–1979), Ch. (1979–80), Past Ch./Chap. Asm. Rep. (1980–81). ALA: *Amer. Libs.* Ed. Adv. Bd. (1976–78). Sierra Club. **Pubns.:** Reviews. **Activities:** 9, 14-Resrch. Lib. Coop.; 17, 20 **Addr.:** Center for Research Libraries, 5721 S. Cottage Grove Ave., Chicago, IL 60637.

Petersen, Nancy Anne (Jl. 13, 1940, Eugene, OR) Cat. Libn., Portland Pub. Schs., 1972–. **Educ.:** Univ. of OR, 1958–62, BA (Grmn., Russ.), 1971–72, MLS. **Orgs.:** ALA: AASL, Com. on Sch. Media Srvs. to Chld. with Spec. Needs (1980–81). OR Educ. Media Assn.: Legis. Co-Ch. (1979–80). Multnomah-Clackamas Educ. Media Assn.: Pres. (1977–78). Portland Assn. of Sch. Libns.: Pres. (1978–79). Portland Assn. of Tchrs. OR Assn. of Tchrs. **Honors:** Phi Beta Kappa, 1962. **Pubns.:** Jt. ed., *Directory of Blind College Students in U.S. and Canada* (1966); *Directories of Portland Area Librarians* (1972–80). **Activities:** 10; 55, 72, 92 **Addr.:** Portland Public Schools, Library Technical Services, 501 N. Dixon St., Portland, OR 97227.

Petersen, Toni (My. 13, 1933, New York, NY) Libn., Bennington Coll. Lib., 1980–; Exec. Ed., RI LA, Intl. Repertory of the Lit. of Art, 1972–80; Catlgr. of Rare Bks., Clark Art Inst., 1972; Catlgr., Williams Coll. Lib., 1969–72; Catlgr., Andover-Harvard Theo. Lib., 1959–68. **Educ.:** Brooklyn Coll., 1952–56, BA (Eng.); Simmons Coll., 1961–63, MLS. **Orgs.:** ARLIS/NA: Art and Archit. Thesaurus Proj., Proj. Dir.; Plng. Proj. for a Biog. Dictionary of Photographers, Adv. Panel. **Pubns.:** *Indexing in Art and Architecture: An Investigation and Analysis; Report to the Council on Library Resources* (1981); "Computer-Aided Indexing in the Arts," *Art Libs. Jnl.* (Fall 1981); various sps. **Addr.:** Crossett Library, Bennington College, Bennington, VT 05201.

Peterson, Anita R. (Mr. 6, 1943, San Diego, CA) Libn. for Srvs. to Span. Speaking, Inglewood Pub. Lib., 1975–. **Educ.:** Univ. of San Diego, 1960–64, BA (Rom. Lang.); Univ. of South. CA, 1973–75, MA (LS); Univ. of Madrid, 1964–65 (Hisp. Std.). **Orgs.:** ALA. CA LA. AZ LA. REFORMA. CA Eth. Srvs. Task Frc.: Ch. (1979–80). Los Angeles World Affairs Cncl. **Pubns.:** *Library Service to the Spanish Speaking* (1977). **Activities:** 9; 15, 16, 39; 66 **Addr.:** 4982 W 59th St., Los Angeles, CA 90056.

Peterson, Arlene C. (Ap. 24, 1926, Elizabeth, NJ) Mgr., Resrch. Info. Syst., Merck Sharp and Dohme Resrch. Labs., 1976–, Sect. Head, 1973–76, Pubns. Coord., 1971–73, Sr. Info. Sci., 1967–71. **Educ.:** Upsala Coll., 1943–47, BS (Chem.); Rutgers Univ., 1965–69, MLS. **Orgs.:** ASIS. Natl. Micro. Assn. Word Prcs. Assn. **Honors:** Beta Phi Mu. **Pubns.:** Jt. auth., "MSDRL Project Information Network," *Procs. ASIS* (1975); jt. auth., "1,250,000 Pages of Biological Information to Microstorage," *Procs. ASIS* (1969). **Activities:** 12; 17, 30, 39; 58, 60, 87 **Addr.:** P.O. Box 2000, R-50A3, Rahway, NJ 07065.

Peterson, Carolyn Sue (Je. 23, 1938, Carthage, MO) Head, Chld. Dept., Orlando Pub. Lib., 1970–; Instr., Grad. Lib., Media Prog., Univ. of CO, 1968–70; Lab. Sch. Libn., Instr., Northwest MO State Coll., 1962–68; Chld. Libn., Town and Country Reg. Lib., 1960–62. **Educ.:** Univ. of MO, 1957–59, AB (Eng.); Univ. of Denver, 1959–60, MA (Libnshp.); Univ. of MO, 1964–66, (Educ.). **Orgs.:** ALA: ALSC/Prog. Pubns. Support Com. (1978–); Lib. Srvs. to Chld. with Spec. Needs Com. (1981–83); Caldecott Com. (1980–). SELA: Pre-Conf. Consult., Instr. (1978). FL LA: Chld. Caucus (Pres., 1976–77); Int. Frdm. Com. (1979–). Natl. Leag. of Amer. Penwomen. Orlando Leag. of Amer. Penwomen. Natl Writers Club. **Honors:** FL LA, Outstan. Lib. Dev. Awd., 1973; ALA, John Cotton Dana Awd., 1978. **Pubns.:** *Story Programs: A Handbook of Materials* (1980); *Index to Children's Songs* (1979); "Parent Education," *FL Libs.* (N.–D. 1978); "Sharing Literature with Children," *Sch. Lib. Jnl.* (F. 1975); "Sharing Literature with Children," *Start Early for an Early Start* (1976); various bks., articles, filmstp. **Activities:** 9, 11; 21, 24, 26; 63, 89 **Addr.:** Orlando Public Library, 10 N. Rosalind, Orlando, FL 32801.

Peterson, Charles Buckley, III (O. 3, 1936, Lancaster, PA) Sr. Map Catlgr., Lib. of Congs., 1975–. **Educ.:** Northwest. Univ., 1954–58, BA (Geo.); Univ. of WA, 1958–60, MA (Geo.), 1960–62, PhD (Geo.); Cath. Univ., 1975, MS (LS). **Orgs.:** DC LA. West. Assn. of Map Libs. SLA. N. Amer. Cartograph. Info. Socty. Various other orgs. Assn. of Amer. Geographers. Amer. Name Socty. **Pubns.:** "The Nature of Soviet Place-Names," *Names–Jnl. of the Amer. Name Socty.* (Mr. 1977). **Activities:** 4; 20; 70 **Addr.:** 1030 31st St. N.W., Washington, DC 20007.

Peterson, Dennis Roy (S. 21, 1949, Red Oak, IA) Pub. Srvs. Libn., Palmer Coll. Lib., 1978–; Asst. Acq. Coord., Jackson Metro. Lib. Syst., 1976–78. **Educ.:** IA West. Cmnty. Coll., 1967–69, AS (Engin.); IA State Univ., 1969–74, BA (Phil.); Univ. of IA, 1975–76, MALS. **Orgs.:** ALA. Med. LA. Leag. of Amer. Wheelmen. Quad Cities Bicycle Club. **Pubns.:** Reviews. **Activities:** 1; 15, 39, 44; 58, 80, 95-Chiropractic. **Addr.:** 4618 Main St., Davenport, IA 52806.

Peterson, Donald G. (Mr. 31, 1913, Duluth, MN) Lib. Dir., Judson Coll., 1973–; Catlgr./Tech. Srvs., Wheaton Coll., 1971–73. **Educ.:** Bethany Coll., 1939–40, BA (Hist.); Bethel Theo. Semy., 1934–37, B Th; North. IL Univ., 1967–72, MA (LS); Bethel Theo. Semy., 1973, MDiv. **Orgs.:** IL LA. SAA. ALA. Christ. Libns. Flwshp. **Activities:** 1; 17, 20, 39; 90, 92 **Addr.:** 316 Dodson St., Geneva, IL 60134.

Peterson, Dorothy S. (D. 23, 1922, Inkster, MI) Med. Libn., Kerrville State Hosp., 1980–; Head Libn., Gillespie Cnty. Lib., 1977–80; Head Libn., Sch. of Theo., Univ. of St. Thomas, 1969–77; Asst. Cur., MI Hist. Col., Univ. of MI, 1947–50. **Educ.:** Univ. of MI, 1942–45, BMus (Msc.); TX Woman's Univ., 1973–75, MLS. **Orgs.:** ALA. Med. LA. ATLA. Cath. LA. Girl Scouts. Gamma Phi Beta: Panhellenic (1957–59). **Honors:** Beta Phi Mu, 1976. **Activities:** 1, 9; 17, 39, 46; 80, 90, 92 **Addr.:** 443 Valley Dr., Kerrville, TX 78028.

Peterson, Francine (F. 15, 1940, Treston, ID) Media Coord., M. Lynn Bennion Sch., 1977–; Libn., Webster Sch., 1964–77; Tchr., Kearns Jr. High, 1963–64. **Educ.:** UT State Univ., 1958–63, BS (Eng., Educ.); Brigham Young Univ., 1977–80, MLS; Univ. of UT, 1980 (Media). **Orgs.:** ALA. UT LA. Salt Lake City Sch. Libns. Salt Lake Tchrs. UT Educ. Assn. Natl. Educ. Assn. Alpha Delta Kappa: Secy. **Honors:** Kiwanis, Tchr. of the Month, 1979. **Activities:** 10; 21, 32, 46; 56, 63 **Addr.:** M. Lynn Bennion Sch., Granger, UT 84120.

Peterson, Fred McCrae (D. 29, 1936, Minneapolis, MN) Dir. of Libs., Cath. Univ. of Amer., 1977–, Asst. Prof., Assoc. Ch., Sch. of LS, 1973–77; Assoc. Dir., IA State Univ. Lib., 1969–70, Asst. Dir., 1968, Head, Cat. Dept. & Asst. Dir., 1964–67; Asst. to Dir., 1961–64. **Educ.:** Univ. of MN, 1954–58, BA (Intl. Rel.), 1959–60, MA (LS); IN Univ., 1970–73, PhD (LS). **Orgs.:** ALA. AALS: Natl. Anl. Mtg., Prog. Plng. (Ch., 1976); Gvt. Rel. Com. (Ch., 1976–78). Cath. LA. DC LA. Cncl. of Comm. Socties.: AALS Rep. (1976–78). **Honors:** Beta Phi Mu, 1971. **Pubns.:** *Motivation: A Vital Force in the Organization: A Home Based Study Course For Library and Information Professionals* (1977); *ALA Glossary of Library and Information Sciences* forthcoming. **Activities:** 1; 17, 26 **Addr.:** 2210 Greenery Ln. #302, Silver Spring, MD 20906.

Peterson, Harold Patrick (Ag. 27, 1935, Chicago, IL) Libn., Ed.-in-chief, Minneapolis Inst. of Arts, 1972–; Ref. Libn., Simmons Coll. Lib., 1970–72. **Educ.:** Harvard Coll., 1954–58, AB (Eng.); Univ. of WI, 1968–70, MA (LS). **Orgs.:** ALA. SLA. ARLIS/NA. Bibl. Socty. of Amer. Ampersand Club. **Pubns.:** Ed., *Chinese Jades* (1977); ed., various exhibition cats. **Activities:** 15, 17, 37; 55 **Addr.:** 333 Oak Grove, Minneapolis, MN 55403.

Peterson, Jean (My. 26, 1946, New York, NY) Sr. Asst. Branch Libn., New York Pub. Lib., 1980–, Ref. Libn., 1978–80; Info. Asst., 1969–78. **Educ.:** Herbert H. Lehman Coll., 1966–69, AB (Sp., Thea.); Pratt Inst., 1974–76, MLS. **Orgs.:** NYLA: Un. Staff Org. RT, Prog. and Legis. Com. (1981). **Honors:** Beta Phi Mu, 1976. **Activities:** 9; 15, 31, 39; 50, 66 **Addr.:** Countee Cullen Branch Library, 104 W. 136 St., New York, NY 10030.

Peterson, Jean S. (Ja. 2, 1929, Pittsburgh, PA) Div. Head, Tech. Info. Div., Ctrl. Resrch. and Dev. Dept., E. I. du Pont de Nemours and Co., 1973–, Sect. Supvsr., Tech. Info. Div., 1966–73, Tech. Info. Spec., 1959–66, Chem., 1950–59. **Educ.:** IN Univ., 1946–50, BS (Chem.). **Orgs.:** ASIS. Amer. Chem. Socty. Ed. Adv. Bd. of Chemical Abs. (1975–). **Pubns.:** "Replacement of an In-House Current Awareness Bulletin by Chemical Abstracts Section Groupings," *Jnl. of Chemical Info. and Comp. Sci.* (1975). **Activities:** 12; 17; 60 **Addr.:** Du Pont Experimental Station, Bldg. 301, Wilmington, DE 19898.

Peterson, Kenneth Gerard (My. 30, 1927, Brooklyn, NY) Dean of Lib. Affairs, South. IL Univ., 1976–; Assoc. Univ. Libn., Univ. of VA, 1968–76; Libn., Pac. Luth. Theo. Semy., 1963–66; various positions as instr., 1949–62. **Educ.:** Drew Univ., 1944–46, BA (Hist.); Yale Univ., 1946–49, MDiv (Theo.); Univ. of CA, Berkeley, 1962–63, MLS, 1963–68, PhD (LS). **Orgs.:** ALA: ACRL, Pubns. in Libnshp., Ed. Bd. (Ed., Ch., 1972–77), Pubns. Com. (1972–81). ARL: ILL Com. (1978–). IL LA: IACRL-IBHE Liaison Com. (1977–); Resrc. Sharing Subcom. (1978–). Midwest Reg. Lib. Netwk.: Bd. of Dirs. (1976–). Various other orgs. Ulysses S. Grant Assn.: Bd. of Dirs., Exec. Com. (1976–). **Honors:** Pi Gamma Mu, 1946; Beta Phi Mu, 1963. **Pubns.:** *An Introductory Bibliography for Theological Students* (1964); *The University of California Library at Berkeley, 1900–1945* (1970); "Twenty-five Years of Library Development in the Southeast," *VA Libn.* (Jl.–Ag. 1976); "Computer-Supported Activities in Library Affairs at Southern Illinois University-Carbondale," *IL Libs.* (Ap. 1978); "Trends in Library Organization: A Look at the Past, Present, and Future," *Emerging Trends in Library Organization: What Influences Change* (1978); various other bks., articles, reviews. **Activities:** 1, 12; 17, 26, 37; 63, 90, 92 **Addr.:** 911 Briarwood Dr., Carbondale, IL 62901.

Peterson, Mahlon N. (Je. 10, 1937, Moline, IL) Univ. Libn., St. Lawrence Univ., 1972–; Dir., Wartburg Coll., 1968–72; Asst. Libn., Lafayette Coll., 1966–68, Acq. Libn., 1964–66. **Educ.:** Augustana Coll., 1958–62, BA (Phil.); Univ. of IL, 1962–64; MLS. **Orgs.:** ALA: ACRL. **Honors:** Phi Alpha Theta. **Activities:** 1; 17, 31 **Addr.:** 22 Governeur St., Canton, NY 13617.

Peterson, Paul A. (Je. 16, 1948, Chicago, IL) Ref. and Exch. Libn., Linda Hall Lib., 1980–, Ref. Libn., Slavic Bibl., 1977–80; Ref. Libn., Kansas City MO Pub. Lib., 1975–76, Head, Circ./Regis., 1973–74. **Educ.:** Univ. of MO, 1966–72, BA (Russ.), minor in Jnlsm., 1976–77, MALS. **Orgs.:** SLA. Univ. of MO Grad. Sch. of Lib. and Info. Sci. Adv. Cncl.: Spec. Libs. Subcom. (Ch., 1978–); Exec. Bd. (1978–). **Pubns.:** Ed., *Linda Hall Library Miscellany* (1980–). **Activities:** 9, 12; 34, 39, 45; 57, 91 **Addr.:** Linda Hall Library, 5109 Cherry, Kansas City, MO 64110.

Peterson, Randall T. (Ag. 27, 1944, Sioux City, IA) Dir. of Law Lib., Asst. Prof. of Law, John Marshall Law Sch., 1977–; Assoc. Law Libn., Brigham Young Univ., 1972–77. **Educ.:** Brigham Young Univ., 1966–68, BS (Psy.); Univ. of UT, 1968–72, JD (Law); Brigham Young Univ., 1972–74, MLS. **Orgs.:** AALL: AV Com. (1973–79). Chicago Assn. of Law Libs.: Admin. Code Com. (1979–). ASIS. **Pubns.:** "Legal Research Instructional Package" media and print (1975–77). **Activities:** 1, 12; 17, 31, 39; 77, 78

PROFESSIONAL ACTIVITIES: Institutions: 1. Acad. lib.; 2. Arch.; 3. Assn.; 4. Fed./Gvt. lib.; 5. Inst. lib.; 6. Mfr./Suppl.; 7. Milit. lib.; 8. Musm.; 9. Pub. lib.; 10. Sch. lib.; 11. Sch. of lib. sci.; 12. Spec. lib.; 13. State lib.; 14. (other). **Functions/Activities:** 15. Acq./Col. dev.; 16. Adult srvs.; 17. Admin.; 18. Apprais.; 19. Archit./Bldgs.; 20. Cat./Class.; 21. Chld. srvs.; 22. Circ.; 23. Cons./Pres.; 24. Consult.; 25. Cont. ed.; 26. Educ. lib. sci.; 27. Ext. srvs.; 28. Fund/Grants; 29. Gvt. pubs.; 30. Indx./Abs.; 31. Instr. lib. use; 32. Media srvs.; 33. Micro.; 34. Netwks./Coop.; 35. Persnl.; 36. PR; 37. Publshg.; 38. Recs. mgt.; 39. Ref. srvs.; 40. Repro.; 41. Resrch.; 42. Review.; 43. Secur.; 44. Serials; 45. Spec. col.; 46. Tech. srvs.; 47. Trustees/Bds.; 48. YA srvs.; 49. (other).

Addr.: John Marshall Law School Library, 315 S. Plymouth Ct., Chicago, IL 60604.

Peterson, Sandra C. (D. 6, 1931, Beatrice, NE) Media Dir., Hastings Sr. HS, 1969–; Libn., Shelby Pub. Schs., 1967–68. **Educ.:** NE Wesleyan Univ., 1967, BA (Educ.); Purdue Univ., 1968–69, MS (Educ.). **Orgs.:** ALA. NE LA. NE Educ. Media Assn. Mt. Plains LA. **Activities:** 10; 15, 17, 32 **Addr.:** Hastings Senior High, 1100 W. 14th, Hastings, NE 68901.

Peterson, Sandra K. (N. 21, 1941, McCook, NE) Docum. Libn., Coll. of William and Mary, 1974–; Docum. Libn., Univ. of North. IA, 1970–74; Ref. Libn., Oberlin Coll., 1968–70; Ref. Libn., WV State Lib., 1967–68. **Educ.:** Kearney State Coll., 1959–63, BA (Hist.); Univ. of Pittsburgh, 1966–67, MLS; George Washington Univ., 1976–78, MS (Human Resrcs.). **Orgs.:** VA LA: Coll. and Univ. Sect. (Secy., 1980–81); Mem. Com. (1980–81); Pub. Docum. Forum, Secy. (1978–79), Coord. (1979–80). ALA: GODORT, Elec. Com., (Ch. 1979–80); Secy. (1980–82). AAUP. Williamsburg Area Women's Ctr. Williamsburg Task Frc. on Battered Women. Women's Fac. Caucus, Coll. of William and Mary. **Activities:** 1; 29, 39; 92 **Addr.:** Documents Department, Swem Library, College of William and Mary, Williamsburg, VA 23185.

Peterson, Sara (Sally) R. (Ag. 23, 1926, Lancaster, PA) Vetny. Med. Libn., Assoc. Prof., IA State Univ., 1971–, Ref. Libn., 1971–73. **Educ.:** Vassar Coll., 1944–47, BA (Zlgy.); Univ. of IL, 1948–52, MS (Bot.); Univ. of IA, 1970–71, MA (LS). **Orgs.:** Med. LA: Vetny. Med. Libns. Sect. (Ch., 1976–77); Intl. Coop. Com. (Ch. 1981). Midwest HSLN. **Pubns.:** "Evolution of a Veterinary Medical Library," *Bltn. of the Med. LA* (1979). **Activities:** 1, 12; 15, 17, 39; 56, 58, 80 **Addr.:** Veterinary Medical Library, Iowa State University, Ames, IA 50011.

Peterson, Stephen Lee (Ja. 31, 1940, Lindsborg, KS) Libn., Yale Dvnty. Sch. Lib., 1980–; Actg. Libn., Libn., Yale Beinecke Rare Bk. Lib., 1978–80; Libn., Yale Univ. Dvnty. Lib., 1972–78; Asst. Dir. for Bibl. Srvs., Jt. Univ. Libs., 1971–72; Dvnty. Libn., Vanderbilt Dvnty. Lib., 1969–71, Acq. Libn., 1968–69. **Educ.:** Bethel Coll., 1962, BA; Vanderbilt Univ., 1975, PhD (Relig.); Colgate Rochester Dvnty. Sch., 1965, BD; Univ. of MI, 1968, AMLS; 1967, AM (Near East. Lang. and Lit.). **Orgs.:** ATLA: Bd. of Dirs. (1979–82); Com. on Stans. of Accred. (Ch., 1980–81). Com. for Theo. Lib. Dev. Amer. Socty. of Missiology: Bd. of Pubn. (1976–80). Intl. Assn. of Missn. Std.: Stdg. Com. on Bibl., Documtn. and Arch. (1980–). **Honors:** Assn. Theo. Schs., Lilly Fellow, 1976; Cncl. on Lib. Resrcs., Fellow, 1976; Beta Phi Mu. **Pubns.:** Jt. ed., *Missionary Periodicals from the China Mainland* (1977); "Collection Development in Theological Libraries: A New Model-A New Hope," *Essays on Theological Librarianship* (1980); "Documenting Christianity: Towards a Cooperative Library Collection Development Program," *Procs. of ATLA* (1978); "The Subject Approach to Theology: An Alternative System for Libraries," *Procs. of ATLA* (1977); "Patterns of Use of Periodical Literature," *Coll. & Resrch. Libs.* (1969). **Activities:** 1, 2; 15, 17; 90 **Addr.:** Yale Divinity School Library, 409 Prospect St., New Haven, CT 06510.

Peterson, Trudy Huskamp (Ja. 25, 1945, Estherville, IA) Chief, Legis. and Nat. Resrcs. Branch, Natl. Arch. and Recs. Srv., 1980–, Asst. to Deputy Archvst. of the U.S., 1977–80, Archvst., Ofc. of Pres. Libs., 1974–77; Archvst., IA State Univ., 1973. **Educ.:** IA State Univ., 1963–67, BS (Eng., Hist.); Univ. of IA, 1968–75, MA, PhD (Hist.). **Orgs.:** SAA: 1980 Prog. Com., Co-Ch.; Ed. Bd. *Amer. Archvst.* Mid-Atl. Reg. Arch. Conf. Amer. Hist. Assn. Org. of Amer. Histns. Agr. Hist. Socty. Amer. Socty. of Access Profs. **Honors:** SAA, Fellow, 1980; SAA, Gondos Prize, 1974; Natl. Arch. and Recs. Srv., Commendable Srv. Awd., 1979. **Pubns.:** *Agricultural Exports, Farm Income, and the Eisenhower Administration* (1979); ed., *Farmers, Bureaucrats, and Middlemen: Historical Perspectives on American Agriculture* (1980); "Education and Research in Archival Administration," *Encyclopedia of Library Science* (1980); "After Five Years: An Assessment of the Amended U.S. Freedom of Information Act," *Amer. Archvst.* (Spr. 1980); "Using the Freedom of Information Act to Acquire Archival Material," *Law Lib. Jnl.* (Fall 1979); "The Gift and the Deed," *Amer. Archvst.* (Ja. 1979); Various other articles. **Activities:** 2; 17, 18, 26 **Addr.:** 810 Massachusetts Ave. N.E., Washington, DC 20002.

Peterson, Vivian A. (O. 15, 1919, Blooming Prairie, MN) Dir., Lib. Srvs., Concordia Tchrs. Coll., 1974–; Dir., Lib., Midland Lutheran Coll., 1960–74; Cat. Libn., Luther Coll., 1952–60; Serials Catlgr., IA State Univ., 1949–52. **Educ.:** Augsburg Coll., 1937–41, BA (Eng.); Univ. of Denver, 1949, MA (LS); Columbia Univ., 1955–71, Cert. of Advnc. Std. (LS). **Orgs.:** ALA: Cnclr. (1976–79). NE LA: Treas., VP, Pres. (1966–68, 1971–73). Mt. Plains LA. AAUP: VP (1969–71). Common Cause. **Pubns.:** "Nebraska Library Association," *Encyc. of Lib. and Info. Sci.* (1976); "Nebraska State Reports," *ALA Yrbk.* (1977–80). **Activities:** 1, 10; 15, 17, 34; 63, 90 **Addr.:** 1103 Kolterman, Seward, NE 68434.

Peterson St. Aubin, Kendra J. (Mr. 8, 1946, Minneapolis, MN) Ref. Libn., Wheaton Coll. Lib., 1980–; Head Ref. Libn., Fairleigh Dickinson Univ. Lib., 1979–80, Docum. Libn., 1976–79; Sr. Libn., NY Pub. Lib., 1973–76, Libn., 1970–73. **Educ.:** Macalester Coll., 1964–68, BA (Grmn.); Univ. of Denver, 1968–69, MA (Libnshp.); Fairleigh Dickinson Univ., 1976–79, MA (Hist.). **Orgs.:** ALA: GODORT. **Honors:** Beta Phi Mu; Phi Beta Kappa; Phi Alpha Theta. **Pubns.:** *The Lowell Mill Girls' Defense of their Rights: Genteel and Militant Approaches* (1979); Ed., *Mid-Manhattan News* (1971–75). **Activities:** 1, 9; 29, 39; 92 **Addr.:** 646 Delano Rd., Marion, MA 02738.

Pethybridge, Arthur E. (Ag. 20, 1924, Leominster, MA) Dir., Lib. Srv., Northwestern CT Cmnty. Coll., 1965–; Libn., Glastonbury HS, 1956–65; Pubns. Libn., Racine Pub. Lib., 1953–56; Asst. Ref. Libn., Providence Pub. Lib., 1951–53. **Educ.:** Boston Univ., 1942–48, AB (Eng.); Simmons Coll., 1950–51, MSLS; Univ. of London, 1949, Cert. (Eng.). **Orgs.:** ALA. CT LA. Northwestern CT Lib. Grp.: Pres. (1977–79). **Honors:** Beta Phi Mu, 1954. ALA, John Cotton Dana Awd., 1955. **Pubns.:** "Racmil – Five Years Later," *Lib. Jnl.* (N. 1, 1954); "The Community College: Connecticut's Newest Academic System," *CT Libs.* (Fall, 1970). **Activities:** 1, 10; 15, 17, 39 **Addr.:** 212 Glendale Ave., Winsted, CT 06098.

Petrak, Cliff M. (S. 6, 1942, Chicago, IL) Media Ctr. Dir., Brother Rice HS, 1977–, Math. Tchr., 1964–76. **Educ.:** DePaul Univ., 1960–64, BS (Math.); Chicago State Univ., 1965–69, MS (Math.), 1976–81, MLS. **Orgs.:** Cath. LA. IL Baseball Coaches Assn. IL HS Assn. Chicago Cath. Hockey Leag. **Pubns.:** "The Strategy and Techniques of the Hit and Run Play," *Scholastic Coach* (F. 1974); "Who's on First (Coaching, That Is)!" *Scholastic Coach* (Ap. 1974); "The 20 Most Prevalent Rule Myths of Baseball," *Scholastic Coach* (Mr. 1975). **Activities:** 10; 17 **Addr.:** Brother Rice High School, 10001 S. Pulaski Ave., Chicago, IL 60642.

Petrie, Claire (N. 7, 1948, Brooklyn, NY) Libn., Pratt Inst., Art and Archit. Dept., 1980–; Libn., Un. Leag. Club, 1979–80; Libn., Brooklyn Pub. Lib., Art and Msc. Dept., 1977–79. **Educ.:** Skidmore Coll.; Adelphi Univ., 1966–71 (Eng.); Columbia Univ., 1976–77, MLS. **Orgs.:** ALA. SLA: Musm., Arts and Hum. (Ch.). ARLIS/NA. Amer. Prtg. Hist. Assn. Columbia Univ. Alum. Assn. **Activities:** 1; 55 **Addr.:** Pratt Institute Library, Art & Architecture Dept., 200 Willoughby Ave., Brooklyn, NY 11238.

Petrone, Anthony F. (Mr. 24, 1950, Springfield, IL) Resrch. Libn., Info. Ctr., DeSoto, Inc., 1979–; Head, Interpretive Srvs., Lib., Med. Coll. of GA, 1977–79, Ref. Libn., 1975–77. **Educ.:** East. IL Univ., 1968–72, BS (Zlgy.); Case West. Rsv. Univ., 1974–75, MSLS; Med. Lib. Assn., 1976, Cert. **Orgs.:** SLA. Med. LA. GA Hlth. Sci. LA: Ch. (1976–77). **Pubns.:** "Health Sciences Librarianship in Transition," *Cath. Lib. World* (N. 1976). **Activities:** 5, 12; 31, 39, 41; 59, 80, 91 **Addr.:** Information Center - De Soto, Inc., 1700 S. Mt. Prospect Rd., Des Plaines, IL 60018.

Petrowski, Ruth Kawai (Ja. 10, 19–, Honolulu, HI) Libn., Koko Head Elem. Sch., 1973–; Libn., Aliiolani Elem. Sch., 1971–73; Tchr., Elem. Schs. in HI, WI, CO, MN. **Educ.:** Univ. of HI, 1950–54, BEd (Elem. Educ.), 1954–55, Dipl. (Elem. Educ.), 1974, MLS. **Orgs.:** HI Assn. of Sch. Libns.: Pres. (1981–82). Univ. of HI Grad. Sch. of Lib. Std. Alum. Grp.: Pres. (1976–77). ALA. HI State Tchrs. Assn. Liliuokalani Sch. Tchr.-Parent-Student Assn.: Pres. (1980–81). New Kaimuki Japanese Lang. Sch. Parent-Tchr. Assn. Amer. Contract Bridge Leag. **Honors:** Beta Phi Mu. **Activities:** 10; 21 **Addr.:** 3350 Sierra Dr. #602, Honolulu, HI 96816.

Pettas, William A. (My. 24, 1935, Buffalo, NY) Libn., Laney Coll., 1964–; Consult., Tech. Libnshp., UNESCO, 1974–75; Sr. Libn., Oakland Pub. Lib., 1962–64; Ref. Libn., Enoch Pratt Lib., 1959. **Educ.:** Univ. of Buffalo, 1953–57, BA (Educ., Eng. Lit.); Rutgers Univ., 1957–58, MLS (Libnshp.); Univ. of CA, Berkeley, 1968–72, PhD (Libnshp.). **Orgs.:** CA Clearinghse. on Lib. Instr.: North. Reg. Strg. Com. Mod. Grk. Std. Assn. **Pubns.:** *The Giunti of Florence* (1980); "The Cost of Printing a Florentine Incunable," *La Bibliofilia* (1973); "Nikolaos Sophianos and Greek Printing in Rome," *The Lib.* (1974); "An International Renaissance Publishing Family," *Lib. Qtly.* (1974); various slide-tape kits (1972–77). **Activities:** 1; 17, 24, 26 **Addr.:** Laney College Library, 900 Fallon St., Oakland, CA 94607.

Pettem, Douglas (D. 17, 1928, Kingston, ON) Coord. of Lib. Resrcs. N. York Bd. of Educ., 1980–, Coord., Media Srvs., 1973–80, Coord., Lib. Srvs., 1967–73; Head Libn., Don Mills Collegiate, 1959–67; Tchr.-Libn., Earl Haig Sec. Sch., 1956–59. **Educ.:** Univ. of Toronto, 1948–52, BA (Eng.), 1952–53, MA (Eng.), 1953–54 HS Spec. Cert. (Eng.); 1975, MEd (Curric.); Spec. Cert. in Sch. Libnshp.; Supervisory Ofcr. Cert. **Orgs.:** Can. LA. ON LA. Assn. for Media and Tech. in Educ. in Can. AECT. ON Sec. Sch. Tchrs. Fed. **Activities:** 10; 17, 24, 32; 63, 67, 93 **Addr.:** 85 Peckham Ave., Willowdale, ON M2R 2V4 Canada.

Pettengill, George Ewald (Je. 5, 1913, Cambridge, MA) Retired, 1973–; Libn., Amer. Inst. of Archit., 1951–73; Asst., Libn., Franklin Inst., 1945–51; Ref. Libn., Reading (PA) Pub. Lib., 1937–45; Ref. Asst., New York Pub. Lib., 1935–37. **Educ.:** Bowdoin Coll., 1929–33, AB; Columbia Univ., 1933–35, BS MS (LS). **Orgs.:** SLA: Arch. Com. (Ch. 1940–43); Philadelphia Chap., Exec. Bd. (1939–40), Pres. (1946–47); D.C. Chap., Dir. (1957–59), 2nd VP (1961–62). ALA: ACRL. Bibl. Socty. of Amer. SAA. Hist. Socty. of Berks Cnty. Arlington Hist. Socty. **Honors:** Amer. Inst. of Archits.; Hon. Mem., 1962, Amer. Inst. of Archits., Libn. Emeritus, 1973. **Pubns.:** "Contributions to a Bibliography of Arlington County," *Arlington Hist. Mag.* (1959–80); "Reading and Berks County Authors; A Bibliography," *Hist. Review of Berks Cnty.* (Ja., Ap. 1943); "The History of the Society's Library," *HRBC* (Ja. 1945); "Franklin, Priestley and the Samuel Vaughan, Jr., Manuscripts, 1775-1782," *Jnl. of the Franklin Inst.* (Mr. 1947); "Walter Rogers Johnson," *JFI* (Ag. 1950); various other articles. **Activities:** 5, 12; 17, 20, 39 **Addr.:** 4102 3rd Rd. N., Arlington, VA 22203.

Petter, Christopher Gordon (D. 3, 1945, Stourbridge, Worcs., Eng.) Archvst. Libn., Univ. of Victoria, 1975–. **Educ.:** Univ. of Victoria, 1963–67, BA (Eng.); Univ. of Leeds, 1968–69, MA (Eng.), 1969–72, MPhil (Eng.), 1972–, PhD Cand. (Eng.); Univ. of West. ON, 1974–75, MLS; Univ. of WA, 1976, Cert. (Arch.). **Orgs.:** Assn. of BC Archvsts.: VP (1977–78). Assn. of Can. Archvsts.: Com. on Autom. (1979–). Univ. of Victoria Lib. Prof. Staff Assn.: Pres. (1980–81); Secy. (1978–79). Univ. of Victoria Fac. Assn. **Pubns.:** *Eastward Ho! by Ben Jonson, John Marston and G. Chapman* (1974); *A Critical Old Spelling Edition of the Works of Edward Sharpham.....* (1981); *"Personae:* From Manuscript to Print," *Std. in Bibl.* (D. 1981). **Activities:** 1, 2; 18, 23, 45; 56, 57, 85 **Addr.:** Special Collections, McPherson Library, Victoria, BC V8V 3H5 Canada.

Pettit, Katherine Denshaw (My. 22, 1925, Beaver Falls, PA) Biblgphr., Spec. Cols. Libn., Trinity Univ. Lib., 1979–, Acq. Libn., 1970–78, Serials Libn., 1968–70. **Educ.:** St. Francis Hosp. Sch. of Nursing, 1943–47, Dip.; Univ. of PA, 1949–51, BA (Eng.); Our Lady of the Lake Univ., 1967–68, MSLS. **Orgs.:** ALA. SLA. Bexar LA: Pres.-Elect (1979). TX LA: Dist. 10, Mem. Com. (Ch., 1978–79). Amer. Nurses Assn. SAA. Texas Nurses Assn. AAUP. **Honors:** Trinity Univ. Lib., Srv. to the Univ., 1979. **Pubns.:** Various sps. **Activities:** 1, 2; 23, 38, 45; 55, 57, 85 **Addr.:** Trinity University Library, San Antonio, TX 78284.

Pettitt, Kenneth I. (F. 3, 1929, Berkeley, CA) Supvsg. Libn., Ref. Srvs., CA State Lib., 1980–, Supvsg. Libn., CA Sect., 1972–80, Supvsg. Libn., Admin. Legis. Ref. Srv., 1962–71, Legis. Ref. Libn., 1961–62, Admin. Ref. Libn., 1961; Libn. 7, Sr. Ref. Asst., Resrch. Asst., Yale Univ. Lib. 1958–61, Libn. 6, Microtext Rm., 1956–58; Libn. 1, Docum. Dept., Univ. of CA, Berkeley, 1954–56. **Educ.:** Univ. of CA, Berkeley, 1946–50, AB (Eng.), 1953–54, BLS. **Orgs.:** SLA. SAA. Socty. of CA Archvsts. Oral Hist. Assn. CA Heritage Prsrvn. Comsn.: Vice-Ch. (1978–80). **Activities:** 13; 15, 39, 49-ILL; 73 **Addr.:** 2909 Hillegass Ave., Berkeley, CA 94705.

Pettus, Eloise S. (Ja. 19, 1926, Jackson, MS) Asst. Prof., Sam Houston State Univ., 1978–; Libn., Kenwood Sch., 1975–77; Libn., NortNorton Park Sch., 1965–74, Tchr., 1963–65. **Educ.:** MS Coll., 1942–45, AB (Mod. Lang.); Emory Univ., 1970–72, MLn (LS); FL State Univ., 1974–77, PhD (LS). **Orgs.:** ALA. TX LA. SWLA. AALS. Various other orgs. TX Assn. of Coll. Tchrs. AAUP. AAUW. **Activities:** 10, 11; 20, 21, 26; 65, 90 **Addr.:** Library Science Dept., Sam Houston State University, P.O. Box 2236, SHSU Station, Huntsville, TX 77341.

Peurye, Lloyd Martin (N. 12, 1949, Chicago, IL) Corporate Resrch. Dir., Eastman and Beaudine, Inc., 1980–; Dir. of Resrch., Mgr. of Resrch. Dept., Marquis Who's Who, Inc., 1976–80, Resrch. Libn., 1974–76. **Educ.:** Univ. of IL, Chicago, 1967–71, BA (Hist.); Rosary Coll., 1972–74, MALS. **Orgs.:** SLA. ALA: ACRL. **Activities:** 12; 17, 37, 41 **Addr.:** 4935 W. Crain St., Skokie, IL 60077.

Peyton, Anne (S. 12, 1946, Elizabethton, TN) Asst. to Dir., Major Gifts, Campaign for Dartmouth, 1981–; Asst. Branch Libn., Dartmouth Coll., 1977–81, Ref. Libn., 1977; Media Resrcs. Adv., Hampshire Coll., 1972–77. **Educ.:** Amer. Univ., 1967–68, BA (Soclgy.); Syracuse Univ., 1970–72, MSLS; Med. LA, 1976, Cert.; ARL, 1978, Consult. Trng. Prog. **Orgs.:** Med. LA. New Eng. Reg. Med. Lib. Srv.: Educ. Com. N. Atl. Hlth. Sci. Libs.: Educ. Com. Ch. Cornish Rescue Squad. Natl. Registry, Emergency Med. Tech. **Activities:** 1, 12; 17, 24, 25; 58, 80, 92 **Addr.:** Campaign for Dartmouth, Dartmouth College, Hanover, NH 03755.

Pfaff, Eugene Edwin, Jr. (Mr. 29, 1948, Greensboro, NC) Oral Hist. and Ref. Libn., Greensboro (NC) Pub. Lib., 1975–; Ext. and Ref. Libn., Wake Cnty. (NC) Pub. Libs., 1974; Ref. Libn., Morris Harvey Coll., 1973. **Educ.:** Univ. of NC, Greensboro, 1967–70, BA (Hist.), 1970–71, MA (Hist.); Univ. of NC, Chapel Hill, 1972–73, MSLS. **Orgs.:** NC LA. SELA. **Pubns.:** "Educational Brokering Agencies: A New Service to the Public," *Southeast. Libn.* (Win. 1978); "Oral History: A New Challenge for Public Libraries," *Wilson Lib. Bltn.* (My. 1980). **Activities:** 9; 16, 39, 41; 50, 86 **Addr.:** Greensboro Public Library, Drawer X-4, Greensboro, NC 27402.

Pfaffenberger, Ann (Jl. 16, 1941, Clarkesville, AR) Coord. of Extramural Srvs., TX Coll. of Osteopathic Med., 1979–; Asst. Ref. Libn., TX Christ. Univ., 1978–79; Ref. Libn., Engin. and Phys. Sci. Lib., Univ. of MD, 1977–78; Sr. Catlgr.,

Special Subjects/Services: 50. Adult educ.; 51. Advert./Mktg.; 52. Aerosp.; 53. Agric.; 54. Area std.; 55. Arts/Hum.; 56. Autom.; 57. Bibl./Prtg.; 58. Bio. sci.; 59. Bus./Fin.; 60. Chem.; 61. Copyrt.; 62. Documtn.; 63. Educ.; 64. Engin.; 65. Env.; 66. Eth. grps.; 67. Film; 68. Food/Nutr.; 69. Geneal.; 70. Geo.; 71. Geol.; 72. Handcpd.; 73. Hist.; 74. Int. frdm.; 75. Info. sci.; 76. Insr.; 77. Law; 78. Legis.; 79. Math./Comp. sci.; 80. Med.; 81. Metals; 82. Nat. resrcs.; 83. Newsp.; 84. Nuc. sci.; 85. Oral hist.; 86. Petr./Energy; 87. Pharm.; 88. Phys./Astr./Math.; 89. Readg.; 90. Relig.; 91. Sci./Tech.; 92. Soc. sci.; 93. Telecom.; 94. Transp.; 95. (other).

Div. for the Blind and Phys. Handcpd., Lib. of Congs., 1976; Lib. Spec., George Washington Univ., 1975–76. **Educ.:** CA State Polytech. Univ., 1959–64, BS (Home Ec. Ed.); Univ. of Pittsburgh, 1974–75, MLS. **Orgs.:** ALA. TX LA. N.E. TX OLUG. **Honors:** Beta Phi Mu. **Pubns.:** "Substitution of SCISEARCH and SOCIAL SCISEARCH for Their Print Versions in an Academic Library," *Data Base* (Mr. 1980). **Activities:** 1; 24, 27, 39; 56, 64, 80 **Addr.:** 2323 Edwin St., Fort Worth, TX 76110.

Pfann, Mary L. (Ag. 11, 1922, Omaha, NE) Libn., RCA Astro-Electronics Lib., 1973–; Ref. Libn., Resrch. Info. Srvs., Rutgers Univ., 1973; Pres., Bd. of Trustees, Bedminster-Far Hills Pub. Lib., 1970–71, Actg. Libn., 1969. **Educ.:** Univ. of Omaha, 1939–43, BA (Chem.); Rutgers Univ., 1971–73, MLS. **Orgs.:** SLA. AAAS: Info., Comp. and Comm. (Secy.). **Activities:** 9, 12; 17, 39, 47; 52, 64, 93 **Addr.:** RCA Astro-Electronics Library, Box 800, Princeton, NJ 08540.

Pfarrer, Theodore (Ted) R. (Je. 13, 1928, New York City, NY) Online Srch. Coord., Univ. of Ctrl. FL, 1978–; Resident Ctr. Coord., FL Tech. Univ., 1976–78; Asst. Dir., Leesburg Pub. Lib., 1976. **Educ.:** FL Tech. Univ., 1972–74, BSBA (Finance); FL State Univ., 1974–75, MSLS, 1981, Advnc. MS. **Orgs.:** ELA: Spec. Lib. Sect. (Ch. Elect., 1981–82); Awds. com. (1979–80). FL LA: Cit. and Awds. Com. (Ch., 1978–79); Online Srchrs. Caucus (Ch., 1979–80). SLA. Ctrl. FL Libns. Air Force Aid Socty. Air Force Sergeants Assn. **Honors:** Phi Kappa Phi; Beta Phi Mu. **Activities:** 1; 15, 39, 41; 59, 77, 80 **Addr.:** 2493 Whitehall Cir., Winter Park, FL 32792.

Pfau, Julia G. (Ap. 15, 1924, Mobile, AL) Cat. Libn., Lister Hill Lib. of the Hlth. Sci., Univ. of AL, Birmingham, 1973–, Asst. Catlgr., 1973. **Educ.:** Univ. of AL, 1940–44, AB (Soclgy.), 1971–72, MLS. **Orgs.:** Med. LA: Cert. Examination Review Com. (1979); Murray Gottlieb Prize Subcom. (Ch., 1982); Hons. and Awds. Com. (Ch., 1981–82). SELA. AL LA: Pubns. Com. (1979–80); Mem. Com.; CUS Com. (Ch., 1977). Hlth. Sci. OCLC User Grp. AL Hlth. Libs. Assn. Friends of Ballet UAB. **Honors:** Beta Phi Mu, 1974. **Pubns.:** Various sps. **Activities:** 1, 5; 20; 80, 95-Dentistry. **Addr.:** 4100 Crescent Rd., Birmingham, AL 35222.

Pfeffer, Anne Kalichman (F. 24, 1947, Bergen-Belsen, Germany) Head Libn., Charles E. Smith Jewish Day Sch. of Washington, 1980–; Head Libn., Hebrew Acad. of Washington, 1977–80; Acq. Libn., Undergrad. Lib., Cornell Univ., 1969–71. **Educ.:** Hunter Coll., 1964–67, BA (Pol. Sci.); Cornell Univ., 1967–68, MAT (Hist.); Syracuse Univ., 1968–70, MLS. **Orgs.:** AJL. Cncl. of Jewish Libns. of Grt. Washington. Assn. of Indp. Sch. Libns. **Activities:** 1, 10; 15, 21 **Addr.:** Charles E. Smith Jewish Day School of Washington, 1901 E. Jefferson St., Rockville, MD 20852.

Pfeifer, Ruth-Ann F. (Mr. 26, 1927, Wuppertal, Germany) Head, Grmn. Sect., Shared Cat. Div., Lib. of Congs., 1966–; Asst. Head Catlgr., Univ. of WI, Milwaukee, 1965–66; Catlgr., Univ. of Chicago, 1961–65; Catlgr., Loyola Univ., 1957–61. **Educ.:** Univ. of Dubuque, 1949–51, BA (Eng. Lit.); Marquette Univ., 1951–56, MA (Eng. Lit.); Univ. of Chicago, 1959–61, MA (LS). **Activities:** 4; 20 **Addr.:** 3003 Van Ness St., N.W., Washington, DC 20008.

Pfeister, Susan Selby (My. 8, 1947, Trenton, NJ) Instr., Columbia Univ., 1979–; Ref. libn., McGraw-Hill, Inc., 1974–79; Ref. Supvsr., Enoch Pratt Free Lib., 1973–74; Ref. Libn., Univ. of IL Lib., 1971–73. **Educ.:** Univ. of IL, 1965–69, BA (Russ.), 1969–71, MS (LS); Columbia Univ., 1981, DLS; various crs. **Orgs.:** SLA. **Honors:** Beta Phi Mu. **Activities:** 12; 26, 29, 39; 51, 59 **Addr.:** 73 Kensington Rd., Bronxville, NY 10708.

Pfister, Fred C. (Ap. 10, 1930, Great Falls, MT) Assoc. Prof., Dept. of Lib. Std., Univ. of S. FL, 1976–; Assoc. Prof., N. TX State Univ., 1974–76; Assoc. Prof., TX Woman's Univ., 1973–74; Assoc. Prof., West. KY Univ., 1970–73. **Educ.:** North. MT Coll., 1948–56, BA (Soc. Sci., Educ.); Univ. of MI, 1960–70, MA, PhD (LS). **Orgs.:** ALA: AASL. AALS. Southeastern LA. FL Assn. for Media in Educ.: Bd. of Dir. (1980–83). Various orgs. **Honors:** Beta Phi Mu; Phi Delta Kappa. **Pubns.:** *School District Professional Libraries in Michigan* (1970); jt. auth., "The Undergraduate Student: An Opportunity and Obligation," *Jnl. of Educ. for Libnshp.* (Fall 1975); jt. auth., "Exceptions to Regular Admissions in Accredited Library School Programs," *Jnl. of Educ. for Libnshp.* (Spr. 1980); jt. auth., "Student Book Collection Contests in American Colleges and Universities," *Coll. and Resrch. Libs.* (Jl. 1980); "Kentucky Sub-Committee on Certification of School Media Libraries," *KY LA Bltn.* (Win. 1973); various articles. **Activities:** 10, 11; 17, 32, 35; 63 **Addr.:** 2518 Campus Hill Dr., Tampa, FL 33612.

Pflueger, Kenneth E. (Ap. 22, 1949, Omaha, NE) Dir., Lib. Srvs., Concordia Theo. Semy., 1980–, Assoc. Dir., 1976–80; Per. Libn., Cmnty. Coll. of Baltimore, 1975–76; Per. Libn., Maricopa Tech. Cmnty. Coll., 1974–75; Head, Circ. Dept., Univ. of MD, Baltimore Cnty. Campus, 1972–74. **Educ.:** Valpariaso Univ., 1969–71, BA (Theo.); AZ State Univ., 1974–75, MAE (Educ.); Concordia Theo. Semy., 1977–79, MDiv (Theo.); West. MI Univ., 1980–81, MLS. **Orgs.:** IN Coop. Lib. Srv. Athrty.: Bd. of Dirs. Area III, Area Lib. Srv. Athty.: Exec. Com. (Secy.). ATLA. ALA. **Pubns.:** Various relig. bk. reviews, *Lib. Jnl.* (1980–). **Activities:** 1; 56, 90, 92 **Addr.:** 3 Wycliffe Pl., Fort Wayne, IN 46825.

Pflueger, Margaret Lois (Ap. 12, 1916, Franklin Furnace, OH) Deputy Asst. Mgr. for Info. Srvs., US Dept. of Energy Tech. Info. Ctr., 1979–; Chief, Ref. Branch, US Energy Resrch. and Dev. Admin., Tech. Info. Ctr., 1972–79; Asst. Chief, Tech. Srvs. Branch, US Atomic Energy Comsn., Tech. Info. Ctr., 1967–72, Ref. Libn., 1948–67; Cat., Army Lib., Washington, DC, 1945–48; Libn., Metallurgical Proj. Lib., Univ. of Chicago, 1944–45. **Educ.:** Capital Univ., 1935–37, BA (Fr.); OH State Univ., 1940–41, MA (Fr.); Univ. of Chicago, 1942–43, BLS. **Orgs.:** SLA: Oak Ridge Chap. (Pres., 1958–59); Bylaws Com. (Ch., 1968). ASIS: Stan. Com. (Ch., 1974–76). Frnds. of the Oak Ridge Pub. Lib.: Pres. (1977–78). **Honors:** U.S. Atomic Energy Comsn., Superior Performance Awd., 1965. **Pubns.:** "Recent Technical Information Activities of the US Atomic Energy Commission," *Spec. Libs.* (Mr. 1957); "Availability of Research and Development Reports," *Literature of Nuclear Science: Its Management and Use* (1962); "Bibliographic Control of Conference Literature," *Spec. Libs.* (Ap. 1964); "Dissemination of AEC Technical Information Outside the United States," *UNESCO Bltn. for Libs.* (Jl. 1964). **Activities:** 4; 17, 39; 91 **Addr.:** US Department of Energy, Technical Information Center, P.O. Box 62, Oak Ridge, TN 37830.

Phelan, Daniel Frank (Ap. 2, 1947, Charleston, WV) Ref. Libn., Coord. Dafoe Comp. Srch. Srvs., Elizabeth Dafoe Lib., Ref. and Dafoe Col., Univ. of MB, 1977–; Ref., AV Libn., Undergrad. Lib., McGill Univ., 1974–77. **Educ.:** WV Univ., 1965–72, BA (Hist.); McGill Univ., 1972–74, MLS. **Orgs.:** ALA. Can. LA. MB OLUG. MB LA: Dir. (1979–80); Bltn. Ed. (1980–81); Nsltr. Ed. (1978–79). **Pubns.:** "Word Processing in Libraries," *MB LA Bltn.* (Je. 1980); "As Others See Us–Image of Librarians in the Media," *MB LA Bltn.* (D. 1980). **Activities:** 1; 31, 39; 56, 67, 92 **Addr.:** University of Manitoba Libraries, Winnipeg, MB R3T 2N2 Canada.

Phelan, Jody (S. 7, 1946, Brooklyn, NY) Dean, TX Woman's Univ., Sch. of LS, 1977–; Supvsr. of Pub. Srvs., Mesquite Pub. Lib., 1972–76. **Educ.:** Cap. Univ., 1964–68, BA (Educ.); TX Woman's Univ., 1971–73, MLS. **Orgs.:** ALA: Hosplty. Com. (Co-Ch., 1979); PLA, Conf. Prog. Com. (1982–84). TX LA: Exhibits Com. (1982). Dallas Cnty. LA. ASIS. **Honors:** Beta Phi Mu. **Activities:** 9, 11; 25, 26, 39; 56, 63, 75 **Addr.:** Texas Woman's University, School of Library Science, Box 22905, Denton, TX 76204.

Phelps, John M. (Mr. 30, 1920, Cold Spring, NY) Coord., Instr. Mtrls. Ctrs., Sweet Home HS, 1958–; Part-time Instr., Canisius Coll., 1959–63; Part-time Instr., SUNY, Buffalo, 1959; Libn., Canisius Coll. 1947–58; Libn., Roswell Park Meml. Inst., 1946–47. **Educ.:** Canisius Coll., 1937–41, AB (Eng.); Columbia Univ., 1945–46, MLS; Canisius Coll., 1948–50, MA (Eng.); SUNY, Buffalo, 1958, (Educ., LS). **Orgs.:** Sch. Libns. Assn. of W. NY. West. NY Educ. Comm. ALA. NYSUT. Sweet Home Educ. Assn. **Honors:** Phi Delta Kappa. **Activities:** 1, 10; 15, 17, 24; 55, 61, 75 **Addr.:** 114 Moore Ave., Buffalo NY 14223.

Phelps, Jonathan O. (D. 7, 1948, Holden, MA) Catlgr., Univ. of MA Med. Ctr., 1976–. **Educ.:** Leicester Jr. Coll., 1969–71, AA (Liberal Arts); New England Coll., 1971–73, BA (Hist.); FL State Univ., 1974–75, MSLS. **Orgs.:** ALA. MLA. Natl. Trust for Hist. Prsrvn. **Activities:** 1, 12; 20; 58, 80 **Addr.:** 36 Walnut Terr., Holden, MA 01520.

Phelps, Lillie Mae (O. 3, 1933, Sinton, TX) Head Libn., Lakeview Elem. Sch., 1974–; Libn., Blue Ridge Elem. Sch., 1973–74; Libn., Dulles HS, 1972–73, Eng. Tchr., 1960–72. **Educ.:** SW TX State Tchrs. Coll., 1950–54, BA (Eng.); Sam Houston State Univ., 1974–75, MLS; Prof. Tchrs. Cert.; Provisional Lib. Cert. **Orgs.:** TX LA: Chld. RT (Secy./Treas., 1978–79). ALA. TX Assn. of Sch. Libns. SWLA. TX State Tchrs. Assn.: Exec. Com. (1968–69). Delta Kappa Gamma Socty.: Secy.-Treas. (1978–79). Classrm. Tchrs. Assn. Ord. of the East. Star. **Honors:** **Activities:** 10; 21 **Addr.:** 2414 Lazy Ln., Rosenberg, TX 77471.

Phelps, Ralph Huyett (Jl. 5, 1905, Monmouth, IL) Libn. St. Andrews Presbyterian Church, Lib., 1969–; Dir., Engin. Socty. Lib., 1946–68; Libn. War Metallurgy Com., Natl. Acad. of Sci., Natl. Resrch. Cncl., 1943–45; Tech. Libn., Birmingham Pub. Lib., 1940–42. **Educ.:** Monmouth Coll., 1923–28, BS (Chem.); Carnegie Inst. of Tech., 1934–38, BS (LS). **Orgs.:** ALA. SLA: Treas. (1962–64). Church and Synagogue LA. AAAS: Fellow (1956–68). Engin. Indx.: Bd. of Dir. (1955–68); VP (1956–62); Pres. (1962–68). Amer. Stan. Assn.: Z–39 Com. on Standardization in Lib. Wk. and Documtn. (Ch., 1954–55). **Pubns.:** "Service to Industry by Professional and Trade Association Libraries," *Lib. Trends* (Ja. 1966); "Engineering Bibliography," *Lib. Trends* (Ap. 1967); "Engineering Information–All is Not Lost," *Mech. Engin.* (D. 1958). **Activities:** 9, 12; 17, 30, 39; 64, 81, 91 **Addr.:** 1474 Fairway Dr., Dunedin, FL 33528.

Phelps, Thomas C. (Ag. 18, 1944, Salt Lake City, UT) Asst. Dir., Div. of Pub. Progs., Natl. Endow. for Hum., 1980–; Deputy Dir., Salt Lake City Pub. Lib., 1975–80, Adult Srvs. Coord., 1972–78, Dir., PR, 1968–72. **Educ.:** UT State Univ., 1964–68, BFA (Thea. Arts); Univ. of OR, 1972, MLS; Univ. of Denver, 1974, Cert. (Bibl. Retrieval). **Orgs.:** ALA: Lib. Admin. Div., PR Com. (1969–72); SRRT; Clearinghouse Ed. (1971–74). UT LA: various coms. (1969–). NCLIS: Eth. Minorities Com. (1980–). Cnsrtm. for Pub. Lib. Innovation: Natl. Coord. (1976–79). **Pubns.:** *User and Non User Study* (1974); "Independent Study Project," *Forcast* (N. 1975); "PR Design and Community Resources," *Pac. NW. Qtly.* (Spr. 1972). **Activities:** 3, 9; 16, 24, 28; 50, 55 **Addr.:** National Endowment for the Humanities, 806 15th St., N.W., MS 406, Washington, DC 20506.

Philbrick, John A (III) Pres., Bd. of Trustees, Free Lib. of Philadelphia, 1978–, VP, Bd. of Trustees, Treas. **Educ.:** Yale Univ. 1949, BA. **Orgs.:** ALA. PA LA. **Honors:** Orpheus Club, Pres.; Assurex Int'l, Past Pres. **Addr.:** C/O H. C. Knight and Co., 320 Walnut St., Philadelphia, PA 19106.

Philippsen, John Joseph (N. 24, 1915, Milwaukee, WI) Serials Bibl. Consult., Univ. of Notre Dame, Meml. Lib., 1979–, Head, Acq. Dept., 1960–78, Asst. Head, 1957–59; Instr., Marquette Univ., Dept. of Mod. Lang., 1954–57; Lib. Asst., Marquette Univ. Lib., 1948–51. **Educ.:** George Washington Univ., 1937–42, Jr. Coll. Cert.; Marquette Univ., 1945–47, PhB (Grmn., Fr.); Univ. of WA, 1947–48, BA (Libnshp.); Marquette Univ., Grad. Sch., 1954–57, MA (Grmn.); various crs. **Orgs.:** ALA: ACRL; RTSD; LITA. State Hist. Socty. of WI. Knights of Columbus. John Henry Newman Hon. Socty. **Honors:** Delta Phi Alpha; Phi Eta Sigma. **Pubns.:** *Library Science Abstracts*; transl. of articles in *Zentralblatt für Bibliothekswesen* in abs. (1965–67). **Activities:** 1; 15, 44; 55, 56 **Addr.:** Memorial Library, University of Notre Dame, Notre Dame, IN 46556.

Phillips, Ann G. (Je. 17, 1929, Jackson, MI) Head, Hum. and Fine Arts Dept., King Lib., Miami Univ., 1978–; Ref. Libn., Auburn Univ., 1972–74; Med. Libn., Penrose Hosp., 1970–72. **Educ.:** MI State Univ., 1949–51, BS (Home Econ.); Univ. of CT, 1956–58, MA (Educ.); Univ. of Denver, 1966–68, MA (LS). **Orgs.:** Acad. LA of OH. **Honors:** Beta Phi Mu. **Activities:** 1; 17, 39; 55, 75 **Addr.:** King Library, Miami University, Oxford, OH 45056.

Phillips, Brian F. (Mr. 9, 1930, New Westminster, BC) Head, Soc. Sci. Div., Simon Fraser Univ. Lib., 1965–; Libn. I, Vancouver Pub. Lib., 1963–65; Libn., Toronto Pub. Lib., 1955–57. **Educ.:** Univ. of BC, 1948–53, BA (Hist.); Toronto Univ., 1953–54, BLS. **Orgs.:** SLA: Geo. and Map Div. (Ch., 1976–77); By-Laws Com. (1978–82). Can. LA. BC LA. Royal Astronomical Socty. of Can. **Pubns.:** "Computer-produced Map Catalogs," *Drexel Lib. Qtly.* (O. 1973); "Filling in the Map. Maps and Mapping in British Columbia Since 1850," *BC Lib. Qtly.* (O. 1971). **Activities:** 1; 39; 70, 92 **Addr.:** Simon Fraser University Library, Burnaby, BC V5A 1S6 Canada.

Phillips, Carol B. (Ap. 4, 1945, Ontario, OR) Head Ref. Libn., Univ. of TX Med. Branch, Moody Med. Lib., 1980–, Data Base Coord., 1977–80; Ref. Libn., Srch. Anal., Houston Acad. of Med., TX Med. Ctr. Lib., 1974–77; Ext. Libn., Univ. of TX Med. Branch, Moody Med. Lib., 1972–74; Pub. Srvs. Libn., Vanderbilt Med. Ctr. Lib., 1969–72. **Educ.:** OR State Univ., 1965–67, BS (Educ.); Univ. of OK, 1968–69, MLS. **Orgs.:** SLA. Med. LA. **Activities:** 1, 12; 17, 39; 58, 80 **Addr.:** Moody Medical Library, The University of TX Medical Branch, Galveston, TX 77550.

Phillips, Charles A. (S. 28, 1937, Baltimore, MD) Biling. Libn., James F. Oyster Biling. Sch., 1973–. **Educ.:** Univ. of Pittsburgh, 1957–60, BA (Econ.); Univ. of MD, 1970–72, BA (LS, Educ.), 1972–73, MLS. **Orgs.:** Reforma. Amer. Socty. for Aerosp. Educ. **Honors:** Meyer Fndn., DC Pub. Schs., CBC Exemplary Prac., 1977. **Activities:** 4, 10; 21, 24, 45; 52, 66, 74 **Addr.:** 13010 N. Commons Way, Potomac, MD 20854.

Phillips, Clifford R. (Jl. 24, 1944, Los Angeles, CA) Head, Tech. Srvs., City of Inglewood Pub. Lib., 1971–. **Educ.:** Univ. of CA, Los Angeles, 1966–68, BA (Hist.), 1970–71, MLS, 1975–80, MBA (Integrative Mgt.). **Orgs.:** ALA. CA LA. South. CA Tech. Prcs. Grp.: Secy.-Treas. (1981–82). CA Socty. of Libns. UCLA Grad. Sch. of Mgt. Assn. **Pubns.:** *Formats Used in the Library Multimedia Union Catalog* (1979); jt. auth., *Library Technical Procsses Procedures* (1972). **Activities:** 9; 17, 46; 59, 75 **Addr.:** Inglewood Public Library, 101 W. Manchester Blvd., Inglewood, CA 90301.

Phillips, Don (F. 18, 1930, Brinkman, OK) Catlgr., Univ. of CA, Los Angeles, 1979–, Asst. Msc. Libn., 1976–78; Asst. Msc. Libn., Univ. of IL, 1973–75; Msc. Libn., North. IL Univ., 1968–73; Libn., Cary-Grove Sr. HS, 1967–68. **Educ.:** TX Tech. Coll., 1947–51, BA (Hist.); North. IL Univ., 1966–68, MA (LS); Univ. of IL, 1969–73, Cert. Adv. Std. (LS). **Orgs.:** Msc. LA: Mem. Com. (Ch., 1973–78); Admin. Com. (1967–71); Midwest Chap., Secy. (1969–71), Prog. Ch. (1970); South. CA, Chap., Nsltr. Co-ed. (1977–78); Pubn. Com. (Ch., 1977). LA of the Univ. of CA. Natl. Educ. Assn. Natl. Cncl. of Tchrs. of Eng. **Pubns.:** *A Selected Bibliography of Music Librarianship* (1974); *A Bibliography of Creativity* (1970); *A Preliminary Directory of Music Librarians in the U.S. and Canada* (1976); *An Expandable Classification Scheme for Phonorecord Libraries* (1969); *The*

PROFESSIONAL ACTIVITIES: Institutions: 1. Acad. lib.; 2. Arch.; 3. Assn.; 4. Fed./Gvt. lib.; 5. Inst. lib.; 6. Mfr./Suppl.; 7. Milit. lib.; 8. Musm.; 9. Pub. lib.; 10. Sch. lib.; 11. Sch. of lib. sci.; 12. Spec. lib.; 13. State lib.; 14. (other). **Functions/Activities:** 15. Acq./Col. dev.; 16. Adult srvs.; 17. Admin.; 18. Apprais.; 19. Archit./Bldgs.; 20. Cat./Class.; 21. Chld. srvs.; 22. Circ.; 23. Cons./Pres.; 24. Consult.; 25. Cont. ed.; 26. Educ. lib. sci.; 27. Ext. srvs.; 28. Fund/Grants; 29. Gvt. pubs.; 30. Indx./Abs.; 31. Instr. lib. use; 32. Media srvs.; 33. Micro.; 34. Netwks./Coop.; 35. Persnl.; 36. PR; 37. Publshg.; 38. Recs. mgt.; 39. Ref. srvs.; 40. Repro.; 41. Resrch.; 42. Review.; 43. Secur.; 44. Serials; 45. Spec. col.; 46. Tech. srvs.; 47. Trustees/Bds.; 48. YA srvs.; 49. (other).

Sound of Music in Illinois Libraries (1972). **Activities:** 1, 10; 15, 17, 20, 39, 46; 55 **Addr.:** 10938 Barman Ave., Culver City, CA 90230.

Phillips, Donna M. (My. 29, 1942, Vermillion, SD) Dir., Hlth. Sci. Lib., Marian Hlth. Ctr., 1977–; Sch. of Nursing Libn., St. Joseph Mercy Hosp., 1974–77. **Educ.:** Wayne State Coll., 1969–72, BA (Eng.); Emporia State Coll., 1973–74, ML (Libnshp.). **Orgs.:** Med. LA. Siouxland Hlth. Sci. Lib. Cnsrtm.: Coord. (1976–). **Pubns.:** Ed. Bd., *Basic Library Management for Health Science Librarians* (forthcoming). **Activities:** 5, 12; 17, 19, 34; 68, 80, 92 **Addr.:** Health Science Library, Marian Health Center, 2101 Court St., Sioux City, IA 57104.

Phillips, Edith B. (Mr. 24, 1921, Shelby, MI) Assoc. Prof., Div. of Lib. Sci., Wayne State Univ., 1968–; Bk. Sel. Coord., MI State Lib., 1968–68, Head, Cat. Sect., 1962–65; Asst. Sch. Libn., Grandville (MI) Pub. Sch. 1958–62; Asst. Dir., Cat., Kent Cnty. (MI) Lib. Syst., 1953–55. **Educ.:** East. MI Univ., 1938–42, BA (Eng., Educ.); Univ. of MI, 1946–49, AMLS. **Orgs.:** ALA: RTSD, Com. on Educ. for Resrcs. and Tech. Srvs. (1976–78); PLA, Cat. Needs of Pub. Libs. Com. (1977–79). MI LA: Tech. Srvs. Sect., (Ch. Elect, 1972; Secty.-Treas., 1954–55). Women's Natl. Bk. Assn.: Detroit Chap., (Pres., 1977–79). AALL. WHCOLIS. Leag. of Women Voters: MI State Bd., 1971–73; Southfield Pres. (1974–75). Amer. Cvl. Liberties Un. **Honors:** Kappa Delta Pi, 1942; Pi Gamma Mu, 1942. **Pubns.:** Co-ed., *Background Readings in Building Library Collections* (1979); *Management and Use of State Documents in Indiana* (1970); "The Cellar Book Shop," *LEADS* (Je. 1977); various reviews. **Activities:** 11; 15, 20, 46; 61, 74 **Addr.:** Division of Library Science, 315 Kresge Library, Wayne State University, Detroit, MI 48202.

Phillips, Frances M. (S. 3, 1924, Iuka, KS) Chief Libn., Grace Hosp. Div., Harper-Grace Hosps., 1979–, Asst. Libn., 1971–79. **Educ.:** Wayne State Univ., 1961–64, BS (Educ.), 1965–70, MSLS; Med. LA, 1974, Cert. (Med. Libn.). **Orgs.:** Med. LA. SLA. Metro. Detroit Med. Lib. Grp.: Participating Lib. Adv. Com. (1980–81). Ward Presby. Church of Livonia: Chancel Choir. **Honors:** Pi Lambda Theta, 1964. **Activities:** 12; 15, 17, 39; 80 **Addr.:** 562 25556 Shiawassee, Southfield, MI 48034.

Phillips, Janet C. (Ap. 29, 1933, Pittsfield, IL) Asst. Ed., AALS, Exec. Secy., 1970–; Asst. Ed., Univ. of IL Lib., 1954–61, Ed. Asst., PR, 1952–54; Rpt., *Quincy Herald Whig,* 1951–54. **Educ.:** Univ. of IL, 1950–54, BS (Jnlsm.). **Addr.:** 471 Park Ln., State College, PA 16801.

Phillips, Jerry Clyde (F. 10, 1943, Shreveport, LA) Asst. Tech. Srvs. Libn., Univ. of NM, Sch. of Law Lib., 1974–; Visit. Libn., Coleg Harlech, Harlech, N. Wales, 1972–73; AV, Msc. Cat., Plymouth State Coll., 1969–74. **Educ.:** Brigham Young Univ., 1961–64, BA (Lit.); LA State Univ., 1967–69, MS (LS); Univ. of NM, 1974–79, MA (Geo.). **Orgs.:** AALL: Cat. and Class. Com. (1976–80). The Soclgy. of Wales Grp. **Pubns.:** "The Use of the Welsh Language as a Measurement of the Dimensions of Welshness" (1979). **Activities:** 1, 12; 20, 41, 44; 54, 70, 77 **Addr.:** Star Rt., Box 375, Placitas, NM 87043.

Phillips, Linda L. (Je. 12, 1937, Baltimore, MD) Tech. Info. Coord., Rochester Gas and Electric Corp., 1976–; Asst. Chld. Libn., Avon Free Lib., 1976; Nursery Sch. Tchr., Dir., Avon Un. Methodist Church, 1972–75. **Educ.:** SUNY, Geneseo, 1974–75, BA (Eng.), 1975–76, MLS; Microfilm Info. Syst. 1979, Con. Ed. Cert. **Orgs.:** SLA. Natl. Micro. Assn. Rochester Reg. Resrch. Lib. Cncl.: Engin. Stan. Com., Union List of Serials Com. (1979). Rochester OLUG: Producer of ROUG Dir. Standardized Nuclear Unit Power Plants Syst.: Rec. Mgt. Com. (1977–79; Ch., 1979). Nuclear Recs. Mgt. Assn. **Honors:** Sigma Tau Delta, 1975. **Pubns.:** "The New Look in Libraries–RG&E's Technical Information Center," *RG and E News* (Ja.–F. 1979); review clmn., *RG and E News,* 1979–. **Activities:** 12; 17, 38, 39; 64, 84, 91 **Addr.:** Rochester Gas and Electric Corporation, 89 East Ave., Rochester, NY 14649.

Phillips, Linda Lucille (Jl. 11, 1947, OH) Head, Undergrad. Lib. Ref. Dept., Assoc. Prof., Univ. of TN, 1977–; Libn., Agr. Tech. Inst., OH State Univ., 1972–77, Asst. Head, Quick Editing Div., 1971–72, Cat., Spec. Purchases Proc. Unit, 1970–71. **Educ.:** WV Univ., 1965–69, AB (Eng.); Rutgers Univ., 1969–70, MLS. **Orgs.:** ALA: ACRL/Sci. and Tech. Sect. (Secty., 1977–78), Bylaws Com. (Ch., 1978–79), Nom. Com. (Ch., 1979–80), Bibl. Instr. Sect., Policy and Plng. Com. (1978–80), Undergrad. Libns. Discuss. Grp. (Ch., 1977–78); RASD. **Honors** Phi Beta Kappa, 1969. **Pubns.:** Jt. Auth., "Comparing Methods for Teaching Use of Periodical Indexes," *Jnl. of Acad. Libnshp.* (Ja. 1979); "Making Library Instruction More Palatable," *Amer. Vocational Jnl.* (Ap. 1977); "The Library–An Ag Teaching Resource," *Agr. Educ.* (Mr. 1975). **Activities:** 1, 10; 17, 31, 39; 58, 65, 91 **Addr.:** UGL Reference Dept., University of TN, Knoxville, TN 37916.

Phillips, Marilyn Payne (S. 26, 1953, Melrose Park, IL) Chld. Libn., W. Belmont Branch, Chicago Pub. Lib., 1979–81, Chld. Libn., Lincoln Park Branch, 1978–79, Chld. Libn., Marshall Sq. Branch, 1976–78. **Educ.:** Univ. of IL, 1971–74, BA (Eng.); Rosary Coll., 1975–77, MALS. **Orgs.:** ALA: ALSC, Intl. Rel. Com. (1979–81). IL LA. **Pubns.:** "A Survey by Kids–for Kids," *Sch. Lib. Jnl.* (S. 1979); various reviews, *Sch. Lib. Jnl.* **Activities:** 9; 21, 42, 48; 67, 89 **Addr.:** 6983 Cornell, University City, MO 63130.

Phillips, Mildred W. (N. 25, 1928, Reform, AL) Exec. Bd., ALA, Pub. Lib. Srv., 1975–; Ch., Trustees and Frnds., AL, 1979–80; Pres., Frnds., Decatur, AL, 1976–78. **Educ.:** Univ. of Montevallo, 1946–50, AB (Hist.). **Orgs.:** AL LA. SELA. ALA. **Activities:** 5, 13; 28, 36, 47; 55, 78 **Addr.:** 2308 Country Club Rd., Decatur, AL 35601.

Phillips, Ray S. (My. 17, 1953, New York NY) Asst. Coord., MO State Lib., 1978–; Libn., Free Lib. of Philadelphia, 1976–78. **Educ.:** St. John's Univ., New York City, 1971–74, BA (Eng. Educ.); Pratt Inst., 1975–76, MLS; 1975, Pub. Libns. Prof. Cert., Tchg. Cert. **Orgs.:** ALA: ASCLA, various com. SLA. Grt. St. Louis Lib. Club. MO LA: Comp. and Info. Tech. Com. (Ch., 1980). Amer. Socty. of Pub. Admin. Assn. for Chld. with Lrng. Disabilities: Bd. of Dir. (1980–82). **Honors:** Lib. of Congs., Intern Nominee, 1976. **Pubns.:** "What's New at Wolfner," *Show-Me Libs.* (My. 1979). **Activities:** 12, 13; 17, 24, 36; 56, 72 **Addr.:** 24 Sylva Ln., Staten Island, NY 10305.

Phillips, Thelma Lee McDaniel (Mr. 27, 1924, Rock Hill, SC) Assoc. Dir., Pub. Srvs., Arlington Pub. Lib., 1978–, Lib. Supvsr., Branches and Ext. Srvs., 1975–78, Ext. Coord., 1973–75; Gillespie Cnty. Libn., Pioneer Meml. Lib., 1966–73; Libn., St. Mary HS, Fredericksburg, TX, 1964–66; Hosp. Libn., Vets. Admin. Hosp., 1950–52; Ref. Libn., Tuskegee Inst., 1946–50. **Educ.:** NC Coll., 1945, AB (Soc. Sci., LS); Univ. of Chicago, 1945–46, BLS. **Orgs.:** ALA. TX LA: Dist. VII, Ch. (1979–80); Ch.-Elect (1973–75). SWLA. Dist. and Area Lib. Assns.: Treas.; Dist. Assn. Pres. Various civic orgs. **Honors:** TX LA, TX Libn. of the Yr., 1971. **Activities:** 1, 9; 17, 27, 35 **Addr.:** Arlington Public Library, 101 E. Abram, Arlington, TX 76010.

Phillips, Theodore D. (Je. 13, 1929, Kansas City, MO) Univ. Libn., Mt. Allison Univ., 1980–; Univ. Libn., Meml. Univ. of NF, 1974–80; Assoc. Libn., Queen's Univ., 1969–74, Asst. Chief Libn., 1967–69; Lib. Mgr., SDD, IBM Corp., San Jose, CA, 1966; Asst. Libn., IBM Corp., Los Gatos, CA, 1963–65; Libn., Fed. Rsv. Bank of Kansas City, MO, 1957–63. **Educ.:** Univ. of NM, 1956, BBA (Bus.); Univ. of Denver, 1956–57, MA (Libnshp.). **Orgs.:** Can. LA. Atl. Prov. LA. **Honors:** SLA, John Cotton Dana Lectr., 1968. **Pubns.:** various articles. **Addr.:** Box 188, Sackville, NB E0A 3C0 Canada.

Phillips, Vicki W. (D. 10, 1945, Okmulgee, OK) Head Docum. Libn., OK State Univ., 1975–, Asst. Soc. Sci. Libn., 1969–75. **Educ.:** OK City Univ., 1964–68, BA (Hist.); Univ. of OK, 1968–69, MLS; OK State Univ., 1970–73, MA (Hist.). **Orgs.:** OK LA: Constn. and Bylaws Com. (1976–79); Ref. Div. (Ch. Elect, 1979–80). ALA. Socty. of Southwest Archvsts. **Honors:** Beta Phi Mu; Phi Kappa Phi; Phi Alpha Theta. **Activities:** 1, 2; 29, 39; 63, 78, 92 **Addr.:** OK State University Library, Stillwater, OK 74078.

Phillips, Virginia (N. 4, 1922, Quantico, MD) Asst. Dir. for Branch Srvs., Univ. of TX, Austin, 1975–; Coord. of Ref. Srvs., Univ. of MD, 1970–75, Soc. Sci. Libn., 1958–70, Asst. Ref. Libn., 1946–57. **Educ.:** West. MD Coll., 1939–43, BA (Econ., Hist.); Emory Univ., 1945–46, BALS; Amer. Univ., 1956–59, MA (U.S. Hist.); Univ. of MD, 1963–69, (U.S. Hist.). **Orgs.:** ALA: ACRL. MD LA: Pres. (1971–72); First VP, Pres.-Elect (1970–71); Coll. and Resrch. Libs. Div. (Ch.-Elect, 1969–70); Fin. Com. (1971–73); Constn. Com. (1972–76); Persnl. Com. (Ch., 1974–75). SWLA. TX LA. **Honors:** Phi Kappa Phi. **Activities:** 1; 17, 39; 92 **Addr.:** Apt. 218, 222 E. Riverside Dr., Austin, TX 78704.

Phillpot, Clive James (Je. 26, 1938, Thornton Heath, Surrey, Eng.) Dir. of Lib., The Musm. of Mod. Art, 1977–; Libn., Chelsea Sch. of Art, London, 1970–77; Libn.-in-Charge, Ctrl. Lending Libs., Hastings Pub. Lib., 1963–70. **Educ.:** Polytech. of N. London, 1964–67, ALA; Univ. of London, 1970–74, Dip. HA. **Orgs.:** The Lib. Assn. (Untd. Kingdom). The Art Libs. Socty. (Untd. Kingdom). Secy. (1970–72); Cncl. (1972–74). The Art Libs. Socty. of N. Amer.: Secty. (1979–81). SLA. Arch. of Amer. Art: Natl. Adv. Com.; Ctr. for Bk. Arts, Bd. of Dir. **Pubns.:** "ARUS/NA–The Art Libraries Society of North America: Present Structure and Some Recent History," *INSPEL* (Ja. 1981). Contrib., *Art Library Manual* (1977); "Chelsea School of Art Library Classification Scheme," *Art Libs. Jnl.* (Sum. 1978); "Art Periodicals, Indexes and Abstracts and Modern Art," *ARLIS Nsltr.* (Je. 1974); *"ARLIS*–The Art Libraries Society," *ARLIS/NA Nsltr.* (F. 1973). **Activities:** 12; 15, 17, 45; 55, 74, 89 **Addr.:** The Museum of Modern Art, 11 W. 53rd St., New York, NY 10019.

Philpott, Emalee Ewing (D. 19, 1921, Charlotte, NC) Media Dir., Thatcher HS, 1955–; Tchr./Libn., Pima Pub. Sch., 1951–55; Tchr., Dunean HS, 1950–51; Chief of Libs., Engin. Resrch. and Dev. Libs., Ft. Belvoir, VA, 1948–50; Catlgr., Indus. Coll. of the Armed Srvs., Natl. War Coll., 1947–48; Ref. Libn., Lib. of Congs., 1945–47; Army and Hosp. Libn., U.S. Army, 1944–45; Libn., Corey Meml. Lib., Oceana, VA, 1943–44. **Orgs.:** ALA: AASL, Com. on Int. Frdm. Rel. and Persnl. (1977–79). AZ LA: *AZ Libn.* Ed. (1961–63); Pres. (1963–64); Int. Frdm. Com. (Ch., 1977–79). AZ Educ. Media Assn. AECT. Various other orgs. Marquis Biog. Lib. Socty. Amer. Biog. Inst. Ord. of the East. Star. Duncan Meth. Church. **Honors:** AZ State Dept. of Educ., AZ Mstr. Tchr., 1971. **Pubns.:** Various articles. **Activities:** 10; 17, 24, 48; 63, 74 **Addr.:** P. O. Box 577, Safford, AZ 85546.

Phinazee, Annette L. Hoage (Jl. 25, 1920, Orangeburg, SC) Dean, Sch. of LS, NC Ctrl. Univ., 1970–; Assoc. Dir., Coop. Coll. Lib. Ctr., Atlanta, 1969–70; Prof., Sch. of Lib. Srv., Atlanta Univ., 1963–69; Head, Spec. Srvs., Trevor Arnett Lib., 1962–67; Asst. Catlgr., South. IL Univ., 1957–62; Asst. Prof., Sch. of Lib Srv., Atlanta Univ., 1946–57; Jnlsm. Libn., Lincoln Univ., 1942–44. **Educ.:** Fisk Univ., 1937–39, BA (Mod. Frgn. Langs.); Univ. of IL, 1941, BSLS, 1948, MSLS; Columbia Univ., 1961, DLS. **Orgs.:** ALA: Stdg. Com. on Lib. Educ. (Ch., 1978–80). AALS: Cncl. of Deans and Dirs. (Ch., 1977). SELA: Treas. (1981–). WHCOLIS: NC Del. (Official Del., Leader, 1979). Various other orgs. AAUP. AAUW. NC Cult. Adv. Cncl. NC Ctrl. Univ. Musm. Bd. Various other orgs. **Honors:** Eno Bus. and Prof. Women's Club, Woman of the Yr., 1976; Phi Beta Sigma, Recog. for Contribs. to Educ., 1976; Durham Cnty. LA, Disting. Lib. Srv. Awd., 1977; ALA, Black Caucus Awd., 1978; other hons. **Pubns.:** *Black Librarians in the Southeast* (forthcoming); jt. cmplr., *Newspapers and Periodicals by and about Black People: Southeastern Holdings* (1978); "Remembrance of Things Past," *NC Libs.* (Fall 1979); "Bench Marks and the Challenges Ahead," *Musings* (1979); "Centralized Library Purchasing and Technical Processing for Six Colleges in Alabama and Mississippi: A Report," *Coll. & Resrch. Libs.* (Jl. 1969); various articles. **Activities:** 46; 63, 66 **Addr.:** School of Library Science, North Carolina Central University, 1801 Fayetteville St., Durham, NC 27707.

Phinney, Hartley K., Jr. (N. 15, 1938, Ames, IA) Dir., Lib., CO Sch. of Mines, 1977–; Chief, Ref. and Circ., U.S. Geol. Srvy., 1974–77; Supvsr., Chevron Oil Fld. Resrch. Co., 1970–74; Geol., Bio. Libn., Princeton Univ., 1966–70. **Educ.:** Univ. of CT, 1960, BA (Geol.); Univ. of Pittsburgh, 1966, MLS; various crs., sems. **Orgs.:** Amer. Geol. Inst.: Bd. of Gvrs. (1974). Ctrl. CO Lib. Syst.: Bd. of Dirs. (1978–); Ch. (1980–81). CO Alliance of Resrch. Libs.: Ch. (1980–81). CO Cncl. of Acad. Libs.: Ch. (1979–80). Various other orgs. Geol. Socty. of Amer.: Jt. Tech. Prog. Com. (1972–73). Geosci. Info. Socty.: Pres. (1973). **Pubns.:** "The Arthur Lakes Library: A Mineral Industries Resource," *CO Miner* (Volume 1, No. 4). **Activities:** 1; 17 **Addr.:** Arthur Lakes Library, Colorado School of Mines Golden, CO 80401.

Phipps, Barbara Helen (Je. 1, 1915, Hinsdale, IL) Retired, 1981. Half-time Libn., Pac. Un. Coll., 1981– Assoc. Libn., Ref., 1961–81; Libn., Andrews Univ., 1958–61, Asst. Libn., 1945–58; Asst. Libn., SDA Theo. Semy., 1943–45; Tchr., Libn., Adelphian Acad., 1942–43; Tchr., Libn., IN Acad., 1939–40. **Educ.:** Andrews Univ., 1934–39, BA (Eng., Fr.); Univ. of MI, 1941–42, ABLS, 1945, AMLS. **Orgs.:** ALA. CA LA. **Pubns.:** "Library Instruction for the Undergraduate," *Coll. and Rsrch. Libs.* (S. 1968); "Library Instruction for College Freshmen," *Jnl. of Adventist Educ.* (F.–Mr. 1974); Various articles. **Activities:** 1; 26, 31, 39 **Addr.:** Pacific Union College Library, Angwin, CA 94508.

Phipps, Michael (Jl. 6, 1944, Boone, IA) Dir., Waterloo Pub. Lib., 1972–; Dir., Cattermole Meml. Lib., 1969–72; Resrch. Asst., Univ. of IA, Sch. of Lib. Sci., 1967–69; Tchr., Des Moines, Tech. HS, 1966–67. **Educ.:** Univ. of North. IA, 1962–66, BA (Eng.), 1967–69, MALS. **Orgs.:** ALA: Cncl. (1975–79). IA LA: Exec. Bd., (1975–79); Legis. Com. (Ch., 1976). Gvr. Adv. Cncl. on Lib. Srvs. **Pubns.:** *Reference/Information Services in Iowa Public Libraries* (1969). **Activities:** 9; 17; 74, 78 **Addr.:** Waterloo Public Library, 415 Commercial St., Waterloo, IA 50701.

Picard, Gilles (Mr. 8, 1943, Shawinigan, PQ) Dir. des Bib. Sci., Univ. de Montréal, 1977–; Dir. de la Bib., CEGEP Vieux, Montréal, 1976–77; Dir., Ctr. des Media, CEGEP Thetford Mines, 1967–76. **Educ.:** Univ. de Montréal, BACC (Arts), 1966–67, BACC (Bibliothéconomie). **Orgs.:** ASTED: Com. de Dir. de la Comsn. des Bibs. de Recherche et Spéc. (1979–). **Activities:** 1; 17, 19, 35; 58, 88, 91 **Addr.:** 480 des Chênes, Beloeil, PQ J3G 2H7 Canada.

Picciano, Jacqueline L. (Jl. 19, 1928, Los Angeles, CA) Ed., *Intern Nursing Indx.,* 1973–; Libn., Sophia F. Palmer Lib., 1971–; Libn., Acad. of Med. of NJ, 1960–71; Libn., Hoffmann-LaRoche, Inc., 1956–57; Ref. Libn., Armed Forces Med. Lib., 1950–55; various wkshps. **Educ.:** Trinity Coll., 1946–50, BA (Chem. Bio.); Cath. Univ. of Amer., 1950–52, MS (LS). **Orgs.:** Med. LA: Handbook Adv. Panel (1976); Med. Socty. Grp. (Ch., 1980); Nursing Libs. Grp. (Ch., 1975); *Med. LA News* Ed. Com. (Ch., 1978); Nom. Com. (1977). ASIS. ALA: ASCLA, Bd. of Dir. (1968–71). AAUW: Bloomfield, NJ Fund-raising Ch.; Bd. Mem. **Pubns.:** Jt. Auth., "Nursing libraries and literature," *Encyc. of Lib. and Info. Sci.* (1977); "How to get an A on Your Term Paper, or, Using The Library to Succeed," *Imprint* (S. 1980); "Continuing Information, Continuing Education," *MCN* (S.–O. 1978); "Personnel problems in small medical libraries," *Bltn. Med. LA* (O. 1965); "Buffalo Telephone Network" audiotape (1974). **Ac-**

Special Subjects/Services: 50. Adult educ.; 51. Advert./Mktg.; 52. Aerosp.; 53. Agric.; 54. Area std.; 55. Arts/Hum.; 56. Autom.; 57. Bibl./Prtg.; 58. Bio. sci.; 59. Bus./Fin.; 60. Chem.; 61. Copyrt.; 62. Documtn.; 63. Educ.; 64. Engin.; 65. Env.; 66. Eth. grps.; 67. Film; 68. Food/Nutr.; 69. Geneal.; 70. Geo.; 71. Geol.; 72. Handcpd.; 73. Hist.; 74. Int. frdm.; 75. Info. sci.; 76. Insr.; 77. Law; 78. Legis.; 79. Math./Comp. sci.; 80. Med.; 81. Metals; 82. Nat. resrcs.; 83. Newsp.; 84. Nuc. sci.; 85. Oral hist.; 86. Petr./Energy; 87. Pharm.; 88. Phys./Astr./Math.; 89. Readg.; 90. Relig.; 91. Sci./Tech.; 92. Soc. sci.; 93. Telecom.; 94. Transp.; 95. (other).

Who's Who in Library and Information Services

tivities: 5, 12; 17, 30, 39; 57, 80 **Addr.:** 380 Essex Ave., Bloomfield, NJ 07003.

Piccolo, Vincent (Mr. 21, 1925, Somerville, MA) Fac., Media Dept., Worcester State Coll., 1964–; Supvsr., Tech. Srvs., Providence Pub. Lib., 1957–64; Sr. Catlgr., Rutgers Univ. Lib., 1953–57; Head, Serials Unit, US Dept. of State Lib., 1951–53. **Educ.:** Tufts Univ., 1946–50, AB (Econ.); Simmons Coll., 1950–51, MSLS (Libnshp.); Boston Univ., 1973–74, MEd (Instr. Tech.). **Orgs.:** New Eng. Educ. Media Assn.: Educ. Com. (Ch., 1973–75). New Eng. Tech. Srvs. Libns.: Pres. (1970). MA Assn. for Educ. Media: Prof. Stan. Com. (Ch., 1977–79). New Eng. LA: Bibl. Com. (Ch., 1972–74). Various orgs. MA Dept. of Educ.: Prof. Adv. Grp. on Sch. Lib. and Media Certs. (Ch., 1977–79). **Activities:** 1, 10; 26, 31, 46; 74, 75 **Addr.:** 100 Richmond Ave., Worcester, MA 01602.

Pichette, William H. (Je. 16, 1937, Sturgeon Bay, WI) Assoc. Prof., Sch. of LS, Sam Houston State Univ., 1975–; Lib. Supvsr., WI Dept. of Pub. Instr., 1970–74; Libn., Premontre HS, 1962–70. **Educ.:** St. Norbert Coll., 1958–62, BA (Amer. Hist.); Univ. of WI, 1962–63, MALS, 1974–75, PhD (Educ. Admin.). **Orgs.:** ALA: Legis. Netwk. Com. (1971); AASL. TX LA: Mem. Com. (1976). TX Assn. for Educ. Tech. AALS. AAUP. TX Assn. for Coll. Tchrs. **Pubns.:** Jt. producer, *Experience Is The Child of Thought* TV series, WHA, Madison (1973); ed., *A Tribute to Rachel K. Schenk* (1963); "New Emphasis in the Elementary Secondary Education Act—Title II," *WI Lib. Bltn.* (S.–O. 1970); "The Community Resource File," *WI Lib. Bltn.* (Mr.–Ap. 1971); "The Right to Read," *WI Lib. Bltn.* (S.–O. 1971); various articles, sps., pamphlets. **Activities:** 10, 11; 15, 17, 19; 63, 74, 78 **Addr.:** Box 151, Elkins Lake, Huntsville, TX 77340.

Pickenpaugh, Treva A. (Je. 20, 1944, Canton, OH) Branch Libn., Chld. Libn., Dayton and Montgomery Cnty. Pub. Lib., 1971–, Chld. Libn., 1967–71. **Educ.:** OH Univ., 1962–66, BA (Eng.); Case West. Rsv. Univ., 1966–67, MSLS. **Orgs.:** ALA. OH LA: Right to Read Task Frc. (Co-Ch., 1973); Div. VIII, Srv. to Chld. and Young Teens (Asst. Coord., 1976–77; Coord. 1977–78). **Honors:** Beta Phi Mu. **Activities:** 9; 17, 21 **Addr.:** Huber Heights Branch Library, 6363 Brandt Pike, Dayton, OH 45424.

Pickens, Lynne Roberson (S. 17, 1944, Savannah, GA) Head, Ctrl. Chld. Dept., Atlanta Pub. Lib., 1971–, Asst. Head, 1969–71, Chld. Libn., 1968–69; Chld. Libn., Boston Pub. Lib., 1967–68. **Educ.:** Lewis and Clark Coll., 1962–66, BA (Eng.); Emory Univ., 1966–67, MLN (Libnshp.). **Orgs.:** ALA: ALSC, Newbery/Caldecott Com. (1977), Mem. Com., *Multimedia Approach to Chld. Lit.* Rev. Com. (1980–82). SELA. GA LA: Chld. and Young People's Sect. (Vice-Ch., 1971–73). **Activities:** 9; 21 **Addr.:** Atlanta Public Library, Children's Dept., 1 Margaret Mitchell Sq., Atlanta, GA 30303.

Pickering, James Herman (Jl. 23, 1919, Orangeburg County, SC) Consult.; Dir., Cuyahoga Cnty. Dist. Libs., 1976–78; Dir., Clark Cnty. Dist. Libs., 1965–76; Dir., Muskingum Cnty. Libs., 1958–65. **Educ.:** Univ. of SC, 1945–47, AB (Educ.); Emory Univ., 1947–48, (LS). **Orgs.:** OH LA: Finance and Admin. Div. (Coord., 1976–77). ALA: Legis. Com. (1978–80); PLA/Stan. Com. (Ch., 1969). Cleveland Area Bd. of Realtors. OH Assn. of Realtors. Natl. Assn. of Realtors. **Pubns.:** "A Second Look," *OH Lib. Trustee* (Jl. 1980); "Computers or Word Processors?" *OH Lib. Bltn.* (Ap. 1976); "Do Your Policies Encourage Employee Efficiency?" *OH Lib. Trustee* (Jl. 1975). **Addr.:** 10117 Lynn Dr., Cleveland, OH 44133.

Pickett, Doyle C. (Greencastle, IN) VP Mktg., Baker and Taylor Co., 1967–, Dir., Prog. Srvs., 1976–80, Natl. Mgr., Acad. Sales, 1974–76, Mgr.-Approval Prog., 1972–74, Mgr., Spec. Proj., 1971–72, Asst. to Pres., 1967–71. **Educ.:** Wabash Coll., AB (Econ.); IN Univ., MBA (Mgt.); 1977–78 Cert. (Creat. Wrtg.); W. R. Grace Exec. Dev. Prog., 1980, Dip. **Orgs.:** ALA. SLA. TX LA. ASIS. Wabash Coll.: Class Agt. (1975–80). Am. Mktg. Assn. Socty. for Schol. Pubshg. Natl. Trust for Hist. Prsrvn. Assn. of MBA Exec., Inc. **Pubns.:** Co-Auth., *Approval Plans and Academic Libraries: An Interpretative Survey* (1977); "Assessment of the Approval Plan Concept," *Tech. Srvs. Nsltr.* (Je. 13, 1980). **Activities:** 14-Bk. Wholesaler; 17 **Addr.:** 240 Great Hills Rd., Bridgewater, NJ 08807.

Pickett, Mary Joyce (Jl. 18, 1940, Ottumwa, IA) Head, Pub. Srv., Augustana Coll. Lib., 1980–81, Ref. Libn., 1975–80; Catlgr., East Lansing Pub. Lib., 1969; Asst. Ref. Libn., Purdue Univ. Libs., 1967–68, Jr. Asst., 1965–67; Asst. Ref. Libn., Jackson Cnty. Pub. Lib., 1963–65. **Educ.:** Simpson Coll., 1958–62, BA (Phil., Relig.); Univ. of IL, 1962–63, MSLS. **Orgs.:** ALA. IL LA. Leag. of Women Voters. **Honors:** Beta Phi Mu, 1963. **Activities:** 1; 31, 39 **Addr.:** 327 8th St., Downers Grove, IL 60515.

Pickworth, Margaret Hannah Simmons (Ag. 4, 1949, Auburn, AL) Actg. Libn., Coll. of Librarian, Univ. of KY, 1981–; Sub. Libn., Fayette Cnty. Schs., 1979–81; freelnc. consult., 1978– Mtrls. Spec., Univ. of KY, 1978. **Educ.:** Southwestern at Memphis, 1967–71, BA (Intl. Std.); Univ. of KY, 1976–77, MSLS. **Orgs.:** ALA. KY LA. KY Sch. Media Assn. Beta Phi Mu: VP, Pres. Elect (1979–). Univ. of KY Med. Auxillary: pediatric storyteller and puppet maker (1977–). **Pubns.:** Jt. creat., *Picadilly Pickle Parade,* TV storyhour for chld. (1979); various bk. reviews. **Activities:** 10, 12; 21, 24, 32 **Addr.:** 461 Woodland, Lexington, KY 40508.

Picquet, D. Cheryn (My. 20, 1947, Knoxville, TN) Asst. Prof. and Asst. Law Libn., Univ. of TN, 1976–. **Educ.:** Univ. of TN, 1969, BA (Eng.), 1974, MLS (Lib. and Info. Sci.); AALL Cert. **Orgs.:** AALL. Southeatern Assn. of Law Libs.: Mem. Com. (Ch., 1980–82); Dupls. Exch. Com. (1981–82). SELA.: Regis. Com. (1976). TN LA: Regis. Com. (1980). Univ. of TN Fac. Women's Club. **Honors:** Pi Sigma Alpha. **Pubns.:** Ed. Asst., *Constitutional Rights of the Accused;* "Tennessee Legislative Information: Where and How to Obtain It," *Judicial Nsltr.* (Spr. 1979); "Tennessee Legislative Information," *Southeastern Law Libn.* (F. 1979); contributor, *American Indian Legal Materials: A Union List, Current Publications in Legal and Related Fields* (Ap./O. issues, semi-annually). **Activities:** 1, 12; 15, 29, 46; 62, 77, 78 **Addr.:** University of Tennessee Law Library, 1505 W. Cumberland Ave., Knoxville, TN 37916.

Pidala, Veronica C. (O. 23, 1944, New York, NY) Lib./Recs. Admin., EBASCO Srvs. Inc., 1981–; Lib. Admin., Intl. Nickel Co. Inc., 1966–. **Educ.:** Hunter Coll., CUNY, 1961–65, BA (Eng.); Columbia Univ., 1970–74, MLS. **Orgs.:** SLA: Nsltr. (VP., Ed., 1976–78); Managing Ed., NY Area Dir. (1979–80); NY Chap., Dir. of Pubns. (1981–83). NY Lib. Club: Cncl. Mem. (1977–81). **Pubns.:** Various sps. **Activities:** 12; 38; 59, 77, 81 **Addr.:** 213-E. 66St. (4B), New York, NY 10021.

Piedracueva, Haydee N. (Cordoba, Argentina) Latin Amer. Biblgphr., Columbia Univ., 1968–, Latin Amer. Catlgr., 1965–68. **Educ.:** Univ. Nacional De Cordoba, Argentina, 1951–55, Cert. (Lang.); Columbia Univ., 1963–65, MLS. **Orgs.:** SALALM: Com. on Bibl. (1968–); Subcom. on Coop. with the Org. of Amer. States (Ch., 1976–78); Com. on Lib. Opers. and Srvs. (1976–78); Subcom. on Bibl. Actv. (Ch., 1972–74). Inter-Amer. Assn. of Agr. Libns. and Docmlsts. **Pubns.:** Ed., *A Bibliography of Latin American Bibliographies, 1975–1979* (1982); assoc. ed., *A Bibliography of Latin American Bibliographies. First Supplement* (1979); jt. auth., *Index to the SALALM Progress Reports, 1956–1970* (1975); various papers. **Activities:** 1, 5; 15, 39, 41; 54, 57 **Addr.:** 423 W. 120th St., New York, NY 10027.

Piele, Linda J. (Jl. 26, 1941, La Grande, OR) Head, Pub. Srvs. Div., Univ. of WI, Parkside, 1978–, Actg. Head, Media Srvs. Div., 1977–78, Media Libn., 1976–77. **Educ.:** Univ. of WA, 1962–63, BA (Fr.); Univ. of OR, 1963–65, MA (Fr.); Univ. of WI, Milwaukee, 1974–75, MLS. **Orgs.:** WI Assn. of Acad. Libns. WI LA. ALA: RASD, Bus. Srvs. Com. (1979–81); ACRL/Bibl. Instr. Sect., Pre-Conf. Plng. Com. (1980–81), AV Com. (1980–82). **Pubns.:** *Materials and Methods for Business Research* (1980). **Activities:** 1; 17, 31, 39; 59, 64, 75 **Addr.:** Library/Learning Center, University of Wisconsin, Parkside, Box 2000, Kenosha, WI 53141.

Pien, Shui-Hsien (My. 15, 1935, Nanking, China) Serials Docum. Libn., Mansfield State Coll., 1970–; Head, Serials, Miami Univ., 1968–70, Asst. Acq. Libn., 1965–68. **Educ.:** Natl. Taiwan Normal Univ., 1954–58, BA (Eng. Lang.); Univ. of Pittsburgh, 1964–65, MLS; Elmira Coll., 1974–75, MEd (Educ.). **Orgs.:** PA LA. Chin. Amer. **Pubns.:** Chin. transl., *A Brief Introduction to Piaget* (1980); "A Chinese Translation of Entry of Serials," *Jnl. of Lib. and Info. Sci.* (O. 1977). **Activities:** 1; 15, 44 **Addr.:** 1127 Country Ln., Pine City, NY 14871.

Pieratt, Asa B. (Ag. 30, 1938, Kalamazoo, MI) Head, Acq. Dept., Univ. of DE, 1974–; Head, Acq., Univ. of New Haven, 1968–73; Serials Libn., Bowling Green State Univ., 1966–67; Pers. Libn., Miami-Dade Jr. Coll., 1965–66. **Educ.:** Kalamazoo Coll., 1957–61, BA (Pol. Sci.); Univ. of MI, 1964–65, AMLS. **Orgs.:** ALA. DE LA. ALA: ACRL, DE Valley Chap. Philadelphia Acq. Info. Netwk.: Coord. (1978–). **Pubns.:** *Kurt Vonnegut: A Descriptive Bibliography* (1974); *Donald Barthelme: A Descriptive Bibliography* (1978); "Henri Cassiers: Belgian Painter," *Hobbies Mag.* (Je. 1975); "Third World Acquisitions: A Report on the Workshop at LC," *Lib. Jnl.* (My. 1, 1977); "Halloween Customs on Postcards," *Hobbies Mag.* (O. 1978). **Activities:** 15, 33, 44 **Addr.:** University of Delaware, Library, Newark, DE 19711.

Pierce, Anton R. (Mr. 12, 1939, Newark, NJ) Plng., Resrch. Libn., VA Polytech. Inst., State Univ., 1975–; Info. Sci., Bell Lab., 1969–75. **Educ.:** Rutgers Univ., 1959–63, AB (Phys.); McMaster Univ., 1965–70, PhD (Phsy.); Rutgers Univ., 1972–75, MLS. **Orgs.:** ALA. VA Assn. Educ. Data Syst.: Pres. (1978–79). Assn. Comp. Machines: Data base Bibl. Grp. (Ch., 1975). Inst. of Electrical and Electronics Engin. **Pubns.:** Jt. auth., "Design Principles for a Comprehensive Library System," *Jnl. of Lib. Autom.* (Je. 1981); jt. auth., "Determination of Unit Costs for Library Services," *Coll. and Resrch. Libs.* (My. 1979); jt. auth., "A Model for Cost Comparison of Automated Cataloging Systems," *Jnl. of Lib. Autom.* (Mr. 1978); Ed., "Planning for Tomorrow's Educational Data Systems" microfiche (1979). **Addr.:** Newman Library, VA Tech., Blacksburg, VA 24061.

Pierce, Gayle Louise (N. 26, 1938, Kalamazoo, MI) Cat. Libn., Meridian Jr. Coll., 1973–; Libn., Meridian Pub. Schs., 1967–71; Tchr., Virginia Beach Pub. Schs., 1963–65; Station Libn., U.S. Nvl. Base, Guantánamo Bay, Cuba, 1961–63. **Educ.:** Kalamazoo Coll., 1956–60, BA (Span.); West. MI Univ., 1969–70, MLA, 1977, SpA (Libnshp.). **Orgs.:** ALA. MS LA: Two Year Colls. RT (Secy., 1980–81). Intl. Student Assn.: Fac. Adv. (1980–81). **Activities:** 1; 20 **Addr.:** Meridian Junior College, Meridian, MS 39301.

Pierce, Mildred L. (N. 30, 1928, GA) Proprietor, Resrch., Tech. Info. Srvs., 1977–; Tech. Writer, Info. Spec., Walker-Wassuk Arts Alliance, 1973–77; Ref. Consult., Mother Lode Lib. Syst., 1967–68; Tech. Libn., Radiological Sci. Lib. Reynolds Electric Co., 1965–67; Libn., Mineral Cnty. Elem. Schs., 1964–65, Chld. Bkmobile. Libn., 1956–64. **Educ.:** SUNY, Geneseo, 1947–51, BS (Educ., LS); Univ. of Denver, 1954–55, MA (LS); Univ. of UT, Univ. of NV, 1956–58, (Hist., Educ.). **Orgs.:** ALA. NV LA: Secy. NV Assn. Sch. Libns.: Ch. AAUW. Natl. Educ. Assn. **Activities:** 10, 12; 21, 24, 28; 55, 67, 83 **Addr.:** Technical Information Service, P.O. Box 1721, Hawthorne, NV 89415.

Pierce, Miriam Dickey (S. 13, 1928, Berlin, PA) Assoc. Libn., Life Sci., PA State Univ. Libs., 1977–, Coord., Acad. Unit Working Col., 1966–77, Ref. Asst., 1958–61; various libn. positions, 1956–58; Asst. Libn., Juniata Coll., 1952–56; Tchr., Hollidaysburg Sr. HS, 1949–52. **Educ.:** Juniata Coll., 1945–49, BA (Latin, Eng.); Case-West. Rsv. Univ., 1952–55, MS (LS). **Orgs.:** SLA: Ctrl. PA Chap., Exec. Bd. AALS. **Honors:** Beta Phi Mu; HQ Area Cmnd. Lib., US Army, Europe, Merit. Achvmt. Awd., 1957. **Pubns.:** *Penn State Publications: a Finding Guide, 1855–1975* (1976); "Bibliography of Studies on the Economic Development of Pennsylvania and Its Regions," *PA Bus. Srvy.* (1962–65); Intro. to *Review of Plant Pathology* slide-tape prog. (1979). **Activities:** 1; 31, 39, 41; 58, 68, 91 **Addr.:** 437 E. Fairmount Ave., State College, PA 16801.

Pierce, Sydney (My. 2, 1943, Providence, RI) Visit. Assoc. Prof., Emory Univ., Div. of Libnshp., 1981–; Sr. Fulbright Lectr., Fed. Univ. of Minas Gerais, Belo Horizonte, Brazil, 1977–79; Asst. Prof., Emory Univ., Div. of Libnshp., 1974–77; Assoc. Libn., SUNY, Albany, 1968–74. **Educ.:** Russell Sage Coll., 1960–64, BA (Eng.); Univ. of Rochester, 1964–72, MA, PhD (Eng.); SUNY, Albany, 1969, 1973–74, MLS. **Orgs.:** ALA: Ofc. for Lib. Persnl. Resrcs., Equal Empl. Oppt. Subcom. (Ch., 1976–77); Louise Giles Minority Schol. Task Frc. (1980). Ctr. for Intl. Exch. of Schols.: LS Adv. Com. (1979–). **Honors:** Fulbright-Hayes Lectrshp., 1974–77. **Activities:** 11; 15, 39; 55, 92 **Addr.:** P.O. Box 33, Campton Village, NH 03223.

Pierce, William Sutherland (Jl. 23, 1930, Pittsburgh, PA) Facilities Plng. Offcr., PA State Univ. Libs., 1956–; Ref. Libn., NY Pub. Lib., 1954–56. **Educ.:** WV Wesleyan Coll., 1948–52, AB (Hist., Eng. Lit.); Carnegie Inst. of Tech., 1952–54, MLS. **Orgs.:** ALA. PA LA: Nom. Com. (1960–61, 1961–62); Natl. Lib. Week (Exec. Dir., 1962–63); Treas. (1964–68); Bldg. and Equip. RT (Ch., 1971–72, 1979–80); Lcl. Exhibits Com. (Ch., 1972); Bldgs. and Equip. RT, Session Ch. Lib. Bur., Inc.: Prof Adv. Bd. **Pubns.:** *Furnishing the Library Interior* (1980); "Equipment, Libraries," *Encyc. of Lib. and Info. Sci.* (1972); "Furniture and Equipment," *ALA Yearbook* (1976, 1977, 1980, 1981); various papers. **Activities:** 1; 19, 24, 33 **Addr.:** 437 E. Fairmount Ave., State College, PA 16801.

Piermatti, Patricia Ann (Mr. 5, 1948, Passaic, NJ) Pharm. Resrc. Libn., Lib. of Sci., Med., Rutgers Univ., 1971–. **Educ.:** Mary Washington Coll., 1966–70, BS (Bio.); Univ. of KY, 1970–71, MSLS; Med. LA, 1972, Cert. Level 1. **Orgs.:** Amer. Assn. of Coll. of Pharm.: Libs. and Educ. Resrcs. Sect., Basic Pharm. Booklist Com., Ch. Med. LA: NY Reg. Grp. SLA: NJ Chap. **Honors:** Beta Phi Mu, 1972. **Pubns.:** "Planning Online Search Service in a State University," *Sci. and Tech. Libs.* (Fall 1980). **Activities:** 1; 15, 39; 68, 87 **Addr.:** Library of Science/Medicine, Rutgers University, P.O. Box 1029, Piscataway, NJ 08854.

Pierobon, Nancy Elizabeth (Ja. 21, 1950, Toronto, ON) Libn., ON Mnstry. of Energy, 1979–; Libn., Fallonbridge Nickel Mines, 1977–79. **Educ.:** Queen's Univ., 1969–73, BA (Geo.); Univ. of West. ON, 1976–77, MLS. **Orgs.:** Can. Assn. Info. Sci.: PR Com. (1979–80). Sheridan Park Lib. and Info. Sci. Com.: Nom. Com. (Secy., 1979–80). ON Gvt. Libns. Cncl. SLA: Toronto Chap., Networking Ch. (1979–80), Prog. Ch. (1980–81), Nom. Com. (1980–81), Consult. Com. (Ch., 1981–82), Lib. Arts. Adv. Com. (Ryerson Polytech. Inst. Rep., 1981–82) Networking Com. (Rep., 1979–80); Petr. and Energy Resrcs. Div. (Treas., 1980–82), Consult. Srv. Com. (1981–83). Intl. Geo. Un. **Pubns.:** Various sps. **Activities:** 13; 15, 17, 39; 64, 84, 86 **Addr.:** Ontario Ministry of Energy Library, 12th Floor, 56 Wellesley St. W., Toronto, ON M7A 2B7 Canada.

Pierson, Elizabeth Anne (Betty) (Ja. 21, 1942, Washington, DC) Head, Tech. Srvs., Our Lady of the Lake Univ., 1970–79; Head Catlgr., Miami-Dade Cmnty. Coll., 1969–70, Catlgr., 1967–69. **Educ.:** FL State Univ., 1959–65, BMEd (Msc. Educ.), 1965–67, MSLS; N. TX State Univ., 1979–, PhD in Prog.

Orgs.: ALA. Msc. LA. SWLA. TX LA. Activities: 1, 11; 26, 35, 46; 55, 70, 90 Addr.: School of Library and Information Sciences, North Texas State University, Box 13796, Denton, TX 76203.

Pierson, Robert Malcolm (Ja. 1, 1927, Greencastle, IN) Schol.-in-Residence, Cath. Univ. of Amer., 1980–; Assoc. Dir., Univ. of MD, 1972–80, Asst. Dir., Admin., 1966–72, Hum. Libn., 1957–66, Cat., 1956–57 Asst. Circ. Libn., 1955–56, Instr. in Eng., 1952–55; Instr. in Eng., OH State Univ., 1949–52. **Educ.:** De-Pauw Univ., 1942–46, AB (Eng.); Duke Univ., 1946–49, PhD (Eng.); Cath. Univ. of Amer., 1953–55, MSLS. **Orgs.:** ALA: Ref. and Subscrpn. Bks. Review Com. (Ch., 1979–). MD LA. NM LA. **Pubns.:** "Conventional Titles," *LRTS* (Fall 1961); "Entries for Works Related to Periodicals," *LRTS* (Sum. 1962); "Roles, Symbols, Awards," *Jnl. Acad. Libnshp.* (Ja. 1977); "On Reference Desks," *RQ* (Win. 1977); "Noxious Weeds in the Groves of Academe," *Crab* (Ap. 1978); various articles. **Activities:** 1, 11; 15, 17, 39; 55, 74 **Addr.:** Graduate School of Library and Information Science, The Catholic University of America, Washington, DC 20064.

Pierson, Roscoe Mitchell (S. 21, 1921, Crenshaw, MS) Libn., Prof. of Relig. Bibl., Lexington Theo. Semy., 1950–; Libn., Lexington Theo. Semy., 1950. **Educ.:** Centre Coll., 1947, (Bio.); Univ. of KY, 1947–50, (LS, Zlgy.). **Orgs.:** KY LA: Pres. (1964). ATLA: Pres. (1965). Disciples of Christ Hist. Socty.: Secty. 1954–81). **Honors:** Phi Beta Kappa; KY LA, Outstan. Spec. Libn., 1965; ATLA, Sr. Libn. Flwshp., 1965. **Pubns.:** *West Indian Church History, a Bibliography* (1968); *Lexington Kentucky Imprints* (1950); "Alexander Bedward," *Black Apostles* (1978); "Denominational Collections in Theological Seminaries and Church Historical Society Libraries," *Lib. Trends* (O. 1960); various articles, bibl. **Activities:** 1; 15, 20, 41; 90 **Addr.:** Lexington Theological Seminary, S. Limestone, Lexington, KY 40508.

Pieschel, Terri J. (D. 7, 1948, Radway, AB) Supvsr., Lib. and Exploration Recs., Chevron Stan. Limited, 1976–; Tchr.-Libn., Calgary Sep. Sch. Bd., 1975–76. **Educ.:** Univ. of Calgary, 1968–72, BEd (Eng.); Dalhousie Univ., 1973–75, MLS. **Orgs.:** Can. LA: Can. Assn. of Spec. Libs. and Info. Srvs., Calgary Chap., Secy.-Treas., (1979–80), Pres. (1980–81). **Activities:** 12; 17, 38; 64, 82, 91 **Addr.:** Chevron Standard Ltd., 400–5th Ave. S.W., Calgary, AB T2P 0L7 Canada.

Pietris, Mary K. Dewees (Ag. 12, 1941, Los Angeles, CA) Chief, Subj. Cat. Div., Lib. of Congs., 1978–, Asst. Chief, 1977–78; Head, Cat. Dept., Northwest. Univ. Lib., 1970–76; Subj. Catlgr., Lib. of Congs., 1966–69, Spec. Rcrt., 1965–66. **Educ.:** Swarthmore Coll., 1959–63, BA (Pol. Sci., Intl. Rel.); Univ. of WA, 1964–65, MLibr. **Orgs.:** ALA: RTSD, Ad Hoc. Com. on New Dirs. (1972–73) Cat. and Class. Sect., Exec. Com. (1975–78), Subj. Analysis Com. (1973–77); Lib. Admin. Div./ Lib. Org. and Mgt. Sect., Stats. for Tech. Srvs. Com. (1970–74). Pac. NWLA. **Activities:** 4; 17, 20 **Addr.:** 5973 Jan-Mar Dr., Falls Church, VA 22041.

Piety, John S. (S. 7, 1938, Lampasas, TX) Dir., Graselli Lib., John Carrol Univ., 1980–; Acq. and Syst. Libn., PanAmer. Univ. Lrng. Resrc. Ctr., 1975–80; Tech. Libn., Comp. Sci. Corp., 1974–75; Col. Dev. Ofcr., Univ. of WI, Green Bay, 1968–74. **Educ.:** Univ. of AZ, 1956–60, BA (Anthro.); Univ. of OK, 1967–68, MLS. **Orgs.:** SLA. ALA. OH LA. **Honors:** Beta Phi Mu, 1968. **Activities:** 1, 12; 15, 17, 34; 56, 75, 91 **Addr.:** Grasselli Library, John Carroll University, University Heights, OH 44118.

Piggford, Roland R. (Ja. 28, 1926, Monongahela, PA) Dir., MA Bd. of Lib. Comsns., 1981–, Head, Lib. Info. Srvs., 1979–81, Coord., Plng. and Resrch., 1974–79; Asst. Prof., Sch. of Lib. and Info. Sci., SUNY, Albany, 1967–73; Proj. Dir., US Agency for Intl. Dev., Guidelines Proj. for Bk. and Lib. Dev. Progs., 1968–70; Visit. Prof., Grad. Sch. of Lib. and Info. Sci., Pratt Inst., 1969; Asst. Dir., Intl. Lrng. Resrcs. and Info. Srvs., Ctr. for Intl. Std. and World Affairs, SUNY, 1966–67; Libn., Intl. Lib. Info. Ctr., Univ. of Pittsburgh, 1964–66. **Educ.:** WV Wesleyan Coll., 1942–48, BA (Eng.); Univ. of Pittsburgh, 1963–64, MLS. **Orgs.:** ALA: Com. on Equivalencies and Reciprocity (1967–72); Com. on the Compar. Std. of the Admin. of State Lib. Agencies (Ch., 1975). MA LA: Com. on Interlib. Coop. (1974). New Eng. LA. **Honors:** Beta Phi Mu. **Pubns.:** Jt. auth., *Manual on Book and Library Activities in Developing Countries* (1971); jt. auth., "International Responsibilities of College and University Libraries" in *Reader in Comparative Librarianship* (1976). **Activities:** 11, 13; 18, 25, 42; 55, 93 **Addr.:** MA Board of Library Commissioners, 648 Beacon St., Boston, MA 02215.

Pike, Esther M. (S. 23, 1930, Pasadena, CA) Acq. Libn., Jackson Lib., Stanford Univ., 1974–, Serials Libn., 1973–74, Cat. Libn., 1969–73. **Educ.:** Univ. of CA, Berkeley, BA (Hist.), MLS. **Orgs.:** SLA. ALA. **Activities:** 1, 12; 15, 17; 59 **Addr.:** J. Hugh Jackson Library, Graduate School of Business, Stanford University, Stanford, CA 94305.

Pike, Kermit J. (Je. 19, 1941, Cleveland, OH) Dir., Hist. Lib., West. Rsv. Hist. Socty., 1975–; Adjunct Prof., Lib. Sci., Case West. Rsv. Univ., 1975–; Chief Libn., West. Rsv. Hist. Socty., 1969–75, Cur. of Mss., 1966–68, Resrch. Asst., 1965–66. **Educ.:** Adelbert Coll., West. Rsv. Univ., 1959–63, BA (Soc. Std.); Grad. Sch., West. Rsv. Univ., 1963–65, MA (Amer. Hist.). **Orgs.:** SAA: Prog. Com. (1971). Socty. of OH Archvsts.: Co-fndr. (1968); Pres. (1971–72). Org. of Amer. Histns. Amer. Assn. for State and Lcl. Hist. **Pubns.:** *A Guide to the Manuscripts and Archives of the Western Reserve Historical Society* (1972); *A Guide to Shaker Manuscripts in the Library of the Western Reserve Historical Society* (1974); "Western Reserve's Norton Collection," *Mss.* (Fall 1968); "Shaker Manuscripts and How They Came to be Preserved," *Mss.* (Fall 1977). **Activities:** 2, 12; 15, 17, 28; 55, 57, 66 **Addr.:** 3985 Orchard Rd., Cleveland Heights, OH 44121.

Pike, Mary L. (Mr. 18, 1946, Duluth, MN) Deputy Dir. of Mem. Servs., Natl. Assn. of Housing and Redevelopment Officials, 1981–, Libn., 1970–81; Asst. Docum. Libn., Univ. of Denver Libs., 1969–70. **Educ.:** Macalester Coll., 1964–68, BA (Hist.); Univ. of Denver, 1968–69, MA (LS). **Orgs.:** SLA: Soc. Sci. Div. (Ch., 1980; Ch. elect, 1979); Urban Affairs Sect. (Ch., 1976); DC Chap., Corres. Secy. (1978). Cncl. of Plng. Libns: Pubn. Com. (1978–). DC LA. Natl. Assn. of Housing & Redevelopment Officials: Natl. Mem. Srvs. Com. Liaison (1979–). **Honors:** Beta Phi Mu. **Pubns.:** *Citizen Participation in Community Development: A Selected Bibliography* (1975); Ed., *Update 76: Selected Recent Works in the Social Sciences* (1976); *Housing Code Bibliography* (1972); *Housing Management Bibliography* (1971); "Annual Index," *Jnl. of Housing,* (1972–); various articles. **Activities:** 12; 17, 39; 92 **Addr.:** National Association of Housing and Redevelopment, Officials Library, 2600 Virginia Ave. N.W., Suite 404, Washington, DC 20037.

Pike, Roberta Eláine (N. 17, 1947, Brooklyn, NY) Cat., Asst. Prof., Long Island Univ., Brooklyn Ctr., 1980–; Asst. Chld. Libn., NY Pub. Lib., George Bruce Branch, 1980; Non-Print Cat., Tchr. Coll., Columbia Univ., 1978–80; Cat., Instr., Long Island Univ., Brooklyn Ctr., 1975–78; Tech. Asst., Acq., Coll. of Physicians and Surgeons, Columbia Univ., 1972; various cat. positions, Long Island Univ., Brooklyn Ctr., 1971, 1973–75; Tchr., Pub. Sch., 81K, Brooklyn, 1969–70. **Educ.:** Hunter Coll., CUNY, 1965–69, AB (Msc., Educ.); New York Univ., 1971–72, MA (Msclgy.); Pratt Inst., 1973–75, MLS. **Orgs.:** ALA. **Honors:** Beta Phi Mu, 1975. **Activities:** 1, 9; 20, 21, 44; 55, 63 **Addr.:** 25 Bay 29th St., Brooklyn, NY 11214.

Pilachowski, David Michael (Ag. 25, 1949, Springfield, MA) Head, Ref. Srvs., Colgate Univ., 1981–; Coord. of Online Srv., Univ. of VT, 1977–81; Ref. Libn., 1973–. **Educ.:** Univ. of VT, 1967–71, BA (Pol. Sci.); Univ. of IL, 1972–73, MLS. **Orgs.:** ALA: RASD/Machine Asst. Ref. Sect., Com. on Eval. VT LA. **Honors:** Phi Beta Kappa, 1971. **Pubns.:** "USP9D: United States Political Science Documents," *Database* (D. 1979); "Introducing Online Bibliographic Service," *Online* (O. 1978); "Bibliographic Geographique Internationale," *Ref. Srvs. Review* (Ap.–Je. 1979). **Activities:** 1; 39, 49-Online, bibl. retrieval. **Addr.:** Reference Department, Case Library, Colgate University, Hamilton, NY 13346.

Pilgrim, Michael Eugene (O. 10, 1952, Lewistown, PA) Supervisory Archvst., Natl. Arch. and Recs. Srv., 1981–, Archvst., 1977–81, Arch. Tech., 1975–77. **Educ.:** Shippensburg State Coll., 1971–74, BS (Educ., Hist.); George Washington Univ., 1975–79 (Hist.). **Orgs.:** Natl. Arch. Asm.: Tech. Com. (Ch., 1980–). Manassas Lodge. **Pubns.:** Ed., *Internal Revenue Tas Assessment Lists for the Territory of Nevada, 1863–1866* (1980); Ed., *Internal Revenue Tax Assessment Lists for the Territory of New Mexico, 1862–1874* (1980). **Activities:** 2, 4; 17, 38, 43; 56, 74, 75 **Addr.:** 9434 Taney Rd., Manassas, VA 22110.

Pilley, Catherine Moore (Mrs. John A.) (Mr. 7, 1914, Nashville, TN) Ed., *The Catholic Periodical & Literature Index*, Cath. LA, 1966–; various positions as legal secty. **Educ.:** Vanderbilt Univ., 1932–36, BA (Hist.); Villanova Univ., 1964–66, MSLS (Libnshp.). **Orgs.:** Cath. LA: Coll. and Resrch. Libns. Assn. ATLA. Booksellers Assn. of Philadelphia. Gamma Phi Beta Sorority. Daughters of the Amer. Revolution. **Activities:** 12; 20, 30, 37; 90 **Addr.:** Merion Manor Apartments, J–2, Idris Rd., Merion Station, PA 19066.

Pillon, Nancy Bach (Jl. 28, 1917, Jackson, KY) Prof. of Lib. Sci., IN State Univ., 1969–; Asst. Prof., Lib. Sci., Univ. of KY, 1965–69; Instr., Lib. Sci., North. IL Univ., 1960–65; Libn., Breathitt Cnty. HS, 1952–60, 1939–42. **Educ.:** West. KY State Univ., 1937–39, BA (Eng.); Univ. of KY, 1955–59, (LS). **Orgs.:** ALA: AASL; YASD. Assn. of IN Media Educ.: Netwk. Com. (Ch., 1979–). Alliance Francaise. **Pubns.:** *Indiana School Libraries–A Decade of Progress* (1974); "The Media Specialist Works with Teachers at the Rio Grande Open School," *Hoosier Sch. Libs.* (D. 1975); "Media Specialists Work with Teachers," *Drexel Univ. Lib. Qtly.* (Jl. 1973); Consult., "Study Skills: Using Reference Materials" 6 Cassettes (1976). **Activities:** 1, 10; 17, 21, 48; 55, 72, 89, 90 **Addr.:** 2375 Ohio Blvd., Terre Haute, IN 47803.

Pillsbury, Penelope Ellen DeLaire (Ja. 5, 1949, Bristol, CT) Ref. Libn., Fletcher Free Lib., 1980–; Ref. Libn., Univ. of VT, 1973–80. **Educ.:** Univ. of VT, 1967–71, BA (Ancient Hist.); Univ. of MI, 1971–73, AMLS. **Orgs.:** ALA. New Eng. LA: Schol. Com. (1976–77). New Eng. ACRL: Bibl. Instr. Com. (1978–80). VT LA: Conf. Ch. (1976); Northwest Sect. (Pres., 1975–76); Nsltr. Ed. (1977–); Nom. Com. (Ch., 1976). **Honors:** Phi Beta Kappa, 1971; Mortar Board, 1971. **Pubns.:** Ed., *VT LA Nsltr.,* 1977–. **Activities:** 1; 30, 31, 39; 55, 57, 69 **Addr.:** 25 University Terr., Burlington, VT 05401.

Pimsler, Martin (N. 14, 1943, Chicago, IL) Biblgphr., Ctr. for the Std. of Ethics in the Profs., IL Inst. of Tech., 1977–. **Educ.:** Roosevelt Univ., 1961–67, BM (Msc.); Univ. of Toronto, 1970–71, MA (Hist.); Univ. of London, Eng., 1971–75, PhD (Hist.). **Orgs.:** ALA: GODORT. **Pubns.:** "Solidarity in the Medieval Village? The Evidence of Personal Pledging at Elton, Huntingdonshire," *Jnl. of Brit. Std.* (Fall, 1977); jt. cmplr., *A Selected Annotated Bibliography of Professional Ethics and Social Responsibility in Engineering* (1980). **Activities:** 12; 15, 20; 55, 57, 92 **Addr.:** 7060 N. Sheridan Rd. #307, Chicago, IL 60626.

Pinch, Glen E. (O. 7, 1933, Moose Jaw, SK) Pres., BC Sch. Libns. Assn., 1979–80, VP, 1978–79, Visit. Lectr., Fac. of Educ., Univ. of BC, 1980–81, Rec. Secy., 1976–77. **Educ.:** SK, 1951–56; BEd; Toronto, 1958–59, BA (Hist.), 1964–65, BLS. **Orgs.:** Can. Sch. LA. BC Sch. Lib. Assn.: Past Pres. (1980–82). BC Tchrs. Fed. **Activities:** 10, 11; 15 **Addr.:** British Columbia School Librarian's Association, Box 253, White Rock, BC V4B 5C6 Canada.

Pincoe, Grace Lillian (Je. 22, 1906, Toronto, ON) Retired Libn., pvt. resrch.; Libn., Frnds. House, Socty. of Frnds., 1972–79; Hist. Libn., Educ. Ctr. Lib., 1968–72; Head, Tech. Srvs., Etobicoke Pub. Lib., 1957–67; Libn., Art Gallery of ON, 1944–57; Libn., Toronto Pub. Lib., 1927–44. **Educ.:** Univ. of Toronto, 1926–30, BA (Gen.); ON Lib. Sch., 1926; various crs. **Orgs.:** ON LA: "Who's Who in ON Art" Com. (1947–51). **Pubns.:** Ed., *Canadian Quaker History 1974–78;* "Early Quakers in the Maritimes," *Frnds. House* (Je. 1975); "Locating the Pennfield Settlement, New Brunswick and Burial Ground," *Frnds. House* (O. 1974); various articles. **Activities:** 2; 30; 57, 69, 85 **Addr.:** 12 Boustead Ave., Toronto, ON M6R 1Y8 Canada.

Pineda, Conchita J. (Manila, Philippines) Mgr., Lib. Dir., Citibank, N. Amer., Fncl. Lib., 1977–, Asst. Dept. Head, 1972–77, Sr. Catlgr., 1969–72; Adult Srvs. Libn., Brooklyn Pub. Lib., 1966–69. **Educ.:** Univ. of the E., Manila, Philippines, 1958–63, BSE (LS, Eng.); Univ. of Pittsburgh, 1965–66, MLS. **Orgs.:** Asian/Pac. Amer. Libns. Assn.: Treas. (1980–82). SLA. NY Tech. Srvs. Libns. NY Lib. Club. **Activities:** 12; 15, 17, 20; 59, 95-Econ. **Addr.:** Citibank, North America, Financial Library, 399 Park Ave., New York, NY 10043.

Pings, Vern Matthew (Ap. 10, 1923, Sauk City, WI) Dir. of Libs., Wayne State Univ., 1971–, Med. Libn., 1961–71; Assoc. Prof., Univ. of Denver, 1960; Libn., OH North. Univ., 1959; Asst. Engin. Libn., Univ. of WI, 1955–58; Dir., Univ. Farms, Amer. Univ. of Beirut, Lebanon, 1952–54; Works Ofcr., Untd. Nations Relief and Works Agency, 1950–51; Env. Sanitation, Amer. Frnds. Srvs. Com., Gaza, Palestine, 1949–50. **Educ.:** Univ. of Chicago, 1944–46, PhB; Univ. of WI, 1946–47, BA (Zlgy.); Columbia Univ., 1948–52, MA (Educ.); Univ. of WI, 1954–55, MA (LS), 1956–58, PhD (Educ.). **Orgs.:** ALA. Med. LA. SLA. MI LA. AAAS. **Pubns.:** "Improvement Document Delivery Service," *Lib. Trends* (Jl. 1974); "President's Page," *Bltn. of the Med. LA* (Jl. 1975); "The Michigan Library Consortium: Why It Is, What It Has Accomplished, and Its Future," *MI Libn.* (Sum. 1976); "Reference Services Accountability and Measurement," *RQ* (Win. 1976); "Reference Services Accountability and Measurement," *The Purposes of Reference Measurement* (1978); "Management Conflict in Network Development," *Spec. Libs.* (F. 1979); various other articles, reviews. **Activities:** 1; 17; 75, 80, 92 **Addr.:** 1248 Navarre Pl., Detroit, MI 48207.

Pinkerton, Marjorie Jean (Je. 15, 1934, Chicago, IL) Actg. Dir. and Asst. Libn., Asst. Prof., Lib. Sci., William Woods Coll., 1973–; Sub. Tchr., Libn., Columbia Pub. Schs., 1965–73; HS Tchr., Span., Eng., Preble HS, 1958–59. **Educ.:** Carroll Coll., 1952–56, BA (Span.); Univ. of WI, 1959–64, MA (Span.); Univ. of MO, 1969–73, MA (LS). **Orgs.:** Beta Phi Mu: Psi Chap. (Pres. 1973–75). ALA. Univ. of MO Sch. of Lib. and Info. Sci.: Adv. Cncl. (1976–81). MO LA. Frdm. to Read Fndn. UN Com. of Columbia: Pres. (1970–). Columbia Safety Cncl.: Pres. (1969–70). Leag. of Women Voters: VP (1967–68). Natl. Cncl. of Tchrs. of Eng. **Honors:** New Dem. Coal., Columbia, MO, Outstan. Young Woman, Srv. in Cmnty., 1975. **Pubns.:** Ed., *Missouri Union List of Audio-Visuals on Library Education* (1979); jt. auth., *Outdoor Recreation and Leisure: A Reference Guide and Selected Bibliography* (1969); "Library School Training for Children's and Young Adult Services." *Show-Me Libs.* (O.–N. 1979); "Suplemento a una bibliografía de Eduardo Mallea," *Revista Iberoamericana* (Jl.–D. 1964). **Activities:** 1; 15, 26, 32; 63 **Addr.:** 1014 Westport Dr., Columbia, MO 65201.

Pinkett, Harold T. (Ap. 7, 1914, Salisbury, MD) Consult. Archvst. and Historian, Legis. and Nat. Resrcs. Branch, Natl. Arch., Washington, DC, 1980–, Chief Archvst., 1971–79, Deputy Dir., Rec. Apprais. Div., 1968–71. **Educ.:** Morgan Coll., 1931–35, AB (Hist.); Univ. of PA, 1936–38, AM (Hist.); Amer. Univ., 1950–53, PhD (Hist.); Columbia Univ., 1939–40 (Hist.). **Orgs.:** SAA: Ed., *Amer. Arch.* (1968–71). Forest Hist. Socty.: Pres. (1976–78). Amer. Hist. Assn. Intl. Cncl. on Arch. Various orgs. Agr. Hist. Socty.: Exec. Com. (1972–75). Amer. Socty. for Env.

Special Subjects/Services: 50. Adult educ.; 51. Advert./Mktg.; 52. Aerosp.; 53. Agric.; 54. Area std.; 55. Arts/Hum.; 56. Autom.; 57. Bibl./Prtg.; 58. Bio. sci.; 59. Bus./Fin.; 60. Chem.; 61. Copyrt.; 62. Documtn.; 63. Educ.; 64. Engin.; 65. Env.; 66. Eth. grps.; 67. Film; 68. Food/Nutr.; 69. Geneal.; 70. Geo.; 71. Geol.; 72. Handcpd.; 73. Hist.; 74. Int. frdm.; 75. Info. sci.; 76. Insr.; 77. Law; 78. Legis.; 79. Math./Comp. sci.; 80. Med.; 81. Metals; 82. Nat. resrcs.; 83. Newsp.; 84. Nuc. sci.; 85. Oral hist.; 86. Petr./Energy; 87. Pharm.; 88. Phys./Astr./Math.; 89. Readg.; 90. Relig.; 91. Sci./Tech.; 92. Soc. sci.; 93. Telecom.; 94. Transp.; 95. (other).

Hist.: Exec. Com. (1978–80). Org. of Amer. Hist. US Capitol Hist. Socty.: Active Bd. of Trustees (1972–). **Honors:** Natl. Arch., Admin. Excep. Srv. Awd., 1979. **Pubns.:** *Gifford Pinchot, Private and Public Forester* (1970); Co-ed., *Research in the Administration of Public Policy* (1975); "Investigations of Federal Record Keeping," *Amer. Archvst.* (Ap. 1958); "The Archival Product of a Century of Federal Assistance to Agriculture," *Amer. Hist. Review* (Ap. 1964); "Accessioning Public Records: Anglo-American Practices and Possible Improvements," *Amer. Archvst.* (O. 1978); various articles. **Activities:** 2; 17, 24, 39; 65, 68, 82 **Addr.:** 5741 27th St., N.W., Washington, DC 20015.

Pinkham, Eleanor H. (Chicago, IL) Coll. Libn., Kalamazoo Coll., 1971–, Asst. Libn., Pub. Srvs., 1967–70, Circ. Supvsr., 1964–67. **Educ.:** Kalamazoo Coll., 1944–48, BA; West. MI Univ., 1964–67, MSL. **Orgs.:** Beta Phi Mu: Kappa Chap. (Pres., 1968); various coms. ALA: ACRL, Chap. Com. (1977–79); Chap. Cncl. (1979–). MI LA: Bd. of Dir. (1977–78); Exec. Bd. (1976–). MI Lib. Cnstrm. Pres. (1977–78); various ofcs. Various orgs. AAUP. **Pubns.:** "Information Technology in the Small College Library," *Kalamazoo Coll. Mag.* (Ag. 1977); "Cooperation: A View From the Private Sector," *MI Libn.* (Spr. 1974). **Activities:** 1; 17, 34, 45 **Addr.:** Kalamazoo College Library, Thompson and Academy St., Kalamazoo, MI 49007.

Pinkney, Gertrude (Mrs) (S. 15, 1916, Brooklyn, NY) Consult., 1976–; Head Ref., ILL, Wayne Oakland Lib. Fed., 1974–76; Org., Head, Mncpl. Ref. Lib., Detroit Pub. Lib., 1966–74, 1945–49. **Educ.:** Univ. of MI, 1933–36, 1936–37, (LS). **Orgs.:** SLA. MI LA. ALA. **Pubns.:** "Fund Sources for Library Programs in the Arts," *Library and The Contemporary Arts* (1977); "DPL & MRL," *Gvt. Pubns. Review* (1975); "So You're Going to Start a Municipal Reference Library," *Spec. Libs.* (1973). **Activities:** 9, 12; 28, 39, 41 **Addr.:** 10725 Borgman, Huntington Woods MI 48070.

Pinkus, Deborah A. (Ap. 27, 1934, New York, NY) Libn., YA Ref., W. Orange Pub. Lib., 1980–, Ref. Libn., 1978–80; Consult., Curric. Asst., Montclair Bd. of Educ., 1974; Adj. Instr., Educ., Montclair State Coll., 1973–80; Asst. to Readg. Help Coord., Sch. Volun. Prog., NY City Bd. of Educ., 1968–71; Corrmay. Readg. Tchr., ESEA Title I, NY City, 1967–71; HS Tchr., NY City Schs., 1956–70. **Educ.:** Smith Coll., 1951–55, BA (Amer. Std.); Harvard Univ., 1955–56, MA (Tchg.); Rutgers Univ., 1978–79, MLS; NY City HS Tchrs. Cert. (Soc. Std.); NJ Tchg. Cert. (K–12, Soc. Std.); Cert. (NJ Educ. Media Spec.); NJ Prof. Libn. Cert. **Orgs.:** NJ LA. ALA. NJ YA Alert Corp. **Honors:** Phi Beta Kappa, 1955; Pi Lamda Theta, 1956; Beta Phi Mu, 1979. **Activities:** 9; 16, 39; 63, 92 **Addr.:** 42 Porter Pl., Montclair, NJ 07042.

Piontek, Frank P. (Ap. 6, 1943, Detroit, MI) Ref. Supvsr., Beverly Hills Pub. Lib., 1979–; Head, Adult Srvs., Altadena Lib. Dist., 1973–78; Instr. Media Spec., Benedictine HS, 1969–72; Tchr., St. Marys of Redford Jr. HS, 1966–72. **Educ.:** Univ. of Detroit, 1962–66, AB (Hist.); Univ. of MI, 1966–69, MALS. **Orgs.:** CA LA. Cath. LA. **Activities:** 9, 10; 16, 39; 59, 68, 90 **Addr.:** 976 Palm Ave., Los Angeles, CA 90069.

Piper, Nelson A. (O. 5, 1925, Vacaville, CA) Asst. Univ. Libn., Cols., Univ. of CA, Davis, 1972–, Asst. Univ. Libn., Tech. Srv., 1966–72, Asst. Libn., Tech. Srvs., 1962–66, Head, Acq. Dept., 1958–62, Asst. Head, Acq. Dept., 1956–58; Serials Libn., Univ. of NE, 1955–56, Asst. Acq. Libn., 1954–56; Soc. Sci. Ref. Libn., Univ. of CA, Berkeley, 1953–54. **Educ.:** Univ. of CA, Davis, 1946–48 (Chem.); Univ. of CA, Berkeley, 1948–51, BA (Hist.), 1951–52 (Hist.), 1952–53, BLS (LS). **Orgs.:** ALA: ACRL, Lib. Mtrls. Price Index Com. (Ch., 1981–82); LAMA; LITA; RSTD. CA Acad. and Resrch. Libns. CA LA: Col. Dev. Chap. **Honors:** Phi Alpha Theta, 1951. **Activities:** 1; 15, 17, 45; 54, 56, 74 **Addr.:** 635 Del Oro Pl., Davis, CA 95616.

Piper, Patricia Baker (Ap. 9, 1929, Norman, OK) Asst. Law Libn., Univ. of CA, Davis, 1965–; Asst. Law Libn., Univ. of OK, 1959–65; Law Libn., Tulsa Univ., 1958–59. **Educ.:** Univ. of OK, 1947–51, BA (Jnlsm.), 1956–58, Mstr. (LS). **Orgs.:** AALL: Secy. (1973–77); Mem. Com. (Ch., 1962–64, 1968–70); Educ. Com. (Ch., 1972–73); Com. on the WHCOLIS (Jt. Coord., 1978–); Law Netwk. Com. (1978–); Schol. Com. (Co-Ch., 1970–72). Univ. of CA, Davis: Athl. Com. (Ch., 1974–75); Law Sch. Affirmative Action Com. (Ch., 1974–75). **Honors:** Phi Beta Kappa, 1950. **Pubns.:** Jt. auth., *A Manual on KF, the Library of Congress Classification Schedule for Law of the United States* (1972); jt. auth., "Cataloging and Classification Practices in Law Libraries," *Law Lib. Jnl.* (Ag. 1978). **Activities:** 12; 46; 77 **Addr.:** 635 Del Oro Pl., Davis, CA 95616.

Piper, Robert William (Ag. 11, 1939, Fort William, ON) Sch. Libn., Fort Garry Sch. Div. #5, 1966–; Consult., Sch. Lib. Srvs., MB Dept. of Educ., 1977–78. **Educ.:** Lakehead Univ., 1962–65, BA (Eng., Psy.); Univ. of MB, 1965–66, Cert. Educ., 1970, BEd (Sch. Lib.); Univ. of AB, 1972–73, BLS. **Orgs.:** Can. LA. Can. Sch. LA. MB LA: Dir. (1973–74); VP (1974–75). MB Sch. Lib. AV Assn.: Secy. (1978–79); MB Display Days Com. (1978–79). MB Tchrs. Socty.: Prof. Dev. Com. (1970–71). **Honors:** Assn. of Prof. Libns., Univ. of AB, Mary Alice Scott Awd. in Acad. Libnshp., 1973. **Activities:** 10; 21, 31, 32 **Addr.:** 66 E. Wildwood Pk., Winnipeg, MB R3T 0C8 Canada.

Pipkin, Michael B. (O. 3, 1934, Mena, AR) Reg. Lib. Consult., U.S. Intl. Comm. Agency, 1973–; Dir., Charles Taylor Meml. Lib., 1967–73; Libn., Olmsted Air Frc. Base, PA, 1964–67; Libn. I, Free Lib. of Philadelphia, 1962–64. **Educ.:** Univ. of MD, 1959–61, BA (Eng.); Univ. of NC, 1961–62, MS (LS). **Orgs.:** India LA. Indian Assn. of Spec. Libs. and Info. Ctrs. ALA: PLA/Armed Frcs. Sect., Exhibits Com. (Ch., 1966–67). VA LA: JMRT (Ch., 1972). **Activities:** 4, 12; 17, 24, 34; 54, 75, 92 **Addr.:** New Delhi (ICA), Dept. of State, Washington, DC 20520.

Pipkin, Wade Lemual, Jr. (Ap. 9, 1945, Seminole, OK) Lib. Dir., Kilgore Coll., 1981–, Acq. Libn., 1977–81; Ref. Libn., GA South. Coll., 1974–77, Cat. Libn., 1973–74. **Educ.:** Univ. of OK, 1963–67, BA (Hist.), 1967–70, MA (Hist.), 1972–73, MLS. **Orgs.:** TX LA: Natl. Lib. Week Com. (1979–80). Lions Club of Kilgore. First Christ. Church. TX Jr. Coll. Tchrs. Assn. **Honors:** Beta Phi Mu. **Activities:** 1; 15, 17; 61 **Addr.:** 2603 Spruce, Kilgore, TX 75662.

Pisha, Louis John (Ja. 23, 1951, Yonkers, NY) Ref. Libn., C.W. Post Ctr., Long Island Univ., 1976–; Actg. Adult Srvs. Libn., Nanuet Pub. Lib., 1975–76; Actg. Libn., Indus. and Labor Rel. Sch. Lib., Cornell Univ., 1975; Biblgphr., Ivory Coast Proj., Amer. Geo. Socty., 1975. **Educ.:** Rockland Cmnty. Coll., 1969–71, AA (Liberal Arts); SUNY, Geneseo, 1971–73, BA (Hist., Anthro.), Rutgers Univ., 1973–75, MLS; Columbia Univ., 1977–, DLS (LS). **Orgs.:** ALA: LHRT. **Honors:** Beta Phi Mu, 1974; Phi Alpha Theta, 1972. **Activities:** 1; 31, 39; 63, 70, 92 **Addr.:** 796 Brookridge Dr., Apt. 57, Valley Cottage, NY 10989.

Pistorius, Marie (Ja. 24, 1923, Prague, Czechoslovakia) Head, Cat. Dept., Sawyer Lib., Williams Coll., 1980–, Catlgr., 1968–79; Catlgr., Sterling and Francine Clark Art Inst., Lib., 1963–68; Asst. Catlgr., Lafayette Coll. Lib., 1961–63. **Educ.:** Realgymnasium, Prague, Czechoslovakia, 1934–42, Matura; State Lib. Sch., Prague, 1943–44, Dip. (LS); Charles Univ., Prague, 1945–48, Staats-exam MA (Hist., Fr.); Un. Fr. des Organismes de Documtn., Paris, 1950, Cert. de Documentn. gén. **Pubns.:** various transls. **Activities:** 1; 20, 46; 55 **Addr.:** 54 Cluett Dr., Williamstown, MA 01267.

Pita, Lorene S. (Ag. 24, 1921, Oklahoma City, OK) Dir., Lib. Srvs., Provident Hosp., Inc., 1967–. **Educ.:** Univ. of Denver, 1954–58, BA (Sci. Area), 1958, MA (Libnshp.); 1969, Cert. Med. Libn. **Orgs.:** Med. LA: Mem. Com. (1978–80). SLA: Baltimore Chap. Pres. (1977–78), Pres.-Elect (1976–77), Secy. (1974–76), Nom. Com. (1980–81), Bltn. Ed. (1975–76). MD Assn. for Hlth. Sci. Libns.: Nom. Com. (1977–79). Baltimore Cnsrtm. for Resrc. Sharing: Ch. (1979–80). Baltimore Heritage, Inc.: Dir. (1981–82). **Activities:** 14-Hosp.; 17; 80 **Addr.:** Library Services, Provident Hospital, Inc., 2600 Liberty Heights Ave., Baltimore, MD 21215.

Piternick, Anne B. (Blackburn, Lancashire, Eng.) Prof., Sch. of Libnshp., Univ. of BC, 1978–, Asst. Prof., Assoc. Prof., 1966–78; Info. Ofcr., Can. Uranium Res. Fndn., 1961–64; Various Lib. Positions, Univ. of BC Lib., 1956–61. **Educ.:** Univ. of Manchester, 1945–48, BA (Eng.); Assoc. of the LA, 1955. **Orgs.:** Can. LA: Pres. (1976–77). Can. Assn. of Spec. Libs. and Info. Srvs.: Pres. (1969–70). ASIS. Natl. Lib. of Can.: Adv. Bd. (1978–); Com. on Bibl. and Info. Srvs. (Ch., 1979). SSHRCC Adv. Acad. Panel (1981–). **Honors:** Cncl. on Lib. Resrcs., Flwshp., 1979–80. **Pubns.:** Ed.-in-Chief, *Proceedings, National Conference on the State of Canadian Bibliography* (1977); "Resource Sharing With the Community," *Jnl. Acad. Lib.* (Jl. 1979); "Financing of Canadian A&I Services," *Can. Lib. Jnl.* (D. 1977); "Effects of binding policy...on availability of journal issues," *Med. Libr. Assn. Bltn.* (Jl. 1976); various articles, rpts. **Activities:** 12; 30, 39; 56, 62 **Addr.:** School of Librarianship, University of BC, Vancouver, BC V6T 1W5 Canada.

Piternick, George (Ap. 5, 1918, New York, NY) Prof., Sch. of Libnshp., Univ. of BC, 1965–; Asst. Dir., Libs., Univ. of WA, 1961–65; Cat., Cat. Anal., Lib. Admin. Anal., Univ. of CA, Berkeley, Gen. Lib., 1947–61. **Educ.:** Univ. of CA, Berkeley, 1935–39, AB (Zlgy.); Univ. of HI, 1939–40; Univ. of CA, Berkeley, 1946–47, BLS (Libnshp.). **Orgs.:** Can. LA. ALA. CALS. BC LA. **Honors:** Phi Beta Kappa, 1939; Cncl. on Lib. Resrcs., Flwshp. **Pubns.:** *Providing Library Services to Extramural Students in British Columbia* (1979); *General Issues Involved in the Bibliographical Control of Stored Materials* (1979); "Periodicals and Interlibrary Lending," *Quill and Quire* (Je. 1979); "Librarians' Views of PLR," *Lib. Trends* (Spr. 1981) various articles, papers. **Activities:** 1, 11; 17, 26, 46; 91 **Addr.:** School of Librarianship, Univ. of BC, Vancouver, BC V6T 1W5 Canada.

Pitkin, Gary M. (D. 30, 1947, Manitowoc, WI) Assoc. Univ. Libn., Appalachian State Univ., 1981–; Coord., Lib. Syst., Sangamon State Univ., 1977–81; Head, Serials Dept., Instr., Bibl., Univ. of Akron, 1974–77; Serials Libn., Coord. Tech. Srvs., Kearney State Coll., 1972–74, Head, Cat. Dept., 1971–72; various positions as consult. **Educ.:** Univ. of WI, Milwaukee, 1968–70, BA (Eng.), 1970–71, MA (LS). **Orgs.:** ALA: RTSD/Serials Sect., Medium-sized Resrch. Libs. Discuss. Grp. (Ch., 1979–80), Com. to Std. Serials Recs. (1979–80), Ad Hoc Com. to Std. Feasibility of Estab. Core Lists of Serials (1979–); ACRL/Univ. Lib. Sect., San Francisco Prog. Com. (1980–81); LITA. **Pubns.:** *Serials Automation in the United States: A Bibliographic History* (1976); jt. auth., "A Method for Cooperative Serials Selection and Cancellation through Consortium Activities," *Jnl. of Acad. Libnshp.* (S. 1978); "Serials Automation at Kearney State College," ERIC (My. 1976); "A Good, Workable Combination for the Cataloging and Classification of Recordings," *Mt. Plains Lib. Qtly.* (1972); news ed., *The Serials Libn.* (1976–); various papers. **Activities:** 1; 17, 24, 46; 56 **Addr.:** Appalachian State University, Boone, NC 28608.

Pitkin, Patricia A. (O. 6, 1951, Rochester, NY) Actg. Dir. of Libs., Wallace Meml. Lib., Rochester Inst. of Tech., 1981–, Head, Autom. and Tech. Srvs., 1979–, Head, Lib. Systs. Dev., 1977–79, Data Base Mgr., Orig. Catlgr., 1974–77. **Educ.:** SUNY, Geneseo, 1969–73, BA (Phil.), 1973–74, MLS. **Orgs.:** ALA: RTSD, Tech. Srvs. Costs (1980–82). **Activities:** 1; 17, 46; 56 **Addr.:** Wallace Memorial Dr., Rochester Institute of Technology, Rochester, NY 14623.

Pittaro, Mauro John, Jr. (S. 5, 1935, New York, NY) Asst. Mgr., Ed. Div., Engin. Indx., Inc., 1980–, Supvsr.-level Positions, Ed. Div., 1972–80, Ed., Abs. and Indexing, Ed. Div., 1967–72; Electronics Ed., Cambridge Comm. Corp., 1966–67. **Educ.:** Columbia Coll., 1953–56, AB (Pre-Engin.); Columbia Univ., 1956–58, BS (Electrical Engin.), 1958–59, MS (Electrical Engin.), 1959–64, (Electrical Engin.); CUNY, 1971–76, Cert. (Lib., Info. Sci.). **Orgs.:** Amer. Socty. of Indxrs.: Pres.-Elect (1981–82); NY Chap., Ch.-Elect (1980–81); various coms. ASIS: Metro. NY Chap., Ch.-Elect (1979–80), Treas. (1975–79); Spec. Interest Grp. on Info. Generation and Publshg., Secy.-Treas. (1980–81); various coms. Inst. of Electrical and Electronics Engin. Amer. Socty. for Engin. Educ. **Honors:** Tau Beta Pi, 1957; Eta Kappa Nu, 1957. **Pubns.:** Indx. Dsgn., "Annual Index," *JASIS* (1973). **Activities:** 14-Abs. and Indexing Srv.; 17, 30, 37; 64, 91 **Addr.:** Engineering Index, Inc., 345 E. 47th St., New York, NY 10017.

Pittman, Louise Minervino (Ag. 31, 1947, Niagara Falls, NY) Dir., Kenosha (WI) Pub. Lib., 1981–; Dir., Troy (NY) Pub. Lib., 1977–; Dir., Adams Cnty. Pub. Lib., 1974–77, Ref., Bkmobile Libn., 1972–74. **Educ.:** Univ. of IA, 1971, BA (Hist.), 1971–72, MLS. **Orgs.:** ALA. NY LA. **Activities:** 9; 17, 35, 36; 55, 75 **Addr.:** c/o Kenosha Public Library, 7979-38th Ave., Kenosha, WI 53104.

Pittman, Marie Estella McGhee (Ap. 17, 1923, Mt. Olive, MS) Resrch., ILL Libn., NC A and T State Univ., 1975–, Asst. Prof., Lib. Educ., 1969–75, Head Cat. Libn., 1964–69; Msc. Libn., NC Ctrl. Univ., 1959–64, Asst. Cat. Libn., 1952–64. **Educ.:** NC Ctrl. Univ., 1948–52, BS (Bus. Educ.); Atlanta Univ., 1957–58, MSLS (Acad. Libnshp.); NC A and T Mgt. Trng. Sem., 1967–74, Cert.; various crs. **Orgs.:** ALA. NC Assn. of Educ.: A and T Unit (Secy., 1977–). Frnds. of the NC A and T African Heritage Ctr. Natl. Assn. of Negro Bus. and Prof. Women, Inc.: Reidsville Club (Pres., 1978–). Natl. Epicureans: Greensboro Chap. (Treas., 1975–79). Delta Sigma Theta, Inc.: Rec. Secy. (1959–64, 1970–72). **Honors:** Reidsville Bus. and Prof. Women Club, Prof. Achvmt. Awd., 1977; Natl. Assn. Bus. and Prof. Women Clubs, Cert. of Recog., 1979. **Activities:** 1; 20, 31, 39; 55, 57, 63 **Addr.:** 415 B Lindsay St., Greensboro, NC 27401.

Pivarnik, Janis G. (Je. 11, 1949, Louisville, KY) Head, Gvt. Pubns. Dept., Univ. of KY Libs., 1979–; Asst. Libn., Gvt. Pubns., IN Univ., 1977–79; Ref., ILL Libn., James Madison Univ., 1973–77. **Educ.:** IN Univ., 1967–71, BA (Eng.), 1971–72, MLS. **Orgs.:** ALA: Gvt. Docum. RT. KY LA. **Activities:** 1; 17, 29, 39; 62 **Addr.:** Government Publications Dept., University of KY Libraries, Lexington, KY 40506.

Pizer, Irwin H. (O. 16, 1934, Wellington, New Zealand) Univ. Libn., Reg. Med. Lib. Dir., Reg. VII, Prof. of Lib. Admin., Univ. of IL, Med. Ctr. 1971–; Dir. of Libs., Prof., SUNY, Buffalo, 1969–71, Dir. of Lib. and Prof. of Med. Hist., SUNY Upstate Med. Ctr., Syracuse, 1964–69; Assoc. Libn. for Machine Methods, WA Univ. Sch. of Med. Lib., 1961–64; Intern, Natl. Lib. of Med., 1960–61. **Educ.:** Antioch Coll., 1954–57, BS (Bio.); Columbia Univ., 1959–60, MS (LS). **Orgs.:** Med. LA: Bd. of Dir. (1975–78). IFLA: Sect. of Bio. and Med. Sci. Libs. (Ch., 1977); Div. of Spec. Libs. (Secy., 1979). IL ACRL–IL Bd. of Higher Educ.: Liaison Com. on Lib. Comp. Syst. Gov. and Mgt. Various Orgs. Univ. of IL Press Bd. Bibl. Retrieval Srvs., Inc.: User Adv. Bd. (1979). Biomedical Comm. Netwk.: Bd. of Dir. (1979). Various Orgs. **Honors:** Med. LA, Murray Gottlieb Prize–Best Med. Hist. Essay, 1964; Med. LA, Ida and George Eliot Prize, 1966. **Pubns.:** "Physical Access to Materials," *Handbook of Medical Library Practice* (1981); "Medical Libraries' *ALA World Encyc. of Libnshp.* (1980); "A Regional Medical Library Network," *Bltn. of the Med. LA* (1969); "New Library Buildings–Library of the Health Sciences," *Bltn. of the Med. LA* (1976); "The Doctor's Bag," *Bltn. of the Med. LA* (1963); various articles, chap., sp., papers. **Activities:** 1, 12; 17, 24, 34; 56, 58, 80 **Addr.:** Library of the Health Sciences, University of IL at the Medical Center, P.O. Box 7509, Chicago, IL 60680.

PROFESSIONAL ACTIVITIES: Institutions: 1. Acad. lib.; 2. Arch.; 3. Assn.; 4. Fed./Gvt. lib.; 5. Inst. lib.; 6. Mfr./Suppl.; 7. Milit. lib.; 8. Musm.; 9. Pub. lib.; 10. Sch. lib.; 11. Sch. of lib. sci.; 12. Spec. lib.; 13. State lib.; 14. (other). **Functions/Activities:** 15. Acq./Col. dev.; 16. Adult srvs.; 17. Admin.; 18. Apprais.; 19. Archit./Bldgs.; 20. Cat./Class.; 21. Chld. srvs.; 22. Circ.; 23. Cons./Pres.; 24. Consult.; 25. Cont. ed.; 26. Educ. lib. sci.; 27. Ext. srvs.; 28. Fund/Grants; 29. Gvt. pubs.; 30. Indx./Abs.; 31. Instr. lib. use; 32. Media srvs.; 33. Micro.; 34. Netwks./Coop.; 35. Persnl.; 36. PR; 37. Publshg.; 38. Recs. mgt.; 39. Ref. srvs.; 40. Repro.; 41. Resrch.; 42. Review.; 43. Secur.; 44. Serials; 45. Spec. col.; 46. Tech. srvs.; 47. Trustees/Bds.; 48. YA srvs.; 49. (other).

Pizzimenti, Benette (D. 13, 1947, Brooklyn, NY) Asst. Lib. Dir., Concord Pub. Lib., 1976–, Actg. Lib. Dir., 1978–79, Supvsr., Adult Srvs., 1973–76. **Educ.:** SUNY, Buffalo, 1966–70, BA (Art Hist.); Univ. of WA, 1970–71, MLS. **Orgs.:** ALA. New Eng. LA. NH LA: Pres. (1980–81); VP (1979–80). Leag. of NH Craftsmen. **Honors:** ALA, JMRT, 3M/JMRT Prof. Dev. Grant, 1981. **Activities:** 9; 16, 17, 36 **Addr.:** Concord Public Library, 45 Green St., Concord, NH 03301.

Place, Philip A. (My. 10, 1939, Lorain, OH) Dir., Manatee Cnty. Pub. Lib. Syst., 1974–; Dir., Prince William Cnty. Pub. Lib., 1970–74; Assoc. Dir., Cabell Cnty. Pub. Lib., 1968–70; Prof., Lib. Sci., Marshall Univ., 1970; Ref. Libn., San Francisco Pub. Lib., 1966–68. **Educ.:** Taylor Univ., 1963, BS (Hist.); Univ. of South. CA, 1967, MLS. **Orgs.:** ALA. FL LA. **Pubns.:** "Serving the Elderly in West Virginia," *WV Libs.* (D. 1969). **Activities:** 9; 17 **Addr.:** Manatee County Public Library System, Central Library, 1301 Barcarrota Blvd. W., Bradenton, FL 33505.

Placek, Joseph Anthony (O. 14, 1929, Detroit, MI) Head, Slavic Div., Tech. Srv., Univ. of MI, 1967–; Head, Ref. Dept., OH State Univ., 1965–67; Libn., DC Tchrs. Coll., 1963–65; Ed., Cath. LA, 1960–63. **Educ.:** St. Mary's Coll., MI, 1947–48; Univ. of Detroit, 1950–53, AB (Eng.); Cath. Univ., 1953–56, MS (LS); Georgetown Univ., 1960–65, MS (Russ.). **Orgs.:** ALA: ACRL/Slavic and E. European Subsect. (1965–66); Vice-Ch., Ch. (1968–71). ARL: Slavic Bibl. and Documtn. Ctr., Adv. Com. Amer. Assn. for the Advnc. of Slavic Std. **Pubns.:** Ed., *Catholic Periodical Index* (1961–62); "University of Michigan," *East Central and Southeast Europe; a handbook of library and archival resources in North America* (1976). **Activities:** 1; 15, 20, 39; 54 **Addr.:** 9 Lois Ct., Ann Arbor, MI 48103.

Plachta, Helen B. (Hartford, CT) Head, Serial and Acq. Srvs., NY Acad. of Med. Lib., 1980–, Head, Serials Dept., 1974–80, First Asst., 1973–74; Libn., Milton Helpern Lib. of Legal Med., 1972–73. **Educ.:** Queens Coll., CUNY, 1964–70, BA (Pathology); Pratt Inst., 1970–71, MLS (Lib. and Info. Sci.); Med. LA, 1972, Cert. (Med. Libnshp.). **Orgs.:** Med. LA: NY Reg. Grp., Pubcty. Com. (1972–73), Regis. Com. (1974–75), Nsltr. Com. (1975–76, 1980–81). **Honors:** Beta Phi Mu, 1972. **Activities:** 12; 15, 44; 58, 80 **Addr.:** New York Academy of Medicine, 2 E. 103rd St., New York, NY 10029.

Plair, Norman V. (Ja. 3, 1943, Cincinnati, OH) Coord., Cmnty. Rel. Srvs. and Persnl. Rcrt., Dayton and Montgomery Cnty. Pub. Lib., 1975–; Branch Head, Pub. Lib. of Cincinnati and Hamilton Cnty., 1971–75, Outreach Libn., 1968–70. **Educ.:** Univ. of Cincinnati, 1968, BSc (Eng., Hist.); Univ. of IL, 1970–71, MSLS; Miami Univ., 1973, Cert. (Exec. Dev. Prog. for Lib. Admin.). **Orgs.:** ALA. OH LA: Bd. of Dir. (1979–82). OH State Lib. Adv. Com. Inst. Lib.: Vice-Ch. (1977–78); Ch. (1978–79). OH Prog. in the Hum.: Com. Mem. (1978–). **Honors:** Beta Phi Mu, 1971. **Activities:** 5, 9; 17, 35, 36; 66, 75 **Addr.:** Comm. Rels. Serv. & Personnel Recruiting, Dayton and Montgomery County Public Library, 215 E. 3rd St., Dayton, OH 45402.

Planton, Stanley P. (D. 15, 1947, Norwood, MA) Head Libn., OH Univ., Chillicothe Campus, 1979–; Dir. of Lrng. Resrcs., Dakota Wesleyan Univ., 1977–79; Dir. of Tech. Srvs., Kearney State Coll., 1975–76, Ref. Libn., 1974–75. **Educ.:** Beloit Coll., 1965–69, BA (Hist.), 1969–70, MAT (Educ.); Univ. of WI, 1973–74, MALS; SD State Lib., 1978, **Orgs.:** OH Acad. LA. ALA. Coll. of Mid-Amer. Libns. Cncl.: Pres.-Elect (1978–79). NE LA: Mem. Com. (Ch., 1975–76). Mitchell Area Arts Cncl.: Adv. Cncl. (1978–79). Scioto Valley Arts Cncl.: Ch. (1981–82). **Pubns.:** "A Decision-Making Strategy in Serials," *Resrcs. in Educ.* (1977); contrib., *Abs. of Pop. Culture* (1978–79); reviews. **Activities:** 1; 15, 32, 39; 56 **Addr.:** Stevenson Library, Ohio University– Chillicothe Campus, Chillicothe, OH 45601.

Platau, Gerard Oscar (Je. 29, 1926, Potsdam, Germany) Sr. Asst., Ed. Opers., Chemical Abs. Srv., 1979–, Asst. Managing Ed., 1971–79, Mgr. Sel. and Abs., 1961–71, Sr. Assoc. Ed., 1950–61. **Educ.:** Brooklyn Coll., 1942–46, BA (Liberal Arts); Purdue Univ., 1946–50, MS, PhD (Chem.). **Orgs.:** ASIS: Cnclr. (1966–70, 1976–1980); Conf. and Mtgs. Com. (Ch., 1969–76); Budget and Finance Com. (1968–70, 1976–80); Exec. Com. (1979–80); Mem. Com. (Ch., 1980–82); Natl. ASIS Mtg. (Vice Ch., 1982). Amer. Chemical Socty.: *Chemical Rec.* (Ed., 1960–63). Natl. Fed. of Abstracting and Indexing Srvs.: Conf. Com. (1975–82). **Honors:** Amer. Socty. for Info. Sci., Watson Davis Awd., 1980. **Pubns.:** various articles, *Jnl. of the Amer. Chemical Socty., Jnl. of the Amer. Socty for Info. Sci.* **Activities:** 12, 14-Abstracting & Indexing Srv.; 17, 30, 37; 56, 60, 75 **Addr.:** Chemical Abstracts Service, P.O. Box 3012, Columbus, OH 43210.

Plate, Kenneth H. (Je. 8, 1939, Richmond, CA) Visit. Assoc. Prof., Univ. of South. CA, Los Angeles, 1981–; Visit. Assoc. Prof., Univ. of CA, Los Angeles, 1978–81; **Educ.:** Assoc. Prof., Univ. of Toronto, 1969–78; Tchg. Asst., Rutgers Univ., 1968; Chem. Libn., Columbia Univ., 1966. **Educ.:** Univ. of CA, Berkeley, 1957–62, AB (Eng.); Rutgers Univ., 1965–66, MLS, 1967–69, PhD (LS). **Orgs.:** ALA. ASIS. SLA. AALL. **Pubns.:** *Management Personnel in Libraries* (1970); "Factors Affecting Librarian's Job Satisfaction," *Lib. Qtly.* (1974); "Matrix Approach to Position Classification," *Coll. and Resrch. Libs.* (1975); "Career Patterns of Ontario Librarians," *Can. Lib. Jnl.* (1979). **Activities:** 12; 35 **Addr.:** Suite 109–194, 7985 Santa Monica Blvd., Los Angeles, CA 90046.

Platt, Glenn E. (Mr. 11, 1920, Ellwood City, PA) Dir., Lib. Srvs., Flagler Coll., 1975–; Asst. Libn., Andover Newton Theo. Sch., 1965–75. **Educ.:** Geneva Coll., 1946–48, BA (Liberal Arts); Wheaton Coll., 1951–53, MA (Relig.); Simmons Coll., 1965–67, MSLS; Boston Coll., 1965–67, (Grmn.); Amer. Univ. 1974, (Introduction to Mod. Arch.). **Orgs.:** ATLA. FL LA. **Activities:** 1; 15, 17, 20; 56, 63, 90 **Addr.:** Flagler College Library, King St., St. Augustine, FL 32084.

Plavchan, Ronald J. (Ag. 4, 1942, Cleveland, OH) Supervisory Archvst., Natl. Arch. and Recs. Srv., 1979–, Archvst., 1974–79; Asst. Prof., Clarke Coll., 1970–72; Instr., Florissant Valley Cmnty. Coll., 1970; Instr., Forest Park Cmnty. Coll., 1967–68. **Educ.:** Univ. of Dayton, 1962–64, BA (Hist.); Miami Univ., OH, 1964–66, MA (Hist.); St. Louis Univ., 1966–69, PhD (Hist.). **Orgs.:** SAA: *Amer. Archvst.* (Dept. Ed., 1976–). Natl. Arch. Asm.: Phys. Plant Com. (Co-ch., 1980–). Amer. Hist. Assn. Knights of Columbus. Org. of Amer. Histns. South. Hist. Assn. North. VA Assn. of Histns. Various orgs. **Honors:** U.S. Gen. Srvs. Admin., Commendable Srv. Awd., 1977, 1981. **Pubns.:** *A History of Anheuser-Busch, Inc., 1852–1933* (1976); Indxr., *Compiled Service Records of Volunteer Soldiers Who Served During the Mexican War in Organizations from the State of Pennsylvania* (1976); *Inventory, Calendar, and Index of the Hiram Strong Papers, 1862–63* (1964); Dept. Ed., "International Scene," *Amer. Archvst.* (1976–); Assoc. Ed., *Intl. Jnl. on Arch.* (1980–). **Activities:** 2; 17, 39, 44; 54, 62 **Addr.:** National Archives and Records Service, 8th & Pennsylvania Ave., N.W., Washington, DC 20408.

Plessner, Joan E. (Ap. 4, 1940, St. Louis, MO) Pub. Info. Dir., NM State Lib., 1979–; Owner, Joan Plessner Advert./PR, 1975–78; Ref. Head, Hemet Pub. Lib., 1974–75; Newswriter, Washington Univ., 1963–67; Branch Head, Riverside Cnty. Lib. Syst., 1968–70; Rpt., Photographer, Riverside Press-Enterprise, 1967–69; various lib. positions, Clayton Pub. Lib., 1954–71. **Educ.:** Washington Univ., 1959–63, AB (Pol. Sci.); Univ. of South. CA, 1977–78, MSLS. **Orgs.:** NM LA. ALA. PR Socty. of Amer. Santa Fe Press Club: Bd. of Dir. **Activities:** 9, 13; 36, 39 **Addr.:** 825 Calle Mejia #122, Santa Fe, NM 87501.

Pletscher, Josephine M. (Muscatine, IA) Fine Arts Coord., Pasadena Pub. Lib., 1964–; Per. Libn., Immaculate Heart Coll., 1963–64, Acq. Libn., 1962–63. **Educ.:** Immaculate Heart Coll., 1959–62, BA (Art), 1962–64, MA (LS). **Orgs.:** CA LA. ARLIS/NA. Immaculate Heart Coll. Alum. Assn. Women's Club, Pasadena. Pasadena Art Cncl. Los Angeles Cnty. Musm. of Art. **Honors:** Pasadena Pub. Lib., Recog. Awd., 1968. **Pubns.:** Poster for *Wilson Lib. Bltn.* (N. 1969). **Activities:** 9; 17, 32, 39; 55, 67 **Addr.:** 1917 Rodney Dr., Los Angeles, CA 90027.

Plette, Lorraine T. (S. 30, 1915, Gardner, MA) Asst. Libn., Anna Maria Coll., 1978–, Libn., 1951–78. **Educ.:** Anna Maria Coll., 1946–48, BS (Educ.); Cath. Univ. of Amer., 1948–56, MS (LS). **Orgs.:** Cath. LA. **Activities:** 1; 15, 17, 20 **Addr.:** Anna Maria College, Paxton, MA 01612.

Pletz, Frances H. (My. 24, 1920, Chicago, IL) Exec. Dir., MI LA, 1969–. **Educ.:** MI State Univ., 1939–81, BA (Comm.). **Orgs.:** ALA: Chap. Rel. Com. (1973–77; Ch., 1975–77); Legis. Com. (1975–77); WHCOLIS Com. (1975–). Zonta Clb. of Lansing. Theta Alpha Phi. Pi Kappa Delta. **Honors:** MI LA, Frances H. Pletz Awd., 1978. **Pubns.:** "Lobbying and the Librarian," *Media Spectrum* (Sum. 1976); "Stroke the Legislators," *Amer. Libs.* (N. 1977); Ed., *MI Libn.* **Activities:** 3; 49-Assn. mgt. **Addr.:** Michigan Library Assn., 226 W. Washtenaw, Lansing, MI 48933.

Pletzke, Chester J. (S. 26, 1941, Bay City, MI) Dir. Lrng. Resrcs. Ctr., Uniformed Srvs., Univ. Hlth. Sci., 1978–; Coord., Reg. Dev., Midwest Hlth. Sci. Lib. Netwk., 1972–78; Asst. Libn., The John Crerar Lib., 1972–78; Dir., Lib. Srvs., Will Rogers Hosp., 1969–72. **Educ.:** Duquesne Univ., 1960–64, BA; The Univ. of MI, 1964–65, AMLS; Yeshiva Univ., Ferkauf Grad. Sch., 1965–67 (Psy.). **Orgs.:** Med. LA: various coms. **Pubns.:** *Analysis of the Midwest Medical Union Catalog* (1975); *Basic Library Management for Health Science Librarians* (1975); "Continuing Education," *Jnl. of Med. Educ.* (Jl. 1973). **Activities:** 1, 12; 17, 32, 34; 75, 80, 74 **Addr.:** 8214 Beech Tree Rd., Bethesda, MD 20814.

Pletzke, Linda (N. 18, 1941, Cleveland, OH) Head, Spec. Ord. Sect., Lib. of Congs., 1978–; Head, Ord. Dept., Northwestern Univ. Lib., 1976–78, Asst. Ord. Libn., 1974–76; Adult Srvs. Libn., Brooklyn Pub. Lib., 1965–67. **Educ.:** Case West. Rsv. Univ., 1959–63, BA (Eng., Psy.); Univ. of MI, 1964–65, AMLS. **Orgs.:** ALA: RTSD/Bookdealer Lib. Rel. Com. (1978–); RTSD-AAP Jt. Com. (1981–). ACRL. **Honors:** Beta Phi Mu, 1965. **Activities:** 1, 4; 15, 17, 46 **Addr.:** 8214 Beech Tree Rd., Bethesda, MD 20817.

Pleune, B. Joyce (N. 18, 1921, Grand Rapids, MI) Assoc. Dir., Kent Cnty. Lib. Syst., 1978–, Dir., 1959–78, Sch. Srvs. Consult., 1953–58, Bkmobile. Libn., 1951–52; Tchr., Grand Rapids Bd. of Educ., 1945–50. **Educ.:** Calvin Coll., 1941–45, AB (Educ.); West. MI Coll., 1950–51, Cert. (LS); Univ. of MI, 1958, MA (LS). **Orgs.:** MI LA. ALA. **Activities:** 9; 17, 35 **Addr.:** Kent County Library System, 775 Ball N.E., Grand Rapids, MI 49503.

Plitt, Jeanne Given (Ag. 27, 1927, Whitehall, NY) Dir., Alexandria Libs., 1970–, Asst. Dir., 1968–70, Ref. Libn., 1967–68; Tchr., Sec. Schs., MD, VA, 1951–67. **Educ.:** St. Lawrence Univ., 1945–47; Univ. of MD, 1947–49, AB (Eng.); Amer. Univ., 1960–61; Cath. Univ., 1968, MSLS; Tchrs. Licn., MD, VA. **Orgs.:** VA LA. Cncl. of Gvts.: Libns. Tech. Com. (Ch., 1971–72); Exec. Bd. (1980–81). North. VA Cnsrtn.: Ch. (1976–77). **Addr.:** 717 Queen St., Alexandria, VA 22314.

Plotkin, Nathan (F. 1, 1928, Detroit, MI) Libn., Ventura School, 1981–; Pub. Srvs. Libn., CA Maritime Acad., 1975–81; US army career, 1952–72. **Educ.:** Univ. of IL, 1949–52, AB (Soclgy.); KS State Univ., 1960–64, MA (Geo.); Univ. of IL, 1972–73, MS (LS); Univ. of CA, Berkeley, 1973–74, (Lib. and Info. Sci.). **Orgs.:** ALA: ACRL. CA LA. Chap. of Acad. and Resrch. Libs. ACLU: Bd. Mem., Contra Costa Cnty., CA. **Honors:** Beta Phi Mu, 1973; Gamma Theta Upsilon, 1963. **Activities:** 1; 22, 31, 39; 91, 94, 95-maritime indus. **Addr.:** Ventura School Library, 3100 Wright Rd., Camarillo, CA 93010.

Plotnik, Arthur (O. 1, 1937, White Plains, NY) Dir., Ed. Dev., 1979–, Ed., Amer. Libs., ALA, 1975–; Assoc. ed., *Wilson Lib. Bltn.*, H.W. Wilson Co., 1969–74; Ed. and info. spec., Lib. of Congs., 1967–69. **Educ.:** SUNY, Binghamton, 1958–60, BA; Univ. of IA, 1960–61, MA (Eng.); Columbia Sch. of Lib. Srv., 1965–66, MS (LS). **Orgs.:** ALA. The Amer. Bk. Awds.: Bd. of Dirs. (1980–). **Honors:** Educ. Press Assn. of Amer., Cert. of Excel. (3), 1973; Educ. Press Assn. of Amer., Cert. of Excel. (1), 1977. **Pubns.:** *The Elements of Editing* (1982); *Library Life–American Style; A Journalists Field Report* (1975); "Great American Library Success Story," *NY Times Supplement* (1976); various articles, sps., 1966–. **Activities:** 12; 17, 37; 50, 51, 52 **Addr.:** American Libraries, 50 E. Huron St., Chicago, IL 60611.

Plotz, Judith C. A. (Jl. 29, 1948, Cleveland, OH) Freelnc. Info. Spec., 1981–; Ed., *RI Lib. Assn. Bltn.*, 1977–80; Soc. Work Libn., Univ. of Pittsburgh, 1975–77; Consult., Pittsburgh Reg. Lib. Ctr., 1974–76; Libn., Heller Sch. Brandeis Univ., 1972–73. **Educ.:** Brandeis Univ., 1966–70, BA (Eng. lit.); Simmons Coll., 1970–71, MLS; Grad. Sch. of Lib. and Info. Sci., Univ. of Pittsburgh, 1975–77, Advnc. Cert. **Orgs.:** SLA. RI LA. New Eng. LA. **Honors:** Beta Phi Mu, 1977. **Pubns.:** *A Library Guide for Social Workers* (1979); "Legislative Activity for RI Librarians," *RILA Bltn.* (Je. 1979); various articles in *RI LA*, 1977–. **Activities:** 1, 12; 24, 25, 36; 92 **Addr.:** Rhode Island Library Association, 104 11th St., Providence, RI 02906.

Plotzke, Robert Francis (Ap. 26, 1947, Chicago, IL) Exec. Dir., Rolling Prairie Lib. Syst., 1978–; Dir., Lib. Srvs., Johnson City Pub. Lib., 1973–78; Dir., Lib. Srvs., St. John's River Jr. Coll., 1970–73. **Educ.:** Univ. of WI, Whitewater, 1965–69, BBA (Bus. Admin.); FL State Univ., 1969–70, MLS; E. TN State Univ., 1975–78, MBA (Bus. Admin.). **Orgs.:** ALA. IL LA. Rotary Club of Decatur. **Activities:** 9, 13; 17; 59 **Addr.:** Rolling Prairie Library System, 345 W. Eldorado St., Decatur, IL 62522.

Plum, Dorothy A. (Je. 16, 1900, Cherry Valley, NY) Retired, 1965–; Bibl., Spec. Col., Vassar Coll. Lib., 1927–65; Asst., Columbia Univ. Sch. of Lib. Srv., 1926–27. **Educ.:** NY State Coll., Vassar Coll., 1919–22, AB (Hist., Latin); NY State Lib. Sch., 1923–26, BLS. **Orgs.:** ALA. NY LA. N. Country Resrch. and Ref. Essex Cnty. Hist. Socty.: Lib. Head (1970–). Adirondack Mt. Club: Bibl. Com. (Ch., 1950–75). **Honors:** Adirondack Musm., Silver plate with inscription re: *Adirondack Bibliography*, 1979. **Pubns.:** *Bibliography of American College Library Administration* (1973); jt. auth., *The Great Experiment* (1961); jt. auth., *The Magnificent Enterprise* (1961). **Activities:** 1, 2; 39; 57 **Addr.:** East Hill, Keene, NY 12942.

Plunkett, Donnaleen Nettles (O. 26, 1944, Greenville, SC) Upper Sch. Media Spec., Savannah Country Day Sch., 1980–; Media Spec., May Howard Sch., 1979–80; Media Spec., Largo Tibet Sch., 1969–72; Libn., U.S. Spec. Srvs., Korea, 1967–68. **Educ.:** Columbia Coll., 1962–65, BA (LS); Univ. of GA, 1969–71, MED (Lib. Educ.). **Orgs.:** ALA. GA LA. Delta Kappa Gamma: Pres. (1979–81). Jr. Leag. of Savannah. Bradley Point Garden Club. **Honors:** Delta Kappa Gamma, 1969; Delta Kappa Pi, 1971; Phi Kappa Phi, 1971. **Activities:** 10; 32, 39, 48; 63 **Addr.:** 706 Bradley Point Rd., Savannah, GA 31410.

Pluscauskas, Martha (Mr. 18, 1939, Newmarket, ON) Coord., Lib. Srvs., E. York Bd. of Educ., 1979–; Libn., Overlea Sec. Sch., 1977–79. **Educ.:** Univ. of Toronto, 1972, MLS. **Orgs.:** ON LA. Can. LA. ON Sec. Sch. Tchrs. Fed. **Pubns.:** Ed., *Canadian Books in Print;* Ed., *Canadian Serials Directory.* **Activities:** 10; 17; 63 **Addr.:** 840 Coxwell Ave., Toronto, ON M4C 2V3 Canada.

Poarch, Margaret E. (S. 18, 1922, Louisville, KY) Lectr., Sch. of Lib. and Info. Sci., SUNY Coll. of Arts and Sci., Geneseo, 1973–, Asst. Dean, 1979–80; Coord. of Chld. and Young People's Srvs., Memphis and Shelby Cnty. Pub. Lib. and Info. Ctr.,

Special Subjects/Services: 50. Adult educ.; 51. Advert./Mktg.; 52. Aerosp.; 53. Agric.; 54. Area std.; 55. Arts/Hum.; 56. Autom.; 57. Bibl./Prtg.; 58. Bio. sci.; 59. Bus./Fin.; 60. Chem.; 61. Copyrt.; 62. Documtn.; 63. Educ.; 64. Engin.; 65. Env.; 66. Eth. grps.; 67. Film; 68. Food/Nutr.; 69. Geneal.; 70. Geo.; 71. Geol.; 72. Handcpd.; 73. Hist.; 74. Int. frdm.; 75. Info. sci.; 76. Insr.; 77. Law; 78. Legis.; 79. Math./Comp. sci.; 80. Med.; 81. Metals; 82. Nat. resrcs.; 83. Newsp.; 84. Nuc. sci.; 85. Oral hist.; 86. Petr./Energy; 87. Pharm.; 88. Phys./Astr./Math.; 89. Readg.; 90. Relig.; 91. Sci./Tech.; 92. Soc. sci.; 93. Telecom.; 94. Transp.; 95. (other).

1971–73; Lib. Dev. Consult., State Lib. of OH, 1968–70; Supervsg. Chld. Libn., San Mateo Cnty. Lib. Syst., 1961–68; Army Libn., US Army, Europe (France, Germany), 1955–57; various chld. libn. positions, 1943–61. **Educ.:** Averett Coll., 1939–41, (Soc. Std.); Radford Univ., 1941–43, AB (Sec. Educ., Soc. Std.); Simmons Coll., 1946–47, BS (LS, Pub. Libnshp.); Univ. of WI, 1970–71, MA (LS, Spec. Cert. in Libnshp.); various crs. **Orgs.:** ALA: Cncl (1971–72), Newbery-Caldecott Com. (1963–64); ALSC/Chld. Srvs. Div. (Dir., 1971–72), Nom. Com. (1953, 1968); PLA, Strategy for Pub. Lib. Change, Strategy III, Resrch. and Prototypes (1972–75); Int. Frdm. RT (1972–). AALS. Amer. Assn. of State Libs. Frnds. of the Osborne and Smith Col., Toronto Pub. Lib., Frnds. of the US Sect. Intl. Bd. of Bks. for Youth. Natl. Bk. Assn. **Pubns.:** *For Storytellers and Storytelling* (1968); "Ghosts and the Supernatural," *WI Lib. Bltn.* (S.–O. 1971); "A Case of Storytelling," *Young Reader's Review* (Ja. 1967); "Katherine B. Shippen–'A Fluent Sense of History'," *Top of the News* (Ja. 1965); "A Librarian Visits Mainland China," *Top of the News* (Spr. 1980). **Activities:** 9, 11; 17, 21, 24; 54, 66, 74 **Addr.:** School of Library and Information Science, SUNY College of Arts and Science, Geneseo, NY 14454.

Pobst, Mary Jane (N. 4, 1920, Georgetown, OH) Chief, Support Srvs., Columbia Univ. Libs., 1980–; Assoc. Dir. for Resrch. and Plng., WA State Lib., 1972–80; Head, Comp. Applications Sect., NY State Lib., 1969–72; Fulbright Lectr., Univ. of Tehran, Fac. of Educ., 1971–72; Lectr., Grad. Sch. of LS, SUNY, Albany, 1969–70; Head, Tech. Srvs., Rensselaer Polytech. Inst., 1968–69, Head of Cat., 1967–68, Cat. Libn., Skidmore Coll., 1961–66. **Educ.:** Antioch Coll., 1938–43, BA (Soc. Sci., Psy.); Antioch-Putney Grad. Sch., 1953–55, MA (Educ.); SUNY, Albany, 1966–67, MLS. **Orgs.:** ALA: LIRT/Bd. of Dirs. (1977–79). ASIS. WA LA. Pac. NW LA. Amer. Cvl. Liberties Un. Common Cause. **Honors:** Beta Phi Mu. **Pubns.:** Jt. auth., *A Network Management Tool: Computer Simulation of Interlibrary Lending* (1979); "Library Automation," *Anl. Review of Info. Sci. and Tech.* (1979); jt. auth., *Study for the Design of an Optimum System for Mail Order Book Delivery Service in the State of Washington* (1974); *Books by Mail Services: Moving the Library to Disadvantaged Adults* (1974); jt. auth., *Nepal in Transition* (1968); various articles. **Activities:** 1, 13; 17, 24, 41; 56, 62, 75 **Addr.:** Columbia University Libraries, Butler 210, 535 W. 114th St., New York City, NY 10027.

Pochciol, Judith Rae Applegate (Mr. 5, 1940, Sharon, PA) Med. Libn., St. Agnes Hosp., 1975–; Asst. Libn., Med. and Chirurgical Fac. of MD, 1970–71; Asst. Libn., West. Psyt. Inst., Univ. of Pittsburgh, 1965–70. **Educ.:** Grove City Coll., 1958–62, BA (Educ.); Univ. of Pittsburgh, 1964–66, MLS; Med. LA, 1976, Cert. (Med. Libnshp.). **Orgs.:** Med. LA. MD Assn. of Hlth. Sci. Libns.: Rec. Secy. (1977–79). **Activities:** 5, 12; 17, 39, 46; 80 **Addr.:** Health Sciences Library, St. Agnes Hospital, 900 Caton Ave., Baltimore, MD 21229.

Podboy, Alvin M., Jr. (F. 10, 1947, Cleveland, OH) Libn., Baker and Hostetler, 1978–; Assoc. Law Libn., Pub. Srvs., Case West. Rsv. Univ. Sch. of Law, 1974–78; Law Libn., Geauga Cnty. Bar Assn., 1973–74. **Educ.:** OH Univ., 1965–69, AB (Gvt.); Case West. Rsv. Univ., 1969–72, JD (Law), 1974–77, MS (LS, Law) AALL, 1977, Cert. Law Libn. **Orgs.:** AALL: *Law Lib. Jnl.* Com. OH Reg. Assn. of Law Libs.: Guidelines Com. Amer. Bar Assn.: Intl. Law Sect. Cleveland Bar Assn.: Law Ofc. Econ. Com. **Pubns.:** "Book Appraisal," *Law Lib. Jnl.* (F. 1978). **Activities:** 1, 5; 17, 24, 41; 74, 77 **Addr.:** Baker and Hostetler, 3200 National City Center, Cleveland, OH 44114.

Podell, Diane K. (Ap. 5, 1931, New York, NY) Pub. Srvs. Libn., Pers. Dept., C.W. Post Coll., 1979–; Visit. Lectr., Queens Coll. Sch. of LS, 1980–; Ref. Libn., Syosset (NY) Lib., 1978–79; Asst. Dir., Maywood (NJ) Lib., 1975–78; Ref. Libn., Englewood (NJ) Lib., 1974–77. **Educ.:** City Coll. of New York, 1948–51, BS (Educ., Soc.); Queens Coll., 1974–75, MLS. **Orgs.:** ALA. NY LA. Nassau Cnty. LA. **Activities:** 1, 9; 16, 20, 44 **Addr.:** Periodicals Dept., C.W. Post College, Greenvale, NY 11545.

Poggi, Patricia Kelly (N. 8, 1941, Boston, MA) Dir., Instr. Srvs., Rockland Cnty. BOCES, 1980–; Admin. Asst. to Dir., North. Westchester BOCES, 1970–80; Consult., Adj. Instr., Dutchess Cmnty. Coll., 1978–80, Facilitator, Grantsmanship Wkshps., 1976–77; Instr., Soclgy. Dept., SUNY, New Paltz, 1972–74; various positions, in educ. 1957–79. **Educ.:** Cornell Univ., 1963, AB (Anthro., Hist.); SUNY, New Paltz, 1974, MS (Soclgy., Educ.); Columbia Univ., 1977, MEd (Curric., Tchg.), 1978, EdD (Instr. Tech.); NY State, Permanent Cert. (Soc. Std., 7–12; Elem. Tchg., N–6). **Orgs.:** Rockland Cnty. LA. Sch. LA of NY State. Educ. Comm. Dir. of NY State. NY LA. AECT. Natl. Assn. of Reg. Media Ctrs. Amer. Sociological Assn. East. Sociological Assn. Various orgs. **Honors:** Ford Fndn., Hist. Grant, 1958; Carnegie and Rockefeller Fndns., Grants for Anthro. Resrch., 1962; Phi Delta Kappa. **Pubns.:** "Anthropological Field Notes," *Human Rel. Area File* (1962); various articles in lcl. pubns. **Activities:** 10; 17, 32; 63 **Addr.:** Salt Point Turnpike, Pleasant Valley, NY 12569.

Pogue, Basil G. (Mr. 5, 1944, Ballymena, North. Ireland) Head, Info. Srvs., Regina Pub. Lib., 1979–, Ref. Libn., 1974–79; Ref. Libn., Univ. of Waterloo Lib., 1973–74; Indxr., Prov. Arch. of AB, 1972. **Educ.:** Univ. of St. Andrews, 1962–67, MA (Geo., Pol. Econ.); Univ. of Calgary, 1967–70, MA (Geo.); Univ. of AB, 1971–72, BLS. **Orgs.:** Can. Assn. of Pub. Libs.: Secy.-Treas. (1975–77). SK LA: Treas. (1976–78); Cont. Ed. Com. (Conv., 1978–). **Activities:** 9; 25, 29, 39; 70 **Addr.:** Information Services, Regina Public Library, 2311–12th Ave., Regina, SK S4P 0N3 Canada.

Pohl, Gunther E. (Jl. 22, 1925, Berlin, Germany) Chief, Lcl. Hist. and Geneal. Div., NY Pub. Lib., 1969–, Asst. Lcl. Hist. and Geneal. Div., NY Pub. Lib., 1948–69. **Educ.:** NY Univ., 1942–46, BA (Hist.), 1948, MA (Hist.); Columbia Univ., 1951, MS (LS). **Orgs.:** ALA: Geneal. Com. (Ch., 1971–73); Hist. Com. (1975–77). **Pubns.:** Cmplr., *New York State Biographical, Genealogical and Portrait Index* card index. **Activities:** 9; 15, 17, 39; 55, 69, 85 **Addr.:** 24 Walden Pl., Great Neck, NY 11020.

Pointer, Beth L. (Jl. 17, 1951, Columbus, GA) Adult Srvs. Libn., Homewood Pub. Lib., 1976–. **Educ.:** Memphis State Univ., 1974, BMsc (Msc. Hist.); Univ. of AL, 1974–75, MLS. **Orgs.:** AL LA: JMRT (1980–81). ALA. SELA. **Activities:** 9; 15, 16, 39; 55, 92 **Addr.:** Homewood Public Library, Birmingham, AL 35209.

Pointer, Jean Marie (F. 6, 1927, Clatskanie, OR) Admin., Instr. Support Systs., Norwalk-La Mirada Unfd. Sch. Dist., 1966–; Part-time Instr., CA State Univ., Long Beach, 1970–; Dist. Libn., Buena Park Sch. Dist., 1962–66; Jr. High Libn., Little Lake Sch. Dist., 1961–62; Tchr., CA Schs., 1959–61. **Educ.:** Reed Coll., 1944–46 (Hum.); Whitman Coll., 1957–59, BS (Hist.); Univ. of OR, Univ. of South. CA, 1962–66, MLS; U.S. Intl. Univ., 1976–79, PhD (Educ., Admin.); CA State Univ., Long Beach, 1975–76 Admin. Cred. **Orgs.:** ALA. CA Media/Lib. Educ. Assn.: Pres. S. Sect. (1982). South. CA Cncl. of Lit. for Chld. and Youth. Claremont Readg. Conf.: Recog. of Merit Com. (1970–). Assn. of CA Sch. Admin. **Honors** CA State Univ., Long Beach, Dept. of Instr. Media, Disting. Srv. Awd., 1977; Parent-Tchrs. Assn., Hon. Life for Contrib. to Libs. and Readg., 1973. **Pubns.:** "Children Vote for Their Favorite Books in the Young Reader Medal Contest," *CA Media and Lib. Educ. Assn. Jnl.* (Fall 1977). **Activities:** 10; 17, 26, 32; 63 **Addr.:** 145 Emerald Bay, Laguna Beach, CA 92651.

Poiré, Joseph A. (Mr. 10, 1938, Worcester, MA) Acq. Libn., Instr., Keene State Coll., 1977–; Dir. of Libs., Becher-Leicester Jr. coll., 1973–77; Ref. libn., Worcester Tech., 1972–73. **Educ.:** Assumption Coll., 1956–60 BA (Eng.); Assumption Coll., 1961–64, MAT (Eng.); Simmons Coll., 1970–72, MLS (Lib.). **Orgs.:** ALA. MA LA: Int. Frdm. Com. NLA. NH LA. New Eng. LA. **Honors:** Beta Phi Mu, 1972. **Pubns.:** "Teaching Film," *Film Socty. News* (Fall 1967); "Beach Movies," *Screen Educ. News* (Spr. 1966). ; 11, 18, 35; 58, 62. **Addr.:** 21 Arletta Ave., Worcester, MA 01602.

Poisson, Ellen Hull (O. 13, 1946, New London, CT) Sr. Asst. Ref. Libn., Cornell Univ. Med. Col. Lib., (1980–); Libn., UN Dev. Prog., Teheran, Iran, 1975–78; Instr. of Eng., Teheran Univ. of Tech., Teheran, Iran, 1971–72. **Educ.:** Smith Coll., 1964–68, BA (Relig., Pre-Med.); Teheran Univ., Teheran, Iran, 1970–72, MA (LS). **Orgs.:** MLA: NY Reg. Grp. UN Dev. Prog., Teheran: Staff Assn. (Ch., 1978). **Pubns.:** *A Selective Directory of Libraries in Iran* (1977); *Sources of Information in Teheran* (1976); "The Teheran Collection," *UN Dev. Prog. News* (S.–O. 1977). **Activities:** 1, 12; 17, 26; 56, 80, 95-Libnshp. in dev. countries. **Addr.:** Cornell University Medical College Library, 1300 York Ave., New York, NY 10021.

Pokorski, Sr. Marie Cecile (Je. 2, 1937, Philadelphia, PA) Archvst., Bernardine Srs., OSF, 1977–; Tchr., various Cath. schs. 1957–80; Prin., St. Peter Sch., Pottstown, PA, 1970–76. **Educ.:** Villanova Univ., 1955–66, AB (Latin), 1972–75, MA (Educ.); various arch. wkshps. **Orgs.:** Cath. LA: Neumann Chap., Arch. Sect. (Ch.-elect, 1981). Mid-Atl. Reg. Arch. Conf. **Activities:** 2, 10; 17, 38; 63, 66, 90 **Addr.:** Maryview, 647 Spring Mill Rd., Villanova, PA 19085.

Polach, Frank J. (Ja. 4, 1944, Muskogee, OK) Assoc. Libn., Lib. of Sci. and Med., Rutgers Univ., 1980–, Agr. and Bot. Resrc. Libn., 1979–80, Agr. Libn., Agr. Lib., 1977–78; Plant Info. Ofcr., NY Bot. Garden, 1975–76; Asst. Prof., NY State Agr. Exper. Station, Cornell Univ., 1971–74. **Educ.:** Ctrl. State Univ., 1962–66, BS (Bio.); Univ. of CA, Davis, 1967–71, PhD (Plant Pathology); Columbia Univ., 1975–76, MS (LS). **Orgs.:** ALA: ACRL/Sci. and Tech. Sect., Nom. Com. (Ch., 1980–81), Oberly Awds. Com. (1977–81). Cncl. on Bot. and Horticult. Libs. NY Lib. Club. Assocs. of Natl. Agr. Lib. AAUP. NY Acad. of Sci. **Pubns.:** "Current Survey of Reference Sources in Agriculture," *Ref. Srvs. Review* (1979). **Activities:** 1; 15, 17, 39; 58, 65, 82 **Addr.:** Library of Science and Medicine, Rutgers University, P.O. Box 1029, Piscataway, NJ 08854.

Polacheck, Demarest Lloyd (Jl. 13, 1918, Milwaukee, WI) Head, Adult Srvs., Stark Cnty. Dist. Lib., 1968–. **Educ.:** Univ. of Chicago, 1935–47, AA, PhB (Eng.); Yale Univ., 1947–50, MFA (Thea.); Kent State Univ., 1962–67, MLS; OH State Univ., 1942–43, ASTP Cert. (Italian). **Orgs.:** OH LA. ALA: AFL-CIO-ALA Jt. Com. on Lib. Srv. to Labor Grps., (Ch., 1973–76). RASD Notable Books Council (1981–82). **Pubns.:** "Outreach Planning for Special Interest Groups," *OLA Bltn.* (Ap. 1978); "Library Service to Labor Groups," *ALA Yearbook* (1976); "Measuring Reference Service," *OLA Bltn.* (Ap. 1976); "A Method of Adult Book Selection for a Public Library System," *RQ* (Spr. 1977). **Activities:** 9; 15, 16, 22; 55 **Addr.:** 36 Fourth St. S.E., Massillon, OH 44646.

Polakof, Susan (Ap. 24, 1948, Los Angeles, CA) Head, OCLC/Autom. Cat. Unit, Univ. of WY, 1977–; Cat., SUNY, Albany, 1975–77; Lib. Asst. III, AZ State Univ., 1970–73. **Educ.:** CO State Univ., 1966–70, BA (Pol. Sci.); Univ. of South. CA, 1973–74, MSLS. **Orgs.:** ALA: Chap. Cnclr. (1979–82); Mem. Com. (1977–81). **Activities:** 1; 17, 20; 56, 92 **Addr.:** 1516 Grand Ave., #108, Laramie, WY 82070.

Poland, Ursula H. (Anker) (Je. 11, 1922, Düsseldorf, Germany) Libn., Prof. of Med. Lib. Sci., Albany Med. Coll., 1964–, Lab. Asst., 1957–61; Sch. Meals Supvsr., Surrey Cnty. Cncl., Eng., 1944–46; Cafeteria Mgr., Messrs Rootes Secur. Ltd., Eng., 1942–44. **Educ.:** SUNY, Albany, 1961–63, BA (Eng.), 1963–64, MLS; King's Coll. of Household and Soc. Sci., Univ. of London, 1940–42 Dip. (Inst. Mgt.); various crs. **Orgs.:** Albany Area Hlth Lib. Afflt.: Ch. (1974–75). IFLA: Sect. of Bio. and Med. Sci. Libs., Spec. Proj. for World Dir. of Hlth. Sci. Libs. (Ch., 1979). Med. LA: Intl. Coop. Com. (Ch., 1974–77); Ad Hoc Com. Med. LA Grp. Structure Impl. (Ch., 1978–81); Upstate NY and ON Reg. Grp. (Ch., 1967–68). Capital Dist. Lib. Cncl.: Bd. of Trustees (1969–73). SUNY Biomed. Comm. Netwk.: Users Task Force Com. (Ch., 1974–75). Reg. Med. Lib. Prog.: Adv. and Plng. Com. (Ch., 1979). Albany Med. Coll. Fac. Org.: Secty., Treas. (1974–78). **Honors:** Med. LA, Eliot Prize, 1979. **Pubns.:** "The Medical Library Association's Internat. Fellowship Programs," *Bltn. Med. LA* (1978); "New Library Buildings," *Bltn. Med. LA* (1974); jt. auth., "Three-Way Catalog Division Combined with Conversion to Medical Subject Headings (MeSH) in a medium-sized Medical Library," *Bltn. Med. LA* (1974). **Activities:** 1; 17, 34; 58, 80 **Addr.:** Schaffer Library of Health Sciences, Albany Medical College, Albany, NY 12208.

Polansky, Patricia A. (Ap. 6, 1944, Billings, MT) Russ. Bibl., Univ. of HI, Hamilton Lib., 1976–, Head, Out-of-Print Unit, 1971–76, Cat., 1969–71; Cat., NUS Corp., 1967–68. **Educ.:** Univ. of HI, 1963–67, BA (Russ. Lang.), 1968–69, MLS; Inst. on Slavic Libnshp., 1970. **Orgs.:** Amer. Assn. for the Advnc. of Slavic Std.: Bibl. and Documtn. Com. (1979–82). Intl. Assn. of Orientalist Libns.: Nom. Com. (Ch., 1980). ALA. West. Slavic Assn. **Honors:** Cncl. on Lib. Resrcs., Flwshp., 1979. **Pubns.:** *Russian Writings on the South Pacific area* (1974); "Russian sources on Asia: a guide to the literature," *Intl. Assn. of Orientalist Libns. Bltn.* (1977); "The Russian Collection at the Univ. of Hawaii," *HLA Jnl.* (1980); "Russians in the Pacific: A Review of New Books, 1974–1979," *Pacific Std.* (1980). **Activities:** 1; 15, 20, 39; 54 **Addr.:** University of Hawaii, Hamilton Library, 2550 The Mall, Honolulu, HI 96822.

Polardino, Linda S. (My. 1, 1952, New York, NY) Chief, Lib. Srv., F.D.R. Hosp., Vets. Admin., 1978–; Libn., Vets. Admin. Med. Ctr., Northport, 1977–78; Libn., Vets. Admin. Med. Ctr., Brockton, MA, 1976–77. **Educ.:** Hofstra Univ., 1970–74, BA (Eng.); Long Island Univ., 1974–75, MLS; 1976, Med. Libnshp. **Orgs.:** Med. LA. ALA: ASCLA. **Activities:** 4, 12; 15, 16, 17; 58, 80 **Addr.:** Library Service, F.D.R. Hospital, Veterans Administration, Montrose, NY 10548.

Polcari, Ann Linda (F. 19, 1943, New York, NY) Univ. Libn. III, Ref., Univ. of CT Lib., 1968–; Biblgphr., Comp. Sci. Dept., PA State Univ., 1966–67. **Educ.:** Queens Coll., CUNY, 1959–63, BA (Fr.); Univ. of Pittsburgh, 1967–68, MLS; NY Univ., 1975–79, MA (Fr.). **Orgs.:** New Eng. OLUG. ACRL: New Eng. Chap. New Eng. LA. Amer. Assn. of Tchrs. of Fr. **Honors** Beta Phi Mu. **Pubns.:** Various articles in lcl. pubns. **Activities:** 31, 39; 56 **Addr.:** U–5R Reference, University of CT Library, Storrs, CT 06268.

Polette, Nancy J. (My. 18, 1930, St. Louis, MO) Assoc. Prof., Educ., Lib. Consult., Wkshp. leader, speaker, auth., Lindenwood Coll., 1980–; Dir., Resrc. Ctrs., Pattonville Sch. Dist., 1964–79. **Educ.:** William Woods Coll., 1948–50, AA (Drama); Washington Univ., 1964, BS (Educ.); South. IL Univ., 1966–68, MS (Educ.). **Orgs.:** ALA: AASL. Mod. Lang. Assn. MO Assn. Sch. Libs. Chld. Readg. RT. Chld. Lit. Assn. **Honors:** MO Assn. Sch. Libns., Disting. Srv. Awd., 1976; William Woods Coll., Disting. Alum. Awd., 1980. **Pubns.:** *The Modern School Library* (1976); *E Is For Everybody* (1976); *Celebrating with Books* (1977); *Katie Penn* (1978); *Exploring Books with Gifted* (1980). **Activities:** 11, 12; 21, 24, 26 **Addr.:** 203 San Jose, O'Fallon, MO 63366.

Polhamus, Julia Elizabeth (F. 1, 1941, Detroit, MI) Acq. Libn., Wayne Cnty. Cmnty. Coll., 1977–; Tchr., Taylor Sch. Dist., 1972–74; Ref. Libn., Campbell-Ewald Co., 1969–70; Head Libn., Riverview Pub. Lib., 1964–69. **Educ.:** Univ. of MI, 1958–62, BA (Eng.), 1962–66, MALS; 1970–72, Tchg. Cert. (Eng.). **Activities:** 1; 15, 32, 39 **Addr.:** 15235 Harrison, Allen Park, MI 48101.

PROFESSIONAL ACTIVITIES: Institutions: 1. Acad. lib.; 2. Arch.; 3. Assn.; 4. Fed./Gvt. lib.; 5. Inst. lib.; 6. Mfr./Suppl.; 7. Milit. lib.; 8. Musm.; 9. Pub. lib.; 10. Sch. lib.; 11. Sch. of lib. sci.; 12. Spec. lib.; 13. State lib.; 14. (other). **Functions/Activities:** 15. Acq./Col. dev.; 16. Adult srvs.; 17. Admin.; 18. Apprais.; 19. Archit./Bldgs.; 20. Cat./Class.; 21. Chld. srvs.; 22. Circ.; 23. Cons./Pres.; 24. Consult.; 25. Cont. ed.; 26. Educ. lib. sci.; 27. Ext. srvs.; 28. Fund/Grants; 29. Gvt. pubs.; 30. Indx./Abs.; 31. Instr. lib. use; 32. Media srvs.; 33. Micro.; 34. Netwks./Coop.; 35. Persnl.; 36. PR; 37. Publshg.; 38. Recs. mgt.; 39. Ref. srvs.; 40. Repro.; 41. Resrch.; 42. Review.; 43. Secur.; 44. Serials; 45. Spec. col.; 46. Tech. srvs.; 47. Trustees/Bds.; 48. YA srvs.; 49. (other).

Poli, Rosario (Je. 20, 1940, Cleveland, OH) Info. Spec., Asst. Prof., Mechanized Info. Ctr., OH State Univ. Libs., 1973–, Head Ref., Educ. Lib., 1967–73; Ed., OH Educ. Assn., 1970–72; Lib. Asst. to Asst. Dir., Case West. Rsv. Univ., ILL, 1964–67, 1963–64; Tchr., Cleveland Bd. of Educ., 1962–63. **Educ.:** Case West. Rsv. Univ., 1958–62, BA (Eng., Chem.), 1963–66 (Educ., Guid.), 1965–67 (Coll. Libs. Documtn.). **Orgs.:** OH Acad. LA: Bd. (1979–81). Columbus Area OLUG: Strg. Com.; Prog. Com. Assn. of Info. and Dssm. Ctrs. ALA. Phi Delta Kappa: OH State Univ. Chap. (Secy., 1970–). **Honors:** Phi Delta Kappa, Srv. Key, 1978. **Pubns.:** Jt. auth., *Design for Library Research* (1980); jt. auth., "To Be or Not To Be," *Jnl. of Acad. Libnshp.* (Mr. 1976); jt. producer, "The Mechanized Information Center," audio slide tape (1977); various articles, bks., edshps. **Activities:** 1, 12; 25, 31, 39; 62, 63, 75 **Addr.:** 60 Broadmeadows, Apt. 300, Columbus, OH 43210.

Polishuk, Bernard (F. 24, 1927, Seattle, WA) Coord., Chld. Srvs., King Cnty. Lib. Syst., 1958–; Chld. Libn., Seattle Pub. Lib.; Chld. Libn. Multnomah Cnty. Lib.; Cat., Spokane Cnty. Lib. **Educ.:** Univ. of WA, BA, MLS; Columbia Univ., MA. **Orgs.:** NLA: WA State Chap., Coores. Secy. WA LA: Soc. Resp. Sect., Ch.; various com. Amer. Cvl. Liberties Un. WA State Chap.; various com. **Pubns.:** various articles. **Activities:** 9; 21, 42; 50, 74, 89 **Addr.:** King County Library System, Service Center, 300 8th North, Seattle, WA 98109.

Politis, John Valentine (S. 15, 1944, New Britain, CT) Libn., A. Philip Randolph Skills Ctr., 1975–; Libn., Moorestown Frnds. Sch., 1972–75. **Educ.:** Univ. of PA, 1962–66, BA (Eng.); Drexel Univ., 1970–71, MLS. **Orgs.:** Assn. of Philadelphia Sch. Libns.: Prog. Com. (1972–). PA Sch. LA. ALA. PA Citizens for Better Libs. **Pubns.:** "Mediatmosphere," *Amer. Libs.* (My. 1979); "Selecting Music for YA Collections," *YA Alternative Nsltr.* (N. 1978); Ed., *Rockingchair* (1977–). **Activities:** 10; 31, 32, 48 **Addr.:** 966 N. Randolph St., Philadelphia, PA 19123.

Polivka, Wendy (Ja. 23, 1950, Albany, CA) Data Prcs. Mgr., Aircraft Tech. Publshrs., 1979–; Asst. Lib. Dir., Libs., Amer. Samoa, 1976–77; Outrch. Libn., Berkeley Pub. Lib., 1975–76; Elem. Sch. Libn., Fairfield-Suisun Sch. Dist., 1972–75. **Educ.:** Univ. of CA, Berkeley, 1969–71, BA (Soc. Sci.), 1971–72, MLS. **Orgs.:** SLA. HI LA. CA Assn. of Sch. Libns. **Pubns.:** *Bound Catalog of Audiovisual Materials Available from Library of American Samoa* (1977). **Activities:** 12; 17; 52, 56, 93 **Addr.:** 595 Merritt Ave. #5, Oakland, CA 94610.

Pollack, Beth (Mr. 3, 1951, Brooklyn, NY) Libn., Ogilvy and Mather, Inc., 1979–; Libn., Brooklyn Pub. Lib., 1974–79; Film Cat., Amer. Musm. of Nat. Hist., 1973. **Educ.:** SUNY, Stony Brook, 1968–71, BS (Bio.); Pratt Inst., 1972–73, MLS. **Orgs.:** SLA. Country Dance and Song Socty. of Amer. Pinewoods Folk Msc. Club. **Pubns.:** Photographs pubsh. in *The Red Balloon* (1970–71); *Against The Grain* (1977). **Activities:** 12; 20, 39, 41; 51, 59 **Addr.:** 832 Union St., Brooklyn, NY 11215.

Pollack, Carol (O. 22, 1938, Detroit, MI) Chief Libn., Asst. Cashier Detroitbank Corp., 1974–; Libn., MI Bell Telephone Co., 1971–74; Ref. libn., Detroit News, 1971; Info. Spec., Wayne Cnty. Intermediate Sch. Dist., 1968–70. **Educ.:** Wayne State Univ., 1957–60, BFA (Art), 1960, MA (Art), 1968–70, MSLS. **Orgs.:** SLA: Bank Libns. RT (Mdrtr., 1980); Pre-conf. Cont. Ed. Sem. (Coord., 1980). Assoc. Info. Mgrs. Downtown Detroit Lib. Netwk. Womens Econ. Club. Assn. of Women in Finance. Penn Ctrl. Passenger Assn.: Treas. Fndrs. Socty., Detroit Inst. of Arts. Various orgs. **Pubns.:** Various papers. **Activities:** 12; 15, 17, 24, 35, 39, 46; 54, 59 **Addr.:** Detroitbank Corp., Research Library, 211 W. Fort St., Detroit, MI 49226.

Pollack, Pamela D. (Je. 19, 1948, New York, NY) Bk. Review Ed., *Sch. Lib. Jnl.*, 1971–, Assoc. Ed., 1974–80, Asst. Ed., 1971–74. **Educ.:** Queens Coll., CUNY, 1966–69, BA (Eng.), 1969–71, MLS. **Orgs.:** ALA: ALSC, Hans Christian Andersen Awds. Com. (1980), Mildred Batchelder Com. (1977), Newbery-Caldecott Awds. Com. (1978). Natl. Bk. Critics Cir. Women's Natl. Bk. Assn.: NY Chap, Bd. of Mgrs. (1976–78). Amer. Bk. Awds.: Nom. Com. for Chld. Bk. Awds. (1979). Natl. Cncl. of Christs. and Jews: Com. to Choose "Human Fam." Booklist (1980–). **Pubns.:** *Books by the Numbers: The Mass-Market Children's Book* (1980); *Best of the Best: A Second Look at SLJ's Best Books '66–'78* (1979). **Activities:** 10, 11; 21, 42, 48; 74, 89 **Addr.:** *School Library Journal*, R.R. Bowker Co., 1180 Ave. of Americas, New York, NY 10036.

Pollak, Sally (Ag. 30, 1943, New Orleans, LA) Asst. Dir. for Pub. Srvs., Univ. of TX Hlth. Sci. Ctr., San Antonio, 1979–; Asst. to Dir. for Staff Dev., Houston Acad. of Med.-TX Med. Ctr. Lib., 1978–79, Head, Circ. Srvs., 1974–78; Acq./Ref. Libn., Schaffer Lib. of Hlth. Sci., 1972–74. **Educ.:** Oberlin Coll., 1961–63; SUNY, Albany, 1967–69, BA, magna cum laude (Eng.); 1969–70, MLS; Med. LA, 1973, Cert. **Orgs.:** Med. LA: Schol. Com. (Ch., 1981–82). SLA: TX Chap. (Pres., 1981–82). **Pubns.:** "Classification of Support Staff in Consortium Medical Library," *Bltn. of the Med. LA* (Ap. 1979). **Activities:** 12; 17, 39; 80 **Addr.:** University of Texas Health Science Center at San Antonio Library, 7703 Floyd Curl Dr., San Antonio, TX 78284.

Pollard, Elizabeth Blitch (Je 16, 1939, Valdosta, GA) Subj. Spec., Fine Arts, Lang. and Lit., Nursing, Asst. Prof. of Bibl., Lib., Univ. of AL, 1970–; Pers. Libn., Stack Supvsr., Theo. Lib., Emory Univ., 1968–70, Rsv. Rm. Libn., 1967–68. **Educ.:** Emory Univ., 1957–61, BA (Fine Arts), 1967–70, MLn (LS); various crs. in msclgy. **Orgs.:** Msc. LA: Southeastern Chap. Coll. Art Assn.: Art Libns. Sect. Amer. Musicological Socty. AAUP: Chap. Pres.; VP; State Conf. Nom. Com. (1978–79). **Honors:** Amer. Biog. Inst., Personalities of the S. Awd., 1975–76. **Pubns.:** "State of the Art Survey of Reference Sources in the Fine Arts and Crafts," *Ref. Srvs. Review* (Jl.–S. 1977 O.–D. 1978 O.–D. 1979); various bk. reviews in *Choice, Lib. Jnl., Reprint Bltn. Bk. Reviews* (1972–). **Activities:** 1; 15, 20, 31; 55, 80 **Addr.:** Library, University of AL in Huntsville, P.O. Box 2600, Huntsville, AL 35899.

Pollard, Frances Marguerite (O. 7, 1920, Florence, AL) Exec. Asst. for Lib. Srvs., Booth Lib., East. IL Univ., 1979–, Ch., Dept. of LS, 1970–79, Admin. Asst., Booth Lib., 1963–70; Head Libn., G.W. Trenholm Meml. Lib., AL State Coll., 1961–63, Asst. Libn., 1949–61. **Educ.:** Selma Univ., 1936–38; AL State Coll., 1939–41, BS (Educ., Eng.); West. Rsv. Univ., 1948–49, MSLS; Columbia Univ., 1952–54 (LS); West. Rsv. Univ., 1959–63, PhD (LS, Soclgy.). **Orgs.:** ALA: Cncl. (1972–73). IL LA: Exec. Bd. (1978–79). IL ACRL: Pres. (1978–79). AALS. Amer. Sociological Assn. Socty. for Appld. Anthro. Amer. Acad. of Pol. and Soc. Sci. **Honors:** Alum. Assn. of the Sch. of LS, Case West. Rsv. Univ., Hon. for Outstan. Achvmt. and Srv. to the Lib. Prof., 1979. **Pubns.:** Contrib., *Major Problems in the Education of Librarians* (1954); "News from Illinois Library Schools: Eastern Illinois University," *IASL News for You* (Win. 1973); ed., *Proceedings of the Personnel Evaluation Institute, Held at Eastern Illinois University, October 24-26, 1975* (1976); "Reflections on a Workshop," *Sum and Substance, Corn Belt Lib. Syst. News* (N.–D. 1979); jt. auth., *Illinois Literary Reflections of the Bicentennial Year: What Reading Does for People* ERIC (1977); various other articles. **Activities:** 1, 11; 15, 17, 26; 56, 63, 92 **Addr.:** 1330 A St., Charleston, IL 61920.

Pollard, Richard C. (Mr. 3, 1941, Fresno, CA) Asst. Dir. for Tech. Srvs., Univ. of Chicago Lib., 1981–; Assoc. Dir. for Tech. Srvs., Univ. of TN, 1977–81; Asst. Chief Admin., Cat. Dept., Stanford Univ. Libs., 1972–77, Catlgr., 1966–72. **Educ.:** Stanford Univ., 1959–63, BA (Hist.), 1963–65, MA (Hist.); Univ. of South. CA, 1965–66, MSLS. **Orgs.:** ALA: RTSD; ACRL; LITA;LAMA. North. CA Tech. Prcs. Grp.: Secy., Treas. (1969–70). **Activities:** 1; 17, 46; 56, 70 **Addr.:** University of Chicago Library, Chicago, IL 60637.

Pollard, Russell O. (Ap. 17, 1947, Princeton, IN) Head, Tech. Srvs., Andover-Harvard Theo. Lib., Harvard Dvnty. Sch., 1979–; Cat. Libn., Episcopal Dvnty. Sch., Weston Sch. of Theo. Lib., 1975–79. **Educ.:** Wabash Coll., 1965–69, BA (Pol. Sci.); Simmons Coll., 1976–78, MS (LS); grad. work in MDiv prog. **Orgs.:** ATLA. ALA: RTSD. New Eng. LA. MA LA. **Activities:** 1; 17, 34, 46; 90 **Addr.:** Andover-Harvard Theological Library, 45 Francis Ave., Cambridge, MA 02138.

Pollard, Stanley C. (Je. 16, 1945, Prince Albert, SK) Asst. Resrcs. Coord., Lrng. Resrcs. Ctr., 1979–, Tchr., Lib. Aides Prog., 1977–80; Libn., Kay Bingham Elem., 1977–79; Libn., John Tod Elem., 1974–77. **Educ.:** Univ. of BC, 1980, BED (Lib.). **Orgs.:** BC Sch. Libns. Assn.: Kamloops, VP (1974), Pres. (1975), Couns. (1976), Reviewer (1974–80). **Activities:** 10, 12; 15, 17, 34; 63 **Addr.:** 1185 McInnes Pl., Kamloops, BC V2B 5T7 Canada.

Pollard, William C. (Ag. 22, 1923, Farmville, NC) Coll. Libn., Mary Baldwin Coll., 1977–; Libn., Coll. of William and Mary, 1966–77; Libn., Old Dominion Univ., 1954–66; Soc. Sci. Libn., Univ. of GA, 1950–54, Biblgphr., 1949–50. **Educ.:** Davidson Coll., 1944–46; Univ. of NC, 1946–48, BA (Comp. Lit.); FL State Univ., 1948–49, MA (LS). **Orgs.:** VA LA: Pres. (1968); Treas. (1961–64); Actv. Com. (1963). SELA: Bd. (1965–67). VA State Bd. for Cert. of Libns. VA State Hist. Recs. Adv. Bd. **Activities:** 1; 15, 17, 39 **Addr.:** Grafton Library, Mary Baldwin College, Staunton, VA 24401.

Pollet, Miriam (New York, NY) Head, Ref. Dept., Downstate Med. Ctr., 1979–; Libn., Sci. Div., Mid-Manhattan Lib., 1978–79; Sci. Biblgphr., Hunter Coll., 1978; Sci. Ref. Biblgphr., Brooklyn Coll., 1970–77. **Educ.:** Brooklyn Coll., City Coll. of NY, 1942–46, BA (Hist.), 1952–60, BS (Bio., Chem.); Columbia Univ., 1968–69, MS (LS); NY Univ., 1971–72, MA (Bio. Educ.). **Orgs.:** LA CUNY. NY Lib. Club. Med. LA: NY Reg. Grp. AAAS. **Activities:** 1, 12; 39; 58, 80 **Addr.:** 100 W. 94 St., New York, NY 10025.

Pollis, Angela R. (Pittsburgh, PA) Staff Supvsr., Tech. and Sci. Info., U.S. Steel Corp. Resrch. Lab.; Instr., Chem., Carnegie Mellon Univ.; Visit. Lectr., Univ. of Pittsburgh, Sch. of Lib. and Info. Sci., 1979–82. **Educ.:** Carnegie Mellon Univ., BS (Chem.); Univ. of Pittsburgh, MLS. **Orgs.:** SLA. ASIS: Mid-Yr. Mtg. (Co-Ch., 1980); Pittsburgh Chap. Ofcr. Amer. Iron and Steel Inst.: Subcom. of Spec. Libs. and Info. Ctrs. Amer. Socty. of Metals: Metals Info. Com. (Secy., 1978–81; Ch., 1981–83). **Activities:** 12; 17, 41; 65, 81, 91 **Addr.:** U.S. Steel Corporation, Research Laboratory, Technical Information Center MS #88, Monroeville, PA 15146.

Pollock, James Wilson (Mr. 21, 1922, Assiut, Egypt) Libn., Near E. Std., Catlgr., Near E. Mtrls., IN Univ. Lib., 1961–; Mnstr., Untd. Presby. Church, Eskridge, KS, 1956–57; Missn., Untd. Presby. Bd. of Frgn. Missns., 1945–56. **Educ.:** Monmouth Coll., 1940–43, 1945, BA (Phil., Psy.); Pittsburgh Theo. Semy., 1943–45, MDiv (Relig.); Andover Newton Theo. Sch., 1951–52, STM (Pastoral Psy.); Hartford Semy. Fndn., 1957–61, MA (Arabic, Islamics); IN Univ., 1961–64, MA (LS). **Orgs.:** Mid. E. Libns. Assn.: Ed. (1973–75, 1976–78). ALA. ATLA. Intl. Assn. of Orientalist Libns. **Pubns.:** "On a Working Leave, 1980," *Mid. E. Libns. Assn. Notes* (F. 1981); "Guidelines for Non-Specialist Library Collections on the Middle East: Lime-lines in the Tall Grass," *Mid. E. Libns. Assn. Notes* (O. 1977); "What is a Middle East Librarian, or, Who Are We?" *Mid. E. Libns. Assn. Occasional Papers* (1981). **Activities:** 1; 15, 20, 39; 54, 90 **Addr.:** Indiana University Library, Bloomington, IN 47405.

Pollock, Joseph J. (Mr. 11, 1943, Coventry, Eng.) Sr. Assoc. Info. Sci., Chemical Abs. Srv., 1969–; Visit. Asst. Prof., Purdue Univ., 1968–69. **Educ.:** St. Andrews Univ., Scotland, 1961–64, BSc (Chem.), 1965–68, PhD (Chem.). **Orgs.:** ASIS. Assn. for Comp. Ling. Assn. for Comp. Mach. Amer. Chemical Socty. **Pubns.:** various papers, articles. **Activities:** 12; 20, 30, 41; 56, 60, 75 **Addr.:** Chemical Abstracts Service (Dept. 23), Box 3012, Columbus, OH 43210.

Polson, Billie Mae (N. 6, 1932, St. Louis, MO) Cat. Libn., James Dickinson Lib., Univ. of NV, 1959–; Los Angeles Pub. Lib., 1956–59. **Educ.:** Univ. of NV, 1950–54, BA (Eng.); Univ. of South. CA, 1957–58, MS (LS). **Orgs.:** ALA: NV Mem. Com. (Ch., 1978–). NV LA. CA LA. Mt. Plains LA. NV State Adv. Cncl. on Libs.: Subcom. on Autom. (1980–81); Nom. Com. (1980). NV State Hist. Recs. Recs. Comsn. Adv. Bd. **Pubns.:** "History of the Nevada Library Association," *Encyc. of Lib. and Info. Sci.* (1976). **Activities:** 1; 17, 20, 26; 56, 89 **Addr.:** Dickinson Library, University of Nevada, 4505 Maryland Pkwy., Las Vegas, NV 89154.

Polster, Joanne F. (F. 3, 1930, New York City, NY) Head Libn., Amer. Craft Cncl. Lib., 1973–; Sch. Libn., Brooklyn Ethical Culture Sch., 1971–72; YA Libn., Brooklyn Pub. Lib., 1970; Prod. Dept., Rand McNally and Co., 1953–62. **Educ.:** Hunter Coll., 1948–52, (Eng. Lit.); Pratt Inst., 1970–73, (LS). **Orgs.:** SLA: NY Pic. Div. (Ch., 1974). Art Libs. Socty. of N. Amer.: Prog. Ch. (1978); NY Chap. (Ch., 1979). **Pubns.:** "Reference Books" in *Contemporary Crafts Market Place* (1975); "Periodicals," "Services" in *Contemporary Crafts Market Place 1977–78* (1977); *Crafts Business Bookshelf* (1977); *Grant References for the Craftsman* (1978); jt. auth., *Master's Theses: Crafts* (1976); various bibl. **Activities:** 5; 15, 17, 20; 55, 57 **Addr.:** American Craft Council Library, 44 W. 53rd St., New York, NY 10019.

Pomahac, Gertrude Cecile (My. 22, 1934, Vina, AB) Asst. Univ. Archvst., Univ. of AB Arch., 1974–; Prof. Ofcr., Sch. of LS, Univ. of AB, 1968–74. **Educ.:** Univ. of AB, 1964–67, BA (Hist.); Univ. of WA, 1967–68, ML (Libnshp.). **Orgs.:** Assn. Can. Archvsts.: Salaries and Benefits Com. (1976–). SAA. Assn. of Recs. Mgrs. and Admins. Can. Micro. Socty. Hist. Socty. of AB. Univ. of AB Acad. Women's Assn. **Pubns.:** Various bk. reviews, guides. **Activities:** 2; 23, 39, 45; 55, 73 **Addr.:** University of Alberta Archives, 1–19 Rutherford Library S., Edmonton, AB T6G 2J4 Canada.

Pomerance, Deborah Sue (Ag. 20, 1950, New York, NY) Stats. Info. Spec., Data Use and Access Labs., 1977–; Assoc., Mariscal and Co., 1975–77; Head Libn., Amer. Pharm. Assn., 1973–75. **Educ.:** George Washington Univ., 1968–72, BA (Eng.); Univ. of MI, 1972–73, MLS. **Orgs.:** Assn. of Popltn. Libs. and Info. Ctrs. Intl. Assn. for Soc. Sci. Info. Srv. and Tech. Data for Dev. **Pubns.:** *Ethnic Statistics: A Compendium of Reference Sources* (1978); jt. auth., "Federal Policy About Machine-Readable Statistical Documents," *Gvt. Pubns. Review* (1981). **Activities:** 12; 24, 39, 41; 75, 92, 95-Popltn., demog. **Addr.:** 7319 Cedar Ave., Takoma Park, MD 20912.

Pommer, Michelle A. (Je. 2, 1949, Oakland, CA) Libn., Hawaiian Telephone Co., 1976–; Asst. Libn., Bank of HI, 1975–76; Lib. Consult., Ctr. for Labor-Mgt. Educ., Univ. of HI, 1975. **Educ.:** Univ. of HI, 1967–71, BA (Fr.), 1973–74, MLS (Lib. Std.). **Orgs.:** SLA: Hawaiian-Pac. Chap. (Pres., 1979–80). HI LA: Exhibits Com. (1978–79, 1979–80). ALA. **Honors:** Phi Beta Kappa, 1967; Beta Phi Mu, 1974. **Activities:** 12; 20, 39, 41; 59, 93 **Addr.:** Hawaiian Telephone Co., Library, P.O. Box 2200, Honolulu, HI 96841.

Pomrenze, Seymour Jacob (S. 1, 1916, Brusilov, Kiev, Ukraine) Dir., Disting. Adjunct Prof., Rec. Mgt., Amer. Univ., 1955–79; Consult., Rec. Mgt. and Arch.; Archvst. of US Army, Dir., Rec. Mgt. Prog., Dept. of US Army, 1950–77; Archvst., US Natl. Arch., 1941–42, 1946–49. **Educ.:** IL Inst. of Tech., 1932–36, BS (Hist., Econ. Acct.); Univ. of Chicago, 1936–38, MA (Hist., Frgn. Rel.), 1938–40, (Hist., Frgn. Rel.). **Orgs.:** Inst. of Cert. Rec. Mgrs.: Pres.; VP; Bd. of Regents (1970–79). Assn. of Rec. Mgrs. Admin.: Speaker. SAA: Fellow; various coms. **Ho-**

Special Subjects/Services: 50. Adult educ.; 51. Advert./Mktg.; 52. Aerosp.; 53. Agric.; 54. Area std.; 55. Arts/Hum.; 56. Autom.; 57. Bibl./Prtg.; 58. Bio. sci.; 59. Bus./Fin.; 60. Chem.; 61. Copyrt.; 62. Documtn.; 63. Educ.; 64. Engin.; 65. Env.; 66. Eth. grps.; 67. Film; 68. Food/Nutr.; 69. Geneal.; 70. Geo.; 71. Geol.; 72. Handcpd.; 73. Hist.; 74. Int. frdm.; 75. Info. sci.; 76. Insr.; 77. Law; 78. Legis.; 79. Math./Comp. sci.; 80. Med.; 81. Metals; 82. Nat. resrcs.; 83. Newsp.; 84. Nuc. sci.; 85. Oral hist.; 86. Petr./Energy; 87. Pharm.; 88. Phys./Astr./Math.; 89. Readg.; 90. Relig.; 91. Sci./Tech.; 92. Soc. sci.; 93. Telecom.; 94. Transp.; 95. (other).

nors: Secy. of Army., Decor. Excep. Civilian Srv.; Secy. of Defense, Merit. Civilian Srv. Medal. **Pubns.:** Jt. auth., *Federal Records of World War II; Guide to Civil Affairs/Military Govt Records; Selected Readings in Records Management;* various bk. reviews, circulars, articles. **Activities:** 2, 4; 38, 43; 74, 74, 92 **Addr.:** 1904 Spruce Dr. N.W., Washington, DC 20012.

Pond, Patricia Brown (Ja. 17, 1930, Mankato, MN) Assoc. Dean and Prof., Sch. of Lib. and Info. Sci., Univ. of Pittsburgh, 1977–; Assoc. Prof., Sch. of Libnshp., Univ. of OR, 1972–77, Asst. Prof., Sch. of Libnshp., 1967–72; Ch., Women's Std. Prog., Univ. of OR, 1974–76; Tch., Asst., Grad. Lib. Sch., Univ. of Chicago, 1965–67; Asst. Prof., East. WA State Coll., Sum. 1964; Ref. Asst., Univ. of MT Lib., 1963–65; Asst. Prof., Lib. Sch., Univ. of MN, 1962–63; various sch. libn. positions, 1952–62. **Educ.:** Coll. of St. Catherine, 1948–52, BA (Eng., LS); Univ. of MN, 1954–55, MA (LS); Univ. of Chicago, 1965–67, Cert. Advnc. Std., 1971, Ph.D., 1981 (LS). **Orgs.:** ALA: Cncl. (1970–74; 1979–82); Com. on Accred. (1973–78); Ofc. for Lib. Persnl. Res. Adv. Bd. (Ch., 1980–82); YA Srvs. Div. (Exec. Bd., 1970–74). AASL. Sch. Media Quarterly (Cons. Ed., 1976–82). LITA. YASD. AALS: Org. and By-Laws Com. (Ch., 1978–80). ASIS. AECT. **Pubns.:** *Science in Nineteenth Century Children's Books* (1966), "Networks, Data Bases and Media Programs," Co-ed. *Sch. Media Qtly.* (Fall 1977); "Development of a National Professional School Library Association," *Sch. Media Qtly.* (Fall 1976); "The American Assn. of Sch. Librarians: The Origins and Development of a National Professional Assn. for Sch. Librarians, 1896–1951." **Activities:** 10, 11; 17, 26, 32; 55, 63, 89 **Addr.:** School of Library and Information Science, University of Pittsburgh, Pittsburgh PA 15260.

Ponsell, Barbara A. (D. 2, 1935, Wilmington, DE) Resrch. Libn., E. I. DuPont de Nemours and Co., 1966–, Catlgr., 1967–72; Resrch. Asst., A. I. Du Pont Inst., Nemours Fndn., 1960–62; Lab. Tech., Atlas Powder Co., 1957–60. **Educ.:** Univ. of DE, 1953–57, BA (Bio.); Univ. of PA, 1962–64 (Classical Std.); Drexel Inst. of Tech., 1965–66, MS (LS). **Orgs.:** SLA. DE Valley Jaguar Club. Classic Car Club of Amer. Classic Jaguar Assn. Antiq. Auto Club of Amer. **Activities:** 12; 39, 41; 64 **Addr.:** E. I. Du Pont de Nemours & Co., Inc., Technical Library, Louviers, Wilmington, DE 19898.

Pontius, Jack E. (O. 9, 1940, Fort Wayne, IN) Head, Micro. Sect., PA State Univ. Lib., 1976–; Ref. Libn., 1972–76; Assoc. Libn., Ref. Sect., SUNY, Stony Brook, 1968–72. **Educ.:** IN Univ., 1959–64, AB (Hist.); Columbia Univ., 1968, MLS. **Orgs.:** ALA: Reprodct. of Lib. Mtrls. Sect., Exec. Com. (Secy., 1979–81); RLMS Stan. Com. (1979–); Resrcs. Sect., Micropublishing Com. (Ch., 1981–); Subcom. to Monitor the Quality of Micropublications (Ch., 1979–); RTSD/Adhoc Subcom. on Monitoring Micro. Advert. (1978–79). **Pubns.:** "Public Service of Large Microforms Collections," *Micro. Review,* (Win. 1981); "The Microforms Area Seven Years Later," *RPI Nsltr.,* (Spr. 1980). **Activities:** 1, 2; 31, 33, 39; 57, 83, 93 **Addr.:** E 5 Pattee Library, PA State University Library, University Park, PA 16802.

Pool, Jane (N. 13, 1932, Nevada, TX) Asst. Prof., Cath. Univ., 1977–; Asst. Prof., Univ. of South. CA, 1972–77; Instr., N. TX State Univ., 1968–71; Sci. Ref. Libn., South. Meth. Univ., 1961–65; Elem. Sch. Libn., TX Schs., 1953–60. **Educ.:** N. TX State Univ., 1950–53, BA (Lib. Srv., Educ.); Univ. of IL, 1960–61, MS (LS), 1965–72, PhD (LS). **Orgs.:** ALA: ASCLA, Patient Libs. Plng. Com. (1978–79)/Lib. Srv. to Prisoners Sect., Nom. Com. (1981–82). Med. LA. AALS: Curric. Sect. (Coord., 1978–80). DC LA: Gvt. Docum. Int. Grp. (Coord., 1980–81). **Honors:** Delta Kappa Gamma; Beta Phi Mu. **Pubns.:** Ed., *Library Services to the Blind and Physically Handicapped: A Bibliography* (1978); ed., "Library Services to Correctional Institutions Issue," *Lib. Trends* (Sum. 1977); "Public Library Services to Prisons," *Lib. Trends* (1977). **Activities:** 5, 12; 16, 17, 24; 72, 80 **Addr.:** 3601 Connecticut Ave., Washington, DC 20008.

Poole, Connie (N. 2, 1951, Manhattan, KS) Asst. to Dir., Lib., Amer. Hosp. Assn., 1978–, Staff Spec./Info. Anal., 1977–78; Clinical Ctr. Libn., MI State Univ., 1976–77, Sci. Libn., 1974–77. **Educ.:** Grinnell Coll., 1969–73, BA (Bio., Anthro.); Univ. of MI, 1973–74, AMLS; Med. LA, 1975, Cert. Grade 1. **Orgs.:** Med. LA: *MLA News* Assoc. Ed. (1979–); Com. on Srvys. and Stats. (1978–81); Midwest Reg. Grp., Pres. (1979), Exec. Com. (1976–78); *MIDLINE* Ed. (1978–79); Fall Mtg. (Prog. Coord., 1975). **Honors:** Beta Phi Mu, 1974. **Pubns.:** Cmplr., *Administrator's Collection* (1978). **Activities:** 1, 12; 17, 39; 80, 91, 95-Hlth. Admin. **Addr.:** Library of the American Hospital Association, 840 N. Lake Shore Dr., Chicago, IL 60611.

Poole, Frazer G. (N. 5, 1915, Federalsburg, MD) Lib. Bldg. and Interior Plng. Consult., 1965–; Prsrvn. Ofcr., Coord. of Bldg. Plng., Lib. of Congs., 1967–78; Dir. of Libs., Univ. of IL, Chicago, 1963–67; Proj. Dir. of Lib. Tech., ALA, Chicago, 1959–63. **Educ.:** Catawba Coll., 1933–37, AB (Bio., Math.); Univ. of CA, Berkeley, 1948–49, BLS. **Orgs.:** ALA: various coms. (1950–). SAA. Natl. Micro. Assn. Amer. Inst. for Cons. Intl. Inst. for the Cons. of Artistic and Hist. Objects. **Honors:** St. John Fisher Coll., Rochester, NY, Doctor of Humane Letters, 1975; Lib. of Congs., Awd. for Disting. Srv., 1978; Catawba Coll., Alum. Assn., Disting. Srv. Awd., 1975. **Pubns.:** "Planning the College Library—Process and Problems," *Coll. Libnshp.* (1981); "Preservation," *Lib.-Arch. Rel.* (1976); "The Selection and Evaluation of Library Bookstacks," *Lib. Trends* (1965). **Activities:** 1, 2; 19, 23, 24 **Addr.:** 1502 River Farm Dr., Alexandria, VA 22308.

Poole, Jay Martin (Ag. 6, 1934, Clinton, OK) Dir., Col. Dev., TX A & M Univ., 1981–; Ed., *CHOICE Mag.,* 1979–81; Head Libn., Undergrad. Lib., Univ. of TX, 1974–79; Head, Ref. Dept., SUNY, Buffalo, 1973–74; Spec. Prog. Libn. Univ. of WA, 1973–74, Ref. Libn., Undergrad. Lib., 1970–73. **Educ.:** Univ. of Tulsa, 1957, BA (Eng.); Univ. of OK, 1970, MLS. **Orgs.:** ALA: ACRL, Undergrad. Libns. Discuss. Grp. (Ch., 1978–79). Socty. for Schol. Publshg. Natl. Bk. Critics Cir. Amer. Bk. Awds.: Nom. Com. (1980). **Honors:** Phi Mu Alpha; Theta Alpha Phi; Univ. of OK Sch. of LS, Cit. for Outstan. Srv. to Libnshp., 1979. **Activities:** 1; 15, 17, 39; 67, 75, 90 **Addr.:** Texas A & M University Library College Station, TX 77843.

Poole, L. Sandra (Je. 23, 1938, New Orleans, LA) Asst. Dir., Wicomico Cnty. Free Lib., 1980–, Coord. Pub. Srvs., 1975–80; Ref. Libn., Kansas City, KS Pub. Lib., 1968–75; Acq. Libn., Univ. of MO, 1965–68; Pub. Lib. Consult., MI State Lib., 1964–65; Acq. Libn., Park Coll., 1962–64; Ref. Libn., Kansas City, MO Pub. Lib., 1961–62. **Educ.:** Mary Washington Coll., 1956–60, BA (Eng.); LA State Univ., 1960–61, MS (LS). **Orgs.:** MD LA. ALA. Amer. Mgt. Assn. Wicomico Cnty. Bd. of Educ.: Adv. Com. on Adult Educ. (1980–). **Pubns.:** "Books of the Times," wkly. clmn. *Salisbury Times.* **Activities:** 9; 16, 17, 21 **Addr.:** 518 Pine Bluff Rd., Salisbury, MD 21801.

Poole, Mary Elizabeth (O. 20, 1914, Troy, NC) Retired, 1981–; Docum. Libn., NC State Univ., 1944–80; Docum. Libn., VA Polytech. Inst., 1943–44; Docum. Libn., Duke Univ., 1936–43. **Educ.:** Duke Univ., 1931–35, AB (Hist.); Univ. of NC, 1935–36, ABLS. **Orgs.:** NC LA. ALA: GODORT. **Honors:** Delta Kappa Gamma; ALA, GODORT, James Bennett Childs Awd., 1978; Univ. of NC, Sch. of LS, Alum. Assn. of Sch. of Lib. Sci., Disting. Alum. Awd., 1981. **Pubns.:** Cmplr., *Documents Office Classification* (1976); jt. cmplr., *Documents Office Classification for Cuttered Documents 1910–1924* (1960); cmplr., *"History" References from the Industrial Arts Index, 1913–1957* (1958); cmplr., *1909 Checklist, Correlation Index* (1973); contrib., "Classes Added," *Hickcox's Monthly Catalog of U.S. Government Publications, 1885–1894;* contrib., "Classes Added," *Monthly Catalog 1895–1924.* **Activities:** 1; 29, 33, 39 **Addr.:** 326 E. Main St., Troy, NC 27371.

Poole, Ralph W. III (Je. 3, 1952, Boston, MA) Info. Mgr., Bain and Co., 1979–; Info. Spec., Boston Consult. Grp., 1977–79; Serials Libn., Simmons Coll., 1975–77. **Educ.:** Ithaca Coll., 1970–74, BA (Eng.); Simmons Coll., 1975–77, MLS. **Orgs.:** SLA. Info. Indus. Assn. Assoc. Info. Mgrs. **Activities:** 12; 17, 24, 41; 59, 60, 86 **Addr.:** Bain & Company, 3 Faneuil Hall, Market Pl., Boston, MA 02109.

Pooley, Beverley John (Ap. 4, 1934, London, Eng.) Prof. of Law, Dir. of Law Lib., Univ. of MI Law Sch., 1962–65; Lectr., Univ. of Ghana, Legon, Ghana, 1960–62. **Educ.:** Cambridge Univ., Eng., 1953–56, BA (Law), 1956–57, LLB (Law); Univ. of MI, 1957–60, SJD (Law), 1963–64, MALS. **Orgs.:** Intl. Assn. of Law Libs. **Pubns.:** *Planning and Zoning in the United States* (1959); *Evolution of British Planning Legislation* (1961); various law, bk. reviews. **Activities:** 1; 17; 77 **Addr.:** University of MI Law School, S-180 Legal Research Bldg., Ann Arbor, MI 48109.

Pope, Andrew Tracey (Ag. 17, 1945, Salem, MA) Head Libn., Educ. Resrc. Ctr., Univ. of NB, 1976–, Asst. Libn., 1974–76. **Educ.:** New Sch. for Soc. Resrch., 1965–67, BA (Phil.); Univ. of NB, 1969–70, BEd; Univ. of Toronto, 1972–74, MLS. **Orgs.:** ALA. ASIS. Can. LA. **Pubns.:** "Bradford's Law and the Periodical Literature of Information Science," *Jnl. of the Amer. Socty. for Info. Sci.* (Jl.–Ag. 1975). **Activities:** 1; 17, 39, 41; 63, 75, 92 **Addr.:** 94 Topcliffe Crescent Fredericton, NB E3B 4P9 Canada.

Pope, Betty Frances (Mr. 9, 1927, Brookhaven, MS) Asst. Catlgr., Msc., N. TX State Univ., 1969–; Msc. Prof., Truett-McConnell Jr. Coll., 1963–66; Msc. Tchr., LA Bapt. Chld. Home, 1957–63; Piano Tchr., City HS, Kosciusko, MS, 1952–54. **Educ.:** Copiah-Lincoln Jr. Coll., 1945–47, Cert. (Msc.); William Carey Coll., 1947–49, BA (Piano); New Orleans Bapt. Theo. Semy., 1954–57, MRel (Educ.); N.E. LA State Coll., 1957–63, MMus (Msc. Educ.); N. TX State Univ., 1968–69, MLS. **Orgs.:** Msc. LA. **Pubns.:** "The Stone Rolled Away," poem *Christ. Single* (My. 1980); "A Day in Egypt," *Christ. Single* (forthcoming). **Activities:** 1; 20; 55 **Addr.:** 724 Bolivar St., Denton, TX 76201.

Pope, Nannette M. (Chicago, IL) Head, Lib. Srvs. Div., Armed Forces Radiobiology Resrch. Inst., 1968–; Order Libn., Natl. Insts. of Hlth. Lib., 1966–68; Libn., Vets. Admin. Hosp. (Denver), 1964–66. **Educ.:** Barat Coll., 1940–44, BA (Eng., Hist.); Univ. of Denver, 1964–66, MA (LS). **Orgs.:** Interlib. Users Assn. (Washington–Baltimore): Bd. Dir. (1969–; Pres. 1979–81). Med. LA: Milit. Med. Libns. Metro. Washington Lib. Cncl. Navy Cncl. of Sci. and Tech. Libs., East. **Pubns.:** Ed., *Journal Holdings of the Washington-Baltimore Area* (1978). **Activities:** 4, 5; 17, 29; 80, 74, 84 **Addr.:** Armed Forces Radiobiology Research Institute - Library, National Naval Medical Center, Bethesda, MD 20814.

Pope, Nolan F. (Ja. 1, 1949, Decatur, IL) Head, Syst. Comp.-Based Opers., Univ. of FL Libs., 1978–, Srch. Anal., Ref. Dept., 1977–78, Circ. Coord., 1975–77. **Educ.:** IL State Univ., 1967–71, BA (Grmn., Fr.); Rutgers Univ., 1974–75, MLS. **Orgs.:** ALA: ACRL; RTSD; LITA; LRRT; JMRT. ASIS: Spec. Interest Grps., Lib. Autom. and Netwks., Prog. Com. (1980–81), *BASIS* Rpt. (1978–81), User On-Line Interface, various coms. SLA: Info. Tech. Div., Proj. Com. (Ch. 1977–78), Conf. Plng. Com. (1977–78), Tech. Applications Com. (Ch., 1979–81); FL Chap. (Pres., 1980–81), Empl. Com. (Ch., 1977–78), Mem. Com. (Ch., 1978–79), Pres.-Elect (1979–80), Pres. (1980–81). CLSI User Grp. Various other orgs. Univ. of FL Acad. Sen. **Honors:** Beta Phi Mu, 1975. **Pubns.:** Jt. auth., *Thesauri Used by SLA Documentation Division Members* (1978); "SIG/LAN at ASIS-78," *Bltn. of ASIS* (F. 1979); "Networking via Automated Circulation Systems: Problems and Potentials," *Bltn. of ASIS* (Je. 1979); jt. auth., "On-line Databases in Chemistry Literature Education," *Jnl. of Chem. Educ.* (S. 1979); jt. auth., "SIG/LAN at ASIS-79," *Bltn. of ASIS* (F. 1980); various articles. **Activities:** 1, 12; 34, 38, 46; 56, 75, 93 **Addr.:** 505 Library W., University of Florida, Gainesville, FL 32611.

Popecki, Joseph Thomas (N. 25, 1924, Saginaw, MI) Dir. of Lib., St. Michael's Coll., 1967–; Actg. Dir. of Libs., Cath. Univ. of Amer., 1965–67, Fndr., Pres., Mid-Atl. Assoc., Consult., 1960–67; Asst. Dir. of Libs., 1958–65. **Educ.:** Sacred Heart Semy., 1942–45, BA (Phil.); Cath. Univ. of Amer., 1947–49, MSLS. **Orgs.:** ALA. VT LA: Past Pres.; Treas.; Mem. Ch. New Eng. LA. VT Archaeological Socty. Pres. (1968–73); Treas. (1976–). VT Hist. Socty. Amer. Mgt. Assn. **Honors:** Beta Phi Mu, 1964. **Pubns.:** *Near-print Duplication and Photographic Reproduction* (1954); jt. ed., *Union List of Serials of the Libraries of the Consortium of Libraries, Washington, DC* (1964). **Activities:** 1; 17, 24, 32; 56, 85, 94 **Addr.:** 33 Woodridge Dr., Burlington, VT 05401.

Popinsky, Sydelle (N. 8, 1935, Newburgh, NY) Mgr., Cont. Educ. and Consult. Dept., TX State Lib., 1976–; Coord., White Hse. Conf. in TX, 1977–; Consult., Coord. of the Persnl. Enrichment Prog., North. IL Lib. Syst., 1973–76; Ref. Libn. II, W. FL Reg. Lib., 1972–73; Ref. Libn. I, Rockford Pub. Lib., 1971–72; Tchr., various positions as tchr., 1957–69. **Educ.:** SUNY, Buffalo, 1954–56; Univ. of WI, 1956–57, BS (Elem. Educ.), 1970–71, MLS. **Orgs.:** ALA: Pub. Lib. Rpt. (Ch., 1974–76); ASCLA, Multi-Lib. Coop., Exec. Bd., Proj. Dev. Com. (Ch., 1978–); White Hse. Conf. (1977–79); Beta Phi Mu Awds. Com. (1974–76). TX LA: Cont. Educ. Com. (1976–78). Austin Lib. Club. CLENE: VP (1980–81). Various other orgs. Mathews Cmnty. Sch., Austin, TX: Adv. Cncl. (Vice-Ch., 1979–). Leag. of Women Voters. **Honors:** Beta Phi Mu. **Activities:** 13; 17, 24, 25; 50, 63, 89 **Addr.:** 1004 Eason, Austin, TX 78703.

Popovich, Charles J. (Johnstown, PA) Mgt., Econ. Libn., SUNY, Buffalo, 1972–, Core Ref. Libn., 1972–73; Sales Rep., NCR Corp., 1968–70. **Educ.:** Youngstown State Univ., 1965–68, BS (Bus.); Univ. of KY, 1971–72, MSLS; Xavier Univ., 1970–72, MBA (Bus.). **Orgs.:** ALA: RASD/Bus. Ref. Srvs. Com. (1974–78); Ch. (1976–78). SLA: Bus. and Finance Div., Nsltr. Ed. (1974–77); Treas. (1977–79). **Pubns.:** "The Characteristics of a Collection for Research in Business Management," *Coll. and Resrch. Libs.* (Mr. 1978); "Business Data Bases: The Policies and Practices of Indexing," *RQ* (Fall 1978); "A Bibliographic Guide to Small and Minority Business Management," *RQ* (Sum. 1979); various papers. **Activities:** 1; 15, 31, 39; 59, 75 **Addr.:** 6307 Town Line Rd., N. Tonawanda, NY 14120.

Popp, Mary Frances Pagliero (N. 29, 1949, Gary, IN) Head, Halls of Residence Libs., IN Univ., 1979–, Asst. Libn., Grad. Lib. Sch. Lib., 1973–79. **Educ.:** IN Univ., 1967–71, BS (Educ.), 1972–73, MLS, 1976–81, MS (Adult Educ.). **Orgs.:** IN LA. ALA: JMRT, *Cognotes* Com. (1976–78); LIRT, PR/Mem. Com. (1980–81). Stone Hills Area Lib. Srvs. Athrty.: VP (1980–82); Pres. (1981–82). Pi Lambda Theta: Iota Chap. (Corres. Secy., 1974–77). IN Univ. Libns. Assn.: Pubns. Com. (Ch., 1975–76); VP (1977–78); Pres. (1978–79); Mem. Com. (Ch., 1979–80). **Honors:** Beta Phi Mu. **Activities:** 1; 15, 17; 50, 75 **Addr.:** 4031 N. Crider Dr., Bloomington, IN 47401.

Popplestone, John A. (O. 30, 1928, Louisville, KY) Dir., Child Dev. Film Arch., Univ. of Akron, 1976–, Dir., Arch. of Hist. of Amer. Psy., 1965–, various admin. positions, 1966–73, Prof., Psy., 1967–, Assoc. Prof., 1963–67, Asst. Prof., 1961–63; Asst. Prof., West. MI Univ., 1958–61; Psychologist, Neuropsyt. Clinic of St. Louis, 1954–58; Consult., Bur. for the Blind, State of MO, Div. of Welfare, 1954–58; various positions as psychologist, 1952–58. **Educ.:** Univ. of MI, 1946–49, BA (Eng. Hist.); Wayne State Univ., 1950–53, MA (Clinical Psy.); Washington Univ., 1953–58, PhD (Clinical Psy.); State of MI, 1960–63, Cert.; State of OH, 1961–73, Cert.; various crs. **Orgs.:** SAA: Com. on Arch. of Prof. Orgs. (1968–73). OH Psy. Assn.: Com. on the Tchg. of Psy. (1961–62); Com. of Psychologists in Acad. Empl. (Ch., 1967–69). Amer. Psy. Assn.: Div. 26 Hist. (Secy.–Treas., 1966–72; Pres., 1977–78), Com. on Fellows (Ch., 1966–80), Jt. Ed., *Nsltr.* (1967–77); Cncl. of Reps. (1975–77, 1981–83); Ad Hoc Com. on Amer. Psy. Assn.–Lib. of Congs.

PROFESSIONAL ACTIVITIES: Institutions: 1. Acad. lib.; 2. Arch.; 3. Assn.; 4. Fed./Gvt. lib.; 5. Inst. lib.; 6. Mfr./Suppl.; 7. Milit. lib.; 8. Musm.; 9. Pub. lib.; 10. Sch. lib.; 11. Sch. of lib. sci.; 12. Spec. lib.; 13. State lib.; 14. (other). **Functions/Activities:** 15. Acq./Col. dev.; 16. Adult srvs.; 17. Admin.; 18. Apprais.; 19. Archit./Bldgs.; 20. Cat./Class.; 21. Chld. srvs.; 22. Circ.; 23. Cons./Pres.; 24. Consult.; 25. Cont. ed.; 26. Educ. lib. sci.; 27. Ext. srvs.; 28. Fund/Grants; 29. Gvt. pubs.; 30. Indx./Abs.; 31. Instr. lib. use; 32. Media srvs.; 33. Micro.; 34. Netwks./Coop.; 35. Persnl.; 36. PR; 37. Publshg.; 38. Recs. mgt.; 39. Ref. srvs.; 40. Repro.; 41. Resrch.; 42. Review.; 43. Secur.; 44. Serials; 45. Spec. col.; 46. Tech. srvs.; 47. Trustees/Bds.; 48. YA srvs.; 49. (other).

Arch. (Co-ch., 1978); various coms. Socy. for Resrch. in Child Dev. Sigma Xi: Univ. of Akron Chap. (Pres., 1977–78). Various orgs. **Honors:** Amer. Psy. Assn./Natl. Sci. Fndn., Visit. Sci., 1966–68; Psi Chi, Cert. of Recog., 1970; Unitarian-Universalist Assn., Fac. Awd. of Student Relig. Liberals, 1964. **Pubns.:** Jt. auth., *Readings for General Psychology* (1965, 1967, 1970); Jt. auth., *Workbook to Accompany General Psychology* (1973); Jt. auth., "The Vitality of the Leipzig Model of 1880–1910 in the United States in 1950–80," *Wundt Studies* (1980); "The Influence of the Apparatus of the Leipzig Laboratory in the United States: 1880–1910," *Wilhelm Wundt—progressives Erbe, Wissenschaftsentwisklung und Gegenwart* (1980); Jt. auth., "Pioneer American Psychology Laboratories in Clinical Settings," *Historiography of Modern Psychology* (1980); various articles, bk. reviews. **Activities:** 2; 15, 41, 45; 92 **Addr.:** Archives of the History of American Psychology, Bierce Library, University of Akron, Akron, OH 44325.

Porcella, Brewster (Ap. 30, 1922, Cranford, NJ) Libn., Trinity Evang. Dvnty. Sch., 1973–; Head, Acq. Dept., Univ. of IA Libs., 1966–68, Asst. Acq. Libn., 1964–66; Pastor, Twin City Bible Church, Urbana, IL, 1953–63. **Educ.:** Wheaton Coll., 1939–43, AB (Bible), 1946–48, AM (Theo.); Faith Theo. Semy., 1948–50, BD (Ministerial); Univ. of IL, 1963–64, MS (LS), 1968–73, PhD (LS). **Orgs.:** ALA. Assoc. Christ. Libns. Chicago Area Theo. LA: Ch. (1980–81). Evang. Theo. Socty. **Activities:** 1; 17, 31, 39; 90 **Addr.:** 3 Lexington Dr., Vernon Hills, IL 60061.

Pormen, Paul E., Jr. (F. 10, 1943, Youngstown, OH) Media Coord., Austintown Lcl. Schs., 1965–. **Educ.:** Youngstown Univ., 1961–65, BSEd (Eng., Soc. Std.), 1969–71, MSEd (Sec. Admin.); Kent State Univ., 1972–80, EdS (Media), MLS (LS). **Orgs.:** OH Lib. Media Assn. AECT. ALA: AASL. Phi Delta Kappa. **Activities:** 10; 17; 56, 63, 92 **Addr.:** Austintown Local Schools, 4560 Falcon Dr., Youngstown, OH 44515.

Port, Idelle (D. 11, 1937, Chicago, IL) Lib. Syst. Spec., Chancellor's Ofc., CA State Univ. and Coll., 1973–; Actg. Asst. Dir., CA State Univ., 1979–80; Sr. Admin. Anal., Univ. of CA, Los Angeles, 1976–77; Syst. Anal., Univ. of South. CA, 1972–73; Consult., Data Prcs., Kaiser Permanente, 1972. **Educ.:** Northwestern Univ., 1955–59, BS (Math.); Univ. of CA, Los Angeles, 1969–72, MSIS (Lib. and Info. Sci.). **Orgs.:** ALA: CA Reg. Ch. (1979–81). ASIS: Mem. Promo. Task Force. **Honors:** Beta Phi Mu. **Pubns.:** "Developing a Strategy for Retrospective Conversion of a Card Catalog to a Machine Readable Data Base in Three Academic Liraries (Small, Medium, and Large): Two Alternatives Considered," *Into. Storage and Retrieval* (My. 1973); various papers. **Activities:** 1; 17, 24, 35; 56, 75 **Addr.:** 680 Kingman Ave., Santa Monica, CA 90402.

Port, Jane S. (S. 12, 1949, New York City, NY) Dir., Gustave L. and Janet W. Levy Lib., Mt. Sinai Med. Ctr., 1980–, Assoc. Dir., 1977–79, Assoc. Libn., Pub. Srvs., 1975–77; Supvsg. AV Libn., Coll. of Med. and Dentistry of NJ, 1973–75. **Educ.:** Queens Coll., CUNY, 1966–69, BA (Psy.); Columbia Univ., 1969–70, MSLS (Med.), 1973–76, Cert. (Advnc. Libnshp.). **Orgs.:** Med. LA: Com. on AV Stan. and Prac. (1978–81); NY Reg. Grp., Exec. Com. (1979–81). Hlth. Sci. Comm. Assn.: Bd. of Dir. (1979–80). **Pubns.:** "The growth of the Levy Library's audio-visual services to the medical center," *Mt. Sinai Jnl. Med.* (Jl.–Ag. 1979); "Continuing education in information retrieval techniques for clinicians," *Bltn. Med. Lib. Assn.* (Ap. 1980); "Faculty attitudes toward the use of audio-visuals in continuing education," *Jnl. of Biocomm.* (N. 1980); Jt. Auth., "Public information services at state-supported medical school libraries; a brief survey," *Bltn. Med. LA* (O. 1976); Jt. Auth., "Brief survey of public information services at privately-supported medical school libraries," *Bltn. Med. LA* (Ap. 1977). **Activities:** 12; 17, 26, 35; 80 **Addr.:** Gustave L. and Janet W. Levy Library, Mt. Sinai Medical Center of NY, 5th Ave. and 100 St., New York, NY 10029.

Portal, Doreen Y. (Ag. 30, 1925, New Westminster, BC) Docum./Serials Libn., Reed Coll. Lib., 1980–; Head of Readers Srvs., OR Coll. of Educ., 1974–80; Ref. Libn., OR State Lib., 1972–74, Head of Docum./Serials Div., 1967, Catlgr., 1966; Cat. Proj. Dir., OR Div. of Vocational Rehab., 1960–61; Head, Docum. Div., OR State Lib., 1955–59; Ref. Libn., Multnomah Cnty. Lib., 1954–55; Head, Docum. Sect., Univ. of IL, 1952–54. **Educ.:** Univ. of BC, 1944–48, BA (Hist., Eng.); Clark Univ., 1948–49, MA (Hist., Intl. Rel.); Univ. of MI, 1949–52, MALS. **Orgs.:** ALA. Pac. NW LA. OR LA. **Honors:** Phi Kappa Phi, 1952, Beta Phi Mu, 1953. **Pubns.:** *A Guide for Cataloging Rehabilitation Literature in Rehabilitation Agencies and Facilities* (1961). **Activities:** 1, 13; 29, 31, 39; 54, 92 **Addr.:** 6023 S.E. 43rd, Portland, OR 97206.

Porter, Barry L. (O. 3, 1942, Cedar City, UT) State Libn., State Lib. Comsn. of IA, 1973–; Ref. Libn., UT State Lib. Comsn., 1968–73. **Educ.:** South. UT State Coll., 1960–67, BS (Math., Pol. Sci.); Brigham Young Univ., 1969–70, MLS. **Orgs.:** ALA. IA LA. UT LA: Exec. Secty. (1972). **Pubns.:** *Distinctive Function of School Media Centers and Public Libraries* (1978). **Activities:** 13; 17, 25 **Addr.:** State Library Commission of IA, Historical Bldg., Des Moines, IA 50319.

Porter, Kathryn W. Co. Libn., Aetna Life and Casualty, 1981–; Town Libn., Bethel Pub. Lib., 1977–81; Asst. Town Libn., Trumbull Lib., 1973–77; Asst. Head, Bus. and Tech. Dept., Bridgeport Pub. Lib., 1971–73. **Educ.:** Univ. of CA, Davis, 1964–68, BA (Pol. Sci.); Univ. of IL, 1968–69, MLS. **Orgs.:** CT LA: Prog. Ch. (1975–76); Mem. Ch. (1976–77); Ed. Com. (1977–80). New Eng. LA: Housatonic Valley Lib. Admins. Grp. (1977–80). Fairfield Lib. Admins. Grp.: Vice-Ch. (1979–80). SW CT Lib. Cncl.: Reg. 4, Bd. (1979–). Leag. of Women Voters. Bridgeport Archit. Conservancy. Proj. OWN, Bridgeport. **Honors:** Beta Phi Mu, 1969. **Pubns.:** *U.S. Office of Education Report* (1969); "Dope Users Can't Find," *Wilson Lib. Bltn.* (N. 1971); ed., "From Around the State," *CT Libs.* (1979–80); ed., *CT LA Memo* (1978–79). **Activities:** 9, 12; 15, 17, 25; 50, 59, 76 **Addr.:** Company Library, Aetna Life & Casualty Co., 151 Farmington Ave., Hartford, CT 06156.

Porter, Maria V. (Jl. 31, 1935, Louisville, KY) Branch Libn., South Bend Pub. Lib., 1977–, Ref. Libn., 1975–77; Lib. Resrch., Encyc. Britannica, 1956–75. **Educ.:** Ursuline Coll., 1952–56, BA (Eng.); IN Univ., 1974–75, MA (LS). **Orgs.:** ALA. IN LA. **Activities:** 9; 17 **Addr.:** 1523 Crestwood Blvd., South Bend, IN 46635.

Porter, Susan F. (Je. 28, 1919, Bradford, AR) Dir., Curric. Mtrls. Ctr., Assoc. Prof., LS, McNeese State Univ., 1967–; Elem. Libn., Little Rock Pub. Schs., 1963–66, Tchr.-Libn., 1948–63; Tchr., various AR HS's, 1941–44. **Educ.:** AR State Tchrs. Coll., 1936–40, BSE (Home Econ.); Univ. of AR, 1950–52, MSE (Educ.); LA State Univ., 1965–66, MS (LS). **Orgs.:** ALA. LA LA: Modisette Awds. Com. (Ch., 1980); LA Tchrs. of LS, Ch. Calcasieu Libns. Assn.: Past Pres. McNeese State Univ. Lib. Com. **Honors:** Alpha Delta Kappa. **Activities:** 10, 11; 17, 26, 32; 63 **Addr.:** 734 Helen St., Lake Charles, LA 70601.

Portsch, Joanne (NMI) (Ap. 26, 1933, Mt. Vernon, NY) Supvsr., Lib. Srvs., Raytheon Co. Equip. Div., 1974–, Sr. Libn., 1970–74, Market Resrch. Libn., 1959–70; Ref. Libn., White Plains Pub. Lib., 1955–59. **Educ.:** CT Coll., 1951–54, BA (European Hist.); Syracuse Univ., 1954–55, MLS. **Orgs.:** SLA: New Eng. Chap., various ofcs. Mystery Writers of Amer. **Honors:** Beta Phi Mu. **Activities:** 12; 15, 17, 20 **Addr.:** Raytheon Co. Equipment Div., Technical Information Center, Boston Post Rd., Wayland, MA 01778.

Portteus, (Mrs.) Elnora M.) (Rosendale, Dir., Dir., Educ. Media Srvs., Cleveland Pub. Sch., 1965–; Adjunct Assoc. Prof. Sch. of Lib. Sci., Kent State Univ., 1976–, Asst. Prof., 1958–65, Actg. Ch., 1965; Dir., NDEA Inst., 1965; Libn., Findlay City Schs., 1949–58; Asst. Libn., Indus. Rel. Couns., 1948–49; Asst. Libn., Fed. Rsv. Bank, 1942–43; Visit. Lectr., Appalachian State Univ., Clarion State Coll., Edinboro State Coll., Univ. of TN. **Educ.:** Oshkosh State Coll., 1937–39; Univ. of WI, 1939–41, BS (Eng., Soc. Std.); Kent State Univ., 1951–54, MLS; various crs. **Orgs.:** ALA: Hammond Chap. Ch.; AASL/Disting. Lib. Sci. Awd. for Sch. Admin. (Ch., 1977–78), Supvsr. Sect., Nom. Com. (Ch., 1978–79), First VP (1971–72), Pres. (1972–73). OH Assn. of Sch. Libns.: Pres. (1958–59). Beta Phi Mu: Rho Chap. (Pres., 1976–77). Cuyahoga Cmnty. Coll.: Adv. Bd. (1965–). Women's Natl. Bk. Assn.: Cleveland Chap. (V.P., 1977–79). AAUW: OH Div. (Bd. Mem., 1955–59). **Honors:** OH LA, Libn. of The Year, 1972; AASL, Encyc. Britannica, Sch. Lib. Prog., 1972; ALA, John Cotton Dana Awd., 1969, 1967; OH Assn. of Sch. Libns Cit., 1972; Kent State Univ., Disting. Alum. Awd., 1972. **Pubns.:** "Media Center Facilities," *AASL Media Ctr. Facilities Dsgn.* (1978); "Supervisory Interface: Reality and Action," *Drexel Lib. Qtly.* (Jl. 1978); "A Practical Look at Media Supervision and Curriculum," *Sch. Media Qtly.* (Spr. 1979); Jt. Adv., *Encyc. Britannica* (1971–72); *Film Learning With Todays Media* (1971–72). **Activities:** 10 **Addr.:** 7357 Westlake Blvd., Kent, OH 44240.

Portugal, Rhoda E. (New York City, NY) Dir., Lyndhurst Pub. Lib., 1979–, Asst. Libn., 1979; Art, Msc. Libn., Bayonne Pub. Lib., 1977–79; Ref. Libn., N. Bergen Pub. Lib., 1976–77. **Educ.:** Montclair State Coll., 1969–73, BA (Psy.); SUNY, Geneseo, 1973–74, MLS. **Orgs.:** NJ LA. ALA. Bergen-Passaic LA. NJ Gvr. Conf.: Alternate Del. (1979). **Activities:** 9; 16, 39; 55 **Addr.:** 35 Lopez Rd., Cedar Grove, NJ 07009.

Poses, June Axelrod (Ja. 12, 1952, New York, NY) Asst. Libn. for Pub. Srvs., Lib., Coll. of Physicians of Philadelphia, 1981–; Head Libn., Sch. of Nursing, MA Gen. Hosp., 1979–81, Assoc. Libn., 1977–79, Asst. Libn., 1976–77; Ref. Asst., Northeast. Univ., 1975–76. **Educ.:** CT Coll., 1969–73, BA, Hist. Hons. (European Hist., Art Hist.); Simmons Coll., 1974–75, MSLS. **Orgs.:** Med. LA. SLA. NE Reg. Cncl. on Lib. Resrcs. for Nurses. CT Coll. Club of Boston. CT Coll. Alum. Assn. **Pubns.:** *A Guide to Slide and Photograph Collections of Primitive Art from Boston to Washington, DC* (1975); *A Guide to Slide and Photograph Collections of Primitive Art in Midwestern United States* (1976). **Activities:** 1, 12; 15, 17, 39; 58, 80, 92 **Addr.:** Library, College of Physicians of Philadelphia, 19 S. 22nd St., Philadelphia, PA 19103.

Posey, Sr. Lauretta (D. 30, 1921, Greensburg, PA) Media Spec., Elizabeth Seton HS Media Ctr., 1968–; Libn., Cardinal McCloskey HS, 1958–68; Eng. Tchr., Libn., Immaculate Conception Acad., 1956–58. **Educ.:** St. Joseph's Coll., Emmitsburg, MD, 1938–42, AB (Hist.); Cath. Univ. of Amer., 1955–56, MS (LS). **Orgs.:** ALA. MD LA. Cath. LA: Washington-MD Unit, HS Sect., Ch. (1975–78), Treas. (1979–81). **Activities:** 10; 17, 32 **Addr.:** Elizabeth Seton High School Media Center, 5715 Emerson St., Bladensburg, MD 20710.

Poska, Valentine J. (My. 21, 1918, Chicago, IL) Assoc. Libn., San Antonio Coll., 1968–; Libn., Eisenhower Mid. Sch., 1966–67; Libn., Christ. Brothers Coll., Memphis, TN, 1949–66; Libn., Christ. Brothers HS, St. Joseph, MO, 1947–49. **Educ.:** St. Mary's Coll., Winona, MN, 1936–40 (Eng.); MN Univ., 1944–46, BSLS (Lib.), 1950–53, MA (Sp., Thea.); Memphis State Univ., 1962–65, MA (Educ.); Our Lady of the Lake, San Antonio, TX, 1970–72, MA (Lib.). **Orgs.:** ALA. TX LA: Coll. Div., Arch. RT; Coll. and Univ. Libs. Div., Info. Com. (1978). Bexar LA: Julia Grothaus Nom. Com. (1979–80); Treas. (1980–81). Frnds. of the Pub. Lib. AAUP. TX Jr. Coll. Tchrs. Assn. San Antonio Coll. Lib.: Various ofcs. Sp. Arts Assn. of San Antonio. Various other orgs. **Honors:** TX Jr. Coll. Tchrs. Assn., Lib. Sect., Ten Yr. Cit., 1980. **Pubns.:** "Oral Communication and the Librarian," *TX Jr. Coll. Tchrs. Assn. Lrng. Resrcs. Notes* (Fall 1980); various bk. reviews, Station KSYM, San Antonio Coll. (1975–81); *Authors on Book Jackets; A Miniature Books Reader; Collecting Miniature Books; Subject Guide to Current Periodicals* (rev. every two yrs.); various bks., guides, sps. **Activities:** 1, 10; 39, 44; 57 **Addr.:** 234 Windcrest Dr., San Antonio, TX 78239.

Posner, Marcia Joan (Je. 4, 1930, Trenton, NJ) Judaica Lib. Consult., Juvenile Jewish Bk. Spec., Bd. of Jewish Educ., Jewish Bk. Cncl., 1979–; Adj. Lectr., Dept. of LS, Queens Coll., CUNY, 1974–77; Asst. Dir., Chld. Libn., Hillside Pub. Lib., 1967–74; Dir., Shelter Rock Jewish Ctr. Lib., 1968–; various wkshps. **Educ.:** City Coll. of NY, 1947–51, BS (Educ.); Queens Coll., CUNY, 1962–67, MLS; NY Univ., 1976–80, PhD (Comm. in Educ., Media). **Orgs.:** AJL: Exec. Cncl. (1980–82). Long Island AJL: Pres. (1980–). ALA. **Honors:** Women's Amer. ORT, North Hills, Woman of the Yr., 1975; Kappa Delta Pi, 1950; Beta Phi Mu, 1976. **Pubns.:** "Jewish Children's Books: Pidyon Hashevuyim: Ransoming of the Captives," *Long Island Jewish World* (F. 6–12, 1981); "The Elderly Portrayed in Jewish Children's Books," *Long Island Jewish World* (F. 20–26, 1981); "Hillel's Rule" super 8 mm. film (1978); "Using Media in Children's Programs," *AJL Bltn.* (Spr. 1977); *Jewish Americans and Their Backgrounds; Sources of Information* (1975); various bk. reviews in *Jewish Bookland* (1976–), *AJL* (1975–), *Sch. Lib. Jnl.* (1970–), *Women's Amer. ORT Bltn.* (1970–), *Shelter Rock Jewish Ctr. Bltn.* (1967–), articles. **Activities:** 10, 12; 21, 24, 25; 57, 66, 90 **Addr.:** 19 Brookfield Rd., New Hyde Park, NY 11040.

Post, J(eremiah) B(enjamin) (N. 17, 1937, Rochester, NY) Map Libn., Free Lib. of Philadelphia, 1965–, Ref. Asst., Lit. Dept., 1964. **Educ.:** Univ. of Rochester, 1956–60, AB (Phil.); Columbia Univ., 1960–61, MSLS (Libnshp.); Amer. Univ., 1973, Cert. (Arch.). **Orgs.:** SLA: Geo. and Map Div. (Ch., 1977–78). Pvt. LA. Philobiblon Club. Philadelphia Sci. Fiction Socty.: Pres. (1966–67); Secy. (1968). The Francis Grose Socty.: Archvst. (1976–). **Pubns.:** *An Atlas of Fantasy* (1973); ed., spec. map issue *Drexel Lib. Qtly.* (O. 1973); "Indexing the Hexamer Surveys," *Spec. Libs.* (Mr. 1977); various reviews, articles. **Activities:** 9; 15, 20, 39; 57, 70 **Addr.:** Map Collection, Free Library of Philadelphia, Philadelphia, PA 19103.

Post, Joyce Arnold (Ja. 10, 1939, Harrisburg, PA) Indxr., *Academic American Encyclopedia*, Arete Publshg. Co., 1979–; Indxr., *TV Guide* mag., Triangle Pubns., 1976–77; Resrch. Assoc., Grad. Sch. of Lib. Sci., Drexel Univ., 1971–75; Indxr., info. broker, libn., freelnc., 1971; Tech. Srvs. Libn., Readr. Dev. Prog., Free Lib. of Philadelphia, 1965–67; Libn., Frgn. Trade Lib., Philadelphia Civic Ctr., 1963–65; Libn. I, Free Lib. of Philadelphia, 1961–62. **Educ.:** Susquehanna Univ., 1956–60, AB (Eng. Lit.); Drexel Univ., 1960–61, MSLS; Natl. Cash Regis., 1967, Cert. (Comp. Prog.). **Orgs.:** Amer. Socty. of Indxrs.: Bd. of Dir. (1979–82); Ed., *ASI Newsletter*. ASIS. ALA. The Philadelphia Sch. Assn.: Mid. Sch. VP. (1979–80). **Honors:** Beta Phi Mu, 1961. **Pubns.:** Jt. auth., *Travel in the United States: A Guide to Information Sources* 1981; Indxr., *The Private Library* (1977); Jt. Auth., "Indexing the *Hexamer General Surveys*," *Spec. Libs.* (Mr. 1977); "Background Reading on Total Community Library Service," *Total Community Library Service* (1973); jt. auth., *The Blue Collar Adult's Information Needs, Seeking Behavior and Use* (1976); various mono. **Activities:** 14-freelnc., publshr.; 24, 30, 41; 75, 92, 93 **Addr.:** 4613 Larchwood Ave., Philadelphia, PA 19143.

Poston, Teresa Gayle (F. 22, 1945, Hemingway, SC) Libn., Media Spec., Window Rock Elem. Sch., Navajo Indian Reservation, 1981–; Asst. Prof. of LS, Univ. of TX, Austin, 1978–81; Asst. Prof. of LS, Peabody Coll., 1976–78; Media Spec., Longwood Coll. Campus Sch., 1969–74; Tchr., Briggs Elem. Sch., 1966–68. **Educ.:** Winthrop Coll., 1963–66, BS (Educ.); Univ. of KY, 1968–69, MS (LS); FL State Univ., 1974–76, PhD (LS). **Orgs.:** ALA: ALSC, Notable Filmstp. Eval. Com. (1978–80); AASL. AALS. SWLA. TX LA. **Honors:** Phi Kappa Phi, 1976; Beta Phi Mu, 1969. **Pubns.:** Rev. com., *A Multimedia Approach to Children's Literature;* "Preadolescent Needs and Problems as

Seen in Family Life Fiction:. .," *Top of The News* (Sum. 1978); "The Concept of the School Media Center and Its Services," *Peabody Jnl. of Educ.* (Ap. 1978). **Activities:** 11; 21, 26, 32; 63 **Addr.:** 220 E. Nizhoni Blvd. Apt. 25, Gallup, NM 87301.

Potash, Loree E. (D. 16, 1951, Cleveland, OH) Assoc. Law Libn., Pub. Srvs., Case West. Rsv. Univ. Law Lib., 1980–, Head, Pub. Srvs., 1978–80, Catlgr., 1975–78. **Educ.:** OH State Univ., 1970–74, BA (Eng.); Case West. Rsv. Univ., 1974–75, MS (LS); Cleveland-Marshall Sch. of Law, 1976–80, JD (Law). **Orgs.:** OH Reg. Assn. of Law Libs.: Lcl. Arrange. (Ch., 1980); Actv. Com. (1979–80). AALL: Educ. Com. (1979); *Law Lib. Jnl.* Com. (1977–78, 1980). Case West. Rsv. Univ. Sch. of LS Student Org. **Pubns.:** Ed., *OH Reg. Assn. of Law Libs. Nsltr.* (1981). **Activities:** 1; 15, 17, 39; 56, 77, 78 **Addr.:** Case Western Reserve University, Law Library, 11075 E. Blvd., Cleveland, OH 44106.

Poteet, Susan S. (O. 9, 1944, Chester, PA) Head of Cat. Dept., Morris Lib., South. IL Univ., 1979–, Actg. Head of Cat., 1978–79, Head of Orig. Cat. Sect., 1975–78, Asst. to Head of OCLC Cat., 1974–75, Catlgr., 1970–74. **Educ.:** OH Wesleyan Univ., 1962–63; Stetson Univ., 1963–66, BA (Fr.); Univ. of Strasbourg, France, 1965–66, Dip.; George Peabody Coll., 1969–70, MLS. **Orgs.:** ALA. IL LA. OCLC Users Grp. (Secy., 1980–81). **Activities:** 1; 20 **Addr.:** Cataloging Dept., Morris Library, Southern Illinois University, Carbondale, IL 62901.

Potter, Corinne J. (F. 2, 1930, Edmonton, AB) Dir., Lrng. Resrc. Ctr., St. Ambrose Coll., 1978–, Ref. Libn., 1977–78; Branch Libn., Rock Island Pub. Lib., 1967–74. **Educ.:** Augustana Coll., 1948–52, BA (Hum.); Univ. of IL, 1975–76, MS (LS). **Orgs.:** ALA. IA LA. IA Educ. Media Assn.: Jt. Com., IA LA/IA Educ. Media Assn. Coop. (Ch. 1980–81). IA ACRL: Spr. Wkshp. (Ch., 1978, 1981); VP (1980–81). **Activities:** 1, 9; 17, 32, 39; 55, 56, 59 **Addr.:** St. Ambrose College Learning Resource Center, 518 W. Locust St., Davenport, IA 52803.

Potter, Robert Ellis (Mr. 16, 1937, Knoxville, TN) Head, Tech. Srvs., Dunedin Pub. Lib., 1980–; Head, Bus., Sci. and Tech. Dept., Hialeah John F. Kennedy Lib., City of Hialeah Lib. Div., 1966–80; various lib. asst. positions. **Educ.:** Univ. of TN, 1955–58, 1959–61, BSJ (Jnlsm.), 1975–78, MSLS; various crs. **Orgs.:** ALA: PLA/New Libs. Col. Com. (1976–1980); SORT, *SORT Bltn.*, (Ed., 1971–74). Steering Com. (1974–75); SELA. FL LA. Dade Cnty. LA: VP (1969–70); Pres. (1970–71); Ed., *DCLA Nsltr.* (1970–75). City of Hialeah Lib. Div. Staff Assn., Pres. (1974–75). Univ. of TN Natl. Alum. Assn.: Miami Chap., Bd. of Dir. (1972–74), VP (1974–75), Pres. (1975–77). Miami Lakes Congregational Church: Church Pres., Church Cncl. Ch. (1977). The Socty. of Prof. Jnlsts., Sigma Delta Chi. Hist. Assn. of South. FL. **Pubns.:** "500 Science (500–540's), 600 Applied Science (600–635's, 660's–670's)," *Books for Public Libraries: Nonfiction for Small Collections* (1981); "Title and Key Words Index to Small Business Administration Bibliography Series," *RQ* (1972); "Libraries in Florida," *FL Libs.* (1976); *Florida Union List of Serials: A Statewide Compilation of Periodicals and Selected Serials* 2 Vols. **Activities:** 9; 16, 17, 39; 59, 91, 92 **Addr.:** 1441 Norwood Ave., Clearwater, FL 33516.

Potter, William Gray (F. 18, 1950, Duluth, MN) Head, Acq., Univ. of IL, 1979–, Asst. to Dir., Tech. Srvs., 1978–79; Systs. Libn., Univ. of WI, Whitewater, 1977–78, Ref. Libn., Catlgr., 1975–77. **Educ.:** South. IL Univ., 1968–73, BA (Eng.); Univ. of IL, 1974–75, MS (LS), 1973–75, MA (Eng.). **Orgs.:** ALA: LITA, Prog. Plng. Com. (1979–83); RTSD/Cat. and Class Sect., Nom. Com. (1982–84). **Pubns.:** Ed., *Serials Automation: Acquisition and Inventory Control* (1981); ed., *Lib. Trends* (Sum. 1981); "Form or Function: an Analysis of the Serials Department in the Modern Library," *Serials Libn.* (Fall 1981); "Lotka's Law Revisited," *Lib. Trends* (Sum. 1981); "Automated Acquisition Systems in Academic Libraries," *IL Libs.* (S. 1980); various articles. **Activities:** 1, 11; 15, 17, 46; 56 **Addr.:** Acquisitions, 214 Library, University of Illinois Library, 1408 W. Gregory, Urbana, IL 61801.

Potts, Rinehart Skeen (Jl. 13, 1927, Philadelphia, PA) Asst. Prof., Lib. Sci., Glassboro State Coll., 1964–; Chief Libn., Aero Srv. Corp., 1958–64, Prod. Cntrl., Plng., 1953–58. **Educ.:** Temple Univ., 1949–53, AB (Psy.); Rutgers Univ., 1961–64, MLS; Indus. Coll. of the Armed Forces, 1961–62, Cert. **Orgs.:** ALA: ACRL; PLA. NJ LA: PR Com. ASIS. Gloucester Cnty. Lib. Comsn. (Ch., 1977–). Glassboro Pub. Lib. Bd. of Trustees: Pres. (1975–). Various Orgs. AAUP. Amer. Fed. of Tchrs. Human Srvs. Coal. Sci. Fiction Resrch. Assn. **Pubns.:** *Graduate Education in Librarianship at Glassboro State College* (1975); *Library Services for the Martian Exploration Expedition* (1963). **Activities:** 11, 12; 26, 31, 47; 63, 69, 90 **Addr.:** 1223 Glen Terr., Glassboro, NJ 08028.

Potvin, Claude (Ag. 18, 1943, Bagotville, PQ) Reg. Libn., Albert-Westmorland-Kent Reg. Lib. 1970–, Asst. Reg. Libn., 1967–70; Ref. Libn., Univ. de Moncton, 1966–67. **Educ.:** Univ. Laval, 1964, BA; Univ. of Ottawa, 1965–66, BLS; McGill Univ., 1971, MLS. **Orgs.:** Atl. Prov. LA: NB VP (1979–81); Adv. Bd., *Bltn. of the Assn.* (1971–72); various com. Cncl. of Head Libns. of NB: Ch. (1974–76); Secy. (1980–); various com. Assn. Can. des Bibtcrs. de Lang. Fr.: Cnclr. (1968–71); Com. on Aims and Objectives (1971); various com. Ctr. Culturel de Moncton: Interim Exec. (Ch., 1973–74). Dept. of Educ. of NB: Task Force on Sch. Libs. (1976–77). Intl. Bd. on Bks. for Young People: Can. Sect., Interim Com. (1977–79). Comm.-Jeunesse. various org. **Pubns.:** Jt. Cmplr., *Répertoire des bibliothèques du Nouveau-Brunswick/ Directory of New Brunswick Libraries* (1976, 1977, 1979); *La littérature de jeunesse au Canada français* (1972); *Livres de langue française pour les centres de développement de l'enfant et les maternelles* (1969); "Ma crotte au coeur," *Atl. Prov. LA Bltn.* (D. 1966); "Recent Acadiana: An Annotated List," *Atl. Prov. LA Bltn.* (Jl.–S. 1980); various articles, transl., papers. **Activities:** 9; 74, 89 **Addr.:** 358 Hennessey, Moncton NB E1A 4Y5 Canada.

Poulos, Angela (Mr. 8, 1942, Kokomo, IN) Col. Dev. Libn., Bowling Green State Univ., 1978–, Actg. Asst. Dir., 1977–78, Head, Ref. Dept., 1974–77, Hum. Libn., 1969–78, Ref. Libn., 1968–69; Ref. Libn. Indianapolis Pub. Lib., 1965–67. **Educ.:** IN Univ., 1960–64, BA (hist.), 1964–65, MALS; Bowling Green State Univ., 1970–73, MA (Eng.). **Orgs.:** ALA. Acad. LA of OH: Nom. Com. (1977). **Honors:** Beta Phi Mu, 1965. **Pubns.:** Bibl., *Mod. Lang. Assn. Intl. Bibl.* (1979–81); "The Best of Both Worlds," *Jnl. of Acad. Libnshp.* (1981); various papers, bk. reviews. **Activities:** 1; 15, 39; 55 **Addr.:** 610 Knollwood Dr., Bowling Green, OH 43402.

Pouncey, Lorene (O. 18, 1921, North Little Rock, AR) Assoc. Prof., Emerita, Univ. of Houston Libs., 1978–, Bibl. Spec., Assoc. Prof., 1976–78, Rare Bk. Catlgr., 1972–76, Cat. Libn., 1956–72; Biblgphr., Gifts and Exch., Lib. of Congs., 1955–56, Bibl. Asst., Map Div., 1954; Biblgphr., Acq., Johns Hopkins Univ. Lib., 1952–53; Catlgr., Univ. of IL Lib., 1949–51; Jr. Catlgr., Henry E. Huntington Lib., 1947–49. **Educ.:** Univ. of TX, 1944–46, BA (Fr.); Univ. of CA, Berkeley, 1946–47, BLS; Univ. of IL, 1949–51, (LS); Univ. of Houston, 1958–63, MA (Eng.). **Orgs.:** Bibl. Socty. of Amer. Bibl. Socty. (London). ALA: ACRL/ Rare Bk. and Mss. Sect. TX LA. Latin Amer. Std. Assn. **Pubns.:** "Printed Research Materials in the Huntington Library," *LIBRI* (1958); *The William B. Bates Collection of Texana and Western Americana* exhibition cat. (1965); "The Fallacy of the Ideal Copy," *The Lib.* (1978); "The Library of the Convent of Ocopa," *Latin Amer. Resrch. Review* (1978); "An Analysis of Hopkins' 'Terrible' Sonnet No. 65, No Worst," *The Critical Srvy.* (Sum. 1966); reviews. **Activities:** 1, 4, 20, 30, 45; 57 **Addr.:** 2815 Jarrard, Houston, TX 77005.

Pouncy, Mitchell L. (Ap. 3, 1930, Palestine, TX) Head, Tech. Srvs., South. Univ., 1976–, Cat. Libn., 1965–76, Circ. Libn., 1961–65, Acq. Libn., 1959–61. **Educ.:** Prairie View A and M Univ., 1947–51, AB (Hist.); Atlanta Univ., 1954–55, MSLS; LA Tech. Univ., 1970, Cert. (Data Prcs.). **Orgs.:** ALA. Cmnty. Assn. for the Welfare of Sch. Chld. **Activities:** 1; 17, 20, 46 **Addr.:** Box 10031, Southern Branch Post Office, Baton Rouge, LA 70813.

Pound, Mary Elizabeth (Je. 9, 1932, Houston, TX) Pubns. Coord., Spec. Asst., Univ. of TX, 1976–, Head Libn., Serials Cat. Unit, 1975–76, Head Libn., Ctrl. Serials Rec. Unit, 1975, Head Libn., Serials Unit, 1973–75, Chief Cat. Libn., 1970–73, Serials Catlgr., 1955–70. **Educ.:** Rice Univ., 1950–54, BA (Eng.); Univ. of TX, 1954–56, MLS. **Orgs.:** TX LA: Ed., *TX Lib. Jnl.* Ed. (1965–75). ALA: Cncl. Com. on Publshg. (1975–76); RTSD/Cat. and Class. Sect. (1970–73); *RTSD Nsltr.* Ed. (1976–79); *Coll. and Resrch. Libs.* Ed. Bd. (1977–80). Unvsl. Serials & Bk. Exch.: Bd. of Dirs. (1977–78). Beta Phi Mu: Beta Eta Chap. (Pres., 1977–78). **Pubns.:** "Year's Work in Serials," *Lib. Resrcs. & Tech. Srvs.* (Spr. 1970–72); State Report: "Texas", *ALA Yrbk.* (1976–79); "Cataloging and Classification," *ALA Yrbk.* (1978). **Activities:** 1; 36, 37, 39 **Addr.:** General Libraries, The University of Texas at Austin, Austin, TX 78712.

Poundstone, Sally Hill (Ap. 7, 1933, Washington, DC) Dir., Mamaroneck Free Lib., Emelin Thea. for the Performing Arts, 1966–; Libn., Bedford Hills Elem. Sch., 1965–66; Chief, Acq. Dept., White Plains Pub. Lib., 1960–62; Libn., Folger Shakespeare Lib., 1959–60; Lib. Sci. Instr., Coll. of New Rochelle, 1970–71; Lib. Sci. Instr., NY Univ. Ctr. for Cont. Ed. 1968–71. **Educ.:** Univ. of KY, 1950–54, BA (LS), 1954–55, MA (LS). **Orgs.:** NY Metro. Ref. and Resrch. Lib. Agency: Trustee (1979–); Copyrt. Com. (1979–). Admin. Srvs. (Ch., 1977–79). Pratt Inst. Grad. Sch. of Lib. and Info. Sci.: Westchester Adv. Cncl. (1979–). Westchester LA: Pres. (1977–78). NY LA: Pub. Lib. Sect. (VP, 1980–81; Pres., 1981–); Adult Srvs. Sect. (Secy., Treas., 1970–72). Mamaroneck Hist. Socty.: Pres. (1976–77); Bd. of Trustees, (1978–). Larchmont-Mamaroneck Film Cncl.: Pres. (1971–72); Hon. VP (1972–). Garden Club of Mamaroneck: Pres. (1969–70); Bd. of Dir. (1968–). Cham. of Cmrc. **Honors:** Phi Beta Kappa, 1953; Beta Phi Mu, 1954. **Pubns.:** various bk. reviews in *Lib. Jnl.* (1962–70). **Activities:** 9; 17, 34; 55, 61, 75 **Addr.:** Mamaroneck Free Library, Library Ln., Mamaroneck, NY 10543.

Pourciau, Lester J., Jr., (S. 6, 1936, Baton Rouge, LA) Dir., Libs., Memphis State Univ., 1970–; Ref. Srvs. Coord., Coll. Lib., Univ. of FL, 1966–67; Ref. Tech. Srvs. Libn., Florence Cnty. Pub. Lib., 1964–65; Asst. Ref. Libn., Univ. of SC, 1963–64. **Educ.:** LA State Univ., 1959–62, BA (Grmn. lang.), 1962–64 MS (LS); IN Univ., 1967–70, PhD (LS). **Orgs.:** ALA. SELA: Gvtl. Rel. Com. (1975–76). TN LA: Grievance Com. (1979–80); Ch. (1974–75); Legis. Com. (Ch., 1975–76); Fed. Rel. Coord. (1975–76). Memphis Lib. Cncl., TN Higher Educ. Comsn. Lions Intl.: Memphis Univ. Lions Club (Secty. 1978–80). Natl. Assn. of Watch and Clock Col. Antique Auto. Club of Amer. **Pubns.:** "The Role of Beginning Academic Librarians," *The Expected Role of Beginning Librarians: A Comparative Analysis from Administrators, Educators, and Young Professionals* (1979); "The Mobility of American Library School Faculty to 1964," *Southeastern Libn.* (Sum. 1968); "The Second Master's Degree in Academic Librarianship," *TN Libn.* (Win. 1978); "Coping with Inflation," *TN Libn.* (Spr. 1981); "Development and Management of Microform Serials Collections," *The Impact of Serials on Collection Development* (1981); various reviews. **Activities:** 1; 17, 26 **Addr.:** Memphis State University Libraries, Memphis, TN 38152.

Pourron, Eleanor Korman (Ap. 26, 1937, Johnstown, PA) Coord., Adult/YA Srvs. and Volun., Arlington Cnty. Lib., 1969–; Head, YA Dept., Hyattsville Branch, Prince George's Cnty. Meml. Lib., 1966–69; YA Libn., Youngstown, Mahoning Cnty. Lib. 1960–66. **Educ.:** Susquehanna Univ., 1955–59, AB (Eng.); Syracuse Univ., 1959–60, MSLS (Ref.). **Orgs.:** ALA: YASD (Pres., 1979–80); Best Bks. for YA Com. (Ch., 1973–74). VA LA: Chld. and YA RT (Ch., 1974–75). DC LA. CLENE. Arlington Film Wkshp.: Pres. (1973–80). North. VA Folk Fest. Assn.: Bd. Mem.; Nsltr. Ed. (1978–). Mensa. **Pubns.:** "Best Books for Young Adults," anl. list, *Libraries and Young Adults* (1979). **Activities:** 9; 36, 42, 48; 50, 67, 89 **Addr.:** Arlington County Library, 1015 N. Quincy St., Arlington, VA 22201.

Pouzar, Frank A. (D. 16, 1951, Dallas, TX) Sci. Ref. Libn., Dallas Pub. Lib., 1976–. **Educ.:** Univ. of TX, Austin, 1970–74, BA (Eng.), 1974–76, MLS. **Orgs.:** ALA. SLA: Cont. Educ. Com. (1979–80). TX LA: GODORT (Vice-Ch., Ch., 1979–80); Mncpl. Docum. Srvy. Com. (1978–79). **Pubns.:** "Dallas Public Library Offers Patrons Course On Using Government Documents," *Pub. Docum. Highlights for TX* (Win. 1979). **Activities:** 9, 12; 15, 29, 39; 56, 60, 91 **Addr.:** Dallas Public Library, Business and Technology Div., 1954 Commerce St., Dallas, TX 75201.

Povsic, Frances F. (S. 29, 1923, Ribnica, Slovenia, Yugoslavia) Head, Curric. Resrc. Ctr., Bowling Green State Univ. Libs., 1973–, Ref. Libn., Educ., 1964–73, Gvt. Docum. Libn., 1963–64; Elem. Sch. Tchr., Cleveland Sch. Syst., 1954–62. **Educ.:** Tchrs. Coll., Slovenia, Yugoslavia, 1940–44, Dip.; John Carroll Univ., 1957–60, BS, cum laude (Educ., Hist.); Case West. Rsv. Univ., 1962–63, MS (LS). **Orgs.:** ALA: ACRL; ALSC. OH Educ. Lib. Media Assn.: Mem. Com. Acad. LA of OH: Frnds. of Intl. Bd. on Bks. for Young People. Socty. for Slovene Std. **Pubns.:** "Bilingualism in American Education–Implications for Ethnic Schools," ERIC (Je. 1978); "Czechoslovakia: Children's Fiction in English," *Readg. Tchr.* (Mr. 1980); "Poland: Children's Fiction in English," *Readg. Tchr.* (Ap. 1980); "Russian Folk and Animal Tales," *Readg. Tchr.* (D. 1981); "Non-Russian Tales from the Soviet Union," *Readg. Tchr.* (N. 1981); various bk. reviews, articles. **Activities:** 1; 15, 17, 39 **Addr.:** Curriculum Resource Center, Bowing Green State University Libraries, Bowling Green, OH 43403.

Powell, Anice Carpenter (D. 2, 1928, Moorhead, MS) Dir., Sunflower Cnty. Lib., 1962–; Eng. Instr., Humphreys Cnty. Schs., 1961–62; Libn., Sunflower Pub. Lib., 1958–61. **Educ.:** Delta State Coll., 1959–61, BS (Eng. Educ.); Delta State Univ., 1974, MLS. **Orgs.:** MSLA: Nom. Com. (1981); MS Gvr. Lib. Conf., Adv. Com., S. Delta Dist. (Ch., 1978–79); Legis. Com. (1981); various coms. MS Lib. Comsn.: Lib. Srv. to Disadv. Wkshp. (Ch., 1974); Adv. Cncl. for Title IV–A (1967–71); LSCA Adv. Bd. (1978–80). Sunflower Methodist Church. Sunflower Cnty. Heart Assn.: Town of Sunflower (Ch., 1963–73). Sunflower Cnty. Hist. Assn. Sunflower Cnty. Welfare Dept.: Title XX Adv. Com. Various orgs. **Honors:** H. W. Wilson, ALA, John Cotton Dana Spec. Awd., 1972; MSLA, Best Year-Round Spec. Proj., 1981; Kappa Delta Pi; MSLA, Cert. of Apprec., 1975. **Activities:** 9; 17 **Addr.:** Sunflower County Library, 201 Cypress Dr., Indianola, MS 38751.

Powell, James Edwin (S. 28, 1935, McComb, MS) Dir., Lib. Srvs., Mid-Amer. Bapt. Theo. Semy., 1980–, Resrch. Libn., 1977–80; HQ Libn., Pike-Amite Lib. Syst., 1968–72; HS Libn., Enterprise HS, 1965–66. **Educ.:** MS Coll., 1953–56, BA (Eng., Classics, Lang.); New Orleans Bapt. Theo. Semy., 1956–59, MDiv; Mid-Amer. Bapt. Theo. Semy., 1975–79, ThD (New Testament); George Peabody Coll. for Tchrs., 1978–79, MLS. **Orgs.:** Memphis Lib. Cncl.: Ch. (1981–82); Interlib. Coop. Com. (Ch., 1980–81). ALA: RTED, Dupl. Exch. Un. Com. (1981–82). ATLA. SELA. Various other orgs. **Honors:** Beta Phi Mu. **Activities:** 1, 12; 15, 17, 31; 90 **Addr.:** Mid-America Baptist Theological Seminary, 1255 Poplar Ave., Memphis, TN 38104.

Powell, James Raymond, Jr. (D. 29, 1937, Pittsburgh, PA) Sr. Info. Sci., Corp. Tech. Lib., The Upjohn Co., 1977–, Actg. Head, Info. Sci., 1976–77, Info. Sci., 1974–76; Assoc. Prof., Microbiology, PA Coll. of Optometry, 1971–73; Asst. Prof. Bio., DE Valley Coll., 1967–71; Sr. Sci., Rohm and Haas Co., 1965–67. **Educ.:** Juniata Coll., 1955–59, BS (Bio.); Univ. of Richmond, 1959–61, MA (Bio.); VA Polytech. Inst., 1961–65, PhD (Myco., Microbiology); Drexel Univ., 1973, MS (Lib. and Info. Sci.). **Orgs.:** SLA: West. MI Chap. (Pres., 1980–81); MI Chap. Secty.,

PROFESSIONAL ACTIVITIES: Institutions: 1. Acad. lib.; 2. Arch.; 3. Assn.; 4. Fed./Gvt. lib.; 5. Inst. lib.; 6. Mfr./Suppl.; 7. Milit. lib.; 8. Musm.; 9. Pub. lib.; 10. Sch. lib.; 11. Sch. of lib. sci.; 12. Spec. lib.; 13. State lib.; 14. (other). **Functions/Activities:** 15. Acq./Col. dev.; 16. Adult srvs.; 17. Admin.; 18. Apprais.; 19. Archit./Bldgs.; 20. Cat./Class.; 21. Chld. srvs.; 22. Circ.; 23. Cons./Pres.; 24. Consult.; 25. Cont. ed.; 26. Educ. lib. sci.; 27. Ext. srvs.; 28. Fund/Grants; 29. Gvt. pubs.; 30. Indx./Abs.; 31. Instr. lib. use; 32. Media srvs.; 33. Micro.; 34. Netwks./Coop.; 35. Persnl.; 36. PR; 37. Publshg.; 38. Recs. mgt.; 39. Ref. srvs.; 40. Repro.; 41. Resrch.; 42. Review.; 43. Secur.; 44. Serials; 45. Spec. col.; 46. Tech. srvs.; 47. Trustees/Bds.; 48. YA srvs.; 49. (other).

1977–79). Drug Info. Assn. The Kalamazoo Singers: Fndr.; Pres. (1976–79). **Pubns.:** Co-ed., "The Prostaglandins Bibliography; Suppl. 4, 1979" (1980); Co-ed., "The Prostaglandins Bibliography; Suppl. 3, 1978" (1979); "Excerpta Medica (EMBASE) On-line-A Reacquaintance," *ONLINE* (1980); "Evaluation of Excerpta Medica On-Line," *Spec. Libs.* (1976). **Activities:** 12; 17, 30, 41; 58, 75, 87 **Addr.:** Corporate Technical Library, The Upjohn Company, Kalamazoo, MI 49001.

Powell, Janice J. (O. 25, 1953, Rahway, NJ) Head, Cat., Uniformed Srvs., Univ. of the Hlth. Sci./LRC, 1978–. **Educ.:** Kean State Coll., 1971–75, BA, summa cum laude (Tchr., Libn.); Univ. of MD, 1975–76, MLS; 1976, Med. Libn. Cert. **Orgs.:** Med. LA: Milit. Med. Libns. (Vice-Ch.). DC LA. **Activities:** 4, 12; 17, 20, 32; 56, 75, 80 **Addr.:** 5112 Parklawn Terr. #101, Rockville, MD 20852.

Powell, Lawrence Clark (S. 3, 1906, Washington, DC) Prof. in Residence Emeritus, Univ. of AZ, 1971–; Dean, Grad. Lib. Sch., Univ. of CA, Los Angeles, 1960–66, Dir., Clark Lib., 1944–66, Univ. Libn., 1944–61. **Educ.:** Occidental Coll., 1928, AB; Univ. of Dijon, 1932, PhD; Univ. of CA, 1937, MLS. **Orgs.:** ALA: Cncl.; various coms. CA LA: Pres. (1950). Bibl. Socty. of Amer.: Pres. (1954–56). Various orgs. **Honors:** Guggenheim Fellow, 1950, 1966; Phi Beta Kappa; various hon. docts. **Pubns.:** Various pubns. **Addr.:** Library A349, University of Arizona, Tucson, AZ 85721.

Powell, Margaret S. (S. 27, 1936, Brooklyn, NY) Asst. Libn., Docum., Ref., Coll. of Wooster, 1980–, various positions in tech. srvs., Andrews Lib., 1972–80; Libn., Cat. Dept., Univ. of WI, 1960–62. **Educ.:** Oberlin Coll., 1954–58, AB (Eng. Lit.); Univ. of IL, 1958–59, MS (LS). **Orgs.:** ALA. Amer. Name Socty. Univ. of IL Lib. Sch. Assn. **Pubns.:** Asst. Ed., Catlgr., *Author, Title, and Subject Catalog, Atlanta University/Bell and Howell Black Culture Collection* (1973–74); Jt. auth., "Place-name Literature, United States and Canada 1971–1974, 1975, 1979," *Names* (D. 1974, D. 1975, D. 1979). **Activities:** 1; 20, 29, 39; 57, 92 **Addr.:** Andrews Library, College of Wooster, Wooster, OH 44691.

Powell, Martha Caroline (Ja. 12, 1936, Gillette, WY) Msc. Libn., Adj. Prof. of Church Msc., South. Bapt. Theo. Semy., 1969–; Prof., Msc., Big Sky Bible Coll., Lewiston, MT, 1967–68; Instr., Msc., Roberts Wesleyan Coll., 1962–64. **Educ.:** Univ. of WY, 1953–57, BMus (Msc., Math.); Univ. of Rochester, 1957–60, MMus (Hist.); Rutgers Univ., 1968–69, MLS. **Orgs.:** Msc. LA: Midwest Chap., Cat. Com. (1979–80). Assn. of Christ. Libns. Hymn Socty. of Amer. **Pubns.:** *A Selected Bibliography of Church Music and Music Reference Materials* (1977); indxr., *Christ. Per. Indx.* **Activities:** 1; 15, 20, 31; 55 **Addr.:** Southern Baptist Theological Seminary, 2825 Lexington Rd., Louisville, KY 40280.

Powell, Ronald R. (My. 24, 1944, Columbia, MO) Asst. Prof., Sch. of LS, Univ. of MI, 1979–; Lib. Dir., Univ. of Charleston, 1976–79; Resrch. Assoc., Lib. Resrch. Ctr., Univ. of IL, 1974–75; Asst. Circ. Libn., Univ. of IL Lib., 1969–71, Acq. Biblgphr., 1968–69. **Educ.:** Univ. of MO, 1962–67, AB (Hist.); West. MI Univ., 1967–68, MS (LS); Univ. of IL, 1971–76, PhD (LS). **Orgs.:** ALA: ACRL. MI LA. AALS. **Honors:** Beta Phi Mu, 1968. **Pubns.:** Jt. auth., *Basic Reference Sources; A Self-Study Manual* (1981); "An Investigation of the Relationships between Quantifiable Reference Service Variables and Reference Performance," *Lib. Qtly.* (Ja. 1978); "A Study of Reference Services and Librarians in Selected Illinois Public Libraries," *IL Libs.* (My. 1978); "A Comparison of Resident and Non-Resident Student Library Use," *WV Libs.* (Spr. 1979); "Women's Studies Resources," *The Women's Yellow Pages; West Virginia Edition* (1979); various other articles. **Activities:** 1, 11; 15, 26, 39; 61, 74 **Addr.:** 1433 E. Park Pl., Ann Arbor, MI 48104.

Powell, Ruth Ann (F. 22, 1939, Fairmont, WV) Tech. Srvs. Libn., Asst. Prof. of Lib. Sci., Fairmont State Coll., 1975–, Acq. Libn., 1971–75, Circ. Libn., Asst. Ref., 1966–71; HS Libn., Mannington HS, 1965–66; Tchr., Dept. Ch., 1961–65. **Educ.:** Fairmont State Coll., 1957–61, AB Ed (Soc. Sci., Eng.); Kent State Univ., 1962–67, MLS; WV Univ., 1974. **Orgs.:** ALA: Cncl. of State Pres. (1977–78); Tri-State ACRL: Secty., Treas. (1976–77); Nom. Com. (Ch., 1977–78); Constn. ByLaws Com. (Ch., 1978–79). Southeastern LA: Com. of State Pres. (1977–78). WV LA: Pres. (1977–78). Soroptimist: Secty. (1977–78). Delta Kappa Gamma: Audit. Com. (1977–78); Schol. and World Flwshp. Com. (1978–79); Nom. Com. (1979–80); Resrch Com. (Ch., 1980–81). Eastern Star. First United Presbyterian Church. **Pubns.:** *The History of the Fairmont State College Library* (1967); various articles in *WV Libs.* (1973–). **Activities:** 1; 15, 17, 46; 63, 85, 92 **Addr.:** Fairmont State College Library, Fairmont, WV 26554.

Powell, Ted F. (F. 2, 1935, Rexburg, ID) Dir., Micro. Div., Geneal. Socty. of UT, 1980–, Dir., Lib. Srvs. Div., 1975–80, Mgr., Acq. and Fld. Oper., 1972–75, Supvsr., Granite Mt. Vault, 1970–71, Supvsr., Geneal. Socty. Lib., 1967–70. **Educ.:** Univ. of UT, 1958–62, BS (Acct.), 1967–68, (LS); Various crs. on microphotography. **Orgs.:** Natl. Micro. Assn.: Intermountain Chap. (Pres., 1977). Intl. Cncl. on Arch.: Microfilm Com.; Dev. Arch. Com. **Honors:** Natl. Microfilm Assn., Outstan. Srv. Awd., 1977. **Pubns.:** "Saving the Past for the Future," *The Amer. Archvst.* (Jl. 1976); "Quality Control–Micrographics System," *Microfilm Com. Bltn.* (1979). **Activities:** 2, 12; 15, 17, 33; 67, 69, 85 **Addr.:** Micrographics Division, Genealogical Society of UT, Salt Lake City, UT 84150.

Powell, Virginia L. (S. 13, 1931, Wheaton, IL) Libn. of Msc., Educ., AV, Buswell Lib., Wheaton Coll., 1972–. **Educ.:** West. MI Univ., 1957–63, BS (Elem. Educ.); Rosary Coll., 1974–75, MLS (Acad. Libs.); Grand Rapids Sch. of the Bible and Msc., 1951–55, Cert. (Msc., Missn.). **Orgs.:** Evangelical Church LA: Wkshp. Tchr. AV Users' Grp. Christ. LA. OCLC Msc. Users' Grp. Msc. LA. Mid-west Msc. LA. **Activities:** 1; 20, 31, 32; 55, 63, 70 **Addr.:** Buswell Memorial Library, Wheaton College, Wheaton, IL 60187.

Powell, Wyley L. (Halifax, VA) Biling. Dcmlst., UTLAS, 1980–; Tech. Asst., Docum., Office of Lib. Coord., Cncl. of ON Univs., 1979–80; Biling. Catlgr., Transl., Bibliocentre, Centennial Coll., 1979–79; Ref. Libn., Ryerson Polytech. Inst., 1978–79. **Educ.:** Coll. of William & Mary, 1959–60, 61–63, BA (Fr.); Trinity Coll., Univ. of Dublin, 1960–61, (Gen. Std.); New York Univ., 1965–67, MA (Fr.); Yale Univ., 1968–72, MPhil (Fr.); Univ. of Toronto, 1976–78, MLS; Univ. of Toronto, 1975–78, Dip. (Trans.). **Orgs.:** Can. LA. ON LA. ASTED. UNICAT/TELECAT. **Honors:** Beta Phi Mu, 1978. **Pubns.:** Jt. Cmplr., *Canadian Energy: Volume 1, A Directory* (1980); Jt. Cmplr., *The Ontario Energy Catalogue;* Cmplr and Ed., *UTLAS Users' Exchange* (1980); Cmplr and Ed., *UTLAS Plans and Progress* (1981). **Activities:** 1, 6; 20, 44, 46; 56, 62 **Addr.:** 142 Cambridge Ave., Toronto, ON M4K 2L8 Canada.

Power, Colleen J. (O. 26 1943, Fort Sill, OK) Ed. Bd., *Topics in Tech. Srvs.,* Coord., Ref. Srvs. CA State Univ., Chico, 1980–, Instr., Col. Dev., Sci. Libn., 1979–80, Col. Dev. Libn., 1978–79; Sci. Col. Dev. Libn., AZ State Univ., 1976–78, Life Sci. Libn., 1974–76; Sci. Libn., Humboldt State Univ., 1970–74; Head Libn., Fisheries-Oceanography Lib., Univ. of WA, 1967–70. **Educ.:** Univ. of OK, 1961–66, BS (Zlgy.) BA (Eng., Hist), 1966–67, MLS. **Orgs.:** ALA. Gvr.'s Conf. on Human Resrcs. **Pubns.:** *Science and Natural Resources Literature Searches* (1975); "Automated Circulation ...and User Satisfaction," *Jnl. of Lib. Autom.* (D. 1978); reviews. **Activities:** 1, 11; 15, 24, 39; 53, 58, 91 **Addr.:** P.O. Box 336, Richvale, CA 95974.

Power, Mary F. (Ag. 6, 1950, Boston, MA) Coord., Ref. Srvs., NRTA-AARP Natl. Grntlgy. Resrc. Ctr., 1979–, Ref. Libn., Asst. Head Libn., 1978–79, Actg. Head Libn., 1977–78, Acq. Libn., 1975–77. **Educ.:** Cath. Univ. of Amer., 1968–72, BA (Russ.), 1974–76, MLS (Lib., Info. Sci.). **Orgs.:** Grntlgcl. Libns. Com.: Ch. (1978–80). SLA: Soc. and Human Srvs. (Ch., 1979–80); Soc. Sci. Sect. (Ch.-Elect, 1981–82); DC Chap., Jt. Spr. Wkshp., Pubcty. (1976), Elec. Ch. (1977–78), Corres. Secy. (1980–81), Cont. Educ. Com. (1980–81). Grntlgcl. Socty.: Educ. Com. (1979–81). Beta Phi Mu: DC Chap. (Ch.-Elect, 1980–81). **Honors:** Sigma Epsilon Phi, 1972. **Pubns.:** "Close Encounters in Gerontology," *Lib. Jnl. Spec. Rpt. #6* (1978); ed., *Grntlgcl. Libns. Nsltr.* (1976–77); ed., *GERONET* (1980–81). **Addr.:** NRTA-AARP National Gerontology Resource Center, 1909 K St. N.W., Washington, DC 20049.

Powers, Beatrice H. (D. 28, 1925, New York, NY) Head, Ref. Dept., San Diego Cnty. Lib., 1963–; Chld. Libn., Mineola Meml. Lib., 1957–63; Chld. Libn., NY Pub. Lib., 1952–57. **Educ.:** Taylor Univ., 1945–49, AB (Eng. Lit.); Pratt Inst., 1951–52, MSLS; 1952, NY State Prof. Libns. Cert. **Orgs.:** NY LA. Nassau Cnty. Lib. Syst.: Chld. Srvs. Com. (1957–63). CA LA: Palomar Chap. **Activities:** 9; 20, 21, 39 **Addr.:** San Diego County Library Headquarters, 5555 Overland Ave., Bldg. 15, San Diego, CA 92123.

Powers, Esther B. (Ap. 3, 1912, Fairmont, WV) Retired; Libn., E. Fairmont HS, 1949–75; Actg. Chief Libn., AV Aids Dept., WV Univ., 1949; Actg. Asst. Libn., Fairmont State Coll., 2 yrs.; Instr., WV Univ., 1960; various wkshps. **Educ.:** Fairmont State Coll., 1929–33, AB (Eng., Soc. Sci.); WV Univ., 1947–48, Lib. Cert.; George Peabody Coll. for Tchrs., 1957–59, MS (LS). **Orgs.:** WV LA. CSLA. Delta Kappa Gamma Socty. Intl.: Corres. Secy. (1974–77). WV Assn. of Retired Sch. Empls. **Honors:** WV LA, Dora Parks Awd., 25 Yrs. of Outstan. Srv. to Libs. and Libnshp. in WV, 1976. **Activities:** 10, 12; 17, 32, 48; 63, 90 **Addr.:** 805 Pittsburgh Ave., Fairmont, WV 26554.

Powers, Sr. (Mary) Luella Prof. Emeritus, Rosary Coll. Grad. Sch. of LS, 1972–, Prof., 1967–72, Dir., 1949–59, Instr., 1944–59, 1931–41; Libn., Dominican Educ. Ctr., Sinsinawa, WI, 1965–67; Prof., Univ. of Portland Dept. of LS, 1962–65; Libn., Pius XII Inst., Florence, Italy, 1959–62; Lectr., Cath. Univ. Grad. Dept. of LS, 1942–44. **Educ.:** Marquette Univ., 1921–24 (Bot.); Rosary Coll., 1924–25, 1927, BA (Bot.); Univ. of MI, 1930–31, BA (LS), 1932–34, MA (LS); Univ. of Chicago, 1940–42, 1945, PhD (LS); Columbia Univ., 1949 (LS); various crs. **Orgs.:** ALA. Cath. LA. IL LA. Amnesty Intl. Bread for the World. Common Cause. **Pubns.:** "Carleton Bruns Joeckel," *ALA World Ency. of Lib. and Info. Sci.;* "Catholic Commercial Publishing in the US," *Cath. Lib. World* (Ap.–My. 1946); ed., *Cath. Booklist* (1945–49, 1957–58). **Activities:** 1; 26, 31, 46; 57 **Addr.:** Rosary College, Graduate School of Library Science, 7900 W. Division St., River Forest, IL 60305.

Powers, Martha Ammidon (Mr. 19, 1940, Boston, MA) Coord., Berkeley Info. Netwk., Berkeley Pub. Lib., 1979–; Archvst., Dolby Labs., 1979–; Consult., ATARI, 1981–; Ref. Libn., BALIS Weekend Lib. Line, 1978–; various positions as freelnc. libn., libn. consult., Univ. of CA, Berkeley, Princeton Univ., Princeton Pub. Lib., Boston Univ., Com. on Chld. TV, collective bookstore, others, 1973–. **Educ.:** Univ. of CA, Riverside, 1958–63, BA (Fr., Eng.); Rutgers Univ., 1966–67, MA (LS). **Orgs.:** ALA. CA LA. SLA. **Pubns.:** Jt. ed., *While You're Up, Get Me a Grant* (1976); "The Migrants—Library Project for Migrant Workers," *NJ Libs.* (F. 1974); ed., Publshr., *Nsltr. For NJ Libns. for Soc. Resp.* (1969–72). **Activities:** 9, 12; 16, 24, 39; 56, 62, 75 **Addr.:** Berkeley Information Network, Berkeley Public Library, 2090 Kittredge St., Berkeley, CA 94704.

Poyer, Robert K. (Jl. 18, 1951, Queens, NY) Coord., Pub. Srvs., Med. Univ. of SC, 1975–; Catlgr., SUNY Upstate Med. Ctr., 1974–75. **Educ.:** Ball State Univ., 1969–73, BS (Soc. Sci.); Case West. Rsv. Univ., 1973–74, MSLS. **Orgs.:** Med. LA. **Pubns.:** "Inaccurate references in signifant journals of Science," *Bltn. Med. LA* (1979); "Improved library service through user education," *Bltn. Med. LA* (1977). **Activities:** 1; 22, 36, 39; 80, 87 **Addr.:** Library, Medical University of SC, 171 Ashley Ave., Charleston, SC 29425.

Praeger, Frederick A. (S. 16, 1915, Vienna, Austria) Adj. Prof., Grad. Sch. of Libnshp., Univ. of Denver, 1976–; Pres., Publshr., Westview Press, 1975–; Gen. Mgr., Ed. Praeger/Schuler Verlag Munchen, Grmn. Fed. Repub., 1970–75; Ch., Phaidon Publshrs. London, 1967–68; Pres., Praeger Publshrs., New York City, 1950–68. **Educ.:** Univ. of Vienna, 1933–38. **Orgs.:** AAP: Exec. Com.; Sci., Med., Tech. Grp. Socty. for Schol. Publshg. **Honors:** Carey Thomas Awd., Creat. Publshg., 1957. **Activities:** 11, 14-Pubshg.; 92, 89-Ed. **Addr.:** Westview Press, 5500 Central Ave., Boulder, CO 80301.

Pragnell, Terence Richard (N. 15, 1943, Winnipeg, MB) Law Libn., Pac. Lighting Corp., 1977–; Asst. Ref. Libn., Los Angeles Cnty. Law Lib., 1970–77. **Educ.:** Univ. of CA, Los Angeles, 1961–66, BA (Eng.); Univ. of South. CA, 1974–76, MLS. **Orgs.:** AALL. ALA. SLA. South. CA Assn. of Law Libs.: Consult. Com. (Ch., 1978–80). **Pubns.:** "The Private Law Library," *The Lawyer's Assistant* (1977); "Space Planning: A Case Study," *Private Law Library, 1980's and Beyond* (1979). **Activities:** 5, 12; 24, 39, 41; 77 **Addr.:** Pacific Lighting Corp., Law Library ML 615, 810 S. Flower St., Los Angeles, CA 90017.

Pralle, Ruth I. (S. 20, 1951, McAllen, TX) Tech. Srvs. Libn., Alma Coll., 1981–; Ref. Libn., 1979–; Libn., WI Dept. of Pub. Instr. Lib., 1978; Ref., Instr. Libn., Univ. of WI, Stout, 1976–78. **Educ.:** St. Olaf Coll., 1969–73, BA (Phil., Relig.); Univ. of IL, 1975–76, MS (LS). **Orgs.:** ALA. WI LA: WI Assn. of Acad. Libns., Com. on Educ. in Lib. Use (1977–78). MI LA. MI State Lib. Task Frc. on ILL. **Activities:** 1; 31, 34, 39; 63, 90 **Addr.:** Alma College Library, Alma, MI 48801.

Pratchett, Patricia A. (Je. 5, 1948, Havana, Cuba) Mgr., Corporate Lib., Untd. Srvs. Auto. Assn., 1979–; Head, Autom. Serials Sect., Univ. of Houston, 1978–79, Asst. Serials Libn., 1975–78; Resrch. Assoc., Reeves of TX, 1974. **Educ.:** LA State Univ., 1966–70, BA (Span.), 1972, MS (LS). **Orgs.:** SLA: TX Chap. (Secy., 1981–82), OLUG, San Antonio Lcl. Plng. Grp. (1980–82); Insr. and Empl. Benefits Div.; Bus. and Fin. Div.; Lib. Mgt. Div. TX LA: Cont. Ed. Com. (1977–78). Univ. Without Walls/Hispanic Intl. Univ.: Bd. (1977–78), Acad. Com. (1977). **Honors:** Beta Phi Mu, 1972. **Activities:** 1, 12; 24, 39, 46; 56, 59, 76 **Addr.:** USAA Corporate Library and Information Center, USAA Bldg., San Antonio, TX 78288.

Pratt, Allan D. (S. 26, 1933, Traverse City, MI) Prof., Grad. Lib. Sch., Univ. of AZ, 1981–; Assoc. Prof., Grad. Lib. Sch., IN Univ., 1975–81, Asst. Prof., 1969–75. **Educ.:** Univ. of MI, 1951–55, BA (Eng.); West. Rsv. Univ., 1958–59, MS (LS); Univ. of Pittsburgh, 1970–74, PhD (LS). **Orgs.:** ASIS. SLA. **Honors:** Comsn. for Educ. Exch., Fulbright Professorship, Copenhagen, 1976. **Pubns.:** *The Information of The Image* (1981); "The Use of Microcomputers in Libraries," *Jnl. of Lib. Autom.* (Mr. 1980); "Danish and American Publishing Patterns," *Lib. Resrch.* (Spr. 1979); "The Analysis of Library Statistics," *Lib. Qtly.* (Jl. 1975). **Activities:** 11; 24, 26, 41; 56, 75, 93 **Addr.:** Graduate Library School, Univ. of AZ, 1515 E. 1st St., Tucson, AZ 85721.

Pratt, Dana J. (D. 9, 1926, Cambridge, MA) Dir. of Publshg., Lib. of Congs., 1978–; Asst. Dir., Yale Univ. Press, 1966–78; Exec. Secy., Assn. of Amer. Univ. Presses, 1962–66; Staff Assoc., Amer. Bk. Publshrs. Cncl., 1959–62; Fld. Consult., Franklin Bk. Prog., 1955–59; Sales Mgr., Univ. of IL Press, 1953–55; Sales Asst., Princeton Univ. Press, 1950–53. **Educ.:** Tufts Univ., 1948 (Hist.). **Orgs.:** Socty. for Schol. Publshg. Art Dir. Club. **Pubns.:** "Publishing the Children of Pride," *Schol. Publshg.* (O. 1973); "Publishing at the Library of Congress," *Schol. Publshg.* (Jl. 1981). **Activities:** 1, 4; 15, 37, 45; 70, 75, 89 **Addr.:** Library of Congress, Washington, DC 20540.

Special Subjects/Services: 50. Adult educ.; 51. Advert./Mktg.; 52. Aerosp.; 53. Agric.; 54. Area std.; 55. Arts/Hum.; 56. Autom.; 57. Bibl./Prtg.; 58. Bio. sci.; 59. Bus./Fin.; 60. Chem.; 61. Copyrt.; 62. Documtn.; 63. Educ.; 64. Engin.; 65. Env.; 66. Eth. grps.; 67. Film; 68. Food/Nutr.; 69. Geneal.; 70. Geo.; 71. Geol.; 72. Handcpd.; 73. Hist.; 74. Int. frdm.; 75. Info. sci.; 76. Insr.; 77. Law; 78. Legis.; 79. Math./Comp. sci.; 80. Med.; 81. Metals; 82. Nat. resrcs.; 83. Newsp.; 84. Nuc. sci.; 85. Oral hist.; 86. Petr./Energy; 87. Pharm.; 88. Phys./Astr./Math.; 89. Readg.; 90. Relig.; 91. Sci./Tech.; 92. Soc. sci.; 93. Telecom.; 94. Transp.; 95. (other).

Who's Who in Library and Information Services

Pratt, V. Lorraine (Je. 15, 1919, Trenton, MI) Dir., Lib. and Resrch. Info. Srvs., SRI Intl., 1948–; Libn., Redwood City Pub. Lib., 1945–48; Engin. Aide, Untd. Aircraft Corp., 1944–45. **Educ.:** Wayne State Univ., 1937–42, BS (Bus. Admin.); Univ. of Denver, 1944–45, BLS. **Orgs.:** SLA: San Francisco Bay Reg. Chap. (Pres., 1958–59). ASIS. Natl. Micro. Assn. Amer. Rec. Mgt. Assn. Inst. of Mgt. Sci. Med. LA. Amer. Mgt. Assn. **Pubns.:** "Analysis of Library Systems: A Bibliography," *Spec. Libs.* (D. 1964). **Activities:** 12; 17, 38, 39; 64, 91, 92 **Addr.:** SRI International, Library and Research Information Services, 333 Ravenswood Ave., Menlo Park, CA 94025.

Preble, Leverett L., III (Jl. 24, 1943, Brooklyn, NY) Prof., Law, Head Law Libn., Cap. Univ. Law Sch., 1980–; Consult., Law Libn., Law Firm of Rackemann, Sawyer and Brewster, 1980; Branch Law Libn., Boston Univ. Law Sch., 1973–1980; Consult., Lib., Instr., Legal Resrch., Middlesex Coll., 1975–80; Instr., Legal Resrch., Boston Univ., 1975–80. **Educ.:** Norwich Univ., 1961–66, BA (Gvt.); Boston Univ., 1966–72, JD (Doctor of Law); Simmons Coll., 1975–78, MLS. **Orgs.:** AALL. Law Libns. of New Eng. OH Reg. Assn. of Law Libs. Amer. Bar Assn. Assn. of Amer. Law Schs. **Activities:** 1, 12; 17, 24; 77 **Addr.:** Capital University Law School Library, 665 S. High St., Columbus, OH 43215.

Preibish, André (Mr. 23, 1923, Wroniawy, Poland) Dir., Cols. Dev. Branch, The Natl. Lib. of Can., 1973–; Head, Area Std. Dept., Syracuse Univ., 1969–72; Cols. Libn., La Trobe Univ. 1966–69; Serials Catlgr., Univ. of BC, 1964–66; Tchr. of Frgn. Lang., Polish HS, Les Ageux, France, 1948–51; Freelnc. Jnlst., Paris, 1947–49, Catlgr., Lib., Univ. of New Eng., Australia, 1957–63. **Educ.:** Univ. of New Eng., Australia, 1955–62, BA (Grmn., Hist.); Univ. of BC, 1965–66, BLS; LA of Australia, 1959, Regis. Cert. **Orgs.:** LA of Australia. ALALM. Shastri Indo-Can. Inst.: Lib. Com., Ch.; Bd. of Dirs. (1973–); Exec. Com. (1976–78). **Honors:** Univ. of BC, Marian Harlow Prize in Libnshp. for Leadership and Resrch. Ability in Spec. Flds., 1966; Beta Phi Mu, 1966. **Pubns.:** *Music Resources in Canadian Collections* (1980); *Directorio/Guia de las Bibliotecas en Ecuador* (1979); "Canadian Book Exchange Centre: A Contribution to Library Resources Development," *Australian Acad. and Resrch. Libs.* (1979); "Polish Libraries: Their Structure, Organization and Aims," *Intl. Lib. Review* (No. 9, 1977); ed., *Research Collections in Canadian Libraries, I Universities, V. 6, Canada* (1973); various articles, bks. **Activities:** 1, 4; 15, 17, 34; 54, 55, 57 **Addr.:** #2106-665 Bathgate Dr., Ottawa, ON K1K 3Y4 Canada.

Preisman, Sophia (O. 27, 1910, Lemberg, Poland) Retired, Indp. Rsrch., 1978–; Col. Libn., Univ. of Victoria, 1967–78; Ed., Can. LA, 1960–67; Circ. Libn., Hamilton Pub. Lib., 1952–59. **Educ.:** Hochschule für Welthandel Wien, Diplom Kaufman, 1933; Inst. Sci. Econ. and Cmrce. (Florence, Italy), 1935, Doctor; McGill Univ., 1952, BLS. **Orgs.:** Can. LA. **Pubns.:** *Canadian Index to Periodicals* (1963); *Canadian Library Horizons* (1963–67); various reviews and articles. **Addr.:** Ste. 206, 1625 Richmond Ave., Victoria, BC V8R 4P7 Canada.

Premont, Jacques O. C. (O. 10, 1926, Quebec, PQ) Chief Libn. Legis. Lib., Natl. Asm. of PQ, 1970–; Clerk of the Exec. Cncl. of PQ, 1962–70; Law Clerk of the Natl. Asm. of PQ, 1960–62. **Educ.:** Jesuits' Coll., 1938–46, BA; Laval Univ., 1946–49, LLL; Oxford Univ., 1958–60, MA (Jurisprudence). **Orgs.:** ASTED. Can. LA. Can. ALL. PQ LA. Various other orgs. Barreau du PQ. **Activities:** 13; 17; 77, 78, 92 **Addr.:** Legislative Library of Quebec, National Assembly of Quebec, Parliament Bldgs., Quebec, GIAIA5 Canada.

Prendergast, Sr. Rita (Ja. 19, 1931, Curragh, Ireland) Archvst., Congregation of the Srs. of Charity of the Incarnate Word, 1975–; Instr., Fr., Incarnate Word Coll., Dunmore, Ireland, 1973–75; Asst. Prof., Eng. Dept., Incarnate Word Coll., San Antonio, TX, 1970–73; Prin., Incarnate Word Coll., Dunmore, Ireland, 1963–70. **Educ.:** Cath. Univ. of Amer., 1957–59, BA (Eng.), 1960–61, MA (Eng.); Natl. Univ. of Ireland, 1963–64, Dip. (Educ.); Georgetown Univ., 1971, Cert. (Ling.). **Orgs.:** SAA. Socty. of SW Archvsts. TX Cath. Hist. Socty. **Honors:** Phi Beta Kappa, 1959. **Activities:** 2; 18, 23, 41; 73 **Addr.:** Incarnate Word Archives, 4503 Broadway, San Antonio, TX 78209.

Prentice, Ann E. (Jl. 19, 1933, Cambridgeport, VT) Dir., Grad. Sch. of Lib. and Info. Sci., Univ. of TN, 1978–; Asst. Prof., SUNY, Albany, 1972–78; Visit. Lectr., Pratt Inst., 1972; Lectr., SUNY, Albany, 1967–68. **Educ.:** Univ. of Rochester, 1950–54, AB (Pol. Sci.); SUNY, Albany, 1958–64, MLS; Columbia Univ., 1968–72, DLS. **Orgs.:** ALA: Cncl. (1979–83); Prof. Ethics Com. (1981–83). ASIS: E. TN Chap. (Ch. Elect, 1980–81); Tech. Prog. (Ch., 1981–82); SELA. Lib. Educ. Sect. (Ch., 1980–84). Girl Scouts of Amer.: Dutchess Cnty. Treas. (1973–76). **Honors:** Keuka Coll., Hon. Doctor of Letters. **Pubns.:** *Strategies for Survival Library Management Today* (1979); *Public Library Finance* (1977); *The Library Trustee, Image and Performance in Funding* (1973); "Continuing Education for Academic Librarians," *Coll. and Resrch. Libs.* (N. 1978); "Grapevine plus hard Data plus Duplicator equals Staff News Letter," *RQ* (Ja. 1968); various bks., articles, papers. **Activities:** 9, 11; 17, 24, 26; 59, 75 **Addr.:** Graduate School of Library and Information Science, University of TN, 804 Volunteer Blvd., Knoxville, TN 37916.

Prentice, Barbara S. (My. 4, 1929, Rockford, IL) Dir. of Resrch, Eval., Tucson Pub. Schs., 1971–; Trustee, Tucson Pub. Lib., 1970–; various univ. tchg. positions, 1968–74; various tchg. positions, Tucson Unified Sch. Dist., Tchr., Rockford Pub. Schs., 1959–61; various consult. **Educ.:** Rockford Coll., 1958–62, BA (Chld. Dev.); Univ. of AZ, 1962–70, PhD (Educ., Psy.); various crs. **Orgs.:** ALA: ALTA, Prog. Ch. (1976–78); Pres. (1978–79). AZ LA: Trustee Liaison (1972–). SWLA. Amer. Educ. Resrch. Assn.: Div. H, Prog. Com. (Ch., 1978); Affirmative Action Ch. Tucson Educ. Assn.: Area Dir. (1965–67). AAUW. Amer. Assn. of Mental Deficiency. **Pubns.:** Bd. Ed. Adv., *Educ. Resrchr.* (1980–83); "Right to Read/Right to Know," *Pub. Libs.* (Spr. 1974); various papers. **Activities:** 9; 41, 47; 63 **Addr.:** 1933 E. 3rd St., Tucson, AZ 85719.

Prentice-Naqvi, Joan Patricia (Je. 11, 1941, Pangman, SK) Libn., Inland Waters Directorate, Env. Can., 1980–; Head Libn., Plains Hlth. Ctr., 1974–79; Docum. Libn., Univ. of Regina, 1969–74. **Educ.:** Univ. of SK, 1958–61, BA (Eng.); Univ. of WA, 1967–69, MLS; Univ. of MB, 1964–65, Tchg. Cert. **Orgs.:** Can. LA: Can. Assn. of Coll. and Univ. Libs.; Can. Assn. of Spec. Libs. and Info. Ctrs. **Activities:** 1, 12; 17, 29, 39; 80 **Addr.:** 3949 - 17th Ave., Regina, SK S4S 0B7 Canada.

Presby, Richard Allan (N. 5, 1936, Manila, Cmwlth. of Philippine Islands) Dir., Libs. JHK and Assocs. Tech. Libs., 1978–, Libn., JHK Lib. San Francisco, 1975–78; Asst. Libn., Resrch., Subiaco Libs., 1973–74; Biblgphr., Lectr., Frgn. Acq., Claremont Colls., Honnold Lib., 1969–73. **Educ.:** U.S. Army Lang. Sch., Monterey, CA, 1956–57 (Russ., Ukranian); CA State Polytech. Univ., 1966–68, BS (Info. Dev.); Fullerton State Univ., 1968–70, MA (Lang.), MS (Info. Sci.). **Orgs.:** SLA: Educ. Com. (Lectr., 1978–80). CA LA. CA Inst. of Libs. Third Ord. of St. Benedict. **Honors:** Papal Cit., Estab., Pubn. of Incunabula Col., 1974; Pres. Cit., 1959. **Pubns.:** Jt. auth., *A Selected Bibliography for High Occupancy Vehicle Facility Development, etc.* (1980); *A Reference Bibliography for Traffic Signal Warrants from Gap Detection Data* (1980); *Passenger Car Equivalents/Truck Equivalents: Reference List;* "Zero Growth/Zero Service," *Spec. Libs.* (Ja. 1981); *Stray Cats'* poetry (1976); various bibls. **Addr.:** JHK & Associates Technical Libraries, 5801 Christie Ave. #220, Emeryville, CA 94608.

Preschel, Barbara M. (Ja. 22, 1929, New York, NY) Indx. Mgr., Funk and Wagnalls, 1980–; Indx. Supvsr., Arete Publshg. Co., 1978–80; Instr., Queens Coll. Grad. Sch. of Lib. and Info. Std., 1971–77; Ed., Bibl., Info. Ctr. on Crime and Delinquency, 1961–66. **Educ.:** Columbia Univ., 1945–49, BS (Lit.), 1959–61, MS (LS), 1974, Cert. (Advnc. Libnshp.). **Orgs.:** Amer. Socty. of Indxrs.: Pres. (1973–75); Dir. (1980–83). ASIS: Metro. NY Chap. (Ch., 1979–80). Cncl. of Natl. Lib. and Info. Assns.: Secy., Treas. (1977–1981). **Honors:** Beta Phi Mu. **Pubns.:** Various indxs., articles. **Activities:** 11, 14-Publshr.; 17, 30, 37; 50, 75 **Addr.:** 400 E. 56 St., New York, NY 10022.

Prescott, Katherine (Je. 2, 1912, Cleveland, OH) Retired, 1977– Reg. Libn. for Blind and Phys. Handcpd., Cleveland Pub. Lib., 1965–77, Branch Libn., 1950–65, Asst. Branch Libn., 1940–50, YA Libn., 1937–40, Asst. Libn., 1935–37. **Educ.:** Vassar Coll., 1930–34, AB (Msc.); West. Rsv. Univ., 1934–35, BS (LS), 1959, MS (LS). **Orgs.:** ALA: Staff Org. RT (Ch., 1948–50); Hlth. Rehab. Srvs. Div. (Co-Pres., 1974–75); Com. To Review Stan. for Lib. Srv. to Blind and Phys. Handcpd. (Ch., 1977–79). OH LA. Cleveland Socty. for the Blind: Bd. of Trustees (1969–74, 1976–78). Amer. Assn. of Workers with the Blind. Natl. Fed. of the Blind Assn. Women's City Club of Cleveland. **Honors:** Natl. Fed. of the Blind of OH, Sighted Ohioan of the Year, 1976; ALA, Hlth. and Rehab. Srvs. Div., Exceptional Srv. Awd., 1978. **Pubns.:** Jt. Auth., *Standards of Service for the Library of Congress Network of Libraries for the Blind and Physically Handicapped* (1979). **Activities:** 9; 16, 17, 49-Srvs. to Blind and Phys. Handcpd.; 56, 72, 75 **Addr.:** 3617 Meadowbrook Blvd., Cleveland, OH 44118.

Preslan, Kristina I. (F. 15, 1945, Dresden, Germany) Lib. Supvsr., Colton Pub. Lib., 1976–; Lib. Supvsr., Pomona (CA) Pub. Lib., 1974–76; Head, Chld. Dept., Decatur (IL) Pub. Lib., 1973–74. **Educ.:** Univ. of WI, 1966–71, BA (Eng. Langs.), 1971–73, MLS; Cnsrtm. for CA State Colls. and Univs., Pomona, 1978 (Pub. Admin.); 1979–, Cmnty. Coll. Tchg. Cred. **Orgs.:** CA LA: Cmnty. Rel. Com. (Ch., 1977–79). Inland Lib. Syst., CA: PR Com. (1979–). Zonta Intl. Amer. Socty. for Pub. Admin. **Pubns.:** *Group Crafts for Teachers and Librarians on Limited Budgets* (1980); "Swingin' on a Comic Book Budget," *IL Libs.* (Ja. 1975); "Laura Ingalls Wilder Lives On," *CA Libn.* (Ap. 1975). **Activities:** 9; 17, 21, 36; 50, 89 **Addr.:** 259 Sherwood Pl., Pomona, CA 91768.

Presseau, Jane Todd (Mr. 4, 1938, Clinton, SC) Student Srvs. Libn., Asst. Prof., Lib. Sci., Presbyterian Coll., 1970–; Libn., Hughes Jr. HS, 1964–70; Visit. Instr., Lib. Sci., Univ. of SC, 1970–72; Visit. Instr., Lib. Sci., Eurman Univ., 1969; Elem. sch. tchr., pub. schs., Greewood, SC, Nashville, TN, Bowie, MD, Greenville, SC, 1959–64. **Educ.:** Erskine Coll., 1956–59, BA (Educ., Soc. Sci.); George Peabody Coll., 1960–61, MA (Educ.); Univ. of NC, 1967–69, MS (LS); various crs. **Orgs.:** SC LA: Coll. and Univ. Sect. (Ch., 1978–79). SC Educ. Assn.: SC Assn. of Sch. Libns. (Pres., 1969–70). Southeastern LA. ALA. Alpha Delta Kappa. **Honors:** Kappa Delta Pi. **Pubns.:** "Student Services in the Four-Year College," *SC Libn.* (Fall 1972). **Activities:** 1, 10; 16, 31, 39; 57, 63, 92 **Addr.:** James H. Thomason Library, Presbyterian College, Clinton, SC 29325.

Presseault, Jacques (Mr. 8, 1949, Charlesbourg, PQ) Coord., Fr. Lang. Srvs., Northeast. Reg. Lib. Syst., 1979–; Dir., Edmundston Pub. Lib., 1978–79; Libn., PQ Real Estate Assn., 1978. **Educ.:** Coll. Jean-de-Brébeuf, 1965–69, Bac ès Arts; Univ. of Montréal, 1969–74, Msc (Pol. Sci.), 1976–78, Msc (LS). **Orgs.:** ON LA: Fr. Lang. Srvs. Gld. Exec. (1980–). Can. LA. ASTED. Atl. Prov. LA. Club Richelieu. **Activities:** 9, 13; 15, 17, 24; 56, 67 **Addr.:** Northeastern Regional Library System, 6 Al Wende Ave., Kirkland Lake, ON P2N 3G9 Canada.

Presser, Carolynne (Ja. 14, 1941, New York, NY) Asst. Libn., Engin., Math. and Sci. Lib., Univ. of Waterloo, 1975–, Head, Gvt. Pubns. Dept., 1971–75; Libn., Ref. and Info. Srvs., ON Inst. for Std. in Educ., 1969–71; Ref. Libn., Per. Libn., Circ. Libn., Temple Univ., 1963–69. **Educ.:** Hunter Coll., 1958–62, AB (Soclgy.); Pratt Inst., 1962–63, MLS. **Orgs.:** Can. LA: Gvt. Pubns. Com. (Conv., 1975–77). ALA. **Pubns.:** *Report on the Installation of an Automated Circulation System* (1980); "CODOC, Co-operative Government Documents," *Coll. & Resrch. Libs.* (Mr. 1978); "Organization of a Separate Government Documents Collection," *Gvt. Pubns. Review* (1975); "Canadian Provincial and Municipal Publications, the Mystery Explained?" *Gvt. Pubns. Review* (1975). **Activities:** 1; 15, 17, 19; 56 **Addr.:** Engineering, Mathematics & Science Library, University of Waterloo, Waterloo, ON N2L 3G1 Canada.

Pressing, Kirk L. (F. 4, 1932, Pittsburgh, PA) Supvsr., Ctr. Lib. Srv., Milwaukee Pub. Lib., 1973–; Coord., Lib. Srv., London, ON, Pub. Lib., 1969–73; Dir., Northport Pub. Lib., 1961–69; Admin. Asst., Grt. Neck Pub. Lib., 1959–61, Branch Libn., 1957–59, Jr. Libn. 1956–57; Ref. Libn. Wilmington Inst. Free Lib., 1954. **Educ.:** Univ. of DE, 1949–53, BA (Hist.); Drexel Univ., 1953–54, MSLS; various crs. **Orgs.:** ALA: PLA/PLSS Ad Hoc Com. on Comm. (1979–80); PLA/MLS Nom. Com. (1980–81). WI LA: Natl. Lib. Week, Asst. State Dir. (1974), State Dir. (1975); Int. Frdm. Com. (1973–76). WI Assn. Pub. Libns.: Bd. (1978–80). Suffolk Cnty. LA: Corres. Secty. (1963–64); VP (1964–66); Pres. (1967–69). Milwaukee Area Socty. of Pub. Admin.: Prog. Com. Research Clearinghouse Metro. Milwaukee (Pres. 1980–82). **Honors:** Beta Phi Mu, 1954. **Pubns.:** Cmplr., *Milwaukee Public Library–Book Selection Criteria* (1975); Cmplr., *London Public Library–Book Selection Policy* (1970). **Activities:** 9, 13; 16, 17, 34; 50, 74 **Addr.:** 709 E. Juneau Ave., Apt. 406, Milwaukee, WI 53202.

Pressnall, Patricia Elizabeth (Mr. 17, 1925, Detroit, MI) Libn., Media Spec., Cornell Elem. Sch., 1975–, 1958–63; various other positions. **Educ.:** Univ. of CA, Berkeley, 1952, BA (Art, Eng.), 1957–58, MLS (Educ.); State of CA, 1957–58, Sch. Lib. Tchg. Cred. **Orgs.:** ALA. CA LA. CA Media and Lib. Educs. Assn. Natl. Educ. Assn. Folk Dance Fed. **Honors:** Phi Beta Kappa, 1952; Parent Tchr. Assn., Hon. Life Mem. for Srv. to Chld., 1963. **Activities:** 10; 15, 21, 31; 55, 63, 75 **Addr.:** Cornell Elementary School, 920 Talbot Ave., Albany, CA 94706.

Preston, Jean F. (Bournemouth, Eng.) Cur. of Mss., Princeton Univ., 1977–; Cur. of Mss., Huntington Lib., 1960–77; Osborn Libn., Beinecke Lib., Yale Univ., 1965–66; Mss. Cat., Folger Lib., 1957–60. **Educ.:** Bristol Univ., Eng., BA (Hist.); Liverpool Univ., Eng., Dip. (Arch.); Dip. (Std. of Rec. Admin. of Arch.). **Orgs.:** SAA: various coms. Socty. of CA Archvsts.: Co-fndr. (1972); VP. Mid-Atl. Reg. Arch. Cncl.: Cncl. (1979). Mss. Socty. Medvl. Assn. of Pac.: Cnclr. (1974–77). **Pubns.:** "Books Before Printing," *Review* (1979); "Medieval Manuscripts at Huntington," *Chronica* (Fall 1977); various articles. **Activities:** 1; 45; 55 **Addr.:** Princeton University Library, Princeton, NJ 08544.

Preston, Jenny (Jl. 24, 1939, Monett, MO) Sr. Libn., McDonnell Douglas Autom. Co., 1980–; Supvsr., Tech. Srvs., St. Louis Pub. Lib., 1978–80, Spec. Proj. Libn., 1974–78; Coord., Info. Srvs., WY State Lib., 1972–73, Fld. Consult., 1969–72; Ref. Libn., Pub. Lib. of Stockton and San Joaquin Cnty. 1964–69. **Educ.:** Lindenwood Coll., 1962, BA (Fr.); Univ. of CA, Berkeley, 1965–68, MLS (Libnshp.); various crs. **Orgs.:** ALA. MO LA. Natl. Org. for Women. Vict. Socty. in Amer. **Honors:** Beta Phi Mu. **Pubns.:** Ed., *Missouri Union List of Serial Publications* (1978); *Collection Development in St. Louis Area Libraries, A Survey* (1975); "Starting a Library at McDonnell Douglas Automation Co.," *Show-Me Libs.* (Jl. 1978); "Cooperative Collection Development," *Show-Me Libs.* (O.–N. 1978); "The Carnegie Library in Wyoming" slide-tape (1972). **Activities:** 9, 13; 24, 25, 44, 46; 56 **Addr.:** 1835 Lafayette Ave., St. Louis, MO 63104.

Preston, Linda D. (Ja. 19, 1940, Blytheville, AR) Libn., Natl. Climatic Ctr., 1978–, Jr. HS AV Libn., Tampa, FL, 1974–78. **Educ.:** Univ. of S. FL, 1971–74, BA (LS, AV), 1977–78, MA (LS). **Orgs.:** SLA: NC Chap., Geog. and Map. Div. West. NC LA. Common Cause. Pilot Club Intl. **Activities:** 4; 49-One-Person Prof. Lib.; 88, 91 **Addr.:** National Climatic Center, Federal Building, Asheville, NC 28801.

PROFESSIONAL ACTIVITIES: Institutions: 1. Acad. lib.; 2. Arch.; 3. Assn.; 4. Fed./Gvt. lib.; 5. Inst. lib.; 6. Mfr./Suppl.; 7. Milit. lib.; 8. Musm.; 9. Pub. lib.; 10. Sch. lib.; 11. Sch. of lib. sci.; 12. Spec. lib.; 13. State lib.; 14. (other). **Functions/Activities:** 15. Acq./Col. dev.; 16. Adult srvs.; 17. Admin.; 18. Apprais.; 19. Archit./Bldgs.; 20. Cat./Class.; 21. Chld. srvs.; 22. Circ.; 23. Cons./Pres.; 24. Consult.; 25. Cont. ed.; 26. Educ. lib. sci.; 27. Ext. srvs.; 28. Fund/Grants; 29. Gvt. pubs.; 30. Indx./Abs.; 31. Instr. lib. use; 32. Media srvs.; 33. Micro.; 34. Netwks./Coop.; 35. Persnl.; 36. PR; 37. Publshg.; 38. Recs. mgt.; 39. Ref. srvs.; 40. Repro.; 41. Resrch.; 42. Review.; 43. Secur.; 44. Serials; 45. Spec. col.; 46. Tech. srvs.; 47. Trustees/Bds.; 48. YA srvs.; 49. (other).

Preston, Lola Marie (Ap. 25, 1943, Oakland, NE) Media Dir., Libn., Newcastle Pub. Sch., 1979–; Media Dir., Libn., Manning Cmnty. Sch., 1976–79; Media Dir., Libn., Mallard Cmnty. Sch., 1975–76; Media Dir., Libn., Alta Cmnty. Sch., 1969–75. **Educ.:** Buena Vista Coll., 1961–65, BA (Eng., Frgn. Lang.); Univ. of IA, (1967–69); MA (Grmn., Fr., LS). **Orgs.:** IA Educ. Media Assn. NE Educ. Media Assn. ALA. Natl. Educ. Assn. Newcastle Educ. Assn. NE State Educ. Assn. **Activities:** 10; 21, 32, 48; 63 **Addr.:** Box 162, Newcastle, NE 68757.

Pretty, Ella Patricia (S. 29, 1912, Vancouver, BC) Trustee, Hon. Life Mem., Fraser Valley Reg. Lib., 1957–. **Educ.:** Columbian Coll., 1927–30 (Arts). **Orgs.:** BC Lib. and Trustees Assn.: Secy. Pac. NW LA: Trustee Sect. (Pres., 1975–77). Can. LA. Fraser Valley Sch. Trustees Assn. **Honors:** Pac. NW LA, Hon. Life Mem., 1978; ALA, Trustee Cit., 1979; Fraser Valley Reg. Lib. Bd., Hon. Life Mem., 1979. **Activities:** 28, 47 **Addr.:** Box 28 - 15500 Morris Valley Rd., Harrison Mills, BC V0M 1L0 Canada.

Prewitt, Barbara G. (Jl. 13, 1939, Abington, PA) Resrch. Lib. Mgr., Rohm and Haas Co., 1981–, Admin. Supvsr., Lib., 1976–81; Info. Chem., 1967–76, Chem., 1961–67. **Educ.:** Ursinus Coll., 1957–61, BS (Chem.); Drexel Univ., 1967–70, MS (Info. Sci.). **Orgs.:** Amer. Chem. Socty.: Div. of Chem. Info., Secy. (1978–80), Ch.-Elect (1981–); Com. on Pubns. (1981–). SLA: Phila. Chap. (Mem. Ch., 1978–79). ASIS: Philadelphia Chap. (Past Secy., 1971–72). PA LA. Chem. Abs. Srvs.: Ed. Adv. Bd. (1980–). AAAS. **Honors:** Iota Sigma Pi; Alpha Chi Sigma; Beta Phi Mu. **Pubns.:** "Online Searching of Computer Data Bases," *Jnl. of Chem. Docum.* (1974); "Searching the Chemical Abstracts Condensates Data Base via Two On-line Systems," *Jnl. of Chem. Info. and Comp. Sci.* (1975); jt. auth., "Application of System 2000 Data Base Management Software at Rohm and Haas Company Research Libraries," *The Information Age in Perspective, Proceedings of the ASIS Annual Meeting* (1978); jt. auth. "Online Data Base Searching via Telephone Conferencing," *Online Mag.* (Ap. 1979). **Activities:** 12; 17, 44; 60, 61, 75 **Addr.:** Rohm and Haas Co., P.O. Box 718, Bristol, PA 19007.

Price, Alvis H. (O. 31, 1934, Tyler, TX) Assoc. Persnl. Ofcr., Univ. Lib., Univ. of CA, Los Angeles, 1970–, Asst. Head, Circ. Dept., 1968–70; Dir. of Lib., Jarvis Christ. Coll., 1966–68; Branch Libn., Boston Pub. Lib., 1965–66. **Educ.:** Univ. of South. CA, 1952–56, BS (Bus.); Simmons Coll., 1961–62, MS (LS). **Orgs.:** ALA: Cncl. Com. on Org. (1974–76). CA LA: Int. Frdm. Com. (1976–77); PR Com. (1970–71). Amer. Mgt. Assn. Amer. Socty. for Trng. and Dev. **Honors:** Cncl. on Lib. Resrcs., Flwshp., 1977; Univ. of MD Lib. Admin. Dev. Prog., Flwshp., 1974. **Pubns.:** "Management Development Programs for Librarians: Strategies for Entering the Marketplace," *CA Libn.* (Jl. 1977). **Activities:** 1; 17, 35 **Addr.:** 13940 Chandler Blvd., Van Nuys, CA 91401.

Price, Bennett J. (O. 2, 1942, Brooklyn, NY) Sr. ADP Systs. Anal., Div. of Lib. Autom., Univ. of CA, 1978–. **Educ.:** Brooklyn Coll., CUNY, 1960–65, BA (Grk.); Univ. of CA, Berkeley, 1965–75, PhD (Classics), 1977–78, MLS. **Orgs.:** ALA: LITA; RTSD. ASIS. Amer. Philological Assn. **Pubns.:** Various articles on Grk. and Latin Classics. **Activities:** 1, 10; 17, 46; 55, 56, 93 **Addr.:** Univ. of CA, Division of Library Automation, 186 University Hall, Berkeley, CA 94720.

Price, Cheryl A. (Mr. 14, 1944, Oak Park, IL) Pol. Sci., Law Libn. North. IL Univ., 1979–; Law Libn., Du Page Cnty. Law Lib., 1973–79. **Educ.:** MO Valley Coll., 1966, BS (Hist.); North. IL Univ., 1968–71, MA (Hist.); Rosary Coll., 1976–78, MA (Acad. Libs.). **Orgs.:** AALL. Smithsonians. Bus. and Prof. Women. **Pubns.:** "Document Examination in American Archives," *Spec. Libs.* (S. 1977); "Key to Legal Research," *NIU Libs.* (Fall 1980). **Activities:** 1, 12; 15, 31, 41; 77, 78, 95-Pub. Admin. **Addr.:** 833 Ridge #311, Dekalb, IL 60115.

Price, (Sr.) Consuelo (D. 21, 1918, Wilmington, NC) Dir., Media Ctr., Bishop Walsh HS, 1968–; Asst. Libn., Instr. of Lib. Sci., Ursuline Coll., 1964–68; Tchr., Libn., Our Lady of Lourdes Sch., 1958–64; Tchr., Libn., Cath. HS, Columbia, SC, 1956–58. **Educ.:** Ursuline Coll., 1956, AB (Eng.); Cath. Univ. of Amer., 1964, MS (LS). **Orgs.:** ALA. AASL. Cath. LA. KY LA: Lib. Educ. Com. (1964–68). Educ. Media Assn. of MD. MD-DC Cath. LA. MD LA. **Pubns.:** "What Do First Graders Like to Read?" *Cath. Sch. Jnl.* (1967); "The Books They Think We Ought to Read," *KY Lib. Bltn.* (Spr. 1960). **Activities:** 10; 17, 39 **Addr.:** 109 N. Smallwood St., Cumberland, MD 21502.

Price, David M. (F 4, 1943, Corpus Christi, TX) Lib. Dir., Aurora (CO) Pub. Lib., 1977–; Asst. Dir., Austin (TX) Pub. Lib., 1971–77; Budget Anal., Mncpl. Ref. Libn., City of Fort Worth, 1966–71. **Educ.:** TX A & I Univ., 1962–66, BA (Eng., Educ.); N. TX State Univ., 1966–71, MLS; Southwest. Bapt. Theo. Semy., 1968–69, Cert. (Couns.). **Orgs.:** ALA: Legis. Com. (1980–81). CO LA: Pres. (1980–81); VP (1979–80). CO Cncl. on Lib. Dev.: Pub. Lib. Rep. (1979–82). TX LA: Dist. 3 Ch. (1976); Pub. Lib. Div. (Secy., 1977). **Honors:** TX LA, Lib. Proj. of the Yr., 1975. **Pubns.:** "IRVING: An Automated Circulation System for the Denver Metropolitan Area Public Libraries," *CO Libs.* (Je. 1979). **Addr.:** Aurora Public Library- Administration, 14949 E. Alameda Dr., Aurora, CO 80012.

Price, Douglas S. (Ap. 17, 1927, Norfolk, VA) Deputy Dir., Natl. Comsn. on Libs. and Info. Sci., 1975–; Deputy Dir., ERIC Prcs. and Ref. Facility, 1970–75; Sr. Syst. Engin., Disclosure, Inc., 1968–70; Spec. Asst. to Dir., NASA Sci. and Tech. Info. Facility, 1962–68. **Educ.:** Hampden-Sydney Coll., 1944–48, BS (Math., Phys.); Univ. of FL, 1948, (Phys.). **Orgs.:** ASIS: Treas. (1974–77); Spec. Interest Grp. on Costs, Budgeting and Econ. (Ch., 1972–73). ALA. SLA. DCLA. Stans. Engin. Socty. WA Sect. (Vice-Ch., 1961–62). Socty. for Schol. Publshg. Assoc. Info. Mgrs. Frnds. of Libs.–USA. **Honors:** Chi Beta Phi, 1948. **Pubns.:** Various sp., papers. **Activities:** 4; 17, 24, 41; 56, 61, 75 **Addr.:** National Commission on Libraries and Information Science, 1717 K St., N.W., Suite 601, Washington, DC 20036.

Price, Joseph W. (S. 28, 1945, Meridian, MS) Chief, Sci. and Tech. Div., Lib. of Congs., 1981–; Deputy Asst. Dir., Autom. Syst. Ofc., 1978–81, Chief, MARC Dev. Ofc., 1977–78, Chief, Serial Rec. Div., 1975–77, Asst. Chief, Serial Rec. Div., 1974–75. **Educ.:** Sam Houston State Univ., 1963–66, BM (Msc.); Univ. of TX, Austin, 1967–68, MLS; Amer. Univ., 1974–76, MS (Pub. Admin.), 1977–79, Advnc. Grad. Cert. (Oper. Resrch.). **Orgs.:** ALA: FLRT (Pres., 1974–75). Jt. Com. on Un. List of Serials: Lib. of Congs. Liason (1975–77). IFLA: Stdg. Com. on Serials (1974–80). Intl. Serials Data Syst.: Tech. Adv. Com. (1973–). **Honors:** Alpha Chi; Pi Kappa Lambda. **Pubns.:** "International Cooperation in Serials: Progress and Prospects," *Drexel Lib. Qtly.* (Jl. 1975); "The National Serials Data Program," *New Serials Titles 21 Year Cummulation: Classed Subject Edition.* **Activities:** 1, 4; 17, 24, 34; 56 **Addr.:** Science and Technology Division, Library of Congress, Washington, DC 20540.

Price, M. Kathleen (F. 28, 1942, Buffalo, NY) Dir., Law Lib., Prof., Law, Univ. of MN, 1980–; Law Libn., Prof., Law, Duke Univ., 1975–80; Assoc. Attorney, Ross, Hardies, O'Keefe, 1973–75; Asst. Law Libn., Univ. of IL, 1970–73; Asst. Law Libn., Univ. of AL, 1967–70. **Educ.:** Univ. of FL, 1960–63, BA (Pol. Sci.); FL State Univ., 1966–67, MS (LS); Univ. of IL, 1970–73, JD (Law). **Orgs.:** AALL: Exec. Bd. (1978–81); Ethics Com. (Ch., 1977–78); Rcrt. Com. (Ch., 1972–73); CLENE Liaison. SE Assn. of Law Libs. MN Assn. of Law Libs. AALS: Lib. Com. (1979–82). **Honors:** *Guide to Law Reviews and Other Related Periodicals in the University of Alabama Law Library* (1970); "Death and Dying: A Bibliographic Essay," *Law Lib. Jnl.* (1978); "Degree-Oriented Study Among Law Librarians," *Law Lib. Jnl.* (1971). **Activities:** 1, 12; 17, 26, 49-Legal educ.; 77 **Addr.:** University of Minnesota Law Library, 229 19th Ave. S., Minneapolis, MN 55455.

Price, Mary Sauer (Ap. 5, 1939, Winona, MN) Asst. Dir. for Prcs. Systs., Netwk. and Autom. Plng., Lib. of Congs., 1980–, Chief, Serial Rec. Div., 1977–80, Asst. Chief for Natl. and Intl. Opers., 1976–77, Head, Natl. Serials Data Prog. Sect., 1975–76, Sr. Ed., 1972–75; Dir. of Lib. for Serials, St. Louis Univ., 1970–72; Catlgr., Descr. Cat. Div., Lib. of Congs., 1965–69. **Educ.:** WA Univ., 1957–61, BA (Psy.); Univ. of IL, 1964–65, MSLS. **Orgs.:** ALA: RTSD, Cat. Code Rev. Com. (1975–77), Policy and Resrch. Com. (Lib. Congs. Liason, 1976–80), Ad Hoc Com. Std. Serial Recs. (1972–77). IFLA: Stans. Com. Serials (U.S. Mem., 1981–). Potomac Tech. Prcs. Libn.: Vice–Ch. (1976–77). Amer. Natl. Stans. Inst.: Z39 Com., Various coms. Jt. Com. Un. List Serials: Lib. of Congs. Rep. (1977–79). Various other orgs. **Honors:** Beta Phi Mu, 1965. **Pubns.:** Jt. auth., *MARC Serials Editing Guide: CONSER Edition* (1975); "National Serials Data Program," *Drexel Lib. Qtly.* (Jl. 1975); "Key Title and Rules for Entry," *Lib. Resrcs. & Tech. Srvs.* (Fall 1975); "Automated Serials Control: Cataloging Considerations," *Jnl. of Lib. Autom.* (Mr. 1976); "National Serials Data Program," *Bowker Anl. of Lib. and Bk. Trade Info.* (1979). **Activities:** 1, 4; 34, 44, 46; 56, 75 **Addr.:** Processing Systems, Networks and Automation Planning, Processing Services, Library of Congress, Washington, DC 20540.

Price, Maureen Beatrice (Ja. 31, 1942, Johannesburg, Transvaal, S. Africa) Head, Tech. Srvs., John Abbott Coll., 1975–; Chem. Libn., Univ. of Toronto, 1966–70. **Educ.:** Univ. of the Witwatersrand, 1960–62, BA (Eng., Psy.), 1963, Dip.; Univ. of WI, Madison, 1973–74, MALS (Libnshp.). **Orgs.:** Can. LA.: Cmnty. and Tech. Coll. Sect., Secy (1978–80), Ch. (1980–81). S. African LA. Corp. of Prof. Libns. of PQ. **Honors:** Beta Phi Mu. **Pubns.:** *Children's Books in English in an African Setting, 1914-1964* (1965); *Directory of Community and Technical College Libraries and Resource Centers in Canada* (1980); prod. and layout mgr., cmplr., *Directory of Community and Technical College Libraries and Resource Centers in Canada* (1981). **Activities:** 1; 15, 20, 39 **Addr.:** 4816 Lake Rd., Dollard-Des-Ormeaux, PQ H9G 1G8 Canada.

Price, May Evelyn (Ap. 15, 1925, Lamar, AR) Cat. Libn., Head, Cat., Hlth. Sci. Lib., Univ. of CA, Davis, 1966–, Cat. Libn., 1965–66; Cat. Libn., San Fernando Valley State Coll., 1963–65; Supvsg. Libn., U.S. Army Spec. Srvs., Berlin, Fulda, Germany, 1961–63; Cat. Libn., San Fernando Valley State Coll., 1959–61. **Educ.:** Fresno State Coll., 1954–58, AB (Eng.); Univ. of CA, Berkeley, 1958–59, MLS. **Orgs.:** Med. LA. SLA: Sierra NV Chap., Mem. Com. (1981), Nom. Com. North. CA Med. Lib. Grp. North. CA Tech. Prcs. Grp. Various other orgs. **Activities:** 12; 20, 46; 80, 74 **Addr.:** Health Sciences Technical Services Dept., University of California, Davis, CA 95616.

Price, Mrs. Olive Bishop (N. 7, 1912, Arkville, NY) Exec. Secy., Bd. Mem., O'Connor Fndn., 1965–; Dept. Branch Chief, Info. Ctrs. Libs., Near East, S. Asia, Africa, Dept. of State USIA, 1949–60; Base Libn., US Navy Libs., 1943–47; Ref. Libn., VA Polytech. Inst., 1939–42. **Educ.:** Colby Jr. Coll., 1932–34, ABA (Hist.); Cornell Univ., 1934–36, BA (Eng. Hist.); Albany Law Sch., 1947–48; Syracuse Univ., 1938–39, BS (LS); Georgetown Univ., 1955–56, (Span.). **Orgs.:** ALA: IRRT (1958–). DC LA: Prog. Com. Ch. Pratt Inst. Grad. Sch. Lib. and Info. Sci. Bd. of Visit. (1980). SUNY, Binghamton: Cncl. (1970–78). Cornell Univ.: Cncl. (1974–). Syracuse Univ.: Trustee. **Honors:** Hon. Harper Forum. **Activities:** 1, 4; 15, 17, 47; 77, 74 **Addr.:** Dolphin House, DeLancey, NY 13752.

Price, Pamela Anita (N. 30, 1952, Washington, DC) Asst. Dir. of Lib. Srvs., Mercer Cmnty. Coll., 1981–; Coord., Evening Readr. Srvs., William C. Jason Lib. Lrng. Ctr., DE State Coll., 1976–81; Serials Catlgr., Univ. of MD, 1975–76; Proj. Asst., Univ. of WI, 1974–75. **Educ.:** NC Agr. and Tech. State Univ., 1970–74, BS (Early Chld. Educ.); Univ. of WI, 1974–75, MS (LS); Columbia Univ., 1979, (Lib. Admin.). **Orgs.:** ALA. DE LA. Kappa Delta Pi: Resol. Com. (1978–80). Assn. for Chld. Educ. Intl. Delta Sigma Theta Sorority, Inc.: Dover (DE) Alum. Chap. (VP 1978–80). **Activities:** 1; 17, 31, 39; 63 **Addr.:** 800 Bacon Ave., Dover, DE 19901.

Price, Robert W. (Ja. 11, 1939, Arnprior, ON) Dir., Gloucester Pub. Lib., 1975–; Head, Campus Resrc. Ctr., Algonquin Coll., 1973–75; Chief Libn., Brockville Pub. Lib., 1969–73. **Educ.:** Univ. of Ottawa, 1957–60, BA (Classics); Univ. of Toronto, 1968–69, BLS; Univ. of West. ON, 1977–80, MLS. **Orgs.:** ON LA. Can. LA. **Addr.:** 3310 Southgate Rd., Unit 182, Ottawa, ON K1V 8X4 Canada.

Price, William S., Jr. (Ja. 19, 1941, Asheboro, NC) Dir., NC Div. of Arch. and Hist., 1971–. **Educ.:** Duke Univ., 1959–63, AB (Hist.); Univ. of NC, 1967–71, PhD (US Hist.). **Orgs.:** SAA: Ethics Com. (1978–). **Pubns.:** *NC Higher-Court Minutes, 1709–1723* (1977); *NC Higher-Court Records, 1702–1708* (1974); "N.C. versus B.C. West, Jr.," *Amer. Archvst.* (Ja. 1978). **Activities:** 2; 17, 35; 55 **Addr.:** Division of Archives & History, 109 E. Jones St., Raleigh, NC 27611.

Pridham, Sherman C. (Ja. 4, 1943, Portsmouth, NH) Dir., Portsmouth Pub. Lib., 1973–; Ref. Libn., Meml. Hall Lib., 1971–73; Gen. Srvs. Libn., Boston Pub. Lib., 1970–71; Eng. Instr., Mitchell Jr. Coll., 1968–70. **Educ.:** Univ. of NH, 1961–65, BA (Eng.); Ctrl. MI Univ., 1965–66, MA (Eng.); Simmons Coll., 1971–73, MLS. **Orgs.:** ALA. New Eng. LA: Exec. Cncl. NH LA. **Activities:** 9; 17 **Addr.:** Portsmouth Public Library, Portsmouth, NH 03801.

Pries, Nancy R. (Ag. 16, 1944, Elizabeth, NJ) Bibl. Spec., Assoc. Prof., Soc., Bhvl. Sci., Seattle Pac. Univ., 1979–, Bibl. Spec., Asst. Prof., Soc., Bhvl. Sci., 1974–78. **Educ.:** Stetson Univ., 1962–66, BA, cum laude (Eng.); Univ. of PA, 1966–72, PhD (Amer. Cvlztn.); FL State Univ., 1973–74, MS (LS). **Orgs.:** ALA. SLA. Amer. Std. Assn. **Pubns.:** Cmplr., *American Studies: An Annotated Bibliography of Reference Works for the Study of the United States* (1978). **Activities:** 1; 15, 31, 39; 59, 63, 92 **Addr.:** Weter Memorial Library, Seattle Pacific University, Seattle, WA 98119.

Priestly, Diana M. (S. 24, 1922, Calgary, AB) Law Libn. and Prof., Univ. of Victoria, 1974–; Legal Ofcr., Dept. of Justice, Gvt. of Can., 1972–74; Assoc. Prof., Fac. of Law, Univ. of West. ON, 1970–72, Asst. Law Libn. and Asst. Prof., York Univ., 1967–70; Law Libn. and Asst. Prof., Univ. of Toronto, 1964–67. Lectr., Sch. of Lib. and Info. Scis., Univ. of West. ON, 1970–72; **Educ.:** Univ. of BC, 1946–50, BA (Hist., Eng.), LLB; Univ. of WA, 1952–53, MLL. **Orgs.:** Can. ALL: Pres. (1969–70). AALL. **Pubns.:** Ed., *C.A.L.L. Nsltr.* (1970–74). **Activities:** 1; 15, 17; 77 **Addr.:** University of Victoria Law Library, Victoria, BC V8W 3B1 Canada.

Prime, Eugenie E. (Ap. 11, 1945, San Fernando, Trinidad, W. Indies) Dir., Med. Lib., Exec. Ed., Cumulative Indx. to Nursing and Allied Hlth. Lit., Glendale Adventist Med. Ctr., 1977–, Managing Ed., CINAHL, 1976–77; Head, Hist. Dept., Naparima Girls' HS, Trinidad, W. Indies, 1969–72. **Educ.:** Univ. of W. Indies, BA (Hist., Soclgy.); Andrews Univ., 1972–73, MA (Hist.); Drexel Univ., 1974–75, MS (LS). **Orgs.:** Med. LA: Hosp. Lib. Sect., PR Com. (1981–). Amer. Socty. of Indxrs. Natl. Assn. of Female Execs. **Honors:** Univ. of W. Indies, Post-grad. Resrch., 1962; Phi Alpha Theta, 1972. **Activities:** 12; 17, 30; 80 **Addr.:** Glendale Adventist Medical Center, 1509 Wilson Terr., Glendale, CA 91206.

Prince, Jack (S. 12, 1931, Cheyenne, WY) Coord., Instr. Resrcs., WY Dept. of Educ., 1976–; Acct. Exec., Columbia Broadcasting Syst., 1974–76; Media Distribution Supvsr., Univ. of CO, 1973–76; Asst. Prof., East. NM Univ., 1970–73. **Educ.:**

Special Subjects/Services: 50. Adult educ.; 51. Advert./Mktg.; 52. Aerosp.; 53. Agric.; 54. Area std.; 55. Arts/Hum.; 56. Autom.; 57. Bibl./Prtg.; 58. Bio. sci.; 59. Bus./Fin.; 60. Chem.; 61. Copyrt.; 62. Documtn.; 63. Educ.; 64. Engin.; 65. Env.; 66. Eth. grps.; 67. Film; 68. Food/Nutr.; 69. Geneal.; 70. Geo.; 71. Geol.; 72. Handcpd.; 73. Hist.; 74. Int. frdm.; 75. Info. sci.; 76. Insr.; 77. Law; 78. Legis.; 79. Math./Comp. sci.; 80. Med.; 81. Metals; 82. Nat. resrcs.; 83. Newsp.; 84. Nuc. sci.; 85. Oral hist.; 86. Petr./Energy; 87. Pharm.; 88. Phys./Astr./Math.; 89. Readg.; 90. Relig.; 91. Sci./Tech.; 92. Soc. sci.; 93. Telecom.; 94. Transp.; 95. (other).

Univ. of North. CO, 1956–58, BA (Educ.), 1958–59, MA (Educ.); Media Specs. Inst., Level III, 1965. **Orgs.:** WY LA. WY Assn. for Educ. Comm. and Tech. **Pubns.:** "How Our Schools Can Handle Censorship," *WY Educ.* (S. 1981). **Activities:** 10; 17, 24, 32; 63 **Addr.:** Instructional Resources, Wyoming Dept. of Education, Hathaway Bldg., Rm. 236, Cheyenne, WY 82002.

Prince, William W. (F. 4, 1943, Greenport, NY) Head, Ref., Univ. of TN at Chattanooga, 1981–; Head, Undergrad. Lib., SUNY, Buffalo 1979–81; Head, Gen. Ref. Div., VA Polytech. Inst. and State Univ., 1976–79, Asst. Soc. Sci. Libn., 1973–76. **Educ.:** Lafayette Coll., 1961–65, BA (Amer. Cvlztn.); IN Univ., 1968–70, MAT (Hist.); Univ. of IL, 1972–73, MS (LS). **Orgs.:** ALA: LAMA/Bldg. and Equipment Sect., Equip. Com. (1981–83); ACRL/Bibl. Instr. Sect., Exec. Cncl. (1979–81), various coms.; Com. on Coop., Subcom. on Clearinghses. (Ch., 1978–79); LIRT, Cont. Educ. Com. (1978–79). VA LA: Cncl. (1978); various coms., ofcs. NY LA: Coord. Cncl. of the Lib. User Educ. RT (1980–). SELA: Various coms. Amer. Leg. **Honors:** Beta Phi Mu, 1981. **Pubns.:** "Annotated Bibliography on Library Guidance Systems," *Sign Systems for Libraries: Solving the Wayfinding Problem* (1979); "An Approach to Freshman Library Instruction: Computer Produced/Scored Exercises," Contrib. *Directions For the Decade: Library Instruction in the 1980's* 1981; *Directory of Academic Library Instruction Programs in Virginia* (1977); contrib., *Funding for Continuing Education Available to Individuals in the Field of Librarianship* ERIC (1979); "Library Instruction: A Column of Opinion," *Jnl. of Acad. Libnshp.* (My. 1980); various jt. authshps., edshps. **Activities:** 1; 15, 17, 39; 59, 92 **Addr.:** University Library, University of Tennessee, Chattanooga, TN 37402.

Prins, Johanna Winterwerp (Eelde, Netherlands) Slide Cur., Syracuse Univ., 1979–, Ref. Libn., Soc. Sci. and Hum., Syracuse Univ., 1974–79. **Educ.:** Univ. of Amsterdam, 1955, (Psy.); Syracuse Univ., 1974, MLS, 1978, MFA. **Orgs.:** ARLIS/NA. Art Libs. Socty. of West. NY: Secty., Treas. (1979–81). **Activities:** 1; 55 **Addr.:** Syracuse University, Fine Arts Dept., Bird Library, Syracuse, NY 13210.

Pritchard, Eileen E. (S. 20, 1938, Red Bluff, CA) Sci. Libn., Assoc. Libn., CA Polytech. State Univ., 1973–; Asst. Prof. of Bot., North. AZ Univ., 1967–70. **Educ.:** CA State Univ., Chico, 1957–61, BA (Bio. Sci.); Univ. of KS, 1962–67, PhD (Bot.); Emporia State Univ., 1971–72, ML (Libnshp.). **Orgs.:** ALA: ACRL. CA LA. Socty. of Amer. Zoologists. The Amer. Socty. of Plant Taxonomists. **Pubns.:** "Teaching Science Citation Index for a Library Orientation," *Jnl. Tech. Writing and Comm.* (1979). **Activities:** 1; 39; 91 **Addr.:** University Library, CA Polytechnic State University, San Luis Obispo, CA 93407.

Pritchard, John Allen (F. 12, 1950, Abingdon, VA) Dir., Catawba Cnty. Lib., 1977–; Dir., Polk Cnty. Pub. Lib., 1975–77. **Educ.:** Univ. of TN, 1969–72, BA (Relig. Std.), 1974–75, MSLS. **Orgs.:** ALA: Natl. Afflt., Jr. Mem. RT. Southeastern LA: PR Com. NC LA: Pub. Lib. Sect., Gvtl. Rel. Com. Ch. **Activities:** 9; 17, 19, 47 **Addr.:** Catawba County Library, 115 W. "C" St., Newton, NC 28658.

Pritchett, John Christopher (My. 17, 1945, Mobile, AL) Head, Pub. Srvs., Duke Lib., Furman Univ., 1981–; Admin. Resrch. Libn., Univ. of AL, 1980–, Ref. Libn., Educ. Lib., 1979–80; Asst. to Dir., Mobile Pub. Lib., 1979, Asst. to Supvsr. of Ext. Dept., Mobile Pub. Lib., 1974–78; Eng. Instr., Troy State Univ., 1969–73. **Educ.:** Livingston Univ., 1968, BA (Eng.); Univ. of MS, 1969, MA (Eng.); Univ. of AL, 1974, MLS, 1978, EdS (LS); various crs. **Orgs.:** ALA. ALLA: Auth. Awds. Com. (1975, 1976, 1980). Southeastern LA. Natl. Trust for Hist. Prsrvn. AL Hist. Assn. **Honors** Sigma Tau Delta, 1972; Beta Phi Mu, 1974; Phi Delta Kappa, 1981. **Activities:** 12; 15, 17, 39; 50, 63 **Addr.:** James B. Duke Library, Furman University, Greenville, SC 29613.

Proctor, Betty C. (N. 30, 1924, Chester, NJ) Dir., New Providence Meml. Lib., 1953–. **Educ.:** Rutgers Univ., 1943–46, BA (Eng.), 1961–64, MLS. **Orgs.:** Morris-Un. Fed.: Exec. Secy. (1974, 1980). **Pubns.:** "New Providence," *Americana Encyc.* (1961). **Activities:** 9; 15, 16, 17; 63, 88 **Addr.:** 14 Edgewood Ave., New Providence, NJ 07974.

Proctor, Martha Jane (O. 12, 1941, Panama City, FL) Pub. Lib. Consult., Stats., State Lib. of FL, 1978–; Law Libn., Arnall, Golden and Gregory, 1977–78; Soc. Sci. Sect. Head, Windsor Pub. Lib., 1973–75; Resrch. and Dev. Ctr., Pratt and Whitney Div., Untd. Aircraft, 1970–72; Ref. Libn., Engin. and Phys. Lib., Univ. of FL Libs., 1967–70; Extension Libn., Northwest Reg. Lib., 1966–67; Ref. libn., Atlanta Pub. Lib., 1966; various ed. positions. **Educ.:** FL State Univ., 1961–63, BA (Soc. Sci.), 1964–65, MS (LS); various crs. **Orgs.:** FL LA: PR Com. (Ch., 1979). ALA: LAMA/PR Sect., Stats. Sect., Com. on PR Srvs. to State Libs. and State Lib. Assns. (1979–80). SLA: FL Chap. Bltn. Ed. (1969–71); VP Elect (1972–73). Atlanta Assn. of Law Libs. AALL. The High Musm. of Art. Young Careers Grp. The Can. Fed. of Univ. Women: Windsor, ON Branch: Corres. Secty. (1974). AAUP: Gainesville, FL Branch, Pres. (1970). **Pubns.:** *1979 Florida Directory with Statistics for 1978* (1979); *1980 Florida Directory with Statistics for 1979* (1980); article on "Florida libraries," *The ALA Yearbook* (1979, 1980, 1981); "The Orange Seed," monthly nsltr. (1978–81). **Activities:** 9, 13; 24, 37, 39; 64, 77, 92 **Addr.:** State Library of FL, RA Gray Bldg., Tallahassee, FL 32301.

Prodrick, Robert Gerald (Jl. 31, 1920, Ottawa, ON) Prof., Sch. of Lib. and Info. Sci., Univ. of West. ON, 1969–; Asst. Libn., Hum. and Soc. Scis., Univ. of Toronto Lib., Jt. Bank-Fund Lib., 1961–69; Biblgphr., Intl. Monetary Fund, 1956–60. **Educ.:** Univ. of Toronto, 1938–42, BA, hons. (Pol. Sci., Econ.), 1948–50, MA (Econ.); Columbia Univ., 1955–56, MS; Univ. of MD, 1967, Cert. (Lib. Admin.). **Orgs.:** AALS: Liaison Com. with IFLA (1973–75); Task Frc. on Accred. Issues (1976–78). ALA: Panel of Profs. for Accred. Visits (1973–). Can. Assn. of Lib. Schs.: Nom. Com., Ch. (1973); Pres., (1978–80). Inst. of Prof. Libns. of ON: Dir. (1969–70); *IPLO Qtly.* Ed. (1976). Various other orgs. Can. Assn. of Univ. Tchrs. Harold Innis Fndn. Quadrats. **Honors:** Beta Phi Mu, 1956. **Pubns.:** *Economic Libraries in Canada, 1977* (1978); jt. auth., "Education for Librarianship in Canada, 1960–75; A Selected Bibliography: Continuing education," *IPLO Qtly.* (Ja. 1975); jt. auth., "Planning Process and Trade-offs," *Media Ctr. Facilities Dsgn.* (1978); "Economic Libraries in Canada," *INSPEL* (1/2 1978); "The Utilization of Public Library Personnel in Canada," *A Can. Pub. Lib. Enquiry; Resrch. Dsgn.* (1976). **Activities:** 1, 12; 17, 19, 34; 59, 75, 92 **Addr.:** 774 Riverside Dr., London, ON N6H 2S4 Canada.

Proehl, Karl H. (N. 10, 1947, Alexandria, MN) Map Libn., PA State Univ., 1977–; Map Libn., SUNY, Stony Brook, 1974–77. **Educ.:** Southwest MO State, 1967–68, BA (Hist.); Univ. of MO, 1971–73, MA (Geo.), 1973–74, MLS. **Orgs.:** SLA: Geo. and Map Div., Mem. Com. (Ch., 1977–78). PA LA: Spec. Libns. Div. (Ch., 1979–). West. Assn. of Map Libs. Amer. Geo. Socty. Assn. of Amer. Geo. Amer. Name Socty. Natl. Cncl. for Geo. Educ. **Pubns.:** "The Soil Survey: An Annotated Cartographic Tool," *SLA Geo. and Map Div. Bltn.* (Mr. 1979); "The Map Interpretation File," *Spec. Libs.* (D. 1977). **Activities:** 1, 12; 20, 39; 54, 70 **Addr.:** Pattee Library–Maps, Penn State Univ., University Park, PA 16802.

Proeschel, Diana C. (F. 5, 1930, Chicago, IL) Fld. Srvs. Libn., HQ Dept. of the Army, Washington, DC, 1977–; Lib. Dir., HQ USAGO (Okinawa), 1974–77; Chief Libn., HQ USARSUP-THAI (Thailand), 1972–74; Staff Libn., HQ USASETAF (Italy), 1966–71; Staff Libn., HQ USACOMZ (France), 1964–66; Area Lib. Supvsr., HQ USAEUR (Germany), 1958–64; Supervisory Libn., HQ USAREUR (Germany), 1955–58; various libn. positions, 1950–55. **Educ.:** West. MI Univ., 1946–50, BS(Educ., LS); Univ. of CA, Berkeley, 1971–72, MLS; Loyola Univ., Chicago, 1951–54(Educ.). **Orgs.:** ALA: John Cotton Dana Com. (1979–81). Lib. PR Cncl. **Honors:** ALA, Hon. Mention, John Cotton Dana, 1976; HQ Dept. of the Army, Outstan. Performance Awd., 1966, 1967. **Pubns.:** "Getting Started: Ideas for Library Public Relations," *The Unabashed Libn.* Issue 26; "Etcetera," qtly. clmn. in *Pub. Libs.* (1977–). **Activities:** 4, 9; 16, 17, 35; 54, 74, 92 **Addr.:** 7605 Cosgrove Pl., Springfield, VA 22151.

Progar, Dorothy R. (S. 14, 1924, Bruceville, TX) Dir. of Libs., Waco-McLennan Cnty. Lib., 1961–, Assoc. Dir., 1972–78, Asst. Dir., 1969–72, Ext. Libn., 1968–69, Ref. Libn., 1967–68, YA Libn., 1965–67, Circ. Libn., 1961–65. **Educ.:** Baylor Univ., MI State Univ., 1941–46, 1967–68, BA (LS); TX Women's Univ., 1975 (LS). **Orgs.:** ALA: Com. on Educ. of Lib. Trustees (1976). TX LA: Natl. Lib. Week Com. (1975); Legis. Com. (1975–77); PR Com. (1976–79); Nom. Com. (1978–79); Awds. Com. (1979–80); Pub. Lib. Div., Ch. (1981–82), Vice-Ch. (1980–81); Com. on PR (1980–81). SWLA. TX Mncpl. Libns. Assn. McLennan Cnty. Hist. Comsn.: Bd. Advert. Club of Waco. TX Conf. on Lib. and Info. Srvs.: Del. (1978). **Pubns.:** *Friends' Organizations: The Supportive Element Essential to Libraries* (1975). **Activities:** 9; 17, 35, 36; 63, 89 **Addr.:** Waco-McLennan County Library, 1717 Austin Ave., Waco, TX 76701.

Prokop, Jana M. (Mrs.) (Ap. 2, 1942, Domazlice, Czechoslovakia) Ref. Libn., Univ. of Toronto, 1973–; Libn., York Univ., 1971–72; Lectr., Dept. of Jnlsm., Charles Univ., Prague, 1965–68; News Ed., Czechoslovak Radio, Prague, 1963–65. **Educ.:** Dept. of Jnlsm., Charles Univ. Prague, 1959–65, PhD (Jnlsm.); Univ. of West. ON, 1970–71, MLS. **Orgs.:** Can. Assn. Info. Sci.: 1980 Conf. Prog. Com. (1979–80). Intl. Assn. for Soc. Sci. Info. Srvs. and Tech. Libns. Assn. of the Univ. of Toronto: Secy. (1980–82); Prog. Com. (1979–80). **Pubns.:** Various sps. **Activities:** 1; 31, 39, 49-Online Retrieval Srvs.; 56, 77, 92 **Addr.:** Reference Department, John P. Robarts Research Library, University of Toronto, Toronto, ON M5S 1A1 Canada.

Pronko, Eugene (S. 10, 1929, Scranton, PA) Sr. Prog. Mgr., Intl. Sci. Info. Actv., Natl. Sci. Fndn., 1961–, Prog. Dir., Natl. and Intl. Coord. (Sci. Info.), 1973–77; Exec. Secty., Com. on Sci. and Tech. Info., Fed. Cncl. for Sci. and Tech., Exec. Ofc. of the Pres., 1971–73; Prog. Dir., Frgn. Sci. Info., Natl. Sci. Fndn., 1966–71; UNESCO Tech. Consult., 1963–64. **Educ.:** St. Basil's Coll., 1948–50, (Phil.); Univ. of Scranton, 1947–48, BA (Phil., Psy.), 1950–52; Amer. Univ., 1953–54, (Soc. Psy.). **Orgs.:** ASIS. Assn. for Comp. Mach. Assn. for Comp. Ling. AAAS. Amer. Watchmaker's Inst. **Honors:** St. Basil's Coll., Thomas Aquinas (Medal), 1950. **Pubns.:** Ed., *Federal Scientific and Technical Communication Activities–Progress Report* (1975, 1976, 1977); Ed., *Current Research and Development in Scientific Documentation* (1961–68); *US–USSR Copyright Negotiations on Scientific and Technical Journals* (1974); "Present State of Mechanized Information Processing in the US," *Info. and Documtn.* (1966). **Activities:** 4; 17, 28, 41; 75, 93 **Addr.:** Division of International Programs, National Science Foundation, Washington, DC 20550.

Pronovost, Muriel A. (N. 17, 1924, Waterbury, CT) Assoc. Prof., LS, South. CT State Coll., 1974–, Dir., Demonstration Lib., 1968–74, Lab. Sch., 1954–68; Darcey Sch., Cheshire, CT, 1952–54. **Educ.:** West. CT State Coll., 1949–52, BS (Elem. Educ.); Univ. of CT, 1957, MA (Educ. Admin.), 1962, 6th Yr. Cert.; South. CT State Coll., 1974, MLS. **Orgs.:** New Eng. LA. CT Educ. Media Assn. CT LA: Chld. Srvs. Prog. Com. (1979–). Chld. Lit. Assn. **Honors** Phi Delta Kappa; Delta Kappa Gamma Intl; Fulbright Exch. Tchr., Eng., 1961–62. **Pubns.:** Contrib., *Ehanna Woyakapi, History and Culture of the Sisseton-Wahpeton Sioux Tribe* (1975). **Activities:** 11; 21, 26, 31; 63 **Addr.:** Division of Library Science & Instructional Technology, Southern Connecticut State College, 501 Crescent St., New Haven, CT 06515.

Proper, David Ralph (F. 22, 1933, Stoneham, MA) Libn., The Meml. Libs., 1970–; The Henry N. Flynt Lib., Historic Deerfield, Inc., Chief, Acq. Dept., Wallace Mason Lib., Keene, NH State Coll., 1968–70; Libn., The Essex Inst., 1962–67; Grad. Asst., Lib. Sch., Simmons Coll., 1960–62. **Educ.:** Univ. of NH, 1951–55, BA (Lang.); Univ. of Besançon (France), 1956–57, Cert. d'etudes; Middlebury Coll., 1958–60, AM (Fr.); Simmons Coll., 1960–62, MS (LS). **Orgs.:** Bibl. Socty. of Amer. SAA. Pocumtuck Valley Meml. Assn.: Libn. (1970–). Franklin Cnty. MA Lib./Media Grp.: Treas. (1977–). Various Orgs. Natl. Assn. of Watch and Clock Collectors. NH Hist. Socty. Assn. of Hist. Socties. of NH: Pres. (1976–78). NH Amer. Revolution Bicent. Comsn. (1969–). **Honors:** Fulbright Schol. Awd. (France), 1955; Univ. of NH Syst., Granite State Awd., Keene State Coll., 1979. **Pubns.:** *Monadnock Sampler; Historical Sketches* (1976); *Story of Wright's Silver Cream, 1873–1973* (1973); *History of the First Congregational Church, Keene, NH* (1973); *History of the First Baptist Church of Keene, NH* (1966); various articles, sp. **Activities:** 2, 5; 15, 41, 45; 55, 69 **Addr.:** The Memorial Libraries, PO Box 53, Deerfield, MA 01342.

Propp, Dale William (Ja. 4, 1947, MI) Mgr., Pub. Srvs. Dept., TX State Lib., 1979–, Docum. Libn., 1977–79, State Docum. Libn., 1974–77, Acq. Libn., 1974. **Educ.:** Univ. of SC, 1965–69, BA (Hist.); Univ. of TX, Austin, 1972–74, MLS. **Orgs.:** TX LA: Docum. RT (Ch., 1978); Spec. Libs. Div. (Vice-Ch., 1979). ALA. State Agency Libs. of TX. **Pubns.:** *Texas State Documents Index 1977, Vol. II: Agency* (1979); *Texas State Documents Depository Survey, 1977: Findings and Results* (1978); *Texas State Documents: The Development of a Program* (1978). **Activities:** 13; 17, 29, 39; 77, 78 **Addr.:** Public Services Dept., Texas State Library, Box 12927 Capitol Station, Austin, TX 78711.

Prosser, Judith Margaret (Je. 20, 1938, Chicago, IL) Coord., Interlib. Coop. Head, Tech. Srvs., WV Lib. Comsn., 1969–; Libn., Univ. Arch. and Spec. Col. Univ. of FL, 1963–69; Lib. Asst., Bus. Lib., Columbia Univ., 1962–63. **Educ.:** Winthrop Coll., 1959–61, BA (Eng.); Columbia Univ., 1961–62, MLS; Amer. Univ., 1966, Cert. (Arch. Mgt.); Univ. of IL, 1967, Cert. (Info. Sci.); USDE Inst. on Info. Sci., Univ. of S. CA, 1968, Cert. **Orgs.:** ALA: Cnclr. (1974–79); ASCLA/State-wide Borrowers Card Std. Com. (Ch., 1978–79); Tech. Srvs. WV LA. Costs Com. (Chap. Cnclr., 1975–77). Guild of Bookworkers. Amer. Socty. of Indxrs. **Pubns.:** "Councilor's Report," *WV Libs.* (Win. 1979). **Activities:** 13; 24, 34, 46; 56, 75, 93 **Addr.:** WV Library Commission, Cultural Center, Charleston, WV 25305.

Prostano, Emanuel T. (O. 12, 1931, New Haven, CT) Dir. Div. of LS and Instr. Tech., South. CT State Coll., 1974–, Assoc. Prof., LS, 1969–74; Sch. Lib. Supvsr., Hartford Pub. Schs., 1966–69. **Educ.:** South. CT State Coll., 1949–53, BS (LS, Educ.), 1953–55, MS (Educ., LS); Univ. of CT, 1955–58, Dip. (Admin.), 1958–62, PhD (Curric., Supvsn.). **Orgs.:** ALA. New Eng. LA. CT LA. New Eng. Educ. Media Assn. CT Educ. Media Assn. **Pubns.:** Jt. auth., *School Library Media Centers* (1977); *School Media Programs* (1974); jt. auth., *Law Enforcement: Bibliography* (1974); *AV Media and Libraries* (1972); jt. auth., "Library Schools and Educational Technology," *AV Instr.* (S. 1979). **Addr.:** Division of Library Science and Instructional Technology, Southern Connecticut State College, New Haven, CT 06515.

Prottsman, Mary Fran (Je. 24, 1949, Opp, AL) Chief, Lib. Srv., Vets. Admin. Med. Ctr., 1975–; Serials, Ref., Univ. of AR Hlth. Sci. Lib., 1972–75. **Educ.:** Univ. of AL, 1967–71, BS (Bio.); Emory Univ., 1971–72, MLS; Med. LA, 1972, Cert. **Orgs.:** Med. LA: S. Ctrl. Reg. Grp. AR LA. **Activities:** 4; 17, 31, 39; 56, 80 **Addr.:** Rte. 2, Box 454, Fayetteville, AR 72701.

Proudfoot, Linda G. (N. 12, 1947, Philippi, WV) Chief, Cat. Sect., US Dept. of Justice, Main Lib., 1979–; Cat., The Army Lib., The Pentagon, 1974–79, Lib., 1973–74; Lib. intern, 1st US

PROFESSIONAL ACTIVITIES: Institutions: 1. Acad. lib.; 2. Arch.; 3. Assn.; 4. Fed./Gvt. lib.; 5. Inst. lib.; 6. Mfr./Suppl.; 7. Milit. lib.; 8. Musm.; 9. Pub. lib.; 10. Sch. lib.; 11. Sch. of lib. sci.; 12. Spec. lib.; 13. State lib.; 14. (other). **Functions/Activities:** 15. Acq./Col. dev.; 16. Adult srvs.; 17. Admin.; 18. Apprais.; 19. Archit./Bldgs.; 20. Cat./Class.; 21. Chld. srvs.; 22. Circ.; 23. Cons./Pres.; 24. Consult.; 25. Cont. ed.; 26. Educ. lib. sci.; 27. Ext. srvs.; 28. Fund/Grants; 29. Gvt. pubs.; 30. Indx./Abs.; 31. Instr. lib. use; 32. Media srvs.; 33. Micro.; 34. Netwks./Coop.; 35. Persnl.; 36. PR; 37. Publshg.; 38. Recs. mgt.; 39. Ref. srvs.; 40. Repro.; 41. Resrch.; 42. Review.; 43. Secur.; 44. Serials; 45. Spec. col.; 46. Tech. srvs.; 47. Trustees/Bds.; 48. YA srvs.; 49. (other).

Army, 1972–73; Dist. libn., 8th US Army, Korea, 1970–71. **Educ.:** WV Univ., 1965–69, BS (Educ.); George Peabody Coll., 1969–70, MLS. **Orgs.:** FEDLINK OCLC Qual. Cntrl. Com.: Ch. (1979–). SLA. AALL. ALA. **Honors:** U.S. Dept. of Justice, Meritorious Awd., 1980; The Army Lib., The Pentagon, Outstan. Rating, 1976; Beta Phi Mu. **Pubns.:** *Input of Monographic Cataloging* (1978); *Searching the OCLC data base* (1978). **Activities:** 4; 20, 26, 46; 56, 77, 92 **Addr.:** 860 S. Harrison St., Arlington, VA 22204.

Provan, Jill E. (F. 3, 1948, Boston, MA) Consult., Owen Grad. Sch. of Mgt., Mgt. Lib., Vanderbilt Univ., 1981–; Consult., Vets. Admin. Med. Ctr. Lib., Nashville, 1980–81; Media Libn., State Univ. Coll. of NY, Buffalo, 1976–80; Consult., Career Info. Lib., State Univ. Coll. of NY, Brockport, 1978; Prog. Dir., Job Info. and Adult Indp. Learner Ctr., NIOGA Lib. Syst., 1976; Ref. Libn., Niagara Falls Pub. Lib., 1976; Area Coord., Browsing Lib. Msc. Rm., SUNY, Buffalo, 1974–76. **Educ.:** Amer. Univ., 1966–70, BA (Elem. Educ.); SUNY, Buffalo, 1973–75, MLS. **Orgs.:** ALA. EFLA. TN LA. NYLA (1975–80). Cnsrtm. Univ. Film Ctrs. AECT. Un. Univ. Professions. TN AV Assn. Nashville Lib. Clb. **Pubns.:** Jt. auth., *Management Media Directory* (1982); jt. auth., *In House Training and Development Programs: A Guide for Business Executives and Human Resource Managers* (1981); "50 Best Renters," *Leader* (Spr. 1980); "Resume Writing," "Job Searching," videotapes (1976); "Drug and Alcohol Use and Abuse: A Recommended List," *Previews* (Ja. 1980); various film reviews. **Activities:** 1, 12; 15, 17, 42; 67 **Addr.:** 309 Greenway Ave., Nashville, TN 37205.

Provenzano, Dominic (Ja. 25, 1951, Manhattan, NY) Ref. Libn., White House Resrch. Branch, Executive Office of the President Library, 1981–; Gvt. Docum. Libn., Georgetown Univ., 1980–81; Ref. Libn., Baker Lib., Dartmouth Coll., 1978–80; Adult Srvs. Libn., Harborfields Pub. Lib., 1978. **Educ.:** Hobart Coll., 1968–72, BA (Pol. Sci.); Georgetown Univ., 1973–75, MSFS (Intl. Rel.); Palmer Grad. Lib. Sch., Long Island Univ., 1977–78, MLS. **Orgs.:** Palmer Grad. Lib. Sch. Alum. Assn.: Secy. (1978). ALA: RASD, Machine-Assisted Ref. Srvs. Com. on Costs and Effectiveness of Comp. Lit. Srch. (1979–81). **Honors:** Pi Gamma Mu, 1972; Beta Phi Mu, 1978. **Pubns.:** "Bakers Federal Population Census Schedules," *Dartmouth Coll. Lib. Bltn.* (N. 1979); *Locating US Government Publications in the Dartmouth College Library Eric* (1979). **Activities:** 1, 9; 16, 29, 39; 54, 63, 92 **Addr.:** Executive Office of the President Library, Room 308, OLD Executive Office Building, Washington, DC 20500.

Prucha, Isabel De La Rosa (San Antonio, TX) Instr., Libn., W. Valley Cmnty. Coll., 1975–; Tchr., Crittenden Jr. HS, 1973–75. **Educ.:** San Jose State Univ., 1971–73, BA (Hist., Span.), 1973–75, MA (LS); State of CA, 1975, Biling. Bicult. Proficiency Cert. **Orgs.:** CA LA: VP, Pres.-Elect (1981). CA Clearinghse. for Lib. Instr.: Com. Mem. La Raza Fac. Assn. of CA Cmnty. Coll. AAUW. CA Women in Higher Educ. Natl. Women's Pol. Caucus: Exec. Com. **Honors:** W. Valley Cmnty. Coll., Curric. Dev. Grant, 1978, 1980. **Pubns.:** Ed., *Natl. Women's Pol. Caucus Nsltr.* Producer, Developer, "How to Use the Reader's Guide to Periodical Literature" slide/tape kit (1980); "How to Use the Card Catalog" slide/tape kit (1979); "Searching the On-Line Catalog" vid. (1980). **Addr.:** West Valley Community College Library, 14000 Fruitvale Ave., Saratoga, CA 95070.

Prud'Homme, François (Je. 16, 1910, Montreal, PQ) Archvst. for Les Clercs de St-Viateur de Montréal, 1969–; Archvst. for Les Clercs de St-Viateur, Gen. Hse., (Rome, Italy), 1967–69. **Educ.:** Univ. of Montreal, BA; Univ. of Louvain, LPh; Scuola Vaticana di Archivistica, 1969, Dip. **Orgs.:** Assn. des Archvsts. du PQ: Head of Hist. Arch. Sect.; Bd. of Admin. Assn. of Can. Archvsts. **Pubns.:** *Notre-Dame de Lourdes de Rigaud, 1874–1974* (1974); "The Archives of 'Les Clercs De St. Viateur," *Arch.* (1973, 1976); "Une Expérience en Microfilm," *Arch.* (1977). **Activities:** 2 **Addr.:** 450, Ave. Querbes, Montreal, PQ H2V 3W5 Canada.

Pruett, Barbara J. (My. 8, 1942, Madison, IN) Head, Tech. Srvs., US Intl. Trade Comsn., 1979–; Head, Soc. Sci. Lib., Cath. Univ. of Amer., 1975–79; Head, Info. Resrch. Ctr., Untd. Farm Workers of Amer., 1972–75; Head, Plng. Lib., Santa Clara Cnty. Plng. Dept., 1969–72. **Educ.:** IN Univ., 1960–66, BS (Soc. Sci.); Univ. of CA, San Jose, 1969–71, MA (Libnshp.). **Orgs.:** ALA: Cncl. (1980–83); Action Cncl. (1980–83); SRRT Farm Labor Task Force (Ch., 1973–); LAMA/PRS Com. DC LA. Ordway-Porter Dev. Assn.: Gen. Partner. Natl.-Capital Labor Hist. Socty., Pres. (1980–81). **Activities:** 4, 12; 17, 39, 46; 54, 59, 92 **Addr.:** Technical Services, US International Trade Commission, Washington, DC 20436.

Pruett, Nancy Jones (O. 28, 1948, Syracuse, NY) Ref. Libn., Tech. Lib., Sandia Natl. Lab., 1981–; Head, Geol.-Geophys. Lib., Univ. of CA, Los Angeles, 1977–81; ILL Libn., S. TX Lib. Syst., 1976; Libn., South. Meth. Univ., 1972–75. **Educ.:** Rice Univ., 1966–70, BA (Geol.); TX Woman's Univ., 1971–72, MLS; South. Meth. Univ., 1973–76, MBA (Mgt.). **Orgs.:** Geosci. Info. Socty.: Pres. (1980–81); VP/Pres.-Elect (1979–80); Ad Hoc Com. on USGS Open File Rpts. (Ch., 1979); Lcl. Arrange. Com. (Ch., 1979). SLA: TX Chap., Cont. Educ. Com. (Ch., 1973–74); Treas. (1974–75); Mem. Ch. (1975–76). West. Assn. Map Libs. ALA. ASIS. Cartographic Users Adv. Cncl. **Honors:** Beta Phi Mu, 1972. **Pubns.:** "Geoscience Information Reviewed," *Geotimes* (F. 1981); ed., *Keeping Current with Geoscience Information, GIS Procs.* (1981); "The Geological Perspective," clmn. *WAML Info. Bltn.* (1980–); "Collection Development in a Geology-Geophysics Research Collection," *Geosci. Info. Socty. Procs.* (1979); "U.S. Geological Survey Open-File Reports," *West. Assn. Map Libs. Info. Bltn.* (Je. 1979); various other articles. **Activities:** 1, 12; 17, 31, 39; 70, 86, 91 **Addr.:** 3144 Technical Library, Sandia National Laboratories, Albuquerque, NM 87185.

Pryor, Judith M. (Je. 18, 1941, Plymouth, IN) Coord. of Instr., Univ. of WI, Parkside, 1968–; Elem. Sch. Libn., Metro. Sch. Dist., Wayne Twp., Indianapolis IN, 1967–68; Elem. Sch. Libn., Metro. Sch. Dist., Martinsville, IN, 1965; Elem. Sch. Libn., Sch. City of Crown Point, IN, 1964. **Educ.:** MacMurray Coll., 1959–61; IN Univ., 1961–64, BS (Educ.), 1967, MSLS. **Orgs.:** ALA: ACRL/Coll. Libs. Sect., Ad Hoc Com. on Stan. and Guidelines (1979–81). WI LA: Com. on Lib. Educ. (1975–77). WI Assn. of Acad. Libns. **Pubns.:** *Methods and Materials for Sociology* (1980). "Competency Based Education and Library Instruction," *Lib. Trends* (Sum. 1980); jt. auth., "Parkside Teaches Library Use," *WI Lib. Bltn.* (Jl. 1977); jt. auth., "Public Service Policy," *WI Lib. Bltn.* (My–Je. 1975). **Activities:** 1; 31 **Addr.:** University of Wisconsin-Parkside, Library/Learning Center, Kenosha, WI 53141.

Ptacek, William H. (Ag. 24, 1950, Chicago, IL) Dir., ID Falls Pub. Lib., 1979–; Dist. Chief, Chicago Pub. Lib., 1978–79, Asst. Dir., Persnl., 1977–78, Head, Systemwide Circ., 1976–77. **Educ.:** Univ. of IL, 1970–72, BA (Eng., Psy.); SUNY, Geneseo, 1973–74, MLS; Univ. of Chicago, 1976–79, Cert. (Advnc. Std.). **Orgs.:** ALA: Com. on Status of Women in Libnshp. (1979–); PLA, Human Srvs. Com. (1978–). ID LA. **Activities:** 9; 17, 35; 56, 92 **Addr.:** 375 Buckboard Ln., Idaho Falls, ID 83401.

Puckett, Elizabeth Ann (N. 10, 1943, Evansville, IN) Asst. Reader Srvs. Libn., South. IL Univ., Sch. of Law Lib., 1978–; Acq./Reader Srvs. Libn., Univ. of KS Law Lib., 1977–78. **Educ.:** East. IL Univ., 1961–64, BS Ed. (Eng.); Univ. of IL, 1974–77, JD, MS (Law, LS); Mem., KS and IL Bars. **Orgs.:** AALL: *Law Lib. Jnl.* Com. (1977–); Law Lib. Srv. to Inst. Residents Spec. Interest Sect. (Vice-Ch./Ch.-Elect, 1979–80). Mid-Amer. Assn. of Law Libs.: Prog. Com. (Ch., 1980). Amer. Bar Assn. Jackson Cnty. Bar Assn. **Honors:** Univ. of IL Coll. of Law, Rickert Awd., 1977. **Activities:** 1; 29, 39; 77, 78 **Addr.:** School of Law Library, Southern Illinois University, Carbondale, IL 62901.

Puckett, Marianne (Ap. 12, 1949, Monroe, LA) Circ. Libn., LA State Univ. Med. Sch., 1976–; Geneal. Libn., Shrene Meml. Lib., 1975–76, Ref. Libn., 1973–75; ILL, Green Gold Lib. Syst., 1972–73; ILL, Trail Blazer Lib. Syst., 1971–72. **Educ.:** LA Tech. Univ., 1967–71, BS (Eng., LS); LA State Univ., 1973–76, MLS; Med. LA, 1976, Cert. **Orgs.:** LA LA: LA Conf., New Mems. RT, Prog. Com. (1981). Med. LA: S. Ctrl. Reg. Grp. LA Lib. Conf.: Pubcty. Com. (Co-ch., 1981). **Honors:** Beta Phi Mu; Phi Kappa Phi. **Activities:** 1; 22, 31, 39; 80 **Addr.:** 109 E. Southfield, Apt. 181, Shreveport, LA 71105.

Puffer, Nathaniel H. (F. 3, 1938, Nashua, NH) Asst. Dir., Libs., Univ. of DE, 1970–, Head, Acq. Dept., 1967–70, Asst. Acq. Libn., 1964–67. **Educ.:** Bates Coll., 1957–61, BA (Hist.); Univ. of Denver, 1961–62, (LS). **Orgs.:** ALA: LAMA/PR Sect., Com. (1981); ACRL. Bibl. Socty. of Amer. **Pubns.:** Three articles in *Publishers for Mass Entertainment in 19th Century America* (1980). **Activities:** 1; 15, 17, 45; 55, 57, 92 **Addr.:** University of Delaware Library, Newark, DE 19711.

Puffer, Yvonne L. (S. 29, 1940, Windsor, CO) Libn., Newark Free Library, 1975–, Ref. Libn., 1968–70; Libn., New Castle Jr. HS, 1964–67; Ref. Libn., Fort Gordon Army Lib., 1963–64. **Educ.:** Univ. of North. CO, 1958–62, BA (Eng.); Univ. of Denver, 1962, MLS. **Orgs.:** DE LA: Pub. Lib. Div. (Pres., 1976–77). ALA. **Activities:** 9; 17, 39, 46 **Addr.:** Newark Free Library, 750 Library Ave., Newark, DE 19711.

Pugh, Ellen (Tiffany) (Je. 2, 1920, Cleveland, OH) Serials Catlgr., WA State Univ., 1969–; Sr. Catlgr., Univ. of Rochester, 1965–68; Sr. Catlgr., Univ. of OR, 1963–65; Head, Ord. Dept., Univ. of NE, 1958–63; Rare Bk. Catlgr., Cincinnati Pub. Lib., 1955–58; Catlgr., Northwest. Univ., 1945–47, Catlgr., 1943–45. **Educ.:** Case West. Rsv. Univ., 1938–43, AB (Eng.), 1943–45, BLS; Northwest. Univ., 1945–47, MA (Eng.). **Orgs.:** ALA: Amer. Lib. Srv. to Schs. and Chld. Div., Intl. Rel. Com. Spokane Writers Gld. Ord. of East. Star. Westerners Intl. **Pubns.:** *Tales From the Welsh Hills* (1968); *Brave His Soul; The Story of Prince Madog of Wales and His Discovery of America in 1170* (1970); *More Tales From the Welsh Hills* (1971); *The Adventures of Yoo-Lah-Teen* (1975). **Activities:** 1; 20, 44, 46 **Addr.:** SW600 Crestview, Apt. 25, Pullman, WA 99163.

Pugh, Mary Jo (Je. 16, 1944, Polson, MT) Ref. Archvst., MI Hist. Cols., Univ. of MI, 1969–. **Educ.:** Univ. of Chicago, 1962–66, AB (Hist.); Univ. of MI, 1967–68, AM (Hist.), 1968–69, AMLS. **Orgs.:** MI Arch. Assn.: Pres. (1974–76); Exec. Com. (1976–78); Ed. (1974–). SAA: Ref. and Access Com. (1970–78); Inst. Eval. Com. (1978–); Prog. Com. (1981). Hist. Socty. of MI. Org. of Amer. Histns. **Pubns.:** "1900–1920," *Pictorial History of Ann Arbor, MI 1824–1974* (1974); "Oral History in the Library: Levels of Commitment," *Drexel Lib. Qtly.* (O. 1979). **Activities:** 2; 39; 61, 86 **Addr.:** Michigan Historical Collections, Bentley Historical Library, University of Michigan, 1150 Beal Ave., Ann Arbor, MI 48109.

Pugsley, Roger Franchis Hook (Ag. 1, 1932, Lincoln, NE) Adj. Libn., Pub. Srvs. Libn., CUNY, Medgar Evers Coll. Lib., 1978–. **Educ.:** Syracuse Univ., 1952–55, BA (Hist.); Princeton Theo. Semy., 1959–63, MDiv (Theo.); Westminster Theo. Semy., 1969–71, ThM (New Testament); NY Univ., 1970–75, MA (European Hist.); Pratt Inst., 1975–76, MLS. **Orgs.:** ALA. NJ LA. ATLA. LA of CUNY. Frnds. of the Princeton Univ. Lib. **Pubns.:** "Sound of New Testament Greek," *Westminister Theo. Jnl.* (Win. 1976). **Activities:** 22, 31, 39; 55, 90, 92 **Addr.:** 2 Elena Pl., Belleville, NJ 07109.

Pugsley, Sharon Gayle (O. 26, 1939, Detroit, MI) Univ. Archvst., Reg. Hist. Mss. Libn., Univ. of CA, Irvine, 1977–; Mss. Libn., Univ. of UT, 1973–77; Ref. Libn., NJ Hist. Socty. 1971–73. **Educ.:** Univ. of UT, 1957–61, BS (Educ.); Rutgers Univ., 1970–72, MLS; Natl. Arch. and Amer. Univ., 1975, Cert. Arch. Admin.; OH Hist. Socty., 1973, Cert., arch. lib. inst.; Case Western Rsv. Univ., 1971, Cert. coll. and univ. arch. inst., **Orgs.:** SAA: Lcl. Arrange. Com. for 1977 Anl. Mtg. (1975–77); Finding Aids Com. (1975–79); Task Force on Dev. of Model Finding Aid Syst. for Coll. and Univ. Arch. (1978–79). Prof. Afnty. Grps., Coll. and Univ. (1980–), Cons. (1980–). South. CA Consrtm. Heritage Proj.: Adv. Com. (1979–). Univ. of CA Archvsts. Cncl. Socty. of CA Archvsts: Secy. and Council Mem. (1981–). South. CA Lcl. Hist. Cncl. West. Hist. Assn. Amer. Assn. for State and Lcl. Hist. Mormon Hist. Assn. **Honors:** Yale Univ. Lib., NEH flwshp. prsrvn. of lib. mtrls. 1979; Beta Phi Mu, 1972. **Pubns.:** "A Checklist of New Jersey Periodicals in the Library of the New Jersey Historical Society," *NJ Hist. Socty.* (1973). **Activities:** 1, 2; 23, 45; 95-local history. **Addr.:** Special Collections, 105 Library, P.O. Box 19557, University of CA, Irvine, CA 92713.

Pullen, June Waller (Je. 8, 1938, Coweta Cnty., GA) Libn., Barstow Lib., Berry Acad., 1970–; Libn., Hilsman Jr. HS, 1969–70; Libn., Chld., YA, Roddenbery Meml. Lib., 1965–68; Libn., Durham City Schs., 1960–63. **Educ.:** LaGrange Coll., 1956–59, AB (Hist.); FL State Univ., 1966–69, MSLS. **Orgs.:** Natl. Assn. of Indp. Schs.: Lib. Sect. Mid-S. Assn. of Indp. Schs.: Lib. Sect. (Ch., 1978–79). **Honors:** Beta Phi Mu, 1969. **Activities:** 10; 17, 32, 48 **Addr.:** Barstow Memorial Library, Mt. Berry, GA 30149.

Pulleyblank, Mildred Corine (Je. 24, 1938, Windsor, ON) Archvst., Toronto Dominion Bank, 1978–; Libn., Untd. Church Arch., 1973–78. **Educ.:** Univ. of Windsor, 1968–72, BA, hons. (Art Hist.); Univ. of West. ON, 1972–73, MLS. **Orgs.:** Toronto Area Archvsts. Grp. Assn. Can. Archvsts. SAA. **Activities:** 2, 12; 17, 41, 45; 59, 69, 92 **Addr.:** Toronto Dominion Bank, P.O. Box 1, Toronto Dominion Centre, Toronto, ON M5K 1A2 Canada.

Pullmann, David E. (Ag. 11, 1944, Detroit, MI) Head, Serials Cat. Unit, US Copyrt. Ofc., 1980–, Head, Performing Arts Cat. Unit, 1978–79; Prod. Coord., MARC Ed., Lib. of Congs., 1977–78; Coord., Tech. Support for COPICS, U.S. Copyrt. Ofc., 1973–76. **Educ.:** Sherwood Msc., Univ. of Chicago, 1962–66, BME (Educ.); Amer. Univ., 1969–72, MA (Msclgy.); Cath. Univ., 1977–78, MLS; LaSalle Univ., 1973–76, LlB (Law). **Orgs.:** ALA: LITA. Lutheran Church LA. **Honors:** Beta Phi Mu. **Pubns.:** *A Catalogue of the Keyboard Works of Baldassare Galuppi* (1972); "An Inside Look at the Copyright Office Cataloging System," *Jnl. of Lib. Autom.* (Je. 1978). **Activities:** 4, 12; 15, 20, 44; 55, 61, 77 **Addr.:** US Copyright Office, Library of Congress, Washington, DC 20540.

Purcell, Gary R. (Ap. 22, 1936, Idaho Falls, ID) Prof., Grad. Sch. of Lib. and Info. Sci., Univ. of TN, 1978–, Dir., 1971–77; Instr., Sch. of LS, Case West. Rsv. Univ., 1965–71; Instr., Sch. of Libnshp., West. MI Univ., 1961–65; Lib. Asst., Enoch Pratt Free Lib., 1959–61. **Educ.:** Univ. of UT, 1953–57, AB (Pol. Sci.); Univ. of WA, 1958–59, MLS (Libnshp.); Case West. Rsv. Univ., 1965–69, MA (Pol. Sci.), 1965–75, PhD (Lib. and Info. Sci.). **Orgs.:** AALS: Pres. (1978–79). TN LA: Pres. (1977–78). ALA: Cncl. (1969–71, 1980–); LRRT, Strg. Com., Ch. **Honors:** Case West. Rsv. Univ., Sch. of LS, Outstan. Alum. Awd., 1979; Beta Phi Mu. **Pubns.:** "The Use of Tennessee State Government Publications," *TN Libn.* (Spr. 1980); "U.S. Government Publication Collection Development for Non-Depository Libraries," *Gvt. Pubns. Review* (Volume 8–A). **Activities:** 11; 25, 26, 41; 75, 92 **Addr.:** Graduate School of Library and Information Science, University of Tennessee, Knoxville, TN 37916.

Purdy, Victor William (Mr. 4, 1926, Milwaukee, WI) Asst. Prof., Sch. of Lib. and Info. Sci., Brigham Young Univ., 1967–, Asst. Dir., Readers Srvs., Col. Dev., Ch., Bk. Sel. Com., Lib., 1964–66, Subj. Libn., Hist., Relig., Phil., 1963, 1958–61, Actg. Ord. Libn., 1961, 1959, Serials Libn., 1954–58; Serials and Asst. Circ. Libn., Fresno State Coll. Lib., 1953–54. **Educ.:** Brigham Young Univ., 1952, BS (Hist.); Columbia Univ., 1957, MS (Lib. Srv.); various grad. crs. **Orgs.:** ALA. UT LA. Mormon Hist.

Special Subjects/Services: 50. Adult educ.; 51. Advert./Mktg.; 52. Aerosp.; 53. Agric.; 54. Area std.; 55. Arts/Hum.; 56. Autom.; 57. Bibl./Prtg.; 58. Bio. sci.; 59. Bus./Fin.; 60. Chem.; 61. Copyrt.; 62. Documtn.; 63. Educ.; 64. Engin.; 65. Env.; 66. Eth. grps.; 67. Film; 68. Food/Nutr.; 69. Geneal.; 70. Geo.; 71. Geol.; 72. Handcpd.; 73. Hist.; 74. Int. frdm.; 75. Info. sci.; 76. Insr.; 77. Law; 78. Legis.; 79. Math./Comp. sci.; 80. Med.; 81. Metals; 82. Nat. resrcs.; 83. Newsp.; 84. Nuc. sci.; 85. Oral hist.; 86. Petr./Energy; 87. Pharm.; 88. Phys./Astr./Math.; 89. Readg.; 90. Relig.; 91. Sci./Tech.; 92. Soc. sci.; 93. Telecom.; 94. Transp.; 95. (other).

Assn. Soc. Sci. Hist. Assn. **Activities:** 11; 26; 90, 92 **Addr.:** 1740 N. 500 E., Provo, UT 84604.

Purdy, Virginia C. (Ag. 1, 1922, Columbia, SC) Ed., *Amer. Archvst.,* SAA, 1978–81; Women's Hist. Spec., Natl. Arch., 1976–, Dir., Educ. Div., 1969–75; Keeper, Cat. of Amer. Portraits, Natl. Portrait Gallery, Smithsonian Inst., 1967–69. **Educ.:** Univ. of SC, 1938–42, AB (Hist.); George Washington Univ., 1958–70, MA, PhD (Hist.). **Orgs.:** SAA. Amer. Hist. Assn. Org. of Amer. Histns. Assn. for Std. of Afro-Amer. Hist. & Life. Socty. for Schol. Pubn. **Honors:** Phi Beta Kappa, 1942; Pi Gamma Mu, 1960. **Pubns.:** *Clio Was a Woman: Studies in the History of American Women* (1980); *Presidential Portraits* (1968); "Automation of the Catalog of American Portraits," *Smithsonian Inst. Info. Syst. Innovations* (S. 1969); "The Arts of Diplomacy," *Amer. Heritage* (F. 1974). **Activities:** 2; 37; 73 **Addr.:** National Archives, Washington, DC 20408.

Pursch, Lenore D. (Ap. 8, 1944, Camden, NJ) Med. Libn., St. Elizabeth's Med. Ctr., 1980–; Ref. Libn., Washington Twp. Pub. Lib., 1980; Med. Libn., U.S. Army Med. Ctr., Okinawa, 1970–71; Head Libn., Sukiran Ref. Lib., Okinawa, 1969–70. **Educ.:** Ursinus Coll., 1962–66, BA (Eng., Hist.); Villanova Univ., 1966–68, MSLS. **Orgs.:** Med. LA. **Addr.:** Health Sciences Library, St. Elizabeth's Medical Center, 601 Miami Blvd. W., Dayton, OH 45408.

Purucker, Mary I. (F. 2, 1934, Lynn, MA) Libn., Media Spec., Juan Cabrillo Elem. Sch., Santa Monica/Malibu Unfd. Sch. Dist., 1965–; Visit. Lectr., Univ. of CA, Los Angeles, Grad. Sch. of Lib. and Info. Sci., 1981–; Instr., Chld. Lit., Santa Monica Coll., 1980–81; Instr., Chld. Lit., Univ. of CA, Los Angeles, 1976; Instr., Chld. Lit., CA State Univ., Los Angeles, 1975; Libn., Los Angeles Pub. Lib., Chld. Rm., 1964–65. **Educ.:** Boston Coll., 1952–55, AA (Eng.); CA State Univ., Los Angeles, 1959–62 (Eng.); Univ. of CA, Los Angeles, 1962–63, AB (Eng.), 1963–64, MLS; Libnshp. Creds.; Stan. Tchg. Creds. (Specs. in Elem. and Sec.); Cmnty. Coll. Instr. Creds.; Cmnty. Coll. Libn. Creds. **Orgs.:** ALA: AASL; ALSC. CA Media and Lib. Educs. Assn.: *South. Sect. Nsltr.* Ed.; Soc. Ch.; Elec. Ch. South. CA Cncl. on Lit. for Chld. and Young People: Awds. Com. Sch. and Chld. Libns. Assn.: Treas. Santa Monica Classrm. Tchrs. Assn. Natl. Educ. Assn. Santa Monica Unfd. Sch. Dist. Mariposa Cnty.-Fish Camp Town Plng. Adv. Cncl. **Pubns.:** Various bk., media reviews and articles in *Sch. Lib. Jnl., Previews, Highlights for Chld., Los Angeles Times, K-Eight, Early Yrs., Malibu Surfside News, CA Sch. Libs., Wilson Lib. Bltn.* **Activities:** 9, 10; 21, 31, 32; 63, 67, 89 **Addr.:** 6636 Wandermere Rd., Malibu, CA 90265.

Purvis, Mary Cecilia Grobe (My. 30, 1945, Bastrop, LA) Libn., Gonzales Primary Sch., 1978–79; Libn., One Sandel Lib., 1976–77; Libn., Rayville HS, 1974–75; Ref. Libn., Denrose Pub. Lib., 1969–70. **Educ.:** LA Tech. Univ., Ruston, 1963–65, (Educ.); NW LA Univ., Monroe, 1965–67, BA (Educ.); LA State Univ., 1976–80, Lib. Cert. **Orgs.:** SLA: LA Chap. LA LA. ALA: JMRT, Mid. Career Awd. Com. (1980). Pilot Club., New Orleans. Alpha Omicron Pi: Alum. Chap. **Honors:** Mu Sigma, 1962. **Activities:** 1, 10; 15, 21; 50, 55, 63 **Addr.:** 369 W. Madison St., Bastrop, LA 71220.

Puryear, Dorothy S. (Ag. 13, –, Rochester, PA) Adult Interagency Spec., Nassau Lib. Syst., 1980–; Asst. Dir., EIC Prog., NY, State Educ. Dept. of NY, 1979–80; Adult Indp. Learner, Nassau Lib. Syst., 1978–79; Job Info. Ctr., Gen. Asst., Brooklyn Pub. Lib., 1977–78. **Educ.:** Queens Coll., CUNY, 1971–74, BA (Soclgy.), 1974–77, MLS (Libnshp.). **Orgs.:** Nassau Cnty. LA. ALA: Mem. Task Force (1975–79); PLA/Info. and Ref. Srvs. Com., Subcom. to Draft Guidelines (Ch., 1978), Cmnty. Info. Srvs. Exec. Steering Com.; SRRT/Action Cncl. (1978, 1979), Liaison to Mem. Com. (1979–). NYLA: Info. and Ref. Com. of RASD (1976–80). NY State Info. and Ref. Assn.: Adv. Bd. Nassau Assn. for Cont./Cmnty. Educ.: Exec. Bd. Literacy Volunteers of Long Island: Exec. Bd. NY Tech. Srvs. Libn. **Honors:** Elmcor Cmnty. Org., Cmnty. Srv. Awd., 1975; RASD, NY LA, "Activist Libn.", 1978. **Pubns.:** "Guidelines for Establishing I&R Services in Public Libraries," *Pub. Libs.* (Fall 1979); various sp. **Activities:** 9, 13; 16, 17, 24; 50, 75, 89 **Addr.:** 99–07 23rd Ave., E. Elmhurst, NY 11369.

Purzycki, Marianne Howald (Ag. 28, 1954, Lakewood, OH) Tech. Ref. Libn., Bell Labs., 1979–; Libn., Warner and Swasey Co., Resrch. Div., 1977–79. **Educ.:** St. Mary's Coll., Notre Dame, 1972–76, BA (Hist.); Case West. Rsv. Univ., 1976–77, MSLS. **Orgs.:** SLA: NJ Chap. (Sec. VP; Prog. Ch.). NJ OLUG. **Honors:** Beta Phi Mu; Kappa Gamma Pi. **Activities:** 12; 15, 39; 56, 91, 93 **Addr.:** Bell Laboratories, Rm. 1G–114, 6 Corporate Pl., Piscataway, NJ 08854.

Pyke, Carol June (Renville) (Mr. 20, 1944, Miami, FL) Dir. of Lib., Urban Inst., 1978–81; Asst. Dir./Tech. Srvs. Libn., 1972–78, Catlgr., 1970–72; Asst. Libn., Mt. Vernon Coll., 1968–70. **Educ.:** Amer. Coll. in Paris, 1962–64; George Washington Univ., 1964–66, BA (Anthro.); Cath. Univ., 1966–68, MS in LS; George Washington Univ., 1973, MA (Anthro.). **Orgs.:** SLA: Rep. to DC LSCA Com. (1979–). DC LA. Frnds. of the Natl. Zoo. Parent and Child, Inc. Nature Conservancy. Suncoast Seabird Sanctuary. **Honors:** Beta Phi Mu, 1968. **Activities:** 12; 17; 92 **Addr.:** Library, The Urban Institute, 2100 M St., N.W., Washington, DC 20037.

Pyle, Claire (S. 17, 1917, Johnstown, PA) Head, Pop. Lib., Carnegie Lib. & Pittsburgh, 1980–, Head, Branch Srvs., 1969–80, Head, Ref. Dept., 1966–69, Head, Gen. Ref. Div., 1962–66; Treas., Cambria Savings and Loan Assn., 1942–57; Tchr., Johnstown Pub. Evening Sch., 1939–42. **Educ.:** Univ. of Pittsburgh, 1935–39, AB (Educ.); Carnegie Inst. of Tech., 1957–58, MLS; Amer. Savings & Loan Inst., IN Univ., 1950–52, Grad. Dip. **Orgs.:** ALA: Ref. and Subscrpn. Bks. Review Com. (1973–77); Guest Reviewer, (1977–). PA LA. Beta Phi Mu: Pittsburgh Chap., Past Pres. Altrusa Intl.: Pittsburgh Club, Past Pres. Cambria Savings and Loan Assn.: Bd. of Dir. (1970–77). **Honors:** Phi Theta Kappa; Pi Lambda Theta. **Activities:** 9; 16, 17, 39; 55, 59 **Addr.:** 4733 Centre Ave., Apt. 3D, Pittsburgh, PA 15213.

Pyle, Lola Anne (D. 22, 1952, Oshkosh, WI) Instr., Univ. of AR, 1976–. **Educ.:** Univ. of WI, Oshkosh, 1971–75, BS (LS); Univ. of IL, 1975–76, MS (LS). **Orgs.:** ALA. AR LA. AR Cncl. on Lib. Educ. AR AV Assn. Various other orgs. **Honors:** Phi Delta Kappa; Kappa Delta Pi, Phi Beta Sigma Awd., 1975. **Activities:** 1, 11; 17, 26, 31; 63, 75 **Addr.:** 1278 Elmwood Ave., Oshkosh, WI 54901.

Pyles, Rodney A. (Je. 21, 1945, Morgantown, WV) Dir., Arch. and Hist. Div., WV Dept. of Culture and Hist., 1977–; Asst. Cur., Arch., WV Univ. Lib., 1971-77; Instr. of Pol. Sci., Alderson Broaddus Coll., 1969–71. **Educ.:** WV Univ., 1963-67, BA (Pol. Sci.), 1967–69, MA (Pol. Sci.). **Orgs.:** WV LA. Midwest Arch. Conf. SAA. Mid Atl. Arch. Conf. Amer. Assn. for State and Lcl. Hist. Amer. Assn. of Musms. Midwest Musm. Conf. WV Hist. Socty. **Pubns.:** "The New Department of Culture and History," *WV Hist. Qtly.* (Jl. 1977). **Activities:** 2, 13; 17, 23, 29; 55, 69, 83 **Addr.:** Archives and History Division, Department of Culture and History, Charleston, WV 25305.

Pypcznski, Penny (Ap. 28, 1949, Trenton, NJ) Info. Consult., Pennfield Assoc.; Instr., Prison Educ., Mercer Cnty. Cmnty. Coll., 1978–79; Instr., Media Comm., Trenton State Coll., 1974–79; Sr. Libn., Monmouth Cnty. Lib., 1972–74. **Educ.:** Trenton State Coll., 1967–71, BS (Media Comm.); George Peabody Coll., Vanderbilt Univ., 1971–72, MLS; Nova Univ., 1976–79, EdD (Curric., Instr.). **Orgs.:** NJ LA: Adult/YA Div., Pres.; Educ. for Libnshp. Com., Ch.; Natl. Lib. Wk. in NJ, Exec. Dir. NJ Educ. Media Assn. Monmouth Cnty. Libns. Assn. **Honors:** Kappa Delta Pi, Compatriot in Educ. 1976; Phi Delta Kappa; Beta Phi Mu. **Activities:** 10, 11; 21, 25, 26; 50, 55 **Addr.:** Pennfield Associates, 26 Brenwal Ave., Ewing, NJ 08618.

Q

Quain, Julie R. (Ja. 9, 1952, New York, NY) Asst. RML Libn., NY and NJ Reg. Med. Lib., 1981–; Sr. Asst. Libn., Downstate Med. Ctr., SUNY, 1980–81; Clinical Libn., St. Francis Hosp. and Med. Ctr., Hartford, CT, 1977–79; Med. Libn., Pubns. Mgr., Biospherics Inc., 1976–77; Med. Libn., Luth. Hosp. of MD, 1975–76. **Educ.:** Hofstra Univ., 1970–74, BA, magna cum laude (Eng. Lit.); Univ. of MD, 1974–75, MLS; various crs. **Orgs.:** CT Assn. of Hlth. Sci. Libs.: Mem. Com. (1978–79). Med. LA: NY Reg. Grp., Nsltr.; Cont. Ed. Crs. 36, Instr.; NY and NJ Chap.; Upstate NY and ON Chap. **Honors:** Phi Kappa Phi, 1976; Beta Phi Mu, 1975; Phi Beta Kappa, 1974. **Activities:** 12; 31, 39, 49-Clinical Libnshp.; 80 **Addr.:** 130 E. 18th St., New York, NY 10003.

Quattlebaum, Marguerite Rebecca (Mrs. Charles A.) (O. 14, 1909, Garrett, IN) Volun. Work, 1976–; Tech. Pubns. Plng. Ofcr., Lib. of Congs., 1970–76, Head, Ed. Sect., 1963–76, Ed., Subj. Headings, 1948–63, Asst. Ed., Subj. Headings, 1943–48, Shelflister, Shelflist Rev., 1938–43. **Educ.:** IN Univ., 1927–31, AB (Latin); George Washington Univ., 1936–39, AB (LS). **Orgs.:** ALA. DC LA. IN Univ. Alum. Assn. George Washington Univ. Alum. Assn. Arlington Ridge Civic Assn. **Honors:** Eta Sigma Phi, 1929; Pi Lamda Theta, 1930; Phi Beta Kappa, 1930. **Pubns.:** Cmplr., Ed., *Period Subdivisions Used under Names of Places in the Library of Congress Subject Headings* (1950, 1975). **Addr.:** 1022 S. 26th Rd., Arlington, VA 22202.

Quay, Richard H. (Ap. 27, 1940, Washington, PA) Soc. Sci. Libn., Educ. Biblgphr., Miami Univ., OH, 1971–. **Educ.:** Waynesburg Coll., 1958–63, BA (Psy., Educ.); Univ. of South. CA, 1967–69, MS (Educ. Psy.); Univ. of Pittsburgh, 1970–71, MLS. **Orgs.:** Amer. Educ. Std. Assn. Acad. LA of OH. Assn. for the Bibl. of Hist. **Honors:** Beta Phi Mu, 1971. **Pubns.:** *In Pursuit of Equality of Educational Opportunity: A Selective Bibliography and Guide to the Research Literature* (1977); *Index to Anthologies on Postsecondary Education, 1960–1978* (1980); *Research in Higher Education: A Guide to Source Bibliographies* (1976). **Activities:** 1; 39, 41; 63, 92 **Addr.:** King Library, Miami University, Oxford, OH 45056.

Queinnec, Young-Hee (Gwon) (Danchun, Hamkyungnamdo, Korea) Chief, Can. MARC Ofc., Natl. Lib. of Can., 1980–, Head, Serials Cat. Sect., 1978–80, Head, Gvt. Docum. Cat. Sect., 1977–78, Serials Catlgr., 1976–77, Bibl. Srch. Ed., 1976; Chief Libn., Coady Intl. Inst., 1971–75; Lectr., IL State Univ., 1970–71; various lib. positions, 1960–70. **Educ.:** Seoul Natl. Univ., 1952–56, BA (Phil.); George Peabody Coll. for Tchrs., 1958–59, MA (LS). **Orgs.:** Can. LA. ALA. **Activities:** 4, 12; 17, 46; 56, 62, 75 **Addr.:** Canadian MARC Office, National Library of Canada, Ottawa ON K1A 0N4 Canada.

Quick, Richard Christian (D. 4, 1926, Montclair, NJ) Dir., Coll. Libs., SUNY, Geneseo, 1968–; Dir., Lib. Srvs., North. AZ Univ., 1965–68; Asst. to Dir., Libs., Univ. of DE, 1959–65, Asst. to Libn., 1956–59, Head, Circ., Univ. of DE, 1954–56; Libn., OH Coll. of Chiropody, 1953–54. **Educ.:** Kenyon Coll., 1948–52, AB (Eng.); Case West. Rsv. Univ., 1953–54, MSLS. **Orgs.:** ALA: ACRL/Coll. Libs. Sect. (Ch., 1973–74), Com. on Cmnty. Use of Acad. Libs. (Ch., 1970–71), Nom. Com. (Ch., 1969–70). AZ LA: Coll. and Univs. Lib. Sect. (Pres., 1967–68). DE LA: Pres. (1958–60). Archaeological Socty. of DE. **Pubns.:** Jt. auth., *The House on the Kerby Tract, Better Known as Carson's Or, the Buck Tavern ca. 1728–1821 and 1821–1961* (1976); "The Library As Continuum: A Commentary to Honor John M. Dawson," *Univ. of DE News* (Je. 1979); "Coordination of Collection Building By Academic Libraries," *New Dimensions For Academic Library Service* (1975); "H. Geiger Omwake's Archeological Writings: A Commemorative Bibliography, 1934–1972," *Archaeological Socty. of DE Bltn.* (1978); ed., *DE Lib. Bltn.* (1962–65); various edshps. **Activities:** 1; 15, 17, 34; 50, 56, 57 **Addr.:** College Libraries, Geneseo, NY 14454.

Quigg, Agnes B. (My. 3, 1934, Pittsburgh, PA) Head Libn., Kamehameha Schs., MidKiff Lrng. Ctr., 1979–; Lib. Consult., Trust Territory Gvt. Arch. Proj., Saipan, Sum. 1981; Asst. Libn., Honolulu Cmnty. Coll., 1978; Lib. Consult., Congs. of Micronesia, Ponape, E.C.I., 1978; Libn., Pac. Urban Std. and Plng., Univ. of HI, 1975–78. **Educ.:** Univ. of HI, 1975–76, BA (Eng. Lit.), 1977–78 MLS. **Orgs.:** ALA. HI LA. HI Assn. of Sch. Libs. Grad. Sch. of Lib. Std. Alum. Grp.: Exec. Bd. (1979–). **Honors:** Beta Phi Mu, 1978. **Pubns.:** *Guide to Library Resources in Urban and Regional Planning* (1978). **Activities:** 1, 4; 15, 17, 22; 65, 82, 92 **Addr.:** Kamehameha Schools, MidKiff Learning Center, Kapalama Heights, Honolulu, HI 96817.

Quimby, Harriet B(owman) (F. 16, 1920, Winchester, MA) Assoc. Prof., Div. of Lib. and Info. Sci., St. John's Univ., 1970–; Coord., Chld. Srvs., Brooklyn Pub. Lib., 1959–70, Branch Libn., 1955–59, Asst. to Supt. of Branches, 1954–55, Chld. Libn., 1942–54. **Educ.:** Simmons Coll., 1938–42, BS (LS); Trchs. Coll., Columbia Univ., 1951, MA (Educ. Psy.). **Orgs.:** ALA: Chld. Srvs. Div., Bd. of Dir. (1964–67), VP (1969–70), Newbery-Caldecott Com. (Ch., 1976); ALSC, Bd. of Dir. (1979–82); Awds. Com., Louise Giles Schol. Awd. (1981); various ofcs. Natl. Sci. Tchrs. Assn.: Chld. Bk. Cncl., Sci. Bk. Com. (1971–). NY LA: Mem. Com. (1977). Various org. Intl. Readg. Assn.: Awds. for 1st Bk. (Judge, 1974–75). **Pubns.:** Jt. auth., *Building a Children's Literature Collection: a Suggested Basic Reference Collection for Academic Libraries* Bibl. (1978); jt. auth., *Illustrators of Children's Books: 1967–1976* (1978); "Children's Periodicals in the US," *Serials Libn.* (Spr. 1981); "Regina Medalists: Rarest of the Best," *Cath. Lib. World* (F. 1975). **Activities:** 9; 21, 24, 42; 63, 89 **Addr.:** 115 Washington Pl., New York, NY 10014.

Quinlan, David James (F. 5, 1926, Wabeno, WI) Lib., Media Dir., Kewaunee Sch. Dist., 1976–, Elem. Sch. Libn., 1974–76, HS Libn., 1966–74; Band Dir., Abbott Pennings HS, 1959–64. **Educ.:** WI State Coll., 1951, BS (Educ.); Univ. of WI, Milwaukee, 1969, MLS (Lib.), 1972–77, (AV). **Orgs.:** Northeast WI Intertype Libs.: Bd. of Dir. (1972–80; 1981–); Mem. and Dues Com. (1974–77); Grant Com. (1977–79); Pubns. Com. (1979–80). Intertype Libns. of Kewaunee Cnty.: Pres. (1976–78). Msc. LA. Kewaunee Educ. Assn., Pres. (1980–81); Cath. Ord. of Foresters. Knights of Columbus. **Pubns.:** "New System for Music Festivals," *WI Sch. Musician* (1955). **Activities:** 10; 15, 17, 32; 63, 89 **Addr.:** Kewaunee School District, Marquette School, 317 Dorelle St., Kewaunee, WI 54216.

Quinly, William J. (O. 1, 1921, Kansas City, KS) Prof., Coord. of Media Educ., FL State Univ., 1975–, Dir., Media Ctr., 1960–75, Asst. Prof., Lib. Sci., 1957–60; Head, AV Dept., Chicago Tchrs. Coll., 1953–57; Asst. State Libn., MO State Lib., 1950–53. **Educ.:** Univ. of MO, 1939–43, BA (Hist., Pol. Sci.); Univ. of Denver, 1947–48, MA (Lib.). **Orgs.:** ALA: AVRT, Ch.; JMRT, Stats. Com. Ch. AECT: Cat. Com., Ch. Accred. Com.; Mem. Com.; Info. Syst. Div., Pres. Cnsrtm. of Univ. Film Ctrs.: Pres.; Data Base Com., Ch. **Pubns.:** *The Selection, Acquisition and Utilization of Audio Visual Materials* (1977, 1979, 1980); *Standards for Cataloging Nonprint Materials* (1968, 1972, 1973, 1976). **Activities:** 1; 17, 26; 63 **Addr.:** Dept. of Educational Research, Development and Foundations, College of Education, FL State University, Tallahassee, FL 32306.

Quinn, Allan S. (D. 3, 1927, El Paso, TX) Dir., Info. Srvs. Div., TX State Lib., 1978–, Mgr., Netwk. Dev. Dept., 1976–78; Head, Bus. Info. Dept., Cleveland Pub. Lib., 1972–76; Lib. Mgr., Mid. S. Srvs., 1970–72. **Educ.:** Univ. of TX, Austin, 1948–53, BA (Econ.); LA State Univ., 1969–70, MLS. **Orgs.:** ALA: ASCLA/Multitype Lib. Coop. Sect., Pubns. Com. (1979–), Rep. to GODORT (1979–80). SLA: LA Chap., Exec. Com. (1972). TX LA.

PROFESSIONAL ACTIVITIES: Institutions: 1. Acad. lib.; 2. Arch.; 3. Assn.; 4. Fed./Gvt. lib.; 5. Inst. lib.; 6. Mfr./Suppl.; 7. Milit. lib.; 8. Musm.; 9. Pub. lib.; 10. Sch. lib.; 11. Sch. of lib. sci.; 12. Spec. lib.; 13. State lib.; 14. (other). **Functions/Activities:** 15. Acq./Col. dev.; 16. Adult srvs.; 17. Admin.; 18. Apprais.; 19. Archit./Bldgs.; 20. Cat./Class.; 21. Chld. srvs.; 22. Circ.; 23. Cons./Pres.; 24. Consult.; 25. Cont. ed.; 26. Educ. lib. sci.; 27. Ext. srvs.; 28. Fund/Grants; 29. Gvt. pubs.; 30. Indx./Abs.; 31. Instr. lib. use; 32. Media srvs.; 33. Micro.; 34. Netwks./Coop.; 35. Persnl.; 36. PR; 37. Publshg.; 38. Recs. mgt.; 39. Ref. srvs.; 40. Repro.; 41. Resrch.; 42. Review.; 43. Secur.; 44. Serials; 45. Spec. col.; 46. Tech. srvs.; 47. Trustees/Bds.; 48. YA srvs.; 49. (other).

Who's Who in Library and Information Services

Honors: Beta Phi Mu, 1970. **Activities:** 9, 13; 17, 34, 39; 59 **Addr.:** 6818 Hanover Ln., Austin, TX 78723.

Quinn, Carol J. (Ap. 7, 1939, Minneapolis, MN) Assoc. Libn., Readrs. Srvs., Hoover Lib., West. MD Coll., 1972–; Hum. Libn., Univ. of FL Libs., 1968–70; Ref. Libn., Jacksonville Pub. Lib., 1966–67. **Educ.:** Univ. of FL, 1956–61, BA (Eng.); Univ. of MN, 1963–65, MLS; Univ. of FL, 1967–69, MA (Eng.). **Orgs.:** MD LA. **Activities:** 1; 29, 31, 39; 55 **Addr.:** Hoover Library, Western MD College, Westminster, MD 21157.

Quinn, Patrick M. (Ag. 22, 1942, Lake Geneva, WI) Lectr., Rosary Coll. Grad. Sch. of Lib. Sci., 1975–; Univ. Archvst., Northwestern Univ., 1974–; Asst. Univ. Archvst., Univ. of WI, 1972–74; Asst. Cur. of Mss., State Hist. Socty. of WI, 1967–71. **Educ.:** Univ. of WI, 1960–64, BS (Eng.), 1964–67, (Hist.); Amer. Univ., 1970, Cert. (Arch. Admin.). **Orgs.:** SAA: Coll. and Univ. Arch. Prof. Afnty. Grp., Vice-Ch. Midwest Arch. Conf.: Pres. Mss. Socty. IL Labor Hist. Socty. Chicago Urban Hist. Grp. **Pubns.:** Various articles, reviews. **Activities:** 1, 2; 17, 26, 38; 62, 63, 75 **Addr.:** University Archivist, Northwestern University Library, Evanston, IL 60201.

Quint, Barbara E. (D. 31, 1943, Los Angeles, CA) Head, Ref. Srvs., Rand Corp., 1968–, Asst. Head Cat., 1966–68. **Educ.:** Immaculate Heart Coll., 1961–65, BA (Hist.), 1965, MLS. **Orgs.:** South. CA OLUG: Fndr.; Conv. (1978–80). SLA: South. CA Chap. (Elect. Ch., 1973). **Honors:** SLA, South. CA Chap., Cert. of Merit, 1979. **Pubns.:** "Online Users Groups," *Knowledge Industry Publication* forthcoming. **Activities:** 12; 39, 49-Online Srv.; 56, 74, 92 **Addr.:** Rand Corp., 1700 Main St., Santa Monica, CA 90406.

Quint, Mary D. (Dorothea) (Ja. 4, 1913, Worcester, MA) Sr. Consult., Lib. Manpower, IL State Lib., 1972–; Dir., Lib. Careers, 1968–72; Lib., Info. Spec., Syracuse Univ. Resrch. Corp., 1966–68; Asst. Chief, Tech. Lib. Branch, U.S. Air Resrch. and Dev. Cmnd., 1961–64; Admin. Libn., U.S. Army Spec. Srvs., Seoul, Korea, 1960–61; Supervisory Libn., Ref., U.S. Air Resrch. and Dev. Cmnd., Cambridge Resrch. Ctr., 1955–60; Proj. Lincoln, MA Inst. of Tech., 1952–55; Head Libn., Amer. Optical Co., 1946–52; various consult., lib. positions, 1937–52. **Educ.:** Worcester State Coll., 1932–36, BSE (Educ.); Simmons Coll., 1951–55, MLS; Boston Coll., 1964–66, MS (PR). **Orgs.:** ALA: ASCLA, Ad Hoc Statewide Lib. Card Com. (1978); PLA, Lib. Coop. Com. (1974–75). SLA: Boston Chap.; Upstate NY Chap., Exec. Bd. (1968–71). IL LA: Cont. Educ. Com. (1978–79); Schol. Com. (1973–77). NY LA. Bus. and Prof. Women. Zonta. **Honors:** H.W. Wilson Co., Lib. Rcrt., 1971. **Pubns.:** Jt. ed., *Directory of Libraries in Worcester and Worcester County* (1952); "Documents at the Air Force Cambridge Research Center Technical Library," *Lib. Resrcs. & Tech. Srvs.* (Fall 1950); ed., *Directory of Library Resources in Central New York* (1969); various articles, *IL Libs.* (1972–). **Activities:** 4, 5; 17, 24, 25; 91, 93 **Addr.:** 2202 Westchester Blvd., Springfield, IL 62704.

Quiring, Virginia M. (D. 21, 1921, Metz, MO) Assoc. Dir., Pub. Srvs., KS State Univ. Libs., 1979–, Asst. Dir., 1974–79, Head, Serials Dept., 1973–74, Asst. Hum. Libn., 1972–73, Cat., 1971–72. **Educ.:** Ottawa Univ., 1939–43, BA (Fr. Lang. and Lit.); Emporia State Univ., 1970–71, ML (Libnshp.), 1975–78, MS (Educ. Admin.). **Orgs.:** ALA:ACRL/Cncl., (Ch., 1980). KS LA: Pres. (1979–80); VP (1978–); Coll. and Univ. Lib. Sect., Nom. Com. (Ch., 1979). various other orgs. Beta Phi Mu: Epsilon Chap., Pres. (1975–76), VP (1974–75). AAUW: 3rd VP (1974–76). Creat. Cookery Interest Grp.: Ch. (1978–79). Delta Kappa Gamma Socty.: Rec. Secty. (1978–80). various other orgs. **Pubns.:** "Orientation to COM Catalogs" KS State Univ. cassette tape series (1980). **Addr.:** 1121 Pioneer Ln., Manhattan, KS 66502.

Qureshi, Naimuddin (Je. 1, 1942, Agra, U.P., India) City Libn., Bell Pub. Lib., 1979–; Asst. Prof., CA State Univ., 1976–78; Libn., Intl. Lib. Info. Ctr., Univ. of Pittsburgh, 1973–76, Sr. Resrch. Asst., 1971–72. **Educ.:** Univ. of Karachi, Karachi, Pakistan, 1957–61, BS (Phys., Chem., Math.), 1962–64, MA (LS); Pratt Inst., 1969–70, MLS; Univ. of Pittsburgh, 1970–71, Advnc. Cert. (LS), 1972–, PhD. **Orgs.:** AALL: Stan. Com. (1977–79). South. CA Assn. of Law Libs.: Grants and Cont. Ed. Com. (1977–78). NLA: Prof. Educ. Com. (1978–). Karachi Univ. Lib. Sci. Alum. Assn.: Secty.-Gen. (1966–68). Pakistan LA: Cnclr. (1968–69). **Honors:** Beta Phi Mu, 1970. **Pubns.:** "The Development of Library and Information Services in Pakistan," *The Bowker Annual* (1978); "Standards for Libraries," *Encycl. of Lib. and Info. Sci.* (1980); "The Education and Training of Librarians and Information Scientists in Pakistan," *LIBRI* (1979). **Activities:** 1, 9; 17, 26, 39; 56, 77, 88 **Addr.:** 600 Langsdorf Dr., Apt. #C-12, Fullerton, CA 92631.

R

Rabban, Elana G. (Ap. 10, 1922, USSR) Dir., Lib. Media, AV, Scarsdale Pub. Schs., 1972–, Libn., 1964–72. **Educ.:** Brooklyn Coll., 1939–43, BA (Psy.); Columbia Univ., 1947–49, MA (Hist.). **Orgs.:** Westchester LA. ALA: Intl. Rel. Com. Frnds. of Scarsdale Pub. Lib.: Pres. Scarsdale Parent-Tchr. Assn.: Prog. Ch. **Pubns.:** *Books from Other Countries* (1972); *Use of Paperbacks with Elementary School Children*. **Activities:** 9, 10; 21, 32; 92, 93 **Addr.:** 123 Brite Ave., Scarsdale, NY 10583.

Raber, Nevin W. (Jl. 18, 1918, Fowlerton, IN) Bus. Libn., IN Univ., 1962–; Asst. Dir., Indianapolis–Marion Cnty. Pub. Lib., 1957–62, Bus. Libn., 1953–57, Sr. Libn., 1952–53. **Educ.:** Purdue Univ., 1938–42, BS (Gen. Sci.); IN Univ., 1946–52, MA (Hist.), 1951–52, MA (LS). **Orgs.:** IN LA: Audit. Com. (Ch., 1967–68, 1970); Insr. Com. (Ch., 1968–69); Nom. Com. (Ch., 1976). SLA: Bylaws Com. (1978–81); Bus. and Fin. Div., various coms., bds. (1967–77); IN Chap. (Pres., 1971–72), various coms., ofcs. (1968–79). Aerosp. Resrch. Applications Ctr: Exec. Bd. (1962–67). IN State Lib.: Adv. Cncl. (Spec. Libs. Rpt. 1970–72). IN Info. Retrieval Srv.: Consult. (1971–72). IN Univ., Grad. Lib. Sch.: Adv. Cncl. Spec. Libs. Rpt. (1972–75). **Honors:** Beta Phi Mu; Beta Gamma Sigma; Cncl. on Lib. Resrcs., Grant, 1970; Fndn. for Econ. and Bus. Stds., Grant, 1963. **Pubns.:** *Marketing, A Selected List of Current Titles* (1972); prin. investigator, *Special Library Resources Study, 1970–71* (1972). **Activities:** 1, 9; 17, 19, 39; 59 **Addr.:** 3701 Morningside Dr., Bloomington, IN 47401.

Rabinowitz, Renee (D. 27, 1934, Chicago, IL) Educ. Media Spec., Cleveland Bd. of Educ., 1967–. **Educ.:** Roosevelt Univ., 1952–55, BA (Educ.); Case West. Rsv. Univ., 1971–74, MLS. **Orgs.:** OH Educ. Lib. Media Assn. ALA. Comp. Users Grp. Alum. Org., Case West. Rsv. Univ. Sch. of LS. Cleveland Pub. Schs. Readg. Cir. **Honors:** Beta Phi Mu. **Pubns.:** Reviewer of nonprint media, *Sch. Lib. Jnl.* (1975–). **Activities:** 10; 15, 21, 32; 63, 67, 90 **Addr.:** 3570 Shannon Rd., Cleveland Hts., OH 44118.

Rabins, Joan R. (Ap. 22, 1931, New York, NY) Archvst. II, Arch. of Labor and Urban Affairs, Wayne State Univ., 1979–. **Educ.:** Long Island Univ., 1949–53, BA (Hist.); Columbia Univ., 1953–55, MA (Hist.); Univ. of WI, 1956–59; various crs. **Orgs.:** SAA. Midw. Arch. Conf. MI Arch. Assn. **Addr.:** 29988 Fernhill Dr., Farmington Hills, MI 48018.

Raburn, Josephine Riling (D. 6, 1929, Norman, OK) Asst. Prof., Cameron Univ., 1972–; Instr., 1968–71; Ref. Libn., Cameron Agr. and Mech. Jr. Coll., 1967–68; Ref./Circ. Libn., Morris Sweatt Tech. Lib., 1966–67; Instr., OK Univ., 1966–67; Ref./Admin. Libn., Spec. Srvs., Fort Sill, OK, 1964–66. **Educ.:** OK Univ., 1949–50, BS (Nutr.), 1963–64, MLS; 1969– (Educ. Tech.). **Orgs.:** ALA. AECT. OK LA: Rcrt. Com. (1979–80); Com. to Study Cert. for Sch. Libns. (1975–77); Lib Educ Div. Secy., (1975, 1980–81), Gvrs. Conf. on Libs. (Del., 1978). Lawton Pub. Lib. Trustees. Other orgs. Alpha Delta Kappa. Delta Kappa Gamma. AAUW. Cameron Dames. Other orgs. **Honors:** Beta Phi Mu; Phi Kappa Phi, Disting. Fac. Awd. **Pubns.:** "Public Relations for a "Special" Public," *Spec. Libs.* (D. 1969); jt.-auth., "A New "Double Your Career Options" Program," *Improving Coll. and Univ. Tchng.* (In Process); "Editor and Student Views on the Censorship Game," ED 173 841 (Apr. 1979); "The Sequoyah Children's Book Award," *OK Tchr.* (J. 1973). **Activities:** 1; 24, 26, 47; 63, 74 **Addr.:** 511 N. W. 40th St., Lawton, OK 73505.

Rachfalski, Sr. Marie (Ag. 27, 1938, Philadelphia, PA) Lib. Dir., Neumann Coll., 1975–, Assoc. Dir., 1970–75. **Educ.:** Our Lady of Angels Coll., 1956–68, AB (Eng.); Cath. Univ. of Amer., 1968–73, MSLS. **Orgs.:** ALA: Tri-State Coll. Lib. Coop. (Secy., 1980–81); ACRL. Cath. LA. **Addr.:** Neumann College Library, Aston, PA 19014.

Rachow Louis August (Ja. 21, 1927, Shickley, NB) Cur., Libn., Walter Hampden-Edwin Booth Thea. Col. and Lib. 1962–; Asst. Libn., Univ. Club, NY, 1958–62. **Educ.:** York Coll., 1944–48, BS (Chem.) Columbia Univ., 1957–59, MLS. **Orgs.:** ALA. Cncl. of Natl. Lib. and Info. Assns.: Secy.-Treas. (1970–71); Bd. of Dir. (1974–77). NY Lib. Club: Pres. (1979–80); VP (1978–79); Cncl. (1973–77). Thea. Lib. Assn: Pres (1967–72, 1981–). Other orgs. and ofcs. Amer. Natl. Thea. and Acad. Amer. Thea. Assn. Amer. Socty. for Thea. Resrch. Amer. Thea. Co.: Bd. of Dirs. (1974). Other orgs. **Honors:** Theta Alpha Phi, Medallion of Honor, 1976. **Pubns.:** "Performing Arts Research Collections in New York City," *Performing Arts Resrcs.* (1974); "International Federation for Theatre Research Congress Review," *Innovations in Stage and Thea. Design* (1972); "The Players," *Performing Arts Rev.* (1971); "The Walter Hampden Memorial Library," Wilson Lib. Bltn. (Ap. 1964); Reviews; other articles; various editorships. **Activities:** 12; 41, 45; 55, 95-Theatre. **Addr.:** 16 Gramercy Pk., New York, NY 10003.

Racine, B. Rose (My. 27, 1943, Wilmington, NC) Libn., Cham. of Cmrce. USA, 1968–; Libn., James Blair HS, 1966–68. **Educ.:** E. Carolina Univ., 1963–66, BS (Educ.); 1963–66, Cert. (LS). **Orgs.:** SLA: Bus. and Advert. (1968–81). Law Libns. Socty. of Washington, DC. **Addr.:** Library, Chamber of Commerce USA, 1615 H St. N.W., Washington, DC 20062.

Racki, David Kenneth (Ag. 24, 1943, Bridgeport, CT) Clinical Prof., Fld. Coord., Univ. of ND, Lib. Trng. Inst., 1979–; Ref. Libn., West. MI Univ., 1978–79; Spec. Srvs. Libn., Van Buren Cnty. Lib., 1977–78. **Educ.:** South. CT State Coll., 1967–71, BA (Soclgy., Grmn.); West. MI Univ., 1978–79, MSL. **Orgs.:** ALA. ND LA. **Activities:** 4, 11; 24, 25, 26; 50, 63, 66 **Addr.:** 180 Fresh Meadow Ln., Milford, CT 06460.

Rademacher, Richard J. (Ag. 20, 1937, Kaukauna, WI) Dir. of Libs., Wichita Pub. Lib., 1976–; Dir., Salt Lake City Pub. Lib., 1969–76; Dir., Eau Claire Pub. Lib., 1966–69; Dir., Kaukauna Pub. Lib., 1964–66. **Educ.:** Ripon Coll., 1955–59, AB (Econ.); Univ. of WI, 1960–61, MSLS. **Orgs.:** ALA. KS LA. Mt. Plains LA. Girl Scouts. KS Com. for the Hum. **Activities:** 9; 16, 17, 47; 50, 55, 74 **Addr.:** Wichita Public Library, 223 S. Main St., Wichita, KS 67202.

Rader, Hannelore B. (D. 19, 1937, Berlin, Germany) Dir., Lib. Lrng. Ctr., Univ. of WI, Parkside, 1980–; Coord., Educ. Psy. Div., East. MI Univ., 1976–80, Orien. Libn., Head, Orien. Prog., 1970–76, Asst. Hum. Libn., 1968–70. **Educ.:** Univ. of MI, 1956–60, BA (Russ., Span.), 1968, MLS, 1968 (Tchg. Cert.). **Orgs.:** ALA: ACRL/Educ. and Bhvl. Sci. Sect., Bibl. Instr. for Educ. Com. (Ch., 1977–79). WI LA. AAUP. Mod. Lang. Assn. **Honors:** Cncl. on Lib. Resrcs., Flwshp., 1979; MI LA, Walter H. Kaiser Awd., 1978. **Pubns.:** *Faculty Involvement in Library Instruction* (1975); *Library Instruction in the Seventies* (1976); "Reference Services as a Teaching Function," *Lib. Trends* (Sum. 1980); "Library Orientation and Instruction 1979," *Ref. Srvs. Review* (Ja.–Mr. 1980); various other articles. **Activities:** 1; 17, 41 **Addr.:** 2826 14th Ln., Kenosha, WI 53140.

Rader, Jennette S. (My. 12, 1929, Providence, RI) Bus., Econ. Libn., Joseph Regenstein Lib., Univ. of Chicago, 1980–, Libn., Human Resrcs. Ctr., 1975–80, Ref. Libn., 1972–75. **Educ.:** Duke Univ., 1947–51, BA (Psy.); Univ. of IL, 1957, MA (Indus. Rel.); Rosary Coll., 1972, MA (LS). **Orgs.:** ALA. SLA. Indus. Rel. Resrch. Assn. **Honors:** Phi Beta Mu, 1972. **Activities:** 1; 15, 17, 39; 59 **Addr.:** Joseph Regenstein Library, 1100 E. 57th St., Chicago, IL 60637.

Rader, Joe C. (Mr. 5, 1938, Nashville, TN) Head, Rsv. Dept., Undergrad. Lib., Univ. of TN, 1978–; Head, Readers Srv., Knoxville Coll., 1976–78, Ref. Libn., 1975–76. **Educ.:** Mid. TN State Univ., 1956–60, BS (Eng.); Defense Lang. Inst., 1962, Cert. (Grmn.); Univ. of TN, 1974–75, MLS. **Orgs.:** ALA: ACRL, Mem. Com. (1980–). E. TN LA. TN LA: Coll. and Univ. Sect. (Ch., 1979–80). AAUP. Univ. of TN GSLIS Alum. Assn. **Pubns.:** Assoc. ed., *TN Libn.* (1980–). **Activities:** 1; 15, 22, 31; 51, 83, 93 **Addr.:** Undergraduate Library, Reserve Dept., University of Tennessee, Knoxville, TN 37996-1000.

Rader, Ronald A. (My. 28, 1951, Newark, NJ) Info. Systs. Sci., MITRE Corp., 1978–; Info. Spec., Gillette Med. Eval. Lab., Gillette Corp., 1976–78, Resrch. Chem., Bio-Conversion Labs., 1974–76. **Educ.:** Univ. of MD, 1969–73, BS (Microbio.), 1976–79, MLS. **Orgs.:** ASIS. Drug Info. Assn. Amer. Chem. Socty.: Div. of Chem. Info. **Pubns.:** *The Chemical Information Resources Directory* (1980); "Information Retrieval for the Safety Evaluation of Cosmetic Products," *Spec. Libs.* (My.–Je. 1976); "The Chemical Information Resources Directory: An Integrating Component of the Chemical Substances Information Network," *Jnl. Chemical Info. and Comp. Sci.* (forthcoming). **Activities:** 12, 14-Consult.; 24, 39, 41; 58, 60, 87 **Addr.:** 8219 Flower Ave., Takoma Park, MD 20912.

Radmacher, Camille J. (Ap. 14, 1917, Monmouth, IL) Exec. Dir., W. IL Lib. Syst., 1966–; Head Libn., Warren Cnty. Lib., 1948–, Circ. Libn., 1943–48. **Educ.:** Monmouth Coll., 1935–38, (Sp.). **Orgs.:** ALA: IL Mem. Ch. (1963–65); PLA, Pub. Lib. Actv. Com. (1973–76). IL State Lib. Adv. Com. Monmouth Coll. Cmnty. Msc. and Lect. Series Altrusa Club. Daughters of the Amer. Revolution. **Honors:** IL LA, Libn. of Yr., 1967. **Pubns.:** "National Library Week in Illinois," *IL Libs.* (Mr. 1961); "Bookmobile Service to Rural Areas," *IL Libs.* (Ag. 1955). **Activities:** 9; 17, 31, 47; 56, 59, 78 **Addr.:** Western Illinois Library System, 58 Public Sq., Monmouth, IL 61462.

Radmacher, Mary (N. 24, 1915, Monmouth, IL) Chief Libn., Skokie Pub. Lib., 1956–; Head, Ref. Dept., Gary Pub. Lib., 1951–56, Ref. Libn., 1946–51; Asst. Agr. Libn., Univ. of IL Agr. Lib., 1946; Adult Ref., Circ. Libn., Warren Cnty. Lib., 1941–43, Chld. Libn., 1936–41. **Educ.:** Univ. of IL, 1943–45, BA (Eng.), 1945–46, BS (LS). **Orgs.:** ALA. Chicago Lib. Club. IL LA. Frnds. of Lit. Various other orgs., coms., ofcs. Art Inst. of Chicago. Skokie Fine Arts Comsn. Leag. of Women Voters. Socty. of Midland Auths. **Honors:** IL LA, Libn. of the Yr. Cit., 1970; Beta Phi Mu. **Pubns.:** "Skokie Public Library," *An Architectural Strategy For Change* (1976); "Mary Radmacher, Chief Librarian, Skokie Public Library, Skokie, Illinois, Statement," *In Our Opinion; Regional Hearings Before the National Commission on Libraries and Information Service* (1973); "Questionable Medical Literature and the Library: A Symposium," *Bltn. of Med. LA* (O. 1963); "Interlibrary Organization of Reference Service," *Library as a Community Information Center* (Allerton Park Inst. No. 4). **Activities:** 9; 17, 19, 35; 55, 59, 74 **Addr.:** Skokie Public Library, 5215 Oakton St., Skokie, IL 60077.

Radoff, Leonard I. (Ja. 9, 1927, Houston, TX) Chief, Branch Srvs., Houston Pub. Lib., 1971–; Dir., Pasadena Pub. Lib.,

Special Subjects/Services: 50. Adult educ.; 51. Advert./Mktg.; 52. Aerosp.; 53. Agric.; 54. Area std.; 55. Arts/Hum.; 56. Autom.; 57. Bibl./Prtg.; 58. Bio. sci.; 59. Bus./Fin.; 60. Chem.; 61. Copyrt.; 62. Documtn.; 63. Educ.; 64. Engin.; 65. Env.; 66. Eth. grps.; 67. Film; 68. Food/Nutr.; 69. Geneal.; 70. Geo.; 71. Geol.; 72. Handcpd.; 73. Hist.; 74. Int. frdm.; 75. Info. sci.; 76. Insr.; 77. Law; 78. Legis.; 79. Math./Comp. sci.; 80. Med.; 81. Metals; 82. Nat. resrcs.; 83. Newsp.; 84. Nuc. sci.; 85. Oral hist.; 86. Petr./Energy; 87. Pharm.; 88. Phys./Astr./Math.; 89. Readg.; 90. Relig.; 91. Sci./Tech.; 92. Soc. sci.; 93. Telecom.; 94. Transp.; 95. (other).

1966–71; Head, Pub. Srvs., Abilene Pub. Lib., 1964–66. **Educ.:** Rice Univ., 1944–49, BA (Hist.); Univ. of TX, 1963–65, MLS. **Orgs.:** TX LA: Dist. 8 (Ch., 1970–71). TX Mncpl. LA: Pres. (1969–70). ALA. SWLA. **Honors:** Beta Phi Mu, 1965. **Activities:** 9; 17, 24, 27; 50, 89 **Addr.:** 4013 Gano St., Houston, TX 77009.

Radovancev, Estela (Jl. 19, 1942, Monterrey, N.L., Mexico) Lib., Media Spec., Natl. Coll. of Educ., 1979–; Tchr., Libn., Chicago Bd. of Educ., 1977–79; Latin Amer. Serials Libn., Univ. of IL, 1974–76; Ref. Libn., Champaign Pub. Lib., 1973–74. **Educ.:** Univ. of IL, 1965–67, BA (Eng., Span. Educ.), 1970–71, MSLS; State of IL, 1971, Media Spec. Cert. **Orgs.:** IL LA. Tchrs. of Eng. to Speakers of Other Lang. **Activities:** 1, 10; 32, 39, 44; 55, 56, 66 **Addr.:** 1249 S. 49th Ct., Cicero, IL 60650.

Radtke, Bruce W. (D. 17, 1940, Williston, ND) Outrch. Libn., Bellingham Pub. Lib., 1973–. **Educ.:** Concordia Sr. Coll., 1960–62, BA (Hist.); Concordia Semy., 1962–66, MDiv; Univ. of IA, 1971–72, MA (LS). **Orgs.:** WA LA: Outrch. Progs. for Essential Needs Interest Grp., Strg. Com. (1975–77). ALA: Com. on World of Work Brochure for Pres. Com. on Empl. of Handcpd. NLA. Whatcom Cnty. Cncl. on Aging: Secy. (1979–). UN Assn./USA (Whatcom Cnty.): Vice-Ch. (1977–78); Ch. (1981–). **Pubns.:** Media reviewer, *Rockingchair Mag.* (1979–). **Activities:** 9; 16, 27; 72, 90 **Addr.:** Bellingham Public Library, P. O. Box 1197, Bellingham, WA 98227–1197.

Rae, E. Ann (Je. 6, 1944, Toronto, ON) Cat. Libn., Univ. of Victoria Law Lib., 1975–; KE Proj. Libn., Natl. Lib. of Can., 1973–75; Cat., York Univ. Law Lib., 1969–72. **Educ.:** Univ. of Toronto, 1963–66, BA (Eng.), 1968–69, BLS, 1972–73, MLS. **Orgs.:** Can. ALL: Tech. Srvs. Com. (Ch., 1979–). AALL: Cat. and Class. Com. (1976–79). Can. LA. ALA. Can. Assn. of Univ. Tchrs.: Acad. Libns. Com. (1980–). Confederation of Univ. Fac.: Cncl. (1979–80). Assns. of BC. Prof. Staff Assn.: Pres. (1979–80). **Pubns.:** *Library of Congress Classification; Class K, Subclass KE, Law of Canada* (1976). **Activities:** 1, 12; 17, 20, 34; 77, 78 **Addr.:** University of Victoria, Law Library, P.O. Box 2300, Victoria, BC V8W 3B1 Canada.

Rafael, Ruth Kelson (O. 28, 1929, Wilmington, NC) Archvst., West. Jewish Hist. Ctr., Judah L. Magnes Meml. Musm., 1968–; Libn., Congregation Beth Sholom, San Francisco, CA, 1965–; Tchr., Horace Mann Jr. HS, 1955–57. **Educ.:** San Francisco State Coll., 1951–53, BA (Lang. Arts), 1953–54, MA (Lang. Arts); Univ. of CA, Berkeley, 1967–68, MLS (Lang.); San Francisco State Univ., 1953–54, Sec. Tchg. Cred. **Orgs.:** North. CA Assn. of Jewish Libns.: Pres. (1977–79). Socty. of CA Archvsts.: Rep. to Lcl. Pres. White Hse. Com. SAA: 1980 Conv., Panelist. AJL: Lcl. Prog. Com., Ch. Various ofcs. Musm. Socty., San Francisco. Musm. of Mod. Art, San Francisco. Judah Magnes Musm., Berkeley. CA Hist. Socty. Various other orgs. **Honors:** Jewish Bk. Cncl., Beth Sholom Lib. Recipient of Solomon Schechter Awd. and Cert. **Pubns.:** *Continuum, A Selective History of San Francisco Eastern European Jewish Life, 1880–1940* (1977); ed. bd., *West. States Jewish Hist. Qtly.* (1978–); "Ernest Bloch at the San Francisco Conservatory of Music," *West. States Jewish Hist. Qtly.* (Ap. 1977); various bk. reviews. **Activities:** 2, 5, 12; 17, 39, 45; 66, 69, 86 **Addr.:** Western Jewish History Center, Judah L. Magnes Memorial Museum, 2911 Russell St., Berkeley, CA 94705.

Rafferty, Eve G. (My. 10, 1927, Ilbeshausen, Rhineland, W. Germany) Coord., Acq., Natl. Grntlgy. Resrc. Ctr., NRTA-AARP, 1977–; Acq., Urban Inst. Lib., 1972–77; Acq., George Washington Univ. Lib., 1961–72. **Educ.:** Coburg Tchrs. Coll., 1957–61, BS (Educ.); Cath. Univ. of Amer., 1972–76, MS (LS); various mgt. wkshps., online and grntlgy. wkshps., sems. **Orgs.:** SLA: DC Chap., SS Grp. (Treas., 1979–80), Hosplty. Ch. (1980–81). Grntlgcl. Libns. Adv. Com.: Grntlgcl. Socty. Anl. Mtg. (Actg. Ch., 1980). **Pubns.:** *Variable Work Time: A Selected Bibliography* (1974); "Aged: Close Encounters in Gerontology," *Lib. Jnl. Spec. Rpt. # 6* (1978); various presentations. **Activities:** 12; 15, 34; 95-Soc. grntlgy. **Addr.:** National Gerontology Resource Center, NRTA-AARP, 1909 K St. N.W., Washington, DC 20049.

Rahal, M. Patricia (Ag. 30, 1942, St. John's, NF) Libn., Coll. of Trades and Tech., 1975–; Chief Catlgr., NF Pub. Lib. Srvs., 1971–75; Acq. Libn., Brock Univ., 1970–71; various positions, Meml. Univ. of NF, 1964–70. **Educ.:** Meml. Univ. of NF, 1959–63, BA (Eng.); McGill Univ., 1963–64, BLS. **Orgs.:** NF LA: Pres. (1975–76). Atl. Provs. LA: NF VP (1965–66, 1975–76, 1980–82). Can. LA. **Activities:** 1, 9; 15, 16, 17 **Addr.:** 16 London Rd., St. John's, NF A1B 2G8 Canada.

Rainey, Laura J. Mgr., Tech. Info. Ctr., Rocketdyne Div., Rockwell Intl. Corp., 1972–, Head Libn., 1970–72, Tech. Prcs. Libn., Power Systs. Div., 1969–70, Catlgr., Sci. Ctr., 1965–69; Catlgr., Rand Corp., 1965–66; Libn., Foote Cone and Belding, Advert., 1958–64; Libn., Braun and Co., Mgt. Consults., 1950–58. **Educ.:** Univ. of CA, Los Angeles, 1944–48, BA (Hist.), 1948–50, MA (Hist.), 1964–65, MLS. **Orgs.:** SLA: South. CA Chap. (Pres.-Elect, Pres., 1978–79); Bylaws Ch. (1980–81); Awds. Ch. (1980–81); Anl. Conf., Lcl. Arrange. Com. (1967–68); Gvt. Info. Srvs. Com. (1967–69); *Sci.-Tech. News* (Bus. Mgr., 1968–70); Lib. Mgt. Div. (Treas., 1978–80); Sci.-Tech. Div., Nom. Com. (1978–80); Aerosp. Div. (Ch., 1969–70), PR Dir. (1972–73); Bus. and Fin. Div. (Secy., 1968–69); Mem. Dir. (1973–); various ofcs. Depos. Lib. Adv. Cncl. to the Pub. Printer. **Pubns.:** "User Experiences with the New TEST," *Spec. Libs.* (Ja. 1970); "Microforms in a Corporate Information System," *Micro Image Nsltr.* (Ja. 1975). **Activities:** 12; 17, 46; 52, 64, 91 **Addr.:** 15127 Lemay St., Van Nuys, CA 91405.

Rainey, Melvyn Daniel (O. 17, 1930, Regina, SK) Asst. Prof., Fac. of Educ., Univ. of BC, 1973–; Tchr.-Libn., Vernon Sr. Sec. Sch., 1970–72; Tchr.-Libn., Dept. of Natl. Defence, Can. Frcs., Germany, 1966–69; Tchr.-Libn., Estevan Collegiate Inst., 1960–66; various positions, elem. and sec. tchg. **Educ.:** Univ. of SK, 1969 (Educ., Hist., Lib.); Univ. of WA, 1972–73, MLS; SK, BC, Tchg. Certs. **Orgs.:** BC Sch. LA: Past Pres. (1973–74); Mem. Ch. (1973–77, 1979–80). Can. Sch. LA: Educ. for Sch. Libns. (1979–80). Can. LA: Mem. Com. (1975–78). Pac. NW LA. Various other orgs. SK Educ. Assn. of Media Specs. **Pubns.:** Contrib., "Technical Services in School Libraries," *BC Sch. Lib. Manual* (S. 1977); "Report on the California School Librarians' Association Conference," *Bookmark* (Mr. 1977); "School Libraries in British Columbia," *CA Sch. Libs.* (Ja. 1977); "Food for a Hungry World," *CA Sch. Libs.* (Win. 1976); "Revision of the Anglo-American Cataloguing Rules," *Bookmark* (Je. 1976); various articles, reviews. **Addr.:** Faculty of Education, University of British Columbia, Vancouver, BC V6T 1W5 Canada.

Raithel, Frederick J. (N. 20, 1949, Jefferson City, MO) Head, Access Srvs., Ellis Lib., Univ. of MO, Columbia, 1981–; Netwk. Coord., Mid-MO Lib. Netwk., 1978–81; Ref. Libn., Daniel Boone Reg. Lib., 1974–78; Ref. Libn., MO State Lib., 1974. **Educ.:** Lincoln Univ., 1968–72, BA (Phil.); Univ. of MO, 1972–73, MA (Lib. and Info. Sci.); Tech. Sch., 1975–77, Certs., (Data Prcs., Electronics Tech.). **Orgs.:** ALA. MO LA: Comp. and Info. Tech. Com. (Ch., 1978–79). Univ. of MO Grad. Sch. of Lib. and Info. Sci. Alum. Assn. **Pubns.:** "Personal Microcomputers in the Library Environment," *Jnl. of Lib. Autom.* (S. 1980); "The Implications of Microcomputers for Libraries," *Show-Me Libs.* (Mr. 1978). **Activities:** 12, 14-Netwk.; 17, 28, 34; 56, 75, 93 **Addr.:** Ellis Library, University of Missouri, Columbia, MO 65211.

Raitt, Mildred Dandridge (N. 30, 1924, Baltimore, MD) Chief, Acq. Srvs., Smithsonian Inst., 1972–, Ord. Libn., 1963–72; Asst. Libn., Cham. of Cmrce. of the U.S., 1958–62; Ref. Asst., Folger Shakespeare Lib., 1957–58; Asst. Libn., Principia Coll., 1955–57, Ord. Libn., 1948–54. **Educ.:** Goucher Coll., 1943–47, AB (Eng.); Columbia Univ., 1947–48, BS (LS), 1954–55, MA (Eng.). **Orgs.:** ALA. DC LA. Eng. Speaking Un. Tilden Gardens Inc. **Activities:** 1, 4; 15, 39, 44; 55, 58, 59 **Addr.:** 3024 Tilden St., N.W., Washington, DC 20008.

Rajec, Elizabeth Molnár (Jl. 23, 1931, Bratislava, Czechoslovakia) Assoc. Prof., City Coll. of CUNY, 1964–. **Educ.:** Columbia Univ., 1957–63, BS (Grmn.); Rutgers, 1963–64, MLS; CUNY, 1967–75, PhD (Grmn.). **Orgs.:** ALA. Amer. Name Socty. NY LA: Resrcs. and Tech. Srvs. Sect., Tech. Com. (1979–). LA of CUNY: Grants Com. (1979–); Com. on Prof. Excel. (1978–); Progs. Sems. and Soc. Actv. Com. (1978–). PhD Alum. Assn. CUNY: Treas. (1979–). AAUP. Kafka Socty. of Amer. Mod. Lang. Assn. **Honors:** Delta Phi Alpha. **Pubns.:** *Namen und ihre Bedeutungen im Werke Franz Kafkas* (1977); *Literarische Onomastik* (1977); *The Study of Names in Literature* (1978); "Kafkas Erzählung 'Blumfeld, einällerer Junggeselle'," *Beiträge zur Namenforschung* (1976); "Franz Kafka and Philip Roth: Their Use of Literary Onomastics," *Literary Onomastics Stds.* (1980). **Activities:** 1; 15, 46; 55, 95-Onomastics Languages. **Addr.:** 500 E. 77 St. Apt. 216, New York, NY 10021.

Rake, Anthony Ifor (Je. 19, 1944, Wimbledon, Eng.) Libn., AV Dir., Wauconda HS, 1968–. **Educ.:** IL State Univ., 1964–68, BS (LS); Univ. of KY, 1970–73, MSLS. **Orgs.:** IL Assn. for Media in Educ. ALA: AASL. IL Assn. For Educ. Comm. Tech. Wauconda Fed. Church. **Honors:** Alpha Beta Alpha. **Activities:** 10; 15, 20, 32; 63 **Addr.:** Wauconda High School Library, 555 N. Main St., Wauconda, IL 60084.

Rakow, Lawrence J. (Ap. 4, 1947, New York City, NY) YA, Sec. Sch. Spec., Cuyahoga Cnty. Pub. Lib., 1976–; Lib., Media Spec., Madison HS, 1974–76; Med. Libn., Cleveland State Hosp., 1971–73. **Educ.:** SUNY, Buffalo, 1965–69, BA (Hist., Eng.); Case West. Rsv. Univ., 1973–74, MLS (Lib., Media). **Orgs.:** ALA: Best Bks. for YA's (Ch., 1981). OH Educ. Lib./Media Assn. OH LA. **Pubns.:** "Meditation and Spiritual Practice: A YA Bibliography," *Top of the News* (Sum. 1977); "Television and Library Service for YA's," *Sch. Lib. Jnl.* (Mr. 1978). **Activities:** 9, 10; 15, 32, 48; 67 **Addr.:** Cuyahoga County Public Library, 4510 Memphis Ave., Cleveland, OH 44144.

Rambler, Linda K. (Ja. 18, 19–, Londonderry Twp., PA) Resrch. and Documtn. Libn., PA State Univ., 1981–, Ref., Soc. Sci. Libn., 1976–81, Soc. Sci. Subj. Spec., 1974–76, Asst. to Dean, Libs., 1972–74, Asst. to Chief Acq. Libn., 1971–72; Sci. Ref. Libn., Lehigh Univ., 1968–71, Cat., Ref. Libn., 1966–68; Admin. Libn., U.S. Army Spec. Srvs., Germany, 1964–66; Libn. Jr.-Sr. HS, Selinsgrove Area Sch. Dist., 1961–63. **Educ.:** Millersville State Coll., 1957–61, BS (LS, Eng., Sec. Educ.); Case West. Rsv. Univ., 1961–64, MS (LS); Lehigh Univ., 1967–70, MA (Eng.); Simmons Coll., 1976–78, DA (Lib. Admin.). **Orgs.:** ALA: PLA, Resrch. Mtrls. Com. (1979–82), Ed. (1978–80). SLA: Ctrl. PA Chap., Exec. Bd. (1979–80); Netwk. Ch. (1980–81). PA Human Rel. Comsn. **Honors:** Beta Phi Mu, 1964. **Pubns.:** Jt. auth., "Collection Development Policy; A Survey of Attitudes," *Collection Development in Libraries; A Treatise* (1980); "Syllabus Study: Key to a Responsive Academic Library," *Jnl. of Acad. Libnshp.* (1982); various reviews, abs., *Serials Review* (1979–), *Women Std. Abs.* (1974–); "An Index to Beryl Rowlands' *Companion to Chaucer Studies*," *Companion to Chaucer Studies* (1979). **Activities:** 1 **Addr.:** 614 S. Pugh St., State College, PA 16801.

Rambo, Helen M. (Ja. 29, 1927, Hutchinson, KS) Cat. Libn., NW Nazarene Coll., 1957–; Sch. Libn., Miller Jr. High, 1954–57; Sch. Libn., Bly HS, 1953–54; Sch. Libn., Merrill HS, 1952–53. **Educ.:** NW Nazarene Coll., 1945–49, AB (Hist.); Univ. of WA, 1953–57, ML (Libnshp.). **Orgs.:** ID LA: Pres. (1980–81); Pres.-Elect (1979–80); Coll. Univ. Div. (Ch., 1978–79). ALA. Pac. NW LA. AAUW. Nampa Pub. Lib. Bd. of Trustees. SW ID Reg. Lib. Syst.: Bd. of Trustees (1976–80). **Activities:** 1, 9; 20, 46, 47; 54, 55, 90 **Addr.:** 703 Elder, Nampa, ID 83651.

Ramer, Faye Padgett (Mr. 10, 1930, Darlington, FL) Coord. of Media Srvs., Bay Cnty. Sch. Syst., 1977–; Media Spec., Bay HS, 1971–77; Media Spec., Everitt Jr. HS, 1966–71; Libn., Cove and Cedar Grove Elem. Schs., 1963–66; Tchr., Millville Elem. Sch., 1959–63. **Educ.:** FL State Univ., 1959–61, BS (Elem. Educ.), 1963–66, MS (LS), 1973–75, EdS (Educ. Admin.). **Orgs.:** FL Assn. for Media in Educ.: Bd. of Dirs. (1977–); Prod. and Pubns. Com. (Ch., 1979–80). FL Cncl. for Libs. Assn. of Bay Cnty. Sch. Media Specs.: Pres. (1966–67); Treas. (1975–77). AECT. ALA: AASL. FL Assn. of Dist. Instr. Mtrls. Admins. FL Assn. for Supvsn. and Curric. Dev. FL Assn. of Sch. Admins. Various other orgs. **Honors:** Alpha Delta Kappa; FL Congs. of Parents–Tchr. Assns., Apprec. Awd., 1970. **Activities:** 10; 17, 28, 32; 63, 93 **Addr.:** 4625 N. Lakewood Dr., Panama City, FL 32401.

Ramer, James David (Jl. 14, 1927, Metropolis, IL) Dean, Grad. Sch. of Lib. Srvs., Univ. of AL, 1971–; Assoc. Prof., Div. of Libnshp., Emory Univ., 1968–71; Dir. of the Lib., Univ. of NC, Charlotte, 1964–68; Head, Engin. and Phys. Scis. Libs., Columbia Univ., 1959–64. **Educ.:** Occidental Coll., 1948–51, AB (Phil.); Univ. of Paris, 1949–50, Cert. (Fr.). Columbia Univ., 1956–57, MS (LS), 1959–64, DLS. **Orgs.:** AALS. ALA: AL Chap. (Cnclr., 1980–82); Educ. Com. (Ch., 1977–79). Amer. Prtg. Hist. Assn. Frnds. of the Earth. **Honors:** Phi Beta Kappa, 1951. **Pubns.:** Ed., *AL Libn.* (1976–78); *Bibliography on Plasma Physics and Magnetohydrodynamics* (1959); "Library/Media Education in Alabama," *The AL Libn.* (My–Je. 1978); "The Book Budget in Academic Libraries," *Southeast. Libn.* (Spr. 1965). **Activities:** 1, 11; 26, 39, 45; 50, 55, 57 **Addr.:** Graduate School of Library Service, P.O. Box 6242, University, AL 35486.

Ramirez, William L. (Ag. 17, 1925, San Francisco, CA) Dir., Ctrl. Lib., San Francisco Pub. Lib., 1972–, Dir., Bay Area Ref. Ctr., 1970–72; Consult., Natl. Educ. Resrcs. Inst., Inc., DC, 1971–72; Consult, Latin Amer. Lib., Oakland Pub. Lib., 1966–70; Libn., Rare Bks. and Spec. Cols., San Francisco Pub. Lib., 1963–70, Branch Libn., 1959–63; Catlgr., Salvation Army Trng. Sch., 1958–62. **Educ.:** Univ. of San Francisco, 1944–48, BS (Hist., Pol. Sci.); Univ. of CA, 1952–54, BLS; various mgt. progs. and crs., 1951–. **Orgs.:** ALA: PLA, Pub. Lib. Actv. Com. (1972–77); RASD, ILL Com. (1973–75), Com. on Mtrls. for the Span. Speaking (1972–75). REFORMA: Treas. (1971–74). Pub. Lib. Execs. of Ctrl. CA: Pres. (1972–73). CA LA: Golden Gate Dist. (Pres., 1970). Various other orgs., ofcs. Image. **Honors:** Beta Phi Mu. **Pubns.:** Jt. auth., "The San Francisco Public Library: A History," *Ency. of Lib. and Info. Sci.* (1979); guest ed., "Libraries and the Spanish Speaking," *Wilson Lib. Bltn.* (Mr. 1970); "Problems of the Public Library in Services to its Spanish-Speaking Population," *XII SALALM* (Je. 1967). **Activities:** 9; 16, 17, 24; 66 **Addr.:** San Francisco Public Library, Civic Center, San Francisco, CA 94102.

Ramm, Dorothy V. (N. 12, 1936, Chicago, IL) Ref., Pers. Libn., Transp. Lib., Northwest. Univ., 1960–. **Educ.:** Swarthmore Coll., 1954–58, BA (Fr.); McGill Univ., 1958–59, BLS. **Orgs.:** ALA. SLA. **Pubns.:** *Police Administration Bibliography* (1979); *Containerization: A Bibliography* (anl.); *Police Personnel Administration: Selected References Since 1965* (1974); *Traffic Restraint: A Bibliography* (1974). **Activities:** 1, 12; 30, 39; 77, 94 **Addr.:** 2319 Commonwealth Ave., Chicago, IL 60614.

Ramquist, Raymond C. (Ap. 14, 1938, Berwyn, IL) Head, Dept. LS and Educ. Media, James Madison Univ., 1975–; Asst. Prof., LS, St. Cloud State Univ., 1970–75; Instr., Educ. Media, Univ. of UT, 1969–70; Dir., AV Srvs., Univ. of IL, Chicago, 1965–67. **Educ.:** DePaul Univ., 1958–64, PhB (Geo.); IN Univ., 1967–74, EdD (Instr. Tech.); Univ. of MN, 1971–74, MA (LS). **Orgs.:** VA LA. VA Educ. Media Assn. ALA. AECT. **Honors:** Phi Delta Kappa. **Activities:** 11; 17, 26, 32; 63, 74, 93 **Addr.:** Dept. Library Science, James Madison University, Harrisonburg, VA 22807.

PROFESSIONAL ACTIVITIES: Institutions: 1. Acad. lib.; 2. Arch.; 3. Assn.; 4. Fed./Gvt. lib.; 5. Inst. lib.; 6. Mfr./Suppl.; 7. Milit. lib.; 8. Musm.; 9. Pub. lib.; 10. Sch. lib.; 11. Sch. of lib. sci.; 12. Spec. lib.; 13. State lib.; 14. (other). **Functions/Activities:** 15. Acq./Col. dev.; 16. Adult srvs.; 17. Admin.; 18. Apprais.; 19. Archit./Bldgs.; 20. Cat./Class.; 21. Chld. srvs.; 22. Circ.; 23. Cons./Pres.; 24. Consult.; 25. Cont. ed.; 26. Educ. lib. sci.; 27. Ext. srvs.; 28. Fund/Grants; 29. Gvt. pubs.; 30. Indx./Abs.; 31. Instr. lib. use; 32. Media srvs.; 33. Micro.; 34. Netwks./Coop.; 35. Persnl.; 36. PR; 37. Publshg.; 38. Recs. mgt.; 39. Ref. srvs.; 40. Repro.; 41. Resrch.; 42. Review.; 43. Secur.; 44. Serials; 45. Spec. col.; 46. Tech. srvs.; 47. Trustees/Bds.; 48. YA srvs.; 49. (other).

Ramsaur, Barbara Ann Meyer (Mr. 23, 1936, Cincinnati, OH) Media Ctr. Spec., Elkton Mid. Sch., 1973–; Elem. Media Spec., Cecil Cnty. Pub. Schs., 1971–73; Catlgr., Narragansett Pub. Lib., 1963–64; Libn. II, Educ., Rel., and Phil., Enoch Pratt Free Lib., 1959–62. **Educ.:** Hanover Coll., 1954–58, AB (Eng., Fr.); Columbia Univ., 1958–59, MSLS; Towson State Univ., Univ. of MD, 1971–78, Cert. (Educ. Media Admin.). **Orgs.:** MD Lib. Assn.: *Crab,* Ed. Com. (1981–). ALA: AASL. Frnds. of the Cecil Cnty. Pub. Lib.: Secy. (1977–78); Pres. (1978–). Cecil Cnty. Speak Out on Libs. Com.: Co-ch. (1978–79). League of Women Voters. Natl. Educ. Assn. MD State Tchrs. Assn. Cecil Cnty. Classroom Tchrs. Assn. **Pubns.:** "Finding Your ID in I.D.," *AV Educ.* (D. 1974). **Activities:** 9, 10; 31, 32, 34; 63, 89 **Addr.:** 108 Jarmon Rd., Elkton, MD 21921.

Ramsey, Donna Elaine (O. 10, 1941, Charlotte NC) Asst. Serials Libn., NM State Univ., 1977; Head Libn., Friendship Jr. Coll., 1973–77; Ref./Circ./Serials Libn., Barber Scotia Coll., 1971–73. **Educ.:** Johnson C. Smith Univ., 1964–69, AB (Fr.); Atlanta Univ., 1970–71, MSLS. Additional course work at Kent State Univ., Univ. of NC, and NM State Univ., 1973–. **Orgs.:** Border Regional LA: News Corres. (1980–1981). ALA: LAMA, Women Admin. DG (Strg. Com., 1981–); Mem. Promo. Tsk. Frc. (1979–); SORT Mem. Ch., (1979–); SRRT, Task Frc. on Woman (Strg. Com., 1977–78). ALA Black Caucus: Const. and By-Laws Com. (1978–79); Southwest News Rpt. (1980–). NMLA. Other orgs. AAUW. AAUP. NAACP. Delta Sigma Theta. **Honors:** ACRL, Mellon/ACRL Mgt. Intern, 1975–76. **Pubns.:** *Brief Guide to Job Power* (1980). **Activities:** 1; 17, 33, 44 **Addr.:** Box 26495, El Paso, TX 79926.

Ramsey, Inez L. (Ap. 25, 1938, Martins Ferry, OH) Asst. Prof., Dept. of LS/Educ. Media, James Madison Univ., 1975–; Libn., Lucy Simms Elem. Sch. (Harrisonburg, VA), 1974–75; Libn., Iroquois Ctrl. Sr. HS (Elma, NY), 1971–73. **Educ.:** SUNY at Buffalo, 1968–71, BA (Hist.), 1971–72, MLS; Univ. of VA, 1974–80, EdD. **Orgs.:** ALA: AASL. VA LA: Chld. and YA RT, Exec. Bd. VA Educ. Media Assn.: Secy. (1981–82); Schol. and Awds. Com. (Ch., 1978–80); numerous other coms. VA State Lib. Bd. (1978–). Other orgs. Phi Beta Kappa(Shenandoah Reg.): Pres. (1980–81). MidAtl. Reg. Oral Hist. Assn. Natl. Assn. for the Prsrvn. and Perpet. of Storytel. **Honors:** Beta Phi Mu; Phi Delta Kappa. **Pubns.:** "Invite a Puppet to Your Classroom," *VA Eng. Bltn.,* (Win. 1979); "Children's Literature in the Child Development Curriculum," *Tips and Topics in Home Econ.* (Fall, 1979); "Puppetry," *AV Instr.* (S. 1979); "Information Sources," *Encyc. of Prof. Mgt.* (1978); oral hist. tapes and storyteller and puppeteer presentations. **Activities:** 10, 11; 17, 21; 86 **Addr.:** Dept. of Library Science & Educational Media, James Madison University, Harrisonburg, VA 22807.

Ramsey, Jack A. (Je. 12, 1922, Kansas City, KS) Dir., Glendale (CA) Pub. Libs., 1966–; Chief, Cust. Rel., H.W. Wilson Co., 1959–66; Dir., Glendale Pub. Libs., 1952–59; Libn., Solano Cnty. (CA) Libs., 1949–52 Admin. Asst. to Libn., Stockton and San Joaquin Cnty. Libs., 1948–49; Libn., NY Pub. Lib., 1947–48. **Educ.:** Univ. of KS, 1940–45, BA (Pol. Sci.); Univ. of IL, 1945–46, MS (LS), 1946–77, MS (Pol. Sci.). **Orgs.:** ALA. CA LA. SLA. Beta Phi Mu: Pres. (1966). **Activities:** 9; 17, 24, 37; 55, 56, 80 **Addr.:** 222 E. Harvard St., Glendale, CA 91205.

Rancer, Susan Plate (Ap. 6, 1942, Milwaukee, WI) Media Spec., McLeansville Mid. Sch., 1979–; Asst. Prof., LS, Appalachian State Univ., 1974–78; Libn., Marinette Cath. Ctrl. High, 1971–74; Tchr., Grade 5, St. Mark's, 1971; Tchr., various elem. schs., 1963–70. **Educ.:** Marian Coll. of Fond du Lac, 1959–68, BA (Elem. Educ.); Univ. of WI, Oshkosh, 1970–74, MA (LS); various post-grad. courses, 1976–78. **Orgs.:** ALA. Cath. LA. NC LA. SELA. NC Assn. of Educs. Educ. Media Assn. (NC). **Pubns.:** "Accountability and the School Media Center Director," *SEast. Libs.* (Spr. 1978). **Activities:** 10; 21, 32, 48; 55, 63 **Addr.:** 4000 Annie Laurie Dr., Greensboro, NC 27408.

Rancilio, James M. (Jl. 19, 1954, Detroit, MI) Branch Libn., Mt. Morris Branch Lib., Genesee Dist. Lib., 1981–; Lib., Media Spec., Grand Blanc Cmnty. Schs., 1976–81. **Educ.:** Wayne State Univ., 1972–76, BS (Educ.), 1977–80, MSLS. **Orgs.:** MI Assn. for Media in Educ.: Reg. Pres. (1979–80). ALA. MI LA. Puppeteers of Amer. Flint Area Readg. Assn. **Pubns.:** "The Puppets Are Coming," *Puppetry in Educ.* (D. 1978); "Creative Library/Media Programming," *Media Spectrum* (Win. 1978). **Activities:** 10; 15, 17, 31; 63 **Addr.:** 6098 Westknoll, Apt. 382, Flint, MI 48507.

Rand, Duncan Dawson (O. 28, 1940, Biggar, SK) Chief Libn., Lethbridge Pub. Lib., 1974–; Actg. Dir., London Pub. Lib. and Art Musm., 1973–74, Asst. Dir., 1971–73; Asst. Chief Libn., Regina Pub. Lib., 1969–71. **Educ.:** Univ. of SK, 1960–63; McGill Univ., 1963–64, BLS; 1965–68, Cert. (Persnl. Admin.). **Orgs.:** Can. Assn. of Pub. Libs.: Ch. (1976–77). Can. LA: Bd.; Cncl. (1976–77); Proj. Progress Strg. Com. (1975–80). LA AB: VP (1980–81). Rotary Club of Lethbridge. SK Geneal. Socty.: Pres. (1970–71). Lethbridge Cham. of Cmrce. **Pubns.:** Jt. ed., *Proceedings Prairie Conference on Library Standards for Canadian Schools* (1968); "Preventative Maintenance," *Can. Lib. Jnl.* (N.–D. 1973); "Library Management Views Library Unions," *Inst. of Prof. Libns. of ON Qtly.* (Ja.–Mr. 1974). **Activities:** 9; 25 **Addr.:** Lethbridge Public Library, 810 - 5 Ave. S., Lethbridge, AB T1J 4C4 Canada.

Rand, Paula D. (Mr. 14, 1949, Toronto, ON) Phys., Chem. Libn., Memorex Corp., 1979–; Head Libn., James F. Maclaren Limited, 1975–78; Catlgr., Univ. of Toronto, 1975. **Educ.:** McMaster Univ., 1968–72, BA (Geo.); Univ. of Toronto, 1973–75, MLS. **Orgs.:** SLA: San Andreas Chap. (Archvst., 1980–); San Fran. Bay Area Chap. **Pubns.:** *Quito: The Face of God* (1972). **Activities:** 12; 20, 30, 39; 60, 65, 88 **Addr.:** Memorex Corp. M.S. 00–27, 1200 Memorex Dr., Santa Clara, CA 95052.

Rand, Robin M. (Ag. 28, 1949, Hanover, NH) Dir. Lib. Srvs., ME Med. Ctr. Lib., 1981–; Med. Libn., Saginaw Hlth. Sci. Lib., 1977–81; Coord., Biomed. Lib. Prog., Univ. of CA, Ctrl. San Joaquin Valley, 1976–77; Ref. Libn., Univ. of CA, Los Angeles, Biomed. Lib., 1972–76. **Educ.:** Skidmore Coll., 1967–71, BA (Bio.); Univ. of Denver, 1971–72, MA (Libnshp.). **Orgs.:** Med. LA. MI Hlth. Sci. Libns.: Treas. (1979–). **Activities:** 12; 17, 36, 39; 58, 80 **Addr.:** Maine Medical Center Library, 22 Bramhall, Portland, ME 04102.

Randall, Ann Knight (New York City, NY) Asst. Univ. Libn., Brown Univ., 1977–; Asst. Prof., Chief Instr. Mtrls. Ctr., Brooklyn Coll., 1973–76; Lectr., Columbia Univ. Sch. of Lib. Srv., 1970–73; Instr., Ref. Libn., Queens Coll., CUNY, 1967–69. **Educ.:** Barnard Coll., 1959–63, BA (Pol. Sci.); Columbia Univ., 1965–67, MLS, 1969–77, DLS; various grad. crs. **Orgs.:** ALA: Cncl. (1980–84); ACRL/Educ. and Bhvl. Sci. Sect. (Ch., 1980–81). N. Atl. Hlth. Sci. Libns.: Ch. (1979–80). Med. LA: Chap. Cncl. Alternate. **Honors:** Beta Phi Mu, 1967. **Activities:** 1; 17 **Addr.:** Brown University, Sciences Library, Box I, Providence, RI 02912.

Randall, Doris (Cairns) (Ag. 17, 1921, Mazomanie, WI) Ref. Libn., Tulare Cnty. Lib., 1964–; Branch Libn., Rubidoux Riverside Cnty., City Lib., 1960–62; Cat., MI State Univ. Lib., 1957–59; Ref. Libn., Educ. Dept., Los Angeles Pub. Lib., 1951–52; Ref. Libn., Educ. Lib., Univ. of South. CA, 1950–51; Ref. Libn., Lansing Pub. Lib., 1946–50; Ref. Libn., Soc. Sci. Sect., IN Univ. Lib., 1944–46. **Educ.:** Univ. of WI, 1939–43, BA (Compar. Lit.), 1943–44, BLS. **Orgs.:** CA LA. ALA. United Methodist Women: CA-NV Conf., Nom. Com., (1979–81). Pub. Empl. Assn. of Tulare Cnty.: Treas. (1978–79). **Activities:** 1, 9; 16, 29, 39 **Addr.:** 2800 W. Laurel Ave., Visalia, CA 93277.

Randall, Gordon E. (Ap. 30, 1914, South Haven, MI) Retired, 1977–; Resrch. Div. Libn., IBM, 1960–77; Tech. Info. Branch Mgr., ARO, Inc., 1952–60; Asst. Chief, Ref. Branch, USAEC, 1948–52. **Educ.:** Univ. of Chicago, 1931–38, BA (Hum.); Univ. of IL, 1938–39, BS (LS). **Orgs.:** SLA: Bd. of Dirs. (1965–67); Sci.-Tech. Div. (Ch., 1962–63); *Sci.-Tech. News* Ed. (1958–60, 1964–67). **Pubns.:** 3 chaps., *Special Librarianship, A New Reader* (1980); chap., *Information Age* (1976); "Into the Information Age," *Jnl. of Lib. Hist.* (Win. 1980); "Budgeting for Libraries," *Spec. Libs.* (Ja. 1976). **Activities:** 12; 17 **Addr.:** 201 Sheri Dr., Martinez, GA 30907.

Randall, Michael H. (Ap. 3, 1945, Tulsa, OK) Asst. Head, Serials Dept., Univ. of CA, Los Angeles, 1975–, Catlgr., 1974–75; Catlgr., Univ. of CA, Santa Barbara, 1968–73. **Educ.:** Univ. of CA, Riverside, 1963–67, AB (Eng.); Univ. of CA, Los Angeles, 1967–68, MLS, 1973–75, MBA. **Orgs.:** ALA: AV Com. (1969–71). ASIS: Los Angeles Chap., Elec. Com. (Ch., 1981). CA Acad. and Resrch. Libns.: Secy. (1972–73). CA LA: Bylaws Com. (Ch., 1970–71); CA Socty. Libns. (Actg. Pres., 1971); Com. on Org. (1970–71); Lib. Dev. and Stans. Com. (1981); Tech. Srvs. Chap. (Treas., 1980). **Pubns.:** *Chicano Studies: Serials Holdings at UCLA* (1976); "Detective Magazines," *Serials Review* (O.–D. 1980); indxs., *CA Libn.* (1969–73); "Movie Magazines," *Serials Review* (Ap.–Je. 1980); "The Student Grades the Teacher," *Jnl. of Educ. for Libnshp.* (Fall 1968). **Activities:** 1; 33, 44, 46; 55, 83, 92 **Addr.:** Serials Dept., University Research Library, University of California, Los Angeles, CA 90024.

Randazzo, Corinne Ohlsen (S. 23, 1932, Vidalia, LA) Dir., Lib. Media Srvs., Natchez Adams Pub. Schs., 1966–; Instr., Univ. of South. MS, 1961–76; Libn., Natchez Adams HS, 1959–66; Libn., St. Martinville HS, 1954–59. **Educ.:** Univ. of Southwest. LA, 1950–54, BA (Elem. Educ., LS); LA State Univ., 1955–58, MS (LS); Univ. of South. MS, 1977–78, AAA Cert. (Educ. Media). **Orgs.:** MS Assn. of Media Educs. ALA. AECT. **Honors:** *Encyc. Britannica,* Natl. Finalist, Sch. Lib. Awd., 1969. **Activities:** 10; 17, 24; 63 **Addr.:** P.O. Box 1188, Natchez Schools, Natchez, MS 39120.

Randich, Karla Marlene (F. 7, 1950, Kingsport, TN) Dir., Pub. Srvs., Ref., CA West. Sch. of Law, 1973–. **Educ.:** Univ. of Cincinnati, 1968–72, BA (Grmn.); Kent State Univ., 1972–73, MLS; CA West. Sch. of Law, 1975–80, JD (law). **Orgs.:** AALL. South. CA Assn. of Law Libs. Lawyers Club: San Diego Women Lawyers. **Pubns.:** *Catalog of the Cryptography Collection at Kent State University* (1973). **Activities:** 1, 10; 31, 33, 39; 55, 77, 78 **Addr.:** California Western School of Law 350 Cedar St., San Diego, CA 92101.

Randolph, Virginia S. (My. 12, 1932, Huntsville, AL) Head of Pub. Srvs., Spec. Col. Libn., Pepperdine Univ., 1979–; Head, Spec. Col., Morehead State Univ., 1975–79 and Dept. of LS, 1974–79; Eng. Dept., Pepperdine Univ., 1968–70. **Educ.:** Pepperdine Univ., 1966–68, BA (Eng.); Morehead State Univ., 1971–73, MA (Eng.); Univ. of KY, 1974–1976, MS (LS). **Orgs.:** SAA. CA LA. Phi Alpha Theta. **Honors:** Beta Phi Mu; Phi Kappa Phi. **Activities:** 1; 39, 45, 49-Univ. Eng. Dept. tchr.; 55, 63, 85 **Addr.:** 43 North Pinewood Ave., Agoura, CA 91301.

Raney, Leon (Ja. 14, 1939, Charleston, AR) Dean of Libs., SD State Univ., 1972–; Asst. Dir. for Tech. Srvs., Univ. of OK, 1967–69, Acq. Libn., 1966–69; Head, Cat. Dept., AR State Univ., 1964–66; Head Libn., Grant Par. (LA)., 1962–64; Tchr., Paris (AK) HS, 1960–61. **Educ.:** Univ. of Ctrl. AR, 1956–60, BS (Hist.); LA State Univ., 1961–62, MS (LS); IN Univ., 1969–72, PhD (LS). **Orgs.:** ALA: Cncl. (1978–). SD LA: Acad. Sect. (Ch., 1974). Mt. Plains LA. Bibl. Ctr. for Resrch, Inc.: Bd. of Dirs. (1977–). SD State Lib.: Adv. Cncl. (1976–). Rotary. **Honors:** Beta Phi Mu; Phi Delta Kappa; Phi Kappa Phi. **Pubns.:** *Adaptibility of an Approval Plan to Medium-sized Academic Library* (1972); *South Dakota Farm and Home Research* (1976). **Activities:** 1; 17, 19, 46; 56, 63, 92 **Addr.:** 2021 Derdall Dr., Brookings, SD 57006.

Rankin, Jocelyn A. (O. 12, 1946, Raleigh, NC) Dir., Med. Lib., Mercer Univ. Sch. of Med., 1974–; Actg. Dir., Georgetown Univ. Med. Ctr. Lib., 1972–73, Pub. Srvs. Libn., 1969–74; Asst. Libn., Med. Coll. of GA Lib., 1968–69. **Educ.:** Amer. Coll., Paris, 1963–65, Dip.; Hollins Coll., 1965–67, BA (Eng.); Emory Univ., 1967–68, MS (LS); Med LA, 1975, Cert. **Orgs.:** Assn. of Acad. Health Sci. Lib. Dirs. GA Hlth. Scis. LA: Ch. (1980–81); Ch.–Elect (1979–80); Secy. (1978–79). GA LA: Constn. and Bylaws Com. (1980–81). Hlth. Sci. Libs. of Ctrl. GA: Secy. (1975–77); Statistician (1979–). Southeast. Reg. Med. Lib. Prog.: Adv. Com. Various other assns. **Pubns.:** "The Library Consortium – Service for Community Hospitals in Georgia," *Jnl. of the Med. Assn. of GA* (D. 1980); "Georgia's Newest Consortium – HSLCG," *GA Libn.* (My. 1977); "The New Look in Manuscripts," *Spec. Libs.* (1970). **Activities:** 1, 12; 15, 17, 34; 80 **Addr.:** Medical Library, Mercer University School of Medicine, Macon, GA 31207.

Ransom, Christina Roxane (O. 28, 1951, Manhattan, NY) Mgr., Info. Ctr., Ayerst Labs., Inc., 1979–; Consult., Sci. and Tech. Info. Ctr., Corning Glass, 1978; Tax Libn., White and Case, 1976–78; Lib. Asst., Winthrop, Stimson, Putnam and Roberts, 1974–76. **Educ.:** Bard Coll., 1969–73, BA (Chem.); Columbia Univ., 1973–74, MLS; 1979–80, Trng. in Dialog, SDC, BRS, Chem. Abs. **Orgs.:** Pharm. Mfrs. Assn.: Info. Subsect. SLA. ASIS. Med. LA. Assoc. Info. Mgrs. **Activities:** 12; 15, 17, 20; 87 **Addr.:** Information Center, Ayerst Labs., Inc., Rouses Point, NY 12979.

Ransom, Stanley Austin Jr. (Ja. 24, 1928, Winsted, CT) Dir., Clinton-Essex-Franklin Lib. Syst., 1974–; Dir., Huntington (NY) Pub. Lib., 1958–74, Asst. Dir., 1956–58; Catlgr., NY Pub. Lib., 1951–56. **Educ.:** Yale Univ., 1951, BA (Hist., Eng.); Columbia Univ. 1951–53, MLS. **Orgs.:** NY LA: Pres. (1972–73); VP (1971–72); State Mem. Ch. (1970–71); Vice-Ch., Legis. Com. (1977–80). ALA. N. Country Ref. and Resrch. Resrcs. Cncl., Secy., Bd. of Trustees, (1976–). Pub. Lib. Syst. Dirs. Org. (Secy., 1977–78). Numerous other orgs. and ofcs. Olympic and Win. Sports Musm.: Chrt. mem., Bd. of Trustees (1979–). Plattsburgh Rotary Club. Clinton Cnty. Hist. Assn. Kent DeLord Hse. Musm. **Honors:** Amer. Assn. for State and Lcl. Hist., Cert. of Cmdn., 1972. **Pubns.:** *America's First Negro Poet; Jupiter Hammon of Long Island* (1970); "The Rural Imperative: New York's Public Library Systems Face the Challenge," *Bkmark* (Spr. 1980); Jt. auth., "An Apple Every Day; Kids and Computers in the Public Library," *Bkmark* (Spr. 1981); jt. auth., "An Apple a Day; Microcomputers in the Public Library," *Amer. Libs.* (D. 1980); Ed., *Suffolk Cnty. LA Data* (1957–58, 1961–62). **Activities:** 9; 17, 23, 34; 56, 89, 93 **Addr.:** P.O. Box 570, Plattsburgh, NY 12901.

Ranz, Jim (Jl. 21, 1921, Atlanta, NE) Dean of Libs., Univ. of KS, 1975–; VP for Acad. Affairs, Univ. of WY, 1964–75; Univ. Libn., Univ. of BC, 1962–64; Dir. of Libs., Univ. of WY, 1955–62. **Educ.:** NE State Coll., 1938–42, BS; Univ. of MI, 1946–48, MALS; Univ. of IL, 1955–1960, PhD (LS). **Orgs.:** Bibl. Ctr. for Resrch.: Trustee (1979–). OCLC Inc.: Users' Cncl. (1979–). KS Lib. Netwk.: Cncl.; Pres.–Elect (1980). N. Ctrl. Assn. of Colls. and Sec. Schs.: Comsn. (1972–75); Consult. and Examiner (1969–). **Pubns.:** *Printed Book Catalogues in American Libraries: 1723-1900* (1964). **Activities:** 1; 15, 17, 20 **Addr.:** 516 Rock Fence, Lawrence, KS 66044.

Raper, James E. Jr. (Ag. 14, 1945, Rocky Mount, NC) Tech. Srvs. Libn., Levy Lib., Mt. Sinai Med. Ctr., 1980–; Reg. Coord., Tech. Srvs., NY and NJ Reg. Med. Lib. Prog., NY Acad. of Med., 1979–80; Head, Tech. Srvs., Med. Lib. Ctr. of NY, 1970–80; various positions, Univ. of NC, 1965–70. **Educ.:** Univ. of NC, 1963–67, BA (Eng.), 1968–70, MSLS; Columbia Univ., 1973 (Biomed. Comm.). **Orgs.:** ALA. Med. LA: Natl. Issues Adv. Cncl. (1979–); Com. on Cat. Descr. and Access (Rep., 1979–); various coms., NY Reg. Grp., Jt. Legis. Com. (Ch., 1979–80), Exec. Com. (1978–79), Regis. Com. (Ch., 1975). Hlth. Sci. OCLC Users Grp.: Cat. Code Rev. Com. (Ch., 1979–81); Secy.-Treas. (1977–78). NY Tech. Srvs. Libns. **Honors:** Beta Phi Mu,

Special Subjects/Services: 50. Adult educ.; 51. Advert./Mktg.; 52. Aerosp.; 53. Agric.; 54. Area std.; 55. Arts/Hum.; 56. Autom.; 57. Bibl./Prtg.; 58. Bio. sci.; 59. Bus./Fin.; 60. Chem.; 61. Copyrt.; 62. Documtn.; 63. Educ.; 64. Engin.; 65. Env.; 66. Eth. grps.; 67. Film; 68. Food/Nutr.; 69. Geneal.; 70. Geo.; 71. Geol.; 72. Handcpd.; 73. Hist.; 74. Int. frdm.; 75. Info. sci.; 76. Insr.; 77. Law; 78. Legis.; 79. Math./Comp. sci.; 80. Med.; 81. Metals; 82. Nat. resrcs.; 83. Newsp.; 84. Nuc. sci.; 85. Oral hist.; 86. Petr./Energy; 87. Pharm.; 88. Phys./Astr./Math.; 89. Readg.; 90. Relig.; 91. Sci./Tech.; 92. Soc. sci.; 93. Telecom.; 94. Transp.; 95. (other).

1970. **Pubns.:** Ed., *Union Catalog of Medical Monographs and Multimedia,* (1979); prod. coord., *Union Catalog of Medical Audiovisuals* (1979); " 'The Centralized Automated Cataloging of Health Science Materials...,' Buying New Technology," *Lib. Jnl.* (1978); "Centralized Automated Cataloging of Health Science Materials in the MLC/SUNY/OCLC Shared Cataloging Service," *Bltn. Med. LA* (Ap. 1977); cmplr., *PHILSOM Coding Manual* (1973); ed., *Author Catalog of Monographs* (1972); ed., *Periodicals and Other Serials Held by the Libraries of the University of North Carolina* (1970); ed., various mono. **Activities:** 1, 12; 15, 20, 44; 56, 75, 80 **Addr.:** Levy Library, The Mount Sinai Medical Center, 100th St. and 5th Ave., New York, NY 10029.

Raphael, Molly (N. 4, 1945, Columbus, OH) Asst. to the Dir., DC Pub. Lib., 1981–, Asst. Libn. and Chief, Phil. Div., 1979–81; Chief, Phil. Div., 1978–79, Chief, Telephone Ref. Div., 1977–78, Readers' Adv., Biog. Div., 1972–77 Chld. Libn., Chevy Chase Br., 1970–72; Asst. Libn., Wilbraham (MA) Pub. Lib., 1969–70. **Educ.:** Oberlin Coll., 1963–67, AB (Psy.) Simmons Coll., 1968–69 MSLS. **Orgs.:** ALA: ASCLA/Lib. Srv. to the Deaf Sect., Strg. Com. (1978–80), Com. on Lib. Srv. to the Deaf (1976–78); RASD, Srvs. to Adults Com. (1977–81); LAMA/LOMS: Budgeting, Acctg. & Costs Com. (1981–); PLA/MLS: Fiscal Emergency Com., (1980–). DC LA. Metro Washington Cncl. of Gvts.: Task Frc. on Lib. Srv. to the Deaf (1977–). Public Citizen. Common Cause. Consumers Un. **Pubns.:** "Deaf Awareness at the District of Columbia Public Library," PLA *Nsltr.* (Win.-Spr. 1976); "Serving the Deaf: A New Section Strong," *Interface* (Fall 1979). **Activities:** 9; 16, 17, 39; 72 **Addr.:** District of Columbia Public Library, 901 G Street, N.W., Washington, DC 20001.

Rapp, Barbara A. (N. 10, 1953, Cincinnati, OH) Online Spec., Inst. for Sci. Info., 1980–; Libn., Natl. Lib. of Med., 1978–80. **Educ.:** IL State Univ., 1971–75, BA (Fr.); Univ. of IL, 1977–78, MS (LS). **Orgs.:** ASIS: Mem. Com. (1979–80); Prof. Com. (1980–81); IL Student Chap. Org. and Pres., (1978). **Pubns.:** Jt. auth., "Automated Information Retrieval in Science and Technology," *Sci.* (Ap. 4, 1980); jt. auth., "Searching MEDLINE in English: A Prototype Interface with Natural Language Query, Term Weighting, and Relevance Feedback", Prcs. ASIS Anl. Mtg. (1979). **Activities:** 4; 30, 41; 56, 75, 80 **Addr.:** National Library of Medicine, 8600 Rockville Pike, Bethesda, MD 20209.

Rapp, Robert Franz (F. 4, 1949, Milwaukee, WI) Outrch. Srvs. Libn., Maude Shunk Lib., 1977–. **Educ.:** Univ. of WI, 1967–71, BA (Phil.), 1973–74, MA (LS), 1978, Sem. on Lib. Srv. to Aging. **Orgs.:** WI LA: Outrch. Srvs. RT (VP, 1979; VP/Pres.-Elect, 1981–82); Bylaws Rev. Com. (Ch., 1979). **Activities:** 9; 16, 27, 39; 55, 72, 95-Aging/Grntlgy. **Addr.:** Maude Shunk Public Library, P.O. Box 347, Menomonee Falls, WI 53051.

Rappaport, Gersten (D. 1, 1920, New York, NY) Asst. Libn., Fordham Univ. Law Lib., 1973–; Acq. Libn., Upsala Coll., 1967–73; Asst. Libn., Cornell Univ. Law Lib., 1966–67; Ref. Libn., Columbia Univ. Law Lib., 1963–66. **Educ.:** IN Univ., 1938–42, AB (Hist.); Yale Univ., 1942–47, JD; Columbia Univ., 1962–63, MLS. **Activities:** 77 **Addr.:** 26 Kendall Ave., Maplewood, NJ 07040.

Rappaport, Miriam W. (Jl. 29, 1923, New York, NY) Consult., Self-empl., 1980–; Mgr., Tech. Data Ctr., OSHA, Dept. of Labor, 1977–79, 1971–75; Conf. Planner, White Hse. Conf. on Handcpd., 1977; Chief, Natl. Clearinghse. on Child Abuse and Neglect, HEW, 1975–77. **Educ.:** Rutgers Univ., 1938–42, LittB (Jnlsm.); Amer. Univ., 1971, MA (Spec. Educ.); Stanford Univ., 1974, Cert. (Soc. Mgt. of Tech.); Univ. of WA, 1974, Cert. (Phys. Therapy). **Orgs.:** ASIS. **Honors:** Univ. of WA, Flwshp., 1973. **Pubns.:** Jt. auth., *Fire Extinguishment in Oxygen Enriched Atmospheres* (1972); *ASRDI Fire Safety Information Activities* (1971–72); "Technology for the Handicapped," *Procs. of White Hse. Conf. on Handcpd.* (Ap. 1977); "Information Services and Assistance for Transshippers of Hazardous Materials," *Natl. Resrch. Cncl.* (O. 1975); "Citation Patterns in Selected Core Journals," *Ctr. for Appld. Ling.* **Activities:** 4; 17, 24, 36; 58, 72, 91 **Addr.:** 8904 Connecticut Ave., Chevy Chase, MD 20015.

Rappelt, John F. (Ja. 11, 1927, Brooklyn, NY) Libn., Jr. HS, Brentwood Pub. Schs., 1973–; Cnty. Law Libn., Supreme Ct. Law Lib., Riverhead, NY, 1973; Libn., Jr. High, S. Huntington Schs., 1965–72; YA Libn., Los Angeles Pub. Lib., 1965; Bkmobile. Libn., San Jose Pub. Lib., 1964; Libn., Jr. High, Uniondale Pub. Schs., 1961–64; Libn., Ref., Readrs. Adv., Franklin Sq. Pub. Lib., 1961. **Educ.:** St. John's Univ., NY, 1949–52, BBA (Mktg.); NY Univ., 1952–55, MS (Rtl.), 1955–57, MA (Educ.); Pratt Inst., 1959–61, MLS. **Orgs.:** ALA: Rcrt. Netwk. (1963–67); Conf.-Within-A-Conf. (1963). Nassau-Suffolk Sch. LA: Mem. Ch. (1971–72). Nassau Lib. Syst.: YA Bk. Review Com. (1962–64). Various cmnty. orgs. **Activities:** 9, 10; 17, 31, 48; 63, 77 **Addr.:** 17 Milland Dr., Northport, NY 11768.

Rapport, Leonard (Ja. 24, 1913, Durham, NC) Archvst., Natl. Arch., 1949–, Assoc. Ed., Documentary Hist. of the Ratif. of the Fed. Constn., Natl. Hist. Pubns. Comsn., 1958–69; Writer, Ed., South. Reg. Writers' Proj., 1938–41; Ed., Univ. of NC Press, 1935–38. **Educ.:** Univ. of NC, 1933–35, AB (Eng.); George Washington Univ., 1951–57, MA (Hist.). **Orgs.:** SAA. Ms. Socty. Org. of Amer. Histns. Amer. Assn. for State and Lcl. Hist. **Honors:** SAA, Fellow, 1970; NEH, Sr. Grant, 1970–71. **Pubns.:** Jt. auth., *Rendezvous With Destiny* (3rd ed., 1976); "Night the Bucket Fell," *VA Qtly. Review* (Sum. 1936); "Printing of the Constitution," *Prologue* (Fall 1970); "Dumped From a Wharf Into Casco Bay," *Amer. Archvst.* (Ap. 1974); "Fakes and Facsimiles," *Amer. Archvst.* (Ja. 1979); "No Grandfather Clause: Reappraising Accessioned Records," *Amer. Archvst.* (Spr. 1981); various articles. **Activities:** 2; 57, 62 **Addr.:** 3510 Macomb St. N.W., Washington, DC 20016.

Rapske, Arnold (Ja. 17, 1928, Berestowitz, Wolyn, Poland) Libn., N. Amer. Bapt. Coll. Lib., 1977–, Prof., Christ. Educ., 1958–77; Pastor, Flwshp. Bapt. Church, Camrose, AB, 1956–58. **Educ.:** Univ. of AB, 1952, BA; North. Bapt. Theo. Semy., 1952–55, BD, 1955–56, ThM; South. Bapt. Theo. Semy., 1962–63, MRE; Univ. of AB, 1971, BEd, 1977–, MLS Cand. **Orgs.:** AB Cncl. of Coll. Libns. AB Christ. Libns. Flwshp. Christ. Libns. Flwshp. **Pubns.:** *Objectives of Christian Education* (1967); "Preparing a Building Proposal Statement," *Christ. Libn.* (F. 1980). **Activities:** 1, 2; 15, 17, 19; 90 **Addr.:** North American Baptist College/ Divinity School Library, 11523–23 Ave., Edmonton, AB T6J 4T3 Canada.

Rasche, Richard R. (Ap. 20, 1916, Uhrichsville, OH) Cur., Hist. of Med., Arch., Univ. of TX, Galveston, 1974–; Serials Catlgr., South. IL Univ., Carbondale, 1965–74. **Educ.:** AZ State Univ., Tempe, 1961–64, BA (Hum.); Univ. of IL, 1964–65, MSLS. **Orgs.:** ALA: ACRL. West. Hist. Assn. West. Lit. Assn. E. End Hist. Dist. Assn. **Activities:** 1; 20, 45; 80 **Addr.:** 1203 Broadway, Galveston, TX 77550.

Rasmussen Gordon E. (D. 13, 1932, Highland Park, MI) Circ. Libn., North. IL Univ., 1961–; Tchr., Adams Cnty., CO, Wheaton Pub. Schs., 1955–60. **Educ.:** N. Ctrl. Coll., 1950–54, BA (Eng.); Univ. of Denver, 1960–61, MA (LS); Univ. of IL, 1966–67, Cert. Advnc. Std. (LS). **Orgs.:** ALA. IL LA. AAUP. **Activities:** 1; 22, 27 **Addr.:** Circulation, Library, Northern Illinois University, DeKalb, IL 60115.

Rasmussen, Jane Hoffman (Ap. 4, 1939, Chicago, IL) Libn. Chemical Mfrs. Assn., 1976–; Libn., Tehran Amer. Sch., 1972–74; Libn., Inst. for Adult Litcy. Methods, 1971–72; Libn., Sidwell Frnds. Sch., 1970. **Educ.:** Georgetown Univ., 1956–60, BSFS (Intl. Rel.); Univ. of Valladolid, 1961–62, Cert. (Span.); Univ. of MD, 1967–69, MLS. **Orgs.:** SLA Law Libns. Soc. of Wash., DC. **Honors:** Beta Phi Mu. **Activities:** 12; 60, 77 **Addr.:** Library, Chemical Manufacturers Association, 2501 M St., N.W., Washington, DC 20037.

Rasmussen, Lane D. (My. 14, 1940, Murray, UT) Asst. Soc. Sci. Libn., VA Polytech. Inst. and State Univ., 1977–; Asst. Bus. Libn., IN Univ., 1971–77. **Educ.:** Brigham Young Univ., 1958–60, 1963–66, BA (Russ.); IN Univ., 1966–69, MA (Slavic), 1969–71, MLS. **Orgs.:** SLA: Bus. and Fin. Div.; VA Chap. VA LA. **Honors:** Phi Eta Sigma; Phi Kappa Phi. **Activities:** 1; 15, 39; 59 **Addr.:** Newman Library, Virginia Polytechnic Institute and State University, Blacksburg, VA 24061.

Rassam, G. N. (Jl. 11, 1943, Iraq) Chief Ed., GeoRef., Amer. Geo. Inst., 1973–; Geo. Resrch., Elf Oil Co., 1970–71; Comsn., Iraq Atomic Energy Comsn., 1969–71; Geologist Iraq Natl. Oil Co., 1969–70; Asst. Prof., Youngstown State Univ., 1966–69. **Educ.:** Baghdad Univ., 1956–60, BS (Geol.); Miami Univ., 1961–63, MS (Geol.); Univ. of MN, 1963–67, PhD (Geol.); George Washington Univ., 1978–81 (Bus. Admin.). **Orgs.:** ASIS. Assn. of Earth Sci. Eds. Geosci. Info. Socty. Geol. Socty. of Iraq: Pres. (1969). **Honors:** Fulbright Schol., 1961. **Pubns.:** "Computer-assisted Editing," *Geosci. Info.* (1979); "A Joint Database in Geology," *Intl. Geol. Congs.* (1980). **Activities:** 11, 12; 24, 30; 57, 82, 86 **Addr.:** American Geological Institute, 5205 Leesburg Pike, Falls Church, VA 22041.

Rast, Elaine Kirkpatrick (Ag. 28, 1933, Chicago, IL) Head, Autom. Recs. Dept., North. IL. Univ., 1980–; Asst. Head, 1970–80; Head, Reg. Campus, Tech. Srvs., OH State Univ., 1968–70, Gen. Catlgr., 1966–67; Ref. Libn., Kansas City (MO) Pub. Lib., 1964–66. **Educ.:** Concordia Coll., 1951–56, BS (Educ.); Rosary Coll., 1956–63, MALS. Northwest. Univ., 1959–60. **Orgs.:** OCLC Serials Cntrl. Adv. Com. OCLC Users Cncl. ALA. IL LA: Nom. Com. (1979–80). IL OCLC Users Grp.: Ch. (1980–81). Fed. of Bus. and Prof. Women. AAUW. Audubon Socty. **Honors:** Beta Phi Mu. **Pubns.:** "Library Services to Library Branch Campuses," *Lib. Resrcs. and Tech. Srvs.* (Fall, 1980). "Data Processing in the University Libraries," *NIU Libs.* (Spr. 1977). "Library Cooperation and Networking," *NIU Libs.* (Spr. 1979). "Conversation Strategies for a Machine-Readable Data Base" *IL. Libs.* (S. 1980). **Activities:** 1; 20, 44, 46; 70, 75, 82 **Addr.:** 304 Forsythe Ln., DeKalb, IL 60115.

Ratcliff, Marcia Goldstein (Ja. 18, 1948, Brooklyn, NY) Dir., CBS News Ref. Lib., 1977–; Mgr. of Lib. Srvs., 1972–77, Serials Libn., 1971–72. **Educ.:** State Univ. Coll. of NY Geneseo, 1966–70, BSLS; Univ. of Pittsburgh, 1970–71, MLS. **Orgs.:** SLA: NY City Chap., Finance Com. (1978–80), Audit Ch. (1979–80); Telecom. Div. Ch. (1979–80), Prog. Ch. (1977–78); Advert./Mktg. Div. Secy. (1976–78), PR Com. Ch. (1979–80), others. **Pubns.:** Ed. Bd., *What's New in Advertising and Marketing* (SLA) (1974–). **Addr.:** CBS News Reference Library, 524 W. 57th St., New York, NY 10019.

Rathbun, Margo C. Trumpeter (O. 21, 1943, Akron, OH) Asst. to the Dean for Mgt., Univ. of NM, Gen. Lib., 1978–; Lib. Dir., Lucius Beebe Meml. Lib., Wakefield, MA, 1974–78, Asst. Dir., 1972–74, Greenwood Branch Libn., 1971–72; Asst. Libn., Comm. Lib., Univ. of IL, 1970–71, Resrch. Assoc., Lib. Resrch. Ctr., 1967–70. **Educ.:** Muskingum Coll., 1961–65, AB (Fr.); Univ. of IL, 1965–67, MLS; Inst. for Amer. Univ., Aix-en-Provence, France, 1963–64, Cert. (Frgn. Std.). **Orgs.:** ALA: Stan. Com. on Lib. Educ., Trng. of Lib. Supportive Staff Subcom. (1978–81). State of NM: Cont. Lib. Educ. Adv. Cncl. (1980–81). SLA. NM LA. **Activities:** 1, 9; 17, 25, 35; 92 **Addr.:** University of New Mexico, General Library, Albuquerque, NM 87131.

Rather, Lucia J. (S. 12, 1934, Durham, NC) Dir. for Cat., Lib. of Congs., 1976–, Asst. Chief, MARC Dev. Ofc., 1973–76, Grp. Leader, 1966–73, Ref. Libn., 1964–66, Catlgr., 1957–64. **Educ.:** Westhampton Coll., 1951–53; Univ. of NC, 1953–55, AB (Hist.), 1955–57, MSLS. **Orgs.:** ALA. IFLA. UNIMARC Working Grp. (1971–75); Working Grp. on Corporate Headings (1976–79); Stdg. Com. on Cat. (Ch., 1977–79). **Honors** Phi Beta Kappa. **Pubns.:** Jt. auth., *The MARC II Format* (1968); "Exchange of Bibliographic Information in Machine Readable Form," *Lib. Trends* (Ja. 1977). **Activities:** 4; 17, 20, 34 **Addr.:** 10308 Montgomery Ave., Kensington, MD 20895.

Ratliff, Neil (Ag. 22, 1936, Greenville, MS) Fine Arts Libn., Head, Msc. Lib., Univ. of MD, 1980–; Acq., Ref. Libn., Msc. Div., NY Pub. Lib., 1963–80. **Educ.:** Southeast. LA Univ., 1955–59, BM (Msc.); IN Univ., 1959–63, (Msclgy.); Columbia Univ., 1965–68, MS (LS). **Orgs.:** Msc. LA: Pubns. Com. (1978–); Jt. Com. with Msc. Publshrs. Assn. (1978–). Intl. Assn. of Msc. Libs.: *Fontes Artis Musicae* Amer. Correspondent (1968–74); U.S. Exec. Bd. (1981). Mod. Grk. Std. Assn. The Bohemians. Amer. Msclgy. Socty. NY Musicians Club. **Pubns.:** Jt. ed., *The Little Book of Louis Moreau Gottschalk* (1976); "Introduction," *Handbuch der musikalischen Litteratur* reprint (1975); "Resources for Music Research in Greece," *Msc. LA Notes* (S. 1979); "Music Libraries in Greece," *Diavazo* (Ag.-S. 1979); "Modern Greek Folk Music and Dance in The New York Public Library," *Msc. LA Notes* (Je. 1974). **Activities:** 1, 9; 15, 17; 57, 66, 95-Msc. **Addr.:** Hornbake Library, University of Maryland, College Park, MD 20742.

Ratliff, Priscilla (D. 26, 1940, Uniontown, PA) Supvsr., Tech. Info., Ashland Chem. Co., 1978–, Resrch. Chem., Info. Spec., 1976–78; Tech. Writer, Warren-Teed Pharm., 1973–76; Info. Sci., Battelle-Columbus Labs., 1967–73; Asst. Ed., Chem. Abs. Srv., 1964–67. **Educ.:** Maryville Coll., 1958–62, BS (Chem.); Vanderbilt Univ., 1962–64, MS (Chem.). **Orgs.:** ASIS. SLA. Frnds. of the Libs. of OH State Univ.: Corp. rep. (1978–). Amer. Chem. Socty. **Activities:** 12; 17, 39; 60 **Addr.:** Ashland Chemical Co., P.O. Box 2219, Columbus, OH 43216.

Raudenbush, Jeanne Caldwell (Mr. 20, 1947, New York City, NY) Pres., Info. Mgt. Specs., Inc., 1974–. **Educ.:** CT Coll., 1965–69, BA (Bot.); Univ. of Denver, 1971–72, MA (Libnshp.). **Orgs.:** CO LA: Legis. Com. (1978–80). Frnds. of the Denver Pub. Lib.: Pres. (1979–80). ASIS. Assn. of Recs. Mgrs. and Admins. Denver Intl. Film Fest. **Honors:** Beta Phi Mu, 1972. **Pubns.:** Jt. auth., *COIN: An Indexed Checklist of Colorado State Publications* (1976–80). **Activities:** 14-Consult.; 24, 38, 39; 65, 77, 91 **Addr.:** Information Management Specialists, Inc., 1816 Race St., Denver, CO 80206.

Raum, Hans L. (Jl. 26, 1940, Philadelphia, PA) Assoc. Libn., Middlebury Coll., 1975–; Head of Pub. Srvs., Castleton State Coll., 1971–75; Assoc. Undergrad. Libn., PA State Univ., 1967–71, Ref. Asst., 1965–67. **Educ.:** PA State Univ., 1958–62, BA (Pol. Sci.); Drexel Univ., 1962–64, MSLS. **Orgs.:** ALA: RASD/Hist. Sect. (Secy., 1979–). New Eng. LA: Coll. Libs. Sect. (Ch., 1974). VT LA: Int. Frdm. Com. (1975–76). **Pubns.:** Jt. auth., *Directory of State and Local History Periodicals* (1977). **Activities:** 1; 29, 39 **Addr.:** Starr Library, Middlebury College, Middlebury, VT 05753.

Rausch, G. Jay (Ap. 9, 1930, Aurora, IL) Dean of Libs., KS State Univ., 1973–; Dir. of Libs., Drake Univ., 1968–73; Chief, Soc. Sci. Div., Lib., WA State Univ., 1962–68. **Educ.:** N. Ctrl. Coll., 1949–55, BA (Psy.); Univ. of IL, 1955–61, MA (Hist.), PhD (Hist.), MLS. **Orgs.:** ALA. KS LA. **Pubns.:** *The Detective Short Story: A Bibliography and Index* (1974); various articles. **Activities:** 1; 17, 34 **Addr.:** Farrell Library, Kansas State University, Manhattan, KS 66506.

Rausch, Lynn L. (J. 7, 1946, St. Paul, MN) Head. Tech. Srvs. Loras Coll., 1979–; Acq. Libn. Law Sch. Lib., Univ. of Notre Dame, 1973–76; Ref. Libn., Great Falls (MT) Pub. Lib., 1972–73. **Educ.:** Trinity Coll., 1966–68, AB (Hist.) University of MD, 1971–72, MLS; IA State Univ.; 1976–79, MA (Eng.). **Orgs.:** ASIS. SLA: Lib. Mgt. Div. Story County Open Line. **Pubns.:** "Economic Challenges and the Manager of the Small Library" *Lib. Mgmt. Bltn.* (Sp. 1981). **Activities:** 1, 12; 17, 41, 46; 56, 62, 75 **Addr.:** Wahlert Library, Loras College, Dubuque, IA 52001.

PROFESSIONAL ACTIVITIES: Institutions: 1. Acad. lib.; 2. Arch.; 3. Assn.; 4. Fed./Gvt. lib.; 5. Inst. lib.; 6. Mfr./Suppl.; 7. Milit. lib.; 8. Musm.; 9. Pub. lib.; 10. Sch. lib.; 11. Sch. of lib. sci.; 12. Spec. lib.; 13. State lib.; 14. (other). **Functions/Activities:** 15. Acq./Col. dev.; 16. Adult srvs.; 17. Admin.; 18. Apprais.; 19. Archit./Bldgs.; 20. Cat./Class.; 21. Chld. srvs.; 22. Circ.; 23. Cons./Pres.; 24. Consult.; 25. Cont. ed.; 26. Educ. lib. sci.; 27. Ext. srvs.; 28. Fund/Grants; 29. Gvt. pubs.; 30. Indx./Abs.; 31. Instr. lib. use; 32. Media srvs.; 33. Micro.; 34. Netwks./Coop.; 35. Persnl.; 36. PR; 37. Publshg.; 38. Recs. mgt.; 39. Ref. srvs.; 40. Repro.; 41. Resrch.; 42. Review.; 43. Secur.; 44. Serials; 45. Spec. col.; 46. Tech. srvs.; 47. Trustees/Bds.; 48. YA srvs.; 49. (other).

Rauschenberger, Douglas B. (Ja. 28, 1952, Sellersville, PA) Dir., Haddonfield Pub. Lib., 1981, Head, Ref. Srvs., 1974–81. **Educ.:** Gettysburg Coll., 1969–73, AB (Hist.); Drexel Univ., 1973–74, MS (LS). **Orgs.:** NJ LA: Ref. Sect., Treas. (1979–80), VP (1980–81), Pres. (1981–82). ALA. **Honors:** Beta Phi Mu. **Activities:** 9; 15, 16, 39 **Addr.:** Haddonfield Public Library, Haddonfield, NJ 08033.

Rawlins, Gordon Webb (My. 24, 1941, Logan, UT) Asst. Dean, Head Bibl. Resrcs. and Srvs., PA State Univ., 1979–, Dir., Lib. Comp. Srvs., 1977–79, Chief of Systs. Dev., 1969–79; Systs. Anal., Brigham Young Univ., 1968–69. **Educ.:** Brigham Young Univ., 1963–66, BA (Span.), 1966–68, MLS (Lib. and Info. Srv.). **Orgs.:** ALA: LITA. Pittsburgh Reg. Lib. Ctr.: Trustee (1975–). **Activities:** 1; 17, 34, 46; 56, 75, 91 **Addr.:** E511 Pattee Library, University Park, PA 16802.

Rawls, Molly Grogan (F. 18, 1949, Winston-Salem, NC) Mgr., Mgt. Info. Srvs., R. J. Reynolds Indus., Inc., 1979–, Mgt. Info. Lib., 1976–79, Mktg. Resrch. Libn., 1973–75. **Educ.:** Univ. of NC, 1969–71, BA (Eng.), 1971–72, MSLS. **Orgs.:** SLA: Sec. VP (1980–81). Natl. Micro. Assn.: Secy. (1977). Assn. of Recs. Mgrs. and Admins. **Activities:** 12; 17, 33, 38; 51, 59 **Addr.:** R.J. Reynolds Industries, Inc., 401 N. Main St., Winston-Salem, NC 27102.

Rawski, Conrad H. (My. 25, 1914, Vienna, Austria) Prof., Dean Emeritus, Sr. Resrch. Schol., Lib. and Info. Sci., Case West. Rsv. Univ., 1980–, Dean, Sch. of LS, 1977–80, Prof., 1967–80, Assoc. Prof., Coord., PhD Prog., 1962–67; Head, Fine Arts Dept., Cleveland Pub. Lib., 1957–62; Head, Fac. Lib. Com., Ithaca Coll., 1943–56, Col. Dev., Msc., Art, Phil., 1940–42; Widener Fellow, Harvard Univ., 1939–40; Asst., Austrian Natl. Lib., 1934–37; various tchg. positions, 1937–78. **Educ.:** Univ. of Vienna, Austria, 1932, AB, 1932–36, MA (Msclgy., Hist.), 1932–37, PhD (Msclgy., Hist.); Austrian Inst. for Hist. Resrch., 1938, Cert. (Libnshp.); Case West. Rsv. Univ., 1957, MS (LS); various grad. crs. **Orgs.:** Msc. LA. ASIS. ALA: ACRL/Spec. Sect., Art (Ch., 1964–65). AALS: Resrch. Com. (1970–). Various other orgs. Amer. Musicological Socty.: West. NY Chap. (Ch., 1948–56). Amer. Socty. for Aesthetics. West. Rsv. Univ.: Various coms. Case West. Rsv. Univ.: Various coms., chs. **Honors:** Fund for the Advnc. of Educ., Ford Fndn., Resrch. Fellow, 1952–53; Beta Phi Mu, Awd., 1979; Pi Kappa Lambda, 1955; Natl. Endow. for Hum., Resrch. Flwshp., 1979. **Pubns.:** "The Scientific Study of Subject Literatures," *Visible Language* (1977); "The Study of Medieval Music; An Analytic Approach to a Subject Literature," *Std.* (1976); "Notes on the Rhetoric in Petrarch's *Invective contra medicum*," *Francis Petrarch, Six Centuries Later: A Symposium* (1975); *Toward a Theory of Librarianship. Papers in Honor of Jesse H. Shera* (1973); contrib., ed., *Fundamental Issues of Librarianship* (1972); various reviews, *Boston Evening Transcript, Ithaca Jnl., Fine Msc., Musical Leader, Jnl. of the Amer. Musicological Socty., Cleveland Plain Dir.*, other pubns.; various articles and essays, *Jnl. of Educ. for Libnshp., Bltn. of the Cleveland Med. LA, Bibliophage*, other pubns.; various transls., TV and radio contribs. **Activities:** 9, 12; 26, 39, 41; 55, 62, 93 **Addr.:** The Matthew A. Baxter School of Information & Library Science, Case Western Reserve University, Cleveland, OH 44106.

Ray, C. Burnelle M. (Je. 3, 1950, Boston, MA) Instr., Instr. Libn., Gallaudet Coll., 1977–; Ref., Instr. Libn., Univ. of WI, Parkside, 1974–77. **Educ.:** Ripon Coll., 1968–72, BA (Span., Hist.); Univ. of WI, Milwaukee, 1973, MALS. **Orgs.:** ALA: Black Caucus, Orien. Com. (Ch. 1979–). DC LA. MA LA. Assn. of Black Interpreters. **Honors:** Inst. on Multicultural Libnshp., 1976. **Pubns.:** Jt. Auth., "Public Service Policy: U. of Wisc.-Parkside," *WI Lib. Bltn.* (My.-Je. 1975); *Library Skills Units* (1978); *A Study of Library Instruction Programs in Post-Secondary Facilities with Programs for the Deaf* (1980). **Activities:** 1, 12; 26, 31, 39; 63, 72 **Addr.:** Gallaudet College Library, 7th Street and Florida Ave. N.E., Washington, DC 20002.

Ray, David Tryon (Ap. 1, 1910, NY, NY) Asst. Prof. Emeritus, South. IL Univ., 1978–, Asst. Prof., 1959–78; Catlgr., Smithsonian Inst., 1953–59; Serials Biblgphr., U.S. Natl. War Coll., 1951–53; Frgn. Srv. Ofcr., U.S. Dept. of State, 1938–46. **Educ.:** Univ. of CA, Los Angeles, 1927–31 AB (Econ.); Yale Univ., 1947–49 (Ling.); Cath. Univ., 1946, BS (LS); South. IL Univ., 1961–67, MA (Phil.), 1973–79, MA (Ling.). **Orgs.:** ALA. Amer. Oriental Socty. Assn. for Asian Std. Audubon Socty. Amer. Assn. of Retired Persons. Un. Nations Assn. of the U.S.A. Frnds. of Buddhism. Various other orgs. **Honors:** Phi Kappa Phi. **Pubns.:** *Typeface Frequencies in Seven Indic Regional Scripts* (1964). **Activities:** 1; 20, 31, 44; 54, 55, 74 **Addr.:** 502 Orchard Dr., Carbondale, IL 62901.

Ray, Dee Ann (Mr. 28, 1938, Tulsa, OK) Lib. Dir., West. Plains Lib. Syst., 1966–; Dir. of Demonstration Srvs., MO State Lib., 1964–66; Fld. Consult. Libn., OK Dept. of Libs., 1960–63; Bkmobile. Libn., Tulsa City Cnty. Lib., 1959. **Educ.:** Univ. of Tulsa, 1956–59, BA (Mod. Lang.); Univ. of OK, 1959–60, MLS. **Orgs.:** OK LA: Treas. (1969–71); Pres.-Elect. (1971–72); Pres. (1973). ALA: Cnclr. at Lg. (1975–78); Small Libs. Pubn. Com. (1975–78); Newberry Caldecott Com. (1976–77). Bus. and Prof. Women's Assn. Custer Cnty. Hist. Socty. OK Hist. Socty. **Honors:** Person of the Yr., Clinton Cham. of Cmrce., 1980; OK LA, Disting. Srvs. Awd., 1974; Delta Kappa Gamma. Beta Sigma Phi, First Lady of Yr., 1974; Bus. and Prof. Women, Woman of the Yr. for Clinton, 1977. **Pubns.:** "Oklahoma Image," *RQ*; various articles, radio progs. **Activities:** 9; 17, 24, 36 **Addr.:** P.O. Box 1027, Clinton, OK 73601.

Ray, Inez Poe (Mr. 16, 1915, Apex, NC) Coord., Curric. Mtrls. Ctr., NC State Univ., 1965–; Libn., Wake Forest HS, 1963–65; KY Dam Libn., TN Valley Athrty., 1940–42; Libn., Reg. IV, Farm Secur. Admin., 1938–40. **Educ.:** Meredith Coll., 1931–35, AB (Eng.); Univ. of NC, 1937–38, AB (LS), 1965–70, MA (Eng.). **Orgs.:** ALA. NC LA. Leag. of Women Voters: Raleigh Chap. **Activities:** 1, 10; 15, 17, 48; 55, 63, 67 **Addr.:** 3401 Noel Ct., Raleigh, NC 27607.

Ray, Jean Meyer (S. 20, 1915, Cambridge, MA) Map and Asst. Sci. Libn., South. IL Univ. Lib., 1968–; Spec. Asst., U.S. Info. Srv. Lib., Bamako, Mali, 1967–68; Asst. Cat. Libn., South. IL Univ., 1961–66; Sr. Catlgr., Descr. Cat. Div., Lib. of Congs., 1950–59; Sr. Catlgr., Yale Univ., 1947–50; Catlgr., OR State Syst. Higher Educ., 1945–47. **Educ.:** Simmons Coll., 1932–36, BS (LS); Columbia Univ., 1941–45, MS (LS); South. IL Univ., 1969–76, MA (Geo.). **Orgs.:** ALA. SLA: Geo. and Map Div., Hons. Com. (1979–81). IL LA. IFLA: Non-voting Del. (1976). AAUP. AAUW. **Pubns.:** "The Future Role of the Academic Librarian," *New Horizons for Acad. Libs.* (1979); "From Aberdeen and Aberystwyth to Rome, from Lisbon to Helsinki," *SLA Geo. and Map Div. Bltn.* (Je. 1979); "Southern Illinois University Map Library," *ICarbS* (Spr.–Sum. 1978); "Who Borrows Maps from a University Library Map Collection - and Why?" *Spec. Libs.* (Mr. 1974; Ja. 1978); various other articles. **Activities:** 1, 4; 20, 39; 70, 91 **Addr.:** Morris Library, Southern Illinois University, Carbondale, IL 62901.

Ray, Joyce M. (D. 29, 1948, Mobile, AL) Spec. Cols. Libn., Univ. of TX Hlth. Sci. Ctr. at San Antonio, 1977–; Tech. Srvs. Libn., Tusculum Coll., 1974–76; Proj. Dir. of Archs. Grant for Natl. Hist. Pubns. and Recs. Comsn., 1976. **Educ.:** Univ. of Houston, 1967–70, BA (Eng.); Univ. of TX, Austin, 1972–74, MLS. **Orgs.:** SAA. Assn. of Libns. in the Hist. of the Hlth. Scis. Socty. of Southw. Archvsts. Med. LA: S. Ctrl. Reg. Grp. **Activities:** 1, 2; 23, 36, 45; 80, 85 **Addr.:** The Univ. of Texas Health Science Center Library, 7703 Floyd Curl Dr., San Antonio, TX 78284.

Ray, Kathryn Collison (N. 6, 1950, Washington, DC) Acq. Libn., The Brookings Inst., 1976–; Resrch. Libn., Agency for Intl. Dev., 1975–76; YA Libn., Arlington Cnty. VA Pub. Lib., 1974–75. **Educ.:** Mary Washington Coll., 1968–72, BA (Amer. Std.); Cath. Univ. of Amer., 1973–75, MS (LS); George Washington Univ., 1976–, PhD (Amer. Std.), 1980, MPhil. **Orgs.:** DC LA: Nom. Com. (1981); Hosplty. Ch. (1979–80); Docum. Grp. Prog. Com. (1978–79). SLA. ALA. Amer. Std. Assn. Frnds. of the Mary Washington Coll. Lib. Adv. Bd. Mid. E. Inst. Oral Hist. Assn. **Honors:** Pi Gamma Mu, 1972; Beta Phi Mu, 1975. **Activities:** 12; 15, 17, 29; 54, 92 **Addr.:** 1400 20th St., NW, #715, Washington, DC 200360.

Ray, Kenlee (My. 7, 1945, Allegan, MI) Head Libn., Exec. Dirs. Lib., World Bank, 1977–, Legal Libn., 1975–77; Libn., Sutherland, Asbill and Brennan, 1971–75; Libn., U.S. Cvl. Srv. Comsn., 1969–71. **Educ.:** Univ. of MI, 1963–67, BA (Soc. Std.), 1967–68, MLS. **Orgs.:** SLA: DC Chap. (Corres. Secy., 1979–80). Law Lib. Socty. of DC: Treas. (1973–75). Univ. of MI Club of DC. **Activities:** 2, 3; 17, 30, 39; 62, 77, 92 **Addr.:** World Bank Law Library, 1818 H St., N.W., Washington, DC 20433.

Rayburn, June H. (Je. 19, 1925, O'Donnell, TX) Libn., Meth. Hosp. and Sch. of Nursing, 1963–; Asst. Libn., Monterey HS, 1957–63. **Educ.:** Wayland Bapt. Coll., 1975–77, BS (Mgt.); various crs. **Orgs.:** Med. LA: S. Ctrl. Reg. Grp. (Secy.-Treas., 1976–77); Nursing Sect. (Ch., 1973–74). Meth. Hosp. Sch. of Nursing Fac. Org. Pilot Intl. **Activities:** 5, 12; 15, 16, 17; 61, 63, 80 **Addr.:** Methodist Hospital Library, 3615 19th St., Lubbock, TX 79410.

Raymond, Boris (D. 18, 1925, Harbin, Manchuria, China) Assoc. Prof., Sch. of Lib. Srvs., Dalhousie Univ., 1974–; Lectr. in Soclgy, Univ. of Winnipeg, 1970–74; Asst. Dir. of Libs., Univ. of MB, 1967–70; Serials Libn., Univ. of NV, 1966–67; Russ. Biblgphr., Univ. of CA, Berkley, 1964–66. **Educ.:** Univ. of CA, 1949, BA (Soclgy.), 1954, MA (Soclgy.), 1955, MLS; Univ. of MB, 1971, MA (Russ. Hist.); Univ. of Chicago, 1978, PhD (Libnshp.). **Orgs.:** ALA: LHRT. Can. LA. **Pubns.:** *Krupskaya and Soviet Librarianship* (1979). **Addr.:** Dalhousie University, School of Library Service, Halifax, NS B3H 4H8 Canada.

Rayward, W. Boyd (Je. 24, 1939, Inverell, New S. Wales, Australia) Dean., Grad. Lib. Sch., Univ. of Chicago, 1980–, Assoc. Prof., 1978–, Asst. Prof., 1975–78, Ed., *Lib. Qtly.*, 1975–79. **Educ.:** Univ. of Sydney, 1956–59, BA, hons. (Eng.); Univ. of New S. Wales, 1962–64, Dip. (LS); Univ. of IL, 1964–65, MS (LS); Univ. of Chicago, 1965–73, PhD (LS). **Orgs.:** ALA: ALSC, Resrch. Com. (1977–80); Lcl. Arrange. Com., Anl. Conf. (1978); PLA, Educ. for Pub. Libns. Com. (1979–80), Pub. Lib. Prins. Task Frc. (1980–) LA Australia: Assoc. **Honors:** Cncl. on Lib. Resrcs., Fellow, 1978. **Pubns.:** Ed., *The Variety of Librarianship; Essays in Honour of John Wallace Metcalf* (1976); ed., *The Public Library: Circumstances and Prospects* (1978); *The Universe of Information: The Work of Paul Otlet for Documentation and International Organisation* Russ. transl., *Universum informatsii Zhizn' i deiatl' nost ' Otle* (1975); various other articles. **Activities:** 11; 17, 26, 41; 57, 62 **Addr.:** Graduate Library School, University of Chicago, 1100 E. 57th St., Chicago, IL 60637.

Razer, Robert L. (Ap. 15, 1949, Little Rock, AR) Head, Tech. Srvs., Ctrl. AR Lib. Syst., 1976–; Ref. Libn., Univ. of TN Law Lib., 1973–76; Libn., AR Geol. Comsn., 1972–73. **Educ.:** Hendrix Coll., 1967–71, BA (Soc. Sci.); Univ. of TN, 1973–75, MSLS, 1974–76, MA (Hist.). **Orgs.:** ALA: Cncl. (1980–); Mem. Task Frc. (1980–). Natl. Libns. Assn.: Exec. Bd. (1980–); AR Mem. Coord. (1978–). SWLA. AR LA: Treas. (1979); PR Com. (Ch., 1979); various other ofcs., coms. AR Hist. Assn. Pulaski Cnty. Hist. Assn. Prepared Childbirth Inc. **Pubns.:** Ed., *AR Libs.* (1981–); "Good Reads: A Review of Recent Arkansiana," *AR Libs.* (S. 1979); "Arkansas Books and Authors," pamphlet (1977); ed., "Arkansas Books and Authors," *AR Libs.* (1976–); reviews. **Activities:** 9; 17, 42, 46; 59, 77, 92 **Addr.:** 2905 Dalewood, Little Rock, AR 72207.

Rea, Jay W. (O. 13, 1935, Litchfield, IL) Univ. Archvst., East. WA Univ., 1972–, Docum. Libn., 1972–, Cat. Libn., 1970–72. **Educ.:** Stanford Univ., 1953–57, BA (Hist.); Amer. Bapt. Semy. of the W., 1958–62, MDiv (Theo.); Univ. of OR, 1969–70, MLS (Arch. Admin.); various grad. crs. **Orgs.:** ALA: ACRL. SAA: Com. on Tech. for Cntrl. and Descr. of Arch. and Mss. (1972–74). NW Archvsts. Amer. Recs. Mgt. Assn.: Inland Empire Chap. (Secy., 1979–80). WA State Hist. Recs. Adv. Bd. Spokane Cnty. Inland Empire Cult. Ctr. WA State Data Netwk. East. WA Univ. Governance: Various coms., ofcs. **Pubns.:** Ed., *The Inland Empire In The Pacific Northwest: Historical Essays and Sketches* (1981); "The California State Archives: Administration, Legal Basis, Organization," ERIC (O. 1971); "The California State Archives: History and Resources," ERIC (O. 1971); "Subject Filing: A Review and Critique," ERIC (O. 1971); "The Record Group Concept," ERIC (O. 1971); various articles, presentations, reviews, edshps. **Activities:** 1, 2; 29, 38, 45; 83, 92, 95-Arch. admin. **Addr.:** Archives and Special Collections, Eastern Washington University Library, Cheney, WA 99004.

Read, Dennis Emory (Ja. 29, 1945, Orange, CA) Managing Ed., Indxs., Info. Access Corp., 1977–; Info. Srvs. Dept. Head, MS Lib. Comsn., 1976–77; Branch Mgr., Jackson Metro. Lib. Syst., 1973–76; Head, Tech. Lib., Litton Indus., 1972–73; Head, Ref. Srvs., Head, Mktg., Hughes Aircraft Co., 1967–72. **Educ.:** Univ. of OK, 1965–67, BA (LS), 1973–75, MLS. **Orgs.:** ASIS: South. Chap. (Ch., 1976–77); Chap. Asm. Rep. (1976–78); Outstan. Chap. Awd. Com. (1977–78). MS LA: Ctrl. W. Reg. (Ch., 1976–77); Int. Frdm. Com. (Ch., 1976–77); JMRT (Vice-Ch., 1974–75); various coms. Cnsrtm. for Lib. Autom. in MS. Bay Area OLUG. Lions Intl. **Honors:** MS LA, Outstan. Lib. Prog., 1975; MS LA, Outstan. Lib. Week Prog., 1975. **Pubns.:** *Manual of Indexing for Information Access Corporation Databases* (1978); chap., *Educational Media Yearbook* (1978); "State-wide Interlibrary Network: A Usage Study," *MS Lib. News* (1978); "Computer/Microform System for State Documents," *MS Lib. News* (1977); "America the Beautiful: A Slide/Tape Presentation" (1976). **Activities:** 9, 12; 17, 30, 39; 59, 75 **Addr.:** Information Access Corporation, 404 6th Ave., Menlo Park, CA 94025.

Read, Glenn F., Jr. (Mr. 13, 1931, Cincinnati, OH) Latin Amer. Std. Area Spec., IN Univ. Libs., 1976–; Latin Amer. Libn., Cornell Univ. Libs., 1964–76; Ref. Libn., Latin Amer. Hist., Amer. Hist. Div., NY Pub. Lib., 1962–64. **Educ.:** Univ. of CA, Berkeley, 1951–53, 1957–59, AB (Hist.), 1960–61, MA (Latin Amer. Hist.), 1961–62, MLS. **Orgs.:** ALA. SALAM: Bibl. Com. (Ch., 1967–70); Exec. Bd. (1970–73); VP (1970–71); Pres. (1971–72); Com. on Coop. Cat. (Ch., 1976–79); Nom. Com. (Ch., 1976–77); various coms. Latin Amer. Std. Assn. **Honors:** Beta Phi Mu. **Pubns.:** "Guidelines for Library Relations with Book Dealers," *SALALM Final Rpt. and Working Papers* (1976); "SALALM: Thoughts on the Birth and Development of an Organization," *Acquisitions from the Third World* (1975); "Latin American Studies and the University Libraries," *Cornell Univ. Libs. Bltn.* (Ja.–F. 1975); "Development of Criteria for Collections in Support of Area Studies Programs: With Emphasis on Latin America," *SALALM Final Rpt. and Working Papers* (1967); "The Inter-American Development Bank and Its Role in Supportive Economics and Development Research," *Gvt. Pubns. Review* (1979). **Activities:** 1, 11; 15, 26, 39; 54, 57, 75 **Addr.:** Indiana University Libraries E660, Bloomington, IN 47405.

Ready, William Bernard (S. 16, 1914, Cardiff, Wales) Univ. Libn. Consult., Prof. Emeritus, 1980–; Univ. Libn., McMaster Univ., 1966–80; Prof., Marquette Univ., 1956–65. **Educ.:** Wales Univ., 1935–39, BA; Univ. of MB, MA; Univ. of West. ON, MLS; Rutgers Univ., Radcliffe Univ., Dip. (Arch., Lib. Admin.). **Honors:** Univ. of Prince Edward Island, Litt. D., 1974; McMaster Univ., DLitt, 1980; Univ. of West. ON, D. Litt., 1980; Fellow, Libn., Royal Socty. 1974. **Pubns.:** "Losers Keepers," (1979); *Lib. Autom.* (1979); *Tolkien Relation* (1970); "Aegean Adventure" tape rec. (1978). **Activities:** 2, 11; 15, 16, 19; 50, 57, 77 **Addr.:** 2641 Capital Hts., Victoria, BC V8T 3M1 Canada.

Special Subjects/Services: 50. Adult educ.; 51. Advert./Mktg.; 52. Aerosp.; 53. Agric.; 54. Area std.; 55. Arts/Hum.; 56. Autom.; 57. Bibl./Prtg.; 58. Bio. sci.; 59. Bus./Fin.; 60. Chem.; 61. Copyrt.; 62. Documtn.; 63. Educ.; 64. Engin.; 65. Env.; 66. Eth. grps.; 67. Film; 68. Food/Nutr.; 69. Geneal.; 70. Geo.; 71. Geol.; 72. Handcpd.; 73. Hist.; 74. Int. frdm.; 75. Info. sci.; 76. Insr.; 77. Law; 78. Legis.; 79. Math./Comp. sci.; 80. Med.; 81. Metals; 82. Nat. resrcs.; 83. Newsp.; 84. Nuc. sci.; 85. Oral hist.; 86. Petr./Energy; 87. Pharm.; 88. Phys./Astr./Math.; 89. Readg.; 90. Relig.; 91. Sci./Tech.; 92. Soc. sci.; 93. Telecom.; 94. Transp.; 95. (other).

Reagan, Agnes Lytton (Ag. 12, 1914, Fayetteville, AR) Prof., Grad. Sch. of Lib. and Info. Sci., Univ. of TX, Austin, 1975–; Accred. Ofcr., Com. on Accred., ALA, 1969–75, Asst. Dir., Ofc. for Lib. Educ., and Exec. Secy., Lib. Educ. Div., ALA, 1967–69; Assoc. Prof., Div. of Libnshp., Emory Univ., 1958–1967, Asst. Prof., 1947–1958; Readers Libn., Wellesley Coll., 1946–1947, Circ. Libn., 1943–1946; Asst. in Lib., Agnes Scott Coll., 1939–1942; LS visit. lectr. positions and other earlier positions. **Educ.:** Univ. of AR, 1931–35, BA (Math.); Emory Univ., 1935–36, MA (Hist.), 1938–1939, AB in LS; Univ. of IL, 1942–1943, MS (LS), 1952–1957, PhD (LS). **Orgs.:** ALA: Cncl. (1963–66); ACRL; Lib. Educ. Div.; RASD; numerous ofcs. and coms. AALS: numerous ofcs. and coms. SLA: TX LA. Numerous other orgs. AAUP. Amer. Hist. Assn. Kappa Kappa Gamma. **Honors:** SLA, GA Chap., Dogwood Awd. for service, 1960; Phi Kappa Phi; Beta Phi Mu; Pi Mu Epsilon. **Pubns.:** *A Study of Factors Influencing College Students to Become Librarians* (1958); "Recent Research in the Division of Librarianship, Emory University", *Southeast. Libn.* (Spr. 1966); "The Literature of Recruiting," *Lib. Jnl.* (O. 1, 1962); "Needed Research in Education for Librarianship," *ALA Bltn.* (Ap. 1962); "The Relationships of Professional Associations to Library Schools and Libraries," *Targets for Research in Library Education* (1973); other articles. **Activities:** 1, 11; 26, 29, 39; 92 **Addr.:** Graduate School of Library and Information Science, University of Texas at Austin, Austin, TX 78712.

Reagan, Michael J. (Ja. 7, 1943, Los Angeles, CA) Sr. Libn., Glendale Pub. Lib., 1972–; Soc. Worker, Cnty. of Los Angeles, 1969–71. **Educ.:** St. John's Semy. Coll., Camarillo, CA, 1960–64, BA (Phil.); Univ. of CA, Los Angeles, 1971–73, MLS. **Orgs.:** CA LA: Ad Hoc Com. on Cert. (1976–77). CA Socty. of Libns.: Com. on Prof. Stan. (Ch., 1975–76). ALA: Com. on Prof. Ethics (1977–79). UCLA Sch. of Lib. Srv. Students Assn.: Pres. (1971–72). Glendale City Empl. Assn.: Pres. (1978–79). **Honors:** Beta Phi Mu. **Pubns.:** "Mandatory Certification–a Proposal That Lost," *Lib. Jnl.* (S. 1977). **Activities:** 9; 16, 17, 35 **Addr.:** 737 S. Oakland Ave., Pasadena, CA 91106.

Ream, Diane F. (Je. 18, 1944, Miami, FL) Dir., Hlth. Sci. Lib., Bapt. Hosp. of Miami, 1976–; Branch Libn., Miami Pub. Lib., 1968–69, Chld. Libn., 1967–68. **Educ.:** Univ. of Miami, 1964–66, BA (Eng.); FL State Univ., 1966–68, MS (LS); Med. LA, 1980, Cert.; various online trng. crs. **Orgs.:** FL Med. Libns.: VP/Pres.-Elect (1980–81). Miami Hlth. Sci. Lib. Cnstrm.: Ch. (1978–79). Med. LA. St. Simon's Episcopal Church. **Honors:** ALA, Best Pubcty., 1980; FL Hosp. Assn., PR Awd. for Jnl. Holdings List, 1980. **Pubns.:** "Author! Author! Day. A National Library Week Success Story," *Hosp. Libs.* (Spr. 1980) **Activities:** 5; 34, 39; 75, 80 **Addr.:** Baptist Hospital of Miami, Health Sciences Library, 8900 S.W. 88 St., Miami, FL 33176.

Reams, Bernard D., Jr. (Ag. 17, 1943, Lynchburg, VA) Prof. of Law; Law Libn., Washington Univ. (St. Louis), 1974–; Asst. Prof. and Law Libn., Univ. of KS, 1969–74; Asst. Libn., Rutgers Univ.-S. Jersey, 1966–69. **Educ.:** Lynchburg Coll., 1961–65, BA (Eng.); Drexel Univ., 1965–66, MS (LS); Univ. of KS, 1969–72, JD. **Orgs.:** AALL: Nom. Com. (Ch., 1979). ALA. SLA. Southwest. Assn. of Law Libs.: Pres. (1977–79). Other orgs. Amer. Bar Assn. AALS: Com. on Libs. (1980–83). Phi Delta Phi: Province IX (Pres.). **Honors:** Kappa Delta Phi; Beta Phi Mu. **Pubns.:** Jt. auth., *Congress and the Courts: A Legislative History 1787-1977* (1978); *Reader in Law Librarianship* (1976); jt. auth., *Historic Preservation Law: An Annotated Bibliography* (1976); "Federal Economic Regulation Through Wage and Price Control Programs 1917–1980," *Law Lib. Jnl.* (Win. 1981); "European Economic Community Depository Libraries and Documentation Centers in the United States," *Gvt. Pubns. Review* (Fall 1974); others. **Activities:** 12; 17, 24, 37; 76, 77, 78 **Addr.:** Campus Box 1120 - Washington University Law Library, Lindell & Skinker, St. Louis, MO 63130.

Rearden, Phyllis L. (F. 11, 1931, Enid, OK) Coord., Pub. Srvs., East. IL Univ., 1980–, Catlgr., 1970–80. **Educ.:** OK State Univ., 1949–52, BS (Bacteriology); Univ. of IL, 1968–70, MS (LS), 1972–74, CAS (LS). **Orgs.:** IL LA: Resrcs. and Tech. Srvs. Sect. (Pres., 1981); Bd.; Subcom. on Fin. (1981). East. IL Univ. Fac. Sen. **Honors:** Beta Phi Mu, 1975. **Pubns.:** "Library Services Survey of Eastern Illinois University Extension Classes," *IL Libs.* (Ap. 1980). **Activities:** 1; 20, 39, 46; 80, 92 **Addr.:** Booth Library, Eastern Illinois University, Charleston, IL 61920.

Reavis, Jennifer John (S. 9, 1946, Houston, TX) Pres., Freelnc., Inc., 1980–; Chief Exec. Ofcr., Freelnc. Resrch. Srv., Inc., 1977–; Ref. Libn., Col. Dev. Spec., Houston Pub. Lib., Bus. Tech. Dept., 1975–77, Ref. Libn., 1971–73. **Educ.:** Sarah Lawrence Coll., 1965–67 (Liberal Arts); Univ. of Houston, 1967–70, BA (Eng. Lit.); Univ. of TX, 1974–75, MLS. **Orgs.:** SLA: TX Chap., Cont. Educ. Com. (1976–78). Intl. Word Prcs. Natl. Micro. Assn. Productivity Cncl. (1980). ASIS: TX Chap., Secy.-Treas. (1979–80), Ch.-Elect (1980–81), Assn. Liaison Com. (1979–80), Awds. Com. (1979–80). Grt. Houston Conv. Cncl. Houston Cham. of Cmrce. Assn. of Recs. Mgrs. and Admins. **Pubns.:** Various sps., SLA, ASIS, Assn. of Recs. Mgrs. and Admins. **Activities:** 9, 12; 15, 17, 24 **Addr.:** Freelance Research Service, 1006 Missouri, Houston, TX 77006.

Rebenack, John H. (F. 10, 1918, Wilkinsburg, PA) Libn.-–Dir., Akron-Summit Cnty. Pub. Lib., 1967–; Assoc. Libn., Akron Pub. Lib., 1965–67, Asst. Libn., 1957–65; Libn., Elyria Pub. Lib., 1953–57; Libn., Salem (OH) Pub. Lib., 1950–53; Ref. Asst., Carnegie Lib. of Pittsburgh, 1947–1950. **Educ.:** Univ. of Pittsburgh, 1937–42, AB (Eng.); Carnegie Inst. of Tech., 1946–47, BS (LS); Miami Univ., Exec. Dev. Prog. for Lib. Admin., 1970. **Orgs.:** ALA: Legis. Assm. (Ch., 1976–77); LAMA/BES (Ch., 1971–73); PAS (Ch., 1966–67); Sch. Lib. Manpower Proj. (Adv. Com., 1967–73). OH LA: Legis. Com. (Ch., 1965–66, 1970–72, 1976–80); Pres. (1966–67); Exec. Bd. (1957–60). Pres. Com. on the Empl. of the Handicapped: Lib. Com. (1967–73, Ch. 1973–80). State Lib. of OH: Adv. Cncl. on Fed. Lib. Progs. (1975–79). Univ. of Pittsburgh, Grad. Sch. of Lib. and Info. Sci.: Bd. of Visitors (1968–74). U.S. Book Exch.: Bd. of Dirs. (1972). **Honors:** OH Lib. Assn., Libn. of the Year, 1979. Untd. Funds and Cncls. of Amer., Newton D. Baker Cit., 1968. **Pubns.:** "Contemporary Libraries in the United States," in *Encyclopedia of Library and Information Science* (1978). **Activities:** 9; 17; 78 **Addr.:** 2095 Brookshire Rd., Akron, OH 44313.

Rebman, Elisabeth Huttig (Je. 20, 1941, Miami, FL) Head, Msc. Cat. Unit, Stanford Univ., 1979–, Msc. Catlgr., 1971–79, Ref. Libn., Meyer Undergrad. Lib., 1969–71; Hum. Ref. Libn., East. MI Univ., 1967–69. **Educ.:** Oberlin Coll., 1959–63, AB (Msc. Hist.); Staatliche Hochschule Für Musik, Frankfurt A.M., 1963–64 (Keybd. Msc.); Univ. of MI, 1965–67, MALS; Stanford Univ., 1981, MA (Msc. Hist.). **Orgs.:** Msc. LA: Autom. Com. (1980–); Nom. Com. (1972); North. CA Chap., Secy.-Treas. (1970–72), Ch. (1979–81). Intl. Assn. of Msc. Libs. Assn. of Rec. Snd. Cols. ALA. Amer. Musicological Socty. **Pubns.:** "The Undergraduate Library," *Lib. Trends* (Ja. 1975); "Undergraduate Libraries," *Encyc. of Lib. and Info. Sci.* (1981). **Activities:** 1; 20, 34; 55, 56 **Addr.:** Music Library, The Knoll, Stanford University, Stanford, CA 94305.

Record, William J. (Je. 21, 1931, New York, NY) Libn., Intl. Proj., Assn. for Voluntary Sterilization, 1981–; Dir. of Lib., Misericordia Hosp., 1976–81; Libn., Fordham Hosp., 1973–76; Pers. Libn., Metro. Hosp., 1971–72; Admin. of Educ. Srvs., Odyssey House, 1970. **Educ.:** George Peabody Coll. for Tchrs., 1958–61, BA (Hist.); Pratt Inst., 1963–65, MLS. **Orgs.:** Med. LA: NY Reg. Grp., Small Hlth. Scis. Com. (1978–80). **Activities:** 12; 17, 25, 39; 80 **Addr.:** International Project, Association for Voluntary Sterilization, 708 Third Ave., New York, NY 10017.

Reddy, Alla R. (Ja. 7, 1935, Nellore, Andhra Pradesh, India) Assoc. Prof., Lib., Head of Ref. and Circ. Dept., Cheyney State Coll., 1966–, Actg. Dir. of Lib. Srvs., Gvt. Docum. 1977–79, Head, Ref. and Gvt. Docum. Depts., 1970–77, Asst. Prof., 1966–70. **Educ.:** Madras Univ. (India), 1956–59, BA (Phil.), 1959–60, MA (Phil.); S.V. Univ., India, 1959–60, MA (Metaphys.); West. MI Univ., 1965–66, MLS; Univ. of Pittsburgh, 1968–73 Advnc. Cert. (Lib. and Info. Scis.). **Orgs.:** PA LA. Assn. of PA State Coll. Univ. Fac. PA State Educ. Assn. AAUP. **Activities:** 1, 4; 29, 31, 39; 63, 75, 92 **Addr.:** L. P. Hill Library, Cheyney State College, Cheyney, PA 19319.

Reddy, Sigrid Robinson (Ag. 5, 1925, Peiping, Hopei, China) Dir., Watertown Pub. Lib., 1971–; Dir., Bedford Pub. Lib., 1962–71; Asst., Boston Pub. Lib., 1947–52. **Educ.:** Wellesley Coll., 1943–47, AB (Hist.); Simmons Coll., 1963–66 (LS). **Orgs.:** ALA: PLA, Legis. Com. (1979–81). New Eng. LA: Prog. Com. (1967–68); Mem. Com. (1969–71); Exec. Bd. (1972–73). MA LA: Pres. (1972–73); VP (1971–72); Prog. Com. (Ch., 1971–72); Secy. (1968–70); Rcrt. Com. (Ch., 1964–66); Educ. Com. (1968–70). Mt. Auburn Hosp. Cmnty. Hlth. Info. Netwk. Mt. Auburn Hosp. Cmnty. Hlth. Educ. Voluns. Proj. **Pubns.:** Ed., *Crossroads on the Charles* (1980); "Massachusetts Library Association," *Encyc. of Lib. and Info. Sci.* (1976); "History of the Massachusetts Library Association: The More Things Change...," *MLA: Bylaws, History, Directory* (1974); "Bedford: An Encounter with the Censors," *Bay State Libn.* (O. 1970). **Activities:** 9, 11; 17, 28, 36; 55, 74, 78 **Addr.:** 19 Buckingham St., Cambridge, MA 02138.

Redinger, Sarah S. (O. 6, 1944, New York, NY) Libn., Visit. Nurse Assn. of Chicago, 1974–; Libn., Loyola Univ., Chicago, 1972–73. **Educ.:** Transylvania Univ., 1962–66, BA (Elem. Educ.); Wayne State Univ., 1971–72, MSLS. **Orgs.:** Med. LA. SLA. **Activities:** 12; 15, 17, 39; 63, 80 **Addr.:** Visiting Nurse Association of Chicago, 310 S. Michigan Ave. Chicago, IL 60610.

Redlich, Barry (Je. 22, 1933, New York, NY) Sr. Ref. Libn., Art and Msc. Dept., Newark Pub. Lib., 1972– Positions in Advert. Dsgn., 1961–71. **Educ.:** Princeton Univ., 1951–1954, (Soclgy.); Columbia Univ., 1955–57, BS (Soclgy.); Pratt Inst., 1958–1961, (Advert. Dsgn.); Columbia Univ., 1971–72, MLS. **Orgs.:** Art Libs. Socty. of NJ: Treas. (1976–). Art Libs. Socty. of NY: Exhibition Pubns. Acq. Com. (Ch., 1979–). **Pubns.:** "Antiques, Collectibles and the Public Art Librarian," *ARLIS/NA Nsltr.* (Sum. 1980); "Message By Design," *NJ Msc. and Arts* (Ja. 1974). **Activities:** 9; 20, 39, 41; 55 **Addr.:** 45 West 10th St. - Apt. 4H, New York, NY 10011.

Redmond, Angela Dierking (Je. 17, 1952, Clinton, MO) Gvt. Docums./Micro. Libn., Tulane Univ. Law Sch. Lib., 1979–; Ref. Libn. and Head of Tech. Srvs., Norman Mayer Lib. Tulane Univ., 1977–79; Ref. Libn., Baylor Univ. Lib., 1976–77. **Educ.:** Ctrl. MO State Univ., 1970–74, BA (Fr.); TX Woman's Univ., 1974–75, MLS; Tulane Univ., 1978–, (Bus. Admin.). **Orgs.:** SLA: LA Chap. (Treas., 1979–; Consult. Ofcr., 1978–1979). SWLA: Coll. and Univ. Libs. Interest Grp. (Secy., 1978–). ALA: ACRL; GODORT. Tulane Univ. Women's Assn. LA State Univ. Dental Wives Assn. **Honors:** Beta Phi Mu. **Activities:** 12; 29, 33, 39; 51, 59, 77 **Addr.:** 4417 Sonfield St., Metairie, LA 70002.

Redmond, Donald A. (My. 19, 1922, Owosso, MI) Prin. Libn., Geol., Ref., Queen's Univ., 1978–, Chief Libn., 1966–77; Sci. and Engin. Libn., Asst. Dir. of Libs., Pub. Srvs., Univ. of KS, 1961–65; Dir. of Lib., Mid. E. Tech. Univ., Ankara, 1959–60; Tech. Lib. Adv., Ceylon Inst. for Sci. and Indust. Resrch., Colombo, 1957–58; Libn., NS Tech. Coll., 1949–60. **Educ.:** Mt. Allison Univ., 1939–42, BSc (Chem., Eng.); McGill Univ., 1946–47, BLS; Univ. of IL, 1947–48, MS (LS). **Orgs.:** ALA. Can. LA: Parlmt. Can. Assn. of Coll. and Univ. Libs.: Ch. (1969). SLA: Metals/Mtrls. Div. (Ch., 1965). Baker Street Irregulars. Sherlock Holmes Socty. of London. Bootmakers of Toronto. Natl. Model Railroad Assn. **Pubns.:** *Checklist of the Arthur Conan Doyle Collection, Metropolitan Toronto Library* (1973); Ed., *Bigelow on Holmes* (1974); various articles on Conan Doyle, Sherlock Holmes. **Activities:** 1; 17, 30; 70, 91 **Addr.:** 178 Barrie St., Kingston, ON K7L 3K1 Canada.

Reeb, Richard C. (S. 2, 1951, Belleville, IL) Head of Serials Unit, Cat. Dept., GA State Univ., 1977–, Cat. Libn., Mono. Unit, 1976–77. **Educ.:** Loyola Univ. (Chicago), 1969–73, BA (Phil.); Univ. of IL, 1975–76, MSLS. **Orgs.:** ALA. GA LA: Resrcs. and Tech. Srvs. Div. (Vice Ch., 1979–81 and Ch., 1981–83). Metro. Atlanta LA. **Activities:** 1; 20, 44 **Addr.:** William Russell Pullen Library, Georgia State University, 100 Decatur St., S.E., Atlanta, GA 30303.

Reece, Motoko B. (Kyoto, Japan) Libn./Subj. Spec., John G. White Dept. of Folklore, Orientalia and Chess, Cleveland Pub. Lib., 1973–; Japanese transl. for Ch. of Fine Arts Dept., IN Univ., 1970–71; Admin. Asst., U. S. Geol. Srvy., 1964–68; Admin. Asst., Syntron FL Sales Co., 1958–63. **Educ.:** Univ. of Tampa, 1958–60, BA (Eng., Pol.Sci.); IN Univ., 1968–1971, MA (Japanese Lit.), 1971–73, MLS; Univ. of MI, 1976–1979, PhD (LS); Eng. Tchr. Licn., 1953. **Orgs.:** ALA: ACRL/Asian and African Sect. (1981–); Rare Bks. and Mss. Sect. (1981–). OH LA: Resrch. and Plng. Com. (1980–). AALS. Socty. of OH Archvsts. Assn. for Asian Std.: E. Asian Std. (1969–). Frnds. of Cleveland Pub. Lib. Univ. of MI Alum. Assn. IN Univ. Alum. Assn. **Honors:** Univ. of MI, Oppt. Awd., 1978. **Pubns.:** *John Griswold White, Trustee, and the White Collection in the Cleveland Public Library,* (1979); *Tayama Katai and His Novel Entitled Futon ("The Quilt"),* (1971); "A Microform System as a Personalized Medium for Information Control," *Reprography Collected Papers,* (1977). **Activities:** 9; 39, 41, 45; 66, 92, 95-Folklore, Orientalia, and Chess. **Addr.:** 12530 Lake Ave., Apt. 212, Lakewood, OH 44107.

Reece, Nancy Jones (Ap. 28, 1918, Cattaraugus, NY) Retired, 1980–; Media Spec., Roosevelt HS, Portland, OR, 1977–80; Indian River HS, 1973–76; Head Libn., Lakewood HS, 1956–73; Libn., Tchr., East. MI Univ., Ypsilanti, 1954–56; Asst. Libn., Lakewood HS, 1944–54. **Educ.:** OH State Univ., Columbus, 1935–39, BA, BSc (Educ.); Case West. Rsv. Univ., 1944–45, BSc (LS); 1950–52 MA (Educ.). **Orgs.:** ALA. OR Educ. Media Assn. **Activities:** 10; 31, 48 **Addr.:** 7006 S.W. Brier Pl., Portland, OR 97219.

Reed, Donald Anthony (N. 22, 1935, New Orleans, LA) Law Libn., Arthur T. Berggren (Los Angeles), 1979–; Libn., Woodbury Univ., 1972–79; Libn., Los Angeles Valley Coll., 1966–68; Legal Asst., J. B. Tietz (Los Angeles), 1968–71; Instr., Hist., CA Inst. of the Arts, 1965–66. **Educ.:** Loyola Univ., Los Angeles, 1953–57, BS (Hist.); Univ. of South. CA, 1957–58, MSLS, 1965–68, JD. **Orgs.:** ALA. AALL. Beta Phi Mu: Univ. of South. CA Chap. (Pres.). Acad. of Sci. Fiction, Fantasy and Horror Films: Pres. (1972–). Count Dracula Socty.: Pres. (1962–). **Honors:** Horace Walpole Gold Medal; Mrs. Ann Radcliffe Lit. Awd.; Acad. Awd. **Pubns.:** *Robert Redford* (1975); *Admiral Leahy at Vichy France* (1966). **Activities:** 1, 12; 15, 32, 41; 67, 77, 92 **Addr.:** 334 W. 54 St., Los Angeles, CA 90037.

Reed, James R. (Je. 23, 1944, Berea, OH) Dir. of Libs. and Cur. of Spec. Cols., MO Bot. Garden, 1972–; Ref. Libn., Pub. Hlth. Lib., Univ. of MI, 1971–72, Resrch. Assoc., Maternal and Child Hlth., 1970–71. **Educ.:** Fort Lewis Coll., 1963–67, BA (Hist.); Univ. of MI, 1969–70, MLS. **Orgs.:** Bk. Club of CA. Gld. of Bk. Workers. ALA. Cncl. of Bot. and Horticultural Libs.: Pres. (1980–81). Other orgs. SAA. MO Musms. Assocs.: Exec. Cncl. (1973–76, 78–80); Pres. (1977–78). Midwest Musms. Conf.: VP (1978–79). Amer. Inst. for Cons. **Honors:** Med. LA, Rittenhouse Awd., 1971. **Pubns.:** Jt. auth., *Henry Shaw:His Life and Legacy* (1977); numerous articles. **Activities:** 2, 12; 17, 23, 28; 58 **Addr.:** Missouri Botanical Garden, P.O. Box 299, St. Louis, MO 63166.

PROFESSIONAL ACTIVITIES: Institutions: 1. Acad. lib.; 2. Arch.; 3. Assn.; 4. Fed./Gvt. lib.; 5. Inst. lib.; 6. Mfr./Suppl.; 7. Milit. lib.; 8. Musm.; 9. Pub. lib.; 10. Sch. lib.; 11. Sch. of lib. sci.; 12. Spec. lib.; 13. State lib.; 14. (other). **Functions/Activities:** 15. Acq./Col. dev.; 16. Adult srvs.; 17. Admin.; 18. Apprais.; 19. Archit./Bldgs.; 20. Cat./Class.; 21. Chld. srvs.; 22. Circ.; 23. Cons./Pres.; 24. Consult.; 25. Cont. ed.; 26. Educ. lib. sci.; 27. Ext. srvs.; 28. Fund/Grants; 29. Gvt. pubs.; 30. Indx./Abs.; 31. Instr. lib. use; 32. Media srvs.; 33. Micro.; 34. Netwks./Coop.; 35. Persnl.; 36. PR; 37. Publshg.; 38. Recs. mgt.; 39. Ref. srvs.; 40. Repro.; 41. Resrch.; 42. Review.; 43. Secur.; 44. Serials; 45. Spec. col.; 46. Tech. srvs.; 47. Trustees/Bds.; 48. YA srvs.; 49. (other).

Reed, Janet S. (Mr. 16, 1940, Rochester, NY) Asst. Mgr., Info. Srvs. Div., Continental IL Natl. Bank, 1980–, Ref. Supvsr., 1978–80; Libn., Sch. of Bus. Admin. Lib., Univ. of CT, 1973–78; Sr. Asst. Libn., Grad. Sch. of Bus., Cornell Univ., 1970–73; Asst. to Dir. of Libs., PA State Univ., 1968–70. **Educ.:** Middlebury Coll., 1957–61, AB (Amer. Lit.); Univ. of Pittsburgh, 1967–68, MLS. **Orgs.:** SLA: Bus. and Fin. Div. (Treas., 1981–83); various Chap. Ofcs. (1970–); Schol. Com. (Ch., 1978–79). **Honors:** Beta Phi Mu, 1968. **Activities:** 12; 17, 39; 59 **Addr.:** 2800 N. Lake Shore Dr., #2305, Chicago, IL 60657.

Reed, Virginia R. (Ja. 13, 1937, Chicago, IL) Sci. Biblgphr., Serials Libn., Northeastern IL Univ., 1971–; BioMed. Ref. Libn., Univ. of Chicago, 1969–71; Libn., Inst. Mario Negri Milan, 1967–69; Ref. Libn., Upjohn Co., 1960–67. **Educ.:** St. Mary-of-the-Woods Coll., IN, 1954–58, BA (Eng.); Univ. of Chicago, 1958–60, MA (LS); Med LA 1978, Cert. **Orgs.:** SLA: IL Chap. Nsltr. (Ed., 1972–74). ALA: Ref. and Subscrpn. Bks. Com. (1979–). Med. LA: Conv. Regis. Com. (1978). Chicago Lib. Club. **Honors:** Istituto diRicerche Faimacologiche/Mario Negri, Srv. Recog., 1969. **Activities:** 1; 30, 39, 44; 58, 80, 91 **Addr.:** Serials Dept./Library, Northeastern IL University, 5500 N. St. Louis, Chicago, IL 60657.

Reed-Scott, Jutta R. (My. 5, 1936, Leipzig, Germany) Dir., Col. Dev., Bibl. Cntrl., Dartmouth Coll. Lib., 1980–; Cols. Dev. Libn., MA Inst. of Tech., 1975–80, Assoc. Hum. Libn., 1972–75; Head, Ref. Dept., George Washington Univ., 1968–71. **Educ.:** Univ. of MD, 1966, BA (Hist.), 1967, MA (LS). **Orgs.:** ALA: ACRL, Resrch. Libs. Grp., Col. Mgt. and Dev. Com. (1980–), Com. on Lib. Tech. Systs. and Bibl. Cntrl. (1980–). **Honors:** Beta Phi Mu, 1967. **Pubns.:** "Collection Development of Serials on Microform," *Micro. Review* (Spr. 1980); "Collection Analysis Project in the M.I.T. Libraries," *New Horizons for Acad. Libs.* (1979); "Cost Comparison of Periodicals in Hard Copy and On Microform," *Micro. Review* (Jl. 1976). **Activities:** 1; 17 **Addr.:** Dartmouth College Library, Hanover, NH 03755.

Reeling, Patricia Glueck (Je. 6, 1939, Cincinnati, OH) Assoc. Prof., Grad. Sch. of Lib., Info. Std., Rutgers Univ., 1967–; Instr., AJ Sems., 1980–; Eval., Mid. States Assn., Comsn. on Higher Educ., 1975–; Educ. Consult., Reeling Assocs., Inc., 1969–; Tchg. Asst., Columbia Univ., SLS, 1964–67; Asst. to Dir., Boston Coll. Libs., 1962–63; Ref. Libn., OH State Univ. Libs., 1961–62. **Educ.:** Edgecliff Coll., 1956–60, BA (Grmn.); Univ. of Vienna, Austria, 1959, Cert. (Advnc. Grmn.); IN Univ., 1960–61, MA (LS); Columbia Univ., 1963–69, DLS. **Orgs.:** ALA: Beta Phi Mu Awd. Jury (Ch., 1980–81); Lib. Educ. Div., Nom. Com. (1974–75), Asia Fndn. Grants Com. (1967–71); GODORT, various coms. NJ LA: Pub. Lib. Self-eval. Subcom. (Ch., 1977–78); Educ. for Libnshp. Com. (1972–74, 1977–78); various coms., chs. Gvt. Docum. Assn. of NJ: Pres. (1981–82); VP (1980–81); Exec. Com. (1978–); Archvst. (1979–); various coms. SLA. Various other orgs. AAUP. Amer. Assn. for Higher Educ. **Honors:** Beta Phi Mu. **Pubns.:** Contrib., *Research Issues on Women in Librarianship* (1981); columnist, *Documents to the People* (1978–); ed., *Documents to the People* (1977–78); ed. bd., *RQ* (1980–); ed. adv. bd., *Index to U.S. Gvt. Pers.* (1979–). **Activities:** 11; 24, 26, 29; 63, 78 **Addr.:** 129 Drake Rd., Somerset, NJ 08873.

Rees, G. Marjorie (Je. 5, 1924, Reading, PA) Assoc. Dir., Scranton Pub. Lib., 1971–; Cmnty. Rel. Libn., Osterhout Free Lib., 1969–71; Asst. Dir., Keystone Jr. Coll., 1962–69. **Educ.:** Kutztown State Coll., 1939–43, BS (LS); Marywood Coll., 1967–68, MLS. **Orgs.:** PA LA: Cnty.–Pub. Div. Ch. (1980–1981); State Ch., Natl. Lib. Wk. (1974–75). ALA: Frnds. Com. (1971–1977, 1981–1983). **Pubns.:** 3 articles, *PA Lib. Bltn.* **Activities:** 9; 17, 24, 27 **Addr.:** Scranton Public Library, Vine St. at N. Washington Ave., Scranton, PA 18503.

Rees, Joe C. (O. 15, 1930, Ripley, MS) Ref. Libn., Duke Univ., 1973–, Engin. Libn., 1967–73; Ref. and ILL Libn., NC State Univ. Lib., 1966–67; Hum. Libn., Simon Fraser Univ., 1965–66. **Educ.:** Univ. of MS, 1955–57, BA (Eng.); Univ. of NC, 1959–62, MSLS. **Orgs.:** SLA: Ch., Engin. Div. (1971–72). SELA. NC LA: Const. Com. (1976–77); Ref. and Adult Srvs. Sec. (Dir., 1979–81). Socty. for the Prsrvn. of the Eno River Valley: Fndr. and Ed., *Eno* (1973–76). **Pubns.:** "High Speed Ground Transportation Literature," *High Speed Ground Transp. Jnl.* (Fall 1976); Reviews, *High Speed Ground Transp. Jnl.* (1969–76). **Activities:** 1; 26, 39; 55, 57, 92 **Addr.:** Reference Department, Duke University Library, Durham, NC 27706.

Rees, Marian Janet (Jl. 3, 1934, Oak Park, IL) Dir., Stanford Univ. Energy Info. Ctr., 1974–; Ch., Frgn. Lang. in Elem. Sch., Wheaton Sch. Dist., MD, 1967–69. **Educ.:** IN Univ., 1952–56, BA (Psy., Econ.); CA State Univ., San Jose, 1971–73, MA (Libnshp.). **Orgs.:** SLA. Energy Libns. of the Bay Area: Ch. (1979–80). West. Info. Netwk. on Energy: Vice-Ch. (1980–81). Coop. Info. Netwk. **Pubns.:** *Energy Modeling: A Selected Bibliography* (1977). ed., *Stanford University Energy Information Center Selected Acquisitions List* (1974–); "Energy Modeling at Stanford," *West. Info. Netwk. on Energy Nsltr.* (Sum. 1979). **Activities:** 1, 12; 15, 17, 20; 64, 65, 82 **Addr.:** Energy Information Center, Bldg. 500 Rm. 500C, Stanford University, Stanford, CA 94305.

Rees, Pamela Clark (Mr. 1, 1948, Shenandoah, IA) Med. Dir., State Lib. Comsn. of IA, Med. Lib., 1978–, Actg. Med. Dir., 1974–78, Libn. I, AV Dept., 1973–74. **Educ.:** MacMurray Coll., 1966–70, BA (Hist.); Univ. of MI, 1971–72, MALS; Med. LA, 1977, Cert. Med. Libn. **Orgs.:** Med. LA. IA LA: Hlth. Sci. Sect., VP (1974–75), Pres. (1976–77). Polk Cnty. Biomed. Cnsrtm. **Activities:** 13; 15, 17, 39; 58, 80 **Addr.:** Iowa State Medical Library, Historical Bldg. E. 12th and Grand, Des Moines, IA 50319.

Rees, Philip A. (O. 19, 1931, Manitowoc, WI) Art Libn., Univ. of NC, 1968–; Readers Srvs. Libn., Sarah Lawrence Coll., 1962–68; Libn., Musm. of the City of New York, 1959–62; Ref. Libn., Union Coll. 1955–58. **Educ.:** Denison Univ., 1950–54, BA (Art); Case West. Rsv. Univ., 1954–55, MS (LS); Univ. of NC, 1971–79, MA (Art Hist.). **Orgs.:** ARLIS/NA. Coll. Art Assn. Socty. of Archit. Histns. **Activities:** 1; 15, 39, 45; 55 **Addr.:** University of North Carolina at Chapel Hill, Ackland Art Center 003-A, Chapel Hill, NC 27514.

Rees, Thomas H., Jr. (F. 17, 1929, Mansfield, OH) Readers srvs. libn., SUNY at Stony Brook, 1979–, Libn., Dept. of Psyt., 1973–79; Consult. Libn., Nassau/Suffolk Reg. Med. Prog., 1971–73; Med. Ctr. Libn., Univ. of Cincinnati, 1964–71; Med. Libn., Dalhousie Univ., 1961–64; Resrch. Assoc., Ctr. for Documtn. and Comm. Resrch., West. Rsv. Univ., 1955–61. **Educ.:** Denison Univ., 1947–51, BS (Pre-med.); West. Rsv. Univ., 1956–58, MS (LS). **Orgs.:** SLA: Bio. Scis. Div. (Ch., 1978–79). Med. LA: Com. on Curric. (Ch., 1974–75). **Pubns.:** "Use of the Library of Congress' MARC II format for a union list of serials," *Proc. of the III Intl. Congs. of Med. Libnshp.* (1970). **Activities:** 1; 24, 39, 46; 56, 58, 80 **Addr.:** P.O. Box 832, Stony Brook, NY 11790.

Reese, Anne O. (Jl. 15, 1943, Niagara Falls, NY) Head Libn., Toledo Musm. of Art, 1965–. **Educ.:** Univ. of MI, 1960–64, BA (Art Hist.), 1964–65, AMLS. **Orgs.:** SLA. ARLIS/NA. Art Resrch. Libs. of OH: Ch. (1975–77). Coll. Art Assn. **Activities:** 5; 15, 17, 20; 55 **Addr.:** Toledo Museum of Art, Box 1013, Toledo, OH 43697.

Rees-Potter, Lorna K. (Je. 4, 1942, Montreal, PQ) Doct. Student, Sch. of Lib., Info. Sci., Univ. of West. ON, 1979–; Dir., Documtn. Ctr., Can. Cncl. on Soc. Dev., 1969–79; Chief, Cat., Can. Dept. of Natl. Hlth. and Welfare, Ottawa, 1967–69. **Educ.:** Univ. of NB, 1959–63, BA (Soclgy.); McGill Univ., 1965–67, MLS. **Orgs.:** ASIS. SLA: Montreal Chap. (Treas., 1978); Soc. Welfare Sect. (Ch., 1973). Can. Assn .of Libs. and Info. Ctrs. Can. Assn. of Info. Sci. ON Prov. Lib. Cncl. **Activities:** 12; 92 **Addr.:** Rm. 114, School of Library Information Science, University of Western ON, London, ON N6A 5B9 Canada.

Reeves, Marjorie Ann (Je. 21, 1935, Oceanside, CA) Law Libn., TRW Electronics, 1979–; NE Rep., Coutts Lib. Srvs., 1977–78; Asst. Dir., Tech. Srvs., IA State Univ., 1974–77; Asst. Dir., Lib. Srvs., OR State Lib., 1972–74; Head, Tech. Prcs., Univ. of CA, Irvine, 1966–71, Head, Acq., 1965–66, Staff Libn., 1964–65; various other prof. positions, 1959–64. **Educ.:** Chapman Coll., 1952–56, BA (Hist., Lit.); Univ. of CA, Berkeley, 1958–59, MLS. **Orgs.:** ALA. South. CA Assn. of Law Libns. **Addr.:** TRW Electronics, 10880 Wilshire Blvd., Suite 510, Los Angeles, CA 91202.

Regan, Muriel (Jl. 15, 1930, New York, NY) Libn., Rockefeller Fndn., 1969–; Libn., Booz, Allen & Hamilton, 1968–69; Deputy Chief Libn., Boro. of Manhattan Cmnty. Coll., 1967–68; Libn., Rockefeller Fndn., 1962–67, Asst. Libn., 1955–1962. **Educ.:** Hunter Coll., 1946–50, BA (Hist.); Columbia Univ., 1950–52, MSLS; Pace Univ., 1982– (Mgt.) (MBA). **Orgs.:** SLA: NY Chap., Pres. (1979–80) Treas. (1975–77); Educ. Com. Ch. (1978–79); others. ALA: Com. on Accred. (1979–). Cnsrtm. of Fndn. Libs.: Ch. (1974–75). Universal Serials and Bk. Exch.: Bd. of Dirs., (1976–78). Numerous other orgs. and coms. Archons of Colophon. Columbia Univ. Sch. of LS Alum. Assn.: Pres. (1979–80). NY Lib. Club. **Honors:** Phi Beta Kappa. **Pubns.:** Ed., *Union List of Serials Currently Received by Members of the Consortium of Foundation Libraries* (1975); ed., *Serials, Advertising, Business, Finance, Marketing, Social Science, in Libraries in the New York Area* (1974); *Information Sources on International and Foreign National Documents* (1977); *Selected Recent Works in the Social Sciences* 1976; "Cooperation among Foundation Libraries in the New York Area," (S. 1976). **Activities:** 12; 17, 39; 92 **Addr.:** 792 Columbus Ave., New York, NY 10025.

Regazzi, John J. (Je. 8, 1948, Brooklyn, NY) Dir., Info. Srvs., Ctr. of Alchl. Std., Rutgers Univ., 1979–; Dir., Ed. Srvs., The Fndn. Ctr., 1976–79; Mgr., Systs. and Plng. Dept., North. IL Univ., 1974–76. **Educ.:** St. John's Univ., 1965–69, BA (Psy.); Columbia Univ., 1974, MS (LS); Univ. of IA, 1972, MA (Relig.); Grmn. Lang. Inst., Goethe Inst., Munich, 1971, Cert. **Orgs.:** ASIS: Tech. Prog. Com. (1978). Amer. Socty. of Indxrs.: *The Indxr.* Ed. Bd. (1979–). Columbia Univ. Alum. Assn.: Bd. of Dirs. (1977–79). **Honors:** Beta Phi Mu, 1974; Columbia Univ., Joseph Wheeler Awd., 1974; St. John's Univ., Pres. Awd., 1969. **Pubns.:** *A Guide to Indexed Periodicals in Religion* (1974); "Information Systems as an Alternative," *What Else You Can Do With a Library Degree* (1980); "Evaluating Indexes: A Review Since Cranfield," *The Indxr.* (Spr. 1980); "Queues and Reference Service: Some Implications for Staffing," *Coll. and Resrch. Libs.* (S. 1978); jt. auth., "Online Services and Continuing Education for Special Librarians," *SLA Jnl.* (My–Je. 1978); various articles. **Activities:** 4, 12; 17, 24; 75, 90, 91 **Addr.:** Center of Alcohol Studies, Smithers Hall, Rutgers University, New Brunswick, NJ 08903.

Regenstreif, I. Gene (Mr. 22, 1929, Sault Ste. Marie, MI) Ed., Libn., Hlth. Admin. Press, 1975–; Libn., Hosp. Admin., Univ. of MI, 1970–75. **Educ.:** Univ. of MI, 1947–51, AB (Bio.), 1969, AMLS. **Orgs.:** SLA. Med. LA. ASIS. S. Ctrl. MI Hlth. Sci. Libs. Assn.: Pres. (1980). **Honors:** Beta Phi Mu, 1969. **Pubns.:** *A Literature Review of Performance Measurement in Hospitals* (1972). **Activities:** 1, 12; 30, 37, 39; 57, 62, 95-Hlth. admin. **Addr.:** Health Administration Press, University of Michigan, Ann Arbor, MI 48109.

Reger, Brenda Sue (S. 16, 1943, Ft. Wayne, IN) Dir., Frdm. of Info., Natl. Secur. Cncl., 1980–; Branch Chief, Supervisory Archvst., Recs. Declass. Div., Natl. Arch. and Recs. Srv., 1972–80, Archvst., Dwight D. Eisenhower Lib., 1969–72. **Educ.:** North. AZ Univ., 1962–66, BS (Hist.), 1967–69, MA (Hist.). **Orgs.:** SAA: Ref. and Access Policy Com. (1972–80); Prog. Com. (1980). Natl. Class. Mgt. Socty.: Chap. Secy. (1980–). **Activities:** 17, 38, 39; 54, 95-Natl. secur. **Addr.:** National Security Council, Rm. 395, OEOB, Washington, DC 20506.

Rehkopf, Charles F. (D. 24, 1908, Topeka, KS) Reg. and Archvst., Episcopal Dio. of MO, 1947–, Archdeacon and Exec. Secy., 1953–76; Rector, St. John's Episcopal Church, 1944–52; Rector, Trinity Episcopal Church, 1935–44. **Educ.:** Washburn Coll., 1926–32, BS (Engin.); Episcopal Theo. Sch., Cambridge, MA, 1932–35, Cert. (Theo.). **Orgs.:** SAA. Assn. of St. Louis Area Archvsts.: Pres. (1976–78). Hist. Socty. of the Episcopal Church: Bd. of Dirs. (1973–). **Pubns.:** "Grassroots Ecumenism," *Witness Mag.* (1965); "Reactions of a Bishop and Diocese to Events of the 1960's," *Hist. Mag. of the Episcopal Church* (D. 1978). contrib., *Bltn. of MO Hist. Socty.* (1955–62). **Addr.:** 642 Clark Ave., Webster Groves, MO 63119.

Rehrauer, George P. (F. 26, 1923, Union City, NJ) Prof., Grad. Sch. of Lib. and Info. Std., Rutgers Univ., 1969–; AV Consult., Prentice Hall, 1967–69; Prin., Mahway Jr.-Sr. HS, 1965–67; Prin., Plainview Sr. HS, 1963–65; Tchr., Hartsdale Jr.-Sr. HS, 1949–63. **Educ.:** Newark Coll. of Engin., 1939–43, BS (Cvl. Engin.); Columbia Univ., 1948–49, MA (Tchg.), 1953–58, EdD (Educ. Admin.). **Orgs.:** ALA. AECT. NJ LA. Cath. LA. NJ Educ. Media Assn. **Pubns.:** *Cinema Booklist* (Volume I, 1972, Volume II, 1974, Volume III, 1977); *The Short Film* (1975); *The Film User's Handbook* (1975); film sect., *Arts in America: A Bibliography* (1980); various articles, *Sch. Lib. Jnl., Cath. Lib. World, Lib. Jnl.,* other pubns. **Activities:** 10, 11; 26, 32, 42; 63, 67, 93 **Addr.:** Graduate School of Library & Information Studies, 4 Huntington St., New Brunswick, NJ 08903.

Rehring, Margaret Cecilia (Mr. 21, 1912, Cincinnati, OH) Supvsr. of Libs. and Frgn. Langs., Cincinnati Pub. Schs., 1956–; Libr., Woodward (Cincinnati) HS, 1953–56, Libn., Withrow (Cincinnati) HS 1938–53; Visit. Instr., various insts., 1938–. **Educ.:** Univ. of Cincinnati, 1930–34, BA (Span.), 1934–37, MA (Span.); Univ. of IL, 1935–37, BS (LS). **Orgs.:** ALA: AASL (Bd. of Dirs., 1954–56). Cath. LA: High Sch. Sect. (Bd. of Dirs., 1977–82). OH Assn. of Sch. Libns.: (Pres., 1953–54). Delta Kappa Gamma. **Honors:** State Awd. of Merit, OH Educ./Lib. Media Assn., 1978. **Pubns.:** Various articles in lib. prof. jnls. **Activities:** 10; 17, 26, 32; 55, 63, 89 **Addr.:** 2884 Pineridge Ave., Cincinnati, OH 45208.

Reich, David Lee (N. 25, 1930, Orlando, FL) Exec. Secy., New Eng. Lib. Bd., 1980–; Dir. of the Cmwlth. of MA Bd. of Lib. Comsns., 1978–80; Visit. Lectr., Univ. of MI, 1978; Comsn., Chief Libn., Chicago Pub. Lib., 1975–78, Deputy Chief Libn., 1973–74; Deputy Dir./Assoc. Dir. for Pub. Srvs., Dallas Pub. Lib., 1968–73; Dir. of Lib. Resrcs., Monroe Cnty. Cmnty. Coll., 1965–68; Asst. to Dir. of Libs., Miami-Dade Jr. Coll., 1964–65; various prof. positions in LS and educ., 1961–64. **Educ.:** Univ. of Detroit, 1957–61, PhB, magna cum laude (Eng.); Univ. of MI, 1962–63, AMLS. **Orgs.:** ALA: Natl. Lib. Week Com. (1966–72); Cncl. (1968–72, 1975–79); ACRL/Jr. Coll. Lib. Sect. (Secy., 1968–69); Lcl. Arranges., ALA Conf. (Ch., 1969–71); PLA/Stans. Com. (1972–74); Lcl. Arranges., Cent. Conf. Plng. Com. (Co-Ch., 1974–76). IL State Lib. Adv. Com. (1977–78). MA LA: Exec. Bd. (1979). New Eng. Lib. Bd.: Vice-Ch. (1979). Various orgs., ofcs., adv. bds. (1963–). **Honors:** Univ. of MI, Sch. of LS, Disting. Alum. Awd., 1978. **Pubns.:** Jt. auth., *The Public Library in Non-Traditional Education* (1974); chap. in *Managing Academic Change* (1975); chap. in *Junior College Libraries: Development, Needs, and Perspectives* (1969); "Cooperation Begins at Home: The Basis of Networking," *UT Libs.* (Fall 1976); "Helpful Hints for Getting Ahead in the Library Field," *Bay State Libn.* (Sum. 1979). **Activities:** 9, 13; 17, 19, 24; 50, 51 **Addr.:** New England Library Board, 2 Central Plz., Augusta, ME 04330.

Reich, Kathleen Johanna Weichel (My. 1, 1927, Mannheim, Germany) Asst. Dean of Fac., Rollins Coll., 1981–; Assoc. Prof., Lib. Srvs. and Acq. Libn., 1971–81; Bur. Chief, FL Dept. of State, Div. of Lib. Srvs., 1968–71; Admin., FL Bk. Prcs.

Special Subjects/Services: 50. Adult educ.; 51. Advert./Mktg.; 52. Aerosp.; 53. Agric.; 54. Area std.; 55. Arts/Hum.; 56. Autom.; 57. Bibl./Prtg.; 58. Bio. sci.; 59. Bus./Fin.; 60. Chem.; 61. Copyrt.; 62. Documtn.; 63. Educ.; 64. Engin.; 65. Env.; 66. Eth. grps.; 67. Film; 68. Food/Nutr.; 69. Geneal.; 70. Geo.; 71. Geol.; 72. Handcpd.; 73. Hist.; 74. Int. frdm.; 75. Info. sci.; 76. Insr.; 77. Law; 78. Legis.; 79. Math./Comp. sci.; 80. Med.; 81. Metals; 82. Nat. resrcs.; 83. Newsp.; 84. Nuc. sci.; 85. Oral hist.; 86. Petr./Energy; 87. Pharm.; 88. Phys./Astr./Math.; 89. Readg.; 90. Relig.; 91. Sci./Tech.; 92. Soc. sci.; 93. Telecom.; 94. Transp.; 95. (other).

Ctr., 1962–68; Head, Tech. Prcs. and Instr., Trinity Univ., 1961–62; Head, Tech. Prcs., Muskegon Pub. Lib., 1960–61; Catlgr. and Instr., Univ. of Detroit, 1957–60; Head, Tech. Prcs., Orlando Pub. Lib., 1955–57; Libn., Inst. for Pre-hist., Univ. of Leipzig, 1948–50. **Educ.:** Deutsche Buchhändler Lehranstalt, 1945–48, Antiq. Dip.; Univ. of Leipzig, 1948–50, Cand. Phil. (Pre-hist.); Univ. of Mainz, 1950–54, Cand. Phil. (Pre-hist., LS), Rollins Coll. 1973–76, MAT (Eng.), 1981, EdS. **Orgs.:** ALA. FL LA: Exec. Com. (RT Ch., 1963–65). SELA. African Lit. Assn. AAUP. **Honors:** Kappa Delta Pi, 1976. **Pubns.:** *African Literature of the French Expression* (1973, 1975). **Activities:** 1, 9; 15, 31, 41; 57, 63, 75 **Addr.:** 211 Fawsett Rd., Winter Park, FL 32789.

Reich, Nancy B. (Jl. 3, 1924, New York City, NY) Asst. Prof., Manhattanville Coll., 1975–; Asst. Prof., Rubin Acad. of Msc., Jerusalem, 1976; Adj. Asst. Prof., Msc. and Educ., NY Univ., 1972–75. **Educ.:** Queens Coll., CUNY, 1941–45, BA (Msc.); NY Univ., 1967–72, PhD (Msc.). **Orgs.:** Msc. LA: Grt. NY Chap. (Ch., 1975–77). Amer. Musicological Socty. Coll. Msc. Socty.: Cncl. (1977–80). **Honors:** Natl. Endow. for Hum., Flwshp. for Coll. Tchrs., 1982; Amer. Phil. Socty., Penrose Grant, 1978; Grmn. Acad. Exch. Srv., Travel-Std. Grant 1978. **Pubns.:** *Resources in Music* (1975); *Catalog of the Works of William Sydeman* (1968); "The Subject is Computers," *Msc. Educs. Jnl.* (F. 1969); "The Rudorff Collection," *Msc. LA Notes* (D. 1974); cmplr., introduction, *Selected Songs of Louise Reichardt* (1981); various articles. **Activities:** 1; 31, 41; 55, 57 **Addr.:** 121 Lincoln Ave., Hastings-on-Hudson, NY 10706.

Reich, Victoria Ann (My. 21, 1953, Romulus, NY) Sci. Ref. Libn., Lib. of Congs., 1980–; Head Libn., Univ. of MI, Mental Hlth. Resrch. Inst., 1978–79; Asst. Libn., Head Ref., Circ., Univ. of MI Nat. Sci. Lib., 1977–78; Lit. Srch., The Upjohn Co., 1976–77. **Educ.:** Goucher Coll., 1970–75, BA (Bio.); Univ. of MI, 1975–76, AMLS; 1976, Cert. of Med. Libnshp. **Orgs.:** ALA: RASD/Machine-Assisted Ref. Sect., Educ. of Online Systs. End Users (1981–). ASIS. **Pubns.:** "Influence of Online Bibliographic Services on Student Behavior," *JASIS* (forthcoming); cmplr., *Drug Research on Human Subjects* (Ag. 1980); *Low-level Ionizing Radiation-health Effects* (Jl. 1980); complr., *Career Opportunities in Science and Technology* (Jn. 1981); *Computers* (Feb. 1981). **Activities:** 1, 4; 16, 39, 41; 56, 80, 91 **Addr.:** Division of Science and Technology, Library of Congress, Washington, DC 20540.

Reichard, Elaine Louise Allentown, PA) Catlgr., Rare Bk. Dept., Free Lib. of Philadelphia, 1976, Libn. II, 1974–76, Libn. I, 1973–74. **Educ.:** Dickinson Coll., 1965–70, BA (Eng.); Syracuse Univ. 1970–72, MLS. ALA: RTSD; ACRL/Rare Bks. and Mss. Sect. **Honors:** Free Lib. of Philadelphia, Travel Grant, 1978. **Pubns.:** "The Rare Book Department of the Free Library of Philadelphia," *Bltn. of the PA Classical Assn.* (Spr. 1980). **Activities:** 9; 20, 39, 45; 55, 57, 77 **Addr.:** Rare Book Dept., Free Library of Philadelphia, Logan Sq., Philadelphia, PA 19103.

Reichel, Mary (Jl. 7, 1946, Kansas City, MO) Head, Ref. Dept., GA State Univ., 1980–; Sr. Ref. Libn., Undergrad. Lib., SUNY, Buffalo, 1976–80; Soc. Sci. Ref. Libn., Univ. of NE (Omaha), 1974–76; Ref. Libn., Free Pub. Lib., Elizabeth, NJ, 1972–74. **Educ.:** Grinnell Coll., 1964–68, BA (Hist.); Univ. of Denver, 1971–72, MA (Libnshp.); Univ. of Wales, Aberyswyth, MScEcon (Intl. Rel.). **Orgs.:** ALA: ACRL, Undergrad. Libs. Discuss. Grp. (Ch., 1979–80), Acad. Status Com. (1980–82); ACRL/Bibl. Instr. Sect., Policy and Plng. Com. (1977–79), Exec. Com. (1980–82). **Pubns.:** Jt. auth., "Conceptual Frameworks for Bibliographic Instruction," *Jnl. of Acad. Libnshp.* (May 1981); jt. auth., "Needs Assessment Checklist," *Bibliographic Instruction Handbook* (1979); jt. auth., "Term Paper Clinic," *Experimenter* (F. 1976). **Activities:** 1; 17, 31, 39; 54, 63, 92 **Addr.:** Reference Dept., William Russell Pullen Library, 100 Decatur St. S.E., Atlanta, GA 30303.

Reichmann, Felix (S. 14, 1899, Vienna, Austria) Prof. Bibl., Emeritus, Cornell Univ., 1972–; Asst. Dir. Cornell Univ. Libs., retired 1972. **Educ.:** Univ. of Vienna, 1923, PhD (Art Hist.); Univ. of Chicago, 1942, MA (LS). **Honors:** Fulbright Fellow, 1955; Guggenheim Fellow, 1955. **Pubns.:** "German Printing in Maryland, A Check List, 1768-1950," *Socty. for the Hist. of the Germans in MD Report* (1950); Jt. auth., *Ephrata as seen by contemporaries,* (1953); *Sugar, Gold, and Coffee; Essays on the History of Brazil,* (1959); Jt. auth., *Bibliographic Control of Microforms,* (1972); *Sources of Western Literacy-The Middle Eastern Civilizations* (1980). **Addr.:** Cornell University Libraries, Ithaca, NY 14850.

Reid, Camilla Brown (Ap. 30, 1952, Union Springs, AL) Sr. Libn., W. Ctrl. GA Reg. Hosp. Lib., 1977–; Ref. Asst., Hlth. Scis. Lib., Univ. of NC, 1974–75. **Educ.:** Samford Univ., 1970–73, AB (Fr.); Univ. of NC, 1974, (Compar. Lit.), 1975–76, MSLS; Cert. Med. Libnshp., 1976; cont. ed. crs. **Orgs.:** Med. LA: South. Reg. Grp.; various coms. GA Hlth. Scis. LA. Hlth. Scis. Libs. of Ctrl. GA: Un. List Ch. (1978–79); Ch. (1979–80). Southeast. Conf. of Hosp. Libns.: Nom. Com. (1978–79). Others. Univ. of NC Sch. of LS Alum. Assn. AAUW. **Honors:** Beta Phi Mu; Phi Kappa Phi; Pi Delta Phi; Kappa Delta Epsilon; others. **Activities:** 4, 5; 17, 20, 39; 80, 92 **Addr.:** 1415 Pagoda Dr., Columbus, GA 31907.

Reid, Elizabeth A. (Je. 29, 1948, Toronto, ON) Dir., Hlth. Scis. Lib., Toronto West. Hosp., 1981–, Chief Med. Libn., 1974–81; Lib. Asst., ON Cancer Inst., 1973. **Educ.:** Univ. of Toronto, 1967–71, BSc (Life Sci.), 1971–72, BEd (Educ.), 1972–74, MLS; Med. LA, 1975, Cert. Med. Libn. (Med. Libnshp.). **Orgs.:** SLA. Can. LA. Med. LA. CHLA. Toronto Med. Libs. Grp.: Pres., 1981–82. Art Gallery of ON. **Honors:** Victoria Univ., The Lillian Massey Treble Gold Medal in Life Sci., 1971; Imperial Oil Limited, Imperial Oil Limited Higher Educ. Awd., 1967–70. **Pubns.:** "New Books Catalogued," (1975–). **Activities:** 12; 17, 39, 46; 80 **Addr.:** Health Sciences Library, Toronto Western Hospital, 399 Bathurst St., Toronto, ON M5T 2S8 Canada.

Reid, John C. (Mr. 7, 1938, Detroit, MI) Dir. of Lib. Srvs., West Bend Cmnty. Meml. Lib., 1970–. **Educ.:** Coll. of Wooster, 1955–59, MA (Econ.); Case West. Rsv. Univ., 1969–70, MSLS. **Orgs.:** WI LA: Admin. RT (Ch., 1978–80). ALA. West Bend Rotary Clb.: Secy. (1975–80). **Activities:** 9; 17, 28, 39 **Addr.:** West Bend Community Memorial Library, 230 S. 6th Ave., West Bend, WI 53095.

Reid, Judith P. (Prowse) (Ap. 16, 1945, Greenville, KY) Ref. Libn., Lcl. Hist. and Geneal. Sect., Lib. of Congs., 1977–; Asst. Legis. Resrch. Libn., IL State Lib., 1972–76, Asst. Ref. Libn., 1969–70. **Educ.:** Lindenwood Coll., 1963–67, AB (Hist., Pol. Sci.); MO, 1967, Life Cert. (Sec. Educ.); Univ. of MO, 1967–69, MA (Pol. Sci.); Univ. of IL, 1971–72, MLS; Natl. Inst. on Geneal. Resrch., 1979. **Orgs.:** ALA: Hist. Sect., Preconf. on Geneal. Resrcs. (1981). Natl. Geneal. Socty. DC LA: Geneal. Com. (Prog. Ch., 1980–). Midwest Pol. Sci. Assn. KY Hist. Socty. Amer. Pol. Sci. Assn. Lincoln Comsn. of the NY Ave. Presby. Church. **Pubns.:** "Guide to Genealogical Periodical Indexes in the Local History and Genealogy Room," Lib. of Congs. bibl. finding aid (1981); "Guide to Periodicals Abstracts and Indexes in the Main and Thomas Jefferson Reading Rooms," Lib. of Congs. bibl. finding aid (1979); various articles, *Lib. of Congs. Info. Bltn.* **Activities:** 4; 39; 56, 69, 92 **Addr.:** Local History & Genealogy Section, Library of Congress, Washington, DC 20540.

Reid, Margaret Bachman (Je. 15, 1945, Philadelphia, PA) Libn., OH Univ., Ironton, 1981; Head, Chld. Dept., Lynchburg Pub. Lib., 1974–81; PR Libn., Jefferson-Madison Reg. Lib., 1973–74; Chld. Libn., Shephard Meml. Lib., 1969–71; Chld. Coord., Richland Cnty. Pub. Lib., 1968–69; Chld. Libn., Lansdowne Pub. Lib., 1967–68. **Educ.:** Geneva Coll., 1963–67, AB (Hist., Pol. Sci.); Villanova Univ., 1967–68 (LS); Emory Univ., 1972, MLn (Libnshp.). **Orgs.:** ALA: ALSC, Com. to Ref. *Multi-Media Approach to Children's Literature* (1980–); PLA, Srv. to Chld. Com. (1980–82). NC LA: Chld. Srvs. Div. (Co-Ch., 1970–71). VA LA: Chld./YA RT (Ch., 1978–80). Charlottesville-Albemarle Kennel Club. Nelson Beekeepers Assn. **Honors:** Beta Phi Mu. **Pubns.:** Ed., *VA LA: Chld./YA RT Nsltr.* (1980). **Activities:** 9; 21, 27, 36; 53, 55, 89 **Addr.:** Rte. 1, Box 100, Willow Wood, OH 45696.

Reid, Marion T. (O. 27, 1944, Baltimore, MD) Asst. Dir., Tech. Srvs., LA State Univ. Lib., 1978–, Head, Ord. Dept., 1969–78; Actg. Asst. Acq. Libn., Australian Natl. Univ. Lib., 1975; Supvsr., Bk. Prcs., LA State Univ. Lib., 1968–69. **Educ.:** Millsaps Coll., 1962–64, Univ. of IL, 1964–66, BS (Eng.), 1966–68, MS (LS). **Orgs.:** ALA: RTSD, Bkdlr. Lib. Rel. Com. (1977–80)/Resrcs. Sect., Exec. Com. (1980–82), Tech. Srvs. Admins. of Medium-Sized Resrch. Libs. Discuss. Grp. (Ch., 1980). SWLA. LA LA. Leag. of Women Voters. **Honors:** Beta Phi Mu; Cncl. on Lib. Resrcs., Fellow, 1974–75; LA State Univ., Exec. Prog. Fellow, 1980–81, 1983. **Pubns.:** Jt. auth., "The Role of the Academic Librarian in Library Governance," *Prcs. Papers of the First ACRL Conference, Boston* microfiche (1979); jt. auth., "A Study of Performance of Five Book Dealers Used by Louisiana State University Library," *Lib. Resrcs. & Tech. Srvs.* (Spr. 1978); "'The Tyranny of Distance' and Other Australian Acquisitions Problems," *Lib. Resrcs. & Tech. Srvs.* (Spr. 1977); "Effectiveness of OCLC Data Base for Acquisitions Verification," *Jnl. of Acad. Libnshp.* (Ja. 1977); various other articles. **Activities:** 1; 15, 17, 46; 75 **Addr.:** Louisiana State University Library, Baton Rouge, LA 70803.

Reid, Richard H. (Jl. 30, 1940, Clarendon, AR) Asst. Dir. of Libs., Univ. of AR, 1974–, Circ. Head, 1970–74, Serial and Binding Head, 1969–70, AV Head, 1968–69. **Educ.:** Univ. of AR, 1958–63, BS (Zlgy.); Univ. of AR, 1963–64, Cert. (Tchg.); LA State Univ., 1967–69, MS (LS). **Orgs.:** ALA: Chap. Cnclr. (1978–82); Int. Frdm. Com. (1979–81). SWLA: Exec. Bd. (1977); SLICE Proj. Cncl. (Ch., 1977–78). WHCOLIS: Del. (1979). AK LA: Pres. (1977); other ofcs. various other orgs. AAUP: Various coms., ofcs. N. AR Symph. Socty. Univ. of AR Campus Cncl. **Honors:** Beta Phi Mu, 1969. **Pubns.:** "Comparison of State Library Assoc. Membership Dues," *AR Libs.* (S. 1977); "The Place of the University Library in the State," *AR Libs.* (D. 1976). **Activities:** 1; 17, 49-Pub. srvs.; 58, 61, 74 **Addr.:** University of Arkansas, Fayetteville, AR 72701.

Reifel, Louie Elizabeth (Ag. 1, 1913, Curve, TN) Retired, 1981–; Consult., TERA, Inc., 1981–; Part-time Libn., Holy Spirit Episcopal Sch., 1981–; Consult., Houston IN Sch. Dist., 1978–; Volun. Libn., Church of the Holy Spirit, 1977–; Exec. Dir. Instr. Media Srvs., Houston IN Sch. Dist., 1974–77, Supvsr., Lib. Srvs., 1961–74, Libn., 1953–61; Tchr., Libn., Aldine Jr. High, 1945–53. **Educ.:** Memphis State Univ., 1931–33 (Latin); Univ. of Houston, 1946–47, BS (Educ., Latin); Sam Houston State Tchrs. Coll., 1949, Sch. Libn. Cert.; Univ. of TX, 1950–55, MLS (Instr. Media), 1961–62, Supvsrs. Cert., 1973–74, Admins. Cert. **Orgs.:** Houston LA: Pres. (1966–67). ALA: Cncl. (1972–73); Reg. VI, Sch. Libns. (Dir., 1970–72); various coms., chs. TX LA: Sch. Libns. (Pres., 1963–64); various coms., chs. Kappa Delta Pi: Alum. Chap. (Pres., 1974–76). Delta Kappa Gamma: Eta Gamm Chap. (VP, 1974–76). Houston Assn. Retired Tchrs. Univ. Grad. Sch. Alum. Assn. **Activities:** 10, 12; 17, 20, 24; 64, 90, 91 **Addr.:** 12118 Queensbury, Houston, TX 77024.

Reilly, Catherine R. (Jl. 22, 1949, Cooperstown, NY) Sec. VP, Mgr., Info. Ctr., Chase Manhattan Bank, 1981–, Asst. Treas., Mgr., Bus. Resrch., Micro., 1977–81, Supvsr., Bus. Resrch. Lib., 1975–77, Libn., 1972–75. **Educ.:** Coll. of Mt. St. Vincent, 1966–70, BA (Pol. Sci.); Pratt Inst., 1971–72, MS (Info. Sci.). **Orgs.:** SLA: B&F Div. Nsltr. Ed. (1980–81); NY Chap. (Prog. Ch., 1980–81); Bank RT (Ch., 1979–). Indus. Info. Assn.: Plng. Com. ALA. ASIS. **Activities:** 12; 17, 59 **Addr.:** The Information Center, The Chase Manhattan Bank, New York, NY 10081.

Reilly, Francis S. III (N. 6, 1932, Pittsburgh, PA) Ref. Libn., U.S. Dept. of Transp., 1967–; Ref. Libn., Free Lib. of Philadelphia, 1966–67; Statistician, U.S. Bureau of The Census, 1958–65. **Educ.:** St. Vincent Coll., 1949–53, BA (Sci.); Univ. of Pittsburgh, 1965–66, MLS; Cath. Univ. of Amer., 1973–77, Post-MLS Cert. **Orgs.:** SLA. DC LA. **Honors:** Beta Phi Mu, 1966. **Activities:** 4; 17, 34, 39; 59, 91, 94 **Addr.:** 2500 Q St. N.W., Apt. 245, Washington, DC 20007.

Reilly, James H. (Ap. 2, 1933, San Francisco, CA) Asst. Chief, Systs. Libn., San Francisco Pub. Lib., 1972–, Head, Sci. and Gvt. Docum. Dept., 1971–72, Head, Parkside Branch, 1970–71, Libn. II, Sci. and Gvt. Docum., 1965–70. **Educ.:** Univ. of San Francisco, 1950–54, BA (Phil.); Univ. of CA, Berkeley, 1962–63, MLS. **Orgs.:** CA LA: Golden Gate Chap. (Secy., 1971). SLA: Conf., Info. Com. (Ch., 1971). **Pubns.:** "The Exposé Exposed," *RQ* (Spr. 1972). **Activities:** 9; 17; 56, 91 **Addr.:** San Francisco Public Library, Civic Center, San Francisco, CA 94102.

Reilly, Jane A. (Jl. 10, 1920, Chicago, IL) Adult Srvs. Libn., Chicago Pub. Lib., 1980–; Asst. Prof. (LS), Sam Houston State Univ., 1977–80; Asst. Prof. (Instr.), Northeast. IL Univ., 1975–77; Head, Adult Bk. Sel., Chicago Pub. Lib., 1974–75, Coord., "Study Unlimited," 1972–74. **Educ.:** DePaul Univ., BA; Rosary Coll., BS (LS); Loyola, Chicago, MA; St. John's Univ. (MN), MA; Univ. of Chicago, CAS (LS): Un. Grad. Sch., PhD. **Orgs.:** IL LA. ALA. **Pubns.:** "Study Unlimited," *Educ. Media Yrbk.* (1976); *The Public Librarian as Adult Learners' Advisor* (1981). **Activities:** 9, 11; 16, 17, 26; 50, 63, 75 **Addr.:** Legler Branch Library, 115 S. Pulaski, Chicago, IL 60624.

Reilly, S. Kathleen (Mr. 6, 1940, Monterey Park, CA) Lib. Mgr., Cap. Resrch. Co., 1978–; Data Libn., Jet Propulsion Lab., 1976–78; Libn., World Trade Lib., 1974–76; Resrch. Libn., Larwin Grp., 1972–74. **Orgs.:** SLA: Chap. Pres. (1981–82), Chap. Pres.-Elect (1980–81), Prog. Com. (1978–79), Handbk. Com. (Ch., 1976–78), Secy. (1975–76), Cmnty. Rel. Dir. (1979–80). Frnds. of the Altadena Lib.: Dir. (1979–82), Secy. (1981–82). **Activities:** 12; 15, 17, 39; 59 **Addr.:** Capital Research Co., Research Library, 333 S. Hope St., 51st Floor, Los Angeles, CA 90071.

Reinhardt, Sr. Eileen (Ja. 7, 1919, Ridgefield Park, NJ) Media Spec./Dir., Paramus Cath. HS, 1971–; Prin., Bayley-Ellard HS, 1967–70; Tchr., Eng. and Latin, DePaul HS, 1956–66; Teacher, Eng. and Latin, St. Joseph HS, 1948–55. **Educ.:** St. Elizabeth Coll., Convent, NJ, 1939–43, AB (Latin); Seton Hall Univ., 1954–57, MA (Eng.); Villanova Univ., 1965–70, MLS. **Orgs.:** ALA. Cath. LA: N. NJ Chap., Secy., Bd. Bergen Cnty. Sch. Libns. Assn. **Activities:** 1, 10; 15, 17, 20; 63, 90 **Addr.:** 425 Paramus Rd., Paramus, NJ 07652.

Reinhold, Edna Jones (Je. 15, 1935, Clinton, IL) Chief Libn., Hum./Soc. Scis., St. Louis Pub. Lib., 1973–, Chief Libn., Readers' Srvs., 1970–73, Prin. Libn., Circ., 1968–70; Supvsr., Adult Srvs., Decatur (IL) Pub. Lib., 1966–68, Actg. City Libn., 1966, Chief, Ctrl. Pub. Srvs., 1965–66, Ref. Dept. asst., 1961–1965, Circ. Dept. asst., 1958–61. **Educ.:** MacMurray Coll. for Women, 1954–58, BS (Bus., Econ.); Univ. of IL, 1961–65, MSLS; Washington Univ., 1970–71, (Mgt.); Univ. of MO-St. Louis, 1975, (Educ.). **Orgs.:** SLA. MO LA. Grt. St. Louis Lib. Club. Natl. Org. for Women. **Honors:** Alpha Lambda Delta. **Activities:** 9; 16, 39; 51, 59, 92 **Addr.:** 2051 Maury, Apt. 5, St. Louis, MO 63110.

Reinke, Carol M. R. (Ap. 20, 1935, Saginaw, MI) Branch Head, Saginaw Pub. Libs., 1972–, Adult Srvs., 1971–72, 1957–62. **Educ.:** East. MI Univ., 1952–56, BS (Educ.); Univ. of MI, 1965,

PROFESSIONAL ACTIVITIES: Institutions: 1. Acad. lib.; 2. Arch.; 3. Assn.; 4. Fed./Gvt. lib.; 5. Inst. lib.; 6. Mfr./Suppl.; 7. Milit. lib.; 8. Musm.; 9. Pub. lib.; 10. Sch. lib.; 11. Sch. of lib. sci.; 12. Spec. lib.; 13. State lib.; 14. (other). **Functions/Activities:** 15. Acq./Col. dev.; 16. Adult srvs.; 17. Admin.; 18. Apprais.; 19. Archit./Bldgs.; 20. Cat./Class.; 21. Chld. srvs.; 22. Circ.; 23. Cons./Pres.; 24. Consult.; 25. Cont. ed.; 26. Educ. lib. sci.; 27. Ext. srvs.; 28. Fund/Grants; 29. Gvt. pubs.; 30. Indx./Abs.; 31. Instr. lib. use; 32. Media srvs.; 33. Micro.; 34. Netwks./Coop.; 35. Persnl.; 36. PR; 37. Publshg.; 38. Recs. mgt.; 39. Ref. srvs.; 40. Repro.; 41. Resrch.; 42. Review.; 43. Secur.; 44. Serials; 45. Spec. col.; 46. Tech. srvs.; 47. Trustees/Bds.; 48. YA srvs.; 49. (other).

AMLS. **Orgs.:** MI LA: Mem. Com. (1979–); Awds. Com. (1980). ALA. MI Assn. for Media in Educ. Univ. of MI Alum.: Hist. Leag. of Women Voters. **Activities:** 9; 15, 16, 17 **Addr.:** Zauel Memorial Library, 3100 N. Center Rd., Saginaw, MI 48603.

Reisner, Genevieve (S. 11, 1922, Hidalgo, IL) Grp. Srvs. Libn., Vigo Cnty. Pub. Lib., 1966–. **Educ.:** McKendree Coll., 1943–46, AB (Hist.); IN State Univ., 1955–57 (LS); State of IN, 1957, Pub. Libn. IV Cert.; IN Plan of Adult Educ., 1979, Cert. Trainer. **Orgs.:** IN LA: Grant Proposal Com. (1977). ALA. Area Sr. Srvs. Adult Educ. Assn. of IN: Nsltr. Ed. (1970–71); Reg., Addictions Com. Bd. of Dirs. (1974–75). Grt. Terre Haute Church Fed.: Bd. of Dirs. (1976–). Vigil Cnty. Cncl. on Aging: Secy. (1969–73). Various other orgs. **Pubns.:** "Survey and Serve," *Focus* (Je. 1969); "The Public Library as Pusher," *ALA Adult Srvs. Div. Nsltr.* (Spr. 1971); "Humanities Project Planning," *IN Com. for the Hum. Nsltr.* (Ap. 1974). **Activities:** 9; 16, 24, 48; 50 **Addr.:** R.R. 3, Box 44, Rosedale, IN 47874.

Reister, John F. (Mr. 28, 1928, Peshastin, WA) Circ. Srvs. Libn., CA State Univ., Chico, 1973–; Asst. Libn., E. OR State Coll., 1963–73. **Educ.:** Pac. Univ., 1948–52, BA (Relig.); San Jose State Univ., 1960–63, MALS; Univ. of Pittsburgh, 1969–70, Cert. (Lib. Admin.). **Orgs.:** CA LA: State and Univ. Colls. Chap. **Honors:** Phi Delta Kappa; Beta Phi Mu. **Activities:** 1; 17, 22; 56 **Addr.:** Library, California State University, Chico, CA 95929.

Reitano, Maimie V. (My. 16, 19–, Rochester, NY) Sr. Tech., Info. Spec., Eastman Kodak Co., Hlth., Safety and Hum. Factors Lab., 1977–, Toxicology and Chem. Info. Spec., 1967–77; Lit. Chem., E.I. du Pont de Nemours, Ctrl. Res., 1954–66. **Educ.:** Nazareth Coll., 1947–51, BS (Chem.); Fordham Univ., 1952–54, MS (Organic Chem.). Intl. Sch. of Corres., 1976–77, Mgt. **Orgs.:** Med. LA. Monroe Cnty. Lib. Club. Amer. Chem. Socty. 42; 53, 60, 71. **Addr.:** Eastman Kodak Company, Health, Safety & Human Factors Laboratory, Bldg. 320, Kodak Park, Rochester, NY 14650.

Reiter, Berle G. (Mrs.) (D. 16, 1926, Dowagiac, MI) Math. Libn., MI State Univ., 1969–, Asst. Serials Libn., 1968–69. **Educ.:** Univ. of IL, 1944–48, BA (Grmn.), 1948–49, MA (Grmn.); West. MI Univ., 1963–67, MS (LS). **Orgs.:** SLA: MI Chap., Nom. Com. (1976–78); Phys.-Astr.-Math. Div. (Treas., 1973–74). MI LA. **Pubns.:** "State of the Art Survey of Reference Sources in Mathematics and Statistics," *Ref. Srvs. Review* (Jl.–S. 1978). **Activities:** 1; 15, 39; 88 **Addr.:** Mathematics Library, Michigan State University, East Lansing, MI 48824.

Reiter, Harriet (My. 9, 1939, New York, NY) Ref. Libn., Judaica Spec., Univ. of MD - Undergrad. Lib., 1977–; Libn., Temple Sinai, 1976–77; Instr. of Biblical Hebrew, Univ. of OK, 1975–76. **Educ.:** Univ. of MI, 1971, BA (Near East); Univ. of OK, 1975–76, MLS. **Orgs.:** Cncl. of Jewish Libs. of Washington Metro. Area: Pres. (1979–80). AJL. DC LA. **Pubns.:** *Judaica: Selected Reference Works* (1979). **Activities:** 1; 15, 31, 39; 95-Jewish Std. **Addr.:** 1960 Dundee Rd., Rockville, MD 20850.

Reith, Jeannie Murray (O. 19, 1922, Scotland, Britain) Sch. Libn., Brentwood Sch., 1971–; Tchr., Sch. Libn., Pub. Schs., Saanich, 1969–80; **Educ.:** Univ. of Victoria, 1967–72, BEd; Univ. of HI, 1976–77, MLS; Brit. Cvl. Srvs. 1940–45, Cert. (Intelligence Srvs.). **Orgs.:** BC LA: BC Sch. Libns. Assn.: Prov. Exec. (1972–78); Saanich Chap., VP 1974–76), Pres. (1978–80). Can. Girl Guides: Leader; Dist. Comsn.; Div. Comsn. (1950–63). Natl. Cncl. Girl Guides of Can.: Intl. Rep. (1965). **Honors:** Boy Scouts of Can., Cert. of Merit, 1968; Girl Guides of Can., Medal of Merit, 1967; Scotland Educ., Medal of Merit, 1940. **Pubns.:** Various briefs, educ. media progs. **Addr.:** 6882 Wallace Dr., Brentwood Bay, BC V0S 1A0 Canada.

Reith, Mariana K. (Mr. 10, 1926, Los Angeles, CA) Dir., Tech. Srvs., Los Angeles Pub. Lib., 1977–, Mgr., Bus. and Econ. Dept., 1965–76, Asst., 1958–65; Head, Bus. Lib., Caterpillar Tractor Co., 1954–58, Asst., 1951–54; Instr., Gvt. Docum., Univ. of South. CA, 1967–68. **Educ.:** Univ. of WI, 1945–49, BS (Educ.); Univ. of WI, 1950–51, MA (LS). **Orgs.:** SLA: Bus. Div. (Ch., 1957–58); Bus. and Fin. Div. (Ch., 1967–68). CA LA: Docum. Sect. (Pres., 1969). ALA. **Activities:** 9, 12; 15, 17, 39; 51, 59 **Addr.:** Los Angeles Public Library, 630 W. 5th St., Los Angeles, CA 90071.

Reith, Marjorie C. (O. 27, 1951, Atlanta, GA) Asst. Dir., Carroll Cnty. Pub. Lib. (MD), 1980–; HQ Libn., Forsyth Cnty. Pub. Lib., 1978–80, Head, Bus.-Sci. Ref. Dept., 1976–77, Ref. Libn., 1975–76. **Educ.:** Earlham Coll., 1970–73, BA (Psy.); Univ. of NC, 1973–74, MSLS. **Orgs.:** ALA. SELA. NC LA: Docum. Sect. (Secy.-Treas., 1977–79). NC State Data Ctr.: Adv. Bd. (1979). **Activities:** 9; 16, 17, 29; 59 **Addr.:** Carroll County Public Library, Westminster, MD 21157.

Reitz, Aelene Blodwen (O. 31, 1938, Caledon, Cape Province, S. Africa) Film Spec., Windsor Pub. Lib., 1979–, Asst. Libn., 1973–79, 1969–70; various soc. work positions. **Educ.:** Univ. of Cape Town, 1956–59, BSocSc (Soclgy., Soc. Work), 1957–59, Cert. of Prof. Competence (Soc. Worker), 1959–62, MSocSc (Soclgy.); Wayne State Univ., 1968–69, MSLS. **Orgs.:** ON LA. Can. LA. Helping Hand. Can. Un. of Pub. Empls. Windsor Pub. Lib. Staff Assn. **Activities:** 9; 16, 21; 50, 67, 92 **Addr.:** 122 Montrose, Windsor, ON N8X 1A3 Canada.

Reitzel, Hilda M. (My. 9, 1921, Pittsburgh, PA) Libn., Mine Safety Appliances Co., 1956–; Head, Ref. Dept., Univ. of Pittsburgh, 1954–56; Libn., Mine Safety Appliances Co., 1952–54; Ref. Asst., Univ. of Pittsburgh, 1945–52. **Educ.:** Univ. of Pittsburgh, 1939–43, BA (Eng.); Carnegie Inst. of Tech., 1943–45, BS in LS; Univ. of Pittsburgh, 1949–52, MA (Geog.). **Orgs.:** SLA: Pres., Pittsburgh Chap. (1958–59). PA LA: Ed., PLA *Bltn.*, (1961–72). Pittsburgh Lib. Club: Pres. (1950–51). **Honors:** PA LA, Cert. of Merit, 1967. **Activities:** 12; 17, 39; 59 **Addr.:** Mine Safety Appliances Co., Library, 600 Penn Center Blvd., Pittsburgh, PA 15235.

Remi, Daniel (D. 12, 1944, Ordizan, France) Ref. Libn., Univ. de Montréal, 1968–. **Educ.:** Univ. de Montréal, 1966–68, BA (Libnshp.), 1969–74, BSc (Pol. Sci.), 1974–76, MALS; École des Hautes Etudes Cmrcl. (Can.), 1976–79, DSA (Admin.). **Orgs.:** ASTED. **Pubns.:** *Guide de la Documentation en Science Politique* (1979); *Guide de la Documentation en Relations Industrielles* (1979). **Activities:** 1; 39; 59, 77, 92 **Addr.:** Bibliotheque des Sciences Humaines et Sociales, Case postale 6202, Succursale A, Montréal, PQ H3C 3T2 Canada.

Remington, David Gray (Ap. 21, 1937, Worcester, MA) Chief, Cat. Distribution Srv., Lib. of Congs., 1976–, Asst. Chief, Subj. Cat. Div., 1973–76; Dir. of Lib. Srvs., Bro-Dart Inc., 1964–73; Head, Tech. Srvs., Summit Free Pub. Lib., 1961–64. **Educ.:** Wesleyan Univ., 1955–59, BA (Eng. Lit.); Rutgers Univ., 1959–61, MLS. **Orgs.:** ALA: Cnclr.-at-Lg. (1974–78); RTSD/Cncl. of Reg. Grps. (Vice-ch., Ch., 1978–82), Cmrcl. Prcs. Srvs. Com. (1974–80), AV Mtrls. in Libs. Com. (Ch., 1970–73), Cat. and Class. Sect., various coms. (1964–77); ASCLA/Multitype Lib. Coop. Sect., Prog. Com. (1979–80); Info. Sci. and Autom. Div., Plng. Com. (1968–69). Amer. Natl. Stans. Inst.: Various coms. (1965–). Appalachian Trail Conf. Natl. Cathedral Assn. Potomac Appalachian Trail Club. **Pubns.:** Various articles, *Lib. Resrcs. & Tech. Srvs.* and other jnls.; various non-print presentations. **Activities:** 1, 9; 34, 46, 49-Info. mktg.; 51, 56, 93 **Addr.:** Library of Congress, Washington, DC 20540.

Remmerde, Barbara L. (Ag. 22, 1920, Seattle, WA) Ref. Libn. and Admin. Asst. to the Univ. Libn., East. WA Univ., 1970–. **Educ.:** Univ. of WA, 1965, BA (Gen. Std.), 1969–70, MLS. **Orgs.:** WA LA. Pac. NW LA. ALA: ACRL. WA State Bd. for Cert. of Libns.: Gvr.'s Appt. Amer. Inst. of Archlg. **Pubns.:** Jt. auth., "Availability of Machine-Readable Cataloging," *Lib. Resrch.* (Fall 1979). **Activities:** 1, 13; 17, 39, 41; 92 **Addr.:** The Library, Eastern Washington University, Cheney, WA 99004.

Renaud, Robert (D. 31, 1952, Montreal, PQ) Anal., UTLAS, 1980–; Catlgr., McGill Univ., 1976–78. **Educ.:** Vassar Coll., 1973–76, AB (Hist.); Univ. of Toronto, 1978–80, MLS. **Orgs.:** ALA. Can. LA. **Pubns.:** *Automated Cataloguing: The Origins and Development of the MARC Format* (1980). **Activities:** 14; 34; 56 **Addr.:** UTLAS, 130 St. George St., Toronto, ON M5S 1A5 Canada.

Renaud-Frigon, Claire (Ottawa, ON) Chief, Dept. Lib., Secy. of State, Can., 1980–; Asst. Chief, Lib. Documtn. Ctr., Natl. Lib. of Can., 1974–80, Ref. Libn., 1971–74, Catlgr., 1966–67. **Educ.:** Univ. of Ottawa, 1961–65, BA; Univ. of Toronto, 1965–66, BLS; Univ. Laval, 1967–70, Lich. Lettres. **Orgs.:** ASTED. **Pubns.:** Jt. auth, "Canada," *Library Service to Children* (1978); "La Dispenibilité Universelle des Publications," *Documtn. et bibs.* (Mr. 1979); other articles. **Activities:** 12; 15, 30, 39; 62, 75 **Addr.:** Departmental Library, Secretary of State, Terrasses de la Chaudiere, Ottawa, ON K1A 0N5, Canada.

Rendell, Kenneth W. (My. 12, 1943, Boston, MA) Pres., The Rendells, Inc., 1966–; Dir., Charles EDE, Ltd., 1981–; Pres., Kenneth W. Rendell, Eng., 1970–; Pres., Kingston Galleries, Inc., 1959–65. **Orgs.:** The Ms. Socty.: Bd. of Dirs. (1966–72); Pres. (1972). Intl. Leag. Autograph and Ms. Dlrs.: Pres. (1975–77). New Eng. Ant. Booksellers Assn.: Pres. (1975–77). The Grolier Club. Assn. Intl. de Bibliophiles. Syndicat de La Lib. Ancienne et Mod. **Pubns.:** Jt. ed., *Autographs and Manuscripts: A Collector's Manual* (1978); *Fundamentals of Autograph Collecting* (1972); various articles, *Mss., The Antiq. Bk. Monthly Review,* "Principles of Appraisals" (1978); "Techniques of Appraising Manuscripts" (1978). **Activities:** 6; 18, 19, 20 **Addr.:** The Rendells, Inc., 154 Wells Ave., Newton, MA 02159.

Reneker, Maxine H. (D. 2, 1942, Chicago, IL) Persnl., Bus. Libn., Univ. of CO, 1978–; Persnl. Libn., Univ. of Chicago Lib., 1971–73, Asst. Acq. Libn., 1970–71, Classics Libn., 1967–70. **Educ.:** Carleton Coll., 1960–64, BA (Latin); Univ. of Chicago, 1964–70, MA (LS); Univ. of CO, 1975–79 (Bus. Admin.). **Orgs.:** ALA. Mt. Plains LA. CO LA. **Honors:** Phi Beta Kappa; Beta Phi Mu; Cncl. on Lib. Resrcs., Acad. Lib. Mgt. Intern, 1980. **Pubns.:** *A Study of Book Thefts in Academic Libraries* (1970); "Paralibrarians - Co SCLP Presentation," *CO Libs.* (D. 1964). **Activities:** 1; 17, 35 **Addr.:** Norlin Library, University of Colorado, Boulder, CO 80309.

Renner Melinda L. Swett (My. 12, 1946, Atlanta, GA) Lib. Prog. Ofcr. for Trng., US Intl. Comm. Agency, 1979–; Asst. to Prog. Dir., WHCOLIS, 1979; Pub. Srvs. Libn., DeKalb Cmnty. Coll., 1975–79, Serials and Micro. Libn., 1969–75; Adj. Fac. (LS), Emory Univ., 1971. **Educ.:** Emory Univ. 1966–68, BA (Lit.); 1968–69, M Ln; Atlanta Univ., 1974–76 (LS); Cath. Univ., 1980–81, (Online, Law Libns.). **Orgs.:** SE LA: Lcl. Arrange. Com. (1970); Mem. Com. (1972–74). GA LA: JM RT (Vice-Ch., 1973–74); Gvtl. Rel. Com. (Ch., 1976–79). Metro Atlanta LA: Int. Frdm. Com. (Ch., 1976–77). DC LA: Legis. Com. (1979–); various other coms. Various other orgs. AAUW. MENSA. High Musm. of Art. Jazz Forum of Atlanta. **Honors:** Beta Phi Mu. **Pubns.:** *Union List of Periodicals and Newspapers Held in Georgia Two-Year Colleges* (1976); "A Peaceful Invasion," *GA Libn.* (N. 1978); "Legislative Day-1979" *GA Libn.* (A. 1979). **Activities:** 1, 4; 25, 33, 39; 50, 54, 55 **Addr.:** 1406 21st St., N.W., Washington, DC 20036.

Rensch, Gloria Katherine (Ap. 11, 1919, Omaha, NE) Sr. Catlgr., Vigo Cnty. Pub. Lib., 1969–; Ref. and Art Libn., Wilmette Pub. Lib., 1963–68; Asst. Prof. and Catlgr., Northwest. Univ., 1960–63. **Educ.:** Northwest. Univ., 1935–39, AB (Latin), 1939–40, MA (Latin); Univ. of IL, 1957–59, MA (Art Hist.); Rosary Coll., 1959–60, MALS. **Orgs.:** IN LA. Chi Omega Alum. Assn.: Patroness. Sigma Alpha Iota Swope Art Gallery. **Honors:** Phi Beta Kappa, 1939. **Pubns.:** Reviews. **Activities:** 1, 9; 15, 20 **Addr.:** Vigo County Public Library, One Library Sq., Terre Haute, IN 47807.

Renshawe, Michael Lawrence (My. 6, 1939, Washington, DC) Law Area Libn., McGill Univ., 1976–; Law Libn., The Baltimore Bar Lib., 1971–76; Ref. Spec., The Lib. of Congs., 1968–71. **Educ.:** Univ. of MD, 1967, BA, 1968, MLS, 1975, JD. **Orgs.:** Can. ALL. AALL. Assn. of McGill Univ. Libns. ALA. McGill Assn. of Univ. Tchrs. **Activities:** 1; 17; 77 **Addr.:** 3644 Peel St., Montreal, PQ H3A 1W9 Canada.

Renter, Lois I. (O. 23, 1929, Lowden, IA) Head Libn., Amer. Coll. Testing Prog., 1968–; Span. Tchr., Mt Vernon HS, 1965–67. **Educ.:** Cornell Coll., 1961–65, BA (Span.); Univ. of IA; 1967–68, MALS. **Orgs.:** ALA. SLA. ASIS. Assoc. Info. Mgrs. **Honors:** Phi Beta Kappa, 1964. **Activities:** 12; 17, 39; 63 **Addr.:** American College Testing Program, Box 168, Iowa City, IA 52243.

Rentof, Beryl L. (S. 2, 1946, New York City, NY) Ref. Libn., Fashion Inst. of Tech., 1977–; Ref. Libn., BBDO Advert. Agency, 1976–77; Evening Ref. Libn., Coll. of Insr. 1976; Evening Ref. Libn., Polytech. Inst. of NY, 1975–76. **Educ.:** NY Univ., 1964–68, BS (Bus. Admin.); Bernard M. Baruch, Grad. Sch. of Pub. Admin., 1969–74, MPA (Pub. Admin.); Queens Coll., CUNY, 1974–75, MLS. **Orgs.:** SLA: NY Chap., Advert. and Mktg. Grp., Ch. (1980–81), Vice-Ch., (1979–80). CUNY LA: Com. on Coop. and Coord. (1980–82). SUNY LA. Fashion Inst. of Tech. Fac. Assn. Fashion Inst. of Tech. Lib./Media. **Pubns.:** Asst. ed., *Special Libraries Directory of Greater New York* (1980). **Activities:** 1, 12; 31, 39; 51, 59 **Addr.:** Fashion Institute of Technology Library, 227 W. 27 St., New York, NY 10001.

Renton, Jeanne Livingston (F. 25, 1927, Jacksonville, FL) HS Lib. Media Spec., Fairview Jr./Sr. HS, 1972–. **Educ.:** PA State Univ., 1945–47; Cleveland State Univ., 1968–70, BA (Eng.); Case West. Rsv. Univ., 1970–72, MSLS. **Orgs.:** ALA: AASL OH Educ. Lib./Media Assn.: Sr. High Interest Grp. OH Educ. Assn. NEA. **Honors:** Phi Beta Mu. **Pubns.:** "Books Unlimited: A School-Wide Reading Program," *Jnl. of Readg.* (N. 1978). **Activities:** 10; 20, 39, 48; 63, 89 **Addr.:** 9800 Memphis Villas Blvd., Brooklyn, OH 44144.

Rentschler, Cathy D. (N. 2, 1947, Anniston, AL) Ed. of *Lib. Lit.*, H. W. Wilson Co., 1974–; Catlgr., *Cumulative Bk. Index,* 1971–74; Elem. Tchr., DeArmanville Jr. HS (AL) 1969–70. **Educ.:** Jacksonville State Univ. (AL), 1965–69, BA (Eng., Math.); FL State Univ., 1970–71, MLS. **Orgs.:** ALA. SLA. NY LA. Women's Natl. Bk. Assn.: NY Chap., Bd. of Mgrs. (1978–81). **Activities:** 14-publshr.; 30, 37 **Addr.:** 60 W. 66th St. 16A, New York, NY 10023.

Renz, James H. (O. 23, 1928, Columbus, OH) Assoc. Dir. for Tech. Srvs., Univ. of FL, 1970–; Assoc. Dir., Coll. of William and Mary, 1960–69; FL Col. Libn., Miami Pub. Lib., 1957–60. **Educ.:** OH State Univ., 1949–53, BA (Grmn.); Univ. of MI, 1956–57, AMLS. **Orgs.:** ALA. VA LA: Coll. and Univ. Sect. (Ch., 1966); Lcl. Arranges. Com. (Ch., 1966); Coll. and Univ. Sect. on Acq. (Mdrtr., 1968). FL LA: Ref. Sect. (Ch., 1960). Univ. of FL Staff Assn.: Pres. (1972–73). Intl. Richard Wagner Socty. **Honors:** Delta Phi Alpha, Goethe Prize, 1953; Beta Phi Mu. **Pubns.:** *The Sources for the Music Dramas of Richard Wagner* (1967); "Floridiana Collection," *Lib. Jnl.* (1958); "Acquisitions," *VA Libn.* (15:2); "Richard Wagner and the Music Drama" radio progs. (1967); "Hart Crane, Voyages I, II, III, IV, V" rec. (1969). **Activities:** 1; 15, 17, 20 **Addr.:** 2602 S.W. 14 Dr., Gainesville, FL 32608.

ReQua, Eloise Gallup (D. 1, 1902, Chicago, IL) Exec. Dir., Lib. of Intl. Rel., 1932–; Org., World Trade Ref. Lib., Intl.

Special Subjects/Services: 50. Adult educ.; 51. Advert./Mktg.; 52. Aerosp.; 53. Agric.; 54. Area std.; 55. Arts/Hum.; 56. Autom.; 57. Bibl./Prtg.; 58. Bio. sci.; 59. Bus./Fin.; 60. Chem.; 61. Copyrt.; 62. Documtn.; 63. Educ.; 64. Engin.; 65. Env.; 66. Eth. grps.; 67. Film; 68. Food/Nutr.; 69. Geneal.; 70. Geo.; 71. Geol.; 72. Handcpd.; 73. Hist.; 74. Int. frdm.; 75. Info. sci.; 76. Insr.; 77. Law; 78. Legis.; 79. Math./Comp. sci.; 80. Med.; 81. Metals; 82. Nat. resrcs.; 83. Newsp.; 84. Nuc. sci.; 85. Oral hist.; 86. Petr./Energy; 87. Pharm.; 88. Phys./Astr./Math.; 89. Readg.; 90. Relig.; 91. Sci./Tech.; 92. Soc. sci.; 93. Telecom.; 94. Transp.; 95. (other).

Hse., New Orleans, 1946; Pubcty. Ofc., Bryn Mawr Coll., 1933–34. **Educ.:** Bryn Mawr Coll., 1924, AB (Pol., Econ., Hist.); Sch. of Intl. Std., Geneva, Switzerland, 1928. **Orgs.:** SLA: PR Com. (Ch., 1944–46); Intl. Rel. Com. (1948–50); Com. for Coop. with Latin Amer. (1940). The Fortnightly. IL Socty. for Mental Hygiene. The Arts Club. Bryn Mawr Coll.: Various ofcs. **Honors:** Chicago Cncl. on Frgn. Rel., World Understan. Awd., 1952; The Eloy Alfaro Intl. Fndn. of Panama, Medal for "Contrib. to Informing Students and Free Men in This Country," 1962; Intl. Hse., New Orleans, LA, Plaque for "Outstan. Contrib. to Intl. Understan.," 1968; City Cncl. of Chicago, Mayor Richard J. Daley, Cert. of Merit, 1973. **Pubns.:** Jt. auth., *The Developing Nations: A Guide to Information Sources Concerning Their Economic, Political, Technical and Social Problems* (1965); various bibls., booklists, radio and TV interviews, sps., articles and bk. reviews, *ALA Bltn., Chicago Schs. Jnl., Export News, IL Libs., Chicago Daily Law Bltn., Ref. Spotlight on Intl. Affairs,* other pubns. **Activities:** 12; 54, 92 **Addr.:** Library of International Relations, 666 Lake Shore Dr., Chicago, IL 60611.

Reslock, Mary H. (Mr. 6, 1914, Hancock, MI) Managing Ed., MMI Press, MI Molec. Inst., 1979–; Resrch. Spec., Info. Sci. Dept., Dow Chem. Co., 1978–79, Mgr., Ctrl. Rpt. Index, Internal Info., 1975–78, Mgr. Chemical Lib., 1971–77, Resrch. Logician Info. Sci. Dept., 1964–71. **Educ.:** MI Tech. Univ., 1934–38, BS (Gen. Sci.); Univ. of MI, 1966–68, MALS. **Orgs.:** SLA: Nom. Com. (1974). Amer. Chem. Socty.: Div. Chem. Info., Ch. (1978), Secy. (1974–77). ASIS. Chem. Notation Assn.: Pres. (1979); Cncl. (1969–); Secy.-Treas. Soc. Schol. Publshg. Zonta Intl.: Srv. Com. (Ch., 1979). Sigma Xi: Mem. Com. (1973–76); Nom. Com. (1975–). Midland Pub. Lib.: Adv. Lib. Bd. (Secy., 1979–81). **Pubns.:** Collaborating ed., *Wisevesser Line Formula Notation* (1968); various articles, *JASIS* (1967–71); ed. adv. bd., *Jnl. of Chem. Info. and Comp. Sci.* (1977–79). **Activities:** 12; 17, 37, 41; 60, 75, 91 **Addr.:** 530 N. Saginaw Rd., Midland, MI 48640.

Resnick, Rhoda (Ap. 17, 1949, Toronto, ON) Libn., Can. Broadcasting Corp., 1979–; Msc. Libn., Metro Toronto Lib., 1976–79; Msc. Catlgr., 1974–76. **Educ.:** Univ. of Toronto, 1967–71, BA (Msclgy.), 1971–73, MLS. **Orgs.:** Can. Assn. of Msc. Libs.: Secy. (1978–79). **Pubns.:** Ed., *Minerva's Diary: A History of Jarvis Collegiate Institute* (1979). **Activities:** 9, 12; 20, 30, 39; 55 **Addr.:** 33 Carl Shepway, Willowdale, ON M2J 1X3 Canada.

Restrepo, Fabio (Jl. 13, 1936, Manizales, Colombia) Proyecto, *LEER* Coord., Sch. of LS, TX Woman's Univ., 1980–; Unesco Consult., Banco del Libro, Venezuela, 1979; Visit. Prof., Sch. of LS, Peabody Coll., 1978; Coord. of OAS Multinatl. Proj., Escuela Interamer. de Bibliotecologia, Colombia, 1976–77; Educ. Coord., IL Migrant Cncl., 1975; Ref. Libn., Rock Island Pub. Lib. (IL), 1969–1974; Ref. Libn., Multnomah Cnty. Lib. (OR), 1967–1969; Prof., Escuela Interamer. de Bibliotecologia 1964–1966; other. **Educ.:** Escuela Interamer. de Bibliotecologia, 1957–60, Lic. (LS); Univ. of IL, 1962–63, BS (Educ.), 1963–64, MS (LS); TX Woman's Univ., 1978–, PhD Cand. (LS). **Orgs.:** ALA: Lib. Servs. to the Span.-speaking Com. Ch. (1981); AASL. ASIS. TX LA. AALS. Others. Aircraft Owners and Pilots Assn. Phi Sigma Iota. **Honors:** Rockefeller Fndn., Grant (MLS), 1962–64. **Pubns.:** *Bibliotecas Especializadas: Su Organizacion y Funcionamiento* (Transl. from Eng.) (1968); "Conference Profile", *Amer. Libs.* (N. 1980); "Projects of Interest", *Proyecto LEER Bltn.* (N. 1980); "School Libraries in Latin America", *Intl. Assn. of Sch. Libnshp. Nsltr.* (Ap. 1980); ed. and fndr., *Revista Interamericana de Bibliotecologia.* **Activities:** 9, 10; 17, 24, 26; 54, 63, 66 **Addr.:** TWU Box 24255, Denton, TX 76204.

Retfalvi, Andrea A. (Je. 2, 1947, Budapest, Hungary) Resrch. Libn., Dept. of Fine Art, Univ. of Toronto, 1977–, Resrch. Asst., 1972–77. **Educ.:** Univ. of Toronto, 1966–70, BA (Fine Art), 1970–71, MA (Hist. of Art), 1974–76, MLS. **Orgs.:** ARLIS/NA. **Pubns.:** Cmplr., *Canadian Illustrated News (Montreal): Index to Illustrations* (1977–); "Les expositions de l'année au Canada/The Year's Exhibitions in Canada," *Can. Art Libs. Nsltr.* (D. 1979). **Activities:** 1; 15, 20, 41; 55 **Addr.:** Dept. of Fine Art, University of Toronto, 100 St. George St., Toronto, ON M5S 1A1 Canada.

Rettig, James R. (N. 11, 1950, Chicago, IL) Ref. Libn., Univ. of Dayton, 1978–; Head Ref. Libn., Murray State Univ., 1977–78, Asst. Ref. Libn., 1976–77. **Educ.:** Marquette Univ., 1968–72, BA (Eng.), 1972–74, MA (Eng.); Univ. of WI, 1975, MALS. **Orgs.:** ALA: Ref. and Subscrpn. Bks. Review Com. (1979–83), Ad Hoc Anls. Subcom. (Ch., 1980–81); RASD, Coop. Ref. Srvs. Com. (1979–81), Darmouth Medal Awd. Com. (Ch., 1981–82); ACRL. Acad. LA of OH. **Pubns.:** "The Status of Reference Librarians, or Waiting for the Revolution," *Ref. Libn.* (forthcoming); "A Classification Scheme for Local Government Documents Collections," *Gvt. Pubns. Review* (1980); "Rights, Resolutions, Fees, and Reality," *Lib. Jnl.* (F. 1981); "Road Maps and Tourist Information for the States and Canada," *RQ* (1977); "Beyond the MLA International Bibliography," *Ref. Srvs. Review* (1979); various articles. **Activities:** 1; 29, 31, 39; 55, 57, 83 **Addr.:** Roesch Library, University of Dayton, 300 College Park, Dayton, OH 45469.

Retzack, Lawrence (Larry) Francis (D. 6, 1940, Plover, WI) Libn., Sagamihara Sch. EMC, 1976–; Multiplex Newscaster, TV-Asahi, Tokyo (Japan), 1979–; Tchr./Asst. Prin., Predischarge Educ. Prog., Open Lrng. Ctr., Camp Fuji (Japan), 1975–76; Libn., Mid. Sch./Sullivans Sch., Yokosuka Nvl. Base, 1974–75. **Educ.:** Univ. of WI, Eau Claire, 1959–63, BA (Msc. Educ.); North. IL Univ., 1964–66, MM (Msc. Educ.), 1970–72, MA (LS); Northw. Univ., 1972–73, (Msc. Educ.); PH.D. Cand. (Msc. Ed.); Dept. of Army and U.S. Air Frc., 1978–79, Certs. (five). **Orgs.:** Msc. LA. Msc. Educs. Natl. Conf.: Student Chap. (Pres., 1963). **Pubns.:** ".... and in Tokyo," *Msc. Educs. Jnl.* (D. 1974); Contrib., "Contempory Nonsense," *Partisan Review* (1971). **Activities:** 10; 21, 32, 46; 55, 63, 95-Broadcast Jnlism. **Addr.:** Sagamihara School EMC, APO San Francisco 96343.

Reuber, Margaret L. J. (Ag. 29, 1928, Springfield, ON) Cat. Supvsr., Inst. for Hist. Micro Reproductions, 1980–; Proj. Coord., Micro., Univ. of West. ON, 1978–79, Sr. Ref. Libn., 1976–78, Ref. Libn., 1972–76. **Educ.:** Univ. of West. ON, 1946–50, BA (Hist.), 1967–68, MLS. **Orgs.:** Can. LA. ON LA: Lcl. Arrange. (1978); Prog. (1979). ON and PQ Wkshp. on Lib. Orien.: Strg. Com. (1976–78). Parkwood Hosp., London, ON: Bd. of Dir. (1975–78). Maycourt Club of Can.: London Branch (Bd. of Dir., 1976–78). **Pubns.:** *Two Walking Tours of London* (1978); **Activities:** 1, 12; 17, 20, 33; 54, 55 **Addr.:** 6 Lakeview Terr., Ottawa, ON K1S 3H4 Canada.

Revesz, Gabrielle Sophie Stern (My. 4, 1927, Budapest, Hungary) Pres., Info./Consult., 1979–; VP, Pubns., Inst. for Sci. Info., 1962–79; Resrch. Asst., Temple Univ. Sch. of Med., Sch. of Pharm., 1960–62. **Educ.:** Univ. of Zurich, Switzerland, 1947–50, (Chem.); Temple Univ., 1956–60, MA (Chem.). **Orgs.:** Amer. Chemical Socty.: Div. Chemical Info. Ch. (1979); Prog. Ch. (1978). ASIS: Pubns. Com. (1974–75). Info. Sci. Abs.: Bd. of Dir. (1974–75). Amer. Stan. Inst.: Z 39 Subcom. (1968–69). Amer. Inst. of Chem.: Philadelphia Chap. (Ch., 1981). Chemical Notation Assn. **Honors:** Sigma Xi. **Pubns.:** Jt. auth., "The Synthetic Chemical Literature from 1960–1969," *Nature* (1973); jt. auth., "One-letter Notation for Calculating Molecular Formulas and Searching Long-Chain Peptides in the Index Chemicus Registry System," *Jnl.Chemical Docum.* (1970); jt. auth., "Index Chemicus Registry System: Pragmatic Approach to Substructure Chemical Retrieval *Jnl. Chemical Docum.* (1970); jt. auth., "Retrieving Chemical Information with Index Chemicus," *Jnl. Chemical Docum.* (1969); jt. auth., "Effects of Mechanization on a Chemical Information Service," *Jnl. Chemical Docum.* (1968); various articles, sps., ed. positions. **Activities:** 14-Pvt. Consult.; 24, 30, 37, 46; 60, 87, 91 **Addr.:** P.O. Box 204, Bala Cynwyd, PA 19004.

Reyes, Helen Marie (D. 29, 1950, Fairfield, CA) Med. Libn., John Muir Meml. Hosp., 1975–; Acq. Libn., Holy Names Coll., 1975; Sch. Libn., Los Angeles Unfd. Sch. Dist., 1973–74. **Educ.:** Holy Names Coll., 1969–73, BA (Psy.); Univ. of South. CA, 1973, MSLS; Med. LA, 1975, 1981, Cert. **Orgs.:** North. CA Med. Lib. Grp.: Mem. Com. (Ch., 1977); Nom. Com. (1978–79). CA LA: Rep. to WHOLIS (1978). Med. LA. ALA. SLA. **Pubns.:** *Art of Bibliotherapy* (1974). **Activities:** 12; 17, 34, 39; 80, 87, 92 **Addr.:** Health Sciences Library, John Muir Memorial Hospital, 1601 Ygnacio Valley Rd., Walnut Creek, CA 94598.

Reynen, Richard Gerard (Mr. 20, 1954, St. Paul, MN) Libn., Deloitte Haskins and Sells, 1976–; Night Libn., Coll. of St. Catherine, 1976–78; Libn., Peat, Marwick, Mitchell and Co., 1975–76. **Educ.:** Coll. of St. Thomas, 1972–76, BA (Bus. Admin., LS); Univ. of MN, 1978–82, MA (LS). **Orgs.:** SLA: MN Chap., Dir. (1978–79), *Bltn.* Ed. (1978–80), Asst. Ed. (1977–78), Student Liaison Ch. (1980–81), Pres.-Elect, Pres. (1981–83). **Activities:** 12; 15, 39, 41; 59 **Addr.:** Deloitte Haskins & Sells Library, 625 4th Ave. S., Minneapolis, MN 55415.

Reynolds, Betty Blakslee (Ja. 11, 1943, Watertown, NY) Tech. Srvs. Libn., NM Tech, 1981–; Head Catlgr., Univ. of MO–Kansas City, 1974–81; Head Catlgr., Inst. of Food and Agr. Scis., Univ. of FL, 1972–73; Assoc. Libn. for Tech. Srvs., Coll. of the VI, 1969–72; Descr. Serials Catlgr., Lib. of Congs., 1966–69. **Educ.:** North. IL Univ., 1961–65, BA (LS, Soc. Scis.); Univ. of Denver, 1965–66, MA (LS); Univ. of MO–Kansas City, 1974–76, MBA (Acct.). **Orgs.:** SLA: Rio Grande Chap. (Treas., 1978–1980). **Activities:** 1; 20, 44; 55, 91 **Addr.:** Martin Speare Library, New Mexico Tech, Socorro, NM 87801.

Reynolds, Catharine J. (Ap. 3, 1919, Erie, PA) Head, Gvt. Pubn. Lib., Univ. of CO, 1966–; Head, Gvt. Docum. Dept., Univ. of IA Libs., 1950–66; Ref./Circ./Docum. Libn., Allegheny Coll., 1947–50. **Educ.:** Villa Maria Coll., 1937–41, BA (Eng., Soclgy.); Columbia Univ., 1946–47, BS (LS); UNITAR (Geneva, Switzerland), 1974, Cert. (Intl. Documtn.). **Orgs.:** ALA: Pub. Docum. Com. CO LA. Assn. of Intl. Libns. *Micro. Review* Bd. of Eds. (1972–). **Honors:** Cncl. on Lib. Resrcs., Flwshp., 1976–77; ALA, GODORT, James Bennett Childs Awd., 1979. **Pubns.:** "League of Nations Documents and Serial Publications 1919–1946," *Micro. Review* (O. 1973); "Declassified Documents Reference System," *Micro. Review* (Mr. 1977); "Discovering the Government Document Collection in Libraries," *RQ* (Spr. 1975); "Planning Space for the Government Documents Collections in Research Libraries," ERIC (1977); "The Public Documents Department Microfiche Information Retrieval System," *Micro. Review* (O. 1974, S. 1978); various articles, reviews. **Activities:** 1; 29; 62 **Addr.:** 850 20th St., Boulder, CO 80302.

Reynolds, Diane Carol Hall (O. 13, 1946, New York, NY) Head, Ref. Libn., Los Angeles Cnty. Law Lib., 1978–, Asst. Head Ref. Libn., 1976–78, Ref. Libn., 1972–76, Ord. Libn., 1969–72. **Educ.:** CA State Univ., 1964–68, BA (Amer. Std.); Univ. of South. CA, 1968–69, MLS; Southwestern Univ., 1970–74, JD. **Orgs.:** CA LA. AALL. South. CA Assn. of Law Libs. CA Women Lawyers. Women Lawyers of Los Angeles. Amer. Cvl. Liberties Un. Amer. Bar Assn. **Pubns.:** Resrch. Ed., *Southwestern Univ. Law Review* (1973). **Activities:** 1, 12; 22, 39, 41; 74, 77, 78 **Addr.:** Los Angeles County Law Library, 301 W. 1st St., Los Angeles, CA 90012.

Reynolds, Judith Arlene (F. 26, 1942, Minneapolis, MN) Catlgr., Kenosha Pub. Lib., 1978–; Ref. Libn., 1970–78; Elem. Libn., Sheboygan Pub. Schs., 1968–69; HS Libn., Sheboygan Falls Pub. Schs., 1967–68; HS Libn., New Glarus Pub. Schs., 1966–67; Span. Tchr., Elcho Pub. Schs., 1965–66. **Educ.:** Augsburg Coll., 1960–65, BA (Span.); Univ. of WI, Oshkosh, 1969–70, MA (LS). **Orgs.:** ALA. WI LA. Women Lib. Workers. Natl. Org. for Women: Secy. (1979–). AAUW: Secy. (1976–78). **Pubns.:** "Pamphlets in Public Libraries," *WI Lib. Bltn.* (My.–Je. 1979). **Activities:** 9; 15, 16, 20 **Addr.:** 5947 Seventh Ave., Kenosha, WI 53140.

Reynolds, Judith (Judy) L. (Jl. 10, 1944, Long Beach, CA) Lib. Instr. Coord., San Jose State Univ. Lib., 1973–; Ref. Libn., San Mateo Pub. Lib., 1971–73; Hum. Ref. Libn., Long Beach State Univ., 1970–71; Head of Cat., Notre Dame Univ. (BC), 1969–70. **Educ.:** San Francisco State Univ., 1964–66, BA (Eng.); Univ. of CA, Berkeley, 1968–69, MLS; San Jose State Univ., 1974–76, MA (Eng.). **Orgs.:** ALA: LIRT; ACRL/Bibl. Instr. Sect., Preconf. Plng. Com. Co-ch. (1980–81). CA Clearhse. on Lib. Instr.: North. Strg. Com. Ch. (1979–81). CA LA: State Univ. and Coll. Libns. Chap. Ch. (1977). CA Postsec. Educ. Comsn. **Pubns.:** Jt. auth., "Experiences with Faculty Status in Academic Libraries," *CA Libn.* (Ja. 1976); "Personnel Plan for Librarians," *CA Libn.* (O. 1977). **Activities:** 1; 15, 31, 39; 55 **Addr.:** San Jose State University Library, 250 S. 4th St., San Jose, CA 95192.

Reynolds, Martha L. (Ap. 20, 1928, Indianapolis, IN) Dir., Frederick Cnty. Pub. Libs., 1967–; Asst. Chief, Pub. Srvs., Montgomery Cnty. Dept. of Pub. Libs., 1963–67; Head, Adult Srvs., Vigo Cnty. Pub. Lib., 1955–63. **Educ.:** Hanover Coll., 1946–50, BA (Eng., Math.); IN Univ., 1955, MSLS. **Orgs.:** MD Assn. of Pub. Lib. Admins.: Ch. (1970). MD LA. ALA: PLA, Goals, Guidelines and Stans. (1975–78); Notable Bks. Cncl. (1964–66, 1975–78). MD Mtrls. Ctr.: Adv. Bd. (1978). MD Pub. Info. Plng. Com. (1979–81). AAUW: Info. Ofcr. (1979). Leag. of Women Voters. Frederick Woman's Civic Club. **Activities:** 9; 17, 19, 47; 50 **Addr.:** Frederick County Public Libraries, 110 E. Patrick St., Frederick, MD 21701.

Reynolds, Maryan E. (F. 17, 1913, Minneapolis, MN) Retired, 1975–; State Libn., WA State Lib., 1951–75; Dir., Richland Pub. Lib., 1950–51; Consult., WA State Lib., 1943–50. **Educ.:** Univ. of MN, 1931–36, BA (Hist.); Univ. of South. CA, 1939–40, BS (LS). **Orgs.:** Amer. Assn. of State Libns.: Pres. (1965–66). ALA: Various ofcs., coms. PC NW LA: VP (1967–68); Pres. (1969–71). AAUW: Olympia Branch (Pres., 1962–64). State Cap. Hist. Socty.: Pres. (1964–66). **Honors:** Delta Kappa Gamma, 1967; State Arts Comsn. Awd., "Quality in pub. arts and enrich. of gvt. through the written word," 1967; Matrix Woman of Achvmt., 1975; Univ. of South. CA, Sch. of LS, Disting. Alum. Awd., 1975. **Pubns.:** *Study of Library Network Alternatives for the State of Washington* (1971); *Authority and Responsibilities of a Network Director* (1970). **Activities:** 13; 17, 24 **Addr.:** 3128 Villa Ct. S.E., Lacey, WA 98503.

Reynolds, Michael M. (D. 8, 1924, New York, NY) Prof., Univ. of MD Coll. of Lib. and Info. Srvs., 1970–, Assoc. Dean/Actg. Dean, 1969–70; Prof., Sch. of LS, SUNY, Albany, 1968–69; Prof., Asst. Dir. of Libs., IN Univ., 1964–68; Actg. Dir. of Libs., WV Univ., 1963, Asst. to Assoc. Dir. of Libs., 1957–64, Asst. Prof., Pol. Sci., 1962–64; Chief Ref. Libn., LA State Univ, 1955–57. **Educ.:** Hunter Coll., 1950, AB; Columbia Univ., 1952, MSLS; Amer. Univ., 1954, MA (Pub. Admin.); Univ. of MI, 1964, PhD. **Orgs.:** ALA: ACRL, Legis. Com. (1969–74); Ref. Srvs. Div., ILL Com. (1963–65); Cncl. (1966–70); Lib. Admin. Div., Com. on Lib. Admin. Dev. (1962), Insr. Com. (1959). WV LA: Pres. (1963). AAUP. **Honors:** Phi Beta Kappa; Pi Gamma Mu; Pi Sigma Alpha. **Pubns.:** *Maryland: A Guide to Information and Reference Sources* (1976); *Guide to Theses and Dissertations: An Annotated Bibliography of Bibliographies* (1975); "Library Cooperation: The Ideal and the Reality," *Coll. and Resrch. Libs.* (1974); jt. ed., *Reader in Library and Information Services* (1974); ed., *Reader in Library Cooperation* (1973); various articles. **Addr.:** Univ. of Maryland, College Park, MD 20742.

Reynolds, Ruth H. (D. 1, 1910, Kossee, TX) Chief, Tech. Lib., HQ, TRADOC Combined Arms Test Activity, Fort Hood, TX 1972–; Lib. Dir., Ctrl. TX Coll., 1967–72; Head Libn.–Franklin Schs., (Ridgewood, NJ), 1964–67; Libn., Houston Sch., (Port

PROFESSIONAL ACTIVITIES: Institutions: 1. Acad. lib.; 2. Arch.; 3. Assn.; 4. Fed./Gvt. lib.; 5. Inst. lib.; 6. Mfr./Suppl.; 7. Milit. lib.; 8. Musm.; 9. Pub. lib.; 10. Sch. lib.; 11. Sch. of lib. sci.; 12. Spec. lib.; 13. State lib.; 14. (other). **Functions/Activities:** 15. Acq./Col. dev.; 16. Adult srvs.; 17. Admin.; 18. Apprais.; 19. Archit./Bldgs.; 20. Cat./Class.; 21. Chld. srvs.; 22. Circ.; 23. Cons./Pres.; 24. Consult.; 25. Cont. ed.; 26. Educ. lib. sci.; 27. Ext. srvs.; 28. Fund/Grants; 29. Gvt. pubs.; 30. Indx./Abs.; 31. Instr. lib. use; 32. Media srvs.; 33. Micro.; 34. Netwks./Coop.; 35. Persnl.; 36. PR; 37. Publshg.; 38. Recs. mgt.; 39. Ref. srvs.; 40. Repro.; 41. Resrch.; 42. Review.; 43. Secur.; 44. Serials; 45. Spec. col.; 46. Tech. srvs.; 47. Trustees/Bds.; 48. YA srvs.; 49. (other).

Arthur, TX), 1960–64. **Educ.:** TX Univ., 1958–60, BS cum laude (Soc. Sci.); George Peabody Coll., 1960–63, MA (LS); Permanent Prof. Tchg. Cert., 1957–60; Other crs., 1975–. **Orgs.:** Natl. Educ. Assn. TX Educ. Assn. TX LA. ALA. **Honors:** Pi Lambda Theta; Phi Alpha Theta. **Activities:** 1, 12; 15, 17, 30; 56, 74, 91 **Addr.:** 210 Live Oak Dr., Harker Heights, TX 76541.

Rezak, Sheila Ann (O. 1, 1949, Gary, IN) Educ. Resrc. Ctr. Libn., Purdue Univ., Calumet Lib., 1976–, Admin. Asst., Ref. Dept., 1971–76. **Educ.:** Purdue Univ., 1967–71, BA (Elem. Educ.); IN Univ., Bloomington, 1972–74, MLS; Purdue Univ., 1975–81 (LS). **Orgs.:** ALA. Rosary Socty. Pilgrimage Socty. of IN. **Honors:** Alpha Lambda Delta, 1967. **Pubns.:** Reviews. **Activities:** 1; 15, 34, 39; 63, 91, 92 **Addr.:** Library, Purdue University, Calumet, Hammond, IN 46323.

Rheay, Mary Louise (Mr. 8, 1920, Montgomery, AL) Dir., Cobb Cnty. Pub. Lib., 1975–; Asst. Dir., Atlanta Pub. Lib., 1963–75; Instr., GA State Univ., 1960–70; Instr., Emory Univ. Lib. Sch., 1960–68; Head, Chld. Dept., 1956–63, Asst. Head, Chld. Dept., 1953–56, Sch. Work, 1942–53. **Educ.:** AL Coll., 1937–40, AB (Hist.); Emory Univ., 1940–41, AB (LS), 1957–59, MS (LS). **Orgs.:** ALA: Chap. Cnclr. (1979–82); ALSC, Frederick Melcher Schol. Com. (1978–80); Jury on Cit. of Trustees (1972–73); Newbery-Caldecott Awd. Com. (1962). SE LA: Com. on Objectives (Ch., 1976–80); various coms., ofcs. (1963–). GA LA: Pres. (1973–75). Metro-Atlanta LA: Pres. (1964–65). Delta Kappa Gamma: Alpha Chap. (Pres., 1967–68). Women's Gld. of Cobb Cmnty. Symph.: Sec. VP (1979–80). **Honors:** Atlanta, Woman of the Yr.–Profs., 1962; PA LA, Allie Beth Martin Awd. (1980). **Activities:** 9; 17 **Addr.:** 4555 Meadow Valley Dr., N.E., Atlanta, GA 30342.

Rhee, Susan F. (N. 10, 1946, Escondido, CA) Head, Cat. Dept., Univ. of CA, San Diego, 1979–; Prin. Catlgr., 1977–79, Head Serials Catlgr., 1974–77; Catlgr., San Diego State Univ., 1968–72. **Educ.:** San Diego State Univ., 1964–68, AB (Grmn.); Univ. of CA, Los Angeles, 1972–73, MLS. **Orgs.:** ALA: RTSD; LITA. CA LA. **Activities:** 1; 17, 20, 46; 56 **Addr.:** Central University Library, CO7SK, University of California, San Diego, La Jolla, CA 92093.

Rhew, David T. (Jl. 31, 1941, Corpus Christi, TX) Libn., Grand Canyon Coll., 1971–; Catlgr., Southwest. Bapt. Semy., 1968–70; Catlgr., TX State Lib., 1966–68; Catlgr., Tarleton State Univ., 1964–66; Ref. Libn., Univ. of Corpus Christi, 1963–64. **Educ.:** Univ. of Corpus Christi, 1959–62, BA (Eng.); N. TX State Univ., 1962–65, MLS; Southwest. Bapt. Theo. Semy., 1968–71, MDiv. **Orgs.:** ALA. AZ State LA. **Activities:** 1; 15, 17; 90 **Addr.:** 3300 W. Camelback Rd., P.O. Box 11097, Phoenix, AZ 85061.

Rhoades, Marjorie H. (F. 22, 1921, New York City, NY) Engin. Sci. Libn., CO State Univ., 1969–; Libn., Fernbank Sci. Ctr., 1967–69; Sci. Ref., Tech. Rpts. Libn., GA Inst. of Tech., 1962–67; Libn., FL Geol. Srvy., 1961–62. **Educ.:** OK State Univ., 1956–59, BS (Sci. Educ.); FL State Univ., 1960–61, MS.; various crs. **Orgs.:** ALA. SLA. Amer. Socty. for Engin. Educ.: Engin. Libs. Div. (Dir., 1979). AAUP: Vice-Ch. (1970–71). **Honors:** CO State Univ., Disting. Libnshp. Awd., 1978; Phi Kappa Phi. **Pubns.:** Ed., *Water and Soil in Arid Regions* (1977); *Water and Soil in Arid Regions* (forthcoming). **Addr.:** Colorado State University Libraries, Morgan Library Bldg. 214, Fort Collins, CO 80523.

Rhoads, James Berton (S. 17, 1928, Sioux City, IA) Retired 1979–; Archvst. of the U. S., Natl. Archs. and Recs. Srv., 1968–79, Deputy Archvst. of the U. S., 1966–68, other Arch. and managerial positions, 1952–66. **Educ.:** Univ. of CA, Berkeley, 1947–50, BA (Hist.), 1950–52, MA (Hist.); Amer. Univ., 1953–65, PhD (Hist.). **Orgs.:** Intl. Cncl. on Archs.: Pres. (1976–79). SAA: Pres. (1974–75). Assn. of Recs. Mgrs. and Admins. Amer. Hist. Assn. Org. of Amer. Histns. **Honors:** Gen. Srvs. Admin., Disting. Srv., 1966, 1979; Rockhurst Coll., Hon. Doct., 1975; Juniata Coll., Hon. Doct., 1976. **Pubns.:** "The Papers of the Presidents", *Proc. of the MA Hist. Socty.* (1977); "Alienation and Thievery. . .", *Amer. Archvst.* (Ap. 1966). **Activities:** 2; 17, 24 **Addr.:** 6502 Cipriano Rd., Lanham, MD 20706.

Rhodes, Glenda M. (Ag. 24, 1942, Sioux Rapids, IA) Dir., Pub. Srvs., Salt Lake City Pub. Lib., 1981–, Head, Fine Arts Dept., 1975–81, Head, YA Dept., 1970–75; Libn., Del Valle Jr. HS (TX), 1964–66. **Educ.:** Univ. of SD, 1960–64, BA (Eng.); CO Coll., 1967–1969, MA (Eng.); The Univ. of TX at Austin, 1973–74, MLS. **Orgs.:** UT LA: New Perspectives RT (Vice-Ch., 1976–77); Natl. Lib. Week Com. (1973–74); Nom. Com. (1980–81). ALA: YASD, Publshrs. Liaison Com. (1974–75). ARLIS/NA. UT Heritage Fndn.: Resrch. Com. (1978–79). **Honors:** Beta Phi Mu; Phi Beta Kappa. **Activities:** 9; 15, 17, 25; 55 **Addr.:** Salt Lake City Public Library, 209 E. Fifth South, Salt Lake City, UT 84103.

Rhodes, J. (Mr. 2, 1921, Sheffield, Yorks., Eng.) Chief Libn., Collins Bay Fed. Medium Secur. Inst. 1969–; Libn., Joyceville Fed. Medium Secur. Inst., 1967–69. **Educ.:** Queens Univ., Kingston, Sch. of Libnshp., 1968; Univ. of BC Lib. Sch., 1977 (Legal Bibl.). **Orgs.:** Can. LA: Prison Lib. Srv. Com. (Ch., 1977–79). Can. Assn. Spec. Lib. and Info. Sci. Kingston LA. **Honors:** The H.W. Wilson Co., John Cotton Dana Lib. PR Awd., 1971; Can. Lib. Resrch. and Dev. Com., Spec. Awd., 1974. **Pubns.:** *Federal Penitentiary Library Survey* (1975); reviews. **Activities:** 12; 36; 50, 74 **Addr.:** Collins Bay Institution, Library Dept., Box 190, Kingston, ON K7L 4V9 Canada.

Rhodes, Lelia G. (O. 21, 1925, Jackson, MS) Dir., Libs., Jackson State Univ., 1976–, Assoc. Dir., 1973–76, Assoc. Head Libn., 1966–73, Cat. Libn., 1957–66; Libn., Jackson Pub. Schs., 1953–57. **Educ.:** Jackson State Univ., 1940–44, BS (Educ.); Atlanta Univ., MSLS; FL State Univ., 1975, PhD (LS). **Orgs.:** SELA. ALA: ACRL, Plng. Com. (1979–81), Ad Hoc Com. on Racism and Sexism Subj. Analysis (1977). MS LA: Pres. (1980); VP (1979); Secy. (1973); Int. Com. (Ch., 1978); ILL Code (Ch., 1981); Nom. Com. (Ch., 1977). Natl. Hist. Pubns. and Recs. Comsn.: Adv. Bd. (1980). MS Hist. Socty. **Honors:** Omega Psi Phi, Citizen of the Yr., 1980; *Amer. Libs.*, Contemporary Libn., 1978; *Essence*, Cited as Career Woman, 1976; Jackson State Univ. Natl. Alum., Inc., Alum. of the Yr., 1973. **Pubns.:** *Jackson State University: First Hundred Years, 1877–1977* (1979); contrib., *Research on Women in Librarianship* (forthcoming); "Not the Triumph, but the Struggle," *MS Libs.* (Win. 1980). **Activities:** 1, 2; 15, 17, 41; 86, 92, 93 **Addr.:** Jackson State University, P.O. Box 17745, Jackson, MS 39217.

Rhodes, Marion E. (Mr. 15, 1922, Pittsburgh, PA) Retired, 1981–; Asst., Lib. Srvs., NY State Lib., 1980–81; Sr. Libn., NY State Lib. for Blind and Visually Handcpd., 1975–80, Sr. Libn., Film Lib., 1968–75. **Educ.:** Univ. of Miami, 1939–43, AB (Art, Educ.); SUNY, Oneonta, 1960–65, MSed (Elem. Educ.); SUNY, Albany, 1965–66, MLS (Lib). **Orgs.:** ALA. NY LA. CLENE. Christ. Libns. Flwshp. **Pubns.:** Various articles on 16mm. film, *Bookmark* (1968–75). **Activities:** 12, 13; 16, 25, 32; 67, 72, 90 **Addr.:** 25 Sandalwood Ln., Scotia, NY 12302.

Rhodes, Yvonne Margaret (S. 4, 1919, Edinburgh, Scotland) Admin. Libn., Med. Tech. Lib., Fitzsimons Army Med. Ctr., 1978–, Libn., 1974–78; Libn., U.S. Army Med. Resrch. and Nutr. Lab., 1954–74. **Educ.:** Loretto Hts. Coll., 1974, BA (Fr.); Univ. of Denver, 1974–76, MA (LS); Med. LA 1977, Cert. **Orgs.:** SLA: Treas. (1970–72). Med. LA. CO Cncl. of Med. Libns. Eng.-Speaking Un. Alliance Francaise de Denver. **Activities:** 4, 14-Hosp.; 17, 39, 46; 80, 74, 91 **Addr.:** 1031 Kingston St., Aurora, CO 80010.

Rhone, Virginia S. (S. 1, 1924, Port Arthur, TX) Lib. Dir., Boyd Meml. Lib., Port Neches Pub. Lib., 1975–. **Educ.:** Lamar Univ., 1973, BBA (Bus.); Sam Houston State Univ., 1980, MLS. **Orgs.:** ALA. TX LA: Legis. Com. (1978–79); Dist. 8 (Treas., 1979–80). Jefferson Cnty. LA. Houston Area Lib. Syst.: Autom. Com. (1976–79). Port Neches Bus. Prof. Women. **Activities:** 9; 15, 17, 26; 75, 78 **Addr.:** George T. Boyd Memorial Library, 635 Ave. C, Port Neches, TX 77651.

Rhydwen, David A. (Je. 14, 1918, Scarborough, ON) Ed. Admin., *The Globe And Mail,* 1981–, Sales Mgr., Info. Globe Div., 1979–80, Chief Libn., 1938–79. **Educ.:** Scarborough Collegiate, 1932–37. **Orgs.:** SLA. Can. LA. ASIS. Can. Micro. Assn. **Honors:** SLA, Newsp. Div., Jack Burness Meml. Awd., 1965; Roll of Hon., 1979. **Pubns.:** "Newspaper Library Computerization," *Spec. Libs.* (F. 1977). **Activities:** 12; 83 **Addr.:** The Globe And Mail, Toronto, ON M5V 2S9 Canada.

Ricard, Richard Joseph, Jr. (D. 15, 1942, Knoxville, TN) Head, Rom. Langs. Sect. I, Descr. Cat. Div., Lib. of Congs., 1975–, Asst. Sect. Head, 1971–75, Sr. Descr. Catlgr., 1969–71, Descr. Catlgr., 1966–69, Lib. Asst., 1964–66. **Educ.:** Lawrence Univ., 1960–64, BA (Hist.). **Orgs.:** ALA. SALALM. **Pubns.:** Jt. auth., "AACR 1 as Applied by Research Libraries for Determining Entry and Heading," *Lib. Resrcs. and Tech. Srvs.* (1980); various contribs. to *Lib. of Congs. Info. Bltn.*; transl., "Graham Greene," by Marie-Béatrice Mesnet in *The Politics of 20th Century Novelists* (1971). **Activities:** 4; 20 **Addr.:** Descriptive Cataloging Division, Library of Congress, Washington, DC 20540.

Ricci, Patricia Rose (D. 30, 1941, St. Paul, MN) Sr. Ref. Libn., J.J. Hill Ref. Lib., 1975–, Ref. Libn., 1965–75. **Educ.:** Coll. of St. Catherine, 1959–63, BA (LS); Univ. of MN, 1963–65, MA (LS). **Orgs.:** MN LA: Spec. Lib. RT (Ch., 1976–78). ALA: SLA/Liason to MN LA (1974–79). MN LUG: Nsltr. Com.; Strg. Com. (1980–). Twin Cities Stans. Coop.: Coord. (1969–). **Pubns.:** "Product and Engineering Standards," *RQ* (Sum. 1979); "At Ease with Computerese," *Minitex Messenger* (Je. 1978). **Activities:** 14-Pvt. Ref.; 31, 36, 39; 59 **Addr.:** James J. Hill Reference Library, 80 W. 4th St., St. Paul, MN 55102.

Rice, Anna Carolyn (S. 21, 1922, Elizabeth, NJ) Educ. Media Spec., Libn., Head, Ref. Lib., Media Ctr., Elizabeth HS, 1977–; Libn., Educ. Media Spec., Battin HS, 1972–77; Supvsg. Libn., Head, Circ., Adult and YA Srvs., Elizabeth Pub. Lib., 1962–72, Prin. Libn., Adult Prog. Coord., 1960–62, Head, Readers Adv. Srv., 1954–60, Sr. Libn., Circ., 1950–54. **Educ.:** NJ Coll. for Women, Rutgers Univ., 1943–45, AB (Eng., Hist.); Columbia Univ., 1947–50, BSLS; State of NJ, Cert. (Prof. Libn.), 1950, 1972, Cert. (Sch. Libn./Educ. Media Spec.), 1979, Cert. (Prin., Supvsr.). **Orgs.:** NJ LA: Human Rel. Com. (Ch., 1968–70); Hist. and Bibl. Sect. (Treas., 1968–71); Adult Educ. Com. (1965–68); Nsltr. NJ Educ. Media Assn.: Com. to Rev. "Eval. of Media Specs." (1979). Un. Cnty. Sch. LA: Secy. (1974); Pres. (1975). NJ State Lib.: Task Frc. on Stans. for NJ Libs. AAUW. Elizabeth Adult Sch. Mayor's Comsn. on Human Rel. Rutgers Grad. Sch. of Educ. Alum. Assn. Various other orgs. **Honors:** Kappa Delta Pi, 1972; Alpha Kappa Alpha; Jt. Ed., *Elizabeth NJ NAACP Nsltr.*, Awd. for Best in its Class, 1963–64. **Pubns.:** Jt. cmplr., *New Jersey and the Negro: A Bibliography 1917–1966* (1967); "The Tyranny of the Bells," *Lib. Jnl.* (Mr. 15, 1978); various articles, *NJ Libs., Adult Srvs. Nsltr.*, other pubns.; reviews, *Lib. Jnl.* **Activities:** 10; 15, 31, 39; 63, 75 **Addr.:** Reference Library and Media Center, Elizabeth High School, 600 Pearl St., Elizabeth, NJ 07202.

Rice, Barbara A. (F. 21, 1936, Northampton, MA) Prin. Libn., Ref. Srvs., NY State Lib., 1981–; Coord., Bibl. Dev., SUNY at Albany, 1977–81, Sci. Biblgphr., 1974–77; Docums. Libn., Knolls Atomic Power Lab., 1968–74; Libn., Richfield Oil Co., 1960–61; Chem. Abs. Abstctr., 1961–62; Chem.-Tech. Files, Shell Oil Co., 1958–60. **Educ.:** Univ. of MA, 1953–57, BS (Chem.); Univ. of CA, Berkeley, 1966–67, MLS; NY State Assoc. Libn. (Med.), 1979; NY State Prin. Libn., 1980. **Orgs.:** SLA: Upstate NY Chap., Dir. Com. (1975), Consult. Com. (1976), Asst. Ed. Chap. Bltn. (1978–81). Capital Dist. Lib. Cncl. **Honors:** Phi Kappa Phi; Beta Phi Mu. **Pubns.:** "Bibliographic Data Bases in Collection Development," *Col. Mgt.* (1979); "Science Periodicals Use Study," *Serials Libn.* (1979); "Weeding in Academic and Research Libraries," *Col. Mgt.* (1978); "The Development of Working Collections in University Libraries," *Coll. and Resrch. Libs.* (1977); "Teaching Bibliographic Reference in a Reports Collection," *Spec. Libs.* (1973). **Activities:** 1, 12; 15, 39, 44; 58, 60, 88 **Addr.:** New York State Library, Cultural Education Center, 6th Floor, Empire State Plz., Albany, NY 12230.

Rice, Cecelia E. (Endicott, NY) Mgr. Tech. Info., Xerox Corp., 1965–; Head Libn., GAF Corp., 1956–65; Asst. Libn., SUNY-Binghamton, 1953–56. **Educ.:** Cornell Univ., 1941–45, AB (Hist.); Syracuse Univ., 1955–56, MSLS. **Orgs.:** SLA. ALA. Assoc. Info. Mgrs. Natl. Assn. of Accts. Natl. Micro. Assn. Intl. Word Prcs. Assn. **Activities:** 12; 17, 39; 51, 59 **Addr.:** Xerox Corporation, Technical Information Center, Rochester, NY 14644.

Rice, Dorothy F. (D. 19, 1928, Denton, TX) Admin. Srv. Libn., Univ. of NV, Reno 1979–, Tech. Srvs. Libn., 1974–79, Serials Libn., 1971–74, Serials Libn., Aeromedical Lib., USAF Sch. of Aerospace Med. 1965–70; Cat. Libn., U.S. Army Engineer School, 1962–65; Libn., U.S. Army Bd. for Aviation Accident Resrch., 1959–62. **Educ.:** N. TX State Univ., 1944–47, BA (Eng.), 1947–50, BS (LS). Med. LA Cert. (1966–). **Orgs.:** NV LA: Conf. Prog. Ch. (1978); Coll. and Resrch. Libs. Sect. (1975–76); Anl. Mtg. Lcl. Arrange. Ch. (1974). Mt. Plains LA: Nom. Com. (1979). ALA. CA LA. **Honors:** NV LA, Spec. Cit., 1978. **Pubns.:** "Portrait of a Network User: University of Nevada, Reno Library," *RLIN Nsltr.* (1979); guest ed., Spec. Issue on Indxng. of NV Newsps., *Highroller* (Ja. 1978); "The Impact of Automation on the UNR Library," *Highroller* (Jy. 1977). **Activities:** 1; 17, 28, 49-Stats.; 55, 56 **Addr.:** University of Nevada Library, Reno, NV 89557.

Rice, James G., Jr. (Je. 18, 1946, Durham, NC) Asst. Prof., LS, West. MI Univ., 1978–; Dir., Instr. Mtrls. Ctr., Univ. of MO, Columbia, 1977–78; Ref. Libn., Bradley Univ., 1972–76; Probation Ofcr., Juvenile Ct. of Marion Cnty. (IN), 1968–70. **Educ.:** Macalester Coll., 1964–68, BA (Eng., Phil.) IN Univ., 1970–71, MLS; Univ. of MO, 1976–78, PhD (LS). **Orgs.:** ALA: ACRL/Bibl. Instr. Sect., Resrch. Com. AALS: Conf. Plng. Com. (1980). **Pubns.:** "Optical Chameter Recognition: The Impending Revolution in Machine Readable Conversion," *Lib. Jnl.* (S. 1981); *Teaching Library Use: A Guide to Library Institution* (1981); "Fiber Optics: A Bright Information Future," *Lib. Jnl.* (My. 1980); "Alternative Careers for Library School Graduates," *Wilson Lib. Bltn.* (S. 1979); "To Fee or Not to Fee," *Wilson Lib. Bltn.* (My. 1979). **Activities:** 1, 11; 26, 32; 56 **Addr.:** School of Librarianship, Western Michigan University, Kalamazoo, MI 49008.

Rice, Sher (Jl. 2, 1951, Milwaukee WI) Libn.-in-Charge, Rebecca Kauffman Meml. Lib., Congregation Kesher Israel, 1981–; Libn.-in-Charge, Raymond A. Lemmon Lib., Downington Indus. and Agr. Sch., 1980–; Dir./Co-Fndr., EemeeBeetee Lib. of the Jewish Woman, 1979–; Libn.-in-Charge, Isadore Gruskin Meml. Lib. of Congregation B'nai David (Southfield, MI), 1975–79. **Educ.:** Univ. of WI, Milwaukee, 1968–73, BA (Eng.); Wayne State Univ., 1974–75 MSLS. **Orgs.:** AJL: Bltn. (Contr. and Asst. Ed., 1977–). Jewish Libns. Caucus: Pubcty. Ch. (1978). Jewish LA of Metro. Detroit: Secy.-Treas. (1976–77); Pres. (1977–78); Pubcty. and Prtg. (Ch., 1978–79). CSLA: Wkshp. Leader (1978). Hadassah. **Honors:** Jewish LA of Metro. Detroit Apprec. Awd., My. 1979. **Pubns.:** "Macedonian Ethnic Library Preserves Yugoslavian Culture," *Amer. Libs.* (O. 1980); "Wanted: 2 Full-Time Professional Jobs," *Amer. Libs.* (Je. 1976); various articles in *AJL Bltn.* (1977–). **Activities:** 12; 24, 36, 39; 63, 66 **Addr.:** Eemee Beetee Library, 190 Apple Dr., Exton, PA 19341.†

Special Subjects/Services: 50. Adult educ.; 51. Advert./Mktg.; 52. Aerosp.; 53. Agric.; 54. Area std.; 55. Arts/Hum.; 56. Autom.; 57. Bibl./Prtg.; 58. Bio. sci.; 59. Bus./Fin.; 60. Chem.; 61. Copyrt.; 62. Documtn.; 63. Educ.; 64. Engin.; 65. Env.; 66. Eth. grps.; 67. Film; 68. Food/Nutr.; 69. Geneal.; 70. Geo.; 71. Geol.; 72. Handcpd.; 73. Hist.; 74. Int. frdm.; 75. Info. sci.; 76. Insr.; 77. Law; 78. Legis.; 79. Math./Comp. sci.; 80. Med.; 81. Metals; 82. Nat. resrcs.; 83. Newsp.; 84. Nuc. sci.; 85. Oral hist.; 86. Petr./Energy; 87. Pharm.; 88. Phys./Astr./Math.; 89. Readg.; 90. Relig.; 91. Sci./Tech.; 92. Soc. sci.; 93. Telecom.; 94. Transp.; 95. (other).

Richard, Harris M. (Ap. 1, 1939, Newark, NJ) Head Libn., San Juan Coll., 1981–; Dir., Lib. Srvs., Coll. of Ganado, 1975–81; Sci. Libn., Univ. of AZ, 1972–75, Serials Libn., 1969–72; Ref. Libn., Plainfield (NJ) Pub. Lib., 1965–69. **Educ.:** Rutgers Univ., 1957–60, BA (Eng.), 1963–65, MLS. **Orgs.:** ALA. SWLA. Indian LA. NM LA. **Activities:** 1; 15, 17, 31; 66 **Addr.:** 3701 Zuni Dr., Apt. 4, Farmington, NM 87401.

Richard, John B. (N. 2, 1932, MS) Dir., E. Baton Rouge Par. Lib., 1977–; Head Libn., LA State Univ., Alexandria, Hum. Div., 1959–60, Prep. Dept., 1959. **Educ.:** Perkinson Jr. Coll., 1950–52; MS South. Coll., 1952–54, BS (Eng.); LA State Univ., 1957–59, MS (LS). **Orgs.:** ALA. SWLA. LA LA: Lit. Awds. Com. (Ch., 1964–67); Coll. and Ref. Sect. (Ch., 1968–69); First VP and Pres. (1968–69, 1969–70); Nom. Com. (Ch., 1971–72); Conf. Ch. (1975, 1979). Kent Hse. Fndn.: Bd. of Dirs. (1971–76). Ctrl. LA Art Assn.: Bd. of Dirs., (1971–76). Baton Rouge Rotary Club. United Way, Agency Srv. Div. Other orgs. **Honors:** Alexandria Daily Town Talk, Outstan. Citizen of Year Awd., 1975. **Pubns.:** "The Financial Plight of Louisiana's Libraries," *LA LA Bltn.* (Spr. 1970); "Survey of Louisiana Libraries - College Library Reaction," *LA LA Bltn.* (Spr. 1968); "The Louisiana Literary Award Medal," *LA LA Bltn.* (Sum. 1967); "The 1965 Louisiana Literary Award," *LA LA Bltn.* (Spr. 1966); Cmplr., Ten exhibition cats. for LSUA Lib. "Meet the Artist" series. **Activities:** 1, 9; 15, 17, 24; 55, 63, 69 **Addr.:** East Baton Rouge Parish Library, 7711 Goodwood Blvd., Baton Rouge, LA 70806.

Richards, Benjamin Billings II (Mr. 24, 1917, Dubuque, IA) Dir., West. NY Lib. Resrcs. Cncl., 1973–; Libn., TX Woman's Univ., 1969–72; Libn., Chatham Coll., 1963–69; Prof., Ch., Div. Lib. Educ. and Lib. Srvs., KS State Tchrs. Coll., 1959–63; Libn., William Allen White Meml. Lib., 1959–63; Asst. Libn., Pomona Coll. Lib., 1949–56; Libn., Knox Coll., 1946–58. **Educ.:** Loras Coll., 1934–36, AB; Univ. North IA, 1939, BS (LS); Case West. Rsv. Univ., 1941, MA (Amer. Std.); Claremont Grad. Sch., 1951; various crs. **Orgs.:** Midwest Acad. Libns. Conf.: Ch. (1955–56). NY LA: Assn. Coll. and Resrch. Libs. (Tri-State Pres., 1966–67). AAUP: TX Woman's Univ. Chap. (VP, Pres. Elect, 1972–73). Carl Sandburg Assn. Ord. Bookfellows. Various other orgs. **Honors:** Sigma Tau Delta; Beta Phi Mu. **Pubns.:** *CA Gold Rush Merchant: The Journal of Stephen Davis* (1956); ed., *The Stepladder* (1952–58). **Activities:** 1, 13; 15, 17, 34; 55, 63, 89 **Addr.:** Western New York Library Resources Council, Lafayette Sq., Buffalo, NY 14203.

Richards, Berry G. (D. 2, 1930, Newark, NJ) Dir. of Univ. Libs., Lehigh Univ., 1977–, Actg. Dir., 1976–77, Assoc. Libn., 1969–76; Head Libn., Sprague Electric Co., 1957–69. **Educ.:** Vassar Coll. 1948–52, AB (Lib. Arts); SUNY, Albany, 1966–68, MLS; Drexel Univ., 1976– (LS). **Orgs.:** Interlib. Del. Srv. of PA: VP (1980–81). ALA: ACRL, DE Valley Chap. (Pres., 1980–81). PA LA: Coll. and Resrch. Div. Secy. (1980–81), Vice-Ch., Ch.-Elect. (1981–82), Ch. (1982–83). ASIS. AAUP. **Pubns.:** Jt. auth., *Magazines for Libraries* 3d ed. (1978); jt. sci. ed., *Magazines for Libraries* 2d ed. (1972, 1974); reviews. **Activities:** 1; 17; 64, 91 **Addr.:** Linderman Library, Lehigh University, Bethlehem, PA 18015.

Richards, Louise Carr (S. 22, 1923, Philadelphia, PA) Head, Tech. Srvs., Randolph-Macon Coll., 1973–; Orig. Catlgr., Univ. of VA, 1970–73; Chem., Amer. Cyanamid Co., 1946–54. **Educ.:** Wilson Coll., 1941–45, BA (Chem.); Syracuse Univ., 1969–70, MSLS. **Orgs.:** ALA. VA LA. Potomac Tech. Prcs. Libns. AAUP. **Honors:** Beta Phi Mu, 1970. **Activities:** 1; 20, 46; 60 **Addr.:** Page Library, Randolph-Macon College, Ashland, VA 23005.

Richards, Pamela Spence (Je. 2, 1941, New York, NY) Asst. Prof., Grad. Sch. of Lib. and Info. Std., Rutgers Univ., 1977–; Ref. Libn., Westchester Cmnty. Coll., 1976–77; Resrch. Assoc., Columbia Bus. Sch., 1973–76. **Educ.:** Harvard Univ., 1959–63, BA (Grmn.); Columbia Univ., 1963–66, MA (Grmn.), 1969–71, MLS, 1974–79, DLS. **Orgs.:** ALA. Amer. Prtg. Hist. Assn. Bibl. Socty. of Amer. **Pubns.:** *The Dutch in America* (1972); *The Netherlands: A Chronicle and Factbook* (1973); "Gathering Enemy Scientific Information in Wartime", *Jnl. of Lib. Hist.* (Win./Spr. 1981); ed., *Jnl. of Rutgers Univ. Libs.* (1980–). **Activities:** 11; 26, 37; 57 **Addr.:** Rutgers University, Graduate School of Library and Information Studies, 4 Huntington St., New Brunswick, NJ 08903.

Richards, Vincent Philip Haslewood (Ag. 1, 1933, Sutton Bonington, Nottinghamshire, Eng.) Dir. of Libs., Edmonton Pub. Lib., 1977–; Chief Libn., Red Deer Coll., 1967–77; Asst. Dir., Fraser Valley Reg. Lib., 1958–67; Asst. Branch Libn., Peace River, Pub. Lib. Comsn., Dawson Creek, 1956–57; various positions in pub. libs., 1949–56. **Educ.:** Univ. of OK, 1966, BLStd.; Royal Army Educ. Corps, Sch. of Army Ed., 1951–52, Cert. (Tchg.). **Orgs.:** LA UK. Can. Assn. of Coll. and Univ. Libs.: Dir. (1972–74). Can. LA. Pac. NW LA: Secy. (1959). Various ofcs., orgs. Rotary. **Pubns.:** "Reform - not schism," *BC Lib. Qtly.* (O. 1965); various papers. **Activities:** 1, 9; 15, 17, 32, 39; 55, 56, 90 **Addr.:** 7 Sir Winston Churchill Sq., Edmonton, AB T5J 2V4 Canada.

Richardson, Donna Lynn (S. 6, 1950, Detroit, MI) Asst. Dir. for Pub. Srvs., Boys Town Ctr. for the Study of Youth Dev., 1980–, Ref. Libn., 1979–80; Dist. Libn., Sch. Dist. 64 (N. Chicago), 1974–79; Elem. Libn., Homewood Sch. (Pittsburgh), 1972–73. **Educ.:** Drake Univ., 1967–70, BS (Educ.); Univ. of MI, 1971–72, AMLS; Univ. of IL, 1978–, Advnc. Study (LS). **Orgs.:** ALA. SLA. Univ. of MI Sch. of LS Alum. Assn. **Activities:** 12; 30, 39; 63, 92 **Addr.:** 11729 Fowler, Omaha, NE 68164.

Richardson, John V. Jr. (D. 27, 1949, Columbus, OH) Asst. Prof., Grad. Sch. of Lib. and Info. Sci., Univ. of CA, Los Angeles, 1978–; Assoc. Instr., IN Univ., 1975–76; Head, ILL Srvs., Univ. of KY, 1973–74, Docum. Libn., 1972–73. **Educ.:** OH State Univ., 1968–71, BA (Soc.); Peabody Coll., 1971–72, MLS; IN Univ., 1975–78, PhD (Libnshp). **Orgs.:** ALA: H.W. Wilson Per. Awd. Com. (1977). ASIS. AALS. Amer. Statistical Assn. Amer. Soc. Assn. **Honors:** Beta Phi Mu, 1973. **Pubns.:** *Municipal Government Reference Sources* (1978); "Theory vs. Practice," *Jnl. of Educ. for Libnshp.* (Spr. 1981); *The Spirit of Inquiry in Library Services* (ALA mono. 42); jt. auth., *Calligraphic Resources* (forthcoming); various articles, reviews. **Activities:** 1, 11; 26, 29, 41; 57, 75, 92 **Addr.:** University of California, Los Angeles, Graduate School of Library and Information Science, Los Angeles, CA 90024.

Richardson, Robert J. (Je. 8, 1937, Gregory, MI) Non-Print Media Libn., Montclair State Coll., 1976–; Ref. Libn., SUNY, Brockport, 1973–76; Bio. Libn., Univ. of Notre Dame, 1970–73. **Educ.:** William Jewell Coll., 1955–59, AB (Hist.); West. MI Univ., 1968–70, MLS; MI State Univ., 1967–69, MA (Hist.). **Orgs.:** ALA: ACRL. **Honors:** Beta Phi Mu, 1970. **Activities:** 1; 31, 32, 33; 67 **Addr.:** Sprague Library, Montclair State College, Upper Montclair, NJ 07043.

Richardson, Selma K. (O. 23, 1931, Allison Park, PA) Assoc. Prof., LS, Univ. of IL, 1974–; Dir., Media Srvs., Oak Park and River Forest (IL) HS, 1970–74; Asst. Prof., Ball State Univ., 1969–70; Libn., Oak Park (MI) Pub. Schs., 1960–69; Tchr., Berkley (MI) Pub. Schs., 1953–60. **Educ.:** St. Olaf Coll., 1951–53, BM (Msc.); Univ. of MI, 1959, MA (Educ.), 1962, AMLS, 1969, PhD (Educ.). **Orgs.:** ALA: Cncl. (1972–76), Awds. Com. (1974–76); ALSC, Nom. Com. (1971–72), Com. on Natl. Plng. for Spec. Cols. (Ch., 1978–79); AASL, Prof. Dev. Com. (1974–78). AALS: Tsk. Frc. on Sixth Yr. Prog. (1975–77). IL LA: IL Assn. for Media in Educ. Various other coms., ofcs. Chld. Lit. Assn. Chicago Chld. Readg. RT. **Honors:** Phi Kappa Phi; Pi Lambda Theta; Beta Phi Mu. **Pubns.:** Ed., *Children's Services of Public Libraries* (1978); "The Study and Collecting of Historical Children's Books," *Lib. Trends* (Spr. 1979); *Research about Nineteenth-Century Children and Books: Portrait Studies* (1980); *Periodicals for School Media Programs* (1978); "Audiovisual Materials for Young Adults," *Lib. Trends* (Ap. 1974); "The Media Specialist as Activist," *IALS News for You* (Mr. 1973); various other pubns. **Activities:** 10, 11; 21, 26, 45; 55, 63, 89 **Addr.:** University of Illinois, Graduate School of Library and Information Science, 410 David Kinley Hall, 1407 W. Gregory Dr., Urbana, IL 61801.

Richardson, Thomas George (S. 22, 1936, Missoula, MT) Head Libn., Mercer Island Pub. Lib., 1969–; Head Libn., Kent Pub. Lib., 1967–69; Head Libn., Forest Park (WA) Pub. Lib., 1966–67. **Educ.:** Univ. of Omaha, 1960–61, BEd (Amer. Lit.); West. MI Univ., 1965–66, MSLS. **Orgs.:** WA LA. NLA: WA Chap. (Pres., 1979–80). **Activities:** 9; 16, 36, 39; 55 **Addr.:** Mercer Island Library, 4400 88th Ave. S.E., Mercer Island, WA 98040.

Richardson, William H. (Ap. 28, 1923, Wooster, OH) Libn., Engin. Resrch. Lib., Detroit Diesel Allison Div., Gen. Motors Corp., 1963–; Ref. Libn., Sandia Corp., 1956–63; Libn., Coll. of Engin., Washington Univ. (St. Louis), 1954–56; Asst. Ref. Libn., Univ. of Denver, 1952–54. **Educ.:** Univ. of NM, 1948–51, BS (Bio.); Univ. of Denver, 1951–52, MA (LS). **Orgs.:** SLA: Rio Grande Chap., Pres. (1960–61); IN Chap., Pres. (1968–69); Aerosp. Div., Ch. (1970–71). **Pubns.:** "Circulation control," *Spec. Libs.* (N. 1960). **Activities:** 12; 20, 22, 39; 52 **Addr.:** Library, S5, Detroit Diesel Allison Div., General Motors Corp., P.O. Box 894, Indianapolis, IN 46206.

Richburg, Verdie Farmer (N. 14, 1944, Wilson, NC) Supvsr., Jefferson Par. Lib., 1980–, Branch Mgr., 1979–80; Chld. Libn., DC Pub. Lib., 1971–77; Lib. of Congs., 1968–69. **Educ.:** NC Ctrl. Univ., 1964–67, BS (Hlth. Educ.), Univ. of MD, 1971–72, MLS. **Orgs.:** ALA. LA LA. Phi Beta Lamda Bus. Club. **Honors:** Delta Sigma Theta. **Activities:** 4, 9; 16, 21, 22; 57, 80, 95-Jail lib. srv. **Addr.:** 4820 Zenith St., Metairie, LA 70001.

Richer, Suzanne (O. 25, 1943, Hull, PQ) Dir. of Documtn., Trans. Bur., Gvt. of Can., 1977–; Liaison Ofcr., Ntwks. Bur., Natl. Lib. of Can., 1976–77; Reg. Libn. (Prov. of PQ), Env. Can., 1974–76, Libn., Laurentian Forest Resrch. Ctr., 1966–74; Tech. Libn., Comp. Devices of Can. Ltd. 1965–66. **Educ.:** Univ. de Montreal, 1960–64, BA; Univ. of Ottawa, 1964–65, BLS. **Orgs.:** Corp. des Bibtcrs. Prof. du PQ. Can. LA. ASTED. Can. Assn. for Info. Sci. Intl. Wildlife Fed. **Pubns.:** *La Gestion de la Documentation au Bureau des Traductions du Gouvernement du Canada* (1980); *Le macrothésaurus des Sciences et des Techniques* (1979); *French-English Index of Subject Headings* **Activities:** 4; 17 **Addr.:** Documentation Directorate, Translation Bureau, Ottawa, ON K1A 0M5 Canada.

Richer, Yvon (Jl. 2, 1943, Hull, PQ) Univ. Chief Libn., Univ. of Ottawa, 1978–, Asst. Dir. of Lib. Syst., 1976–77; Asst. Dir., Systs., Cat. Branch, Natl. Lib. of Can., 1975–76; Head, Procs. Div. Tech. Srvs., Univ. Laval Lib., 1974–75, Head of Cat. Dept., 1968–72, Asst. Head of Cat., 1966–68, Catlgr., 1965–66. **Educ.:** Univ. of Ottawa, 1959–64, BA (Arts), 1964–65, BLS; Univ. of Toronto, 1969–70, MLS. **Orgs.:** ASTED: Can. LA: ALA. Corp. des bibl. prof. du PQ. Can. Assn. Info. Sci. **Activities:** 1; 17; 56 **Addr.:** University of Ottawa, 65 Hastey St., Ottawa, ON K1N 9A5 Canada.

Richert, Paul (Ag. 31, 1948, Elwood, IN) Law Libn., Univ. of Akron Sch. of Law, 1978–, Visit. Asst. Prof., LS, Kent State Univ. Sch. of LS, 1980; Asst. Law Libn., 1977–78; Circ. Libn., Yongson Lib., 1972–74. **Educ.:** Univ. of IL, 1966–70, AB (Hist.), 1970–71, MS (LS); Tulane Univ., 1974–77, JD (Common Law). **Orgs.:** AALL: Rcrt. Com. (1979–81). OH Reg. Assn. of Law Libs.: Nom. Com. (1980–81). Akron Bar Assn. Amer. Bar Assn. **Pubns.:** "Update on Ohio Judicial Reporting," *OH State Law Jnl.* (1980). **Activities:** 1; 17, 31, 39; 77 **Addr.:** Law Library, School of Law, C. Blake McDowell Law Center, The University of Akron, Akron, OH 44325.

Richeson, Marian E. (O. 31, 1940, Rahway, NJ) Mgr., Instr. Srvs., Justice Inst. of BC, 1978–; Dir., Pub. Legal Educ. and Legal Info. Srvs., Legal Srvs. Comsn., 1975–78; Actng. Dir., Lib. and Info. Srvs., Mnstry. of the Attorney–Gen., 1976–77; Bus. Libn., Univ. of AB, 1973–74; Asst. Dir., AB Rural Libs. Proj., 1972–73; Sessional Lectr., Lib. Sch., Univ. of AB, 1971–72; Asst. Ed., *Can. Jnl. of Agr. Econ.,* 1969–71; Pubns. Dir., Dept. of Agr. Econ. and Rural Soclgy., Univ. of AB, 1966–70. **Educ.:** Coll. of Wooster, 1961–63, BA (Eng.); Univ. of AB, 1970–71, BLS, 1978, MLS. **Orgs.:** Can. LA: Int. Frdm. Com. (Conv., 1976–80). ALL: Access to Law Com. (1978–). ASIS. Can. Law Info. Cncl: Pub. Legal Educ. and Info. Com. Pac. Legal Educ. Assn.: Dir. (1979–). Can. Cmnty. Law Jnl.: Ed. Bd. (1977–80). **Honors:** Sch. of LS, Univ. of AB, Gold Medal in LS, 1971. **Pubns.:** "Library Development in the Prairies," *Can. Libnshp.* (1976); *Canadian Rural Sociology Bibliography* (1971); "Student Impressions of the Western International Library Conference," *MB Lib. Bltn.* (1971). "Legal Information Services," *Emergency Libn.* (1977); "Legal Information Services in B.C.," *The Advocate* (1977). **Activities:** 1, 12; 17, 32, 39; 50, 74, 77 **Addr.:** Justice Institute of BC, 4180 W. 4th Ave., Vancouver, BC V6R 4J5 Canada.

Richey, Alice L. (O. 22, 1926, Enid, OK) Zollars Libn., Phillips Univ., 1963–; Catlgr., Bass Bapt. Hosp. Nursing Sch., 1962–63; Libn., Vance Air Frc. Base, 1954–55; Libn., Carnegie (Enid, OK) Pub. Lib., 1948–49. **Educ.:** Phillips Univ., Univ. of OK, 1943–47, BA (LS), 1974–76, MLS. **Orgs.:** OK LA: Lib. Educs. Div. (Secy., 1978–80). Garfield Cnty LA: Rpt. (1977–78). SW LA. Phillips Univ. Fed. Credit Un., Keowettes Ext. Homemakers. **Honors:** Beta Phi Mu, 1976. **Activities:** 1, 11; 17, 26, 35; 57, 63, 74 **Addr.:** 2701 E. Cherokee, Enid, OK 73701.

Richmond, Le Roy I. (Ja. 5, 1938, Tacoma, WA) Head Msc. Catlgr., NY Pub. Lib., 1971–; Msc. Catlgr., 1968–71, Msc. Libn., 1967–68, Chld. Libn., 1966–67. **Educ.:** Univ. of WA, 1955–61, BA (Msc.), 1965–66, MLS. **Orgs.:** Msc. LA: Cat. Cncl., Exec. Com. (1976–). **Honors:** H. W. Wilson Awd., 1966. Beta Phi Mu. **Activities:** 9; 20; 55 **Addr.:** The New York Public Library, 8 E. 40th St., New York, NY 10016.

Richmond, Phyllis Allen (Ja. 5, 1921, Boston, MA) Prof., LS, Case West. Rsv. Univ., 1970–; Prof., LS, Syracuse Univ., 1969–70; Info. Systs. Spec., Univ. of Rochester, 1966–68, Supvsr., River Campus Sci. Libs., 1960–66, Serials Catlgr., 1955–60. **Educ.:** Mather Coll., West. Rsv. Univ., 1938–42, AB (Hist.); Univ. of PA, 1945–46, MA (Hist. of Sci.), 1948–49, PhD (Hist. of Sci.); West. Rsv. Univ., 1952–56, MSLS. **Orgs.:** ALA: Various ofcs., coms. SLA. ASIS: Jnl. Ed. Bd. (1962–78). Class. Resrch. Grp. (London). *Intl. Class.* Ed. Bd. (1977–). Hist. of Sci. Socty. Amer. Assn. for the Hist. of Med. Amer. Assn. of Variable Star Observers: Solar Flare Ptl. **Honors:** Phi Beta Kappa, 1942; ASIS, Awd. of Merit, 1972; ALA, Margaret Mann Cit., 1977; Cncl. on Lib. Resrcs., Mid–Career Flwshp., 1977. **Pubns.:** *Introduction to PRECIS for North American Usage* (1981); *Index to Scientific Journal Title Abbreviations in the Physical Review* (1964); various articles (1942–). **Activities:** 1, 11; 20, 26, 41; 56, 75, 91 **Addr.:** Baxter School of Information and Library Science, Case Western Reserve University, Cleveland, OH 44106.

Richter, Anne F. (O. 7, 1930, Oakland, CA) Asst. Ed., *Lib. Jnl.* 1978–; Ed. Asst., Reviews, 1977–78, Asst. Ed., *Subj. Guide to Bks. in Print* 1975–77. **Educ.:** Reed Coll., 1948–53, BA (Lit.); Columbia Univ., 1972–75, MS with honors (LS). **Orgs.:** ALA. **Honors:** Phi Beta Kappa. **Activities:** 14-Publishr.; 20, 37, 41 **Addr.:** Library Journal, 1180 Ave. of the Americas, New York, NY 10036.

Richter, John Henry (N. 25, 1919, Vienna, Austria) Head, Docum. Unit, Serials Div., Univ. of MI, 1980–, Asst-.Docum. Acq. Libn., 1976–80; Serials Catlgr., 1972–76, Head, Tech. Docum. Srv., Willow Run Labs., 1956–72; various libn.

PROFESSIONAL ACTIVITIES: Institutions: 1. Acad. lib.; 2. Arch.; 3. Assn.; 4. Fed./Gvt. lib.; 5. Inst. lib.; 6. Mfr./Suppl.; 7. Milit. lib.; 8. Musm.; 9. Pub. lib.; 10. Sch. lib.; 11. Sch. of lib. sci.; 12. Spec. lib.; 13. State lib.; 14. (other). **Functions/Activities:** 15. Acq./Col. dev.; 16. Adult srvs.; 17. Admin.; 18. Apprais.; 19. Archit./Bldgs.; 20. Cat./Class.; 21. Chld. srvs.; 22. Circ.; 23. Cons./Pres.; 24. Consult.; 25. Cont. ed.; 26. Educ. lib. sci.; 27. Ext. srvs.; 28. Fund/Grants; 29. Gvt. pubs.; 30. Indx./Abs.; 31. Instr. lib. use; 32. Media srvs.; 33. Micro.; 34. Netwks./Coop.; 35. Persnl.; 36. PR; 37. Publshg.; 38. Recs. mgt.; 39. Ref. srvs.; 40. Repro.; 41. Resrch.; 42. Review.; 43. Secur.; 44. Serials; 45. Spec. col.; 46. Tech. srvs.; 47. Trustees/Bds.; 48. YA srvs.; 49. (other).

positions, Lib. of Congs., 1950–56. **Educ.:** Univ. of CA, Berkeley, 1946–49, BA (Pol. Sci.), 1949–50, BLS. **Orgs.:** SLA: Gvt. Info. Srvs. Com. (Ch., 1977–79). ALA: GODORT. Depos. Lib. Cncl. to the Pub. Printer, (1978–81). Amer. Topical Assn.: *Topical Time* Ed. Bd. **Honors:** Amer. Topical Assn., Disting. Srv. Awd., 1963. **Pubns.:** Cumulative index, 1954–61, *The Holy Land Philatelist* (1975); *Judaica on Postage Stamps* (1974). cumulative index, 1949–72, *The Israel Philatelist* (1973). Various articles in prof., hist., and philatelic pers. **Activities:** 1; 15, 29, 44 **Addr.:** P.O. Box 7978, Ann Arbor, MI 48107.

Richter, Sarah Jane (Mr. 9, 1947, Baltimore, MD) Catlgr., U.S. Gvt. Prtg. Ofc., 1977–; Catlgr., Ref. Libn., Midland Pub. Lib., 1974–77; Catlgr., Jt. Univ. Libs., Nashville, TN, 1969–72. **Educ.:** Hiram Coll., 1965–69, BA (Hist.); George Peabody Coll., 1970–72, MLS. **Orgs.:** SLA. Smithsonian Resident Assoc. **Activities:** 4; 20, 29; 78 **Addr.:** Government Printing Office, N. Capitol and H. Sts., NW, Washington, DC 20401.

Rick, Thomas C. (O. 26, 1944, Milaca, MN) Cat. Libn., Harris-Stowe State Coll., 1981–; Coord. of Cat. Conversion, Christ Semy., 1978–81, Dir. of Tech. Srvs., 1974–78; Dir. of Tech. Srvs., Concordia Semy., 1971–74. **Educ.:** Concordia Semy., 1966–70, MDiv; Univ. of IL, 1970–71, MLS. **Orgs.:** ALA. ATLA: Com. on Cat. and Class. (Ch., 1974–1976). Univ. of IL Alum. Assn. **Honors:** Beta Phi Mu. **Activities:** 1; 20, 46; 90 **Addr.:** 4140 Castleman, St. Louis, MO 63110.

Rickards, Doris J. (Mr. 23, 1944, Delaware County, PA) Med. Libn., Paoli Meml. Hosp., 1972–. **Educ.:** Westminster Coll., 1962–66, BA (Educ.); Drexel Univ., 1967–70, MSLS; Med. LA, Cert. (Med. Libnshp.). **Orgs.:** Med. LA: Philadelphia Reg. Grp. (Bd. of Dir., 1977–78). Cnsrtm. for Hlth. Info. and Lib. Srvs.: Exec. Com. (1976–); VP. (1978–79); Pres. (1979–81). **Pubns.:** "Providing Health Care Information to Patients in a Small Hospital," *Bltn. Med. LA* (Jl. 1978). **Activities:** 12; 39, 46; 50, 80 **Addr.:** Robert M. White Memorial Library, Paoli Memorial Hospital, Paoli, PA 19301.

Rickert, Carol A. (Je. 20, 1953, Waukegan, IL) Cmnty. Srvs. Libn., Arlington Heights Meml. Lib., 1978–; Asst. Chld. Libn., Mt. Prospect Pub. Lib., 1976–78. **Educ.:** Cornell Coll., 1971–75, BSS (Grmn., Hist.); Univ. of IL, 1975–76, MLS. **Orgs.:** ALA. IL LA: Chld. Libns. Sect. (Secy., 1979–80); Jr. Mem. RT, Treas. (1978–79); Mem.-at-Large (1979–80). NLA. N. Suburban Lib. Syst.: Reg. Lib. Adv. Cncl., Chld. Libns. Unit (Secy., 1978–79). **Activities:** 9; 27, 36; 72 **Addr.:** 514 S. Circle, Barrington, IL 60010.

Ricklefs, Dale Lynne Rogers (Jl. 29, 1953, Chicago, IL) Lib. Dir., Round Rock Pub. Lib., 1980–; Libn., Radian Corp., 1975–80. **Educ.:** IL Wesleyan Univ., 1971–74, BA (Phil., Relig.); Univ. of TX, Austin, 1976–77, MLS, 1978–, PhD (Mgt.). **Orgs.:** TX Mncpl. Leag.: Lib. Dirs. Div. (1981). ALA. SLA: TX Dir. (1977–), Asst. Ed. (1977–); Austin Cont. Educ. Com. (1978–79). ASIS: TX Nom. Com. (1978–), TX Nsltr. Ed. (1978–79). Various other orgs. **Honors:** Beta Phi Mu, 1977; Phi Kappa Phi, 1977. **Activities:** 9, 12; 17, 31, 36; 56, 75, 91 **Addr.:** Round Rock Public Library, 216 E. Main, Round Rock, TX 78664.

Rickling, Iraida Badillo (S. 13, 1932, Aguada, PR) Libn., FL Solar Energy Ctr., 1975–; Asst. to the Libn., Kennedy Space Ctr. Lib., 1970–72; Head, Ref. Dept., FL Tech. Univ., 1968–69; Libn., Aerosp. Corp./ETRO Ofc., 1961–68; Tech. Catlgr. and Resrch. Libn., Martin Co. (Orlando), 1959–61; Ref. Libn., U.S. Army War Coll., 1956–59; Post Libn., Camp Losey (PR), 1955–56; Catlgr., Univ. of PR Lib., 1954–55. **Educ.:** Univ. of PR, 1949–52, BA (Hum.); Carnegie Lib. Sch., 1953–54, MLS. **Orgs.:** SLA. FL LA. AAUW. **Honors:** Phi Kappa Phi; Beta Phi Mu. **Activities:** 12, 13; 17, 39; 52, 64, 86 **Addr.:** 347 Jack Dr., Cocoa Beach, FL 32931.

Ricks, Bonnie Bouchard (Mr. 27, 1921, South Bend, IN) U.S. Army Post Libn., Ft. Greely, AK, 1976–; Elem. Libn., Gary IN Pub. Sch., 1971–76; Libn., AV Coord., Niles Cmnty. Sch., MI, 1969–71; LS Instr., Lake MI Coll., 1968–69; Elem. Libn., South Bend Cmnty. Sch., 1965–69; Slayton Sch., 1961–65; Libn. and Tchr., Bertha, MN, 1958–61. **Educ.:** IN Univ., 1938–42, BS (Soc. Std.); 1965–66, MLS; Univ. of OK, 1967; Univ. of AK, Fairbanks, 1977 (LS). **Orgs.:** IN Sch. LA. ALA. AK LA. **Addr.:** P.O. Box 70, Delta Junction, AK 99737.

Riddle, Raymond E. (N. 9, 1947, Orlando, FL) Dir., Cass Cnty. Pub. Lib., 1978–; Dir., Humphreys Cnty. Lib., 1975–78. **Educ.:** St. Andrews Presby. Coll., 1965–69, BA (Psy.); Univ. of MS, 1971–75, MLS, 1971–74, (Psy.). **Orgs.:** ALA: JMRT; LAMA; LITA; PLA; various ofcs., coms., sects. Kansas City Area Wide Org. of Libns.: Exec. Com. (Ch., 1979). MO LA: Jr. Mems. RT (Ch., 1981); others. Natl. Micro. Assn. Other orgs. Amer. Cancer Socty. Cass Cnty. (MO) Hist. Socty. LIONS Club Intl. Cham. of Cmrce. (Harrisonville). Other orgs. **Honors:** Phi Delta Kappa. **Pubns.:** "Mini-Library: A Versatile Concept," *Show-Me Libs.* (Jl. 1980); "Belzoni-Humphreys County, Miss.," *Delta Tour Guide and Picture Book* (1979); "The Encounter," *Lagniappe: A Jnl. of the Old South* (Sum., 1975); "Getting Ready For NLW?" *Show-Me Libs.* (Mr. 1979). **Activities:** 9; 17, 32, 33; 50, 56 **Addr.:** Cass County Library Headquarters, 103 Oriole St., Harrisonville, MO 64701.

Riddles, James A. (N. 2, 1917, Cleveland, OH) Libn.-at-Lg., Univ. of The Pac., 1979–; Dir. of Libs., 1965–79, Ref. Libn., 1960–65; Branch Libn., San Diego Pub. Lib., 1950–60. **Educ.:** AZ State Coll., 1936–40, BA (Msc.); Univ. of South. CA, 1945–46, MS (LS). **Orgs.:** CA Lib. Athrty. For Systs. and Srvs.: Athrty. Adv. Cncl. (1977–80). CA LA: Golden Empire Dist. Pres. (1968–69); Com. on Acad. Status (1967–68). Amer. Cvl. Liberties Un.: Stockton Chap. Pres. (1967–68, 1977–78). **Honors:** Cncl. on Lib. Resrcs., Flwshp., 1971. **Activities:** 1; 17, 34, 39; 74, 90, 92 **Addr.:** Irving Martin Library, University of The Pacific, Stockton, CA 95211.

Rider, Lillian M. (Ag. 31, 1939, Sherbrooke, PQ) Ref. Libn., McGill Univ., 1969–; **Educ.:** Bishop's Univ., Lennoxville, PQ 1956–59, BA; McGill Univ., 1967–69, MLS. **Orgs.:** Can. LA: Cnclr. (1974–77). PQ LA: Cnclr. (1976–78). Assn. of McGill Libns.: Pres. (1975–76). **Pubns.:** "The State of Canadian Bibliography: A CACUL Report," *Can. Lib. Jnl.* (Ag. 1975); jt. ed., *The Reference Interview; Proceedings of the CACUL Symposium..-.Montreal...1977* (1979); *Canadian Resources at McGill: A Guide to the Collections* (1980); *Training Program for Reference Desk Staff* ERIC. **Activities:** 1; 40, 50-Staff trng.; 56, 93, 89-Can. std. **Addr.:** Reference Dept., McLennon Library, McGill University, 3459 McTavish St., Montreal, PQ H3A 1Y1 Canada.

Ridge, Alan D. (O. 2, 1926, Brighton, Sussex, Eng.) Prov. Archvst., Prov. Arch. of AB, 1968–; Univ. Archvst., McGill Univ., 1962–68; Div. Head, Rec. and Regist. Srv., Natl. Coal Bd., Yorkshire, Eng., 1958–62. **Educ.:** Univ. of London, 1944–47, BA (Hist.); Sch. of Libnshp. and Arch., Univ. Coll., London, 1947–48, Dip. (Arch.); Inst. of Cert. Recs. Mgrs., 1977, Cert. Admin. Recs. Mgr. **Orgs.:** Inst. of Cert. Recs. Mgrs.: Bd. of Regents (1979–). Assn. of Recs. Mgrs. and Admin. Assn. Can. Archvsts.: Educ. Com. (1975–). SAA: Coll. and Univ. Arch. Com. (1965–68); State and Lcl. Recs. Com. (1970–78); Com. on Terminology (1972–75); Sub-Com. on Frdm. of Info. (1976–78); various coms. Hist. Socty. of AB: Chap. Pres. (1971–73); Pres. (1978–80). **Honors:** Assn. of Recs. Mgrs. and Admin. Informatics Awd., 1979. **Pubns.:** "What Training Do Archivists Need?" *Can. Archvst.* (1965); "Chairman's Letter," *Can. Archvst.* (1966); *The McGill University Archives* (Ap. 1967); "Arranging the Archives of the School of Nursing of the Montreal General Hospital," *Journal Socty. of Archvsts.* (O. 1968); "C. C. McCaul, Pioneer Lawyer," *AB Hist. Review,* (Win. 1973); various reviews, articles. **Activities:** 2, 11; 15, 23, 38; 50, 62, 78 **Addr.:** Provincial Archives of AB, 12845–102 Ave., Edmonton, AB T5N 0M6 Canada.

Ridge, Davy-Jo Stribling (Ja. 16, 1932, Anderson, SC) Assoc. Dir. of Libs., Univ. of SC, 1975–, Asst. Dir. for Ref. Srvs., 1973–75, Head, Ref. Dept., 1965–73; Head, Ref. Dept., DeKalb Cnty. Lib. Syst. (GA), 1956–64; Instr. in Cat., Univ. of GA Lib. 1955–1956. **Educ.:** Queens Coll. (NC), 1950–54, BA (Eng.); Emory Univ., 1954–55, MLn; Cert., Med. LA, 1957. **Orgs.:** ALA. SELA: Constn. and By Laws Com. (Ch., 1981–83). SC LA: PR Com. (Ch., 1972–73); ILL Com. (Ch., 1974); Legis. Com. (Ch., 1976); Lcl. Arrange. Com. (Ch., 1976); Ed. Com. (1980–82). S. Caroliniana Socty. Natl. Audubon Socty. Columbia Audubon Socty. Palmetto Cat Club. **Pubns.:** *Rare Books in the McKissick Memorial Library of the University of South Carolina* (1966); *A Checklist of Microforms in the University of South Carolina Libraries* (1971); "The Southeastern Survey and Academic Libraries in South Carolina," *SC Libn.* (1976); "Letters about a Little Lost Book," *RQ* (Win. 1969); Reviews. **Activities:** 1; 17, 39 **Addr.:** 112 Carriage Hill Apts., Columbia, SC 29206.

Ridgeway, Patricia M. (O. 27, 1948, Patuxent River, MD) Head, Ref. Dept. and Assoc. Prof., Ida Jane Dacus Lib., Winthrop Coll., 1981–; Head, Ref. Dept. and Asst. Prof., 1973–80, Ref. Lib. and Instr., 1971–73. **Educ.:** Radford Coll., 1965–69, BS (LS, Eng.); FL State Univ., 1969–70, MS (LS); Winthrop Coll., 1972–77, MA (Eng.). **Orgs.:** SC LA: Pub. Srvs. Sec. Ch. (1980), Vice-Ch., (1976–80). SELA: Orien. and Bibl. Instr. Subcom. (1976–80); Ref. and Adult Srvs. Div./Nom. Com. (1976). AAUP. **Honors:** Beta Phi Mu, 1971. **Pubns.:** "Here's 'How We Notify Our Faculty Good'," *The UNABASHED Libn.* (Fall 1974); "The State of Interlibrary Loan in South Carolina," *SC Libn.* (Fall 1974); "Orientation/Instruction Round-Up: Southeastern Clearinghouse Established, PC and USC Grant Program Reports," *SC Libn.* (Fall 1977); "Orientation/Instruction Round-Up: South Carolina in SELA Directory," *SC Libn.* (Fall 1978); "Orientation/Instruction Round-Up: Services for the Blind," *SC Libn.* (Spr. 1979); various sps., articles, abs., reviews. **Activities:** 1; 31, 39, 49-Online Srch.; 55, 61, 63 **Addr.:** Reference Dept., Winthrop College Library, Rock Hill, SC 29733.

Riechel, Rosemarie Adele (N. 29, 1937, Landau, Germany) Head, Info., Pub. Cat. and Telephone Ref. Div., Queens Boro. Pub. Lib. 1968–, Asst. Head, 1967–68, Libn., Lang. and Lit. Div., 1966–67, Libn., Auburndale Branch, 1965–66; Gen. Asst., Butler Lib., Columbia Univ., 1961–65. **Educ.:** Hunter Coll., 1955–59, BA (Grmn., Hum.); Columbia Univ., 1962–65, MS (LS), Cert. Advnc. Libnshp., 1981. **Orgs.:** ALA. NY LA. Cath. LA. NY Lib. Club. Metro. Opera Gld. Queens Hist. Socty. Frdm. to Read Fndn. **Pubns.:** "Public Libraries: A Method of Survival Through Preservation," *Catholic Lib. World* (N. 1979). **Activities:** 9; 16, 17, 39; 55, 56, 75 **Addr.:** 151-31 25 Ave., Whitestone, NY 11357.

Riedesel, Laureen Falk (Je. 1, 1951, Wakefield, NE) Dir., Beatrice Pub. Lib., 1977–; Youth Libn., Dunklin Cnty. Lib., 1974–76, Pub. Srv. Libn., 1976–77. **Educ.:** Wheaton Coll., 1969–73, BA (Educ.); Univ. of MO, 1973–74, MALS; IL, 1973, Tchrs. Cert. **Orgs.:** Mt. Plains LA. NE LA: Natl. Lib. Week Com. (1979–80); Legis. Com. (1981–82); Pub. Lib. Sect. (Secy., 1979–80). ALA: PLA, Srvs. to Chld. Com. (1978–82); LAMA. NE Lib. for the Blind and Phys. Handcpd. Adv. Cncl.: Secy. (1978). Soroptimists Intl.: Dir. (1979–82); Cmnty. Srvs. Com. (Ch., 1980–82). AAUW. SE NE Geneal. Socty. Nebraskans for Peace. **Pubns.:** "Suit Yourself—With a Pattern From the Library," *NE LA Qtly.* (Sum. 1980); "Nebraska News—Junior High Volunteer Program," *Lib. Outrch. Coop. Nsltr.* (Jl. 1979). **Activities:** 9; 15, 17, 36; 63, 69, 89 **Addr.:** 218 N. 5th St., Beatrice, NE 68310.

Riggs, Dean Edward (D. 13, 1936, Hutchinson, KS) Acq. and Col. Dev. Libn., Asst. Prof. of Lib. Admin., Univ. of Toledo, 1974–; Acq. Libn., Univ. of MO, Kansas City, 1968–74; Libn., U.S. Dependents Schs. European Area, Dept. of Defense, 1963–74; Libn., Seaman Rural High Sch., 1960–62; Libn., Norton Comnty. High Sch., 1959–60. **Educ.:** Dodge City Coll., 1955–57, AA; Emporia State Univ., 1957–59, BS (Soc. Sci., Educ., LS), 1959–63, MS (LS). **Orgs.:** ALA. Acad. Lib. Assn. of OH. North. OH Tech. Srvs. Libn. Inter-Univ. Lib. Cncl. Univ. of Toledo Lib. Faculty: Com. on Elects. and Bylaws Rev. **Activities:** 1; 15, 34 **Addr.:** 3709 Woodmont Rd., Toledo, OH 43613.

Riggs, Donald E. (My. 11, 1942, Middlebourne, WV) Univ. Libn., AZ State Univ., 1979–; Dir. of Libs., Univ. of CO, Denver, Metro. State Coll., Cmnty. Coll. of Denver (Auraria Campus), 1976–79; Dir., Libs. & Media Srvs., Bluefield State Coll., Concord Coll., 1970–76. **Educ.:** Glenville State Coll., 1960–64, BA (Bio.); WV Univ., 1964–66, MA (Admin.); Univ. of Pittsburgh, 1967–68, MLS; VA Polytech. and State Univ., 1973–75, Ed.D, Univ. of CO, 1977–78 (Leadership). **Orgs.:** ALA: ACRL/Urban Univ. Libs. Sect. (1977–). AZ LA: Coll. and Univ. Div. (Pres., 1981–). CO LA: Pres. (1978–79). Mesa Pub. Lib.: Bd. of Trustees (1980–). AZ State Lib. Adv. Cncl. SWLA. Other orgs. Kiwanis. **Honors:** OH Cnty. Schs., Outstand. Young Educ., 1966; Jaycees, Spec. Ed. Awd., 1975; Beta Phi Mu; Phi Delta Kappa; other hons. **Pubns.:** Contrib., *Libraries in the Political Process* (1980); ed., *Leadership in Librarianship: A Futuristic View* (1981); assoc. ed., *Southeast. Libn.* (1973–75); chief ed., *WV Libs.* (1973–75); various other articles. **Activities:** 1, 9; 17, 28, 41; 56, 78, 93 **Addr.:** Library, Arizona State University, Tempe, AZ 85287.

Rigney, Janet M. (Je. 6, 19–, Yonkers, NY) Libn., Cncl. on Frgn. Rel., 1976–, Asst. Libn., 1960–75. **Educ.:** Hunter Coll., 1953–57, BA (Hist.); Columbia Univ., 1957–60, MLS. **Orgs.:** SLA: Bd. of Dirs. (Treas., 1970–76; Pres.-Elect (1981–82); Pres. (1982–83). NY Metro. Ref. and Resrch. Lib. Agency: Trustee (1980–). NY Lib. Club. **Activities:** 5, 12; 17, 45; 54, 92 **Addr.:** Council on Foreign Relations Library, 58 E. 68th St., New York, NY 10021.

Rike, Galen E. (O. 12, 1942, Wooster, OH) Assoc. Prof. of LS, Ball State Univ., 1977–; Spec., Resrch. and Stats., IL State Lib., 1973–77; Visit. Lectr., Grad. Lib. Sch., IN Univ., 1972–73; Doct. Fellow, Sch. of LS, FL State Univ., 1969–72; Resrch. Assoc., Lib. Resrch. Ctr., Univ. of IL, 1967–69; Biblgphr., Acq. Dept., Univ. of IL Lib., 1966–67. **Educ.:** Ashland Coll., 1960–63, BA (Hist.); Univ. of IL, 1964–66, MS (LS); FL State Univ., 1976, PhD (LS). **Orgs.:** ALA: ASCLA, Resrch. Com., Ch. (1979–81); LAMA, Stats. for Pub. Lib. Com. Ch. (1979–80), Stats. for Nonprint Media Com., Ch. (1977); LRRT, Rep. to CLENE (1976–79), Nom. Com., Ch. (1975); LAD/LOMS Stats. for State Lib. Agencies Com. (1975–77). ASIS. AALS. IN LA. **Honors:** Beta Phi Mu; Phi Kappa Phi. **Activities:** 1, 13; 17, 24, 41; 57, 78, 92 **Addr.:** P.O. Box 3083, Muncie, IN 47302.

Riley, Eileen V. (Hartford, CT) Chief, Acq. Branch, U.S. Dept. of Labor Lib., 1973–; Chief, Tech. Prcs. Unit, U.S. Vets. Admin. Ctrl. Ofc., 1971–73; Selector, Area Spec., Natl. Lib. of Med., 1966–71; Ref. Libn., 1970–71, Selector, 1961–66, Catlgr., 1960–61, Intern, 1959–60. **Educ.:** Boston Univ., 1950–54, AB (Econ.); Columbia Univ., 1958–59, MSLS (Lib. Srv.); 1959–81, various certs. (mgt. trng. crs.). **Orgs.:** SLA. ALA: Lib. Admin. Div. (Volun. Recruiter, 1963–65). DC LA: Asst. Secy. (1962–63). Fed. Lib. Com.: Subcom. on Procurement (1976); Subcom. on the Autom. of Acq. (1976–79). Various other orgs. Potomac Lily Socty. Washington Daffodil Socty. **Honors:** U.S. Dept. of Labor, Admin. Prog. Dir., Cert. of Apprec., 1980; U.S. Dept. of Labor, Lib. Dir., Cert. of Apprec., 1980; U.S. Dept. of Labor, Grp. Spec. Achvmt. Awd., 1976; U.S. Vets. Admin., Grp. Spec. Achvmt. Awd., 1973. **Activities:** 4; 15, 39, 44; 80, 92 **Addr.:** U.S. Dept. of Labor Library, Acquisitions, Rm. N2439, 200 Constitution Ave. N.W., Washington, DC 20210.

Riley, Mary F. (O. 17, 1925, New York, NY) Chief Ref. Libn., Fordham Univ. Lib., 1967–; Ref. Asst., 1965–67; Ref. Asst., Scarsdale Pub. Lib., 1964–65; Prof. Intern, Columbia

Special Subjects/Services: 50. Adult educ.; 51. Advert./Mktg.; 52. Aerosp.; 53. Agric.; 54. Area std.; 55. Arts/Hum.; 56. Autom.; 57. Bibl./Prtg.; 58. Bio. sci.; 59. Bus./Fin.; 60. Chem.; 61. Copyrt.; 62. Documtn.; 63. Educ.; 64. Engin.; 65. Env.; 66. Eth. grps.; 67. Film; 68. Food/Nutr.; 69. Geneal.; 70. Geo.; 71. Geol.; 72. Handcpd.; 73. Hist.; 74. Int. frdm.; 75. Info. sci.; 76. Insr.; 77. Law; 78. Legis.; 79. Math./Comp. sci.; 80. Med.; 81. Metals; 82. Nat. resrcs.; 83. Newsp.; 84. Nuc. sci.; 85. Oral hist.; 86. Petr./Energy; 87. Pharm.; 88. Phys./Astr./Math.; 89. Readg.; 90. Relig.; 91. Sci./Tech.; 92. Soc. sci.; 93. Telecom.; 94. Transp.; 95. (other).

Who's Who in Library and Information Services

Univ., Grad. Sch. of Bus. Lib., 1963–64. **Educ.:** Coll. of New Rochelle, 1945–47; Fordham Univ., 1947–49, BS (Eng.); Columbia Univ., 1960–63, MLS. **Orgs.:** ALA. NY LA: Coll. and Univ. Sect., Legis. Com. (1978–79). METRO(NY Metro. Ref. and Resrch. Lib. Agency): Legis. Com. (1978–); Pub. Srvs. Com. (1977–). **Pubns.:** Jt. auth., *Dissertations in Philosophy Accepted at American Universities,1861-1975* (1978). **Activities:** 1, 9; 39; 78 **Addr.:** Fordham University Library, Bronx, NY 10458.

Rimmer, Anne Hammond (F. 1, 1944, Marfa, TX) Asst. Libn., Tech. Srv., Univ. of TX Law Lib., 1976–; Chief Libn., Dept. of Hlth., NZ, 1976; Deputy Chief Catlgr., Parlmt. Lib., NZ, Head, Serials, Acq. **Educ.:** Univ. of NC, 1962–66, BA (Educ.); NZ Lib. Sch., 1972 (LS). **Orgs.:** AALL: Com. on Rel. with Publshrs.; Com. on Index Legal Pers. Southwest. Assn. of Law Libs. ALA. NZ LA: Assoc. (1976–). **Pubns.:** *Bibliography of New Zealand Library School Bibliographies* (1975); *Standards for Hospital Libraries in New Zealand* (1977); "White Paper on Health Care and its Affect on the Standards for Hospital Libraries in New Zealand," *NZ Libs.* (Ap. 1976). **Activities:** 1; 15, 37; 77 **Addr.:** University of Texas, Tarlton Law Library, 2500 Red River, Austin, TX 78705.

Rine, Joseph Leon (F. 10, 1944, South Bend, IN) Chief Libn., Minneapolis Cmnty. Coll., 1977–; Dir., Urban Campus Lib., Natl. Coll. of Educ., 1972–77; Catlgr., Bar Ilan Univ., 1970–72; Libn., Kibbutz Sde Eliyahu, 1969–70; Tchr., Sch. Libn., Chicago Pub. Schs., 1966–69. **Educ.:** Jewish Univ. of Amer., 1961–63, AA; Natl. Coll. of Educ., 1963–65, BEd; Spertus Coll. of Judaica, 1974–77, BJS (Judaica); Rosary Coll., 1967–69, MALS; Laurence Univ., 1975–81, EDD (Educ.). **Orgs.:** ALA: ACRL/Educ. and Bhvl. Sci. Sect., Cntrl. and Access to Educ. Mtrls./Cmnty. and Jr. Coll. Libns., Srvs. to Disadv. Students Com.; JMRT; ALSC; LAMA/Bldg. and Equip. Sect. (1980–82); YASD, Legis. Com. (1982–84). MN LA: Chld. and Young People Div. (Pres., 1980–81); various coms. Natl. Libns. Assn.: Conf. Coord. (1979). MN Gvr.'s Pre-WHCOLIS: Hosplty. and Reg. Com. (1978). Kenesset Israel Congregation. Minneapolish Jewish Fam. Srv. **Activities:** 1; 15, 17, 22; 66 **Addr.:** 7316 W. 22nd St. Apt. 309, St. Louis Park, MN 55426.

Rineer, A. Hunter, Jr. (Je. 24, 1931, Rohrerstown, PA) State Libn., MA State Lib., 1973–80; Dir., Gen. Lib., PA State Lib., 1968–73; Dir., Lower Merian Lib. Assn., 1961–68; Ref. Libn., Free Lib. of Philadelphia, 1956–61. **Educ.:** Franklin and Marshall Coll., 1948–52, AB (Hist.); Columbia Univ., 1952–54, MSLS. **Orgs.:** MA LA. New Eng. LA. ALA. AALL. Cncl. on Abandoned Milit. Posts. **Activities:** 2, 13; 15, 17, 23; 77, 78, 83 **Addr.:** 7 Stonehill Dr., Stoneham, MA 02180.

Rinehart, Constance O. (Jl. 21, 1922, Huntington, WV) Asst. Dean, Univ. of MI, Prof., LS, 1969–, Head, European Langs. Unit, Subj. Cat. Div., Lib., 1958–69, Cat. Libn., 1948–57, Asst. Catlgr., Goucher Coll. Lib., 1944–45. **Educ.:** Marshall Univ., 1939–43, AB (Psy.); Univ. of MI, 1943–44, ABLS, 1946–48, AMLS. **Orgs.:** ALA. MI LA: Tech. Srvs. Sect. (1977–78). AALS. **Pubns.:** *Library Technical Services; An Annotated Bibliography* (1977); "Selection for Preservation," *Lib. Resrcs. & Tech. Srvs.* (Win. 1980); "Success in Library School," *Jnl. of Educ. for Libnshp.* (Win. 1979). **Activities:** 1; 20, 26, 46 **Addr.:** School of Library Science, University of Michigan, Ann Arbor, MI 48109.

Rinehart, Jeanne R. (D. 30, 1921, Kendallville, IN) Head, Chld. Rm., Ferguson Lib., 1970–; Head Libn., Nepean HS Lib. (Ottawa, ON), 1968–69; Head Lib., Staples HS., 1964–67; Elem. Sch. Lib., Milford Pub. Sch., 1961–63. **Educ.:** Goshen Coll., 1940–44, BA (Eng.); South. CT State Coll., 1960–62, MLS. **Orgs.:** CT LA: Prog. Com. (1976–79). ALA. Target: Chld.–Urban Five Libs.: Treas. (1978–79). Leag. of Women Voters: Mem. Com. (1978–79). **Pubns.:** Jt. ed., *Toys to Go: A Guide to the Use of Realia in Public Libraries* (1975). **Activities:** 9, 10; 21, 48 **Addr.:** Ferguson Library, 96 Broad St., Stamford, CT 06901.

Rinehart, Mitzi M. (N. 20, 1934, Ogden, UT) Asst. Dir., Maricopa Cnty. Lib., 1977–; Libn. II, Bus., Sci., Tech., Phoenix Pub. Lib., 1976–77, Libn. I, Chld., 1974–76; Libn., Paul Revere Elem. Sch., 1972–74. **Educ.:** Univ. of South. CA, 1953–56 (Soclgy.); CA State Coll., Fullerton, 1968–70, BA (Geo.), 1970–72, MLS. 1978, Cert. (Cmnty. Analysis); 1979, Cert. (Grantsmanship Trng. Prog.); 1979, Cert. (Performance Based Mgt.). **Orgs.:** ALA: Starter List for New Branch Cols. Com. (1981–83). SWLA. CA LA. AZ State LA: Nsltr. Ed. (1980–82); Conf. Ch. (1979–80); AZ Hwys. 5 Yr. Index Com. (Ch., 1978–79); Pub. Lib. Div., Secy.-Treas. (1977–78), Conf. Treas. (1977–78); Jr. AZ Mems., Vice-Ch. (1976–77), Pres. (1977–78); AZ Hwys. 1 Yr. Index Com., Ch. (1976–77), Conf. Secy. (1976–77). Toastmasters Intl.: Educ. VP (1979); Educ. Pres. (1980). AAUW. **Pubns.:** Various reviews, *Lib. Jnl.* (1979–80). **Activities:** 9; 15, 17, 36 **Addr.:** 702 E. Chilton Dr., Tempe, AZ 85283.

Ring, Joan S. (Jl. 1, 1941, Oak Park, IL) Acq. Libn., Stormont-Vail Reg. Med. Ctr., 1979–; Actg. Persnl. Libn., Univ. of WI, Madison, 1978–79, Acq. Libn., Med. Lib., 1967–70; Mss. Catlgr., Keats-Shelley Meml. Lib., Rome, Italy, 1968. **Educ.:** Lake Forest Coll., 1959–63, BA (Eng.); Univ. of WI, 1966–67, MA (LS). **Orgs.:** ALA. Med. LA. **Honors:** Phi Beta Kappa, Beta Phi Mu. **Pubns.:** "Manuscript Catalog," *Book and Manuscript Catalog of the Keats-Shelley Memorial House Library* (1969). **Addr.:** Health Sciences Library, Stormont-Vail Regional Medical Center, 1500 W. 10th St., Topeka, KS 66606.

Rink, Bernard C. (O. 22, 1926, Avon, OH) Lib. Dir., Northwest. MI Coll., 1957–; Demonstration Proj., MI State Lib., 1955–57; Ref. Libn., Univ. of Detroit, 1952–55; Cnty. Libn., Sandusky Cnty., 1949–52. **Educ.:** John Carroll Univ., 1944–48, AB (Eng.); West. Rsv. Univ., 1948–49, MSLS. **Orgs.:** MI LA: Pres. (1971). ALA. Amer. Socty. of Enologists. **Activities:** 1 **Addr.:** Osterlin Library, Northwestern Michigan College, Traverse City, MI 49684.

Rioux, Jean-Louis (Ap. 13, 1944, Mont-Joli, PQ) Dir., Srv. de la Consult., de la recherche, Microfor Inc., 1975–; Supt. Consult. Inf. Sci., Univ. Tanal, 1975–, 1973–75; Docmlst., Ctr. de Documtn., L'Inst. Coop. Desgardins, Lévis, 1966–68; Resp., Banque d'Info., Bur. d'Aménagement de l'Est du PQ Inc., Mont-Joli, 1965–66. **Educ.:** Univ. d'Ottawa, 1962–64, BA (Phil.); Univ. de Montréal, 1964–65, BBibl, 1968–73, BSc (Comp. Sci.). **Orgs.:** ASTED: VP (1974–75); Del. to Féd. Intl. de Documtn. (1975–79). Féd. de l'Info. du PQ Inc. Ordre des Ingénieurs Forestiérs du PQ. **Honors:** Assn. Can. des Bibtcrs. de Lang. Fr., Grolier Schol., 1964. **Pubns.:** *Manuel Pratique de Classement des Fiches de Catalogue* (1969); "Le Monde," *Nouvelles de l'ASTED* (Je./Ag. 1978); *La Documentation dans un centre Residential d'Education des Adults* (1968). **Activities:** 6, 12; 17, 37, 49; 56, 75, 83 **Addr.:** Microfor Inc., 265, rue de la Couronne, Bureau no 505, Québec, PQ G1K 6E1 Canada.

Ripma, Mary Austin (Ag. 7, 1952, St. Johns, MI) Dir., Publshg. Opers., Info. Access Corp., 1977–; Volun. Ref. Libn., Menlo Park Pub. Lib., 1978–. **Educ.:** MI State Univ., 1970–74, BA (Eng., Jnlsm.); San Jose State Univ., 1976–77, MLS. **Orgs.:** SLA. **Activities:** 14-Database producer; 37; 56, 62, 93 **Addr.:** 2121 Manzanita Ave., Menlo Park, CA 94025.

Rippel, Jeffrey A. (Je. 19, 1945, Moberly, MO) Deputy Dir., Greenville Cnty. Lib., 1978–; Dir., Victoria, TX Pub. Lib., 1976–78; Branch Libn., Waco Pub. Lib., 1974–76. **Educ.:** FL State Univ., 1965–67, BA (Eng.); Univ. of TX, Austin, 1972–73, MLS. **Orgs.:** SC LA: Lib. Admin. Sect. (Ch., 1980). ALA. Piedmont LA. Metro. Arts Cncl. (Greenville, SC). Appalachian Reg. Comp. Comsn.: Exec. Com. (1980–81). **Honors:** City of Victoria (TX), Disting. Srvs., 1978. **Activities:** 9; 17, 35, 47; 50, 56, 72 **Addr.:** Greenville County Library, Greenville, SC 29601.

Riser, Virginia Marie (LaCrosse, WI) Prin./Supt., Assumption Sch., Minneapolis, 1981–; Media Generalist, Derham Hall HS, 1971–81; Dir., Instr. Systs. Lab., Univ. of MN, 1975–76; Dir., Fox Lake Pub. Lib., 1970–71. **Educ.:** State Univ. of IA, 1960–64, BA (Soc. Sci.); Rosary Coll., 1969–70, MALS; Univ. of MN, 1972–73, Media Generalist, 1981, PhD (Curric. and Instr. Systs., Educ. Admin.). **Orgs.:** ALA. MN Educ. Media Assn. Assn. for Supvsn. and Curric. Dev. Natl. Educ. Assn. **Honors:** Phi Beta Mu; Lansing, IA, Jaycees, Educ. of the Yr., 1965. **Pubns.:** Various media and educ. kits. **Activities:** 1, 10; 15, 17, 41; 63, 75, 92 **Addr.:** 1440 Randolph, Apt. 104, St. Paul, MN 55105.

Risner, Thomas (D. 23, 1933, Phoenix, AZ) Dir., Natl. Info. Ctr. for Educ. Media, Univ. of South. CA, 1966–; Consult., Self-empl., 1956–65. **Educ.:** AZ State Univ., 1950–54, BS (Pol. Sci.); Univ. of CA, Univ. of South. CA, 1958–72, MA, Phd (Comm.). **Orgs.:** ASIS. AECT. **Pubns.:** "Compaction of Data through the Use of Micrographics," *Micro. Jnl.* (1971); "Information Center Profile," *Info. Hotline* (1976); "A Brief Overview of NIMIS I/II: Implications for Future Dissemination," *Jnl. of Spec. Educ. Tech.* (1978). **Activities:** 12; 15, 20, 24; 56, 63 **Addr.:** National Information Center for Educational Media, NICEM, University of Southern California, Los Angeles, CA 90007.

Ristow, Walter W. (Ap. 20, 1908, La Crosse, WI) Retired, 1978–; Chief, Geo. and Map Div., Lib. of Congs., 1968–78, Asst. Chief, Assoc. Chief, 1946–68; Chief, Map Div., NY Pub. Lib., 1937–46. **Educ.:** Univ. of WI, 1927–31, BA (Geo.); Oberlin Coll., 1931–33, MA (Geo., Geol.); Clark Univ., 1933–35, 1937, PhD (Geo.). **Orgs.:** SLA. Assn. of Amer. Geographers. Socty. for the Hist. of Discoveries. Amer. Congs. on Surveying and Mapping. **Honors:** SLA, Geo. and Map Div., Hons. Awd., 1963. **Pubns.:** *Emergence of Maps in Libraries* (1980); jt. auth., *Nautical Charts on Vellum in the Library of Congress* (1977); contrib., *The Map Librarian in the Modern World, Essays in Honour of Walter W. Ristow* (1979). **Activities:** 4, 9; 17, 24, 35; 70 **Addr.:** 6621 Claymore Ct., McLean, VA 22101.

Ritter, Philip Wayne (My. 29, 1945, Ft. Myers, FL) Dir., Gaston–Lincoln Reg. Lib., 1980–; Dir., Ctrl. NC Reg. Lib., 1976–80; Ext. Libn., Wake Cnty. Dept. of Lib., 1972–76; Libn., Sside VA Cmnty. Coll., 1971–72. **Educ.:** Atl. Christ. Coll., 1963–67, BA (Hist.); Vanderbilt Univ., 1967–70, MDiv (Church Hist.); Univ. of NC, 1970–71, MSLS; various cont. ed. wkshps. (1975–80). **Orgs.:** ALA. SELA. NC Pub. Lib. Dirs. Assn. NC LA: Sec. VP (1979–81). Pub. Rel. Com. (1975–77); Mem. Com. (Ch., 1979–). Gvtl. Rel. Com. (1977–79); Pub. Lib. Sect. (Secy., 1977–79; various coms., 1973–). Various coms. and adv. concls. (1978–). **Honors:** Beta Phi Mu, 1972. **Pubns.:** Jt. auth., *Information Resources: An Analysis of Community Needs and an Evaluation of Library Services in Chatham and Alamance Counties* (1978). **Activities:** 9; 17, 35, 47 **Addr.:** Gaston–Lincoln Regional Library, 1555 E. Garrison Blvd., Gastonia, NC 28052.

Rivera-Alvarez, Miguel Angel (F. 26, 1951, San Juan, PR) Libn., UPR Sch. of Law Lib., 1981–; Legal Libn., Dept. of Justice, 1980–81; Dir., Sch. of Nursing Lib., 1980–80. **Educ.:** Univ. of PR, 1977, BA (Arch./Math.); 1978–79, MLS; Urban Plng., 1977–78. **Orgs.:** Sociedad de Bibters. de PR. Asociacion de Bibters. de Derecho. Amer. Assn. of Law Libns. PR Olympic Com.: Publshg. Ofcr. PR Chess Fed.: Actv. Dir. PR Tennis Assn. **Pubns.:** *An art and graphic design thesaurus* (1979). **Activities:** 4, 12; 16, 19, 24; 51, 55, 77 **Addr.:** Del Rio 124, Santurce, PR 00911.

Rivera-Davis, Carlos Juan (N. 21, 1932, Carolina, PR) Dir., Law Lib., Interamer. Univ. Sch. of Law, 1977–, Rcrt., Promo. and Place. Ofcr., Ctr. of Criminal Justice, 1976–77, Asst. Dir., Sch. of Law, 1972–76; Ref. Libn., Night Shift, Univ. of PR Sch. of Law, 1966–72. **Educ.:** Univ. of PR, 1950–61, BA (Soc. Sci.); Interamer. Univ., 1972–75, JD; AALL, 1975, Cert. of Competence (Law Libnshp.). **Orgs.:** AALL. AECT. Amer. Assn. of Law Libns. Assn. of PR Law Libs. **Activities:** 1, 12; 19; 77, 78 **Addr.:** Interamerican University of Puerto Rico, School of Law Library, 1610 Fernández Juncos Ave., P.O. Box 8897, Santurce, PR 00910.

Rivera-Davis, Vilma L. (Je. 15, 1930, Carolina, PR) Dir., Lib., Grad. Sch. of Libnshp., Univ. of PR, 1979–, Prof., LS, 1972–, Circ., Ref. Libn., Dir., Circ. Ref. Dept., 1966–79, Ref. Libn., Gen. Lib., 1965–66, Dir., Contact Srv. Dept., Lib. Coll. of Agr., Mayaguez Campus, 1965–66, Catlgr., Tech. Srv. Dept., 1962–63, Prof., Span. Lit., Grammar, 1962; various positions as prof., 1950–58. **Educ.:** Univ. of PR, 1950, BA (Span. Lit.); Pratt Inst., 1965, MLS; AALL, 1973, Cert. Law Libn.; various grad. crs. **Orgs.:** Assn. of Caribbean Univ. and Resrch. Libs. Inst. Libs.: Pubn. Com. (1975–); Exec. Cncl. (1977–80). SBPR: Pubn. Com. (1980–). SALALM. ALA. Various other orgs., confs. **Honors:** PR State Bar Assn., Valuable Bibl. Contrib. to PR Law Lit., 1973; Mnstry. of Educ., Cumaná, Venezuela, Hons. for Prof. Civic Work with Student and Cmnty., 1960. **Pubns.:** Collaborator, *Revista del Colegio de Abogados de Puerto Rico; Photographic Methods in Libraries Instead of Microforms* (1964); *The Puerto Rico Public Library System : Carnegie Public Library and Others* (1964); *Report on Materials for Children : An Aspect of Children Literature* (1964); "The Storytelling Programs for Children in Public Library," *Bltn. de la SBPR* (Ap. 1964); various mono. **Activities:** 1, 11; 15, 17, 26; 56, 85 **Addr.:** Library, Graduate School of Librarianship, University of Puerto Rico, P.O. Box 21906, San Juan, PR 00931.

Rivera de Ponce, Blanca Nilda (O. 3, 1931, Garrochales, Barceloneta, PR) Dir., Pub. Lib. Syst., Dept. of Educ., 1977–, Pub. Sch. Dir., 1975–77; Acad. Lib. Supvsr., Interamer. Univ., 1975–77; Asst. Prof., Univ., of PR, 1969–70; Dir., Sch. Libs., Dept. of Educ., 1955–75. **Educ.:** Univ. of PR, 1968–70, Mstr. (Libnshp.), 1970–71, Mstr. (Supvsn. and Admin.). **Orgs.:** PR Libns. Assn. ALA. PR Tchrs. Assn. **Pubns.:** Various confs. **Activities:** 4, 5; 15, 16, 17, 25; 50, 63, 72 **Addr.:** José B. Acevedo St. 456, Los Maestros, Rio Piedras, PR 00926.

Rivin, Robert J. (O. 28, 1926, Sioux City, IA) Trustee, NW IA Reg. Lib. Syst., 1976–; Trustee, Pres. (2 yrs.), Sioux City Pub. Lib., 1963–70. **Educ.:** Univ. of NM, 1945–48, BA (Psy.); Univ. of TX, 1949–50 (Psy.); Univ. of SD, 1979– (Bus. Mgt.). **Orgs.:** ALA: Legis. Com. (1978–79); ALTA. Amer. Rental Assn. **Honors:** Amer. Rental Assn., Merit. Srv., 1980. **Activities:** 9, 13; 47; 50, 59, 74 **Addr.:** Sioux City, IA 51104.

Rivoire, Helena G. (Mr. 22, 1917, Everett, WA) Chief, Tech. Srvs., Bucknell Univ. Lib., 1969–, Cat. Libn., 1963–69, Asst. Cat. Libn., 1960–63, Asst. Ord. Libn., 1957–59; Libn., Sr. Grade, Univ. of CA, Berkeley, 1944–45, Libn., Jr. Grade, 1939–44. **Educ.:** Reed Coll., 1933–35; Univ. of CA, Berkeley, 1935–37, BA (Fr.), 1937–38, MA (Fr.), 1938–39, Cert. (LS); Univ. de Paris, 1948, Cert. (Fr.). **Orgs.:** ALA. PA LA: Tech. Srv. RT, Nom. Com. (1977–78); Susquehanna Valley Chap. (Secy., 1967–69). Assoc. Colls. of Ctrl. PA: Nom. Com. (1972, 1976); Strg. Com. (1978–80). ASIS. AAUP: State Com. W (1979–); Triennial Mtg. (Del., 1976, 1979). **Honors:** Phi Beta Kappa, 1937. **Activities:** 1; 15, 20, 46; 55, 56, 75 **Addr.:** Box 222, RD 1, Lewisburg, PA 17837.

Roach, James Kenneth (F. 13, 1935, Mt. Pleasant, TX) Dir. of Libs. and Instr. Media, Abilene Christ. Univ., 1977–; Media Spec., Dallas Pub. Lib., 1974–77; Assoc. Libn. Pub. Srvs., TX Womans Univ., 1973–74; Dir. of Lib., Howard Coll., 1961–73. **Educ.:** Abilene Christ. Coll., 1954–58, BA (Eng.); Univ. of TX, Austin, 1960–61, MLS; N. TX State Univ., 1973–81, PhD (Educ. Admin.). **Orgs.:** TX LA: Lib. Plng. Com. (1976–78); Legis. Com. (Ch., Dist. I, 1977–79). **Pubns.:** "The Media Specialist's Position in the Dallas (Texas) Public Library," *New Media in Public Libraries; a survey ...* (1976); "Learning Resource Centers in Academic Libraries," *Readings in Academic Administration* (1977). **Activities:** 1; 17, 19, 24; 63 **Addr.:** Margaret and Herman

PROFESSIONAL ACTIVITIES: Institutions: 1. Acad. lib.; 2. Arch.; 3. Assn.; 4. Fed./Gvt. lib.; 5. Inst. lib.; 6. Mfr./Suppl.; 7. Milit. lib.; 8. Musm.; 9. Pub. lib.; 10. Sch. lib.; 11. Sch. of lib. sci.; 12. Spec. lib.; 13. State lib.; 14. (other). **Functions/Activities:** 15. Acq./Col. dev.; 16. Adult srvs.; 17. Admin.; 18. Apprais.; 19. Archit./Bldgs.; 20. Cat./Class.; 21. Chld. srvs.; 22. Circ.; 23. Cons./Pres.; 24. Consult.; 25. Cont. ed.; 26. Educ. lib. sci.; 27. Ext. srvs.; 28. Fund/Grants; 29. Gvt. pubs.; 30. Indx./Abs.; 31. Instr. lib. use; 32. Media srvs.; 33. Micro.; 34. Netwks./Coop.; 35. Persnl.; 36. PR; 37. Publshg.; 38. Recs. mgt.; 39. Ref. srvs.; 40. Repro.; 41. Resrch.; 42. Review.; 43. Secur.; 44. Serials; 45. Spec. col.; 46. Tech. srvs.; 47. Trustees/Bds.; 48. YA srvs.; 49. (other).

Brown Library, Abilene Christian University, Station ACU, Box 8177, Abilene, TX 79699.

Roach, Linda C. (Ag. 4, 1943, Chattanooga, TN) Libn., Morgan, Lewis and Bockius, 1972–, Asst. Libn., 1970–72. **Educ.:** FL State Univ., 1961–65, BA (Span., Fr.); various crs. **Orgs.:** SLA: Philadelphia Chap., Dirs. Com. (1980). Grt. Philadelphia Law LA: Pres. (1974–75); Nom. Com. (Ch., 1979–80). AALL: Pvt. Law Lib. Spec. Interest Sect., Nom. Com. (1980). **Activities:** 12; 17, 39, 41; 59, 77, 78 **Addr.:** Morgan, Lewis & Bockius, 2100 Fidelity Bldg., Philadelphia, PA 19109.

Roach, Margaret Anne (O. 13, 1937, Presque Isle, ME) Coord. of Pub. Srvs., Head of Ref., Wright State Univ., 1981–; Sr. Ref. Libn., 1979–81, Actg. Head, Ref., 1974–75, 1967–68, Ref. Libn., 1966–79; Ref. Libn., Battelle Meml., 1965–66; Resrch. Tech., Univ. of Pittsburgh, 1962–64; Resrch. Assoc., Mellon Inst., 1961–62. **Educ.:** Notre Dame Coll., Staten Island, NY, 1955–59, BA (Chem.); Duquesne Univ., 1959–61, MS (Biochem.); Univ. of Pittsburgh, 1963–65, MLS. **Orgs.:** SLA: Chem. Div. (Mem. Ch., 1974–76); Dayton Chap., Rcrt. Com. (Ch., 1968–69), Consult. Com. (Ch., 1976–77), Educ. Com. (1975–77), Pres. (1972–73); Ctrl. OH Chap., Pres (1978–79), Archvst. (1973–), Nom. Com. (1980–81). Acad. LA of OH: Secy. (1981–82); Asst. Secy. (1980–81); Prog. Com. (1978–80). OH LA: Various coms. **Honors:** Kappa Gamma Pi; Beta Phi Mu. **Pubns.:** Indxr., *America: Religion and Religions* (1981); indxr., *Sons of the Fathers: The Civil Religion of the American Revolution* (1977); indxr., *Christian Criticism in the Twentieth Century: Theological Approaches to Literature* (1975). **Activities:** 1; 31, 39, 49-Online srvs.; 58, 60, 91 **Addr.:** 4110 Kinsey Rd., Englewood, OH 45322.

Roads, Clarice Jane (S. 20, 1923, Dallas, TX) Coord., Lib. Resrcs., Innovation and Support Progs., OK State Dept. of Educ., 1977–; Lib. Media Spec., Elem., Edmond Pub. Schs., 1970–77; Lib. Media Spec., Sec., OK City Pub. Schs., 1967–70; Branch Libn., OK Cnty. Libs., 1966–67. **Educ.:** Ctrl. State Univ., 1962–64, BS (Elem. Educ. LS); Univ. of OK, 1965–66, MLS. **Orgs.:** OK LA: Exec. Bd. (1979–80); Sequoyah Com. (1977–); Cont. Ed. Com. (1978–79). Edmond Readg. Cncl.: Treas. (1976–77). Lib. Tech. Assts. Prog.: Adv. Com. (1981–82). **Honors:** Beta Phi Mu, 1966; Alpha Chi. **Activities:** 9, 10; 21, 24, 32; 63, 72, 89 **Addr.:** Oklahoma State Department of Education, Library and Learning Resources, Oliver Hodge Bldg., 2500 N. Lincoln, Oklahoma City, OK 73105.

Robbin, Alice R. (Ap. 10, 1944, New York City, NY) Head, Data and Prog. Lib. Srv., Univ. of WI, Madison, 1969–. **Educ.:** Rutgers Univ., 1961–66, BA (Pol. Sci.); Sorbonne, Univ. de Paris, 1963–64; Univ. of WI, 1967–68, MA (Pol. Sci.). **Orgs.:** SAA. ASIS. Intl. Assn. for Soc. Sci. Info. Srv. and Tech.: Pres. (1979–82). **Pubns.:** "The Pre-Acquisition Process: A Strategy for Locating and Acquiring Machine-Readable Data," *Drexel Lib. Qtly.* (Ja. 1977); "Strategies of Improving Utilization of Computerized Statistical Data by the Social Scientific Community," *Soc. Sci. Info. Std.* (1981). **Activities:** 12; 17, 39, 41; 56, 75, 92 **Addr.:** Data and Program Library Service, 4452 Social Science Bldg., University of Wisconsin, Madison, WI 53706.

Robbins, Donald C. (Ag. 24, 1933, Lockport, NY) Asst. Proj. Dir., Cornell Univ., 1978–; Msc. Catlgr., Cornell Univ., 1971–78 Msc. Tchr., Binghamton (NY) Schs., 1962–70. **Educ.:** Eastman Sch. of Msc., 1951–55, BMus.; Univ. of MI, 1955–59, M.Mus.; SUNY Albany, 1970–71, MLS. **Orgs.:** Msc. LA. Intl. Assn. of Msc. Libs. **Pubns.:** "EDP Applications to Musical Bibliography," *Spec. Libs.* (S. 1972); "Current resources for bibliographic control of sound recordings," *Lib. Trends* (Jy. 1972). **Activities:** 1; 17, 20, 30; 55 **Addr.:** 801 Mitchell St., Ithaca, NY 14850.

Robbins, G. Daniel (F. 8, 1940, Rocky Mount, NC) Dir., Info. Div., Oak Ridge Natl. Lab., 1978–; Mgr., UCCND Key Persnl. Dev. Prog., Un. Carbide Corp., Nuc. Div., 1976–78; Dir., Ofc. of Prof. and Univ. Rel., Oak Ridge Natl. Lab., 1974–78, Coord., PhD Rcrt., 1973–74. **Educ.:** Univ. of NC, 1962, BS (Chem.); Princeton Univ., 1964, MS (Chem.), 1966, PhD (Chem.). **Orgs.:** ASIS. **Honors:** Princeton University Resrch. Flwshp., 1964; Norway, Fulbright Post Doct. Fellow, 1966–67. **Activities:** 5, 12; 17 **Addr.:** Oak Ridge National Laboratory, P.O. Box X, Oak Ridge, TN 37830.

Robbins-Carter, Jane (S. 13, 1939, Chicago, IL) Prof. and Dir., Lib. Sch., Univ. of WI-Madison, 1981–; Dean, Grad. Sch. of LS, LA State Univ., 1979–81; Assoc. Prof., 1977–79; Lib. Consult., 1974–77; Assoc. Prof., Div. of Libnshp., Emory Univ., 1973–74; Asst. Prof. Grad. Sch. of Lib. and Info. Sci., Univ. of Pittsburgh, 1972–73; Ref. Libn., Transp. Lib., Northwestern Univ., 1968–69; Descr. Catlgr., Lib. of Congs., 1967; Ref. Libn., Map Lib., Dept. of the Army, 1966. **Educ.:** Wells Coll., 1957–61, BA (Soclgy.); West. MI Univ., 1964–66, MLS; Univ. of MD, 1969–72, PhD (Libnshp.). **Orgs.:** ALA: Cncl. (1972–73, 1976–80), Lib. Resrch. RT, Ch. (1977–78). AALS: Dir. (1978–81). CLENE: Adv. Com., Ch. (1977–79). AAUP: LA State Univ. Chap., Secy. (1979–80). Amer. Civil Liberties Un. **Honors:** Beta Phi Mu, 1966. **Pubns.:** *Public Library Policy and Citizen Participation* (1975); "State Librarianship," *Jnl. of Educ. for Libnshp.* (Sp. 1980); "Multicultural Graduate Library Education," *Jnl. of Educ. for Libnshp.* (Sp. 1978); "The Reference Librarian: A Street-Level Bureaucrat?", *Lib. Jnl.* (April 15, 1971). **Activities:** 9, 13; 17, 34, 41; 78 **Addr.:** Library School, University of Wisconsin-Madison, Madison, WI 53706.

Roberts, Ammarette (Je. 24, 1923, Oakalla, TX) Mgr., Tech. Info., Mobil Resrch. and Dev. Corp. Exploration and Prod. Div., Fld. Resrch. Lab., 1978–, Info. Spec., 1969–78; Mgr., Info. Srvs., Lone Star Gas, 1956–69. **Educ.:** Mary Hardin-Baylor Univ., 1940–43, BS (Chem.); various grad. crs. in LS. **Orgs.:** SLA: TX Chap. (Pres., 1968–69); various ofcs., coms. ASIS: TX Chap., Treas. Amer. Rec. Mgrs. and Admins.: Dallas Chap. (Pres., 1966–67); Reg. V (VP, 1967–68). Assoc. Info. Mgrs. Amer. Chem. Socty. Desk and Derrick Club. **Pubns.:** "Starting A Records Management Program," *Special Librarianship: A New Reader* (1980); "How to Check Your Ideas," *Petr. Mgt.* (Ap. 1965); jt. auth., "Blood Coagulation Abnormalities Associated with Leukemia," *Blood* (1956); jt. auth., "An Unusual Coagulation Inhibitor Encountered in Refractory Hemophilia," *Jnl. of Lab. and Clinical Med.* (1956); jt. auth., "Hemorrhagic Diathesis Associated with Hyperheparinemia," *Jnl. of Lab. and Clinical Med.* (1955); various articles. **Activities:** 12; 38, 49-Mgt. tech. info.; 86 **Addr.:** Technical Information, Mobil Research and Development Corp., FRL, 3600 Duncanville Dr., Dallas, TX 75236.

Roberts, Anne F. (Je. 20, 1937, San Diego, CA) Comms. Projs. Libn. SUNY Albany, 1980–; Coord., Lib. Instr., 1972–80, Ref. Libn., 1967–72; Chld. Libn., Albany Pub. Lib., 1966–67. **Educ.:** Stanford, Univ. of CA Berkeley, Long Beach State, SUNY Albany, 1966, BA (Eng.); SUNY Albany, 1966–67, MLS, 1972–75, MA (Amer. Lit.), 1979–, (Chld. Lit. Hist.), 1981. **Orgs.:** ALA: Dewey Awd. Jury (1978); Com. on Accred. (1979–); RASD, Stans. Com. (1974–79); ACRL/Bibl. Instr. Sect. Ch. (1981–83), Cont. Ed. Com. Ch. (1977–79); ACRL, East. NY Chap. Fndr., Ch. (1975). NY Lib. Instr. Clearhse.: Adv. Bd. (1976–1980). Albany Women's Forum. N. East. Mod. Lang. Assn.: Women in Lit. Sect. Ch. (1976–77). **Honors:** Beta Phi Mu; Chancellor's Awd. for Excel. in Libnshp., 1977; Cncl. on Lib. Resrcs. Flwshp., 1978. **Pubns.:** *Library Instruction For Librarians* (in press 1981); "Changing Role of Academic Instruction", *Cath. Lib. World* (F. 1980); "How to Generate User Interest in Library Instruction," *Bookmark* (Fall 1979); "Prescriptive, Descriptive, or Proscriptive?", *RQ* (Spr. 1978); slide/tapes on univ. lib. **Activities:** 1, 9; 24, 31, 39 **Addr.:** University Library, 1400 Washington Ave., Albany, NY 12222.

Roberts, Don L. (Ag. 13, 1938, Dodge City, KS) Head Msc. Libn., Northwest. Univ., 1969–; Instr., LS, Rosary Coll., 1972–; Fine Arts Libn., Univ. of NM, 1963–68. **Educ.:** Frnds. Univ., 1958–61, BA (Msc.); Univ. of MI, 1961–63, AMLS. **Orgs.:** Assn. for Rec. Snd. Cols.: Pres. (1971–74). IFLA: Lib. Schs. Strg. Com. (1978–). Msc. LA: Bd. (1977–79); Midwest Chap. (Ch., 1971–73); *Nsltr.* Ed. (1971–73). Intl. Assn. of Msc. Libs.: Cncl. (1975–); U.S. Branch (Secy.-Treas., 1975–). Socty. for Ethnomsclgy.: Treas. (1978–); Cnclr. (1969–72, 1974–76, 1977–80); Jnl. Rec. Rev. Ed. (1969–71). New World Recs.: Ed. Com. (Ch., 1975–79). **Honors:** Cncl. on Lib. Resrcs., Flwshp., 1972; Woodrow Wilson Flwshp., 1961. **Pubns.:** "The Ethnomusicology of the Eastern Pueblos," *New Perspectives on the Pueblos* (1972); "A Calendar of Eastern Pueblo Ritual Dramas," *Southwest. Indian Ritual Drama* (1980). **Activities:** 1, 11; 15, 17; 55 **Addr.:** Northwestern University Library, Evanston, IL 60201.

Roberts, Elizabeth P. (Ja. 17, 1928, St. Louis, MO) Head, Owen Sci. and Engin. Lib, WA State Univ., 1972, Head, ILL, 1970–72, Actg. Chief, 1969–70, Head, Serial Rec. Sect., 1963–69, Actg. Chief, 1965–66, Ref. Libn., 1957–64; Ref. Libn., A.W. Calhoun Med. Lib., Emory Univ., 1956–57. **Educ.:** William Woods Coll., 1945–47, AA (Arts and Sci.); Univ. of MO, 1947–49, BA (Bot.); Emory Univ., 1954–55, MLS. **Orgs.:** WA LA: Women's Caucus (Ch., 1979–80). ALA. Pac. NW LA. AAUP: WA State Univ. Chap. (VP, 1979). Sierra Club. **Pubns.:** *Guide to Literature on Agricultural Engineering* (1971); "The Science and Engineering Library," *West. Vetn.* (Je. 1977); "Selecting Materials for the Engineering Library," *Engin. Educ.* (1971); "Reclassification from Dewey Decimal to LC in Subject Blocks," *Spec. Libs.*, (1969); "A Visit to the Czechoslovak Academy of Sciences Library," *Open Stacks* (volume 12); various articles. **Activities:** 1; 17; 64, 91 **Addr.:** Box 2114 C.S., Pullman, WA 99163.

Roberts, Gerald F. (Ja. 24, 1938, Detroit, MI) Spec. Cols. Libn., Berea Coll., 1975–; Asst. Prof. of Hist., Univ. of MO, Rolla, 1967–73; Instr. in Hist., Georgetown Coll., 1963. **Educ.:** Murray State Coll., 1955–59, BA (Hist.); Univ. of KY, 1959–62, MA (Hist.); MI State Univ., 1964–70, PhD (Hist.); Wayne State Univ., 1973–74, Visit. Doct. Guest (Arch. and Mss. Admin.). **Orgs.:** KY Cncl. on Arch.: Ch. (1979–80). SAA. Org. of Amer. Histns. Amer. Std. Assn. West. Hist. Assn. West. Amer. Lit. Assn. Various hist. orgs. **Honors:** Phi Alpha Theta. **Activities:** 2, 12; 15, 17, 45; 92 **Addr.:** Special Collections, Berea College Library, Berea, KY 40404.

Roberts, Gerrard Jude (O. 21, 1936, Big Rapids, MI) Lib. Dir., Cleveland Electric Illuminating Co., 1979–; Lib. Asst., Cleveland Pub. Lib., 1977–78; Indp. Info. Broker, 1969–75. **Educ.:** Aquinas Coll., 1955–62, BA (Hist.); Univ. of MI; 1957–60, AB (Msc. Hist.); Case West. Rsv. Univ., 1975–77, MS (LS), 1975–77, MA (Hist.); Cleveland State Univ., 1977–79, MPA; Case West. Rsv. Univ., 1978–, (LS). **Orgs.:** ALA. SLA. NLA. ASIS. Amer. Socty. for Pub. Admin. Student Org., Sch. of Lib. Sci., Case West. Rsv. Univ. **Honors:** Beta Phi Mu, 1979. **Pubns.:** Review. **Activities:** 1, 12; 17, 39, 41; 59, 86, 91 **Addr.:** 4300 Euclid Ave., #509, Cleveland, OH 44103.

Roberts, Gloria A. (F. 16, 1924, New York, NY) Head Libn., Planned Parenthood Fed. of Amer., Inc., 1978–; Assoc. Libn., 1973–78; Libn., SEDFRE 1971; Acq. Libn., NY State Psyt. Inst., 1967–70. **Educ.:** Vassar Coll., 1941–44, BA (Chld. Psy.); Columbia Univ., 1965–67, MLS; Med. Libn. Cert., 1969. **Orgs.:** SLA. Med. LA. Assn. for Popltn./Fam. Plng. Libs. and Info. Ctrs.: Intl. Pubns. Ofcr. (1979–82). **Activities:** 12; 17, 34, 39; 80, 92 **Addr.:** 215 E. 68th St., #5M, New York, NY 10021.

Roberts, Mrs. Hazel J. (Ap. 8, 1925, Calgary, AB) Head Libn., Assn. of Univs. and Colls. of Can., 1974–; Catlgr., Stats. Can., 1973–74; Libn., Secy. of Bd., Fort Smith, N.W.T. Pub. Lib., 1964–67. **Educ.:** Brandon Univ., Univ. of MB, 1946–48, BA (Econ.); Univ. of Ottawa, 1972–73, BLS. **Orgs.:** Can. Assn. Info. Sci.: Chap. Dir. (1980). Indexing and Abs. Socty. of Can.: Fndn. Dir. (1978–80). SLA. Can. LA: 1979 Conf., Lcl. Arrange. Com.; Can. Assn. of Univ. and Coll. Libns., Exec. Com. (1974–). Various other orgs. Univ. Women's Club, London, ON. Univ. Women's Club, Ottawa, ON. **Pubns.:** Jt. cmplr., *Bibliography of Higher Education in Canada* (1981); *Faculty Collective Bargaining in Canadian Universities 1974–1979: A bibliography* (1980); *Select Bibliography on Higher Education* (Qtly. 1964–). **Activities:** 1, 12; 17, 30, 38; 63 **Addr.:** Association of Universities and Colleges of Canada, 151 Slater St., Ottawa, ON K1P 5N1 Canada.

Roberts, Helene Emylou (Mr. 23, 1931, Seattle, WA) Cur. of Visual Cols., Harvard Univ., 1970–; Slide Libn., Dartmouth Coll., 1968–70, Art Libn., 1964–68. **Educ.:** Univ. of WA, 1948–53, BA (Drama), 1956–57, MA (Drama), 1959–61, ML. **Orgs.:** ARLIS/NA. Resrch. Socty. in Vict. Pers.: Treas., (1968–1973); Adv. Ed. (1975–). SLA. Amer. Socty. of Pic. Profs.: Boston Chap. (Secy., 1978–). **Pubns.:** *American Art Periodicals of the Nineteenth Century* (1963); "British Art Periodicals of the 18th and 19th centuries," *Vict. Pers. Nsltr.* (1970); "The Exquisite Slave," *Signs* (1977); "Marriage, Redundy or Sin," *Suffer and Be Still* (1972); "Submission, Masochism, Narcissism" *Women's Lives* (1977). **Activities:** 1; 15, 17, 20; 55, 95-Vict. Std. **Addr.:** Fine Arts Library, Fogg Art Museum, Harvard University, Cambridge, MA 02138.

Roberts, Justine Turner (S. 4, 1927, Chicago, IL) Head, Systs. Ofc., Univ. of CA, San Francisco Lib., 1967–, Catlgr., 1965–66. **Educ.:** Univ. of CA, Berkeley, 1944–48, AB (Soclgy.), 1962–64, MLS; Med. LA, 1970, Cert.; Univ. of CA, Berkeley, 1975–78, MBA. **Orgs.:** Med. LA: *Bltn.* Ed. Com. (1978–81); North. CA Med. Lib. Grp.: Pres. (1979–80). ASIS: Bay Area Chap. (Pres., 1977–78). Assn. for Comp. Mach.: Golden Gate Chap. Exec. Bd. (1974–76). SLA. ALA. Various other orgs., ofcs. Alexander Graham Bell Assn. for the Deaf. **Honors:** Beta Phi Mu, 1964, Washington Univ. Sch. of Med. Lib., St. Louis, MO, Fellow, Biomed. Libnshp., **Pubns.:** "Mechanization of Library Procedures in the Medium-Sized Medical Library," *Bltn. of the Med. LA* (Ja. 1968); "Grant Information via a Shared Data Base," *Jnl. of Lib. Autom.* (S. 1973); "PLEA; A PL/1 Efficiency Analyzer," *Jnl. of Lib. Autom.* (S. 1973); "Circulation (US.) Photocopy: Quid Pro Quo," *Bltn. of the Med. LA* (Jl. 1980). **Activities:** 1, 12; 17, 41; 56, 58, 80 **Addr.:** 152 Sycamore Ave., Mill Valley, CA 94941.

Roberts, Patricia S. (N. 25, 1939, Missouri Valley, IA) Libn., Lib. and Archs. facility, Reorganized Church of Jesus Christ of LDS, 1976–; Soclgy. Instr., Staten Island Cmnty. Coll., 1974–76; Acq. Libn., Univ. of North. IA, 1972–73. **Educ.:** Graceland Coll., 1967, BA (Soclgy.); LA State Univ., 1969, MLS; Univ. of North. IA, 1972, MA (Soclgy.). **Orgs.:** ALA. ATLA: KS City Chap. (Secy., 1977–78; Pres., 1978–79). Amer. Cvl. Liberties Un. Natl. Org. of Women. East. Jackson Cnty. Women's Pol. Caucus. **Honors:** Beta Phi Mu. **Pubns.:** "Do You Have a Church Library?" *INSIGHT* (Ag. 1977). **Activities:** 1, 12; 15, 17; 90, 92 **Addr.:** Library & Archives, Reorganized Church of Jesus Christ of L.D.S., The Auditorium - Box 1059, Independence, MO 64051.

Roberts, Sallie H. (Ag. 29, 1928, Washington, DC) Asst. Prof., Curric. and Instr., Coll. of Educ., OH Univ., 1980–, Instr., 1976–80, Lectr., Educ. Media, 1974–76, Supvsr., Educ. Media Ctr., 1968–78. **Educ.:** OH Univ., 1946–50, BA (Eng.), 1966–70, MA (Eng.); Kent State Univ., 1976–78, MLS, 1978–80 (Sixth Yr. LS). **Orgs.:** ALA: YASD, Educs. Grp. (1979–81). OH Educ. Lib. Media Assn.: Int. Frdm. Ch. (1980–81). OH LA: Educs. Grp. (1980–81). **Honors:** Phi Delta Kappa. **Activities:** 14-State univ.; 20, 39, 48; 63, 74 **Addr.:** College of Education, Ohio University, Athens, OH 45701.

Roberts, Susan Neal (Ap. 19, 1954, DeLand, FL) Asst. Libn., Waycross Jr. Coll., 1978–. **Educ.:** St. Johns River Jr. Coll., 1972–74, AA (Gen.); Univ. of S. FL, 1974–76, BA Honors (Eng.), 1976–78, MA (LS). **Orgs.:** ALA. GA LA. AAUW. Leag.

Special Subjects/Services: 50. Adult educ.; 51. Advert./Mktg.; 52. Aerosp.; 53. Agric.; 54. Area std.; 55. Arts/Hum.; 56. Autom.; 57. Bibl./Prtg.; 58. Bio. sci.; 59. Bus./Fin.; 60. Chem.; 61. Copyrt.; 62. Documtn.; 63. Educ.; 64. Engin.; 65. Env.; 66. Eth. grps.; 67. Film; 68. Food/Nutr.; 69. Geneal.; 70. Geo.; 71. Geol.; 72. Handcpd.; 73. Hist.; 74. Int. frdm.; 75. Info. sci.; 76. Insr.; 77. Law; 78. Legis.; 79. Math./Comp. sci.; 80. Med.; 81. Metals; 82. Nat. resrcs.; 83. Newsp.; 84. Nuc. sci.; 85. Oral hist.; 86. Petr./Energy; 87. Pharm.; 88. Phys./Astr./Math.; 89. Readg.; 90. Relig.; 91. Sci./Tech.; 92. Soc. sci.; 93. Telecom.; 94. Transp.; 95. (other).

of Women Voters. Girl Scouts of the U.S.A. **Honors:** Phi Kappa Phi; Beta Phi Mu. **Pubns.:** "Stepping into the ALA," *FL Media Qtly.* (Fall 1977); Jt. auth., "Exceptions to Regular Admissions in ALA Accredited Library Schools," *Jnl. of Educ. Libnshp.* (Spr. 1979). **Activities:** 1; 22, 31, 39; 55, 85, 92 **Addr.:** 704 Richmond Ave., Waycross, GA 31501.

Robertson, Ann Morris (S. 25, 1945, Independence, KS) Assoc. Prof., Head, Sci. and Engin. Ref. Dept., Univ. of Houston, 1975–; Asst. Prof., 1974–75, Asst. Prof., Phys. Sci. Libn., 1973–74, Instr., 1971–73, Instr., Asst. Sci. Libn., 1970–71; Libn., Fluor Corp., 1969–70. **Educ.:** TX Woman's Univ., 1963–67, BA (LS), 1968–69, MLS. **Orgs.:** ALA. SLA: Phys.-Astr.-Math. Div (Proj. Ch., 1974–76); TX Chap., Cabinet (1975–77), Pres. (1977–78); various coms., ofcs. SWLA. TX LA. Houston OLUG. Various other ofcs., coms. AAUP. TX Assn. Coll. Tchrs. **Pubns.:** Jt. auth., "Chemistry 411, the Literature of Chemistry," *SLA Sci.-Tech. News* (Jl. 1978); "Solar Energy," *SLA Phys.-Astr.-Math. Div. Bltn.* (My. 1976); "Current Awareness and Search Services Offered Through the ... University of Houston Libraries," *SLA, TX Chap. Bltn.* (Mr. 1972); "Scientific and Technical Libraries in Texas," *SLA, TX Chap. Bltn.* (Mr. 1972). **Activities:** 1, 12; 15, 17, 39; 60, 88, 91 **Addr.:** 4310 Briarbend, Houston, TX 77035.

Robertson, Betty May (My. 26, 1934, New York, NY) Recs. Mgt. Supvsr., Expl. & Prod. Div., Mobil Oil Corp., 1980–; Info. Spec., Esso Inter-Amer., 1978–80; Info. Spec., Stan. Oil Co. (IN), 1974–75; Geologist and Supvsr., Resrch. and Legal Lib., Amoco Intl., 1962–65; Asst. to VP, Conorada Petr. Corp., 1955–62. **Educ.:** CUNY, 1951–55, BA (Geol.); Univ. of Dijon, 1968–69, Dip. (Fr. Lang. and Culture). **Orgs.:** SLA. Geosci. Info. Socty. SALALM. Amer. Assn. of Petr. Geologists. Geo. Socty. of Amer. Assn. of Recs. Mgrs. and Admins. **Activities:** 12; 24, 41, 46; 71-Geol., 77, 86 **Addr.:** Exploration & Producing Div., Mobil Oil Corp., 150 E. 42nd St., New York, NY 10017.

Robertson, Howard W. (S. 19, 1947, Eugene, OR) Cat. Libn., Biblgphr., Univ. of OR, 1975–. **Educ.:** Univ. of OR, 1966–70, BA (Grmn., Russ.); Univ. of South. CA, 1974–75, MSLS; Univ. of OR, 1976–78, MA (Compar. Lit.). **Orgs.:** ALA. Amer. Assn. for the Advnc. of Slavic Std. **Honors:** Phi Beta Kappa, 1970. **Pubns.:** "What Every Serials Publisher Should Know about Unnecessary Title Changes," *Serials Libn.* (Sum. 1979); various articles, poems. **Activities:** 1; 15, 20, 44; 54, 55 **Addr.:** 765 E. 18th. Ave. #10, Eugene, OR 97402.

Robertson, Ina N. (D. 9, 1925, Decatur, IL) Instr. Srvs. Libn., Sangamon State Univ., 1980–; Instr., Grad. Sch. LS, Univ. of IL, 1979–80, Coord., AV Lab., 1976–78; Dir., Media Srvs., Ball Elem. Sch., 1970–76, Tchr., 1968–70. **Educ.:** Univ. of IL, 1943–47, AB (Admin.); Sangamon State Univ., 1970–72, MA (Comm.); 1972, Cert. (Supervisory Sch. Media Spec.); Sangamon State Univ., 1974–75, MA (Educ. Admin.); 1975, Cert. (Gen. Admin., Elem. and Sec. Schs.); Univ. of IL, 1976–77, LS, 1977–80, PhD (Educ.). **Orgs.:** ALA: AASL; ALSC. IL LA: Legis. and Lib. Dev. Com. (1976–79). IL Assn. for Media in Educ.: Legis. Netwk. (Ch., 1975–77); Pub. Affairs Com. (Ch., 1975–77); Prof. Rel. Com. (Ch., 1978–80). AAUW. Natl. Cncl. of Tchrs. of Eng. **Honors:** Beta Phi Mu; Phi Delta Kappa; Kappa Delta Pi; Phi Kappa Phi; other hons. **Pubns.:** "Betsy Byars—Writer for Today's Child," *Lang. Arts* (Mr. 1980); jt. auth., "Facsimiles of Historic Children's Books," *Lib. Trends* (Spr. 1979); "It's Up to You," AV prod. (1979); "Flannel Boards—Back to the Basics in Audiovisual Materials, Too," ERIC. **Activities:** 1, 10; 21, 31, 48; 57, 63, 92 **Addr.:** 96 Fox Mill Ln., Springfield, IL 62707.

Robertson, Linda L. (F. 17, 1940, Columbus, IN) Dir., Wabash Carnegie Pub. Lib., 1970–; Head, Ext. Srvs. and Dist. Talking Bk. Ctr., Bartholomew Cnty. (IN) Pub. Lib., 1968–70; Libn., N. Fort Myers (FL) Jr.-Sr. HS, 1965–68, Tchr. (Eng., Jnlsm.), 1962–65. **Educ.:** Ball State Univ., 1958–62, BS (Sec. Educ.); IN Univ., 1968–70, MLS. **Orgs.:** ALA. IN LA: Treas. (1976–77); Legis. Com., Ch. (1977–80). IN Coop. Lib. Srv. Athrty.: Secy. (1979–80). IN Oral Hist. RT: Pres. (1973). **Pubns.:** *Index of Wabash County History, 1914* (1979); *History of Wabash County, Indiana* (1976); "No, We'll Remodel, Too - Wabash," *Focus on IN Libs.* (Sum. 1972). **Activities:** 9, 10; 17, 34, 39; 69, 78, 85 **Addr.:** 13 Bonbrook Dr., Wabash, IN 46992.

Robertson, Louise (Montreal, PQ) Head, Tech. Srvs., McGill Univ. Law Lib., 1979–, Head, Acq., 1973–79, Cat., McLennan Lib., 1971–73. **Educ.:** McGill Univ., 1969, BA (Classics), 1969–71, MLS. **Orgs.:** AALL. Assn. of McGill Univ. Libns.: Secty. (1977–78). Can. ALL. SLA. Can. LA. McGill Assn. of Univ. Tchrs. **Activities:** 1; 46; 52, 77 **Addr.:** McGill University Law Library, 3466 Peel St., Montreal, PQ H3A 1W9 Canada.

Robertson, Marion Aletta Root (Mrs. John W.) (Ap. 25, 1920, Craftsbury Common, VT) Sch. Lib. Media Spec., W. Hills Elem. Sch. (Knoxville), 1964–; Lib. Asst., Tchrs. Coll., Columbia Univ., 1946–49; Instr., SUNY, Plattsburg, 1945–46; Tchr., Brattleboro (VT) HS, 1942–44; Tchr., Bristol (VT) HS, 1941–42. **Educ.:** Univ. of VT, 1937–41, BS (Home Econ.); Tchrs. Coll. Columbia Univ., 1944–45, MA (Educ.); Univ. of TN, 1960–79, (LS). **Orgs.:** ALA: Amer. Issues Forum Chlds. Bk. List Sel. Com. (1975); AASL; ALSC, Newbery–Caldecott Awds. Sel. Com. (1974), Intl. Rels. Com. (1975–78), Laura Ingalls Wilder Awd. Sel. Com. (1971–75), Prog. Support Pubns. Com. (1979–). TN LA. Intl. Assn. of Sch. Libnshp. Frnds. of Intl. Bd. of Bks. for Young People. Other orgs. Natl. Educ. Assn. Delta Kappa Gamma Natl. Assn. of Tchrs. of Eng. Natl. Assn. for the Prsrvn. of Storytel. Other orgs. **Honors:** Univ. of VT, Mortar Bd.; TN LA, Louise Meredith Sch. Lib. Media Srv. Awd., 1979. **Pubns.:** Idea Exchange Column *Sch. Media Qtly.* (1972–79); Sel. com. for H.W. Wilson *Children's Catalog* (1975–); Consult. for vol. of Brewton's *Subject Index to Poetry for Children* (1978); Asst. ed., *Sch. Media Qtly.* (1972–79), Ed. bd., *The Source* (Knoxville Sch. Libns. Jnl.) (1976–). **Activities:** 10; 15, 21, 31, 36; 55, 89 **Addr.:** 7117 Downing Dr., Knoxville, TN 37919.

Robertson, May Rose (My. 17, 1924, Donaldsonville, LA) Retired, O. 1979–; Chief, Tech. Prcs. Branch, U. S. Dept. of Transp. Lib., 1971–79, Chief, Acq. Sect., Dept. of Transp. and Fed. Aviation Admin. Libs., 1967–71; Catlgr., U. S. Food and Drug Admin. Med. Lib., 1965–67; Sel. Ofcr., Natl. Agr. Lib., 1962–1965; Command Libn., HQ, North. Area Command, U. S. Army, Europe (Frankfurt, Germany), 1955–1962; Libn. (various titles), U. S. Army, Air Frc. (Germany, GA, NY, KS), 1946–1955; Libn., LA State Univ. Lib., 1944–46. **Educ.:** LA State Univ., 1939–43, BS (Eng., Fr.), 1943–44, BS (LS). **Orgs.:** ALA. SLA. DC LA. ASIS. Other orgs. DAR. Animal Protection Inst. of Amer. Amer. Horticultural Socty. Socty. of Descendants of Francis Epes of VA. **Honors:** U. S. Dept. of Transp. Lib., Dist. Career Srv. Awd., 1979; Alpha Lambda Delta; Phi Kappa Phi; Beta Phi Mu; other hon. socty. **Activities:** 4; 15, 44, 46; 56, 74, 94 **Addr.:** 3341 Ardley Ct., Falls Church, VA 22041.

Robertson, Patsy (O. 10, 1942, Liberty, NY) Lib.-Media Spec., Greece Ctrl. Sch. Dist., 1975–; Tchr., Livingston Manor Ctrl., 1966–75. **Educ.:** SUNY, New Paltz, 1966, BA (Eng., Educ.); SUNY, Geneseo, 1974, MLS; various crs. **Orgs.:** Grt. Rochester Area Sch. Media Spec.: Exec. Bd. (1980–81). NY LA: Sch. Lib. Media Spec. ALA. Natl. Educ. Assn.: Bd. of Dir. (1980–81). Greece Tchrs. Assn.: Secy. (1976–79). Delta Kappa Gamma: Pi State, Beta Eta Chap. (Parlmt., Legis. Ch.). **Activities:** 10; 15, 32, 39 **Addr.:** Hoover Dr. Jr. High School, 133 Hoover Dr., Rochester, NY 14615.

Robertson, Peter D. W. (Jl. 28, 1944, Moncton, NB) Hist. Resrch. Ofcr., Pub. Arch., Can., 1967–. **Educ.:** Univ. of West. ON, 1962–66, BA (Eng., Hist.). **Orgs.:** Assn. Can. Archvsts. Can. Aviation Hist. Socty.: Ottawa Chap. (Prog. Ch., 1975–76). **Pubns.:** *Relentless Verity: Canadian Military Photographers Since 1885* (1973); "Canadian Photojournalism During the First World War," *History of Photography* (1978); "More Than Meets the Eye," *Archivaria* (Sum. 1976). **Activities:** 2; 15, 18, 41; 55 **Addr.:** Public Archives of Canada, 395 Wellington St., Ottawa, K1A 0N3 Canada.

Robertson, W. Davenport (O. 10, 1947, Hickory, NC) Head Libn., Natl. Inst. of Env. Hlth. Scis., 1977–; On-site Supvsr., EPA/UNC Lib. Intern Prog., Env. Protection Agency, 1975–77. **Educ.:** Univ. of NC, 1965–69, AB, honors (Hist.), 1973–75, MLS. **Orgs.:** SLA: NC Chap., Bltn. Mgr. (1979–). NC OLUG. **Honors:** Natl. Insts. of Hlth., Awd. of Merit, 1980. Beta Phi Mu, 1976. Phi Beta Kappa, 1968. **Pubns.:** "User-Oriented Approach to Setting Priorities for Library Services," *Spec. Libs.* (Ag. 1980); "UNC-EPA Internship Presents Unique Opportunity for Students," *Spec. Libs.* (Ag. 1976). **Activities:** 4, 12; 17, 39; 56, 58, 65 **Addr.:** National Institute of Environmental Health Sciences Library, P.O. Box 12233, Research Triangle Park, NC 27709.

Robin, Madeleine (Ja. 5, 1945, Port Alfred, PQ) Art Libn., Acq. and Ref., Laval Univ. Lib., 1978–; Lib. Tech., CEGEP of Jonquière, 1970–72. **Educ.:** CECEP de Jonquiere, 1966–68, DEC (Bibliotechnique); Univ. d'Aix en Provence, France, 1973–75 (Art Hist.); Montreal Univ., 1975–76, BA (Art Hist.); Univ. de Montreal, 1976–78, MA (LS). **Orgs.:** ASTED: Com. Prix Marie Claire Daveluy (1979). **Activities:** 1; 15, 19, 24; 55, 85 **Addr.:** Bibliothéque Générale Universite Laval, Division des Collections en Sciences Humaines et Sociales (C.S.H.S.), Local 4530 C. Pavillon Bonenfant, Ste Foy, PQ G1K 7P4 Canada.

Robins, Barbara K. (F. 26, 1949, Parsons, KS) Hum. Libn., Emporia State Univ., 1972–, Catlgr., 1968–71. **Educ.:** KS State Tchrs. Coll., 1959–63, BME (Msc.), 1963–64, MM (Msc.), 1965–68, MLS. **Orgs.:** KS LA: Coll. and Univ. Libs. Sect. (Ch., 1978–79); Exec. Com. (1978–79). Msc. LA. ALA. AAUP. **Activities:** 1; 31, 39; 55 **Addr.:** University Library, Emporia State University, Emporia, KS 66801.

Robinson, Barbara M. (F. 11, 1945, Summit, NJ) Dir., Metro. WA Lib. Cncl., Metro. WA Cncl. of Gvts., 1977–; Exec. Secy., Cncl. for Computerized Lib. Netwks., 1979–; Consultant, Machlup Info. Resrch., 1976–77; Resrch. Assoc., Natl. Enquiry into Scholary Comm., 1976; Actng. Asst. Libn. for Spec. Projs., Princeton Univ., 1975–76; Dir., Info. Ctr., Pub. Tech., Inc., 1973–75; Ref. and Young Adult Libn., Princeton Pub. Lib., 1971–73; Ed. Assoc., Juvenile Div., Puffin, Penguin Books, 1970–71; various prof. positions and consults. (1969–72). **Educ.:** Mt. Holyoke Coll., 1962–66, BA (Eng.); Simmons Sch. of LS, 1968–69, MLS. **Orgs.:** ALA: ASLCA/Multitype Lib. Coop. Sect., Prog. Com. (co–ch., 1980); Nom. Com. (1979–80). SLA: DC Chap. ASIS. Assoc. Info. Mgrs. of the Info. Indus. Assn. Various State LAs. **Honors:** Beta Phi Mu. **Pubns.:** "Funding for Library Networks: Types and Sources of Available Funds," *Critical Issues in Cooperative Library Development a Conference on Networks for Networkers* (1980); "Municipal Library Services 1977," *The Municipal Yearbook* (1979); "Much More About Laminated Posters at the Princeton Public Library," *The Unabashed Libn.* (Win. 1973); "Moving the Library Outside its Walls: A Case Study of South Boston," *Bay State Libn.* (O. 1969); "A Tutorial Project for Poor Students," *Jnl. of Marriage and the Family,* (Win. 1964); various other rpts. (1965–1977). **Activities:** 14-Reg. Plng. Org.; 17, 28, 34; 63, 94 **Addr.:** Director, Metropolitan, Washington Library Council, 1875 Eye St. N.W., Suite 200, Washington, DC 20006.

Robinson, Barrie John (My. 30, 1926, Cornwall, ON) Dir. Secy. Treas., Lake ON Reg. Lib., 1967–; Ref. Coord., Mid York Lib. Syst., 1966–67; Chief Libn., Massena Pub. Lib., 1965–66; HS Tchr. Libn., N. Essex Sch., 1958–63. **Educ.:** Toronto/Leeds/Sir George Williams Mtl., 1945–51, BSc (Textiles, Bio.); McGill Univ., 1963–64, BLS (Lib.); NY State Permanent Cert. Pub. Lib., 1966. **Orgs.:** ALA. Can. LA. ON LA. ON Geneal. Socty.: Kingston Branch Ch. (1980–81); Secy. (1973–75); Treas. 1976–77); Vice-Ch. (1978–79); Cncl. (1978–79). Geneal. Socty. **Pubns.:** Various articles in *ON Lib. Review.* **Activities:** 2, 9; 19, 24, 37; 57, 69, 70 **Addr.:** 192 Churchill Crescent, Kingston, ON K7L 4N2 Canada.

Robinson, Betty Ann (F. 19, 1929, Des Moines, IA) Tech. Srvs. Libn., Cmnty. Coll. of Denver, 1969–; Tchr. (Elem.), Volusia Cnty. (FL) Bd. of Educ. 1959–68; Tchr. (Elem.), Garfield Hts. (OH) Bd. of Educ. 1955–59; Soc. Worker Cuyahoga Cnty. (OH) Welfare Dept. 1953–54. **Educ.:** Stetson Univ., 1947–50, BA (Hum.) Univ. of Denver, 1968–69, MA (LS), South. Bapt. Theo. Semy. 1951–53, MRE (Relig. Educ.). **Orgs.:** CO LA: Acq. Sect., Tech. Srvs. RT Ch. (1978–79). ALA. Assn. of CO Cmnty. Coll. Lrng. Resrc. Ctrs.: Pres. (1972–73). Altrusa Intl. Amer. Assn. of Women in Cmnty. and Jr. Colls. **Activities:** 1; 15, 20, 46; 50, 66, 72 **Addr.:** Learning Materials Center, Community College of Denver, North Campus, 3645 W. 112th Ave., Westminster, CO 80030.

Robinson, Chantal (F. 6, 1952, Gaspé, PQ) Ref. Libn., Ofc. de la Lang. Fr., 1980–; Ref. Libn., Srv. Gen. des Moyens d'Enseignement, 1978–80; Ref. Libn., École des Hautes Etudes Cmrcl., 1976–77. **Educ.:** Univ. de Montréal, 1970–73, Bac. (Hist., Art), 1975–77, MLS. **Orgs.:** Assn. Can. des Sci. de l'Info.: Secy. (1979–80); Montreal Chap. (Pres., 1980–81). Corp. des Bibtcrs. Prof. du PQ: Com. Élec. (1978–79), com. du Droit à l'Exercise de la Prof. (1980–82). **Activities:** 4; 17, 39; 55, 78, 91 **Addr.:** 5055 Roslyn, apt. 410, Montréal, PQ H3W 2L7 Canada.

Robinson, Charles W. (F. 27, 1928, Peking, China) Dir., Baltimore Cnty. Pub. Lib., 1963, Assoc. Dir., 1959–63; Admin. Asst. to Dir., Free Lib. of Philadelphia, 1955–59, Libn. I, 1953–59. **Educ.:** Colby Coll., 1946–50, AB (Soc. Sci.); Simmons Coll., 1950–51, MS (LS). **Orgs.:** ALA: Cncl. (1979–82); various coms. MD LA: Various coms. **Honors:** MD LA, Awd., 1977. **Pubns.:** Various articles. **Activities:** 9; 17, 34 **Addr.:** Baltimore County Public Library, 320 York Rd., Towson, MD 21204.

Robinson, Christopher Derek (Je. 25, 1941, Poole, Dorset, Eng.) Catlgr., ON Hydro Lib., 1980–; Info. Sci. Consult., 1976–80; Chief Subj. Anal., Coll. Bibliocentre, 1973–76; Head, PRECIS Indexing Team, Brit. Natl. Bibl., 1970–72, Subj. Rev., 1968–70, Catlgr., 1967–68. **Educ.:** Univ. of Bristol, 1960–63, BA, hons. (Eng.); Northwest. Polytech., 1966, ALA (LS). **Orgs.:** LA (UK). Assn. of Asst. Libns. **Pubns.:** *PRECIS Authority File* (1975); *PRECIS: An Annotated Bibliography* 2nd ed. (1977); "Indexing Nonbook Materials by PRECIS," *Prcs. Intl. PRECIS Wkshp.* (1976); "PRECIS Canada: Achievements and Prospects," *Can. Jnl. Info. Sci.* (1979). **Activities:** 12; 20, 30; 56, 75 **Addr.:** 572 Greenwood Ave., Toronto, ON M4J 4A9 Canada.

Robinson, Elizabeth Anne (Mr. 8, 1929, New York NY) Libn. Good Samaritan Hosp. and Hlth. Ctr., 1974–; Libn., Chld.'s Med. Ctr., 1966–74; Lib. Asst., Miami Valley Hosp., 1961–66; Indxr., Squibb Inst. Med. Resrch, 1959–59; Resrch. Asst., Ortho Resrch. Fndn., 1951–55. **Educ.:** Hope Coll., 1946–50, BA (Bio.); Rutgers Univ., 1950–52, MS (Bacteriology), 1952–53, (Bio.); Wright State Univ., 1971–75, (LS). **Orgs.:** Med. LA: Mid W. Reg. Grp.; Hosp. Lib. Sect. Miami Valley Assn. of Hlth. Scis. Libs. **Honors** Sigma XI, 1952. **Activities:** 12; 15, 17, 39; 80 **Addr.:** 6452 Greenbrook Dr., Dayton, OH 45426.

Robinson, Evelyn Rose (Mr. 15, 1909, Boston, MA) Retired Dir. of Lib. Sch., South. CT State Coll., 1962–; Assoc., Prof. of LS, 1962–74; Instr., Clark Univ., 1955–62; Visit. Lectr., Wheaton Coll., MA, 1962, Lectr., Sec. Eng., Boston Univ., 1956–59; Instr., LS, Queens Coll., 1956–59; Asst. Prof. of LS, SUNY, Albany, 1954–56; Visit. Assoc. Prof., LS, Univ. of TN, 1955; various positions in lib. work with chld. and YA. **Educ.:** Columbia Univ. Sch. of Lib. Srv., 1940–45, 55; Boston Univ., 1950, BS (Sec. Eng. Educ.), 1950–51, EdM, 1962, EdD. **Orgs.:** ALA: Cncl. CA LA. CT LA: VP, Pres. (1970–72). MA LA. Natl.

PROFESSIONAL ACTIVITIES: Institutions: 1. Acad. lib.; 2. Arch.; 3. Assn.; 4. Fed./Gvt. lib.; 5. Inst. lib.; 6. Mfr./Suppl.; 7. Milit. lib.; 8. Musm.; 9. Pub. lib.; 10. Sch. lib.; 11. Sch. of lib. sci.; 12. Spec. lib.; 13. State lib.; 14. (other). **Functions/Activities:** 15. Acq./Col. dev.; 16. Adult srvs.; 17. Admin.; 18. Apprais.; 19. Archit./Bldgs.; 20. Cat./Class.; 21. Chld. srvs.; 22. Circ.; 23. Cons./Pres.; 24. Consult.; 25. Cont. ed.; 26. Educ. lib. sci.; 27. Ext. srvs.; 28. Fund/Grants; 29. Gvt. pubs.; 30. Indx./Abs.; 31. Instr. lib. use; 32. Media srvs.; 33. Micro.; 34. Netwks./Coop.; 35. Persnl.; 36. PR; 37. Publshg.; 38. Recs. mgt.; 39. Ref. srvs.; 40. Repro.; 41. Resrch.; 42. Review.; 43. Secur.; 44. Serials; 45. Spec. col.; 46. Tech. srvs.; 47. Trustees/Bds.; 48. YA srvs.; 49. (other).

Cncl. of Tchrs. of Eng.: Com. on Cert. and Prep. of Tchrs. of Eng. (1963–68). Amer. Red Cross: Ambulance Driver (1943–45). Natl. Leag. of Amer. Pen Women: Secy. (1976–78). Photo-Travelers Club **Honors:** Pi Lambda Theta, 1951; CT Sch. LA, Rheta A. Clark Awd., 1974; **Pubns.:** Ed., *Reading About Children's Literature* (1966); "Multi-Media Appraoch to Teaching Children's Literature," *Educ. Horizons* (Sum. 1967); various Bibls., articles. **Activities:** 9, 13; 21, 26, 27; 63 **Addr.:** 727 Sapphire St., Apt. 110, San Diego, CA 92109.

Robinson, Judith Braunagel (S. 18, 1947, Meridian, MS) Assoc. Prof., SUNY, Buffalo, 1975–; Catlgr., FL State Univ., 1973; YA Libn., Monroe Cnty. Pub. Lib., 1972–73; Asst. to Head, Dept. Libs., OH State Univ., 1970–72. **Educ.:** Manatee Jr. Coll., 1965–66, AA (Liberal Arts); FL State Univ., 1967–68, BA (Eng.), 1969–70, MLS, 1973–75, PhD (LS). **Orgs.:** ALA: Srv. to Aging Popltn. (1977–79); Stdg. Com. on the Status of Women (1976–78). AALS. **Honors:** *Amer. Libs.*, 1st Prize, Round 5, Prize Article Contest, 1979; Beta Phi Mu, 1970; Phi Theta Kappa, 1966. **Pubns.:** Jt. auth., *The Librarian and Reference Queries* (1980); "Job Mobility of Men and Women Librarians," *Amer. Libs.* (D. 1979); "Using Student Submitted Questions for Practice in Answering Reference Questions," *Jnl. of Educ. for Libnshp.* (Sum. 1978). **Activities:** 11; 26 **Addr.:** 201 Lawrence D. Bell Hall, School of Information & Library Studies, SUNYAB, Amherst, NY 14260.

Robinson, Karen M. (Jl. 7, 1951, Washington, DC) Grad. Theo. Libn., Dir., Holy Spirit Resrch. Ctr., Oral Roberts Univ., 1979–, Coord., 1975–78; Elem. Tchr., Lone Star Sch., 1974–75. **Educ.:** Oral Roberts Univ., 1969–74, BA (Educ.); Emporia State Univ., 1978–79, MLS (Acad., Spec. Libnshp.). **Orgs.:** OK LA: OK JMRT (1979–); Coll. and Univs. Div. (1979–). ALA. KS JMRT (1978–79). Socty. for Pentecostal Std. **Honors:** Oral Roberts Univ., Lib. Sch. Fac., Nom. to Intl. Lib. of Congs. Internship Prog., 1979; OK Dept. of Libs., Dorothea Dale Schol., 1980; Beta Phi Mu, 1979. **Pubns.:** "Pentecostal Research Center—Oral Roberts University," *Socty. for Pentecostal Std. Nsltr.* (Ap. 1977); "I Love My Job!" *Reach Mag.* (F. 1976); *An Annotated Bibliography of Catholic Charismatic Materials in The Holy Spirit Research Center at Oral Roberts University* (1978); bk. review ed., *PNEUMA* (1980–81), ed. com. *Socty. for Pentecostal Std. Nsltr.* (1976–79). **Activities:** 1, 12; 15, 17, 45; 57, 62, 90 **Addr.:** Oral Roberts University, 7777 S. Lewis, Tulsa, OK 74171.

Robinson, Wendy J. (Ag. 10, 1946, Long Branch, NJ) Adult Libn., Free Lib. of Philadelphia, 1977–; Adult Libn., New Castle Lib., 1974–76. **Educ.:** Douglass Coll., 1964–67, Boston Univ., 1967–68, BA (Soclgy.); Drexel Univ., 1976–77, MS (LS). **Orgs.:** ALA. DE LA: Pub. Lib. Div. (VP, 1975–76). AAUW: Secty. (1981–). **Honors:** Beta Phi Mu, 1977. **Pubns.:** "A Comparison of the Guides to Abstracting and Indexing Services Provided by Katz, Chicorel, and Ulrich," *RQ* (Sum. 1978); "Meeting the Psychological and Social Needs of Older Adults: The Library's Role," *Drexel Lib. Qtly.* (Ap. 1979). **Activities:** 9; 16; 56, 85 **Addr.:** 41 Woodale Rd., Philadelphia, PA 19118.

Robinson, William Chandler (O. 25, 1939, Bakersfield, CA) Assoc. Prof., Univ. of TN, 1972–; Asst. Prof., Univ. of South. CA, 1970–71, Head, World Affairs Lib., 1966–67, Admin. Asst. to Univ. Libn., 1965–66. **Educ.:** Claremont Men's Coll., 1957–61, BA magna cum laude (Pub. Affairs); Tufts Univ., 1961–62, AM (Intl. Rels.); Univ. of South. CA, 1964–65, MSLS; Univ. of IL, 1967–72, PhD (LS). **Orgs.:** TN LA: Int. Frdm. Com. (Ch., 1975–1976); Educ. Sect. (Ch., 1974–1975); Legis. Com. (1973–1975). AALS: Ed. Bd. (1976–); Conv., Resrch. Interest Grp. (1977); others. E. TN LA: Nom. Com. (Ch., 1979). SLA. Amer. Prtg. Hist. Assn. **Honors:** Tufts Univ., Woodrow Wilson Flwshp.; Univ. of South. CA, H.W. Wilson Flwshp. **Pubns.:** "The Utility of Retail Site Selection for The Public Library," *Univ. of IL Grad. Sch. LS Occasional Paper 122* (Mr. 1976); "The Role of Library Schools in Continuing Education," *Southeast. Libn.* (Fall 1976); "Local Government Publications in Larger Tennessee Public and Academic Libraries," *TN Libn.* (Fall 1976); jt. auth., "Time lag in The 1972 Monthly Catalog of United States Government Publications," *Gvt. Pubns. Review* (1976); other articles; Ed., *TN Libn.* (1977–). **Activities:** 11; 15, 26, 41; 57, 63, 92 **Addr.:** Graduate School of Library & Information Science, University of Tennessee, 804 Volunteer Blvd., Knoxville, TN 37916.

Robison, Carolyn Love (Ag. 9, 1940, Orlinda, TN) Assoc. Univ. Libn., GA State Univ., 1976–, Asst. Univ. Libn., 1971–75, Head of Circ. Dept., 1967–71; Asst. Libn./Lectr., GA Inst. of Tech., 1965–67; Tchr. (Eng., Hist.), Dag Hammarskjold Jr. HS, (Wallingford, CT), 1962–1964. **Educ.:** Dickinson Coll., 1958–60; Denison Univ., 1960–1962, BA (Eng.); Emory Univ., 1964–65, M. Libn.; GA State Univ., 1973–, (Educ. Leadershp.). **Orgs.:** GA LA. SELA. ALA. AAUP. Delta Kappa Gamma. **Activities:** 1; 17 **Addr.:** William Russell Pullen Library, Georgia State University, 100 Decatur St., S.E., Atlanta, GA 30303.

Robison, Dennis E. (D. 6, 1934, Ft. Wayne, IN) Univ. Libn., Univ. of Richmond, 1974–; Asst. Dir., Pub. Srvs., Univ. of S. FL, 1970–74, Ref. Libn., 1966–70, Asst. Ref. Libn., 1962–66. **Educ.:** St. Petersburg Jr. Coll., 1957–58; FL State Univ., 1958–60, BS (Hist.), 1960–62, MLS; Univ. of S. FL, 1969, MA (Soc. Sci.). **Orgs.:** VA LA: Coll. and Univ. Sect. (Ch., 1979–80). ALA: ACRL, Bibl. Instr. Com. (1971–76); RASD, Afflt. Grp. Com. (1969–73); Chap. Rel. Com. (1972–78). FL LA: Pres. (1973–74); Chrt. and Bylaws Com. (1970); Ref. RT (1966–67). Southeast. Lib. Netwk.: Bd. of Dirs. (1977–80). **Honors:** Phi Alpha Theta, 1960; Beta Phi Mu, 1962; ARL, Ofc. of Mgt. Libs., Consult. Trng. Prog., 1979. **Pubns.:** "Chapter and By-Laws Committee Revisions," *FL Libs.* (1973); "Evaluating the Community Study," *FL Libs.* (1972); jt. auth., "Who's Teaching Chemical Literature Courses These Days?" *Jnl. of Chem. Documtn.* (1969). **Addr.:** 1406 Westridge Rd., Richmond, VA 23229.

Robison, Juanita F. (Mr 25, 1914, Columbus, OH) Retired, 1981–; Lib. Tech. Srvs. Admin., Phoenix Pub. Lib., 1955–81; Catlgr., OH State Lib., 1954–55, Lib. Dir., Lake Air Frc. Base, 1941–43, Catlgr., Cincinnati Pub. Lib., 1940–41; Ref. Libn., Catlgr., OH State Lib., 1936–40. **Educ.:** OH State Univ. 1931–35, BA (Eng.); West. Rsv. Univ., 1935–36, MA (LS). **Orgs.:** AZ LA. SWLA. ALA. Ladies Oriental Shrine. East. Star. **Activities:** 9; 17, 20, 46; 56, 75 **Addr.:** 4320 E. Piccadilly Rd., Phoenix, AZ 85018.

Robson, John Marquis (Ja. 23, 1950, Covington, KY) Head, Tech. Srvs., VA Milit. Inst., 1979–; Catlgr., Univ. of WI, La Crosse, 1972–76. **Educ.:** Kent State Univ., 1968–71, BS (Educ.), 1971–72, MLS; Univ. of WI, 1976– (LS). **Orgs.:** ALA. VA LA: Int. Frdm. Com. (1980–). **Activities:** 1; 15, 17, 20; 74, 75, 91 **Addr.:** Preston Library, Virginia Military Institute, Lexington, VA 24450.

Rocafort, María de los A. (O. 6, 1938, San Juan, PR) Dean, Lrng. Resrcs., PR Jr. Coll., 1980–, Assoc. Dean, Lrng. Resrcs., 1979–80, Lib. Dir., 1974–78; Acq. Dir., Interamer. Univ., 1973–74; Cat. Dir., Corp. for Econ. Dev. of the Caribbean, 1965–68. **Educ.:** Univ. of PR, 1955–58, BA (Psy.), 1974–76, MLS. **Orgs.:** ALA: AECT. Assn. para las Comms. y la Tech. Educ. SBPR. **Pubns.:** Various copy for TV scripts, videocassettes (1979). **Activities:** 1; 17, 20 **Addr.:** Calle 25 #1313, Urb. Montecarlo, Río Piedras, PR 00924.

Rocha, Guy Louis (S. 23, 1951, Long Beach, CA) NV State Archvst., State, Cnty. and Mncpl. Arch., State of NV, 1981–Interim Dir., NV Hist. Socty., 1980–81, Interim Asst. Dir., 1980, Cur., Mss., 1976–81; Hist. Instr., West. NV Cmnty. Coll., 1976; Sub. Tchr., Reno-Sparks Pub. Schs., 1975–76; Evening Tchr., Camp Pendleton Refugee Camp, 1975. **Educ.:** Syracuse Univ., 1973, BA (Soc. Std.); San Diego State Univ., 1975, MA (Amer. Std.); Univ. of NV, 1976–, ABD (Hist.); various wkshps. **Orgs.:** SAA. Conf. of Intermt. Archvsts.: Cncl. (1979–81). NV State Adv. Cncl. on Libs. State Hist. Recs. Adv. Bd. Washoe Cnty. Hist. Socty. **Pubns.:** "Coney Island on the Truckee," *Reno Mag.* (Jl. 1980); "Boomer Fights," *NV Mag.* (S.–O. 1980); "Marvin Hart vs. Jack Root: The Heavyweight Championship Fight That Time Forgot," *Boxing Digest* (S. 1980); "Rhyolite: 1900–1940, An Historical Overview," "Tonopah: 1900–1940, An Historical Overview," *Nye County History Project* (1980); "The IWW and the Boulder Canyon Project," The Death Throes of American Syndicalism," *At The Point Of Production: The Local History of the IWW* (1981); various articles, reviews, presentations. **Addr.:** Nevada State County Municipal Archives, 101 S. Fall St., Capitol Complex, Carson City, NV 89710.

Rochell, Carlton C. (N. 2, 1933, Lawrenceburg, TN) Dean of Libs., NY Univ., 1976–; Dir., Atlanta Pub. Lib., 1968–76; Dir., Pub. Lib. of Knoxville and Knox Cnty., 1965–67; Dir., Anniston-Calhoun Cnty. Pub. Lib., 1963–65; Dir., Hattiesburg - Forrest Cnty. Pub. Lib., 1961–1963; Spec. Asst., Nashville Pub. Lib., 1959–1960. **Educ.:** George Peabody Coll., 1959, BS (Math.); FL State Univ., 1961, MS (LS); GA State Univ., 1973, MS (Urban Std.); FL State Univ., 1974, Advnc. MS (Libnshp., Gvt.), 1976, PhD (LS, Gvt.). **Orgs.:** NY Metro. Ref. and Resrch. Agency: Pres., (1979–80). NY State Bd. of Regents: Adv. Cncl. for Libs. (Ch., 1979–); Comsn. Com. on Statewide Lib. Dev. (1980–). NY LA: WHCOLIS Task Frc., Ch. (1978–). **Honors:** ALA, John Cotton Dana Pubcty. Awd., 1976; NY Chap. Amer. Mktg. Assn., Effie Awd. of Excel., 1976; Advert. Club of NY, Andy Awd. of Merit, 1976; CLR Fellow 1973–74, Fellow to Int. Inst. Adm. Sci. (Brussels) (1980–81). **Pubns.:** *Practical Administration of Public Libraries,* (1980); "Library Development & Legislation: A Call for Unity," *Lib. Jnl.* (S. 15, 1979); "The Research Collections Program of NEH," *LJ* (S. 1, 1979); "Libraries and the Humanities: NEH on the Move," *LJ* (Ap. 1, 1979). **Activities:** 1, 9; 17, 28, 36; 50, 78, 93 **Addr.:** New York University, 70 Washington Sq. So., New York, NY 10012.

Rochlin, Phillip (Mr. 24, 1923, New York, NY) Tech. Info. Spec./Chem., Env. and Energy Ofc., Nvl. Ordnance Station, 1979–; Instr., LS, Charles Cnty. Cmnty. Coll., 1973–; Dir., Tech. Info. Div./Supvsry. Chem., Nvl. Ordnance Station, 1969–78; Chief, Accession and Indexing Branch, Natl. Highway Safety Inst., Documtn. Ctr., FHWA, 1968–69; Dir., Tech. Info. Div./Supvsry. Chem., Nvl Propellant Plant, Nvl. Ordnance Station, 1963–68. Sci. Anal./Engin. Spec., Natl. Referral Ctr. for Sci. and Tech., Lib. of Congs., 1963; Resrch. Chem., Picatinny Arsenal, 1950–63. **Educ.:** City Coll. of New York, 1939–43, BS (Chem.); New York Univ., 1944–49, MS (Chem.); Rutgers Univ., 1957–60, MLS. **Orgs.:** Cncl. of Navy Sci. and Tech. Libns., E.: NPP/NAVORDSTA rep. (1963–68, 1969–78; Ch., 1976–78); Com. on Trng. for Lib. Techs. (Ch., 1973–78); Instr., Ref. (1970–78). SLA: DC Chap./Transp. Grp. (Ch., 1968–69); Milit. Grp. (Ch., 1971–72). Amer. Chem. Socty. Com. on Info. Hang-ups. Assn. for Recorded Snd. Cols. **Pubns.:** *Fremont for the Philatelist: A Catalog* (1971, 1981); "Micro Media in the Library," *Jnl. of Micro.* (Ja. 1973); Ed., *Philatelic Lit. Review* (1956–60). **Activities:** 4, 12; 17, 24, 26; 60, 74, 91 **Addr.:** Environmental and Energy Office, Naval Ordnance Station, Indian Head, MD 20640.

Rockman, Ilene F. (N. 9, 1950, Yonkers, NY) Ref. Libn., CA Polytech. State Univ., San Luis Obispo, 1975–; Educ. Libn., WA State Univ., 1974–75. **Educ.:** Univ. of CA, Los Angeles, 1968–72, BA (Hist.); Univ. of South. CA, 1973–74, MSLS; CA Polytech. State Univ., 1976–78, MA (Educ.). **Orgs.:** ALA: RASD, Cat. Use Com. (Ch., 1978–80); ACRL/Educ. and Behav. Sci. Sect., Exec. Bd. (1981–82), Bibl. Instr. for Educs. Com. (1977–80), Cont. Educ. Com. (1981–83); Com. on Instr. (1977–79); SRRT; LIRT. CA LA: Int. Frdm. Com. (1976–78). Bay Area Educ. Libns. Total Interlib. Exch.: Pres. (1979–80). **Honors:** Phi Delta Kappa; Kappa Delta Pi. **Pubns.:** "The Potential of Online Circulation Systems as Public Catalogs: An Introduction," *RQ* (Fall 1980); "Where's the Catalog? An Introduction," *RQ* (Fall 1979); "The Educational Needs of Pilipino American Children," *Educ. Libs.* (Spr.–Sum. 1979); "Censorship: Are You Prepared To Resist It?" *Kappa Delta Pi Rec.* (Ap. 1978); jt. auth., "An Interim Solution to an Overcrowded Academic Library," *CA Libn.* (Ap. 1977). **Activities:** 1; 31, 32, 39; 56, 63, 66 **Addr.:** University Library, California Polytechnic State University, San Luis Obispo, CA 93407.

Rockwood, D. Stephen (D. 10, 1946, Philadelphia, PA) Dir., Lib., Mt. St. Mary's Coll., 1981–; Head, Pers., Albion Coll., 1975–80; Serials Recorder, Univ. of Chicago, 1972–75. **Educ.:** OH Wesleyan Univ., 1964–68, BA (Hist.); Miami Univ., 1968–72, MA, PhD (Hist.); Rosary Coll., 1974–75, MLS. **Orgs.:** ALA. **Pubns.:** Jt. ed., *College Librarianship* (1981); "Collection Development from a College Perspective," *Coll. & Resrch. Libs.* (Jl. 1979); "The Use and Abuse of Psychohistory," *Jnl. of Psyt.* (Sum. 1977). **Addr.:** Hugh Phillips Library, Mt. St. Mary's College, Emmitsburg, MD 21727.

Rockwood, Ruth Humiston (O. 15, 1906, Chicago, IL) Prof. Emeritus, Sch. of LS, FL State Univ., 1979–, Prof., 1953–79; Visit. Asst. Prof., IN Univ. Lib. Sch., 1958–59; Fulbright Lectr., Chulalongkorn Univ., Bangkok, Thailand, 1952–53; Admin. Asst., Instr., Univ. of IL Lib. Sch., 1949–52. **Educ.:** Wellesley Coll., 1927, AB (Eng., Hist.); Univ. of IL, 1949, MS (LS); IN Univ., 1960, EdD (Adult Educ.). **Orgs.:** ALA. FL LA: Pres.; Secy. SELA. FL Assn. for Media in Educ. Pilot Club. Sierra Club. FL Trail Assn. AAUP. **Honors:** Beta Phi Mu, 1949. **Pubns.:** *The Relationship Between the Professional Preparation and Subsequent Types of Library Positions Held by a Selected Group of Library School Graduates* ACRL microcard series (1952); various articles in prof. pers. (1954, 1960, 1961–73). **Activities:** 9; 16, 20, 26; 50, 63, 89 **Addr.:** 1616 Woodgate Way, Tallahassee, FL 32312.

Rocque, Bernice L. (Ag. 28, 1950, Norwich, CT) Coord., Corp. Lib. Netwk., Texaco Inc., 1979–; YA/Ref. Libn., Simsbury Pub. Lib., 1976–79. **Educ.:** Univ. of CT, 1968–72, BA (Eng.); Syracuse Univ., 1974–75, MLS. **Orgs.:** Pratt Inst., Westchester Adv. Comm. SLA. ASIS. ALA. CT LA. **Honors:** Beta Phi Mu. **Activities:** 12; 17, 34; 56, 59, 86 **Addr.:** 33 Pine Hill Ave., Stamford, CT 06906.

Rod, Donald Olaf (Jl. 14, 1915, Roland, IA) Dir., Lib. Srvs., Univ. of North. IA, 1953–; Libn., Augustana Coll., IL 1943–53; Asst. Libn., Assoc. Libn., Luther Coll., IA; Bldg. Consult., various colls. and univs. 1940–43. **Educ.:** Luther Coll., 1934–38, AB (Latin); Univ. of MI, 1938–40, ABLS; various grad. crs. in LS. **Orgs.:** IA LA: Pres. (1958–59). N. Ctrl. Assn.: Consult./Examiner (1973–). ALA: Cncl. (1961–65); ALA/Amer. Inst. of Archits. Lib. Bldgs. Awd. Jury (1974); Univ. Lib. Bldgs. Com. (Ch., 1970–71); ACRL, Coll. Lib. Stans. Com. **Honors:** Luther Coll., Dist. Srv. Awd., 1969. **Pubns.:** "Research Libraries in Scandinavia," *Coll. & Resrch. Libs.* (O. 1949); various bk. reviews, *Lib. Qtly.* **Activities:** 1; 17, 19, 24 **Addr.:** Library Services, University of Northern Iowa Library, Cedar Falls, IA 50613.

Rodda, Dorothy J. (Ja. 29, 1922, Philadelphia, PA) Exec. Secy., Church and Synagogue LA, 1973–; Asst. Libn., Harcum Jr. Coll., 1976–77; Libn., The Lankenau Sch., 1969–74; Asst. Libn., Harcum Jr. Coll., 1967–69; Exec. Secty., Church and Synagogue LA, 1967–71. **Educ.:** Univ. of PA, 1939–43, AB (Econ.); Drexel Univ., 1963–67, MS (LS). **Orgs.:** Church and Synagogue LA: Treas. (1967–71). DE Valley Chap.: Treas. (1972–73); Pres. Elect (1973–74); Pres. (1974–75). Cncl. of Natl. Lib. and Info. Assns.: Cnclr. (1978–). First Presbyterian Church Ardmore: Libn. (1964–76); Christ. Educ. Com. (1971–76); Pastor Nom. Com. (1976–77, 1980–81). **Honors:** Phi Beta Kappa, 1942; Pi Gamma Mu, 1943; Beta Phi Mu, 1967; Phi Kappa Phi, 1967. **Pubns.:** Jt. cmplr., *Church and Synagogue Library Resources* (1975, 1979); Jt. Cmplr., *Directory of Church and Synagogue Libraries* (1965); Contrib., "The Church and Synagogue Library Association,"

Special Subjects/Services: 50. Adult educ.; 51. Advert./Mktg.; 52. Aerosp.; 53. Agric.; 54. Area std.; 55. Arts/Hum.; 56. Autom.; 57. Bibl./Prtg.; 58. Bio. sci.; 59. Bus./Fin.; 60. Chem.; 61. Copyrt.; 62. Documtn.; 63. Educ.; 64. Engin.; 65. Env.; 66. Eth. grps.; 67. Film; 68. Food/Nutr.; 69. Geneal.; 70. Geo.; 71. Geol.; 72. Handcpd.; 73. Hist.; 74. Int. frdm.; 75. Info. sci.; 76. Insr.; 77. Law; 78. Legis.; 79. Math./Comp. sci.; 80. Med.; 81. Metals; 82. Nat. resrcs.; 83. Newsp.; 84. Nuc. sci.; 85. Oral hist.; 86. Petr./Energy; 87. Pharm.; 88. Phys./Astr./Math.; 89. Readg.; 90. Relig.; 91. Sci./Tech.; 92. Soc. sci.; 93. Telecom.; 94. Transp.; 95. (other).

Church and Synagogue Libraries (1980). **Activities:** 10; 17, 21, 26; 63, 90 **Addr.:** 1812 Manor Rd., Havertown, PA 19083.

Rodda, Reddy R. (D. 5, 1945, Guntur, Andhra Pradash, India) Asst. Prof. and Engin. Libn., Univ. of TN, 1978–; Cols. Dev. Libn., Univ. of West. ON, 1974–78; Ref. Libn., McGill Univ. 1973–74. **Educ.:** Andhra Univ. (India), 1962–68, BE (Electronics); Univ. of KS, 1969–70, MS (Electrical); Univ. of West. ON, 1972–73, MLS. **Orgs.:** ALA. Can. LA. SELA. Assn. for Comp. Machinery. **Activities:** 1, 12; 15, 16, 39; 56, 64, 75, 88, 91 **Addr.:** University of Tennessee, Science - Engineering Library, Knoxville, TN 37916.

Rodeffer, Georgia Hester (S. 13, 1946, New Orleans, LA) Head Textile Libn., NC State Univ., 1976–; Instr., Textiles, CO State Univ., 1970–71. **Educ.:** SEast. LA Univ., 1964–68, BS (Home Econ.); CO State Univ., 1968–70, MS (Textiles); Univ. of IL, 1974–75, MS (LS). **Orgs.:** Textile Info. Users Cncl.: Exec. Bd. (1977–). SLA. ALA. **Honors:** Omicron Nu. **Pubns.:** "Information Networking in the Textile Industry," *Proceedings, General Motors Res. Lab., Conf. on Spec. Lib. Role in Netwks.* (My. 1980); "United Nations Publications as a Source of Textile Related Information," *Proceedings, Textile Info. Users Cncl. Mtg.* (Ap. 1978); "Resource Utilization by the Texturing Industry," *Proceedings, Textured Yarn Assn. of Amer. Tech. Conf.* (F. 1978); "Information Services at the NCSU Textiles Library," *Proceedings, Textile Info. Users Cncl.* (O. 1976). **Activities:** 1, 12; 15, 17, 39; 55, 91 **Addr.:** School of Textiles Library, North Carolina State University, Box 5006, Raleigh, NC 27650.

Roden, Ruth N. (O. 26, 1931, Florence, AL) Head, Cat. Dept., Univ. of CA, Irvine, Lib., 1979–; Head, Cat. Dept., CA State Polytech. Univ., Pomona, Lib., 1973–79; Cat. Libn., W. Liberty State Coll. Lib., 1970–73; Maps Catlgr., Sci. Lib., Univ. of GA, 1969–70; Congs. Com. Liaison, Docum. Expediting Proj., Lib. of Congs., 1968–69. **Educ.:** Univ. of AL, 1950–52, BA (Eng.); Univ. of NC, 1966–68, MSLS; CA State Polytech. Univ., Pomona, 1974–76, MA (Eng.). **Orgs.:** ALA: RTSD; ACRL; LITA. CA LA. South. CA Tech. Prcs. Grp. Common Cause. Amer. Cvl. Liberties Un. Amnesty Intl. Sierra Club. **Honors:** Sigma Tau Delta, 1952; Alpha Beta Alpha, 1965. **Activities:** 1; 17, 20, 46; 56, 65, 70 **Addr.:** Library, University of California, P.O. Box 19557, Irvine, CA 92713.

Roderer, Nancy K. (S. 12, 1946, Oak Park, IL) VP, Opers., King Rsrch., Inc., 1979–, Sr. Rsrch. Assoc., 1975–79; Lib. and Info. Spec., Westaf, Inc., 1973–75. **Educ.:** Univ. of Dayton, 1964–67, BS (Math., Comp. Sci.); Univ. of MD, 1971–73, MLS. **Orgs.:** ASIS: Spec. Interest Grp. on Fndns. of Info. Sci. (Ch., (1978–79); various other offices, SIG/FIS (1972–79). **Pubns.:** Jt. ed., *Key Papers in the Economics of Information* (forthcoming); jt. auth., *Cost Model for Determining Optimum Document Reproduction Policies at NTIS* (F. 1980); "Electronic Processes: A Solution to the Economic Difficulties Facing Small Journals," *Jnl. of Rsrch. Comm. Stds.* (O. 1979); jt. auth., *The Journal in Scientific Communication: The Roles of Authors, Publishers, Libraries, and Readers in a Vital System* (My. 1979); *U.S. Expenditures for Biomedical Communication, 1960–1985* (A. 1979); various articles, monos., and conf. presentations (1973–). **Activities:** 12; 24, 41; 75 **Addr.:** King Research, Inc., 6000 Executive Blvd., Rockville, MD 20852.

Rodger, Elizabeth A. (Je. 29, 1943, Lanark Twp., ON) Libn. II, User Srvs., Toronto Pub. Lib., 1970–, Libn. I, Pub. Srvs., 1967–70. **Educ.:** Queen's Univ., 1961–64, BA (Eng., Fr., Relig.); Univ. of Toronto, 1966–67, BLS. **Orgs.:** ON LA. Can. LA. **Activities:** 9; 16, 22, 39 **Addr.:** 15 Walmer Rd., Apt. 307, Toronto, ON M5R 2X1 Canada.

Rodgers, Clarence Wilbur (O. 20, 1925, North Platte, NE) Sr. Libn., Queens bor. Pub. Lib., 1963–. **Educ.:** Univ. of NE, 1955–59, BA (Econ.); FL State Univ., 1962–63, MS (LS). **Orgs.:** ALA. NY Lib. Club. NY Tech. Libns. Econ. Hist. Assn. AAUP. **Activities:** 9; 16, 39, 48 **Addr.:** 485 Front St. Apt. 315, Hempstead, NY 11550.

Rodgers, Frank (Jl. 28, 1927, Darlington, Cnty. Durham, Eng.) Dir. of Libs., Univ. of Miami, 1979–; Dir. of Lib., Portland State Univ., 1969–79; Asst. Dir., Pub. Srvs., PA State Univ., 1966–69, Chief Ref. Libn., 1965–66; Asst. Ref. Libn., Univ. of IL, 1959–64. **Educ.:** King's Coll., Durham Univ., 1944–47, BA, hons. (Eng.); Univ. Coll., London Univ., 1950–51, Postgrad. Dip. (LS); LA of UK, 1952, Assoc., 1955, Fellow. **Orgs.:** ALA. LA UK. OR LA: VP (1973–74); Pres. (1974–75); various com. chs. (1971–79). PA LA: Gvt. Docum. Com. Ch., 1966–68). Pac. NW Bibl. Ctr.: Bd. of Dirs. (1973–77). **Honors:** Cncl. on Lib. Resrcs., Ofcr.'s Grant, 1975; Univ. of Southampton, Visit. Fellow, 1975–76. **Pubns.:** *Guide to British Government Publications* (1980). *Serial Publications in the British Parliamentary Papers 1900–1968* (1971); jt. auth., *Guide to British Parliamentary Papers* (1967); *Index to National Diet Library Directory of Japanese Learned Periodicals* (1963). **Activities:** 1; 17, 34, 39 **Addr.:** 5630 Twin Lakes Cir., South Miami, FL 33143.

Rodgers, Patricia M. (N. 27, 1947, Charleston, WV) Coord., Tech. Srvs., Biomed. Lib., Univ. of S. AL, 1980–, Assoc. Dir., 1979; Cat. Libn., 1976–79. **Educ.:** Clemson Univ., 1966–70, BA (Sec. Educ.); Univ. of SC, 1974–75, MLS. **Orgs.:** Med. LA. AL LA: Legis. Com. (1978–79). **Activities:** 12; 15, 46; 80 **Addr.:** P.O. Box U-1207 USA, Mobile, AL 36688.

Rodich, Nancy Ann (Ag. 15, 1931, Fresno, CA) Tech. Srvs. Libn., Mid-MS Reg. Lib. Syst., 1976–; Instr., Univ. of MD Coll. of Lib. and Info. Srvs., 1974–76; Tech. Srvs. Libn., Georgetown Univ. Med. Sch. Lib., 1974–75; Cat. Libn., Univ. of OR Med. Sch. Lib., 1968–73. **Educ.:** Univ. of OR, 1949–53, BA (Math.), 1967–68, MLS. **Orgs.:** ALA. ASIS. MS LA. **Activities:** 9; 20, 34, 46; 55, 56 **Addr.:** Technical Services Librarian, Mid-Mississippi Regional Library System, Kosciusko, MS 39090.

Rodrigues, Ronald J. (O. 26, 1947, Alameda, CA) Ref. Libn., Oakland Pub. Lib., 1972–; Ref. Libn., Berkeley/Oakland Srv. Syst., 1974–78. **Educ.:** CA State Univ., Hayward, 1972–75, BA (Geo.); Univ. of CA, Berkeley, 1975–76, MLS. **Orgs.:** West. Assn. Map Libns. **Activities:** 9; 39; 65, 70 **Addr.:** 10124 Voltaire Ave., Oakland, CA 94603.

Rodriguez, Jose F. (D. 14, 1922, Caibarien, Las Villas, Cuba) Pub. Srvs. Libn., Univ. of GA Law Lib., 1967–. **Educ.:** Marist Coll. (Caibarien), 1936–40, A&SB (Arts, Scis.); Univ. of Havana, 1940–45, Dr. (Law); KS State Tchrs. Coll., 1965–67, MS (LS). **Orgs.:** AALL: Frgn. Law Com. (1971–73); Rcrt. Com. (1977–78); Southeast. Chap., Minority Libns. Com. **Activities:** 1; 77 **Addr.:** University of Georgia Law Library, School of Law, Athens, GA 30606.

Roe, Eunice M. (D. 8, 1942, Watertown, WI) Proj. Assoc., Inst. for Resrch. on Land and Water Resrcs., PA State Univ., 1978–; Asst. Libn., Life Scis. Lib., PA State Univ., 1974–77, Proj. Spec., Env. Scis., Univ. of WI, 1967–68. **Educ.:** Univ. of WI, 1960–64, BS (Bot., Zlgy.); Univ. of OR, 1972–73, MLS. **Orgs.:** SLA: Ctrl. PA Provis. Chap. (Mem. Ch., 1979–81). Mid–State Litcy. Cncl. **Honors:** Beta Phi Mu. **Pubns.:** Ed., "Problems of Publishing" *Science* (1981); ed., *Membership and Resources Directory*, Central PA Chptr., Spec. Libs. Assoc. (1981); Jt. auth., *The Flowering phenology of North American plants: A bibliography* (1975); jt. auth., *Guide to the Flowering Seasons of the United States and Southern Canada.* (1972). **Activities:** 12; 15, 17, 39; 65, 82 **Addr.:** Research Library, Inst. for Research on Land & Water Resources, Land & Water Research Bldg., Pennsylvania State University, University Park, PA 16802.

Roe, Keith E. (Ag. 25, 1937, Williams, IA) Head, Life Scis. Lib., PA State Univ., 1977–; Sr. Asst. Libn., Life Scis., 1973–77; Biblgphr. for Nat. Scis., St. Mary's Coll. of MD, 1973. **Educ.:** IA State Univ., 1956–60, BS (Horticult.); Univ. of WI, 1962–69, MS, PhD (Bot.); Univ. of OR, 1972–1973, MLS. **Orgs.:** ALA: ACRL/ Sci. and Tech. Sect., Prog. Plng. Com. (1980–); Oberly Awds. Com. (1978–80). Cncl. of Bot. and Horticult. Libs. Dictionary Socty. of N. Amer. Amer. Inst. of Bio. Scis. **Pubns.:** Chaps. in 2 bks.; various articles; reviews. **Activities:** 1; 15, 17, 39; 58, 68, 53-Agr. **Addr.:** Life Sciences Library, E205 Pattee, The Pennsylvania State University, University Park, PA 16802.

Roe, Margaret D. (My. 16, 1947, Wahoo, NE) Coord. for Southeast. Lib. Netwk., NE Lib. Comsn., 1976–. **Educ.:** NE Wesleyan Univ., 1965–69, BS (Soclgy.); Univ. of CA, Los Angeles, 1973–76, MLS (Ref.). **Orgs.:** ALA. Mt. Plains LA. NE LA. Lincoln Hlth. Scis. Lib. Cnsrtm.: Com. on AV Grant to Natl. Lib. of Med. (Co–Ch., 1979–); Cat. Com. (Ch., 1978–). **Activities:** 13; 24, 34, 47 **Addr.:** Nebraska Library Commission, 1420 P St., Lincoln, NE 68508.

Roeckel, Alan G. (My. 18, 1947, Brooklyn, NY) Ref. Libn., Incorporated Vlg. of Garden City, 1976–; Asst. Ref. Libn., E. Meadow Pub. Lib., 1971–76. **Educ.:** King's Coll., 1965–69, BA (Eng.); SUNY, Albany, 1970–71, MLS; various crs. **Orgs.:** ALA. ASIS. Assoc. Info. Mgrs. **Activities:** 9; 16, 17, 39; 55, 56, 94 **Addr.:** 29 Washington St., Hicksville, NY 11801.

Roe–Coker, Kathy Juanita (O. 7, 1951, Vallejo, CA) Apprais. Archvst. III, SC Dept. of Arch. and Hist., 1976–; Asst. Archvst., Winthrop Coll. Arch., 1974–76. **Educ.:** Winthrop Coll., 1970–74, BA, magna cum laude (Hist.), 1974–76, MA (Hist.); Univ. of SC, 1977–79, ML; Natl. Arch. and Recs. Srv., 1976, Cert. (Arch. Admin.), 1978, Cert. (Arch. Admin.); 1980–, Advnc. Grad. Std. in Hist. **Orgs.:** SAA: Acq. Task Frc. ALA. Socty. of GA Archvsts.: Bk. Review Com. SC LA: Arch. and Spec. Cols. RT (Vice-Ch./Ch.-Elect, 1981–82). Bk. and Key Club: VP (1974). WHCOLIS: Del.–at–Lg. (1978). **Honors:** Phi Alpha Theta; Phi Kappa Phi. **Pubns.:** "Lady Traveller in Skirts," *Historicus* (N. 1978); various reviews (1976–80). **Activities:** 2; 15, 18; 73-Hist.; 92 **Addr.:** South Carolina Department of Archives and History, P.O. Box 11,669 Capitol Station, 1430 Senate St., Columbia, SC 29211.

Roedde, William A. (My. 10, 1925, Vancouver, BC) Dir., Prov. Lib. Srv., ON Dept. of Educ., 1960–81, Asst. Dir., 1958–60; Dir., Northwest. ON Reg. Lib. Coop., 1953–58; Libn., Ft. William Pub. Lib., 1951–53. **Educ.:** Univ. of BC, 1950, BA; McGill Univ., 1951, BLS. **Orgs.:** Can. LA. ON LA. **Addr.:** Libraries and Community Information, 77 Bloor St. West, 2nd Floor, Toronto, ON M7A 2R9 Canada.*

Roehm, Jane D. (Jl. 21, 1916, Gary, IN) Archvst., Fairfield Hist. Socty., 1978–; Ch., Lib. Com., Fairfield Country Day Sch., 1956–64; Ch., Frnds. of the Lib., Bethel, CT, 1950–55; Docum. and Comms. Ofcr., U.S. Nvl. Rsv., 1942–45. **Educ.:** Northwest. Univ., 1938, BA (Eng., Hist.); Pratt Inst., 1967, MLS. **Orgs.:** SAA. Amer. Assn. for State and Lcl. Hist. **Activities:** 2; 23, 41, 45; 55, 62 **Addr.:** 43 Wells Hill Rd., Weston, CT 06883.

Roesch, Gay Ellen (O. 20, 1948, Denver, CO) Libn., Davis, Graham and Stubbs, 1977–; Asst. Libn., 1976–77; Lib. Asst. Arapahoe Reg. Lib. Dist. 1975–76; Head, Ref., Univ. of MD Law Lib., 1972–74. **Educ.:** Univ. of CO, 1966–70, BA (Intl. Rel.); Univ. of Denver, 1971–72, MA (LS). Univ. of MD, 1973–74 (Law). **Orgs.:** AALL: Ethics Com. (1972–73). CO Cnsrtm. of Law Libs.: Pres. (1979–80); Pubn. Com. Ch. (1977–78). Rocky Mt OLUG: Pres. (1980–81). SLA: Rocky Mt. Chap. Nsltr. Ed. (1976–77). Other orgs. and Ofcs. Mental Hlth. Assn. **Activities:** 12; 17, 20, 39; 77 **Addr.:** 2605 Ingalls #205, Edgewater, CO 80214.

Rogalski, Leonore G. (Je. 28, 1926, Wheeling, IL) Lib. Supvsr., UOP, Inc. 1955–; Libn., Intl. Minerals and Chemical Co., 1952–55; Resrch. Chem., Dr. Wagner's Lab., Northwestern Univ. Med. Sch., 1948–52. **Educ.:** Northwestern Univ., 1944–48, BS (Chem.), 1948–50, MS (Chem.). **Orgs.:** SLA. ASIS. Amer. Petr. Inst.: Ctrl. Abs. and Indexing Srv., Adv. Com. Amer. Chemical Socty. **Pubns.:** "On-Line Searching of the American Petroleum Institute's Databases," *Jnl. of Chemical Info. and Comp. Sci.* (1978); jt. auth., "Bengilide and its Reduction by Lithium Aluminum Hydride," *Transactions IL Acad. Sci.* (1975); "Technical Information Activities of a Petroleum Research Library," *Spec. Libs.* (O. 1958); jt. auth., "Esterification of Serum Cholesterol. III. Hypercholesterolemic Rabbit," *Jnl. Lab. Clinical Med.* (1952); jt. auth., "Esterification of Serum Cholesterol. II. Influence of Phosphatides and Other Factors," *Jnl. Lab. Clinical Med.* (1952). **Activities:** 12; 17; 60, 64, 86 **Addr.:** UOP, Inc., 10 UOP Plz., Des Plaines, IL 60016.

Rogers, A. Robert (S. 9, 1927, Moncton, NB) Dean, Sch. of LS, Kent State Univ., 1978–, Actg. Dean, Sch. of LS, 1977–78, Prof. of LS, 1969–; Visit. Prof. of LS, Pahlavi Univ., 1976–77; Dir. of Lib., Bowling Green State Univ., 1964–1969, Actg. Dir. of Lib., 1961–1964, Asst. to the Dir. of Lib., 1959–61; Adult Asst., Detroit Pub. Lib., 1957–59; various positions in Acad. Libs., 1951–56. **Educ.:** Univ. of NB, 1944–48, BA (Phil., Hist.); Univ. of Toronto, 1948–50, MA (Phil.); Univ. of London, 1950–53, Post grad. dip. (LS); Univ. of MI, 1957–64, PhD (LS). **Orgs.:** ALA: Cncl. (1972–76). AALS: Cncl. of Deans and Dirs./Nom. Com. (1979–80). OH LA: Bd. (1968–76); Pres. (1979–80). Bibl. Socty. of Can. Can. LA. Lib. Assn. of Grt. Brit. **Honors:** OH LA, Libn. of the Year, 1976. **Pubns.:** *The Humanities: A Selective Guide to Information Sources* (1974, 1980); *The White Monument* (1955); jt. auth., "Education for Librarianship at Pahlavi University, Shiraz, Iran," *Intl. Lib. Review* (Ap. 1979); jt. auth. "Library Education in a Developing Country: Pahlavi University, (Shiraz, Iran) as a Case Study," *Unesco Jnl. of Info. Sci., Libnshp. and Arch. Admin.* (Fo 1982); "Ohio's Support of Library Services," *Libraries in the Political Process* (1980); various articles and chaps. (1953–). **Activities:** 1, 11; 17, 26, 39; 55, 78 **Addr.:** 1965 Pine View Dr., Kent, OH 44240.

Rogers, Dr. Bonnie L. (Ap. 14, 1940, Olive Hill, KY) Dean, Instr. Resrcs., Palomar Cmnty. Coll., 1979–, Asst. Dean, Instr., Lib. Srvs., 1977–79, Coord., Lib. Pub. Srv., 1969–77; Asst. Head Ref. Libn., U.S. Intl. Univ., 1968–69; Cat. Libn., U.S. Nvl War Coll., 1967–68. **Educ.:** Morehead State Univ., 1957–61, BA (Econ., Soclgy., Fr.); Univ. of MD, 1968, MLS (Lib., Info. Sci.); Univ. of South. CA, 1980, EdD (Educ. Admin. and Supvsn., Comm., Coll. Admin.); various wkshps. **Orgs.:** Cmnty. Coll. Assn. for Instr. and Tech.: West. Reg. Dir. (1980–82). CA LA: Cmnty. Coll. Libns. Chap. (Pres., 1979). Lrng. Resrcs. Assn. of CA Cmnty. Colls.: Bd. of Dirs. (1980–82). San Diego Cmnty. Coll. Lrng. Resrcs. Cnsrtm.: Pres. (1978–80). Assn. of CA Cmnty. Coll. Admins. **Honors:** Beta Phi Mu. **Pubns.:** "Management Consciousness for Library Administrators," *INTERCOM* (O. 1980); "A Cooperative Effort That Works," *INTERCOM* (D. 1980); "Do You Have A Problem—Employee," *INTERCOM* (Ja. 1981); "The Merit System and Collective Bargaining," *Univ. of South. CA Rpt.* (1977); various rpts. **Activities:** 1; 17, 32, 35; 63, 66, 93 **Addr.:** Instructional Resources, Palomar Community College, 1140 W. Mission Rd., San Marcos, CA 92069.

Rogers, Brian D. (Je. 26, 1937, New London, CT) Coll. Libn., CT Coll., 1975–; Head, Pub. Srvs., Wesleyan Univ. Lib., 1969–75, Ref. Libn., 1967–69; Asst. Regis., Salem Coll., 1964–66. **Educ.:** Alfred Univ., 1955–59, BA (Hist.); U.S. Army Lang. Sch., 1961–62 (Czech); Rutgers Univ., 1966–67, MSLS. **Orgs.:** ALA: Legis. Netwk. (1979–); ACRL. New Eng. Chap. ACRL: Bd. of Dirs. (1978–). State Adv. Cncl. on Libs.: Ch. (1977). Southeast. CT LA: Exec. Com. (1976–); Pres. (1979–80). CT LA. Untd. Way. Columbiad Club. **Honors:** Beta Phi Mu. **Pubns.:** "Connecticut College Library," *Lib. Jnl. Spec. Rpt. #16* (1980). **Activities:** 1; 17, 39, 45; 55, 57 **Addr.:** Connecticut College Library, New London, CT 06320.

Rogers, Deborah (O. 7, 1948, Pittsburgh, PA) Asst. Libn., American Heritage Pub. Co., 1981–; Asst. Libn., Rockefeller

PROFESSIONAL ACTIVITIES: Institutions: 1. Acad. lib.; 2. Arch.; 3. Assn.; 4. Fed./Gvt. lib.; 5. Inst. lib.; 6. Mfr./Suppl.; 7. Milit. lib.; 8. Musm.; 9. Pub. lib.; 10. Sch. lib.; 11. Sch. of lib. sci.; 12. Spec. lib.; 13. State lib.; 14. (other). **Functions/Activities:** 15. Acq./Col. dev.; 16. Adult srvs.; 17. Admin.; 18. Apprais.; 19. Archit./Bldgs.; 20. Cat./Class.; 21. Chld. srvs.; 22. Circ.; 23. Cons./Pres.; 24. Consult.; 25. Cont. ed.; 26. Educ. lib. sci.; 27. Ext. srvs.; 28. Fund/Grants; 29. Gvt. pubs.; 30. Indx./Abs.; 31. Instr. lib. use; 32. Media srvs.; 33. Micro.; 34. Netwks./Coop.; 35. Persnl.; 36. PR; 37. Publshg.; 38. Recs. mgt.; 39. Ref. srvs.; 40. Repro.; 41. Resrch.; 42. Review.; 43. Secur.; 44. Serials; 45. Spec. col.; 46. Tech. srvs.; 47. Trustees/Bds.; 48. YA srvs.; 49. (other).

Fndn., 1978–80; Admin. Asst., Metro. Musm. of Art, 1977–78; Base Libn., Ankara Air Station, U.S. Air Frc., 1976–77; Ref. Libn., Carnegie Lib. of Pittsburgh, 1972–76. **Educ.:** Univ. of Pittsburgh, 1966–69, BA (Eng. Lit.), 1971–72, MLS. **Orgs.:** SLA. **Honors:** Beta Phi Mu. **Activities:** 9, 12; 39, 41; 54, 55, 92, 95-Online Srch. **Addr.:** American Heritage Publishing Company, 10 Rockefeller Plz., New York, NY 10020.

Rogers, Dorothy (Smith) (My. 15, 1938, Buffalo, NY) Head of Cat., Carleton Univ., Ottawa, 1976–; Libn. (Part-Time), Map Lib., Univ. of Toronto, 1974–75; Libn. (Part-time), Arch., Untd. Church of Can., 1967–73; Actg. Head of Cat., Med. Lib., Yale Univ., 1966–67. **Educ.:** Wellesley Coll., 1955–59, BA (Zlgy.); Univ. of Toronto, 1960–61, BLS; Yale Univ., 1966–68, MA (Hist. of Sci.). **Orgs.:** Can. LA: Anl. Conf. Wkshp. (Ch., 1977). Can. Assn. of Coll. and Univ. Libs. Can. Assn. of Spec. Libs. and Info. Srvs. Med. LA: New Eng. Reg. Grp. (Anl. Conf. Ch., 1964). Various other orgs. **Honors** Beta Phi Mu, 1961. **Pubns.:** "A Calendar of the Fergusson Papers," *Jnl. Hist. of the Bio. Sci.* (1964). **Activities:** 1; 20; 70, 80, 91 **Addr.:** 24 Second Ave., Ottawa, ON K1S 2H3 Canada.

Rogers, Earl M. (My. 2, 1938, Moline, IL) Asst. Mss. Libn., Univ. of IA, 1970–; Catlgr., Univ. of UT, 1967–70. **Educ.:** IA State Univ., 1957–61, BS (Hist.); Univ. of CA, Berkeley, 1966–67, MLS. **Orgs.:** ALA. IA Hist. Mtrls. Prsrvn. Socty.: VP (1976–77). Midwest Arch. Conf.: Lcl. Arrange. (Ch., Fall 1977). SAA. Agr. Hist. Socty. Org. of Amer. Histns. **Pubns.:** Cmplr., *A Bibliography of the History of the University of Iowa, 1847–1978* (1979); ed., *The Wallace Papers, An Index to the Microfilm Editions of the Henry A. Wallace Papers....* (1975); "The Papers of Henry A. Wallace," *Bks. at IA* (N. 1974). **Activities:** 2; 45 **Addr.:** University of Iowa Library, Iowa City, IA 52242.

Rogers, Elaine S. (Ja. 21, 1929, Detroit, MI) Libn., Tax Sect. Lib., Gen. Motors Corp., 1979–81; Ref. Libn., Grosse Pointe Pub. Lib., 1976–78; Law Libn., Clark, Klein, Winter, Parsons and Prewitt, 1973–75. **Educ.:** Wayne State Univ., 1948–71, BA (Hist.), 1971–73, MSLS. **Orgs.:** AALL. OH Reg. Assn. of Law Libns. **Activities:** 12; 15, 29, 39; 59, 77, 92†

Rogers, Frank Bradway, (D. 31, 1914, Norwood, OH) Consult. 1974–; Libn., Univ. of CO Med. Ctr., 1963–74; Dir., Natl. Lib. of Med. 1949–63. **Educ.:** Yale Univ., 1932–36, AB (Pre-Med.); OH State Univ., 1938–42, MD; Columbia Univ. Sch. of Lib. Srvs., 1948–49, MS (LS). **Orgs.:** Med. LA: Pres. (1962–63). Jt. Com. on the Un. List of Serials: Ch. (1960–63). Amer. Assn. for the Hist. of Med.: Pres. (1966–68). **Honors:** Med. LA, Marcia Noyes Awd., 1961; ALA, Melvil Dewey Medal, 1963; LA UK, Barnard Prize, 1964. **Pubns.:** *Selected Papers of John Shaw Billings* (1965); "Computerized Bibliographic Retrieval Services," *Lib. Trends* (1974); *The Index Medicus in the Twentieth Century* (forthcoming); *The Origins of MEDLARS* (forthcoming). **Activities:** 1, 12; 17; 80 **Addr.:** 1135 Grape St., Denver, CO 80220.

Rogers, Gerald Blane (Je. 10, 1929, Whitehorse, OK) Dir., Media and Tech., Educ. Srv. Ctr., Reg. XVII, 1967–; Dir., W. TX Coop. AV Srvs., 1965–67; Asst. Prin., Monterey HS, 1962–65, Dir., Student Actv., AV Coord., 1960–62. **Educ.:** TX West. Coll., 1950–52, BA (Phys. Educ.), 1952–55, MA (Educ.); Amarillo Coll., 1947–50, AAS (Liberal Arts). **Orgs.:** TX Assn. for Educ. Tech.: Pres. (1968–69). EFLA: Bd. (1977–80); VP (1980). AECT: Conv. Treas. (1977); Mem. Com. (1975). Natl. Assn. of Reg. Media Ctrs. **Activities:** 10, 12; 17, 22, 32; 63, 67, 93 **Addr.:** Media and Technology, Education Service Center, Region XVII, 4000 — 22nd Pl., Lubbock, TX 79410.

Rogers, James E. (Je. 11, 1935, Warren, OH) Dir., E. Cleveland Pub. Lib., 1977–; Dir. of Urban Srvs., Cleveland Pub. Lib., 1971–76; Exec. Dir., 21st Congsnl. Dist. Caucus, 1969–71. **Educ.:** Azusa-Pac. Coll., 1964–66, BA (Soc. Sci.); Case West. Univ., 1971–72, MSLS, 1973–77, PhD (Info. Sci.); Miami Univ., 1978, Cert. (Lib. Admin.). **Orgs.:** ALA. ASIS. OH LA. **Honors:** Lubrizol Corp., Awd., 1972. **Pubns.:** "The Change Goes On," *The Open Shelf* (Ap.–Je. 1973). **Activities:** 9, 11; 24, 26, 47; 63, 66, 75 **Addr.:** East Cleveland Public Library, 14101 Euclid Ave., East Cleveland, OH 44112.

Rogers, JoAnn V. (Jl. 28, 1940, Pittsburgh, PA) Assoc. Prof., Univ. of KY, 1974; Media Spec., White Plains HS, 1967–71; Tchr., Eng., Port Chester Pub. Schs., 1962–66; Pic. Libn., Amer. Heritage Publshg. Co., 1962. **Educ.:** CT Coll., 1958–62, BA (Eng.); Columbia Univ., 1966–67, MLS; Univ. of Pittsburgh, 1972–77, PhD (LS). **Orgs.:** ALA: AASL, Intl. Rel. Com. (1979–); YASD, Bylaws Com. (Ch., 1976–77); LRRT, Resrch. Dev. Com. (Ch., 1979). AALS: Resrch. Forum (Ch., 1980); Conf. Plng. Com. (1980). **Honors:** Beta Phi Mu, Ctr. for Dev. Change, Flwshp., 1977. **Pubns.:** *Libraries and Young Adults* (1979); "Young Adults and Libraries," *Ency. of Lib. and Info. Sci.* (1981); "Nonprint Cataloging: A Call for Standardization," *Amer. Libs.* (Ja. 1979); various other articles. **Activities:** 11; 20, 32, 48 **Addr.:** College of Library Science, University of Kentucky, Lexington, KY 40506.

Rogers, Nancy H. (Mr. 8, 1946, Birmingham, AL) Southeast. Sales Rep., EBSCO Subscrpn. Agency, 1978–; Dir., Sch. of Nursing Lib., Samford Univ., 1972–78; Serials Libn., Univ. of AL, 1968–72; Bkmobile. Libn., Birmingham Pub. Lib., 1966–68. **Educ.:** Univ. of AL, 1970–74, BA (Eng.); FL State Univ., 1974–75, MSLS; Emory Univ., 1977, Med. LA Cert. (Med. Libnshp.). **Orgs.:** SELA. ALA. SLA. AL LA: Various coms., chs. Various other orgs. **Honors:** Natl. Bus. Womens Assn., Awd., 1975; EBSCO Subscrpn. Agency, Outstan. Sales Rep., 1979. **Activities:** 1; 17, 33, 44; 55, 80 **Addr.:** 128 Cambrian Way, Birmingham, AL 35243.

Rogers, Rutherford David (Je. 22, 1915, Jesup, IA) Univ. Libn., Yale Univ., 1969–; Dir. of Univ. Libs, Stanford Univ., 1964–69; Deputy Libn. of Congs., Lib. of Congs., 1957–64; Chief, Ref. Dept., New York Pub. Lib., 1955–57; Dir., Rochester Pub. Lib., 1952–54; Dir., Gosvenor Lib., 1948–52; Resrch. Anal., Smith, Barney and Co., 1946–48; Actng. Libn. and Libn., Columbia Coll. Columbia Univ., 1941–42; various prof. positions, 1938–42. **Educ.:** Univ. of North. IA, 1932–36, BA (Eng.); Columbia Univ., 1936–38, MA (Eng., Comp. Lit.), 1937–38, BS (LS). **Orgs.:** Resrch. Libs. Grp., Inc.: Ch. of Bd. (1979–). ALA: VP, Exec. Bd. (1961–66); Natl. Union Cat. Com. (1973–); various ofcs. and coms. H. W. Wilson Fndn.: Trustee (1969–). H. W. Wilson Co.: Bd. of Dirs. (1969–). Various orgs. and ofcs. (1950–). **Honors:** IFLA, Medal, 1977; King of Belgium, Officier de l'Ordre de la Couronne, 1977; Amer. Acad. of Arts and Sci., Fellow; Univ. of Dayton, Dr. of Lib. Admin., *honoris causa,* 1971. Various other honors. **Pubns.:** Jt. auth., *University Library Administration* (1971); "An Essay on the Use and Advantages of the Fine Arts by John Trumbull," *Thirteen Colonial Americana* (1977); "An American Dictionary of the English Language, by Noah Webster," *76 United Statesiana* (1976); "Organization and Decision Making in Research Libraries," *Issues in Library Administration* (1974); "College and University Libraries," *World Book Encyclopedia* (1974); various articles, chaps., reviews, and consults. (1941–). **Activities:** 1, 4; 17 **Addr.:** Yale Univ. Library, Box 1603A Yale Station, New Haven, CT 06520.

Roggenkamp, Alice Mary (Ap. 6, 1917, New York, NY) Asst. mgr., Info. Resrc. Ctr., Amer. Telephone and Telegraph Co., 1978–, Head Libn., 1974–77, Libn. for Ref. Col. and PR, 1967–74, Asst. Libn. Tech. Srvs., 1960–67, Asst. Libn. Cat., 1954–60. **Educ.:** Hunter Coll., 1936–40, BA (Econ. and Stats.); Columbia Univ., 1944–45, MA (Educ.), 1969–71, MSLS. crs. **Orgs.:** SLA: Pub. Utils. Div. (1977 Conv. session Ch.). NY LA. Smithsonian Inst. Episcopal Church Women. NY Hist. Socty. NY Bot. Socty. Other orgs. **Activities:** 12; 17, 39, 41; 59, 92, 93 **Addr.:** American Telephone and Telegraph Co., 195 Broadway, Rm. 30C-1240, New York, NY 10007.

Rogofsky, Murray (D. 16, 1929, Bronx, NY) Chief, Cat. Branch, Support Div., Defense Mapping Agency, Hydrographie/Topographic Ctr., 1980–, Tech. Info. Spec., 1978–80, Chief Libn., 1977–78; Chief Libn., Nvl. Oceanographic Ofc., 1967–77; Chief Libn., Vitro Lab., 1967; Docmlst., Xerox Corp., 1965–67; Chief Libn., Nvl. Appld. Sci. Lab., 1958–65; Head Catlgr., Yeshiva Univ., 1957–58. **Educ.:** Brooklyn Coll., 1946–50, BA (Hist.); Univ. of MO, 1950–52, MA (Hist.); Columbia Univ., 1956–58, MSLS. **Orgs.:** ASIS. SLA: Washington DC Chap., Sci.–Tech. Grp., Ch. (1972). Sigma Xi. Inst. of Electronic and Electric Engins. **Pubns.:** "Naval Oceanographic Office Library," *NODC Nsltr.* (Ap. 1969). **Activities:** 1, 4; 17, 39, 46; 64, 70, 91 **Addr.:** 2901 Tarragon Ln., Bowie, MD 20715.

Rohde, Nancy J. (Freeman) (F. 13, 1936, Hibbing, MN) Asst. Prof., Univ. of MN Lib. Sch., 1968–; Asst. Prof., North. IL Univ. Dept. of LS, 1972–73; Instr., Asst. to Dir., Univ. of MN Lib. Sch., 1962–68; Sr. Libn., NY Pub. Lib., 1960–62, Libn., NY Pub. Lib., 1958–60. **Educ.:** Univ. of MN, 1954–57, BA (Interdept.), 1957–58, MA (LS); Univ. of WI, 1968–71, Spec. Cert. (Lib. Educ.). **Orgs.:** AALS: Org. and Bylaws Com. (Ch., 1980–81); Secy.-Treas. (1976–79). ALA. MN LA. ASIS. AAUP. MN Assn. for Cont. Adult Educ. **Honors** Beta Phi Mu, 1958; Phi Beta Kappa, 1957. **Pubns.:** "Gratia Alta Countryman: Librarian and Reformer," *Women of Minnesota: Selected Biographical Essays* (1977); "Educating the Adult Services Librarian," *RQ* (Spr. 1979); ed., *Library Services in North Dakota: Report of a Survey Conducted for the State Library Commission and the State Historical Society* (1966); "The Education of Adult Services Librarians," *Adult Srvs.* (Fall–Win. 1971). **Activities:** 11; 26 **Addr.:** University of Minnesota Library School, 419 Walter Library, 117 Pleasant St. S.E., Minneapolis, MN 55455.

Rohdy, Margaret A. (Ag. 7, 1945, Keokuk, IA) Head, Tech. Srvs., St. Lawrence Univ. Lib., 1978–; Cat. Libn., Rosary Coll. Lib., 1975–78; Catlgr., Mncpl. Ref. Lib., 1972–75; Instr., Fr., Univ. of SD, 1968–71. **Educ.:** Univ. of North. IA, 1963–67, BA (Fr.); Middlebury Coll., 1967–68, MA (Fr.); Univ. of Chicago, 1971–73, AM (LS). **Orgs.:** ALA. SUNY/OCLC Netwk. Adv. Cncl.: Pvt. Higher Educ. (Rep., 1980–82). SUNY/OCLC Serials Adv. Cncl. **Pubns.:** Various reviews. **Activities:** 1; 17, 46 **Addr.:** Owen D. Young Library, St. Lawrence University, Canton, NY 13617.

Rohlf Robert H. (My. 14, 1928, Minneapolis, MN) Dir., Hennepin Cnty. Lib., 1969–; Dir. of Admin., Lib. of Congs., 1968–69, Coord. of Bldg. Plng., Lib. of Congs., 1966–1968; Dir., Dakota-Scott Reg. Lib., 1959–66; Dir., IL Lib. Dev. Proj., 1963; various positions, Minneapolis Pub. Lib., 1953–58; Libn., Fresh.–Soph. Lib., Univ. of MN, 1951–53, Libn., Inst. of Agr., 1950–1951. **Educ.:** Coll. of St. Thomas, 1945–49, BA (Hist., Econ.); Univ. of MN, 1949–50, BSLS, 1950–53, MA (Lib. Admin., Pub. Admin.), 1954, Cert. Pub. Admin. **Orgs.:** ALA: Lib. Admin. Div./Bldg. and Equip. Sect. (Exec. Bd. and Ch.); Cncl. (1963–66, 1971–75); PLA (Pres., 1981–1982); others. MN LA: (Pres., 1958–1959); Legis. Com. (Ch., 1956–59; Co-Ch., 1972–73). WHCOLIS: Del. NCLIS: Consult. (1976–78). Other orgs. Rotary Intl. Intl. Jr. Cham. of Cmrce.: VP (1958–1959). MN Hum. Comsn. Minneapolis Jr. Cham. of Cmrce. **Honors:** Amer. Inst. of Archits., Cert. of Awd., 1979; MN LA, Libn. of Yr., 1966. **Pubns.:** *A Plan for Public Library Development in Illinois* (1964); Jt. auth., *Interim Standards for Small Public Libraries* (1962); "Library - Public Libraries," *Americana Encyc.* (1976); "Library Management," *ALA Yrbk.* (1977–80); other articles. **Activities:** 4, 9; 17, 19, 24; 78 **Addr.:** Hennepin County Library, 70th and York, Edina, MN 55435.

Rohrlick, Ruth (O. 30, 1932, Montreal, PQ) Head, Norris Lib., Concordia Univ., 1979–, Head, Drummond Sci. Lib., 1976–79, Ref., Sel. Libn., Phys. and Math., 1975–76; various positions in med. resrch., 1954–73. **Educ.:** McGill Univ., 1949–53, BSc (Biochem., Psy.), 1973–75, MLS. **Orgs.:** SLA: East. Can. Chap., Co-ch., Lcl. prog. ASIS. Can. LA. Can. Assn. Info. Sci. various orgs. Can. Amateur Msc. Assn. Amer. Recorder Socty. Prov. of PQ Socty. for the Protection of Birds. St. George's Sch. of Montreal: Bd. of Dir. (Secy. 1977–79). **Honors:** Montreal Chap. Spec. Libn. Assn. Prize, 1975. **Pubns.:** Contrib., "Preferential Uptake of D-Glucose by Isolated Human Erythrocyte Membranes," *Biochem.* (1971); jt. auth., "D-Glucose Uptake by Isolated Human Erythrocyte Membranes Versus D-Glucose Transport by Human Erythrocytes," *Jnl. of Bio. Chem.* (1972); Contrib., "Involvement of Phospholipids in the D-Glucose Uptake Activity of Isolated Human Erythrocyte Membranes," *Jnl. of Biochem.* (1972); jt. auth., "Evidence for an Asymetric Distribution of Phospholipids in the Human Erythrocyte Membrane," *Can. Jnl. of Biochem.* (1974); jt. auth., "Studies on the Mechanism and Reversal of the Phospholipase A2 inactivation of D-Glucose Uptake by Isolated Human Erythrocyte Membranes," *Can. Jnl. of Biochem.* (1974). **Activities:** 1; 17, 22, 39; 55, 91, 92 **Addr.:** 1455 De Maisonneuve Blvd. W., Norris Bldg., Rm. N-620-2, Montreal, PQ H3G 1M8 Canada.

Roldan, Maria Antonia (F. 21, 1921, Havana, Cuba) Archvst., Recs. Mgr., Org. of Amer. States, Recs. Mgt. Ctr., 1979–, Catlgr., Columbus Meml. Lib., 1962–79; Catlgr., Cath. Univ. of Villanova, Havana, Cuba, 1960–61; Catlgr., Mnstry. of Frgn. Rel. of Intl. Orgs., Havana, Cuba, 1959–60; Catlgr., Lib. of the Socty. Econ. de Amigos del País, 1956–59. **Educ.:** Escuela Cubana de Bibtcrs., Havana, Cuba, 1955–56, Libn. (LS); Havana Bus. Univ., 1957–58 (Arch. Std.); Havana Univ., 1959–60, BLS; various grad. crs. **Orgs.:** ALA: Lib. Resrcs. and Tech. Srvs. (1969–). DC LA: Gvt. Docum. Grp. (1963–). Assn. of Recs. Mgrs. and Admins.: Grt. DC Chap. (1980–). ASIS: Lib. Autom. and Netwks. (1976–). **Pubns.:** "Las formas de la literatura infantil," *Bltn. de la Assn. Cubana de Bibtcrs.* (Je. 1958). **Activities:** 3; 20, 38, 39; 54, 62 **Addr.:** 2401 Calvert St., N.W., Washington, DC 20008.

Rollins, Jane Gray (O. 11, 1924, Bangor, ME) Consult., Coord. Statewide ILL Prog., NY State Lib., 1968–; Head, Readers Srvs., Skidmore Coll., 1957–67; Asst. Head, Circ., Mount Vernon (NY) Pub. Lib., 1951–57; Ref. Libn., Bard Coll., 1948–51. **Educ.:** Colby Coll. 1943–47, BA (Hist.); Simmons Coll., 1947–48 BS (LS); Univ. of ME, 1964–65, (Hist.). **Orgs.:** ALA: RASD, ILL Com. (1979–81; 1981–83); ILL Discuss. Grp., Co–Ch. (1981–83). NY LA: Coll. and Univ. Libs. Sect. (1971–73). SUNY/OCLC: Advisory Com. on Interlibrary Loan (1979–82). **Activities:** 1, 13; 34, 39, 44; 55, 56, 61 **Addr.:** New York State Library, Bureau of Specialist Library Services, Cultural Education Center, Empire State Plz., Albany, NY 12230.

Rollins, Ottilie Hirt (N. 18, 1915, Vienna, Austria) Head Libn./Assoc. Prof., Clarkson Coll. of Tech., 1967–, Actg. Libn./Asst. Prof., 1966–67, Asst. Libn./Asst. Prof., 1960–66, Asst. Libn. and Catlgr., 1956–60, Lectr., Grmn, 1950–56; Instr. in Phys. Educ., Russell Sage Coll. 1945–1948, Asst., Grmn. Dept., 1942–1945; Acad. Secy. and Teacher of Grmn., Putney Sch. 1935–42. **Educ.:** Russell Sage Coll., 1940–45, BS (Phys. Educ.); West. Rsrv. Univ., 1957–60, MLS. **Orgs.:** ALA: ACRL/East. NY Chap. NY LA: Legis. Com. (1973); Coll. and Univ. Lib. Sect. (Dir., 1972). SLA: NY Chap. (Rpt., 1976–; Dir., 1978–). N. Country Ref. and Rsrch. Resrcs. Cncl.: Trustee (1976–82); various ofcs. and coms. (1978–80). Amer. Socty. for Engin. Educ.: Liaison with SLA. Northern Folk Dancers. AAUW: Pres. (1954–56); Intl. Rel. Com. (Ch., 1956–57); Art. Com. (Ch., 1958–59). **Honors:** Beta Phi Mu (1961). **Pubns.:** Various Contribs. to ASEE Nsltrs. SLA/Upstate NY Chap. Bltn.; "The Enviable Librarian in Her Quiet Domain" in *Twenty-Seven to One* (1970); Contrib., *Experiment in International Living. Letters to the Founder* (1977); Ed., *The North Country Reference & Research Resources Council, 1964–1967, A Record of Achievement* (1977). **Activities:** 1; 17, 20, 46; 63, 75, 91 **Addr.:** Harriet Call Burnap Memorial Library, Clarkson College of Technology, Potsdam, NY 13676.

Special Subjects/Services: 50. Adult educ.; 51. Advert./Mktg.; 52. Aerosp.; 53. Agric.; 54. Area std.; 55. Arts/Hum.; 56. Autom.; 57. Bibl./Prtg.; 58. Bio. sci.; 59. Bus./Fin.; 60. Chem.; 61. Copyrt.; 62. Documtn.; 63. Educ.; 64. Engin.; 65. Env.; 66. Eth. grps.; 67. Film; 68. Food/Nutr.; 69. Geneal.; 70. Geo.; 71. Geol.; 72. Handcpd.; 73. Hist.; 74. Int. frdm.; 75. Info. sci.; 76. Insr.; 77. Law; 78. Legis.; 79. Math./Comp. sci.; 80. Med.; 81. Metals; 82. Nat. resrcs.; 83. Newsp.; 84. Nuc. sci.; 85. Oral hist.; 86. Petr./Energy; 87. Pharm.; 88. Phys./Astr./Math.; 89. Readg.; 90. Relig.; 91. Sci./Tech.; 92. Soc. sci.; 93. Telecom.; 94. Transp.; 95. (other).

Rollins, Stephen J. (Mr. 10, 1950, Providence, RI) Circ. Libn., Gen. Lib., Univ. of NM, 1979–; Circ. Supvsr., Univ. of RI, 1973–79. **Educ.:** Providence Coll., 1968–72, BA (Eng.); Univ. of RI, 1972–75, MLS. **Orgs.:** ALA: Ad Hoc Subcom. on Copyrt. Grt. Albuquerque LA: Constn. and By-Laws Com. NM LA. **Pubns.:** "Why CLSI at URI", *RI LA Bltn.* (Jl./Ag. 1979); "Network Update . . . Automated Circulation at UNM" *NMLA Newsltr.* (Aug. 1980); "OCLC/ILL in New Mexico" *NMLA Newsltr* (O. 1980); "OCLC/ILL in New Mexico–some expectations" *NMLA Newsltr* (Mr. 1981). **Activities:** 1; 22, 34; 56, 61 **Addr.:** Zimmerman Library, Univ. of New Mexico, Albuquerque, NM 87131.

Rollock, Barbara T. (New York, NY) Coord., Chld. Srvs., NY Pub. Lib., 1974–, Asst. Coord., 1971–74, Chld. Spec., Bronx Boro., 1965–71. **Educ.:** Hunter Coll., 1940–44, BA (Classics); Columbia Univ., 1945–48, BLS (Libnshp.). **Orgs.:** ALA: Prof. Ethics Com. (Ch., 1977–81); Chld. Srvs. Div. (Pres., 1974). NY LA: Chld. and YA Sect. (Pres., 1969). **Pubns.:** Ed., *The Black Experience in Children's Literature* (1974, 1979); "Caveat Lector," *Cath. Lib. World* (O. 1974); "Public Library/School Cooperation....," *The Bookmark* (Sum. 1978); "Children's Services in the Public Library: Meeting Challenges...," *The Bookmark* (Fall 1980). **Activities:** 9; 21; 55, 66 **Addr.:** New York Public Library, Office of Children's Services, 8 E. 40th St., New York, NY 10016.

Rolnick, Nancy (D. 22, 1924, Atlantic City, NJ) YA Libn., Croton Free Lib., 1969–. **Educ.:** Douglass Coll., 1942–46, BA (Hist., Pol. Sci.); Columbia Univ., 1967–69, MLS. **Orgs.:** ALA: YASD, Best Bks. Com. (1979–); YASD, Outstanding Fiction for the Coll. Bound Comej, Publishers Liaison com., Youth Participation in Library Decision Making Com. Westchester LA: Crossections Ch. (1977–80). NY LA: Ref. and Adult Srvs. Sect., Prisons Com. (Ch., 1977–1978). **Pubns.:** Jt. auth., "Creating a Community Video Event," *Film Lib. Qtly.*, (1977). **Activities:** 9; 39, 48 **Addr.:** 30 E. 9 St., Apt. 5MM, New York, NY 10003.

Rolon, Lawrence Jay (S. 6, 1951, Los Angeles, CA) Lib. Admin. Asst., San Mateo Pub. Lib., 1981–; Mem., Bd. of Trustees, Huntington Beach Pub. Lib., 1977–81. **Educ.:** Univ. of South. CA, 1976–79, BS (Pub. Admin.), 1981, MPA, MSLS. **Orgs.:** ALA. SLA. CA LA: Gvt. Rel. Com. (1978). ASIS. **Activities:** 4, 9; 17, 28, 47; 78, 74 **Addr.:** 5081 Robinwood Dr., Huntington Beach, CA 92649.

Román, Elba I. (Ag. 28, 1950, Moca, PR) Head, Tech. Srvs., Univ. of PR, Aguadilla Reg. Col., 1978–, Libn., Cat., 1975–77, Asst. Libn., 1972–74; Sch. Libn., Dept. of Educ., Aguadilla, 1971. **Educ.:** Univ. of PR, 1967–70, BA (Soc. Sci.), 1975, MLS. **Orgs.:** SBPR. Assn. para las Comm. y Tech. Educ. de PR. Assn. de Bib. Univ. y de Investigación del Caribe. **Activities:** 1; 15, 20 **Addr.:** Urbanización Extención Villa Marbella, Calle 4 No. 342, Aguadilla, PR 00603.

Roman, Susan (Je. 4, 1939, St. Louis, MO) Consult., Dev. of Chld. Col., Hubbard Woods Sch., 1979–; Head, Chld. Srvs., Northbrook Pub. Lib., 1978–; Head, Chld. Srvs., Deerfield Pub. Lib., 1975–78, Chld. Prog., Adult Ref., 1971–75. **Educ.:** WA Univ., St. Louis, MO, 1957–61, AB (Psy., Soclgy.); Rosary Coll., 1972–76, MALS (Pub. Libs.); Univ. of Chicago, 1981–. **Orgs.:** ALA: 1980 Newbery Com. (1980–81); 1978 Chicago Conf. Lcl. Arrange. Com. (1977–78); Rochester Conf. on Media Eval., The Grp. Prcs. (Mr. 1979); various com. IL LA: Chld. Libns. Sect. (Secy., 1977–78); various coms. Lib. Admins. Cncl. of North. IL: various com. Reg. Lib. Adv. Cncl.: N. Suburban Lib. Syst., Chld. Libns. Unit, Exec. Com. (Ch., 1977–78), Bk. Discuss. Bk. Eval. Com. (Ch., 1977); various coms. Girl Scouts of Amer.: Badge Leader (1974–78). Parent-Tchr. Org.: Lcl. Secty. (1974–75). **Pubns.:** "Foundations of Quality: Guidelines for Public Library Service to Children," *IL Libs.* (D. 1980); jt. auth., "Standards for Children's Services in North Suburban Library System Member Libraries," (Mr. 1978); jt. auth., "A Survey of Library Services for Children in Illinois 1960 to the Present," *IL Libs.* (Mr. 1978). **Activities:** 9; 17, 21, 48; 57, 67, 89 **Addr.:** Northbrook Public Library, 1201 Cedar Ln., Northbrook, IL 60062.

Romanansky, Marcia Canzoneri (Ap. 22, 1941, Brooklyn, NY) Mgr., Prog. Srvs., Baker and Taylor Co., 1981–; Asst. Mgr., Cust. Srv., Baker & Taylor Co., 1980–81; Chief Libn., Approval Prog., 1972–80; Libn., Roselle HS, 1967–71; Acq. Libn., St. Peter's Coll., 1963–66. **Educ.:** Coll. Misericordia, 1958–62, BA (Hist.); Pratt Inst., 1967–69, MLS; Seton Hall Univ., 1971–74, MA (Educ.); Fairleigh Dickinson Univ., 1979– (Bus.). **Orgs.:** ALA. **Honors:** Beta Phi Mu, 1969. **Pubns.:** "The Approval Plan Concept and the Community College Library," *Emanations* (Win. 1980). **Activities:** 1, 6-Mfr./Suppl.; 15, 17, 46; 51, 59, 63 **Addr.:** 994 Oakland Ave., Plainfield, NJ 07060.

Romo, Rolando M. (O. 27, 1947, Houston, TX) Sr. Libn., Austin Pub. Lib., 1974–; Trng. Coord., City of Austin, 1972–74; Job Couns., Univ. of Houston, 1972; Soc. Welfare Worker, Harris Cnty. Chld. Welfare, 1970–71. **Educ.:** Univ. of TX Austin, 1965–70, BA (Pol. Sci.); Univ. of AZ, 1978–79, MLS. **Orgs.:** ALA. Reforma: Austin Chap. Actg. Pres. (1980). Sociedad Genealogica: Bd. of Dirs. Treas. (1980–81). **Honors:** Beta Phi Mu. **Pubns.:** numerous works of poetry (1972–). **Activities:** 9; 15, 16, 17; 66 **Addr.:** P.O. 4482, Austin, TX 78765.

Ronen, Naomi (My. 30, 1937, St. Joseph, MI) Asst. Libn. for Acq., Harvard Law Sch. Lib., 1981–, Micro. Proj. Libn., 1978–81; Asst. Life Scis. Libn., Purdue Univ., 1977; Lib. Asst. in Tech. Srvs., Harvard Law Sch. Lib., 1976–77; Clasfr., Jewish Natl. and Univ. Lib. (Jerusalem), 1971–76; Catlgr., IN Univ. Reg. Campus Libs., 1968–69. **Educ.:** Oberlin Coll., 1955–59, AB (Hist.); IN Univ., 1964–68, MA (LS). **Orgs.:** AALL: Stans. Com. (1980–). Law Libns. of New Eng. ALA: ACRL. **Pubns.:** Co-cmplr., *Law & Science: A Selected Bibliography* (1978), (1980). **Activities:** 1; 33; 62, 77 **Addr.:** Harvard Law School Library, Langdell Hall, Cambridge, MA 02138.

Roney, Raymond G. (Philadelphia, PA) Deputy Dir., Univ. of DC, 1970–; Instr., Grad. Sch., U.S. Dept. of Agr.; Dir., Lib. Srvs., WA Tech. Inst., Ch., Media Tech. Prog., 1970–77, Dir., Lib. Srvs., Natl. Leag. of Cities/U.S. Conf. of Mayors, 1967–70. **Educ.:** Ctrl. State Univ., 1959–63, BA (Pol. Sci.); Pratt Inst., 1964–65, MLS; Cath. Univ., PhD Cand. **Orgs.:** ALA: ACRL/Jr. Coll. Sect., Bibl. Com. (Ch., 1973–75); Lib. Educ. Div., Lib./Media Tech. Assts. Com. (1974–75), Educ. and Trng. of Lib. Supportive Com. (1976–). Natl. Org. for Media/Lib. Tech. Assts.: Cncl. on Lib. Tech. (Bd., 1976–). Cncl. on Lib./Media Tech. Assts.: VP, Pres.-Elect (1980–). Socty. of Lib. and Info. Techs.: Bd. (1976–). Various other orgs. **Honors:** DC Cncl., Cert. of Appt., 1975; DC Fed. of Civic Assns., Grass Roots Awd., 1975; Phi Delta Kappa. **Pubns.:** *The NLC/USCM Library Classification System: Index for an Urban Studies Collection* (1968); jt. auth., *Introduction to A V for Technical Assistants* (1981); jt. auth., *1981 Directory of Programs for the Training of Library Media Technical Assistants* (1981). **Activities:** 1, 12; 17, 26, 39; 63, 92 **Addr.:** University of DC, Learning Resources, 4200 Connecticut Ave. N.W., Washington, DC 20012.

Rooks, Dana Collier (Ap. 5, 1947, Oklahoma City, OK) Bus./Econ. Libn., Univ. of Houston, 1980–; Head of Instr. and Resrch. Srvs., Univ. of MO-St. Louis, 1976–80, Ref. Libn., 1975–76; Lower Div. Libn., Univ. of OK, 1970–73. **Educ.:** LA State Univ., 1967–69, BA (Eng.), 1969–70, MS (LS); Univ. of OK, 1970–73, MA (Pub. Admin.). **Orgs.:** ALA: ACRL OK LA: Soc. Resp. Com. (1971); Nom. Com. (1972). **Pubns.:** *PERT: Program Evaluation and Review Technique, 1964-1974* (1975); "Management Training for Librarians," *OK Libn.* (O. 1975). **Activities:** 1; 17, 39; 59, 92 **Addr.:** 15330 Torry Pines, Houston, TX 77062.

Rooney, Paul M. (Ap. 16, 1918, Buffalo, NY) Dir., Buffalo and Erie Cnty. Pub. Lib., 1975–, Deputy Dir., 1963–75, Asst. Deputy Dir., 1961–63, Head, Tech. Dept., 1959–61; Head, Ref. Dept., Grosvenor Lib., 1946–59, Ref. Asst., 1945–46; Branch Libn., Buffalo Pub. Lib., 1940–42. **Educ.:** NY State Tchrs. Coll., 1934–38, BS (Educ.); Univ. of Buffalo, 1938–40, BS (LS). **Orgs.:** ALA. NY LA: Constn. Rev. Com. (Ch., 1976–77); various other coms. West. NY Lib. Cncl.: Trustee (1966–); Pres. (1969–70). Pub. Libn.'s Cert. Com.: Ch. (1959–60). Buffalo and Erie Cnty. Hist. Socty.: Bd. of Mgrs. (1975–). Comsn. of Educ. Com. on Statewide Lib. Dev. (1980–). **Pubns.:** "New York State Public Librarians' Certification Program," *Lib. Jnl.* (S. 15, 1958); "Buffalo Bridges Its Site," *LJ* (D. 1, 1965; "Federated Public Library Systems" *Bookmark* (Spr. 1980). **Activities:** 9; 17 **Addr.:** 522 Ashland Ave., Buffalo, NY 14222.

Rooney, Sieglinde E. H. (S. 3, 1940, Hamburg-Harburg, Germany) Head, Acq., Univ. of AB Lib., 1979–, Tech. Srv. Libn., 1971–79, Syst. Anal., 1968–71, Ref. Libn., 1965–68; Cat., York Univ., 1963–65. **Educ.:** Univ. of SK, 1959–62, BA (Grmn., Hist.); Univ. of Toronto, 1962–63, BLS; Univ. of AB, 1971–78, MA (Grmn. Lit.). **Orgs.:** ASIS. Can. LA: Coll. and Univ. Libs. (Treas., 1975–78); Subcom. Srvy., Acad. Status Com., Ch., AB LA. IFLA: Stdg. Com. Univ. Libs. (1981–84). Can. Assn. of Univ. Tchrs. Can. Assn. of Univ. Tchrs. of Grmn. Acad. Assn. of Univ. of AB: Welfare Com. (1978–). Salary Com. (1976–79). **Pubns.:** Various abs. in *Can. Review of Compar. Lit.* **Activities:** 1; 15, 17, 46; 55, 56, 75 **Addr.:** Head, Acquisitions Division, Library, Univ. of AB, Edmonton, AB Canada.

Roose, Tina (D. 15, 1944, Pomona, CA) Dir., Ref., N. Suburban Lib. Syst., Wheeling, IL, 1975–, Ref. Libn., 1974–75; Branch Head, Ft. Lauderdale Pub. Lib., 1972–74, Ref. Libn., Head, PR, 1971–72; Dir., Oakland Park Pub. Lib., 1971; Catlgr., Grad. Lib., Univ. of MI, 1968–70; Catlgr., West. MI Univ., 1967–68. **Educ.:** Kalamazoo Coll., 1962–66, BA (Eng.); Univ. of MN, 1966–67, MA (LS). **Orgs.:** ALA: RASD, Dir.-at-Lg. (1981–84), Conf. Prog. Com., Philadelphia 1982 (1981–82), Prototype Wkshp. on Performance Improvement for Ref. Libns. (Ch., 1978–), Dartmouth Medal Awd. Com. (Ch., 1976)/Machine-Asst. Ref. Sect., Pub. Libs. Com. (1979–83), Plng. Com. (1981–82); ASCLA, Plng. Org. and Bylaws Com. (1980–81); SRRT, Task Frc. on Women (1973–), Cent. Conf. Plng. Com. (1975–76). LITA; LAMA; RTSD. IL LA: Various sects., RTs. IL Reg. Lib. Cncl. ASIS. Various other orgs. Amer. Cvl. Liberties Un. Sierra Club. Women Employed. Women in Mgt. Natl. Org. for Women. **Honors:** Beta Phi Mu. **Pubns.:** Jt. auth., ed., *Infopass/Datapass Procedures Manual and Directory* (1977–81); jt. auth., "Library Resources Are More than Materials," *Col. Bldg.* (1979); "Reference Services—an Essential Type of Resource Sharing," *Cath. Lib. World* (F. 1981); ed. bd., *RQ* (1980–82). **Activities:** 13; 17, 24, 39; 59, 75, 92 **Addr.:** North Suburban Library System, 200 W. Dundee Rd., Wheeling, IL 60090.

Root, Nina J. (D. 22, New York, NY) Ch., Dept. of Lib. Srvs., Amer. Musm. of Nat. Hist., 1981–, Chief Libn., 1970–81; Mgt. Consult., Nelson Assocs., Inc., 1966–70; Head, Ref. and Lib. Srvs. Sect., Lib. of Congs. Sci. and Tech. Div., 1964–66; Chief Libn., Amer. Inst. of Aeronautics and Astronautics, 1962–64. **Educ.:** Hunter Coll., 1951–55, BA (Intl. Rel.); Pratt Inst., 1958–59, MLS; CUNY Grad. Sch., U.S.D.A. Grad. Sch. 1964–. **Orgs.:** ALA: RTSD/Prsrvn. of Lib. Mtrls. Sect. (Ch., 1980–81). Archons of Colophon: Conv. (1979). SLA: Various offices. ASIS. Others. AAAS. NY Acad. of Scis.: Archs. Com.; Pubn. Com. (1976–80). Amer. Assn. of Musms. Socty. for the Bibl. of Nat. Hist.: Amer. Rep. **Honors:** Lib. of Congs., Merit. Srv. Awd., 1965. **Pubns.:** "The Rare Book & Manuscript Collection of the American Museum of Natural History Library," *CURATOR* (1977); "The Library of the American Museum of Natural History," *Jnl. of the Socty. for the Bibl. of Nat. Hist.* (Ap. 1980). **Activities:** 2, 8-Musm.; 17, 23, 37; 57, 95-Nat. Hist., Rare Bks. Mss. **Addr.:** American Museum of Natural History, Dept. of Library Sciences, CPW at 79th St., New York, NY 10024.

Roper, Fred W. (My. 15, 1938, Hendersonville, NC) Asst. Dean and Assoc. Prof., Sch. of LS, Univ. of NC, 1977–, Asst. Prof., 1971–77; Head of Pub. Srvs., Chicago State Coll. Lib., 1967–68; Resrch. Assoc., Inst. for Lib. Resrch., Univ. of CA, Los Angeles, 1966–67, Biomed. Machine Methods Libn., Biomed. Lib., 1963–66. **Educ.:** Univ. of NC, 1956–60, AB (Eng.), 1960–62, MS (LS); Biomed. Lib. Trng. Prog., Univ. of CA, Los Angeles, 1962–63, Cert.; IN Univ., 1968–71, PhD (LS). **Orgs.:** Med. LA: Com. on Cont. Ed. (Ch., 1973–74); *MLA News* Ed. Com. (Ch., 1974–76); *Bltn. of the MLA* Consult. Ed. (1974–77), Pubns. Panel (1976–79); Hlth. Sci. Lib. Techs. Com. (1976–79); Cert. Exam. Rev. Com. (1980–83). SLA: Bd. of Dirs. (1978–80); Chap. Cabinet (Ch., 1979–80); NC Chap. (Pres., 1976–77). AALS. NC LA: Various coms., ofcs. (1974–79). **Honors:** Beta Phi Mu, 1962. **Pubns.:** Ed., *Alfred William Pollard: A Selection of His Writings* (1976); "Health Sciences Libraries," *Resources of South Carolina Libraries* (1976); jt. auth., *Introduction to Reference Sources in the Health Sciences* (1980); jt. auth., "Publication Patterns of Scientific Serials," *Amer. Documtn.* (Ap. 1965); "A Computer-based Serials Control System for a Large Biomedical Library," *Amer. Documtn.* (Ap. 1968); various other articles (1968–79). **Activities:** 11, 12; 26, 39; 80, 91 **Addr.:** School of Library Science, Manning Hall 026-A, University of North Carolina, Chapel Hill, NC 27514.

Rorick, William C. (Je. 23, 1941, Elyria, OH) Msc. Ref. Libn., Queens Coll., CUNY, 1974–; Cur., Performance Msc. Col. Ofc. Mgr., Ref. Asst., Manhattan Sch. of Msc. Lib., 1970–74. **Educ.:** OH Wesleyan Univ., 1959–63, BA (Econ.); Univ. of UT, 1966–68, BM (Msc. Hist.); Northwest. Univ., 1968–70, MM (Msc. Hist.); Pratt Inst., 1972–74, MLS; NY Univ., 1972– (Msclgy.). **Orgs.:** Msc. LA: Subcom. on Basic Msc. Col. (1977–79); Mem. Com. (Ch., 1979–); Grt. NY Chap., Prog. Ch. (1977–79); Secy.-Treas. (1979–81). LA of CUNY: Grants Com. (Ch., 1978–80); Pubns. Com. (1979–81). Amer. Musicological Socty. Assn. for Rec. Snd. Cols. **Honors:** CUNY, Resrch. Awd., 1981–82; Beta Phi Mu, 1974. **Pubns.:** "Intrumental Methods and Studies," *A Basic Music Library: Essential Scores and Books* (1978); ed., *LA of CUNY Directory* (1980–81); "The Horatio Parker Archives in the Yale University Music Library," *Fontes artis musicae* (O.–D. 1979); "Index to Record Reviews: Manufacturers' Numerical Index to Volume 37, September 1980 Through June 1981," *Notes* (Je. 1981); various bk. reviews. **Activities:** 1; 15, 17, 39; 55 **Addr.:** Music Library Queens College, CUNY, Flushing, NY 11367.

Rorvig, Mark Evan (S. 20, 1950, Spokane, WA) Sr. Consult., Appld. Info. Sci., 1979–; Visit. Fac., Glendale Cmnty. Coll., 1980–; Adj. Fac., Queens Coll., CUNY, 1979; Sr. Systs. Anal., Baker and Taylor Co., 1978–79; Consult., Dept. of Lib., Arch. and Pub. Recs., State of AZ, 1976–77; Systs. Anal., Brodart Indus., 1975–76 Progmr. Anal., Gen. Resrch. Corp., 1974; Asst. Ref. Libn., Univ. de las Amér. Puebla, Mex., 1972–73. **Educ.:** Seattle Univ., 1969–72, BA (Eng.); Univ. de las Amer., 1973 (Phil.); Columbia Univ., 1973–74, MS (Info. Sci.); various grad. crs. **Orgs.:** ASIS. Bk. Indus. Stans. Adv. Com.: Telecom. Subcom. (1978–79). **Pubns.:** *Microcomputers in Libraries* (1981); "The Effect of Federal and State Grants on Local Library Funding Support," *Roadrunner* (Ja. 1977); jt. auth., *Specifications for a National Manpower Law Enforcement Labor Relations Data Base* (1979); jt. auth., *User Reference Manual and Data Base Search Guide: Criminal Justice Manpower Planning Data Bank* (1980); jt. auth., "A Report on Data Collection Operations for Analysis of Court System Impacts of the Revised Arizona Criminal Code," *Seminar on Information Systems and Court Statistics* (1980); various mono., articles. **Activities:** 14-Freelnc. consult. srvs.; 24; 56, 75 **Addr.:** 16422 N. 36th Pl., Phoenix, AZ 85032.

Rosasco, Joan M. (F. 4, 1952, San Francisco, CA) Chief Libn., Bechtel Ctrl. Lib., 1975–. **Educ.:** Univ. of CA, Davis, 1970–74, BA (Eng.); Univ. of CA, Los Angeles, 1974–76, MLS; 1976, Cert. of Spec. in Corp. Libs. **Orgs.:** ALA. CA LA. SLA: Bay

PROFESSIONAL ACTIVITIES: Institutions: 1. Acad. lib.; 2. Arch.; 3. Assn.; 4. Fed./Gvt. lib.; 5. Inst. lib.; 6. Mfr./Suppl.; 7. Milit. lib.; 8. Musm.; 9. Pub. lib.; 10. Sch. lib.; 11. Sch. of lib. sci.; 12. Spec. lib.; 13. State lib.; 14. (other). **Functions/Activities:** 15. Acq./Col. dev.; 16. Adult srvs.; 17. Admin.; 18. Apprais.; 19. Archit./Bldgs.; 20. Cat./Class.; 21. Chld. srvs.; 22. Circ.; 23. Cons./Pres.; 24. Consult.; 25. Cont. ed.; 26. Educ. lib. sci.; 27. Ext. srvs.; 28. Fund/Grants; 29. Gvt. pubs.; 30. Indx./Abs.; 31. Instr. lib. use; 32. Media srvs.; 33. Micro.; 34. Netwks./Coop.; 35. Persnl.; 36. PR; 37. Publshg.; 38. Recs. mgt.; 39. Ref. srvs.; 40. Repro.; 41. Resrch.; 42. Review.; 43. Secur.; 44. Serials; 45. Spec. col.; 46. Tech. srvs.; 47. Trustees/Bds.; 48. YA srvs.; 49. (other).

Area Reg. Chap., Finance Ch. Mechanics Inst. Lib. **Pubns.:** "Politics & Economics: Impact on Building a Corporate Library Network," (1979). **Activities:** 12; 15, 17, 41; 59, 64, 91 **Addr.:** Bechtel Central Library, 50 Beale St., San Francisco, CA 94119.

Rose, Dianne Elizabeth (Ag. 19, 1954, Trenton, NJ) Hosp. Libn., Frankford Hosp., 1977–. **Educ.:** Rider Coll., 1972–76, BA (Hist.); Drexel Univ., 1976–77, MS (LS). **Orgs.:** Med. LA: Philadelphia Reg. Grp. SLA. Yardley Hist. Socty. **Pubns.:** Indxr., *Geriatric Foot Care* (1979). **Activities:** 5, 12; 15, 20, 39; 77, 80, 92 **Addr.:** 2002 Sylvan Terr., Yardley, PA 19067.

Rose, Isabel A. (S. 26, 1937, Timmins, ON) Head, Msc. Dept., Asst. Head, Lib., Metro. Toronto Lib., 1974–; Asst. Msc. Libn., Yale Univ., 1970–74; Asst. Msc. Libn., Msc. Catlgr., Vassar Coll., 1968–70; HS Tchr., ON, 1961–66. **Educ.:** Univ. of Toronto, 1955–59, BA (Msc.); Syracuse Univ., 1967–68, MSLS; Assoc. Royal Cnsvty. of Msc., Toronto, 1955. **Orgs.:** Msc. LA: Micro. Com. (1971); NY-ON Chap. (Ch., 1977-78). CAML: Pres. (1978–80). **Pubns.:** "What! No Music?" *Expression* (N.–D. 1979). **Activities:** 1, 9; 15, 17, 24; 55 **Addr.:** Metropolitan Toronto Library, 789 Yonge St., Toronto, ON M4W 2G8 Canada.

Roselle, William Charles (Je. 30, 1936, Vandergrift, PA) Prof. and Dir. of Lib., Univ. of WI–Milwaukee, 1971–; Asst. Dir. of Libs., Univ. of IA, 1969–71, Lib. Admin. Asst., 1966–69, Engin. and Math. Libn., 1965–66; Asst. Cat. Libn., PA State Univ., 1963–1965; Lib. Trainee, State Lib. of PA, 1962–1963; Fac. Mem., Milton Hershey Sch., 1960–1962. **Educ.:** Thiel Coll., 1954–58, BA (Eng.); Univ. of Pittsburgh, 1962–63, MLS; Univ. of MD, Lib. Admins. Dev. Prog. 1973, Cert. **Orgs.:** ALA. SLA. WI LA. Cncl. of WI Libns. (Ch., 1973–74); other orgs. and ofcs. Socty. for Tympanuchus Cupido Pinnatus. Milwaukee Cvl. War RT. Univ. of WI-Milwaukee Alum. Assn. **Honors:** Amer. Geo. Socty., Hon. Fellow, 1978; SLA, Spec. Cit., 1979; Beta Phi Mu; Phi Kappa Phi. **Pubns.:** Various articles and reviews; Ed. Bd. of *Jnl. of Lib. Admin.* (1979–); Consult. Ed. for *Current Geo. Pubns.* 1978–). **Activities:** 1; 17, 19, 46; 57, 70, 91 **Addr.:** The Golda Meir Library, University of Wisconsin Milwaukee, P.O. Box 604, Milwaukee, WI 53201.

Rosenbaum, Solomon (O. 18, 1908, W. New Brighton, NY) Ch., Panel of Couns., New Eng. Lib. Bd., 1980–, Ch., MA Bd. of Lib. Comsns., 1979–; Vice-Ch., 1979; Vice-Ch., MA Bd. of Lib. Comsns., 1978, Ch., Budget Com., 1978, Mem., 1976; Fund., Rosenbaum Eth. Heritage Rm., Fitchburg Pub. Lib., 1976; various org. appts., 1949–75; Former Asst. Dir., Resrch., State Bar of CA; Former Prof., Law, New Eng. Sch. of Law. **Educ.:** Univ. of South. CA, 1930, BA, 1930, Bachelor of Laws; 1931, JD; various grad. crs.; various bar mems. **Orgs.:** ALA: ALTA. MA LA: IF RT (1978); Int. Frdm. Com. (1974–). MA Lib. Trustee Assn.: Pres. (1975); 1st VP, Pres.-Elect (1972–75); Bd. of Trustees (1965–). Fitchburg Pub. Lib.: Bd. of Trustees, Ch. (1969–76), Treas. (1960–69). Various other orgs. B'nai B'rith: Various ofcs., coms. Natl. Conf. on Citizenship: Natl. VP (1974–); Natl. Bd. of Dirs. (1968–). Cvl. Liberties Un. of MA. Amer. Bar Assn. Various other orgs. **Honors:** B'nai B'rith, Natl. Cit. for Disting. Hum. Srvs., 1974; B'nai B'rith, Natl. Comsn. on Cmnty. Volun. Srvs., 1969; Phi Kappa Phi; Ord. of the Coif; other hons. **Pubns.:** *Manual on the Observance of National Holidays* (1954); "Leading Decisions of the 1971–1972 Term of the United States Supreme Court," *New Eng. Law Review* (Fall 1972); ed., *South. CA Law Review*; ed., bd. of annotators, *Restatement of the Law of Contracts;* various articles, *Natl. Jewish Monthly*; sps., confs., sems. **Activities:** 5, 13; 47, 49; 66, 74, 77 **Addr.:** 18 Mechanic St., Fitchburg, MA 01420.

Rosenberg, Diane Lynne (My. 19, 1945, Pittsburgh, PA) Corp. Libn., Paul, Weiss, Rifkind, Wharton and Garrison, 1973–; Circ. and Ref. Libn., Antioch Sch. of Law, 1972–73; Asst. Libn., Circ. and Ref. Libn., Georgetown Univ. Sch. of Law, 1968–72. **Educ.:** PA State Univ., 1963–66, BA (Fr.); Univ. of Pittsburgh, 1967–68, MLS. **Orgs.:** SLA. AALL. **Activities:** 12; 17, 30, 39; 56, 59, 77 **Addr.:** Paul, Weiss, Rifkind, Wharton and Garrison Law Firm, 345 Park Ave., New York, NY 10022.

Rosenberg, John Edward (F. 4, 1916, Philadelphia, PA) Chief, Tech. Lib., Harry Diamond Labs., 1951–. **Educ.:** Univ. of PA, 1933–38, BA (Eng.); Drexel Univ., 1949–51, MS (LS). **Orgs.:** SLA. ALA. DC LA. **Honors:** Phi Kappa Phi, 1951. **Activities:** 4; 15, 17; 64, 74, 91 **Addr.:** 4501 Connecticut Ave., N.W., Apt. 803, Washington, DC 20008.

Rosenberg, Kenyon Charles (S. 9, 1933, Chicago, IL) Asst. Dir. of Univ. Libs., Kent State Univ., 1976–, Assoc. Dir., Ctr. for Lib. Std., 1971–76, Asst. Prof., Sch. of LS, 1968–71; Dir., Tech. Info. Srvs., Ampex Corp., 1966–68; Head, Tech. Lib. Srvs., Hughes Aircraft Co., 1965–66, Supvsr., Tech. Docs. Ctr., 1963–65, Asst. Supvsr., Tech. Docs. Ctr., 1962–63; Law Lib. Consult., AL State Court Syst., 1962; various positions in law libs. and as assoc. prof., 1955–. **Educ.:** Los Angeles City Coll., 1955–57, AA (Latin); Univ. of CA, Los Angeles, 1957–59, AB (Eng.); Univ. of South. CA, 1959–61, MS (LS). **Orgs.:** ALA: Com. on Insr. for Libs. ASIS: San Francisco Chap. (Pres.). Natl. Secur. Indus. Assn.: Task Force on Info. Analysis Ctrs. (Ch.) Msc. Critics Assn. **Honors:** Beta Phi Mu; Alpha Mu Gamma, 1957; Chi Delta Pi, 1959. **Pubns.:** Jt. auth., *Young People's Literature in Series: Fiction* (1972); jt. auth., *Young Peopple's Literature in Series: Non-Fiction and Publishers' Series* (1973); jt. auth., *Watergate: An Annotated Bibliography* (1975); jt. auth., *Media Equipment: A Guide and Dictionary* (1976); jt. auth., "Why Admittees to Library Schools Fail to Attend: or, Is It All Their Fault?," *Jnl. of Educ. for Libnshp.* (Win. 1975); various articles, reviews, and editorships (1968–); various poetry and msc. criticism. **Activities:** 1, 4, 12; 17, 26, 37; 55, 75, 91 **Addr.:** 2154 White Pond Dr., Stow, OH 44224.

Rosenberg, Melvin Harold (Je. 19, 1925, Detroit, MI) Coord., YA Srvs. Los Angeles Pub. Lib., 1971–, Prin. Libn., 1971, Branch Libn., 1968–71, YA Libn., 1965–68. **Educ.:** Wayne State Univ., 1943–47, BA (Eng. Lit.); Immaculate Heart Coll., 1964–65, MALS; Sch. of Letters, IN Univ., 1951, grad. crs. **Orgs.:** ALA: YASD, Selected Films for YAs Com. (1979–). CA LA. YA Reviewers of South. CA: Pres. (1972). **Pubns.:** "Fathers, Daughters, and FOREVER," *VOICE OF YOUTH Advocates* (O. 1979); "Thinking Poor: The Non-library Review Media," *Top of The News* (Win. 1979). **Activities:** 9, 11; 24, 26, 48 **Addr.:** Young Adult Services, Los Angeles Public Library, Los Angeles, CA 90071.

Rosenberg, Murray D. (F. 9, 1940, Philadelphia, PA) Head, Tech. Info. Facility, Philip Morris U.S.A. Resrch. and Dev. Ctr., 1977; Dir., Info. Resrch., Randex Corp., 1975–77; Mgr., Qual. Assurance, Systs. Dutch Boy Paints Div., 1972–75; Sr. Info. Sci., Inst. for Sci. Info., 1969–72; Resrch. Chem., 1963–69. **Educ.:** Temple Univ., 1959–63, BA (Chem.), 1968–71, MBA; Amer. Inst. of Chems., 1976, Cert. Prof. Chem. **Orgs.:** ASIS. SLA. Drug Info. Assn. Chem. Notation Assn.: PR Com. (Ch., 1979–). Various other assns. Amer. Chem. Socty.: Chem. Lit. Div. AAAS. NY Acad. of Sci. **Honors:** Amer. Inst. of Chems., Fellow, 1975; Sigma Xi. **Pubns.:** "Chemical Substructure Index - A New Research Tool," *Jnl. Chem. Info. and Comp. Sci.* (1971); "Synthesis of Amino-5-Arylsulfonyl-Pyrimidines-I," *Jnl. Heterocyclic Chem.* (1971); "A Practical Synthesis of Protoslephanine," *Jnl. of Organic Chem.* (1967); "Eine Neue Synthese von 3,5,4',5' - Tetramethoxy-Diphensaure," *Helvetica Chimica Acta* (1966); various other articles in chem. **Activities:** 6, 12; 17, 30, 33; 56, 60, 91 **Addr.:** Technical Information Facility, Research & Development Center, Philip Morris U.S.A., P.O. Box 26583, Richmond, VA 23261.

Rosenberg, Neil V. (Mr. 21, 1939, Seattle, WA) Dir., Mem. Univ. of NF Folklore and Lang. Arch., 1976–, Archvst., 1968–76; Catlgr., Arch. of Traditional Msc., IN Univ., 1966–68. **Educ.:** Oberlin Coll., 1957–61, BA (Hist.); IN Univ., 1961–64, MA; 1964–70, PhD (Folklore). Socty. for Ethnomsc.: Cncl. (1971–73); Ed. Bd. (1968–73). Can. Oral Hist. Assn.: Treas. (1975–77); VP (1977–78). Amer. Folklore Socty.: Exec. Bd. (1978–81). Folklore Std. Assn. of Can.: Secy (1977–78); Pres.-Elect (1978–79); Pres. (1979–80). **Pubns.:** *Folklore and Oral History* (1978); *Bill Monroe and His Blue Grass Boys* (1974); "From Sound To Style: The Emergence of Bluegrass," *Jnl. of Amer. Folklore* (1967) "Goodtime Charlie and the Bricklin: A Satirical Song in Context," *Jnl. of the Can. Oral Hist. Assn.* (1978); jt. ed., *"Folk-Songs of America": The Robert Winslow Gordon Collection, 1922–1932* (1978). *Hills and Home: Thirty Years of Bluegrass* (1976). **Activities:** 2; 15, 17, 20; 66, 85 **Addr.:** Memorial University of Newfoundland Folklore and Language Archive, Department of Folklore, Memorial University, St. John's, NF A1C 5S7 Canada.

Rosenberg, Victor (Mr. 20, 1942, Lansdale, PA) Assoc. Prof., Univ. of MI, 1977–; Visit. Prof., Fed. Univ. of Minas Gevais, Belo Horizonte, Brazil, 1976–77; Asst. Prof., Univ. of CA, Berkeley, 1970–76. **Educ.:** Lehigh Univ., 1959–64, BA (Eng.), 1964–66, MS (Info. Sci.); Univ. of Chicago, 1966–70, PhD (LS). **Orgs.:** ALA. ASIS: MI Chap. (Ch., 1978). Latin-Amer. Std. Assn. Amer. Assn. for the Advnc. of Appropriate Tech. **Pubns.:** "The Scientific Premises of Information Science," *Jnl. of the Amer. Socty. for Info. Sci.* (Jl.–Ag. 1974); "Teaching Information Science to Non-Scientists," *Jnl. of Educ. for Libnshp.* (1972); "Aikido for a Media Center" film (1974). **Activities:** 11; 26, 41; 56, 75, 93 **Addr.:** School of Library Science, University of Michigan, Ann Arbor, MI 48109.

Rosenberg–Pene, Florence Henriette (Ag. 27, 1931, Addis-Abeba, Ethiopia) Actng. Head, Ref. Dept., Bapst Lib., Boston Coll., 1980–, Ref. Libn., 1976–80; Assoc. Libn., Fr. Lib., Boston, 1975; Psychologist, France, 1953–57. **Educ.:** Univ. of Strasbourg, 1947–51, BA (Psy.), 1951, MA (Psy.); Univ. de Paris, 1951–53, Dips. (Appld. Psy.); Simmons Coll., 1970–74, MLS. **Orgs.:** ALA: ACRL. SLA. New Eng. OLUG. ASIS. Newton Mental Hlth. Assn. **Honors:** Fulbright/Smith–Mundt Schol., 1954. **Pubns.:** Jt. auth., "Essai sur l'illusion de la mediane des angles," *Archives de Psy.* (1955); "Le bilinguisme," *La Caravelle* (1963). **Activities:** 1; 31, 39, 49-On-Line Srch.; 55, 63, 72 **Addr.:** 18 Hazelton Rd., Newton Centre, MA 02159.

Rosenblum, Richard Seth (My 1, 1944, Newark, NJ) Dir., W. New York (NJ) Pub. Lib., 1978–; Dir., Roselle Park (NJ) Pub. Lib., 1976–78; Actg. Dir. of Evening Srvs. and Ref. Libn., Seton Hall Univ. Lib., 1974–76; Sch. Libn., Newark Schs., 1974; Part-time Ref. Libn., Upsala Coll., 1974; Catlgr., Scotch Plains Pub. Lib. 1973. **Educ.:** Upsala Coll., 1963–66, BA (Fr.); W.M. Paterson Coll., 1969–73, MAT (Elem. Educ.); Pratt Inst., 1973–74, MLS; Univ. of WI, Bryn Mawr Coll. (in France), West. Rsv. Univ., 1966–68, Grad. Std. (Fr.). **Orgs.:** ALA. NJ LA: Mem. Com. (1973–74); Gvt. Rel. Com. (1975–76); Educ. for Libnshp. Com. (1976–77); Del. at Lg. (1977–78); Trustee Rel. Com. (1977–80); Constn. Com. (1978–80). B'nai Brith. Alpha Kappa Psi. **Pubns.:** "The MacManus Collection", *NJ Libs.* (Mr. 1976); "Service to Handicapped in W. New York," *NJ Libs.* (D. 1979/ Ja. 1980); "A Review of School Zone", *Lib. Jnl.* (F. 15, 1976); Ed. staff, *NJ Libs.* (1974–75). **Activities:** 9; 17, 35, 36; 59, 63, 72 **Addr.:** West New York Public Library, West New York, NJ 07093.

Roseneder, Janette M. (Je. 14, 1948, Brisbane, Queensland, Australia) Biblgphr., Spec. Col., Univ. of Calgary Lib., 1979–, Head, Info. Ctr., 1975–79, Head, ILL, 1974–75; Chief Cat., Univ. of Winnipeg Lib., 1973–74, Cat., 1972–73; Ref. Libn., SK Prov. Lib., 1969–71. **Educ.:** Univ. of AB, 1966–68, BA (Hist.), 1968–69, BLS. **Orgs.:** Can. LA. Can. Art Libs. Assn. LA of AB: Lib. Legis. Com. (1975–76). Foothills LA: Treas. (1976–77). Various orgs. AB Geneal. Socty.: Prov. Libn. (1977–79). W. Surrey Fam. Hist. Socty. Can. Assn. of Univ. Tchrs. Alcuin Socty. **Pubns.:** Jt. Ed., *Winnipeg: A Centennial Bibliography* (1974); "Portrait miniatures in Canada," *Can. Art Libs. Nsltr.* (S. 1978); "Family Portrait Galleries," *Relatively speaking* (Win. 1976); various reviews, *Can. Bk. Review Anl.* (1975–77). **Activities:** 1, 12; 30, 45; 57, 69 **Addr.:** Special Collections, Library, University of Calgary, Calgary, AB T2N 1N4 Canada.

Rosenfeld, Joel C. (Je. 16, 1939, Brooklyn, NY) Exec. Dir., Rockford Pub. Lib., 1980–; Exec. Dir., Metro. Lib. Srv. Agency, 1974–79; Dir., Urbana Free Lib., 1968–74; Adult Srvs. Consult., Lincoln Trail Libs., 1967–68; Branch Libn., Flint Pub. Lib., 1962–66. **Educ.:** Univ. of MI, 1959–61, AB (Eng.), 1962–64, AMLS. **Orgs.:** IL LA. ALA: PLA (Dir.-at-Lg., 1980–81); Metro. Lib. Sect. (Pres., 1979–80). MN LA: Legis. Com. (Ch., 1976–78). Amer. Interprof. Inst. **Activities:** 4, 9; 16, 17, 34; 50, 78, 93 **Addr.:** Rockford Public Library, 215 N. Wyman St., Rockford, IL 61101.

Rosensteel, J. Randall (Ja. 16, 1939, Mount Union, PA) Admin. Asst. to Dir., Free Lib. of Philadelphia, 1969–, Asst. Libn., Bk. Sel., 1965–69, Libn., Fiction Dept., 1964–65, 1961. **Educ.:** Maryville Coll., 1956–60, BA (Eng.); Drexel Univ., 1960–61, MSLS. **Orgs.:** ALA: Intl. Rel. Com. (1971–74). PA LA. The Philobiblon Club. **Activities:** 9; 17 **Addr.:** Office of the Director, The Free Library of Philadelphia, Logan Sq., Philadelphia, PA 19103.

Rosenstein, Philip (F. 5, 1922, Montreal, PQ) Dir. of Libs., Coll. of Med. and Dentistry of NJ, 1956–; Dir., Brooklyn Coll. of Pharm., Long Island Univ., 1955–56; Ref. Asst., NY Acad. of Med., 1952–55. **Educ.:** Univ. of CA, Los Angeles, 1946–48, BA (Anthro.); Columbia Univ., 1948–50, MA (Anthro.), 1952–55, MSLS, 1973, Cert. Advnc. Libnshp. **Orgs.:** Med. LA: NY Reg. Grp., Ch. (1966–67); Pharm. Grp., Ch. (1959); various coms. (1972–78). NY–NJ Reg. Med. Lib.: Adv. Com. (1969–). SLA: NY Chap. (Ch.). Med. Lib. Ctr. of NY: Adv. Com., Ch. (1973–76). NY Acad. of Scis. **Pubns.:** "A Medical Librarian's Bag of Tricks," *Bltn. of Med. LA* (Ap. 1975); "Some Implications for Libraries of the Recent Williams and Wilkins Decision", *Spec. Libs.* (My./Je. 1972); "Changing Objectives of the Pharmacy College Library," *Bltn. of Med. LA* (Spr. 1963). **Activities:** 1, 12; 17, 24; 80 **Addr.:** College of Medicine and Dentistry of New Jersey, 100 Bergen St., Newark, NJ 07040.

Rosenthal, Faigi (S. 6, 1936, Montreal, PQ) Asst. Head Libn., NY Post, 1978–; Libn., NY Cnty. Lawyers Assn., 1973–78; Libn., The Conf. Bd., 1960–66; Head Libn., McGill Univ. Sch. of Soc. Work, 1958–60. **Educ.:** McGill Univ., 1953–57, BA; 1957–58, MLS. **Orgs.:** SLA. **Activities:** 12, 14-newsp.; 30, 39, 41; 75 **Addr.:** 4 Washington Sq. Village, New York, NY 10012.

Rosenthal, Joseph A. (Ag. 11, 1929, Pittsburgh, PA) Univ. Libn., Univ. of CA, Berkeley, 1979–, Actg. Univ. Libn., 1978–79, Assoc. Univ. Libn., Tech. Srvs., 1971–79; Chief, Prep. Srvs., NY Pub. Lib., 1964–70. **Educ.:** Dickinson Coll., 1949, BA (Pol. Sci.); PA State Univ., 1951, MA (Pol. Sci.); Columbia Univ., 1957, MSLS; various grad. crs. **Orgs.:** NY Tech. Srvs. Libns.: Pres. (1968–69); VP (1967–78); Prog. Com. (Ch., 1963–64). ARL: Task Frc. on Cat. Cutoff (Ch., 1974). ASIS: Various coms. ALA: RTSD, Bd. of Dirs. (1970–73), Info. Sci. and Autom. Div., VP (1975–76), Pres. (1976–77)/Cat. and Class. Sect., Cat. Policy and Resrch. Com., Secy. (1969–70), Ch. (1971–72), Ref. Srvs. Div., various coms.; ACRL, Appts. and Nom. Com. (1969–70). Various other orgs. Archons of Colophon. Pub. Affairs Info. Srv.: Bd. of Trustees (1971–). Lib. of Congs.: Bibl. Adv. Com. to the Nationwide Data Base Dsgn. Proj. (1978–). Amer. Natl. Stans. Inst.: Com. Z–39, Subcom. on Indexing (1964–68). **Honors:** Phi Beta Kappa, 1948; Beta Phi Mu, 1957. **Pubns.:** "Planning for the Catalogs: A Managerial Perspective," *Jnl. of Lib. Autom.* (S. 1978); "Network Brew: Hints from a Misty Crystal Ball," *Jnl. of Lib. Autom.* (Je. 1977); "Non-professionals and Cataloging: A Survey of Five Libraries," *Lib. Resrcs. & Tech. Srvs.* (Sum. 1969); "Planning a Library's Automation Effort," *Colloque sur les implications administratives de l'automatisation dans les grandes bibliothèques/Institute on Automation in Large Libraries: Im-*

Special Subjects/Services: 50. Adult educ.; 51. Advert./Mktg.; 52. Aerosp.; 53. Agric.; 54. Area std.; 55. Arts/Hum.; 56. Autom.; 57. Bibl./Prtg.; 58. Bio. sci.; 59. Bus./Fin.; 60. Chem.; 61. Copyrt.; 62. Documtn.; 63. Educ.; 64. Engin.; 65. Env.; 66. Eth. grps.; 67. Film; 68. Food/Nutr.; 69. Geneal.; 70. Geo.; 71. Geol.; 72. Handcpd.; 73. Hist.; 74. Int. frdm.; 75. Info. sci.; 76. Insr.; 77. Law; 78. Legis.; 79. Math./Comp. sci.; 80. Med.; 81. Metals; 82. Nat. resrcs.; 83. Newsp.; 84. Nuc. sci.; 85. Oral hist.; 86. Petr./Energy; 87. Pharm.; 88. Phys./Astr./Math.; 89. Readg.; 90. Relig.; 91. Sci./Tech.; 92. Soc. sci.; 93. Telecom.; 94. Transp.; 95. (other).

plications for the Administrator and the Manager (1968); various bk. reviews, *Lib. Resrcs. & Tech. Srvs., Lib. Jnl., Drexel Lib. Qtly., Coll. & Resrch. Libs.;* various bibls. **Activities:** 1; 17, 35 **Addr.:** 51 Buena Vista Terr., San Francisco, CA 94117.

Rosenwinkel, Heather Gail (D. 8, 1938, Montreal, PQ) Acq., Libn., OR Hlth. Sci. Univ. Lib., 1977–, Head, Ref. Dept., 1976–77, Actg. Dir., 1975–76, Head, Ref. Dept., 1966–75, Asst. to Catlgr., 1965–66. **Educ.:** Bishop's Univ., Lennoxville, PQ, 1957–59, BA (Eng., Hist.), 1959–60, HS Tchg. Cert.; Univ. of MN, 1964–66, MA (LS, Anthro.). **Orgs.:** Med. LA: Intl. Coop. Com. (1975–79). Frnds. of the Multnomah Cnty. Lib.: Bd. Secy. (1978–81). SLA: OR Chap. (Pres., 1977–78). OR LA: Schol. Com. (Ch., 1979–80). Univ. of OR Hlth. Sci. Ctr. Sch. of Med. Amer. Youth Hostels, Inc. **Activities:** 1, 12; 15, 39, 45; 56, 80, 92 **Addr.:** Acquisitions Dept., Oregon Health Sciences University Library, P.O. Box 573, Portland, OR 97207.

Rosignolo, Beverly Ann (S. 12, 1950, New York, NY) Assoc. Libn., Coll. of Insr., 1981–, Catlgr., 1977–81; Catlgr./Indxr., H.W. Wilson Co., 1975–77. **Educ.:** Queens Coll., 1970–74, BA (Psy.), 1974–75, MLS. **Orgs.:** ALA. SLA: Insr. Div. **Honors:** Beta Phi Mu, 1975. **Pubns.:** Jt. ed., *Chld.'s Cat. Supplement* (1977); Indxr.: *Insr. Pers. Index* (1978–); Contrib., *Insr. Lit.* (1978–). **Activities:** 1, 12; 20, 39; 59, 76 **Addr.:** The College of Insurance Library, 123 William St., New York, NY 10038.

Roslien, Sharon Esther (Ap. 12, 1937, Mason City, IA) Head Media Spec., Mariner HS, 1981–, Media Spec., 1978–80; Media Spec., Ctrl. Jr. HS, 1968–78; Tchr., Faribault Pub. Schs., 1962–66; Tchr. and Tchr.-Libn., Virogua Pub. Schs., 1959–62. **Educ.:** St. Olaf Coll., 1955–59, BA, magna cum laude (Hist., Span.); Univ. of MN, 1967–68, MA (LS), 1979, Media Generalist. **Orgs.:** ALA: AASL. MN Educ. Media Org. **Honors:** Phi Beta Kappa, 1959. **Activities:** 10; 32, 39, 48 **Addr.:** 3654 Auger Ave., White Bear Lake, MN 55110.

Ross, Alexander D. (Ag. 3, 1941, New York, NY) Head Libn., Art and Archit. Lib., Stanford Univ., 1975–; Assoc. Libn., Cleveland Musm. of Art, 1971–75, Asst. Fine Arts Libn., Columbia Univ., 1968–71. **Educ.:** Columbia Univ., 1966, AB (Eng.), 1968, MS (LS), 1971, MA (Art Hist.). **Orgs.:** ARLIS/NA. Coll. Art. Assn. **Pubns.:** "Abstracts and Indexes," *Art Lib. Manual* (1977); reviews. **Activities:** 1, 12; 15, 31, 39; 55 **Addr.:** Art and Architecture Library, Stanford University, Stanford, CA 94305.

Ross, Annie V. (N. 27, 1919, Uniontown, PA) Cat. Libn., Univ. of AZ, 1961–; Libn., NY Phoenix Sch. of Dsgn., 1946–47; Catlgr., Columbia Univ., 1942–46. **Educ.:** Univ. of Pittsburgh, 1937–41, BA (Hist.); Columbia Univ., 1941–42, BS (LS). **Orgs.:** AZ State LA. **Activities:** 1; 20 **Addr.:** 5667 W. Flying M St., Tucson, AZ 85713.

Ross, BevAnne (Ag. 20, 1921, San Francisco, CA) Pubn. Consult., Self-empl., 1977–; Sr. Resrch. Assoc., Assoc. Consults., Inc., 1979–; Indexing Tchr.; Managing Ed., Amer. Stats. Index, Congsnl. Info. Srv., 1976–77; Lead Ed., Issue Brief Syst., Congsnl. Resrch. Srv., Lib. of Congs., 1974–76; Chief, Ed. Branch, Human Resrcs. Resrch. Org., 1973–74; Tech. Ed., Meteorological Abs., Amer. Meteorological Socty., 1969–73; various positions in wrtg., ed., wkshps. on indexing. **Educ.:** George Washington Univ., 1977–78, BA (Pol. Sci.); Upper IA Univ., 1977–78, BPA (Pub. Admin.); 1980, Paralegal Dip.; various sems., grad. crs. **Orgs.:** Amer. Socty. of Indxrs.: Natl. Pres. (1977–78); Bd. of Dirs. (1976–); Documtn. Abs., Bd. of Dirs. (1979–). Bus. and Prof. Women: DC State Pres. (1979–80). Natl. Fed. of Press Women. Natl. Assn. Parlmts. **Honors:** U.S. Navy, Outstan. Performance, 1959; Bus. and Prof. Women, DC, Woman of the Yr., 1977–78; Pan Amer. Liaison of Women, Woman of Achvmt., 1975. **Pubns.:** Ed., prin. writer, *Amer. Socty. of Indxrs. Nsltr.* (1978–80); ed., prin. writer, *Potomac BPW Nsltr.* (1980–); various articles, indxs., abs., bibls., transls., std. prog. in indexing. **Activities:** 14-Self-empl.; 24, 30; 56, 75, 91 **Addr.:** 4405 Dolphin Ln., Alexandria, VA 22309.

Ross, Delanie Mitchum (D. 25, 1945, Miami, FL) First Asst., Hist. and Travel Dept., Memphis/Shelby Cnty. Pub. Lib. and Info. Ctr., 1981–, Ref. Libn., Spec. Cols., 1975–81; in other fields. **Educ.:** Agnes Scott Coll. and Southwestern-at-Memphis, 1963–67, BA (Hist.); MS State Univ., 1971–72, MSS (Hist., Soclgy., Anthro.); George Peabody Coll., 1974–75, MLS. **Orgs.:** ALA. TN LA: W. TN Coord., Legis. Netwk; Legis. Action Com. TN Archvsts. Assn.: Nom. Com. **Pubns.:** Bk. reviews, *TN Lib. Jnl.* **Activities:** 2, 9; 23, 39, 45 **Addr.:** Memphis Room (History Dept), Memphis/Shelby County Public Library & Information Center, 1850 Peabody Ave., Memphis, TN 38104.

Ross, Deryck A. (Jl. 13, 1942, Montreal, PQ) Info. Sci., Dept. of Natl. Defence, 1977–, Prog. Coord. Ofcr., 1976–77, Info. Sci., 1975–76; Sci. Ed., Defence Resrch. Bd., 1971–75. **Educ.:** Bishop's Univ., Lennoxville, PQ 1959–63, BSc (Chem., Phys.); Univ. of West. ON, 1963–65, MSc (Chem.). **Orgs.:** Socty. for Tech. Comm.: Ch. (1976–78); Prog. Div. (1974); Nom. Com. (Intl. Exec., Dir., 1981–82). Can. Assn. Info. Sci.: Pubcty. Dir. (1979–80); Prog. Com. (1979–80). Chem. Inst. of Can. **Activities:** 4, 12; 30, 39, 45; 52, 74, 91 **Addr.:** National Defence Headquarters, 101 Colonel By Drive, ATTN: CRAD/DSIS, Ottawa, ON K1A 0K2 Canada.

Ross, Gary McCane (Mr. 23, 1952, Hicksville, NY) Asst. Head, Automated Prcs. Div., Ohio State Univ., 1978–; Libn., Ctrl. City Bus. Inst., 1975–76; Sci. Catlgr. and Asst. Supvsr., VA Polytech. Inst., 1976–78. **Educ.:** Cornell Univ., 1970–74, BS (Agr. Econ.); Syracuse Univ., 1975–76, MLS. **Orgs.:** ALA. ASIS. **Pubns.:** "Rights and Responsibilities in Interlibrary Cooperation," *SEast. Libn.* (Win. 1980). **Activities:** 1; 15, 20, 34; 56, 75, 93 **Addr.:** Ohio State University Libraries, 1858 Neal Ave. Mall, Rm. 040S, Columbus, OH 43210.

Ross, Nina M. (Ja. 8, 1923, Parkersburg, WV) Info. Retrieval Spec., Univ. of Pittsburgh, 1975–, Instr., Sch. of Lib. and Info. Sci., 1980–. **Educ.:** Chatham Coll., 1939–43, AB (Econ., Soclgy.); Univ. of Pittsburgh, 1972–74, MLS. **Orgs.:** ASIS. PA LA. Pittsburgh OLUG. **Honors:** Beta Phi Mu, 1974. **Pubns.:** Jt. auth., "An Exercise in Utility," *ONLINE* (Ja., 1980). **Activities:** 11; 25, 26, 34; 56, 63, 75 **Addr.:** 120 Merrie Woode Dr., Pittsburgh, PA 15235.

Ross, Pamela A. (S. 26, 1945, Rahway, NJ) Head, Circ. Dept., Boston Coll., 1979–; Head, Circ. Dept., Columbia Univ., 1974–77, Asst. Libn., 1971–74. **Educ.:** Vassar Coll., 1963–67, AB (Pol. Sci.); Fordham Univ., 1967–68, AM (Hist.); Columbia Univ., 1970–71, MSLS. **Orgs.:** ALA. Lexington (MA) Chld. Ctr. Vassar Club of Boston Alum.: Admis. Com. (1978–). **Activities:** 1; 17, 22, 43 **Addr.:** 34 Meadowbrook Rd., Bedford, MA 01730.

Ross, Patsy S. (N. 30, 1950, Sebree, KY) Head, Serials Dept., Univ. of AL Lib., 1979–; Libn., Crete-Monee HS, 1973–74. **Educ.:** Murray State Univ., 1968–72, BS (Psy., LS); Univ. of AL, 1977–79, MLS. **Orgs.:** ALA. SELA. AL LA. **Activities:** 1; 17, 44, 46; 56, 75 **Addr.:** University of AL Library, Serials Dept., Drawer S, University, AL 35486.

Ross, Robert Donald (Mr. 28, 1931, New York, NY) Lib. Dir., Ridgewood Pub. Lib., 1973–; Lib. Dir., S. Brunswick Pub. Lib., 1969–73; Reader Srvs. Libn., Suffolk Cnty. Coll., 1966–69; Ref. Libn., Brooklyn Pub. Lib., 1965. **Educ.:** City Coll. of NY, 1948–54, BA (Eng. Lit.); Rutgers Univ., 1965–66, MLS, Columbia Univ., 1968, Post Mstrs. Cert. (LS). **Orgs.:** ALA: LAMA/Bldgs. and Equipment Sect., Archit. for Pub. Libs. Com. NJ LA: Lib. Dev., Educ. For Libnshp. Com., Ch. Natl. Adv. Com. for Film and the Hum., Natl. Endow. for the Hum.: Exec. Bd. (1973–76). **Pubns.:** "Paying for Library Service Promotion," *UNABASHED Libn.* (Sum. 1973). **Activities:** 9; 17, 24, 31; 55, 63, 75 **Addr.:** Ridgewood Public Library, 125 N. Maple Ave., Ridgewood, NJ 07450.

Ross, Rodney Anson (Jn. 14, 1943, Chicago, IL) Archvst., NARS:Nixon Pres. Mtrls. Proj., 1977–; Leg. Asst., U.S. Rep. Tim L. Hall, 1975–77; Lectr. (African Hist.), IN Univ. Northwest, 1972; Instr. Wilberforce Univ., 1967–69. **Educ.:** Knox Coll., 1961–65, BA (Hist.); Univ. of Chicago, 1965–75, MA, Ph.D. (Amer. Hist.). **Orgs.:** SAA. Mid-Atl. Reg. Arch. Conf. Org. of Amer. Histns. **Honors:** Ford Fndn., Flwshp., 1972. **Pubns.:** "Black Americans and Italo-Ethiopian Relief, 1935–1936," *Ethiopia Observer* (1972); "Mary Todd Lincoln, Patient at Bellevue," *Jnl. of the IL State Hist. Socty.* (1970). **Activities:** 2, 4; 42; 92 **Addr.:** 1311 Delaware Ave., S.W., Apt S849, Washington, DC 20024.

Ross, Ryburn M. (F. 22, 1920, Warrensburg, NY) Asst. Univ. Libn., Cornell Univ. Libs., 1964–; Dir. of Lib., Aerospace Corp., 1962–64; Dir. of Chinese Proj. and Assoc. Dir. Exec. Ofcr., Sci. Lib., M.I.T. Lib., 1957–69; Libn., U.S. Nvl. Trng. Devices Ctr., 1952–57; Asst. Prof. and Asst. Librn., U.S. Nvl. Postgrad. Sch., 1950–51. **Educ.:** City Coll. of NY, 1939–42; Columbia Univ., 1946–47, BS (Educ.), 1947–48, MA, 1948–49, MSLS. **Orgs.:** ALA. **Pubns.:** "CONSER: A New Approach to Building a Serials Information Data Base," *Cornell Univ. Libs. Bltn.* (S./O. 1975); "Cost Analysis of Technical Services," *Proc. of the 1976 Clinic on Lib. Applications of Data Procs.* (1977). **Activities:** 1; 17, 24, 34; 56, 75 **Addr.:** Assistant University Librarian, Cornell University Libraries, Ithaca, NY 14853.

Rosse, Rosanna H. (Ja. 18, 1920, The Hague, Netherlands) Head, Reader Srvs., Clarkson Coll. of Tech., 1967–; Ref. Libn., Contra Costa Cnty. Lib., 1965–67; Elem. Tchr., Pacifica and San Francisco, 1961–63; Secy., Stanford Resrch. Inst., 1949–53; Secy., U.S. Info. Srv., (The Hague), 1945–46; Secy., Koninklijke Bibliotheek (The Hague), 1941–1945; numerous positions as secy. in various fields, 1946–64. **Educ.:** San Francisco State Coll., 1953–58, BA (Art), 1959–61, Elem. Tchg. Cred.; Univ. of CA, Berkeley, 1964–65, MLS; crs. and cert. in photography, 1963–73. **Orgs.:** SLA. ALA: ACRL. N. Country Ref. and Resrch. Resrcs. Cncl.: Prog. Com. (1971–73). AAUW: St. Lawrence Branch (Secy., 1969–75). Sierra Club. Coms. at Clarkson Coll. **Pubns.:** Photographs for illustrations in two bks. (1975). **Activities:** 1; 22, 31, 39; 59, 91 **Addr.:** 122 Leroy St., Potsdam, NY 13676.

Rossell, Glenora E. (O. 6, 1925, Johnstown, PA) Dir., Univ. Libs., Univ. of Pittsburgh, 1970–, Actg. Dir., 1970, Asst. Dir., Univ. Libs., 1967–69, Adj. Asst.Prof. of Bus. Bibl., 1966–67, Asst. to the Dir., 1965–66, Bus. Libn., 1961–65, Docum. Libn., 1958–61; Ref. and Educ. Libn., Brooklyn Coll., 1954–57; other prof. positions, 1947–53. **Educ.:** Juniata Coll., 1943–47, AB (Span., Hist.); Columbia Univ., 1951–52, MS (LS); Univ. of Pittsburgh, Post-masters work. **Orgs.:** ALA. PA LA. SLA. Pittsburgh Bibliophiles. Pittsburgh Cncl. on Higher Educ.: Lib. Com. **Pubns.:** *Pittsburgh Regional Library Center Newspaper List* (1976); *Major Microform Holdings in Eight Pittsburgh Regional Library Center Libs.* (1973); Ed., *Pennsylvania Newspapers, A Bibliography & Union List* (1978); article in *Encyclopedia of Library and Information Science.* **Activities:** 1; 17, 63 **Addr.:** 1433 Beulah Rd., Pittsburgh, PA 15235.

Rossman, Renee (My. 17, 1937, Trenton, NJ) Adult Srvs. Libn., Ref., Progs., Portage Pub. Lib., 1976–; Ref. Libn., Kalamazoo Valley Cmnty. Coll., 1976. **Educ.:** IN Univ., 1955–59, BA (Thea., Eng.); West. MI Univ., 1975, MSL. **Orgs.:** ALA: ASCLA/Lib. Srv. to the Deaf, Exec. Com. (1980–82), Stans. for Lib. Srv. to the Deaf (1978–80). Natl. Assn. of the Deaf. MI Assn. of the Deaf. AAUW. Hadassah. **Honors:** MI LA, Loleta D. Fyan Awd., 1978; MI State Bd. of Educ., Cert. of Apprec. for Native Amer. Week, 1979; Lib. PR Cncl., Awd., 1979. **Pubns.:** "Programs For All," *Colt Nsltr.* (O. 9, 1979); wkly. lib. clmn., *Portage Headliner News* (1976–); various indxs. **Activities:** 9; 16, 30, 39; 50, 72 **Addr.:** Portage Public Library, 300 Library Ln., Portage, MI 49002.

Rosswurm, Kevin Michael (N. 16, 1949, New Haven, IN) Head, Phil., Relig. and Educ. Div., Akron-Summit Cnty. Pub. Lib., 1977–, Ref. Libn., 1975–77. **Educ.:** Ctrl. MI Univ., 1968–72, BS Ed (Hist.); Kent State Univ., 1972–75, MA (Hist.), 1974–75, MLS. **Orgs.:** ALA: RASD, Outstan. Ref. Srcs. Com. (1980–82), Dartmouth Medal Com. (1979–80); JMRT, Exec. Bd. (1980–82), Com. on Governance (1979–80), *Footnotes* (Ed., 1980–82), Anl. Conf. Soc. Com. (Ch., 1979). OH LA. **Pubns.:** "Professional Reading...The World According to Gore," *OLA Bltn.* (Ja. 1979); "Shaping Our Image in Cleveland, October 12–14, 1978," *OLA Bltn.* (Ja. 1979); various reviews. **Activities:** 9; 16, 17, 39; 50, 63, 92 **Addr.:** Philosophy, Religion and Education Division, Akron-Summit County Public Library, 55 S. Main St., Akron, OH 44305.

Roston, John B. (Jl. 18, 1945, Montreal, PQ) Assoc. Dir., Instr. Comm. Ctr., McGill Univ. 1978–, Distribution Supvsr., 1972–78, Media Resrcs. Consult., 1970–72; Film Producer, Roha Motion Pics. Limited, 1968–70; Assoc. Publshr., *Take One Mag.,* 1966–68. **Educ.:** McGill Univ., 1974–76, BA (Film), grad. work (Comm.). **Orgs.:** EFLA. Assn. for Media and Tech. in Educ. in Can. AECT. Film Stds. Assn. of Can. **Pubns.:** Producer, "Rainy Day Woman" feature film (1970); "A Model for the Development of the Canadian Feature Film Industry," *Working Papers in Comm.* (1981). **Activities:** 10; 17, 32, 34; 55, 67, 93 **Addr.:** Instructional Communications Centre, McGill University, 815 Sherbrooke St. W., Montreal, PQ H3A 2K6 Canada.

Roten, Paul (Ja. 14, 1920, Maryville, TN) Libn., Assoc. Mennonite Biblical Semys., 1965–; Asst. Prof. of Sp., Manchester Coll., 1959–64; Assoc. Prof. of Sp. and Drama, Sioux Falls Coll., 1953–59. **Educ.:** Ottawa Univ., KS, 1937–41, BA (Eng.); Univ. of MI, 1946–53, MA (Sp.), 1963, PhD (Sp.), 1964–65, MALS. **Orgs.:** ATLA. ALA. Chicago Area Theo. LA: VP (1972–73); Pres. (1973–74). **Activities:** 1; 15, 17, 20; 90 **Addr.:** 2800 Benham, Elkhart, IN 46514.

Rotenberry, Julia Ward (D. 16, 1922, Tuscaloosa, AL) Assoc. Prof. and Head, Tech. Srvs., Univ. of Montevallo, 1954–; Archit. and Arts Libn., Auburn Univ., 1946–47; Circ. Asst., Knoxville Pub. Lib., 1945–46. **Educ.:** AL Coll., 1941–44, AB (Hist.); Univ. of NC, 1944–45, BS (LS). **Orgs.:** AL LA: Pres. (1981–82); Secy. (1974–75); Nom. Com. (Ch., 1979–80); Rcrt. Com. (1977–78); Awds. and Cits. Com. (Ch., 1974–); Coll. Univ. and Spec. Libs. Div. Secy., (1968–69), Ch., (1973–74). Socty. of AL Archvsts. **Pubns.:** Jt. ed., *AL Review Index* (1979); "Assembly Line Cataloging," *AL Libn.* (Ja. 1970); "What is the *Alabama Review?,*" *AL Libn.* (My.–Je. 1979). **Activities:** 5; 20 **Addr.:** 249 Highland St., N., Montevallo, AL 35115.

Roth, Britain G. (Ja. 20, 1952, Scranton, PA) Med. Libn., Vets. Admin. Med. Ctr., 1977–; Med. Libn., Resrch. Fndn., SUNY, Buffalo, 1975–77. **Educ.:** Syracuse Univ., 1969–73, BA (Hist., Anthro.); SUNY, Buffalo, 1975–77, MLS; Med. LA, 1977, Med. Libnship. Cert. **Orgs.:** ALA. Med. LA. **Pubns.:** "Perspective: Graduating the Truly Professional," *Natl. Libn.* (My. 1979); "Health Information for Patients: The Hospital Library's Role," *Bltn. of the Med. LA* (Ja. 1978); "Patient Health Education Programs" tape (1978). **Activities:** 4, 12; 15, 39, 41; 58, 68, 80 **Addr.:** Medical Library/142D, Veterans Administration Medical Center, 1201 N.W. 16th St., Miami, FL 33124.

Roth, Charles P. (Mr. 2, 1950, Philadelphia, PA) Head, Tech. Srvs., Philadelphia Coll. of Pharm. and Sci., 1979–; Col. Dev. Libn., Head, Acq., La Salle Coll., 1977–79; Srchr., NY Times Data Bank, Free Lib. of Philadelphia, 1977; Bibl. Asst. Hum. and Soc. Sci., Drexel Univ., 1975–77. **Educ.:** St. Joseph's Univ., 1968–72, BA (Eng.); Drexel Univ., 1974–76, MS (LS); various crs. **Orgs.:** ATLA. Med. LA. ALA. **Honors:** Beta Phi Mu, 1976. **Activities:** 1, 12; 15, 20, 44; 87, 90 **Addr.:** Joseph W. Eng-

PROFESSIONAL ACTIVITIES: Institutions: 1. Acad. lib.; 2. Arch.; 3. Assn.; 4. Fed./Gvt. lib.; 5. Inst. lib.; 6. Mfr./Suppl.; 7. Milit. lib.; 8. Musm.; 9. Pub. lib.; 10. Sch. lib.; 11. Sch. of lib. sci.; 12. Spec. lib.; 13. State lib.; 14. (other). **Functions/Activities:** 15. Acq./Col. dev.; 16. Adult srvs.; 17. Admin.; 18. Apprais.; 19. Archit./Bldgs.; 20. Cat./Class.; 21. Chld. srvs.; 22. Circ.; 23. Cons./Pres.; 24. Consult.; 25. Cont. ed.; 26. Educ. lib. sci.; 27. Ext. srvs.; 28. Fund/Grants; 29. Gvt. pubs.; 30. Indx./Abs.; 31. Instr. lib. use; 32. Media srvs.; 33. Micro.; 34. Netwks./Coop.; 35. Persnl.; 36. PR; 37. Publshg.; 38. Recs. mgt.; 39. Ref. srvs.; 40. Repro.; 41. Resrch.; 42. Review.; 43. Secur.; 44. Serials; 45. Spec. col.; 46. Tech. srvs.; 47. Trustees/Bds.; 48. YA srvs.; 49. (other).

land Library, Philadelphia College of Pharmacy and Science, Philadelphia, PA 19104.

Roth, Claire Jarett (New York, NY) Lib. Dir., Mercantile LA, 1977–; Freelnc. Ed., 1975–77; Lib. Dir., Finch Coll., 1973–75; Lib. Coord., Eng.-Speaking Un., 1971–72; Libn., Fac. Mem., Sch. of Nursing, E.O. Gen. Hosp., 1956–64; Libn., NY Univ., 1946–51. **Educ.:** Univ. of NC, 1943, BA (European Hist.); Columbia Univ., 1945, MLS; NY Univ., 1950, MA (Guid., Persnl. Admin.). **Orgs.:** Archons: Nom. Com. (1980). NY LA: Exhibits Com. (1978–). NY Metro. Ref. and Resrch. Lib. Agency: DDC 19 Task Frc. (1979). ALA: Interagency Cncl. on Lib. Tools for Nursing (1962–64); Stans. for Nursing Libs. (Resrc. Person, 1963). METRO: Strg. Com., Coop. Acq. Prog. (1974–75); Resrcs. Dev. Com. (1975–76). NY Lib. Club. Various other orgs. NY Rug Socty. Long Island Antique Dlrs. Assn. **Pubns.:** Consult. ed., *Antique Shops and Dealers–USA* (1976); *Hospital Health Services* (1964); *Art Careers* (1963); "Keep Personal References Informed," *Lib. Jnl.* (Mr. 15, 1966); reviews, *LJ* (1948–65). **Activities:** 12; 17, 28, 35; 50, 55 **Addr.:** 28 Station Plz., Great Neck, NY 11021.

Roth, Dana Lincoln (Mr.) (O. 23, 1935, Hollywood, CA) Scis. Libn., CA Inst. of Tech., 1965–; Info. Ofcr., Stirling Univ. (Scotland), 1975–76; Lib. Adv., IIT - Kanpur (India), 1971–72. **Educ.:** Univ. of CA, Los Angeles, 1959–62, BS (Chem.); CA Inst. of Tech., 1962–64, MS (Chem.); Univ. of CA, Los Angeles, 1964–65, MLS. **Orgs.:** ASIS. CA Acad. and Resrch. Libns. Amer. Chem. Socty. Amer. Inst. of Bio. Sci. Sigma Xi. **Pubns.:** *Serials and Journals in the Caltech Libraries* (1979); *An Index Guide to Beilstein, Gmelin ...* (1972); "Innovative Uses of OCLC Records," *Jnl. Lib. Autom.* (1978); "The Needs of Library Users," *UNESCO Bltn. Libs.* (1974); "Scientific Serials List," *Jnl. Lib. Autom.* (1972). **Activities:** 1, 12; 15, 31, 39; 58, 60, 91 **Addr.:** 2023 Rose Villa St., Pasadena, CA 91107.

Roth, Elaine G. (My. 3, 1932, Chicago, IL) Dir., Media Srvs., Oak Park and River Forest HS, 1979–; Head Libn., New Trier E. HS, 1974–79; Libn., Niles Twp. HS, 1969–74; Lect., Rosary Coll., 1981–. **Educ.:** IN Univ., 1949–53, BS (Educ.); Rosary Coll., 1968–69, MA (LS); De Paul Univ., 1979–80, Admin. Cert. **Orgs.:** IL LA: Mem. Com. (1978–79). IL Assn. for Media in Educ.: Cert. Com. (Ch., 1976–80); Exec. Bd. (1981–82). Chicago Lib. Club: Secy. (1980–81). **Honors:** Beta Phi Mu; Phi Delta Kappa. **Pubns.:** "Response to a Case Study," *IL Libs.* (My. 1978). **Activities:** 10; 17, 32, 35; 63, 67 **Addr.:** 155 N. Harbor Dr., Chicago, IL 60601.

Roth, Eris E. (F. 25, 1923, Willow Lakes, SD) Head, Tech. Srvs., Soc. Secur. Admin. Lib., 1974–; Catlgr., Natl. Agr. Lib., 1970–74; Assoc. Libn. for Tech. Srv., Univ. of MD, 1969–70; Law Catlgr., Univ. of South. CA, Law Ctr., 1967–69; Lib. Consult., Xerox Prof. Lib. Srvs., 1967; Head, Tech. Srvs., Whittier Pub. Lib., 1963–66. **Educ.:** CA State Univ., Fullerton, 1958–62, BA (Bio. Sci.); Univ. of South. CA, 1963–64, MSLS, 1969 (Info. Sci.). **Orgs.:** ALA: Exec. Bd., Fed. Libns. RT (1979, 1980); GODORT, Micro. Task Frc. (Coord., 1977, 1978). MD LA: Tech. Srvs. Div. (VP/Pres.-Elect., 1979). South. CA Tech. Prcs. Grp.: Mem. and Hosplty. Com. (Ch., 1963–64). **Honors:** Soc. Secur. Admin. Ofc. of Mtrl. Resrcs., Superior Performance, 1979. **Activities:** 4, 9; 17, 20, 46 **Addr.:** 7907 Brookford Cir., Baltimore, MD 21208.

Roth, Frances Regina (Gina) (Ap. 14, 1947, Carshalton, Surrey, Eng.) Cat. Libn., CA State Polytech. Univ., Pomona, 1979–; Documtn. Asst., Lee Pharms., 1975–76; Archvst., Boosey and Hawkes Msc. Publshrs. (London), 1971–74; Mss. Catlgr., Huntington Lib. and Art Gallery, 1969–71. **Educ.:** Univ. of CA, Los Angeles, 1967–69, BA (Eng.); Univ. of South. CA, 1976–77, MSLS. **Orgs.:** Msc. LA: South. CA Chap. CA LA: Tech. Srvs. Chap.; Tech Prcs. Grp. Msc. OLUG. CA State Polytech. Univ. Lute Socty. (Eng.). **Honors:** Beta Phi Mu. **Pubns.:** "Literature Search: Labeling of Living Cells by Means of Ferritin and Polymeric Microspheres," *Jnl. of Immunological Methods* (1977). **Activities:** 1; 20, 46; 55 **Addr.:** Library, California State Polytechnic University, 3801 W. Temple Ave., Pomona, CA 91768.

Roth, Harold Leo (F. 25, 1919, New York, NY) Dir., The Bryant(Roslyn) Lib., 1978–; Natl. Accts. Mgr., Univ. Microfilms Int., 1977–78; Dir., Nassau Cnty. Resrch. Lib., 1970–77; VP, Lib. and Inst. Rel., Baker and Taylor Co., 1967–70; Dir., E. Orange Pub. Lib., 1954–67. **Educ.:** NY Univ., 1946–48, BA (Hist.); Columbia Univ., 1948–50, MS (LS). **Orgs.:** ALA: LAMA/Bldg. and Equip. Sect. (Ch., 1962–63), Lib. Facilities Com. (Ch., 1981), Equip. Com. (1979–). NY LA: Exhibits Com. (Ch., 1978–80). NJ LA: Pres. (1966–67). Lib. PR Cncl.: Pres. (1967–68). Lib. Dirs., Nassau Lib. Syst. Optimist Club of E. Orange. Archons of Colophon: Conv. (1974–75). **Honors:** Phi Beta Kappa, 1948; Beta Phi Mu, 1966. **Pubns.:** Ed., *Books, Publishing and Libraries Series* (1978–); ed., *Library Trends, An Analysis and Survey of Commercial Library Supply Houses* (1976); ed., *Planning Library Buildings for Service* (1964); "Education for Special Librarianship," *Jnl. of Educ. for Libnshp.* (1966–67). **Activities:** 9; 15, 17, 19; 56, 76, 95-Consult. **Addr.:** 28 Station Plz., Great Neck, NY 11021.

Roth, Helga (My. 12, 1920, Salzburg, Austria) Chief, Clearinghse. on the Handcpd., Dept. of Educ., 1977–; Dir., Clearinghse., Natl. Ctr. for Voluntary Action, 1969–76; Chief, Soc. Sci. and Cmnty. Progs., Sci. Info. Exch., 1960–69. **Educ.:** Maximilian's Univ., Munich, Germany, 1938–43, PhD (Psy.); New Sch. for Soc. Resrch., 1954–57, MA (Psy.). Young Men's Christ. Assn. Natl. Easter Seal Socty. **Pubns.:** "Information And Referral for Handicapped Individuals," *Drexel Lib. Qtly.* (1981); jt. auth., "Annual Review of Rehabilitation," *Info. Delivery in Rehab.* (1982); various sps., confs. **Activities:** 4, 12; 17, 28; 72, 92 **Addr.:** 3107 Kent St., Kensington, MD 20895.

Rothberg, Ryna H. (Ap. 22, 1936, Hartford, CT) Coord., Chld. Srvs., Newport Beach Pub. Lib., 1973–, Balboa Branch Supvsr., 1972–73; Chld. Libn., Ventura City and Cnty. Lib., Simi Branch, 1964–69; various tchg. positions. **Educ.:** Univ. of CT, 1954–58, BA (Eng., Educ.); Univ. of WA, 1971, MLS (Chld. Srvs.); Univ. of CT, (Eng.); Stan. Tchg. Cred., (Sec. Tchg.). **Orgs.:** CA LA: Chld. Srvs. Chap. (Pres., 1974, 1980); various ofcs., coms. YA Reviewers of South. CA: Pres. (1981); Treas. (1977–78); various ofcs. Santiago Lib. Syst.: Chld. Srvs. Div., Exec. Bd. (1973–); Pres. (1977–78); various ofcs. South. CA Cncl. on Lit. for Chld. and Young People: Awds. Com. (1976); various ofcs.; various orgs. Orange Cnty. March of Dimes: Reading Olympics Adv. Com. (1979). Orange Cnty. UNICEF Chap.: Intl. Year of the Child Adv. Com. (1979). Newport Beach Frnds. of the Lib. **Honors:** Kappa Delta Phi, 1958, Beta Phi Mu, 1971. **Pubns.:** "A Selected Bibliography of Juvenile Fiction Portraying the Handicapped," (1979); "Outreach to the Unserved: Children's Services Can Lead the Way", *CA Libn.* (Jl. 1975); "Don't Underrate Service to Children!" *CA Libn.* (Ap. 1976); Bibl., *Books and The Teen-Age Reader.* **Activities:** 9; 17, 21, 48 **Addr.:** 12271 Oakwood St., Garden Grove, CA 92640.

Rothberger, Fred A. (Je. 15, 1927, Austin, TX) Gifts Biblgphr., Gen. Libs., Univ. of TX, Austin, 1974–; Head, Circ. Dept., 1967–74, Educ. and Psy. Libn., 1960–67; Libn., Fulmore Jr. HS (Austin), 1953–60; Libn., Menard Sr. HS (TX), 1951–1952. **Educ.:** Southw. TX State Univ., 1948; Univ. of TX, Austin, 1949–51, BS (Educ.), 1952–53, MLS. **Orgs.:** Socty. of Univ. of TX Libns. TX Assn. of Coll. Tchrs. **Honors:** Phi Alpha Theta. **Activities:** 1, 10; 15, 22, 36; 63 **Addr.:** 2106 Airole Way, Austin, TX 78704.

Rothenberger, James (N. 12, 1935, Logansport, IN) Head, Gvt. Pubns. Dept., Lib., Univ. of CA, Riverside, 1970–; Pub. Docum. Libn., Yale Univ. Lib., 1967–70. **Educ.:** Univ. of CA, Berkeley, 1960, AB (Geo.); Univ. of OK, 1967, MLS. **Orgs.:** ALA. **Activities:** 1; 29, 39, 46; 70, 77, 92 **Addr.:** Government Publications Dept., Library, University of CA, Riverside, CA 92507.

Rothlisberg, Allen Peter (N. 15, 1941, Jamaica, NY) Dir. of Lrng. Resrcs., Northland Pioneer Coll., 1975–; Dir., Yavapai Cnty. Lib. Syst., 1968–74; Dir., Prescott Pub. Lib., 1963–68. **Educ.:** San Diego State Univ., 1959–63, AB (Liberal Arts); Our Lady of the Lake Univ., 1968–70, MS (LS). **Orgs.:** ALA. AZ LA: Pres. (1964). Cath. LA. CSLA. Lions. Kiwanis. Elks. **Honors:** AZ LA, Libn. of the Yr., 1966, 1967. **Pubns.:** *We've a Story to Tell to the Nations* (1975). **Activities:** 1; 15, 20, 32; 50, 72, 89 **Addr.:** 1417 Greer Ave., Holbrook, AZ 86025.

Rothman, John (Ap. 21, 1924, Berlin, Germany) Dir. of Resrch. and Info. Tech., NY Times Co., 1975–, Dir. of Info. Srvs., 1967–75; Ed., *NY Times Index*, 1964–67, Asst. Ed., 1950–64, Indxr., 1946–50. **Educ.:** Queens Coll., 1941–46, BA summa cum laude (Eng.); NY Univ., 1946–49, MA (Eng.); Columbia Univ., 1949–56, PhD (Compar. Lit.). **Orgs.:** ASIS. Info. Indus. Assn.: Dir. (1974–); Privacy Task Frc. Ch. (1971–5); Proprietary Rights Com. (1973–). NY Metro. Resrch. and Ref. Lib. Agency: Trustee (1975–). Copyrt. Clearance Ctr.: Adv. Bd. (1977–). U.S. Natl. Comsn. for Intl. Cncl. of Sci. Uns. Abs. Bd. (1978–); Amer. Natl. Stans. Inst. Com. Z-39: Subcom. on indexes, Ch. (1964–75). (NY St. Commissioner's Com. for Long-Range Lib. Development (1980–). **Honors:** Info. Indus. Assn., Hall of Fame, 1979. **Pubns.:** *Dramatic Criticism in The New York Times, 1851-1880* (1949); *Schiller's Dramatic Technique* (1956); "Index, Indexer, Indexing", *Encyc. of Lib. and Info. Sci.* (1972); "The New York Times Information Bank", *Spec. Libs.* (1972); Ed., *NY Times Thesaurus of Descriptors* (1968–71); Speeches. **Activities:** 12, 14-Cmrcl. publshr.; 17, 24, 30; 62, 75, 83 **Addr.:** The New York Times Co., 229 W. 43rd St., New York, NY 10036.

Rothrock, Ilse Skipsna (F. 17, 1928, Riga, Latvia) Libn., Kimbell Art Musm., 1967–; Head of Cat. Dept., TX Christ. Univ., 1955–65; Catlgr., Univ. of TX, Austin, 1951–54. **Educ.:** N. TX State Univ., 1950–51, AB (LS); Univ. of TX, Austin, 1951–54, MLS; Hunter Coll., 1965–67, MA (Anthro.). **Orgs.:** ARLIS/NA. SLA. TX Inst. of Letters. **Pubns.:** Four volumes of fiction in Latvian. **Activities:** 1, 8-Musm.; 15, 20, 39; 55 **Addr.:** Kimbell Art Museum Library, P.O. Box 9440, Ft. Worth, TX 76107.†

Rothstein, Pauline M. (Je. 24, 1944, New York, NY) Sr. Coord./Lib. Srvs., *ERIC* Clearhse. on Urban Educ., 1977–; Educ./Ref. Libn., Lehman Coll., 1969–75; Eng. Tchr., HS of Fashion Indus., 1965–68. **Educ.:** New York Univ., 1961–65, BS (Eng.); Hunter Coll., 1965–68, MA (Eng.); Pratt Inst., 1968–69, MLS; Fordham Univ., 1975–80, PhD (Educ.). **Orgs.:** ASIS. SLA: Anl. Conf. Contrib. Papers Com. (1977); Conf. session mdrtr. (1977); Educ. Div. Ch. (1979), Nom. Com. Ch. (1974), Jt. Prog. Com. (1977), Lcl. Rep. Anl. Conf. (1977). Amer. Educ. Resrch. Assn. **Pubns.:** Jt. ed., *Directory of Special Libraries of Interest to Educators* (1979); "Women: A Selected Bibliography of Books," *Bltn. of Bibl. and Mag. Notes* (Ap.–Je. 1975); "A Classification System and Procedure Manual for Cataloging Textbooks in a Univ. Lib. Curriculum Lab. Collection," *Research in Education* (S. 1975); Reg. Columnist "News from ERIC" in *Educ. Libs.* (1978–). **Activities:** 1, 12; 30, 31, 39; 62, 63, 92 **Addr.:** 350 W. 24th St., Apt. 19B, New York NY 10011.

Rothstein, Samuel (Ja. 12, 1921, Moscow, Russia) Prof., Sch. of Libnshp., Univ. of BC, 1961–, Dir., 1961–70, Actg. Univ. Libn., 1961–62, Assoc. Univ. Libn., 1959–61, Asst. Univ. Libn., 1954–59, Head, Acq. Dept., 1945–51, Ref. Libn., 1947–48. **Educ.:** Univ. of BC, 1937–39, BA (Fr., Eng.), 1939–40, MA (Fr., Eng.); Univ. of CA, 1946–47, BLS (Libnshp.); Univ. of IL, 1951–54, PhD (Libnshp.). **Orgs.:** BC LA: Pres. (1959–60); various ofcs. Pac. Northwest LA: Pres. (1963–64); various ofcs. Can. LA: Cncl. Lib. Educ. Com., Ch. AALL: Pres. (1968–69). Various orgs. Vancouver Jewish Cmnty. Ctr.: Pres. (1972–74); various ofcs. Can. Jewish Congs.: Pac. Div. (VP., 1971–76). Natl. Resrch. Cncl. of Can.: Assoc. Com. on Sci. Info. (1961–70); Adv. Bd. on Sci. and Tech. Info. (1970–74). **Honors:** BC LA, Dr. Helen Gordon Stewart Awd., 1970; York Univ., Doctor of Letters, 1971. **Pubns.:** *The Development of Reference Services* (1955); jt. Auth., *Training Professional Librarians for Western Canada* (1957); jt. Auth., *As We Remember It* (1970); Jt. Auth., *The University–The Library* (1972); various bk. chaps., articles, bk. reviews, encyc. contrib. **Activities:** 1; 15, 26, 39; 50, 55, 74 **Addr.:** School of Librarianship, University of BC, 831–1956 Main Mall, Vancouver, BC V6T 1W5 Canada.

Roulston, William Wray (Mr. 7, 1946, Sudbury, ON) Bus. Libn., Kitchener Pub. Lib., 1981–; Ind. Rel. Libn., ON Mnstry. of Labour Resrch. Lib., 1981–; Libn., Natl. Ofc. for Can., Untd. Steelworkers of Amer., 1981–; Libn., Grt. Lakes/Seaway Task Force, ON Mnstry. of Transp. and Comm. 1980–81; Chief Libn., Newman Indus. Rel. Lib., Ctr. for Indus. Rel., Univ. of Toronto, 1977–80; Asst. Head, Acq. Sect., Serials Dept., John P. Robarts Resrch. Lib., Univ. of Toronto, 1974–77; Head, Adult, Info. Srvs., City of Brampton Pub. Lib. and Art Gallery, 1971–74; Asst. Libn., Harbord Collegiate Inst., 1970–71. **Educ.:** Univ. of Toronto, 1964–68, BA (Hist.), 1969–70, BLS, 1970–74, MLS, 1968–69, (Hist., Sch. Libnshp.). **Orgs.:** Can. LA: Mem. Com. (1977–78). ON LA. SLA. Com. of Indus. Rel. Libns.: Subj. Headings Com. (1977–80). Kinsmen Club of Erin Mills. Soc. Plng. Cncl. of Peel: Hlth. Issues Com. (1980–). **Pubns.:** Various papers. **Activities:** 1, 12; 15, 30, 41; 59, 62, 83 **Addr.:** 2928 Council Ring Rd., Mississauga, ON L5L 1L2 Canada.

Rounds, Joseph B. (My. 24, 1909, Knightstown, IN) Secy., Grosvenor Socty. (Frnds. of Buffalo-Erie Cnty. Pub. Lib.), 1976–, and Dir. Emeritus, Buffalo-Erie Cnty. Pub. Lib., 1978–; Lectr. (Info. and Lib. Std.), SUNY Buffalo, 1976–78; Dir., Buffalo-Erie Cnty. Pub. Lib., 1954–75; Dir., Erie Cnty. Pub. Lib., 1947–54; Dir., Grosvenor Lib., 1941–1947; Assoc. Prof. and Dir., Lib. Sch., Univ. of Buffalo, 1940–45; Consult., ILO Lib. (Geneva, Switzerland), 1938–39; Libn., Earlham Coll., 1931–36; others. **Educ.:** Earlham Coll., 1926–30, AB; Univ. of MI, 1930–31, AB (LS), 1937–38, MA (LS). **Orgs.:** NY State Regents Adv. Cncl. on Libs. ALA. NY LA. Buffalo and Erie Cnty. Hist. Socty. Buffalo Socty. of Nat. Scis. Saturn Club. **Honors:** Rockefeller Fndn. Flwshp. (Geneva), 1938–39; Buffalo Evening News Outstan. Citizen Awd., 1954. **Pubns.:** *Research Facilities of the International Labor Office* (1939); various articles. **Activities:** 9, 11; 17, 24, 26 **Addr.:** 140 North St., Buffalo, NY 14201.

Roundtree, Elizabeth S. (Jl. 27, 1925, Plaquemine, LA) Coord., Tech. Srvs., LA State Lib., 1969–, Asst. Coord., Tech. Srvs., 1966–69, Head Catlgr., 1963–66, Asst. Catlgr., 1960–63, Asst. Serials Libn., 1953–58, Gift and Exch. Libn., 1953, Catlgr. 1951–53, Acq., 1947–51. **Educ.:** LA State Univ., 1941–44, BS (Hist.), 1945–46, BSLS. **Orgs.:** SWLA. ALA: RTSD, Esther Piercy Awd. Jury (1981–82), Margaret Mann Cit. Com. (1972–73), Tech. Srv. Dirs. of Prcs. Ctrs. Discuss. Grp. (Ch., 1970, 1981); GODORT, Name Athrty. Coop. Proj. (Ch., 1980–81). LA LA: LA Numerical Regis. Com. (1968–); LA Un. Cat. Com. (Ch., 1980–). Baton Rouge Lib. Club. **Pubns.:** "One Year Later," LA LA *Bltn.* (Spr. 1970). **Activities:** 13; 20, 29, 46; 56, 69, 86 **Addr.:** 1852 Pollard Pkwy., Baton Rouge, LA 70808.

Rountree, Elizabeth Coffee (Jl. 13, 1937, Alto, GA) Asst. City Libn., New Orleans Pub. Lib., 1977–; Dir., Brunswick-Glynn Cnty. Reg. Lib., 1972–77; Dir., N.E. GA Reg. Lib., 1965–72; Dir., Piedmont Coll. Lib., 1959–65. **Educ.:** Piedmont Coll., 1955–58, AB (Eng.); Univ. of IL, 1958–59, MA (LS) Emory Univ., 1970–71, Dip. Advnc. Std. (Libnshp.). **Orgs.:** ALA. SWLA. LA LA. Grt. New Orleans Lib. Club. **Honors:** Beta Phi Mu. **Pubns.:** "New Orleans Public Library Survey," *Amer. Libs.* (S. 1979). **Activities:** 9; 17, 46 **Addr.:** New Orleans Public Library, 219 Loyola St., New Orleans, LA 70140.

Rouse, Charlie Lou (S. 9, 1924, Boynton, OK) Libn., Stillwater Mid. Sch., 1973–; Lib. Media Wkshp. Dir., Phillips Univ.,

Special Subjects/Services: 50. Adult educ.; 51. Advert./Mktg.; 52. Aerosp.; 53. Agric.; 54. Area std.; 55. Arts/Hum.; 56. Autom.; 57. Bibl./Prtg.; 58. Bio. sci.; 59. Bus./Fin.; 60. Chem.; 61. Copyrt.; 62. Documtn.; 63. Educ.; 64. Engin.; 65. Env.; 66. Eth. grps.; 67. Film; 68. Food/Nutr.; 69. Geneal.; 70. Geo.; 71. Geol.; 72. Handcpd.; 73. Hist.; 74. Int. frdm.; 75. Info. sci.; 76. Insr.; 77. Law; 78. Legis.; 79. Math./Comp. sci.; 80. Med.; 81. Metals; 82. Nat. resrcs.; 83. Newsp.; 84. Nuc. sci.; 85. Oral hist.; 86. Petr./Energy; 87. Pharm.; 88. Phys./Astr./Math.; 89. Readg.; 90. Relig.; 91. Sci./Tech.; 92. Soc. sci.; 93. Telecom.; 94. Transp.; 95. (other).

1978; Libn., Stillwater HS, 1970–73; Asst. Circ. Libn., Baylor Univ., 1960–63; Supvsr. of Libs., Connally HS, Lake Air and Elm Mott Elem. Schs., 1952–54; Asst. Ref. Libn., Univ. of OK Lib., 1951–52; Eng. Tchr., Northeast. OK State Univ. 1949–51; Libn. and Eng. Tchr., Moore HS, 1946–47. **Educ.:** E. Ctrl. OK State Univ., 1942–45, BA (Eng., Sp.); Univ. of OK, 1945–46, LS, 1947–48, MEd. **Orgs.:** ALA: LAMA/Lib. Org. Mgt. Sect., Com. on Stats. for Sch. Libs. (1975–79); Bldgs. and Equip. Sect., Sch. Lib. Facilities Com. (1979–81), AASL: Del. to Afflt. Asm. (1976–77, 1977–78). OK LA: Awds. Com. (1976–77). OK Assn. of Sch. Lib. Media Specs.: Constn. and Bylaws Com. (1975–76); Com. on Ofcs. Handbk. (Vice Ch./Ch., 1977–78). FLA. Various other orgs. Natl. Educ. Assn. OK Educ. Assn.: Stillwater Educ. Assn. AAUW. **Honors:** Stillwater Mid. Sch., Tchr. of the Yr., 1978; Gvr. of the State of OK, Ambassador of Goodwill, O. 1979; Kappa Delta Pi, 1948–; Pi Kappa Delta, 1943–. **Pubns.:** "School Library Media News," *OK Libn.* (1977–78). **Activities:** 10; 17, 31, 32; 63, 78 **Addr.:** 2623 Black Oak Dr., Stillwater, OK 74074.

Rouse, David A. (N. 8, 1946, Lafayette, IN) Head, Bus. Info. Ctr., Chicago Pub. Lib., 1976–. **Educ.:** Purdue Univ., 1964–68, BS (Psy.); IN Univ., 1973, MLS. **Orgs.:** SLA: IL Chap., Prog. Com. (1980–81). Chicago Lib. Club. **Honors:** Frnds. of the Chicago Pub. Lib., Outstan. Srv. Awd., 1979; Beta Phi Mu. **Activities:** 9, 12; 15, 31, 39; 51, 59 **Addr.:** 1272 W. Victoria, Chicago, IL 60660.

Rouse, Roscoe, Jr. (N. 26, 1919, Valdosta, GA) Univ. Libn., OK State Univ., 1967–, Univ. Libn. and Head, Dept. of LS, 1967–74; Dir. of Libs., SUNY, Stony Brook, 1963–67; Univ. Libn. and Ch., Dept. of LS, Baylor Univ., 1953–63; Actg. Libn., Northeast. State Coll., 1948–51, Asst. Libn., 1948–49. **Educ.:** Univ. of OK, 1945–48, BA (LS), 1951–52, MA (Eng. Lit.); Univ. of MI, 1953–58, MA (LS), 1956–62, PhD (LS), Rutgers Univ., Sem. for Lib. Admins., Spr. 1956, Cert. **Orgs.:** ALA: Cncl. (1971–72, 1976–80), Cncl. Budget and Plng. Asm. (1978–79), Cncl. Com. on Coms. (1979–80); ACRL/Univ. Libs. Sect., Exec. Com. (Ch., 1969–70); LAMA/Exec. Bd. (1972–74)/Lib. Org. and Mgt. Sect. (Ch., 1973–75), Nom. Com. (Ch., 1978–79); various coms. (1976–81). IFLA: Various coms. (1976–80). SWLA: Various coms., ofcs. (1958–80). OK LA: Various coms., ofcs. (1969–80). Stillwater Rotary Club. Univ. of MI Sch. of LS Alum. Socty: Pres. (1979–80). Archons of Colophon. **Honors:** Beta Phi Mu, 1958; ALA, Natl. Lib. Week Awd., 1970; OK LA, Disting. Srv. Awd., 1979. **Pubns.:** *Organization Charts of Selected Libraries* (1973); *A History of the Baylor University Library* (1962); "International Report: Meeting in a Communist State," *Amer. Libs.* (1978); "The ALA Councilor Reports," *OK Libn.* (1976–80); "The University Library," *The Legal Aspects of Oklahoma Higher Education* (1978); various articles, reviews and edshps. (1951–). **Activities:** 1; 17, 19, 24; 54, 55 **Addr.:** Oklahoma State University Library, Stillwater, OK 74078.

Rouse Sandra H. (S. 29, 1947, Newport, RI) Sr. Resrch. Sci., GA Inst. of Tech., 1981–; Info. Sci., Univ. of IL, 1974–81; Visit. Sr. Resrchr., Delft Univ. of Tech., The Netherlands, 1979–80. **Educ.:** RI Coll., 1965–69, BA (Eng., Soc. Sci.); Simmons Coll., 1970–71, MA (Eng.); 1971–73, MS (LS). **Orgs.:** ASIS: Lib. Autom and Networks Spec. Interest Grp. Nsltr. Ed. (1975–77); Comp. Retrieval Srvs. Spec. Int. Grp. Nsltr. Ed. (1974–76). **Pubns.:** Jt. auth., *The Management of Library Networks* (1980); Jt. auth., *Computer Readable Bibliographic Data Bases: A Directory and Data Sourcebook* (1976); "Computer-Based Manuals for Procedural Information," *IEEE Trans. on Systems, Man, and Cybernetics* (Ag. 1980); Various other articles, papers, and rpts. **Activities:** 14-Univ. Resrch. Lab.; 41; 56, 75, 95-Info. Syst. Design. **Addr.:** Center for Man–Machine Systems Research, School of Industrial and Systems Engineering, Georgia Institute of Technology, Atlanta, GA 30332.

Rousseau, Denis (F. 4, 1944, St-Narcisse, PQ) Docmlst., Bur. de Surveillance du Cin., 1979–; Docmlst., Socty. Radio-Can., 1977–79; Pubcty. Dir., ASTED, Inc., 1974–76; Dir., Lib. Sch. Lib., Univ. de Montreal, 1969–74. **Educ.:** Univ. of Montreal, 1968, BA (Libnshp.), 1964, BA (Phil.); Ecole Vincent D'Indy, 1971, Dip. (Msc.); Univ. of Montreal, 1975, MALS. **Orgs.:** ASTED. Corp. des Bibtcrs. Prof. du PQ. **Pubns.:** Contrib., *Bibliotheque et Cultore Quebecoise; Melanges Offerts à Edmond Desrochers, S.J.* (1977); "Documentation et Bibliotheques à Interroge SES Lecteurs," *Documtn. et Bibs.* (Jl. 1976). **Activities:** 12; 17, 37, 41 **Addr.:** Bureau de Surveillance du Cinema, 360, Rue McGill, Montreal, PQ Canada.

Rousseau, Yvelte Henry (F. 12, 1945, Paris, France) Tchr., Univ. de Montreal, 1979–; Ingénieur Docmlst., C.N.R.S. (France), 1969–78. **Educ.:** Univ. de Paris, Dip. (Math.), 1968–69, Dip. (Comp. Sci.), 1969–70, Dip. (Comp. Sci.). Féd. de Info. du PQ. **Pubns.:** *Elaboration d'un Thésaurus Français d'Informatique* (1976); *Rapport sur la Documentation en Suéde* (1978); *PASCAL-VIRA, Manuel d'Utilisation* (1977). **Activities:** 11, 12; 30, 34, 39; 56, 57, 75 **Addr.:** Université de Montréal, Ecole de Bibliothéconomie, C.P. 6128, Montreal, PQ H3C 3J7 Canada.

Rovelstad, Howard (Mr. 5, 1913, Elgin, IL) Dir. of Lib. Emeritus, Univ. of MD, 1975–; Lib. Consult., 1960–; Dir. of Libs. and Prof. of LS, Univ. of MD, 1946–75, Ref. and Loan Libn., 1942–43, Acq. Libn., 1940–42. **Educ.:** Univ. of IL, 1932–36, BA (Eng.), 1936–37, MA (Eng.); Columbia Univ., 1939–40, BSLS. **Orgs.:** ALA: Cncl. (1961–65); Constn. and Bylaws Com. (Ch., 1961–65); Bldgs. Com. (Ch., 1954–56); ACRL/Lib. Bldgs. Com. (Ch., 1952). Mid. Atl. Reg. Lib. Conf. MD LA. DC LA. **Pubns.:** Jt. ed., *Guidelines for Library Planners* (1960); ed., *The University and the Wise Mann* (1959); "College and University Library Buildings in Contemporary Library Design," *Frontiers in Libnshp.* (1958); various jnl. articles. **Activities:** 1; 17, 19, 24; 63, 91, 93 **Addr.:** 11 Banbury Rd., Gibson Island, MD 21056.

Rovelstad, Mathilde V. (Ag. 12, 1920, Kempten, Germany) Prof. of LS, Cath. Univ. of Amer., 1960–; Sch. Libn., Gonzaga HS, 1959; Sch. Libn., Amer. Dependent Sch., Japan, 1953–56; Catlgr., Mt. St. Mary's Coll., 1953. **Educ.:** Tuebingen Univ., Germany, 1953, PhD (Mod. Lang. and LS); Cath. Univ. of Amer., 1960, MSLS. **Orgs.:** ALA: Intl. Rel. Com. (1978–79). AALS. IFLA: Stdg. Adv. Com. for Lib. Schs. **Honors:** Beta Phi Mu, 1960. **Pubns.:** *Bibliotheken in den Vereinigten Staaten, Muenchen, Verlag Dokumentation* (1974); various articles, transls., reviews. **Activities:** 11; 26 **Addr.:** 11 Banbury Rd., Gibson Island, MD 21056.

Rovira, Anna (S. 25, 1920, Montreal, PQ) Consult., Dollard-Des-Ormeaux/Pierrefonds, 1980–; Consult., Montreal N. Pub. Lib., 1968–73; Dir., Bib. Mncpl. LaSalle, 1960–. **Educ.:** Ecole des Beaux-Arts de Montreal, 1939–44; Univ. of Ottawa, 1964–66, Cert.; Sheffield Univ., 1966, Cert.; Coll. Ste-Marie, 1966–68 (Admin.). **Orgs.:** Natl. Lib. Adv. Bd. (1981–84). Assn. des Bibtcrs. du PQ: Pres. (1971, 1978–79). Pub. de L'Ile de Montreal: VP (1978–). Assn. Can. Des Bibtcrs. de Lang. Fr.: Dir. (1970–72) Can. LA: Rep. to Assn. des Bibtcrs. du PQ (1978–79). Various other orgs. Socty. Hist. Cavelier de LaSalle. **Pubns.:** "Pour l'Autonomie des Bibliothèques Publiques," *La Revue de L'Assn. Bibtcrs. PQ* (1971); "Automatisation de la Bibliothèque de Montreal-Nord," *Bltn. de L'Assn. Can. Bibtcrs.* (1970). **Activities:** 9; 17, 19, 24 **Addr.:** 2332 Menard St., LaSalle, PQ H8N 1J5 Canada.

Rovira, Carmen (Je. 13, 1919, Santiago de Cuba, Oriente, Cuba). Chief, Lib. and Arch. Dev. Prog., Org. of Amer. States, 1978–, Sr. Spec., 1971–78, Libn. Spec., 1960–71; Chief Libn., Cath. Univ. of St. Tomás de Villanueva, Havana, 1953–60. **Educ.:** Univ. of Havana, 1938–41, PhD (Art Hist.), School of Libnshp., 1950–52, Bibtcr. Cath. Univ. of Amer., 1962–71, MSLS. **Orgs.:** ALA: Lib. Educ. Div., Equivalences and Reciprocity Com. (1968–71); Spec. Com. on Coop. with Latin Amer. Catlgrs. and Clasfrs. (1954–56). Colegio Nacional de Bibtcrs. Univ.: Exec. Com. (1955–59). SALALM: Com. on Dues and Fees (1977–79). **Pubns.:** *Lista de encabezamientos de materia para bibliotecas* (1967); *Los epígrafes en el catálogo diccionario* (1966); "Spanish Language Cataloging," Lib. Rescrs. and Tech. Srvs. (Win. 1958); various articles and reviews in *Cuba Bibliotecológica* (1953–59). **Activities:** 4; 17, 24, 41; 54, 57, 75 **Addr.:** 3001 Veazey Terr., N.W., Washington, DC 20008.

Rovirosa, Dolores Fermina (D. 6, 1926, Matanzas, Cuba) Libn., Latin Cham. of Cmrce., Miami, 1981–; Clerk of Cts., Admin. Judge, Cvl. Div., Cnty. Ct., 1977–; Instr., Miami Dade Cmnty. Coll., 1974–75; Libn., Lourdes Acad., 1971–75; Cat. Libn., Univ. of TX, 1964–70; Instr., South. IL Univ., 1963–64; Asst. Cat. Libn., Univ. of NV, 1962–63; Prof. of Cat., Univ. of Havana, 1961; Head, Cat. Dept., Natl. Lib., Havana, 1959–61; various prof. positions in Cuba. **Educ.:** Univ. of Havana, 1945–49, PhD (Hist.), 1950–51, MLS; Univ. of Miami, 1971–75, MEd (Lib., AV); FL Tchr. Cert., Media spec. **Orgs.:** ALA. Cuban Women Club. AAUW. **Pubns.:** *Jose Marti: Reference Sources. Jose Marti: Fuentes para su estudio* (1981); *Bibliografía Martiana del Exilio, 1959–1981* (1981); *Ana Rosa Nuñez: Vida y obra* (1981); *Calixto García; A Tentative Bibliography. Calixto García; Ensayo de una bibliografía* (1979); *Catalogacion y clasificacion simplificada para bibliotecas pequeñas* (1960); *Las enciclopedias como instrumentos de consulta y referencia* (1956); various articles (1955–72). **Activities:** 1, 9; 17, 20, 39; 57, 77, 85 **Addr.:** 2301 S.W. 24 Terr., Apt. 1, Miami, FL 33145.

Rowe, Dorothy B. (Mr. 10, 1939, Lafayette, IN) Head Libn., Ctrl. DuPage Hosp., 1974–; Head, Southampton Free Lib., 1970–73; Cat. Libn., NJ State Lib., 1968–69; Ref. Libn., East. MI Univ., 1967–68; Cat. Libn., Willow Run Pub. Lib., 1966–67; Cat., Univ. of MI, 1964–65; Serials Libn., Purdue Univ., 1962–64. **Educ.:** Purdue Univ., 1957–61, BS (Eng.); Univ. of MI, 1966–66, AMLS; Med. LA: 1976, Cert. **Orgs.:** ALA. Med. LA. Hlth. Sci. Libns. IL.: Pres. Elec. (1981). DuPage Libns. Assn. Various orgs. Maplebrook Homeowners Assn.: Mem. Com. (Asst. Coord., 1980). Fox Valley Hlth. Sci. Libs.: VP. (1975–77). Rush Afflts. Info. Netwk.: Secty. **Pubns.:** "Open Medical Library," *Hosp.* (D. 16, 1980); "$50,000 Grant for the Central DuPage Hospital Library," *Hosp. Libs.* (Sum. 1979). **Activities:** 12; 17, 24, 44; 80 **Addr.:** Central DuPage Hospital Medical Library, Winfield, IL 60190.

Rowe, Gladys Elaine (N. 9, 1934, Merton, WI) Ref. Libn., Sandia Natl. Labs., 1966–; Libn., North. IL Gas Co., 1965–66; Libn., Lockheed Aircraft Intl., 1962–65; Catlgr., Aerojet–Gen. Corp., 1962; Assoc. Libn., Labs. for Appld. Sci., Univ. of Chicago, 1960–62; Asst. Libn., Fld. Enterprises Educ. Corp., 1957–60. **Educ.:** Coll. of St. Catherine, St. Paul, MN, 1952–56, BA (Eng., Fr.); Univ. of Chicago, 1956–60, MA (LS). **Orgs.:** SLA. **Honors:** Phi Beta Kappa, 1956; Beta Phi Mu, 1960. **Pubns.:** "Thinking Small in a Big Way," *Coll. & Resrch. Libs.* (N. 1979). **Activities:** 12; 15, 39, 49-Online srch.; 82, 84, 86 **Addr.:** Sandia National Laboratories Technical Library Div. 3144, Albuquerque, NM 87185.

Rowe, Harry M., Jr. (O. 15, 1921, Vallejo, CA) Lib. Consult., 1979–; Cnty. Libn., Orange Cnty. (CA) Lib., 1968–79; City Libn., Fullerton (CA) Pub. Lib., 1957–68; Cnty. Libn., Solano Cnty. (CA) Lib., 1952–57; Dist. Libn., Coalinga (CA) Dist. Lib., 1949–52; Libn., Coalinga HS and Jr. Coll., 1948–49; Ref. Libn., Coalinga Dist. Lib., 1947–48; various positions coll. and univ. lectr., 1949–78. **Educ.:** Univ. of CA, Berkeley, 1940–46, BA (Hist.), 1946–47, MLS, 1952–55 (LS). **Orgs.:** ALA: Cncl. (1972–76); various coms. CA LA: Pres. (1966); Yosemite Dist. (Pres., 1952); Golden Gate Dist. (Pres., 1954); South. Dist. (Pres., 1962). Orange Cnty. LA: Pres. (1975–76). Pub. Lib. Admins. of Orange Cnty.: Pres. (1959, 1969). Various other orgs., ofcs. Kiwanis. Solano Cnty. Hist. Socty.: Chrt. Pres. (1955). Orange Cnty. Hist. Comsn.: Secy. (1973–79). **Honors:** Parent-Tchr. Assn., CA Cncl., Life Mem., 1968. **Pubns.:** *California, Here We Came* (1965); various articles in *CA Libn.* **Activities:** 9, 11; 17, 26; 74 **Addr.:** 5009 Woodman Ave. #112, Sherman Oaks, CA 91423.

Rowe, Judith S. Assoc. Dir., Acad. Data and Prog. Srvs., Princeton Univ. Comp. Ctr., 1979–, Assoc. Dir., Soc. Sci. User Srvs., 1971–79; Mgr., Princeton-Rutgers Census Data Proj., 1971–; Asst. Dir, Princeton Univ. Ofc. for Srvy. Resrch. and Stats. Std., 1966–71; Freelnce. Resrch. Consult., 1956–66; Fld. Dir., A. S. Bennett-Cy Chaikin, Inc., 1953–56. **Educ.:** Drew Univ., 1948–51, BA, magna cum laude; Yale Univ., 1951–53, MA, ABD. **Orgs.:** ALA: RTSD/CCRC, Subcom. on Cat. of Machine-Readable Data Files (1970–); RASD/RTSD/ASCLA Pub. Docum. Com., Subcom. on Census Data (Ch., 1973–76); GODORT, Ad Hoc Task Frc. on Machine-Readable Data Files, Coord. (1973–77), Asst. Coord. (1977–79), Strg. Com. (1973–77). Intl. Assn. for Soc. Sci. Info. Srv. and Tech.: U.S. Secy. (1974–); Admin. Com. (1974–); Pre-conf. Wkshp. (Instr., 1980). SLA. ASIS. Various other orgs. Intl. Srvy. LA: Adv. Cncl. (Ch., 1978–); Princeton Univ. Rep. (1977–). Com. of Prof. Assns. for Fed. Stats. Assn. of Pub. Data Users: Organizing Com.; Acq. Com., Ch.; Bd. (1978–); Conf. Mdrtr. (1979); Pres. (1981–82). Amer. Assn. of Pub. Opinion Resrch. Various other orgs. **Pubns.:** "Machine-Readable Data Files of Government Publications," *Gvt. Pubns. Review* (1980); jt. auth., "A Model Bibliographic Information System for Machine-Readable Data Files in the Humanities and Social Sciences," *Data Bases in the Humanities and Social Sciences* (1980); "Privacy Legislation: Implications for Archives," *Archivists and Machine-Readable Records* (1979); "Publicly Available Machine-Readable Data Files," *Popltn. Index* (O. 1979); jt. auth., "Using Secondary Analysis for Quasi-experimental Research," *Soc. Sci. Info.* (1979); various articles, edshps. positions, confs., sps.

Rowe, Kenneth E. (Ap. 15, 1937, Coaldale, PA) Meth. Resrch. Libn., Drew Univ., 1970–. **Educ.:** Drew Univ., 1955–59, AB (Hist.); Yale Univ., 1959–62, BD (Relig.); Drew Univ., 1966–69, PhD (Church Hist.); Rutgers Univ., 1969–70, MLS. **Orgs.:** ATLA: Pubns. Com. (1971–); ATLA Mono. Series Ed. (1972–); ATLA Bibl. Series Ed. (1974–); Bd. of Dirs. (1977–80). Meth. Libns. Flwshp.: Pres. (1977–79). **Honors:** Assn. of Theo. Schs. in the U.S. and Can., Lib. Staff Dev., 1977. **Pubns.:** *Methodist Union Catalog* (1975–). **Activities:** 1, 2; 45; 90 **Addr.:** Rose Memorial Library, Drew University, Madison, NJ 07940.

Rowe, Mary Lou (Ag. 12, 1933, Kempner, TX) City Libn., Beverly Hills Pub. Lib., 1977–; Asst. City Libn., Anaheim Pub. Lib., 1963–77; Docum. Libn., Hughes Aircraft, 1959–63; Info. Spec., Sylvania Electronics, 1958–59; Tech. Libn., Ampex Corp., 1957–58, Docum. Resrch. Inst., 1956–57, Elem. Sch. Libn., Dallas Indp. Sch. Dist., 1953–56. **Educ.:** N. TX State Univ., 1950–53, BA (LS); Univ. of South. CA, 1962–63, MLS. **Orgs.:** ALA. CA LA: Anl. Conf. Ch. (1972); Forums Com. (Ch., 1978); Cnclr. (1974–78); Lib. Dev. and Awds. Com. (Ch., 1973); Grt. Los Angeles Chap. (Pres., 1974–75). Libns. Sodalitas: Bd. (1977–81). **Activities:** 9; 17, 35 **Addr.:** 5009 Woodman Ave. #112, Sherman Oaks, CA 91423.

Rowell, John A. (S. 29, 1929, Grand Rapids, MI) Prof. and Dir., Sch. Lib. and Pub. Progs., Case West. Rsv. Univ., 1965–State Dir., Sch. Libs., PA Dept. of Pub. Instr., 1960–65; State Sch. Lib. Consult., MI State Lib., 1958–60; various consults. **Educ.:** Harvard Univ., 1947–51, AB; Univ. of Denver, 1954, MS (LS). **Orgs.:** ALA: AASL (Pres., 1969–70). Amer. Assn. of Sch. Lib. Supervsrs. (Pres., 1965–66). Natl. Educ. Assn. Women's Natl. Book Assn. **Honors:** Univ. of Denver, Hon. LL.D., 1962; PA LA, Awd. of Merit, 1966; Amer. Socty. of Pub. Admins., Man of Year (PA Chap.), 1965; Bur. Ind. Pubs. and Distributors, Awd., 1963; various other awds. **Pubns.:** *Glad Eden: The Organization and Operation of Educational Media Selection Centers* (1971); Ed., *Sch. Libs.;* various fiction and screenplays. **Activities:** 10, 11; 21, 26, 48; 63, 67, 89 **Addr.:** 19121 S. Woodland Rd., Shaker Heights, OH 44122.

PROFESSIONAL ACTIVITIES: Institutions: 1. Acad. lib.; 2. Arch.; 3. Assn.; 4. Fed./Gvt. lib.; 5. Inst. lib.; 6. Mfr./Suppl.; 7. Milit. lib.; 8. Musm.; 9. Pub. lib.; 10. Sch. lib.; 11. Sch. of lib. sci.; 12. Spec. lib.; 13. State lib.; 14. (other). **Functions/Activities:** 15. Acq./Col. dev.; 16. Adult srvs.; 17. Admin.; 18. Apprais.; 19. Archit./Bldgs.; 20. Cat./Class.; 21. Chld. srvs.; 22. Circ.; 23. Cons./Pres.; 24. Consult.; 25. Cont. ed.; 26. Educ. lib. sci.; 27. Ext. srvs.; 28. Fund/Grants; 29. Gvt. pubs.; 30. Indx./Abs.; 31. Instr. lib. use; 32. Media srvs.; 33. Micro.; 34. Netwks./Coop.; 35. Persnl.; 36. PR; 37. Publshg.; 38. Recs. mgt.; 39. Ref. srvs.; 40. Repro.; 41. Resrch.; 42. Review.; 43. Secur.; 44. Serials; 45. Spec. col.; 46. Tech. srvs.; 47. Trustees/Bds.; 48. YA srvs.; 49. (other).

Rowell, Margaret Kenny (Je. 11, 1906, Fall River, MA) Retired, 1976–; Chief Libn., Prof., Grad. Sch. and Univ. Ctr., CUNY, 1965–76; Chief Cat. Libn., Assoc. Prof., Brooklyn Coll., 1942–64; Cat. Libn., Hunter Coll., 1937–42. **Educ.:** Brown Univ., 1923–27, AB (Eng. Lit.); Boston Univ., 1932–33, MEd (Educ., Eng.); Columbia Univ., 1936–37, BLS, high hons. (Cat.). **Orgs.:** ASIS. NY Tech. Srvs. Libns. NY Lib. Club. LA CUNY: Secy. (1938–41); Pres. (1948–49). **Honors:** Beta Phi Mu, 1954. **Pubns.:** Ed., cmplr., *Union List of Periodicals in the Libraries of the City University of New York* (1966, 1968); "College Library" in "Technical Services Division in Libraries: A Symposium," *Coll. & Resrch. Libs.* (Ja. 1949); "The Library Participates in Faculty Day," *C&RL* (1954); "Case Studies: A Large Research Library," *Catalog Use Study* (1958). **Activities:** 1; 17, 20, 44 **Addr.:** 67–38 108th St., Forest Hills, NY 11375.

Rowland, Arthur Ray (Ja. 6, 1930, Hampton, GA) Libn., Augusta Coll., 1961–, Prof., 1976–; Lectr., Lib. Educ., Univ. of GA, 1962–68; Assoc. Prof., Augusta Coll., 1961–76; Libn., Jacksonville Univ., 1958–61; Head, Circ. Dept., Auburn Univ., 1956–58; Libn., Armstrong Coll., 1954–56; Circ. Libn., GA State Coll., 1952–54. **Educ.:** Mercer Univ., 1946–51, AB (Hist.); Emory Univ., 1951–52, MLn (LS). **Orgs.:** ALA: ACRL; RTSD; RASD. GA LA: Sec. VP (1965–67, 1971–73); First VP (1973–75); Pres. (1975–77); Budget Com. (Ch., 1977–79); Adv. to Pres. (1979–). Gvr. Conf. on GA Libs. and Info. Srvs.: Ch. (1977). WHCOLIS: Del. (1979). Various assns., ofcs. and consults. Richmond Cnty. Hist. Socty.: Pres. (1967–69); Cur. (1964–); GA Hist. Socty. GA Bapt. Hist. Socty. GA Trust for Hist. Prsrvn. **Pubns.:** Jt. auth., *A Bibliography of the Writing on Georgia History 1900–1970* (1978); *The Librarian and Reference Service* (1977); *The Catalog and Cataloging* (1969); *CSRA Library Association Union List of Serials* (1967); *A Bibliography of the Writings on Georgia History* (1966); various mono., articles in LS, **Activities:** 1; 17 **Addr.:** 1339 Winter St., Augusta, GA 30904.

Rowland, Eileen (O. 27, 1928, NY, NY) Chief Libn., John Jay Coll. of Criminal Justice, 1975–; Head, Tech. Srvs., 1971–75; Asst. Supt, Acq., Queens Borough Pub. Lib., 1968–71, other Tech. Srvs. positions, 1966–68. **Educ.:** Queens Coll., City Univ. of NY, 1963, BA (Hist.); Columbia Univ., 1966, MS (LS); New Sch. for Soc. Resrch., 1975, MA (Lib. Stds.); NY Univ., 1981, MA (Hist.). NY Univ., Prof. Arch. Cert., 1981. **Orgs.:** ALA. NY LA. Metro. Ref. and Resrch. Libs.: Tech Srvs. Com. (1978–), Archvsts. RT. Other orgs. **Activities:** 1, 2; 15, 17, 45; 77 **Addr.:** John Jay College of Criminal Justice Library, 445 W. 59th St., New York, NY 10019.

Roxas, Savina A. (N. 3, 1916, New York, NY) Consult., Self-Empl., 1975–; Prof., LS Dept., Clarion State Coll., 1971–74; Instr. and Tchg. Fellow, Univ. of Pittsburgh, 1964–70; Catlgr., Duquesne Univ., 1962–64; Ref. Libn., Carnegie Tech., 1960–62. **Educ.:** Duquesne Univ., 1957, BA (Psy., Eng. Lit.); Carnegie Tech, 1960, MLS; Univ. of Pittsburgh, 1970, PhD (Lib. and Info. Sci.). **Orgs.:** ALA: Com. on Equivalency and Reciprocity of Qualifications (1968–70); Intl. RT (Secy.-Treas., 1968–70). PA LA. AAUP. Pittsburgh Bibliophiles. Women's Assn. of Pittsburgh Symph. Socty. **Honors:** Psi-Chi; Sigma-Tau-Delta; Beta Phi Mu. **Pubns.:** *Library Education in Italy; an Historical Survey* (1971); "Bibliographical Societies," *Encyc. of Lib. and Info. Sci.;* "The London Bibliographical Society," "Thomas Franklin Currier," *Encyc. of Lib. and Info. Sci.;* "Librarians–Italian Style," *Lib. Review* (Win. 1976–77); various articles. **Activities:** 1, 11; 20, 24, 26, 54, 55, 85 **Addr.:** 265 Sleepy Hollow Rd., Pittsburgh, PA 15216.

Roy, Donald Edward (D. 22, 1932, Omaha, NE) Dir. of Lib., NY Med. Coll., 1972–; Libn., Westchester Acad. of Med., 1964–72; Libn., Mercy Hosp. of Pittsburgh, 1960–64; Catlgr., Falk Lib., Univ. of Pittsburgh, 1959–60. **Educ.:** Creighton Univ., 1949–53, BS (Eng.); Carnegie Inst. of Tech. 1955–56, MS (LS). **Orgs.:** Med. LA: NY Reg. Grp., Exec. Bd. and Treas. (1968–71); Pittsburgh Reg. Grp. Ch. (1963). SLA. Hlth Info. Libs. of Westchester: Fndr. and Ch., (1966–1970); Ed., Un. List; Exec. Bd., (1974–). NY Acad. of Scis. Reg. Med. Lib.–Natl. Lib. of Med.–Reg. II-NY: Adv. and Plng. Com., (1974–); Nom. Com. (1981–). **Pubns.:** "Books for the Hospital Emergency Service," *Bltn. of the Med. LA* (1966); "Westchester Medical Center Library," *Westchester Med. Bltn.,* (1979). **Activities:** 1, 12; 17, 23, 45; 65, 80, 91 **Addr.:** Edgewood, 35 Di Rubbo Dr., Peekskill, NY 10566.

Roy, E. Irene (F. 21, 1926, Hull, PQ) Retired, 1982–; Chief Libn., Law Reform Comsn. of Can., 1972–81; Chief Libn., Pub. Srv. Staff Rel., Bd. of Can., 1967–71; Chief Libn., Judge Advocate Gen. Natl. Defence, Ottawa, 1956–67. **Educ.:** Univ. d'Ottawa, 1956–61, Cert. (LS), 1956–67, Inc. **Orgs.:** Can. ALL. Can. LA: Can. Assn. of Spec. Libs. and Info. Srvs. **Activities:** 4; 77 **Addr.:** Law Reform Commission of Canada, 130 Albert St., Rm. 809, Varette Bldg., Ottawa, K1A 0L6 Canada.

Roy, Jean-Luc (O. 7, 1931, Lac-Mégantie, PQ) Bibtcr., Ctr. D'Animation, de Dév. et de Resrch. en Educ., 1971–. **Educ.:** Univ. de Montréal, 1964–65, BLS; Univ. d'Ottawa, 1969–70. **Orgs.:** Corp. des bibtcrs. prof. du PQ: conseil d'admin.; various coms. ASTED: Bur. d'admin.; various coms. **Pubns.:** *Thésaurus de descripteurs pour l'éducation* (1981). **Activities:** 1, 10; 17, 24, 39; 50, 63, 75 **Addr.:** C.A.D.R.E., 1940, Boul. Henri-Bourassa Est, Montréal, PQ H2B 1S2 Canada.

Roy, Saktidas (O. 11, 1935, Murshidabad, West Bengal, India) Dir. of Univ. Libs., SUNY at Buffalo, 1977–, Asst. Dir. for Tech. Srvs., 1973–77; Head, Preps. Div., VA Polytech. Inst. and State Univ., 1972–73; Head, Serial Recs. Div., Harvard Univ. Libs., 1969–72; Asst. Acq. Libn., Univ. of CA, Santa Cruz, 1968–69; Chief Libn., Lib. of Congs., New Delhi, India, 1967–68; Libn., Amer. Std. Resrch. Ctr., Hyderabad, India, 1965–67; Serials Catlgr., Baker Lib., Harvard Bus. Sch., 1960–65. **Educ.:** Calcutta Univ., 1954–58, BA (Econ., Hist.); Simmons Coll., 1960–64, MS (LS). **Orgs.:** West. NY Lib. Resrcs. Cncl.: Bd. of Trustees. Five Associated Univ. Libs.: Pres., Bd. of Dirs. ALA. **Activities:** 1; 17, 24, 46; 54, 57, 75 **Addr.:** 4547 Chestnut Ridge Rd. Apt. #206, Amherst, NY 14221.

Royal, Norma McCoy (Mr. 1, 1932, Mt. Olive, NC) Media Coord., Eno Valley Sch. 1977–; Media Consult., NC Dept. of Pub. Instr., 1974–77; Media Coord., Durham City Schs., 1970–74; Circ. Libn., NC Ctrl. Univ., 1968–70. **Educ.:** NC Ctrl. Univ., 1950–54, AB (Soc. Std.), 1961, MA (LS); Univ. of NC, 1968, MSLA. **Orgs.:** ALA: Chap. Cnclr. (1977–), Orien. Comm; Status of Women Com. NC LA: Exec. Com. (1977–). NC Ctrl. Univ. Sch. of LS Alumn. Assn.: Curric. Com. (1979–); Exec. Com. (1978–). Durham City Human Rel. Comsn.: Pub. Actv. Com. Y.W.C.A. NC Assn. of Educs.: Div. of Individualized Pupil Srvs. (Secy., 1977–79); Natl. Educ. Assn. **Activities:** 11; 21, 31, 32; 63, 66 **Addr.:** 2217 Apex Hwy., Durham, NC 27707.

Royce, Robert H. (O. 16, 1923, Seattle, WA) Coord., Lrng. Resrcs. Ctrs., World Univs., Inc., 1976–; Head Libn., Intl. Inst. of the Amer., San Juan, PR, 1960–73; Libn., Inter Amer. Univ., PR, 1960–65; Acq. Libn., Univ. of ID, 1957–60. **Educ.:** Ctrl. WA Coll., 1951–53, BA (Eng.); Univ. of Denver, 1954–55, MA (Libnshp.). **Orgs.:** ALA. World Inst. of Info. Srvs.: Bd. Natl. Micro. Assn. Intl. Inst. of the Amer. Bd. of Trustees, World Univs., Inc.: Bd. of Gvrs. World Univ.-Miami: Bd. of Gvrs. WA Intl. Coll.: Bd. of Gvrs. Educ. Advnc. Fund-Intl.: Bd. of Dirs. **Activities:** 1; 15, 17, 33 **Addr.:** World University, Ave. Barbosa, esq. Guayama, Hato Rey, PR 00917.

Royer, Jenny Lynch (Je. 16, 1941, Kokomo, IN) Actg. Libn., Rapides Par. Lib., 1980–, Asst. Libn., 1978–80, Tech. Srvs. Libn., 1974–78; Head of Cat. Dept., E. Baton Rouge Par. Lib., 1971–73; Sr. Libn., Cat. Dept., Univ. of New Orleans, 1967–1970; Asst. Cur. Map Div., Dept. of Geol. and Geo., LA State Univ., 1966–1967. **Educ.:** LA State Univ., 1959–66, BA (Psy.), 1966–67, MS (LS). **Orgs.:** ALA. SWLA. LA LA: Secy. (1977); Lit. Awd. Com. (Ch., 1978–1980). AAUW. Alexandria Bar Assn. Auxiliary. Alexandria Musm. Ctrl. LA Girl Scout Cncl.: Bd. (1975). Other orgs. **Activities:** 1, 9; 17, 20, 46; 69, 83 **Addr.:** 606 Fendler Pkwy., Pineville, LA 71360.

Royle, Mary Anne (Ag. 24, 1952, Vancouver, WA) Law Lib. Dir., Washoe Cnty. Law Lib., 1978–; Libn., GA Admin. Ofc. Cts., 1978; Actg. Libn., Natl. Judicial Coll., 1976–77. **Educ.:** Willamette Univ., 1971–73, BA (Pol. Sci.); Emory Univ., 1977–78, MLn (Libnshp.). **Orgs.:** AALL: Stans. Com. (1979–81); various other coms. SLA: Sierra NV, Natl. Place. Ch. (1980–81). Amer. Frnds. Srv. Com.: Legis. Com., Aid Abused Women (1980). Planned Parenthood: NV State Pub. Affairs (Ch., 1976–77). **Pubns.:** "Law Books in Nevada," *InterAlia: Jnl. of NV State Bar* (Je. 1980). **Activities:** 4, 12; 17, 28, 34; 75, 77, 78 **Addr.:** Washoe County Law Library, Courthouse, Box 11130, Reno, NV 89520.

Royster, Vivian Hall (F. 21, 1951, Monticello, FL) Asst. Dir./Head Acq., Univ. of MD, 1980–; Assoc. Univ. Libn., FL State Univ., 1974–80. **Educ.:** FL A&M Univ., 1969–73, BS (Lib. Media); Atlanta Univ., 1973–74, summa cum laude MSLS; various cont. ed. crs. **Orgs.:** ALA: ACRL; JMRT (1973–), Liason for FL State Univ. Sch. of LS (1975–77). Tallahassee Urban Leag. FL A&M Univ. Alum. Chap., Tallahassee. Natl. Assn. of Negro Women. NAACP. **Honors:** Alpha Kappa Alpha; Beta Phi Mu. **Activities:** 1; 39, 41, 42; 54, 59, 63 **Addr.:** Frederick Douglass Library, University of Maryland, Eastern Shore, Princess Anne, MD 21853.

Rozene, Janette B. (J. 29, 1952, Bridgeport, CT) Spec. Col., Non-print Catlgr., Fashion Inst. of Tech., 1981–; Ref. Libn., Musm. of Mod. Art, 1977–81; Ref. Lib., Art Dept., Newark Pub. Lib., 1975–77; Spec. Libn., Lowenstein Dsgn. Resrch. Lib., 1975. **Educ.:** Brandeis Univ., 1970–72; Boston Univ., BA (Art Hist.); Columbia Univ., 1974–75, MLS; Hunter Coll., City Univ. of New York, 1976– (Art hist.). **Orgs.:** ARLIS/NA. SLA. **Honors:** Natl. Gallery of Art intern, 1975. **Pubns.:** Reviews. **Activities:** 9, 12; 31, 39, 42; 55, 57 **Addr.:** 2 Riverside Dr., New York, NY 10023.

Rozniatowski, David William (Ag. 11, 1941, Forfar, Scotland) Libn., Winnipeg Art Gallery, 1977–; Indxr., Agr. Can. Lib., 1977; Biblgphr., MB Dept. of Educ., Sch. Lib. Srvs., 1975; Libn., St. John's HS, 1971–73. **Educ.:** Univ. of MB, 1959–62, BA (Eng.), 1974, MEd (Educ. Fndns.), 1970, BEd (Sch. Libnshp.); Univ. of BC, 1974–76, MLS. **Orgs.:** ARLIS/NA. Can. LA. MB LA. Frnds. of the Met. Univ. of MB Alum. Assn. **Pubns.:** *A Banquet of Books* (1975). **Activities:** 12; 15, 20, 39; 55 **Addr.:** Clara Lander Library, Winnipeg Art Gallery, 300 Memorial Blvd., Winnipeg, MB R2K 0P3 Canada.

Ruark, Ardis L. (S. 9, 1927, Huron, SD) Dir. of Lib. Media and ESEA Title IV–B, Div. of Elem. and Sec. Educ., 1975–; Sch. Libn., Mitchell Jr. HS, 1969–75; Tchr., Vermillion HS, 1965–67; Libn./Instr., Mitchell Jr. HS, Dakota Wesleyan Univ., 1960–65. **Educ.:** Huron Coll., 1945–48, BA (Hist.); Univ. of SD, 1964–68, MA (Eng.); various crs. **Orgs.:** SD Sch. Lib. Media Assn.: Pres. (1974–75). SD Sch. Libns. RT: Pres. (1966–67). SD Educ. Media RT: Pres. (1967–68). SD Assn. for Comm. and Tech.: Secy. (1981). Various other orgs. Delta Kappa Gamma: Chap. Pres. (1969–70). Intl. Toastmistress Club. **Honors:** Leader of Amer. Sec. Educ., Outstan. Educ., 1971, 1973. **Pubns.:** *Kangaroo Kapers: How to Jump into Library Service for the Handicapped* (1978); *South Dakota Adventures: Bibliography* (1981). **Activities:** 10, 13; 17, 24; 63, 74 **Addr.:** Library Media and ESEA Title IV–B, Division of Elementary and Secondary Education, Kneip Bldg., 700 N. Illinois St., Pierre, SD 57501–2281.

Rubens, Charlotte C. (S. 15, 1950, New York, NY) Asst. Chief of Ctrl. Circ., Cecil H. Green Lib., Stanford Univ., 1979–; Catlgr., Margaret Clapp Lib., Wellesley Coll., 1978–79; Asst. Catlgr., Monroe C. Gutman Lib., Harvard Univ., 1976–78. **Educ.:** SUNY, StonyBrook, 1968–72, BA (Span. Lit.); Simmons Coll., 1976–78, MLS. **Orgs.:** ALA: ACRL; LAMA; RTSD. CA Acad. and Resrch. Libns.: Mem. Com. (1981–). CA LA. **Honors:** Beta Phi Mu, 1978; SUNY (StonyBrook), Span. Awd., 1972. **Pubns.:** Ed., *SULA Nsltr.* (1980–81). **Activities:** 1; 17, 20, 22; 55, 56 **Addr.:** Cecil H. Green Library, Central Circulation Dept., Stanford University, Stanford, CA 94305.

Rubens, Jane Cora (Je. 5, 1945, Richmond, VA) Assoc. in Charge of Lib., Libn., Coudert Brothers, 1970–; Ref. Libn., Fordham Univ., 1968–70. **Educ.:** Vassar Coll., 1963–67, AB (Eng.); Columbia Univ., 1967–68, MS (LS); Fordham Univ., 1979, JD (Law). **Orgs.:** AALL: SLS Nom. Com. (1980–81). Law LA of Grt. NY: Treas. (1973–75). SLA. Amer. Bar Assn. Assn. of the Bar of the City of New York. **Activities:** 1, 12; 77 **Addr.:** Coudert Brothers, 200 Park Ave., New York, NY 10166.

Rubin, Rhea Joyce (Je. 14, 1950, Chicago, IL) Lib. Consult., 1981–; Hum. Prog. Rep., Natl. Cncl. on the Aging, Inc., 1978–81; Instr., Kent State Univ., Sch. of LS, 1980, 1978; Consult., Natl. Inst. on Lib. Srvs. to Jail Popltns., ALA, 1980; Grant Reviewer, Natl. Endow. for the Hum., Pub. Lib. Progs., 1979; Trainer, OK Dept. of Libs., Correct. Inst. Libs. Wkshp., 1979; Dir., Reg. Lib. for the Blind and Phys. Handcpd., OR State Lib., 1977–78; Spec. Srvs. Libn., Pierce Cnty. Lib., 1977; Proj. Dir., Cook Cnty Correct. Proj., Chicago Pub. Lib., 1973–75. **Educ.:** Univ. of WI, 1968–72, BA (Psy.), 1972–73, MA (LS). **Orgs.:** ALA: Cnclr. (1978–82), Cncl. Orien. Com. (1980–82); ASCLA, Cont. Ed. Com. (1978–80), Biblther. Com. (Consult., 1976–80)/ Lib. Srvs. to the Blind and Phys. Handcpd. Sect., Bylaws Com. (1978–79), Women Lib. Workers 1976–), various coms.; Hlth. and Rehab. Lib. Srvs. Div., Nom. Com. (1976–77). West. Grntlgcl. Socty. OK Adult and Cont. Ed. Assn.: Gvr.'s Conf. on the Adult Learner. Amer. Correct. Assn. **Honors:** Shaw Awd., 1980; Natl. Fed. of the Blind of OR, Spec. Cit., 1978. **Pubns.:** Jt. auth., *Reading for Older Adults* (forthcoming); "Packaging Programs: New Mode of Public Library Service to Older Adults," *Pub. Lib. Qtly.* (Spr. 1980); "The Bibliographic Structure of Bibliotherapy and the Role of the Journal in its Development," *The Serials Libn.* (Fall 1980); *Using Bibliotherapy: A Guide to Theory and Practice* (1978); *Bibliotherapy Sourcebook* (1978); various chaps., articles. **Activities:** 5, 9; 24, 25, 27; 55, 72, 95-Bibliother. **Addr.:** 2753 Chelsea Ln., Oakland, CA 94611.

Rubin-Cohen, Ina M. (My. 10, 1954, Philadelphia, PA) Judaica Libn., Hebrew Un. Coll., 1978–; Asst. Libn., Baltimore Hebrew Coll., 1976–78. **Educ.:** Univ. of PA, 1971–75, BA (Intl. Rel.; Near E. Stds.); Columbia Univ., 1975–76, MLS. **Orgs.:** Assn. of Jewish Libs.: Conv. Com. (1980–81); Resrch. Div. Nsltr. Ed. (1980–81). NY Area Theo. Libs. Assn.: Nom Com. (1979–81). ALA. **Pubns.:** "American Jewish Fiction Books," *Jewish Bk. Anl.* (1979, 1980). **Activities:** 1; 19, 20, 39; 54, 95-Jewish Stds. **Addr.:** Klau Library, Hebrew Union College - Jewish Institute of Religion, 1 W. 4th St., New York, NY 10012.

Rubinstein, Sallie (Salem, NJ) Assoc. Univ. Libn., FL State Univ., 1970–; Asst. Libn., Hialeah Pub. Lib., 1969–70. **Educ.:** Rollins Coll., BMus; Univ. of MI, 1969–70, MMus, MLS. **Orgs.:** Msc. OCLC Users Grp. Southeast. Msc. LA. **Activities:** 1, 9; 15, 44, 46; 55 **Addr.:** 2334 Jim Lee Rd., Tallahassee, FL 32301.

Rubinstein, Stanley (Jn. 7, 1938, Cleveland, OH) Prog. Dev. Ofcr., Intl. Comm. Agency, 1981–, Acad. Exch. Ofcr., Latin Amer., 1980–81; Supvsr. Acad. Exch. Ofcr., Africa, 1979–80, Acad. Exch. Ofcr., 1978–79, Prog. Dev. Asst., 1973–78; Ref. Libn., U.S. Info. Agency, 1970–73; Bibl., Lib. of Congs., 1969–70, Subj. Spec., Enoch Pratt Free Lib., 1966–69. **Educ.:** OH State Univ., 1956–60, BA (Hist.); Kent State Univ., 1964, BS (Educ.); George Washington Univ., 1969–78, PhD (Amer. Stds.); Rutgers Univ., 1964–66, MLS; West. Rsv. Univ., 1961–63, MA (Hist.). **Orgs.:** ALA. Immigration Hist. Assn. **Honors:** Phi Alpha Theta. **Pubns.:** "Enoch Pratt Free Library and Black Patrons," *Jnl. of*

Special Subjects/Services: 50. Adult educ.; 51. Advert./Mktg.; 52. Aerosp.; 53. Agric.; 54. Area std.; 55. Arts/Hum.; 56. Autom.; 57. Bibl./Prtg.; 58. Bio. sci.; 59. Bus./Fin.; 60. Chem.; 61. Copyrt.; 62. Documtn.; 63. Educ.; 64. Engin.; 65. Env.; 66. Eth. grps.; 67. Film; 68. Food/Nutr.; 69. Geneal.; 70. Geo.; 71. Geol.; 72. Handcpd.; 73. Hist.; 74. Int. frdm.; 75. Info. sci.; 76. Insr.; 77. Law; 78. Legis.; 79. Math./Comp. sci.; 80. Med.; 81. Metals; 82. Nat. resrcs.; 83. Newsp.; 84. Nuc. sci.; 85. Oral hist.; 86. Petr./Energy; 87. Pharm.; 88. Phys./Astr./Math.; 89. Readg.; 90. Relig.; 91. Sci./Tech.; 92. Soc. sci.; 93. Telecom.; 94. Transp.; 95. (other).

Lib. Hist. (V. 15) (Fall 1980). **Activities:** 4; 73 **Addr.:** 249 Rolling Ave. #T3, Rockville, MD 20852.

Rubinton, Phyllis (Mr. 24, 1927, New York, NY) Libn., Payne Whitney Psyt. Clinic, 1975–; Libn., NY Psychoanalytic Inst., 1970–74, Asst. Libn., NY State Psyt. Inst., 1967–69. **Educ.:** Wellesley Coll., 1945–49, BA (Phil.); Pratt Inst., 1964–67, MLS. Columbia Univ., 1969 (Med. Lib.); Med. LA, 1969, Cert. **Orgs.:** Med LA: Vital Notes (1969–74). ALA. SLA. Reg. Med. LA: Cont. Educ. (1972–74). **Honors:** Beta Phi Mu, 1967. **Pubns.:** Jt. auth., *Resources for the Psychoanalyst* (1979); jt. auth., "On searching the literature," *Jnl. of Psyt. Educ.* (1980); jt. cmplr., "Collection of psychoanalytic classics," *Jnl. of the Amer. Psychoanalytic Assn* (1979); jt. auth. "Ilse Bry–A Tribute," *Bltn. MLA* (1976); "Writings of Berta Bornstein," *Psychoanalytic Study of the Child* (1973); various articles and reviews (1973–78). **Activities:** 1, 12; 15, 17, 39; 80, 92 **Addr.:** Payne Whitney Psychiatric Clinic Library, New York Hospital–Cornell Medical College, 525 E. 68th St., New York, NY 10021.

Ruby, Carmela M. (S. 7, 1933, San Francisco, CA) Lib. Consult., CA State Lib., 1973–; Lectr., Lib. Sch., Cath. Univ., 1974; Lectr., Lib. Sch., Univ. of CA, Berkeley, 1973, Lib. Progs. Coord., NM State Lib., 1969–73; Ref. Lab. Libn., 1966–68. **Educ.:** Univ. of CA, Berkeley, 1951–57, BA (Lit.); Univ. of CA, Los Angeles, 1964–65, MLS; Univ. of London, Cert. of Completion (17th/18th Century Lit. and Art Prog.); various grad. crs. **Orgs.:** ALA: ASCLA (Pres., 1980–81). CLENE: Adv. Bd. (1978–). CA LA: Cont. Educ. Com. (Ch., 1975–). Amer. Socty. for Trng. and Dev. **Pubns.:** "What To Do Till the Money Comes," *News Notes of CA Libs.* (1977). **Activities:** 13; 24, 25; 50, 72, 93 **Addr.:** 2240 Meer Way, Sacramento, CA 95822.

Ruby, Lois F. (S. 11, 1942, San Francisco, CA) Libn., Temple Emanu-El, 1973–; Art, Msc. Libn., Univ. of MO, 1967–68; YA Libn., Dallas Pub. Lib., 1965–67. **Educ.:** Univ. of CA, Berkeley, 1960–64, BA (Eng.); CA State Univ., San Jose, 1964–65, MA (LS). **Orgs.:** ALA. AJL. CS LA: S. Ctrl. KS Chap., 1st Secy. **Honors:** ALA, Best Bks. for YAs List, (1977). **Pubns.:** "Rites of Passage," *Top of the News* (Win. 1980); *Arriving at a Place You've Never Left* (1977); *What Do You Do in Quicksand?* (1979). **Activities:** 9, 12; 15, 20, 21; 63, 90 **Addr.:** 6200 Perryton, Wichita, KS 67220.

Rucker, Laura Allen (Ag. 17, 1911, Edmond, OK) Asst. Dir. and Head Info. Srvs., Univ. of OK Hlth. Scis. Ctr. Lib., 1967–; ILL Libn., Univ. of OK Lib., 1965–67. **Educ.:** OK City Univ., 1932, BA (Math.); Univ. of OK, 1964–65, MLS; Med. LA, 1968, Cert. **Orgs.:** Med LA: S. Ctrl. Reg. Grp. (1970–). OK Hlth. Scis. LA. OK LA. Assn. of Libns. in the Hist. of the Hlth. Scis.: Chrt. Mem. (1976–). Higher Educ. Alum. Cncl. of OK. P.E.O. **Honors:** Phi Gamma Delta. Beta Phi Mu, 1965. **Pubns.:** Jt. auth., "Government Publications in Oklahoma Public Libraries," *OK Libn.* (Jl. 1966); "New Tools and Networks in Medical Librarianship," *Nsltr. SLA, OK Chap.* (Jl. 1970). **Activities:** 12; 16, 17, 45; 56, 80 **Addr.:** University of Oklahoma Health Sciences Center Library, P.O. Box 26901, Oklahoma City, OK 73190.

Ruckman, Stanley N. (Ja. 16, 1936, Scottsbluff, NE) Dir., Lrng. Srvs., Linn-Benton Cmnty. Coll., 1972–; Asst. Dir., Ref., OR State Lib., 1970–72; Ref. Libn., The Coll. of ID, 1964–70; Sr. Libn., LA of Portland, 1963–64; Libn., Vandenberg Jr. HS, 1961–63; Libn., OR City HS, 1958–61. **Educ.:** Univ. of OR, 1953–57, BEd (Educ.); Univ. of Denver, 1957–58, MA (Libnshp.). **Orgs.:** ALA: Cncl. from OR (1979–82); ACRL/Cmnty. and Jr. Coll. Sect. (Secy., 1974–75). OR LA: Treas. (1976–77). OR Cmnty. Coll. LA: Ch. (1974–75). SLA: OR Chap. (Pres., 1973–74). OR Educ. Media Assn. **Activities:** 1; 17, 32, 46; 50, 56 **Addr.:** 736 N.W. Fox Pl., Corvallis, OR 97330.

Rucks, Frances Burell (Mr. 4, 1918, Galva, IL) Ed., Bibl. Pubns., Air Univ. Lib., 1968–; Catlgr., Bus. Lib., Univ. of AL, 1943–68; Circ. and Bibl. Asst., Univ. of AZ, 1942–43; Cat. Asst., Univ. of ID, 1941–42. **Educ.:** Univ. of AZ, 1936–39, AB (Eng., Grmn.); Peabody Lib. Sch., 1939–40, BS (LS); Univ. of AL, 1954–58, MA (Eng.). **Orgs.:** SLA: Adv. Cncl. (1962–63); AL Chap. (Pres., 1962–63). SELA: Resrcs. and Tech. Srvs. Sect. (Secy., 1968–70). AL LA. Women in Comms., Inc. **Honors:** Phi Beta Kappa; Phi Kappa Phi. **Pubns.:** Ed., *Publications at the University of Alabama* (1954–64); "Centralized Cataloging and the Departmental Library," *Jnl. of Cat. and Class.* (Sum. 1951). **Activities:** 1, 4; 30, 37, 46; 57, 59, 74 **Addr.:** 3427 Audubon Rd., Montgomery, AL 36111.

Rudd, Amanda S. Deputy Comsn., Chicago Pub. Lib., 1975–, Asst. Chief Libn., Cmnty. Rel. and Spec. Progs., 1975; Consult., Field Enterprises Educ. Corp., 1970–75; Asst. Supvsr., Sch. Libs., Cleveland Pub. Schs., 1965–70. **Educ.:** FL A&M Univ., BS; West. Rsv. Univ., MLS. **Orgs.:** ALA: Cncl. (1978–82); Plng. Com. (1980–82), Plng. and Budget Asm. (1981–82); PLA, Exec. Com. (1980–83), Nom. Com. (1981–83); Int. Frdm. RT, Exec. Com. (1979–81). IL Lib. Syst. Dirs. Org.: Presiding Ofcr. IL LA: Legis.-Lib. Dev. Com. (1981–83); Pub. Lib. Sect., Ad Hoc Com. to Plan for Implementation of Multitype Library Systs., Stans. Com. (1981–). Case West. Rsv. Sch. of LS: Visit Com. of the Bd. of Overseers (1979–81); Alum. Assn. (Pres., 1979–81). IL WHCOLIS: Chicago Reg. Conf., Ch.; Core Com. on Reg. Confs. Other actv. **Pubns.:** Ed. consult., *School and Public Library Media Programs for Children and Young Adults* (1976); jt. auth., *Selection of Materials and Program Development for Various Minority/Ethnic Groups* (1974). **Addr.:** Chicago Library System, 425 N. Michigan Ave., Chicago, IL 60611.

Rudd, Hynda L. (My. 20, 1936, Salt Lake City, UT) Archvst., Univ. of South. CA, 1979–; Libn., Los Angeles Herald Examiner, 1978–79; Recs. Supvsr., Univ. of UT, 1974–78, Soc. Work Libn., 1973–74, Co-fndr., Jewish Archs., Univ. of UT Lib., 1972. **Educ.:** Univ. of UT, 1965–74, BS (Hist.), 1974–78, MS (Hist.); Univ. of South. CA, 1979–80, MSLS; Inst. for Mod. Archs. Admin., 1975. **Orgs.:** SAA: Com. for Natl. Conv. (1977). Conf. of Intermt. Archvsts.: Com. for Conv. (1977). UT Women's Hist. Assn.: Fndr. (1977–78). AJL. **Pubns.:** Asst. ed., *Directory of Career Resources for Women* (1979); Asst. ed., *Directory of Career Training and Development Programs* (1979); *Mountain West Jewry- The Pioneer Period: A Source Book* (1979); "Samuel Newhouse: Utah Mining Magnate, Land Developer," *West. States Jewish Hist. Qtly.* (Jl. 1979); Film- *History of the Jews of Utah:1854-1977* (1978); various other articles. **Activities:** 1, 2; 25, 37, 39; 67, 86, 91 **Addr.:** 10634 Valparaiso St. #36, Los Angeles, CA 90034.

Ruddick, Brian P. (N. 4, 1939, Langley Moor, Eng.) Asst. Dir., Tech. Srvs., Cleveland State Univ. Lib., 1977–, Head, Tech. Srvs., 1974–77, Asst. Head, Tech. Srvs., 1970–74; Head, Gifts and Exch., Cleveland Pub. Lib., 1964–69 Ed., Asst. Secy., North. Reg. Lib. Bureau, Newcastle upon Tyne, Eng., 1963-64; Branch Libn., Eng., 1961–63. **Educ.:** Cleveland State Univ., 1964–69 BA (Eng.), Case West. Rsv. Univ., 1970–71, MSLS. LA (UK), 1960–61, Associateship. **Orgs.:** ALA: RTSD, Price Index Com. (1973–75); ACRL, Tri-State Chap. Ch. (1980–81). North. OH Tech. Srvs. Libns.: Pres. (1978–80). Acad. LA of OH: Nom. Com. (1979). **Activities:** 1; 17, 34, 46; 56, 57, 93 **Addr.:** Cleveland State University Library, 1860 E. 22 St., Cleveland, OH 44115.

Ruddick, Patsy Ruth (D. 16, 1932, Arma, KS) Dir. of Lib. Srvs., Garden City Cmnty. Coll., 1963–; Eng. Tchr., Garden City Jr. HS, 1954–63. **Educ.:** Labette Cmty. Cmnty. Coll., 1950–52, AA (Eng.); Pittsburg (KS) State Univ., 1952–54, BS Ed. (Lang., Lit.); Univ. of Denver, 1963, MA (LS); 1959–77, various crs., **Orgs.:** ALA: ACRL. KS LA: Coll. and Univ. Libs./Nom. Com. (1976). Finney Cnty. LA. KS State Netwk. Athrty. (1979–80). Natl. Educ. Assn. KS–Natl. Educ. Assn.: KS State Readg. Cir. KS Higher Educ. Assn.: State Del. (1977–79). Delta Kappa Gamma: State Conv. Ch. (1970). **Activities:** 1; 17, 39, 46 **Addr.:** Garden City Community College, 801 Campus Dr., Garden City, KS 67846.

Ruder, Clarice Marie (My 31, 1948, Marshfield, WI) Asst. Head Spec. Col. Dept., Tampa–Hillsboro. Cnty. Pub. Lib., 1976–; Adult Srvs. Libn., Palm Beach Cnty. Pub. Lib., 1974–76; Lib. Tech., Mem. Lib. Univ. of WI, 1971–74; Lib. Tech., Legis. Ref. Bur. Lib., 1970–71. **Educ.:** Univ. of WI, Oshkosh, 1966–70, BS (LS); Univ. of WI, Madison, 1972–73, MS (LS). **Orgs.:** FL LA: Gvt. Docums. Caucus (Ch., 1979–80). ALA: GODORT. **Activities:** 1, 9; 16, 29, 39; 69, 78 **Addr.:** 9404 N. 10th St., Tampa, FL 33612.

Rudkin, David William (Ag. 16, 1936, Windsor, ON) Univ. Archvst., Univ. of Toronto, 1971–; Coord. of Pre-Confederation, Can. Recs., Mss. Div., Pub. Arch. of Can., 1967–70, Archvst., Post-Confederation Sect., Mss. Div., 1961–63. **Educ.:** Univ. of Windsor, West. ON, 1957–61, BA (Hist.), 1973, MA (Can. Hist.). **Orgs.:** Assn. Can. Archvsts.: VP. (1976–77); Pres. (1977–78); various ofcs., coms. SAA: Com. on Coll. and Univ. Arch. (1971–). Toronto Area Archvsts. Grp.: Co-fndr. (1973); Ch. (1975). Assn. of Rec. Mgrs. and Admin. Various orgs. Archit. Cons. of ON. ON Musm. Assn. Brit. Rec. Assn. Intl. Cncl. on Arch. **Pubns.:** "Henry Boys," *Dictionary of Canadian Biography* (1976); "University Archives: An Academic Question," *Archivaria* (Sum. 1979). **Activities:** 2; 15, 17, 39; 63, 86 **Addr.:** University of Toronto Archives, 120 St. George St., Toronto, ON M5S 1A5 Canada.

Rudnik, Sr. Mary Chrysantha (D. 2, 1929, Winona, MN) Head Libn., Felician Coll., 1957–, Dir., Dev., PR, 1975–, Instr., Good Couns. HS, 1957–; Tchr., Holy Fam. Sch., WI, 1954–56. **Educ.:** DePaul Univ., 1957–58, PhB (Eng.); Rosary Coll., 1960–62, MALS. **Orgs.:** Cath. LA: Various coms. and ofcs. Cncl. on Lib. Tech. Assts.: Various coms. and ofcs. IL WHCOLIS: Del. (1978). Copernicus Fndn. **Pubns.:** Various reviews, *Curric. Review;* jt. ed., *Job Description and Certification for Library Technical Assistants* (1970); *Coming of Age of LTAs* (1971). "Library Supervisors," *Cath. Lib. World* (F. 1976); various other reviews. **Activities:** 1; 15, 17, 20 **Addr.:** Felician College Library, 3800 W. Peterson Ave, Chicago, IL 60659.

Rudolph, L. C. (D. 24, 1921, Jasper, IN) Cur. of Bks., Lilly Lib. of IN Univ., 1978–, Head of Tech. Srvs., 1970–78; Rare Bks. Biblghr., Van Pelt Lib., Univ. of PA, 1969–70; Prof. of Church Hist., Louisville Presby. Semy., 1954–69. **Educ.:** DePauw Univ., 1946–48, AB (Hist.); Louisville Presby. Semy., 1948–51, BD (Hist.); Yale Univ., 1952–58, PhD (Hist.); IN Univ., 1967–68, MLS. **Orgs.:** ALA: ACRL/Rare Bks. and Mss. Sect., Exec. Com. (1979–). Amer. Socty. of Church Hist. Presby. Hist. Socty: Trustee (1970–); VP (1977–); Pres. 1980–). **Honors:** Amer. Assn. of Theo. Schs., Rockefeller Flwshp., 1960; Presby. Hist. Socty., Thomas–Kuch Awd. for *Hoosier Zion,* 1963; IN Univ. Writers' Conf., Best Bk. Published on IN, 1964. **Pubns.:** *Indiana Letters* (1979); *Francis Asbury* (1966); *Hoosier Zion* (1963); "Writing a History of Your Church," *Jnl. of Presby. Hist.* (Win. 1975). **Activities:** 1, 12; 17, 45; 57 **Addr.:** Lilly Library of Indiana University, Bloomington, IN 47405.

Ruffier, Arthur J. (Ap. 11, 1930, Maximo, OH) Ref. Libn., WA State Law Lib., 1968–; Acq. Libn., Univ. of CA, Davis, Law Lib., 1966–67; Tech. Srvs. Libn., WA State Law Lib., 1964–66; Acq. Libn., Univ. of WA Law Lib., 1960–64, Circ. Libn., 1959–64. **Educ.:** OH Univ., 1949–56, BFA; Univ. of WA, 1958–59, MLS. **Orgs.:** AALL: Schol. Com. (1969–72). **Activities:** 13; 39; 77 **Addr.:** Temple of Justice, Olympia, WA 98504.

Rugge, Sue (Mr. 7, 1941, CA) Pres., Info. on Demand, 1979–; Partner, Info. Unlimited, 1972–79; Head Libn., Singer Bus. Machines, 1969–72; Head Libn., Dalmo Victor, 1964–69; Head Libn., Phys. Intl., Inc., 1963–65, Asst. Libn., Gen. Motors Defense Resrch. Labs., 1961–63. **Orgs.:** SLA. Info. Indus. Assn. ASIS. Women Entrepeneurs. **Pubns.:** "Document Delivery," *Online* (Ja. 1977); *Union List of Standards and Specifications* (1976); various sps. **Activities:** 12; 17; 51, 59, 80 **Addr.:** P.O. Box 9550, Berkeley, CA 94709.

Ruiz de Nieves, Angela Margarita (O. 2, 1940, Santurce, PR) Chief, Cat. Dept., Univ. PR, Humacao Univ. Coll., 1979–; Head, Cat. Lib. Dir., 1973–78, Head, Acq. Dept., 1969–72, Dept., 1967–69. **Educ.:** Univ. of PR, 1958–62, BA, BS (Home Econ.); Syracuse Univ., 1966–67, MSLS. **Orgs.:** SBPR. **Honors:** Phi Delta Kappa. **Addr.:** Calle 3, H2, Urb. Los Rosales, Humacao, PR 00661.

Rule, Judy K. (D. 13, 1944, Beech Glen, WV) Asst. Dir., Cabell Cnty. Pub. Lib., 1967–. **Educ.:** Concord Coll., 1962–66, BS (Educ.); IN Univ., 1966–67, MLS. **Orgs.:** ALA: PLA Starter List for Branch Libs. (1965–80). SELA: Exec. Bd. (1978–). WV LA: VP (1979–80), Pres. (1980–81). Quota Club of Huntington. Cmnty. Mental Hlth. Ctr. **Pubns.:** *Books for Public Libraries* (1975, 1980). **Activities:** 9; 17, 20, 21; 55, 68 **Addr.:** Cabell County Public Library, 455th St. Plz., Huntington, WV 25701.

Rundell, Walter, Jr. (N. 2, 1928, Austin, TX) Prof., Hist., Univ. of MD, 1971–; Ch., Prof., Hist., IA State Univ., 1969–71; Prof., Hist., Univ. of OK, 1967–69; Srvy. Dir., Natl. Arch., 1965–67. **Educ.:** Univ. of TX, Austin, 1948–51, BJ, BS (Jlsm., Msc.); Amer. Univ., 1954–57, MA, PhD (Hist.). **Orgs.:** SAA: Pres. (1977–78). Amer. Hist. Assn.: Com. on Info. Srvs. (Ch., 1971–74). Org. of Amer. Histns.: Com. on Bibl. and Resrch. Needs (Ch., 1968–73). West. Hist. Assn.: Pres. (1982–83). **Honors:** SAA, Waldo G. Leland Prize, 1971; Univ. of TX, Arlington, Webb-Smith Awd., 1975; Univ. of MD, Student Awd. for Outstan. Tchg., 1979. **Pubns.:** *Military Money: A Fiscal History of the U.S. Army Overseas in World War II* (1980); *Early Texas Oil: A Photographic History, 1866–1936* (1977); *In Pursuit of American History: Research and Training in the United States* (1970); "Walter Prescott Webb as Businessman," *The Grt. Plains Jnl.* (1979); "Photographs as Historical Evidence: Early Texas Oil," *Amer. Archvst.* (1978). **Activities:** 1; 55, 86 **Addr.:** Dept. of History, University of Maryland, College Park, MD 20742.

Runkel, Phillip M. (N. 4, 1946, Waukesha, WI) Asst. Archvst., Marquette Univ., 1977–; Bibl. Resrch. Asst., Newberry Lib., 1975. **Educ.:** Carroll Coll., 1965–69, BA (Hist.); Marquette Univ., 1970–72, MA (Hist.); Peabody Coll., 1972–1973, MLS; Univ. of Denver, 1971, Cert. Arch. Admin. **Orgs.:** SAA. Midwest Archs. Conf. Waukesha Cnty. Hist. Socty. Milwaukee Cnty. Hist. Socty. State Hist. Socty. of WI. **Pubns.:** *Alfred Lunt and Lynn Fontanne: A Bibliography* (1978). **Activities:** 1, 2; 45 **Addr.:** 601 N. 20th St., Apt. 201, Milwaukee, WI 53233.

Runkle, Martin (O. 18, 1937, Cincinnati, OH) Dir., Univ. Lib., Sr. Instr., Grad. Lib. Sch., Univ. of Chicago, 1980–, Asst. Dir., Tech. Srvs., Lib. 1979–80, Head Cat. Libn., 1975–79, Lib. Systs. Anal., 1970–75. **Educ.:** Muskingum Coll., 1955–59, BA (Eng.); Univ. of Pittsburgh, 1962–64, MA (Eng.); Univ. of Chicago, 1969–70, MA (LS). **Orgs.:** ALA: Head Catlgrs. Discuss. Grp. (Ch., 1979). **Honors:** U.S. Dept. of Educ., Fulbright Tchg. Grant, Greece, 1965. **Pubns.:** "Authority in On-line Catalogs," *IL Libs.* (S. 1980). **Activities:** 1; 17, 26, 46; 56 **Addr.:** University of Chicago Library, 1100 E. 57th St., Chicago, IL 60637.

Runkle, Susan M. (O. 29, 1931, Columbus, OH) Libn., Waterloo Cmnty. Schs., 1974–. **Educ.:** Case West. Rsv. Univ., 1949–53, BA (Pol. Sci., Eng.); Univ. of North. IA, 1969–72, MA (LS). **Orgs.:** IA LA. IA Educ. Media Assn. Cedar Falls Pub. Lib.: Bd. of Trustees (Secy., 1972). Waterloo Educ. Assn. IA Educ. Assn. Natl. Educ. Assn. **Honors:** Phi Beta Kappa, 1953. **Activities:** 9, 10; 31, 32, 47 **Addr.:** 1616 Picturesque Dr., Cedar Falls, IA 50613.

Runyon, Constance L. (Mr. 31, 1945, Meadville, PA) Asst. Branch Mgr., Kings Park Lib., Fairfax Cnty. Pub. Lib., 1977–, Ref. Libn., 1977, Ref. Libn., Ctrl. Lib., 1972–77, Catlgr., 1969–72; Srch., Ed., *Natl. Regis. of Micro. Mstrs.,* U.S. Lib. of

PROFESSIONAL ACTIVITIES: Institutions: 1. Acad. lib.; 2. Arch.; 3. Assn.; 4. Fed./Gvt. lib.; 5. Inst. lib.; 6. Mfr./Suppl.; 7. Milit. lib.; 8. Musm.; 9. Pub. lib.; 10. Sch. lib.; 11. Sch. of lib. sci.; 12. Spec. lib.; 13. State lib.; 14. (other). **Functions/Activities:** 15. Acq./Col. dev.; 16. Adult srvs.; 17. Admin.; 18. Apprais.; 19. Archit./Bldgs.; 20. Cat./Class.; 21. Chld. srvs.; 22. Circ.; 23. Cons./Pres.; 24. Consult.; 25. Cont. ed.; 26. Educ. lib. sci.; 27. Ext. srvs.; 28. Fund/Grants; 29. Gvt. pubs.; 30. Indx./Abs.; 31. Instr. lib. use; 32. Media srvs.; 33. Micro.; 34. Netwks./Coop.; 35. Persnl.; 36. PR; 37. Publshg.; 38. Recs. mgt.; 39. Ref. srvs.; 40. Repro.; 41. Resrch.; 42. Review.; 43. Secur.; 44. Serials; 45. Spec. col.; 46. Tech. srvs.; 47. Trustees/Bds.; 48. YA srvs.; 49. (other).

Congs., 1968–69, Ed., *Natl. Un. Cat.,* 1968. **Educ.:** WV Wesleyan Coll., 1963–67, BS (LS); Cath. Univ. of Amer., 1967–68, MS (LS). **Orgs.:** ALA: ASCLA, Lib. Srv. to the Deaf Sect., Pubns. Com. (1980–82). VA LA. Metro. WA Cncl. of Gvt. Lib. Srv. to the Deaf. WA Ear, Bd. North. VA Regis. of Interpreters for the Deaf. **Activities:** 9; 16, 17, 39; 72 **Addr.:** 2304 Mcgregor Ct., Vienna, VA 22180.

Runyon, Robert S. (Je. 28, 1934, Summit, NJ) Lib. Dir., Univ. of NE (Omaha), 1978–; Assoc. Dir., Univ. of UT Lib., 1973–78; Tech. Srv. Libn., Johns Hopkins Univ., 1966–73. **Educ.:** Wesleyan Univ., 1952–56, BA (Phil.); Rutgers Univ., 1958–61, MLS; Univ. of UT 1975–, PhD Cand. **Orgs.:** ALA: Chap. Cnclr. (1978–80); Lib. Admin. Div./Lib. Org. Mgt. Sect., Ref. Stats. Com. (1976–78). Mt. Plains LA: Acad. Lib. Sect. (Ch., 1976). **Pubns.:** "Power and Conflict in Academic Libraries," *Jnl. of Acad. Libnshp.* (S. 1977); jt. auth., "Computers: Equipment and Services," *Lib. Trends* (Ap. 1976). **Activities:** 1; 17 **Addr.:** University Library, University of Nebraska at Omaha, Omaha, NE 68182.

Runyon-Lancaster, K. Elizabeth (D. 26, 1942, Ellwood City, PA) Asst. Prof., Univ. South. CA Sch. of LS, 1978–; PR Libn., Univ. of UT Libs., 1974–78, Catlgr., 1971–74. **Educ.:** Stanford Univ., 1960–64, BA (Japanese); SUNY, Geneseo, 1969–70, MLS; Univ. of UT, 1973–79, PhD (Comm.). **Orgs.:** ALA: JMRT, Afflts. Cncl. (Sec. VP, 1977–78); Ed. Adv. Com. for *Amer. Libs.* (1977–1979); SRRT, Action Cncl. (1978–1979). West. Sp. Comm. Assn. **Pubns.:** "U.L.A.: History and Current Trends," *UT Libs.* (1978); Ed., *Mt. Plains LA Nsltr.* (1976–78), *Univ. of UT Libs. Nsltr.* (1976–78), *Biblio Billboard* (1974). **Activities:** 1, 11; 17, 26, 35, 36, 41; 92, 93 **Addr.:** 2492 Amherst Ave., Los Angeles, CA 90064.

Rupert, Elizabeth A. (Jl. 12, 1918, Emlenton, PA) Dean, Sch. of LS, Clarion State Coll., 1961–; Libn., Tchr., Eng., Oil City (PA) Area Schs. 1959–61; various positions in bus., 1939–69. **Educ.:** Altoona Sch. of Cmrce., 1935–36 (Bus.); Clarion State Coll., 1956–59, BS (LS, Eng.); Syracuse Univ., 1959–62, MS (LS); Univ. of Pittsburgh, 1962–70, PhD (LS). **Orgs.:** PA LA: Dir. (1975–78). PA Sch. LA: Com. on Prof. Stans. (1976–77) ALA: AASL, Com. on Cert. (1975–77). Gvr.'s Pre-WHCOLIS: Strg. Com. (1976–77). **Honors:** Clarion State Coll., Disting. Fac. Awd., 1976, Beta Phi Mu. **Pubns.:** "Clarion State College, School of Library Science," *Ency. of Lib. and Info. Sci.* (1980). **Activities:** 10, 11; 17, 26, 39; 55, 63, 92 **Addr.:** School of Library Science, Clarion State College, Clarion, PA 16214.

Ruppe, Carol V. (F. 22, 1923, Menlo, IA) Ref. Libn., AZ State Univ., 1972–, Head, Ref. Dept., 1975–78, Part-Time Ref. Libn., 1962–72. **Educ.:** Univ. of NM, 1940–45, BA (Anthro.); Univ. of Denver, 1957–59, MLS. **Orgs.:** ALA. ACRL. AZ LA: Coll. and Univ. Div., VP (1977–78), Pres. (1978–79). Online Users. Heard Musm. Lib. **Activities:** 1; 39, 49-Online Srch.; 55, 66, 92 **Addr.:** Reference Department, Library, Arizona State University, Tempe, AZ 85281.

Rupprecht, Leslie P. (Je. 9, 1923, Newark, NJ) Supvsg. Libn. (Ref.), Newark Pub. Lib., 1970–; Prin. Libn., 1960–69, Sr. Libn., 1956–60, Jr. Libn., 1952–56. **Educ.:** Seton Hall Univ., 1946–49, BS (Soc. Std.); Columbia Univ., 1950–51, MLS. **Orgs.:** ALA. SLA. AFSCME. **Pubns.:** Ed., *Business Literature.* **Activities:** 9, 12; 17; 59 **Addr.:** Newark Public Library, Business Library, 34 Commerce St., Newark, NJ 07102.

Rupprecht, Theodore A., Jr., (S. 22, 1923, Cleveland, OH) Libn., Bendix Corp., Advnc. Tech. Ctr., 1981–; Mgr., Lib. Srvs., Bendix Corp., Resrch. Labs., 1962–80; Dept. Head, Tech. Docum. Dept., Chrysler Missile Div., 1956–61; Libn. I, II, Detroit Pub. Lib., 1953–56. **Educ.:** Univ. of IL, 1948–51, BLS, 1953–54, MLS. **Orgs.:** SLA: MI Chap., Pres. (1969–70), Prog. Com. (Ch., 1967–68), Treas. (1964–65); various ofcs. Oakland Cmnty. Coll.: Lib. Tech. Citizens Adv. Com. (1964–80). Oakland Cnty. Libs.: Task Force for Coop. Efforts (1979). **Activities:** 12; 16, 17, 30; 64, 81, 91 **Addr.:** 10756 Green Mountain Cir., Columbia, MD 21044.

Ruschin, Siegfried (My. 18, 1925, Schoenlanke, Germany) Libn. for Col. Dev., Linda Hall Lib., 1978–; Serials Libn., 1964–77, Actg. Serials Libn., 1963–1964, Asst. Serials Libn., 1960–63; Readers Adv., Topeka Pub. Lib., 1958–59. **Educ.:** Washburn Univ., 1954–58, BA (Phys.); Emporia State Univ., 1959–60, MS (LS). **Honors:** Tau Delta Pi; Pi Gamma Mu. **Activities:** 12; 15, 39; 91 **Addr.:** 5322 Charlotte, Kansas City, MO 64110.

Rush, James E. (Jl. 18, 1935, Warrensburg, MO) Dir. of Rsrch., OCLC, Inc., 1973–; Assoc. Prof., Comp. and Info. Sci., OH State Univ., 1969–73, Asst. Prof., 1968–69; Tech. Liason Ofcr., Chem. Abs. Srv., 1967–68, Asst. Head., Chem. Info. Procs. Dept., Resrch. and Dev. Div., 1965–67, Asst. Ed., Organic Index Ed. Dept., 1962–65. **Educ.:** Ctrl. MO State Coll., 1956, BS (Chem., Math.); Univ. of MO, 1962, PhD (Chem.). **Orgs.:** Amer. Natl. Stans. Com. Z39, Lib. and Info. Sci. and Rel. Pub. Pracs.: Exec. Cncl. (1978–80). ASIS: Spec. Interest Grp. on Lib. Automation and Netwks. (Ch., 1976–77); Pubs. Com. (Ch., 1973–74); Ctrl. OH Chap. (1970). Intl. CODEN Srv.: Adv. Com. (1977–). Amer. Chem. Socty.: Div. of Chem. Lit. (Ch., 1973). Amer. Mgt. Assn. **Honors:** ASIS, Best Paper Awd., 1977. **Pubns.:** Jt. auth., *Guide to Information Science* (1979); jt. auth., *Information Retrieval and Documentation in Chemistry* (1974); jt. auth., "The Modeling of a Large On-Line, Real-Time Information System," *Proceedings of the 10th Annual Simulation Symposium* (1977); Jt. auth., "A Simulation Model for Information System Design, Evaluation, and Planning," *Proceedings of the 12th Annual Simulation Symposium* (1979); jt. auth., "Design and Implementation of a Fault-Tolerant Data Base Processor System," *Proceedings of the Ninth Annual Seminar for Academic Computing Services* (1978); various articles, presentations, and consults. in LS and chem. (1962–). **Activities:** 11, 6-Mfr./Suppl.; 17, 41, 49-comp. mgt. 51, 60, 75 **Addr.:** OCLC, Inc., 1125 Kinnehr Rd., Columbus, OH 43212.

Rush, Rita S. (My. 21, Brooklyn, NY) Head Libn., Erasmus Hall HS; Tchr. **Educ.:** Brooklyn Coll., BA (Eng.), MA (Educ.); St. John's Univ., MLS; Columbia Univ., (LS). **Orgs.:** NY City Sch. LA: VP (1968–70); Pres. (1970–72). NY Lib. Club: VP (1973–74); Pres. (1974–75). NY LA: Awds. Com. (1973–75); Persnl. Admin. Com. (Ch., 1977–79). ALA: Various coms. **Honors:** ALA, Del., LIB./USA, NY World's Fair, 1964; NY State Gvr.'s Conf., Del., 1978; NY State Regents Reg. Conf., Del., 1977–80. **Pubns.:** *How to Develop the Librarian's Role in Career Education* (1975); ed., *1980 Salary Survey, NY State College and University Library* 1981; ed., *SLMSgram Nsltr.* (1978–79). **Activities:** 10; 17, 31, 48; 55, 95-Career educ. **Addr.:** 72A Marlborough Rd., Brooklyn, NY 11226.

Rush, Stephan (Ag. 3, 1920, Meahyhirya, Ternopil, Ukraine) Chief Libn., Dept. of Indus., Trade and Cmrce., 1969–; Libn. Spec., Natl. Lib. of Can., 1968–69, Head, Newsp. Sect., 1967–68, NST Coord., 1963–67, Ref. Libn., 1962–63. **Educ.:** Ukrainian Cath. Semy., Culemborg, 1943–49, BA (Phil.); Univ. of Ottawa, 1963–68, MLS (Ref.), 1966–68, MA (Ling.), 1976–, PhD (Compar. Lit.). **Orgs.:** SLA. ASIS. **Pubns.:** *Union List of Non-Canadian Newspapers Held by Canadian Libraries* (1968, 1977); various articles. **Activities:** 4, 12; 15, 17, 24; 59, 75, 91 **Addr.:** 1166 Field St., Ottawa, K2C 2P8 Canada.

Rusiewski, Charles B. (N. 4, 1935, DuBois, IL) Media Ctr. Dir., Nashville Cmnty. HS, 1967–, Adult Educ. Instr., Bus. Educ., Kaskasia Jr. Coll., 1975; Bus. Educ. Tchr., Libn., 1958–67; Bus. Educ. Tchr., Libn., Nokomis HS, 1957–58. **Educ.:** South. IL Univ., 1953–57, BS (LS, Bus. Admin.), 1965–67, MS (Instr. Media); Pub. Lib. Admin., Media Spec., Tchg. K-12 1963–67 (Cert.). **Orgs.:** IL LA: Rev. Com. IL Assn. Media Educ.: Exec. Bd. (1982–83); Budget Com. (Treas., 1972). ALA: AASL; various nsltr. exhibits; Nsltr. Eds. Discuss. RT (Ch., 1976). IL AECT. Natl. Educ. Assn. IL Educ. Assn. Nashville Cmnty. Sch. Bd. St. Ann's Cath. Church: Par. Cncl. (1967–76). **Honors:** IL Ofc. of Educ. Recipient, Auth. of Spec. Grant LIFE, 1975; IL Assn. for Media in Educ., Named Ch. of Anl. Conf. Reservation and Regis. Com. "Entering the 80s," 1980. **Pubns.:** Ed., *IL Assn. Media Educ. News For You* (1975–); various reviews, *Sch. Lib. Jnl.* **Activities:** 10; 32, 46, 48; 59, 75, 92 **Addr.:** 207 E. Chester St., Nashville, IL 62263.

Ruskell, Virginia A. (Je. 4, 1948, Nashville, TN) Ref. Coord., W. GA Coll., 1980–, Coord. of Bibl. Instr., 1977–80, ILL Libn., 1970–77. **Educ.:** Emory Univ., 1967–69, BA (Hist.); George Peabody Coll., 1969–70, MLS; W. GA Coll., 1971–75, MA (Eng.). **Orgs.:** GA LA: Int. Frdm. Com. (1980). Southeast. LA. AAUP. **Honors:** Beta Phi Mu, 1970; Cncl. on Lib. Resrcs., Lib. Srvs. Enhancement Grant, 1976–77. **Activities:** 1; 31, 39; 55, 70 **Addr.:** Box 844, Carrollton, GA 30117.

Russ, Marjorie Jaris (F. 7, 1926, Los Angeles, CA) Supvsr. of Recs., Long Beach Pub. Lib., 1976–; Gen. Libn., Los Altos Branch Lib., 1975–76; Sub. Libn., Long Beach Pub. Lib., 1974–75. **Educ.:** CA State Univ., 1969–71, BA (Hist.); Univ. of South. CA, 1971–73, MS (LS). **Orgs.:** Lib. Sodalitas: Secy. (1980–81); Treas. (1981–). CA LA. Msc. LA. Amer. Hist. Assn. Oral Hist. Assn. **Activities:** 9, 11; 16, 26, 39 **Addr.:** P.O. Box 3064, Newport Beach, CA 92663.

Russell, David A. (Ag. 15, 1934, Wichita, KS) Instr., LS, Univ. of WY, 1980–; Dir. of Educ. Media, IA City Cmnty. Sch. Dist., 1972–80; Libn., Grand Blanc HS, 1970–72; Staff Spec., Libs., Flint Cmnty. Sch. Dist., 1967–70, Tchr., 1959–67. **Educ.:** Univ. of MI, 1954–56, AB (Eng.), 1960–66, AM (Educ.), 1958–59, Tchr. Cert., 1968–71, AMLS. **Orgs.:** ALA: AASL/Disting. Lib. Srvs. Awd. for Sch. Admins. Com. (1979–81), PR (Unit 5 Head, 1981–). AECT: Div. of Educ. Media Mgt./VP–Pres. Elec. (1978–79), Pres. (1979–80), Bd. (1976–78); Cncl. (1978–80). **Pubns.:** "Application of Accountability to School Media Programs," *AV Instr.* (D. 1975). **Activities:** 10, 11; 17, 26, 32; 63, 89 **Addr.:** 1121 Park Ave., Laramie, WY 82070.

Russell, Dolores E. (D. 16, 1926, Duquesne, PA) Mgr., Recs. and Files Oper., Westinghouse Electric Corp. Nuclear Energy Systems, 1980–, Tech. Adv. to QA Mgr., 1978–80, Mgr., Recs. and Files Oper., 1976–78, Mgr., Files Oper., 1973–76, Syst. Anal., 1970–73; Recs. Admin., W. Penn Power Co., 1954–70. **Educ.:** Westminster Coll., 1944–48, BA (Psy.); Univ. of Pittsburgh, 1964–67, MLS. **Orgs.:** SLA. Assn. of Recs. Mgrs. and Admins.: VP, Reg. I (1970–71). Assn. for Syst. Mgt.: Pres., Pittsburgh Chap. (1978–79). **Honors:** Assn. of Recs. Mgrs. and Admins., Awd. of Merit, 1976; Assn. for Syst. Mgt., Achvmt. Awd., 1980. **Pubns.:** "Library and Records Management by Objective," *Recs. Mgt. Qtly.* (1977); "A Records Managers View of Micrographics," *The Office* (1975); other articles. **Activities:** 17, 33, 38; 64, 84 **Addr.:** Westinghouse Nuclear Energy Systems, P. O. Box 355, Pittsburgh, PA 15230.

Russell, Dorothy W. (My. 20, 1946, Philipsburg, PA) Assoc. Dir., PALINET, 1982–, Coord., Netwk. Srvs., 1976–82; Bibl. Asst., Un. Lib. Cat. of PA, 1972–76. **Educ.:** PA State Univ., 1964–68, BA (Jrnlsm); Drexel Univ., 1974–76, MLS. **Orgs.:** ALA: ASCLA. PA LA: PA Un. List of Serials Adv. Com. **Honors:** Beta Phi Mu. **Pubns.:** "Bibliographic Networks," *Bltn. of the Amer. Socty. for Info. Sci.* (Je. 1979); "Interlibrary Loan in a Network Environment: The Good and the Bad News," *Spec. Libs.* (Ja. 1982); *Index to the Union Library Catalogue on Microfilm* (1976). **Activities:** 24, 34; 56, 62, 75 **Addr.:** PALINET, 3420 Walnut St., Philadelphia, PA 19104.

Russell, Flora L. (Ag. 9, 1940, Brundidge, AL) Asst. Dean, Lrng. Resrcs., Cmnty. Coll. of Allegheny Cnty. North, 1969–; Tchr., 1961–65. **Educ.:** AL State Coll., 1957–61, BS (Sci.); Univ. of Pittsburgh, 1967–68, MLS, 1973–(LS); Doct. Student. **Orgs.:** PA LA: Tech. Arrange. Com. (1974, 1980). ALA. PA Lrng. Resrcs. Assn. Assn. for the Std. of Afro-Amer. Life and Hist.: Secy.-Treas. (1974–). Zonta: Secy. (1981). Assn. of Lrng. Ctrs. in Higher Educ.: Pres. (1980–81). **Activities:** 1, 12; 17, 22, 39; 58, 89, 91 **Addr.:** Community College of Allegheny County, Center North, 1130 Perry Ave., Pittsburgh, PA 15237.

Russell, J(ohn) Thomas (Ag. 27, 1935, Washington, DC) Dir., Natl. Defense Univ., 1976–; Assoc. Libn., U.S. Milit. Acad., 1971–76, Asst. Libn., 1968–71, Chief, Spec. Col. Div., 1964–68, Spec. Col. Libn., 1963–64; Reader Srvs. Libn., U.S. Nvl. Weapons Lab., 1961–63; Pub. Srvs. Libn., Washington and Lee Univ., 1959–61. **Educ.:** Kenyon Coll., 1954–57, AB (Hist.); Univ. of MI, 1958–59, MALS. **Orgs.:** SLA: Treas.; Milit. Libns. Div. Archons of Colophon. Fed. Lib. and Info. Netwk.: Exec. Adv. Cncl. (Ch., 1979–80). Army Lib. Cncl. **Honors:** U.S. Army (W. Point), Outstan. Performance Awd., 1967, U.S. Army (Nat'l Defense Univ.), Outstan. Performance Awd., 1978, 1980. **Pubns.:** *West Point Thayer Papers, 1808–1833* (1964); *Edgar Allan Poe, The Army Years* (1972); various bibls. and poems. **Activities:** 1, 2, 4; 17, 23, 34, 35, 39, 45; 55 **Addr.:** National Defense University Library, Fort Lesley J. McNair, 4th and P Sts., S.W., Washington, DC 20319.

Russell, Jane Dexter (D. 17, 1928, Teaneck, NJ) Ast. Law Libn., Univ. of NC at Chapel Hill, 1980–; Ast. Law Libn., Univ. of MO, Kansas City, 1978–79; Asst. Law Libn., Univ. of FL, 1974–78; Assoc. Dir., Lake City Cmnty. Coll., 1970–72. **Educ.:** Univ. of FL, 1967–69, BAE (Educ., LS); 1969–70, MEd; FL State Univ., 1973–74; Advnc. MLS; 1975, crs. completed for PhD. **Orgs.:** ALA. AECT. AALL. Mensa: Lib. Spec. Interest Grp. (Coord.). **Honors:** Beta Phi Mu, 1975. **Pubns.:** Ed., "Biblio Mania," *Mensa Nsltr. for Libns.* (1977–79); numerous reviews. **Activities:** 1; 20, 32, 33; 56, 77, 93 **Addr.:** 2861 Rue Sans Famille, Raleigh, NC 27607.

Russell, Jane Dexter (D. 17, 1938, Teaneck, NJ) Asst. Law Libn., Head Cat., Law Lib. Univ. of NC (Chapel Hill), 1980–; Asst. Law Libn., Head Tech. Srvs., Bloch Law Lib., Univ. MO (Kansas City), 1978–79; Asst. Law Libn., Ref., Holland Law Lib., Univ. FL, 1974–78, LS Instr., 1973; Assoc. Dir., Lrng. Resrc. Ctr., Lake City Cmnty. Coll., 1970–72. **Educ.:** Univ. of FL, 1967–69, BA (Educ.), 1969–70, MEd; FL State Univ., 1973–74, MLS; Cert. Law Libn., 1979. **Orgs.:** ALA: ACRL, Nonprint Ed. Bd. (1981–). NC LA. AALL. AECT. AAUW. Mensa: Libn. Spec. Interest Grp., Nsltr. Ed. and Coord. (1977–79). **Honors:** Beta Phi Mu, 1975; Pi Lambda Theta, 1968; Phi Kappa Phi, 1969. **Pubns.:** Reviews. **Activities:** 1, 12; 20, 32; 77 **Addr.:** 2861 Rue Sans Famille, Raleigh, NC 27607.

Russell, John S. (Ja. 21, 1923, Winnipeg, MB) City Libn., Winnipeg Pub. Lib., 1979–, Asst. City Libn., 1979; Chief Libn., St. James-Assiniboia Pub. Lib., 1956–78; Chief Libn., St. Boniface Pub. Lib., 1952–56. **Educ.:** Univ. of MB, 1942–46, BA; Univ. of Toronto, 1949–50, BLS. **Orgs.:** MB LA. Can. LA. **Pubns.:** Jt. auth., "Library Amalgamation: The Winnipeg Experience," *Can. Lib. Jnl.* (Je. 1980). **Activities:** 9; 17 **Addr.:** Winnipeg Public Library, 251 Donald St., Winnipeg, MB R3C 3P5 Canada.

Russell, Joyce R. (N. 6, 1920, Chicago, IL) Sr. Resrch. Info. Sci., E.R. Squibb, 1980–, Supvsr. Lib. Opers., 1973–80; Tech. Libn., Thiokol Chem. Corp., 1969–73; Chem. Libn., Univ. FL, 1967–69. **Educ.:** Univ. of KY, 1939–42, BS (Chem.); Rosary Coll., 1966–67, MLS. **Orgs.:** SLA: Princeton Trenton Chap., Hosplty. Ch., Prog. Ch., Secy., Dir., VP, Pres. (1971–81). Amer. Chem. Socty.: Trenton Sect., Bus. Mgr., Secy., Dir. (1969–79). **Honors:** Beta Phi Mu, 1967; Mortar Bd., Sigma Pi Sigma, 1942; Chi Delta Phi; Pi Sigma Alpha, 1942. **Pubns.:** Ed., *Preservation of Library Materials* (1980); "Microforms Pro and Con, Microform Review," (forthcoming); various sps. **Addr.:** 343 Berwyn Ave., Trenton, NJ 08618.

Special Subjects/Services: 50. Adult educ.; 51. Advert./Mktg.; 52. Aerosp.; 53. Agric.; 54. Area std.; 55. Arts/Hum.; 56. Autom.; 57. Bibl./Prtg.; 58. Bio. sci.; 59. Bus./Fin.; 60. Chem.; 61. Copyrt.; 62. Documtn.; 63. Educ.; 64. Engin.; 65. Env.; 66. Eth. grps.; 67. Film; 68. Food/Nutr.; 69. Geneal.; 70. Geo.; 71. Geol.; 72. Handcpd.; 73. Hist.; 74. Int. frdm.; 75. Info. sci.; 76. Insr.; 77. Law; 78. Legis.; 79. Math./Comp. sci.; 80. Med.; 81. Metals; 82. Nat. resrcs.; 83. Newsp.; 84. Nuc. sci.; 85. Oral hist.; 86. Petr./Energy; 87. Pharm.; 88. Phys./Astr./Math.; 89. Readg.; 90. Relig.; 91. Sci./Tech.; 92. Soc. sci.; 93. Telecom.; 94. Transp.; 95. (other).

Russell, Keith W. (J. 2, 1945, Pittsfield, IL) Prog. Assoc., Cncl. on Lib. Resrcs., 1981–; Head, Sci.-Engin. Lib., The Univ. of AZ, 1980–81; Asst. Staff and Fiscal Srv. Libn., Univ. of TX, Austin, 1977–79; Resrch. Libn., Houston Acad. of Med.–TX Med. Ctr. Lib., 1974–76; Serials Libn., 1972–74. **Educ.:** IL State Univ., 1962–66, BS (Bio.) Univ. of IL, 1969–71, MS (Bot.); 1971–72, MS (LS). **Orgs.:** Med. LA: Mem. Com. (1973–76). ALA: ACRL, Leg. Com. (1978–); Un. Rel. for Mgrs. Com. (1979–). ASIS. AAAS. **Honors:** Beta Phi Mu. **Pubns.:** Jt. auth., *Costs and their assessment to users of a medical library* (1977); Articles on plant ecology. **Activities:** 1, 12; 17, 25, 35; 58, 80, 91 **Addr.:** Council on Library Resources, One Dupont Cir., Washington, DC 20036.

Russell, Mary A. (S. 18, 1940, Rochester, NY) Head Libn., Timberland Reg. Lib., 1972–, Head Libn., Bldg. Supvsr., Chehalis Branch, 1970–72. **Educ.:** Bucknell Univ., 1958–62, BA (Psy.); Univ. WA, 1969–70, MLS. **Orgs.:** ALA: State Mem. Com. (Ch., 1974–76). WA LA: Mem. Com. (1979–81). Pac. NW LA. Zonta Club of Olympia: Pres. (1981–82); 1st VP, Pres.-Elect (1980–81), 2nd VP (1979–80); Rec. Secy. (1978–79). AAUW: Olympia Branch (Treas., 1974–76); PR Com. (1974); various other ofcs. Thurston Cnty. Litcy. Cncl.: Various coms. Voluntary Action Ctr.: Various coms. **Honors:** Beta Phi Mu, 1970. **Activities:** 9, 14-Reg. syst.; 17, 36, 47; 62, 75 **Addr.:** Lacey Public Library, 4516 Lacey Blvd., Lacey, WA 98503.

Russell, Mattie Underwood (My. 14, 1915, Randolph, MS) Cur. of Mss., Duke Univ., 1952–, Asst. Cur. of Mss., 1948–52; Visit. Assoc. Prof., Univ. of NC, 1969–78; Asst. Prof., Mars Hill Coll., 1943–46; Tchr., three MS HS, 1937–43. **Educ.:** Univ. of MS, 1933–37, BA (Hist.), 1937–40, MA (Hist.); Duke Univ., 1946–56, PhD (Hist.). **Orgs.:** ALA: ALA/SAA Jt. Com. on Lib.–Arch. Relshps. (Ch., 1974–78). SAA Com. on Educ. and Prof. Dev. (1977–80). South. Hist. Assn.: Natl. Arch. Adv. Cncl., Rep. (1977–). Hist. Socty. of NC: Pres., 1974–75. NC Literary and Hist. Assn.: R. D. W. Connor Awd. Bd. (1962, 1972). **Honors:** SAA, Fellow, 1979. **Pubns.:** Jt. ed., "Essays in Southern History in Honor of Robert H. Woody," *S. Atl. Qtly.* (Win. 1974); "NC Ruling Menaces Manuscript Collections," *Amer. Libs.* (O. 1977); "The Manuscript Department in the Duke University Library," *Amer. Archvst.* (Jl. 1965); "Organization of Materials Within the Library," *Materials by and about American Negroes. Papers Presented at an Institute Sponsored by the Atlanta University School of Library Service* (1967); various articles in LS and hist. jnls. (1949–79). **Activities:** 1; 17, 45 **Addr.:** 2209 Woodrow St., Durham, NC 27705.

Russell, Ralph E. (Ja. 25, 1938, Bradenton, FL) Univ. Libn., GA State Univ., 1975–; Dir. of Lib. Srvs., E. Carolina Univ., 1973–75; Dir., Sci. Lib., Univ. of GA, 1968–71; Head Libn., FL Jr. Coll. at Jacksonville, 1966–68; Asst. Circ., Asst. Acq. Libn., Univ. of South. CA, 1964–66. **Educ.:** FL State Univ., 1957–60, AB (Eng.), 1960–61, MS (LS); NY Univ., 1961–62, MA (Eng.); FL State Univ., 1971–73, PhD (LS). **Orgs.:** Southeast. Lib. Netwk.: Bd. of Dirs. (Ch., 1979–81). SELA: Coll. and Univ. Sect. (Ch., 1978–80). ALA: ACRL, Com. on Acad. Status, Univ. Libs. Strg. Com. OCLC User's Cncl. **Honors:** Beta Phi Mu; Omicron Delta Kappa. **Pubns.:** "Growing Pains," *Proc. of First ACRL Conf.* (1978); "Search for Identity," *TN Libn.* (Fall 1979). **Activities:** 1; 17, 34 **Addr.:** Pullen Library, Georgia State University, 100 Decatur St., S.E., Atlanta, GA 30303.

Russell, Richard A. (Ja. 1, 1928, Buffalo, NY) Mgr., Cat. Dept., Brodart, Inc., 1965–; Cat., Buffalo and Erie Cnty. Pub. Lib., 1958–65; Circ. Libn., Niagara Univ., 1956–57; Libn. Bkmobile. Sci., Buffalo Pub. Lib., 1955–56; Lectr., Lib. Sci., Williamsport Area Cmnty. Coll., 1965–68. **Educ.:** SUNY, Geneseo, 1952–55, BS (LS); Canisius Coll., 1955–56, MA (Eng.). **Orgs.:** ALA. **Activities:** 12; 20, 21, 46; 74, 75, 91 **Addr.:** Brodart, Inc., 1609 Memorial Ave., Williamsport, PA 17705.

Russo, Mary Townsend (Mr. 10, 1923, Providence, RI) Spec. Cols. Libn.–Broadsides, John Hay Lib., Brown Univ., 1977–, Asst. Spec. Cols. Libn., 1966–77. **Educ.:** RI Coll., 1941–45, EdB (Educ.); Univ. of RI, 1964–66, MLS. **Orgs.:** ALA. RI LA. New Eng. Archvsts. Amer. Prtg. Hist. Assn.: New Eng. Chap. RI Hist. Socty. N. Smithfield Heritage Assn. Women Admins. of Brown Univ. Friends. of the Lib. Brown Univ. **Activities:** 1; 15, 20, 45; 55, 57 **Addr.:** 57 Morse Ave., North Smithfield, RI 02895.

Ruthven, Patricia Evelyn (D. 11, 1938, Dorking, Surrey, Eng.) Head, Ref. Dept., Harriet Irving Lib., Univ. of NB, 1976–, Ref. Libn., 1967–76; Chld. Libn., Chiswick Pub. Lib., 1964–67; Lib. Asst., Kensington Pub. Lib., 1961–63. **Educ.:** King's Coll., London, 1957–60, BA (Grmn.); LA (UK), Assoc. **Orgs.:** LA (UK). Can. LA. Can. Assn. of Coll. and Univ. Libns. Atl. Prov. LA. Indexing and Abs. Socty. of Can. **Activities:** 1; 31, 39; 55 **Addr.:** Reference Dept., Harriet Irving Library, University of NB, P.O. Box 7500, Fredericton, NB E3B 5H5 Canada.

Rutkowski, Hollace A. (N. 16, 1951, Cleveland, OH) Mgr., Resrch. and Ref. Srvs., Franklin Mint Corp., 1976–; Libn. Handcpd., RI Dept. State Lib. Srv., 1974–76. **Educ.:** Cleveland State Univ., 1969–74, BA (Soclgy.); Univ. RI, 1974–76, MLS. **Orgs.:** SLA: Philadelphia Chap., Pres. (1980–81); Pres.-Elect (1979–80), Secy. (1978–79); Awd. Com. (1977–78). PA Citizens for Better Lib. Free Lib., Haverford Twp., Lib. Gld. **Activities:** 12; 39, 41; 51, 59, 61 **Addr.:** Information Research Services, The Franklin Mint, Franklin Center, PA 19091.

Rutledge, Deborah Toomey (Je. 29, 1950, Bellows Falls, VT) Talking Bk. Libn., Albany-Dougherty Pub. Lib., 1979–; Shared Srv. Libn., Lake Blackshear Reg. Lib., 1977–79; Fld. Srv. Libn., FL Reg. Lib. Blind and Phys. Handcpd., 1976–77; Asst. Supvsr., Resrc. Coord. Unit, Lib. of Congs., 1974–76. **Educ.:** Windham Coll., 1968–72, BA (Hist.); Univ. of MD, 1973–74, MLS. **Orgs.:** ALA: ASCLA, Lib. Srv. Blind Phys. Handcpd., Exec. Com. (1980–81), Org. Handbk. Com. (1978–79), Radio Readg. Srv. Com.; Hlth. Rehab. Lib. Srv., Intl. Rel. Com. (1977–78). South. Conf. Libn. Srvg. Blind and Phys. Handcpd.: Vice–Ch. (1979–81). GA LA: RT Blind Phys. Handcpd. Bus. and Prof. Women's Club. **Honors:** Windham Coll., Blue Key Hon. Socty., 1972. **Pubns.:** *Toys, Games and Gift Ideas for the Blind and Physically Handicapped* (1976). **Addr.:** 1922 W. Highland Ave., Albany, GA 31707.

Rutstein, Joel Stephen (S. 5, 1940, Burlington, VT) Col. Dev. Libn., CO State Univ. Libs., 1979–, Soc. Sci. Libn., 1971–79; Asst. Cat. Libn., Univ. of NH Lib., 1969–71, Asst. Ref. Libn., 1967–69. **Educ.:** Univ. of VT, 1958–62, BA (Pol. Sci.); Boston Univ., 1962–63, AM (Hist.); Simmons Coll., 1966–67, MS (LS), Banaras Hindu Univ. (India), 1979–80, Cert. **Orgs.:** ALA. CO LA. **Pubns.:** "The Role of Newspapers as an Information Resource," *Lib. Scene;* jt. auth., "The Politics of Book Fund Allocation," *New Horizons for Acad. Libs.* (1979). jt. auth., "Educating Large Numbers of Users in University Libraries," *Progress in Educating the Library User* (1978); "Climbing Everest: A History," *Climbing Mag.* (Je. 1973). **Activities:** 1; 15, 34; 54 **Addr.:** Colorado State University Libraries, Ft. Collins, CO 80523.

Ruwell, Mary Elizabeth (Jl. 4, 1949, Cynwyd, PA) Archvst., Univ. Musm. of the Univ. of PA, 1981–; Archvst., Natl. Arch., 1977–81; Archvst., INA Corp., Philadelphia, 1972–76. **Educ.:** Georgetown Univ., 1966–70, BS (Fr.); Univ. of PA, 1972–, MA (Amer. Cvlztn.); Natl. Arch. Inst. for Arch. Admin., 1972. **Orgs.:** SAA: Bus. Arch. Com. (1973–77); Lcl. Arrange. Com. (1975). Mid Atl. Reg. Arch. Conf.: Strg. Com. (Ch., 1979–81). **Pubns.:** *Guide to INA Corporation Archives* (1976); "Fire Insurance Records: A Versatile Resource," *Amer. Archvst.* (Ja. 1975). **Activities:** 2; 24, 45; 55 **Addr.:** 2116 Spruce St., Philadelphia, PA 19103.

Ryan, Christine (Ap. 25, 1951, CT) Ref. Libn., Dartmouth Coll. Lib., 1977–; Ref. Libn., Wesleyan Univ. Lib., 1975–77. **Educ.:** Univ. of CT, 1970–74, BS (Psy.); Simmons Coll., 1974–75, MS (LS); Dartmouth Coll., 1978–80, MALS (Liberal Std.). **Orgs.:** CT LA: Coll. and Univ. Sect. (Secy., 1976–77). **Activities:** 1; 31, 33, 49-Online sch.; 55, 63, 92 **Addr.:** Reference Department, Baker Library, Dartmouth College, Hanover, NH 03755.

Ryan, Clare E. (Je. 17, 1927, Springfield, MA) Dir. of Tech. Srvs., NH State Lib., 1968–; Head, Cat. Dept., Carnegie Lib. of Pittsburgh, 1961–68; Dir. of Tech. Srvs., Arlington Cnty. Lib., 1960–61; Dir. of Tech. Srvs., Racine Pub. Lib., 1956–60. **Educ.:** Coll. of Our Lady of the Elms, 1945–49, AB (Eng. Lit., Hist.); Carnegie Lib. Sch., 1953–54, MLS. **Orgs.:** ALA: RTSD; PLA, Resrch. Com. (1977–80), Dewey Decimal Ed. Policy Com. (1970–79). **Activities:** 13; 15, 29, 46 **Addr.:** 203 Loudon Rd., Bldg. 1, Apt. 21, Concord, NH 03301.

Ryan, Frederick William (Mr. 16, 1941, Highland Park, MI) Asst. Dir. of Lib., CA State Univ., 1977–; Head of Lrng. Resrc. Ctr., South. Alberta Inst. of Tech., 1971–77; Slavic Biblgphr., Univ. of IL, 1965–71. **Educ.:** Univ. of CA, Riverside, 1959–63, BA (Russ.); Univ. of IL, 1964–65, MA (Slavic Langs. and Lits.), 1965–68, MS (LS). **Orgs.:** ALA: ACRL/Slavic Sect., ASIS. AECT. CA LA. Other orgs. **Pubns.:** "Four Days for Four Years", *Can. Lib. Jnl.* (Ag. 1976). **Activities:** 1; 17, 32, 46; 54, 56, 75 **Addr.:** California State University - Library, Chico, CA 95929.

Ryan, L.(oretta) Dolores (Jl. 8, 1913, Cleveland, OH) Retired, 1979–; Head, Pub. Srvs., Cleveland State Univ. Lib., 1971–79, Head, Coll. Lib. Spec. Srvs., 1969–71, Undergrad. Libn., 1965–69. **Educ.:** Case West. Rsv. Univ., 1931–35, BS, 1942–43, MSLS; IBM 1965, Cert. (Lib. Autom.); Case West. Rsv. Univ., 1976–77, Cont. Ed. Cert. **Orgs.:** ALA: Ref. Bks. of the Year Com. (1964–70); Hist. Sect. (Secy., 1968–70). Tri-State ACRL: Secy., Treas. (1970–71). AAUW. Womens Natl. Bk. Assn. Cuyahoga Cmnty. Coll.: Various coms. Case West. Rsv. Univ. Sch. of Lib. Sci. **Honors:** Kiwanis Club Awd., 1960. **Pubns.:** *Rudiments of Research* (1965); *Bibliography for Social and Industrial Relations: Instructional Materials Lab.* **Activities:** 1, 12; 17, 31, 39; 56, 61, 63 **Addr.:** 12540 Edgewater Dr. #909, Lakewood, OH 44107.

Ryan, Mary Annette (Je. 15, 1942, St. Louis, MO) Head, Ellis Lib. Ref. Srvs., Univ. of MO–Columbia Libs., 1977–, Head, Undergrad. Lib., 1974–77, Ref. Libn., 1972–74. **Educ.:** St. Louis Univ., 1960–64, BS magna cum laude (Hist.); Univ. of IL, 1968–69, MA (Pol. Sci.), 1970–71, MS (LS). **Orgs.:** ALA. MO LA. **Activities:** 1; 39; 92 **Addr.:** Ellis Library Room 202D, University of Missouri - Columbia Libraries, Columbia, MO 65201.

Ryan, Pamela Ann (N. 27, 1952, La Jolla, CA) Chld. Libn., Contra Costa Cnty. Lib., 1979–; Serials Un. List Libn., Stanford Univ. Libs., 1978–79; Catlgr., Santa Clara Cnty., Hlth. Dept. Lib., 1976–78. **Educ.:** Univ. of Santa Clara, 1971–74, BA (Gen. Hum.); San Jose State Univ., 1975–77, MA (LS). **Orgs.:** ALA. CA LA. Assn. of Chld. Libns. **Activities:** 1, 9; 20, 21, 42; 56, 80, 89 **Addr.:** 331 Soto St., Martinez, CA 94553.

Ryan, Patricia M. (Ag. 31, 1950, Philadelphia, PA) Lib. Dir. and Chld. Libn., Ridley Twp. Pub. Lib., 1977–; Ref. Libn., Haverford Twp. Free Lib., 1973–76. **Educ.:** West Chester State Coll., 1968–72, BA (Eng.); Drexel Univ., 1972–73, MS (LS). **Orgs.:** ALA. PA LA: SE Chap. (Vice Ch./Ch. Elect, 1979–81). DE Cnty. Libs. Assn.: Chld. Srvs. Div. (Ch., 1978–79). **Activities:** 9; 17, 21, 28 **Addr.:** Ridley Township Public Library, MacDade Blvd. and Morton Ave., Folsom, PA 19033.

Ryan, R. Paul (F. 10, 1948, Philadelphia, PA) Chief, Closed Lit., Sci. Tech. Info. Branch, U.S. Army Ballistic Resrch. Lab., Aberdeen Proving Ground, MD, 1975–; Libn., Sci., Engin., U.S. Army Picatinny Arsenal, Dover, NJ, 1972–75. **Educ.:** Villanova Univ., 1966–70, BS (Math.); Drexel Univ., 1970–72, MS (Info. Sci.). **Orgs.:** ASIS: Lib. Autom. Netwks. Spec. Interest Grp. (1971–). SLA: Milit. Libns. Div. Defense RDT and E Online Syst. Users Grp.: VP (1980–82). **Honors:** Phi Beta Mu. **Pubns.:** "Managing Libraries in the 1990s," *Procs., Milit. Libns. Div., SLA* (1979). **Activities:** 4; 17; 75, 74 **Addr.:** U.S. Army Ballistic Research Laboratory/ ARRADCOM, ATT: DRDAR-TSB-S, Aberdeen Proving Ground, MD 21005.

Ryan, Richard W. (N. 28, 1930, Columbus, OH) Cur. Bk., William L. Clements Lib., Univ. MI, 1978–; Head, Spec. Col., OH Univ., 1970–78; Libn., and various other positions, Denison Univ., 1964–70; Spec. Rcrt. and various other positions, Lib. of Congs., 1960–63. **Educ.:** OH State Univ., 1956, BA (Hist.); Case West. Rsv. Univ., 1960, MSLS. **Orgs.:** Bibl. Socty. Bibl. Socty. Amer. **Pubns.:** "Peter Edes," *Boston Printers, Publishers and Booksellers, 1640–1800* (1980); "Checklist Peter DeVries and Wilfrid Sheed," *First Printings of American Authors* (1979). **Activities:** 1; 23, 45; 57 **Addr.:** William L. Clements Library, University of Michigan, Ann Arbor, MI 48109.

Rycombel, Judith T. (Mr. 13, 1947, Chicago, IL) Ref. Libn., DePaul Univ. Lib., 1971–; Tchr., Komarek Sch., 1969–71. **Educ.:** DePaul Univ., 1965–69, BM (Msc.); Rosary Coll., 1975–77, MALS. **Orgs.:** SLA. **Activities:** 1; 15, 31, 39; 51, 59 **Addr.:** DePaul University Library, 25 E. Jackson, Chicago, IL 60604.

Ryd, Beverly J. (Ag. 3, 1935, Boston, MA) Asst. VP, Libn., First Boston Corp. 1965; Asst. Catlgr., Fed. Rsv. Bank of NY 1964–65; Ref. Libn., Cornell Univ., 1959–64; Law Libn., CT Gen., 1957–58. **Educ.:** Simmons Coll., 1953–7, BS (LS); Columbia Univ., 1958–59, MS (LS). **Orgs.:** SLA: NY Chap. Pres. (1977–78), other activities. Bus. and Finance Div. NY Lib. Club. WHCOLIS: Del. (1979). NY Gvrs. Conf. on Libs.: Del. (1978). NY Metro. Ref. and Resrch. Lib. Agency: Pub. Srvs. Com. (1978). **Activities:** 12; 17, 39; 59 **Addr.:** 39 Cinderella Ln., East Setauket, NY 11733.

Ryder, Valerie Jeanne (F. 21, 1949, New York, NY) Mgr., Info. Resrcs. Ctr., Westinghouse Water Reactors Div., 1981–; Mgr., Info. and Recs. Systs., Westinghouse Nuclear Srv. Div., 1977–81, Tech. Lib., Nuclear Europe, 1975–77, Tech. Lib., Nuclear Energy Systs., 1971–75; Autom. and Info. Science Lib., OH State Univ., 1970–71. **Educ.:** Univ. of Rochester, 1965–69, AB (Math.); Univ. of Pittsburgh, 1969–70, MLS. **Orgs.:** ASIS. SLA: Nuc. Sci. Div. (Ch., 1974–75); Pittsburgh Chap. (Secy., 1972–74). Assn. of Recs. Mgrs. and Admins. **Honors:** Phi Beta Kappa, 1969; Beta Phi Mu, 1970; ASIS, Outstan. Young Prof., 1977. **Pubns.:** "Impressions of the International Atomic Energy Agency Nuclear Information Resources," *Sci-Tech News* (1977). **Activities:** 12; 17, 38; 56, 75, 84 **Addr.:** Westinghouse Water Reactors Division, P. O. Box 355, Pittsburgh, PA 15230.

Ryken, Jorena (O. 17, 1938, Oskaloosa, IA) Asst. Lib. Dir., Wheaton Coll., 1969–; HS Eng., Sp. Tchr., Libn., Pella Christ. HS, 1964–69; Elem. Tchr., Zeeland Christ. Sch., 1959–62. **Educ.:** Wheaton Coll., 1961–63, AB (Eng.); Univ. of IA, 1963–69, MA (LS); Nova Univ., 1977–80, EdD (Higher Educ.); Central Coll., 1967–68, HS Tchrs. Cert. **Orgs.:** ALA. IL LA: ACRL, Nsltr. Ed. (1978–80). LIBRAS: VP (1977–78); Pres. (1978–79); Treas. (1975–76). **Activities:** 1; 15, 17, 31; 90 **Addr.:** 530 Aurora Way, Wheaton, IL 60187.

Ryland, John A. (S. 21, 1943, Cullman, AL) Libn., Hampden-Sydney Coll., 1979–; Col. Dev. Ofcr., SUNY, Binghamton, 1976–79; Anglo-Germanic Biblgphr., Univ. of VA, 1971–76; Clasfr., Socialhøjskolen (Sch. of Soc. Welfare), Copenhagen, 1970–71. **Educ.:** FL State Univ., 1961–64, BA (Gvt.), 1967–69, MA (Hist.); Danmarks Biblioteksskole (Royal Coll. of Libnshp.), 1969–71, Dip. **Orgs.:** ALA: RTSD/Resrcs. Sect., Col. Dev. Com. (Consult., 1978–82); ACRL, West. European Langs. Specs. Discuss. Grp. Ch., 1977–79)/West. European Specs. Sect., Nom.

PROFESSIONAL ACTIVITIES: Institutions: 1. Acad. lib.; 2. Arch.; 3. Assn.; 4. Fed./Gvt. lib.; 5. Inst. lib.; 6. Mfr./Suppl.; 7. Milit. lib.; 8. Musm.; 9. Pub. lib.; 10. Sch. lib.; 11. Sch. of lib. sci.; 12. Spec. lib.; 13. State lib.; 14. (other). **Functions/Activities:** 15. Acq./Col. dev.; 16. Adult srvs.; 17. Admin.; 18. Apprais.; 19. Archit./Bldgs.; 20. Cat./Class.; 21. Chld. srvs.; 22. Circ.; 23. Cons./Pres.; 24. Consult.; 25. Cont. ed.; 26. Educ. lib. sci.; 27. Ext. srvs.; 28. Fund/Grants; 29. Gvt. pubs.; 30. Indx./Abs.; 31. Instr. lib. use; 32. Media srvs.; 33. Micro.; 34. Netwks./Coop.; 35. Persnl.; 36. PR; 37. Publshg.; 38. Recs. mgt.; 39. Ref. srvs.; 40. Repro.; 41. Resrch.; 42. Review.; 43. Secur.; 44. Serials; 45. Spec. col.; 46. Tech. srvs.; 47. Trustees/Bds.; 48. YA srvs.; 49. (other).

Com. (Ch., 1979–80). **Activities:** 1; 15, 17, 28; 54, 57 **Addr.:** Eggleston Library, Hampden-Sydney College, Hampden-Sydney, VA 23943.

Rystrom, Barbara B. (Je. 26, 1936, Chicago, IL) ILL Libn., Univ. of GA, 1977–; Libn. Commerce (GA) HS, 1975–77. **Educ.:** Univ. of CA, Berkeley, 1954–57, BA, (Eng.), 1966–68, MLS. **Orgs.:** ALA. SELA. GA LA: ILL Coop. RT. Common Cause/GA: Governing Bd. League of Women Voters. **Activities:** 1; 34, 61 **Addr.:** Interlibrary Loan Service, University of Georgia Libraries, Athens, GA 30602.

Rzepecki, Arnold M. (Jl. 1, 1931, Detroit, MI) Libn., Sacred Heart Semy., 1963–, Asst. Libn., 1954–63. **Educ.:** Wayne State Univ., 1949–53, BA (Eng.); Univ. MI, 1953–54, AMLS; Wayne State Univ., 1956–58, MA (Eng.). **Orgs.:** ALA: ALA/Cath. LA Jt. Com. (1971–72); RTSD, Cert. Code Rev. Com. (1975–76). MI LA: Nom. Com. (1970–72); PR Com. (1976–78). Cath. LA: CPLI Com. (1966–73, 1976–); Exec. Bd. (1973–75); various other coms. Polish Amer. LA: Various ofcs. MI Cath. LA: Various ofcs. N. Rosedale Park Civic Assn.: Exec. Bd. (1978–80). **Honors:** Detroit Pub. Lib., Alma Josenhans Awd., 1953. **Pubns.:** Ed., *Book Review Index to Social Science Periodicals* (1979–); ed., *Index to Free Periodicals* Volume 1 (1975–); *Literature and Language Bibliographies from The American Yearbook* (1970); various other pubns. **Activities:** 1; 15, 16, 20; 55, 90 **Addr.:** Sacred Heart Seminary, 2701 Chicago Blvd., Detroit, MI 48206.

Rzeszutko, Judith A. (Ap. 8, –.) Head Catlgr., Worcester (MA) Pub. Lib., 1979–, Catlgr., 1976–79. **Educ.:** Bridgewater State Coll., 1971–75, BA (Anthro.); SUNY, Albany, 1975–76, MLS. **Orgs.:** ALA. New Eng. LA. MA LA: Tech. Srvs. Sect., Prog. Com. (1979–80). **Activities:** 9; 17, 20, 46; 92 **Addr.:** Cataloging Section, Worcester Public Library, Salem Sq., Worcester, MA 01608.

S

Sabatini, Joseph D. (O. 25, 1942, Bronx, NY) Head, Main Lib., Albuquerque Pub. Lib., 1980–, Cmnty. Resrcs. Spec., 1977–79, Head, Info. Srvs., 1973–77; Asst. Libn., Univ. of NM Law Sch. Lib., 1968–73. **Educ.:** Univ. of CA, Los Angeles, 1960–64, BA (Pol. Sci.), 1964–65, MLS. **Orgs.:** NM LA: Pres. (1980–81); 1st VP (1980); 2nd VP (1979–80); Pub. Lib. Div. (Ch., 1976); Legis. and Int. Frdm. Com. (Ch., 1972–74, 1978). **Pubns.:** *American Indian Law: A Bibliography* (1973); jt. auth., "Legislative Support of Library Services in New Mexico," *Libraries in the Political Process* (1980); various articles in *NM Libs. Nsltr.* **Activities:** 9; 16, 17, 39; 78 **Addr.:** 3514 6th St. N.W., Albuquerque, NM 87107.

Sable, Martin H. (S. 24, 1924, Haverhill, MA) Prof., Sch. of Lib. Sci., Univ. of WI, Milwaukee, 1968–; Asst. Resrch. Prof., Latin Amer. Ctr., Univ. of CA, Los Angeles, 1965–68; Ref. Libn., Los Angeles Cnty. Lib., 1964–65; Hum. Ref. Libn., CA State Univ., 1963–64; Ref. Libn., Northeastern Univ., 1959–63. **Educ.:** Boston Univ., 1943–46, AB (Span., Fr.), 1949–52, MA (Latin Amer. Std.); Natl. Univ. of Mex., 1952, Dr en Letras (Span.); Simmons Coll., 1958–59, MS (LS). **Orgs.:** ALA: RASD; LED; Phi Beta Mu Awd. Com. (1975–76); Com. on Lib. Srv. to the Span.-Speaking (1977). AALS. SALAM: Subcom. on Nonprint Mtrls. (1976–79); Lib., Bookdealer, Pubcty. Com. (1979–). Shorewood Lib. Plng. Bd. Midwest Cncl. of Latin Amer. Std. **Honors:** Assn. of Libns. of Colombia, Hon. Mem., 1962. **Pubns.:** Cmplr., *International and Area Studies Librarianship: Case Studies* (1973); *Master Directory for Latin America* (1965); *A Guide to Nonprint Materials for Latin American Studies* (1979); *Latin American Urbanization* (1971); *Exobiology: A Research Guide* (1978); *A Guide to Nonprint Materials for Latin American Studies* (1979); *A Guide to Latin American Studies* (1967); various bks., mono., articles. **Activities:** 11; 26, 39; 54, 55, 57 **Addr.:** 4518 N. Larkin St., Shorewood, WI 53211.

Sabsay, David (S. 12, 1931, Waltham, MA) Dir., Sonoma Cnty. Lib., 1965–; City Libn., Santa Rosa Pub. Lib., 1956–65; Circ. Supvsr., Richmond (CA) Pub. Lib., 1955–56. **Educ.:** Harvard Coll., 1949–53, AB; Univ. of CA, Berkeley, 1954–55, BLS, 1955–56, grad. std. **Orgs.:** ALA: Legis. Com. (1969–73). CA LA: Pres. (1971); Lib. Dev. and Stans. Com. (Ch., 1960–61); Gvt. Rel. Com. (1963–64, 1971–72, 1979–80); Com. Org. (Ch., 1970). N. Bay Coop. Lib. Syst. CA Pub. Lib. Dev. Bd. Various other orgs. Harvard Club of San Francisco Cmwlth. Club. **Honors:** Assoc. Harvard Clubs, Harvard Prize Bk., 1948; CA LA, Cert. of Apprec., 1971, 1980. **Pubns.:** *A Comprehensive Library Services Study for the County of Monterey* (1981); *The National Legislative Network for Libraries: A Master Plan* (1973); *Statistical Study of Public Library Systems, 1963–1968* (1969); "The North Bay Cooperative Library System," *News Notes of CA Libs.* (Sum. 1963); "Regional Library Service," *The Library Reaches Out* (1965); various other pubns. **Activities:** 9, 14-Indp. consult. 13, 19, 34; 74, 78, 95-Lib. fin. **Addr.:** Sonoma County Library, Third & E St., Santa Rosa, CA 95404.

Sacco, Concetta Norma (Ja. 23, 1935, New Haven, CT) Dir., West Haven Pub. Lib., 1971–; Supvsr., Srch. Sect., Bibl. Dept., Yale Univ. 1968–71, Sr. Ref. Asst., 1963–68. **Educ.:** South. CT State Coll., 1952–56, BS (Educ., LS); Syracuse Univ., 1959–62, MSLS. **Orgs.:** ALA: RASD, Cat. Use Com. (Ch., 1970–74), Nom. Com. (1970, 1974–75); PLA, Stans. Com. Task Frc. Adult Srv. (1972–73); various coms. CT LA: Secy. (1962–63); Fed. Coord. (1963–66); Rep. Lg. (1973–75). New Eng. LA. South. CT Lib. Cncl.: Various ofcs. Various other orgs. W. Haven Cncl. of the Arts: Secy. (1974–80). W. Haven Cmnty. Hse.: Bd. of Trustees (1972–). **Honors:** Beta Phi Mu. **Pubns.:** "Book Catalog Use Study," *RQ* (Spr. 1973). **Activities:** 1, 9; 16, 17, 39; 56, 57, 67 **Addr.:** West Haven Public Library, 300 Elm St., West Haven, CT 06516.

Sachse, Gladys M. (Jl. 21, 1918, Shawnee, OK) Assoc. Prof., LS, Asst. Libn., Univ. of Ctrl. AR, 1948–; Actg. Asst. Libn., AR State Lib., Comsn., 1947–48; Cnty. Libn., Yell Cnty. Lib., 1943–47; Tchr., Belleville HS, 1940–43; Tchr., Dardanelle HS, 1939–40. **Educ.:** AR Polytech. Coll., 1936–37; Univ. of Ctrl. AR, 1937–39, BSE (Hist.); LA State Univ., 1943–46, BSLC (LS); Univ. of AR, 1952–55, MEd (Educ. Admin.); various crs. **Orgs.:** ALA. AR LA: Pres. (1951–52). SW LA: Educ. Com. (1956–57, 1965–68); Prog. Com. (1958). AR Cncl. on Lib. Educ.: Ch. (1967–69). AAUW. **Honors:** Univ. of Ctrl. AR, Pres. Achvmt. Awd., 1974; Beta Phi Mu; Phi Kappa Phi; Kappa Kappa Iota. **Pubns.:** *Manual for the Elementary School Library in Arkansas* (1954); "Library Education and Certification–Considerations and Goals," *AR Libs.* (D. 1977). **Activities:** 1; 26 **Addr.:** 358 Farris Rd., Conway, AR 72032.

Sadler, Graham H. (Ag. 17, 1931, Sikeston, MO) Lib. Dir., Cnty of Henrico Pub. Lib., 1978–; Asst. Libn./Dir. of Cmnty. Srvs., Denver Pub. Lib., 1970–77; Assoc. Prof., Div. of Libnshp., KS State Tchrs. Coll., 1967–69; Dir., Ft. Lewis Coll. Lib., 1966–67; Adm. Libn., Kinderhook Reg. Lib., 1961–66; Asst. Libn., SE MO State Coll., 1954–61. **Educ.:** SE MO State Coll., 1949–52, BS (Bus. Adm); Emory Univ., 1955–57; MALS. **Orgs.:** ALA: Adv. Com., Ofc. of Lib. Srvs. to Disadv. (1978–); Subcom. on Lib. Srvs. to Rural and Appalachia Poor (Ch., 1979–). VA LA. SE LA. **Pubns.:** "Denver Public Library Offers Something for Everyone," *The Right To Read and The Nation's Libraries* (1974); "Library Administration," *Encyc. of Educ.* (1969). **Activities:** 9; 17, 36, 47; 50, 89 **Addr.:** County of Henrico Public Library, P.O. Box 27032, Richmond, VA 23273.

Sadler, Judith DeBoard Donnalley (Charleston, WV) Assoc. Prof., LS, E. Carolina Univ., 1969–; Head Catlgr., Morris Harvey Coll., 1966–69; Libn., Univ. of Pittsburgh; Resrch. Libn., Catlgr., WV Lib. Comsn.; Tchr., Anne Arundel Cnty. Schs. **Educ.:** Morris Harvey Coll., 1956–60, (PE, Soc. Sci.); Univ. of Pittsburgh, 1965–66, (LS, Info. Sci.); various crs. in LS, comp. sci. **Orgs.:** AALS. NC LA. SE LA. **Pubns.:** "The Organization of Slides," *Picturescope* (Win. 1974); "What's in a Description? ISBD–An Overview," *Cath. Lib. World* (F. 1982). **Activities:** 1, 10; 20, 26, 34; 56 **Addr.:** Dept. of Library Science, East Carolina University, Greenville, NC 27834.

Sadler, Philip A. (N. 26, 1929, Sikeston, MO) Asst. Prof., Chld. Lit., Ctrl. MO State Univ., 1963–; Eng., Sp. Tchr., Edison HS, 1954–63; Elem. Tchr., Sikeston, MO Pub. Schs., 1949–50. **Educ.:** Southeast MO State Coll., 1947–52 BS (Educ., Eng.); Trinity Univ., 1959–62, MA (Eng. Sp.); FL State Univ., 1966–68, ABD. **Orgs.:** MOLA. MO Assn. of Sch. Libns. Mark Twain Awd. Com. Chld. Lit. Assn. Phi Delta Kappa: Nsltr. Ed. **Honors:** MO Writer's Gld., Cert. of Recog., 1972. **Pubns.:** "History Lives in Books for Children," *Sch. and Cmnty.* (Ja. 1975); "Realism in YA Books: Is It Here To Stay?" *Show-Me Libs.* (O.–N. 1979); consult., reviewer, *Elem. Tchr.* (1976–78). contrib., *Dictionary of Literary Biography on American Writers for Children.* **Activities:** 1, 10; 21, 26, 42; 55, 89 **Addr.:** College of Education and Human Services, Central Missouri State University, Warrensburg, MO 64093.

Sadler, Rowena S. (Ap. 20, 1921, Spokane, WA) Chief, Lib. Srvs., Info. Branch, Soc. Secur. Admin., 1978–; Chief, Lib. Srvs., Dept. of Defense, Overseas Europe, Schs., 1973–76; Asst. Exec. Secy., ASL, 1972–73; Asst. Proj. Ofcr., Intl. Rel. Ofc., ALA, 1970–72. **Educ.:** Mills Coll., 1939–43, BA (Eng.); Cath. Univ., 1947–48, BSLS. **Orgs.:** Assn. of Info. Mgrs. SLA. ALA. **Honors:** Soc. Secur. Admin., Comsn. Cit., 1980; Dept. of the Army, Cert. of Outstan. Performance, 1976. **Activities:** 10, 12; 17; 74, 92 **Addr.:** Library Services and Information Branch, Rm. 571, Altmeyer Bldg., Baltimore, MD 21235.

Sadlier Mary Ann (O. 24, 1916, Lima, OH) Dir., Lima Pub. Lib., 1980–, Asst. Dir., 1972–80, Head, Cat. Dept., 1960–80; Libn., Lima Ctrl. Cath. HS, 1958–60; Chld. Libn., Lima Pub. Lib., 1940–42. **Educ.:** Mary Manse Coll., 1933–37, AB (Educ.); Carnegie Inst. of Tech., 1939–40, BS (LS). **Orgs.:** ALA. North. OH Tech. Srvs. Libns.: Secy. (1968). OH LA: Staff Dev. Com. (Ch., 1970–71); Int. Frdm. Com., Ch.; Tech. Srvs. Div. (Ch., 1968); Anl. Reg. Mtg. (Ch., 1974). Lima State Hosp.: Lib. Adv. Com. (1971–). **Activities:** 5, 9; 15, 17, 20; 72, 74, 75 **Addr.:** 2028 W. High St., Lima, OH 45805.

Saenz, Mercedes (Ap. 7, 1939, Santurce, PR) Dir., Col. Puertorriqueña, Univ. of PR, 1977–, Admin., Dirección Colección Puertorriqueña, 1977; Prof., Dirección Com. de Pubns. de la SBPR, 1976–77; Libn., Ref. Dept., Univ. of PR, 1975–76, Consult., Com. Financiero del Gobernador, 1975; Catlgr., Tech. Srvs., 1973–74; Docente, Estudios Hispánicos, 1962–64. **Educ.:** Coll. Sacro Corde Santurce, 1960, BA; Univ. of PR, Rio Piedras, 1974, MLS; Sussex Univ., UK, 1977, D Litt; Oxford Univ., 1975, Doctor of Classics Lit. **Orgs.:** SBPR. Assn. de Bibs. Univ. y de Investigación del Caribe. Socty. de Hipnólogos de PR. Metro. Opera Gld. **Pubns.:** *Acercamiento a José de Diego y Luis Palés Matos* (1976); *Bécquer: poeta innovador* (1976); *Bibliografía anotada: revistas y periódicos de Puerto Rico* (1974); *El desarrollo económico de Puerto Rico a través de una bibliografía anotada* (1975); *Introducción a Fray Luis de León* (1976); various bks., rpts., articles. **Activities:** 1, 2; 23, 24, 37; 50, 55, 83 **Addr.:** P.O. Box 22828, University of Puerto Rico Station, San Juan, PR 00931.

Safford, Herbert D. (Jl. 27, 1942, Burlington, VT) Assoc. Dir., Lib., Bowie State Coll., 1979–; Dir., Lib., North. MT Coll., 1978–79; Prep. Libn., VA Polytech. Inst., State Univ., 1973–75, Hum. Catlgr., 1972–73. **Educ.:** Univ. of VT, 1961–65, BA (Phil.); Yale Univ., 1965–66, 1968–69, MA (Phil.); Columbia Univ., 1971–72, MLS; various crs. **Orgs.:** ALA. MD LA. MT LA. VT LA. Potomac Tech. Prcs. Libns. **Activities:** 1, 12; 15, 17, 46; 55, 56, 90 **Addr.:** 105-B Donzen Dr., Bel Air, MD 21014.

Safran, Franciska K. (Ag. 22, 1935, Ujkécske, Hungary) Assoc. Libn., Ref., SUNY, Fredonia Reed Lib., 1973–; Chief Biblgphr., Univ. of VA, Alderman Lib., 1970–72; Acq. Libn., Monmouth Coll., Guggenheim Meml. Lib., 1966–70; Lib. Clerk, Syracuse Univ., Carnegie Lib., 1959–66. **Educ.:** Syracuse Univ., 1959–65, AB (Eng. Lit.), 1965–66, MSLS; various crs. **Orgs.:** NY LA: Resrcs. and Tech. Srvs. Sect., Resrcs. Com. (Ch., 1980). West. NY ACRL: ON Chap. (1976). SUNY LA: 2nd VP (1979). Amer. Assn. for State and Lcl. Hist. **Honors:** Mncpl. Arch. of Amsterdam, The Netherlands, Resrch. Grant, 1981; Beta Phi Mu; Phi Alpha Theta. **Pubns.:** "Defensive Ordering," *Library Acquisitions: Practice and Theory* (1979). **Activities:** 1; 15, 39; 54, 55 **Addr.:** State University of New York, Reed Library, Reference Dept., Fredonia, NY 14063.

Sage, Mary D. (Je. 12, 1947, Marysville, CA) Asst. Dir., Metro. WA Lib. Cncl., 1977–. **Educ.:** Univ. of CA, Santa Barbara, 1965–69, BA (Combined Soc. Sci.); Univ. of MD, 1974–75, MLS. **Orgs.:** ALA: ASCLA/Multitype Lib. Coop. Sect., Pubns. Com. (1979–80). DC LA: (1979). ASIS. SLA. **Pubns.:** *Model Management Curriculum for Special Libraries* (1979); *Continuing Library Education: An Interdisciplinary Approach Women and Factors Affecting their Development* (1975). **Activities:** 12; 17, 25, 34 **Addr.:** Metropolitan Washington Library Council, COG, 1875 Eye St. N.W., Washington, DC 20006.

Sager, Donald J. (Mr. 3, 1938, Milwaukee, WI) Comsn., Chicago Pub. Lib., 1978–; Dir., Pub. Lib. of Columbus, Franklin Cnty., 1975–78; Dir., Mobile Pub. Lib., 1971–75; Dir., Elyria Pub. Lib., 1966–71; Dir., Kingston Pub. Lib., 1964–66; Sr. Docmlst., AC Electronics Div., Gen. Motors Corp., 1958–63; Engin. Tech., Resrch. and Dev., Dept. of Cutler-Hammer, Inc., 1956–58. **Educ.:** Univ. of WI, Milwaukee, 1958–63, BS (Eng., Amer. Lit.); Univ. of WI, Madison, 1963–64, MS (LS); Kent State Univ., 1967, (Lib. Admin.); various crs. **Orgs.:** ALA: Legis. Asm. (Ch., 1979–81); Constn. and Bylaws Com. (1971–73); PLA, VP/Pres.-Elect (1981–82), Ch., (1979–81), Bd. of Dirs. (1974–78); various other coms.; Info. Sci. and Autom. Div., Vid. Comm. and CATV Srvs., Legis. Com. (1979). IL State Lib. Adv. Com. IL LA: Various coms. OH LA: Bd. of Dirs. (1969–71); various ofcs. various other orgs. OCLC, Inc.: Bd. of Dirs., (Secy., 1976–78). Columbus Area CATV Comsn.: Bd. of Dirs. (Ch., 1976–78). Rotary Club of Chicago: Youth Srvs. Com. (1979–81); Prog. Com. (1979–81). Chicago Educ. and Cult. CATV Cnsrtm.: Bd. of Dirs. (Ch., 1981–82). various other orgs. **Pubns.:** *Reference: A Programmed Instruction* (1970); *Participatory Management* (1981); "National Periodicals Center: Too Limited a Goal," *Amer. Libs.* (S. 1979); "Answering the Call for Health Information," *Amer. Libs.* (S. 1978); "Case History in Cooperation: Northern Ohio Film Circuit," *OH LA Bltn.* (Jl. 1968); various articles. **Activities:** 9; 17, 35, 47; 56, 75, 78 **Addr.:** Chicago Public Library, 425 N. Michigan Ave., Chicago, IL 60611.

Sager, Naomi (Mr. 21, 1927, Chicago, IL) Sr. Resrch. Sci., NY Univ., 1966–, Adj. Prof. Ling., 1974–, Dir., Ling. String Proj., 1966–; various positions in engin. **Educ.:** Columbia Univ., 1953, BS (Electrical Engin.); Univ. of PA, 1968, PhD (Ling.). **Orgs.:** ASIS. Assn. Comp. Mach.: SIG Lang. Analysis (1975–78). Std. in Hum. Info. Syst.: Adv. Bd. (1974). Biophys. Socty.: Fndn. Mem. Assn. for Comp. Ling. Amer. Jnl. Comp. Ling.: Ed. Bd. (1974). **Pubns.:** *Natural Language Information Processing: A Computer Grammar of English and Its Applications* (1981); "Natural Language Information Formatting: The Automatic Conversion of Texts to a Structured Data Base," *Advnc. in Comp.* (1978); "Syntactic Analysis of Natural Language," *Advnc. in Comp.* (1967); various jnl. pubns. **Activities:** 41; 75, 80, 95-Lang. **Addr.:** 251 Mercer St., New York, NY 10012.

Sager, Rochelle (Ap. 16, 1944, Chicago, IL) Pub. Srv. Libn., Univ. of AK (Juneau), 1978–; Ref. Libn., Univ. of AK (Fairbanks), 1975–78; Ref. Libn., Chicago State Univ., 1969–75. **Educ.:** Univ. of IL, 1962–66, BA (Eng. Lit.), 1968–69, MSLS;

Special Subjects/Services: 50. Adult educ.; 51. Advert./Mktg.; 52. Aerosp.; 53. Agric.; 54. Area std.; 55. Arts/Hum.; 56. Autom.; 57. Bibl./Prtg.; 58. Bio. sci.; 59. Bus./Fin.; 60. Chem.; 61. Copyrt.; 62. Documtn.; 63. Educ.; 64. Engin.; 65. Env.; 66. Eth. grps.; 67. Film; 68. Food/Nutr.; 69. Geneal.; 70. Geo.; 71. Geol.; 72. Handcpd.; 73. Hist.; 74. Int. frdm.; 75. Info. sci.; 76. Insr.; 77. Law; 78. Legis.; 79. Math./Comp. sci.; 80. Med.; 81. Metals; 82. Nat. resrcs.; 83. Newsp.; 84. Nuc. sci.; 85. Oral hist.; 86. Petr./Energy; 87. Pharm.; 88. Phys./Astr./Math.; 89. Readg.; 90. Relig.; 91. Sci./Tech.; 92. Soc. sci.; 93. Telecom.; 94. Transp.; 95. (other).

Loyola Univ., 1971–75, MEd (Educ. Psy.). **Orgs.:** ALA: ACRL; RASD. AK LA: Pac. NW LA. Frnds. of the Lib. Grp. Juneau Leag. of Woman Voters. Natl. Assn. for Women. **Pubns.:** Various articles, *Sourdough, Jnl. AK LA;* reviews. **Activities:** 1; 16, 31, 39; 63, 92 **Addr.:** 326 4th, Apt. 1109, Juneau, AK 99801.

Sahak, Judy Harvey (O. 27, 1942, Owensboro, KY) Libn., Ella Strong Denison Lib., Asst. Dir., Libs., Claremont Colls., 1976–, Asst. Dir. for Ctrl. Srvs., Honnold Lib., 1972–76; Head, Ref. Dept., Univ. of CA, Riverside, 1970–72; Sr. Ref. Libn., Lib. of Congs., 1965–70. **Educ.:** Scripps Coll., 1960–64, BA (European Std.); Univ. of WA, 1964–65, MLibnshp. **Orgs.:** ALA: ACRL/Univ. Libs. Sect. (Secy. 1980–82), South. CA Chap., Nom. Com. (Ch., 1977). CA LA: PR Com. (1976–77). *Nwsltr.,* Chap. of Acad. and Resrch. Libns. (Ed., 1979). Socty. of CA Archvsts. **Activities:** 1; 15, 17, 45; 55, 57, 92 **Addr.:** Ella Strong Denison Library, Scripps College, Claremont, CA 91711.

Sahli, Nancy A. (Ja. 4, 1946, Beaver Falls, PA) Arch. and Info. Consult., 1981–; Coord., Guide Proj., Natl. Hist. Pubn. and Rec. Comsn., 1976–81, Archvst., 1975–76. **Educ.:** Vassar Coll., 1963–67, AB (Hist.); Univ. of PA, 1968–74, MA (Hist.), PhD; Twelfth Anl. Sem. for Hist. Admin., 1970–70, Cert.; Mod. Arch. Inst., 1973, Cert. **Orgs.:** SAA: Com. Status of Women (Ch., 1980–); Task Frc. Natl. Info. Syst. (1979–). SPINDEX Users' Netwk.: Exec. Bd. (1979–). Berkshire Conf. of Women Hist. Org. of Amer. Histns. **Honors:** Gen. Srv. Admin., Cmdn. Srv. Awd. Cit., 1978, 1979. **Pubns.:** Ed., *Directory of Archives and Manuscript Repositories in the U.S.* (1978); *SPINDEX: An Introduction for New and Prospective Users* (1980); "Finding Aids: A Multi-Media, Systems Perspective," *Amer. Archvst.* (Win. 1981); "Local History Manuscripts: Sources, Uses, and Preservation," *Hist. News* (My. 1979) "The NHPRC and a Guide to Manuscript and Archival Materials in the United States," *Amer. Archvst.* (Ap. 1977); various other hist. articles. **Activities:** 2, 4; 17, 28; 55, 56, 73 **Addr.:** 9 Indian Spring Dr., Silver Spring, MD 20901.

Sahli, Sue (S. 25, 1927, Beaver Falls, PA) Asst. Prof., Dept. of LS, North. IL Univ., 1978–; Assoc. Dir., Col. Dev., Cleveland State Univ., 1970–76, Asst. Dir. for Col. Dev., 1969–70, Head, Soc. Sci. Div., 1967–69; Asst. Head, Hist. Dept., Cleveland Pub. Lib., 1956–66. **Educ.:** Denison Univ., 1946–49, BA (Eng.); Columbia Univ., 1949–50, (Eng.); West. Rsv. Univ., 1951–52, MSLS; Case West. Rsv. Univ., 1973–81, PhDC (Lib. and Info. Sci.); various crs. **Orgs.:** ALA: RASD, Nom. Com. (1964), Hist. Sect. (Secy., 1965–67); RTSD, Com. on Col. Dev. (1973–74). OH LA: Ref. Srvs. RT (Secy., 1968–70); OH Dupl. Exch. Prog. (Ch., 1969–76); Lib. Dev. Com. (1973–74). ASIS. SLA: Cleveland Chap., Prog. Com. (1970–72). AAUP: Cleveland State Univ. Chap., Com. on Econ. Status (1972–73); Chap. Secy. (1973–74); Nom. Com. (Ch., 1976). Women's Natl. Bk. Assn.: Cleveland Chap., Secy. (1960–62); Pres. (1970–71); VP (1971–74). **Activities:** 11; 26 **Addr.:** Department of Library Science, Northern Illinois University, DeKalb, IL 60115.

Sahu, Krushnapriya (D. 9, 1950, Bargarh (Sambalpur), Orissa, India) Dir., Lib., Univ. of Osteopathic Med. and Hlth. Sci., 1974–. **Educ.:** Women's Coll., Sambalpur, Orissa, India, BA (Eng., Econ., Oriya Home Sci.); Women's Coll., Sambalpur, Orissa, India, BEd (Educ.); Univ. of WI, 1972–73, MALS. **Orgs.:** Med. LA. Polk Cnty. Biomed. Cnsrtm.: Serials Com.; Medline Com. (1974); Insrv. Com. (1980–81). IA LA: Hlth. Sci. Sect., Governing Bd. (1976–77). Midwest Hlth. Sci. Lib. Netwk.: Cncl. of the Hlth. Sci. Lib., Governing Bd. (1976–78). **Activities:** 1, 12; 17, 20, 39 **Addr.:** University of Osteopathic Medicine & Health Sciences Library, 3200 Grand Ave., Des Moines, IA 50265.

St. Clair, Guy L. (Jl. 21, 1940, Montgomery County, VA) Lib. Dir., Univ. Club Lib., NY, 1979–; Dir., Cult. Progs., Un. Leag. Club, 1969–79; Libn., Univ. Coll., Univ. of Richmond, 1967–69; Ref. Libn., Richmond Pub. Lib., 1965–67; Serials Asst., Univ. of IL, 1964–65. **Educ.:** Univ. of VA, 1958–63, BA; Univ. of IL, 1964–65, MS (LS). **Orgs.:** SLA: Musms., Arts and Hum. Div. (Ch., 1976–77). **Pubns.:** "The One-Person Library: An Essay on Essentials," *Spec. Libs.* (My.–Je. 1976). **Activities:** 1, 5; 17, 39, 45; 55, 59 **Addr.:** University Club Library, 1 W. 54th St., New York, NY 10019.

St. Clair, Helen D. (Jl. 29, 1927, Prince Albert, SK) Med. Libn., Wilmington Med. Ctr., 1970–; various med. positions. **Educ.:** Univ. of BC, 1944–48, BSc (Bacteriology); Drexel Univ., 1969–70, MS (LS); various crs. **Orgs.:** Med. LA: Philadelphia Reg. Grp., Ch. (1977–78), Prog. Ch. (1976–77); various ofcs. DE LA: Coll. and Resrch. Libs. Div. (Ch., 1981–82); Prog. Com. (1980–81). DE Lib. Cnsrtm. Wilmington Area Biomed. Lib. Cnsrtm. various other orgs. Gvr.'s Adv. Cncl. on Libs., DE (1976–80). Wilmington Trail Club: Cncl. (1976–79). Unitarian Flwshp. of Newark: Secy. (1977–78, 1979–80); Pres. (1981–82). **Pubns.:** "Teaching Residents a Personal Filing System," *Bltn. Med. LA* (Jl. 1981). **Activities:** 12; 15, 34, 39; 80 **Addr.:** Medical Library, Delaware Division, Wilmington Medical Center, Box 1668, Wilmington, DE 19899.

St. Onge, Jacques (S. 1, 1948, Contrecoeur, PQ) Media Spec., Daniel Johnson HS, 1976–. **Educ.:** Univ. of PQ, 1969–72, BA (Hist.); Univ. of Montreal, 1972–76, MA (Hist.); McGill Univ., 1974–76, MLS; Univ. of Montreal, 1979– (Educ. Tech.). **Orgs.:** Corp. of Prof. Libns. of PQ: Com. of Sch. Libns. Can LA: Sch. Sect. ASTED: Sch. Sect. (Treas., 1978–). Can. Wildlife Fed. Natl. Geo. Socty. Amer. Musm. of Nat. Hist. Natl. Audubon Socty. Various other orgs. **Pubns.:** "La Formation Documentaire à La Mediatheque," *Bltn. des Enseignants de Fr. du Sec.* (S. 1979). **Activities:** 10; 17, 31, 32 **Addr.:** 5333 East, Sherbrooke St., Apt. 152A, Montreal, PQ H1T 3V8 Canada.

Saito, Shiro (Mr. 11, 1928, Pahala, HI) Col. Consult., Soc. Sci., Univ. of HI Lib., 1979–, Assoc. Univ. Libn., 1974–79, Soc. Sci. Biblgphr., 1971–74, Soc. Sci. Ref., Head, 1966–71. **Educ.:** Univ. of HI, 1947–51, BEd (Educ.); Univ. of MN, 1955–56, MA (Lib. Std.); 1952–53, 5th Yr. Tchg. Cert. **Orgs.:** Assn. for Asian Std.: Com. on Resrch. Mtrls. on SE Asia, Ref. Aids Subcom. (Ch., 1974–75); Philippine Std. Grp., Exec. Bd. HI LA. HI Com. for the Hum. **Honors:** Fulbright Resrch. Grant, 1967; Cncl. on Lib. Resrcs. Flwshp., 1977; Natl. Endow. Hum., Proj. Dir., SE Asian Resrch. Tools Proj., 1977; Beta Phi Mu. **Pubns.:** *Philippine Ethnography: A Critically Annotated and Selected Bibliography* (1972); *Filipinos Overseas: A Bibliography* (1977); "Sociology of Marriage and Family Behavior: 1957–1962: Area Editor: The Philippines," *Current Soclgy.* (1969). **Activities:** 1; 15, 28; 92 **Addr.:** University of Hawaii Library, 2550 The Mall, Honolulu, HI 96822.

Saiz, John Thomas (Mr. 17, 1932, New York, NY) Law Libn., Asst. Prof. of Law, St. John's Univ., Sch. of Law, 1967–; Actg. Law Libn., 1971–72, Asst. Law Libn., 1967–71. **Educ.:** Univ. of Notre Dame, 1950–52, 1957–59, BA (Mod. Lang.); Columbia Univ., 1966–67, MS (LS); St. John's Univ., 1968–72, JD (Law). **Orgs.:** AALL. Law Lib. Assn. of Grt. NY: Pres. (1974–75); VP (1973–74). Amer. Bar Assn. NY State Bar Assn. **Activities:** 15, 17, 35; 77 **Addr.:** St. John's University, School of Law, Grand Central and Utopia Pkwys., Jamaica, NY 11439.

Sakovich, Musya (Ap. 23, 1918, Moscow, Russia) Libn., Consult., Sonoma Cnty. Ofc. of Educ., 1971–; Libn., San Francisco Unfd. Sch. Dist., 1965–71; various positions in tchg. **Educ.:** Univ. of CA, Berkeley, 1936–38; San Francisco State Univ., 1938–40, BA, 1955–58, MA; Univ. of San Francisco, 1962–64; Admin. Cred.; CA Cmnty. Coll., Instr. Cred. **Orgs.:** CA Media and Lib. Educ. Assn. ALA. Intl. Assn. of Sch. Libn. Assn. of Chld. Libns. Various other orgs. Delta Kappa Gamma: Resrch. Com. (1980–1981). Delta Phi Upsilon: Secy. AAUW. Amer. Topical Assn. **Activities:** 10, 14-Cnty. ofc.; 21, 24, 31; 61, 66, 89 **Addr.:** Sonoma County Office of Education, County Administration Center, Rm. 111E Education Bldg., 410 Fiscal Dr., Santa Rosa, CA 95401.

Salabiye, Velma S. (Je. 29, 1948, Bellemont, AZ) Libn., Amer. Indian Std. Ctr., Univ. of CA, Los Angeles, 1977–; Navajo Resrch. and Stats. Ctr., Navajo Nation, 1975–77; Spec. Educ. Tchr., St. Michaels' Sch. for Handcpd. Chld., 1972–74. **Educ.:** Univ. of AZ, 1966–72, 1973–74, NY Univ., 1970, (Jnlsm. Intern). **Orgs.:** SLA: Rio Grande Chap. (1974–77). Conf. of Intermt. Archvsts. Navajo Sci. Com.: Educ. Subcom. (1975–76). ALA: RASD (1978–); Lib. Srv. to the Disadv. (1979–). Univ. of CA, Los Angeles: Eth. Libs. Eval. Task Frc. CA Eth. Srvs. Task Frc. Col. Eval. Com. **Pubns.:** "The Library Experience–A Native American Viewpoint," *Amer. Indian Libs. Nsltr.* (Win. 1978); "Library and Information Services," *Guide to Community-Based Research in Indian Communities* (forthcoming). **Activities:** 1; 15, 16, 17; 55, 66, 75 **Addr.:** 3220 Campbell Hall, 405 Hilgard Ave., Los Angeles, CA 90024.

Saley, Stacey (Jl. 24, 1942, New York, NY) Chief Med. Libn., Mt. Sinai Srvs. City Hosp. Ctr., Elmhurst, NY 1969–; Med. Libn., Hillside Div. of Long Island, Jewish/Hillside Med. Ctr., 1964–69. **Educ.:** SUNY, Geneseo, 1960–63, BS (Educ.); Queens College, NY 1967–69, MLS. **Orgs.:** Brooklyn, Queens Staten Island Hlth. Sci. Grp.: Pres. (1981–83); Prog. Ch. (1977–79). Med. LA: NY Reg. Grp., Pubcty., Past Ch. **Activities:** 1, 5; 15, 17, 31; 58, 80 **Addr.:** Medical Library, City Hospital Center, 79-01 Broadway, Elmhurst, Queens, NY 11373.

Salinas, Kathleen Heinemann (Je. 5, 1943, Sacramento, CA) Consult., Los Angeles Cnty. Supt. of Schs., 1979–; Prof., CA State Univ., Los Angeles, 1975–; Libn., Catlgr., Montebello Unfd. Sch. Dist., 1973–. **Educ.:** Stanford Univ., 1961–64 (Classics); Univ. of Denver, 1965, BA (Hist.); Univ. of South. CA, 1972–73, MS (LS). **Orgs.:** ALA. CA Media and Lib. Educ. Assn.: Com. on Copyrt. and Off-Air Video Rec. (1979). Amer. Socty. for Trng. and Dev.: Educ. Inst. Liaison Com. (1981); Media Interest Grp. (1981). Stanford Alum. Assn. Univ. of South. CA Lib. Sch. Alum. Assn. **Honors:** Stanford Univ., Ford Fndn. Flwshp., 1964. **Pubns.:** "Copyright and Off-Air Videotaping," *CA Media and Lib. Educ. Assn. Jnl.* (Spr. 1979); *Subject Index For Cataloging Educational Films* (1980). **Activities:** 10, 11; 26, 32, 46; 61, 63 **Addr.:** 1360 Blackstone Rd., San Marino, CA 91108.

Salley, Landrum (My. 27, 1928, Stewart, MS) Dir., Norton Meml. Lib., LA Coll., 1973–; Pastor, 1st Bapt. Church, Kentwood, LA, 1956–71; Pastor, Kilmichael Bapt. Church, Kilmichael, MS, 1952–56; Tchr., Chamberlain-Hunt Acad., 1949–50. **Educ.:** MS State Univ., 1944–48, BS (Eng., Soc. Std.); LA State Univ., 1948–49, MA (Hist.); New Orleans Bapt. Theo. Semy., 1951–54, BD (Theo.); George Peabody Coll., Vanderbilt Univ., 1972–73, MLS; various crs. **Orgs.:** LA LA: Exhibits Com. (Ch., 1975); LA Un. Cat. Com. (1977–80). SW LA. First Bapt. Church, Pineville, LA. **Activities:** 1; 15, 31, 35 **Addr.:** 303 Iris Park Dr., Pineville, LA 71360.

Salmon, Kay H. (N. 2, 1935, Raymond Alta, AB) Lib. Dir., Corvallis Pub. Lib., 1970–; Branch Libn., Salt Lake Cnty. Lib. Syst., 1967–70; Tchr., Granite Sch. Dist., 1963–67; Tchr., Duchesne Sch. Dist., 1962–63. **Educ.:** Brigham Young Univ., 1958–62, BA (Msc. Educ.), 1969–70, MLS. **Orgs.:** Pac. NW LA: Treas. (1977–81). ALA: PLA, Mem. Com. OR LA: Dev. Com. (1972–77); Legis. Com. (1973–77); Conf. Ch. (1974); Pres. (1975–76); various ofcs., coms. Kiwanis: Exec. Bd. (1973–74). **Activities:** 9; 17, 25, 47 **Addr.:** Corvallis Public Library, 645 N.W. Monroe Ave., Corvallis, OR 97330.

Salmon, Stephen R. (Ja. 28, 1933, Brownsville, TN) Asst. VP, Lib. Plans and Policies, Univ. of CA, Systemwide Admin., 1976–; Dir. of Libs., Univ. of Houston, 1971–75; Pres., Xerox Bibls., 1969–71; Asst. Dir., Prcs. Srvs., Lib. of Congs., 1966–69; Assoc. Dir., Libs., Washington Univ., 1964–66; Asst. Chief, Photodup. Srv., Lib. of Congs., 1962–64, Admin. Asst., 1961–62; Libn., George Mason Univ., 1959–61; various libn. positions, 1957–59. **Educ.:** Univ. of CA, Berkeley, 1955–57, AB (Eng.), 1957–58, MLS (Libnshp.). **Orgs.:** CA Lib. Athty. for Systs. and Srvs.: Bd. of Dirs., Ch. (1980–), Vice-Ch. (1978–79). ALA: Cncl. (1965–67, 1974–78); LITA, Pres. (1966–67), Bd. of Dirs. (1966–68), various coms.; ACRL, various coms.; AALS, Cont. Lib. Educ. Netwk. (1972–73); various ofcs., coms. **Honors:** Lib. of Congs., Superior Srv. Awd., 1968. **Pubns.:** *The University of California Libraries: A Plan for Development* (1977); *Library Automation Systems* (1975); "User Resistance to Microforms in the Research Library," *Micro. Review* (Jl. 1974); "Implementing Planning for Computing in Libraries," *Planning for Computing in Higher Education* (1980); various mono., articles. **Activities:** 1; 17, 34; 56, 93 **Addr.:** 2915 Shasta Rd., Berkeley, CA 94708.

Salmond, Margaret A. (S. 19, 1940, Bienfait, SK) Law Catlgr., Law Lib., Univ. of Victoria, 1979–; Micromtrls. Libn., Univ. of AB, 1969–77; Catlgr., North. IL Univ., 1965–68. **Educ.:** Victoria Coll., 1958–62, BA (Eng., Psy.); Univ. of Denver, 1964–65, MA (Libnshp.). **Orgs.:** Can. LA. Can. ALL. AALL. **Activities:** 1; 20, 33; 77, 83 **Addr.:** University of Victoria, Law Library, P.O. Box 2300, Victoria, BC V8W 3B1 Canada.

Salo, Annette C. (S. 7, 1944, Biwabik, MN) Supvsr. of Vid. Comm. Ctr., St. Paul Pub. Lib., 1975–, Coord. of Frnds. of the Lib., 1975–77. **Educ.:** Metro. State Univ., 1972–74, BA (Comm.); Univ. of MN, 1978–81 (LS); Tech. Vocational Inst. of St. Paul, 1976, Cert. (Basic Instr. Trng.). **Orgs.:** ALA: Vid. Cable Comm. Sect., Legis. Com. (1980–82). MN LA: Media RT (Ch., 1980–81). Metro. Lib. Srv. Org.: AV Com. (1974–). Com. Open Media: St. Paul Cable Comm. Task Frc. (1974–81). MN Educ. Media Org.: Telecom. Com. (1980–81). **Pubns.:** Various media prods. **Activities:** 9; 15, 28, 32; 67, 78, 93 **Addr.:** The St. Paul Public Library, 90 W. Fourth St., St. Paul, MN 55102.

Salonen, Ethel Margaret (F. 1, 1951, New York, NY) Resrch. Lib., Arthur D. Little, Inc., 1980–; Asst. Libn., Phys. Sci. Lib., Univ. of CA, Riverside, 1978–80. **Educ.:** SUNY, Stony Brook, 1969–74, BA (Earth, Space Sci.); 1974–77, MA (Liberal Std.); C.W. Post Coll., 1976–77, MS (LS). **Orgs.:** SLA. ALA. New Eng. OLUG. Soumi Seura. Finlandia Fndn. **Activities:** 1; 29, 31, 39; 60, 70, 91 **Addr.:** Research Library, Arthur D. Little, Inc., 15 Acorn Park, Cambridge, MA 02140.

Salter, Jeffrey L. (D. 9, 1950, Starkville, MS) Asst. Dir., Shreve Meml. Lib., 1980–; Dir., Catahoula Par. Lib. Syst., 1978–80. **Educ.:** Southeast. LA Univ., 1976, BA (Eng.); LA State Univ., 1976–77, Math.). LA State Bd. Lib. Examiners, 1981, Exec. Cert. **Orgs.:** LA LA: Dues Std. Com. (1978); Modisette Awd. Com. (1980); Anl. Conf. Regis. (Ch., 1980–81). Ctrl. LA Lib. Trustee Assn.: Secy. (1979). **Pubns.:** "Where Have All the Readers Gone? A Per Capita Circulation Study," *LA LA Bltn.* (Sum. 1980). **Activities:** 9; 17, 35, 49-Pub. Srvs. **Addr.:** Shreve Memorial Library, 424 Texas St, Shreveport, LA 71101.

Salton, Gerard (Mr. 8, 1927, Nuremburg, Germany) Prof., Comp. Sci., Cornell Univ., 1965–; Asst. Prof., Harvard Univ., 1960–65. **Educ.:** Brooklyn Coll., 1947–50, BA (Math.); Harvard Univ., 1955–58, PhD (Appld. Math.). **Orgs.:** ASIS. Assn. Comp. Math.: Cncl. (1971–78). **Honors:** Phi Beta Kappa; Guggenheim Flwshp., 1962; ASIS Awd., Best Info. Sci. Paper, 1970, 1975. **Pubns.:** *Dynamic Information and Library Processing* (1975); *Automatic Information Organization and Retrieval* (1968); "The SMART System," *Encyc. Lib. Info. Sci.* (Volume 28); various other articles. **Activities:** 11, 14-Univ.; 41; 75, 79 **Addr.:** Computer Science Department, Cornell University, Ithaca, NY 14853.

Saltzer, Benjamin Arden (Ag. 14, 1943, Los Angeles, CA) Head, Info. Systs. and Tech. Prog., Nvl. Ocean Systs. Ctr., 1973–; Pres., Saltzer, Sutton, and Endicott, Inc., 1980–; Head, Systs. Dev. Branch, Nvl. Ocean Systs. Ctr., 1972–76; Head, Tech. Info. Dept., Nvl. Undersea Ctr., 1973–74, Head, Acoustical Imaging Prog., 1969–73, Head, Divers' Navigation Syst. Proj.,

PROFESSIONAL ACTIVITIES: Institutions: 1. Acad. lib.; 2. Arch.; 3. Assn.; 4. Fed./Gvt. lib.; 5. Inst. lib.; 6. Mfr./Suppl.; 7. Milit. lib.; 8. Musm.; 9. Pub. lib.; 10. Sch. lib.; 11. Sch. of lib. sci.; 12. Spec. lib.; 13. State lib.; 14. (other). **Functions/Activities:** 15. Acq./Col. dev.; 16. Adult srvs.; 17. Admin.; 18. Apprais.; 19. Archit./Bldgs.; 20. Cat./Class.; 21. Chld. srvs.; 22. Circ.; 23. Cons./Pres.; 24. Consult.; 25. Cont. ed.; 26. Educ. lib. sci.; 27. Ext. srvs.; 28. Fund/Grants; 29. Gvt. pubs.; 30. Indx./Abs.; 31. Instr. lib. use; 32. Media srvs.; 33. Micro.; 34. Netwks./Coop.; 35. Persnl.; 36. PR; 37. Publshg.; 38. Recs. mgt.; 39. Ref. srvs.; 40. Repro.; 41. Resrch.; 42. Review.; 43. Secur.; 44. Serials; 45. Spec. col.; 46. Tech. srvs.; 47. Trustees/Bds.; 48. YA srvs.; 49. (other).

Who's Who in Library and Information Services

1966–69. **Educ.:** CA Inst. of Tech., 1961–65, BS (Engin.); Univ. of South. CA, 1966–67, MS (Engin.); MA Inst. of Tech., 1976–77, PhD (ABD) (Org. Behavior and Comp. Sci.). **Orgs.:** Natl. Micro. Assn. ASIS. AAAS. Inst. of Electrical and Electronic Engin. **Pubns.:** "A Catalog of State-of-the-Art Components and Techniques for the Advanced Records Technologies and Systems (ARTS) Project," *NOSC TN 495* (1978); jt. auth., "Office of the Future - Several Viewpoints," *IBM Resrch. Rpt.* (Je. 1980); various sps. **Activities:** 14-Fed. R&D lab.; 17, 24, 41; 56, 64, 95-Org. behavior. **Addr.:** 3205 Talbot St., San Diego, CA 92106.

Salvadore, Maria B. (S. 21, 1949, Washington, DC) Coord., Chld. Srvs., Cambridge Pub. Lib., 1978–; Chld. Libn., DC Pub. Lib., 1976–78, 1973–76. **Educ.:** Univ. of MD, 1967–71, BS (Educ.), 1971–73, MEd (Educ.), 1975–76, MLS. **Orgs.:** ALA: Filmstp. Eval. Com. (1979–81). New Eng. LA: Adv. Exec. Com., RT of Chld. Libns. (1979–). MA LA. Chld. Lit. Assn. Assn. for Childhood Educ. Intl.: Ref. Bk. Review Com. (1978–81). **Activities:** 9, 11; 17, 21, 42; 63, 72 **Addr.:** Children's Services, Cambridge Public Library, 449 Broadway, Cambridge, MA 02138.

Salvatore, Lucy V. (Ap. 11, 1922, Providence, RI) Assoc. Prof., Grad. Lib. Sch., Univ. of RI, 1963–; Coord., Lib. Srvs., Weston Pub. Sch., 1959–64; Libn., Stoneham HS, 1958–59; Asst. Libn., Univ. HS, Univ. of IL, Urbana, 1957–58, Catlgr., Cat. Rev., 1955–57; Catlgr., Brown Univ. Lib., 1951–54. **Educ.:** Brown Univ., 1939–43, AB (Mod. Langs.); Univ. of IL, 1956–58, MSLS; Univ. of Sarasota, Doct. in prog. (Educ.). **Orgs.:** ALA: AASL. AALS: Liaison for GLS (1977–). New Eng. LA: Secy. (1966); Exec. Bd. (1978). New Eng. Media Assn.: Exec. Bd. (1979–80). **Honors:** Beta Phi Mu, 1957. **Pubns.:** "Children's Services in RI," *RI LA Bltn.* (F. 1979). **Activities:** 10; 21, 32, 48; 63 **Addr.:** 58 Rebecca Ln., Osterville, MA 02655.

Salzer, Elizabeth M. (S. 5, 1944, Providence, RI) Head Libn., J. Henry Meyer Meml. Lib., Stanford Univ., 1975–; Head, Ref. Srvs. Dept., Univ. Libs., SUNY, Albany, 1973–75, Head, Gvt. Pubns. Dept., 1972–73, Bibl. Srvs. Libn., Univ. Libs., 1971–72, Actg. Sci. Bibl., 1971–72, ILL Libn., 1967–71. **Educ.:** Coll. of St. Rose, Albany, NY, 1962–66, BA (Eng.); Univ. of MI, 1966–67, AMLS. **Orgs.:** ALA: ACRL, Stan. and Accred. Com. 1977–81); LAMA; LITA; RASD. CA LA. SUNY LA: Pres. (1973–75). **Pubns.:** "A View from Stanford University," *Jnl. of Acad. Libnshp.* (Jl 1979). *A Selected Bibliography of Books on Women in the Libraries of the SUNY Albany* ERIC (Jl. 1972). **Activities:** 1; 17 **Addr.:** J. Henry Meyer Memorial Library, Stanford University, Stanford, CA 94305.

Sammons, Christa (Jl. 9, 1942, Gloucester, MA) Cur., Yale Col. of Grmn. Lit., Yale Univ., 1980–, Libn., 1970–80, Asst. to Libn., 1969–70. **Educ.:** Mt. Holyoke Coll., 1960–64, BA (Grmn.); Yale Univ., 1964–68, PhD (Grmn.); South. CT State Coll., 1970–77, MLS. **Orgs.:** ALA. Goethe Socty. of N. Amer. **Pubns.:** "Hermann Broch Archive, Yale University Library," *Mod. Austrian Lit.* (1972); "The German Literature Collection," *Yale Univ. Lib. Gazette* (1974); "The Dukes of Brunswick–-Lüneburg: A Commemorative Collection," *Yale Univ. Lib. Gazette* (1977); "Goethe as Librarian," *Yale Univ. Lib. Gazette* (1978); "Faust at Yale," *Yale Univ. Lib. Gazette* (1979); various articles. **Activities:** 1; 15, 20, 45; 55 **Addr.:** Beinecke Rare Book and Manuscript Library, 1603A Yale Station, New Haven, CT 06520.

Samore, Theodore (Jl. 27, 1924, Sioux City, IA) Prof., Sch. LS, Univ. of WI (Milwaukee), 1966–; Coll. Lib. Spec., U.S. Ofc. of Educ., 1962–66; Chief, Tech. Srv., Livonia Pub. Sch., 1960–62; Pers. Libn., Ball State Univ., 1957–60. **Educ.:** Univ. of MO, 1946–49, BA (Phil.); Univ. of MI, 1952–53, MA (LS), Univ. of MI, 1950–52, MA (Phil.). **Orgs.:** ALA: Lib. Admin. Div., Stats. Com. Colls. and Univs. (Ch., 1970–75). WI LA: Int. Frdm. Com. (1972–74). SLA: WI Chap., Rcrt. Com. (Ch., 1971–74). Lib.-Coll. Assoc.: Secy. (1966–67). Com. for a Free Press in WI: Treas. (1969). **Honors:** Phi Beta Kappa, 1949. **Pubns.:** Ed., *Problems in Library Classification: Dewey 17 and Conversion* (1968); ed., *Acquisition of Foreign Materials for U.S. Libraries* (1973); "Milwaukee: Small Town Metropolis," *OH LA Bltn.* (O. 1979); "Arts and Humanities Resources in Wisconsin," *WI Lib. Bltn.* (My.–Je. 1980). **Activities:** 1, 4; 17, 20, 29; 55, 57, 77 **Addr.:** University of Wisconsin - Milwaukee, School of Library and Information Science, P.O. Box 4;3, Milwaukee, WI 53201.

Sampier, Judith M. (S. 12, 1939, Portsmouth, IA) Elem. Sch. Libn., 1977–; Elem. Sch. Libn., Jefferson and Beals Schs., 1977–81; various tchg. positions, 1961–77. **Educ.:** Duchesne Coll., 1957–61, BA (Hist.); Univ. of Denver, 1974–78, MA (LS). **Orgs.:** ALA. NE LA. NE Educ. Media Assn. Mt. Plains LA. Omaha Educ. Assn. NE State Educ. Assn. Natl. Educ. Assn. **Honors:** Beta Phi Mu, 1978. **Activities:** 10; 21, 31, 32 **Addr.:** 12111 Shirley St., Omaha, NE 68144.

Sampson, Daphne Babbitt (Ag. 11, 1943, Milwaukee, WI) Chief, Readers' Srvs., Fed. Trade Comsn. Lib., 1980–; Sr. Ref. Libn., White Hse. and E.D.P. Info. Ctr., 1978–80; Sr. Ref. Libn., U.S. Dept of State, 1968–78; Ref. Libn., Defense Intelligence Agency, 1966–68. **Educ.:** Univ. of WI, 1962–65, BA (Pol. Sci., Hist.), 1965–66, MA (LS). **Orgs.:** SLA. ASIS. **Activities:** 12; 17, 39, 41; 54, 78, 92 **Addr.:** 5838 Wyomissing Ct., Alexandria, VA 22303.

Sampson, Karen L. (N. 1, 1950, Savanna, IL) Asst. to Dir., Univ. of NE, 1979–; Actg. Asst. to Dir., Pub. Srvs., Univ. of IL, 1978–79, Bookstacks Libn., 1974–78. **Educ.:** Univ. of IL, 1968–71, BS (Eng.), 1971–74, MS (LS); St. Louis Inst. of Msc., 1968, (Piano Cert.). **Orgs.:** ALA: LAMA, Women Admin. Discuss. Grp., Strg. Com. (1978–79). Mt. Plains LA. NE LA: NE LA/Mt. Plains LA Jt. Conf., Plng. Subcom. (Ch., 1980); NE Cons. of Lib. and Arch. Mtrls. Plng. Com. (Ch., 1980). Rock Island Cnty. Hist. Socty.: Lib. Bldg. Com. (Consult., 1980–). **Honors:** Univ. of IL Lib., Resrch. and Pubn. Com., Std. Grant, 1978. **Pubns.:** Contrib., *Ancestors of Mette Kirstine Andersen and Michael (Srugies) Sampson and Their Descendents* (1980); cmplr., *Nebraska Library and Archival Conservation Information* (1980); "Karen Sampson of UNO Comments on a Pre-Conference Session That Was Cancelled," *NE LA Qtly.* (Win. 1980); "Planning for Conversation of Nebraska Library and Archival Resources," *NE LA Qtly.* (Sum. 1981); various mono. **Activities:** 1; 17, 35, 36; 63, 69, 75 **Addr.:** University Library, University of Nebraska at Omaha, Omaha, NE 68182.

Samuel, Harold E. (Ap. 12, 1924, Hudson, WI) Msc. Libn., Prof. of Msc., Yale Univ., 1971–; Msc. Libn., Assoc. Prof. of Msc., Cornell Univ., 1957–71. **Educ.:** Univ. of MN, 1946–49, BA (Msc. Hist.), 1949–50, MA (Msclgy.); Univ. of Zurich, 1950–51, (Msclgy.); Cornell Univ., 1951–55, PhD (Msclgy.); Univ. of Erlangen, Germany, 1955–57, (Msclgy.). **Orgs.:** Msc. LA: Bd. of Dirs. (1973–75). Intl. Assn. of Msc. Libs.: US Branch (Pres., 1978–81). Amer. Musicological Socty.: Cncl. (1969–71). Coll. Msc. Socty. **Honors:** Fullbright, Flwshp., 1955–57; Martha Baird Rockefeller, Grant, 1961–62; Amer. Cncl. of Resrch. Soctys., Travel Grant, 1978; Amer. Phil. Socty., Grant, 1978. **Pubns.:** *The Cantata in Nuremberg During the 17th Century* (1963); ed.-in-chief, *Notes* (1965–70); various articles, *Groves Dictionary of Music and Musicians* (1980); "Yale's DMA: a Progress Report," *Symp., Jnl. of the Coll. Msc. Socty.* (1978); "Musicology and the Music Library," *Lib. Trends* (1977); various articles. **Activities:** 1; 15, 17, 24; 55 **Addr.:** 101 Santa Fe Ave., Hamden, CT 06517.

Samuels, Alan R. (S. 12, 1942, New York, NY) Asst. Prof., LS Educ. Tech. Dept., Univ. of NC, 1979–; Head Ref. Libn., Hofstra Univ., 1974–75, Ref. Libn., 1972–73, Catlgr., 1970–71; Adult Srvs. Libn., Brooklyn Pub. Lib., 1969–70. **Educ.:** NY Univ., 1960–64, BA (Latin); Univ. of Chicago, 1964–68, MA (Hist.); Pratt Inst., 1969–70, MLS; Rutgers Univ., 1975–79, PhD (LS). **Orgs.:** ALA. ASIS. AALS. NC LA. Amer. Hist. Assn. **Honors:** Beta Phi Mu, 1970. **Pubns.:** *A Program Planning and Evaluation Self Instructional Manual* (1975); "Assessing Organizational Climate in Public Libraries," *Lib. Resrch.* (Fall 1979); *Strategies in Library Administration* (1981). **Addr.:** Library Science/Education Technology Division, School of Education, University of North Carolina at Greensboro, McNutt Hall, Greensboro, NC 27412.

Samuels, Lois A. (O. 25, 1934, Mullica Hill, NJ) Info. Sci., Ethicon, Inc., 1971–; Ref. Libn., Un. Carbide, Bound Brook, 1967–71; Sr. Resrch. Libn., Firestone Tire and Rubber, 1965–67; Tech. Libn., Shell Chem., 1962–64; Chem., E.I. Dupont de Nemours, 1959–62. **Educ.:** Rutgers Univ., 1952–56, BA (Nat. Sci.), 1969–71, MLS. **Orgs.:** SLA: Pharm. Div. (Ch., 1978–79); NJ Chap. (Dir., 1975–77). ASIS. Med. LA. Amer. Rec. Mgt. Assn. Amer. Chem. Socty. AAAS. **Activities:** 12; 17, 30, 39; 60, 80, 87 **Addr.:** 740 Watchung Rd., Bound Brook, NJ 08805.

Samuelson, Richard T. (S. 14, 1969, Jamestown, NY) Lib. Dir., Colonie Town Lib., 1976–; Assoc. Prof., Libn., F.H. La Guardia Cmnty. Coll., 1970–76; Lib. Dir., Somerset Cnty. Coll., 1967–70; Lib. Dir., Asst. Prof., Alfred Agr. and Tech. Coll., 1965–67; Lib. Consult., Chamberlayne Jr. Coll., 1967–68; Asst. Libn., Trenton State Coll., 1964–65; Libn., Instr. Mtrls. Ctr., Mt. Lakes HS, 1962–64; Med. Resrch. Libn., Squibb Inst. for Med. Resrch., 1959–62; various tchg., engin. positions, 1946–59. **Educ.:** Alfred Univ., 1935–39, BA, 1956–59, MS; Rutgers Univ., 1959–63, MLS; 1976, Libnshp. Cert. #8224. **Orgs.:** NJ Cmnty. Coll. LA: Pres. (1968–69). NJ Cmnty. Coll. Lib. Dirs. Assn: Pres. (1969–70). ALA. NY LA. Rotary Intl.: Dir. SUNY at Albany's Cap. Dist. Hum. Prog.: Adv. Bd. (1978–). Colonie Hist. Socty.: Trustee. NY Lib. Club. **Pubns.:** Contrib., *Instructional Materials Centers* contrib., *The Chicorel Index Series;* various articles. **Activities:** 1, 9; 17, 19, 24; 57, 63, 77 **Addr.:** Colonie Town Library, 629 Albany Shaker Rd., Loudonville, NY 12211.

Sanchez, Dino Moro (My. 14, 1936, Witherbee, NY) Co-owner, Quantum Press, 1981–; Owner, Dino Moro Sanchez Bk. Dir., 1976; Assoc. Libn., Univ. CA, Los Angeles, 1968–76. **Educ.:** Univ. CA, Los Angeles, 1960, BA (Eng., Hist.), 1968, MLS, 1971, MA (Latin Amer. Hist.), 1973–; PhD (Latin Amer. Hist.). **Orgs.:** SALALM. Latin Amer. Std. Assn. **Pubns.:** Various pubns. in phil. and educ. **Addr.:** Bookdealer, P.O. Box 8730, Universal City, CA 91608.

Sanchez, Raymond G. (My. 19, 1934, Dallas, TX) Dir., Career Dev. Ctr., San Antonio Indp. Sch. Dist., 1978; Lectr., San Antonio Cmnty. Coll. Dist., 1967–81; Dir., Soc. Srv., Mex. Amer. Unity Cncl., 1973–78; various other positions as exec. dir. for educ. projs. **Educ.:** St. Mary's Univ., 1952–56, BA (Pol. Sci.), 1959–66, MA (Pol. Sci.). **Orgs.:** San Antonio Pub. Lib.: Bd. Trustees, Ch. (1978–80), Vice-Ch. (1976–78); 75th Anniv. Com. (1978–79). SWLA: Exhibits, Conf. (Ch., 1962). Bexar LA: Mem. Dir. (Ch., 1963). San Antonio Toastmasters Club: Pres. (1963). Alamo City Toastmasters Club: Pres. (1968). Bexar Cnty. Hist. Comsn.: Marker Com. (Ch., 1981). San Antonio Musm. Assn.: Adv. Com. (1980–81). **Honors:** City San Antonio, Outstan. Mem. Bd. Trustees, 1981; other hons. **Pubns.:** Various articles on coll. entrance. **Activities:** 10; 17, 32, 47; 63 **Addr.:** 3310 Herlinda Ave., San Antonio, TX 78228.

Sanchis, Evidia Blanco (O. 8, 1921, Havana, Cuba) Prof., Catlgr., Univ. of Miami Lib., 1962–; Libn., Banfai I, 1955–60; Asst. Prof., Catlgr., Univ. de la Habana Eseuela de Bibtcr., 1959–60. **Educ.:** Inst. de la Habana, 1944–48, Bachiller Letters; Univ. de la Habana, 1948–52, PHD (Lit.), 1952–55, Libn. (LS). **Orgs.:** ALA. FL LA. Assn. of Caribbean Univ. and Resrch. Libs. Cuban Women Club. Univ. of Miami Lib. Staff Assn.: Pres. (1965). **Pubns.:** *Manuel Pérez Beato y Blanco: Suvida y obra bibliográfica* (1966); "De Nuestra Literatura," *Ascr. de Vec. del Repaeto Kalhy* (1955–59); "En Doscientas yalabras precisamente," *Cubamena* (1941–43). **Activities:** 1; 20, 41, 46; 56, 57 **Addr.:** 7600 S.W. 19 St., Miami, FL 33155.

Sandberg, Joy E. (Ag. 11, 1951, Scottsbluff, NE) Info. Ctr. Mgr., Mt. States Empls. Cncl., 1975. **Educ.:** NE Wesleyan Univ., 1970–73, BA (Pol. Sci.); Simmons Coll., 1974–75, MS (LS). **Orgs.:** SLA. Leag. of Women Voters. **Pubns.:** "Record Retention and Posting Requirements of the Federal Government," *Prsnl. Admin.* (Ap. 1979). **Activities:** 12; 17, 39, 41; 59, 78 **Addr.:** Mountain States Employers Council, P.O. Box 539, Denver, CO 80206.

Sandberg, Nina Eve (Ap. 12, 1953, Salt Lake City, UT) Temporary Msc. Catlgr., Oberlin Coll. Cnsvty. Msc. Lib., 1981–; Msc. Libn., Middlebury Coll., 1980–81; Supvsr., Msc. Resrc. Ctr., Univ. of Akron, 1978–80. **Educ.:** Wilson Coll., 1971–75, BA (Msc.); Case West. Rsv. Univ., 1975–77, MSLS, MA(Msc. Hist.). **Orgs.:** Msc. LA. Msc. OCLC Users Grp. Amer. Musicological Socty. **Activities:** 1, 12; 15, 17, 20; 55 **Addr.:** 3205 Ashwood Rd., Cleveland, OH 44120.

Sanders, Brian (Ja. 17, 1937, Kingston-on-Thames, Surrey, Eng.) Sr. Ref. Libn., Srch. Anal., U.S. Dept. of State, 1974–; Assoc. libn., Col. Dev., Lehigh Univ., 1969–73; Soc. Sci. Biblgphr., MI State Univ., 1967–69; Admin. Asst., Univ. of London, 1963–65. **Educ.:** Univ. of Nottingham, Eng., 1956–59, BA (Hist.); Univ. of London, 1959–63, MA (Hist., Intl. Rel.); Rutgers Univ., 1965–67, (Lib. Srv.). **Orgs.:** SLA. Smithsonian Inst. **Pubns.:** *British Foreign Policy in the Far East and Relations with the United States 1903–1911* (1964); *New Channels; A Report on Broadcasting* (1962); "Commitment in Film Criticism," *Gong* (1958). **Activities:** 1, 4; 15, 17, 39; 54, 75, 92 **Addr.:** U.S. Dept. of State Library, Rm. 3239, 2201 C St., N.W., Washington, DC 20520.

Sanders, Nancy P. (Ap. 24, 1945, Lawrence, KS) Resrch. Asst., OCLC, Inc., 1979–; Budget and Plng. Ofcr., IN Univ., 1977–79, Admin. Asst. to Dean, 1974–77; Serial Recs. Dept. Head, AZ State Univ., 1972–74, Gvt. Docum. Dept. Head, 1970–72; Gvt. Docum. Dept. Head, FL Atl. Univ., 1969, Ref. Libn., 1968. **Educ.:** KS Univ., 1963–67, BA (Span.); Denver Univ., 1967–68, MA(LS); various crs. **Orgs.:** ALA: Com. on Econ. Status, Welfare and Fringe Benefits (1976); Budgeting, Acct. and Costs Com. LENE. FL LA. AZ LA. Various other orgs. **Pubns.:** Jt. ed., "Online Subject Access: The Human Side of the Problem," *RQ* (Fall 1980); jt. ed., "Research," *ALA Yrbk., 1980* (1981); jt. ed., *Municipal Publications: Reference Sources Relating to Selected U.S. Cities* (1978); *Survey of the Automated Activities in Libraries of the World* (1970–73); "Continuing Education and Staff Development: Needs Assessment, Comprehensive Program Planning and Evaluation," *Jnl. of Acad. Libnshp.* (Jl. 1978); various articles. **Activities:** 1, 2; 17, 34, 41; 56, 75 **Addr.:** 6565 Frantz Rd., Dublin, OH 43017.

Sandhu, Roopinder K. (D. 31, 1932, Lahore, Punjab, India) Asst. Catlgr. and Asst. Prof., OK State Univ., 1973–, Instr., Asst. Catlgr., 1973–78. **Educ.:** Punjab Univ. (Chandigarh, India), 1954–68, BS (Phil. and Psy.); Univ. of West. ON, 1968–71, MLS; Univ. of S. FL, 1965–67 (Educ., LS). **Orgs.:** OK LA: Minority Rcrt. Com. (1974–75). ALA. Edmon Low Lib. Fac. Assn.: Lib. Fac. Org. Com. (1974–76); Cont. Educ. Com. (1979–); Reappt. Promo. Tenure Com. (1981). **Honors:** Univ. of S. FL, Gold Key Awd., 1966. **Pubns.:** "Villages With and Without Libraries in India," *Intl. Lib. Review* (1979); "Job Perceptions of University Librarians and Library Students," *Can. Lib. Jnl.* (N.D. 1971). **Addr.:** 43 Yellow Brick Dr., Stillwater, OK 74074.

Sandifer, Patricia Ann (Ap. 27, 1943, Urbana, IL) Dir. Media Ctr., E. Alton Wood River HS, 1974; Libn., Ctrl. Jr. HS, 1967–74; Libn., Richwoods HS, 1966–67; Libn., South. IL Univ., (Sums.) 1967–79. **Educ.:** South. IL Univ., 1961–65, BS (Hist.); Univ. IL, 1965–66, MS (LS); South. IL Univ., 1967–78 (Instr. Mtrls.). **Orgs.:** IL LA. ALA. IL Assn. Media Educ. IL AECT. Ord. Whites Shrine Jerusalem: Worthy High Priestess (1980–81).

Special Subjects/Services: 50. Adult educ.; 51. Advert./Mktg.; 52. Aerosp.; 53. Agric.; 54. Area std.; 55. Arts/Hum.; 56. Autom.; 57. Bibl./Prtg.; 58. Bio. sci.; 59. Bus./Fin.; 60. Chem.; 61. Copyrt.; 62. Documtn.; 63. Educ.; 64. Engin.; 65. Env.; 66. Eth. grps.; 67. Film; 68. Food/Nutr.; 69. Geneal.; 70. Geo.; 71. Geol.; 72. Handcpd.; 73. Hist.; 74. Int. frdm.; 75. Info. sci.; 76. Insr.; 77. Law; 78. Legis.; 79. Math./Comp. sci.; 80. Med.; 81. Metals; 82. Nat. resrcs.; 83. Newsp.; 84. Nuc. sci.; 85. Oral hist.; 86. Petr./Energy; 87. Pharm.; 88. Phys./Astr./Math.; 89. Readg.; 90. Relig.; 91. Sci./Tech.; 92. Soc. sci.; 93. Telecom.; 94. Transp.; 95. (other).

Ord. East. Star: Worthy Matron (1972). **Activities:** 10; 15, 32, 48 **Addr.:** 610 Oregon, Bethalto, IL 62010.

Sandock, Mollie A. (Je. 27, 1950, South Bend, IN) Asst. Ref. Libn., Univ. of IL, Chicago, Lib., 1979–; Ref. Libn., Univ. of KY Libs., 1976–78; Branch Libn., Cranston Pub. Lib., 1973–74. **Educ.:** Brown Univ., 1968–72, AB (Human Std.); Univ. of Chicago, 1974–76, MA (Libnshp.); 1978–79, MA (Eng. Lit.), 1979–, PhD Prog. (Eng. Lit.). **Orgs.:** ALA: RASD; ACRL. **Honors:** Beta Phi Mu, 1976. **Pubns.:** *Student Awareness and Use of Reference Services in a Large University Library* ERIC (1976); "A Study of University Students' Awareness of Reference Services," *RQ* (Sum. 1977); various bk. reviews. **Activities:** 1; 31, 39; 55, 56, 57 **Addr.:** 5559 S. Kimbark, Apt. 2, Chicago, IL 60637.

Sandrock, Dorothy M. (Je. 17, 1917, Canby, MN) Libn., Media, Mid. Sch., Line St. Sch., 1972–; Libn., Media, Pine Jr. HS, 1960–71; Libn., Media, Baden-Econ. Jr. High, 1959–60; Libn., D.T. Watson Home/Crippled Chld., 1953–59; Libn., Bethel Twp. Jr.-Sr. HS, 1939–41. **Educ.:** Grove City Coll., 1935–39, BA (LS, Eng., Latin, Fr.); IN State Univ., 1959–60, (AV Aids, Dev. Readg.); Univ. of GA, 1966 (LS); Univ. of Pittsburgh, 1971 (LS). **Orgs.:** ALA. Suburban Sch. Libns.: Pres. PA State Sch. Libns. Natl. Educ. Assn. PA Educ. Assn. GA Educ. Assn. **Addr.:** 202 Briarwood Dr., Calhoun, GA 30701.

Sands, George A., Jr. (N. 28, 1946, Cohoes, NY) Admin., Caroline Cnty. Pub. Lib., 1975–; Supvsr. of Ctrl. Lib., Palm Beach Cnty. Pub. Lib., 1974–75; Readers Srv. Libn., Palm Beach Atl. Coll., 1972–74. **Educ.:** C. W. Post Coll., 1969, BA (Eng.); Long Island Univ., 1970–72, MS (LS). **Orgs.:** ALA. MD LA. Palmer Grad. Lib. Sch. Alum. Assn. East. Shore Reg. Lib. Adv. Cncl. Denton Rotary Club: VP. Mid Shore Symph. Socty.: Pres. Caroline Cnty. Cncl. of Arts: Treas. **Addr.:** Caroline County Public Library, 100 Market St., Denton, MD 21629.

Sands, Nathan J. (Jl. 3, 1923, St. Louis, MO) Mgr., Info. Srv., Singer Librascope, 1954–; Head, Accessioning, Lib. Congs., 1946–48, 1942–43. **Educ.:** Univ. CA, Los Angeles, 1948–49, BA (Hist.); Univ. South. CA, 1951–53, MS (LS). **Orgs.:** SLA: South. CA Chap. (Pres., 1960–61). ASIS: Mem. Com. (1960–66); Natl. Conv. Treas. (1973). **Activities:** 12; 17, 20, 41; 52, 56, 64 **Addr.:** Singer Librascope, 833 Sonora Ave., Glendale, CA 91201.

Sandy, John H. (O. 27, 1943, St. Cloud, MN) Sci. Libn., Univ. of TX, Austin, 1979–; Asst. Prof., Univ. of NE, 1976–79; Head, Ext. Srvs., Billings Pub. Lib., 1974–76. **Educ.:** St. Cloud State Univ., 1965–69, BA (Geog.); South. IL Univ., 1969–71, MS (Earth Sci.); Univ. of MO, 1972–74, MLS. **Orgs.:** NE LA: *NE LA Qtly.* Ed. Bd. (1976–79). ALA. **Honors:** Univ. of NE, Resrch. Cncl. Grant, 1978; Beta Phi Mu. **Pubns.:** Jt. auth., *Geological Literature of Nebraska, 1843–1976* (1980); "One Card Everywhere," *NE LA Qtly.* (1978); "Recruiting the Public Library Director," *Pub. Libs.* (1981). **Activities:** 1, 9; 17, 35, 41; 70, 88, 91 **Addr.:** 901 Chisholm Valley, Round Rock, TX 78664.

Sanfilippo, Jane V. (D. 23, 1947, Newport, RI) Branch Libn., Curric. Support Lib., Nvl. Educ. and Trng. Ctr., 1974–; Ref. Libn., RI Jr. Coll., 1974; Ref. Libn., Newport Pub. Lib., 1973. **Educ.:** Univ. of RI, 1969–71, BA (Phil.), 1971–72, MLS. **Orgs.:** ALA: JMRT (Afflt. Cncl. Rep., 1977–78). RI SLA: Secy. (1979–80). RI LA. RI JMRT: Pres. (1979–80). **Activities:** 12; 15, 17, 39; 74, 90, 91 **Addr.:** 16B Bliss Mine Rd., Middletown, RI 02840.

Sanfilippo, Mary Helena (Sr. of Mercy) (Mr. 13, 1929, Buffalo, NY) Archvst., CA/AZ Srs. of Mercy, 1978–; various positions tchg., hosp. Trustee. **Educ.:** San Francisco Coll. for Women, 1957, BA (Hist.); Univ. of San Francisco, 1967, MA (Hist.); Univ. of Notre Dame, 1972, PhD (Amer. Hist.). **Orgs.:** SAA. Socty. of CA Archvst.: Cncl. Amer. Cath. Hist. Socty. **Pubns.:** "Personal Religious Expressions of Roman Catholicism: A Transcendental Critique," *Cath. Hist. Review* (Jl. 1976). **Activities:** 2; 15, 17, 23; 86, 90, 92 **Addr.:** 2300 Adeline Dr., Burlingame, CA 94010.

Sangwine, Eric V. (My. 9, 1950, Regina, SK) Asst. Libn., Support Srvs., Wentworth Lib.; 1978–. **Educ.:** Simon Fraser Univ., 1970–72, BA (Hist.), 1972–75, MA (Hist.); Univ. of Toronto, 1975–77, MA (LS). Folio Bk. Socty. **Pubns.:** "The Private Libraries of Tudor Doctors," *Jnl. of the Hist. of Med. and Allied Scis.* (Ap. 1978); "Spell it Snow," CBC radio talk (1978). **Activities:** 9; 55, 56 **Addr.:** Wentworth Library, 69 Sanders Blvd., Hamilton, ON L8S 3J8 Canada.

Santiago-Rodríguez, Gladys (Ja. 12, 1929, Guaynabo, PR) Libn., Bur. of the Budget, Ofc. of Gvr., 1960–; Ref. Libn., InterAmer. Univ., 1972–75; Asst. Libn., PR Dept. of Hlth., 1949–60. **Educ.:** Univ. of PR, 1946–55, BA (Educ.), 1970–71, MLS (Spec. Libs.). **Orgs.:** SBPR. **Activities:** 4; 17, 29, 39 **Addr.:** Box 3228, San Juan, PR 00904.

Santiago Rodríguez, Gladys (Ja. 12, 1929, Guaynabo, PR) Dir., Ofc. of Budget and Mgt., 1975–, 1961–72; Dir., Ref. Dept., Inter-Amer. Univ., 1972–75; Asst. Libn., Dept. of Hlth., 1949–60. **Educ.:** Univ. of PR, 1946–51, BA (Educ.), 1971–72, MLS. **Orgs.:** PR Lib. Socty. Natl. Educ. Assn. PR Tchrs. Assn. WHCOLIS: Liason. **Honors:** WHCOLIS, Cert., 1981. **Activities:** 4, 12; 15, 20, 41; 59, 78, 92 **Addr.:** Urb. Monte Verde, 4th St. H-25, Toa Alta, PR 00758.

Santo-Tomas, María B. (Ja. 23, 1932, Moron, Camagüey, Cuba) Cat. Libn. II, Auburn Univ. 1970–, Sci. and Tech. Ref. Libn., 1967–70; Sch. Libn., H.H. Filer Jr. HS, 1962–65; Chld. Libn., Bibtcr. Natl. (Havana, Cuba), 1960–61. **Educ.:** Univ. of Havana (Cuba), 1959–60, Libn. Degree; Emporia State Univ. 1965–67, BS; Auburn Univ., 1969–71, MA (Span.); FL, 1973–83, Tch. Cert. **Orgs.:** AL LA: Rcrt. Com. (1979–80). SELA. Frnd. of the Lib., Auburn, AL. Partners of the Amérs. **Honors:** Sigma Delta Pi. **Activities:** 1, 10; 20, 39, 46; 63, 70, 92 **Addr.:** 605 Green St., Auburn, AL 36830.

Santo-Tomas, Raul A. (Mr. 1, 1922, Guanajay, Pinar del Rio, Cuba) Cat. Libn., Libn. II, Auburn Univ., 1974–, Gen. Biblgphr., 1967–74; Soc. Worker, FL State Dept. of Pub. Welfare, 1962–65; Attorney at Law, Self-Empl., 1943–61. **Educ.:** Vedado Inst., Havana, Cuba, 1935–39, BS, BA; Univ. of Havana, Cuba, 1939–43, Dr. of Laws; Emporia State Univ., 1965–67, MLS (Libnshp.); Auburn Univ., 1969–71, MA (Span.); US Dept. of HEW, 1969, Dip. (Lincoln-Marti); Univ. of FL, 1974–76, Law Cert. (Cuban Lawyers). **Orgs.:** AL LA: Bibl. Com. (1979–81). SE LA. SALALM: Subcom. on Cuban Bibl. Caribbean Std. Assn. Frnds. of the Lib.: VP (1969–70). Southeast. Conf. on Latin Amer. Std. AAUP. **Pubns.:** *A Selected Checklist of Works by Latin American Authors* typescript (1969). **Activities:** 1, 12; 15, 20, 46; 57, 66, 77 **Addr.:** 605 Green St., Auburn, AL 36830.

Sapienza, Diane Goodland (Mr. 12, 1947, Cambridge, MA) Libn., Kadison, Pfaelzer, Woodard, Quinn and Rossi, 1978–, Consult. Libn., 1977–81; Libn., Wyman, Bautzer, Rothman and Kuchel, 1976–77. **Educ.:** George Washington Univ., 1965–73, BA (Art Hist.); Univ. of South. CA, Los Angeles, 1975–76, MLS. **Orgs.:** AALL. South. CA Assn. of Law Libs.: Audit and Budget Com. (1979–80). **Pubns.:** Jt. auth., "Gerontology and the Law: A Selected Bibliography," *Law Lib. Jnl.* (Spr. 1980). **Activities:** 12; 17, 24, 39; 77 **Addr.:** 27104 Shorewood Rd., Rancho Palos Verdes, CA 90274.

Saracevic, Tefko (N. 24, 1930, Zagreb, Croatia, Yugoslavia) Prof., Sch. of LS, Case West. Rsv. Univ., 1969–, various resrch. and tchg. positions, 1962–66. **Educ.:** Univ. of Zagreb, 1952–57; Case West. Rsv. Univ., 1961–62, MS (LS), 1966–69, PhD (Info. Sci.). **Orgs.:** ASIS: Cnclr. (1970–73). **Pubns.:** *Introduction to Information Science* (1970); "Information Systems in Latin America," *Ann. Review of Info. Sci. and Tech.* (1979); "Relevance: A Review of and a Framework for the Thinking in Information Science," *JASIS* (N.–D. 1975); "An Essay on the Past and Future (?) of Information Science Education," *Info. Prcs. and Mgt.* (Ja. 1979). **Activities:** 11; 26, 41; 54, 75 **Addr.:** Matthew A. Baxter School of Information and Library Science, Case Western Reserve University, Cleveland, OH 44106.

Saraidaridis, Susan Bridget (S. 21, 1951, Cleveland, OH) Libn., Med. Electronics Div., Hewlett-Packard Co., 1978–; Libn., Cleveland Metro Gen. Hosp., 1977–78; Libn., Highland View Hosp., 1974–77. **Educ.:** OH Univ., 1969–73, BA (Eng.); Case West. Rsv. Univ., 1974–78, MS (LS); Northeast. Univ., 1979–, BS (Info. Systs.). **Orgs.:** Med. LA. SLA. New Eng. OLUG. Inst. of Electrical and Electronics Engins. **Pubns.:** "Measurement of Service at a Public Library," *Pub. Lib. Qtly.* (Sum. 1980). **Activities:** 12; 15, 17, 38; 59, 75, 80 **Addr.:** 6 Sesame St., Wakefield, MA 01880.

Sarangapani, Chetluru (Mr. 15, 1933, Chitvel, Andhra Pradesh, India) Coord., Autom. and Circ., Univ. of DC Lib., 1978–; Assoc. Dir., WA Tech., Inst., 1974–77, Pers. Libn., 1972–73; Catlgr., Xerox Bibls., 1971–72; Dir., Comp. Div., Viswa Bharati Inst., Bangalore, India, 1969–70; Libn., Embassy of India, 1967–69; various cat. positions, 1963–67; Abstctr., Coder, Documtn. Ctr., West. Rsv. Univ., 1962; Libn., V.S.R. Coll., India, 1955–58. **Educ.:** Madras Univ., India, 1948–53, BS (Chem.), 1954–55, Dip. (LS); Univ. of South. CA, Los Angeles, 1958–59, MS (LS); IN Univ., 1962–63, MS (Educ.); Amer. Med. LA, 1965, Cert. (Med. Libnshp.); Comp. Lrng. Ctr., 1971, Cert. (Systs. Analysis Prog.). **Orgs.:** ALA: LITA. Grt. WA Telugu Cult. Socty.: Pres. (1979–80), VP (1978–79). Assn. of Indians in Amer.: Secy. (1978). **Activities:** 1; 17, 46; 75 **Addr.:** 12329 Palermo Dr., Silver Spring, MD 20904.

Sarenius, Ann E. (Ap. 1, 1949, Traverse City, MI) Chld. Libn., Comstock Twp. Lib. (MI), 1977–. **Educ.:** West. MI Univ., 1969–73, BS (Eng.), 1976–77, MLS. **Orgs.:** ALA. MI LA: Salary Srvy. Com. (1980–81); Share Your Success II Com. (1981–82); Chld. Srv. Caucus. Univ. West. MI, Sch. LS Alum. Assn.: Treas. (1979–81). **Activities:** 9; 21 **Addr.:** 1328 Howland Ave., Kalamazoo, MI 49001.

Sargent, Charles W. (D. 18, 1925, Shelburn, IN) Ch., Hlth. Comm. Dept., Dir., Educ. Resrcs. Div., TX Tech. Univ. Hlth. Sci. Ctr., 1972–; Ch., Info. Sci. Dept., Univ. of MO, 1971–72, Assoc. Prof., 1968–71; Deputy Libn., Univ. of NM Med. Sch., 1967–68. **Educ.:** MI State Univ., 1948–51, BA (Hist.), 1950–51, MA (Hist.); Univ. of MI, 1952–53, MALS; Univ. of NM, 1961–64, PhD (Econ. Hist.); Med. LA, 1968, Cert., Grade III. **Orgs.:** ASIS: Liaison to Hlth. Sci. Comm. Assn. (1976–79). CLENE. SLA: Stan. Com. (1970–74, 1974–76); Copyrt. Com. (1970–72); Rio Grande Chap., Pres.; various coms. Med. LA: Bd. (1972–75); S. Ctrl. Reg. Grp. (Pres., 1976–77); Nom. Com. (Pres., 1981–82); various other coms. Intl. TV Assn. Assn. of Acad. Hlth. Sci. Lib. Dirs. Assn. of Biomed. Comm. Dirs. Hlth. Sci. Comm. Assn. **Honors:** Phi Kappa Phi, 1951; Phi Alpha Theta, 1950; Beta Phi Mu, 1970. **Pubns.:** "Individual Conscience," *Bltn. Amer. Socty. for Info. Sci.* (1978); "Zero Based Budgeting and the Library," *Bltn. Med. LA* (1978). **Activities:** 1; 17; 80 **Addr.:** 5213 26th St., Lubbock, TX 79407.

Sargent, Margaret Patterson (Ap. 6, 1948, Salt Lake City, UT) Media Coord., Salt Lake Sch. Dist., 1974–80; Media Coord., Belmont Sch. Dist., 1972–74. **Educ.:** UT State Univ., 1966–70, BA (Hist.); Boston Univ., 1971–73, MEd (Instr. Media). **Orgs.:** UT LA: Sch. Sect. Ch. (1980–81), Vice-Ch. (1979–80), Secy. (1978–79). UT Educ. Media Assn. ALA. AECT: 1975 Conv., Prog. Eval. Jr. Leag. of Salt Lake. Salt Lake Sch. Dist. Media Coord.: In-Srv. Leader (1978–80); Pres. (1977–78). **Activities:** 10; 17, 21, 22; 63, 89 **Addr.:** 6822 Pine View Cir., Salt Lake City, UT 84121.

Sargent, Seymour H. (Ap. 23, 1932, Concord, NH) Asst. Prof., Univ. of WI Oshkosh, 1971–. **Educ.:** Univ. of NH, 1950–54, BA (Eng.); Univ. of MN, 1958–71, MA, PhD (Eng.); Univ. of WI, 1973–74, MA (LS). **Orgs.:** ALA. AALL. WI LA. **Pubns.:** "Wargames: A Modest Defense," *Top of the News* (Fall 1980); "The Uses and Limitations of Trueswell," *Coll. and Resrch. Libs.* (S. 1979). **Activities:** 11; 16, 26, 41; 55, 67 **Addr.:** Library Science Dept., University of WI Oshkosh, WI 54901.

Sarick, Judy (S. 14, 1939, Toronto, ON) Pres., Chld. Bk. Store, 1974–; Actg. Head of Sch. Lib., Toronto Bd. of Educ., 1972–74; Tchr. Libn., Cent. Sch. (Frontenac), 1970–72; Lib. Consult., Etobicoke Bd. of Educ., 1964–66; Chld. Libn., Forest Hill Pub. Lib., 1962–64. **Educ.:** Univ. of Toronto, 1957–61, BA (Phil.), 1961–62, BLS. **Orgs.:** Can. LA: Can. Mtrls. Ed. Bd. (1974–). Chld. Bk. Ctr.: Bd. of Dirs. (1979–). ON LA. **Honors:** Can. Publshr. Prof. Assn., Bk. Seller of the Yr., 1979. **Pubns.:** "The Children's Book Store," *Horn Bk.* (Ap. 1977); "Children's Book Awards," *Emergency Libn.* (Spr. 1980). **Addr.:** The Children's Book Store, 604 Markham St., Toronto, ON M6G 2L8 Canada.

Sarkis, Jeanne M. (D. 13, 1945, Albuquerque, NM) Clinical Med. Libn., Univ. of MO-Kansas City, Hlth. Sci. Lib., 1979–; Oncology Nurse, Penrose Hosp. (Colorado Springs), 1975–78; Supvsr. Libn., Prcs. Ctr., Sch. Dist. #1 (Colorado Springs), 1968–72. **Educ.:** Bethany Coll., 1965–67, BA (Span.); Emporia State Univ., 1967–68, MLS; Beth-El Sch. of Nursing (Colorado Springs), 1972–75, Dip. (Regis. Nurse). **Orgs.:** Med. LA. New Eng. Reg. Cncl. on Lib. Resrcs. for Nurses. Hlth. Sci. Lib. Grp. of Grt. Kansas City. Kansas City OLUG. **Honors:** Beta Phi Mu; Beta Tau Sigma; Phi Theta Kappa. **Activities:** 1, 12; 39, 49-Clinical med. libnshp. srvs.; 80 **Addr.:** University of Missouri (Kansas City), Health Sciences Library, 2411 Holmes, Kansas City, MO 64108.

Sarna, Helen H. (Ag. 3, 1923, London, Eng.) Asst. Libn., Hebrew Coll., 1966–. **Educ.:** Columbia Univ., BS (Hist.); Simmons Coll., 1965–66, MLS; Hebrew Coll., MHL; Boston State Coll., 1967, MA Tchr. Lic. **Orgs.:** AJL: Boston Branch (VP, 1970–71). **Addr.:** 35 Everett St, Newton Center, MA 02159.

Sarris, Shirley (Jl. 25, 1938, New York, NY) Pres., Sarris Bkmktg. 1978–; Mktg. Dir. R.R. Bowker, 1975–78; Mktg. Dir., Franklin Watts, 1974–75; Mktg. Dir., Arno Press, 1974–74; Mgr., Lib. Mktg., John Wiley and Sons, 1970–74. **Educ.:** City Coll. of NY, 1955–66, BA (Eng. Lit.); Univ. of Chicago, 1966–67, MA (Eng.). **Orgs.:** ALA: RTSD/Assn. of Amer. Publshrs. Com. (Co-Ch., 1977–78). SLA. Assn. of Amer. Publshrs.: Small Publshrs. Grp. (Consult., 1978–); Lib. Com. (Ch., 1975–78); Educ. for Publshg. Com. (1980–81). **Activities:** 14-Consult. firm; 24, 37; 93 **Addr.:** 23 E. 26th St., New York, NY 10010.

Sartorius, Richard C. (N. 1, 1923, St. Louis, MO) Info. Anal., Gulf Oil Chem. Co, 1979–, Bus. Anal., 1974–78, Systs. Prog., 1970–73, Tech. Srv., 1959–69. **Educ.:** WA Univ., St. Louis, Mo, 1953, BS (Nat. Sci.), 1956, MBA. **Orgs.:** SLA. **Activities:** 1, 2; 60, 75, 91 **Addr.:** Polymer Research Lab. Library, Gulf Oil Chemicals Co., P.O. Box 79070, Houston, TX 77079.

Sarvis, Andrew Rust (O. 27, 1946, Evanston, IL) Asst. Ref. Libn., Northwest. Univ. Law Lib., 1980–; Tchg. Asst., Hist. Dept., Doct. Cand., Univ. IL, Chicago, 1980–; Head Libn., St. Ignatius Coll. Prep., 1976–80; Ref. Libn., Felician Coll. Lib., 1975–76; Asst. Acq. Libn., Lake Cnty. Pub. Lib. Syst., 1975. **Educ.:** Macalester Coll., 1964–68, BA, magna cum laude (Hist.); Case West. Rsv. Univ., 1968–69, 1972–73, MA (Hist.); Rosary Coll., 1973–75 (LS). **Orgs.:** ALA: YASD, YA Com. TV (1978, 1980). Cath. LA: HS Sect., North. IL, Co-Ch. Amer. Assn. Adv. Slavic Std. Amer. Hist. Assn. **Honors:** Phi Beta Kappa, 1968. **Activities:** 1, 2 **Addr.:** 2023 N. Sheffield, Chicago, IL 60614.

Sass, Samuel (Ap. 15, 1911, Tarnoruda, Ukraine, Russia) Mem., MA Bd. of Lib. Comsn., 1978–; Libn., Gen. Electric Co.,

PROFESSIONAL ACTIVITIES: Institutions: 1. Acad. lib.; 2. Arch.; 3. Assn.; 4. Fed./Gvt. lib.; 5. Inst. lib.; 6. Mfr./Suppl.; 7. Milit. lib.; 8. Musm.; 9. Pub. lib.; 10. Sch. lib.; 11. Sch. of lib. sci.; 12. Spec. lib.; 13. State lib.; 14. (other). **Functions/Activities:** 15. Acq./Col. dev.; 16. Adult srvs.; 17. Admin.; 18. Apprais.; 19. Archit./Bldgs.; 20. Cat./Class.; 21. Chld. srvs.; 22. Circ.; 23. Cons./Pres.; 24. Consult.; 25. Cont. ed.; 26. Educ. lib. sci.; 27. Ext. srvs.; 28. Fund/Grants; 29. Gvt. pubs.; 30. Indx./Abs.; 31. Instr. lib. use; 32. Media srvs.; 33. Micro.; 34. Netwks./Coop.; 35. Persnl.; 36. PR; 37. Publshg.; 38. Recs. mgt.; 39. Ref. srvs.; 40. Repro.; 41. Resrch.; 42. Review.; 43. Secur.; 44. Serials; 45. Spec. col.; 46. Tech. srvs.; 47. Trustees/Bds.; 48. YA srvs.; 49. (other).

1945–76; Sr. Div. Libn., Univ. of MI, 1941–45, various positions, 1938–41; Head, Sci. Lib., Univ. of KS, 1937–38. **Educ.:** Univ. of KS, 1931–34, AB (Soclgy.); Univ. of MI, 1939–41, AMLS (Libnshp.). **Orgs.:** SLA: Prof. Stans. Com. (1965–68); various other coms. MA LA. Berkshire Cnty. Hist. Socty.: Secy. (1978–). **Honors:** SLA, Hall of Fame, 1977. **Pubns.:** *Bibliography of Electron Microscopy* (1950); "Library Technicians–Instant Librarians?" *Lib. Jnl.* (Je. 1, 1967); "Must Special Librarians Be Parasites?" *Spec. Libs.* (Ap. 1959); "The Library in Industry," *MI Bus. Review* (Mr. 1956); "Everyone Is a (Bad) Librarian," *Spec. Libs.* (1956). **Activities:** 1, 12; 17, 39; 64, 91 **Addr.:** 523 Crane Ave., Pittsfield, MA 01201.

Sauer, Tim D. (F. 6, 1946, St. Catharines, ON) Asst. Head, Tech. Srvs., Univ. of Guelph Lib., 1979–, Asst. Head, Prcs. Div., 1978–79, Head, Bibl. Srch. Sect., 1976–78, Orig. Catlgr., 1972–76. **Educ.:** Univ. of Waterloo, 1964–68, BSc, hons. (Chem.), 1969–71, MSc (Organic Chem.); Univ. of West. ON, 1971, MLS. **Orgs.:** Can. LA. **Pubns.:** "On-line Acquisitions/Circulation Interfaces of the University of Guelph," *Lib. Acq. Prac. and Theory* (1980); "Beekeeping Manuscript Mentioned in Thomas Isham's Latin Diary," *Bibl. Socty. of Amer. Papers* (1979); "Predicting Book Fund Expenditures: A Statistical Model," *Coll. & Resrch. Libs.* (1978). **Activities:** 1; 15, 17, 46 **Addr.:** Technical Services, University of Guelph Library, University of Guelph, Guelph, ON N1G 2W1 Canada.

Saul, Beverly Joan (Field) (Ja. 19, 1936, Eldorado, IL) Coord., Lib. Srvs., Thompson Sch. Dist. R2–J, 1978–, Elem. Lib. Coord., 1970–78, Elem. Libn., 1963–70. **Educ.:** South. IL Univ., 1954–58, Educ. (Eng., LS, Sp.); Univ. of CO, 1971–73, MA (Lib. Media); CO State Univ., 1977–79, Type D (Sch. Admin., Elem. Prin.). **Orgs.:** ALA. AECT: Conv. eval. (1978). CO Educ. Media Assn.: Conv. eval. (1978). CO LA: Sch. Lib. Div. (Ch., 1977); Mem. Com. (Ch., 1979). CO Assn. of Sch. Execs.: Bd. of Dept. Educ. Specs. (1976–80); *The Medium* Ed. Bd. Loveland Musm. Bd.: Ch. (1979); Bd. (1975–79). Phi Delta Kappa: Secy. (1981). **Activities:** 10; 17, 21, 24 **Addr.:** 2207 Frances Dr., Loveland, CO 80537.

Saulmon, Sharon Ann (Je. 13, 1947, Blackwell, OK) Ref., Spec. Projs. Libn., Oscar Rose Jr. Coll., 1980–; Asst. Chief, Ext. Srvs., Metro. Lib. Syst., 1977–80, Coord., Pub. Srvs., 1974–77, Chld. Libn., 1969–74. **Educ.:** Ctrl. State Univ., 1968–69, BA (Eng., LS); Univ. of OK, 1971–74, MLS; North. OK Coll., 1965–67, ABA (Eng.); various wkshps. **Orgs.:** ALA. OK LA: Chld. and Young People's Div. (Ch., 1976–77); Natl. Lib. Week Com. (Ch., 1977–78); Hum. Com. (1977–79). South. Hills Un. Meth. Church: Organist (1978–); Chld. Coord. (1976–77). Urban Leag. of Grt. OK City: Educ. Task Frc. (1977–80). Mental Hlth. Assn. of OK Cnty: Prog. Com. (1978–79). Amer. Inst. of Discuss.: Mdrtr. (1973–77). **Pubns.:** *Task-Oriented Staff Allocation* (1981); *Task-Oriented Library Staff Allocation* (1978); "Realistic Allocation of Branch Library Staff," *Lib. Jnl.* (F. 1, 1979); "Utilizing Art with Storytelling" videocassette (1973); "Sage Age" newsp. clmn. (1977–80); *Community Analysis Report, Paris, Texas* (1980). **Activities:** 1, 9; 17, 27, 36; 50, 51, 66 **Addr.:** Little Ltd. Consultants, P.O. Box 12071, Oklahoma City, OK 73157.

Saunders, Allene W. (Mr. 7, 1927, Omaha, NE) Catlgr., Span. and Portuguese Mtrls., Univ. of Pittsburgh, 1970–; Libn., Mono. Col., Acq., Cat., Ref., Westinghse. Bettis Atomic Power Lab., 1969–70. **Educ.:** Univ. of CA, Berkeley, 1945–48, AB (Gen. Curric.); NY Theo. Semy., 1949–51, MRE (Relig. Educ.); Univ. of Pittsburgh, 1968–69, MLS. **Orgs.:** ALA. Assn. of Univ. Libns.: Secy. (1977–78); Budget Policies Com. (1977); Exec. Com. (1979–81); Hlth. & Welfare Com. (1981–82). Univ. of Pittsburgh: Peer Review Com. (1979–81); Docum. Rev. Subcom. (1979–81). Beta Phi Mu: Pi Chap., VP (1977), Pres. (1978), Schol. Com. (1980–81). **Activities:** 1; 20; 54, 55 **Addr.:** Hillman Library, G–49, University of Pittsburgh, Pittsburgh, PA 15260.

Saunders, E. Stewart (Ap. 3, 1936, Bradenton, FL) Ref., Liaison Libn., Purdue Univ. Libs., 1978–; Sr. Ref. Libn., OH State Univ., 1969–77, Docum. Libn., 1967–68, Soc. Sci. Biblgphr., 1965–67, Lib. Intern, 1964–65. **Educ.:** DePauw Univ., 1954–59, BA (Premed. Sci.); Ball State Univ., 1961–62, MA (Hist.); IN Univ., 1963–64, MLS; OH State Univ., 1970–80, PhD (Hist.). **Orgs.:** ALA. Socty. for Fr. Hist. Std. Popltn. Assn. of Amer. **Pubns.:** "The Archives of the Academie des Sciences," *Fr. Hist. Std.* (Fall 1978). **Activities:** 1; 15, 39; 54 **Addr.:** Purdue University Libraries, Stewart Center, Purdue University, West Lafayette, IN 47907.

Saunders, Laurel B. (Ag. 17, 1926, Ainsworth, NE) Chief Libn., White Sands Missile Range, 1975–, Chief, Cat. and Acq., 1965–74; Supvsr. Libn., U.S. Army Air Defense Sch. Clasfd. Lib. (Ft Bliss, TX), 1962–64; Base Libn., Biggs Air Frc. Base, (TX), 1953–62. **Educ.:** Univ. of SD, 1944–48, BA (Pol. Sci.); Univ. of MI, 1948–50, MA (LS). **Orgs.:** Border Reg. LA: Bylaws Com. (1972). NM LA. SWLA. SLA. Ord. of the East. Star: NM Renich Chap., Worthy Matron (1970). First Untd. Meth. Church, El Paso TX: Admin. Bd. (1981). NM Farm Bur. **Honors:** Biggs Air Frc. Base (TX), Outstan. Performance, 1961–62; U.S. Army Ft. Bliss (TX), Outstan. Performance, 1964; White Sands Missile Range, Outstan. Performance, 1976, 1978. **Activities:** 4; 15, 17, 20; 64, 88, 91 **Addr.:** Rte. 1 Box 329, Anthony, NM 88021.

Saunders, Laverna M. (S. 22, 1948, Brush, CO) Dir. of Lrng. Resrc. Ctr., Un. Coll., 1978–; Cat. Libn., Drew Univ., 1976–78. **Educ.:** Univ. of North. CO, 1966–70, BA, magna cum laude (Eng.); Rutgers Univ., 1974–76, MLS; Drew Univ., 1976–81, MA (Eng.). **Orgs.:** AECT. KY AECT: Secy. (1980–81). KY LA. Delta Omicron Intl. Msc. Fraternity. **Honors:** ALA, JMRT, Shirley Olofson Meml. Awd., 1977; Beta Phi Mu. **Activities:** 1; 17, 20, 32 **Addr.:** Union College, Box 453, Barbourville, KY 40906.

Saunders, Lelia B. (Roanoke, VA) Lib. Dir., Arlington Cnty. Pub. Lib., 1979–; Asst. Lib. Dir., Arlington Cnty. Dept. of Libs., 1958–79; Branch Libn., Enoch Pratt Free Lib., 1952–58; Army Libn., US Armed Srvs., Germany, 1949–52; Bkmobile. Libn., Lib. of HI, 1946–48; Circ. Libn., Roanoke City Pub. Lib., 1942–46; Cnty. Libn., Dickinson Cnty., VA, 1941–42. **Educ.:** Roanoke Coll., 1935–39, BA (Eng.); Columbia Univ., 1939–40, BLS. **Orgs.:** VA LA: VP (1979); Pres. (1980). ALA: Cncl. (1964–68, 1970–72, 1979); RASD, Bd. (1979). DC LA: Ref. Interest Grp. (1978–79). AAUW: Womens Issues Ch. (1977–81). Frnds. of Women Prisoners: VP (1979–80). Presby. Mtg. Hse. (Elder, 1976–79). Alexandria VA Comsn. on Status of Women: Ch. (1978–79). **Activities:** 9; 15, 16, 17 **Addr.:** 1015 N. Quincy St., Arlington, VA 22201.

Saunders, William B. (O. 3, 1927, Smithers, WV) Ref., Dir., External Coord., Antioch Univ. Ctr., 1971–; Educ. Biblgphr., Ref. Libn., Temple Univ., 1970–72; AV, Curric. Mtrls. Libn., Cheyney State Coll., 1969–70; Dir. of Lib. SVS Inst. for the Advnc. of Bio-Med. Comm. Univ. Sci. Ctr., 1968–69, Dir., Lib. Srvs., Mktg. Sci. Inst., 1963–68; Libn., Bus. Lib., Temple Univ., 1959–63; Libn., Free Lib. of Philadelphia, 1957–59. **Educ.:** Bluefield State Coll., 1943–47, BS (Sec. Educ.); WV Univ., 1947–48, MA (Educ., Soc. Sci.); Univ. of Pittsburgh, 1956–57, MSLS (Gen. Libnshp.). **Orgs.:** SLA: Philadelphia Chap. Pres., (1966–67); Pres. Com. on Empl. of the Handcpd., SLA Rep. Educ. Libn. of Grt. Philadelphia: Co-Fndr. (1974). DE Valley Chap. ACRL. PA LA. AAUP. Amer. Assn. of Higher Educ. PA Abolition Socty. Frnds. of the Chapel of the Four Chaplains. **Honors:** Chapel of the Four Chaplains, Awd., 1978. **Pubns.:** Various bk. reviews, articles. **Activities:** 1, 12; 17, 31, 39; 63, 72, 92 **Addr.:** 337 W. Mt. Airy Ave., Philadelphia, PA 19119.

Sauter, Hubert Eugene (Ja. 10, 1923, Dietenheim, Germany) Admin., Defense Tech. Info. Ctr., 1973–, Deputy Admin., 1972–73; Asst. to Dir., Natl. Tech. Info. Syst., Dept. of Cmrce., 1970–72; Dir., Clearing Hse. for Fed. Sci. and Tech. Info. Srv., 1967–70, Deputy Dir., 1965–67; Chief, Tech. Srvs. Sci. and Tech. Div., NASA, 1961–65; Resrch. Info. Spec., Aircraft Nuc. Propulsion Div., Gen. Electric; Lectr., LS Depts., Cath. Univ., Amer. Univ. **Educ.:** Marquette Univ., 1949, BEE (Electrical Engin.); Univ. of WI, 1949–50, BLS. **Orgs.:** Amer. Mgt. Assn. ASIS. SLA. Adv. Grp. for Aerosp. Resrch. and Dev., NATO: Tech. Info. Panel (Ch. 1980); Deputy Ch. (1978–80). Various other orgs. **Honors:** Defense Logistics Agency Defense Tech. Info. Ctr., Outstan. Performance, 1974–80. **Pubns.:** "The Place of Research/Classified Reports in a Special Library," *A New Reader* (1980); *Advisory Group for Aerospace Research and Development, Technical Information Panel Members Guide* (Ja. 1981); contrib., *Encyc. of Lib. and Info. Sci.* (1971); various papers. **Activities:** 4, 12; 15, 30, 34; 75, 74, 91 **Addr.:** Defense Technical Information Center, Cameron Station, Alexandria, VA 22032.

Savage, Gretchen S. (Ja. 15, 1934, Seattle, WA) Pres., Savage Info. Srvs., 1977–; Consult., Info. Syst. Dsgn. and Dev., Self-Empl., 1965–77; Mgr., Online Srch., Admin. on Aging Thesaurus Proj. various Gvt. Contracts, Documtn. Assn., 1975–77; Mgr., Pubns. and Data Control Dept., NASA Facility, Documtn., Inc., 1963–65; Head Libn., Lib. Supvsr., Douglas Aircraft Co., 1957–63. **Educ.:** Univ. of CA, Los Angeles, 1951–55, BA (Educ.); LaVerne Coll., Univ. of CA, Santa Barbara, 1956–72, (LS, Math., Educ.); State of CA, Life Cred. (Libnshp.). **Orgs.:** SLA: Mem. Com. (1978–79); Info. Tech. Div., Secy. ASIS: ASIS 80 Conf., Hosplty. Com. South. CA OLUG: Strg. Com. (1978–). AAUW. Alpha Phi: Soc. Com., various com. **Honors:** Phi Beta Kappa, 1955; Delta Phi Upsilon, 1954–55; Pi Lambda Theta, 1954–55. **Pubns.:** *Study of Online Bibliographic Database Services in California* (1977); "Scisearch on Dialog," *Database* (S. 1978); "Experience in Man and Machine Relationships in Library Mechanization," *Amer. Documtn.* (Jl. 1964); "The Education of Library Staff and Library Users for Mechanization," *Spec. Libs.* (Ap. 1964); ed., *ASIS Los Angeles Nsltr.* various articles, sps., papers. **Activities:** 12, 14-consult.; 17, 24, 46 **Addr.:** 30000 Cachan Pl., Rancho Palos Verdes, CA 90274.

Savard, Réjean (N. 12, 1950, PQ) Asst. Prof., Ecole de Bibliotheconomie, Univ. de Montréal, 1981; Libn., Bib. Natl. Du PQ, 1975–81. **Educ.:** Laval Univ., 1970–73, BA (Phil.); Univ. of Montréal, 1973–75, MLS; various crs. **Orgs.:** Corp. of Prof. Libns. of PQ: Ed. (1976–77); Bd. of Dirs. (1976–81). **Activities:** 4, 9; 33, 36, 41 **Addr.:** 8313 Berri, Montréal, PQ Canada.

Savaro, Josephine (Ja. 14, 1915, Scranton, PA) Lib. Dir., St. Joseph's Univ., 1964–; Head of Soc. Scis. Lib., Cath. Univ. of Amer., 1963–64; Head Libn. and Fndr., Wheeling Coll., 1954–63; Asst. Prof., Grad. Lib. Sch., Cath. Univ. of Amer., 1953–54; Instr., Grad. Lib. Sch., Marywood Coll., 1951–53; Head Libn., Univ. of Scranton, 1947–51; Visit. Lectr., Cath. Univ. of Amer. Grad. Lib. Sch., (Sums.) 1950–1964; Head Cat. Libn., Manhattanville Coll., 1944–47. **Educ.:** Marywood Coll., 1933–37, BA, magna cum laude (Fr., Italian, Eng.), 1942–43, BS (LS); Columbia Univ., 1944–50, MS (LS); Univ. of IL, 1968, Cert. (Lib. Autom.). **Orgs.:** Cath. LA: Bd. (1966–72); Coll. Sect. (Ch., 1965–66); Cat. Sect. (Ch., 1957–59). ALA. PA LA. SAA. AAUP. **Pubns.:** Various reviews, rpts. **Activities:** 1, 2; 15, 17, 19; 55, 56, 57 **Addr.:** Library, Saint Joseph's University, 5600 City Ave., Philadelphia, PA 19131.

Savig, Norman I. (O. 6, 1928, Boston, MA) Coord., Msc. Lib., Univ. of North. CO, 1968–; Msc. Catlgr., Univ. of CO, 1962–68; Msc. Libn., Milwaukee Pub. Lib. 1955–62. **Educ.:** Univ. of Denver, 1948–52, BA (Eng.), 1948–53, BA (Msc.), 1954–55, MLS (Libnshp.). **Orgs.:** Msc. LA: Rocky Mt. Chap. Greeley Philharmonic Orch.: Violoncellist (1968–). Greeley Concerts Assn.: Treas. (1970–73). **Honors:** Phi Beta Kappa, 1952. **Pubns.:** *Checklist of Music Serials in 18 Libraries of the Rocky Mountain Region* (1970); *Uniform Titles for Music, a Compilation* (1977). **Activities:** 1, 12; 15, 20, 39 **Addr.:** Music Library, University of Northern Colorado, Greeley, CO 80639.

Savit, Madeleine Elise Kolisch (N. 8, 1951, Roslyn Heights, NY) Clinical Libn., Health Scis. Ctr., State Univ. of NY at Stonybrook, 1980–; Clinical Info. Coord., Dept. of Orthopaedic Surgery, Beth Israel Hosp., 1978–; Ref./Clinical Libn., Bibl. Instr. Coord., Yale Med. Lib., 1976–78. **Educ.:** SUNY, Plattsburgh, 1973–74, BA (Span., Ling.); Univ. of MI, 1975–76, AMLS (Med. Libnshp.); Med. LA 1976, Cert. **Orgs.:** Med. LA. **Pubns.:** "A System for Managing Clinical Information," *Jnl. of Med. Educ.* forthcoming; "Clinical Information Coordinator: A New Information Specialist Role for Medical Librarians," *Bltn. Med. Lib. Assn.* (O. 1980); "Evaluation of a Clinical Medical Librarian Program at the Yale Medical Library," *Bltn. of the Med. LA* (Jl. 1978). **Activities:** 1, 12; 17, 28, 39; 75, 80, 91 **Addr.:** 200 Carmen Ave., 15D, East Meadow, NY 11554.

Savitzky, Evelyn Robbins (D. 28, 1920, Yonkers, NY) Asst. Mgr., Corporate Lib., Perkin-Elmer Corp., 1966–; Libn., Westport HS, 1960–66. **Educ.:** SUNY, 1939–43, BA (BioChem.); South. CT State Coll., 1960–64, MS (LS). **Orgs.:** SLA. ASIS. Southwest. CT Lib. Cncl.: Prog. Ch. (1980–81). Wilton Pub. Lib.: Bd. of Trustees; Resrch. and Dev. (Ch., 1978–80). Assn. of Info. Mgrs. **Activities:** 12; 17, 34, 39; 52, 60, 91 **Addr.:** Perkin Elmer Corp., Main Ave., Norwalk, CT 06856.

Savoie, Guy (Je. 29, 1935, Lac Etchemin, PQ) Dir. du Ctr. de Documtn., Univ. du PQ-Télé-Univ., 1978–, Attaché d'Admin., 1975–78; Prof. de Lit. Québécoise, Univ. du PQ, Rouyn, 1972–74; Prof., 1959–66. **Educ.:** Univ. d'Ottawa, 1948–57, BA (Phil.), 1957–58, LPh (Phil.); Univ. Laval, 1966–68, LesL, 1969–71, Dip. (Péd.), 1969–72, MA (Lit. Can.); Univ. de Montréal, 1974–76, MBibl. **Orgs.:** Corp. des Bibtcrs. Prof. du PQ. ASTED. Caisse Pop. les Etchemins: Admin. (1980–). Assn. des Cadres de la Télé-Univ.: Secy./Tréas. (1980). **Pubns.:** *Bio-bibliographie de Norbert Thibault (1840–1881)* (1968); *Le Réalisme du Cadre Spatio-temporel de "Bonheur d'Occasion"* (1972). **Activities:** 12; 17, 25, 32; 50, 63, 93 **Addr.:** Télé-université, Centre de documentation, 214, ave St-Sacrement, Québec, PQ G1N 4M6 Canada.

Sawin, John S. (Mr. 2, 1915, Wakefield, MA) Libn., Archvst., Simpson Lib., Christ. and Missn. Alliance, Intl. HQ, 1976–; Pastor, Missn., USA and Vietnam, 1938–75. **Educ.:** Myack Coll., 1932–35; Gordon Coll., 1936–38, ThB (Theo.); Gordon-Conwell Semy., 1939–59, MDiv (Theo.); Ball State Univ., 1941–43; West. Rsv. Univ., 1943–45. **Orgs.:** ATLA. **Activities:** 2, 12; 23, 45; 90 **Addr.:** Christian & Missionary Alliance International Headquarters, Box C, Myack, NY 10940.

Sawyer, Deborah Christine (Ja. 28, 1953, Ince-in-Makerfield, Lancashire, Eng.) Creat. Dir., Info. Plus, 1979–; Ed., Can. Educ. Indx. and Dir. of Educ. Std. in Can., Can. Educ. Assn., 1976–79. **Educ.:** Univ. of Toronto, 1970–74, BA (Ling., Russ., Chinese), 1974–76, MLS (Info. Srvs. for Law, Sci., Bus., Gvt.), 1977, Cert.; McGill Univ., 1979, Cert. **Orgs.:** Can. LA. Can. Assn. Info. Sci. Indx. Abs. Socty. Can.: Nom. Com. (1978). Freelnc. Eds. Assn. of Can. **Pubns.:** Ed., *Canadian Education Subject Headings* (1979); ed., volume 12, 13, 14, *Canadian Education Index* (1977–79); ed., *Directory of Education Studies in Canada* (1978–79); "The Canadian Education Index: A View of Index Editing," *Can. Lib. Jnl.* (Ag. 1978); "A Potential Canadian Data Base–The Canadian Education Index," *CSSE News* (My. 1978); various articles. **Activities:** 14-Info., Resrch. Srv.; 24, 30, 41; 56, 63, 92 **Addr.:** Information Plus, P.O. Box 287, Postal Station P, Toronto, ON M5S 2S8 Canada.

Sawyer, Edmond J. (My. 12, 1936, Tarrytown, NY) Tech. Info. Spec., US Gen. Acct. Ofc., 1977–; Chief, Ref. Branch, Fed. Energy Admin., 1975–77; Supvsr., Info. Srvs., Babcox and Wilcox Co., 1971–75; Lexicographer, Leasco Systs. and Resrch. Corp., 1970–71. **Educ.:** Univ. of MD, 1965, BA, 1969, MLS.

Special Subjects/Services: 50. Adult educ.; 51. Advert./Mktg.; 52. Aerosp.; 53. Agric.; 54. Area std.; 55. Arts/Hum.; 56. Autom.; 57. Bibl./Prtg.; 58. Bio. sci.; 59. Bus./Fin.; 60. Chem.; 61. Copyrt.; 62. Documtn.; 63. Educ.; 64. Engin.; 65. Env.; 66. Eth. grps.; 67. Film; 68. Food/Nutr.; 69. Geneal.; 70. Geo.; 71. Geol.; 72. Handcpd.; 73. Hist.; 74. Int. frdm.; 75. Info. sci.; 76. Insr.; 77. Law; 78. Legis.; 79. Math./Comp. sci.; 80. Med.; 81. Metals; 82. Nat. resrcs.; 83. Newsp.; 84. Nuc. sci.; 85. Oral hist.; 86. Petr./Energy; 87. Pharm.; 88. Phys./Astr./Math.; 89. Readg.; 90. Relig.; 91. Sci./Tech.; 92. Soc. sci.; 93. Telecom.; 94. Transp.; 95. (other).

Orgs.: ASIS: Couns.-at-Large (1980–82). **Activities:** 4; 17, 29, 30; 75 **Addr.:** 9317 Madison St., Laurel, MD 20810.

Sawyer, Katherine H. (Jl. 11, 1908, Cleveland, OH) Retired; Cur., Sophia Smith Col., Smith Coll., 1970–71; Consult., Med. Sci. Lib., Mnstry. of Hlth. (Guyana), 1966–68; Med. Libn., St. Luke's Hosp. (Pittsfield, MA), 1965–66; Hosps. and Insts. Dept., Cleveland Pub. Lib., 1956–62. **Educ.:** Smith Coll., 1926–30, BA (Eng. Lit.); Case West. Rsv. Univ., 1955–56, MS (LS); 1973, Cert. (Archvst.). **Orgs.:** SLA. Frnds. West. Rsv. Hist. Lib.: Ch. (1972–77); Trustee (1980–). **Activities:** 9, 11; 17, 27, 45; 72, 80 **Addr.:** 17485 Shelburne Rd., Cleveland, OH 44118.

Sawyer, Ruth (McMullen) (Ag. 26, 1914, Dallas, TX) Retired, 1981–; Libn., Lib. Sch. Lib., The Gen. Libs., Univ. of TX, Austin, 1954–81; Libn., Jefferson HS, 1938–39; Libn., J.P. Elder Jr. HS, 1937–38; Libn., Tchr., Alvin HS, 1935–37. **Educ.:** TX Woman's Univ., 1931–35, BS, BA (LS); various crs. **Orgs.:** ALA. TX LA: Natl. Lib. Week Com. (1974–75). CS LA: Lib. World Liaison (Ch., 1977–79). Child Nurture Club: Austin Area Chap., Sponsor; Treas.; Exec. Cncl. (1978–). **Honors:** Univ. of TX Grad. Sch. of LS Alum. Assn., Plaque: a Salute for Srv. to Students and Fac., 1976. **Activities:** 1, 11; 15, 26, 39; 50, 89, 90 **Addr.:** 2826 San Gabriel St., Austin, TX 78705.

Sawyers, Elizabeth J. (D. 2, 1936, San Diego, CA) Dir., Hlth. Sci. Lib., OH State Univ., 1975–; Asst. Dir. of Lib. for Tech. Srvs., SUNY at Stony Brook, 1973–75; Spec. Asst. to the Assoc. Dir. for Lib. Opers., Natl. Lib. of Med., 1969–73, Spec. Asst. to the Chief, Tech. Srvs. Div., 1966–69, Head, Acq. Sect., 1963–66, Asst. Head, Acq., 1962–63, Libn. Intern, 1961–62. **Educ.:** Univ. of CA, Los Angeles, 1957–59, BA (Bacteriology); 1960–61, MLS; Glendale Jr. Coll., 1954–57, AA (Gen.). **Orgs.:** Med. LA: MLA/NLM Liaison Com. (1981–); 1983 Natl. Prog. Com. (Assoc. Ch., 1980–); Pubn. Com. (1971–73); Com. on Vital Notes (1964–73). ASIS: Ctrl. OH Chap. (Secy., 1977–78). SLA: Ctrl. OH Chap. (Pres., 1979–80). OH LA. Various other orgs. OH Acad. Sci.: Sect. S, Info. LS (VP, 1981–82). **Pubns.:** "Union List Development: Control of the Serial Literature," *Bltn. of the Med. LA* (Jl. 1972). **Activities:** 17, 34, 46; 56, 80 **Addr.:** Health Sciences Library, Ohio State University, 376 W. Tenth Ave., Columbus, OH 43210.

Saxe, Minna Claire (S. 16, 1938, Providence, RI) Chief, Serials, Lib., Grad. Sch., CUNY, 1970–; Slavic Catlgr., Harvard Coll., 1960–69. **Educ.:** Brown Univ., 1956–60, AB (Pol. Sci.); Simmons Coll., 1962–64, MSLS. **Orgs.:** ALA. NY LA. NY Tech. Srvs. Libns. NY Lib. Club. **Pubns.:** "Great Faith and a Few Big Questions: Notes from a Librarian Using the CONSER Base," *Amer. Libs.* (Ja. 1977). **Activities:** 1; 20, 44, 46 **Addr.:** 230 E. 48 St., New York, NY 10017.

Saye, Jerry D. (My. 3, 1946, Sheboygan, WI) Asst. Prof., Sch. of Lib. and Info. Sci., Drexel Univ., 1977–; Tchg. Fellow, Grad. Sch. of Lib. and Info. Sci., Univ. of Pittsburgh, 1977; Head Catlgr., Instr., Fairmont State Coll., 1972–75, Asst. Catlgr., Instr., 1971–72. **Educ.:** Univ. of WI, Sheboygan, 1964–66; WI State Univ., Oshkosh, 1966–68, BS, magna cum laude (Hist.); Univ. of Pittsburgh, 1970–71, MLS, 1975–78, PhD (LS). **Orgs.:** ALA.: ACRL, DE Valley Chap; LITA; RTSD. AALS. Bibl. Socty. of the Univ. of VA. **Honors:** Phi Alpha Theta; Kappa Delta Pi; Beta Phi Mu, 1971. **Pubns.:** *An Examination of the Bibliographic Control Devices of the Library of American Civilization,* ERIC (1978). **Activities:** 1, 11; 20, 26, 46; 56, 57, 75 **Addr.:** School of Library and Information Science, Drexel University, Philadelphia PA 19104.

Sayers, Winifred F. (O. 28, 1936, St. Louis, MO) Mgr., Parsippany Info. Ctr., GPU NUC. Corp., 1981–; Syst. Libn., GPU Srv. Corp., 1979–81, Libn., 1975–79. **Educ.:** AZ State Univ., 1973, BA (Elem. Educ.); Rutgers Univ., 1975, MLS; Fairleigh Dickinson Univ., 1980, MBA. **Orgs.:** SLA: NJ Chap., Pres. (1979–80), 1st VP (1978–79), 2nd VP (1977–78); Pub. Util. Div., Bltn. Ed. (1980–81); Secy. (1978–80). AAUW. **Activities:** 12; 17, 34; 95-Electric util. bus. **Addr.:** Parsippany Information Center, GPU Nuclear Corporation, 100 Interpace Pkwy., Parsippany, NJ 07054.

Sayles, Jeremy Whitman (Je. 9, 1937, Schenectady, NY) Head, Pub. Srvs., GA Coll., 1979–; Head, Ref. Dept., Fitchburg State Coll., 1972–79; Head, Ref. Div., West. CT State Coll., 1970–72. **Educ.:** Allegheny Coll., 1956–60, BA (Art Hist.); Simmons Coll., 1967–70, MS (LS). **Pubns.:** "Bookman's Folly; A Hymn to Reference as Information Service," *RQ* (Win. 1978); "An Opinion About Librarian Instruction," *The Southeast. Libn.* (Win. 1980). **Activities:** 1; 22, 31, 39; 75 **Addr.:** Russell Library, Georgia College, Milledgeville, GA 31061.

Saylor, Chris (Priscilla H.) (F. 2, 19–, Canton, OH) Elem. Media Spec., Columbus Pub. Schs., 1969–; Sch. Libn., Medina Jr. High, 1960–69; Sch. Libn., Van Wert HS, 1959–60. **Educ.:** OH State Univ., 1955–59, BSEd (Eng., Educ.); various crs. **Orgs.:** ALA. OH LA: Div. VIII (Secy., 1976). OH Educ. Lib. Media Assn.: Lcl. Arrange. (Ch., 1972); Legis. Com. WHCOLIS: Alternate Del. (1979). AAUW. **Honors:** Delta Kappa Gamma. **Activities:** 10; 21, 31, 32 **Addr.:** 53 Deland Ave., Columbus, OH 43214.

Saylor, Helen Howe (F. 19, 1934, Lincoln, NE) Med. Libn., Presby. Hosp. Ctr., 1975–; Med. Libn., Passavant Hosp., 1972–74; Libn., Jacksonville HS, 1971–72. **Educ.:** Midwest Bible Coll., 1950–54, ThB (Christ. Educ.); Taylor Univ., 1954–56, BS (Sec. Educ.); South. IL Univ., 1967–68; Univ. of NM, 1980– (Educ. Fdn.). **Orgs.:** NM LA. Albuquerque Area Hosp. Med. Lib. Med. LA: Exch. Com. (1979–); S. Ctrl. Reg. Grp., Bylaws Com. (1978–80), Prog. Com. (1980–81, 1983), Hosp. Libns. SIG (Pres., 1979–80); SCRG, Mem. Com. (1982). Albuquerque Cham. of Cmrce.: Educ. Com. (1978–79). **Pubns.:** "Six Steps to Easier Record-keeping," *Hosp. Lib.* (Je. 1978). **Activities:** 12, 14-Hosp.; 15, 17, 39; 80 **Addr.:** Presbyterian Hospital Center Medical Library, 1100 Central Ave. S.E., Albuquerque, NM 87102.

Sayre, Edward C. (Ag. 15, 1923, Longview, WA) Dir., Mesa Pub. Lib., 1979–; Coord., Serra Coop. Lib. Syst., 1978–79; Coord., Ctrl. CO Lib. Syst., 1972–78; Syst. Coord., NM State Lib., 1970–72; Dir., Roswell Pub. Lib., 1969–70; Dir., Lib. Srvs., Thomas Nelson Cmnty. Coll., 1968–69. **Educ.:** Coll. of Grt. Falls, 1953–55, BA (Hist.); Univ. of ID, 1958–61, MA (Eng.); Univ. of MD, 1967–68, MLS. **Orgs.:** ALA: Lib. Admin. Div., Compar. Lib. Org. (Ch., 1970–71). Mt. Plains LA. NM LA: Pres.-Elect (1972). Santa Fe LA: Pres. (1971). **Pubns.:** *Library Services in a Regional Services Authority* (1973); "Cost Accounting Model for Public Libraries," *Pub. Productivity Review* (Ja. 1978); "Five Factors for Interlibrary Cooperation," *Lib. Jnl.* (D. 1975). **Activities:** 9, 12; 17, 35, 47; 54, 55, 74 **Addr.:** Mesa Public Library, Los Alamos, NM 87544.

Sayre, John Leslie (Mr. 28, 1924, Hannibal, MO) Dir., Univ. Libs., Phillips Univ., 1971–, Semy. Libn., Assoc. Prof., Theo. Bibl., 1962–71; Campus Mnstr., The Univ. of TX, Austin, Univ. Christ. Church, 1957–62; Campus Mnstr., OK State Univ., First Christ. Church, 1950–57. **Educ.:** Univ. of OK, 1942–43, AB (Relig.); Phillips Univ., 1943–46, AB (Relig.); Yale Univ., 1946–50, MDiv (Relig.); Univ. of TX, Austin, 1962–63, Mstrs. (LS), 1971–73, Doctor of Phil. **Orgs.:** ALA. ATLA: Bd. of Dirs. (1973–76); Mem. Com. (Ch., 1970). OK LA: Constn. Com. (1967–68); Lib. Educ. Div. (Pres., 1976–77). SW LA: Constn. Com. (1976–77). Disciples of Christ Hist. Socty. **Honors:** Phi Kappa Phi; Beta Phi Mu; Theta Phi. **Pubns.:** *A Manual of Forms for Term Papers and Theses* (1977); *An Index of Festschriften in Religion* (1970); *An Illustrated Guide to the Anglo-American Cataloging Rules* (1972); *The Personalized System of Instruction in Higher Education: Readings in P.S.I.–The Keller Plan* (1972); *Tools for Theological Research* (1978). **Activities:** 1, 11; 15, 17, 20; 90 **Addr.:** Box 2212, University Station, Enid, OK 73702–2212.

Sayre, John Richard (Mr. 9, 1953, Stillwater, OK) Ref., Instr. Libn., Undergrad. Lib., IN Univ., 1979–, Ref. Libn., 1978–79, ERIC 'Probe' Libn., 1977–79; Asst. Libn., OK Coll. of Osteopathic Med. and Surgery, 1977. **Educ.:** Phillips Univ., 1971–75, BA (Hist.); Univ. of OK, 1975–76, MLS. **Orgs.:** ALA. IN LA: Ad Hoc Com. on Bibl. Instr. (1979–80). IN–Bloomington Lib. Fac. Cncl. IN Univ. Libns. Assn.: Natl. Lib. Week Com. (Ch., 1979–81). **Pubns.:** "The Communication Way," *Lrng. Today* (Spr. 1976); jt. auth., *The United States Congress: A Bibliography* (1981). **Activities:** 1; 31, 39 **Addr.:** Undergraduate Library, Indiana University, Bloomington, IN 47401.

Sayre, Samuel R. (Ag. 25, 1951, Fairfield, IA) Asst. Ref. Libn., ID State Univ., 1977–; Dir., Shoshone Bannock Lib. and Media Ctr., 1975–77. **Educ.:** Reed Coll., 1969–74, BA (Intl. Std.); Univ. IL, 1974–75, MSLS. **Orgs.:** ID LA: VP, Pres.-Elect (1980–81). ALA. Pac. NW LA. ID Hlth. Info. Assn. ID Educ. Media Assn. **Activities:** 1; 39; 92 **Addr.:** Idaho State University Library, Pocatello, ID 83209.

Scales, Patsy R. (Ag. 28, 1944, Mobile, AL) Libn., Greenville Mid. Sch., 1972–; Libn., Metcalf Lab. Sch., IL State Univ., 1970–72. **Educ.:** AL Coll., 1962–66, BS (Elem. Educ.); George Peabody Coll., 1969–70, MLS. **Orgs.:** SC LA: Sch. Sect., Past Ch.; Frdm. Com.; Budget Com.; SC Assn. of Sch. Libs.: Bk. Awd. Com. SELA: Sch. and Chld. Sect., Ch. Frnds. of the Lib.: Greenville Cnty. Pub. Lib. Syst., Bd. **Honors:** Outstan. Leaders in Elem. and Sec. Educ., Outstan. Young Educ. of the Yr., 1976. **Pubns.:** "Call An Author" *American Education* TV interview (1976); "Spotlighting Readers and Writers," *Sch. Lib. Jnl.* (O. 1976). **Activities:** 10; 21, 24, 48; 63, 74, 89 **Addr.:** Apt. 16-G Yorktown Apts., Greenville, SC 29615.

Scanlan, Jean M. (Ap. 6, 1945, Portland, ME) Dir. of the Info. Ctr., Price Waterhse. and Co., 1976–; Bus. Ref. Libn., Univ. of MA, 1973–76; Head, Reader Srvs., Babson Coll., 1969–73. **Educ.:** Univ. of ME, 1963–67, BA (Eng.); Simmons Coll., 1968–69, MSLS. **Orgs.:** ALA: Bus. Ref. Srvs. Com. (Ch., 1979–80). SLA: Boston Chap. (Treas., 1978–79). **Pubns.:** "Profile of Information Information Manager Center," (D. 1978). **Activities:** 1, 12; 17, 39; 59 **Addr.:** Price Waterhouse & Co., One Federal St, Boston, MA 02110.

Scanland, Roger (Ag. 22, 1941, Wichita Falls, TX) Serials and Gvt. Docum. Catlgr., Brigham Young Univ. Lib., 1980–; Sr. Catlgr., Geneal. Socty. of UT Lib., 1975–80, Sect. Head, Gen. Ref. Sect., 1973–75, Asst. Coord. of Branch Lib., 1971–73. **Educ.:** Midwest. State Univ., 1959–63, BMEd (Msc. Educ.); Brigham Young Univ., 1970–71, MLS. **Orgs.:** UT LA: Cont. Educ. Com. (1981–82). Assn. of Prof. Genealogists: Bd. of Trustees (1979–80) ALA. Brigham Young Univ. Lib. Sch. Assn. Frnds. of the Orem Pub. Lib. **Honors:** Assn. of Prof. Genealogists, Disting. Srv. Awd., 1980. **Pubns.:** "Ethnic Materials in the Genealogical Society of Utah Library," *Ethnic Genealogical Librarianship* (forthcoming); fndn. ed., *APG Nsltr. Assn. Prof. Genealogists* (1979–80); contrib. ed., *Geneal. Jnl.* (1977–). **Activities:** 1, 12; 20, 29, 44; 69 **Addr.:** 6380 HBLL, Brigham Young University, Provo, UT 84602.

Scannell, Elizabeth F. (O. 14, 1917, Boston, MA) Admin. Libn., Boston Pub. Sch., 1965–; Asst. Head, Cat. and Class., Ref. Div., Boston Pub. Lib., 1960–65, Ref. Libn., Kirstein Bus. Branch, 1953–60, Lieutenant (s.g.), USNR Spec. Devices Div., Ofc. of Nvl. Resrch., 1943–46. **Educ.:** Simmons Coll., 1934–38, BS (LS); Boston State Coll., 1970, MEd, 1972, CAGS (Admin.). **Orgs.:** ALA. New Eng. LA. MA Assn. for Educ. Media: Treas. (1966–72). Leag. of Women Voters of Boston. **Activities:** 10, 12; 17, 32, 39; 63 **Addr.:** Administration Library, Boston Public Schools, 26 Court St., Boston, MA 02108.

Scannell, Francis X. (D. 15, 1917, Boston, MA) State Libn., MI State Lib., 1968–; Libn., Ref. Lib., MI State Univ., 1965–68; Head, Reader Srvs., MI State Lib., 1953–65; Asst. Chief, Ref., Detroit Pub. Lib., 1948–53, Ref. Asst., 1946–48; Ref. Asst., Boston Pub. Lib., 1943–46. **Educ.:** Harvard Univ., 1938–42, AB (Lit.); Columbia Univ., 1942–43, BS (Fr., Latin, Grk.). **Orgs.:** ALA. Amer. Socty. of Pub. Admin. **Honors:** MI Constitutional Conv., Cit. for Lib. Srv. **Pubns.:** *Michigan Novelists* (1964). **Addr.:** 3627 Colchester Rd., Lansing, MI 48906.

Scantland, Jean-Marie (Mr.) (My. 28, 1922, Angers, PQ) Chief, Spec. Cols. Div., Laval Univ. Lib., 1978–, Asst. Chief Libn., 1963–78; Chief Libn., Gvt. Pubns., Gvt. Can., 1960–63; Ref. Libn., Gvt. Pubns., Parlmt. Lib. (Can.), 1950–60. **Educ.:** Univ. Ottawa, 1936–44, BA, BAPH (Phil.), 1950–54, BLS; Univ. MD, 1969, Lib. Admin. Dev. Prog. **Activities:** 1; 32, 45; 67, 70 **Addr.:** Special Collections Division, Laval University Library, Bonenfant Bldg., Ste Foy, PQ G1K 7P4 Canada.

Scarborough, Ella Butler (Je. 3, 1946, Sumter, SC) Tech. Libn., Duke Power, 1975–; Jr. HS Libn., Charlotte/Mecklenburg, 1973–75; Lib. Asst., Lincoln HS, Sumter Sch. Dist. #17, 1965–67; Lib. Asst., Ofc. of the Internal Revenue Srv., 1968–69. **Educ.:** SC State Coll., 1967–71, BS (LS Educ.); SLA, 1976–81, Cont. Ed., Lib. Mgt. **Orgs.:** SLA: Pub. Util. Div. (Ch., 1979–81). NC SLA: Sec. VP-Elect (1981–82). Metrolina LA. NC LA: Gvr.'s Com. on Libs. for the White Hse. Conf. (1978). SC State Alum. Chap.: Pres. (1977–79). Women's Pol. Caucus: Bd. **Activities:** 12; 17, 20, 30; 65, 84, 91 **Addr.:** 801 Braxfield Dr., Charlotte, NC 28210.

Scarborough, Ruth Ellen (Mr. 31, 1917, Scranton, PA) Dir., Lrng. Resrcs., Centenary Coll., 1946–; Ref. Libn., Post Lib., 1943–46; Head Libn., Monmouth Jr. Coll., 1940–43. **Educ.:** Marywood Coll., 1935–39, BS (Educ., Soc. Std.); Syracuse Univ. 1939–40, BS (LS); Rutgers Univ., 1969–72, MLS (Lib., Info. Sci.). **Orgs.:** ALA: ACRL. NJ LA. Hackettstown Hist. Socty.: Pres. (1975–78). AAUW: Hackettstown Chap. (Pres., 1980–82); Prog. VP (1971–72). Leag. of Women Voters. 1968–1977. **Honors:** Phi Beta Mu, 1972. **Pubns.:** "Statistics for Junior College Libraries," *Assn. Coll. and Resrch. Libs.* (Ja. 1956, Ja. 1957). **Activities:** 1; 17, 31, 39; 63, 75, 85 **Addr.:** 504 E. Valley View Ave., Hackettstown, NJ 07840.

Scarfia, Angela M. (Ap. 20, 1950, Rochester, NY) Asst. Libn., Pennwalt Pharm. Div. Resrch. Lib., 1976–. **Educ.:** Nazareth Coll. of Rochester, NY, 1968–72, BA (Eng.); SUNY Geneseo, 1977–79, MLS. **Orgs.:** SLA: Schol. Com. (1981). Med. LA. Rochester Reg. Resrch. Lib. Cncl.: Un. List of Serials Com.; ILL Com. Rochester Area Lib. in Hlth. Care. Rochester Area OLUG. **Activities:** 12; 29, 39, 44; 58, 80, 87 **Addr.:** Research Library, Pennwalt Pharmaceutical Division, P.O. Box 1710, Rochester, NY 14603.

Scarlett, Jane H. (Mr. 28, 1931, Gastonia, NC) Assoc. Libn., Head, Serials Cat., FL State Univ., 1975–, Asst. Libn., Serials Cat., 1973–75; Cnty. Lib. Srvs. Coord., Mid-MS Reg. Lib., 1967–68; Catlgr., Cumberland Cnty. Pub. Lib., 1964–66. **Educ.:** Univ. of MS, 1951–53, AB (Hist.); FL State Univ., 1972–73, MS (LS), 1977–79, Advnc. Mstrs. (LS, Mgt.). **Orgs.:** ALA. FL LA. SELA. Frnds. of the Lib.: Strozier Lib. Women of Presby. Church: Histn. (1978). **Pubns.:** "Catalog Assistance at Florida State University," *FL Libs.* (Fall 1977); "Random Reading," clmn. *Fayetteville Observer* (1964–66). **Activities:** 1, 9; 20, 44, 46 **Addr.:** 1919 Rhonda Dr., Tallahassee, FL 32303.

Scarry, Patricia (Jl. 22, 1949, Cleveland, OH) Chap. Rel. Ofcr., ALA, 1980–; Dir., Cnty. Libs., Sussex Cnty., DE, 1975–80; Libn., Fairfield Cnty., SC, 1972–75. **Educ.:** WV Univ., 1967–71, AB (Eng.); FL State Univ., 1971–72, MS (LS). **Orgs.:** ALA. DE LA: Pres. (1979–80). WHCOLIS: Del. WV Alum. Assn. FL State Univ. Alum. Assn. **Honors:** Beta Phi Mu; Natl. Assn. of Cntys., Achvmt. Awd., 1977, 1978. **Activities:** 9, 12; 17, 24, 25 **Addr.:** American Library Association, 50 E. Huron St., Chicago, IL 60611.

PROFESSIONAL ACTIVITIES: Institutions: 1. Acad. lib.; 2. Arch.; 3. Assn.; 4. Fed./Gvt. lib.; 5. Inst. lib.; 6. Mfr./Suppl.; 7. Milit. lib.; 8. Musm.; 9. Pub. lib.; 10. Sch. lib.; 11. Sch. of lib. sci.; 12. Spec. lib.; 13. State lib.; 14. (other). **Functions/Activities:** 15. Acq./Col. dev.; 16. Adult srvs.; 17. Admin.; 18. Apprais.; 19. Archit./Bldgs.; 20. Cat./Class.; 21. Chld. srvs.; 22. Circ.; 23. Cons./Pres.; 24. Consult.; 25. Cont. ed.; 26. Educ. lib. sci.; 27. Ext. srvs.; 28. Fund/Grants; 29. Gvt. pubs.; 30. Indx./Abs.; 31. Instr. lib. use; 32. Media srvs.; 33. Micro.; 34. Netwks./Coop.; 35. Persnl.; 36. PR; 37. Publshg.; 38. Recs. mgt.; 39. Ref. srvs.; 40. Repro.; 41. Resrch.; 42. Review.; 43. Secur.; 44. Serials; 45. Spec. col.; 46. Tech. srvs.; 47. Trustees/Bds.; 48. YA srvs.; 49. (other).

Scepanski, Jordan Michael (N. 21, 1942, Yonkers, NY) Dir., Ctrl. Lib., Vanderbilt Univ., 1978–; Mgt. Intern, Jt. Univ. Libs., 1977–78; Asst. Dir., Lib., Univ. of NC, Charlotte, 1974–78; various staff positions, ALA, 1970–73. **Educ.:** Manhattan Coll., 1960–64, BS (Soc. Sci.); Emory Univ., 1966–67, MLn (Libnshp.); Univ. of TN, Nashville, 1978–, MBA cand. **Orgs.:** ALA: Natl. Lib. Week Com., Ch.; J. Morris Jones Awd. Jury (1980); Melvil Dewey Cand. Jury (1979); SCMAI Com., 1976; various ACRL and LAMA coms. SELA. TN LA: Grievance Com. (1979–80); Int. Frdm. Com. (1979–81); Regis. Ch., 1979 Anl. Conv. Nashville Lib. Club. AAUP. **Honors:** Beta Phi Mu, 1968; ARL, Consult. Trainee, 1979; Fulbright Lectr., Turkey, 1981–82. **Pubns.:** *Children's Area Space Allocation in Selected Public Libraries* (1972); ed., *Planning Libraries for Media Services, Presentations Made at the LAD Buildings and Equipment Section Program 1971* (1972). **Activities:** 1; 17, 24, 35; 54 **Addr.:** Central Library, Vanderbilt University, Nashville, TN 37203.

Schaaf, Robert Warren (Je. 6, 1926, Rochester, NY) Sr. Spec., Untd. Nations and Intl. Docum., Lib. of Congs., 1978–, Head, Un. Cat., Intl. Orgs. Ref. Sect., 1970–78, Head, Intl. Orgs. Sect., 1966–70, Asst. Head, 1956–65. **Educ.:** Hamilton Coll., 1946–50, BA (Hist., Pol. Sci.); Johns Hopkins Univ., 1950–52, MA (Intl. Rel.). **Orgs.:** ALA: GODORT (Secy, 1976–78); Intl. Docum. Task Frc (Coord., 1978–80); Law and Pol. Sci. Subsect. (Secy., 1964–67). Assn. of Intl. Libs. DC LA. **Honors:** Phi Beta Kappa, 1949; Lib. of Congs., Outstan. 4 Performance Awds. **Pubns.:** *Documents of International Meetings, 1953* (1959); contrib., *International Scientific Organizations* (1962); "International Documentation in the Library of Congress," *Gvt. Pubns. Review* (1975); various reviews. **Activities:** 4; 15, 39; 54 **Addr.:** 7247 Reservoir Rd., Springfield, VA 22150.

Schaafsma, Carol A. (Ja. 9, 1937, Ft. Wayne, IN) Head, Acq. Div., Univ. of HI Lib., 1974–, Head, Sel. and Srch. Sect., 1969–74, Jr. Lib. Spec., 1968–69. **Educ.:** IN Univ., 1956–58, BS (Educ.); Univ. of HI, 1967–68, MLS, 1970–77, MBA. **Orgs.:** ALA. HI LA: Conf. Exhibits Com. (Ch., 1977–). **Activities:** 1; 15, 17, 44 **Addr.:** Acquisitions Division, University of Hawaii Library, 2550 The Mall, Honolulu, HI 96822.

Schabas, Ann H. (My. 14, 1926, Toronto, ON) Assoc. Prof., Fac. of LS, Univ. of Toronto, 1978–, Asst. Prof., 1966–78; Ref. Libn., Toronto Bd. of Educ., 1964–66. **Educ.:** Univ. of Toronto, 1948, BA (Phys.); Smith Coll., 1949, AM (Phys.); Univ. of Toronto, 1964, BLS; Univ. of London, 1970, MA (LS), 1979, PhD (LS). **Orgs.:** ASIS. Can. Assn. Info. Sci. AALS. Can. Assn. of Coll. and Univ. Libs. Can. Assn. of Lib. Sch. Can. LA: Nom. Com. (Ch., 1974). Various other orgs. Can. Assn. of Univ. Tchrs. Univ. of Toronto Fac. Assn. **Honors:** Sigma Xi; Beta Phi Mu. **Pubns.:** Jt. auth., "The Imprint Date in the Anglo-American Cataloging Rules," *Lib. Resrcs. & Tech. Srvs.* (Spr. 1976); jt. auth., "Indexing," *Access to the Law: a Study Conducted for the Law Reform Commission of Canada* (1975); "Technical Services and Technology: Technological Advance," *A Century of Service: Librarianship in the United States and Canada* (1976); jt. auth., "A Role for the Minicomputer in Library Education," *Applications of Minicomputers to Libraries and Related Problems* (1974); "Machine Searching of UK MARC on Title, Library of Congress Subject Headings, and PRECIS for Selective Dissemination of Information," *The PRECIS Index System: Principles, Applications, and Prospects* (1977). **Activities:** 20, 30; 56, 62, 75, 91 **Addr.:** Faculty of Library Science, University of Toronto, 140 Saint George St., Toronto, ON M58 1A1 Canada.

Schabel, Donald (My. 20, 1937, Chicago, IL) Dir., Tech. Srvs., Chicago Pub. Lib., 1979–, Asst. Dir., Tech. Srvs., 1977–79, Dir., Cult. Ctr., 1974–77, Chief, Hist. and Travel Dept., 1971–74. **Educ.:** North. IL Univ., 1955–59, BS (Msc. Educ., LS); Rosary Coll., 1966–67, MALS; Amer. Mgt. Assn., 1979 (Fundamentals of Data Prcs. for the Non-Data Prcs. Exec.). **Orgs.:** IL LA: Resrcs. and Tech. Srvs. Sect., Cont. Ed. Com. (1980–). Lib. Admin. Conf. of North. IL: Tech. Srvs. Sect., Prog. Com. (1978–80). ALA: Metro. Area Lib. Srv. Com. (1976–77). Phi Mu Alpha Sinfonia; Intl. Visitors Ctr. **Pubns.:** "Experience with a Computer Produced Catalog," *IL Libs.* (S. 1980); "From Shambles to Showplace," *Amer. Libs.* (D. 1977). **Activities:** 9; 15, 23, 46; 56 **Addr.:** Technical Services, Chicago Public Library, 425 N. Michigan Ave., Chicago, IL 60611.

Schacht, John N. (F. 24, 1943, Chicago, IL) Libn. II, Univ. of IA, 1977–; Interviewer, Univ. of IA Comm. Workers of Amer. Oral Hist. Proj., 1968–72. **Educ.:** Wesleyan Univ., 1960–64, BA (Hist.); Univ. of IA, 1964–66, MA (Hist.), 1966–77, PhD (Hist.); Univ. of IL, 1976–77, MS (LS). **Orgs.:** ALA. **Honors:** Phi Beta Kappa. **Pubns.:** Ed., *Three Progressives from Iowa: Gilbert N. Haugen, Herbert C. Hoover, Henry A. Wallace* (1980); ed., *Three Faces of Midwestern Isolationism* (1981); "Toward Industrial Unionism: Bell Telephone Workers and Company Unions, 1919–1937," *Labor Hist.* (Win. 1975). **Activities:** 1; 39; 85 **Addr.:** Reference Dep., University of Iowa Libraries, Iowa City, IA 52242.

Schad, Jasper G. (Jl. 29, 1932, Los Angeles, CA) Dean of Libs. and Media Resrcs. Ctr., Wichita State Univ., 1971–; Assoc. Dir. of Libs., CA State Univ., Northridge, 1970–71, Asst. Dir. for Tech. Srvs., 1969–70, Head Acq. Libn., 1966–69, Head Bibl. Libn., 1964–66, Soc. Sci. Libn., 1961–66. **Educ.:** Occidental Coll., 1950–54, BA (Hist.); Stanford Univ., 1956–57, MA (Hist.); Univ. of CA, Los Angeles, 1960–61, MLS. **Orgs.:** AECT. ALA: Com. on Stans. (Ch., 1979–); ACRL, Stan. for Coll. Libs. Rev. Com. (1977–81); ACRL Rep. to the Assn. of State Lib. Agencies, Stan. Review Com. (1976–81); Subcom. to Rev. the 1959 Stan. for Coll. Libs. (1973–75); ACRL/ARL Jt. Com. on Univ. Lib. Stans., (1973–74); Com. on Stans. and Accred. (Ch., 1972–1976). **Honors:** Phi Alpha Theta, 1953; Phi Kappa Phi, 1976. **Pubns.:** "The Evolution of College and University Library Standards," *Libraries and Accreditation In Institutions of Higher Education* (1981); jt. auth., *Problems in Developing Academic Library Collections* (1974); "Missing the Brass Ring in the Iron City," *Jnl. of Acad. Libnshp.* (My. 1979); "Allocating Materials Budgets in Institutions of Higher Education," *Jnl. of Acad. Libnshp.* (Ja. 1978); "Allocating Book Funds: Control or Planning?" *Coll. & Resrch. Libs.* (My. 1970); jt. auth., "Book Selection in Academic Libraries: A New Approach," *Coll. & Resrch. Libs.* (S. 1969). **Activities:** 1; 15, 17 **Addr.:** Library/Media Resources Center, Box 68, Wichita State University, Wichita, KS 67208.

Schaeder, Patricia Ann (Ap. 3, 1951, Brooklyn, NY) Coord., Chld. Srvs., Lower Merion LA, 1981–; Chld. Libn., YA Spec., 1978–; Chld. Libn., Sch. Libn., Bala Cynwyd Lib., Bala Sch., 1974–78. **Educ.:** St. Francis Coll., 1969–73, BS (Educ.); Drexel Univ., 1974–76, MS (LS). **Orgs.:** PA LA: New Libn. RT (Pres., 1981–82). ALA. DE Valley YA Libn.: Fndn. Mem. (1980). **Activities:** 9; 21, 24, 48 **Addr.:** Lower Merion Library Association, Bryn Mawr, PA 19010.

Schaefer, Barbara K. (Ap. 5, 1932, Buffalo, NY) Visit. Lectr., Sch. of Lib. and Info. Sci., State Univ. Coll., Geneseo, 1971–; Assoc. Libn., Ref. Dept., Univ. of CA, Irvine, 1979; Asst. Prof., Grad. Sch. of Lib. and Info. Sci., SUNY, Albany, 1963–67; Head Libn., Jr. Coll. of Albany, 1957–63. **Educ.:** Eastman Sch. of Msc., Univ. of Rochester, 1950–56, BMus (Msc.); SUNY, Albany, 1956–57, MLS; Univ. of Pittsburgh, 1964–72, PhD (LS). **Orgs.:** ALA. ASIS. AALS. NY LA. AAUP. **Pubns.:** *Using the Mathematical Literature: A Practical Guide* (1979); *Classification of the Literature of Mathematics: A Competative Analysis* (1972); "Set Theory," *Encyc. of Lib. and Info. Sci.* (1979); "Mathematics Literature," *Encyc. of Lib. and Info. Sci.* (1976); "The Phoenix Schedule 510 in Dewey 18," *Lib. Resrcs. & Tech. Srvs.* (Win. 1975). **Activities:** 1, 11; 20, 26, 39; 55, 75, 91 **Addr.:** 5259A Devel Rd., Honeoye, NY 14471.

Schaefer, Elizabeth K. (Jl. 10, 1923, Chicago, IL) Libn., St. Vincent Ferrer Sch. Lib., 1966–; Gifts and Exch. Libn., John Crerar Lib., 1950–55; Libn., Sci. Lib., De Paul Univ., 1950, Asst. Libn., Liberal Arts Lib., 1949; Asst. Libn., River Forest Pub. Lib., 1945–49; Army Libn., 1944–45; Asst. Catlgr., Northwest. Univ., 1944; various part-time positions. **Educ.:** Rosary Coll., 1940–44, BA (LS); Univ. Chicago, 1947–48, BLS. **Orgs.:** ALA: Serials RT, *Serial Slants* Ed. (1952–55); Lib. Pers. RT, Nom. Com. (1954); Div. Cat. Class., Pubns. Com. (1954–59) IL LA: Constn. Rev. Com. (1954–55); Rcrt. Schol. Com. (1975–77). Cath. LA. IL AV Assn. Elmwood Pub. Lib.: Bd. Dirs. (1963–81); Pres. (various yrs.); VP (various yrs.); Secy. (various yrs.). Chicago Lib. Club: Treas. (1951–52); Mem. Com. (Ch., 1952–53). Grad. Lib. Sch. Alum. Assn.: Secy.–Treas. (1950–51). Rosary Coll. Alum. Assn.: First Anl. Bk. Fair (Ch., 1972). **Honors:** Rosary Coll., Mem. Theotokoeian, 1940–44; St. Vincent Ferrer Sch., Tchr. Yr. Awd., 1978; State Bd. Educ. IL, Hon. Mention Excel. Educ., 1978. **Pubns.:** Jt. auth., *Read to Learn, A Right to Read Project* (1973); "College Librarian and the Library Committee," *Lib. Qtly.* (Ap. 1951); "Special Library Problems," *Spec. Libs.* (Jl.–Ag. 1953). **Activities:** 1, 9, 10; 17, 21, 44; 92 **Addr.:** 1722 N. 74th Ct., Elmwood Park, IL 60635.

Schaefer, Patricia (Ap. 23, 1930, Fort Wayne, IN) Asst. Dir., Muncie Pub. Lib., 1959–. **Educ.:** Northwest. Univ., 1947–51, BM (Piano); Univ. of IL, 1957–58, MM (Msclgy.); Univ. of MI, 1960–63, MALS. **Orgs.:** IN LA: Awds. & Hons. Com., Ch. (1977–80); Treas. (1973–75); Lib. Plng. Com. (Ch., 1969–73); Div. of Women in IN Libs., Bd. ALA. Mu Phi Epsilon. Natl. Leag. of Amer. Pen Women. Amer. Recorder Socty. Muncie Matinee Musicale. **Pubns.:** Reviews; concert prog. annotator; wkly. newsp. clmn. **Activities:** 9; 32, 36; 67, 95 **Addr.:** Muncie Public Library, Audio-Visual Center, 200 E. Main St., Muncie, IN 47305.

Schaeffer, Lorraine Dey (D. 14, 1946, Philadelphia, PA) Asst. State Libn., State Lib. of FL, 1978–, Fed. Grants Coord., 1971–78; Ext. Dir., Santa Fe Reg. Lib., 1969–71. **Educ.:** FL State Univ., 1964–68, BA (LS, Hist.), 1968–69, MS (LS). **Orgs.:** FL LA: Secy. (1978–79); Mem. Com. (Ch., 1975–77); Caucus Org. Com. (Ch., 1974–75). SELA: Exec. Bd. (1976–80). ALA: Com. on Org. (1979–83); ASCLA, Plng., Org. & Bylaws Com. (Ch., 1976–80), Bd. (Dir., 1980–82). Amer. Socty. for Pub. Admin. **Honors:** Beta Phi Mu, 1969. **Activities:** 13; 17, 28, 35 **Addr.:** State Library of Florida, R. A. Gray Bldg., Tallahassee, FL 32301.

Schafer, Gerald (Jay) (Ap. 20, 1942, El Paso, TX) Libn., Skidmore, Owings and Merrill, 1981–; Branch Lib. Mgr. II, Denver Pub. Lib., 1978–81, Asst. Head, Sci. and Engin., 1977–78, Ref. Libn., Sci. and Engin., 1976–77; Resrch. Info. Sci., Denver Resrch. Inst., Univ. of Denver, 1974–76. **Educ.:** Univ. of TX, El Paso, 1968–71, BA (Eng.); Univ. of Denver, 1972–73, MA (LS). **Orgs.:** ALA. Univ. of Denver, Grad. Sch. of Libnshp. Alum.: Treas. (1979–); Rocky Mt Chap., Pres. (1975–77). **Honors:** Beta Phi Mu, 1973. **Pubns.:** *A Case Study of Technology Transfer: Cardiology* (1974); jt. auth., *An Evaluation of the Aurora (County) Public Library: Resources, Services, and Facilities* (1973). **Activities:** 9; 17, 19 **Addr.:** 1675 Broadway, Denver, CO 80202.

Schafer, Marilyn E. (S. 7, 1942, Toronto, ON) Mgr., East. Can., Infomart, 1979–; Head, Pub. Srvs., Intl. Dev. Resrch. Ctr., 1974–79; Libn., Multilingual Div., Trans. Bur., Secy. of State, 1974; Branch Head, Nepean Pub. Lib., 1970–73. **Educ.:** Univ. of Toronto, 1961–65, BA (Fr., Span.), 1965–66, BLS. **Orgs.:** Can. LA: Pres. Can. Assn. of Spec. Libs. and Info. Srvs. (1980–81). Can. Assn. Info. Sci.: Ottawa Chap., Bd. of Dirs. (1976–78). ASIS: *JASIS* Ed. Bd. (1979–81). Univ. Women's Club of Ottawa. Match Intl. Ctr. **Pubns.:** "Administrative Accountability for Funds and Functions," *Can. Lib. Jnl.* (F. 1981); jt. auth., "The International Development Research Centre and Computerized Retrieval Services," *Procs. of the Fourth Can. Conf. on Info. Sci.* (1976). **Activities:** 6, 12; 25, 36, 39; 54, 56, 58 **Addr.:** Infomart, 300–141 Laurier Ave. W., Ottawa, ON K1P 5J3 Canada.

Schaffer, Ellen G. (Ag. 17, 1949, New York, NY) Ref. Libn., Org. of Amer. States, 1976–; Rom. Lang. Descr. Catlgr., Lib. of Congs., 1973–76. **Educ.:** SUNY, Albany, 1966–71, BA (Span., Latin Amer. Std.); Columbia Univ., 1972–73, MLS. **Orgs.:** SLA: Intl. Affairs Sect. DC LA. **Pubns.:** *Guide to Latin American Business Information Sources* (1977); "A Selective Guide to Law Related Publications of Latin America and the Caribbean," *Intl. Jnl. of Law Libs.* (1978). **Activities:** 14-Intl. org.; 28, 29, 39; 92, 95-Inter-Amer. std., intl. rel. **Addr.:** Columbus Memorial Library, Organization of American States, 17th and Constitution Ave., Washington, DC 20008.

Schaffer, Evelyn Joan (Ja. 12, 1947, Albany, NY) Chief, Lib. Srv., U.S. Vets. Admin. Med. Ctr., Huntington, WV, 1971–. **Educ.:** SUNY, Albany, 1964–68, BA (Hist.), 1969–71, MLS. Med. LA, 1980, Cert. **Orgs.:** ALA. Med. LA.: Mid. Atl. Reg. Grp., Reg. Adv. Cncl. (1979–81). WV LA: JMRT, Exec. Bd. (1974–77); Spec. Libs. Sect. (Secy., 1976–79); Nom. Com. (Ch., 1979). Various other orgs. Fed. Jewish Charities of Huntington, WV. Hadassah. Huntington Galleries Lib. Voluns. Frnds. of WPBY-TV. **Activities:** 4, 12; 15, 17, 32, 39; 72, 80 **Addr.:** Veterans Administration Medical Center, Library Service 142D, 1540 Spring Valley Dr., Huntington, WV 25704.

Schalit, Michael (Mr. 10, 1930, Munich, Germany) Resrch. Libn., Sandia Labs., 1968–; Chem., Great West. Sugar Co., 1956–68; Resrch. Chem., Eastman Kodak Co., 1953–56. **Educ.:** Univ. of Denver, 1948–53, BSc (Chem.), 1965–68, MA (Libnshp.). **Orgs.:** SLA. ASIS. Amer. Socty. of Sugar Beet Tech. **Pubns.:** *Heinrich Schalit; The Man and His Music* (1979); *Fused Salts; A Bibliography* (1972); *Guide to the Literature of the Sugar Industry* (1970). **Activities:** 12; 29, 39, 41; 81, 84, 91 **Addr.:** 451 Bell Ave., Livermore, CA 94550.

Schallert, Ruth Fortun (Mr. 31, 1920, Whitehall, WI) Bot. Libn., Smithsonian Inst. Libs., 1966–; Ref. Libn., U.S. Nvl. Oceanograph. Lib., 1963–66; Libn. Pac. Salmon Investigations Lab., 1954–57; Art Libn., State Univ. of IA, 1943–48. **Educ.:** Luther Coll., 1938–42, BA (Eng.); Univ. of MI, 1942–43, MLS. **Orgs.:** Socty. for the Bibl. of Nat. Hist. SLA. Cncl. on Botanical and Horticult. Libs: Governing Bd. (Pres., 1972–73). Univ. of MI LS Alums. **Activities:** 4; 15, 39; 91 **Addr.:** 1210 Laurel Dr., Accokeek, MD 20607.

Schanck, Peter C. (My. 7, 1938, Chicago, IL) Lib. Dir., Assoc. Prof., Univ. of Detroit, Sch. of Law, 1978–; Head, Ref. Dept., Univ. of MI, Law Lib., 1974–78; Ref. Libn., 1972–74; Sr. Legal Spec., Law Lib., Lib. of Congs., 1969–71, Asst. Chief, Amer.-Brit. Law Div., 1968–69, Legal Spec., 1965–68. **Educ.:** Dartmouth Coll., 1956–60, BA (Phil.); Yale, 1960–63, JD (Law); Univ. of MD, 1971–72, MLS. **Orgs.:** AALL: Contemporary Soc. Problems Spec. Interest Sect. (Ch., 1980–81); Readers' Srvs. Spec. Interest Sect., (1978–); Law Lib. Srv. MI Assn. of Law Libs.: Pres. (1979–80). OH Reg. Assn. of Law Libs. **Honors:** Beta Phi Mu, 1972. **Pubns.:** *A Guide to Legal Research in the University of Michigan Law Library* (1976, 2nd ed. 1978); "'Ordinary Joe' in the Decision-making Process: The Viability of Staff Participation in Law Library Administration," *Law Lib. Jnl.* (Sum. 1980); "Unauthorized Practice of Law and the Legal Reference Librarian," *Law Lib. Jnl.* (Win. 1979); "Of Gregory, Gold and Greeley," *Qtly. Jnl. of the Lib. of Congs.* (O. 1969). **Activities:** 1, 14-Law Lib.; 15, 17, 39; 77, 78, 92 **Addr.:** University of Detroit School of Law, 651 E. Jefferson Ave., Detroit, MI 48226.

Schandorff, Esther May Dech (Ag. 9, 1923, Modoc, IN) Dir. of Lrng. Srvs., Point Loma Coll., 1980–, Acq. Libn., 1978–80, Actg. Head Libn., 1977–78, Acq. Libn., 1975–77; Head Libn., Pasadena Coll., 1968–75. **Educ.:** Pasadena Coll., 1941–44, 1949–51, AB (Eng.); Univ. of South. CA, 1953–54, MS (LS). **Orgs.:** ATLA SAA. Christ. Libn. Assn. West. Theo. LA. CT Socty. of Genealogists. Lehigh Cnty. (PA) Hist. Socty. Holt Cnty. (ND) Hist. Socty. San Diego Geneal. Socty. **Activities:** 1, 2; 15, 17, 45; 57, 69, 90 **Addr.:** 4930 Del Mar, #205, San Diego, CA 92107.

Special Subjects/Services: 50. Adult educ.; 51. Advert./Mktg.; 52. Aerosp.; 53. Agric.; 54. Area std.; 55. Arts/Hum.; 56. Autom.; 57. Bibl./Prtg.; 58. Bio. sci.; 59. Bus./Fin.; 60. Chem.; 61. Copyrt.; 62. Documtn.; 63. Educ.; 64. Engin.; 65. Env.; 66. Eth. grps.; 67. Film; 68. Food/Nutr.; 69. Geneal.; 70. Geo.; 71. Geol.; 72. Handcpd.; 73. Hist.; 74. Int. frdm.; 75. Info. sci.; 76. Insr.; 77. Law; 78. Legis.; 79. Math./Comp. sci.; 80. Med.; 81. Metals; 82. Nat. resrcs.; 83. Newsp.; 84. Nuc. sci.; 85. Oral hist.; 86. Petr./Energy; 87. Pharm.; 88. Phys./Astr./Math.; 89. Readg.; 90. Relig.; 91. Sci./Tech.; 92. Soc. sci.; 93. Telecom.; 94. Transp.; 95. (other).

Scharlock, Nidia Thomas (O. 18, 1930, Buffalo, NY) Head, Info. Srvs., Hlth. Sci. Lib., Univ. NC at Chapel Hill, 1980–; Readers' Srvs. Libn., Edward G. Miner Lib., Univ. of Rochester Sch. of Med. and Dentistry, 1974–80, Serials Libn., 1972–74; Serials Libn., Milne Lib., State Univ. Coll. at Geneseo, 1970–72, Visit. Prof., Sch. of Lib. & Info. Sci., 1973–79. **Educ.:** Univ. of Buffalo, 1947–50, BA (Psy.), 1950–52, MA (Psy.); State Univ. Coll. at Geneseo, 1968–70, MLS; Med. LA, 1973, Cert. Grade II. **Orgs.:** Med. LA: Mid-AtL. Reg. **Honors:** Beta Phi Mu, 1970. **Pubns.:** "A preliminary study to develop a more discriminating F plus ratio," *Jnl. of Clinical Psy.* (1954). **Activities:** 11, 12; 17, 26, 39; 75, 80, 92 **Addr.:** 805 Powell St., Chapel Hill, NC 27514.

Schatzman, Erna E. (S. 19, 1932, Berlin, Germany) Data Srvs. Libn., Univ. of WI, 1975–, Ref. Libn., 1973–75. **Educ.:** Univ. of WI, 1968–72, BA (Grmn., Art Hist.), 1972, MALS (Lib., Info. Sci.). **Orgs.:** ALA. ASIS. WI LA. Beta Ro: Pres. (1978–79). **Honors:** Beta Phi Mu. **Pubns.:** "Data Base Services at the University of Wisconsin-Milwaukee Library," *WI Lib. Bltn.* (My.–Je. 1977). **Activities:** 1; 39; 56 **Addr.:** P.O. Box 604, University of Wisconsin-Milwaukee, Milwaukee, WI 53201.

Schatzman, Louise G. (F. 2, 1924, Auburn, NY) Sr. Syst. Engin., Fluor Engins. and Constructors, 1974–; Ofc. Mgr., Astromatics, Inc., 1961–71; Cvl. Engin., Tidewater Oil Co., 1955–58. **Educ.:** CA State Univ., Fullerton, 1972, BA (Math.), 1973, MSLS. **Orgs.:** ASIS: Los Angeles Chap. (Treas., 1979–80). Natl. Micro. Assn. Toastmstrs. Intl., Club 124: Pres. (1979). **Pubns.:** "Retrieval Systems," *Engineering and Industrial Graphics Handbook* (1980); "A Systems Approach of Coordinating Technologies," *Jnl. of Micro.* (S.-O. 1979). **Activities:** 12; 30, 38; 64, 75, 86 **Addr.:** 3333 Michelson Dr., Irvine, CA 92730.

Schaub, Theresa F. (Ap. 3, 1923, Lake Leelanau, MI) Chld. Libn., Traverse City Pub. Lib., 1963–; Chld. Libn., Ext. Dept., Saginaw Pub. Lib., 1961–63; Chld. Libn., Carnegie Lib. of Pittsburgh, 1951–61. **Educ.:** Aquinas Coll., 1942–50, AB (Hist.); Univ. of MI, 1950–51, AMLS. **Orgs.:** MI LA: Chld. Lib. Srvs. RT (Ch., 1969). ALA: Ref. and Subscrpn. Bks. Review Com. (1971–72). **Activities:** 9; 21, 31 **Addr.:** Traverse City Public Library, 322 6th St., Traverse City, MI 49684.

Schauman, Claudia J. (O. 23, 1947, St. Louis, MO) Branch Libn., Pub. Lib. of Nash and Davidson Cnty., 1980–, Spec. Projs. Coord., 1975–80; Libn., Jr. HS, Charlotte/Mecklenburg Sch. Syst., 1970–74; Libn., Sr. HS, Anderson Cnty. Sch. Syst., 1969–70. **Educ.:** Univ. of TN, 1967–69, BS (Educ.), 1974–75, MLS. **Orgs.:** ALA. SELA. TN LA: Pub. Lib. Sect. (Secy.–Treas., 1979–80). **Activities:** 9, 10; 15, 16, 27; 50, 66, 72 **Addr.:** 8th Ave. N. & Union, Public Library of Nashville and Davidson County, Nashville, TN 37201.

Schear, Thomas W. (Ja. 13, 1925, Elizabeth, NJ) Lib. Dir., Passaic Pub. Lib., 1961–; Coord. of Adult Prog., Elizabeth Pub. Lib., 1951–60. **Educ.:** Seton Hall Univ., 1947–49, BS (Eng.); Columbia Univ., 1949–51, MS (LS), 1953–55, Cert. (Advnc. Libnshp.). **Orgs.:** NJ LA: Pres. (1973–74). ALA. **Activities:** 9; 15, 16, 17; 50, 55, 66 **Addr.:** Passaic Public Library, 195 Gregory Ave., Passaic, NJ 07055.

Schebora, John Charles (Jl. 1, 1945, Chicago, IL) Libn., Broward Cnty. Pub. Lib., 1980–; Libn./Info. Res., U.S. Army Resrch. Inst. of Env. Med., 1977–79; Div. Libn./Info. Ctr., U.S. Army Corps of Engin., Atlanta, 1976–77; Libn., U.S. Army Corps of Engin., Memphis, 1973–76. **Educ.:** FL Atl. Univ., 1970–71, BS (Educ.); FL State Univ., 1972–75, MS (LS). **Orgs.:** Memphis Lib. Com. SLA: Memphis Chap., Nom. Com. (Ch., 1975). ALA. FL LA. **Activities:** 4, 9; 15, 33, 46; 64, 80, 95 **Addr.:** 321 Carolina Ave., Ft. Lauderdale, FL 33312.

Schechter, Maureen S. (Mr. 17, 1949, Norwich, CT) Trng. Prog. Spec., Ofc. of Mgt. Std., ARL, 1980–; Asst. to Dir. for Persnl., Univ. of MD Libs., 1979–80, Asst. Persnl. Libn., 1977–79. **Educ.:** Univ. of MD, 1972–74, BA (Hist.), 1974–76, MS (LS). **Orgs.:** ALA: LAMA/Persnl. Admin. Sect., Econ. Status, Welfare, and Fringe Benefits Com. (1979–83); ACRL, Persnl. Ofcrs. of Lg. Resrch. Libs. Discuss. Grp. MD LA. DC LA. **Activities:** 1; 17, 35; 85 **Addr.:** Office of Management Studies, Association of Research Libraries, 1527 New Hampshire Ave. N.W., Washington DC 20036.

Scheckter, Stella J. (N. 30, 1926, Philadelphia, PA) Dir., Ref. & Loan Div., NH State Lib., 1958–; Sr. Asst., Bus. & Econ. Dept., Enoch Pratt Free Lib., 1956–58, Jr. Asst., Lang. & Lit. Dept., 1954–56; Asst. Branch Libn., Hartford Pub. Lib., 1953–54, Jr. Asst. Ref. Dept., 1952–53. **Educ.:** Temple Univ., 1944–48, AB (Hist.); Drexel Inst. of Tech., 1949–52, MS (LS). **Orgs.:** ALA: Mem. Ch. for NH (1964–69). New Eng. LA: Bibl. Com. (Ch., 1971–72). NH LA: Cncl., PR Com. (1971). NH Assn. for Mental Hlth.: Bd. (1979–). Cmnty. Concert Assn. Concord Cmnty. Players. Concord Msc. Club. **Honors:** New Eng. Thea. Conf., Best Set Dsgn. Awd., 1968. **Activities:** 13; 39 **Addr.:** 27 Church St., Concord, NH 03301.

Scheeder, Donna Wills (N. 8, 1947, Buffalo, NY) Coord. of Congs. Ref. Srvs., Congs. Resrch. Srv., Lib. of Congs., 1979–, Team Leader, 1978–79, Sr. Ref. Spec., 1975–78, Ref. Libn., 1969–75. **Educ.:** Georgetown Univ., 1965–69, BSFS (Intl. Affairs). **Orgs.:** ALA. SLA: Fndn. Com. on Legis. Awareness, DC Chap. Lib. of Congs. Prof. Org. **Activities:** 4; 17, 29, 39; 78 **Addr.:** Congressional Reference Division, Library of Congress, 1st & Independence Ave., S.E., Washington, DC 20540.

Scheele, Barbara (Mr. 24, 1942, New York, NY) Coord., Online Srch. Srv., Brooklyn Coll., 1980–, Pers. and Micro. Libn., 1971–80, Gift Acq. Libn., 1968–71; Ref. Libn., Columbia Univ., 1966–68. **Educ.:** Hunter Coll., 1959–63, BA (Eng.); Simmons Coll., 1965–66, MS (LS); NY Univ., 1974–78, MA (Eng.). **Orgs.:** ALA: Prog., Lcl. Arrange. (1980). LA CUNY: Pres. (1980–81); Secy. (1970–71). NY LA: RTSS, Resrcs. Com. (1979–81). **Activities:** 1; 17, 39; 55, 63, 67 **Addr.:** 54 Orange St., Brooklyn, NY 11201.

Scheer, Jon Frederic (Mr. 23, 1949, Detroit, MI) Branch Head, Jackson (MS) Metro. Lib., 1977–; Asst. to Dir., Un. Cnty. Pub. Lib., 1975–77. **Educ.:** Univ. of MI, 1966–70, AB (Thea.); Wayne State Univ., 1973–74, MSLS; MS Coll., 1978–, MBA in prog. **Orgs.:** ALA: PLA (Dir., 1979–80); Small and Medium-Sized Libs. Sect., Nom. Com. (Ch., 1979–80); Pubcty. (Ch., 1979). MS LA: Legis. Com. (1979–); JMRT (Treas., 1980). MS Gvr.'s Conf. on Libs.: Del. (1979). Un. Cnty. Cmnty. Concert Assn. **Honors:** Wayne State Univ., H. W. Wilson Awd., 1974. **Pubns.:** Reviews. **Activities:** 9; 16, 17, 39 **Addr.:** South Hills Library, 515 W. McDowell Rd., Jackson, MS 39204.

Scheer, Malcolm E. (F. 28, 1933, New York, NY) Lib. Dir., NY Sch. of Interior Dsgn., 1979–; Lib. Dir., New Sch. for Soc. Resrch., 1974–78, Asst. Chief Libn., 1969–74, Sr. Libn., 1963–69, Catlgr., 1961–63. **Educ.:** City Coll. of NY, 1951–54, BA (Econ.); Columbia Univ., 1959–60, MSLS. **Orgs.:** ALA. SLA. NY Lib. Club. **Activities:** 1; 17; 55, 92 **Addr.:** 345 E. 52nd St., New York, NY 10022.

Scheetz, George Henry (Jl. 27, 1952, Columbus, OH) Head, Lakeview Branch, Peoria Pub. Lib., 1979–, Head, Bus., Sci. & Tech. Dept., 1978–79; Ref. Libn., Biblgphr., Bradley Univ., 1977–78; Resrch. Asst., Dept. of Eng., Univ. of IL, 1976–77. **Educ.:** Univ. of IL, 1970–74, BA, with distinction (Eng.), 1975–76, MS (LS). **Orgs.:** ALA. IL LA. IL Valley Lib. Syst.: Adv. Cncl. Task Frc. on Per. (1977–79); Adv. Cncl. Task Frc. on Phonorecords (1978). Natl. Socty., Sons of the Amer. Rev. Peoria Advert. & Selling Club. Alpha Phi Omega Natl. Srv. Fraternity. Amer. Philatelic Socty. **Honors:** Sigma Tau Delta; Omicron Delta Kappa. **Pubns.:** "Peoria, USA," *Papers of the North Central Names Institute* (1980); "Tennis Philately," *Jnl. of Sports Philately* (Jl. Ag. N.D. 1979); "Onomasticon," *Word Ways, the Jnl. of Recreational Ling.* (Ag. 1977, F. 1979); "A Collacon on 'Collacon,'" *Word Ways* (N. 1976); bk. reviews, *Lib. Jnl.* (1979–). **Activities:** 1, 9; 17, 39, 46; 67, 91, 95 **Addr.:** 710A W. Moss Ave., #3, Peoria, IL 61606.

Scheffler, Diana (Je. 6, 1943, Newcastle-on-Tyne, Eng.) Head of Tech. Srvs., San Diego Cnty. Lib., 1979–, Head of Cat. Sect., 1977–79, Ref. Libn., 1974–77. **Educ.:** Univ. of MB, 1960–64, BA (Hist.); Simmons Coll., 1969–70 MLS; 1978–83, CA Cnty. Libns. Cert. **Orgs.:** ALA. ASIS: Tech. Srvs. Chap. CA LA: Cnclr. (1981–83); Palomar Chap. (Pres., 1977). Natl. Org. for Women. **Pubns.:** "Subject Headings for Information and Referral," *CA Libn.* (Jl. 1979). **Activities:** 9; 20, 22, 46; 56 **Addr.:** San Diego County Library, 5555 Overland Ave., Bldg. 15, San Diego, CA 92014.

Scheffler, Frederic L. (Ja. 4, 1936, Richmond, IN) Exec. Ofcr., Dayton Tech. Transls., 1980–; Tech. Ed., Libn., SofTech, Inc., 1979–; Proj. Supvsr., Info. Systs. Sect., Univ. of Dayton, 1961–79. **Educ.:** Purdue Univ., 1953–57, BS (Chem. Engin.); Univ. of MI, 1957–59, MS (Engin.); 1964–71, various crs. in info. sci. **Orgs.:** ASIS: Pubn. (Ch., 1975–80); Ch. (1972–73); Treas. (1975–76). **Honors:** ASIS, Outstan. Mem., 1977; ASIS, Spec. Recog., Nsltr. Ed., 1980. **Pubns.:** Jt. auth., "Technical Information Retrieval—What Do We Really Want?" *Procs. of the ASIS 5th Mid-Yr. Mtg.* (1976); jt. auth., "Significance of Titles Abstracts and Other Portions of Technical Documents for Information Retrieval," *IEEE Transactions on Prof. Comm.* (Mr. 1974). **Activities:** 9, 14-Tech. transl. srvs.; 17, 46, 49-Transls.; 62, 91, 95-Tech. transls. **Addr.:** Dayton Technical Translators, 677 Meadowview Dr., Dayton, OH 45459.

Scheide, Benton F. (F. 3, 1918, Kennard, NE) Dir. of Libs., CA State Coll., 1968–; Supvsr., Pub. Srvs., Lib., San Diego State Coll., 1962–68; Dir. of Libs., Head LS Div., N.E. MO State Tchrs. Coll., 1956–62; Head, Circ. Dept., AL Polytech. Inst., Lib., 1952–56; Asst. Circ. Libn., OR State Coll. Lib., 1949–51. **Educ.:** CO A and M Coll., CO Coll., 1937–40; Univ. of Denver, 1947–48, BA (Econ.), 1948–49, MA (LS); Case West. Rsv. Univ., 1973, PhD (LS). **Orgs.:** CA LA. SLA. Amer. Socty. for Pub. Admin.: Bakersfield Chap. (Secy., 1981–). **Activities:** 1; 17 **Addr.:** Library, California State College, 9001 Stockdale Hwy., Bakersfield, CA 93309.

Schein, Lorraine Sandra (Ja. 29, 1933, Brooklyn, NY) Head Libn., Polytech. Inst. of NY, Long Island Ctr., 1970–; Libn., Grumman Aerosp., 1966–67; Patent Liaison/Libn., Leesona-Moos Labs., 1960–66; Lit. Chem., Sci. Dsgn. Co., 1956–60. **Educ.:** Adelphi Univ., 1950–54, BA (Chem.); NY Univ., 1954–58, MS (Chem.); Brooklyn Coll., 1957–60 (Math.); Long Island Univ., 1962–67, MS (LS). **Orgs.:** Nassau Cnty. LA. ASIS. SLA. Beta Phi Mu: Beta Mu Chap. (Treas., 1979–81). Amer. Chem. Socty. Assn. for Comp. Mach. NY Acad. of Sci. Hadassah. **Honors:** Gamma Sigma Epsilon, 1953; Delta Phi Alpha, 1953; Delta Tau Alpha, 1953. **Activities:** 1, 12; 16, 17, 39; 52, 60, 64 **Addr.:** 17 Admiral Ln., Hicksville, NY 11801.

Schell, Dorothy B. (Mrs. Russell S.) (Ap. 22, 1924, Brooklyn, NY) Branch Libn., Schenectady Cnty. Pub. Lib., 1978; Chld. Libn., 1977–78; Consult., Natl. Cmrcl. Bank, 1962–63; Instr., SUNY, Albany, Sch. LS, 1958–60; Consult., Srs. of St. Colman's Home, 1958–59; Sch. Libn., Menands Pub. Sch., 1957–65; Sch. Libn., N. Colonie Ctrl. Sch., 1950–51; Instr., Eng., Green Mt. Coll., 1947–50; various positions in tchg. **Educ.:** SUNY, Albany, 1943–47, BA (Eng.), 1947, MSLS; Un. Coll., 1964–65, (Amer. Std.); NY State, Perm. Sec. Tchg. Licn., Sch. Libn. Cert. **Orgs.:** NY LA. East. Mohawk LA. **Activities:** 9, 11; 15, 16, 17; 50, 95-Sr. citizens prog. **Addr.:** 1913 Union St., Schenectady, NY 12309.

Schell, Irene I. (Ag. 10, 1918, Montreal, PQ) Lib. Dir., Gloucester City Lib., 1972–, Ref. Libn., Catlgr., 1970–72. **Educ.:** Rutgers Univ., Camden, 1961–69, BA (Soc. Sci.); Drexel Univ., 1969–71, MS (LS); 1972, Cert. Med. Libn., Grade 1; 1971, NJ Cert. Prof. Libn.; various crs., wkshps. **Orgs.:** ALA. NJ LA: PR Com. (1973–74); Admin. Sect., Nom. Com. (1978). Libs. Unlimited: VP (1972–73). Mid. Atl. Reg. Lib. Fed. Camden-Gloucester Area Lib. Srv. Cncl.: AV Ch. (1974); Strg. Com. (Ch., 1977-78). Various other orgs. Rutgers Univ. Alum. Assn. AAUW. Leag. of Women Voters. Evergreen Ave. Sch. Parent-Tchr. Assn. **Honors:** Lib. PR Cncl., Hon. Mention, 1972. **Pubns.:** Contrib., *Library Programs Worth Knowing About* (1977); "Library 'Storytellers' Bring 30 Handicapped Students Joy," *NJ Interact* (My. Je. 1976); "Storytellers Visit Homebound Children," *Sch. Lib. Jnl.* (N. 1976). **Activities:** 9; 15, 17, 25; 55, 92 **Addr.:** Gloucester City Library, Railroad Ave. between Hudson & Monmouth Sts., Gloucester City, NJ 08030.

Schell, Joan Bruning (Je. 9, 1932, New York, NY) Book Sel. Coord., Pub. Lib. of Cincinnati & Hamilton Cnty., 1979–, Bus. Ref. Libn., 1973–79; Sci./Tech. Ref. Libn., Dallas Pub. Lib., 1971–73. **Educ.:** Wittenberg Univ., 1950–54, AB (Bus., Econ.); Univ. of Pittsburgh, 1966–68, MLS. **Orgs.:** SLA: Cincinnati Chap. (Treas., 1977); Prog. Com. (1978); Bylaws Com. (1979); Educ. Com. (1980). ALA. ASIS. **Honors** Beta Phi Mu, 1968. **Activities:** 9; 15, 16, 39; 51, 59 **Addr.:** Book Selection Room, Public Library of Cincinnati & Hamilton County, 800 Vine St., Cincinnati, OH 45202.

Schell, Rosalie Faye (Je. 13, 1929, Martinsville, MO) Dir. of Reader Srvs., Ctrl. MO State Univ., 1973–, Soc. Sci. Libn., 1968–73; Libn., SW Harrison HS, 1963–68; Libn., N. Harrison HS, 1960–63. **Educ.:** NW MO State Univ., 1955–60, BS (Educ.); KS State Tchrs. Coll., 1965–68, MLS; Ctrl. MO State Univ., 1972–75, EdS (Lrng. Resrcs.); Cert. Instr. Tech.; Cert. Lrng. Resrc. Dir. **Orgs.:** MO LA. ALA. Kansas City Metro. Lib. Netwk.: Policy Dev. Com. (1980). Daughters of Amer. Revolution. **Activities:** 1; 17, 31, 39; 59, 77, 92 **Addr.:** 301 Olive, Windsor, MO 65360.

Schellhorn, Mary Ann (Decatur, IL) Head of Cat., Gvrs. State Univ., 1973–; Libn., Thornton Cmnty. Coll., 1969–72; Serials Libn., Univ. of IA, 1968–69. **Educ.:** Univ. of ND, 1964–66, BA (Hist.); Univ. of IA, 1967–68, MA (LS); Gvrs. State Univ., 1971–73, MA (Soc. Sci.). **Orgs.:** ALA. **Activities:** 1; 15, 17, 20; 55, 92, 93 **Addr.:** 773 Aberdeen Dr., Crete, IL 60417.

Schenck, William Ziegler (My. 2, 1945) Head, Acq., Dept., Univ. of NC, 1976–; Acq. Libn., Yale Univ., 1972–76. **Educ.:** Johns Hopkins Univ., 1963–67, AB; Univ. of NC, 1967–72, MA, MLS. **Orgs.:** ALA: Various coms. **Honors:** Beta Phi Mu. **Activities:** 1; 15, 23, 46 **Addr.:** Acquisitions Dept., Wilson Library, Univ. of North Carolina, Chapel Hill, NC 27514.

Schenk, Margaret T. (Ja. 23, 1919, Albany, NY) Assoc. Libn., Col. Dev., Bibl. Instr., SUNY, Buffalo, 1969–; Ref. Libn., Cornell Aeronautical Lab., 1960–69; Head Cat. Sect., Bell Aerosysts. Co., 1954–60; Resrch. Libn., Am. Optical Co., 1945–48. **Educ.:** Univ. of Buffalo, 1936–40, BA (Hist.), 1940–41, BLS. **Orgs.:** SLA: Upstate NY Chap.; (Pres., 1975–76), Env. Info. Div. (Ch., 1978–79). West. NY Lib. Resrcs. Cncl.: Cont. Ed. Com. **Pubns.:** Jt. complr., *Selected Properties of Silicon: An Annotated Bibliography* (1975); "Academic Science/Engineering Library's Experience with the New York (State) Loan Network," *Spec. Libs.* (My. Je. 1976). **Activities:** 1; 15, 31, 39; 64 **Addr.:** State University of New York at Buffalo, Science and Engineering Library, Capen Hall, Amherst Campus, Buffalo, NY 14260.

Schepis, Frank J. (Ag. 27, 1943, Weatherford, TX) Dir., Libs., Natrona Cnty. Pub. Lib., 1981–; Asst. Dir., Springfield-Greene Cnty. Lib., 1978–; Asst. Dir., Hurst Pub. Lib., 1977–78; Branch Mgr., Audelia Rd. Branch, Dallas Pub. Lib., 1972–76, First Asst., 1971–72, First Asst., Hampton-IL Branch, 1971. **Educ.:** Univ. of Dallas, 1963–65, BA (Hist.); N. TX State Univ., 1969–70, MLS. **Orgs.:** ALA: LAMA. MO LA: Lib. Dev. Com.

PROFESSIONAL ACTIVITIES: Institutions: 1. Acad. lib.; 2. Arch.; 3. Assn.; 4. Fed./Gvt. lib.; 5. Inst. lib.; 6. Mfr./Suppl.; 7. Milit. lib.; 8. Musm.; 9. Pub. lib.; 10. Sch. lib.; 11. Sch. of lib. sci.; 12. Spec. lib.; 13. State lib.; 14. (other). **Functions/Activities:** 15. Acq./Col. dev.; 16. Adult srvs.; 17. Admin.; 18. Apprais.; 19. Archit./Bldgs.; 20. Cat./Class.; 21. Chld. srvs.; 22. Circ.; 23. Cons./Pres.; 24. Consult.; 25. Cont. ed.; 26. Educ. lib. sci.; 27. Ext. srvs.; 28. Fund/Grants; 29. Gvt. pubs.; 30. Indx./Abs.; 31. Instr. lib. use; 32. Media srvs.; 33. Micro.; 34. Netwks./Coop.; 35. Persnl.; 36. PR; 37. Publshg.; 38. Recs. mgt.; 39. Ref. srvs.; 40. Repro.; 41. Resrch.; 42. Review.; 43. Secur.; 44. Serials; 45. Spec. col.; 46. Tech. srvs.; 47. Trustees/Bds.; 48. YA srvs.; 49. (other).

Who's Who in Library and Information Services

(1978–79); Legis. Com. (1979–80); Anl. Conf., Hosplty. Com. (Ch., 1979). TX LA: Conf. Treas. (1978). WY LA: Legis. Com. Various other orgs. Amer. Socty. for Pub. Admin. **Activities:** 9; 17, 35 **Addr.:** Natrona County Public Library, 307 E. 2nd St., Casper, WY 82601–2598.

Scherma, George W. (O. 31, 1919, Cleveland, OH) Dir., Rocky River Pub. Lib., 1967–; HD Libn., Univ. Hts. Branch, Cleveland Hts.-Univ. Hts. Pub. Lib., 1964–67; HD Libn., Nottingham Branch, Cleveland Pub. Lib., 1960–64. **Educ.:** Case-West. Rsv. Univ., 1938–42, BA (Fr.), 1946–47, BS (LS), 1966–67, MS (LS). **Orgs.:** OH LA. ALA. Rocky River Hist. Socty. Cowan Pottery Musm. of Rocky River. **Activities:** 9; 15, 17, 35; 55, 59 **Addr.:** Rocky River Public Library, 1600 Hampton Rd., Rocky River, OH 44116.

Schertz, Morris (My. 3, 1929, New York, NY) Dir. of Lib., Univ. of Denver, 1969–; Assoc. Dir. of Tech. Srvs., Univ. of MA, 1964–69; Libn., State Univ. Coll. at Buffalo, 1962–64; Rare Bk. Libn., Colby Coll., 1958–62. **Educ.:** NY Univ., 1948–52, BA (Hist.); Pratt Inst., 1955–56, MLS. **Orgs.:** ALA. CO LA. Mt. Plains LA. **Pubns.:** "A Periodical Use Study," *Lib. Jnl. Spec. Rpt. #11* (N. 11, 1979). **Activities:** 1; 15, 17 **Addr.:** Penrose Library, 2150 E. Evans, Denver, CO 80208.

Scheuerman, Luanne J. (Mr. 20, 1929, Otis, KS) Head Libn., West HS, Wichita, KS, 1965–; Asst. Libn., Catalina HS, Tucson, AZ, 1959–65; Tchr., Bus. Educ. & Eng., Safford HS, 1956–59; Tchr., Bushton HS, 1954–56. **Educ.:** Ft. Hays KS State Coll., 1947–51, BA (Eng.); Univ. of AZ, 1957–59, MEd (LS); Emporia State Univ., 1974–79, MLS. **Orgs.:** Wichita Assn. of Sch. Libns.: Ch. (1978–79); Lcl. Arrange. Com. (Spr. Conv., 1979). KS Assn. of Sch. Libns. ALA: AASL, Com. on Accred. (1979). AAUW: Bd. (1978–79). **Honors:** Delta Kappa Gamma. **Pubns.:** Jt. auth., "Over the Editor's Desk," *Childhood Educ.* (F. 1973); poetry. **Activities:** 10; 15, 17, 48; 55, 63, 92 **Addr.:** 951 S. Bleckley Ave., Apt. 109, Wichita, KS 67218.

Schexnaydre, Linda C. (Ja. 24, 1947, Baton Rouge, LA) Fac. Mem., Sch. of LS, Emporia State Univ., 1979–; Freelnc. Ed. and Indxr., 1978–; Ed., LA State Univ. Press, 1978–79; Ed., Lrng. Concepts, 1976–77; Mgr., Cont. Educ. Dept., TX State Lib., 1974–76; Head, Soc. Work Lib., Univ. of TX, 1969–72. **Educ.:** LA State Univ., 1964–67, BA (Eng.); Univ. of TX, Austin, 1970–72, MLS, 1972–73, 6th Yr. Cert. (LS). **Orgs.:** ALA: ASCLA/Lib. Srv. Prisoners Sect., Co-Ch., Prog. Com. (1980). Mt. Plains LA: Prof. Dev. Grants Com. (1980). KS LA: *KS LA Nsltr.* Ed. (1980–). KS Cont. Educ. Task Frc.: Ch. (1980–). **Pubns.:** *Workshops for Jail Library Service: A Planning Manual* (1981); *Planning Audiovisual Services in Public Libraries* (1975); *Adult Basic Education: A Guide to Library Materials* (1975); *Establishing Library Learning Centers for Adult Basic Education* (1974); "A Model for Public Library Service in the Mexican American Community," *Library Services to Mexican Americans* ERIC (1978); various other pubns. **Activities:** 9, 11; 25, 26, 30; 50 **Addr.:** School of Library Science, Emporia State University, Emporia, KS 66801.

Schey, Samuel (Je. 22, 1909, Passaic, NJ) Trustee, Passaic, NJ Lib. Bd., 1977–; Prin., Dir., Adult Educ., Wilson Jr. HS, Sch. Prin., Passaic Pub. Sch., 1944–74. **Educ.:** Panzier Coll., Montclair State Coll., Upsala Coll., 1928–32; Rutgers Univ. 1946–50, MA (Educ.). **Orgs.:** NJ Lib. Trustee Assn. NJ LA. ALA. **Honors:** Passaic Cham. of Cmrce., Disting. Srv. Awd., 1974; NJ Congs. of Parents and Tchrs., Life Mem. Awd., 1969. **Activities:** 47; 50, 63 **Addr.:** 17 Tennyson Pl., Passaic, NJ 07055.

Schick, Frank L. (F. 4, 1918, Vienna, Austria) Chief, Lrng. Resrcs. Branch/DMES, Dept. of Educ., Natl. Ctr. for Educ. Stats., 1971–; Dir., Sch. of LS, Univ. of WI, Milwaukee, 1966–71; Asst. Dir., Lib. Srvs. Branch, U.S. Ofc. of Educ., 1958–66; Asst. Libn., Biblgphr., Wayne State Univ. Libs., 1955–58; Asst. to Dean, Sch. of Lib. Srv., Columbia Univ., 1954–55. **Educ.:** Wayne State Univ., 1940–46, BA (Gvt.); Univ. of Chicago, 1946–47, BLS, 1947–48, MA (Pol. Sci.); Univ. of MI, 1951–55, MLS, 1955–57, PHD (LS). **Orgs.:** ALA: Cncl. (1968–72, 1976–80); Stat. Coord. Com. (Ch., 1969–71). SLA: Prof. Stans. Com. (Ch., 1977–). Fed. Lib. Com. Ch., Stats. Com. (1975–78). IFLA: Com. on Stats., Secy. (1972–75); Ch. (1976–80). Amer. Natl. Stan. Inst. Sect. Com. Z39, Lib. Stats. Subcom. (Ch., 1966–68); Per. Stats. Com. (1977–78). Intl. Org. for Standardization Tech. Com. 46: Stat. Com. (Ch., 1964–71). UNESCO Intl. Conf. on Lib. Stats.: Pres. (1970). **Pubns.:** *North American Library Education Directory* (1969–71); *Directory of Health Science Libraries* (1969); *Survey of Special Libraries Serving the Federal Government* (1968); "Problems of Research in Cooperative and International Library Science," *Cooperative and International Library Science* (1977); "The Standardization of International Library Statistics: 1853–1977," *ALA Yrbk.* (1978); various other articles. **Activities:** 4; 17, 18; 95-Stats. **Addr.:** 2809 Blazer Ct., Silver Spring, MD 20906.

Schick, Renee (My. 30, 1919, Vienna, Austria) VP, Cap. Systs. Grp., 1980–; Proj. Dir., Arthritis Info. Clearinghse., 1978–; Sr. Info. Spec., Cap. Systs. Grp., 1973–80; Hlth. Info. Spec., Technomics, Inc., 1971–72; Proj. Coord., Hlth. Sci. Lib. Srvy., Amer. Med. Assn., 1968–70. **Educ.:** Wayne State Univ., 1945–48, Med. Tech.; Univ. WI, 1969–71, BA (Soclgy.); Univ. MD (Info. Sci.). **Orgs.:** ASIS. Med. LA. Amer. Pub. Hlth. Assn. **Pubns.:** Ed., *Directory of Online Information Services* (1979); "On Demand Information Services," *Bowker Anl. Lib. Info. Srv.* (1980). **Activities:** 12; 17, 24, 30; 56, 75, 80 **Addr.:** Capital Systems Group, 11301 Rockville Pike, Rockville, MD 20795.

Schickler, Clairann G. (Je. 4, 1942, Seattle, WA) Asst. Head, Serials Div., Univ. of WA, 1976–, Actg. Head, Serials Div., 1977–78, Serials Catlgr., 1967–76; Catlgr., Univ. of CA, Irvine, 1965–67. **Educ.:** Univ. of WA, 1960–64, BA (Pol. Sci.), 1964–65, MLibr. **Orgs.:** ALA: RTSD, Subj. Anal. Com. (1973–74). **Activities:** 1; 20, 44 **Addr.:** Serials Division, Suzzallo Library FM-25, University of Washington, Seattle, WA 98195.

Schiffenbauer, Zelda Rosenfeld (Ap. 4, 1948, New York, NY) Exec. Dir., IL Reg. Lib. Cncl., 1979–81; Proj. Ofcr., 1977–78; Dir., Montgomery-Floyd Reg. Lib., VA, 1976–77, Asst. Dir., 1975–76; Head Libn., Salem (VA) Pub. Lib., 1973–75; Adults Libn., Boston Pub. Lib., 1972–73. **Educ.:** Brooklyn Coll., 1964–68, BA (Span., Econ.); Simmons Coll., 1971–72, MS (LS). **Orgs.:** ALA: ASCLA/Multitype Lib. Coop. Sect., Plng. Com. (1979–80); Cont. Ed. Com. (1979–80); Assn. of State Lib. Agencies, Interlib. Coop. Com. (1978–79). SLA. IL LA. CLENE. **Pubns.:** Jt. cmplr., *Directory of Human Resources* (1979). **Activities:** 9, 13; 17, 25, 34 **Addr.:** 2029 N. Racine, Chicago, IL 60614.

Schiller, Anita R. (New York, NY) Ref. Libn., Biblgphr., Univ. of CA, San Diego, 1970–; Ralph R. Shaw Visit. Schol., Rutgers Univ., Grad. Sch. of LS, 1978, Visit. Prof., 1974; various positions in resrch., Univ. of IL, Lib. Resrch. Ctr., 1963–70. **Educ.:** NY Univ., 1949, BA (Econ.); Pratt Inst., 1959, MLS. **Orgs.:** ALA: Cncl. (1972–76); LITA; ACRL; LRRT (Secy–Treas., 1978). ASIS. **Honors:** Cncl. on Lib. Resrcs., Flwshp., 1976. **Pubns.:** *Characteristics of Professional Personnel in College & University Libraries* (1969); "The Potential of Online Systems: The Librarians Role," *The On-line Revolution in Libraries* (1978); "Women in Librarianship," *Advncs. in Libnshp.* (1974); "The Disadvantaged Majority," *Amer. Libs.* (Ap. 1970); ed., "Aware," *Amer. Libs.* (1971–72); various ed. bds. **Activities:** 1; 15, 39, 41; 56, 92 **Addr.:** C-075R University of California San Diego, LaJolla, CA 92093.

Schimansky, Donya Dobrila (Kavadar, Yugoslavia) Musm. Libn., Metro. Musm. of Art Lib., 1973–; Asst. to the Ch., The Cloisters, NY, 1969–73; Resp. for Cult. Affairs, Frgn. Consulate in W. Germany, 1953–67. **Educ.:** Univ. at Belgrade (Yugoslavia), BA (Art Hist.), MA (Art Hist.); CUNY, MLS; Univ. at Hamburg (West Germany), PhD in progress (Art Hist.). **Orgs.:** ARLIS/NA: NY Chap., Com. Cont. Educ. (Ch., 1980); NY City Chap., Prog. Ch. (1979). SLA: Musm. Art Hist. Div., NY Chap., (Secy.–Treas., 1978). Intl. Ctr. Medvl. Art: Secy. (1969–74); Adv. Bd. (1975–). Yugoslav Amer. Artist Assn.: Bd. Dirs. (1979–). **Pubns.:** Ed., *Metropolitan Museum of Art Subject Headings and the Art Thesaurus* (forthcoming); "The Metropolitan Museum of Art Library Classification System," *ARLIS/NA Nsltr.* (1976); "Museum Art Libraries Collection Development Policy in the United States," *Art Libs. Jnl.* (Win. 1981); various articles on art hist. **Addr.:** Metropolitan Museum of Art, The Library, 82nd and 5th Ave., New York, NY 10028.

Schimmelbusch, Johannes Severich (Mr. 19, 1935, Vienna, Austria) Tech. Info. and Engin. Subjs. Spec., 1981–, Chief, Lib. Branch, Bonneville Power Admin., 1969–80, Actg. Libn., 1968–69, Asst. Libn., 1966–67; Engin. Lib., Puget Snd. Nvl. Shipyard, 1966–67; Libn., McNeil Island Fed. Penitentiary, 1965–66. **Educ.:** Univ. WA, 1959–64, BA (Grmn. Lit.), 1964–65, MA (LS). **Orgs.:** SLA. ASIS. **Honors:** Delta Phi Alpha, 1964; Phi Delta Kappa, 1964. **Activities:** 4; 39; 56, 91 **Addr.:** Bonneville Power Administration, 1002 N.E. Holladay St., P.O. Box 3621, Portland, OR 97208.

Schindel, Morton (Ja. 9, 1918, Newark, NJ) Pres., Weston Woods Studios, Inc., 1953–; Attaché, U.S. Embassy, Ankara, Turkey, Dept. of State, 1951–53. **Educ.:** Univ. of PA, 1935–39, BS (Econ.); Columbia Univ., 1947–49, MA (Curric.). **Orgs.:** ALA. Natl. Assn. for the Perpet. and Prsrvn. of Storytel. **Honors:** Cath. LA, Regina Medal, 1979. **Pubns.:** *Storytelling in the Audiovisual Media* (1981); *Children's Literature on Film From the Audiovisual Era to the Age of Telecommunications* (1981); various motion pics., filmstps., recs. based on outstan. chld. bks. (1956–81). **Activities:** 21, 32, 37; 63, 67, 93 **Addr.:** Weston Woods, Weston, CT 06883.

Schipma, Peter B. (O. 24, 1941, Chicago, IL) Sci. Adv. & Mgr., IL Inst. of Tech. Resrch. Inst., 1972–, Resrch. Sci., 1970–72, Assoc. Sci., 1968–70, Asst. Sci., 1967–68. **Educ.:** IL Inst. of Tech., 1959–65, BS (Phys.), 1965–67, MS (Sci. Info.). **Orgs.:** ASIS: Chicago Chap. (Ch., 1977). Assn. of Sci. Info. Diss. Ctrs.: Stdg. Com. (1970–81); Secy./Treas. (1976). AAAS. **Pubns.:** Jt. auth., "Design and Operation of a Computer Search Center for Chemical Information," *Jnl. of Chem. Documtn.* (1969); jt. auth., "Comparison of Document Data Bases," *Jnl. of the Amer. Socty. for Info. Sci.* (S., O., 1971); "Computer Search Center Statistics on Users and Data Bases," *Jnl. of Chem. Documtn.* (F. 1974); "Generation and Uses of Machine-Readable Data Bases," *Anl. Review of Info. Sci. and Tech.* (1972); various other articles, sps. **Activities:** 14-Resrch. Ctr.; 24, 28, 41 **Addr.:** Info. Sci. 11TR1, 10 W 35, Chicago, IL 60616.

Schlachter, Gail Ann (Ap. 7, 1943, Detroit, MI) Dir., Amer. Bibl. Ctr., 1981–; Asst. Univ. Libn., Pub. Srvs., Univ. of CA, Davis, 1976–81; Head, Soc. Sci. Dept. Lib., CA State Univ., Long Beach, 1974–76; Asst. Prof., Lib. Sch., Univ. of South. CA, 1971–74; Head, Soc. Sci. Grad. Ref. Ctr., Univ. of WI, 1967–68. **Educ.:** Univ. of CA, Berkeley, 1962–64, BA (Hist., Soc. Sci.); Univ. of WI, 1964–66, MA (Hist., Educ.), 1966–67, MA (LS); Univ. of MN, 1968–71, PhD (LS); Univ. of South. CA, 1975–79, MPA (Pub. Admin.), **Orgs.:** ALA. AALS. SLA. NLA. Various other orgs. **Honors:** *Choice,* Outstan. Ref. Bk. Awd., 1978. **Pubns.:** *Directory of Financial Aids for Women* (1978); *Minorities and Women: A Guide to Reference Literature in the Social Sciences* (1977); *Directory of Internships* (1975); *Library Science Dissertations, 1925–1972* (1974); bk. review ed., *RQ* (1980–); various articles. **Activities:** 1; 17, 39 **Addr.:** American Bibliographical Center, ABC-Clio, 2040 A.P.S., Santa Barbara, CA 93103.

Schlaerth, Sally Gallagher (My. 23, 1928, Erie, PA) Head Libn., *Buffalo Evening News,* 1973, Sch. Libn., Grand Island Sch., 1968–73. **Educ.:** D'Youville Coll., 1946–50, BA, cum laude (Eng.); Univ. Buffalo, 1965–68, MLS. **Orgs.:** SLA: Newsp. Div. Advert. Women of Buffalo. Various msc. grps. **Honors:** Kappa Gamma Pi. **Pubns.:** Reviews; various articles, *Buffalo Evening News.* **Activities:** 12, 14-Newsp.; 17, 32, 35; 83 **Addr.:** Buffalo Evening News Library, One News Plz., Buffalo, NY 14240.

Schlaf, Suzanne S. (Jl. 10, 1935, Chicago, IL) Head Ref. Adult Srvs., Poplar Creek Pub. Lib. Dist., 1979; Head Libn., Bloomingdale Pub. Lib., 1974–78; YA Libn., Long Beach Pub. Lib., 1972–73; HS Libn., Fullerton HS, 1971–72. **Educ.:** CA State Univ., Long Beach, 1962–69, BA (Eng.); Univ. South. CA, 1969–71, MLS. **Orgs.:** ALA. IL LA. **Activities:** 9; 15, 16, 17; 56 **Addr.:** 5 N. 425 Eagle Terr., Itasca, IL 60143.

Schleifer, Harold B. (O. 22, 1942) Asst. Dir., Libs. for Tech. Srvs., SUNY, Stony Brook, 1976–; Chief, Acq. Div., Assoc. Prof., Herbert H. Lehman Coll. Lib., CUNY, 1968–76; Head, Acq. Dept., NY Univ. Libs., 1967–68; Lectr., Pol. Sci. Dept., Coll. Liberal Arts and Sci., Brooklyn Coll., CUNY, 1966–67; Actg. Head, Bibl. Dept., NY Univ. Libs., 1966–67; Soc. Sci., Educ., Gvt. Docum. Ref. Libn. and Instr., Brooklyn Coll. Lib., CUNY, 1965–66. **Educ.:** City Coll., CUNY, 1959–63, BA (Pol. Sci.); Columbia Univ., 1963–65, MS (LS); CUNY, 1965–72, PhD (Pol. Sci.); various crs. **Orgs.:** ALA: ACRL; LAMA; LITA; RASD; RTSD; Com. on Accred. (1980–). ASIS. CA LA. Can. LA. various other orgs., confs. **Honors:** Phi Beta Kappa; Beta Phi Mu. **Pubns.:** Jt. auth., *Puerto Rican Authors: A Biobibliographic Handbook* (1974); jt. auth., "CUNY Libraries: A Proposal for Self-Study," *LACUNY Jnl.* (Spr. 1972); jt. auth., "An Annual Library Research Award for CUNY Undergraduates: A Proposal," *LACUNY Jnl.* (Fall 1975); jt. auth., "'Books in Print' on Microfiche: A Pilot Test," *Micro. Review* (Ja. 1976); jt. auth., "Research Libraries in Transition: What Faculty Members Should Know about Changing Patterns of Library Service," *AAUP Bltn.* (My. 1978); various reviews. **Addr.:** 33–24 77th St., Jackson Heights, NY 11372.

Schlesinger, Deborah Lee (S. 13, 1937, Cambridge, MA) Dir., S. Park Twp. Lib., 1977–; Head Libn., Carnegie Free Lib. of Swissvale, 1973–77; Ref. Libn., Bentley Coll., 1964–65. **Educ.:** Univ. of MA, 1955–60, BA (Hist.), Simmons Coll., 1962–74, MSLS. **Orgs.:** ALA: PLA: LITA; LAMA; Lib. Media RT, Exec. Bd. PA LA: Legis. Com.; SW Chap. Site, Ch. S. Hills LA.: Admin. LSCA Video Grant (1979); Trustee Strg. Com. PA Dist. Adv. Cncl. **Activities:** 9; 17, 36, 49-Vid.; 91, 93, 95-Vid. **Addr.:** South Park Township Library, 2575 Brownsville Rd., Library, PA 15129.

Schlessinger, Bernard S. (Mr. 19, 1930, Toronto, ON) Dean, Grad. Lib. Sch., Univ. of RI, 1977–; Prof., Coll. of Libnshp., Univ. of SC, 1975–77; Prof., Assoc. Dir., Div. of LS, South. CT State Coll., 1968–75; Sr. Info. Assoc., Olin Corp., 1966–68; Head, Subj. Indexing, Chem. Abs., 1958–66. **Educ.:** Roosevelt Univ., 1946–50, BS (Chem.); Miami Univ., 1950–52, MS (Chem.); Univ. of WI, 1952–55, PhD (Chem.); Univ. of RI, 1975, MLS. **Orgs.:** ALA: Com. Accred. (1979–). SLA. RI LA. AALS. **Honors:** Beta Phi Mu, 1975; Sigma XI, 1955; Univ. of RI Grad. Lib. Sch., Oustan. Alumn., 1979. **Pubns.:** Jt. auth., "Papers Presented at a Workshop on the Integrated Core Curriculum," *Jnl. of Educ. for Libnshp.* (Fall 1978); jt. auth., "Continuing Education-General Considerations with Application to School Librarians," *Excellence in School Media Programs* (1979); jt. auth., "English Language Articles in German Journals," *Sci. and Tech. Libs.* (Win. 1980); "Teaching of Scientific Literature," *Jnl. Chem. Educ.* (Fall 1980); "Report of Planning Conference for Rhode Island Libraries in The Eighties," *RI LA Bltn.* (Mr. 1981); various other bks., articles. **Activities:** 11, 12; 17, 26, 30; 56, 75, 91 **Addr.:** Graduate Library School, University of Rhode Island, Kingston, RI 02881.

Schlichting, Catherine Fletcher Nicholson (N. 18, 1923, Huntsville, AL) Assoc. Prof., Ref., ILL, Bibl. Instr.,

Special Subjects/Services: 50. Adult educ.; 51. Advert./Mktg.; 52. Aerosp.; 53. Agric.; 54. Area std.; 55. Arts/Hum.; 56. Autom.; 57. Bibl./Prtg.; 58. Bio. sci.; 59. Bus./Fin.; 60. Chem.; 61. Copyrt.; 62. Documtn.; 63. Educ.; 64. Engin.; 65. Env.; 66. Eth. grps.; 67. Film; 68. Food/Nutr.; 69. Geneal.; 70. Geo.; 71. Geol.; 72. Handcpd.; 73. Hist.; 74. Int. frdm.; 75. Info. sci.; 76. Insr.; 77. Law; 78. Legis.; 79. Math./Comp. sci.; 80. Med.; 81. Metals; 82. Nat. resrcs.; 83. Newsp.; 84. Nuc. sci.; 85. Oral hist.; 86. Petr./Energy; 87. Pharm.; 88. Phys./Astr./Math.; 89. Readg.; 90. Relig.; 91. Sci./Tech.; 92. Soc. sci.; 93. Telecom.; 94. Transp.; 95. (other).

Docum., OH Wesleyan Univ., 1965–; Asst. Libn., Ctr. for Chld. Bks., Univ. of Chicago, 1950–52; Libn., Hinsdale HS, 1945–49; Libn., Sylacauga HS, 1944–45. **Educ.:** Univ. of AL, 1941–44, BS (Educ.); Univ. of Chicago, 1946–50, MALS; AL, IL, 1944, 1945, Tchrs. Cert. **Orgs.:** Acad. LA of OH. ALA. Midwest Acad. Libn. Conf. AAUP: Exec. Bd., Lcl. Chap. (1967–70). OH Wesleyan Univ.: Exec. Com.; Acad. Status Com. OH Wesleyan Univ. Woman's Club. Various other orgs. **Honors:** OH Wesleyan-Mellon Fndn., Grantee, 1972–73; Gt. Lakes Coll. Assn., Tchg. Fellow, 1976–77. **Pubns.:** *Introduction to Bibliographic Research: Basic Sources* (1978); *Introduction to Bibliographic Research: Script and Slide Catalog* (1978); "New OWV Library Instructional Program Aids Students in Efficient Use of Literary Resources," *OH Wesleyan Mag.* (N. 1974); *Audio-Visual Aids in Bibliographic Instruction* (1976); snd./Slide and videotape shows. **Activities:** 1; 31, 39, 41; 54, 77, 92 **Addr.:** 414 N. Liberty St., Delaware, OH 43015.

Schlipf, Frederick A. (S. 14, 1941, Fargo, ND) Exec. Dir., Urbana Free Lib., 1974–; Adj. Prof., Univ. of IL Lib. Sch., 1974–, Asst. Prof., 1970–74; Instr., Grad. Lib. Sch., Univ. of Chicago, 1966–70. **Educ.:** Carleton Coll., 1959–63, AB (Hist.); Univ. of Chicago, 1963–73, AM, PhD (LS). **Orgs.:** IL State Lib. Adv. Com., Vice Ch. (1980–). ALA. IL LA. Champaign Cnty. (IL) Hist. Musm.: Bd. of Dirs. (1979–); Pres. (1981). **Pubns.:** Ed., *Collective Bargaining in Libraries* (1975); various articles, reviews. **Activities:** 9, 11; 17, 26 **Addr.:** The Urbana Free Library, 201 S. Race St., Urbana, IL 61801.

Schloeder, Mary C. (N. 25, 1918, Kansas City, MO) Libn., Frgn. Srv. Inst., Dept. of State, 1970–, Asst. Libn., 1963–70; Sr. Decimal Clasfr., Dewey Decimal Ofc., Lib. of Congs., 1961–63; Asst. Chief, Cat., Dept. of State Lib., 1959–61, various cat. positions, 1951–59; Asst. to Pres., Thomas More Bk. Shop, 1944–45; Bibl. Asst., Univ. of Chicago Grad. Lib. Sch., 1944–45; various positions, Cath. Univ. of Amer. Lib. Sch., 1942–44; Asst. Libn., St. Mary Coll., Leavenworth, KS, 1941–42. **Educ.:** St. Mary Coll., 1938–40, AB (Eng., Soc. Sci.); St. Teresa's Coll., Kansas City, MO, 1936–38, AA; Cath. Univ. of Amer., 1942–44, MS (LS). **Orgs.:** SLA. ALA. DC LA. Potomac Tech. Prcs. Libns. **Honors:** Delta Epsilon Sigma, 1956; Beta Phi Mu, 1958. **Pubns.:** *Index to Books on Trial* (1945–46); *Index to Papal Documents on Mary* (1954). **Activities:** 4; 17, 20, 39; 54, 55, 92 **Addr.:** 3426 Gunston Rd., Alexandria, VA 22302.

Schlosser, Anne Griffin (D. 28, 1939, New York, NY) Lib. Dir., The Amer. Film Inst., 1969–; Head Libn., Univ. of CA, Los Angeles, Thea. Arts Lib., 1964–69. **Educ.:** Wheaton Coll., MA, 1958–62, BA (Hist.); Simmons Coll., 1963–64, MLS; Amer. Univ., 1970, Cert. (Arch. Admin.). **Orgs.:** SAA. Socty. of CA Archvsts. Thea. LA. **Pubns.:** *Motion Pictures, Television, and Radio: A Union Catalogue of Manuscript and Special Collections in the Western United States* (1977). **Activities:** 1, 5; 15, 20, 39; 67, 93 **Addr.:** The American Film Institute, Attn: Louis B. Mayer Library, 2021 N. Western Ave., Los Angeles, CA 90027.

Schmidt, Bruce K. (N. 17, 1938, Detroit, MI) City Libn., Southfield Pub. Lib., 1967–; First Asst., Chase Branch, Detroit Pub. Lib., 1965–67, Libn. I, II, Hubbard Branch, 1963–65; Adj. Lectr., Univ. of MI, Sch. of LS, 1979, 1975–76. **Educ.:** Wayne State Univ., 1957–62, AB (Hist.); Univ. of MI, 1962–63, AMLS. **Orgs.:** Detroit Suburban Libns. RT: Ch. (1976–77, 1981–82). ALA. MI LA: Cont Ed. Com. (1974); Conf. Com. (1976); CATV Task Frc. (1981). Natl. Lib. Week: State Exec. Dir. (1966). Southfield Arts Cncl. Black Sheep Repertory Thea. **Honors:** Beta Phi Mu, 1963. **Pubns.:** "Reaching the Unserved," *MI Libn.* (S. 1973). **Activities:** 9, 11; 17, 26, 35; 55 **Addr.:** Southfield Public Library, Civic Center, 26000 Evergreen Rd., Southfield, MI 48076.

Schmidt, C. James (Je. 27, 1939, Flint, MI) Univ. Libn., Brown Univ., 1979–; Dir. of Libs., SUNY, Albany, 1972–79; Head, Undergrad. Libs., Asst. Prof., OH State Univ., 1967–70; Assoc. Libn., SW TX State Univ., 1965–67. **Educ.:** Flint Cmnty. Jr. Coll., 1957–59; Cath. Univ., 1959–62; BA, Columbia Univ., 1963, MS (LS); Univ. of TX, 1966–67 (Pol. Sci.); OH State Univ., 1968–70 (Pol. Sci.); FL State Univ., 1974, PhD (LS). **Orgs.:** ALA: ACRL, Bd. of Dirs. (1975–77) Univ. Libs. Sect., (Ch., 1976–77); Acad. Status Com. (1973–77); Ad Hoc Srch. Com. for ACRL Exec. Secy. (1976–77). Ctr. for Resrch. Libs.: Bd. of Dirs. (1978–81). ARL: Task Frc. on Natl. Per. Supt. (Ch., 1978–80). ASIS. AAUP. Amer. Cvl. Liberties Un. Amer. Mgt. Assn. **Honors:** Pi Sigma Alpha, 1969; Beta Phi Mu, 1971. **Pubns.:** "An Alternative Model of a Profession for Librarians," *Coll. Resrch. Libs.* (My. 1975); "Collective Bargaining and Academic Librarians: A Review of the Decisions of the NLRB," *Coll. & Resrch. Libs. News* (Ja. 1976); "Introduction," *Collective Bargaining in Higher Education* (1976); "The Three Faces of Eve: Or The Identity of Academic Librarianship A Symposium," *Jnl. of Acad. Libnshp.* (Ja. 1977); "Lobbying the Academic Library Budget: The Care & Filling of the Bottomless Pit," *Amer. Libs.* (N. 1977); various other articles, reviews. **Activities:** 1; 17, 24; 56, 90, 92 **Addr.:** Brown University, Providence, RI 02912.

Schmidt, Charles J. (F. 11, 1944, Philadelphia, PA) Dir., Mid. GA Reg. Lib., 1970, Assoc. Dir., 1970–71; Admin. Asst. to Dir., Mobile Pub. Lib., 1969–70, Ext. Libn., 1968–69; Libn., Intl. Trade Lib., Port Mobile, 1966–68. **Educ.:** Univ. of Houston, 1965, BA (Hist.); LA State Univ., 1966, MA (LS); GA Coll., 1975, MBA. **Orgs.:** GA LA. SELA. Macon Civitan: Pres. (1981). **Activities:** 2, 9 **Addr.:** Middle Georgia Regional Library, 1180 Washington Ave., Macon, GA 31202.

Schmidt, Donald T. (S. 13, 1919, Brighton, IL) Dir., Lib. Arch., Hist. Dept., Church of Jesus Christ of Latter-day Saints, 1972–; Asst. Dir., Lib., Brigham Young Univ., 1966–72, Ref. Libn., 1965–66; Head, Pub. Srvs., Geneal. Socty. Lib., 1964–65. **Educ.:** Univ. of IA, 1943–47, BA (Hist.); 1947–49, MA (Hist.); Univ. of Denver, 1962–64, MA (Libnshp.); Arch. Admin. Inst., 1973. **Orgs.:** Mt. Plains LA: Exec. Bd. (1976–79). ALA. SLA. SAA: Relig. Arch. Com. (1975–). Various other orgs. **Addr.:** Historical Dept., 50 E. North Temple St., Salt Lake City, UT 84150.

Schmidt, Elizabeth (Je. 24, 1925, Detroit, MI) Sr. Info. Sci., NALCO Chem. Co., 1969–; Patent Info. Srvs., Ethyl Corp., 1956–68; Patent Info. Srvs., Dow Corning Corp., 1952–56; Patent Info. Srvs., Dow Chem. Co., 1947–52. **Educ.:** MI State Coll., 1943–47, BS (Chem.); Case-West. Rsv. Univ., 1968–69, MLS. **Orgs.:** ASIS. ALA. Chem. Notation Assn. Amer. Chem. Socty. **Activities:** 12; 30, 39, 49-Online Srch.; 60 **Addr.:** NALCO Chemical Co. - Naperville Technical Cntr.–Information Srvs., 1801 Diehl Rd., Naperville, IL 60540.

Schmidt, Janet Anne (Jl. 31, 1945, Brooklyn, NY) Mgr., Mktg. Srvs., Predicasts Inc., 1979–; Mgr., Info Srvs., EIC, 1978–79; Market Rep., Disclosure Inc., 1977–78; Mgr., Bus. Info Ctr., Amer. Can Co., 1971–77. **Educ.:** Pace Univ., 1968–72, BA (Bus.). **Orgs.:** SLA: Hudson Valley Chap. (Pres., 1977–78). Southwest. CT Lib. Grp.: Pres. (1973–74); VP (1972–73). Natl. Info. Conf. Exposition: Plng. Com. (1979–80). Chem. Club. Alfa Romeo Owners Club. **Pubns.:** "How to Promote Online Services to People Who Count," *Online* (Ja. 1977); "Public Relation Programs for Libraries & Information Centers," *Online* (O. 1978); "Microfilm Today," *Info. Mgr.* (1978); "Laws Demand," *Info. World* (1979). **Activities:** 12; 17, 24, 41; 51, 59, 91 **Addr.:** Oak Hill, Bridgewater, CT 06752.

Schmidt, Jean M. (My. 25, 1951, Minneapolis, MN) Archvst./Ref. Libn., MT State Univ., 1975–; Libn., Sch. of Jnlsm., Univ. of MN, 1974. **Educ.:** Macalester Coll., 1969–73, BA (Hist.); Univ. of Denver, 1973–74, MA (Libnshp.); MT State Univ., 1977–81, MA (Hist.). **Orgs.:** MT LA: Acad. and Spec. Libs. Div., (1979–80). SAA. NW Archvsts. MT Hist. Recs. Adv. Cncl. **Activities:** 1, 2; 38, 39, 45 **Addr.:** Renne Library - Archives, Montana State University, Bozeman, MT 59717.

Schmidt, Judith Goacher (Ap. 22, 1946, Cincinnati, OH) Tech. Ofcr., Acq., Cat. and Prcs. Srvs., Lib. of Congs., 1979–, Supvsr., Ident. and Srch. Unit, Copyrt. Ofc., 1978–79, Sr. Descr. Catlgr., 1970–78, Intern, 1969–70. **Educ.:** Miami Univ., 1964–68, BA (Classical Hum.); Case West. Rsv. Univ., 1968–69, MSLS. **Orgs.:** ALA: FLRT, Nsltr. Ed. (1977–78); LITA, *Jnl. of Lib. Autom.* Bk. Review Ed. (1978–79); Advert. Ed. (1979–). Women's Natl. Bk. Assn. **Activities:** 4; 15, 20, 46; 61 **Addr.:** 1408 D. St., S.E., Washington, DC 20003.

Schmidt, Kim McHenry (Ja. 27, 1951, Lakewood, OH) Instr. Coord., OCLC, Inc., 1978–; Visit. Prof., Kent State Univ., 1979; Ref., Soc. Sci., Miami Univ., 1977–78; Catlgr., Cuyahoga Cnty. Pub. Lib., 1976–77. **Educ.:** Miami Univ., 1969–73, BA (Relig.); Kent State Univ., 1975–76, MLS. **Orgs.:** ALA: RTSD/Descr. Cat. Com. (1978–80). Acad. LA of OH. **Honors:** Beta Phi Mu, 1976; Omicron Delta Kappa, 1973. **Pubns.:** "Interlibrary Loan with OCLC" videotape (1979); "The OCLC Interlibrary Loan Subsystem" slide/tape (1979). **Activities:** 14-Networking; 15, 20, 34; 56, 75 **Addr.:** User Services Division, OCLC, Inc., 1125 Kinnear Rd., Columbus, OH 43212.

Schmidt, Mary Ann (D. 3, 1944, Milwaukee, WI) Libn., Milwaukee Sch. of Engin., 1980–, Libn. for Info. Srvs., 1979–80, Asst. Libn., 1978–79; Tech. Libn., Bostrom Div. UOP, 1976–78. **Educ.:** Valparaiso Univ., 1962–67, BA (Msc.); Univ. of WI, Milwaukee, 1975–77, MA (LS). **Orgs.:** SLA: WI Chap. (Pres.-Elect, 1980–81). WI LA. Amer. Socty. for Engin. Educ. Resrch. Clearinghse. of Metro. Milwaukee. **Addr.:** Milwaukee School of Engineering, Walter Schroeder Library, P.O. Box 644, Milwaukee, WI 53201.

Schmidt, Mary Morris (Je. 28, 1926, Minneapolis, MN) Libn., Marquand Lib., Princeton Univ., 1977–; Fine Arts Libn., Columbia Univ., 1969–77; Ed., Art Index, H. W. Wilson Co., 1966–69, Indxr., Art Index, 1958–66. **Educ.:** Univ. of MN, 1945–47, BA (liberal Arts.), 1952–53, BS (LS), 1955, MA (Art Hist.); Fulbright Student, Paris, 1956–57 (Art Hist.). **Orgs.:** ARLIS/NA: Pubns. Com. (1975). Art Libs. Socty. of NY: Ch. (1975–76); Awds. Com. (1974–75). Coll. Art Assn. of Amer. **Activities:** 1; 15, 17, 30 **Addr.:** Marquand Library, McCormick Hall, Princeton University, Princeton, NJ 08544.

Schmidt, Nancy J. (My. 17, 1936, Cincinnati, OH) Libn., Tozzer Lib., Harvard Univ., 1977–; Visit. Assoc. Prof. of Anthro., Univ. of IL, 1974–77; Assoc. Prof. of Anthro., Rockford Coll., 1971–74; Asst. Prof. of Anthro., Stanislaus State Coll., 1968–70. **Educ.:** Oberlin Coll., 1954–58, BA (Soclgy.); Univ. of MN, 1958–61, MA (Intl. Rel.); Northwest. Univ., 1962–65, PhD (Anthro.); IN Univ., 1970–71, MLS. **Orgs.:** ALA. SLA. African Std. Assn. African Lit. Assn. Amer. Anthro. Assn. Amer. Ethnological Socty. **Honors:** Beta Phi Mu, 1971. **Pubns.:** *Children's Fiction About Africa in English* (1981); *Supplement to Children's Books on Africa and Their Authors* (1979); *Children's Books on Africa and Their Authors* (1975); "All Africa Folklore," *Children's Bks. Intl. 4* (1979); "The Development of Written Literature for Children in Subsaharan Africa," *Zeitschrift fur Kulturaustrauch* (1979). **Activities:** 1; 15, 17, 30; 66, 92 **Addr.:** Tozzer Library, 21 Divinity Ave., Cambridge, MA 02138.

Schmidt, Robert R. (Jl. 3, 1941, Denver, CO) Dir. of the Law Lib., Hall of Justice Law Lib., 1977–; Law Libn., City and Cnty. of San Francisco, 1972–77; Law Libn., Cornell Univ. Sch. of Law, 1971. **Educ.:** Univ. of Denver, 1960–63, BA (Russ.), 1966–69, JD (Law), 1970–71, MA (Libnshp.). **Orgs.:** AALL: Exch. of Dupls. (1979–80). ALA. Frnds. of San Francisco Pub. Lib. AAUP. North. CA Srv. Leag.: Bd. of Dirs. (1979–80). Musm. Socty. San Francisco Opera. **Pubns.:** *Legislative Procedures in Colorado* (1968); "Courses for Tear Gas Law Permit," *The Recorder* (Mr. 9, 1979); "Preservation & Restoration of Rare Books," *San Francisco Pub. Lib. Bltn.* (1975); "Administration of Public Libraries," *Pseudographia* (1974). **Activities:** 12, 13; 15, 17, 20; 77 **Addr.:** Hall of Justice Law Library, 850 Bryant St., Rm. 305, San Francisco, CA 94103.

Schmidt, Sherrie (D. 19, 1948, Columbus, OH) Asst. Dir., Lib. Srvs., Univ. of TX, Dallas, 1979–, Coord., Pub. Srvs., 1978–79; Head, User Srvs., Amigos Bibl. Cncl., 1975–78; Catlgr., Univ. of FL, 1974–75. **Educ.:** OH State Univ., 1968–70, BA (Soclgy.); Emory Univ., 1973–74, MLn (Libnshp.). **Orgs.:** ALA: LITA, Prog. Plng. Com. (1977–81); AALS. **Activities:** 1; 17, 20, 34 **Addr.:** 315 Brookwood Dr., Richardson, TX 75080.

Schmidt, Susan K. (N. 16, 1948, Detroit, MI) Exec. Dir., SWLA, 1979–; Dir., Southeast. OH Reg. Lib., 1978–79; Proj. Dir., Mideast. OH Lib. Org., 1976–78; Coord., Lib. Inst. Series, AAEC, Morehead State Univ., 1973–76. **Educ.:** Wayne State Univ., 1966–70, BA (Classics), 1972–73, MS (LS). **Orgs.:** CLENE: Mem. Com. (Ch., 1978); Nom. Com. (1975); Secy. (1980–81). ALA: PLA/Alternative Educ. Progs. Sect., Pres. (1981–82), VP (1980–81), Basic Educ. Com. (Ch., 1977–79); Ofc. for Lib. Outrch. Srvs., Rural Poor and Appalachian People (Ch., 1975–77). Wayne State LS Assn: Staff Liaison (1973). **Pubns.:** Ed., *Library Service Guide Series* pamphlet series (1977); *Books by Mail Services* (1977); *Utilizing Volunteers in Expanding Library Services to Disadvantaged Adults* (1977); "A History of ABE Services in Public Libraries," *Drexel Lib. Qtly.* (O. 1978); "Planning Library Services for Disadvantaged Adults" videotape (1976). **Activities:** 3, 9; 24, 25, 34; 50, 85, 89 **Addr.:** P.O. Box 23713, TWU Station, Denton, TX 76204.

Schmidt, Valentine Lucille (D. 21, 1919, New York, NY) Lib. Dir., Ringling Musm. of Art, 1965–; Lib. Dir., Babcock & Wilcox Co. - Atomic Energy Div., 1962–64; Admin. Libn., Army Lib. Srv., Germany, 1960–62; Asst. Libn., Main Post Lib., Ft. Bragg, NC, 1957–58. **Educ.:** Cnsvty. of Musical Art, 1935–39, Dip.; Rutgers Univ., 1936–40, BSc (Math.); Univ. of NC, 1958–60, MSLS; various crs. **Orgs.:** SLA: FL Chap., Archvst. (1970), VP (1972), Pres. (1973). FL LA. ALA. Amer. Socty. for Metals. Amer. Nuc. Socty. **Honors:** Beta Phi Mu, 1960. **Pubns.:** "The Art Research Library of the Ringling Museum of Art," *FL Libs.* (S. 1970); jt. auth., "Twentieth Century Illustrated Books," (1967); *Rare Books of the 16th, 17th, and 18th Centuries From the Library of the Ringling Museum of Art* (1969). **Activities:** 12; 17, 20, 39; 55 **Addr.:** 2624 Reserve Pl., Bradenton, FL 33507.

Schmitt, Damaris Ann (D. 5, 1948, St. Louis, MO) Head, Ref. Dept., St. Louis Cmnty. Coll., Meramec, 1972–. **Educ.:** Univ. of MO, St. Louis, 1967–71, BA (Eng. Lit.); Univ. of MO, Columbia, 1971–72, MA (LS); Webster Coll., 1975–78, MA (Media-Film); Anglo-Amer. Lib. Sem., Oxford, 1977. **Orgs.:** ALA: ACRL/Cmnty. & Jr. Coll. Sect., Comm. Com., Ch. MO LA: Ref. RT, Cofndr. (1976). MO ACRL: Pres. (1976–77); Instr. Resrcs. Sect. (Ch., 1974). Beta Phi Mu: Psi Chap. (Pres., 1976–77). Meramec Fac. Fndn. Women's Assn., St. Louis Symph. Socty. **Pubns.:** "Staff Response to the COM Catalogue," *Instr. Resrcs. Nsltr.* (Ja. 1980); "Prototype" film (1978). **Activities:** 1; 31, 39 **Addr.:** Reference Dept., 11333 Big Bend Blvd., Kirkwood, MO 63122.

Schmitt, Florence (nee Bauer) (Ja. 21, 1930, New York, NY) Sch. Lib. Med./Spec., Plainedge Sch. Dist., 1960–; Libn., Sec. Level, Riverhead, NY, First Supvsy. Dist., 1958–60; Spec. Libn., Westinghse. Electronic Tube Div., 1957–58; Tchr., HS Eng., Cowanesque Valley Dist., PA, 1956–57; Tchr., Eng., Stuyvesant HS, 1950–51. **Educ.:** Hunter Coll., NY, 1947–50, BA (Eng. Lit); Long Island Univ., 1967, MLS; Adelphi Univ., Syracuse Univ., (LS, Educ.). **Orgs.:** Nassau/Suffolk Sch. LA: Secy. (1961). ALA. NY LA. Nassau/Suffolk Sch. Media Assn. **Addr.:** Packard Junior High School of Plainedge School District, North Idaho and Central Ave., North Massapequa, NY 11758.

Schmitt, Margaret S. (Ap. 25, 1927, La Crosse, WI) Lib. Dir., Alsip-Merrionette Park Pub. Lib., 1974–; Asst. Libn., La Grange Pub. Lib., 1972–74, Ref. Libn., 1971–72. **Educ.:** Univ. of WI, 1944–48, BA (Hisp. Std.); Rosary Coll., 1969–70, MALS.

Orgs.: ALA. IL LA. S. Suburban LA. **Honors:** Phi Beta Kappa, 1948; Beta Phi Mu, 1971; Sigma Delta Pi, 1947; Phi Kappa Phi, 1948. **Activities:** 9; 17, 39 **Addr.:** 1409 53rd Pl., La Grange, IL 60525.

Schmittroth, John, Jr. (Jl. 5, 1949, Detroit, MI) Ed., Gale Resrch. Co., 1972–. **Educ.:** Wayne State Univ., 1968–72, BA (Eng.). **Orgs.:** ASIS. European Assn. of Info. Srvs. Intl. Assn. for Soc. Sci. Info. Srv. and Tech. **Pubns.:** Jt. ed., *Ency. of Info. Systs. and Srvs.* (1981). **Activities:** 14-Publshr.; 37; 49-Online Srvs.; 56 **Addr.:** Gale Research Company, Book Tower, Detroit, MI 48226.

Schmitz, Eugenia E. (Grand Rapids, MI) Prof. of LS, Univ. of WI, Oshkosh, 1968–, Ch., Dept. of LS, 1968–80; Asst. Prof. of LS, Univ. of MI, 1967–68, Lectr., Dept. of LS, 1963–67. **Educ.:** West. MI Univ., AB (Latin, Eng.); Coll. of St. Catherine, BSLS; Univ. of MI, AMLS; Univ. of MI, 1966, PhD (LS). **Orgs.:** ALA. AALS. WI LA. **Honors:** Phi Beta Kappa; Phi Kappa Phi; Beta Phi Mu; Pi Lambda Theta; Sigma Pi Epsilon. **Pubns.:** Reviews. **Activities:** 11; 20, 39; 57 **Addr.:** University of Wisconsin-Oshkosh, Dept. of Library Science, Oshkosh, WI 54901.

Schmoll, Donavon M. (Jl. 17, 1929, Geneseo, IL) Lib. Dir., Wartburg Coll., 1975–; Lib. Dir., St. Leo Coll., 1970–75, Tech. Srvs. Libn., 1967–70; Tchr., Namilyango Coll., Kampala, Uganda, 1961–65. **Educ.:** IL State Univ., 1947–51, BSEd (Soc. Sci.); NY Univ., 1955–58, MA (Pol. Sci.); Columbia Univ., 1958–61 (Educ. Admin.); Univ. of WI, 1965–67, MSLS. **Orgs.:** ALA. IA LA. AAUP. Bread for the World. **Honors:** U.S. Agency for Intl. Dev., E. Africa Trng. Flwshp., 1961; Beta Phi Mu. **Activities:** 1; 15, 17, 39; 54, 63, 75 **Addr.:** 1316 W. 18th St., Cedar Falls, IA 50613.

Schmuch, Joseph J. (Mr. 9, 1928, Lynn, MA) Libn., Belmont Pub. Lib., 1961–; Libn., Reading Pub. Lib., 1958–61. **Educ.:** Bowdoin Coll., 1945–48, AB (Classics); Simmons Coll., 1957–59, MSLS; Brown Univ., 1950–52, MA (Classics). **Activities:** 9; 15, 17, 35 **Addr.:** Belmont Public Library, P.O. Box 125, 336 Concord Ave., Belmont, MA 02178.

Schnaitter, Allene F. (N. 19, 1921, Sandusky, OH) Dir. of Libs., WA State Univ., 1976–; Dir. of Libs., Gvrs. State Univ., 1973–76, Asst. Dir. of Libs., 1970–73; Head, Ord. Dept., Univ. of MO, 1961–67; Asst. Head, Ord. Dept., Univ. of MI Law Lib., 1954–61; Sci. & Msc. Libn., Antioch Coll., 1953–54; Head, Current Serials Unit, Univ. of MI Gen. Lib., 1950–53. **Educ.:** Univ. of MI, 1945–49, AB (Grmn.), 1950–52, AMLS; IN Univ., 1967–70, PhD (LS). **Orgs.:** WA Lib. Netwk.: Exec. Cncl. (Ch., 1977–78). ALA. WA LA. Pac. NW LA. AAUW. Assn. for Fac. Women, WA State Univ. **Activities:** 1; 17, 34, 39 **Addr.:** P.O. Box 2337 C.S., Pullman, WA 99163.

Schnare, Mary Kay W. (N. 12, 1945, Pittsburgh, PA) Dir. of Opers., Sch. of Bus. Admin., Univ. of CT, 1980–, Dir., Sch. of Bus. Admin., Lib., 1978–80; Assoc. Libn., Dutchess Cmnty. Coll., 1973–78; Ref. Libn., MBA Lib., Univ. of CT, 1971–73; Ref. Libn., W. Hartford Pub. Lib., 1970–71; Head, Bus., Indus., Sci. Dept., Providence Pub. Lib. 1968–70; Tech., Mine Safety Appliances Lib., 1962–67. **Educ.:** Carlow Coll., 1963–67, BA (Hist.); Univ. of Pittsburgh, 1967–68, MLS; Univ. of CT, 1972–75, MBA (Persnl.). **Orgs.:** SLA: CT Valley Chap., Corres. Secy. (1980–), Asst. Bltn. Ed. (1979). CT LA. NY LA. Hartford Women's Netwk. Socty. for the Advnc. of Mgt. **Honors:** Hartford YWCA Women in Leadership Recog. Awd., 1980; Outstan. Young Women of Amer., Nominee for "Woman of the Yr.," 1980; Dutchess Cmnty. Coll., Bene Merenti Awd., 1978; Beta Phi Mu, 1968. **Activities:** 1; 17, 35, 39; 51, 59, 76 **Addr.:** 69 Gillett St., Apt. 309, Hartford, CT 06105.

Schnare, Robert Edey Jr. (D. 31, 1944, Morristown, NJ) Asst. Libn. for Spec. Cols., U.S. Milit. Acad., 1973–; Ref. Libn. for Hist. and Geneal., CT State Lib., 1967–73. **Educ.:** William Paterson Coll. of NJ, 1963–67, BA (Soc. Sci.); Univ. of Pittsburgh, 1967–68, MLS; Univ. of CT, 1971, MA (Amer. Hist.); Amer. Univ. and Natl. Arch., 1976, Intro. to Modern Arch. Admin.; Columbia Univ., 1978, Inst. Dev. Admin. Prsrvn. Prog. **Orgs.:** NY LA: RTSS, Cons. Com. (Ch., 1977–79). ALA. New Eng. Archvsts. New Eng. Cons. Assn. OCLC: Task Frc. on Mss. (1978–). Assn. Std. CT Hist.: Pres. (1978–80). Amer. Inst. Cons. CT Leag. Hist. Socty. Various other orgs. **Pubns.:** *Bibliography of Resources for the Conservation of Library Materials* (1979); *Sources of Supply and Information for the Conservation of Library Materials* (1979); *Local Historical Resources in Connecticut: A Guide to Their Use* (1975); "Buried Treasure: 20th Century Governors Records in Connecticut State Library," *Amer. Archvst.* (O. 1971); assoc. ed., *Cons. Admin. News* (1979–). **Activities:** 1, 4; 17, 23, 45; 57, 70, 74 **Addr.:** Special Collections, United States Military Academy Library, West Point, NY 10996.

Schneider, Adele G. (My. 13, 1924, New York, NY) Assoc. Prof., Kingsborough Cmnty. Coll. Lib., CUNY, 1972–, Asst. Prof., 1970–72, Instr., 1965–70, Ed., Brooklyn Coll. Alum. Qtly., 1961–65; various positions in soc. srv. **Educ.:** Brooklyn Coll., 1941–45, BA (Eng.); Pratt Inst., 1961–65, MLS; Long Island Univ., 1967–71, MA (Eng.); Columbia Univ., Univ. WI, New Sch. Soc. Resrch., 1946–79 (various crs.). **Orgs.:** ALA: ACRL; RTSD. NY Tech. Srvs. Libns. LA CUNY: Exec. Cncl. (1979–80); Bibl. Instr. Com. (1975–80); Pubns. Com. (1980–81). AAUP. **Honors:** Beta Phi Mu, 1965. **Pubns.:** Adv. bd., *Urban Acad. Libn.* (1981). ed., *Op. Cit.* (1966–74); ed. bd., *LA CUNY Jnl.* (1972). **Activities:** 1; 31, 39, 46; 55 **Addr.:** Kingsborough Community College Library, 2001 Oriental Blvd., Brooklyn, NY 11235.

Schneider, Beverly Bury (Ja. 1, 1953, Lexington, VA) Lib. Dir., Campbell Cnty. Pub. Lib., 1977–, Asst. Libn., Campbell Cnty. Pub. Lib., 1976–77. **Educ.:** Longwood Coll., 1971–75, BA (Fr., Grmn.); Univ. of KY, 1975–76, MSLS. **Orgs.:** KY LA: Pub. Lib. Sect. (Ch., 1980–81). SELA. ALA. Leag. of Women Voters. Frnds. of the Campbell Cnty. Pub. Lib. **Activities:** 9; 17 **Addr.:** Campbell County Public Library, 4th & Monmouth St., Newport, KY 41071.

Schneider, D. W. (F. 15, 1935, Middleton, OH) Assoc. Dir., LA State Univ., 1975–; Undergrad. Libn., Univ. of NC, 1970–75, Head, Bus. Admin./Soc. Sci. Div., 1967–70. **Educ.:** Kalamazoo Coll., 1959–61, BA (Econ.); IN Univ., 1961–63, MBA (Fin.), 1964–67, MA (LS). **Orgs.:** Cont. Lib. Educ. Adv. Cncl.: Ch. (1979–). LA LA: Audit. Com. (1978); Cont. Ed. Com. (1978–). ALA: LAMA/Lib Org. and Mgt. Sect, Prog. Com. (1979–). **Honors:** Beta Phi Mu, 1967. **Activities:** 1; 17, 25, 39; 56, 95-Lib. Coop. **Addr.:** Louisiana State University Library, Baton Rouge, LA 70803.

Schneider, Hennie Rand (Jl. 6, 1922, Baltimore, MD) Supervisory Ref. Libn., U.S. Intl. Trade Comsn., 1980–; Biblgphr.-Indxr.-Ref. Libn., U.S. Dept. of Transp. Lib., 1975–80; Libn.-Biblgphr., Amer. Stats. Index, 1972–75; Supvsr. Ref. Libn., U.S. Bur. of the Census Lib., 1965–70; Ref. Libn., Natl. Agr. Lib., 1962–65; Ref. Libn., Branch Libn., Prince George Cnty. Meml. Lib., 1957–62. **Educ.:** Johns Hopkins Univ., 1938–40; Univ. of MD, 1940–42; Simmons Coll., 1961, MSLS. **Orgs.:** ALA. SLA. Law Libns. Socty. of DC. DC LA. Federally Employed Women. **Pubns.:** Cmplr., *Where to Look Next: Subject Guide to Reference Sources* (1971); cmplr., *International Statistical Sources: A Bibliography* (1968). **Activities:** 4, 12; 30, 37, 39; 57, 93, 94 **Addr.:** 11430 Lockwood Dr., Silver Spring, MD 20904.

Schneider, J. Kaye Proj. Dir., West. OH Reg. Lib. Dev. Syst., 1973–; Sci. Ref. Libn., Detroit Pub. Lib., 1967–72. **Educ.:** OH State Univ., 1961–65, BS (Educ.); Univ. of MI, 1966–67, MALS; various cont. educ. crs. in LS, comps., admin. **Orgs.:** ALA: ASLA Prog. (1977–79). OH LA: Stans. Com. (Ch., 1976–79). OH State Lib.: Adv. Com. Outrch. (1976–81). **Activities:** 9, 14-Syst.; 17, 24, 34 **Addr.:** Worlds, 640 W. Market, Lima, OH 45801.

Schneider, John H. (S. 29, 1931, Eau Claire, WI) Dir., Intl. Cancer Resrch. Data Bank Prog., Natl. Cancer Inst., 1974–; Sci. and Tech. Info. Ofcr., 1967–, Sci. and Tech. Info. Spec., 1964–67. **Educ.:** Univ. of WI, 1950–53, BS (Chem.); Univ. of WI, 1953–58 PhD (Experimental Oncology). **Orgs.:** ASIS: Potomac Valley Chap. (VCh., 1971–1972); (Ch. 1972–1973). Amer. Assn. for Cancer Resrch. AAAS. **Honors:** Pub. Hlth. Srv., Sustained High Quality Wk. Performance, 1971; Pub. Hlth. Srv., Awd. to ICRDB Grp. for Spec. Achvmt., 1978. **Pubns.:** "CANCERGRAMS: A Large-Scale System for Selective Dissemination of Information to Cancer Researchers," *Proc. of the ASIS Anl. Mtg.* (1978); "Information Services of the International Cancer Research Data Bank (ICRDB) Program in Cancer Chemotherapy and Pharmacology," *Adv. in Pharm. and Chemotherapy* (1980). **Activities:** 12; 17, 30, 49-Tech. Info. Syst. Operation; 56, 58, 75 **Addr.:** National Cancer Institute, Westwood Building, Rm. 10A-18, Bethesda, MD 20205.

Schneider, Robert Allan (Ag. 18, 1942, Milwaukee, WI) Lib. Dir., North. KY Univ. Lib., 1972–; Assoc. Libn. and Head of Readers' Srvs., Northwest. Coll., 1970–72. **Educ.:** Univ. of WI, Milwaukee, 1960–65, BS (Soc. Work), 1965–66, MS (Soclgy.); Univ. of HI, 1969–70, MLS. **Orgs.:** ALA. KY LA. Grt. Cincinnati Lib. Cnsrtm.: Resrcs. Com. (Ch., 1979–). Frnds. of Campbell Cnty. Pub. Lib.: Pres. (1979–80). **Honors:** Beta Phi Mu, 1970. **Activities:** 1; 15, 31, 46; 92 **Addr.:** W. Frank Steely Library, Northern Kentucky University, Highland Heights, KY 41076.

Schnelder, Stewart P. (N. 8, 1924, Orange, NJ) Assoc. Prof., Sch. LS, Univ. RI, 1968–; Head, Ref. Dept., Univ. RI Lib., 1964–68; various positions in publshg. and tchg. **Educ.:** Haverford Coll., 1942–44, BA (Eng.); Columbia Univ., 1946–48, 1949–50, MA (Eng.), 1963–64, MS (LS), 1972–74, Cert. (Adv. LS). **Orgs.:** ALA: RASD, Ref. Subscrpn. Bks. Review Com. (1971–75). RI LA: Mem. Com. (1977–); Cont. Educ. Com. (1978–). AALS. RI Hist. Socty. Steamship Hist. Socty. Amer. **Honors:** Phi Beta Kappa, 1948; Beta Phi Mu, 1964. **Pubns.:** "Employment Survey of 1977 GLS Graduates," *RI LA Bltn.* (N. 1978); "Employment Survey of 1978 GLS Graduates," *RI LA Bltn.* (F. 1980); reviews. **Activities:** 11; 29, 39; 78, 94 **Addr.:** Graduate Library School, University Rhode Island, Kingston, RI 02881.

Schnick, Rosalie A. (S. 23, 1942, Owatonna, MN) Tech. Info. Spec., Natl. Fishery Resrch. Lab., 1967–. **Educ.:** Univ. of MN, 1961–65, BA (Hist.), 1965–67, MA (LS). **Orgs.:** SLA. **Pubns.:** fourteen articles and tech. rpts. on fishery chems., fish culture, and fish cntrl. **Activities:** 4; 29, 39, 41; 58, 65, 82 **Addr.:** National Fishery Research Laboratory, U.S. Fish and Wildlife Service, P.O. Box 818, La Crosse, WI 54601.

Schock, Richard George (Je. 17, 1929, Oak Park, IL) Lib. Dir., Moody Bible Inst., 1971–, Actg. Dir., 1970, Asst. to Dir., 1969. **Educ.:** Northwest. Univ., 1948–51, BS (Psy.); North. IL Univ., 1967–70, MALS. **Orgs.:** Assn. Christ. Libns.: Pres. (1978). ALA. **Activities:** 1, 2; 17; 90 **Addr.:** Moody Bible Institute, 820 N. LaSalle Dr., Chicago, IL 60610.

Schoenly, Steven Browning (Ag. 12, 1949, Nashville, TN) Asst. Prof., Sch. LS and Info. Sci., Univ. of MS, 1978–; Resrch. Asst., Univ. of IL Arch., 1977–78; various positions in tchg. **Educ.:** MA Inst. of Tech., 1967–69; Vanderbilt Univ., 1969–71, BA (Phil.); South. IL Univ., 1971–76, MA, PhD (Phil.); Univ. of IL, 1977–78, MSLS. **Orgs.:** ALA. SLA. MS LA. SELA: *The Southeast. Libn.* Mgr. Ed. (1978–). Various other orgs. Socty. of MS Archvsts. **Honors:** Phi Kappa Phi, 1972; Beta Phi Mu, 1978. **Pubns.:** Jt. auth., *A Conservation Bibliography for Librarians, Archivists, and Administrators* (1979); "Automation on a Small Scale," *MS Lib.* (Fall 1979). **Activities:** 11; 26, 41; 55, 56, 75 **Addr.:** Graduate School of Library and Information Science, University of Mississippi, University, MS 38677.

Schoenthaler, Jean A. (S. 15, 1941, Newark, NJ) Head, Tech. Srvs. Div., Drew Univ., 1971–, Catlgr., 1968–71; Asst. Libn., Tech. Srv., Rocky Mt. Coll., 1964–68. **Educ.:** Tusculum Coll., 1959–63, BA (Eng.); Pratt Inst., 1963–64, MLS. **Orgs.:** ALA. NJ LA. Caldwell Pub. Lib. Bd. of Trustees: Treas. (1981–). **Activities:** 1, 9; 23, 33, 46 **Addr.:** 21 Park Ave., Caldwell, NJ 07006.

Schoenung, James G. (N. 14, 1945, Cincinnati, OH) Exec. Dir., PALINET/ULC, 1979–; Instr. Srvs. Supvsr., OCLC, Inc., 1978–79; Cat. Libn., Wayne State Univ., 1973–75. **Educ.:** Xavier Univ., 1963–67, BS (Eng.); Drexel Univ., 1971–73, MS (LS), 1975–78, PhD (Info. Sci.). **Orgs.:** ALA: LITA, Com. on Educ. (1979–). ASIS. NJ LA. PA LA. Amer. Socty. for Trng. and Dev. Cncl. for Comp. Lib. Netwks: Secy. (1979–80). **Honors:** Beta Phi Mu, 1973. **Pubns.:** *The Ohio College Library Center: An Overview* (1974); "Cable Television: A Bibliographic Review," *ALA Packet* (1973). **Activities:** 11, 14-lib. networks; 20, 34, 41; 56, 75 **Addr.:** 19 Burd Ave., Upper Darby, PA 19082.

Scholberg, Henry (My. 29, 1921, Darjeeling, Bengal, India) Libn., Ames Lib. of S. Asia, Univ. of MN, 1961–; Libn., Columbia Hts. HS, 1954–61. **Educ.:** Univ. of IL, 1940–43, BA (Hist.); Univ. of MN, 1960–62, MA (LS). **Orgs.:** ALA: ACRL, African Asian Sect. (Secy., 1970–73), Ch. (1974–75). MN LA: Acad. Sect. (Ch., 1966–67). S. Asia Micro. Proj.: Exec. Bd. (Ch., 1976–77). **Pubns.:** "The Asia Library in Its University Setting," *Foreign Acq. Nsltr.* (Spr. 1972); "The Records of Portuguese India," *AIIS Nsltr.* Monsoon (1976); cat. ed., *Ames Library of South Asia* (1981); "Indian Libraries: An American View," *Indian Librarianship: Perspectives and Prospects* (1981); "The Encyclopedias of India," *Professor T.K. Venkataraman's 81st Birthday Commemoration Volume* (1981); various bibls. **Addr.:** Ames Library of South Asia, S-10 Wilson Library, University of Minnesota, Minneapolis, MN 55455.

Scholten, Frances (Je. 2, 1919, New Hurley, NY) Libn., Amer. Cyanamid Co., 1974–; Libn., Glen Rock Jr. HS, 1958–74. **Educ.:** Wilson Coll., 1936–40, AB, cum laude (Chem.); Rutgers Univ., 1957–61, MLS; Columbia Univ., 1949–51. **Orgs.:** ALA. NJ LA: Rcrt. Com. (1969–70); Elec. Com. (Ch., 1973–). NJ Sch. Media Assn.: Rcrt. Com. (Ch., 1969–70); Nom. Com. (1970–71). NJ Educ. Assn.: Del. Asm. (1971–74); Pension Policy Com. (1971–); various other coms. Wilson Coll.: Alum. Bd. Dir. (1964–67); Class Pres. (1960–65); Club North. NJ (Pres., 1953–55). **Honors:** Beta Phi Mu, 1961. **Activities:** 12; 15, 17, 39; 65, 80, 91 **Addr.:** 39 Lake Dr. W., Wayne, NJ 07470.

Scholz, Dell DuBose (Mrs.) (Gonzales, TX) Lib. Prog. Coord., LA State Lib., 1979–, Head, Films & Recs. Sect., 1960–79; Libn., LA State Univ. Law Lib., 1954–59; Supvsr., Msc., Webster Groves Sch. Syst., St. Louis, MO, 1949–51. **Educ.:** SW TX State Coll., 1942, BS (Msc.); LA State Univ., 1960, MS (LS). **Orgs.:** ALA. SWLA. LA LA. **Honors:** Beta Phi Mu. **Pubns.:** *Manual for the Cataloging of Recording in Public Libraries.* **Activities:** 1, 13; 17, 20, 32; 55, 67 **Addr.:** Louisiana State Library, P.O. Box 131, Baton Rouge, LA 70821.

Schon, Barbara Margaret (Sandwich, ON) Chief Libn., Newcastle Pub. Lib., 1980–; Area Libn., Toronto Pub. Lib., 1978–80, Head, Sanderson Branch, 1976–78, Admin. Asst. for Bd. and Com., 1975–76; **Educ.:** York Univ., 1965–69, BA, hons. (Eng.); Univ. of West. ON, 1973, MLS. **Orgs.:** Can. LA: Lcl. Arrange. Com. (1975). ON LA. ON Film Assn. **Pubns.:** Coord., *Goals, Objectives and Priorities Study: Toronto Public Libraries* (1975); "Community Participation and Library Planning," *ON Lib. Review* (Je. 1976). **Activities:** 9; 16, 17, 19; 67, 69, 89 **Addr.:** 28 Nesbitt Dr., Toronto, ON M4W 2G3 Canada.

Special Subjects/Services: 50. Adult educ.; 51. Advert./Mktg.; 52. Aerosp.; 53. Agric.; 54. Area std.; 55. Arts/Hum.; 56. Autom.; 57. Bibl./Prtg.; 58. Bio. sci.; 59. Bus./Fin.; 60. Chem.; 61. Copyrt.; 62. Documtn.; 63. Educ.; 64. Engin.; 65. Env.; 66. Eth. grps.; 67. Film; 68. Food/Nutr.; 69. Geneal.; 70. Geo.; 71. Geol.; 72. Handcpd.; 73. Hist.; 74. Int. frdm.; 75. Info. sci.; 76. Insr.; 77. Law; 78. Legis.; 79. Math./Comp. sci.; 80. Med.; 81. Metals; 82. Nat. resrcs.; 83. Newsp.; 84. Nuc. sci.; 85. Oral hist.; 86. Petr./Energy; 87. Pharm.; 88. Phys./Astr./Math.; 89. Readg.; 90. Relig.; 91. Sci./Tech.; 92. Soc. sci.; 93. Telecom.; 94. Transp.; 95. (other).

Schon, Isabel (Ja. 19, 19–, Mexico City, Mex.) Assoc. Prof., AZ State Univ., 1974–; Eval., Biling. Educ. Mtrls., Univ. of CO, 1973; Educ. Eval., Sch. of Bus Admin., Natl. Univ. of Mex., 1972; Dir., Educ. Media Ctr., Amer. Sch. Fndn., Mexico City, 1958–72. **Educ.:** Univ. Nacional Autónoma de Méx., 1967–70; Mankato State Coll., 1971, BS; MI State Univ., 1972, MA (Educ.); Univ. of CO, 1974, PhD (Lib. Media). **Orgs.:** ALA: AASL; LITA. AZ LA. Amer. Educ. Resrch. Assn. **Honors:** ALA, Herbert W. Putnam Hon. Awd., 1979. **Pubns.:** *A Hispanic Heritage: A guide to juvenile books about Hispanic people and cultures.* (1980); *Books in Spanish for Children and Young Adults* (1978); *A Bicultural Heritage: Themes for the Exploration of Mexican and Mexican-American Culture through Books for Children and Adolescents* (1978); "Legends and Folktales from Spanish-speaking Countries," *Chld. Books Intl.* (1979); "A Heartfelt Plea: Notes on Books for Children and Adolescents from Spain," *Eng. Jnl.* (Mr. 1977); various other bks., articles, filmstps. **Activities:** 10, 11; 15, 26, 41; 56, 57, 63, 66 **Addr.:** Arizona State University, College of Education, Tempe, AZ 85281.

Schonbrun, Rena (N. 3, 1940, New York, NY) Libn., West. Reg. Resrch. Ctr., Agr. Resrch. Srv., US Dept. of Agr., 1971–; Syst. Anal., Natl. Agr. Lib., 1970–71, Libn., Syst. Dev. 1968–70; Info. Chem., Lederle Labs., 1967–68, Lit. Chem., Cat., 1963–67. **Educ.:** Queens Coll., CUNY, 1958–62, BS (Chem.); Case West. Rsv. Univ., 1962–63, MLS. **Orgs.:** ASIS San Francisco Bay Reg. Chap. (Treas. 1971–72). SLA: Info. Tech. Div., Ch., Nom. Com. (1968–69), Treas. (1972–74, 1980–82); various other coms., ofcs. Amer. Chem. Socty. **Honors:** Beta Phi Mu, 1963. **Activities:** 4, 12; 17, 46, 49, Online srch. srvs.; 60, 62, 91 **Addr.:** 66 Las Moradas Cir., San Pablo, CA 94806.

Schoonover, David E. (N. 15, 1944, Abilene, TX) Cur., Yale Col. of Amer. Lit., Yale Univ., 1980–; Biblgphr., Schol.-Libn., Northwest. Univ. Lib., 1978–80; Asst. Prof. of Eng., Jundi Shapur Univ., Ahwaz, Iran, 1975–77. **Educ.:** Univ. of TX, 1963–67, BS (Eng.); Univ. of MI, 1970–71, AM (Eng.); Princeton Univ., 1971–75, PhD (Eng.); Univ. of TX, 1977–78, MLS. **Orgs.:** ALA: ACRL/Rare Bks. and Mss. Sect. Mod. Lang. Assn. Grolier Club. Caxton Club of Chicago. **Pubns.:** "The Pots of Normandy in English Printed Books," *Direction Line* (Fall 1978); Reviews. **Addr.:** Yale University Library, New Haven, CT 06520.

Schormann, Victor (D. 21, 1918, Staplehurst, NE) Asst. Serials Libn., North. IL Univ., 1966–; Pers. Libn., West. IL Univ., 1951–66; Circ. and AV Libn., Augustana Coll., 1950–57; Ord. Libn., Knox Coll., 1949–50. **Educ.:** Univ. of IL, 1947–48, AB (Grmn.), 1948–49, MSLS. **Orgs.:** ALA: ACRL, Constn. Bylaws Com. (1978–), Univ. Lib. Sect. IL LA. Amer. Fed. Tchr.: Lcl. Treas. Natl. Educ. Assn. AAUP. **Activities:** 1; 15, 44 **Addr.:** 821 Sharon Dr., DeKalb, IL 60115.

Schorr, Alan Edward (Ja. 7, 1945, New York, NY) Lib. Consult., Sheldon Jackson Coll. (Sitka), 1981; Dir., Lib. and Media Srvs., Univ. of AK, Juneau, 1978–; Gvt. Pubns. and Map Libn., Univ. of AK, Fairbanks, 1973–78. **Educ.:** Hunter Coll., 1962–66, BA; Syracuse Univ., 1966–67, MA (Hist.); Univ. of IA, 1967–71 (Hist.); Univ. of TX, 1972–73, MLS. **Orgs.:** ALA: Cnclr. at Lg. (1977–81, 81–85); Ref. and Subscrpn. Bks. Review Com. (1975–78); ACRL, Pubns. Com. (1976–80); Isidore Gilbert Mudge Cit. Com. (1977–79). Pac. NW LA: Jobline Com. (1977–78). AK LA: Juneau Chap. (Pres., 1981–82); *SOURDOUGH* Ed. (1974–75); Exec. Bd. (1974–75, 1980–82). Bk. Club of CA. Explorers Club of NY. Dartmouth Medal Com., 1980–81. Lippincott Awd. Com., 1981–82. **Pubns.:** *Alaska Place Names, 2d ed.* (1980); *Directory of Special Libraries in Alaksa* (1975); *Bibliography of Alaskana 1969–73* (1974); "Alaskan-Polar Resources," *Arctic Bltn.* (Mr. 1978); "Education Index and CIJE," *Jnl. of Acad. Libnshp.* (Jl. 1976); various other bks., articles, reviews. **Activities:** 1; 17, 29; 70 **Addr.:** Library and Media Services, University of Alaska, Juneau, 11120 Glacier Hwy., Juneau, AK 99803.

Schorrig, Claudia M. (Ja. 24, 1943, Frankfort, Germany) Lib. Dir., Siemons Corp., 1980–; Asst. Dir., FL Atl. Univ., 1972–80; Asst. to Head, Approval Dept., Otto Harrassowitz, 1970–72. **Educ.:** Univ. WA, 1962–66, BA (Ling.); Murray State Univ., 1967–69, MA (Grmn.); Univ. KY, 1969–70, MLS. **Orgs.:** ALA. SLA. FL LA. **Honors:** Beta Phi Mu; Sigma Delta Pi. **Activities:** 1, 12; 17, 28, 36; 55, 75, 93 **Addr.:** 275 N.W. 9th St., Boca Raton, FL 33432.

Schrader, Alvin M. (Mr. 11, 1944, Bentley, AB) Assoc. Instr., IN Univ., Sum. 1980–81; Deputy Branch Head, Chinguacousy Brampton Pub. Lib., 1977–79; Info. Resrc. Consult., Cncl. of Mnstrs. of Educ. (Can.), 1975–76. **Educ.:** Univ. of AB, 1962–66, BA, hons. (Hist.); Carleton Univ., 1966–67, MA (Hist.); Univ. of Toronto, 1973–75, MLS; IN Univ., 1979–, PhD Cand. **Orgs.:** AALS. ALA. ASIS. NLA. **Honors:** Beta Phi Mu. **Pubns.:** Jt. auth., *The Search for a Scientific Profession: Library Science Education in the U.S. and Canada* (1978); "Teaching Bibliometrics," *Lib. Trends* (1981); "Performance Measures for Public Libraries: Refinements in Methodology and Reporting," *Lib. Resrch.* (1980–81); "The Role of the PhD Dissertation in Library Science," *Lib. Resrch.* (1979); "Library Science Education in Canada; The Knowledge Bank of Library Science as Indicated by Course Reading Lists in Canadian Library Schools," *IPLO Qtly.* (1976). **Activities:** 15, 26, 39; 62 **Addr.:** 11 Bain Ave., Toronto, ON M4K 1E5 Canada.

Schrader, Sr. Marion, (My. 22, 1928, St. Louis, MO) Hum. Catlgr., Asst. Prof. of Lib. Admin., Univ. of IL Lib., 1972–; Head libn., Cardinal Ritter Lib., St. Louis, 1970–72; Asst. Prof. of Classics, Notre Dame Coll., St. Louis, 1963–67; Prin., St. Alphonsus Sch., McComb, MS, 1958–63; Tchr., Sacred Heart Schs., New Orleans, 1948–58. **Educ.:** Notre Dame Coll., 1945–48, AB (Latin); Loyola Univ., New Orleans, 1948–58; St. Louis Univ., 1959–64, AM (Latin); Univ. of IL, 1967–69, MS (LS). **Orgs.:** ALA. Cath. LA. **Honors:** Beta Phi Mu, 1969. **Pubns.:** "Prospects for Change in Bibliographic Control," *Univ. of IL Lib. Staff Bltn.* (D. 1976). **Activities:** 1; 15, 20, 46; 55, 90 **Addr.:** 1405 W. Park St., Urbana, IL 61801.

Schrager, Benjamin M. (Jl. 15, 1943, St. Louis, MO) Lib. Srvs. Mgr., Addison-Wesley Publshg. Co., 1978–; Sales Mgr., Elsevier N. Holland Publshg. Co., 1973–77; Sales Rep., Acad. Press, 1971–73; Asst. Sales Mgr., Hayden Bk. Co., 1968–71. **Educ.:** Univ. of S. FL, 1961–65, BA (Hist.). **Orgs.:** ALA. SLA. Publshrs. Lib. Promo. Grp. **Pubns.:** Various sps. **Activities:** 6, 14; 17; 51 **Addr.:** Library Services Manager, Addison-Wesley Publishing Co., Reading, MA 01867.

Schramm, Betty V. (O. 17, 1923, St. Louis, MO) Asst. Dir., Lib. Srvs., 1981–; Supvsr. of Branches, St. Louis Cnty. Lib., 1974–80, Supvsr. of Readers' Srv., 1970–74, Supvsr. of Tech. Prcs., 1961–70, Supvsr. of Nat. Bridge Branch, 1960–61. **Educ.:** Washington Univ., 1964, BS (Eng.); Univ. of MO, 1972, MA (LS). **Orgs.:** ALA: Gvt. Docum. Com. (1973–). MO LA: Legis. Com. (1973–79); Gvt. Docum. Com. Coord. (1974–76); Treas. (1979–80). SLA: St. Louis Metro. Area, Secy. (1976–77), Pres. (1978–79). St. Louis Reg. Lib. Netwk.: VP (1978–79). **Addr.:** St. Louis County Library, 1640 S. Lindbergh Blvd., St. Louis, MO 63131.

Schramm, Jeanne Vannoy (Ag. 31, 1941, Wilmington, DE) Asst. Libn., Ref., W. Liberty State Coll., 1972–; Tchr., Chem., Triadelphia HS, 1967–68; Instr., Foods and Nutr., W. Liberty State Coll., 1965–67. **Educ.:** Univ. of DE, 1959–63, BS (Educ.); Univ. of TN, 1964–65, MS (Foods, Nutr.); Univ. of Pittsburgh, 1970–72, MLS. **Honors:** WV LA. **Pubns.:** "The Great Computer Hoax," *Lib. Lit. 6–the Best of 1975* (1975); "The Search for Chief Joseph," *WV Libs.* (Sum. 1979); "Don't You Care About the Future of Our Civilization?" *WV Libs.* (Sum. 1978); "Take What You Want - Return When Finished," *UNABASHD Libn.* (1976). **Activities:** 1; 31, 39 **Addr.:** Box 102, W. Liberty, WV 26074.

Schrank, H. Paul, Jr. (O. 21, 1927, Akron, OH) Vice-Ch., Bd. of Trustees, OCLC Online Comp. Lib. Ctr., Inc., 1980–; Univ. Libn., Univ. of Akron, 1965–80; Admin. Asst. to the Dir., GA Inst. of Tech. Libs., 1963–65. **Educ.:** OH Univ., 1946–49, BSC (Cmrce.); Univ. of IL, 1962–63, MS (LS). **Orgs.:** OH LA: Constn. Com. (1972); Legis. Com. (1971–72, 1976–80); Dev. Com. (1976–77) ALA: ACRL, Coll. Univ. Lib. Bldgs. Sect., Strg. Com.; Univ. Sect. (1978–81). SLA. ASIS. Netwk. Adv. Com. to Lib. Congs. (1980–). OH Coll. Lib. Ctr.: Trustee (1972–); Vice-Ch. (1972–75), Ch. (1975–80). Inter-Univ. Lib. Cncl. OH: (Ch., 1968–69). Various other orgs. **Honors:** OH Libn. of the Yr., 1978; Beta Phi Mu; Omicron Delta Kappa. **Activities:** 6, 14-Comp. based lib. srv. corp.; 17, 34 **Addr.:** OCLC Online Computer Library Center, 6565 Frantz Rd., Dublin, OH 43017.

Schreiber, Adrian H. (My. 4, 1943, Butler, PA) Dir., Ofc. Tech. Grp., Duffy, Inc., NY, 1981–; Mgr., Info. Srvs., NJ Educ. Comp. Netwk., Inc., 1978–81; Intern, Bell Telephone Labs., 1976–77; Intelligence Ofcr., U.S. Navy, 1966–76. **Educ.:** Rutgers Univ., 1961–65, BA (Hist.), 1976–78, MLS; Sch. of Grad. Std., Old Dominion Univ., 1974–75, Cert. (Strategy & Policy). **Orgs.:** ASIS: NJ Ctrl. Chap., Educ. Com. (Ch., 1979–). Assoc. Info. Mgrs.: Prog. Coord. (1980–). Assn. for Comp. Mach. Natl. Arts Club. **Pubns.:** Jt. auth., *BTL Software: The Published Record, 1966–1976* (1977); various sps., articles. **Activities:** 14-Comp. Netwk.; 26, 34, 37; 56, 62, 93 **Addr.:** 27 Landry Rd., Somerset, NJ 08873.

Schreiber, Marilyn P. (S. 14, 1937, Orange, NJ) Head of Branch, Northfield Branch Lib., 1978–; Ref. Libn., Wilmette Pub. Lib., 1977–78; Asst. Dir., Clearinghse. Adult Educ., 1976–77; Libn., ERIC Clearinghse. in Career Educ., 1974–76. **Educ.:** Kent State Univ., 1972, BA (Art Hist.); Univ. of TX, 1973, MLS. **Orgs.:** ALA. IL LA. **Pubns.:** Jt. auth., *Key Resources in Career Education* (1977); ed., *Directory of Vocational Information Resources in the United States* (1975); "Through the Clearinghouse," *Career Educ. Digest* (Ja.–F., Mr. 1974). **Activities:** 4, 9; 16, 21, 22 **Addr.:** Northfield Branch Library, 1785 Orchard Ln., Northfield, IL 60093.

Schreiber, Robert Edwin (My. 3, 1919, Oak Park, IL) Asst Prof., Head, Educ. Mtrls. Ctr. Libn., North. IL Univ. Libs., 1954–; Asst. Prof., Glassboro, NJ State Coll., 1953–54; Dir., AV Srv., Instr., Educ., Univ. of ME, Orono, 1949–53; Supvsr., Tchg. Aids, Mishawka Pub. Schs., 1947–49; Supvsr., AV Srvs., Stephens Coll., 1943–45. **Educ.:** Northwest. Univ., 1939–41, BS (Psy.); Univ. of IL, 1941–42, MS (Educ. Psy.); Univ. of Chicago, 1945–47, (AV Mtrls.); North. IL Univ., 1975, IL Cert. K-12 Media Spec. (LS). **Orgs.:** ALA. AECT. Amer. Film Inst. **Honors:** Phi Delta Kappa. **Pubns.:** *Building an Audio-Visual Program* (1946); *EFLA Redbook of Audio-Visual Equipment* (1949); "Visual Education," *Britannica Jr.* (1947–); "Audio-Visual Instruction," *New Stan. Encyc.* (1960–); various edshps., articles, mono. **Activities:** 1, 10; 15, 17, 32; 63, 67, 75 **Addr.:** University Libraries, Northern Illinois University, DeKalb, IL 60115.

Schremser, Robert F. (Ap. 19, 1942, Fort Wayne, IN) Consult. for Netwks. and Inst. Libs., AL Pub. Lib. Srv., 1977–81; Lib. Dir., Alexander City State Jr. Coll., 1971–77. **Educ.:** Univ. of WI, 1968–69, BS (Psy.), 1969–71, MLS; Auburn Univ. 1972–75, (Vocational Educ.); Univ. of NC at Chapel Hill, 1981, Doct. Student. **Orgs.:** ALA: Multitype Lib. Coop. Sect. (Secy., 1979–80); ACRL/Cmnty. and Jr. Coll. Sect. (1971–). AL LA: Plng. Com. (1974–76); Legis. Dev. Com. (Ch., 1977–78). AL Jr. Coll. LA: Pres. (1973–74). Natl. Educ. Assn. AL Educ. Assn. Amer. Vocational Assn. **Honors:** Beta Phi Mu, 1971. **Pubns.:** Jt. auth., "Binocular Coordination in Reading," *Jnl. Appld. Psy.* (Je. 1971); *Proceedings of Conference on the New ACRL-AECT-AACJC Guidelines for Two-Year College Learning Resources Programs* (1973). **Activities:** 1, 13; 17, 24, 34; 56, 63 **Addr.:** 103 Pinegate Cir., Apt. 11, Chapel Hill, NC 27514.

Schreyer, Alice D. (Ag. 7, 1947, New York, NY) Ref. Libn., Rare Bk. and Ms. Lib., Columbia Univ., 1975–; Libn., Oskar Diethelm Hist. Col., Cornell Med. Coll., 1975–75. **Educ.:** Barnard Coll., 1964–68, AB (Eng.); Yale Univ., 1968–69, MAT (Eng.); Emory Univ., 1971–75, PhD (Eng.); Columbia Univ., 1974–75, MS (LS). **Orgs.:** ALA: ACRL/Rare Bk. Mss. Sect. Amer. Prtg. Hist. Assn.: Prog. Ch. (1980–81); Trustee (1981–). Prtg. Hist. Socty. Grolier Club. Bibl. Socty. of Amer. **Honors:** Columbia Univ., Sch. of Lib. Srv., R. Krystyna Dietrich Awd. for Scholastic Excel., 1975. **Pubns.:** Ed., *The Centenary of John Masefield's Birth* (1978); "Scuffy, Tootles and Other Creations by Tibor Gergely," *Columbia Lib. Clmns.* (F. 1979); "Anthony Trollope as Novelist and Preacher," *Columbia Lib. Clmns.* (My. 1977); asst. ed., *Prtg. Hist.*; reviews. **Activities:** 1; 39, 45 **Addr.:** 180 West End Ave. Apt. 12C, New York, NY 10023.

Schriefer, Kent (D. 21, 1933, Schriever, LA) Head, Tech. Srvs., Univ. of CA Law Sch., 1972–; Asst. Dir., Libs., SUNY, Buffalo, 1957–72; Assoc. Libn., Univ. of CO Med. Sch., 1955–57; Head, Cat. Dept., Tulane Univ., 1950–55. **Educ.:** Univ. of MO, 1953–57, AB (Eng.); Univ. of CA, Berkeley, 1958–60, MLS (Libnshp.). **Orgs.:** AALL: Cat. Com. (1974–). Med. LA: Reprint Com. (1955–58). **Pubns.:** "Compact Book Storage: Mechanized Systems," *Lib. Trends* (Ja. 1971); "Reclassification at Berkeley," *Law Lib. Jnl.* (F. 1974); "Ballots at Boalt," *Law Lib. Jnl.* (Spr. 1980). **Activities:** 1; 15, 20, 46; 77, 78 **Addr.:** Law School Library, Boalt Hall, University of California, Berkeley, CA 94720.

Schrock, Nancy Carlson (O. 27, 1946, New York, NY) Bookbinder, Consult. on Lib. Cons., 1979–; Visual Cols. Libn., MA Inst. of Tech., Rotch Lib., 1976–78; Rare Bk. Libn., Winterthur Musm., 1972–75. **Educ.:** Brown Univ., 1964–68, AB (Art); Simmons Coll., 1970–71, MLS; Univ. of DE, 1973–77, MA (Art Hist.). **Orgs.:** Amer. Inst. for Cons. ARLIS/NA. MA Com. for the Prsrvn. of Archit. Recs.: Secy., Proj. Dir. (1978–). Amer. Prtg. Hist. Assn. Gld. of Bk. Workers. Socty. of Archit. Histns. **Honors:** Beta Phi Mu, 1971. **Pubns.:** *Records in Architectural Offices* (1980); introduction, bibl., index, *History of Wood Engraving in America 1882* (1976); "Joseph Andrews: A Swedenborgian Justification," *Winterthur Portfolio 12* (1977); Contrib., *Handbook on Picture Librarianship* (1981). **Activities:** 1; 23, 24, 45; 55 **Addr.:** 11 S. Crescent Circuit, Brighton, MA 02135.

Schroeder, Edwin M. (Je. 25, 1937, New Orleans, LA) Law Libn., Prof., Asst. Dean, FL State Univ. Coll. of Law, 1969–; Asst. Law Libn., Univ. of TX Law Lib., 1968–69; Asst. Prof., Univ. of CT Sch. of Law, 1965–68; Tchg. Fellow, Boston Coll. Law Sch., 1964–65. **Educ.:** Gregorian Univ., Rome, Italy, 1957–59, PhB (Phil.), 1959–61 (Theo.); Tulane Univ., 1961–64, JD (Law); FL State Univ., 1969–70, MS (LS). **Orgs.:** AALL: Stan. Com. (Ch., 1970–72); AV Com. (Vice-Ch., 1976–). Sect. on Legal Resrch. and Wrtg. (Ch., 1976); Southeast. Chap., Place. Com. (Ch., 1972–). ALA. SLA. Natl. Micro. Assn. **Honors:** Ord. of the Coif Legal Hon., 1964; Beta Phi Mu, 1970. **Pubns.:** Assignments, instr. manual *Fundamentals of Legal Research* (1977); ed., *FL Supreme Court Records and Briefs* (1974–); "Standards for Law Libraries," *Law Lib. Jnl.* (1971); reviews. **Activities:** 1, 12; 17, 19, 33; 77 **Addr.:** Florida State University, College of Law, Tallahassee, FL 32306.

Schroeder, Janet K. (Ja. 25, 1934, Two Rivers, WI) Dir. of Lib., Duluth Pub. Lib., 1977–, Asst. Dir., 1968–77, Head, Ref. and Adult Srv., 1965–68, Ref. and Gvt. Docum. Libn., 1963–65. **Educ.:** Univ. of WI, Madison, 1951–52, BA (Eng.); Univ. of MN, 1961–63 (Eng.), 1972–73, MALS. **Orgs.:** ALA. MN LA: Pres. (1977), VP (1976); MN Hum. Comsn. **Honors:** Beta Phi Mu, 1974. **Pubns.:** "Studying Popular Culture in the Public Library," *Drexel Lib. Qtly.* (Jl. 1980); "Little Bookie!...What Kind of Library," *MN Lib.* (Fall 1973). **Activities:** 9; 17 **Addr.:** 830 E. Second St., Duluth, MN 55805.

PROFESSIONAL ACTIVITIES: Institutions: 1. Acad. lib.; 2. Arch.; 3. Assn.; 4. Fed./Gvt. lib.; 5. Inst. lib.; 6. Mfr./Suppl.; 7. Milit. lib.; 8. Musm.; 9. Pub. lib.; 10. Sch. lib.; 11. Sch. of lib. sci.; 12. Spec. lib.; 13. State lib.; 14. (other). **Functions/Activities:** 15. Acq./Col. dev.; 16. Adult srvs.; 17. Admin.; 18. Apprais.; 19. Archit./Bldgs.; 20. Cat./Class.; 21. Chld. srvs.; 22. Circ.; 23. Cons./Pres.; 24. Consult.; 25. Cont. ed.; 26. Educ. lib. sci.; 27. Ext. srvs.; 28. Fund/Grants; 29. Gvt. pubs.; 30. Indx./Abs.; 31. Instr. lib. use; 32. Media srvs.; 33. Micro.; 34. Netwks./Coop.; 35. Persnl.; 36. PR; 37. Publshg.; 38. Recs. mgt.; 39. Ref. srvs.; 40. Repro.; 41. Resrch.; 42. Review.; 43. Secur.; 44. Serials; 45. Spec. col.; 46. Tech. srvs.; 47. Trustees/Bds.; 48. YA srvs.; 49. (other).

Schroeder, John Robert (N. 30, 1939, Ansley, NE) Head, Cat. Unit, Geo. Map Div., Lib. of Congs., 1977–; Head of Map Sect., U.S. Geol. Srvy. Lib., 1975–77; Map Catlgr., Geo. Map Div., Lib. Congs., 1969–75. **Educ.:** West. WA Univ., 1964–67, BA (Geo.); Univ. of WA, 1968–69, MLS. **Orgs.:** SLA: Geo. Map Div., Ch. (1980–), Ch.-Elect (1979–80); DC Chap., Geo. Map Div., Ch. N. Amer. Cartograph. Info. Socty.: Org. Com. (1980–). Assn. Can. Map Libs. West. Assn. Map Lib. Various other orgs. Assn. of Amer. Geographers: S.E. Div. OCLC Task Frc. on Map Cat.: Ch. (1976). **Pubns.:** Jt. auth., "Bibliographical Control of Geological Maps," *Geoscience Information: An International State-of-the Art Review* (1979); "Perspectives on Map Cataloging and Classification," *Lib. Trends* (Win. 1981). **Activities:** 4; 17, 20, 34; 70 **Addr.:** Library of Congress, Geography and Map Division, Washington, DC 20540.

Schroeder, Marvin (Ag. 14, 1932, Milwaukee, WI) VP, Treas., Inst. for Sci. Info., 1968–; Proj. Controller, Auerbach Assocs., 1966–68; Systs. Anal., The Singer Co., Diehl Div., 1965–66; Proj. Coord., Royal Typewriter Co., 1956–64. **Educ.:** Univ. of CT, 1950–54, BA (Gvt.), 1964–66, MBA. **Orgs.:** Info. Indus. Assn. ASIS. AAAS. Amer. Mgt. Assn. Assn. for Corporate Growth. **Activities:** 6; 17, 37; 59, 61, 76 **Addr.:** 3501 Market St., University City Science Center, Philadelphia, PA 19104.

Schroether, Marian R. (Ap. 5, 1919, Davenport, IA) Coord., Waukegan Pub. Lib., 1944–; Chld. Libn., Winona Pub. Lib., 1942–44. **Educ.:** Cornell Coll., 1937–41, BA (Eng.); West. Rsv. Univ., 1941–42, BS (LS, Chld. Libnshp.). **Orgs.:** IL LA: Chld. Lib. Sect. (Ch., 1950–51). ALA: Chld. Srvs. Div., Melcher Schol. Fund (Ch., 1955–56); Newbery-Caldecott Com. (1957–61, 1973–74); Bk. Eval. Com. (Ch., 1960–61). AAUW. Luth. Church Women. **Honors:** Phi Beta Kappa, 1941. **Pubns.:** "A Practical Approach to Book Selection," *IL Libs.* (S. 1961); "Promoting Reading For Fun," *IL Libs.* (N. 1966); consult., *Children's Catalog* (1954–); consult., *Index to Poetry for Children and Young People* (1965–). **Addr.:** Waukegan Public Library, 128 N. County St., Waukegan, IL 60085.

Schroyer, Helen Q. (Je. 7, 1924, Terre Haute, IN) Ref. Libn. for Gvt. Docum., Purdue Univ. Libs., 1978–, Docum. and Spec. Col. Libn., 1974–78, Arch. Spec., 1966–74; Tchr., Mt. Vernon HS, VA, 1953–54. **Educ.:** IN State Univ., 1941–43, 1945–46, BS (Math); Purdue Univ., 1966–71, MS (Media Sci.); Univ. of Denver, 1969–69, Cert. of Arch. Std. **Orgs.:** SLA: Gvt. Info. Srvs. Com. (1975–79); IN Chap. (Secy., 1979–80). ALA: GODORT. Tri Kappa Sorority. **Pubns.:** *Guide to a Course in Government Publications* occasional paper No. 135, Univ. of IL (1978); "Contributions to the Development of Management Thought," *Procs., Acad. of Mgt.* (1975); "What's Wrong with the Superintendent of Documents Classification System," *Docum. to the People* (1979); "Management and Use of U.S. Government Documents," *Procs.* SLA conf. (1976). **Activities:** 1 **Addr.:** Purdue University Libraries, West Lafayette, IN 47907.

Schuegraf, Ernst T. (S. 24, 1943, Bamberg, W. Germany) Assoc. Prof., St. Francis Xavier Univ., 1968–. **Educ.:** Univ. of Erlangen, (W. Germany, 1962–68, MSC (Math.); Univ. of AB, 1971–74, PhD (Comp. Sci.). **Orgs.:** ASIS. Can. Assn. Info. Sci.: Publ. Com. (Ch., 1975–77). Assn. for Comp. Mach. Can. Info. Prcs. Socty. **Pubns.:** Jt. auth., "Determination of the Number of Unambiguous Bit Matrices," *Intl. Jnl. of Comps. and Info Scis.* (S. 1977); "A Survey of Data Compression Methods for Non Numeric Records," *Can. Jnl. of Info. Sci.* (1977); "Compression of Large Inverted Files with Hyperbonic Term Distribution," *Info. Prcs. and Mgt.* (1976); "Query Processing in a Retrospective Document Retrieval System That Uses Word Fragments As Language Elements," *Info. Prcs. and Mgt.* (1976). **Activities:** 11; 24, 26, 41; 56, 63 **Addr.:** Box 55, St. Francis Xavier University, Antigonish, NS B2G 1C0 Canada.

Schuller, Carla N. Vasquez (O. 13, 1944, Dunsmuir, CA) Admin., Lewiston City Lib., 1978; Asst. Dir., El Paso Pub. Lib., 1974–76; Persnl. Libn., Sacramento City Cnty. Lib., 1971–74; Libn., Instr., Sacramento City Coll. Lib., 1969–71. **Educ.:** CA State Univ. 1963–66, BA (Eng.); Univ. CA, Berkeley, 1968–69, MLS; CA, Stan. Tchg. Cert.; Cmnty. Coll. Student Persnl. Worker Cert.; other certs. **Orgs.:** ALA. CA LA. ID LA. NLA. AAUW. **Activities:** 9; 17, 35, 36 **Addr.:** c/o Lewiston City Library, 428 Thain Rd., Lewiston, ID 83501.

Schuller, Nancy Shelby (Ag. 20, 1942, Austin, TX) Cur. of Visual Arts, Lectr., Dept. of Art, Univ. of TX, Austin, 1977–, Libn., 1967–77, Hum. Resrch. Assoc., 1965–67. **Educ.:** Univ. of TX, 1958–63, BFA (Art), 1964–69, MA (Art Hist.). **Orgs.:** ARLIS/NA: TX Chap., Pres., *The Medium* Ed. (1979–81). TX Conf. of Art Histns. Coll. Art Assn.: Prog. Dir. for Visual Resrcs. (1980–81); Acad. Sect., Stan. Com. (Ch., 1979–81). **Honors:** Phi Kappa Phi, 1967. **Pubns.:** Ed., *Guide for Management of Visual Resource Collections* (1979); "Conservation," *MA-CAA Slides and Photographs Nsltr.* (Fall 1979); "Report of MA-CAA Slide and Photograph Curators' Meeting," *Worldwide Art & Lib. Nsltr.* (Ja. 1974); "Slide Collections," *TX Lib. Jnl.* (S. 1971). **Activities:** 1, 14-Visual Resrcs.; 15, 17, 23; 55, 67 **Addr.:** University of Texas at Austin, Slide & Photo Collections, Department of Art, Fine Arts Bldg., Austin, TX 78712.

Schulte, Linda A. (My. 28, 1954, Santa Monica, CA) Dir., Law Lib., Southwest. Univ. Sch. of Law, 1980–, Head, Ref. Libn., 1978–80. **Educ.:** Univ. of CA, Irvine, 1972–76, BA (Art Hist.); Univ. of CA, Los Angeles, 1976–78, MLS; Southwest. Univ., 1979–, JD. **Orgs.:** AALL. South. CA Assn. of Law Libs. **Pubns.:** "A Survey of Computerized Legislative Information Systems," *Law Lib. Jnl.* (1979); "Computer Crime, a Bibliography," *Comp./Law Jnl.* (1980). **Activities:** 1, 12; 17, 39; 77, 78 **Addr.:** Southwestern University School of Law Library 675 S. Westmoreland Ave., Los Angeles, CA 90005.

Schulte, Sr. Teresa M. (Mr. 6, 1910, Jefferson City, MO) Libn., St. Alphonsus Sch. (Greendale, WI), 1971–; various positions in tchg. and admin. **Educ.:** De Paul Univ., 1930–42, BA (Educ.); Fordham Univ., 1956–61, MA (Educ.); Lang. Inst., Cuernavaca, Mexico, 1966–67; State WI, 1970–, Cert. (Libn.). **Orgs.:** WI LA. Cath. LA: Adv. Cncl. (1979–81). WI Cath. LA: Pres. (1979–81). Natl. Cath. Educ. Assn. **Activities:** 10; 21, 22, 35; 89 **Addr.:** 5085 S. Greenbrook Terr. #2101, Greenfield, WI 53220.

Schulte-Albert, Hans G. (Jl. 26, 1931, Gelsenkirchen, Westphalia, Germany) Assoc. Prof., Univ. West. ON, 1978, Asst. Prof., 1971–78; Supvsr., Shelflist Conversion Proj., Case West. Rsv. Univ., 1968–69, Sr. Cat. Libn., 1964–68, Catlgr., 1958–63. **Educ.:** Kent State Univ., 1951–56, BA (Grmn.), BS (Educ., Hist.); Case West. Rsv. Univ., 1956–65, MS (LS), MA (Hist.), 1966–72, PhD (LS). **Orgs.:** IFLA: Com. Lib. Theory Resrch. (1981–). Can. LA. ALA. ON LA. Can. Assn. Lib. Schs. AALS. Assn. of Can. Archvsts. **Honors:** Beta Phi Mu, 1957. **Pubns.:** "Classificatory Thinking from Kinner to Wilkins: Classification and Thesaurus Construction," *Lib. Qtly.* (Ja. 1979); "Cyprian Kinner and the Idea of a Faceted Classification," *Libri* (1974); "Gottfried Wilhelm Leibniz and Library Classification," *Jnl. of Lib. Hist.* (Ap. 1971); "Leibniz, Gottfried Wilhelm (1646–1716)," *ALA World Encyc. of Lib. and Info. Srv.* (1980). **Activities:** 11; 15, 20, 26; 62, 66, 92 **Addr.:** School of Library and Information Science, University of Western Ontario, London, ON N6A 5B9 Canada.

Schultz, Barbara A. (Pittsburgh, PA) Chief, Lib. Srv., VA Med. Ctr., Chillicothe, OH, 1977–; Patients Libn., VA Med. Ctr., Sepulveda, CA, 1975–76; Patients Libn., VA Med. Ctr., Denver, CO, 1970–75; Coord., Adult Srvs., Cuyahoga Cnty. Pub. Lib., 1968–69; Branch Libn., Prince George's Cnty. Meml. Lib., 1963–67. **Educ.:** Univ. of MD, 1957–61, BA (Hist.); Case West. Rsv. Univ., 1962–63, MSLS. **Orgs.:** Med. LA. Hlth. Sci. Comm. Assn. AAUW. Federally Employed Women. **Pubns.:** *Bicycles and Bicycling* (1979). **Activities:** 4, 12; 16, 17, 39; 80 **Addr.:** Library Service, (142D), VA Medical Center, 17273 State Rte. 104, Chillicothe, OH 45601.

Schultz, Charles R. (D. 6, 1935, Giddings, TX) Univ. Archvst., TX A&M Univ., 1971–; Libn., G. W. Blunt White Lib., Mystic Seaport, 1967–71, Keeper of Mss., 1963–67. **Educ.:** TX Luth. Coll., 1954–58, BA (Hist., Eng.); Bowling Green State Univ., 1958–60, MA (Hist.); OH State Univ., 1960–63, PhD (Hist.). **Orgs.:** SAA: Acq. PAG (Ch., 1979–81). Socty. of SW Archvsts.: VP (1976–78); Pres. (1978–80). Oral Hist. Assn.: Natl. Wkshp. (Ch., 1977). TX LA. TX State Hist. Assn. TX Assn. of Coll. Tchrs. **Pubns.:** *"Making Something Happen": Texas A&M University Libraries 1876–1976* (1979); *Life on Board American Sailing Ships during the 19th Century* (1977); "Erasmus Gest and the Cincinnati, Wilmington and Zanesville Railroad," *Railway Hist. Socty. Bltn.* (Aut. 1977); "Last Great Conclave of the Whigs," *MD Hist. Mag.* (D. 1968); "Glimpses into Cincinnati's Past: The Gest Letters, 1834–1842," *OH Hist.* (Sum. 1964); various other articles. **Activities:** 1, 2; 15, 45; 53, 85 **Addr.:** University Archives, Texas A&M University, College Station, TX 77843.

Schultz, Claire K. (N. 17, 1924, Etters, PA) Prof. Info. Sci. and Dir. of Libs., Med. Coll. of PA, 1972–; Freelnc. Consult., 1970–72; Inst. for the Advnc. of Med. Comm., Resrch. Sci., 1961–70; Sperry Rand UNIVAC, Sr. Syst. Anal., 1958–61; Merch, Sharp and Dohme, Libn., 1949–57; Visit. Assoc. Prof., Drexel Inst., 1962–70. **Educ.:** Juniata Coll., 1941–44, BS (Pre/Med.); Drexel Univ., 1949–52, MS (LS). **Orgs.:** ASIS: Pres. (1962); Prog. Com. (1954, 1961). SLA: Pharm. Sect. (Ch., 1954). Med. LA: Goals Com. (1978–). Assn. of Info. Mgrs. **Honors:** ASIS, Awd. of Merit, 1980. **Pubns.:** Ed., cmplr., *Thesaurus of Information Science Terminology* (1978); ed., *H.P. Luhn: Pioneer of Information Science* (1967); various articles. **Activities:** 1, 11; 24, 26, 41; 56, 75, 80 **Addr.:** Line Lexington, PA 18932.

Schultz, Erich R. W. (Je. 1, 1930, Rankin, ON) Univ. Libn. and Archvst., Wilfrid Laurier Univ., 1959–. **Educ.:** Waterloo Coll. 1947–51, BA; Waterloo Luth. Semy., ON, 1951–54, BD; Knox Coll., 1957–58, MTh; Univ. of Toronto, 1958–59, BLS. **Orgs.:** ON LA: Pres. (1968–69). Can. LA. ATLA: Pres. (1975–77). Assn. of Can. Archvst. Various other orgs. East. Can. Synod Luth. Church in Amer.: Archvst. Waterloo Hist. Socty.: 1st VP (1980–). **Pubns.:** Ed., *Vita Laudanda - Essays in Memory of Ulrich S. Leupold* (1976); transl., *Getting Along With Difficult People by Friedrich Schmitt* (1970); ed., *Ambulatio Fidei; Essays in Honour of Otto W. Heick* (1965). **Activities:** 1, 2; 17; 90 **Addr.:** Wilfrid Laurier University, Waterloo, ON N2L 3C5 Canada.

Schultz, Jon S. (My. 3, 1941, Hastings, NE) Dir. and Prof. of Law, Univ. of Houston, 1975–; Dir. and Assoc. Prof. of Law, Univ. of SC, 1972–75; Asst. Law Libn. and Asst. Prof. of Law, IN Univ., 1970–72; Asst. Prof. Law, OR State Univ., 1966–69. **Educ.:** Kearney State Coll., 1959–63, BA (Fr., Eng.); The Sorbonne, Univ. of Paris, 1962, Cert. (Fr.); Univ. of Denver, 1963–66, JD (Law); Univ. of WA, 1969–70, MLL (LS). **Orgs.:** AALL: Com. on Stans. (Ch., 1975–77); Com. on Exch. (Ch., 1973–75). Intl. Assn. of Law Libs. **Honors:** Beta Phi Mu, 1970. **Pubns.:** *Comparative Statutory Sources* (1978); jt. auth., *South Carolina Legal Research* (1976); ed., *Criminal Justice Systems Review* (1975); various articles, reviews. **Activities:** 1, 12; 17, 19, 24; 77 **Addr.:** University of Houston Law Library, 4800 Calhoun, Houston, TX 77004.

Schultz, Lois B. (O. 19, 1935, Cutchogue, NY) Lectr., Chld. Mtls. Srv., North. IL Univ., 1973– Asst. Prof., LS, Univ. of IL, 1964–72; Chld. Libn., Dayton Montgomery Cnty. Pub. Lib., 1961–63; Sch. Libn., Dansville Elem. Sch., 1957–61. **Educ.:** SUNY, Geneseo, 1953–57, BS (Educ., LS); Univ. of IL, 1963–64, MS (LS). **Orgs.:** ALA. IL LA. Luth. Church LA: Chicago Chap., VP (1980–81), Pres. (1981–82). **Activities:** 9, 10; 21, 32; 90 **Addr.:** 501 Andrus Rd., Downers Grove, IL 60516.

Schultz, Lois Eileen (Ap. 13, 1947, Monticello, KY) Head of Cat., North. KY Univ., 1978–; Catlgr., Xavier Univ., 1976–78; Catlgr., Thomas More Coll., 1974–76. **Educ.:** Univ. of KY, 1965–69, BS (Home Econ.), 1971–74, MSLS. **Orgs.:** ALA. KY LA. OH Valley Grp. of Tech. Srv. Libns.: Regis. Com., (Treas., Ch., 1981). Beta Phi Mu: Pres., Upsilon Chap. (1978). AAUP. AAUW. **Activities:** 1; 20 **Addr.:** W. Frank Steely Library, Northern Kentucky University, Highland Heights, KY 41076.

Schultz, Susan A. (D. 22, 1911, Mountain Lake, MN) Emeritus, Retired Dir. Lib. Srv., Asbury Theo. Semy., 1978–, Dir., 1949–78. **Educ.:** John Fletcher Coll., 1937–40, BA (Hist.); Northwest. Univ., 1944–45; Univ. IL, 1945–46, BLS, 1947–49, MLS. **Orgs.:** ATLA: Exec. Secy. (1967–71); Bd. Dirs. (1975–78). Wesleyan Theo. Socty. Withers Meml. Lib.: Bd. Trustees (1964–77), Assoc. Mem. (1980–). First Alliance Church: Exec. Com. (1956–76, 1981–). **Honors:** KY Lib. Trustee Assn., Outstan. Spec. Libn. Yr., 1967; Asbury Theo. Semy., Disting. Srv. Awd., 1973; Houghton Coll., Hon. Doctor Letters, 1974; Christ. Libn. Flwshp., Emily Russell Awd., 1974. **Activities:** 1; 17 **Addr.:** 308 Maxey, Wilmore, KY 40390.

Schulz, Elizabeth Lee (S. 21, 1944, Chicago, IL) Branch Libn., Boston Pub. Lib., 1978–, Adult Libn., 1977–78, Chld. Libn., 1973–77; Tchr., pvt. and pub. schs. in Boston, 1965–72. **Educ.:** Radcliffe Coll., 1960–64, BA (Hist.); Columbia Tchrs. Coll., 1964–65, MA (Hist.); Simmons Coll., 1972–73, MLS. **Orgs.:** ALA. MA LA. Cambridge Leag. of Women Voters: Bd., Voter Srv. Cambridge Elec. Comsn. **Honors:** Beta Phi Mu, 1973; ALA, JMRT, Shirley Olafson Meml. Awd., 1976. **Pubns.:** Ed., Boston Pub. Lib. Prof. Tri-Weekly Staff Assn. *Real Sheet* (1975–); Consult., WGBH ZOOM (1976–78). **Activities:** 9, 13; 16, 21, 24; 72, 74 **Addr.:** 295 Harvard St., Cambridge, MA 02139.

Schulze, Suzanne S. (Ja. 14, 1922, Detroit, MI) Docum. Libn., Univ. of North. CO, 1972–; Ref. Libn., Bryant Coll. of Bus., 1971–72. **Educ.:** Univ. of MI, 1940–44, BA (Pol. Sci.); Wayne Univ., 1946–47, MPA (Pub. Admin.); Univ. of RI, 1969–71, MLS. **Orgs.:** CO LA: Gvt. Docum. RT (Ch., 1977–78). ALA: GODORT, Educ. Task Frc. (Secy., 1979–80). Leag. of Women Voters. Amer. Cvl. Liberties Un. **Pubns.:** *Century of the Colorado Census* (1977); various articles. **Activities:** 1; 29 **Addr.:** Michener Library, University of Northern Colorado, Greeley, CO 80639.

Schulzetenberg, Anthony C. (O. 17, 1929, Melrose, MN) Prof., Lib. and AV Educ., St. Cloud State Univ., 1974–, Asst. Dean, Lrng. Resrcs., 1965–74; Instr., Pub. Sch., Ely, MN, 1956–65; Instr., Pub. Sch., Holdingford, MN, 1954–56. **Educ.:** St. John's Univ., MN, 1947–51, BA (Hist.); St. Cloud State Univ., 1960–65, MEd (Educ.); Univ. of MN, 1960–69, MA (LS); Univ. of ND, 1969–70, EdD (Higher Educ.). **Orgs.:** ALA: ACRL, Nonprint Ed. Bd. (1978–80). MN LA: Tech. Srvs. Div. (Ch., 1967). MN Educ. Media Org.: Pres.-Elect (1977–78); Pres. (1978–79). AECT: Tchr. Educ. Com. (Ch., 1979–81); Nom. and Elec. (1980–81). Phi Delta Kappa. **Pubns.:** Contrib., *Nonprint Media in the Academic Library* (1975); *The College Learning Resources Center* (1978). **Activities:** 1, 11; 17, 26, 41; 63, 89, 93 **Addr.:** Center for Library and Audiovisual Education, Saint Cloud State University, Saint Cloud, MN 56301.

Schumacher, Carolyn Sutcher (Jl. 8, 1933, Oak Park, IL) Proj. Dir., Arch. of Pittsburgh Bd. of Educ., 1981–; Instr., Hist., Asst. Dir., Arch. Prog., Duquesne Univ., 1979–81; Resrch. Assoc., Hist., Carnegie-Mellon Univ., 1977–80; Instr., Women's Std., Univ. of Pittsburgh, 1977–78. **Educ.:** Univ. of WI, 1951–52; Univ. of IL, 1952–54, BS (Educ.); Univ. of WA, 1955–58, MA (Hist.); Univ. of Pittsburgh, 1965–69 (LS), 1969–77, PhD (Hist.). **Orgs.:** SAA. Mid-Atl. Reg. Archvsts. Conf. Amer. Hist. Assn. Hist. of Educ. Socty. **Activities:** 2; 63 **Addr.:** 1212 Denniston St., Pittsburgh, PA 15217.

Special Subjects/Services: 50. Adult educ.; 51. Advert./Mktg.; 52. Aerosp.; 53. Agric.; 54. Area std.; 55. Arts/Hum.; 56. Autom.; 57. Bibl./Prtg.; 58. Bio. sci.; 59. Bus./Fin.; 60. Chem.; 61. Copyrt.; 62. Documtn.; 63. Educ.; 64. Engin.; 65. Env.; 66. Eth. grps.; 67. Film; 68. Food/Nutr.; 69. Geneal.; 70. Geo.; 71. Geol.; 72. Handcpd.; 73. Hist.; 74. Int. frdm.; 75. Info. sci.; 76. Insr.; 77. Law; 78. Legis.; 79. Math./Comp. sci.; 80. Med.; 81. Metals; 82. Nat. resrcs.; 83. Newsp.; 84. Nuc. sci.; 85. Oral hist.; 86. Petr./Energy; 87. Pharm.; 88. Phys./Astr./Math.; 89. Readg.; 90. Relig.; 91. Sci./Tech.; 92. Soc. sci.; 93. Telecom.; 94. Transp.; 95. (other).

Who's Who in Library and Information Services

Schuman, Patricia Glass (Mr. 15, 1943, New York, NY) Pres., Neal-Schuman Publshrs., Inc., 1976–; Sr. Acq. Ed., R. R. Bowker Co., 1973–76; Assoc. Ed., *Sch. Lib. Jnl.,* 1970–73; Asst. Prof., Acq. Libn., NYC Cmnty. Coll., 1966–70. **Educ.:** Univ. of Cincinnati, 1960–63, AB (Eng.); Columbia Univ., 1964–66, MS (LS). **Orgs.:** ALA: *ACRL News* Ed. Bd. (1980–); NY Conf. Lcl. Arrange. Com. (Ch., 1979–80); Cncl. (1971–79); Com. on Org. (1975–78); SRRT, Action Cncl. (Coord., 1970–71). NY LA: Int. Frdm. Com. (1970–74). CLENE. Women Lib. Workers. Various other orgs. Women's Natl. Bk. Assn. **Pubns.:** *Social Responsibility and Libraries* (1976); *Materials for Occupational Education: An Annotated Source Guide* (1971); "Becoming a Publisher," *What Else You Can Do With A Library Degree* (1980); "The Women Arisen," *Amer. Libs.* (Je. 1979); "Publishers of Library Science Books and Monographs," *Drexel Lib. Qtly.* (Ja. 1979); various other bks., articles. **Activities:** 1, 6, 14; 15, 25, 37; 61 **Addr.:** Neal-Schuman Publishers, 23 Cornelia St., New York, NY 10014.

Schur, Barbara S. (S. 16, 1928, New York, NY) Dir. of Lib., Brentwood Hosp., 1978–; Dir. of Lib., St. Alexis Hosp., 1972–78; Msc. Libn., Cleveland Heights-Univ. Heights Pub. Lib., 1963–72; Libn., Mt. Sinai Hosp., Cleveland, 1970–72; Libn., Allen Med. Lib., 1959–60; Msc. Libn., Chicago Pub. Lib., 1957–58; Patents Libn., Armour and Co., 1952–53. **Educ.:** Univ. of Cincinnati, 1946–49, AB (Eng.); Univ. of MN, 1950–51, BSLS; Med. LA Cert., 1962; Cincinnati Cnsvty. of Msc., 1948–50, (Msclgy.); Chicago Musical Coll., 1952–53 (Msclgy.). **Orgs.:** Med. LA of Northeast. OH: Pres. (1961–62); VP (1981–82); Biomed. Serials Com. (Ch., 1980–). Participating Lib. Adv. Com.: Ch. (1978–81). ALA. Med. LA. **Activities:** 5, 9; 15, 17, 39; 55, 80, 95 **Addr.:** Brentwood Hospital, 4110 Warrensville Center Rd., Cleveland, OH 44122.

Schuster, Ronald J. (Je. 15, 1939, Melrose, MN) Dir., Sandstone Vocational Sch., 1974–; Media Coord., 1972–74; Libn., MN State Reformatory, 1967–72; State Correct. Libn., MN Dept. of Corrections, 1972–. **Educ.:** St. Cloud State Univ., 1965–70, BA (Soclgy., Psy.), 1970–71, MS (Info. Media); Univ. of MN, Duluth, 1975–79, (Admin. Educ.). **Orgs.:** ALA: Lib. Srvs. to Prisoners (1978); Secur. Guidelines Com. (1979). Amer. Corrections Assn. ACA/ALA Jt. Com. (1974, 1977, 1979). Ofc. of Pub. Libs. and Interlib. Coop.: Adv. Cncl. (1973–78). AECT. Corrections Educ. Assn. Natl. Assn. of Vocational Educ. **Activities:** 5, 13; 16, 17, 24; 50, 63, 66 **Addr.:** Sandstone Vocational School, P.O. Box "P", Sandstone, MN 55072.

Schut, Grace W. (O. 17, 1922, New York, NY) Assoc. Dir., Pub. Srv., St. Peter's Coll., 1947–; Libn., NY Pub. Lib., 1945–47. **Educ.:** Hunter Coll., 1939–43, BA (Hist.); NY Univ., 1943–44, MA (Hist.); Columbia Univ., 1946–47, MLS, 1954–60 (Hist.). **Orgs.:** ALA: Various coms. Cath. LA: Various coms. NJ LA: Bibl. Hist. Com.; various coms. Metro. Cath. Coll. Libns.: Various coms. AAUP. Hunter Coll. Alum.: Schol. Welfare Fund; Bd. Dirs. AAUW. Various other orgs. **Honors:** NJ LA, Coll. Univ. Sect., Disting. Srv. Awd., 1972; Hunter Coll., Hall of Fame, 1977; St. Peter's Coll., Cent. Medal, 1972; St. Peter's Coll., Bene Merenti Medal, 1967. **Pubns.:** Jt. ed., *NJ and The Negro: A Bibliography 1715–1966* (1967); jt. ed., *Checklist for NJ Public Library Histories* (1979). **Activities:** 1; 17, 31, 39; 55, 57, 92 **Addr.:** 129 Pelton Ave., Staten Island, NY 10310.

Schuurman, Guy (Ag. 22, 1931, Utrecht, Holland) Dir., Salt Lake Cnty. Lib. Syst., 1971–; Dir., Weber Cnty. Lib., Ogden, UT, 1966–71; Chief Libn., UT State Lib., Div. for the Blind, 1961–66, Supvsr. of Tech. Srvs., 1959–60; Sch. Libn., Sonora HS, 1958–59. **Educ.:** Univ. of UT, 1953–58, BA (Hist.); Univ. of WA, 1960–61, MLS. **Orgs.:** UT LA: Exec. Secy. (1958–70); Pres. (1976). Mt. Plains LA. ALA. Amer. Socty. for Pub. Admin.: Bd. of Dirs. (1979–81). **Honors:** H. W. Wilson Co., Lib. PR Awd., 1974–75; UT LA, Disting. Srv. Awd., 1979. **Activities:** 9; 17, 19, 24; 51, 56, 75 **Addr.:** c/o Salt Lake County Library System, 2197 E. 7000 S., Salt Lake City, UT 84121.

Schwab, Bernard (N. 25, 1920, Brooklyn, NY) Dir., Madison Pub. Lib., 1957–; Asst. Dir., 1954–57; Chief, Ext. Dept., DC Pub. Lib., 1953–54, Actg. Chief, Acq. Dept., 1952–52, Srv. Expediter, 1952–52, Chief, Bus. and Econ. Div., 1950–52, Supvsr., Ctrl. Circ. Div., 1947–52. **Educ.:** Coll. of the City of New York, 1937–43, BSS (Econ.); Pratt Inst., 1946–47, BLS. **Orgs.:** ALA: Cncl. (1960–64). WI LA: Pres. (1966–67). Madison Area Lib. Cncl.: Pres. (1970–72, 1977). WI Cncl. for Lib. Dev.: Ch. (1973–74). **Honors:** WI LA, Libn. of the Yr., 1970. **Addr.:** Madison Public Library, 201 W. Mifflin St., Madison, WI 53703.

Schwalb, Ann Weiss (Jl. 17, 1949, Modena, Italy) Ref. Libn., Tredyffrin Pub. Lib., 1979–; Head, Chld. Dept., 1973–79; Sch. Libn., Akiba Day Sch., 1972–73. **Educ.:** Univ. of Rochester, 1967–71, BA (Lit.); Drexel Univ., 1971–73, MSLS. **Orgs.:** PA LA. ALA. **Pubns.:** "Puppets for loan," *Sch. Lib. Jnl.* (F. 1978); *Puppet Corner in Every Library* (1978); *Puppetry in Pre-School Education* (1980); *Puppetry and the Art of Story Creation* (1980). **Activities:** 9; 15, 32, 39; 63, 89, 95-Puppetry. **Addr.:** c/o Tredyffrin Public Library, 582 Upper Gulph Rd., Strafford, PA 19087.

Schwartz, Barbara A. (Ja. 5, 1950, Philadelphia, PA) Coord., Instr. Prog., Undergrad. Lib., Univ. of TX, 1979–, Instr. and Ref. Libn., 1978–79; Ref. Libn., Zahn Instr. Mtrls. Ctr., Temple Univ., 1974–78. **Educ.:** Temple Univ., 1968–71, BA (Soclgy.); Drexel Univ., 1973–74, MS (LS). **Orgs.:** ALA: ACRL/Bibl. Instr. Sect., Educ. for Bibl. Instr. Com. (1978–80); Policy and Plng. Com. (Secy., 1981–82). Women Lib. Workers. **Pubns.:** Jt. auth., "Hiring the Best Librarian," (1979); jt. auth., *Teaching Library Skills in Freshman English: An Undergraduate Library's Experience* (Univ. of TX Gen. Libs. (1981). **Activities:** 1; 25, 31, 39; 63, 92 **Addr.:** Undergraduate Library, The General Libraries, The University of Texas at Austin, Austin, TX 78712.

Schwartz, Carolyn S. (Candy) (D. 17, 1947, Toronto, ON) Asst. Prof., Simmons Coll., Sch. of Lib. and Info. Sci., 1980–; Sessional Lectr., McGill Univ., Sch. of LS., 1979–81; Cat. Libn., Concordia Univ., 1974–77. **Educ.:** McGill Univ., 1964–69, BA (Ling.), 1972–74, MLS; Syracuse Univ., 1977– (Info. Transfer). **Orgs.:** Can. LA. Can. Assn. Info. Sci. Amer. Socty. of Indxrs. ASIS. SLA. **Honors:** Montreal Chap. SLA, Awd., 1974; Beta Phi Mu. **Pubns.:** "Human-Assisted Thesaurus Generation," *ASIS Procs.* (1978); "Indexing Behavior," *ASIS Procs.* (1977); "Simules," *Jnl. of Educ. for Libnshp.* (Spr. 1977). **Activities:** 1; 20, 26, 30; 56, 75 **Addr.:** School of Library and Information Science, Simmons College, 300 The Fenway, Boston, MA 02115.

Schwartz, Diane G. (Jl. 24, 1941, Weehawken, NJ) Coord. User Educ., Alfred Taubman Med. Lib.; Assoc. Libn., Med. Ctr. Lib., Univ. of MI, 1978–; Head Ref. Libn., NY Botanical Garden Lib., 1973–78, Ref., Resrch. Libn., 1972–73, Archvst., Ms. Cat., 1970–72. **Educ.:** Douglass Coll., Rutgers Univ., 1959–63, AB (Pol. Sci., Hist.); Queens Coll., CUNY, 1971–72, MLS. **Orgs.:** SLA. Cncl. on Botanical and Horticult. Libs.: Nsltr. Ed. (1977–78). S. Ctrl. MI Hlth. Sci. LA. Mod. Lang. Assn. **Honors:** Beta Phi Mu, 1972. **Pubns.:** *Nutrition: A Selected Annotated Bibliography* (1980); *Adaptation; Guide to the Health Sciences Literature* bibl. (1979); *Rhododendrons; Selected annotated Bibliography* (1978); *Catalog of the Manuscript and Archival Collections and Index to the Correspondence of John Torrey* (1973); "The Indoor Gardener's Essential Library," *Good Housekeeping Mag.* (Ja. 1976); "Plant Pollution Reading List," *Grounds Maintenance* (My. 1973); various bibls., articles. **Activities:** 1, 12; 15, 31, 39; 58, 80, 82 **Addr.:** Alfred Taubman Medical Library, University of Michigan, Ann Arbor, MI 48109.

Schwartz, Eleanor Elving (Je. 15, 1920, Bronx, NY) Coord., Lib./Media Prog., Assoc. Prof., Kean Coll. of NJ, 1971–, Ch., LS Dept., 1967–71, Adj. Fac., 1964–67; Libn. in Charge of Sch. Libs., Newark Bd. of Educ., 1966–67, Admin., 1952–66; Head, Lib./AV Ctr., S. Side High, Newark, 1953–63; Elem. Libn., Dayton St. Sch., Newark, 1952–53; AV Libn., Newark Bd. of Educ. 1949–51. **Educ.:** Douglass Coll., 1938–42, BA (Eng., LS); Rutgers Univ., 1961–63, MLS, 1963–64, (LS); various crs. **Orgs.:** ALA: AASL, Bibl. Com. for N.D.E.A., Title III (1959). NJ LA: PR Com. (1979–80); Nat. Lib. Week Com. (1978–79); Lib. Educ. Com. (1974–76). Educ. Media Assn. of NJ: Int. Frdm. Com. (1975–76); Exec. Bd. (1974–75). Newark Sch. Libns. Assn.: Pres. (1965–66). Various other orgs. Jewish Pubn. Socty. of Amer. NJ Hist. Socty. AAUP. Amer. Assn. for Higher Educ. Various other orgs. **Pubns.:** Contrib., *American Reference Books Annual* (1975–); "The New Copyright Law," *Infokineticator* (N.D. 1976); "Developing Methods of Inquiry," *Sch. Media Qtly.* (Spr. 1975); Ed., "Mediaviews," *NJEA Review* (1973–); "That Terrible Ten-Letter Word," *Lib. Scene* (Sum. 1972); various other bks., articles, radio and TV progs. **Activities:** 1, 10, 14; 26, 32, 42; 66, 67, 95-TV. **Addr.:** Library/Media Program, Department of Communication Sciences, Kean College of New Jersey, Union, NJ 07083.

Schwartz, Gloria Duckman (N. 12, 1926, New York, NY) Media Spec., Jupiter Mid. Sch., 1978–; Libn., FL Atl. Univ., 1977–78; Media Spec., Palm Beach Cnty. Schs., 1975–77. **Educ.:** Queens Coll., 1943–46, 1967–69, BA (Educ.), 1969–71, MLS. **Orgs.:** ALA. FL LA. Educ. Media Assn. AAUW. **Activities:** 10; 15, 20, 21 **Addr.:** Apt. M1-205 1605 U.S. Hwy. #1, Jupiter, FL 33458.

Schwartz, Helen (N. 29, 1924, Scranton, PA) Libn., Frederick Douglass Instr. Mtrls. Ctr., 1972–; Asst. Head, Ctrl. Chld. Dept., Free Lib. Philadelphia, 1971–72, Catlgr., 1968–71; Libn., Conwell Mid. Sch. (Philadelphia), 1967–68. **Educ.:** Waynesburg Coll., 1942–44, 1946–48 BA, magna cum laude (Eng.); PA State Univ., 1949–50; Drexel Univ., 1968, MLS. **Orgs.:** ALA. PA Sch. Libns. Assn.: Legis. Com. (1977); Mem. Com. (1975). Assn. Philadelphia Sch. Libns.: Mem. Com. (1981); Treas. (1980). AECT. PA Lrng. Resrc. Assn. Natl. Assn. Propagation and Prsrvn. Storytel. **Honors:** Beta Phi Mu, 1969; Phi Alpha Theta, 1948. **Addr.:** 1458 Higbee St., Philadelphia, PA 19149.

Schwartz, Irving Lloyd (Mr. 1, 1919, Brooklyn, NY) Assoc. Prof., Sinclair Cmnty Coll., 1979–; Chief of Protocol, Aeronautical Systs. Div., U.S. Air Frc., 1950–79. **Educ.:** Univ. of Dayton, 1939–42, BA (Hist.); Miami Univ., 1947–49, MA (Hist.); Univ. of Florence, 1946–47, Dip. **Orgs.:** Dayton and Montgomery Cnty. Lib. Syst. Bd. of Trustees. ALA: Int. Frdm. Com. (1978–79). City of Dayton Plng. Bd. Aviation Hall of Fame: Exec. **Honors:** U.S. Air Frc., Excep. Civilian Srv. Awd., 1973, 1975, 1979. **Pubns.:** *Dayton, Ohio During the Civil War* (1946). **Activities:** 1, 9; 36; 83, 85, 91 **Addr.:** 2033 Burroughs Dr., Dayton, OH 45406.

Schwartz, James H. (Cleveland, OH) Fncl. Info. Anal., Bank of Amer., 1980–, Lib. Supvsr., 1978–80; Mgr., Lib. Srvs., Dynapol, 1972–78; Info. Sci., Celanese Corp., 1969–72. **Educ.:** Marietta Coll., BS (Chem.); Univ. of Santa Clara, MBA (Fin.). **Orgs.:** SLA. Amer. Chem. Socty. **Pubns.:** "Factors Affecting the Comparison of Special Libraries," *Spec. Libs.* (Ja. 1980); "Improving the Image of the Special Library," *Spec. Libs.* (D. 1980); "What Has Been Published? — More Patents than Journal Literature," *Jnl. Chem. Educ.* (1976); "A Union List of Books on Toxicology," *Spec. Libs.* (Mr. 1976); "Technical Books: Appraisal of Selection Policy and Use by Creative Chemists," *Spec. Libs.* (F. 1974); various articles. **Activities:** 12; 17, 39, 41; 59, 60, 91 **Addr.:** Corporate Electronic Banking Administration, Bank of America, Box 37000, San Francisco, CA 94137.

Schwartz, Joan (O. 14, 1928, New York, NY) Lib. Promo. Mgr., Cambridge Univ. Press, 1976–. **Educ.:** IN Univ., 1945–49, AB (Tex. Merch.); Manhattanville Coll., 1967–70, MAT (Eng.). **Orgs.:** ALA. Women's Natl. Bk. Assn. Common Cause. **Activities:** 6; 37, 49-Lib. Promo. **Addr.:** Cambridge University Press, 510 North Ave., New Rochelle, NY 10801.

Schwartz, Joan M. (Je. 7, 1951, Brooklyn, NY) Photo-archvst., Natl. Photography Col., Pub. Arch. of Can., 1977–. **Educ.:** Univ. of Toronto, 1969–73, BA (Geo.); Univ. of BC, 1973–77, MA (Geo.). **Orgs.:** Assn. of Can. Archvsts. Can. Assn. of Geo. **Honors:** Can. Cncl., Explorations Grant, 1979. **Pubns.:** "Beyond the Gallery and the Archives," *Acadiensis,* (Spr. 1981); contrib. ed., *Photo Communique;* "The Photograph as Historical Record: Early British Columbia," *Jnl. of Amer. Culture,* (Spr. 1981); "Double Vision: The Stereo Views of James Esson," *Photo Communiqué* (Mr. Ap. 1979); "G.R. Fardon, Photographer of Early Vancouver Island," *Afterimage* (D. 1978); "The Photographic Record of Pre-Confederation British Columbia," *Archivaria* (Win. 1977–78). **Activities:** 2; 15, 41; 73, 95 **Addr.:** National Photography Collection, Public Archives of Canada, 395 Wellington St., Ottawa, ON K2P 0Z6 Canada.

Schwartz, S. Arlene (Ag. 27, 1947, Atlanta, GA) Mgr., ILLINET Bibl. Data Base Srv., IL State Lib., 1978–, Coord. for Fld. Srvs., 1975–78, Head, Serials Sect., 1974–75; Instr., Ctrl. Tech. Prcs., Miami-Dade Cmnty. Coll., 1969–78. **Educ.:** Emory Univ., 1965–68, BA (Grmn.), 1968–69, MLn. **Orgs.:** ALA: Cncl. (1981–85); ASCLA; ERT; ACRL; JMRT; LITA; RTSD. IL OCLC Users Grp.: Exec. Bd. (1976–). Cncl. of Computerized Lib. Netwks. OCLC Users Cncl.; Secy. (1979–80); VP (1980–81). IL Bd. of High Educ. Lib. Task Frc.: Subcom. on Circ. Systs. (1977–79). **Pubns.:** "OCLC Services: A Vehicle for Cooperation in Illinois," *IL Libs.* (S. 1979). **Activities:** 1, 13; 17, 34, 46; 56, 63 **Addr.:** Illinois State Library, ILLINET Bibliographic Data Base Service, Centennial Bldg., Springfield, IL 62756.

Schwartz, Steven M. (Jl. 12, 1938, Detroit, MI) Sr. VP, Dir. Mktg., Franklin Watts Inc., 1976–, Natl. Sales Mgr., 1973–76; Sales Rep., McGraw-Hill, 1967–72. **Educ.:** Univ. of Detroit, 1957–60; Wayne State Univ., 1960–61, BS (Educ.), 1962–65, MA (Educ.); Inst. for Human Potential, 1971, Cert.; Pace Univ., 1979–, MBA (Exec. Mgt.). **Orgs.:** ALA: ERT, Bd. of Dirs. Amer. Mgt. Assn. NY Mktg. Assn. NY Bk. Leag. Amer. Mktg. Assn. **Activities:** 14-Publshr.; 17, 25, 37; 50, 51 **Addr.:** Franklin Watts Inc., 730 5th Ave., New York, NY 10019.

Schwarz, Betty P. (S. 25, 1940, Brooklyn, NY) Info. Sci., Calgon Corp., 1980–; Libn., Info. Spec., Alcoa Labs., 1973–80; Info. Chem., Shell Chem. Corp., 1968–71. **Educ.:** Chestnut Hill Coll., 1958–62, BS (Chem.); Villanova Univ., 1965, MS (Chem.); Univ. of Pittsburgh, 1973, MS (LS). **Orgs.:** ASIS: Pittsburgh Chap., Ch.-Elect (1980–81), Ch. (1981–82). SLA: Awds. Com. (Ch., 1976); Liason to Pittsburgh Reg. Lib. Ctr. (1979–81). Amer. Chem. Socty. **Pubns.:** Adv. com., *PA Union List of Serials* (1981). **Activities:** 12; 20, 39, 46; 60, 65, 91 **Addr.:** Calgon Corp., Information Center, P.O. Box 1346, Pittsburgh, PA 15230.

Schwarz, Philip J. (Je. 13, 1940, Mazomanie, WI) Spec. Asst. to Autom. and Micro. Libn., Univ. of WI, 1975–, Autom. Coord., 1971–74, Serials Libn., 1968–74, Actg. Circ. and Serials Libn., 1967–68; Pub. Srvs. Libn., Univ. of Puget Snd., 1963–67. **Educ.:** Univ. of WI, 1958–62, BS (Hist.); Univ. of Denver, 1962–63, MA (LS); Univ. of WI, 1968–75, MS (Media Tech.). **Orgs.:** Natl. Micro. Assn. WI LA. WI Assn. of Acad. Libns. **Honors:** Cncl. on Lib. Resrcs., Flwshp., 1976. **Pubns.:** "COM: Decisions and Applications in a Small University Library," ERIC (Jl. 1977); ed., *Wisconsin Public Documents: Cumulated Keyword Title and Personal Author Index* (1974); ed., *Wisconsin Public Documents: Cumulated Keyword Title and Personal Author Index, 1968–1973* (1975); ed., *University of Wisconsin System Videotape Catalog* (1975); cmplr., *Conversion of Periodical Holdings to Microform: A Rating Form* ERIC (Jl. 1973); various mono., articles. **Activities:** 1; 17, 24, 33; 56 **Addr.:** Rte. 1, Box 214, Menomonie, WI 54751.

Schwarzkopf, LeRoy C. (D. 9, 1920, Sebewaing, MI) Head, Docum., Maps Unit, Univ. of MD Libs., 1977–, Gvt. Do-

PROFESSIONAL ACTIVITIES: Institutions: 1. Acad. lib.; 2. Arch.; 3. Assn.; 4. Fed./Gvt. lib.; 5. Inst. lib.; 6. Mfr./Suppl.; 7. Milit. lib.; 8. Musm.; 9. Pub. lib.; 10. Sch. lib.; 11. Sch. of lib. sci.; 12. Spec. lib.; 13. State lib.; 14. (other). **Functions/Activities:** 15. Acq./Col. dev.; 16. Adult srvs.; 17. Admin.; 18. Apprais.; 19. Archit./Bldgs.; 20. Cat./Class.; 21. Chld. srvs.; 22. Circ.; 23. Cons./Pres.; 24. Consult.; 25. Cont. ed.; 26. Educ. lib. sci.; 27. Ext. srvs.; 28. Fund/Grants; 29. Gvt. pubs.; 30. Indx./Abs.; 31. Instr. lib. use; 32. Media srvs.; 33. Micro.; 34. Netwks./Coop.; 35. Persnl.; 36. PR; 37. Publshg.; 38. Recs. mgt.; 39. Ref. srvs.; 40. Repro.; 41. Resrch.; 42. Review.; 43. Secur.; 44. Serials; 45. Spec. col.; 46. Tech. srvs.; 47. Trustees/Bds.; 48. YA srvs.; 49. (other).

cum. Libn., 1967–77. **Educ.:** Yale Univ., 1940–43, BA (Hist.); Univ. of MI, 1949–51, MA (Educ.); Rutgers Univ., 1966–67, MLS. **Orgs.:** ALA: GODORT, Fed. Docum. Task Frc., Secy. (1973–75), Coord. (1975–77), Clearinghse. Ch. (1977–79); Map and Geo. RT. AALL: Gvt. Docum. Com. (1975–76). DC LA: Gvt. Docum. Interest Grp. MD LA: Gvt. Docum. Div. Various other orgs. The Retired Ofcrs. Assn. **Honors:** Beta Phi Mu, 1967. 5th Anl. CIS/Godort/ALA Docum. to the People, Awd., 1981. **Pubns.:** *Pricing of GPO Sales Publication* (1976); *Regional Libraries and the Depository Library Act of 1962* (1972); "The Depository Library Program and Access by the Public to Official Publications of the U.S. Government," *Gvt. Pubns. Review* (1978); "The Monthly Catalog and Bibliographic Control of U.S. Government Publications," *Drexel Lib. Qtly.* (Ja.–Ap. 1974); ed., *Documents to the People* (1978–); various articles. **Activities:** 1; 29; 70, 78 **Addr.:** University of Maryland Libraries, College Park, MD 20742.

Schwass, Earl R. (D. 26, 1920, Muskegon Heights, MI) Lib. Dir., Nvl. War Coll., 1970–; Asst. Dean, Univ. of RI Ext. Div., 1967–68; Asst. Dir., Coll. of Nvl. Cmnd., Nvl. War Coll., 1963–67. **Educ.:** Northwest. Univ., 1938–42, BA (Eng. Lit.); Georgetown Univ., 1946–49, JD (Law); Univ. of RI, 1969–70, MLS. **Orgs.:** ALA. RI LA: Persnl. Com. (Ch., 1979–). Cnsrtm. of RI Acad. and Resrch. Libs.: Ch. (1978–). SLA. Various other orgs. **Honors:** Phi Beta Kappa, 1942; Cncl. on Lib. Resrcs., Flwshp., 1975. **Activities:** 1; 17, 34, 35; 74 **Addr.:** Naval War College, Newport, RI 02840.

Schweizer, Linda S. (Ja. 30, 1950, Detroit, MI) Asst. Bus. Libn., MI State Univ., 1978–; Urban Policy and Plng. Libn., 1977–78; Tech. Srvs. Libn., Thomas M. Cooley Law Sch. Lib., 1973–77. **Educ.:** MI State Univ., 1968–72, BA (Amer. Std.); Univ. of MI, 1972–73, AMLS; AALL, 1979, Cert. **Orgs.:** MI Assn. of Law Libs.: VP (1977–78); Pres. (1978–79). MI LA: Legis. Com. (1979–). OH Reg. Assn. of Law Libs. AALL. **Pubns.:** "Directory of Michigan Law Libraries," *MI State Bar Jnl.* (N. 1977). **Activities:** 1, 12; 31, 39, 46; 51, 59, 77 **Addr.:** Business Library, Eppley Center, Michigan State University, East Lansing, MI 48824.

Schweizer, Susanna (Je. 19, 1949, Yonkers, NY) Asst. Prof., Grad. Sch. of Lib. and Info. Sci., Simmons Coll., 1980–; Tchg. Fellow, Interdisciplinary Dept. of Info. Sci., Univ. of Pittsburgh, 1976–79; Libn., Yonkers Pub. Lib., 1971–75. **Educ.:** SUNY, 1967–71, BA (Hist.); Columbia Univ., 1971–73, MS (LS); Univ. of Pittsburgh, 1975–78, MSIS; PhD cand. **Orgs.:** ASIS. New Eng. OLUG: Mgt. Com. **Honors:** Phi Beta Mu, 1973. **Pubns.:** Jt. auth., *A Directory of Automated Systems for Career Planning and Placement Offices* (1979); jt. auth., *Online Bibliographic Searching: A Learning Manual.* **Activities:** 9, 11; 24, 26, 41; 56, 75, 93 **Addr.:** 10 Dennis Dr., Burlington, MA 01803.

Schwenke, Eszter L. K. (D. 26, 1937, Lèva, Bars/Hont, Hungary) Head Libn., Sci. Lib., Univ. of NB, 1980–; Head, Msc. Sect., York Reg., Fredericton, NB, 1978–80; Asst. and Ref. Libn., Macdonald Coll. Lib., McGill Univ., 1973–77; Head, Tech. Srvs., Vanier Coll., CEGEP, 1970–72; Catlgr., McGill Med. Lib., 1962–64. **Educ.:** McGill Univ., 1958–61, BA, 1962, BLS. **Orgs.:** Can. LA. Széchényi Socty. Univ. of NB Assn. of Libns. **Pubns.:** Various bk. reviews, *Daily Gleaner.* **Activities:** 1, 9; 17, 20, 39; 58, 60, 91 **Addr.:** 171 Saunders St., Fredericton, NB E3B 1N4 Canada.

Schwerin, Kurt (Ap. 17, 1902, Beuthen, Oberschlesien, Germany) Prof. of Law Emeritus, Law Libn. Emeritus, Northwest. Univ., 1970–, Prof. of Law, Law Libn., 1972–73, 1964–70, Head, Frgn. and Intl. Law Sects., 1948–64; Dept. Head, Univ. of VA Law Lib., 1946–48; Catlgr., Columbia Univ. Law Lib., 1942–46. **Educ.:** Univ. of Breslau, Germany, 1930–34; New Sch. for Soc. Resrch., 1940, MSSc; Columbia Univ., 1943, BSLS, 1955, PhD (Hist.). **Orgs.:** AALL: Frgn. Law Com. (Ch., 1957–63); Intl. Assn. of Law Libs.: Bd. of Dirs. (1965–71); AALL Rep. (1960–70). Excerpta Criminologica, Amsterdam: Ed. Bd. (1961–64). Leo Baeck Inst.: Bd. of Dirs. (1972–). Amer. Frgn. Law Assn.: Chicago Chap. (Pres., 1963–68). Selfhelp of Chicago, Inc.: Bd. of Dirs. (1967–). **Honors:** AALL, Ford Fndn. Grant, 1957–58. **Pubns.:** *Bibliographie rechtswissenschaftlicher Schriftenreihen* (1978); *Classification for International Law and Relations* (1969); "German Compensation for Victims of Nazi Persecution," *Northwest. Univ. Law Review* (S.–O. 1972); "Foreign Law Selection and Acquisition: Sources and Problems," *Law Lib. Jnl.* (F. 1970); "Foreign Legal Periodicals in American Law Libraries," *Law Lib. Jnl.* (My. 1961). **Activities:** 1, 12; 17, 20, 41; 57, 77, 92 **Addr.:** Northwestern University School of Law, 357 E. Chicago Ave., Chicago, IL 60611.

Schwob, Elizabeth W. (S. 11, 1923, Edmonton, AB) Head, Circ. Srvs. & Undergrad. Lib., Univ. of AB, 1980–, Head, Undergrad. Lib., 1974–80, ILL Libn., 1970–74, Asst. Ref. Libn., 1969–70. **Educ.:** Univ. of AB, 1941–44, BA, 1968–69, BLS. **Orgs.:** Can. LA. ALA. LA of AB: Secy. (1972). **Pubns.:** "Library Program Shows 'Gratifying' Results," *Feliciter* (F. 1977). **Activities:** 1; 17, 31, 39 **Addr.:** Cameron Library, The University of Alberta, Edmonton, AB T6G 2J8 Canada.

Scilken, Marvin (D. 7, 1926, New York, NY) Lib. Dir., Orange Pub. Lib., 1963–. **Educ.:** Univ. of CO, 1944–48, BA (Econ.); Pratt Inst., 1959–60, MLS. **Orgs.:** NJ LA: Exec. Bd. ALA: Various coms. Lib. PR Cncl.: Pres., Exec. Bd. Various other orgs. Beta Phi Mu: Pratt Chap., Pres., Exec. Bd. **Pubns.:** Ed., publshr., *The UNABASHED Libn.* contrib., *Farewell to Alexandria* (1976); contrib., *Best of Library Literature* (1977); contrib., *Nature and The Future of the Catalog* (1979). **Activities:** 9; 15, 17, 20 **Addr.:** General PO Box 2631, New York, NY 10001.†

Sclar, Herbert (N. 3, 1931, Brooklyn, NY) Pres., Updata Pubns., Inc., 1973–; Consult., Lockheed Dialog, 1973–77; Consult., Holt Info. Systs., 1971–73; Dir., Comp. Info. Systs., CCM Info., 1968–71. **Educ.:** Brooklyn Coll., 1955–61, BA (Eng.); New Sch. for Soc. Resrch., 1961–64, AAS (Info. Prcs.). **Orgs.:** ASIS: Conf. Exhibits Ch. (1980). SLA: South. CA Chap. (Advert. Mgr., 1979–80). Tech. Transfer Assn. Natl. Micro. Assn. various other orgs. **Pubns.:** *Libraries and Microforms* (1975); "Think Small," *Careers* (1977). **Activities:** 6; 29, 33, 37; 56, 75, 91 **Addr.:** Updata Publications Inc., 1756 Westwood Blvd., Los Angeles, CA 90024.

Scofield, James Steve (S. 26, 1928, Cincinnati, OH) Chief Libn., St. Petersburg Times and Evening Indp., 1962–; Dir., FL Suncoast Publshrs., 1960–62. **Educ.:** Univ. of IL, 1954, BS, with hons. (Jnlsm.); Amer. Press Inst. Newsp. Lib. Sem., 1967, Cert. **Orgs.:** SLA: Div., Intl. Ch. (1970–71). Autom. Com. (Ch., 1979–80). ASIS. FL LA. Grk. Orthodox Archdio. of N. and S. Amer.: Cncl. (1970–72; 1974–). Grk. Orthodox Archdio. Press: Pubn. Bd. (Secy., 1971–72); Adv. Bd. (1974–). Ord. of Ahepa. **Honors:** SLA, Newsp. Div., Awd. of Merit, 1971; Silver Key Awd. to the City of Athens, Greece, 1968. **Pubns.:** "Where the Past Is Prologue: Library Has 'Tomorrow Look'," *Ed. and Publshr. Mag.* (O. 25, 1969); "Public Service," *Guidelines For Newspaper Libraries* (1974); ed., *Basic Specifications for a Full–Text Online Automated Newspaper Library System* (1980). **Activities:** 12; 17, 24, 41; 56, 83 **Addr.:** Times - Independent, P. O. Box 1121, St. Petersburg, FL 33731.

Scoles, Clyde S. (Ap. 14, 1949, Columbus, OH) Asst. Dir., Toledo-Lucas Cnty. Pub. Lib., 1978–; Dir., Zanesville Pub. Lib., 1974–78; Consult., Legis. Ref. Statehse., OH, 1972–77; Libn., Columbus Pub. Lib., 1971–74. **Educ.:** OH State Univ., 1967–71, BS (Soc. Sci.); Univ. of MI, 1972, AMLS; Miami Univ., 1976 (Lib. Exec. Prog.). **Orgs.:** OH LA: Legis. (1975–78); Lib. Dev. (1978–; Ch., 1981–). ALA: PLA, Legis. (1980–83). Rotary. Amer. Socty. Pub. Admin. **Honors:** Zanesville Jaycees, Man of Year, 1976. **Pubns.:** *A Survey of the Business Community—Columbus Public Library* (1974); "The LRB, a service to Legislators," *OH LA Bltn.* (Ap. 1974). **Activities:** 9; 17, 32, 47; 59, 78, 93 **Addr.:** 325 Michigan, Toledo, OH 43–.

Scollard, Robert Joseph (Ag. 15, 1908, Toronto, ON) Archvst., Univ. of St. Michael's Coll., 1975–, Per. Libn., 1969–75; Libn., St. Basil's Semy., Toronto, 1968–69, Secy. Gen., The Basilian Fathers, Toronto, 1954–68; Libn., St. Basil's Semy.; Libn., Pontifical Inst. of Medvl. Std., 1932–51. **Educ.:** Univ. of Toronto, 1924–28, BA (Gen.), 1938–39, BLS; Univ. of MI, 1939–41, AM (LS); ON Coll. of Educ., 1929–30, HS Tchrs. Cert.; St. Basil's Semy., 1929–33, (Theo.). **Orgs.:** ON LA: Cat. Grp. Can. LA: Resol. and Nom. Com. ALA. Cath. LA. Can. Cath. Hist. Assn.: Secy. (1970–73). Assn. of Can. Archvsts. Toronto Area Archvsts. Grp. **Honors:** Can. Cath. Hist. Assn., Clerk Medal, 1975. **Pubns.:** *Dictionary of Basilian Biography, 1822–1968* (1969); *A Calendar of the Deceased Bishops and Priests of the Archdiocese of Toronto* (1975); contrib., *New Catholic Encyclopedia* (1967); contrib., *Dictionary of Canadian Biography* (1972); "A List of Photographic Reproductions of Mediaeval Manuscripts in the Library of the Pontifical Institute of Mediaeval Studies," *Medvl. Std.* (1942); various edshps. **Activities:** 1, 2; 15, 17, 20; 55, 90 **Addr.:** 50 St. Joseph St., Toronto, ON M5S 1J4 Canada.

Scollie F. Brent (Ap. 20, 1940, Thunder Bay, ON) Chief Libn., Resrc. Econ. Lib., Dept. of Energy, Mines and Resrcs., 1980–; Head, Per. Sect., Natl. Lib. of Can., 1977–80, Chief, Can. Theses Div., 1976–77, Cat. in Pubn. Proj. Ofcr., 1975–77, Subj.-Anal. Reviewer, 1973–75; Asst. Prof., LS, Lakehead Univ., 1972–73. **Educ.:** Queen's Univ., 1958–62, BA (Eng., Fr.); Univ. of Toronto, 1970, BLS, 1973, MLS; ON Tchrs. Cert. **Orgs.:** Can. LA: Can. Assn. of Spec. Libs. and Info. Sci.: Ottawa Chap. (Ch., 1978–79); Review Com. Can. Per. Index (1976). Can. Sch. LA: Adv. Com. on Pubns. (Ch., 1974). Prof. Inst. of the Pub. Srv. of Can.: LS Grp. (Ch., 1975–76). **Pubns.:** *Fort William, Port Arthur, Ontario, and Vicinity, 1857–1969: An Annotated List of Maps* (1971); "Every Scrap of Paper: Access to Ontario's Municipal Records," *Can. Lib. Jnl.* (Ja. F. 1974); "Regional Planning in Ontario: An Introduction to the Literature," *ON Lib. Review* (Mr. 1973); "Canadian Cataloguing in Publication Program," *ON Lib. Review* (S. 1976). **Activities:** 4; 17, 20, 44; 82, 86 **Addr.:** 2431 Clementine Blvd., Ottawa, ON K1V 8E1 Canada.

Scott, Alice H. (Jefferson, GA) Dir., Cmnty. Rel. and Spec. Prog., Chicago Pub. Lib., 1977–; Dir., Woodson Reg. Lib., 1974–77, Libn., Woodlawn Branch Lib., 1968–72, Libn., Pullman Branch Lib. 1967–68, Libn., Hall Branch Lib., 1961–66; Libn. I, Brooklyn Pub. Lib., 1958–59. **Educ.:** Spelman Coll., 1954–57, AB (Eng., Fr.); Atlanta Univ., 1957–58, MLS; Univ. of Chicago, 1976–, Phd Cand. **Orgs.:** ALA: Cncl. (1981–85); OLOS Adv. Com. (1980–82); ASCLA/Lib. Srv. to the Blind and Phys. Handcpd. Sect., Constn. and Bylaws Com. Ch. (1981–82). IL LA: Nom. Com. (1979–80). Chicago Lib. Club. **Activities:** 9; 17; 50, 66 **Addr.:** The Chicago Public Library, 425 N. Michigan, Chicago, IL 60611.

Scott, Barbara Grace (Mr. 16, 1942, Bellingham, WA) Dir., Lrng. Ctr./Lib., Birmingham-South. Coll., 1974–; Acq. Libn., Gustavus Adolphus Coll., 1967–74. **Educ.:** Univ. of WA, 1962–64, AB (Hist.), 1966–67, MLN (Libnshp.). **Orgs.:** AL LA: Secy. (1978–79); Conv. Ch. (1979–80). SELA. ALA. Altrusa Club of Birmingham. **Activities:** 1; 15, 17; 50 **Addr.:** Box A-20, Birmingham-Southern College, 800 8th Ave. W., Birmingham, AL 35204.

Scott, Bettie H. (Mr. 26, 1938, Raleigh, NC) Assoc. Libn., Univ. of CA, Los Angeles, 1981–; Assoc. Libn., Univ. of CA, Davis, 1975–81, Chld. Libn., Montgomery Cnty. Pub. Lib., 1967–70. **Educ.:** Univ. of NC, 1956–59, BA (Compar. Lit.); Univ. of HI, 1974–75, MLS (Lib. Std.); Univ. of Pac., 1977–81, JD (Law). **Orgs.:** ALA. AALL: Com. on Indexing Per. Lit. (1980–81); W. Pac. Chap. CA Acad. and Resrch. Libs. Acad. Staff Org. **Pubns.:** "Price Index to Legal Publications," *Law Lib. Jnl.* (F., 1976–81); "Price Index to Legal Publications—Summary," *AALL Nsltr.* (D. 1977–80). **Activities:** 1, 12; 22, 33, 39; 77 **Addr.:** Law Library, University of California, 405 Hilgard Ave., Los Angeles, CA 90024.

Scott, Catherine D. (Je. 21, 1927, Washington, DC) Chief Libn., Natl. Air and Space Musm., Smithsonian Inst., 1972–; Chief Tech. Libn., Bellcomm. Inc., Amer. Telephone and Telegraph Co., 1962–72; Asst. Libn., Ref. Libn., Natl. Assn. of Home Builders, 1955–62; Asst. Libn., Export-Import Bank of the U.S., 1950–55. **Educ.:** Cath. Univ. of Amer., 1946–50, AB (Eng.), 1951–55, MS (LS); various crs. **Orgs.:** Natl. Comsn. on Libs. and Info. Sci.: Vice-Ch. (1972–73); various coms. SLA: Aerosp. Div. (Ch., 1980–81); Ch.-Elect, 1979–80; Secy., 1968–69), Proj. Com. (Ch., 1977–79); DC Chap. (Pres., 1971–72; 1st VP, 1970–71), Sci.-Tech. Grp. (Ch., 1969–70), Corres. Secy. (1966–67), Consultation Com. (Ch., 1976–81), various coms. ASIS: Pub. Affairs Com. (1979–80); various coms. IFLA: Various confs. Cath. Univ. of Amer. LS Club: Pres. (1975–76). Cath. Univ. of Amer. Libs.: Bd. of Visitors. Cath. Univ. of Amer.: Frnds. of the Libs. Republican Natl. Com. Various orgs. **Honors:** Smithsonian Inst., Secys. Superior Performance Awd., 1976; Cath. Univ. of Amer., Alum. Achvmt. Awd. for Pub. Info., 1977; Natl. Aeronautics and Space Admin., Apollo Achvmt. Awds., 1969. **Pubns.:** Ed., *International Handbook of Aerospace Awards and Trophies* (1978, Supplement, 1981); "National Air and Space Museum Library," *Bowker Anl. of Lib. and Bk. Trade Info.* (1976); various presentations. **Addr.:** 700 7th St. S.W., Apt. 435, Washington, DC 20024.

Scott, Donald John (Jl. 17, 1940, Florence, NS) Prov. Libn., PEI Prov. Lib., 1971–; Libn., PEI Dept. of Dev., 1968–71; Asst. Dir., Northeast. Reg. Lib. Syst., 1966–68. **Educ.:** Mt. Allison Univ., 1959–63, BA (Hist.), BLS; McGill Univ., 1963–64, BLS. **Orgs.:** Atl. Prov. LA: Pres. (1972–73). Can. LA. Cncl. of Prov. and Territorial Libs.: Dir. **Activities:** 4, 9, 10, 12, 13; 15, 17, 35; 78 **Addr.:** Co Provinciol Library, University Ave., Charlottetown, PEI C1A 7N9 Canada.

Scott, Dorothea Hayward (London, Eng.) Lectr., Univ. of WI Lib. Sch., 1964–; E. Asian Biblgphr., Cornell Univ. Libs., 1962–63; Asst. to Dir., Columbia Univ. Libs., 1960–62; Univ. Libn., Hong Kong Univ., 1950–60; Brit. Cncl. Libn., Nanking, China, 1947–50. **Educ.:** Univ. of London Sch. of Libnshp. and Arch., 1932–35, ALA (Libnshp.). **Orgs.:** LA (Gt. Britain). ALA. WI LA. Amer. Prtg. Hist. Assn. Assn. of Asian Std. **Honors:** Carnegie Corp., Travel Flwshp., 1957. **Pubns.:** *Chinese Popular Literature and the Child: An Outline History* (1980); "Pollock's Toy Theatres," *Horn Bk. Mag.* (O. 1979); "LU HSüN and Chinese Literature for Children," *Intl. Lib. Qtly.* (1975); reviews. **Activities:** 1, 11; 21, 26, 45; 54, 55, 57 **Addr.:** Residence Le Musset Bat H., Rte. de Vauvenarques, 13100 Aix–en–Provence, France.

Scott, Edith (D. 19, 1918, Uniontown, KY) Chief, Cat. Instr. Ofc., Lib. of Congs., 1964–; Asst. Dir., Tech. Srvs., Univ. of OK, 1953–64, Assoc. Prof., Sch. of LS, 1959–64; Tech. Srvs. Libn., Ball State Univ., 1945–53; First Asst. Catlgr., Univ. of AL, 1944–45; Catlgr., Lawrence Coll., 1943–44; Catlgr., Natl. Coll. of Educ., 1941–43. **Educ.:** West. KY Univ., 1936–39, AB (Hist.); George Peabody Coll., 1939–41, BS (LS); Univ. of MI, 1951, AM (LS); Univ. of Chicago, 1970, PhD (LS). **Orgs.:** ALA: RTSD, Cncl. of Reg. Grps. (Ch., 1958–60) Univ. Libs. Sect. (Secy., 1958–59); Tech. Srvs. Admin. in Medium-Sized Resrch. Libs. (Ch., 1957–58). **Pubns.:** "J. C. M. Hanson," "Charles Martel," *ALA Encyc.* (1981); "Hanson, J. C. M.," *Encyc. of Lib. and Info. Sci.* (1973); "The Evolution of Bibliographic Systems in the United States, 1876–1945," *Lib. Trends* (Jl. 1976); "IFLA and FID—History and Programs," *Lib. Qtly.* (Ja. 1962). **Activities:** 1, 4; 20, 26, 31 **Addr.:** 9002 Clifford Ave., Chevy Chase, MD 20015.

Scott, Edward Alderman (My. 14, 1943, Mobile, AL) Dir., Lib. and Info. Systs., Keene State Coll., 1981–; Dir., Lib. and Lrng. Resrcs., Castleton State Coll., 1978–81; Dir., Instr. Mtrls. Ctr., Winthrop Coll., 1973–77, Ch., LS, 1970–75; Libn., FL State

Special Subjects/Services: 50. Adult educ.; 51. Advert./Mktg.; 52. Aerosp.; 53. Agric.; 54. Area std.; 55. Arts/Hum.; 56. Autom.; 57. Bibl./Prtg.; 58. Bio. sci.; 59. Bus./Fin.; 60. Chem.; 61. Copyrt.; 62. Documtn.; 63. Educ.; 64. Engin.; 65. Env.; 66. Eth. grps.; 67. Film; 68. Food/Nutr.; 69. Geneal.; 70. Geo.; 71. Geol.; 72. Handcpd.; 73. Hist.; 74. Int. frdm.; 75. Info. sci.; 76. Insr.; 77. Law; 78. Legis.; 79. Math./Comp. sci.; 80. Med.; 81. Metals; 82. Nat. resrcs.; 83. Newsp.; 84. Nuc. sci.; 85. Oral hist.; 86. Petr./Energy; 87. Pharm.; 88. Phys./Astr./Math.; 89. Readg.; 90. Relig.; 91. Sci./Tech.; 92. Soc. sci.; 93. Telecom.; 94. Transp.; 95. (other).

Univ. Std. Ctr., Florence, Italy, 1969–70; Asst. Soc. Sci. Libn., FL State Univ., Tallahassee, 1966–69. **Educ.:** FL State Univ., 1961–65, BS (Instr. Mtrls.), 1966–66, MS (LS); Univ. of SC, 1975–77, PhD (Instr. Dsgn.). **Orgs.:** ALA. VT Educ. Media Assn. VT LA: VP/Pres.-Elect (1980–81). SC Assn. for Educ. Comm. and Tech.: Pres.-Elect (1977); Secy. (1976); Leadership Dev. Ch. (1975); Conv. Dir. (1976–77); Reg. Rep. (1974). Castleton State Coll. Fac. Asm.: Pres. (1979–80). **Honors:** AECT, Leadership Dev. Flwshp, 1976; SC Assn. for Educ. Comm. and Tech., Educ. Media Person of the Yr., 1976. **Pubns.:** "Index to Florida Education," *FL Educ.* (1965–70). **Activities:** 1, 10, 11; 17, 19, 26, 32; 59, 61, 63 **Addr.:** 44 Jefferson St., Rutland, VT 05701.

Scott, Jack William (Jl. 30, 1938, Akron, OH) Head, Tech. Srvs., Kent State Univ., 1968–; Dir., Lrng. Resrcs., Lorain Cnty. Cmnty. Coll., 1964–68; Catlgr., Akron Law LA, 1962–64. **Educ.:** Heidelberg Coll., 1957–60, BA (Phil. Classics); West. Rsv. Univ., 1960–62, MSLS. **Orgs.:** ALA. SLA. OH LA: Com. on Fringe Benefits (1974); Com. on Lib. Dev. (1972–73). ASIS. Amer. Fed. of Musicians. **Pubns.:** "OCLC and Management in a Medium-sized University," *OCLC: A National Library Network* (1979); "Integrated Computer-based Technical Processing Systems," *Jnl. of Lib. Autom.* (Fall 1968); "U.S. Documents In an Online Union Catalog," *Serials Libn.* (Fall 1978). **Activities:** 1, 12; 17, 34, 46; 56, 74, 77 **Addr.:** Kent State University Libraries, Kent, OH 44242.

Scott, James F. (F. 20, 1932, Wheatland, WY) Dir. of Lib., Multnomah Sch. of the Bible, 1979–; Asst. Libn., Dallas Theo. Semy., 1969–79. **Educ.:** Greenville Coll., 1958–60, AB (Hist.); E. TX State Univ., 1970–71, MA (LS); Dallas Theo. Semy., 1977, MABS (Bible, Theo.). **Orgs.:** ATLA. Christ. Libns. Flwshp. **Pubns.:** *An Analytical Index to Bibliotheca Sacra from 1934 Through 1970* (1971); indxr., various bks. **Activities:** 1; 17, 30, 31; 90 **Addr.:** 11303 N.E. Siskiyou, Portland, OR 97220.

Scott, John E. (Ag. 12, 1920, Washington, GA) Dir. of Lib. Resrcs., WV State Coll., 1957–; Asst. Ref. Libn., Univ. of KS, 1956–57; Circ. Libn., VA State Coll., 1955–56; Libn., KS Tech. Inst., 1949–55. **Educ.:** Morehse. Coll., 1946–48, AB (Soclgy.); Atlanta Univ., 1948–49, BSLS; Univ. of IL, 1950–55, MSLS. **Orgs.:** ALA: Cncl. (1964–68); ACRL/Coll. Libs. Sect. (Ch., 1969–70). WV LA: Coll. Libs. Sect., Ch. (1959–60); Pres. (1961–62). SELA: Mem. Com. (1978–79); Treas. (1979–80). Alpha Phi Alpha: Secy. (1962–). **Honors:** WV LA, Cert. of Merit, 1975. **Pubns.:** "Fees and Modified Privileges for Outside Borrowers," *Coll. & Resrch. Libs.* (My. 1967); "Circulation of Materials to Outside Borrowers," *Coll. & Resrch. Libs.* (My. 1970); "Changes in College Libraries in the Seventies," *WV Libs.* (Spr. 1971). **Activities:** 1; 17 **Addr.:** P.O. Box 303, Institute, WV 25112.

Scott, Joseph W. (Je. 13, 1949, Providence, RI) Asst. Msc. Libn., Univ. of CT, 1976–; Msc. Libn., CT Coll., 1973–76. **Educ.:** Brown Univ., 1967–71, AB (Msc.); Simmons Coll., 1971–72, MSLS. **Orgs.:** Msc. LA: New Eng. Chap., Ch. (1978–79); Vice-Ch./Prog. Ch. (1977–78); Pubns. Ch. (1975–77). Msc. OCLC Users Grp.: Mtg. Host (1981). NELINET Msc. Users Grp.: Mtg. Host (1979); Strg. Com. (1981). **Pubns.:** Cmplr., "Directory of Music Libraries and Collections in New England," (1974, 1977). **Activities:** 1, 12; 17, 20, 46; 55, 56 **Addr.:** Music Library, U-12, University of Connecticut, Storrs, CT 06268.

Scott, Marianne Florence (D. 4, 1928, Toronto, ON) Dir. of Libs., McGill Univ., 1975–, Law Area Libn., 1973–74, Lectr., Legal Bibl., Fac. of Law, 1964–74; Law Libn., 1955–73. **Educ.:** McGill Univ., 1949, BA, 1952, BLS. **Orgs.:** CARL: Pres. (1978-79); Exec. Bd. (1980-81). Can. LA: First VP, Pres.-Elect (1980-81). Can. ALL: Pres. (1963-69); Archvst.; Exec. Bd. (1973-75). Intl. Assn. of Law Libs.: Bd. (1974-77). Various other orgs., coms. **Pubns.:** Ed., *Index to Canadian Legal Periodical Literature* (1963–); *Canadian Library Handbook 1979–80* (1979); "Law Library Resources and Planning in Canada," *Intl. Jnl. of Law Libs.* (1975); "Indexing Legal Periodicals," *Procs. of the Can. Assn. of Libs.* (1974); "1971 Statistical Survey of Canadian Law Libraries and Librarians," *Law Lib. Jnl.* (1973); various other articles. **Activities:** 1; 17; 30, 31; 77 **Addr.:** Office of the Director of Libraries, McGill University, 3459 McTavish St., Montreal PQ H2X 1Y1 Canada

Scott, Mary Ellen (Mr. 14, 1926, Hutchinson, KS) Catlgr. and Archvst., Clifford E. Barbour Lib., Pittsburgh Theo. Semy., 1967–. **Educ.:** Sterling Coll., 1943–47, BA (Msc.); Univ. of Pittsburgh, 1966–68, MLS. **Orgs.:** Pittsburgh Reg. Lib. Ctr.: Secy. (1977–78). ATLA. MARAC. **Honors:** Beta Phi Mu. **Activities:** 1, 2; 17, 20, 45; 90 **Addr.:** 327 Hillcrest Ave., Pittsburgh, PA 15237.

Scott, Mary Woods (Ja. 16, 1943, Chattanooga, TN) Sci., Engin. Biblgphr., Ref. Libn., Chester Fritz Lib., Univ. of ND, 1973–; Res. Asst., ND Geol. Srvy., 1970–73; Biblgphr., ND Water Resrc. Resrch. Inst., 1970–73; Geol. Libn., Univ. of ND Geol. Dept., 1967–70. **Educ.:** Muskingum Coll., 1961–65, BS (Geol.); Univ. of ND, 1966–72, MS (Geol.). **Orgs.:** Geosci. Info. Socty.: Secy. (1976–77); VP, Pres. (1981–82). ND State LA. AAUW. **Honors:** Sigma Gamma Epsilon. **Pubns.:** *Annotated Bibliography of the Geology of North Dakota 1960–1979* (1981); *Bibliography and Index of North Dakota Water Resources 1878–1970* (1976); *Annotated Bibliography of the Geology of North Dakota 1806–1959* (1972); "North Dakota Regional Environment Assessment Program," *Geosci. Info. Socty. Proc.* (1978); "Geolibrarianship," *The Compass* (1970). **Activities:** 1; 15, 29, 39; 64, 70, 71 **Addr.:** Bibliography Dept., Chester Fritz Library, University of North Dakota, Grand Forks, ND 58202.

Scott, Patricia Lyn (D. 7, 1950, Rigby, ID) Asst. Hum. Head, Salt Lake City Pub. Lib., 1978–, State Docum. Libn., 1977–78, Asst. Branch Libn., Rose Park Branch, 1973–76. **Educ.:** Ricks Coll., 1969–71, AA (Hist.); South. UT State Coll., 1971–73, BA (Hist.); Wayne State Univ., 1976–77, MSLS; Univ. of UT, 1977– (Hist.). **Orgs.:** SAA: Lib.-Arch. Rel. Com. (1978–79). ALA: JMRT, Orien. Com. (1978); SRRT, Mtrls. Exch. Task Frc., Arch. Com. (1978). UT LA: Asst. Histn. (1975–76); Resrch. Com., Secy. (1979–80); Spec. Lib. Sect., Vice-Ch. (1980–81), Ch. (1980–). Conf. of Intermt. Archvsts. Various other orgs. UT Women's Hist. Assn.: Prog. Com. (1979–80). UT Hist. Socty. ID Hist. Socty. Amer. Assn. for State and Lcl. Hist. Various other orgs. **Honors:** Wayne State Univ., H. W. Wilson Awd., 1977. **Pubns.:** "The History of Rigby, 1885–1914," *Snake River Echoes* (Win. 1973); "The Train Comes to the Upper Valley," *Snake River Echoes* (Sum. 1975); series of bibl. on UT hist. (1979–); *The Hub of Eastern Idaho: The History of Rigby, Idaho, 1885–1976* (1976). **Activities:** 2, 9; 16, 23, 39; 57, 66, 69 **Addr.:** Humanities Dept., Salt Lake City Public Library, 209 E. 500 S., Salt Lake City, UT 84111.

Scott, R. Neil (O. 27, 1952, Montgomery, AL) Ref. Libn., Stetson Univ., 1980–; Pub. Srvs. Libn., William Carey Coll., 1977–80; Assoc. Syst. Writer, Burroughs Corp., 1976–77; Comp. Oper., Sav-A-Stop-Data Prcs., 1974–75. **Educ.:** Univ. of S. FL, 1972–74, BA (Eng.); FL State Univ., 1975–76, MLS; Stetson Univ., 1980–82; MBA (Mgmt.). **Orgs.:** MS LA. SELA. FL LA. **Honors:** Beta Phi Mu, 1976. **Pubns.:** "The 'Duplicate Books Collection' of LC's Gift and Exchange Division," *The Southeast. Libn.* (Sum. 1980); bk. reviews. **Activities:** 1; 17, 39, 42; 57, 59, 75 **Addr.:** Box 528, Richton, MS 39476.

Scott, Ralph L. (Jl. 23, 1942, New York, NY) Ref. Libn., Coord. Online Srch., E. Carolina Univ., 1970–. **Educ.:** Columbia Univ., 1960–68, BA (Hist.), 1968–70, MS (LS); E. Carolina Univ., 1975–79, MA (Hist.). **Orgs.:** ALA. SLA. NC LA. Amer. Hist. Assn. Sierra Club. **Honors:** Beta Phi Mu; Phi Alpha Theta; NY Lib. Club, Anl. Awd., 1970; Columbia Univ., Tauber-Bergman Awd., 1972. **Pubns.:** "A Glossary of Library Binding Terms," *Library Binding Manual* (1972); "A Computer Based Census and Local Handlist for Incunabula," *Comps. and the Hum.* (1971); "Jeffersonian Americana," *Micro. Review* (1975); "A $1,000 Misunderstanding: UM's Index to its *Dissertation Abstracts International*," *Wilson Lib. Bltn.* (1971); "Phonefiche," *Micro. Review* (1977); various articles, abs., reviews. **Activities:** 1; 15, 39, 49-Online srch.; 56, 59, 72 **Addr.:** East Carolina University, J. Y. Joyner Library, Greenville, NC 27834.

Scott, Thomas L. (Jl. 30, 1943, Council Bluffs, IA) Syst. Dir., Plum Creek Lib. Syst., 1980–; Reg. Lib. Dir., Ctrl. FL Reg. Lib., 1971–79; Head, Ref. Dept., Omaha Pub. Lib., 1968–71. **Educ.:** Univ. of NE, 1961–65, BA (Hist.); Univ. of IL, 1966–68, MS (LS). **Orgs.:** ALA. FL LA: Legis. and Plng. Com. (Ch.); Pre-White Hse. Conf. Plng. Com. Early-Risers Kiwanis Club. **Pubns.:** Ed., *FL Libs.* **Activities:** 9; 17, 34, 35, 39; 56, 74, 75 **Addr.:** 844 Winifred, Worthington, MN 56187.

Scott, William H. Oliver (O. 20, 1922, Chicago, IL) Docum. Libn., Assoc. Prof., West. WA Univ., 1971–, Circ. Libn., 1960–70; Visit. Asst. Prof., Sch. of Libnshp., Univ. of WA, 1959–60; Assoc. Libn., LA Polytech. Inst., 1956–59; Asst. Libn., Waco Pub. Lib., 1955–56; Chief Couns. Libn., Assoc. Libn., Univ. of IL, Chicago, 1951–55; Asst. Ref. Libn., Univ. of FL, 1949–51. **Educ.:** West. MI Coll. of Educ., 1943–45 (Soc. Std.); Univ. of MI, 1945–46, AB (Eng. Lit.), 1947–48, AM (Amer. Lit.), 1948–49, AMLS. **Orgs.:** ALA: GODORT; ACRL. WA LA. Pac. NW LA. Frnds. Bellingham Pub. Lib.: VP (1969–71, 1977–79); Pres. (1971–73). Amer. Cvl. Liberties Un. Amer. Fed. of Tchrs. Amer. Humanist Assn. Bellingham Unitarian Flwshp. Various other orgs. **Honors:** Beta Phi Mu, 1953. **Pubns.:** *Statistics in Washington State Government Publications; A Bibliography...* (1979); ed., *Recommended East Asian Core Collections for Children's, High School, Public, Community College, and Undergraduate College Libraries* (1974); "Ethics and Red China," *Reflections* (1963); jt. auth., "Waco Public Library," *TX Libs.* (D. 1955); "Counselor Librarianship," *ILA Rec.* (S. 1953); various bibls. **Activities:** 1; 29, 31, 39 **Addr.:** 518 Everglade Rd., Bellingham, WA 98225.

Scott, Willodene Alexander (Mrs. Ray D.) (S. 4, 1922, Ethridge, TN) Dir., Instr. Mtrls. and Lib. Srvs., Metro. Nashville-Davidson Cnty. Sch. Syst., 1973, Supvsr., Instr. Mtrls. Ctr., 1966–73; Libn., McCann Elem. Sch., 1963–66; Libn., Howard HS, 1954–62; Libn., Waverly Belmont Jr. HS, 1951–54; Libn., Sylvan Park Elem. Sch., 1947–51. **Educ.:** George Peabody Coll., 1941–46, BA (Eng.), 1946–47, BS in LS, 1947, MA (Geo.), 1949 EdS (LS). **Orgs.:** ALA. SELA: Schol. Com. (1968–70). TN LA: Mem. Ch. (1955, 1964); Treas. (1977–78). Nashville Lib. Club: Pres. (1952–53). TN Educ. Assn.: Lib. Sect. (Pres., 1954). Metro. Nashville Educ. Assn. Natl. Educ. Assn. Daughters of Amer. Revolution. George Peabody Coll. for Tchrs.: Bd. of Trustees (1977–81). **Pubns.:** "Metropolitan Nashville-Davidson Instructional Materials Center County Schools," *TN Libn.* (Spr. 1969); "Experiencing Literature with Children," *Elem. Eng.* (O. 1968). **Activities:** 10; 17, 21, 48; 63 **Addr.:** 525 Clematis Dr., Nashville, TN 37205.

Scribner, Sara A. (Ja. 18, 1947, Macon, GA) Supvsg. Libn., Branch Supvsn., San Jose Pub. Lib., 1980–, Coord., YA Srvs., 1979–80, Branch Libn., 1977–79; Dir., Plymouth (MA) Pub. Lib., 1974–76; Libn., Asa Griggs Candler Lib., Emory Univ., 1972–74. **Educ.:** Vassar Coll., 1964–68, AB (Drama); Simmons Coll., 1971–72, MS (LS). **Orgs.:** ALA. CA LA: Cmnty. Rel. Com. (1979–81). Concerned Lib. Activist Workers: Strg. Com. (1977–79). East. MA Reg. Lib. Syst.: Exec. Bd. (1974–76). Muncpl. Empls. Fed.: Pres. (1979). **Activities:** 9; 17, 25, 48; 74, 95-YA lit. **Addr.:** San Jose Public Library, 180 W. San Carlos St., San Jose, CA 95125.

Scroggins, John M., Jr. (Ag. 14, 1942, Minneapolis, MN) Dir., Prcs. Impr. Div., Natl. Arch. and Recs. Srv., 1980–, Dir., Prog. Mgt. and Coord. Div., 1979–80, Dir., Prog. Coord. Staff, 1974–79, Prog. Anal., Chief, Plng. and Anal. Branch, Ofc. of the Exec. Dir., 1968–74, Archvst., 1964–68. **Educ.:** Jamestown Coll., 1961–64, BA (Hist.); Amer. Univ., 1964–72, MA (Pub. Admin.). **Orgs.:** SAA. Amer. Socty. for Pub. Admin. Org. of Amer. Histns. **Honors:** Gen. Srvs. Admin., Commendable Srv. Awd., 1968. **Activities:** 2; 17, 38; 56 **Addr.:** 3408 Weltham St., Suitland, MD 20746.

Scudamore, Rosemary Joy (Ap. 6, 1927, Vancouver, BC) Coord., Grt. Vancouver Lib. Fed., 1976–; Deputy Chief Libn., Burnaby Pub. Lib., 1973–75; Branch Head, Vancouver Pub. Lib., 1959–75; Consult., Lib. Dev. Comsn., 1972–73. **Educ.:** Univ. of BC, 1946–50, BA (Hist.); McGill Univ., 1950–51, BLS. **Orgs.:** BC LA: Pres. (1969–70). Can. Assn. of Pub. Libns.: Dir. (1974–76). Pac. NW LA: Secy. (1978–80); Pres. (1981–82). Assn. of BC Libns.: Dir. (1965); VP, Pres.-Elect (1980–82). Univ. Women's Club. **Pubns.:** Jt. ed., *Focus, Directory of Libraries in BC* (1980); "Gulf, Partnership in Cooperation," *BC LA Rpt.* (Je. 1980). **Activities:** 9; 17, 24, 34; 50 **Addr.:** 3206 W. 32nd Ave., Vancouver, BC V6L 2C3 Canada.

Scudder, Mary Clayton (N. 29, 1928, Tuscaloosa, AL) Lib. Dir., Lynchburg Coll., 1975–; Asst. Libn. for Pub. Srvs., 1969–75; Atl. Christ. Coll., 1956–58; Asst. Libn., Woman's Coll. Lib., Duke Univ., 1961–67, 1959–60; Asst. Libn., Kinston Pub. Lib., 1954–55; Catlgr., Margaret I. King Lib., Univ. of KY, 1953–54; Pers. Libn., Amelia Gayle Gorgas Lib., Univ. of AL, 1952–53. **Educ.:** Univ. of AL, 1947–52, BS (Educ); Geo. Peabody Coll. for Tchrs., 1974, MLS. **Orgs.:** ALA. SE LA. VA LA: Reg. II, (Ch., 1978–79). **Honors:** Alpha Beta Alpha, 1952; Beta Phi Mu, 1976. **Activities:** 1, 2; 17, 20, 22; 50 **Addr.:** 3229 Landon St., Lynchburg, VA 24503.

Scull, Roberta A. (O. 2, 1940, Ft. Benning, GA) Assoc. Libn., LA State Univ., 1969–; Tchr., New Castle Spec. Sch. Dist., 1963–67; Tchr., Alexandria (VA) Sch. Syst., 1962–63. **Educ.:** Univ. of TN, 1960–62, BLA (Eng.); LA State Univ., 1968–69, MLS. **Orgs.:** ALA: GODORT, Educ. Task Frc. Com. (1979). SLA: Bus. and Fin. Div. LA LA: Docum. Com., Exec. Com. (1978–81). **Honors:** Beta Phi Mu. **Pubns.:** *Bibliography of United States Government Bibliographies 1974–1976* (1979); "Keeping Current in Business with Government Bibliography," *Spec. Libs.* (Ja. 1979); "Information for Louisiana Business Through Federal, State, and Local Sources," *LA Bus. Review* "Bibliography of U.S. Government Bibliographies," *Ref. Srvs. Review* (1974, 1975, 1976); "More Reference Sources," *TX Libs.* (Sum. 1976); various sps. **Activities:** 1, 4; 24, 29, 39 **Addr.:** BA/DOCS Dept. Library, Louisiana State University, Baton Rouge, LA 70803.

Scully, Mark Francis (O. 3, 1943, Riverside, NJ) Supervisory Libn., Supt. of Docum., U.S. Gvt. Prtg. Ofc., 1981–; Tech. Info. Spec., U.S. Gen. Acct. Ofc., 1980–81; Lib. Dir., U.S. Con. Prod. Safety Comsn., 1977–80, Tech. Srvs. Libn., 1973–77; Libn., Natl. Lib. of Med., 1971–73. **Educ.:** Rutgers Univ., 1961–65, AB (Soc. Sci.); Univ. of MD, 1969–71, MLS; Amer. Univ., 1975–77, MPA (Pub. Admin.). **Orgs.:** SLA. **Honors:** Beta Phi Mu, 1971; Pi Alpha Alpha, 1977. **Pubns.:** Ed., *Washington Consortium of Universities Union List of Serials* (1974). **Activities:** 4, 12; 17, 34, 36; 56, 59, 92 **Addr.:** 2203 Darrow St., Silver Spring, MD 20902.

Seab, Myra McGraw (F. 13, 1947, Baton Rouge, LA) YA Libn. IV, East Baton Rouge Par. Lib., 1969–. **Educ.:** LA State Univ., 1965–69, BS (Educ.), 1971–72, MS (LS). **Orgs.:** LA LA: YA Interest Grp. (Ch., 1976–79). SW LA. ALA. **Activities:** 9; 48 **Addr.:** 9535 El Cajon Dr., Baton Rouge, LA 70815.

Seal, Robert A. (Je. 9, 1948, Canton, OH) Dir., Lib. Pubn. Srvs., Univ. of OK Lib., 1981–; Dir., Admin. Srvs., Univ. of VA Lib., 1976–81, Sci., Tech. Circ. Libn., 1975–76, Autom. Libn., 1974–76, Engin. Libn., 1974–75, Assoc. Engin. Li[illegible], 1973–74, Circ. Libn., 1972–73. **Educ.:** Northwestern Univ., 1966–71, BA (Astronomy); Univ. of Denver, 1971–72, MLS. **Orgs.:** SLA: VA Chap. (Treas., 1975–77); Phys.-Astr.-Math. Div. (Ch., 1978–79); Stans. Com. (1978–81); ALA: ACRL, Pubns. in Libnshp., Ed. Bd.

PROFESSIONAL ACTIVITIES: Institutions: 1. Acad. lib.; 2. Arch.; 3. Assn.; 4. Fed./Gvt. lib.; 5. Inst. lib.; 6. Mfr./Suppl.; 7. Milit. lib.; 8. Musm.; 9. Pub. lib.; 10. Sch. lib.; 11. Sch. of lib. sci.; 12. Spec. lib.; 13. State lib.; 14. (other). **Functions/Activities:** 15. Acq./Col. dev.; 16. Adult srvs.; 17. Admin.; 18. Apprais.; 19. Archit./Bldgs.; 20. Cat./Class.; 21. Chld. srvs.; 22. Circ.; 23. Cons./Pres.; 24. Consult.; 25. Cont. ed.; 26. Educ. lib. sci.; 27. Ext. srvs.; 28. Fund/Grants; 29. Gvt. pubs.; 30. Indx./Abs.; 31. Instr. lib. use; 32. Media srvs.; 33. Micro.; 34. Netwks./Coop.; 35. Persnl.; 36. PR; 37. Publshg.; 38. Recs. mgt.; 39. Ref. srvs.; 40. Repro.; 41. Resrch.; 42. Review.; 43. Secur.; 44. Serials; 45. Spec. col.; 46. Tech. srvs.; 47. Trustees/Bds.; 48. YA srvs.; 49. (other).

(1981–); RASD, Subcom. on ILL (Rep., 1979–). VA LA: Reg 6 (Ch., 1977–78). Intl. Astr. Un.: Comsn. 5, Documtn., Consult. Mem. **Honors:** Beta Phi Mu, 1973. **Pubns.:** *A Guide to the Literature of Astronomy* (1977). **Activities:** 1; 17, 34, 35; 57, 88 **Addr.:** Library Dean's Office, Bizzell Library, University of Oklahoma, Norman, OK 73019.

Seamon, Judith Ann (N. 28, 1946, Cooperstown, NY) Assoc. Dir., Lrng. Resrcs. Ctr., Hudson Valley Cmnty. Coll., 1980–; Dir., Lib. Media, Educ. Comms., Norwich City Schs., 1978–80; Lib. Media Spec., Utica City Schs., 1973–78; Libn., Ilion Ctrl. Schs., 1968–70. **Educ.:** Univ. of Denver, 1965–68, BA (Eng.); Syracuse Univ., 1974–76, MLS, 1976–79, MS (Educ. Admin.); various crs. **Orgs.:** Ctrl. NY LA: Pres. (1979–80); Secy. (1978–79). Sch. Lib. Media Supvsrs. of NY State: VP, Pres.-Elect (1979–80). NY LA: Sch. Lib. Media Sect., Parents as Readg. Partners Prog., Ad Hoc Com. (Ch., 1980–81). Various other orgs., confs. NY Lib. Pilot Proj. at DE Genango BOCES: Strg. Com., Ch. Natl. Org. of Women. Natl. Assn. of Female Execs. Sch. Admins. Assn. of NY. Various other orgs. **Honors:** Beta Phi Mu, 1976. **Pubns.:** Ed., *Ctrl. NY LA Nsltr.* (1979–80); ed., *SLMS Promotes Parents as Reading Partners* (1980); *Central New York Library Association Directory* (1979–80); "ITV: Uses and Abuses" videotape (1979); *Center for Learning–Your School Library Media Center* (1979); various brochures, rpts. **Activities:** 10; 17, 28, 32; 63, 92, 93 **Addr.:** Hudson Valley Community College, 80 Vandenburgh Ave., Troy, NY 12180.

Searcy, David L. (Ja. 30, 1951, Thomaston, GA) Head Branch Libn., Atlanta Pub. Lib., 1977–, Pub. Srv. Libn., 1976–77. **Educ.:** Morris Brown Coll., 1969–73, BA (Eng.); Atlanta Univ., 1975–76, MSLS. **Orgs.:** GA LA: Gvtl. Rel. Com. (1977–79). Metro Atlanta LA: Secy. (1977–78); VP, Pres.-Elect (1979–81). SELA. ALA: JMRT, Minorities Rcrt. Com. (Ch., 1979–81); SRRT; LIRT; Adv. Com. to ALA Ofc. for Lib. Outrch. Srvs. (1979–82); Black Caucus, Prof. Dev. and Rcrt. Com. (1978–81). Beta Phi Mu: Zeta Chap. (Pres., 1978–79); Natl. Adv. Cncl. (1978–80). **Activities:** 9; 16, 17, 48; 50, 55, 66 **Addr.:** 703 Durant Pl., N.E., Atlanta, GA 30308.

Searle, Jo-Anne M. (N. 5, 1945, Elizabeth, NJ) Dir., Lib. Srvs., Morristown Meml. Hosp., 1979–; Libn., Mountainside Hosp., 1970–79. **Educ.:** Newark State Coll., 1966–69, BA (Elem. Educ.); Pratt Inst., 1974–76, MLS. **Orgs.:** Med. LA. Hlth. Sci. LA of NJ: Bylaws Com. (1980); Stan. Com. (1972). Cosmopolitan Biomed. Lib. Cnsrtm.: Pres. (1980); Secy. (1974). **Activities:** 12; 17, 34, 39; 80 **Addr.:** 41 Wetmore Ave., Morristown, NJ 07960.

Searls, Eileen Haughey (Ap. 27, 1925, Madison, WI) Prof. Law, St. Louis Univ., 1964–, Assoc. Prof., 1956–64, Asst. Prof., 1953–56, Instr., 1952–53, Law Libn., 1952–. **Educ.:** Univ. of WI, 1944–48, BA (Hist.), 1948–50, JD (Law), 1950–51, MS (LS), 1967–68, (LS). **Orgs.:** ALA. AALL. Cath. LA. WI Bar Assn. Landmarks. **Activities:** 1, 12; 15, 17, 34; 77, 78 **Addr.:** Law Library, Saint Louis University, 3700 Lindell Blvd., Saint Louis, MO 63108.

Seaton, Elaine (My. 6, 1928, New York, NY) Dir., Manhasset Pub. Lib., 1972–; Dir., SUNY Old Westbury Coll. Lib., 1968–72; Head, Ref. and Adult Srvs., Shelter Rock Pub. Lib., 1963–68. **Educ.:** Univ. of Chicago, PhB (Soclgy., Psy.); Long Island Univ., MSLS. **Orgs.:** ALA: Lib. Admin. Div./Persnl. Admin. Sect., Staff Dev. Com. (1974–) PR Sect., Frnds. of Lib. Com. (1979–); various coms. NY LA: Pub. Libs. Sect., Prof. Dev. Com. (Ch., 1974); Coll. and Univ. Sect. (1968–72). Nassau Cnty. LA: Coll. and Univ. Libs. Sect., Exec. Bd. (1971). SUNY Head Libns. Assn.: Exec. Com. (1970–71). Nassau Cnty. Lib. Dirs. Assn.: (1973–77). Various other orgs., confs. Long Island Univ.: Palmer Grad. Sch., Adv. Com. (1974–75); Srch./Adv. Com. (1974–75); Srch./Sel. Com. for New Dean (1976). **Honors:** Beta Phi Mu. **Pubns.:** "With Friends like These....," *Organizing the Library's Support: Donors, Volunteers, Friends* (N. 1979). **Activities:** 1, 9; 17, 36 **Addr.:** 333 E. 49th St., New York, NY 10017.

Seavey, Charles A. (Ag. 21, 1941, New York, NY) Head, Gvt. Pubns. and Maps Dept., Univ. of NM, 1979–; Docum. and Maps Libn., Univ. of North. IA, 1975–79. **Educ.:** Univ. of MA, 1963–67, BA (Hist.); Univ. of KY, 1973–74, MSLS. **Orgs.:** ALA: Map and Geo. RT (Co-fndr., 1980), Ch. (1981–82). SLA: Geo. and Map Div., Mem. Com. (Ch., 1978–79), Cartograph. Users Adv. Com. (1977–79); Cartograph. Users Adv. Cncl. (Ch., 1980–). Midwest Acad. Libns. Conf.: Pubcty. Ch. (1976). NM LA: Docum. RT, (Ch.-Elect, 1980–). **Honors:** SLA, Geo. and Map Div., Bill M. Woods Awd., 1977; Beta Phi Mu, 1974. **Pubns.:** "Collection Development for Government Map Collections," *Gvt. Pubns. Review* (1981); "Practically Speaking: An Inexpensive Map Collection," *Sch. Lib. Jnl.* (Ag. 1980); jt. auth., "Government Publications for Geographic Education," *Geo. Perspectives* (Fall 1979); "Maps of the American State Papers," *SLA Geo. Map Div. Bltn.* (Mr. D., 1977); "A Bibliographic Addendum to Carl I. Wheat's *Mapping the Transmississippi West, 1540–1861*," *Geo. and Map Div. Bltn.* (S. 1976); various articles. **Activities:** 1; 15, 29, 37; 70 **Addr.:** Government Publications and Maps Dept., General Library, University of New Mexico, Albuquerque, NM 87131.

Seay, Jean A. (F. 10, 1929, San Jose, CA) Libn., Prof. Lib., Portland Pub. Schs., 1974–81; Lib. Media Spec., Salem Pub. Schs., 1970–74; Elem. Tchr., Alum Rock Elem. Sch. Dist., 1967–70. **Educ.:** San Jose State Coll., 1946–50, BA (Span.); Portland State Univ., 1974–77, MS (Educ.); CA State Univ., 1965–67, Elem. Tchg. Cred. **Orgs.:** SLA: OR Chap., Mem. Ch. (1978–80; Pres-Elect (1980–81). ASIS. ALA: LITA. **Activities:** 2, 12; 15, 39, 41; 55, 63 **Addr.:** 1669–J Belleville Way, Sunnyvale, CA 94087.

Seba, Douglas B. (Ap. 24, 1941, Columbus, OH) Exec. Secy., Sci. Adv. Bd., U.S. Env. Protection Agency, 1978–, Dir., Natl. Info. Ctr. for Enforcement, 1972–77; Pvt. Consult., Info. and Env. Sci., 1965–71. **Educ.:** Cap. Univ., 1959–63, BS (Env. Sci.); Univ. of Miami, 1963–79, MS (Env. Sci.), PhD (Env. Sci.). **Orgs.:** ASIS. Acad. of Marine Sci.: VP. Amer. Chem. Socty. **Honors:** U.S. Env. Protection Agency, Bronze Medal, 1977, 1981. **Pubns.:** "On-Line Environmental Information Goes to Court," *Special Librarinship–A New Reader* (1980); ed., "Management Outpost," *ONLINE* (1976–). **Activities:** 4, 14-Non-Profit Fndn.; 24; 65, 75, 91 **Addr.:** Science Advisory Board, U.S. Environmental Protection Agency, A–101M, Washington, DC 20460.

Seckelson-Simpson, Linda Eve (Ag. 29, 1945, Chicago, IL) Art, Msc., Film Libn., Evanston Pub. Lib., 1975–; Ref., Pers., Libn., Northwest. Univ. Lib., 1971–75, Libn., Poetry and Listening Rm., 1970–71. **Educ.:** Grinnell Coll., 1963–67, BA (Msc.); Univ. of CA, Los Angeles, 1969–70, MLS (Lib. Srv.). **Orgs.:** ALA: RASD, Info. Retrieval Com. (1975–78). **Activities:** 9; 32; 55, 67 **Addr.:** Evanston Public Library, 1703 Orrington Ave., Evanston, IL 60201.

Secor, John R. (Ap. 22, 1939, Malden, MA) Pres., The Country Schol., Inc., Natl. Lib. Bookjobber, 1976–, Pres., Yankee Bk. Peddler, Inc., 1971–; Dir., Sales Trng., Dev., Prentice-Hall Pubshg. Co., 1965–71. **Educ.:** Boston Coll., 1957–60. **Orgs.:** ALA: Booksellers Discuss. Grp. (Ch., 1980). New Eng. LA. US Jaycees: Past Natl. Dir. MA Jaycees: Past VP. **Addr.:** Pleasant St., Westford, MA 03229.

Sedgwick, Dorothy L. Head Libn., Price Waterhse. and Co., 1978–; Resrch. Assoc., Univ. of Toronto, 1976–78; Ref. Libn., Town of Markham Pub. Libs., 1974–76; Asst. Ed., *Quill and Quire*, 1971–74. **Educ.:** Univ. of Toronto, 1945–49, BA (Phil.), 1967–71, MA (Eng.), 1972–74, MLS. **Orgs.:** SLA: Toronto Chap., Cont. Ed., Ch. Can. LA: Pubns. Com. (1975–80). Indexing and Abs. Socty. of Can. Bibl. Socty. of Can. *Thea. Hist. in Can.*: Bd. of Mgt. Assn. for Can. Thea. Hist. **Pubns.:** *Bibliography of Canadian Theatre History and Drama in English* (1976). **Activities:** 12; 15, 17, 39; 59 **Addr.:** National Library, Price Waterhouse & Co., Box 51, Toronto-Dominion Centre, Toronto, ON M5K 1G1 Canada.

Sedgwick, Frederica M. (D. 11, 1932, Long Beach, CA) Dir. of Law Lib., Prof. of Law, Loyola Law Sch., Los Angeles, CA, 1975–, Actg. Dir., 1974, Asst. Law Libn., Ref. Libn., 1970–73, Acq., Ref., 1966–69, Cat. Libn., 1964–66; Pers. Libn., Univ. of CA, Los Angeles, 1963–64; Sci. Libn., Univ. of South. CA, 1961–63, Circ. Libn., 1959–61. **Educ.:** Long Beach State Coll., 1952–54, BA (Hist.), 1955–57, MA (Soc. Sci.); Univ. of South. CA, 1957–59, MSLS; Loyola Univ., 1966–70, JD (Law). **Orgs.:** AALL: Com. on Exch. of Dupls, Pubns. Com. South. CA Assn. of Law Libs.: Treas. (1974–75), VP (1975–76); Pres. (1976–77). South. CA Tech. Prcs. Grp. Cath. LA: SW Branch. Intl. Geranium Socty.: Treas. (1977–79); Rec. Secy. (1979–). **Honors:** Alpha Sigma Nu, 1970; Beta Phi Mu. **Activities:** 1; 15, 17, 31; 77 **Addr.:** Loyola Law School, Law Library, 1440 W. 9th St., Los Angeles, CA 90015.

Sedney, Frances V. (Je. 21, 1928, Boston, MA) Coord., Chld. Srvs., Harford Cnty. Lib., 1968–; Volun. Ch., Lib. Com. Staff, St. Margaret Sch., Bel Air, 1956–68; Chld. Libn., Carnegie Lib., 1950–51; Chld. Libn., NY Pub. Lib., 1949–50. **Educ.:** St. Joseph Coll., Emmitsburg, MD, 1944–48, AB; Carnegie Inst. of Tech., 1948–49, MLS. **Orgs.:** MD LA: Chld. Srv. Div., Prog. Ch., Ch.-Elect (1975); Actg. Ch. (1976); Ch. (1977). ALA: ALSC, Boy Scouts Adv. Com. (Ch., 1978–80); PLA, Bylaws Com. (1979–80); YASD. St. Joseph Coll. Alum.: Treas. (1974–78); Pres.-Elect (1980). **Activities:** 9; 21 **Addr.:** Harford County Library, 100 Pennsylvania Ave., Bel Air, MD 21014.

Seeds, Robert Stewart, III (Ja. 1, 1946, Altoona, PA) Hlth. Sci. Libn., PA State Univ., 1974–, Med. Coll. Ref. Libn., 1971–74, Head, Reg. Med. Prog. Info. Srv., 1969–71. **Educ.:** PA State Univ., 1963–67, BS (Zlgy.); Univ. of Pittsburgh, 1967–68, MLS; Univ. of TN, 1968–69, Cert. (LS); Med. LA, 1969, Cert. Grade II (Med. Libnshp.). **Orgs.:** Med. LA. SLA. Ctrl. PA Hlth. Sci. LA: Fndr., Ch. (1973–74). **Pubns.:** Jt. auth., "Literature Searching with the CAIN Online Bibliographic Database," *BioSci.* (D. 1975); jt. auth., "Development of SDI Service," *Bltn. of the Med. LA* (D. 1974); ed., *Resource Directory of Central Pennsylvania Health Sciences Libraries* (1978); jt. auth., "Interest among Librarians to Participate in Library-Related Instruction at the Pennsylvania State University Libraries," *PA LA Bltn.* (My. 1976); "Literature Searching with the CAIN On-line Bibliographic Data Base," *BioSci.* (D. 1975); various papers, articles, rpts. **Activities:** 1, 12; 15, 31, 39; 58, 68, 80 **Addr.:** E205 Pattee Library, University Park, PA 16802.

Seegraber, Frank J. (O. 8, 1916, Boston, MA) Spec. Cols. Libn., Boston Coll., 1975–; Lectr., LS, Northeast. Univ., 1966–75, Consult. and Sr. Lectr., 1976; Libn., Sch. of Mgt., Boston Coll., 1968–75; Libn., Univ. of MA, Boston, 1965–68; Libn., Merrimack Coll., 1958–65; Ref. Libn., Boston Coll., 1948–58; Educ. Couns., Grolier Socty., 1947. **Educ.:** Holy Cross Coll., 1934–38, AB (Eng., Amer. Lit.); Columbia Univ., 1941–43, BS (LS); Harvard Univ., 1952–53, (Bibl.). **Orgs.:** ALA. New Eng. LA: Bibl. Com. (1967–69). MA LA: Educ. Com. (Ch., 1974–75). Bibl. Socty. of Amer. Bibl. Socty., Univ. of VA. **Activities:** 1, 11; 24, 26, 45; 50, 55, 57 **Addr.:** 79 Winthrop Ave., Wollaston, MA 02170.

Seeley, Catherine R. (Jl. 31, 1922, New York, NY) Assoc. Libn., SUNY Upstate Med. Ctr. Lib., 1969–; Anal. Chem., Bristol Labs., 1951–52; Anal. Chem., Gen. Foods, 1946–51; Anal. Chem., Bell Telephone Labs., 1944–45. **Educ.:** Hunter Coll., SUNY, 1939–43, BA (Chem.); Syracuse Univ., 1968–69, MSLS (Lib., Info. Sci.). **Orgs.:** ASIS: Upstate NY Chap., Secy.-Treas. (1972–73), Ch. (1976–77). SLA: Upstate NY Chap., Prog. Ch. (1972–73), Pres. (1974–75). Med. LA: 1979 Anl. Mtg., Prog. Ch. Biomed. Comm. Netwk.: Subcom. on Netwk. Oper. (1975–76). Various other orgs. Amer. Chem. Socty.: Div. of Chem. Info. **Honors:** Beta Phi Mu, 1969. **Pubns.:** "Information Transfer Limitations, Titles of Chemical Document," *Jnl. Chem. Docum.* (O. 1970). **Activities:** 1, 12; 39, 41; 56, 58, 80 **Addr.:** SUNY Upstate Medical Center, Library, 766 Irving Ave., Syracuse, NY 13214.

Seely, Edward (Ja. 1, 1933, Cleveland, OH) Head, Tech. Srvs., Cleveland Pub. Lib., 1978–, Head, Acq., 1976–78; Exec. Dir., INFO Libs., Cnsrtm. - Lorain and Medina Cntys., 1972–76; Head, Tech. Srvs., Lorain Pub. Lib. 1971–72. **Educ.:** Kent State Univ., 1951–55, BA (Eng.); Case West. Univ., 1970–71, MLS; various grad. crs. **Orgs.:** OH LA: Mem. Com. (Ch., 1980–81). Cleveland Area Metro. Lib. Syst.: Tech. Srvs. Interest Grp. (Ch., 1979–81). Pub. Libs. Empls. Credit Un. **Activities:** 9, 13; 15, 17, 46; 56, 75, 93 **Addr.:** 325 Superior Ave., Cleveland, OH 44114.

Seely, Nora P. (Mr. 4, 1928, Cebu City, Cebu, Philippines) Serials Libn., Asst. to Serials Dept. Head, Fordham Univ., 1978–, Acq., 1970–76, Serials Catlgr., 1970. **Educ.:** Univ. of the Philippines, 1947–51, BS (Educ.); Ateneo de Manila Univ., 1953–60, MA (Eng. Lit.); Univ. of AB, 1966–68, MA (Eng.); Univ. of MN, 1969–70, MA (Lib.); various grad. crs. **Orgs.:** Can. LA: Can. ACRL (1977–). AB Tchrs. Assn. Philippine Assn. of Univ. Women. Assn. on Amer. Std., Philippines. **Pubns.:** Resrchr., *The Wordsworth Collection; a Catalogue of Dove Cottage Papers Facsimiles of the University of Alberta* (1971). **Activities:** 1; 15, 44, 46; 55, 63, 92 **Addr.:** 2280 Olinville Ave., Apt. 103, Bronx, NY 10467.

Segal, Jo An S. (S. 14, 1930, Brooklyn, NY) Interim Exec. Dir., Bibl. Ctr. for Resrch., 1980–, Resrc. Sharing Prog. Mgr., Div. Head, 1978–80; various consult. positions, 1976–78; Libn., West. Interstate Comsn. for Higher Educ., 1970–76; Actress, Instr., Trident Thea., 1963–68; Libn., Inst. of Math. Sci., NY Univ., 1955–58; Libn., Bergen Jr. Coll., 1953–55; various lib. positions, 1951–53. **Educ.:** Rutgers Univ., Douglass Coll., 1947–51, BA (LS); Columbia Univ., 1952–55, MS (LS); Univ. of CO, 1974–78, PhD (Comm.). **Orgs.:** ALA. SLA: Rocky Mt. Chap. (Pres., 1981–82); Educ. Div. (Ch., 1981–82). Mt. Plains LA. CO LA. Various other orgs. Sp. Comm. Assn. Natl. Org. for Women. **Honors:** Beta Phi Mu, 1955. **Pubns.:** "Mind, Body and Spirit in the 1976 Colorado Shakespeare Festival," *CO Shakespeare Fest. Anl.* (1976); jt. auth., *A Methodology for Describing Federal Programs that Support Adult Learning Opportunities* (1977); *Learning Opportunities for Adults: A Literature Review. Boulder, Colorado* (1977); "Group Development in the Casts of the 1977 Colorado Shakespeare Festival," *CO Shakespeare Fest. Anl.* (1977); *Library Manual in Lifelong Learning* (1978); various papers, bks., articles. **Activities:** 12, 14-Netwk.; 17, 25, 34; 56, 75, 93 **Addr.:** 630 Pennsylvania Ave., Boulder, CO 80302.

Segal, Ronald (O. 7, 1938, Philadelphia, PA) Dir., Info. Systs. Div., Essex Corp., 1981; Dir., Resrch. and Dev., EDUCOM, 1975–81; Instr., NY Univ., 1972–75; Lectr., Univ. of PA, 1970–72; Systs. Anal., Gen. Electric Co., 1960–70. **Educ.:** PA State Univ., 1956–60, BS (Engin. Sci.); Univ. of PA, 1967–70, MS (Info. Systs.); 1973, Cert. (Data Prcs.); various grad. crs. **Orgs.:** ASIS: Spec. Interest Grp. on Lib. Autom. and Networking (Cabinet Rep.). Assn. for Comp. Mach.: Spec. Interest Grps. in Comm., Performance Measur., and Simulation. **Pubns.:** "Technical Considerations in Planning for a Nationwide Library Network," *Bltn. of the Amer. Socty. for Info. Sci.* (Je. 1980); "Likely Characteristics of a National Computer Network for Higher Education and Research," *The Reality of National Networking* (1979); Prin. auth., "Simulation and Gaming Project for Inter-Institutional Computer Networking," *Final Report to the National Science Foundation on Grant #MC S75–03634* (1979); Jt. auth., "Control of Computing Funds and Resources in a Networking Environment," *Proc.: Natl. Comp. Conf.* (1979); various monos., articles. **Activities:** 14; 24, 34, 41; 56, 59, 91 **Addr.:** 34 Norton Rd., Monmouth Junction, NJ 08852.

Special Subjects/Services: 50. Adult educ.; 51. Advert./Mktg.; 52. Aerosp.; 53. Agric.; 54. Area std.; 55. Arts/Hum.; 56. Autom.; 57. Bibl./Prtg.; 58. Bio. sci.; 59. Bus./Fin.; 60. Chem.; 61. Copyrt.; 62. Documtn.; 63. Educ.; 64. Engin.; 65. Env.; 66. Eth. grps.; 67. Film; 68. Food/Nutr.; 69. Geneal.; 70. Geo.; 71. Geol.; 72. Handcpd.; 73. Hist.; 74. Int. frdm.; 75. Info. sci.; 76. Insr.; 77. Law; 78. Legis.; 79. Math./Comp. sci.; 80. Med.; 81. Metals; 82. Nat. resrcs.; 83. Newsp.; 84. Nuc. sci.; 85. Oral hist.; 86. Petr./Energy; 87. Pharm.; 88. Phys./Astr./Math.; 89. Readg.; 90. Relig.; 91. Sci./Tech.; 92. Soc. sci.; 93. Telecom.; 94. Transp.; 95. (other).

Segal, Sheryl A. (N. 6, 1947, Philadelphia, PA) Lib. Dir., Fed. Comm. Comsn., 1979–; Head, White Hse. Law Lib., 1979; Asst. Libn., US Tax Ct., 1974–78. **Educ.:** Boston Univ., 1965–69, BA (Hist.); Univ. of MD, 1973–75, MLS. **Orgs.:** Law Libns. Socty. of Washington DC: Educ. Com. (Ch., 1979–81). **Activities:** 4; 17, 26, 34; 56, 77, 93 **Addr.:** 2144 California St. N.W., Washington, DC 20008.

Seger, Robert M. (D. 16, 1926, Detroit, MI) Dir., Clinton Pub. Lib., 1967–; Libn., Presque Isle Cnty. Lib., 1960–67; Dir., Northland Lib. Syst., 1965–67; Ref. Libn., St. Clair Cnty. Lib., 1956–59. **Educ.:** West. MI Univ., 1953–56, BA (Educ.); Univ. of MI, 1959–60, AMLS. **Orgs.:** ALA. IA LA. Kiwanis. **Activities:** 9; 17 **Addr.:** Clinton Public Library, 306 8th Ave. S., Clinton, IA 52732.

Segesta, James Edward (N. 12, 1934, Detroit, MI) Ref. Libn., CA State Coll., 1970–; Head, Cat. Srvs., Prof. Lib. Srvs., 1968–69; Head, Tech. Srvs., CA State Coll., San Bernardino, 1963–66; Asst. Acq. Libn., CA State Coll., Long Beach, 1959–63. **Educ.:** Univ. of MI, 1952–56, BA (Eng.); Univ. of South. CA, 1958–59, MS (LS), 1967–68, MA (Eng.). **Orgs.:** CA LA. **Activities:** 1; 39 **Addr.:** California State College Library, 9001 Stockdale Hwy., Bakersfield, CA 93309.

Segre, M. Rose (N. 13, 1924, Italy) Head, Acq. Dept., Adelphi Univ., 1968–; Catlgr., 1963–68; Catlgr., McGill Univ., 1955–62; Asst. Fine Arts Libn., Columbia Univ., 1948–55. **Educ.:** Sir George Williams Univ., 1953–55, BA (Hist. of Art); Columbia Univ., 1947–48, Cert. (LS). **Orgs.:** ALA. NC LA. **Pubns.:** "University Libraries in Italy," *Coll. & Resrch. Libs.* (My. 1974). **Activities:** 1; 15, 20; 55 **Addr.:** Adelphi University Library, Garden City, NY 11530.

Seibert, Donald C. (O. 3, 1929, Los Angeles, CA) Head, Fine Arts Dept., Bird Lib., Syracuse Univ., 1975–, Msc. Biblgphr., 1968–75; Asst. Libn., Msc. Catlgr., Juilliard Sch., 1967–68; Msc, Libn., SUNY, Stony Brook, 1965–67; Asst. Libn., Msc. Catlgr., Juilliard Sch., 1962–65. **Educ.:** George Pepperdine Univ., 1947–51, BA (Hist.); Columbia Univ., 1958–61, MS (Lib.). **Orgs.:** CNLIA: Jt. Com. on Spec. Cat. (Ch.). Msc. LA: Cat. Com. **Pubns.:** *S L A C C; The Partial Use of the Shelf List As Classed Catalog* (1973); *The Hyde Timings, a Collection of Timings Made at Concerts in New York City between 1894 and 1928* (1964); Reviews. **Activities:** 1; 15, 20, 39; 55 **Addr.:** Music Collection, E. S. Bird Library, Syracuse University, Syracuse, NY 13210.

Seibert, Karen S. (F. 1, 1944, Fort Wayne, IN) Head, Ref., Univ. of IL, Chicago, 1978–; Asst. Dept. Head, Ctrl. Ref. Libn., Univ. of AZ, 1977, Hum. Libn., 1970–76. **Educ.:** IN Univ., 1962–69, BA (Eng.), 1969–70, MLS. **Orgs.:** ALA: ACRL/Bibl. Instr. Sect., Educ. for Bibl. Instr. Com. (Secy., 1978–80), Nom. Com.; LAMA; RASD. IL LA. AZ State LA. **Honors:** Beta Phi Mu, 1970. **Pubns.:** Jt. auth., "The Involvement of the Librarian in the Total Educational Process," *Lib. Trends* (Sum. 1980). **Activities:** 1; 17, 31, 39; 56 **Addr.:** University of Illinois at Chicago Circle, Main Library, Box 8198, Chicago, IL 60680.

Seidel, Richard Reynolds (Jl. 26, 1937, Teaneck, NJ) Tech. Srvs. Libn., The Newberry Lib., 1971–; Acq. Libn., Univ. of IL, Chicago, 1966–71; Asst. Ord. Libn., Rutgers Univ., 1963–66. **Educ.:** Rutgers Univ., 1955–59, BA (Hist.), 1963–65, MLS. The Caxton Club, Chicago: Secy. (1972–). Vestry, St. Peter's Episcopal Church (1978–). **Pubns.:** Contrib., *Magazines for Libraries* (1972, 1978). **Activities:** 1, 5; 15, 17, 18 **Addr.:** The Newberry Library, 60 W. Walton St., Chicago, IL 60610.

Seidenberg, Edward (Ja. 18, 1949, Rochester, NY) Planner, TX State Lib., 1979–, Outrch. Inst. Consult., 1976–79; Libn., TX Dept. of Corrections, Asst. Prof., Sam Houston State Univ., 1974–75; Libn., Alameda Cnty. Juvenile Hall, 1973–74; Media Lab. Supvsr., SUNY, Buffalo, 1971–72. **Educ.:** SUNY, 1966–70, BA (Soclgy.), 1971–72, MLS; SW TX State Univ., 1979, MPA (Pub. Admin.). **Orgs.:** ALA: ASCLA (Pres., 1979–80); Lib. Srv. to Prisoners Sect. (Ch., 1976–78). TX LA. SWLA. Austin Lib. Club. Amer. Correct. Assn. TX Corrections Assn. **Pubns.:** "Public Library Budgets: Taxes and Tactics," *TX Lib. Jnl.* (Spr. 1979); ed., *Library Developments;* various articles, rpts. **Activities:** 5, 13; 24, 27, 49-Plng., Eval.; 50, 72 **Addr.:** Texas State Library, Box 12927 Capitol Station, Austin, TX 78711.

Seidler, Louise M. (Ja. 21, 1928, Baytown, TX) Supvsr., Lib. Info. Ctr., Amoco Prod. Co., 1977–; Math. Libn., Tulane Univ., 1964–77; Lib. Asst., Loyola Univ., 1962–64. **Educ.:** Edgewood Park Jr. Coll., Univ. of TX, Austin, 1944–46, (Merchandising, Psy., Soclgy.); New Orleans Acad. of Art, 1947–49, Dip. (Cmcrl. Art). **Orgs.:** SLA: Los Angeles Chap., VP, Pres.-Elect (1978–79), Pres. (1979–80); PAM Div. (Secy., 1975–77). LA LA: Subj. Spec. Div. (Secy., 1976). SWLA. Alliance for Good Gvt. WYES, Pub. TV: Mem. Dr. (1974–79). **Activities:** 12; 17; 86, 88 **Addr.:** Amoco Production Co., Central Library, P.O. Box 50879, New Orleans, LA 70150.

Seidman, Ruth K. (My. 29, 1938, St. Catharines, ON) Libn., U.S. Env. Protection Agency Reg. I, New Eng., 1970–; Sci./Ref. Asst., Sears Lib., Case Inst. 1966–68; Libn., Russ. Resrch. Ctr., Harvard Univ., 1964–65. **Educ.:** Brown Univ., 1956–60, AB (Pol. Sci.); Harvard Univ., 1960–62, AM (Soviet Std.); Case West. Rsv. Univ., 1966–68, MSLS. **Orgs.:** Fed. Lib. Com.: New Eng. Rep. (1974–). SLA: Boston Chap., Secy. (1978–79), Pres.-Elect (1980–81), Pres. (1981–82); Sci./Tech. (Ch., 1977–78). New Eng. Lib. Bd. Panel of Couns.: MA Spec. Lib. Rep. (1977–); Exec. Bd. (1978). **Honors:** Phi Beta Kappa, 1959; Beta Phi Mu, 1968; U.S. Env. Protection Agency, Intl. Women's Yr. Awd., 1975. **Pubns.:** "The EPA Library System–A Field Librarian Views the Development of A Network," *Spec. Libs.* (S. 1978); "Access to Environmental Information Through EPA," *Educ. Libs.* (Win. 1979); jt. ed., "Recycling of Metals and Materials," ERIC (1972). **Activities:** 4, 12; 29, 34, 39; 64, 65, 91 **Addr.:** Region I Library, U.S. Environmental Protection Agency, 2100-B JFK Bldg., Boston, MA 02203.

Seifert, Jan E. (Je. 16, 1938, Pittsburg, KS) Hd., Branch Libs., Fine Arts Libn., Univ. of OK, 1981–, Assoc. Dir., Pub. Srvs., 1976–81; Coord. of Undergrad. Lib. Srvs., Univ. of IL, 1963–76. **Educ.:** KS State Coll., 1956–60, BMus, 1960–61, MS Mus; Univ. of IL 1963–64, MSLS. **Orgs.:** ALA. OK LA. SW LA. **Activities:** 1 **Addr.:** 3713 Red Oaks Dr., Norman, OK 73069.

Seiser, Virginia (Ag. 9, 1948, Anchorage, AK) Educ., Psy. Libn., Portland State Univ. Lib., 1974–; Libn. I, LA of Portland, 1973–74. **Educ.:** Reed Coll., 1966–69; Univ. of OR, 1970–71, BA (Psy.); Univ. of Chicago, 1971–73, MALS. **Orgs.:** ACRL: OR Chap. (Pres., 1980–81). OR LA: Acad. Div. (Ch., 1980–81); Job Place. Com. (Ch., 1974–75). Pac. NW LA: Jobline Com. (Co-Ch., 1977–78). Portland Area Spec. Libns.: Secy. (1980–81); Pres. (1976–77). AAUP. Mazamas. **Honors:** Beta Phi Mu, 1973. **Pubns.:** "Oregon Library'/Media Jobline...Who, What and Where," *PNLA Qtly.* (Spr. 1977); various reviews, articles. **Activities:** 1; 39, 41, 42; 63, 92 **Addr.:** Portland State University Library, P.O. Box 1151, Portland, OR 97207.

Sekerak, John M. (N. 2, 1917, Cleveland, OH) Bio.-Ag. Col. Dev., Ref. Libn., Univ. of CA, Davis, 1953–, Agr. Lib. Consult., UN Food and Agr. Org., Dacca, Bangladesh, 1979; Agr. Lib. Consult., Untd. Nations Food and Agr. Org., Khartoum, Sudan, 1974; Dir. of Libs., Amer. River Coll., 1963–66; various HS tchg. positions, 1951–53. **Educ.:** Cleveland State Univ., 1936–41, AB (Soc. Sci. Educ.); Univ. of CA, Davis, 1945–48, BS (Ani. Sci.); Univ. of CA, Berkeley, 1952–53, BLS (Libnshp.); States of OH, CA, 1941–50, Tchg. Creds. **Orgs.:** ALA: ACRL/ Bio. and Agr. Subsect. (Vice-Ch., 1960–61). CA LA: North. Sect. Coll. Univ. and Resrch. Libs. (Secy., 1954). Amer. Inst. of Bio. Sci. Intl. Assn. of Agr. Libns. and Doncmlsts. Natl. Educ. Assn. Assn. of Higher Educ. **Pubns:** *Grapes, Viticulture, Wine and Wine-Making: a Bibliography* (1975). **Activities:** 1; 39, 45; 58, 68, 91 **Addr.:** 2120 Camino Ct., Davis, CA 95616.

Sekerak, Robert J. (F. 10, 1942, Cleveland, OH) Head, Tech. Srvs., Univ. of VT Med. Lib., 1981–, Ref. Libn., 1977–81, Dir., Hosp. Lib. Dev. Srvs., 1972–77; Insr. Underwriter, Allstate Insr. Co., 1970–71; Sec. Sch. Tchr., Willoughby S. HS, 1969–70; Ofc. Supvsr., Allstate Insr. Co., 1967–69; various tchg. positions, 1963–67. **Educ.:** John Carroll Univ., 1959–63, BS (Hist.); Case West. Rsv. Univ., 1971–72, MSLS (Libnshp.). **Orgs.:** Med. LA: ILL, Resrc. Sharing Stan. Com. (1978–). New Eng. Reg. Med. Lib. Adv. Cncl.: Exec. Bd., Ch.-Elect (1979), Ch. (1980); Hosp. Lib. Stan. Com. (1979–81). N. Atl. Hlth. Sci. Libs.: Prog. Com. (1976). Hlth. Sci. Libs. of NH and VT: Bylaws Com. (1979–81). Boy Scouts of Amer.: VT Troop, Exec. Com. (1978–). **Pubns.:** "Cooperation Strengthens Small Hospital Libraries," *Bltn. Med. LA* (Jl. 1979); "Hospital Library Development Services," *VT Libs.* (Mr.–Ap. 1975). **Activities:** 1, 12; 17, 27, 39 **Addr.:** University of Vermont, Charles A. Dana Medical Library, Burlington, VT 05405.

Selander, Sandy E. (Mr. 30, 1952, New York, NY) Systs. Anal., RDW Systs. Inc., 1981; Systs. Engin., MITRE Corp., 1979–81; Libn., Anal., Eval. Resrch. Corp., 1978–79; Libn., Coord. Sci. Lab., 1977–78. **Educ.:** SUNY, Albany, 1970–73, BA magna cum laude (Psy.); Univ. of IL, 1977–78, MS (Info. Sci.); various grad. crs. **Orgs.:** ASIS: Pub. Pvt. Interface; Lib. Autom.; Numeric Databases. **Pubns.:** Jt. auth., *Reference Guide for the Integrated Library System: Using the Help System* (1980); *A User's Guide to Maintaining the Master Bibliographic File of the Integrated Library System* (1980); Jt. auth., "Comparative Analysis of the Quality of OCLC Serials Cataloging Records as a Function of Contributing CONSER Participant and Field as Utilized by Serials Catalogers at the University of Illinois," *Serials Libn.* (Sum. 1979). **Activities:** 13; 75, 77 **Addr.:** RDW Systems Inc., 8200 Greensboro Dr., McLean, VA 22102.

Self, George Anah (O. 29, 1927, Bulls Gap, TN) Circ. Libn., Carson-Newman Coll., 1969–. **Educ.:** Tusculum Coll., 1946–48, BA cum laude (Span.); Univ. of TN, 1968–69, MSLS; various grad. crs. **Orgs.:** SELA. TN LA: Staff Dev. Task Force (1977–78); Coll. and Univ. Sect., Nom. Com. (1979). ALA. E. TN LA: Secy. (1972). Gvt. Docum. Org. of TN. **Honors:** Pi Lambda Theta. **Activities:** 1; 22, 29, 39 **Addr.:** Rte. 4, Box 355B, Talbott, TN 37877.

Self, James R. (My. 14, 1944, Greeneville, TN) Head, Undergrad. Lib., IN Univ., 1978–, Head, Ref., Reg. Campus Libs., 1973–78, Ref. Libn., 1971–73. **Educ.:** Univ. of TN, 1964–67, BS (Hist.), 1968–70, MA (Hist.); Univ. of Denver, 1970–71, MA (Libnshp.). **Orgs.:** ALA: RASD, Cat. Use Com. (1979–83); LAMA, Compar. Lib. Org. Com. (1979–81). IN LA: Copyrt. Liaison to ALA (1979–80). **Pubns.:** "Library Instruction in the Real World," *Procs.* (1980). **Activities:** 1; 15, 31, 39; 61, 92 **Addr.:** 201 E. 12th St., Bloomington, IN 47401.

Self, Phyllis C. (D. 5, 1946, Moline, IL) Asst. Dir. for Life Sci. Libs. and Hlth. Sci. Libn., Univ. of IL, 1977–, Various positions as lectr., 1978–79; Asst. Hlth. Sci. Libn., 1975–77, Asst. Phys. Educ. Libn., 1974–75; Tchr., HS Libn., Northwest. HS, 1971–73; Unit Libn., Rockridge Sch. Unit, 1970–71; Jr. Libn., Rock Island Pub. Lib., 1969–70. **Educ.:** Univ. of IL, 1967–69, BS (Bio.), 1973–75, MS (LS); Med. LA, 1975, Cert. I; various grad. crs. **Orgs.:** IL LA: Hlth. and Rehab. Lib. Srvs. Com. (Ch., 1977–78); Spec. Lib. Srvs. Sect., Actg. Pres. (1978), Pres. (1978–79); Exec. Bd., Subcom. on the Exec. Ofc. (1978–79); Com. on Prog. Eval. and Support (1978–79). Med. LA: Midwest Reg. Grp., Pres.-Elect (1979–80), Pres. (1980), Exec. Com. (1978–80), Nom. Com. (Ch., 1979); various coms. MEDLINE Users Grp. of the Midwest. Midwest Hlth. Sci. Lib. Netwk. various orgs. Univ. of IL at Urbana: Various coms. Univ. of IL at the Med. Ctr.: various coms. **Honors:** Beta Phi Mu, 1974. **Pubns.:** Jt. auth., "Funding—and its Dollars," *Jnl. of the IL AV Assn.* (Mr. 1978); "Illinois Public Libraries Providing Services for Persons with Handicaps," *IL State Lib. Rpt. No. 4* (My. 1978); Jt. auth. "Library of the Health Sciences, Urbana-Champaign; an example of cooperation and Resource Sharing," *IL Libs.* (1979); Jt. auth., "User-Computer Interface Designs for Information Systems: A Review," *Lib. Resrch.* (1980–81); Jt. auth., "A Quality Assurance Process in Health Science Libraries," *Bltn. Med. LA* (1980); various articles. **Activities:** 1; 31; 72, 80 **Addr.:** Library of the Health Sciences, University of Illinois, 102 Medical Sciences Bldg., 506 S. Mathews, Urbana, IL 61801.

Sell, Betty M. (O. 31, 1928, Coplay, PA) Dir., Lib. Srvs., Catawba Coll., 1970–; Acq. Libn., Livingstone Coll., 1968–70; Asst. Libn., FL State Univ., 1966–68. **Educ.:** Ursinus Coll., 1946–50, BS (Math.); Lancaster Theo. Semy., 1951–53, MRE (Relig. Educ.); Inst. de Lenguas Espanolas, San Jose, Costa Rica, 1957–58, Cert. (Span.); FL State Univ., 1965–67, MS (LS); FL State Univ., 1975–76, AMD (LS), 1976–81, PhD (LS). various crs. **Orgs.:** ALA: ACRL; LAMA. NLA. NC LA. Docum. Libns. of NC: Treas. (1974–75). Various other orgs. AAUP: Catawba Coll. Chap. (Pres., 1979–80); NC St. Exec. Com. (1980–). Assn. of Couples for Marriage Enrich.: Natl. Treas. (1979–81). Rowan Cnty. Fam. Life Cncl.: Pres. (1978–81). Groves Conf. on Marriage and Fam. Various other orgs. **Honors:** Beta Phi Mu, 1967; Delta Kappa Gamma, 1979; ALA, Outstan. Ref. Bk. Com., Outstan. Ref. Bk. of the Yr., 1978. **Pubns.:** Jt. auth., *Divorce in the United States, Canada and Great Britain: A Guide to Reference Sources* (1978); jt. auth., *Suicide; A Guide to Information Sources* (1980); series jt. ed., *Information Guide on Social Problems and Social Issues* (1976–); contrib., *Library Effectiveness: a State of the Art* (1980). **Activities:** 1; 17 **Addr.:** Catawba College Library, Salisbury, NC 28144.

Sell, MaryGrace (Ja. 9, 1951, Pittsburgh, PA) Coord., Ref. and Pub. Srv., Westmoreland Cnty. Cmnty. Coll., 1978–; Chld. Libn., Carnegie Lib. of Pittsburgh, 1976–78, Libn., YA, Chld. and Adult, 1974–76. **Educ.:** Univ. of Pittsburgh, 1968–72, BA (Fr.), 1972–74, MLS; Univ. of Pittsburgh, MBA in progress. **Orgs.:** PA LA: Chld., Young People's and Sch. Libns. Div. (Ch., 1979–80); New Libns. RT (1978–79); Task Force on YA Srvs. in PA (1976); Com. for the Survival of Lib. Srvs. to Chld. and Young People in PA (1977–78). **Honors:** PA LA, New Libns. Hon. Awd., 1979. **Activities:** 1, 9; 21, 31, 39 **Addr.:** Reference & Public Service, Learning Resources Center, Westmoreland County Community College, Youngwood, PA 15697.

Selle, Donna M. (S. 12, 1941, Evansville, IN) Coord., WA Cnty. Coop. Lib. Srvs., 1975–; HS Libn., Ctrl. HS, 1967; Legal Libn., Richard Ernst Hse. Couns., Pac. Maritime Assn., 1965–66. **Educ.:** IN Univ., 1960–63, BS (Educ.); (Lang. Arts, LS) Portland State Univ., 1978; various crs. **Orgs.:** Pac. NW LA: 2nd VP (1979–81). OR LA: Cont. Ed. Com. (Ch., 1979–80). Pac. NW Bibl. Ctr.: Bd. (1979–81). OR State Adv. Cncl. on Libs. Various other orgs. Jr. Leag. of Portland: Pub. Affairs Dir. (1976–77). AAUW: VP (1975–76). **Pubns.:** *Guidelines for Jail Library Services in Oregon* (1977). **Activities:** 9; 17, 25, 34; 56, 72, 93 **Addr.:** Washington County Cooperative Library Services, P.O. Box 5129, Aloha, OR 97006.

Sellen, Betty-Carol (Mr. 28, 1934, Seattle, WA) Assoc. Libn., Ref. Srvs. Col. Dev., Brooklyn Coll. Lib., 1964–; Circ. Libn., Univ. of WA Law Lib., 1961–63; Adult Srvs., Brooklyn Pub. Lib., 1959–60. **Educ.:** Univ. of WA, 1952–56, BA (Hist.), 1958–59, ML (Libnshp.); NY Univ., 1972–74, MA (Eng.). **Orgs.:** ALA: Leroy Merritt Humanitarian Fund (Trustee, 1976–79); Joseph Lippincott Awd. Com. (1977–78); Melvil Dewey Awd. Com. (1977–78); various coms., ofcs.; ACRL, Prog. Com. (1973–74); RTSD; IFRT; SRRT. NY LA. Frdm. to Read Fndn.: Bd. of Trustees (1974–76). LA CUNY: Pres. (1969–71); Exec. Cncl. (1971–72, 1973–74); various coms. various orgs. Amer. Prtg. Hist. Assn. NY Lib. Club. **Pubns.:** *What Else You Can Do With A Library Degree* (1980); Contrib., Ed. Bd., *Serials for*

PROFESSIONAL ACTIVITIES: Institutions: 1. Acad. lib.; 2. Arch.; 3. Assn.; 4. Fed./Gvt. lib.; 5. Inst. lib.; 6. Mfr./Suppl.; 7. Milit. lib.; 8. Musm.; 9. Pub. lib.; 10. Sch. lib.; 11. Sch. of lib. sci.; 12. Spec. lib.; 13. State lib.; 14. (other). **Functions/Activities:** 15. Acq./Col. dev.; 16. Adult srvs.; 17. Admin.; 18. Apprais.; 19. Archit./Bldgs.; 20. Cat./Class.; 21. Chld. srvs.; 22. Circ.; 23. Cons./Pres.; 24. Consult.; 25. Cont. ed.; 26. Educ. lib. sci.; 27. Ext. srvs.; 28. Fund/Grants; 29. Gvt. pubs.; 30. Indx./Abs.; 31. Instr. lib. use; 32. Media srvs.; 33. Micro.; 34. Netwks./Coop.; 35. Persnl.; 36. PR; 37. Publshg.; 38. Recs. mgt.; 39. Ref. srvs.; 40. Repro.; 41. Resrch.; 42. Review.; 43. Secur.; 44. Serials; 45. Spec. col.; 46. Tech. srvs.; 47. Trustees/Bds.; 48. YA srvs.; 49. (other).

Libraries (1979); "Collection Development and the College Library," *Col. Bldg.* (1978); "Urban Homesteading: the Tenant Co-op," *Booklegger* (Sum. 1976); Ed. Bd., *Col. Bldg.* (1979–); various articles. **Activities:** 1; 15, 17, 39 **Addr.:** Reference Services & Collection Development, Brooklyn College Library, Brooklyn, NY 11210.

Sellers, Jesse Leroy (Ag. 14, 1913, Van Buren, AR) Ref., Info. Libn., Sun City Lib., 1973–; Libn.-in-Charge, George Westinghouse Vocational and Tech. HS, 1958–73; Tchr. of Lib., Brooklyn HS of Automotive Trades, 1955–58; Tchr. of Lib., Franklin K. Lane HS, 1953–55; Tchr. of Lib., Far Rockaway HS, 1952–53. **Educ.:** Hofstra Coll., 1947–50, BA (Eng.); Columbia Univ., 1950–54, MS (Lib. Srv.). **Orgs.:** SLA. Frnds. of the Lib. of Sun City, AZ: Pres. (1981). **Addr.:** 10105 Cameo Dr., Sun City, AZ 85351.

Sellers, Phyllis Fox (F. 6, 1925, Des Moines, IA) Libn., N. HS, 1961–; First Asst., Circ., Pub. Lib. of Des Moines, 1959–61; Libn., Resrch., World Bk. Encyc., 1950–55; Chld. Libn., Winnetka, IL, 1948–50. **Educ.:** IA State Univ., 1943–47, BS (Earth Sci.); Univ. of Chicago, 1947–48, BLS. **Orgs.:** ALA. Natl. Educ. Assn. IA State Educ. Assn. Des Moines Educ. Assn. **Activities:** 10; 32, 48 **Addr.:** 3416–57th St., Des Moines, IA 50310.

Sellers, Rose (Zakarin) (Ja. 25, 1910, Brooklyn, NY) Ref. Libn., Sun City (Az.) Lib., 1973–; Assoc. Prof., Brooklyn Coll., 1965–72, Assoc. Libn., 1956–65, Asst. Libn., 1948–56, Lib. Asst., 1934–48. **Educ.:** Hunter Coll., 1926–30, AB (Latin); Columbia Univ., 1932–33, BS (Lib. Srv.); NY Univ., 1945–50, AM (Higher Educ.). **Orgs.:** LA of the City Colls. of NY: Pres. (1950–51). NY Lib. Club: Pres. (1954–55). LA CUNY: Pres. (1963–64). SLA: Mus. Div. (Pres., 1966–67). Frnds. of the Sun City Lib.: Pres. (1980). Fac.-Hillel Assocs. at Brooklyn Coll.: Pres. (1968–70). Fac. Club at Brooklyn Coll.: VP (1964–65). Phi Sigma Sigma: Metro. Bd. (Adv., 1954–60). **Honors:** Wilson Lib. Bltn. and ALA, PR Com., John Cotton Dana Pubcty. Awd., 1948, 1951; Lib. PR Cncl., Anl. Awd. For Achvmt. in PR, 1952. **Pubns.:** "A Different Drummer: Thoughts on Library Education," *Jnl. of Educ. for Libnshp.* (Win., 1966); introduction, *Conference on Reference Services for Foreign Area Studies* (1965); "One Bold Step Forward and Two Cautious Steps Back," *Jnl. of Educ. for Libnshp.* (Jl. 1949); "Recruiting in College Libraries," *Lib. Jnl.* (My. 1962). **Activities:** 1; 17, 31, 36 **Addr.:** 10105 Cameo Dr., Sun City, AZ 85351.

Sellers, Wayne C. (Mr. 10, 1916, Brady, TX) Consult., Newsp., 1980–; Ed., Pubshr., Palestine TX Herald-Press, 1966–79; Pubshr., Rock Hill SC Herald, 1958–66. **Educ.:** TX Tech. Coll., 1934–38, BA (Jnlsm.); Univ. of TX, 1940–41 (Jnlsm.). **Orgs.:** Palestine Carnegie Lib.: Vice-Ch.; Trustee. TX for Libs. TX LA. Bks. for Texans: Strg. Com. (Ch.). TX Press Assn.: Dir. (1980). TX Daily Newsp. Assn.: Pres. (1974). **Honors:** Mass Comm. Dept., TX Tech. Univ., Hall of Fame, 1979; TX LA, Awd. for Outstan. Service to TX Pub. Libs., 1981. **Activities:** 9; 28, 36; 83 **Addr.:** Rte. 3, Box 319W, Palestine, TX 75801.

Sellin, Jon B. (Ag. 6, 1937; OK City, OK) Map Libn., U.S. Geol. Srvy., 1978–; Sci. Biblgphr., Lib. of Congs., 1977–78; Cat. Proj. Mgr., Informatics, Inc., 1976–77. **Educ.:** TX Christ. Univ., 1955–60, BA (Geol.); Cath. Univ. of Amer., 1975–76, MSLS. **Orgs.:** SLA: Geo. and Map Div.; Petr. and Energy Resrcs. Div. (1975–). DC LA. ALA. Geosci. Info. Socty. **Activities:** 4; 46; 70, 82, 86 **Addr.:** 9108 Edmonston Rd., Apt. 103, Greenbelt, MD 20770.

Selmer, Marsha L. (D. 13, 1945, Winamac, IN) Map Libn., Univ. of IL, Chicago, 1971–; Cartographer, Resrch. Anal., Defense Mapping Agency Aerosp. Ctr., 1967–70. **Educ.:** IN Univ., 1963–67, AB (Geo.); West. MI Univ., 1970–71, MSL (LS). **Orgs.:** SLA: IL Chap., Mem. Dir. Com., (1976–78); Geo. and Map Div., Hon. Com. (1976–77), Stan. Com. (1979–80), Lcl. Arrange. Com. (1974–75). West. Assn. Map Libs. (1974–). Assn. Can. Map Libs. (1977–). Chicago Map Socty.: Bd. of Dirs. (1976–); Rec. Secy. (1978–79); Hosplty. Com. (Ch., 1976–77); Nom. Com. (1979); Prog. Com. (1976–77); Pubns. Com. (1978–79). Amer. Geo. Socty. (1974–79). **Pubns.:** "A Policy for Withdrawal from the Map Collection," *SLA Geo. and Map Div. Bltn.* (Je. 1979); "Map Cataloging and Classification Methods: A Historical Survey," *SLA Geo. and Map Div. Bltn.* (Mr. 1976); various bk. reviews, *SLA Geo. and Map Div. Bltn.* (1977–). **Activities:** 1; 15, 17, 39; 70 **Addr.:** University of Illinois at Chicago Circle, The Library–Map Section, Box 8198, Chicago, IL 60680.

Seltzer, (Bowen), Ada M. (Je. 7, 1942, Kempton, PA) Asst. Dir., Pub. Srvs., Med. Ctr. Lib., Univ. of S. FL, 1979–, Head, Srvs. to Pub., 1974–79, Libn., Ref. Dept., 1971–74, Assoc. Libn., Ref. Dept., Univ. Lib., 1969–71, Asst. Libn., 1965–69. **Educ.:** Kutztown State Coll., 1960–64, BS (Lib. Educ., Eng.); FL State Univ., 1964–65, MS (LS); Univ. of S. FL, 1969–71, MA (Soclgy., Jr. Coll. Educ.). **Orgs.:** ALA. Med. LA: South. Chap. (Secy., Treas., 1977–78); Bylaws Com. (Ch., 1979–81). SELA: Mem. Com. (1974–76). FL LA: Pres. (1981–82); Exec. Bd. (Dir., 1978–80); Ref. RT, various ofcs. (1967–70); Various other orgs. Univ. of S. FL Alum. Assn.: Multi-Campus Chap. (VP, 1981–82). FL State Univ. Alum. Assn. FL Cncl. on Aging. FL Med. Libns. **Honors:** Kappa Delta Pi; Beta Phi Mu. **Pubns.:** Ed., *Florida Union List of Serials* (1973); "The FLA Economic Juncture: True Grit," *FL Libs.* (1980); "Online Health Information News," nsltr. clmn. *FL Online* (1980); "On-Line Literature Retrieval as a Continuing Medical Education Course," *Bltn. of the Med. LA* (1977); "Freedom Corner I–IV," *FL Libs.* (1974–75); "Activities for and about Aging," *FL Libs.* (1974); various articles. **Activities:** 1, 12; 17, 39, 41; 58, 80, 93 **Addr.:** Medical Center Library, University of South Florida, 12901 N. 30th St., Box 31, Tampa, FL 33612.

Selvar, Jane Cumming (Lincoln, NE) Dir., Bronxville Pub. Lib., 1979–; Asst. Dept. Head, Adult Reader, Info. Srvs., White Plains Pub. Lib., 1978–79, Libn., Adult Srvs., 1974–78. **Educ.:** Univ. of NE, 1967, BA (Eng., Sp.); South. IL Univ., 1969, MA (Sp.); West. MI Univ., 1973, MSL (LS). **Orgs.:** ALA: LAMA; RASD, Notable Bks. Cncl. Ch. (1980–82). NY LA. Westchester LA. **Honors:** Phi Kappa Phi, 1969. **Activities:** 9; 15, 17; 55, 85 **Addr.:** Bronxville Public Library, 201 Pondfield Rd., Bronxville, NY 10708.

Selzer, Nancy S. (Ap. 30, 1953, Melrose Park, PA) Libn., E. I. DuPont de Nemours and Co., Haskell Lab., 1977–; Head Reg. Photocopy, Coll. of Physicians, 1975–77. **Educ.:** Mt. Holyoke Coll., 1971–75, BA (Eng.); Drexel Univ., 1975–77, MS (LS); Med. LA, 1978, Cert. Med. Libn. **Orgs.:** Med. LA: Philadelphia Reg. Grp., Cont. Ed. Com. SLA: Phila. Chap. Pres-Elect. (1980–81); Pres. (1981–82). **Honors:** Beta Phi Mu, 1978. **Activities:** 12; 17, 39; 80, 91 **Addr.:** E. I. DuPont de Nemours & Co., Haskell Laboratory for Toxicology and Industrial Medicine, Elkton Rd., Newark, DE 19711.

Semler, Evelyn Williams (S. 7, 1921, Utica, NY) Assoc. Cur., Heineman Col., Supvsr., Readg. Rm., Pierpont Morgan Lib., 1970–; Ref. Libn., Musm. of Mod. Art, 1968–70, Catlgr., 1964–68, Asst., Dept. of Egyptian Art, Metro. Musm. of Art, 1947–59; Catlgr., Farnsworth Art Musm., Wellesley Coll., 1946–47. **Educ.:** Mt. Holyoke, 1940–44, BA (Art); Columbia Univ., 1957–61, MS (LS). **Orgs.:** SLA: Musm. Div. Archvsts. RT of Metro. NY. Msc. LA. Amer. Musicological Socty. Columbia Sch. Lib. Srv. Alum. Assn. Mt. Holyoke Club of NY. Blue Hill Troupe. **Activities:** 39, 45; 55 **Addr.:** 162 E. 80th St., New York, NY 10021.

Semler, George Herbert, Jr. (O. 28, 1924, New York, NY) Sr. Ref. Libn., Bus. Lib., Newark Pub. Lib., 1966–; Cat. Libn., Swirbul Lib., Adelphi Univ., 1964–66; Jr. Libn., Scarsdale Pub. Lib., 1958–64. **Educ.:** Bard Coll., 1947–50, BA (Gvt.); Columbia Univ., 1956–58, MS (LS). **Orgs.:** Msc. LA: NY Chap., Secy.-Treas. (1961–62), Ch. (1965–67). Amer. Musicological Socty. **Activities:** 13; 20, 39; 55 **Addr.:** 162 E. 80th St., New York, NY 10021.

Seng, Mary A. (Ja. 15, 1932, Appleton, WI) Head, Spec. Srvs. Dept., Gen. Libs., Univ. of TX, Austin, 1977–; Head, Bus. Admin., Econ. Lib., 1968–77; Bus. Libn., Univ. of WI, 1966–68. **Educ.:** Univ. of WI, Milwaukee, 1950–54, BA (Eng., Educ.); Univ. of WI, Madison, 1965–66, MA (LS). **Orgs.:** ASIS. SLA: TX Chap., Austin Lcl. Plng. Grp., Ch. **Pubns.:** "Reference Service Upgraded," *Spec. Libs.* (Ja. 1978); "Business Reference Titles Since 1972," *SLA TX Chap. Bltn.* (1976); *Computer-based Reference Services in Selected Texas Libraries* (1980). **Activities:** 1; 17, 31, 46; 59, 75 **Addr.:** General Libraries, PCL 1.102, University of Texas, Austin, TX 78712.

Senner, Rachel B. (N. 10, 1921, Henderson, NE) Lib. Srvs. Dir., Hesston Unfd. Sch. Dist. 460, 1967–; Pub. Libn., Buhler Pub. Lib., 1956–66. **Educ.:** Bethel Coll., 1939–43, BS (Home Econ.); Emporia State Univ., 1966–69, ML (LS); various crs. **Orgs.:** KS Assn. of Sch. Libns.: Dist. III (Dir., 1979–80). KS Netwk. Athrty. Cncl. KS Assn. of Educ. and Tech. Gvr. Carlin's Com. on Lib. Resrcs. Buhler Mennonite Church. **Activities:** 10; 20, 34, 48; 61, 74, 78 **Addr.:** 221 W. Ave. B, Buhler, KS 67522.

Senzig, Donna Mae (S. 9, 1940, Green Bay, WI) Actg. Dir., Coll. Lib., Univ. of WI, 1980–, Assoc. Dir., Coll. Lib., 1976–80, Chief, Prcs. Dept., Meml. Lib., 1970–75, Head, Germanic Cat., 1967–70, Serials Catlgr., 1963–66. **Educ.:** Univ. of WI, 1958–62, BA (Eng.), 1962–63, MLA (LS). **Orgs.:** WI LA: Bd. (1981–). WI Assn. of Acad. Libns.: Ch.-Elect (1981); Ch. (1982). ALA: Representation in Machine-Readable Form of Bibl. Info. Interdiv. Com. (1980–); RASD; ACRL/Bibl. Instr. Sect., Coop. Com. (1979–81); LAMA, Circ. Syst. Eval. Com. (1979–81). **Pubns.:** Contrib., *Turnkey Automated Circulation Systems: Aids for Libraries in the Marketplace* (1980); Jt. auth., "Mission of an Undergraduate Library," *Coll. and Resrch. Libs. News* (N. 1979); "Bibliographic Instruction in the Discipline Associations," *Coll. and Resrch. Libs. News* (N. 1980). **Activities:** 1; 17, 31, 46; 56, 75 **Addr.:** College Library, University of Wisconsin-Madison, 600 N. Park St., Madison, WI 53706.

Sepehri, Abazar (Ap. 11, 1939, Rezaiyeh, Iran) Head Libn., Mid. E. Col., Gen. Libs., Univ. of TX, Austin, 1979–; Asst. Head, Mid. E. Coll., Univ. of Chicago Lib., 1975–79; Mid. E. Biblgphr., Princeton Univ. Lib., 1974–75; Chief Libn., Dropsie Univ., 1972–74. **Educ.:** Tabriz Univ., Iran, 1961–64, BA; Tehran Univ., Iran, 1967–69, MLS; Univ. of Pittsburgh, 1971–72, Advnc. Cert. (Lib., Info. Sci.); various crs. **Orgs.:** ALA. Mid. E. LA: Tech. Prcs. Com. (1980–). **Pubns.:** *Iranian Corporate Headings with References* (1976); *Directory of Libraries in Northwest Iran* (1970); "Academic Libraries in Iran," *Unesco Bltn. for Libs.* (Mr.–Ap. 1978); various articles. **Activities:** 1; 15, 17, 20; 54 **Addr.:** 7207 Daugherty, Austin, TX 78757.

Serban, William M. (S. 28, 1949, Canton, OH) Gvt. Docum. Libn., LA Tech. Univ. Lib., 1978–. **Educ.:** Purdue Univ., 1967–71, BA (Pol. Sci.); OH Univ., 1971–73, MA (Pol. Sci.); Univ. of Pittsburgh, 1977–78, MLS. **Orgs.:** ALA: GODORT (1978–). LA LA: Docum. Com. (1979–). Stained Glass Assn. of Amer. Glass Art Socty. **Pubns.:** Jt. auth., *Stained Glass: A Guide to Information Sources* (1980); Jt. ed., *Stained Glass Index: 1906–1977* (1979); "Louisiana Documents Depository Legislation," *LA LA Bltn.* (Win. 1981); "Computerized Bibliographic Retrieval: The Louisiana Connection," *LA LA Bltn.* (Spr. 1980). **Activities:** 1; 29, 39; 55, 91, 92 **Addr.:** Government Documents Dept., Prescott Memorial Library, Louisiana Technological University, Ruston, LA 71272.

Serebnick, Judith (Ap. 23, 1929, New York, NY) Asst. Prof., Grad. Lib. Sch., IN Univ., 1977–; Adj. Fac., Grad. Sch. of Lib. Srv., Rutgers Univ., 1973–77; Ref. Libn., Brooklyn Bus. Lib., 1972–75; Bk. Ed., *Lib. Jnl.*, 1969–72; Asst. Ord. Libn., Princeton Univ., 1966–69; Core Libn., Northwest. Univ., 1965–66; Asst. Bk. Ed., *Lib. Jnl.*, 1957–64. **Educ.:** City Coll., New York, 1949–52, BS (Eng.); PA State Univ., 1952–54, MA (Eng.); Univ. of CA, Los Angeles, 1964–65, MLS; Rutgers Univ., 1972–78, PhD (LS). **Orgs.:** ALA. ASIS. AALS. IN LA. **Honors:** Ford Fndn., Travel-Std. Grant, 1974. **Pubns.:** Ed., *Lib. Jnl. Bk. Review* (1970–72); "A Review of the Research Related to Censorship in Libraries," *Lib. Resrch.* (Sum. 1979); "An Analysis of the Relationship Between Book Reviews and the Inclusion of Potentially Controversial Books in Public Libraries," *Collection Building* (1979); "The 1973 Court Rulings on Obscenity: Have They Made a Difference?" *Wilson Lib. Bltn.* (D. 1975). **Activities:** 1, 9; 15, 16, 26; 63, 74, 92 **Addr.:** Graduate Library School, Indiana University, Bloomington, IN 47401.

Servis, Willie (Mae) D(earing) (Mr. 29, 1923, Aberdeen, MS) Ref. Libn., Sandia Lab., 1958–; Tech. Libn., The BDM Corp., 1971–75; Tech. Libn., Dikewood Corp., 1970–71; Catlgr., KAFB Spec. Srvs. Lib., 1970–70; Libn., Sandia Labs., 1958–70; Tech. Libn., Natl. Bur. of Stans., 1956–57; Tech. Libn., Rohm and Haas Co., Redstone Arsenal Resrch. Div., 1950–55. **Educ.:** MS State Coll., 1943–49, BS (Chem. Engin.); Univ. of WA, 1949–50, BS (LS). **Orgs.:** SLA. NM LA. Amer. Chem. Socty. **Activities:** 4, 12; 17, 20, 39; 60, 64, 81 **Addr.:** Rte. 4 Box 1162, Los Lunas, NM 87031.

Sessa, Frank Bowman (Je. 11, 1911, Pittsburgh, PA) Prof. Emeritus, Univ. of Pittsburgh, 1980–, Prof., Sch. of Lib. and Info. Sci., 1966–79, Actg. Dean, 1971–73, Ch., Com. of Doct. Std., 1966–76; Dir., Miami Pub. Lib., 1951–66; Asst. Prof., Hist., Univ. of Miami, 1950–51, Instr., Hist., 1947–50. **Educ.:** Univ. of Pittsburgh, 1929–33, AB (Hist.), 1933–34, MA (Hist.); Carnegie Inst. of Tech., 1942, BS (LS); Univ. of Pittsburgh, 1950, PhD (Hist.). **Orgs.:** ALA: Treas. (1972–76); Cncl. (2X). SELA: Pub. Lib. Sect., Ch. FL LA: Pres. (1957). FL Hist. Socty.: Pres. (1962–64). AAUP. Beta Phi Mu: Pres. (1970); Natl. Exec. Secy. (1975–80). **Honors:** Univ. of Pittsburgh/Carnegie Lib. Sch., Alum. Assn. Hon. Grad., 1977. **Pubns.:** "History of the Public Library," *Encyc. of Lib. and Info. Sci.* (1978); "The Miami Public Library," *Encyc. of Lib. and Info. Sci.* (1976); "Fire in Libraries," *Encyc. of Lib. and Info. Sci.* (1972); *Survey: Beaver County Federated Library System: An Assessment* (1978); *Library Services in Clearfield County: A Review* (1978). **Activities:** 9, 11; 17, 19, 24 **Addr.:** 2849 Northwood Blvd., Orlando, FL 32803.

Sessions, Judith Ann (D. 16, 1947, Lubbock, TX) Dir., Lib. and Lrng. Resrc. Ctr., Mt. Vernon Coll., 1977–; Head Libn., Univ. of South. CA, Salkehatchie Campus, 1974–77; Asst. Libn., Pub. Srvs., Univ. of South. CA, Spartenburg, 1971–74. **Educ.:** FL Tech. Univ., 1966–70, BA (LS); FL State Univ., 1970–71, MS. **Orgs.:** WA Metro. Cncl. Gvts.: Lib. Cncl. (Coll. Rep., 1979–80). WHCOLIS: Info. Ctr. Volun. (1979). ALA: Couns.-At-Large (1982–86); LITA/Vid. and Cable Comm. Sect. (Secy., 1979–81); JMRT (Pres., 1981–82). DC LA: Secy. (1979–81). **Honors:** ALA, Shirley Olafson Meml. Awd., 1978. **Pubns.:** "Finding Libraries in the Video Maze," *American Libraries* (My. 1981); various bk. reviews. **Activities:** 1, 2; 17, 39; 74, 78, 93 **Addr.:** Mt. Vernon College Library, 2100 Foxhall Rd., Washington, DC 20007.

Sessions, Vivian S. (D. 15, 1920, Ossining, NY) Dir., Prof., McGill Univ., Grad. Sch. of Lib. Sci., 1976–; Dir., Assoc. Prof., CUNY, Ctr. for the Advnc. of Lib./Info. Sci., 1969–76, Proj. Dir., Resrch. Fndn., 1965–69; Libn., Sr. Libn., NY Pub. Lib., 1959–65. **Educ.:** Univ. of MI, 1945, AB (Letters, Law), 1948, MA (Hist.); Columbia Univ., 1959, MS (LS). **Orgs.:** ASIS: SIG/BSS, Ch. SLA. Corp. of Prof. Libns. of PQ: VP (1979–80); Bd. (1977–81). Can. LA. various orgs. Can. Cncl. of Lib. Schs.: Ch. (1980–). **Honors:** Beta Phi Mu; Cncl. of Plng. Libns., Disting. Srv. Awd. **Pubns.:** *Data Bases in the Social and Behavioral Sciences* (1974); "The Graduate School of Library Science of McGill University," *Argus* (S.–D. 1980); "Continuing Education: Courses Are Few and Disparate," *Can. Lib. Jnl.* (Je. 1979); "URBANDOC: Lessons for Urbanists and Documentalists," *Documentation for*

Special Subjects/Services: 50. Adult educ.; 51. Advert./Mktg.; 52. Aerosp.; 53. Agric.; 54. Area std.; 55. Arts/Hum.; 56. Autom.; 57. Bibl./Prtg.; 58. Bio. sci.; 59. Bus./Fin.; 60. Chem.; 61. Copyrt.; 62. Documtn.; 63. Educ.; 64. Engin.; 65. Env.; 66. Eth. grps.; 67. Film; 68. Food/Nutr.; 69. Geneal.; 70. Geo.; 71. Geol.; 72. Handcpd.; 73. Hist.; 74. Int. frdm.; 75. Info. sci.; 76. Insr.; 77. Law; 78. Legis.; 79. Math./Comp. sci.; 80. Med.; 81. Metals; 82. Nat. resrcs.; 83. Newsp.; 84. Nuc. sci.; 85. Oral hist.; 86. Petr./Energy; 87. Pharm.; 88. Phys./Astr./Math.; 89. Readg.; 90. Relig.; 91. Sci./Tech.; 92. Soc. sci.; 93. Telecom.; 94. Transp.; 95. (other).

Urban Management, Proceedings of a Symposium at OECD...1975 (1979); "Library and Information Services for Urban Professionals," *ALA Yearbook* (1976). **Activities:** 11, 12; 17, 26; 75, 92 **Addr.:** McGill University, Graduate School of Library Science, 3459 McTavish St., Montreal PQ H3A 2M1 Canada.

Settanni, Joseph Andrew (Ag. 15, 1954, New York City, NY) Assoc. Archvst., The Salvation Army Arch. and Resrch. Ctr., 1977–. **Educ.:** Manhattan Coll., 1972–76, BA (Hist.); NY Univ., 1976–77, MA (Hist.), NY Univ., 1977–78, Cert. (Arch.); Assn. of Recs. Mgrs. and Admins., Inc., 1980, Recs. Mgt. Cert.; Amer. Assn. for State and Lcl. Hist., 1981, Docums. Exhibition Cert. **Orgs.:** SAA: Relig. Arch. Com. (1979); Descr. Com. (1979). Mid-Atl. Reg. Arch. Conf. Long Island Arch. Conf. Amer. Assn. for State and Lcl. Hist. **Honors:** Phi Alpha Theta, 1974; Manhattan Coll., McGoldrick Medal for Hist., 1976; Kappa Delta Pi, 1975; Epsilon Sigma Pi, 1975. **Pubns.:** "Unethical Ethical Destruction," *Univ. Bookman* (Sum. 1979); *A Report on the Manuscript Department of The New-York Historical Society* (1977); bk. reviews *Modern Age*. **Activities:** 2; 20, 23, 45; 62, 75, 92 **Addr.:** The Salvation Army Archives and Research Center, 145 W. 15th St., New York, NY 10011.

Settel, Barbara A. (Jl. 29, 1949, New Haven, CT) Adj. Fac., Sch. of Info. Std., Syracuse Univ., 1980–; Serials Libn., Asst. Un. List Ed., Ctrl. NY Lib. Resrcs. Cncl., 1979–80; Ref. Libn., Syracuse Univ. Libs., 1977–79; Asst. Libn., SUNY Coll. of Env. Sci. and Forestry, 1977. **Educ.:** Univ. of Rochester, 1967–71, BA (Hist.); Syracuse Univ., 1971–76, MA (Hist.), MLS. **Orgs.:** Assn. for Asian Std. ASIS. **Honors:** Beta Phi Mu. **Pubns.:** Jt. auth., *Self Study Guide on Urban Problems and Urbanism in South Asia* (1974); "Getting through the Journal Literature: Computerized Literature Searches," *S. Asia Lib. Notes and Queries* (Je. 1979); jt. auth., "Characteristics of Book Indexes for Subject Retrieval in the Humanities and Social Sciences," *Indxr.* (Ap. 1978). **Activities:** 1, 12; 34, 39, 41; 54, 92 **Addr.:** RD #1, Lafayette, NY 13084.

Sever, Eileen D. (Winnipeg, MB) Branch Libn., Los Angeles Pub. Lib., 1979–, Sr. Libn., Bus. and Econ. Dept., 1977–79, Ref. Libn., 1973–77; Mgr., Info. Ctr., South. CA Libs., 1971–73; Bibl. Ed., *Anl. Review of Info. Sci. and Tech.*, 1968–70; Catlgr., Los Angeles Law Lib., 1966–68. **Educ.:** Univ. of CA, Los Angeles, 1954–58, AB (Soclgy.), 1965–66, MLS, 1968–69, Tchg. Cert. **Orgs.:** ALA. ASIS. SLA: S. CA Chap., Salary Srvy. Com. (1978–79). **Honors:** Beta Phi Mu, 1966. **Pubns.:** *Bibliography of Information Science and Technology* (1968–69); jt. auth., *1979 Salary Survey, SLA Southern California Chapter* (1979); "Dialogue at the Top," *Communicator* (Mr. 1975); "Performance Evaluations," *Communicator* (F.–Mr. 1977). **Activities:** 9, 12; 16, 17, 34; 50, 59, 95-Resrc. Location. **Addr.:** 2920 Overland Ave., Los Angeles, CA 90064.

Severance, Malcolm D. (F. 25, 1918, Spring Lake, NJ) Pres., The Turner Subscrpn. Agency, Inc., 1946–; Circ. Mgr., Hearst Mag., Inc., 1944–46. **Educ.:** Univ. of PA, 1936–39 (Bus. Admin.). **Orgs.:** ALA. SLA. Audit Bus. of Circ. **Activities:** 1, 5; 15, 44 **Addr.:** The Turner Subscription Agency, Inc., 235 Park Ave. S., New York, NY 10003.

Severance, Robert W. (D. 13, 1907, Florence, SC) Retired, Dir. Emeritus, Air Univ. Lib., 1974–, Dir., 1957–74; Spec. Asst. to Dir., for designing new bldg., Natl. Lib. of Med., 1956–57; Deputy Dir., The Army Lib., Pentagon, 1953–56; Dir., Baylor Univ. Lib., 1940–53; Dir., Lib., Prof. Lib. Sci., Stetson Univ., 1936–40; Circ. Libn., NC State Coll., 1934–36; Cnty. Libn., Knoxville Pub. Lib., 1933–34. **Educ.:** Furman Univ., 1925–28, BA (Hist.); Univ. of VA, 1928–29, MA (Hist.); George Peabody Coll., 1932–33, BS (LS); various grad. crs. **Orgs.:** ALA: Com. on Bds. and Coms. (1954–55); Com. on Org. (Ch., 1957–62); Spec. Com. on Reorg. (1955); Cncl.; ACRL (Pres., 1952–53); PLA/Armed Forces Lib. Sect. (Pres., 1960–69); FLRT, Founder, Org. SWLA. SELA: Com. on Org. (Ch., 1970). AL LA: Pres. (1970). FL LA: Pres. (1938–40). various orgs. Milit. Libns. Wkshp.: Org. (1957). **Honors:** PLA, Armed Forces Lib. Sect., Cit., 1974; US Air Force, Decor. for Excep. Civilian Srv., 1974. **Pubns.:** Ed., *TX Lib. Jnl.* (1940–49). **Activities:** 1, 4; 17, 19, 35; 52, 70, 74 **Addr.:** 168 Carol Woods, Chapel Hill, NC 27514.

Severtson, Susan, M. O. (Ag. 29, 1943, Eau Claire, WI) Exec. Ed., Resrch. Pubns., Inc., 1974–; Asst. Libn., Tech. Srvs., Middlebury Coll., 1971–74; Dir., Lib., Franconia Coll., 1968–71; Asst. to Lib. Dir., Hampshire Coll., 1967–68. **Educ.:** Univ. of MN, 1961–64, (Eng. Lit., Phil.); Univ. of Chicago, 1966–67 (LS). **Orgs.:** ALA: Reprodct. of Lib. Mtrls. Sect., Exec. Com. (1978–). ASIS. ARL: Natl. Adv. Bd. for Std. of Bibl. Cntrl. of Micro. (1979–80). **Pubns.:** "Toward the Library/Bookstore," *Lib. Jnl.* (Ja. 15, 1971). **Activities:** 14-Publshg.; 23, 33, 37; 55, 56 **Addr.:** Research Publications, Inc., 12 Lunar Dr., Woodbridge, CT 06525.

Sewell, Robert George (Ag. 28, 1942, Stillwater, OK) Japanese Biblgphr., Assoc. Prof., Univ. of IL, 1970–; Lib. Assoc., Meml. Lib., Univ. of WI, 1967–69. **Educ.:** Univ. of WI, 1960–64, BS (Asian Std.); Columbia Univ., 1964–67, MA (Japanese Lit.); Univ. of IL, 1971–76, PhD (Compar. Lit.). **Orgs.:** Assn. for Asian Std.: Com. on E. Asian Libs., Subcom. on Japanese Mtrls. (1978–80). **Honors:** Univ. of WI, Ford Fndn. Schol., 1969; Japan Fndn., Japan Fndn. Prof. Flwshp., 1977. **Pubns.:** Jt. auth., "A Project for the Publication of Japanese Government Documents in Microfiche," *Jnl. of Intl. Micro. Congs.* (1979); "Old and Rare Japanese Books in U.S. Collections," *Coll. & Resrch. Libs.* (My. 1978); "Art as Imitation: The Theories of Aristotle's *Mimesis* and Zeami's *Monomane*," *Hikaku bungaku kenkyu/Etudes de littératures comparées* (D. 1978); "Printers and Printing: Japanese Printing," *Encyc. of Lib. and Info. Sci.* (1978); "The Path of the Poet-Priest Saigyo," *Denver Qtly.* (Sum. 1977). **Activities:** 1; 15, 39, 45; 54, 55 **Addr.:** Asian Library, University of Illinois Library, Urbana, IL 61801.

Sewell, Winifred (Ag. 12, 1917, Newport, WA) Consult., 1970, Ed., *Gale Info. Guides*, Hlth. Affairs, 1972; Adj. Asst. Prof., Pharm., Univ. of MD, Sch. of Pharm., 1970–, Adj. Lectr., Coll. of Lib. and Info. Srvs., 1969–; Head, Drug Lit. Prog., Natl. Lib. of Med., 1965–70, Subj. Heading Spec., Deputy Chief, Bibl. Srvs. Div., 1961–65; Sr. Libn., Squibb Inst. for Med. Resrch., 1946–1961; Libn., Wellcome Resrch. Labs., 1942–46. **Educ.:** State Univ. of WA, 1938, BA; Columbia Univ., 1940, BSLS, MS; various crs. **Orgs.:** Amer. Assn. of Colls. of Pharm.: Libs./Educ. Resrcs. Sect. (Ch., 1979–80); Cncl. on Sects. Admin. Bd. (1980–82). Med. LA: Pub. Hlth. and Hlth. Admin. Libs. Sect. (Ch., 1979–80); Recert. Com. (Ch., 1979–80); Rittenhse. Awd. Subcom. (Ch., 1975–76). SLA: Pres. (1960–61); SIG Class. Resrch., Ch. Drug Info. Assn.: Pres. (1970–71). Amer. Socty. of Hosp. Pharmacists. Amer. Hlth. Plng. Assn. Amer. Chem. Assn. Various other orgs. **Honors:** Philadelphia Coll. of Pharm. and Sci., Doctor of Sci., Honoris Causa, 1979; Med. LA, Ida and George Eliot Prize, 1977; Med. LA, Flwshp., 1978. **Pubns.:** *Guide to Drug Information* (1976); jt. auth., *Using MeSH for Effective Searching: A Programmed Guide* (1976); *Reader in Medical Librarianship* (1973); "Medical Subject Headings," *Index Medicus* (Ja. 1963); jt. auth., "Integrating Library Skills Teaching into the Pharmacy School Curriculum," *Amer. Jnl. of Pharm. Educ.* (F. 1980); various rpts. **Activities:** 11, 14-Consult.; 24, 26, 31; 80, 87, 92 **Addr.:** 6513 76th Pl., Cabin John, MD 20818.

Seymour, Whitney North, Jr. (Jl. 7, 1923, Huntington, WV) Secy., Ntl. Citizens for Pub. Libs., 1980–; Secy., Natl. Citizens Emergency Com. to Save our Pub. Libs., 1976–79; Trustee, NY Pub. Lib., 1967–76; US Attorney, S.D.N.Y., 1970–73; NY State Sen., 1966–68; Attorney, 1950–66. **Educ.:** Princeton Univ., 1941–47, AB (Politics); Yale Univ., 1947–50, LLB (Law). **Orgs.:** ALA. Urban Libs. Cncl.: Exec. Bd. **Pubns.:** Jt. Auth., *For The People: Fighting for Public Libraries* (1979); *Why Justice Fails* (1972). **Activities:** 3 **Addr.:** 1 Battery Park Plz., New York, NY 10004.

Shaaban, Marian T. (Americus, GA) Intl. Docum. Libn., IN Univ. Lib., 1971–, Asst. Ref. Libn., 1969–71; Asst. Ref. Libn., Univ. of TN, 1962–68. **Educ.:** GA Southwest. Coll., 1956–58; Univ. of GA, 1958–60, BA (Pol. Sci.); FL State Univ., 1960–62, MLS. **Orgs.:** ALA. IN LA. **Pubns.:** Jt. auth., "United Nations Documentation: An Introductory Guide," *DEA News for Tchrs. of Pol. Sci.* (Spr. 1980); "Examination of Published and Unpublished Manuals and Handouts on United Nations Documentation," *Gvt. Pubns. Review* (1979); jt. ed., "U.N. and Other International Organizations," *Gvt. Pubns. Review*. **Activities:** 1, 12; 15, 29, 39; 54, 57, 92 **Addr.:** Documents Department, Indiana University Library, Bloomington, IN 47405.

Shabowich, Stanley A. (N. 17, 1932, Byelorussia) Acq. Libn., Pan Amer. Univ., 1981–; Acq. Libn., Purdue Univ., Calumet, 1971–81; Tech. Srvs. Libn., NC Wesleyan Coll., 1971; Dir. of Tech. Srvs., E. Carolina Univ., 1969–70; Acq. Libn., SW TX State Univ., 1967–69; Slavonic and Germanic Langs. Biblgphr., MI State Univ., 1966–67. **Educ.:** Wayne State Univ., 1957–62, BA (Russ.); West. MI Univ., 1965–66, MSLS. **Orgs.:** ALA. IN LA. **Pubns.:** "An Approach to Assessment of Quality of a University Library 1975 Collection," ERIC (1975, 1977). **Activities:** 1; 15, 44, 46; 54, 65 **Addr.:** Library Acquisitions, Pan American University, Edinburg, TX 78539.

Shackleton, Suzanne Marie (S. 5, 1950, Quincy, IL) Libn. II, IL State Bd. of Educ., 1976–; Libn., IL Env. Protection Agency, 1974–76; Libn., Notre Dame HS, 1973–74. **Educ.:** IL State Univ., 1970–72, BA (LS, Hist.); Univ. of IL, 1972–73, MSLS; 1973, Tchrs. Cert. **Orgs.:** IL LA. SLA. IL Vocational Assn. **Honors:** Phi Alpha Theta, Beta Phi Mu. **Activities:** 12, 13; 20, 30, 39; 50, 63, 65 **Addr.:** 800 Durkin, Springfield, IL 62704.

Shadwick, Virginia Ann Greer (N. 10, 1942, Danville, KY) Col. Dev. Libn., San Francisco State Univ., 1976–, Head, Circ. Dept., 1972–76, Catlgr., 1969–72, Cat./Ord. Libn., 1968–69. **Educ.:** MI State Univ., 1960–64, BA (Hist); Univ. of KY, 1967, MSLS. **Orgs.:** ALA. CA LA: State Coll. and Univ. Libns. Chap. San Francisco State Univ.: State Sen. (Vice-Ch., 1978–); various other coms., ofcs. Sch. Persnl. Comsns. Assn. North. CA: Pres.-Elect (1981); VP (1980). **Activities:** 1; 15, 31, 35; 66 **Addr.:** 483 Andover Drive, Pacifica, CA 94044.

Shaevel, Evelyn F. (N. 23, 1947, Gary, IN) Exec. Dir. YASD, ALA, 1975–; Branch Head, Highland Pub. Lib., Lake Cnty. Pub. Lib., 1974–75, Asst. Coord., Adult/YA Srvs., 1972–74; Sch. Libn., Gary Pub. Schs., 1970–71. **Educ.:** Purdue Univ., 1965–67; Univ. of WI, 1967–69, BS (Amer. Hist., Educ.); Rutgers Univ., 1969–70, MLS; Brit. Inst., Florence, Italy, 1972 (Art Hist.). **Orgs.:** IL Reg. Lib. Cncl.: IL White Hse. Conf. Proj. Com. (1980–). ALA: YASD, Mem. Com. (1975). IL LA. WHCOLIS: Facilitator (1979). Adlsnt. Lit. Asm. of Natl. Cncl. of Tchrs. of Eng. Amer. Cvl. Liberties Un. **Pubns.:** Jt. ed., *Cooperative Seminar for School and Public Librarians Working with Young Adults* (1980); "Professional Awareness: Keeping Up with the News," *Libraries and Young Adults* (1979); "How Old Is A Young Adult," *Sch. Lib. Jnl.* (My. 1978). **Activities:** 3, 9; 15, 27, 48; 89, 95-YA lit. **Addr.:** Young Adult Services Division, American Library Association, 50 E. Huron St., Chicago, IL 60611.

Shafer, Anne Elise (N. 23, 1937, Hampton, IA) Michael Resrc. Ctr. Libn., Evanston Twp. HS, 1967–; Libn., Iowa Falls HS and Jr. High, 1962–66; Eng. Tchr., Libn., Osage Cmnty. HS, 1960–62. **Educ.:** Univ. of North. IA, 1956–60, BA (LS); West. MI Univ., 1966–67, MSL (Libnshp.); Northwest. Univ., 1977, Admin. Cert. (Educ.). **Orgs.:** Intl. Assn. of Sch. Libnshp.: Treas., Exec. Bd. (1981–84). ALA: AASL Rec. Secy., Exec Bd. (1972–73), Int. Frdm. Com. (Ch., 1972–75), Legis. Com. (1976–79); Pres. Awd. Sel. Com. (Ch., 1980–81), Nom. Com. (1974–75, 1976–77), Intl. Rel. Com. (1973–76; 1979–83). IL Assn. for Media in Educ. IL LA. Natl. Educ. Assn. IL Educ. Assn. Chicagoland Assn. for Media in HS. **Honors:** Kappa Delta Pi, 1960; Beta Phi Mu, 1967. **Activities:** 10; 17, 31, 32; 56, 63, 92 **Addr.:** Evanston Township High School, 1600 Dodge Ave., Evanston, IL 60204.

Shafer, Marcia (Anolik) (Ag. 8, 1939, New York, NY) Head, Youth Dept., Ann Arbor Pub. Lib., 1976–, Asst. Branch Libn., 1971–76. **Educ.:** City Coll. of NY, 1957–62, BS (Educ.); Univ. of MI, 1966–69, AMLS. **Orgs.:** ALA. Chld. Lit. Assn. MI LA. Natl. Affiliation for Lit. Advnc. **Activities:** 9; 15, 17, 21; 63, 89 **Addr.:** Ann Arbor Public Library, Youth Dept., Ann Arbor, MI 48104.

Shaffer, Dallas Y. (Je. 18, 1940, Spokane, WA) New Carrollton Area Branch Libn., Prince George's Cnty. Lib., 1981–; Info. Srvs. Ofcr., 1979–81, Exec. Asst. to Dir., 1975–79; Acq. Ed., Congsnl. Info. Srv., 1973–75; Dir., NE Pubns. Clearinghse., NE Lib. Comsn., 1970–73; Freelnc. Resrch., Indexing, 1967–70; Catlgr., U.S. Dept. of the Interior, 1966–67; Chld. Libn., King Cnty. Lib. Syst., 1965–66. **Educ.:** Stanford Univ., 1958–62, BA (Hist.); Univ. of WA, 1964–65, MLS. **Orgs.:** MD LA: Pres. (1980–81); *The Crab* Nsltr. Ed. (1977–78). ALA: LAMA/Persnl. Admin. Sect. (Ch., 1979–80), Legis. Asm. (Ch., 1978–79); GODORT, *Documents to the People* Ed. (1973–74). *Gvt. Pubns. Review*: Ed. Adv. Bd. (1975–77). **Pubns.:** "Nebraska: A Case Study of State Document Depository Legislation," *Gvt. Pubns. Review* (Ag. 1973). **Activities:** 9, 13; 17, 29, 36; 51, 78, 95-Stats. **Addr.:** 11505 Soward Dr., Wheaton, MD 20902.

Shaffer, Jack Wave (N. 9, 1930, Toledo, OH) Dir., Hlth. Sci. Lib., St. Vincent Hosp. and Med. Ctr., 1972–. **Educ.:** OH State Univ., 1954–58, BA (Anthro.); Univ. of Toledo, 1968–70, MALS; various wkshps. **Orgs.:** Hlth. Sci. Libns. NW OH: Pres. (1974–76). Med. LA: Midwest Reg. Grp. OH Acad. of Med. Hist. St. Vincent Hosp. Sch. of Nursing Alum. Assn. **Honors:** Univ. of Toledo Cmnty. and Tech. Coll., Cert. of Apprec. for Adv. Com. Srv. to the Lib. Media Tech. Prog., 1976. **Activities:** 5, 12; 15, 17, 36; 59, 80 **Addr.:** Health Science Library, St. Vincent Hospital and Medical Center, 2213 Cherry St., Toledo, OH 43608.

Shaffer, Margaret M. (S. 20, 1940, New Orleans, LA) Head Libn., Terrebonne Par. Lib., 1973–, Asst. Libn., 1965–73. **Educ.:** Nicholls State Univ., 1960–63, BA (Hist.); LA State Univ., 1963–65, MA (LS). **Orgs.:** LA LA. ALA. SWLA. Delta Kappa Gamma. Bus. and Prof. Women's Club. **Activities:** 9; 17, 35, 47 **Addr.:** Terrebonne Parish Library, 424 Roussell St., P.O. Box 510, Houma, LA 70361.

Shaffer, Norman John (Mr. 1, 1936, Lyons, NE) Chief, Photodup. Srv., Lib. of Congs., 1980–, Chief, Prsrvn. Ofc., 1978–80, Natl. Prsrvn. Prog. Ofcr., 1977–78, Asst. Chief for Bibl. Srv., Photodup. Srv., 1973–77, Assoc. Dir. of Libs. for Tech. Srvs., Univ. of NE, 1970–73, Asst. Dir. of Libs. for Pub. Srvs., 1969–70; Prsrvn. Microfilming Ofcr., Lib. of Congs., 1968–69, Prsrvn. Proj. Libn., 1967–68. **Educ.:** Cornell Univ., 1954–56 (Romanian); Univ. of NE, 1958–61, AB (Phil., Hist.); Univ. of WA, 1965–66, M Libr (Libnshp.). **Orgs.:** SAA. ALA: RTSD, Pres. (1982–83), Prsrvn. Microfilming Com. (Ch., 1981); Plng. Com. (1973–76), Micropublshg. Proj. Com. (1971–76)/Resrcs. Sect., Bkdlr.-Lib. Rel. Com. (1975–77); RTSD/Reprodct. of Lib. Mtrls Sect. (Ch., 1977–78), Policy and Resrch. Com. (Ch., 1973–76, 1971–76). IFLA: Sect. on Cons., Stdg. Com. (1981–85). Amer. Natl. Stans. Inst.: Lib. of Cong. Rep. to PH5 Com. (1973–). **Honors:** Phi Beta Kappa, 1961. **Pubns.:** "A National Preservation Effort, Hopes and Realities," *Preservation of Paper and Textiles of Historic and Artistic Value-II* (1981); "Library of Congress Pilot Preservation Project," *Coll. & Resrch. Libs.* (Ja. 1969). **Activities:** 4; 33, 39; 40; 62 **Addr.:** Photoduplication Ser-

PROFESSIONAL ACTIVITIES: Institutions: 1. Acad. lib.; 2. Arch.; 3. Assn.; 4. Fed./Gvt. lib.; 5. Inst. lib.; 6. Mfr./Suppl.; 7. Milit. lib.; 8. Musm.; 9. Pub. lib.; 10. Sch. lib.; 11. Sch. of lib. sci.; 12. Spec. lib.; 13. State lib.; 14. (other). **Functions/Activities:** 15. Acq./Col. dev.; 16. Adult srvs.; 17. Admin.; 18. Apprais.; 19. Archit./Bldgs.; 20. Cat./Class.; 21. Chld. srvs.; 22. Circ.; 23. Cons./Pres.; 24. Consult.; 25. Cont. ed.; 26. Educ. lib. sci.; 27. Ext. srvs.; 28. Fund/Grants; 29. Gvt. pubs.; 30. Indx./Abs.; 31. Instr. lib. use; 32. Media srvs.; 33. Micro.; 34. Netwks./Coop.; 35. Persnl.; 36. PR; 37. Publshg.; 38. Recs. mgt.; 39. Ref. srvs.; 40. Repro.; 41. Resrch.; 42. Review.; 43. Secur.; 44. Serials; 45. Spec. col.; 46. Tech. srvs.; 47. Trustees/Bds.; 48. YA srvs.; 49. (other).

vice, 10 1st St., S.E., Library of Congress, Washington, DC 20540.

Shaffer, Robert Stanley (Je. 16, 1916, Spencerville, OH) Phys. Sci. and Engin. Libn., U.S. Air Frc. Acad., 1956–; Math and Sci. Cat. Proj., Kaman Sci. Corp., 1966; Catlgr., Reynolds, Ward and Carey, 1957–60; 1st Asst. Libn., Bus. and Tech. Dept., Tacoma Pub. Lib., 1951–55; Instr., Air Univ., 1946–48. **Educ.:** Bowling Green State Univ., 1935–39, BS (Math, Phys. Sci.); Harvard Univ., MA Inst. of Tech., 1942–43, Cert. (UHF Tech. and Radar); IN Univ., 1950–51, MA (LS). **Orgs.:** SLA: Puget Snd. Chap., Lcl. Prog. Ch. (1953). Milit. Libns. Wkshp.: *Procs.* Ed. (1975). CO LA. U.S. Air Frc. Rsv. Flight A: Prin. Instr. (1963–69). **Honors:** U.S. Air Frc. Acad., Sustained Superior Performance, 1958. **Pubns.:** *Astronautics 1966–1975* (1976); *Astronautics 1960–1966* (1966). **Activities:** 1, 12; 24, 39; 52, 64, 88 **Addr.:** 1632 N. Prospect St., Colorado Springs, CO 80907.

Shalat, Herbert (My. 10, 1924, New York, NY) Bd. Pres., Shelter Rock Pub. Lib., 1981–, Bd. VP, 1978–80, Bd. Mem., 1962–77. **Educ.:** Cooper Un., 1946–49, Cert. (Arch.); Yale Univ., 1949–51, MArch. **Orgs.:** ALA. NY LA. Nassau Cnty. LA. Amer. Inst. of Archits. NY State Assn. of Archits. NY Socty. of Archits. **Honors:** Queens Cham. of Cmrce., Excel. in Dsgn., 1966; East Side Cham. of Cmrce., Excel. in Dsgn., 1968. **Activities:** 9; 19, 47 **Addr.:** 55 Deepdale Pkwy., Roslyn Heights, NY 11577.

Shaloiko, John L. (D. 26, 1951, Lockport, NY) Pilot Proj. Coord., Rochester Area Resrc. Exch., 1979–; YA Libn., Gates Pub. Lib., 1978–79; Ref. Libn., St. John Fisher Coll., Rochester, NY, 1974–78. **Educ.:** St. John Fisher Coll., Rochester, NY, 1969–73, BA (Hist.); State Univ. Coll., Geneseo, 1973–74, MLS. **Orgs.:** NY LA. ALA. **Activities:** 14-Netwk.; 24, 25, 34 **Addr.:** Rochester Area Resource Exchange, 339 East Ave. Rm. 300, Rochester, NY 14604.

Shama, Christine Anne (Jl. 26, 1950, Lima, OH) Sr. Staff Assoc., Pub. Affairs Dept., Borden Inc., 1980–; Dir., Columbus Reg. Info. Srv., Columbus Area Cham. of Cmrce., 1979–80; Dir., Clermont Cnty. Pub. Lib., 1978–79; Asst. Dir., Westerville Pub. Lib., 1974–77; Info. Writer, OH Arts Cncl., 1972–73. **Educ.:** Miami Univ., 1968–72, BA (Eng.); IN Univ., 1973–74, MLS. **Orgs.:** OH LA. ALA. Columbus Landmarks Fndn. **Honors:** Intl. Assn. of Bus. Communicators, Awd. for Copywrtg., 1973. **Activities:** 9, 12; 17, 35, 36; 55, 59 **Addr.:** 473 Oakland Park Ave., Columbus, OH 43214.

Shanafelt, Ellen M. (O. 1, 1943, Evart, MI) Media Spec., Powell/Romeo Cmnty. Schs., (1971); Tchr., Fremont Pub. Schs., 1966–68. **Educ.:** Ctrl. MI Univ., 1961–65, BA (Hist.); Univ. of Vienna, Austria, 1965; Univ. of MI, 1970–71, AMLS; Wayne State Univ., 1977–79 (Spec. in Curie.). **Orgs.:** MI Assn. for Media in Edu.: Int. Frdm. Com., Vice-Ch., Ch. ALA: AASL. Right of Read Fndn. MI Assn. for Comp. Users in Lrng. MI Assn. for Affective Educ. Romeo Educ. Assn.: Treas. (1974); Secy. (1976); Bd. of Dirs. (1980–81). Lcl. 1 Educ. Assn.: Acad. Frdm. Com. MI Educ. Assn. Amer. Cvl. Liberties Un. **Pubns.:** "Media Selection Policy-A New Approach," *Media Spectrum* (Ap. 1980). **Addr.:** 72875 McIntosh Ct., Romeo, MI 48065.

Shank, Russell (S. 2, 1925, Spokane, WA) Univ. Libn. and Prof., Univ. of CA, Los Angeles, 1977–; Dir. of Libs., Smithsonian Inst., 1967–77; Assoc. Prof., Columbia Univ., 1966–67; Sr. Lectr., 1964–66; Asst. Univ. Libn., Univ. of CA, Berkeley, 1959–64; Engin.-Phys. Sci. Libn., Columbia Univ., 1953–59; Chief, In-Srv. Trng. and Persnl. Cntrl., Milwaukee Pub. Lib., 1953. **Educ.:** Univ. of WA, 1943–46, BS (Elec. Engin.), 1947–49, BA (Libnshp.); Univ. of WI, 1949–52, MBA; Columbia Univ., 1964–66, DLS. **Orgs.:** SLA. ALA: Pres. (1978–79); Exec. Bd. (1974–80); Cncl. (1961–65, 1974–80, 1980–84); ACRL (Pres., 1972–73); LITA/Info. Sci. and Autom. Sect. (1968–69). AAAS. **Honors:** Cncl. on Lib. Resrcs., Fellow, 1973; Univ. of WA, Sch. of Libnshp., Disting. Alum., 1968. **Activities:** 1; 17, 34 **Addr.:** Library Administrative Office, University Research Library, University of California, Los Angeles, CA 90024.

Shanks, Maudean Wright (N. 21, 1925, Jamestown, TN) Supvsr., Tech. Lib., Head of Cat., Un. Carbide Nuc. Corp., Oak Ridge Natl. Lab. Lib. Syst., 1971–, Asst. Libn., 1954–71; Libn.-Tchr., Alvin C. York Inst., 1949–54; Tchr., Fentress Cnty. Bd. of Educ., 1947–49. **Educ.:** Carson-Newman Coll., 1943–47, AB, cum laude (Eng.); Univ. of TN, 1949–50, Tchr.-Libn. Cert. **Orgs.:** SLA: PR (Ch., 1963–64; 1969–70); Secy. (1964–65); Rcrt. (Ch., 1971–72; 1972–73). Ord. of the East. Star. **Activities:** 10, 12; 20, 39, 46; 75, 84, 91 **Addr.:** 101 Timbercrest Dr., Clinton, TN 37716.

Shannon, Coe (Jl. 16, 1926, Pittsburgh, PA) Coord. of Lib. Srvs., Wilkinsburg Sch. Dist., 1969–; Tchr., Wilkinsburg Sch. Dist., 1951–66; Tchr., Coronado Pub. Sch., 1949–50. **Educ.:** Coll. of Wooster, 1944–49, BA (Eng.); Univ. of Pittsburgh, 1950–52, MEd (Educ.); Cert., Supvsr. (LS). **Orgs.:** PA Sch. Libns. Assn.: Prof. Stans. Com. (1974–80). ALA: Student Involvement in Media Ctrs. (1974–78). Frnds. of the Living Lib. of Wilkinsburg: Sch. Liason Rep. (1976–80). Wilkinsburg Hist. Socty. **Activities:** 10; 17, 24; 63 **Addr.:** 1515 Penn Ave., Pittsburgh, PA 15221.

Shannon, Dwight W. (Ap. 5, 1918, Dayton, OH) Assoc. Dir. of Libs., Assoc. Dean for Lrng. Resrcs., CA State Univ., Chico, 1974–, Dir. of Tech. Srvs., 1962–74, Circ. Libn., 1960–62; Sci. Libn., Sacramento State Coll., 1958–60; Asst. Dir., Dayton and Montgomery Cnty. Pub. Lib., 1956–58, Head, Ref. Dept., 1949–56; Asst. Univ. Libn., TX A & M Univ., 1948–49; Libn., TX Engin. Lib., 1947–48. **Educ.:** Univ. of Dayton, 1934–38, BS (Educ., Hist.); VA Polytech. Inst., 1938–39 (Agr.); Univ. of IL, 1941–42, BSLS. **Orgs.:** ALA. CA LA: State Adv. Cncl. (Ch., 1964). **Activities:** 1; 17 **Addr.:** 479 Redwood Way, Chico, CA 95926.

Shannon, Michael Owen (Je. 1, 1938, New York, NY) Chief, Ref. Div., Herbert Lehman Coll., CUNY, 1980–, Docum. Libn., 1967–80; Docum. Libn., Hunter Coll., 1966; Mncpl. Ref. Libn., Mncpl. Ref. Lib., 1965–66; Libn., Manhattan Coll. Lib. of Plant Morphogenesis, 1964–65. **Educ.:** Manhattan Coll., 1957–61, BA (Pol Sci.); Columbia Univ., 1964–65, MS (LS). **Orgs.:** AALL. ALA: Law and Pol. Sci. Sect. (Del., 1971–72); Law and "Pol. Sci." Sect. (Prog. Ch., 1970). Gvt. Docum. Assn of NJ. SLA. Amer. Socty. of Intl. Law. Amer. Assn. of State and Lcl. Hist. Amer. Prtg. Hist. Assn. Art Students Leag. **Pubns.:** *Oman and Southeastern Arabia* (1978); *Modern Ireland* (1981); "Collection Development," *Gvt. Pubns. Review* (1981); "Local Legislation and Municipal Law," *Gvt. Pubns. Review* (1978); "Ebbing of Municipal Documents," *Gvt. Pubns. Review* (1976); various other articles. **Activities:** 1; 29, 39; 77, 92 **Addr.:** 41 Pleasant Ave., Bergenfield, NJ 07621.

Shannon, Sr. Theresa Marie, R.S.M. (Je. 14, 1919, Brookville, PA) Libn., Upper Sch., Walsingham Acad., 1971–; Libn., St. Hubert HS, Philadelphia, 1968–71; Libn., Tchr., Hallahan HS, 1962–68; Libn., Tchr., St. Hubert HS, Philadelphia, 1955–62; Elem. Tchr., Philadelphia Archdio. Syst., 1940–55. **Educ.:** Villanova Univ., 1940–53, AB, 1953–58, MSLS (Educ.); various crs. **Orgs.:** Cath. LA: East. PA Unit Secy.; Nsltr. Ed. ALA: Com. on Guidelines for Persnl. Working with People in Spec. Situations (1969–74). VA LA. **Pubns.:** *Early Childhood Media* booklet; *Guidelines for Personnel Working with "The Special Patron"* booklet. **Activities:** 10; 31 **Addr.:** Walsingham Academy, P. O. Box 159, Jamestown Rd., Williamsburg, VA 23187.

Shannon, Zella J. (Jl. 4, 1921, Tokio, ND) Assoc. Dir., Minneapolis Pub. Lib., 1951–, Head, Hist. Dept., 1975–77, Head, N. Reg. Lib., 1972–75, Libn., INFORM, 1970–72. **Educ.:** Univ. of MN, 1964–67, BA (Hist.), 1967–68, MLS. **Orgs.:** MN LA: Lib. Mgt. RT (Ch., 1979). ALA: LAMA, Stats. Sect. Com. (1981–83); PLA/Metro. Libs. Sect., Fiscal Emergency Com. (1981–83). SLA: MN Chap. (Pres., 1975). Zonta. **Pubns.:** "Public Library Service to the Corporate Community," *Spec. Libs.* (Ja. 1974). **Addr.:** Minneapolis Public Library and Information Center, 300 Nicollet Mall, Minneapolis, MN 55401.

Shapiro, Beth J. (Jl. 18, 1946, Boston, MA) Asst. Dir., Resrch. Srvs., MI State Univ., 1981–; Coord., Soc. Sci. Cols., 1979–81, Urban Policy and Plng. Libn., 1972–79. **Educ.:** MI State Univ., 1964–68, BS (Soclgy.), 1969–71, MA (Soclgy.); West. MI Univ., 1972–74, MSL (LS); MI State Univ., 1975–81, PhD (Soclgy.). **Orgs.:** ALA: ACRL/Bibl. Instr. Sect., Policy and Plng. Com. (1978–80), 1981 Prog. Plng. Com. (Ch., 1979–81); RTSD/Resrcs. Sect., Lib. Mtrls. Price Indx. Com. (1980–82); SRRT, Eth. Mtrls. Info. Exch. Task Force (Prog. Co-Ch., 1978). Amer. Sociological Assn. N. Ctrl. Soclgy. Assn. **Pubns.:** *Directory of Ethnic Studies Librarians* (1976); *Directory of Ethnic Publishers and Resource Organizations* (1976); "Training the Radical Researcher," *Insurgent Sociologist* (Win. 1978); "Teaching Sociology Graduate Students Bibliographic Methods for Document Research," *Jnl. of Acad. Libnshp.* (My. 1979). **Activities:** 1; 15, 39; 66, 92 **Addr.:** Michigan State University Libraries, E. Lansing, MI 48824.

Shapiro, Leila C. (Jl. 14, 1932, Brooklyn, NY) Asst. Reg. Libn., Montgomery Cnty. Pub. Libs., 1977–, Chld. Libn., 1972–77. **Educ.:** George Washington Univ., 1950–54, AB (Eng. Lit.); Cath. Univ. of Amer., 1970–72, MSLS. **Orgs.:** ALA: YASD, Adv. Com. to the Col. Dev. Sect. of the Lib. of Congs. (1978–). DC LA: Prog. Com. (1975). MD LA. Cath. Univ. of Amer. Sch. of Lib. and Info. Sci. Alum.: Pres. (1981–82). **Honors** Beta Phi Mu, 1972; J.Morris Jones—ALA, Goals Awd., "Students to Dallas," 1971. **Pubns.:** Reviews. **Activities:** 9; 16, 17, 21 **Addr.:** 9602 Hillridge Dr., Kensington, MD 20795.

Shapiro, Leonard Philip (Jl. 15, 1940, New York, NY) Dir., Lib. Srvs., CA Coll. of Podiatric Med., 1970–; Sr. Catlgr., Univ. of San Francisco, 1967–70; Asst. Catlgr., Fed. Rsv. Bank of NY, 1965–67. **Educ.:** The Amer. Univ., 1958–62, BA (Hist.); Pratt Inst., 1964–66, MLS. **Orgs.:** Med. LA: Exch. Com. (1978–81). SLA: San Francisco Bay Reg. Chap. Nsltr. (Advert. 1973). North. CA Med. Lib. Grp.: Pres. (1972–73); Exch. Com. (Ch., 1979–). **Honors:** CA Coll. of Podiatric Med., Cert. of Apprec., 1977. **Activities:** 1, 12; 15, 17, 46; 58, 80 **Addr.:** CA College of Podiatric Medicine, Schmidt Medical Library, P.O. Box 7855, Rincon Annex, San Francisco, CA 94120.

Shapiro, Lillian L. (O. 11, 1913, Jamaica, NY) Sch. Lib. Consult., 1975–; Dir. of Media Srvs., Untd. Nations Intl. Sch., 1974–75; Asst. Prof., St. John's Univ. Lib. Sch., 1969–73; Supvsr., Sr. HS Libs., Bd. of Educ., New York City, 1963–65; Head, various HS libs., New York City, 1965–69, 1948–63. **Educ.:** Hunter Coll., 1928–32, BA (Latin); Columbia Univ., 1938–40, BSLS, 1968–69, MSLS. **Orgs.:** ALA: Nom. Com. (1975); SRRT, Bd. NY LA: 2nd VP (1970–71); Lib. Educ. Sect. (Pres., 1972). New York City Sch. Libns. Assn.: VP (1955); Pres. (1956–58). NY Lib. Club: Pres. (1968). Women's Natl. Bk. Assn.: Bd. (1968–69); 2nd VP (1969–70); Pres. (1971–72). Booksellers' Leag.: Bd. (1970–71, 1977–). **Honors:** Beta Phi Mu, 1954; Cath. LA, HS Div., Cert. of Merit, 1976. **Pubns.:** *Fiction for Youth* (1980); *Teaching Yourself in Libraries* (1978); *Serving Youth* (1975); "Celebrations and Condolences," *Sch. Lib. Jnl.* (D. 1979); "Libraries for Tomorrow's Children," *Lib. Jnl.* (Ja. 1, 1976); various other articles, reviews. **Activities:** 10, 11; 26, 32, 48; 63, 89 **Addr.:** 307A Heritage Hills, Somers, NY 10589.

Shapiro, Ruth Thomson (F. 22, 1925, Cincinnati, OH) Lib. Consult., Southwest. PA AHEC, 1980–81; Lib. Consult., Allegheny Cnty. Dept. of Dev., 1979–80; Lib. Consult., Allegheny Cnty. Dept. of Plng. and Dev., 1971–79; Lib. Consult., Allegheny Cnty. Dept. of Hlth., 1971–75. **Educ.:** Northwest. Univ., 1945–47, BMus (Voice); Univ. of Pittsburgh, 1969–71, MLS. **Orgs.:** SLA: Pittsburgh Chap. Treas.; Pres. (1980–81). Cncl. of Plng. Libns. West. PA Law Libns. Assn. West. PA Med. Libs. Assn. Bennington Coll. Alum. Assn. Leag. of Women Voters. **Activities:** 4; 17, 29, 38; 50, 77, 78 **Addr.:** 6212 Hampton St., Pittsburgh, PA 15206.

Shapiro, S. R. (Ag. 30, 1911, New York, NY) Pres., S.R. Shapiro Co., Bks. for Libs., 1935–. **Educ.:** NY Univ., 1931–33, ScB (Hist. Sci.); Columbia Univ., 1933–34, MA (Int. Hist.); Univ. of London, 1934–35, (Bibl.). **Orgs.:** ALA: ACRL/Rare Bk. and Mss. Sect. Bibl. Socty. of Amer. Bibl. Socty. of Eng. Prtg. Hist. Socty. various other orgs. The Junketeers. Socty. for the Advnc. of the Graph. Arts. Ctr. for the Bk. Arts: Bd. of Dirs. (1974–78). **Pubns.:** Ed. in Chief, *U.S. Cumulative Book Auctions Records* (1945–51); *Check-List of the Rarest and Most Valuable Books Designed by Bruce Rogers* (1956); *Bruce Rogers of Indiana* (1957); various articles. **Activities:** 9; 24, 47 **Addr.:** 29 E. 10th St., New York, NY 10003.

Shappe, Ellen (O. 22, 1944, New York, NY) Mgr., Lib. Srvs., Natl. Assn. of Accts., 1974–; Libn., Syracuse Univ., 1973–74; Libn., Brooklyn Pub. Lib., 1972–73. **Educ.:** Brooklyn Coll., 1962–67, BA (Psy.); Pratt Inst., 1970–72, MLS; Pace Univ., 1976–81, MBA (Acct.). **Orgs.:** SLA. ASIS. **Pubns.:** *The Bookshelf* (1977, 1978); *Industry Accounting Manuals* (1978, 1980). **Activities:** 12; 15, 17, 30; 56, 59 **Addr.:** 249 E. 48 St., New York, NY 10017.

Share, Carol R. (D. 15, 1928, New York, NY) Head Branch Libn., Memphis Pub. Lib., 1969; Head Branch Libn., Cleveland Hts.-Univ. Hts. Pub. Lib., 1964–69, Ref. Libn., 1963–64. **Educ.:** Brooklyn Coll., 1946–49, AB (Lit.); West. Rsv. Univ., 1960–63, AM (LS). **Orgs.:** ALA. TN LA. SE LA. W. TN LA. Univ. of TN Fac. Wives. **Activities:** 9; 16, 17, 36; 50, 59, 89 **Addr.:** 340 Shady Woods Cove, Memphis, TN 38119.

Sharify, Nasser (S. 23, 1923, Tehran, Iran) Dean and Prof., Grad. Sch. of Lib. and Info. Sci., Pratt Inst., 1968–; Trustee, Brooklyn Pub. Lib., 1973–; Dir., Intl. Libnshp. and Documtn. Intl. Std. and World Affairs, SUNY, 1966–68. Consult. for Intl. Std. and World Affairs, 1965–66; Dir., Intl. Lib. Info. Ctr., Univ. of Pittsburgh, 1964–66, Assoc. Prof., Grad. Sch. of Lib. and Info. Sci., 1966, Asst. Prof., 1963–66, Asst. Prof. of Intl. Educ., 1965–66. **Educ.:** Univ. of Tehran, 1944–47, Lic. es Lettres (Fr. Lit.); Columbia Univ., 1953–54, MSLS, 1954–58, DLS (LS). **Orgs.:** ALA: Nom. Com. (1970–71); Lib. Educ. Div., Com. on Equivalencies and Reciprocity (Ch., 1965–71); Intl. Educ. Com., Mid. E. Resrc. Panel (Ch., 1969–). AALS: Nom. Com. (Ch., 1977–79); Long Range Plng. Com. (1973–). **Honors:** Sch. of Lib. Srv., Columbia Univ., Grolier Socty. Flwshp., 1956; Ford Fndn., Schol., 1953–54. **Pubns.:** *The Pahlavi National Library of the Future, Resources, Services, Programs and Building Requirements-17 vols.* (1976); *The Pahlavi National Library of the Future, A Summary of Its Origins, Its Planning, Its Objectives, and Its Services* (1976); *MAROC - Plan d'ensemble pour la creation d'une ecole des sciences de l'information* (1974); *MAROC - Creation de l'Ecole des sciences de l'information (ESI)* (1974); *Beyond the Bridge* (1973). **Activities:** 11, 14-Natl. Libs.; 17, 24, 26; 54, 62, 63 **Addr.:** Graduate School of Library and Information Science, 215 Ryerson St., Brooklyn NY 11205.

Sharma, Millicent M. Mineola, NY) Fine Arts Libn., Pasadena Pub. Lib., 1973–; Instr., Eng., OR State Univ., 1965–70. **Educ.:** Univ. of CA, Los Angeles, 1954, BA (Eng.), 1958–60, MA (Eng.), 1971–72, MLS. **Orgs.:** ARLIS/NA: Art Bk. Awds. Com. (1979). CA LA. ALA. **Activities:** 9; 15, 19, 39; 55, 63, 67 **Addr.:** 1520 Rose Villa St., Pasadena, CA 91106.

Sharma, Ramesh C. (My. 15, 1937, India) OCLC Coord., Tech. Srvs., Pittsburg (KS) State Univ., 1978–; Head Cat. and Prcs. Branch, IL State Lib., 1975–78; Asst. Cat. Libn., Head OCLC Ed. Sect., SUNY, Buffalo, 1972–75; Libn., Panjab Univ. Lib., India, 1960–70. **Educ.:** Panjab Univ., India, 1952–57, BA (Eng. Lit.), 1957–58, BEd (Educ.); Banaras Univ., India,

Special Subjects/Services: 50. Adult educ.; 51. Advert./Mktg.; 52. Aerosp.; 53. Agric.; 54. Area std.; 55. Arts/Hum.; 56. Autom.; 57. Bibl./Prtg.; 58. Bio. sci.; 59. Bus./Fin.; 60. Chem.; 61. Copyrt.; 62. Documtn.; 63. Educ.; 64. Engin.; 65. Env.; 66. Eth. grps.; 67. Film; 68. Food/Nutr.; 69. Geneal.; 70. Geo.; 71. Geol.; 72. Handcpd.; 73. Hist.; 74. Int. frdm.; 75. Info. sci.; 76. Insr.; 77. Law; 78. Legis.; 79. Math./Comp. sci.; 80. Med.; 81. Metals; 82. Nat. resrcs.; 83. Newsp.; 84. Nuc. sci.; 85. Oral hist.; 86. Petr./Energy; 87. Pharm.; 88. Phys./Astr./Math.; 89. Readg.; 90. Relig.; 91. Sci./Tech.; 92. Soc. sci.; 93. Telecom.; 94. Transp.; 95. (other).

1958–59, Dip. (LS); Panjab Univ., India, 1960–62, MA (Soc. Sci.), 1967–69, MA (Pub. Admin.); KS State Tchrs. Coll., 1971–72, MLS. **Orgs.:** KS LA. ALA: ACRL; LITA; RTSD. **Activities:** 1; 17, 26, 46; 56, 75, 92 **Addr.:** 490 Fieldcrest Dr., Pittsburg, KS 66762.

Sharma, Ravindra Nath (O. 22, 1944, Jullundur, Panjab, India) Head Libn., PA State Univ., Beaver Campus, 1981–; Ref. Libn., Colgate Univ., 1971–81; Lib. Mgt. Intern, SUNY, Buffalo; Asst. Libn., Asst. Prof., Lib. Sci., Coll. of the Ozarks, 1970–71; Staff Libn., N. TX State Univ., 1968–70; Rep., Sports Correspondent, Can. India Times, Toronto, 1967–68. **Educ.:** Univ. of Delhi, India, 1960–63, BA hons. (Hist.), 1963–65, MA (Hist.); N. TX State Univ., 1968–70, MLS; SUNY, Buffalo, 1978–, PhD Cand. (LS, Higher Educ.). **Orgs.:** ALA: ACRL/Univ. Sect., Asian/African Sect. Asian/Pac. Amer. Libns. Assn.: Schol. and Rcrt. Com. (1980–82). AR LA: Pubns. Com. (1970–71). Ctrl. NY Lib. Resrcs. Cncl.: Prof. Dev. Com. (1977–78). Can. Stats., Toronto, ON. Sem. Srvs. for West. NY's Higher Educs. NY Conf. for Asian Std. **Honors:** Amer. Inst. of Indian Std., Flwshp., 1975–76. **Pubns.:** *Indian Librarianship: Perspectives and Prospects* (1981); *India and Indians: A Bibliography* (1974); "Copyright — U.S.A.: The Librarian's View," *Libri* (Mr. 1981); "Bibliographic Education: An Overview," *Libri* (D. 1979); US Corresp., *Indian Libn.*; various bk. reviews, articles. **Activities:** 1; 17, 24, 39; 54, 57, 92 **Addr.:** Penn State University, Beaver Campus, Brodhead Rd., Monaca, PA 15061.

Sharp, Jo Gardner (O. 5, 1926, Ridgely, TN) Fusion Energy Div. Libn., Oak Ridge Natl. Lab., 1979–, Acq. Libn., 1972–79, Bio. Div. Libn., 1970–72, Lib. Liaison for Info. Ctrs., 1964–70, Ref. Libn., 1959–64, Acq., 1949–59. **Educ.:** Univ. of TN, 1944–47, BA (Chem., Soclgy.). **Orgs.:** ASIS. SLA: Bd. of Dirs. (1979); Hosplty. Com.; Nom. Com.; *Radiations.* Ed. **Activities:** 12; 15, 17, 39; 56, 88, 91 **Addr.:** Rte. 2 Box 178A, Lake Breeze Ln., Ten Mile, TN 37880.

Sharp, Linda Carlson (Jl. 24, 1952, Lafayette, IN) Catlgr., IN Hist. Socty. Lib., 1980–, Mss. Libn., 1978–80. **Educ.:** IN Univ., 1970–74, BA (Hist., Anthro.), 1975–77, MLS, 1977–, MA in progress (Eng. Hist.). **Orgs.:** Ctrl. IN Area Lib. Srvs. Athty.: Bd. of Dirs. (1979–81); Cont. Educ. Com. (1979–81). IN Coop. Lib. Srvs. Athty.: Bd. of Dirs. (1981–). ALA. Socty. of IN Archvsts. Amer. Prtg. Hist. Assn. Morgan Cnty. IN Hist. Socty. IN Hist. Socty. Prtg. Hist. Socty., London. **Pubns.:** Contrib., "Indiana and the Old Northwest," *IN Hist. Socty. Bltn.* (1980); Ed., *IN Pro-Choice Action Leag. Nsltr.* (1979–81). **Activities:** 12; 23, 41, 45; 55, 73 **Addr.:** Indiana Historical Society Library, 315 W. Ohio St., Indianapolis, IN 46202.

Sharplin, C. David (Je. 1, 1932, London, Eng.) Asst. Ref. Libn., Univ. of AB, 1970–, Actg. Head, J. A. Weir Law Lib., 1969–70, Libn., Anal., Cameron Lib. Systs., 1967–69. **Educ.:** Univ. of AB, 1962–66, BA hons. (Soclgy.); Univ. of Toronto, 1966–67, BLS. **Orgs.:** ASIS. LA of AB. **Activities:** 1; 15, 31, 39; 92 **Addr.:** Reference Services, 2–102 N. Rutherford Library, University of Alberta, Edmonton, AB T6G 2J4 Canada.

Sharrow, Marilyn J. (Oakland, CA) Dir. of Libs., Univ. of MB, 1979–; Assoc. Dir., Univ. of WA Libs., 1978–79, Asst. Dir.,/Undergrad. Lib. Srvs., 1975–77; Dir., Roseville Pub. Lib., 1973–75; Head, Fine Arts Dept., Syracuse Univ. Libs., 1970–73; Ref. Libn., Detroit Pub. Lib., 1968–70. **Educ.:** Univ. of MI, 1967, BS (Desgn.-Art), 1968–69, MALS. **Orgs.:** ALA: RASD, Mem. Com. (1979–83); LAMA/Stats. Sect., Dev., Organ., Plng. and Prog. (1979–82). MB LA: Exec. Bd., Dir.; Cont. Educ. Com. (Ch., 1981–82). Can. LA: Can. Assn. of Resrch. Lib., Exec. Bd., (1980–81). Natl. Lib. of Can.: Adv. Bd. Resrc. Netwk. Com. (1981–). Bus. and Prof. Women's Club of Winnipeg. Univ. of MB Press Bd. **Honors:** Brit. Cncl. Grant, Travel in UK, 1981. **Pubns.:** "Academic Libraries in Great Britain, 1981," *MB LA Bltn.* (S. 1981); "The Climate of Librarianship: A Forecast for the 80's," *MB LA Bltn.* (Je. 1980). **Activities:** 1, 9; 17, 24, 35; 55 **Addr.:** University of Manitoba, Dafoe Library, Winnipeg, MB R3T 2N2 Canada.

Shaughnessy, Thomas W. (My. 3, 1938, Pittsburgh, PA) Asst. Dir., Pub. Srvs. and Col. Dev., Univ. of Houston, 1978–; Assoc. Dean, Lib. Sch., Univ. of South. CA, 1974–78; Lib. Dir., Rutgers Univ., 1971–74, Asst. Dean, Lib. Sch., 1969–71; Resrch. Dir., Chicago Pub. Lib. Srvy., 1968–69. **Educ.:** St. Vincent Coll., 1959–61, AB (Phil.); Univ. of Pittsburgh, 1963–64, MLS; Rutgers Univ., 1965–70, PhD. **Orgs.:** ALA: Action Cncl., SRRT (1970–71). NJ LA: Cncl. (1971–74). TX LA. **Honors:** Beta Phi Mu, 1964; Cncl. on Lib Resrcs., Flwshp., 1974. **Pubns.:** *Library Response to Urban Change* (1969); "Library Administration in Support of Emerging Services", *Lib. Trends* (O. 1979); "Redesigning Library Jobs," *Jnl. of Amer. Socty. for Info. Sci.* (Jl. 1978); "Technology and Job Design in Libraries," *Jnl. of Acad. Libnshp.* (N. 1977); "Particpative Management, Collective Bargaining and Professionalism," *Coll. & Resrch. Libs.* (Mr. 1977). **Activities:** 1; 15, 17, 26; 57, 92 **Addr.:** 12019 Wedgehill Ln., Houston, TX 77077.

Shaver, Donna B. (Ag. 2, 1946, Redmond, OR) Info. Spec., NW Reg. Educ. Lab., 1976–; Reader's Srvs. Libn., Pac. Univ., 1973–76. **Educ.:** Univ. of OR, Eugene, 1964–68, BA (Hist.), 1972–73, MLS, 1968–69, Tchg. Cert. (Soc. Std.). **Orgs.:** SLA: OR Chap. (Pres., 1980–81). ASIS. OR OLUG: Coord. (1978–). E. African Wild Life Socty.: OR Rep. (1980–). **Honors:** Beta Phi Mu, 1973. **Pubns.:** *Directory of Special Libraries in Oregon and Southwest Washington* (1978). **Activities:** 12; 34, 39; 63 **Addr.:** Information Center/Library, Northwest Regional Educational Laboratory, 300 S.W. 6th, Portland, OR 97204.

Shaver, Eleanor Ann (Je. 9, 1944, Greenville, SC) Media Srvs. Consult., Sch. Dist. of Greenville Cnty., 1975–; Media Coord., Piedmont Sch. Proj., 1973–75; Lib. Media Spec., Hughes Mid. Sch., 1970–73; Lib. Media Spec., Davenport Jr. High, 1967–69. **Educ.:** Winthrop Coll., 1963–67, BA (LS); FL State Univ., 1969–70, MLS. **Orgs.:** SC LA: Chld. and Young People's Sect. (Ch., 1979–80). AECT of SC: Secy. (1976–77); Mem. Ch. (1975–76, 1978–79). Southeast. Reg. Media Leadership Cncl.: SC Rep. (1976–78). ALA: Supvsrs. Sect., Prog. Com. (1976–77). Various other orgs. **Honors:** Alpha Delta Kappa; SC AECT, Media Person of the Yr., 1978; Beta Phi Mu; Kappa Delta Phi; Phi Kappa Phi. **Activities:** 10; 17, 24, 32; 63, 89 **Addr.:** Rte. 4 Hudson Rd., Greer, SC 29651.

Shaw, Courtney Ann (F. 10, 1946, Hagerstown, MD) Head, Art Lib., Univ. of MD, 1976–; Head, Fine Arts Lib., Lake Placid Sch. of Art, 1975–76; Ref. Spec., AZ State Univ., 1975. **Educ.:** Univ of WI, 1966–68, BA (Eng.); Case West. Rsv. Univ., MSLS; Univ. of MD, 1979–, MA, PhD (Art Hist.). **Orgs.:** ARLIS/NA: WA Art Libs. Resrc. Com.: Ch.; various ofcs. WA Cons. Gld. **Pubns.:** various presentations. **Activities:** 1; 15, 17, 23 **Addr.:** Art Library, University of Maryland, College Park, MD 20742.

Shaw, Debora J. (Mr. 22, 1950, Grand Rapids, MI) Visit. Lectr., Sch. of Lib. and Info. Sci., IN Univ., 1980–; Proj. Mgr., Online Un. List of Serials Proj., IN Univ. Libs., 1979–80; Netwk. Libn., INCOLSA, 1976–79; Asst. Serials Libn., Youngstown State Univ., 1974–76. **Educ.:** Univ. of MI, 1968–71, BA (Hist. of Ideas); 1972–74, MA (LS); IN Univ., 1980–, Doct. Student. **Orgs.:** ASIS: IN Chap., Secy. (1977–78), Ch. (1979–80). ALA. **Honors:** Beta Phi Mu. **Pubns.:** Jt. auth., "Relative Percentages of Fiction and Non-Fiction in Selected Canadian and American Public Libraries," *Pub. Lib. Qtly.* (Sum. 1979); jt. auth., "Cooperative Cataloging and Automated Bibliographic Networks: Considerations for Public Libraries," *Pub. Lib. Qtly.* (Win. 1981); "A Review of Developments Leading to Online Union Listing of Serials," *The Serials Libn.* spec. mono. supplement (1981); jt. auth., "Collection Overlap as a Function of Library Size," *Jnl. of the Amer. Socty. for Info. Sci.* (Ja. 1979); jt. auth., "Contributions of Small Libraries to State-wide Resource Sharing," *Pub. Lib. Qtly.* (Fall 1979). **Activities:** 1, 11; 26, 34; 75 **Addr.:** School of Library and Information Science, Indiana University, Bloomington, IN 47405.

Shaw, Pamela Anne (N. 1, 1945, New Kensington, PA) Head Libn., Winchester–Thurston Sch., 1980–; Asst. Msc. Libn., Univ. of Pittsburgh, 1973–80, Undergrad. Msc. Adv., 1973–80; Organist-Choirmstr., St. Philomena's Church, 1979–81. **Educ.:** Nyack Coll., 1964–67, BA, cum laude (Soc. Sci.); Univ. of Pittsburgh, 1969–70, MA (Msc.), 1970–71, MLS. **Orgs.:** Msc. LA: PA Chap., Mem. Com. (1979). Amer. Gld. of Organists. Natl. Assn. of Pastoral Musicians. Kasamon Ballet Co.: Dancer and Dir. of PR (1976–). **Honors:** Beta Phi Mu, 1971. **Activities:** 1, 10; 15, 17, 20; 55, 66, 92 **Addr.:** 225 Melwood Ave., Apt. 46, Pittsburgh, PA 15213.

Shaw, Renata Vitzthum (Jl. 21, 1926, Mänttä, Häme, Finland) Bibl. Spec., Lib. of Congs., 1971–, Supvisory Ref. Libn., 1967–71, Ref. Libn., 1962–67. **Educ.:** Univ. of Helsinki, Finland, 1945–47; Wittenberg Coll., 1947–48; Univ. of Chicago, 1948–49, MA (Art. Hist.); Univ. of Helsinki, Finland, 1950–51, Magister Philosophiae; Ecole de Louvre, Paris, France, 1951–52, Dip. (Msclgy.); Univ. of Paris, France, 1952–54; Cath. Univ., 1961–62, MLS. **Orgs.:** SLA: Bd. of Dirs. (1976–78); Div. Cabinet (Ch., 1977–78); Pic. Div. (1963–). ARLIS/NA. Washington Art Lib. Resrcs. Com.: Ch. (1981). **Honors:** Lib. of Congs., Merit. Srv. Awd., 1975; Beta Phi Mu, 1962. **Pubns.:** Cmplr., *Graphic Sampler* (1979); cmplr., *A Century of Photographs, 1846–1946* (1980); *Picture Searching: Techniques and Tools* (1973); "Visual Materials and the Use of Foreign Languages in Picture Research," *The Fed. Ling.* (Mr. 1978); various other articles. **Activities:** 4, 12; 15, 37, 44; 55, 57, 75 **Addr.:** Prints and Photographs Division, Library of Congress, James Madison Memorial Bldg., Washington, DC 20540.

Shaw, Robert B. (Je. 26, 1945, New Haven, CT) Sr. Libn., CA Dept. of Justice Lib., 1974–; Ref. Libn., Coll. Lib., Univ. of CA, Los Angeles, 1971–74. **Educ.:** Whittier Coll., 1963–67, BA (Pol. Sci.); Univ. of CA, Los Angeles, 1969–70, MA (Pol. Sci.), 1970–71, MLS; West. State Univ. Coll. of Law, 1976–80, JD (Law). **Orgs.:** AALL. South. CA Assn. of Law Libs. **Pubns.:** Jt. auth., *A Bibliography for the Study of African Politics* (1973). **Activities:** 4, 12; 77, 78 **Addr.:** California Dept. of Justice Library, Suite 600, 110 W. "A" St., San Diego, CA 92101.

Shaw, Ruth Jean (Ja. 12, 1943, Glasgow, MT) Mgr., Lib. Resrcs., Anchorage Sch. Dist., 1979–; Spec. Projs. Libn., WA State Univ., 1971–78; Lib. Dir., Coll. of Grt. Falls, 1968–70; Libn., E. TX State Univ., 1966–67. **Educ.:** E. TX State Univ., 1963–66, BS (Msc.); Univ. of OK, 1966–67, MLS. **Orgs.:** AK LA: Cont. Educ. Com. (1981–); Anchorage Chap. (Secy., 1981–). AAUW. Anchorage Keyboard Tchrs. Assn. **Pubns.:** Ed., *AAUW Nsltr.* (1981–). **Activities:** 1, 10; 15, 17, 20; 50, 63, 82 **Addr.:** Library Resources, 1800 Hillcrest Dr., Anchorage, AK 99503.

Shaw, Sarah J. (Mr. 14, 1947, Chicago, IL) Art Catlgr., Brown Univ., 1981–, Sheet Mss. Catlgr., 1980–81; Libn., Art and Msc. Dept., Providence Pub. Lib., 1978–80; Actg. Branch Libn., Pullman Branch, Chicago Pub. Lib., 1972–76. **Educ.:** Occidental Coll., 1964–68, AB, cum laude (Msc.); Univ. of CA, Berkeley, 1970–71, MLS, 1968–70, (Msc.). **Orgs.:** ALA. RI LA. Msc. LA. ARLIS/NA. **Honors:** Phi Beta Kappa, 1964. **Activities:** 9; 15, 20, 39; 55 **Addr.:** 22 Eames St., Providence, RI 02906.

Shaw, Spencer Gilbert (Ag. 15, 1916, Hartford, CT) Prof., Libnshp., Sch. of Libnshp., Univ. of WA, 1970– Consult., Lib. Srv. to Chld., Nassau Cnty. Lib. Syst., 1959–70; Prog. Coord., Storytel. Spec., Dept. of Work with Chld., Brooklyn Pub. Lib., 1949–59; Branch Libn., Hartford Pub. Lib., 1945–48, 1940–43; various visit. fac. positions, 1958–79. **Educ.:** Hampton Inst., 1936–40, BS (Eng., Soc. Std.); Univ. of WI, 1940–41, BLS; Univ. of Chicago, 1948–49 (Advnc. Std.). **Orgs.:** ALA: Cncl. (1969–71); Awds. Com. (Ch., 1969–71); ALSC, Bd. of Dirs. (1974–77), Pres. (1975–76), VP, Pres.-Elect (1974–75), various coms.; ASCLA; Chlds. Srvs. Div., various coms.; PLA, Lib. Srv. to Chld. Com. (Ch., 1971–74); HRLSD; AASL. WA LA: Awds. Com. (1980–). Pac. NW LA. NY LA: Chld. and YA Srvs. Sect., Bd. of Dirs. (1951–53). various orgs. Natl. Cncl. of Tchrs. of Eng. World Bk.-Childcraft Intl. Inc.: Ed. Adv. Bd. (1972–). Frnds. of the Seattle Pub. Lib. Child Std. Assn. of Amer. various orgs. **Honors:** Hampton Inst., Disting. Alum. Awd., 1960; Beta Phi Mu, 1949; Brooklyn Pub. Lib., Frnds. of the Lib. Awd., 1955; Carnegie Fndn., Carnegie Flwshp., 1940. **Pubns.:** "Ethnicity and Cultural Diversity: Legacies for Use in Literature for Children," *Arts in Cultural Diversity* (1980); "Augusta Baker, a Profile" *ALA World Encyclopedia of Library and Information Services* (1980); "Children's Services Operating Under 'Systems' Organization," *Lib. Trends* (Jl. 1973); "Shall we break the glass walls of illiteracy?" *Motivation and the Right to Read Conf. Proc.* (1973); "Where Do We Go from Here?" *Issues: Background Papers* (1978); "The Children's Librarian as Viewed by Library School Educators," *Children's Services of Public Libraries* (1978); various articles, monos., sps., film narrations, bk. reviews. **Activities:** 9, 11; 21, 25, 26; 55, 66, 72 **Addr.:** School of Librarianship, Suzzallo Library FM–30, University of Washington, Seattle, WA 98195.

Shawcross, Nancy M. (O. 15, 1952, Rahway, NJ) Mss. Libn., Dance Col., NY Pub. Lib., 1978–; Libn., Env. Psy. Prog., Grad. Ctr., CUNY, 1976–78; Ref. Libn., Un. Coll., 1976. **Educ.:** Middlebury Coll., 1970–74, BA (Eng., Drama); Rutgers Univ., 1975–76, MLS, 1976–80, MA (Comp. Lit.). **Orgs.:** SAA. **Activities:** 2, 12; 15, 23, 45; 55, 67 **Addr.:** 1408 Blvd., Westfield, NJ 07090.

Shea, Rev. Joseph J., S.J. (Je. 25, 1908, Boston, MA) Archvst., Coll. of the Holy Cross, 1966–, Prof. of Phil., 1939–78, 1932–34. **Educ.:** Boston Coll., 1925–29, AB (Phil.); Gregorian Univ., 1935–39, LST (Theo.); Amer. Univ., 1966, Cert. (Introduction to Mod. Arch. Admin.). **Orgs.:** SAA. Amer. Phil. Assn. Cath. Theo. Assn. **Pubns.:** *Synthesis of Philosophical Psychology* (1950); *Record Holdings of Holy Cross Archives* (1970). **Activities:** 1, 2; 15, 18, 20; 55, 63 **Addr.:** Archives, Holy Cross College, Worcester, MA 01610.

Shea, Joseph T. (Jl. 22, 1942, Boston, MA) Libn., Boston Tech. HS, 1969–; Libn., Boston Latin Sch., 1968–69; Visit. Lectr., Lib. Sci., Boston State Coll., 1971–72; Tchr., William E. Russell Sch., 1964–68. **Educ.:** Boston State Coll., 1960–64, BSEd (Sci. Educ.); Univ. of RI, 1964–68, MLS. **Orgs.:** ALA. New Eng. LA. MA LA. Boston Tchrs. Un. **Honors:** Boston State Coll., Alum. Achvmt. Awd., 1969. **Addr.:** Boston Technical High School, 205 Townsend St., Boston, MA 02121.

Shea, Larry L. (Ap. 18, 1945, Garden City, KS) Chief, Lib. Srv., Vets. Admin., 1980–; Head, Circ. Srvs., Instr., Lib. Sci., Univ. of OK Hlth. Sci. Ctr., 1976–80; Dir., Libs., OK Dept. of Corrects., 1974–76; Head Libn., Capitol Hill Branch, OK Cnty. Libs., 1970–74. **Educ.:** Oklahoma City Univ., 1965–70, BA (Sp., Thea.); University of OK, 1972–74, MLS. **Orgs.:** Med. LA. OK LA: Right to Read Com. (1974); Lib. Week Com. (1975). **Honors:** John Cotton Dana PR Awd., 1980. **Pubns.:** *Needs Assessment of the Oklahoma Department of Corrections Libraries* (1975). **Activities:** 4; 17, 39; 58, 80 **Addr.:** Library Service (142D), Memorial Station, Honor Heights Dr., Muskogee, OK 74401.

Shea, Regina Kram (My. 26, 1944, Philadelphia, PA) Asst. Head Ref. Libn., Univ. of Chicago Lib., 1979–, Asst. Ref. Libn., 1968–79. **Educ.:** Wheeling Coll., 1962–66, BA (Hist.); Univ. of Chicago, 1966–70, MA (LS). **Orgs.:** Chicago Area OLUG. ALA: ACRL; RASD; GODORT; LIRT. Intl. Crane Fndn. **Activities:** 1; 29, 31, 39; 55, 57, 92 **Addr.:** 2851 M.L.King Dr., Chicago, IL 60616.

Shearer, Benjamin F. (S. 12, 1949, Dayton, OH) Dir., Thomas Byrne Meml. Lib., Spr. Hill Coll., 1981–; Gvt. Docum./Law Libn., E. TN State Univ., 1978–81; Gvt. Docum. and Asst. Ref. Libn., St. Louis Univ., 1975–77, Browsing & Rsv. Libn., 1974–75. **Educ.:** St. Louis Univ., 1968–71, BA (Phil.), 1973–75, AM (Amer. Hist.), 1975–78, PhD (Hist. of Ideas); Univ. of IL, 1977–78, MS in LS. **Orgs.:** TN LA. **Honors:** Natl. Endow. for the Hum., Grant, 1977. **Pubns.:** *Finding the Source: A Thesaurus Index to the Reference Collection* (1981); *Aspects of Health in the Technological Society; A Bibliography* (1980); *Communications Technologies and Society; A Bibliography* (1979); "Canadian Collections in the United States," *Gvt. Pubns. Review* (1979); "Students' Army Training Corps at the University of Illinois," *Jnl. of the IL State Hist. Socty.* (Ag. 1979); various other articles. **Activities:** 1; 29, 30, 39; 55, 57 **Addr.:** 4582 Hawthorne Pl., Mobile, AL 36608.

Shearer, Gary W. (F. 9, 1941, Lockwood, MO) Spec. Cols. Libn., Loma Linda Univ., La Sierra Campus, 1981–, Ref. Libn., 1970–81, Pub. Srvs. Libn., 1969–70. **Educ.:** Andrews Univ., SW MO State, Un. Coll., Lincoln, NE, 1960–65, BA (Soc. Sci., Relig.); Emporia State Univ., 1968–69, ML (LS). **Orgs.:** ALA: ACRL; RASD. SAA. Assn. of Seventh-Day Adventist Histns. Assn. of West. Adventist Histns. Mormon Hist. Assn. UT State Hist. Socty. **Activities:** 1; 39, 45; 70, 90, 92 **Addr.:** 5341 Sierra Vista, Riverside, CA 92505.

Shearer, Kenneth D. (Jl. 9, 1937, Far Rockaway, NY) Prof., Sch. of LS, NC Ctrl. Univ., 1974–; Asst. Prof., Sch. of LS, Univ. of NC, 1968–74; Asst. Branch Chief, Jefferson Branch Lib., Detroit Pub. Lib., 1967–68, Libn., Bk. Sel., 1964–67. **Educ.:** Amherst Coll., 1955–59, AB (Math.); Rutgers Univ., 1962–63, MLS, 1963–69, PhD (LS). **Orgs.:** ALA: *Pub. Libs.* Ed. (1978–); PLA, Exec. Bd. (1978–); LAMA/Stats. Sect., Exec. Com. (1978–). NC LA: Dev. Com. (Ch., 1976–78). Durham Cnty. LA.: Pres. (1974–75). AALS: Prog. Com. (1978–79). AAUP. **Honors:** Beta Phi Mu, 1963. **Pubns.:** *The Collection and Use of Public Library Statistics by State Library Agencies* (1978); "Legislative Support of Library Service in North Carolina," *Libraries in the Political Process* (1980); "The Impact of Research on Librarianship," *Jnl. of Educ. for Libnshp.* (Fall 1979); "PLA's Seminar on *A Planning Process for Public Libraries*," *Pub. Libs.* (Win. 1979); various other articles. **Activities:** 9, 11; 26, 37, 41 **Addr.:** School of Library Science, North Carolina Central University, Durham, NC 27707.

Shearer, Susan (O. 20, 1946, Philadelphia, PA) Lib. Srvs. Coord., Natl. Trust for Hist. Prsrvn., 1980–, Adv. Srvs. Asst., 1979; Visual Srvs. Libn., Frances Loeb Lib., Grad. Sch. of Dsgn., Harvard Univ., 1976–78, Photograph, Slide Catlgr., Fogg Musm., Fine Arts Lib., 1968–76. **Educ.:** Mt. Holyoke Coll., 1964–68, BA (Art Hist.); Simmons Coll., 1974–76, MLS; Boston Univ., 1976–78, MA (Prsrvn. Std.). **Orgs.:** ARLIS/NA. SLA. Assn. of Archit. Libns. Socty. for Cmrcl. Archlg.: Bd. of Dirs. (1979–). Assn. for Prsrvn. Tech. Socty. of Archit. Histns. Amer. Assn. for State and Lcl. Hist. **Honors:** Beta Phi Mu, 1976. **Pubns.:** Jt. auth., *Guide to Resources Use in Historic Preservation Reasearch* (1978); *The National Trust for Historic Preservation:Manual of Procedures* (1978); Jt. auth., "Acquistion of Print and Audiovisual Materials for Historic Prservation Collections," *Natl. Trust for Hist. Prsrvn.* (1978). **Activities:** 12; 15, 17, 20; 55 **Addr.:** National Trust for Historic Preservation, 1785 Massachusetts Ave. N.W., Washington, DC 20036.

Sheary, Edward J. (Ag. 4, 1953, Asheville, NC) Dir., Northwest. Reg. Lib., 1981–, Area Consult., 1979–81; Ref. Libn., Cannon Meml. Lib., 1977–79. **Educ.:** Univ. of NC, Asheville, 1971–75, BA (Pol. Sci.); Univ. of NC, 1975–76, MS (LS). **Orgs.:** ALA. NC LA. **Activities:** 9; 17, 24 **Addr.:** Northwestern Regional Library, 111 N. Front St., Elkin, NC 28621.

Shedd, Jeanne H. (O. 30, 1919, Honolulu, HI) Ref. Libn., Northport Pub. Lib., 1970–; Asst. Dir., Huntington Hist. Socty., 1965–67. **Educ.:** Middlebury Coll., 1936–39; Univ. of HI, 1939–41, BA (Lang., Lit., Art); Long Island Univ., 1967–70, BSLS. **Orgs.:** ALA. ARLIS/NA. Suffolk Cnty. LA. Huntington Hist. Socty. Northport Hist. Socty. Bishop Musm. Assn. AAUW. **Honors:** Phi Kappa Phi, 1941. **Pubns.:** *Selected Serials in European Languages: The Language Problem* (1978); "Education at Huntington Historical Society," *Museologist* (S. 1966); "Our Hawaiian Idol," *Huntington Hist. Socty. Qtly.* (1965). **Addr.:** Northport Public Library, Reference Dept., Northport, NY 11768.

Shediac, Margaret C. (O. 6, 1951, Bryn Mawr, PA) Libn., Howard, Rice, Nemerovski, Canady and Pollak, 1978–; Asst. Libn., Morgan, Lewis and Bockius, 1976–77. **Educ.:** Defiance Coll., 1971–74, BA (Eng., Psy.); Univ. of NC, 1974–75, MS (LS). **Orgs.:** SLA. Assn. of Recs. Mgrs. and Admins. AALL: Conf. of Newer Law Libns., Treas. (1979), Co-ch. (1981–82); Pvt. Law Lib. Spec. Interest Sect. (Com. Ch., 1979–80; Co-Ch., 1981–82). North. CA Assn. of Law Libs.: Co-fndr. (1980). **Pubns.:** "Greater Philadelphia Law Library Association 1977 Survey," *Law Lib. Jnl.* (F. 1978) "Private Law Library Special Interest Section 1979 Salary Survey," *Law Lib. Jnl.* (Win. 1980). **Activities:** 12; 17, 38; 77 **Addr.:** Howard, Rice, Nemerovski, Canady & Pollak, 650 California St., Suite 2900, San Francisco, CA 94108.

Sheehan, Sr. Helen, S.N.D. (Jl. 25, 1904, Manchester, NH) Libn. Emeritus, Trinity Coll., 1972–, Libn., 1934–72; Tchr., Libn., New Eng. Schs., 1931–34; Libn., Cathedral Lib., 1930–31; Libn. in Charge of Branches, City Lib., Manchester, NH, 1926–30; Rpt., *Manchester Mirror*, 1924–25. **Educ.:** Trinity Coll., Washington, DC, 1920–24, BA (Math., Eng.); Simmons Coll., 1925–26, MS (LS). **Orgs.:** ALA: Brotherhood Week, Jt. Com. ALA and Cath. LA (Ch., 1971–73); ACRL, Ed. Bd. *Choice* (Ch., 1966–69). Cath. LA: Exec. Bd. (1959–65); VP (1967–69); Pres. (1969–71). Lib. Coll. Assocs.: Ed. Bd. *L-C Jnl.* (1967–72). Cncl. of Natl. Lib. Assns.: Bd. (1969–71). Trinity Coll. Bd. of Trustees. **Honors:** US Steel, Resrch. Awd. for Std. of Small Coll. Libs., 1956; Simmons Coll. Sch. of Lib. Sci. Alum. Achvmt. Awd., 1973; Pro Ecclesia Medal, 1965; Trinity Coll., Lib. Renamed and Dedicated as Sr. Helen Sheehan Lib., 1979. **Pubns.:** *The Small College Library* (1963); "The Library-College Idea; Trend of the Future," *Lib. Trends* (Jl. 1969); "The Student and the Library-College," *Lrng. Today* (Spr. 1976); "Experimentation and the College Library," *MD Libs.* (Fall 1966); "Automated Alternatives to the Card Catalog," *Cath. Lib. World* (S. 1975); various articles. **Activities:** 1; 17 **Addr.:** Trinity College, Washington, DC 20017.

Sheehan, John T. (F. 22, 1913, Boston, MA) Consult., Sci. Info., Squibb Inst. for Med. Resrch., 1978–, Sr. Resrch. Info. Sci., 1973–78, Sr. Resrch. Investigator, 1942–73; Resrch. Chem., Winthrop Chem. Co., 1940–42. **Educ.:** Boston Coll., 1930–34, AB (Phil.), 1934–35, MS (Chem.); Fordham Univ., 1935–39, PhD. **Orgs.:** EFLA: Fest. Juror and Ch. (1964–79). Middlesex (NJ) Free Pub. Lib.: Trustee (1975–79). Amer. Chem. Socty.: Film Ofcr. (1938–); NJ Sect., Educ. Com. (1970–78). **Addr.:** Squibb Institute for Medical Research Library, Rte. 206 & Province Line Rd., Box 4000, Princeton, NJ 08540.

Sheehan, Robert Charles (Ap. 24, 1930, Pittsburgh, PA) Sr. Prin. Libn., Mid-Manhattan Lib., NY Public Lib., 1973–, Prin. Libn., 1967–73, Readers Adv., New York Pub. Lib., 1961–67, Sr. Libn., Donnell Lib., NY Pub. Lib., 1957–60; Sr. Libn., Riverside Branch, 1954–55, Gen. Adult libn., 1953–54. **Educ.:** Duquesne Univ., 1948–52, BPed (Eng.); Carnegie Inst. of Tech., 1952–53, MLS; U.S. Army Chem. Bio. Radiological Spec. Sch., 1954, Cert. **Orgs.:** ALA: AV Com. (1960–63). METRO: Ref. Libns. RT LEX Wkshp. Conf. (Ch., 1978). **Pubns.:** Jt. ed., *Consumer Bibliography* (1972). **Activities:** 9; 63, 92, 95-Readers' adv. **Addr.:** 372 Central Park W., Apt. 2W, New York, NY 10025.

Sheehan, William John (Ja. 1, 1937, Syracuse, NY) Asst. Libn., Woodstock Theo. Ctr. Lib., Georgetown Univ., 1976–; Univ. Libn., Univ. of St. Thomas, Houston, TX, 1968–75. **Educ.:** Univ. of Toronto, 1954–60, BA (Eng., Phil.), 1963–66, STB (Theo.); Case West. Rsv. Univ., 1967–68, MS in LS. **Orgs.:** ALA. **Activities:** 1; 17, 19, 39; 90 **Addr.:** 3700 Massachusetts Ave., N.W., Washington, DC 20016.

Sheehy, Eugene P. (O. 10, 1922, Elbow Lake, MN) Head, Ref. Dept., Columbia Univ. Libs., 1965–, Ref. Asst., 1953–65; Ref. Libn., Georgetown Univ. Lib., 1952–53. **Educ.:** St. John's Univ., Collegeville, MN, 1947–50, BA (Eng.); Univ. of MN, 1950–51, MA (Eng.), 1951–52, BS in LS. **Orgs.:** ALA: Com. on Wilson Indxs. (1965–72). **Honors:** ALA, Isadore Gilbert Mudge Cit., 1981. **Pubns.:** *Yvor Winters; a Bibliography* (1959); *Frank Norris; a Bibliography* (1959); *Sherwood Anderson; a Bibliography* (1960); supplements 1-3 to *Guide to Reference Books* 8th and 9th eds. (1968–72, 1976, supplement 1979); "Selected Reference Books," *Coll. & Resrch. Libs.* (1964–); various other bks. **Activities:** 1; 39; 55, 57 **Addr.:** 185 W. End Ave., New York, NY 10023.

Sheerr, Lucy Bethel (N. 7, 1949, Stoneham, MA) Pub. Srvs. Libn., Colby-Sawyer Coll., 1978–; Tech. Srvs. Libn., Richards Lib., Newport, NH, 1976–78; Resrch. Libn., Amer. Assn. of Advert. Agencies, 1973–76. **Educ.:** CT Coll., 1967–71, BA (Eng. Lit.); South. CT State Coll., 1972–73, MS (LS); Simmons Coll., Certs. in Autom. Circ., Docum. Cons., Lib. Grantsmanship, other certs. **Orgs.:** ALA: NH-JMRT Rep. (1980–82). SLA. New Eng. LA: Secy. (1980–81); Pubns. Bd. (Ch., 1980–). NH LA: NH/JMRT (Pres., 1979); Nom. Com. (Ch., 1980); Cont. Ed. Com. (1978–). Various other orgs. Grantham Lib.: Bd. of Trustees (Ch., 1979–). Lib. Arts Ctr.: Bd. of Trustees (Treas./Secy., 1977–79). **Honors:** ALA, JMRT, Shirley M. Olofson Awd., 1980. **Activities:** 1; 17, 31, 39; 51, 59 **Addr.:** P.O. Box 242, Grantham, NH 03753.

Sheets, Janet Elizabeth (Ja. 25, 1943, Winston-Salem, NC) Ref. Libn., Baylor Univ., 1977–; Coord. of Pub. Srvs., N.E. LA Univ., 1975–77; Ref. Libn., Jt. Univ. Libs., 1973–75; Ref. Libn., Duke Univ. Lib., 1968–72. **Educ.:** Coll. of William and Mary, 1961–65, AB (Ancient Lang.); Univ. of NC, 1965–67, MS in LS; Scan. Sem., 1972–73. **Orgs.:** ALA: RASD, Outstan. Ref. Books Com. (1978–82); RASD, Bibl. Com. (1977–81). **Honors** Beta Phi Mu; Phi Beta Kappa. **Pubns.:** Jt. auth., "The RASD Outstanding Reference Sources Committee: Retrospect and Prospect," *RQ* (Sum. 1981). **Activities:** 1; 17, 31, 39; 55, 90, 92 **Addr.:** Reference Dept., Moody Library, Baylor University, Waco, TX 76706.

Sheets, Shirley H. (D. 1, 1934, Fort Worth, TX) Asst. Libn., Tech. Srv., Univ. of TX, Arlington, 1977–, Mono. Libn., 1972–77, Catlgr., Head Catlgr., 1963–72; Catlgr., TX Wesleyan Coll., 1962–63; Asst. Catlgr., N. TX State Univ., 1955–62. **Educ.:** N. TX State Univ., 1952–55, BA (LS), 1967–70, MLS. **Orgs.:** ALA. TX LA: Coll. and Univ. Div., Legis. Com. (1980–82). SWLA. **Honors:** Sigma Alpha Iota. **Activities:** 1; 17, 46 **Addr.:** Box 19497, University of Texas, Arlington, TX 76019.

Sheinwald, Franette (Ap. 8, 1948, Long Beach, NY) Sr. Libn. (Law), NY State Dept. of Law Lib., 1981–; Sales/Cust. Rel., Readex Microprint Corp., 1979–81; Asst. Libn., NY State Lib., 1973–77; Reg. Ref. Libn., New Bedford Free Pub. Lib., 1970–72. **Educ.:** Fairleigh Dickinson Univ., 1965–69, BA (Hist.); Syracuse Univ., 1969–70, MSLS; Russell Sage Coll., 1974–75; Baruch Coll., 1977–79, MPA. **Orgs.:** ALA: GODORT. NY LA: Cont. Ed. Com., Ref. and Adult Srv. Sect. (1977). SLA. AALL. **Honors:** Amer. Socty. for Pub. Admin., Pi Alpha Alpha, 1979. **Activities:** 29, 34, 39; 77, 78, 92 **Addr.:** New York State Dept. of Law Library, 2 World Trade Center, New York, NY 10047.

Shelar, James W. (O. 17, 1943, Charlottesville, VA) Libn., Arnold and Porter, 1975–; Libn., Squire, Sanders and Dempsey, 1971–75. **Educ.:** Thiel Coll., 1961–65, BA (Eng.); Carnegie Mellon Univ., 1965–67, MA (Eng.); Case West. Rsv. Univ., 1969–71, MSLS; Cath. Univ., 1977–81, JD (Law). **Orgs.:** AALL. DC Law Libns. Socty. **Activities:** 12; 17; 77, 78 **Addr.:** Arnold & Porter—Library, 1200 New Hampshire Ave., N.W., Washington, DC 20036.

Sheldon, Brooke Earle (Ag. 29, 1931, Lawrence, MA) Dean, Sch. of LS, Actg. Provost, TX Woman's Univ., 1977–; Head, Tech. Srvs. and Trng., AK State Lib., 1973–75; Trng. Dir., Leadership Trng. Inst., FL State Univ., 1972–73; Head, Lib. Dev., NM State Lib., 1969–72. **Educ.:** Acadia Univ., 1948–52, BA (Eng. Econ.); Simmons Coll., 1953–54, MS in LS; Univ. of Pittsburgh, 1975–77, PhD (LS). **Orgs.:** ALA: Exec. Bd. (1979–84); Cncl. Mem. at Lg. (1977–80); Assn. of State Lib. Agencies, Exec. Bd. (1972–73, 1975–77); HQ Visit. Com. (1979–80); Nom. Com. (1972). TX LA. SWLA: Pub. Lib. Sect. (Ch., 1970). **Honors:** Beta Phi Mu, 1977. **Pubns.:** "Personnel Administration in Libraries," *LAMA* (1980); *Regional Library Cooperation in Ohio* (1977); *Illinois Interlibrary Cooperation (Consultant) Program* (1981); *Proposal Writing Handbook* (1976); ed. bd., *Pub. Lib. Qtly.* (1979–); various other pubns., articles. **Activities:** 11, 13; 17, 24, 26, 28; 50, 63, 89 **Addr.:** Texas Woman's University, Denton, TX 76204.

Sheldon, Paul C., Jr. (O. 9, 1938, Denver, CO) Head, Cat. Dept., Univ. of CO, 1978–, Head, Cat. Maintenance and Prsrvn. Dept., 1968–78; Cat. Libn., Regis Coll., 1965–68. **Educ.:** Univ. of CO, 1964, BA (Geo.); Univ. of Denver, 1965, MA (Libnshp.). **Orgs.:** ALA: RTSD/Reprodct. of Lib. Mtrls. Sect., Policy and Resrch. Com. (1974–78). CO LA. SLA: CO Chap. (Secy., 1969–70). **Activities:** 1; 20, 23, 46; 70 **Addr.:** University of Colorado, Boulder Libraries, Box 184, Boulder, CO 80309.

Sheldon, Ted P. (Oak Park, IL) Assoc. Dir., Libs., SUNY, Binghamton, 1981–; Head, Col. Dev., Univ. of KS, 1979–81, Ref. Libn., Hist. Biblgphr., 1977–79. **Educ.:** Elmhurst Coll., 1960–64, BA (Hist.); IN Univ., 1964–76, MA, PhD (Hist.); Univ. of IL, 1976–77, MSLS. **Orgs.:** ALA: RASD, Bibls. and Indxs. Com. (1979–81); ACRL; RTSD Org. of Amer. Histns. Amer. Hist. Assn. **Pubns.:** *Population Change in the Southern Low Countries, 1300–1525* (1976). **Activities:** 1; 15, 17; 57, 73 **Addr.:** Glenn G. Bartle Library, State University of New York at Binghamton, Binghamton, NY 13901.

Shelkrot, Elliot L. (Je. 24, 1943, Pittsburgh, PA) State Libn., State Lib. of PA, 1980–; Chief, Pub. Srvs. Support, Baltimore Cnty. Pub. Lib., 1976–80; Spec. in Cmnty. Srvs., Div. of Lib. Dev. and Srvs., MD Dept. of Educ., 1969–76; Branch Head and Asst. Head, Free Lib. of Philadelphia, 1966–69. **Educ.:** Oberlin Coll., 1961–65, BA; Univ. of Pittsburgh, 1965–66 MLS. **Orgs.:** ALA: PLA, Goals, Guidelines and Stans. for Pub. Libs. (1979–83); Int. Frdm. Com. (1975–79); ASCLA; Cncl. Mem. from MD (1972–78). COSLA. PA LA. PA Sch. Libns. Assn. **Activities:** 13; 17; 78, 95-Plng. **Addr.:** State Library of Pennsylvania, Box 1601, Harrisburg, PA 17105.

Shellaby, Suzanne (Mr. 26, 1946, Waban, MA) Assoc. Libn., Univ. of CA, Los Angeles, 1972–; Libn., Johannes-Gutenberg-Univ., Mainz, West Germany, 1971–72; Bk Dlr., Otto Harrassowitz, Wiesbaden, West Germany, 1969–71. **Educ.:** Univ. of CA, Santa Cruez, 1965–67, BA (Hist.); Univ. of CA, 1968–69, MLS. **Orgs.:** ALA. CA LA. **Activities:** 1; 17, 39, 46; 66 **Addr.:** Library Task Force, 145A Powell Lib., University of California, Los Angeles, CA 90403.

Shelley, Leo E. (F. 26, 1942, Snyder Cnty., PA) Ref. Libn., Millersville State Coll., 1967–; Ref. Cat. Libn., Cuttington Univ. Coll., Liberia, 1965–67. **Educ.:** Millersville State Coll., 1960–64, BS (Lib. Educ.); Univ. of Pittsburgh, 1967–70, MLS. **Orgs.:** Lancaster Cnty. LA: Pres. (1973–74). PA LA. ACRL: DE Chap. PA Grmn. Socty. Lancaster Hist. Walking Tour. Ephrata Cloister Assocs. West Lancaster Jaycees. **Honors:** West Lancaster Jaycee of the Yr., 1977. **Pubns.:** *Newspapers in Microform owned by*

Special Subjects/Services: 50. Adult educ.; 51. Advert./Mktg.; 52. Aerosp.; 53. Agric.; 54. Area std.; 55. Arts/Hum.; 56. Autom.; 57. Bibl./Prtg.; 58. Bio. sci.; 59. Bus./Fin.; 60. Chem.; 61. Copyrt.; 62. Documtn.; 63. Educ.; 64. Engin.; 65. Env.; 66. Eth. grps.; 67. Film; 68. Food/Nutr.; 69. Geneal.; 70. Geo.; 71. Geol.; 72. Handcpd.; 73. Hist.; 74. Int. frdm.; 75. Info. sci.; 76. Insr.; 77. Law; 78. Legis.; 79. Math./Comp. sci.; 80. Med.; 81. Metals; 82. Nat. resrcs.; 83. Newsp.; 84. Nuc. sci.; 85. Oral hist.; 86. Petr./Energy; 87. Pharm.; 88. Phys./Astr./Math.; 89. Readg.; 90. Relig.; 91. Sci./Tech.; 92. Soc. sci.; 93. Telecom.; 94. Transp.; 95. (other).

State Colleges and Indiana U of PA (1978). **Activities:** 1; 31, 39 **Addr.:** 225 Redwood Dr., Lancaster, PA 17603.

Shelton, Clara S. (Ag. 23, 1929, Logan, IA) Retired, 1981; Serials Libn., SD State Univ. Lib., 1977–81, Acq. Libn., 1971–77, Circ. Libn., 1969–71, Pers. Libn., 1966–69. **Educ.:** Univ. of NE, Omaha, 1956–64, BA (Hist.); Univ. of Denver, 1964–65, MALS. **Orgs.:** ALA. Mt. Plains LA. SD LA. AAUW. Org. of Amer. Histns. **Pubns.:** Coord., *South Dakota Union List of Serials* (1978). **Activities:** 1; 44 **Addr.:** c/o Mrs. Calvin C. Hughes, Box 239, Glidden, IA 51443.

Shelton, John L. (F. 21, 1934, Terre Haute, IN) Lib. Dir., Lake Lanier Reg. Lib., 1978–; Adult Srvs. Coord., Chattahoochee Valley Reg. Lib., 1972–78; Lib. Dir., Charlotte Cnty. Libs., 1970–72; Coord. of Lib. Srvs., Lake Ridge Sch., Griffith, IN, 1965–69. **Educ.:** IN State Univ., 1956–59, BS (Liberal Arts), 1960–62, MS (Educ.); FL State Univ., 1970–71, MS (LS). **Orgs.:** ALA. GA LA. SELA. ASIS. GA Adult Educ. Assn. Socty. of GA Archvsts. GA Hist. Socty. Natl. Micro. Assn. **Pubns.:** "Cultivating the Library Habit," *Wilson Lib. Bltn.* (S. 1975). **Activities:** 9; 16, 17, 27 **Addr.:** Lake Lanier Regional Library, 275 Perry St., Lawrenceville, GA 30245.

Shen, I-yao (N. 9, 1926, China) Fac.-Libn., Univ. of DC, 1977–; Fac.-Libn., DC Tchrs. Coll., 1971–77; Libn., Lib. of Congs., 1970–71; Libn., Univ. of MD, 1961–70. **Educ.:** Sun Yatsen Univ., 1945–49, BA (Hist.); Columbia Univ., 1957–60, MA (Soc. Sci.); Rutgers Univ., 1960–61, MLS. **Orgs.:** ALA. DC LA. MD LA. AAUP. **Pubns.:** *A Century of Chinese Exclusion Abroad* (1970, 2nd ed. 1980); *A Century of American Immigration Policy Toward China* (1974); "Ten points of Proposal for Library Modernization in China," *China Daily News* (Ja. 15, 1979); "Some Problems of Orientation in Library Modernization in China," *China Daily News* (Ja. 1981). **Activities:** 1, 4; 26; 56, 75, 92 **Addr.:** University of DC Lib., 9005 Acredale Ct., College Park, MD 20001.

Sheng, Jack T. (N. 15, 1929, Hsiang-Yin, Hunan, China) Chief Law Libn., Duval Cnty. Law Lib., 1975–; Instr., FL Jr. Coll., 1975–; Asst. Law Libn., Asst. Prof. of Law, OH North. Univ. Coll. of Law, 1972–75; Head Libn., Assoc. Prof. of Law, Soochow Univ., 1970–72; Libn. I and II, Cat., Detroit Pub. Lib., 1967–70. **Educ.:** Soochow Univ., 1958–63, LLB (Chinese Law); Yale Univ. Law Sch., 1964–66, LLM (Intl. Law); LA State Univ., 1966–67, MS (LS); Wayne State Univ., 1967–69, JD, 1968, AALL, 1973, Libns. Prof., Cert., JD (Amer. Law); Law Libnshp. Cert.; FL Jr. Coll., 1976, Tchrs. Cert. **Orgs.:** AALL. Chinese-Amer. Libns. Assn. Duval Cnty. LA: Constn. and Bylaws Com. (1979–80). FL Jr. Coll. Adv. Com. (1977–80). **Honors:** Phi Dau Phi, 1971; OH North. Univ., Willis Socty., 1974. **Pubns.:** *Index to Chinese legal Periodicals 1963–70* (1972); contrib., *Library of Congress and National Union Catalog Author Lists, 1942–62* (1970); "Soochow University Library" handbk. (1970). **Activities:** 12; 41; 77 **Addr.:** 220 Courthouse, Jacksonville, FL 32202.

Shenholm, Daisy S (O. 29, 1924, Milwaukee, WI) Lib. Dir., Douglass Lib., Rutgers Univ., 1969–; Instr., Grad. Sch. of LS, Rutgers Univ., 1968–69. **Educ.:** Rutgers Univ., 1940–44, BA (Langs.), 1966–68, MLS. **Orgs.:** ALA. NJ LA. NJ Cncl. of Coll. and Univ. Libns.: Pres. (1979–80). **Activities:** 1; 17, 31, 32; 56 **Addr.:** Douglass Library, Rutgers University, New Brunswick, NJ 08903.

Shenk, Margaret Mae (F. 15, 1919, Elida, OH) Cat. Libn., Head, East. Mennonite Coll., 1973–, Head Libn., 1961–73; Libn., Amer. Collegiate Inst., Izmir, Turkey, 1960–61; Asst. Libn., East. Mennonite Coll., 1950–60, Tchr. 1940–45. **Educ.:** East. Mennonite Coll., 1938–40, 1948–49, BA (Eng.); George Peabody Coll., 1949–50, MALS. **Orgs.:** ALA. SE LA. VA LA. **Honors:** Pi Gamma Mu, 1950. **Activities:** 1 **Addr.:** Eastern Mennonite College, Harrisonburg, VA 22801.

Shenton, Kathleen Edwina (O. 18, 1954, Hackensack, NJ) Mgr., Phys. Sci. Info. Srvs., SDC Srch. Srv., 1980–; Resrch. Chemist, Alerting and Srchg. Grp., Exxon Resrch. and Engin. Co., 1977–80; Chemist, Lipton Tea Co., 1976. **Educ.:** Princeton Univ., 1972–76, AB (Chem.); Yale Univ., 1976–77 MS (Chem.). **Orgs.:** ASIS. SLA. Amer. Chemical Socty. **Pubns.:** Chap. 2, *An Information Managers Guide to Online Services* (1980); "Conference Searching at 1200 Baud," *Online* (1981); various sps. **Activities:** 6, 12; 15, 41, 46; 60, 64, 86 **Addr.:** System Development Corp., 2520 Colorado Ave., Santa Monica, CA 90406.

Shepard, David H. (O. 22, 1940, New York, NY) Spec. Projs. Ofcr., Dirs. Gld. of Amer., 1976–; VP, Blackhawk Films Inc., 1973–76; Assoc. Archvst., Amer. Film Inst., 1969–73; Asst. Prof., PA State Univ., 1965–68. **Educ.:** Hamilton Coll., 1958–62, AB (Phil., Relig.); Univ. of PA, 1962–63, MA (Amer. Std.); Syracuse Univ., 1963–65, PhD cand. **Orgs.:** Intl. Film Sems., Inc.: Trustee (1977–81); Adv. (1971–77). Socty. for Cin. Std.: Trustee (1980–83). Univ. Film Assn. EFLA. various other orgs. Los Angeles Intl. Film Exposition: Prog. Consult. (1971–). Los Angeles Cinemathèque: Bd. of Advs. (1979–). Emmanuel Evang. Free Church. **Honors:** Natl. Acad. of TV Arts and Scis., Emmy, 1973; Socty. for Cinephiles, Ltd., Cineward, 1970. **Pubns.:** Jt. ed., *The American Film Heritage* (1972); "Authenticating Textual Sources in Film," *Qtly. Jnl. of Lib. of Congs.* (Spr. 1980); "When Is A Movie *The* Movie," *Amer. Film* (Mr. 1979); "The Victor Animatograph Company and the Beginnings of Nontheatrical Film," *Bks. at IA* (Ap. 1976); producer, various TV series. **Activities:** 2, 12; 15, 16, 23; 67, 93 **Addr.:** 4236 Klump Ave., N. Hollywood, CA 91602.

Shepard, Margaret E. (O. 5, 1941, Detroit, MI) Libn., Transp. and Traffic Sci., Gen. Motors Resrch. Labs., 1972–, Acq. Libn., 1966–68. **Educ.:** Alma Coll., 1959–63, BA (Educ.); Univ. of MI, 1964–67, AMLS. **Orgs.:** SLA. Cncl. of Plng. Libns. GODORT of MI. **Honors:** Beta Phi Mu. **Pubns.:** *Annotated Bibliography of the Application of Behavior and Attitude Research to Transportation System Planning and Design* (1976); *Handicapped Persons in the U.S. and Public Transportation Travel Demand: A Literature Review and Annotated Bibliography* (1978). **Activities:** 12; 30, 39, 44; 57, 94 **Addr.:** Transportation & Traffic Science Dept., General Motors Research Laboratories, Warren, MI 48090.

Shepard, Marietta Daniels (Ja. 24, 1913, Mt. Washington, MO) Consult., 1978–; Chief, Lib. and Arch. Dev. Prog., Org. of Amer. States, 1959–78, Assoc. Libn., Columbus Meml. Lib., 1948–58; Spec. Asst. to Libn. of Congs., Lib. of Congs., 1946–48; Lib. Dir. and Prof. of LS, Escuela Normal, Panama, 1943–46; Chief of Circ., Lib., Washington Univ., 1938–43. **Educ.:** Univ. of KS, 1931–33, BA (Rom. Lang.); Columbia Univ., 1939–43, BSLS; Washington Univ., 1939–45, MA (Rom. Lang.). **Orgs.:** ALA: Cncl. (1956–60, 1969–74); Exec. Bd. (1968–72); Budget Asm. (1973–74); RTSD, Bd. (1963–69). DC LA: Pres. (1957–58). SALALM: Exec. Bd. (1956–). IFLA. Various other orgs., coms. AAUW. Latin Amer. Std. Assn. Altrusa Intl. **Honors:** Sociedad Colombiana Panamer., Achvmt. in Inter-Amer. Libnshp., 1948; ALA, Letter Awd. for Achvmt. in Intl. Libnshp. 1954; Spanish Bk. Indus., Contrib. to Publshg., 1972; Beta Phi Mu. **Pubns.:** *Bases for Developing an Inter-American Library and Information System* (1981); *La infraestructu bibliotecológica de sistemas nacionales de información* (1972); "Organization of American States," *ALA Yrbk.* (1978–); "Organization of American States," *ALA Encyc.* (1980); "Centralized Cataloging Services for Latin America," *Libri* (D. 1978); various other bks., articles. **Activities:** 12, 14-Lib. dev.; 24, 34; 54, 62, 89 **Addr.:** P. O. Box 331, Bedford, PA 15522.

Shepherd, Antoinette (O. 19, 1943, Galveston, TX) Catlgr., Rosenberg Lib., 1970–; Circ./Acq. Libn., Univ. of TX Med. Branch, 1965–69. **Educ.:** Our Lady of the Lake Coll., 1961–65, BA (LS). **Orgs.:** TX LA. SWLA: Catlgrs. Secy. (1978–81). ALA. AAUW. **Honors:** Beta Sigma Phi. **Activities:** 9; 20, 46; 56 **Addr.:** 1912-54th St., Galveston, TX 77550.

Shepherd, Clayton A. (My. 16, 1929, Washington, DC) Assoc. Prof., IN Univ., 1967–; Assoc. Dir., Documtn. Srv., Amer. Socty. Metals, 1963–67; Mgr., Info. Retrieval, Univac Div. Sperry Rand, 1961–63, Sr. Systs. Anal., 1959–61. **Educ.:** Univ. of MD, 1947–52, AB (Eng.), 1954–56, MA (Soclgy.). **Orgs.:** ASIS. Assn. Comp. Mach. SLA. AALS. **Honors:** ASIS, IN Chap., Mem. of the Yr., 1978. **Activities:** 12; 26, 33, 34; 56, 62, 75 **Addr.:** School of Library and Information Science, Indiana University, Bloomington, IN 47401.

Shepherd, Murray C. (Jl. 31, 1938, Saskatoon, SK) Univ. Libn., Univ. of Waterloo, 1973–, Assoc. Libn., 1971–73, Head of Tech. Srvs., 1969–71; Head of Cat. Dept., Regina Campus, Univ. of SK, 1967–69, Asst. Educ. Libn., 1964–67. **Educ.:** Univ. of SK, 1963, BEd (Eng.); Univ. of Denver, 1968, MA (LS). **Orgs.:** CARL. ON Cncl. of Univ. Libs.: Ch. (1975–76). Bd. for Lib. Coord. Can. LA. SK Assn. of Sch. Libs.: Pres. (1967–68). **Honors:** Beta Phi Mu. **Pubns.:** "Increasing Library Effectiveness," *Quill and Quire* (Jl. 1977). **Activities:** 1; 17 **Addr.:** Dana Porter Arts Library, University of Waterloo, Waterloo, ON N2L 3G1 Canada.

Sheppard, Yvonne Christine (D. 21, 1924, Brantford, ON) Retired, 1980; Coord. of Lrng. Resrcs., Wentworth Cnty. Bd. of Educ., 1970–79; Lib. Consult., Halton Cnty. Bd. of Educ., 1968–69; Lib. Consult., Burlington Bd. of Educ., 1962–68, Tchr.-Libn., 1957–62. **Educ.:** McMaster Univ., 1953–59, BA (Psy.); Miami Univ., 1963–67, MEd (LS); Heed Univ., 1973–75, EdD (Admin.); Elem. and Sec. Tchg. Cert. **Orgs.:** Can. LA: Com. on Pubns. (1976). Can. Sch. LA. ON LA. ON Sch. LA. ON Tchrs. Fed. ON Sec. Sch. Tchrs. Fed. Fed. of Women Tchrs. Assn. of ON. ON Coord. Assn. **Activities:** 10; 17, 24, 32; 63, 67, 89 **Addr.:** 308 W. 2nd St., Hamilton, ON L9C 3H2 Canada.

Shera, Jesse Hauk (D. 8, 1903, Oxford, OH) Dean Emeritus, Sch. of LS, Case West. Rsv. Univ., 1972–, Prof., 1971–72, Dean, 1952–70; Assoc. Prof., Grad. Lib. Sch., Univ. of Chicago, 1947–52; Assoc. Dir., Univ. of Chicago Libs., 1944–47; Deputy Chief, Ctrl. Info. Div., U.S. Ofc. of Strategic Srvs., 1941–44; Chief, Census Lib. Proj., Lib. of Congs., 1940–41; Biblgphr., Scripps Fndn. for Resrch. in Popltn. Problems, Miami Univ., 1928–40. **Educ.:** Miami Univ., 1921–25, AB (Eng. Lit.); Yale Univ., 1925–27, MA (Eng. Lit.); Univ. of Chicago, 1938–40, 1944, PhD (LS). **Orgs.:** ALA: Cncl. (1964–68). AALS: Pres. (1963–64). OH LA: Pres. (1963–64). Beta Phi Mu: Natl. Pres. (1970–71). AAAS. Caxton Club (Chicago). Rowfant Club (Cleveland). Prof. Men's Club (Cleveland). **Honors:** Phi Beta Kappa; Univ. of Chicago, Alum. Prof. Achvmt. Awd., 1977; Ball State Univ., LLD, 1976; ALA, Joseph W. Lippincott Awd., 1973; Melvil Dewey Medal, 1968; other hons. **Pubns.:** *The Sociological Foundations of Librarianship* (1970); *Foundations of Education for Librarianship* (1972); *Knowing Books and Men* (1973); *Introduction to Library Science* (1976); jt. auth., *Dictionary of American Library Biography* (1978); various other bks., articles. **Activities:** 1, 11; 17, 20, 26; 62, 63, 92 **Addr.:** School of Library Science, Case Western Reserve University, Cleveland, OH 44106.

Sherby, Louise S. (F. 2, 1947, Bridgeton, NJ) Head Ref. Libn., RI Coll., 1977–, Asst. Libn., Ref., 1973–77; Adjunct Prof., Univ. of RI Grad. Lib. Sch., 1981–; Libn. I, Adult Srvs., Chicago Pub. Lib., 1970–73. **Educ.:** Hofstra Univ., 1967–69, BA (Soclgy.); Univ. of Denver, 1969–70, MA (Libnshp.); Columbia Univ., 1979–, DLS Cand. **Orgs.:** ALA: ACRL/Coll. Libs. Sect., Nom. Com. (Ch., 1980–81); New Eng. Chap., Bibl. Instr. Com. Guide Subcom. (Ch., 1977–79). NLA: Prof. Educ. Com. (1977–80); Nom. Com. (1979–80). RI LA: Exec. Bd. (1975–77); Prof. Com. (Ch., 1976–77); various coms., ofcs. SLA: RI Chap. Bylaws Com. (1975–76); Secy. (1976–78). various orgs. Amer. Fed. of Tchrs. AAUP. **Pubns.:** "Academic Librarians and the Peer Evaluation Process," *Essays From the New England Academic Librarians' Writing Seminar* (1980); "Academic Librarian: Librarian or Faculty Member?" *Jnl. of Acad. Libnshp.* (N. 1978); Jt. auth., "Unionization at RIC and the Librarians," *RI LA Bltn.* (F. 1976); "Long-Range Plan Implementation Committee Report," *RI LA Bltn.* (My. 1976); "Pursuit of Faculty Status," *RILA Bltn.* (N. 1981). **Activities:** 1, 11; 17, 26, 39; 63, 92 **Addr.:** Rhode Island College Library, 600 Mt. Pleasant Ave., Providence, RI 02908.

Sheridan, Helen Adler (O. 3, 1937, Kansas City, MO) Head Libn., Kalamazoo Inst. of Arts, 1977–, Libn., 1975–77; Inst., Coll. of Gen. Std., West. MI Univ., 1968–75, Instr., Dept. of Eng., 1966–68; Pubns. Writer, Space Tech. Labs., TRW, 1960–65. **Educ.:** Univ. of KS, 1955–59, BA (Eng., Hum.); Univ. of CA, Los Angeles, 1961–64, MA (Eng.); West. MI Univ., 1975–77, MLS (Libnshp.). **Orgs.:** ARLIS/NA: MI Chap., VP, Pres., 1977–79. ALA. Beta Phi Mu: Kappa Chap. (VP, Pres., 1979–81). Coll. Art Assn. MI Musm. Assn. Amer. Assn. of Musms. **Honors:** Phi Beta Kappa, 1959; Beta Phi Mu, 1977. **Pubns.:** Ed., *German Expressionist Art in Western Michigan Collections* (1979); Ed., *Kalamazoo Collects Photography* (1980). **Activities:** 5, 8; 17, 39, 41; 55 **Addr.:** Kalamazoo Institute of Arts, 314 S. Park St., Kalamazoo, MI 49007.

Sheridan, John Brian (Ag. 20, 1947, New York, NY) Head Libn., Transylvania Univ., 1977–; Tech. Srvs. Libn., Knox Coll., 1975–77; Acq. Libn., Kearney State Coll., 1974–75, Cat. Libn., 1973–74. **Educ.:** City Coll. of NY, 1965–70, BA (Classics); IN Univ., 1970–72, AM (Classics); Univ. of WI, Milwaukee, 1972–73, MA (LS). **Orgs.:** ALA: ACRL/Coll. Lib. Sect., Com. on Impact of Natl. Dev. and Policies (Ch., 1979–); San Francisco Conf. Prog. Plng. Com. (1980–81); SRRT, Peace Info. Task Frc. (1979–). Southeast. Lib. Netwk.: Discuss. Grp. of Small Acad. Users (1979). KY Gvr.'s Pre-White Hse. Conf. on Libs.: Task Frc. on Delivery of Srvs. (1978–79). KY LA: Com. on Autom. (1980–). Various other orgs. Fayette Coop. Nursery and Kindergarten. Metro. Env. Improvement Comsn. Lexington-Fayette Co. Urban Cnty. Gvt.: 8th Dist. Comsn. (1977–81). **Pubns.:** "Example Five-Francis (sic) Thomas Library," *Zero-base Budgeting in Library Management* (1980). **Activities:** 1; 17, 34, 46 **Addr.:** Transylvania University Library, Lexington, KY 40508.

Sheridan, Leslie W. (D. 18, 1935, Jamaica, NY) Dir., Univ. Libs., Univ. of Toledo, 1975–; Assoc. Law Libn., Univ. of TX, Austin, 1971–75; Dir., Lib., Coll. of St. Vincent, Grad. Sch. of Theo., 1963–71; Asst. to Dir., Mary Immaculate Coll., 1961–63. **Educ.:** St. Joseph's Coll., Princeton, NJ, 1953–55, AA (Liberal Arts); Mary Immaculate Coll., Northampton, PA 1957–59, BA (Phil.); Cath. Univ. of Amer., 1968–69, STL (Theo.); St. John's Univ., Jamaica, NY, 1967–71, MLS (Libnshp.). **Orgs.:** Acad. LA of OH: Prog. Com. (1979–80). Amer. Lib. Hist. RT: Nom. Com. (1979–80); Com. on Soc. Problems (1973–74). AALL: Com. on Autom. and Sci. Dev. (1972–76). ALA: ACRL, Com. on Legis. Netwk.; Sect. on Law and Pol. Sci., Prog. Plng. Com. (1976–77), Nom. Com. (Ch., 1977–78). various orgs. Inter-Univ. Lib. Cncl., OH: Vice-Ch., Ch.-Elect (1977–79); Ch. (1978–79). OHIONET: Bd. of Trustees (1977–79). **Pubns.:** Jt. auth., *A Manual on Medical Literature for Law Librarians* (1973); *Canon Law Bibliography* (1971); "People in Libraries as Security Agents," *Lib. and Arch. Secur.* (Spr. 1980); "On Turning Over a New Leaf," *The Lib. Chronicle* (Fall 1972); "Legal-medical Studies," *The TX Bar Jnl.* (N. 1972); various articles, bk. reviews. **Activities:** 1, 14-Netwk.; 17, 28, 34; 90, 93 **Addr.:** William S. Carlson Library, University of Toledo, Toledo, OH 43606.

Sheridan, Robert Neal (Mr. 28, 1930, Greenwood, SC) Dir., Suffolk Coop. Lib. Syst., 1976–; Dir., Levittown Pub. Lib., 1964–76; Chief of Branch, Queens Boro. Pub. Lib., 1962–64; various positions, 1957–62. **Educ.:** Univ. of SC, 1948–52, AB (Hist), 1953–54, MA (Hist.); Rutgers Univ., 1956–57, MLS. **Orgs.:** ALA: PLA, Leg. Com. (1974–77); RASD, Pub. Liaison

PROFESSIONAL ACTIVITIES: Institutions: 1. Acad. lib.; 2. Arch.; 3. Assn.; 4. Fed./Gvt. lib.; 5. Inst. lib.; 6. Mfr./Suppl.; 7. Milit. lib.; 8. Musm.; 9. Pub. lib.; 10. Sch. lib.; 11. Sch. of lib. sci.; 12. Spec. lib.; 13. State lib.; 14. (other). **Functions/Activities:** 15. Acq./Col. dev.; 16. Adult srvs.; 17. Admin.; 18. Apprais.; 19. Archit./Bldgs.; 20. Cat./Class.; 21. Chld. srvs.; 22. Circ.; 23. Cons./Pres.; 24. Consult.; 25. Cont. ed.; 26. Educ. lib. sci.; 27. Ext. srvs.; 28. Fund/Grants; 29. Gvt. pubs.; 30. Indx./Abs.; 31. Instr. lib. use; 32. Media srvs.; 33. Micro.; 34. Netwks./Coop.; 35. Persnl.; 36. PR; 37. Publshg.; 38. Recs. mgt.; 39. Ref. srvs.; 40. Repro.; 41. Resrch.; 42. Review.; 43. Secur.; 44. Serials; 45. Spec. col.; 46. Tech. srvs.; 47. Trustees/Bds.; 48. YA srvs.; 49. (other).

Who's Who in Library and Information Services

Com. (Ch., 1966–69), Prog. Eval. and Budget Com. (1970–72). NY LA. Nassau Cnty LA. Long Island Libs. Resrcs. Cncl. U.S. Nvl. Inst. Navy Recs. Socty. Intl. Nautical Resrch. Org. **Pubns.:** Jt. ed., *The Future of Adult Books and Reading in America* (1970); jt. auth., *Results of Tests to Determine the Need for a Book Theft Deterrent Device and the Ability of the "Tattle Tape" Electronic Book Detection System to Reduce Book Theft* (1972). **Activities:** 9; 17 **Addr.:** Robert N. Sheridan, 154 Parkwood St., Ronkonkoma, NY 11779.

Sherman, Jacob Ross (Ap. 29, 1943, Harrisburg, PA) Asst. Libn., Rutland Free Lib., 1977–; Tech. Srvs. Libn., 1972–76; PR Writer, Saratoga Performing Arts Ctr., 1970–71; Writer, Albany *Times -Un.*, 1967–70. **Educ.:** Univ. of PA, 1960–64, BA, hons. (Eng. Lit); SUNY, Albany, 1970–71, MLS; Simmons Coll., Wkshp. in PR, 1977. **Orgs.:** New Eng. LA: PR Com. (Ch., 1976–78). VT LA: State Rep. to NELA Cncl. (1976–80); Pubcty. and Pubns. Com. (Ch., 1974–76). ALA. Crossrds. Arts Cncl. of Rutland. B'nai B'rith Lodge #1608 of Rutland. Appalachian Mt. Club. Green Mt. Club. **Pubns.:** "New England Libraries Serve Ethnic Americans," *Lib. Scene* (Spr. 1976); "Book Theft: How Bad a Problem for Vermont Libraries," *VT Libs.* (S. 1974). **Activities:** 9; 15, 36, 46; 55, 70 **Addr.:** 48 Morse Pl., Rutland, VT 05701.

Sherman, James Glen (F. 20, 1950, Los Angeles, CA) Sr. Ref. Libn., South. Meth. Univ., 1979–; Lib. Dir., Asst. Prof., San Fernando Valley Coll. of Law, 1972–79; Law Libn., Greenberg, Bernhard, Weise, and Karma, 1973–75; Asst. Libn., Univ. of South. CA, Law Lib., 1971–72. **Educ.:** Univ. of South. CA, 1968–72, BA (E. Asian Std.), 1976–77, MS (LS); San Fernando Valley Coll. of Law, 1972–76, JD (Law). **Orgs.:** AALL: Ethics (1977–78). South. CA Assn. of Law Libs.: Nsltr. (1977); Constn. Rev. (1978). **Honors:** Delta Theta Phi. **Pubns.:** "A Note on Sources of Scientific Research for Lawyers," *Law Lib. Jnl.* (My. 1977). **Activities:** 1; 17, 31, 39; 77 **Addr.:** 4630 Cole Ave., #19, Dallas, TX 75205.

Sherman, Jean G. (Ja. 28, 1930, Camp Hill, AL) Asst. Dir., Dept. of Sch. Libs., Detroit Pub. Schs., 1975–, Catlgr., 1973–75, Sum. Lectr., Univ. of MI Sch. of Lib. Sci., 1970–72; Tchr. Prog. Coord., EDPA Detroit Pub. Schs., 1970–71, HS Libn., 1962–69; Elem. Sch. Libn., 1956–62. **Educ.:** AL State Univ., 1947–51, BS (Eng.), Univ. of MI, 1953–55, MLS, 1969–70, Post Mstrs. (Lib., Instr. Media). **Orgs.:** ALA: AASL, Lib. Media Srv. to the Disadv. (1976–77). MI Assn. for Media in Educ.: Anl. Jt. Conf. Com. (1977–78, 1979–80). Chld. Bk. Fair Cncl. of Metro. Detroit: Ch. (1978–79); Transp. Com. (1975–78); Current Bk. Sel. (1975–81). Wayne Cnty. Intermediate Sch. Dist. Reg. Educ. Media Ctr. Adv. Cncl.: Co-ch. (1980–81); Film Sel. Com. (1977–81). NAACP. Alpha Kappa Alpha: Asst. Secy. (1966–68); Secy. (1970–74); Exec. Bd. (1980–81). AL State Univ. Alum. Univ. of MI Lib. Sci. Alum. **Honors:** AL State Univ. Alum., Alum. of the Year, 1963; AL State Univ. Alum., Alum. Pres. of the Year, 1977; Phi Delta Kappa. **Pubns.:** "Media Centers: Libraries Provide Source Materials," *The Detroit Readg. Review* (Nov. 30, 1979). **Activities:** 10; 17, 20, 32; 63 **Addr.:** 4036 Cortland, Detroit, MI 48204.

Sherman, Madeline (Schnabel) (F. 13, 1946, Monticello, NY) Libn., Proctor Jr.-Sr. HS, 1973–; Ref. Libn., Bethlehem Pub. Lib., Delmar, NY, 1971–73; Asst. Libn., Mechanicville Pub. Lib., 1970–71. **Educ.:** SUNY, Albany, 1964–68, BA (Hist.), 1970–71, MLS; NY, 1971, Pub. Libn. Cert., VT, 1973, Cert., Sch. Libn. **Orgs.:** ALA. VT Educ. Media Assn. VT LA. New Eng. LA. VT Educ. Assn. Natl. Educ. Assn. New Eng. Educ. Media Assn. Rutland Hlth. Cncl. **Activities:** 10; 31, 32, 39; 75, 83, 92 **Addr.:** 48 Morse Pl., Rutland, VT 05701.

Sherman, Stuart Capen (O. 30, 1916, Amherst, MA) Rare Bk. Libn., Prof., Bibl., Brown Univ., 1968–; Dir., Providence Pub. Lib., 1968–; Libn., 1957–68, Assoc. Libn., 1954–57, Asst. Libn., 1945–54, Branch Supvsr., 1943–45; Branch Libn., Enoch Pratt Free Lib., 1940–43; various visit. lectr. positions. **Educ.:** Brown Univ., 1935–39, AB (Geol.); Columbia Univ., 1939–40, BS (LS). **Orgs.:** Bibl. Socty. of Amer. ALA: Pres. (1947–49). Ms. Socty. RI Hist. Socty. Amer. Antiq. Socty. Corp. of Providence Pub. Lib. Frnds. of John Hay Lib. various orgs. **Honors:** Phi Beta Kappa, Brown Univ., LLD. **Pubns.:** *The Voice of the Whaleman* (1965); Preface, *History of the American Whale Fishery; The First Ninety Years of the Providence Public Library*; Ed., *Books at Brown* (1947–48, 1977–81). **Activities:** 45; 57 **Addr.:** 654 Angell St., Providence, RI 02906.

Sherr, Merrill F. (O. 5, 1941, New York, NY) Head Libn., *NY Post*, 1976–; Asst. Libn., Univ. of Buffalo, 1972–76; Adj. Asst. Prof., Queensboro. Cmnty. Coll., 1969–72; Lectr., City Coll., 1966–69. **Educ.:** Queens Coll., 1959–63, BA (Hist.); Columbia Univ., 1963–64, MA (Hist.); NY Univ., 1964–69, PhD (Hist.); Columbia Univ., 1971–72, MS (LS). **Orgs.:** SLA: Comm. Chap. (Ch., 1980–81). Amer. Hist. Assn. Conf. on Brit. Std. Newsp. Gld. **Pubns.:** "Bishop Edwin Bonner: A Quasi Erasmian," *Hist. Mag. of the Prot. Episcopal Church* (1974); "Religion and The Legal Profession: A Study of the Religious Sensibilities of 16th-century London Lawyers," *Hist. Mar. of the Prot. Episcopal Church* (1976); "Bishop Edwin Bonner: A Biblio-

graphical Essay," *Univ. of Newcastle Hist. Jnl.* (1975). **Activities:** 1; 83 **Addr.:** 322 W. 57th St., Apt 26K, New York, NY 10019.

Sherry, Barbara Ann (Ap. 23, 1941, Oakland, CA) Libn. Lower Columbia Coll., 1977–; Chief Med. Libn., Orthopaedic Hosp., 1967–74. **Educ.:** Whittier Coll., 1958–62, BA (Bio.); Univ. of South. CA, 1964–68, MS (LS); Medline Trng., 1972, 1979; Med. LA, Hlth. Sci. Libn. Cert. **Orgs.:** WA OLUG. OR OLUG. Med. LA. Med. Lib. Grp. of South. CA and AZ: VP, Pres.-Elect (1969–70). **Activities:** 1, 12; 17, 31, 39, 49-Online srch.; 63, 80 **Addr.:** Lower Columbia College, Longview, WA 98632.

Sherwood, Arlyn K. (N. 12, 1948, Elgin, IL) Ref. Coord., Map Catlgr., IL State Lib., 1980–, Map, Legis. Ref. Libn., 1976–80, Map, Gen. Ref. Libn., 1974–76, Gen. Ref. Libn., 1972–74. **Educ.:** Valparaiso Univ., 1966–70, BA (Eng.); Univ. of IL, 1970–71, MLS; Sangamon State Univ., 1976–80, MA (Lit.). **Orgs.:** IL LA: GODORT (1981). SLA: ALA. Cartographic Info. Socty. IL Mapping Adv. Com. **Honors:** Beta Phi Mu, 1971. **Pubns.:** "Maps at the Illinois State Library," *IL Libs.* (F. 1976). **Activities:** 13; 20, 29, 39; 70, 78 **Addr.:** Illinois State Library, Centennial Bldg., Springfield, IL 62756.

Sherwood, Betty R. (Sioux Falls, SD) Ref. Libn., Lib., NASA, Ames Resrch. Ctr., 1974, Supervisory Libn., Life Sci. Lib., 1965–74; Libn., Consult. to IL State Hosp. Libs., Psyt. Inst., Chicago Prof. Lib., IL State, 1960–65; Assoc. Libn., Asst. Prof., Univ. of NE, Coll. of Med. Lib., 1955–60; Asst. Libn., Vanderbilt Univ. Sch. of Med. Lib., 1952–55. **Educ.:** Augustana Coll., 1939–41; Berea Coll., 1941–43, BA (Bio.); Univ. of NC, 1951–52, BSLS; various crs. **Orgs.:** Med. LA. ALA. SLA: Bay Area Un. List of Serials Com. (1973–75). **Honors:** NASA, Ames Resrch. Ctr., Spec. Achvmt. Awd., 1976. **Pubns.:** "Charles F. and Olga C. Moon Collection on Obstetrics and Gynecology," *Med. LA Bltn.* (Jl. 1960); "Chemical Evolution and the Origin of Life–Bibliography Supplement," *Space Life Sci.* (Ap. 1973); cmplr., *Ames Research Center Publications, Jl. 1971–D. 1973* (1975); cmplr., *Ames Research Center Publications, 1974* (1976); "Chemical Evolution and the Origin of Life-Bibliography Supplement," *Origins of Life* (Jl.–O. 1974); various ed. projs. **Activities:** 4; 12; 29, 37, 39; 52, 80, 91 **Addr.:** 1220 Vienna Dr. #494, Sunnyvale, CA 94086.

Shields, Caryl L. (Mr. 30, 1950, Wichita, KS) Ref., ILL Libn., U.S. Geol. Srvy., 1979–; Geologist, U.S. Bur. of Mines, 1978–79, Asst. Libn., 1977–78; Consult., Amer. Geol. Inst., 1978–79. **Educ.:** Univ. of NH, 1968–72, BA (Geol.); Univ. of DE, 1972–75 (Geol.); Univ. of MI, 1974–75, AMLS. **Orgs.:** Geosci. Info. Socty.: Secy. (1978–80). ALA. SLA. Univ. of MI LS Alum. Socty. Geol. Socty. of Amer. **Activities:** 4; 34, 39, 49-Online Srch.; 65, 82, 91 **Addr.:** 510 22nd St., Boulder, CO 80302.

Shields, Dorothy M. (Ag. 7, 1930, Rochester, PA) Asst. Prof., Lib. and Info. Sci., Brigham Young Univ., 1974–; Head Libn., Church Coll. of NZ, 1968–72; Head Libn., Liahona HS, Tonga, 1965–68; Elem. Sch. Libn., Pub. Schs., Lexington, MA, 1964–65; Lib. Consult., Oberlin Coll., 1964; Jr. HS Libn., Highlands Intermediate Sch., 1961–62. **Educ.:** Muskingum Coll., 1948–52, BA (Home Econ. Educ.); OH State Univ., 1953, Elem. Tchg. Cert.; Univ. of HI, 1958–61, Prof. Sec. Cert.; West. Rsv. Univ., 1963–64, MLS Brigham Young Univ., 1972–77, EdD (Sec. Curric., Instr.). **Orgs.:** ALA. Mt. Plains LA. UT LA. Chld. Lit. Assn. of UT. UT Educ. Media Assn. Brigham Young Univ. LA. **Honors:** Beta Phi Mu; Delta Kappa Gamma. **Pubns.:** Jt. auth., "Evaluation in Library Media Centers," *School Library Media Centers: Studies and State of the Art* (1981); "A Look at ALA's Failure to Attract Utah Librarians," *UT Libs.* (Fall 1978). **Activities:** 10, 11; 21, 26, 48 **Addr.:** 5042 HBLL, Brigham Young University, Provo, UT 84601.

Shields, Gerald Robert (N. 24, 1925, Waukeegan, IL) Asst. Dean, Sch. of Info. and Lib. Std., SUNY, Buffalo, 1973–; Ed., *Amer. Libs.*, ALA, 1968–73; Head, Soc. Sci. Dept., Dayton and Montgomery Cnty. Pub. Libs., 1964–68; Ref. Libn., Marquette Univ. Libs., 1961–64. **Educ.:** Univ. of WI, Milwaukee, 1960, BS (Sp.); Univ. of WI, Madison, 1960–61, MALS. **Orgs.:** ALA: Cnclr.-at-Lg. (1974–78, 1980–84); IFRT, Bd. (1975–76); SRRT (Treas., 1975–77); Com. on Prog. Eval. and Support (Ch., 1979–81). NY LA: Awds. Com. (Ch., 1980–81). NLA: Bd. of Dirs. (1977–79). Various other orgs., coms. **Honors:** ALA, H. W. Wilson, Outstan. Per., 1967; Educ. Press Assn., Outstan. Ed. Wrtg., 1972–73. **Pubns.:** Jt. auth., *Freedom of Access in Libraries* (1982); jt. ed., *Budgeting for Accountability in Libraries* (1974); "The National and State Library Periodicals," *Drexel Lib. Qtly.* (Ja. 1979); "David Horace Clift," *Dict. of Amer. Lib. Biog.* (1978); "Intellectual Freedom: Justification for Librarianship," *Lib. Jnl.* (S. 1977); various other pubns. **Activities:** 9, 11; 15, 39; 74, 92 **Addr.:** 546 College Ave., Niagara Falls, NY 14305.

Shields, Joyce F. (Jl. 18, 1930, Leland, IL) Lib. Dir., Niagara Falls Pub. Lib., 1979–; Assoc. Lib. Dir., Nioga Lib. Syst., 1975–79; Ref., Interloan Coord., Suburban Lib. Syst., IL, 1969–73; Head Catlgr., Wright State Univ. Lib., 1966–68. **Educ.:** Lawrence Coll., 1948–52, BA (Grmn.); Columbia Univ., 1952–54, MS (LS). **Orgs.:** ALA. NY LA. Frnds. of the Niagara Falls Pub. Lib. **Honors:** Phi Beta Kappa, 1951. **Pubns.:** *Make It; an Index to Projects and Materials* (1975); *Union List of Serials*

in the Libraries in the Miami Valley (1968). **Activities:** 9 **Addr.:** 546 College Ave., Niagara Falls, NY 14305.

Shields, Sr. M. Jean Ellen, B.V.M. (Ap. 30, 1912, Rock Island, IL) Libn., Don Bosco Tech. Inst., 1972–; Ref. Libn., Burbank Pub. Lib., 1969–72; Ref. Libn., Notre Dame Univ., 1968; Tchr., Libn., Bellarmine-Jefferson HS, 1962–72; various tchg. positions, 1933–62. **Educ.:** Marquette Univ., 1936–45, BA (Hist.); St. Louis Univ., 1949–54, MA (Hist.); Rosary Coll., 1958–62, MA (LS). **Orgs.:** Los Angeles Archdio. Strg. Com. ALA. Cath. LA: SW Unit, *Clasp* Ed. (1964–66); Vice-Ch. (1966–69), Ch. (1969–71); HS Sect. (Ch., 1964–66); Coll. Ch. (1977–80); Natl. Cath. Student Lib. Assts. (West. Ch., 1969–72). CA Media and Lib. Educ. Assn. Burbank Interfaith Cncl.: Secy. (1967–72). **Honors:** Burbank Interfaith Cncl., Brotherhood Awd., 1969. **Activities:** 1; 15, 17, 39; 64, 91 **Addr.:** 121 W. Glenoaks Blvd., Glendale, CA 91202.

Shiflett, Orvin Lee (Ag. 1, 1947, Melbourne, FL) Asst. Prof., LA State Univ., 1979–; Coord., Tech. Srvs., Univ. of WI, LaCrosse, 1976–78, Col. Dev. Libn., 1971–74. **Educ.:** Univ. of FL, 1965–69, BAE (Eng.); Rutgers Univ., 1970–71, MLS; FL State Univ., 1974–79, PhD (LS). **Orgs.:** ALA. LA LA. AALS. **Honors:** Beta Phi Mu. **Pubns.:** *The Origins of American Academic Librarianship* (1981). **Activities:** 1, 11; 15, 17, 29; 57, 78, 92 **Addr.:** School of Library and Information Science, Louisiana State University, Baton Rouge, LA 70803.

Shih, Philip C. (Jl. 6, 1943, Hung-Chong, Hunan, China) Dir., Logansport-Cass Cnty. Pub. Lib., 1973–; Ref. Libn., Whichita State Univ., 1969–73. **Educ.:** Tunghai Univ., 1961–65, BA (Econ.); FL State Univ., 1967–68, MS (LS). **Orgs.:** ALA. IN LA. Rotary Club. **Activities:** 9; 17, 24; 59, 63, 76 **Addr.:** 2020 Westgate Dr., Logansport, IN 46947.

Shill, Harold B. (O. 9, 1944, Philadelphia, PA) Head Libn., Evansdale Lib., Asst. Prof. of Lib. Sci., WV Univ., 1980–, Chief Circ. Libn., Asst. Prof., 1976–80, Ref. Libn., 1975–76; Lib. Consult., Costabile Assocs., 1975. **Educ.:** Rutgers Univ., 1962–66, AB (Hist.); Univ. of NC, 1966–71, PhD (Pol. Sci.); Univ. of MD, 1974–75, MLS. **Orgs.:** WV LA: Coll. and Univ. Sect. (Ch., 1980–81). ALA. WV Pol. Sci. Assn. Amer. Pol. Sci. Assn. **Honors:** Beta Phi Mu, 1975; Phi Kappa Phi, 1975. **Pubns.:** *Insurgency* (1970); "The Library Re-Visited," *Tchg. Pol. Sci.* (Ap. 1979); "Open Stacks and Library Performance," *Coll. & Resrch. Libs.* (My. 1980); Series ed., *Gale Information Guide Series in American Government and History* (1977–81). **Activities:** 1; 15, 17, 31; 91, 92 **Addr.:** Evansdale Library, West Virginia University, Morgantown, WV 26506.

Shilstone, Marian Ruth (Mr. 8, 1943, Morristown, NJ) Col. Dev. Libn., CT Coll. Lib., 1981–; Serials Libn., 1971–81, Asst. Serials Libn., 1969–71. **Educ.:** Rutgers Univ., 1961–65, BA (Russ. Std.), 1968–69, MLS; CT Coll., 1975–80, MA (Russ. Std.). **Orgs.:** CT LA: Prog. Com., Co-ch. (1980–81), Asst. Co-ch. (1979–80). ALA: ACRL, Natl. Chap., New Eng. Chap. AAUP. **Honors:** Beta Phi Mu, 1969. **Pubns.:** "Transition Abroad, 1927–1938," *CT Coll. Lib. Bltn.* (Win. 1981); "Faculty and the Academic Library," *CT Libs.* (Spr. 1979); Jt. auth., "Current Bibliographies in Russian-Soviet Area Studies, 1976–1977," *Russ. Review* (Jl. 1978). **Activities:** 1; 15, 39, 44; 54, 55, 83 **Addr.:** Connecticut College Library, New London, CT 06320.

Shinn, Allen Edward (Ap. 30, 1942, Elmira, NY) Asst. Preps. Libn., VA Polytech. Inst. and State Univ., 1979–; Hum. Cat. Supvsr., 1974–79; Asst. Chief Catlgr., Bro-Dart Corp., 1970–74. **Educ.:** Dickinson Coll., 1960–64, AB (Span.); Middlebury Coll., 1964–67, MA (Span.); Columbia Univ., 1969–70, MSLS. **Orgs.:** ALA. VA LA. Potomac Tech. Prcs. Libns. **Honors:** Beta Phi Mu, 1970. **Activities:** 1; 17, 20 **Addr.:** Preparations Dept., Carol M. Newman Library, Virginia Polytechnic Institute and State University, Blacksburg, VA 24061.

Shiotani, Nancy W. (Ap. 5, 1947, Akron, OH) Head, Tech. Srvs., Lane Med. Lib., Stanford Univ., 1981–, Head, Cat. Dept., 1977–80, Ref., Cat. Libn., 1973–76; Ref. Libn., OH State Univ., 1971–72. **Educ.:** Univ. of CA, Berkeley, 1965–69, AB (Hist.), 1970–71, MLS; Med. LA, 1975, Cert. **Orgs.:** Med. LA. SLA. North. CA Med. Lib. Grp. **Honors:** Beta Phi Mu, 1971. **Pubns.:** "Obsolescence in Biomedical Journals: Not an Artifact of Literature Growth," *Lib. Resrch.* (1980–81). **Activities:** 1, 12; 15, 17, 20; 80 **Addr.:** Lane Medical Library, Stanford University Medical Center, Stanford, CA 94035.

Shipman, George W. (Ap. 9, 1939, Monroe, MI) Univ. Libn., Univ. of OR, 1980–; Assoc. Dir. of Libs., Univ. of TN/ Knoxville, 1971–80; Admin. Ofcr., Card Div., Lib. of Congs., 1969–71, Asst. Head, Amer.-Brit. Exch. Sect., 1968–69, Catlgr., Span./Portuguese, Shared Cat., 1968, Spec. Rcrt., 1967–68; Instr., Hist., InterAmer. Univ. of PR, 1965–66. **Educ.:** Albion Coll., 1963, BA (Hist.); West. MI Univ., 1965, MA (Hist.); Univ. of MI, 1967, MALS. **Orgs.:** ALA. Pac. NW LA. OR LA. AAUP. **Activities:** 1, 4; 17 **Addr.:** University of Oregon, Eugene, OR 97403.

Shires, Leslyn Mary (Ap. 11, 1939, Hartford, WI) Asst. Supt. Lib. Srvs., State of WI, 1981–; Dir., Wauwatosa Pub. Lib.,

1974–81; Coord., Adult Srvs., Milwaukee Pub. Lib., 1972–74, Branch Head, 1964–72, Proj. Dir., "Over 60" Srv., 1967–69, Ref. Libn., 1963–67; Ref. Libn., Pub. Admin. Srv., 1962–63. **Educ.:** Univ. of WI, 1957–61, BA (Hist.); Columbia Univ., 1961–62, MSLS. **Orgs.:** WI LA: Ref. and Adult Srvs. (Ch., 1974); Pres. (1979). ALA: RASD, Com. on Aging (1967–74); Hist. Sect., Exec. Bd. (1979–81). Milwaukee Cncl. for Adult Lrng. Delta Kappa Gamma: Secy. (1972–74). Zonta Club of Milwaukee. Univ. of WI-Milwaukee Lib. Sch. Adv. Com. **Honors:** WI LA, Spec. Srvs. Awd., 1981. **Pubns.:** "Aging and the Aged," *Lib. Occurrent* (F. 1972); "Educational Library Service to the Aging," *AHIL Qtly.* (Spr.–Sum. 1972); Cmplr., "Autumnal Face" booklist (1971). **Activities:** 9; 16, 17; 50 **Addr.:** 5430 Greening Ln., Madison, WI 53705.

Shirk, Frank Charles (Ap. 2, 1917, Englewood, NJ) Asst. Acq. Libn., VA Polytech. Inst. and State Univ., 1971–; Consult., State Cncl. of Higher Educ. for VA, 1970–71; Lib. Dir., VA Polytech. Inst. and State Univ., 1961–70, Assoc. Dir., 1955–61. **Educ.:** Rutgers Univ., 1935–39, BA (Eng.); Drexel Univ., 1939–40, BSLS. **Orgs.:** SLA: VA Chap. (Pres., 1968–69). VA LA: Pres. (1965). Montgomery-Radford Lib. Bd.: Ch. (1954–61). AAUP: VA Tech. Chap. (Pres., 1962–63). Blacksburg Dist. Cmnty. Fed.: Pres. (1951–52). **Pubns.:** "DDT to Combat Silverfish," *Lib. Jnl.* (My. 1, 1952); "Virginia Tech's New $2,000,000 Library," *Mineral Indus. Jnl.* (S. 1955); reviews. **Activities:** 1, 9; 15, 17, 46; 56, 64, 70 **Addr.:** 111 Country Club Dr., S.E., Blacksburg, VA 24060.

Shirk, Gary M. (Ap. 14, 1946, Downey, CA) Head of Bk. Acq., Univ. of MN Libs., 1977–, Coord. of Budget and Mgt. Plng., 1976–77; Lib. Mgt. Anal., Hennepin Cnty. Lib. Syst., 1973–75. **Educ.:** Univ. of CA, Riverside, 1964–68, BA (Comp. Lit.); Univ. of CA, Berkeley, 1970–72, MLS. **Orgs.:** ALA: Com. on Resrch. (1980–82); PLA, Conf. Prog. Coord. Com. (Ch., 1980–81, 1980–82); LAMA/Lib. Org. and Mgt. Sect., Budgeting, Acct. and Costs Com. (1980–82); H. W. Wilson Co. Lib. Per. Awd. Com. (1979). MN LA: Treas. (1977–79); Lib. Mgt. RT (Ch., 1975–77); Budget and Fin. Com. (Ch., 1977–79). Metronet Adv. Com. **Honors:** Phi Beta Kappa, 1968. **Pubns.:** "Applying Standards for Public Library Evaluation," *Cath. Lib. World* (F. 1977); "Academic Library Materials: Budgeting and Allocation" ERIC (1976); "Metropolitan Public Library Funding and Intergovernmental Fiscal Relations" ERIC (1979). **Addr.:** Central Technical Services, University of Minnesota, 170 Wilson Library, 309-19th Ave. S., Minneapolis, MN 55455.

Shirk, Virginia B. (Mr. 31, 1950, Owatonna, MN) Corporate Libn., MN Gas Co., 1972–. **Educ.:** Coll. of St. Catherine, 1968–72, BA (LS, Math.). **Orgs.:** SLA: Pub. Util. Div. (Treas., 1977–79); MN Chap. (Dir., 1980–81), Mem. Ch. (1977–80), Secy. (1976–77), Bltn. Ed. (1975–76). MN LA: Spec. Libs. RT (Ch., 1974–75); Nom. Com. (1977–78). Amer. Gas Assn.: Lib. Srvs. Com. (1973–). **Pubns.:** "Gas Libraries: An Industry-Wide Network," *Sci. and Tech. Libs.* (Win. 1980). **Activities:** 12; 15, 17, 39; 59, 86 **Addr.:** Minnesota Gas Co. Library, 733 Marquette Ave., Minneapolis, MN 55402.

Shirley, Sherrilynne (D. 18, 1945, Mishawaka, IN) Assoc. Dir., Norris Med. Lib., Univ. of South. CA, 1974–, Pub. Srvs. Libn., 1977–78, Head, Ref. Sect., 1974–77; Info. Anal., Brain Info. Srv., Biomed. Lib., Univ. of CA, Los Angeles, 1972–74. **Educ.:** IN Univ., 1963–67, BA (Bio.), 1968–69, MLS; Univ. of South. CA, PhD in Prog. (Lib. and Info. Mgt.). **Orgs.:** Biomed. Comm. Netwk.: Bd. of Dirs. (1978–). CA Lib. Athrty. for Systs. and Srvs.: Adv. Com. (1978–). Med. Lib. Grp. of South. CA and AZ: Secy. (1976–77). **Pubns.:** "The Application of Document Data Management Techniques to Quality Filtering of Scientific Literature," *ASIS Procs.* (1981); "A Survey of Computer Search Service Costs in the Academic Health Sciences Library," *Bltn. Med. LA* (1978); "An Annotated Bibliography of Education for Medical LIbrarianship, 1940–1968," *Bltn. Med. LA* (1969). **Activities:** 1; 17, 35, 41; 58, 80, 87 **Addr.:** Norris Medical Library, University of Southern California Health Sciences Campus, 2025 Zonal Ave., Los Angeles, CA 90033.

Shisler, Shirley M. (Mr. 15, 1931, McGregor, IA) Head, Ref. Dept., Pub. Lib. of Des Moines, 1964–, First Asst., Ref. Dept, 1959–64; Libn., Hist. and Travel Dept., Enoch Pratt Free Lib., 1957–59; Sch. Libn., Elbow Lake Pub. Sch., 1954–55; Tchr. Libn., Sleepy Eye Pub. Sch., 1952–54. **Educ.:** Hamline Univ., 1948–52, BA (Soc. Std. Educ.); Columbia Univ., 1956–57, MS (LS). **Orgs.:** ALA: Cnclr. (1970–74); Ref. and Subscrpn. Bks. Review Com. (1974–81); Ref. Srv. Div., Bd. (1970–72). IA LA: Johnson Brigham Plaque Com. (Ch., 1968–71); Adult Srvs. Div. (Secy., 1971–72). Des Moines Metro. Area LA. Intl. Altrusa AAUW. Leag. of Women Voters. Women's Pol. Caucus. **Activities:** 9; 39 **Addr.:** 3523 University, Apt. 10-A, Des Moines, IA 50311.

Shiverdecker, Darlene J. (Ag. 23, 1948, Celina, OH) Libn., Media Spec., Aiken HS, 1975–; Libn., Media Spec., Crest Hills Jr. High, 1971–75; Libn., Media Spec., Merry Jr. High, 1969–71. **Educ.:** Bowling Green State Univ., 1967–69, BS (LS, Hist., Pol. Sci.); Miami Univ., 1977–78, MS (Educ. Media), 1978, Supvsn. Cert. **Orgs.:** OH Educ. Lib./Media Assn.: HS Div. (Ch., 1980–82); HS Com. (1978–80); Conv. Lcl. Arrange. Com. (1978); PR Com. (1977). OH Assn. of Sch. Libns.: Bd. of Dirs. (1974–76); Affiliations Com. (1975–76). ALA: AASL; YASD; JMRT. Cincinnati Fed. of Tchrs. Amer. Fed. of Tchrs.: OH Fed. of Tchrs. **Pubns.:** "Favorite Reference Books for the Senior High School Library," *OH Media Spectrum* (Fall 1979); "Reference Books for American History Classes," *OH Media Spectrum* (Fall 1980). **Activities:** 10; 20, 31, 48 **Addr.:** 72 Twilight Dr., Fairfield, OH 45014.

Shlapak, (Mrs.) Irene (F. 10, 1946, Goslar, Germany) Mgr., Lib. Srvs., ON Mnstry. of Cmnty. and Soc. Srvs., 1974–; Catlgr., ON Mnstry. of Nat. Resrcs., 1971–74. **Educ.:** Univ. of Waterloo, 1966–69, BA (Soclgy.); Univ. of Toronto, 1969–70, BLS. **Orgs.:** SLA. Can. LA. ON Gvt. Libns. Cncl.: Ch. (1977–78); Vice-Ch. (1976–77). **Activities:** 4; 15, 17, 24; 72, 92 **Addr.:** Library Services, Ontario Ministry of Community and Social Services, 880 Bay St., Rm. 663, Toronto, ON M7A 1E9 Canada.

Shockley, Ann Allen (Louisville, KY) Assoc. Libn. for Spec. Cols., Univ. Archvst., Fisk Univ., 1980–, Assoc. Libn. for Pub. Srvs., Assoc. Prof., LS, 1967–80; Asst. Libn., DE State Coll., 1959–60; Asst. Libn. and Cur., Negro Col., Univ. of MD, East. Shore, 1966–69. **Educ.:** Fisk Univ., 1944–48, BA (Hist., Eng.); Case West. Rsv. Univ., 1958–59; Univ. of MD, 1974, Lib. Admin. Dev. Inst. Cert. Oral Hist. Assn.; SAA: Com. on Collecting Personal Papers Mss. (1971–75); Natl. Prog. Com. (1977–78). ALA: Black Caucus. Assn. for the Std. of Afro-Amer. Life and Hist. TN Lit. Arts Assn. Mod. Lang. Assn. **Honors:** ALA, Black Caucus, Spec. Awd., 1975. **Pubns.:** Jt. ed., *Handbook of Black Librarianship* (1977); jt. auth., *Living Black American Authors* (1973); various other bks., articles, filmstp. **Activities:** 1, 2; 24, 37, 41; 66 **Addr.:** Fisk University Library, Nashville, TN 37203.

Shockley, Cynthia W. (Mr. 23, 1950, Fresno, CA) Consult., Indp., 1979–; Sr. Assoc., Comp. Performance Assn., 1977–79; Mgr., Info. Systs. Div., Info. Plng. Assn., 1976–77; Sr. Proj. Anal., Appld. Mgt. Sci., 1974–76; Info. Anal., Gen. Electric Corp., 1972–74; Musm. Tech., Smithsonian Inst., 1968–72. **Educ.:** George Washington Univ., 1969–72, BA (Hist.); Univ. of MD, 1978–81, MLS. **Orgs.:** ASIS. **Pubns.:** various tech. rpts. **Activities:** 4, 12; 24, 46, 49-Online Srvs.; 56, 78, 92 **Addr.:** 7535 Spring Lake Dr., Bethesda, MD 20817.

Shoemaker, Betty G. (Ap. 23, 1925, Zeeland, MI) Biog., Lang. Lit., Dept. Head, Grand Rapids Pub. Lib., 1973–, First Floor Supvsr., Dept. Head, 1967–75, Readers Adv., 1957–67; Tchr., SW MN Christ. HS, 1954–57; Tchr., Lynden Christ. HS, 1947–54. **Educ.:** Calvin Coll., 1943–47, AB (Educ.); Univ. of MI, 1957–59, MALS; Permanent Tchg. Cert.; MI, Permanent Prof. Lib. Cert.; Mid. Mgt. Cert. **Orgs.:** CS LA. MI LA. Grand Rapids Libns. Club: Various coms. Zeeland Lib. Bd.: Secy.; Pres. Zeeland I Christ. Ref. Church: Libn. **Honors:** Beta Phi Mu, 1959. **Activities:** 9, 12; 16, 34, 47; 55, 72, 90 **Addr.:** 257 S. Wall St., Zeeland, MI 49464.

Shoffit, Judith Kay Miller (Ap. 9, 1948, Clarinda, IA) Coord. for Prcs., TX Woman's Univ., 1975–, Head Catlgr., 1974–75, Asst. Catlgr., 1971–74, Dallas Ctr. Nursing Sch. Libn., 1970. **Educ.:** IA West. Cmnty. Coll., 1966–68, AA; TX Woman's Univ., 1968–70, BA (Eng.), 1970–71, MLS. **Orgs.:** ALA: RTSD. Assn. for Higher Educ.: Ch. (1977–79); Cat. Sect. Dallas Acad. of Karate (Black Belt). **Pubns.:** Contrib., *On Equal Terms* (1977). **Activities:** 1; 17, 20, 46; 56, 75 **Addr.:** 120 Forest, Denton, TX 76201.

Shoffner, Ralph M. (D. 18, 1932, Punxysutawney, PA) Pres. & Consult., Ringgold Mgt. Syst., Inc., 1981–, VP, 1974–80; Dir. of Mktg., Dir. of Resrch. & Dev., Richard Abel & Co., 1972–74; Proj. Mgr. & Coord., Inst. of Lib. Resrch., Univ. of CA, Berkeley, 1965–72; Sr. Syst. Anal., Informatics, Inc., 1964–65; Project Engin., 1955–64. **Educ.:** MA Inst. of Tech., 1955, SB (Bus. & Engin. Admin.); Carnegie Inst. of Tech., 1960, MS (Indus. Admin.); Univ. of CA, Berkeley, 1972, DLS. **Orgs.:** ALA: Info. Sci. & Autom. Div., VP (1971–72); Pres. (1972–73). ASIS. Assn. for Comp. Mach. WA Athletic Club. Oper. Resrch. Socty. of Amer. **Pubns.:** Jt. auth., *British Columbia Library Network* (1980); jt. auth., *The Dobis and Washington Library Network Systems* (1980); "Comparative Cost Analysis," *Proceedings, American Society for Information Science,* (1975); "Outlook for the Future of Library Automation" in *Library Automation–A State of the Art Review,* (1975); "Concepts of Operations Research in Libraries," *Proc. LARC Inst. on Oper. Resrch.* (1973); various other articles. **Activities:** 6; 17, 24; 56, 59, 75 **Addr.:** Ringgold Management Systems, Inc., Box 368, Beaverton, OR 97075.

Shold, Rosemary Kay (Ag. 31, 1941, Webster City, IA) Supvsr., WLN Bibl. Maintenance, WA State Lib., 1979–, Serials, Acq. Libn., 1970–79, Catlgr. 1968–70. **Educ.:** Ellsworth Jr. Coll., 1960–62, AA (Liberal Arts); Univ. of IA, 1962–64, BA (Fr.); Rosary Coll., 1966–68, MALS. **Orgs.:** Pac. NW LA: Tech. Srvs. Div., Nom. Com. (1980–81). ALA: RTSD/Serials Sect., Exec. Com. (1974–75). WA LA. **Activities:** 13; 20, 34, 44 **Addr.:** WLN Bibliographic Maintenance, Washington State Library, Olympia, WA 98504.

Sholtz, Katherine J. (Jl. 14, 1931, Waukegan, IL) Assoc. Dir., Mayo Clinic Med. Lib., 1972–, Comp. Applications Libn., 1967–72. **Educ.:** Univ. of IL, 1949–52, BS (Chem.), 1952–53, MS (Chem.); SUNY, Albany, 1964–67, MLS; 1978, Cert. Med. Libn. **Orgs.:** Med. LA. SLA. MN Hlth. Sci. LA. **Pubns.:** Jt. auth., "The Mayo Clinic Author Catalog: A Living Repository of Medical Knowldge," *Bltn. Med. LA* (Ap. 1973); jt. auth., "Library Automation at the Mayo Clinic Library, Rochester, Minnesota," *LARC Series on Automated Activities in Health Science Libraries* (1975); jt. auth., "The Importance of Journal Publication in Information Transfer for the Health Sciences," *Hosp. Libs.* (N. 15, 1976); jt. auth., "The Impact of a Document Delivery Service on a Medical Library and its Patrons," *Med. Mktg. and Media* (D. 1975); jt. auth., "The Controlled Circulation Journal in Medicine: Rx or Rogue?" *Serials Libn.* (Fall 1979); various articles. **Activities:** 1, 12; 15, 17, 36; 61, 80, 91 **Addr.:** 5801 Sumac Ln. N.E., Rochester, MN 55901.

Shong, Joy C. (D. 29, 1948, Minneapolis, MN) Coord. of Lrng. Ctr., St. Francis Hosp., 1978–; Libn., Oconomowoc Meml. Hosp., 1974–78. **Educ.:** Univ. of WI, Eau Claire, 1967–71, BA (Geo., LS); Univ. of WI, Stout, Menomonie, 1971–73, MS (AV Comm.). **Orgs.:** WI Hlth. Sci. Libns. Assn.: Pres. (1979–81). SLA: Serials List Com. SE WI Hlth. Sci. LA: Coord. (1979–81). Intl. TV Assn.: Pres. (1977–80). **Honors:** Phi Kappa Phi, 1970. **Activities:** 12; 15, 17, 32; 80 **Addr.:** St. Francis Hospital, 3237 S. 16th St., Milwaukee, WI 53215.

Shoniker, Fintan Raymond (N. 13, 1914, Rochester, NY) Dir. of Libs., St. Vincent Coll. and Archabbey, 1972–; various admin. positions in lib., fac., 1936–72. **Educ.:** St. Vincent Coll., 1934–38, BA (Phil.); Univ. of Notre Dame, 1939–40 (LS); St. Vincent Semy., 1938–42 (Theo.); St. Vincent Coll., 1940, MA (Phil.); Rosary Coll., 1941–43, BSLS; Columbia Univ., 1944–47 (LS). **Orgs.:** ALA: Bldgs. and Equip. Sect., Nom. Com. (1960–61); ACRL, Tri-State Chap. (Pres., 1962–63); Exec. Bd. (1963–64); Nom. Com. Ch., (1958–59). Cath. LA: Exec. Cncl. (1959–61); various ofcs. PA LA: Coll. and Ref. Sect., Nom. Com. (Ch., 1959–60); various ofcs. SLA: Pittsburgh Chap., Univ. and Coll. Grp. (Ch., 1945–46). St. Vincent Archabbey Benedictine Socty.: Human Resrcs. Cncl. (Exec. Secy., 1980–83); various ofcs. Roman Cath. Church: Ordained Priest (1942). Mid. States Assn.: Eval. Teams (1945–). Amer. Benedictine Acad.: LS Sect. (Ch., 1948–50). various other orgs. **Honors:** Amer. Benedictine Acad. LS Sect., Cit., 1970; Sen. of PA, Cit., 1976, Gannon Univ., LLD (Hon.), 1970. **Pubns.:** Jt. cmplr., *Seton Hill College-Saint Vincent College. Cooperative Program Handbook of Guidelines* (1980); (1980); *The Saint Vincent College Library 1965–1966 to 1974–1975* (1976); "St. Vincent Archabbey," *Dizionario degli Istituti de Perfezione* (1974–); "St. Vincent College," *New Cath. Encyc.* (1967); "St. Vincent College Library," *Guidelines for Library Planners* (1959); various articles. **Activities:** 1, 17 **Addr.:** St. Vincent College Library, Latrobe, PA 15650.

Shook, Suzanne (S. 29, 1941, Utica, NY) Rare Bk. Libn., VA State Lib., 1979–, Coord., VA Gvr. Conf. on Lib. and Info. Srvs., 1978–79; Coop. Prog. Libn., 1974–78; Libn., Chesterfield Cnty. Pub. Lib., 1970–74. **Educ.:** Randolph-Macon Woman's Coll., 1960–64, AB (Hist.); Syracuse Univ., 1968–70, MSLS. **Orgs.:** VA LA: Treas. (1973–75); JMRT (Ch., 1972–73). ALA: ASCLA, Interlib. Coop. Com. (1975); JMRT Exec. Bd. (1974–75). SE LA. **Honors:** Beta Phi Mu, 1970. **Pubns.:** *ASLA Directory of Interlibrary Cooperative Projects* (1976); *Middle Peninsula–Northern Neck Library Survey* (1975); various articles, *VA Libn.* **Addr.:** Virginia State Library, 11th and Capitol St., Richmond, VA 23219.

Short, John T. (N. 5, 1926, Detroit, MI) Reg. Mgr., Coronet, 1967–. **Educ.:** George Williams Coll., 1947–51, BS (Admin.). **Orgs.:** ALA: ALTA (Pres., 1975–76). Assn. of CT Lib. Bds.: Pres. (1972–76). CT State Lib. Adv. Com.: Ch. (1973–76). WHCOLIS: Adv. Com. Grosse Pointe (MI) Bd. of Educ.: VP and Treas. (1966–69). **Pubns.:** "Library Trustee Guidelines," *PLA Bltn.* (Mr. 1975); "ALTA Afloat in the Sargasso Sea," *Lib. Jnl.*. **Activities:** 9, 10; 24, 37, 47; 78, 89 **Addr.:** Box E, Avon, CT 06001.

Short, Sylvia I. (My. 6, 1938, Georgetown, DE) State Libn., DE Div. of Libs., 1977–; DE Legis. Cncl. Lib., 1974–77; DE Div. of Libs., 1972–73; Indian River Sch., Lib. Dist., 1971–72. **Educ.:** Duke Univ., 1955–59, AB (Pol. Sci.); Drexel Univ., 1966–67, MSLA (Lib.). **Orgs.:** DE LA. ALA. DE Sch. Lib. Media Assn. Leag. of Women Voters. **Activities:** 13; 17, 24, 36 **Addr.:** Delaware Division of Libraries, P.O. Box 639, 43 S. du Pont Hwy., Dover, DE 19901–0639.

Short, Virginia (S. 7, 1929, Rome, Italy) Syst. Dir., Mt.-Valley Lib. Syst., 1976–; Ref. Coord., Mt.-Valley Info. Ctr., 1968–75; Libn., US Air Force, Italy, 1963–67; Ref. Libn., Univ. of CA, Davis, 1962; Libn., US Air Force, Italy, 1960–61; Libn., US Air Force, Eng., 1958–60; Ref. Libn., Sacramento State Coll., 1952–58. **Educ.:** Univ. of CA, Berkeley, 1946–50, BA (Hum.); Sacramento State Coll., 1950–51, Tchg. Cred.; Case West. Rsv. Univ., 1951–52, MS (LS). **Orgs.:** ALA. SLA. CA LA: Cnclr. (1980–82). **Activities:** 9, 13; 17, 34, 39; 75 **Addr.:** Mountain-Valley Library System, 828 I St., Sacramento, CA 95814.

PROFESSIONAL ACTIVITIES: Institutions: 1. Acad. lib.; 2. Arch.; 3. Assn.; 4. Fed./Gvt. lib.; 5. Inst. lib.; 6. Mfr./Suppl.; 7. Milit. lib.; 8. Musm.; 9. Pub. lib.; 10. Sch. lib.; 11. Sch. of lib. sci.; 12. Spec. lib.; 13. State lib.; 14. (other). **Functions/Activities:** 15. Acq./Col. dev.; 16. Adult srvs.; 17. Admin.; 18. Apprais.; 19. Archit./Bldgs.; 20. Cat./Class.; 21. Chld. srvs.; 22. Circ.; 23. Cons./Pres.; 24. Consult.; 25. Cont. ed.; 26. Educ. lib. sci.; 27. Ext. srvs.; 28. Fund/Grants; 29. Gvt. pubs.; 30. Indx./Abs.; 31. Instr. lib. use; 32. Media srvs.; 33. Micro.; 34. Netwks./Coop.; 35. Persnl.; 36. PR; 37. Publshg.; 38. Recs. mgt.; 39. Ref. srvs.; 40. Repro.; 41. Resrch.; 42. Review.; 43. Secur.; 44. Serials; 45. Spec. col.; 46. Tech. srvs.; 47. Trustees/Bds.; 48. YA srvs.; 49. (other).

Shorthouse, Thomas James (Mr. 23, 1933, Nelson, BC) Law Libn., Univ. of BC, 1966–, Ref. libn., Curric. Lab., 1965–66; Tchr., Surrey, BC and Vancouver Schs., 1955–64. **Educ.:** Univ. of BC, 1951–54, BA (Hist., Eng.), 1964–65, BLS; BC, 1954–55, Tchrs. Cert. **Orgs.:** Can. ALL: Pres. (1977–79). BC LA: Treas. (1967–68). **Activities:** 1; 17; 77 **Addr.:** Law Library, University of British Columbia, 1822 E. Mall, Campus, Vancouver, BC V6T 1W5 Canada.

Shortreed, Vivian H. (Je. 10, 1933, Wabash Cnty., IN) Dir., Lib. Srvs., Quinebaug Valley Cmnty. Coll., 1978–, Asst. Dir., 1971–78; Instr., Univ. of WI, Waukesha, 1967–68; Lectr., Univ. of WI, Milwaukee, 1965–67; Coord., Cmnty. Discuss. Progs., Univ. of Chicago, 1961–62; Instr., North. IL Univ., 1960–61; Instr., Elmhurst Coll., 1959–60. **Educ.:** Manchester Coll., 1950–54, BA (Lang. Arts); Northwest. Univ., 1958–59, MA (Comm. Std.); Univ. of RI, 1969–72, MLS. **Orgs.:** ALA. CT LA: 2nd VP (1979–80); Legis. Com. (Co-ch., 1979–80); Fed. Rel. Coord. (1979–). Coop. Lib. Srv. Units Review Bd.: Exec. Com. (Ch., 1978–80). CT Autom. Coord. Com. (1980–). ALA: ACRL, New Eng. Chap., Nom. Com. (1980). Sp. Comm. Assn. **Honors:** Beta Phi Mu. **Pubns.:** Entries for Elizabeth Oakes Smith and Jane Grey Swisshelm, *American Women Writers* (forthcoming). **Activities:** 1; 17 **Addr.:** Quinebaug Valley Community College Library, Danielson, CT 06239.

Shosid, Norma J. (N. 9, 1937, Dallas, TX) Asst. Prof., Univ. of CA, Berkeley, 1976–; Instr., Vanderbilt Univ.; Consult., Woodview Psyt. Hosp. Lib., 1969–; Consult., Whittaker Corp. Mktg. Resrch. Div., 1969; Consult., Loyola Univ., Los Angeles, Coll. of Bus. Admin., 1968–; Head, Crocker Lib. of Bus. Admin., Univ. of South. CA, 1964–68; Libn., Stan. Oil, NJ, 1963–64. **Educ.:** Barnard Coll., 1956–58, AB (Hist.); Columbia Univ., 1962–64, MS (LS); Univ. of South. CA, 1964–68, MPA (Pub. Admin.); Univ. of CA, Los Angeles, PhD (Soclgy.). **Orgs.:** ALA. SLA. Amer. Soclgy. Assn. **Activities:** 1, 9; 16, 17, 24 **Addr.:** University of California School of Library and Information Studies, Berkeley, CA 94720.

Shouse, Margaret Elizabeth (Betty) (F. 27, 1926, Kansas City, MO) Supvsr. of Pub. Srvs., Kansas City Pub. Lib., 1978–, Coord. of Ctrl. Ref., 1974–78, Coord. of Adult Srvs., 1970–74, Supvsr., Reader Srvs., 1967–70. **Educ.:** William Jewell Coll., 1944–48, BA (Lit.); Univ. of Denver, 1949–50, MA (LS). **Orgs.:** ALA: Ref. and Subscrpn. Bks. Reviews Com. (1970–72). MO LA: Pub. Lib. Div., Pres.-Elect; Adult Educ. Com. (1969). NM LA: Secy. (1960). SLA: Heart of America Chap., Treas. (1977–81). **Activities:** 9; 16, 17, 35; 50, 55, 59 **Addr.:** 4618 Warwick, Kansas City, MO 64112.

Shouse, Robert E. (Ap. 30, 1939, Winston-Salem, NC) Head Ref. Libn., Towson State Univ., 1976–, Asst. Ref. Libn., 1966–75; Asst. Libn., Harford Cmnty. Coll., 1965–66; Libn., Garinger HS, 1963–65. **Educ.:** Wake Forest Univ., 1957–61, BA (Educ.); Univ. of NC, 1966, MS in LS. **Orgs.:** ALA. **Activities:** 1, 10; 31, 39 **Addr.:** Cook Library, Towson State University, Baltimore, MD 21204.

Shove, Raymond H. (S. 20, 1906, Howard, SD) Prof. Emeritus, Univ. of MN Lib. Sch., 1975–, Prof., 1948–75; Head, Acq. Dept., Univ. of MN Lib., 1937–48; Asst. Acq. Dept., Univ. of IL, 1930–37. **Educ.:** Morningside Coll., BA (Lang., Lit.); Univ. of IL, MA (LS). **Pubns.:** *Cheap Book Production in the United States, 1870–1891* (1937); jt. auth., *The Use of Books and Libraries* 10th and earlier eds. (1963); "The University of Minnesota Library School," *Encyc. of Lib. and Info. Sci.*;"Frank K. Walter," *Encyc. of Lib. and Info. Sci.* **Activities:** 1; 15, 26, 31; 57 **Addr.:** University of Minnesota Library School, Minneapolis, MN 55414.

Shreve, Doris L. (D. 18, 1900, West Point, NE) Retired; Dir., Pub. Srv. Careers Prog., St. Louis Pub. Lib., 1970–73; Acq. Libn., MO State Lib., 1954–70; Dir., Rolla Free Pub. Lib., 1950–54. **Educ.:** Univ. of WI, 1920–24, BA (Fr.); Univ. of Chicago, 1926; Univ. of Paris, 1934; Carnegie Tech., 1947–48, BS (LS). **Orgs.:** MO LA: Pub. Lib. Div., Past Ch. ALA: ASCLA; ALSC. Women's Intl. Leag. for Peace and Frdm. Orchesis. St. Louis Coal. of the Env. Peace Resrch. various orgs. **Honors:** Phi Beta Kappa, 1924. **Pubns.:** Various articles. **Activities:** 9, 13; 15, 25 **Addr.:** Chesterfield, MO 63017.

Shreve, Irene M. Strieby (S. 6, 1894, Converse, IN) Indp. Lib. Consult., 1959–; Tchr., LS, Columbia Univ., 1957; Libn., Eli Lilly and Co., 1934–59; Inst. for Resrch. in Soc. Sci., Univ. of NC, 1933-34; Libn., PR Dir., Riverside Milit. Acad., 1929–32. **Educ.:** Brenau Coll., 1912–16, AB (Eng., Sci.); Univ. of WI, 1930, Cert. (LS); Univ. of NC, 1932–33, BS (LS). **Orgs.:** SLA: Pres. (1947–48). Cncl. of Natl. LAs. Med. LA: Fellow (1975–). ALA: Various coms., ofcs. Amer. Pharm. Assn.: Various coms. Indianapolis Musm. of Art: Life Trustee (1973–). IN Hist. Assn.: Com. on Geneal. (1941–47); various other coms., ofcs. various lcl. hist. and geneal. assns. **Honors:** SLA, Prof. Awd., 1956; Hall of Fame, 1959; Med. LA, Hon. Mem., 1959; Med. LA, Fellow, 1978; Purdue Univ., Pres. Cncl., Disting. Fellow, 1980–; other hons. **Pubns.:** "All The King's Horses," *Spec. Libs.* (N. 1959); "Looking Around: The Company Library," *Harvard Bus. Review* (My.–Je. 1959); "Public Relations Activities of Special Libraries," *Lib. Trends* (O. 1958); "The Pharmaceutical Library of the Future," *Bltn. Med. LA* (O. 1953); jt. auth., *Scientific and Technical Libraries* (1972); various other articles in hobby mags. and prof. lib. mgt., pharm. jnls. **Activities:** 12; 17, 24, 26; 60, 69, 87 **Addr.:** Westminster Village, Apt. 3216, 2741 N. Salisbury St., West Lafayette, IN 47906.

Shreve, Joan Marie (N. 15, 1950, Gary, IN) Asst. Prof., Comp. Tech., Kent State Univ., Trumbull Campus, 1982–; Lib. Dir., Asst. Prof., Lib. Admin., E. Liverpool Campus, 1980–82; Buhl Libn., Buhl Dept. Lib., Univ. of Pittsburgh, 1977–80. **Educ.:** Capital Univ., 1968–71, BA (Soclgy., Soc. Work); Kent State Univ., 1976–77, MLS; Univ. of Pittsburgh, 1978–80, CASIS. **Orgs.:** SLA. ALA. Amer. Anthro. Assn. Amer. Folklore Socty. **Honors:** Beta Phi Mu, 1977; Kappa Alpha Pi, 1972. **Pubns.:** *Lois Jaffe: Social Worker, Clinician, Teacher: Biography and Annotated Bibliography* (1981); "Images of Aging in Literature," *Images of Aging No. 2* (Sum. 1981); "Selected Readings and Bibliography," *Genesis of Structures in African Narrative Volume II: Dahomean Narrative* (1981). **Addr.:** Library, Trumbull Campus, Kent State University, 4314 Mahoning Ave., Warren, OH 44483.

Shubert, Joseph F. (S. 17, 1928, Buffalo, NY) State Libn., Asst. Comsn. for Libs., NY State Lib., 1977–; State Libn., State Lib. of OH, 1966–77; Asst. Dir., Intl. Rel. Ofc., ALA, 1962–66; State Libn., NV State Lib., 1959–61. **Educ.:** NY State Univ. Coll., 1951, BS; Univ. of Denver, Grad. Sch. of Libnshp., 1957, MA. **Orgs.:** ALA: Legis. Com.; Pub. Docum. Com. Chief Ofcrs. of State Lib. Agencies: Ch. (1977–78). Pub. Printer, US Gvt.: Adv. Cncl. WHCOLIS: Com. (1977–79). OCLC, Inc.: Bd. of Trustees (1977–78). New Eng. Lib. Bd. Panel of Couns. **Activities:** 13; 17, 24; 78 **Addr.:** New York State Library, Cultural Education Center, Rm. 10C34, Empire State Plz., Albany, NY 12230.

Shuchman, Hedvah L. (O. 7, 1932, Newark, NJ) Dir., Ctr. for Tech. Assessment, Prof., NJ Inst. of Tech., 1981–; Mgr., Sci. Policy Std., The Futures Grp., 1976–81; Resrch. Assoc. Prof., NY Univ., 1979–80; Sr. Resrch. Assoc., The Futures Grp., 1976–78. **Educ.:** Univ. of PA, 1949–52, BA (Pol. Sci.), 1952–54, MA (Intl. Pol.); George Washington Univ., 1971–77, PhD (Pol. Sci.). **Orgs.:** ASIS. AAAS. APSA. **Pubns.:** *Information Transfer in Engineering* (1981), *Self-Regulation in the Professions* (1981). **Activities:** 12; 41; 64, 91, 92 **Addr.:** 300 Mercer St., Apt. 24N, New York, NY 10003.

Shuey, Andrea Lee (N. 2, 19–, Oakland, CA) Branch Mgr., Dallas Pub. Lib., 1976–; st Asst. to Branch Mgr., 1968–76; Libn., GA Inst. of Tech., 1966–68. **Educ.:** LA State Univ., 1965, BA (Hist.), 1966, MLS. **Orgs.:** ALA. TX LA. Dallas Cnty. LA. Hist. Prsrvn. Leag. **Pubns.:** Contrib., *Twentieth Century Authors* (1982); various bk. reviews *Lib. Jnl.* (1977–80). **Activities:** 9; 16, 17, 42; 50, 85 **Addr.:** 6006 Lomo Alto, Dallas, TX 75205.

Shufeldt, Patricia Smith (Je. 6, 1945, Valparaiso, IN) Acq., Data Prcs. Libn., Greenville Cnty. Lib., 1978–, Reg. Ref. Libn., 1974–78, 1972–73, Asst. Head, Bus., Sci., Tech. Div., Docum. Libn., 1973–74, Ref. Libn., Cmrce. Lib., OH State Univ. Libs., 1968–72. **Educ.:** Macalester Coll., 1963–67, BA (Econ.); Rutgers Univ., 1967–68, MLS. **Orgs.:** ALA: Bus. Ref. Srvs. Com. (1970–73). SLA: S. Atl. Chap., Dir. (1976–78). SE LA. Piedmont Libs. Assn.: Pres. (1977–78). **Honors:** H.W. Wilson Co., John Cotton Dana Lib. PR Awd., 1976. **Pubns.:** Jt. auth., "Direction for the future," *OH LA Bltn.* (Jl. 1973); Jt. auth., "Oliver Hudson Kelley: Minnesota Pioneer, 1849–1868," *MN Hist.* (Fall 1967). **Activities:** 9; 15; 56 **Addr.:** Greenville County Library, 300 College St., Greenville, SC 29601.

Shulman, Frank Joseph (S. 20, 1943, Boston, MA) Head, E. Asia Col., Univ. of MD Libs., 1976–; Bibl., Libn., Ctr. for Japanese Std., Univ. of MI, 1970–75; Asst. Ed., *Bibliography of Asian Studies* Assn. for Asian Std., 1970–72. **Educ.:** Harvard Univ., 1961–64, BA (Hist.); Univ. of MI, 1968, MA (E. Asian Std.), MA, (LS); various PhD crs. **Orgs.:** Assn. for the Bibl. of Hist. DC LA. Intl. Assn. of Orien. Libns. Mid. E. Libns. Assn. Assn. for Asian Std.: Com. on E. Asian Libs.; Mid-Atl. Reg., Reg. (Mem.-at-Large, 1977–78), Com. on Acad. Resrcs. (1978–), Prog. Com. (1979–), v.p. (1980–), **Honors:** Phi Kappa Phi, 1969; Beta Phi Mu, 1969; Univ. of MI, Carnegie LS Endow. Flwshp., 1969. **Pubns.:** Ed., cmplr., *Doctoral Dissertations on Asia: An Annotated Bibliographical Journal of Current International Research* (1980); Adv. Ed., Ref. Bks., *Asian Std. Series* G.K. Hall and Co. (1977–); asst. ed., *Mid-Atlantic Directory to Resources for Asian Studies* (1980); *Doctoral Dissertations on China, 1971–1975: A Bibliography of Studies in Western Languages* (1978); jt. auth., *East Asian Resources in American Libraries* (1977); "Doctoral Research on Malaya and Malaysia, 1895–1977: A Comprehensive Bibliography and Statistical Overview," *Malaysian Studies: Present Knowledge and Research Trends* (1979); various other bks., articles, rpts., reviews. **Activities:** 1; 17, 39, 49; 54, 57 **Addr.:** E. Asia Collection, McKeldin Library, University of Maryland, College Park, MD 20742.

Shumaker, Earl R. (S. 20, 1948, Winnfield, LA) Head, Gvt. Pubns. Dept., Univ. Libs., North. IL Univ., 1978–; Head, Gvt. Docum. Dept., OH Univ., Athens, 1975–78; Docum. Libn., West. KY Univ., 1972–75. **Educ.:** Yuba Coll., 1966–68, AA (Hist.); Portland State Univ., 1968–70, BS (Soc. Sci.); LA State Univ., 1970–71 (LS); OH Univ., 1977, Cert. (Sem. for Mgrs.). **Orgs.:** ALA: RASD/Hist. Sect., Bibl. and Indxs. Com. Ofc. for Lib. Srv. to the Disadv., Subcom. on Lib. Srv. for the Amer. Indian People (1977–79). IL LA. KY LA. **Pubns.:** *Municipal Government Reference Sources: Publications and Collections* (1978); "Kentucky Serials: a Selective Bibliography," *KY LA Bltn.* (Spr. (1976); jt. auth., "Kentucky Kaleidoscope" clmn. *KY LA Bltn.* (1975–76); reviews. **Activities:** 1; 29, 39, 46; 70, 75, 78 **Addr.:** 1524 Timberwood Ct., Sycamore, IL 60178.

Shuman, Bruce A. (Jl. 16, 1941, Chicago, IL) Assoc. Prof., Queens Coll. CUNY, Grad. Sch. of Lib. and Info. Std., 1979–; Assoc. Prof., Univ. of OK, 1977–79; Asst. Prof., IN Univ., 1971–77. **Educ.:** Univ. of Chicago, 1959–63, AB (Eng., Fr.), 1963–65, AM (LS); Rutgers Univ., 1968–73, PhD (LS). **Orgs.:** AALS. ASIS. ALA. IFRT, Ch. (1981–), Dir. (1979–). World Future Socty. **Pubns.:** *The River Bend Casebook: Problems in Public Library Service* (1981); "Sex Magazines: Problems of Acquisition, Retention, Display and Defense in Public and Academic Libraries," *The Serials Libn.* (1981). **Activities:** 11; 26, 39, 49-Database Srch. **Addr.:** Queens College, CUNY, Grad. Sch. of Lib. & Info. Studies, Flushing, NY 11367.

Shumer, Barbara Lee (N. 27, 1952, Royal Oak, MI) Branch Head, N. Durham Branch, Durham Cnty. Lib., 1980–; Dept. Head, Ext. Srvs., Farmington Cmnty. Lib., 1979–80; Head Libn., Oakland Cnty. Lib. for the Blind, 1979–80; Dept. Head, Chld. Srvs., Farmington Cmnty. Lib., 1976–79. **Educ.:** Univ. of MI, 1970–74, BA (Eng., Hist.), 1974–75, AMLS. **Orgs.:** ALA: ALSC, Com. on Liaison with Natl. Orgs. Srvg. the Child (1978–); Caldecott Com. (1981). MI LA: Chld. Srvs. Caucus (Ch., 1979–80). Durham Cnty. LA. NC LA. Natl. Assn. for the Prsrvn. & Perpet. of Storytel. NC Assn. for Cmnty. Educ. **Honors:** MI LA, Loleta D. Fyan Awd., 1980. **Pubns.:** "Library Display—Charity Christmas Cards," *Wilson Lib. Bltn.* (O. 1979). **Activities:** 9; 16, 17, 21 **Addr.:** 5219-F Penrith Dr., Durham, NC 27713.

Shurman, Richard L. (My. 23, 1950, Los Alamos, NM) Autom. Coord., DuPage Lib. Syst., 1979–, Spec. Srvs. Libn., 1974–79. **Educ.:** Univ. of WA, 1969–72, BA (Anthro.), 1973–74, MLS. **Orgs.:** ALA: Lib. Srv. to the Deaf Sect., Strg. Com. (1979–80). IL LA. Metro. Coal. for Lib. Srv. to the Hearing Impaired. **Honors:** Beta Phi Mu, 1974. **Pubns.:** Reviews. **Activities:** 9, 13; 17, 24, 28; 55, 56, 72 **Addr.:** DuPage Library System, P.O. Box 268, 127 S. 1st St., Geneva, IL 60134.

Shurtleff, Carl H. (Mr. 21, 1915, Harrisville, UT) Asst. Libn., Augusta Coll., 1976–; Circ. Libn., Brigham Young Univ., 1974–76; Cmnty. Srvs./AV, Augusta-Richmond Cnty. Pub. Lib., 1972–74. **Educ.:** George Washington Univ., 1956–60, BA (Intl. Rel.); Brigham Young Univ., 1971–72, MSLIS; Air Cmnd. and Staff Coll., 1955–56 (Mgt. and Intl. Rel.) **Orgs.:** ALA. GA LA. Ctrl. Savannah River LA. Retired Ofcrs. Assn. Kiwanis Club. **Activities:** 1, 9; 16, 22, 39 **Addr.:** REESE Library, Augusta College, Augusta, GA 30910.

Shutt, Thelma Miller (Ag. 12, 1926, Indianapolis, IN) Libn., Ft. Benjamin Harrison, IN, 1979–; Supvisory Libn., U.S. Nvl. Avionics Ctr., 1977–79; Libn., Franklin Ctrl. HS, 1963–77; Libn., Greenfield HS, 1958–63; Tchr. Libn., Charlottesville HS, 1955–58; Tchr., 1950–54. **Educ.:** IN Univ., 1944–45; Butler Univ., 1948–50, AB (Eng., Span., Latin); Univ. of CO, 1950–53, MED (Educ.); IN Univ., 1958–63, MLS; Sch. Libn. Cert.; Med. Libn. Cert.; Pub. Libn. Licn.; various crs. **Orgs.:** IN Sch. Libns. Assn. SLA. Parents Without Partners. Loyal Ord. of the Moose. **Honors:** Beta Phi Mu, 1963. **Activities:** 10, 12; 17, 39, 48; 63, 64, 74 **Addr.:** 8845 Fountainview, Apt. 508, Indianapolis, IN 46226.

Sibia, Tejinder S. (Ag. 20, 1937, Raipur, Punjab India) Head, Bio. and Agr. Sci. Dept., Shields Lib., Univ. of CA, Davis, 1979–; Head, Sci. and Tech. Dept., VA Polytech. and State Univ., 1970–79; Head, Sci. and Tech. Dept., KS State Univ., 1967–70; Ref. Libn., Linda Hall Lib., 1965–67. **Educ.:** Punjab Agr. Univ., 1955–59, BSC (Agr.); KS State Univ., 1960–63, MS (Horticulture); Emporia State Univ., 1964–65, MS (Libnshp.). **Orgs.:** SLA. Intl. Assn. of Agr. Libns. and Docmlsts. Assocs. of the Natl. Agr. Lib., Inc. **Activities:** 1; 58, 65, 68 **Addr.:** Biological & Agricultural Sciences Dept., Shields Library, University of California, Davis, CA 95616.

Sibley, Marjorie H. (Ap. 23, 1920, Longview, IL) Ref. Libn., Assoc. Prof., Augsburg Coll., 1978–, Head Libn., 1971–78, Ref. Libn., 1961–71; Acq. Libn., Macalester Coll., 1959–61. **Educ.:** Univ. of IL, 1938–42, AB (Soclgy.), 1942–43, MA (Soclgy.); Univ. of MN, 1958–59, MA (LS); various grad. crs. **Orgs.:** MN Ofc. of Pub. Libs. and Lib. Coop. Adv. Cncl. MN Educ. Comp. Cnsrtm. Lib. Com. ALA: ACRL/Coll. Sect. (Pres., 1976–77); SCMAT Review Com. (1977–78). MN LA: Long Range Plng. Com.; various coms. AAUP. MN Women in Higher Educ. Women's Intl. Leag. for Peace and Frdm. Univ. of MN Lib. Sch. Adv. Com. **Honors:** MN LA, Cert. of Merit, 1964; Beta Phi Mu, 1959; Phi Beta Kappa, 1941. **Pubns.:** Jt. cmplr., "Recent Publications of Political Interest," *Amer. Pol. Sci. Review* (bimonthly, 1944–48). **Addr.:** 2018 Fairmount Ave., St. Paul, MN 55105.

Special Subjects/Services: 50. Adult educ.; 51. Advert./Mktg.; 52. Aerosp.; 53. Agric.; 54. Area std.; 55. Arts/Hum.; 56. Autom.; 57. Bibl./Prtg.; 58. Bio. sci.; 59. Bus./Fin.; 60. Chem.; 61. Copyrt.; 62. Documtn.; 63. Educ.; 64. Engin.; 65. Env.; 66. Eth. grps.; 67. Film; 68. Food/Nutr.; 69. Geneal.; 70. Geo.; 71. Geol.; 72. Handcpd.; 73. Hist.; 74. Int. frdm.; 75. Info. sci.; 76. Insr.; 77. Law; 78. Legis.; 79. Math./Comp. sci.; 80. Med.; 81. Metals; 82. Nat. resrcs.; 83. Newsp.; 84. Nuc. sci.; 85. Oral hist.; 86. Petr./Energy; 87. Pharm.; 88. Phys./Astr./Math.; 89. Readg.; 90. Relig.; 91. Sci./Tech.; 92. Soc. sci.; 93. Telecom.; 94. Transp.; 95. (other).

Sibley, Richard P., Jr. (O. 27, 1942, Melrose, MA) Libn., Dir., Waterville Pub. Lib., 1976–; Head Libn., Dir., Millinocket Meml. Lib., 1974–76. **Educ.:** Univ. of MA, 1960–64, BA (Hist.); Emory Univ., 1964–65, MAT (Sec. Educ.); Univ. of MO, 1973–74, MALS. **Orgs.:** ME LA: Secy. (1976–81); Legis. Com. (1975–76). New Eng. LA. ALA. **Pubns.:** "Bright or Muted Decor in Libraries?" *Downeast Libs.* (Ja. 1977). **Activities:** 9; 16, 17, 22 **Addr.:** 71 High St., Waterville, ME 04901.

Sibulkin, Lucille (Jl. 3, 1925, Cleveland, OH) Cat. libn., RI Coll., 1976–, Head of Tech. Srvs., 1972–76, Cat. and Ref. Libn., 1966–72. **Educ.:** West. Rsv. Univ., 1943–46, BA (Soclgy.); Univ. of RI, 1964–66, MLS. **Orgs.:** ALA. New Eng. LA. RI LA: Conf. Com. (1977–). SLA. **Pubns.:** "Comments on Several Academic Libraries in London," *RI LA Bltn.* (Ap. 1978). **Activities:** 1; 20, 39, 46 **Addr.:** Adams Library, Rhode Island College, Providence, RI 02908.

Sichel, Beatrice (My. 26, 1934, Nuremburg, Germany) Head, Phys. Sci. Lib., West. MI Univ., 1977–, Sci. Catlgr., 1974–77; Libn., Kalamazoo Spice Extraction Co., 1973–74. **Educ.:** CUNY, 1951–55, BS (Sci.); Brandeis Univ., 1955–57, MA (Chem.); West. MI Univ., 1970–72, MLS. **Orgs.:** SLA: Sci.-Tech. Div. (Mem. Ch., 1976–77); Phys./Astr./Math. Div. Geosci. Info. Socty. Beta Phi Mu: Kappa Chap., Nom. Com. (1977–78). **Honors:** Phi Beta Kappa, 1955. **Pubns.:** Reviews. **Activities:** 1; 17, 22, 39; 56, 71, 88 **Addr.:** Physical Sciences Library, Western Michigan University, Kalamazoo, MI 49008.

Sickles, Linda C. (My. 7, 1947, Detroit, MI) Dir., Orion Twp. Pub. Lib., 1980–; Asst. Head, Adult Srvs., Avon Twp. Pub. Lib., 1977–80; Asst. Head, Ref. Dept., YA Coord., Baldwin Pub. Lib., 1973–77; Ref., Serials Libn., Tufts Med./Dental Sch. Lib., 1970–72. **Educ.:** East. MI Univ., 1965–69, BA (Pol. Sci., Sec. Educ.); West. MI Univ., 1969–70, MSL (LS). **Orgs.:** MI LA: JMRT, Bd. (1976–77), Ch. (1977–78); Conf. Plng. Com. (1981). ALA. Wayne Oakland Lib. Fed.: Adult Ref. Com. (1978–). **Activities:** 9; 16, 17, 39; 50, 59, 69 **Addr.:** Orion Township Public Library, 845 S. Lapeer Rd., Lake Orion, MI 48035.

Sickles, Robert C. (F. 7, 1938, Rochester, NY) Bio. Sci./Agr. Biblgphr., IA State Univ., 1971–, Sci. Biblgphr., 1968–71; Tech. Prcs. Libn., Univ. of CA, Irvine, 1967–68; Sci. Div. Libn., ID State Univ., 1966–67; Math. Tchr., Greensburg HS, 1964–65. **Educ.:** Sterling Coll., 1959–63, BS (Math.); Syracuse Univ., 1965–66, MS (LS). **Orgs.:** ALA: RASD, Info. Retrieval Com. (1972–76). SALALM. **Honors:** Pi Gamma Mu. **Activities:** 1; 15, 17, 39; 53, 58, 68 **Addr.:** Iowa State University Library, Ames, IA 50011.

Sieben, Regina Monks (Mr. 31, 1939, Orange, NJ) Info. Sci., Gen. Foods, 1980–; Serials Libn., Rutgers Univ., 1976–80; Libn., Monmouth Cnty. Lib., 1974–76. **Educ.:** Caldwell Coll., 1956–60, BA (Chem.); Rutgers Univ., 1971–74, MLS. **Orgs.:** NJ SLA: Exec. Bd. (1980–). ACRL/NJ LA: Coll. and Univ. Sect. (Secy.-Treas., 1977–80). AAUW. **Pubns.:** Reviews. **Activities:** 12; 30, 33, 38; 60, 68, 91 **Addr.:** 86 River Edge Dr., Little Silver, NJ 07739.

Siebersma, Daniel J. (F. 24, 1955, Sioux Center, IA) Dir., George Amos Meml. Lib., 1981–, Asst. Dir., 1980–81, Info. Srvs. Libn., 1979–80; Branch Mgr., Sioux City Pub. Lib., 1976–78. **Educ.:** Morningside Coll., 1973–76, BA (Eng.); Univ. of Denver, 1978–79, MA (Libnshp.). **Orgs.:** ALA. Mt. Plains LA: Pub. Lib. Sect. (Secy., 1980–81). WY LA: Gvt. Docum. Interest Grp. (Ch., 1980–81). Sci. Fiction Resrch. Assn. Cncl. of Cmnty. Srvs. **Activities:** 9; 17, 29, 39; 55, 78, 89 **Addr.:** George Amos Memorial Library, 412 S. Gillette Ave., Gillette, WY 82716.

Sieburth, Janice F. (Ja. 26, 1927, Ellensburg, WA) Ref., Biblgphr., Phys. and Engin. Sci., Univ. of RI Lib., 1974–, Classfd. Libn., Cat., 1972–74. **Educ.:** WA State Univ., 1945–49, BS (Home Econ.), 1949–51, MS (Food and Nutr.); Univ. of RI, 1969–72, MLS. **Orgs.:** RI LA: Conf. Com. (Co-Ch., 1976–78); NELA Cnclr. (1978–80). New Eng. LA: RI Rep. on Exec. Bd. (1978–80); Mem. Com. (1980–). Amer. Socty. for Engin. Educ.: Anl. Conf. (Session Ch., 1980). Gvrs. Conf. on Libs. and Info. Srvs.: Del. (1979). various orgs. Leag. of Women Voters. Univ. of RI: various coms. S. Kingstown Pub. Lib.: Bd. of Trustees (1975–80). Kingston Free Lib.: Bd. of Trustees (1974–76). **Honors:** Univ. of RI Resrch. Com., Grant-in-Aid. **Pubns.:** "Book Publishing in Biochemistry—Volume and Costs," *Spec. Cols.* (forthcoming); "The NELA Connection," *RI LA Bltn.* (N. 1980); "Online Data Base Searching—Who Needs It? What Do You Get Out of It? What Does It Cost?" *RI LA Bltn.* (Jl.–Ag. 1979); "Talk-Back—A Tool for Public Relations," *RQ* (1977). **Activities:** 1; 15, 31, 39; 60, 64, 91 **Addr.:** Reference Dept., University of Rhode Island Library, Kingston, RI 02881.

Siegel, Elliot R. (My. 31, 1942, New York, NY) Sr. Sci., Lister Hill Natl. Ctr. for Biomed. Comm., Natl. Lib. of Med., 1976–; Sci. Affairs Ofcr., Amer. Psy. Assn., 1975–76, Pubns. Dev., Dept., Mgr., 1972–74, Resrch. Assoc., Ofc. of Comm., 1970–72. **Educ.:** Brooklyn Coll., CUNY, 1960–64, BA (Psy.); MI State Univ., 1964–66, MA (Psy.), 1966–69, PhD (Comm.). **Orgs.:** ASIS: Bhvl. and Soc. Sci. SIG (Ch., 1974–75). Intl. Comm. Assn. Amer. Psy. Assn. AAAS. **Honors:** Psy Chi. **Pubns.:** "Transfer of Information to Health Practitioners," *Progress in Communication Sciences, Vol. 3* (1981); "Use of Computer Conferencing to Validate and Update NLM's Hepatitis Knowledge Base," *Electronic Communication: Technology and Impacts* (1980); jt. auth., "The Hepatitis Knowledge Base: A Prototype Information Transfer System," *Annals of Internal Medicine* (Jl. 1980); "The Evaluation of Innovations in APA Publications Activities: The Case of the Journal Supplement Abstract Service," *Amer. Psychologist* (1976). **Activities:** 4; 41; 56, 75, 93 **Addr.:** Lister Hill National Center for Biomedical Communications, National Library of Medicine, 8600 Rockville Pike, Bethesda, MD 20209.

Siegel, Henry J. (Ag. 31, 1951, Buffalo, NY) Dir., CBS News Arch., CBS Inc., 1978–, Supvsr., CBS News Film/Video-Tape Lib., 1978, Libn., CBS News Film Lib., 1976–77; Media Instr., SUNY, Buffalo, Sch. of Info. and Lib. Std., 1975–76. **Educ.:** SUNY, Buffalo, 1969–73, BA (Psy.), 1975–76, MLS; CBS Sch. of Mgt., 1980. **Orgs.:** ALA. SLA. ASIS. Amer. Film Inst. Nat. Geo. Socty. Smithsonian Inst. Radio and TV News Dirs. Assn. **Pubns.:** "Preserve Nonprint Too," *Lib. Jnl.* (S. 1, 1979); "Printed Book Catalogs" slide/tape lrng. package (1976). **Activities:** 2, 12; 17, 30, 37; 93 **Addr.:** 360 Central Park West, New York, NY 10025.

Siegfried, Dorothy E. (S. 27, 1921, Massillon, OH) Tech. Info. Spec., U.S. Coast Guard, Resrch. and Dev., Ctr. Lib., 1979–; Assoc. Libn., Sacred Heart Univ., 1967–78. **Educ.:** Seton Hall Univ., 1960–64, AB (Hist.); Columbia Univ., 1965–68, MLS; Paris Cnsvty. Msc., 1952–53. **Orgs.:** SLA. Southeast. CT Assn. CT LA. CT Coll. Lib. Frnds. of the Lib. Fulbright Alum. Assn. **Honors:** Fulbright Schol., 1952–53. **Activities:** 4, 5; 17, 39, 41; 60, 64, 74 **Addr.:** U.S. Coast Guard R & D Center, Avery Point, Groton, CT 06340.

Siegrist, Edith B. (My. 9, 1925, McIntosh, SD) Asst. Prof., Lib., Univ. of SD, 1961–; Libn., Everett HS, 1955–61; Asst. Libn., North. State Coll., 1954–55; Elem. Sch. Tchr., SD Pub. Schs., 1950–53, 1945–48. **Educ.:** Huron Coll., 1943–45, 1948–50, BA (Eng.); Univ. of Denver, 1953–54, MA (LS). **Orgs.:** ALA: YASD. Mt. Plains LA: Awds. Com. (1979). SD LA: Cert. and Accred. Com. (Ch., 1975–). **Honors:** Delta Kappa Gamma; Phi Delta Kappa; Huron Coll., Disting. Alum. Awd., 1973. **Pubns.:** Jt. ed., *Reading for Young People: The Great Plains* (1979); *Instructional Media Catalog* (1979); ed., *Good Words: Notable Books on the American Indian* (1973); "The Learning Resources Laboratory - A Decade of Service," *Univ. of SD Educ. Jnl.* (Fall 1979); "Library Media," *Univ. of SD Educ. Jnl.* (Spr. 1978); various slide tape shows. **Activities:** 1, 10; 20, 26, 48; 63, 74, 89 **Addr.:** 854 Eastgate Dr., Vermillion, SD 57069.

Sievert, Mary Ellen (N. 20, 1941, Springfield, MA) Resrch. Asst. and Lectr., Sch. of Lib. and Info. Sci., Univ. of MO, 1977–, Asst. Instr., Eng. Dept., 1973–77. **Educ.:** Emmanuel Coll., 1959–63, BA (Eng.); Univ. of IA, 1963–65, MA (Eng.); Univ. of MO, 1975–77, MA (LS). **Orgs.:** SLA: Mid-MO Chap. (Secy./Treas., 1979–80). Jane Addams Chld. Bk. Awd. Com. (1972–). **Pubns.:** "Philosopher's Index on DIALOG," *Database* (Mr. 1980). **Activities:** 11; 26; 56, 75 **Addr.:** School of Library & Informational Science, Stewart Hall, University of Missouri, Columbia, MO 65211.

Sieving, Pamela Carey (D. 7, 1948, Shreveport, LA) Litigation Docum. Mgr., Kirkland and Ellis, 1979–; Ref. Libn., Univ. of IL, Chicago Cir. Lib., 1974–79; ILL Spec., Yale Univ. Lib. **Educ.:** Valparaiso Univ., 1966–70, BA (Eng.); Univ. of WI, Madison, 1970–71, MA (Eng.); South. CT State Coll., 1972–74, MSLS. **Orgs.:** Chicago OLUG: Treas. (1979), Vice-Ch. (1979–80). ASIS. ALA: RASD/Machine-Assisted Ref. Sect., Bylaws Com. (1978), Nom. Com. (Ch., 1979), Prog. Com. (Ch., 1981–82). Frnds. of the Oak Park Lib.: Exec. Bd. (1979–83). Chicago Acad. Lib. Cncl. Ref. Subcom. (Ch., 1976–77). Valparaiso Univ. Gld.: Chap. Secy. (1976–79); Pres. (1979–83). **Activities:** 1, 12; 30, 39; 56 **Addr.:** 1163 S. Lyman, Oak Park, IL 60304.

Sigel, Efrem J. (Ap. 29, 1943, New York, NY) Exec. VP, Ed.–in–Chief, Knowledge Indus. Pubns., 1978–, VP, Ed.–in–Chief, 1974–78. **Educ.:** Harvard Coll., 1960–64, AB (Soc. Sci.); Harvard Univ., 1966–68, MBA, 1969–70, Sheldon Travelling Flwshp. **Orgs.:** Auths. Gld. **Pubns.:** *Videotext: The Coming Revolution in Home/Office Information Retrieval* (1980); *Video Discs: The Technology, the Applications, and the Future* (1980); *Crisis: The Taxpayer Revolt and Your Kids' Schools* (1978); various articles in lit., comp., and other jnls. and newsps. **Activities:** 6; 37; 75, 93 **Addr.:** Knowledge Industry Publications, 701 Westchester Ave., White Plains, NY 10604.

Sigel, John A. (Ap. 27, 1927, Los Angeles, CA) Law Libn. CA Supreme Ct. Lib., 1967–, Asst. Law Libn., 1961–67; Sr. Libn., Admin., Legis. Ref. Sect., CA State Lib., 1958–61. **Educ.:** Pomona Coll., 1947–51, BA (Mod. Grmn. Lit.); Univ. of CA, Berkeley, 1951–52, MA (Mod. Grmn. Lit.), 1952–53, BLS; AALL, 1969, Cert. (Law Libn.). **Orgs.:** AALL: Nom. Com. (1981–82); Lcl. Arrange. (Ch., 1979); State, Ct. and Cnty. Law Libns. Spec. Interest Sect. (Ch., 1979–80); West.-Pac. Chap., Prog., 1980 Anl. Mtg.; North. CA Chap., Strg. Com. (1979–80). **Activities:** 13; 15, 17, 20; 77, 78 **Addr.:** Library, Supreme Court of California, State Bldg. Annex, Rm. 4241, 455 Golden Gate Ave., San Francisco, CA 94102.

Siggins, Jack A. (Jl. 11, 1938, Arp, TX) Assoc. Dir., Libs. for Pub. Srvs., Univ. of MD, 1977–, Asst. Dir., Reader Srvs., 1975–77, Head, E. Asia Col., 1970–75; Libn., Far East. Lib., Univ. of Chicago, 1969–70; Resrch. Anal., Lib. of Congs., 1965–66, Serials Biblgphr., 1965; Japanese Interpreter, Transl., U.S. Army, 1961–64. **Educ.:** Princeton Univ., 1956–60, BA (Rom. Lang.); Amer. Univ., 1966–68, MA (Far East. Std.); Defense Lang. Inst., 1961–62, Japanese Lang. Cert.; Univ. of Chicago, 1967–70, MA (LS). **Orgs.:** ALA: Staff Org. RT, Strg. Com. (Ch., 1979). MD LA. Assn. for Asian Std. **Honors:** Amer. Univ., Ford Fndn. Flwshp., 1966–67. **Pubns.:** "University of Maryland Japanese Collection," *Assn. for Asian Std. Nsltr.* (D. 1970); "The East Asia Collection," *Frgn. Acq. Nsltr.* (Spr. 1971). **Activities:** 1; 15, 17, 28; 54, 74 **Addr.:** 3203 "S" St. N.W., Washington, DC 20007.

Sigler, Ronald F. (D. 12, 1932, New York, NY) Class. and Rating Admin. Bd., Motion Pic. Assn. of Amer., 1981–; Asst. Prof., Sch. of LS, Univ. of WI, Milwaukee, 1975–81; Coord., AV Srvs., Los Angeles Cnty. Pub. Lib. Syst., 1965–73; Pub. Lib. and AV Consult., MI State Lib., 1964–65; Dept. Head, AV Dept., Buena Park Lib. Dist., (CA), 1958–64, Libn., Gen. Ref., Recs., Msc., 1957–58. **Educ.:** Queens Coll., 1951–56, BA (Msc.); Univ. of South. CA, 1962–63, (Cin.); Univ. of CA, Los Angeles, 1963–64, MLS; FL State Univ., 1974–75, Adv. MLS, 1975–77, PhD (LS). **Orgs.:** AALS: Conf. Com. (1979–80). ALA: LITA/AV Sect. (Vice-Ch., Ch.-Elect, 1978–80); LITA Rep. to Frdm. to Read Fndn. (1979–); LITA, Nom. Com. (1981–82); PLA, AV Com. (1972–74). EFLA: Frdm. to View Com. (Ch., 1977–). AECT. Film Lib. Info. Cncl.: Bd. of Dirs. (Vice-Ch., 1971–73). Various other orgs., coms. CA Ctr. of Films for Chld.: Bd. of Dirs. (1969–73). AAUP. **Pubns.:** "Using EFLA's Intellectual Freedom Document," *Sightlines* (Fall 1979); "Librarians Win Relief in 'Harmful Matter' Law," *Sightlines* (Spr. 1980); "A Rationale for the Film as a Public Library Resource and Service," *Lib. Trends* (Sum. 1978); "A Study in Censorship: The Los Angeles '19'," *Film Lib. Qtly.* (Spr. 1971); ed., "Freedom to View," clmn. *Sightlines* (1977–). **Activities:** 9, 11; 17, 26, 32; 67, 74, 93 **Addr.:** Motion Picture Association of America, Classification & Rating Administration, 8480 Beverly Blvd., Hollywood, CA 90048.

Silberberg, Sophie C. (My. 15, 1913, Rochester, NY) Dir., Fund For Free Expression, 1979–; Dir., Lib. Mktg., Random Hse., 1977–78; Dir. Promo. and Advert., Chld. Bks., Thomas Y. Crowell, 1968–77; Dir., Lib. Promo., Rand McNally and Co., 1964–1968; Dir., PR, Nassau Lib. Syst., 1959–64. **Educ.:** Hunter Coll., 1931–35, BA (Hist., Pol. Sci.). **Orgs.:** ALA: ALSC, Presch. Com. (1975–77); ALTA, Subcom. Int. Frdm. (Ch., 1969–72). Frdm. to Read Fndn.: Bd. of Trustees (1969–72, 1973–79). Lib. PR Cncl.: Pres. (1962–64). Chld. Bk. Cncl.: Pres. (1972). Assn. of Amer. Pubshrs.: Libs. Com. (1974–77). **Pubns.:** "Let's Learn from the Schools," *ALA Bltn.* (1960); Producer, Scriptwriter, "Working Together: Nassau Builds Better Library Service" 12 minute film. **Activities:** 9, 10; 21, 36, 37; 51, 74 **Addr.:** 70 E. 10 St., New York, NY 10003.

Silcox, Nancy Victoria Noyes (My. 8, 1945, Fergus Falls, MN) Chld. Libn., Asst. Branch Libn., Arlington Cnty. Lib., 1973–, Chld. Libn., 1972–73. **Educ.:** Univ. of MN, 1963–67, BA (Sp., Thea.); Univ. of MI, 1971–72, MALS. **Orgs.:** VA LA: Chld. and YA RT (Ch., 1977–78). ALA: ALSC/Filmstp. Eval. Com. (Ch., 1979–80). **Activities:** 9; 17, 21 **Addr.:** 4835 S. 8th St., Arlington, VA 22204.

Sillito, John R. (S. 8, 1948, Salt Lake City, UT) Archvst. and Asst. Prof. of Libs., Lib., Weber State Coll., 1977–; Sr. Catlgr., LDS Church Hist. Dept., 1974–77; Asst. Recs. Mgr., Univ. of UT, 1971–74. **Educ.:** Univ. of UT, 1966–70, BS (Hist.), 1973, BS (Pol. Sci.), Amer. Univ. Natl. Arch., 1973, Cert. (Arch. Admin.); Univ. of UT, 1974–77, MA (Hist.). **Orgs.:** Conf. of Intermt. Archvsts.: Cncl. (1975–). SAA. Natl. Hist. Pubns. and Recs. Comsn.: UT Recs. Com. (1979–81). UT Gvr.'s Conf. on Lib. and Info. Srvs.: Spec. Libs. Plng. Com. (1979). Org. of Amer. Histns. Hist. Socty. Mormon Hist. Assn. UT Womens Hist. Assn. **Pubns.:** "Franklin Spencer Spalding and the Mormons: A Documentary Approach," *Sunstone* (Jl. Ag. 1979); reviews. **Activities:** 1, 2; 15, 17; 85 **Addr.:** Stewart Library, Weber State College, Ogden, UT 84408.

Silver, Barbara Ceizler (Mr. 4, 1940, Los Angeles, CA) Ref. and ILL Libn., Univ. of CA, Santa Barbara, 1967–; Catlgr., Conf. Bd., 1966–67; Chld. Libn., NY Pub. Lib., 1963–65. **Educ.:** Univ. of CA, Los Angeles, 1957–61, BA (Eng.); Univ. of CA, Berkeley, 1962–63, MLS. **Orgs.:** CA State Lib.: Srvs. Working Grp. ALA: RASD, ILL Com. Univ. of CA Libns. Assn. **Activities:** 1; 17, 34, 39 **Addr.:** 643 Willowglen Rd., Sta. Barbara, CA 93105.

Silver, Linda R. (Ja. 25, 1940, Cleveland, OH) Head, Chld. Srvs., Cuyahoga Cnty. Pub. Lib., 1980–, Instr., Chld. Lit., Kent State Univ., 1981–; Asst. Coord., Chld. Srv., Cuyahoga Cnty. Pub. Lib., 1979–80, Branch Libn., 1976–79, Chld. Libn., 1973–76. **Educ.:** Cleveland State Univ., 1959–63, BS (Educ.); Case West. Rsv. Univ., 1963–64, MLS. **Orgs.:** ALA: ALSC

PROFESSIONAL ACTIVITIES: Institutions: 1. Acad. lib.; 2. Arch.; 3. Assn.; 4. Fed./Gvt. lib.; 5. Inst. lib.; 6. Mfr./Suppl.; 7. Milit. lib.; 8. Musm.; 9. Pub. lib.; 10. Sch. lib.; 11. Sch. of lib. sci.; 12. Spec. lib.; 13. State lib.; 14. (other). **Functions/Activities:** 15. Acq./Col. dev.; 16. Adult srvs.; 17. Admin.; 18. Apprais.; 19. Archit./Bldgs.; 20. Cat./Class.; 21. Chld. srvs.; 22. Circ.; 23. Cons./Pres.; 24. Consult.; 25. Cont. ed.; 26. Educ. lib. sci.; 27. Ext. srvs.; 28. Fund/Grants; 29. Gvt. pubs.; 30. Indx./Abs.; 31. Instr. lib. use; 32. Media srvs.; 33. Micro.; 34. Netwks./Coop.; 35. Persnl.; 36. PR; 37. Publshg.; 38. Recs. mgt.; 39. Ref. srvs.; 40. Repro.; 41. Resrch.; 42. Review.; 43. Secur.; 44. Serials; 45. Spec. col.; 46. Tech. srvs.; 47. Trustees/Bds.; 48. YA srvs.; 49. (other).

Newbery/Caldecott (1978); Andersen (1979); Bd. of Dirs. (1980–); Resrch. and Dev. (1976–79). Chld. Lit. Assn. Women's Natl. Bk. Assn. **Pubns.:** "Criticism, Reviewing, and the Library Review Media," *Top of the News* (Win. 1979); "Judging Books Is Our Business," *Sch. Lib. Jnl.* (Ja. 1979); "From Baldwin to Singer—Authors for Kids and Adults," *Sch. Lib. Jnl.* (F. 1979); "Standards and Free Access: Equal but Separate," *OH LA Bltn.* (O. 1979); "One Book to Win: The Continuing Story of the Newbery-Caldecott Awards," *Top of the News* (Fall 1979); various articles. **Activities:** 9, 11; 17, 21, 42; 55 **Addr.:** Cuyahoga County Public Library, 4510 Memphis Ave., Cleveland, OH 44144.

Silver, Martin Arnold (Je. 12, 1933, New York, NY) Msc. Libn., Univ. of CA, Santa Barbara, 1967–; Msc. Resrch. Div., NY Pub. Lib., 1964–67. **Educ.:** Coll. of the City of NY, 1951–55, BA (Msc.); Columbia Univ., 1961–64, MLS. **Orgs.:** Assn. for Rec. Snd. Cols.: Secy., Bd. (1981–83). Msc. LA: Bd. of Dirs. (1977–79). South. CA Msc. LA: Ch. (1971–72); VP/Pres. Elect (1981–83). Intl. Assn. of Msc. Libs. **Pubns.:** Various reviews in *Notes, Lib. Jnl., Amer. Rec. Guide* (1965–79). **Activities:** 1; 15, 36, 39; 55 **Addr.:** Music Library, University of California, Santa Barbara, CA 93106.

Silvernail, Patricia Wand (Mr. 28, 1942, Portland, OR) Head, Access Srvs., Hum. and Hist. Div., Columbia Univ. Libs., 1977–; Asst. Prof., Lib. Dept., Coll. of Staten Island, CUNY, 1972–77; Asst. Libn., Wittenberg Univ. Lib., 1967–69; Tchr., Caro HS, 1969–70; Tchr., Langley Jr. High, 1965–67; Peace Corps Volun., Rural Cmnty. Dev., Colombia, S. Amer., 1963–65. **Educ.:** Seattle Univ., 1960–63, BA (Hist.); Antioch Grad. Sch., 1965–67, MAT (Soc. Sci.); Univ. of MI, 1968–72, AMLS; various anthro. crs. **Orgs.:** NY Metro. Ref. and Resrch. Lib. Agency: METRO Task Force to Std. NYSILL (1980–81); METRO Jt. Task Force on Fncl. Aspects of Personal Access (1978–79). LA CUNY: Lib. Instr. Com. (1974–77). ALA: ACRL/Bibl. Instr. Sect. (Secy., 1980–81), various coms./Anthro. and Soclgy. Sect., Lcl. Arrange. for NY Conf. (1979–80), Nom. Com. (Ch., 1977–78)/Two-Year Coll. Sect., Instr. in Use Com. (1976–78); RTSD/Reprodct. of Lib. Mtrls. Sect., Subcom. to Monitor Advert. of Micros. (1977–79), Rep. to Bylaws Com. (1977–81). Natl. Educ. Assn. Staten Island Dance Thea. Inc. **Pubns.:** "A Third Opinion," in "Library Instruction; a Column of Opinion" *Jnl. of Acad. Libnshp.* (N. 1979); "Library Instruction Material in CUNY; A Review," *LACUNY Jnl.* (Fall 1975); Reviews. *Lib. Jnl.* (1976–79). **Activities:** 1; 16, 17, 31; 63, 92 **Addr.:** Columbia University Libraries, New York, NY 10027.

Silverstein, Diane L. (F. 10, 1946, Newark, NJ) Biling. Chld. Libn., Providence Pub. Lib., 1979–; Tchr., 1970–74. **Educ.:** PA State Univ., 1963–67, BA (Educ.); SUNY, Buffalo, 1967–70, MA (Fr.); Simmons Coll., 1975–78, MLS, 1977, Cert. (Eng. as a Sec. Lang.). **Orgs.:** RI LA. ALA. Intl. Hse. RI. RI Snd.-Barbershop Chorus. **Honors:** Pi Sigma Iota. **Activities:** 9; 21, 42; 66, 95-Langs. **Addr.:** Knight Memorial Library, 935 Pontiac Ave., Providence, RI 02907.

Silvester, Elizabeth (N. 27, 1935, Vienna, Austria) Head, Ref. Dept., McLennan Lib., McGill Univ., 1965–, Asst. Head, Ref. Dept., 1963–64, Ref. Libn., 1962–63, Catlgr., 1961–62. **Educ.:** McGill Univ., 1954–58, BA (Hist.), 1961, BLS, 1967, MLS; London Sch. of Econ., MA, 1968 (Intl. Hist.). **Orgs.:** ALA: Ref. and Subscrpn. Bks. Review Com. (1972–76). Corp. of Prof. Libns. of PQ: Bur. (1978–80). Can. LA: Coll. Univ. Libs. Sect. (Secy., 1966–67). SLA: Montreal Chap., Rep. on Inter-Assn. Com. on Copyrt. (1977–78). **Honors:** Univ. Coll., London, Sch. of Lib. Arch. and Info. Std., Hon. Resrch. Fellow, 1980–81. **Pubns.:** Jt. auth., *McGill University Thesis Directory* (1975–76); *A Preliminary Guide to the Papers of D.O. Hebb* (1977); *Some Aspects of Honorary Cooperation with Province of Quebec* (1966); "Reference Collection Policy Development in Academic Libraries," *Expression* (1978); reviews. **Activities:** 1; 17, 39 **Addr.:** 418 Pine Ave. W #36, Montreal, PQ H3A 1Y1 Canada.

Sim, Yong Sup (Mr. 20, 1935, Korea) Asst. Prof., Ref. Libn., Mercer Cnty. Cmnty. Coll., 1968–. **Educ.:** Konkuk Univ., Seoul, Korea, 1958–62, BA (Lit.); Atlanta Univ., 1965–68, MSLS; Nova Univ., 1973–77, EdD (Educ.). **Orgs.:** ALA. Natl. Educ. Assn. NJ Educ. Assn. **Pubns.:** "Library Work Order Processing System," *Resrcs. in Educ.* (1976); "A Study of the Status of the Library Technical Assistant," *Resrcs. in Educ.* (1977). **Activities:** 1; 39 **Addr.:** Mercer County Community College Library, P.O. Box B, 1200 Old Trenton Rd., Trenton, NJ 08690.

Siman, Bliss Beckman (Ja. 21, 1943, Brooklyn, NY) Asst. Prof., Lib. Instr. Srvs., Baruch Coll., CUNY 1980–, Acq. Libn./Col. Dev. Coord., 1971–80, Catlgr., 1968–71; Cat./Ref. Libn., Mann Lib., Cornell Univ., 1966–68; Ref. Libn., Half Hollow Hills Pub. Lib., 1965–66. **Educ.:** Ithaca Coll., 1959–63, BFA (Thea.); Drexel Univ., 1964–65, MLS; Hunter Coll., 1970–73, MA (Hist.); Grad. Ctr., City Univ. of NY, 1974–, PhD Cand. (Hist.). **Orgs.:** ALA. NY LA. SLA. Amer. Hist. Assn. **Activities:** 1; 15, 41, 46; 56, 92 **Addr.:** 9 Norwood Ave., Upper Montclair, NJ 07043.

Simard, Denis (Jl. 16, 1940, St-Joachim, Montmorency, PQ) Coord. du Ctr. De Documtn., Coll. de Trois-Rivières, 1978–; Dir. du Srv. du Prêt, Univ. Laval, 1968–78. **Educ.:** Univ. Laval, 1952–66, BAC (Arts); Univ. de Montréal, 1966–68, BAC (Bibl.). **Orgs.:** Corp. des Bibtcrs. Prof. du PQ. ASTED: Cnsl. d'Admin. (1979–80). **Activities:** 1, 10; 17, 22, 34; 56, 89 **Addr.:** CEGEP de Trois-Rivières, 3500 de Courval, Trois-Rivières, PQ G9A 5E6 Canada.

Simek, Ione V. (F. 24, 1921, Minot, ND) Pres., Cnty. Lib. Bd., Bottineau Cnty. Lib., 1979–; Asst Prof., West. IL Univ., 1969–75; Head HS Libn., Croton-on-Hudson, NY, 1967–69; Head HS Libn., Spackenkill Dist., NY, 1959–67. **Educ.:** SUNY, Albany, 1955–59, BA (Eng., Math., LS), 1959–62 (LS); Columbia Univ., 1969–71 (LS). **Orgs.:** ALA. ND LA. **Addr.:** 1302 Bennett, Bottineau, ND 58318.

Simeone, Henrietta M. (Mr. 27, 1922, Brooklyn, NY) Sch. Libn., Solvay HS, 1968–; Sch. Libn., N. Syracuse HS, 1953–68; Serials Catlgr., Syracuse Univ., 1948–52. **Educ.:** Coll. of New Rochelle, 1940–43, BA (Fr.); Columbia Univ., 1944–45 (LS); Syracuse Univ., 1952–53, MS (LS). **Orgs.:** ALA. Syracuse Univ. Women's Club. Untd. Tchrs. **Activities:** 10; 15, 20, 48 **Addr.:** 839 Cumberland Ave., Syracuse, NY 13210.

Simmons, Beatrice Elaine Tomei (N. 10, 1920, Stroudsburg, PA) Educ. Prog. Spec., U.S. Dept. of Educ., Ofc. of Libs. and Lrng. Resrcs., 1976–; Dir., Lrng. Resrcs., SUNY, 1973–76; Dir., Instr. Resrcs., Drexel Univ., 1971–73; PA Lib. Career Consult., PA State Lib., Drexel Univ., 1969–71; Educ. Prog. Spec., U.S. Ofc. of Educ., Reg. 2, 1968–69; Dir., Sch. Libs., Abington Sch. Dist., 1961–68; various tchg., libn. positions, 1942–61. **Educ.:** E. Stroudsburg State Coll., 1938–42, BS (Hlth. Educ.); Drexel Univ., 1961–65, MLS; Temple Univ., 1967–70, MEd (Educ. Comm.); Millersville State Coll., 1953–56, State Cert. (LS). **Orgs.:** PA LA: Rcrt. Com. (Ch., 1963–64); Conf. Site and Exhibits (Ch., 1964–68). ALA: Com. on Paperbacks for Chld. (Ch., 1968–72); Com. on Lib. Facilities (1967–68); Com. on Sel. of Outstan. Sch. Admin. (1968–69). Cath. LA. AECT. Bus. and Prof. Womens Org.: Pres. (1953–55, 1957–58); Dist. Dir. (1959–61). Booksellers of Philadelphia. Booksellers of New York City. Lib. PR of Grt. Philadelphia: VP (1970–71); Pres. (1971–72). **Honors:** Dept. of HEW, Outstan. Contrib. Cmnty., 1976; Phi Delta Kappa, Outstan. Contrib. to Educ., 1977. **Pubns.:** *Aids to Media Selection for Students and Teachers* (1979); "Reference Skills" workbk. (1979); "Library Skills" workbk. (1976, 1979); "Fiscal Management in the Academic Library: Challenge and Opportunity," *Cath. Lib. World* (1979); various articles. **Activities:** 17; 24, 26; 50, 63, 93 **Addr.:** Office of Libraries and Learning Resources, 400 Maryland Ave. S.W., Rm. 3125–B (ROB–3), Washington, DC 20202.

Simmons, Joseph M. (Ap. 6, 1921, Fairfield, CT) Dir., Lib./Info. Ctr., Towers, Perrin, Forster and Crosby, 1969–; Instr., Rosary Coll., 1964–69; Libn., *Chicago Sun-Times*, 1960–69; Lib. Spec., Lib. Bur., 1954–60. **Educ.:** Georgetown Univ., 1945–47, BSFS (Econ.); Columbia Univ., 1951–52, MLS. **Orgs.:** SLA: Chap. Liaison Ofcr. (1967–69); IL Chap. (Pres., 1964–65). ASIS. Amer. Compensation Assn. Assn. of Info. Mgrs. Admin. Mgt. Socty. **Honors:** West. MI Univ., John Cotton Dana Lectr., O. 1965. **Activities:** 12; 17; 59, 76 **Addr.:** Towers, Perrin, Forster & Crosby, Inc., 600 3rd Ave., New York, NY 10016.

Simmons, Robert M. (O. 2, 1941, Providence, RI) Curric. Libn., Bridgewater State Coll., 1971–; Documn. Libn., RI Coll., 1967–71. **Educ.:** Univ. of RI, 1960–64, BA (Eng.), 1965–66, MA (Eng.), 1968–73, MLS. **Orgs.:** ALA: IFRT. NLA: Cert. Stan. Com. (1976–). MA LA: Int. Frdm. Com. (1979–). New Eng. LA. Natl. Educ. Assn. **Pubns.:** *A Library User's Guide to ERIC* (1980); *Organizing and Servicing a Collection of Standardized Tests: a Manual for Librarians* (1980); "Finding That Government Document," *RQ* (Win. 1972); "Handling Changes in Superintendent of Documents Classification," *Lib. Resrcs. and Tech. Srvs.* (Spring 1971); *State Minimum Competency Testing: a Survey* (1980); Other articles. **Activities:** 1; 21, 31, 33; 57, 63, 74 **Addr.:** Bridgewater State College, Bridgewater, MA 02324.

Simmons, Sharon Phelps (D. 1, 1940, Clinton, IL) Libn., Media Spec., Clinton HS, 1964–; Libn., Clinton Jr. HS, 1962–64. **Educ.:** IL State Univ., 1958–62, BSEd (Eng., Lib.), 1970–73, MSEd (Info. Sci.). **Orgs.:** Vespasian Warner Pub. Lib.: Bd. of Dirs. (1969–); Secy. (1970–74); Pres. (1974–76); various coms. E. Ctrl. IL AV Assn.: Pres. (1973–75). IL AECT: State Secy. (1978–80); Leadership Conf., Resrc. Person (1975), Jr. Co-Ch. (1976), Sr. Co-Ch. (1977); Leadership Dev. Com. (Ch., 1977–78, 1980–82). Rolling Prairie Lib. Syst.: Bd. of Dirs. (1972–79); Pres. (1977–79); Dir.-Sel. Com. (Ch., 1978); various coms. various orgs. Natl. Educ. Assn. Amer. Bus. Women's Assn.: Woman-of-the-Year Awd. Com. IL Educ. Assn. Clinton Educ. Assn. **Honors:** Phi Delta Kappa, 1980; IL AV Assn., Pres. Awd., 1978. **Pubns.:** Various articles. **Activities:** 9, 10; 32, 47, 48; 63, 74, 85 **Addr.:** P.O. Box 64, Clinton, IL 61727.

Simon, Bradley Alden (Mr. 9, 1929, Meriden, CT) City Libn., Chula Vista Pub. Lib., 1978–; City Libn., Newport Beach Pub. Lib., 1977–78; Lib. Bldg. Consult., City Libn., Pomona Pub. Lib., 1971–77; Lib. Dir., Scottsdale Pub. Lib., 1966–71. **Educ.:** South. CT State Coll., 1947–51, BS (Educ.); FL State Univ., 1954–55, MSLS. **Orgs.:** ALA: PLA (Dir., 1974–78). Pub. Lib. Film Circuit of South. CA: VP (1974–75), Pres. (1975–76). AZ State LA: Pub. Lib. Div. (Pres., 1969–70). Pub. Lib. Execs. of South. CA: Secy.–Treas. (1974); Pres. (1975). Rotary Club: Nsltr. Ed. **Honors:** John Cotton Dana Pubns. Awd., 1973–74, Grand Prize, 1975. **Pubns.:** "Whats That?" *AZ Libn.* (Win., 1969); "Southwestern Flavor for Scottsdale," *Lib. Jnl.* (D. 1969); various other articles. **Activities:** 9, 13; 17, 19, 24; 74, 75, 93 **Addr.:** P.O. Box 1843, Chula Vista, CA 92012.

Simon, Jeffrey Jonathan (Jl. 16, 1951, Lackawanna, NY) Info. Systs. Spec., Bell Telephone Labs., 1980–; Lib. Syst. Anal. II, OCLC, Inc., 1978–80; Coord./Prog. Mgr., Cattaragus Cnty. BOCES (Olean, NY), 1976–78; Outreach Coord., Olean Public Library, 1975–76. **Educ.:** Empire State Coll., 1976, BS (Educ.); Syracuse Univ., 1977–78, MLS. **Orgs.:** ASIS. Cattaraugus Cnty. Coop. Ext. Assn.: Human Resrc. Com. (1977). **Honors:** ASIS, Prof. Leadership Dev. Conf., 1979. **Activities:** 6; 34, 46, 49-Syst. anal. and design; 56 **Addr.:** Bell Telephone Laboratories, Rm. 6A–315, 600 Mountain Ave., Murray Hill, NJ 07974.

Simon, Marie-Louise (Jl. 11, 1930, Port-Au-Prince, Haiti) Head Libn., St. Laurent Mncpl. Lib., 1980–; Asst. Head Libn., R.J.P. Dawson Lib., 1978–79, Fr. Libn., 1974–79. **Educ.:** Univ. de Montréal, 1951–54, B (Ped. Fam.); Northwest. Univ., 1956–57, MA (Sp.); Univ. de Montréal, 1972–74, MLS. **Orgs.:** PQ LA: Pres. (1980–81). Can. LA: Cnclr. (1980–81). Corp. des Bibtcrs. du PQ: Rcrt. Com. (1979–). SLA. Concordia Univ. Adv. Bd. of Lib. Std. Conf. des Dirs. des Bibs. Pub. de L'Ile de Montreal: VP. **Pubns.:** "Un Budget de $1000 Pour une Collection de Disques," *Biblio Contact* (Win. 1979); "En Marge du Plan Quinquenal," *ABQ/PQ LA Bltn.* (S.–D. 1979). **Activities:** 9; 17, 26 **Addr.:** 2830 Marcel, St. Laurent, PQ H4R 1B1 Canada.

Simon, Matthew J. (Mr. 9, 1948, Indianapolis, IN) Assoc. Prof., Chief Libn., Queens Coll., City Univ. New York, 1980–; Lehman Libn., Columbia Univ., 1977–80, Chem. Libn., 1976–77; Head, Evening and Weekend Srv. Div., Hunter Coll. Lib., 1974–76; Gvt. Docum. Libn., Kean Coll., 1973–74; Asst. Libn. for Econ. and Pol. Sci., IN Univ., 1972–73, Econ. and Pol. Sci. Catlgr., 1971–73. **Educ.:** IN Univ., 1970, BA (Pol. Sci.), 1973, MLS, 1975, MA (Pol. Sci.); Columbia Univ., 1978–80, (Acct.). **Orgs.:** ALA: LAMA, Mid. Mgt. Disc. Grp.; ASCLA; LRRT. **Pubns.:** *You'll Manage: Becoming a Boss–Best Tips*, (1980); Various speeches. **Activities:** 1, 12; 17, 34, 43; 59, 92 **Addr.:** Queens College of the City University of New York, 65–30 Kissena Blvd., Flushing, NY 11367.

Simon, Patricia Beth (Je. 30, 1932, Newark, NJ) Sr. Libn., Adult Srv., New City Lib. 1973–; Libn., 1971–73. **Educ.:** Bucknell Univ., 1950–54, BA (Gen.); Columbia Univ., 1969–71, MLS. **Orgs.:** Rockland Cnty. Pub. LA: Treas. (1977–79). NY LA: RASS, Pres. (1978–79); Com. Concerns of Women (1976–78). ALA: RASD; SRRT; Task Force on Women. Unitarian Socty. Rockland Cnty.: Bd. Worship (1975–79); Nom. Com. (1980); Minstry. Rel. Com. (1980–). **Honors:** Phi Beta Kappa, 1954; Beta Phi Mu, 1971. **Activities:** 9; 15, 16, 39; 55 **Addr.:** 289 Haverstraw Rd., Suffern, NY 10901.

Simon, Ralph Charles (F. 17, 1932, New York, NY) Dir., Lrng. Resrc. Media Ctr., Prof., Michael J. Owens Tech. Coll., 1978–; Dir. of Lib., Prof., Technion, Israel Inst. of Tech., 1974–78; Assoc. Engin. Libn., Assoc. Prof., Purdue Univ. Libs., 1965–74; Libn., Lect., IBM Syst. Resrch. Inst., 1961–65; Resrchr., Univ. of HI Grad. Lib. Sch., 1964–65; Libn., Cncl. on Frgn. Rel., 1961. **Educ.:** City Coll. of New York, 1954–58, BA (Pol. Sci.); Columbia Univ., 1960–62, MS (LS); CA Cmnty. Coll. Cert., Chief Admin. Ofcr., Supvsr., Libn., 1978; ARL, Lib. Mgt. Skills Inst., 1976; Various courses, workshops. **Orgs.:** OH LA: Task Force Com. on Weeding (1979); Instr. & Use Com. ALA Coll. & Univ. Libs. Bldg. Com. Intl. Assn. of Tech. Univ. Libs.: Bd. of Dir. (1975–78). Acad. LA of OH. Israel Socty. of Spec. Libs. & Info. Ctrs.: Bd. of Auditors (1978). Other orgs. AAUP: Pres., IN Fed. (1977–78). Socty. for Gen. Syst. Resrch. Amer. Assn. for Higher Educ. Assn. for Comp. Mach. **Pubns.:** "The Audio - Visual Centre Library, Technion-Israel Institute of Technology Haifa," *IATUL Bltn.* (1977); Ed., *Haifa Bltn.* (1978); "Synthesis of IATUL Conference -Belguim," *IATUL Proc.* (1977–78); "Collective Bargaining & Higher Education," *Purdue Alum.* (D. 1972); "A Delphi Approach to a Selected Book Retirement Policy," *ERIC* (1973). **Activities:** 1, 10; 17, 41; 63, 91, 92 **Addr.:** 2704 Thoman Pl., Toledo, OH 43613.

Simon, Ralph R. (D. 9, 1950, Cleveland, OH) Congregational Libn., Archvst., Temple Emanu El, 1977–; Educ. Media Spec., Cleveland Pub. Schs., 1975–78. **Educ.:** John Carroll Univ., 1970–74, BA (Hist.); Case West. Rsv. Univ., 1974–75, MSLS, 1978–, Doct. Cand. **Orgs.:** ALA. Assn. of Jewish Libs. of South. CA. AJL: Schol. Com. (Ch., 1980–). Jewish Libns. Assn. of Grt. Cleveland: Secy. (1980–). **Activities:** 12; 15, 16, 17; 90 **Addr.:** 2200 S. Green Rd., Cleveland, OH 44121.

Simon, Rose Anne (Je. 23, 1947, Westfield, NY) Dir. of Lib., Salem Acad. and Coll., 1979–; Coord. of Ref. and Bibl. Instr., Guilford Coll., 1975–79. **Educ.:** Univ. of Rochester, 1965–69, AB (Eng.); Univ. of VA, 1969–70, MA (Eng.); NY State Sec. Tchg. Cert., 1969–70 (Eng.); Univ. of Rochester,

Special Subjects/Services: 50. Adult educ.; 51. Advert./Mktg.; 52. Aerosp.; 53. Agric.; 54. Area std.; 55. Arts/Hum.; 56. Autom.; 57. Bibl./Prtg.; 58. Bio. sci.; 59. Bus./Fin.; 60. Chem.; 61. Copyrt.; 62. Documtn.; 63. Educ.; 64. Engin.; 65. Env.; 66. Eth. grps.; 67. Film; 68. Food/Nutr.; 69. Geneal.; 70. Geo.; 71. Geol.; 72. Handcpd.; 73. Hist.; 74. Int. frdm.; 75. Info. sci.; 76. Insr.; 77. Law; 78. Legis.; 79. Math./Comp. sci.; 80. Med.; 81. Metals; 82. Nat. resrcs.; 83. Newsp.; 84. Nuc. sci.; 85. Oral hist.; 86. Petr./Energy; 87. Pharm.; 88. Phys./Astr./Math.; 89. Readg.; 90. Relig.; 91. Sci./Tech.; 92. Soc. sci.; 93. Telecom.; 94. Transp.; 95. (other).

1970–77, PhD (Eng.); Univ. of NC (Chapel Hill), 1977–78, MS (LS). **Orgs.:** ALA. NC LA. **Honors:** Phi Beta Kappa, 1969; Beta Phi Mu, 1979; Cncl. on Lib. Resrc., Lib. Srv. Enhancement Prog. Grant Proj. Libn., 1977. **Activities:** 1; 17, 31; 55 **Addr.:** Gramley Library, Salem College, Winston-Salem, NC 27108.

Simon, Vaughn L. (Ag. 21, 1938, Menomonie, WI) Chief of Prcs., Enoch Pratt Free Lib., 1976–; Chief of Prcs., Dartmouth Coll., 1968–76; Libn., Cowles Fndn., 1966–68. **Educ.:** Univ. of MN 1961–63, BA (Russ.); South. CT St. Coll., 1966–68, MS (LS); Johns Hopkins Univ., 1977–81, MAS (Admin.). **Orgs.:** ALA. MD LA: Mem. Com. (1977–79). Potomac Tech. Prcs. Libn. **Activities:** 9; 17, 46 **Addr.:** 610 Jasper St., Baltimore, MD 21201.

Simone, M. Janet (My. 2, 1944, Pittsburgh, PA) Prof., Kutztown State Coll., 1978–; Sch. Lib. Media Spec., Churchill Sch. Dist., Pittsburgh, 1977–78, 1970–76; Elem. Tchr., Little Lake City Sch. Dist., Santa Fe Spring, CA, 1968–69; Elem. Sch. Libn., Chartiers Valley School Dist., 1966–68. **Educ.:** Clarion State Coll., 1962–66, BS (Elem. Ed., LS); Univ. of Pittsburgh, 1969–70, MLS, 1974–77, PhD (LS). **Orgs.:** ALA: AASL, Disting. Lib. Srv. Awd. (1977–78); Legis. Com. (1978–80). AALS. Berks Cnty. Sch. Libns. Assn. PA Sch. Libns. Assn.: Conf. Com. (1970–79); Ch., Legis. Com. (1979–). **Honors:** Beta Phi Mu, 1970. **Pubns.:** "Centralized Processing of Print and Non-Print Materials for Elementary School Libraries," *Lrng. and Media* (Aut. 1978). **Activities:** 11; 26, 37, 42; 75, 78, 92 **Addr.:** Kutztown State College, Library Science Department, Kutztown, PA 19530.

Simoneau, Paul-André - P.A. (Jl. 30, 1928, Thetford Mines, PQ) Regis., Mnstry. of Transp., 1979–, Head Libn., 1976–79; Lib. Coord., Mnstry. of Justice, 1973–76; Lib. Dir., Mnstry. of Comm., 1971–73. **Educ.:** Univ. Ottawa, 1968, BA, (LS), 1970, MALS; Univ. Laval, 1966, BA. **Orgs.:** Corp. des Bibtcrs. Prof. du PQ. ASTED. Socty. des Archvsts. du PQ. **Activities:** 4, 13; 17, 29, 41; 62, 78, 94 **Addr.:** 8660 Ave. Hautevue, Charlesbourg, PQ G1G 5A6 Canada.

Simonis, James J. (D. 5, 1941, Toledo, OH) Dir. of Libs., Mansfield State Coll., 1967–, Circ. Libn., 1966–67; AV Libn. I, Brooklyn Pub. Lib., 1965–66. **Educ.:** Findlay Coll., 1959–63, AB (Hist.); Pratt Inst., 1963–65, MLS, magna cum laude. **Orgs.:** ALA: ACRL. Cncl. of PA State Coll. and Univ. Lib. Dirs.: Stan. Com. on Interlib. Coop. and Resrc. Sharing (Ch. 1974–76, 1979–, Secy., 1976–78). Susquehanna Lib. Coop.: Ch. (1973); Stan. Com. on Dev. (Ch., 1974–). Amer. Cvl. Liberties Un. **Honors:** Beta Phi Mu. **Activities:** 1; 17; 56, 74, 75 **Addr.:** Box 44, Mansfield, PA 16933.

Simons, Wendell W. (N. 10, 1928, Independence, MO) Libn., Judson Baptist Coll., 1980–; Assoc. Univ. Libn., Univ. CA, Santa Cruz, 1973–80; Libn., Sum. Inst. of Ling., (Papua New Guinea), 1972; Asst. Univ. Libn., Univ. CA, Santa Cruz, 1963–71; Asst. Libn., Srv., Univ. CA, Santa Barbara 1954–63. **Educ.:** Univ. CA, Berkeley, 1945–49, AB (Art); 1953–54, BLS; Fuller Theo. Semy., 1974–80, MA (Theo.). **Orgs.:** ALA: ACRL, AV Com. (1967–69); LAD, Com. Phys. Facilities (1968–69), Equip. Com. (1966–69). Fuller Theo. Semy.: San Francisco Bay Area Ext., Strg. Com. (1978–80). **Pubns.:** *A Slide Classification System for the Organization and Automatic Indexing of Interdisciplinary Collections of Slides and Pictures* (1970); "The Spiritual Clairvoyance of a Late Renaissance Man," *Christ. Today* (O. 1979); "Automated Indexing for a Classified 2x2 Slide Collection," *LARC Reports* (Je. 1969); "Choosing Audio-Visual Equipment," *Lib. Trends* (Ap. 1965). **Activities:** 1; 17, 19, 24; 55, 90 **Addr.:** Judson Baptist College Library, 9201 N.E. Fremont, Portland, OR 97220.

Simonton, Wesley (Je. 22, 1921, Cincinnati, OH) Dir., Lib. Sch., Univ. of MN, 1974–, Prof., Assoc., Asst. Prof., 1956–74, Chief Cat. Libn., Lib., 1949–56. **Educ.:** Univ. of Cincinnati, 1937–41, AB (Eng.); Columbia Univ., 1946, BSLS, 1948, MSLS; Univ. of IL, 1960, PhD (LS). **Orgs.:** ALA: RTSD (Pres., 1965–67). AALS: Secy.-Treas. (1960–64). ASIS. MN LA. AAUP. **Pubns.:** Jt. auth., *AACR 2 and the Catalog: Theory—Structure—Changes* (1981); Jt. Ed., *Information Retrieval with Special Reference to the Biomedical Sciences* (1966); "AACR 2: Antecedents, Assumptions, Implementation," *Advances in Librarianship* (1980); "An Introduction to ACCR 2," *Lib. Resrcs. & Tech. Srvs.* (Sum. 1979); "Serial Cataloging Problems: Rules of Entry and Definition of Title," *Lib. Resrcs. & Tech. Srvs.* (Fall 1975); various articles. **Activities:** 11; 20, 26; 56, 75 **Addr.:** Library School, University of Minnesota, 419 Walter Library, 117 Pleasant St. S.E., Minneapolis, MN 55455.

Simpkins, Alice G. (Mr. 5, 1916, Fishersville, VA) Pub. Srvs. Libn., Mary Baldwin Coll., 1962–; Circ. Libn., Wilson Mem. HS, 1961–62; Libn., U.S. Nvl. Hosp., 1944–45; Asst. Libn., Actg. Libn., Staunton Pub. Lib. 1941–44; Libn, C. H. Frnd. HS, 1939–41; Libn., Powhatan HS, 1938–39. **Educ.:** Mary Baldwin Coll., 1933–37, BA (Eng.); Simmons Coll. 1937–38, BS (LS). **Orgs.:** ALA. VA LA. Augusta Cnty. Hist. Assn. Hist. Staunton Fndn. Delta Kappa Gamma: Resrch. Com. (1980–81). Frnds. of the Augusta Cnty. Lib. Lib. Assocs.: Martha S. Grafton Lib.–Mary Baldwin Coll. **Activities:** 1; 31, 39 **Addr.:** P.O. Box 309, Fishersville, VA 22939.

Simpkins, Irwin F. (Ap. 18, 1924, New York, NY) Dir., Lib. Srv., Dekalb Cmnty. Coll.–S. Campus, 1979–, Ref. Libn., 1972–79; Ref. Libn., Emory Univ., 1961–72; Ref. Libn., Flint Pub. Lib., 1958–61. **Educ.:** Univ. of MO, 1948–51, AB (Eng.); Univ. of MI, 1957–58, MALS. **Orgs.:** ALA. GA LA: Coll. and Univ. Sect. (Ch., 1973–74). Metro-Atlanta Lib.: VP (1966–67). **Honors:** Phi Beta Kappa; Sigma Xi; Beta Phi Mu. **Pubns.:** "Selective Dissemination of Information," *Coll. & Resrch. Lib.* (Ja. 1967); "The National Collection, Its Growth," *The Acad. Lib.* (1974). **Activities:** 1; 15, 17, 39 **Addr.:** 1243 Briarwood Dr. N.E., Atlanta, GA 30306.

Simpkins, Marjory Grace (N. 24, 1933, Hamilton, OH) Ed., Un. Cat. of the Atlanta-Athens Area, 1972–; Ref. Libn., Atlanta Pub. Lib., 1960–61; Pub. Srvs. Libn., Flint Coll. of the Univ. of MI, 1958–59; Slide Catlgr., Sch. of Archit. & Design, Univ. of MI, 1957–58; Asst., Msc. Dept., St. Louis Pub. Lib., 1956–57; Ref. Asst., Art & Msc., Cincinnati Pub. Lib., 1955–56. **Educ.:** Capital Univ., 1950–51; Miami Univ., 1951–54, BA (Eng.); Columbia Univ., 1954–55, MS (LS). **Orgs.:** GA LA: Ch., Nom Com. of Spec. Lib. Sect. (1979). Metro. Atlanta LA. SLA: S. Atl. Chap. **Pubns.:** "Pioneer in Cooperation: The Union Catalog of the Atlanta Athens Area," *GA Libn.* (My. 1978). **Activities:** 14-Interlib. Coop.; 17, 34, 36; 75 **Addr.:** Union Catalog of the Atlanta- Athens Area, Candler Library Bldg.; Emory University, Atlanta, GA 30322.

Simpson, Barbara (Ap. 6, 1947, Cleveland, OH) Dir., Lrng. Resrcs., Cuyahoga Cmnty. Coll., 1977–; Dir., Lib., 1976–77, Libn., 1972–76. **Educ.:** OH State Univ., 1964–68, BS (Educ.); Kent State Univ., 1968–71, MLS; Inst. for Educ. Mgt., 1968, Cert. **Orgs.:** ALA. OH Educ. Media Assn. AECT. Acad. LA of OH. Other orgs. Assn. of Women Deans. Amer. Assn. of Cmnty. and Jr. Coll. Amer. Assn. of Higher Educ. Assn. for Supvsn. and Curric. **Pubns.:** *Evaluating Nonprint Material* (1971); *Teaching Techniques and Methods for the Culturally Deprived* (1968); "Evaluating Media," *Booklist* (Ja. 1979); "Media Centers," *Probe* (Mr. 1969); Contrib., *Managing Multimedia Libraries* (1975). **Activities:** 1; 17; 50, 63, 93 **Addr.:** Cuyahoga Community College, 4250 Richmond Rd., Warrensville Twp., OH 44122.

Simpson, Charles W. (Mr. 17, 1940, Colorado Springs, CO) Cat. Libn., Univ. of IL, Chicago Circle, 1980–; Asst. Msc. Libn. for Tech. Srvs., Northwestern Univ., 1974–80, Msc. Catlgr., 1972–73; Libn., Msc. Dept., Chicago Pub. Lib., 1969–72. **Educ.:** Univ. of Denver, 1962–66, BM (Msc.), 1968–69, MA (Libnshp.); Northwestern Univ. 1970–76, (Msc. hist., lit.). **Orgs.:** ALA: RTSD. Intl. Assn. of Msc. Libs. Assn. for Recorded Snd. Col.: Del. to ALA Com. on Cat.: Descr. and Access; Ch., Bibl. Access to Snd. Rec. Com. (1977–); Second VP (1975–77). Msc. LA: Bd. of Dir. (1981–); Autom. Com. (1978–81); Co-Ch., MARC Format Subcom. (1980–81); Midwest Chap., Ch., Cat. Com. (1978–80); Other Coms. Amer. Musicological Socty. **Activities:** 1, 12; 17, 20, 46; 55 **Addr.:** 8517 Kimball Ave., Skokie, IL 60076.

Simpson, Donald Bruce (D. 13, 1942, Ithaca, NY) Dir., The Ctr. for Resrch. Libs., Inc., 1980–; Exec. Dir., Bibl. Ctr. for Resrch., 1975–80; Head, Cat. Ctr., State Lib. of OH, 1971–75; Asst. Libn., Keuka Coll., 1970–71. **Educ.:** Corning Cmnty. Coll., 1961–62, AA (Gen. Hum.); Alfred Univ., 1962–64, BA (Eng. Lit.); Syracuse Univ., 1969–70, MS (LS); 1971–74, (Pub. Admin.). **Orgs.:** Assn. of State Lib. Agencies: Pres. (1977–78). ALA: Cnclr. at Lg. (1979–). Cncl. for Comp. Lib. Netwks.: Legis. Com. (Ch., 1979–80). OCLC, Inc. Users Cncl.: Del. (1978–80); VP (1979–80). Various other orgs. Satellite Netwk. Adv. Bd. Telefac. Netwk. Adv. Bd. **Honors:** Beta Phi Mu, 1970. **Pubns.:** "Association of State Library Agencies," *ALA Yrbk.* (1978); *BCR, A High Growth, Multi-Program, Library Services Network* (1976); "Bibliographic Processing Centgrs," *ALA Yrbk.* (1978); "The National Library and Information Science Network: A View from the Bottom," *Jnl. of Lib. Autom.* (D. 1977); jt. auth., *Networking for On-Line Information Retrieval Services–METRO Information Retrieval Network* (1976); various articles, chaps., rpts. **Activities:** 1; 14-Coop. Netwk.; 17, 24, 34; 56, 78, 93 **Addr.:** 2603 S. Balsam St., Lakewood, CO 80227.

Simpson, Imogene (N. 7, 1927, Louisville, KY) Prof., Lib. Sci., West. KY Univ., 1962–, Ref. Libn., 1960–62; Libn., Hillwood HS, 1959–60; Libn., Ocala Jr. HS, 1955–59 Tchr., Ft. McCoy HS, 1954–55; Tchr., Bartow HS, 1953–54; Tchr., Franklin-Simpson HS, 1950–53. **Educ.:** West. KY Univ., 1945–51, AB (Eng.); George Peabody Coll., 1956–61, MA (LS), 1971–73, (Educ. Spec., LS). **Orgs.:** ALA. SELA. KY LA. AAUW. **Honors:** AAUW, Flwshp. Name Grant, 1980. **Pubns.:** "A Survey: The Influence of Censorship...," *Southeast. Libn.* (S. 1974); "Will Today's Fiction Literature for Young People Last?" *KY LA Bltn.* (S. 1977); "Chained Libraries," *KY LA Bltn.* (S. 1979). **Activities:** 11; 26 **Addr.:** Library Media Education, Helm Library, Western Kentucky University, Bowling Green, KY 42101.

Simpson, Mildred W. (Mr. 15, 1939, Bethlehem, PA) Libn., Photography Col., Atl. Richfield Co., 1978–; Libn., Acad. of Motion Pic. Arts and Sci., 1968–78, Asst. Libn., 1964–68; Asst. Circ. Libn., Univ. of South. CA, 1962–64. **Educ.:** Univ. of DE, 1959–60, BA (Fr.); Univ. of South. CA, 1960–62, MSLS. **Orgs.:** Socty. of CA Archvsts.: Cncl. (1976–78); VP (1979–80). SLA: South. CA Chap. (Cmnty. Rel. Dir., 1977–78). ALA. **Honors:** Beta Phi Mu, 1962; Phi Kappa Phi, 1960. **Pubns.:** Ed. adv. bd., *American Film Institute Catalog* (1971–); adv. com., *A Union Catalogue of Manuscript and Special Collections* (1977). **Activities:** 32, 36; 67, 82, 86 **Addr.:** Atlantic Richfield Co., Rm. 16103, 515 S. Flower St., Los Angeles, CA 90071.

Simpson, Rolly L., Jr. (Ja. 30, 1945, Atlanta, GA) Head, Prod. Info. Sect., Tech. Info. Dept., Burroughs Wellcome Co., 1973–; Readers Srv. Libn., GA Inst. of Tech., 1970–72, Asst. Resrch. Sci., 1970–70. **Educ.:** Oglethorpe Univ., 1966–69, BS (Bio.); Emory Univ., 1969–70, MLn, (LS); Univ. of TN Med. Units, 1972–73, (Cert. Sci., LS) **Orgs.:** SLA: NC Chap., Treas. (1978–). ASIS: NC Chap., Treas. (1979–80). NC OLUG. **Activities:** 12; 30; 80, 87 **Addr.:** Burroughs Wellcome Co., 3030 Cornwallis Rd., Research Triangle Park, NC 27709.

Sims, Martha J. (O. 29, 1946, Portsmouth, VA) Lib. Dir., VA Beach Pub. Lib., 1976–, Asst. Lib. Dir., 1974–76, Branch Libn., 1971–74; Art, Msc. Libn., Richmond Pub. Lib., 1969–71. **Educ.:** Mary Baldwin Coll., 1964–68, BA (Eng.); Univ. of NC, 1968–69, MS (LS); Old Dominion Univ., 1975–79, MA (Pub. Admin.). **Orgs.:** VA LA: Secy. (1977–78); Legis. Com. (1979–). SE LA: Mem. Com. (1978–). ALA. VA Beach Arts Ctr.: Bd. (1972–); Treas. (1974–76). *New VA Review* Adv. Bd. (1979–). **Activities:** 9; 17, 28, 34; 55, 59, 78 **Addr.:** Virginia Beach Public Library, Operation's Bldg., Municipal Center, Virginia Beach, VA 23456.

Sims, Oscar L. (Je. 23, 1925, Uniontown, PA) Soc. Sci. Biblgphr., Univ. of CA, Los Angeles, 1970–. **Educ.:** Howard Univ., 1946–49, BS (Psy.); Univ. of CA, Los Angeles, 1969–70, MLS; Fisk Univ. Inst. on Building Col. of Black Lit., 1971; Fisk Univ., Internship in Black Std. Libnshp., 1973, Cert. **Orgs.:** ALA: Black Caucus. CA Libns. Black Caucus. Assn. for the Std. of Afro Amer. Life and Hist. **Activities:** 1; 15; 66, 92 **Addr.:** 1531 Corinth Ave., Apt. "A", West Los Angeles, CA 90025.

Sims, Phillip W. (Jl. 16, 1925, Fort Smith, AR) Msc. Libn., Assoc. Prof. of Msc. Bibl., Southwest. Bapt. Theo. Semy., 1967–; Minister of Msc., First Baptist Church, Helena, AR, 1959–61; Minister of Msc. & Asst. Pastor, Arcadia Baptist Church, Dallas, TX, 1955–59; Minister of Msc., Church of the Air, Inc., Billings, MT, 1954–55. **Educ.:** Ouachita Bapt. Univ., 1946–50, BA (Voice); Southwest. Bapt. Theo. Semy., 1950–53, BSM (Voice), 1955–56, MSM (Voice), 1961–70, DMA (Church Msc.); N. TX State Univ., 1970–73, MLS. **Orgs.:** Alpha Lambda Sigma. Msc. LA: TX Chap., Long Range Proj. Com. (1974–75); Ch., Nom. & Mem. Com. (1978–79). Church Msc. Conf., South. Bapt. Conv. **Pubns.:** Jt. auth., "Psalters in the Maurice Frost Collection at Southwestern," *The Hymn*, (Ap. 1979); "Hymnology in the New Grove Dictionary of Music and Musicians, 1980 Edition," *The Hymn* (Jl. 1981). **Activities:** 1, 12; 15, 17, 24; 55, 90 **Addr.:** Southwestern Baptist Theological Seminary, P.O. Box 22,000, Fort Worth, TX 76122.

Sinclair, Dorothy (My. 24, 1913, Baltimore, MD) Prof. Emeritus, Sch. of LS, Case West. Resrv. Univ., 1980–; Prof. of LS, 1965–80; Coord., Adult Srvs., Enoch Pratt Free Lib., 1961–65; Prin. Libn. Field Srvs., CA State Lib., 1955–60; Asst. Coord., Adult Srvs., Enoch Pratt Free Lib., 1950–55, Head, Hist., Travel, Biog. Dept., 1943–50. **Educ.:** Goucher Coll., 1929–33, AB (Eng.); Columbia Univ., 1942, BS (LS); Johns Hopkins Univ., 1950, MA (Medvl. Hist.); Case West. Resrv. Univ., 1970, PhD (LS). **Orgs.:** ALA: Cncl. (1950–53, 1960–67); Budget Asm. (1974–); PLA, Pres. (1974–76); Ref. Srvs. Div., Pres (1966–67); Bd. of Dir. (1967–67); other coms. OH LA: Com. on Lib. Educ. (1979–). Adult Educ. Cncl. of Grt. Cleveland. **Pubns.:** *Administration of the Small Public Library* (1965, 1979); "Growth Patterns of Public Libraries," in *Toward a Theory of Librarianship*, (1973); "The Education of Tomorrow's Public Librarian," in *Toward the Improvement of Library Education* (1973); "Services Offered Within the Library" in *Local Public Library Administration* (1981); "Materials to Meet Special Needs," *Lib. Trends* (Jl. 1968); Other books, articles, reviews. **Activities:** 9, 11; 16, 24, 34 **Addr.:** 3960 Elmwood Rd., Cleveland Heights, OH 44121.

Sineath, Timothy W. (My. 21, 1940, Jacksonville, FL) Dean, Prof., Coll. of LS, Univ. of KY, 1977–; Assoc. Prof. & Dir. of Doc. Std., Simmons Coll., 1975–77, Asst. Prof., 1970–75; Acad. Coord of Ext. in LS, Univ. of IL, 1966–68; Cat. Libn., Univ. of GA, 1964–66, Ref. Libn., 1963–64. **Educ.:** FL State Univ., 1958–62, BA (Hist.), 1962–63, MS (LS); Univ. of IL, 1966–70, PhD. **Orgs.:** ALA: Resrch. Com. (1975–77); LRRT, Vice/Ch., (1974–75); Ch. (1975–76); Lib. Educ. Div., Pubns. Com. (1968–72); Resrch. Com. (1971–75). ASIS: Ch., Spec. Events 1975 Anl. Conf. Com. Beta Phi Mu: Beta Beta Chap., Secy., Treas. (1973–74). Episcopal Diocese of MA: Org. Dev. Consult. (1974–77). **Pubns.:** Contrib. Auth., *Library Education Statistics* (1980–); Various articles. **Activities:** 1, 11; 17, 24, 26 **Addr.:** Univ. of Kentucky, College of Library Science, 459 P.O.T., Lexington, KY 40506.

PROFESSIONAL ACTIVITIES: Institutions: 1. Acad. lib.; 2. Arch.; 3. Assn.; 4. Fed./Gvt. lib.; 5. Inst. lib.; 6. Mfr./Suppl.; 7. Milit. lib.; 8. Musm.; 9. Pub. lib.; 10. Sch. lib.; 11. Sch. of lib. sci.; 12. Spec. lib.; 13. State lib.; 14. (other). **Functions/Activities:** 15. Acq./Col. dev.; 16. Adult srvs.; 17. Admin.; 18. Apprais.; 19. Archit./Bldgs.; 20. Cat./Class.; 21. Chld. srvs.; 22. Circ.; 23. Cons./Pres.; 24. Consult.; 25. Cont. ed.; 26. Educ. lib. sci.; 27. Ext. srvs.; 28. Fund/Grants; 29. Gvt. pubs.; 30. Indx./Abs.; 31. Instr. lib. use; 32. Media srvs.; 33. Micro.; 34. Netwks./Coop.; 35. Persnl.; 36. PR; 37. Publshg.; 38. Recs. mgt.; 39. Ref. srvs.; 40. Repro.; 41. Resrch.; 42. Review.; 43. Secur.; 44. Serials; 45. Spec. col.; 46. Tech. srvs.; 47. Trustees/Bds.; 48. YA srvs.; 49. (other).

Singer, Blanche Ladenson (Ja. 17, 1926, Chicago, IL) Libn., Docum. Delivery, ILL, Hlth. Sci. Lib., Univ. of WI, 1979–; Libn., Ref., ILL, 1968–79, Libn., 1967–68. **Educ.:** Univ. of IL, 1943–47, AB (Fr., Psy.); Univ. of WI, 1964–67, MA (LS). **Orgs.:** Med. LA: Midwest Reg. Grp. **Activities:** 1, 12; 34, 39; 58, 80, 91 **Addr.:** Health Sciences Library, University of Wisconsin, 1305 Linden Dr., Madison, WI 53706.

Singer, Carol A. (Mr. 13, 1953, Tarentum, PA) Gvt. Docum. Coord., Wayne State Coll., 1981–, Ref. Srvs. Coord., 1980–81, Info. Resrcs. Libn., 1979–80. **Educ.:** Bowling Green State Univ., 1971–75, BA (Fr.); IN Univ., 1978–79, MLS. **Orgs.:** ALA: ACRL; GODORT. **Pubns.:** "Easy Promotion of Government Documents", *Pub. Docum. Highlights* (O. 1980); "Major Monographic Literature on Government Documents," *Gvt. Pubns. Review* (1980, 1981); Doing Research with United States Government Documents in the U.S. Conn Library, ERIC; "Federal Information Centers," *Gvt. Pubns. Review* (1982). **Activities:** 1; 29, 31, 39 **Addr.:** Box 17, WSC, Wayne, NE 68787.

Singer, Philip (F. 2, 1947, Toronto, ON) Libn. Supvsr., N. York Pub. Lib., 1980–; Gen. Libn., 1971–80. **Educ.:** Univ. of Guelph, 1966–70, BA (Eng., Econ., Pol. Std.); Univ. of West. ON, 1970–71, MLS. **Orgs.:** ON LA. Can. LA. **Activities:** 9, 12; 16, 29, 39 **Addr.:** 35 Canyon Ave. #912, Downsview, ON M3H 4Y2 Canada.

Singer, Susan Arnett (Je. 1, 1929, Philadelphia, PA) Pres., Info. Assoc., Ltd., 1979–; Branch Mgr., Tucson Pub. Lib., 1975–79; Instr., Univ. of AZ GSLS, 1978; Head, Ctrl. Ref. Srv., Morris Cnty. Free Lib., 1968–75; Libn., Lyons Vets. Admin. Hosp., 1966–68. **Educ.:** Univ. of Rochester, 1947–51, AB (Applied Econ.); Rutgers Univ., 1965–67, MLS; Univ. of AZ, 1976–, (Mgt.). **Orgs.:** AZ LA: Ch., Pub. Lib. Div. Stan. Com. (1978–); Secy.-Treas., Pub. Lib. Div. (1978–79). NJ LA: Ch., Nom. Com. Ref. Sect. (1973). Assoc. Info. Mgrs. ALA. Tucson Bus. & Prof. Women. Prof. Allies of Tucson. Metro. Tucson Cham. of Cmrc. **Pubns.:** *Union List of Periodicals, Morris County, NJ* (1975). **Activities:** 14-Info. Brokerage; 17, 39, 41; 59, 75, 77 **Addr.:** 92 West End Ave., North Plainsfield, NJ 07060.

Singh, Jaswant (Mr.) (My. 5, 1932, Jagraon, Punjab, India) Dir., Reg. Educ. Media Ctr., Cooper Country Intermediate Sch. Dist., 1975–; Head Libn., Ontonagon Area Schs., 1971–75; Sr. Soc. Std. Tchr., Brooks Sch. Dist., AB, Canada 1966–67; Sr. Soc. Std. Tchr., AV Mtrls. Supvsr., Red Deer Roman Cath. Sch. Dist., AB, Can., 1967–70; Sr. Soc. Std. Tchr., Brooks Sch. Dist., 1966–67; Air-Photo Interpreter, Dept. of Geo., Univ. of AB, 1965–66; Tchr., Bonnyville Sch. Div., 1964–65; Lectr., Geo., Malwa Coll. of Educ., Ludhiana, India, 1961–63; Map Interpreter, Cmplr., Natl. Atlas of India, 1960–61; various positions in tchg., 1953–59, 1963. **Educ.:** Panjab Univ., Solan, India, 1949–53, BSc hons. (Geo.); Calcutta Univ., India, 1957–60, MSc (Geo.); Univ. of AB, 1964–68, MA (Geo.); West. MI Univ., 1970–71, MSL (LS); various grad. crs. **Orgs.:** ALA. Indian LA. AECT. MI Intermediate Media Assn.: Eval. Com. for the MI's Reg. Educ. Media Ctrs. (Ch., 1978–); Pres. (1980–81). MI Assn. of Sch. Libs.: U.P. Branch (1972–73). Indian Adult Educ. Assn. MI Assn. for Media in Educ. **Honors:** Phi Delta Kappa, 1968. **Activities:** 10; 15, 17, 24; 67, 72 **Addr.:** Regional Educational Media Center 1, 600 Hecla St., Hancock, MI 49930.

Singleton, Christine M. (Mr. 30, 1932, Liverpool, Eng.) Resrch. Libn., New York Univ. Med. Ctr., Inst. Env. Med., 1972–; Info. Sci., Untd. Glass Ltd., 1965–67; Tech. Abstctr./Srchr., Imperial Chem. Indus. Ltd., 1956–63; Asst. Info. Ofcr., Untd. Kingdom Atomic Energy Authrty. Indus. Grps., 1954–56. **Educ.:** Univ. of Liverpool, 1950–53, BSc (Chem./Phys.); Cert. in Libnshp., Untd. Kingdom, 1963. **Orgs.:** SLA: Secy./Treas., Hudson Valley Chap. (1979–81). Hlth. Info. Libs. of Westchester (Treas., 1981–). Med. LA. Lib. Assn. (London). Inst. of Info. Sci. (UK). **Activities:** 1, 12; 15, 17, 20; 65, 80, 91 **Addr.:** Institute of Environmental Medicine Library, New York University Medical Center, Long Meadow Rd., Tuxedo, NY 10987.

Sink, Robert E. (Ap. 14, 1944, Waco, TX) Sr. Archvst., Brooklyn Rediscovery, 1979–, Asst. Archvst., 1978–79. **Educ.:** Rutgers Univ., 1962–66, BA (Hist.); City Coll. of New York, 1977, MA (Amer. Hist.); Pratt Inst., 1974–77, MA (LS); Natl. Arch., 1980, Cert. (Arch. Admin.). **Orgs.:** SAA. Mid-Atl. Reg. Arch. Conf.: Strg. Com. (1980–). Archvsts. RT of New York City: Prog. Com. (1979–). Org. of Amer. Histns. Amer. Assn. for State and Lcl. Hist. **Pubns.:** *A Guide to Brooklyn Manuscripts in the Long Island Historical Society* (1980); "The Photographic Collections of the Consulate General of Israel," *Picturescope* (Fall/Win. 1975); "Oral Memoir of Richard S. Childs" audio tape (1975); "Affirmative Action at Pratt" videotape (1975); Reviews. **Activities:** 2; 38, 41, 45; 73, 92 **Addr.:** 37 1/2 St. Marks Pl., New York, NY 10003.

Sink, Thomas R. (Mr. 28, 1950, Roanoke, VA) Dir. of Lib. & AV, Mercy Hosp., Toledo, OH, 1981–; Serials Libn., Med. Coll. of OH at Toledo, 1976–81, Ref. Libn., 1974–76. **Educ.:** VA Cmwlth. Univ., 1968–72, BS (Premed.); Univ. of MI, 1973–74, AMLS; Med. LA, 1975, Cert. **Orgs.:** Med. LA: ILL and Resrc. Sharing Stan. and Prac. Com. (1981–); Midwest Chap. Acad. LA of OH: Exec. Bd. (1976–78). Hlth Sci. Libns. of Northwest. OH: Pres. (1976–78); Ch., Prog. Com. (1978–80). Hlth. Sci. OCLC Users Grp.: Ch., Ad Hoc Com. on Un. List of Serials (1980–1981). OHIONET: Ch., Serials Cntrl. Cncl. (1978–80). Other orgs. **Pubns.:** *Health Science Librarians of Northwestern Ohio Union List of Serials* (1977). **Activities:** 12; 17, 32, 39; 58, 80 **Addr.:** E. L. Burns Health Sciences Library, Mercy Hospital, 2200 Jefferson Ave., Toledo, OH 43624.

Sinnott, Gertrude M. (Mr. 15, 1919, Brooklyn, NY) Ref. Libn., U.S. Geol. Srvy., Lib., 1978–; Ref. Libn., Rider Coll., 1968–78. **Educ.:** Radcliffe Coll., 1937–41, BA (Geol.); Rutgers Univ., 1965–68, MLS. **Orgs.:** SLA. Geosci. Info. Socty: Arch. Com. (1980–81). **Honors:** Beta Phi Mu, 1968. **Activities:** 1, 4; 15, 39; 70, 82 **Addr.:** U.S. Geological Survey Library, National Center, Mail Stop 950, Reston, VA 22092.

Sintz, Edward F. (F. 6, 1924, New Trentin, IN) Dir., Miami-Dade Pub. Lib. Syst., 1968–; Assoc. Dir., St. Louis Pub. Lib., 1966–68; Asst. Dir., Kansas City Pub. Lib., 1964–66, Head, Various Dept., 1954–64. **Educ.:** Univ. of KS, 1949–50, BA (Eng.), 1953–54, MA (LS); Univ. of MO, 1963–65, MS (Pub. Admin.). **Orgs.:** ALA: Const. & Bylaws Com. (1968–70). MO LA: Ed., *MO Lib. Qtly.* (1956–58). FL LA: Legis. & Plng. Com. (1970–74); Pres. (1976). SELA: Site Sel. Com. (1974–78). **Activities:** 9; 17, 24, 25, 35, 47; 50 **Addr.:** Miami-Dade Public Library, One Biscayne Blvd., Miami, FL 33132.

Sipe, Lynn F. (N. 4, 1942, Denver, CO) Head Libn., Von KleinSmid Lib., Univ. of South. CA, Los Angeles, 1968–, Head, Bibl. Srch. Sect., 1966–68. **Educ.:** Amer. Univ., 1960–64, BA (Intl. Rel.); Columbia Univ., 1964–66, MLS; Univ. of South. CA, Los Angeles, 1968–74, MPA. **Orgs.:** ALA: ACRL; Gvt. Docums. RT. SLA: South. CA Chap.: Calendar Coord. (1978–79); Archvst. (1979–80). Natl. Gay Arch.: Bd. of Dirs. **Pubns.:** Cmplr., *Classification System for the National Gay Archives* (1980); cmplr., *International and Public Affairs Index* (1974–); cmplr., *An Annotated Directory of Abstracts, Indexes and Continuing Bibliographies Relevant to Public Administration* (1981); *The Western Sahara; A Comprehensive Bibliography* (forthcoming). **Activities:** 1, 12; 15, 30, 39; 54, 92 **Addr.:** Von KleinSmid Library, University of Southern California, University Park, Los Angeles, CA 90007.

Sipkov, Ivan (O. 24, 1917, Sofia, Bulgaria) Chief, European Law Div., Law Lib., Lib. of Congs., 1980–, Asst. Chief 1969–80, Sr. Legal Spec., 1963–69, Legal Spec., 1952–63; US Dept. of State, 1952. **Educ.:** Univ. Law Sch., Sofia, Bulgaria, 1936–40, LLB (Law); Univ. Law Sch., Berlin, Germany, 1941–43, MA (Law); Univ. Law Sch., Innsbruck, Austria, 1945–47, DJ (Law); George Washington Univ., 1952–55, MCL (Law). **Orgs.:** Law Libns. Socty. AALL: Com. on Indx. to Frgn. Legal Per. (1961–). Intl. Assn. Law Libs.: Secy.–Treas. (1967–71); Sec. VP (1980–83); *Intl. Jnl. of Law Libs.* (Ed.–in–Chief). Amer. Socty. of Intl. Law: Com. on the Lib. (1969–). **Pubns.:** *Legal Sources and Bibliography of Bulgaria* (1956); *The Costumes of France in the Library of Congress* (1977); "Postwar Nationalizations and Alien Property in Bulgaria," *Amer. Jnl. of Intl. Law* (1958); "Settlement of Dual Nationality in European Communist Countries," *Amer. Jnl. of Intl. Law* (1962); *The Civil Aviation Law of Bulgaria* (1976); various monos., articles. **Activities:** 4, 12; 29, 41; 77 **Addr.:** 4917 Butterworth Pl., N. W., Washington, DC 20016.

Sirkin, Arlene Farber (My. 30, 1949, Boston, MA) Requirements Ofcr., US Army AV Ctr., 1980–, Chief, Still Photo Lib., 1979–80; Nonprint Libn., Univ. of MD, 1976–79; Dir., Lib. Media Ctr., Rye Country Day Sch., 1974–75. **Educ.:** Simmons Coll., 1967–71, AB (Educ.); Columbia Univ., 1973–74, MS (Lib.); New Sch. for Soc. Resrch., 1974–76, MA (Media). **Orgs.:** ALA: LITA/Vid. and Cable Comm. Sect. (Vice-ch., Ch., 1980–82), Prog. Plng. Com. (1979–83). SLA: Washington Pic. Grp. (Vice-ch., Ch., 1980–82). **Pubns.:** Jt. ed., *Serial Automation* (1981); *Video and Cable Programming* (forthcoming); "Academic Libraries Struggle to Provide Video Services," *Amer. Libs.* (O. 1980); "Cable TV: Channels of Information," *Amer. Libs.* (My. 1980); Ed. Bd., *Jnl. of Lib. Autom.* (1979–83); various articles. **Activities:** 2, 4; 32; 67 **Addr.:** 108 9th St., S.E., Washington, DC 20003.

Sirois, Dorothy (Ja. 25, 1926, Detroit, MI) Med. Libn., Montreal Chld. Hosp., 1969–; Dir., Gvt. Pubns., Bib. Natl., 1967–69; Ref. Libn., Intl. Cvl. Aviation Org., 1956–67. **Educ.:** Marianopolis Coll., 1942–46, BA; McGill Univ., 1969–71, BLS. **Orgs.:** Med. LA. Can. Hlth. Libs. Assn. ASTED. **Addr.:** Montreal Children's Hospital Medical Library, 2300 Tupper St., Montreal, PQ H3H 1P3, Canada.

Sirois, France Boutin (F. 28, 1914, Bienville, PQ) Dir., Cat., Barreau de PQ, 1980–; Archvst., Ville de PQ, 1970–79. **Educ.:** Univ. Laval, 1967–70, licn. és lettres. **Orgs.:** Assn. of Can. Archvsts.: Coll. and Univ. Arch. Com. Assn. des Archvsts. du PQ. **Activities:** 2, 15-PQ Bar; 20; 77 **Addr.:** 1194, rue Colbert #406, Ste-Foy, PQ G1V 3Y8 Canada.

Sirskyj, Wasyl (F. 12, 1921, Sokoliwka, Ukraine) Head Catlgr., Wilfrid Laurier Univ. Lib., 1972–; Slavic Spec., Univ. of Waterloo, 1962–72. **Educ.:** Univ. of Toronto, 1961, BA (Russ. Philology), 1963, BLS; Univ. of Waterloo, 1967, MA (Russ. Philology); Ukrainian Free Univ., Munich, 1971, PhD (Russ., Ukrainian Philology). **Orgs.:** Can. LA. Can. Assn. of Slavists. Ukrainian Hist. Assn. **Pubns.:** "Ideological Overtones in Gopol's Taras Bulba," *Ukrainian Qtly.* (Fall 1979); various articles. **Addr.:** 336 Batavia Pl., Waterloo, ON N2L 3W2 Canada.

Sissenwine–Zaleski, Ilene Z. (S. 26, 1946, Worcester, MA) Assoc. Ed., Oceanographic Lit. Review, 1977–; Libn., Univ. of RI Lib., 1973–75, Asst. Circ. Libn., 1972–73; Sci. Tchr., Narragansett Jr. HS, 1970; HS Bio. Tchr., Northampton Sch. for Girls, 1969–70; Pk. Ranger Naturalist, Cape Cod Natl. Seashore, 1968–69. **Educ.:** Univ. of MA, 1964–68, BS cum laude (Zlgy.); Univ. of RI, 1971–73, MLS, 1968–70, 1973–74, (Oceanography, Marine affairs); MA Maritime Acad., 1976, (AV Educ.). **Orgs.:** ALA. MA LA. Intl. Assn. of Marine Sci. Libns. and Info. Ctrs. New Eng. Estuarine Resrch. Socty. **Honors:** RI State Empl. Incentive Awd., 1973. **Pubns.:** Abs., Oceanographic Lit. Review (1979–); Reviews. **Activities:** 6; 30, 37, 42; 58, 91, 95-Oceanography. **Addr.:** 46 Miami Ave., Falmouth, MA 02540.

Sistrunk, James Dudley (Ag. 13, 1919, Jayess, MS) Dir., Lib. Srvs., Campbell Univ., 1964–; Admin. Libn., Southeast. Bapt. Theo. Semy., 1959–64, Circ. Libn., 1957–59. **Educ.:** Baylor Univ., 1952–54, BA (Relig., Greek); Southwest. Bapt. Theo. Semy., 1954–57, BD (Relig. & Greek), Masters of Divinity, 1978; N. TX State Univ., 1957–59, BSLS; Univ. of NC, 1959–64, Post Grad. **Orgs.:** NC LA. SELA. NC Assn. of Indp. Coll. Cnsrtm.: Exec. Com. Sen. of Campbell Univ. **Activities:** 1, 2; 15, 17, 21; 50, 63, 90 **Addr.:** Carrie Rich Memorial Library, Box 98, Buies Creek, NC 27506.

Sites, Katherine P. (Mr. 31, 1947, Henderson, KY) Chief Libn., Quartermaster Ctr. & Ft. Lee MSA Lib., 1980–; Libn., Ft. Monroe Post Lib., VA, 1978–80; Libn., Ft. Shafter Post Lib., HI, 1975–77; Libn., Ft. Monroe Post Lib., VA, 1973–75. **Educ.:** West. KY Univ., 1965–69, BA (Eng.); Univ. of KY, 1969–70, MSLS. **Orgs.:** ALA. VA LA. AAUW. **Activities:** 4; 17, 34; 74 **Addr.:** US Army Quartermaster Center and Fort Lee, MSA Library, Bldg. P–9023, Ft. Lee, VA 23801.

Sitkin, Ann G. (Mr. 26, 1944, New York, NY) Asst. Head of Cat., Harvard Law Lib., 1981–, Catlgr., 1978–81; Catlgr., Andover-Harvard Lib., 1972–78; Catlgr., Widener Lib., 1970–71. **Educ.:** Macalester Coll., 1962–67, BA (Grmn.); Columbia Univ., 1968–69, MLS. **Orgs.:** ALA. AALL. ATLA. **Activities:** 1; 20 **Addr.:** Harvard Law School Library, Technical Services, Langdell Hall, Cambridge, MA 02138.

Sitter, Clara M. L. (Je. 28, 1941, Watonga, OK) Media Spec., Harrison HS, Colorado Springs, CO, 1973–; Libn., St. Mary's HS, 1971–73; Assoc. Dir. of Libs., Amarillo Coll., 1968–71; Catlgr., W. TX State Univ., 1967–68; Actg. Libn., Univ. of TX Rare Books Lib., 1966, Catlgr., 1965. **Educ.:** Univ. of OK, 1959–62, BA (Amer. Std.); Univ. of TX, 1962–66, MLS; Univ. of CO, 1971–, PhD in progress (Educ.); Univ. of Denver, Cert. in Adv. Std., 1981 (Info. Mgmt.). **Orgs.:** CO LA. CO Educ. Media Assn. ALA. AAUW. **Activities:** 1, 10; 15, 17, 48; 63 **Addr.:** 5030 W. Rowland Ave., Littleton, CO 80123.

Sitzman, Glenn L. (Ag. 23, 1920, Corn, OK) Serials Catlgr., Clarion State Coll., 1974–, Assoc. Libn., 1969–73; Chief Libn., Univ. of Guyana, 1967–68; Deputy/Actg. Libn., Makerere Univ., Uganda, 1966–67; Ref. Libn., Natl. Lib. of Nigeria, 1963–65; Asst. Head Catlgr., Univ. of PR, 1961–63; Catlgr., Columbia Univ., 1955–60, Lectr., Part-time, Sch. of LS, 1959–60. **Educ.:** OK Bapt. Univ., 1942, BA (Eng.); Baylor Univ., 1945–47, MA (Eng.); Columbia Univ., 1954–56, MS (LS). **Orgs.:** ALA. PA LA. Nigerian LA. E. African LA. **Pubns.:** "Uganda's University Library," *Coll. & Resrch. Libs.* (My. 1968). **Activities:** 20, 39, 44 **Addr.:** P. O. Box 507, Clarion, PA 16214.

Sivak, Marie Rose (S. 24, 1935, Chicago, IL) State Sch. Lib. Media Supvsr., IL State Bd. of Educ., 1974–; Lib. Coord. K-12, Kentwood (MI) Schs., 1973–74; Lib. Dir. K-12, River Valley Schs., Three Oaks, MI, 1964–74; Eng. Dept. Head/Libn., Three Oaks Schs., 1959–64; Tchr./Libn., Bloomingdale Schs., 1957–59. **Educ.:** West. MI Univ., 1953–57, BA (Educ.), 1958–62, MA (Eng.), 1969–72, SpA (Libnshp.); Various courses, Educ. Admin. **Orgs.:** ALA: AASL, By Laws Com. (1978–81). Springfield (IL) Lib. Club: Pres. (1978); VP (1977). Lib. Book Sel. Srv.: Ch. of Bd. (1979–80). Alpha Delta Kappa. **Pubns.:** "State of the Art - School Library/Media Development in Illinois," *IL Libs.* (Je. 1976); "Suggested Program for Library/Media Technical Assistants," *Career Educ. Jnl.* (Ap. 1976); "Many Hats of Max & Marian" slide program (1979); "Instructional Boards for the Classroom Teacher," *Readgs. in Lrng. Resrc.* (1980). **Activities:** 17, 24; 63, 89 **Addr.:** Illinois State Board of Education, 100 N. First St., Springfield, IL 62777.

Sive, Mary Robinson (Ag. 9, 1928, Berlin, Germany) Dir., INFORMEDIA, Ed., MEDIA MONITOR, 1977; Free-lnc. wrtg., 1973–; Dir., Sch. & Lib. Dept., Env. Info. Ctr., 1972–73; Consult., Westchester BOCES, 1972; Sch. libn., S. Orangetown, Clarkstown, 1964–69. **Educ.:** CT Coll., 1948, BA (Amer. Hist., Pol. Sci.); Columbia Univ. 1948–49, (Pub. Law); Rutgers Univ., 1962, MLS; New York Univ., 1968–69, (Educ. Admin.). **Orgs.:** Curric. Adv. Srv.: Adv. Bd. (1979–). Amer. Film Fest.: Juror

Special Subjects/Services: 50. Adult educ.; 51. Advert./Mktg.; 52. Aerosp.; 53. Agric.; 54. Area std.; 55. Arts/Hum.; 56. Autom.; 57. Bibl./Prtg.; 58. Bio. sci.; 59. Bus./Fin.; 60. Chem.; 61. Copyrt.; 62. Documtn.; 63. Educ.; 64. Engin.; 65. Env.; 66. Eth. grps.; 67. Film; 68. Food/Nutr.; 69. Geneal.; 70. Geo.; 71. Geol.; 72. Handcpd.; 73. Hist.; 74. Int. frdm.; 75. Info. sci.; 76. Insr.; 77. Law; 78. Legis.; 79. Math./Comp. sci.; 80. Med.; 81. Metals; 82. Nat. resrcs.; 83. Newsp.; 84. Nuc. sci.; 85. Oral hist.; 86. Petr./Energy; 87. Pharm.; 88. Phys./Astr./Math.; 89. Readg.; 90. Relig.; 91. Sci./Tech.; 92. Soc. sci.; 93. Telecom.; 94. Transp.; 95. (other).

(1977–). Adirondack Mt. Club. Ramapo Orienteering Club. NY-NJ Trails Conf. Frnds. of the Earth. Other orgs. **Pubns.:** *Educators Guide to Media Lists* (1975); *Environmental Legislation* (1976); *Selecting Instructional Media* (1978); Clmn., *Curric. Review* (1978–); Various articles; reviews. **Activities:** 14-info. srv.; 24, 37, 41; 63, 95-curric. subj., instr. mtrls. **Addr.:** P.O. Box 7130, Ardsley-on-Hudson, NY 10503.

Sivigny, Robert J. (Mr. 17, 1945, Meriden, CT) Libn., Melodyland Sch. of Theo., 1980–, Ref. Libn., 1978–79; Catlgr., Charles River Assoc., 1978. **Educ.:** Barrington Coll., 1963–67, BA (Gen. Lang.); Gordon-Conwell Theo. Semy., 1967–70, MDiv; Simmons Coll., 1975–77, MLS. **Orgs.:** ATLA. Christ. Libn. Assn. Orange Cnty. LA. Laubach Litcy. Assoc. **Activities:** 1, 5; 20, 41, 46; 66, 89, 90 **Addr.:** P.O. Box 8686, Anaheim, CA 92802.

Sizemore, William Christian (Je. 19, 1938, South Boston, VA) Dean, Prof., S. GA Coll., 1971–, Libn., Assoc. Prof., 1966–71; Assoc. Libn., Southeast. Bapt. Theo. Semy., 1964–66. **Educ.:** Univ. of Richmond, 1956–60, BA (Eng.); Southeast. Bapt. Theo. Semy., 1960–63, BD (Hist.); Univ. of NC, 1963–64, MSLS; FL State Univ., 1970–71, Adv. MSLS, 1971–73, PhD (Educ. Admin.). **Orgs.:** ALA: ACRL, Pubns. Com. (1969–71). SELA: Ref. Srvs. Div. Nom. Com. (1968–69). GA LA: Gvt. Rel. Com. (1969–71); Educ. for Libnshp. Sect., Vice-ch. (1971–73); Natl. Lib. Week Exec. Com. (1968). S. GA Assoc. Libs.: Secy. (1966–67). Amer. Assn. for Higher Educ. Natl. Cncl. on Lrng. Natl. Cncl. of Instr. Admin. South. Assn. of Coll. and Schs. **Honors:** Beta Phi Mu, 1963. **Pubns.:** *Resources of South Carolina Libraries* (1976); Ed., *Serial Holdings of South Georgia Associated Libraries* (1971); "Experimental College Programs and Implications for Library Service," *Southeast. Libn.* (1972); "A Revision of 'Baptist' Entries in the Library of Congress and Pettee's Subject Heading Lists," *ATLA Nsltr.* (1965). **Activities:** 1; 17, 24, 34; 56, 63, 78 **Addr.:** 212 Red Bird Trail, Douglas, GA 31533.

Skallerup, Harry R. (Mr. 20, 1927, Chicago, IL) Dir. of Libs., FL Atl. Univ., 1977–; Assoc. Libn., US Nvl. Acad., 1967–77; Head Cat. Dept.; Engin. Libn., Univ. of IA, 1962–67; Asst. Mgr., Walter J. Johnson, Inc., Antiquarian Books, 1959–62; Chief Sci. Div., South. IL Univ., 1955–59; Physics Libn., Univ. of IL, 1954–55. **Educ.:** Univ. of IL, 1948–52, BS (Bot.); Washington Univ., 1952–53, AM (Bot.); Univ. of MN, 1953–54, MA (LS). **Orgs.:** ALA: ACRL. FL LA. Beta Phi Mu: Treas. (1955–56). SELA. Bibl. Socty. of Amer. Nautical Resrch. Guild. Steamship Hist. Socty. of Amer. **Honors:** Sigma Xi. **Pubns.:** *Books Afloat & Ashore;* (1974); Various articles. **Activities:** 1; 17, 37, 45; 57, 73, 91 **Addr.:** University Library, Florida Atlantic University, Boca Raton, FL 33431.

Skanse, Ruth Thompson (Jy. 16, 1923, Round Prairie, MN) Cat. Libn., Downers Grove Cmnty. HS N, 1970–; Church Libn., Evangel Bapt. Church, Wheaton, IL, 1967–; Head Libn., Wheaton Acad., 1967–70, Instr. (Eng.), 1965–67; Instr. (Eng.), Grade Ch., Richfield, (MN) HS, 1962–65; Asst. Dir., Hosp. Lib., The Mayo Clinic 1960–62. **Educ.:** Wheaton Coll., 1945–48, AB (Eng.); Rosary Coll., 1966–69, MALS; Northwest. Bible Sch. 1941–45, Dipl., Cert. **Orgs.:** IL LA. DuPage LA. Evangelical Church LA: Intl. Pres. (1975–). Natl. Educ. Assn. IL Educ. Assn. Downer's Grove Educ. Assn. **Pubns.:** "Church Library Series," *Libns. World* (forthcoming); Reviews. **Activities:** 10, 12; 20, 42, 47; 57, 63, 90 **Addr.:** 425 East Oak Ave., Wheaton, IL 60187.

Skarr, Robert John (My. 13, 1941, Washington, DC) Libn., Jack Faucett Assocs., 1975–; Asst. Head, Circ. Srvs.; Univ. of MD, Undergrad. Lib., 1973–75; Libn., Transp. Inst., 1970–73. **Educ.:** Univ. of MD, 1959–63, BA (Eng.), 1967–68, MA (Amer. Std.), 1969–70, MLS. **Orgs.:** SLA. Metro. WA Lib. Cncl. Assoc. Info. Mgrs. Natl. Acad. of Sci.: Transp. Resrch. Bd. **Honors:** Beta Phi Mu, 1970. **Activities:** 1, 12; 17, 39, 41; 59, 86, 94 **Addr.:** 3744 Patuxent Manor Rd., Davidsonville, MD 21035.

Skeith, Mary Elizabeth (New Dayton, AB) Asst. Libn., Prsnl., Queen's Univ. (ON), 1978–, Head, Cat. Div., 1966–78; Head, Tech. Srvs., Univ. of Calgary, 1960–66; Catlgr., McGill Univ., 1958–60; Genl. Libn., Univ. of West. ON, 1955–58; Libn., *Lethbridge Herald* (AB), 1950–54. **Educ.:** Queen's Univ., 1946–50, BA (Hist.); McGill Univ., 1954–55, BLS; 1968, MLS; Bryn Mawr, Summer Inst. for Women in Higher Educ. Admin., 1978. **Orgs.:** Can. LA. ALA: LAMA; LITA; RTSD. **Activities:** 1; 20, 35, 46; 92 **Addr.:** Douglas Library, Queen's University, Kingston, ON K7L 5C4 Canada.

Skerrett, Claire Marie (Ap. 27, 1946, Boston, MA) Dir., Cabrini Coll. Lib., 1981–; Coord., of Chld. Srvs., Lower Merion LA, 1976–81; Branch Libn., Free Lib. of Philadelphia, 1973–76; Asst. Dir., Limestone Coll., 1971–73; Ref. Libn., Bridgewater (MA) Pub. Lib., 1969–71. **Educ.:** Boston Univ., 1964–69, BA (Soclgy.); Simmons Coll., 1969–71, MS (LS). **Orgs.:** ALA: ACRL; ALSC, Newbery-Caldecott Alternatives (1980). PA LA: Awds. Com. (1977). Main Line Libns.: Nsltr. Com. (1980–81). **Honors:** Beta Phi Mu. **Activities:** 1, 9; 15, 17, 21 **Addr.:** 24 Mary Watersford Rd., Bala Cynwyd, PA 19004.

Skerritt, Elizabeth (Ja. 20, 1932, New York City, NY) Head Libn., NY HQ, Corporate Info. Ctr., Intl. Paper Co., 1977–; Head Libn. and Indx. Mgr., Amer. Banker, 1973–75; Regis. Libn., E.V. Thaw, 1972–73. **Educ.:** Smith Coll., 1950–54, BA (Gvt.); Columbia Univ., 1965, MA (Art Hist.), 1973, MLS. **Orgs.:** SLA: Musms., Arts, and Hum. Ch., (1977–78); Newsp. Grp. (Ch., 1974–75); Bicent. Com. (Ch., 1976). Info. Mgt. Com. Columbia Univ. Grad. Fac. Alum. Com.: Dir.; Prog. Com. (1976–78). Columbia Univ. Alum. Fed. Com.: Com. on Qual. of Student Life; Lib. Com. (1978). various other orgs. **Pubns.:** *Subject Guide to Sources in New York City and Environs on the American Revolutionary Period* (1976); ed., *1974 Annual to American Banker Index* (1974). **Activities:** 12; 15, 17, 41; 55, 59, 93 **Addr.:** International Paper Co., Corporate Information Center 1910, 220 E. 42nd St., New York City, NY 10017.

Skidmore, Carolyn B. (My. 20, 1942, WV) Coord. of Libs. & Lrng. Resrcs., WV Dept. of Educ., 1971–; Media Spec., Carver Career and Tech. Ctr., 1970–71; Media Supvsr., Mason Cnty. Bd. of Educ., 1968–70; Elem. Tchr., Greenbrier Cnty. Bd. of Educ., 1964–68. **Educ.:** Fairmont State Coll., 1962–64, BA (Elem Educ.); WV Univ., 1964–66, MA (AV Educ.); VA Polytech. Inst. and State Univ., 1974–, (Cmnty. Coll. Admin.); Supvsrs. cert., 1968–70, Other courses. **Orgs.:** AECT: Pres. (1979–80); Secy. Treas. (1974–77); Ch., Cncl. Strg. Com. (1973). WV Educ. Media Assn.: Pres. (1976–78). WV LA: Bd. of Dir. (1976–) ALA: AASL. Alpha Delta Kappa. Amer. Socty. for Trng. and Dev. **Honors:** Region V, AECT, Edgar Dale Awd., 1975. **Activities:** 10, 14-State Dept of Educ.; 17, 24, 25, 32; 63 **Addr.:** WV Department of Education, Room B 346, 1900 Washington St., Charleston, WV 25305.

Skillin, Glenn B. (Ag. 8, 1931, Worcester, MA) Libn. II, Free Lib. of Philadelphia, 1975–; Dir., War Lib. and Musm. of the Loyal Legion of the U.S., 1975; Asst. Libn., The Balch Inst., 1972–75; Asst. Libn., St. Francis Coll. Lib., 1970–72; Asst. Dir., George Arents Resrch. Lib., Syracuse Univ., 1969–70, Lectr., Sch. of LS, 1970, Assoc. Cur. of Mss. Spec. Cols., 1968–69; Dir. and Libn., ME Hist. Socty., 1965–68. **Educ.:** Univ. of VT, 1959, BA (Eng., Hist.); Columbia Univ., 1959–60, MS (LS). **Orgs.:** SAA. Philobiblon Clb. Colonial Socty. of MA. Appalachian Mt. Clb. Green Mt. Club. **Pubns.:** Ed., *ME Hist. Socty. Nsltr.,* (My. 1966–Ag. 1968), reviews. **Activities:** 1, 12; 15, 39, 45; 55, 57, 66 **Addr.:** Northeast Regional Library, Cottman & Oakland Sts., Philadelphia, PA 19149.

Skinner, Aubrey E. (Mr. 19, 1928, Vernon, TX) Chem. Libn., Univ. of TX, Austin, 1951–. **Educ.:** Kilgore Jr. Coll., 1945–47, AA; N. TX State Coll., 1948–51, BA (LS); Univ. of TX, Austin, 1975–77, MLS. **Orgs.:** ALA. TX LA. SLA. SWLA. TX State Hist. Socty. **Pubns.:** *The Rowena Country* (1973); Ed., *Reminiscences of a Texas Ranger* (1967); "The Academic Departmental Library - Is It Special," *Special Libnshp.: A New Reader* (1980); "Wilson, Halsey William," *ALA World Ency. of Lib. and Info. Srvs.* (1980); Reviews and other articles. **Activities:** 1; 15, 17, 39; 58, 60, 68 **Addr.:** John W. Mallet Chemistry Library, University of Texas, Austin, TX 78712.

Skinner, Robert Gordon (Ja. 9, 1948, Austin, TX) Msc. and Fine Arts Libn., South. Meth. Univ., 1979–; Recorded Sound Libn., Harvard Univ., 1977–79. **Educ.:** N. TX State Univ., 1974, BA (Msc.), 1977, MLS. **Orgs.:** Assn. for Recorded Sound Arch. Intl. Assn. of Msc. Libs. Msc. LA: Rep. to ALA AACR 2 Preconf. (1979); TX Chap., Organizational Com. (1974). Amer. Musicological Socty. **Honors:** Beta Phi Mu, 1977; Pi Kappa Lambda. **Pubns.:** Jt. cmplr., *A checklist of Texas composers* (1980); "A Randall Thompson Discography," *ARSC Jnl.* (1980); "A Selective Guide to Dealers and Distributors Specializing in Foreign Sound Recordings," *Notes of the MLA* (D. 1978); Other articles, reviews. **Activities:** 1; 15, 17; 55 **Addr.:** Music Library OAC, Southern Methodist University, Dallas, TX 75275.

Skinner, Vicki F. (N. 29, 1948, Lebanon, MO) Popular Lib. Supvsr., Libn. III, Austin Pub. Lib., 1979–, Prints, Rec., Chld. Srvs. Supvsr., Libn. III, 1977–79, Prints, Recs. Supvsr., Libn. II, 1974–77. **Educ.:** N. TX State Univ., 1966–70, BM (Msc.); 1971–73, MLS; TX State Univ., 1979– (Pub. Admin.). **Orgs.:** Msc. LA: Lcl. Arrange. Com. (1980); TX Chap. (Secy., 1978–79), Proj. Com. (Ch., 1976–80). ALA. TX LA: Arts. RT (Secy.-Treas., 1976–77). Autom. Lib. Info. Exch.: Mem. at Large (1979–80). **Honors:** Beta Phi Mu. **Pubns.:** Ed., *Union List of Music Periodicals* (Msc. LA: TX Chap.) (1978). **Activities:** 9; 17, 22, 39; 55 **Addr.:** Austin Public Library, P.O. Box 2287, Austin, TX 78768.

Skipsna, Alvin (Ja. 20, 1925, Riga, Latvia) Prof. & Ch., Lib. Dept., Skidmore Coll., 1969–, Head, Tech. Srvs., 1961–69; Sr. Catlgr., New York Pub. Lib., 1956–61. **Educ.:** Friedrich-Alexander Univ., Erlangen, 1946–48, (Law, Philology); City Coll. of New York, 1952–54, BA (Eng.); Columbia Univ., 1955–56, MS (LS). **Orgs.:** Capital Dist. Lib. Cncl.: Bd. of Trustees, Pres. (1972–74). NY LA: Coll. & Univ. Lib. Sect., Pres. (1977–78). ALA: ACRL. AAUP: Pres., Skidmore Coll. Chap. (1967–68). Pali Text Socty. **Honors:** Phi Beta Kappa; Beta Phi Mu; Grolier Socty., Highest Acad. Achvmt. **Pubns.:** Jt. auth., "Title II-A Bargain At the Price: A Symposium," *Jnl. of Acad. Libnshp.* (S. 1979); "The Role of Academic Libraries in the 3-R's Systems," *Bookmark* (Spr. 1979). **Activities:** 1; 15, 17, 34; 54, 55, 92 **Addr.:** Skidmore College Library, Saratoga Springs, NY 12866.

Skirrow, Helena (Mrs.) (O. 15, 1925, Neerlandia, AB) Coord. of Lib. Srvs., AB Dept of Educ., 1970. **Educ.:** Calvin Coll., 1947–50, BA (Educ.); Univ. of AB, 1969–70, BLS; Univ. of BC, 1977–78, MLS; Tchg. Cert., AB. **Orgs.:** Can. Lib. Trustee Assn.: Secy. (1979–80). Can. Sch. LA: Ch., Handbook Com. (1972–74). Edmonton LA: VP (1972). LA of AB: Cnclr. (1975–77). Phi Delta Kappan. Delta Kappa Gamma Socty. Intl.: Prov. Pres. (1979–81). **Activities:** 4; 17, 20, 47; 63, 72 **Addr.:** Alberta Education Library, 7120-95 Ave., Edmonton, AB T6B 1B2 Canada.

Sklar, Hinda F. (Mr. 9, 1946, Philadelphia, PA) Head, Tech. Srvs., Loeb Lib., Grad. Sch. of Dsgn., Harvard Univ., 1979–, Catlgr., 1975–79; Lib. Asst. (Intern), Houghton Lib., Harvard Univ., 1972–75, Asst. to the Cur., Thea. Col., 1970–72. **Educ.:** IN Univ., 1964–68, BA (Thea. Eng.); Simmons Coll., 1972–74, MS (LS); grad. crs. at various univs. **Orgs.:** ALA. ARLIS/NA. **Honors:** Beta Phi Mu. **Pubns.:** "Buildings for Books and Books for Building" exhibit cat. (1976). **Activities:** 1, 17, 20; 46; 55 **Addr.:** Frances Loeb Library, Graduate School of Design, Harvard University, Cambridge, MA 02138.

Skolnik, Herman (Mr. 22, 1914, Harrisburg, PA) Consult., 1980–; Mgr., Tech. Info. Div., Hercules Inc., 1952–80, Supvsr., Lit. Resrch., 1946–51, Resrch. Chem., 1942–45. **Educ.:** PA State Univ., 1933–37, BS (Chem. Engin); Univ. of PA, 1939–42, PhD (Org. Chem.). **Orgs.:** SLA. ASIS. Amer. Chem. Socty: Div. of Chem. Info. (Ch., 1961); DE Sect. (Ch., 1962); Ed., *Jnl. Chem. Info. Comp. Sci.* (1960–). **Honors:** Austin M. Patterson Awd. in Chem. Document., 1969; Amer. Chem. Socty., Div. of Chem. Info., Outstan. Contrib., 1976. **Pubns.:** Jt. auth., *A Century of Chemistry* (1976); Jt. auth., *Sulfur-Sulfur and Sulfies - Oxygen Five and Six-Membered Heterocycles* (1967); Various articles. **Activities:** 12; 17, 41; 56, 60, 75 **Addr.:** 402 Foulk Rd., Apt. 1A3, Wilmington, DE 19803.

Skoog, Anne C. (Ja. 21, 1917, Rochester, PA) Fine and Rare Bks. Libn., Carnegie-Mellon Univ., 1966–, Assoc. Catlgr., 1966–76, Asst. Catlgr., 1950–66; Soc. Rel. Branch Libn., Carnegie Inst. of Tech., 1946–50, Asst. Bus. Libn., 1944–46; Catlgr., Westminster Coll. Lib., 1940–44. **Educ.:** Carnegie Inst. of Tech., 1935–39, BS (Eng.), 1939–40, BS (LS). **Orgs.:** ALA: ACRL/Rare Bks. and Mss. Sect. Tri-State ACRL. PA LA: Bltn. Ed. (1957–60), Bibl. Socty. of Amer. Pittsburgh Bibliophiles. Hist. Socty. of West. PA. Pittsburgh Hist. and Landmarks Fndn. **Honors:** Phi Kappa Phi. **Pubns.:** "Fore-edge Painting," "Colophons," *Ency. of Lib. and Info. Sci.* (1971, 1973); jt. auth., "A Slide Collection Classification," *PA LA Bltn.* (Ja. 1969). **Activities:** 1; 45; 55, 57 **Addr.:** 5604 Fifth Ave., Apt. 206, Pittsburgh, PA 15232.

Skopp, Samuel Robert (F. 11, 1942, New York, NY) Tech. Srvs. Coord., Portland Pub. Schs., 1979–; Head, Tech. Srvs., Beverly Hills Pub. Lib., 1975–79, Catlgr./Ref. Libn., 1973–75. **Educ.:** CA State Univ., Long Beach, 1963–65, BA (Hist.), 1970–74, MA (Hist.); Univ. of CA, Los Angeles, 1972–73, MLS. **Orgs.:** OR Educ. Media Assn. ALA. **Activities:** 10; 17, 20, 46 **Addr.:** Portland Public Schools, Educational Media Dept., P.O. Box 3107, Portland, OR 97208.

Skrzeszewski, Stan E. (Ja. 3, 1947, Godalming, Eng.) Reg. Libn., Parkland Reg. Lib., 1975–; Branch Supvsr., Wapiti Reg. Lib., 1974–75; Chief Libn., Lincoln Pub. Lib., 1971–73. **Educ.:** Brock Univ., 1967–70, BA (Phil.); Univ. of West. ON, 1970–71, MLS. **Orgs.:** Polish-Can. Libns. Assn.: Ch. (1981–82). Inst. of Prof. Libns. of ON: Mem. Ch. (1972–73). Can. LA. SK LA: Mem. Ch. (1975–76). West. Dev. Musm. Bd.: Exec. Com. (1979–81). Yorkton Cent. Com.: Ch. (1982). **Activities:** 9; 17, 35, 47; 55, 66, 89 **Addr.:** Parkland Regional Library, 95A Broadway W., Yorkton, SK S3N 0L9 Canada.

Skuja, Lucija (N. 26, 1922, Prode, Latvia) Head, Msc., Art and Phil./Relig. Dept., Grand Rapids Pub. Lib., 1969–, Head, Ref., 1959–69, Catlgr., 1957–59. **Educ.:** Univ. Riga, Latvia, 1942–44 (Baltic Lang); Univ. Kiel, Germany, 1945–49, BA (Grmn., Phil., Art Hist.); Univ. of MI, 1954–58, AMLS. **Orgs.:** ALA: Mem. Com. ARLIS/NA: MI Chap. (Ch., 1979–). MI LA. Amer. Latvian Assn. Grand Rapids Hist. Socty. Grand Rapids Art Musm. Womens Natl. Book Assn. **Honors:** Beta Phi Mu. **Pubns.:** Ed., *Union List of Serials for Grand Rapids Area Libraries* (1976); ed., *Arts Organization Directory* (1981). **Addr.:** 1852 Crescent Dr. N.E., Grand Rapids, MI 49503.

Slack, Kenneth T. (Mr. 4, 1920, Toquerville, UT) Dir., Univ. Libs., Marshall Univ., 1972–; Assoc. Dir. of Libs., Univ. of UT, 1967–72; Asst. Libn., AZ State Univ., 1965–67; Libn., Church Coll. of HI, 1955–65; Asst. Libn., East. OR Coll., 1953–55; Libn., Smile Jr. HS, Denver, CO, 1952–53; Libn., Byers Jr. HS, Denver, CO, 1952. **Educ.:** UT State Univ., 1949, BS (Pol. Sci.); Univ. of Denver, 1952, MA (Libnshp.); Univ. of UT, 1964, EdD (Educ. Admin.). **Orgs.:** ALA: Cncl. Mem., HI (1958). HI LA: Treas. (1957–58). WV LA: Ch., Coll. & Univ. Sect. (1974). Phi Delta Kappa. UT Acad. of Sci., Arts and Letters: Exec. Secy. (1971–72). **Pubns.:** "Our Buildings Shape Us," *ALA Bltn.* (Je. 1968); "A New Library For a New College," *Coll. & Resrch.*

PROFESSIONAL ACTIVITIES: Institutions: 1. Acad. lib.; 2. Arch.; 3. Assn.; 4. Fed./Gvt. lib.; 5. Inst. lib.; 6. Mfr./Suppl.; 7. Milit. lib.; 8. Musm.; 9. Pub. lib.; 10. Sch. lib.; 11. Sch. of lib. sci.; 12. Spec. lib.; 13. State lib.; 14. (other). **Functions/Activities:** 15. Acq./Col. dev.; 16. Adult srvs.; 17. Admin.; 18. Apprais.; 19. Archit./Bldgs.; 20. Cat./Class.; 21. Chld. srvs.; 22. Circ.; 23. Cons./Pres.; 24. Consult.; 25. Cont. ed.; 26. Educ. lib. sci.; 27. Ext. srvs.; 28. Fund/Grants; 29. Gvt. pubs.; 30. Indx./Abs.; 31. Instr. lib. use; 32. Media srvs.; 33. Micro.; 34. Netwks./Coop.; 35. Persnl.; 36. PR; 37. Publshg.; 38. Recs. mgt.; 39. Ref. srvs.; 40. Repro.; 41. Resrch.; 42. Review.; 43. Secur.; 44. Serials; 45. Spec. col.; 46. Tech. srvs.; 47. Trustees/Bds.; 48. YA srvs.; 49. (other).

Libs. (N. 1960); "Wanted: A State Librarian," *HI LA Jnl.* (N. 1961); "Oasis in Arizona," *Lib. Jnl.* (D. 1966); "The Emerging Education Requirements for Academic," *Proc. of UT Acad. of Sci., Arts and Letters,* (1969); Other articles. **Activities:** 1; 17, 28, 35; 56, 75 **Addr.:** 348 Cherokee Trail, Huntington, WV 25705.

Slade, Alexander (Sandy) (My. 15, 1946, Victoria, BC) Ext. Libn., Univ. of Victoria, 1980–; Supvsr., ILL, Univ. of Waterloo, 1974–80, Ref. & Col. Dev. Libn., 1971–80. **Educ.:** Univ. of Victoria, 1964–68, BA (Soclgy.); Univ. of BC, 1970–71, BLS. **Orgs.:** Can. LA: Copyright Com. (1979–). Can. Assn. of Coll. and Univ. Libs. **Pubns.:** *A Bibliography of Works by and about Thomas S. Szasz, M.D., 1947–1975* (1976); "Cumulative Indexes to Trend Reports & Bibliographies," *Current Soclgy.* (1976); "Standardizing Spine Information on Bound Serial Volumes," *Serials Libn.* (1981). **Activities:** 1; 15, 39, 49-ILL; 61, 92 **Addr.:** McPherson Library, University of Victoria, Victoria, BC V8W 3H5 Canada.

Slaight, Wilma R. (Ja. 20, 1944, Ithaca, NY) Archvst., Wellesley Coll., 1972–; Arch. Asst., Case West. Rsv. Univ., 1971–72. **Educ.:** SUNY, Oneonta, 1962–66, BA (Soc. Std. Educ.); Case West. Rsv. Univ., 1966–68, MA (Hist.), 1968–74, PhD (Hist.). **Orgs.:** SAA: Coll. and Univ. Arch. Prof. Afnty. Grp. (1976–). New Eng. Archvsts.: Pres. (1978–79); VP (1977–78). **Activities:** 2 **Addr.:** Wellesley College Archives, Wellesley, MA 02181.

Slaney, Robert W. (Jl. 14, 1938, Chicago, IL) Dir., Lib. Srvs., Coll. of the Mainland, 1970–; Libn., Roosevelt Jr. HS, 1968–69; Libn., Sandia HS, 1967–68. **Educ.:** AZ State Univ., 1960–65, BS (Hist.); FL State Univ., 1969–70, MLS. **Orgs.:** ALA: ACRL/Cmnty. and Jr. Colls. Sect., Nom. Com. (1979). TX LA. TX Jr. Coll. Tchrs. Assn. **Pubns.:** "Book Circulation in Texas Two-Year Colleges," *TX Lib. Jnl.* (Fall 1977); "The Libraries of Galveston County," *TX Lib. Jnl.* (Mr. 1972). **Activities:** 1; 17; 56 **Addr.:** Learning Resources Center, College of the Mainland, Texas City, TX 77590.

Slater, Frank (Butler, PA) Mgr., Lib. Systs. Dev., Univ. of Pittsburgh, 1969–; Mgr., Ctrl. Srvs. and Systs., 1966–69; Mgr., Systs. and Prcs., H.I.P. Div. H.K. Porter Co., 1964–65; Syst. Anal., Tubular Prod., Div. Babcock and Wilcox Co., 1957–64. **Educ.:** Thiel Coll., 1948–52, BS (Econ.); Univ. of Pittsburgh, 1967–69, MLS. **Orgs.:** ASIS: Natl. Tres. (1980–83); Chap. Asm. Cnclr. (1974–78); Constn. and Bylaws Com. (Ch., 1978–79); Pittsburgh Chap. (Ch., 1970–71); Tech. Prog. Com., Mid. Yr. Mgt. (Ch., 1972); Lcl. Arrange., Mid. Yr. Mgt. (Ch., 1974). **Honors:** ASIS, Watson Davis Awd., 1979. **Pubns.:** Ed., *Cost Reduction for Special Libraries and Information Centers* (1973). **Activities:** 1; 17; 56, 59, 93 **Addr.:** G-33 Hillman Library, University of Pittsburgh, Pittsburgh, PA 15260.

Slater, Jack (N. 14, 1926, New York, NY) Assoc. Dir. of Libs., Drexel Univ., 1966–; Head, Acq. Dept., 1964–66; Catlgr., Elizabethtown Coll., 1962–64. **Educ.:** City Coll. of NY, 1946–50, BS (Econ.); Univ. of MI, 1960–62, MALS; Wayne State Univ., 1958–59, Tchr. Cert. **Orgs.:** ALA. **Pubns.:** Jt. auth., "Searching at the Drexel Institute of Technology Libraries," *HI LA Jnl.* (1967). **Activities:** 1; 17, 19, 46; 75 **Addr.:** Drexel University Libraries, 32nd and Chestnut Sts., Philadelphia, PA 19104.

Slavens, Thomas P. (N. 12, 1928, Cincinnati, IA) Prof., Sch. of LS, Univ. of MI, 1964–; Libn., Dvnty. Sch., Drake Univ., 1960–64; various positions as pastor, 1953–60. **Educ.:** Phillips Univ., 1948–51, AB (Bible); Un. Theo. Semy., 1952–54, MDiv (New Testament); Univ. of MN, 1960–62, AM(LS); Univ. of MI, 1963–65, PhD (LS); Univ. of Oxford, Eng., 1980 (Theo. Lib). **Orgs.:** AALS: Pres. (1972). ALA: Dartmouth Medal Com. (Ch., 1976–77); Lib. Educ. Div., Exec. Bd. (1971–72); Media Resrch. Com. (Ch., 1965–71). Fac. Assoc., Ctr. for Resrch. on Lrng. and Tchg., Univ. of MI. AAUP. **Honors:** Univ. of MI, Warner G. Rice Fac. Awd. in the Human., 1977; H. W. Wilson Fellowship, 1961. **Pubns.:** *Informational Interviews and Questions* (1978); *Library Problems in the Humanities* (1981); *The Retrieval of Information in the Social Science and the Humanities* (1981); *Sources of Information in the Humanities* (forthcoming); *The Development and Testing of CAI in the Education of Reference Librarians* (1970); various articles, bibls. **Activities:** 11; 24, 26, 41; 55, 90, 92 **Addr.:** School of Library Science, The University of Michigan, Ann Arbor, MI 48109.

Slavin, Suzy Margot (Je. 1, 1940, Cleveland, OH) Asst. Head, Ref. Dept., McLennan Lib., McGill Univ., 1971–, Ref. and ILL Libn., 1969–71; Congressional Ref. libn., Lib. of Congs., 1968–69, Chld. Lit. Catlgr., 1967–69. **Educ.:** Antioch Coll., 1959–63, BA (Hist.); West. Resrv. Univ., 1964–65, MLS. **Orgs.:** ALA: ACRL/Anthro. Sect. (Secy., 1975–77). **Pubns.:** "Excerpts From An East Asian Journal," *ARGUS* (N./D. 1976). **Activities:** 1; 17, 39; 83 **Addr.:** Reference Department, McLennan Library, McGill University, 3459 McTavish St., Montreal, PQ H3A 1Y1 Canada.

Sleep, Esther Louise (Ap. 22, 1937, Toronto, ON) Head, Serials Dept., Brock Univ. Lib., 1970–; Sci. Serials Libn., Sci. Lib., McMaster Univ., 1969–70, Serials Libn., Mill Meml. Lib., 1968–69; Catlgr., Tanganyika Lib. Srvs., Dares Salaam, Tanzania, 1965–67. **Educ.:** Univ. of Toronto, 1956–60, BA (Hist.); McMaster Dvnty. Coll., 1960–61, Dip. (Christ. Educ.); McGill Univ., 1964–65, BLS, 1967–68, MLS. **Orgs.:** Can. LA. Can. Univ. Srv.: Overseas Ch. (1972–73). **Pubns.:** "Wither the Issn? A Practical Experience," *Can. Lib. Jnl.* (Ag. 1977). **Activities:** 1, 9; 15, 20, 44 **Addr.:** Brock University Library, Decew Campus, St. Catharines, ON L2S 3A1 Canada.

Slezak, Eva (S. 3, 1946, Prague, Czechoslovakia) Afro Amer. Spec., Ref. Libn., MD Dept., Enoch Pratt Free Lib., 1977–, Ref. Libn., Hum. Dept., 1969–77. **Educ.:** West. MD Coll., 1964–68, BA (Fr.); Drexel Inst. of Tech., 1968–69, MS (LS). **Orgs.:** Amer. Socty. Indxrs. SLA. MD LA. MD Hist. Socty. MD Geneal. Socty.: Bltn. Ed. (1980–). **Pubns.:** *Of the Dawn of Freedom* (1979); "Czechs in Maryland: Before 1900," *MD Geneal. Socty. Bltn.* (Win. 1980). **Activities:** 9; 41, 45; 66, 69 **Addr.:** Enoch Pratt Free Library, 400 Cathedral St., Baltimore, MD 21201.

Slick, Myrna Hays (Ja. 13, 1932, Greensburg, PA) Libn., Johnstown Vo-Tech Sch., 1970–; Libn., Conemaugh Twp. HS, 1967–70. **Educ.:** Hood Coll., 1949–53, AB (Msc.); Univ. of Pittsburgh, 1967–69, MLS, 1974–77, PhD (LS). **Orgs.:** ALA: Amer. Vocational Assn./AASL com. (1978–80). PA LA: Ch., Mem. (1977–78); Ad hoc Dues Com. (1977–78); Nom. Com. (1978–79); Juniata-Conemaugh Chap., Pres. (1978–79). PA Sch. Libns. Assn. State Adv. Cncl. for Lib. Media Prog., PA Dept. of Educ. Natl. Educ. Assn. PA State Educ. Assn. PA Vocational Assn. **Honors:** Beta Phi Mu. **Pubns.:** "Recreational Reading Materials for Special Education Students," *ERIC* (1969); "Periodicals for a Vocational-Technical High School," *ERIC* (1974); Jt. ed., *Vocational-Technical Bibliography* (1981). **Activities:** 10; 25, 31, 39; 63, 68, 91 **Addr.:** R. D. #2, Box 226, Holsopple, PA 15935.

Slingerland, Charmaine Kinsley (Ag. 2, 1930, Albany, NY) Head Circ. Libn., Miami Univ. Lib., 1980–, Head Serials Libn., 1972–80; Per. Libn., SUNY, Albany, 1968–72. **Educ.:** Bates Coll., 1949–53, BA (Psy.); SUNY, Albany, 1968–72, MLS; Miami Univ., Exec. Dev. Prog. for Lib. Admin., 1976; Other courses. **Orgs.:** OH LA: Coord., Div. VI Staff Dev. (1979–80). Ohio Valley Grp. Tech. Srvs. Libns.: Secy. (1977). Miami Univ. Lib.: Persnl. Com., Secy. (1978–81). Natl. Fed. of Bus. & Prof. Womens Clubs. Preble Cnty. Hist. Socty. **Honors:** Natl. Fed. of Bus. & Prof. Womens Clubs, Highway Safety Prog. Awd., 1978. **Pubns.:** *King's Kuisine* (1979). **Addr.:** 2841 Camden-College Corner Rd., Camden, OH 45311.

Slingluff, Deborah H. (Ag. 12, 1950, Raleigh, NC) Agency Head, Patterson Pk. Branch, Enoch Pratt Free Lib., 1980–, Evening Libn., Univ. of MD, Hlth. Sci. Lib., 1981–; Admin. Asst., 1979–80, YA Libn., 1978–79; Head of Ref., Ctrl. NC Reg. Lib., 1977–78, Ext. Libn., Chatham Cnty., 1973–77. **Educ.:** Univ. of NC, 1970–71, AB (Eng. Educ.), 1972–73, MSLS; NC and MD, Pub. Lib. Cert. **Orgs.:** ALA. MD LA. **Activities:** 9; 16, 27, 48; 50, 89 **Addr.:** 3521 N. Calvert St., Baltimore, MD 21218.

Slivka, Enid Miller (My. 24, 1927, Buffalo, NY) Libn., R.W. Beck & Assoc., 1979–; Libn. II, Tech., 1971–78, Branch Libn., 1958–67; Seattle Pub. Lib.; 1st Asst., Hum. Div., Univ. of NE Libs., 1953–56; Libn. US Army Spec. Srv., Austria, 1950–53; Ref. Libn. I, Denver Pub. Lib., 1949–50. **Educ.:** Univ. of CO, 1944–48, BA (Fr.); Univ. of Denver, 1949–50, MALS; Univ. of Vienna, 1951–52; Univ. of WA, 1957–58. **Orgs.:** SLA: Pac. NW Chap. Pres. (1979–80); Educ. Com., Ch., (1969–70); Secy./Treas. (1970/71); Nom. Com., Ch. (1972/73); Ad Hoc Restaurant Com. (1977–79); Bltn. co-ed. (1976–79). ASIS. Pac. NW LA. WA LA. NW Chamber Orchestra. **Pubns.:** "Public Service and Cataloging at the University of Nebraska," *Lib. Resrcs. and Tech. Servs.* (Sum. 1959). **Activities:** 12; 17, 39; 56, 64, 91 **Addr.:** R.W. Beck and Associates, Tower Building, Seventh Ave. at Olive Way, Seattle, WA 98101.

Sloan, Andrew James, Jr. (Jl. 18, 1923, Preston Cnty., WV) Retired, 1981–; Dir., Warsaw Cmnty. Pub. Lib., 1956–81; Dir., Portland-Jay Cnty. Pub. Lib., 1955–56; Head, Gvt. Sect., MI State Lib., 1952–55; Ref. Libn., MI State Lib., 1950–52. **Educ.:** Miami Univ., 1942, 1946–48, AB (Eng.); West. Rsv. Univ., 1949–50, MS (LS); IN, Libn. I Cert. **Orgs.:** ALA. IN LA: Various coms. North. IN Lib. Admins. RT. Kosciusko Cnty. Hist. Socty. Rotary. Amer. Legion. Kosciusko Cnty. Mental Hlth. Assn. **Pubns.:** "History of the Warsaw Community Public Library," *Kosciusko Cnty. Hist. Bltn.* (Sum. 1966); "Do You See?" poem *Wilson Lib. Bltn.* (Ap. 1950); various articles. **Activities:** 9, 13; 15, 17, 36; 69, 83, 89 **Addr.:** 1403 W. Oriole Dr., Warsaw, IN 46580.

Sloan, Elaine F. (My. 20, 1938, Pittsburgh, PA) Dean of Univ. Libs., IN Univ., 1980–; Assoc. Univ. Libn., Pub. Srv., Univ. of CA, Berkeley, 1977–; Asst. Dir., Libs. for Mgt. and Dev., Smithsonian Inst. Libs., 1976, Asst. to Dir. for Plng. and Resrch., 1973–75, Smithsonian Predoct. Fellow, 1970–72; various resrch. asst. positions, 1959–70. **Educ.:** Chatham Coll., 1955–59, BA (Psy.); Univ. of Pittsburgh, 1960–62, MA (Hist.); Univ. of MD, 1968–70, MLS, 1970–73, PhD (Lib. and Info. Srv.). **Orgs.:** ASIS. Cont. Libns. Educ. Netwk. Exch. ALA: Cncl. (1978–79); Publshg. Com. (1977–78, 1979–80); ACRL/Univ. Libs. Sect., Nom. Com. (Ch., 1977), PLA Interlib. Coop. (ACRL Rep., 1972–76), Com. on Cmnty. Use of Acad. Libs. (1972–74); RTSD Resrcs. Sect., Col. Dev. Com. (Consult., 1975–77); various other coms. Various other orgs. **Honors:** Phi Alpha Theta, 1962; Beta Phi Mu, 1972; Univ. of MD, Beta Phi Mu Awd. for Outstan. Univ. of MD Grad., 1972. **Pubns.:** "Academic Library Cooperation," *ALA Encyc.* (1980); jt. auth., "Relative Use Patterns of Libraries Serving Medical School Populations," *Information in the Health Sciences: Working to the Future* (1973); jt. auth., "The Governance of National Libraries and Information Services at the Federal Level," *Lib. Trends* (Fall 1977). **Activities:** 1; 17 **Addr.:** Main Library, Indiana University, Bloomington, IN 47401.

Sloan, Gwendolyn G. (My. 27, 1929, Truro, NS) Consult., Comp. Index Systs. for Media, 1970–; "Foreign Broadcast Info. Srv.", NewsBank, Inc., 1979–80; TV Commercials, Color Microfiche, J. Walter Thompson Co., 1977–79; Radio and TV Progs., Musm. of Broadcasting, 1975–77; Coord. of Resrch. Mtrls., McKinsey and Co., Inc., 1966–70. **Educ.:** Mt. Allison Univ., 1947–50, BA (Hist.); Columbia Univ., 1953–54, MLS. **Orgs.:** SLA. Thea. LA. **Activities:** 2, 12; 20, 30, 33; 56, 62, 67 **Addr.:** 235 W. 76th St., New York, NY 10023.

Sloan, Patricia K. (D. 31, 1949, Lincoln, NE) Fed. Docum. Libn., NE Lib. Comsn., 1972–. **Educ.:** Univ. of NE, Lincoln, 1968–72, BS (Soc. Sci.). **Orgs.:** ALA: GODORT, Elect. Com. (Ch., 1977–78); Asst. Ch. (1978–79 - 1979–80); Awards Com. (1981–82). Depos. Lib. Cncl. to the Pub. Printer: (1979–80 - 1981–82). NE LA. Natl. Micro. Assn.: Cornhusker Chap. **Activities:** 13; 29, 33 **Addr.:** Nebraska Library Commission, 1420 P St., Lincoln, NE 68508.

Sloan, William J. (N. 11, 1927, Regina, SK) Libn., Circulating Film Lib., Dept. of Film, The Musm. of Modern Art, 1980–; Head, Film Lib., New York Pub. Lib., 1958–80, Libn., Picture Col., 1954–57; Assoc. Prof., Pratt Inst. Grad. Sch. of Lib. & Info. Sci., 1966–. **Educ.:** Mt. Allison Univ., 1946–50, BA (Eng., hist.); Columbia Univ., 1953–54, MS (LS). **Orgs.:** ALA. NY LA. **Pubns.:** Ed., *Film Lib. Qtly.* (1967–). **Addr.:** Circulating Film Library, Department of Film, The Museum of Art, 11 W. 53rd St., New York, NY 10019.

Slocum, Grace Payson (Jl. 7, 1922, Wilmington, NC) Admin., Cecil Cnty. Pub. Lib., 1974–; Asst. Dir., Enoch Pratt Free Lib., 1964–74; Persnl. Ofcr., Free Lib. of Philadelphia, 1959–64; Supt., Work with YA, Brooklyn Pub. Lib., 1953–59; YA Libn., Enoch Pratt Free Lib., 1947–1953; Eng. tchr., Chestnut St. Sch., Wilmington, NC, 1943–1946. **Educ.:** Univ. of NC, 1939–43, AB (Eng.); Columbia Univ., 1946–47, BS (LS). **Orgs.:** MD LA: Pres. (1967–68). MD Adv. Cncl. on Libs. Frdm. to Read Fndn.: Trustee (1973–75, 1978–80). ALA: Lib. Admin. Div., Pres. (1972–1973); Int. Frdm. Com. (1976–1980); Cncl. (1954–61, 1974–); Exec. Bd. (1978–); Other coms. Cecil Cnty. Cncl. of Soc. Agencies: Ch. (1978–79). **Honors:** MD LA, Anl. Awd., 1979. **Activities:** 9; 17, 35, 48; 63, 74, 78 **Addr.:** Cecil County Public Library, 135 E. Main St., Elkton, MD 21921.

Slocum, Hester B. (O. 4, 1909, Corning, KS) Actg. Dir., Xavier Univ. Lib., 1981–; Asst. City Libn., New Orleans Pub. Lib., 1970–77, Head, Tech. Srvs., 1969–70, Admin. Asst., Ref. Libn., and Div. Head, 1967–69. **Educ.:** Baker Univ., 1927–32, BA (Econ.); Univ. of MO Law Sch., 1939–41; LA State Univ., 1956–67, MS (LS). **Orgs.:** ALA: PLA, Mem. Com. (1976–78); ALTA, Prog. Com (1978–). SWLA: Nsltr. Ed. (1968–70); Exec. Bd. (1972–1974–76). LA LA: Stat. Com. (Ch., 1970–72); Stan. Com. (1974–76). (1978–). Frnds. of New Orleans Pub. Lib., Pres. (1978–80). Frnds. of Univ. of New Orleans. **Honors:** Phi Kappa Phi, 1967; Beta Phi Mu, 1978–80; LA LA, Essae M. Culver Awd., 1977. **Addr.:** 6800 Morrison Rd., Apt. 105, New Orleans, LA 70126.

Slocum, Patricia A. (Jl. 7, 1930, Springfield, IL) Educ. Consult., Exper. and Demonstration Ctrs. Prog., MI Dept. of Educ., 1981–, Sch. Lib./Media Consult., State Lib., 1972–80; Head, Hum. Dept., Meml. Lib., Univ. of Notre Dame, 1968–71; Tchr., Bloomington Pub. Schs., 1952–54. **Educ.:** IL State Univ., 1948–52, BS (Elem. Educ.); West. MI Univ., 1966–67, MSLS. **Orgs.:** ALA: AASL, Afflt. Asm. (1978–80); Lib. Educ. Com. (1978–82); ASCLA, Legis. Com. (1977–79); LAMA, Stats. for Sch. Lib. Media Ctrs. (1979–81). AECT: State Afflt. Pres. (Ch., 1978); various coms. Natl. Assn. of State Educ. Media Profs.: Pres.-Elect (1980); Pres. (1980–81); Resol. Com. (1978–80). MI Assn. for Media in Educ.: Pres.-Elect (1977); Pres. (1978); Past Pres. (1979); Non-Per. Pubns. Com. (Ch., 1976–80). Various other orgs. MI Readg. Assn. MI Assn. for Supvsn. and Curric. Dev. MI Assn. of State/Fed. Prog. Spec. MI Intermediate Media Assn. **Pubns.:** "ESEA, Title IV–B, Supports Instructional Purposes," *MASCD Jnl.* (Fall 1981); "Educational Services for the State Library," *MI in Bks.* (Win. 1980); "Regional Educational Media Centers—Today and Tomorrow," *Media Spectrum* (1979); "In Their Opinion—The Conference and Money," *Media Spectrum* (1977); "Getting in on the Action—Grants for School Media Centers," *MI Libn.* (Sum. 1975). **Activities:** 10, 13; 17, 24, 32; 55, 63, 74 **Addr.:** 1370 Lakeside Dr., East Lansing, MI 48823.

Slocum, Robert Bigney (Ap. 6, 1922, Brockton, MA) Assoc. Cat. Libn., Cornell Univ. Libs., 1954–; Catlgr., Univ. of IL,

Special Subjects/Services: 50. Adult educ.; 51. Advert./Mktg.; 52. Aerosp.; 53. Agric.; 54. Area std.; 55. Arts/Hum.; 56. Autom.; 57. Bibl./Prtg.; 58. Bio. sci.; 59. Bus./Fin.; 60. Chem.; 61. Copyrt.; 62. Documtn.; 63. Educ.; 64. Engin.; 65. Env.; 66. Eth. grps.; 67. Film; 68. Food/Nutr.; 69. Geneal.; 70. Geo.; 71. Geol.; 72. Handcpd.; 73. Hist.; 74. Int. frdm.; 75. Info. sci.; 76. Insr.; 77. Law; 78. Legis.; 79. Math./Comp. sci.; 80. Med.; 81. Metals; 82. Nat. resrcs.; 83. Newsp.; 84. Nuc. sci.; 85. Oral hist.; 86. Petr./Energy; 87. Pharm.; 88. Phys./Astr./Math.; 89. Readg.; 90. Relig.; 91. Sci./Tech.; 92. Soc. sci.; 93. Telecom.; 94. Transp.; 95. (other).

Who's Who in Library and Information Services

Instr., 1951–54; Asst. to Dir., Simmons Coll. Lib., 1950–51; Libn. intern, Lib. of Congs., 1949–50. **Educ.:** Boston Univ., 1940–43, 1945–46, BA (Hist.); Columbia Univ., 1946–47, MA (European Hist.); Simmons Coll., 1948–49, BS (LS). **Orgs.:** ALA. Amer. Hist. Assn. AAUP. Common Cause. **Pubns.:** *Biographical Dictionaries and Related Works* (1967); 1st supplement (1972); 2d (1978); "Bibliographer's Lament," *Cornell Univ. Lib. Bltn.* (Ap. 1978); "Making a Catalog Department manual," *Lib. Resrcs. & Tech. Srvs.* (Fall 1960); *Sample Cataloging Forms* (3rd Edit.) (1980); "Printed National Union Catalog," *Lib Resrcs. & Tech. Svrs.* (Win. 1959); Other books, articles. **Activities:** 1; 20; 57 **Addr.:** Catalog Department, Olin Library, Cornell University Libraries, Ithaca, NY 14853.

Small, Doris (Mr. 14, 1953, Los Angeles, CA) Head, Tech. Srvs., Rand Corp., 1980–; Head, Cat. Sect., 1979–80, Asst. Head, Cat., 1978–79; Catlgr., Univ. of South. CA Law Ctr. Lib., 1975–78. **Educ.:** CA State Univ., Northridge, 1970–74, BA (Pol. Sci.); West. MI Univ., 1974–75, MSL (LS). **Orgs.:** ALA. SLA. South. CA Tech. Prcs. Grp. South. CA OLUG. **Activities:** 12; 46 **Addr.:** Rand Corporation Library, 1700 Main St., Santa Monica, CA 90406.

Small, Henry Gilbert (Je. 17, 1941, Chicago, IL) Dir. of Corporate Resrch., Inst. for Sci. Info., 1972–; Actg. Dir., Ctr. for Hist. and Phil. of Phys., Amer. Inst. of Phys., 1969–72. **Educ.:** Univ. of IL, 1959–63, BA (Chem.); Univ. of WI, 1964–69, PhD (Hist. of Sci. and Chem.). **Orgs.:** Socty. for Soc. Std. of Sci.: Cncl. (1979); Nsltr. Ed. ASIS. AAAS. Hist. of Sci. Socty. **Honors:** Phi Beta Kappa, 1962. **Pubns.:** "Cited Documents as Concept Symbols," *Soc. Std. of Sci.* (1978); jt. auth., "Specialties in Science and Social Science," *Scientometrics* (1979); various articles, reviews. **Activities:** 12; 28, 41; 75, 91, 95-Cit. Analysis/Bibliometrics. **Addr.:** Institute for Scientific Information, 3501 Market St., Philadelphia, PA 19104.

Small, Sandra (Ap. 2, 1945, Bishop's Stortford, Hertfordshire, Eng.) Head, Adult Srvs., Haverhill Pub. Lib., 1980–; Supvsr., AV Srvs., Cary Meml. Lib., 1977–80, Ref. Libn., 1970–77; Lib. Asst., Emma S. Clark Meml. Lib., 1966–69. **Educ.:** Adelphi Univ., 1967–69, BA (Arts); Univ. of HA, 1969–70, MLS. **Orgs.:** ALA. MA LA. New Eng. LA. Film Lib. Info. Cncl. Cmnty. Hlth. Info. Netwk.: Rep. (1978–80). Lexington Selectmen's Adv. Com. on Cable Comms. (1974–80). **Honors:** Beta Phi Mu. **Pubns.:** "Part of the Parcel: Reciprocal Borrowing and System Development in Massachusetts," *Bay State Libn.* (Ap. 1973). **Activities:** 9; 32, 34, 39; 55, 67, 80 **Addr.:** 99 Main St., Haverhill, MA 01830.

Smalley, Ann Walker (N. 17, 1951, Evanston, IL) Resrch. Sci., Battelle Meml. Inst., 1978–; Admin. Asst., State Lib. of OH, 1974–78. **Educ.:** OH State Univ., 1969–73, BFA (Art Hist.); Kent State Univ., 1973–75, MLS; Miami Univ. Exec. Dev. Wkshp. for Lib. Admins., 1975. **Orgs.:** OH LA: Mem. Com. (1977–79); Reg. Prog. (Ch., 1979); OH JMRT (Coord., 1979). Franklin Cnty. LA: Secy. (1978). ALA: ASCLA/State Lib. Agency Sect., various ofcs. and coms.; JMRT (Ch., 1978), Students to ALA (Ch., 1978). Assn. for Women in Sci. **Pubns.:** Ed., *The State Library Agencies Survey* (1981); *Manual Circulation Handbook* (1981); "Implementing the Circulation System," videotape (1981); auth., *The Administration of LSCA Title I* (1981); jt. auth., *The Budget Process in State Library Agencies* (1980). **Activities:** 13, 14-Resrch. inst.; 17, 24, 41; 72, 95-Cmnty. analysis needs assess. **Addr.:** Battelle Columbus Laboratories, 505 King Ave., Columbus, OH 43201.

Smalley, Topsy N. (D. 5, 1943, Boston, MA) Sr. Asst. Libn./Ref. Srvs., Feinberg Lib., SUNY, Coll. at Plattsburgh, 1980–; Asst. Dir., Lib., Clinton Cmnty. Coll., 1978–79; Actg. Head, Ref. Srvs., Feinberg Lib., Plattsburgh State Univ. Coll., 1975–76; Libn., Miner Inst. for Man and Env., Chazy, NY, 1973–75; Asst. Libn., Ref. Srvs., Feinberg Lib., SUNY, Coll. at Plattsburgh, 1970–72; Head Libn., Greenville Area (PA) Pub. Lib., 1967–70. **Educ.:** Pomona Coll., 1960–66, BA (Phil./Hist.); Univ. of CA, Los Angeles, 1966–67, MLS; Cath. Univ., 1976–77, Post-Masters Cert. (LS). **Orgs.:** Educ. Media Assn. of the Two-Year Coll. of the State of NY: Secy. (1979–). N. Country Ref. and Resrc. Resrcs. Cncl.: Coop. Acq. Com. ALA. NY LA. **Pubns.:** "Political Science: The Discipline, The Literature and The Library," *Libri* (Mr. 1980); "How to Find Out About Consumerism: A Library Research Guide," *Readers Adv. Srv.* (1979); "Bibliographic Instruction in Academic Libraries: Questioning Some Assumptions," *Jnl. of Acad. Libnshp.* (N. 1977); "Collection Building in the Environmental Sciences," *Spec. Libs.* (Ap. 1975). **Activities:** 1; 31, 39; 65, 92 **Addr.:** Reference Services, Feinberg Library, State University of New York, College at Plattsburgh, Plattsburgh, NY 12901.

Smalls, Mary L. (O. 12, 1947, Salley, SC) Col. Org. Spec., SC State Coll., 1977–; Ref. Libn., Voorhees Coll., 1975–77, Instr. of Chld. Lit., 1976–77. **Educ.:** SC State Coll., 1971–74, BS (Educ.), Univ. of SC, 1974–75, ML (Libnshp.), Cont. Educ. Credit, 1977. **Orgs.:** ALA. SC LA: Secy., Tech. Srvs. Div. (1980). SELA. Alpha Beta Alpha: Alpha Omega Chap., Pres. (1973–74). Alpha Kappa Mu. SC State Empl. Assn. **Activities:** 1; 20, 41, 46; 56, 63, 75 **Addr.:** 1813 State Coll., Orangeburg, SC 29117.

Smallwood, Ann C. H. (D. 11, 1930, Tifton, GA) Med. Lib. Consult., AL Hosp. Assn., 1979–; Ref. Libn., Maxwell Air Force Base Lib., 1977–79; Dir. of Libs., Sch. of Nursing Libn., Troy State Univ., Montgomery, 1973–77; Libn., Montgomery Acad., Montgomery AL, 1965–71. **Educ.:** Univ. of AL, 1950–53, BS (Educ., LS); Sam Houston State Univ., 1958–59, MEd (Educ.); Emory Univ., 1971–72, MLN (Libnshp.); Med. Lib. Cert., 1974–75. **Orgs.:** Med. LA. AL LA: Sch. Libns. (Secy., 1967). Montgomery Cnty. LA: Secy. (1978). Alpha Beta Alpha. Phi Kappa Delta. **Activities:** 1, 12; 20, 24, 34; 63, 80 **Addr.:** P.O. Box 17081, Montgomery, AL 36117.

Smardo, Frances Antoinette (My. 8, 1947, Baltimore, MD) Libn., Early Chld. Srvs., Dallas Pub. Lib., 1979–, st Asst., Youth Libn., 1976–79, Chld. Libn., 1972–76; Tchr., Baltimore City Pub. Schs., 1969–71; Adj. Fac., TX Woman's Univ., 1981–. **Educ.:** Towson State Univ., 1965–69, BA (Eng., Early Chld. Educ.); Univ. of Denver, 1971–72, MA (Libnshp.); N. TX State Univ., 1973–78, PhD (Early Chld. Educ., Libnshp.). **Orgs.:** ALA: ALSC, Presch. Srvs. & Parent Ed. Com. (1981–83), Lib. Srv. to Chld. with Spec. Needs Com. (1980–82); PLA, Resrch. Com. (1980–82), Plng. Prcs. for Pub. Libs. Adv. Com. (1980–). Assn. for Chld. Educ. Intl. Natl. Assn. for the Educ. of Young Chld. **Honors:** Phi Delta Kappa; Phi Beta Mu. **Pubns.:** "Early Childhood Development Cooperative Relationships," *TX Lib. Jnl.* (Spr. 1974); "Are Children's Librarians Prepared to Serve the Young Child?" *Jnl. of Educ. for Libnshp.* (Spr. 1980); "Public Library Programs for Young Children," *Pub. Lib. Qtly.* (Sum. 1979); "What Research Tells Us About Programs for Young Children," *Pub. Libs.* (Spr. 1980); "Public Library Services for Young Children" *Chld. Today* (My–Je. 1980); "Before the Stork and After Big Bird," *TX Lib. Jnl.* (Win. 1980). **Activities:** 9; 21, 48; 63, 92 **Addr.:** Dallas Public Library, 1954 Commerce St., Dallas, TX 75201.

Smart, Martha J. (S. 9, 1945, Ann Arbor, MI) Asst. Dir., Farmington Cmnty. Lib., 1981–, Head, Ext. Srvs. Dept., 1980–81; Elem. Media Ctr. Coord., Mason Pub. Schs., 1970–78. **Educ.:** Univ. of MI, 1963–67, BA (Pol. Sci.), 1968–68, MLS, 1978–, PhD Cand. (LS). **Orgs.:** MI LA: Legis. Com. (Secy., 1980–81). ALA: ASCLA/Lib. Srv. Deaf, Rel. with Outside Orgs. Com. (1980–82); Lib. Srv. Impaired Elderly Sect., Clearinghse. of Info. Com. (1980–82). **Honors:** Beta Phi Mu, 1968. **Activities:** 4, 9; 17, 21, 27; 63, 72, 78 **Addr.:** Farmington Community Library, 32737 W. Twelve Mile Rd., Farmington Hills, MI 48018.

Smellie, Don C. (S. 17, 1937, Buhl, ID) Head, Instr. Tech. Dept., UT State Univ., 1967–; Instr./Prod. Supvsr., IN Univ., 1963–66. **Educ.:** Brigham Young Univ., 1960, BS (Indus. Educ.); IN Univ., 1961, MEd, 1967, EdD. **Orgs.:** AECT: Nom. Com. (1978). UT Educ. Media Assn. Mt. Plains Leadership. Symp. Assn. for Multi-Image. Instr. Media Assn. **Honors:** IN Univ., L.C. Larsen Awd., 1978. **Pubns.:** "Videodisc Innovation Projects," *Professional Development and Educational Technology* (1980); jt. auth., "Videodisc: Implications and Anticipated Effects on the Field of Media Management," *DEMM Nsltr.* (Win. 1981); "The Professional Dilemma: Information, Media or Technology-A Review of Definitions," *Intl. Jnl. of Instr. Media* (1979–80); "Integrated Media to ID, The Only Way to Go," *Intl. Jnl. of Instr. Media* (1977–78); various videotapes. **Activities:** 10; 17, 26, 32; 63, 67 **Addr.:** Department of Instructional Technology, Utah State University, Logan, UT 84322.

Smelser, Lawrence Byron (Jl. 25, 1928, Grandin, MO) Prof., Ctr. for Lib. and AV Educ., St. Cloud State Univ., 1969–. **Educ.:** SW MO State Univ., 1950–54, BS (Elem. Eng., Educ.); WA Univ., St. Louis, MO, 1959–62, MA (Educ. Admin.); Univ. of OK, 1957–59, EdD (Educ. Media). **Orgs.:** ALA. AECT: Tchr. Educ. Com. (1978). MN Educ. Media Org.: Pres., Past Pres. (1977–78). State of MN Interfac. Org.: Del. to Conv.; Exec. Bds. MN Educ. Assn. Amer. Educ. Assn. MN Indp. Republican Party: State Conv. Del.; Ward Ch. **Honors:** St. Cloud State Univ., 10 Yr. Srv. Awd., 1979; St. Cloud State Univ., Outstan. Tchr. Awd., 1974, 1978. **Pubns.:** "Government Publications in Secondary School Libraries in Minnesota," *Gvt. Pubn. Review* (1979). **Activities:** 1, 11; 26, 32, 41; 63 **Addr.:** Centennial Hall, St. Cloud State University, St. Cloud, MN 56301.

Smid, Marcelyn J. (O. 24, 1932, George, IA) Dir., Lib., St. Paul Bible Coll., 1966–; Libn., Monroe Jr. HS, 1961–66; Tchr. (Eng.), Harris Sch. Dist., 1957–59. **Educ.:** St. Paul Bible Coll., 1950–54, BMus; Westmar Coll., 1955–57, BA (Eng.); Univ. of MN, 1959–61, MA (LS). **Orgs.:** Assn. of Christ. Libns.: Secy. (1969–76), Exec. Secy. (1976–). ALA. MN LA. Msc. LA. **Pubns.:** Indxr., *Christian Per. Index.* **Activities:** 1; 15, 17, 44; 63, 90, 92 **Addr.:** St. Paul Bible College Library, Bible College, MN 55375.

Smiraglia, Richard Paul (Mr. 18, 1952, New York, NY) Msc. Cat. Libn., Asst. Prof., Lib. Admin., Univ. of IL, 1978–, Asst. Msc. Cat. Libn., 1974–78. **Educ.:** Lewis & Clark Coll., 1970–73, BA (Msc.); IN Univ., 1973–74, MLS. **Orgs.:** Msc. LA: Cat. Com. 1980–). Intl. Assn. of Msc. Libs. Msc. OCLC Users Grp. IL OCLC Users Grp. Amer. Musicological Socty. **Activities:** 1; 17, 20, 46; 55, 56 **Addr.:** Music Cataloguing, 2136 Music Building, University of Illinois at Urbana-Champaign, 1114 W. Nevada, Urbana, IL 61801.

Smith, Alice G. (D. 5, —, Farmington, MI) Prof., LS, Univ. of S. FL, 1965–, Prof., Ch., Dept. of Lib., Media, & Info. Std., 1965–73; Asst. Prof., LS, Wayne State Univ., 1958–65; Sch. Libn., Detroit Pub. Schs., 1947–57. **Educ.:** Wayne State Univ., 1932, BA (Eng., Sp.), 1933, MI Life Cert., 1957, MEd (LS), 1965, EdD (Tchr. Educ. for LS); Post doct. workshop, Univ. of Chicago, 1974. **Orgs.:** FL LA: Coll. and Resrch. Sect. (Secy., 1969–71). FL Assn. of Sch. Libns. AALS. ALA: Natl. Com. on Lib. Educ.; Chld. Srvs. Div., Ident. of Col. in Chlds. Lit.; Ch., Resrch. in Chld. Lit., ASCLA, Bibliother. Com. (1979–80); Bibliother. Discuss. Grp. (Ch., 1979–81). AAUP. AAUW. Assn. for Childhood Educ. Intl. Natl. Educ. Assn. Other orgs. **Honors:** Women of Wayne State Alum. Awd., 1950; Outstan. Tchr., Wayne State Univ., 1964, Univ. of S. FL, 1969. **Pubns.:** *Literature for Children through School and Public Libraries Programs* (Ja., F. 1981); Clmn., *Ref. Srvs. Review*; "Library Materials for Children in Southeastern United States," *Southeast. Libn.* (Je. 1977); Other articles, reviews. **Activities:** 10, 11; 21, 26, 45; 63, 89, 95-Biblther. **Addr.:** 7 Barcelona Dr., Land o' Lakes, FL 33539.

Smith, Ann Montgomery (Ja. 18, 1941, Denver, CO) Consult. for Lib. Srvs. to the Blind & Phys. Handcpd., MA Bd. of Lib. Comsn., 1980–; Resrch. Libn., Natl. Assessment & Dssm. Ctr., 1976–79; Ref. Libn., Winchester Pub. Lib., 1969–76. **Educ.:** Radcliffe Coll., 1959–63, BA (Rom. Langs./Lits.); Simmons Coll., 1964–69, MLS. **Orgs.:** MA LA: VP (1980–81); Secy. (1977–79); Prog. Ch. (1975–77); Ed., Bay State Letter (1978–81); Ch. (1972–74), Adult Srvs. RT. ALA: ASCLA Outrch. consult. discuss. grp. (1981–). **Pubns.:** Jt. auth., "Evaluation of Reference Service: Qualitative," *Bay State Libn.* (O. 1977); Other articles. **Activities:** 9, 13; 16, 24, 39; 54, 66, 72 **Addr.:** Massachusetts Board of Library Commissioners, 648 Beacon St., Boston, MA 02215.

Smith, Barbara Green (F. 8, 1946, Denver, CO) Head Catlgr., New Orleans Pub. Lib., 1971–; Soc. Sci. Libn., Univ. of Southwest. LA Lib., 1969–71. **Educ.:** Marietta Coll., 1964–66; Univ. of MI, 1966–68, AB (Russ. Hist.); Univ. of MI, 1968–69, AMLS. **Orgs.:** ALA. LA LA: Ad Hoc Com. to Std. Ofc. of Exec. Secy. (1977). Southeast. Lib. Netwk. (SOLINET): Data Base Qual. Cntrl. Com. (1977–79). **Activities:** 9; 17, 20, 46 **Addr.:** New Orleans Public Library, 219 Loyola Ave., New Orleans, LA 70140.

Smith, Barbara J. (Ap. 14, 1939, Jersey Shore, PA) Coord., Campus Libs., PA State Univ., 1970–, Ref. Libn., 1970–74. **Educ.:** PA State Univ., 1957–61, BS (Educ.); SUNY, Oswego, 1965–67, MS (Educ.); Univ. of Pittsburgh, 1969–70, MLS; PA State Univ., 1974–81, D.Ed. (Higher Educ.). **Orgs.:** PA LA: Coll. and Resrch. Div., Bd. of Dir. (1977–81). ALA: ACRL. Pittsburgh Reg. Lib. Ctr.: Bd. of Trustees (1978–). NE Assn. of Inst. Resrchrs. Natl. Univ. Ext. Assn. **Honors:** Beta Phi Mu, 1970; Phi Delta Kappa, 1979. **Pubns.:** "The State of Library User Instruction in Colleges and Universities in the U.S.," *Peabody Jnl. of Educ.* (Jl. 1980); "Dear Part-time Student, Higher Education is Beginning to Love You," *Peabody Jnl. of Educ.* (1978); "The Community College Impact on Academic Libraries and Librarians," *Jnl. of Acad. Libnshp.* (1978); "Status of Continuing Education in Libraries," *Adult Leadership* (Je. 1977); "Reference Tools for the Study of Modern China," *Jnl. of Gen. Educ.* (Fall, 1974); Other articles. **Activities:** 1; 17, 31, 39; 50, 63 **Addr.:** E505 Pattee Library, Pennsylvania State University, University Park, PA 16802.

Smith, Barbara J. (Ap. 23, 1929, Windsor, ON) Coord., Media Srvs., Peel Bd. of Educ., 1968–; Prof. (LS), Univ. of West. ON, 1966–68; Dir., Elem. Sch. Libs., ON Mnstry. of Educ., 1959–68; Chief Libn., Port Credit Pub. Lib., 1956–59. **Educ.:** Univ. of Toronto, 1948–52, BA (Eng.), 1952–53, BLS; 1965–68, MEduc. **Orgs.:** ON LA: Pres. (1981–82). Bk. and Per. Dev. Cncl.: Can. LA Rep. (1978–81). Can. Sch. LA: Budget Com. for Stans. ALA: Newbery-Caldecott Awds. Com. (1967). **Pubns.:** Lib. adv. com., *World Bk. Encyc.* (1978–); "Elementary School Libraries in Ontario" film (1966). **Activities:** 10, 13; 17, 19, 32; 63, 67, 74 **Addr.:** Peel Board of Education, Media Centre, 166 Windy Oaks Dr., Mississauga, ON L5G 1Z3 Canada.

Smith, David D. (Jl. 15, 1951, Dallas, TX) Ref. Libn., Bell Labs., 1980–; Head, Correct. Srvs., Clarence Darrow Lib., Chicago Lib. Syst., 1978–80. **Educ.:** Milton Coll., 1973–76, BA (Bio., Chem.); Univ. of WI, 1976–77, MLS; IL Benedictine Coll., 1980–, MBA. **Orgs.:** ALA: ACRL/Lib. Srvs. to Prisoners Sect., Prog. Com. (1980), Lcl. Jails Resol. Com. (1979). Chicago OLUG. ASIS. SLA. **Activities:** 12; 15, 39, 41; 56, 91, 93 **Addr.:** Technical Library, Bell Laboratories, Naperville, IL 60566.

Smith, David R. (O. 13, 1940, Pasadena, CA) Archvst., Walt Disney Prod., 1970–; Ref. Libn., Univ. of CA, Los Angeles, 1965–70; Exch. Libn., Lib. of Congs., 1963–65. **Educ.:** Univ. of CA, Berkeley, 1960–62, BA (Hist.), 1962–63, MLS. **Orgs.:** SAA: Ch., Bus. Arch. Com. (1972–74). Mss. Socty.: Bd. of Dir. (1977–80); VP (1980), Exec. Dir. (1980–); South. CA Chap., VP (1973–75); Pres. (1977–79). Socty. of CA Archvsts.: Cncl. (1973–75). South. CA Lcl. Hist. Cncl. Intl. Animated Film Socty. **Honors:** Intl. Animated Film Socty., Cert. of Merit, 1979. **Pubns.:** *Jack Benny Checklist* (1970); *The Monitor & The Merrimac; a Bibliography* (1968); "Disney Before Burbank," *Fun-*

PROFESSIONAL ACTIVITIES: Institutions: 1. Acad. lib.; 2. Arch.; 3. Assn.; 4. Fed./Gvt. lib.; 5. Inst. lib.; 6. Mfr./Suppl.; 7. Milit. lib.; 8. Musm.; 9. Pub. lib.; 10. Sch. lib.; 11. Sch. of lib. sci.; 12. Spec. lib.; 13. State lib.; 14. (other). **Functions/Activities:** 15. Acq./Col. dev.; 16. Adult srvs.; 17. Admin.; 18. Apprais.; 19. Archit./Bldgs.; 20. Cat./Class.; 21. Chld. srvs.; 22. Circ.; 23. Cons./Pres.; 24. Consult.; 25. Cont. ed.; 26. Educ. lib. sci.; 27. Ext. srvs.; 28. Fund/Grants; 29. Gvt. pubs.; 30. Indx./Abs.; 31. Instr. lib. use; 32. Media srvs.; 33. Micro.; 34. Netwks./Coop.; 35. Persnl.; 36. PR; 37. Publshg.; 38. Recs. mgt.; 39. Ref. srvs.; 40. Repro.; 41. Resrch.; 42. Review.; 43. Secur.; 44. Serials; 45. Spec. col.; 46. Tech. srvs.; 47. Trustees/Bds.; 48. YA srvs.; 49. (other).

nyworld (Sum. 1979); "The Beast of New Orleans," *Mss.* (Win. 1979); "A Mouse is Born," *Coll. & Resrch. Libs.* (N. 1978); Other articles. **Activities:** 2; 17, 39, 45; 67, 95-Entertainment. **Addr.:** Walt Disney Productions, 500 S. Buena Vista St., Burbank, CA 91521.

Smith, David Rexford (Jl. 29, 1934, Anamosa, IA) Assoc. Dir., Hennepin Cnty. Lib., 1975–, Dir. of Cmnty. Lib. Srvs., 1970–75; Dir., Cedar Rapids Pub. Lib., 1967–70; Head Libn., Hopkins Pub. Lib., MN, 1963–67; Pub. Lib. Consult., 1968–. **Educ.:** IA State Univ., 1952–56, BS (Soclgy., Eng.); Univ. of IA, 1958–60, (Pol. Sci.); Univ. of MN, 1961–63, MS (LS). **Orgs.:** ALA: Cnclr. (1971–72); Bd. of Dir. (1971–72); LAMA VP/Pres. Elect (1981–82); LAMA/Bldg. Equipment Sect., Ch. (1977–78). MN LA: Pres. (1972–73); Pub. Lib. Sect., Treas. (1966–67), Ch. (1965–66). Ofc. of Pub. Libs. and Interlib. Coop., MN: Pub. Lib. Goals Review Com. (1977–79). MN Educ. Media Org. **Activities:** 9; 17, 19, 35 **Addr.:** Hennepin County Library, 12601 Ridgedale Dr., Minnetonka, MN 55343.

Smith, Denis James (F. 3, 1951, Chicago, IL) Pres., Smith Consults., 1978–. **Educ.:** Wright Coll., 1970–71; Northeast. IL Univ., 1971–73, BA (Hist.); FL State Univ., 1975–76, MS (LS). **Orgs.:** ALA. FL LA. Tau Kappa Epsilon: Lcl. Chap. Pres., VP, Secy., Histn. **Honors:** Phi Alpha Theta. **Activities:** 12; 24, 39, 41; 54, 78 **Addr.:** 5106 S. Mayfield, Chicago, IL 60638.

Smith, Diane Harvey (F. 29, 1952, Worcester, MA) Head, Docum. Sect., PA State Univ., 1981–, Sr. Asst. Libn., 1976–. **Educ.:** Mary Washington Coll., 1970–74, BA (Intl. Rel.); Univ. of NC, 1974–76, MLS; PA State Univ., 1980–, (Bus.). **Orgs.:** PA LA: GODORT (Ch., 1979–80). ALA: GODORT, Mem. Com. (Ch., 1980–82). **Pubns.:** "Analysis of Reader Microprint and Alternate Sources of Non-Depository Publications," *Docum. to the People* (Ja. 1980); reviews. **Activities:** 1; 29, 31, 39; 77, 78, 92 **Addr.:** Pattee Library, Penn State University Libraries, University Park, PA 16801.

Smith, Donald Raymond (S. 25, 1946, Highland, IL) Educ. Libn., South. IL Univ., Edwardsville, 1978–, Lib. Instr., 1973–78, Acad. Adv., 1970–73; Soc. Sci. Tchr., Triad HS, 1968–69. **Educ.:** South. IL Univ., Edwardsville, 1964–68, BA (Hist.), 1968–72, MA (Hist.); Univ. of MO, 1974–76, MA (LS); South. IL Univ., 1973–78, MS (Instr. Tech.). **Orgs.:** Lib-Coll. Assoc. NLA. South. IL Univ., Edwardsville Fed. of Univ. Tchrs. IFT, AFT, AFL-CIO. **Pubns.:** *Edwardsville Intelligencer Index, 1976–77* (1977, 1978); "Comment," *Cath. Lib. World* (D. 1978); *Newspaper Indexing Handbook for Small Libraries* (1978). **Activities:** 1; 31, 33, 39; 56, 63, 75 **Addr.:** 205 Ladue Rd., Belleville, IL 62223.

Smith, Donald T(ait) (Ap. 11, 1923, Brooklyn, NY) Asst. Univ. Libn. for Admin. Srvs., Univ. of OR, 1980–, Actg. Univ. Libn., 1979–80; Asst. Univ. Libn., 1963–79; Asst. Dir. of Libs. for Reader Srvs., Boston Univ., 1961–63, Admin. Asst. to the Dir. of Libs., 1958–61; Head Libn., Wagner Coll., 1955–58. **Educ.:** Wesleyan Univ., 1949, BA (Phil.), 1949–50, MA (Phil.); Columbia Univ., 1950–51, MS (LS). **Orgs.:** ALA. Pac. NW LA. OR LA. AAUP. **Activities:** 1; 17, 19 **Addr.:** University of Oregon Library, Eugene, OR 97403.

Smith, Dorothy B. Frizzell (D. 9, 1901, Moundridge, KS) Retired, 1968–; Coll. Libn., Long Beach City Coll., 1938–67; Cryptographer, U.S. Army Signal Corps, 1943–45; Instr. (Eng.), Carroll Coll., 1932–37; Head, Eng. Dept., Holland HS, 1930–31; Collator, Chaucer Mss., Univ. of Chicago, 1929–30; Tchr., Seoul (Korea) Frgn. Sch., 1926–27; Visit. Libn., Intl. Christ. Univ., Tokyo, 1953; Isabella Thoburn Coll., India, 1965. **Educ.:** Southwest. Coll., 1920–24, AB (Fr., Eng.); Univ. of Chicago, 1928–29, AM (Amer. Lit.); Cambridge Univ., 1930, 1936; Columbia Univ., 1937–38, BS (LS). **Orgs.:** ALA. AAUP. P.E.O. AAUW. Natl. Retired Tchrs. Assn. Various other orgs. **Pubns.:** *Subject Index To Poetry For Children And Young People* (1957; 1977); jt. auth., *College Handbook for Freshman English* (1934). **Activities:** 1; 39 **Addr.:** 650 W. Harrison Ave., Claremont, CA 91711.

Smith, Dorothy Brand (O. 4, 1922, Beaumont, TX) Libn./Lrng. Resrcs. Spec., Katherine A. Cook Elem. Sch., 1974–; Libn., Highland Park Elem. Sch., Austin, TX, 1966–74, Tchr., 1962–66; Tchr., Beaumont, TX, 1954–62. **Educ.:** Lamar Univ., 1954, BS (Soc. Sci.); Univ. of TX, 1969–71, MLS; Postgrad. Work, SW TX Univ., Univ. of TX. **Orgs.:** ALA. TX LA: Ch., Dist. 13 div.; Secy., Chld. RT. TX Assn. Sch. Libns.: Secy. Austin Lib. Club: Pres. Phi Delta Kappa. Delta Kappa Gamma. **Pubns.:** *Texas in Children's Books* (1974); "Libraries Will Never Be the Same Again," *TX Outlook* (My. 1976). **Activities:** 10; 24, 25; 95 **Addr.:** 6108 Mountainclimb Dr., Austin, TX 78731.

Smith, Dorothy C. (Ja. 3, 1924, Shawmut, AL) Assoc., Lib. Srvs., NY State Lib., 1963–; Adult Srvs. Libn., Richland Cnty. Pub. Lib., 1961–63; Fld. Consult., SC State Lib. Bd., 1957–61; Libn., Horry Cnty. Meml. Lib., 1952–57; Ref. Asst., Pub. Lib. of Charlotte and Mecklenburg Cnty., 1951–52. **Educ.:** Randolph-Macon Woman's Coll., 1944, AB (Hist.); Univ. of SC, 1947, MA (Hist.); Univ. of NC, 1951, BSLS. **Orgs.:** ALA. NY LA. **Honors:** Phi Beta Kappa. **Activities:** 13; 24, 34, 47; 50 **Addr.:** Library Development, New York State Library, Empire State Plz., Albany, NY 12230.

Smith, Earl P. (S. 30, 1931, Detroit, MI) Assoc. Prof., Auburn Univ., 1975–; Asst. Prof., Univ. of VA, 1969–75; Tchr. (Art, Math.), Southfield Pub. Schs., 1957–68. **Educ.:** MI State Univ., 1949–53, BA (Art), 1956–57, MA (Art); Syracuse Univ., 1966–69, PhD (Instr. Comm. and Tech.). **Orgs.:** AL Instr. Media Assn. AL Educ. Assn. Natl. Educ. Assn. **Pubns.:** "Preparation of Mediabased Materials for Career Education," *Monograph of the College Placement Council, Inc.* (1975); jt. auth., "Perceptions of Role of the School Library Media Specialist by Teachers, Administrators and Media Specialists," *Sch. Media Qtly.* (1981); "Comparison of Role Perceptions of the School Media Specialist Among Administrators, Teachers and Library Media Specialists," *Southeast. Libn.* (Sum. 1978). **Activities:** 11; 17, 26; 54, 63, 93 **Addr.:** Department of Educational Media, 3058 Haley Center, Auburn University, AL 36849.

Smith, Eldred Reid (Je. 30, 1931, Payette, ID) Univ. Libn., Prof., Univ. of MN, 1976–; Dir. of Libs., Prof., SUNY at Buffalo, 1973–76; Assoc. Univ. Libn., Head, Loan Dept., Univ. of CA, Berkeley Libs., 1969–72, Head, Search Div., Biblgphr., 1960–69; Ref. Libn., San Francisco State Coll. Lib., 1959–60; Acq. Ref. Libn., Long Beach State Coll., 1957–59. **Educ.:** Univ. of CA, Berkeley, 1956, BA (Eng.); Univ. of South. CA, 1957, MSLS; Univ. of CA, Berkeley, 1962, MA (Eng.). **Orgs.:** ALA: ACRL, Pres. (1977–78); Bd. of Dir. (1976–79); Univ. Libs. Sect. Strg. Com., Ch. (1974–75); Comm. on Acad. Stat. (1969–74). ARL: Bd. of Dir. (1979–82). Ctr. for Resrch. Libs.: Bd. of Dir. (1975–78). Midwest Reg. Lib. Network: Bd. of Dir. (1977–). Other orgs., coms. **Honors:** Cncl. on Lib. Resrcs. Flwshp., 1970. **Pubns.:** "Academic Status for College and University Librarians - Problems and Prospects," *Coll. and Resrch. Libs.* (Ja. 1970); "Librarians' Organizations as Change Agents," *Focus on IN Libs.* (D. 1970); "The Impact of the Subject Specialist Librarian on the Organization and Structure of the Academic Research Library," In *The Academic Library: Essays in Honor of Guy R. Lyle,* (1974); "Changes in Higher Education and the University Library," In *New Dimensions in Academic Library Service,* (1975); "The Specialist Librarian in the Academic Research Library," in SALALM, *Final Report and Working Papers* (1975); Other articles. **Activities:** 1; 17 **Addr.:** 499 Wilson Library, 309 19th Ave. S., Minneapolis, MN 55455.

Smith, Eleanor Touhey (Ja. 4, 1910, Portland, OR) Consult., Lib. and Adult Educ., 1975–; Reg. Lib. Srvs. Prog. Ofcr., U.S. Ofc. of Educ., 1967–75; Coord., Adult Srvs., Brooklyn Pub. Lib., 1954–67, Dir., Persnl., 1952–54. **Educ.:** Univ. of OR, 1928–30, BA (Eng.); Los Angeles Lib. Sch., 1931–32, Cert. (LS); Columbia Univ., 1951–52, MS (LS). **Orgs.:** ALA: Adult Srvs. Div. (Pres. 1964–65). NY LA: Pres. (1969–70). NY Lib. Club: Pres. (1960–61). Lib. PR Cncl.: Pres. (1955–56). Various other orgs., ofcs. Women's Natl. Bk. Assn.: Secy. (1964–65). Bookseller's Leag. of NY: Pres. (1980–81). Litcy. Voluns. of Amer.: Bd. (1975–); Secy. (1980–81). **Honors:** Phi Beta Kappa; Brooklyn Pub. Lib., Frnds. Awd. for Disting. Libnshp., 1961. **Pubns.:** *Psychic People* (1968); "Libraries and Their Use," *Materials and Methods in Continuing Education* (1976); "Education Needed for Selecting Public Library Materials," *Library School Teaching Methods' Courses* (1969); "Advocates for Literacy? The Library Situation," *Cath. Lib. World* (S. 1980); "Library Education Responds to Needs of Older Adults," *Cath. Lib. World* (F. 1979); various other articles. **Activities:** 4, 9; 16, 24, 25; 50, 89, 95-Aging. **Addr.:** 96 Fifth Ave., Apt. 2M, New York, NY 10011.

Smith, Elizabeth Martinez (Ap. 14, 1943, Upland, CA) Cnty. Libn., Orange Cnty. Pub. Lib., 1979–; Chief, Pub. Srvs., Los Angeles Cnty. Pub. Lib., 1979; Reg. Admin., 1975–78; Prin. Libn., 1973–75. **Educ.:** Univ. of CA, Los Angeles, 1961–65, BA (Latin Amer. Std.); Univ. of South. CA, 1965–66, MSLS. **Orgs.:** ALA. CA LA. Univ. of CA, Los Angeles, Cncl., Sch. of Info. Sci. Assn. of Mex.-Amer. Educ. Women in Gvt. **Honors:** Natl. Assn. of Span. Speaking Libns., Sanchez Awd., 1976. **Pubns.:** "Pensamentos," *CA Libn.* (Ja. 1973); "Chicana Bibliography," *New Directions in Education* (1974); jt. ed., *Wilson Lib. Bltn.,* (N. 1978). **Activities:** 9; 17; 66 hisp. **Addr.:** 1677 N. Upland Ave., Upland, CA 91786.

Smith, Elizabeth Sandness (D. 28, 1939, Two Harbors, MN) Spec. Libn., 3M Corp., 1977–; Media Spec., White Bear Mariner HS, 1975–77; Spec. Prog's. Instr., Hennepin Cnty. Pub. Lib., 1976; Tchr., Aitkin Pub. Sch., 1962–64. **Educ.:** Univ. of MN, St. Paul, 1958–62, BS (Home Econ.), 1964–66, MS (Textiles); Univ. of MN, Minneapolis, 1971–73, MA (LS), St. Cloud State Univ., 1976, Cert. (Media). **Orgs.:** SLA. Amer. Chem. Socty. **Honors:** Beta Phi Mu. **Pubns.:** (As Elizabeth S. French) *Exploring the Twin Cities with Children* (1975, 1977, 1982). **Activities:** 10, 12; 21, 29, 39; 60, 69, 91 **Addr.:** 3M, Technical Library 201-2S, St. Paul, MN 55144.

Smith, Elizabeth Ward (O. 10, 1923, Tilden, NE) Asst. Prof., Lectr. (LS), SUNY, Buffalo, 1968–78; Asst. Prof. (LS), CA State, San Jose, 1961–67; Ref. Libn., San Jose Pub. Lib., 1962–63; Libn., Stauffer Chem. Co., 1963; Med. Libn., Santa Clara Cnty. Hosp., 1956–58; Asst. Supvsr., Cat. Clerical Staff, 1949–54; Asst. Catlgr., Univ. of PA Lib., 1948–49; Tchr., 1944–48. **Educ.:** James Madison Univ., 1940–44, AB (Eng.); CA State Univ., San Jose, 1959–61, MA (LS); SUNY, Buffalo, 1978, PhD (Educ.). **Orgs.:** NY LA. Socty. for Prev. of Cruelty to Animals. **Pubns.:** "Josephus Larned," *Dictionary of American Library Biography* (1978). **Activities:** 11, 12 **Addr.:** 197 Smallwood Dr., Snyder, NY 14226.

Smith, Emilie Varden (F. 4, 1925, Lexington, KY) Head, Cat. Dept., Univ. of KY Lib., 1967–, Head, Mono. Cat., 1956–67, Asst. Serials Cat., 1947–56, Asst. Cat., 1946–47. **Educ.:** Univ. of KY, 1942–46, AB (LS); Univ. of IL, 1950–53, MS (LS). **Orgs.:** ALA. KY LA. OH Valley Grp. of Tech. Srv. Libns.: Pres. (1956–57). **Activities:** 1; 17, 20 **Addr.:** 329 Greenbriar Rd., Lexington, KY 40503.

Smith, Esther Arnold (Jl. 29, 1930, Watford, Herts., UK) Col. Dev. Libn., Ctr. for Resrch. Libs., 1975–, Acq. Libn., 1964–75, Asst. Acq. Libn., 1959–64. **Educ.:** Mt. Holyoke Coll., 1947–49, Bryn Mawr Coll., 1949–51, BA (Classical Archlg.); Univ. of Chicago, 1951–53, MA (Classical Archlg.); Amer. Sch. of Classical Std., Athens, Greece, 1953–54. Archaeological Inst. of Amer. **Pubns.:** Cmplr., *Rarely Held Scientific Serials in the Midwest Inter-Library Center* (1963–68). **Activities:** 12; 15, 33 **Addr.:** 5334 Kimbark, Chicago, IL 60615.

Smith, Frederick E. (Ja. 17, 1932, Detroit, MI) Law Libn., Univ. of CA, Los Angeles, 1967–; Assoc. Dir., Univ. of MI, Law Lib., 1963–67, Ref. Libn., 1961–63. **Educ.:** Yale Univ., 1950–53, BA (Eng.); Univ. of MI, 1957–60, LLB (Law), 1960–61, MALS. **Orgs.:** AALL. South. CA Assn. of Law Libs. Intl. Assn. of Law Libs. **Pubns.:** Contrib., *How to Find the Law* (1976). **Activities:** 1; 17; 77 **Addr.:** Rm. 1444 Law Bldg., University of California, Los Angeles, 405 Hilgard Ave., Los Angeles, CA 90024.

Smith, Frederick E. (My. 24, 1941, Harrisburg, PA) Lib. Dir., Westminster Coll., 1975–, Asst. Libn., 1974–75; Head, Circ. Dept., MI State Univ., 1971–74, Admin. Asst. to the Dir., 1969–71, Head, Order Sect., 1968–69. **Educ.:** Muhlenberg Coll., 1959–67, BA (Soc. Sci.); Univ. of Pittsburgh, 1967–68, MLS. **Orgs.:** ALA: Com. on Comp. Lib. Org. (1977–79). PA LA: Four-Cnty. Chap., Ch. (1979–80), Ch.-Elect & Prog. Ch. (1978–79). Pittsburgh Reg. Lib. Ctr.: Treas., Ch., Audit, Budget, and Finance Com., Exec. Cncl. (1979–81). **Honors:** Beta Phi Mu, 1969. **Activities:** 1; 17, 34; 61 **Addr.:** McGill Library, Westminster College, New Wilmington, PA 16142.

Smith, Gary Lee (N. 13, 1939, Joplin, MO) Asst. Libn., Ref., Resrch., South. CA Edison Co., 1971–. **Educ.:** KS State Coll., 1957–62, BM (Msc.); Tulsa Univ., 1962–63, MM (Msc.); Univ. of South. CA, Los Angeles, 1969–71, MSLS. **Orgs.:** SLA. Msc. LA. Amer. Gld. of Organists: Los Angeles Chap. Amer. Philatelic Socty. **Activities:** 12; 20, 22, 39; 59, 64, 91 **Addr.:** P. O. Box 65064, Los Angeles, CA 90065.

Smith, Hardin E. (F. 11, 1922, Daisy, OK) Dir., Jackson Cnty. Lib. Syst., 1971–; Dir., Clark Cnty. Lib., 1969–71; Dir., E. Chicago (IN) Pub. Lib., 1956–69; Supvsr., Branches and Bkmobiles., Jackson Cnty. (MO) Lib., 1951–55. **Educ.:** Univ. of OK, 1946–49, BLS. **Orgs.:** OR LA. Pac. NW LA. ALA. Assn. of OR Cnty. Libns.: Pres. (1979–). **Activities:** 9; 17, 19, 25 **Addr.:** Jackson County Library System, 413 W. Main St., Medford, OR 97501.

Smith, Harold F. (Jl. 9, 1923, Kansas City, MO) Lib. Dir., Park Coll., 1964–; Soc. Sci. Libn., South. IL Univ., 1957–64; Acq. Libn., Univ. North. CO, 1952–57; Pub. Srv. Libn., Univ. NE, 1951–52. **Educ.:** Park Coll., 1940–44, AB (Hist.); Univ. Denver, 1949–50, AM (LS); Univ. KS, 1945–46, AM (Hist.); South. IL Univ., 1958–63, PhD (Educ.). **Orgs.:** ALA: various com. (1965–). Mt Plains LA: Various com. (1953–). MO LA: Various com. (1967–). Amer. Assn. Higher Educ. Oral Hist. Assn. Org. Amer. Hist. **Pubns.:** *American Travellers Abroad: An Annotated Bibliography* (1969); "Cleopatra's Needle Comes to New York," *Amer. Hist. Illustrated* (O. 1967); "Bread for The Russians," *MN Hist.* (Sum. 1970); Other hist. articles. **Activities:** 1; 17, 34, 44; 51, 61, 85 **Addr.:** Mid-America Inter Library Services, Park College, Parkville, MO 64152.

Smith, Henry Bradford (N. 24, 1936, Philadelphia, PA) Asst. Head, Ref., Gvt. Docum., ILL, Univ. of Rochester, 1970–, Asst. Ref. Libn., 1966–70, Asst. Libn., 1965–66; Tchr., Batavia Jr. HS, 1964. **Educ.:** Hamilton Coll., 1955–59, AB (Hist.); Cornell Univ., 1959–60 (Law); Univ. of Rochester, 1960–63, MA (Amer. Hist.); Syracuse Univ., 1965–69, MSLS. **Orgs.:** Rochester OLUG. Amer. Hist. Assn. **Pubns.:** jt. auth., "Rochester's Turbulent Transit History," *Rochester Hist.* (Jl. 1968). **Activities:** 1; 15, 31, 39; 55, 77, 92 **Addr.:** 74 Montaine Park, Rochester, NY 14617.

Smith, Hope C. (My. 14, 1923, Tunbridge Wells, Kent, Eng.) Libn., ABC-Clio, Inc., 1976–; Libn., Intl. Volun. Srv., Swaziland Coll. of Tech., Swaziland, 1971–75; Head, Ord. Dept., Univ. of CA, Santa Barbara, Lib., 1968–70, Catlgr., 1964–67. **Educ.:** San Jose State Coll., 1959–62, BA (Soc. Srv.); Syracuse Univ., 1962–63, MSLS. **Orgs.:** LA UK. ALA. CA LA. Santa Barbara Mineral and Gem Socty. **Honors:** Beta Phi Mu. **Ac-**

Special Subjects/Services: 50. Adult educ.; 51. Advert./Mktg.; 52. Aerosp.; 53. Agric.; 54. Area std.; 55. Arts/Hum.; 56. Autom.; 57. Bibl./Prtg.; 58. Bio. sci.; 59. Bus./Fin.; 60. Chem.; 61. Copyrt.; 62. Documtn.; 63. Educ.; 64. Engin.; 65. Env.; 66. Eth. grps.; 67. Film; 68. Food/Nutr.; 69. Geneal.; 70. Geo.; 71. Geol.; 72. Handcpd.; 73. Hist.; 74. Int. frdm.; 75. Info. sci.; 76. Insr.; 77. Law; 78. Legis.; 79. Math./Comp. sci.; 80. Med.; 81. Metals; 82. Nat. resrcs.; 83. Newsp.; 84. Nuc. sci.; 85. Oral hist.; 86. Petr./Energy; 87. Pharm.; 88. Phys./Astr./Math.; 89. Readg.; 90. Relig.; 91. Sci./Tech.; 92. Soc. sci.; 93. Telecom.; 94. Transp.; 95. (other).

tivities: 1, 6; 15, 20, 44; 91 85. **Addr.:** 515 Red Rose Ln., Apt. 12, Santa Barbara, CA 93109.

Smith, Howard McQueen (Jl. 25, 1919, Charlotte, NC) City Libn., Richmond Pub. Lib., 1959–; Persnl. Officier, Free Lib. of Philadelphia, 1955–59; Head, Films Dept., Enoch Pratt Free Lib., 1953–55, Exec. Asst. to Dir., 1951–53. **Educ.:** Univ. of VA, 1937–41, BA (Eng.); Univ. of MI, 1941–46, ABLS, 1946–47, MPA. **Orgs.:** ALA: Lib. Admin. Div./Persnl. Admin. Sect. (Ch., 1957–58). VA LA: Pres. (1973–74). SE LA: Bd. (1968–72). **Activities:** 9; 17 **Addr.:** 4120 Hillcrest Rd, Richmond, VA 23225.

Smith, Jane Fulton (Ap. 16, 1935, Lowell, MA) Exec. Dir., S. East. Lib. Resrc. Cncl., 1971–; various positions in ed. and dealing bks. **Educ.:** Skidmore College, 1953–57, AB (Eng.); Long Island Univ., 1971–73, MLS. **Orgs.:** ALA. NY LA. Dutchess Cnty. LA. **Pubns.:** Ed., *A Union List of Serials* (1968); Ed., *A Directory of Southeastern NY Libraries* (1969). **Activities:** 4; 17 **Addr.:** Southeastern NY Library Resources Council, Lady Washington House #3, 20 Academy St., Poughkeepsie, NY 12601.

Smith, Jean Chandler (Ap. 13, 1918, Philadelphia, PA) Retired, 1981–; Resrch. Assoc., Smithsonian Inst., 1981–; Asst. Dir. of Libs. for Reader Srv./Smithsonian Inst. Libs., 1965–, Acting Dir., 1977–79; Actg. Chief Acq., Ref. Libn., Natl. Inst. of Hlth., 1959–63; Ref. Libn., Yale Univ., 1947–1958. **Educ.:** Bryn Mawr Coll., 1935–39, AB (Rom. lang.); Yale Univ., 1950–53, MS (Zlgy.); Cath. Univ., 1973, MS (LS). **Orgs.:** ALA. SLA. Universal Serials & Book Exch.: Bd. Bryn Mawr Coll.: Frnds. of the Lib. Com. **Pubns.:** "Bibliography on the Metabolism of Endoparasites," *Exper. Parasitology* (1965); "Bibliography on the Biochemistry of Endoparasites," *Exper. Parasitology* (1968). **Activities:** 1, 4; 15, 17, 39; 58 **Addr.:** 3601 Connecticut Ave. N.W., Washington, DC 20008.

Smith, Jeanette M. (F. 15, 1938, Palacios, TX) Dir. of Lib. Media Srv., Forsyth Country Day Sch., 1975–, Lower Sch. Lib. Media Specialist, 1973–75; Chld. Libn., Forsyth Cnty. Pub. Lib., 1972; Head, Acq., Wake Forest Univ. Lib., 1970–72, Actg. Head, Baptist Col., 1969–70; Sch. Libn., Madison, WI, 1963–65. **Educ.:** Univ. of WI, 1959–62, BA (Eng.), 1962–63, MA (LS); Wake Forest Univ., Tchr. Cert., 1973; Various courses. **Orgs.:** ALA: AASL/Non Pub. Sch. Sect. (Ch. elect, 1981–82). NC LA: Secy.-Treas. (1979–80); Local Arrange. Com. for Biennial Conf. (Ch. 1978). Del. to AASL Afflt. Asm. (Je. 1978). Wake Forest Univ. Club: Pres. and various com. Wake Forest Baptist Church Diaconate, Bd. of Educ. **Honors:** Phi Beta Kappa, 1962; Beta Phi Mu, 1963. **Pubns.:** "It's Quite a Job," in *A Tribute to Rachel Katherine Schenk* (1963); Jt. ed., *Lib. Connection–Local* (1979–). Ed., *News of FCDS* (1976–). **Activities:** 10; 15, 32, 48 **Addr.:** 2988 Ormond Dr., Winston-Salem, NC 27106.

Smith, Jessie Carney (Greensboro, NC) Univ. Libn., Prof., Fisk Univ., 1965–; Coord. of Lib. Srvs., Asst. Prof., TN State Univ., 1963–65, Head Catlgr., Instr., 1957–60; Visit. Prof., George Peabody Coll., 1980–. **Educ.:** NC Agri. & Tech. State Univ., 1946–50, BS (Home Econ.); Cornell Univ., 1950–51, (Textiles); MI State Univ., 1954–55, MA (Child Dev.); George Peabody Coll., 1956–57, MALS, Univ. of IL, 1960–64, PhD (Lib. Admin.). **Orgs.:** ALA: Cncl. (1969–71); Black Caucus, Strg. Com. (1970–72); *Choice* Ed. Bd. (1969–75); Ch., HW Wilson Per. Awd. Com. (1974). TN LA: Coll. and Univ. Sect. (Ch., 1969–70). Beta Phi Mu: Pres. (1976–77). SELA. Other orgs. and coms. Links, Inc.: VP. (1979–81). NAACP. AAUP. African Std. Assn.: Arch. Lib. Com., Bd. of Dir. (1976–). **Honors:** Cncl. on Lib. Resrcs., Flwshp., 1969; Natl. Urban Leag., Fellow, 1968, 1976. **Pubns.:** "Librarianship and Black Studies–A Natural Relationship," in: *Library and Information Services for Special Groups* (1973); "Arna Bontemps," in *Dictionary of American Library Biography* (1978); "Acquiring Afro-American Literature," in *Bibliographical Control of Afro-American Literature* (1977); "Special Collections of Black Literature in the Traditionally Black College," *Coll. and Resrch. Libs.* (S. 1974); "Blacks and Libraries," in: ALA *Yearbook* (1977–81); *Black Academic Libraries and Research Collections*, (1977); Other books, articles, reviews. **Activities:** 1; 24, 28; 66 **Addr.:** Fisk University Library, Fisk University, Nashville, TN 37203.

Smith, Jessie Cottman (N. 15, 1928, Pocomoke, MD) Dir., Lib. Srvs., Univ. of MD, East. Shore, 1972–; Ref. Libn., 1966–72; Libn., Worcester HS, 1951–66. **Educ.:** Univ. of MD, East. Shore, 1950, AB (Hist., Gvt.); Columbia Univ., 1959, MSLS; various crs. **Orgs.:** ALA: ACRL; Black Caucus. MD LA. Various other orgs. Untd. Meth. Women. Natl. Educ. Assn. MD State Tchrs. Assn. AAUW. **Honors:** ACRL-Mellon Fndn. Intern, 1974–75, Stanford Univ. **Pubns.:** "Managerial Case Studies," ERIC (1975); reviews. **Activities:** 1, 4; 25; 56, 63, 85 **Addr.:** Frederick Douglass Library, University of Maryland Eastern Shore, Princess Anne, MD 21853.

Smith, Jewell G. (Ap. 11, 1922, St. Joseph, MO) Dir., Springfield-Greene Cnty. Lib., 1977–, Asst. Dir., 1967–77; Ref. Libn., Ozark Pioneer Lib. Syst., 1965–67; Asst. Libn., Daniel Boone Reg. Lib., 1962–65. **Educ.:** William Jewell Coll., 1940–44, BA (Eng.); TX Woman's Univ., 1961–62, MLS. **Orgs.:** ALA: Notable Books Cncl. (1980–82). MO LA: VP (1970); Pres. (1971). Springfield Area LA: Pres. (1970–72). Soroptimist Club of Springfield. SW MO Musm. Assoc. **Addr.:** Springfield-Greene County Library, Box 737, Springfield, MO 65801.

Smith, Jo Therese (O. 25, 1932, Chicago, IL) Chief Info. Chem. & Mgr. Lib. Srvs., Witco Chem. Corp., 1967–; Lib. Mgr., Lever Bros., 1965–67; Info. Anal., Natl. Acad. Sci., 1963–65; Chief Info. Chem., Mobil Chem. Co., 1960–63. **Educ.:** Univ. of WI, 1949–53, BS (Chem.); Univ. of TX, 1954–55, (Chem.). **Orgs.:** SLA. **Activities:** 12; 15, 17, 18; 60, 64, 86 **Addr.:** Witco Chemical Corp., Corporate Technical Center, 100 Bauer Dr., Oakland, NJ 07436.

Smith, John Brewster (Je. 26, 1937, Bryan, TX) Dir. of Libs., Dean of Lib. Srvs., SUNY, Stony Brook, 1974–; Dir. of Libs., TX A & M Univ., 1969–74, Asst. Dir. for Pub. Srvs., 1966–69; Asst. Law Libn., Columbia Univ., 1965–66, Circ. Libn., Law, 1963–65. **Educ.:** TX A & M Univ., 1955–60, BA (Eng.); Columbia Univ., 1961–63, MS (LS); 1964–66 (Law). **Orgs.:** ALA: ACRL, Com. on Cmnty. Use of Acad. Libs. (Ch., 1970–71), Com. on Legis. (1977–79); SUNY Cncl. of Head Libns.: Vice-Ch./Ch. (1979–). Suffolk Cnty. LA: Bd. of Dirs. (1979–). Long Island Lib. Resrcs. Cncl.: Bd. of Trustees (1976–). Bibl. Retrieval Svrs. User Bd.: Ch. (1977–79). **Honors:** TX LA, Libn. of the Yr., 1972. **Pubns.:** "Copyright Reexamined . . .," *The Bookmark* (Sum. 1979); "Research Libraries in Transition," *AAUP Bltn.* (May 1978). **Activities:** 1, 2; 17, 28; 55, 77 **Addr.:** State University of New York at Stony Brook, Frank Melville Jr. Memorial Library, Stony Brook, NY 11794.

Smith, John W. V. (N. 30, 1914, Springfield, CO) Histn./Archvst., Gen. Asm., Church of God, 1957–; Prof. (Church Hist.), Assoc. Dean, Anderson Sch. of Theo., 1952–80; Prof. (Theo.), Warner Pac. Coll., 1949–52. **Educ.:** Northwest. OK State Univ., 1934–38, AB (Hist.); OK Univ., 1939–41, MA (Hist.); Univ. of South. CA, 1946–54, PhD (Relig., Hist.). **Orgs.:** SAA: Relig. Arch. Com. (1970–); Relig. News *Amer. Archvst.* Rpt. (1978–80). Amer. Socty. of Church Hist.: Spr. 1980 Mtg. Prog. Ch. Conf. on Faith and Hist. Amer. Acad. of Ecumenists. **Honors:** Northwest. OK State Univ., Outstan. Alum., 1979. **Pubns.:** *Heralds of A Brighter Day* (1955); *A Brief History of the Church of God Reformation Movement* (1976); *The Quest for Holiness and Unity: A Centennial History of the Church Of God* (1980); "Holiness and Unity," *Wesleyan Theo. Jnl.* (Spr. 1975); various other articles. **Activities:** 2; 15, 17, 38; 85, 90 **Addr.:** Anderson College, Anderson, IN 46012.

Smith, Juanita J. (Je. 11, 1923, Muncie, IN) Spec. Col. Libn., Assoc. Prof., Ball State Univ., 1975–, Ref. Libn., 1971–75, Head Cat. Libn., 1969–71, Cat. Libn., 1949–69. **Educ.:** Ball State Univ., 1940–41, 1943–45, BS in ED (Bus. Educ., Soc. Sci.); Univ. of MI, 1950–51, AMLS, 1958, (LS, Hist.). **Orgs.:** ALA: ACRL. IN LA. SAA. Socty. of IN Archvist. AAUP. AAUW. Leag. of Women Voters. Delta Kappa Gamma Socty. **Pubns.:** Assoc. Ed., *Steinbeck Qtly., Steinbeck Monograph Series;* "The Steinbeck Collection at the Bracken Library, Ball State University," *Steinbeck Qtly.* (Sum. Fall 1978); Reviews. **Activities:** 1, 2; 45, 49 **Addr.:** Special Collections, Bracken Library, Ball State University, Muncie, IN 47306.

Smith, Julia B. (D. 21, 1947, Newnan, GA) Media Spec., Dolvin Elem. Sch., 1980–; Media Spec., Newtown & Hopewell Elem. Schs., 1972–80; Media Spec., N. Roswell Elem., 1970–72; Media Spec., Harris St., 1969–70. **Educ.:** LaGrange Coll., 1964–68, AB (Elem. Educ.); Emory Univ., 1968–69, MLn (LS); Univ. of GA, 1974–76, EDS (Lib. Educ.). **Orgs.:** ALA. GA LA. SELA. GA Lib. Media Dept., GA Assn. of Educ.: 5th dist. - Secy.-Treas. (1979–80). Natl. Educ. Assn. GA Assn. of Educ. Fulton Cnty. Assn. of Educ. **Activities:** 10; 21, 31, 32 **Addr.:** 1270 Mission Hill Ct., Roswell, GA 30075.

Smith, Julie L. (My. 11, 1954, Burbank, CA) Dir., Lib. Srvs., Burlew Med. Lib., St. Joseph Hosp., Orange, CA, 1979–; Prin. Lib. Asst., Cedars-Sinai Med. Ctr, Los Angeles, 1977–79. **Educ.:** Univ. of CA, Irvine, 1972–76, BA Summa Cum Laude (Eng.); Univ. of South. CA, 1976–77, MLS; Med. LA, 1979, Cert. **Orgs.:** Med. Lib. Grp. of South. CA and AZ: Cont. Educ. Com., Salary Survey Com. (Ch.) Med. LA. Nursing Info. Cnsrtm. of Orange Cnty.: Persnl. Com. (Ch.). **Honors:** Beta Phi Mu; Phi Beta Kappa, 1976. **Activities:** 12; 15, 17, 39; 80, 87, 92 **Addr.:** Burlew Medical Library, Saint Joseph Hospital, 1100 W. Stewart Dr., Orange, CA 92667.

Smith, Karen Leigh (Mr. 9, 1941, London, ON) Head, Lib. Srvs., Sir Adam Beck HS, 1978–82; Head, Lib. Srvs., Sir Frederick Banting HS, 1972–77; Tchr./Libn., Emily Carr Pub. Sch., 1970–72; Tchr./Libn., Sherwood Forest Pub. Sch., 1970; Tchr./Libn., Masonville Pub. Sch., 1970; Tchr./Libn., Thames HS, 1968–70; Tchr., Ingersoll Dist. Collegiate Inst., 1962–65. **Educ.:** Univ. of West. ON, 1962–66, BA (Hist.), 1967–68, MLS; 1967, ON Tchrs. Cert.; Queens Univ., 1977–78, MEduc. **Orgs.:** Can. LA: *Lib. Jnl.* Ed. Bd. (1978–80), Cncl. (1976–77); *On Line* (Ed., 1973–74). Can. Sch. LA: *Moccasin Telegraph* Ed. (1973–76). ON LA: *Focus* Ed. (1978–79); Glds. Com. (Ch., 1978–79); Pres. (1977–78); various other ofcs. ON Sch. LA. Phi Delta Kappa. ON Sec. Sch. Tchrs. Fed. London Pub. Lib. Trustees. **Honors:** ON Lib. Trustees Assn., Awd. of Merit, 1975. **Pubns.:** "Basic Media Skills Through Games: A Review," *Can. Lib. Jnl.* (Ap. 1980); "Libraries and Young Adults: Media, Services, and Librarianship: a Review," *Can. Lib. Jnl.* (F. 1980); "The Canadian Library Association and Canadian School Library Association," *Emergency Libn.* (My.-Ag. 1979); "Info Is Power," *Focus* (D. 1978); various other articles. **Activities:** 10; 31, 32, 48; 63 **Addr.:** Sir Adam Beck Secondary School, 1250 Dundas St., E., London, ON N5W 5P2 Canada.

Smith, Katherine de Dory (Ja. 6, 1923) Lib. Consult., Amer. Secur. Cncl. Educ., 1979–; Chief Catlgr., Fndn. Lib., U.S. Army Coastal Engin. Resrch. Ctr., 1978–; Supvsr. Libn., U.S. Army Engin. Ctr., 1970–77; Ref./Resrch. Libn., West Point Lib., 1969, 1964–67; Libn., Bien Hoa Air Base (Vietnam), 1967–68. **Educ.:** Msc. Cnsvty., 1948–52, BA (Msc.); Univ. KY, 1958–62, MSLS; 1962, NY Prof. Libns. Cert.; various crs. **Orgs.:** Cath. LA. SLA. Amer. Acad. of Soc. and Pol. Scis. Assn. for Asian Std. Alliance Francaise. Org. of Amer. States. The Asia Socty. Various other orgs. **Activities:** 1, 4; 24, 31, 39; 57, 74, 92 **Addr.:** 6833 Pacific Ln., Annandale, VA 22003.

Smith, Kent A. (S. 3, 1938, Boston, MA) Deputy Dir., Natl. Lib. of Med., 1979–, Asst. Dir., Admin., 1971–79; Exec. Ofcr., Div. of Resrch. Resrcs., 1968–71, Admin. Ofcr., 1965–68; Mgt. Anal., Dept. of HEW, 1962–65. **Educ.:** Hobart Coll., 1956–60, BA (Math., Econ.); Cornell Univ., 1960–62, MPA (Pub. Admin.). **Orgs.:** Med. LA: Natl. Lib. of Med., Liaison Com. (1979–). ASIS. Amer. Mgt. Assn. Amer. Socty. for Pub. Admin.: Chap. Ch. (1971). **Honors:** Natl. Lib. Med. Dept. of HEW Superior Srv. Awd., 1974; Natl. Lib. Med., Outstan. Performance, 1978. **Pubns.:** "Lister Hill National Center," *ALA Yrbk.* (1980); "National Library of Medicine," *ALA Yrbk.* (1979–80). **Activities:** 4; 17, 34; 56, 80, 93 **Addr.:** National Library of Medicine 8600 Rockville Pike, Bethesda, MD 20209.

Smith, LaMar Ralph (S. 12, 1923, Logan, UT) Educ. Libn., Univ. of NV - Reno, 1963–, Circ. Libn., 1955–63. **Educ.:** Univ. of NV, 1946–50, BA (Hist.); Univ. of OK, 1954–55, MLS. **Orgs.:** NV LA: Rcrt. Com. (Ch., 1960–1961); Audit Com. (Ch., 1960–1963); NV Authors, NV LA Conv. (Ch., 1963); Acad. & Spec. Lib. Sect. (Vice-Ch., 1970–72); NW Dist., Co-Ch., Prog. Com. (1977–78); Silver Circle, Juvenile Sect. (Ch., 1978–1979). ALA. Intl. Reading Assn. Natl. Aerosp. Educ. Assn.: Natl. Bd. Mem. (1972–1976); Cncl. (1975–1976); Natl. Exec. Adv. Cncl. (1975–1977). **Honors:** Natl. Aerosp. Educ. Assn., Outstan. person in Aerosp. Educ., 1972. **Activities:** 1; 21, 39; 52, 63 **Addr.:** 1201 Ralston St., Reno, NV 89503.

Smith, Lena Denham (Je. 29, 1932, Vanceburg, KY) Catlgr., Tchr., Centralized Lib. Tech. Srvs., Spalding Coll., 1974–; Libn., Media Spec., Bruce Mid. Sch., 1971–74; KY Reception Ctr., 1968–71; Lewis Cnty. HS, 1962–68. **Educ.:** Morehead State Univ., 1960–61, AB (Educ., LS); Univ. of KY, 1971, MSLS. **Orgs.:** ALA. KY LA: State Adv. Bd. Jefferson Cnty. Sch. Media Assn. KY Sch. Media Assn. Crescent Hills Cmnty. Cncl. Natl. Educ. Assn. KY Educ. Assn. Jefferson Cnty. Tchrs. Assn. **Activities:** 11; 20, 32, 46 **Addr.:** 102 Crescent Ct., Louisville, KY 40206.

Smith, Lester K. (Jl. 25, 1925, San Diego, CA) Arts Libn., North. IL Univ., 1980–, Assoc. Dir., Pub. Srvs., 1973–80; Lib. Dir., Concord Coll., 1970–73; Head, Hum. Div., San Diego State Univ., 1962–67, Ref. Libn., 1957–61. **Educ.:** San Diego State Univ., 1945–49, BA (Art); Univ. of South. CA, 1956–57, MLS, 1967–70, PhD (LS). **Orgs.:** ALA: RASD, Com. on State & Reg. Grps. (1977–79); LAMA/Bldgs. and Equipment Sect., BCUL Com. (1979–). IL LA: IL ACRL, Cont. Educ. Com. (1978–79). AAUP. Amer. Civil Liberties Un. **Pubns.:** "Northern Illinois University Libraries" in *Encyclopedia of Library and Information Sciences* (V. 20.); "Copying for Reserve Reading-A Differing Viewpoint," *Coll. & Resrch. Lib. News* (My. 1978); "Data Processing at the Northern Illinois University Libraries," *IL Libs.* (Ap. 1978). **Activities:** 1; 17, 19, 39; 55, 74 **Addr.:** 6 Pheasant Run, DeKalb, IL 60115.

Smith, Linda Cheryl (Ja. 27, 1949, Rochester, NY) Asst. Prof., Grad. Sch. of LS, Univ. of IL, 1977–; Lit. srchr., Lib., GA Inst. of Tech., 1974–75; Trainee in comp. libnshp., Lib., Washington Univ. Sch. of Med., 1972–73. **Educ.:** Allegheny Coll., 1967–71, BS (Physics & Math); Univ. of IL, 1971–72, MS (LS); GA Inst. of Tech. 1973–75, MS (Info. & Comp. Sci.); Syracuse Univ., 1975–77, PhD (Info. Transfer); Washington Univ., 1972–73, Cert. (Syst. & Data Prcs.). **Orgs.:** ASIS: Mem. Com. (1978–); Educ. Com. (1979–); Fac. adv., Univ. of IL Student Chap. (1977–). SLA. Med. LA. AALS. AAAS. Assn. for Comp. Mach. **Honors:** Med. LA, Rittenhouse Awd., 1973; ASIS, Student Mem. Paper Contest Awd., 1974; Beta Phi Mu; Phi Beta Kappa. **Pubns.:** Jt. Auth., "Science, Scholarship and the Communication of Knowledge," *Lib. Trends,* (Win. 1979); "Artificial Intelligence in Information Retrieval Systems," *Info. Prcs. and Mgt.* (1976); "Systematic Searching of Abstracts and Indexes in Interdisciplinary Areas," *Jnl. of ASIS* (N.-D. 1974); "The Medical Librarian and Computer-Assisted Instruction," *Bltn. of the Med. LA* (Ja. 1974). **Activities:** 11; 26, 41; 56, 75, 91 **Addr.:** Graduate School of Library Science, 410 David Kinley Hall, University of Illinois, Urbana, IL 61801.

Smith, Linda L. (Ap. 19, 1948, Jacksonville, FL) Head, Cat. Dept./Assoc. Univ. Libn., Univ. of N. FL Lib., 1972–, Asst. Catlgr., 1972–75. **Educ.:** Hollins Coll., 1966–70, AB (Hist.); Univ. of NC, 1971–72, MSLS; Sorbonne, 1968–69, Cert. (Fr.). **Orgs.:** ALA. SELA. FL LA. **Honors:** Phi Beta Kappa, 1970; Beta Phi Mu, 1972. **Activities:** 1; 17, 20, 46; 92 **Addr.:** Thomas G. Carpenter Library, University of N. Florida Library, P.O. Box 17605, Jacksonville, FL 32216.

Smith, Lora (N. 9, 1936, Ava, MO) Lib. Media Spec., West Plains R-7 Sch. Dist., 1973–; Tchr., Mt. View Sch. Dist., 1962–65; Elem. Tchr., Ellington Sch. Dist., 1957–60. **Educ.:** SW MO State Univ., 1961, BS; Emporia State Univ., 1979, MLS. **Orgs.:** MO Assn. Sch. Libns.: Pres. (1981–82); VP (1980–81); Legis. Ch. (1978–80). ALA: AASL, Afflt. Asm. (Del., 1980–82). MO State Tchrs. Assn. Gen. Fed. of Womens Clubs. **Honors:** Delta Kappa Gamma. **Activities:** 10; 15, 17, 48 **Addr.:** Rte. 3, Box 597, West Plains, MO 65775.

Smith, Sr. Louise (D. 9, 1928, Rawlins, WY) Col. Libn. for Msc., Univ. of West. ON, 1974–. **Educ.:** Our Lady of Victory Coll., 1954, BA (Msc.); Catholic Univ. of Amer., 1968, MA (Msclgy.); N. TX State Univ., 1972, MLS. **Orgs.:** Msc. LA. Can. Assn. of Msc. Lib.: Treas. (1980–). **Pubns.:** Reviews. **Activities:** 1; 15, 42; 55 **Addr.:** The Music Library, University of Western Ontario, London, ON N6A 3K7 Canada.

Smith, Lynn Suzanne (S. 30, 1945, Honolulu, HI) Spec. Projs. Libn., Col. Dev. Dept., Univ. of CA, Riverside, 1979–, Head, Serials Dept., 1975–79, Serials Catlgr., 1968–75. **Educ.:** Univ. of Redlands, 1963–67, BA (Eng.); Univ. of CA, Los Angeles, 1967–68, MLS. **Orgs.:** ALA. CA LA. South. CA Tech. Prcs. Grp. Frdm. to Read Fndn. South. CA Coal. for Int. Frdm.: Secy. (1979–). Amer. Cvl. Liberties Un.: Riverside Chap., Strg. Com. (1979–). Costume Socty. of Amer. **Pubns.:** *A Practical Approach to Serials Cataloging* (1978); "To Classify or Not to Classify...," *Serials Libn.* (Sum. 1978). **Activities:** 1; 15, 20, 44; 55, 74 **Addr.:** 552 Highlander, Riverside, CA 92507.

Smith, M. Patricia Murphy (O. 1, 1923, Washington, DC) Asst. Libn., Natl. Geo. Socty. Mag., 1964–; ILL, Circ. Libn., TRW/STL, 1957–63; Milit. Libn., US Army, Spec. Srvs., 1949–53. **Educ.:** St. Mary's Coll., Notre Dame, 1941–45, BA (Hist.); Immaculate Heart Coll., Los Angeles, CA, 1963–64, MLS; various cont. ed. crs. **Orgs.:** SLA: Geo. and Map Div. (Mem. Ch., 1966–68). DC LA. Smithsonian Assn. Frnds of the Zoo. St. Mary's Alum. Assn.: Immaculate Heart Assn. Alum. Natl. Hist. Assn. **Activities:** 4, 12; 15, 16, 17; 55, 70, 91 **Addr.:** 8133 Marcy Ave., West Springfield, VA 22152.

Smith, Marian J. (N. 21, 1941, Brooklyn, NY) Libn., Online Srvs., Gen. Electric Co., Main Lib., 1979–, Lit. Srchr., 1967–79; Catlgr., Siena Coll., 1964–67. **Educ.:** St. Bonaventure Univ., 1959–63, BA (Hist.); SUNY, Albany, 1963–64, MLS; various courses, workshops. **Orgs.:** SLA: Upstate NY Chap., PR Ch. (1976–77); Prog. Ch. (1978); Nom. Com. Ch. (1979). Capital Dist. Lib. Cncl.: Comp. Based Ref. Srv. Com. (Secy., 1979–80). AAUW. **Activities:** 12; 15, 39; 59, 64, 81 **Addr.:** Main Library, General Electric Co., One River Rd., Schenectady, NY 12345.

Smith, Murphy D. (O. 16, 1920, Birmingham, AL) Assoc. Libn., Amer. Phil. Socty. Lib., 1971–, Asst./Mss. Libn., 1961–71, Mss. Libn., 1951–61. **Educ.:** Univ. of TN, 1946–49, BA (Hist.), 1949–50, MA (Hist.); Univ. of PA, 1950–55, (Hist.); Amer. Univ., 1955, (Arch.). **Orgs.:** SAA: Ch., Papers of Sci. (1962–63). Mss. Socty. Amer. Hist. Assn. **Pubns.:** *Sherman Day, Artist, Forty Niner, Engineer* (1980); *Oak from an Acorn: History of the American Philosophical Society Library to 1803* (1976); *Guide to Archives and Manuscripts Collections of the Amer. Phil. Soc.* (1966); "Darwin and the Library of the Amer. Phil. Soc.", *Mss.* (1977); "The Stephen Girard Papers", *Mss.* (1977); Other articles. **Addr.:** American Philosophical Society Library, 105 South Fifth St., Philadelphia, PA 19105.

Smith, Nathan McKay (Ap. 22, 1935, Wendell, ID) Assoc. Prof., Lib. & Info. Sci., Brigham Young Univ., 1973–, Life Sci. Libn., 1966–73; Jr. High Sci. Tchr., OR Schs., 1961–66. **Educ.:** East. OR State Coll., 1957–61, BS (Sci. Educ.); OR State Univ., 1964–65, MS (Sci. Educ.); Brigham Young Univ., 1966–69, MLS, 1969–72, PhD (Zlgy.). **Orgs.:** ALA. AALS. Mt. Plains LA. UT LA. N. Amer. Socty. for Adlerian Psy. Herpetologists League. Socty. for the Study of Amphibians & Reptiles. **Honors:** Beta Phi Mu, 1976; Sigma Xi, 1969; Phi Kappa Phi, 1975. **Pubns.:** *SPSS as a Library Research Tool* (1977); Jt. auth., "Vertical-Horizontal Relationships: Their Application for Librarians", *Spec. Libs.* (1975); Jt. auth., "Recognizing and Coping with the Vertical Patron", *Spec. Libs.* (1976); Jt. auth., *Index to Herpetologica 1956–1975 (vol. 12-31)* (1977); "The Librarian As Counselor: Detroit Revisited", *Top of the News* (1978); Other articles. **Activities:** 11; 39, 41; 91 **Addr.:** Brigham Young University, School of Library and Information Sciences, Room 5042 HBLL, Provo, UT 84602.

Smith, Nicholas N. (D. 25, 1926, Malden, MA) Dir., Ogdensburg Pub. Lib., 1969–; Adult consult., N. Country Lib. Syst., 1965–69, Film Libn., 1961–65; Dir., Peekskill Pub. Lib., 1959–61. **Educ.:** Univ. of ME, 1946–50, BA (Hist.); Columbia Univ., 1957–59, MLS. **Orgs.:** NY LA. ALA: Mem. Com. (1974–75). Indep. Cntrl. Lib. Assn.: Ch., Stan. com. (1972–74); VP (1976); Pres. (1977–80). St. Lawrence Cnty. Litcy. Volun. Indian Creek Nature Ctr. **Honors:** Natl. Musm. of Can., grant, Comput. Bibl. in Canadian Ethnology, 1967. **Pubns.:** "Film Care", *Bookmark* (Mr. 1968); "Wabanaki Bibliography," *Man in the NE* (Fall 1977); 16mm film, River Rendezvous (1971); other articles, films. **Activities:** 9; 17, 24, 28, 35; 57, 66 **Addr.:** Ogdensburg Public Library, Ogdensburg, NY 13669.

Smith, Patricia Kathleen (Mr. 15, 1953, Austin, TX) Info. Consult., 1976–; Lect., Cath. Univ., 1980–; Co-Proj. Dir., NSF Contract to train Egyptian info. spec., 1979–81; Ref. Libn., Daniel Boone Reg. Lib., 1974–75. **Educ.:** Univ. of MO, 1971–75, BA (Econ.); Univ. of MD, 1975–76, MLS. **Orgs.:** ASIS: Co-fndr., Spec. Int. Grp. on Mgt. (1976). SLA. Natl. Assn. of Female Exec. Washington Women's Network. **Honors:** Beta Phi Mu, 1976. **Pubns.:** *Society for Technical Communication Cumulative Index* (1978); "Marketing Online Services", *ONLINE* (Ja. 1980, Ap. 1980); *Solar Energy Information Locator* (1978); "On Preparing a Persuasive and Technical Information Presentation," In: *Proc., ASIS,* (1977); "Management–The Neglected Tool" In: *Proc., SLA* (1976). **Activities:** 14-Consult.; 24, 38, 41; 75, 80, 86 **Addr.:** P.O. Box 23737, L'Enfant Plaza, Washington, DC 20024.

Smith, Patricia L. (O. 10, 1931, Otley, Yorkshire, Eng.) Chief, Lib. Srvs., Gvt. of NT, 1965–; Branch Libn., Gvt. of BC, 1959–65; Interne Libn., Toronto Pub. Libs., 1955–57; Sr. Asst., W. Riding Cnty. Libs., 1953–55. **Educ.:** Univ. of Toronto, 1957–59, BA (Fr.); Assoc. of Lib. Assn. (UK), 1954. **Orgs.:** Can. LA. Lib. Assn. (UK). Prov. & Territorial Lib. Dir. Cncl.: Secy. (1980–81). **Pubns.:** Contrib., *Can. Libs. in Their Changing Environment,* (1977); "Beyond the City: Library Services to Children in the Northwest Territories," *Intl. Lib. Review* (1975); "The Library is People" Videotape (1973–74). **Activities:** 13; 17, 24, 34; 66 **Addr.:** P.O. Box 1100, Hay River, NT X0E 0R0 Canada.

Smith, Raymond W. (S. 25, 1923, Deposit, NY) Dir., Four Cnty. Lib. Syst., 1978–, Asst. Dir., 1967–78; State Libn., State of DE, 1965–66; Asst. Dir., South. Tier Lib. Syst., 1961–65. **Educ.:** Syracuse Univ., 1946–50, BA (Eng.), 1950–51, MS (LS). **Orgs.:** ALA. NY LA: Mem. Com. (1967–76); Ch., Pub. Libs. Sect. Mem. Com. (1976); VP, Pub. Libs. Sect. (1977); Pres., Pub. Libs. Sect., (1978). Binghamton Rotary Club. **Activities:** 9; 16, 17, 39; 72 **Addr.:** Four County Library System, Clubhouse Rd., Binghamton, NY 13903.

Smith, Reginald Weldon (Ap. 12, 1925, Pittsburgh, PA) Assoc. Dir., Coll. of Med. & Dentistry of NJ, 1968–; Adj. Fac., Rutgers Grad. Sch. of Lib. and Info. Std., 1972–; Head, Drug Info., Wampole Labs., Stamford, CT, 1967–68; Libn., Inst. for the Advnc. of Med. Comm., 1965–67; Libn., Wyeth Labs., Radnor, PA, 1961–65. **Educ.:** Univ. of Pittsburgh, 1946–49, BS (Pharm.); West. Resrv. Univ., 1955–57, MSLS. **Orgs.:** Med. LA: Progr. Com. (1977–78); Cont. Educ. Com. (1977–79). SLA: Ch., Pharm. Div. (1973); Ch., NJ Chap. (1976). **Pubns.:** Jt. auth., "Evolving the 90 Pharmaceutical Library," *Spec. Libs.* (F. 1970). **Activities:** 1; 17, 26, 31; 80 **Addr.:** College of Medicine and Dentistry of New Jersey, 100 Bergen St., Newark, NJ 07103.

Smith, Richard D. (My. 1, 1927, S. Bethlehem, PA) Pres., Wei T' o Assocs., 1972–; Instr. (LS), Univ. of Chicago, 1976–; Consult., Pub. Arch. of Can., 1976–; Asst. Prof. (LS), Univ. of WA, 1971–74; Engin., 1952–63. **Educ.:** PA State Univ., 1948–52, BS (Ceramic Sci.); Univ. of Denver, 1963–64, MA (LS); Univ. of Chicago, 1964–71, PhD (LS); Regis. Prof. Engin. (OH). **Orgs.:** SAA: Prsrvn. Methods Com. (1972–). SLA: Resrch. Com. (Ch., 1972–74). ALA. Natl. Arch. Adv. Com. on Prsrvn. (1980–). Various other orgs. Amer. Chem. Socty. Mss. Socty. Inst. of Paper Cons. **Pubns.:** Jt. ed., *Deterioration and Preservation of Library Materials* (1970); "A Comparison of Paper in Identical Copies of Books from the Lawrence University, The Newberry, and The New York Public Libraries," *Restaurator* (Suppl. 2, 1972); "Design of a Liquified Gas Mass Deacidification System for Paper and Books," *Preservation of Paper and Textiles of Historic and Artistic Value* (1977); "Preservation: Library Need and Industry Opportunity," *Lib. Scene* (D. 1979, Mr. 1980); various other articles, patents, reviews. **Activities:** 6, 11; 23, 24, 26; 59, 64 **Addr.:** Wei T'O Associates, P.O. Box 40, Matteson, IL 60443.

Smith, Robert Charles (N. 24, 1943, McComb, MS) Assoc. Prof., Dept. of LS and Instr. Media, West. KY Univ., 1973–; Media Libn., Park Elem. Sch., Baton Rouge, LA, 1971–73; Media Spec., BCT Com. Grp., Ft. Ord, CA, 1969–70; Par. Libn., Assumption Par. Lib. Demonstration, Napoleonville, LA, 1967–68. **Educ.:** Southeast. LA Coll., 1962–66, BA (Hist. & Geo.); LA State Univ., 1967–75, MEd (LS), MA (Educ. Admin.), MS (LS), EdD (Admin.-Media). **Orgs.:** ALA. AECT. KY LA: Ed., *KY Libs.* (1979–82); Pubns. Com. (1978–82); Lib. Educ. Sect., Ch., (1977–78); Exec. Bd. (1977–78). SELA: Outstan. Auth. Awds. Com., (1979–80). **Pubns.:** "The Effects of Economic Inflation on Local Public Library Support in Kentucky", *ERIC* (1978); Jt. auth., *Library Personnel Education Report.* (1978); "Accreditation and the Profession," *Southeast. Libn.* (Spr. 1979); "The 'Boob Tube': What School Media Librarians Can Do", *KY LA Bltn.* (Spr. 1978); "Some Effects of Federal Funding upon Public Library Services in Louisiana," *LA LA Bltn.* (Win. 1976). **Activities:** 10, 11; 24, 26, 27; 63, 67, 93 **Addr.:** Dept. of Library Science/Inst. Media, Helm 5A, Western Kentucky University, Bowling Green, KY 42101.

Smith, Robert S. (S. 4, 1943, Pittsburgh, PA) Adult Ref., Branch Mgr., Cuyahoga Cnty. Pub. Lib., 1980–, 1979–80, Coord., YA Srvs., 1976–79, Branch Head, 1971–75; Head Libn., Richland Pub. Lib., 1967–70. **Educ.:** Duquesne Univ., 1961–66, BA (Classics); Univ. of Pittsburgh, 1966–67, MLS, 1968–78, Advnc. Cert., (LS); Gestalt Inst. of Cleveland, 1973–75, Cert. (Psy.). **Orgs.:** ALA: Cncl. (1981–84); PR for Libs. (1979–); Alternative Educ. Prog. Sect. (1976–77); Liaison for YASD to RASD (1979–); Ch., Discuss. grp. for YA Coord. (1976–). OH LA: Stan. Revision (1977–79). PA LA. Cath. LA. Youth Srvs. Coord. Cncl. SW Youth Cncl. Berea Cmnty. Ctr.: Trustee (1974–77). **Honors:** Jaycees, Outstan. Young Men, 1975. **Pubns.:** "YA Programming Roundup II", *Top of The News* (Fall 1978); "Politicking", *Sch. Lib. Jnl.* (D. 1977). **Activities:** 9; 16, 17, 48; 50 **Addr.:** 388 Pattie Dr., Berea, OH 44017.

Smith, Roger Grant (O. 23, 1946, Burlington, VT) Mgr., Affirmative Action Plng., Merck and Co., Inc., 1979–, Patent/Tech. Srvs. Coord., 1974–79, Patent/Licn. Info. Coord., 1972–74, Patent Info. Spec., 1969–72; Tech. Info. Sci., Intl. Flavors and Fragrances, 1968–69. **Educ.:** Seton Hall Univ., 1964–68, BC (Chem.), 1970–74, MBA, 1974–75, Cert. (Intl. Bus. Mgt.); U.S. Patent Ofc., 1974, Cert. Patent Agent. **Orgs.:** ASIS: Ctrl. NJ Chap. (Ch., 1979–80). Pharm. Mfrs. Assn.: Sci. Info. Sect., Patent Info. Com. (Ch., 1977–79). Mfr. Chem. Assn.: Tech. Info. Retrieval Com. (1970–78). Derwent Pubns. Adv. Bd. (1974–79). Amer. Chem. Socty. **Pubns.:** Various jnl. articles on patent info., online retrieval, legal info. **Activities:** 12; 17, 35, 49-Plng.; 56, 87, 95-Int. property. **Addr.:** Merck and Co. Inc., R60-120 P.O. Box 2000, Rahway, NJ 07065.

Smith, Roger J. (Je. 15, 1938, Orpington, Kent, Eng.) Assoc. Prof., Sch. Libnshp. Dept., Fac. of Educ., Univ. of Toronto, 1970–; Head Libn., Cedarbrae Collegiate, 1965–69, Asst. Libn., 1963–65. **Educ.:** Univ. of Toronto, 1959–62, BA (Gen. Arts), 1969–70, BLS, 1973–76, MLS; HS Asst. Cert., Coll. of Educ., Univ. of Toronto, 1962–63, Spec. Cert. in Sch. Lib., 1966. **Orgs.:** Can. LA. ON LA: Educ. Com. (1979). ON Lib. Educ. Assn. **Pubns.:** Jt. ed., *"Canadian Stories of Action and Adventure"* (1978); *"The Library or How I Learned to Love Melvil Dewey"* (1976); "Ontario School-Housed Public Libraries," in *The Canadian School-Housed Public Library* (1979); Jt. auth., "Combination School and Public Libraries; An Attitudinal Study" *Can. Lib. Jnl.* (Je. 1976); Reviews. **Activities:** 10, 11; 25, 26, 48; 50, 63, 67 **Addr.:** Faculty of Education, 371 Bloor St. West, Toronto, ON M5S 2R7 Canada.

Smith, Rosemary Romaker (Ap. 26, 1926, Liberty Ctr., OH) Libn., Nappanee Mid. Sch., Wakarusa K-8, Nappanee, IN, 1978–; Asst. Libn., Assoc. Mennonite Biblical Seminaries, 1971–78. **Educ.:** Bowling Green State Univ., 1944–48, BScEd (Soc. Std.); IN Univ., South Bend; West. MI Univ., 1970–71, MSL. **Orgs.:** ALA. Psi Chi. AAUW. Natl. Educ. Assn. IN State Tchrs. Assn. **Honors:** Beta Phi Mu. **Activities:** 1, 10; 17, 20, 48; 63, 90, 92 **Addr.:** 2606 Wood St., Elkhart, IN 46514.

Smith, Ruth Camp (O. 10, 1916, Washington, DC) Chief, Lib. Branch, Div. of Resrch. Srvs., Natl. Inst. of Hlth., 1973–; Dir., Sci. Docum. Div., Nvl. Ship Syst. Cmnd., 1971–73; Head, Info. Anal. and Prcs. Branch, Nvl. Ship R & D Ctr., 1968–71, Thesaurus Coord., 1965–68; Head, Tech. Prcs. Sect., Bur. of Ships Tech. Lib., 1961–65, Head, Cat. Sect., 1949–61; Asst. Branch Libn., Libn., New York Pub. Lib., 1942–48; Serials Libn., Howard Univ., 1939–41. **Educ.:** Howard Univ., 1933–37, AB; Hampton Inst., 1937–38, BS (LS); Columbia Univ., 1941–45, MLS; Amer. Univ., 1960–67, Cert.; Cornell Univ., 1969, Cert. **Orgs.:** IFLA: Secy., Bio. and Med. Libs. Sect., Spec. Libs. Div. (1977–81). Med. LA: Com. on Bibl. Proj. and Problems (1974–76); Ch., Bibl. and Info. Srvs. Assess. Com. (1976–77). SLA: Docum. Div., (Treas., 1974–1976); (Ch., 1977–1978). Fed. Libns. Assn.: Ed., *FLA Nsltr.* (1975). Other orgs. **Honors:** Navy Merit. Civilian Srv. Awd., 1973; DHEW Sr. Mgt. Cit., 1978. **Pubns.:** *Bureau of Ships Thesaurus of Descriptive Terms and Code Book.* (1964); "SHARP: Experiences in Library Automation," *Spec. Libs.* (1973). **Activities:** 4; 17, 24, 34; 58, 60, 80 **Addr.:** National Institutes of Health Library, 9000 Rockville Pike, Building 10, Rm. 1L25G, Bethesda, MD 20205.

Smith, Ruth (Lillian) Schluchter (O. 18, 1917, Detroit, MI) Chief, Ofc. of Cust. Srvs., Natl. Tech. Info. Srv., 1981–; Mgr., Tech. Info. Srvs., Inst. for Defense Analyses, 1975–81, Head Libn., 1967–75, Chief, Unclasfd. Lib. Sect., 1965–67, Ref. Libn., Chief, Reader Srvs., 1961–65; Libn., Bethesda Meth. Church, 1955–61; Resrch. Asst., Moore Sch. Electrical Engin., Univ. of PA, 1946–47; Jr. Libn., Detroit Pub. Lib., 1942–43. **Educ.:** Wayne Univ., 1935–39, AB (Eng.); Univ. of MI, 1941–42, ABLS. **Orgs.:** Com. on Info. Hang-ups: Coord. (1969–). Fed. of Info. Users: VP (1973–75). SLA: Dir. (1981–83); Div. Cabinet (Ch., 1980–81); Lib. Mgt. Div. (Ch., 1978–79); Aerosp. Div. (Ch., 1975–76); Nom. Com. (1977–78); Gvt. Info. Srvs. Com. (Ch., 1971–75). CSLA: Pres. (1967–68); Pubns. Com. (Ch., 1969–75). Various other orgs. **Honors:** SLA, John Cotton Dana

Special Subjects/Services: 50. Adult educ.; 51. Advert./Mktg.; 52. Aerosp.; 53. Agric.; 54. Area std.; 55. Arts/Hum.; 56. Autom.; 57. Bibl./Prtg.; 58. Bio. sci.; 59. Bus./Fin.; 60. Chem.; 61. Copyrt.; 62. Documtn.; 63. Educ.; 64. Engin.; 65. Env.; 66. Eth. grps.; 67. Film; 68. Food/Nutr.; 69. Geneal.; 70. Geo.; 71. Geol.; 72. Handcpd.; 73. Hist.; 74. Int. frdm.; 75. Info. sci.; 76. Insr.; 77. Law; 78. Legis.; 79. Math./Comp. sci.; 80. Med.; 81. Metals; 82. Nat. resrcs.; 83. Newsp.; 84. Nuc. sci.; 85. Oral hist.; 86. Petr./Energy; 87. Pharm.; 88. Phys./Astr./Math.; 89. Readg.; 90. Relig.; 91. Sci./Tech.; 92. Soc. sci.; 93. Telecom.; 94. Transp.; 95. (other).

Awd., 1979. **Pubns.:** *Setting Up a Library; How to Begin or Begin Again* (CSLA Guide No. 1) (1979); *Cataloging Made Easy; How to Organize Your Congregation's Library* (1978); "Interaction Within the Technical Reports Community," *Sci. and Tech. Libs.* (Sum. 1981); "About GPO and the Depository Library Council," *Spec. Libs.* (Jl. 1976); "Government Information—Problems and Options," *Spec. Libs.* (N. 1973); "User Group Technique in Action," *Spec. Libs.* (Ja. 1973); various pamphlets. **Activities:** 4, 12; 17, 29, 36; 62, 75, 91 **Addr.:** 5304 Glenwood Rd., Bethesda, MD 20814.

Smith, S. Mary (Denver, CO) Archvst., Salve Regina - Newport Coll., 1974–, Prof., Asst. prof., 1973–74; Lect., Santa Monica Bus. Sch., 1969–72; Tchr., Feehan HS, 1966–71. **Educ.:** Cath. Tchrs. Coll., 1940–44, BEd (Educ.); Bryant Coll., 1944–46, BA (Bus. Educ.); Cath. Univ., Notre Dame Univ., 1946–50, MA (Bus. Admin.); Case-West. Univ., 1947, Cert. (Econ.). **Orgs.:** SAA. Northeast. Socty. of Archvsts. RI Socty. of Archvsts. **Activities:** 1, 2; 15, 17, 28; 55, 63, 92 **Addr.:** Salve Regina College, Newport, RI 02840.

Smith, Sallye Wrye (N. 11, 1923, Birmingham, AL) Asst. Prof./Ref. Libn., Univ. of Denver Lib., 1980–, Pres., CO Resrchs., Inc., 1979–; Instr./Ref. Libn., 1972–80, Head, Sci.-Engin. Lib., 1969–72. **Educ.:** Univ. of AL, 1942–45, AB (Psy.); Univ. of Denver, 1968–69, MA (LS). **Orgs.:** SLA. ASIS. Rocky Mt. OLUG: Ch. (1979). Beta Phi Mu: Phi Chap. (Pres., 1977). **Honors:** Phi Beta Kappa. **Pubns.:** Indxr., *Statistical Abstract of Colorado 1976–77* (1976); "Venn Diagramming for On-Line Searching," *Spec. Libs.* (N. 1976). **Activities:** 1; 39, 49-Online srch.; 91 **Addr.:** 1666 S. Fairfax St., Denver, CO 80222.

Smith, Sharman B. (S. 2, 1951, Lambert, MS) Head, Info. Srvs., MS Lib. Comsn., 1978–; Dir., Lincoln-Lawrence-Franklin Reg. Lib., Brookhaven, MS, 1977–78, Asst. Dir., 1975–77; Libn., Clinton (MS) Pub. Lib., 1972–74. **Educ.:** MS Univ. for Women, 1969–72, BS (LS); George Peabody Coll., 1974–75, MLS; Tchrs. Cert., 1972. **Orgs.:** MS LA: Int. Frdm. Com. Ctrl. MS Lib. Cncl.: Ch. (1980). **Activities:** 4, 9; 17, 22, 39 **Addr.:** Mississippi Library Commission, P.O. Box 3260, Jackson, MS 39207.

Smith, Sharon E. (Mr. 5, 1950, Las Vegas, NM) Asst. Acq. Libn., Univ. of Houston, 1979–; Serials Libn., Wright State Univ., 1978–79; Tech. Reports/Docum. Libn., TX A & M Univ., 1977–78, Serials Libn., 1972–77. **Educ.:** NM Highlands Univ., 1967–71, BA (Eng/Jnlsm.); Univ. of TX, 1971–72, MLS. **Orgs.:** TX LA: Acq. RT (Ch., 1976–77); Rcrt. Com. (1977–78); Cncl. (1976–77). Acad. LA of OH: Serials Forum, Ch. (1981); Nom. Com. (1979). **Pubns.:** Jt. Cmplr., *TX Lib. Jnl. Index, 1924–75* (1977); "Telephone Directory Acquisitions," *TX Lib. Jnl.* (N. 1976); "Serials Songsheet", *Amer. Libs.* (F. 1976). **Activities:** 1; 15, 29, 44 **Addr.:** 9267 Imogene Houston, TX 77036.

Smith, Susan Christine (Ja. 22, 1946, Detroit, MI) th Yr. Spec. Prog. Student, Wayne State Univ., 1981–; Archvst., Harper-Grace Hosp., 1979–81; Libn., Grace Hosp. Sch. of Nursing, 1971–79. **Educ.:** Univ. of MI, 1964–69, BA; Wayne St. Univ., 1969–70, MSLS; Med. LA, Cert. (Grade I), 1973; Wayne St. Univ., 1979–80, (Arch.). **Orgs.:** Med. LA. CSLA. Allen Park United Presby. Church: Church Lib. (Ch. 1978–). **Activities:** 2, 12; 17; 80 **Addr.:** 15 E. Kirby, Apt. 704, Detroit, MI 48202.

Smith, Susan Perry (S. 1, 1942, Asheboro, NC) Actg. Dean, Lib. Srvs., Evergreen State Coll., 1981–, Lib. Coord. of Media Srv., 1978–81, Lib. Coord. of User Srv., 1975–78, Head of Circ., 1972–75; Order Libn., Univ. of NC (Chapel Hill), 1970–72; Med. Ref. Libn., VA Hosp. (Durham, NC), 1968–70; Ref. Libn., Multnomah Cnty. Lib. (Portland, OR), 1967; Head of Circ., Gleason Lib., Univ. San Francisco, 1966; Ext. Libn., Fort Bragg, NC, Spec. Srv. Lib., 1965. **Educ.:** Wake Forest Univ., 1960–63, BA (Hist.); Univ. of NC (Chapel Hill), 1963–64, MSLS. **Orgs.:** ALA. WA Lib. Ntwk. Exec. Cncl.: Ch. (1979). **Honors:** WHCOLIS, Del., 1979. **Activities:** 1; 17, 31, 32; 66, 92, 95-Women's Std. **Addr.:** Library, Evergreen State College, Olympia, WA 98501.

Smith, Susanna R. (Shelbyville, IN) Hosp. Libn., Flint Pub. Lib., 1976–, Cat. Libn., 1974–76, Ref. Libn., 1969–74; Sch. Libn., Potterville Pub. Sch., 1968–69. **Educ.:** Kalamazoo Coll., 1956–60, BA (Fr.); Univ. of MI, 1964–67, AMLS, 1960–62, AM. **Orgs.:** NLA. **Pubns.:** "Beginning Positions and Training Programs in Genesee, Lapeer and Shiawassee Counties" rpt. (1974). **Activities:** 5, 9; 16, 21, 27; 80 **Addr.:** Flint Public Library, 1026 E. Kearsley, Flint, MI 48502.

Smith, Thelma Paterson (My. 20, 1927, Detroit, MI) Libn., Alamo Heights Jr. Sch., 1973–; Libn., Cambridge Elem. Sch., 1968–73; Ed. Asst., USAFSS, 1950–52; Tchr., Jefferson Intermediate Sch., 1948–50. **Educ.:** Wayne State Univ., 1944–48, BS (Educ.), 1948–51, MS (Educ.); Our Lady of the Lake Coll., San Antonio, TX, 1967–73, MLS; various crs. **Orgs.:** TX LA. ALA. Bexar LA. TX Assn. Sch. Libns.: Schol. Com. (Ch., 1980–81). Alamo Heights Tchrs. Assn. Frnds. of San Antonio Pub. Lib. TX State Tchrs. Assn. Natl. Educ. Assn. Various other orgs. **Activities:** 10; 15, 21, 32 **Addr.:** 2911 Belvoir, San Antonio, TX 78230.

Smith, Thomas A. (S. 16, 1947, Canton, OH) Cur. of Mss., Rutherford B. Hayes Presidential Ctr., 1981–; Mss. Libn., Rutherford B. Hayes Lib., 1974–81; Tchg. Fellow, Dept. of Hist., Miami Univ., 1972–74. **Educ.:** Bowling Green State Univ., 1965–69, BS (Hist.), 1969–71, MA (Hist.); Miami Univ., 1971–74, (Hist.). **Orgs.:** SAA: Strg. Com., Mss. Prof. Afnty. Grp. (1979). Socty. of OH Archvsts.: Cncl. (1978–80); Ed. Adv. Bd. (1979). Socty. of OH Archvsts.: Pres. (1981–82). Org. of Amer. Histns. OH Acad. of Hist. Phi Alpha Theta. Phi Kappa Phi. **Pubns.:** "Ohio's Favorite Son: Rutherford B. Hayes," *The Western Reserve Magazine* (Jl.-Ag., 1981); "Before Hyde Park: The Rutherford B. Hayes Library," *The American Archivist* (Fall, 1980); "The Firelands and the Settlement of Vermillion," *The Western Reserve Magazine* (Mr.-Ap., 1980); "A Northwest Ohioan's View of California", *NW OH Qtly.* (Sum., 1979); "The Hayes Library," *Socty. of OH Archvsts. Nsltr.* (Fall, 1979). **Activities:** 2, 12; 15, 33, 45; 69, 92 **Addr.:** The Rutherford B. Hayes Presidential Center, Spiegel Grove, Fremont, OH 43420.

Smith, Valerie M. (F. 14, 1947, Mt. Pleasant, PA) Supvsr., Chld. Srvs., Lorain Pub. Lib., 1974–; Adult Srvs. Libn., Garfield Hts. Lib., 1973–74; YA Libn., Parma-Show Lib., 1970–71. **Educ.:** Bowling Green State Univ., 1965–68, BA (Educ., LS); Kent State Univ., 1971–72, MLS. **Orgs.:** OH LA: Prog. Peddler Com.; Hi/Lo Task Force (1979–80). ALA. **Addr.:** Lorain Public Library, 351 6th St., Lorain, OH 44052.

Smith, Virginia Carlson (Je. 30, 1944, Pasadena, CA) Consult., 1976–; Ref. Libn., Univ. of CA, Santa Barbara, 1974–76, Art Libn., 1969–74. **Educ.:** Univ. of CA, Santa Barbara, 1962–66, BA (Art Hist.); Univ. of CA, Berkeley, 1968–69, MLS, 1967–68 (Art Hist.). **Orgs.:** ARLIS/NA. Natl. Audubon Socty. Sierra Club. **Pubns.:** "Microforms," *Art Library Manual* (1977); *Juan de Borgoña and His School: A Bibliography* (1973); "Computerized Approach to Art Exhibition Catalogs," *Lib. Trends* (Ja. 1975); "Art Exhibition Catalog Program of U.C.S.B.," *ARLIS/NA Nsltr.* (Ap. 1973). **Activities:** 1; 24, 30, 39; 55, 56 **Addr.:** 1708 N. Nevada Ave., Colorado Springs, CO 80907.

Smith, Wilfred Irvin (My. 20, 1919, Port La Tour, NS) Dominion Archvst., Pub. Arch. of Can., 1970–, Actg. Dominion Archvst., 1968–70, Asst. Dominion Archvst., 1966–70, Dir., Hist. Branch, 1965–66, Chief, Ms. Div., various other positions, 1950–65; Instr., Hist. Dept., Univ. of SK, 1948–50. **Educ.:** Acadia Univ., 1940–43, BA (Hist.), 1945–46, MA (Hist.); Univ. of MN, 1946–48, PhD (Hist.). **Orgs.:** Intl. Cncl. on Arch.: Exec. Com. (1972–76); Deputy Secy. Gen. (1976–). Can. Hist. Assn.: Arch. Com. (1967–68); Hist. Booklets Ed. (1965–68). SAA: Cncl.; VP (1968–72); Pres. (1972–73); various com. ch. Natl. Lib. Adv. Bd. various org. Hist. Sites and Monuments Bd. of Can. Can. Heraldry Socty.: Hon. VP. Ord. of St. John. Untd. Empire Loyalist Assn. of Can.: Hon. Pres., Hon. VP. **Honors:** Can. Decor., Cent. Medal, 1967, Jubilee Medal, 1977; Acadia Univ., Hon. DCL, 1975; SAA, Fellow. **Pubns.:** Various articles on arch., rec. mgt. and hist. in prof. jnls. **Activities:** 2; 17 **Addr.:** Public Archives of Canada, 395 Wellington St., Ottawa, ON K1A 0N3 Canada.

Smith, William Keith (F. 2, 1935, Adrian, MI) Asst. Prof., West. MI Univ., 1967–; Dir., Coldwater Pub. Lib., 1965–66, Dir., Branch Cnty. Lib., 1964–66; Coord., Pub. Srvs., Genesee Cnty. Lib., 1961–63. **Educ.:** Univ. of MI, 1953–55; West. MI Univ., 1955–57, AB (Pol. Sci.), 1960–61, MA (Libnshp.), 1970, SpA (Lib. Mgt.). **Orgs.:** ALA: Lippincott Awd. Jury (Ch., 1974–75). AALS: Adult Srvs. Interest Grp. MI LA: PR Com. (1971–72); Nom. Com. (1971–72); Recreation and Schol. Com., Ch.; Cnty. and Reg. Secy. (Ch., 1966–67); Dist. I (Ch., 1966–67); Legis. Com. (Ch.-Elect, 1965–66). **Honors:** Phi Mu Alpha Sinfonia; Beta Phi Mu. **Activities:** 9, 11; 16, 17, 39; 50, 66 **Addr.:** 3514 Edinburgh Dr., Kalamazoo, MI 49007.

Smith, Yvonne B. (S. 6, 1937, Ft. Wayne, IN) Sr. Lit. Chem., Intl. Flavors and Fragrances, 1978–; Libn., Amer. Can Co., 1973–78; Libn., RCA Corp., 1972–73. **Educ.:** IN Univ., 1955–59, AB (Math.); Drexel Univ., 1967–71, MS (Info. Sci.). **Orgs.:** SLA: Princeton/Trenton Nsltr. Ed. (1974–75). ASIS: NJ Mem. Com. (1979–80). Tech. Assn. Pulp and Paper Indus.: Info. Retrieval Com. (1974–78). **Activities:** 12; 39, 49-Lit. Srch., 60, 64 **Addr.:** Intl. Flavors and Fragrances, R&D, TIC, 1515 St. Hwy. 36, Union Beach, NJ 07735.

Smithee, Jeannette P. (Ja. 9, 1946, Cleveland, OH) Lib. Dir., Onondaga Free Lib., 1981–; Libn., Laubach Litcy. Intl., 1975–81; Ref. Libn., Coord. Litcy. Prog., Savannah Pub. Lib., 1973–75, Ref. Libn., 1970–71; Libn., Rickards Sr. HS, 1968–70. **Educ.:** FL State Univ., 1964–68, BA (LS); Syracuse Univ., 1975–77, MLS. **Orgs.:** ALA: PLA/Alternative Educ. Progs. Sect., Org. Com. (1979–). SLA: Upstate NY Chap., Student Papers Com. (1979–80), Nsltr. Rpt. (1980–). Natl. Affiliation for Litcy. Advnc. Leag. of Women Voters. **Pubns.:** "TV and Literacy: British Programming Bequeaths Sound Advice," *Litcy. Advnc.* (Fall 1981); "National NALA Library Supports Councils," *Litcy. Advnc.* (Fall 1981); "NALA's Loan Library Expands," *Litcy. Advnc.* (Spr. 1980); "LLI-NALA Library Collection," *Litcy. Advnc.* (Fall 1978); "Resource Materials for a Shoestring Budget," *Litcy. Advnc.* (Win. 1976). **Activities:** 6, 12; 17, 41, 46; 50, 89 **Addr.:** Onondaga Free Library, 4840 W. Seneca Turnpike, Syracuse, NY 13215.

Smithson, Paul G. (Ag. 15, 1946, Deposit, NY) Asst. Dir., Kalamazoo Coll., 1972–, Head, Tech. Srvs., 1971–, Head, Ref. Srvs., 1971. **Educ.:** Kalamazoo Coll., 1964–68, BA; West. MI Univ., 1968–72, MSL. **Orgs.:** ALA. OCLC, Inc. MI Lib. Cnsrtm. Cat. Peer Cncl. Beta Phi Mu: Kappa Chap. Bach Fest. Socty. of Kalamazoo. **Activities:** 1; 17, 20, 46 **Addr.:** Kalamazoo College Library, Thompson and Academy Sts., Kalamazoo, MI 49007.

Smoke, Lillian H. (Ja. 12, 1909, Baltimore, MD) Libn. Emerita, Gettysburg Coll. Pres. Bd. of Trustees, Adams Cnty. (PA) Lib. Syst., 1981–; Head Libn., Gettysburg Coll., 1959–74; Actg. Libn., Juniata Coll. 1942–44, Asst. Libn., 1931–41. **Educ.:** Juniata Coll., 1927–31, AB (Eng., Latin); Columbia Univ., 1934–35, BLS. (Acad. Libnshp.). **Orgs.:** ALA. PA LA: Coll. and Resrch. Div. (Ch., 1970–72). AAUW: Bylaws Com. (Ch., 1950–54) Educ. Com. (Ch., 1950–54). **Honors:** PA LA, Cert. of Merit, 1972. **Activities:** 1, 9; 17, 34, 47; 54, 55, 57 **Addr.:** 249 N. Washington St., Gettysburg, PA 17325.

Smolin, Judith R. (Je. 2, 1951, Miskolc, Hungary) Prin. Ofcr., Knowledge Exchange, Inc., 1980–; Info. Srvs. Libn., Natl. Acad. of Sci., 1979–80; Libn., Natl. Clearinghouse for Biling. Educ., 1978–79; Libn., Vets. Admin., Ctrl. Ofc., 1978; Libn., Tele-Sec Lib. Srv. Grp., 1976–78. **Educ.:** OH State Univ., 1969–73, BS (Educ.); Univ. of Pittsburgh, 1975–76, MLS (Lib., Info. Sci.). **Orgs.:** ALA. ASIS. SLA. Bnai Brith Women. **Pubns.:** *Guide to Professional Organizations* (1979); "Directory of Library Associations Serving Ethnic and Minority Communities," *Educ. Libs.* (Spr.–Sum. 1979). **Activities:** 4, 12; 34, 39, 49-Online Srvs.; 56, 80, 91 **Addr.:** 12630 English Orchard Ct., Silver Spring, MD 20906.

Smutny, Ernestine S. (Ag. 14, 1920, S. Norfolk, VA) Serials Libn., Univ. of the Pac. Lib., 1963–; Ref. Libn., Catlgr., Stockton San Joaquin Pub. Lib., 1955–63; Catlgr., Univ. of NM, 1953–55; Libn. 1, Prin. Lib. Asst., Univ. of CA, Berkeley, 1950–53. **Educ.:** Coll. of William and Mary, 1937–41, BA (Latin, Grk.); Columbia Univ., 1946–47, MA (Latin); Univ. of CA, Berkeley, 1950–53, BLS. **Orgs.:** ALA. CA LA: Tech. Srvs. Chap. (Treas., 1979). **Honors:** Phi Beta Kappa, 1941; Phi Kappa Phi, 1964. **Pubns.:** Ed., *Union List of Serials in the 49/99-CAL Cooperative Library System* (1968–); Bk. Review Ed., *Pac. Histn.* (Fall 1973–80). **Activities:** 1; 39, 44; 56 **Addr.:** Library, University of the Pacific, Stockton, CA 95211.

Smythe, Alvetta Denise (O. 26, 1953, Washington, DC) Supervisory Libn., Taylor Nvl. Ship R and D Ctr., 1976–, Acq. Libn., 1975–76. **Educ.:** Amer. Univ., 1971–74, BA (Soclgy., Latin Amer. Std.); Catholic Univ. of Amer., 1974–75, MSLS; various wkshps. **Orgs.:** ASIS. CLENE. SLA. **Pubns.:** Ed., *EEO Gazette* (1978). **Activities:** 4, 12; 15, 17, 39; 81, 91, 92 **Addr.:** 3144 Apple Rd., N.E., Washington, DC 20018.

Snapp, Elizabeth M. (Mr. 31, 1937, Lubbock, TX) Actg. Dir., Lib., TX Woman's Univ., 1979–, Asst. to Provost, Grad. Sch., 1977–79, Coord. of Readers Srvs., Lib., 1974–77, Head, Acq., 1971–74, Cat. Libn., 1969–71. **Educ.:** N. TX State Univ., 1966–68, BA (LS), 1968–69, MLS, 1972–77, MA (Hist.). **Orgs.:** ALA: ACRL. TX LA: Prog. Com. (1978), Post-conf. Coord. (1978). TX Cncl. for State Univ. Libns.: Prsrvn. of Lib. Mtrls. Com. (1980–81). AAUP: TX Rep. to Natl. Coal. Against Censorship (1975–76). TX Assn. of Coll. Tchrs.: Nom. Com. (1977–78). Assn. Higher Educ. of N. TX: AV Un. List Std. Com. (Ch., 1981). Beta Phi Mu: Natl. Dir. (1980–82); Natl. Adv. Asm. Pres. (1979–80), Secy. (1978–79). **Pubns.:** "Government Patronage of the Press in St. Louis, Missouri: 1829-1832," *MO Hist. Review* (Ja. 1980); "The Acquisition of the Vollbehr Collection of Incunabula for the Library of Congress," *Jnl. of Lib. Hist.* (Ap. 1975). **Activities:** 1, 11; 17, 20, 26; 56, 57, 83 **Addr.:** Box 24093, Texas Woman's University Station, Denton, TX 76204.

Snead, Barbara J. (Jl. 9, 1948, Wadsworth, OH) Lib. Dir., Hiram Coll., 1979–, Head, Tech. Srvs., 1976–79, Serials/Ref. Libn., 1974–76. **Educ.:** Oberlin Coll., 1967–71, BA (Grmn.); Kent State Univ., 1973–74, MLS. **Orgs.:** Acad. LA of OH: Secy. (1979–81). Northeast. OH Libs. Assn.: Trustee (1981). ALA. **Honors:** Phi Beta Kappa. **Activities:** 1; 17, 31, 46; 95-Women's std. **Addr.:** Hiram College Library, P.O. Box 98, Hiram, OH 44234.

Snedeker, Sherrill A. (Mr. 18, 1952, Salem, OH) Info. Spec., Tech., BF Goodrich Co., 1979–; Info. Spec., Babcock & Wilcox Co, 1974–79. **Educ.:** Hiram Coll., 1970–74, BA (Math); Kent State Univ., 1975–, (LS). **Orgs.:** SLA: Cleveland Chap. ASIS: Rec. Secy. (1977–78); OH ASIS Rep. (1979–81). Cleveland Area OLUG. Alliance Cmnty. Concert Assn. **Activities:** 5; 30, 41, 49-On line srch.; 60, 64, 91 **Addr.:** BF Goodrich Co. - Dept. 0045, Bldg. 10-D, 500 S. Main St., Akron, OH 44318.

Snell, Mary Kay Holmes (Ag. 13, 1936, Sayre, OK) Asst. City Libn., Amarillo Pub. Lib., 1979–, Head, Ref. and Adult Readrs. Srv., 1977–79; Asst. Geneal. Libn., TX State Lib., 1974–77. **Educ.:** Univ. of TX, Austin, 1969–73, BA (Hist.), 1973–76, MLS. **Orgs.:** ALA. TX LA: Dist. VII (Pres., 1980). Soroptimist Intl. Natl. Geneal. Socty. **Honors:** Phi Beta Kappa, 1976; Phi Kappa Phi, 1976. **Pubns.:** Ed., *Bibliography of the Bush/FitzSimon/McCarty Collections on the Southwest* (1979).

PROFESSIONAL ACTIVITIES: Institutions: 1. Acad. lib.; 2. Arch.; 3. Assn.; 4. Fed./Gvt. lib.; 5. Inst. lib.; 6. Mfr./Suppl.; 7. Milit. lib.; 8. Musm.; 9. Pub. lib.; 10. Sch. lib.; 11. Sch. of lib. sci.; 12. Spec. lib.; 13. State lib.; 14. (other). **Functions/Activities:** 15. Acq./Col. dev.; 16. Adult srvs.; 17. Admin.; 18. Apprais.; 19. Archit./Bldgs.; 20. Cat./Class.; 21. Chld. srvs.; 22. Circ.; 23. Cons./Pres.; 24. Consult.; 25. Cont. ed.; 26. Educ. lib. sci.; 27. Ext. srvs.; 28. Fund/Grants; 29. Gvt. pubs.; 30. Indx./Abs.; 31. Instr. lib. use; 32. Media srvs.; 33. Micro.; 34. Netwks./Coop.; 35. Persnl.; 36. PR; 37. Publshg.; 38. Recs. mgt.; 39. Ref. srvs.; 40. Repro.; 41. Resrch.; 42. Review.; 43. Secur.; 44. Serials; 45. Spec. col.; 46. Tech. srvs.; 47. Trustees/Bds.; 48. YA srvs.; 49. (other).

Activities: 4, 9; 17, 30, 39; 57, 69 **Addr.:** 2220 Milam, Amarillo, TX 79109.

Snell, Patricia P. (Ap. 11, 1943, Santa Fe, NM) Head, Bindery Prep., Los Angeles Cnty. Law Lib., 1977–, Catlgr., 1976–77, Ord. Libn., 1972–76; Acq. Libn., Univ. of NM Sch. of Law Lib., 1971–72; Asst. Law Libn., Univ. of Miami Sch. of Law Lib., 1970–71; Med. Libn., Bedford Vets. Admin. Hosp. Lib., 1968–69; Asst. Educ. Libn., Univ. of South. CA Educ. Lib., 1966–68. **Educ.:** Univ. of NM, 1961–65, BA (Hist., Educ.); Univ. of South. CA, 1965–66, MSLS. **Orgs.:** ALA. CA Assn. of Resrch. Libs. South. CA Assn. of Law Libs. Beverly Hills Presby. Church. **Honors:** Pi Lambda Theta, 1964; Phi Alpha Theta, 1964. **Activities:** 12, 13; 23, 46; 77 **Addr.:** Los Angeles County Law Library, 301 W. 1st St., Los Angeles, CA 90012.

Snezek, P. Paul (S. 4, 1936, Vermilion, OH) Dir., Lib. and Instr. Media, Wheaton Coll., 1970–, Dir. of Lib., Moody Bible Inst., 1969–70. **Educ.:** Philadelphia Coll. of Bible, 1960–62, BS (Christ. Educ.); N. TX Univ., 1967–68, BA (Hist.); Dallas Semy., 1962–66, MTh (Theo.); North. IL Univ., 1971–72, MA (LS); Univ. of Chicago, 1973, CAS (LS). **Orgs.:** ALA: ACRL. IL ACRL. LIBRAS: Pres.-Elect (1981). Conf. on Christianity and Lit. Pvt. Coll. of IL: Pres.-Elect (1981). Faith and Hist. Socty. for the Std. of Relig. under Communism: Bd. of Dirs., Ch. **Activities:** 1; 17, 35, 45; 57, 90, 93 **Addr.:** Buswell Library, Wheaton College, Wheaton, IL 60187.

Snider, David P. (My. 22, 1948, Highland Park, MI) Lib. Dir., Casa Grande Pub. Lib., 1977–; Head, Pub. Srvs., Mesa Pub. Lib., 1974–77. **Educ.:** Amer. Univ. of Beirut, Lebanon, 1970–72, BA (Eng. Lit.); Wayne State Univ., 1972–74, MSLS. **Orgs.:** AZ State Lib. Assn.: Anl. Conf. (Ch., 1975, 1977); Chap. Cnclr. to ALA (1976, 1978–82). ALA: PLA, Org. Com. (1978–80). Casa Grande Police Athl. Leag. Casa Grande Valley Hist. Socty. **Pubns.:** "Arizona," *Libraries in the Political Process* (1980); "Pop-Rock Sexist Scene," *Voice of Youth Advocates* (Je. 1979); "Libraries and the Popular Music Periodical," *Rockin' in the Fourth Estate* (Sum. 1978). **Activities:** 9; 16, 28, 48; 54 **Addr.:** Casa Grande Public Library, 405 E. 6th St., Casa Grande, AZ 85222.

Snodgrass, Wilson D. (Ja. 15, 1932, Angleton, TX) Assoc. Dir., Ctrl. Univ. Libs., South. Meth. Univ., 1980–, Assoc. Dir., Prcs. Srvs., 1977–79, Asst. Dir., 1969–77, Head, Cat. Dept., 1960–69, Catlgr., 1959–60; Catlgr., Univ. of TX, El Paso, 1956–59; Docum. Libn., Sam Houston State Univ., 1954. **Educ.:** Sam Houston State Univ., 1949–52, BS (LS); Univ. of TX, Austin, 1952–54, MLS. **Orgs.:** ALA: RTSD, Bylaws Com. (1971–73); Cncl. of Reg. Grps. (1964–65); Dallas Conf. Prog. Com. (1978–79)/CCS, Dallas Conf. Prog. Com. (1970–71). AMIGOS Bibl. Cncl.: South. Meth. Univ. Tech. Srvs. Liaison (1975–). TX LA: Spec. Com. on Round Tables (Ch., 1965–66); TX Reg. Grp. of Catlgrs. and Clasfrs., Ch. (1964–65); Exec. Com. (1970–71). Various org. Univ. of TX Grad. Sch. of Lib. Sci. Alum. Assn. Interuniv. Cncl. of the N. TX Area: Spec. Com. for a Reg. Lib. Ctr. (1973–74); Eval. Adv. Com., Interuniv. Cncl./OCLC Netwk. Eval. Std. (1974–75); Lib. Com., Subcom. to Std. Coop. Prcs. (1970–71). **Honors:** Beta Phi Mu, 1954. **Pubns.:** "Music Libraries and Collections in Texas," *TX Lib. Jnl.*, (S. 1957); "Crowds in San Antonio," *Opera News* (Ap. 5, 1954); various msc. reviews, criticism in *Musical Amer.* (1957–59). **Activities:** 1; 15, 17, 20; 55, 56 **Addr.:** P.O. Box 1505, Southern Methodist University, Dallas, TX 75275.

Snoke, Helen Lloyd (My. 20, 1926, Miami, OK) Prof., LS, Univ. of MI, 1977–, Assoc. Prof., LS, 1971–77, Asst. Prof., LS, 1969–71; Dir., Sch. Media Srvs., OK City Pub. Schs., 1966–69; Asst. Prof., OK State Univ., 1965–66, Instr., 1963–65; Sch. Libn., OK City Pub. Schs., 1956–63; Asst. Libn., Glendale Un. HS, 1952–53. **Educ.:** Univ. of OK, 1945–48, BA (Drama); Lindenwood Coll., 1944–45; Univ. of OK, 1956–60, MLS, 1965–68, PhD (Educ.). **Orgs.:** ALA: Com. on Restructuring ALA (1977–78); Publshg. Com. (1978–); AASL, Bd. of Dirs. (1968–69, 1973–76); Pres. (1974–75), various ofcs.; ALSC, various coms.; LAMA, various coms. AECT. AALS. MI Assn. for Media in Educ.: Bd.; *Media Spectrum* Ed. (1980); Int. Frdm. Com. (Ch., 1975–77). Various other orgs. Assn. for Supvsn. and Currie. Dev. **Honors:** Beta Phi Mu; Univ. of OK, Sch. of LS, Disting. Alum., 1979. **Pubns.:** "The Future of School Libraries and Librarianship," *OK Libn.* (Ja. 1980); "Leadership Beyond the Building Level," *Sch. Media Qtly.* (Spr. 1979); "Children and Television—Concerns for Library School Library Media Specialists," *Sch. Media Qtly.* (Spr. 1977); "1974 Status Report of the University of Michigan–Experimental Program in School Library Media Education," *Evaluation of Alternative Curricula, Approaches to School Library Media Education* (1975); "Final Report of the University of Michigan Experimental Program in School Library Media Education, 1971–1973," *Curriculum Alternatives, Experiments in School Library Media Education* (1974). **Activities:** 10, 11; 21, 26, 32 **Addr.:** School of Library Science, University of Michigan, 580 Union Dr., Ann Arbor, MI 48109.

Snow, Bonnie S. (S. 10, 1947, Akron, OH) Head, Ref. Srvs., Srch. Anal., Philadelphia Coll. of Pharm. and Sci., 1977–, Ref. and Serials Libn., 1976–77; Tchr., Spec. Educ. Prog., Waterville Pub. Schs., 1973–74. **Educ.:** Wellesley Coll., 1965–69, BA (Eng. Lit.); Drexel Univ., 1974–77, MSLS. **Orgs.:** Med. LA: Pharm. Spec. Interest Grp. (Ch., 1978–80); Cont. Ed. Instr. (1979–). Amer. Assn. of Colls. of Pharm.: Sect. of Libs., Educ. Resrcs. Ch.-Elect (1979–80), Ch. (1980–81). Philadelphia Area Ref. Libns. Info. Exch.: Ref. Srvs. Coord. (1979–80). SLA: Rep. to PA State ILL Code Dev. Grp. (1978–79). Drexel Lib. Sch. Alum. Assn.: Nom. Com. (1979–80). AAUP. Drug Info. Assn. **Honors:** Beta Phi Mu, 1977. **Pubns.:** "Drug Information Requests at the Philadelphia College of Pharmacy and Science," *Amer. Jnl. of Pharm. Educ.* (My. 1979); ed., *Joseph W. Eng. Lib. Nsltr.* (1976–); various papers, Amer. Assn. of Colls. of Pharm. (1977–78). **Activities:** 1, 12; 25, 31, 39; 58, 80, 87 **Addr.:** 4306 Chestnut St. Apt. 404, Philadelphia, PA 19104.

Snowball, George J. (Ap. 24, 1926, Streatham, Eng.) Lectr., Concordia Univ., 1975–, Actg. Asst. Dir., Lib., Sr. Libn., 1967–; Visit. Lectr., McGill Univ., 1971–74; Abstctr., Indxr., Amer. Geol. Inst., 1967–69; Tech. Rec. Ofcr., Geol. Srvy. of Zambia, 1957–67; Extra-Mural Lectr., Leicester Univ., 1950–54; Keeper of Geol., Leicester Musm. and Art Gallery, 1949–57, Asst. Keeper of Geol., 1947–49. **Educ.:** Univ. Coll., London, Eng., 1944–47, BSc (Geol.); McGill Univ., 1969–71, MLS. **Orgs.:** ALA. PQ LA: Treas. (1974–76). Can. LA: Stats. Com. (1971); Can. Assn. of Coll. and Univ. Libs., Wkshp. on Col. Dev. (Ch., 1972, 1973), Wkshp. on Graph. in the Lib. (Ch., 1974). Geosci. Info. Socty. Intl. Geol. Congs.: Montreal Mtg. (1972); Exhibits Com. (1969–72). Musms. Assn.: Musms. Assts. Grp. (Secy., 1948–49). Leicester Lit. and Phil. Socty. Assn. of African Geol. Srvys. Various org. **Honors:** Geologists Socty. of London, Fellow. **Pubns.:** "Application of the Triangular Diagram to the Presentation of Library Data," *Can. Lib. Progress* (1973); Jt. Auth., "Selection of Periodicals for Return to Prime Space from a Storage Facility," *Can. Lib. Jnl.* (N.–D. 1973); Jt. Cmplr., "Bibliography of the Geology of Leicestershire (to 1970)," *Mercian Geologist* (D. 1973); "A Preliminary Account of the Planning, Carrying Out and Results of a Survey of Library Users on the Sir George Williams Campus of Concordia University," *Conf. Proc. PQ LA* (1975); Jt. Auth., "Control of Book Fund Expenditures Under an Accrual Accounting System," *Col. Mgt.* (Spr. 1979); various articles, presentations, reviews. **Activities:** 1; 17, 19, 26; 57, 63, 95-Stats. **Addr.:** 4866 Cote Des Neiges, # 1106, Montreal, PQ H3V 1H1 Canada.

Snowden, Deanna (F. 5, 1942, near Ozark, AR) Asst. Dir., Libs., MS Cnty. Lib. Syst., MS Cnty. Cmnty. Coll. Fac., 1977–; Libn., Carnegie Lib. of Pittsburgh, Msc. & Art Dept., Gen. Ref. Dept., 1972–77; Asst. Libn., Msc. Lib., Univ. of Pittsburgh, 1970–71, Asst. Libn., Bus. Lib., 1969–70; Asst. Libn., Hazelwood Sch. Dist., 1967–69, Tchr., 1965–67; Tchr., Pangburn, AR, 1964–65. **Educ.:** Harding Univ., 1960–64, BA (Elem. Educ., Soc. Sci., Hum.); Univ. of Pittsburgh, 1969–71, MLS; various libn. crs. **Orgs.:** ALA: LAMA (State Rpt., 1979). AR LA. SWLA. ARLIS/NA. MS Cnty. Cmnty. Coll. Concert Com. NE AR Amer. Cancer Socty. AR Cmnty. Coll. Libs. Assn. **Activities:** 1, 9; 17, 36, 46; 63, 75 **Addr.:** 200 N. 5th, Blytheville, AR 72315.

Snyder, Bette T. (My. 27, 1937, Colfax, WA) Corporate Fin. Assoc., Underwood, Neuhaus and Co., 1975–; Libn., Oppenheimer and Co., 1969–74; Asst. Libn., Morgan Stanley and Co., 1966–68; Libn., Indus. Rel. Couns., 1962–66. **Educ.:** Univ. of OR, 1957–59, BA (liberal Arts); Univ. of WA, 1955–57; Columbia Univ., 1961–62, MLS. **Orgs.:** SLA. Assn. for Corporate Growth. **Activities:** 12; 17; 59 **Addr.:** Underwood, Neuhaus & Co., Inc., 724 Travis, Houston, TX 77002.

Snyder, Carolyn Ann (N. 5, 1942, Elgin, NE) Assoc. Dean, Pub. Srvs., IN Univ. Libs., 1977–, Persnl. Libn., 1973–77; Asst. Dir., Readr. Srvs., various other positions, Univ. of NE, 1970–73; Admin. Army Libn., Europe, 1968–70. **Educ.:** Kearney State Coll., 1961–64, BS (Home Econ.); Univ. of Denver, 1964–65, MA (Libnshp.). **Orgs.:** NE LA: Natl. Lib. Week (Exec. Dir., 1973); various com. IN LA: Autom. RT (Secy., 1973–74); various com. ALA: ACRL, various com.; LAMA, Bd. of Dir. (1977–78), VP, Pres.-Elect (1980–81), various com.; RASD, ILL Com. (1978–79); various com., ofcs. FTRF. Various org. IN Univ. Club. IN Univ. Women's Fac. Club. AAUP. AAUW. **Pubns.:** Jt. Auth., "Continuing Education/Staff Development: Needs Assessment, Comprehensive Program Planning, and Evaluation," *Jnl. of Acad. Libnshp.* (Jl. 1978); Jt. Auth., "Flexible Scheduling: The Indiana University Experience," *Lib. Jnl.* (Ap. 1, 1976); Ed. Bd. *Jnl. of Acad. Libnshp.* (1980–); IN LA Pubns. Bd. (1980–). **Activities:** 1; 17, 35, 39; 61, 63 **Addr.:** Library Administration, IN University Libraries, Bloomington, IN 47405.

Snyder, Louise Cathey (Mr. 20, 1928, Seattle, WA) Dir., Sterling Coll., 1973–; Libn., Hutchinson HS, 1972–73; Prin., Intl. Sch., 1958–66; Tchr., 1950–55. **Educ.:** Wheaton Coll., 1946–50, BA; Univ. of Denver, 1970–72, MA (Libnshp.); Univ. of Denver, 1978–81, CAS. **Orgs.:** ALA: ACRL. KS LA. **Honors:** Beta Phi Mu, 1973. **Activities:** 1; 17; 63, 90 **Addr.:** Sterling College, Sterling, KS 67579.

Snyder, Patricia B. (Je. 4, 1932, Detroit, MI) Info. Srvs. Rep., Shell Dev. Co., 1977–; Sci. Libn., Wesleyan Univ., 1970–77; Ad Hoc Fac., South. CT State Coll. Lib. Sch., 1972–75; Head, Syst. Dept. Lib., Untd. Tech., 1967–70. **Educ.:** Univ. of NC, 1961–66, BS (Eng.), 1966–70, MLS; Rensselear Polytech. Inst., 1968–71, MCS (Comp. Sci.); Univ. of CT, 1974–77, MBA (Bus. Admin.). **Orgs.:** SLA: CT Valley Chap. (Pres., 1972–73), Hosplty. Com. (Treas., Secy.), Consult. Intl. Toastmistress Inc. Assn. of MBA Exec. **Pubns.:** *Connecticut Union List of Serials* (1973); various articles in: *Spec. Libs.* (1974). **Activities:** 1, 12; 17, 38, 41; 56, 59, 91 **Addr.:** Shell Development Co., P.O. Box 4248, Modesto, CA 95352.

Snyder, Rena M. (Jl. 28, 1949, Fairmont, MN) Dir., of Lib. Srvs., Un. Meml. Hosp., 1978–; Ref./Circ. Libn., Med. and Chirurgical Fac. of the State of MD, 1977–78. **Educ.:** OH State Univ., 1967–71, BA (Soclgy.); Univ. of MD, 1975–76, MLS; Med. LA, 1977, Cert. **Orgs.:** MD Assn. of Hlth. Scis. Libns.: Pres. (1980–81). Natl. Lib. of Med. Reg. IV: Adv. Cncl., Exec. Bd. (1979–80). Med. LA: Mid. Atl. Reg., Prog. Com. (1980–81). **Activities:** 12; 17; 80 **Addr.:** The Union Memorial Hospital, 201 E. University Pkwy., Baltimore, MD 21218.

Snyder, Richard L. (F. 18, 1927, Toronto, ON) Dir., Libs., Drexel Univ., 1965–; Assoc. Dir., MA Inst. of Tech., 1962–64, Sci. Libn., 1959–62; Sci. Libn., IN Univ., 1958–59, Bio. Libn., 1955–58, Dept. of Geol., Geol. Srvy. Libn., 1953–55. **Educ.:** Univ. of Toronto, 1945–49, BA (Phys. Sci.); IN Univ., 1949–52, MALS. **Orgs.:** ALA: ACRL, DE Valley Chap./Subj. Spec. Sect., Ch. (1967–68), Pres. (1969–71); Bd. of Dirs. (1968–73). SLA: Boston Chap., Sci. Tech. Grp. (Ch., 1963–64). Documtn. Abs., Inc.: Treas., Actg. Bus. Mgr. (1966–70); Bd. of Dirs. (1966–70). EDUCOM: Drexel Univ. Rep. (1967–73). PALINET: Bd. of Trustees, Ch. (1972–75); Pres. (1980–81). various other orgs. Unitarian Flwshp., Bloomington, IN: Bd. of Dirs. (1956–57). Q. T. Inc., Boston: Bd. of Dirs., (1960–61). Various other orgs. **Honors:** Cncl. on Lib. Resrcs., Flwshp., 1971–72. **Pubns.:** jt. cmplr., *International Union List of Communist Chinese Serials* (1963); "Scientific and Technical Books of 1966. One Hundred Outstanding Titles for a General Collection," *Lib. Jnl.* (Mr. 1, 1967); jt. auth., "Searching at the Drexel Institute of Technology Libraries," *HI LA Jnl.* (1967); various reviews. **Activities:** 1; 17; 75, 91 **Addr.:** Drexel University Libraries, 32nd & Chestnut Sts., Philadelphia, PA 19104.

Snyder, William E. (N. 12, 1930, Johnsonburg, PA) Head Libn., OH State Univ., Newark Campus, 1976–; Head, Admin. Srvs., SUNY, Albany, 1972–76; Head Libn., OH State Univ., Mansfield Campus, 1970–72, Ref. Libn., Lima Campus, 1969–70; Libn., Turkey Foot Valley Area Schs., 1966–68, Tchr., 1964–66. **Educ.:** PA State Univ., 1948–52, BA (Soclgy.); Univ. of Pittsburgh, 1967–69, MLS. **Orgs.:** ALA. Acad. LA of OH. **Honors:** Beta Phi Mu, 1969. **Activities:** 1; 15, 17; 63, 92 **Addr.:** OH State University, Newark Campus, Founders Hall, University Dr., Newark, OH 43055.

Snyder, William E., Jr. (Jl. 31, 1949, Baltimore, MD) Dir., Sampson-Clinton Pub. Lib., 1975–; Adult Srvs. Libn., Wilson Cnty. (NC) Pub. Lib., 1971–74. **Educ.:** E. Carolina Univ., 1967–71, BS (Hist.), 1971–73, MLS; Univ. of Miami, 1978 (LS, Lib. Admin. Dev.). **Orgs.:** ALA. NC LA: JMRT, Ch. SELA. NC Pub. Lib. Dir. Assn. **Activities:** 9; 17, 19, 47 **Addr.:** Sampson-Clinton Public Library, Connestee St., Clinton, NC 28328.

Snyder, William H. (My. 27, 1920, Grand Rapids, MN) Lib. Dir., City/Cnty. Lib. of Missoula, 1970–; Ext. Libn., Jackson Cnty. Lib. Syst., 1968–70. **Educ.:** Seattle Pac. Coll., 1950–54, BA (Hist.); Univ. of Dubuque, 1954–57, MA (Theo.); Univ. of OR, 1966–67, MA (LS). **Addr.:** City-County Library of Missoula, 101 Adams, Missoula, MT 59801.

Snyderwine, L. Thomas (Ja. 27, 1943, Sharon, PA) Dir., The Nash Lib., Gannon Univ., 1980–; Asst. Dir., 1979–80; Dir., Relig. Educ., St. Patrick Church, 1976–79; Guid. Instr., Cathedral Prep., 1971–76. **Educ.:** St. Mary's Semy. & Univ., 1962–64, BA (Phil.); Cath. Univ. of Amer., 1964–68, MA (Educ.); Nova Univ., 1972–75, EdD (Supvsn.); Case West. Rsv. Univ., 1979–80, MSLS. **Orgs.:** ALA. NW Interlib. Coop. Assn. of PA: Treas. (1980–82). US Coast Grd. Auxiliary. **Pubns.:** "The Future of the Card Catalog," *Educ. Media Sci.* (Sum. 1980). **Activities:** 1, 2; 17, 24, 35; 56, 63, 92 **Addr.:** Nash Library, Gannon University, Perry Sq., Erie, PA 16541.

Soapes, Thomas F. (N. 11, 1945, Independence, MO) Archvst., Oral Histn., Ofc. of Pres. Libs., Natl. Arch. and Rec. Srv., 1978–; Dir., Eleanor Roosevelt Oral Hist. Proj., Franklin D. Roosevelt Lib., 1977–78; Oral Histn., Dwight D. Eisenhower Lib., 1975–77, Archvst., 1973–75. **Educ.:** Univ. of MO, 1963–67, BSEd (Soc. Std.), 1967–69, AM (Hist.), 1969–73, PhD (Hist.). **Orgs.:** Oral Hist. Assn. **Pubns.:** "The Federal Writer's Project Slave Interviews: Useful Data or Misleading Source," *Oral Hist. Review* (1977); "The Fragility of the Roosevelt Coalition: The Case of Missouri," *MO Hist. Review* (O. 1977). **Activities:** 2, 4; 15, 39, 45; 56, 73, 85 **Addr.:** Office of Presidential Libraries, National Archives and Records Service, Washington, DC 20408.

Sobkowski, Nikoletta Taminen (N. 22, 1943, Chicago, IL) Asst. Libn., Univ. of MI, 1977–, Lectr., 1976–79, Sr. Instr. Assoc., 1973–75; Elem. Sch. Tchr., Seattle Sch. Bd., 1967–68. **Educ.:** MI State Univ., 1961–67, BA (Hist.); Rosary Coll., 1971–72, MALS. **Orgs.:** ALA. Frnds of the Ann Arbor Pub. Lib. AAUW: Legis. Ch. (1978–79); Bk. Sale (Co-Ch., 1979–80). **Ac-**

Special Subjects/Services: 50. Adult educ.; 51. Advert./Mktg.; 52. Aerosp.; 53. Agric.; 54. Area std.; 55. Arts/Hum.; 56. Autom.; 57. Bibl./Prtg.; 58. Bio. sci.; 59. Bus./Fin.; 60. Chem.; 61. Copyrt.; 62. Documtn.; 63. Educ.; 64. Engin.; 65. Env.; 66. Eth. grps.; 67. Film; 68. Food/Nutr.; 69. Geneal.; 70. Geo.; 71. Geol.; 72. Handcpd.; 73. Hist.; 74. Int. frdm.; 75. Info. sci.; 76. Insr.; 77. Law; 78. Legis.; 79. Math./Comp. sci.; 80. Med.; 81. Metals; 82. Nat. resrcs.; 83. Newsp.; 84. Nuc. sci.; 85. Oral hist.; 86. Petr./Energy; 87. Pharm.; 88. Phys./Astr./Math.; 89. Readg.; 90. Relig.; 91. Sci./Tech.; 92. Soc. sci.; 93. Telecom.; 94. Transp.; 95. (other).

Who's Who in Library and Information Services

tivities: 1, 12; 15, 20, 39; 63, 66, 92 **Addr.:** 1606 Brooklyn, Ann Arbor, MI 48104.

Soergel, Dagobert (Ja. 7, 1940, Freiburg, Germany) Prof. (LS), Univ. of MD, 1976–, Visit. Lectr., Assoc. Prof., 1970–76; Head, Documtn. Dept., DATUM, Bad Godesberg, 1969–70; Head, Documtn. Dept., Stiftung Wissenschaft und Politik, Ebenhausen, 1967–69. **Educ.:** Univ. of Freiburg, 1958–60, BS equivalent (Phys.), 1960–64, MS equivalent (Math., Phys.), 1964–70, PhD (Pol. Sci.), 1966–67, Tchg. Cert. **Orgs.:** ASIS: Educ. Com. (Ch., 1978–79). Assn. Comp. Mach. AALS. Deutsche Gesellschaft fur Dokumentation. **Pubns.:** *Indexing Languages and Thesauri* (1974); *Dokumentation und Organisation des Wissenschaft* (1971); "Is User Satisfaction a Hobgoblin?" *Jnl. of ASIS* (Jl. 1976); "Mathematical Analysis of Documentation Systems," *Info. Storage and Retrieval* (Jl. 1967); various other articles. **Activities:** 11; 20, 30, 49-Info. needs Std.; 75 **Addr.:** College of Library and Information Services, Hornbake Library, University of Maryland, College Park, MD 20742.

Sohl, Marjorie Ann (F. 27, 1919, Hammond, IN) Head, Adult Srvs., Hammond Pub. Lib., 1946–. **Educ.:** IN Univ., 1937–44, AB (Eng.); Univ. of IL, 1944–46, BS (LS). **Orgs.:** ALA. IN LA. CSLA. IN Hist. Socty. Hammond Hist. Socty. Altrusa Club of Hammond. **Activities:** 9; 16, 39; 67 **Addr.:** Hammond Public Library, Hammond, IN 46320.

Sokol, Christine W. (Mr. 18, 1946, Cincinnati, OH) Dir., Franklin Pub. Lib., 1975–; Chld. Libn., Rockville Ctr. Pub. Lib., 1974–75; Chld. Libn., Elmont Pub. Lib., 1973–74; Chld. Libn., Baltimore Cnty. Pub. Lib., 1971–73. **Educ.:** Univ. of Cincinnati, 1965–68, BA (Eng.); Univ. of KY, 1970, MSLS. **Orgs.:** ALA. NE LA. NH LA. **Activities:** 9; 15, 17, 21; 89 **Addr.:** 310 Central St., Franklin Public Library, Franklin, NH 03235.

Solbrig, Dorothy J. (Mr. 14, 1945, Baltimore, MD) Libn., Bio. Labs., Harvard Univ., 1971–. **Educ.:** Goucher Coll., 1962–66, AB (Bio.); Univ. of MI, 1966–69, AM (Bot.); Simmons Coll., 1970–72, MS (LS). **Orgs.:** ALA: LITA; ACRL; RTSD. New Eng. OLUG. **Pubns.:** Jt. Auth., *Introduction to Population Biology and Evolution* (1979). **Activities:** 1; 15, 20, 39; 58 **Addr.:** Biological Labs. Library, Harvard University, 16 Divinity Ave., Cambridge, MA 02138.

Sollenberger, Julia F. Gingrich (O. 15, 1950, Lancaster, PA) Systs. Libn., Tech. Srvs. Div., Natl. Lib. of Med., 1978–, Lib. Assoc., 1977–78; HS Tchr. (Math), 1972–76. **Educ.:** Manchester Coll., 1968–72, BA, magna cum laude (Math.); IN Univ., 1976–77, MLS. **Orgs.:** Med. LA. SLA. **Honors:** Beta Phi Mu, 1977; Kappa Mu Epsilon. **Activities:** 4; 17, 46; 56, 80, 91 **Addr.:** National Library of Medicine, 8600 Rockville Pike, Bethesda, MD 20209.

Solloway, Athalie Bel Macfarlane (Victoria, BC) Trustee, Richmond Pub. Lib., 1976–. **Educ.:** Royal Bus. Coll., Victoria, BC, (Acct., Bus. Admin.); Univ. of BC, BA (Psy., Eng.). **Orgs.:** Can. LA. Can. Lib. Trustee Assn.: 2nd VP. (1979–80); Pres. (1981–82). Can. Assn. of Pub. Libs.: Ad Hoc Com. on Future of Lib. Bds. (1979–80). ALA: ALTA, Pubcty. Com. (1978–80); State Assn. Com., 1978–80); Reg. VP, Reg. X (1980–82). Univ. Women's Club of Richmond, BC. Can. Fed. of Univ. Women: Cncl. Rep. Kappa Kappa Gamma: Alum. Assn. of Vancouver. **Pubns.:** *Residential and Commercial Library Information Survey of the Municipality of Richmond* (1975). **Activities:** 9; 36, 47; 95-User & non-user Surveying Policy. **Addr.:** 9751 #3 Rd., Richmond, BC V7A 1W2 Canada.

Solomon, Seena L. (Jl. 20, 1926, Brooklyn, NY) Dir., Bergen-Passaic Reg. Film Ctr., Johnson Pub. Lib., 1974–, Asst. to Dir., 1972–74; Sch. Libn., Norwood Pub. Sch., 1970–72; Sch. Libn., Emerson Sch., 1968–70. **Educ.:** Brooklyn Coll., 1943–47, BA (Rom. Lang.); William Peterson Coll., 1955–57, Cert. (Elem. Tchrs. Licn.), 1968–70, Tchrs.-Libn. Cert.; Columbia Univ., 1970–72, MA (Instr. Tech.); Long Island Univ., 1972–77, MLS. **Orgs.:** NJ LA: AV Sect., Corresp. Secy. NJ Gvrs. Conf. on Lib. and Info. Srv.: Rep. (1979). **Honors:** Beta Phi Mu, 1977. **Activities:** 9; 15, 17, 32; 67 **Addr.:** Bergen-Passaic Regional Film Center, Johnson Public Library, 275 Moore St., Hackensack, NJ 07601.

Solomon Shiff, Linda A. (Mr. 2, 1952, Montreal, PQ) Head Libn., Can. Nurses Assn., 1980–; Lib. Dir., Can. Hosp. Assn., 1977–80; Libn., Centraide, 1976–77; Asst. Libn., Cote St. Luc Pub. Lib., 1975–76. **Educ.:** Smith Coll., 1969–73, AB (Fr.); McGill Univ., 1973–75, MLS. **Orgs.:** SLA. Med. LA. CHLA. **Pubns.:** Ed., *The Health Administrator's Library* (1978, 1st supplement 1979). **Addr.:** Canadian Nurses Association, 50 Driveway, Ottawa, ON K2P 1E2 Canada.

Solow, Linda I. (O. 14, 1947, New York, NY) Msc. Libn., Msc. Catlgr., MA Inst. of Tech., 1972–; Msc. Sect., Descr. Cat. Div., Lib. of Congs., 1971–72; various positions as tchr., consult., 1966–80. **Educ.:** Grt. NY Inst. of Msc., 1956–68 (Piano Flute); Brooklyn Coll., CUNY, 1968, BA (Msc.), 1970, MA (Musicology); Univ. of MI, 1971, AMLS; various crs. **Orgs.:** Msc. LA: Bd. of Dir. (1976–78); Pubns. Cncl. (Ch., 1978–); Nom. Com. (1980); various com.; New Eng. Chap., various com., ch. Intl. Assn. of Msc. Libs.: Bd. of Dir., US Branch (1978–80); Nom. Com., (1978); various com. Assn. of Rec. Snd. Cols.: Mem. Dir. Com. (1980–). Amer. Socty. of Indxrs. various org. The Word Gld. Amer. Msclgy. Socty. **Honors:** Intl. Assn. of Msc. Libs., US Branch, Travel Grant, 1976, 1978, 1980. Amer. Socty. of Indxrs., H. W. Wilson Co. Indexing Awd., 1979; Beta Phi Mu, 1971; H. W. Wilson Co., Lib. Awd., 1970. **Pubns.:** Jt. Auth., "IAML Convenes in Cambridge," *Msc. LA Nsltr.* (1980); "Education for Music Librarianship in the United States," *Fontes Artis Musicae* (1979); "IAML Meets in Lisbon," *Msc. LA Nsltr.* (1978); "An Index to Publishers, Engravers, and Lithographers and A Bibliography of the Literature Cited in the IAML *Guide for Dating Early Published Music,*" *Fontes Artis Musicae* (1977); "Qualifications of a Music Librarian, A Statement prepared by the Members of the Committee on Professional Education," *Fontes Artis Musicae* (1974); *Checklist of Music Bibliographies* (1974); various articles, indxs., ed. positions. **Activities:** 1; 15, 17, 30, 39, 42; 57, 95-Music. **Addr.:** Music Library (14E-109), Massachusetts Institute of Technology, Cambridge, MA 02139.

Solt, George (Ap. 2, 1913, Pecs, Baranya, Hungary) Chief Prov. Law Libn., Dept. of the Attorney Gen., 1969–81; Actg. Law Libn., Univ. of AB, 1968–69, 1964–65; Head, Legal Dept., Mnstry. of Chemical Indus., Hungary, 1952–56. **Educ.:** Univ. of Pecs, Hungary, 1931–35, Dip. (Law); Acad. of Cmrce., Vienna, Austria, 1935–37, Dip. (Cmrce.); Budapest Bar Assn., 1945–47, PhD (Law); Univ. of AB, 1968–69, Cert. (LS). **Orgs.:** Can. ALL: Com. on Law Socty. Libs. (1970–72); Place. Com. (1973). Edmonton Law Libs. Assn. AALL. Various org. Hungarian Cult. Socty.: VP (1970–73); Exec. Secy. (1975–79). **Honors:** Gvt. of the Prov. of AB, AB Achvmt. Awd. of Excel., 1978. **Addr.:** Attorney General & Law Society of Alberta Library, Edmonton, AB T5J 0R2 Canada.

Soltow, Martha-Jane (Jl. 9, 1924, PA) Libn., Sch. of Labor and Indus. Rel., MI State Univ., 1961–; Head, Corp. Recs., Sch. of Bus. Admin., Harvard Univ., 1958–59. **Educ.:** Dickinson Coll., 1942–46, PhB (Psy.); Pratt Inst., 1952–53, MLS. **Orgs.:** ALA. Com. of Indus. Rel. Libns. Indus. Rel. Resrch. Assn. **Pubns.:** "University Industrial Relations Libraries; An Overview," *Spec. Libs.* (Ap. 1976); *American Labor History; a Guide to Sources in the Michigan State University Libraries* (1980); jt. auth., *Industrial Relations and Personnel Management; Selected Information Sources* (1979); *American Women and the Labor Movement, 1825–1974; an Annotated Bibliography* (1976); *Women in the American Labor Movement, 1825–1935; an Annotated Bibliography* (1972); various articles. **Activities:** 1; 39, 41; 95-Labor and Indus. Rel. **Addr.:** Libraries, Michigan State University, East Lansing, MI 48824.

Somers, (Mrs.) Carin A. (Mr. 18, 1934, Frankfurt/Main, Hesse, Germany) Dir., Libs., NS Prov. Lib., 1974–, Supvsr., Pub. Libs., 1973–74; Chief Libn., Halifax Cnty. Reg. Lib., 1967–73, Asst. Libn., 1964–67; Libn. Tech. Srvs., Halifax City Reg. Lib., 1961–64; Regis., Saint Mary's Univ., Halifax, 1956–58, Fr. Lectr., 1956–60. **Educ.:** Newton Coll. of the Sacred Heart, Newton, MA, 1953–55, BA (Mod. Lang.); Dalhousie Univ., 1955–56, MA (Fr.); Univ. of Toronto, 1960–61, BLS. **Orgs.:** Atl. Prov. LA: Past-Pres. (1969–70). Can. LA: 2nd VP (1974–75); Mem. Com. (Ch., 1971–73); Aims and Objectives Com. (1970–71). Can. Nat. Fed. NS Bird Socty. **Honors:** Can., Queen Elizabeth II Jubilee Medal, 1977; Can., Gvr. Gen. Medal, 1953. **Pubns.:** "The Public Library Scene in Nova Scotia," *Atl. Prov. Bltn.* (Win. 1974). **Activities:** 9, 13; 17, 34, 47 **Addr.:** Nova Scotia Provincial Library, 5250 Spring Garden Rd., Halifax, NS B3L 4K5 Canada.

Somers, Janet Schlein (Ap. 20, 1942, Stockton, CA) Ref. Libn., Westfield Meml. Lib., 1979–; Catlgr., Juilliard Sch., 1970–79; Art and Msc. Ref. Libn., Newark Pub. Lib., 1969–70; Msc. Catlgr., Cornell Univ., 1966–69. **Educ.:** San Francisco State Coll., 1960–64, BA (Msc.); Univ. of CA, Berkeley, 1965–66, MLS. **Orgs.:** Msc. LA: Com. on the Msc. LA Arch. (1981); Grt. NY Chap. (Ch., 1971–72); Lcl. Arrange. Com. (1974). Intl. Assn. of Msc. Libs. Irvington Symph. Orch. **Activities:** 12; 20, 23, 39; 55 **Addr.:** 168 Madison Ave., Westfield, NJ 07090.

Somerville, Arleen N. (S. 23, 1937, Milwaukee, WI) Head, Sci. & Engin. Libs., Univ. of Rochester, 1976–, Head, Chem., Bio., Geol., Math., Sci. Libs., 1967–76; Head, Bibl. Rec. Grp., Chemical Abs. Srv., 1965–67; Ref. and Per. Libn., Case West. Rsv. Univ., 1962–65. **Educ.:** Univ. of WI, 1955–59, BS (Chem.), 1959–60, MSLS. **Orgs.:** SLA. ASIS. Amer. Chemical Socty. **Honors:** Natl. Sci. Fndn., grant for "Integrated Chemical Info. Curric.," 1979–81. **Pubns.:** "Place of the Reference Interview in Computer Searching: The Academic Setting," *Online* (O. 1977); "Academia and the Environment:...," *Jnl. Chem. Info. Comp. Sci.* (F. 1976). **Activities:** 1; 17, 31, 39; 60, 64, 91 **Addr.:** University of Rochester Library, Rochester, NY 14627.

Somerville, Mary Robinson (Ag. 16, 1941, Fairfield, AL) Coord., Chld. Srvs., Louisville Free Pub. Lib., 1978–; Coord., Young People's Srvs., Lincoln City Libs., 1973–78, Ref., Docum. Libn., 1971–73. **Educ.:** Univ. of NC, 1961–63, BA (Eng.); Univ. of CO, 1964–67, MA (Eng.); Univ. of OK, 1970–1971, MLS. **Orgs.:** NE LA: Sch., Chld. and Young People's Sect. (Ch., 1977–78); Conv. Com. (Ch., 1976). ALA: YASD, Biog. for the Coll. Bound Com. (1979–); ALSC, Boy Scout Adv. Com. (1976–80); ALSC Bd. (1981–84); Managing Chlds. Srvs. Discuss. Grp. (Ch., 1980–82). **Honors:** Phi Beta Kappa, 1963. **Pubns.:** "An Interview with Ruth Rosekrans Hoffmann," *NE LA Qtly.* (Win. 1978); "Recent Trends in Children's Work," *NE LA Qtly.* (Sum. 1978); "How to Knock the Stuffings out of Your Summer Reading Program," *Top of the News* (Spr. 1981). **Activities:** 9; 17, 21, 48 **Addr.:** Louisville Free Public Library, 4th and York Sts., Louisville, KY 40203.

Sommer, Ronald R. (Ag. 18, 1936, Apple Creek, OH) Assoc. Prof., Med. Bibl., Head, Readrs. Srvs., Univ. of TN Ctr. for the Hlth. Sci., 1974–; Hlth. Sci. Libn., Assoc. Prof., Med. Bibl., Northeast LA Univ., 1972–74; Assoc. Prof. Med. Bibl., Assoc. Libn., LA State Univ. Med. Ctr. Sch. of Med., 1968–72; Dir. of Genesys Libs./Assoc. Prof., Univ. of FL, 1967–68, Ref. Libn., Instr., Engin. and Phys. Lib., 1965–67; Libn., Hernando HS, 1961–63; Acad. Instr., Libn., FL Sch. for Boys, 1959–61. **Educ.:** FL State Univ., 1954–58, BS (Eng. Educ.), 1964–65, MS (LS); 1969, Cert. (Med. Libnshp.). **Orgs.:** SLA: Chap. Cabinet (1975–76); Natl. Adv. Cncl. (1970–72); LA Chap., Pres. (1971–72); Exec. Bd. (1970–73); Memphis Prov. Chap., Pres. (1975–76). TN LA: Spec. Libs. Sect., Ch. (1978–79). Memphis Lib. Cncl.: Ch. (1976–77); Treas. (1975–76). LA LA: Lib. Dev. Com. of LA, Northeast LA Reg. (Coord., 1973–74). Various org. AAUP: Dept. Mem. Rep. (1976–78). **Pubns.:** Indxr., "Roentgenographic Diagnosis of Renal Mass Lesions," *Modern Concepts of Radiology Series* (1971); "The Tennessee Library Legislative Network," *TN Libn.* (Spr. 1979); "Bibliographic Control for Tennessee Now: A Look at The Tennessee Numerical Register," *TN Libn.* (Win. 1977); "A Brief Look at Numerical Registers," *Information 2* (Win. 1977); "Public Services in the Library of the LSU Medical School in Shreveport," *Bltn. of the Shreveport Med. Socty.* (Ag. 1971). **Activities:** 1, 12; 17; 56, 80, 87 **Addr.:** University of Tennessee Center for Health Sciences, 800 Madison Ave., Memphis, TN 38163.

Sommer, Susan Thiemann (Ja. 7, 1935, New York, NY) Lectr., Lib. Srv., Columbia Univ. Sch. of Lib. Srv., 1970–. Head, Spec. Cols., Msc. Div., NY Pub. Lib., 1968–; **Educ.:** Smith Coll., 1956, BA magna cum laude (msc.); Columbia Univ., 1956–75, MA, MPhil (Musicology), 1967, MLS. **Orgs.:** Msc. LA: Bd. of Dir. (1974–75); Ed., Notes (1981–). Intl. Assn. of Msc. Libs.: US Bd. of Dir. (1979–81). CNLIA: Secy.-Treas. (1978–79); Nom. Com. (1979); Com. on Coms. (1980). Amer. Musicological Socty.: Com. on Internal Inventory of Musical Srcs. (1970–); Cncl. (1980–82). **Honors:** Phi Beta Kappa, 1955; Fulbright Schol., 1960–61. **Pubns.:** Bk. Review Ed., *Notes* (1978–). **Activities:** 1, 11; 26, 45; 55 **Addr.:** Special Collections, Music, New York Public Library, 111 Amsterdam Ave., New York, NY 10023.

Son, Lark Lee (Ja. 12, 1933, Hwame-dong, Kyungbuk-do, Korea) Acq. Libn., Asst. Ferris State Coll., 1980–, Cat. Libn., Asst. Prof., 1973–80, Asst. Libn., Cat., 1967–73. **Educ.:** Sook-Myung Women's Univ., Seoul, Korea, 1956–60, BA (Educ.); Spaulding Coll., 1965–67, MLS. **Orgs.:** ALA: RTSD. MI LA: Acad. Div. (1974–). MI Lib. Cnsrtm.: Trustee (1979). Nat. Educ. Assn. **Activities:** 1; 20, 44, 46 **Addr.:** 620 Lilac, Big Rapids, MI 49307.

Songe, Alice H. (Je. 15, 1914, Morgan City, LA) Lib., Resrch. Consult., Auth., 1975– Ref. Libn., Natl. Inst. of Educ. Lib., 1973–75; Educ. Spec., Lib., US Dept. of HEW, 1963–73; Educ. Spec., Lib. of Congs., Legis. Ref. Srv., 1956–63; Chief, Ref. Dept., Cath. Univ. of Amer. Lib., 1952–56; various positions as libn. in schs., lib. syst. in LA, NC. **Educ.:** Univ. of Southwestern LA, 1932–36, BA (Liberal Arts); LA State Univ., 1936–37, BS (LS); Cath. Univ. of Amer., 1954–56, MA (Educ.). **Orgs.:** ALA. Amer. Socty. of Indxrs. **Pubns.:** *The Land-Grant Idea in American Higher Education: A Guide to Information Sources* (1980); *American Universities and Colleges: A Dictionary of Name Changes* (1978); Jt. Auth., "Professional Associations at the National Level: A Survey of Their Major Interests," *IFLA Jnl.* (1976); Indxr., *Understanding Church Growth and Decline* (1979); Jt. Auth., *International Guide to Library, Archival and Information Science Associations* (1980); various articles. **Activities:** 14-Consult.; 30; 63, 75 **Addr.:** 4500 Connecticut Ave. N.W. Apt. 608, Washington, DC 20008.

Songstad, Virginia H. (Ja. 5, 1941, Washington, IN) Sr. Ed., Prod. Specifications and Srvs., Chemical Abs. Srv., 1963–. **Educ.:** Marian Coll., 1959–63, BS (Math.). **Orgs.:** ASIS. Amer. Chemical Socty. N. Broadway Chld. Ctr. **Activities:** 6; 30, 46; 56, 60, 75 **Addr.:** Chemical Abstracts Service, P.O. Box 3012, Columbus, OH 43210.

Sonin, Hille (Jl. 13, 1937, Tallinn, Estonia) Head, Acq. Dept., Univ. of San Francisco, 1969–; Head, Srch. Sect., Brandeis Univ., 1968–69; Libn., Berklee Sch. of Msc., 1967–68; Spec. Proj. Libn., Harvard Law Sch. Lib., 1965–66. **Educ.:** Univ. of Toronto, 1957–61, BA (Eng.), 1963–64, BLS (Libnshp.). **Orgs.:** ALA: ACRL; RTSD. Bk. Club of CA. **Honors:** Beta Phi Mu. **Activities:** 1; 15 **Addr.:** Acquisitions Dept., R.A. Gleeson Library, University of San Francisco, San Francisco, CA 94117.

Sonnet, Susan (Ag. 24, 1942, New York, NY) Asst. Msc. Libn., Univ. of CA, Santa Barbara, 1968–; Msc. Catlgr., Yale

PROFESSIONAL ACTIVITIES: Institutions: 1. Acad. lib.; 2. Arch.; 3. Assn.; 4. Fed./Gvt. lib.; 5. Inst. lib.; 6. Mfr./Suppl.; 7. Milit. lib.; 8. Musm.; 9. Pub. lib.; 10. Sch. lib.; 11. Sch. of lib. sci.; 12. Spec. lib.; 13. State lib.; 14. (other). **Functions/Activities:** 15. Acq./Col. dev.; 16. Adult srvs.; 17. Admin.; 18. Apprais.; 19. Archit./Bldgs.; 20. Cat./Class.; 21. Chld. srvs.; 22. Circ.; 23. Cons./Pres.; 24. Consult.; 25. Cont. ed.; 26. Educ. lib. sci.; 27. Ext. srvs.; 28. Fund/Grants; 29. Gvt. pubs.; 30. Indx./Abs.; 31. Instr. lib. use; 32. Media srvs.; 33. Micro.; 34. Netwks./Coop.; 35. Persnl.; 36. PR; 37. Publshg.; 38. Recs. mgt.; 39. Ref. srvs.; 40. Repro.; 41. Resrch.; 42. Review.; 43. Secur.; 44. Serials; 45. Spec. col.; 46. Tech. srvs.; 47. Trustees/Bds.; 48. YA srvs.; 49. (other).

Univ., 1966–68. **Educ.:** City Coll., CUNY, 1960–64, BA (Msc.); Columbia Univ., 1964–66, MLS; Univ. of CA, Santa Barbara, 1972–76, MA (Msclgy.). **Orgs.:** Msc. LA: Place. Com. (Ch., 1966–70); Bd. of Dir. (1974–75); Com. on Educ. (1979). Intl. Assn. of Msc. Libns. Assn. of Rec. Snd. Cols. **Activities:** 1, 2; 15, 20, 39; 55 **Addr.:** Arts Library, University of California, Santa Barbara, CA 93106.

Sonntag, Edith Ericson (Mr. 3, 1943, Durham, NC) Trng. Spec., Enoch Pratt Free Lib., 1980–; Ref. Libn., Soc. Work, IN Univ. 1976–80; Tchg. Asst., Univ. of IA, 1973–75; Acq. Libn., St. Mary's Coll., MD, 1971–72. **Educ.:** Coe Coll., 1960–65, BA (Phil.); SUNY, Geneseo, 1970–71, MLS; Univ. of IA, 1973–76, MA (Urban, Reg. Plng.). **Orgs.:** ALA: GODORT, State and Lcl. Docum. Task Frc. (Secy., 1978–79); Com. of 8 (1978–80). Urban and Reg. Info. Syst. Assn. Ctrl. IN Area Lib. Srvs. Athrty.: Plng. and Eval. Com. (1977–78); PR Com. (1979). IN Info. and Ref. Assn.: Bylaws Com. (1980). Various other orgs. IA Chld. Lobby: Bd. (1974–76); Secy. (1975–76). IA City 4C's. **Activities:** 1, 9; 15, 25, 39; 56, 92 **Addr.:** 2525 Eutaw Pl., 7H, Baltimore, MD 21217.

Sonntag, Iliana Leonor (Ag. 28, 1924, Buenos Aires DF, Argentina) Latin Amer. Biblgphr., San Diego State Univ. Lib., 1981–; Ref. Libn., Span.-Amer. Spec., Univ. of AZ, 1977–, Head, LS Col., 1973–77, Catlgr., 1971–73. **Educ.:** State Univ. of CA, Northridge, 1970, BA (Eng.); Univ. of CA, Los Angeles, 1970–71, MLS; Univ. of AZ, 1973–78, MA (Latin Amer. Std.). **Orgs.:** AZ State LA: Cont. Educ. Com. SWLA: Subcom. on Exch. of Libns., Ch. REFORMA: AZ Chap. (Pres., 1978–79). SALALM: Nsltr.; HAPI Indexing Proj.; Com. on Lib. Srvs. (1976–); Exec. Bd. (1981–). Latin Amer. Std. Assn. Beta Phi Mu: Beta Pi Chap. (Secy., 1979–80). **Pubns.:** Ed., *Guide to Chicano Resources at the University of Arizona Library* (1976); "Bibliografía de escritoras chicanas," *La Palabra* (Sum. 1980); reviews. **Activities:** 1; 15, 31, 39; 54, 66 **Addr.:** 9652 Seth Ln., Santee, CA 92071.

Soo, Sze (F. 20, 1938, Macao) Tech. Srvs., Ref. Libn., Hartnell Coll., 1974–; Tech. Srvs. Libn., DE Tech. and Comm. Coll., 1968–73; Acq. Libn., Worcester Polytech. Inst., 1966–68; Ref. Libn., Indxr., Xerox Corp., 1964–66; Ref. Libn., Linda Hall Lib., 1963–64. **Educ.:** Natl. Taiwan Univ., 1955–60, BS (Phys.); KS State Univ., 1962–63, MS (LS); Univ. of DE, 1968–71, MS (Stats.). **Orgs.:** CA Tchrs. Assn. SLA. Chinese Amer. Citizens Alliance. **Honors:** Delta Kappa Gamma. **Activities:** 1; 15, 20 **Addr.:** 325 Primavera Way, Salinas, CA 93901.

Soong, Samson C. (D. 26, 1945, Hsiangtan, Hunan, China) Actg. Dir., Tech. Srvs., Rutgers Univ., 1981–, Head, Soc. Sci. Cat., 1979–81, Cat. Libn., 1977–79, Actg. Head, E. Asian Lib. 1974–75, Chinese Catlgr., 1971–77; Calligrapher, Harvard-Yenching Lib., Harvard Univ., 1970. **Educ.:** Natl. Taiwan Univ., 1966–68, BA (Pol. Sci.); Tufts Univ., 1969–70, MA (Intl. Rel.); Cath. Univ. of Amer., 1970–71, MSLS; Rutgers Univ., 1976–80, MBA (Mgt.). **Orgs.:** ALA: ACRL. NY Tech. Srvs. Libns. Chinese-Amer. Libns. Assn.: Prog. Com. (1979–81). Assn. for Asian Std. **Pubns.:** *A Chinese-English Glossary of International Relations Terminology* (1976); "Building of East Asian Collections," *Nsltr. of the Com. on E. Asian Libs.* (1974); "Suggestions for the Establishment of a Graduate School of Library Service in Taiwan," *Bltn. of the Natl. Ctrl. Lib.* (1973). **Activities:** 1; 17, 20, 46; 54, 59, 92 **Addr.:** Alexander Library, Rutgers University, New Brunswick, NJ 08903.

Soper, Marley Huber (N. 11, 1934, Leslie, MI) Ch., LS Dept., Andrews Univ., 1967–; Tchr./Libn., WI Acad., 1961–67; Tchr./Libn., Stanton Un. HS, 1958–61. **Educ.:** Andrews Univ., 1953–58, BA (Eng.); Univ. of WI, 1961–67, MALS; Andrews Univ., 1973–77, MA (Hist.). **Orgs.:** ALA. MI LA. MI Acad. of Arts, Scis., Letters. **Pubns.:** "UNSER Seminar," *Adventist Heritage Mag.* (Sum. 1977). **Activities:** 1; 22, 26; 63, 90 **Addr.:** Library, Andrews University, Berrien Springs, MI 49104.

Soper, Mary Ellen (Je. 12, 1934, Wichita, KS) Asst. Prof., Sch. of Libnshp., Univ. of WA, 1972–; Serials Libn., Univ. of NM, 1963–67; Catlgr. Univ. of IL, 1961–63. **Educ.:** Univ. of IL, 1951–55, BA (Soclgy.), 1961–63, MS (LS), 1967–72, PhD (LS). **Orgs.:** ALA: RTSD, Nom. Com. (1975)/Serials Sect., Com. to Study Serials Cat. (1980–82); LITA/AVS, Bd. (1979–81). SLA: Pac. Northwest Chap. (Student Liason, 1975–78). WA LA: Tech. Srvs. Interest Grp. (Ch., 1978–80). AALS: Prog. Plng. Com. (1976, 1978). Various org. AAUP. **Honors:** Phi Beta Kappa, 1954; Beta Phi Mu, 1962. **Pubns.:** "Trends in Bibliographic Control: International Issues," *Lib. Trends* (Ja. 1977); "Characteristics and Use of Personal Collections," *Lib. Qtly.* (O. 1976) "Entry of Serials," *Serials Libn.* (Fall 1976); "Anglo-American Cataloging Rules: Revision of Chapter 6: a Review," *Pac. Northwest LA Qtly.* (Win. 1975); "Description and Entry of Serials in AACR2," *Serials Libn.* (Win. 1979). **Activities:** 1, 11; 20, 26, 44; 61, 62 **Addr.:** School of Librarianship, FM–30, University of Washington, Seattle, WA 98195.

Sopinsky, Philip (S. 29, 1926, Philadelphia, PA) Sr. VP, Prodct. Opers., Inst. for Sci. Info., 1965–; Dir., Data Prcs., Food Fair Stores, Inc., 1961–65; Mgr., Programming, Curtis Publshg. Co., 1959–61; Mgr., Comp. Opers., U.S. Army Signal Corps, 1950–59. **Educ.:** Temple Univ., 1944–49, BS (Cmrce.), 1955–58, EdM (Bus. Educ.). **Orgs.:** ASIS. Data Prcs. Mgt. Assn. GUIDE: Subcom. on Oper. Stats. Assn. for Comp. Mach. various other orgs. **Activities:** 14; 17, 30, 37; 56, 57, 75 **Addr.:** 225 Susan Dr., Elkins Park, PA 19117.

Sorensen, Richard J. (O. 2, 1935, Madison, WI) State Sch. Lib. Media Supvsr., WI Dept. of Pub. Instr., 1972–; Dir., Sch. Libs., Verona Area Pub. Schs., 1967–72, Tchr. (Eng., Latin), 1960–67. **Educ.:** St. Francis Major Semy., Milwaukee, WI, 1955–58, BS (Phil.); Univ. of WI, 1958–59, MS (Educ.), 1965–68, MS (LS). **Orgs.:** ALA: AASL. WI LA. WI AV Assn. Natl. Assn. of State Educ. Media Profs. **Pubns.:** "The Role of School Media Programs in Networks," *Networks for Networkers* (1980); ed., *The Role of the School Library Media Program in Networking* (1978); "The Place of School Libraries/Media Centers in Library Networks," *Lib. Acq.: Prac. and Theory* (1978). **Activities:** 10, 13; 24, 32, 34 **Addr.:** Wisconsin Department of Public Instruction, 125 S. Webster St., P.O. Box 7841, Madison, WI 53707.

Sorkow, Janice R. (S. 20, 1954, Killeen, TX) Mgr., Dept. of Photograph. Srvs., Musm. of Fine Arts, Boston, 1980–, Slide Libn., 1977–80, Catlgr., Slide Lib., 1976–77. **Educ.:** WA Univ., 1972–76, AB (Art Hist.); Simmons Coll., 1977–79, MS (LS). **Orgs.:** Coll. Art Assn.: Prof. Stans. Com. (Grp. Leader, 1978–). ARLIS/NA: Visual Resrcs. Spec. Interest Grp. (Coord., 1981). SLA. Amer. Assn. of Musms. New Eng. Musm. Assn. Amer. Socty. of Pic. Profs. **Pubns.:** "Archival Storage of Visual Resources on a Videodisc," *Videodisc News* (Mr. 1981); vid. disc proj., Msm. of Fine Arts, Boston (1980). **Activities:** 12; 22, 45; 55 **Addr.:** Museum of Fine Arts, 465 Huntington Ave., Boston, MA 02115.

Soroka, Allen H. (Jl. 11, 1938, New York, NY) Asst. Law Libn., Univ. of BC Law Sch., 1969–; Attorney, Criminal Trial Div., Legal Aid Socty. of NY, 1964–69; Attorney, Fed. Rsv. Bank of NY, 1963–64. **Educ.:** Columbia Univ., 1954–58, BA (Arts); Univ. of VA Law Sch., 1958–61, LLB (Law); Columbia Univ., 1967–69, MLS. **Orgs.:** Can. ALL. Can. LA: Copyrt. Com. (Ch., 1973–75). **Pubns.:** *Basic Legal Research* (1979). **Activities:** 1; 15, 39, 41; 61, 77 **Addr.:** University of BC Law Library, 1822 East Mall, Vancouver, BC V6T 1W5 Canada.

Sorrentino, Sherrill O. (My. 3, 1941, Tulare, CA) Proj. Dir., Jonsson Comprehensive Cancer Ctr., Univ. of CA, Los Angeles, 1981–; Med. Libn., Rancho Los Amigos Hosp., 1980; Asst. Med. Libn. to Actg. Dir., Los Angeles Cnty. Harbor-Univ. of CA, Los Angeles, Med. Ctr., 1976–80. **Educ.:** Univ. of CA, Davis, 1964, BA (Psy.); Univ. of CA, Los Angeles, 1969, MA (Zlgy.), 1976, MLS. **Orgs.:** Med. LA: South. CA and AZ Grp., Prog. Com. (Pres.-Elect, 1980–81), PR Com. (Ch., 1979–80). Cancer Libns. Con. Hlth. Info. Prog. and Srvs.: Adv. Bd. (1979–). **Pubns.:** Jt. auth., "CANCERLIT: A New Look," *Natl. Lib. of Med. Tech. Bltn.* (My. 1978); jt. auth., "Cataloging Procedures and Catalog Organization for Patient Education Materials," *Bltn. Med. LA.* (Ap. 1979); jt. auth., "CATLINE as an Acquisitions Tool for Health and Patient Education Materials," *Bltn. Med. LA* (O. 1979). **Activities:** 14-Prog. coord.; 17, 34, 36; 80 **Addr.:** Jonsson Comprehensive Cancer Center, 1100 Glendon Ave., Suite 844, Los Angeles, CA 90049.

Soto, Raymond (Jl. 31, 1944, Needles, CA) Ref. Libn., Univ. of CA, San Diego, 1980–, Serials Catlgr., 1977–79. **Educ.:** Univ. of CA, Los Angeles, 1962–66, BA (Eng.), 1975–77, MLS. **Orgs.:** CA Clearinghse. on Lib. Instr.: South. Strg. Com. (Secy., 1980–81). ALA. **Activities:** 1; 20, 31, 39; 55, 92 **Addr.:** 2777 Dwight St., San Diego, CA 92104.

Soubers, Richard Rodney (F. 3, 1947, Yakima, WA) Archvst., Dwight D. Eisenhower Lib., 1975–. **Educ.:** Ctrl. WA State Univ., 1967–72, BA (Pol. Sci.), 1973–74, MA (Hist.); West. WA State Univ., 1974–75 (Arch. Admin.). **Orgs.:** SAA. Org. of Amer. Histns. KS State Hist. Socty. **Activities:** 2, 4; 39, 42, 45; 55, 67, 92 **Addr.:** 901 N. Olive, Abilene, KS 67410.

Souder, Edith I. (Jl. 22, 1937, DeKalb Cnty., IN) Info. Consult., Info. Resrch. Anals., 1979–; Info. Consult., InfoSrc., 1978–80; Systs. Dsgn./Anal., R. Thornburgh's Campaign for Gvr., 1977–78. **Educ.:** Univ. of Pittsburgh, 1972–77, BS (Info. Sci.), 1977–79, MSIS; Chatham Coll., 1979, Cert. (Entrepreneurship). **Orgs.:** ASIS. Assoc. Info. Mgrs. Pittsburgh Online Users Forum. Natl. Assn. of Women Bus. Owners Natl. Assn. of Bus. Economists. **Honors:** Alpha Sigma Lambda. **Activities:** 12; 24, 25, 41; 56, 59, 80 **Addr.:** Information Research Analysts, 41 Lebanon Hills Dr., Pittsburgh, PA 15228.

Souders, Marilyn Naomi (Jl. 28, 1941, Harmony, NJ) Acq. Libn., Newsweek, Inc., 1980–; Bus. Ref. Libn., Univ. of NC, 1978–80; Dev. Coord., Pratt Inst., 1977–78; Bus. Libn., Brooklyn Pub. Lib., 1976–77; Dir., Resrch., Long Island Hist. Socty., 1972–74. **Educ.:** Pratt Inst., 1960–64, BS (Art), 1973–75, MLS. **Orgs.:** SLA. NC OLUG. **Honors:** Beta Phi Mu, Theta Chap. Awd., 1975. **Activities:** 1; 28, 31, 39; 51, 59, 75 **Addr.:** Newsweek, Inc. Library, 444 Madison Ave., New York, NY 10022.

Souffront, Blanche L. (S. 26, 1931, St. Thomas, VI) Asst. Dir., Bur. of Libs., Musms. and Arch. Srvs., 1976–, Prof. Libn. IV, 1969–76, Chief Libn., 1965–69. **Educ.:** Inter-Amer. Univ., 1952–55, BA cum laude (Eng.); Univ. of MI, 1955–56, MSLS. **Orgs.:** St. Thomas/St. John LA. Enid M. Baa Schol. Fndn. Inc.: Treas. (1979–). **Activities:** 9; 17, 35 **Addr.:** P. O. Box 785, Charlotte Amalie, St. Thomas, VI 00801.

Soule, Harvey G. (O. 8, 1925, Philadelphia, PA) Assoc. Prof., Ref. Libn., Coord., Comp. Info. Srvs., Kent State Univ., 1967–; Ref. Libn., Univ. of MD, 1962–67; Ref. Libn., Univ. of South. CA, 1961–62. **Educ.:** Univ. of TN, 1946–49, BS (Sec. Educ.); Los Angles State Coll., 1955–59, MA (Educ. Admin.); Univ. of South. CA, 1961–62, MS (LS). **Orgs.:** ALA: ACRL, Com. on Bibl. Instr. for Coll. Educs. OH LA. **Pubns.:** Various bibls. **Activities:** 1; 15, 31, 33; 56, 63 **Addr.:** Kent State University, Kent, OH 44240.

Soule, Maria J. (Je. 14, 1944, Kenosha, WI) Libn., FL Keys Cmnty. Coll., 1980–; Ref., Instr. Libn. Univ. of WI, Parkside, 1975–80, Cat. Spec., 1970–75; Campus Libn., Univ. of WI, Kenosha, 1968–71. **Educ.:** Univ. of WI, Milwaukee, 1964–66, BA (Eng., Fr.), 1966–68, MALS. **Orgs.:** ALA: ACRL. FL LA. SELA. **Honors:** Sigma Tau Delta. **Pubns.:** various reviews in *Magill's Survey of Cinema* (1980). **Activities:** 1; 15, 31, 39; 55, 67 **Addr.:** Learning Resources Center, Florida Keys Community College, Key West, FL 33040.

Soules, Aline Elisabeth (F. 2, 1948, Broughty Ferry, Angus, Scotland) Coord. of Extramural Lib. Srvs., Leddy Lib., Univ. of Windsor, 1976–; Libn., Lawrence Inst. of Tech., 1973–76. **Educ.:** Univ. of Windsor, 1965–69, BA (Eng.), 1969–70, MA (Eng.); Wayne State Univ., 1972–73, MSLS. **Orgs.:** ALA: LAMA, Upper MI and ON Rep. Can. LA. MI LA. ON LA. Frnds. of the Detroit Pub. Lib. **Pubns.:** "Off-campus Library Services: Those Inbetween Years," *Procs. of 1st Anl. Conf. of ACRL* (1979). **Activities:** 1; 27 **Addr.:** 24332 Heritage Dr., Woodhaven, MI 48183.

Souter, Thomas A. (My. 16, 1930, Adel, GA) Assoc. Dir., VA Tech., 1975–; Asst. Dir., IN Univ., 1969–75, Head, Circ. Dept., 1962–69; Head Libn., NM Milit. Inst., 1960–62; Soc. Sci. Libn., FL State Univ., 1959–60, Asst. Acq. Libn., 1957–59. **Educ.:** FL State Univ., 1947–50, BS (Soc. Sci.), 1954–57, MLS. **Orgs.:** ALA. SELA. VA LA. **Honors:** Phi Delta Kappa. **Pubns.:** Asst. Ed., *Lib. and Arch. Secur.* (1974–76). **Activities:** 1; 15, 17, 19; 56, 59, 92 **Addr.:** 906 Elliott Dr., Blacksburg, VA 24060.

Southcombe, Patricia A. (Jl. 23, 1939, Kalamazoo, MI) Sch. Lib. Media Spec., Park Rd. Elem. Sch., Pittsford Ctrl. Schs., 1968–; Sch. Lib. Media Spec., Greece Ctrl. Sch. Dist. #1, 1965–68; Sch. Lib. Media Spec., Un.-Endicott Ctrl. Sch. Dist. #1, 1961–65. **Educ.:** State Univ. Coll., Geneseo, 1957–61, BSEd (Lib.), 1962–67, MLS. **Orgs.:** Grt. Rochester Area Sch. Media Specs.: VP (1978–79); Pres. (1979–80); Sch. Lib. Media Specs. Conf. Plng. Com. (1978); Media Madness Com. (1977–81). NY LA. ALA: AASL; YASD; ALSC. Pittsford Dist. Tchrs. Assn. Geneseo Alum. Assn. **Honors:** State Univ. Coll., Geneseo, Disting. Alum. Awd., 1971. **Activities:** 10; 15, 21, 31; 63 **Addr.:** 906 Eastbrooke Ln., Rochester, NY 14618.

Sowders, Jeannette B. (My. 20, 1932, Winchester, KY) Asst. Prof., Educ., Libn., Media Spec., Model Lab. Sch., East. KY Univ., 1968–; Tchr., KY Pub. Schs., 1955–68; various positions as consult. **Educ.:** BA (Sec. Educ.); MA (Educ., LS); various grad. crs. **Orgs.:** KY Sch. Media Assn. ALA: YASD. Assn. for Childhood Educ. KY AV Assn. KY Assn. for Curric. Dev. **Honors:** Phi Delta Kappa; Delta Kappa Gamma. **Pubns.:** Jt. Auth., *Comprehensive Child-Centered Social Studies Curriculum Handbook* (1975–76); Jt. Auth., *Modified Phase-Elective Communication Curriculum* (1976); "Role of the Librarian in Environmental Education," *Sch. Media Nsltr.* (My. 1974); "The Gifted—What Do We Do?" *Lexicom* (Mr. 1978); Jt. Ed., "Free and Inexpensive Materials" (1972); various reviews, presentations. **Activities:** 10; 21, 32, 48; 63 **Addr.:** Model Laboratory School, Eastern Kentucky University, Richmond, KY 40475.

Sowell, Steven L. (Ap. 4, 1949, Jamestown, OH) Assoc. Dir., Pub. Srvs., TX Coll. of Osteopathic Med., 1978–, Ref. Libn., 1978; Asst. Ref. Libn., Georgetown Univ. Med. Ctr., 1976–78. **Educ.:** Univ. of MD, 1970–75, BS (Zlgy.), 1975–76, MLS. **Orgs.:** Med. LA: Copyrt. Com. (1979–81); Legis. Com., Subcom. to Draft the Copyrt. Brochure (1978). Metroplex Cncl. of Hlth. Sci. Libns. Northeast TX OLUG. **Honors:** Phi Beta Kappa, 1975. **Pubns.:** "LATCH at the Washington Hospital Center, 1967–1975," *Bltn. of the Med. LA* (Ap. 1978). **Activities:** 1; 17, 35, 39; 58, 61, 80 **Addr.:** Library, Texas College of Osteopathic Medicine, Camp Bowie at Montgomery, Fort Worth, TX 76107.

Spahn, Theodore Jurgen (O. 11, 1931, Chicago, IL) Assoc. Prof., Sch. of Lib. and Info. Sci., Rosary Coll., 1972–; Lectr., Lib. Sci., Univ. of MI, 1967–69; Visit. Asst. Prof., Lib. Sci., Rosary Coll., 1966–67; Chief Biblgphr., Univ. of IL, Chicago, 1966–67, Biblgphr., 1965–66, Asst. Ref. Libn., 1965. **Educ.:** Northwestern Univ., 1949–53, BS, MA (Hist.); Univ. of Chicago, 1954–56 (Hist.); Rosary Coll., 1964–65, MA (LS); University of MI, 1967–79, PhD (LS). **Orgs.:** Chicago Lib. Club. Cath. LA: North. IL Unit. Chicago Area Cons. Grp. CSLA. **Pubns.:** *From Radical Left to Extreme Right* (1970–76); Copy Ed., *Jnl. of Lib. and Info. Sci.* (1978). **Activities:** 11; 15, 39, 45; 55, 57, 90 **Addr.:**

Special Subjects/Services: 50. Adult educ.; 51. Advert./Mktg.; 52. Aerosp.; 53. Agric.; 54. Area std.; 55. Arts/Hum.; 56. Autom.; 57. Bibl./Prtg.; 58. Bio. sci.; 59. Bus./Fin.; 60. Chem.; 61. Copyrt.; 62. Documtn.; 63. Educ.; 64. Engin.; 65. Env.; 66. Eth. grps.; 67. Film; 68. Food/Nutr.; 69. Geneal.; 70. Geo.; 71. Geol.; 72. Handcpd.; 73. Hist.; 74. Int. frdm.; 75. Info. sci.; 76. Insr.; 77. Law; 78. Legis.; 79. Math./Comp. sci.; 80. Med.; 81. Metals; 82. Nat. resrcs.; 83. Newsp.; 84. Nuc. sci.; 85. Oral hist.; 86. Petr./Energy; 87. Pharm.; 88. Phys./Astr./Math.; 89. Readg.; 90. Relig.; 91. Sci./Tech.; 92. Soc. sci.; 93. Telecom.; 94. Transp.; 95. (other).

School of Library and Information Science, Rosary College, River Forest, IL 60305.

Spain, Frances Lander (Mr. 15, 1903, Jacksonville, FL) Retired, 1971–; Dir., Lib. Srvs., Ctrl. FL Cmnty. Coll., 1961–71; Coord., Chld. Srvs., NY Pub. Lib., 1953–61; Asst. Dir., Lib. Sch., Univ. of South. CA, 1949–53; Head, LS Dept., Winthrop Coll., 1936–48, Libn., 1945–48; Asst., Chld. Rm., Jacksonville Pub. Lib., 1918–21. **Educ.:** Winthrop Coll., 1921–25, AB (Phys. Educ.); FL State Coll. for Women, 1935 (Soc. Sci.); Emory Univ., 1935–36, AB (LS); Univ. of Chicago, GLS, 1939, MA, 1944, PhD. **Orgs.:** ALA: Pres. (1960–61); Bd. of Educ. for Libnshp. (1950–53); Dutton-McCrae Awd. Com. (Ch., 1952–54); Lib. Educ. Div. (Pres., 1959–60). SC LA: VP (1946); Pres. (1947). South. Assn. of Colls. and Sec. Schs.: Lib. Comsn. (1940–49). SELA. Various other orgs. AAUW. U.S. Ofc. of Educ.: Conf. on Lib. Stats. (1946). SC Dept. of Educ. **Honors:** Beta Phi Mu; Whos Who in Amer. and Who's Who in Women, Bds., Outstan. Woman in Libnshp., 1960; Winthrop Coll., Mary Mildred Sullivan Alum. Achvmt. Awd., 1981; Fulbright Fndn., Grant to Thailand, 1951–52; Rockefeller Fndn., Grant to Thailand, 1964–65; other hons. **Pubns.:** "Application of School Library Standards," *Library in General Education;* "High Schools in the South," *Secondary Education in the South* (1946); past ed., *Reading without Boundaries;* past ed., *The Contents of the Basket;* various articles. **Activities:** 1, 9; 17, 21, 26 **Addr.:** P.O. Box 128, Anthony, FL 32617–0128.

Spalding, Helen H. (My. 18, 1950, Kansas City, MO) Head, Tech. Srvs., Univ. of MO, Kansas City, 1979–; Head, Serials Cat./Asst. Prof., IA State Univ. Lib., 1978–79, Coord., Serials Cat./Asst. Prof., 1977–78, Serials Catlgr./Instr., 1976–77, Serials Rec. Libn./Instr., 1974–76. **Educ.:** Univ. of IA, 1969–72, BA (Eng.), 1973–74, MA (LS). **Orgs.:** ALA. IA LA. MO LA: Mem. Ch. (1981). Kansas City OLUG. AAUP. Soroptimists. **Honors:** Phi Beta Kappa. **Pubns.:** "A Computer-Produced Serials Book Catalog with Automatically Generated Indexes," *Lib. Resrcs. & Tech. Srvs.* (Fall 1980); reviews. **Activities:** 1; 17, 44, 46 **Addr.:** Library, University of Missouri, 5100 Rockhill Rd., Kansas City, MO 64110.

Sparks, Claud Glenn (O. 21, 1922, Commerce, TX) Prof., Dean, Grad. Sch. of Lib. and Info. Sci., Univ. of TX, Austin, 1971–; Dean, School of Lib. and Info. Sci., N. TX State Univ., 1967–71; Dir., Libs., TX Christ. Univ., 1953–65; Asst. Ref. Libn., Univ. of IL, 1952–53; Pub. Srvs. Libn., TX Coll. of Arts and Indus., 1951–52. **Educ.:** E. TX State Univ., 1939–43, BS (Bus. Admin.); TX Christ. Univ., 1948–49, MA (Eng.); Univ. of OK, 1949–50 (Eng.); Univ. of TX, Austin, 1950–51, MLS; Univ. of MI, 1961–63, 1965–67, PhD (LS). **Orgs.:** ALA. AALS: Exec. Bd (1972–75). SWLA: CE Adv. Cncl. (1973–). TX LA: Cncl. (1971–73); Gvrs. Conf. (Del., 1978). TX Cncl. on Lib. Educ.: Ch. (1974–76). **Honors:** Phi Beta Kappa; Beta Phi Mu; Phi Kappa Phi; Univ. of MI, Bishop Lectr., 1971. **Pubns.:** *William Warner Bishop, A Biography* (1967); assoc. ed., ed., *Jnl. of Lib. Hist.* (1976, 1980–81). **Activities:** 1, 11; 17, 26, 39; 57 **Addr.:** 4213 Prickly Pear Dr., Austin, TX 78731.

Sparks, Marie Catherine (Je. 13, 1951, Tiffin, OH) Lib. Dir./Assoc. Prof. of Dental Lit., IN Univ. Sch. of Dentistry, 1980–; Serial Acq. Libn., Univ. of OK Hlth. Sci. Ctr. Lib., 1976–80, ILL Libn., 1975–76, Spec. Proj. Libn., 1974–75, Reg. Med. Libn., 1973–74. **Educ.:** OH North. Univ., 1969–72, BA (Bio.); Univ. of OK, 1973–74, MLS, 1977–80, MPH (Hlth. Admin.); Med. LA, 1975, Cert. **Orgs.:** IN Hlth. Scis. Libns. Med. LA: Midwest Reg. Grp. SLA. Amer. Assn. of Dental Schs. Amer. Dental Assn. **Honors** Beta Phi Mu. **Pubns.:** "Trials and Tribulations of Serials," *Ebsco Bltn. of Serial Changes* (1979). **Activities:** 1, 12; 15, 17, 36; 56, 80 **Addr.:** Indiana University School of Dentistry Library, 1121 W. Michigan St., Indianapolis, IN 46202.

Spaulding, Barbara J. (O. 17, 1945, Akron, OH) Cat. Libn., Brown Univ., 1973–. **Educ.:** Muskingum Coll., 1963–67, BA (Liberal Arts, Hist.); Yale Univ., 1967–69, MA (Southeast Asian Std.); Univ. of Chicago, 1969–72, MA (LS). **Orgs.:** ALA. New Eng. LA. RI LA. Assn. for Asian Std. **Activities:** 1; 20, 45; 54, 55 **Addr.:** John D. Rockefeller Jr. Library, Brown University, Providence, RI 02912.

Spaulding, Frank H. (Jl. 12, 1932, Danielson, CT) Head, Lib. Oper., Bell Telephone Labs., 1970–, Grp. Supvsr., Lib. Tech. Prcs., 1965–70; Adjunct Prof., Drexel Univ., Grad. Sch. of Lib. Srv., 1964; Supvsr., Info. Srvs., Colgate-Palmolive Co., 1961–65. **Educ.:** Brown Univ., 1954–57, AB (Eng.); Case West. Rsv. Univ., 1960–61, MSLS. **Orgs.:** ALA. SLA: Lib. Mgt. Div. (Ch., 1981–82); NJ Chap. (Pres., 1977–78). ASIS: Docum. Abs. Inc., Bd. of Dir. (VP, 1980–81). Rutgers Univ. Grad. Sch. of Lib. and Info. Std.: Adv. Assoc. PALINET: Bd. of Dir. (1979–81). **Pubns.:** "Computer-Aided Selection in a Library Network" *Jnl. of the Amer. Socty. for Info. Sci.* (S.–O. 1976). **Activities:** 12; 17, 34; 56, 93 **Addr.:** Bell Telephone Labs., Rm. 3B-202, Holmdel, NJ 07733.

Spaulding, Nancy Jo (O. 4, 1937, Cincinnati, OH) Dir., Media, Round Rock Indp. Sch. Dist., 1977–, Libn., 1974–77, Elem. Tchr., 1972–74; Elem. Tchr., Austin Indp. Sch. Dist., 1969–72; Instr., Univ. of TX, 1968–69; Elem., Jr. HS Tchr., Austin Indp. Sch. Dist., 1959–68. **Educ.:** Univ. of TX, 1955–59, BS (Home Econ.), 1959–63, MEd (Elem. Educ.), 1963–76 (LS, Educ.); Provisional Cert. (Sec. Educ., Elem. Educ.); Prof. Lrng. Resrcs. Specs. Cert. **Orgs.:** TX LA. ALA. Assn. for Supvsn. and Curric. Dev. Lrng. Resrcs. Prog. Dir. of TX. Delta Kappa Gamma: Kappa Lambda Chap. (Treas., 1977–80). Natl. Educ. Assn. TX State Tchrs. Assn.: Constn. Com. (1967). **Activities:** 10; 17, 32 **Addr.:** 1300 N. Mays, Round Rock, TX 78664.

Spawn, Carol M. (D. 16, 1928, Worcester, MA) Ms., Arch. Libn., Acad. of Nat. Sci. of Philadelphia, 1978–; Actg. Libn., Philadelphia Yearly Mtg. of the Socty. of Frnds., 1975–76; Supvsr., Microfilming Proj., Free Lib. of Philadelphia, Rare Bk. Dept., 1973–74; Catlgr., Consult., PA Hosp., 1973–75; Libn. 1, Rare Bk. Dept., Free Lib. of Philadelphia, 1958–61. **Educ.:** Brown Univ., 1946–50, AB (Intl. Rel.); Columbia Univ., 1956–57, MSLS. **Orgs.:** SAA. Mid-Atl. Reg. Archvsts. Conf. Bibl. Socty. of Amer. **Activities:** 2, 12; 23, 39, 45 **Addr.:** Academy of Natural Sciences of Philadelphia, 19th and the Parkway, Philadelphia, PA 19103.

Spaziani, Carol (N. 12, 1930, Toledo, OH) Cmnty. Srvs. Libn., IA City Pub. Lib., 1968–; Ref. Libn., Univ. of IA Lib., 1961–62. **Educ.:** Univ. of CA, Los Angeles, 1950–53, BA (Pre-Libnshp.); Univ. of IL, 1959–60, MS (LS). **Orgs.:** Frnds. of the Iowa City Pub. Lib.: Staff Liaison. ALA. IA LA: Gvt. Docum. Sect. (Ch., 1979); Legis. Com. (1971–75); Non-User Com. (1978–80); Bks. Behind Bars Com. (1977–78). IA Gvrs. Conf. on Libs. and Info. Sci.: Del. (1979). Various org. IA Cvl. Liberties Un. Johnson Cnty. Women's Pol. Caucus. Natl. Org. for Women. Leag. of Women Voters. Various org. **Pubns.:** *Getting Started on Library Service to Jails* (1978); *Learning Resources for non-English Speaking People Available to Iowa Libraries* (1980). **Activities:** 9; 16, 27, 39; 72, 89, 92 **Addr.:** Iowa City Public Library, College & Linn Sts., Iowa City, IA 52240.

Spear, Jack B. (Mr. 18, 1918, Ashley, IL) Assoc., Lib. Srvs., Sect. Head, Lib. Dev., NY State Lib., 1977–, Head, Auxiliary Srvs. Sect., 1961–77, Head, Traveling Libs., 1953–61; Dir., Amer. Heritage Proj., ALA, 1952–53; Dir., Fld. Srvs., Lib. Ext. Div., NY State Lib., 1950–52; Asst. Libn., Ext., Gary Pub. Lib., 1947–50; Asst. Libn., IL State Hist. Lib., 1946–47, Lib. Asst., 1941–42; various libn. positions, 1938–41. **Educ.:** Univ. of South. IL, 1935–39, BEd (Educ.); Univ. of IL, 1939–40, BS (LS); Columbia Univ., 1947–56, MLS. **Orgs.:** ALA: Pub. Lib. Div. (Pres., 1954–55). NY LA: Natl. Lib. Week (Ch., 1960–61). Pres. Empl. of the Handcpd.: Lib. Sect. (1963–). Lions Club of Albany, NY. Free and Accepted Masons. DeMolay Adv. Bd. Sight Cons. Socty. of Northeastern NY. **Pubns.:** *Film Catalog of the New York State Library* (1966, 1968, 1970, 1973); various articles. **Activities:** 13; 24, 32, 47; 50, 55, 67 **Addr.:** Bureau of Specialist Library Services, New York State Library, Cultural Education Center, Rm. 10B41, Albany, NY 12230.

Spear, Louise S. (Je. 5, 1948, Green Bay, WI) Assoc. Dir., IN Univ. Arch. of Traditional Msc., 1971–. **Educ.:** WI State Univ., 1966–70, BA (Eng.); Univ. of WI, 1970–71, MA (LS). **Orgs.:** Msc. LA. IN Univ. Libns. Assn. Assn. for Rec. Snd. Cols. Intl. Assn. of Snd. Arch. Amer. Folklore Socty. Socty. for Ethnomsclgy. **Pubns.:** "The Indiana University Archives of Traditional Music: An Interview with George List," *Discourse in Ethnomusicology: Essays in Honor of George List* (1978); "Phonorecordings of Indiana Folk Music and Folklore in the Archives of Traditional Music," *IN Univ. Libns. Assn. Qtly.* (1978); "Current Bibliography and Discography," discography sect. *Ethnomsclgy.: Jnl. of the Socty. for Ethnomsclgy.* (1978–). **Activities:** 1, 2; 17, 32, 39; 55, 66, 85 **Addr.:** Archives of Traditional Music, Maxwell Hall 057, Indiana University, Bloomington, IN 47405.

Specht, Alice Wilson (Ap. 3, 1948, Caracas, Venezuela) Assoc. Dir., Univ. Libs., Hardin-Simmons Univ., 1981–; Syst. Coord., Big Country Lib. Syst., 1975–79; Ref. Libn., Lubbock City Cnty. Lib., 1973–75; Asst. Soc. Sci. Libn., N. TX State Univ., 1971–73. **Educ.:** Univ. of Pac., 1966–69, BA (Soc. Sci.); Emory Univ., 1969–70, MLn (LS). **Orgs.:** ALA. Southwestern LA: PR Com. (Secy., 1978–80). TX LA: PR Com. (Ch., 1977–78). TX Conf. on Libs.: Del. (1978). **Honors:** H.W. Wilson Co., ALA, John Cotton Dana Awd., 1979. **Activities:** 9, 13; 24, 25, 28; 50, 92 **Addr.:** 918 Grand, Abilene, TX 79605.

Specht, Joe W. (F. 8, 1945, Marlin, TX) Dir., McMurry Coll., 1975–; Ref. Libn., Soc. Sci., TX Tech. Univ., 1973–75; Prof. Lib. Asst., N. TX State Univ., 1972–73. **Educ.:** N. TX State Univ., 1963–68, BA (Hist.), 1971–72, MLS, 1971–73, MA (Hist.). **Orgs.:** TX LA: Dist. I. (Ch., 1978–79); Cnclr. (1979–81) SWLA. TX State Hist. Assn. **Honors** Phi Alpha Theta; Beta Phi Mu. **Pubns.:** "Hoyle Nix the West Texas Cowboy," *Old Time Music* (1980–81); "Slim Willet," *West Texas Historical Association Yearbook* (1981). **Activities:** 1; 15, 17, 28 **Addr.:** Box 237 McMurry Station, Abilene, TX 79697.

Speed, William J. (Jl. 30, 1921, Ponca City, OK) Prin. Libn., Mgr. Media Dept., Los Angeles City Pub. Lib., 1950–; Mgr., Media Dept., Univ. of CA, 1945–50. **Educ.:** Univ. of South. CA, 1955–60, BA (Comm.), 1960–61, MLS. **Orgs.:** CA LA: AV Chap. (Pres., 1960). EFLA: Bd. of Dir. (1964–73). Film Lib. Cncl.: Pres. (1972). **Honors:** EFLA, Blue Ribbon Awd., 1973; Can. Gvt., Cert. of Srv., 1976; CA LA, Boyle-Hutchinson Awd., 1974. **Pubns.:** Ed., *International Index to Multi-media Information* (1969–); "Have you been 'propositioned—the impact of Prop. 13 on California Public Libraries," *Media Digest* (F. 1979). **Activities:** 9; 32; 67 **Addr.:** 4819 Regalo Rd., Woodland Hills, CA 91364.

Speisman, Stephen A. (My. 17, 1943, Toronto, ON) Dir., Can. Jewish Congs. ON Reg. Arch., Jewish Arch., 1973–. **Educ.:** Univ. of Toronto, 1963–68, BA (Hist.), 1968–69, MA (Hist.), 1969–75, PhD (Hist.). **Orgs.:** Assn. Can. Archvsts.: Relig. Arch. Pubn. Com. (1979–80). Toronto Area Archvsts. Grp.: Prog. Com. (1977–78). ON Musm. Assn. SAA. Can. Hist. Assn. Org. of Amer. Histns. Amer. Jewish Hist. Socty. Can. Jewish Hist. Socty.: Bd. of Dir. (1976–); Prog. Com. (Ch., 1976–77); Contrib. Ed., *Jnl.* (1977–). **Pubns.:** *The Jews of Toronto: A History to 1937* (1979); "Munificent Parsons and Municipal Parsimony," *ON Hist.* (Mr. 1973); Resrchr., "History of the Jews of Canada" Filmstp. (1979). **Activities:** 2; 15, 17, 23; 66, 73, 85 **Addr.:** 150 Beverley St., Toronto, ON M5T 1Y6 Canada.

Spence, Melville R. (Jl. 26, 1919, Hamilton, ON) Head, Gvt. Docum. Col., Bowling Green State Univ. Lib., 1977–, Dir., Libs., 1970–77; Assoc. Dir., Libs., Univ. of OK, 1967–70, Asst. Dir., Libs., 1960–67, Actg. Dir., Libs., 1963–64, Actg. Dir., Sch. of Lib. Sci., 1963–65, Acq. Libn., 1958–60; Gen. Libn., Univ. of ID, 1953–56. **Educ.:** Beloit Coll., 1947–50, BA (Psy.); Case West. Rsv. Univ., 1950–51, MALS; various crs. **Orgs.:** ALA: RTSD/RLMS, Exec. Com. (Secy., 1970–73), Budgeting, Acct. and Costs Com. (1968–71). SWLA: Exec. Bd. (1966–70); various com. OK LA: Bus. Mgr., *OK Libn.* (1961–70); Coll. and Univ. Sect. (Ch., 1961–62); Exec. Bd. (1966–70); various com., ch. Acad. LA of OH: Exec. Bd. (1975–78). Various org. Beta Phi Mu: Lambda Chap. (Pres., 1968–69). **Pubns.:** *A Bibliographic Guide to US and Ohio Documents* (1979); *The American Indian in Government Documents* (1979). **Activities:** 1; 17, 29, 31 **Addr.:** 219 Evergreen Ln., Apt. 47, Bowling Green, OH 43402.

Spence, Paul H. (D. 25, 1923, Geraldine, AL) Libn., Univ. of AL, in Birmingham, 1970–; Assoc. Dir., Pub. Srvs., Univ. of GA, 1966–70; Hist., Pol. Sci. Libn., Univ. of IL, 1963–66; Asst. Dir., Soc. Std., Univ. of NE, 1960–63; Asst. Dir., Soc. Std., Univ. of Notre Dame, 1959–60; Dir., Lib., Air Force Inst. of Tech., 1957–58; Per. Ref., Air Univ., 1953–56; Asst. Ref. Libn., Emory Univ., 1950–53. **Educ.:** Emory Univ., 1946–48, AB (Hist.), 1948–50, MA (Libnshp.); Univ. of IL, 1958–59, PhD (LS). **Orgs.:** ALA: Cncl. (1976–78); Ref. Bk. Com. (1969–73). SELA: VP, Pres.-Elect (1978–80). AL LA: Treas. (1975–76); Coll., Univ. and Spec. Div. (Ch., 1972–73). Southeastern Lib. Netwk.: Bd. of Dir. (1973–75); Secy. (1974–75). **Activities:** 1; 17; 92 **Addr.:** Mervyn H. Sterne Library, University of Alabama, University Station, Birmingham, AL 35294.

Spence, Theresa Sanderson (Ja. 25, 1949, Detroit, MI) Univ. Archvst./Spec. Cols. Libn., MI Tech. Univ., 1978–; Instr. Asst., Wayne State Univ., 1977–78. **Educ.:** North. MI Univ., 1969–71, BA (Hist.), 1971–73, MA (Hist.); Wayne State Univ., 1976–78, MA (LS). **Orgs.:** SAA. ALA. MI Arch. Assn.: Nom. Com. (1980), Model Theft Law (1980). Hist. Socty. of MI. Houghton Cnty. Hist. Socty. Keweenaw Cnty. Hist. Socty. Amer. Assn. State and Lcl. Hist. Leag. of Women Voters. Various other orgs. **Pubns.:** "MTU Archives Collects Historical Documents," *WUPPDR Nsltr.* (Mr.-Ap. 1980); "Lone Archivist," *Open Entry* (Sum. 1980). **Activities:** 1, 2; 15, 17, 45; 69, 91 **Addr.:** Library, Michigan Technological University, Houghton, MI 49931.

Spencer, Dorothy Ann (Ag. 31, 1947, Yonkers, NY) Chief, AV Srvs., Med. Coll. of GA Lib., 1971–79; Libn., Rombout Mid. Sch., 1970–71. **Educ.:** Hope Coll., 1965–69, BA (Pol. Sci.); West. MI Univ., 1969–70, MSL (Libnshp.); Univ. of NE, 1979– Doct. Cand. **Orgs.:** Med. LA: Hlth. Sci. Comm. Assn. Liaison (1977–79); Hlth. Sci. AV Grp. (Ch., 1973–75); Consult. Ed., *Med. LA Bltn.* (1976–79). Hlth. Sci. Comm. Assn.: Bd. of Dir. (1975–77); Elec. Com. (Ch., 1976–77); Ed. Review Bd., *Jnl. of Biocomm.* (1977–80). GA Assn. of Instr. Tech.: Mem. Com. (1978–79). GA LA. **Pubns.:** Jt. Auth., *Source List for Patient Education Materials* (1978); "Descriptive Cataloging Elements for Use in Bibliographic Control of Nonprint Materials," *Jnl. of Biocomm.* (1977); "Rank and Promotion of Library Faculty in a Health Sciences University," *Med. LA Bltn.* (1977); "Model Universe: The Librarian's Role," *Biomed. Comm.* (1976); "Media Notes" clmn. *Med. LA News.* (Je. 1974–Ja. 1978). **Activities:** 1, 12; 17, 25, 32; 50, 80, 93 **Addr.:** Biomedical Communications, University of NE Medical Center, 42nd & Dewey Ave., Omaha, NE 68105.

Spencer, Leon P. (O. 10, 1943, Roanoke Rapids, NC) Archvst./Assoc. Prof. (Hist.), Talladega Coll., 1970–. **Educ.:** Wake Forest Univ., 1961–65, BA (Pol., Gvt.); IN Univ., 1965–67, MA (African Std.); Syracuse Univ., 1966–75, PhD (African Hist.); Amer. Univ.-Natl. Arch., 1977, Dip. **Orgs.:** Socty. AL Archvsts.: Pres. (1978–79). SAA. African Std. Assn.: Arch.-Libs. Com., Exec. Bd. (1977–79, Deputy Ch. (1980–81), Ch. (1981–82). Socty. for African Church Hist. Kenya Hist. Assn. **Pubns.:** *Christianity and Politics in Kenya* (forthcoming); *Re-*

PROFESSIONAL ACTIVITIES: Institutions: 1. Acad. lib.; 2. Arch.; 3. Assn.; 4. Fed./Gvt. lib.; 5. Inst. lib.; 6. Mfr./Suppl.; 7. Milit. lib.; 8. Musm.; 9. Pub. lib.; 10. Sch. lib.; 11. Sch. of lib. sci.; 12. Spec. lib.; 13. State lib.; 14. (other). **Functions/Activities:** 15. Acq./Col. dev.; 16. Adult srvs.; 17. Admin.; 18. Apprais.; 19. Archit./Bldgs.; 20. Cat./Class.; 21. Chld. srvs.; 22. Circ.; 23. Cons./Pres.; 24. Consult.; 25. Cont. ed.; 26. Educ. lib. sci.; 27. Ext. srvs.; 28. Fund/Grants; 29. Gvt. pubs.; 30. Indx./Abs.; 31. Instr. lib. use; 32. Media srvs.; 33. Micro.; 34. Netwks./Coop.; 35. Persnl.; 36. PR; 37. Publshg.; 38. Recs. mgt.; 39. Ref. srvs.; 40. Repro.; 41. Resrch.; 42. Review.; 43. Secur.; 44. Serials; 45. Spec. col.; 46. Tech. srvs.; 47. Trustees/Bds.; 48. YA srvs.; 49. (other).

Who's Who in Library and Information Services

cords of Black Organizations: A Guide to Preservation (1978); jt. auth., *People's Day, Black Missions, and a Hanging: Black History and Historical Analysis* (1974); "Africana Archival and Manuscript Materials at Predominately Black Institutions," *GA Arch.* (Fall 1978); various articles on African hist. **Activities:** 2; 41, 45; 55, 66, 85 **Addr.:** The Historical Collections, Talladega College, Talladega, AL 35160.

Spencer, Marjorie Hall (Je. 17, 1926, Union City, PA) Lib., Media Spec., Dundee Ctrl. Sch., 1971–; Soc. Std. Tchr., 1967–71, Elem. Tchr., 1951–67; Primary Tchr., Savona Ctrl. Sch., 1950–51. **Educ.:** SUNY, Cortland, 1948, BE; SUNY, Geneseo, 1962, MLS; various grad. crs. **Orgs.:** ALA. Yates Cnty. LA. Delta Kappa Gamma: Beta Phi Chap. (Pres., 1981–83). Ord. of the East. Star. **Activities:** 10; 21, 28, 31 **Addr.:** 6 Hollister St., Dundee, NY 14837.

Spensley, Malcolm C. (S. 27, 1919, Town of Coeymans, NY) Asst. Head, Info. Pub. Cat., Telephone Ref., Queens Boro. Pub. Lib., 1966–; Sr. Asst., Educ. Dept., Enoch Pratt Free Lib., 1955–61. **Educ.:** Hartwick Coll., 1939–43, BA (Relig., Psy.); Columbia Univ., 1953–55, MS (LS), 1963–65, MA (Psy.). **Orgs.:** ALA. Assn. for Resrch. and Enlightenment. **Pubns.:** *Adult Independent Learner Bibliography* (1976). **Activities:** 1, 9; 16, 25, 39; 75, 90 **Addr.:** 434 W. 120th St. Apt. 3A, New York, NY 10027.

Sperl, Virginia R. (Ja. 3, 1920, Orange, NJ) Assoc. Prof., Dowling Coll., 1961–, Actg. Dir., 1975–76, Asst. Dir., 1961–68; Chief Catlgr., Albert Einstein Coll. of Med., 1958–60; Tech. Srv. Consult., NY State Wkshp. for Inst. Libns., 1956–58; Serials Catlgr., Asst. Cat. Libn., Med., Columbia Univ., 1947–58; Asst., PA Sch. of Soc. Work, 1947; Asst., Harvard Law Lib., 1945–46. **Educ.:** Randolph-Macon Woman's Coll., 1939–42, BA (Eng.); Univ. of MN, 1944–45, BS (LS). **Orgs.:** SLA. NY LA. Long Island Arch. Conf. ALA: RTSD, Code Rev. Com. (Rep., 1961–65). AAUW. AAUP. **Activities:** 46 **Addr.:** Dowling College Library, Oakdale, NY 11769.

Sperry, Kip (My. 25, 1940, Chardon, OH) Supvsr., Libn., Amer. Ref. Sect., Geneal. Socty. of UT, 1981–, Sr. Resrch. Spec., 1976–81, Sr. Ref. Consult., 1971–76. **Educ.:** Brigham Young Univ., 1971, BS (Geneal.), 1974, MLS. Geneal. Socty. of UT, 1971, Accred. Genealogist. UT Geneal. Assn.: Bd. of Dir. 1976–81). New Eng. Hist. Geneal. Socty. Natl. Geneal. Socty. **Honors:** Natl. Geneal. Socty., Awd. of Merit, 1981. **Pubns.:** *Index to Genealogical Periodical Literature, 1960–1977* (1979); *A Survey of American Genealogical Periodicals and Periodical Indexes* (1978); *Connecticut Sources for Family Historians and Genealogists* (1980); various articles, bk. reviews; Ed., *Geneal. Jnl.* (1975–). **Activities:** 12; 30, 37, 41; 69, 73 **Addr.:** P. O. Box 11381, Salt Lake City, UT 84147.

Spicer, Erik John (Ap. 9, 1926, Ottawa, ON) Parliamentary Libn., Lib. of Parlmt., 1960–; Deputy Libn., Ottawa Pub. Lib., 1954–60; Pub., Univ. Libn., 1949–54. **Educ.:** Victoria Univ., 1946–49, BA; Univ. of Toronto, 1949–50; Univ. of MI, 1959, BLS, MALS; Can. Cncl. Flwshp.; various crs. **Orgs.:** Can. LA: 1st VP, Pres.-elect (1978–79); Pres. (1979–80); Can. Assn. Spec. Libs. Info. Srvs. ON LA: Pres. (1962–63). FTRF. IFLA: Spec. Libs. Sect. (Dir., 1967–73); Parliamentary and Admin. Libs. Sect. (Pres., 1973–76); Gen. Resrch. Libs. Div., Parliamentary Libs. Sect. (Pres., 1976–79); Voting Del. to various confs. (1966–81). Various org. Inst. of Pub. Admin. of Can. Intl. Pol. Sci. Assn. Can. Pol. Sci. Assn. ON Hist. Socty. Various org. **Honors:** Phi Kappa Phi; Univ. of MI, Disting. Alum. Awd., 1959; Beta Phi Mu, 1960; Cent. Medal, 1967; Queen's Silver Jubilee Medal, 1977. **Pubns.:** "It's Your Business," clmn. *Feliciter* (S. 1979–); "Universal Availability of Publications (UAP) and Parliamentary Libraries," *IFLA Jnl.* (1978); "The International Federation of Library Associations and Parliament," *Parlmt.* (Ja. 1977); "Canadian Library of Parliament," *Parlmt.* (Jl. 1976); "State Senates: Are They Really Necessary?" *State Gvt.* (Sum. 1975); various sp., articles, monos. **Activities:** 9, 13; 17, 35, 36; 74, 95-Politics. **Addr.:** Library of Parliament, Ottawa, ON K1A 0A9 Canada.

Spiegel, Martha Robb (Ap. 17, 1934, Utica, NY) Ed., Interdok Corp., 1969–; Libn., IBM Sci. Ctr., 1968; Head, Acq. Dept., Engin. Soctys. Lib., 1961–67, Ref. Libn., 1959–61. **Educ.:** Oberlin Coll., 1951–55, BA (Eng. Lit.); Univ. of MI, 1955–57, AMLS. **Orgs.:** SLA: Hudson Valley Chap., Bd. Amer. Socty. of Indxrs: NY Chap., Ch. Elect. ASIS. **Pubns.:** Ed., Indxr., *Dir. of Published Proc. of Confs.* **Activities:** 6; 37; 75 **Addr.:** 85 Storer Ave., Pelham, NY 10803.

Spiess, Johanna M. (Ap. 5, 1927, Brooklyn, NY) Prin. Libn., Brooklyn Pub. Lib., 1961–, Supvsg. Libn., Sr. Libn., Libn., 1949–61; Exch. Libn., Hamburger Oeffentliche Buecherhallen, Hamburg, Germany, 1956–57. **Educ.:** Brooklyn Coll., 1945–49, BA (Functional Major); Pratt Inst., 1949–50, MLS. **Orgs.:** NY Lib. Club. Thea. LA. **Activities:** 9; 17, 39; 55 **Addr.:** Brooklyn Public Library, Ingersoll Bldg., Grand Army Plz., Brooklyn, NY 11238.

Spigai, Frances Dana Gage (S. 29, 1938, Salina, KS) Pres., Database Srvs., 1980–; Mktg. Dir., Dialog Info. Retrieval, 1976–80; Asst. to Dir., OR Higher Educ. Lib. Cncl., 1974–76; Systs. Mktg., Richard Abel Bookseller, 1973–74; Ed., *Adv. Tech./Libs.*, Becker and Hayes, Inc., 1971–72; Staff Engin., MA Inst. of Tech., 1970–71; Asst. Prof., Lib. and Comp. Ctr, OR State Univ., 1969–70; Instr., Lib., 1967–68. **Educ.:** City Coll. of NY, 1956–60, BS (Gen. Sci); Cath. Univ. of Amer., OR State Univ., Univ. of OR, 1965–70 (LS). **Orgs.:** ALA. SLA. ASIS. Natl. Micro. Assn. **Pubns.:** *Electronic Publishing; A Guide for Print Publishers in Dealing with Online and Videotex Systems* (1981); managing ed., *Print Samples. A Series of Online User Aids* (1980–); *The Invisible Medium; A State of the Art of Microforms* (1973); jt. auth., "Micrographics," *Annual Review of Information Science and Technology* (1976). **Activities:** 14-Consult. info. co.; 24, 25, 39; 56, 62, 75 **Addr.:** Database Services, 885 N. San Antonio Rd., Los Altos, CA 94022.

Spina, Marie Cimino (S. 2, 1945, New York, NY) Lcl. Hist. Libn., Libn., Hist., Relig., Brooklyn Pub. Lib., 1969–. **Educ.:** Hunter Coll., CUNY, BA; Columbia Univ., MS (Lib. Srv.). **Orgs.:** SLA. Mid. Atl. Reg. Arch. NY Arch. RT. NY Cons./Prsrvn. Grp. **Pubns.:** "Brooklyn: as it was," *Brooklyn Mag.* (O. 1978); Lcl. Hist. Slide Presentations (1979–81). **Activities:** 2, 9; 23, 39, 41; 55, 90, 95-Photographs. **Addr.:** History Division, Brooklyn Public Library/ Grand Army Plz., Brooklyn, NY 11238.

Spindler, Ruth A. (Jl. 27, 1928, Tanta, Egypt) Sr. Info. Spec., BF Goodrich Co., 1978–; Cmrcl. Libn., Sherwin-Williams Co., 1973–78; Sch. Libn., Cleveland Pub. Schs., 1968–73. **Educ.:** Monmouth Coll., 1946–50, BS (Chem.); Kent State Univ., 1969–72. **Orgs.:** SLA: Cleveland Chap. Mem. (1979–80); Employ. Ch. (1981–82). Cleveland OLUG: Coord. (1979–81). ASIS: Cleveland Chap. (Treas., 1974–76), Alt. Chap. Rep. (1981–82). **Activities:** 12; 30, 39, 41; 59, 60, 64 **Addr.:** 7302 Trevor Ln., Parma, OH 44129.

Spinks, Paul (Mr. 7, 1922, London, Eng.) Dir. of Libs., Nvl. Postgrad. Sch., Monterey, CA, 1975–, Assoc. Libn., 1961–74, Tech. Rpts. Libn., 1959–61. **Educ.:** Royal Socty. of Arts Dip., 1939; Univ. of OK, 1952–58, BA (Pol. Sci., Hist.), 1958–59, MLS. **Orgs.:** Coop. Info. Netwk.: Bd. of Dirs. (1976–80). SLA. ASIS. **Honors:** Beta Phi Mu, 1959. **Activities:** 1; 17; 63 **Addr.:** Dudley Knox Library, Naval Postgraduate School, Monterey, CA 93940.

Spiro, Louise M. (My. 26, 1931, Cleveland, OH) Branch Libn., Cleveland Pub. Lib., 1972–, various positions as asst. branch libn., 1973–77; Elem. Sch. Tchr., Cleveland Hts., E. Cleveland, 1953–65. **Educ.:** OH State Univ., 1949–51 (Readg.); Case West. Rsv. Univ., 1951–53, BS (Elem. Educ.), 1966–69, MS (LS). **Orgs.:** OH LA: Int. Frdm. Com. (1979–82). ALA. Cleveland Pub. Lib. Staff Assn. **Activities:** 9; 16, 21, 48; 89, 90, 92 **Addr.:** 14342 Cedar Rd. 106B, University Heights, OH 44121.

Spirt, Diana L. (F. 22, 1925, Waterbury, CT) Prof., LS, Long Island Univ., Grad. Lib. Sch., 1965–; Visit. Prof., Univ. of WA, 1975; Visit. Prof., Dalhousie Univ., 1974, 1970; Visit. Prof., Kent State Univ., 1971; Sch. Libn., Brookville, NY, 1958–65. **Educ.:** Cornell Univ., 1946, BS; Long Island Univ., 1959, MS, 1961, MS (LS); NY Univ., 1970, PhD. **Orgs.:** Nassau-Suffolk Sch. LA: Pres. (1961). ALA. AECT. NY Lib. Club. **Honors:** Pi Lambda Theta; Kappa Delta Pi; NY LA, Awd., 1962. **Pubns.:** *Library-Media Manual* (1979); *A Guide to Books About Children's Books* (1981); jt. auth., *Paperback Books for Young People* (1972); jt. auth., *The Young Phenomenon* (1972); jt. auth., *Creating a School Media Program* (1973); various articles in lib., educ. jnls., cats., edshps. **Addr.:** Graduate Library School, Long Island University, Greenvale, NY 11548.

Spivack, Jane Elizabeth (Jl. 24, 1925, New York, NY) Place Dir., Sch. of Lib. and Info. Sci., Drexel Univ., 1976–; Libn., Devereux Fndn., 1975–76; Mgr. Ed., *Drexel Lib. Qtly.*, Drexel Univ., 1972–75. **Educ.:** Hunter Coll., CUNY, 1948–50, BA (Anthro.); Columbia Univ., 1950–51, (Anthro.); Drexel Univ., 1969–72, MSLS. **Orgs.:** ASIS: Mem. Com., Task Frc. Place. (Head, 1979–). Assoc. Info. Mgrs. ALA. Mid–Atl. Place. Assn. **Honors:** Phi Beta Kappa, 1950; Beta Phi Mu, 1972. **Pubns.:** "101 Jobs for Information Scientists," *ASIS Bltn.* (O. 1980). **Activities:** 11; 26; 56, 75, 93 **Addr.:** School of Library and Information Science, Drexel University, Philadelphia, PA 19104.

Sprankle, Anita T. (Je. 10, 1944, Bellefonte, PA) Non-Bk. Mtrls. Libn., Kutztown State Coll., 1967–; Tech. Srvs. Libn., Cmwlth. Campuses Lib., PA State Univ., 1966–67. **Educ.:** PA State Univ., 1962–65, BA (Geo.); Drexel Univ., 1965–66, MSLS, 1978–79, Cert. of Advnc. Std. (LS). **Orgs.:** SLA. PA LA: AV Com. (1970–71, 1977–78). Assn. of Amer. Geographers. PA Cncl. for Geo. Educ. **Activities:** 1; 15, 20, 32; 70 **Addr.:** 406 E. Smith St., Topton, PA 19562.

Sprinkle, Michael D. (N. 23, 1939, Elkin, NC) Dir., Bowman Gray Sch. of Med., Wake Forest Univ., 1972–; Assoc. Dir., Med. Ctr. Lib., Univ. of KY, 1970–71; Dir., Un. Cat. of Med. Per., Med. Lib., Ctr., 1967–69. **Educ.:** Univ. of NC, 1958–62, AB (Eng.), 1965–66, MSLS; Pre-doctoral Fellow in Comp. Libnshp., WA Univ. Sch. of Med., 1966–67. **Orgs.:** Med. LA: Com. on Med. Educ. (1966–71). SLA. ASIS. ALA: Frnds. of Amer. Libs. Plng. Com. (1978). Amer. Assn. for the Hist. of Med. Hlth. Sci. Comm. Assn. Assn. for the Dev. of Comp.-Based Instr. Syst. Hastings Inst. of Socty., Ethics and Life Sci. Various org. **Pubns.:** "Regional Utilization of the Union Catalog of Medical Periodicals System," *Bltn. of the Med. LA* (Jl. 1969); "New Concepts of Media and their Management at the University of Kentucky Medical Center," *Drexel Lib. Qtly.* (Ap. 1971); "Extending Library Services Utilizing a New Technology," *Bltn. of the Med. LA* (Ap. 1972); "Oral History in a Medium-Sized Medical School Library," *Frontiers in Health Sciences Librarianship: Extended Abstract Proceedings* (1976); "Emergency Medicine Audiovisual Satellite Library at Bowman Gray School of Medicine," *Bltn. of the Med. LA* (O. 1981). **Activities:** 1, 12; 17, 28, 33; 80, 86, 93 **Addr.:** Libraries, Bowman Gray School of Medicine, Wake Forest University, Winston-Salem, NC 27103.

Sprug, Joseph Wm. (Ap. 9, 1922, Fort Smith, AR) Dir., Lib., St. Edward's Univ. Lib., 1973–; Gimbel Aeronautical Hist. Libn., US Air Force Acad., 1971–73; Dir., Lib., Loretto Hts. Coll., 1964–71; Head, Tech. Prcs., St. Vincent Coll., Latrobe, PA, 1962–64; Head, Tech. Prcs., Fresno Cnty. Free Lib., 1961–62; Ed., *Cath. Per. Indx.*, Cath. Univ. of Amer., 1952–61, Catlgr., Head Catlgr., Lib., 1947–52; various positions in tchg., lib. **Educ.:** St. Meinrad Coll., 1940–46, BA (Phil.), Cath. Univ. of Amer., 1946–47, BSLS, 1947–49, MA (Phil.). **Orgs.:** Cath. LA: Various com. TX LA. TX Cath. Hist. Assn. Amer. Stan. Assn.: Various com. **Honors:** Beta Phi Mu; ALA, Resrch. Grant; Cath. LA, Resrch. Grant; Cath. Univ. of Amer., Resrch. Grant. **Pubns.:** *An Index to G. K. Chesterton* (1966); *Index to the Twentieth Century Encyclopedia of Catholicism* (1971); Jt. Cmplr., *A Bibliography of Time Perception* (1974); *Index to American Reference Books 1969–73* (1974); *Index to Nutrition-and-Health* (1981); various indxs., bk. reviews. **Activities:** 1, 2; 15, 17, 30; 55, 68, 90 **Addr.:** 403 Riley Rd., Austin, TX 78746.

Sprules, Marcia Lynn (Jl. 13, 1948, Kearny, NJ) Coord., Comp. Assisted Bibl. Srv., Univ. of SD, 1980–; Asst. Ref. Libn., Fairleigh Dickinson Univ., 1976–80; Jr. Libn., Ref., Newark Pub. Lib., 1972–74; Asst. Slavic Catlgr., OH State Univ., 1971–72. **Educ.:** Cornell Univ., 1966–70, AB (Russ. Lit.); Case West. Rsv. Univ., 1970–71, MS (LS); Fairleigh Dickinson Univ., 1976–79, MA (Intl. Std.). **Orgs.:** ALA: ACRL. SD LA. **Honors:** Beta Phi Mu, 1971; Phi Alpha Theta, 1979. **Activities:** 1; 29, 31, 39; 54 **Addr.:** 1D Weeks Library, University of South Dakota, Vermillion, SD 57069.

Sprung, George (O. 3, 1926, New York, NY) Ref. Supvsr., Coll. of Med. and Dentistry of NJ, 1976–; Libn., Jersey City Med. Ctr., 1970–75; Dental Libn., Coll. of Med. and Dentistry of NJ, 1970–; Reg. Ref. Libn. NY, North. NJ, Reg. Med. Lib., 1969–70; Circ. Coord., NY Acad. of Med., 1968–69. **Educ.:** NY Univ., 1943–49, BS (Bus. Admin.); Long Island Univ., 1965–67, MLS. Med. LA. NJ Hlth. Sci. LA. **Pubns.:** Reviews. **Activities:** 12, 13; 15, 39; 80, 87 **Addr.:** 255 W. 88th St., New York, NY 10024.

Spulber, Pauline (S. 8, 19–, Paris, France) Assoc. Ref. Libn., & Comp. Srch. Anal., IN Univ., 1970–. **Educ.:** IN Univ., 1961–63, BA high distinction (Slavic Lang., Lit.), 1964–67, MA (Fr., Italian), 1969–70, MLS, 1975, PhD (Fr., Italian). **Orgs.:** ALA. IN Univ. LA. **Honors:** Phi Beta Kappa, 1963. **Activities:** 1; 15, 39; 56 **Addr.:** Reference Dept., Main Library, Indiana University, Bloomington, IN 47401.

Spurling, Norman K. (D. 15, 1948, Raleigh, NC) Sr. Biblgphr., Raven Syst. and Resrch., 1978–; Peace Corps Libn., Tutume-McConnell Cmnty. Coll., 1976–77; Peace Corps Libn., Moeng Coll., 1976; Asst. Libn., Fed. Home Loan Bank Bd. Resrch. Lib., 1974–75. **Educ.:** Coll. of William and Mary, 1966–70, BA (Anthro.); Duke Univ., 1970–73, MA (Anthro.); Univ. of NC, 1971–73, MS (LS). **Orgs.:** ALA. DC LA. **Pubns.:** "Information Needs and Bibliographic Problems of the Anthropology Departments at U.N.C. and Duke University," ERIC (O. 1974). **Activities:** 12; 20; 65, 75 **Addr.:** 5225 Connecticut Ave. N.W., Apt. 202, Washington, DC 20815.

Spurlock, Sandra E. (S. 24, 1947, Chardon, OH) Dir., Lib. Srvs., Long Island Jewish-Hillside Med. Ctr., 1979–; Life Sci. Libn., MA Inst. of Tech. Sci. Lib., 1976–79; Resrch. Assoc., Ctr. for Blood Resrch., 1972–76; Lab. Tech., MI State Univ., 1970–72. **Educ.:** Marietta Coll., 1965–69, BS (Bio.); MI State Univ., 1969–70 (Microbio.); Simmons Coll., 1974–76, MSLS. **Orgs.:** ALA: ACRL. Med. LA: NY Reg. Grp. N. Atl. Hlth. Sci. Libs.: Prog. Com. (1978–79). ASIS: New Eng. Chap. (Mem. Ch., 1979). **Pubns.:** "A Study of Life Sciences Book Use in the MIT Science Library: Budgetary Implications," *Quantitative Measurement and Dynamic Library Service* (1978); "Applications of an Operations Research Model to the Study of Book Use in a University Library: Implications for Library Management," *New Horizons for Acad. Libs.* (1979). **Activities:** 1, 12; 15, 17; 58, 80, 91 **Addr.:** Health Sciences Library, Long Island Jewish-Hillside Medical Center, New Hyde Park, NY 11042.

Spurrier, Laura J. (S. 15, 1941, Detroit, MI) Catlgr./Tech. Info. Spec., Lawrence Berkeley Lab., 1979–, Biblgphr., 1978–79. **Educ.:** Univ. of MI, 1959–63, BA (Hist.); Univ. of WI, 1963–64, MA (Indian Std.), 1969–71, MA (Hist.); Univ. of CA, Berkeley, 1973–75, MLS. **Orgs.:** SLA. Assn. for Asian Std. **Honors:** Fulbright-Hays Awd., 1970. **Pubns.:** Jt. auth., *Accounting Practices and Financial Reporting in the Petroleum Industry, a Bibliogra-*

Special Subjects/Services: 50. Adult educ.; 51. Advert./Mktg.; 52. Aerosp.; 53. Agric.; 54. Area std.; 55. Arts/Hum.; 56. Autom.; 57. Bibl./Prtg.; 58. Bio. sci.; 59. Bus./Fin.; 60. Chem.; 61. Copyrt.; 62. Documtn.; 63. Educ.; 64. Engin.; 65. Env.; 66. Eth. grps.; 67. Film; 68. Food/Nutr.; 69. Geneal.; 70. Geo.; 71. Geol.; 72. Handcpd.; 73. Hist.; 74. Int. frdm.; 75. Info. sci.; 76. Insr.; 77. Law; 78. Legis.; 79. Math./Comp. sci.; 80. Med.; 81. Metals; 82. Nat. resrcs.; 83. Newsp.; 84. Nuc. sci.; 85. Oral hist.; 86. Petr./Energy; 87. Pharm.; 88. Phys./Astr./Math.; 89. Readg.; 90. Relig.; 91. Sci./Tech.; 92. Soc. sci.; 93. Telecom.; 94. Transp.; 95. (other).

phy (1979); "Use of RLIN in Cataloging Conference Literature," *Procs. of the Wkshp. on Conf. Lit. in Sci. and Tech.* (forthcoming). **Activities:** 4; 46; 56, 59 **Addr.:** 1281 Queens Rd., Berkeley, CA 94708.

Spyers-Duran, Peter (Ja. 26, 1932, Budapest, Hungary) Dir., Lib., CA State Univ., Long Beach, 1976–; Prof., Head, Lib. Sci. Prog., Dir., Libs., FL Atl. Univ., 1970–76; Prof., Lib. Sci., Dir., Libs., West. MI Univ., 1967–70; Assoc. Dir., Libs., Assoc. Prof., Univ. of WI, Milwaukee, 1963–67; Prof. Asst. to Exec. Secy., ALA, 1962–63; Head, Circ. Dept., Instr., Univ. of Wichita Lib., 1960–62; Ref. Libn., Chicago Pub. Lib., 1959–60; Cat. Dept., Univ. of Chicago, Law Lib., 1957–59; various positions as visit. prof., lectr., 1965–70. **Educ.:** Univ. of Chicago, 1956–60, MA (LS); Nova Univ., 1972–75, EdD (Higher Educ., Finance); CA State Univ., Long Beach, 1977, Cert. (Admin. Inst.); various grad. crs. **Orgs.:** ALA: ACRL, Com. on Upper Div. Univ. Libs. (Ch., 1973–), Com. on Stan. (1965–69), Pubns. Com. (1977–); Lib. Admin. Div./Sect. on Circ. Srvs., Nom. Com. (1977–78)/ Persnl. Admin. Sect. (Ch., 1970–72), Com. on Econ. Status (Ch., 1967–69), PR Com., various com. FL LA. SELA. CA LA. CA State Univ.: Various com., ofcs. FL Assn. of Pub. Jr. Colls. Untd. Fund of Boca Raton. Univ. of Chicago GLS Alum. Assn. **Pubns.:** "Plans for Acquisition of Current Library Materials: Approval Plans," *Encyc. of Lib. and Info. Sci.* (1977); Jt. Ed., "Management Problems in Serials Work," *Proc. of the Conf. on Mgt. Problems in Serials Work* (1973); "Proposed Model Budget Analysis System and Quantative Standards," ERIC (Je. 1973); "Curriculum Development for Library Technicians in Junior Colleges," ERIC (1973); "Faculty Studies: A Survey of Their Use in Selected Libraries," *Coll. and Resrch. Libs.* (Ja. 1968); various articles, monos., reviews. **Activities:** 1; 15, 17, 24; 59, 63 **Addr.:** 11221 Weatherby Rd., Los Alamitos, CA 90720.

Srednicki, Joseph Norton (F. 3, 1951, Norwich, CT) Asst. Chief, Tech. Srvs., Boston Athen., 1977. **Educ.:** CT Coll., 1969–73, AB (Fr.); Simmons Coll., 1976–77, MSLS. **Orgs.:** New Eng. Lib. Info. Netwk.: Rare Bks. and Ms. Users Grp. (Secy., 1979–); Qual. Cntrl. and Cat. Adv. Com. (1979–); Stans. Com. (1979–). ALA: ACRL/Rare Bk. and Mss. Sect. **Honors:** Beta Phi Mu, 1978. **Activities:** 2; 20, 45; 55, 56, 57 **Addr.:** The Boston Athenaeum, 10 1/2 Beacon St., Boston, MA 02108.

Srikantaiah, Taverekere (Taverekere, India) Documtn. Syst. Anal., World Bank, 1977–; Assoc. Prof., CA State Univ., Fullerton, 1977, Asst. Prof., 1973–77. **Educ.:** Ctrl. Coll., India, 1954–58, BS (Chem., Geo.); Karnatak Univ., India, 1958–60, MS (Geo.); Univ. of South. CA, 1964–65, MS (LS), 1968–71, MPA (Pub. Admin.), 1968–73, PhD (LS). **Orgs.:** ALA. ASIS. Assoc. Info. Mgrs. **Pubns.:** *Systems Analysis in Libraries: A Question and Answer Approach* (1979); *Quantitative Research Methods for Librarians* (1977). **Activities:** 11, 12; 26, 30, 38; 56, 59, 75 **Addr.:** 4515 Willard Ave., Apt. 715, Chevy Chase, MD 20015.

Staas, Gretchen Lee (O. 1, 1938, Dallas, TX) Consult., Lib. and Media Srvs., Garland Indp. Sch. Dist., 1978–, Sch. Libn., 1974–78, Classrm. Tchr., 1967–74. **Educ.:** TX Christ. Univ., 1959–61, BS (Home Econ., Educ.); E. TX State Univ., 1971–74, MS (LS); N. TX State Univ., 1980– (Doct. Std.). **Orgs.:** ALA: AASL, Com. on Critical Issues Discuss. Grp. (1980–81); Lcl. Arrange. (1979). Lrng. Resrcs. Prog. Dirs. of TX: Pres.-Elect (1981–82). TX LA. TX Assn. for Educ. Tech. Delta Kappa Gamma: Chap. VP (1979–80). AAUW. E. TX State Univ. Lib. Sch. Alum.: Pres. (1980–81). **Honors:** Phi Delta Kappa. **Activities:** 10, 12; 17, 24; 63 **Addr.:** Learning Resources, Garland Independent School District, 720 Stadium Dr., Garland, TX 75040.

Staats, Joan (Jl. 31, 1921, Chicago, IL) Sr. Staff Sci., Libn., Jackson Lab., 1947–; Actg. Instr., Univ. of IL, 1945–47; Exper. Pharmacologist, Armour Labs., 1944–45; Resrch. Asst., Wilson Labs., 1943–44. **Educ.:** Univ. of IL, 1943, BS (Psy.), 1945–47, MS (Zlgy.). **Orgs.:** Med. LA: Various com., ch. N. Atl. Hlth. Sci. Libs.: Ch. (1963). Hlth. Sci. Libs. and Info. Coop. New Eng. Reg. Med. Lib. Srv.: Adv. Cncl.; Exec. Cncl. AAUW. AAAS. Genetics Socty. of Amer. **Honors:** Sigma Delta Epsilon, 1947. **Pubns.:** "Inbred strains: mouse," *Biology Data Book* (1972); Jt. Auth., "Standardized nomenclature for inbred strains of rats, fourth listing," *Transplantation* (1973); "Diabetes in the mouse due to two mutant genes—a bibliography," *Diabetologia* (1975); "Standardized nomenclature for inbred strains of mice, sixth listing," *Cancer Resrch.* (1976); Jt. Auth., "Behavioral studies using genetically defined mice — a bibliography," *Bhvl. Genetics* (Jl. 1976–Ag. 1978); various articles, bibl. **Activities:** 12; 17, 24, 39; 58, 80 **Addr.:** The Jackson Lab., Bar Harbor, ME 04609.

Stachura, Leonard Richard (Ag. 26, 1923, Chicago, IL) Lib. Dir., St. John Vianney Coll./Semy. 1978–; Various positions as tchr., par. worker, libn. **Educ.:** St. Ambrose Coll., 1943–45, BA (Fr.); Univ. of IL, 1946–49, MA (Educ.); Cath. Univ. of Amer., 1951–54. **Orgs.:** ALA. Cath. LA. **Activities:** 1; 15, 17, 39; 55, 66, 90 **Addr.:** Saint John Vianney College-Seminary 2900 S.W. 87 Ave., Miami, FL 33165.

Stack, Betty Buyck (O. 24, 1925, St. Matthews, SC) Ed., *The Msc. Indx.*, Info. Coords., Inc., 1955–; Ref. Libn., Msc., Detroit Pub. Lib., 1954–56; Catlgr., Copyrt. Div., Lib. of Congs., 1949–54; Msc. Catlgr., Boston Pub. Lib., 1947–49. **Educ.:** Univ. of NC, 1942–46, BSM (Msc.); New Eng. Cnsvty. of Msc., 1946–48, MM (Msc. Theory); Drexel Univ., 1953–54, MSLS. **Orgs.:** Msc. LA. ALA. Greenville Civic Band. Crescent Msc. Club. **Activities:** 14; 30; 55 **Addr.:** 22 Primrose Ln., Greenville, SC 29607.

Stack, Robert J. (Ap. 18, 1949, Milwaukee, WI) Dir., Granite City Pub. Lib., 1978–; Asst. Dir., Clinton Pub. Lib., 1975–78. **Educ.:** Lakeland Coll., 1967–71, BA (Hist.); Univ. of WI, 1974, MA (LS). **Orgs.:** ALA. IL LA. IA LA: Empl.-Empl. Rights and Resp. Com. (1976–78); IA JMRT, Vice-Ch. (1976–77), Ch. (1977–78). Granite City Rotary Club. **Honors:** Beta Phi Mu. **Activities:** 9; 15, 17, 24 **Addr.:** 3105 Wayne, Granite City, IL 62040.

Stackpole, Laurie E. (Je. 27, 1934, Schenectady, NY) Chief, User Srvs. Branch, Natl. Oceanic and Atmospheric Admin., Env. Sci. Info. Ctr., 1980–, Head Libn., Silver Spring Ctr., 1978–80, Ref. Libn., 1977–78. **Educ.:** Trinity Coll., 1952–56, AB (Phys.); Smith Coll., 1956–57, MA (Phys.); Cath. Univ., 1974–77, MLS. **Orgs.:** ASIS. ALA. SLA. **Honors:** Beta Phi Mu, 1977. **Pubns.:** Jt. Auth., "Beyond the Sci-Tech Pub—Providing Oceanic and Atmospheric Decision Makers with Information Syntheses," *The Information Age in Perspective* (1979); Jt. Auth., "Managing for Results—A Case Study in Coalition Building," *New Horizons for Acad. Libs.* (1979); "A Meteorological Library," *Weatherwise* (1979); "NOAA Library and Information Services — A National Resource for Atmospheric Research," *Bltn. of the Amer. Meteorological Socty. 61* (D. 1979). **Activities:** 4, 12; 17, 39; 65, 91 **Addr.:** 6009 Executive Blvd., Rockville, MD 20852.

Stading, Gerald Frederick (Mr. 4, 1935, Richardton, ND) Libn., Media Dir., Stdg. Rock Cmnty. Elem. Sch., 1978–; Libn., US Dept. of the Interior, Bur. of Land Mgt., 1977–78; Instr., Adult Basic Educ., Miles City, MT, Fort Yates, ND, 1977–; Libn., Archvst., Ord. of the Holy Cross, W. Park, NY, 1969–76; Asst. Cur., Mss., MN Hist. Socty., 1967–69; Lib. Dir., Pub. Lib., Faribault, MN, 1965–67; Film Tech., Denver Pub. Lib., 1963–64; Lib. Dir., Pub. Lib., Detroit Lakes, MN, 1961–63; Libn., Sr. HS, Detroit Lakes, MN, 1960–1961. **Educ.:** Univ. of ND, 1953–56; Valley City State Coll., 1956–57, 1959–60, BS (Soc. Sci.); Univ. of Denver, 1963–64 (Libnshp.). **Orgs.:** ALA: AASL. ND LA. MPLA. Mensa. Natl. Educ. Assn. ND Educ. Assn.: Lib. Media Sect. (Treas., 1980–81). **Activities:** 4, 10; 21, 33, 45; 57, 66, 69 **Addr.:** P. O. Box 179, Fort Yates, ND 58538-0179.

Staggs, Edwin A. (N. 11, 1929, Cleveland, OH) Sr. Lit. Sci., Head Libn., Riker Labs., Inc., 3M Co., 1967–, Lit. Sci., 1962–67, 1961–62; Chem., Calbiochem., Los Angeles, CA, 1958–59; Resrch. Asst., Univ. of CA, Citrus Exper. Station, Riverside, 1955–58. **Educ.:** Univ. of CA, Santa Barbara, 1947–51, AB (Chem.); Univ. of CA, Los Angeles, 1952–55, MS (Organic Chem.); Immaculate Heart Coll., Los Angeles, CA, 1963–65, MALS. **Orgs.:** SLA: Chap. Treas. (1974–75); Pharm. Div. (Treas., 1969–72). ASIS. Drug Info. Assn. Amer. Chem. Socty.: Div. of Chem. Lit. **Pubns.:** Abs., *Unlisted Drugs* SLA (1966–); various sci. articles. **Activities:** 12; 15, 17, 39; 60, 80, 87 **Addr.:** Riker Laboratories, Inc. - Library, 19901 Nordhoff St., Northridge, CA 91324.

Stahl, Hella (Ag. 10, 1941, Hamburg, W. Germany) Mgr., Tech. Info. Sect., Pulp and Paper Resrch. Inst. of Can., 1980–, Tech. Info. Spec., 1978–80; Docmlst., M.A.M.R., 1975–78. **Educ.:** Concordia Univ., 1963–73, BA (Langs.); McGill Univ., 1973–75, MLS. **Orgs.:** SLA: East. Can. Chap., Networking Com. (Ch., 1979–). Montreal OLUG: Ch. (1979–). Can. Assn. Info. Sci. **Pubns.:** *Directory of Educational Facilities for the Mentally Handicapped in Montreal* (1977). **Activities:** 12; 17, 30, 39, 49-Online srch.; 82, 86, 91 **Addr.:** 570 St. John's Blvd., Pointe Claire, PQ H9R 3J9 Canada.

Stahl, Milo D. (Mr. 27, 1930, Cocolamus, PA) Dir., Lrng. Resrcs., East. Mennonite Coll., 1960–, Asst. Dean, Coll. Men, 1957–60; Ofc. Coord., of Instr. Dev. and Tech. Acad. Prog., MI State Univ., 1977. **Educ.:** East. Mennonite Coll., 1951–53, 1956–58, BS (Chem.); Case West. Rsv. Univ., 1961–62, MS (LS); MI State Univ., 1965–69, 1976–77, (Instr. Dev. and Tech.). **Orgs.:** AECT: Conv. Eval. (1981). VA Educ. Media Assn. EFLA. VA LA: Mgt. Wkshp. Planner (1973). VA Gvrs. Conf. on Lib. and Info. Srvs.: Del. (1979). Various other orgs. Phi Delta Kappa: Shenandoah Valley Chap. (Secy., 1978–). **Honors:** Phi Delta Kappa, Srv. Key, 1980. **Pubns.:** Ed., *Selected Mennonite History Media Productions* (1980); ed., *Resources to Aid in the Growth and Enrichment of Families with Teenagers* (1979); ed., *Resources to Aid in Meeting Today's Marriage and Home Needs* (1976); ed., *A Selected List of Films for and about Peacemaking* (1975); various slide-tape prods. **Activities:** 1; 32, 40; 63, 67, 93 **Addr.:** 1140 Parkway Dr., Harrisonburg, VA 22801.

Stahlschmidt, Agnes D. (S. 22, 1943, St. Charles, MO) Asst. Prof., Sch. of LS, Univ. of IA, 1979–. **Educ.:** South. IL Univ., 1968–72, BS (Educ.); Univ. of IL, 1973–74, MS (LS); Univ. of IL, EdD, 1981. **Orgs.:** ALA. Chld. Lit. Assn. NCTE. **Honors:** Phi Delta Kappa; Univ. of IA, Old Gold Fellow. **Pubns.:** Jt. auth., "Facsimiles of Historical Children's Books," *Lib. Trends* (Spr. 1979). **Activities:** 10, 11; 21, 26, 31; 55, 63, 89 **Addr.:** School of Library Science, University of Iowa, Iowa City, IA 52242.

Stair, Fred G. (Ap. 27, 1948, Kansas City, MO) Libn. for Info. Srvs., Cities Srv., Tulsa, OK, 1981–; Ref. Libn., CO Sch. of Mines, 1978–81. **Educ.:** Univ. of WA, 1973–74, BA (Educ., Pol. Sci., Chem.); 1975–77 (Libnshp.). **Orgs.:** SLA: Rocky Mt. Chap. (Secy., 1979–80). ASIS: 1981 Mid-Yr. Mtg., Exec. Com. CO OLUG. Amer. Chem. Socty. **Pubns.:** *Mineral Resources and Mining in the American States: A Bibliography of Bibliographies* (1980); "Searching the Mineral Industries" audio-cassette (1979). **Activities:** 1, 12; 31, 32, 39; 60, 64, 86 **Addr.:** ERG Research Library, P.O. Box 3908, Tulsa, OK 74102.

Stajniak, Elizabeth T. (Ja. 26, 1947, Poland) Dir., Lib. Srvs., Detroit Bar Assn., 1973–; Ref. Libn., Detroit Pub. Lib., 1969–73. **Educ.:** Detroit Inst. of Tech., 1966–69, BA (Hist.); Wayne State Univ., 1969–71, MLS; Univ. of Detroit, 1975–80, JD (Law). **Orgs.:** AALL. OH Reg. Assn. of Law Libs. MI Assn. of Law Libs.: Treas. (1980–). **Activities:** 3, 12; 15, 17, 41; 56, 77, 78 **Addr.:** Detroit Bar Association, Foundation Library, 600 Woodward, Detroit, MI 48226.

Staley, Valeria S. Howard (My. 5, 1925, Georgetown, SC) Ref., Info. Spec., SC State Coll., 1978–, Acq. Libn., 1968–78, Asst. Libn., 1958–68; Sch. Libn., Howard HS, 1949–57; Ref. Libn., FL A&M Univ., 1946–49. **Educ.:** Talladega Coll., 1941–45, BA (Eng.); Univ. of Chicago, 1945–46, BLS; various crs. **Orgs.:** Orangeburg Cnty. Lib. Comsn.: Ch. (1980). SC LA. SE LA. ALA: Black Caucus. AAUP. SC Empl. Assn. NAACP. Talladega Coll. Alum. Assn. Various other orgs. **Honors:** Alpha Beta Alpha; Delta Sigma Theta. **Activities:** 1; 15, 39; 66, 75, 93 **Addr.:** South Carolina State College, Box 1947, Orangeburg, SC 29117.

Stalker, John C. (Mr. 9, 1945, Buffalo, NY) Head, Pub. Srvs., Atlanta Univ. Lib., 1979–, Acq. Libn., 1975–79, Biblgphr., Ref. Libn., 1973–75; Visit. Asst. Prof., Eng., NC Ctrl. Univ., 1972. **Educ.:** Canisius Coll., 1962–66, BA (Eng.); Univ. of NC, 1966–69, MA (Eng.), 1970–72, MSLS, 1972–78, PhD (Eng.). **Orgs.:** ALA: Ref. and Subscrpn. Bks. Review Com. (1976–80); Ref. Srvs. in Lg. Acad. Libs. Com. (1974–). SE LA. **Activities:** 1; 17; 55, 57, 89 **Addr.:** Trevor Arnett Library, Atlanta University, 223 Chestnut St., Atlanta, GA 30314.

Stallings, Elizabeth A. (S. 30, 1927, Washington, DC) Reg. Lib. Liaison and Proj. Libn., U.S. Dept. of Housing and Urban Dev., 1981–, Reg. Liaison, Ref. Libn., 1975–81, Circ., ILL Libn., 1974–75, Cat., Acq. Libn., 1968–74. **Educ.:** Wellesley Coll., 1945–49, BA (Eng.); Cath. Univ. of Amer., 1964–68, MS (LS); various crs. **Orgs.:** Beta Phi Mu: Iota Chap., Treas. (1978–79), VP. (1979–80), Pres. (1980–81). SLA: Soc. Sci. Div., Urban Affairs Sect., Vice-Ch., (1980–81), Ch. (1981–82); DC Chap. (Treas., 1981–84); Fed. Interagency Fld. Libns. Wkshp.: Various ofcs. WA Wellesley Club: 1949 Class Secy. (1969–74). Amer. Cancer Socty.: Reach-to-Recvy. Prog. (Volun., 1978–). **Honors:** Beta Phi Mu, 1968; U.S. Dept. of Housing and Urban Dev., Cert. of Spec. Achvmt., 1978, 1980. **Activities:** 4; 17; 55, 92 **Addr.:** U.S. Dept. of Housing & Urban Development, Library, Rm. 8141, 451 7th St., S.W., Washington, DC 20410.

Stam, David H. (Jl. 11, 1935, Paterson, NJ) Andrew W. Mellon Dir., The Resrch. Libs., NY Pub. Lib., 1978–; Lib., Johns Hopkins, 1973–78; Assoc. Libn., Newberry Lib., 1967–73; Libn., Marlboro Coll., 1964–67. **Educ.:** Wheaton Coll., 1951–55, BA (Eng.); Rutgers Univ., 1962, MLS; Northwest. Univ., 1978, PhD (Hist.). **Orgs.:** ALA. Resrch. Lib. Grp.: Bd. of Gvrs. Grolier Club. Caxton Club. Amer. Hist. Assn. Renaissance Socty. of Amer. **Honors:** Brit. Acad., Overseas Fellow, 1975. **Pubns.:** *Wordsworthian Criticism 1964–1973* (1974). **Activities:** 12; 17, 23, 45; 55, 57, 90 **Addr.:** 1 Fraser St., Pelham, NY 10803.

Stam, Deirdre C. (Ag. 13, 1940, Everett, MA) Exec. Secy., Bibl. Socty. of Amer., 1980–; Art Ref. Libn., SUNY, Purchase, 1979–80; Cur. Asst., Tutankhamen Show, Metro. Musm. of Art, 1978–79; NEH Proj. Coord., Baltimore Cnty. Pub. Lib., 1977–78; Tchr., Bryn Mawr Sch., 1974–76; Asst. Cur., Ancient Art, Art Inst. of Chicago, 1972–73. **Educ.:** Radcliffe Coll., 1958–62, BA, cum laude (Fine Arts); Inst. of Fine Arts, NY Univ., 1962–64, MA (Egyptian Art); Johns Hopkins Univ., 1974–76, MEduc; Cath. Univ., 1976–78, MLS. **Orgs.:** ARLIS/NA: Pubn. Com. (Ch., 1980–); NY Chap., *News* Ed. (1978–). Coll. Art Assn. ALA. Amer. Assn. of Musms. **Pubns.:** Ed., *Rembrandt after Three Hundred Years, a Symposium* (1975); "Burne-Jones and the *Golden Legend*," *Newberry Lib. Bltn.* (Ag. 1978). **Activities:** 55 **Addr.:** 1 Fraser St., Pelham, NY 10803.

Stamenkovich, Slobodanka (Boba) (D. 13, 1943, Belgrade, Serbia, Yugoslavia) Exch. Libn., USDA/SENAL, 1976–. **Educ.:** Cath. Univ. of Amer., 1971–73, MS (LS). **Orgs.:** ASIS. **Pubns.:** "International Exchange Program," *ALIN* (S. 1978); *Slavic Serials in Agricultural Sciences—A Bibliography* (1978). **Activities:** 4, 12; 15, 36; 53 **Addr.:** USDA/SE Exchange, National Agricultural Library, Beltsville, MD 20705.

Standrod, Garland L. (Jl. 15, 1940, Fort Smith, AR) Tech. Info. Spec., Agency for Intl. Dev., 1977–; Env. Policy Biblgphr., Lib. of Congs., 1976–77; Ref., Docum. Libn., U.S. Info.

PROFESSIONAL ACTIVITIES: Institutions: 1. Acad. lib.; 2. Arch.; 3. Assn.; 4. Fed./Gvt. lib.; 5. Inst. lib.; 6. Mfr./Suppl.; 7. Milit. lib.; 8. Musm.; 9. Pub. lib.; 10. Sch. lib.; 11. Sch. of lib. sci.; 12. Spec. lib.; 13. State lib.; 14. (other). **Functions/Activities:** 15. Acq./Col. dev.; 16. Adult srvs.; 17. Admin.; 18. Apprais.; 19. Archit./Bldgs.; 20. Cat./Class.; 21. Chld. srvs.; 22. Circ.; 23. Cons./Pres.; 24. Consult.; 25. Cont. ed.; 26. Educ. lib. sci.; 27. Ext. srvs.; 28. Fund/Grants; 29. Gvt. pubs.; 30. Indx./Abs.; 31. Instr. lib. use; 32. Media srvs.; 33. Micro.; 34. Netwks./Coop.; 35. Persnl.; 36. PR; 37. Publshg.; 38. Recs. mgt.; 39. Ref. srvs.; 40. Repro.; 41. Resrch.; 42. Review.; 43. Secur.; 44. Serials; 45. Spec. col.; 46. Tech. srvs.; 47. Trustees/Bds.; 48. YA srvs.; 49. (other).

Agency, 1974–75; Libn. Consult., Ctr. for Econ. Dev. and Admin., Kathmandu, Nepal, 1971–73; Ref., Sel. Lib., U.S. Dept. of the Interior, 1968–71. **Educ.:** Tulane Univ., 1958–62, BA (Phil.); Univ. of MD, 1967–68, MLS; Un. Grad. Sch., 1969–74, PhD (Info. Sci.). **Orgs.:** ALA. Assoc. Info. Mgrs. WA Indp. Writers. **Honors:** Phi Beta Kappa, 1962; Beta Phi Mu, 1968. **Pubns.:** Jt. auth., *Information Resources on Nepal* (1973); *The Automation of Fish Processing and Handling: A Bibliography* (1970); "Libraries in Nepal," *ALA World Encyc. of Lib. and Info. Srvs.* (1980); ed., *A.I.D. Resrch. and Dev. Abs.* (1977–); ed., *Nepal Documtn.* (1970–73). **Activities:** 4, 12; 15, 30, 39; 54, 57, 65 **Addr.:** 2135 Newport Pl., N.W., Washington, DC 20037.

Stanford, Edward B. (Mr. 31, 1910, Moorhead, MN) Prof. Emeritus, Univ. of MN, 1977–, Prof., Lib. Sch., 1971–77, Prof., Dir., Univ. Libs., 1951–71, Asst. Univ. Libn., 1946–51. **Educ.:** Dartmouth Coll., 1927–32, AB (Biog., Compar. Lit.) Univ. of IL, 1933–34, BS (LS); Williams Coll., 1936–39, MA (Eng. Lit.); Univ. of Chicago, 1939–42, PhD (LS). **Orgs.:** ALA: Cncl.; Bd. on Persnl. Admin., Ch.; ACRL/Univ. Libs. Sect., Ch., Bd. of Dirs. ARL: Bd. of Dirs. **Pubns.:** *Library Extension Under the W.P.A.* (1942); various articles, *Amer. Libs., Lib. Jnl.* **Activities:** 1, 11; 17, 19, 26; 57, 85 **Addr.:** Rose Mall Apts. #306, 2220 N. Pascal St., Roseville, MN 55113.

Stanger, Keith Judd (D. 8, 1946, New York, NY) Instr. Libn., East. MI Univ., 1977–, Asst. Educ./Psy. Libn., 1974–77. **Educ.:** Harpur Coll., 1964–68, BA (Psy.); OH State Univ., 1970–72, MA (Psy.); Univ. of IL, 1973–74, MLS. **Orgs.:** ASIS: MI Chap. (Treas., 1978–80). MI LA: Ref. Sect. (1977–78). ALA. **Honors:** Beta Phi Mu. **Activities:** 1; 31, 39; 63, 92 **Addr.:** Library, Eastern Michigan University, Ypsilanti, MI 48197.

Stanley, Judith R. (New York, NY) Ref. and Col. Dev. Lib., Kennedy Sch. of Gvt., Harvard Univ., 1979–; Soc. Sci. Biblgphr., Univ. of CA, Irvine, 1974–79. **Educ.:** Univ. of CA, Los Angeles, 1963–68, BA (Hist.), 1971–72, MA (Hist.); Univ. of South. CA, 1973–74, MSLS. **Orgs.:** ALA. SLA. AALL. **Honors:** Phi Beta Kappa, 1968; Phi Gamma Mu, 1967. **Pubns.:** "Personnel Rotation - A Personal View," *The Unabashed Libn.*. **Activities:** 1; 15, 31, 39; 92 **Addr.:** Kennedy School of Government Library, Harvard University, 79 Boylston St., Cambridge, MA 02138.

Stanley, Nancy Nell (N. 26, 1924, Blum, TX) Mgr., Jenkins Lib. and Arch. Ctr. For. Missn. Bd., SBC, 1960–; Asst., Missn. Pers. Dept., 1958–60; Youth Educ. Dir., Rel. Educ., First Bapt. Church, 1957–58. **Educ.:** Baylor Univ., 1956, BA (Eng.); VA Cmwlth. Univ., 1960–62 (LS); Amer. Univ., 1974 Arch. Mgt.). **Orgs.:** ALA. VA LA: Spec. Libs. Grp. (Mem. Ch., 1970). SAA: Rel. Arch. Sect., Com. on Funding (1977–78). South. Bapt. Hist. Socty. VA Bapt. Hist. Socty. **Honors:** Alpha Chi, 1956; Sigma Tau Delta. **Activities:** 2; 17, 23, 41; 54, 90 **Addr.:** 3806 Monument Ave., Richmond, VA 23230.

Stanley, William T. (N. 29, 1926, Whiteville, NC) Dir., Lib., CA Bapt. Coll., 1981–; Asst. Prof., Sch. of LS, Univ. of South. CA, 1973–80; Head Libn., Rio Hondo Coll., 1972–73; Hum., Soc. Sci. Libn., CA Tech., 1953–69. **Educ.:** Univ. of CA, Los Angeles, 1947–49, BA (Eng.); Univ. of CA, Berkeley, 1949–51, MA (Eng.); Univ. of South. CA, 1969–76, PhD (LS). **Orgs.:** ALA. CA LA. SLA. ASIS. Eng.-Speaking Un. **Pubns.:** *Broadway in the West End* (1978). **Activities:** 1; 17, 31 **Addr.:** 6511 Short Way, Los Angeles, CA 90042.

Stansfield, Agnes (Jl. 7, 1940, Sanford, FL) Serials Libn., Loyola Univ., N., 1978–, Sci. Libn., 1974–78; Asst. Libn., E. Carolina Univ., 1972–73; Ref. Libn., Med. Univ. SC, 1971–72; various positions, Tulane Med., 1964–70. **Educ.:** FL State Univ., 1958–62, BS (Educ.), 1970–71, MS (LS); Med. LA, 1972, Cert. **Orgs.:** SLA: Various chap. ofcs. (1975–). ALA. Med. LA. Amer. Pub. Hlth. Assn. **Pubns.:** Ed., *Spec. Libs. LA Chap. Bltn.* (1975–78). **Activities:** 1, 12; 33, 39, 44; 58, 80 **Addr.:** 711 Fern St., New Orleans, LA 70118.

Stansfield, Cynthia M. (D. 7, 1940, Yonkers, NY) Libn., St. Mary's Episcopal Church, Manchester, CT, 1974–; Cat., Univ. Libn. III, Univ. of CT Lib., 1966–; Cat., Uni. Tech. Corp., 1963–66. **Educ.:** Univ. of CT, 1958–62, BA (Hist.); Syracuse Univ., 1962–63, MSLS. **Orgs.:** SLA: CT Valley Chap., Rcrt. Com., Ch. (1963–68); Rec. Secy. (1968–69). CS LA: Sec. VP (1976–77); CT Chap., Pres. (1977–78), PR Ch. (1978–), Secy. (1977–78), 1980 Natl. Conf., Pubcty. Com. **Honors:** Beta Phi Mu, 1963. **Pubns.:** "Instructing Your Library Patrons," *Church and Synagogue Libs.* (Ja.–F. 1978); photographer *Workshop Planning* (1979); various photographs, *Church and Synagogue Libs.* **Activities:** 1, 12; 20, 33, 36; 55, 90 **Addr.:** Cataloging Department, University of Connecticut Library, U–5B, Storrs, CT 06268.

Stansfield, George James (Mr. 8, 1917, Oak Park, IL) Sr. Histn., HQ, U.S. Army Materiel Dev. and Readiness Cmnd., 1980–; Chief, Spec. Cols. and Hist. Branch, Natl. Defense Univ. Lib., 1978–80, Histn., 1976–78; Histn., Natl. War Coll., 1965–76, Lib. Dir., 1961–73. **Educ.:** MA Inst. of Tech., 1934–35; Harvard Coll., 1936–40, SB (Hist.); Amer. Univ., 1940–44, 1961–64, (Arch. Admin.); George Washington Univ., 1965–66 (Intl. Rel.). **Orgs.:** SAA: Schol. Subcom. (1980–82). SLA. Alexandria Lib. Co. Amer. Milit. Inst.: Libn. (1944–63); Bk. Review Ed. (1944–63). Alexandria Hist. Recs. Adv. Comsn.: Ch. (1975–). **Honors:** Amer. Milit. Inst., Fellow, 1967; Natl. Defense Univ., Srv. Awd., 1980. **Pubns.:** *Alexandria, a Town in Transition* (1977); "The Libraries of Military Educational Systems in the U.S.," *Spec. Libs.* (Mr. 1960); "History JAGD Department of the Army," *Milit. Affairs* (F. 1945); "(Civil War): Impact on the Army Educational System," *Army Info. Digest* (Ap. 1961). **Activities:** 1, 2; 17, 38, 45; 54, 74 **Addr.:** 512 Duke St., Alexandria, VA 22314.

Stanton, Lee W. (D. 3, 1944, Fulton, NY) Sr. Libn., NY State Lib., 1979–; Archvst. III, NY State Arch., 1978–79, Archvst. II, 1977–78, Asst. Libn., NY State Lib., 1968–77. **Educ.:** SUNY, Oswego, 1962–66, BS (Hist.); SUNY, Albany, 1966–68, MLS; various grad. crs. **Orgs.:** SAA: Com. on Access. ALA. NY LA. NY State Hist. Assn. **Activities:** 2, 13; 17, 39; 55, 69 **Addr.:** Humanities Reference Service, New York State Library, Albany, NY 12204.

Stanton, Mattie (Ja. 10, 1941, Memphis, TN) Div. Asst., Info. Support Srvs., St. Louis Pub. Schs., 1963–, Div. Asst. MIIS, 1977–79, Admin. Asst., Eval., 1976–77, Tchr., 1963–76. **Educ.:** Harris Tchrs. Coll., 1959–63, BA (Educ.); St. Louis Univ., 1970–72, MA (Spec. Educ.); various grad. crs. **Orgs.:** SLA. Assn. of Educ. Data Systs. **Honors:** East. Star, Woman of the Yr., 1979; Phi Delta Kappa; Sigma Gamma Rho. **Activities:** 2, 12; 17, 20, 30 **Addr.:** St. Louis Public Schools, Information Support Services, 911 Locust, St. Louis, MO 63101.

Stanton, Robert O. (N. 15, 1926, Pittsburgh, PA) Head, Internal Tech. Info. Dept., Bell Telephone Labs., 1981–, Head, Info. Systs. Dept., 1976–81, Head, Lib. Opers. Dept., 1964–75, Head, Pubn. Prod. Dept., 1963–64. **Educ.:** Univ. of Pittsburgh, 1944–49, BS (Zlgy.); Carnegie-Mellon Univ., 1949–50, MLS. **Orgs.:** ASIS: Ctrl. N. Chap. (Ch., 1978–79); Mem. Com. (1979–80), Prof. Com. (Ch., 1980–81). **Pubns.:** "Computer-Aided Selection in a Library Network," (w F. H. Spaulding) *Jnl. of the Amer. Socty. for Info. Sci.* (N. 1975); "Applying the Manage. by Obj. Tech. in an Industrial Library," *JASIS* (S. 1976). **Activities:** 12; 17, 56, 61 **Addr.:** Bell Telephone Labs., 600 Mountain Ave., Rm. MH 6A–316, Murray Hill, NJ 07974.

Stanton, Ruth Paré (D. 10, 1946, New York, NY) Sr. Ref. Libn., Assoc. Prof., N. VA. Cmnty. Coll., 1973–; Libn., Grad. School of LS, Simmons Coll., 1970–73; Asst. Ref. Libn., Brandeis Univ., 1969–70. **Educ.:** Bates Coll., 1965–68, BA (Eng.); Simmons Coll., 1968–69, MSLS; Cath. Univ., 1974 (Educ.). **Orgs.:** VA LA. ALA. Natl. Socty. for Performance and Instr. AAUP. **Honors:** Beta Phi Mu. **Pubns.:** Jt. auth., *Lib. Skills Module* (1976–77); "Walking Tour of the Annandale Campus Library" cassette (1974, 1976, 1979). **Activities:** 1; 15, 31, 39; 50 **Addr.:** Annandale Campus, Northern Virginia Community College, 8333 Little River Turnpike, Annandale, VA 22003.

Stanton, Vida Cummins (Ag. 3, 1930, Holyrood, KS) Asst. Prof., Sch., of LS, Univ. of WI, Milwaukee, 1972–; Asst. Prof., Dept. of LS, North. IL Univ., 1970–72; Supvsr., Sch. Libs., Hutchinson Pub. Schs., 1965–67; Ref. Libn., KS State Univ., 1964–65; Catlgr., Univ. of WY, 1963–64; Sch. Libn., Laramie Jr. Sr. HS, 1958–61. **Educ.:** Univ. of KS, 1947–52, BS (Educ.); Univ. of WI, 1956–60, MS (LS); IN Univ., 1972, PhD (Higher Educ., LS). **Orgs.:** AALS. WI LA: Educ. Sect. (Ch., 1978–79); VP (1981); Pres. (1982). ALA: Lib. Educ. Div./Tchrs. Sect. (Secy., 1972–75). AAUP. Natl. Cncl. of Tchrs. of Eng. AECT. **Honors:** Beta Phi Mu. **Pubns.:** "The Library School: Its Role in Teaching the Use of the Library," *Progress in Educating the Library User* (1978); "Volunteers: Another View," *WI Lib. Bltn.* (S.–O. 1978); "Roadmaps through Information Sources," *Cath. Lib. World* (Mr. 1979). **Activities:** 11; 21, 25, 31 **Addr.:** School of Library Science, University of Wisconsin, Milwaukee, WI 53201.

Stanton, Virginia Barbara (Ja. 7, 1931, Flushing, NY) Dir., Garden City Pub. Lib., 1977–; Asst. Dir., Rockville Ctr. Pub. Lib., 1964–77; Head, Adult Srvs., Bethpage Pub. Lib., 1963; Supvsg. Army Libn., U.S. Army, Germany, 1961–63; Asst. Head, Bus. Sci. Ind. Dept., Free Lib. of Philadelphia, 1960, Asst. Head, Mercantile Lib., 1958–60, Sr. Ref., Libn. Gen. Info. Dept., 1957, Ref. Libn., Lcl. Hist. and Geneal. Dept., 1955–56; various libn. positions, 1952–54. **Educ.:** Douglass Coll., 1948–52, BA (Hist.); Columbia Univ., 1952–53, MSLS (Lib.); various grad. crs. **Orgs.:** ALA. NY LA. Nassau Cnty. LA. Rockville Ctr. Mayor's Bicent. Comsn. **Honors:** Village of Rockville Ctr., Mayor's Bicent. Awd., 1976. **Activities:** 9; 17 **Addr.:** Garden City Public Library, 60 7th St., Garden City, NY 11530.

Stanwood, Cheryl J. (Ap. 27, 1947, San Diego, CA) Law Libn., Ct. of Appeal, 2nd Dist., 1978–; Libn., CA West. Law Sch., 1977–78; Lectr., Chelmer Inst. of Higher Educ., 1974–77; Lectr., Univ. of the W. Indies, 1971–72. **Educ.:** Univ. of CA, San Diego, 1965–69, BA (Eng. Lit.); Univ. of MO, 1972–73, MLS. **Orgs.:** AALL. ALA. **Activities:** 13; 15, 17, 41; 77 **Addr.:** Ct. of Appeal Library, 2nd District, 3580 Wilshire Blvd., Rm. 448, Los Angeles, CA 90010.

Stanylewich, Roberta J. (Ja. 26, 1948, Beacon, NY) Media Spec., Roy C. Ketcham Sr. HS, 1975–; Libn., Rocliff Jansen Ctrl. Sch., 1970–73. **Educ.:** State Univ. Coll., Geneseo, 1966–70, BS (LS); Pratt Inst., 1973–75, MLS; New Sch. for Soc. Resrch., 1977, MMS (Media). **Orgs.:** ALA. Southeast. NY LA. Dutchess Cnty. LA. **Activities:** 10; 15, 31, 32; 56, 63, 93 **Addr.:** Roy C. Ketcham Sr. HS, Myers Corners Rd., Wappingers Falls, NY 12590.

Staples, Loretta T. (Ja. 16, 1932, Washburn, ME) Lib. Dept. Ch., Nashua HS, 1975–; Libn., Pelham HS, 1974–75; Head Libn., N. Plainfield HS, 1969–74; Libn., Canton HS, 1966–69. **Educ.:** Colby Coll., 1949–53, BA (Eng.); Univ. of RI, 1964–67, MLS; various crs. **Orgs.:** ALA. New Eng. Educ. Media Assn. NH Educ. Media Assn.: Mem. Ch.; Exec. Bd. **Activities:** 10; 17, 32, 48; 92 **Addr.:** Madison Ln., Amherst, NH 03031.

Stapleton, Sr. Mary Mauricita (Jl. 6, 1939, Fall River, MA) Dir., The Newport Coll., Salve Regina, 1979–, Actg. Libn., 1978–79, Asst. Libn., Pub. Srvs., 1976–78, Lib. Staff, 1974–76; Elem., Sec. Tchr., Dio. of Providence, RI and Fall River, MA, 1962–74. **Educ.:** Salve Regina Coll., 1957–62, BA (Math.); RI Coll., 1966–71, MEd (Educ.); George Peabody Coll., 1975–77, MLS (Acad. Lib.); RI Tchr. Cert.; MA Tchr. Cert. **Orgs.:** ALA. New Eng. ACRL. RI LA. Cnsrtm. of RI Acad. and Resrch. Libs. Beta Phi Mu: Secy. (1980–81). Mercy Higher Educ. Colloquium. Assn. of RI Hlth. Sci. Libns. **Activities:** 1; 17, 31, 39; 63, 75, 89 **Addr.:** The Newport College, Salve Regina, Ochre Point Ave., Newport, RI 02840.

Stark, Bruce P. (Ag. 7, 1940, New London, CT) Archvst., Arch. and Mss. Sect., Sterling Meml. Lib., Yale Univ., 1982–; Head, Spec. Cols., SUNY, Plattsburgh, 1978–82; Asst. Prof., Hist., Univ. of CT, Southeast. Branch, 1970–75. **Educ.:** Brown Univ., 1958–62, AB (Hist.); Univ. of CT, 1966–70, PhD (Amer. Hist.); South. CT State Coll., 1976–78, MLS. **Orgs.:** SAA: Mss. Prof. Afnty. Grp., Strg. Com. (1980–). NY LA: Resrcs. and Tech. Srvs. Sect., Cons. Com. (1978–79). CT LA. New Eng. Archvsts. Amer. Hist. Assn. CT Hist. Socty. Org. of Amer. Histns. Inst. of Early Amer. Culture. **Honors:** SUNY, Resrch. Fndn., Grant, 1981. **Pubns.:** *Lyme, Connecticut: From Founding to Independence* (1976); *Connecticut Signer: William Williams* (1975); "The Election of 1740 in Connecticut," *CT Hist.* (Ja. 1981); "Stephen Johnson: Patriot Minister," *CT Hist. Socty. Bltn.* (Ja. 1979); "The Redford Crown Glass Company, Clinton County, New York," *Reflections: The Story of Redford Glass* (1978); various articles. **Activities:** 1; 15, 23, 39; 69, 73 **Addr.:** Sterling Memorial Library, Yale University, Beaver Brook Rd., Lyme, CT 06371.

Stark, Lucile S. (Chicago, IL) Lib. Dir., West. Psyt. Inst. and Clinic, 1974–; Ed., *Bhvl. and Soc. Scis. Libn.* (1981–). **Educ.:** Univ. of Chicago, BA (Geo.); Univ. of MO, MA (LS); Univ. of Pittsburgh various crs. in LS. **Orgs.:** ALA. Amer. Psyt. Assn.: Mental Hlth. Libns. Grp. Med. LA: Legis. Com. (Ch., 1982); Mental Hlth. Libns. Grp. (Secy., 1976–77); Pittsburgh Chap. (Ch., 1980). SLA: Ref. Update, Psy. and Mental Hlth. (1980). **Activities:** 12; 15, 17, 24; 57, 75, 95-Psyt. **Addr.:** Western Psychiatric Institute and Clinic, 3811 O'Hara St., Pittsburgh, PA 15261.

Starkey, Edward D. (O. 21, 1942, Oswego, NY) Head, Ref., Univ. of Dayton, 1979–; Coll. Libn., Urbana Coll., 1976–79; Coll., HS Eng. Tchr., 1968–75. **Educ.:** Stonehill Coll., 1960–65, BA (Phil.); Gregorian Univ., Rome, Italy, 1965–66 (Theo.); SUNY, Albany, 1966–68, MA (Eng.); Univ. of KY, 1975–76, MSLS. **Orgs.:** Miami Valley Lib. Org.: Dayton-Miami Valley Cnsrtm., Univ. Liaison (1976–). ALA: ACRL. Otto Multitype Interlib. Coop. Com. (Vice-Ch., 1980–). **Honors:** Beta Phi Mu, 1976. **Activities:** 1; 31, 34, 39; 54, 55, 90 **Addr.:** Roesch Library, University of Dayton, Dayton, OH 45469.

Starr, Carol Lynn (Ap. 3, 1945, Pittsburgh, PA) Alameda Cnty. Lib./Pleasanton Branch Mgr.; Coord., YA Srvs., Alameda Cnty. Lib., 1973–81; YA Libn., Menomonee Falls, WI, 1970–72; YA Dept. Head, Bowie Branch, Prince George Cnty. Lib., 1967–70; Guest Instr. for Adlsnt. Lit., Univ. of WI, 1972–73. **Educ.:** Univ. of WI, Madison, 1963–66, BA (Hist.), 1966–67, MALS. **Orgs.:** ALA: Amer. Libs. Ed. Adv. Com. (1976–78); YASD (Pres., 1975); Bd. (1974–76); various coms. Bay Area YA Libns.: Bk. Review Ed. (1976–78); Pres. (1978–79). CA LA: CA Socty. of Libns. Bd. (1976–79); Cncl. (1976–79). **Pubns.:** "Effects of Proposition 13 on Youth Services in California," *Top of the News* (Win. 1979–80); "Young Adult Services," *ALA Yrbk.* (1975); jt. auth., "Sex–Ask the Librarian," *Lib. Jnl. Spec. Rpt. #6* (1978); ed., *WLW Jnl.*, 1980–; ed./publshr., *Young Adult Alternative Nsltr.*, 1973–79. **Activities:** 9; 25, 37, 48; 74, 89 **Addr.:** Alameda County Library/ Pleasanton Branch, 4333 Black Ave., Pleasanton, CA 94566.

Starr, Daniel A. (D. 19, 1952, Chicago, IL) Assoc. Libn., Cat., Musm. of Mod. Art, 1979–; Ref., Cat. Libn., Art Inst. of Chicago, 1977–79. **Educ.:** Univ. of Chicago, 1971–74, BA (Grmn. Lit.), 1975–77, MA (LS). **Orgs.:** Art Libs. Socty. NY. ARLIS/NA. **Pubns.:** Bibl., *Joseph Cornell* (1980); ed. "Cataloging and Indexing Special Interest Group," clmn. *ARLIS/NA Nsltr.* (1979–); "Choice of Main Entry for Art Exhibition Catalogs," ERIC (1977). **Addr.:** Museum of Modern Art Library, 11 W. 53rd St., New York, NY 10019.

Special Subjects/Services: 50. Adult educ.; 51. Advert./Mktg.; 52. Aerosp.; 53. Agric.; 54. Area std.; 55. Arts/Hum.; 56. Autom.; 57. Bibl./Prtg.; 58. Bio. sci.; 59. Bus./Fin.; 60. Chem.; 61. Copyrt.; 62. Documtn.; 63. Educ.; 64. Engin.; 65. Env.; 66. Eth. grps.; 67. Film; 68. Food/Nutr.; 69. Geneal.; 70. Geo.; 71. Geol.; 72. Handcpd.; 73. Hist.; 74. Int. frdm.; 75. Info. sci.; 76. Insr.; 77. Law; 78. Legis.; 79. Math./Comp. sci.; 80. Med.; 81. Metals; 82. Nat. resrcs.; 83. Newsp.; 84. Nuc. sci.; 85. Oral hist.; 86. Petr./Energy; 87. Pharm.; 88. Phys./Astr./Math.; 89. Readg.; 90. Relig.; 91. Sci./Tech.; 92. Soc. sci.; 93. Telecom.; 94. Transp.; 95. (other).

Stear, James R. (My. 1, 1937, Peoria, IL) Staff Syst. Anal., Env. Sci. Info. Ctr., Natl. Oceanic and Atmospheric Admin., 1977–, Chief, User Srvs. Branch, 1976–77, Chief, Syst. Branch, Tech. Info. Div., 1973–77; Tech. Info. Spec., Vets. Admin., 1969–73. **Educ.:** Bradley Univ., 1954–58, BSME (Mech. Engin.); St. Louis Univ., 1958–60, MS (Meteorology); Amer. Univ., 1978–80, MPA (Pub. Admin.). **Orgs.:** ASIS. Natl. Fed. of Abs. and Indexing Srv.: Educ. Com. (1974–75). Tape Users Grp: Fed. Lib. Com. (Ch., 1977–79). Natl. Fed. of Schols. **Honors:** Sigma Tau, 1958; Tau Beta Pi, 1973; Pi Alpha Alpha, 1980. **Pubns.:** Jt. auth., *General Systems Analysis and Design for an Automated Library and Information System* (1979); *Management Review and Analysis Program for Library and Information Services Division* (1977); jt. ch., "Sounding in the Eye of Hurricane Arlene to 108,000 Feet," *Jnl. of Appld. Meteorology* (1965); "OASIS, A One-Stop Information Service," *Procs. 9th Anl. Mtg. of Geosci. Info. Socty.* (1975); "OASIS, A NOAA Service to Users of Marine Information," *Procs. of 10th Anl. Marine Tech. Conf.* (1972). **Activities:** 4, 12; 17, 41; 56, 93 **Addr.:** 15305 Emory Ln., Rockville, MD 20853.

Stearns, Norman S. (O. 17, 1923) Assoc. Dean, Cont. Educ., Prof., Tufts Univ. Sch. of Med., 1973–. **Educ.:** Harvard Coll., 1943 (Bio.); Boston Univ. Sch. of Med., 1947 (Med.); Boston Univ. Grad. Sch., 1950, Pharmgy. **Orgs.:** Boston Med. Lib.: Trustee, VP (1974–77). Amer. Coll. of Physicians: *Annals of Internal Med.* Pubn. Com. (1973–77). Amer. Fed. for Clinical Resrch. Amer. Med. Assn. Assn. for Hosp. Med. Educ.: Pres. (1976–78), various other ofcs. Various other orgs. **Honors:** Med. LA, Hon. Mem., 1978; other med. hons. **Pubns.:** Jt. auth., *Library Practice in Hospitals; A Basic Guide* (1972); various pubns. in med. **Activities:** 1, 5; 17, 25; 50, 80 **Addr.:** Office of Continuing Education, Tufts University School of Medicine, 136 Harrison Ave., Boston, MA 02111.

Stearns, Susan M. (My. 9, 1949, Urbana, IL) Prod. Mgr., C. L. Systs., Inc., 1978–; Corporate Libn., Abt Assocs., Inc., 1975–78; Corporate Libn., Untd. Brands Co., 1974–75; Ref., Circ. Libn., VA Un. Univ., 1972–73. **Educ.:** Mt. Holyoke Coll., 1967–71, AB (Hist.); Simmons Coll., 1973–74, MS (LS). **Orgs.:** SLA: Boston Chap., Consult. Com. 1978–81). **Activities:** 6; 24, 49-Prod. Mgr.; 56, 77, 92 **Addr.:** CL Systems, Inc., 81 Norwood Ave., Newtonville, MA 02160.

Steben, (Wright) Florence Ethel (N. 3, 1924, Malta, IL) Sch. Libn., E. Baton Rouge Par. Schs., Glasgow Mid. Magnet, 1979–, Sch. Libn., Prescott Jr. High, 1969–79; Asst. Libn., Soc. Sci., Bus., Chico State Univ., 1965–69; Catlgr., Spring Valley-LaMesa Sch. Dist., 1965; Asst. Libn., Willson Jr. High, 1961–64. **Educ.:** N. Ctrl. Coll., 1942–46, BA (Eng.); LA State Univ., 1970–72, MS (LS). **Orgs.:** ALA. LA LA. Natl. Educ. Assn. LA Assn. of Educ. **Pubns.:** "An Academic Parable, A Modern Day Tale," *LA Assn. of Educ. Jnl.* (My. 1979). **Activities:** 10; 15, 17, 20; 63 **Addr.:** 342 Jennifer Jean, Baton Rouge, LA 70808.

Steckler, Phyllis B. (My. 15, 1933, New York, NY) Pres., Oryx Press, 1973–; Ed. Dir., Holt Info. Syst., 1971–73; Proj. Dir., Macmillan Info., 1969–71; Ed., Dir., Current Bibl.; R.R. Bowker Co., 1954–69. **Educ.:** Hunter Coll., BA (Eng.); NY Univ., MA (Comm.). **Orgs.:** ALA. SLA. ASIS. AZ LA. Various other orgs. **Activities:** 6; 17, 30, 37; 57, 63, 75 **Addr.:** 2214 N. Central at Encando, Phoenix, AZ 85004.

Steele, Anitra T. (Ja. 22, 1949, Concord, CA) Chld. Spec., Mid-Continent Pub. Lib., 1976–; Young People's Libn., Livingston Cnty. Meml. Lib., 1972–76. **Educ.:** Ctrl. MO State Univ., 1967–70, BS (Eng.); Univ. of OK, 1971–72, MLS. **Orgs.:** MO LA: Chld. Srvs. RT (Ch., 1979–80); Women in Libs. Spec. Com. (1977–79). ALA: ALSC, Notable Chld. Bks. 1971–75 Com. (1979–80); Media Re-eval. Com. (1977–78); Sexism in Lib. Mtrls. for Chld. Discuss. Grp. (1975–78); Soc. Issues in Lib. Mtrls. for Chld. Discuss. Grp. (Coord., 1978). AAUW. Amer. Cvl. Liberties Un. **Pubns.:** Ed., *Chld. and YA Bk. Sel. Com. Nsltr.* (1975–); "How to Produce — Library Slide Tape Show," *Show-Me Libs.* (Jl. 1979). **Activities:** 9; 15, 21, 25; 55 **Addr.:** Mid-Continent Public Library, 15616 E. 24 Hwy., Independence, MO 64050.

Steele, Apollonia (O. 2, 1944, Leobersdorf, Austria) Spec. Cols. Libn., Univ. of Calgary, 1979–, Spec. Cols. Catlgr., 1974–78, Gifts and Exch. Libn., 1972–74; Catlgr., Univ. of West. ON Lib., 1968–72. **Educ.:** Univ. of Windsor, 1963–67, BA, hons. (Eng.); Univ. of Toronto, 1967–68, BLS; various crs. **Orgs.:** Can. LA. AB LA. Foothills LA. Bibl. Socty of Can. Various other orgs. **Activities:** 1; 45 **Addr.:** Arts and Humanities Library, 2500 University Dr., N.W., Calgary, AB T2N 1N4 Canada.

Steele, Carl L. (Ag. 22, 1934, Patoka, IL) Dir., Educ. Resrcs. Ctr., Rock Valley Coll., 1968–; Tchr., Forrest-Strawn-Wing HS, 1959–61; Tchr., Richwoods Cmnty. HS, 1961–66; Asst. Dir., Instr. Mtrls., Lib. Srvs., Sauk Valley Coll., 1966–68. **Educ.:** South. IL Univ., 1952–56, BS (Eng.), 1959–60, MS (Educ. Admin.); North. IL Univ., 1970–71, MA (LS). **Orgs.:** ALA: ACRL, Cont. Educ. Com. (1979–81). AECT: Conv. Eval. (1978–79). IL LA. IL AV Assn.: Conv. Com. (1975). Cncl. on Lib. Tech. **Pubns.:** "Eighth Annual Conference—Junior College Libraries," *IL AV Assn. Jnl.* (S. 1973); "Library Technicians—The Big Controversy," *Spec. Libs.* (Ja. 1969); "Audiovisual Trends in Illinois Community Colleges," *IL Libs.* (Ap. 1969); "A Survey of the Need for Library Technicians," *Resrch. in Educ.* (Ja. 1973). **Activities:** 1, 12; 17; 63, 75, 95-Multimedia. **Addr.:** 5758 Weymouth Dr., Rockford, IL 61111.

Steele, Margaret E. (Peggy) (Ap. 24, 1945, Worcester, MA) Head, Serials Dept., Northwest. Univ. Lib., 1980–, Sr. Serial Catlgr., 1978–80, Head, Bindery and Marking Dept., 1971–78. **Educ.:** Amer. Univ., 1962–66, BA (Pol. Sci.); Simmons Coll., 1967–68, MS (LS). **Orgs.:** ALA. **Addr.:** Serials Dept., Northwestern University Library, Evanston, IL 60201.

Steele, Robert Scott (N. 7, 1917, Butler, PA) Dir., Film Dept., Prof. (Film), Boston Univ., 1959–81; BBC, London, 1955–58; various tchg. positions at Tufts Univ., MA Inst. of Tech., and Lang. Sch., Landour, India. **Educ.:** OH Wesleyan Univ., 1936–40, BA; Hartford Fndn., 1941–44, MD; at Univ. of London, Columbia Univ., others (grad. std.). **Orgs.:** EFLA. Socty. of Cinema Std.: Various ofcs. **Pubns.:** *Cataloguing of Cinema Literature* (1967); dir., writer, various films. **Activities:** 1, 2; 20, 41; 50, 93†

Steen, Barbara J. (F. 4, 1953, Des Moines, IA) Elem. Sch. Media Spec., J.C. Hoglan Elem. Sch., 1976–; Jr.-Sr. HS Libn., Glidden-Ralston Cmnty. Sch., 1975–76. **Educ.:** Univ. of North. IA, 1971–75, BA (Educ.), 1975–79, MA (LS). **Orgs.:** ALA. IA Educ. Media Assn.: Legis. Com. (Ch., 1979–81); ALA Legis. Hotline Contact (1979–81). IA State Educ. Assn.: Del. Asm. Rep. (1976); Resrch. Info. Gathering Syst. Contact (1980). Marshalltown Educ. Assn. **Activities:** 10; 21, 31, 32; 61, 63, 89 **Addr.:** J.C. Hoglan Elementary School, S. 3rd Ave. and Southridge Rd., Marshalltown, IA 50158.

Steensland, Ronald Paul (D. 16, 1946, Dothan, AL) Dir., Lexington Pub. Lib., 1977–; Dir., Los Alamos Cnty. Lib., 1976–77; Dir., Hidalgo Cnty. Lib., 1973–76; Dir., Davidson Cnty. Lib., 1970–73. **Educ.:** FL State Univ., 1965–69, BA (LS), 1969–70, MS (LS); Univ. of MD, 1980, Cert. (Lib. Admin. Dev. Prog.). **Orgs.:** ALA: LAMA/PR Sect., John Cotton Dana Awd. Com. (Ch., 1977), Exec. Com. (1979–80); Ref. and Subscrpn. Bks. Review Com. (1974–76). KY LA Pub. Lib. Sect. (Treas., 1978–79). SELA: Com. on Coms. (1980). Rotary. Assn. of U.S. Army. U.S. Chess Fed. Hidalgo Cnty. Red Cross. **Pubns.:** " 'We Won!' Library PR As Viewed By a John Cotton Dana Awards Judge," *OH Media Spectrum* (My. 1977); "Report of The Task Force On Librarian Certification," *TX Lib. Jnl.* (Win. 1975); "Management In Public Libraries," *NC Libs.* (Win. 1974). **Activities:** 9; 17, 19, 24; 56 **Addr.:** 1309 Golf Course Cir., Lexington, KY 40502.

Steere, Paul Joseph (O. 15, 1940, Grant Pass, OR) Cult. Affairs Ofcr., Amer. Inst. in Taiwan, Taipei, Taiwan, 1979–; Chief, Lib. Prog., U.S. Intl. Comm. Agency, 1978–79; Chief, Lib. Srvs., U.S. Info. Agency, DC, 1977–78; Reg. Lib. Consult., SW Asia, U.S. Info. Srvs., Karachi, Pakistan, 1975–77; Reg. Lib. Consult., U.S. Info. Agency, DC, 1974–75; Chief, Ctrl. Cat., U.S. Army Libs. Europe, Aschaffenburg, W. Germany, 1971–74, Admin. Libn., Erlangen, W. Germany, 1970–71; Head Libn., Instr., Seattle Cmnty. Coll., WA Branch Campus, 1969–70. **Educ.:** Univ. of MD Far E. Div., 1963–66; Defense Lang. Inst., Monterey, CA, 1964–65, Dip. (Chin. Mandarin); Univ. of WA, 1967–68, BA (Far East. Pol. Sci.), 1968–69, MLS (Libnshp.). **Orgs.:** ALA: ACRL/Law and Pol. Sci. Sect., Nom. Com. (1975); FLRT (1976–); IRRT (1970–); LAMA (1978–). UNESCO Gen. Info. Prog.: U.S. Natl. Com., Chrt. Del. (1978); Alternate Del. (1979). Amer. Frgn. Srv. Assn. Vietnam Vets. of Amer. Univ. of WA Alum. Assn. **Honors:** Beta Phi Mu, 1970; U.S. Dept. of the Army, Outstan. Performance Awd., 1973. **Activities:** 4, 12; 17, 24, 49-Cult. exch. progs.; 54, 66, 74 **Addr.:** AIT Taipei, American Cultural Center, P. O. Box 1612, Washington, DC 20013.

Stefancic, Emil J. (S. 18, 1916, Cleveland, OH) Assoc. Dir., Cleveland State Univ., 1969–, Libn., 1966–69; Head Libn., Fenn Coll., 1955–65, Asst. Libn., 1945–55, 1941–42. **Educ.:** Miami Univ., 1937–40, BA (Hist.); Case West. Rsv. Univ., 1940–41, BSLS. **Orgs.:** ALA: Mtg. Rm. Subcom. (1961). OH LA: Coll. and Univ. RT (Vice-Ch., Ch., 1963–65). N.E. OH Acad. Libs.: Prog. Ch. (1963). Cleveland Comsn. on Higher Educ. **Activities:** 1; 17, 35 **Addr.:** 25504 Chatworth, Euclid, OH 44117.

Stefani, Carolyn R. (S. 4, 1935, Newton, MA) Ref. Libn., Nassau Lib. Syst., 1981–; Libn., North. Parkway Elem. Sch., 1979–81; Libn., Buckley Country Day Sch., 1977–79; Ref., Cat., Baldwin Pub. Lib., 1976–; Lib. Media Spec., Belmont Elem. Sch., 1971–73; Ref., Cat., Turner Lib., 1966–68; Ref., Watertown Pub. Lib., 1964–65; Libn., Holliston HS, 1961–62; Educ. Dept., Boston Pub. Lib., 1960–61. **Educ.:** Wheaton Coll., 1955–57, AB (Fr.); Long Island Univ., 1971–74, MSLS. **Orgs.:** ALA. Long Island Sch. Media Assn. Hudson Valley LA. **Activities:** 9, 10; 20, 31, 39 **Addr.:** 1450 Little Whaleneck Rd., North Merrick, NY 11566.

Steffen, Rev. Francis J. (N. 18, 1931, Platteville, WI) Libn., Holy Name Semy., 1964–. **Educ.:** Loras Coll., 1949–53, BA (Classics); Univ. of WI, 1964–68, MA (LS). **Orgs.:** Madison Area Lib. Cncl.: Bd. of Dirs. (1969–70). WI Cath. LA: Pres. (1973–75). WI Assn. of Sch. Libns.: Pres. (1970–71); Nsltr. Ed. (1971–72); Communique Ed. (1972–74). **Addr.:** Holy Name Seminary, 3577 High Point Rd., Madison, WI 53711.

Stegh, Leslie J. (My. 21, 1944, Cleveland, OH) Archvst., Deere and Co., 1977–; Univ. Archvst., Dir. of Amer. Hist. Resrch. Ctr., Kent State Univ., 1972–77, Tchg. Fellow, 1969–72; Tchr., Columbus Bd. of Educ., 1967–69. **Educ.:** Kent State Univ., 1962–66, BS (Educ.); OH State Univ., 1966–67, MA (U.S. Hist.); Kent State Univ., 1969–75, PhD (U.S. Hist.); OH Hist. Socty. Arch., Lib. Inst., 1973. **Orgs.:** Midwest Arch. Conf. Assn. of Recs. Mgrs. and Admins. SAA: Bus. Arch. Com. (1977–). Socty. of OH Archvsts.: Cncl. (1975–77); Com. on Coll. and Univ. Arch. (Ch., 1974–75). Amer. Assn. for State and Lcl. Hist. Org. of Amer. Histns. Bus. Hist. Conf. **Pubns.:** *Trinity Lutheran Church, 1877–1977, A Centennial History* (1978); reg. ed., *Guide to Manuscripts Collections and Institutional Records in Ohio* (1974); "A Paradox of Prohibition: Election of Robert J. Bulkley as Senator from Ohio," *OH Hist.* (Sum. 1974). **Activities:** 2; 15, 17, 38; 64, 68, 91 **Addr.:** Deere and Co., John Deere Rd., Moline, IL 61265.

Steidel, Hermann (N. 1, 1926, Maunabo, PR) Dir., Acq. Dept., Univ. of PR, Cayey Univ. Coll., 1977–, Dir. Cat. Dept., 1973–77; Dir., Pub. Libs., PR Dept. of Educ., 1971–73; Coord. of Med. Libs., Univ. of PR, Med. Campus, 1969–70; Lib. Dir., Univ. Ctrl. De Bayamon, 1968–69; Sch. Admin., Dept. of Educ., 1956–60; Asst. Dir., Elem. Sch., Univ. of PR, 1961–63. **Educ.:** Univ. of PR, 1954–56, BAE; 1958–59, Prof. Dip. (Sch. Admin.); Univ. of Syracuse, 1967–68, MSLS. **Orgs.:** SBPR: Past Pres. (1970–71). Assn. de Maestros de PR. Org. de Profs. Univ. Exch. Club: Past Pres. (1972–73). **Pubns.:** "Reto del Libro en la Sociedad Puertorriqueña," *Revista Cayey* (S. 1979); "Busca información? Orientese," *Revista Cayey* (1980). **Activities:** 1, 9; 15, 17, 24; 63, 75, 85 **Addr.:** P.O. 2085, Cayey, PR 00633.

Steiger, Monte L. (F. 28, 1940, Colfax, WA) Asst. Dir. Tech. Srvs., Univ. of ID, 1982–; Sr. Tech. Srvs. Libn., North. AZ Univ. Libs., 1975–81; WA State Univ. Lib., 1969–75. **Educ.:** Ctrl. WA Univ., 1965–68, BS (Hist.); Univ. of WA, 1968–69, MLS (Libnshp.); AZ Game and Fish Dept., 1979 Cert. Firearms Safety Instr. **Orgs.:** AZ State LA. Amer. Canoe Assn. Benevolent and Protective Ord. of Elks. **Honors:** Beta Phi Mu. **Pubns.:** Jt. auth., *The Card Catalog: A Guide* (1980); *The Colfax Public-Colfax High School: A History* (1975). **Activities:** 1; 17, 20, 46; 95-Recreation/outdoors. **Addr.:** Technical Services, Library, University of Idaho, Moscow, ID 83843. Flagstaff, AZ 86001.

Stein, Janice L. (Jl. 25, 1949, Toronto, ON) Prof. Consult., Francophone Srvs., N. Ctrl. Reg. Lib. Syst., 1978–; Libn., Media Sel., Sch. Lib. Srvs., West. Australia, 1975–77; Resrch. Asst., Educ., Univ. of West. Australia, 1973–74. **Educ.:** Univ. of Toronto, 1968–72, BA (Latin Amer. Std.); West. Australian Inst. of Tech., 1974, Grad. Dip. (LS). **Orgs.:** Can. LA. ON LA. Prov. Lib. Srvs.: Chld. Srvs. Com. (1979); *OLR in Review* Bk. Reviewer. **Pubns.:** Rpt., *Northern Life* (1979–80); ed., *N. Ctrl. Reg. Lib. Mag.*; ed., *Rapport* reg. bltn; producer, cable TV lib. prog. (1979). **Activities:** 9, 13; 21, 24, 37; 54, 55 **Addr.:** N. Central Regional Library System, 334 Regent St., Sudbury, ON P3C 4E2 Canada.

Stein, Lenore A. (Je. 27, 1934, Pittsburgh, PA) Photo-Text Libn., Intl. Comm. Agency, Press and Pubns., 1975–; Libn., Defense Int. Agency Sch., 1969; Reg. Overseas Libn., U.S. Info. Agency, 1967; Chld. Libn., Carnegie Lib. of Pittsburgh, 1957. **Educ.:** Duquesne Univ., 1952–56, BA (Soclgy.); Univ. of Pittsburgh, 1956–57, MSLS. **Orgs.:** SLA: Pic. Div., DC Pic. Grp. (Ch., 1980–81). **Pubns.:** "Image-Bearing Catalog Cards for Photolibraries," *Spec. Libs.* (N. 1979). **Activities:** 4, 12; 23, 30, 37; 55 **Addr.:** International Communication Agency, Rm. 460, 1776 Pennsylvania Ave., N.W., Washington, DC 20547.

Stein, Rita M. (F. 20, 1928, New York, NY) Consult., Libs., Lrng. Resrcs., RI Dept. of Educ. 1978–; Sch. Media Spec., Barrington Mid. Sch., 1975–78; Sch. Libn., E. Prov. Sch., 1971–73; Sch. Libn., Turn of River Jr. HS., 1969–70. **Educ.:** Brooklyn Coll., 1945–49, BA (Langs.); Columbia Univ., 1953–55, MA (Hist.); Pratt Inst., 1969–71, MLS; RI, Prof. Life Cert., Tchr. of LS. **Orgs.:** New Eng. Educ. Media Assn.: Bd. (1979–). Com. on Pub. and Sch. Libs.: Co-Ch. (1979). RI Sch. LA: Mem. Ch.; Secy. RI Sch. Media Assn.: Conf. Com., Secy. Various other orgs. RI Educ. Media Assn.: Pres. (1980–81). Temple Habonim Lib.: Ch., Libn. (1974–). Leag. of Women Voters. Rochambeau Celebration Com. **Honors:** Beta Phi Mu. **Pubns.:** "Federal Funding, What's Ahead," *Bltn. of the RI LA* (Ap. 1980). **Activities:** 14-Dept. of educ.; 21, 24, 28; 63 **Addr.:** Rhode Island Dept. of Education, 235 Promenade St., Providence, RI 02908.

Stein, Roger R. (Ap. 2, 1942, New York, NY) Lib. Media Spec., New York City Bd. of Educ., 1979–, Lib. Media Spec., 1973–76, 1970–73; Lib. Media Spec., Massapequa, J.P. McKenna Jr. HS., 1964–70; Lib. Media Spec., Hicksville, Foric Ln. Sch., 1963–64. **Educ.:** C.W. Post Coll., 1959–63, BA (Msc., Educ.), 1963–65, Sch. Lib. Cert., Pub. Libns. Cert.; Hofstra Univ., 1965–67, MS (Sec. Educ.); NY Univ., 1972–76 (Comm. in Educ.). **Orgs.:** New York City Sch. LA. Long Island Sch. Media Assn. Nassau-Suffolk Sch. LA: Nsltr. Ed. (1967–69). AECT. Various other orgs. Metro. Opera Gld. New York City Opera Gld. WNET/Thirteen. **Activities:** 10, 12; 15, 17, 20 **Addr.:** 33–47 91 St., Jackson Heights, NY 11372.

PROFESSIONAL ACTIVITIES: Institutions: 1. Acad. lib.; 2. Arch.; 3. Assn.; 4. Fed./Gvt. lib.; 5. Inst. lib.; 6. Mfr./Suppl.; 7. Milit. lib.; 8. Musm.; 9. Pub. lib.; 10. Sch. lib.; 11. Sch. of lib. sci.; 12. Spec. lib.; 13. State lib.; 14. (other). **Functions/Activities:** 15. Acq./Col. dev.; 16. Adult srvs.; 17. Admin.; 18. Apprais.; 19. Archit./Bldgs.; 20. Cat./Class.; 21. Chld. srvs.; 22. Circ.; 23. Cons./Pres.; 24. Consult.; 25. Cont. ed.; 26. Educ. lib. sci.; 27. Ext. srvs.; 28. Fund/Grants; 29. Gvt. pubs.; 30. Indx./Abs.; 31. Instr. lib. use; 32. Media srvs.; 33. Micro.; 34. Netwks./Coop.; 35. Persnl.; 36. PR; 37. Publshg.; 38. Recs. mgt.; 39. Ref. srvs.; 40. Repro.; 41. Resrch.; 42. Review.; 43. Secur.; 44. Serials; 45. Spec. col.; 46. Tech. srvs.; 47. Trustees/Bds.; 48. YA srvs.; 49. (other).

Steinbach, Mary Anna Belle (N. 26, 1938, Baton Rouge, LA) Med. Libn., U.S.P.H.S. Hosp., 1970–; Lib. Asst., E. Baton Rouge Par. Lib., 1968–70. **Educ.:** Webster Coll., 1957–60, AB (Eng.); LA State Univ., 1960–63, MS (LS), LA State Univ., 1975, Cert. (Med. Libn.). **Orgs.:** Med. LA: S. Ctrl. Reg. Grp., Hosp. Lib Grp., Treas. Hlth. Sci. LA of LA. ALA. LA LA. Phys. Limited Assn. for a Constructive Env.: Baton Rouge Chap., Secy. (1977–79), VP (1980). Amer. Legion Auxilliary. **Honors:** Pilot Club of Baton Rouge, Outstan. Handcpd. Prof. Woman of the Yr., 1977; Phys. Limited Assn. for a Constructive Env., Intl. Baton Rouge Chap., Srv. Awd. 1979. **Activities:** 4, 12; 39, 41, 45; 58, 80, 92 **Addr.:** Medical Library, U.S. P.H.S. Hospital, Carville, LA 70721.

Steinberg, David L. (Ag. 22, 1943, Rolla, MO) Asst. Prof., Dept. of LS and Educ. Media, James Madison Univ., 1975–; Instr., Ref. Libn., Mesa Cmnty. Coll., 1973–75; Instr., Sch. of Lib. and Info. Sci., Univ. of MO, 1969–71; Asst. Libn., Instr., LS, William Woods Coll., 1968–73; Elem. Sch. Libn., Waynesville-Fort Leonard Wood Schs., 1963–66. **Educ.:** Ctrl. MO State Univ., 1959–63, BS (Math.); Univ. of NC, 1966–68, MSLS; grad. work in educ. tech. **Orgs.:** ALA: AASL. AALS: Assoc. Mem. AECT: Div. of Instr. Dev. VA Educ. Media Assn.: Prog. Com.; Reg. Mtg. Com. (Presentor, 1978–81). **Honors:** Beta Phi Mu, 1968; Phi Delta Kappa, 1976; Pi Lambda Theta, 1975. **Pubns.:** Various convs., papers, wkshps. **Activities:** 1, 10; 26, 32, 41; 55, 63, 75 **Addr.:** Dept. of Library Science & Educational Media, James Madison University, Harrisonburg, VA 22807.

Steinberg, Eileen (My. 26, 1941, Philadelphia, PA) Libn., Meehan Mid. Sch., 1972–; Libn., M.M. Bethune Elem. Sch., 1970–72; Libn., M. H. Stanton Elem. Sch., 1967–70; Tchr., Harrison Elem. Sch., 1966–67. **Educ.:** Temple Univ., 1959–63, BS (Elem. Educ.); Drexel Univ., 1967–70, MS (LS). **Orgs.:** Assn. of Philadelphia Sch. Libns.: Treas. (1974–76). PA Sch. Libns. Assn. ALA. **Activities:** 10; 21, 32, 42 **Addr.:** 7043 Dorcas St., Philadelphia, PA 19111.

Steinberger, Pearl Judith (N. 18, 1925, Scranton, PA) Supvsr., Sch. Lib. Srv., Sch. Dist. 8, NY City, 1971–, Tchr., LS, P.S. 93 (Bronx), 1964–71, Tchr., LS, Jr. HS 22 (Manhatten), 1959–64, Tchr., 1949–59; Tchr., Eng. as a Sec. Lang., 1951–71. **Educ.:** Brooklyn Coll., 1943–49, BA (Psy.); City Coll., NY, 1951–59, MS (Elem. Educ.); Queens Coll., 1970, MLS; various other crs. **Orgs.:** ALA. NY LA. NY City Sch. Libns. Assn. Cncl. of Supvsrs. and Admins. **Activities:** 10 **Addr.:** School District 8, 650 White Plains Rd., Bronx, NY 10473.

Steiner, Janet E. (S. 24, 1947, Racine, WI) Exec. Dir., S. Ctrl. Resrch. Lib. Cncl., 1980–; Admin. Libn., Elk Grove Village Pub. Lib., 1975–80, Head, Adult Srvs., 1974–75; Instr., LS, Coll. of Racine, 1971–74. **Educ.:** Dominican Coll., 1965–69, BA (Eng.); Univ. of WI, 1969–70, MA (LS); Marquette Univ., 1970–72, MA (Eng.). **Orgs.:** ALA: LAMA, Prog. Com. (1979–81). IL LA: Conf. Com. (1977). Reg. Lib. Adv. Cncl.: Pres. (1978–79). Suburban Libs. Untd. for Reg. Plng.: Ch. (1977–80). Grt. O'Hare Assn. of Indus. and Cmrce.: Bd. of Dirs. (1977–80), Bylaws Com. (Ch., 1978). **Activities:** 9, 14-Netwk.; 17, 34 **Addr.:** 215 N. Cayuga, Ithaca, NY 14850.

Steinfirst, Susan (Ag. 22, 1940, Pittsburgh, PA) Asst. Prof., Univ. of NC, 1976–; Head Libn., Butler Lib., State Univ. Coll. 1970–73; Libn., City Schs. Buffalo, NY, 1971–73; Libn., City Schs., Baltimore, 1966–67. **Educ.:** Sarah Lawrence Coll., 1958–62, BA (Fine Arts); Univ. of MD, 1967–68, MLS; Univ. of Pittsburgh, 1973–76, PhD (LS). **Orgs.:** ALA: ALSC, Caldecott Com. (1980–81); YASD. AALS. Natl. Cncl. of Tchrs. of Eng. Chld. Lit. Assn. **Pubns.:** Jt. auth., *A History of Children's Literature* (1980); "More About the Funny Bone," *Sch. Lib. Jnl.* (Ja. 1980); "Education of the Young Adult Librarian," *Libraries and Young Adults* (1979). **Activities:** 11; 21, 26, 48 **Addr.:** University of North Carolina, School of Library Science, Manning Hall 026–A, Chapel Hill, NC 27514.

Steininger, Ellen (Je. 3, 1943, Chicago, IL) Head Libn., Marsteller Inc., 1968–. **Educ.:** Thiel Coll., 1966, BA (Hist.); Univ. of IL, 1968, MSLS. **Orgs.:** SLA: IL Chap., Pres., Treas. (1973–75); Food And Nutr. Div., Secy. (1977–78), Prog. Ch. and Lcl. Rep. (1975); Advert. and Mktg. Div., Bd. of Dirs. (1976–78), Ch. (1975–76). IL Reg. Lib. Cncl.: Voting Rep. (1972–). **Activities:** 17, 39 **Addr.:** One E. Wacker Dr., Chicago, IL 60601.

Steinke, Cynthia A. (Mr. 14, 1937, Oak Park, IL) Sci. Libn., Univ. of IL, Chicago, 1970–; Sci. Libn., Chief, Ref. Srvs., IL Inst. of Tech., John Crerar Lib., 1966–70. **Educ.:** MI State Univ., 1955–59, BA (Fr. Lang., Lit.); Univ. de Paris, Inst. de Phonetique, La Sorbonne 1957–58, Cert. d'Etudes Pratiques de Prononciation Francaise; Univ. of IL, 1964–66, MS (LS). **Orgs.:** SLA: Sci. and Tech. Div., Ch.-Elect (1980–81), Ch. (1981–82); IL Chap. (Dir., 1979–80). ALA. ASIS. **Honors:** Beta Phi Mu, 1966. **Pubns.:** Jt. cmplr., *Standards, Specifications and Codes Available in the Chicago Area; A Union List* (1980); "Standards, Specifications and Codes; A Union List Approach to Resource Sharing in the Chicago Metropolitan Area," *Sci. and Tech. Libs.* (Win. 1980). **Activities:** 1, 12; 15, 17, 26; 91 **Addr.:** Science Library, University of Illinois at Chicago Circle, Box 7565, Chicago, IL 60680.

Steinmann, Betty Edna (My. 20, 1922, Freeport, IL) Msc., Hum. Catlgr., North. IL Univ., 1963–; Head Libn., Monroe Pub. Lib., 1959–60; Cat., Ref. Libn., Evanston Pub. Lib., 1961–62; Libn., Univ. of Dubuque, 1962–63; Catlgr., Msc., Hum., North. IL Univ., 1963. **Educ.:** MacMurray Coll., 1940–44, BA (Soc. Sci.); Univ. of WI, 1958–59, MA (LS); Univ. of FL, 1968, 6th Yr. Cert. (LS). **Orgs.:** ALA. IL LA: Pubns. Com. (1970–72). Msc. LA: Msc. Users Grp. OCLC, Consult. DeKalb Bus. and Prof. Womens Club: Pres. (1970–72). DeKalb-Sycamore AAUW: Secy. (1969). Leag. of Women Voters. **Activities:** 1; 20; 55 **Addr.:** Northern Illinois University Library, DeKalb, IL 60115.

Stell, Melvina Wall (Mr. 18, 1927, Washougal, WA) Head Libn., Good Samaritan Hosp. and Med. Ctr., 1973–; Libn., WA Cnty. Schs., 1969–73; Libn., Josephine Cnty. Schs., 1964–69; Sch. Tchr., 1949–64. **Educ.:** East. WA Univ., 1945–49, BA (Educ.); Portland State Univ., 1961 (LS). **Orgs.:** OR Hlth. Scis. LA: Pres. (1980); Com. on Lib. Consult. and Dev. (1978–82). Med. LA: Hosp. Libs. Sect. (Treas., 1981); Pac. NW Reg. Grp., Legis. Com. (1980–84); 1977 Conv. (Hosp. Com.). OR LA. NW OR Cncl. of Hosp. Ad Hoc. Com. on Telecom. (1979–82). Various other orgs., ofcs. **Activities:** 12; 15, 17, 24; 50, 63, 80 **Addr.:** Good Samaritan Health Sciences Library, 1015 N.W. 22nd Ave., Portland, OR 97210.

Stellhorn, Donald V. (O. 27, 1942, Orange, NJ) AV Spec., Parsippany HS, 1973–; Night Dir., Media Ctr., Montclair State Coll., 1978–; AV Dir., East Orange HS, 1968–73; AV Coord., East Orange, Title I Prog., 1970–73. **Educ.:** Montclair State Coll., 1960–64, BA (Soc. Std.), Seton Hall Univ., 1979– (Media). **Orgs.:** Educ. Media Assn. of NJ. Parsippany Troy Hills Educ. Assn. Morris Cnty. Educ. Assn. NJ Educ. Assn. Natl. Educ. Assn. **Activities:** 10; 17, 32, 46; 63, 67, 93 **Addr.:** Media Center, Parsippany High School, Parsippany, NJ 07054.

Stellmacher, Nancy Sifdol (My. 11, 1945, Eugene, OR) Sr. Libn., PPG Indus., Chem. Div., Spec. Prods. Unit, 1977–; Div. Head Lib. Non-Print and Lrng. Resrcs. Div., Univ. of MN, Duluth, 1974–77; Libn., Chemplex Co., 1969–74. **Educ.:** Univ. of Exeter, Devon, Eng., 1964–65, (Eng. Lit.); Univ. of OR, 1965–67, BA (Eng.); Univ. of MN, 1967–69, MALS; Univ. of OR, 1967–70, Cert. (HS Eng.). **Orgs.:** SLA: Chicago Chap., Soc./Dinner Com. (1971). ASIS. Amer. Chem. Socty.: Co. Rpt., *Chicago ACS Bltn.* **Activities:** 1, 12; 17, 39, 46; 59, 60, 91 **Addr.:** PPG Industries, Chemical Division - USA, Specialty Products Unit, P.O. Box 66251, AMF O'Hare - 12555 W. Higgins Rd., Chicago, IL 60666.

Stenberg, Beth M. (Ag. 6, 1948, Brownsville, TX) Med. Libn., San Antonio State Hosp., 1979–; Ref. Back-Up Libn., S. TX Lib. Syst., 1978–79, Med. Libn., Driscoll Fndn., Chld. Hosp., 1977–78. **Educ.:** Univ. of TX, 1969–70, BA (Eng.), 1973–74, MLS. **Orgs.:** ALA. TX LA. **Honors:** Phi Beta Kappa, 1969. **Activities:** 9, 12; 15, 39; 55, 80 **Addr.:** 933 Fredericksburg Rd., New Braunfels, TX 78130.

Stenstrom, Patricia Fitzgerald (Chicago, IL) Lib. and Info. Sci. Libn., Univ. of IL, Urbana/Champaign, 1981–, Serial Consult., 1980, Head, Rapid Cat., 1979, Serial Catlgr., 1967–78; Lib. Tech. Asst., IL Nat. Hist. Srvy., 1962–67; Asst. Libn., Educ. Lib., Univ. of IL, Urbana/Champaign, 1957–58, Asst. Libn., Undergrad. Lib., 1957; Ref. Libn., Gary Pub. Lib., 1954–55. **Educ.:** Univ. of IL, 1950–54, BA (Hist.), 1957, MS. **Orgs.:** ALA. **Pubns.:** "Serial Use by Social Science Faculty," *Coll. & Resrch. Libs.* (S. 1979). **Activities:** 1; 20, 44, 46; 56, 92 **Addr.:** University of Illinois Library, 306, Urbana, IL 61801.

Stepanovich, Mitch M. (Ag. 7, 1948, Minden, Germany) Instr., Lib., Ln. Cmnty. Coll. Lib., 1980–, Cat. Asst., 1974–. **Educ.:** Univ. of OR, 1966–77, BS (Soc. Sci.), 1977–78, MLS (Libnshp., Aut.), 1978–81, MS (Educ. Admin.); Lane Cmnty. Coll., 1978, AS (Comp. Sci.). **Orgs.:** OR LA: Autom. Com. (1981–). OR Cmnty. Coll. LA: Nsltr. Co-ed. (1978–). NLA: NW Chap. (Treas., 1981–). Lane/Douglas Reg. Lib. Cnsrtm.: Strg. Com. (Ch., 1979–). Ln. Cmnty. Coll. Empls. Fed.: Rec. Ofcr. (1978–79); Pres. (1979–). **Pubns.:** Indxr., *Oregon Times, 1971–75* (1978); ed., jt. indxr., *Eugene Register–Guard* (1979–80). **Activities:** 1, 9; 30, 34, 46; 56, 63, 75 **Addr.:** Lane Community College Library, 4000 E. 30th Ave., Eugene, OR 97405.

Stephan, Sandra S. (Ag. 1, 1944, Recife, Brasil) Spec., Staff Dev. and Cont. Educ., Div. of Lib. Dev., MD Dept. of Educ., 1979–; Asst. Area Branch Libn., Prince George's Cnty. Meml. Lib., 1975–79, Volun. Srvs. Supvsr., 1972–75, YA Dept. Head, 1970–72. **Educ.:** Univ. of Madrid, 1964–65, Dip.; George Washington Univ., 1965–67, BA (Span.); Cath. Univ. of Amer., 1967–68, MLS. **Orgs.:** ALA: ASCLA/State Lib. Agency Sect. (1981–82). CLENE: Bd. of Dirs. (1980–82). MD LA: Pres. (1981–82). **Pubns.:** "Volunteers in Management," *Cath. Lib. World* (S. 1973). **Activities:** 9, 13; 24, 25 **Addr.:** Division of Library Development and Services, Maryland State Department of Education, 200 W. Baltimore St., Baltimore, MD 21201.

Stephen, Ross G. (Je. 14, 1938, Sacramento, CA) Coll. Libn., Rider Coll., 1980–; Assoc. Dir., Univ. of WI, Oshkosh, 1977–80; Acq. Libn., William Rainey Harper Coll., 1971–77; Instr., Sp., Dir., Thea., Wright Coll., 1967–69; Instr., Sp., Thea., SUNY, Albany, 1962–66. **Educ.:** Willamette Univ., 1956–60, BA (Sp., Drama); OH Univ., 1960–62, MFA (Thea.); Univ. of IL, 1969–71, MSLS; Simmons Coll., 1974–76, DA (LS). **Orgs.:** ALA: LAMA, Bd. of Dirs. (1978–), Pubn. Com. (1980–); RASD, Notable Bks. Cncl. (1974–78), Cat. Use Com. (1978–80). WI LA: ACRL Chap., Prog. Plng. Com. (1978–80). Natl. CLSI Users Grp.: Pres. (1978–80). **Pubns.:** Ed., *LAMA Nsltr.* (1978–); reviews. **Activities:** 1; 15, 17, 34; 56, 95-Org. dev. **Addr.:** F. F. Moore Library, Rider College, 2083 Lawrenceville Rd., Lawrenceville, NJ 08648.

Stephens, Alice Gerald (Ja. 6, 1946, Clanton, AL) Head, Lib. Opers., AL Pub. Lib. Srv., 1980–, Head, Tech. Srvs., 1975–80, Resrch. and Dev. Ofcr., 1974–75, Fld. Rep. Consult., 1971–74. **Educ.:** Univ. of AL, 1964–68, BA (Hist.); Univ. of NC, 1968–69, MS (LS). **Orgs.:** AL LA: Secy. (1979–80); Auth. Awd. Com. (Ch., 1977–78); JMRT (Secy., 1974–75); Mdrtr. (1975–76). ALA: JMRT, Orien. Com. (1975–76); Hosplty. Com. (1976–77). AAUW: Montgomery Hosplty. Ch. (1976–77); Fam. Facing Change Com. (Ch., 1979–80). **Honors:** Phi Beta Kappa, 1968. **Activities:** 13; 17, 20, 24; 56 **Addr.:** Alabama Public Library Service, 6030 Monticello Dr., Montgomery, AL 36130.

Stephens, Arial Avant (Jl. 23, 1932, Charlotte, NC) Dir., Pub. Lib. of Charlotte and Mecklenburg, 1971–, Asst. Dir., 1962–71. **Educ.:** Charlotte Coll., 1950–52, AA (Liberal Arts); Univ. of NC, 1956–60, BA (European Hist.), 1961–62, MSLS. **Orgs.:** Mecklenburg Cnty. LA: Pres. (1965–66). Metrolina LA: Pres. (1965–67). NC LA: Pub. Lib. Sect. (Ch., 1977–79); Exhibit Ch., Conf. Mgr. (1967–81); JMRT (Ch., 1963–65). NC State Lib.: Lib. Srvs. and Construct. Act Adv. Cncl. (1975–79); various coms. Mecklenburg Cmnty. Exec. Congs.: Ch. (1970–72). Arts and Sci. Bd. **Activities:** 9; 17, 34, 35; 56, 78 **Addr.:** 810 Sunnyside Ave., Charlotte, NC 28204.

Stephens, Gretchen (My. 7, 1948, Nashville, TN) Vetny. Med. Libn., Asst. Prof., LS, Purdue Univ., 1977–, Asst. Life Sci. Libn., 1976–77; ILL Libn., Univ. of GA, 1976, Asst. Sci. Ref. Libn., 1974–76, Asst. Ref. Libn., 1973–74, Asst. Soc. Sci. Libn., 1970–73. **Educ.:** George Peabody Coll., 1966–69, BA (Hist., Math.), 1969–70, MLS; Med. LA, 1980, Cert. (Hlth. Sci. Libn.). **Orgs.:** Med. LA: Midwest Chap., Bylaws Rev. Com. (1978–80); Vetny. Med. Sect., Bylaws Com. (Ch., 1979–). IN Hlth. Sci. Libns. Assn.: Secy.-Treas. (1980–81). SLA: Bio. Sci. Div. (Mem. Ch., 1977–79); various ofcs. Midwest Hlth. Sci. Lib. Netwk.: Cncl. of the Hlth. Sci. Libs., Un. List Com. (Locator, 1980–). ALA: IN JMRT, Mem. Com. (1980–81). Purdue Women's Club: Thea. Grp. (Secy., 1979–80). **Honors:** Pi Gamma Mu, 1968; Beta Phi Mu, 1970. **Pubns.:** Jt. asst. ed., *Library Management, 1979* (1980); "Information Services for Indiana Veterinarians," *Purdue Vetny. Notes* (Jl. 1980); "Information Resources for Veterinary Medical Education: Addendum III," *Jnl. of Vetny. Med. Educ.* (Spr. 1980); ed., *Lib. Mgt. Bltn.* (1980); rpt., "Workshop V: Cost/Benefit Analysis in the Special Library," *Lib. Mgt. Bltn.* (1979). **Activities:** 1, 12; 15, 17, 39; 58, 80 **Addr.:** Veterinary Medical Library (108 Lynn Hall), Purdue University, West Lafayette, IN 47907.

Stephens, James T. (Ap. 14, 1939, Birmingham, AL) Pres., EBSCO Subscrpn. Srvs. **Educ.:** Yale Univ., 1957–61, BA (Hist.); Harvard Univ., 1962–64, MBA. **Orgs.:** ALA. **Addr.:** EBSCO Subscription Services, P.O. Box 1943, Birmingham, AL 35201.

Stephens, Jerry W. (S. 10, 1949, Birmingham, AL) Asst. Dir., Admin., Mervyn H. Sterne Lib., Univ. of AL in Birmingham, 1974–. **Educ.:** Univ. of AL, 1972–74, BS (Acct.), 1974–76, MBA (Bus.), 1976–77, MLS, 1977–, (Admin. in Higher Educ.). **Orgs.:** SELA: Site Sel. Com. (1981–82); Conf. Treas. (1980). AL LA: Treas. (1977); Budget Com. (1976–79). ALA: JMRT Handbk. Com. (1976–77). Amer. Mgt. Assn. Univ. Coll. Sen. **Pubns.:** "The Integrated Library System," *Library Acquisitions: Practice and Theory* (1980). **Activities:** 1; 17, 24, 38; 56, 59, 75 **Addr.:** Sterne Library, University Station, Birmingham, AL 35294.

Stephens, John Richard, Jr. (Ja. 21, 1940, Rome, GA) Dir., Instr. Resrcs. Ctr., Univ. of GA, 1979–, Coord., Instr. Resrcs., 1975–79, Supvsr., Oper. IRC, 1970–75, Coord., Instr. TV, 1965–70. **Educ.:** Univ. of GA, 1957–61, ABJ (Radio, TV, Film). **Orgs.:** AECT. Intl. TV Assn.: Videotape Exch. Coord. GA Assn. for Instr. Tech. Athens Jaycees: Pres. (1972–73). GA Jaycees: VP (1971–72). U.S. Jaycees: U.S. Dir. (1973–74). Clarke Assn. for Talented and Gifted Chld: Pres. (1979). Various other orgs. **Honors:** U.S. Jaycees, First Place, Ed., State Pubn., 1976. **Pubns.:** Various sps. **Activities:** 5, 11; 32, 46; 50, 67, 93 **Addr.:** P.O. Box 1021, Athens, GA 30603.

Stephens, Jon Kent (Ap. 11, 1937, Delta, CO) ILL/Ref. Libn., CA State Univ., Chico, 1975–, Ref. Libn., Coord., 1974–75, Sci. Tech. Libn., 1961–74, Gvt. Pubns. Libn., 1964–71, Asst. Soc. Sci. and Bus. Libn., 1960–61. **Educ.:** West. State Coll., 1955–59, BA (Hist.); Univ. of Denver, 1959–60, MA (LS). **Pubns.:** *Matches, Flumes and Rails: The Diamond Match Company in the High Sierras* (1977); *Index to Locomotive Rosters 1965–1978* (1979); "Yreka Western Railroad," *The Short Line*

Special Subjects/Services: 50. Adult educ.; 51. Advert./Mktg.; 52. Aerosp.; 53. Agric.; 54. Area std.; 55. Arts/Hum.; 56. Autom.; 57. Bibl./Prtg.; 58. Bio. sci.; 59. Bus./Fin.; 60. Chem.; 61. Copyrt.; 62. Documtn.; 63. Educ.; 64. Engin.; 65. Env.; 66. Eth. grps.; 67. Film; 68. Food/Nutr.; 69. Geneal.; 70. Geo.; 71. Geol.; 72. Handcpd.; 73. Hist.; 74. Int. frdm.; 75. Info. sci.; 76. Insr.; 77. Law; 78. Legis.; 79. Math./Comp. sci.; 80. Med.; 81. Metals; 82. Nat. resrcs.; 83. Newsp.; 84. Nuc. sci.; 85. Oral hist.; 86. Petr./Energy; 87. Pharm.; 88. Phys./Astr./Math.; 89. Readg.; 90. Relig.; 91. Sci./Tech.; 92. Soc. sci.; 93. Telecom.; 94. Transp.; 95. (other).

(Mr., Ap., Jl./Ag. 1978); Many other articles on railrd. hist. **Activities:** 1; 15, 39; 65, 91, 94 **Addr.:** California State University, Chico, CA 95929.

Stephens, Joycelyn Gunn (Jl. 1, 1941, Monroe, LA) Mgr., Info. Ctr., DeSoto, Inc., 1974–; Info. Spec., Chem., Food and Drug Admin., 1969–72; Sci. Libn., Lib. of Congs., 1968–69; Info. Spec., Chem., Herner and Documtn., 1966–68. **Educ.:** Xavier Univ., 1959–63, BS (Chem.); Amer. Univ., 1969–71, MS (Info. Retrieval); Northwest. Univ., 1979, MBA (Mktg.). **Orgs.:** IL Reg. Lib. Cncl.: CACIC Chicago Area Comp. Info. Ctrs. (1978–). Cntrl. Data Corp.: Midwest Adv. Bd. on Tech. Transfer. Univ. of Chicago: Indus. Rel. Dept., Adv. Cncl. on Lib. Mgt. (1978–). OLUG: Plng. Com. (1978–). Amer. Chem. Socty. Fed. of Socty. for Coatings Tech.: Tech. Info. Systs. Com. **Pubns.:** "Automation in Illinois Special Libraries," *IL Libs.* (Ap. 1978); "Countercurrent Distribution of Labeled Anomeric Methyl D-arabinosides and Methyl d-D-Mannoside," *Jnl. of Chromatograyph* (1967). **Activities:** 4, 12; 17, 30, 34; 51, 60, 91 **Addr.:** 245 Eddy St., Chicago Heights, IL 60411.

Stephens, Lola W. (F. 14, 1913, Traverse City, MI) Libn., Little Falls Church, 1975–81; Chief, Law Branch, The Army Lib., 1969–75, Ref. Libn., 1965–69; Chld. Libn., Arlington Cnty. Lib., 1964–65; Libn., Little Falls Church, 1954–64; Ref. Libn., Bur. of Ships Tech. Lib., Washington, DC, 1949–52; Libn., Sel. Srvs. Syst., 1948–49; Libn., Ofc. of Vocational Rehab., 1946–48. **Educ.:** Univ. of WA, Seattle, 1932–36, BA (Pol. Sci), 1936–37, BALS; U.S. Cvl. Srvs. Comm. Inst. on Legis. Function; 1970, Cert., Univ. of VA, Mgt. Dev. Inst., 1974. **Orgs.:** SLA: Bylaws Com. of Milit. Libns. Div. (1972–73). Law Libns. Soc. of DC: Un. List of Legis. Hist. (1971–72); Panel Mem. on Lessons in Libnshp. (1971). North. VA Church and Synagogue Lib. Cncl.: Histn. (1978–); Resrc. Ident. Wkshp. (Panel Rep., 1979). Arlington Cnty. 4H Leaders Assn.: Pres. (1978–79); 4H Rep. to Arlington Cnty. Fair (1978); Treas. (1978). Rock Springs Ext. Homemakers Club: Con. Affairs Ch. (1979); Achvmt. Day Ch. (1980). **Pubns.:** Ed., *Union List of Serials in Naval Libraries of the Washington Area* (1952); jt. cmplr., *Employment of the Physically Handicapped–Selected References* (1948); "County Library Service," *OR State Bltn.* (1941); "Novel Installation Service," *Church and Synagogue Libs.* (Mr.–Ap. 1979); Cmplr., *Bibliography for "Rehabilitation of the Physically Handicapped* (1947). **Addr.:** 6218 N. 31st St., Arlington, VA 22207.

Stephens, Norris L. (D. 14, 1930, Charleroi, PA) Msc. Libn., Asst. Prof., Univ. of Pittsburgh, 1968–. **Educ.:** Carnegie-Mellon Univ., 1950–57, BFA, MFA (Msc); Un. Theo. Semy., 1954–56, SMM (Sacred Msc.); Univ. of Pittsburgh, 1962–66, PhD (Msclgy.), 1967–68, MLS. **Orgs.:** ASIS. Msc. LA. Intl. Msc. LA. Amer. Musicological Socty. **Pubns.:** Contrib., *Grove's Dictionary of Music & Musicians;* contrib., *Encyclopedia of Library and Information Science.* various msc. pubns., articles. **Activities:** 1; 15, 20, 23, 26, 37; 55 **Addr.:** 106 Candlewyck Dr., Glenshaw, PA 15116.

Stephenson, Lillian VanArkadie (O. 16, 1915, Norfolk, VA) Retired, 1978–; Elem. Sch. Libn., Lott Carey Elem. Sch., 1973–78; Ref. Libn., Norfolk State Coll., 1961–65; Libn., Lee Elem. Sch., 1963–70; Libn., Bowling Park Elem. Sch., 1953–63; various tchg. positions, 1936–52. **Educ.:** VA State Coll., 1934–36, 1940–42, 1949, BS (Elem. Educ.); Syracuse Univ., 1952–59, MS (LS); Kent State Univ., 1965, Cert. (Elem. Sch. Lib. Plng.); Hampton Inst., 1970, Cert. (Educ. Media). **Orgs.:** VA Educ. Assn.: Sch. Libns. Dept., Pres. (1973–75); VP (1971–73); Prof. Affairs Com. (Ch., 1967–71). VA Educ. Media Assn.: Exec. Com. (1975–77). **Honors:** VA Educ. Media Assn., Plaque for Srv. to Org., 1975; Sch. Libns. Dept VA Educ. Assn., Cert. for Srv., 1974; VA Educ. Media Assn., Plaque and Life Mem. Cert., 1978. **Pubns.:** Ed., *Libra Chat* (1973–75). **Activities:** 1, 10; 21, 31, 32; 50, 66, 89 **Addr.:** 1061 Vista St., Norfolk, VA 23504.

Stephenson, Martin W. (Ag. 26, 1941, San Pedro, CA) Asst. Dir., Corvallis Pub. Lib., 1972. **Educ.:** Riverside City Coll., Univ. of CA, Riverside, 1962–66, BA (Hist.), 1966–68, MA (Hist.); Univ. of OR, 1971–72, MLS. **Orgs.:** ALA. Pac. NW LA. OR LA: Exhibits Ch. (1976–78), Legis. Com. (Ch., 1978), Treas. (1979–81), VP-Elect (1981). Benton Cnty. Juvenile Srvs. Comsn.: Ch. (1980–81). **Activities:** 9; 15, 17, 27; 92 **Addr.:** Corvallis Public Library, 645 N.W. Monroe, Corvallis, OR 97330.

Stephenson, Phillip Anthony (O. 11, 1937, Mineral, OH) Dir., Sec. Educ., Vandalia-Butler City Schs., 1980–, Dir., Instr. Media, 1968–80; Coll. Instr., Wright State Univ., 1969–75; Jr. High Tchr., Libn., Vandalia-Butler City Schs., 1965–67; Jr. High Tchr., Tipp City Vlg. Schs., 1959–65. **Educ.:** OH Univ., 1955–59, BS (Sec. Educ.), 1959–61, MEd (Admin.); IN Univ., 1967–68, MLS. **Orgs.:** ALA: AASL. OH Educ. Lib. Media Assn. Buckeye Assn. of Sch. Admins. Assn. for Supvsn. and Curric. Dev. **Activities:** 1, 10; 17, 20, 32; 50, 63 **Addr.:** Vandalia Butler City Schools, 306 S. Dixie Dr., Vandalia, OH 45377.

Stephenson, Richard W. (N. 22, 1930, Washington, DC) Head, Ref. and Bibl. Sect., Geo. and Map Div., Lib. of Congs., 1970–, Head, Acq. Sect., 1966–70, Ref. Libn., 1954–66. **Educ.:** Wilson Tchrs. Coll., 1949–54, (Geo.); George Washington Univ., 1955–66, BA (Geo.); Cath. Univ. of Amer., 1973–76, MS (LS). **Orgs.:** SLA: Geo. and Map Div., Vice-Ch. (1971–72), Ch. (1972–73); DC Chap., Ch. (1970–71), Vice-Ch. (1968–70), 2nd VP (1979–80). Assn. Can. Map. Libns. West. Assn. of Map Libs. Amer. Congs. on Surveying and Mapping. Assn. of Amer. Geographers. Socty. for the Hist. of Discoveries. Columbia Hist. Socty. **Honors:** Gamma Theta Upsilon, 2952; Lib. of Congs., Merit. Srv. Awd., 1968; Beta Phi Mu, 1976; SLA Geo. and Map Div., Hons. Awd. for Outstan. Achvmt. in Geo. and Map Libnshp., 1977. **Pubns.:** *The Cartography of Northern Virginia* (1981); *Civil War Maps* (1961); *Land Ownership Maps* (1967); *Selected Maps and Charts of Antarctica* (1959); ed., *Federal Government Map Collecting; A Brief History* (1969); jt. auth., *Map Collections in the United States and Canada* (1978); various articles. **Activities:** 4, 11; 26, 39, 45; 70 **Addr.:** Geography and Map Division, Library of Congress, Washington, DC 20540.

Stephenson, Shirley E. (F. 28, 1922, Cass City, MI) Assoc. Dir., Oral Hist. Prog., Dir., Oral Hist. Arch., CA State Univ., Fullerton, 1972–; Ref. Lib. Volun., Golden W. Coll., 1971. **Educ.:** Golden W. Coll., 1966–68, AA (Liberal Arts); CA State Univ., Fullerton, 1968–71, BA (Hist.), 1971–73, MS (LS), 1975–80, MA (Hist.); Bus. Coll., Detroit, MI, 1942–43, Dip.; CA Cmnty. Coll., Libn. Cred., Instr. Cred. **Orgs.:** Orange Cnty. LA. CALA: Socty. of Libns. Orange Cnty. Hist. Socty. Socty. of CA Archvsts.: Com. of 1980s. Natl. SW Oral Hist. Assn.: VP (1981–). CA State Univ.: Fullerton Alum. Assn. Phi Delta Gamma: Hist. (1972); Regis. (1973–74); Adv., (1975–); Pres. (1978–79); Liaison (1980). **Honors:** Phi Kappa Phi, 1973; Phi Alpha Theta, 1974. **Pubns.:** Jt. ed., *A Guide for Oral History Programs* (1973); "Oral History: Today's Approach to the Past," *Cath. Lib. World* (N. 1976); "Keep Reaching!" *Phi Delta Gamma Jnl.* (Je. 1980); "Understanding Our Past, Present, and Future: Oral History," *Phi Delta Gamma Jnl.* (Je. 1979); "Oral History & The Genealogist," *Orange Cty. CA Genealogical Soc. Q* (M. 1977); various interviews. **Activities:** 1; 17, 24, 37; 86 **Addr.:** Oral History Program, California State University, Fullerton, 800 N State College Blvd., Fullerton, CA 92634.

Sterling, Sheila Linden (Ap. 15, 1952, London, Eng.) Head Libn., E. F. Hutton and Co., Inc. 1977–; Libn., Standard and Poor's Corp., 1974–77. **Educ.:** NY Univ., 1969–73, BA (Eng.); Columbia Univ., 1973–74, MS (LS). **Orgs.:** SLA. **Activities:** 12; 17; 59 **Addr.:** E. F. Hutton & Co., Inc., Research Library, One State St. Plz., New York, NY 10004.

Sterman, Betsy L. (F. 18, 1927, Parkersburg, WV) Sch. Lib. Media Spec., Todd Elem. Sch., Briarcliff Manor, NY, 1968–; Chld. Lit. Consult., Empire State Coll., 1980–81; various positions as reader/eval., 1977–81; Tchr., Buffalo Pub. Schs., 1949–54. **Educ.:** Univ. of Buffalo, 1944–48, BA, cum laude (Eng. Lit.), 1951–53, MA (Eng. Lit.); SUNY, Geneseo, 1965–66, MLS. **Orgs.:** Westchester LA: Exec. Bd., Chld./YA Sect. (Ch., 1980–82). NY LA: Sch. Lib. Media Sect. Sch. Lib. Media Specs. of Southeast. NY. ALA. Jane Austen Socty. of N. Amer. **Pubns.:** *Libraries Are For Finding Out: Using the Encyclopedia* (1977); *Libraries Are For Finding Out: Using the Card Catalog* (1978); *Libraries Are For Finding Out: Using Reference Books* (forthcoming); *Libraries Are For Finding Out: Playing Library Skills Games* (forthcoming); various presentations. **Activities:** 10; 15, 31, 32 **Addr.:** 56 Commodore Rd., Chappaqua, NY 10514.

Stern, Helene C. (Mrs. Myron B.) (O. 3, 1942, Ashtabula, OH) Msc. Libn., Univ. Hts. Pub. Lib., 1974–; Msc. Libn. Case West. Rsv. Univ., Rec. Catlgr., Cleveland Inst. of Msc., 1969–73. **Educ.:** West. Rsv. Univ., 1960–64, BA (Eng.), 1968–69, MSLS; various crs. **Orgs.:** Msc. LA: Natl. Chap.; Midwest Chap. OCLC Msc. Users Grp. North. OH Tech. Srvs. Libns. OH LA. OH Cham. Orch.: Bd. of Trustees (1979–). Cmnty. Temple: Lib. Bd. (1979–). Cham. Msc. Socty. Cmnty. Temple Parent, Tchrs. and Student Assn.: Bk. Sale (Ch., 1978–); Pubcty. Ch. (1979–). Cleveland Cham. Msc. Socty.: Bd. of Trustees (1981–). **Honors:** Beta Phi Mu, 1969. **Activities:** 9; 15, 16, 20 **Addr.:** 3297 Enderby Rd., Shaker Heights, OH 44120.

Stern, Richard Elliot (My. 4, 1945, Bronx, NY) Libn., Gordon Hurwitz Butowsky et al, 1980–; User Consult., Volun., Electronic Info. Exch. Syst., 1979–; Ref., Docum. Libn., Rutgers Univ., 1974–79; Libn., ERIC Clearinghse. on Lib. and Info. Srvs., 1973–74; Libn., Port Athrty. of NY, NJ 1973; Volun., Peace Corps, Liberia, 1968–70. **Educ.:** Antioch Coll., 1963–68, BA (Soclgy.); Columbia Univ., 1972, MLS; Rutgers Univ., 1975–, Phd (LS); various crs. **Orgs.:** ALA: RASD, Stans. Com. (1979–82). Gvt. Docum. Assn. of NJ: Treas. (1975–76); Frdm. of Info. Task Frc. (Ch., 1976–81). ASIS. Fortune Socty. Sierra Club. **Pubns.:** Various presentations. **Activities:** 1, 12; 29, 39, 46; 75, 92, 93 **Addr.:** 210 Franklin St. #207, Bloomfield, NJ 07003.

Sternberg, Virginia A. (Ag. 27, 1922, Lawrence, MA) Lib. Consult., Lawrence Berkeley Lab., 1977–; Mgr., Tech. Info., Westinghse., Bettes' Atomic Power Lab., 1970–75, Libn., 1950–70; BioAssayist, Cutter Lab., 1946–49. **Educ.:** Univ. of DE, 1940–43, BA (Chem.); Drexel Univ., 1949–50, MLS; Univ. of Pittsburgh, 1963–70, PhD. **Orgs.:** SLA. ASIS. AAAS. Amer. Chem. Socty.: Chem. Lit. Div. Socty. of Tech. Writers and Publshrs. Various other orgs. **Activities:** 12; 17, 24, 39; 84, 86, 91 **Addr.:** 1100 Ptarmigan Dr. #6, Walnut Creek, CA 94595.

Sternfeld, Ruth Schwartz (O. 6, 1913, Chicago, IL) Retired, 1980–; Archvst., Rockefeller Univ., 1970–; Serial Catlgr., Harvard Univ., 1959–70; Libn., Temple Israel, Boston, 1958–70. **Educ.:** Northwest. Univ., 1934–36, PhB (Zlgy.); Simmons Coll., 1957–58, MLS. **Orgs.:** SAA: Sci. Com. (1976–). Mid-Atl. Reg. Arch. Conf.: Mem. Com. (Ch., 1977–78); NY State Mailing Rep. (1974–76). AJL: Grt. Boston Chap. (Ch., 1968–69). **Activities:** 1, 2; 15, 20, 45; 58, 80, 91 **Addr.:** 1385 York Ave., New York, NY 10021.

Steuben, Larry R. (D. 15, 1943, Chicago, IL) Dir., Lib. Srvs., Columbia Coll., 1976–; Media Coord., Ref. Libn., Ohlone Coll., 1972–76; Ref., ILL Libn., CA State Univ., Hayward, 1968–72. **Educ.:** Univ. of CA, Santa Barbara, 1963–67, BA (Pol. Sci.); Univ. of CA, Los Angeles, 1967–68, MLS; various grad. crs. **Orgs.:** CA LA: Cmnty. Coll. Libns. Chap. (Pres., 1978). CA Cmnty. Coll. Media Assn. ALA. **Activities:** 1; 15, 17, 31; 73 **Addr.:** 10999 Faun Ct., Sonora, CA 95370.

Steuermann, Clara (F. 10, 1922, Los Angeles, CA) Archvst., Arnold Schoenberg Inst., 1975–; Libn., Cleveland Inst. of Msc., 1966–75; Catlgr., Juilliard Sch., 1965–66. **Educ.:** Los Angeles City Coll., 1939–41; Univ. of CA, Los Angeles, 1941–43, BA (Msc.), 1943–44, MA (Msc.); Columbia Univ., 1962–64, MLS. **Orgs.:** Msc. LA: VP/Pres.–Elect (1974); Pres. (1975–76); Rep. Intl. Assn. of Msc. Libs. SAA. CA Socty. of Archvsts. **Pubns.:** Reviews. **Activities:** 2, 12; 17, 23, 45; 55 **Addr.:** Arnold Schoenberg Institute, University of Southern California, Los Angeles, CA 90007.

Stevens, Albert David (Ag. 5, 1942, Burlington, VT) Mem., VT Bd. of Libs., VT Dept. of Libs., 1978–; Pres., Trustees of the Baldwin Meml. Lib., 1972–80. **Educ.:** Univ. of VT, 1960–64, BS (Dairy Sci.); Saint Michael's Coll., 1979–, Mstrs. (Admin.). **Orgs.:** VT Lib. Trustees Assn.: Pres. (1974–78); Gvt. Rel. Ch. (1978–80). VT LA: Int. Frdm. Com. (1974–80); Gvt. Rel. Ch. (1974–80). New Eng. Lib. Bd.: Panel of Couns. (Ch., 1976–77). **Activities:** 9, 13; 47; 74, 78 **Addr.:** Sunset Hill Farm, Wells River, VT 05081.

Stevens, Christine L. (O. 5, 1948, St. Louis, MO) Ref. Libn., IN Univ. Sch. of Law, 1976–; Asst. Dir., Readers Srvs., 1974–76; Actg. Dir., 1972–74, Asst. Dir., Tech. Srvs., 1971–72. **Educ.:** West. MI Univ., 1966–70, BA (Eng.); IN Univ., 1970–71, MLS. **Orgs.:** AALL: Rcrt. Com. (1972–76); Readers Srvs. Spec. Interest Sect. (1979–); Model Bibl. (Ch., 1975–76, 1978–80); Legis. Com. (1976–78). OH Reg. Assn. of Law Libs. SLA. **Pubns.:** Ch., *Orall Model Bibl. of Texts for Law Libs.* (1979); *Res Gestae Yearly Index* IN State Bar Assn. (1971). **Activities:** 1, 12; 15, 29, 39; 77, 78 **Addr.:** Indiana University - School of Law: Indianapolis 735 W. New York St., Indianapolis, IN 46202.

Stevens, Elizabeth A. (Je. 9, 1925, Morgantown, WV) Sch. Lib. Media Spec., Gen. Elwell S. Otis Sch., #30, 1971–. **Educ.:** Coll. of Wooster, 1943–47, BA (Eng. Lit.); SUNY, Geneseo, 1970–71, MLS (Sch. Libs.); various crs. **Orgs.:** ALA: Sch. Lib. Media Prog. of Yr. Com. (1979). NY LA. Grt. Rochester Area Sch. Media Spec.: Legis. Com. (1978–79). Rochester Sch. Lib. Cncl.: Lib. Adv. Com. (Ch., 1979–80). Parsells Ave. Cmnty. Church: Treas. (1979–80). Girl Scouts: Co-Leader (1979–80). Rochester Meml. Art Gallery. Rochester Musm. and Sci. Ctr. Various other orgs. **Activities:** 10; 21, 31, 32; 63 **Addr.:** 1694 Blossom Rd., Rochester, NY 14610.

Stevens, Glenda Bailey (Ag. 1, 1938, Brookhaven, MS) Archvst., Amistad Resrch. Ctr., 1977–. **Educ.:** MS Coll., 1957–60, BS (Home Econ.); SW MO State Univ., 1969–75, MA (Hist.); various crs. **Orgs.:** SAA. Frnds. of Amistad. Frnds. of the Arch. of LA. **Activities:** 2; 39, 41, 45; 66, 85 **Addr.:** 4209 Seminary Pl., New Orleans, LA 70126.

Stevens, Jane (Je. 4, 1928, New Orleans, LA) Head, LA Col., Tulane Univ. Lib., 1981–, Head, Cat. Dept., 1965–81, Catlgr., 1955–65; Catlgr., Loyola Univ. Lib., 1950–55. **Educ.:** Loyola Univ., 1945–49, PhB (Soclgy.); LA State Univ., 1949–50, BSLS. **Orgs.:** LA LA: LA Un. Cat. Com. (1972–77, 1981–); LA Numerical Regis. Com. (1974–). Grt. New Orleans Lib. Club. Sierra Club. **Activities:** 1; 20, 34, 45; 69, 73 **Addr.:** Louisiana Collection, Howard-Tilton Memorial Library, Tulane University, New Orleans, LA 70118.

Stevens, Jane E. (Ag. 28, 1917, LaSalle, NY) Assoc. Prof., Sch. of Lib. Srv., Columbia Univ., 1976–; various lectr. positions, 1959–75; Ed., *Lib. Lit.,* H. W. Wilson, 1963–73; Assoc. Libn., SUNY Brockport, 1949–63; Asst. Libn., Scarsdale HS, 1947–49; Libn., Haverling HS, 1942–47; Libn., Oakfield HS, 1939–42; **Educ.:** Univ. of Rochester, 1933–37, AB (Eng.); SUNY, Geneseo, 1937–41, BS (LS); Middlebury Coll., Bread Loaf Sch., 1950–53, MA (Eng.); Columbia Univ., 1958 (LS). **Orgs.:** ALA. NY LA: Resrcs. and Tech. Srvs. Sect. (Pres., 1972–73). Amer. Socty. of Indxrs.: Bd.; CNLIA Rep. (1970–80). NY Tech. Srvs. Libs.: Pres. (1973–74). Various other orgs. AAUP. Amer. Cvl. Liberties Un. **Activities:** 11; 20, 30 **Addr.:** School of Library Service, Columbia University, New York, NY 10027.

Stevens, Nicholas G. (O. 30, 1911, Pittsburgh, PA) Prof. Emeritus, Kutztown State Coll., 1977–, Prof., Dir., LS, 1955–77,

PROFESSIONAL ACTIVITIES: Institutions: 1. Acad. lib.; 2. Arch.; 3. Assn.; 4. Fed./Gvt. lib.; 5. Inst. lib.; 6. Mfr./Suppl.; 7. Milit. lib.; 8. Musm.; 9. Pub. lib.; 10. Sch. lib.; 11. Sch. of lib. sci.; 12. Spec. lib.; 13. State lib.; 14. (other). **Functions/Activities:** 15. Acq./Col. dev.; 16. Adult srvs.; 17. Admin.; 18. Apprais.; 19. Archit./Bldgs.; 20. Cat./Class.; 21. Chld. srvs.; 22. Circ.; 23. Cons./Pres.; 24. Consult.; 25. Cont. ed.; 26. Educ. lib. sci.; 27. Ext. srvs.; 28. Fund/Grants; 29. Gvt. pubs.; 30. Indx./Abs.; 31. Instr. lib. use; 32. Media srvs.; 33. Micro.; 34. Netwks./Coop.; 35. Persnl.; 36. PR; 37. Publshg.; 38. Recs. mgt.; 39. Ref. srvs.; 40. Repro.; 41. Resrch.; 42. Review.; 43. Secur.; 44. Serials; 45. Spec. col.; 46. Tech. srvs.; 47. Trustees/Bds.; 48. YA srvs.; 49. (other).

Who's Who in Library and Information Services

Assoc. Prof., Hist. and LS, 1949–55; Tchr., Pittsburgh Pub. Schs., 1946–48, 1936–42; various tchg. positions, 1954–64; Investigator, PA Dept. of Pub. Assistance, 1935–36. **Educ.:** Univ. of Pittsburgh, 1930–33, AB (Hist.), 1936–40, AM (Hist.); Univ. of MI, 1948–49, AMLS. **Orgs.:** PA LA: Pres. (1963–64); Educ. and Cert. Com. (Ch., 1961–62). ALA: Cnclr. (1968–69); Lib. Educ. Div., Tchrs. Sect., Ch. Wilson Educ. Index Rev. Com. (1968–69); Ad Hoc Com. on Flood Damage Libs. in PA (1972–73). Lions Club of Kutztown: Pres. (1958–59). PA Sch. Libns. Assn. PA Educ. Resrch. Assn. "75" Club of PA Educs. **Honors:** PA Dept. of Educ., Disting. Educs. Awd., 1964; Kutztown State Coll., Twenty-five Yrs. Srv. Awd., 1975; PA Assn., Awd. of Merit, 1976; PA LA, Disting. Srv. Awd., 1977; other hons. **Pubns.:** *Kutztown Bulletins: School Libraries–How To Increase Their Use* (1956); *Elementary Libraries: A Basic Beginning* (1957); *The Total Task of a School Librarian* (1960); *Educational Trends, Innovations, Technology, Multi-Media, Taxonomies of Learning, Librarianship: A Bibliographic Checklist. 1965–1971* (1972); *Adult, Continuing, and In-Service Education and the Library in Higher Education: A Bibliographic Checklist* (1973). **Activities:** 10, 11; 26, 39, 41; 63, 89, 92†

Stevens, Norman D. (Mr. 4, 1932, Nashua, NH) Univ. Libn., Univ. of CT Lib., 1968–; Actg. Univ. Libn., Rutgers Univ. Lib., 1966–68, Assoc. Libn., 1963–68; Actg. Dir., Univ. Libs., Howard Univ. Lib., 1961–63; Instr., Resrch. Assoc., Rutgers Univ., Grad. Sch. of Lib. Srv., 1959–61, Instr., 1957–59. **Educ.:** Amer. Univ., 1949–51; Univ. of NH, 1951–54, BA (Gvt.); Rutgers Univ., 1955–57, MLS, 1959–61, PhD (LS). Victoria Univ. Coll., Wellington, NZ, 1954. **Orgs.:** OCLC Users Cncl.: Exec. Com. (1979–). NELINET: Exec. Com. (1969–78); Vice-Ch. (1972–73); Ch. (1973–74, 1974–75, 1978–79); Controller (1977–78); Bd. of Trustees (1978–79). The Molesworth Inst.: Dir. (1957–). **Pubns.:** Jt. ed., *Landmarks of Library Literature* (1976); jt. ed., *The Librarian* (1976); ed., *Essays for Ralph Shaw* (1975); ed., *Library Humor* (1971); various articles. **Activities:** 1, 2; 17, 34, 41; 62 **Addr.:** University Library, University of Connecticut, Storrs, CT 06268.

Stevens, Patricia (Ja. 3, 1929, Oak Park, IL) Dir., Lib., Principia Coll., 1979–; Mgr., Bus. Info. Srvs., The Coca-Cola Co., 1975–79; Dept. Libn., MA Dept. of Educ., 1968–72; Bibl. Srch., Brandeis Univ., 1967–68. **Educ.:** Boston Univ., 1961–63, BA (Classical Cvlztn.); Simmons Coll., 1965–67, BSLS. **Orgs.:** ALA. IFLA. SLA: VP, Pres.-Elect (1978–79). various other orgs. Leag. of Women Voters: Lincoln, MA VP, Pres.-Elect (1964–65). Lincoln Hist. Socty., Etc. **Honors:** Phi Beta Kappa. **Activities:** 1; 17, 45 **Addr.:** 3 Dogwood Ln., Elsah, IL 62028.

Stevens, Richard C. (Je. 25, 1923, Alexandria, MN) Ref. Libn., CO State Univ. Libs., 1962–; Libn., AV Spec., Santa Monica Unfd. Sch. Dist., 1961–62; various positions in educ., cmrcl. broadcasting. **Educ.:** St. Olaf Coll., 1946–49, BA (Hist., Eng.); Univ. of Denver, 1951–53, MA (RadioBroadcasting), 1960–61, MA (LS). **Orgs.:** ALA. CO LA. AAUP. **Pubns.:** Jt. auth., *AIMLO: Auto-Instructional Media for Library Orientation* ERIC (1974); jt. auth., "Evaluating the AIMLO Project," *Evaluating Library Use Instruction* (1975). **Activities:** 1; 17, 31, 39; 93 **Addr.:** Colorado State University Libraries, Ft. Collins, CO 80523.

Stevens, Robert David (Ag. 11, 1921, Nashua, NH) Lectr., Grad. Sch. of Lib. Std., Univ. of HI, 1980–; Chief, Copyrt. Cat. Div., Lib. of Congs., 1975–80; Dean, Grad. Sch. of Lib. Std., Univ. of HI, 1969–75, Assoc. Dean, Lib. Actv., 1965–69; Dir., Resrch. Cols., E.-W. Ctr., 1964–65; various libn. positions, Lib. of Congs., 1947–64. **Educ.:** Syracuse Univ., 1938–42, AB (Eng. Lit.); Columbia Univ., 1946–47, BS (LS); Amer. Univ., 1949–64, Phd (Pub. Admin.); Nvl. Sch. of Oriental Langs., 1943, Dip. (Japanese). **Orgs.:** ALA: Cncl. (1967–70); Adv. Com. on Liason with Japanese Libs. (Ch., 1974–78); Reprodct. of Lib. Mtrls. Sect., Policy and Resrch. Com. (Ch., 1978–80). HI LA: Pres. (1966–67). DC LA: Treas. (1955–56). Intl. Affairs Forum: Honolulu. **Honors:** Phi Beta Kappa, 1942; Pi Sigma Alpha, 1957. **Pubns.:** Ed., *Japanese and U.S. Libraries at the Turning Point* (1977); *Documents of International Organizations* (1974); "Past as Prologue," *Wilson Lib. Bltn.* (D. 1976). **Activities:** 1, 4; 17, 20, 39; 54, 56, 61 **Addr.:** 3265 Paty Dr., Honolulu, HI 96822.

Stevens, Robert R. (Mr. 10, 1952, Chicago, IL) Archvst./Rare Bk. Libn., Rosenberg Lib., 1979–, Ref. Libn., 1979–80. **Educ.:** Cornell Coll., 1970–74, BA (Hist.); Univ. of IA, 1974–76, MA (Hist.); Univ. of WI, 1977–78, MLS. **Orgs.:** ALA. TX LA. Smithsonian Inst. **Activities:** 2, 9; 15, 23, 39; 92 **Addr.:** Rosenberg Library, 2310 Sealy St., Galveston, TX 77550.

Stevens, Roberta Ann (S. 27, 1948, Pittsburgh, PA) Assoc. Dir., Tech. Opers. Fairfax Cnty. Pub. Lib., 1979 Ch., Media Srvs. Dept., Natl. Tech. Inst. for the Deaf, 1977–78; Coord., Resrc. Ctr., Genesee-WY Bd. of Coop. Srvs., 1974–77; Media Lab. Supvsr., SUNY, Buffalo, 1973–74. **Educ.:** SUNY, Buffalo, 1966–70, BA (Psy., Eng.); SUNY, Binghamton, 1970–72, MA (Eng.); SUNY, Buffalo, 1973–74, MLS (Media, LS). **Orgs.:** ALA. VA LA. AAUW: Bd. of Dirs. (1979–80). Beta Phi Mu: Bd. of Dirs. (1975–76). SUNY Buffalo: Sch. of Info. and Lib. Std. Alum. Assn. (Adv., 1976–77). **Pubns.:** *Multimedia Occupational Materials; An Annotated Bibliography* (1976); "Encouraging the Stereotype," *Lib. Jnl.* (N. 15, 1979); "Learning Resource Center Handles Occupational Materials," *Amer. Vocational Jnl.* (Ap. 1976); "Principles for Effective Group Media Presentations," *Intl. Jnl. of Instr. Media* (Win. 1975); "Cluster Classroom Attitude Survey" multi-media presentation (1978); "A Computer-Based Equipment Inventory" multi-media presentation (1978); various multi-media presentations. **Activities:** 1, 9; 17, 32, 46; 67, 91, 93 **Addr.:** 10355 Pond Spice Terr., Burke, VA 22015.

Stevens, Rolland E. (Ap. 7, 1915, St. Louis, MO) Prof. Emeritus, Grad. Sch. of LS, Univ. of IL, 1980–, Prof., 1963–80; Assoc. Dir., Tech. Prcs., OH State Univ. Libs., 1960–63, Asst. Dir., Tech. Prcs., 1953–60, Head, Acq. Dept., 1950–53; Asst. to Dir., Head, Ref., Univ. of Rochester Lib., 1946–48. **Educ.:** WA Univ., St. Louis, 1935–39, AB (Grk.); Univ. of IL, 1939–40, BS (LS), 1940–42, MS (LS), 1948–50, PhD. **Orgs.:** OH Valley Grp. of Tech. Srv. Libns.: Ch. (1960–61). ALA: ACRL, *Mono.* Ed. (1956–60); RTSD/Acq. Sect. (Ch., 1957–58)/Serials Sect. (Ch., 1963–64); LR RT (Ch., 1972–73); Ed. Com. (1965–68). Amer. Documtn. Inst.: Ctrl. OH Chap. (Ch., 1962–63). Phi Beta Kappa: Epsilon of OH (Secy., 1957–60). Phi Beta Kappa: Gamma, IL Fncl. Secy. (1964–69); Pres. (1968–69). **Honors:** Beta Phi Mu, Good Tchg. Awd., 1968. **Pubns.:** *Reference Books in the Social Sciences and Humanities* (1977); *A Feasibility Study of Centralized and Regionalized Interlibrary Loan Centers* (1973); jt. auth., "Interlibrary Loan in Tennessee," *The Southeast. Libn.* (Fall 1977); "A Study of Interlibrary Loan," *Coll. & Resrch. Libs.* (S. 1974); "Resources in Microform for the Research Library," *Micro. Reviews* (Ja. 1972); various mono., articles, bk. reviews. **Activities:** 1; 15, 23, 39 **Addr.:** 305 Burkwood Ct. W., Urbana, IL 61801.

Stevens, Sharon G. (Jl. 4, 1949, Bryn Mawr, PA) Tech. Prog. Rep., Baker and Taylor Co., 1979–; Asst. Libn., Tech. Srvs., Univ. of NH, 1976–79; Sel. Cntrl. Libn., Approval Prog., Baker and Taylor Co., 1973–76. **Educ.:** Georgetown Univ., 1967–71, BSL (Fr.); Drexel Univ., 1971–72, MLS; Univ. de Dijon, Dijon, France, 1969 (Fr.). **Orgs.:** ALA. New Eng. LA. NY LA. **Honors:** Beta Phi Mu. **Activities:** 1; 15, 46 **Addr.:** Baker and Taylor Co., 6 Kirby Ave., Somerville, NJ 08876.

Stevens, Stanley David (N. 10, 1933, San Francisco, CA) Map Libn., Univ. Lib., Univ. of CA, Santa Cruz, 1965–. **Educ.:** San Jose State Univ., 1951–60, BA (Pol. Sci.); various crs. **Orgs.:** ALA. West. Assn. Map Libs.: Pres. (1967–68); Treas. (1969–); Pubns. Ed. (1971–). SLA: Hons. Com. (Ch., 1977); Cartograph. Users Adv. Cncl. (1978–). Natl. Micro. Assn.: Stans. Com. on Cartograph. Micro. (1974–). Assn. Can. Map Libs.: Assoc. Mem. CA Hist. Socty. CA Map Socty. **Honors:** SLA, Geo. and Map. Div., Hons. Awd. for Outstan. Achvmt., 1981. **Pubns.:** "Planning a Map Library? Create a Master Plan!" *Spec. Libs.* (Ap. 1972); "Maps in the Local History Collection," *West. Assn. of Map Libs. Info. Bltn.* (Jl. 1972); "Lighthouse Point: Discovery of Historical Land Use through Maps, Photos, and Text," *SLA Geo. and Map Div. Bltn.* (Je. 1973); "Map and Aerial Photo Collections in the United States: Survey of the Seventy Largest Collections," *Lib. Trends* (WIN. 1981); "The Sherman Day 1850 Map of San José and How to Correct LC Cataloging," *West. Assn. of Map Libs. Info. Bltn.* (N. 1981); various articles, reviews. **Activities:** 1; 23, 37, 45; 54, 70 **Addr.:** 231 13th Ave., Santa Cruz, CA 95062.

Stevenson, Grace Thomas (Ja. 27, 1900, Morganfield, KY) Retired; Deputy Exec. Dir., ALA, 1952–65, Dir., ALA Amer. Heritage Proj., 1951–52; Head, Adult Educ. Dept., Seattle Pub. Lib., 1945–51; Head, Persnl. Dept., Hunter's Point Nvl. Shipyard, 1943–44, Asst., Long Beach Pub. Lib., 1926–27; Asst., Evansville Pub. Lib., 1918–21. **Educ.:** Mt. St. Joseph's Acad., St. Joseph, KY, 1912–17. **Orgs.:** Pac. NW LA: Adult Educ. Com., Ch. Adult Educ. Assn. of U.S.: Bd. (1956–60); Pres. (1957–58). EFLA. Educ. Media Cncl. Hon. Ord. of KY Colonels. **Honors:** EFLA, The EFLA Awd., 1967; ALA, Cent. Cit., 1976; Univ. of AZ Alum. Assn., Disting. Citizen Awd., 1978. **Pubns.:** *Library Area Reference and Service Center for Pima County* (1973); *ALA Chapter Relationships—National, Regional, and State* (1971); *Arizona Library Survey* (1968); *Serra Regional Library System* (1969); *Library Service Across the Border* (1969); various articles. **Addr.:** 1250 5th St., Imperial Beach, CA 92032.

Steward, Constance R. (Ap. 24, 1949, Sayre, PA) Mgr., Info. Srvs., Gen. Electric Co., Electronics Lab., 1978–; Admin. Asst. to Dean, Sch. of Info. Std., Syracuse Univ., 1976–78; Asst. Ed., SUNY Un. List of Serials, SUNY, 1974–76; Supvsr., Serials and Docum. Receiving, Bird Lib., Syracuse Univ., 1972–74. **Educ.:** Syracuse Univ., 1967–71, BA (Soviet, E. European Std.), 1971–74, MLS (Info. Std.). **Orgs.:** Assoc. Info. Mgrs.: Plng. Com. for 1980 Natl. Info. Conf. and Exposition. ASIS: Upstate NY Chap., Pres. **Pubns.:** Asst. Ed., *Central New York Union List of Serials* (1976); "Expanding Job Market for Information Professionals," *Bltn. of the Amer. Socty. for Info. Sci.* (O. 1979); "Interview with an Information Manager," *The Info. Mgr.* (O. 1979); "Promoting the Use of On-line Services," *Lib. Mgt. Bltn.* (O. 1979). **Activities:** 12; 17, 36, 41; 59, 64, 91 **Addr.:** Electronics Park Library, General Electric Co., Electronics Park 3, Rm. 105, Syracuse, NY 13221.

Stewart, Alan Kleven (O. 16, 1943, Oak Park, IL) Resrch. Info. Sci., Stan. Oil, 1976–; Info. Sci., IL Inst. of Tech. Resrch. Inst., 1971–76; Resrch. Engin., Inland Steel Co., 1967–71. **Educ.:** Purdue Univ., 1961–66, BS (Metal Engin.), 1966–67, MS (Metal Engin.); IL Inst. of Tech., 1971–72, MS (Sci. Info.). **Orgs.:** SLA: Documtn. Div., Com. on Name and Scope (1978). Assn. of Info. and Dissemination Ctrs.: *ASIDIC Nsltr.* Ed. (1975–76). ASIS: Prof. Leadership Com. (Ch., 1979); Awds. and Hons. Com. (1978–79); various other coms., ofcs. **Pubns.:** "The 1200 Band Experience," *Online* (Jl. 1978); jt. auth., "Comparative Analysis of Technical Literature," *Jnl. of Tech. Wrtg. and Comm.* (Sum. 1973); jt. auth., *ASIDIC Survey of Information Center Services* (1972); various presentations. **Activities:** 12; 34, 41; 64, 75, 93 **Addr.:** PO Box 400 (F-1), Naperville, IL 60540.

Stewart, Alva W. (Je. 13, 1931, Marshallville, GA) Ref. Libn., NC Agr. and Tech. State Univ., 1980–; Head, Ref. Dept., Memphis State Univ. Lib., 1977–80; Assoc. Libn., Coll. of William and Mary, 1971–77; Head Libn., NC Wesleyan Coll., 1968–71; Ref. Libn., Univ. of NC, 1965–68. **Educ.:** Univ. of NC, 1951–53, AB (Pol. Sci.); Duke Univ., 1953–54, MA (Pol. Sci.); Vanderbilt Univ., 1956–57, (Pol. Sci); Univ. of NC, 1958–60, MSLS. **Orgs.:** Southeastern LA: Constn. and Bylaws Com. (1979–80). NCLA: ALA-Southeastern LA Mem. Com. (1969–70); Ed., *NC Libs.* (1966–68). NC LA. Natl. Mncpl. Leag.: Correspondent (1963–). **Honors:** Cncl. on Lib. Resrcs., Flwshp., 1972; Beta Phi Mu, 1959. **Pubns.:** *The 1980 Census of Population: A Bibliographic Overview* (1981); *Municipal Extraterritorial Jurisduction: A Bibliographic Survey* (1981); *The National Center for State Courts: A Preliminary Bibliography* (1980); *The National Municipal League: A Bibliographical Survey* (1978); *The All-America Cities Program: A Selected Bibliography* (1979). **Activities:** 1; 17, 39; 72, 77, 83 **Addr.:** 410-C Savannah St., Greensboro, NC 27406.

Stewart, Archibald W. L. (O. 4, 1940, Edmonton, AB) Ref. Libn., Natl. Musm. of Nat. Sci., 1980–; Actg. Libn., Connaught Labs., Ltd., 1979–80; Actg. Libn., St. Thomas Psyt. Hosp., 1979; Purser, Nordair Ltd., 1974–77; Tchr., Art, Edmonton Pub. Sch. Bd., 1969–73. **Educ.:** Univ. of AB, 1960–64, BSc (Bot.), 1964–66, MSc (Bot./Myco.), 1968–69, Grad. Dipl. (Art Educ.); Univ. of Toronto, 1977–79, MLS. **Orgs.:** Can. LA. Geosci. Info. Socty. **Honors:** Beta Phi Mu, 1978; Natl. Resrch. Cncl. of Can., Schol., Sci. LS and Documtn., 1978. **Pubns.:** "Development and Taxonomy of *Apiosporina collinsii*," *Can. Jnl. Bot.* (1967). **Activities:** 1, 12; 15, 17, 39; 58, 80, 91 **Addr.:** 1375 Prince of Wales Dr., Apt. 1809, Ottawa, ON K2C 3L5 Canada.

Stewart, Charles C. (O. 17, 1947, Trenton, NJ) Dir., Prog. Srvs., Baker and Taylor Co., 1981–; Adj. Lectr., Queens Coll. Grad. Sch., 1979–; Mgr. Cont. Srvs., Baker and Taylor Co., 1979–81, Tech. Libn., 1978–79; Info. Srvs. Mgr., NJ Educ. Comp. Netwk., 1976–77. **Educ.:** Harvard Univ., 1969, AB (Amer. Std.); Hartford Semy., 1973, MA (Phil.), 1975, MDiv (Theo., Lib.); Rutgers Univ., 1976, (Lib. Admin.). **Orgs.:** ALA: LITA. ASIS. NJ LA. NY Acad. of Sci. Natl. Youth Sci. Camp: Rep. (1965). **Honors:** Beta Phi Mu, 1976. **Pubns.:** "Women in America 1800–1860," *Micro. Review* (Jl. 1977); various articles. **Activities:** 1, 9; 15, 24, 46; 56, 59, 75 **Addr.:** R.D. #2 Box 64, Pittstown, NJ 08867.

Stewart, Charles M. (D. 7, 1945, Corinth, MS) Lib. Systs. Anal., Resrch. Libs. Grp., 1978–; Sci. and Law Catlgr., Princeton Univ. Lib., 1975–78; Asst. Law libn., O'Melveny and Myers, 1972–74. **Educ.:** MI State Univ., 1963–67, BA (Classics); Univ. of CA, Los Angeles, 1971–72, MLS. **Orgs.:** ALA: RTSD, Bk. Cats. Com. (1976–80), Com. on Cat.: Descr. and Access (1979–). CA LA. ASIS. **Honors:** Beta Phi Mu, 1972. **Activities:** 1; 34, 46; 56 **Addr.:** P. O. Box 2316, Stanford, CA 94305.

Stewart, David Marshall (Ag. 1, 1916, Nashville, TN) Chief Libn., Nashville Pub. Lib., 1960–; Libn., U.S. Gvt., DC, 1948–60; Spec. Asst., Lib. of Congs., 1947. **Educ.:** Bethel Coll., 1934–38, AB (Hist., Eng.); Peabody Coll., 1938–39, BS (LS). **Orgs.:** ALA: PLA, Pres. (1966–67); Stan. Com. (Ch., 1964–65). SELA. TN LA: Pres. (1966–67); Legis. Com. (Ch., 1965–66). Mid. E. TN Chap. Arthritis Assn.: VP (1965–). Coffee Hse. Club, Nashville: Pres. (1964). Cncl. of Cmnty. Agencies, Nashville. Bethel Coll. Alum. Assn. Various other orgs. **Activities:** 9; 17 **Addr.:** Nashville Public Library, 222–8th Ave. N., Nashville, TN 37203.

Stewart, Donald E(dwin) (Ag. 26, 1927, Chicago, IL) Assoc. Exec., Dir. for Publshg., ALA, 1974–; Managing Ed., *Encyc. Britannica*, 1965–73, Assoc. Ed., 1964–65, Managing Ed., *Great Ideas Today*, 1961–63; Asst. to Exec. Ed., 1951–64. **Educ.:** Univ. of Chicago, 1947–50, AB (Liberal Arts). **Orgs.:** ALA. Chicago Bk. Clinic: VP (1978–80); Secy. (1976–78). **Pubns.:** Managing ed., *The ALA World Encyclopedia of Library and Information Services* (1980); assoc. ed., *The ALA Yearbook* (1976–81); "Publishing, ALA," *The ALA Yrbk.* (1976–81). **Activities:** 3, 12; 37; 75, 95-Ref., Prof. publshg. **Addr.:** Publishing Services, 50 E. Huron St., Chicago, IL 60611.

Stewart, George R. (Ag. 19, 1944, Birmingham, AL) Dir., Birmingham Pub. Lib., 1977–, Deputy Dir., 1970–76. **Educ.:** Samford Univ., 1962–66, BA (Hist.), 1966–67, MA (Hist.); Emory Univ., 1967–70, MLS. **Orgs.:** AL LA: Pres. (1976–77).

Special Subjects/Services: 50. Adult educ.; 51. Advert./Mktg.; 52. Aerosp.; 53. Agric.; 54. Area std.; 55. Arts/Hum.; 56. Autom.; 57. Bibl./Prtg.; 58. Bio. sci.; 59. Bus./Fin.; 60. Chem.; 61. Copyrt.; 62. Documtn.; 63. Educ.; 64. Engin.; 65. Env.; 66. Eth. grps.; 67. Film; 68. Food/Nutr.; 69. Geneal.; 70. Geo.; 71. Geol.; 72. Handcpd.; 73. Hist.; 74. Int. frdm.; 75. Info. sci.; 76. Insr.; 77. Law; 78. Legis.; 79. Math./Comp. sci.; 80. Med.; 81. Metals; 82. Nat. resrcs.; 83. Newsp.; 84. Nuc. sci.; 85. Oral hist.; 86. Petr./Energy; 87. Pharm.; 88. Phys./Astr./Math.; 89. Readg.; 90. Relig.; 91. Sci./Tech.; 92. Soc. sci.; 93. Telecom.; 94. Transp.; 95. (other).

SELA. ALA. Indus. Hlth. Cncl. Volun. and Info. Ctr. State Adv. Cncl. on LSCA. Various ofcs. **Honors:** Phi Kappa Phi. **Activities:** 9; 17, 19, 24; 56, 59, 75 **Addr.:** Birmingham Public Library, 2020 Park Pl., Birmingham, AL 35203.

Stewart, Henry R. (Ap. 16, 1944, Wilmington, DE) Assoc. Dean, Lib. Srvs., Old Dominion Univ., 1977–; Asst. Prof., Univ. of AL, 1972–77; Actg. Head, LS Dept., Tasmanian Coll. of Advnc. Educ., 1976; Ref. Libn., AV Dir., Cornell Coll., 1967–69. **Educ.:** Cornell Coll., 1962–66, BA (Pol. Sci., Econ.); Univ. of Denver, 1966–67, MA (Libnshp.); IN Univ., 1969–72, PhD (LS). **Orgs.:** ALA: Lib. Admin. Div./Lib. Org. Mgt. Sect., Stats. Com. on Lib. Educ. (Ch., 1974–76); JMRT, Orien. Prog. (Coord., 1976), JMRT Prog., Mem. Mtg. (Ch., 1978); ERT, Exec. Bd. (1980–83). SE LA: Various coms. AALS: Various coms., ofcs. Beta Phi Mu: Nsltr. Com., Pubcty. Com. (1980–81); Nom. Com. (1979–80). Various other orgs. **Pubns.:** Jt. auth., "Processing and Maintenance of Federal Documents," *Southeast. Libn.* (Win. 1975); "Some of My Best Friends Are Sales Reps," *Amer. Libs.* (Je. 1978). **Activities:** 1; 17, 29, 39; 54, 61, 74 **Addr.:** Old Dominion University Library, Norfolk, VA 23508.

Stewart, James B. (S. 12, 1944, Bryan, TX) Dir., Victoria Pub. Lib., 1978–; Head, Info. Srvs., Corpus Christi Pub. Libs., 1973–78; Ref. Libn., Austin Pub. Lib., 1972. **Educ.:** Univ. of TX, 1963–70, BA (Gvt.), 1971–72, MLS. **Orgs.:** TX LA: Legis. Com. (1979). SW LA: Pubns. Com. (1977). ALA. TX State Hist. Assn. Antient and Random Ord. of the Coo: Ch. (1972). **Activities:** 9; 17 **Addr.:** Victoria Public Library, 302 N. Main, Victoria, TX 77901.

Stewart, Kathryn A. (D. 10, 1942, Springfield, OH) Lib. Srvs. Coord., Brevard Cnty. Lib. Syst., 1975–; Coord. of Lib. Srvs., Volusia Cnty. Pub. Lib. Syst., 1968–75; Ref. Libn., Ctrl. FL Reg. Lib., 1964–68. **Educ.:** FL State Univ., 1964, BA (Amer. Hist.); LA State Univ., 1967, MLS; Pub. Srv. Mgt. Std., Univ. of N. FL, 1979, Cert. of Achvmt.; various crs. **Orgs.:** FL LA. ALA. **Activities:** 9; 17, 28, 35; 50, 67, 74 **Addr.:** Brevard County Library System, 2575 N. Courtenay Pkwy., Rm. 153, Merritt Island, FL 32952.

Stewart, Margaret A. (S. 23, 1944, Clio, AL) Asst. Lib. Dir., Christopher Newport Coll., 1979–; Branch Head, Portsmouth Pub. Lib., 1977–79; Lib. Dir., Enterprise State Jr. Coll., 1974–77, Asst. Lib. Dir., 1968–73. **Educ.:** Univ. of South. MS, 1962–66 (LS); Univ. of AL, 1973–74, MLS. **Orgs.:** ALA: JMRT, Aflt. Rep. (1975–76), Pres. (1977–78), various ofcs.; Exhibits RT, Booth Staffing Ch. (1979–80), Exec. Bd. (1981–82), various coms. AL LA: Nom. Com. (Ch., 1976–77); various ofcs. VA LA: Mem. Ch. (1981–); various coms. Frnds. of Portsmouth Pub. Lib. Various other orgs. AAUW. **Honors:** Beta Phi Mu, 1975; Beta Sigma Phi; Alpha Delta Kappa. **Pubns.:** Ed., *Between Two Covers Newsletter* (1978–79); ed., *Newsnotes* (1977–78). **Activities:** 1; 17, 22, 35 **Addr.:** Christopher Newport College Library, 50 Shoe Ln., Newport News, VA 23606.

Stewart, Sharon Lee (F. 10, 1944, St. Paul, MN) Lib. Instr., Univ. of AL, 1976–, Reclass. Libn., 1972–76. **Educ.:** Cornell Coll., 1962–66, BA (Psy.); Univ. of IA, 1968–69, MA (LS). **Orgs.:** ALA: JMRT, Cognotes Com. Ch. (1976–78), Treas. (1978–80). AL LA: JMRT, Exec. Bd. (1974–75), Wkshp. Com. (Ch., 1987–79), Nom. Com. (Ch., 1979–80); Coll. Univ. and Spec. Libs. Div., Proj. Com. (Ch., 1978–79). Univ. Luth. Chapel: Treas. (1977–79); Congregation Pres. (1981–). Univ. of AL: Fac. Sen. (1978–80); Student Affairs Com. (Ch. 1979–80); Lib. Fac. Org. (Pres., 1980–81). **Pubns.:** Ed., *Cognotes* (1976–78). **Activities:** 1; 31; 50 **Addr.:** P.O. Box S, University, AL 35486.

Stewart, Virginia R. (My. 7, 1944, Chicago, IL) Consult. in Arch. and Hist.; Asst. Ms. Libn., Assoc. Prof., Univ. of IL, Chicago, 1968–78. **Educ.:** Knox Coll., 1961–65, BA (Pol. Sci.); Purdue Univ., 1965–67, MA (Pol Sci.); Amer. Univ., 1971, Cert. (Admin. of Mod. Arch.). **Orgs.:** SAA: Com. on Col. Personal Papers and Mss. (Ch., 1975–78). Midwest Arch. Conf.: Com. Regis. Nom. Com., Ch. Women in the Hist. Prof.: Coord. Com. YWCA of Metro. Chicago: VP; Bd. of Dirs. (1977–) Amer. Assn. for State and Lcl. Hist. Knox Coll. Alum. Assn.: Natl. Alum. Cncl. (Secy., 1977–). **Pubns.:** "The Constituencies of Urban Archives: Donors, Users and Institutions," *Drexel Lib. Qtly.* (O. 1977); "A Primer on Manuscript Field Work," *Midwest. Archvst.* (1976); "Problems of Confidentiality in the Administration of Personal Case Records," *Amer. Archvst.* (Jl. 1974). **Activities:** 2; 15, 24, 45; 55, 92 **Addr.:** 168 Geneva, Elmhurst, IL 60126.

Stewart, William L., Jr. (Ja. 17, 1935, Selma, AL) Assoc. Dir., Tech. Srvs., Univ. of WY, Laramie, 1980–; Asst. Dir., Tech. Srvs., Univ. of TX, San Antonio, 1975–80; Acq. Libn., Univ. of S. FL, 1967–74, Asst. Acq. Libn., 1963–67; Circ. Lib., GA State Coll., 1959–63. **Educ.:** High Point Coll., 1954–57, AB (Soc. Std.); Univ. of NC, 1957–63, MS (LS). **Orgs.:** ALA. **Activities:** 1; 15, 20, 46; 55, 56 **Addr.:** P.O. Box 893, Laramie, WY 82070.

Stibbe, Hugo L. P. (My. 6, 1934, Semarang, Indonesia) Chief, Documtn. Cntrl. Sect., Natl. Map Coll., Pub. Arch. of Can., 1972–; Univ. Map Cur., Univ. of AB, 1966–71. **Educ.:** Univ. of AB, 1960–64, BSc (Geo.); Univ. of Utrecht, Netherlands, 1971–76, PhD (Cartography). **Orgs.:** Assn. Can. Map Libs.: VP (1970–71); Pres. (1971–72); Natl. Un. Cat. Com. (Ch., 1972–74); various ofcs. IFLA: Geo. and Map Libs. Sect., Mem. Stdg. Adv. Com. (1975–); and Stdg. Com. (Ch., 1981–); Spec. Libs. Div., Coord. Bd. (Secy., 1981–); Jt. Working Grp., Ch.; various ofcs. Can. Cartograph. Assn. Anglo-Amer. Cat. Com. for Cartograph. Mtrls. **Pubns.:** "Bibliographic Control of Cartographic Materials in Canada," *Information Is Power: The Ontario Library Association 1978 Conference Papers* (1979); various mono. **Activities:** 1, 2; 17, 20, 41; 56, 62, 70 **Addr.:** National Map Collection, Public Archives of Canada, 395 Wellington St., Ottawa, ON K1A 0N3 Canada.

Stickel, Donald Albert (Je. 27, 1953, Kalamazoo, MI) Asst. Life Sci. Libn., Purdue Univ., 1977–; Ref. Libn., Kearney State Coll., 1976–77. **Educ.:** Kalamazoo Valley Cmnty. Coll., 1971–73; West. MI Univ., 1973–75, BA (Bio.), 1975–76, MSL (Libnshp.). **Orgs.:** SLA: Dir.-At-Lg. (1980–81); Prog. Com. (1979–80). **Activities:** 1, 12; 22, 31, 39; 58, 82, 91 **Addr.:** Life Science Library, Purdue University Libraries, West Lafayette, IN 47907.

Stickel, William Robinson (Ja. 25, 1926, Newark, NJ) Msc. Catlgr., NY Pub. Lib. Cat. Dept., 1980–; Msc. Catlgr., Long Island Univ., Brooklyn Ctr., 1978–80; Catlgr., Msc. Libn., St. Peter's Coll., 1971–78; Ref. Libn., Seton Hall Univ., 1965–66; Art Libn. Asst., Queen's Coll., 1965–66; Ref. Libn., Orange Pub. Lib., 1963–64; Recat. Proj., Bloomfield Coll. Lib., 1962–63. **Educ.:** Princeton Univ., 1947–50, AB (Msc.); Yale Univ., NY Univ., 1951–58, MA; St. John's Univ., 1963–65, MLS; various crs. **Orgs.:** Msc. LA. NJ LA. NY Tech. Srvs. Libns. Assn. Amer. Musicological Socty.: NY Chap. Amer. Gld. of Organists: NJ Chap. **Activities:** 1; 20, 46; 56, 80, 87 **Addr.:** 179 S. Harrison St., Apt. 503, East Orange, NJ 07018.

Stickley, Beverly A. (Je. 12, 1949, Harrisburg, PA) Church Libn., Albany Park Luth. Church, 1975–; Pers. Libn., N. Park Coll., 1972–75; HS Libn., Halifax Area HS, 1970–71. **Educ.:** Shippensburg State Coll., 1967–70, BS (Eng., LS); Univ. of Pittsburgh, 1971–72, MLS (Ref.). **Orgs.:** CSLA. Luth. LA. **Honors:** Beta Phi Mu. **Pubns.:** "For Those Odds and Ends... A Vertical File in Your Library," *Church and Synogogue Libs.* (Ja.–F. 1978); "Pentecost," *Lrng. With* (My. 1981); various reviews. **Activities:** 1, 12; 15, 42, 44; 90 **Addr.:** 5846 N. Spaulding Ave., Chicago, IL 60659.

Stickman, James S. (Ap. 7, 1948, Waverly, IA) RLIN Coord., CO State Univ., 1980–, Asst. Cat. Libn., Bibl. Systs., 1979–, Prin. Proj. Supvsr., HEA Title II–C, Gvt. Docum. Cat. Proj., 1978–81, OCLC Coord., 1977–80, Asst. Cat. Libn., Serials, 1975–79; Asst. Cat. Libn., Univ. of WI, 1972–75. **Educ.:** Univ. of North. IA, 1966–70, BA (Eng.); Univ. of IA, 1970–72, MA (LS). **Orgs.:** ALA. CO LA: Autom. and Tech. Srvs. Div. (VP, Ch.-elect, 1981–); Cat. Interest Grp., Secy. (1977–78), Ch. (1978–79); Tech. Srvs. RT (Secy., 1979–80). **Activities:** 1; 20, 44, 46; 55, 56 **Addr.:** 1625 W. Elizabeth J–1, Fort Collins, CO 80521.

Stieber, Michael Thomas (D. 6, 1943, Peoria, IL) Archvst. and Sr. Resrch. Sci., Hunt Inst. for Bot. Documtn., Carnegie-Mellon Univ., 1977–; Resrch. Assoc., Bot., Carnegie Musm. of Nat. Hist., 1978–; HS Bio. Instr., St. Viator HS, 1974–77; Tech. Asst., Dept. of Bot., Smithsonian Inst., Sum. 1971–72; Bot. Instr., Cath. Univ. of Amer., Sum., 1970; HS Bio. Instr., Bishop McNamara HS, 1967–69. **Educ.:** Cath. Univ. of Amer., 1964–66, AB (Bio.), 1966–67, MS (Syst. Bot.); Univ. of MD, 1970–75, PhD (Syst. Bot.). **Orgs.:** SAA: Arch. of Sci. Com. (1977–79); Mid–Atl. Reg. Arch. Conf. Socty. for the Bibl. of Nat. Hist. Intl. Assn. for Plant Taxonomy. Amer. Socty. of Plant Taxonomists. Assn. for Tropical Bot., Inc. **Honors:** Natl. Sci. Fdn., Resrch. Grant, 1970. **Pubns.:** "The Vascular Flora of Anne Arundel County Maryland," *Castanea* (1971); "Mary Agnes Chase, 1869-1963," *Notable Amer. Women* (1980); jt. auth., "Guide to the Botanical Records and Papers in the Archives of the Hunt Institute, Pt. 1," *Huntia* (1981); various papers, reviews. **Activities:** 2, 5; 15, 41, 45; 85, 95-Biog. and Iconography of Botanists. **Addr.:** Hunt Institute for Botanical Documentation, Carnegie-Mellon University, Pittsburgh, PA 15213.

Stieda, Sieglinde (My. 9, 1942, Stettin, Germany) Ville de Montreal, Bib. Pub., 1981; Radio Can./CBC, Bib., 1981; Sch. Dist. Lib. Supvsr., Roman Cath. Sch. Bd., Humber-St. Barbe, 1972–75; Catlgr., Univ. de Montreal, 1971–72; Tchr., Roman Cath. Sch. Bd., 1969–70; Biblgphr., Humber-St. Barbe, Meml. Univ. of NF, 1969; Chld. Libn., NY Pub. Lib., 1966–68. **Educ.:** Univ. of MB, 1960–62; Univ. of BC, 1962–64, BA (Eng., Grmn. Lit.), 1965–66, BLS; Meml. Univ. of NF, 1975–77, MEd (Educ.); various crs. **Orgs.:** Bibl. Socty. of Can. ASTED. Can. LA: Sch. Dist. Lib. Supvsr. Com. (Ch., 1974–75). Can. Resrch. Socty. for Chld. Lit.: Fndr. (1979), *Nsltr.* Ed. (1979–). Various other orgs. Socty. for Intercult. Educ., Trng., and Resrch. Can. Fed. of Univ. Women. **Pubns.:** *Directory of Canadian School District Library Supervisors* (1975); *A Basic Resource List for the Elementary Schools Under the R.C. School Board* (1973); european correspondent, managing ed., *Film Lib. Qtly.* (1968); "The Book: An Extension of the Eye," *The Muse* (F. 4, 1969); "TV as a Library Medium," *Film Lib. Qtly.* (Spr. 1969); various articles, papers, ed. projs. **Activities:** 1, 9; 21, 37, 41; 56, 57, 67 **Addr.:** 3181 Edouard Montpetit, #16, Montreal, PQ H3T 1K3 Canada.

Stieg, Margaret F. (My. 20, 1942, Utica, NY) Asst. Prof., LS, Columbia Univ., 1975–; Asst. Prof., LS, Univ. of AL, 1972–75; Ref. Libn., Harvard Coll. Lib., 1968–71. **Educ.:** Harvard Univ., 1959–63, AB (Gvt.); Columbia Univ., 1963–64, MS (LS); Univ. of CA, Berkeley, 1964–70, MA, PhD (Hist.). **Orgs.:** ALA: LRRT (Secy.-Treas., 1980–); Ref. and Subscrpn. Bks. Review Com. (1975–79). SAA. Amer. Hist. Assn. **Pubns.:** Ed., *The Diary of John Harington, M.P., 1646-1653* (1977); jt. ed., "Libraries and Society: Research and Thought," *Lib. Trends* (Win. 1979); "The Nineteenth-Century Information Revolution," *Jnl. of Lib. Hist.* (Win. 1980); "In Defense of Problems: The Classical Method of Teaching Reference," *Jnl. of Educ. for Libnshp.* (Win. 1980); "Continuing Education and the Reference Librarian in the Academic and Research Library," *Lib. Jnl.* (D. 15, 1980). **Activities:** 11; 73 **Addr.:** School of Library Service, Columbia University, New York, NY 10027.

Stiegemeyer, Nancy Trustee, Cape Girardeau (MO) Pub. Lib., Pres., 1970, 1978. **Educ.:** SE MO Univ., 1948, BA, 1949, BS. **Orgs.:** ALA: Com. on Appts. (1980–82); ALTA, Pres. (1981–82); VP-Pres. Elect (1980–81); Budget Com. (Ch., 1981); Other coms. MO LA: Trustee Div. (Pres., 1972); Legis. Com. WHCLIS: Del. SE MO Lib. Syst. Bd.: Pres. **Honors:** MO LA, Hon. Awd., 1976. **Pubns.:** Contrib., *Library Trustee* (1979); *Show Me* (1978). **Activities:** 9; 47 **Addr.:** 215 Camellia Dr., Cape Girardeau, MO 63701.*

Stievater, Susan M. (Ja. 6, 1939, Buffalo, NY) Assoc. Libn., Ref., SUNY, Buffalo, 1966–. **Educ.:** Daemen Coll., 1956–63, AB (Soc. Std.); SUNY, Geneseo, 1964–67, MLS. **Orgs.:** ALA. NYLA. West. NY Lib. Resrcs. Cncl.: Cont. Ed. Com. (Ch., 1978–80). SUNY LA. Various other orgs. AAUW: Buffalo Branch (3rd VP, 1978–80). Creat. Educ. Fndn.: Creat. Problem Solving Inst. (Planner, 1972–); (colleague, 1977). **Pubns.:** "Online Revolutions in Creative Studies," *Jnl. of Creat. Behavior* (1980); indxr., biblgphr., *Jnl. of Creat. Bhvr* (1971–). **Activities:** 1; 31, 39, 41; 92 **Addr.:** E. H. Butler Library, SUNY College at Buffalo, 1300 Elmwood Ave., Buffalo, NY 14222.

Stifflear, Allan J. (Ap. 23, 1939, Central Bridge, NY) Dir., Jt. Lib., Episcopal Dvnty. Sch. and Weston Sch. of Theo., 1976–81, Head Catlgr., 1974–75; Head, Tech. Srvs., Newton Coll., 1973–74; Catlgr., Boston Coll., 1970–73. **Educ.:** SUNY, Albany, 1959–61, BS (Educ.); Nashotah Hse., 1962–65, MDiv; SUNY, Albany, 1968–70, MLS. **Orgs.:** ALA. ATLA. **Activities:** 1; 15, 17, 20 **Addr.:** 438 N.E. 7th Ave., Ft. Lauderdale, FL 33301.

Stiffler, Stuart A. (Ja. 16, 1934, St. Louis, MO) Dir., Lib. Srvs., Cornell Coll., 1977–; Dir. of Lib., Behrend Coll., PA State Univ., 1973–77; Dir. of Lib., Findlay Coll., 1968–73; Assoc. Dir., Hiram Coll., 1959–68. **Educ.:** Hiram Coll., 1951–55, BA (Hist.); West. Rsv. Univ., 1956–57, MA (Hist.); MSLS. **Orgs.:** ALA. IA LA. AAUP. **Pubns.:** "The Library, The Scholar and The Book Collection," *Lib. Coll. Jnl.* (1970); "A Philosophy of Book Selection for Smaller Academic Libraries," *Coll. & Resrch. Libs.* (My. 1963); "Notes on an Approach to Book Selection and Library Education," *Jnl. of Educ. for Libnshp.* (Fall 1971). **Activities:** 1; 15, 39 **Addr.:** 314 A Ave. S., Mt. Vernon, IA 52314.

Stiles, Muriel Holm (S. 8, 1927, Gardner, MA) Lib. Dir., Beaman Meml. Pub. Lib., 1969–. **Educ.:** Tufts Coll., 1945–49, BA (Soclgy.); Simmons Coll., 1978, MLS; State Coll. at Worcester, MA, 1967–70 (LS). **Orgs.:** Ctrl. Reg. Adv. Cncl.: Ch. (1975–77). MA LA. New Eng. LA. ALA. Frnds. of Beauman Meml. Pub. Lib.: Liaison (1981–). First Congregational Church: Bd. of Church and Cmnty. (1977–78); Diaconate (1979–). Woman's Club of W. Boylston: 2nd VP (1969–71); 1st VP (1971–73); Pres. (1973–75); Pub. Affairs Ch. (1979–81); Fed. Secy. (1975–77). **Activities:** 9; 17 **Addr.:** 36 Woodland Heights Dr., West Boylston, MA 01583.

Stiles, William G. (D. 3, 1924, London, Eng.) Chief, Info. Dssm. Div., Lib. of Parlmt., 1974–, Agency Libn., Can. Intl. Dev. Agency, 1971–74; Chief Libn., Cmrcl. Prod. Grp., Atomic Energy of Can., 1965–71; Libn., Uplands Branch Natl. Sci. Lib., 1963–65; Catlgr., Natl. Lib. of Can., 1959–63; Libn., Pembroke Pub. Lib., 1958–59; Libn., various libs. in Eng., 1951–58. **Educ.:** Carleton Univ.; LA UK, 1959, Fellow. **Orgs.:** LA UK. SLA: Nuc. Sci. Div. (1969–70), Com. on the Role of the Divs. (1972). Can. LA: Intl. Rel. Com. (Secy., 1972–75). Can. Assn. Info. Sci. Can. Assn. of Spec. Libs. and Info. Srvs.: Awd. Com. (1979–80). Various other orgs. **Pubns.:** "Charging by a Simple Exchange Principle," *LA Rec.* (D. 1957); "Organic and Inorganic," *Asst. Libn.* (Ap. 1958); "Ranganathan Re-focussed," *ON Lib. Review* (N. 1958); "Freedom of Information and our State Libraries," *Can. Lib. Jnl.* (D. 1980); reviews. **Activities:** 4, 12; 17, 30, 39; 57, 78, 92 **Addr.:** Library of Parliament, Parliamentary Bldgs., Ottawa, ON K1A 0A9 Canada.

Still, F. Claire (Je. 29, 1916, Hastings, NE) Med. Ref., Cat. Libn., Stanford Univ., 1969–. **Educ.:** Univ. of NE, 1934–38, AB (Soclgy.); Cath. Univ. of Amer., 1938–39, 1943–44, MSSW (Soc. Work); Univ. of CA, Berkeley, 1968–69, MLS; Med. LA, Cert. **Orgs.:** Med. LA. Stanford Hist. Socty. AAUW. **Pubns.:** "A

PROFESSIONAL ACTIVITIES: Institutions: 1. Acad. lib.; 2. Arch.; 3. Assn.; 4. Fed./Gvt. lib.; 5. Inst. lib.; 6. Mfr./Suppl.; 7. Milit. lib.; 8. Musm.; 9. Pub. lib.; 10. Sch. lib.; 11. Sch. of lib. sci.; 12. Spec. lib.; 13. State lib.; 14. (other). **Functions/Activities:** 15. Acq./Col. dev.; 16. Adult srvs.; 17. Admin.; 18. Apprais.; 19. Archit./Bldgs.; 20. Cat./Class.; 21. Chld. srvs.; 22. Circ.; 23. Cons./Pres.; 24. Consult.; 25. Cont. ed.; 26. Educ. lib. sci.; 27. Ext. srvs.; 28. Fund/Grants; 29. Gvt. pubs.; 30. Indx./Abs.; 31. Instr. lib. use; 32. Media srvs.; 33. Micro.; 34. Netwks./Coop.; 35. Persnl.; 36. PR; 37. Publshg.; 38. Recs. mgt.; 39. Ref. srvs.; 40. Repro.; 41. Resrch.; 42. Review.; 43. Secur.; 44. Serials; 45. Spec. col.; 46. Tech. srvs.; 47. Trustees/Bds.; 48. YA srvs.; 49. (other).

Women's Lib Centennial," *Stanford M.D.* (Spr. 1976). **Activities:** 1; 20, 39; 80, 73 **Addr.:** 440 Ravenswood #8, Menlo Park, CA 94025.

Stillman, June S. (Je. 27, 1929, Webster, FL) Head, Ref. Dept., Univ. of Ctrl. FL, 1968–; Asst. Libn., Orlando Jr. Coll., 1963–68; Libn., Rogers Jr. HS, 1956–57; Libn., Sunrise Jr. HS, 1954–57; Libn., Williston HS, 1951–54. **Educ.:** FL State Univ., 1949–51, BA (LS), 1966, MA (LS). **Orgs.:** ALA. SE LA. FL LA. FL Lib. Orien. Instr. Clearinghse.: Dir. (1977–). **Honors:** Beta Phi Mu, 1966. **Pubns.:** "Library Instruction in Florida's Academic Libraries," *FL Libs.* (Jl. 1977); *Orientation/Instruction in Florida's Academic Libraries–a Directory* (1978). **Activities:** 1; 31, 39 **Addr.:** Library, University of Central Florida, P.O. Box 25000, Orlando, FL 32816.

Stillman, Mary Elizabeth (O. 31, 1929, Philadelphia, PA) Prof., Dir. of Lib., Albright Coll., 1972–; Asst. Prof., Drexel Univ., 1968–72; Dir., Resrch. Lib., Export-Import Bank of the U.S., 1965–68; Dir., Educ. and Libs., U.S. Air Frc., Logistics Cmnd., Ankara, 1960–63; Admin. Libn., Fifth Air Frc., Korea and Japan, 1953–59, Regimental Libn., U.S. Nvl. Trng. Ctr., Bainbridge, MD, 1952–53. **Educ.:** Wilson Coll., 1946–50, AB (Classics); Drexel Univ., 1952–53, MS (LS); Univ. of IL, 1963–65, PhD (LS). **Orgs.:** PA LA: Dir. (1974–79). ALA: Subscrpn. Bks. Review Com. (1969–73, 1975–79). Colloquium on Info. Sci., Inc.: Dir. (1978–80), Treas. (1979–80). Human Rel. Cncl. of Berks Cnty. AAUP. Hist. Socty. of Berks Cnty. **Honors:** H. W. Wilson, Lib. Performance Awd., 1980. PA LA, Cert. of Merit, 1980. **Pubns.:** Ed., *Pacific Air Force Bibliography Project* (1956–58); ed., *Drexel Lib. Qtly.* (1969–72); ed., *PA LA Bltn.* (1974–77, 1978–79). **Activities:** 1; 17 **Addr.:** Albright College, Reading, PA 19604.

Stillwell, Charlotte B. (Wabash Cnty., IL) Ref. Libn., Cook Cnty. Law Lib., 1967–; Libn., U.S. Railroad Retirement Bd., 1955–67; Libn., U.S. P.O. Dept., DC, 1948–55; Chief Clerk, U.S. Attorneys Ofc., N. Dist. of IN, 1929–48. **Educ.:** Univ. of IN; Univ. of IL. **Orgs.:** SLA. AALL. **Pubns.:** Jt. auth., *The Constitution of Illinois: A Selective Bibliography* (1970); "Identifying and Acquiring Federal Government Documents," *Law Lib. Jnl.* 4–15–442. **Activities:** 4, 9; 29, 41; 77 **Addr.:** Cook County Law Library, 2900 Richard J. Daley Civic Center, Chicago, IL 60602.

Stine, Diane (My. 13, 1950, Chicago, IL) Head, Serials Cat. Team, Univ. of NM Lib., 1979–; Catlgr., Ctr. for Resrch. Libs., 1977–79; Copy Catlgr., Northwest. Univ. Lib., 1972–77. **Educ.:** Univ. of IL, 1968–72, BA (Russ.); Northwest. Univ., 1973–74, MA (Slavic Lit., Ling.); Rosary Coll., 1975–77, MLS. **Orgs.:** ALA. NM LA: Pubn. and Mailing Com. (1980–). **Pubns.:** "Cataloging Serials in Microform under AACR 2," *Serials Libn.* (Spr. 1981). **Activities:** 1; 20, 44; 55, 66 **Addr.:** University of New Mexico Library, Albuquerque, NM 87131.

Stines, Joe Robert (Ag. 27, 1952, Gastonia, NC) Chld. Libn., Sheppard Meml. Lib., 1976–, E. Branch Libn., 1974–75. **Educ.:** E. Carolina Univ., 1972–74, BS (LS, Hist.); Univ. of TN, 1975–76, MSLS (Lib. Info. Sci.). **Orgs.:** ALA. NC LA: Chld. Srvs. Sect. (Ch., 1977–79). Chld. Lit. Assn. Natl. Assn. for the Prsrvn. and Perpet. of Storytel. **Pubns.:** *Going It Together; the Library and the Community* (1977). **Activities:** 9; 21 **Addr.:** Sheppard Memorial Library, P.O. Drawer 7207, Greenville, NC 27834.

Stith, Janet Barcley (Jl. 31, 1945, St. Marys, WV) Asst. Dir., Med. Ctr. Lib., Univ. of KY, 1976–, Extramural Coord., 1972–, Head, Pub. Srvs., 1974–76, Ref. Libn., 1973–74, Acq. Libn., 1971–73. **Educ.:** Glenville State Coll., 1965–68, BA (Educ.); Univ. of KY, 1970–71, MSLS; WV Univ., 1968–71, MA (Educ.). **Orgs.:** Med. LA. KY LA: PR (1980–83). SLA: KY Chap. (Pres., 1979–80). **Honors:** Beta Phi Mu. **Pubns.:** "Development and Evaluation of a Small Ready-Reference Library Collection for a Rural Practice," *Bltn. Med. LA* (Ap. 1979). **Activities:** 1, 12; 17, 24; 80 **Addr.:** Medical Center Library, University of Kentucky, Lexington, KY 40536.

Stiverson, Gregory A. (Je. 17, 1946, Tonasket, WA) Asst. State Archvst., MD Hall of Recs., 1975–; Assoc. Resrch. Hist., Colonial Williamsburg Fndn., 1973–75. **Educ.:** Univ. of WA, 1964–68, BA (Hist.); Johns Hopkins Univ., 1968–73, PhD (Hist., U.S., Colonial). **Orgs.:** SAA. Assocs. of the Natl. Agr. Lib.: Adv. Ed. Bd. **Honors:** Phi Beta Kappa, 1968; Ford Fndn., Fellow, 1971; Woodrow Wilson Fndn., Fellow, 1972. **Pubns.:** *Poverty In A Land of Plenty: Tenancy in Eighteenth-Century Maryland* (1977); jt. auth., *Maryland. A New Guide to the Old Line State* (1976); jt. auth., *William Paca. A Biography* (1976); jt. auth., "General Smallwood's Recruits: The Peacetime Career of the Revolutionary War Private," *William and Mary Qtly.* (Jan. 1973); "Books Both Useful and Entertaining: Reading Habits in Eighteenth-Century Virginia," *Southeast. Libn.* (Win. 1975); various articles. **Activities:** 2; 17, 23, 37; 55, 57, 63 **Addr.:** Maryland Hall of Records, P.O. Box 828, Annapolis, MD 21404.

Stock, Sr. Gertrude M. (Ja. 10, 1912, Ottawa, ON) HS Libn., Notre Dame HS, Toronto, 1965–; Prin., St. Patrick's Sch., Rosemere, PQ, 1963–64; Vice-Prin., Darcy McGee HS, 1960–63; Tchr., St. Paul's Acad., Montreal, 1959–60. **Educ.:** Univ. of Ottawa, 1944–47, BA (Eng., Phil.), 1947–51, (Phil., Eng., Math., Fr.); Syracuse Univ., 1968–71, MSLS; Fac. of Educ., Toronto, 1966–68, Intermediate and Spec. Cert. in HS Libnshp.; 1950–75, various tchg. certs. **Orgs.:** Intl. Assn. Sch. Libnshp. Can. LA. ON LA. Metro. Sep. Sch. Bd. Libns. Assn.: HS Div. (Area Rep., 1970). Various other orgs. ON Eng. Cath. Tchrs. Assn.: Dist. Ch. (1956–58); Educ. Resrch. Com. (Ch., 1956–59). Intl. Readg. Assn. Syracuse Univ. Sch. of Info. Sci. Alum. Assn. Youth Corps of Toronto. **Activities:** 10; 15, 39, 48; 66, 89, 90 **Addr.:** Notre Dame High School, 12 Malvern Ave., Toronto, ON M4E 3E1 Canada.

Stock, Jonathan Curtis (Je. 15, 1942, New Haven, CT) Lib. Dir., CT State Lib., Stamford Law Unit, 1979–; Asst. Law Libn., CT State Lib., New Haven Law Unit, 1976–79; Adj. Asst. Prof., Post Coll., Legal Resrch., 1978; Asst. Prof., Sacred Heart Univ., Bridgeport, CT, 1968–75. **Educ.:** Bowdoin Coll., 1960–64, BA (Eng.); South. CT State Coll., 1974–76, MLS; Trinity Coll., Hartford, 1964–65, MA (Eng.); Trinity Coll., Dublin, 1965–68, MLitt (Eng.). **Orgs.:** AALL. South. New Eng. Law LA. ALA. South. CT State Coll.: Alum. Student LA. **Honors:** Beta Phi Mu, 1977. **Pubns.:** "Modern Fiction: The Divided Spirit," *The Relig. Bk. Guide* (Mr.–Ap. 1972); "My Last Will and Testament," *The Dublin Mag.* (Fall 1971); assoc. ed., amer. rep., *The Dublin Mag.* (1971–74). **Activities:** 12, 13; 15, 17, 20; 77 **Addr.:** P.O. Box 1554, Samp Mortar Station, Fairfield, CT 06430.

Stockard, Joan (My. 20, 1930, Woburn, MA) Readers Srvs. Libn., Wellesley Coll., 1972–. **Educ.:** Smith Coll., 1947–51, AB (Eng.); Simmons Coll., 1968–72, MSLS. **Orgs.:** ALA: ACRL/Bibl. Instr. Sect. (Secy., 1979–80), New Eng. Chap., Pres. (1982–83), Nsltr. Ed. (1977–79). **Honors:** Beta Phi Mu, 1972. **Pubns.:** Cmplr., *A Directory of Bibliographic Instruction Programs in New England Academic Libraries* (1978); jt. auth., "Adding to Knowledge about Document Exposure Counts in Three Academic Libraries: Circulation and In-Library Use," *Quantitative Measurements and Dynamic Library Services* (1978); "Selective Survey of MARC Literature," *Lib. Resrcs. & Tech. Srvs.* (1971); contrib., *MLA Intl. Bibl.* (1978–); reviews. **Activities:** 1; 31, 39 **Addr.:** 79 Adams St., Lexington, MA 02173.

Stockdale, Kay Little (N. 3, 1942, Ft. Jackson, SC) Libn., Hist. Fndn. of Presby. and Reformed Churches, 1972–; Eng. Instr., Stillman Coll., 1971–72; Prog. Dir., Ridgecrest Area Residence Hall, Univ. of AL, 1969–71; Tchr., Druid HS, 1968–69; Tchr., Greene Cnty. Ctrl. HS; Tchr., N. Johnston HS. **Educ.:** Atl. Christ. Coll., 1961–65, AB (Eng., Phys. Educ.); Univ. of AL, 1969–72, MA (LS); OH Hist. Socty. Lib. and Arch. Wkshp., 1974. **Orgs.:** ALA. SE LA. WNCLA: Secy. (1981–82). ATLA: Mem. Com. (1979–). Various other orgs. AAUW: Tuscaloosa, AL Branch (Pres., 1970–72); ALA Div. (VP, 1972); Asheville, NC Branch, Bd. (1973–79); NC Div., Bd. (1975–79). **Pubns.:** "Tuscaloosa (AAUW) Branch History," *A Half Century of AAUW in Alabama* (1975); "Preserving Periodicals at The Historical Foundation," *NC Libs.* (Spr. 1979). **Activities:** 12; 44, 46, 49-Photographs; 73, 90 **Addr.:** Historical Foundation of Presbyterian and Reformed Churches, Box 847, Montreat, NC 28757.

Stockey, Edward A. (O. 29, 1949, Pittsburgh, PA) Head, Data Srvs. Dir., IN State Lib., 1979–; Mgr., INCOLSA Prcs. Ctr., 1977–79; Admin. Asst., Lrng. Resrc. Ctr., Cmnty. Coll. of Philadelphia, 1976–77; Lib. and Info. Consult., Boone, Young, and Assocs., 1976–77. **Educ.:** IN Univ., 1967–71, AB (Psy.); Drexel Univ., 1975–76, MLS (Lib., Info. Sci.); Univ. of PA, 1972–75, Mstrs. (Classical Archlg.). **Orgs.:** ALA: RTSD, Prcs. Ctr. Dir. Com. (Vice-Ch., Ch.-Elect, 1978–79)/Cat. and Class. Sect., Nom. Com. IN LA: Plng. Com. (1977–81); Anl. Conf. Com. (1979–80). **Pubns.:** *An Introduction to Data Base Searching: A Self-Instruction Manual* (1977); "Contributions of Small Libraries to State-wide Resource Sharing," *Pub. Lib. Qtly.* (Spr. 1980); "How to Choose a Processing Service," *Hoosier Sch. Libs.* (F. 1978). **Activities:** 13, 14-Netwk.; 15, 41, 46; 56, 75 **Addr.:** Indiana State Library, 140 N. Senate Ave., Indianapolis, IN 46204.

Stockton, Gloria Jean (Ag. 21, 1948, Bakersfield, CA) Chief Libn., Ctrl. Circ., Green Lib., Stanford Univ., 1975–, Selector, Ling., 1975–77, Asst. Engin. Libn., 1972–74. **Educ.:** Univ. of CA, Berkeley, 1966–70, AB (Ling.), 1971–72, MLS; various insts., crs. **Orgs.:** ALA: LAMA/Circ. Srvs. Sect. (Vice-Ch./Ch.-Elect, 1981–82), Prog. Plng. Com. (Ch., 1978–79), Stats. Sect., Circ. Stats. Com. (1978–81). ASIS: Bay Area Chap. SLA: Bay Reg. Chap. Univ. of CA, Berkeley, Grad. Lib. Sch. Alumni Assn.: Bd. of Dirs. (1980–82). AAUP. **Activities:** 1; 17, 22; 55, 75, 92 **Addr.:** Central Circulation Dept., Green Library, Stanford University, Stanford, CA 94305.

Stoddard, William Sanford (Ag. 26, 1922, Kalamazoo, MI) Bus. Libn., MI State Univ., 1975–, Undergrad. Libn., 1969–74, Bus. Libn., 1965–69, Soc. Sci. Libn., 1956–65. **Educ.:** Univ. of MI, 1946–48, BBA (Bus.), 1948–49, MBA (Bus.), 1949–51, AMLS. **Orgs.:** ALA. MI LA: Treas. (1970–77); Acad. Div. (Ch., 1965–66); HQ and Fin. Com. (Ch., 1977–78); Anl. Conf. (Vice-Ch., 1966–67). Corres. Chess Leag. of Amer.: 1st VP (1975–76); Secy., Treas. (1976–). **Pubns.:** *A Selected List of Book and Periodicals in the Field of Business* (1966, 1968); *MI State Univ., Bus. Topics* (1950–69); reviews, various bks. **Activities:** 1; 24, 39, 41; 59, 77, 92 **Addr.:** Graduate School of Business Administration, Michigan State University, East Lansing, MI 48824.

Stoddart, Joan M. (Je. 22, 1947, St. Louis, MO) Ref. Libn., Eccles Hlth. Sci. Lib., Univ. of UT, 1978–; Lib. Mgr., Eimco PMD Resrch. Div., 1977–78; Ref. Libn., Univ. of Cincinnati Med. Ctr. Lib., 1977; Lib. Mgr., Inhalation Toxicology Resrch. Inst., 1973–77. **Educ.:** Univ. of WI, 1965–70, BA (Hist.); Rosary Coll., 1971–72, MALS; Med. LA, 1973, Cert. **Orgs.:** Med. LA. SLA. UT LA. **Activities:** 12; 31, 39; 64, 80, 91 **Addr.:** Eccles Health Sciences Library, University of Utah, Salt Lake City, UT 84112.

Stoffel, Lester L. (Ap. 16, 1920, Lakewood, OH) Exec. Dir., Suburban Lib. Syst., 1967–; Head Libn., Oak Park Pub. Lib., 1955–67; Head Libn., Easton Pub. Lib., 1949–55; Head Libn., Guernsey Cnty. Pub. Lib., 1946–49. **Educ.:** Wittenberg Coll., 1938–42, BA (Pol. Sci.); West. Rsv. Univ., 1946–47, BSLS. **Orgs.:** ALA: Pub. Lib. Div., Com. on Legis. (1965–66); Lib. Adm. Div. (Pres., 1971–72). IL LA: VP (1965). IL State Lib. Adv. Com.: Ch. (1972–74). **Honors:** IL LA, Libn. of the Yr., 1968. **Pubns.:** Jt. auth., *Public Libraries in Cooperative Systems* (1971); "The Suburban Library in the Metropolitan Community," *The Metropolitan Library* (1972). **Activities:** 9; 17, 19, 24, 35 **Addr.:** Suburban Library System, 125 Tower Dr., Burr Ridge, IL 60521.

Stoffle, Carla J. (Je. 19, 1943, Pueblo, CO) Asst. Chancellor for Educ. Srvs., Univ. of WI, Parkside, 1978–, Exec. Asst. to Chancellor, 1978, Asst. Dir., Lib./Lrng. Ctr., 1976–78, Head, Pub. Srvs. Div., 1973–76. **Educ.:** Univ. of CO, 1965, BA; Univ. of KY, 1969, MSLS; Univ. of WI, Madison, PhD Cand. (Educ. Admin.). **Orgs.:** ALA: ACRL, Pres. (1982–83) Coll. Lib. Sect. (Ch., 1979–80)/Bibl. Instr. Sect., Prog. Com. (1977–78), Exec. Com. (1978–81). Midwest Fed. of LA: Prog. Com. (Ch., 1978–79). WI LA: PR Com. (1977–78). WI Assn. of Acad. Libns.: Task Frc. on Instr. in Acad. Libs. (Ch., 1973–75). Various other orgs., ofcs. **Pubns.:** *Materials and Methods for Political Science Research* (1979); *Materials and Methods for History Research* (1978); *Administration of Government Documents Collections* (1974); "The Academic Library as a Teaching Library: A Role for the 1980s," *Lib. Trends* (Win. 1979); various articles. **Activities:** 1; 17, 31, 39 **Addr.:** University of Wisconsin-Parkside, P.O. Box 2000, WLLC 343, Kenosha, WI 53141.

Stoia, Joseph P. (D. 14, 1943, Detroit, MI) Med. Libn., Kettering Med. Ctr., 1972–; Libn., Spr. Valley Acad., 1968–72; Prin., Columbus Jr. Acad., 1966–68. **Educ.:** Andrews Univ., 1962–66, BA (Hist., LS); Wright State Univ., 1969–71, MEd (Sch. Admin., Supvsr. of Instr.); Univ. of Cincinnati, 1979, EEd (Curric., Instr., Hlth. Educ.). **Orgs.:** Med. LA. Miami Valley Assn. Hlth. Sci. Lib. Dayton-Miami Valley Cnsrtm. Dayton Area MEDLINE Cnsrtm. **Activities:** 12; 17, 20, 39; 68, 80 **Addr.:** Medical Library, Kettering Medical Center, 3535 Southern Blvd., Kettering, OH 45429.

Stoller, Irene (Edinburgh, Scotland) Asst. Dir., Madison Pub. Lib., 1980–; Ext. Srvs. Admin., Phoenix Pub. Lib., 1979–80; Head, Ctrl. Lib., Contra Costa Cnty. Lib., 1976–79; Dir., Old Bridge Pub. Lib., 1971–75; Consult., Baker and Taylor, 1970; Dir., Cherry Hill Pub. Lib., 1962–70; Instr., various colls., 1965–71. **Educ.:** Rutgers Univ., 1950–61, BA (Soclgy., Pol. Sci.); Drexel Univ., 1961–62, MSLA; various crs. **Orgs.:** ALA: Adult Srvs. Div.; Assn. of Amer. Publshrs. Liaison Com. (1965–70), ERT (1969–); PLA, Org. Com. (1980–), Fiscal Emergency Com. (1981–). WI LA: Conf. Com. (1981). Various other orgs., ofcs. Amer. Cvl. Liberties Un. Burlington Cnty. Human Rel. Cncl. Frnds. of the Arboretum, Madison, WI. Leag. of Women Voters. **Honors:** Beta Phi Mu. **Pubns.:** Jt. auth., *The Trustee and Personnel* (1971). **Activities:** 9, 11; 15, 17, 26; 67 67. **Addr.:** Madison Public Library, 201 W. Mifflin St., Madison, WI 53703.

Stoller, Janet S. (N. 14, 1943, Aurora, IL) Corporate Libn., Mutual Life Insr. Co. of NY, 1974–; Asst. Med. Libn., Equitable Life Assurance Socty., 1971–74. **Educ.:** Univ. of FL, 1962–66, BA (Educ.); Queens Coll., 1969–71, MLS. **Orgs.:** Law LA Grt. NY. Amer. Socty. of Indxrs. SLA: Insr. Div. (Dir., 1977–78), IPI Online Com. (1979), *Insr. Per. Indx.* Indxr. (1974–79). **Pubns.:** Ed., *Insurance Periodicals Index*, 1979 (1980). **Activities:** 12; 15, 17, 39; 59, 76, 77 **Addr.:** Library 2-36, Mutual of New York, 1740 Broadway, New York, NY 10019.

Stoltz, James R. (Ag. 3, 1928, Stella, NE) Dir., Lib. Srvs., Clatsop Cmnty. Coll., 1976–; Dir., Crosby Lib., Gonzaga Univ., 1973–76; Cat. Libn., Marylhurst Coll., 1966–73; Libn., Molalla Grade Sch., 1959–66. **Educ.:** Peru State Coll., 1946–52, AB (Fr.), 1952–53, AB Educ (Educ.); Univ. of WA, 1964–67, MALibr (LS). **Orgs.:** ALA. OR LA. OR Cmnty. Coll. Libns.: Pres. (1978–79). **Activities:** 1, 10; 15, 17, 39; 55, 67 **Addr.:** 1680 Lexington Ave., Astoria, OR 97103.

Stone, Ann F. (My. 28, 1932, Henderson, NC) Persnl. Libn., Duke Univ., 1979–, Undergrad. Libn., 1959–79. **Educ.:** Wake Forest Univ., 1952–54, BA, summa cum laude (Eng.); Univ. of NC, 1965–70, MS (LS). **Orgs.:** ALA. NC LA. Duke Libns. Asm. **Honors:** Phi Beta Kappa, 1954; Beta Phi Mu, 1970. **Pubns.:** "Long-Range Planning: An Interim Report on the Duke Ex-

Special Subjects/Services: 50. Adult educ.; 51. Advert./Mktg.; 52. Aerosp.; 53. Agric.; 54. Area std.; 55. Arts/Hum.; 56. Autom.; 57. Bibl./Prtg.; 58. Bio. sci.; 59. Bus./Fin.; 60. Chem.; 61. Copyrt.; 62. Documtn.; 63. Educ.; 64. Engin.; 65. Env.; 66. Eth. grps.; 67. Film; 68. Food/Nutr.; 69. Geneal.; 70. Geo.; 71. Geol.; 72. Handcpd.; 73. Hist.; 74. Int. frdm.; 75. Info. sci.; 76. Insr.; 77. Law; 78. Legis.; 79. Math./Comp. sci.; 80. Med.; 81. Metals; 82. Nat. resrcs.; 83. Newsp.; 84. Nuc. sci.; 85. Oral hist.; 86. Petr./Energy; 87. Pharm.; 88. Phys./Astr./Math.; 89. Readg.; 90. Relig.; 91. Sci./Tech.; 92. Soc. sci.; 93. Telecom.; 94. Transp.; 95. (other).

Who's Who in Library and Information Services

perience," *NC Libs.* (Win. 1978). **Activities:** 1; 17, 35; 63 **Addr.:** 5114 Pine Trail Dr., Durham, NC 27712.

Stone, Carl (Je. 18, 19–, Spartanburg, SC) Dir., Anderson Cnty. Lib., 1974–; Ext. Libn., Richland Cnty. Pub. Lib., 1970–74; Ref. Libn., Sci. Lib., Univ. of GA, 1968–70. **Educ.:** Univ. of SC, 1963–67, AB (Hist.); Emory Univ., 1967–68, MLS (Libnshp.). **Orgs.:** SC LA: Admin. Sect. (Strg. Ch., 1978); JMRT (Ch., 1970–71); Pub. Lib. Sect. (Ch., 1980). SE LA: SC Mem. Ch. (1979–80); Ref. and Adult Srvs. Sect., Vice-Ch., Ch. ALA: LAMA, Archit. for Pub. Libs. Com. (1978–80); Chap. Cnclr. (1972–76); various other ofcs. **Activities:** 9; 17, 27; 91 **Addr.:** Anderson County Library, P.O. Box 4047, Anderson, SC 29622.

Stone, Elizabeth W. (Je. 21, 1918, Dayton, OH) Dean, Sch. of Lib. and Info. Sci., Cath. Univ. of Amer., 1981–, Ch., Grad. Dept. of Lib. and Info. Sci., Prof., 1972–80, Asst. to Ch., Assoc. Prof., 1967–71, 1963–67, Instr., Asst. to Ch., 1962–63; Lib. Sub., Pasadena Pub. Lib., 1953–60; Dir. of PR, Asst. to Pres., Univ. of Dubuque, 1942–46. **Educ.:** San Diego State Coll., 1934–36; Stanford Univ., 1936–37, AB (Hist.), 1937–38, MA (Hist.), Sec. Tchg. Cert.; Cath. Univ. of Amer., 1960–61, MLS; Amer. Univ., 1962–68, PhD (Pub. Admin.). **Orgs.:** ALA: Pres. (1981–82); Cncl. (1976–80); Lib. Admin. Div., Staff Dev. Com. (Ch., 1969–72); Prof. Ethics Com. (1976–78). DC LA: Pres. (1966–67), *Qtly. Jnl.* Ed. (1964–65). CLENE: Exec. Dir. (1975–79). AALS: Pres. (1974). SLA: DC Chap. (Pres., 1973–74). Various other orgs., ofcs. **Honors:** CLENE, Designated Fndr., 1980; Amer. Mothers, Inc., DC Mother of the Yr., (1980); Mem., Pres. Com. on Empl. of Handcpd. (1972–). Beta Phi Mu; other hons. **Pubns.:** *American Library Development 1600–1899* (1977); *Continuing Library Education as Viewed in Relation to Other Professional Education* (1975); "Educating Librarians and Information Scientists to Provide Information Services to Disabled Individuals," *Drexel Lib. Qtly.* (Ap. 1980); "Personnel Development and Continuing Education in Libraries," *Lib. Trends* (Jl. 1971); "Continuing Education for Librarians in the United States," *Advances in Librarianship* (1978); various other bks., articles. **Activities:** 9, 11; 17, 25, 41; 63, 72, 73 **Addr.:** School of Library and Information Science, The Catholic University of America, Washington, DC 20064.

Stone, Irene V. (Ja. 25, 1920, Sacramento, CA) Supvsg. Libn., Admin. Legis. Ref. Sect., CA State Lib., 1972–, Sr. Libn., 1971–72, Libn., 1968–71; Ref. Libn., Sacramento City Lib., 1942. **Educ.:** Univ. of CA, Berkeley, 1940, AB (Eng.), 1941–42, Cert. (LS). **Orgs.:** SLA: Legis. Ref. Libns. Sect. (Ch., 1975). Natl. Legis. Conf.: Legis. Ref. Libns. Sect. (Ch., 1974). Natl. Conf. of State Legislatures: Legis. Ref. Libns. Sect., Legis. Info. Needs Com., (1979–). CA State Interdepart. Resrch. Coord. Com.: Ch. (1979). Golden Empire Hlth. Syst. Agency. Sacramento Cnty. Hlth. Cncl. Various ofcs. **Activities:** 13; 15, 24, 39; 63, 78, 92 **Addr.:** Administrative Legislative Reference Section, California State Library, P.O. Box 2037, Sacramento, CA 95809.

Stone, William V. (Ja. 1, 1918, Danbury, CT) Libn. in Charge, St. John's Univ., Staten Island, NY, 1954–; Asst. Libn., Univ. of Bridgeport, 1950–54; Libn., U.S. Vets. Admin., Northport, NY, 1948–49; Libn., NY Pub. Lib., 1947–48. **Educ.:** Yale Univ., 1936–40, BA (Eng.), 1940–42, MA (Eng.); Columbia Univ., 1946–47, BLS. **Orgs.:** Cath. LA. **Honors:** Phi Beta Kappa, 1940; Chi Delta Theta, 1939. **Pubns.:** *The Loveliest and The Best* (1960); *Phantom of False Morning* (1946); jt. collaborator, *Our Pleasant Vices* (1941); *National Poetry Anthology, Teachers and Librarians Edition* (1952–); *Yanks in Britain* (1945). **Activities:** 1, 5, 9; 17, 20 **Addr.:** Loretto Memorial Library, 300 Howard Ave., Staten Island, NY 10301.

Stonehill, Helen (Ag. 18, 1924, Waco, TX) Chief Libn., ICD Rehab. and Resrch. Ctr., 1963–; Volun. Libn., Pub. Sch. 61, Manhattan, 1960–63; Asst. to Pres., Stonehill Art Studio, 1955–63; Mgr., Data Prcs. Unit, Volupte, Inc., 1946–50. **Educ.:** Brooklyn Coll., 1964–68, BA (Soclgy., Psy.); Pratt Inst., 1968–70, MLS (Lib., Info. Sci.); Med. LA, 1975, Cert. Grade 1 (Med. Libnshp); various crs. **Orgs.:** Med. LA: NY Grp., Pubcty. Ch. (1980); Mem. Ch. (1970–71); Hosplty. Ch. (1973). SLA: Soc. Sci. Grp. (Mem. Ch., 1976–77); Prog. Com. (1978–79). NY Lib. Club. Pratt Inst. Alum. Grp. **Pubns.:** Biblgphr., *Tower (Testing, Orientation and Work Evaluation in Rehabilitation)* (1967, 1974). **Activities:** 5, 12; 16, 39, 41; 72, 80, 92 **Addr.:** 245 Ave. C, New York, NY 10009.

Stoney, George Cashel (Jl. 1, 1916, Winston-Salem, NC) Prof., Film/TV, NY Univ., 1970–; Exec. Producer, "Challenge for Change," Natl. Film Bd., Can., 1968–70; Prefector, Germany, India, Japan, Intl. Sch. of Amer., 1967–68; Filmmaker in Residence, Stanford Univ., 1965–67; Pres., George C. Stoney Assocs., 1956–; various positions as consult. **Educ.:** Univ. of NC, 1933–37, AB (Eng.); NY Univ., New Sch. for Soc. Resrch., 1938–40 (Wrtg.); Balliol Coll., Oxford Univ., 1945–46; Univ. of London, 1947–48, Cert. (AV). **Orgs.:** Intl. Film Sems.: Bd. (1979–82). Indp. Cin. Artists and Producers. EFLA. NY State Cncl. on the Arts: Media Panel (1978–). NY Film Cncl.: Pres. (1980–82). **Honors:** 28 Film Fest. Awds., 1949–79; Natl. Fed. of Lcl. Cable Progmrs., Spec. Srv. Awd., 1978; Assn. of Indp. Vid. and Filmmakers, Srv. Awd., 1976; Amer. Film Fest., EFLA, numerous Blue Ribbon awds. **Pubns.:** "A Survey of Social Issue Films 1960 to Present," *Sightlines* (1978); "What Libraries Can Do About Cable TV," *Film Lib. Qtly.* (1975); producer, various films, prof. vid. tapes. **Activities:** 9; 24; 67, 85, 93 **Addr.:** 240 Waverly Pl., New York, NY 10014.

Stoops, Louise (Honolulu, HI) Chief Libn., Lehman Brothers Kuhn Loeb, 1977–; Libn., Baker, Weeks and Co., 1972–76; Libn., Dominick and Dominick, 1971–72; Libn., Cities Srv. Co., 1970–71; Chief Libn., Bache and Co., 1968–70; Chief Libn., U.S. Steel Corp., 1958–68; Libn., Advert. Dept., Eastman Kodak Co., 1954–57; Libn., Enoch Pratt Free Lib., 1952–54. **Educ.:** Univ. of AZ, 1943–46, BA (Eng.); Simmons Coll., 1951–52, MS (LS). **Orgs.:** SLA. NY LA: Dir. (1980–84). ASIS. Fncl. Women's Assn. of NY. **Pubns.:** Indxr., *Dollars and Sense of Business Film* (1956); "Is This a Problem?" *Spec. Libs.* (1964). **Activities:** 51, 59 **Addr.:** Lehman Bros. Kuhn Loeb, Inc., 55 Water St., New York, NY 10041.

Stoppel, Ellen Kaye (Vickers) (D. 27, 1934, Ewing, MO) Asst. Libn., Law Lib. Serials Libn., Assoc. Prof., Drake Univ., 1974–; Acq. Libn., Wilson Coll., 1972–73; Pub. Srvs. Libn., Westminster Coll., 1967–71; Libn., MO Sch. for the Deaf, 1966–67. **Educ.:** NE MO Univ., 1952–54, 1956–58, BS (Educ.); Univ. of Denver, 1969–70, MA (Libnshp.); AALL, 1977, Cert. Law Libn. **Orgs.:** AALL: Com., Index to Legal Per. (1975–78); Com., Rel. with Publshrs. and Dlrs. (1979–); Subcom. Wkshp. Rel. (Ch., 1980–); 1981 Anl. Mtg., Panel Org., Modrtr. AAUP. **Honors:** Beta Phi Mu. **Pubns.:** Reviewer, *Lib. Jnl.* **Activities:** 1; 15, 44, 46; 77 **Addr.:** Drake University, Law Library, Des Moines, IA 50311.

Stoppel, William A. (F. 22, 1934, Chicago, IL) Dir., Libs., Drake Univ., 1973–; Coll. Libn., Shippensburg State Coll., 1971–73; Dir., Jt. Libs., Westminster and William Woods Coll., 1967–71; Coll. Libn., Westminster Coll., 1966–67. **Educ.:** Cornell Coll., 1951–55, BA (Grmn. Lit.); Univ. of IA, 1956–64, MA, PhD (Grmn. Lit.); Univ. of Denver, 1965–66, MA (Libnshp.). **Orgs.:** ALA: ACRL. **Activities:** 1; 17 **Addr.:** 658 56th St., Des Moines, IA 50312.

Storie, Laura Elizabeth (South) (Ag. 18, 1921, Boone, NC) Media Coord., Statesville Sr. HS, 1961–, Tchr., 1960–61; Deputy Clerk, Superior Ct., Watauga Cnty., Boone, NC, 1957–59; Instr., Appalachian State Univ., 1956–57. **Educ.:** Appalachian State Univ., 1938–42, BS (Eng., Hist., Phys. Educ.), 1961–64, MS (LS). **Orgs.:** ALA. SE LA. NC LA: Hon. and Life Mem. Com. (1978–79). NC Assn. of Sch. Libns.: Awds. and Schol. Ch. (1965–71); *NC Assn. Sch. Libns. Bltn.* Ed. (1971–78). Natl. Educ. Assn.: NC Rcrt. Netwk. Rep. (1963–67). Delta Kappa Gamma: Vice-Ch. (1977–80); Eta State, Alpha Xi Chap. (Pres., 1980–82). NC Assn. of Educ.: Dist. Secy. (1963–64); Dist. Dept. Ch. (1965); Unit Treas. (1968–69); Unit Pres. (1970–71). **Honors:** NC Assn. of Educ., Lcl. Sch. Unit, Tchr. of the Yr., 1971. **Pubns.:** "First Library of North Carolina Established in 1715," *NC Libs.* (Spr. 1976). **Activities:** 10; 20, 31, 32, 48 **Addr.:** 514 Lakeside Dr., Statesville, NC 28677.

Stortz, Gene M. (Jl. 9, 1942, Kalamazoo, MI) Info. Retrieval Consult., CO State Lib., 1979–, Cont. Educ. Consult., 1975–77, Inst. Lib. Consult., 1968–75; Chld. Libn., Wayne Cnty. Libs., 1965–67. **Educ.:** MI State Univ., 1960–64, BS (Zlgy.); Univ. of MI, 1964–65, AMLS. **Orgs.:** CO LA: Educ. Com. (1974–77), Awds. Com. (1975–76). SLA: Cont. Educ. Com. (1977–79), Nsltr. Ed. (1978–80). CO Cncl. of Med. Libns. **Activities:** 13; 24, 25, 39 **Addr.:** Colorado State Library, 1362 Lincoln St., Denver, CO 80203.

Story, Allen C. (D. 21, 1950, Suffolk, VA) Asst. Libn., U.S. Internal Revenue Srv., 1980–; Libn., Pension Benefit Guaranty Corp., 1976–80; Dir., Circ. and Supvsr., Ref. Marshall-Wythe Law Lib., Coll. of William and Mary, 1973–75. **Educ.:** Coll. of William and Mary, 1969–73, BBA (Bus. Admin.); Univ. of MD, 1975–76; MLS. **Orgs.:** AALL. DC Law Libns. Socty.: Schols. and Grants Com. (Ch., 1981–82). ALA. DC LA. **Pubns.:** "Microphobia in the Legal Profession," *70 Law Lib. Jnl.* (F. 1977); "Leo in Libraryland," *7 Amer. Libs.* (O. 1976). **Activities:** 4; 17, 46; 59, 77 **Addr.:** U.S. Internal Revenue Service Library, CC: A: LIB: Rm. 4324, 1111 Constitution Ave. N.W., Washington, DC 20224.

Stouffer, Isabelle (D. 31, 1912, Pittsburgh, PA) Asst. Libn., Head Catlgr. Emeritus, Princeton Theo. Semy., 1979–, Asst. Libn., Head Catlgr., 1949–79, Head Catlgr., 1936–49, Spec. Catlgr., 1935–36. **Educ.:** Wilson Coll., 1930–34, AB (Eng. Lit.); Drexel Inst., 1934–35, BS (LS). **Orgs.:** ALA. ATLA: Exec. Com. (1968–70). NY Tech. Srvs. Libns. **Activities:** 1; 20, 46; 90 **Addr.:** 49 Palmer Sq. W., Princeton, NJ 08540.

Stough, Helen E. (Ag. 15, 1949, Zaire) Head, Ext. Srvs., Aurora Pub. Lib., 1979–; Chld. Libn., Helen M. Plum Meml. Lib., 1975–79. **Educ.:** Greenville Coll., 1967–71, BA (Eng.); Rosary Coll., River Forest, IL, 1974–75, MALS. **Orgs.:** IL LA: VP, Pres.-Elect (1979–81). Prairie State Story Leag.: Chld. Libns. Sect. (Pres., 1978–80). Lib. Admin. Cncl. of North. IL: "Rainbow of Resources" Ed. (1978–80). **Activities:** 9; 21, 27, 48; 72 **Addr.:** 1240 Exeter Ct., Wheaton, IL 60187.

Stout, Chester Bernard (My. 31, 1918, Jacksonville, TX) Dir., McKinley Meml. Lib., 1969–; Asst. Libn., Ctrl. MO State Univ., 1963–67. **Educ.:** Auburn Univ., 1957–60, BS (Indus. Mgt.); LA State Univ., 1961–63, MS (LS, Econ.); Ctrl. MO State Univ., 1965–67 (Bus., Econ.); Case West. Rsv. Univ., 1968–76, PhD (Info. Sci., LS). **Orgs.:** ALA: Micro. Task Frc. (Ch., 1970–71). OH LA: Reg. Mtgs. (Ch., 1974). Trumbull Cnty. LA: Pres. (1975). Northeast. OH Reg. Lib. Srv.: Admin. Agent (1975–). Mason. Shriner. Loyal Ord. of Moose. AAUP. **Honors:** Young Men's Christ. Assn., Disting. Srv. Awd., 1972; Kiwanis Intl., Disting. Pres. Awd., 1979; Kiwanis Intl., New Club Bldg. Awd., 1981. **Activities:** 1, 9; 17, 24, 33; 56, 59, 74 **Addr.:** 67 Helen, Niles, OH 44446.

Stout, Doris M. (S. 13, 1924, Oskaloosa, IA) Jr.-Sr. High Media Libn., Clarke Cmnty. Sch., 1972–; Circ. Libn., William Penn Coll., 1964–66; Tchr., Montezuma Cmnty. Sch., 1955–64; Tchr., Oskaloosa Cmnty. Sch., 1952–53; Tchr., Barnes City Consolidated Sch., 1950–52. **Educ.:** William Penn Coll., 1956, BA (Educ., Eng.); Drake Univ., 1956–59, MA (Eng.); State Univ. of IA, 1960–64 (LS). **Orgs.:** ALA: AASL. IA Educ. Media Assn. Natl. Educ. Assn. IA State Educ. Assn. IA Area XIV Libns.: Pres. (1975–76). IA Student Educ. Media Assts.: Sponsor (1975–76, 1978–79). **Honors:** Pi Lambda Theta, 1964. **Activities:** 10; 15, 22, 32 **Addr.:** General Delivery, Montezuma, IA 50171.

Stout, Joan O. (S. 9, 1932, Ft. Madison, IA) Asst. Dean, Lrng. Resrcs. Ctr., Clark Coll., 1980–, Tech. Srvs. Libn., 1968–80; tchr.-libn., sec. sch. **Educ.:** West. IL Univ., 1950–54, BA (Eng.); Univ. of WA, 1968, MSLS; Portland State Univ., 1972, MAT (Soclgy.). **Orgs.:** ALA. WA LA. Cmnty. Coll. Lib. and Media Specs. AAUP. Natl. Educ. Assn. AHE. Various adult educ. orgs. **Honors** Beta Phi Mu. **Activities:** 1, 13; 17, 28, 34; 50, 74, 89 **Addr.:** Learning Resource Center, Clark College, 1800 E. McLoughlin, Vancouver, WA 98663.

Stout, Leon James (O. 10, 1947, Long Branch, NJ) Head, PA State Rm., Sr. Asst. Libn., Spec. Col., PA State Univ., 1974–, Asst. to the Archvst., PA Hist. Col. and Labor Arch., 1972–74. **Educ.:** PA State Univ., 1965–69, BA (Hist.), 1969–72, MA (Hist.); Univ. of Pittsburgh, 1972–74, MLS. **Orgs.:** SAA: Autom. Recs. and Techqs. Com. (1977–). PA LA: Arch. Com. (Ch., 1977–78, 1979–80); Bd. of Dirs. Mid-Atl. Reg. Arch. Conf.: Pubns. Com. (1979–). Socty. for Ch'ing Std. Ctrl. PA Geneal. Socty.: Pres. (1979), Treas. (1977–78). **Pubns.:** "Cartographic Records," *A Manual of Archival Techniques* (1979); "Resources on Twentieth-Century China in Special Collections at the Pennsylvania State University Libraries," *CEAL Bltn.* (1978); "Pennsylvania Town Views, 1850–1922: A Union Catalogue," *West. PA Hist. Mag.* (1975–76); reviews. **Activities:** 1, 2; 15, 17; 45; 56, 69, 95-Hist. of Higher Educ. **Addr.:** C107 Pattee Library, University Park, PA 16802.

Stout, Robert Johnson (Je. 2, 1953, Peoria, IL) Head, Chld. Hosp. Lib., OH State Univ., 1979–; Lrng. Resrcs. Coord., Med. Univ. of SC, 1978–79. **Educ.:** Univ. of IA, 1974–75, BGS (Gen. Std.); Univ. of SC, 1977–78, MLS (Libnshp.). **Orgs.:** Med. LA. Mid-OH Hlth. Sci. LA. AAAS. OH State Univ. Libs. **Pubns.:** "Children's Hospital Libraries; A Report on Average 1980 Collection Size and Budget," *Bltn. of the Med. LA* (O. 1980); "Journal Usage in a Children's Hospital Library," *Hosp. Libs.* (Sum. 1980). **Activities:** 1, 12; 17, 39; 80 **Addr.:** Health Sciences Library, Ohio State University, 376 W. 10th Ave., Columbus, OH 43210.

Stowers, Joel A. (D. 8, 1932, Elberton, GA) Dir., Univ. of TN, Martin, 1970–; Head Libn., Mercer Univ. in Atlanta, 1968–70; Head Libn., Berry Coll., 1962–68; Libn., Reinhardt Coll., 1959–62. **Educ.:** GA South. Coll., 1949–53, BS (Msc. Educ.); Emory Univ., 1958–59, MLn. **Orgs.:** ALA. TN LA. SELA. W. TN LA: Pres. (1976). Southeast. Lib. Netwk.: Bd. of Dirs. (1975–78). **Activities:** 1; 15, 17 **Addr.:** 106 Mockingbird Ln., Martin, TN 38237.

St-Pierre, Michel (D. 8, 1945, Montreal, PQ) Tchr., Tech. of Documtn., Coll. de Maisonneuve, 1971–; Head Catlgr., Discotheque, Can. Broadcasting Corp., 1970–71. **Educ.:** Univ. de Montreal, 1967–69, BLS, 1971–75, MLS. **Orgs.:** ASTED. Corp. des Bibtcrs. Profs. du PQ. **Pubns.:** "Le Marche du Travail en Bibliotechnique," *Documtn. et Bibs.* (Je. 1973); *How to Catalogue LPs* (1971). **Activities:** 11; 26; 62 **Addr.:** Techniques de la Documentation, College de Maisonneuve, Montreal, PQ H1X 2A2 Canada.

Strable, Edward G. (F. 12, 1922, Camden, NJ) VP, Dir., Info. Srvs., J. Walter Thompson Co., 1968–; Exec. Secy., Ref. Srvs. Div., ALTA, ALA, 1964–68; Lib. Dir., J. Walter Thompson Co., 1955–64; Exec. Asst., Chicago Pub. Lib., 1951–55. **Educ.:** Univ. of IL, 1946–48, BS (Jnlsm.); Univ. of Chicago, 1949–51, MALS. **Orgs.:** SLA: Pres. (1972–73). IL Reg. Lib. Cncl.: Dir. (1977–80). Vista Homes Corp.: Bd. of Dirs., Pres., (1978–79); Dir. (1976–79). **Pubns.:** Ed., *Special Libraries: A Guide for Management* (1966); jt. auth., *Subject Headings in Advertising, Marketing and Communications Media* (1964); jt. auth., "Moving Up: A Study of Librarians Who Have Become Officers of Their Organizations," *Spec. Libs.* (D. 1979). **Activities:** 12; 17, 38, 39;

PROFESSIONAL ACTIVITIES: Institutions: 1. Acad. lib.; 2. Arch.; 3. Assn.; 4. Fed./Gvt. lib.; 5. Inst. lib.; 6. Mfr./Suppl.; 7. Milit. lib.; 8. Musm.; 9. Pub. lib.; 10. Sch. lib.; 11. Sch. of lib. sci.; 12. Spec. lib.; 13. State lib.; 14. (other). **Functions/Activities:** 15. Acq./Col. dev.; 16. Adult srvs.; 17. Admin.; 18. Apprais.; 19. Archit./Bldgs.; 20. Cat./Class.; 21. Chld. srvs.; 22. Circ.; 23. Cons./Pres.; 24. Consult.; 25. Cont. ed.; 26. Educ. lib. sci.; 27. Ext. srvs.; 28. Fund/Grants; 29. Gvt. pubs.; 30. Indx./Abs.; 31. Instr. lib. use; 32. Media srvs.; 33. Micro.; 34. Netwks./Coop.; 35. Persnl.; 36. PR; 37. Publshg.; 38. Recs. mgt.; 39. Ref. srvs.; 40. Repro.; 41. Resrch.; 42. Review.; 43. Secur.; 44. Serials; 45. Spec. col.; 46. Tech. srvs.; 47. Trustees/Bds.; 48. YA srvs.; 49. (other).

51, 59 **Addr.:** J. Walter Thompson Company, 875 N. Michigan Ave., Chicago, IL 60611.

Strader, Helen B. (Ja. 19, 1919, St. Lawrence, PA) Supvsr., Outrch. Srvs., Manatee Cnty. Lib. Syst., 1978–; Asst. Prof., LS, Emporia State Univ., 1971–78; AV Asst. Libn., Brooklyn Pub. Lib., 1965–71; Art Libn., Ringling Musm. of Art, 1963–65. **Educ.:** Albright Coll., 1941–45, AB (Eng., Msc.); Pratt Inst., 1965–68, MLS; Univ. of NC, 1946–49 (Drama). **Orgs.:** Film Lib. Info. Cncl. ALA: Visual Litcy. Com. (1981); ASCLA, Prison Access and Censorship Prog. Com. (1981). EFLA: Fest. Juror (1966–77), Pre-Screening Ch. (1973–78). Litcy. Cncl. of Manatee Cnty. Frnds. of the Deaf. **Addr.:** 1631 Hillview St., Sarasota, FL 33579.

Strader, Thomas E. (Ap. 26, 1927, Rittman, OH) Dir., Cook Lib., Towson State Univ., 1970–; Dir. of Libs., Rochester Inst. of Tech., 1956–70; Assoc. Libn., Un. Coll., 1952–56. **Educ.:** OH Univ., 1946–51, AB (Zlgy.); Case West. Rsv., 1951–52, MS (LS). **Orgs.:** ALA. MD LA: Various coms. Coop. Libs. of Ctrl. MD. Cncl. of Acad. Lib. Dirs. **Activities:** 1; 17, 32, 39; 58, 80, 91 **Addr.:** Cook Library, Towson State University, Towson, MD 21204.

Strahler, Clytie Evelyn (Je. 17, 1907, Dayton, OH) Prof., Assoc. Dir., Univ. Libs., Emerita, Wittenberg Univ., 1975–, Prof., Assoc. Dir., 1968–75, Assoc. Prof., Asst. Dir., Reader Srvs., 1964–67, Assoc. Prof., Asst. Head Libn., 1962–64; Coord., Persnl. Srvs., Dayton and Montgomery Cnty. Pub. Lib., 1956–62, First Asst., Ref. Dept., 1949–56, Branch Libn., Sch. Libn., 1932–49. **Educ.:** Wittenberg Coll., 1928–34, AB, cum laude (Hist.); Univ. of IL, 1935–38, BSLS; various crs., extensive travel. **Orgs.:** ALA: Notable Bks. Cncl. (Ch., 1955–59), Cncl. (1958–60), various coms. OH LA: Exec. Bd. (1958–60), Subprof. Trng. Com. (1959–60), Nom. Com. (1974). Dayton and Miami Valley Cnsrtm. Dayton Cncl. on World Affairs. Cincinnati Cncl. on World Affairs. AAUW. AAUP. **Honors:** Beta Phi Mu. **Activities:** 1, 9; 17, 31, 39; 54, 57 **Addr.:** 5340 Brendonwood Ln., Dayton, OH 45415.

Straight, Elsie H. (O. 9, 1914, Cumberland, Eng.) Head Libn., Ringling Sch. of Art and Dsgn., 1974–, Art Libn., 1974–81; Head Libn., Elmhurst Acad., 1969–74; Head Libn., St. Raphael Acad., 1963–69. **Educ.:** Roger Williams Coll., 1970–72, BA (Art); Univ. of RI, 1966–74, MLS; NY Sch. of Appld. Dsgn., 1938–40; Art Inst. of Pittsburgh, 1936–38. **Orgs.:** ARLIS/NA: SE Ch. (1980). FL LA. RI LA. RI Sch. LA: Secy. (1966). Sarasota Art Assn. Manatee Art Leag. **Honors:** Manatee Art Leag., 1st Prize, Sculpture (1979). **Activities:** 10, 12; 15, 23; 55 **Addr.:** 435 Edwards Dr., Sarasota, FL 33580.

Strain, Paula M. (Brooke Cnty., WV) Mgr., Info. Srvs., MITRE Corp., 1970–; Head Libn., Booz Allen Appld. Resrch., 1968–70; Tech. Libn., Intl. Bus. Machines Corp., 1960–68; Sr. Resrch. Anal., Lib. of Congs., 1957–60. **Educ.:** Bethany Coll., AB (Eng. Lit.); Carnegie Inst. of Tech., BS (LS); various crs. **Orgs.:** SLA: Various divs., ofcs. Interlib. Users Assn. Cnsrtm. for Cont. Higher Educ. in North. VA: Lib. Netwk. Com. (1974–). Potomac Appalachian Trail Club: Pres. (1972–74). Appalachian Trail Conf.: Bd. of Mgrs. (1981–). Finger Lakes Trail Conf.: Pres. (1964–66), Bd. of Mgrs. (1962–68). **Honors:** SLA, John Cotton Dana Lectr., 1968. **Pubns.:** *Portrait, With Salary, of Non-Federal Special Libraries in Washington, DC* (1981); *Looking at Union Lists in Washington, DC* (1978). **Activities:** 4, 12; 17, 34, 42; 56, 70, 91 **Addr.:** The MITRE Corporation, 1820 Dolley Madison Blvd., McLean, VA 22102.

Stranc, Sr. Mary Celaine, C.S.S.F. (Buffalo, NY) Lib./Media Spec., Notre Dame HS, Batavia, NY, 1979–; Head Libn., Villa Marie Coll. of Buffalo, 1972–79, Asst. Libn., 1969–72, Coord., Prof. (Lib. Tech. Asst. Prog.), 1966–79; Supvsr., Felician Sch. Libs., 1970–71. **Educ.:** St. Joseph Tchrs. Coll., Buffalo, NY, 1950, BS (Educ.); SUNY, Coll. at Geneseo, 1963–66, MLS; Nazareth Coll., Rochester, NY, 1955–56, Cert. (Educ., LS); NY State Cvl. Srv., 1973, Cert. (Supvsn.). **Orgs.:** Cath. LA: Adv. Bd. (1971–73); Exec. Bd. (1979–81). NY LA: Lib. Educ. Sect. (Ch., 1971–73). West. NY Cath. Libns. Conf.: Vice-Ch. (1969–71); Secy. (1967–68). Natl. Cath. Educ. Assn. **Pubns.:** *Media Handbook* (1976); "The Faculty and the Centralized Library," *Cath. Lib. World* (Mr. 197–). **Activities:** 10; 48 **Addr.:** 600 Doat St., Buffalo, NY 14211.

Strand, Kathryn Anne (My. 28, 1943, San Bernardino, CA) Libn., High Altitude Observatory Lab., 1969–; Ref. Libn., Contra Costa Cnty. Lib. Syst., 1966–68. **Educ.:** Univ. of CA, Santa Barbara, 1961–65, BA (Hist.); Univ. of CA, Berkeley, 1965–66, MLS. **Orgs.:** SLA: Phys./Astr./Math. Div. (Treas., 1978–80). **Activities:** 12; 39, 41, 46, 49-One—person lib.; 88, 95-Solar phys. **Addr.:** High Altitude Observatory Library, P.O. Box 3000, Boulder, CO 80307.

Strassberg, Richard (Ap. 21, 1942, New York, NY) Asst. Dir., M.P. Catherwood Lib., Cornell Univ., 1981–, Dir., Archvst., Labor-Mgt. Documtn. Ctr., 1977–, Assoc. Archvst., 1971–76; Sr. Asst. Archvst., Dept. of Mss. and Arch., Cornell Univ., 1968–70. **Educ.:** William Paterson Coll., 1961–65, BA (Hist.); N. IL Univ., 1965–67, MA (Hist.); Univ. of Denver, 1967–68, MS (Libnshp.); Univ. of Denver, 1968, Cert. (Arch. Admin.). **Orgs.:** NY LA: Prsrvn. Com. (1972–75). SAA: Ad-Hoc Com. on Arch. Manpower (Ch., 1978); Bldg. and Tech. Prcs. Com. (Ch., 1977–80); Labor Arch. Com. (1976–). Assn. of Recs. Mgrs. and Admins.: Arch.-Hist. Com. (1974); Ctrl. NY Chap. (Pres., 1974). Amer. Assn. for the Cons. of Hist. and Artistic Works. NY State Labor Hist. Assn.: Secy. (1976–78); Treas. (1979); Secy.-Treas. (1980–). **Honors:** Beta Phi Mu, 1968. **Pubns.:** Cmplr., *Cornell University Libraries Manual of Manuscript Processing* (1973–75); "The Use of Fumigants in Archival Repositories," *Amer. Archvst.* (Ja. 1978); "Archival and Manuscript Processing Manuals," *GA Arch.* (Sum. 1977); jt. auth., "Anatomy of a Library Emergency," *Lib. Jnl.* (O. 1973); ed., *Cities* (1974–76). **Activities:** 2, 12; 15, 17, 45; 59, 65 **Addr.:** 144 Ives Hall, Cornell University, Ithaca, NY 14853.

Strasser, Dennis K. (Je. 27, 19–, Watervliet, MI) Lib. Dir., Natl. Coll. of Educ., Urban Campus, 1981–, Pub. Srvs. Libn., 1979–81. **Educ.:** West. MI Univ., 1973–75, BS (Educ.), 1977–78, MLS. **Orgs.:** IL LA. Chicago OLUG. **Activities:** 1; 17, 24, 31; 63, 92 **Addr.:** National College of Education, Learning Resource Center, Urban Campus, Chicago, IL 60603.

Stratton, Elaine A. (Miller) (Ap. 27, 1925, Flint, MI) Dir., WRITE–ON, Target Wrtg. Prog., Title IV-C ESEA Prog., 1980–; Dir., Libs. K–12, Highland Cmnty. Unit Dist. #5, 1970–80, Dir., Wrtg. Prog., Elem. Grades, 1979, Org. Volun., 1976–78, Libn., K–6, 1964–70, Elem. Tchr., 1948; Legis. Netwk. Area Person, Lewis and Clark State Syst., 1973–78; HS Tchr., 1945–47. **Educ.:** South. IL Normal Univ., 1943–46, BSEd (Hist.); South. IL Univ., 1965–67, Mstrs. (Instr. Mtrls.), 1974–76, Gen. Admin. Cert. (K–12). **Orgs.:** Amer. Assn. of Sch. Libns.: Media Ctr. Facilities (1979–81); Lib. Media Skills Instr. Ad Hoc Com. (Natl. Ch., 1981). Intl. Assn. of Sch. Libns. Frdm. to Read Fndn. Lib. Bk. Sel. Srv.: Mid. Grade Bks. Consult. (1977–). Various other orgs. Amer. Assn. of Sch. Admins.: Partners' Prog. (Ch., 1979–80). Congregational Church Sch.: Supt. (1965–68). Highland Nite Unit IL Homemakers: Pres. (1962). Highland Hist. Assn.: PR Ch. (1973–79); Bd. of Dirs. **Honors:** *Encyc. Britannica*, State of IL, Sch. Lib. Media Prog. of Yr., 1976; Natl. Comsn. for Tchrs. Educ. and Prof. Stan., Natl. Demonstration Elem. Sch. Lib. Awd., 1965; State of IL, City of Highland, Bicent. Actv. Awds., 1976. **Pubns.:** *Highland Area Bicentennial Historical Calendar* (1975); "Pay Day in the Library," *Sch. Lib. Jnl.* (D. 1974); various articles, radio progs. **Activities:** 10, 11; 15, 17, 21; 54, 85, 89 **Addr.:** Highland Community Unit #5, 1800 Lindenthal Ave., Highland, IL 62249.

Stratton, Frances M. (Ap. 9, 1924, Prospect Park, PA) Leader, Ref. Grp., Amer. Cyanamid Co., 1963–, Asst. Libn., 1950–63; Jr. Chem., E.I. DuPont de Nemours, 1945–49. **Educ.:** Dickinson Coll., 1941–45, BA (Chem.), Drexel Univ., 1949–50, MLS; various cont. educ. and trng. crs. **Orgs.:** SLA: Pharm. Div. (Ch., 1974–75); Sci-Tech Div., Ch. (1967–68), Treas. (1963–64), Secy. (1961–63); Unlisted Drugs (Bus. Mgr., 1953–56). ASIS. Hudson Valley OLUG. Amer. Chem. Socty. Soroptimist Intl. **Honors:** Phi Beta Kappa. **Pubns.:** "Processing Pharmaceutical Product Information," *Abs. of Papers, Amer. Chem. Socty.* (S. 1965). **Activities:** 12; 17, 39, 49-Online srch.; 58, 80, 87 **Addr.:** American Cyanamid Company, Medical Research Division, Lederle Laboratories, Pearl River, NY 10965.

Stratton, George W. (Je. 19, 1940, Ravenna, OH) Asst. Dir., South Bend Pub. Lib., 1978–; AV Consult., C.O.I.N., 1976–78; Dir., Lrng. Resrcs., Univ. Sch., 1975–76; Branch Libn., Cleveland Hts. Pub. Lib., 1972–75. **Educ.:** Kent State Univ., 1958–64, BSEd (Educ.); 1970–72, MLS. **Orgs.:** IN LA: State Mem. Ch. (1980); Dist. I Plng. Com. (Co-Ch., 1981). ALA. **Activities:** 9; 17, 27, 32 **Addr.:** 122 W. Wayne St., South Bend, IN 46601.

Strauch, Helena M. (Jn. 15, 1953, Baltimore, MD) Comm. Dir., Info. Indus. Assn., 1976–; Prodct. Mgr., Natl. Congsnl. Analysis Corp., 1975–76; Staff Asst. to Congressman Charles E. Bennett (D-FL), 1973–75. **Educ.:** Amer. Univ., 1971–75, BA (Comm.). **Orgs.:** ASIS. Assoc. Info. Mgrs. Assoc. Women Consults.: Fndn. Bd. (1978–79). Natl. Org. for Women. WA Socty. for Assn. Execs. **Honors:** *Assoc. Trends*, Excel. in Assn. Pubns., 1979. **Pubns.:** "Managing Your Information Resources," *The Ofc.* (Ja. 1978); "Attention: Career Dead Ends Ahead," *Info. World* (Ap. 1979); various articles. **Activities:** 3; 17, 25, 36; 75 **Addr.:** Information Industry Association, 316 Pennsylvania Ave., S.E., Suite 502, Washington, DC 20003.

Strauch, Katina P. W. (D. 24, 1946, Columbia, SC) Head, Col. Dev., Coll. of Charleston, 1979–; Libn., Low Country Rural Hlth. Cnsrtm., 1978–79; Head Libn., Trident Tech. Coll., 1977–78; Ref., AV Libn., Duke Univ. Med. Ctr., 1975–77; Head Libn., Duke Univ. Sch. of Nursing, 1972–75. **Educ.:** Univ. of NC, 1967–69, BA (Econ.), 1969–72, MS (LS). **Orgs.:** Med. LA. ALA. SE LA. SC LA. Metro. Opera Gld. **Pubns.:** Jt. auth., *Guide to Library Resources for Nurses* (1980); jt. auth., *Theory and Design in Bibliographic Education* (1982); various papers. **Addr.:** Robert S. Small Library, College of Charleston, Charleston, SC 29424.

Straus, Leslie S. (N. 2, 1944, Kaslo, BC) VP, Resrcs., John Coutts Lib. Srvs., 1979–, Exec. Asst., 1972–79; Head, Prcs. Dept., York Univ. Libs., 1969–70, Catlgr., York Univ. Libs., 1966–69. **Educ.:** Univ. of Waterloo, 1962–65, BA (Eng.); Univ. of Toronto, 1965–66, BLS. **Orgs.:** SLA: Publshg. Div. (Bltn. Ed., 1980–81). Can. LA. ALA. Univ. of Toronto Arts Women's Club. Univ. of Toronto Sch. of LS Alum. Assn. **Pubns.:** Contrib., "Directory of Alternative Librarians in Canada," *Can. Lib. Jnl.* (1977); various presentations. **Activities:** 6; 15, 46 **Addr.:** 59 Carney Rd., Willowdale, ON M2M 1T3 Canada.

Strauss, Carol D. (Jl. 29, 1925, Waterloo, IA) Lib. Srvs. Coord., Westlake Cmnty. Hosp., 1978–; Indxr., Amer. Dental Assn., 1975–77; Catlgr., Northwest. Univ. Dental Sch., 1971–75, Catlgr., Northwest. Univ. Med. Sch., 1970. **Educ.:** Cornell Coll., 1943–47, BA (Chem.); Rosary Coll., 1969–71, MALS. **Orgs.:** Med. LA: Rcrt. Com. (1971–73). SLA. Hyde Park-Kenwood Cmnty. Hlth. Ctr. **Pubns.:** "A Suggested Expansion of the NLM Classification Scheme for Dentistry," *Bltn. of the Med. LA* (1973). **Activities:** 12; 15, 20, 30; 80 **Addr.:** 5431 S. Ridgewood Ct., Chicago, IL 60615.

Strauss, Diane Wheeler (F. 14, 1943, Milwaukee, WI) Head, Bus. Admin., Soc. Sci. Ref. Dept., Wilson Lib., Univ. of NC, 1976–, Soc. Sci. Ref. Libn., 1973–76; Legis. Ref. Libn., U.S. Dept. of Labor Lib., 1970–72; Asst. Mtrls. Anal., Lib. Sch., Univ. of WI, 1968–69; YA Libn., Enoch Pratt Free Lib., 1967–68. **Educ.:** Univ. of WI, Milwaukee, 1962–66, BS (Eng.); Univ. of WI, Madison, 1966–67, MSLS. **Orgs.:** NC OLUG: Pres. (1978–79). SLA: NC Chap, Pres. (1981–82); VP, Pres. Elect (1980–81); Com. on PR (Ch., 1979–80); Com. on Career Educ., Ch. SE LA. **Activities:** 1, 4; 25, 29, 39; 59, 75, 92 **Addr.:** 2028 Sprunt Ave., Durham, NC 27705.

Strauss, Richard F. (Ag. 4, 1944, West Reading, PA) Ctr. Cnty. Libn., Bucks Cnty. Free Lib., 1980–; Asst. Dir., Montgomery Cnty.–Norristown Pub. Lib., 1978–80, Head, Tech. Srvs. Dept., 1972–78, Head, Acq. Dept., 1969–72. **Educ.:** Albright Coll., 1962–66, AB (Eng.); Rutgers Univ., 1966–68, MLS; Univ. of Pittsburgh, 1968–69, Advnc. Cert. (Lib., Info. Sci.). **Orgs.:** ALA. PA LA: Tech. Srvs. RT (Ch., 1978–79); Bd. of Dirs. (1978–79). **Honors:** Beta Phi Mu; Phi Alpha Theta; Delta Phi Alpha. **Activities:** 9; 17, 28, 35; 50, 56, 89 **Addr.:** Bucks County Free Library, 50 N. Main St., Doylestown, PA 18901.

Straw, Deah F. (O. 26, 1946, Harrisburg, PA) Libn., Dir., South. Pines Pub. Lib., 1974–; Ref. Libn., Cumberland Cnty. Pub. Lib., 1973–74; Lib. Dir., Camp Humphreys, South Korea, 1972–73; Chld. Libn., Wolfson Meml. Lib., 1970–72. **Educ.:** Mansfield State Coll., 1964–68, BS (LS); Drexel Univ., 1968–70, MSLS. **Orgs.:** NC LA: Cont. Educ. Com. NC Lib. Dirs. Assn. SELA. ALA. NC Netwk. Civic Club. **Activities:** 4, 9; 17, 36, 39; 56, 74, 78 **Addr.:** Southern Pines Public Library, 180 SW Broad St., P.O. Box 780, Southern Pines, NC 28387.

Strazdon, Maureen E. (Ag. 6, 1948, Elizabeth, NJ) Libn., Amer. Coll., 1978–; Ref. Libn., Drexel Univ., 1971–78. **Educ.:** Douglass Coll., 1966–70, BA (Relig.); Rutgers Univ., 1970–71, MLS; Drexel Univ., 1974–78, MBA. **Orgs.:** SLA: Insr. Div., Insr. Database Com. (Ch., 1979–). Philadelphia Area Ref. Libns. Info. Exch.: Strg. Com.: LUG. (Coor., 1978–). ALA. **Honors:** Beta Gamma Sigma, 1978. **Pubns.:** Jt. auth., *Library Management* (1980); "Measuring Students' Preferences for Reference Service: A Conjoint Analysis," *Lib. Qtly.* (Ap. 1980); "Searching Insurance Literature On-Line," *Best's Review P/C* (Mr. 1979). **Activities:** 1, 12; 17, 39, 41; 50, 59, 76 **Addr.:** Lucas Memorial Library, The American College, Bryn Mawr, PA 19010.

Streck, Sr. Helen (Cherryvale, KS) Archvst., Adorers of the Blood of Christ, 1978–, Histn., 1977; Head Libn., KS Newman Coll., 1966–77. **Educ.:** Frnds. Univ., 1931–37, BA (Eng.); Wichita State Univ., 1951–55, B Mus, M Mus Ed (Piano, Msc. Educ.); Rosary Coll., River Forest, ILL, 1964–68, MALS; various arch. wkshps. **Orgs.:** ALA. KS LA. Cath. LA. SAA. Various other orgs. **Honors:** Beta Phi Mu, 1968. **Pubns.:** Various bk. reviews, *Srs. Today* (1978–). **Activities:** 2; 15, 17, 41; 63, 85, 90 **Addr.:** 1400 S. Sheridan, Wichita, KS 67213.

Streeter, David (D. 31, 1929, Los Angeles, CA) Supvsr., Spec. Cols., Pomona Pub. Lib., 1973–; Head, Ref. Dept., Univ. of WI, Parkside, 1970–73; Head, Ref. Dept., Univ. of Denver, 1969–70, Bus. Admin. Libn., 1968–69; Head, Bus. Div., Denver Pub. Lib., 1964–68; Ref. Libn., NM State Univ., 1960–64; Reg. Libn., NM State Lib., 1959–60; various prof. positions, 1957–59. **Educ.:** CO State Coll. of Educ., 1948–54, BA (Bio. Sci., Eng.); Univ. of Denver, 1955–57, MA (LS). **Orgs.:** ALA: Ref. Srvs. Div., Bus. Ref. Srvs. Com. (1967–70). CO LA: Ad Hoc. Comms. and Pubns. Com. (1968–69). SLA: CO Chap. (Pres., 1970). NM LA: Int Frdm. Com. (Ch., 1963–64). Hist. Socty. of Pomona Valley: Pres. (1979). Pomona Valley Geneal. Socty.: Bltn. Ed. (1980–). City of Pomona Cent./Bicent. Com. **Honors:** Pomona Valley Geneal. Socty., Hon. Life Mem., 1977. **Pubns.:** *A Bibliography of Ed Dorn* (1973); *Things My Mother Never Told Me Or How To Boil Water and Other Earthly Delights* (1973); "The Irving Wallace Collection," *Socty. for the Study of Midwest. Lit. Nsltr.* (Fall 1973); various articles. **Activities:** 9; 16, 39, 45; 69, 73 **Addr.:** 866 Hillcrest Dr., Pomona, CA 91768.

Special Subjects/Services: 50. Adult educ.; 51. Advert./Mktg.; 52. Aerosp.; 53. Agric.; 54. Area std.; 55. Arts/Hum.; 56. Autom.; 57. Bibl./Prtg.; 58. Bio. sci.; 59. Bus./Fin.; 60. Chem.; 61. Copyrt.; 62. Documtn.; 63. Educ.; 64. Engin.; 65. Env.; 66. Eth. grps.; 67. Film; 68. Food/Nutr.; 69. Geneal.; 70. Geo.; 71. Geol.; 72. Handcpd.; 73. Hist.; 74. Int. frdm.; 75. Info. sci.; 76. Insr.; 77. Law; 78. Legis.; 79. Math./Comp. sci.; 80. Med.; 81. Metals; 82. Nat. resrcs.; 83. Newsp.; 84. Nuc. sci.; 85. Oral hist.; 86. Petr./Energy; 87. Pharm.; 88. Phys./Astr./Math.; 89. Readg.; 90. Relig.; 91. Sci./Tech.; 92. Soc. sci.; 93. Telecom.; 94. Transp.; 95. (other).

Strehl, Daniel J. (F. 14, 1948, Petosky, MI) Head, Gen. Readg. Srvs., Los Angeles Pub. Lib., 1980–, Sr. Libn., Sci. and Tech., 1976–80, Libn., Bus. and Econ., 1974–76. **Educ.:** Kalamazoo Coll., 1966–70, BA (African Std.); West. MI Univ., 1972–73, MSL (Libnshp.). **Orgs.:** SLA: South. CA Chap. (Advert. Mgr., 1978); Prog. Com. (1980–81). Libns. Gld. (AFSCME Lcl. 2626): Chief Supvsr. Steward (1980–81). **Activities:** 9, 12; 17, 22, 23; 62, 68, 83 **Addr.:** Los Angeles Public Library, 630 W. 5th St., Los Angeles, CA 90071.

Streit, Samuel Allen (F. 9, 1944, Sheffield, AL) Asst. Univ. Lib., Spec. Cols., Brown Univ., 1977–; Archvst., Head of Spec. Cols., City Coll., CUNY, 1972–77; Instr., Appalachian State Univ., 1969–72. **Educ.:** Univ. of N. AL, 1962–65, BA (Hist.); Univ. of Houston, 1965–67, MA (Hist.); Columbia Univ., 1972, MLS. **Orgs.:** SAA: Coll. and Univ. Arch. Com.; Prsrvn. Com.; RBMS Nom. Com. ALA. New Eng. Archvsts. Gld. Bookworkers. Various other orgs. Com. for New Eng. Bibl. Amer. Prtg. Hist. Assn. Bibl. Socty. of Amer. RI Hist. Socty.: Lib. Com. **Activities:** 1, 2; 17, 19, 23; 55, 57 **Addr.:** Brown University, Box A, Providence, RI 02912.

Stretton, Alan M. (O. 8, 1950, Wilmington, DE) Data Prcs. Admin., Progmr., News Bank, Inc., 1979–; Libn. I, Ref., Cat., Maywood Pub. Lib., 1978–79. **Educ.:** Defense Lang. Inst., 1970–71, Cert. (Grmn. Lang.); Univ. of DE, 1973–77, BA (Econ., Grmn.); Columbia Univ., 1977–78, MS (Lib. Srv.). **Orgs.:** ALA. Data Prcs. Mgt. Assn. Assn. of Systs. Mgrs. Grmn. Hon. Socty.: Pres. (1976). Columbia Sch. of Lib. Srv. Student Assn.: Treas. (1977). **Honors:** Econ. Hon. Socty., Cert. for Achvmnt., 1977; Grmn. Hon. Socty., Cert. for Achvmt., 1976. **Pubns.:** Ed. asst., *The Catalog: Its Present and Future* (1979). **Activities:** 14-Publshr.; 17, 37, 46; 56, 83 **Addr.:** 65 Bedford St., #2A, Stamford, CT 06901.

Streuli, Huguette F. (My. 14, 1932, Brasschaat, Antwerp, Belgium) Law Libn., Windels, Marx, Davies and Ives, 1980–; Head Libn., Legal and Tax Depts., Texaco Inc., 1977–80; Ref. Libn., Pace Univ. Sch. of Law, 1977; Gvt. Docum. Libn., Sarah Lawrence Coll., 1972–77. **Educ.:** Inst. Marie Haps, Brussels, 1950–54, BS (Psy.); Pratt Inst., 1970–73, MLS (Lib. and Info. Sci.); AALL, 1980, Cert. (Law Libnshp.). **Orgs.:** AALL. Law LA of Grt. NY. Intl. Assn. of Law Libs. SLA. **Activities:** 1, 12; 17; 59, 75, 77 **Addr.:** Windels, Marx, Davies and Ives, Library, 51 W. 51st St., New York, NY 10019.

Strickland, Albert Carson (Ap. 19, 1920, Savannah, GA) Dir., Hume Lib., Inst. of Food and Agr. Scis., Univ. of FL, 1969–, Catlgr., 1958–69; Libn., U.S. Marine Corps Supply Ctr., Albany, GA, 1955–58. **Educ.:** U.S. Navy Flight Sch., 1945–47 (Nvl. Aviator); FL State Univ., 1951–54, BS (Geo.), 1954–55, MSLS. **Orgs.:** ALA: ACRL/Sci. Tech Sect., Oberly Awd. Com. (1976–77, 1980–). Intl. Assn. of Agr. Libns. and Docmlsts. Cncl. on Bot. and Hort. Libs. Assn. Interamericana de Bibtcrs. y Docmlsts. FL LA: Tech. Srvs. RT (Ch., 1966). **Honors:** Gamma Sigma Delta. **Pubns.:** Review. **Addr.:** Hume Library, University of Florida, Gainesville, FL 32611.

Strickland, Jimmy Ray (S. 4, 1936, Lubbock, TX) Dir., Libs., S. Plains Coll., 1980–, Asst. Libn., 1978–80; Libn., Kermit HS, 1967–78. **Educ.:** Hardin-Simmons Univ., 1955–59, BA (Sp.); Sul Ross State Coll., 1964–67, MEd (Educ.); E. TX State Univ., 1967–72, MSLS. **Orgs.:** TX LA. SWLA. TX State Tchrs. Assn. TX Jr. Coll. Tchrs. Assn. **Honors:** Future Tchrs. of Amer., TX State Advs. Awd., 1978. **Activities:** 1; 15, 17, 22; 93 **Addr.:** South Plains College Library, 1400 College Ave., Levelland, TX 79336.

Strickland, Martha (Ap. 29, 1939, Naples, TX) Libn., Dallas Pub. Lib., 1978–; CELS Proj. Staff, SW LA, 1977–78; Dir., Acton Pub. Lib., 1974–76; Dir., Wolcott Pub. Lib., 1972–74. **Educ.:** E. TX State Univ., 1958–61, BA (Eng.); South. CT State Coll., 1971–73, MLS. **Orgs.:** CT LA: Cont. Ed. Sect. (Ch., 1973–74); Proc. Com. (Ch., 1975–77). New Eng. LA. SW LA. CT Target 1976: Strg. Com.; Stans. Task Grp. Various other orgs. CT LSCA Adv. Cncl. on Libs. **Pubns.:** *TARGET '76: The Library Planning Experience in Connecticut–1970–75* (1977); guest ed., "Continuing Education," *Jnl. of Educ. for Libnshp.* (Win. 1978); ed., *Current Awareness Jnl.* audio cassette (1977–78); *A Continuing Education Needs Assessment of Librarians in the Southwest* (1977); ed. rsrch., *A Guide to Humanities Resources in the Southwest* (1978). **Activities:** 9; 17, 25, 37 **Addr.:** 4130 Emerson, Dallas, TX 75205.

Strickland, Muriel (Je. 8, 1925, Carlisle, Eng.) Map Cur., San Diego State Univ., 1975–. **Educ.:** San Diego State Univ., 1971–73, BA (Geo.), 1973–75, MA (Geo.). **Orgs.:** SLA. West. Assn. of Map Libs.: Nom. Com. (1979), Hosplty. Com. (1978–80). **Pubns.:** "Use of Maps in the Instruction of Remote Sensing Imagery Interpretation," *Bltn. West. Assn. of Map Libs.* (N. 1979); "Library of Congress Summer Project Acquisitions," *Bltn. West. Assn. Map Libs.* (N. 1978). **Activities:** 1, 12; 70 **Addr.:** Library, San Diego State University, San Diego, CA 92182.

Strickland, Nellie B. (D. 12, 1932, Belmont, MI) Chief, Lib. Div., Dept. of Army, 1974–; Dir., U.S. Army Lib., 1972–73, 1971–72; Ft. Benning Lib. Syst., 1969–71. **Educ.:** Murray State Coll., 1950–54, BS (Educ.); Peabody Coll., 1969–71, MLS. **Orgs.:** ALA. Natl. Micro. Assn. **Activities:** 4; 17 **Addr.:** 203 Yoakum Pkwy. #614, Alexandria, VA 22304.

Strickland, Normalie Catherine Richards (Ja. 12, 1938, Effingham, IL) Head Libn., Helen Matthes Lib., 1967–; Lib. Asst., St. Anthony High, 1966–67; Asst., Acq. Dept., Univ. of OK, 1965–66; Actg. Head, Sci. Dept., Phoenix Pub. Lib., 1963–65, Lib. Asst., 1962–63; Lib. Asst., Sci. Dept., Enoch Pratt Free Lib., 1960–62. **Educ.:** Marian Coll., 1956–60, BA (Hist.); Univ. of IL, 1960–61, MSLS. **Orgs.:** IL LA: Pub. Libs. Sect., Exec. Bd. (1976). ALA. **Activities:** 9; 15, 17, 20 **Addr.:** RR #1, Box 176, Effingham, IL 62401.

Striedieck, Suzanne S. (Je. 3, 1945, Medford, MA) Chief, Serials Dept., PA State Univ., 1977–; Head, Serials Dept., SUNY (Buffalo), 1975–77; Serials Catlgr., PA State Univ., 1969–75. **Educ.:** PA State Univ., 1963–66, BA (Pol. Sci.); Univ. of Pittsburgh, 1968–69, MLS. **Orgs.:** ALA. PA LA. **Honors:** Cncl. on Lib. Resrce., Flwshp., 1979. **Activities:** 1; 17, 44, 46 **Addr.:** RD 1, Box 160A, Port Matilda, PA 16870.

Strip, A. C. (Ap. 13, 1936, Antwerp, Belgium) Pres., Urban Libs. Cncl., 1980–; Pres., Pub. Lib. of Columbus and Franklin Cnty., 1979–80. **Educ.:** OH State Univ., 1954–57, BA (Econ.), 1957–60, JD. **Addr.:** 575 S. Third St., Columbus, OH 43215.

Strobel, Susan J. (Jl. 20, 1950, Saginaw, MI) Info. Spec., Price Waterhouse, 1981–; Univ. Libn., FL Intl. Univ., Tamiami Campus, 1980–81; Mgr., Corporate Info., GCC Beverages, Inc., 1978–80; Archit., Engin. Libn., Robert and Co. Assocs. Inc., 1976–78; Gen. Ledger, FICS Libn., Mgt. Sci. Amer., 1976. **Educ.:** Univ. of MI, 1969–71, BA (Jnlsm., Span.), 1972, AMLS. **Orgs.:** SLA. FL LA. S. FL Online Srchs. DC LA. **Activities:** 1; 39; 59 **Addr.:** Price Waterhouse, 3500 One Biscayne Tower, Miami, FL 33131.

Strohecker, Edwin Charles (F. 22, 1923, Allentown, PA) Dean, Libs., Murray State Univ., 1973–, Ch., Dept. of LS, 1972–; Ch., Dept. of LS, Spalding Coll., 1959–72; Head, Tech. Srvs., Chief Catlgr., New Orleans Univ., 1958–59; Asst. Prof., LS, Kent State Univ., 1955–58; Libn., Sch. of Educ., Univ. of MI, 1953–55; Instr., E. TX State Univ., 1950–52; Circ., Ref. Libn., Gettysburg Coll., 1949–50. **Educ.:** Kutztown State Coll., 1946–49, BS (LS); George Peabody Coll., 1949–50, MA (LS); Univ. of MI, 1969, PhD (LS). **Orgs.:** OH Assn. of Sch. Libns.: Resrch. Com. (Ch., 1954–55). KY LA: Natl. Lib. Week, (Exec. Dir., 1960–61); ALA Cncl. Rep. (1967); Lib. Educ. Sect. (Ch., 1975–76); VP, Pres.-Elect (1976–77); various other ofcs. ALA: Lib. Educ. Div./Tchrs. Sect., Nom. Com. (Ch., 1966–67). AALS. Various other orgs. KY Gvr.'s Adv. Cncl. on Libs. KY Cncl. on Higher Educ.: Lib. Task Frc. (1974–76). KY Gvr.'s WHCOLIS: Strg. Com. (1977–79). WHCOLIS: KY Del. (Alternate, 1979). **Honors:** Univ. of MI, Lib. Srv. Fellow, 1952; Beta Phi Mu, 1953; Phi Delta Kappa, 1954. **Pubns.:** *The Library Technical Assistant* (1970); indxr., *Guide to Federal Map and Chart Publications, 1937–1953* (1955); "Manuscripts, Memorabilia and Microfilm," *KY LA Bltn.* (Spr. 1975); "Organize Your Elementary Library," *The Cath. Sch. Jnl.* (F. 1962). **Activities:** 1, 11; 17; 74 **Addr.:** Rte. 7, Box 730, Murray, KY 42071.

Strom, Sara C. (Mr. 28, 1952, Ames, IA) Ref. Libn., Natl. Arch. Lib., 1976–. **Educ.:** Coll. of William and Mary, 1970–74, BA (Hist.); Cath. Univ. of Amer., 1975–77, MSLS. **Orgs.:** SLA. DC LA. **Honors:** Phi Beta Kappa, 1973; Beta Phi Mu, 1979. **Pubns.:** "Writings on Archives, Historical Manuscripts, and Current Records 1975" *Amer. Archvst.* (Jl. 1977); "...1976," *Amer. Archvst.* (Jl. 1978). **Activities:** 2, 4; 22, 29, 39; 55, 57, 69 **Addr.:** 9018 Parliament Dr., Burke, VA 22015.

Stroman, Josh H. (O. 11, 1938, Ardmore, OK) Asst. Dir., Tech. Srvs., Univ. of Tulsa, 1974–; Docum. Catlgr., OK State Univ., 1964–70, Head Docum. Libn., 1970–74. **Educ.:** OK State Univ., 1956–60, BA (Jnlsm.); Univ. of OK, 1964, MLS. **Orgs.:** OK LA: Tech. Srvs. Div. (Ch., 1967–68); Treas. (1974–77). ALA. **Pubns.:** Ed., *OK Libn.* (1967–69). **Activities:** 1; 46 **Addr.:** McFarlin Library, University of Tulsa, 600 S. College, Tulsa, OK 74104.

Stromme, Gary L. (Jl. 8, 1939, Willmar, MN) Law Libn., Pac. Gas and Electric Co., 1974–; Indus. Contracting Attorney, 1973–74; Asst. Libn., Graham and James, 1971–73; Asst. Libn., McCutchen, Doyle, Brown and Enersen Law Firm, 1970–71; Serials Libn., Univ. of MN, 1967–69. **Educ.:** Pac. Luth. Univ., 1965, BLS; Univ. of BC, 1967, JD; Hastings Coll. of Law, 1973; CA Bar, 1973; U.S. Supreme Ct. Bar, 1977. **Orgs.:** AALL. Intl. Socty. Gen. Semantics: San Francisco Chap. (Pres., 1978–80). Amer. Bar Assn.: Lib. Com. Sect., Econs. of Law Prac., Ch. **Pubns.:** *An Introduction to the Use of the Law Library* (1974); *Basic Legal Research Techniques* (1979). **Activities:** 12 **Addr.:** Pacific Gas and Electric Co., 77 Beale St., San Francisco, CA 94106.

Strong, Blondell M. (Ja. 11, 1943, Ft. Pierce, FL) Dir., Lib., Meharry Med. Coll., 1967–; Asst. Catlgr., AV Libn., Indian River Jr. Coll., 1965–67; Libn., Lincoln Jr. Coll., 1964–65, Dir., Msc., 1964–65. **Educ.:** TN State Univ., 1960–64, BS (Msc.); George Peabody Coll., 1965–67, MSLS; Univ. of MI, 1980–, Doct. Student (LS). **Orgs.:** Med LA: South. Reg. Grp., Vice-Ch. (1973–74), Ch. (1974–75); Natl. Lib. of Med., Liaison Com. (1976–77). TN LA: Staff Dev. Com. (Ch., 1975–76); Com. on Long-Range Plng. (1974–75). Mid-State LA for TN: Exec. Cncl. (1972). Southeast. Reg. Med. Lib. Prog.: Exec. Cncl. (1972). NAACP: Nashville Branch, VP (1974), Secy. (1973). **Honors:** Kappa Delta Pi, 1964; Alpha Kappa Alpha, 1964; Beta Phi Mu, 1970; Meharry Med. Coll., Outstan. Srv. Dev. Awd., 1974. **Activities:** 1, 12; 17, 26, 32; 63, 80 **Addr.:** 2569 Stone Dr., Ann Arbor, MI 48105.

Strong, Donald Russell (Mr. 2, 1931, Homer City, PA) Lib. Dir., W. Liberty State Coll., 1964–; Head, Ready Ref., Bkmobile. Srvs., Dayton and Montgomery Cnty. Lib., 1960–64; Readers Adv., Ref., Carnegie Pub. Lib., Pittsburgh, 1958–60. **Educ.:** Univ. of Pittsburgh, 1949–56, BA (Eng. Lit.); Carnegie Inst. of Tech., 1957–58, MLS. **Orgs.:** WV LA: 1st VP (1965). **Pubns.:** "Black's Cabin," *Upper OH Valley Hist. Review* (Fall 1976). **Activities:** 1; 15, 17, 31 **Addr.:** RD #1, Box 104, Wheeling, WV 26003.

Strong, Gary E. (Je. 26, 1944, Moscow, ID) CA State Libn., CA State Lib., 1980–; Deputy State Libn., WA State Lib., 1979–80, Assoc. Dir. for Srvs., 1976–79; Lib. Dir., Everett Pub. Lib., 1973–76; Lib. Dir., Lake Oswego Pub. Lib., 1967–73; Head Libn., Markley Residence Lib., Univ. of MI, 1966–67; Ext. Libn., Latah Cnty. Free Lib., 1966. **Educ.:** Univ. of ID, 1962–66, BS (Educ.); Univ. of MI, 1966–67, AMLS. **Orgs.:** ALA: Legis. Com. (1980–); ASCLA, State Aid Std. Com. (1977–80), various coms. LAMA, Bd. of Dirs. (1980–), Small Libs. Pubn. Com. (1969–73). OR LA: Pres. (1970–71). Pac. NW Bibl. Ctr: Bd. of Dirs., VP (1977–80). Pac. NW LA: Treas. (1974–77); Pres. (1978–79). CA Lib. Athrty. for Systs. and Srvs.: Bd. of Dirs. (1980–); Vice-Ch. (1981–). Thurston-Mason Cnty. Mental Hlth. Ctr.: Bd. of Dirs. (1977–80); Pres. (1979–80). St. Peters Hosp.: Psyt. Task Frc. (1979–80). Everett Area Cham. of Cmrce.: Bd. of Dirs. (1974–76). Sr. Srv. of Snohomish Cnty., Inc.: Bd. of Dirs. (1973–76). Various other orgs. **Pubns.:** *Patterns of Information Requests at the Washington State Library* (1981); cmplr., *PNLA Manual of Procedures* (1980); "Evaluating the Reference Product," *RQ* (Sum. 1980); "The Consortium for Public Library Innovation," *Pub. Lib. Qtly.* (Fall 1979); producer, host, *Signatures* cable TV prog. (1974–76); various articles. **Activities:** 9, 13; 17, 24, 34; 51, 75, 93 **Addr.:** California State Library, P.O. Box 2037, Sacramento, CA 95809.

Stroud, Janet Gossard (Jl. 16, 1939, Tipton, IN) Asst. Prof., Lib., Media and Instr. Dev., Purdue Univ., 1976–, Grad. Instr., 1973–76; Media Spec., Tipton Jr. HS, 1965–73; Tchr., 1964–65; Media Spec., Clinton Ctrl. HS, 1961–64. **Educ.:** Ball State Tchrs. Coll., 1957–61, BS (Eng., LS); Purdue Univ., 1973–76, PhD (Educ.). **Orgs.:** ALA: AASL, Resrch. Com.; YASD, Resrch. Com. AALS: Fac. Liaison. AECT: Eval. of Media Prog. Com. Assn. of IN Media Educs.: Nsltr. Ed. Bd.; Conf. Regis. Com., Co-ch. Delta Kappa Gamma Socty.: World Flwshp. Com.; Resrch. Com., Ch. **Pubns.:** *Purdue Self-Evaluation System for School Media Centers* (1976); *Evaluative Case Studies of School Library Media Center Services: PSES Approach* (1979); "Current Research: Evaluation of School Library Programs," *Sch. Media Qtly.* (Sum. 1979); "Evaluation Tools for Practitioners," *AV Instr.* (F. 1977); "School Media Center Services," *Intl. Jnl. of Instr. Media* (1978–79); "User Needs and Library Services," *Cath. Lib. World* (N. 1977); various articles. **Activities:** 11; 26, 37, 41; 63, 67, 72 **Addr.:** 1833 Summit Dr., West Lafayette, IN 47906.

Strougal, Patricia Greganti (S. 21, 1939, Cleveland, MS) Law Libn., Macey and Zusmann, 1979–; Law Libn., Greene, Buckley, DeRieux and Jones, 1978–79; Ctrl. Libn., Supvsr., Archdio. of Atlanta, 1971–75; Sch. Libn., Christ the King Sch., 1970; Ref. Libn., GA Inst. Tech., 1961–63. **Educ.:** Univ. of IL, 1959–60, BA (Hist.), 1960–62, MS (LS). **Orgs.:** AALL. Atlanta Law LA: Pres. (1982–83), Bylaws Com. (1980). Southeast. Assn. of Law Libs.: Pvt. Law Libs. Com. (1981–83). SLA. **Activities:** 12; 15, 17, 30; 77 **Addr.:** 2304 Montview Dr., N.W., Atlanta, GA 30305.

Stroumtsos, Lorraine Y. (Je. 22, 1947, New Brunswick, NJ) Info. Mgt., Exxon Resrch. and Engin. Co., 1979–; Asst. Ed., Merck and Co., Inc., 1972–79; Info. Sci., G.D. Searle, 1971–72. **Educ.:** Wheaton Coll., 1965–69, BA (Chem.); Univ. of CT, 1969–71, MS (Chem.); Tech. Writers Inst., Rennselaer Polytech. Inst., Cert. **Orgs.:** ASIS: Arrange., Hosplty. Ch. (1980–81); Asm. Rep. (1981–82). Socty. for Tech. Comm. Amer. Chem. Socty. Lioness Club of Cranbury: Pres. (1980–81). Woman's Club of Cranbury: Cookbk. Ed. (1979). **Pubns.:** "Information Retrieval," *Kirk-Othmer Encyclopedia of Chemical Technology* (Mr. 1981); *The Merck Index* 9th ed (1976). **Activities:** 12; 30, 37, 46; 56, 75, 93 **Addr.:** Exxon Research & Engineering Co., P.O. Box 121, Linden, NJ 07036.

Stroup, Betty Anne (Jl. 4, 1923, Pittsburgh, PA) Dir., Mt. Lebanon Pub. Lib., 1968–, Asst. Libn., 1966–68; Instr., Eng. Dept., Univ. of Pittsburgh, 1946–65. **Educ.:** Univ. of Pittsburgh, 1941–45, AB (Eng.), 1945–48, MA (Eng.), 1965–66, MSLS. **Orgs.:** PA LA. ALA. **Activities:** 9; 16, 17, 39 **Addr.:** Mt. Lebanon Public Library, 16 Castle Shannon Blvd., Pittsburgh, PA 15228.

PROFESSIONAL ACTIVITIES: Institutions: 1. Acad. lib.; 2. Arch.; 3. Assn.; 4. Fed./Gvt. lib.; 5. Inst. lib.; 6. Mfr./Suppl.; 7. Milit. lib.; 8. Musm.; 9. Pub. lib.; 10. Sch. lib.; 11. Sch. of lib. sci.; 12. Spec. lib.; 13. State lib.; 14. (other). **Functions/Activities:** 15. Acq./Col. dev.; 16. Adult srvs.; 17. Admin.; 18. Apprais.; 19. Archit./Bldgs.; 20. Cat./Class.; 21. Chld. srvs.; 22. Circ.; 23. Cons./Pres.; 24. Consult.; 25. Cont. ed.; 26. Educ. lib. sci.; 27. Ext. srvs.; 28. Fund/Grants; 29. Gvt. pubs.; 30. Indx./Abs.; 31. Instr. lib. use; 32. Media srvs.; 33. Micro.; 34. Netwks./Coop.; 35. Persnl.; 36. PR; 37. Publshg.; 38. Recs. mgt.; 39. Ref. srvs.; 40. Repro.; 41. Resrch.; 42. Review.; 43. Secur.; 44. Serials; 45. Spec. col.; 46. Tech. srvs.; 47. Trustees/Bds.; 48. YA srvs.; 49. (other).

Stroup, Ruth M. (Ap. 28, 1926, Pittsburgh, PA) Elem. Sch. Libn., W. Mifflin Area Schs., 1951–; Asst. Libn., Carnegie Lib., Pittsburgh, 1948–51. **Educ.:** Westminster Coll., 1943–47, BA (Grmn.); Carnegie-Mellon Univ., 1947–48, BSLS; Univ. of Pittsburgh, 1952–55, MEd (Elem. Educ.). **Orgs.:** ALA. PA LA: Regis. Com., 1980 Conf. PA Sch. Libns. Assn.: Secy. (1966–68). Amer. Fed. of Tchrs. West. PA Geneal. Socty. **Activities:** 10; 21, 32 **Addr.:** Clara Barton Elementary School, 764 Beverly Dr., West Mifflin, PA 15122.

Strowd, Elvin E. (Ja. 22, 1925, Ivor, VA) Univ. Libn., Duke Univ., 1981–, Interim Univ. Libn., 1981–, Asst. Univ. Libn., Readers Srvs., 1978–81, Asst. Univ. Libn., Circ. and Dept. Libs., 1970–78, Head, Circ. Dept., 1955–70. **Educ.:** Guilford Coll., 1942–48, AB (Hist.); Univ. of NC, 1948–50, MA (Mod. European Hist.), 1953–55, BS (LS). **Orgs.:** ALA. SELA: *Southeast. Libn.* Advert. Mgr. (1966–72). NC LA: Exhibits Com. (Ch., 1961, 1963, 1965); Coll. and Univ. Sect. (Secy., 1967–69); Exec. Bd. (Dir., 1961–63); JMRT (Ch., 1957–59); Coll. and Univ. Chap. (Ch., 1977–79); *NC Libs.* Ed. Bd. (1956–61). **Honors:** Beta Phi Mu, 1980; Cncl. on Lib. Resrcs., Grant, Flwshp., 1970. **Pubns.:** "Readers' Services—One and All," *The Librarian and Reference Service, Contributions To Library Literature* (1977). **Activities:** 1; 17, 22 **Addr.:** 220 Perkins Library, Duke University, Durham, NC 27705.

Stroyan, Susan E. (Mr. 16, 1950, Lincoln, IL) Instr., IL State Univ., 1977–; Head of Adult Srvs., Bloomington Pub. Libs., 1974–78. **Educ.:** IL State Univ., 1968–72, BSLS; Univ. of IL, 1972–73, MLS. **Orgs.:** ALA: JMRT, Conf. Arrange. (Dir., 1979–80), Awds., Mem. and Cont. Ed. (Dir., 1980–81); LAMA, Pub. of Small Pub. Libs. Com. (1978–80), Prog. Com. (1978–82). IL LA: JMRT (1978–79); Pres. (1979–80). IL Objectives Com. (1977–78); *Lagniappe* Ed.-Conv. (1977). Bd. of Dir. State Alumni Assn.: Bd. of Dirs.; VP (1980–82). McLean Cnty. Arts Cncl.: VP (1977–78). Alpha Beta Alpha: Mu Chap. (Pres., 1971–72). **Honors:** Beta Phi Mu, 1973. **Activities:** 9, 11; 17, 24, 26; 56, 63, 75 **Addr.:** 2013 E. Talyor St., Bloomington, IL 61701.

Strub, Jeane E. (F. 15, 1947, Ft. Riley, KS) Med. Libn., Lovelace Med. Ctr., 1972–; Med. Libn., Thompson Med. Lib., Nvl. Reg. Med. Ctr., 1971–72. **Educ.:** Univ. of NM, 1965–69, BA (Span.); Univ. of KY, 1970–71, MSLS. **Orgs.:** Med. LA. S. Ctrl. Reg. Med. Lib. Prog.: Reg. Adv. Cncl. (1972–74); Exec. Bd. (1974); Hosp. Libns. Com. (1979–80). Grt. Albuquerque LA: Treas. (1974–75). **Honors:** Beta Phi Mu. **Activities:** 12, 15, 17, 39 **Addr.:** Lovelace Medical Library, 5200 Gibson Blvd. S.E., Albuquerque, NM 87108.

Stuart, Frances C. (Je. 7, 1919, Cameron, SC) Dir., Lib. Srvs., Midlands Tech. Coll., 1966–; Catlgr., SC State Lib., 1957–66; Hosp. Libn., Fort Jackson Post Lib., 1956–57; Asst. Lib., Atlas Powder Co., 1954–54. **Educ.:** Univ. of SC, 1936–40, BA (Hist.); George Peabody Coll., 1941–43, BS (LS), 1970–71, MLS. **Orgs.:** ALA. Frnds. of Richland Cnty. Lib.: Various coms., ofcs. SE LA. SC Tech. Libns. Assn.: Various coms., ofcs. Various other orgs. **Honors:** Beta Phi Mu, 1971. **Activities:** 1, 9; 15, 17, 20; 55, 59, 64 **Addr.:** 3546 Greenleaf Rd., Columbia, SC 29206.

Stuart-Stubbs, Basil Frederick (F. 3, 1930, Moncton, NB) Dir., Sch. of Libnshp., Univ. of BC, 1981–, Univ. Libn., 1964–81, Coord., Cols., 1962–64, Head, Spec. Cols. Div., 1960–62; Ref. Libn., McGill Univ. Lib., 1954–56. **Educ.:** Univ. of BC, 1948–52, BA (Phil.); McGill Univ., 1953–54, BLS (Libnshp.). **Orgs.:** ALA. Can. LA: Copyrt. Com., Ch. BC LA. BC ILL Netwk. Proj.: Dir. Various other orgs. Univ. of BC Press: Bd., Ch. Adv. Bd. for Sci. and Tech. Info. Open Lrng. Inst.: Bd. Vancouver City Arch.: Bd. Various other orgs. **Pubns.:** Jt. auth., *The Northpart of America* (1979); *A Survey and Interpretation of the Literature of Interlibrary Loan* (1976); various articles. **Activities:** 1, 11; 26, 34, 37 **Addr.:** University of British Columbia, School of Librarianship-Library, 1956 Main Mall, Vancouver, BC V6T 1Y3 Canada.

Stubbs, Gordon T. (My. 6, 1918, Manchester, Eng.) Assoc. Prof., Univ. of BC, 1965–; Libn., Como Lake Sec. Sch., 1957–65; various tchg. positions, 1940–57. **Educ.:** Univ. of Manchester, 1935–39, BMus (Msc.); Univ. of Manchester, 1939–40, Tchrs. Dip.; Univ. of BC, 1963–65, BLS, MA (Lib. Educ.). **Orgs.:** ALA. BC Sch. Libns. Assn. Can. LA: Sch. Lib. Stans. Com. (Prov. Consult., 1973–78). **Honors:** Univ. of BC, Marian Harlow Prize in Libnshp., 1964. **Pubns.:** *The Role of Egerton Ryerson in the Development of Public Library Service in Ontario* (1966); jt. ed., *Only Connect; Readings on Children's Literature* (1980). **Activities:** 1, 10; 26, 39; 63, 75 **Addr.:** 4830 Osler St., Vancouver, BC V6H 2Y7 Canada.

Stubbs, Linda T. (Ja. 27, 1947, Port Huron, MI) Supvsr. Libn., MARC Ed. Div., Lib. of Congs., 1980–, Descr. Catlgr., 1976–80, MARC Mono. Verifier, 1975–76; Lib. Tech., McKeldin Lib., Univ. of MD, 1973–75. **Educ.:** MI State Univ., 1965–73, BA (Hum.); Univ. of MD, 1974–76, MLS. **Orgs.:** Lib. of Congs. Prof. Assn.: Secy. (1981). DC LA: Tech. Srvs. Com. (1978–79). SALALM. ALA. **Addr.:** 1830 N. Kirkwood Pl., Arlington, VA 22201.

Stuckert, Mrs. Beatrice Stackhouse (Ja. 12, 1910, Camden, NJ) Retired, 1973–; Dir., Haddonfield Pub. Lib., 1944–73, Asst. Libn., 1936–44, E.R.A. Sum. Sub., 1930–36. **Orgs.:** ALA: Intl. Rel. Com. (1968–); various coms. Lib. PR Assn. of Grt. Philadelphia: Exec. Bd. (1966–68, 1972–74); Prog. Ch. (1968); Nom. Com. (Ch., 1973–74). NJ LA: Secy. (1953); 2nd VP (1965–66); Trustee Relshp. Com. (Ch., 1972–76); Natl. Lib. Week Com. (Exec. Dir., 1966–68); Adult Srvs. Sect. (1st Pres., 1963–64); various coms., ofcs. Libs. Unlimited: Pres. (1968–69); various coms. Various other orgs. Zonta Intl. Batsto Citizens Com. Haddonfield Untd. Meth. Church. Leag. of Hist. Soctys. of NJ. **Honors:** Haddonfield Civic Assn., Woman of the Yr., 1953; Camden Cnty., Good Neighbor Awd., Grolier Awd. for Best Natl. Lib. Week in the Country for NJ LA, 1967; NJ LA, Cert. of Recog., 1967. **Pubns.:** *History of the Haddonfield Public Library* (1978); contrib., indxr., "This is Haddonfield," (1964); ch., ed., *Local Indexes in New Jersey Libraries* (1943); ed., *NJ State Frnds. of the Lib. Bltn.* (1967); various articles. **Activities:** 9; 15, 16, 17 **Addr.:** 265 Hawthorne Ave., Haddonfield, NJ 08033.

Stuckey, Janet H. (Jl. 1, 1945, Buffalo, NY) Dir., Benson Meml. Lib., 1976–, Catlgr., 1972–76; Educ. Dir., Drake Well Musm., 1968–72; Asst. News Dir., WTIV Radio, 1968–74. **Educ.:** Edinboro State Coll., 1963–67, BS (Educ.); Clarion State Coll., 1968–70, (Media); State Lib. of PA, 1974, Prov. Lib. Cert. **Orgs.:** PA LA: Memb. Com. (1975, 1978); Northwest Chap. Secty., Treas. ALA. Northwestern Interlib. Coop. Bus. and Prof. Women. Allegheny Canoe Club of Northwestern PA: Pubcty. Ch. (1970–). Amer. Heart Assn.: Northwest Reg., Info. Ofcr. **Activities:** 9; 17, 36, 47; 85, 86, 95-Rural lib. srvs. **Addr.:** 213 N. Franklin St., Titusville, PA 16354.

Stucki, Curtis William (O. 24, 1928, LaCrosse, WI) Head, Cat. Div., Univ. of WA, 1963–81; Head, Cat. Div., Univ. of IA, 1962–63, Head, Spec. Cols. Div., 1960–62; Ref. Libn., Biblgphr., NY State Sch. of Indus. and Labor Rel., Cornell Univ., 1956–60. **Educ.:** Cornell Coll., 1946–50, BA (Hist.); Univ. of OR, 1950–51, 1953–54, MA (Hist.); Univ. of IL, 1954–56, MS (LS). **Orgs.:** ALA: RTSD, Exec. Bd. (1974–77) Cat. and Class. Sect., Exec. Bd (1969–73); Lib. Admin. Div., Tech. Srvs. Stats. Com. (Ch., 1969–73) Persnl. Admin. Sect., Nom. Com. (1974), Com. on Econ. Status, Welfare and Fringe Benefits (1969–75), Staff Dev. Com. (1974–76). Pac. NW LA. Audubon Socty. Nat. Conservancy. **Honors:** Beta Phi Mu. **Pubns.:** *American Doctoral Dissertations on Asia, 1933–1966* (1968); series ed., *Ethnic Studies Information Guide Series* (1974–). **Activities:** 1; 20, 35, 46; 54, 57, 66 **Addr.:** 517 Carlyon Ave., Olympia, WA 98501.

Stucky, Martha (Ap. 3, 1919, McPherson, KS) Dir., Libs., Bethel Coll., 1975–; Dir., Lib. Media, Unfd. Sch. Dist. 383, Manhattan, KS, 1962–75, Libn., 1956–62; Catlgr., KS State Univ., 1953–56; Tchr.—Libn., Lane Cnty. Cmnty. HS, 1946–51; Tchr.—Libn., Henderson HS, 1943–46. **Educ.:** Bethel Coll., 1938–43, AB (Eng.); Univ. of Denver, 1949–52, MA (LS). **Orgs.:** ALA: ACRL; AASL. KS LA: Pres. (1970); VP (1969); Secy. (1959–60). KS Assn. of Sch. Libns.: Pres. (1962–63); VP (1961–62); Secy. (1958–59). Delta Kappa Gamma: Manhattan Chap. (Pres. 1974–75). AAUW. Bus. and Prof. Women's Club, Inc. **Honors:** Bus. and Prof. Women's Club, Woman of the Yr.; Unfd. Sch. Dist. 383, Nominee for KS Mstr. Tchr., 1971. **Activities:** 1, 10; 15, 17, 34 **Addr.:** 2613 Rosewood, P.O. Box 293, North Newton, KS 67117.

Studdiford, Abigail M. (Ap. 23, 1941, Washington, DC) Exec. Dir., NJ Lib. Assn., 1981–; Assoc. Univ. Libn., Princeton Univ., 1976–80; Univ. Libn., Univ. CA Riverside, 1973–76; Asst. Univ. Libn., 1970–73; Acq. Libn., Univ. CO, 1966–70. **Educ.:** Univ. SC, 1958–62, AB (Eng.); Univ. NC (Chapel Hill), 1962–64, MLS; MI Univ., 1977, Cert. Collective Bargaining; Rutgers Univ., 1978, Cert. Collective Bargaining; Rutgers Univ., 1980–, PhD (LS). **Orgs.:** ALA: Couns. Lg. (1978–81); RTSD/Resrc. Sect. (Ch.), Bk. Dealer Lib. Relations Com. (Ch.). Sierra Club: Desert Sub-Com. (1972–75). **Pubns.:** *FEASTschrift (a cookbook)* (1967); "Ten Years of Progress in Acquisitions," *LRTS* (Sum. 1967); "Acquisitions in 1967," *LRTS* (Spr. 1968); "Acquisition Trends - 1968," *LRTS* (Sum. 1969). **Activities:** 1; 15, 17, 34; 56, 95-Labor Relations. **Addr.:** 170 Old York Rd., Bridgewater, NJ 08807.

Studeny, Robert Louis (Jl. 30, 1948, Yoakum, TX) Media Coord., Charles Rice Early Chld. Ctr., Dallas Indp. Sch. Dist., 1977–, Instr. Facilitator, 1976–77, Lrng. Resrcs. Spec., 1974–76; Head Libn., Pillow Acad., 1973–74; Asst. Libn., Legis. Ref. Bur., MS State Law Lib., 1973. **Educ.:** Univ. of South. MS, 1968–71, BA (Jnlsm.); Univ. of MS, 1973–74, MLS; various crs. **Orgs.:** Dallas Cnty. LA: Pres. (1979–80); VP (1978–79); Pubcty. Ed., Nsltr. Ed. (1975–77). Dallas Assn. of Sch. Libns.: Nsltr. Ed. (1975–76). TX LA: Pubns. Com. (1977–78). MS LA: Cont. Ed. Com. Various other orgs. Dallas Metro. Ballet: VP (1977–78). Classrm. Tchrs. of Dallas: Fac. Rep. (1974–76). Dallas Civic Opera Gld. Delta Psi Omega: VP. **Pubns.:** "Pop Corn," *Read Ability Series* (1980); "How Chewing Gum Is Made," *Read Ability Series* (1979); *Tips for Librarians* (1977). **Activities:** 10; 21, 31, 36; 63, 66 **Addr.:** 8710 Park Ln., Unit H, Dallas, TX 75231.

Studer, Paul A. (N. 17, 1924, Biel, Bern, Switzerland) Assoc. Prof., SUNY, Geneseo, 1971–; Head Libn., Annenberg Sch. of Comm., Univ. of PA, 1967–69; Resrch. Assoc., Inst. for Advnc. of Med. Comm., 1963–67; Proj. Dir., Army Resrch. Ofc., 1963–64; Info. Sci., Wallace Labs., 1959–64. **Educ.:** G. Cesare. Lyc., Rome, Italy, Classical BA; Univ. of Pavia, 1950, PhD (Pharm. and Toxicological Chem.); various crs. **Orgs.:** ASIS: *Fndns.* Ed. (1974–). Amer. Socty. for Cybernetics: *Cybernetics Forum* Assoc. Ed. (1974–). Intl. Comm. Assn. SLA. AAAS. Amer. Chem. Socty.: Div. of Chem. Lit. **Pubns.:** "Information Science and the Phenomenon of Information," *JASIS* (Jl. 1978); "The Natural Evolution of Information Phenomena as Organizing Factor for a typology of information science," *Foundations* (Ag. 1975); "From Multidisciplinary to Interdisciplinary Research: Effects of Information Systems on Formal Organizations," *JASIS* (1972); various papers. **Activities:** 11; 27 **Addr.:** School of Library & Information Science, SUNY, Geneseo, NY 14454.

Studer, William J. (O. 1, 1936, Whiting, IN) Dir. of Libs., OH State Univ., 1977–; Assoc. Dean of Univ. Libs., IN Univ., 1973–76, Dir. of Reg. Campus Libs., 1968–73; Intern and Sr. Biblgphr., Lib. of Congs., 1961–65. **Educ.:** IN Univ., 1954–58, BA (Eng.), 1959–60, MA (LS), 1965–68, PhD (LS). **Orgs.:** ALA: Various coms; ACRL (Bd. mem., 1977–81). OCLC, Inc.: Bd. Mem. (1977–79). OHIONET: Vice Ch. of Bd. (1978–). ARL: Ofc. of Mgt. Std. Adv. Com. (1977–); Task Force on Natl. Lib. Netwk. Dev. (1978–, Ch., 1981–); Task Force on Mem. Criteria (1979–). Lib. of Congs. Netwk. Adv. Com. (1981–). Various other orgs. AAUP. **Honors:** Beta Phi Mu; IN Univ., Louise Maxwell Awd., 1978. **Pubns.:** Jt. complr., *John Fitzgerald Kennedy, 1917-1963* (1964); "Book-oriented SDI Service," *Reader in Library Services and the Computer* (1971); "From Cornucopia to Famine: The Impacts and Implications of Budgetary Decline," *Emerging Trends in Library Organization: What Influences Change* (1978); Chaps. in *A Guide to the Study of the United States of America, Supplement 1956-1965* (1976). **Activities:** 1; 17, 34; 56 **Addr.:** The Ohio State University Libraries, Room 106F Main Library, 1858 Neil Ave. Mall, Columbus, OH 432101286.

Studley, Jeanette A. (Mr. 30, 1933, Saugatuck, MI) Asst. Coord., Young People Srvs., Fairfax Cnty. Pub. Lib., 1978–; Chld. Libn., Meriden Pub. Lib., 1974–75. **Educ.:** MI State Univ., 1949–54, BS (Bacteriology); South. CT State Coll., 1970–73, MLS. **Orgs.:** ALA: Liasion with Natl. Orgs. Srvg. Young Chld. (1979–81); YA Bk. List of Nonfiction for the Coll. Bound (1981–82). VA LA. DC LA: Chld. and YA Discuss. Grp. (Ch., 1981–82). **Activities:** 9; 15, 17, 21 **Addr.:** 2622 Garfield St. N.W., Washington, DC 20008.

Studt, Shirlee A. (F. 20, 1934, Woodland, MI) Art Libn., Hum. Bibl. Coord., MI State Univ., 1973–79, Art, Maps, Micro. Libn., 1973, Head Mono. Srch., 1971–73, Asst. Head, 1970–71. **Educ.:** MI State Univ., 1965–69, BA (Hum.); Univ. of MI, 1969–70, AMLS; MI State Univ., 1971–77, MA (Art Hist.). **Orgs.:** ARLIS/NA: Wittenborn Awd. Com. (1976–); Muehsam Awd. Com. (Ch., 1980–); Educ. Com. (1980). Coll. Art Assn. **Activities:** 1; 15, 17, 39; 55, 70 **Addr.:** R. 1, Woodland, MI 48897.

Studwell, William E. (Mr. 18, 1936, Stamford, CT) Head, Cat. Dept., North. IL Univ., 1970–; Head Libn., Kirtland Cmnty. Coll., 1968–70; Actg. Asst. Ed., Decimal Class. Ofc., Lib. of Congs., 1966–68, Tech. Abstctr., Aerosp. Tech. Div., 1963–66. **Educ.:** Univ. of CT, 1954–58, BA (Hist.), 1958–59, MA (Hist.); Cath. Univ., 1964–67, MSLS. **Orgs.:** ALA. IL LA. IL Assn. of Coll. and Resrch. Libs.: Nsltr. (Ed., 1980–); Ex-Officio Mem. of Exec. Bd. (1980–). **Pubns.:** *Chaikovskii, Delibes, Stravinskii* (1977); "To Hear the Angels Sing," *Jnl. of Church Msc.* (D. 1976); "Wonderful Night," *JCM* (D. 1978); "Glory to the Newborn King," *JCM* (D. 1979); "Cantique de Nöel," *JCM* (D. 1980); various other articles. **Activities:** 1; 17, 20 **Addr.:** Founders Memorial Library, Northern Illinois University, DeKalb, IL 60115.

Stueart, Robert D. (Je. 1, 1935, Monticello, AR) Dean, Prof., Grad. Sch. of Lib. and Info. Sci., Simmons Coll., 1975–; Assoc. Prof., Asst. Dean, Grad. Sch. of Libnshp. and Info. Mgt., Univ. of Denver, 1972–74; Visit. Lectr., Coll. of Libnshp., Wales, 1971–72; Asst. Dir. of Libs. for Systs. and Prcs., PA State Univ., 1966–68; Asst. to Dir., Head of Circ., Univ. of CO, 1962–66. **Educ.:** South. AR Univ., 1953–56, BA (Eng.); LA State Univ., 1960–62, MLS; Univ. of Pittsburgh, 1968–71, PhD (Lib. and Info. Sci.). **Orgs.:** ALA: Cncl. (1978); Com. on Lib. Educ. (1978); Appts. Com. (1977–78); RTSD; ACRL; LAMA. AALS: Bd. of Dirs. (1976-79). Long Range Plng. Com. Ch. (1978–79). ASIS. SLA. Beta Phi Mu: Dir. (1974–76). **Honors:** Melvil Dewey Medal, 1980. **Pubns.:** Ed., *Collection Development in Libraries* (1980); jt. ed., *New Horizons for Academic Libraries* (1979); jt. auth., *Lib. Mgt.* (1977); various articles, *Encyc. of Lib. and Info. Sci., Lib. Resrcs. & Tech. Srvs., Jnl. of Educ. for Libnshp., Bay State Libn., Coll. & Resrch. Libs., Jnl. of Acad. Libnshp., AR Libs., Wilson Lib. Bltn.* **Activities:** 1, 11; 15, 17, 26; 54 **Addr.:** Graduate School of Library and Information Science, Simmons College, 300 The Fenway, Boston, MA 02115.

Stuhlman, Daniel D. (O. 7, 1950, St. Louis, MO) Pres. and head consult., Bet Yoatz Lib. Srvs., 1975–; Judaica Libn., Klau Lib., Hebrew Union Coll.-Jewish Inst. of Relig.; Libn., Solomon Schecter Day Sch. **Educ.:** Columbia Univ., 1968–73, BA (Psy.);

Special Subjects/Services: 50. Adult educ.; 51. Advert./Mktg.; 52. Aerosp.; 53. Agric.; 54. Area std.; 55. Arts/Hum.; 56. Autom.; 57. Bibl./Prtg.; 58. Bio. sci.; 59. Bus./Fin.; 60. Chem.; 61. Copyrt.; 62. Documtn.; 63. Educ.; 64. Engin.; 65. Env.; 66. Eth. grps.; 67. Film; 68. Food/Nutr.; 69. Geneal.; 70. Geo.; 71. Geol.; 72. Handcpd.; 73. Hist.; 74. Int. frdm.; 75. Info. sci.; 76. Insr.; 77. Law; 78. Legis.; 79. Math./Comp. sci.; 80. Med.; 81. Metals; 82. Nat. resrcs.; 83. Newsp.; 84. Nuc. sci.; 85. Oral hist.; 86. Petr./Energy; 87. Pharm.; 88. Phys./Astr./Math.; 89. Readg.; 90. Relig.; 91. Sci./Tech.; 92. Soc. sci.; 93. Telecom.; 94. Transp.; 95. (other).

Jewish Theo. Semy., 1968–73, BHL (Bible); Haim Greenberg Coll., 1970–71, Tchr. cert., Columbia Univ., 1973–74 MS LS. **Orgs.:** ALA. AJL. Kehilath Jacob Beth Samuel: VP, 1979–. **Pubns.:** *My Own Hannukah Story* (1980); *My Own Pesah Story* (1980); *Whole wheat bread recipes* (1979); various reviews. **Activities:** 5, 10; 15, 20, 24; 63, 90 **Addr.:** 6247 N. Francisco, Chicago, IL 60659.

Stull, Sarah Louise (Ag. 3, 1917, Thompsonville, IL) Curric. Libn., CA State Univ., Fresno, 1979–, Curric. Libn. and Prof. of Educ., 1967–78; Head, Soc. Sci. Lib., Univ. of AZ, 1966–67; Curric. Libn., CA State Univ., Fresno, 1959–66; Elem. Sch. Libn., Evanston Pub. Schs., 1958–59. **Educ.:** Univ. of IL, 1949–57, BA (Eng. Lit.), 1957–58, MS (LS). **Orgs.:** ALA: AASL. CA LA. CA Media and Lib. Educs. Assn. CA State Empl. Assn. Internatl. Readg. Assn. **Pubns.:** "Some Materials Centers in the Midwest," *Jnl. of Tchr. Educ.* (D. 1960); "Some Materials Centers in the Midwest: A Further Look," *Jnl. of Tchr. Educ.* (Mr. 1963). **Activities:** 1; 15, 20, 39; 63 **Addr.:** 1274 E. Vartikian, Fresno, CA 93710.

Sturgeon, Mary C. (N. 14, 1920, Conway, AR) Assoc. Prof., LS, Univ. of AR., Little Rock, 1967–. **Educ.:** Univ. of Ctrl. AR, 1937–41, BSE (Eng.); George Peabody of Vanderbilt, 1953–56, MA (LS). **Orgs.:** ALA. AR LA. AR Assn. of Sch. Lib. Media Educs.: Ch. (1980). Phi Delta Kappa. **Addr.:** 6217 Boyle Park Rd., Little Rock, AR 72204.

Sturgis, Cynthia M. (Ag. 7, 1946, Lynchburg, VA) Chld. Libn., Ledding Lib., 1979–; Branch Libn., Adult and Chld. Srv., Multnomah Cnty. Lib., 1976–79; Ref. Libn., Willamette Univ. Lib., 1975–76; Ref. Libn., Tucson Pub. Lib., 1974–75; Branch Chld. Libn., Newton Free Lib., 1971–73. **Educ.:** Lynchburg Coll., 1968–69, BA (Phil.); Simmons Coll., 1971–73, MS (LS). **Orgs.:** ALA: Filmstp. Eval. Com. (1981–83), Boy Scout Adv. Com. (1977–81). OR LA: Chld. Sect. (Ch., 1982–83). **Activities:** 9; 21, 31, 39 **Addr.:** Rowe Children's Library, c/o Ledding Library of Milwaukie, 10660 S.E. 21st Ave., Milwaukie, OR 97222.

Suarez, Celia C. (D. 5, 1943, Habana, Cuba) Assoc. Dean, Lrng. Resrcs., Miami–Dade Cmnty. Coll., N., 1981–, Dir., Lib. Srvs., 1975–81, Ref. Libn., 1973–75; Dir. of Lib., Dade Ctr., FL Atl. Univ., 1971–72, Asst. Dir. of Lib., 1970–71. **Educ.:** Cath. Univ. of Amer., 1961–65, BA (Latin Amer. Hist.), 1968–70, MS (LS). **Orgs.:** FL LA: Cmnty. and Jr. Coll. Caucus (Ch., 1978–79); Nom. Com. (1980). ALA. Dade Cnty. LA. FL Devel. Educ. (VP, 1979; Pres., 1980). FL Assn. of Cmnty. Colls. SE FL Educ. Cnsrtm.: Lib. Task Force (Ch.). **Activities:** 1; 17, 25, 31; 55, 56, 89 **Addr.:** Miami–Dade Community College 11380 N. W. 27 Ave., Miami, FL 33167.

Sublette, Doris L. (Ap. 11, 1934, Belvidere, IL) Libn., IL Nat. Hist. Srvy., 1971–. **Educ.:** Univ. of IL, 1954–56, AB (Soclgy.), 1968–71, MS (LS). **Orgs.:** SLA: Env. Info. Div., Treas. (1979–81), Mem. Ch. (1977–79). Grt. Lakes Env. Info. Sharing. **Activities:** 13; 15, 17, 39; 58, 65, 82 **Addr.:** Illinois Natural History Survey, 607 E. Peabody, Champaign, IL 61820.

Subramanyam, Krishna (S. 23, 1934, Mysore, India) Assoc. Prof., Drexel Univ., 1976–; Sci., Eng. Libn., SUNY, Buffalo, 1975–76; Tchg. Fellow, Univ. of Pittsburgh, 1971–75; Sci. Info. Ofcr., Reg. Resrch. Lab., Bhubaneswar, India, 1964–70. **Educ.:** Univ. of Mysore, 1950–54, BS (Phys.); INSDOC, New Delhi, 1966–67, Dip. (Info. Sci.); Univ. of Pittsburgh, 1971–75, MLS, PhD (LS). **Orgs.:** ALA. SLA. ASIS. AALS. **Honors:** Beta Phi Mu, 1972. **Pubns.:** *Scientific and Technical Information Resources* (1981); jt. auth., *Ion Implantation: An Annotated Bibliography* (1975); jt. auth., *Cooperative Use of Machine—Readable Databases by Publishers of Primary and Secondary Journals: A Preliminary Report* (1977); *Directory of Architecture Periodicals* (1980); *Directory of Environmental Periodicals* (1979); *Directory of Primary Journals in Computer Science* (1976); various bk. reviews in *Title Varies* (1977–79), articles, indxs., mono. **Activities:** 11; 26, 30, 44; 64, 65, 91 **Addr.:** 3900 Chestnut St. #320, Philadelphia, PA 19104.

Sudano, Barbara A. (Mr. 9, 1953, Washington, DC) Curric. Lab. Libn., FL Internatl. Univ., 1977–. **Educ.:** Augustana Coll., 1971–75, AB (Hist.); Univ. of IL, 1975–76, MSLS. **Orgs.:** ALA JMRT/Afflt. Cncl. (Rep., Ap. 1979–). FL LA: JMRT/Afflt. Cncl. (Rep., Ap. 1979–). **Honors:** Phi Beta Kappa; Beta Phi Mu. **Activities:** 1; 31, 39; 63, 85 **Addr.:** Library, Curriculum Laboratory, Florida International University, Bay Vista Campus, North Miami, FL 33181.

Sudduth, Susan F. (Je. 15, 1946, Los Angeles, CA) Libn./Mktg. Anal., IMA, Inc., 1980–; Mgt. Libn., Indus. Rel. Ctr., CA Inst. of Tech., 1979; Head, Ref. Dept., Krannert Lib., Krannert Grad. Sch. of Mgt., Purdue Univ., 1975–78; Head, MSS Dept., OR Hist. Socty., 1972–75. **Educ.:** Univ. of South. CA, 1965–68, BA (Hist.); Univ. of OR 1969–70, MLS; Cert. Arch. Admin., 1969–70. **Orgs.:** SLA: Bus. and Fin. SAA: Bus. Arch. Com. (1975–78). Socty. of NW Archvsts.: Chrt. mem.; VP; Cncl. mem. (1973–75). **Pubns.:** "The Employment of Professionals in Support Positions: a Symposium," *Jnl. of Acad. Libnshp.* (Ja. 1978); "The New York Public Library," ERIC report (1971). **Activities:** 1, 12; 15, 39, 41; 51, 59, 93 **Addr.:** IMA, Inc., 15233 Ventura Blvd./Suite 500, Sherman Oaks, CA 91403.

Suelflow, August Robert (S. 5, 1922, Rockfield, WI) Dir., Concordia Hist. Inst., 1948–, Asst. Cur., 1946–48. **Educ.:** Concordia Semy., 1942–46, BD, 1946–47, STM (Hist. Theo.); Bd. of Cert. of Genealogists, 1966, cert. **Orgs.:** SAA: Relig. Arch. Com. (Ch., 1958–62, 1964–77). Amer. Micro. Acad.: Trustee (1962–75). Amer. Recs. Mgt. Assn.: Com. on Hist. and Arch., (Ch., 1969–72). Luth. Hist. Conf.: Pres. (1964–68, 1970–78); VP (1962–64). Luth. Acad. for Schol. Amer. Assn. for Musms. Natl. Trust for Hist. Prsrvn. Various other orgs. **Honors:** SAA, Fellow, 1964; Concordia Semy., Dr. of Dvnty., 1967; SAA, Sr. M. Claude Lane Awd., 1976. **Pubns.:** *Heart of Missouri* (1954); contrib., *The Lutherans in North America* (1975); contrib., *The Encyclopedia of the Lutheran Church* (1965); assoc. ed., *Concordia Historical Institute Quarterly* (1950–); ed., *Directory of Religious Historical Depositories in America* (1963); various other edships. **Activities:** 2, 5; 17, 28, 35; 55, 69, 90 **Addr.:** Concordia Historical Institute, 801 De Mun Ave., St. Louis, MO 63105.

Sugden, Barbara L. (D. 20, 1945, Mt. Clemens, MI) Head Libn., Barrington Area Lib., 1975–; Chld. Libn., Westport Pub. Lib., 1974–75; Ref. Libn., Fairfield Univ., 1974–75; Dir., Merl Kelce Lib., Univ. of Tampa, 1972–74, Circ. Libn., 1971–72; Chld. Libn., N. Babylon Pub. Lib., 1969–71. **Educ.:** West. MI Univ., 1964–67, BA (Eng.); Univ. of Pittsburgh, 1968–69, MSL; Nwest. Univ., 1980– (Mgt.). **Orgs.:** IL LA: Pub. Lib. Sect./Dir. at Lg. (1978–79), Measures of Qlty. Com. (1979). N. Suburban Lib. Syst.: Reg. Lib. Adv. Cncl. (Bd. Mem., 1980); Legis. Netwk. (Co-Ch., 1978–). ALA. Robert Wood Fndn.: Sr. Srvs. Coord. Proj. (Bd. Mem., 1981–). Barrington Area Arts Cncl. Barrington Woman's Club. Chicago Cncl. on Frgn. Rel. **Honors:** Beta Phi Mu, 1969. **Activities:** 1 5; 17, 21, 36 **Addr.:** Barrington Area Library, 505 N. Northwest Hwy., Barrington, IL 60010.

Suggars, Gary Francis (N. 21, 1947, Pittsburgh, PA) Media Spec., Baltimore City Pub. Schs., 1970–. **Educ.:** Westminster Coll., 1965–69, BA (Hist.); Johns Hopkins Univ., 1971–72, MLA (History of ideas); Univ. of MD, 1973–75, MLS. **Orgs.:** ALA. MD LA. Baltimore Blueprint: Educ. Policy Team. Union Sq. Assn.: Pres. H.L. Mencken Socty: Centennial Plng. Com. **Honors:** ALA, Charles S. Scribners Son's Awd., 1978. **Activities:** 10; 21, 24, 32; 55, 63, 89 **Addr.:** 1404 Hollins St., Union Sq., Baltimore, MD 21223.

Sukiennik, Adelaide Weir (Ag. 16, 1938, Pittsburgh, PA) Women's Std. Biblgphr., Univ. of Pittsburgh, Hillman Lib., 1975–, Educ., Biblgphr., 1972–, Instr., Grad. Sch. Lib. and Info. Sci., 1970–72; Hum. Biblgphr., OH State Univ. Libs., 1966–68; Asst. Libn., S. Hills HS, 1964–66. **Educ.:** Otterbein Coll., 1957–61, BA (Eng., Educ.); Univ. of Pittsburgh, 1963–65, MLS, 1978, PhD (LS). **Orgs.:** ALA. PA Lrng. Resrcs. Assn. Natl. Women's Std. Assn. **Honors:** Beta Phi Mu. **Pubns.:** Cmplr., *Resources in Women's Studies* (1980); "Teachers' Libraries," *Encyc. of Lib. and Info. Sci.* (1980). **Activities:** 1; 15, 31; 63, 92 **Addr.:** G27 Hillman Library, University of Pittsburgh, Pittsburgh, PA 15260.

Sullenger, Lee W. (Ja. 26, 1938, Snyder, TX) Assoc. Dir., Pub. Srvs., Stephen F. Austin State Univ., 1971–; Asst. Ref. Libn., Univ. of TX, Arlington, 1970–71. **Educ.:** TX Tech., 1956–60, BA (Eng.); U.S. Army Lang. Sch., 1961 (Span.); Univ. of TX, Austin, 1964–66, MA (Eng.), 1967–70, MLS. **Orgs.:** TX LA: Dist. 8 (Ch., 1976–77); Cncl. (1976–77). SWLA. ALA: Ad Hoc Copyrt. Subcom. (TX Rep., 1980–). Southwest. Amer. Lit. Assn. **Pubns.:** *A Study of Interlibrary Loan Transactions in the Texas Information Exchange* ERIC (1976); "Publishers of Texas Folklore," *Paisanos; A Folklore Miscellany* (1978). **Activities:** 1; 17, 35; 61 **Addr.:** Ralph W. Steen Library, Stephen F. Austin State University, Nacogdoches, TX 75962.

Sullivan, Janet S. (My. 11, 1943, E. Chicago, IN) Coord., Clinical Lab., Bowling Green State Univ., 1978–, Asst. Prof., 1976–78; Dir., Lrng. Ctr., Sch. Dist. 107, Highland Park, IL, 1969–75; Tchr., Crown Point Pub. Schs., 1967–68; Tchr., Cedar Lake Pub. Schs., 1967. **Educ.:** Purdue Univ., 1961–65, BA (Elem. Educ.), 1968–69, MS (Educ. Media); North. IL Univ., 1977, EdD (Instr. Tech.). **Orgs.:** ALA: Student Involvement in the Media Ctr. Prog. Com. (1979–81). AECT: Cont. Educ. Com. (1975–81); Comp. Application in Educ. Com. (1980–). OH Educ. Lib. Media Assn.: Pubn. Com. (1978–81). **Pubns.:** "Nine Design Factors for Better Learning," *Instr. Innovator* (1981); "Initiating Instructional Design into School Media Programs," *Sch. Media Qtly.* (Sum. 1980); "Media Center Programming—A New Twist," *Sch. Media Qtly.* (Spr. 1980); "The Clinical Lab—A Unique Approach to Learning," *Motor Dev.: Theory Into Prac.* (Spr. 1982); "Design Can Turn Micros Into Maxis!" *Electronic Educ.* (D. 1981); various articles, comp. progs. **Activities:** 10, 12; 17, 24, 26; 63 **Addr.:** Clinical Lab., 215 Education Bldg., Bowling Green State University, Bowling Green, OH 43403.

Sullivan, Josephine E. (O. 28, 1914, Hickman, KY) Chief, Readrs. Srvs. Branch, Army Lib., The Pentagon, 1968–, Asst. Chief, 1962–67, LS Instr., Grad. Level, Univ. of VA, North. VA Ctr., 1964–72; Chief, Pers. Sect., 1953–61; Ref. Libn., U.S. Engin. Sch., 1950–52; Tchr., 1951–68; Sr. Catlgr., Sch. of Advnc. Intl. Std., Johns Hopkins Frgn. Srv. Sch., 1949–50; various libn. positions, 1945–49. Tchr., Hickman HS, 1938–45. **Educ.:** Murray State Univ., 1935–38, BS (Eng., Bus. Educ.); George Peabody Coll., 1944–46, MLS (Coll. Libs.). **Orgs.:** SLA: Milit. Libns. Div., Army Lib., Srv. Rep. (1964). DC LA: Mem. Ch. (1965). Inter-Agency Lib. Proj.: Frgn. Area Std. Bibl. Grp., DC Area (1964–68). **Honors:** U.S. Army, Spec. Act of Srv. Awd., 1962; U.S. Army, Spec. Achvmt. Awd., Sustained, Superior Performance, 1969. **Pubns.:** Cmplr., *Union List of Military Periodicals* (1960); "The College Library," *Wilson Lib. Bltn.* (N. 1949). **Activities:** 1, 4; 25, 39; 63, 64, 74 **Addr.:** 4 W. Howell Ave., Alexandria, VA 22301.

Sullivan, Marjorie E. (O. 30, 1950, Holyoke, MA) Admin. Libn., Vets. Admin. Med. Ctr. (Northampton, MA), 1974–, Libn., 1974; Head Libn., Cathedral High School, 1973–74. **Educ.:** Regis Coll., 1968–72, BA (Hist.); SUNY, Albany, 1972–73, MLS. **Orgs.:** MA Hlth. Sci. Libns. Assn.: Pres. (1979–81); VP (1977–79). West. MA Hlth. Info. Cnsrtm.: Ch. (1978–80). Med. LA. ALA. Hlth. Sci. Comms. Assn. **Pubns.:** Various reviews. **Activities:** 4, 5; 17, 34, 39; 58, 72, 80 **Addr.:** P.O. Box 38, Williamsburg, MA 01096.

Sullivan, Martha J. (Ja. 30, 1942, New Haven, CT) Unit Head, CT State Lib., Law Lib. at New Haven and Law Lib. at Waterbury, 1967–; Asst. Ed., *Who's Who in Library Service*, 1965–66. **Educ.:** Manhattanville Coll., 1959–63, AB (Eng.); South. CT State Coll., 1964–66, MS (LS). **Orgs.:** New Eng. Law Libns. Assn. South. New Eng. Law Libns. Assn. AALL. **Activities:** 13; 15, 17, 39; 77 **Addr.:** Connecticut State Library, Law Library at New Haven, County Courthouse, 235 Church St., New Haven, CT 06510.

Sullivan, Michael Vernon (Ag. 11, 1939, Houston, TX) Head Bio. Libn., Stanford Univ., 1979–, Cat./Ref. Libn., Lane Med. Lib., 1977–79; Ref. Libn., Hlth. Sci. Lib., Univ. of WA, 1975–77. **Educ.:** Univ. of CA, Berkeley, 1963–65, BA (Psy.); Stanford Univ., 1966–71, PhD (Psy.); Univ. of CA, Berkeley, 1973–74, MLS (Libnshp.). **Orgs.:** Med. LA: Prog. Com. (1974–75). ASIS. AAAS. **Honors:** Sigma Xi. **Pubns.:** Cmplr., *Neurogenesis and neural regeneration in fish and amphibia, 1971–1974* (1975); "Obsolescence in Biomedical Journals," *Lib. Resrch.* (Ap. 1980). **Activities:** 1; 15, 17, 39; 58, 80 **Addr.:** Falconer Biology Library, Stanford University, Stanford, CA 94305.

Sullivan, Michele Frances (Ja. 30, 1941, Butte, MT) Docum. Libn., Yale Univ. Lib., 1972–; Head, Ref., Reader Srvs., MT State Lib., 1971–72; Assoc. Docum. Libn., Univ. of KS, 1967–69; Sr. Ref. Libn., Westminister Lib. Syst. London, Eng., 1966–67; Asst. Circ. Libn., CA State Univ., Sacramento, 1964–66. **Educ.:** San Francisco Coll. for Women, 1959–63, BA (Hist., Pol. Sci.); Univ. of CA, Berkeley, 1963–64, MLS; Univ. of London, Univ. Coll., 1969–70, MA (Hist.). **Orgs.:** ALA: GORDORT, Intl. Docum. Task Frc. (Ch., 1976–77). CT GORDORT. Medvl. Acad. of Amer. **Activities:** 1, 12; 16, 29, 39; 62, 78, 92 **Addr.:** 19 Wilkins St., Hamden, CT 06517.

Sullivan, Peggy A. (Ag. 12, 1929, Kansas City, MO) Dean, Coll. of Prof. Std., North. IL Univ., 1981–; Asst. Comsn. for Ext. Srvs., Chicago Pub. Lib., 1977–81; Assoc. Prof. and Dean of Students, Grad. Lib. Sch., Univ. of Chicago, 1974–77; Exec. Secy., Lib. Educ. Div., Dir., Ofc. for Lib. Persnl. Resrcs., ALA, 1973–74; Asst. Prof. and Dir., Sch. Lib. Cert. Prog., Grad. Sch. of Lib. and Info. Scis., Univ. of Pittsburgh, 1971–73. **Educ.:** Clarke Coll., 1946–50, AB (Lang., Lit.); Cath. Univ. of Amer., 1950–52, MS (LS); Univ. of Chicago, 1968–72, PhD (LS). **Orgs.:** ALA: Pres. (1980–81); various coms.; Cncl. (1977–). Chicago Lib. Club: Various coms.; Secy. (1963–75). SLA: IL Chap., Com. on New Spec. Libs. (1976–79). IL LA: various coms. (1973–). AAUW. AAUP. **Honors:** Tangley Oaks Flwshp., 1968. **Pubns.:** *Opportunities in Libraries and Information Science* (1977); *Carl H. Milam and the American Library Association* (1976); *Problems in School Media Management* (1971); Ed., *Realization: The Final Report of the Knapp School Libraries Project* (1968); "Research in Librarianship," *IL Libs.* (My. 1978). **Activities:** 9, 11; 18, 27, 36; 68, 75, 90 **Addr.:** 1777 Longwood Dr., Sycamore, IL 60178.

Sullivan, Robert Coyle (My. 29, 1927, Washington, DC) Chief, Order Div., Lib. of Congs., 1971–, Asst. Chief, Photodup. Srv., 1964–71, Asst. Chief, Order Div., 1960–64, Head, Orders Sect., Card Div., 1960. **Educ.:** Georgetown Coll., 1945–49, BS (Hist.); Cath. Univ., 1955–65, MLS. **Orgs.:** ALA. Natl. Micro. Assn. Amer. Natl. Stans. Inst.: Com. Z–39. SALALM. **Pubns.:** Jt. auth., *Reprographic Services in Libraries* (1975); "The Acquisition of Library Microforms," *Micro. Review* (My. and Jl. 1977); "Microform Developments Related to Acquisitions," *Coll. and Resrch. Libs.* (Ja. 1973); "Developments in Reproduction of Library Materials, 1968," *Lib. Resrcs. and Tech. Srvs.* (Sum. 1969); "Developments in Reproduction of Library Materials, 1969," *LRTS* (Spr. 1970); "Developments in Reproduction of Library Materials, 1970," *LRTS* (Spr. 1971). **Activities:** 4; 15, 17, 33; 56 **Addr.:** 3915 20th Pl., Hillcrest Heights, MD 20748.

Sullivan, Sarah E. (Sarabeth) (Ap. 25, 1927, Lubbock, TX) Div. Head, Bus. and Tech. Div., Dallas Pub. Lib., 1970–, Div. Head, Cmnty. Living Div., 1969–70, 1st Asst. Bus. and

PROFESSIONAL ACTIVITIES: Institutions: 1. Acad. lib.; 2. Arch.; 3. Assn.; 4. Fed./Gvt. lib.; 5. Inst. lib.; 6. Mfr./Suppl.; 7. Milit. lib.; 8. Musm.; 9. Pub. lib.; 10. Sch. lib.; 11. Sch. of lib. sci.; 12. Spec. lib.; 13. State lib.; 14. (other). **Functions/Activities:** 15. Acq./Col. dev.; 16. Adult srvs.; 17. Admin.; 18. Apprais.; 19. Archit./Bldgs.; 20. Cat./Class.; 21. Chld. srvs.; 22. Circ.; 23. Cons./Pres.; 24. Consult.; 25. Cont. ed.; 26. Educ. lib. sci.; 27. Ext. srvs.; 28. Fund/Grants; 29. Gvt. pubs.; 30. Indx./Abs.; 31. Instr. lib. use; 32. Media srvs.; 33. Micro.; 34. Netwks./Coop.; 35. Persnl.; 36. PR; 37. Publshg.; 38. Recs. mgt.; 39. Ref. srvs.; 40. Repro.; 41. Resrch.; 42. Review.; 43. Secur.; 44. Serials; 45. Spec. col.; 46. Tech. srvs.; 47. Trustees/Bds.; 48. YA srvs.; 49. (other).

Tech. Div., 1960–69; Libn., Pulaski Heights Jr. HS, 1958–59. **Educ.:** N. TX State Univ., 1943–47, BS (Lib. Srv.); TX Woman's Univ., 1963–68, MLS. **Orgs.:** SLA: Bus. and Fin. Div. (Dir. 1981–82). Pub. and Gvt. RT (Ch., 1979–80). TX LA: Dist. 5 (Ch., 1971). **Pubns.:** Ed., *Business History Collection, a Checklist* (1974); *A Survey of Patrons of the Science and Industry Department of Dallas Public Library* (1969); ed., *For Your Information* nsltr. (1967); ed., *Business Information for Dallas* nsltr. (1976). **Activities:** 9; 16, 17, 24; 51, 59, 68 **Addr.:** 3715 Durango, Dallas, TX 75220.

Sullivan, Sharon A. (D. 22, 1947, Fitchburg, MA) Persnl. Libn., OH State Univ. Libs., 1980–; Lib. Systs. Anal., OCLC, Inc., 1978–80; Systs. Libn., Harvard Univ. Lib., 1973–78. **Educ.:** Regis Coll., 1965–69, AB (Hist.); Simmons Coll., 1970–73, MS (LS). **Orgs.:** ALA: LITA/Tech. Stans. for Lib. Autom. Com. (1978–80). ASIS. **Activities:** 1, 15, 17, 34; 56, 57 **Addr.:** Ohio State University Libraries, 1858 Neil Ave. Mall, Columbus, OH 43210.

Sullivan, Suzanne E. (Ja. 16, 1930, Hollywood, CA) Asst. Head, Ref., JFK Lib., CA State Univ., Los Angeles, 1981–; Pers. Libn., 1980–81, Coord. Lib. Instr., 1976–81, Head, Curric. Ctr., 1974–81; Chld. Libn., Los Angeles Cnty. Pub. Lib., 1971–74. **Educ.:** CA State Coll., San Bernardino, 1965–69, BA (Hist.); Immaculate Heart Coll., 1969–71, MALS. **Orgs.:** CA LA: Chld. Div., Conf. Prog. (Ch., 1975). YA Reviewers of South. CA: Pres. (1977). CA Clearinghse. on Lib. Instr.: Strg. Com. (1978–79). ALA: ALSC, Mildred L. Batchelder Awd. Sel. Com. (1979); YASD, Srvs. Statement Dev. Com. (1976–77), Mem. Promo. Com. (1978–82), Outstan. Fiction for the Coll. Bound (1979–81). **Activities:** 1; 17, 31, 49-Curric. resrcs.; 55, 63 **Addr.:** John F. Kennedy Library, California State University, Los Angeles, 5151 State University Dr., Los Angeles, CA 90032.

Sullivan, Thomas E(dward) (F. 11, 1921, Worcester, MA) Assoc. Dir., Indexing Srvs., The H.W. Wilson Co., 1961–; Chief, Cat. Dept., John Crerar Lib., 1959–61; Serials Catlgr., Lib. of Congs., 1952–59; Catlgr., Yale Univ. Lib., 1947–49. **Educ.:** Holy Cross Coll., 1939–43, BA (Phil.); Columbia Univ., 1946–47, BS (LS, Libnshp.); Cath. Univ. of Amer., 1949–52, MA (Phil.). **Orgs.:** ALA: RTSD/Cat. and Class. Sect. (Ch., 1970–71). Cath. LA: Fin. Com. (Ch., 1967–69, 1974–79). Lake Placid Educ. Fndn.: Forest Press Com. (1978–). **Activities:** 14-Publshg.; 17, 20, 30; 55, 56, 57 **Addr.:** 10 Waterside Plz., Apt. 15A, New York, NY 10010.

Sullivan, Vicki (Ag. 15, 1949, Washington, DC) Dir., Lib. Resrcs., OK Hist. Socty., 1979–; Asst. OK Pubns. Libn., OK Dept. of Libs., 1978–79; Hist. Socty. Libn., OK Hist. Socty., 1976–78; Libn., 130th Gen. Hosp., Nuernberg, Germany, 1974–75. **Educ.:** Univ. of OK, 1969–73, BSed (Educ., LS), 1973–74, MLS; OK State Univ., 1976–77, MA (Hist.). **Orgs.:** OK LA: Gvrs. Mansion Lib. Com. (1980–81). Socty. of SW Archvsts.: Nsltr. Ed. (1980–81). Amer. Assn. for State and Lcl. Hist. **Honors:** Phi Alpha Theta, 1977. **Pubns.:** Jt. auth., *Index to the 1890 Oklahoma Territorial Census for the Counties of Kingfisher, Payne and Beaver* (1977); "Oklahoma Books," *The Chronicles of OK* (1976–); asst. ed., *OK Gvt. Docum.* (1979–80). **Activities:** 2, 3; 39, 41, 45; 66, 69, 83 **Addr.:** Oklahoma Historical Society, Historical Bldg., Oklahoma City, OK 73105.

Sultana, Pierre (Ja. 27, 1916, Visina, Roumanie) Chief Libn., Univ. de Montréal, Bib. de bibliothéconomie, 1974–, Ref. and Class., Bib. méd., 1962–74. **Educ.:** Univ. de Montréal, 1958–59, Mstr. (Phil.), 1962–63, BLS, 1972–73, MLS. **Orgs.:** Corp. des Bibtcrs. Profs. du PQ. Romanian Assn. of Can. **Activities:** 1; 15, 35, 39 **Addr.:** Bibliothèque de bibliothéconomie, Université de Montréal, C.P. 6128, Succursale "A", Montreal, PQ H3C 3J7 Canada.

Sumler, Claudia Burnett (S. 14, 1947, New York, NY) Dir., Kent Cnty. Pub. Lib., 1974–; Mono. Biblgrphr., Univ. of IL, 1971–73. **Educ.:** Univ. of IL, 1965–69, BA (Hist.), 1969–70, MLS; Univ. of MD, Lib. Admins. Devel. Prog., 1977, Cert. (Mgt.). **Orgs.:** MD LA: Co-ch. exhibits, anl. conf. (1975–78); Plng. and Legis. Com. (1976–77); Adult/Young Adult Srvs. Div. (Pres., 1979). MD Div. of Lib. Devel. and Srvs.: Cont. Lib. Educ. in MD (1977–). **Pubns.:** *Kent County Public Library: A Survey of a Small Public Library and its Community with Recommendations for Future Goals* (1976). **Activities:** 9; 15, 25, 49-Community Analysis. **Addr.:** Kent County Public Library, 408 High St., Chestertown, MD 21620.

Summers, Frank William (F. 8, 1933, Jacksonville, FL) Dean, Coll. of Libnshp., Univ. of SC, 1976–, Asst. Dean, 1971–76; State Libn., FL State Lib., 1965–69; Assoc. Libn., Providence Pub. Lib., 1961–65. **Educ.:** FL State Univ., 1951–55, BA (LS); Rutgers Univ., 1958–59, MLS, 1969–73, PhD (LS). **Orgs.:** ALA: Com. on Prog. Eval. and Support (1977–, Ch., 1981–82); Cncl. (1973–77, 1981–); Com. on Accred. (1968–73, Ch., 1972–73). SC LA: Pres. (1981). Lib. of Congs.: Adv. Com. on Libs. (1976–77). **Honors:** Beta Phi Mu, 1959. **Pubns.:** Issue Ed., *Lib. Trends* (Fall 1977); "The Use of Formulae in Resource Allocations," *Lib. Trends* (Ap. 1975); various lib srvys. and consults. **Activities:** 4, 9, 11; 17, 18, 24; 63, 77, 78 **Addr.:** College of Librarianship, University of South Carolina, Columbia, SC 29208.

Summers, Nancy G. (Mr. 6, 1946, Richmond, VA) Med. Campus Archvst., Med. Coll. of VA, VA Cmwlth. Univ., 1975–81, Med. Catlgr., 1973–75. **Educ.:** Coll. of William and Mary, 1964–68, BA (Eng.); Univ. of IL, 1968–69, MA (Eng.); Mod. Arch. Inst., Amer. Univ., 1979, Cert. (Arch. Admin.). **Orgs.:** SAA. Mid-Atl. Reg. Arch. Conf. **Activities:** 2, 12; 15, 17, 41; 80 **Addr.:** 1004 Francisco Rd., Richmond, VA 23229.

Summers, Robert A. (O. 23, 1939, Sedro–Woolley, WA) Circ. Assoc., Circ. Film Prog., Musm. of Mod. Art, 1977–; Film Prsrvn. Tech. Coord., Lib. of Congs., 1975–77; Dir., NW Film Study Ctr., 1970–72. **Educ.:** Portland State Univ., –69, BA (Gen. Stds.); NY Univ., 1969–75, MA (Cin. Stds.). Socty. for Cin. Stds. Socty. for Motion Pic. and TV Engins. **Activities:** 2, 4; 15, 22, 23; 67, 92 **Addr.:** The Museum of Modern Art, Circulating Film Program, 11 W. 53rd St., New York, NY 10021.

Summit, Roger K. (O. 14, 1930, Detroit, MI) Pres., DIALOG Info. Srvs. Inc., Lockheed Corp., 1981–, Dir., Info. Systs., Lockheed Palo Alto Resrch. Lab., 1978–81, Mgr., DIALOG Info. Retrieval Srvc., 1972–77, Resrch. Sci., 1965–72. **Educ.:** Stanford Univ., 1948–52, AB (Psy.), 1957, MBA (Bus. Admin.), 1965, PhD (Mgt. Systs.). **Orgs.:** Engin. Index: Trustee. Info. Indus. Assn.: Dir. ASIS. Dept. of Cmrce. and MA Inst. of Tech. Natl. Comsn. of Libs. and Info. Sci. **Honors:** Lockheed Corp., Spec. Invention Awd.; Info. Indus. Assn., Info. Prod. of the Yr., 1975. **Pubns.:** "DIALOG Interactive Information Retrieval System," *Encyc. of Lib. and Info. Sci.* (1972); "New Developments in Online Information Retrieval Techniques as Applied to the Uniform Parole Reports," *Abs. on Criminology and Penology* (Ja.–F. 1970); "On-Line Information Retrieval Comes of Age," *ASIS* (O. 1968). **Addr.:** Lockheed Palo Alto Research Lab., Dept. 52-80, B/580 3460 Hillview Ave., Palo Alto, CA 94304.

Sumners, Bill F. (Ap. 15, 1950, Wilsonville, AL) Asst. Archvst., Auburn Univ., Arch., 1977–; Lib. Dir., Shelby Cnty. Lib., 1976–77; Asst. Archvst., Rosenberg Lib., 1975–76. **Educ.:** Samford Univ., 1968–72, BA (Hist.); Univ. of TX, Arlington, 1973–75, MA (Hist., Arch.); 1975, Cert. (Arch. Admin.). **Orgs.:** SAA. Socty. of AL Archvsts.: VP (1979–80); Pres. (1980–81); Nsltr. Ed. (1977–81). **Pubns.:** "Southern Baptists and Women Right to Vote," *Bapt. Hist. and Heritage* (Ja. 1977); "Southern Baptists and Women's Rights," *AL Bapt. Histn.* (Je. 1980). **Activities:** 2; 15, 39, 45; 55, 85, 92 **Addr.:** Auburn University Archives, R.B.D. Library, Auburn University, AL 36849.

Sunday, Donald E. (Ap. 15, 1951, Flint, MI) Libn., Gen. Motors Resrch. Labs., Lib., Tech. Ctr., Warren, MI, 1977–; Libn., Detroit Pub. Lib., 1974–77. **Educ.:** Univ. of MI, 1969–72, BA (Eng.), 1973, AMLS. **Orgs.:** SLA: MI Chap., Educ. Com. (1981). ALA. GODORT of MI. **Activities:** 12; 20, 31, 39; 75, 91, 94 **Addr.:** General Motors Research Labs., Library, GM Technical Center, Warren, MI 48090.

Sundt, Christine Leszczynski (Ja. 11, 1944, Chicago, IL) Cur., Slides and Photographs, Univ. of WI, Madison, Dept. of Art Hist., 1973–. **Educ.:** Univ. of IL, Chicago, 1966–69, BA (Art Hist.); Univ. of WI, Madison, 1969–73, MA (Art Hist.). **Orgs.:** ARLIS/NA: Acad. Sect. (1977–80), Jt. Ad—Hoc Com. on Prof. Stans. for Visual Resrcs. Cols. (Ch., 1980–). ARLIS/NA—Mid–States. Coll. Art Assn. Mid—Amer. Coll. Art Assn.: U–R Com. (Ch. Elect, 1981–82). **Pubns.:** Ed., *Guide to Equipment for Slide Maintenance and Viewing* (forthcoming); "Mounting Color Slide Film Between Glass—For Preservation or Destruction?" *Visual Resrcs.: An Intl. Jnl. of Documtn.* (forthcoming); various articles, *Intl. Bltn. for Photographic Documtn. in the Visual Arts.* **Activities:** 12, 14-Slide/vid. col.; 15, 17, 20; 55 **Addr.:** Dept. of Art History, University of Wisconsin, Madison, 800 University Ave., Madison, WI 53706.

Sundvold, Glenn E. (Jl. 6, 1926, Watertown, SD) Lib. and Educ. Media Dir., Mount Marty Coll., 1969–; Libn. and Span. Tchr., Mount Marty High Sch., 1966–69; Natl. Bank Examiner, US Comptroller of the Currency, 1965–66; Asst. Bank Mgr., First Natl. Bank of San Diego, 1954–65. **Educ.:** Univ. of SD, 1945–48, BA (Span.); Natl. Inst. of Banking, 1954–65, Grad. Cert. (Banking); Emporia State Univ., 1970–71, MLS. **Orgs.:** ALA. SD LA: Acad. Sect. (Ch., 1975–76). Mt. Plains LA: Exec. Bd. (SD Rep., 1976–78). Colls. of Mid–Amer. LA. Amer. Luth. Church. B.P.O. Elks. Sigma Alpha Epsilon. **Honors:** Beta Phi Mu, 1973. **Activities:** 1; 17, 32 **Addr.:** Mount Marty College Library, Yankton, SD 57078.

Sung, Carolyn Hoover (D. 24, 1942, Chester, SC) Exec. Ofcr., Resrch. Srvs., Lib. of Congs., 1980–; Asst. Chief, Photodup. Srv., 1977–80, Head, Ref. and Reader Srvs., Ms. Div., 1971–77, Ms. Lib. Prep. Sect., 1967–71. **Educ.:** Winthrop Coll., 1961–65, BA (Hist.); Univ. of MD, 1967–70, MA (Hist.); George Washington Univ., 1975–, ABD (Amer. Std.); NHPRC Ed. Inst., Univ. of VA, 1975. **Orgs.:** SAA: Nom. Com. (Ch., 1974); Com. on Finding Aids (1973–76); Com. on Ref. and Access Policies (1976–80); Arch. Manpower Proj. (1977); Task Frc. on Stan. Rpt. Pracs. (1980–81); Task Frc. on Copyrt. (1980–81). SLA. Mid—Atl. Reg. Arch. Conf.: Prog. Ch. (1977). Ms. Socty.: DC Chap. (Pres., 1973–74). South. Hist. Assn. **Honors:** Phi Alpha Theta, 1964. **Pubns.:** *Specifications for Microfilming Manuscripts* (1980); "Catharine Mitchill's Letters from Washington, 1806–1812," *Qtly. Jnl. of the Lib. of Congs.* (Jl. 1977); *Register of the Papers of J. Robert Oppenheimer in the Manuscript Division* (1974); "Your Manuscripts and the Scholarly World," *Autographs and Manuscripts: A Collector's Manual* (1978); "Local History: The Genesis of State and National History," *Preserving The Past for the Future: Local History and the Community* (1980). **Activities:** 1, 2; 17, 33, 39; 54, 67, 69 **Addr.:** Research Services, Library of Congress, Washington, DC 20540.

Supple, Sr. Michael P. (Los Angeles, CA) Dir., Instr. Media Ctr., Mt. St. Mary's Coll., 1974–). **Educ.:** Mount St. Mary's Coll., BA; Univ. of MD, –74, MLS. **Orgs.:** ALA. Beta Phi Mu: Beta Chap. CA LA. CA Media and Lib. Educs. Assn. AECT. Cmnty. Coll. Media Assn. of South. CA. **Honors:** US Ofc. of Educ., Grant for the Study of Eth. and Cult. Change. **Activities:** 1; 17, 32 **Addr.:** Mount St. Mary's College, 12001 Chalon Rd., Los Angeles, CA 90049.

Surace, Cecily J. (Je. 9, 1931, Brooklyn, NY) Ed. Lib. Dir., *Los Angeles Times,* 1979–; Lib. Dir., Rand Corp., 1975–79, Deputy Lib. Dir., 1973–75; Syst. Coord., Metro. Coop. Lib. Syst., 1971–73; Deputy Lib. Dir., Rand Corp., 1966–71. **Educ.:** Hunter Coll., 1948–52, BA (Hist.); Columbia Univ., 1952–54, MS (LS). **Orgs.:** SLA: Chap. Advert. Com., Chap. Secy.; Chap. Pres.; Gvt. Info. Srvs. Com. ASIS. ALA. Assn. of Info. Mgrs. CA Lib. Srvs. Bd. **Pubns.:** "PEARL—Periodicals Automation," *Rand P–4627* (1971); "Displays of a Thesaurus," *Rand P–4331* (1970); "Library Circulation Systems," *Rand P–4338* (1970); "The Human Side of Libraries," *Rand P–4005* (1969); "The Current Awareness Bulletin," *Procs. Reg. Wkshp. Rpt. Lit.* (1965). **Activities:** 12; 17, 34; 56, 83, 93 **Addr.:** Editorial Library, *Los Angeles Times,* Times Mirror Sq., Los Angeles, CA 90053.

Surprenant, Thomas T. (My. 3, 1942, Troy, NY) Asst. Prof., Univ. of RI, 1978–; Head Libn., Northland Coll., 1969–78; Supvsr., Tech. Info. Srvs., IL Inst. of Tech. Resrch. Inst., Electromagnetic Compatibility Analysis Ctr., 1965–69. **Educ.:** Siena Coll., 1960–64, BA (Hist., Eng.); Cath. Univ. of Amer., 1964–67, MSLS; Univ. of WI, LaCrosse, 1973–75, MS; Univ. of WI, Madison, 1978–80, PhD (LS, Instr. Tech.). **Orgs.:** ALA: ACRL, New Eng. Chap., Bibl. Instr. Com. (Ch., 1980–81). RI LA: Exec. Bd. (1979–80). World Future Socty. **Activities:** 1, 12; 26, 32, 41; 63, 75, 93 **Addr.:** Graduate Library School, University of Rhode Island, Rodman Hall, Kingston, RI 02881.

Surrency, Erwin C. (My. 11, 1924, Jesup, GA) Prof. of Law, Law Libn., Law Sch., Univ. of GA, 1979–; Asst. Dean, Prof. of Law, Law Libn., Temple Univ., 1950–78. **Educ.:** Univ. of GA, 1945–48, AB (Hist.), 1948–49, JD (Law), MA. **Orgs.:** AALL: Pres. (1973–74). Natl. Micro. Assn. Amer. Socty. for Legal Hist.: Fndr.; Pres. **Pubns.:** *Guide to Legal Research;* various articles, *Amer. Jnl. of Legal Hist.;* ed., various microfilm cols. **Activities:** 12; 24, 30, 33; 61, 77, 78 **Addr.:** Law Library, University of Georgia, Athens, GA 30602.

Sutherland, J. Elizabeth (F. 19, 1943, Brandon, MB) Head, Lib. Srvs., Bedford Inst. of Oceanography, 1980–, Actg. Head, Lib. Srvs., 1979–80, Ref. Libn., 1974–79. **Educ.:** Univ. of AB, 1959–63, BA (Hist.), 1964, Spec. Yr. (Msc.); Dalhousie Univ., 1972–74, MLS. **Orgs.:** Can. LA: Status of Women Com. (1974–76). Atl. Provs. LA: Treas. (1979–81); Cnclr. for Mem. (1978–79). Internatl. Assn. of Marine Sci. Libs. and Info. Ctrs.: VP/Pres. Elec., 1980–81; Local arranges. conv. (1980). NS On–Line Cnsrtm.: Conv. (1976–78). Various other orgs. Heritage Trust of NS. **Honors:** Beta Phi Mu, 1974. **Pubns.:** "The Nova Scotia On-Line Consortium," *APLA Bltn.* (1978). **Activities:** 4; 17, 20, 39; 91 **Addr.:** Library, Bedford Institute of Oceanography, P.O. Box 1006, Dartmouth, NS B2Y 4A2 Canada.

Sutherland, Johnnie David (N. 10, 1942, Pendleton, OR) Map Cur., Univ. of GA Libs., 1976–. **Educ.:** Univ. of OR, 1963–70, BS (Geo.), 1970–72, MA (Geo.); Univ. of GA, 1972–76, (Geo.). **Orgs.:** SLA. West. Assn. Map Libns. OCLC Map Users Grp.: Secy. (1979–). Southeast. Div., Assn. of Amer. Geographers: Com. on South. Map Libs. (1978–); Ed., CSML Nsltr. (1980–); Wkshp. on Map Libs. (Prog. Ch., 1978). **Activities:** 1, 12; 15, 20, 39; 70 **Addr.:** Map Collection, Science Library, University of Georgia Libraries, Athens, GA 30602.

Sutherland, Thomas A. (O. 24, 1940, Owensboro, KY) Dir., Paducah Pub. Lib., 1968–; Exec. Dir., KY LA, 1970–; Reg. Dir., KY Dept. of Libs., 1965–68. **Educ.:** KY Wesleyan Coll., 1959–64, BA (Hist.); Univ. of KY, 1964–65, MSLS. **Orgs.:** ALA: Pub. Lib. Systs. Sect. (Pres., 1977–78); Chap. Rel. Com. (1975–77); Exhibits RT (ERT Nsltr., Ed., 1978–). KY LA: Pres. (1969–70). SELA: Plng. and Devel. Com. KY Gvr.'s Lib. Adv. Cncl.: Ch. (1974–75). **Honors:** KY LA, Outstan. Pub. Libn., 1974; KY Lib. Trustees Assn., Pres.'s Awd., 1971. **Pubns.:** "The Gravesend Press," *Amer. Book Collector* (Ap. 1965); "Art in the Public Library," *SEast. Libn.* (Sum. 1966). **Activities:** 9; 15, 17, 23; 55 **Addr.:** Paducah Public Library, 555 Washington St., Paducah, KY 42001.

Special Subjects/Services: 50. Adult educ.; 51. Advert./Mktg.; 52. Aerosp.; 53. Agric.; 54. Area std.; 55. Arts/Hum.; 56. Autom.; 57. Bibl./Prtg.; 58. Bio. sci.; 59. Bus./Fin.; 60. Chem.; 61. Copyrt.; 62. Documtn.; 63. Educ.; 64. Engin.; 65. Env.; 66. Eth. grps.; 67. Film; 68. Food/Nutr.; 69. Geneal.; 70. Geo.; 71. Geol.; 72. Handcpd.; 73. Hist.; 74. Int. frdm.; 75. Info. sci.; 76. Insr.; 77. Law; 78. Legis.; 79. Math./Comp. sci.; 80. Med.; 81. Metals; 82. Nat. resrcs.; 83. Newsp.; 84. Nuc. sci.; 85. Oral hist.; 86. Petr./Energy; 87. Pharm.; 88. Phys./Astr./Math.; 89. Readg.; 90. Relig.; 91. Sci./Tech.; 92. Soc. sci.; 93. Telecom.; 94. Transp.; 95. (other).

Sutherland, Zena B. (S. 17, 1915, Winthrop, MA) Assoc. Prof., Grad. Lib. Sch., Univ. of Chicago, 1977–; Lectr., 1972–76, Chld. Bk. Ed., *Chicago Tribune*, 1972–; Contrib. Ed., *Saturday Review*, 1966–72; Ed., *Bltn. of the Ctr. for Chld. Bks.*, 1958–. **Educ.:** Univ. of Chicago, 1933–37, BA (Eng.), 1966, MA (LS). **Orgs.:** Intl. Readg. Assn.: Bk. Awd. Com. (Ch., 1981). ALA: ALSC, Dirs. Bd. (1977–80), Newbery—Caldecott Com. (Ch., 1975), Batchelder Awd. Com. (Ch., 1981). Chld. Readg. RT. Intl. Bd. on Bks. for Young People: U.S. Sect. Auths. Gld. Socty. of Midland Auths. Natl. Cncl. of Tchrs. of Eng. Women's Natl. Bk. Assn. **Honors:** Chld. Readg. RT, Anl. Recog. Awd., 1978; Pi Lambda Theta, Best Educ. Bk., 1974; Univ. of Chicago, Zena Sutherland Lectrshp., 1981; Recipient of Festschrift, *Celebrating Children's Books: Essays in Honor of Zena Sutherland* (1981). **Pubns.:** *Children and Books* (1981); *The Best in Children's Books* (1980); ed., *Children and Libraries: Patterns of Access to Materials and Services* (1981); ed., *The Arbuthnot Lectures, 1970–1979* (1980); ed., *Burning Bright*; various bks., articles in *Wilson Lib. Bltn., Lib. Trends, Lib. Qtly., Amer. Libs., Top of the News, Tuesday, Saturday Review, Chicago Tribune, Sch. Lib. Jnl., Chld. Lit. in Educ.*, others. **Activities:** 9, 10; 21, 42, 48; 50, 74, 89 **Addr.:** 1100 E. 57 St., Chicago, IL 60637.

Sutliff, Sandra A. (Jl. 18, 1948, Kingston, PA) Chief Libn., Doyle Dane Bernbach, 1976–; Resrch. Libn., Young and Rubicam; Resrch. Libn., Booz Allen and Hamilton; Ref. Libn., Danbury Pub. Lib. **Educ.:** Marywood Coll., 1966–70, BA (Soc. Std.); Queens Coll., CUNY, 1971–72, MLS. **Orgs.:** SLA: Advert. and Mktg. Div. (Ch., 1981–82); Advert. and Mktg. Grp. (Ch., 1977–78). Assn. of Info. Mgrs. Frnds. of the Ridgefield Pub. Lib.: PR Rec. Secy. **Pubns.:** *Slogans In Print '79* (anl.). **Activities:** 12; 17, 35, 39; 51, 55, 59 **Addr.:** Doyle Dane Bernbach, 437 Madison Ave., New York, NY 10022.

Sutter, Carolyn S. (O. 9, 1942, Kalamazoo, MI) Dir., City of Long Beach Telecom., 1981–; Dir., Long Beach Pub. Lib., 1979–81, Assoc. Dir., Admin. 1978–79, Assoc. Dir., Main Lib., 1977–78; Dir., Lib. Syst. of Southwest. MI, 1974–77. **Educ.:** Calvin Coll., 1960–64, BS (Psy.); West. MI Univ., 1971–72, MLS; CA State Univ., Long Beach, 1981, MPA. **Orgs.:** ALA: LAMA; PLA; LITA; ASCLA; ICMA. Pub. Lib. Execs. of South. CA. Natl. Platform Assn. Cham. of Cmrce.: Bd. of Dirs. Leag. of CA Cities CATV Adv. Com. Natl. Assn. of Telecom. Ofcrs. and Advs. Mgrs. and Admins. of Lg. Cities Cable Com. **Pubns.:** "Neighborhood Libraries," *MI Libn.* (Win. 1973); "Librarians Face 'Jaws II': A New Jarvis Proposition," *Amer. Libs.* (F. 1980). **Activities:** 9; 17 **Addr.:** Long Beach Public Library, 101 Pacific Ave., Long Beach, CA 90802.

Suttle, Linda Faye (N. 1, 1953, Tuscaloosa, AL) Ref. Libn., Univ. of AL, 1976–. **Educ.:** Stillman Coll., 1972–75, BA (Eng.); Atlanta Univ., 1975–76, MSLS. **Orgs.:** ALA: JMRT/Arch. Com. (1978–80); Minorities Rcrt. Com. (1979–80). AL LA: Newsp. Indexing Com. (Secy., 1976–78; Ch., 1978–); Schol. and Loans Com. (1979–80). Delta Sigma Theta Sorority, Inc.: Tuscaloosa Alum. Chap. **Honors:** Beta Phi Mu, 1976. **Addr.:** 4527-18th Ave., E., Apt. 1021, Tuscaloosa, AL 35405.

Sutton, Judith Kay (S. 13, 1947, Salisbury, NC) Assoc. Dir. of Libs., Pub. Lib. of Charlotte and Mecklenburg Cntys., 1977–; Adult/Cont. Educ. Consult., NC Div. of State Lib., 1973–77, Geneal. Ref. Libn., 1972–73, Prcs. Ctr. Libn., 1970–72. **Educ.:** Univ. of NC, Charlotte, 1965–69, BS (Hist.); Univ. of NC, 1969–70, MSLS. **Orgs.:** ALA. SELA. NC LA: JMRT (Secy., 1971–72); Pub. Lib. Sect., Persnl. Com. (Ch., 1979–80). NC Adult Educ. Assn.: Exec. Bd. (1976, 1977). Natl. Cncl. on Aging. **Activities:** 9, 13; 17, 25, 35; 50, 63, 69 **Addr.:** 1004-F North Wendover Rd., Charlotte, NC 28211.

Sutton, Lynn A. Sorensen (Jl. 31, 1953, Detroit, MI) Corporate Dir. of Libs., Detroit-Macomb Hosp. Assn., 1977–; Hosp. Libn., S. Chicago Cmnty. Hosp., 1976–77. **Educ.:** Univ. of MI, 1971–75, AB (Greek), 1975–76, AMLS. **Orgs.:** Med. LA: Copyrt. Com. (1979–80). Metro. Detroit Med. Lib. Grp.: Exec. Bd. (1979–81); ULOSSOM (1978–79); Prog. Com. (1978–79). MI Hlth. Sci. Libns. Assn. **Activities:** 12; 17; 80 **Addr.:** Detroit-Macomb Hospitals Association, 690 Mullett, Detroit, MI 48226.

Suvak, Daniel Stephen (O. 28, 1947, Cleveland, OH) Dir., Mideast. OH Lib. Org., 1980–; Dir., Spec. Srvs., Youngstown Pub. Lib., 1977–80; Libn., South. OH Correct. Facility, 1972–77. **Educ.:** Kent State Univ., -70, BA (Math.), 1971–72, MLS. **Orgs.:** OH LA: Lib. Srvs. to Older Adults. ALA: Fed. Prisons Com. **Honors:** OH LA, Diana Vescelius Awd., 1974; Best Article of Year Awd., 1979. **Pubns.:** *Memoirs of American Prisons: An Annotated Bibliography* (1979); "Images of Libraries in Prison Diaries," *Lib. Jnl.*; "Federal Prison Libraries: The Quiet Collapse," *LJ*. **Activities:** 14-Cooperative; 17, 24, 34 **Addr.:** Mideastern Ohio Library Organization, 808 E. Main St., Louisville, OH 44641.

Suvak, Nancy Jean (D. 31, 1939, Pittsburgh, PA) Resrch. Supvsr., Cmrcl. Info. Ctr., U.S. Steel Corp., 1967–. **Educ.:** Univ. of Pittsburgh, 1966, BS (Bus. Educ.), 1968, MLS. **Orgs.:** SLA: Metals/Mtrls. Div. (Ch., 1981–82); Pittsburgh Chap. (Pres., 1976–77). ALA. Amer. Iron and Steel Inst.: Subcom. of Libs. and Info. Ctrs. (Ch., 1978–80). **Pubns.:** Ed., *Steel Data Sources* (1980); ed., *Metals Mtrls. News* (1976–80). **Activities:** 12; 15, 17, 30; 51, 59, 81 **Addr.:** 600 Grant St., Rm. 1818, Pittsburgh, PA 15230.

Suzuki, Janet M. (F. 19, 1943, Westboro, OH) Comp. Sci. Libn., Bus., Sci., Tech. Div., Chicago Pub. Lib., 1981–, Head, Ref. Unit, Pop. Lib., 1970–81. **Educ.:** Univ. of NE, 1964–68, BS (Hist.); Univ. of Denver, 1968–69, MSLS. **Orgs.:** ALA: Adult Lib. Mtrls. Com. (1975); CODORT: Ofc. of Lib. Persnl. Resrcs. Subcom. (1976–79); PLA, Nom. Com. (1979–80). Asian Amer. Libns. Caucus: Co-fndr. and Ch. (1975–76). SLA. IL LA. Chicago Lib. Club. Japanese Amer. Citizens Leag. Chicago Chap., Bd. of Dirs. (1973–77, 1980–). **Pubns.:** "Asian American Public Librarians," *Opportunities for Minorities in Librarianship* (1977); "Asian Americans and Libraries," *ALA Yrbk.* (1976). **Activities:** 9; 16, 32, 39; 59, 91 **Addr.:** 5701 N. Sheridan, #P-28, Chicago, IL 60660.

Svengalis, Kendall F. (My. 16, 1947, Gary, IN) Asst. Law Libn., RI State Law Lib., 1976–; Ref. Libn., Providence Coll. Lib., 1975–77. **Educ.:** Purdue Univ., 1965–70, BA (Eng. Lit.), 1971–73, MA (Hist.); Univ. of RI, 1974–75, MLS. **Orgs.:** AALL. Law Libns. of New Eng. **Pubns.:** "Theological Controversy among Indiana Lutherans," *Concordia Hist. Inst. Qtly.* (Sum. 1973). **Activities:** 12, 13; 20, 29, 39; 77 **Addr.:** RI State Law Library, Providence County Courthouse, 250 Benefit St., Providence, RI 02903.

Svenonius, Elaine F. (Ja. 9, 1933, Philadelphia, PA) Assoc. Prof., Grad. Sch. of Info. Sci., Univ. of CA, Los Angeles, 1981–; Assoc. Prof., Grad. Sch. of Lib. and Info. Mgt., Univ. of Denver, 1978–81; Actg. Dean, Sch. of Lib. and Info. Sci., Univ. of West. ON, 1977–78, Asst. Dean, 1972–78; Dir., Ctr. Comm. and Info. Resrch., Univ. of Denver, 1970–72. **Educ.:** Barnard Coll., 1950–54, AB (Phil.); Univ. of PA, 1955–57, MA (Phil.); Univ. of Chicago, 1962–65, MA (LS), 1965–1971, PhD (LS). **Orgs.:** ALA: LITA/Info. Sci. and Autom. Sect., Lib. Educ. Div. (Ch., 1972–73); RTSD/Cat. and Class. Sect., Policy and Resrch. Com. (1978–). ASIS: Educ. Com. (Ch., 1973–74); Spec. Interest Grp., Educ. (Secy./Treas., 1973–74, 1976–77); Anl. Doct. Forum (Ch., 1974); Spec. Interest Grp., Class. Resrch. (Ch., 1980–81). AALS: various ofcs. and coms. (1977–). IFLA: various coms. Internatl. Fed. of Documtn.: various ofcs. **Pubns.:** Ed., *String Indexing* (1977); "Directions for Research in Indexing, Classification and Cataloging," *Lib. Resrcs. and Tech. Srvs.* (Ja.–Mr. 1981); "Facets as Semantic Categories," *Klassifikation und Erkenntnis* (1979); "Facet Definition: A Case Study," Internatl. Class. (1978); jt. auth., "Current Issues in the Subject Control of Information," *Lib. Qtly.* (Jl. 1977); various articles and chaps. (1972–77). **Activities:** 20, 26, 30 **Addr.:** School of Library and Information Science, University of California, Los Angeles, Los Angeles, CA 90024.

Svoboda, Joseph G. (Mr., 31, 1930, Pelhrimov, Bohemia, Czechoslovakia) Head, Univ. Arch. and Spec. Col., Univ. of NE, 1976–, Univ. Archvst., 1968–76; Inst. Archvst., Case Inst. of Tech., 1966–68; Archvst., Dept. of Pub. Recs. and Arch., Prov. of ON, 1960–66. **Educ.:** Univ. of Toronto, 1954–58, BA (Hist.); Univ. of Delhi, 1958–59 (Hist.); Amer. Univ., 1963, Cert. (Mgt. of Recs. and Arch.). **Orgs.:** SAA: Coll. and Univ. Arch. Com. (1970–); Eth. Arch. Com. (1976–). Midw. Arch. Conf. NE State Hist. Recs. Bd. **Pubns.:** Ed., *Guide to Ethnic Resource Materials in Great Plains Repositories* (1978); "Czechs: The Love of Liberty," *Broken Hoops and Plains People* (1976). **Activities:** 1, 2; 15, 18, 45; 66, 83, 85 **Addr.:** 303 Love Library, University of Nebraska–Lincoln, Lincoln, NE 68588.

Swade, Susanna L. (Ja. 4, 1939, Monessen, PA) Supvsr., Media Srvs., Sch. Libs., Columbus Pub. Schs., 1974–; Libn., Ft. Cherry Schs., 1973–74; Libn., Classrm. Tchr., Dept. of Defense, Okinawa, Germany, 1970–73; Libn., Tchr., Ringgold Schs., 1965–70. **Educ.:** CA State Coll., California, PA, 1963–65, BS, highest hons. (Elem. Educ.); Univ. of Pittsburgh, 1966–68, MLS; OH State Univ., 1974–75, Supervisory Cert. **Orgs.:** ALA: AASL. OH Educ. Lib./Media Assn.: Conv. Pubcty. Ch. (1980–81); Legis. Ch. (1978–80); Ctrl. Reg. Dir. (1980–82); *Spectrum* Jt. Ed. Franklin Cnty. LA: Treas. (1978–79). Delta Kappa Gamma: Pubcty. Ch. (1977); 1st VP (1980–82); 2nd VP (1978–80); PR Ch. (1973). AAUW. **Honors:** Phi Delta Kappa; Beta Phi Mu, 1968. **Activities:** 10; 17, 21, 48; 63 **Addr.:** 1947 Tamarack Cir. S., #C, Columbus, OH 43229.

Swaim, Elizabeth A. (D. 6, 1933, Carlisle, PA) Spec. Col. Libn. and Univ. Archvst., Wesleyan Univ., 1964–; Antiq. Bookseller, Hamill & Barker, 1969; Rare Book Catlgr., Athenaeum of Philadelphia, 1961–64; Catlgr. and Ref. Libn., Oberlin Coll., 1958–60; Spec. Rcrt., Serials Catlgr., Lib. of Congs., 1956–58. **Educ.:** Dickinson Coll., 1950–54, AB (Eng.); Carnegie Lib. Sch., 1954–55, MLS; Univ. of PA, 1960–64, MA (Eng.). **Orgs.:** ALA: Rare Books and Mss. Sect. (1977–80). SAA. New Eng. Archvsts. CT State Hist. Recs. Adv. Bd. (1976–81). Bibliographical Socty. Bibliographical Socty. of Amer. Amer. Prntg. Hist. Assn. **Honors:** Rotary Foundation Flwshp., 1955. **Pubns.:** "The Auction as a Means of Book Distribution in Eighteenth-Century Yorkshire," *Publshg. Hist.* (S. 1977); "Private Press Books in the College Library," *Choice* (D. 1977). **Activities:** 1, 2; 45; 57, 92 **Addr.:** Wesleyan University Library, Middletown, CT 06457.

Swain, Richard H. (My. 17, 1944, Moscow, ID) Hum. Ref./Biblgrphr., Cleveland State Univ., 1979–; Govt. Docum. and Ref. Lib., North. MI Univ., 1974–79; Instr., Phil., MI State Univ., 1972–73. **Educ.:** Oakland Univ., 1962–66, BA (Phil.); Yale Univ., 1966–68, MA (Asian Stds.), 1968–71, MPhil (Phil.); Univ. of MI, 1973–74, AMLS. **Orgs.:** ALA. OH Acad. LA. AAUP. **Honors:** Beta Phi Mu, 1974; Woodrow Wilson Flwshp., 1966. **Pubns.:** Jt. auth., "The Logic and Ontology of Kung-sun Lung-tzu," *Phil. E. and W.* (Ap. 1970); Transl., "On 'Can the Law of Non–Contradiction be Contravened?'" *Chinese Stds. in Phil.* (Win.–Spr. 1970). **Activities:** 1; 15, 31, 39; 54, 55, 90 **Addr.:** Cleveland State University Libraries, 1860 E. 22nd St., Cleveland, OH 44115.

Swaine, Cynthia A. W. (Jl. 30, 1944, Elkhart, IN) Lib. Instr. Libn., Old Dominion Univ. Lib., 1979–, Ref. Libn., Educ., 1975–79; Tchr., Elkhart Cmnty. Schs., 1966–72. **Educ.:** Goshen Coll., 1962–66, BS (Elem. Educ.); IN Univ., 1972–73, MS (Art Educ.), 1973–75, MLS. **Orgs.:** ALA: ACRL. SELA. VA LA: Mem. Com. (1978–79). **Honors:** Beta Phi Mu. **Pubns.:** "Requests for Ratings of School Systems," *RQ* (Fall 1979); "Fostering Improved User Perceptions of Library Staff through Displays," *Southeast. Libn.* (Spr. 1979). **Activities:** 1; 31, 39; 63 **Addr.:** Old Dominion University, University Library, Norfolk, VA 23508.

Swan, James A. (Ap. 6, 1941, Stockton, CA) Admin., Ctrl. KS Lib. Syst., 1977–; Dir., Pickens Cnty. Lib., 1971–77. **Educ.:** Brigham Young Univ., 1959–67, BA (Span.), 1968–71, MLS. **Orgs.:** ALA: PLA/Nom. Com. (1978), Starter List Com. (1977–1979); LAMA/PRS Pubns. Com. (1979). Mt. Plains LA: Pub. Rel. Com. (Ch., 1979). KS LA. **Honors:** H.W. Wilson and ALA, John Cotton Dana Pub. Rel. Spec. Awd., 1977. **Pubns.:** "New Visibility for the Small PL," *Wilson Lib. Bltn.* (Ja. 1977); "An Answer to the Term Paper Dilemma," *RQ* (Fall 1971); "Library Minus Program Equals Storehouse?" *Top of the News* (N. 1975). **Activities:** 9; 17, 36; 69 **Addr.:** 1409 Williams, Great Bend, KS 67530.

Swanekamp, Joan (My. 20, 1951, Medina, NY) Head, Tech. Srvs., Sibley Msc. Lib., 1980–, Msc. Catlgr., 1980; Msc. and Gvt. Docum. Catlgr., SUNY, Geneseo, 1978–79; Msc. and Rec. Catlgr., Univ. of Miami, 1975–77. **Educ.:** SUNY, Buffalo, 1969–73, BA (Msc.); Univ. of Miami, 1973–75, MM (Msclgy.), 1975, Cert. (Msc. Libnshp.); SUNY, Geneseo, 1977–78, MLA (LS). **Orgs.:** Msc. LA. Amer. Msclgy. Socty. Coll. Msc. Socty. **Pubns.:** *Diamonds and Rust: an annotated bibliography and discography to Joan Baez* (1980). **Activities:** 1, 12; 20, 44, 46; 55 **Addr.:** Sibley Music Library, Eastman School of Music, University of Rochester, Rochester, NY 14604.

Swanigan, Meryl H. (Ap. 1, 1939, Baltimore, MD) Corporate Libn., Atl. Richfield Co., 1977–, Supvsr., Ref. Srvs., 1974–77; Mgr., Tech. Info. Ctr., Douglas Aircraft Co., McDonnell Douglas Corp., 1970–74; Lib. Supvsr., Missile and Space Syst. Div., McDonnell Douglas Corp., 1964–70. **Educ.:** Univ. of NC, 1957–61, BA (Art Hist.); various cont. ed. crs., sems., 1965–. **Orgs.:** SLA: South. CA Chap. (1971–); various ofcs. ASIS. South. CA OLUG: Strg. Com. (1979–). Los Angeles Reg. Tech. Info. Users Cncl. Amer. Petr. Inst.: Subcom. on Tech. Info., Bus. Info. Task Frc. (Ch., 1977–). Univ. of South. CA, Sch. of LS: Bd. of Cnclrs. (1977–). **Honors:** Young Women's Christ. Assn., of Los Angeles, Cert. of Achvmt., 1978. **Pubns.:** "The Impact of Proposition 13 on the Nation and Its Libraries," *California's Proposition 13, Three Viewpoints* (1979); ed., *U.S. Bureau of Mines Document Collections* (1976). **Activities:** 12; 17; 59, 82, 86 **Addr.:** Headquarters Library, Atlantic Richfield Co., 515 S. Flower St., Los Angeles, CA 90071.

Swank, Cynthia G. (My. 14, 1947, New Rochelle, NY) Archvst., J. Walter Thompson Co., 1979–; Asst. Archvst., Ctr. for the Std. of the Cons. Movement, 1978–79; Bank Ofcr., 1969–76. **Educ.:** Muhlenberg Coll., 1965–69, AB (Hist.); NY Univ., 1978, MA (Hist.), 1979, Cert. (Arch. Mgt., Hist. Ed.). **Orgs.:** SAA. Mid-Atl. Reg. Arch. Conf. Assn. of Recs. Mgrs. and Admins. Huguenot-Thomas Paine Hist. Assn. Amer. Assn. for State and Lcl. Hist. **Activities:** 2; 38, 39, 45; 51 **Addr.:** J. Walter Thompson Co., Archives, 420 Lexington Ave., New York, NY 10017.

Swanker, Esther M. (O. 15, 1927, Syracuse, NY) Asst. Comsn., Manpower and Empl. Rel., NY State Dept. of Transp., 1979–; Spec. Asst. to Gvr., NY State, 1975–79; Dir., Gvrs. Conf. on Libs.; Pres., Donovan—Swanker Assocs., 1969–75; Asst. Dir., Urban Educ., NY State Educ. Dept., 1968–69, Asst. to Deputy Comsn., 1967–68, Coord. of Title III, ESEA, 1965–67; Supvsr., Libs., Schenectady Pub. Schs., 1963–65. **Educ.:** Syracuse Univ., 1946–50, AB (Liberal Arts); SUNY, Albany, 1958–63, MLS, 1963–68 (Grad. Std. in Educ.). **Orgs.:** ALA: Sch. Lib. Sect., Pubns. Com. (1964–67). NY LA: Cncl. (1967–69). Citizens Lib. Cncl. of NY State: Ch. (1980); Bd. (1981). WHCOLIS: NY State Del., Strg. Com.; NY State Del. Amer. Red Cross: Emergency Blood Com. (Ch., 1959–62); Pubcty. Com. (Ch., 1959–63). Amer. Assn. of Sch. Admins.: White Hse. Conf. on Chld.: Del. (1970). Natl. Educ. Assn. Various other orgs. **Honors:** Delta Kappa Gamma. **Pubns.:** Contrib., *Phi Delta Kappan, NY State Sch. Bd. Jnl., Cath. Sch. Jnl., Lib. Jnl., Sch. Lib. Jnl., Cath. Sch. Tchr., Sch. Libs., Procs.: Symp., Nonpub. Educ.* **Activities:** 3, 10; 17, 24, 28 **Addr.:** 1470 Grenoside Ave., Schenectady, NY 12308.

PROFESSIONAL ACTIVITIES: Institutions: 1. Acad. lib.; 2. Arch.; 3. Assn.; 4. Fed./Gvt. lib.; 5. Inst. lib.; 6. Mfr./Suppl.; 7. Milit. lib.; 8. Musm.; 9. Pub. lib.; 10. Sch. lib.; 11. Sch. of lib. sci.; 12. Spec. lib.; 13. State lib.; 14. (other). **Functions/Activities:** 15. Acq./Col. dev.; 16. Adult srvs.; 17. Admin.; 18. Apprais.; 19. Archit./Bldgs.; 20. Cat./Class.; 21. Chld. srvs.; 22. Circ.; 23. Cons./Pres.; 24. Consult.; 25. Cont. ed.; 26. Educ. lib. sci.; 27. Ext. srvs.; 28. Fund/Grants; 29. Gvt. pubs.; 30. Indx./Abs.; 31. Instr. lib. use; 32. Media srvs.; 33. Micro.; 34. Netwks./Coop.; 35. Persnl.; 36. PR; 37. Publshg.; 38. Recs. mgt.; 39. Ref. srvs.; 40. Repro.; 41. Resrch.; 42. Review.; 43. Secur.; 44. Serials; 45. Spec. col.; 46. Tech. srvs.; 47. Trustees/Bds.; 48. YA srvs.; 49. (other).

Swanson, Ann (Patricia) (Mr. 18, 1936, Sioux City, IA) Admin., N. Ctrl. Reg. Lib., 1973–; Admin., N. IA Lib. Ext., 1966–73; Dir., Hampton Pub. Lib., 1964–66; Libn., Sioux City, E. HS, 1958–61. **Educ.:** Univ. of North. IA, 1954–58, BA (Langs.); Univ. of SD, 1958, Tchg. Accred. (LS); Univ. of MN, 1966–68, MA (LS). **Orgs.:** IA LA: Legis. Com. (1975–78); Mem. Com. (1978–). P.E.O. **Activities:** 9, 13; 17, 24, 34; 56, 75, 92 **Addr.:** North Central Regional Library, 544 College Dr., Mason City, IA 50401.

Swanson, Don R. (O. 10, 1924, Los Angeles, CA) Prof., Grad. Lib. Sch., Univ. of Chicago, 1963–, Dean, 1977–79, 1963–72; Resrch. Sci., TRW Inc., 1955–63. **Educ.:** CA Inst. of Tech., 1942–45, BS (Phys.); Rice Univ., 1946–47, MA (Phys.); Univ. of CA, Berkeley, 1949–52, PhD (Phys.). **Orgs.:** ASIS. AALS. **Pubns.:** "Libraries and the Growth of Knowledge," *Lib. Qtly.* (Ja. 1979); "Toward a Psychology of Metaphor," *Critical Inquiry* (Fall 1978); "Information Retrieval as a Trial-and-Error Process," *Lib. Qtly.* (1977); "On Force, Energy, Entropy, and the Assumptions of Metapsychology," *Psychoanalysis and Contemporary Science* (1977); "A Critique of Psychic Energy as an Explanatory Concept," *Jnl. Amer. Psychoanalytic Assn.* (1977); various articles, mono., bks. **Activities:** 1; 26, 41; 56, 75 **Addr.:** Graduate Library School, University of Chicago, 1100 E. 57th St., Chicago, IL 60637.

Swanson, Edward (F. 10, 1941, Thief River Falls, MN) Head, Prcs. Dept., MN Hist. Socty., 1977–, Head, Tech. Srvs. Dept., 1969–77, Head, Newsp. Dept., 1968; Asst. Circ. Libn., Macalester Coll., 1960–64, 1967–68. **Educ.:** Macalester Coll., 1960–64, BA (Fr.); Univ. of MN, 1965–69, MA (LS). **Orgs.:** MN LA: Pres. (1972–73); VP (1971–72); Bd. of Dirs. (1971–74, 1979–); various other coms. (1968–). ALA: Com. on Cat.: Descr. and Access (1979–); Cncl. (1979–). OCLC: Users Cncl. (1980–); Cat. Adv. Com. (1979–). MN AACR2 Trainers. Twin City Ms Socty.: Pres. (1972–74). MN World Affairs Ctr.: Bd. of Dirs. (1972–). **Pubns.:** Ed., *Bltn. of the MN LA* (1968–71); Asst. Ed., *Lib. Resrcs. & Tech. Srvs.* (1979–); *A Manual of AACR2 Examples for Manuscripts* (1981); Ed., *A Manual of AACR2 Examples* (1980); Ed., *A Manual of AACR2 Level 1 Examples* (1981); various articles, AACR2 manuals. **Activities:** 12; 20, 44, 46 **Addr.:** 1065 Portland Ave., Saint Paul, MN 55104.

Swanson, Jean R. (D. 16, 1950, Summit, NJ) RLG/RLIN Coord., Rutgers Univ., 1979–, Law Cat. Libn., 1974–79; Info. Sci., Food and Drug Resrch. Labs., 1973–74. **Educ.:** Syracuse Univ., 1968–72, BA (Brit. Lit.); Rutgers Univ., 1972–73, MLS. **Orgs.:** NJ LA: Com. on Coop. and Networking. NY Tech. Srvs. Libns. ALA. AAUP. **Activities:** 1; 17, 20, 34; 56 **Addr.:** 180 E. Cedar St., Livingston, NJ 07039.

Swanson, Patricia Ann (Mr. 18, 1936, Sioux City, IA) Admin., N. Ctrl. Reg. Lib. Syst., 1973–; Admin., N. IA Lib. Ext., 1966–73; Admin., Hampton Pub. Lib., 1964–66; Sch. Libn., Sioux City E. HS, 1958–61. **Educ.:** Univ. of North. IA, 1954–58, BA (Frgn. Lang.); Univ. of MN, 1967–68, MA (LS). **Orgs.:** IA LA: Legis. Com. (1973–75); Mem. Com. (1978–80). ALA. IA Assn. for Life Long Lrng. **Activities:** 9, 13; 17, 19, 24; 50, 75, 93 **Addr.:** North Central Regional Library System, 544 College Dr., Mason City, IA 50401.

Swanson, Patricia K. (My. 8, 1940, St. Louis, MO) Head, Ref. Srvs., Univ. of Chicago, 1979–, Sr. Lectr., Grad. Lib. Sch., 1974–, Ref. Libn., 1970–79; Ref. Libn., Cat., Simmons Coll., 1967–68. **Educ.:** Univ. of MO, 1958–62, BS (Eng. Lit.); Simmons Coll., 1966–67, MLS. **Orgs.:** ALA. Chicago Lib. Club. **Pubns.:** "Reference Services," *ALA Yrbk. 1980* (Spr. 1981); various bk. reviews. **Activities:** 1, 11; 26, 31, 39 **Addr.:** Joseph Regenstein Library, University of Chicago, 1100 E. 57th St., Chicago, IL 60637.

Swanson, Rowena Weiss (Ag. 3, 1928, Brooklyn, NY) Prof. of Libnshp. and Info. Sci., Univ. of Denver, 1970–; Resrch. Admin., Air Frc. Ofc. of Sci. Resrch., 1961–70; Patent Resrch. Spec., US Patent Ofc., Dept. of Cmrce., 1957–61; Acq. Ofcr., Ed., Abstctr., Armed Srvs. Tech. Info. Agency, 1950–57. **Educ.:** Cath. Univ. of Amer., 1945–49, BS ChE (Chem. Engin.); George Washington Univ. Law Sch., 1950–53, JD. **Orgs.:** Inst. of Electrical and Electronics Engins. Assn. for Comp. Mach. ASIS: Educ. Com., Ch.; Frontier Chap., Ch.; Newsltr. Ed.; Spec. Interest Grp./Educ. Rocky Mt. OLUG. AAAS: Eval. Netwk. **Honors:** ASIS, Paper of Yr. Awd., 1975. **Pubns.:** *Cost Analysis and Work Measurement Manual* (1976); *System Analysis plus Work Study equals Library Accountability* (1974); *Information, An Exploitable Commodity* (1968); *Move the Information, A Kind of Missionary Spirit* (1967); *Cybernetics in Europe and the U.S.S.R.* (1966); various articles. **Activities:** 11; 18, 24, 26; 56, 63, 75 **Addr.:** University of Denver, GSLIM-BMC 118, Denver, CO 80208.

Swanson, Sheila (Mr. 10, 1921, Aberdeen, Scotland) Libn., Acad. of Med., Toronto, 1966–; Libn., Dept. of Chem., Univ. of Toronto, 1964–66. **Educ.:** Edinburgh Univ., 1938–42, BSc (Chem.); Univ. of Toronto, 1963–64 BLS; Med. LA, Cert. **Orgs.:** Can. Hlth. LA: Bd. of Dirs. (1979–). Med. LA. Can. LA. **Activities:** 12; 15, 17, 45; 80 **Addr.:** William Boyd Library, Academy of Medicine, Toronto, 288 Bloor St. W., Toronto, ON M5S 1V8 Canada.

Swanton, James E. (Jl. 11, 1941, Springfield, OH) Prin. Assoc., Med. Bibl., Albert Einstein Coll. of Med., 1978–; Temporary positions, Univ. of MO, 1977–78; Asst. Prof., CUNY, 1969–75; Ed., SUNY Un. List of Serials, SUNY, Upstate Med. Ctr., 1968; Assoc., US Natl. Lib. of Med., 1967. **Educ.:** OH State Univ., 1958–62, BA (Bio. Sci.); Univ. of London, Univ. of Paris, 1963–66; Columbia Univ., 1966–67, MS (LS), 1975–79, CAS. **Orgs.:** NY Reg. Med. LA. Med. LA. **Pubns.:** "Qualifications sought by employers of health sciences librarians," *Bltn. of Med. LA* (Ja. 1980). **Activities:** 1, 12; 17, 20, 39; 75, 77, 80 **Addr.:** 1270 5th Ave.–8T, New York, NY 10029.

Swartz, Renee Becker (F. 25, 1935, Newark, NJ) Ch., Lib. Comsn., Monmouth Cnty. Lib., 1966–. **Educ.:** Barnard Coll., 1955, BA (European Hist.). **Orgs.:** WHCOLIS: NJ Del. (Ch., 1980). State Lib. Adv. Cncl. NJ LA: Exec. Com. (1973–77). NJ Lib. Trustee Assn.: Exec. Com. (1976–81); Secy. (1978–81). State Lib. Adv. Cncl. Various other orgs. Rutgers Grad. Sch. of Lib. and Info. Sci.: Trustee (1980–). Barnard Coll. Alum. Assn.: Pres. (1981–). Barnard Coll.: Trustee (1981–). Columbia Univ.: Trustee (1981–). Various other orgs. **Honors:** Natl. Cncl. of Jewish Women, Grt. Red Bank Sect., Hannah G. Solomon Awd., 1979; NJ LA, NJ Trustee of the Yr., 1980. **Pubns.:** "Poised for the Information Age: The White House Conference," *NJ Libs.* (D.–Ja. 1979–80); "A Perspective for the 80's" pamphlet (Mr. 1980); "Implementation: An Imperative of the WHC," *Emanations* (Spr. 1981); "People's Bill of Rights," *NJ Libs.* (Mr. 1979); "Up-date—WHC—A Focus or a Fantasy," *NJ Libs.* (Ap. 1981). **Activities:** 9, 13; 17, 36, 47; 63 **Addr.:** 136 Rumson Rd., Rumson, NJ 07760.

Swartz, Roderick G. (My. 25, 1939, Fairbury, NE) State Libn., WA State Lib., 1975–; Exec. Ofcr., WA Lib. Netwk., 1976–; Deputy Dir., Natl. Comsn. on Libs. and Info. Sci., 1972–74; Assoc. Dir., Tulsa City–Cnty. Lib., 1970–72, Asst. Dir., 1966–70; Lib. Consult., MO State Lib., 1964–66; Asst. to Exec. Secy., Lib. Admin. Div., ALA, 1963–64; Catlgr., Univ. of Chicago, 1962–63. **Educ.:** Univ. of NE, 1958–61, BA (Hist.), 1961–62, MA (Hist.); Univ. of Chicago, 1962–63, MA (LS). **Orgs.:** ALA: Cncl.; Lib. Admin. Div./Stats. Com. for Pub. Libs. (Ch., 1970–72) Bldg. Equip. Sect., Archit. Com. for Pub. Libs. (Ch., 1973–74); various other coms. OK LA: Pres. (1970–). **Honors:** Fulbright Grant, 1975; Cncl. on Lib. Resrcs., Flwshp., 1975; New Worlds Fair Awd., 1965. **Pubns.:** "The Library Change Agent, A State Library Role For The Future," *As Much to Learn as to Teach: Essays In Honor of Les Asheim* (1979); "The Multitype Library Cooperative Response to User Needs," *Multitype Library Cooperation* (1977); "The Need for Cooperation Among Libraries in the United States," *Libraries in Post Industrial Society* (1977); "Progress Toward Goals in Library Resource Sharing: A Response," *Library Resource Sharing* (1977); "Need for Cooperation Among Libraries in the United States," *Lib. Trends* (O. 1975); various chaps., articles, edshps. **Activities:** 9, 13; 17, 25, 34; 75, 78, 93 **Addr.:** WA State Library, AJ-11, Olympia, WA 98504.

Swartzburg, Susan Garretson (Ag. 26, 1938, Summit, NJ) Libn., Gifts and Prsrvn., Rutgers Univ. Libs., 1975–, Actg. Art Libn., 1974–75, Libn., Alexander Lib., 1972–74; Libn., Prsrvn. Proj., Yale Univ. Lib., 1971–72, Libn., CTUW Proj., 1966–71; Bibl. Resrch., NY Pub. Lib., 1964–65; Bibl. Resrch., Univ. of MI Libs., 1963–64. **Educ.:** Wells Coll., 1956–60, BA (Phil.); NY Univ., 1960–62, MA (Eng. Lit.); Simmons Coll., 1965–66, MS (LS); various crs. **Orgs.:** ALA: RTSD/Prsrvn. Lib. Mtrls. Sect., Educ. Com. (1980–); ILL Com. (1971–72). Amer. Prtg. Hist. Assn. ARLIS/NA: NJ Chap. (Secy., 1975–78, 1980); NY Chap. NJ LA: Schol. Com. (Ch., 1975–76); Coll. and Resrch. Libs. Sect. various other orgs. NJ Wells Club: Princeton Ch. (1975–78); NJ Ch. (1979–81). Hist. Socty. of Princeton. Natl. Trust for Hist. Prsrvn. NJ Hist. Socty. various other orgs. **Pubns.:** *Preservation of Library Materials, a Manual* (1980); columnist, "On Preservation," *ARLIS/NA Nsltr.* (1978–); columnist, "On Preservation," *NJ Libs.* (1979); Reg. Ed., *Cons. Admin. News* (1979–); various reviews (1977–). **Activities:** 1, 2; 15, 23, 45; 55 **Addr.:** 38 Evergreen Cir., Princeton, NJ 08540.

Swe, Thein (Ja. 29, 1944, Pegu, Burma) Asst. Dir., Col. Dev., LA State Univ. Lib., Chief Biblgphr., 1975–; Soc. Sci. Biblgphr., Northwest. Univ., 1973–75; Biblgphr., Assn. for Asian Std., 1970–73; Asst. to Univ. Libn., Amer. Univ., 1967–70. **Educ.:** Yale Univ., 1961–64, BA (Pol. Sci.); Amer. Univ., 1964–68, MA (Intl. Rel.); Univ. of MI, 1969–70, AMLS, 1981, PhD (LS). **Honors:** Fulbright, Travel grant, 1961. **Pubns.:** *Bibliography of Asian Studies, 1970* (1972); *Bibliography of Asian Studies, 1971* (1973); "Burma," *ALA World Encyclopedia of Library and Information Science* (1980). **Activities:** 1; 15, 17, 26; 54, 56, 92 **Addr.:** 5127 Heritage Dr., Baton Rouge, LA 70808.

Swearingen, Wilba Shaw (S. 7, 1939, Texarkana, TX) Serials Libn., Marquette Univ., 1978–, Circ. Libn., 1977–78, Serials Tech., 1974–78; Serials Libn., LA State Univ. Dental Lib., 1971–74; Actg. Head of Serials/Lib. Asst., Tulane Univ., 1970–71. **Educ.:** N. TX State Univ., 1961, BS (Educ.), 1966, MA (Eng.); Univ. of WI, Milwaukee, 1977, MLS. **Orgs.:** ALA. Beta Phi Mu: Rho Chap. (Pres.-Elect, 1979–80). Mod. Lang. Assn. Amer. Socty. for 18th Century Std. **Activities:** 1; 15, 44, 46; 55 **Addr.:** Serials Dept., Memorial Library, Marquette University, 1415 W. Wisconsin Ave., Milwaukee, WI 53233.

Sweat, Mary Lee (S. 25, 1946, Indianapolis, IN) Univ. Lib., Loyola Univ. Lib., 1981–, Head, Pub. Srvs., 1977–81, Ref. Libn., 1974–77, Serials Libn., 1970–74, Jr. HS Libn., Intl. Sch. of Brussels, Belgium, 1969–70. **Educ.:** Southwest. at Memphis, 1964–68, BA (Eng.); Univ. of NC, 1968–69, MSLS; Loyola Univ., 1977–81, MBA. **Orgs.:** LA LA: Pubns. Com. (1972–74). ALA: ACRL. SWLA. Loyola Univ. Sen. **Honors:** Loyola Univ., Fac. Resrch. Grant, 1976. **Activities:** 1; 17, 22, 39; 55, 56, 59 **Addr.:** Loyola University Library, 6363 St. Charles Ave., New Orleans, LA 70118.

Sween, Roger David (My. 2, 1940, Montevideo, MN) Ref. Libn., ILL Coord., Instr., Ctr. for Lib. and AV, St. Cloud State Univ., 1978–; Pres., INFOSPEC, Inc., 1981–; Head Libn., Red Wing Pub. Lib., 1976–78; Ref. Coord., Univ. of WI, Platteville, 1965–74; HS Libn., Boscobel Area Pub. Schs., 1964–65; HS Libn., Markesan Dist. Schs., 1963–64. **Educ.:** St. Olaf Coll., 1958–63, BA (Hist.); Univ. of WI, 1963–66, MA (LS); various crs. **Orgs.:** MN LA: Pub. Lib. Div. (Ch., 1979–80). Ctrl. MN Libs. Exch.: Exec. Secy. (1981); Adv. Com. (Secy., 1979–80). **Activities:** 1, 9; 16, 31, 39; 75, 73-History, 95-Sci. Fiction. **Addr.:** Learning Resources, Centennial Hall, St. Cloud State Univ., St. Cloud, MN 56301.

Sweeney, Carolyn Musselman (Ja. 24, 1948, Gettysburg, PA) Info. Mgr., Corp. Lib., Digital Equip. Corp., 1978–, Ref. Libn., 1974–78; Ref. Libn., Arthur D. Little, Inc., 1969–74; Asst. Libn., Morgan Lewis and Bockius, 1968–69. **Educ.:** Gettysburg Coll., 1965–68, BA (Hist.); Drexel Univ., 1969–70, MSLS. **Orgs.:** SLA: Boston Chap. (Pres., 1978–79). MA LA. Assn. for Comp. Mach. Leag. of Women Voters. L.U.U. Bk. Club. **Honors:** MA Inst. of Tech., Matchless Libn. Awd., 1970. **Pubns.:** Jt. auth., "Aptitude Requirements for Library Assistants in Special Libraries," *Spec. LIbs.* (S. 1979). **Activities:** 12; 17, 24, 39; 56, 75, 91 **Addr.:** Digital Equipment Corp., ML4-3/A20, 146 Main St., Maynard, MA 01754.

Sweeney, Del G. (Ja. 10, 1940, Brooklyn, NY) Info. Spec., PA Transp. Inst., PA State Univ., 1976–; Lectr., Hist., Wayne State Univ., 1973–74, Asst. Prof., LS, 1971–72, Arch. Asst., 1970; Asst. Prof., Hist., Univ. of MI, Flint, 1967–69; Assoc. Prof., Hist., Winston-Salem State Univ., 1966–67; Lectr., Hist., Queens Coll., CUNY, 1963–65. **Educ.:** Brooklyn Coll., 1959, BA (Hist.); Wayne State Univ., 1969–70, MSLS; Cornell Univ., 1959–61, 1965–66, PhD (Hist.). **Orgs.:** SLA: Ctrl. PA Chap. (Treas., 1979–); Pubns. Com. (1981–83). Medvl. Acad. of Amer. **Honors:** Phi Beta Kappa, 1960. **Pubns.:** Bk. Review Ed., *Accident Analysis and Prevention* (1978–80); prod. ed., *Transp. Jnl.* (1980–81). **Addr.:** Pennsylvania Transportation Institute, PA State University, Research Bldg. B, University Park, PA 16802.

Sweeney, Mary Jo (F. 18, 1947, Boston, MA) Supvsr., Publshr. Srvs., F. W. Faxon Co., 1980–, Supvsr., Bibl. Ref., 1979–80, Ed., Serials Updating Srv., 1977–79; Lbin., Boston Pub. Lib., 1968–77. **Educ.:** Boston State Coll., 1975, BA (Hist.); Simmons Coll., 1977, MLS. **Orgs.:** SLA. MA LA. New Eng. LA. ALA. Bk. Builders of Boston. **Activities:** 12; 17, 44 **Addr.:** F. W. Faxon Co., 15 Southwest Park, Westwood, MA 02090.

Sweeney, Richard T. (Ja. 22, 1946, Atlantic, NJ) Exec. Dir., Pub. Lib. of Columbus and Franklin Cnty., 1979–; Dir., Genesee Cnty. Lib., 1976–79; Dir., Atl. City Free Pub. Lib., 1971–76; Libn., Cntrl. Jr. High, 1969–70; Tchr., Holy Spirit High, Absecon, NJ 1967–69. **Educ.:** Villanova Univ., 1967, BA (Hum.); Glassboro State Coll., 1970, MA (LS); Drexel Univ., 1972, MLS. **Orgs.:** NJ LA. Cape-Atl. Cnsrtm. ALA: LITA; PLA. OH LA: Legis. Com. various other orgs. Flint Area Rotary. Jaycees, Gt. Atl. City. Kiwanis Clb. of Atl. City. **Activities:** 9, 11; 17, 19, 22; 56, 93 **Addr.:** Public Library of Columbus and Franklin County, 28 S. Hamilton Rd., Columbus, OH 43213.

Sweeney, Urban J. (Ja. 18, 1922, St. John, NB) Chief Libn., Gen. Dynamics Convair Div., 1966–; Chief Libn., Repub. Aviation, 1958–66; Asst. Libn., Sperry Gyroscope, 1957–58; Asst. Libn., Queensboro Pub. Lib., 1956–57. **Educ.:** NY Univ., 1951–55, BS (Educ.); Pratt Inst., 1955–56, MLS. **Orgs.:** SLA: Chap. Pres.; San Diego Div. (Ch., 1973–74); Aerosp. Div. (1978–80). ASIS. Assn. for Comp. Mach. **Pubns.:** Various articles. **Activities:** 12; 52 **Addr.:** General Dynamics Convair Div., P.O. Box 80986, San Diego, CA 92138.

Sweeny, June D. (Ja. 19, 1945, Baltimore, MD) Georgetown Reg. Branch Libn., DC Pub. Lib., 1977–; NE Branch Libn., 1974–77, NE Chld. Libn., 1971–74, SE Asst. Chld. Lib., 1968–71. **Educ.:** Howard Univ., 1963–67, BA (Span.); Univ. of MD, 1970–71, MLS; Dept. of Agr. Grad. Sch. 1973, Cert. (Law Libnshp.); Cuauhnahuae Inst. Colectivo de Lengua y Cultura, Mex. **Orgs.:** Friendship Settlement Hse.: Bd. of Dirs.; Persnl. Com. (1979). ALA: RASD; PLA. Delta Sigma Theta Sorority. **Honors:** Beta Phi Mu, 1971. **Pubns.:** "Librarian's Programatic View" filmstp. (1972). **Addr.:** Georgetown Regional Library, 3260 R. St. N.W., Washington, DC 20007.

Special Subjects/Services: 50. Adult educ.; 51. Advert./Mktg.; 52. Aerosp.; 53. Agric.; 54. Area std.; 55. Arts/Hum.; 56. Autom.; 57. Bibl./Prtg.; 58. Bio. sci.; 59. Bus./Fin.; 60. Chem.; 61. Copyrt.; 62. Documtn.; 63. Educ.; 64. Engin.; 65. Env.; 66. Eth. grps.; 67. Film; 68. Food/Nutr.; 69. Geneal.; 70. Geo.; 71. Geol.; 72. Handcpd.; 73. Hist.; 74. Int. frdm.; 75. Info. sci.; 76. Insr.; 77. Law; 78. Legis.; 79. Math./Comp. sci.; 80. Med.; 81. Metals; 82. Nat. resrcs.; 83. Newsp.; 84. Nuc. sci.; 85. Oral hist.; 86. Petr./Energy; 87. Pharm.; 88. Phys./Astr./Math.; 89. Readg.; 90. Relig.; 91. Sci./Tech.; 92. Soc. sci.; 93. Telecom.; 94. Transp.; 95. (other).

Sweet, Victoria Salls (Ap. 23, 1952, Nyack, NY) Circ., Acq. Dept. Head, U.S. Natl. Aeronautics and Space Admin., 1978–; Catlgr., U.S. Dept. of Agr., 1976–77; Libn., Tele-Sec, Inc., 1975–76. **Educ.:** Muhlenberg Coll., 1970–74, BA (Eng.); Univ. of MD, 1974–75, MLS. **Orgs.:** ALA. SLA. ASIS. **Activities:** 4, 12; 15, 22, 33; 52, 56, 91 **Addr.:** 312 Longwood Dr., Newport News, VA 23606.

Sweeting, Sharon Howe (Ap. 11, 1943, Erie, PA) Spec. Asst. to Dir., Smithsonian Inst. Libs., 1981–, Gift and Exch. Libn., 1972–81. **Educ.:** Syracuse Univ., 1965–71, BS, BA (Eng., LS); Cath. Univ. of Amer., 1973–75, MLS. **Orgs.:** SLA: Musms., Arts, Hum. Div., Ch. (1979–80), *Nsltr.* Ed. (1981–82). DC LA. The Galpin Socty. **Honors:** Beta Phi Mu. **Pubns.:** Ed., *Smithsonian Libs. Nsltr.* **Activities:** 4, 5; 15, 36, 39; 55, 91 **Addr.:** 4112 Gallatin St., Hyattsville, MD 20781.

Sweetland, James Harvey (Ag. 13, 1944, Kalamazoo, MI) Dir., Acad. Srvs., Howard–Tilton Lib., Tulane Univ., 1980–, Dir., Ref. and Bibl. Srvs., 1980–81; Libn., Pub. Srvs., Boys Town Ctr. for Std. of Youth Dev., 1976–80; Ref. Libn., Univ. of NE, 1974–76, Circ. Libn., 1974; Spec. Biblgphr., African Std. Prog., IN Univ., 1973–74. **Educ.:** Providence Coll., 1962–66, AB (Hist.); Univ. of Notre Dame, 1966–76, PhD (US Hist.); IN Univ., 1972–73, MLS. **Orgs.:** ALA: RASD/Mach.-Assisted Ref. Sect. (VP, Pres.-Elect, 1980–), Database Prods. and Srch. Srv. Vendors (Ch., 1979–81); ACRL (1977–). NE LA: Coll. and Univ. Sect. Vice–Ch. (1977–78), Ch. (1978–79); Persnl. Com. (Ch., 1976–77). NE Gvrs. Conf. on Lib. and Info. Srvs: Procs. Com. (Del., 1976). SLA. Natl. Hist. Cmnl. Soctys. Assn. Amer. Hist. Assn. West. Hist. Assn. NE Pre–White Hse Conf: Del. (1979). **Pubns.:** "Using Online Systems in Reference Work," *Online* (Jl. 1979); "Periodicals Loan Policies in Urban Commuter Colleges," *Serials Libn.* (Win. 1978); "Icarian Communism: A Preliminary Exploration in Historiography, Bibliography, and Social Theory," *Intl. Review of Mod. Soclgy.* (Spr. 1976); "Miniseminars in Research Literature," *The Experimenter* (N. 1975); "Seeking the Past: The Wright Bibliography," *Notre Dame Lib. Nsltr.* (Spr. 1972); various reviews in LS and hist. jnls. **Activities:** 1, 12; 15, 31, 39; 56, 92 **Addr.:** Howard-Tilton Memorial Library, Tulane University, New Orleans, LA 70118.

Swerdlove, Dorothy L. (Ja. 4, 1928, New York, NY) Cur., Billy Rose Thea. Col., Performing Arts Resrch. Ctr., NY Pub. Lib., 1980–, st Asst., 1967–80, Libn., Thea. Col., 1961–67; Econ., Caltex Corp., 1955–61; Resrch. Asst., Chase Manhattan Bank, 1954–55; Resrch. Asst., Princeton Univ., 1953–54; Soc. Sci. Anal. Congsnl. Ref. Srv., Lib. of Congs., 1949–53; Resrch. Asst., Fed. Rsv. Bank of NY, 1948–49. **Educ.:** Swarthmore Coll., 1944–48, BA (Econ.); Columbia Univ., 1958–61, MLS. **Orgs.:** Thea. LA: Exec. Bd. (Secy.–Treas., 1966–70, ex officio, 1970–). SLA: Thea. LA Rep. (1970–). NY LA. NY Lib. Club. Archvsts. RT. Amer. Socty. for Thea. Resrch.: Exec. Bd. (1979–). New Drama Forum Assn., Inc.: Treas. (1979–). Amer. Ensemble Co.: Exec. Bd. (1978–). Outer Critics Cir. **Honors:** Phi Beta Kappa, 1948; Beta Phi Mu, 1961. **Pubns.:** Contrib., *Notable American Women, The Modern Period* (1980); contrib., *Notable Names in the American Theatre* (1976); contrib., *Oxford Companion to the Theatre, 3d ed.* (1967, 4th ed. forthcoming); contrib., *Performing Arts International Bibliography* (1976); jt. auth., *Survey of United States International Finance* (1954); asst. ed., *Public Affairs Abstracts* (1950–51). **Activities:** 9, 12; 15, 17, 39; 55, 67, 93 **Addr.:** Billy Rose Theatre Collection, New York Public Library, 111 Amsterdam Ave., New York, NY 10023.

Swift, Ardyce R. (Mr. 28, 1935, Geddes, SD) Lib. Dir., Redmond Pub. Lib., 1975–. **Educ.:** OR Coll. of Educ., 1973–75, BS (Elem. Educ.). **Orgs.:** OR LA: Bd. of Dirs. (1976); Natl. Lib. Week (State Ch., 1978). Libs. of Ctrl. OR: Treas. (1979). Redmond Soroptimists. Redmond Cham. of Cmrce. **Activities:** 9; 16, 17, 21; 69 **Addr.:** Redmond Public Library, 446 S.W. 7th St., Redmond, OR 97756.

Swinburne, Ralph E., Jr. (Mr. 11, 1931, New York, NY) Staff Mgr., Legal Dept., Amer. Telephone and Telegraph, 1979–; Lib. Consult., Telecom. Co. of Iran, Amer. Bell Intl., 1977–79; Supvsr., Whippany Lib., Bell Labs., 1966–77, Tech. Libn., Un. Carbide Corp., 1958–66; Lib. Asst., Sci. and Tech. Div., NY Pub. Lib., 1955–58. **Educ.:** NY Univ., 1950–54, BS (Bio.); Columbia Univ., 1954–56, MLS. **Orgs.:** SLA: Job Place. Com. (Ch., 1969–70); Sci. and Tech. Div. (Ch., 1968–70); West. NY Chap., Prog. Ch. (1963), Rcrt. Ch. (1964); NJ Chap., Bd. of Dirs., (1972–74); various ofcs. (1966–77). **Activities:** 12; 17, 31; 64, 91, 93 **Addr.:** American Telephone and Telegraph Co., 430 Mountain Ave., Murray Hill, NJ 07974.

Swinehart, Denise Cox (S. 3, 1947, Davenport, IA) Head, Chld. Rm., Gary Pub. Lib., 1972–, Chld. Libn., Kennedy Branch, 1970–72. **Educ.:** Augustana Coll., 1966–69, BA (Hist.); Univ. of IA, 1969–70, MS (LS). **Orgs.:** ALA. IN LA: Chld. and Young People's Div., Exec. Bd. (1977–79), Dist. Ch. (1979–1980). Puppeteers of Amer. **Activities:** 9; 21, 48; 95-Puppetry. **Addr.:** Gary Public Library, 220 W. 5th Ave., Gary, IN 46402.

Swint, Katherine Moon (Mrs. J.T.) (D. 7, 1917, Muscogee Cnty., GA) Head, Tech. Prcs., GA Div. of Pub. Lib. Srvs., 1963–; Cat. Libn., Agnes Scott Coll., 1956–61; Libn., Decatur HS, 1954–56; Libn., Tchr.–Libn., Schs. of Fulton, Gwinett and Seminole Cntys., 1938–54. **Educ.:** Oglethorpe Univ., 1938–40, AB (Educ.); George Peabody Coll., 1941–43, BS (LS); various crs. **Orgs.:** ALA. SELA. GA LA: GA Reprints Com. (Ch., 1975). Oakhurst Bapt. Church. Mstr. 4H Club. **Activities:** 1, 10, 20, 44, 46 **Addr.:** 0128 Parkwood Ln., Decatur, GA 30030.

Swinton, Cordelia W. (S. 9, 1939, Pittsburgh, PA) Chief, Lending Srvs., PA State Univ., 1973–, Soc. Sci. Libn., 1972–73, Libn., Human Dev. Lib., 1966–72; Serials Catlgr., Ref. Libn., Dickinson Coll., 1963–66. **Educ.:** Lake Erie Coll., 1958–61, BA (Art Hist.); Univ. of Pittsburgh, 1962–63, MLS. **Orgs.:** ALA: PLA, Mem. Com. (1979–80). PA LA: Mem. Ch. (1979–80); Chap., Mem. Ch. (1977–79). SLA Lcl. Arrange. Com. (1973). **Addr.:** C106 Pattee Library, The Pennsylvania State University, University Park, PA 16802.

Swisher, Christopher Charles (Ja. 21, 1950, Syracuse, NY) Inst. Resrcs. Coord., Drexel Univ., Sch. of Lib. and Inf. Sci., 1981–; Media Libn., Wolfgram Meml. Lib., Widener Univ., 1981; Media/Pub. Srvs. Libn., Krauth Meml. Lib., Lutheran Theo. Semy., 1977–81; Adj. Instr., Drexel Univ., Sch. of Lib. and Info. Sci., 1978–. **Educ.:** W. Chester State Coll., 1968–74, BA (Lit.); Drexel Univ., 1975–77, MSLS. **Orgs.:** ALA. AECT. PA LA: Spec. AV Com. (1977). Drexel Univ., Sch. of Lib. and Info. Sci. Alum. Assn.: Exec. Com. (1980). **Honors:** Beta Phi Mu, 1977; Phi Delta Kappa, 1981. **Pubns.:** AV media reviewer, *Lib. Jnl.;* reviews. **Activities:** 1, 11; 26, 32, 39; 93 **Addr.:** 6232 McCallum St., Philadelphia, PA 19144.

Swist, Ann M. (F. 24, 1942, Paterson, NJ) Info. Anal., Bristol Myers Prods., 1972–; Mktg. Libn., BASF Wyandotte, 1970–72; Libn., Inmont Corp., 1963–70. **Educ.:** Fairleigh Dickinson Univ., 1959–63, BS (Chem.). **Orgs.:** SLA: Dir. (1980–81); Treas. OLUG: Prog. Ch. **Activities:** 58, 60 **Addr.:** Bristol Myers Products, 1350 Liberty Ave., Hillside, NJ 07207.

Switzer, Peri Irish (Ag. 1, 1940, Kendallville, IN) Head, Cat., Wright State Univ., 1978–; Media Catlgr., Univ. of CO, Denver, 1976–78; Cat. Asst., CO Women's Coll., 1974–75; Asst. Catlgr., IN Univ. Reg. Campus Libs. Tech. Srvs., 1970–71. **Educ.:** Franklin Coll. of IN, 1958–62, BA; IN Univ., 1966–70, MLS; Wright State Univ., 1979–, MBA (Bus.). **Orgs.:** CO LA: Ed., *CO Libs.* (1976–78); Mem. Com. (1977–78); PR Com. (1977–78). ALA: LAMA/Persnl. Admin. Sect., Supervisory Skills Com. (1978–). Dayton–Miami Valley Cnsrtm.: Lib. Div./Prsnl. Com. (Ch., 1978–). **Activities:** 1; 20, 46 **Addr.:** Wright State University Library, Dayton, OH 45435.

Swope, Cynthia Diane (Ap. 12, 1949, Lafayette, IN) Head, Lib. Srvs., Harford Cmnty. Coll., 1980–, Catlgr., 1978–80; Media Spec., Franklin Coll., 1977–78; Forms Anal., Fireman's Fund Insr., 1971–75. **Educ.:** IN Univ., 1967–71, AB (Eng.), 1975–76, MLS, 1976–77, EdS (Instr. Tech.). **Orgs.:** MD LA: Fed. Legis. Subcom. (1980–). Congs. of Acad. Libns. ALA: Cmnty. and Jr. Colls. Libs. Comm. (1980–). **Activities:** 1; 15, 17, 32; 63 **Addr.:** Harford Community College, 401 Thomas Run Rd., Bel Air, MD 21082.

Sykora, Jane M. (Mr. 20, 1930, Prague, Czechoslovakia) Dir., Test Dev. Libs., Educ. Testing Srv., 1977–; Head, Ord. Div., Princeton Univ. Lib., 1968–77. **Educ.:** Rutgers State Univ., 1974–75, MLS. **Orgs.:** ALA: LAMA Persnl. Admin. Sect., Econ. Status, Welfare, and Fringe Benefits Com. (1979–83), Hiring and Termination Procs. Subcom. (1979–81). Rutgers Alum. Assn. **Activities:** 1, 12; 17; 61 **Addr.:** Educational Testing Service, Rm. D–423, Princeton, NJ 08541.

Sylvester, Melvin R. (Mr. 25, 1939, New Orleans, LA) Head, Pers. Dept., C.W. Post Ctr., 1964–, Head, Circ. Dept., 1962–64; Ref., Circ. Libn., Dillard Univ., 1961–62. **Educ.:** Dillard Univ., 1957–61, BA (Nat. Sci.); Long Island Univ., 1961–66, MSLS (Lib.), 1970–73, MEd (Educ.). **Orgs.:** NY LA. Nassau Cnty. LA: Secy. (1973–75). Lib. Fac. Persnl. Com.: Pres. (1971–72). Melvil Dui Assn. Palmer Grad. Lib. Sch. Alum. Assn.: VP (1970–71). Glen Cove Schs. Com. on the Handcpd. (1978–). C.W. Post Fac.: Interdisciplinary Com. (1974–75); Fac. Cncl. (1974–76); Student Affairs Appeals Com. (1979–); Space Util. Com. (Ch., 1975–77). Tau Kappa Epsilon Fraternity: Fac. Adv. (1964–77). various other orgs. **Honors:** Tau Kappa Epsilon Fraternity, Srv. and Dedication, 1970; Tau Kappa Epsilon Fraternity, Outstan. Chap. Adv., 1974; Alpha Phi Alpha Fraternity, Recog. of Srv., 1979; Glen Cove Schs., Apprec. for Srv. Plaque, 1981. **Pubns.:** *Negro Periodicals in the United States, 1826–1960* (1975); *A Library Handbook to Basic Source Materials in Guidance and Counseling* (1973); various reviews for *Lib. Jnl., Sch. Lib. Jnl.* (1970–76). **Activities:** 1, 9; 17, 22, 31 **Addr.:** C.W. Post Center, Schwartz Memorial Library, Northern Blvd., P.O. Greenvale, NY 11548.

Sylvestre, Jean Guy (My. 17, 1918, Sorel, PQ) Natl. Libn., Natl. Lib. of Can., 1968–; Assoc. Parlmt. Libn., Lib. of Parlmt., 1953–68; Admin. Ofcr., Dept. Resrcs., 1950–53; Pvt. Secy. to Prime Mnstr. of Can., 1948–50. **Educ.:** Coll. Ste. Marie, Montreal, 1935–37; Univ. of Ottawa, 1937–41, BA, BPh, LPh, MA. **Orgs.:** Can. Assn. Info. Sci.: 1st Pres. (1971–72). FLA: Natl. Libs. Sect. (Ch., 1977–81); Gen. Resrch. Libs. Div. (Ch., 1977–81). Can. LA. ON LA. Various other orgs. Can. Writers Fndn.: Past Pres. Royal Socty. of Can.: Hon. Libn. (1975); Pres. (1973–74). Acad. Can. Fr. Del to various confs. **Honors:** Univ. of Ottawa, LS (Hon.), 1969; Mt. Allison Univ., Litt (Hon.), 1970; Univ. of Toronto, Law (Hon.), 1974; P.E.I., Law (Hon.), 1975. **Pubns.:** *Anthologie de la poesie quôbecoise* (1943–74); *Canadian Writers* (1964); *A Century of Canadian Literature* (1967); various articles. **Activities:** 1, 4; 17, 23; 55, 92 **Addr.:** National Library of Canada, 395 Wellington St., Ottawa, ON Canada.

Sywak, Myron (Jl. 10, 1925, Brooklyn, NY) Assoc. Prof., LS, Long Island Univ., 1979–, Asst. to Dean, Asst. Prof., 1969–79; Libn., Robert Cushman Murphy Jr. HS, 1968–69; Assoc. Libn., Cold Spr. Harbor HS, 1964–68. **Educ.:** C.W. Post Coll., 1959–64, BA (Hist.); Long Island Univ., 1964–66, MS (LS); NY Univ., 1969–70, PhD (Admin. of Higher Educ.). **Orgs.:** ALA. NY LA. Long Island Sch. Media Assn. AALS. **Honors:** Alpha Sigma Lambda; Pi Gamma Mu. **Pubns.:** "Looping the Library," *Lib. Jnl.* (F. 15, 1968); jt. auth., "Results of the Intellectual Freedom Committee's IFG Test," *NY LA Bltn.* (N. 1975); "The Climate of Meaning," *Ventures in Research* (1976). **Activities:** 11; 20, 26, 41; 56, 75 **Addr.:** Palmer Graduate Library School, C.W. Post Center, Long Island University, P.O. Greenvale, NY 11548.

Sywak, Zofia (Mr. 26, 1941, Poland) Dir., Archvst., RI Hist. Recs. Srvy., Gvt. Ofc., 1979–; Archvst., Kelly Inst., St. Francis Coll., 1978–79; Archvst., New Haven Colony Hist. Socty., 1975–78. **Educ.:** Albertus Magnus Coll., 1959–64, BA (Pol. Sci.); St. Johns Univ., Jamaica, NY, 1964–66, MA (Pol. Sci.); 1966–75, PhD (Hist.); Amer. Univ., 1976, Cert. (Arch. Admin.). **Orgs.:** SAA: Status of Women Com. (1980–). Assn. of Recs. Mgrs. and Admins. New Eng. Archvsts.: Nom. Com. (1980): Bylaws Rev. (1979–80). Amer. Hist. Assn. Amer. Assn. for the Advnc. of Slavic Std.: Lcl. Arrange. Com., 1979 Anl. Mtg. Polish Inst. of Arts and Sci. RI Hist. Socty.: Lib. Com. (1980–). **Pubns.:** Jt. auth., *Poles in America: Bicentennial Essays* (1979); amer. ed., *Paderewski* (1980); various reviews, articles. **Activities:** 2, 12; 17, 38; 62, 69, 78 **Addr.:** 31 Thomas Olney Com., Providence, RI 02904.

Szegedi, Laszlo (Jl. 19, 1923, Abony, Hungary) Head Cat. Libn., Loyola Law Sch. Lib., Los Angeles, 1966–; Soc. Sci. Biblgphr., York Univ. Lib., 1964–66; Catlgr., Univ. of Toronto Lib., 1962–64. **Educ.:** Pazmany Univ., Budapest, Hungary, 1943–48, LLB (Law); Univ. of BC, 1958–61, BA (Hist., Geo.); Univ. of Toronto, 1961–62, BLS (Libnshp.). **Orgs.:** AALL: Cat. and Class. (1971–73); Frgn. and Intl. Law (1974–76). South. CA Assn. of Law Libs.: Audit and Budget Com. (Ch., 1976–78). South. CA Tech. Prcs. Grp. Hungarian Reformed Church of Hollywood. **Activities:** 1; 20, 29, 46; 59, 77, 92 **Addr.:** Loyola Law School Library, 1440 W. 9th St., Los Angeles, CA 90015.

Szekely, Yoram B. (Ag. 1, 1943, Tel Aviv, Israel) Libn., Uris Lib., Cornell Univ., 1978–; Head, Undergrad. Lib., SUNY, Buffalo, 1973–78; Circ. Libn., Herbert Lehman Lib., Columbia Univ., 1969–72. **Educ.:** Columbia Univ., 1961–65, BA (Oriental Std.), 1968–69, MLS. Amer. Philatelic Socty. **Honors:** Phi Beta Kappa. **Activities:** 1; 15, 17 **Addr.:** Uris Library, Cornell University, Ithaca, NY 14853.

Szemraj, Edward Richard (Ag. 7, 1934, Buffalo, NY) Lib. Media Coord., K–12, Maryvale Sch. Syst., 1981–; Lib. Media Spec., Maryvale Sr. HS, 1971–, Co-Ch., Eng. Dept., 1968–70, Russ. Tchr., 1966–70, Eng. Tchr., 1960–70; Eng. Tchr., Lyndonville Ctrl. Sch., 1957–59. **Educ.:** Univ. of Buffalo, 1952–56, BA (Eng.); Canisius Coll., 1957–59, MS (Educ.), 1964–68, NY State Cert. (Russ.); SUNY, Geneseo, 1970–71, MLS; various crs. **Orgs.:** ALA. NY LA. Sch. Libns. Assn. of West. NY. Polish Amer. Libns. Assn. West. NY Educ. Comms. Cncl. Permanent Ch. of Polish Cult. at Canisius Coll.: Vice-Ch. (1974–78); Rec. Secy. (1978–). Cheektowaga Pub. Lib. Bd. Kosciuszko Fndn. **Activities:** 10; 15, 20, 48 **Addr.:** 15 Normandy Ave., Buffalo, NY 14225.

Szeplaki, Joseph (Ap. 17, 1932, Hatvan, Hungary) Supvsg. Libn., Head, Tech. Srvs., The Free Pub. Lib. of Elizabeth, NJ, 1981–; Dir., Tech. Srvs., Brookdale Cmnty. Coll., 1979–80; VP, Monitor Systs. Inc., 1977–79; Head, Acq., Asst. Prof., LS, Univ. of MN, 1974–77; Head, Serials Dept., OH Univ., 1969–74; Supvsr., Tech. Srvs., Info. Dynamics Corp., 1967–68; Head, Acq., Brandeis Univ., 1966–67, Actg. Head, Acq., 1965–66, Asst. Acq. Libn., 1963–65; various prof. positions, 1957–63. **Educ.:** Apaczai Csere Janos Coll. of Ped., 1954, MLS; Rutgers Univ., 1962. **Orgs.:** ALA: ACRL/Slavic and E. European Sect. (1974–75). Intl. P. E. N. Intl. Soc. Sci. Hon. Socty. Amer. Assn. for the Std. of Hungarian Hist. Amer. Hungarian Educs. Assn. various other orgs. **Honors:** Cleveland Arpad Acad., Silver Medal, 1972, Gold Medal, 1973, Awd, 1974. **Pubns.:** "Ohio University Pilot Project Analysis of the Processing Work Flow of Serials Department," *LARC Rpts.* (1969); "Planning and Analysing an Automated Library Project," *LARC Rpts.* (1971); *Hungarians in the United States and Canada: A Bibliography* (1977); *Louis Kossuth, "The Nation's Guest"* (1976); *The Hungarians in America, 1583–1974* (1975); various articles, bibls. in LS, Hungarian Cult. (1955–). **Activities:** 1; 17, 41, 46; 56, 57, 66 **Addr.:** 36 Canterbury Rd., Phillipsburg, NJ 08865.

PROFESSIONAL ACTIVITIES: Institutions: 1. Acad. lib.; 2. Arch.; 3. Assn.; 4. Fed./Gvt. lib.; 5. Inst. lib.; 6. Mfr./Suppl.; 7. Milit. lib.; 8. Musm.; 9. Pub. lib.; 10. Sch. lib.; 11. Sch. of lib. sci.; 12. Spec. lib.; 13. State lib.; 14. (other). **Functions/Activities:** 15. Acq./Col. dev.; 16. Adult srvs.; 17. Admin.; 18. Apprais.; 19. Archit./Bldgs.; 20. Cat./Class.; 21. Chld. srvs.; 22. Circ.; 23. Cons./Pres.; 24. Consult.; 25. Cont. ed.; 26. Educ. lib. sci.; 27. Ext. srvs.; 28. Fund/Grants; 29. Gvt. pubs.; 30. Indx./Abs.; 31. Instr. lib. use; 32. Media srvs.; 33. Micro.; 34. Netwks./Coop.; 35. Persnl.; 36. PR; 37. Publshg.; 38. Recs. mgt.; 39. Ref. srvs.; 40. Repro.; 41. Resrch.; 42. Review.; 43. Secur.; 44. Serials; 45. Spec. col.; 46. Tech. srvs.; 47. Trustees/Bds.; 48. YA srvs.; 49. (other).

Szerenyi, Bela Joseph (N. 13, 1914, Budapest, Hungary) Dir., Lib. Srvs., East. IL Univ., 1967–; Dir., Lib. Srvs., Tri-State Univ., 1964–67; Asst. Libn., Engin. Lib., Cornell Univ., 1962–64. **Educ.:** Pazmany Peter Univ., 1934–38, BA (Pol. Sci.); Elizabeth Univ., 1938–40, Doct. (Pol. Sci.); Syracuse Univ., 1960–62, MS (LS). **Orgs.:** ALA: ACRL/Com. on Lib. Instr. (1979). **Pubns.:** *Investment laws of Hungary* (1950); jt. auth., "Booth Library On-line Circulation System," *Jnl. of Lib. Autom.* (1971). **Activities:** 1, 2; 15, 17, 19 **Addr.:** 2200 Cortland Dr., Charleston, IL 61920.

Szmuk, Szilvia E. (O. 13, 1946, Budapest, Hungary) Lib. and Info. Sci. Libn./Spec. Col. Libn., St. John's Univ., 1976–; Ref. Libn., The Resrch. Libs., NY Pub. Lib., 1974–75. **Educ.:** Queens Coll., 1964–68, BA (Latin Amer. Area Std.), 1968–72, MA (Span. Lit.), 1971–72, MLS. **Orgs.:** ALA. SALALM. Bk. Arts Press. Amer. Prtg. Hist. Assn. **Honors:** Phi Beta Kappa, 1968. **Pubns.:** Jt. auth., *A Catalogue of the Comedias Sueltas in the New York Public Library* (1980). **Activities:** 1; 26, 31, 45; 55, 57, 75 **Addr.:** St. John's University, Grand Central & Utopia Pkwys., Jamaica, NY 11439.

Szonyi, Geza (F. 7, 1919, Budapest, Hungary) Sr. Sci., Resrch. Comp. Grp.; Supvsr., Chem. Info. Ctr., Polaroid Corp., 1969–; Head, Tech. Info., CIBA Corp., 1964–69; Sr. Resrch. Chem., Atlas Chem. Indus., 1958–64; Sr. Chem., Allied Chem. and Dye Corp., 1953–57. **Educ.:** Zurich Univ., 1938–43, 1943–45, PhD (Chem.). **Orgs.:** ASIS. Amer. Chem. Socty. **Honors:** Sigma XI. **Pubns.:** "The Use of Central Composite Experimental Designs to Improve Quality Control of Sensitometric Parameters," *Jnl. Appld. Photographic Engin.* (1981); "Experimental Design and Optimization the Easy Way," *Chemtech* (Ja. 1973); jt. auth., "How To Avoid Lying with Statistics," *Chemometrics: Theory and Applications* (1977); "DRS - A User Oriented Information Retrieval System," *Jnl. Chem. Documtn.* (1974); various tech. papers. **Activities:** 12; 17, 41, 46; 56, 60, 95-Appl. Stats. **Addr.:** C/o Polaroid Corporation, 750 Main St., Cambridge, MA 02139.

Szterenfeld, Helen (F. 10, 1953, Katowice, Poland) Head, Documtn. and Info. Srvs., Intl. Planned Parenthood Fed., 1976–. **Educ.:** Brooklyn Coll., CUNY, 1971–75, BA (Span.); Pratt Inst., 1975–76, MLS; Baruch Coll., CUNY, 1979–, MPA (Pub. Admin.). **Orgs.:** Assn. for Popltn./Fam. Plng. Libs. and Info. Ctrs.–Intl.: NY Chap., Secy. (1977–78), Vice-Ch. (1978–79); Ch. (1979–80). SLA. Polish-Amer. Libns. Assn. Dev. Libns. Grp. Amer. Assn. for Pub. Admin. **Honors:** Phi Beta Kappa, 1974; Beta Phi Mu, 1976. **Pubns.:** "Bibliografia sobre Educacion Sexual en America Latina," *Sexualidad Humana y Relaciones Personales* (1980); *IPPF/WHR Family Planning/Population Thesaurus* (1980); *IPPF/WHR Classification Scheme* (1980); "Selection and Acquisitions," *Procs. of Twelfth Anl. Conf., Assn. for Popltn./Fam. Plng. Libs. and Info. Ctrs.–Intl.* (1979); *Family Planning Programes* (1978). **Activities:** 5, 12; 17, 26, 41; 80, 95-Popltn. and Fam. Plng. **Addr.:** Intl. Planned Parenthood Federation, Western Hemisphere Region, 105 Madison Ave., New York, NY 10016.

Sztorc, Sr. Mary Virginia, CSSF (Jl. 5, 1931, Chicago, IL) Libn./Media, St. Joseph HS, 1978–; Libn./Media Spec., Our Lady of Ransom Sch., Niles, IL, 1974–78; Supvsr., Libs., Archdio. of St. Paul, 1972–74; LS Instr., Felician Coll., Chicago, IL, 1972. **Educ.:** DePaul Univ., 1961, PhB (Educ.); Chicago State Univ., 1968–72, MLS. **Orgs.:** Cath. LA: North. IL Unit, MI/Dakota Unit, Elem. Sect. (Vice-Ch., 1972–74); Regina Medal Com. (1976, 1979). Felician Lib. Srv.: Supvsr. (1970–). IL LA: Wkshp. Com. (1974–78). N. Suburban Lib. Syst.: Wkshp. Com. (1976–77). Chicagoland Assn. for Media in HSs. **Honors:** Cath. LA, World Bk.–Childcraft Awd., 1975. **Pubns.:** Various reviews. **Activities:** 10; 17, 32, 39; 63, 90, 92 **Addr.:** St. Joseph High School, 4831 S. Hermitage Ave., Chicago, IL 60609.

Szudy, Thomas Alan (D. 28, 1951, Cleveland, OH) Adult Srvs. Libn., Cuyahoga Cnty. Pub. Lib., 1975–. **Educ.:** OH Univ., 1970–73, BGS (Soclgy.); Case West. Rsv. Univ., 1977–78, MLS. **Orgs.:** ALA: RASD, Prof. Dev. Com. (1980–82). OH LA: Task Frc. on Srvs. to Older Adults (1980). **Activities:** 9; 16, 39, 48; 61, 90, 92 **Addr.:** Cuyahoga County Public Library, Parma Regional Library, 5850 Ridge, Parma, OH 44129.

Szynaka, Edward M. (S. 26, 1948, New York City, NY) Lib. Dir., Pasadena Pub. Lib., 1980–; Dir., Grace A. Dow Meml. Lib., 1977–80; Dir., Massena Pub. Lib., 1973–77; Assoc. Dir., Syracuse Univ. Film Ctr., 1971–73. **Educ.:** SUNY, Fredonia, 1966–70, BA (Pol. Sci.); Syracuse Univ., 1970–71, MLS; 1973, Advnc. Cert. (LS). **Orgs.:** NY LA: Pub. Lib. Div.; Adult Srv. Div. (Pres., 1973–74); JMRT (VP, 1972–73). Amer. Mgt. Assn. **Activities:** 9; 16, 17, 19 **Addr.:** 4336 Toyon Cir., LaVerne, CA 91750.

T

Tabb, D. Winston (O. 10, 1942, Stillwater, OK) Asst. Chief, Gen. Readg. Rms. Div., Lib. of Congs., 1978–, Head, Inquiry Sect., Congsnl. Resrch. Srv., 1977–78, Head, Congsnl. Readg. Rm., 1975–77, Ref. Libn., Congsnl. Ref. Div., 1973–75. **Educ.:** OK Bapt. Univ., 1959–63, BA (Eng.); Harvard Univ., 1963–71, AM (Amer. Lit.); Simmons Coll., 1971–72, MSLS. **Orgs.:** ALA: RASD/Stans. Com. (1980–). DC LA. Metro. WA Lib. Cncl. **Honors:** Beta Phi Mu; Lib. of Congs., Spec. Rcrt., 1972. **Pubns.:** "George F. Bowerman," *Dictionary of Amer. Lib. Biog.* (1975). **Activities:** 4; 16, 17, 39; 69 **Addr.:** General Reading Rms. Div., Library of Congress, Washington, DC 20540.

Taber, Sharon A. (S. 29, 1944, Miami, FL) Head, Circ. Srvs., McKeldin Lib., Univ. of MD, 1978–, Admin. Staff Libn., 1976–78, Soc. Sci. Ref. Libn., 1973–74, Gen. Ref. Libn., 1972–73. **Educ.:** WA State Univ., 1962–65, BA (Langs.); Univ. of MD, 1969–72, MLS. **Orgs.:** ALA: LAMA, Prog. Orien. Com. (1979–81). Beta Phi Mu: Iota Chap. (Treas., 1976–78). **Honors:** Phi Beta Kappa, 1966; Phi Kappa Phi, 1965. **Activities:** 1; 17, 22, 39; 63, 92 **Addr.:** 14700 Willoughby Rd., Upper Marlboro, MD 20870.

Tabler, Patricia W. (Ag. 3, 1929, Oak Park, IL) Church Libn., Silver Spring Presby. Church, 1958–; various temporary appts., Natl. Agr. Lib., 1975–78. **Educ.:** Univ. of IL, 1947–51, BS (LS). **Orgs.:** CSLA: Secy. (1975–76); Mem. Ch. (1979–80). Church Lib. Cncl. (DC): Nsltr. Ed. (1965–67); Treas. (1968–70); VP (1971–73); Pres. (1973–75); Wkshp. Co-ch. (1973–81). **Activities:** 12; 16, 21, 46; 50, 90, 92 **Addr.:** P.O. Box 116, Keedysville, MD 21756.

Taborsky, Theresa Budapest, Hungary) Lib. Dir., Widener Univ., 1980–; Asst. Dir., Eccles Hlth. Sci. Lib., Univ. of UT, 1970–80, Head, Serials and Docum., 1967–80; Ref. Libn., US Milit. Acad., 1964–65; Catlgr., Lib. of Congs., 1962–63. **Educ.:** Trinity Coll., 1952–54, BA (Span.); Columbia Univ., 1958–62, MS (LS); Med. LA, 1972, Cert., Univ. of UT, 1978–80, MPA (Pub. Admin.). **Orgs.:** ALA. PA LA. **Pubns.:** *The Public's Access to Health Sciences Information* (1980); *Use of Government Documents in Medical Libraries* (1979). **Activities:** 1; 17 **Addr.:** Wolfgram Memorial Library, Widener University, Chester, PA 19013.

Tacha, Michael Lee (Ag. 4, 1941, Denver, CO) Dir., Lib. Srvs., Neosho Cnty. Cmnty. Coll., 1973–; Adj. Fac. Mem., Sch. of LS, Emporia State Univ., 1973–; Instr., Unfd. Sch. Dist. 227, 1970–72; Assoc. Dir., Tchr. Corps, Adams State Coll., 1969–70. **Educ.:** KS Wesleyan Univ., 1959–63, BA (Soc. Sci., Elem. Educ.); Adams State Coll., 1968–69, MA (Cult. Std.); Emporia State Univ., 1972–73, MLS. **Orgs.:** KS LA: Pres. (1978); VP/Pres.-Elect (1977); Exec. Cncl. (1974–). ALA: KS Fed. Rel. Coord. (1981–). SE KS Cmnty. Coll. Lib. Cncl.: Co-fndr. (1973). KS Conf. on Lib. and Info. Srv.: State Ch. KS Assn. of Cmnty. Colls.: State Conf. Plng. Com. (1975–78). **Honors:** KS Assn. of Cmnty. Colls., Awd. of Merit, 1979. **Activities:** 1; 17, 26, 34; 63, 75 **Addr.:** Neosho County Community College, Chapman Library, 1000 S. Allen, Chanute, KS 66720.

Tachuk, Roger S. (My. 19, 1952, Detroit, MI) Head, Ref. Dept., Northwest. Univ. Med. Lib., 1981–, Ref. Libn., 1978–80. **Educ.:** Univ. of Detroit, 1970–74, AB (Asian Std.); Univ. of MI, 1977–78, AMLS. **Orgs.:** ALA: ACRL. Med. LA: Com. on Lib. Stans. and Prac. (1981–); Bd. of Dirs. (1980–81). Biomed. Comm. Netwk. Chicago OLUG. Chicago Lib. Club. **Pubns.:** "Bibliography on the Anglo-American Cataloguing Rules, Second Edition," *IL Libs.* (Ap. 1980); ed., *BCN Postings: the Nsltr. of the Biomed. Comm. Netwk.* (1980–81). **Activities:** 1; 17, 31, 39; 56, 75, 80 **Addr.:** Northwestern University Medical Library, 303 E. Chicago Ave., Chicago, IL 60611.

Tackett, Janet Sue (O. 9, 1940, Grahn, KY) Libn., John B. Lowe Elem. Sch., 1974–; Libn., Lyndon Elem. Sch., 1965–75; Libn., S. Park and Auburndale Elem. Schs., 1962–65. **Educ.:** Morehead State Coll., 1958–62, AB (Elem. Educ.); Univ. of KY, 1963–67, MSLS. **Orgs.:** KY Sch. Media Assn.: Pres. (1979–80); Pres.–Elect (1978–79); Nsltr. Ed. (1976–78); Treas. (1975–76); Lcl. Arrange. (1974–75); Nom. Com. (1973–74). KY LA: Exec. Bd. (1978–80). Jefferson Cnty. Sch. Media Assn. ALA: AASL; various coms. KY Educ. Assn. Natl. Educ. Assn. KY Theta of Alpha Delta Kappa: Pres.–Elect (1978–80); Pres. (1980–82); Treas. (1976–78); Secy. (1972–74). **Activities:** 10; 21, 32; 63 **Addr.:** 9378 Loch Lea Ln., Louisville, KY 40299.

Tacy, Gillian (Ag. 14, 1951, Hull, E. Yorkshire, Eng.) Tech. Pres. Libn., Alvin Cmnty. Coll., 1981–; Cnty. Libn./Syst. Coord., San Patricio Cnty. Lib. Syst., 1977–81. **Educ.:** CA State Univ., Long Beach, 1971–75, BA (Hist.); Univ. of South. CA, 1975–76, MLS; 1976, TX Cnty. Libns. Cert. **Orgs.:** TX LA. ALA. SWLA.: Various coms. **Activities:** 9; 17, 25, 36; 85 **Addr.:** 4601 Quail Hollow Dr., #2610, Baytown, TX 77521.

Tagg, Frederick Brister (Jl. 29, 1935, Philadelphia, PA) Assoc. Dir., Educ. Systs., Bur. of Natl. Affairs, 1978–, Dir., Educ. Progs., 1975–78, Comm. Mgr., 1972–75. **Educ.:** LaSalle Coll., Columbia Univ., 1951–56, (liberal Arts); Columbus Sch. of Law, Cath. Univ., 1968–71, JD. **Orgs.:** AALL. Washington Socty. of Law Libs. SLA. ASIS. various other orgs. Amer. Bar Assn.: Com. on Fed. Srv. Labor Law (Secy., 1976–80). VA Bar. Fed. Bar Assn.: Natl. Cncl. (1978–80). Psi Upsilon; Delta Theta Phi. **Pubns.:** Ed., various cont. ed. Crsbks. (1975–80); "Public Employees, The Right To Organize, Bargain, and Strike," *Cath. Univ. Law Review* (Spr. 1970); producer, "Teaching Legal Research" video (1978); "Controlling Inflation" video (1977); "Divorce Taxation" video (1980). **Activities:** 6-Mfr./supplr.; 25, 26, 37; 50, 77, 92 **Addr.:** BNA Education Systems, 1231 25th St. N.W., Suite S-605, Washington, DC 20037.

Taggart, Dorothy T. (Trekell) (Ap. 20, 1917, Harper, KS) Libn., Wellington Sr. HS, 1961– Instr., Lib. Media, North. MI Univ., Sum., 1970; Instr., Eng. and Jnlsm., Wellington HS, 1959–61. **Educ.:** Univ. of KS, 1934–38, BA (Eng., Fr.); Emporia State Univ., 1967–69, ML (LS); Univ. of CO, 1969–, Doct. cand., (Educ.); various crs. **Orgs.:** ALA: AASL, Pubns. Com. (1976). AECT KS AECT. KS Assn. of Sch. Libns.: Sec. Ch. various other orgs. KS Educ. Assn.: VP. Univ. of KS Alum. **Honors:** Mt. Plains LA, Recog. Awd., 1976; Pi Lambda Theta. **Pubns.:** *Management and Administration of the School Library Media Program* (1980); *Guide to Sources in Educational Media and Technology* (1975); "Innovative Programs in Kansas Media Centers," *AV Instr.* (N. 1977); "The Library Media Specialist and Networking," *Action for Libs.* (O. 1979). **Activities:** 10, 11; 17, 26, 34; 57, 93 **Addr.:** 315 N. C St., Wellington, KS 67152.

Taggart, Thoburn (O. 14, 1930, Ft. Worth, TX) ILL Libn., Wichita State Univ., 1972–; Asst. Libn., Nuffield Coll., Oxford Univ., 1971–72; Actg. Dir., Libs., Wichita State Univ., 1969–71, Coord., Pub. Srvs., 1967–69, Chief Ref. Libn., 1964–67, Soc. Sci. Ref. Libn., 1962–64; Asst. Libn., Wayne State Coll., 1961–62; Asst. Libn., Ref./Circ., KS State Univ., 1958–61. **Educ.:** Univ. of the S., 1949–53, BA (Pol. Sci.); George Peabody Coll., 1957–58, MA (LS). **Orgs.:** ALA. KS LA: Int. Frdm. Com. (Ch., 1966–67). AAUP. **Addr.:** 244 N. Yale St., Wichita, KS 67208.

Taggart, William R. (My. 5, 1925, Glasgow, Scotland) Head, Col. Div., Lib., Univ. of Victoria, 1966–; Head, Bibl. Dept., Univ. of SK, 1961–66; Reg. Libn., Vancouver Island Reg. Lib., 1956–61; Lectr., Eng. Dept., Univ. of BC, 1953–55. **Educ.:** University of MB, 1946–49, BA (Gen. Arts); McGill Univ., 1950–51, BLS, 1950–52, MA (Eng.). **Orgs.:** BC LA: Couns. (1958–60). Can. LA: Can. Assn. of Coll. and Univ. Libs. (Dir., 1975–78). **Pubns.:** "Book Selection Librarians in Canadian Universities," *Can. Lib. Jnl.* (O. 1974); "Blanket Approval Ordering–A Positive Approach," *CJL* (Jl.–Ag. 1970); "The Development of the Library Short Course in British Columbia," *BC Lib. Qtly.* (Ja. 1962); various reviews, articles. **Activities:** 1, 9; 15, 17, 45; 55, 57, 92 **Addr.:** Collections Division, University of Victoria Library, Victoria, BC V8W 2Y2 Canada.

Tai, Henry H. (Ap. 16, 1922, Changchow, China) Oriental Libn., Univ. of CA, Santa Barbara, 1966–; Asst. Libn., SUNY, Binghamton, 1964–66; Instr., Slippery Rock State Coll., 1963–64. **Educ.:** Natl. Cheng-chih Univ., Nanking, China, 1945–49, BA Jnlsm.; George Peabody Coll., 1962–63, MA (Libnshp.); Univ. of Chicago, 1969, Cert. Adv. Std. (Far E. Libnshp.). **Orgs.:** ALA. LA China (Taiwan). Assn. Asian Std. **Activities:** 1, 5; 15, 17, 20; 54 **Addr.:** 5532 Tellina Way, Santa Barbara, CA 93111.

Tai-Lauria, Elaine Elizabeth (Je. 27, 1952, St. Andrew, Jamaica) Clinical Libn., Hlth. Info. to Cmnty. Hosps., Univ. of South. CA, Norris Med. Lib., 1979–; Asst. Libn., Hlth. Sci. Lib., SUNY, Buffalo, 1979; Med. Libn., Deaconess Hosp., 1977–79. **Educ.:** St. Bonaventure Univ., 1971–75, BA (Eng.); SUNY, Geneseo, 1975–76, MLS; Med. LA, 1976, Cert. **Orgs.:** West. NY Hlth. Scis. Libns.: Secy. (1978–79); VP–Elect (1979); Nsltr. Co–Ed (1977–78). Med. LA. Med. Lib. Grp. of South. CA and AZ. Untd. Univ. Profs. **Activities:** 1, 5; 15, 24, 39; 58, 80, 87 **Addr.:** Norris Medical Library, Health Sciences Campus, University of Southern CA, 2025 Zonal Ave., Los Angeles, CA 90033.

Taitano, Magdalena S. (Agana, GU) Territorial Libn., Nieves M. Flores Meml. Lib., 1966–; Chief Libn., Univ. of GU, 1964–66; Ref. Libn., Ofc. of Tech. Srvs., Dept. of Cmrce., 1962–64. **Educ.:** Mt. Mary Coll., 1951–55, BA (Bus. Admin.); TX Women's Univ., 1958–59, MLS. **Orgs.:** ALA. GU LA: Ch. (1966–68). Frnds. of the Lib. Soroptomist. **Activities:** 9; 15, 22, 39 **Addr.:** Nieves M. Flores Memorial Library, P. O. Box 652, Agana, GU 96910.

Talar, Sr. Anita (Je. 21, 1942, Trenton, NJ) Dir., Lib. Srvs., Farley Meml. Lib., Georgian Ct. Coll., 1976–; Sch. Libn., Phillipsburg Cath. HS, 1970–76; Sch. Libn., St. Mary HS, South Amboy, NJ, 1968–70, Tchr., 1965–68. **Educ.:** Georgian Ct. Coll., 1961–65, BA (Eng.); Rutgers Univ., 1968–71, MLS (Lib. Srv.); 1978–81, 6th Yr. Spec. Cert. (LS); various crs. **Orgs.:** ALA. NJ LA. LA of Ocean Cnty. **Activities:** 1; 17, 31; 63, 90 **Addr.:** Farley Memorial Library, Georgian Court College, Lakewood, NJ 08701.

Talbot, Elizabeth J. (N. 25, 1947, Frankfurt a/M, Germany) Branch Head, Newark Branch, Alameda Cnty. Lib., 1979–, YA Spec., Fremont Main Branch, 1978–79, YA Spec., Dublin Branch, 1976–78; YA Ref., Richmond City Lib., 1974–76. **Educ.:** San Diego State Univ., Univ. of CA, San Diego, 1965–69, AB (Psy., Soclgy.), 1972–73, MA (Bhvl. Psy.); Univ. of CA, Berkeley, 1973–74, MLS. **Orgs.:** Bay Area YA Libns.: VP, Pres. (1975–76). Coal. to Restore Qual. Lib. Srv.: Treas. (1978–) CA LA. ALA: Cncl. (1981–85); YASD/Legis. Com. (1979–81); Bay

Special Subjects/Services: 50. Adult educ.; 51. Advert./Mktg.; 52. Aerosp.; 53. Agric.; 54. Area std.; 55. Arts/Hum.; 56. Autom.; 57. Bibl./Prtg.; 58. Bio. sci.; 59. Bus./Fin.; 60. Chem.; 61. Copyrt.; 62. Documtn.; 63. Educ.; 64. Engin.; 65. Env.; 66. Eth. grps.; 67. Film; 68. Food/Nutr.; 69. Geneal.; 70. Geo.; 71. Geol.; 72. Handcpd.; 73. Hist.; 74. Int. frdm.; 75. Info. sci.; 76. Insr.; 77. Law; 78. Legis.; 79. Math./Comp. sci.; 80. Med.; 81. Metals; 82. Nat. resrcs.; 83. Newsp.; 84. Nuc. sci.; 85. Oral hist.; 86. Petr./Energy; 87. Pharm.; 88. Phys./Astr./Math.; 89. Readg.; 90. Relig.; 91. Sci./Tech.; 92. Soc. sci.; 93. Telecom.; 94. Transp.; 95. (other).

Who's Who in Library and Information Services

Area SRRT. Women Lib. Workers. **Pubns.:** "Impact of Proposition 13 on Children's and Young Adult Services in CA," *Top of The News* (Win. 1980); "Sex–Ask the Librarian," *Lib. Jnl. Spec. Rpt. No. 6.* **Activities:** 9; 16, 17, 48; 74, 78 **Addr.:** Newark Branch Library, Alameda County System, 37101 Newark Blvd., Newark, CA 94560.

Talbot, Richard Joseph (D. 18, 1932, Lynn, MA) Dir., Libs., Univ. of MA, 1973–, Actg. Dir., 1972–73, Assoc. Dir., 1970–72, Chief, Cat. and Systs., 1968–70. **Educ.:** Manhattan Coll., 1950–54, AB (Phil.); Simmons Coll., 1960–61, MS (LS); Syracuse Univ., 1979–80, MBA. **Orgs.:** ALA: ACRL/Acad. Status Com. (1972–76); Bd.; Exec. Com.; Fin. Com. (Ch., 1980). CRL: Bd.; Exec. Com.; Finance Com. (Ch., 1981). NELINET: Bd. (1981). ARL: Stats. Com. (1980–). **Pubns.:** *Salary structures of librarians in higher education, 1975-1976* (1976); "Cotton Mather's Christian Loyalty, 1727," *Thirteen Colonial American* (1977). **Activities:** 1; 17 **Addr.:** 40 High Point Dr., Amherst, MA 01002.

Talcott, Ann Ward (D. 5, 1945, Chicago, IL) Grp. Supvsr., Murray Hill Lib., Bell Labs., 1976–, Grp. Supvsr., Lib. and Srvs., West. Electric, Naperville, 1976, Grp. Supvsr., Lib. Srvs. and Tech. Ed., 1976, Grp. Supvsr., Indian Hill Lib., 1976, Ref. Libn., 1969–; Catlgr., Alderman Lib., Univ. of VA, 1968–69. **Educ.:** Vanderbilt Univ., 1963–67, BA (Hist.); Univ. of MI, 1967–68, AMLS; various SLA cont. ed. crs., 1979–. **Orgs.:** SLA: NJ Chap./Secy. (1979–81); 1st VP (1981–82); Fin. Com. (Ch., 1977–79). Citizens Adv. Bd., Aurora Coll. DAR. PEO. Cmnty. Congregational Church. **Honors:** Beta Phi Mu, 1968; Fam. Srv. Assn. of DuPage Cnty., Bd. of Dirs., Disting. Srv. Awd., 1976. **Pubns.:** "LSI Microprocessors and Microcomputers: A Bibliography Continued," *Comp.* (Ja. 1976); "LSI Microprocessors and Microcomputers: A Bibliography, 1970 Through April 1974," *Comp.* (Jl. 1974); "The Culture Boom and Art History Libraries," *Spec. Libs.* (S. 1968). **Activities:** 12; 17; 91, 93 **Addr.:** Bell Labs., 600 Mountain Ave., Murray Hill, NJ 07974.

Tallman, Johanna E(leonore) (Ag. 18, 1914, Lübeck, Germany) Dir. of Libs., CA Inst. of Tech., 1973; Coord., Phys. Scis. Libs., Univ. of CA, Los Angeles, 1962–73, Lectr., Sch. of LS, 1961–73, Head, Engin. and Math. Scis. Lib., 1945–73; Asst. Libn. and Libn., Pac. Aeronautical Lib., Inst. of the Aeronautical Scis., 1942–44; Tech. Ref. Libn. and other positions, Los Angeles Cnty. Pub. Lib., 1938–42; Catlgr., Asst. Libn., San Marino Pub. Lib., 1937–38. **Educ.:** Univ. of CA, Berkeley, 1933–36, AB (Fr.), 1936–37 Cert. (LS). **Orgs.:** ALA: ACRL/Engin. Libs. Sect. (Ch., 1949–50); Cncl. (1949–53); Subscrpn. Bks. Com. (1954–56). SLA: Sci.–Tech. Div./Engin.–Aeronautics Sect. (Co–Ch. (1947–48), Ch. (1969–70); S. CA Chap. (Pres., 1965–66); Consult. Com. (1978–80). CA LA: Various ofcs., coms. (1954–81). Libns. Assn., Univ. of CA: Various ofcs. various orgs., ofcs. West. Assn. of Schs. and Colls.: Eval. Teams (1974–). Zonta Club Fine Arts Club of Pasadena. Utd. Srv. Clubs Ofcrs. Assn. various orgs., ofcs., consults. **Honors:** Fulbright Lectr., 1966–67. **Pubns.:** "The budget pinch; coping in university libraries," *Managing under Austerity; a Conference for Privately Supported Academic Libraries. Summary Proceedings* (1976); "Implications of the New Copyright Law for Libraries and Library Users," *IEEE Transactions on Professional Communications* (1977); "One Year's Experience with CONTU Guidelines for Interlibrary Loan Photocopies," *Jnl. of Acad. Libnshp.* (My. 1979); "What is an engineering librarian?" *Queen City Gazette* (S. 1979); "Perils of publishing," *Title Varies* (Mr. 1980); various articles, reviews (1942–). **Activities:** 1; 17; 57, 61, 91 **Addr.:** 4731 Daleridge Rd., La Canada, CA 91011.

Tallman, Karen Dalziel (Ap. 7, 1944, Vinton, IA) Head, Serials Acq., IA State Univ., 1981–, Serials Catlgr., 1978–81. **Educ.:** Univ. of FL, 1976, BA, hons. (Eng.); FL State Univ., 1978, MLS. **Orgs.:** Frdm. to Read Fndn. Can. LA. IA LA. ALA: RTSD; IFRT (1977–); *Amer. Libs.* Ed. Adv. Com., Int. Frdm. Com. (IFRT Liaison, 1981–). various other orgs. **Honors:** Beta Phi Mu, 1979. **Pubns.:** "Sex Magazines: Problems of Acquisition, Retention, Display and Defense in Public and Academic Libraries," *Sex Magazines in the Library Collection: A Scholarly Study of Sex in Serials and Periodicals, A Monographic Supplement to The Serials Librarian, Volume 4, 1979–80* (1981); "Doris Hargrett Clack: Not Subject to Classification," *Amer. Libs.* (S. 1978). **Activities:** 1; 20, 44, 46; 74, 86, 95-Subj. Analysis. **Addr.:** 154 Library–Serials Dept., Iowa State University, Ames, IA 50011.

Tamblyn, Eldon Waldo (N. 19, 1928, Centralia, WA) Head Catlgr., Portland State Univ., 1967–; Head Slavic Catlgr., Asst. Div. Cat. Rev., Stanford Univ., 1964–67; Slavic Catlgr., Duke Univ., 1962–64; Libn., Sch. of LS, Univ. of NC, 1962, Relig. Catlgr., 1961–62. **Educ.:** Univ. of Puget Snd., 1946–51, BA (Fr.); Syracuse Univ. (USAFSS), 1952–53, Cert. (Russ. lang.); Univ. of NC, 1961–64, MS (LS). **Orgs.:** ALA: RTSD/Cat. and Class. Sct., Bylaws Com. (1969–70), Secy. (1971–74), Nom. Com. (1974–75), Margaret Mann Cit. Com. (Ch., 1975–76). CA LA: Tech. Prcs. Libns. RT (Secy., 1966–67). Portland Art Assn. **Honors:** Beta Phi Mu; Sigma Nu. **Pubns.:** "They play it safe; a report of a survey on book selection and censorship in North Carolina public libraries," *Lib. Jnl.* (Je. 1, 1965); index, *CA Libn.* (1966, 1967); anl. index, *Coll. & Resrch. Libs.* (1975–80); 15-yr. index, *Coll. & Resrch Libs.* (1981); index, *Libraries for Teaching, Libraries for Research; Essays for a Century* (1977); various reviews, *C & RL* (1978–80). **Activities:** 1; 20, 30 **Addr.:** 2020 S. W. Main St., Apt. 501, Portland, OR 97205.

Tambo, David C. (My. 1, 1946, Albert Lea, MN) Cur., Stoeckel Arch./Ctr. for Middletown Std., Ball State Univ., 1979–; Asst. Archvst., State Hist. Socty. of WI, 1978–79. **Educ.:** St. Olaf Coll., 1964–68, BA (Hist., Phil.); Univ. of WI, 1971–74, MA (Hist.), 1977–78, MLS, 1978– (Hist.). **Orgs.:** SAA: Strg. Com., Lcl. Gvt. Recs. Sect. (1979–). Midwest Arch. Conf.: Educ. Com. (1979–). Socty. of IN Archvsts. African Stds. Assn.: Arch.–Lib. Com. (1979–). Oral Hist. RT, IN. Hist. Prsrvn. and Rehab. Comsn., Muncie. **Honors:** Phi Beta Kappa, 1968; Fulbright–Hays, Flwshp., 1975. **Pubns.:** "African Historical Dictionaries in Perspectives," *African Std. Assn., Review of Bks.* (1981); "The 'Hill Refuges' of the Jos Plateau: An Historiographical Examination," *Hist. in Africa* (1978); "The Sokoto Caliphate Slave Trade in the Nineteenth Century," *Intl. Jnl. of African Hist. Std.* (1976). **Activities:** 1, 2; 15, 17, 28; 62, 86, 92 **Addr.:** Stoeckel Archives/Center for Middletown Studies, Bracken Library, Ball State University, Muncie, IN 47306.

Tamulonis, Susan (O. 29, 1951, Shenandoah, PA) Asst. Prof./Slide Cur., North. IL Univ., 1979–; Art Slide Cur., Wake Forest Univ., 1976–79. **Educ.:** PA State Univ., 1969–73, BA (Art Hist.); South. Meth. Univ., 1974–75, MA (Art Hist.); Univ. of MO, 1977, Chancellor's Cert. **Orgs.:** Art Libs. Socty./Mid States. ARLIS/NA. Coll. Art Assn. of Amer. various other orgs. **Pubns.:** *Guide for Photographic Collections* (1978); various sp. **Activities:** 1; 49-Slide Lib.; 55 **Addr.:** P.O. Box 164, DeKalb, IL 60115.

Tanaka, Momoe (Mr. 5, 1934, Papaaloa, HI) State Law Libn., Supreme Ct. of HI, 1977–, Asst. Law Libn., 1969–77; Libn., Dept. of Educ., 1958–69. **Educ.:** Univ. of HI, 1952–56, BA; Univ. of WA, 1956–57, MLS. **Orgs.:** AALL: West. Pac. Chap. State, Ct. and Cnty. Law Libs. Soroptimist Intl. of Honolulu. **Addr.:** Supreme Court Law Library, P.O. Box 779, Honolulu, HI 96808.

Tang, Chin-Shih (Ap. 27, 1938, Shanghai, China) Ref. Libn., Law Lib., Univ. of Ottawa, 1971–, Lectr., Fac. of Law, 1975–81. **Educ.:** Natl. Taiwan Univ., 1957–61, LLB (Law); McGill Univ., 1963–67, LLM (Law), 1969–71, MLS. **Orgs.:** Can. ALL. AALL. Inst. of Air and Space Law Assn.: Hon. Secy. (1964–65). **Pubns.:** "The Boundary Question in Space Law," *Ottawa Law Review* (Win. 1973); Reviews. **Activities:** 1; 31, 39; 52, 77 **Addr.:** University of Ottawa Law Library, 57 Copernicus St., Ottawa, ON K1N 6N5 Canada.

Tanguay, Guy (N. 25, 1941, Sherbrooke, PQ) Dir., Bib. de Droit, Univ. de Sherbrooke, 1966–. **Educ.:** Univ. de Sherbrooke, 1960–63, LLL (Law); Univ. de Montréal, 1964–64, Bac. (LS). **Orgs.:** Can. ALL.: Pres. (1971–73). AALL. Intl. Assn. of Law Libs.: Nom. Com. (Ch., 1980). Societé Québécoise d'Info. Juridique: Bd. of Dir. (1976–). **Pubns.:** Jt. ed., *Constitutions of Canada* (1978–); "The Case for the Special Status of the University Law Library," *Law Lib. Jnl.* (1973). **Activities:** 1; 17; 77, 78 **Addr.:** Bibliothèque de Droit, Université de Sherbrooke, Sherbrooke, PQ J1K 2R1 Canada.

Tanis, James Robert (Je. 26, 1928, Phillipsburg, NJ) Dir. of Libs. and Prof. of Hist., Bryn Mawr Coll., 1969–; Lectr., Yale Divnty. Sch., 1967–69; Univ. Libn., Yale Univ., 1965–68; Libn. and Lectr., Harvard Divnty. Sch., 1956–65. **Educ.:** Yale Univ., 1946–51, BA (Hist.); Union Theo. Semy., 1951–54, BD (New Testament); Univ. of Utrecht, 1962–67, DrTheo., highest hons. (Hist.). **Orgs.:** ALA. ATLA. Balch Inst.: Bd. (1979–). Renaissance Socty.: Bd. (1974–). Netherlands Socty.: Vice–Ch. (1980–). **Pubns.:** *Dutch Calvinistic Pietism in the Middle Colonies* (1967); "Reformed Pietism in Colonial America," *Continental Pietism and Early American Christianity* (1976); "Pietism and the Rise of Reformed Missions," *Harvard Theo. Review* (1974); "The Union of Utrecht," *de Halve Maen* (Fall–Win. 1979); "The Dutch Reformed Clergy in the American Revolution," *Wegen en Gestalten* (1976). **Activities:** 1; 15, 17, 45; 57, 90, 73-History. **Addr.:** Office of the Director, Bryn Mawr College Libraries, Bryn Mawr, PA 19010.

Tanis, Norman Earl (Ag. 15, 1929, Grand Rapids, MI) Dir. of Univ. Libs., CA State Univ., Northridge, 1969–; Dir. of Libs., KS State Univ., Pittsburg, 1966–69; Head Libn., Henry Ford Cmnty. Coll., 1963–66, Libn., 1956–63. **Educ.:** Calvin Coll., 1947–51, AB (Eng.); Univ. of MI, 1951–52, MALS, 1954–56, MA (Amer. Hist.), 1957–61, MA (Hist. and Phil. of Educ.). **Orgs.:** ALA: ACRL (Pres., 1973–74); IFRT (1980–); Awds. and Grants (1980–). CA LA: Int. Frdm. Com. (Ch., 1975–77). NLA: Pres. (1980–81); VP (1979–80); Cert. Stans. Com. (Ch., 1977–79). Phi Kappa Phi: Pres. (1974–75). Mss Socty. AAUP: Chap. Pres. (1961–62). Univ. of CA, Los Angeles, Adv. Cncl. (1972–). various other orgs. **Honors:** Univ. of San Fernando, Doctor of Humane Letters, 1973; Mid-Valley Coll. of Law, Doctor of Laws, 1976; Beta Phi Mu, 1974. **Pubns.:** Jt. auth., *India and Its People: A Bibliography* (1980); jt. auth., *China in Books* (1979); "A New Model for Faculty Status," *Jnl. of Acad. Libnshp.* (Jl. 1978); Ed., Santa Susana Press (1975–); Producer, "Famous People of Southern California" (video) (1975–); various articles. **Activities:** 1; 17, 28, 37; 57, 74, 78 **Addr.:** Oviatt Library Administration, California State University, Northridge, 18111 Nordhoff St., Northridge, CA 91330.

Tannehill, Robert S., Jr. (D. 3, 1940, Vicksburg, MS) Lib. Mgr., Chem. Abs. Srv., 1969–; Info. Sci., Actg. Libn., Med. Ctr. Lib., Vanderbilt Univ., 1967–69; Libn., Sadtler Rsrch. Labs., 1966–67. **Educ.:** Univ. of South. MS, 1962, BA (Chem.); Drexel Univ., 1967, MA (Info. Sci.). **Orgs.:** Columbus Area Lib. and Info. Cncl.: Pres. (1978–79). Amer. Natl. Stans. Com. Z39: Cnclr. (1978–80); Alternate Amer. Chem. Socty. Rep. (1970–). ASIS: Stans. Com. (1978–); Spec. Interest Grp. on Lib. Autom. and Networking Vice–Ch. (1978–79), Ch. (1979–80); Networking Com. (1979–); Ctrl. OH Chap., Nswltr. Ed. (1974–), Ch. (1973–74). Natl. Fed. of Abs. and Indexing Srvs.: Various coms. (1974–). Intl. Org. for Stan.: Various coms. (1974–). IFLA: Working Grp. on the Intl. Stan. Bibl. Descr. for Analytics (1978–). Amer. Chem. Socty. *Sci. and Tech. Libs.* Ed. Bd. (1979–). **Pubns.:** "Regional Medical Library Planning in the Southeastern United States," *Coll. & Resrch. Libs.* (1969); "Problems in Accessing Scientific and Technical Serials," *Spec. Libs.* (1977); "CASSI: File for Document Access," *Spec. Libs.* (1978). **Addr.:** Chemical Abstracts Service, P. O. Box 3012, Columbus, OH 43210.

Tannenbaum, Arthur C. (Jl. 5, 1941, New York, NY) Bldg. and Plng. Libn., NY Univ., 1978–, Libn. for Info. Tech., 1973–77, Circ. Libn., 1968–72. **Educ.:** NY Univ., 1963–67, BA (Eng. Lit.); Pratt Inst., 1968–69, MLS; NY Univ., 1970–72, MA (Media Comm.). **Orgs.:** Natl. Micro. Assn. AECT. **Pubns.:** "Microform Room Planning," *Serials Libn.* (1980); "User Environment/User Attitude," *Lib. Jnl.* (O. 15, 1976); various sp. **Addr.:** Elmer Holmes Bobst Library, New York University, 70 Washington Sq. S., New York, NY 10012.

Tannenbaum, Earl (Jl. 30, 1915, Milwaukee, WI) Retired, 1981–; Actg. Dean, Lib. Srvs., IN State Univ., Terre Haute, 1978–81, Dir., Lib. Pub. Srvs., 1969–81, Actg. Dean, Lib. Srvs., 1974–75; Visit. Lectr., Grad. Sch. of Libnshp., Univ. of Denver, 1962–69; Head Libn., Regis Coll., 1961–69; Asst. Hum. Libn., South. IL Univ., 1957–61; Spec. Consult., WI Free Lib. Comsn., 1957; Asst. Libn., WI State Coll., 1953–56. **Educ.:** Univ. of WI, 1934–36, BA (Eng.); Univ. of Chicago, 1946–47, MA (Eng.); IN Univ., 1952–53, MA (LS). **Orgs.:** ALA: RASD/Com. on Ref. Stans. (1969–72). CO LA: VP, Exec. Bd. (1962–63). Bibl. Ctr. for Rsrch., Rocky Mts. Reg.: Treas. (1963–65). **Honors:** Beta Phi Mu, 1960. **Pubns.:** Jt. auth., *Introduction to Cataloging and Classification* (1964); ed., *A Checklist of the Cordell Collection of Dictionaries, Cunningham Memorial Library, Indiana State University* (1971); "Ballast in Balloons: An Addition to O.E.D.," *Notes and Queries* (D. 1963); "The Librarian in the College Library," *Coll. & Resrch. Libs.* (My. 1963). **Activities:** 1; 17, 31, 39; 55, 57 **Addr.:** Indiana State University, Terre Haute, IN 47809.

Tanner, Allan B. (Ap. 24, 1950, Salina, KS) Comp. Mktg. Rep., Radio Shack Comp. Ctr., 1981–; Ref. Libn., Wichita State Univ., 1978–81; Bus. and Sci. Libn., Metro. Lib. Syst., OK City, 1976–78; VISTA Volun., Wichita, KS, 1972–73. **Educ.:** Univ. of KS, 1968–72, BA (Amer. Std.); South. Meth. Univ., 1973–74 (Law); N. TX State Univ., 1974–75, MLS. **Orgs.:** OK LA: Ref. Div. (Ch., 1978). ALA. SWLA. NLA. Midtown Citizens Assn. **Activities:** 1, 9; 16, 39; 59, 77 **Addr.:** 2018 Park Pl., Wichita, KS 67203.

Tanner, Elizabeth Louise (My. 17, 1951, Eldorado, IL) Tech. Libn., Greeley and Hansen, 1981–; Tech. Libn., Brown and Root, Inc., 1976–81. **Educ.:** Monmouth Coll., 1969–73, BA (Latin, Eng.); Rosary Coll., 1973–77, MALS; various sems. **Orgs.:** ALA. SLA: Engin. Div. Ch.–Elect (1979–80), Ch. (1980–81); Construct. Unit Nsltr. Ed. (1977–79). Addison Pub. Lib.: Bd. of Trustees (1979–81). IL Reg. Lib. Cncl.: Cont. Ed. Com. (1977–80). DuPage Lib. Syst.: Afflt. Libns. Com. (1978–79). **Activities:** 12; 17, 39; 64, 86, 91 **Addr.:** 303 Hale, Apt. 2R, Addison, IL 60101.

Tanner, Thomas M. (S. 7, 1951, Francesville, IN) Libn., Lincoln Christ. Coll., 1979–. **Educ.:** Lincoln Christ. Coll., 1969–73, AB (Mnstry.); Lincoln Christ. Semy., 1973–76, MDiv (New Testament); Univ. of IL, 1976–78, MA (Classics), 1978–79, MLS. **Orgs.:** ATLA. Christ. Libns. Flwshp. **Honors:** Beta Phi Mu. **Pubns.:** "A History of Early Christian Libraries from Jesus to Jerome," *Jnl. of Lib. Hist.* (Fall 1979). **Activities:** 1; 15, 39, 41; 90 **Addr.:** Lincoln Christian College, Box 178, Lincoln, IL 62656.

Tanno, John W. (S. 28, 1939, Brooklyn, NY) Asst. Univ. Libn., Univ. of CA, Riverside, 1978–, Head, Mono. Dept., 1972–78, Msc. Libn., 1971–72; Ord. Libn., Honnold Lib., Claremont Colls., 1970; Msc. Libn., SUNY, Binghamton, 1965–68. **Educ.:** AZ State Univ., 1960–63, BA (Msc.); Univ. of South. CA, 1963–65, MA (Msc.), 1969–70, MS (LS). **Orgs.:** Msc. LA: Bd. of Dirs. (1980–82); Pubns. Com. (Ch., 1975–78); Pubns. Cncl. (Ch., 1976–78); Admin. Com. (Ch., 1972–75); Autom. Com. (1972–75). Assn. of Rec. Snd. Cols. Coll. Msc. Socty. Guitar Fndn. of Amer.: Exec. Com. (1976–80). **Honors:** Beta Phi Mu. **Pubns.:** Jt. cmplr., *Directory of Music Library Automation Projects* (1973); "Planning and Moving a Music Library," *Msc. LA*

PROFESSIONAL ACTIVITIES: Institutions: 1. Acad. lib.; 2. Arch.; 3. Assn.; 4. Fed./Gvt. lib.; 5. Inst. lib.; 6. Mfr./Suppl.; 7. Milit. lib.; 8. Musm.; 9. Pub. lib.; 10. Sch. lib.; 11. Sch. of lib. sci.; 12. Spec. lib.; 13. State lib.; 14. (other). **Functions/Activities:** 15. Acq./Col. dev.; 16. Adult srvs.; 17. Admin.; 18. Apprais.; 19. Archit./Bldgs.; 20. Cat./Class.; 21. Chld. srvs.; 22. Circ.; 23. Cons./Pres.; 24. Consult.; 25. Cont. ed.; 26. Educ. lib. sci.; 27. Ext. srvs.; 28. Fund/Grants; 29. Gvt. pubs.; 30. Indx./Abs.; 31. Instr. lib. use; 32. Media srvs.; 33. Micro.; 34. Netwks./Coop.; 35. Persnl.; 36. PR; 37. Publshg.; 38. Recs. mgt.; 39. Ref. srvs.; 40. Repro.; 41. Resrch.; 42. Review.; 43. Secur.; 44. Serials; 45. Spec. col.; 46. Tech. srvs.; 47. Trustees/Bds.; 48. YA srvs.; 49. (other).

Nsltr. (S.–O. 1974); "Locating Guitar Music," *Guitar Fndn. of Amer. Soundbd.* (O. 1975); "The Acoustics of Strings as Related to the Guitar," *Guitar Fndn. of Amer. Soundbd.* (Ag. 1977); "Recent Reference Works on the Guitar," *Soundbd.* (N. 1979); various articles, reviews, edshps. (1968–). **Activities:** 1; 17, 32, 46; 55, 56, 57 **Addr.:** The Library, P.O. Box 5900, University of California, Riverside, CA 92507.

Tanzer, Barbara (Ap. 9, 1939, Brooklyn, NY) Asst. Libn., NY Cnty. Lawyers Assn., 1970–, Catlgr., 1968–70. **Educ.:** City Coll. of New York, 1956–60, BS (Educ., Hist.); Pratt Inst., 1965–68, MLS. **Orgs.:** Law LA of Grt. NY: Pres. (1977–78); VP (1976–77); Bd. of Dirs. (1972–73); Un. List of Pers. (1979). **Activities:** 5; 17, 31, 39; 62, 77 **Addr.:** New York County Lawyers Association Library, 14 Vesey St., New York, NY 10007.

Taoka, Wesley M. (Jl. 29, 1950, San Francisco, CA) UTLAS Mgr., Maruzen Co., Ltd., 1981–; Info. Spec., 1979–81; Info. Spec., Univ. of MD, 1978–79; Ref. Libn., Harvard Univ., 1976–78. **Educ.:** Univ. of CA, Berkeley, 1968–72, AB (Bio., Sci.); Simmons Coll., 1975–76, MS (LS); Med. LA, 1977, Cert. **Orgs.:** Med. LA: Anl. Mtg. Com. (1978). SLA. ASIS. AAAS. **Activities:** 6, 12; 17, 34, 39; 75, 80, 87 **Addr.:** Maruzen Co., Ltd., P.O. Box 5335, Tokyo International 100-31, Japan.

Taplin, Franklin P. (Jl. 28, 1919, Wellesley, MA) Dir., Westfield Athen., 1967–; Dir., West. Reg. Pub. Lib. Syst., 1962–67; Dir., Holyoke Pub. Lib., 1959–62; Asst. Libn., Waltham Pub. Lib., 1959. **Educ.:** Amherst Coll., 1937–39; New Eng. Cnsvty. of Msc., 1939–42, BMus (Msc.); Simmons Coll., 1953–58, MS (LS). **Orgs.:** ALA: Chap. Cnclr. (1970–75). New Eng. LA: Reg. Plng. Cncl. (1963–64). MA LA: Pres. (1963–64). West. MA Reg. Adv. Cncl.: Ch. (1970–72). MA Gvr.'s Conf. on Libs. and Info. Srvs.: Citizens' Adv. Com. (1978–79). Natl. Conf. of Christs. and Jews: Holyoke Chap. Westfield Rotary Club. **Pubns.:** Jt. auth., "Western Massachusetts Regional Library System," *Pub. Lib. Rpt.* (1967). **Activities:** 9; 17, 36, 47; 50, 55, 75 **Addr.:** Westfield Athenaeum, 6 Elm St., Westfield, MA 01085.

Tarakan, Sheldon Lewis (Je. 25, 1942, New York, NY) Head, Info. Srvs., Port Washington Pub. Lib., 1973–; Chief Ref. Libn., Half Hollow Hills Cmnty. Lib., 1969–73; Libn., S. Windsor Pub. Lib., 1968–69; Chief Ref. Libn., Bellmore Meml. Lib., 1967–68. **Educ.:** Queens Coll., CUNY, 1960–65, BA (Msclgy.); Manhattan Sch. of Msc., 1965–66, MA (Msc. Composition); Queens Coll., CUNY, 1966–67, MLS. **Orgs.:** Natl. Micro. Assn. Com. of Small Mags. Eds. and Publshrs. **Pubns.:** Publshr. and ed., *The Tarakan Music Letter* (1979–); ed., *Random House Dictionary of the English Language* (1967); various reviews, *Micro. Review.* **Activities:** 9; 33, 37, 41; 55, 75 **Addr.:** 1 Maple Dr., Great Neck, NY 11021.

Taran, Nadia P. (O. 30, 1947, Karlschrue, W. Germany) Reg. Libn., S. MD Reg. LA, 1979–; Lib. Coord., Free Lib. of Philadelphia, 1978–79, Libn. I, II, 1974–78. **Educ.:** Temple Univ., 1968–72, BA (Eng.); Drexel Univ., 1972–75, MLS. **Orgs.:** CLENE. ALA. MD LA. EFLA. MD Assn. of the Deaf. **Honors:** Beta Phi Mu, 1972. **Pubns.:** Reviews. **Activities:** 9, 14-Reg. Systs.; 17, 32, 49-Staff Dev.; 67, 72 **Addr.:** Southern Maryland Regional Library Association, P.O. Box 1069, La Plata, MD 20646.

Taranko, Walter J. (Jl. 20, 1943, Slonim, Poland) Media Consult., ME State Lib., 1975–; Coord., ESEA IV B, Dept. of Educ. Srvs., 1975–81; Dir., Proj. Lodestone, Reg. Media Ctr., 1971–75; Instr., Univ. of ME, 1969–81. **Educ.:** Gorham State Coll., 1962–66, BS (Educ.); IN Univ., 1968–70, MS (Instr. Systs. Tech.), 1970–71, EdS (Instr. Systs. Tech.). **Orgs.:** AECT: Cert. (1976–80); Accred. (1975–77); Natl. Cncl. (1974). Natl. Assn. of State Educ. Media Profs. ME Educ. Media Assn.: Pres. (1974); Exec. Bd. (1973–81); Treas. (1973). WA Cnty. Supts. Assn. U.S. Jaycees. **Pubns.:** *Maine Resources: Print and Non-Print* (1977). **Activities:** 10, 13; 24, 25, 32 **Addr.:** Media Services, Maine State Library, LMA Bldg., State House Station 64, Augusta, ME 04333.

Tarbox, Ruth Waddell (O. 16, 1911, Mellen, WI) Retired, 1973–; Exec. Secy., ALSC and YASD, ALA, 1966–73; Dir., Sch. and Lib. Srv., Fld. Enterprises Educ. Corp., 1946–65; Dir., Work with Chld., River Forest Pub. Lib. and Pub. Schs., 1943–46; Libn., Cleveland Hts. Pub. Lib., 1942–43; Libn., Roosevelt Elem. Sch., 1935–42; Tchr., Shell Lake HS, 1933–35; Tchr., Libn., Drummond HS, 1932–33. **Educ.:** Northland Coll., 1928–32, BA (Latin); Univ. of MN, 1940–41, BS (LS). **Orgs.:** ALA: ALSC/Newbery Caldecott Com. (1979–80). Chicago UNICEF Bd. **Honors:** Beta Phi Mu. **Pubns.:** Contrib., *ALA Yrbk.* (1976–80); Contrib., *ALA Encyc.* (1980). **Activities:** 9, 10; 17, 21, 48 **Addr.:** 1360 Lake Shore Dr., Chicago, IL 60610.

Tárczy, Stephen István (Ag. 13, 1925, Ungvár, Czechoslovakia) Head, Cat. Div., Univ. of CA, San Francisco, 1969–; Catlgr., Gen. Lib., Univ. of CA, Berkeley, 1963–69; Accot., Airborne Freight Corp., 1957–62; Magyar Beruházási Bank, Budapest, 1951–56. **Educ.:** Pázmány Péter Univ., Budapest, Hungary, 1943–47, Dr (Law, Pol. Sci.); Univ. of CA, Berkeley, 1962–63, MLS. **Orgs.:** ALA: LITA; RTSD. Med. LA. N. CA Grp. Hlth. Sci. OLUG. Univ. of CA Libns. Assn. **Activities:** 1, 12; 17, 20; 58, 80 **Addr.:** University of California, S257 Library, San Francisco, CA 94143.

Tarlton, Shirley M. (Ag. 8, 1937, Raleigh, NC) Dean, Lib. Srvs., Winthrop Coll., 1975–, Assoc. Libn., Tech. Srvs., 1968–74; Head, Tech. Srvs. Div., Univ. of NC, Charlotte, 1961–68. **Educ.:** Queens Coll., 1960, AB (Fr.); Univ. of NC, 1966, MSLS; various wkshps., insts. **Orgs.:** ALA: RTSD/Esther Piercy Awd. Jury (1974–75); Dupl. Exch. Un. Com. (1976–78). SC Adv. Cncl. on Libs.: Ch. (1977–80). SC LA: Coll. and Univ. Sect. (Ch., 1976–77). SOLINET: Bd. of Dirs. (Secy., Vice–Ch., 1976–79); various coms., ofcs. Various other orgs. **Honors:** Beta Phi Mu, 1981. **Pubns.:** "The Future of Library Cooperation in South Carolina," *The SC Libn.* (Fall 1979); various sps., consults. (1976–). **Activities:** 1; 17, 34, 46; 56 **Addr.:** 7406 Windyrush Rd., Matthews, NC 28105.

Tarnawsky, Marta (N. 15, 1930, Lviv, Ukraine) Asst. Libn., Frgn. and Intl. Law, Biddle Law Lib., Univ. of PA, 1977–, Frgn. Law Libn., 1967–77; Libn. II, Free Lib. of Philadelphia, 1966–67, Libn. I, 1964–66. **Educ.:** Temple Univ., 1952–62, BA summa cum laude (Soclgy.); Drexel Univ., 1962–64, MSLS. **Orgs.:** Intl. Assn. of Law Libs. Ukrainian LA. AALL: Cat. and Class. (Vice-Ch., 1972–73); Frgn. and Intl. Law (1973–74); Index to Frgn. Legal Pers. (1976–). Ukrainian Writers' Assn. (SLOVO). Ukrainian Natl. Women's Leag. of Amer. **Honors:** Ukrainian Lit. Fund Prize, 1974. **Pubns.:** *Zemletrus* (1981); *Ostap Tarnavskyi: Bibliohrafichnyi Pokazhchyk* (1980); *Ievheniia Iaroshynska* (1976); *Khvaliu iliuziiu* (1972); "Ukrainian Literature for the American Reader," *World Lit. Today* (Spr. 1978); various articles, reviews, short stories, poetry in LS and Ukrainian press. **Activities:** 1; 20, 39, 45; 57, 77, 95-Ukrainian Lit. **Addr.:** 6509 Lawnton Ave., Philadelphia, PA 19126.

Tashima, Marie (Ap. 11, 1929, Monterey Park, CA) Supvsr., Info. Srvs., Nalco Chem. Co., 1977–; Mgr., Tech. Ctr. Libs., Contl. Can Co., 1967–77; Sci. and Engin. Libn., Univ. of KS, 1966; Tech. Libn., Kaiser Aluminum and Chem. Co., 1963–65; Asst. Libn., Shell Dev. Co., 1958–61; Asst. Resrch. Chem., CA Resrch. Corp., 1950–57. **Educ.:** Whittier Coll., 1946–50, BA (Chem.); West. Rsv. Univ., 1957–58, MSLS; Univ. Coll., London, 1961–62 (LS). **Orgs.:** ALA. ASIS. Assn. of Recs. Mgrs. and Admins. SLA. various other orgs. Amer. Chem. Socty. AAAS. Tech. Assn. of Pulp and Paper Indus. **Honors:** Fulbright Fellow, 1961; Beta Phi Mu. **Activities:** 12; 17, 30, 39; 60, 64, 91 **Addr.:** 880 Lake Shore Dr. 22E, Chicago, IL 60611.

Tashjian, Sharon A. (D. 23, 1947, Pontiac, MI) AV Libn., Metro. Hosps. Inc., 1980–; AV Libn., Consult., AV Video Srvs., Good Samaritan Hosp. and Med. Ctr., 1980; Head of Circ., Ctr. Lib., Univ. of OR Hlth. Scis. Ctr., 1980, Dental Libn., Dental Lib., 1978–79, Co–Dir., Div. of Educ. Resrcs., Sch. of Dentistry, 1978–79; Asst. Libn., Harper Hosp. Lib., 1977–78. **Educ.:** North. MI Univ., 1966–72, BA (Sp.–Drama); Wayne State Univ., 1973–74, MSLS; Med. LA, 1977–81, Cert.; OR Hlth. Scis. LA, 1978–, Consult. Cert. **Orgs.:** ALA. Med. LA: Pac. NW Reg. Grp. OR LA. Portland Area Hlth. Scis. Libns.: ILL Com. (1978–80); AV Interest Grp. (Ch., 1979–). various other orgs. **Honors** Beta Phi Mu, 1977. **Pubns.:** Various sps. (1978–). **Activities:** 1, 12; 17, 32, 46; 56, 80, 93 **Addr.:** 1834 N.E. 51st, Portland, OR 97213.

Tashjian, Virginia A. (S. 20, 1921, Brockton, MA) Lib. Dir., Newton Free Lib., 1970–, Asst. Lib. Dir., 1967–70, Branch Libn., 1945–67. **Educ.:** Simmons Coll., 1939–43, BS (Eng., LS), 1969, MLS; various cont. ed. crs., 1955–79. **Orgs.:** MA LA: Pres. (1973–75). New Eng. LA: VP, Pres. (1977–79). ALA: ALSC/Com. on Chld. Bk. Distribution (1975–77). Women's Natl. Bk. Assn. **Honors:** New Eng. LA, Jordan–Miller Lectureshp., 1973. **Pubns.:** *With a deep sea smile* (1974); *Three apples fell from heaven* (1971); Juba this and Juba that (1969); *Once there was and was not* (1966); *Sing and Pray* (1960). **Activities:** 9; 17, 21, 26; 50, 63, 89 **Addr.:** 278 Belmont St., Watertown, MA 02172.

Tassia, Margaret R. (Ap. 3, 1941, York, PA) Assoc. Prof., Ch., Dept. of LS, Millersville State Coll., 1971–, Asst. Prof., 1971–81; Tchg. Fellow, Sch. of LS, Univ. of Pittsburgh, 1977–78; Elem. Libn., Brecht Sch., Manheim Twp. Sch. Dist., 1964–71; Libn., Solanco Sch. Dist., 1963–64. **Educ.:** Millersville State Coll., 1959–63, BS (Educ., LS); Villanova Univ., 1967–69, MS (LS); Univ. of Pittsburgh, 1976–78, PhD (LS). **Orgs.:** PA Schl. Libns. Assn.: Awds. Com. (Ch., 1976–78); Media Sel. and Review (Ch., 1979–81); Bd. of Dirs. (1979–82). Lancaster Cnty. LA: Secy. (1965–66); various coms. (1963–). ALA: AASL; ALSC. AALL. various other orgs. AAUP. Natl. Educ. Assn. Millersville State Coll. Fac. Assn. PA State Educ. Assn. various other orgs. **Honors:** Phi Delta Kappa; Univ. of Pittsburgh, Univ. Schol., 1979. **Pubns.:** "It's Not Just a Game," *Sch. Lib. Jnl.* (Mr. 1979); jt. auth., "Meet the PSLA Award Winners," *Lrng. and Media* (Fall 1978); "Make Them Aware of Authors," *Instr.* (Mr. 1974); "Make Your Own Dictionary Drill," *Instr.* (Mr. 1975); *Games For Information Skills* (1980). **Activities:** 10; 21, 26, 31; 63 **Addr.:** 12 Nursery Ln., Lancaster, PA 17603.

Tassin, Anthony Gaston (Ja. 14, 1925, Edgard, LA) Circ./Autom./Hum. Libn., Univ. of New Orleans Lib., 1979–, Lib. Systs. Anal., 1972–79, Admin. Asst. to Dir., 1970–72, Spec. Lectr., Eng. Dept., 1970–; Asst. Prof., Eng., St. Joseph Semy. Coll., 1949–68. **Educ.:** Loyola Univ., New Orleans, 1949–52, BS (Educ.); Cath. Univ. of Amer., 1952–55, MA (Educ.); LA State Univ., 1956–66, PhD (Eng.), 1975–78, MLS. **Orgs.:** LA LA. SWLA. ALA. St. Dominic Cath. Par. Boy Scouts of Amer., Troop #27, Bienville Dist. **Addr.:** 6477 Gen. Diaz St., New Orleans, LA 70124.

Tate, Elizabeth L. (Ag. 13, 1917, Portland, OR) Retired, 1976–; Chief, Descr. Cat. Div., Lib. of Congs., 1973–76; Lib. Dir., Natl. Bur. of Stans., 1967–73, Asst. Chief Libn., 1964–67; Info. Resrcs. Anal., Natl. Ref. Ctr. for Sci. and Tech., Lib. of Congs., 1963–64, Head, Preliminary Cat. Sect., 1948–52, Catlgr., Copyrt. Ofc., 1947–48; various prof. positions, (1939–47). **Educ.:** Reed Coll., 1935–39, BA (Lit., Langs.); Pratt Inst., 1941–42, BLS; Univ. of Chicago, 1956–63, PhD (LS). **Orgs.:** ALA: RTSD/Cat. and Class. Sect., Exec. Com. (Ch., 1977–78), Descr. Cat. Com. (Ch., 1970–72); LRRT/Provisional Exec. Com. (1969–70), Strg. Com. (1970–72). DC LA: Com. on Cont. Prof. Educ. (Ch., 1966–68); Pres. (1970–71). Amer. Natl. Stans. Inst.: Stans. Com. Z39/SC33. SLA: Various coms., ofcs. (1972–76). Various other orgs. Litcy. Cncl. of Montgomery Cnty.: VP (1981–); various other ofcs. (1978–81). **Honors:** Phi Beta Kappa, 1939; Beta Phi Mu, 1963. **Pubns.:** "Access Points and Citations," *Lib. Resrch.* (Win. 1979); "Examining the 'Main' in Main Entry Headings," *The Making of a Code* (1980); "International Standards," *Lib. Resrcs. & Tech. Srvs.* (Win. 1976); "The Cataloger's Right Arm: The Library of Congress," *Spec. Libs.* (S. 1975); ed., *Lib. Resrcs. & Tech. Srvs.* (1979–); various articles, edshps. (1959–). **Activities:** 4, 12; 17, 20 **Addr.:** 11415 Farmland Dr., Rockville, MD 20852.

Tate, Horace E. (O. 6, 1922, Elberton, GA) Exec. Secy., GA Assn. of Educs., 1977–, Assoc. Exec. Secy., 1970–77; Exec. Secy., GA Tchrs. and Educs. Assn., 1961–70; Assoc. Prof. of Educ., Fort Valley State Coll., 1959–61; Tchr., GA Sec. Schs., 1942–59. **Educ.:** Fort Valley State Coll., 1943, BS; Atlanta Univ., 1951, MA; Univ. of KY, 1961, PhD. **Orgs.:** NCLIS: Comsn. (1978–). GA Sen.: Mem. (1975–80). Atlanta Bd. of Educ.: Mem. (1965–69). Natl. Educ. Assn. **Honors:** GA Classroom Tchrs., Human Rel. Awd., 1966; Atlanta Bd. of Educ. Awd., 1969. **Pubns.:** *Rising in the Sun* (1966); Various articles in educ. **Activities:** 14-Educ.; 47; 63 **Addr.:** Georgia Association of Educators, 3951 Snapfinger Pkwy., Decatur, GA 30035.*

Tatman, Sandra L. (N. 12, 1944, Dover, DE) Archit. Libn., Athen. of Philadelphia, 1978–; Resrch. Coord. Hist. Comsn, City of Springfield, OR, 1977–78; Asst., Archit. and Allied Arts Lib., Univ. of OR, 1975–77; Libn., Amer. Sch. of Barcelona, Spain, 1973–75. **Educ.:** Univ. of DE, 1961–65, BA (Eng.); Univ. of OR, 1970–73, MLS (Libnshp.), 1975–77, MA (Art Hist.). **Orgs.:** SAA. ARLIS/NA. Socty. of Archit. Histns. Vict. Socty. in Amer. **Pubns.:** Various papers presented at Socty. Archit. Histns. mtgs. **Activities:** 12; 19, 41, 45; 55, 85 **Addr.:** The Athenaeum of Philadelphia, 219 S. 6th St., Philadelphia, PA 19106.

Tatum, George Marvin (O. 23, 1935, Alexandria, VA) Hum. Libn., Cornell Univ. Libs., 1975–; Asst., Assoc., Libn., Acq. Dept., 1966–75; Ref., Acq. Libn., A.G. Bush Lib., Indus. Rel. Ctr., Univ. of Chicago, 1963–66; Asst. Cat. and Acq. Libn., Cornell Univ. Libs., 1960–63. **Educ.:** Lehigh Univ., 1953–57, BA (Gvt.); Univ. of NC, 1958–60, MS (LS); Univ. of Chicago, 1963–66. **Orgs.:** ALA. **Honors:** Beta Phi Mu. **Pubns.:** "The Development of the Cornell University Libraries' Collections on the Near East," *Cornell Univ. Libs. Bltn.* (Ja.–F. 1975); jt. auth., "The Development of Collections in American University Libraries," *Coll. & Resrch. Libs.* (My. 1976); various transls. **Activities:** 1; 15, 39; 55 **Addr.:** 1314 Hanshaw Rd., Ithaca, NY 14850.

Taylor, David C. (Ag. 24, 1936, Savannah, GA) Undergrad. Libn., Univ. of NC, 1975–; Serials Libn., MI State Univ., 1970–75; Ref. Libn., Univ. of RI, 1966–70; Circ. Libn., Un. Theo. Semy., 1964–66. **Educ.:** Phillips Univ., 1953–57, BA (Soc. Sci.); Univ. of Chicago, 1957–61, BD (Mnstry.); Columbia Univ., 1963–65, MA (LS). **Orgs.:** ALA: RTSD/Serials Sect., Policy and Resrch. Com. (1972–74). Libns. Untd. to Fight Costly Silly Unnecessary Serials Title Changes: Hon. Pres. (1973–81). **Pubns.:** Ed., publshr., *Title Varies* (1973–81); "The Serials Librarian as Activist," *Drexel Lib. Qtly.* (Jl. 1975). **Activities:** 1; 37, 44 **Addr.:** 422 Ridgefield Rd., Chapel Hill, NC 27514.

Taylor, Gladys M(iller) (S. 29, 1923, Yonkers, NY) Archvst., Wallace Meml. Lib., Rochester Inst. of Tech. Lib., 1976–, Head, Ref. Dept., 1970–76, Ref. Libn., 1958–70; Libn., Wayland Ctrl. Sch., 1947–57. **Educ.:** SUNY, Geneseo, 1943–47, BS (Educ.), Cornell Univ., 1949–53, MA (Eng.). **Orgs.:** ALA. NY LA. SAA. Monroe Cnty. Lib. Clb.: Pres. (1969, 1972). Rochester Hist. Socty. **Pubns.:** "Deaf Characters in Short Stories," *Deaf Amer.* (My. 1974, Jl.–Ag. 1976). **Activities:** 1; 2; 23, 30, 39; 63, 72, 85 **Addr.:** Rochester Institute of Technology Library, 1 Lomb Memorial Dr., Rochester, NY 14623.

Taylor, Grace Elizabeth "Betty" Woodall (Je. 14, 1926, Butler, NJ) Prof. of Law, Dir. of Law Lib., Univ. of FL Law Lib., 1976–, Law Libn., 1962–76, Asst. Law Libn., 1956–62, Asst. in Lib., Univ. Libs., 1950–56. **Educ.:** FL State Univ., 1946–49, AB (LS), 1949–50, MA (LS); Univ. of FL, 1950–62, JD. **Orgs.:**

Special Subjects/Services: 50. Adult educ.; 51. Advert./Mktg.; 52. Aerosp.; 53. Agric.; 54. Area std.; 55. Arts/Hum.; 56. Autom.; 57. Bibl./Prtg.; 58. Bio. sci.; 59. Bus./Fin.; 60. Chem.; 61. Copyrt.; 62. Documtn.; 63. Educ.; 64. Engin.; 65. Env.; 66. Eth. grps.; 67. Film; 68. Food/Nutr.; 69. Geneal.; 70. Geo.; 71. Geol.; 72. Handcpd.; 73. Hist.; 74. Int. frdm.; 75. Info. sci.; 76. Insr.; 77. Law; 78. Legis.; 79. Math./Comp. sci.; 80. Med.; 81. Metals; 82. Nat. resrcs.; 83. Newsp.; 84. Nuc. sci.; 85. Oral hist.; 86. Petr./Energy; 87. Pharm.; 88. Phys./Astr./Math.; 89. Readg.; 90. Relig.; 91. Sci./Tech.; 92. Soc. sci.; 93. Telecom.; 94. Transp.; 95. (other).

AALL: Exec. Bd. (1981–84); Autom. and Sci. Dev. Com.; Nom. Com.; Place. Com.; Lawnet Com. (Ch. all). Intl. Assn. of Law Libs.: Place. Com., Ch. SOLINET: Exec. Bd. (1981–84). ASIS. Gvr.'s Conf. on Libs. and Info. Sci.: Plng. Com.; Resols. Com., Ch.; Sel. Com. Del., Ch. WHCOLIS: Alternate Del. **Honors:** Phi Beta Kappa, 1978; Beta Phi Mu. **Pubns.:** "Audio Research in the Law: Materials and Cassettes," *Basic American Law* (1978); *Budgeting for Law School Libraries* (1981); various articles, *Law Lib. Jnl.* **Activities:** 1, 12; 15, 17, 24; 56, 75, 77 **Addr.:** Law Library, University of Florida, Gainesville, FL 32611.

Taylor, Hugh A. (Ja. 22, 1920, Chelmsford, Essex, Eng.) Prov. Archvst., Pub. Arch. of NS, 1978–; Dir., Arch. Branch, Pub. Arch. of Can., 1971–77; Prov. Archvst., Prov. Arch. of NB, 1967–71; Prov. Archvst., Prov. Arch. of AB, 1965–67; Cnty. Archvst., Northumberland Cnty. Rec. Ofc., Eng., 1958–65; Archvst., Liverpool Pub. Libs., 1954–58; Archvst., Leeds Pub. Libs., 1951–54. **Educ.:** Oxford Univ., 1946–49, BA (Mod. Hist.), 1949–53, MA (Mod. Hist.); Liverpool Univ., 1950–51, Dip. (Arch. Admin.). **Orgs.:** Socty. of Archvsts. (Eng.): Cncl. (1963–65). SAA: Pres. (1978–79). Can. Hist. Assn.: Arch. Sect. (Ch., 1967–68). **Pubns.:** *Northumberland History: A Brief Guide to Records and Aids* (1963); *New Brunswick History: A Checklist of Secondary Sources* (1971); *The Arrangement and Description of Archival Materials* (1980); "The Discipline of History and The Education of The Archivist," *Amer. Archvst.* (1977); "Documentary Art and The Role of The Archivist," *Amer. Archvst.* (1979); various articles (1972–78). **Activities:** 2; 17 **Addr.:** Public Archives of Nova Scotia, 6016 University Ave., Halifax, NS B3H 1W4 Canada.

Taylor, James B. (Jl. 12, 1944, New York, NY) Head, Bus. and Sci. Dept., Seattle Pub. Lib., 1978–; Head, Ref. Dept., Wichita State Univ., 1976–78, Bus. Libn., 1972–76. **Educ.:** Univ. of CO, 1963–66, BA (Econ.); Univ. of MA, 1966–68, MBA (Bus. Admin.); Univ. of Denver, 1971–72, MALS. **Orgs.:** ALA: Bus. and Ref. Srvs. Com. (1977–81). SLA. **Activities:** 1, 9; 16, 17, 39; 59, 91 **Addr.:** Seattle Public Library, 1000 4th Ave., Seattle, WA 98155.

Taylor, Janet Schmidle (Ap. 12, 1934, Buffalo, NY) Ref. Libn., Milwaukee Stratton Coll., 1981–; Ref. Libn., Univ. of TX Med. Branch, Galveston, 1980–; Ref. Libn., Med. Coll. of WI, 1977–79; Ref. Libn., Northwest. Univ. Dental Sch., 1975–77. **Educ.:** Niagara Univ., 1951–52 (Nursing); D'Youville Coll., 1952–54 (Nursing); Canisius Coll., 1966–71, BA (Phil.); SUNY, Buffalo, 1972–75, MLS (Lib. Std.); 1976, Cert. (Med. Libnshp.). **Orgs.:** Med. LA. SLA. Mensa. Intl. **Activities:** 1, 12; 39; 80 **Addr.:** 2905 W. Wisconsin Ave., #901, Milwaukee, WI 53208.

Taylor, Kathryn E. (Ja. 27, 1944, Jefferson City, MO) Lib. Mgt., Consult., Taylor and Assocs., 1976–; Law Libn., Alameda Cnty. Law Lib., 1975; Libn., ISI Corp., 1971–72; Libn., McKinsey and Co., Inc., 1968–70. **Educ.:** Smith Coll., 1962–66, BA (Hist.); McGill Univ., 1963, Cert. (Fr.); Univ. of MI, 1966–68, MLS. **Orgs.:** SLA. AALL: Bd. of Dirs. Frnds. of the San Francisco Pub. Lib. CA Tomorrow. **Pubns.:** various sems. **Activities:** 12, 13; 19, 24, 35; 76, 77, 78 **Addr.:** Taylor & Associates, 681 Market St., San Francisco, CA 94105.

Taylor, Kenneth I. (Ap. 28, 1926, Springfield, MN) Assoc. Prof., Proj. Dir., State, Reg., Natl. Self Std., Educ. and LS, Villanova Univ., 1975–81; Co–Dir., Sch. Lib. Manpower Proj., Millersville State Coll., 1971–75; Dir., Instr. Mtrls., Madison Pub. Schs., 1964–71; Ch., Instr. Mtrls. Ctr., W. Leyden HS, 1956–64. **Educ.:** Univ. of MN, 1948–52, BS (Educ.); Univ. of IL, 1952–55, MS (LS); Univ. of Chicago, 1965–74, PhD (Curric.); Villanova Univ., 1979–, Post–Doct. Std. (Amer. Phil.). **Orgs.:** ALA: Lib. Admin. Div./Bldgs. and Equip. Sect., Sch. Lib. Quarters Com. (1961–71); Cncl. (1970–73); AASL, Legis. Netwk. Mem. for WI (1965–71), Bd. of Dirs. (1971–72), Spec. Proj. Com. (1972–75). AALS: Educ. of Lib. Support Staff Task Frc. Proj. (1978–81). PA Div. of Tchr. Educ.: Prog. Review Com. (1972–75). N. Ctrl. Assn. of Coll. and Sec. Schs.: Std. of Sch. Lib. Stans. (1967–75). **Honors:** *Atl. Monthly*, Short Story Awd., 1948; MN AV Coords. Assn., M. J. Smith Leadership Awd. in AV Educ., 1967; WI LA, Lib. of the Yr. Awd., 1971. **Pubns.:** Ed. bd., *Lrng. and Media* (1981–); various articles, monos. in LS, curric. and instr., phil. **Activities:** 10, 11; 17, 26, 49-Phil. of Libnshp.; 63, 74, 93 **Addr.:** 211 N. President Ave., Lancaster, PA 17603.

Taylor, Larry D. (Ap. 21, 1945, Hampton, VA) Head, Cat. Dept., Drexel Univ. Libs., 1975–; Asst. Dir. of Libs., St. Charles Borromeo Semy., 1969–75; Reg. Libn., Tulsa City–Cnty. Lib. Syst., 1968–69. **Educ.:** Univ. of Tulsa, 1963–67, BA (Eng.); Drexel Univ., 1967–68, MS (LS); 1981, MS (Human Behavior, Dev.). **Orgs.:** ALA: ACRL, DE Valley Chap. (Treas., 1979–81). Cath. LA: Coll. and Univ. Sect., Bd. of Dirs. (1973–75); East. PA Unit, Coll. and Univ. Sect., Ch. (1973–75), Vice–Ch. (1971–73). PA LA: Mem. Com. (1974–75). Drexel Lib. Sch. Alum. Assn.: Treas. (1977–79); Anl. Prog. Ch. (1976–77). Various other orgs., adv. coms. (1970–). **Pubns.:** "Cooperation and Commitment," *PA LA Bltn.* (My. 1974); "Great Literary Find! The Lilliputian Solution," *Cath. Lib. World* (D. 1972); "The Computer and Theological Materials," *Coll. & Resrch. Libs.* (My. 1969). **Activities:** 1; 17, 20, 46; 56, 75, 92 **Addr.:** Drexel University Libraries, 32nd and Chestnut Sts., Philadelphia, PA 19104.

Taylor, Lillian McCulloch (Mr. 29, 1928, Elizabethtown NC) Dir., Lib. Opers., Columbia Theo. Semy., 1976–, Head Libn., Montgomery Bell Acad., 1970–73; Div. Head, Jt. Univ. Libs., 1963–69; Pub. Sch. Tchr., PA, NJ, 1951–53. **Educ.:** Queens Coll., NC, 1945–49, BA (Relig.); Presby. Sch. of Christ. Educ., 1949–51, MA (Bible); George Peabody Coll., 1962–63, MA (LS), 1969–70, ES (LS). **Orgs.:** ALA. SELA. GA LA. People to People. Atlanta Presby. Task Frc. on Women. **Activities:** 1; 16, 26, 31 **Addr.:** 2669 Rangewood Ct. N.E., Atlanta, GA 30345.

Taylor, Madeline V. (Ap. 25, 1933, New York, NY) Serials Libn., Coll. of Med. and Dentistry, George F. Smith Lib., 1971–; Head, Readers Srvs., Columbia Univ., Harlem Hosp. Ctr. Lib., 1970–71; Med. Indxr./Ref. Libn., Physicians News Srv., 1963–70; Libn., Jewish Chronic Disease Hosp., 1960–63. **Educ.:** Brooklyn Coll., 1950–54, BS (Chem.); Columbia Univ., 1968–70, MLS; NY Sch. of Bible, 1977–79, Cert. (Bible). **Orgs.:** Med. LA: NY Reg. Grp, Ch./Ch.–Elect (1978–80), Exec. Com. (1975–77), Ed./Ed. Bd. (1973–77); Unvsl. Serials and Bk. Exch. Rep. (1977–79). Relig. Educ. Assn. **Activities:** 1; 15, 17, 44; 58, 80, 91 **Addr.:** College of Medicine and Dentistry of New Jersey, George F. Smith Library of the Health Sciences, 100 Bergen St., Newark, NJ 07103.

Taylor, Margaret P. J. (My. 28, 1950, Ottawa, ON) Dir., Lib. Srvs., Chld. Hosp. of East. ON, 1978–; Hlth. Sci., Educ. Libn., Mohawk Coll., 1976–78; Sch. Libn., Metro. Toronto Sch. Bd., 1974–75. **Educ.:** Carleton Univ., 1967–70, BA (Psy.); Univ. of Toronto, 1972–75, MLS; Med. LA, 1975, Cert. **Orgs.:** CHLA. Can. LA. Med. LA. **Pubns.:** *Pediatric Patient Education Directory* (forthcoming). **Activities:** 12; 17, 18, 39; 80, 87, 92 **Addr.:** Library, Children's Hospital of Eastern Ontario, 401 Smyth Rd., Ottawa, ON K1H 8L1, Canada.

Taylor, Margaret T. (Je. 2, 1930, Detroit, MI) Lectr., Sch. of LS, Univ. of MI, 1974–; Asst. Prof., Grad. Sch. of Lib. Std., Univ. of HI, 1964–74; Head, Ord. Prep., Acq., Lib., Univ. of CA, Los Angeles, 1964, Head, Out of Print Srch., 1956–63. **Educ.:** Univ. of MI, 1949–52, AB (Eng.); Univ. of CA, Los Angeles, 1957–61, MA (Eng.), 1961–62, MLS (Lib. Srv.); Univ. of MI, 1975– (LS). **Orgs.:** ALA. AALS. MI LA. **Pubns.:** *Basic Reference Sources; a Self-Study Manual* (1981). "A Self-Study Approach to Reference Sources," *Jnl. of Educ. for Libnshp.* (Spr. 1972). **Activities:** 1, 11; 15, 26, 39; 50, 57, 89 **Addr.:** School of Library Science, University of Michigan, Ann Arbor, MI 48104.

Taylor, Marion R. (F. 9, 1922, Atlanta, GA) Assoc. Prof., Div. of Libnshp., Emory Univ., 1963–; Ed., Un. Cat. of the Atlanta Athens Area, 1951–63. **Educ.:** Wesleyan Coll., 1939–43, AB (Eng., Fr.); Emory Univ., 1951–57, MA (LS); Rutgers Univ., 1966–73, PhD (LS). **Orgs.:** ALA. AALS: Tellers Com. (Ch., 1977–78). SLA: S. Atl. Chap., Pres. (1955–60), Dir. (1960–64), Secy. (1976–78), Bylaws Com. (Ch., 1974–78), Arch. Com. (Ch., 1976–). various other orgs. Altrusa Intl. Altrusa Club of Atlanta: Various ofcs. **Honors:** Beta Phi Mu. **Pubns.:** *Guide to Latin American Reference Materials: A Union List for Use in the Atlanta-Athens Area* (1953); jt. auth., "Adapting an Existing Card Catalog to AACR2, a Feasibility Study," *Lib. Resrcs. & Tech. Srvs.* (Sum. 1980); "Mobility and Professional Involvement in Librarianship," *Collection on Women in Librarianship* (forthcoming). **Activities:** 11; 20, 46; 57, 73-Hist. **Addr.:** 1223 Clifton Rd., N.E., Atlanta, GA 30307.

Taylor, Marion W. (Ag. 9, 1920, Beloit, WI) Ch., Dept. of LS and Comm. Media, Chicago State Univ., 1972–, Prof., 1956–80; Libn., N. Chicago HS, 1955–; Tchr./Libn., Chicago Pub. Schs., 1943–55. **Educ.:** Chicago Tchrs. Coll., 1937–42, BEd, 1955, MEd (LS); South. IL Univ., 1978, PhD. **Orgs.:** IL LA: Exec. Bd. (1970–71). IL Assn. Sch. Libns.: Prog. Ch. (1964); Pres. (1970); Prog. Com. (1980); Stans. Com. (1961–62). IL Ofc. Educ.: Adv. Com. ALA: Cncl. (IL Mem., 1970). **Pubns.:** "What Books Are Our Children Reading," *Chicago Schs. Jnl.* (Ja. 1957); "The Public Library Serves the Gifted Child," *IL Libs.* (Ja. 1959). **Activities:** 11; 17, 26; 63, 72, 89 **Addr.:** 2306 Holiday Ct., Lansing, IL 60438.

Taylor, Merrily E. (My. 24, 1945, Winchester, MA) Dir., Lib. Srvs. Grp., Columbia Univ. Libs., 1978–; Spec. Asst. to Univ. Libn., Yale Univ. Lib., 1977–78; Col. Dev. Libn., Univ. of S. FL Lib., 1974–77, Circ.–Rsv. Libn., 1969–74, Asst. Ref. Libn., 1968–69. **Educ.:** St. Petersburg Jr. Coll., Univ. of S. FL, 1963–67, AA, BA (Eng. Educ.); FL State Univ., 1967–68, MS (LS); Univ. of S. FL, 1971–73, MA (Eng. Lit.). **Orgs.:** ALA: ACRL. Resrch. Libs. Grp.: Pub. Srvs. Com. (Ch., 1979–). NY Metro. Ref. and Resrch. Lib. Agency: Admin. Srvs. Com. (Ch., 1979–). Natl. Org. for Women. Natl. Trust for Hist. Prsrvn. **Honors:** Cncl. on Lib. Resrcs., Acad. Lib. Mgt. Internship, 1976. **Pubns.:** "Introduction," *Conscience: The Search for Truth* (1979); "The Yale University Library 1701–1978," *Ency. of Lib. and Info. Sci.* (1981). **Activities:** 1; 17, 49-Gen. pub. srvs. **Addr.:** 560 Riverside Dr., #15H, New York, NY 10027.

Taylor, Nettie B. (Ag. 6, 1914, Brownsville, TN) Asst. State Supt. for Libs., Div. of Lib. Dev. and Srvs., MD State Dept. of Educ., 1960–, Supvsr. of Pub. Libs., 1948–60; Lib. Dir., Pamunkey Reg. Lib. Syst., 1947–48; Lib. Dir., U.S. Army, US, Germany, 1942–47; Libn., Leon Cnty. HS, 1940–42; Libn., Taylor Cnty. HS, 1936–40. **Educ.:** FL State Univ., 1936, AB, Univ. of NC, 1942, BS (LS); Univ. of MD, 1950–60 (Soclgy.); Johns Hopkins Univ., 1967, MS (Liberal Arts). **Orgs.:** CLENE: Pres. (1976). MD LA: Pres. (1960). ALA: Plng. Com. (1975–79); State LA (Pres., 1969–70); ALTA (Sec. VP, 1965); Nom. Com. (1965); various other coms. (1965–80). Various adv. coms., bds. (1955–81). **Honors:** MD LA, Disting. Srv. Awd., 1979. **Activities:** 13; 17 **Addr.:** MD State Dept. of Education, Div. of Library Development & Services, 200 W. Baltimore St., Baltimore, MD 21201.

Taylor, Phyllis McEwen (My. 30, 1950, Atlanta, GA) Corporate Libn., Ebasco Srvs., Inc., 1978–; Asst. Spec., Cols. Libn., Atlanta Univ., 1977–78; Asst. Law Libn., Univ. of FL Law Lib., 1974–77. **Educ.:** Spelman Coll., 1970–73, BA (Eng.); Atlanta Univ., 1973–74, MSLS. **Orgs.:** SLA: S. Atl. Chap. (Secy., 1979–81). Atlanta Univ. LS Alum. Assn. **Activities:** 1, 12; 15, 17, 39; 55, 77, 91 **Addr.:** 1690-D W. Lake Ct., N.W., Atlanta, GA 30314.

Taylor, Rebecca A. (N. 4, 1952, Gulfport, MS) Asst. Libn., Jefferson Davis Par. Lib., 1981–; Bkmobile., Chld. Libn., St. Charles Par. Lib., 1976–81. **Educ.:** Univ. of South. MS, 1970–74, BA (Hist.); LA State Univ., 1974–75, MLS. **Orgs.:** ALA: JMRT, VP/Pres.–Elect, Afflts. Cncl. (1980–81), Olofson Awd. Com. (1980–81). LA LA: Modisette Awd. for Pub. Libs. (Ch., 1980–81); Com. to Std. Culver Awd. (1979); Pub. Sect. (Parlmt., 1976–77); New Mems. RT (various ofcs., coms., 1976–81). **Activities:** 9; 16, 21, 36 **Addr.:** Jefferson Davis Parish Library, P.O. Box 356, Jennings, LA 70546.

Taylor, Robert S. (Je. 15, 1918, Ithaca, NY) Dean., Sch. of Info. Std., Syracuse Univ., 1972–81, Prof., 1972–; Dir., Lib. Ctr., Prof., Lang. and Comm., Hampshire Coll., 1967–72; Dir., Ctr. for Info. Scis., Lehigh Univ., 1962–67, Assoc. Prof., Head, Div. of Info. Sci., Dept. of Phil., 1962–67, Assoc. Libn., 1956–67. **Educ.:** Cornell Univ., 1935–40, BA (Hist.); Columbia Univ., 1949–50, MS (LS); Lehigh Univ., 1952–54, MA (Hist.). **Orgs.:** ASIS: Exec. Cncl. (1959–61); Prog. Com., Natl. Mtg. (1959); Tech. Sessions, Anl. Mtg. (Co–Ch., 1964); Pres. (1968); Midyr. Mtg. (Ch., 1977); various other coms. ALA: Com. on Accred. (1970–71); LRRT, Exec. Com. (1970–71). NY LA: Various ofcs. AAAS: Cncl. (1975–77, 1979–81); Com. on Fellows, Cncl. (1976–77). Assoc. Info. Mgrs.: Adv. Bd. (1977–). Info. Indus. Assn.: Awds. Com. (1975–77). Natl. Inst. of Hlth.: Biomed. Comm. Std. Sect. (1970–74). Various other orgs. **Honors:** Fulbright Lectr., 1956; ASIS, Awd. for Best Bk. in Info. Sci., 1972. **Pubns.:** Ed., *Economics of Information Dissemination* (1974); *The Making of a Library* (1972); "Educational Breakaway," *Amer. Libs.* (Je. 1979); "Reminiscing About the Future," *Lib. Jnl.* (S. 15, 1979); "Notes Toward a User–Centered Academic Library," *New Dimensions in Academic Library Service* (1975); various articles (1957–). **Activities:** 11; 24, 26; 75 **Addr.:** 5085 Skyline Dr., Syracuse, NY 13215.

Taylor, Rosemarie Kazda (N. 13, 1951, Wilkes-Barre, PA) Dir., Lib. Srvs., Wilkes-Barre Gen. Hosp., 1974–. **Educ.:** Wilkes Coll., 1969–73, BA (Eng.); Univ. of Denver, 1973–74, MALS; Med. LA, 1974; Cert. (Med. Libnshp.). **Orgs.:** Hlth. Info. Lib. Netwk. of Northeast. PA: Vice-Ch. (1979–80); Ch. (1981–). Mid-East. Reg. Med. Lib. Srv.: Com. for Online Coord. (1979–81). Med. LA: Hosp. Lib. Sect., Mem. Com. (1978–80). PA Citizens for Better Libs. **Activities:** 12; 17; 80 **Addr.:** Library, Wilkes-Barre General Hospital, Wilkes-Barre, PA 18764.

Taylor, Sandra J. (My. 12, 1946, Charlottetown, PE) Sch. Lib. Consult., Prov. Lib., PE, 1972–; Chld. Libn., Confed. Ctr. Lib., 1968–72. **Educ.:** Mt. Allison Univ., 1965–67, BA (Eng.); Univ. of Toronto, 1967–68, BLS, 1975–76, MLS. **Orgs.:** Can. LA: Can. Sch. LA; Can. Assn. of Pub. Libs., Amelia Frances Howard Gibbon Awd. Com. (1978–83). Atl. Provs. LA: VP (1977–79); Secy. (1972–73). Intl. Bd. on Bks. for Young People: Can. Sect. (Cnclr., 1980–81). PE Sch. LA. **Honors:** Beta Phi Mu. **Pubns.:** *Teachers, Kids and Education* (1980); *Children, All Different, All the Same* (1979); various articles, jt. edshps. *Sch. Lib. Nsltr.* **Activities:** 10; 24; 63 **Addr.:** Provincial Library, University Ave., Charlottetown, PE C1A 7N9 Canada.

Taylor, Susan Elizabeth (S. 27, 1954, Glendale, CA) Libn., Wyman, Bautzer, Rothman, Kuchel, and Silbert, 1977–; Asst. Libn., Paul, Hastings, Janofsky and Walker, 1976–77. **Educ.:** CA Polytech. State Univ., 1974–76, BA (Hist.); Univ. of South. CA, 1976–77 MLS. **Orgs.:** South. CA Assn. of Law Libs.: Treas. (1979–81); Mem. Com. (1978–79). AALL: Pvt. Law Libs. Spec. Interest Sect., Mem. Com. (1979–80). SLA. Beta Phi Mu: Bd. (1979–). **Pubns.:** *Century City Union List of Serials* (1979, 2nd ed. 1981). *Century City Union List of Looseleaf Services* (1980). **Activities:** 12; 15, 17, 39; 77 **Addr.:** Wyman, Bautzer, Rothman, Kuchel and Silbert, Library, 2049 Century Park E., Los Angeles, CA 90067.

Taylor, Warren G. (My. 8, 1945, Denver, CO) Asst. Dir., Admin., Auraria Lib., 1979–, Asst. Dir., 1976–79, Biblgphr., 1972–76. **Educ.:** Univ. of CO, 1965–70, BA (Soclgy.); Univ. of Denver, 1970–72, MA (Libnshp.); Univ. of CO, 1973–76, MA (Anthro.); various grad. crs. in higher educ. **Orgs.:** ALA: CO Mem. Ch. (1978–83). CO LA: Spec. Cols. RT, Ch. Univ. of

PROFESSIONAL ACTIVITIES: Institutions: 1. Acad. lib.; 2. Arch.; 3. Assn.; 4. Fed./Gvt. lib.; 5. Inst. lib.; 6. Mfr./Suppl.; 7. Milit. lib.; 8. Musm.; 9. Pub. lib.; 10. Sch. lib.; 11. Sch. of lib. sci.; 12. Spec. lib.; 13. State lib.; 14. (other). **Functions/Activities:** 15. Acq./Col. dev.; 16. Adult srvs.; 17. Admin.; 18. Apprais.; 19. Archit./Bldgs.; 20. Cat./Class.; 21. Chld. srvs.; 22. Circ.; 23. Cons./Pres.; 24. Consult.; 25. Cont. ed.; 26. Educ. lib. sci.; 27. Ext. srvs.; 28. Fund/Grants; 29. Gvt. pubs.; 30. Indx./Abs.; 31. Instr. lib. use; 32. Media srvs.; 33. Micro.; 34. Netwks./Coop.; 35. Persnl.; 36. PR; 37. Publshg.; 38. Recs. mgt.; 39. Ref. srvs.; 40. Repro.; 41. Resrch.; 42. Review.; 43. Secur.; 44. Serials; 45. Spec. col.; 46. Tech. srvs.; 47. Trustees/Bds.; 48. YA srvs.; 49. (other).

Denver Grad. Sch. of Libnshp. and Info. Mgt. Alum. Assn. **Pubns.:** "Auraria Libraries Learning Resources Center," *CO Libs.* (1977). **Activities:** 1; 17, 19 **Addr.:** Administration, Auraria Library, University of Colorado at Denver, Lawrence at 11th St., Denver, CO 80204.

Taylor–Vaisey, Robert David (D. 17, 1948, Peterborough, ON) Admin., Retention/Arch., Imperial Oil Limited, 1980–; Arch. Consult., Hamilton Civic Hosps., Upper Can. Coll., 1980–; Asst. Corp. Archvst., Imperial Oil Limited, 1980; Asst. Archvst., Univ. of Toronto Arch., 1977–79. **Educ.:** Trent Univ., 1966–70, BA, hons. (Hist.), 1971–72, MA (Hist.); Univ. of Toronto, 1974–, PhD (Hist. of Law). **Orgs.:** Toronto Area Archvsts. Grp.: Nsltr. Ed. (1980–81). Stans. Cncl. of Can. (TS0154). Can. Assn. Info. Sci. Assn. Can. Archvsts.: Pubns. Com.; Select Com. on Hosp. Admin. and Hist. Recs., Co–ch.; Anl. Conf. (Prog. Coord., 1978). Univ. of Toronto: Various coms. Assn. of Recs. Mgrs. and Admins. **Pubns.:** "The First Century of Cistercian Legislation," *Citeaux Com. Cist.* (1976); "Regulations for the Operations of a Medieval Library," *The Library* (5th Series, 33:1); ed., *Ontario's Heritage, A Guide to Archival Resources Vol. 1* (1978); "The Peterborough Law Society, 1879–1921," *Law Socty. of Upper Can. Gazette* (Je. 1976); various reviews. **Activities:** 2; 55, 62, 75 **Addr.:** 795 Sherbrooke St., Peterborough, ON K9J 2R2 Canada.

Tayyeb, Rashid (N. 20, 1936, Sheikhupur, Uhter Pradesh, India) Head, Tech. Srvs., Patrick Power Lib., St. Mary's Univ., 1979–; Head, Cat. Dept., Leddy Lib., Univ. of Windsor, 1976–79; Resrc. Acq. Ofcr., ON Mnstry. of Educ., 1973–76; Lectr., LS, Univ. of Tabriz, Iran, 1969–72; Asst. Libn., Inst. of Islamic Std., McGill Univ., 1965–69; Cat. Libn., Univ. of Toronto, 1963–65. **Educ.:** Karachi Univ., 1956–60, BA (Econ.); Univ. of Toronto, 1962–63, BLS, 1972–73, MLS. **Orgs.:** ON LA: Cnclr. (1975–79); Assn. of Coll. and Univ. Libs., Nsltr. Ed. Adv. Can. LA: Tech. Srvs. Coord. Grp. (1979). Atl. Provs. LA: BIBCAP Com. on DOBIS Costs, Conv.; AAU/BNA Grp. on Costing. ALA: Reg. X Mem. Com. (Ch., 1979–81). various other orgs. Univ. of Windsor Fac. Assn. **Pubns.:** *A Dictionary of Acronyms and Abbreviations in Library and Information Science* (1979); *AACR-II; A Selected Bibliography* (1979); reg. ed., *Lib. Scene* (1974–); various articles, reviews. **Activities:** 1; 17, 20, 46; 57, 75 **Addr.:** Patrick Power Library, St. Mary's University, Halifax, NS B3H 3C3 Canada.

Tchobanoff, James B. (S. 1, 1946, Detroit, MI). Mgr., Tech. Info. Ctr., Pillsbury Co., 1976–; Sr. Clinical Med. Libn., Univ. of MO, Kansas City, Med. Lib., 1975–76, Clinical Med. Libn., 1972–75; Postgrad. Trainee, Univ. of TN, Med. Units, 1971–72. **Educ.:** Univ. of MI, 1964–68, BS (Chem.), 1970–71, AMLS; Univ. of TN, 1971–72, Cert. (Med. Libnshp.). **Orgs.:** SLA: Com. on Coms. (1980–83); Food and Nutr. Div. (Ch.-Elect, 1981–82); MN Chap. (VP, Pres.–Elect, Prog. Ch., 1978–79); Pres. (1979–80). Med. LA. AAS. Amer. Chem. Socty. **Honors:** Beta Phi Mu, 1971. **Pubns.:** Jt. auth., *The biomedical librarian in the patient care setting; final report on Research Grant NLM-01574* (1975); jt. ed., *Health evaluation: an entry to the health care system* (1974); "The databases of food - a survey of what works best and when," *Online* (Ja. 1980); jt. auth., "A role for clinical medical librarians in continuing medical education," *Jnl. of Med. Educ.* (Je. 1978); various sps. (1973–). **Activities:** 1, 12; 17, 39, 49-On-line srch.; 60, 68, 80 **Addr.:** Technical Information Center, Pillsbury R&D, 311 2nd St. S.E., Minneapolis, MN 55414.

Teague, Edward Hickman (Ja. 5, 1952, Lenoir, NC) Ref. Libn./Hum. Biblgphr., Univ. of NC, Charlotte, 1980–; Ref. Libn., Valdosta State Coll., 1978–80. **Educ.:** Univ. of NC, 1970–73, BFA (Art); Univ. of GA, 1974–76, MA (Art Hist.); Univ. of NC, 1977–78, MSLS. **Orgs.:** ALA. ARLIS/NA. GA LA. SELA. Coll. Art Assn. **Pubns.:** *Henry Moore: Bibliography and Reproductions Index* (1981); Reviews. **Activities:** 1; 30, 39, 42; 55 **Addr.:** Atkins Library, University of North Carolina, Charlotte, NC 28212.

Teather, Linda M. (N. 9, 1946, Ottawa, ON) Head, Cat. Sect., Univ. of Waterloo Lib., 1981–; Head, Serials Dept., Univ. of MB Libs., 1978–, Serials Catlgr., 1976–78, Orig. Catlgr., 1973–76. **Educ.:** Univ. of Victoria, 1964–68, BA (Eng.); Univ. of BC, 1971–73, MLS. **Orgs.:** MB LA: Secy. (1975–76); Treas. (1976–77). Can. LA. ALA. **Activities:** 1; 17, 20, 44; 56, 83 **Addr.:** Cataloging Dept., Dana Porter Arts Library, University of Waterloo, Waterloo, ON N2L 3G1 Canada.

Tebbetts, Diane Ruth (My. 3, 1943, Buffalo, NY) Asst. Ref. Libn., Assoc. Prof., Univ. of NH Lib., 1971–, Cat. Asst., 1965–71. **Educ.:** Univ. of NH, 1961–65, BA (Hist.); Simmons Coll., 1969–72, MLS; Boston Univ., 1974–78, MLA (Hist.). **Orgs.:** New Eng. LA: Bibl. Com. (Co–Ch., 1976–78); Coll. Libns. Sect. (Ch., 1979–80). NH LA: Pres. (1978–79). Acad. Libns. of NH: Secy. (1977–78). ALA: ACRL/New Eng. Chap. (Secy.–Treas., 1979–81). New Eng. Lib. Info. Netwk.: Com. on Interlib. Comm.; ILL Adv. Com. Educ. Resrcs. Info. Ctr.: Vocabulary Review Grp. **Pubns.:** Jt. ed., *A Guide to Newspaper Indexes in New England* (1978); contrib., *New Hampshire's Role in the American Revolution 1763-1789; A Bibliography* (1974); jt. auth., "Undergraduate Reference Aids," *RQ* (Spr. 1973); Cmplr., ed., *Pathfinders;* proj. dir., "New Hampshire Writers View the Small Town" film (1979). **Activities:** 1; 39, 49-On–line srch.; 56, 92 **Addr.:** Reference Dept., University of New Hampshire Library, Durham, NH 03824.

Tebo, Jay D. (O. 6, 1934, Morristown, NJ) Leader, Ref. and Bk. Srvs. Sect., Vitro Labs. Div., Autom. Indus., Inc., 1977–; Lib. Consult., Cloyd Dake Gull and Assocs., Inc., 1977; Lib. Consult., Sierra Club, DC Ofc., 1977; Mgr., Webster Tech. Info. Ctr., Xerox Corp., 1966–76; Ref. Libn., Resrch. Labs. Div., Untd. Techs. Corp., 1964–65; Tech. Libn., AC Spark Plug Div., Gen. Motors Corp., 1959–63. **Educ.:** Lycoming Coll., 1954–56, AB (Chem.); Univ. of IL, 1958–59, MSLS. **Orgs.:** ALA. Amer. Socty. of Indxr.: DC Coord. (1977–78); Treas. (1977–79); Pubn. Com. (Ch., 1979–); Nom. Com. (Co-Ch., 1980). ASIS. SLA: CT Valley Chap., Treas. (1964–65), Rcrt./Mem. Com. (Ch., 1965–66); Upstate NY Chap., (various ofcs., 1967–73). **Activities:** 12; 30, 39, 46; 59, 64, 91 **Addr.:** 2806 Hyson Ln., Falls Church, VA 22043.

Tebo, Marlene K. (N. 7, 1936, Northville, MI) Asst. Dir. for Sci., Tech. and Med. Lib. Resrcs., SUNY, Binghamton, 1979–; Tech. Libn., MITRE Corp., 1975–79; Tech. Libn., Xerox Corp., 1969–75; Sci. Biblgphr., SUNY, Binghamton, 1966–69. **Educ.:** MI State Univ., 1954–59, BS (Chem.); Drexel Univ., 1964–65, MS (LS); various cont. ed. crs., 1975–. **Orgs.:** ASIS. SLA: Div. of Env. Info., Ch.–Elect Past Ch. **Activities:** 1, 12; 17, 29, 39; 65, 82, 91 **Addr.:** Science Library, State University of New York at Binghamton, Binghamton, NY 13901.

Teclaff, Ludwik A. (N. 14, 1918, Czestochowa, Poland) Prof. of Law, Law Libn., Fordham Univ. Sch. of Law, 1959–. **Educ.:** Warsaw Univ., Oxford Univ., 1936–44, Mag.Jur. (Law); Columbia Univ., 1953–54, MLS; NY Univ., 1959–65, JSD. **Orgs.:** AALL: Com. for Liaison with Lib. of Congs. (1968–69). Law Libns. Assn. of Grt. NY: VP (1968–69); Pres. (1969–70). Intl. Law Assn.: Com. on Nat. Resrcs. (1973–). Intl. Cncl. on Env. Law. Intl. Water Law Assn. Polish Inst. of Arts and Scis. in Amer.: Trustee. various other orgs. **Pubns.:** Jt. ed., *Water in a Developing World* (1978); *Legal and Institutional Responses to Growing Water Demand* (1978); "An International Comparison of Trends in Water Resources Management," *Ecol. Law Qtly.* (1979); "Transboundary Ground Water Pollution," *Nat. Resrcs. Jnl.* (1979); *International Groundwater Law* (1981); various bks., mono. in env. law. **Activities:** 1; 17; 65, 77, 82 **Addr.:** Fordham University School of Law, 140 W. 62nd St., Lincoln Center, New York, NY 10023.

Tees, Miriam H. (F. 24, 1923, Montreal, PQ) Assoc. Prof., Grad. Sch. of LS, McGill Univ., 1979–; Chief Libn., Royal Bank of Can., 1953–79; Catlgr., Intl. Cvl. Aviation Assn., 1951–53. **Educ.:** McGill Univ., 1940–44, BA (Econ.), 1950–51, BLS, 1973–75, MLS. **Orgs.:** SLA: Pres. (1975–76); Conf. Ch. (1969); Bd. of Dirs. (1970–73, 1974–77); Educ. Com. (1981–); various lcl. and assn. ofcs. Corp. des Bibtcrs. Prof. du PQ: Pres. (1971–72); various coms., ofcs. (1968–). PQ LA: Pres. (1965–66). IFLA: Sects. on Lib. Schs. Std. Com. (1981–85); 1982 Congs., Prog. Com., Ch. various other orgs. Untd. Church of Can.: Natl. Com. on Liturgy; various other coms. Girl Guides of Can.: Trainer, (1946–66); Comsn. (1960–66); Camp Adv. (1954–60). Can. Amat. Musicians/Musiciens amat. can.: Natl. Bd. (1977–79). Can. Bankers Assn.: Jnls. Com. (1977–79). **Honors:** SLA, John Cotton Dana Lect., 1973. **Pubns.:** "The Corporation of Professional Librarians of Quebec," *IPLO Qtly.* (O. 1973); "Special Libraries," *ALA Yrbk.* (1977, 1978); "Are Librarians Prunes," *Argus* (Ja.–F. 1975); "President's Report, 1975–76," *Spec. Libs.* (S. 1975); "The Information Society," *SL* (S. 1975); various articles, bk. reviews. **Activities:** 11, 12; 17, 25, 26; 59 **Addr.:** McGill University, Graduate School of Library Science, 3459 McTavish St., Montreal, PQ H3A 1Y1 Canada.

Tegler, Patricia (D. 18, 1953, Buffalo, NY) Asst. Ref. Libn., Univ. of IL, Chicago, 1981–; Lib. Std./Comm. Libn., SUNY, Buffalo, 1976–. **Educ.:** SUNY, Buffalo, 1971–75, BA (Eng., Hist.), 1975–76, MLS. **Orgs.:** ALA: ACRL/West. NY/ON Chap. (1977–). SUNY Libns. Assn. **Honors:** Phi Beta Kappa, 1975. **Pubns.:** "The Indexes and Abstracts of Library and Information Science," *Drexel Lib. Qtly.* (Jl. 1979). **Activities:** 1, 11; 15, 31, 39; 62, 75, 93 **Addr.:** University of Illinois, Chicago Circle, Library, Chicago, IL 60680.

Teitelbaum, Gene W. (D. 27, 1935, New York, NY) Law Libn., Prof. of Law, Univ. of Louisville, 1975–; Assoc. Law Libn., Duke Univ., 1973–75; Lawyer, New York City, 1968–72; Assoc. Law Libn., Rutgers Univ., 1961–68. **Educ.:** City Coll. of New York, 1953–57, BA (Gvt.); Pratt Inst., 1959–60, MLS; Rutgers Univ., 1963–68, LLB. **Orgs.:** AALL: Com. on Indexing Legal Pers.; various coms. (1973–). **Activities:** 1; 17, 31; 77 **Addr.:** Law Library, University of Louisville, Belknap Campus, Louisville, KY 40292.

Teitelbaum–Kronish, Priscilla (F. 15, 1926, New York, NY) Pub. Srvs. Libn., Babst Lib., NY Univ., 1979–, Libn. for Instr., Orien. and Bibl. Retrieval, 1976–79, Ref. Libn., Sci. and Info. Sci., 1973–76; Ref. Libn., Air and Water Cons., Amer. Petr. Inst., 1968–73, Ref. Libn., Air and Water Cons., 1966–68; Head, Sci. Lib., NY Univ., 1962–66. **Educ.:** Brooklyn Coll., 1942–46, BS (Bio.); Columbia Univ., 1958–61, MLS. **Orgs.:** SLA: Docum. Grp. (Ch., 1963–64); Docum. Div. (Treas., 1966–68). ASIS: Ch.–Elect, Ch. (1976–78). **Pubns.:** "Use of Multi Databases: A Case Study," *ASIS Procs.* (O. 1975); "Building a Science Collection," *Choice* (Ja. 1966). **Activities:** 1, 12; 31, 39, 49-On-Line Srch.; 75, 88, 93 **Addr.:** 110 Bleecker St., New York, NY 10012.

Telatnik, George M. (S. 24, 1942, Niagara Falls, NY) Dir., Libs., Niagara Univ., 1977–, Acq. Dept. Head, 1976–77, Circ. Dept. Head, Pub. Srvs. Libn., 1973–76; Instr., Hist., Nazareth Coll. of Rochester, 1966–68. **Educ.:** Niagara Univ., 1960–66, BA, MA (Hist.); MI State Univ., 1968–72, ABD (Hist.); SUNY, Buffalo, 1974–76, MLS. **Orgs.:** ALA: ACRL. Cath. LA. NY LA. **Honors:** Beta Phi Mu; Pi Gamma Mu. **Activities:** 1; 17 **Addr.:** 1821 Braley Rd., Youngstown, NY 14174.

Teloh, Mary H. (Mr. 5, 1946, Menomonie, WI) Spec. Cols. Libn., Vanderbilt Med. Ctr. Lib., 1977–, Serials Libn., 1973–77; Sel. Libn., Madison Pub. Schs., 1971–72; Mtrls. Anal., Lib. Mtrls. Resrch. Proj., Univ. of WI, 1969–71. **Educ.:** Univ. of WI, 1964–68, BA (Hist.), 1968–69, MA (LS). **Orgs.:** Med. LA. TN LA. TN Archvsts. Mid.–TN Hlth. Sci. Libns. **Honors:** Beta Phi Mu, 1969. **Pubns.:** "The Moll Collection on Hypnotism at Vanderbilt," *Bltn. of the Med. LA* (Ja. 1977). **Activities:** 1, 2; 23, 36, 45; 68, 80 **Addr.:** 4302 Sneed Rd., Nashville, TN 37215.

Tema, William J. (Je. 23, 1937, Senatobia, MS) Dist. Libn., Altadena Lib. Dist., 1973–; Ref. Libn., Pasadena Pub. Lib., 1962–73; Ref. Libn., Cedar Rapids Pub. Lib., 1960–62. **Educ.:** Univ. of MN, 1955–59, BS (Educ.), 1959–60, MA (LS). **Orgs.:** ALA: PLA, Mem. Com. (1975–78). Pub. Lib. Execs. of South. CA: Pres. (1977). Pub. Lib. Film Circuit: Pres. (1976–77). YA Reviewers of South. CA: Treas. (1969–70). Various other orgs. Altadena Cham. of Cmrce. Altadena Old Fashioned Days Parade. E. Pasadena Little Leag. Altadena Kiwanis Club. **Activities:** 9; 16, 17, 47 **Addr.:** 1115 Sierra Madre Villa, Pasadena, CA 91107.

Temkin, Edward A. (Mr. 12, 1917, Bronx, NY) Asst. Prof., Lib./Media Sci., Kean Coll. of NJ, 1969–; Lib. Dir., Clark Pub. Lib., 1961–69; Sch. Libn., McManus Jr. HS, 1957–65; Jr., Sr., Prin. Bus. Libn., Newark Pub. Lib., 1951–57; Supvsr., Main Readg. Rm., Ref. Div., NY Pub. Lib., 1949–50; Ref. Asst., Bus. and Econ. Dept., Enoch Pratt Free Lib., 1947–48. **Educ.:** Univ. of CT, 1938–42, BA (Pol. Sci.); Syracuse Univ., 1946–47, BLS; Seton Hall Univ., 1961–65, MA (Educ.). **Orgs.:** NJ LA: Educ. Com. (Ch., 1974–78). NJ Assn. for Educ. Media. AECT. Un. Cnty. Educ. Assn. NJ Educ. Assn. Natl. Educ. Assn. Un. Cnty. AV Aids Cmsn.: Vice–Ch. (1979–80). Various other orgs., ofcs. **Pubns.:** "The Library is My Classroom," *Lib. Binder* (Je. 1971). **Activities:** 11; 20, 32, 39; 59, 63 **Addr.:** 15 Lenox Ave., Cranford, NJ 07016.

Temkin, Sara Anne (O. 1, 1912, Hoboken, NJ) Asst. Dir., Cranford Pub. Lib., 1956–; Head, Serials, Ref. Dept., Army Med. Lib., DC, 1944–48; Hosp. Libn., Goldwater Meml. Hosp., 1943–44; Ref. Libn., Linden Pub. Lib., 1930–43. **Educ.:** NJ State Tchrs. Coll., 1942–43; George Washington Univ., 1944–48; 1956, NJ Prof. Libn. Cert. **Orgs.:** NJ LA: Tech. Srvs. Com. (Ch., 1974); *NJ Biblgphr.* Ed. (1961–63); Persnl. Com. (1976–78). Dames of Kean Coll.: VP (1974–75). **Pubns.:** *Jinny Williams, Library Assistant* (1963); *Your Future in Library Science* (1973); "Let Them Read Books," *Lib. Scene* (Win. 1973); "How to Buy an Encyclopedia," *Coronet* (1971); various articles on med. topics. **Addr.:** 15 Lenox Ave., Cranford, NJ 07016.

Templin, Dorothy (F. 17, 1933, Victoria, BC) Dir., Ctrl. ON Reg. Lib. Syst., 1976–, Asst. to Dir., 1969–76; Asst. Dir., Tech. Srvs., York Univ., 1966–69, Head, Acq. Dept., 1965–66, Head, Cat. Dept., 1964–65; Catlgr., Univ. of Toronto, 1959–64. **Educ.:** Univ. of BC, 1950–54, BA; Univ. of Toronto, 1958–59, BLS, 1969, MLS. **Orgs.:** ALA. Can. LA: Tech. Srvs. Sect. (Secy., 1967–68). SLA. ON LA: ON Assn. of Coll. and Univ. Libs. (Secy., 1965–66); Tech. Srvs. Grp. (Ch., 1966–67); Educ. Com. (Ch., 1967–69); Nom. Com. (Ch., 1974–75). Univ. Women's Club. **Pubns.:** "Planning for Technicians," *ON Lib. Review* (S. 1970). **Activities:** 9, 13; 17, 34 **Addr.:** 8111 Yonge St., Unit 1112, Thornhill, ON L3T 4V9 Canada.

Tener, Jean F. (Ap. 27, 1931, London, Eng.) Archvst., Univ. of Calgary, 1974–. **Educ.:** Univ. of Calgary, BA, with distinction (Hist.), MA (Hist.); various cont. ed. crs. (1976–79). **Orgs.:** Assn. Can. Archvsts.: Treas. (1979–80). **Pubns.:** "Accessibility and Archives," *Archivaria* (Sum. 1978). **Activities:** 1, 2; 38, 45; 55, 86 **Addr.:** Special Collections, 12th Floor, Library Tower, University of Calgary, Calgary, AB T2N 1N4 Canada.

Tenney, H. Baird (Ag. 26, 1925, Madison, WI) Pres., State Lib. Bd., State Lib. of OH, 1979–, Mem., State Lib. Bd., 1976–79; Pres., Bd. of Trustees, Cleveland Hts.–Univ. Hts. Pub. Lib., 1974–76. **Educ.:** Northwest. Univ., 1944–47, BS (Bus.); Harvard Univ., 1949–50, MBA. **Orgs.:** OH Lib. Trustees Assn. **Addr.:** 3735 Northampton Rd., Cleveland Hts., OH 44121.

Tenopir, Carol (S. 17, 1952, Whittier, CA) Lib. Systs. Libn., Univ. of HI, 1979–81; VP, Opers., Cibbarelli and Assoc., 1978–79, Supervisory Libn., 1976–78; Libn., COM Ed., Huntington Beach Pub. Lib., 1976–78. **Educ.:** Whittier Coll., 1970–74,

Special Subjects/Services: 50. Adult educ.; 51. Advert./Mktg.; 52. Aerosp.; 53. Agric.; 54. Area std.; 55. Arts/Hum.; 56. Autom.; 57. Bibl./Prtg.; 58. Bio. sci.; 59. Bus./Fin.; 60. Chem.; 61. Copyrt.; 62. Documtn.; 63. Educ.; 64. Engin.; 65. Env.; 66. Eth. grps.; 67. Film; 68. Food/Nutr.; 69. Geneal.; 70. Geo.; 71. Geol.; 72. Handcpd.; 73. Hist.; 74. Int. frdm.; 75. Info. sci.; 76. Insr.; 77. Law; 78. Legis.; 79. Math./Comp. sci.; 80. Med.; 81. Metals; 82. Nat. resrcs.; 83. Newsp.; 84. Nuc. sci.; 85. Oral hist.; 86. Petr./Energy; 87. Pharm.; 88. Phys./Astr./Math.; 89. Readg.; 90. Relig.; 91. Sci./Tech.; 92. Soc. sci.; 93. Telecom.; 94. Transp.; 95. (other).

Who's Who in Library and Information Services

BA, highest hons. (Eng.); CA State Univ., Fullerton, 1974–76, MSLS; Univ. of IL, 1981–, Doct. Student. **Orgs.:** CA Gvr.'s Conf. on Libs. and Info. Srvs.: Mstr. Facilitator; Reg. III Grp. Facilitator. CA LA: Cmnty. Rel. Com. (Ch., 1978–79). HI LA: Coll. and Univ. Sect. (Ch., 1980–81); Exec. Bd. (1980–81). SLA. various other orgs. (1975–). CA State Univ., Fullerton, Alum. Assn.: Bd. (1976–77). **Pubns.:** "Evaluation of Library Retrieval Software," *Procs. of the ASIS Anl. Mtg.* (O. 1980); jt. auth., "OCLC Card Receipts," *Jnl. of Lib. Autom.* (Je. 1980); "Intracorporate Networks," *Procs. of the ASIS Mid-Yr. Mtg.* (My. 1979); jt. auth., "A Retrieval System for Engineering Drawings," *Spec. Libs.* (F. 1979); jt. auth., "LIBNOTES–A Laboratory Notebook Retrieval System," *Procs. of the ASIS Anl. Mtg.* (N. 1978); various articles, sps. (1978–). **Activities:** 1; 17, 26, 49-Autom. plng.; 56, 75 **Addr.:** Graduate School of Library & Information Science, University of Illinois, 410 David Kinley Hall, 1407 W. Gregory Dr., Urbana, IL 61801.

Teo, Elizabeth A. (Mr. 7, 1945, Newark, NJ) Asst. Libn., Moraine Valley Cmnty. Coll., 1973–; Libn. I, Chicago Pub. Lib., 1970–73. **Educ.:** South. IL Univ., 1964–66, BA (Hist.), 1967–69, MA (Hist.); Univ. of Denver, 1969–70, MA (LS). **Orgs.:** IL LA. NLA. **Pubns.:** "Audiovisual Materials in the College and Community College Library: The Basics of Collection Development," *Choice* (Je., Jl./Ag. 1977); reviews. **Activities:** 1; 15, 31, 42 **Addr.:** Learning Resources Center, Moraine Valley Community College, Palos Hills, IL 60465.

Teresinski, Sally Selner (My. 29, 1937, Coleman, WI) Libn., Winneconne HS, 1977–; Curric. Libn., Lib. Fac., Univ. of WI, Oshkosh, 1964–77; Tchr., Oshkosh HS W., 1962–63; Tchr./Libn., Coleman HS, 1959–62. **Educ.:** Univ. of WI, Oshkosh, 1955–59, BS (LS, Eng.); Univ. of WI, 1963–64, MSLS. **Orgs.:** ALA: AASL. WI LA. WI AV Assn. Univ. of WI Grad. Lib. Sch. Alum. Assn.: Secy. (1968–69). Univ. of WI Alum. Assn.: Alum. Bd. AAUW. **Honors:** Beta Phi Mu. **Pubns.:** Jt. auth., *Cataloging, Processing, Administering A V Materials: A Model for Wisconsin Schools* (1972); "Archer Awards for Authors; Wisconsin Children Choose Golden and Little Archers," *WI Lib. Bltn.* (N.–D. 1979). **Activities:** 10; 15, 17, 20; 63, 92 **Addr.:** 6031 Skeleton Bridge Rd., Oshkosh, WI 54901.

Ternberg, Milton G. (Ag. 16, 1947, Fairmont, MN) Bus. Spec., Middleton Lib., LA State Univ., 1981–; Head, Gvt. Pubns. Div., Dallas Pub. Lib., 1977–81, First Asst., Bus. and Tech. Div., 1976–77; Bus. Libn., New Orleans Pub. Lib., 1973–76. **Educ.:** Mankato State Univ., 1965–69, BS (Hist.); Univ. of MN, 1972–73, MA (LS). **Orgs.:** SLA: Pub. and Gvtl. Bus. Libs. RT (1977–78). TX LA: GODORT (Prog. Ch., 1978–79). ALA: Lcl. Arrange. Com., Dallas Conv. (1979). **Honors:** Phi Alpha Theta; New Orleans Pub. Lib., Outstan. Srv. Rating, 1975. **Pubns.:** "Databases Key to Business Research," *Dallas/Fort Worth Bus.* (N. 1977). **Activities:** 1, 9; 17, 29, 39; 59, 91, 92 **Addr.:** Business Administration, Government Documents Department, Middleton Library, Louisiana State University, Baton Rouge, LA 70803.

Terrant, Seldon W. (N. 17, 1918, Cleveland, OH) Head, Resrch. and Dev., Bks. and Jnls. Div., Amer. Chem. Socty., 1972–, Sr. Staff Adv., Chem. Abs. Srv., 1968–72, Managing Ed., Spec. Pubns. and Srvs., 1964–68. **Educ.:** OH Univ., 1936–40, BS (Chem.); Case Inst. of Tech., 1946–48, MS (Chem.), 1948–50, PhD (Chem.). **Orgs.:** ASIS: Com. for Intersocty. Coop. (1978–80). Socty. for Schol. Publshg.: Dir. (1979–80). SLA. Assoc. Info. Mgrs. Amer. Chem. Socty. AAAS. **Pubns.:** "Computers in Publishing," *Annual Review of Information Science and Technology* (1980); "The Computer and Publishing," *Annual Review of Information Science and Technology* (1975); jt. auth., "Evaluation of an Alternative Journal Format," *Procs. of ASIS Mtg.* (1979); jt. auth., "Evaluation of a Dual Journal Concept," *Jnl. of Chem. Info. and Comp. Sci.* (1977). **Activities:** 3-Prof. assn.; 32, 37, 41; 56, 60, 75 **Addr.:** American Chemical Society, 1155 16th St., N.W., Washington, DC 20036.

Terry, Ann Scott (D. 31, 1947, Toronto, ON) Cmnty. Srvs. Libn., York Cnty. Lib., 1979–; Chld. Coord., VA Beach Pub. Lib., 1972–79; Chld. Libn., Petersburg Pub. Lib., 1971–72. **Educ.:** Wesleyan Coll., 1966–70, BA (Elem. Educ.); Univ. of KY, 1970–71, MSLS. **Orgs.:** ALA: JMRT, Dir. (1978–80), Afflt. Cncl. (Pres., 1976); *Footnotes* Ed. (1976–78); LAMA/PR Srvs. to Pub. Libs. Com. (1979–83); PLA/Small and Medium-sized Libs. Sect. VA LA: JMRT, Afflt. Cncl., Rep. (1974–76), Pres. (1976–77); Chld. and YAs Srvs. RT, Pres. (1974–76), Nsltr. Ed. (1976–77); Nom. Com. (1979). SELA. SC LA. Tidewater Cncl. of Camp Fire Girls: Bd. of Dirs. (1975–78). VA Beach Readg. Cncl. **Honors:** ALA, ALSC, Charles Scribner's and Sons Awd., 1975. **Activities:** 9; 16, 21, 36 **Addr.:** York County Library, P.O. Box 10032, Rock Hill, SC 29730.

Terry, Carol Sue (D. 9, 1946, E. Orange, NJ) Visit. Slide Cur., Herron Sch. of Art, IN Univ., 1980–82; Actg. Libn., 1981; Slide Cur., Dept. of Art, Stanford Univ., 1972–80; AV Catlgr., MN Hist. Socty., 1971–72. **Educ.:** Macalester Coll., 1965–69, BA (Hum.); Univ. of MN, 1969–71, MA (LS). **Orgs.:** ARLIS/NA: N. CA Chap. (Ch., 1976–77); Visual Resrcs. Spec. Interest Grp., Com. on Slide Qual. (Ch., 1977–79); Exec. Bd. (West. Reg. Rep., 1978–80); Ad Hoc Com., Stans. for Fine Arts Slide Cols.; Visual Resrcs. Sessions, (Conf. Mdrtr., 1981). Coll. Art Assn.: Adv. Com. of Visual Resrcs. Grp., Rep. **Pubns.:** (Written as Carol T. Ulrich) "The Role of the Library in Public Opinion Formation during World War I," *MnU Bltn.* (O. 1971). **Activities:** 14-Acad. Slide Col.; 15, 20; 55 **Addr.:** Herron School of Art, Indiana University, 6215 N. Washington Blvd., Indianapolis, IN 46220.

Terry, Josephine R. (Jl. 3, 1930, Chicago, IL) Dir., Butte Cnty. Lib., 1968–; Fld. Srvs. Libn., NV State Lib., 1965–68; City Libn., Sierra Madre Pub. Lib., 1961–65; Ref. and Branch Libn., Miami Pub. Lib., 1955–61. **Educ.:** FL State Univ., 1948–53, BS (Geo.), 1954–55, MS (Lib.). **Orgs.:** CA Inst. of Libs.: VP, Pres.-elect (1980–). CA LA: Cncl. (1970–71, 1979–81). ALA. CA State Lib. Adv. Cncl. on Libs. (1976–77). Soroptimist Intl. of Oroville. **Activities:** 9; 19, 34, 35; 70, 74, 92 **Addr.:** Butte County Library, 1820 Mitchell Ave., Oroville, CA 95965.

Terry, Sue (Paonessa) (Ap. 13, 1942, Honolulu, HI) Branch Coord., Alameda Free Lib., 1977–, Chld. Coord., 1971–77, Chld. and Ref. Libn., 1967–71. **Educ.:** Univ. of CA, Santa Barbara, 1961–64, BA (Hist.); Univ. of CA, Berkeley, 1965–66, MLS. **Orgs.:** Assn. of Chld. Libns. of North. CA: Pres. (1979–80). CA LA: Com. on Resrch. (1978). ALA. Frnds. of Intl. Bd. on Bks. for Young People: Amer. Del. to Congs., Prague (1980). Intl. Youth Lib., Munich. Leag. of Women Voters. Alameda Cmnty. Chorus. Goethe Inst. **Pubns.:** "Children's Literature Conference in Klagenfurt," *Frnds. of IBBY Nsltr.* (Sum.–Fall 1980). **Activities:** 9; 17, 21, 27 **Addr.:** c/o Alameda Free Library, 1433 Oak St., Alameda, CA 94501.

Terwilliger, Gloria (S. 30, 1927, Springfield, MA) Dir., Lrng. Resrcs., North. VA Cmnty. Coll., 1969–, Libn., 1968–69; Catlgr., Acq. Libn., Mary Washington Coll., 1966–68; Msc. Tchr./Accompanist, 1955–. **Educ.:** Smith Coll., 1946–50, BA (Liberal. Arts); IN Univ., 1951–53, MA (Msclgy.); Cath. Univ., 1966–68, MLS; Univ. of MD, 1969–75, EdD. **Orgs.:** ALA: ACRL/Cmnty. and Jr. Coll. Sect., Ad Hoc Com. on Instr. Dev. (Ch., 1980–), Jt. Com. on Lrng. Resrcs. Progs. (1973–75); Legis. Com. (1978–82). AECT: Ed. Adv. Com. (1978–80); Div. of Instr. Dev., Mem. Com. (1979–81); Cmnty. Coll. Assn. for Instr. and Tech. (various ofcs., 1971–78). VA LA: Cmnty. Coll. Sect. (Ch., 1970–71). VA Educ. Media Assn.: Various ofcs., coms. (1972–79); Various adv. coms. (1979–81). AAction Cnsrtm.: Instr. AAction Ctr. Adv. Com. (1979–82). Com. on Status of Women in Alexandria. Assn. for Cmnty. and Jr. Colls., Natl. Cncl. on Lrng.: Pres. (1973–74). **Pubns.:** *Resource Identification Workshops: A Report* (My. 1979); ed., *Status Report on TICCIT* (Ag. 1978); jt. auth., *A Report: Resource Identification Workshops* (My. 1978); "Exploring Learning Resources," *New Directions for Community Colleges* (1974); "Personhood...," *Cmnty. and Jr. Coll. Jnl.* (D.–Ja. 1975); various articles, reviews (1971–74). **Activities:** 1; 17, 32, 34 **Addr.:** Northern Virginia Community College, Alexandria Campus, 3001 N. Beauregard St., Alexandria, VA 22311.

Terzian, Shohig Sherry (Constantinople, Turkey) Dir., Mental Hlth. Info. Srv., Neuropsyt. Inst., Univ. of CA, Los Angeles, 1975–, Fac., Dept. of Psyt. and Biobhvl. Scis., 1969–, Libn., Neuropsyt. Inst., 1961–74; Libn., West. Home Ofc., Prudential Insr. Co., 1948–61; Resrch. Libn., Natl. Affairs, Time, Inc., 1947–48; Pic. Ed., Resrch. Asst., US Ofc. of War Info., War Dept. Cvl. Affairs Div., US Dept. of State, Ofc. of Intl. Info., 1943–46; Ref. Asst., Vassar Coll. Lib., 1942–43. **Educ.:** Radcliffe Coll., 1933–37, AB, cum laude (Eng.); Columbia Univ., 1940–42, MS (LS); various cont. ed. crs. **Orgs.:** Assn. of West. Hosps.: Hosp. Libns. Sect., Fndr., Ch. (1966–67), Secy. (1970–71); PR Dir. (1968–78). SLA: South. CA Chap., Pres., 1st Bhvl. Scis. Com., Ch.; various other coms. CA LA: Hosps. and Insts. RT (Ch., 1964–65). Psyt. Libns. of Los Angeles: Fndr., Ch. (1961–63). Various other orgs. Columbia Univ. Alum. of South. CA: Nsltr. Ed.; VP. Assn. for Mental Hlth. Afflt. with Israel: Lib. Com., Ch.; Lib. Resrcs. Com. AAUP. Mental Hlth. Assn. of Los Angeles. various other orgs. **Honors:** Assn. for Mental Hlth. Afflt. with Israel, Hon. Mem. **Pubns.:** "Bibliography of the Writings of George Santayana: 1880 to 1940," (with index) *The Philosophy of George Santayana* (1940); various articles in *South. CA Psyt. Socty. News, South. CA Psyt. Inst. and Socty. Bltn., Los Angeles Times, Lib. Jnl., SLA South. CA Chap. Bltn., News Notes of CA Libs., exCh., CA Libs.,* other prof. pubns. **Activities:** 1, 12; 39, 41, 49-Online srch.; 80, 92 **Addr.:** Neuropsychiatric Institute, University of California at Los Angeles, 760 Westwood Plz., Los Angeles, CA 90024.

Tessier, Louise (F. 17, 1948, Saint-Jerome, PQ) Resp. du Bur. du Depot Legal, Bib. Natl. du PQ, 1972–, Bibtcr. au Srv. des Acq., 1971–72. **Educ.:** Univ. de Montreal, 1961–69, Bacc. (Arts), 1969–71, Bacc. (Bibl.), 1974–78, Cert. (Rel. Pub.), 1978– (Bibl.). **Orgs.:** ASTED: Com. d'Org. Du Cong. (1973; 1975); Com. d'Org. des coms. (1977–); Com. d'Elec. (1979). Can LA. **Pubns.:** "Statistiques de l'Édition au Québec en 1978," *Bltn. de la Bib. Natl. du PQ* (Ap. 1979); "L'Editoria Canadese enl 1973," *Giornale della Libreria* (Ap. 1975); "L'ISBN à la Bibliothèque Nationale du Québec," *Bltn. de la Bib. Natl. du PQ* (D. 1974); various articles. **Activities:** 15, 46 **Addr.:** 10640 Sacre-Coeur # 15, Montreal, PQ H2C 2S9 Canada.

Tessier, Yves (S. 4, 1940, La Pérade, PQ) Chef de la Cartothèque, Bib. de l'Univ. Laval, 1964–. **Educ.:** Univ. Laval, 1961–64, Licence Lettres; Univ. d'Ottawa, 1968–69, BA (Bibliotheconomie); Treas. Univ. Laval, 1970–71, Maîtrise (Hist.). **Orgs.:** Assn. des Cartothèques Can.: Com. du cat. collectif (Pres., 1970–71); Com. de la microreprodct. (Prés., 1976–77). **Pubns.:** Cmplr., *Catalogue collectif des atlas des cartothèques universitaires du Québec* (1976); jt. auth., *Directory of Canadian Map Collections* (1969); "Apprendre à s'informer: les fondements et les objectifs d'une politique de formation documentaire en milieu universitaire," *Documtn. et bibs.* (Je. 1977). **Activities:** 1, 12; 15, 17, 31; 56, 65, 70 **Addr.:** Cartothèque, Bibliothèque de l'Université Laval, Québec, PQ G1K 7P4 Canada.

Testa, Elizabeth Margaret (Saskatoon, SK) Head Libn., CA Postsec. Educ. Comsn., 1975–; Lib. Consult., Haile Sellassie I Univ. (Ethiopia), 1969–71; Crs. Dir., Lib. Tech. Prog., Niagara Coll. (Can.), 1968–69; Libn., Leslie Frost Lib., York Univ., 1964–68; Head, Pub. Srvs., Sir George Williams Univ., 1962–64; Head Libn., Natl. Film Bd. of Can., 1957–1961. **Educ.:** Univ. of SK, BA (Mod. Lang.); Univ. of Toronto, 1952, BLS, 1963, MLS. **Orgs.:** SLA: Sierra Nevada Chap. (Secy. Treas., 1976–78). CA LA. Lib. Admin. Assn. of North. CA: Secy. Treas. (1978–79). ALA. **Activities:** 12; 17, 41; 63 **Addr.:** California Postsecondary Education Commission, 1020 Twelfth St., Sacramento, CA 95814.

Tevis, Ray (Centralia, IL) Assoc. Prof., LS, Ball State Univ., 1977–; Dir., Granite City Pub. Lib., 1974–77; Instr., Sum. Sessions, Sch. of Lib. and Info. Sci., Ext. Div., Univ. of MO, 1975–77; Libn., Granite City HS S., 1973–74. **Educ.:** Greenville Coll., 1965, BA (Hist.), 1966, BS (Educ.); South. IL Univ., Edwardsville, 1970, MA (Hist.); Univ. of MO, 1973, MALS; St. Louis Univ., 1976, PhD (Amer. Hist.). **Orgs.:** ALA. AALS. Assn. of IN Media Educs. IN LA. Org. of Amer. Histns. **Pubns.:** "Academic Library Instruction: The Need for a New Breed," *Cath. Lib. World* (My.–Je. 1974); "Library Cooperation in Granite City: The Public Library and the High Schools, 1975-77," *IL Libs.* (Ja. 1979). **Activities:** 9, 11; 25, 26; 63, 73, 75 **Addr.:** Dept. of Library Science, Ball State University, Muncie, IN 47306.

Thatcher, Mary E. (My. 16, 1927, Concord, NH) Acq. Libn., Univ. of CT Lib., 1960–. **Educ.:** Wheaton Coll., 1945–49, BA (Eng.); Univ. of RI, 1970–73, MLS. **Orgs.:** ALA: ACRL/New Eng. Chap., Bd. of Dirs. (1976–79), Mem. Coord. (1977–79). New Eng LA. CT LA: Coll. and Univ. Sect. (Secy., 1974–75), Nom. Com. (1975), Bylaws Rev. (1976–77), Plng. Com., Gvr.'s Conf. (1975–78). **Honors:** Beta Phi Mu, 1973. **Pubns.:** Various reviews. **Activities:** 1; 15 **Addr.:** P.O.Box 54, Storrs, CT 06268.

Thaxton, Carlton James (My. 23, 1935, Tucson, AZ) Dir., Lake Blackshear Reg. Lib., GA, 1981–, Asst. Dir., 1979–80; Chief, Pub. Lib. Srvs., GA State Dept. of Educ., 1968–79; Dir., Coastal Plain Reg. Lib., GA, 1958–68. **Educ.:** Univ. of GA, 1953–57, ABJ (Jnlsm.); FL State Univ., 1957–58, MS (LS). **Orgs.:** GA LA: Pres. (1981). Natl. Lib. Wk.: Exec. Dir., GA (1965–67). ALA. SELA. **Activities:** 9 **Addr.:** Lake Blackshear Regional Library, 307 E. Lamar St., Americus, GA 31709.*

Thayer, Marlene Parrish (My. 26, 1923, Allegan, MI) Dir., Sch. Media Coord., ESEA Title IV B, State Lib. of MI, 1969–, Lib. Consult., 1969–, Head, Sch. Cat., 1966–69; Libn., St. Joseph Sr. HS, 1961–66; Catlgr., State Lib. of MI, 1960–61; Asst. Libn., Mary H. Weir Lib., 1959–60; Head Libn., Swaney Meml. Lib., 1957–59; Asst. Ref. Libn., Kent State Univ., 1956–57. **Educ.:** Kent State Univ. 1942–45, BA (Hist.), 1949–50, BS (Soc. Std.), 1955–56, MA (LS); various cont. ed. crs., wkshps. **Orgs.:** MI LA: State Treas. (1977–). ALA: ACRL; AASL. Delta Kappa Gamma: Intl. Conv. (1980); Treas. (1978–80); State Treas., 1981–). Beta Zeta: Chrt. Pres. (1964–66); Theta Chap. (Pres. 1970–72). MI Geneal. Cncl.: Mem. Ch. (1975–). Amer. Assn. for State and Lcl. Hist. Various other orgs. **Honors:** USAF Air Defense Team, Ground Observer Corps Srv., Hon. Life Mem., 1959. **Pubns.:** Ed., *Eaton County* (1969). **Activities:** 10, 13; 17, 24, 32; 59, 63, 69 **Addr.:** 6866 Willow Hwy., Grand Ledge, MI 48837.

Theilmann, James William (N. 3, 1937, Chillicothe, MO) Dir., Lib. Srvs., Mesa Cmnty. Coll., 1975–, Ref. Libn., 1969–75; Ref. Libn., Stanford Univ., 1967–69; Tchr., Coronado Jr. HS, 1964–66. **Educ.:** Coll. of Emporia, 1955–60, AB (Eng.); Emporia State Univ., 1966–67, MS (LS). **Orgs.:** ALA. AZ LA. SWLA. AECT. **Activities:** 1; 17, 35, 36; 50, 63, 90 **Addr.:** 1465 E. 8th St., Mesa, AZ 85203.

The-Mulliner, Lian H. N. (N. 27, 1936, Probolinggo, Jawa Timr, Indonesia) Head, SE Asia Col., OH Univ., 1967–; SE Asia Catlgr., Cornell Univ., 1962–67; Bkmobile. Libn., Prince George's Cnty., 1961. **Educ.:** Airlangga Univ., 1957–59, Sarjana Muda (Eng.); Cath. Univ., 1960–61, MA (LS). **Orgs.:** ALA: ACRL. Cncl. on Resrch. Mtrls. on SE Asia: Exec. Com. (1972–74). Assn. for Asian Std. **Pubns.:** *Treasures and Trivia: Doctoral Dissertations on Southeast Asia...in US* (1968); Transl., *Education and Social Change in Colonial Indonesia* (1969); *The Verhandelingen van het Bataviaasch Genootschap: Annotated Content Analysis* (1973); various reviews (1980). **Activities:** 1; 15, 20, 39; 54 **Addr.:** Southeast Asia Collection, Alden Library, Ohio University, Athens, OH 45701.

PROFESSIONAL ACTIVITIES: Institutions: 1. Acad. lib.; 2. Arch.; 3. Assn.; 4. Fed./Gvt. lib.; 5. Inst. lib.; 6. Mfr./Suppl.; 7. Milit. lib.; 8. Musm.; 9. Pub. lib.; 10. Sch. lib.; 11. Sch. of lib. sci.; 12. Spec. lib.; 13. State lib.; 14. (other). **Functions/Activities:** 15. Acq./Col. dev.; 16. Adult srvs.; 17. Admin.; 18. Apprais.; 19. Archit./Bldgs.; 20. Cat./Class.; 21. Chld. srvs.; 22. Circ.; 23. Cons./Pres.; 24. Consult.; 25. Cont. ed.; 26. Educ. lib. sci.; 27. Ext. srvs.; 28. Fund/Grants; 29. Gvt. pubs.; 30. Indx./Abs.; 31. Instr. lib. use; 32. Media srvs.; 33. Micro.; 34. Netwks./Coop.; 35. Persnl.; 36. PR; 37. Publshg.; 38. Recs. mgt.; 39. Ref. srvs.; 40. Repro.; 41. Resrch.; 42. Review.; 43. Secur.; 44. Serials; 45. Spec. col.; 46. Tech. srvs.; 47. Trustees/Bds.; 48. YA srvs.; 49. (other).

Thériault, Michel (D. 2, 1942, Toronto, ON) Chief, Retrospective Natl. Bibl. Div., Natl. Lib. of Can., 1975–; Head, Acq. Dept., Univ. de Montréal, 1969–75. **Educ.:** Univ. de Montréal, 1960–62, B (Phil.); Univ. of Toronto, 1968–69, BLS; Pontifical Univ. of St. Thomas Aquinas, Rome, 1962–67, JCD; McGill Univ., 1974–76, MLS. **Orgs.:** ALA: ACRL/Rare Bks. and MSSSect., Rare Bk. Com. (1974–75). Amtmann Circle. Assn. for the Bibl. of Hist. Canon Law Socty. of Amer. Intl. Canon Law Assn. Can. Canon Law Socty. **Pubns.:** *Choix et Acquisitions des Documents au Québec* (1977); *Néo-vagin et Impuissance* (1971); "Un imprimé en Caractères Grecs à Montréal en 1837," *Paper of the Bib. Socty. of Can.* (1974); "Fleury Mesplet, Printer to the Congress in Montreal," *Forces* (1978); Ed., *Canadiana 1867–1900: Monographs* (1980–); various bks. and articles. **Activities:** 4; 23, 24; 57, 90 **Addr.:** 56-2069 Jasmine Cr., Ottawa, ON K1J 7W2 Canada.

Thibodeau, Patricia L. (Ja. 6, 1952, Nashua, NH) Dir., Hlth. Sci. Info. Ctr., Women and Infants Hosp. of RI, 1977–; Catlgr./Instr., RI Coll., 1976–77. **Educ.:** Univ. of NH, 1970–74, BA (Hist.); Univ. of RI, 1974–76, MLS. **Orgs.:** Assn. of RI Hlth. Scis. Libns.: VP (1979–80). RI LA: Conf. Com. (1976–); Nom. Com. (1979–). ALA: RI Mem. Task Frc. (1976–). Med. LA. Various other orgs. **Activities:** 1, 12; 20, 39, 46; 80, 92 **Addr.:** Health Sciences Information Center, Women and Infants Hospital of Rhode Island, 50 Maude St., Providence, RI 02908.

Thiele, Paul E. (Mr. 10, 1942, Lodz, Poland) Libn., Head, Crane Meml. Lib., Univ. of BC, 1968–; Recreation Dir., Can. Natl. Inst. for the Blind, 1962–65. **Educ.:** Univ. of BC, 1962–65, BA (Langs.), 1965–67, MA (Compar. Lit.). **Orgs.:** Can. LA: Com. on Lib. Srvs. for the Print Handcpd., Ch. Natl. Task Frc. on Educ. Mtrls. for the Handcpd. IFLA: RT on Lib. Srvs. for the Blind. Natl. Lib. of Can.: Task Grp. on Lib. Srvs. for the Blind. Vancouver City Cncl. Com. on the Disabled. Can. Manpower: Outrch. Prog., Dir. **Pubns.:** *Educational Materials for the Handicapped-A Preliminary Union List* (1978); "Formats in Non-Print Media for the Blind and Physically Handicapped," *Library Services for the Blind and Physically Handicapped* (1979); jt. auth., "A Proposal for the Establishment of an International Biography of the Blind in Prominent Positions" (Ag. 1979); "Copyright and Library Materials for the Handicapped," *Rpt. of the Task Grp. of Lib. Srvs. to the Handcpd.* (1976); "Metric Information in Non-Print Form," *The New Outlook* (Je. 1976); various articles, chaps., sps. **Activities:** 1, 10, 12; 17, 24, 32; 61, 72 **Addr.:** University of British Columbia, Charles Crane Memorial Library, 1874 E. Mall, Vancouver, BC V6T 1W5 Canada.

Third, Bettie Jane (Ag. 29, 1929, Fort Bragg, NC) Ed., *Bus. Pers. Index*, H. W. Wilson Co., 1973–; Consult., World Trade Info. Ctr., Port Athrty. of NY and NJ, 1971–72, Chief Libn., 1962–71; Libn., Gen. Electric Co., 1959–62. **Educ.:** E. Carolina Univ., 1951–54, BS (Hist.); Columbia Univ., 1960–61, MLS. **Orgs.:** ALA. Amer. Socty. of Indxrs. ASIS: NY Chap., Treas.; Place. Com. (1979). SLA: Transp. Div. (Ch., 1964); Lib. Info. Div. (Ch., 1978); NY Chap., various ofcs. **Activities:** 6-Mfr./Suppl.; 30; 59 **Addr.:** 2077 Center Ave., Fort Lee, NJ 07024.

Thomas, Carol Jeanet (My. 4, 1949, Richmond, KY) Asst. Prof., East. KY Univ., 1975–; Tchg. Asst., Univ. of KY, 1972–74. **Educ.:** East. KY Univ., 1968–71, BA (Eng.), 1971–72, MA (Eng.); Univ. of KY, 1974–75, MSLS. **Orgs.:** ALA. SELA. KY LA. OH Valley Grp. of Tech. Srvs. Libns. AAUP. AAUW. **Honors:** Phi Kappa Phi; Beta Phi Mu, 1976; Sigma Tau Delta, 1971. **Pubns.:** "An Introduction to the Library of Congress Classification System" videocassette (1975). **Activities:** 1; 20 **Addr.:** Crabbe Library, Catalog Section, Eastern Kentucky University, Richmond, KY 40475.

Thomas, Carol M. (O. 26, 1929, Detroit, MI) Coord., S.W. MI Lib. Coop., 1978–; Sr. Outrch. Srv. Proj. Libn., Kalamazoo Pub. Lib., 1977–78; Libn. and Info. Ofcr., U.S. Info. Srv. (Swaziland), 1974–75; Libn., Intl. Sch. (Pakistan), 1969–70. **Educ.:** Oberlin Coll., 1947–51, BA (Educ.); West. MI Univ., 1974–76, MA (LS). **Orgs.:** ALA. MI LA. Frnds. of the Kalamazoo Pub. Lib. Leag. of Women Voters. Untd. Nations Assn. **Honors:** Beta Phi Mu. **Activities:** 4, 9; 16, 21, 34 **Addr.:** 1416 Academy St., Kalamazoo, MI 49007.

Thomas, Christine F. (D. 29, 1928, Alexandria, VA) Exec. Dir., LA LA, 1967–; Ref. Libn., LA State Lib., 1953–55; Libn., Art Lib., LA State Univ., 1949–51. **Educ.:** LA State Univ., 1945–49, BS (Home Econ.), 1949–53, BSLS. **Orgs.:** Cncl. of Lib. Assn. Execs.: Nom. Com. (Ch., 1979–80). ALA. SWLA. Baton Rouge Lib. Club. LA LA: Exec. Bd.; ex officio; various other coms. **Pubns.:** "Building Service for the Seventies," *LA LA Bltn.* (Spr. 1970); actg. ed., *LALA Bltn.* (Fall–Win., Spr. 1979). **Activities:** 17, 36, 37; 95-Assn Mgt. **Addr.:** Louisiana State Library, P.O. Box 131, Baton Rouge, LA 70821.

Thomas, David A. (F. 4, 1944, Los Angeles, CA) Prof., Law, Law Lib. Dir., Brigham Young Univ., 1974–; Attorney, Christensen, Gardiner, Jensen and Evans, 1973–74; Law Clerk, US Dist. Judge, 1972–73. **Educ.:** Brigham Young Univ., 1961–67, BA (Pol. Sci.); Duke Univ., 1967–72, JD; Brigham Young Univ., 1977, MLS. **Orgs.:** AALL: Stats. Coord. (1978–); Constn. and Bylaws Com. (Ch., 1975–80); Ethics Com. (1975–78); West. Pac. Chap. (Pres., 1979–81). UT LA: Various coms., ofcs. (1976–79). UT Coll. Lib. Cncl.: Ch. (1977–78). Resrch. Libs. Grp.: Law Prog. Cncl. (1979–); Law Adv. Cncl. (1979–). Amer. Bar Assn.: Com. on Significant Legis. (1975–); Com. on Significant Decisions (1979–); Real Property, Probate and Trust Sect. UT State Bar (1972–). UT Heritage Fndn.: Legal Com. (1974–); Nom. Com. (1978). **Pubns.:** Ed., *Micrographics for Law Librarians* (1980); *Utah Civil Procedure* (1980); "1979 Statistical Survey of Law School Libraries and Librarians," *Law Lib. Jnl.* (Spr. 1980); "Legal Issues in the Use and Abuse of Student Records," *The Midwest. Archvst.* (1978); "Administrative Assistants: Key Roles for a Non-Lawyer Non-Librarian in a Law Library," *Law Lib. Jnl.* (Ag. 1977); various articles in law jnls. (1976–77). **Activities:** 1, 12; 15, 17, 33; 61, 77, 78 **Addr.:** Law School, Brigham Young University, Provo, UT 84602.

Thomas, David H. (Je. 22, 1934, Highland Park, MI) Head, Tech. Srvs., MI Tech. Univ. Lib., 1964–. **Educ.:** MI Tech. Univ., 1964–74, BA (Hist.); Univ. of MI, 1974–76, AMLS. **Orgs.:** ALA. MI LA: Legis. Coord., 11th Congs. Dist. (1977). MI Arch. Assn. Hist. Socty. of MI. MI Tech. Univ. Sen.: Sen. (1979). **Pubns.:** Jt. auth., "Michigan Technological University Library Archives," *Hist. Socty. of MI Chronicle* (1st Quarter 1973). **Activities:** 1; 15, 20, 22; 57, 85 **Addr.:** Library, Michigan Technological University, Houghton, MI 49931.

Thomas, Diana M. (Je. 22, 1937, Rossland, BC) Assoc. Prof., Univ. of CA, Los Angeles, 1974–; Visit. Asst. Prof., Univ. of MN, Sums. 1976, 1978; Asst. Coll. Libn., Pub. Srvs., Mills Coll., 1972–74, Actg. Ref. Libn., 1971–72; Actg. Instr., Univ. of CA, Berkeley, Sum. 1968; Libn., Upward Bound Prog., Mills Coll., Sums. 1966, 1967, Asst. Ref. Libn., 1961–65. **Educ.:** Univ. of BC, 1955–59, BA (Eng., Hist.); Univ. of CA, Berkeley, 1960–61, MLS, 1965–67, MA (Eng.), 1967–74, PhD (Libnshp.). **Orgs.:** ALA. CA LA. SLA. CA Acad. and Resrch. Libs. Bk. Club of CA. Rounce and Coffin Club. Hand Bookbinders of CA. **Pubns.:** *Royal Company of Printers and Booksellers of Spain, 1763–1794* (1982); jt. auth., *The Effective Reference Librarian* (1981); "Pedro Rodríguez and the Wooden Printing Press in Spain," *Lib.* (Mr. 1982); "Printing Privileges in Spain," *Publshg. Hist.* (1979). **Activities:** 11; 26, 39, 45; 57 **Addr.:** Graduate School of Library and Information Science, 120 Powell Library Bldg., University of California, Los Angeles, CA 90024.

Thomas, Frankie T. (O. 3, 1922, Samantha, AL) Head, Ref. Dept., Univ. of AL, 1973–, Ref. Libn., 1969–73; Head, Tech. Srvs., Catlgr., AL A and M Coll., 1968–69; Catlgr., Stillman Coll., 1967–68; Ref. Libn., AL A and M Coll., 1961–67; Libn., Boteler HS, 1958–61. **Educ.:** AL State Coll., 1947–49, BS (Elem. Educ.); Univ. of WI, 1958–60, MSLS. **Orgs.:** ALA. SELA. AL LA: Nom. Com. (1972–73); Gvt. Docums. RT, Intl. Docums. Task Frc. (1974–75), Fed. Docums. Task Frc. (1978–79); Newsp. Indexing Com. (1975–); Plng. Com. (1978–81); Int. Frdm. (1969–70). Univ. of AL Lib.: Various coms., ofcs. (1974–). Univ. of AL: Various coms. (1976–). Mt. Galilee Bapt. Church. Benjamin Barnes Branch YMCA. **Activities:** 1; 17, 29, 39; 55, 83, 92 **Addr.:** 1301 Park St., Northport, AL 35476.

Thomas, Jacqueline P. (My. 12, 1947, Joplin, MO) Lrng. Resrc. Dir., Carthage R-9 Pub. Schs., 1977–; Media Technologist, Parkwood HS, 1975–77, Eng. Tchr., 1970–75; Eng. Tchr., Carthage HS, 1969–70. **Educ.:** MO South. State Coll., 1966–69, BS (Educ., Eng.); Pittsburg State Univ. (KS), 1973–76, MS (Educ., LS). **Orgs.:** MO Assn. of Sch. Libns.: Grievance Com. (1979); Exec. Bd. (1979). ALA: LITA; AASL. **Pubns.:** "Library Skills Program to Use Video Tapes," *Show ME Libs.* (Mr. 1979). **Activities:** 10; 17, 20, 31, 32 **Addr.:** Rte. 4, Box 426, Carthage, MO 64836.

Thomas, James L. (My. 29, 1945, Roanoke, VA) Freelnc. Consult., Spec. Lib. Srvs. to Handcpd., 1980–; Asst. Prof., LS, N. TX State Univ., 1977–81; Media Spec., Albemarle Cnty. Schs., 1974–76; Head Libn., Hargrave Milit. Acad., 1971–73. **Educ.:** Lenoir-Rhyne Coll., 1964–67, BA (Eng.); Univ. of TN, 1967–70, MA (Eng.); Univ. of KY, 1971–72, MSLS; Univ. of VA, 1974–77, EdD. **Orgs.:** ALA. TX LA. AECT. **Honors:** Beta Phi Mu. **Pubns.:** *Turning Kids on to Print Using Nonprint* (1978); jt. ed., *Motivating Children and Young Adults to Read* (1979); jt. ed., *Meeting the Needs of the Handicapped* (1980); *Academic Library Services to the Handicapped Student in the US* (1981); *Using Periodicals in School Library Media Centers* (1980). **Activities:** 10; 21, 24, 37; 72 **Addr.:** 1810 Teasley Ln., Denton, TX 76201.

Thomas, John B. (O. 30, 1941, Washington, DC) Dean, Lrng. Resrcs., Davidson Cmnty. Coll., 1971–. **Educ.:** West. Carolina Univ., 1960–64, AB (Hist.); Emory Univ., 1970–71, MLN (Libnshp.). **Orgs.:** ALA. SELA. NC LA: *NC Libs.* Assoc. Ed. (1975–78). NC Lrng. Resrcs. Assn.: Natl. Lrng. Resrcs. Conf., Plng. Com. (1978), Exhibits Ch. (1978); State Lrng. Resrcs. Priorities Com. (1978); Lrng. Resrcs. Automs. Com. (1978). AECT. NC Assn. of Educ. Comm. Tech.: Bd. of Dirs. (1980). **Activities:** 1; 15, 17; 93 **Addr.:** P. O. Box 1287, Lexington, NC 27292.

Thomas, Lucille Cole (O. 1, 1921, Dunn, NC) Asst. Dir., Sch. Lib. Srvs., Bd. of Educ., New York, 1977–; Adj. Prof., LS, Pratt Inst., 1972–; Supvsr., Sch. Lib. Srvs., Dist. 16, Bd. of Educ., New York, 1968–77, Coord., ESEA Title II, Spec. Proj., 1967–68, Libn., Macon Jr. HS, 1956–67. **Educ.:** Bennett Coll., 1937–41, BA (Soc. Std.); NY Univ., 1952–55, MA (Eng.); Columbia Univ., 1955–57, MS (LS); various crs. **Orgs.:** NY LA: Pres. (1977–78); VP (1976–77); Cncl. (1973, 1976–79). ALA: Lcl. Arrange. Com. (1980); Plng. and Budget Asm. (1980–); Cncl. (1979–83); various coms., RTs, ofcs. (1973–79); AASL, various coms., ofcs. (1972–); ALSC, various coms., ofcs.; LAMA. Intl. Assn. of Sch. Libnshp.: Various ofcs. (1974–). NY Lib. Club: Various ofcs. (1974–79). various other orgs., ofcs. Assn. for Supvsrs. and Curric. Devl. Cncl. of Dirs. and Asst. Dirs. Amer. Readg. Cncl.: Trustee (1976–). AAUW. various other orgs. **Honors:** Jessie Owens Elem. Sch., Lib. Named in Hon. of Lucille C. Thomas, 1980; Protestant Bd. of Guardians, Leadership Awd., 1979; NY Black Libns. Caucus, Leadership Awd., 1978; ALA, Black Libns. Caucus, Leadership Awd., 1979; other hons. **Pubns.:** "Mobilizing Parents for Reading," *Bookmark* (Win. 1980); "Evaluating Library Materials," *Cath. Lib. Jnl.* (1979); *Parents are Partners in the Library* (1979); "Once Upon a Time," *Bookmark* (1978); "Once Upon a Time ...," *Phantasm* (1978); various articles, eds., chaps. (1975–77). **Activities:** 10, 11; 25, 26, 32 **Addr.:** Office of Library, Media and Telecommunications, New York City Board of Education, 131 Livingston St., Brooklyn, NY 11201.

Thomas, Patricia M. (Mr. 2, 1931, Hollywood, CA) Head, Tech. Srvs., Burlingame Pub. Lib., 1960–; Libn., San Diego Cnty. Lib., 1957–60; Catlgr., San Diego City Lib., 1956; Circ. Libn., Navy Electronics Lib., San Diego, 1954–55; Libn. I, San Marino Pub. Lib., 1953–54. **Educ.:** Univ. of CA, Los Angeles, 1952, BA (Pre–Libnshp.); Univ. of South. CA, 1953, MS (LS). **Orgs.:** North. CA Tech. Prcs. Grp.: Secy.–Treas. (1974–75). CA LA: Tech. Srvs. Chap. (Pres., 1980). ALA: RTSD/Cat. and Class. Sect., Com. on Cat.: Descr. and Access (1980–). **Activities:** 9; 20, 46 **Addr.:** Burlingame Public Library, 480 Primrose Rd., Burlingame, CA 94010.

Thomas, Patricia Upham (F. 1, 1944, Philadelphia, PA) Dir. of Lrng. Resrcs., Tidewater Cmnty. Coll., 1973–; Libn., Chesapeake Coll., 1969–73; Acq. Libn., Montgomery Cnty.–Norristown Pub. Lib., 1968–69; Libn., Spec. Srvs., Fort Bragg, 1967–68; Libn., Spec. Srvs., Camp Carroll (Korea), 1966–67. **Educ.:** Univ. of PA, 1961–65, BA (Hist.); Drexel Univ., 1965–66, MSLS. **Orgs.:** ALA. VA LA. SELA. Tidewater Cnsrtm. for Higher Educ.: Lib. Dirs. Com. **Activities:** 1, 14-Cmnty. coll. media ctr.; 15, 17, 32 **Addr.:** Tidewater Community College, 1428 Cedar Rd., Chesapeake, VA 23320.

Thomas, Ritchie D. (Ja. 26, 1931, Olympia, WA) Univ. Libn., Wright State Univ., 1976–; Univ. Libn., Amer. Univ. of Beirut, 1973–76, Assoc. Univ. Libn., 1967–73; Coll. Libn., Sacramento City Coll., 1963–67; City Libn., Woodland Pub. Lib. (1959–63); Asst. Libn., *NY Times*, Washington Bur., (1956–59). **Educ.:** Whitman Coll., 1953–55, BA (Eng.); Cath. Univ. of Amer., 1956–59, MS (LS). **Orgs.:** OH Netwk.: Bd. of Trustees. OH Inter–Univ. Lib. Cncl.: Ch. (1979–80). Dayton–Miami Valley Cnsrtm.: Lib. Exec. Cncl. (Ch., 1979–80). OH LA: Int. Frdm. Com. Various other orgs. **Pubns.:** "Some 19th Century Photographers in Syria, Palestine and Egypt," *Hist. of Photography* (Ap. 1979); "Bonfils and Son, Egypt, Greece and the Lavant, 1867–1894," *Hist. of Photography* (Ja. 1979). **Activities:** 1; 17 **Addr.:** 2041 Elsmere Ave., Dayton, OH 45406.

Thomas, Robert C(harles) (Ap. 3, 1925, Detroit MI) Sr. Ed., Gale Resrch. Co., 1960–; Asst. Libn., Serials and Binding Dept., Cornell Univ. Libs., 1956–59. **Educ.:** Univ. of MI, 1953–55, AB (Far East. langs. and lit.), 1955–56, AM (LS). **Orgs.:** Amer. Socty. of Indxrs. Bk. Club of Detroit: Pres. (1973–81). Frnds. of the Detroit Pub. Lib. **Pubns.:** Jt. ed., *Research Centers Directory* (1981); jt. ed., *Business Organizations and Agencies Directory* (1980); ed., *National Directory of Newsletters and Reporting Services* (1978); jt. ed., *Reverse Acronyms and Initialisms Dictionary* (1972); ed., *Book Review Index* cums. (1972–74); various edshps. **Activities:** 6-Mfr./supplr.; 49-Ed.; 95-Ref. bks. **Addr.:** Apt. 1407, Leland House, 400 Bagley Ave., Detroit, MI 48226.

Thomas, Robert D., Sr. (O. 22, 1944, Effingham, IL) Coord., Lrng. Resrcs. Ctr., Assoc. Prof., LS, Sauk Valley Coll., 1970–; Libn., Casey HS, 1968–70; Tchr., Libn., Mt. Auburn HS, 1965–68. **Educ.:** East. IL Univ., 1962–65, BS (Eng.); Univ. of IL, 1966–69, MS (LS); various cont. ed. crs. **Orgs.:** ALA: ACRL. North. WHCOLIS: Reg., State Del. (1979). IL Lib. Syst.: Acad. Libs. Adv. Com. (1977–). Univ. of IL Lib. Sch. Assn. Natl. Educ. Assn. IL Educ. Assn.: State Rep. Asm. (1978–81). Sauk Valley Coll. Fac. Assn. **Pubns.:** "Collecting the 'King's' Records," *Antique Trader Wkly.* (Je. 27, 1979); "White House Conference Report," *Netwk. News* (Ja. 1979); "Valuable, Early Rhythm and Blues Recordings," *Antique Trader Wkly.* (F. 20, 1980); bk. reviewer, *Goldmine Mag.* (1978–). **Activities:** 1; 15, 17, 45; 55, 73, 92 **Addr.:** Learning Resources Center, Sauk Valley College, R # 5, Dixon, IL 61021.

Thompson, Alleen (S. 18, 1919, Waterville, ME) Retired, 1981–; Mgr., Lib., Nuc. Energy Bus. Grp., Gen. Electric Co., 1955–81; Chief Libn., CA State Dept. of Pub. Hlth., 1949–55;

Special Subjects/Services: 50. Adult educ.; 51. Advert./Mktg.; 52. Aerosp.; 53. Agric.; 54. Area std.; 55. Arts/Hum.; 56. Autom.; 57. Bibl./Prtg.; 58. Bio. sci.; 59. Bus./Fin.; 60. Chem.; 61. Copyrt.; 62. Documtn.; 63. Educ.; 64. Engin.; 65. Env.; 66. Eth. grps.; 67. Film; 68. Food/Nutr.; 69. Geneal.; 70. Geo.; 71. Geol.; 72. Handcpd.; 73. Hist.; 74. Int. frdm.; 75. Info. sci.; 76. Insr.; 77. Law; 78. Legis.; 79. Math./Comp. sci.; 80. Med.; 81. Metals; 82. Nat. resrcs.; 83. Newsp.; 84. Nuc. sci.; 85. Oral hist.; 86. Petr./Energy; 87. Pharm.; 88. Phys./Astr./Math.; 89. Readg.; 90. Relig.; 91. Sci./Tech.; 92. Soc. sci.; 93. Telecom.; 94. Transp.; 95. (other).

Who's Who in Library and Information Services

Ref. Libn., Safeway Stores, Inc., 1947–48; Asst. Libn., Freeport Sulphur Co., 1946–47; Engin. Libn., PA State Coll., 1941–43. **Educ.:** Colby Coll., 1936–40, BA (Geol.); Simmons Coll., 1940–41, BS (LS); Univ. of CA, Berkeley, 1951–55 (LS). **Orgs.:** SLA: Dir. (1956–60); Pres. (1965–66); San Francisco Bay Reg. Chap., Secy. (1948–50), Pres. (1954–55); various coms., other ofcs. (1947–). Unvsl. Serials and Bk. Exch. Inc.: (Dir., 1976–78). San Jose State Univ., Dept. of Libnshp.: Adv. Com. (1972–76). San Jose City Coll., Lib. Tech. Prog.: Adv. Com. (1967–70). US Navy: LCDR (1943–46). U.S. Navy Rsv.: LCDR. **Activities:** 12; 17, 39; 84 **Addr.:** Apt. 20, 1681 The Alameda, San Jose, CA 95126.

Thompson, Ann R. (Ja. 16, 1940, Washington, DC) Asst. Dir. of Resrch. and Educ., Intl. Brotherhood of Teamsters, 1978–, Head Libn., 1962–78. **Educ.:** Amer. Univ., 1957–71, BA (Econ.); Cath. Univ. of Amer., 1972–75, MS (LS). **Orgs.:** WA Indus. Rel. Libns. Com. of Indus. Rel. Libns. WA Un. Women. Indus. Rel. Resrch. Assn. **Honors:** Beta Phi Mu, 1975. **Pubns.:** *Teamsters All: Pictorial Highlights in Our History* (1976). **Activities:** 12; 17, 41; 59, 77, 94, 95-Labor rel. **Addr.:** International Brotherhood of Teamsters, 25 Louisiana Ave. N.W., Washington, DC 20001.

Thompson, Benna Brodsky (Je. 15, 1944, New Haven, CT) Info. Ctr. Mgr., Southeast. Area of Agr. Resrch. and Food Safety Inspection Srv., USDA, 1981–; Libn., Richard B. Russell Resrch. Ctr., 1979–81; Sci. Ref. Libn., Univ. of GA, 1978–79, Soc. Sci.–Hum. Ref., 1976–77; Soc. Sci. Ref. and Chld. Libn., Long Beach Pub. Lib., 1971–72; Lib. Mgr., Columbia-Presby. Hosp., 1970–71; Catlgr., Univ. of CA, Berkeley, 1969–70. **Educ.:** Barnard Coll., 1962–66, BA (Russ.); Hebrew Univ., Jerusalem, Israel, 1964–65; Columbia Univ., 1968–69, MLS. **Orgs.:** SLA. **Activities:** 4; 17; 80, 91 **Addr.:** Library, Richard B. Russell Research Center, USDA-SEA, P.O. Box 5677, Athens, GA 30613.

Thompson, Bert Allen (D. 13, 1930, Bloomington, IN) Dir., Lib. Srv., IL Benedictine Coll., 1969–; Dir. of Libs., Kearney State Coll., 1963–69; Instr., Grad. Lib. Sch., North. IL Univ., 1961–63; Head, Ref. Srv., Mankato State Coll., 1959–61. **Educ.:** Ball State Univ., 1949–53, BS (Eng.); IN Univ., 1955–56, AM (LS); Univ. of Denver, 1967, Cert. (Arch. Admin.). **Orgs.:** ALA. IL LA: Various coms. Cath. LA: Acad. Sect. (Natl. Secy. Treas., 1981–). Amer. Pol. Items Collectors. Amer. Lcl. Pol. Items Collectors: Natl. Secy.–Treas. (1976–80). **Honors:** IL LA, de La-Fayette Reid Schol., 1978. **Pubns.:** "History of LIBRAS," *IL Libs.* (My. 1973); "Nurse to Whitman," *Walt Whitman Review* (S. 1969). **Activities:** 1, 2; 17, 34; 73-Hist. **Addr.:** Theodore Lownik Library, Illinois Benedictine College, 5700 College Rd., Lisle, IL 60532.

Thompson, Brent G. (D. 9, 1949, Ogden, UT) Supvsr. of Autom., Latter-day Sts. Church Hist. Dept., 1979–, Sr. Catlgr., Mss., 1975–79; Catlgr., 1973–75. **Educ.:** Univ. of UT, 1967–73, BA (Hist.), 1975–79, MA (Hist.). **Orgs.:** SPINDEX Users' Netwk.: Cncl. Mem. (1979–). SAA. Conf. of Intermt. Archvsts.: Cncl. Mem. (1974–76). **Activities:** 2; 20, 46; 56 **Addr.:** Latter-day Saints Church Historical Department, 50 E. North Temple, Salt Lake City, UT 84150.

Thompson, Deborah Ann (Ag. 28, 1952, Ft. Leavenworth, KS) Libn., Bio. and Med. Scis., Vets. Admin. Med. Ctr., Indianapolis, IN, 1981–; Med. Ref. Libn., Indiana Univ. Sch. of Med. Lib., 1980–81; Interim Life Scis. Libn., Purdue Univ., 1978–80; Clinical Med. Libn., Univ. of MO, Kansas City Med. Sch., 1975–78. **Educ.:** Univ. of MO, Columbia, 1971–74, BA (Hist.), 1974–75, MLS; Med. LA, 1975, Cert. **Orgs.:** Med. LA: Midwest Reg. Grp., Mem. Com. (1980–82); Hlth. Scis. Lib. Techs. Com. (1981–84). SLA: IN Chap., PR Com. (Ch., 1980–81). **Pubns.:** Reviews. **Activities:** 1, 4; 17, 39, 41; 58, 80, 91 **Addr.:** Library Service (142D), Veterans Administration Medical Center, 1481 W. 10th St., Indianapolis, IN 46202.

Thompson, Diane Marie (S. 27, 1945, Aberdeen, WA) Asst. Dir., Pub. Srvs., Pierce Cnty. Lib., 1980–, Coord., Chld. Srvs., 1973–, Chld. Libn., 1968–73. **Educ.:** Univ. of Puget Snd., 1963–67, BA (Hist.); Univ. of WA, 1967–68, MA (LS). **Orgs.:** ALA: Mem. Com. (WA State Ch., 1971–72); ALSC, Lib. Srv. to Disadv. Chld. (1972–74), Newbery Com. (1980–). Puget Snd. Cncl. for Reviewing Chld. Media: Bk. Com. (Ch., 1977–78). WA LA: Chld. and YA Srvs., Strg. Com. (1970–72); Secy., Nsltr. Ed. (1974–76). **Honors:** Beta Phi Mu. **Activities:** 9; 17, 21 **Addr.:** Pierce County Library, 2356 Tacoma Ave. S., Tacoma, WA 98402.

Thompson, Donald D. (O. 31, 1940, Richmond, CA) Mgr., Lib. Resrch. and Dev., Systemwide Admin., Univ. of CA, 1975–; Mgr., Spec. Projs., Gen. Lib., Univ. of CA, Berkeley, 1973–75, Resrch. Asst., Inst. of Lib. Resrch., 1972–73, Resrch. Asst., Sch. of Lib. and Info. Std., 1972–73. **Educ.:** Univ. of CA, Berkeley, 1958–64, AB (Psy.), 1971–72, MLS; various grad. crs. **Orgs.:** ALA. CA LA. ASIS: Lcl. Chap. (Mem. Ch., 1974–75). **Pubns.:** "The Duplication of Monograph Holdings in the University of California Library System," *Lib. Qtly.* (Je. 1975). **Activities:** 1, 13; 24, 34, 41; 56, 95-Bldg. and space plng. **Addr.:** 5521 Panama Ave., Richmond, CA 94804.

Thompson, Donald Eugene (Jl. 10, 1913, McCallsburg, IA) Retired, 1978–; Libn., Wabash Coll., 1955–78; Dir., Libs., MS State Univ., 1948–55; Asst. Dir., Libs., Univ. of AL, 1944–48. **Educ.:** IA State Coll., 1930–35, BS (Econ.); Univ. of IL, 1936–37, BS (LS); Temple Univ., 1937–40, MA (Econ.). **Orgs.:** IN LA: Pres. (1967–68). ALA: ACRL. **Honors:** IN LA, Spec. Srv. Awd., 1979. **Pubns.:** *Indiana Authors and Their Books, 1917–1966* (1974); *Indiana Authors and Their Books, 1967–1980* (1981); *Directory of Special and Subject Collections in Indiana* (1970); various articles. **Activities:** 1, 2; 37; 57 **Addr.:** 1103 W. Pike St., Crawfordsville, IN 47933.

Thompson, Dorothea Mosley (Ag. 2, 1928, Trenton, NJ) Ref. Libn., Carnegie-Mellon Univ., 1973–. **Educ.:** Douglass Coll., 1946–50, BA (Fr.); Univ. of Pittsburgh, 1963–68, MLS, 1968–72, MA (Fr. Lit.). **Orgs.:** ALA: ACRL, Tri-State Chap., Nom. Com. (Ch., 1979–80). ASIS: Pubcty. Com. (Ch., 1978–79, 1979–80); Hosplty. Com. (Ch., 1979–80); 1980 MidYr. Conv. Com. Pittsburgh Reg. Lib. Ctr.: Com. on Clearinghse. for ILL (Secy., 1978–79, 1979–80). Pittsburgh Bibliophiles. Pittsburgh Symph. Socty. Women's Assn. Campaigns (1967, 1968, 1972, 1973). Fox Chapel Racquet Clb. **Pubns.:** "The Correct Use of Library Data Bases Can Improve ILL Efficiency," *Jnl. of Acad. Libnshp.* (My. 1980); "Irma Rombauer," "Caroline Soule," *American Women Writers; A Critical Reference Guide* (1979–); jt. auth., "A Bibliography of Game Theory," *Contributions to the Theory of Games 4* (1959). **Activities:** 1; 15, 34, 39; 55, 59, 92 **Addr.:** Carnegie-Mellon University, Hunt Library, 5000 Forbes Ave., Schenley Park, Pittsburgh, PA 15213.

Thompson, Douglas L. (Je. 24, 1934, Regina, SK) Dir. of Comms., Can. Pharm. Assn., 1980–; Managing Ed., Intl. Pharm. Abs., 1968–79; Prod. Dev. Pharm., Ayerst Labs., Inc., 1965–68; Dir. of Pharm., Nanaimo Reg. Gen. Hosp., 1963–65. **Educ.:** Univ. of BC (Can.), 1954–58, BScP; State Univ. of IA, 1962–63, MSc (Hosp. Pharm.). **Orgs.:** ASIS. Amer. Socty. of Indxrs.: DC Chap. (Ch., 1979). Can. Assn. Info. Sci. Amer. Pharm. Assn. Amer. Socty. of Hosp. Pharmacists. Can. Pharm. Assn. AAAS. **Honors:** Sigma Xi. **Activities:** 14-Prof. socty.; 17, 30, 37; 58, 62, 87 **Addr.:** Canadian Pharmaceutical Association, 1815 Alta Vista Dr., Ottawa, ON K1G 3Y6 Canada.

Thompson, Enid Thornton (D. 24, 1919, Idaho Falls, ID) Adj. Prof., Univ. of Denver, 1977–; Resrch., Freelnc., 1972–77; Head, Lib., State Hist. Socty., CO, 1962–72; Libn., Denver Pub. Lib., 1956–62; Libn., Butte Pub. Lib., 1941–43. **Educ.:** Univ. of MT, 1937–41, BA (Eng. Anthro.); Univ. of Denver, 1956–59, MA (LS); various cont. ed. crs. (1963–69). **Orgs.:** SLA: CO Chap. (Pres., 1968); Musm. Div. (Pres., 1969); Pic. Div. (1976). SAA: Photodup. Com.; Lib.–Arch. Rel. (1969). West. Hist. Assn. MT Hist. Socty. CO Hist. Socty. **Pubns.:** *Local History Collections: A Manual for Librarians* (1978). **Activities:** 2, 11; 18, 23, 26; 55, 63 **Addr.:** 3730 Allison Ct., Wheatridge, CO 80033.

Thompson, Evan Lewis (Ag. 26, 1918, Fall River, MA) Asst. Dir., W. Side Branches, Detroit Pub. Lib., 1973–, Chief, Dept. Lang. and Lit., 1961–73, Chief, Div. Bowen Branch Lib., 1960–61, 1st Asst., 1958–60, Adult Asst., 1955–58; Instr., Eng., Univ. of ME, 1949–51; Instr., Eng., Purdue Univ., 1947–49; Instr., Moses Brown, 1946–47. **Educ.:** Duke Univ., 1936–40, AB (Eng.), 1940–42, MA (Eng.); OH State Univ., 1951–54 (Eng.); Simmons Coll., 1954–55, MS (LS). **Orgs.:** ALA. MI LA. Detroit Lib. Staff Assn.: VP (1958–59); Pres. (1959–60). Lib. Staff Meml. and Flwshp.: Treas. (1963); Pres. (1964–65). various other orgs. Bk. Club of Detroit. Charles Lamb Socty. Parkside Day Care Ctr. Wayne State Univ.: Anl. Playwrtg. Contest, Judge. various other orgs. **Pubns.:** "Thoreau: A Centenary View," *Among Friends* (Spr. 1962). **Addr.:** 4261 Bishop Rd., Detroit, MI 48224.

Thompson, Frances H. (Ja. 1, 1922, Indianola, IA) Lib. Supvsr., Omaha Pub. Schs., 1964–; Libn., Norris Jr. HS, 1959–64; Core Tchr., Monroe Jr. HS, 1958–59; Tchr., West. Hills Elem. Sch., 1954–58; Tchr., Clifton Hill Elem. Sch., 1948–54. **Educ.:** Univ. of Omaha, 1945–48, BS (Educ.), 1948–53, MS (Educ. Admin.); Univ. of Denver, 1969–71, MA (LS). **Orgs.:** ALA: AASL, Com. for Sel. of Pers. for Sec. Schs. (1960). NE LA: Sch. Lib. Sect. (Ch., 1961). NE Educ. Media Assn. Natl. Educ. Assn. Natl. Cncl. of Tchrs. of Eng. Omaha Educ. Assn. NE State Educ. Assn. various other orgs. **Activities:** 10; 17, 21, 24; 89, 95-Budget plng. **Addr.:** Office of Library Services, Omaha Public Schools, 1410 N. 47th St., Omaha, NE 68132.

Thompson, Glenn J. (O. 16, 1936, Sioux Falls, SD) Ch., Dept. of LS and Media Educ., Univ. of WI, Eau Claire, 1970–; Assoc. Prof., St. Cloud State Coll. 1966–70; Libn. and AV Dir., Perham Pub. Schs., 1963–66; Band and Orch. Dir., Wayzata Pub. Schs., 1958–63. **Educ.:** Augustana Coll. 1954–58, BS (Eng., Msc. Educ.); Univ. of MN, 1963–66, MA (LS); Univ. of SD, 1968–69, EdD (Sec. Educ.); MN Cert., Msc., Eng., LS, AV Educ. **Orgs.:** ALA. WI Educ. Media Assn. Luth. Church LA. WI Sch. Lib. Media Assn. Assn. of Univ. of WI Fac. Natl. Educ. Assn. **Activities:** 10, 11; 20, 26, 31 **Addr.:** Rte. 7, Box 76, Menomonie, WI 54751.

Thompson, James A. (O. 3, 1947, Whiteville, NC) Head Circ. Libn., Lister Hill Lib. of the Hlth. Scis., 1973–, Microfilming Supvsr., 1978–81, Biblgphr., Lister Hill Papers, 1976–77; Lectr., Univ. of AL, 1976–77; AL Msm. of the Hlth. Scs., Cur. and Reynolds Libn., Lister Hill Lib. of the Hlth. Scis., 1972–73. **Educ.:** Univ. of AL, Tuscaloosa, 1967–69, BA (Hist.), 1971–72, MLS. **Orgs.:** SLA: Empl.–Career Guid. Com. (1979). Med. LA: South. Reg. Grp. SELA. AL LA: CUS Proj. Com. (1979); Conv. Com. (1978–79); Bylaws Com. (1975); Hlth. Scis. RT Nom. Com. (Mdrtr.–Elect, 1978). Grt. Birmingham Lib. Club. Reynolds Assocs. Oakmont Untd. Meth. Church. **Pubns.:** "The Effects of Journal Cost Inflation Upon the Brandon List," *Bltn. of the Med. LA* (Ja. 1980); "The Graefenberg Medical Institute," *AL Jnl. of Med. Scis.* (O. 1979); jt. auth., "The Suggestion Card as an Alternative to the Suggestion Book," *Bltn. of the Med. LA* (Ap. 1980); jt. auth., "Evaluation of the Xerox 6500 Color Photocopy Machine," *Bltn. of the Med. LA* (O. 1979); jt. auth., "The Southern University Medical College," *AL Jnl. of Med. Scis.* (Jl. 1979); various articles, reviews (1973–79). **Activities:** 1, 12; 22, 32, 40; 75, 80, 91 **Addr.:** Lister Hill Library of the Health Sciences, University of Alabama in Birmingham, University Station, Birmingham, AL 35294.

Thompson, James Craig (Ap. 18, 1945, New Haven, CT) Assoc. Univ. Libn., Rice Univ., 1981–; Asst. Dir., Tech. Srvs., Johns Hopkins Univ., 1977–81; Head, Acq. Dept., Univ. of PA Libs., 1974–77, Data Srvs. Libn., 1974; Orig. Catlgr., Ursinus Coll. Lib., 1972–74. **Educ.:** Princeton Univ., 1963–67, AB (Eng.); Univ. of WI, 1967–71, MA (Eng.), 1971–72, MLS. **Orgs.:** ALA: Ad Hoc Com. on AACR II Implementation (1978–79); ACRL, Alternatives to the Card Cat. Discuss. Grp. (Ch., 1979–80); RTSD, Tech. Srvs. Costs Com. (1978–81), Tech. Srvs. Admins. of Medium-Sized Resrch. Libs. Discuss. Grp. (Ch., 1978–79, 1981–82); LITA/Info. Sci. and Autom. Sect. (Vice-ch., Ch.–Elect, 1981–82; ERT; various other RTs. Bk. Indus. Systs. Adv. Com. CLENE. Cncl. for Comp. Lib. Netwks. various other orgs. **Honors:** Beta Phi Mu, 1972. **Pubns.:** "The 'New' Catalogs and the Unfinished Evolution," *Amer. Libs.* (Je. 1979); "Acquisitions," *ALA World Encyc. of Lib. & Info. Sci.* (1980); fndr., ed., *Alternative Cat. Nsltr.* (1978–80); "Ten Ways to Profit from a Long Engagement," *Amer. Libs.* (O. 1978); "Booksellers and the Acquisition Librarian: A Two-Way Relationship," *Lib. Acq.: Prac. and Theory* (1977); "Current Awareness for Better Library Acquisitions," *Lib. Acq.* (1977). **Activities:** 1; 17, 34, 46; 56, 75, 93 **Addr.:** Rice University Library, Fondren Library, P.O. Box 1892, Houston, TX 77001.

Thompson, James Howard (Ag. 20, 1934, Memphis, TN) Dir. of Libs., Univ. of NC, Greensboro, 1970–; Dir., Undergrad. Lib., Univ. of NC, Chapel Hill, 1968–70; Asst. Prof., Hist., Univ. of CO, 1966–68; Asst. Prof., Hist., Univ. of Southwest. LA, 1965–66; Subj. Catlgr., Duke Univ., 1963–65. **Educ.:** Southwest. Univ., 1952–55, BA (Hist.); Univ. of NC, 1955–61, MA, PhD (Hist.); Univ. of IL, 1961–63, MS (LS). **Orgs.:** ALA: RASD, Notable Bks. Cncl. (1968–70). Southeast. Lib. Netwk.: Bd. of Dirs. (1979–82); Treas. (1981–82); Srch. Com. for Exec. Dir. (1979–80); Com. to Eval. Exec. Dir. (1979–80). **Honors:** Phi Beta Kappa, 1955; Beta Phi Mu; 1963. **Pubns.:** "Ezra Pound: Letters to Elizabeth Winslow," *Paideuma* (Fall 1980); various reviews in LS and hist. jnls. **Activities:** 1; 17 **Addr.:** 3006 New Hanover Dr., Greensboro, NC 27408.

Thompson, Jean Tanner (Je. 15, 1929, San Luis Obispo, CA) Head, Soc. Sci. Div., Univ. Libs., VA Polytech. Inst. and State Univ., 1978–, Asst. Soc. Sci. Libn., 1973–77, HS Libn., Granton HS, 1969–71; HS Libn., Loyal HS, 1967–68. **Educ.:** Boston Univ., 1949–51, AB (Msc.); Univ. of WI, Eau Claire, 1964–67, Sch. Lib. Cert., Columbia Univ., 1972–73, MS (LS); Univ. of VA, 1975–78, MEd. **Orgs.:** ALA: ACRL/Educ. and Bhvl. Sci. Sect. (Secy., 1981–), Psy./Psyt. Com. (1979–). SELA. VA LA: Coll. and Univ. Libs. Sect. (Secy–Treas., 1980–). **Honors:** Phi Delta Kappa; Phi Beta Kappa; Beta Phi Mu. **Pubns.:** Jt.–ed., *Women's Work and Women's Studies 1972* (1973); *Occupational Socialization in Graduate and Professional Education: An Annotated Bibliography* (1979). **Activities:** 1; 15, 33, 39; 50, 63, 92 **Addr.:** Social Science Div., University Libraries, Virginia Polytechnic Institute and State University, Blacksburg, VA 24061.

Thompson, Kathryn Frances (N. 26, 1918, Center, TX) Dir., Lrng. Media Srvs., Spring Branch Sch. Dist., 1968–; Consult., Gulf Coast Sci., Houston Sch. Dist., 1966–68, Libn., Johnston Jr. HS, 1959–66, Sci. Tchr., Long Jr. HS, 1957–59. **Educ.:** Rice Univ., 1934–38, BA (Sci., Eng.); Univ. of Denver, 1961–63, MA (LS). **Orgs.:** Lrng. Resrc. Prog. Dirs. of TX: Pres. (1980–81). TX Assn. Educ. Tech. TX LA. ALA: AASL. TX State Lib.: LSCA Adv. Cncl. (1979–81). AECT. **Honors:** Reg. VII, AECT, William Fulton Leadership Awd., 1976. **Activities:** 10; 24, 25, 32 **Addr.:** 310 Bunker Hill Rd., Houston, TX 77024.

Thompson, Lawrence Sidney (D. 21, 1916, Raleigh, NC) Prof., Classical Std., Univ. of KY, 1948–; Head Libn., Prof. of Span., West. MI Coll., 1946–48; Spec. Agent, Fed. Bur. of Investigation, US Dept. of Justice, 1942–45; Asst. to Libn., IA State Coll., 1940–42. **Educ.:** Univ. of NC, 1932–34, AB (Latin, Grmn.); Univ. of Chicago, 1935, AM (Latin, Grmn.); Univ. of NC, 1936–38, PhD (Latin, Grmn.); Univ. of MI, 1939–40, ABLS. **Orgs.:** ALA: ACRL/Rare Bks. Sect. (Ch., 1968). Bibl. Socty. of Amer.: Cncl. (1970–78). Grolier Club. KY Folklore Socty.: Pres.

PROFESSIONAL ACTIVITIES: Institutions: 1. Acad. lib.; 2. Arch.; 3. Assn.; 4. Fed./Gvt. lib.; 5. Inst. lib.; 6. Mfr./Suppl.; 7. Milit. lib.; 8. Musm.; 9. Pub. lib.; 10. Sch. lib.; 11. Sch. of lib. sci.; 12. Spec. lib.; 13. State lib.; 14. (other). **Functions/Activities:** 15. Acq./Col. dev.; 16. Adult srvs.; 17. Admin.; 18. Apprais.; 19. Archit./Bldgs.; 20. Cat./Class.; 21. Chld. srvs.; 22. Circ.; 23. Cons./Pres.; 24. Consult.; 25. Cont. ed.; 26. Educ. lib. sci.; 27. Ext. srvs.; 28. Fund/Grants; 29. Gvt. pubs.; 30. Indx./Abs.; 31. Instr. lib. use; 32. Media srvs.; 33. Micro.; 34. Netwks./Coop.; 35. Persnl.; 36. PR; 37. Publshg.; 38. Recs. mgt.; 39. Ref. srvs.; 40. Repro.; 41. Resrch.; 42. Review.; 43. Secur.; 44. Serials; 45. Spec. col.; 46. Tech. srvs.; 47. Trustees/Bds.; 48. YA srvs.; 49. (other).

(1966). Rotary Club, Lexington, KY. NC Socty. of the Cincinnati. **Pubns.:** *The New Sabin* (cont., v. 7, 1979); *Bibliography of Dissertations in Classical Studies* (1968, 1976); various articles, *Encyc. of Lib. and Info. Sci.;* publshr., bk. review ed., *Amer. Notes and Queries. Germanic Notes, Appalachian Notes;* various articles, edshps. **Activities:** 1, 6-Mfr./supl.; 18, 24, 33; 55, 57 **Addr.:** 225 Culpepper, Lexington, KY 40502.

Thompson, Marilyn T. (Clinton, MA) Dir. of Lib. Srvs., George Williams Coll., 1967–, Head, Tech. Srvs., 1965–67; Ref. Libn., Aurora Coll., 1964–65; Head, Tech. Srvs., Univ. of Bridgeport, 1958–63. **Educ.:** Larson Jr. Coll., 1941–43, AA (LS); Simmons Coll., 1949–51, BS (LS); Rosary Coll., 1967–69 MLS; George Williams Coll., 1975–79, MS (Admin. and Org. Behavior). **Orgs.:** ALA. IL LA. Pvt. Acad. Libs. of IL: Secy.–Treas. IL Reg. Lib. Cncl.: Com. on Dir. of Human Resrcs., Ch. **Pubns.:** *Management Information: Where to Find It* (1981). **Activities:** 1; 15, 17, 31 **Addr.:** 6421 Dean Dr., Woodridge, IL 60517.

Thompson, Martha (S. 18, 1920, Omaha, NE) Media Spec., Pub. Srvs. Area, Lrng. Resrcs. Ctr., Assoc. Prof., Brookdale Cmnty. Coll., 1969–; Head Libn., Monmouth Cnty. Hist. Assn. Ref. Lib., 1962–68; Libn., Knollwood Pub. Sch., 1961–62; Catlgr., Red Bank Pub. Lib., 1958–61; Head, Film Div., Toledo Pub. Lib., 1953–54, Sr. Asst., Tech. Dept., 1952–53; Sr. Asst., Phil., Relig. and Educ. Dept., Detroit Pub. Lib., 1950–52, Sr. Asst., Home Readg. Dept., 1947–50; various prof. positions, 1943–47. **Educ.:** Univ. of Cincinnati, 1938–41, AB (Grmn.); George Peabody Coll., 1942–43, BS (LS); Univ. of Cincinnati, 1946, MA (Grmn.); various crs. (1970–74). **Orgs.:** ALA. NJ LA: Hist. and Bibl. Sect. (Pres., 1976–77), Lib. Dev. Com. (1961–65). Monmouth Area Lib. Coord. Cncl.: Nsltr. Ed. (1979–). Monmouth Cnty. Hist. Assn.: Lib. and Arch. Com. (1975–). Various other orgs. AAUW: North. Monmouth Cnty. Branch/NJ Hist. Std. Grp. (Ch., 1973–75); Lib. Com. (Ch. 1963–68). NJ Hist. Socty. Little Silver Hist. Socty. **Honors:** Pi Gamma Mu, 1943; Delta Phi Alpha, 1941. **Pubns.:** Jt. cmplr., *Books for Adult Beginners* (1946). **Activities:** 1, 9; 39, 45; 50, 55, 92 **Addr.:** Learning Resources Center, Brookdale Community College, Lincroft, NJ 07738.

Thompson, Mary Tobin (D. 31, 1946, Belvidere, IL) Actg. Head Libn., Downers Grove Pub. Lib., 1979–, Asst. Head Libn., 1977–79; Exec. Dir., Broadview Pub. Lib., 1976–77; Instr. and Coord., Lib. Tech. Prog., Wilbur Wright Coll. Lib., 1973–75; Head, Sch. Media Ctr., MacArthur Jr. HS, 1971–72; Head, Media Ctr., Salt Brook Sch., 1970–71; Head, Lib., WA Jr. HS, 1969–70. **Educ.:** West. IL Univ., 1964–69, BA (Eng.); Rosary Coll., 1972–73, MA (LS), 1979– (Bus. Admin.); various crs. (1971–79). **Orgs.:** IL LA: AV Com. (1976–79). Lib. Admins. Conf. of North. IL. ALA: YASD; ALSC; PLA; RASD; ACRL; LAMA/Persnl. Admin Sect., Ad Hoc Persnl. Dynamics for Supvsrs. Com. (1979–). Frnds. of the Oak Park Pub. Lib. Various other orgs. Leag. of Women Voters. Natl. Org. for Women. Women in Mgt. **Activities:** 1, 9; 17, 24, 35; 51 **Addr.:** 805 N. Harvey, Oak Park, IL 60302.

Thompson, Richard Martin (D. 25, 1947, Grants Pass, OR) Musm. Dir., Info. Spec., GA-Pac. Hist. Musm., 1979–, Info. Spec./Archvst., 1978–79; Secy., OR Electric Railway Hist. Socty., 1975–79; Tchr., U.S. Hist., Soc. Std., Cent. HS, 1974–75; Instr., European Hist., Chapman Coll., 1973. **Educ.:** Univ. of OR, 1966–70, BS (Soc. Sci.), 1970–72, MA (Hist., Eng.); Portland State Univ., 1976–79, Cert. (LS). **Orgs.:** SAA. Portland Area Spec. Libns. OR Educ. Media Assn. Natl. Trust for Hist. Prsrvn. OR Hist. Socty.: Volun. Musm. Guide (1973). Victorian Socty. in Amer.: Reg. VP (1979–80). **Pubns.:** "Eastside Neighborhood Growth: Role of the Streetcar," *Timeimage* (Je. 1979). **Activities:** 2, 12; 17, 36, 39; 95-Forestry and forest prods. hist. **Addr.:** Georgia-Pacific Historical Museum, 900 S.W. 5th Ave., Portland, OR 97204.

Thompson, Shirley L. (Ja. 10, 1928, Seguin, TX) Supvsr., Lib., Shell Oil Co., Woodcreek, 1980–; Supvsr., Lib., Shell Dev. Co., Westhollow Resrch. Ctr., 1975–80; Tech. Libn., Shell Dev. Co., Pipeline Resrch. and Dev. Lab., 1969–75, Libn., 1959–69, Lab. Tech., 1952–59. **Educ.:** TX Coll. of Arts and Indus., 1947–48, BS (Chem.). **Orgs.:** SLA: TX Chap. (Pres., 1980–81); Chem. Div. (Treas., 1978–80). ASIS. Amer. Chem. Socty. **Activities:** 12; 17; 60, 86, 91 **Addr.:** Shell Oil Company, Woodcreek Library, P.O. Box 4423, Houston, TX 77210.

Thompson, Susan Otis (Ag. 9, 1931, Nashville, TN) Assoc. Prof., Sch. of Lib. Srv., Columbia Univ., 1978–, Asst. Prof., 1972–78, Lectr., 1966–72, Asst. Ref. Libn., 1963–64. **Educ.:** Sweet Briar Coll., 1948–52, AB, summa cum laude (Fr.); Columbia Univ., 1962–63, MS (LS), 1964–72, DLS. **Orgs.:** ALA: LHRT (Secy.–Treas., 1976–77). Amer. Prtg. Hist. Assn.: Natl. Bd. Trustee (1974–79). Pvt. Libs. Assn. Bibl. Socty. of Amer. Grolier Club: Lib. Com. (1978–). Beta Phi Mu: Nu Chap. (Pres., 1977–78). William Morris Socty. Typophiles. **Honors:** Phi Beta Kappa, 1952. **Pubns.:** *American Book Design and William Morris* (1977); ed., *Caxton: An American Contribution to the Quincentenary Celebration* (1976); "Paper Manufacturing and Early Books," *Annals of the NY Acad. of Sci.* (O. 20, 1978); "Ownership Marks on Books," *AB Bookman's Wkly.* (Ja. 30, 1978); "The American Library in Paris," *Lib. Qtly.* (Ap. 1964); various chaps., edshps. (1977–). **Activities:** 1, 11; 23, 26, 45; 55, 57, 73-hist. **Addr.:** 516 Butler Library, School of Library Service, Columbia University, New York, NY 10027.

Thompson, William M. (Ag. 13, 1930, Perth Amboy, NJ) Dir., Data Base Srvs., Defense Tech. Info. Ctr., 1975–, Dir., Ofc. of Info. Sci. and Tech., Chief, Syst. Dsgn. Branch, Defense Documtn. Ctr., 1972–75, Chief, Info. Input Branch, 1968–72; Asst. Chief, Mgt. and Sci. Info. Branch, Ofc. of Aerosp. Resrch., 1964–68. **Educ.:** Rutgers Univ., 1948–52, BS (Ceramic Tech.); OH State Univ., 1952–53, MS (Ceramic Engin.). **Orgs.:** ASIS. SLA. **Activities:** 4 **Addr.:** Defense Technical Information Center, DTIC-I, Cameron Station, Alexandria, VA 22314.

Thomson, Ashley (Mr. 27, 1946, Sudbury, ON) Asst. Libn., Laurentian Univ., 1975–; Instr. and Info. Srvs. Libn., Main Lib., Univ. of SK, 1973–75, Circ. Libn., Law Lib., 1972–73. **Educ.:** Univ. of Toronto, 1964–68, BA, hons. (Hist.); McMaster Univ., 1968–69, MA (Hist.), 1969–70, BEd; Univ. of Toronto, 1970–72, MLS. **Orgs.:** Sudbury Pub. Lib. Bd.: Trustee (1977–80). SK LA: Secy., *SK Lib.* Jt. Ed. (1974–75). Can. LA. ON Hist. Socty.: Mem. Ch. (1978–). Laurentian Univ. Fac. Assn. **Honors:** Beta Phi Mu. **Pubns.:** "Interview: Elizabeth Brewster," *SK Lib.* (Spr. 1975); "The Connaught Experiment," *SK Lib.* (Win. 1974); "Keeping Librarians Up-to-Date," *Can. Lib. Jnl.* (1974); "Fire Years Later: Faculty Status at Laurentian," *Can. Lib. Jnl.* (Ag. 1981); various reviews, sps. **Activities:** 1; 31, 42, 47; 92, 95-Collective bargaining. **Addr.:** Laurentian University Library, Sudbury, ON P3E 2C6 Canada.

Thomson, Dorothy F. (N. 15, 1924, McAdam, NB) Asst. Libn., Plng. and Cols., Univ. of Ottawa, 1981–, Asst. Libn., Pub. Srvs. and Cols., 1977–81, Plng. Libn., 1975–77, Head, Bibl. Srch. Srvs., 1973–75, Ref. Libn., 1969–73; Catlgr., Boston Univ., 1967–69; Instr., Secretarial Sci., Mt. Allison Univ., 1950–60. **Educ.:** Acadia Univ., 1944–47, BA (Eng.); Boston Univ., 1951–53, MEd (Bus. Educ.); Mt. Allison Univ., 1960–64, MA (Eng. Lit.); Univ. of MI, 1966–67, AMLS. **Orgs.:** ALA. Can. LA: Can. Assn. of Spec. Libs. and Info. Sci. Mod. Lang. Assn. **Pubns.:** Reviews. **Activities:** 1; 15, 17, 23; 55, 57 **Addr.:** 655 Echo Dr., Ottawa, ON K1S 1P2 Canada.

Thomson, Sarah Katharine (Je. 25, 1928, Statesville, NC) Media Util. Adv., Prof., Bergen Cmnty. Coll., 1976–, Ch./Dir., Lib. Lrng. Resrcs., 1967–76; Ref. Libn., Barnard Coll., 1955–66; Ref. Asst., Mncpl. Ref. Lib., NY Pub. Lib., 1951–55, Sch. and Ref. Asst., Webster Branch, 1950–51. **Educ.:** Agnes Scott Coll., 1947–49, BA (Eng.); Columbia Univ., 1949–50, MS (LS), 1960–67, DLS. **Orgs.:** ALA: ACRL/Coll. Lib. Sect. (Secy., 1971–72), Stans. and Accred. Com. (1973–77), Subcom. for Dev. of Quantitative Stans. for Lrng. Resrc. Ctrs. in Two–Yr. Colls. (1975–78); RASD, ILL Com. Consult. (1967), Ch. (1969–74). ARL: Adv. Com. to ILL Std. (1970–71). Amer. Assn. of Cmnty. and Jr. Colls., AECT, ALA/ACRL: Jt. Com. (1976–77). NCLIS: Adv. Com. on Natl. Pers. Syst. (1978–). various other orgs., ofcs. (1970–). AAUP. AECT. Natl. Educ. Assn. NJ Educ. Assn. **Honors:** Cncl. on Lib. Resrcs., Flwshp., 1973–74. **Pubns.:** *Learning Resource Centers in Community Colleges: A Survey of Budgets and Services* (1975); *Interlibrary Loan Policies Directory* (1975); jt. auth., *NIL: A Study of Unfilled Interlibrary Loan Requests in the NYSILL System* (1970); *Interlibrary Loan Involving Academic Libraries* (1970); *Interlibrary Loan Procedure Manual* (1970); various articles, reviews, video. (1972–80). **Activities:** 1; 24, 34, 41; 75, 80 **Addr.:** P. O. Box 311, Paramus, NJ 07652.

Thorbeck, Jo Anne Stefanski (Jl. 28, 1938, Fairmont, MN) Trustee, MN Pub. Lib., 1976–; Libn., Mounds View HS, 1967–69. **Educ.:** Univ. of MN, 1956–60, BA (Eng.), 1967–69, BS (Educ.), 1967–69, Sch. Lib. Cert. **Orgs.:** ALTA: Speakers Bur. Com. (Ch., 1979–81); White Hse. Conf. Com. (1976–81); Cncl. V Admin. (1981–82). MN Gvr.'s Conf. on Libs.: Plng. Com. (1977–78). WHCOLIS Follow-up: Plng. Com. (1980). Minneapolis Bd. of Estimate and Tax. **Activities:** 9, 10; 47; 72 **Addr.:** 2100 Irving Ave. S., Minneapolis, MN 55405.

Thorkildson, Terry A. (My. 16, 1943, Warren, MN) Dir., Claude Moore Hlth. Sci. Lib., Univ. of VA Med. Ctr., 1979–, Assoc. Dir., 1974–79; Asst. Libn., Lib. of the Med. Sci., Univ. of NM, 1972–74. **Educ.:** Univ. of FL, 1969–71, BA (Eng.); FL State Univ., 1971–72, MS (LS). **Orgs.:** Med. LA: Mid Atl. Reg. Grp., Nom. Com. (1979). Reg. Med. Lib. IV: Reg. Adv. Cncl. (1977–). ALA. VA LA. Amer. Med. Technologists. Amer. Assn. for the Hist. of Med. **Pubns.:** Ed., *VA Un. List of Biomed. Serials* (anl.); ed., *AV Cat.* (anl.); ed., *The Claude Moore Hlth. Sci. Lib. News.* **Activities:** 12; 32, 39, 46; 80 **Addr.:** University of Virginia, Medical Center Box 234, Charlottesville, VA 22908.

Thorne, Bonnie Baker (F. 22, 1928, Houston, TX) Assoc. Prof., Sam Houston State Univ. 1972–, Libn., LS Instr., 1961–70. **Educ.:** Sam Houston State Univ., 1960, BS (LS); TX Womans Univ., 1964, MA (LS), 1975, PhD (LS). **Orgs.:** TX Cncl. of Lib. Educs. AALS. ALA. TX LA: Dist. VIII Secy. (1977–78), Vice Ch. (1978–79), Ch. (1979–80). various other orgs. Delta Kappa Gamma: Schol. Com. (1977–78). AAUW: Various ofcs. (1962–). TX Assn. of Coll. Tchrs.: Various ofcs. (1965–79). **Honors:** Beta Phi Mu, 1975. **Activities:** 1, 2; 20, 24, 45 **Addr.:** 145 Sunset Lake Dr., Huntsville, TX 77340.

Thorne, Marco G. (Jl. 13, 1914, Los Angeles, CA) Ch., Syst. Adv. Bd., Serra Coop. Lib. Syst., 1979–; City Libn., San Diego Pub. Lib., 1970–78, Asst. City Libn., 1949–70; Asst. Dir., Washoe Cnty. Lib., 1946–49. **Educ.:** Stanford Univ., 1935–39, BA (Hist.), 1939–40, MA (Hist.); Univ. of CA, Berkeley, 1941–42, MLS (Libnshp.). **Orgs.:** NV LA: Fndr. (1946); Pres. (1948–49). CA LA: Treas. (1956–57); Palomar Chap. (Pres., 1964). ALA: Cncl. (1947). San Diego Metro. Area Lib. Cncl.: Fndr.; Pres. (1974). Various other orgs. **Pubns.:** *Ride the Ferry* (1958); "San Diego," *Ency. Amer.;* "San Diego Public Library," *Encyc. of Lib. and Info. Sci.* **Activities:** 9; 17, 35 **Addr.:** 4325 W. Overlook Dr., San Diego, CA 92115.

Thornley, Phyllis J. (Je. 30, 1925, Minneapolis, MN) Actg. Dir., Educ. Media Srvs., Minneapolis Pub. Schs., 1980–, Asst. Dir., 1976–81, Libn.–Media Supvsr., 1969–75; Instr., Univ. of MN Lib. Sch., 1968–69; Libn., Univ. of MN HS, 1965–68. **Educ.:** Univ. of MN, 1943–47, BA (Pol. Sci.), 1960–61, BS (Elem. Educ.), 1963–66, MA (LS); various crs. **Orgs.:** ALA. AECT: Int. Frdm. (1976–79). MN Educ. Media Org.: Goals and Long Range Plng. Com. (Ch., 1979–80); Stans. Com. (1976). MN Assn. of Sch. Libns.: Pres. (1971–72). AV Assn. of MN. Pi Lambda Theta: Epsilon Chap., Pres.–Elect (1979–80), Treas. (1968–69). MN Assn. of Admins. and Consults.: Treas. (1979–80). **Activities:** 10; 17, 32; 63, 74 **Addr.:** 974-17 Ave. S.E., Minneapolis, MN 55414.

Thornton, Eileen (Ag. 12, 1909, Wexford, Ireland) Retired, 1971–; Head Libn., Oberlin Coll. Lib., 1956–71; Head Libn., Vassar Coll., 1945–56. **Educ.:** Univ. of MN, 1927–31, BS (LS); Univ. of Chicago, 1942–45, MA (LS). **Orgs.:** ALA: Exec. Com., Pub. Bd. (1968–71); ACRL. OH LA. MN LA. Pub. Affairs Info. Srv.: Bd. of Trustees (1947–71). **Honors:** Univ. of MN, Outstan. Achvmt., 1969. **Activities:** 1, 9; 17, 24, 49-Accred. **Addr.:** 143 E. College St., #318, Oberlin, OH 44074.

Thornton, Michael Vincent (My. 10, 1933, New York, NY) Libn., Mary Immaculate Semy., 1972–; Libn., Semy. of Our Lady of Angels, Albany, NY, 1964–72. **Educ.:** Mary Immaculate Semy. and Coll., 1957, BA (Phil.), 1957–61, Ordination; SUNY, Albany, 1964–66, MLS; Fordham Univ., 1968–70, MA (Relig. Doctrine). **Orgs.:** ATLA. Southeast. PA Theo. LA: Ch. (1976–78). **Pubns.:** "Who Runs ALA?" *Lib. Jnl.* (Ja. 1, 1966); jt. auth., "Who Runs the American Library Association: Implications for Professional Development," *Social and Political Aspects of Librarianship* (1965); ed., *Teamwork.* **Activities:** 1, 12; 17, 20, 39; 55, 90, 92 **Addr.:** Mary Immaculate Seminary, P.O. Box 27, Northampton, PA 18067.

Thorp, Katherine Knox (My. 13, 1925, St. Louis, MO) Ref. Libn., Pius XII Library, St. Louis Univ., 1965–; Bus. Lib. Asst., Sacramento Pub. Lib., 1964–65; Asst. Circ. Libn., OR State Univ., 1950–52; Ref. Libn., Clayton Pub. Lib., 1947–49. **Educ.:** Maryville Coll., 1943–47, AB (Eng.); Columbia Univ., 1949–50, MSLS; St. Louis Univ., 1972–76, MA (Educ.). **Orgs.:** ALA. World Future Socty. **Activities:** 1; 39; 63 **Addr.:** 8714 Warner Ave., St. Louis, MO 63117.

Thorpe, Suzanne (O. 6, 1949, Chicago, IL) Asst. Libn., Law Lib., Hamline Univ. Sch. of Law, 1974–. **Educ.:** Univ. of WI, Madison, 1967–71, BA (Scan. Std.), 1973–74, MA (LS). **Orgs.:** MN Assn. of Law Libs.: Secy./Treas. (1977–79); Prog. Com. (1976–77); Cont. Educ. Com. (1979–). AALL: Job Secur. Com. (1978–79); Mem. Com. (Co–Ch., 1979–80). MN LA. **Honors:** Beta Phi Mu. **Activities:** 1; 20, 46; 77 **Addr.:** Law Library, Hamline University School of Law, St. Paul, MN 55104.

Thrasher, Jerry A. (O. 3, 1942, Fairfield, AL) Dir., Cumberland Cnty. Pub. Lib., 1980–; Assoc. Dir., Forsyth Cnty. Pub. Lib., 1977–80; Dir., Haywood Cnty. Pub. Lib., 1975–77; Libn., City Island Pub. Lib., Volusia Cnty., 1972–74. **Educ.:** Univ. of AL, 1964–69, BA (Intl. Std.); FL State Univ., 1969–70, MSLS. **Orgs.:** NC LA: Pub. Lib. Sect. (Dir., 1979–81). SELA: Pub. Lib. Sect. (Secy., 1981–82). NC Lib. Srvs. and Construct. Act: Adv. Cncl. (1980–81). Fayetteville Kiwanis Club. WFSS Radio Adv. Cncl., Fayetteville State Univ. (1981–82). **Honors:** Beta Phi Mu, 1970. **Activities:** 9; 17 **Addr.:** Cumberland County Public Library, P. O. Box 1720, Fayetteville, NC 28302.

Thrasher, William D. (D. 16, 1928, Evanston, IL) Asst. to Actg. Comsn., Chicago Pub. Lib., 1977–; ILL Libn. and Asst. Prof., Univ. of IL, Chicago, 1969–76; Actg. Dir., Wheaton Coll. Lib., 1966–69; Asst. Ref. Libn., Univ. of IL, Chicago, 1964–66. **Educ.:** Univ. of IL, Urbana, 1946–50, BS (Jnlsm.); Rosary Coll., 1962–64, MALS. **Orgs.:** ALA: PLA. IL LA. Thea. LA. Chicago Lib. Club: Treas. (1977–78). **Activities:** 1, 9; 17, 34, 39; 83 **Addr.:** 1130 N. Dearborn St., Apt. 1106, Chicago, IL 60610.

Thresher, Jacquelyn E. (S. 12, 1947, Oakland, CA) Spec. Srvs. Coord., Westchester Lib. Syst., 1980–, Adult Srvs. Consult., 1975–80; Projs. Coord., Woodbridge Pub. Lib. 1973–75, YA Libn., 1971–73. **Educ.:** FL State Univ., 1965–69, BA, cum laude (Hum., Eng.); Rutgers Univ., 1970–71, MLS, summa cum laude 1973– (Bus. Admin.). **Orgs.:** ALA: PLA/Alternative Educ. Progs. Sect. VP (1978–79), Pres. (1979–80); Educ. of Pub. Libns. Com. (1979–81); Litcy. and Lrng. Com. (1976); Pub. Lib. Resrch. Com. (1975–77); RASD/Adult Lib. Mtrls. Com. (1976–77). NY LA: Adult Learner Com. (Ch.,

Special Subjects/Services: 50. Adult educ.; 51. Advert./Mktg.; 52. Aerosp.; 53. Agric.; 54. Area std.; 55. Arts/Hum.; 56. Autom.; 57. Bibl./Prtg.; 58. Bio. sci.; 59. Bus./Fin.; 60. Chem.; 61. Copyrt.; 62. Documtn.; 63. Educ.; 64. Engin.; 65. Env.; 66. Eth. grps.; 67. Film; 68. Food/Nutr.; 69. Geneal.; 70. Geo.; 71. Geol.; 72. Handcpd.; 73. Hist.; 74. Int. frdm.; 75. Info. sci.; 76. Insr.; 77. Law; 78. Legis.; 79. Math./Comp. sci.; 80. Med.; 81. Metals; 82. Nat. resrcs.; 83. Newsp.; 84. Nuc. sci.; 85. Oral hist.; 86. Petr./Energy; 87. Pharm.; 88. Phys./Astr./Math.; 89. Readg.; 90. Relig.; 91. Sci./Tech.; 92. Soc. sci.; 93. Telecom.; 94. Transp.; 95. (other).

1976–78); various other coms. Westchester LA. NJ LA: Various coms. various other orgs. Litcy. Voluns. of NY: Bd. of Dirs. (1979–80). NY External HS Dipl. Prog.: Reg. Adv. Com. (1978–). NY Educ. Dept.: Educ. Info. Ctr. Adv. Cncl. (1979–); Lib. Srvs. and Construct. Act Adv. Cncl. (Ch., 1978–80). Westchester Litcy. Voluns. Cnsrtm.: Ch. (1977–79). various other orgs., ofcs. **Honors:** Beta Phi Mu, 1971; Westchester/Putnam Assn. of Adult and Cont. Ed.: Outstan. Contrib. to Cont. Cmnty. Educ., 1979. **Pubns.:** "Westchester Library System Services for Adult Learners," *Bookmark* (Spr. 1979); "Public Libraries May Be Natural Homes for Educational Brokering Services, But Are Librarians Natural Brokers?" *Natl. Ctr. for Educ. Brokering Bltn.* (Sum. 1979); jt. auth., *Guidelines for Library Services for Young Adults in New Jersey* (1973); jt. auth., *A Workshop Guide to the Lifelong Learner* (1979); various sps. (1979–). **Activities:** 9, 14-Lib. syst.; 16, 17, 24; 50 **Addr.:** P.O. Box 668, White Plains, NY 10602.

Thurman, Patricia Ann (Mr. 21, 1939, Sterling, KS) Lib./Media Srvs. Coord., Fairbanks N. Boro. Sch. Dist., 1972–; Libn., Ryan Jr. HS, 1969–72; Libn., Augusta Jr. HS, 1965–69; Tchr., Amer. Dependent Sch. (Naha Okinawa), 1963–64; Tchr., Chapman Sch., 1961–63. **Educ.:** Cottey Coll., 1957–59, AA; Ft. Hays State Univ., 1959–61, BS (Elem. Educ.); Emporia State Univ., 1964–65, MS (LS). **Orgs.:** ALA. AK LA: Media RT. AASL. Natl. Educ. Assn. Fairbanks Educ. Assn. **Honors:** Delta Kappa Gamma. **Activities:** 10; 15, 21, 32; 63, 67 **Addr.:** SR #80397, Fairbanks, AK 99701.

Thurston, Minnie G. (Ag. 12, 1926, Jacksonville, FL) Supvsr. of Lib. Srvs., Offshore Power Systs., 1972–; Elem. Sch. Libn., Duval Cnty. Sch. Bd., 1958–72; Sch. Libn., Nassau Cnty. Sch. Bd., 1954–58; Coll. Adult Educ. Tchr., St. John's Cnty. Normal Coll., 1949–52. **Educ.:** FL Normal Coll., 1943–47, BS (Soc. Sci.); Syracuse Univ., 1954–58, MLS; various sems. (1972–80). **Orgs.:** Duval Cnty. LA. SLA: Schol. Com. (Pres., 1980–81); FL Chap., Bd. (1976–79), Minority Rep. (1979), Nom. Com., Ch. Offshore Power Systs. Credit Un. **Activities:** 1, 12; 17, 31, 39; 64, 84, 91 **Addr.:** Offshore Power Systems, 8000 Arlington Expy., Jacksonville, FL 32211.

Thweatt, John Howton (O. 9, 1935, Memphis, TN) Sr. Archvst., TN State Lib. and Arch., 1971–; Instr., Hist., Austin Peay State Univ., 1965–70; Instr., Hist., TX A and I Coll., 1962–64; Instr., Hargrave Milit. Acad., 1960–62. **Educ.:** Baylor Univ., 1955–59, BA (Hist.), 1959–60, MA (Hist.). **Orgs.:** SAA: Acq. Com. (1977–78). TN Archvsts.: Schol. Com. (1979–80). South. Hist. Assn. TN Hist. Socty. **Pubns.:** "James Priestley: Classical Scholar of the Old South," *TN Hist. Qtly.* (Win. 1980); "The James K. Polk Papers," *TN Hist. Qtly.* (Spr. 1974). **Activities:** 2; 20, 30; 69, 86, 92 **Addr.:** Tennessee State Library and Archives, 403 7th Ave. N., Nashville, TN 37219.

Tibesar, Rev. Leo Joseph (D. 7, 1942, St. Paul, MN) Dir., John Ireland Meml. Lib., St. Paul Semy., 1976–; Actg. Archvst., Chancery Arch. and Cath. Hist. Socty., Archdio. of St. Paul and Minneapolis, 1979–; Instr. (Scripture), Dept. of Theo., Coll. of St. Thomas (St Paul), 1973–76, Chaplain, Dept. of Campus Mnstry., 1971–73; Asst. Pastor, Church of St. Rose of Lima, 1968–71. **Educ.:** St. Paul Semy., 1962–64, BA (Scholastic Phil.); Coll. of St. Thomas, 1963–67, MA (Educ. Admin.); St. Paul Semy., 1964–73, MA (Theo.). **Orgs.:** ALA. ATLA. SAA. MN Cnsrtm. of Theo. Schs. MN Hist. Socty. U.S. Diocesan Archvsts. **Activities:** 1, 2; 15, 17, 45; 73, 90 **Addr.:** The St. Paul Seminary, 2260 Summit Ave., St. Paul, MN 55105.

Tice, Wilma L. (O. 20, 1926, St. Joseph, TN) Coord., Lib. Srvs., Metro Schs., Waverly-Belmont Bldg., 1979–; Lib. Consult., All Levels, 1971–79, Libn., McMurray Jr. High, 1964–71, Libn., E. Jr. High, 1959–64, 5th Grade Tchr., Lockeland Sch., 1958–64. **Educ.:** Florence State Coll., 1958, BS; George Peabody Coll., 1961, MS (LS); various grad. crs. **Orgs.:** ALA. SELA. TN LA: Pres. (1979–81). Mid. TN LA. Natl. Educ. Assn. TN Educ. Assn.: Lib. Sect. (Pres., 1970). Delta Kappa Gamma: Secy. (1969); Treas. (1976). Jr. High Tchrs. Assn.: Pres. (1960); Secy. (1964). Various other orgs. **Pubns.:** Various bk. reviews, *TN Tchr.* (1977); various articles, *TN Libn.* (1979–81). **Activities:** 10 **Addr.:** 4846 Corning Dr., Nashville, TN 37211.

Tidemann, Viola (S. 12, 1918, Valley Springs, SD) Head, Ref. Dept., Wichita Pub. Lib., 1953–; Libn., Rapid City Pub. Lib., 1946–52; HS Tchr., Hot Springs, 1942–46; HS Tchr., Canning, 1940–42. **Educ.:** Huron Coll., 1936–40, BA (Eng.); Univ. of Denver, 1952–53, MA (LS). **Orgs.:** Mt. Plains LA. ALA. KS LA. Bus. and Prof. Women's Club: Pres. (1965–66). **Activities:** 9; 39; 69, 73 **Addr.:** 1818 W. 18th St., Apt. 185, Wichita, KS 67203.

Tidman, Jacqueline C. (Boston, MA) Conservator, Hist./Geneal. Dept., Westborough Pub. Lib., 1973–. **Educ.:** Boston Univ., 1946, BA (Eng.), 1976–, MFA (Cons.). **Orgs.:** MA LA: Prog. Com. (Consult., 1978–); Lcl. Hist. and Geneal. Sect., Exec. Bd. (1978–). SAA: Prsrvn. Methods Com. (1977–79); Cons. Prof. Afnty. Grp. (1979–). Natl. Endow. for the Hum.: Review Bd. for Grant Proposals (1977–). Amer. Inst. for Cons. of Hist. and Artistic Works. New Eng. Cons. Assn. Westborough Hist. Comsn. **Pubns.:** *C/P/R Life-Saving Techniques for Your Collection* (1979). **Activities:** 9; 23, 24, 45; 69, 85, 73-Hist. **Addr.:** 8 Pinecrest Dr., Westborough, MA 01581.

Tiefel, Virginia May (My. 20, 1926, Detroit, MI) Head, Undergrad. Libs., Dir. of Lib. User Educ., OH State Univ., 1977–; Assoc. Head Libn., Hiram Coll., 1974–77, Acq. and Ref. Libn., 1969–74; Sch. Libn., S. Euclid/Lyndhurst Sch. Syst., 1968–69. **Educ.:** Wayne State Univ., 1958–62, BA (Elem. Educ.); Univ. of MI, 1965–68, MA (LS). **Orgs.:** Acad. LA of OH: Pres. (1974); Constn. Com. (Ch., 1975). OH LA: Constn. Com. (1970); Div. VII (Coord., 1980). State Lib. of OH: Multitype Interlib. Coop. Com. (1975–80). ALA. AAUP. **Pubns.:** "What is ALAO Anyway?," *OH LA Bltn.* (My. 1975); "Lib. Instr." clmn *Jnl. of Acad. Libnshp.* (S. 1979). **Activities:** 1; 17, 31 **Addr.:** Main Library, Ohio State University Libraries, 1858 Neil Ave. Mall, Columbus, OH 43210.

Tien, Mary Anna (Mr. 4, 1920, Flint, MI) Lib. Bldg. Consult., CT State Lib., 1980–, Srv. Ctr. Dir., 1969–; Head Libn., Jacob Edwards Lib., 1955–69; Asst. Dir., Docums. Dept., IN Univ. Lib., 1948–55; Branch Libn., Flint Pub. Lib., 1945–47. **Educ.:** Univ. of MI, 1943–45, AB (Eng.), 1945–47, MA (Oriental Cvlztn.), 1945–49, BLS; Hartford Coll., 1976–77, Cert. (Admin.). **Orgs.:** CT Coal. for Acad. Frdm.: Ch. (1979–). CT LA: Int. Frdm.; PR; Trustee and Frnds. Awds. Com. (1979–). ALA: Bldg. Critique Com. (1980); Int. Frdm. Com. New Eng. LA: Bibl. Com. (Ch., 1974–76). various other orgs. E. Hampton Multipurpose Bldg. Com. Socty. for Prsrvn. of New Eng. Antiqs. Yesteryrs. Musms. Assn. **Honors:** Bk. of the Month Club, Dorothy Canfield Fisher Hon. Mention, 1963; Southbridge Bus. and Prof. Women, Woman of Achvmt., 1968; CT Leag. of Hist. Soctys., Awd. of Merit, 1974. **Pubns.:** *Chronicle of History* (1966); "ACLB/CLA Trustee and Friends Award," *CT Libs.* (Ja. 1980); ed., *Occasional Notes.* CT State Lib. (1970–); "Between the Bookends" *Southbridge Evening News* (1955–69). **Activities:** 9, 13; 15, 19, 24; 74, 85, 95-Oriental Cvlztn. **Addr.:** Connecticut State Library Service Center, 786 S. Main St., Middletown, CT 06457.

Tierney, Clifford L. (Ap. 7, 1924, St. Paul, MN) Mgr., Tech. Info. Ctr., Whirlpool Corp., 1955–; Ref. Libn., Honeywell Corp., 1953–55. **Educ.:** Univ. of MN, 1946–49, BS (Eng.), 1952–53, MA (LS). **Orgs.:** SLA: West. MI Chap. (Pres., 1981–82). Socty. for Tech. Comm.: St. Joseph Valley Chap. (Ch., 1978–79). Sigma Xi Whirpool Chap. (Secy., 1979–80). **Pubns.:** "A technical information network serving a decentralized manufacturing company," *Managing Data Elements in Information Processing* (1974); "Managing Technical Information Resources in Industry," *Jnl. of the Socty. of Resrch. Admin.* (Spr. 1976); "Written Technical communication involves more than writing," *Jnl. of Coatings Tech.* (Ja. 1978); "Users role in the development of a technical information network," *Procs. of ASIS* (1973). **Activities:** 12; 17; 64 **Addr.:** Whirlpool Corp.–R&E, Monte Rd., Benton Harbor, MI 49022.

Tietjen, Mildred Campbell (My. 26, 1940, Floyd Cnty., GA) Dir. of Lib. Srvs., GA Southwest. Coll., 1964–; Libn., Gordon Lee HS, 1962–64; Libn., GA State Dept. of Educ., Sums. 1963, 1964. **Educ.:** Berry Coll., 1957–61, BA (Eng.); George Peabody Coll., 1961–62, MA (LS). **Orgs.:** ALA. SELA: Mem. Com. (1979–80). GA LA: Sec. VP (1977–79). Delta Kappa Gamma: Alpha Epsilon Chap. (Pres., 1976–77). Daughters of the Amer. Revolution: Cncl. of Safety Chap. **Honors:** Cncl. on Lib. Resrcs., Flwshp., 1975. **Pubns.:** *A Study, Comparison and Evaluation of Instructional Programs at ALA Accredited Graduate Library Schools in the United States and Canada, with Special Attention Focused on Practical Experience or Field Work Provided Within the Curricula* ERIC (1976); "Practice Makes Perfect," *Wilson Lib. Bltn.* (1977); "The Child Goes Forth," *Delta Kappa Gamma Bltn.* (Fall 1976); "Serving Not the Culturally Deprived But the Culturally Different," Lib. Scene (Mr. 1974). **Activities:** 1; 17; 55, 63, 75 **Addr.:** P.O. Box 1145, Americus, GA 31709.

Tieuli, Anthony F. (My. 21, 1941, Boston, MA) Asst. Dir., Malden Pub. Lib., 1973–; Actg. Coord., ESEA, Title II, MA Bur. of Lib. Ext., 1969, Supvsr., Sch. Libs., 1967–69. **Educ.:** Northeast Univ., Boston, 1958–63, BS in Ed (Hist.); 1963, MA Tchr. Cert.; Univ. of RI, 1964–69, MLS; 1968, MA Prof. Libn. Cert. **Orgs.:** ALA. MA LA: Ad Hoc Com. on State Aid (Ch., 1977–80). Men's Libns. Club. Electric Railroaders' Assn. Boston St. Railway Assn. **Honors:** MA LA, PR Awd., 1st Prize, 1978. **Pubns.:** "Update on State Aid Committee," *Bay State Libn.* (Win. 1979). **Activities:** 9; 17, 22, 35; 56 **Addr.:** Malden Public Library, 36 Salem St., Malden, MA 02148.

Tiffany, Constance J. (Ag. 22, 1946, Galesburg, IL) AV Coord., IA City Pub. Lib., 1976–; Ref. Libn., Univ. of WI, Stout, 1974–76. **Educ.:** Univ. of CA, Davis, 1964–69, BA (Eng.); Univ. of WI, 1971–74, MA (LS). **Orgs.:** ALA. IA LA: AV Com. (1980–). Films for IA Libs.: Pres. (1979–80); Secy. (1978–79). US Trotting Assn. Amer. Film Inst. **Honors:** Beta Phi Mu, 1974. **Pubns.:** "Mechanical Misery," *Amer. Libs.* (O. 1978); "War Between the Stacks," *AL* (D. 1978). **Activities:** 1, 9; 15, 32, 39; 55, 67, 93 **Addr.:** 2709 E. Court St., Iowa City, IA 52240.

Tighe, Ruth Liepmann (Jl. 9, 1931, Wurzburg, Germany) Ofc. of Lib. Srvs., Gvt. of N. Mariana Islands, 1981–; Consult., CNMI ofc. of Lib. Srvs., 1981–; Resrch. Assoc., NCLIS, 1979–81; Prog. Coord., WHCOLIS, 1977–79, Resrch. Assoc., 1976–77; Asst. Dir., Fld. Opers., New Eng. Lib. and Info. Netwk., 1972–76; Ref. Libn., Harvard Coll. Lib., 1970–72, Chief Ref. Libn., 1968–70, Ref. Libn., 1967–68. **Educ.:** NY State Coll. for Tchrs., 1949–51, BA (Soc. Std.); Columbia Univ., 1966–67, MLS cum laude. **Orgs.:** ASIS: Pres. Elect, Pres. (1981); various coms., other ofcs. (1970–). ALA: At-Large Cncl. Mem. (1976–84); ASCLA/Multi-type Lib. Coop. Sect. (Ch., 1979–80); LITA, Legis. Com. (Ch., 1978–80), Bd. of Dirs. (1974–77); Com. on Machine-Readable Bibl. Interchange (Ch., 1974–75); RASD/Info. Retrieval Com. (1970–74). **Honors:** ALA/RTSD, Esther J. Piercy Awd., 1976; ASIS, Spec. Apprec., 1975; Beta Phi Mu, 1967. **Pubns.:** Jt. auth., "Networks," *ALA Yrbk.* (forthcoming); "NCLIS and the White House Conference," *Educ. Media Yrbk.* (forthcoming); "National Commission on Libraries and Information Science: Program and White House Conference," *Educ. Media Yrbk. 1978* (1978); "Library and Information Networks," *Annual Review of Information Science and Technology* (1974); jt. ed., *Information Revolution: Proceedings of the ASIS Annual Meeting* (1975); various articles (1974–76). **Activities:** 4; 17, 34; 75, 78, 93 **Addr.:** Office of Library Services, Government of N. Mariana Islands, Saipan, CM 96950.

Tillett, Barbara B. (S. 29, 1946, Galveston, TX) Head, Tech. Srvs., Scripps Inst. of Oceanography Lib., Univ. of CA, San Diego, 1977–, 1973–76, OCLC Coord. (Assoc. Libn.), Univ. of CA, San Diego Libs., 1976–77; Ref. Libn., Sci. and Tech., Head, Ed. and Conversion of Serials Proj., Hamilton Lib., Univ. of HI, 1970–73, Dir., Ocean Sci. Info. Ctr., 1971–73; Bibl. Anal., Tsunami Docum. Retrieval Syst., Jt. Tsunami Resrch. Effort, HI Inst. of Geophys., Univ. of HI, 1970. **Educ.:** Old Dominion Coll., 1964–68, BA (Math.); Univ. of HI, 1969–70, MLS; MEDLINE Trng., 1973, Cert. **Orgs.:** ALA: ACRL; LITA; RTSD. ASIS. CA LA: Palomar Chap., VP; Pres. (1977–78). SLA: HI-Pac. Chap. (Secy., 1972–73). Various other orgs. **Honors:** Beta Phi Mu, 1970. **Pubns.:** "Ocean Science Information Center," *HI LA Jnl.* (D. 1972). **Activities:** 1, 12; 46; 91 **Addr.:** Scripps Institution of Oceanography Library, University of California, San Diego C-075C, La Jolla, CA 92093.

Tilton, James Joseph (O. 1, 1942, Sioux City, IA) Dir., Comp. Srvs. Ctr., Bibl. Ctr. for Resrch., Inc., 1979–, METRO Prog. Mgr., 1978–79; Sr. Ref. Libn., US Dept. of Housing and Urban Dev., 1974–78, Circ./ILL Libn., 1972–74; Head Libn., US Defense Documtn. Ctr., 1971–72, Libn., 1970–71; Consult., Enoch Pratt Free Lib., 1970; Resrch. Info. Spec., Urban Std. Cncl., 1969–70. **Educ.:** CZ Jr. Coll., 1960–62, AA (Hist.); Univ. of VA, 1966–68, BA (Hist.); Univ. of MD, 1968–70, MLS; various cont. ed. crs. (1973–76). **Orgs.:** ALA: SRRT, Task Frc. on Jobs, DC Area Liaison (1971–77), Co-Ch. (1973); FLRT, Legis. Com. (Ch., 1976–78), Nom. Com. (Ch., 1977–78); various other coms. DC LA: Job Resols. Com. (Ch., 1975). Fed. Interagency Field Libns. Wkshp.: Prog. Plng. Com. (1978); Phys. Facilities Com. (Ch., 1976); various other coms. (1972–74). Frdm. to Read Fndn. Smithsonian Assocs. **Pubns.:** "OCLC Terminal Installation," *Action for Libs.* (Ja. 1980); "IR Costs Lowered by Increased Use," *Action for Libs.* (D. 1979); "BCR Training Costs Explained," *Action for Libs.* (Ag. 1979); jt. cmplr., "Housing and Community Development," *Spec. Choice* (My. 1978); cmplr., *Aids to Understanding HUD* (1975, 1978); various edshps. (1972–73). **Activities:** 14-Netwk.; 17, 34, 39; 51, 56, 75 **Addr.:** CSD, Bibliographic Center for Research, Inc., Suite 212, 245 Columbine, Denver, CO 80206.

Timberlake, Evelyn M. (Je. 11, 1940, New York, NY) Ref. Spec., Amer. Lit., Lib. of Congs., 1971–, Ref. Libn., 1968–71, Subj. Catlgr., Eng. Lang., Eng. and Amer. Lit., 1967–68, Rcrt. Prog., 1966–67. **Educ.:** Cap. Univ., 1958–62, BA (Eng.); Simmons Coll., 1965–66, MS (LS). **Orgs.:** DC LA. Animal Protection Inst. of Amer. Amer. Anti-Vivisection Socty. **Honors:** Lib. of Congs., Incentive Awd., 1979. **Pubns.:** Reviews; contrib., *A Guide to the Study of the United States of America* (1976). **Activities:** 4, 14-Natl. lib.; 31, 39, 41; 55, 62, 92 **Addr.:** Library of Congress, General Reading Rms. Division (GRRD), Washington, DC 20540.

Timberlake, Patricia P. (F. 6, 1938, Pomona, CA) Head, Sci. Lib., Univ. of MO, 1981–; Head, Tech. Srvs., MO State Lib., 1979–81, Asst. Coord., Ref. and Loan, 1976–81, Ref. Libn., 1974–76, Asst. Ref. Libn., 1973–74. **Educ.:** Pomona Coll., 1955–59, BA (Soclgy., Eng.); Univ. of MO, 1969–73, MA (LS). **Orgs.:** MO LA: Ref. Com. (Ch., 1976–77); Pub. Lib. Div. (Pres., 1977–79). SLA: Mid-MO Chap. (Pres., 1977–78); Soc. Sci. Div./Legis. Ref. Sect. (Secy-Treas., 1980–82). Beta Phi Mu: Psi Chap. (VP, 1975–76); Soc. Sci. Div., Nom. Com. (1980), Hosplty. Ch. (1981). **Honors:** Alpha Kappa Delta, 1959. **Pubns.:** Ed., *Reference Update* (1977); "State Library Offers Legislative Hotline," *MoBar Bltn.* (D. 1980); "The State Library's Legislative Hotline," *Show-Me Libs.* (D. 1980); "The 1978 Missouri Legislative Session," *Show-Me Libs.* (Je. 1978); "Antique Requests at the Missouri State Library," *Show-Me Libs.* (Ja. 1976); various articles. **Activities:** 13; 20, 39, 46; 77, 78, 92 **Addr.:** Science Library, University of Missouri, Columbia, MO 65201.

Timour, John A. (Ja. 20, 1926, Hartford, CT) Univ. Libn., Thomas Jefferson Univ., 1975–; Dir., Mid-East. Reg. Med. Lib.

PROFESSIONAL ACTIVITIES: Institutions: 1. Acad. lib.; 2. Arch.; 3. Assn.; 4. Fed./Gvt. lib.; 5. Inst. lib.; 6. Mfr./Suppl.; 7. Milit. lib.; 8. Musm.; 9. Pub. lib.; 10. Sch. lib.; 11. Sch. of lib. sci.; 12. Spec. lib.; 13. State lib.; 14. (other). **Functions/Activities:** 15. Acq./Col. dev.; 16. Adult srvs.; 17. Admin.; 18. Apprais.; 19. Archit./Bldgs.; 20. Cat./Class.; 21. Chld. srvs.; 22. Circ.; 23. Cons./Pres.; 24. Consult.; 25. Cont. ed.; 26. Educ. lib. sci.; 27. Ext. srvs.; 28. Fund/Grants; 29. Gvt. pubs.; 30. Indx./Abs.; 31. Instr. lib. use; 32. Media srvs.; 33. Micro.; 34. Netwks./Coop.; 35. Persnl.; 36. PR; 37. Publshg.; 38. Recs. mgt.; 39. Ref. srvs.; 40. Repro.; 41. Resrch.; 42. Review.; 43. Secur.; 44. Serials; 45. Spec. col.; 46. Tech. srvs.; 47. Trustees/Bds.; 48. YA srvs.; 49. (other).

Who's Who in Library and Information Services

Srv., Coll. of Physicians of Philadelphia, 1973–75; Dir., Lib. Srvs., CRMP-Yale Univ., 1969–73; Trng. Dir., Natl. Lib. of Med., 1966–69. **Educ.:** Miami Univ., 1948–51, BA (Jnlsm.); George Washington Univ., 1958–60, MA (Persnl. Mgt.); Univ. of MD, 1967–69, MLS. **Orgs.:** ALA: Hlth. Educ. Com., HLRS (1974–76). Med. LA: Ad Hoc Com. to Std. ILL Pracs. and Problems (1976–77); Bd. of Dirs. (1978–81); Philadelphia Reg. Grp. (Ch., 1975–76). SLA: Bio. Sci. Div. (Ch., 1976–77); Philadelphia Chap. (Pres., 1979–80). Other coms. AAUP. Hlth. Sci. Comm. Assn. Sigma Xi: Jefferson Chap., *Resrch. Bltn.* Ed. **Honors:** Beta Phi Mu; CT Assn. of Hlth. Sci. Libs., Hon. Life Mem. **Pubns.:** Jt. auth., "The role of the field consultant," *Library Practice in Hospitals* (1972); jt. auth., "Are Hospital Libraries Meeting Physicians' Information Needs?" *Spec. Libs.* (My.–Je. 1973); jt. auth., "The MERMLS Leadership Institute for Hospital Librarians: A New Concept in Extension Service," *Bltn. Med. LA* (Ja. 1977); "Use of Selected Abstracting and Indexing Journals in Biomedical Resource Libraries," *Bltn. Med LA* (Jl. 1979); jt. auth., "A Clinical Program for In-service Nurses: A Preliminary Report," *Bltn. Med LA* (Jl. 1980). **Activities:** 1, 12; 17, 25, 28; 56, 80 **Addr.:** Scott Memorial Library, Thomas Jefferson University, 1020 Walnut St., Philadelphia, PA 19107.

Ting, Eunice Tse-feng Chen (Jl. 14, 1935, Chekiang, China) Catlgr., Col. Dev. Libn., Biomed. Lib., Univ. of CA, Los Angeles, 1979–, Mono. Libn., 1969–79; Serials and Docum. Libn., CA State Univ. Lib., Long Beach, 1967–69; Gvt. Pubns. Libn., Fresno State Univ. Lib., 1966–67; Catlgr., OK State Univ. Lib., 1960–66. **Educ.:** Natl. Taiwan Univ., 1953–57, BA (Frgn. Lang. and Lit.); Univ. of OK, 1959–60, MLS. **Orgs.:** CA LA. Chin.–Amer. LA: Bd. of Dirs. (1979–81). Med. LA: Los Angeles Chap., Ad Hoc Com. on Task Analysis (1977–78). Med. Lib. Grp. of South. CA and AZ. South. CA Tech. Prcs. Grp. Natl. Taiwan Univ. Alum. Assn. of South. CA. **Activities:** 1, 12; 15, 20, 29; 58, 68, 80 **Addr.:** Biomedical Library, Center for Health Sciences, University of California, Los Angeles, CA 90024.

Ting, Lee-hsia (Hsu) (F. 7, 1923, Yangchow, Kiangsu, China) Assoc. Prof., Dept. of Lrng. Resrcs., West. IL Univ., 1977–; Assoc. Prof., Asst. Prof., Dept. of LS, North. IL Univ., 1973–77; Lect., Grad. Lib. Sch., Univ. of Chicago, 1969–71; Instr., Ext. Div., Grad. Sch. of LS, Univ. of TX, 1965–66; Libn., Pharr-San Juan-Alamo (TX) Pub. Schs., 1965–1966; various positions as pub. sch. libn., 1959–65; Tchr., Heep Yunn Sch., Hong Kong, 1954–56; Assoc. Ed., U.S. Info. Srv., Hong Kong, 1952–53; various positions in educ., China, 1944–53. **Educ.:** Natl. Ctrl. Univ., China, 1940–44, BA (Eng.); Mt. Holyoke Coll., 1947–48, AM (Eng. Lit.); Univ. of TX, 1964, MLS; Univ. of Chicago, 1967–69, PhD (LS). **Orgs.:** Chin.–Amer. Libns. Assn.: VP/Pres.-Elect (1978–80), Pres. (1980–81), Prog. Com. (Ch., 1979–80); Nom. Com. (Ch., 1981–82); Bd. of Dirs. (1978–84). IL LA. IL Assn. of Educ. in Media: Int. Frdm. Com. (1978–80). ALA: ALSC. Amer. Folklore Socty. **Honors:** Phi Beta Mu. **Pubns.:** *Government Control of the Press in Modern China: 1900-1949* (1975); jt. auth., *Chinese Folk Narratives, A Bibliographical Guide* (1975); "Networks, Data Bases, and School Media Program in Illinois," *Jnl. of the IL Assn. for Educ. Comm. and Tech.* (Ap. 1979); "Chinese Libraries During and After the Cultural Revolution," *Jnl. of Lib. Hist.* (Sum. 1981); various transl. from Eng. into Chin. **Activities:** 11; 21, 26, 39; 54, 57, 74 **Addr.:** 10 Woodland Ln., Macomb, IL 61455.

Tinsman, William A. (Jl. 28, 1927, Lima, OH) Docum. Libn., Pan Amer. Univ. Lib., 1969–; Ref. Libn., IN State Univ. 1967–69; Gen. Libn., Queens Boro. Pub. Lib. Syst., 1964–66. **Educ.:** Kent State Univ., 1948–54, BS (Psy.); Univ. of KY, 1962–64, MS (LS); Yale Univ., 1957, Dip. (Mandarin Chin.). **Activities:** 1; 15, 29, 39; 59, 92 **Addr.:** 1123 W. Samano St., Edinburg, TX 78539.

Tipton, Mary Lynn (F. 26, 1944, Green Bay, WI) Netwk. Coord., WI Lib. Cnsrtm., 1979–; Head Retrospective Conversion Cat., Univ. of VA, 1977–79. **Educ.:** Univ. of WI, 1962–67, BA (Span.), 1974–77, MLS. **Orgs.:** ALA: RASD, Mem. Com. (1979–). WI LA: Awd. and Hons. (1981); Conf. Plng. (1981). WI Assn. of Acad. Libns.: Mem. Com. (1980–). OCLC, Inc.: Internetwk. Qual. Cntrl. Cncl. (1979–). Moravian Msc. Fest. and Sem.: Coord. (1980–81). **Activities:** 14-Netwk. ofc.; 20, 24, 34; 50, 56, 74 **Addr.:** 464 Memorial Library, Wisconsin Library Consortium, 728 State St., Madison, WI 53706.

Tipton, Roberta Louise (Ag. 7, 1950, Dayton, OH) Med. Libn., John F. Kennedy Med. Ctr., 1977–. **Educ.:** OH State Univ., 1968–72, BA (Eng.); Rutgers Univ., 1976–77, MLS; Med. LA, 1977, Cert. **Orgs.:** Med. Resrcs. Cnsrtm. of Ctrl. NJ: Pres. (1978–80). Hlth. Sci. LA of NJ: VP/Pres.-Elect (1981–82); Bd. (1979–81). **Honors:** Beta Phi Mu, 1977. **Pubns.:** Tech. ed., *JFK Med. Ctr. Fam. Prac. Jnl.* (Win. 1979–). **Activities:** 12; 16, 17; 80 **Addr.:** Medical Library, John F. Kennedy Medical Center, Edison, NJ 08818.

Tissing, Robert W., Jr. (Mr. 22, 1946, Chicago, IL) Archvst., Lyndon B. Johnson Pres. Lib., 1975–; Asst. Archvst., Barker TX Hist. Ctr., Univ. of TX, 1973–75. **Educ.:** Baylor Univ., 1964–68, BA (Hist.); Univ. of Oxford, Eng., 1968, Cert. (Hist.); Baylor Univ., 1970–73, MA (Hist.); Univ. of TX, 1971–74, MLS; Inst. on Mod. Arch. Admin., Natl. Arch., 1974, Cert. (Arch. Admin.). **Orgs.:** SAA: Ref. and Access Policies (1975–). Socty. of SW Archvsts. Austin Area Archvst. Assn. TX State Hist. Assn. **Pubns.:** "Stalag-Texas, 1943-1945," *Milit. Hist. of TX and the SW* (1976); "Prisoners of War," *Handbook of Texas. Supplement* (1976); "Oregon Boundary Dispute," *A.W. Library Pathfinder* (1973). **Activities:** 2; 15, 31, 39; 55, 62, 85 **Addr.:** Lyndon B. Johnson Library, 2313 Red River, Austin, TX 78705.

Tissot, Thalia-Manon (F. 12, 1930, Detroit, MI) Chief, Ctrl. Chld. Rm., Brooklyn Pub. Lib., 1979–, st Asst. Branch Libn., 1974–79, Chld. Libn., 1964–74. **Educ.:** Brooklyn Coll., 1948–51, BA (Lit.); Columbia Univ., 1951–54, MLS. **Orgs.:** NY LA. ALA: ALSC, Chld. with Spec. Needs Com. (1973–76), Film Eval. Com. (1976–79), Newbery Awd. Com. (1980). **Pubns.:** Jt. auth., "Cents and Noncents of AV crafts," *Top of the News* (Ja. 1972); "Innovation Through Trial and Error," *Film Lib. Qtly.* (Fall 1969). **Activities:** 9; 21, 32, 42; 63, 67, 72 **Addr.:** Central Children's Rm., Brooklyn Public Library, Grand Army Plz., Brooklyn, NY 11238.

Tisthammer, Dana Jean (N. 8, 1924, Des Moines, IA) Asst. Dir. for Tech. Srvs., St. Louis Univ., Pius XII Meml. Lib., 1964–, Acq. Libn., 1957–64; Ord. Libn., South. Meth. Univ., Fondrin Lib., 1955–57; Catlgr., Univ. of HI, 1954–55. **Educ.:** Univ. of NE, 1948, AB (Eng.); TX Woman's Univ., 1954, BS (LS). **Orgs.:** ALA. Leag. of Women Voters. **Honors:** Beta Phi Mu; Phi Beta Kappa. **Activities:** 1; 46; 54, 55, 75 **Addr.:** St. Louis University, Pius XII Memorial Library, 3655 W. Pine Blvd., St. Louis, MO 63108.

Titus, Elizabeth McKenney (Jl. 5, 1945, Flushing, NY) Assoc. Prof., Coord. of Comp. Srch. Srvs., Oakland Univ., 1969–. **Educ.:** Oakland Univ., 1963–66, BA (Pol. Sci.); Univ. of MI, 1966–69, MALS; Wayne State Univ., 1979, MUP (Mstr. of Urban Plng.). **Orgs.:** MI Database Users Grp.: Treas./Mem. Ch. (1980). Metro. Detroit Med. Libns. Grp.: Nsltr. Ed. (1975–77). AAUP: Oakland Univ. Chap., (VP 1980–). **Honors:** MI LA, Loleta E. Fyan Awd., 1970. **Pubns.:** Jt. auth., *Resources for Third World Health Planners: A Selected Subject Bibliography* (1980); jt. ed., *Oakland County Union List of Serials* (1975, 1976, 1979); jt. auth., "Point of Increasing Returns: A Student Library Committee," *Lib. Jnl.* (D. 15, 1966); jt. auth., "An Interlibrary Loan Primer," ERIC (1977); jt. auth., "Special Libraries: The Problems of Bibliographic Access," ERIC (1975). **Activities:** 1; 31, 39, 49-Online database srvs.; 56, 92 **Addr.:** Oakland University, 102 University Library, Rochester, MI 48063.

Tiwana, Nazar Hayat (N. 27, 1927, Kalra, Punjab, India) Dir., Amer.'s Eth. Heritage Prog., Chicago Pub. Lib., 1979–, Adult Srvs. Libn., Rogers Park Branch, 1976–78, Ref. Libn., Hist. Dept., 1973–75; Admin. Asst., Catlgr., Bensenville Pub. Lib., 1972–73; Ref. Libn., Newberry Lib., 1968–71. **Educ.:** Pembroke Coll., Cambridge, Eng., 1945–46, BA (Econ.); Univ. of Chicago, 1968–71, MA (LS). **Orgs.:** ALA: Ed. & Pub. Rpt. Com. (1977–81). SLA. IFLA. IL LA. Cncl. of Frgn. Rel. Lincoln's Inn, London, Eng. Chicago Map Socty. **Honors:** Beta Phi Mu, 1979; Frnds. of Chicago Pub. Lib., Hon. Mention Cert., 1979. **Pubns.:** Jt. auth., *Integrated Rural Information System* (1976). **Activities:** 4, 9; 16, 29, 39; 54, 66, 70 **Addr.:** 2620 W. Pratt Blvd., Chicago, IL 60645.

Tobin, Carol M. (Jl. 4, 1944, Greenwich, CT) Ref. Libn., Princeton Univ. Lib., 1980–; Asst. Ref. Libn., Univ. of IL, Chicago, 1973–79; Instr., Hist., Shippensburg State Coll., 1967–68. **Educ.:** Trinity Coll., DC, 1962–66, BA (Hist.); Duke Univ., 1966–67, MA (Hist.); Univ. of Chicago, 1972–73, MA (LS). **Orgs.:** Chicago OLUG: Plng. Com. (1978–79). ASIS. ALA: RASD/Machine-Assisted Ref. Sect., Com. on the Educ. and Trng. of Srch. Anals. (1978–81), Nom. Com. (1980–81), Rep. to Hist. Sect., Conf. Prog. Com. (1980–81); ACRL/Bibl. Instr. Sect., Conf. Plng. Com. (1977–78). Philadelphia Area Ref. Libns. Info. Exch. Amer. Hist. Assn. **Honors:** Beta Phi Mu. **Pubns.:** *The Infopass Program: A Referring Library's Experience* (1979); jt. auth., *Guide to Online Computer Searching* ERIC (1980); Reviews. **Activities:** 1; 31, 39, 49-Online Srch.; 55, 92 **Addr.:** General Reference Div., Princeton University Library, Princeton, NJ 08544.

Tobin, Margaret Mary (O. 11, 1928, Scranton, PA) Libn., St. Francis Coll., 1950–, Asst. Prof., 1950–58. **Educ.:** Marywood Coll., 1950, BA; Duquesne Univ., 1958, MEd; PA State Univ., 1962. **Orgs.:** ALA. PA LA. Cath. LA. AAUP. Bus. and Prof. Women's Club. **Pubns.:** *Bibliographic and Library Manual* (1953, 1962). **Addr.:** St. Francis College, Pius XII Memorial Library, Loretto, PA 15940.

Tobin, Richard James (My. 4, 1937, Newark, NJ) Ref. Libn. II, Bapst Lib., Boston Coll., 1981–; Spec., Battig Meml. Lib., Univ. of WI, Sheboygan, 1977–81; Asst. Ed., Retrospective Indexing Proj., *The Philosopher's Index,* Phil. Docum. Ctr., 1977–79. **Educ.:** Fordham Univ., 1955–59, BA (Hist.); Univ. of WI, 1970–75, PhD (Phil.), 1978–79, MLS. **Orgs.:** ALA. Amer. Phil. Assn. Amer. Socty. for Aesthetics. **Pubns.:** Jt. auth., *The Philosopher's Index: A Retrospective Index to Non-U.S. English Language Publications from 1940* (1980); jt. auth., *The Philosopher's Index: A Retrospective Index to U.S. Publications from 1940* (1978). **Addr.:** 64 Myrtle St., Boston, MA 02114.

Todd, Alexander W., Jr. (Ap. 14, 1928, Vandalia, IL) Dir., Fountaindale Pub. Lib. Dist., 1975–; Dir., McCowan Meml. Lib., 1971–75. **Educ.:** US Nvl. Acad., 1947–51, BS (Nvl. Sci.); Drexel Univ., 1969–72, MS (LS). **Orgs.:** Libs. Unlimited, NJ: Pres. (1973–74). IL LA: Legis. Dev. Subcom. (1977–80). ALA. Amer. Red Cross. **Activities:** 9; 15, 17, 19; 56 **Addr.:** Fountaindale Public Library District, 300 W. Briarcliff Rd., Bolingbrook, IL 60439.

Todd, Elizabeth Grace (Ag. 6, 1926, Boston, MA) Head, Cat. Div., The Bancroft Lib., 1964–; Head of Adult Srvs., Orange Pub. Lib., 1962–64; Pers. Libn., Univ. of Miami, 1958–62, Catlgr., 1950–58. **Educ.:** Boston Univ., 1944–48, BS (Hist., Educ.); Simmons Coll., 1948–50, BLS. **Orgs.:** CA LA: CA Lcl. Hist. Bibl. Com. (1971–). Frnds. of The Bancroft Lib. Univ. of CA, Berkeley, Women's Fac. Club. CA Hist. Socty. **Activities:** 1; 20, 45, 46; 57, 73, 92 **Addr.:** 1078 Annerley Rd., Piedmont, CA 94610.

Todd, Fred W. (S. 12, 1936, Timpson, TX) Chief Libn., US Air Frc. Sch. of Aerosp. Med., Brooks Air Frc. Base, TX, 1975–; Asst. Libn., Univ. of TX Hlth. Sci. Ctr., San Antonio, 1970–75; Asst. Dir., Indus. Info. Srvs., South. Meth. Univ., 1967–70; Head Libn., Tech. Info. Srv., Stanford Univ. Libs., 1966–67, Asst. Libn., Engin. Lib., 1965–66. **Educ.:** Stephen F. Austin State Univ., 1954–58, BBA (Gen. Bus. Admin.), 1959–60, MA (Eng.); Univ. of TX, Austin, 1963–65, MLS. **Orgs.:** SLA: TX Chap., Bylaws Com. (Ch., 1976–78); Sci.-Tech. Div. (Secy., 1977–79), Nom. Com. (Ch., 1980–81); various other coms. Med. LA: Lcl. Arrange. Com., 73d Anl. Conf. (Asst. to Ch., 1974). Cncl. of Resrch. and Acad. Libs.: Secy. (1980–82); various coms. Hlth. Oriented Libs. of San Antonio: Pres. (1977–78). **Activities:** 4, 12; 17, 24, 34; 58, 80, 91 **Addr.:** Strughold Aeromedical Library, U.S. Air Force School of Aerospace Medicine, Brooks AFB, TX 78235.

Todd, Kay Moller (Ap. 24, 1946, Chicago, IL) Libn., Kilpatrick and Cody, 1972–; Ref. Libn., GA State Lib., 1970–72; Asst. Ref. Libn., Columbia Univ. Law Lib., 1969–70. **Educ.:** New Coll., 1964–67, AB (Liberal Arts); Columbia Univ., 1967–69, MLS. **Orgs.:** AALL: Pubns. Com. (1978); Mem. Com. (1980); Southeast. Chap., Prog. Com. (1980–81), Nom. Com. (1979). Intl. Assn. of Law Libs. SLA. Atlanta Law Libs. Assn.: Pres. (1976). **Activities:** 12; 24; 77 **Addr.:** Kilpatrick and Cody, 100 Peachtree St., Suite 3100, Atlanta, GA 30043.

Todd, Rose-Aimée (N. 23, Winnipeg, MB) Chief Libn., Natl. Film Bd., 1966–; Libn., Law Firm, 1963–66; Libn., Chld. Lib., 1959–63; Soc. Worker, Chld. Aid Socty., 1958–59. **Educ.:** Univ. of MB, 1955–58, BA; McGill Univ., 1961–63, BLS. **Orgs.:** Can. LA. ASTED. SLA. **Activities:** 4; 15, 17, 20; 55, 67, 92 **Addr.:** National Film Board of Canada, Reference Library, P.O. Box 6100, Station A, Montreal, PQ H3C 3H5 Canada.

Todorovich, Divna (Je. 20, 1940, Belgrade, Yugoslavia) Subj. Catlgr., Lib. of Congs., 1968–; Area Chld. Libn., London Boro. of Newham, Eng., 1966–68; Jr. Libn., Elizabeth Pub. Lib., 1965–66. **Educ.:** NY Univ., 1959–62, BA (Eng. Lit.); Rutgers Univ., 1963–65, MLS. **Orgs.:** ALA: ALSC, Toys, Games, and Realia Com. (1977–81). DC LA. Frnds. of IBBY. **Honors:** Phi Beta Kappa, 1962; Sigma Delta Omicron, 1962. **Pubns.:** *Subject Headings for Children's literature* (1969). **Activities:** 4, 9; 20, 21, 48; 55, 67 **Addr.:** 301 G St., S.W., Washington, DC 20024.

Toifel, Peggy White (Ap. 6, 1944, Atlanta, GA) Head, Ref. Dept., Univ. of W. FL, 1972–, Head, ILL, 1970–72; Assoc. Dir., Adult Srvs., Mobile Pub. Lib., 1967–70, Ref. Libn., 1966–67. **Educ.:** Samford Univ., 1962–65, BA (Eng., Fr.); Univ. of NC, 1965–67, MSLS. **Orgs.:** ALA. SELA. FL LA. **Pubns.:** Ed., *West Florida Union List of Serials* (1972, 1976, 1978). **Activities:** 1; 25, 30, 31; 51, 56, 59 **Addr.:** 900 Langley Ave., Pensacola, FL 32504.

Toifel, Ronald C. (Je. 4, 1933, Mobile, AL) Dir. of Curric. Lab., Coord. of Educ. Srvs., Univ. of W. FL, 1969–; Asst. Dir., Gadsden Pub. Lib., 1968–69; Asst. Head of Ref., Head of Circ., Mobile Pub. Lib., 1967–68, Head of Bkmobiles., 1966–67. **Educ.:** MS South. Coll., 1953–57, BS (Geol.); LA State Univ., 1965–66, MS (LS); FL State Univ., 1978–, EdD. **Orgs.:** SELA. FL Assn. for Media in Educ. FL LA. W. FL LA: Pres. (1972–73). Untd. Fac. of FL: Univ. of W. FL Chap., VP (1976–77), Pres. (1981–82). AAUP: Univ. of W. FL Chap. (Secy., 1975–76). **Activities:** 1, 14-Curric. mtrls. lab.; 15, 17, 20; 63 **Addr.:** John C. Pace Library, The University of West Florida, Pensacola, FL 32504.

Tolbert, Jean F. (Ap. 26, 1925, Fernwood, MS) Ref. Libn., Baylor Univ., 1968–, Relig. Libn., 1964–68, Asst. Serials Libn., 1957–64; Jr. Ln., LA State Univ., 1954–57; Asst. Libn., MS Coll., 1951–54. **Educ.:** MS Coll., 1943–47, BA (Hist., Educ.); Baylor Univ., 1962–63 (LS); TX Woman's Univ., 1963–65, MLS, Post-mstrs. std. (LS). **Orgs.:** ALA. SWLA: Coll. & Univ. Interest Grp. (Ch., 1977–78). TX LA: Ref. RT (1967–68); Pubcty. Com. (1977–79). AAUW: Exec. Com. (1976–79); Pres. (1979–80). Delta Kappa Gamma Intl: Soc. Com. (1979–81). **Honors:** Beta Phi Mu, 1976. **Activities:** 1; 31, 39; 75, 90, 92 **Addr.:** 5206 Lake Arrowhead, Waco, TX 76710.

Special Subjects/Services: 50. Adult educ.; 51. Advert./Mktg.; 52. Aerosp.; 53. Agric.; 54. Area std.; 55. Arts/Hum.; 56. Autom.; 57. Bibl./Prtg.; 58. Bio. sci.; 59. Bus./Fin.; 60. Chem.; 61. Copyrt.; 62. Documtn.; 63. Educ.; 64. Engin.; 65. Env.; 66. Eth. grps.; 67. Film; 68. Food/Nutr.; 69. Geneal.; 70. Geo.; 71. Geol.; 72. Handcpd.; 73. Hist.; 74. Int. frdm.; 75. Info. sci.; 76. Insr.; 77. Law; 78. Legis.; 79. Math./Comp. sci.; 80. Med.; 81. Metals; 82. Nat. resrcs.; 83. Newsp.; 84. Nuc. sci.; 85. Oral hist.; 86. Petr./Energy; 87. Pharm.; 88. Phys./Astr./Math.; 89. Readg.; 90. Relig.; 91. Sci./Tech.; 92. Soc. sci.; 93. Telecom.; 94. Transp.; 95. (other).

Toliver, David E. (N. 19, 1948, Chungking, China) Mgr., OL'SAM Proj., Franklin Inst., 1980–; Adj. Prof., Info. Sci., Drexel Univ. 1979–; Sr. Progmr., Anal., Franklin Inst., 1977–80; Progmr., Nixdorf Comps., 1973–75. **Educ.:** Un. Coll., 1966–73, BS (Math.); Drexel Univ., 1975–77, MS (LS). Comp. Socty. Inst. of Electrical and Electronics Engins. **Honors:** Sch. of Lib. and Info. Sci., Drexel Univ., Alice B. Kroeger Awd., 1977. **Pubns.:** "A Program for Machine-Mediated Searching," *Info. Prcs. and Mgt.* (forthcoming); "An Interactive Retrieval Information System," *Personal Comp.* (N. 1979). **Activities:** 14-Resrch. and dev. facility; 41, 46; 56, 75 **Addr.:** Franklin Research Center, 20th and Race St., Philadelphia, PA 19103.

Toll, Morris Mark (Philadelphia, PA) Chief, Lib. Prcs., Sch. Dist. of Philadelphia, 1969–; Acq. Libn., Free Lib. of Philadelphia, 1954–69, Cur., Thea. Col., 1951–53. **Educ.:** Temple Univ., 1946–49, BS (Educ.); Drexel Univ., 1950–51, MSLS. **Orgs.:** ALA. PA LA. **Activities:** 9, 10; 15, 20 **Addr.:** School District of Philadelphia, 734 Schuylkill Ave., Philadelphia, PA 19146.

Tolliver, Don L. (Mr. 11, 1938, Louisville, IL) Asst. Dir., Univ. Lib., Univ. of MI, 1980–; Dean, Lib. and Lrng. Resrcs., Univ. of WI, Whitewater, 1974–80; Head Instr. Media Resrch. Unit, Libs. and AV Ctr., Purdue Univ., 1970–74, Asst. Head, 1969–70, Instr., Instr. Media, 1965–69. **Educ.:** East. IL Univ., 1956–60, BS (Educ.), 1963–64, MS (Educ.); Univ. of IL, 1965–66, MS (LS); Purdue Univ., 1966–70, PhD (Admin.). **Orgs.:** ALA. ASIS. WI LA: Bd. of Dirs. (1979–). WI Assn. of Acad. Libns.: Ch. (1980). **Pubns.:** "On Scaling Down MRAP for Smaller Libraries," *Jnl. of Acad. Libnshp.* (Ja. 1976); "Citizens May Use Any Tax-Supported Library," *WI Lib. Bltn.* (D. 1976); jt. auth., "Overdue Policies: A Comparison of Alternatives," *Coll. & Resrch. Libs.* (1974); jt. auth., "A General Statistical Model for Increasing Effeciency and Confidence in Manual Data Collection Systems through Sampling," *Jnl. of Amer. Socty. for Info. Sci.* (1974); jt. auth., "The Ohio College Library Center System: A Study of Factors Affecting the Adaptation of Libraries to On-Line Networks," *Lib. Tech. Rpts.* (1976); various other articles, mono. **Activities:** 1; 17 **Addr.:** 818 Hatcher Library, University of Michigan, Ann Arbor, MI 48109.

Tollman, Thomas A. (Mr. 19, 1939, Omaha, NE) Ch., Ref. Dept., Univ. of NE, Omaha, 1979–; Visit. Instr., Univ. of AZ, 1978–79; Ref. Libn., NW MO State Univ., 1974–77; Asst. Dean of the Coll., Carleton Coll., 1968–73; Peace Corps Volun., Colombia, 1962–64. **Educ.:** Carleton Coll., 1956–60, BA (Hist.); Univ. of Chicago, 1964–68, MA (Educ.); Univ. of MN, 1973–74, MA (LS). **Orgs.:** ALA. NE LA. Mt. Plains LA. Phi Delta Kappa: Chap. VP (1975–77). **Honors:** Beta Phi Mu. **Activities:** 1, 11; 15, 31, 39; 54, 63, 92 **Addr.:** 2121 S. 84th St., Omaha, NE 68124.

Tolmachev, Mirjana (Knezevic) (O. 5, 1918, Trogir, Yugoslavia) Actg. Dir., Gen. Lib., PA State Lib., 1979–, Coord., User Srvs., 1974–79, Ref. Libn., 1965–74. **Educ.:** Univ. of Belgrade, 1951–55, BS (Pol. Sci., Econ.); Drexel Univ., 1964–65, MS (LS). **Orgs.:** PA LA. ALA. AAUW. **Addr.:** 2467 Mercer St., Harrisburg, PA 17104.

Tolman, Lorraine E. (Je. 14, 1920, Cambridge, MA) Assoc. Prof., Sch. of Educ., Boston Univ., 1949–; Libn., Worcester State Tchrs. Coll., 1947–49. **Educ.:** Radcliffe, 1939–43, BA (Eng.); Univ. of South. CA, 1948, BS (LS), 1948, MEd; Boston Univ., 1958, DEd. **Orgs.:** MA LA. New Eng. Educ. Media Assn.: Pres. (1974–75). AECT. ALA. **Pubns.:** "High Interest - Low Vocabulary Reading Materials," *Jnl. of Educ.* (Ap. 1967). **Activities:** 5, 10; 26, 32 **Addr.:** 5 Fife Rd., Wellesley Hills, MA 02181.

Tolzmann, Don Heinrich (Ag. 12, 1945, Granite Falls, MN) Ref. Libn., Biblgphr., Grmn., Phil., Univ. of Cincinnati Libs., 1974–. **Educ.:** Univ. of MN, 1963–68, BA (Grmn.); Untd. Theo. Semy. and Northwest. Luth. Theo. Semy., 1968–72, MDiv.; Univ. of KY, 1972–73, MA (LS); Univ. of Cincinnati, 1977– (Hist.). **Orgs.:** ALA. PLA: Multiling. Srvs. Com. (1977–79). Socty. for Grmn.–Amer. Std: Secy. (1977–81); Pres. (1981–). **Honors:** Socty. for Grmn.–Amer. Std., Merit of Achvmt., 1973; Swedish Pioneer Hist. Socty., Sec. Prize in Essay Contest, 1974. **Pubns.:** *German-Americana, A Bibliography* (1975); *America's German Heritage* (1976); *German-American Literature* (1977); "The Minnesota German Book Trade, 1850–1935," *Amer. Bk. Collector* (1974); "The St. Louis Free Congregation Library: A Study of German-American Reading Interests," *MO Hist. Review* (1976). **Activities:** 1; 15, 39; 66 **Addr.:** Reference–Bibliographic Services Dept., Central Library, University of Cincinnati, Cincinnati, OH 45221.

Tom, Chow Loy (Hilo, HI) Assoc. Prof., Univ. of Denver Grad. Sch. of Libnshp. and Info. Mgt., 1969–; Asst. Prof., Coord. LS Prog., Univ. of HI, 1961–68; Lib. Supvsr., Instr., Univ. of HI HS, 1959–61; Actg. Libn., Instr., Univ. of IL HS, 1956–57; Libn., Ref., YA, Chld. Dept., Allentown Pub. Lib., 1945–46; Libn., Armed Srvs. YMCA, Honolulu, 1943–44; Sch. Libn., HI Dept. of Educ., 1942–59. **Educ.:** Univ. of HI, 1937–41, EdB (Educ.); Univ. of IL, 1944–45, BS (LS), 1952–53, MS (LS); OH State Univ., 1965–68, PhD (Educ.). **Orgs.:** ALA: AASL, Treatment of Minorities in Textbks. and Other Instr. Mtrls. Com. (1970–75); Task Frc. on Eng. Speakers of Other Langs. (1978–79); Early Childhood Com. (1980–); ALSC; ASCLA; ACRL; LITA; RASD; YASD; various RTS. HI Assn. of Sch. Libns.: Pres. (1962). Intl. Assn. of Sch. Libnshp. Natl. Micro. Assn.: Rocky Mt. Chap., Bd. of Dirs. (1981–). Various other orgs. AAUP. Assn. for Childhood Educ. Intl. Natl. Cncl. of Tchrs. of Eng. Natl. Educ. Assn. **Honors:** Beta Phi Mu, 1949; Pi Gamma Mu, 1940; Phi Kappa Phi, 1941. **Pubns.:** "An Experimental Program in School Library Media Education, 1971-73: 1974 Status Report," *Evaluation of Alternative Curricula: Approaches to School Library Media Education* (1975); jt. auth., "An Experimental Program in School Library Media Education, 1971–73," *Curriculum Alternatives: Experiments in School Library Media Education* (1974); "Paul Revere Rides Ahead: Poems Teachers Read to Pupils in the Middle Grades," *Lib. Qtly.* (Ja. 1973). **Activities:** 10, 11; 21, 26, 32; 63, 93, 95-Chld. lit. **Addr.:** University of Denver Graduate School of Librarianship and Information Management, Denver, CO 80208.

Tomaselli, Mary Frances (My. 25, 1944, New York, NY) Assoc. Systs. Ofcr., Untd. Nations Info. Syst. Unit, 1979–; Indexing Systs. Consult., Ctr. for Arts Info., 1977–; Indxr./Consult., Index Dsgn., Macy Fndn., 1976–77; Libn./Consult., Info. Srv., NY State Assn. for Retarded Chld., Inc., 1975–. **Educ.:** Queens Coll., CUNY, 1962–66, BA (Comm. Arts), 1972–75, MLS. **Orgs.:** Amer. Socty. of Indxrs.: Com. on Indxr. Econ. (Ch., 1975–); Secy. (1977–79); Mid-Win. Mtg., Prog. Plng. Com. and Panel Ch. (1977); Treas. (1979–81). SLA. ASIS. ALA. Ctr. for Arts Info. Natl. Endow. for the Hum.: Resrch. Mtrls. Prog., Reviewer/Eval. **Honors:** Beta Phi Mu, 1978. **Pubns.:** "Freelance Indexing," *What Else Can You Do With A Library Degree?* (1980); "American Heritage Index," *Amer. Heritage Mag.* (1975–); indxr., *The Magnificent Builders* (1978); indxr., *Infections in the Abnormal Host* (1980). **Activities:** 12; 24, 30; 55, 72, 80 **Addr.:** 146-05 14th Ave., Whitestone, NY 11357.

Tomasulo, Patricia A. (Ag. 16, 1953, New York, NY) Libn., Dept. of Psyt. Lib., Downstate Med. Coll., Kings Cnty. Hosp., 1977–. **Educ.:** Hunter Coll., 1971–75, BA, magna cum laude (Fr.); Pratt Inst., 1975–77, MLS, 1977–. **Orgs.:** Med. LA: NY Reg. Grp., Hosplty. Com. (1978–). Brooklyn–Queens–Staten Island Hlth. Scis. Lib. Grp.: Shared Resrcs. Com. (1978–79). SLA. **Activities:** 12; 15, 20, 39; 80 **Addr.:** 46 W. 76th St., New York, NY 10023.

Tomberlin, Irma R. (Ag. 23, 1920, Baton Rouge, LA) Boyd Prof. of LS, Univ. of OK, 1957–, Asst. Ref. Libn., 1952–57, Art Libn., 1948–52; Resrch. Libn., Esso Labs., 1944–45; Libn., Natchitoches Par. Lib., 1943–44; Asst. Libn., Bossier Par. Lib., 1941–43. **Educ.:** LA State Univ., 1936–41, BA (Eng.), BS (LS); Univ. of OK, 1955–58, MLS. **Orgs.:** SLA: OK Chap. (Pres., 1977). SWLA: Schol. Com. (1973–74). ALA: Chap. Cnclr. (1972–76); Chap. Rel. Com. (1972–76); various other coms. OK LA: Secy. (1951–52); VP (1956–57); Pres. (1957–58); Exec. Bd. (1951–53, 1956–59, 1972–76); various coms. Various other orgs. **Honors:** Phi Kappa Phi; Univ. of OK, Baldwin Awd. for Tchg. Excel., 1972; OK LA, Disting. Srv. Awd., 1976; Univ. of OK, David R. Boyd Disting. Profshp., 1978. **Pubns.:** Jt. auth., *Manual for the Organization of Library Materials I* (1972, 1974); "Oklahoma: State Report," *ALA Yrbk.* (1976–80); jt. auth., "Government Documents Practicum," *Gvt. Pubns. Review* (Win. 1977–78); "Graduate Education for Librarianship at the University of Oklahoma," *OK Libn.* (Ap. 1973); "Organizing Photographs...," *AK Libs.* (Je. 1978); various ERIC docums. **Activities:** 11; 20, 29 **Addr.:** 825 W. Timberdell, Norman, OK 73069.

Tomcak, Jacqueline (D. 1, 1926, St. Louis, MO) Coord./Supvsr., Lib. Tech. Srvs., Shawnee Missn. Pub. Schs., 1968–. **Educ.:** Lindenwood Coll., 1945–47; Univ. of NE, 1947–49, AB (Hist., Eng.); Emporia State Univ., 1968–72, MLS; Univ. of KS, 1973–75, Admin. Cert. **Orgs.:** KS Assn. of Sch. Libns.: Treas. (1979–80). ALA. KS State Lib. Networking: COM Task Frc. (1980). KS LA. KS State Media Dirs. Assn.: Secy.–Treas. (1980–81). Various other orgs. AAUW. Univ. of KS Alum. Assn. Univ. of NE Alum. Assn. Frnds. of the Lib. Various other orgs. **Pubns.:** "Shawnee Mission's Cataloging and Processing of Non-Book Materials," *Mt. Plains* (1972); jt. auth., "On-Line Cataloging: An Elementary Library Project," *Jnl. of Lib. Autom.* (Mr. 1971). **Activities:** 10; 17, 20, 46; 56 **Addr.:** 8711 Meadow Ln., Leawood, KS 66206.

Tomer, Christinger (Jl. 8, 1949, Lorain, OH) Asst. Prof., Case West. Rsv. Univ., 1978–, Lectr., 1976–78; Ref. Libn., U.S. Nvl. War Coll., 1973–75; Ref. Libn., Cuyahoga Cnty. Pub. Lib., 1972–73. **Educ.:** Coll. of Wooster, 1967–71, BA (Eng.); Case West. Rsv. Univ., 1972–78, MS, PhD (LS). **Orgs.:** ALA. **Pubns.:** "Identification, Evaluation, and Selection of Documents for Preservation," *Col. Mgt.* (1979). **Activities:** 23, 39; 57 **Addr.:** School of Library Science, Case Western Reserve University, Cleveland, OH 44106.

Tomlin, Ronald E. (Ja. 1, 1947, Vicksburg, MS) Dir., Div. of Recs. Mgt., MS Dept. of Arch. and Hist., 1981–, Chief, 1978–81. Archvst. II, 1974–78, Archvst. I, 1973–74, Resrch. Asst., 1973. **Educ.:** Univ. of the S., 1965–69, BA (Hist.); Univ. of MS, 1975–77, MLS; Amer. Univ., Mod. Arch. Inst., 1974, Cert. (Arch. Admin.); various crs. **Orgs.:** SAA: Com. on Ref. and Access Policies (1978); Descr. of Arch. and Mss. Prof. Afnty. Grp. (1979–80). Socty. of MS Archvsts.: Exec. Dir. (1978–). MS LA: MS GODORT (Ch., 1979); Arch./Hist. Com. (Ch., 1980). Assn. of Recs. Mgrs. and Admins.: Jackson Chap., Ch., Legis. Com. (1979–80), Bd. of Dirs. (1980–81), VP (1981–82). Natl. Trust for Hist. Prsrvn. MS Hist. Socty. Amer. Assn. for State and Lcl. Hist. **Pubns.:** *Guide to Official Records in the Mississippi Department of Archives and History* (1975); contrib. ed., *Eudora Welty Newsletter* (1976–81); indxr., *Jnl. of MS Hist.* **Activities:** 2; 15, 17, 33; 61, 69, 75 **Addr.:** Mississippi Dept. of Archives & History, 929 High St., Jackson, MS 39202.

Tomlinson, Elizabeth K. (Ap. 19, 1914, Brooklyn, NY) Head, Coord. of Sci. Libs., Carleton/St. Olaf Colls., 1979–; Head, White Meml. Lib., Univ. of MD, 1968–79; Tech. Libn., Scott Paper Co., 1966–68; Tech. Libn., Houdry Process and Chem. Co., 1960–66. **Educ.:** Birmingham-South. Coll., 1950–52, BA (Eng. Lit); Rutgers Univ., 1959–61, MLS. **Orgs.:** SLA. OLUG. Amer. Chem. Socty.: Div. of Chem. Info. **Pubns.:** "Goldmining in the Library," *Chem.* (F. 1974). **Activities:** 1, 12; 15, 17, 39; 58, 60, 88 **Addr.:** Science Library, Carleton College, Northfield, MN 55057.

Tommey, Richard Joseph (Je. 9, 1924, Carnegie, PA) Libn., Gen. Atomic Co., 1960–; Instr., San Diego Cmnty. Coll., Evening Coll., 1977–; Libn., Nuc. Fuels, Olin Mathieson, 1957–60; Ref. Libn., Ctrl. Intelligence Agency, 1951–57; ILL Libn., Cath. Univ. of Amer., 1950–51; YA Libn., Enoch Pratt Lib., 1949–50. **Educ.:** Tarleton Coll., 1943 (Engin.); Loyola Coll., Baltimore, MD, 1946–49, PhB (Hist.); Cath. Univ. of Amer., 1950–51, MS (LS). **Orgs.:** SLA: Chap. Pres. (1964–65); Chap. VP, Bltn. Ed. (1962–63). San Diego Lib. Metro: VP (1979–80). Natl. Mgt. Assn.: Gen. Atomic Co. Chap. (Secy., 1979–80). **Activities:** 4, 12; 15, 17, 39; 64, 81, 84 **Addr.:** 6073 Avenida Chamnez, La Jolla, CA 92037.

Tompkins, Philip (O. 11, 1932, Toledo, OH) Assoc. Dir. of Libs., Univ. of MO, Kansas City, 1974–, Asst. Dir. of Libs., 1973–74, Chief of Pub. Srvs., 1971–74. **Educ.:** St. Meinrad Coll., 1950–54, BA (Phil.); Medvl. Inst., Notre Dame, 1956–57 (Med. Std.); Kenrick Theo. Semy., 1957–60, BD (Theo.); Univ. of MO, Kansas City, 1963–65, MA (Hist.); Univ. of MO, Columbia, 1970–71, MLS. **Orgs.:** ALA. MO LA: Pres. (1980–81). KS City Metro. Lib. Netwk.: Pres. (1978–80). KS City Metro. Info. Netwk.: Proj. Dir. (1976–). Socty. of Archit. Histns. Univ. of MO Kansas City Frnds. of the Lib. **Honors:** Beta Phi Mu, 1971; Phi Kappa Phi, 1975. **Pubns.:** Ed., *Cooperative Collection Development for Multitype Libraries* (1981); ed., *William Morris in Private Press and Limited Edition* (1980); *Proceedings of the Midwest Regional Conference on a National Periodicals Center* (1979); jt. auth., "The Urban University Library: Effectiveness Models for 1989," *New Horizons for Academic Libraries* (1979); "Metropolitan Multitype Library Cooperative Online Searching Networks," *Lib. Jnl. Spec. Rpts. #4* (Ja. 1978). **Activities:** 1; 17, 34, 39, 46 **Addr.:** General Library, University of Missouri-Kansas City, 5100 Rockhill Rd., Kansas City, MO 64110.

Toms, Evelyn Woodward (F. 16, 1921, Waycross, GA) Instr. in Lib. Media and Coll. of Educ. Lrng. Mtrls. Ctr., Univ. of WI, Whitewater, 1967–; Instr., Class., Texas Women's Univ., 1974; Instr., LS, Berea Coll., 1966–67; Sch. Lib. Consult., Grady Cnty. Schs., 1962–66; Elem. Lib. Consult., Thomas Cnty. Schs., 1960–62; HS Libn., Cairo HS, 1956–66; Eng. Tchr., Cook HS, 1952–56; Eng. Tchr., Nahunta HS, 1951–52. **Educ.:** Valdosta State Coll., 1941, AB (Art); FL State Univ., 1958, MA (LS); Univ. of CO, Boulder, 1978, DEd. **Orgs.:** ALA. AECT. WI LA. WI AV Assn. Socty. of Amer. Poets. **Pubns.:** Jt. auth., *The Wisconsin Library Media Skills Guide* (1979). **Activities:** 1; 15, 20, 26; 63, 72 **Addr.:** University of Wisconsin, Library Media Program, Whitewater, WI 53190.

Toms, Merrill F. (Jl. 24, 1929, Kansas City, MO) Branch Supvsr., Kansas City Pub. Lib., 1975–, Admin. Asst., 1970–75, Ref. Libn., First Asst., 1967–70. **Educ.:** Univ. of MO, Columbia, 1948–50, BA (Span.); Emporia State Univ., 1966–67, MLS; Armed Frcs. Info. Sch., 1951, Cert. **Orgs.:** MO LA: Lib. Dev. Com. (1974–75). SLA: Lcl. Chap. (Pres., 1970–71). Natl. Micro. Assn: Lcl. Chap. (Pres., 1979–80). Interamer. Club. **Activities:** 9; 17, 33, 39; 54, 59, 93 **Addr.:** Branch Supervisor, Kansas City Missouri Public Library, 311 E. 12th, Kansas City, MO 64106.

Toney, Stephen Ross (N. 20, 1946, Pigeon Cove, MA) Mgr. for Systs. and Plng., Smithsonian Inst., 1978–; Progmr., Anal., Lib. of Congs., 1975–78; Catlgr., Ref. Libn., King Cnty. Lib. Syst., 1973–75. **Educ.:** Antioch Coll., 1964–69, MA (Art); Univ. of BC, 1973–75, MLS. **Orgs.:** ALA. DC LA. Amer. Mgt. Assn. **Activities:** 4, 12; 17, 19, 41, 49-Systs. analysis; 56 **Addr.:** Smithsonian Institution Libraries, Washington, DC 20560.

Tong, Josephine S. (Je. 17, 1949, Hong Kong, China) Mtrls. Resrc. Ctr. Libn., AB Educ., 1980–; Head, Tech. Srvs., AB Educ. Lib., 1976–80; AV Libn., AB Educ., 1975–76. **Educ.:** Brandon Univ., 1969–72, BA (Psy.); Univ. of AB, 1974–75, BLS, 1980, Tchg. Cert. **Orgs.:** Edmonton LA: VP (1980–81); Pubcty. Cnclr. (1979–80). AB Gvt. Lib. Cncl.: Staff Dev. Com. (1979–80). LA AB. **Activities:** 12, 13; 17; 63, 72 **Addr.:** Materials

PROFESSIONAL ACTIVITIES: Institutions: 1. Acad. lib.; 2. Arch.; 3. Assn.; 4. Fed./Gvt. lib.; 5. Inst. lib.; 6. Mfr./Suppl.; 7. Milit. lib.; 8. Musm.; 9. Pub. lib.; 10. Sch. lib.; 11. Sch. of lib. sci.; 12. Spec. lib.; 13. State lib.; 14. (other). **Functions/Activities:** 15. Acq./Col. dev.; 16. Adult srvs.; 17. Admin.; 18. Apprais.; 19. Archit./Bldgs.; 20. Cat./Class.; 21. Chld. srvs.; 22. Circ.; 23. Cons./Pres.; 24. Consult.; 25. Cont. ed.; 26. Educ. lib. sci.; 27. Ext. srvs.; 28. Fund/Grants; 29. Gvt. pubs.; 30. Indx./Abs.; 31. Instr. lib. use; 32. Media srvs.; 33. Micro.; 34. Netwks./Coop.; 35. Persnl.; 36. PR; 37. Publshg.; 38. Recs. mgt.; 39. Ref. srvs.; 40. Repro.; 41. Resrch.; 42. Review.; 43. Secur.; 44. Serials; 45. Spec. col.; 46. Tech. srvs.; 47. Trustees/Bds.; 48. YA srvs.; 49. (other).

Resource Centre, Alberta Education, 11160 Jasper Ave., 4th Floor, W. Tower, Edmonton, AB T8N 0W9 Canada.

Tonkery, Thomas Daniel (Dan) (Jl. 21, 1946, Fairmont, WV) Assoc. Univ. Libn., Tech. Srvs., Univ. of CA, Los Angeles, 1979–, Lectr., Grad. Sch. of Lib. and Info. Sci., 1979–; Chief, Tech. Srvs. Div., Natl. Lib. of Med., 1976–79, Deputy Chief, Tech. Srvs. Div., 1976–78, Head, Sel., Acq., 1973–76, Spec. Asst. to Assoc. Dir., 1972–73, Netwk. Dev. Staff, 1971–72. **Educ.:** David Lipscomb Coll., 1964–68, BA (Bio.); Univ. of IL, 1969–70, MA (LS). **Orgs.:** ALA. Hlth. Sci. Comms. Assn. Med. LA. CLENE: Bd. of Dirs. (1979–82). Data Prcs. Mgt. Assn. **Honors:** Natl. Inst. of Hlth., Awd. of Merit, 1977. **Activities:** 1, 4; 17, 25, 46; 56, 75, 93 **Addr.:** Technical and Bibliographical Product Services, University of California, 405 Hilgard Ave., Los Angeles, CA 90024.

Toombs, Kenneth Eldridge (Ag. 25, 1928, Colonial Heights, VA) Dir. of Libs., Univ. of SC, 1967–; Dir. of Libs., Prof., LS, Univ. of Southwest. LA, 1963–67, Asst. Dir. in Charge of Pub. Srvs., 1962–63; Mem. of Staff and Fac., LA State Univ., 1955–63. **Educ.:** TN Wesleyan Coll., 1950, AA; TN Polytech. Inst., 1951, BS; Univ. of VA, 1955, MA (Hist.); Rutgers Univ., 1956, MLS; various crs. **Orgs.:** SC LA: Pres. (1976); Exec. Bd. (1981). Assn. of Southeast. Resrch. Libs.: Ch. (1973–75). Southeast. Lib. Netwk.: Vice Ch. (1973–74); Ch. (1974–75); Exec. Bd. (1973–76). SELA: Exec. Bd. (1981). Other orgs. Univ. of South. CA Educ. Fndn.: Bd. of Dirs. (1975–). Wesley Fndn.: Treas. Amer. Fld. Srvs. Intl. Schols.: VP; Bd. of Dirs. AAUP: Secy. various other orgs. **Honors:** SELA, Rothrock Awd., 1978. **Pubns.:** Managing Ed., *SWLA Jnl.* (1963–67); "Intertype Library Cooperation for Large Academic Libraries," *Multitype Library Cooperation* (1977); "University of South Carolina Libraries," *Encyc. of Lib. and Info. Sci.* (1979); ed., *Bltn. LA LA* (1959–62); ed., *SWLA* (1963–67); adv. bd., *Ling. Atlas;* various articles. **Activities:** 1; 17, 19, 24, 28; 56, 70, 85 **Addr.:** 16 Garden Springs Rd., Columbia, SC 29209.

Tooth, John Ernest (Ag. 31, 1947, Winnipeg, MB) Head Libn., MB Dept. of Educ. Lib., 1976–; Tchr.-Libn., St. James Collegiate, 1972–76. **Educ.:** Univ. of Winnipeg, 1966–70, BA, hons (Hist.); Univ. of MB, 1970–71, Cert. (Educ), 1971–73, BEd (Sch. Libnshp.), 1980, MEd (Hist. of Educ.). **Orgs.:** MB LA: Treas. (1978–79); Budget Com. (Ch., 1978–79). Can. LA. Can. Sch. LA: VP (1981–82). MB Sch. Lib. AV Assn.: Gvt. Resrcs. Com. (Ch., 1974–79); Conf. Com. (Ch., 1974–75); VP (1975); Pres. (1975–77). **Pubns.:** *Looking For Manitoba Government Publications* (1978); *Education in Nicaragua* (1979). **Activities:** 12, 13; 25, 29, 32; 63 **Addr.:** 361 Wales Ave., Winnipeg, MB R2M 2S8 Canada.

Tope, Diana Ray (D. 13, 1938, Jacksonville, FL) Dir., Cherokee Reg. Lib., 1981–; Dir., Lib., Robeson Cnty. Pub. Lib., 1975–81; Coord., Srvs., Sandhill Reg. Lib. Syst., 1973–75; Branch Libn., Eden Pub. Lib., 1971–73. **Educ.:** Duke Univ., 1956–59, BA (Eng.); Emory Univ., 1970–71, MLS; NC State Univ., 1976–79, MEd (Adult and Cmnty. Coll. Educ.). **Orgs.:** ALA: Pub. Lib. Systs. Sect., Interlib. Coop. Com. (Ch., 1981). SELA. NC LA: Pub. Lib. Sect., Litcy. Com. (Ch., 1979–81). NC Pub. Lib. Dirs. Assn. GA LA: Int. Frdm. Com. (1982–83). Various other orgs. **Pubns.:** "Public Libraries and Adult Education: Some Representative Programs," *NC Libs.* (Spr. 1979); assoc. ed., contrib. writer, *Robeson County: A Life of Quality* (1981). **Addr.:** Cherokee Regional Library, Box 707, LaFayette, GA 30728.

Topper, Judith M. (New York, NY) Hlth. Sci. Libn., Lawrence Hosp., 1974–; Med. Libn., Beekman Downtown Hosp., 1972–74; Asst. Med. Libn., Jamaica Hosp., Jamaica, NY, 1972. **Educ.:** Barnard Coll., BA (Eng., Psy.); Long Island Univ., MSLS; Med. LA, Cert. **Orgs.:** Med. LA: Com. on Hosp. Lib. Stans. (1978–81); Nom. Com. (1980); Pubns. Panel (1981). Hlth. Info. Libs. of Westchester: Pres. (1977–78); NY Reg. Grp., Exec. Com. (1978–80); Nom. Com. (1977–78); *Bltn.* Consult. Ed. (1981). **Pubns.:** "Management and use of library materials," *Hospital Library Management* (forthcoming); jt. auth., "JCAH accreditation and the hospital library: a guide for librarians," *Bltn. of the Med. LA* (Ap. 1980); "Hospitals as centers for consumer health information," *Bltn. of the Amer. Socty. for Info. Sci.* (Ap. 1978). **Activities:** 5, 12; 15, 17, 25; 80, 87, 92 **Addr.:** 880 5th Ave., New York, NY 10021.

Torkelson, Norma Ruth (Mr. 24, 1928, Hill City, KS) Chief, Lib. Srv., Vets. Admin., 1976–; Head Med. Libn., TX Dept. of Mental Hlth. & Retardation, 1975–76; Instr., Univ. of TX Grad. Sch. of LS, 1976; Chief, Ctrl. Ofc., TX Dept. of Mental Hlth., 1970–75; Head Libn., Vetny. Med. Lib., KS State Univ., 1967–69. **Educ.:** KS State Univ., 1946–50, BS (Home Econ.); Univ. of TX, 1972, MLS; Med. LA 1975, Cert. **Orgs.:** ALA: Netwks. Inst. (1974). SLA: Heart of Amer. Chap., Empl. Com. (Ch., 1978). Med. LA. AAUW. First Bapt. Church. 4-H Leader. Cub Scout Den Mother. Phi Kappa Phi, 1950; Omnicron Nu, 1950. **Pubns.:** "SDI as a Control of Information Overload," *Proc. of the Amer. Socty. for Info. Sci.* (1973). **Activities:** 4, 12; 15, 17, 35; 80, 91, 95-Psyt. **Addr.:** Library Service, Veterans Administration Medical Center, 2200 Gage Blvd, Topeka, KS 66622.

Torkington, Roy B. (Ja. 10, 1940, Rochester, NY) Asst. VP, Secur. Pac. Natl. Bank, 1980–; Syst. Anal., Yale Univ. Lib., 1979–80; Syst. Anal., Intl. Telecom. Un., 1978–79; Syst. Anal., Intl. Labor Ofc., 1973–77; Head, Lib. Systs. Dept., Univ. of CA, San Diego, 1970–73; Syst. Anal., LC MARC Dev. Ofc., 1969–70; Spec. Rcrt., Lib. of Congs., 1968–69; Syst. Anal., Univ. of CA, Berkeley, Inst. of Lib. Resrch., 1968. **Educ.:** Yale Univ., 1957–61 (Phys.); Univ. of CA, Berkeley, 1963–65, BA (Hist.), 1967–68, MLS (Libnshp.). **Pubns.:** "MARC and Its Application to Library Automation," *Advncs. in Libnshp.* (1974); "Cumulating the Supplements to the Seventh Edition of LC Subject Headings," *Jnl. of Lib. Autom.* (D. 1973). **Activities:** 1, 4; 33, 34, 46; 56, 75, 93 **Addr.:** 3525 Buena Vista, Glendale, CA 91208.

Torok, Andrew George (F. 10, 1944, Budapest, Hungary) Assoc. Prof., North. IL Univ., 1973–; Instr., Cuyahoga Cmnty. Coll., 1970–73; Ctr. for Documtn. and Comm. Resrch., Case West. Rsv. Univ., 1968–70. **Educ.:** Univ. of VT, 1962–64, BA (Chem.); Case West. Rsv. Univ., 1965–67, MSLS; Cleveland State Univ., 1967–68, MS (Chem.); Case West. Rsv. Univ., 1968–73, PhD (Lib. and Info. Sci.). **Orgs.:** ALA: RTSD, Educ. Com. (1978–) Reprodct. of Lib. Mtrls. Sect., Policy and Resrch. Com. (1978–); ALA Publshg. Com., Glossary subcom. (1978–). ASIS. AALS. IL LA. **Pubns.:** *Micrographics Education for Librarians* (1978); "Computer Output Microfilm: Technological Implications for Information Management," *Procs. of ASIS Anl. Mtg.* (1977); various other procs. articles. **Activities:** 11; 26, 33, 41; 56, 75, 91 **Addr.:** Northern Illinois University, Library Science Dept., DeKalb, IL 60115.

Torok, Stephen, Sr. (Ag. 2, 1915, Budapest, Hungary) Libn., Coord. of Spec. Proj., SUNY, Oswego, 1966–; Head, Bibl. Srvs., Univ. of VT, Med. Sch., 1963–66; Instr., Admin. Asst., Youngstown State Univ., 1958–63. **Educ.:** State Tchr. Inst., Budapest, 1929–34, Dip. (Elem. Educ.); Cath. Tchrs. Inst., 1934–36, Dip. (Phil.); Penn State Univ., 1955–58, Cert. (Metallurgy); West. Rsv. Univ., 1959–60, MSLS; Case West. Rsv. Univ., 1963, Cert. (Med. Libn.); SUNY, Oswego, 1969–70, MA (Mod. European Hist.); SUNY, Geneseo, 1973–76, 6th Yr. Cert. (LS). **Orgs.:** N. Country 3 R's Resrch. Cncl.: Microfilming and Prog. Com. (1969–81). SUNY LA: Grants and Prof. Dev. Com. (1973–80). NY LA: GODORT (Coord., 1973–80). AAUP. Save Our Shores. Eth. Citizens' Cncl. of Oswego. **Pubns.:** *The Other Catholics* (1978); *Catholics Hungarians in North America* (1978); *Proceedings of the Second International Government Documents Workshop* (1978); "Microform Utilization in Europe," *Jnl. of Micro.* (1976); various articles, reviews, sps. **Activities:** 1; 24, 26, 33; 62, 66, 75 **Addr.:** 11 W. 4th St., Oswego, NY 13126.

Torres, Leida I. (N. 10, 1949, Santurce, PR) Reg. Libn., PR Reg. Lib. for the Blind and Phys. Handcpd., 1978–; Acq. Libn., Interamer. Univ., 1977–78; Prof., Spec. Educ., PR Jr. Coll., 1977–78; Reg. Libn., PR Reg. Lib. for the Blind and Phys. Handcpd., 1974–77; Asst. Dir., Head Tech. Srvs., Univ. of the Sacred Heart, 1973–74. **Educ.:** Univ. of PR, 1967–71, BA (Soc. Sc.), 1972–73, MLS; Lib. of Congs., 1974, Trng. in Lib. Srvs. for the Handcpd.; various crs. in spec. educ. **Orgs.:** PR Socty. of Libns.: Lib. Week Exec. Dir. (1975); Pubns. Com. (1975, 1977). Lib. of Congs./Natl. Lib. Srv. for the Blind and Phys. Handcpd.: Ad-hoc Com. on Span. Dev. Col. (1977–). Assn. of Ex-Alum. of the Grad. Sch. of Libnshp.: Pres. Mem. Com. (1978); Pres. PR Com. (1979–80). PR Socty. for the Prevention of Blindness: Prog. Com. (VP, Pres., 1977); Bd. of Dirs. (1979–80). Com. of the Blind Musicians Fest. Assn. for the Advantage of the Blind and Visually Handcpd. PR Cncl. of the Blind. **Honors:** Assn. for the Advantage of the Blind, Extraordinary Help to the Blind, 1976; PR Socty. of Libns., Recog. of Participation. **Pubns.:** *La Realidad de P.R., lista de tesis presentadas enla U.P.R., desde 1929 hasta 1974* (1973); "Library Services for the Handicapped in P.R.," *Dikta* (Spr. 1976); "What it means to be a librarian for the handicapped in P.R.," *Dikta* (Spr. 1977); "La lectura es para todos y Reading is for everybody" *Carta Informativa ACURIL* (Jan.–Je. 1976); "Servicios bibliotecarios para impedidos," *ACURIL Nsltr.* (1976); various bks., articles, slide shows. **Activities:** 9, 12; 16, 17, 21; 50, 72, 89 **Addr.:** Box 5063, Pta. de Tierra Sta., San Juan, PR 00906.

Torres-Tapia, Manuel Antonio (Ag. 18, 1935, Aibonito, PR) Libn. V, Legis. Lib. of PR, 1967–; Dir., Bkmobile. Srvs., San Juan, Dept. of Educ., 1963–66; Libn. I, Carnegie Lib., San Juan, 1962–63; Sec. Sch. Tchr., 1959–62. **Educ.:** Univ. of PR, 1953–59, BA (Hum., Fine Arts), 1973, MLA, MLS. **Orgs.:** SBPR: Legis. Com.; Lcl. of Directive and Cncl. Assn. de Bibtcrs. de Derecho, San Juan. Coop. de Credito EL Capitolio, San Juan. Coop. de Con. Coop. Rio Piedras. **Pubns.:** *El Ombudsman - Cuaderno Bibliográfico de la Sociedad de Bibliotecarios de Puerto Rico* (1978). **Activities:** 4, 5; 15, 20, 24; 57, 77 **Addr.:** T. Aguilar 760 Los Maestros, Rio Piedras, PR 00923.

Toscano, Lynn Schweitzer (Je. 26, 1947, Milwaukee, WI) Interim Cur., Immigration Hist. Resrch. Ctr., Univ. of MN, 1978–81, Resrch. Fellow, 1974–78; Resrch. Spec., Soc. Welfare Hist. Arch., Univ. of MN, 1972–73. **Educ.:** Univ. of WI, Milwaukee, 1965–69, BA (Italian); Rutgers Univ., 1969–72, MA (Italian). **Orgs.:** SAA. Amer. Italian Hist. Assn. **Pubns.:** *The Italian American Collection* (1977); "The Foreign Language Information Service," "The Common Council for American Unity," and "The American Council for Nationalities Service," *The Greenwood Encyc. of Amer. Insts.: Soc. Srv. Orgs.* (1978). **Activities:** 2; 15, 17, 23; 66 **Addr.:** E. 1926 Joseph Ave., Spokane, WA 99207.

Totten, Herman Lavon (Ap. 10, 1938, Van Alstyne, TX) Assoc. Dean, Prof., Sch. of Lib. and Info. Sci., N. TX State Univ., 1977–; Dean, Prof., Sch. of Libnshp., Univ. of OR, 1974–77; Assoc. Dean, Prof., Coll. of LS, Univ. of KY, 1971–74; Dean, Coll., Prof., Wiley Coll., 1970–71. **Educ.:** Wiley Coll., 1957–61, BA (Msc.); Univ. of OK, 1963–64, MLS, 1964–66, PhD (Educ., LS). **Orgs.:** ALA: Info. Sci. and Autom. Div./AV Sect., Vice-Ch., Ch.-Elect, (1976–78); Beta Phi Mu Awds. Jury (1979–80); Cncl. (1979–83). TX LA: Pubns. Com. (1978–80); AV Interest Grp., Nom. Com. (1979). Beta Phi Mu: Exec. Cncl. (1975–79); Bylaws Rev. Com. (1976–78). **Honors:** Cncl. on Lib. Resrcs., Fellow, 1974–75; Amer. Cncl. on Educ., Fellow, 1970–71; South. Educ. Fndn., Fellow, 1964–66. **Pubns.:** *Administrative Aspects of Education for Librarianship: A Symposium* (1975); "Weapons Against Intolerance and Ignorance," *Jnl. of Lib. Hist.* (Sum. 1978); "Oregon. University of Oregon School of Librarianship," *Encyc. of Lib. and Info. Sci.* (1977); "Survey and Evaluation of Minority Programs in Selected Graduate Library Schools in the United States of America," *Jnl. of Educ. for Libnshp.* (Sum. 1977); jt. auth., "Scope and Content of Nonprint Media Courses Taught in Graduate Library Schools," *Expanding Media* (1977); various articles. **Activities:** 1, 11; 26, 34, 39; 66, 78, 93 **Addr.:** School of Library and Information Sciences, N. Texas State University, Denton, TX 76203.

Towey, Martin G. (F. 11, 1934, St. Louis, MO) Prof. of Hist., Dir. of Arch. and Oral Hist. Ctr., St. Louis Univ., 1975–; Assoc. Prof. of Hist., Univ. of MO, 1970–75; Tchr., Riverview Gardens HS, 1960–70. **Educ.:** St. Louis Univ., 1956–60, BS (Hist., Eng.), AM (Hist.), 1960–71, PhD (Hist.). **Orgs.:** SAA. Amer. Hist. Assn. Socty. of Amer. Histns. **Honors:** Fulbright, Flwshp., 1969; Danforth Fndn., Flwshp., 1965; Freedoms Fndn., Tchr. Awd., 1964. **Pubns.:** *Democracy vs. Totalitarianism* (1964); *St. Louis in the 20th Century* (1973); "The Knights of Father Mathew," *MO Hist. Review* (1980); "Hooverville in St. Louis," *Gateway Heritage* (1980). **Addr.:** St. Louis University, Archives and Oral History Center, St. Louis, MO 63103.

Towles, Anne Slaughter (Ja. 21, 1949, Yazoo City, MS) Law Libn., McCollister, McCleary, Fazio, Mixon, Holliday and Hicks, 1976–; Law Libn., Bank of Amer. Legal Dept., 1970–73. **Educ.:** San Jose State Coll., 1969–70, BS (Admin.); LA State Univ., 1975–76, MLS. **Orgs.:** AALL: Southeast. Chap., Pvt. Law Lib. Com. (1978–80); Secy./Treas. (1980–82). **Honors:** Southeast. Chap. AALL, Lucille Elliot Schol. Awd., 1980; AALL, Grant, 1976. **Pubns.:** "Louisiana Legislative Information," *Southeast. Law Libn.* (Ja. 1977). **Addr.:** Box 2706, Baton Rouge, LA 70821.

Towles, Betty Lorraine (O. 7, 1943, Salt Lake City, UT) Autom. Systs. Libn., Richland Coll., 1972–; Map Libn., South. Meth. Univ., 1968–72; Libn., Campbell Taggart, Resrch., 1967–68. **Educ.:** Brigham Young Univ., 1961–67, BA (Eng., Grmn.), 1968–70, MLS. **Orgs.:** SAA. Arch. Assocs. Dallas Cnty. LA: Treas. (1978–79). ALA: Student Messenger Com. (1972). TX Jr. Coll. Tchrs. Assn. Dallas Cmnty. Coll. Fac. Assn. Richland Coll. Fac. Assn. Goals for Dallas. **Honors:** Leadership Garland, Participant, 1980–81; Fred J. Heath Fndn., Meml. Awd., 1957. **Pubns.:** "A Journal Now," *Fam. Heritage Mag.* (F. 1979); "Search Strategy for On-Line Reference Service" snd.-slide (1977). **Activities:** 1, 2; 23, 31, 32; 56, 69, 85 **Addr.:** Richland College - LRC, 12800 Abrams Rd., Dallas, TX 75243.

Towner, Lawrence W. (Bill) (S. 10, 1921, St. Paul, MN) Pres., Libn., Newberry Lib., 1962–; Fellow, Harvard Univ., 1961–62; Ed., *William and Mary Qtly.*, 1956–61; Assoc. Prof., Hist., Coll. of William and Mary, 1955–62; Asst. Prof., Hist., Instr., MA Inst. of Tech., 1950–55. **Educ.:** Cornell Coll., 1938–42, BA (Hist., Eng.); Northwest. Univ., 1946–50, PhD (Hist.). **Orgs.:** Indp. Resrch. LA: Ch. (1975–77); Exec. Com. (1977–). ALA. Amer. Hist. Assn.: Cncl. Inst. of Early Amer. Hist.: Cncl. **Honors:** Northwest. Univ., LHD, 1965; Lake Forest Coll., LittD, 1965; Cornell Coll., LHD, 1965. **Pubns.:** Jt. auth., *The Flow of Books and Manuscripts* (1969); *"Wrecking" Havoc* (1976); "A Fondness For Freedom: Servant Protest in Puritan Society," *William and Mary Qtly.* (1962); "The Indentures of Boston's Poor Apprentices, 1734-1805," *Colonial Socty. of MA Pubns.* (1966). **Activities:** 14-Indp. resrch. lib.; 17 **Addr.:** The Newberry Library, 60 W. Walton St., Chicago, IL 60610.

Townley, Charles T. (F. 7, 1946, Oklahoma City, OK) Head Libn., PA State Univ., Cap. Campus, 1979–; Proj. Dir., Natl. Indian Educ. Assn. Lib. Proj., 1974–75, Asst. Proj. Dir., 1972–74; Biblgphr./Serials Libn., Univ. of CA, Santa Barbara, 1969–72. **Educ.:** Univ. of OK, 1964–68, BA (Hist.), 1968–69, MLS; Univ. of MD, 1973, Lib. Admin. Dev. Prog.; Univ. of CA, Santa Barbara, 1970–75, MA (Hist.); Univ. of MI, 1975–, PhD Cand. (LS). **Orgs.:** ALA: Cnclr.-at-Large (1973–77); Budget Asm. (1976–77); ACRL; LITA; LAMA, Compar. Lib. Org. Com. (1981–). SLA. West. Hist. Assn. **Honors:** Beta Phi Mu, 1971; ALA, Disting. Srv. Cert., 1977. **Pubns.:** *Management Information Systems, 1972-1975* (1976); "American Indian Library Ser-

Special Subjects/Services: 50. Adult educ.; 51. Advert./Mktg.; 52. Aerosp.; 53. Agric.; 54. Area std.; 55. Arts/Hum.; 56. Autom.; 57. Bibl./Prtg.; 58. Bio. sci.; 59. Bus./Fin.; 60. Chem.; 61. Copyrt.; 62. Documtn.; 63. Educ.; 64. Engin.; 65. Env.; 66. Eth. grps.; 67. Film; 68. Food/Nutr.; 69. Geneal.; 70. Geo.; 71. Geol.; 72. Handcpd.; 73. Hist.; 74. Int. frdm.; 75. Info. sci.; 76. Insr.; 77. Law; 78. Legis.; 79. Math./Comp. sci.; 80. Med.; 81. Metals; 82. Nat. resrcs.; 83. Newsp.; 84. Nuc. sci.; 85. Oral hist.; 86. Petr./Energy; 87. Pharm.; 88. Phys./Astr./Math.; 89. Readg.; 90. Relig.; 91. Sci./Tech.; 92. Soc. sci.; 93. Telecom.; 94. Transp.; 95. (other).

vice," *Advncs. in Libnshp.* (1978); "Policy Negotiations: Simulation as a Tool in Long-Range Library Planning," *Spec. Libs.* (Mr. 1978); "Using SPSS to Analyze Book Collection Data," *Drexel Lib. Qtly.* (Fall 1981). **Activities:** 1, 13; 17, 24, 28; 66, 75, 92 **Addr.:** Richard H. Heindel Library, Penn State University - Capitol Campus, Middletown, PA 17057.

Towns, Rose Mary (Ja. 7, 1934, Houston, TX) Syst. Prog. Coord., N. Bay Coop. Lib. Syst., 1975–; City Libn., Richmond Pub. Lib., 1969–70, Asst. City Libn., 1966–69, Supvsg. Libn., Oakland Pub. Lib., 1962–66, Sr. Libn., 1960–62, Jr. Libn., 1956–60. **Educ.:** San Francisco State Coll., 1955, BA (Soc. Sci.); Univ. of CA, Berkeley, 1956, MLS; CA Cmnty. Colls. Cred. **Orgs.:** ALA. CA LA: Int. Frdm. Com. (Ch., 1968–69); Long-range Plng. Com. (1969); CA Socty. of Libns. (Secy., 1979). CA Libns. Black Caucus, N.: Secy. (1972–73). Black Women Organized for Pol. Action. **Pubns.:** Ed., *NBCLS News Bltn.* (1975–). **Activities:** 9, 14-Coop. lib. syst.; 17, 34, 39; 66 **Addr.:** John F. Kennedy Library (Solano County), 505 Santa Clara St., Vallejo, CA 94590.

Townsend, Eleanor M. (Ap. 9, 1922, Sycamore, IL) Libn., Newark Musm., 1977–78; Libn., Sch. of Visual Arts, 1967–75; Asst. Libn., Cooper Un. Sch. of Art and Archit., 1952–67. **Educ.:** Stanford Univ., 1939–40; Denison Univ., 1940–43, AB (Eng.); Columbia Univ., 1947–48, BS (LS); NY Bot. Garden, 1976–77, Cert. (Bot.). **Orgs.:** ARLIS/NA: NY Chap. (Secy/Treas., 1974–76); Hosplty. Com. (Ch., 1979–80). SLA: NY Chap., Musm. Grp. (Secy., 1960–62); Musm. Div. (Secy./Treas., 1962–63, 1969–71). **Activities:** 1, 12; 15, 20, 39; 55 **Addr.:** 180 Park Row, New York, NY 10038.

Townsend, Patricia Lynn (Je. 4, 1946, Toronto ON) Archvst., Acadia Univ. Arch., 1972–; Archvst., Trent Univ., 1969–70. **Educ.:** Trent Univ., 1965–69, BA, hons., (Can. Hist.). **Orgs.:** Arch. Assn. of Atl. Can.: Secy. (1979–). Assn. Can. Archvsts.: Pubn. Com. (1980–81); Lcl. Arranges. Com. (1980–81). Kings Hist. Socty.: Arch. Prsrvn. Com.; Corres. Secy. **Activities:** 2; 23, 38, 41; 62, 69, 90 **Addr.:** Acadia University Archives, Wolfville, NS B0P 1X0 Canada.

Townsend, Rita M. (D. 16, 1924, Auburn, MA) Chld. Libn., Elem. Sch., St. Bede Sch., 1973–; Sub. Tchr., St. Maurice and St. Bede Schs., 1961–71; Tchr., Elem., St. Maurice Sch., 1959–61. **Educ.:** Cornell Univ., 1942–48, BS (Soclgy.); Univ. of Pittsburgh, 1970–72, MLS. **Orgs.:** Cath. LA: West. PA Chap. (Secy., 1979–83). Cornell Women's Club of Pittsburgh. **Activities:** 10; 21 **Addr.:** 203 Carnegie Pl., Pittsburgh, PA 15208.

Toy, Beverly Marie Johnson (O. 8, 1926, Beloit, WI) Assoc. Univ. Libn., Univ. of CA, Irvine, 1972–, Actg. Univ. Libn., 1979–80, Assoc. Univ. Libn., 1976–79, Head, Cat. Dept., 1972–76; Head, Cat., Serials, Tech Prcs., San Diego State Univ., 1964–72. **Educ.:** Univ. of AK, 1956–62, BA (Eng.); Univ. of CA, Los Angeles, 1962–63, MLS; San Diego State Univ., 1964–72, MA (Eng. Lit.). **Orgs.:** ALA: ACRL, Acad. Status Com. (1969–72). CA LA: Coll. Sect. (Secy., 1965, 1972, 1976). Pac. Coast Conf. on Brit. Std. **Pubns.:** "The Role of the Academic Librarian," *Jnl. of Acad. Libnshp.* (Jl. 1978); "'An Apt Summary,' in a Symposium on Identity of Academic Librarianship," *Jnl. of Acad. Libnshp.* (Ja. 1977); "Updating an Outmoded 'Approach to Academic Status of Librarians'," *CA Libn.* (O. 1968). **Activities:** 1; 17, 20, 31 **Addr.:** Library, University of California, Irvine, CA 92663.

Toyama, Ryoko (Mr. 9, 1938, Dairen, Shangdon, China) Biblgphr., Catlgr. for the Orientalia Col., Univ. of OR Lib., 1973–; Catlgr., U.S. Army Spec. Srvs. Lib., Bangkok, Thailand, 1971–72; Catlgr., Shared Cat. Dept., Lib. of Congs., 1968–70. **Educ.:** Niigata Univ., Japan, 1956–60, BA (Grmn. Lit.); Cath. Univ. of Amer., 1970–73, MSLS; Univ. of OR, Eugene, 1974–76, MA (Ling.). **Orgs.:** ALA: ACRL/OR Chap., Nsltr. Ed. (1976–78). Assn. for Asian Std.: Com. on E. Asian Libs. (1974–); Subcom. on Tech. Srvs. (1979–); Subcom. on Lib. Access. Assn. for Tchrs. of Japanese. Asian Std. in the Pac. Coast: Stdg. Com. (1979–82). **Pubns.:** Jt. auth., *Biographical Sketches of the White Birch School* (1974); "Amerika no Toshokan ni Okeru Shokuin no Taigu," *Gendai no Toshokan: Mod. Libs.* (My. 1979); "Daigaku Toshokan Riyoho," *Gendai no Toshokan: Mod. Libs.* (N. 1978); jt. transl., "The Three Crabs," *The Japan Qtly.* (Jl.–S. 1979). **Activities:** 1; 15, 31, 46; 54, 56 **Addr.:** The Library, University of Oregon, Eugene, OR 97403.

Tozer, Peggy M. (N. 28, 1921, Shell Lake, WI) Lib. Dir., East. NM Univ., 1976–, Asst. Lib. Dir., 1973–76, Pub. Srv. Libn., 1952–73; Libn., Beloit Meml. HS, 1948–52; Tchr., WI Schs., 1943–47. **Educ.:** WI State Coll., Eau Claire, 1939–43, BS (Eng.); Univ. of WI, 1947–48, BLS; Univ. of MI, 1955–59, MALS. **Orgs.:** ALA. SWLA. NM LA: Coll. Univ. and Spec. Lib. Sect., Ch., Schol. Com., Ch., Nom. Com., Ch., VP (1970–71), Pres. (1971–72). Altrusa: Dist. X (Secy., 1962–64). Delta Kappa Gamma: Lcl. Chap. Pres. (1978–80); Theta State Prof. Affairs Com. (1979–81). **Honors:** East. NM Univ., Fac. Senate Awd., 1976. **Pubns.:** Reviews. **Activities:** 1; 17, 39; 51, 59, 63 **Addr.:** 1321 W. 17th Ln., Portales, NM 88130.

Tra, John A. M. (N. 7, 1919, Goirle, North Brabant, Netherlands) Lib. Dir. AV, Divine Word Coll., 1975–; Resrch. Assoc., Libn., Ctr. for Appld. Resrch. in The Apostolate, 1967–74; Prin., HS, Maiwara, Papua, New Guinea, 1963–64; Prin., Tchrs. Coll., Megiar, Papua, New Guinea, 1959–63; Pastoral Work, Bogia/Lae, Papua, New Guinea, 1945–59. **Educ.:** Cath. Semy., Netherlands, 1938–45, (Phil., Theo.); Loyola Univ., 1958–59, MEd; Rosary Coll., 1965–66, MALS; Loyola Univ., 1958–59, Tchr. Cert. **Orgs.:** ALA. IA LA. IA Pvt. Acad. Libs.: Int. Frdm. Com. (1978). Cath. LA: Coll. and Semy. Div., Bd. (1980). Smithsonian Inst. **Honors:** Beta Phi Mu, 1967. **Pubns.:** *National Mission Institute: A Missionary Training Coalition* (1969). **Activities:** 1, 2; 15, 17, 46; 66, 74, 90 **Addr.:** Divine Word College, South Center, Epworth, IA 52045.

Tracy, Joan I. (D. 9, 1928, Tacoma, WA) Asst. Libn., Tech. Srvs., East. WA Univ., 1972–, Head Catlgr., 1969–72, Catlgr., 1967–69; Sch. Libn., Forest Grove, OR, 1960–63; Lectr., Newcastle-upon-Tyne Polytech., Eng., 1977. **Educ.:** Univ. of WA, 1946–50, BA (Educ.), 1961–65, MLS. **Orgs.:** WA LA: Acad. and Resrch. Libs. Interest Grp. (Ch., 1976–77); Bd. of Dirs. (1979–80). ALA. Pac. NW LA. **Pubns.:** "Feminist Periodicals: An Annotated Bibliography...," *Serials Libn.* (volume 3, no. 4); "British Librarianship: An American Point of View," *PNLA Qtly.* (volume 43, no. 2); "Availability of Machine-Readable Cataloging: Hit Rates...," *Lib. Resrch.* (volume 1, no. 3). **Activities:** 1; 17, 44, 46; 56 **Addr.:** The Library, East Washington University, Cheney, WA 99004.

Tracy, Joyce Ann (D. 14, 1932, Berwick, PA) Cur. of Newsp. and Serials, Amer. Antiq. Socty., 1973–; Ed., *Can. Per. Index,* 1970–72, Asst. Ed., 1969–70, Indxr., 1968–69; Catlgr., Bowdoin Coll., 1963–68; Ref. Libn., Sacramento State Coll. Educ. Dept., 1962–63; Soc. Sci. Tchr., ME HSs, 1954–61. **Educ.:** Univ. of ME, 1950–54, BA (Rom. Lang.); Univ. of WI, 1956–57 (Hist.); Univ. of WA, 1961–62, MLS (Libnshp.). **Orgs.:** ALA. New Eng. LA. MA LA. **Honors:** Phi Beta Kappa, 1954; Phi Beta Phi, 1954; Beta Phi Mu, 1962. **Pubns.:** "Indexing at CPI," *CASLIS Nsltr.* (1971); jt. auth., "Periodical Indexes in Canada," *The Indxr.* (1972); "Newspaper Collections at the American Antiquarian Society," *News. and Gazette Rpt.* (1976). **Activities:** 14-Pvt. resrch. lib.; 20, 29, 44; 83 **Addr.:** American Antiquarian Society, 185 Salisbury St., Worcester, MA 01609.

Traill, Susan M. (Mr. 31, 1947, Toronto, ON) Libn., Princess Elizabeth HS, 1976–; Head, Tech. Srvs., Winnipeg Sch. Div. # 1, 1975; Libn., Schol.'s Choice Ltd, 1972–74; Libn., Sch. of Lib. Info. Sci., 1971–72. **Educ.:** Univ. of Toronto, 1965–69, BA; Univ. of West. ON, 1970–71, MLS; Brandon Univ., 1975–76, Tchg. Cert. **Orgs.:** MB Sch. Lib. AV Assn.: Pres. (1978–80). Can. LA. MB LA. Assn. for Media and Tech. in Educ. in Can. MB Tchrs. Socty.: Status of Women in Educ. Com. (1979–). **Pubns.:** *Cataloguing for School Libraries* (1974, 1981); Reviews. **Activities:** 10; 17, 31, 32 **Addr.:** 417 6th St., Brandon, MB R7A 3N7 Canada.

Trainer, Karin Ann (D. 17, 1948, Detroit, MI) Dir., Tech. Srvs., NY Univ., 1978–; Cat. Maintenance Libn., OCLC Oper. Mgr., Princeton Univ., 1974–78, Catlgr., Head of Filing, 1973–74, Catlgr., Head of Serials Srch., 1972–73. **Educ.:** Douglass Coll., 1966–70, BA (Eng.); Bryn Mawr Coll., 1970–71, (Eng.); Drexel Univ., 1971–72, MS (Lib. and Info. Sci.). **Orgs.:** ALA: Rep. in Machine-Readable Form of Bibl. Info. Com. (1974–78); Conser Adv. Bd. (Rep., 1977–78); Tech. Srvs. Dirs. of Large Resrch. Lib. Discuss. Grp. (Ch., 1980–); Esther J. Piercy Awd. Jury (1980–). SUNY/OCLC Netwk.: Adv. Com. (1979–). NY Metro. Ref. and Resrch. Lib. Agency: Tech. Srvs. Com. (1978–). **Honors:** Beta Phi Mu, 1973. **Activities:** 1; 17, 34, 46; 56 **Addr.:** 32 Strongs Ave., Portland, CT 06480.

Trainer, Leona Margaret (Ag. 1, 1935, Winnipeg, MB) Sch. and Lib. Mktg. Coord., Bantam Bks., Can., Inc., 1981–; Educ. and Lib. Sales Coord., Penguin Bks. Can. Ltd., 1975–81, Sales Rep., 1974–75; Dist. Mgr., Instr. Mtrls. Div., *Encyc. Britannica,* 1968–74. **Educ.:** Univ. of MB, 1955–56, Lib. Cert. **Orgs.:** Can. LA: Exec. Com.; Lib. Trustee Rep. (1971–75). Can. Lib. Trustees Assn.: Secy.-Treas., 2nd Vice-Ch., 1st. Vice-Ch. (1971–75). MB LA: Dir. (1970–74). MB Lib. Trustees Assn.: Pres. (1973–75); VP (1971–73). Chld. Bk. Ctr.: Dir. (1979–). Can. Book Publshrs. Cncl.: Trade Grp. (Pres., 1976–77); Lib. Rel. Com. (Ch., 1975–76, 1978–). Can. Assn. of Publshrs. Educ. Reps.: Pres. (1980). Educ. Distributors Assn. of MB: Pres. (1970–75). **Honors:** MB Lib. Trustees' Assn., Life Mem., 1977. **Activities:** 9, 10; 37, 47; 51, 63, 89 **Addr.:** 29–20 Brimwood Blvd., Agincourt, ON M1V 1B7 Canada.

Traister, Daniel H. (My. 24, 1942, New York, NY) Libn., Rare Bks. and Mss. Div., NY Pub. Lib., 1977–; Spec. Proj. Biblgphr., Lehigh Univ., 1977; Intern, Bodleian Lib., Oxford Univ., Untd. Kingdom, 1977. **Educ.:** Colby Coll., 1959–63, AB (Eng. Lit.); NY Univ., 1963–73, MA, PhD (Eng. Lit); Columbia Univ., 1975–76, MS (LS). **Orgs.:** Amer. Prtg. Hist. Assn.: Trustee (1979–); Prog. Ch. (1978, 1979). ALA: ACRL/Rare Bks. and Mss. Sect., Ad Hoc Com. on Secur. (1979–); Cont. Ed. Com. (1980–); Preconf. Ch. (1982). Grolier Club: Com. on Spec. Functions (1979–). Bibl. Socty. of Amer.: Nom. Com. (1981). NE Amer. Socty. for Eighteenth-Century Std. Amer. Bk. Collector: Bk. Review Ed. (1979–). **Honors:** Beta Phi Mu, 1976. **Pubns.:** "Introduction," *American Encyclopaedia of Printing 1871* (reprinted 1981); "Addendum to the Thom Gunn Bibliography," *Pubns. of Bibl. Socty. of Amer.;* "How Much Research Would a Research Librarian Do If a Research Librarian Could Do Research?" *Options for the 80's–The 1981 ACRL 2nd Natl. Conf. Procs.* (forthcoming); various reviews, sps. **Activities:** 9, 14-Indp. resrch. lib.; 24, 39, 45; 57 **Addr.:** Rare Books and Manuscripts Div.-303, The New York Public Library, 5th Ave. & 42nd St., New York, NY 10018.

Tranfaglia, Twyla Lynn (S. 21, 1952, Hinsdale, IL) Law Libn., Kemp, Smith, White, Duncan, and Hammond, 1978–; Circ. Libn., Univ. of TX Law Sch. Lib., 1975–78; Head Cat. Libn., Bryan Pub. Lib., 1974–75; Head Cat. Libn., Biblical Std. Ctr., Austin, TX, 1974. **Educ.:** Univ. of TX, Austin, 1970–73, BA (Gvt.), 1973–74, MLS; Wkshp. on Serial Cat., 1975. **Orgs.:** TX LA. AALL: Pvt. Law Libn. Spec. Interest Sect. (1977–). Southwest. Assn. of Law Libns.: ILL Com. (1978–). **Honors:** Phi Beta Kappa, 1973; Phi Kappa Phi, 1974; Beta Phi Mu, 1974; Pi Sigma Alpha, 1972. **Pubns.:** *The Grand Jury; A Selected Bibliography* (1975). **Activities:** 1, 12; 20, 22, 41; 77, 90, 92 **Addr.:** 7227 N. Mesa #1004, El Paso, TX 79912.

Trapani, Jean-Ellen M. (Ag. 1, 1951, Valley Forge, PA) Libn., Info. Srvs. Coord., Libby, McNeill and Libby, 1977–; Info. Sci., G. D. Searle, 1976–77. **Educ.:** Boston Univ., 1973, BA (Anthro.); Univ. of Pittsburgh, 1974–75, MLS. **Orgs.:** ASIS: Chicago Chap., Secy. Treas. (1976–78); Pubcty. Ch. (1979–80). Assoc. Info. Mgrs. SLA. Chicago OLUG. Chicago Sting Fan Club. Folk Dance Leadership Cncl. **Pubns.:** Jt. auth., "Novice User Training on PIRETS," *Amer. Socty. for Info. Sci., Procs.* (1975). **Activities:** 12; 34, 38, 49-On-line srch.; 68 **Addr.:** Libby, McNeill & Libby, Research & Product Development Center Library, 1800 W. 119th St., Chicago, IL 60643.

Trauth, Eileen M. (Ap. 15, 1951, Cincinnati, OH) Asst. Prof., Bentley Coll., 1980–; Syst. Anal., Univ. of Pittsburgh, Dev. Ofc., 1976–77. **Educ.:** Univ. of Dayton, 1969–72, BSEd (Eng., Sp.); Univ. of Pittsburgh, 1974–76, MSIS (Info. Sci.), 1977–79, PhD (Info. Sci.). **Orgs.:** ASIS. Assn. for Comp. Mach. Assn. of Women in Comp. **Honors:** Beta Phi Mu, 1977; Univ. of Pittsburgh, Catherine Ofiesh Orner Awd., 1979. **Pubns.:** Jt. auth., "On the Shoulders of the Spouses of Scientists," *Soc. Std. of Sci.* (Ag., 1977); various papers. **Activities:** 11; 26; 56, 75, 78 **Addr.:** Computer Information Systems Dept., Bentley College, Waltham, MA 02254.

Trautman, Maryellen (Ag. 13, 1943, Milwaukee, WI) US Gvt. Docum. Libn., Natl. Arch. and Recs. Srv. Lib., 1978–; Reg. US Gvt. Docum. Libn., OK Dept. of Libs., 1968–77, Legis. Ref. Libn., 1967–68; Chld. Libn., Metro. Lib. Syst., Oklahoma City, OK, 1966–67. **Educ.:** Ctrl. State Univ., 1961–65, BA, magna cum laude (Hist., Eng.); Univ. of OK, 1965–67, MLS. **Orgs.:** ALA: GODORT, Fed. Docum. Task Frc. (Secy., 1972–73); Admin. and Org. Work Grp. Forms Clearinghse. (Ch., 1975–78); Assn. of State Lib. Agencies, Info. Needs of State Gvt. Work Grp. (1976–78). Depos. Lib. Cncl. to the Pub. Printer (1972–76). OK LA: Int. Frdm. Com. (1975–76). Interlib. Coop. Com. (1976–78); various other coms. SLA: OK Chap., Secy. (1969–70), Dir. (1970–73); DC Chap. (1978–). Amer. Prtg. Hist. Assn. Amer. Film Inst. Women's Natl. Bk. Assn. Socty. for Hist. in the Fed. Gvt.: Arch. Com. (1981–). Various other orgs. **Honors:** Smithsonian Resident Assoc., 1979–. **Pubns.:** *Directory, U. S. Government Documents Depository Libraries, State of Oklahoma* (1972, 1974, 1975, 1977). **Activities:** 2, 4; 29, 31, 39; 56 **Addr.:** 9207 Chanute Dr., Bethesda, MD 20014.

Travillian, Mary W. (Je. 24, 1938, Memphis, TN) Dir., Media Srvs., Area Educ. Agency 6, 1975–; AV Consult., Marshall Cnty. Sch. Syst., 1965–75; AV and Prog. Plng. Libn., Daniel Boone Reg. Lib., 1962–64. **Educ.:** Memphis State Univ., 1956–59, BA (Bus. Admin); George Peabody Coll., 1961–62, MA (LS). **Orgs.:** AECT: Secy.-Treas.; Bd. of Dirs. IA Educ. Media Assn.: Pres.; Secy. AV Educ. Assn. of IA: Secy.; Pres. Natl. Assn. of Reg. Media Ctrs. Marshalltown Cmnty. Thea. Leag. of Women Voters. AAUW. **Pubns.:** *The Mediators* (1968). **Activities:** 10, 14-Reg. media ctr.; 17, 32; 57, 63, 67 **Addr.:** 1101 W. Main, Marshalltown, IA 50158.

Travis, Irene L. (N. 9, 1940, Austin, TX) Systs. Application Sci., Plng. Resrch. Corp., 1981–; Asst. Prof., Coll. of Lib. and Info. Srvs., Univ. of MD, 1975–81, Lectr., 1972–75; Asst. Spec., Inst. of Lib. Resrch., Univ. of CA, Berkeley, 1968–69; Libn. I, Acq. Dept., Univ. of CA, Berkeley, 1966. **Educ.:** Mills Coll., 1958–62, AB (Msc.); Univ. of CA, Berkeley, 1964–66, MLS, 1966–74, PhD (Libnshp.). **Orgs.:** ALA. ASIS: San Francisco Bay Area Chap. (Treas., 1971–72); Spec. Interest Grp. in Class. Resrch. (Ch., 1980); Ch.-Elect, Prog. Ch. (1979). AALS. MD LA. AIM. ACM. **Honors:** Phi Beta Kappa, 1962; Beta Phi Mu, 1966. **Pubns.:** "Trade Literature at the National Museum of History and Technology," *Spec. Libs.* (Sum. 1979); "Design Equations for Citation Retrieval Systems," *Info. Prcs. and Mgt.* (1977). **Activities:** 11; 24, 41, 49-Tchg.; 56, 62, 75 **Addr.:** 1500 Planning Research Dr., McLean, VA 22101.

PROFESSIONAL ACTIVITIES: Institutions: 1. Acad. lib.; 2. Arch.; 3. Assn.; 4. Fed./Gvt. lib.; 5. Inst. lib.; 6. Mfr./Suppl.; 7. Milit. lib.; 8. Musm.; 9. Pub. lib.; 10. Sch. lib.; 11. Sch. of lib. sci.; 12. Spec. lib.; 13. State lib.; 14. (other). **Functions/Activities:** 15. Acq./Col. dev.; 16. Adult srvs.; 17. Admin.; 18. Apprais.; 19. Archit./Bldgs.; 20. Cat./Class.; 21. Chld. srvs.; 22. Circ.; 23. Cons./Pres.; 24. Consult.; 25. Cont. ed.; 26. Educ. lib. sci.; 27. Ext. srvs.; 28. Fund/Grants; 29. Gvt. pubs.; 30. Indx./Abs.; 31. Instr. lib. use; 32. Media srvs.; 33. Micro.; 34. Netwks./Coop.; 35. Persnl.; 36. PR; 37. Publshg.; 38. Recs. mgt.; 39. Ref. srvs.; 40. Repro.; 41. Resrch.; 42. Review.; 43. Secur.; 44. Serials; 45. Spec. col.; 46. Tech. srvs.; 47. Trustees/Bds.; 48. YA srvs.; 49. (other).

Travis, Julie M. (Ag. 23, 1943, Hackensack, NJ) Supervisory Mgr., Film Srv., Dallas Pub. Lib., 1975–, Adult Libn., Hampton–IL Branch, 1973–75, Admin. Asst. to Chief of the Ctrl. Lib., 1972–73. **Educ.:** Univ. of Dallas, 1966–67, BA (Eng.); N. TX State Univ., 1971–72, MLS. **Orgs.:** TX LA: AV Interest Grp. (Secy., 1978); Prog. Com. (1977). **Activities:** 9; 32; 67 **Addr.:** Dallas Public Library, 1954 Commerce, Dallas, TX 75201.

Treadway, Cleo Carson (Ag. 21, 1928, Henryville, IN) Dir. of Lib. Srvs., Tusculum Coll., 1971–, Interim Actg. Dir., 1970. **Educ.:** Grove City Coll., 1945–49, BMus (Organ); E. TN State Univ., 1969–71, MA (LS). **Orgs.:** ALA: ACRL, Chaps. Com. (Ch., 1978–80) Bibl. Instr. Sect., Exec. Com. (1978–80). SELA: Handbk. Rev. Com. (1974–76). TN LA: Staff Dev. Com. (Ch., 1976–77) Coll. and Univ. Sect. (Ch., 1975–76). Mid-Appalachian Coll. Cnsrtm.: Lib. Sect. (Ch., 1973). Various other orgs. **Honors:** Natl. Endow. for the Hum., Cncl. on Lib. Resrcs., Grant, 1979–1982; Cncl. on Lib. Resrcs., Grant, 1977; Natl. Endow. for the Hum., Grant, 1981–82. **Pubns.:** "The Four R's: Implications for Library Services," *Reform and Renewal in Higher Education: Implications for Library Instruction* (1980); "Reclassification: The Tusculum Way," *TN Libn.* (Win. 1976); various sps. **Activities:** 1, 2; 17, 31 **Addr.:** Box 87, Tusculum College, Greenville, TN 37743.

Treat, Mary Lou S. (Ag. 1, 1927, Steubenville, OH) Head Libn., Northfld. Mt. Hermon Sch., 1972–; Libn., Barlow Sch., 1964–69; Asst. Ed., McGraw Hill Publshg. Co., 1951–54; various positions as consult. **Educ.:** CT Coll., 1945–49, BA (Econ.); Simmons Coll., 1967–74, MLS; various crs. **Orgs.:** Natl. Assn. of Indp. Sch. Libns. ALA: LIRT, Mem./PR Com. (1981–); AASL, Non-Pub. Div; ACRL. New England Educ. Media Assn.: Schol. Com. (1976–77; 1977–78). Franklin Cnty. Lib./Media Assn.: Treas. (1977–78); Pres. (1979–80); Exec. Com. (1980–81). New Eng. LA. MA Bd. of Lib. Comsns.: Adv. Com. on Cert. of Libns. (1976–78). **Honors:** Beta Phi Mu. **Pubns.:** Jt. ed., *Books for Secondary School Libraries* (1981). **Activities:** 10; 15, 17, 24 **Addr.:** Winchester Rd., Northfield, MA 01360.

Tredwell, Irving A., Jr. (O. 31, 1929, Hempstead, NY) Asst. Libn., Pilgrim Psyt. Ctr., 1979–; Lib. Coord., Freeport Fam. Cmnty. Ctr., 1978; Biblgphr., Roosevelt Pub. Lib., 1977–78; Ref. Libn., Queens Boro. Pub. Lib., 1974–76. **Educ.:** Morehouse Coll., 1948–52 (Pre-Med.); Adelphi Univ., 1960–72, BA (Amer. Cvlztn.); St. John's Univ., Jamaica, NY, 1973–74, MLS; 1977, Pub. Libns. Prof. Cert.; Columbia Univ., 1980, (Biblither.). **Orgs.:** ALA: Black Caucus. NY LA. Med. LA: NY Reg. Grp. Bethel AME Church, Westbury, NY. Oper. PUSH. **Pubns.:** *Bibliography on Black Studies.* **Activities:** 5, 13; 32, 39, 49-Programming; 63, 67, 72 **Addr.:** 169 Grant St., Westbury, NY 11590.

Treese, William R. (D. 7, 1931, Burlington, WA) Art Libn., Arts Lib., Univ. of CA, Santa Barbara, 1966–; Coll. Libn., Yuba Coll., 1964–66; Art Libn., Free Lib. of Philadelphia, 1961–64. **Educ.:** Art Inst. of Chicago, 1956–60, BFA (Art); Stanford Univ., 1960–61, MA (Art); Drexel Univ., 1961–64, MLS (Libnshp.). **Orgs.:** ARLIS/NA. **Pubns.:** *Catalog of the Art Exhibition Catalog Collection of the Arts Library of the University of California at Santa Barbara* (1978–); "Computerized Approach to Art Exhibition Catalogs," *Lib. Trends* (Ja., 1975). **Activities:** 1; 15, 17, 39; 55 **Addr.:** Arts Library, University of California, Santa Barbara, CA 93106.

Trefry, Mary G. (D. 5, 1947, Jacksonville, FL) Pub. Srvs. Coord., Kansas City Pub. Lib., 1981–; Head, Ref. and Circ. Depts., 1980–81; various positions as Branch Libn., Fairfax Cnty. Pub. Lib., 1977–79, Chld. Libn., 1974–77. **Educ.:** Agnes Scott Coll., 1965–69, BA (Fr.); Univ. of MD, 1973–74, MLS (Lib. and Info. Srvs.); various trng. progs. **Orgs.:** ALA: Mem. Com. (1975–76); LAMA, Mid. Mgt. Discuss. Grp., Ch. (1980–81), Prog. Ch. (1979–80). VA LA: Chld. and YA Exec. Bd. (1976–78), North. VA Reg. Coord. (1976–78). DC LA: Chld. and YA RT Exec. Com. (1975–76). SELA: Mem. Com. (1975–76). **Honors:** Beta Phi Mu. **Activities:** 9; 17, 22, 39 **Addr.:** 3208 N.E. 71st Terr., Gladstone, MO 64119.

Trefz, Robert O. (Jl. 8, 1927, Iowa City, IA) Cat. Libn., Denver Pub. Lib., 1971–; Catlgr., CO Women's Coll., 1968–71; Catlgr., Denver Pub. Lib., 1955–68; Serials Catlgr., Univ. of WY, 1954–55. **Educ.:** Univ. of CO, 1945–49, BA (Fr.); Univ. of Denver, 1950–52, MA (Eng.), 1953–54, MA (LS). **Orgs.:** ALA: Margaret Mann Awd. Com. (1961). CO LA: Cat. Interest Grp. Org. Com. (1977–78). Univ. of Denver Lib. Sch. Alum. Assn.: Treas. (1969–70). **Honors:** Denver Pub. Lib., Outstan. Empl. of the Yr., 1980; Phi Beta Kappa. **Activities:** 1, 9; 20, 45; 55, 57 **Addr.:** 1901 E. 13th Ave., Denver, CO 80206.

Treger, Rita M. Carmona (Mr. 27, 1947, Miami, FL) Head, Ref. Dept., FL Inst. of Tech., 1981. Asst. Head, Ref. Dept., 1977–1981. **Educ.:** Univ. of FL, 1965–69, BA (Hist.); FL State Univ., 1976–77, MLS. **Orgs.:** FL LA: Online Srch. Caucus; Nsltr. Ed. (1979–80). **Honors:** Beta Phi Mu. **Pubns.:** Selected bib. of U.S. Govt. Docum. (FL LA) (1979). **Activities:** 1; 29, 31, 39 **Addr.:** Library, Florida Inst. of Technology, P.O. Box 1150, Melbourne, FL 32903.

Trejo, Arnulfo D. (Ag. 15, 1922, Durango, Mex.) Prof. of LS, Univ. of AZ, 1966–; Asst. Prof., Sch. of LS, Univ. of CA, Los Angeles, 1965–66; Dir. of Lib., Escuela de Admin. de Negocios para Graduados, USAID, Lima, Peru, 1963–65; Asst. Coll. Libn., Long Beach State Univ., 1959–63. **Educ.:** Univ. of AZ, 1946–49, BA (Educ.); Univ. de las Amers., 1950–51, MA (Span.); Kent State Univ., 1952–53, MA (LS); Natl. Univ. of Mex., 1951–59, PhD (Span. Lang. Lit.). **Orgs.:** ALA: Cncl. (1974–78); Nom. Com. (Ch., 1979–80). AZ LA. SALALM. REFORMA: Pres. (1972–74). Beta Phi Mu: Cnclr. (1979–); Beta Pi Chap. (Pres., 1978–79). AAUP. **Honors:** Kent State Univ., Sch. of LS, Disting. Alum., 1969; AZ LA, Rosenweig Awd., 1976; Phi Delta Kappa; Sigma Delta Pi; **Pubns.:** *The Chicanos–As We See Ourselves* (1979); *Bibliografía Chicana: A Guide to Information Sources* (1975); "Modifying Library Education for Ethnic Imperatives," *Amer. Libs.* (Mr. 1977); jt. auth., "Needed: Hispanic Librarians - A Survey of Library Policies," *Wilson Lib. Bltn.* (N. 1978). **Activities:** 11; 26; 66, 72 **Addr.:** Graduate Library School, University of Arizona, 1515 E. 1st St., Tucson, AZ 85719.

Tremere, Dianne Hendricks (Jl. 15, 1949, Port Clinton, OH) Assoc. Fac., Northland Pioneer Coll., 1979–; Reg. V Chld. Consult., Casa Grande City Lib., 1977–79; Bookseller, The Bk. Mark, 1976–77. **Educ.:** Knox Coll. 1967–69; Lake Forest Coll. 1969–70; Univ. of AZ, 1970–71, BA (Hist.), 1975–76, MLS; 1977, Grantsmanship Cert.; 1978, Consult. Skills Cert.; AZ Cmnty. Coll. 1979. Cert.; **Orgs.:** ALA: ALSC. AZ State LA: Pub. Libs. Div. AZ Libns. for YA Srvs.: Secy.–Treas. (1979–80). **Honors:** Beta Phi Mu, 1976. **Pubns.:** Reviews. **Activities:** 9, 14-Cmnty. coll.; 21, 26, 27; 89 **Addr.:** 716 Kinsley, Winslow, AZ 86047.

Trester, Dorothy Webb (Shreveport, LA) Ref. Libn., Univ. of NM, 1979–, Biblgphr., 1974–79, Gen. Ref. Libn., 1971–74, Serials Libn., 1967–71. **Educ.:** LA State Univ., BS (Educ.), 1962–63, MS (LS). **Orgs.:** NM LA: Various coms. Grt. Albuquerque LA: Various coms. SLA: Rio Grande Chap. AAUP: Univ. of NM Chap. (VP, 1973–), Past Secy. Albuquerque Press Club. **Pubns.:** Reviews. **Activities:** 1, 10; 15, 21, 39 **Addr.:** 1710 Princeton N.E., Albuquerque, NM 87106.

Treyz, Joseph Henry (N. 23, 1926, Binghamton, NY) Dir. of Libs., Univ. of WI, 1971–; Asst. Dir., Univ. of MI Lib., 1965–71; Head, New Campuses Prog., Univ. of CA, 1961–65; Asst. Head, Cat. Dept., Yale Univ. Lib., 1955–61, Admin. Asst., Cat. Dept. 1955; Catlgr., Stevens Inst. of Tech., 1953–54; Catlgr., Columbia Univ. Lib., 1951–53. **Educ.:** Oberlin Coll., 1944–50, BA (Hist.); Columbia Univ., 1950–52, MS (LS). **Orgs.:** ALA: Cnclr. (1970–74, 1977–81); Com. on Coms. (1979–80); Plng. and Budget Asm. (1978–80); ACRL; various coms.; Lib. Admin. Div., various coms.; RTSD, Bd. of Dirs. (1970–74), various coms., ch. ARL: Bd. of Dirs. (1975–78); various coms. Ctr. For Resrch. Libs.: Cncl. (1972–80). Unvsl. Serials and Bk. Exch.: Pres. (1977); Bd. of Dirs. (1976–78). Midwest Reg. Lib. Netwk.: Pres. (1979–80); various coms. Various other orgs. Signature Club. Univ. Club. WI Ctr. for Film and Thea. Resrch.: Bd. of Dirs. (1972–80). Nat. Hist. Musm.: Cncl. (1977–78). **Honors:** ALA, Melvil Dewey Awd. Medal, 1970. **Pubns.:** Jt. ed., *Books For College Libraries* (1967); "The O. P. Market," *CHOICE* (1965); jt. auth., "The New Campuses Program," *Lib. Jnl.* (My. 15, 1965); "F. Bernice Field," *Lib. Resrcs. & Tech. Srvs.* (1967); "The Conservation of Natural Resources," *76 Untd. Statesiana* (1976); various articles. **Activities:** 1; 17, 24, 46; 54, 56, 74 **Addr.:** 843 Farwell Dr., Madison, WI 53704.

Trezza, Alphonse F. (D. 27, 1920, Philadelphia, PA) Dir., Intergvtl. Lib. Coop. Proj., Fed. Lib. Com., Lib. of Congs., 1980–; Exec. Dir., NCLIS, 1974–80; Dir., IL State Lib., 1969–74; Assoc. Exec. Dir., ALA, 1960–69. **Educ.:** Univ. of PA, 1948, BS; Drexel Univ., 1949, Lib. Cert.; Univ. of PA, 1950, MS. **Orgs.:** ALA: Exec. Bd. (1974–79); Publshg. Bd. (1974–78, 1981–); Com. on Plng. (1974–78); Space Needs (1974–). Cncl. (1972–). Joliet Diocesan Bd. of Educ.: Pres. (1966–68). Cath. Bk. Week: Natl. Ch. (1954–56). **Honors:** ALA, ASCLA, Excep. Achvmt. Awd., 1981; IL LA, Libn's. Cit., 1974; IL LA, Spec. Libns. Cit., 1965; Drexel Grad. Sch. of LS, Outstan. Alum. Awd., 1963. **Pubns.:** "Networks," *ALA Yrbk.* (1976–81); "National Commission on Libraries and Information Science," *Bowker Annual of Library and Book Trade Information* (1976); "Toward a National Program for Library and Information Services: Progress and Problems," *Aslib Procs.* (F. 1978); "The Role of State Library Agencies in National Plans for Library and Information Services," *Lib. Trends* (Fall 1978); "Toward a National Cooperative Library and Informational Sciences Network," *Library Acquisitions: Practice and Theory* (1978); various articles. **Activities:** 4, 13; 18, 25, 35; 62, 76, 80 **Addr.:** Intergovernmental Cooperative Library Project, Library of Congress, Washington, DC

Triber, Beverly Finlayson (Ap. 14, 1937, Charlotte, NC) Libn., Media Spec., Virginia Pack Elem. Sch., 1975–; Libn., Media Spec., Logan Elem. Sch., 1973–75; Tchr., John P. Thomas Elem. Sch., 1959–73. **Educ.:** Univ. of SC, 1955–59, AB (Elem. Educ.), 1961–67, ME, 1971–77, MLS. **Orgs.:** SC Sch. Libns.: Pres. (1974–75). SELA. SC LA. ALA. Natl. Educ. Assn. SC Educ. Assn. Richland Cnty. Educ. Assn. **Honors:** Delta Kappa Gamma. **Activities:** 10 **Addr.:** 2016 Dalloz Rd., Columbia, SC 29204.

Tribit, Donald King (O. 19, 1934, Philadelphia, PA) Assoc. Prof., Per. and Micro. Libn., Millersville State Coll., 1961–; Ofcr., Info. and Educ. Ofc., US Nvl. Comm. Station, Guam, 1958–60; Tchr., NE HS, 1955–57. **Educ.:** Shippensburg State Coll., 1952–55, BS (Hist., Geo.); George Peabody Coll., Vanderbilt Univ., 1963–65, MSLS; Millersville State Coll., 1961–62, Mstrs. Equivalency Cert. (LS). **Orgs.:** Lancaster Cnty. LA: VP (1970–71); Pres. (1971–72). PA LA: 1974 Conf., Exhibits Co Ch. ACRL: DE Valley Chap. Phi Delta Kappa: Millersville State Coll. Chap. (Chap. Rep., 1977–); Nom. Com. (1979). Millersville State Coll. Fac. Assn. Assn. of PA State Coll. and Univ. Facs. **Honors:** Beta Phi Mu. **Activities:** 1; 33, 40, 44; 63, 83 **Addr.:** 1101 Little Brook Rd., Lancaster, PA 17603.

Triffin, Nicholas (My. 30, 1942, Boston, MA) Law Libn., Asst. Law Prof., Hamline Univ. Sch. of Law, 1982–; Head of Pub. Srvs., Univ. of CT Sch. of Law, 1977–81; Attorney, DiSesa and Evans, 1973–76; Dean of Students, Johnson State Coll., 1971–73. **Educ.:** Yale Univ., 1960–65, BA, cum laude (Phil.), 1965–68, JD (Law); Rutgers Univ., 1977–78, MLS (Lib. Admin.). **Orgs.:** AALL: Reader Srvs. SIS (Ch., 1980–81). South. New Eng. Law Libns.: Nom. Com. (1979–80). New Eng. Law Libns.: Pres. (1981); Prog. Com. (1979–80). CT Bar Assn.: Young Lawyers Chap. of New Haven, (Pres., 1977). **Honors:** Beta Phi Mu, 1978. **Pubns.:** "Legalized Gambling: A Selectively Annotated Bibliography from 1970–1980," *CT Law Review* (volume 12, no. 4). **Activities:** 1, 12; 17, 22, 39; 56, 77, 78 **Addr.:** Hamline University School of Law, St. Paul, MN 55104.

Trim, Kathryn R. (Mr. 18, 1930, Detroit, MI) Head Media Spec., Ypsilanti HS, 1969–; Adj. Lect. Sch. of LS, Univ. of MI, 1977–; Libn., Grosse Pointe Univ. Sch., 1958–67. **Educ.:** Univ. of MI, 1948–52, BA (Eng.); Wayne State Univ., 1960–62, MED (LS). **Orgs.:** MI Assn. for Media in Educ.: Prof. Educ. (Pres., 1980; Secy./Treas., 1979). Metro Media. ALA. MI Educ. Assn. Delta Kappa Gamma: Pres. (1976–78). **Pubns.:** "Name the Face Contest," *Wilson Lib. Bltn.* (1962). **Activities:** 10; 26, 32, 48 **Addr.:** 1414 Normandy Rd., Ann Arbor, MI 48103.

Trimble, Kathleen L. (O. 10, 1949, Reading, PA) Head Libn., *The Toledo Blade,* 1978–, Asst. Head Libn., 1976–78. **Educ.:** Univ. of Toledo, 1967–72, BA (Eng.), 1973–79, MALIS. **Orgs.:** SLA: Newsp. Div. (Dir., 1979–80; Secy.–Treas., 1980–82); Mem. Com. (Ch., 1979–80); Cont. Educ. (AV Ch., 1978–79); Long-range Plng. Com. (Ch., 1981–82). Zonta Club of Toledo. **Honors:** Phi Kappa Phi, 1971. **Pubns.:** "Newspaper Libraries: Non-Automated Approaches," (1980); "Microfilming Newspaper Clipping Files" slide/tape presentation (1981); "Subject Heading Control" slide/tape presentation (1979). **Activities:** 12; 15, 17, 39; 56, 83 **Addr.:** The *Blade,* 541 Superior St., Toledo, OH 43660.

Trimboli, Sr. Teresa, FMI. (Mr. 7, 1940, Dayton, OH) Assoc. Dir., Law Lib., St. Mary's Univ. Sch. of Law, 1979–, Head, Ref. and Circ. Dept., Univ. of Dayton Sch. of Law, 1977–79; Asst. Law Libn., St. Mary's Univ. Sch. of Law, 1970–77; Libn./Media Spec., St. James The Apostle Elem. Sch., 1965–70; Archvst./Docum. Libn., Provincialate/Marianist Sisters, 1970–. **Educ.:** St. Mary's Univ., 1960–64, BA (Eng.); Our Lady of the Lake, 1966–70, MSLS; TX Tchg. Cert., 1967; Cert. Law Libn., 1977. **Orgs.:** AALL. Southwest. Assn. of Law Libs. TX LA. SAA. Daughters of Mary Immaculate (Marianist Sisters). **Pubns.:** "Cumulative Index 1970-78," *Marianist Resrcs. Comsn.* (D. 1978); "In Response to an Invitation: A Bibliography of Marianist History," *Marianist Resrcs. Comsn.* (Ap. 1976); "Letter Concerning Marianist Archives and Libraries," *Marianist Resrcs. Comsn.* (Je. 1973); other articles. **Activities:** 2, 12; 17, 22, 39; 77, 78 **Addr.:** Law Library, St. Mary's University School of Law, San Antonio, TX 78284.

Trimby, Madeline Jean (Ag. 15, 1943, Ann Arbor, MI) Pres., Dynamic Directions, 1981–; Consult., Managerial Educ. Srvs., Gen. Motors Corp., 1979–80; Assoc. Prof. and Coord. of Lib. Tech. Prog., Ferris State Coll., 1967–79. **Educ.:** Univ. of MI, 1961–65, BA (Eng.); Rutgers Univ., 1965–67, MLS; MI State Univ., 1977–, (Educ. Systems Dev.). **Orgs.:** MI LA: Conf. Co-Ch. (1977); 2nd VP (1976); Acad. Div. (Ch., 1974); AV Sect. (Ch., 1972). Cncl. on Lib. Tech.: Mem. Com. (1976). MI Assn. for Media in Educ.: Reg. II, Alternate Del. (1976). AECT. Other orgs. Bus. and Prof. Women. AAUP: Treas. of Lcl. Chap. (1971–72). **Honors:** Beta Phi Mu, 1967. **Pubns.:** Contrib., *Women's Resource Guide* (1978); "Needs Assessment Models: A Comparison," *Educ. Tech.* (D. 1979); "The Coming of Age of Library Technicians," *MI Libn.* (Fall 1970); "What's Your R.Q.?–Rights Quotient, That Is," Videotape on Title IX (1978). **Activities:** 1; 24, 26, 32; 63, 75, 93 **Addr.:** 2759 Brentwood, East Lansing, MI 48823.

Trimm, Maureen D. (Ag. 22, 1948, Madison, WI) Dir., S. Bay Coop. Lib. Syst., 1978–; Resrc. Dev. Libn., Mt. Valley Lib. Syst., 1975–78; Outrch. Proj. Libn., N. State Coop. Lib. Syst., 1972–75. **Educ.:** Humboldt State Univ., 1966–69, BA (Jnlsm.); UT State Univ., 1970–71, MEd (LS); Univ. of South. CA, 1976–77, MPA (Pub. Admin.). **Orgs.:** CA LA: Forum Com. (Ch., 1980–81). CA Socty. of Libns.: Dir. (1978–81). SLA: Sierra Nevada Chap., Prog. Dir. (1978); Pubcty. Dir. (1977). **Pubns.:** "Mountain Valley Library System Delivery Study," *ERIC*

Special Subjects/Services: 50. Adult educ.; 51. Advert./Mktg.; 52. Aerosp.; 53. Agric.; 54. Area std.; 55. Arts/Hum.; 56. Autom.; 57. Bibl./Prtg.; 58. Bio. sci.; 59. Bus./Fin.; 60. Chem.; 61. Copyrt.; 62. Documtn.; 63. Educ.; 64. Engin.; 65. Env.; 66. Eth. grps.; 67. Film; 68. Food/Nutr.; 69. Geneal.; 70. Geo.; 71. Geol.; 72. Handcpd.; 73. Hist.; 74. Int. frdm.; 75. Info. sci.; 76. Insr.; 77. Law; 78. Legis.; 79. Math./Comp. sci.; 80. Med.; 81. Metals; 82. Nat. resrcs.; 83. Newsp.; 84. Nuc. sci.; 85. Oral hist.; 86. Petr./Energy; 87. Pharm.; 88. Phys./Astr./Math.; 89. Readg.; 90. Relig.; 91. Sci./Tech.; 92. Soc. sci.; 93. Telecom.; 94. Transp.; 95. (other).

(1977); "SLIC in the Sierra Nevada," *Making Cooperation Work, LJ Special Report #9* (1979). **Activities:** 14-Network; 17, 34 **Addr.:** South Bay Cooperative Library System, 2635 Homestead Rd., Santa Clara, CA 95051.

Triolo, Victor Anthony (My. 31, 1932, Brooklyn, NY) Assoc. Prof., Div. of LS, South. CT State Coll., 1975–; Assoc. Prof., Temple Univ., 1971–74, Asst. Prof., 1968–71, Instr., 1966–71; Postdoct. Fellow, Univ. of WI, 1962–66. **Educ.:** Brooklyn Coll., 1950–53, BS (Bio.); Univ. of MA, 1954–56, MA (Zlgy.); Columbia Univ., 1973–74, MS (LS); Univ. of WI, 1957–62, PhD (Med. Hist.). **Orgs.:** ALA: LITA, LRRT. Socty. of Sigma Xi. Amer. Pomological Socty. **Honors:** Natl. Cancer Inst., Resrch. Career Dev. Awd., 1966–71. Natl. Inst. of Hlth., Biomed. Comm. **Pubns.:** Jt. auth., "Continuing Education in On-Line Searching," *Spec. Libs.* (My./Je. 1978); reviews. **Activities:** 11; 26, 30, 41; 56, 58, 91 **Addr.:** Division of Library Science and Instructional Technology, Southern Connecticut State College, 501 Crescent St., New Haven, CT 06515.

Tripplett, M. Glenn (Mr. 6, 1939, Charlotte, NC) Assoc. Dean of Lrng. Resrcs., Miami Dade Cmnty. Coll., New World Ctr. Campus, 1979–; Ref. Libn., Pensacola Jr. Coll., 1977–79; Chief, Bur. of Book Prcs., State Lib. of FL, 1972–77; Dir., Ctrl. Tech. Prcs., Miami-Dade Cmnty. Coll., 1968–71, Chair, Acq. Dept., South Campus, 1966–68. **Educ.:** FL State Univ., 1958–62, BA (Gvt.), 1963–65, MS (LS), 1971–72, (Art Educ.). **Orgs.:** ALA: ACRL/Cmnty. and Jr. Coll. Lib. Sect., Plng. and Procedures Com. (Ch., 1979–81); Srvs. to Disadv. Students Com. (1980–82); ASCLA, Compar. Study of the Admin. Prcs. of State Lib. Agencies Com. (1977–79); Rep., Tech. Stan. for Lib. Autom. Sect. (1976–80); RTSD, Tech. Srvs. Dir. of Prcs. Ctrs. Discuss. Grp. (Ch.). FL LA. **Pubns.:** "Solinet," *Southeast. Libn.* (Win. 1976). **Activities:** 1, 13; 17, 32, 34; 56, 72, 93 **Addr.:** Miami-Dade CC - New World Center Campus, 300 N. E. 2nd Ave., Miami, FL 33132.

Tripp–Melby, Pamela (Ja. 13, 1948, New York, NY) Libn., ACTION 1975–80; Lib. Consult., Peace Corps Volun., Univ. of Iloilo, Philippines, 1973–75; Catlgr., Tchrs. Coll., Columbia Univ., 1971–72. **Educ.:** Tufts Univ., 1966–70, BA (Pol. Sci.); Columbia Univ., 1970–71, MLS. **Orgs.:** SLA: DC Chap. (Hosplty. Ch., 1976–78), Soc. Sci. Grp. (Prog. Ch., Pres.-Elect, 1978–80). **Pubns.:** *A Sampler of Library Forms* (1982). **Activities:** 4, 12; 17, 20, 24; 54, 92 **Addr.:** 40 bis, rue Violet, 75015, Paris, France.

Trivedi, Harish S. (Ahmedabad, Gujarat, India) Dir., Ref. and Resrch., Dayton Newsp. Inc., 1969–; Sr. Resrch. Asst., *The Times of India*, 1963–68; Subed., Vyapar, Bombay, India, 1962–63. **Educ.:** Univ. of Bombay, 1953–57, BA (Econ.), 1962, LLB (Law), 1961, MA (Econ.), 1966, (LS). **Orgs.:** ASIS. SLA: Newsp. Div., Dir. (1978–79); Secy. Treas. (1979–80). Cont. Educ. Com. (1978–80); Awds. Com. (1980–81). **Pubns.:** *Alternate System of Subject Classification for Media Libraries* (1974); *Management thru Change* (1975). **Activities:** 5, 12; 15, 17, 20, 37 **Addr.:** Dayton Newspapers Inc., 37 S. Ludlow St., Dayton, OH 45402.

Trivison, Margaret A. (Ag. 9, 1942, Cleveland, OH) Reg. Lib. Coord., San Diego Cnty. Lib., 1971–; Ref. Libn., Cuyahoga Cnty. Lib., 1969–71; Elem. Sch. Libn., Cleveland Bd. of Educ., 1966–69; Elem. School Instr., Cath. Bd. of Educ., Cleveland, 1964–66. **Educ.:** Notre Dame Coll., Cleveland, 1960–64, BA (Eng. Educ.); Case-West. Resrv. Univ., 1966–69, MS in LS; WA State Univ., "Lib. Outrch. to Minorities", 1971; Tchrs. Coll., Columbia Univ., 1965. **Orgs.:** ALA. CA LA: Palomar Chap. CA Lib. Srvs. Bd.: Rep. for Pub. Libs. (1981); Budget Com.; Data Base Adv. Com. **Activities:** 9, 13; 16, 28, 34; 50, 66, 78 **Addr.:** 6216 Agee St., San Diego, CA 92122.

Tromater, Raymond B. (D. 26, 1939, Ruston, LA) Dir., SW AR Reg. Lib., 1981–; Dir., Green Gold Lib. Syst., 1979–81; Head, Ref. Srvs., Shreve Meml. Lib., 1976–79; Dir., Mid-MS Reg. Lib., 1971–74; Jr. Libn., Queens Boro. Pub. Lib., 1970–71. **Educ.:** LA State Univ., 1959–62, BA (Eng.), 1968–70, MS (LS); LA Tech, 1975–76, MA (Hist.). **Orgs.:** ALA. LA LA. MS LA: Pub. Lib. Sect., (VP, 1973–74). Lions. Shreveport Writers Club. N.W. LA Writers Conf. **Honors:** Beta Phi Mu. **Pubns.:** Various articles. **Activities:** 9; 16, 17, 34 **Addr.:** Rte. 1, Box 22, Hope, AR 71801.

Trombitas, Ildiko D. (O. 3, 1932, Budapest, Hungary) Head, Tech. Info. Dept., Burroughs Wellcome Co., 1970–; Corp. Libn., Becton, Dickinson Co., 1969–70; Resrch. Libn., Smith, Kline and French, 1964–69; Med. Libn., Ciba Co. Ltd., Canada 1961–64. **Educ.:** Eötvös Lorand Univ., Hungary, 1951–56, MSLS; Med. LA, 1967, Cert. (Med. Libnshp.). **Orgs.:** ASIS. Med. LA. Drug Info. Assn. SLA: Pharm. Div., Secy. (1978–80), Ch.-Elect (1979–80), Ch. (1981–82), Lcl. Rep. (1969); NC Chap., Pres.-Elect (1976–77); Pres. (1977–78). **Activities:** 12; 17, 36, 39; 58, 60, 80 **Addr.:** Burroughs Wellcome Co., 3030 Cornwallis Rd., Research Triangle Park, NC 27709.

Trotti, John Boone (D. 11, 1935, Asheville, NC) Libn., Prof. of Bibl., Union Theo. Semy. in VA, 1980–, Libn., Assoc. Prof. of Bibl., 1968–80; Pastor, Altavista Presby. Church, 1964–68; Asst., Assoc. Prof. Randolph-Macon Woman's Coll., 1965–67, 1974; Instr., Yale Dvnty. Sch., 1961–62. **Educ.:** Davidson Coll., 1953–57, BA (Eng.); Union Theo. Semy. in VA, 1957–60, BD (Dvnty.); Yale Univ., 1960–61, MA (Old Testament), 1961–64, PhD (Old Testament); Univ. of NC, 1963–64, MS (LS). **Orgs.:** ATLA: Pres. (1977–78). Presby. LA: Pres. (1973–74). VA LA. Stillman Coll. Bd. of Trustees: Secy. (1977–1978). Hist. Fndn. of Presby. and Reformed Churches: Bd. of Dir. (1979–). **Honors:** Beta Phi Mu. **Pubns.:** *Lesser Festivals 2* (1980); Ed., *Aids to a Theological Library* (1977); Ed., *Scholar's Choice* (1970–); Assoc. Ed., *Interpretation* (1979–); other articles, reviews. **Activities:** 1; 15, 17, 31; 55, 57, 90 **Addr.:** Union Theological Seminary in VA, 3401 Brook Rd., Richmond, VA 23227.

Trottier, Donald H. (Ap. 11, 1942, Salt Lake City, UT) Racquetball Instr., OGDEN Racquet and Swim Club, 1979–; Dir., Corpus Christi Pub. Libs., 1978–79; Dir., Weber Cnty. Lib., Ogden, UT, 1971–78; Exec. Secy., ALTA, 1969–71. **Educ.:** Brigham Young Univ., 1960–65, BA (Eng.); Univ. of WA, 1965–66, MLS. **Orgs.:** ALA: Exec. Bd., Cncl. (1975–). UT LA: Int. Frdm. Com. (Ch., 1976–77). Big Brothers of North. UT: Adv. Bd. (1974–75). Leag. of Women Voters. **Honors:** Mt. Plains LA, Int. Frdm. Awd., 1978; Sch. of Libnshp., Univ. of WA, Ruth Worden Schol. Medal, 1966. **Pubns.:** "Up the Library Organization," *IL Libs.* (1970). **Activities:** 9; 17, 21, 47; 74, 75, 78 **Addr.:** Box 2007, Ogden, UT 84404.

Troutner, Joanne Johnson (S. 9, 1952, Muncie, IN) Media Spec., Meml. Jr. HS, 1979–, Tchr., 1978–79; Media Spec., Jefferson HS, 1974–77. **Educ.:** Purdue Univ., 1970–74, BA (Media), 1974–76, MS (Media). **Orgs.:** ALA: AASL Resrch. Com. (1976–80); Dist. Sch. Admin. (1980–81). ND LA. Assn. for IN Media Educ. ND Press Women. ND Reading Assn. Communiversity: Curric. Com. (1980–81). **Honors:** Finalist, ND Tchr. of the Yr., 1981; Phi Beta Kappa. **Pubns.:** "Media Center Math," *Sch. Lib. Jnl.* (D. 1980); "Videodisc at Memorial," *Videodisc/Teletext* (Ja. 1981); "Videodisc in Education," *ND Outlook* (D. 1980); "A "New" Group of Researchers," *Sch. Media Qtly.* (Fall 1978); "Tracking Down Readers," *Sch. Lib. Jnl.* (Mr. 1978); other articles. **Activities:** 10; 15, 32, 48; 63, 67, 89 **Addr.:** Memorial Jr. High, Rocket Rd., Minot AFB, ND 58704.

Troy, Patricia H. (Je. 3, 1946, Birmingham, AL) Media Srvs. Dir., Chesapeake Acad., 1980–, Co-Fndr., VP, Bd. of Dirs., 1980–; Dir., Severna Park Publshrs., Inc., 1979–; Media Srvs. Coord., Wroxeter-on-Severn Sch., 1978–80; Instr., Lib., Media Educ., Chapman Coll., 1972–75; Asst. Libn., McKendree Coll., 1969–71. **Educ.:** Auburn Univ., 1964–68, BS (Educ.), 1968–69, MEd (Lib. Media). **Orgs.:** ALA. AECT. Severna Forest Cmnty. Assn. San Bernardino Panhellenic. Annapolis Panhellenic. Ft. Severn Daughters of the Amer. Revolution. **Honors:** Norton AFB-OWC, Outstan. Mem. Awd., 1975; San Gorgonio Cncl. Girl Scouts, Recog. Awd., 1976. **Pubns.:** "Media and the Young Child," *News and Views* (1975); "Textbooks vs. the Tube," *Arundel Observer* (1978); "Family Partnership" snd. filmstp. (1976). **Activities:** 10; 17, 32, 37; 63 **Addr.:** Chesapeake Academy, 1185 Baltimore/Annapolis Blvd., Arnold, MD 21012.

Truck, Lorna R. (S. 27, 1947, NJ) Coord. of Ext. Srvs., Pub. Lib. of Des Moines, 1978–, Branch Head S. Side and Franklin Branches, 1976–78, Supvsg. Libn., 1973–76, Libn., 1971–73. **Educ.:** Carleton Coll., 1965–69, BA (Relig.); Univ. of Chicago, 1969–70, MA (LS). **Orgs.:** IA LA: Int. Frdm. Com. (1977–80, Ch. 1979); Bd. of Dirs. (1981–). ALA: SRRT; IFRT, Ad Hoc Subcom. on Copyrt. Legis., liaison for IA. Amnesty Intl. IA Civil Liberties Un. **Activities:** 9; 15, 17, 27; 55, 74, 90 **Addr.:** Public Library of Des Moines, 100 Locust St., Des Moines, IA 50308.

Trucksis, Theresa A. (S. 1, 1924, Hubbard, OH) Dir., NOLA Reg. Lib. Syst., 1974–; Asst. Head, Readers' Adv. Div., Pub. Lib. of Youngstown & Mahoning Cnty., 1973–74, Libn., Boardman Branch Lib., 1972–73. **Educ.:** Youngstown Coll., 1942–45, BS (Educ.); Kent State Univ., 1971–72, MLS. **Orgs.:** OH LA: Bd. of Dir. (1979–81); Coord., Resrch. and Plng. (1978); Lib. for the 70's Com. (Ch., 1976). State Lib. of OH: Multitype Interlib. Coop. Com. (Ch., 1978–1980). ALA: ASCLA. **Pubns.:** "OMICC: Progress Report," *OH LA Bltn.* (O. 1978). **Activities:** 9, 14-Coop. syst.; 17, 25, 34; 56, 63 **Addr.:** 133 Viola Ave., Hubbard, OH 44425.

Trudell, Robert J. (S. 6, 1930, Buffalo, NY) Dir., Greenburgh Pub. Lib., 1976–; Head of Acq., Smithtown Pub. Lib., 1974–76; Dir., Harborfield Pub. Lib., 1970–74; Consult., Chautauqua Lib. Syst., 1966–70; Sr. Libn., Buffalo Pub. Lib., 1960–66. **Educ.:** Univ. of Buffalo, 1956–60, AB (Lit.); Columbia Univ., 1960–61, MS (LS). **Orgs.:** ALA. NY LA. Westchester LA: Exec. Bd. (1979). **Activities:** 9; 17, 24, 39; 50, 55 **Addr.:** 300 Tarrytown Rd., Elmsford, NY 10523.

Truelson, Stanley D., Jr. (Mr. 19, 1929, Cambridge, MA) Dir., AK Hlth. Sci. Lib., 1976–; Libn., Yale Med. Lib., 1966–76; Med. Libn., Edw. G. Miner Lib., Univ. of Rochester, 1963–66; Libn., SUNY Upstate Med. Ctr. Lib., 1960–63; Libn., Tufts Med. and Dental Lib., 1958–60. **Educ.:** Harvard Coll., 1947–51, AB (Eng. Lit.), 1954–55, MAT (Eng. Lit.); Simmons Coll., 1955–56, MS (LS). **Orgs.:** Med. LA: Assoc. Ed. *Bltn. of the Med. LA* (1962–66); Bylaws Com. (Ch., 1974–77); Ed. Com. on the *Handbook of Medical Library Practice* (Ch., 1971–73); Pubs. Com. (Ch., 1966–70); New Eng. Reg. Grp. (Ch., 1971); Upstate NY Reg. Grp. (Ch., 1965). Adv. Com. to the New Eng. Reg. Med. Lib. Srv.: Ch. (1971). **Pubns.:** "Selecting for Health Science Library Collections When Budgets Falter," *Bltn. Med. LA* (Ap. 1976); "The Need to Standardize Descriptive Cataloging," *Bltn. Med. LA* (Ja. 1969); "The Totally Organized Reference Collection," *Bltn. Med. LA* (Ap. 1962). **Activities:** 12, 13; 15, 17; 80 **Addr.:** Alaska Health Sciences Library, 3211 Providence Dr., Anchorage, AK 99504.

Truesdell, Eugenia R. (Ag. 4, 1921, Elmira, NY) Assoc. Prof., Head, Regular Col. Cat., W. Chester State Coll., 1969–; Libn., Tibbetts Jr. HS, Farmington, NM, 1965–68; Asst. Coll. libn., Head, Cat., State University Coll. at Buffalo, 1952–61. **Educ.:** Elmira Coll., 1939–43, AB (Eng., Fr.); Syracuse Univ., 1946–47, BS (LS); Drexel Univ., 1970–72, MS (LS). **Orgs.:** ALA: Commercial Autom. Support for Tech. Srvs. in Medium-Sized Resrch. Libs. Discuss. Grp. (Ch., 1980–82). ASIS. SLA. **Honors:** Phi Beta Kappa, 1943; Beta Phi Mu, 1972. **Pubns.:** "Citation Indexing: History and Applications," *Drexel Lib. Qtly.* (Ap. 1972). **Activities:** 1; 20, 46 **Addr.:** Head, Regular Collection Cataloging, West Chester State College Library, West Chester, PA 19380.

Truesdell, Walter George (O. 22, 1919, New York, NY) Libn., Theo. Semy. of the Reformed Episcopal Church, 1964–; Rector, Church of the Redemption, 1956–; Libn., Shelton Coll., 1951–69; Mnstr., New York City, 1944–54. **Educ.:** Columbia Univ., 1941, BA; Theol. Semy. Reformed Episcopal Church, 1944, BD; Pratt Inst., 1950, BLS; Columbia Univ., 1975, MA. **Orgs.:** Christ. Libns. Flwshp. ALA. PA LA. Pratt Inst. Grad. LA. Assn. of Statisticians of Amer. Relig. Bodies. **Activities:** 1; 15, 17, 20; 56, 88, 90 **Addr.:** The Kuehner Memorial Library, Theological Seminary of the Reformed Episcopal Church, 4225 Chestnut St., Philadelphia, PA 19104.

Trueswell, Richard William (O. 12, 1929, Newark, NJ) Prof. of Indus. Engin., Univ. of MA, 1958–, Head, Dept. of Indus. Engin., 1965–75; Mfg. Engin., Westinghouse, 1954–56. **Educ.:** Stevens Inst. of Tech., 1948–52, ME (Mech. Engin.), 1956–58, MS (Indus. Engin.); Northwestern Univ., 1961–64, PhD (Indus. Engin.). **Orgs.:** ALA. ASIS. Amer. Inst. of Indus. Engin. Oper. Resrch. Socty. of Amer. **Honors:** Tau Beta Pi; Sigma Xi; Alpha Pi Mu. **Pubns.:** "User Circulation Satisfaction versus Size of Holdings at Three Academic Libraries," *Coll. and Resrch. Libs.* (My. 1969); "Article Use and Its Relationship to Individual User Satisfaction," *Coll. and Resrch. Libs.* (Jl. 1970); jt. auth., "Zero Growth: When is NOT-Enough Enough? A Symposium," *Jnl. of Acad. Libnshp.* (N. 1975); "Growing Libraries: Who Needs Them? A Statistical Basis For The No-Growth Collection," In *Farewell To Alexandria: Solutions to Space, Growth and Performance Problems of Libraries* (1976); jt. auth., "The Weighted Criteria Statistic Score; An Approach to Journal Selection," *Coll. and Resrch. Libs.* (Jl. 1978); other articles, speeches. **Activities:** 1, 9; 15, 24, 41; 56, 62, 75 **Addr.:** 3 Kennedy Dr., Hadley, MA 01035.

Trujillo, Gloria N. (S. 19, 1947, Dixon, NM) Elem. Sch. Libn., Fairview Elem. Sch., 1981–, Elem. Sch. Libn., Media Spec., 1980–81; Elem. Sch. Libn., Media Spec., Chimayo Elem. Sch., 1979–80; Elem. Sch. Lib. Supvsr., Espanola Mncpl. Schs., 1976–79; Elem. Sch. Libn., Chimayo Elem. Sch., 1971–73. **Educ.:** NM Highlands Univ., 1965–69, BA (Elem. Educ.), 1969–70, MA (Elem. Educ.), 1969–70, Cert. (LS). **Orgs.:** ALA: AASL. NM LA: Lib. Dev. Com. (1978–79); Exec. Bd. (1979–80); Sch. Libs., Chld. and YA Srvs. Div., Vice-Ch. (1978–79), Ch. (1979–80); Lib. Usage and Info. Srvs. to Span.-speaking Amers. RT. State Lib. Media Adv. Com. (Ch., 1980). NM Media Assn. Parent Tchrs. Assn. **Activities:** 9, 10; 17, 21, 25; 63, 66, 75 **Addr.:** Chimayo, NM 87522.

Trulock, Joy Bostwick (Ag. 8, 1925, Donalsonville, GA) Assoc. Prof. of LS, Asst. Dir. of Lib., Valdosta State Coll., 1964–; Ref. Libn. and Ext. Libn., Savannah Pub. Lib., 1955–64. **Educ.:** Wesleyan Coll., Macon, GA, 1942–46, AB (Psy.); Emory Univ., 1953–54, MAT (Hist.); George Peabody Coll., 1956–58, MA (LS); Med. LA, 1959, Cert. **Orgs.:** ALA. SELA. GA LA. Delta Kappa Gamma. **Honors:** Beta Phi Mu. **Pubns.:** Jt. auth., "Buying an Encyclopedia," *Consumers Resrch. Mag.* (F. 1975). **Activities:** 1; 17, 31, 39; 92 **Addr.:** P. O. Box 2233, Valdosta, GA 31601.

Trumbore, Jean Foight (Mr. 29, 1933, Pittsburgh, PA) Docum. and Maps Libn., Univ. of DE, 1979–, Assoc. Ref. Libn., 1976–79, Asst. Ref. Libn., 1973–75; Asst. in Ref. and ILL, Lincoln Univ., 1969–73; Sch. Libn., Newark Sch. Dist., 1968. **Educ.:** PA State Univ., 1951–55, BS (Home Econ.); Drexel Univ., 1965–67, MS (LS); Univ. of DE, 1970–74, MA (Pol. Sci), 1963–66, sch. lib. cert. **Orgs.:** ALA: ACRL/DE Valley Chap. (Secy./Treas., 1976–78); GODORT. DE LA: Del. to Middle Atl. Reg. Lib. Fed. (1974–77); Nom. Com. (1975); Coll. and Resrch. Libs. Div. Nom. Com. (1976); VP, Pres. elect (1979). Newark Leag. of Women Voters. DE Leag. of Women Voters. AAUP. Newark Mayor's Charter Info. Com. **Honors:** Cncl. on Lib. Resrcs., 1978. **Pubns.:** Jt. ed., *A Bibliography of Delaware,*

PROFESSIONAL ACTIVITIES: Institutions: 1. Acad. lib.; 2. Arch.; 3. Assn.; 4. Fed./Gvt. lib.; 5. Inst. lib.; 6. Mfr./Suppl.; 7. Milit. lib.; 8. Musm.; 9. Pub. lib.; 10. Sch. lib.; 11. Sch. of lib. sci.; 12. Spec. lib.; 13. State lib.; 14. (other). **Functions/Activities:** 15. Acq./Col. dev.; 16. Adult srvs.; 17. Admin.; 18. Apprais.; 19. Archit./Bldgs.; 20. Cat./Class.; 21. Chld. srvs.; 22. Circ.; 23. Cons./Pres.; 24. Consult.; 25. Cont. ed.; 26. Educ. lib. sci.; 27. Ext. srvs.; 28. Fund/Grants; 29. Gvt. pubs.; 30. Indx./Abs.; 31. Instr. lib. use; 32. Media srvs.; 33. Micro.; 34. Netwks./Coop.; 35. Persnl.; 36. PR; 37. Publshg.; 38. Recs. mgt.; 39. Ref. srvs.; 40. Repro.; 41. Resrch.; 42. Review.; 43. Secur.; 44. Serials; 45. Spec. col.; 46. Tech. srvs.; 47. Trustees/Bds.; 48. YA srvs.; 49. (other).

1960–1974 (1976); Jt. auth., "Student Use of Online Bibliographic Services," *Jnl. of Acad. Libnshp.* (Mr. 1978); reviews. **Activities:** 1; 29; 69, 70, 77 **Addr.:** 113 Dallas Ave., Newark, DE 19711.

Tryon, Jonathan S. (Jl. 8, 1933, Boston, MA) Assoc. Prof., Grad. Lib. Sch., Univ. of RI, 1969–; Asst. Prof., Lib. Sch., Pratt Inst., 1966–68; Asst. Libn., Kenyon Coll., 1965–66; Head Readers Srvs., RI Coll. lib., 1963–65. **Educ.:** Brown Univ., 1951–55, AB (Eng.); Columbia Univ., 1962–63, MS (LS); Univ. of RI, 1965–70, MA (Eng.); Columbia Univ., 1968–74, Cert. Adv. Std. (LS); Suffolk Univ. Law Sch., 1977–81, J.D. **Orgs.:** ALA. RI LA: Int. Frdm. Com. (Ch., 1979–). AALS. Assoc. of the John Carter Brown Lib. AAUP. Amer. Civil Liberties Un. **Pubns.:** "Theses and Dissertations," *Lib. Qtly.* (Ap. 1979); "Reuben Aldridge Guild," *Dict. of Amer. Lib. Biog.* (1978); "R.I. URI Graduate Lib. Sch.", *Encyc. of Lib. and Info. Sci.* (1978). **Activities:** 1; 15, 23, 26; 57, 74, 77 **Addr.:** Graduate Library School, University of Rhode Island, Rodman Hall, Kingston, RI 02881.

Tryon, Roy Hugh (S. 11, 1946, Bridgeport, CT) Chief, Bur. of Arch. and Recs. Mgt., State of DE, 1981–; Lib. Dir., Balch Inst. for Eth. Std., 1979–81; Assoc. Arch., State Hist. Socty. of WI, 1976–79; Mss. Prcs. and Catlgr., Bentley Lib., Univ. of MI, 1975–76; Archvst./Libn., Premier's Ofc., St. Vincent, West Indies, 1974. **Educ.:** Sacred Heart Univ., 1964–68, BA (Hist.); Fordham Univ., 1970–72, MA (Am. Hist.); Univ. of MI, 1973–74, MLS. **Orgs.:** ALA. SLA. SAA: Wider Use of Arch. (1977–78); Contemporary Themes (1979–80). Org. of Amer. Histns. **Pubns.:** Cmplr., *A Selected List of Newspaper and Manuscript Holdings* (1979); reviews. **Activities:** 2, 14-Resrch. lib.; 15, 38, 45; 66, 83 **Addr.:** Hall of Records, Dover, DE 19901.

Tsao, James Jui-Chi (Ag. 25, 1935, Li-Shui Hsien, Chekiang Prov., China) Chief, Tech. Srvs., WA State Law Lib., 1970–; Head, Tech. Srvs., AZ State Univ., Coll. of Law Lib., 1969–70, Cat. Libn., 1967–69; Libn. I, Menlo Park Mncpl. Lib., 1967. **Educ.:** Tamkang Coll. of Arts and Sci., Taiwan, 1958–60, BA (Frgn. Lang. and Lit.); San Jose State Coll., 1964–67, MALS. **Orgs.:** AALL. **Activities:** 12, 13; 15, 20, 46; 77 **Addr.:** Washington State Law Library, Temple of Justice, Olympia, WA 98504.

Tseng, Sally C. (Canton, Kwangtung China) Prin. Serials Catlgr., Serials Dept., Univ. Lib., Univ. of CA, Irvine, 1981–; Head, Serials Cat., Univ. of NE - Lincoln, 1977–81, Catlgr., 1968–76. **Educ.:** Soochow Univ., Taipei, Taiwan, 1958–62, BA (Lang., Lit.); Univ. of OR, 1966–68, MLS. **Orgs.:** ALA: ACRL; RTSD; LITA. Asian/Pac. Amer. Libns. Assn.: Mem. Ch. (1980–81). CA LA. Chinese-Amer. Libns. Assn.: Bd. of Dir. (1980–83); Mem. Ch. (1979–80); Treas. (1980–81). **Pubns.:** Contrib., *Getting Ready for AACR 2: The Cataloger's Guide* (1980); *Membership Directory of the Chinese-American Librarians Association* (1980); "Serials Cataloging and AACR 2: An Introduction," *Jnl. of Educ. Media Sci.* (Spr. 1981). **Activities:** 1; 20, 44, 46; 55, 56 **Addr.:** Serials Department, University Library, University of California, Irvine P. O. Box 19557, Irvine, CA 92713.

Tsien, Tsuen-hsuin (D. 1, 1909, Tsi-hsien, Kiangsu China) Prof. and Cur. Emeritus, Univ. of Chicago, 1979–, Prof. in LS and Chinese Lit., 1964–79, Libn. and Cur., Far East. Lib., 1947–78; Visit. Prof., Univ. of HI, 1959; Ed., Natl. Peking Lib., 1937–47. **Educ.:** Univ. of Nanking, 1928–32, BA (Hist.); Univ. of Chicago, 1947–57, AM, PhD (LS). **Orgs.:** Assn. for Asian Std.: Com. on E. Asian Libs. (Ch., 1966–68); Exec. Mem. (1971–74). ALA: Exec. mem., Asian & African Div. (1970–72). Intl. Assn. of Oriental Libns.: Exec. Bd. (1968–72). Amer. Oriental Socty. **Honors:** Natl. Endowment for Hum., Grant, 1977–81; Com. on E. Asian Libs., Assn. for Asian Std., Disting. Srv. Awd., 1978. **Pubns.:** *Written on Bamboo and Silk* (1962); jt. ed., *Area Studies and the Library* (1966); *China: Annotated Bibliography of Bibliographies* (1978); *Paper and Printing in Chinese Civilisation* (1982?); "Trends in Collection Building for East Asian Studies in American Libraries," *Coll. & Resrch. Libs.* (1979); other articles. **Activities:** 1; 17, 26, 41; 54, 55, 57 **Addr.:** 1408 E. Rochdale Pl., Chicago, IL 60615.

Tsuneishi, Warren M. (Jl. 4, 1921, Monrovia, CA) Dir. for Area Std., Lib. of Congs., 1978–, Chief, Asian (Orientalia) Div., 1966–78; Cur., E. Asian Col., Yale Univ. Lib., 1960–66; Head, Far East. Lang. Sect., Descr. Cat. Div., Lib. of Congs., 1957–60; Cur., Far East. Col., Yale Univ. Lib., 1953–57, Catlgr., 1950–52. **Educ.:** Univ. of CA, Syracuse Univ., 1939–43, BA (Pol. Sci.); Columbia Univ., 1946–48, MA (E. Asian Std.), 1949–50, MSLS; Yale Univ., 1952–60, PhD (Pol. Sci.). **Orgs.:** ALA: Intl. Rel. Adv. Com. for Liaison with Japanese Libs. (1967–, ch., 1971–74); ACRL/Subj. Spec. Sect., Asian and N. African Org. Com. (1967–69). ARL: Adv. Com. on the Chinese Resrch. Mtrls. Ctr. (1967–72). Assn. for Asian Std.: Com. on E. Asian Libs., Exec. Grp. (1964–67). Ctr. for Resrch. Libs.: Intl. Std. Adv. Com. (1980–81). Amer. Cncl. of Learned Societies: E. Asian Libs. Strg. Com. (1975–78). Amer. Cncl. on Educ.: Intl. Educ. Proj., Task Force on Lib. and Info. Resrcs. (1973–74). **Pubns.:** Jt. ed., *Issues in Library Administration* (1974); jt. ed., *University and Research Libraries in Japan and the United States* (1972); *Japanese Political Style: an Introduction to Institutions and Processes* (1966); various papers. **Addr.:** 5703 Maiden Ln., Bethesda, MD 20034.

Tsusaki, Edna K.O. (D. 7, 1931, Honolulu, HI) Lib. Dist. Admin., HI State Lib. Syst., 1975–, Reg. Libn., Pearl City, 1969–75, Head, Ref. HI State Lib., 1968–69, Head, Kaimuki Reg. Lib., 1962–69, Head, Bkmobile, 1958–62; Ref. Libn., Hild Reg. Lib., Chicago Pub. Lib., 1955–57. **Educ.:** Univ. of HI, 1949–53, BA (Sp.); Syracuse Univ., 1953–55, MS (LS). **Orgs.:** HI LA: Treas. (1978); Mem. ch. (1979); Handbook Com. (1975); Nom. Com. Ch. ALA. Momilani Jades 4-H Club. Boy Scouts of America. Momilani Cmnty. Assn. Pearl City Aquatics Club. **Honors:** Beta Phi Mu. **Activities:** 9; 17 **Addr.:** 1916 Hoolehua St., Pearl City, HI 96782.

Tu, Carol Chun Jen (Mr. 16, 1937, Harbin, China) Per. Libn. and Instr., WV Inst. of Tech., 1975–; Resrch. Asst., Univ. of Pittsburgh, 1974; Head, Curric. Sect., Chiao-Tung Univ., 1965–67. **Educ.:** Providence Coll., 1958–64, BA (Eng. Lit.); Univ. of Pittsburgh, 1972–73, MLS. **Orgs.:** ALA. WV LA. **Activities:** 1, 9; 20, 44, 46; 56, 83, 91 **Addr.:** West Virginia Institute of Technology, Fayette Pike, Montgomery, WV 25136.

Tubbs, William Johnston (My. 21, 1938, Philadelphia, PA) Asst. Libn., Wesleyan Univ., 1980–, Head of Tech. Srvs., 1977–80, Head of Cat., 1968–77, Reclassification Supvsr., 1967–68, Catlgr., 1966–67. **Educ.:** Davis and Elkins Coll., 1958–60, BA (Math.); Princeton Theo. Semy., 1960–63, MDiv; Columbia Univ., 1965–66, MS (LS). **Orgs.:** CT LA: Resrcs. and Tech. Srvs. Sect. (Secy., 1975–76; Ch., 1977–78); Prog. Com. (1975–). New Eng. LA. New Eng. Lib. Info. Network: Quality Control Com. (1976–79, Ch., 1978–79). ALA: ACRL; LITA; RTSD; LAMA. **Activities:** 1; 17, 22, 46 **Addr.:** 22 Lawn Ave., Middletown, CT 06457.

Tubesing, Richard L. (N. 25, 1937, Kansas City, MO) Asst. Dir., Lib., Progs., Univ. of Toledo Libs., 1981–; Lib. Dir., Lewis Univ., 1978–81; Bus. and Sci. Dept. Head, Atlanta Pub. Lib., 1976–78; Ref. Libn., GA Inst. of Tech. Lib., 1973–76. **Educ.:** Yale Univ., 1955–59, BA (Eng.); Univ. of Chicago, 1964–69, MA (Anthro.); West. MI Univ., 1971–72, MS (Libnshp.). **Orgs.:** ALA. Various state and lcl. orgs. **Honors:** Beta Phi Mu, 1972. **Pubns.:** *Architectural Preservation in the United States, 1941–1975: A Bibliography of Federal, State and Local Government Publications* (1978); "Pre-Columbian Libraries in the Americas," *The Southeast. Libn.* (Fall 1975); fndr., *The Contemporary Print Archives and Gallery,* Lewis Univ. (Dedicated 1981). **Activities:** 1; 17, 28, 37 **Addr.:** Carlson Library, University of Toledo, Toledo, OH 43606.

Tucci, Valerie Karvey (Ag. 25, 1938, Pittsburgh, PA) Mgr., Info. Srvs., Air Products & Chemicals, Inc., 1976–; Supvsr., Lib. Opers., Colgate-Palmolive, 1973–76; Info. Spec., Koppers Co., 1961–73. **Educ.:** Carlow Coll., 1956–60, BA (Chem.); Univ. of Pittsburgh, 1963–68, MLS; Adv. Cert., Info. Srvs., 1968–71. **Orgs.:** SLA: Pharm. Div. (Secy., 1975–76). ASIS: NJ Chap., Mem. (Ch., 1979–80). Assoc. Info. Mgrs. Indus. Tech. Info. Mgrs. Grp. Amer. Chem. Socty. **Honors:** Phi Beta Mu, 1968. **Activities:** 12; 17; 56, 91 **Addr.:** Air Products & Chemicals, Inc., P. O. Box 538, Allentown, PA 18105.

Tuchman, Helene L. (F. 20, 1939, New York, NY) Asst. Dir., Watertown Free Pub. Lib., 1981–, Branch Libn., N. Branch, 1980–81, Ref. Libn., 1967–80; Head Libn., Congregation Mishkan Tefila, 1968–80. **Educ.:** Brooklyn Coll., 1956–60, BA (Hist.); Pratt Inst., 1960–61, MLS. **Orgs.:** New Eng. Jewish LA: Pres. (1970–72). **Pubns.:** *Bibliography of Negro-Jewish Relations* (1968); *Bibliography of Large Print Books and Other Materials of Jewish Interest for the Visually Handicapped* (1981). **Activities:** 9, 10; 15, 16, 30 **Addr.:** Watertown Free Public Library, 123 Main St., Watertown, MA 02172.

Tuchman, Maurice Simon (S. 14, 1936, Brooklyn, NY) Libn., Hebrew Coll., 1966–; Cat. Consult., Mid-Hudson Libs., 1964–66; Asst. Libn., NY State Maritime Coll., 1962–64; Jr. Catlgr., Buffalo and Erie Cnty. Pub. Lib., 1959–60; Fac., Univ. of RI Grad. Lib. Sch., 1979–. **Educ.:** Brooklyn Coll., 1954–58, BA (Hist.); Columbia Univ., 1958–59, MLS; Simmons Coll., 1974–79, DA (Lib. Mgt.); Jewish Theo. Semy. of Amer., 1954–64, BHL (Jewish Hist.). **Orgs.:** CSLA: Pres. (1974–75). AJL: Prog. Com. (1977). AAUP. **Pubns.:** Reviews. **Activities:** 1, 12; 15, 17, 24, 42; 54, 75, 90 **Addr.:** 16 Duffield Rd., Auburndale, MA 02166.

Tucker, Ellis Eugene (S. 15, 1931, Booneville, MS) Prof., Dir., Grad. Sch. of Lib. and Info. Sci., Univ. of MS, 1969–, Asst. Prof., Ch., Dept. of LS, 1974–76; Proj. Dir., AL Lib. Lrng. Ctr., Jacksonville City Schs., 1968–69; Asst. Libn., A-V Coord., Allegany Cmnty. Coll., 1967; Actg. Libn., Frederick Coll., 1965–67, Catlgr., Asst. Libn., 1964–65; Libn., Lepanto City Schs., 1963–64; Libn., Monette HS, 1950. **Educ.:** Univ. of MS, 1950–52, BAE (Eng.); Emory Univ., 1955–58, BD (Old Testament); LA State Univ., 1964–67, MSLS; Emory Univ., 1972, MDiv.; FL State Univ., 1972–73, Adv. MLS, 1972–74, PhD (LS). **Orgs.:** ALA: LITA. SELA. MS LA: Autom. and Networking RT (1979–); Long-Range Plng. Com. (1974–76, 1978–80); Cred. Com. (Ch., 1976); Budget Com. (Ch., 1977–). AALS. Phi Delta Kappa; Phi Kappa Phi; Beta Phi Mu. **Pubns.:** Ed., *Southeast. Libn.* (1979–); "Alabama Library Learning Center Involvement in Improving Education," *AL Libn.* (Ap. 1976); "Accountability In Education: A Bibliography," *ERIC* (1972); reviews. **Activities:** 11; 17, 26, 31; 90 **Addr.:** 601 Manor Dr., Oxford, MS 38655.

Tucker, Florence Ray (Jl. 11, 1921, Henderson, KY) Assoc. Dir. for Support Srvs., Detroit Pub. Lib., 1978–, Resrch. and Grants Coord., 1973–78, Coord. of Cat. Dept., 1966–73, Actg. Chief, Tech. and Sci. Dept., 1966, Asst. Chief, Tech. and Sci. Dept., 1959–66, Ref. Asst., Tech. and Sci. Dept., 1946–59, Ref. Asst., Ref. Dept., 1945–46. **Educ.:** Flint Jr. Coll., 1938–40, AA; Univ. of MI, 1942–44, AB (Hist.), 1944–45, ABLS. **Orgs.:** ALA: Lcl. Arrange., 1977 Detroit Conf. (Ch.); Tech. Srvs. (Ch., 1969); Ref Div. (Secy., 195?). MI LA. SLA. MI Lib. Cnsrtm.: Exec. Cncl. (1974–). Christadelphian Church. **Honors:** Phi Beta Kappa, 1944; Phi Kappa Phi, 1944. **Activities:** 9; 17 **Addr.:** Detroit Public Library, 5201 Woodward Ave., Detroit, MI 48202.

Tucker, Jane C. (D. 17, 1940, Pittsburgh, PA) Chief, Systs. Dsgn., Natl. Bur. of Stans., 1974–; Catlgr., Montgomery Cnty. Pub. Schs., 1971–74; Lib. Systs. Anal., Becker and Hayes, 1970–71; Lib. Systs. Anal., Progmr., Univ. of IL, 1962–70. **Educ.:** Oberlin Coll., 1958–62, BA (Math.); Univ. of IL, 1962–65, MS (LS); various crs. **Orgs.:** ASIS: SIG/CBE Nsltr. Ed. ALA. Amer. Natl. Stan. Inst.: Com. Z39 (1978–). OCLC, Inc.: Users Cncl. (Secty., 1979). FEDLINK-OCLC Users Grp.: Ch. (1978–80). World Future Socty. Seneca Valley Unitarian-Universalist Flwshp.: Bd. of Trustees (1977–80). **Honors:** Beta Phi Mu, 1965. **Pubns.:** *Impact of Copyright Law on a Research Library* (1978); "Guidelines and Standards for Scientific Data," *Sourcebook on Handling Scientific and Technical Data* (Spr. 1980). **Activities:** 1, 4; 17, 34, 46; 56, 75, 91 **Addr.:** 10105 Blue Tee Terr., Gaithersburg, MD 20879.

Tucker, John Mark (O. 25, 1945, Natchez, MS) Ref. Libn., Asst. Prof. of LS, Purdue Univ., 1979–; Ref. Libn., Wabash Coll., 1973–79; Asst. Libn., Volunteer St. Cmnty. Coll., 1972–73; Head Libn., Freed-Hardeman Coll., 1968–71. **Educ.:** David Lipscomb Coll., 1963–67, BA (Eng., Relig.); George Peabody Coll. for Tchrs., 1967–68, MLS, 1971–72, EdS, (LS); Univ. of IL, 1979–, PhD Cand. (LS). **Orgs.:** ALA: ACRL/Bibl. Instr. Resrch. Com., Subcom. on Eval. (1981–); LHRT; LIRT. AALS. SAA. IN LA: JMRT. AAUP. Disciples of Christ Hist. Socty. Students Theo. Flwshp. Assn. for the Bibl. of Hist. **Honors:** H.W. Wilson Schol., 1967; Beta Phi Mu; Phi Kappa Phi. **Pubns.:** "Azariah Smith Root and Social Reform at Oberlin College," *Jnl. of Lib. Hist.* (Spr. 1981); "User Education in Academic Libraries: A Century in Retrospect," *Lib. Trends* (Sum. 1980); "The Origins of Bibliographic Instruction in Academic Libraries, 1876–1914," in *New Horizons in Academic Libraries;* "An Experiment in Bibliographic Instruction at Wabash College," *Coll. and Resrch. Libs.* (My. 1977); "Library School Admissions and the Liberal Arts," *Jnl. of Educ. For Libnshp.* (Win. 1975). **Activities:** 1; 26, 31, 39; 57, 63, 92 **Addr.:** General Library, Purdue University, W. Lafayette, IN 47907.

Tucker, Mae S. (O. 5, 1922, Mount Holly, NC) Asst. Dir., Main Lib. Srvs., Pub. Lib. of Charlotte and Mecklenburg Cnty., 1973–, Head, Main Lib. Pub. Srvs., 1956–73, Ref. Asst., 1945–56. **Educ.:** Appalachian State Univ., 1940–43, BS (Educ.); Univ. of NC, 1944–45, BS (LS). **Orgs.:** ALA: Lib. Admin. Div./Lib. Org. and Mgt. Sect., Stats. for Ref. Srvs. Com. (1973–77); Stats. for Pub. Libs. Com. (1977–79). NC LA: Corres. Secy. (1955–57); Rec. Secy. (1963–65); Pub. Libs. Sect.; JMRT. Metrolina LA. SELA: various ofcs., various orgs. AAUW: Charlotte Branch, Spec. Proj. Com. (Ch., 1978–80). Charlotte Bus. and Prof. Women's Club. **Honors:** Beta Phi Mu. **Pubns.:** *Textiles: A Bibliography* (1952). **Activities:** 9, 12; 16, 25, 39; 50, 57, 74 **Addr.:** Public Library of Charlotte and Mecklenburg County, 310 N. Tryon St., Charlotte, NC 28202.

Tucker, Phillip H. (My. 9, 1952, Perryville, MO) Lrng. Resrcs. Dir., Perry Cnty. Sch. Dist. 32, 1977–, Head Libn., Instr. Media Tech., 1975–77, Asst. Libn., 1974–75. **Educ.:** S.E. MO State Univ., 1972–74, BS (Elem. Educ.), 1974–76, MS (Instr. Media Tech.). **Orgs.:** S.E. MO Libns. Assn.: VP (1977–78); Pres. (1978–79). Perryville Cmnty. Tchrs. Assn. **Pubns.:** "Learning Resources Centers," *Sch. and Cmnty.* (D. 1976). **Activities:** 10; 17, 32, 39 **Addr.:** Learning Resources Program, Perry County School District #32, Perryville, MO 63775.

Tudiver, Lillian (O. 3, 1927, New York, NY) Chief, Soc. Sci. Div., Brooklyn Pub. Lib., 1960–, Asst. Chief, 1957–59, Libn., 1955–57; Branch Libn., Tottenham, Eng. Pub. Lib., 1954–55; Libn., Telephone Ref., Brooklyn Pub. Lib., 1953–54, Libn., 1952–53. **Educ.:** Brooklyn Coll., 1945–48, BA; Columbia Univ., 1951–52, MS (LS). **Orgs.:** ALA. SLA. Thea. LA. NY Lib. Club. Amer. Socty. Thea. Resrch. Thea. Hist. Socty. Amer. Film Inst. Smithsonian Inst. **Pubns.:** Various presentations. **Activities:** 9, 12; 15, 26, 39; 55, 67, 92 **Addr.:** 61 Eastern Pkwy., Brooklyn, NY 11238.

Tudor, Dean F. (My. 26, 1943, Toronto, ON) Ch., Lib. Art Dept., Ryerson Polytech. Inst., 1974–; Branch Dir., Lib., ON Dept. of Revenue, 1968–73; Ref. Libn., York Univ. Libs., 1967–68. **Educ.:** Univ. of Toronto, 1962–65, BA (Hist.); McGill Univ., 1965–67, MLS; George Brown C.A.A.T., 1970–74, Dip. (Food, Wine). **Orgs.:** SLA. ALA. ON Assn. of Lib. Techs. ON LA. Various orgs. Intl. Wine and Food Socty. Guilde de Froma-

Special Subjects/Services: 50. Adult educ.; 51. Advert./Mktg.; 52. Aerosp.; 53. Agric.; 54. Area std.; 55. Arts/Hum.; 56. Autom.; 57. Bibl./Prtg.; 58. Bio. sci.; 59. Bus./Fin.; 60. Chem.; 61. Copyrt.; 62. Documtn.; 63. Educ.; 64. Engin.; 65. Env.; 66. Eth. grps.; 67. Film; 68. Food/Nutr.; 69. Geneal.; 70. Geo.; 71. Geol.; 72. Handcpd.; 73. Hist.; 74. Int. frdm.; 75. Info. sci.; 76. Insr.; 77. Law; 78. Legis.; 79. Math./Comp. sci.; 80. Med.; 81. Metals; 82. Nat. resrcs.; 83. Newsp.; 84. Nuc. sci.; 85. Oral hist.; 86. Petr./Energy; 87. Pharm.; 88. Phys./Astr./Math.; 89. Readg.; 90. Relig.; 91. Sci./Tech.; 92. Soc. sci.; 93. Telecom.; 94. Transp.; 95. (other).

giers. Ragtime Socty. of Can. **Honors:** H. W. Wilson Co., Best Article in 1972 *Spec. Libs.* 1973; *Choice* Best Ref. Bks. of the Year, 1974; ALA, Outstan. Ref. Bk. of 1976, 1977; Can. Cncl., Exploration Awd., 1975, 1979. **Pubns.:** Jt. auth., *Jazz* (1979); jt. auth., *Grass Roots Music* (1979); jt. auth., *Contemporary Popular Music* (1979); jt. auth., *Annual Index to Popular Music Record Reviews* (1972–); jt. auth., *Popular Music Periodicals Index* (1973–); various articles, indxs., reviews, ed., consult. **Activities:** 1, 11; 26, 30, 42; 56, 57, 75 **Addr.:** 51 Gothic Ave., Toronto, ON M6P 2V8 Canada.

Tuke, Donna M. (Jl. 12, 1950, Cincinnati, OH) Chief Libn., Winston & Strawn, 1981–; Law Libn., Freidman and Koven, 1976–81; Asst. Ref. Libn., DePaul Coll. of Law Lib., 1974–76. Adjunct Instr., Rosary Coll. Grad. Lib. Sch., 1979. **Educ.:** IN Univ., 1968–72, BA (Psy., Relig. Std.), 1972–74, MLS; DePaul Coll. of Law, 1975–80, JD (Law). **Orgs.:** Chicago Assn. of Law Libs.: Pres. (1980–81); Secy., Exec. Bd. (1979–80); Educ. Com. (Ch., 1977–78). AALL: Pvt. Law Libs. Spec. Interest Sect., Educ. Com. (Ch., 1978–79). **Pubns.:** "Young Persons in the Legal Literature: Annotated Bibliography," *Law in Amer. Socty.* (S. 1975); Originator, Coord., "Legal Research" clmn. *Chicago Daily Law Bulletin.* **Activities:** 12; 17, 39, 41; 77, 78 **Addr.:** Winston & Strawn, One First National Plz., Chicago, IL 60603.

Tupling, Donald Murray (Mr. 3, 1943, Pembroke, ON) Catlgr., Leddy Lib., Univ. of Windsor, 1966–. **Educ.:** Univ. of Windsor, 1962–66, BA (Hist.); Wayne State Univ., 1970–73, MSLS. **Orgs.:** Can. LA. Bibl. Socty. of Can. Essex Cnty. Hist. Assn. **Pubns.:** Ed., *Canada: A Dissertation Bibliography* (1980); *Conquer the Card Catalogue* (1979). **Activities:** 1, 2; 20, 23, 30 **Addr.:** 4180 Longfellow Ave., Windsor, ON N9G 2B6 Canada.

Turchyn, Andrew (Jl. 17, 1912, Chernytsia, Galicia, Ukraine) Libn. Emeritus, IN Univ. Libs., 1979–, Libn., Slavic Std. Area Spec., 1969–79, Libn., Slavic and E. Asian Cols., 1966–69, Assoc. Head, Cat. Dept., 1959–68, Sr. Catlgr., 1953–59; Prof. Emeritus, Sch. of Lib. and Inf. Sci., IN Univ., 1975–80, Assoc. Prof. 1973–75, Visit. Lectr., 1970–73. **Educ.:** Theo. Acad., L'viv, Ukraine, 1933–38, Dip. (Theo.); Univ. of Munich, Germany, 1946–49, PhD (Phil.); Univ. of MI, 1952–53, MALS; IN Univ., 1955–60, MA (Slavic Std.). **Orgs.:** ALA: ACRL/Subj. Spec. Sect., Nom. Com. (Ch., 1965–66)/Slavic and E. European Sect., Exec. Com. (Ch., 1965–66), Nom. Com. (Ch., 1966–67, 1973–74, 1977–78), Com. on Problems of Access and Cntrl. of Slavic and E. European Lib. Mtrls. Ukranian LA of Amer.: Audit Bd. (Ch., 1963–70); Exec. Com. (1972–). Amer. Assn. for the Advnc. of Slavic Std. Shevchenko Sci. Socty. Ukrainian Hist. Socty. AAUP. **Honors:** Russ. and E. European Inst., IN Univ., travel grant, 1972; Polish Std. Ctr., IN Univ., Warsaw Univ., travel grant, 1978; Russ. and E. European Inst., IN Univ., Intl. Resrch. and Exch. Bd., travel grant, 1974. **Pubns.:** Chapters "Indiana University," *East Central and Southeast Europe: A Handbook of Library and Archival Resources in North America* (1976); "Slavic Publications," *Cataloging and Classification of Non-Western Material: Concerns, Issues and Practices* (1980); "Nearly a Century of Errors," *Lib. Nsltr.* (IN Univ.) (F. 1968); "Needed at the Library of Congress: Classification Changes," *The Ukrainian Qtly.* (Sum. 1973); various articles, bk. reviews. **Activities:** 1; 26; 54, 57, 66 **Addr.:** 3205 Browncliff, Bloomington, IN 47401.

Turk, Beatrice E. (La Crosse, WI) Adjunct Prof., Sch. of Lib. Sci., Case West. Rsv. Univ., 1972–; Media Spec., Elyria City Schs., 1972–; Coord. of Sch. Libs., Bd. of Cath. Educ., Diocese of Cleveland, 1965–72. **Educ.:** Coll. of St. Catherine, St. Paul, MN, 1941–45, BS (Hist., LS); Case West. Rsv. Univ., 1962–65, MS (LS). **Orgs.:** ALA: Com. on Cat. Chld. Mtrls. (1969–72); AASL, Nom. Com. (1972–73), Disting. Admin. Awd. (Ch., 1971). OH Educ. Lib./Media Assn. Natl. Educ. Assn. **Honors:** Jennings Schol., Outstan. Educ. of Grt. Cleveland, 1975–76. **Pubns.:** "The Listening Post," *OH Media Spectrum* (Fall 1979). **Activities:** 10; 21, 31, 32, 48 **Addr.:** 22095 Cottonwood Dr., Rocky River, OH 44116.

Turnbull, R. Keith (My. 23, 1945, Edmonton, AB) Asst. Prov. Libn. (Direct Srvs.), SK Prov. Lib., 1976–, Asst. Prov. Libn., Dev., 1971–76; Chief Libn., Chinook Reg. Lib., 1971–72; Lib. Consult., SK Prov. Lib., 1969–71. **Educ.:** Univ. of AB, 1963–66, BA (Eng.), 1968–69, BLS. **Orgs.:** SK LA: Cnclr. (1972–76). Can. LA. Can. Assn. Info. Sci. **Activities:** 9; 17, 18, 24; 75, 92 **Addr.:** Saskatchewan Provincial Library, 3116 College Ave., Regina SK Canada.

Turner, Ann (Mr. 19, 1925, Warren, OH) Head Libn., Norwich Univ., 1975–, Ref. Libn., 1963–75; Head Pub. Libn., Walden, NY, 1950–52; Ref. Libn., Dartmouth Coll., 1945–47. **Educ.:** Skidmore Coll., 1941–44, AB (Fr.); Columbia Univ., 1944–45, MLS. **Orgs.:** VT LA: Secy. (1981–82). **Pubns.:** "Contribution in Title II-A," *Jnl. of Acad. Libnshp.* (S. 1979). **Activities:** 1; 17, 31, 39; 63, 64, 78 **Addr.:** Norwich University Library, Northfield, VT 05663.

Turner, Anne M. (Ag. 11, 1941, Palo Alto, CA) Dir., Lowell City Lib., 1980–; Dir., Jones Lib., 1975–80; Ref. Libn., Simon's Rock Early Coll., 1973–75; Asst. Dir., Housing Assn. of DE Valley, 1965–70. **Educ.:** Amer. Univ., 1962–64, BA (Hist.); Univ. of PA, 1964–65, (Pol. Sci.); Simmons Coll., 1972–73, MS (LS), 1978–79, DA (Lib. Mgt.). **Orgs.:** ALA. MA LA. **Pubns.:** *Rank and Filing: A Collective Bargaining Game for Library Workers* (1979); "Nonresident Borrowers: A Statistical Study for Amherst's Public Library," *Quantitative Measurement and Dynamic Library Service* (1978); "Why *Do* Department Heads Take Longer Coffee Breaks? A Public Library Staff Evaluates Itself," *Amer. Libs.* (Ap. 1978). **Activities:** 9, 11; 17; 59 **Addr.:** Lowell City Library, 401 Merrimack St., Lowell, MA 01852.

Turner, Carol A. (Ag. 22, 1943, Centralia, IL) Chief Libn., Gvt. Docum. Dept., Stanford Univ. Libs., 1977–, State, Lcl. Docum. Libn., 1974–77, Head, Tech. Info. Srv., 1972–74, Ref. Libn., Meyer Lib., 1968–72; Ref. Libn., Kansas City, MO, Pub. Lib., 1966–68. **Educ.:** Univ. of MO, 1961–65, BA (Eng.); Rutgers Univ., 1965–66, MLS; San Francisco State Coll., 1969–71, MA (Eng.); Univ. of Santa Clara, 1975–78, MBA. **Orgs.:** ALA: GODORT, Intl. Docum. Task Force (Asst. Ch., 1979–80), Stats. Interest Grp. (Ch., 1979–), Frgn. Docum. Work Grp. (Ch., 1978–79); LAMA. **Activities:** 1; 17, 29, 31; 62, 78, 92 **Addr.:** Government Documents Department, Stanford University Libraries, Stanford, CA 94305.

Turner, Elizabeth W. (Je. 17, 1936, Clifton Forge, VA) Ref. Libn., DeKalb Cmnty. Coll., N. Campus, 1979–, Catlgr., Head, Tech. Prcs., 1968–79; Sci. Catlgr., Univ. of AL, 1967; Head Libn., Stillman Coll., 1966–67, Asst. Libn., Instr., 1961–66. **Educ.:** Mary Baldwin Coll., 1954–58, BA (Eng.); Emory Univ., 1959–60, MLn (Libnshp.). **Orgs.:** SE LA. GA LA: Resrcs. and Tech. Srv. Sect. (Ch., 1973–75); Int. Frdm. Com. (1975–77); Ad Hoc Com. on Wkshps. (1977–79). Metro. Atlanta LA. **Activities:** 1; 20, 39, 46; 55 **Addr.:** 2404 Tanglewood Rd., Decatur, GA 30033.

Turner, Frank L. (O. 18, 1929, Little Rock, AR) Prof., Lib. Sci., TX Woman's Univ., 1974–, Assoc. Dir., 1978–80, Actg. Dir., 1976–77; Dir., Libs., Henderson State Univ., 1971–74. **Educ.:** Southwestern at Memphis, 1947–50, BA (Hist.); Univ. of NC, 1950–52, MA (Hist.), 1954–60, PhD (Hist.); LA State Univ., 1970–71, MS (LS). **Orgs.:** ALA: Cncl. (1980–83). TX LA: Cncl. (1979–); Exec. Bd. (1979–). AR LA: Coll. and Univ. Div. (Ch., 1973–74). Beta Phi Mu: Natl. Nom. Com. (1979). **Honors:** Phi Beta Kappa, 1950. **Pubns.:** "Texas Library Association," *Encyclopedia of Library and Information Science* (1980); "Texas Woman's University School of Library Science," *Encyclopedia of Library and Information Science* (1980). **Activities:** 1, 11; 17, 26, 46; 74, 92 **Addr.:** School of Library Science, Texas Woman's University, Denton, TX 76204.

Turner, Gurley (New York, NY) Dir., Info. Srvs., Catalyst, 1974–; Head, Info. and Ref., Inst. of Intl. Educ., 1964–74; Supvsg. Branch Libn., Queens Bor. Pub. Lib., 1949–64. **Educ.:** Hunter Coll., 1938–42, BA (Soclgy.); Columbia Univ., 1947, MLS. **Orgs.:** ALA: Task Force On Women, Strg. Com. NY LA: RT on Women's Concerns, Coord. Cncl. SLA: New York City Chap., Women's Caucus, Ch. Assn. of Fam. Plng. and Popltn. Libs. Women's Natl. Bk. Pubshg. Assn. AAUW. Women Lib. Workers. Women's Info. Sci. Netwk. **Activities:** 9, 12; 15, 16, 17; 63, 92 **Addr.:** Catalyst, 14 E. 60 St., New York, NY 10022.

Turner, Judith Campbell (S. 24, 1950, New York, NY) Musm. Libn., Milwaukee Pub. Musm., 1974–. **Educ.:** Douglass Coll., Rutgers Univ., 1968–72, BA (Eng.); Univ. of Denver, 1972–73, MA (Libnshp.); Univ. of WI, Milwaukee, 1976–79, MBA. **Orgs.:** Lib. Cncl. of Metro. Milwaukee: PR; Org., Funding and Structure; Treas. (1975–76, 1978–79). ALA. SLA. WI LA: WI Assn. of Acad. Libns. Stans. Com. Univ. of Denver Alum. Assn. Univ. of WI–Milwaukee Alum. Assn. **Honors:** Beta Phi Mu, 1973. **Pubns.:** "Milwaukee Public Museum Reference Library," *LCOMM News* (1977); "LORE Readers Write Back: Some Highlights of the Survey," *LORE* (1978). **Activities:** 4, 8; 15, 17, 39; 55, 91 **Addr.:** Milwaukee Public Museum Reference Library, 800 W. Wells St., Milwaukee, WI 53233.

Turner, Lillian M. (D. 9, 1921, Hartland, NB) Libn., York Meml. Collegiate Inst., 1979–; Libn., Vaughan Rd. Collegiate Inst., 1974–79. **Educ.:** Mt. Allison Univ., 1938–42, BA (Latin); Univ. of Toronto, 1972–73, BEd (Sch. Libnshp.), 1975–76, Spec. Cert. (Sch. Libnshp.). **Orgs.:** Can. LA: Can. Mtrls. Reviewer. Can. Sch. LA. ON LA: *The Reviewing Libn.* Reviewer (1980–). ON Sch. LA. Univ. Women's Club. **Pubns.:** Reviews. **Activities:** 10; 15, 17, 42 **Addr.:** 1477 Bayview Ave., Apt. G1, Toronto, ON M4G 3B2 Canada.

Turner, Mary Louise (O. 13, 1925, Quincy, IL) Assoc. Prof., Lib. Sci., Chief, Educ./Info., Lib., Med. Coll. of GA, 1980–; Asst. Prof., Dept. of Lib. and AV Educ., Div. Leader, Instr. Srvs., Lib., St. Cloud State Univ., 1978–79; Dir., Educ. Tech. Ctr., Coll. of Educ., Univ. of NE, 1976–77, Instr., Lib. Sci., Dept. of Lib. Media, 1975–76; AV Educ. Spec., Grad. Sch. of Lib. Sci., Univ. of TX, Austin, 1974–75; Head Libn., El Paso Cmnty. Coll., 1973–74; Libn., Pkwy. N. Sr. HS, 1971–73; Libn., MO Trng. Sch. for Boys, 1969–71. **Educ.:** Univ. of MO, 1962–67, AB (Psy., LS), 1967–68, AM (LS); Univ. of TX, Austin, 1974–75, (Info. Sci.); Univ. of MO, 1978–79, PhD (Curric., Instr.); various crs. **Orgs.:** ALA: Amer. Hosp. and Inst. Libs. Biblther. (Ch., 1971). ASIS. Assn. for Comp. Mach. MN Assn. for Supvsn. and Curric. Dev.: Com. for Resrch. and Dev. (1979–). AECT: Anl. Conf. Eval. (1976, 1980); Anl. Conf. (Presenter, 1979). Amer. Correct. Assn.: Consult. for Self-Eval. and Self-Accred. (1970). MN Educ. Assn. MO Assn. of Classroom Tchrs. MO State Tchrs. Assn. Various orgs. **Honors:** Beta Phi Mu, 1968; Kappa Delta Pi, 1978; Mid-MO Mental Hlth. Ctr., Cert. of Recog. for Volun. Srv., 1967–68. **Pubns.:** *Visual Literacy Assessment of Mediated Instructional Expertise for Educators* (1978); *Library Policy and Procedure Manual for El Paso Community College* (1974); "Two Movements of Healing," "The Profile of a Librarian," *Show-Me Libraries* (1978–79); "Visual Literacy Test, Form A," (1977); *Visual Literacy Test, Form B with Test Administration Manual and Test Manual* (1977); "An Armchair Tour of the MCG Library" TV prod. (1980); "The Role of the Learner in Instructional Development," *AECT Resrch. and Theory Div. Nsltr.* (N. 1977); various articles, reviews, handbks. **Activities:** 1, 14-Medical College; 17, 26, 32; 63, 80, 91 **Addr.:** Education/Information Division, Library, Medical College of Georgia, Augusta, GA 30912.

Turner, Patricia (Je. 17, 1928, Indianapolis, IN) Ref., Biblgphr., Univ. of MN, 1974–; Head, Hum. Div., Univ. of AZ, 1970–73; Chld. Libn., NY Pub. Lib., 1969–70; Instr., Lib. Sch., Univ. of MN, 1967–69; Sr. Hum. Libn., Univ. of AZ, 1963–66; Chld. Libn., NY Pub. Lib., 1960–63; Chld. Libn., Indianapolis Pub. Lib., 1956–60. **Educ.:** Butler Univ., 1946–50, AB (Hist., Pol. Sci.); IN Univ., 1956–60, MA (LS); Univ. of MN, 1977, Spec. Cert. (LS). **Orgs.:** ALA: ACRL; RASD. Chld. Lit. Assn. MN LA. Amer. Pol. Sci. Assn. Natl. Assn. of Negro Musicians. **Honors:** Beta Phi Mu. **Pubns.:** *Afro-American Singers: An Index and Preliminary Discography of Opera, Choral Music, and Song* (1977). **Activities:** 1; 15, 31, 39; 54, 66, 92 **Addr.:** 621 11th Ave., S.E., Minneapolis, MN 55414.

Turner, Philip Michael (N. 26, 1948, Ayer, MA) Asst. Prof., Univ. of AL Grad. Sch. of Lib. Srv., 1977–; Libn., AV, Edison Jr. HS, 1973–76; Co-Partner, VideoGuide Prods., 1972–73; Tchr., Edgewood Jr. HS, 1969–71. **Educ.:** Boston State Coll., 1966–69, BS (Educ., Math.); Univ. of WI, 1970–71, MS (AV); E. TX State Univ., 1976–77, MS (LS, Lib.), 1974–77, EdD (Educ. Media). **Orgs.:** AECT: Schol. Com. (Ch., 1979–); Subcom. for Prod. of the Eval. of Instr. Mtrls. Com. (Ch., 1978); Strg. Com. for Cncl. (Vice-Ch., 1978). AL Instr. Media Assn.: Bd. of Dir. (1977–) Long Range Plng. Com. (Ch., 1977–). AL LA: Pubcty. Com. (Ch., 1977–78). **Honors:** Green Bay Area JayCees; Edison Jr. HS Outstan. Educ., 1974; Natl. Alum. Assn. of the Univ. of AL; Outstan. Commitment to Tchg. Awd., 1979. **Pubns.:** *Handbook for In-School Media Personnel* (1975); "The Relationship Between the Principal's Attitude and the Amount and Type of Instructional Development Performed by the Media Professional," *Intl. Jnl. of Instr. Media* (Volume 7, 2); *Trigger Tapes: Simulation of Classroom Discipline Problems* (1972); "Empathy and the K-12 Instructional Developer," *Intl. Jnl. for Instr. Media* (Volume 7, 3); "Is Misuse of Media Giving us a Black Eye?" *AV Instr.* (O. 1977). **Activities:** 10; 32, 41; 67 **Addr.:** P.O. Box 6242, University, AL 35486.

Turner, R. Ann (Ap. 6, 1944, Duncan, BC) Head, Cat. Recs. Div., Univ. of BC Lib., 1978–, Head, Serials Div., 1973–78, Head, Cat. Prep. Div. 1969–73, Msc. Catlgr., 1968–69, Cat. Maintenance Libn., 1967–68. **Educ.:** Univ. of BC, 1962–66, BMus (Msclgy.); Univ. of WA, 1966–67, MLS (Libnshp.); Toronto Consvty. of Msc., 1964–65, ARCT (Piano performance, Tchg.); Vancouver Cmnty. Coll., 1976–78, Cert. (Bus. Admin.). **Orgs.:** BC Un. Cat. Proj.: Subcom. on Stan. (Ch., 1979–); Serials Task Force (Ch., 1978). Univ. of BC Libns. Assn.: VP. (1976–77). Can. Assn. of Coll. and Univ. Libs.: Nom. Com. (1973). ALA. Various orgs. Univ. of BC Fac. Assn.: Secty. (1972–73). Can. Assn. of Univ. Tchrs. **Pubns.:** *Filing Rules for the Divided Catalogues of the University of British Columbia Library System* (1968); "Comparative Card Production Methods," *Lib. Resrcs. and Tech. Srvs.* (Sum. 1972); "The Effects of AACR2 on Serials Cataloguing," *Serials Libn.* (Win. 1979). **Activities:** 1; 17, 20, 34; 55, 56 **Addr.:** University of BC, Catalogue Records Div., Library Processing Ctr., 2206 East Mall, Vancouver, BC V6T 1Z8 Canada.

Turner, Ruth Elaine (Jl. 28, 1922, Kaysville, UT) Head Gvt. Docum. Dept., Database Srch. Srvs., Weber State Coll. Lib., 1965–, Head, Pub. Srvs. Unit, 1975–79, Head Docum., Per. Depts., Gvt. Docum. Spec., 1973–75, Head, Docum., Curric. Lib., 1971–73, Gen. Col. Dept., Soc. Sci. Libn., 1970–71, Ref., Soc. Sci. Libn., 1969–70, Acq. Libn., 1965–69. **Educ.:** Weber State Coll., 1962–65, BS (Eng.); Brigham Young Univ., 1967–69, MLS. **Orgs.:** ALA: GODORT, *Dir. of Docum. Libns.* (UT Rep., 1972–73); Constn. and By-Laws Com. (1973–74, 1976–77, 1981–82); Elec. Com. (1979–80); ACRL. UT LA: GODORT, Asst. Coord. (1975–77), Coord. (1977–78), various coms. Cnsrtm. of North. UT Hlth. Sci. Libs. ASIS. Various orgs. AAUW: Ogden Branch, 1st VP., Prog. Ch. (1973–75); Stdg. Com. on Status of Women. Natl. Educ. Assn. UT Educ. Assn. Weber State Coll. UT Educ. Assn. Grp.: Bd. Various orgs. **Honors:** Beta Phi Mu, 1969; Lambda Iota Tau, 1964. **Pubns.:** *A Beginner's Manual to Government Documents* (1981); "Copyright Law Status Quo," *UT Libs.* (Fall 1969); "Faculty Status–Do We Deserve It?" *UT Libs.* (Spr. 1976); "Do Local Documents Exist in Utah?" *UT Libs.* (Fall 1976); "Database Subject Searching Comes to Stewart Library" tape/slide (1980). **Activities:** 1;

PROFESSIONAL ACTIVITIES: Institutions: 1. Acad. lib.; 2. Arch.; 3. Assn.; 4. Fed./Gvt. lib.; 5. Inst. lib.; 6. Mfr./Suppl.; 7. Milit. lib.; 8. Musm.; 9. Pub. lib.; 10. Sch. lib.; 11. Sch. of lib. sci.; 12. Spec. lib.; 13. State lib.; 14. (other). **Functions/Activities:** 15. Acq./Col. dev.; 16. Adult srvs.; 17. Admin.; 18. Apprais.; 19. Archit./Bldgs.; 20. Cat./Class.; 21. Chld. srvs.; 22. Circ.; 23. Cons./Pres.; 24. Consult.; 25. Cont. ed.; 26. Educ. lib. sci.; 27. Ext. srvs.; 28. Fund/Grants; 29. Gvt. pubs.; 30. Indx./Abs.; 31. Instr. lib. use; 32. Media srvs.; 33. Micro.; 34. Netwks./Coop.; 35. Persnl.; 36. PR; 37. Publshg.; 38. Recs. mgt.; 39. Ref. srvs.; 40. Repro.; 41. Resrch.; 42. Review.; 43. Secur.; 44. Serials; 45. Spec. col.; 46. Tech. srvs.; 47. Trustees/Bds.; 48. YA srvs.; 49. (other).

29, 31; 75 **Addr.:** Stewart Library 2901, Weber State College, Ogden, UT 84408.

Turner, Susanna J. (Jl. 17, 1940, Allentown, PA) Head, Hum. Ref. Dept., MS State Univ. Lib., 1978–, Head, Circ. Dept., 1976–78; Instr., Lib. Sci. Dept., MS Univ. for Women, 1974–76; Libn., Educ. Lib., Univ. of AL, 1972. **Educ.:** E. Stroudsburg State Coll., 1958–62, BS (Educ.); Univ. of AL, 1971–72, MLS (Lib. Srv.). **Orgs.:** ALA: LIRT (Secy., 1981–82); Prog. Plng. Com. (1978–80), Cont. Educ. Task Force (1978–80). SE LA. MS LA: LIRT (Ch., 1980–81), Ed. Com. (Ch., 1981). **Honors:** Beta Phi Mu. **Pubns.:** Jt. auth., "Bibliographic Instruction: Just Formalizing a Trend?" *MS Libs.* (Sum. 1979). **Activities:** 1; 17, 31, 39; 55, 63 **Addr.:** P.O. Box 4278, Mississippi State, MS 39762.

Turner, Virginia S. (O. 18, 1932, Mobile, AL) Supvsr., Libs., Portsmouth Pub. Schs., 1978–; Supvsr. Ctrl. Prcs., VA Beach Pub. Schs., 1973–78; Resrch. Anal., US Navy, Pentagon, 1958–61. **Educ.:** Amer. Univ., 1951–54, BSS (Intl. Rel.); Pratt Inst., 1970–72, MLIS (LS). **Orgs.:** VA Educ. Media Assn.: PR Com. (1979–80). VA LA: Reg. Nom. Com. (1979–80). ALA: AASL. **Honors:** Beta Phi Mu. **Activities:** 10; 17, 26, 46; 63, 67, 89 **Addr.:** 1365 Baycliff Dr., Virginia Beach, VA 23454.

Turney, Ruth Anderson (N. 27, 1928, New Bedford, MA) Msc. Catlgr., Ferguson Lib., 1978–; Libn., Trinity Par. Lib., 1970–. **Educ.:** Brown Univ., 1945–49, AB (Math.); West. CT State Coll., 1970–75, MA (Eng. Lit.); South. CT State Coll., 1977–78, MLS. **Orgs.:** SLA. CT LA. CS LA: Treas. (1975–79); 2nd VP. (1979–); CT Chap. (Pres., 1978–79). **Activities:** 9, 12; 16, 20, 21; 50, 55, 90 **Addr.:** c/o Trinity Parish Library, 36 Main St., Newtown, CT 06470.

Turock, Betty J. (Je. 12, Scranton, PA) Asst. Prof., Rutgers Univ. Grad. Sch. of Lib. and Info. Std., 1980–; Asst. Dir., Rochester/Monroe Cnty. Lib. Syst., 1978–80; Dir., Montclair Pub. Lib., 1975–77, Asst. Dir., 1973–75; E. Area Head, Forsyth Cnty. Pub. Lib. Syst., 1972–73; Branch Libn., Forsyth Cnty. Pub. Lib. Syst., 1970–72; Educ. Media Spec., Alhambra Pub. Sch. Syst., 1967–70. **Educ.:** Syracuse Univ., 1955, BA (Psy., magna cum laude); Univ. of PA, 1955–56, (Clinical Psy.); Rutgers Univ., 1965–69, MLS (Lib. Srv.), 1978, ABD (Lib. Srv.). **Orgs.:** ALA: Natl. Lib. Week Com. (1976–); PLA, Pub. Lib. Rpt. Com. (Ch., 1979–), Pubns. Com. (1979–); LAMA/Stats. Sect. (Pres., 1982–), Pub. Lib. Stats. Com. (1978–); SRRT, various coms., ofcs. ofcs. NJ LA: various coms. Grass Roots, Inc.: Bd. of Dir., (1974–). Montclair Pub. Sch. Syst.: Title VII Adv. Cncl. on Racial Isolation (1975–77). Rutgers Univ. Grad. Sch. of Lib. and Info. Std. Alum. Assn.: Pres. (1977–78); Exec. Bd. (1976–79); Adv. Assoc. (1977–78); Admis. Com. (1977–78). **Honors:** Beta Phi Mu, 1969; Psi Chi, 1954. **Pubns.:** "Women's Information and Referral Service Asks Community for Answers," *Wilson Lib. Bltn.* (Ap. 1975); "Program Planning for Young Adults; A Response to Young Adult Needs," *Top of the News* (Ja. 1975). **Activities:** 9, 11; 17, 24, 34; 56, 66, 75 **Addr.:** 11 Undercliff Rd., Montclair, NJ 07042.

Turtle, Mary R. (Ap. 29, 1944, South Bend, IN) Pres., AMT Info. Srv., 1979–; Dir., Nat. Resrcs. Lib., TN Valley Arthrty., 1974–79; Acq. Libn., Law Lib., Univ. of Notre Dame, 1966–70. **Educ.:** NM State Univ., 1968–70, BS (Sec. Educ.); Univ. of TN, 1973–74, MSLS (Info. Sci.). **Orgs.:** SLA: South. Appalachian Chap. (Secy., 1976–77). Intl. Assn. of Soc. Sci. Info. Srv. and Tech. **Honors:** Beta Phi Mu, 1974. **Pubns.:** "The Relationship between Time Lag and Place of Publication in Library and Information Science Abstracts and Library Literature," *RQ* (1974); "Library Retrieval Aids Research," *TVA Today* (Jl. 1976). **Activities:** 4, 12; 15, 17, 24; 58, 64, 77 **Addr.:** 629 N. Kellogg, Santa Barbara, CA 93111.

Tuteur, Civia M. (S. 24, 1937, Ware, MA) Chld. Libn., N. Pulaski Branch, Chicago Pub. Lib., 1981–; Asst. Tech. Srvs. Lib., Head Catlgr., Roosevelt Univ., 1974–81; Catlgr., Mundelein Coll., 1969–74; Empl. Couns., Blvd. Empl., 1964–69; Chld. Libn., Franklin Sq. Pub. Lib., 1961–64. **Educ.:** Univ. of MI, 1955–59, BA (Hist.); Pratt Inst., 1959–61, MLS. Roosevelt Univ., 1977, MA (Latin Amer. Std.). **Orgs.:** ALA: LITA; RTSD. IL LA: Rpt., *Resrcs. and Tech. Srv. Nsltr.* (1977–79). Msc. Users' OCLC Grp. Chicago Acad. Lib. Cncl.: Subcom. on Cat. Various orgs. Art Inst., Chicago. AAUP: Roosevelt Univ. Chap. Secy.–Treas. (1975–78). **Honors:** Beta Phi Mu. **Activities:** 1; 20, 46; 54, 56, 66 **Addr.:** 7327 N. Osceola Ave., Chicago, IL 60648.

Tutt, Celestine Claressa (N. 9, 1932, Winston-Salem, NC) Chief Libn., Whitney M. Young, Jr. Meml. Lib. of Soc. Work, Columbia Univ., 1978–, Asst. Libn., 1973–77, Libn., The Urban Ctr., 1971–73. **Educ.:** Winston-Salem Tchrs. Coll., 1949–52, BS (Educ.); Columbia Univ., 1969–71, MLS, various crs. **Orgs.:** ALA. NY LA. Assn. for the Std. of Afro-Amer. Life and Hist. Intl. Conf. on Soc. Welfare. Cncl. on Soc. Work Educ. Natl. Conf. of Christ. and Jews. **Activities:** 1; 15, 17, 39; 92 **Addr.:** 456 Riverside Dr., New York, NY 10027.

Tuttle, Helen Welch (Ap. 13, 1914, Larned, KS) Retired, Asst. Univ. Libn., Tech. Srvs., Princeton Univ. Lib., 1979–, Asst. Univ. Libn., Tech. Srvs., 1968–79; Acq. Libn., Univ. of IL Lib., 1952–68, Asst. Acq. Libn., 1947–52, Biblgphr., Acq. Dept., 1945–47, Jr. Lib. Asst., 1942–45; HS Tchr., Libn., Atlanta (KS) HS, 1936–39. **Orgs.:** ALA: Exec. Bd. (1975–79); Cnclr. (1961–62, 1964–68, 1971–79); Future ALA Structure Com. (Ch., 1976–78); RTSD, various coms., ofcs.; ACRL; RASD. Beta Phi Mu: Pres. (1952–53); Pubns. Com. (Ch., 1962–79. ARL. Cncl. of Natl. Lib. and Info. Assns.: various coms., various orgs. AAUP: Univ. of IL Chap., Exec. Com. (1965–68); Mem. Com. (Ch., 1965–68). Amer. Natl. Stan. Inst.: Com. Z39, Subcom. 22 on Stan. for Lib. Mtrls. Price Indxs. (1969–74). Carey-Thomas Awd. Jury (1973). Frdm. to Read Fndn.: Exec. Bd., (1974–78); Treas., (1976–78); Nom. Com. (Ch., 1976–77). **Honors:** Phi Beta Kappa, 1935; Beta Phi Mu, 1950; Phi Kappa Phi, 1935; Pi Mu Epsilon, 1935. **Pubns.:** Ed., *Beta Phi Mu Chapbook* (1958–79); "From Cutter to Computer: Technical Services in Academic and Research Libraries, 1876–1976," *Libraries for Teaching; Libraries for Research* (1977); "Price Indexes, Library Materials," *Encyclopedia of Library and Information Science* (1977); "Out-of-print Books," *Encyclopedia of Library and Information Science* (1977); "Women in Academic Libraries," *Social Responsibilities and Libraries* (1976); "Coordination of the Technical Services," *Advances in Librarianship* (1975); various articles, papers. **Activities:** 1; 15, 17, 46 **Addr.:** 75 S. Stanworth Dr., Princeton, NJ 08540.

Tuttle, Leah Jane (N. 18, 1921, Lansing, MI) Ref. Dept., Head, Baldwin Pub. Lib., 1962–, Pubcty., 1958–79, Ref. Libn., grp. srvs., and Gen. Asst., 1958–62; Comm. Skills Instr., MI State Univ., 1956–57; Comm. Skills Instr., Heidelberg Coll., 1955–56; Writer, WJIM Radio-TV, 1954–55. Univ. of MI TV Ofc., Univ. of MI, 1953–54; various radio positions, 1945–52. **Educ.:** MI State Univ., 1939–45, BA (Radio, Sp.); Univ. of MI, 1953–55, MA (Sp., TV), 1957–58, AMLS. **Orgs.:** ALA. MI LA: Natl. Lib. Week Pubcty. Com. (1970–72); Ref. Sect., Ch.-Elect (1973–74), Ch. (1974–75); Org. Review Com. (1976–78); Constn. and By-laws Com. (1978–79). Birmingham Hist. Comsn.: VP. (1964–66). Birmingham-Bloomfield League of Women Voters: Finance Adv. Com. (1972–). Alpha Xi Delta Sorority. **Honors:** Beta Phi Mu; Alpha Epsilon Rho; Phi Kappa Phi. **Activities:** 9; 36, 39 **Addr.:** 525 Watkins St., Apt. 103, Birmingham, MI 48009.

Tuttle, Marcia Lee (Ap. 11, 1937, Charlotte, NC) Head, Per. and Serials Dept., Univ. of NC, 1969–, Head, Interlib. Ctr., 1968–69; Head, Ref. Dept., Univ. of VT, 1966–68; Asst. Ref. Libn., Princeton Univ., 1964–66; Catlgr., Princeton Theo. Semy., 1962–64. **Educ.:** Duke Univ., 1955–59, AB (Relig.); Emory Univ., 1959–62, MLn (Libnshp.); Univ. of NC, 1969–74, MA (Geog.). **Orgs.:** ALA: RTSD/Serials Sect. (Ch., 1979–81), Adhoc Cncl. Core Lists of Serials (1978–79). NC LA. **Pubns.:** Jt. Ed., *Title Varies* (1975-79). **Activities:** 1; 15; 39, 44; 70 **Addr.:** Head, Serials Dept., Univ. of NC, Wilson Library 024–A, Chapel Hill, NC 27514.

Tweedy, Albert Vincent (My. 13, 1939, Sparta, MI) Dir., Marion Cnty. Pub. Libs., 1980–; Dir., Alpha Reg. Lib. Syst., 1979–80; Dir., New Martinsville Pub. Lib., 1975–79. **Educ.:** Albion Coll., 1963–67, BA (Hist., Bus. Admin.); Ctrl. MI Univ., 1973–74, MA (Hist.); West. MI Univ., 1974–75, MLS (Libnshp.). **Orgs.:** ALA: PLA/Small and Medium-Sized Lib. Sect. (1978), Exec. Bd. (1980); JMRT, Afflt. Cncl. (WV Rep., 1979–), Orien. Com. (1976–79), Comm. Com. (1976–77), Com. on Governance (1975–77). WV LA: Pub. Lib. Sect. (Pres., 1978–79); various coms., ofcs. lions Club, New Martinsville, WV: Pres. (1979). **Activities:** 9; 17, 34; 52, 55, 91 **Addr.:** Marion County Public Libraries, 321 Monroe St., Fairmont, WV 26554.

Twombly, Carole E. (Ag. 13, 1944, Providence, RI) Libn. Keyes Assocs., 1976–. **Educ.:** Univ. of RI, 1964–70, BA (Soclgy.), 1971–76, MLS. **Orgs.:** SLA: RI Chap., Pres. (1980–81); Pres. Elect (1979–80); Mem. Ch. (1978–79); Treas. (1977–78). Assn. of Recs. Mgrs. and Admins., Inc. **Activities:** 12; 15, 17, 20; 64 **Addr.:** Keyes Associates, 321 S. Main St., Providence, RI 02903.

Tyce, Richard S. (F. 16, 1947, New Britain, CT) Head Libn., PA State Univ., Hazleton Campus Lib., 1981–; Head, Ref. Dept., Wright State Univ. Lib., 1975–81, Soc. Sci. Ref. Libn., 1973–75. **Educ.:** Cornell Univ., 1965–69, BA (Gvt.); Univ. of Pittsburgh, 1971–73, MLS. **Orgs.:** PA LA. Acad. LA of OH: Involvement Com. (Ch., 1976–77). ALA. Bibl. Socty., Univ. of VA. Dayton-Miami Valley Cnsrtm.: Persnl. Com. (Ch., 1975–77); Ref. Srvs. Com. (1976–81). OCLC: ILL Adv. Com. (1979–80). AAUP. Univ. of Pittsburgh/Carnegie Lib. Schs. Alum. Assn.: Secy. (1978–79). **Honors:** Beta Phi Mu. **Pubns.:** *Edward Albee, A Bibliography* (1982); Abstcr., *Abstracts of English Studies* (1972–). **Activities:** 1; 17, 29, 39; 57, 61, 92 **Addr.:** 425 S. Franklin St., Wilkes-Barre, PA 18702.

Tylecki, Mary Frances (Ap. 10, 1950, Lewes, DE) Law Libn., Superior Ct. Law Lib., Sussex Cnty., 1975–; Tech. Prcs. Asst., DE State Coll., Jason Lib. Lrng. Ctr., 1974–75, Circ. Dept. Libn., 1973–74; Libn., Rehoboth Pub. Lib., 1972–73. **Educ.:** Univ. of DE, 1968–72, BA (Amer. Std.). **Orgs.:** DE LA: Nsltr. (1977–79); PR Ch. (1979–80). AALL. Grt. Philadelphia Assn. of Law Libns. **Activities:** 4, 12; 17, 29, 39; 77, 78 **Addr.:** Courthouse, Box 486, Georgetown, DE 19947.

Tyler, Carolyn Smith (Ja. 30, 1923, Culverton, GA) Educ. Libn., Univ. of SC, 1960–; Catlgr., Colleton Cnty. Meml. Lib., 1957–58; Serials Catlgr., Duke Univ., 1956–57; Libn., Div. of Libnshp. Lib., Emory Univ., 1945–56. **Educ.:** GA State Coll. for Women, 1940–44, AB (Eng.); Emory Univ., 1944–45, AB (LS). **Orgs.:** ALA. SC LA. AAUW. **Activities:** 1; 17, 26, 39; 63, 75 **Addr.:** 1100 Eastminster Dr., Columbia, SC 29204.

Tyler, Wilma M. (S. 23, 1922, Plainfield, IA) Elem. Sch. Lib. Media Spec., Dike Elem. Sch., 1970–81; Sch. Libn., Cedar Falls Cmnty. Schs., 1969–70, Sch. Secy., 1960–67; Tchr., Denver (IA) Cmnty. Schs., 1943–44; Tchr., Alta Vista (IA) Cmnty. Schs., 1942–43. **Educ.:** Wartburg Coll., 1940–42, (Elem. Educ.); Univ. of North. IA, 1967–69, BA (LS), 1973–75, MA (LS). **Orgs.:** IA Educ. Media Assn.: State Treas. (1975–77). ALA: AASL; ALA/Encyc. Britannica Com., Sch. Lib. Media Prog. of Year, 1982–. State Dept. of Pub. Instr.: Adv. Com. of Area Educ. Agencies Instr. Media Ctrs. (1978–81). Delta Kappa Gamma Socty.: Lcl. Chap. (Treas., 1978). Natl. Educ. Assn. **Honors:** IA State Dept. of Pub. Instr., IA Educ. Media Assn., IA Rep. for Encyc. Britannica and ALA Awd. for Outstan. Lib. Media Prog. at Elem. Level, 1977, 1979. Kappa Delta Pi. **Activities:** 10, 13; 21, 26, 32; 63, 89 **Addr.:** 31 Carballo Ln., Hot Springs Village, AR 71909.

Tyler-White, Patricia Gayle (O. 8, 1949, Huntsville, TX) Info. Spec., Badische Corp., Resrch. and Dev. Lib., 1979–; Ref. Libn., Houston Pub. Lib., 1976–79; Cnty. Chld. Libn., San Patricio Cnty. Lib. Syst., 1975–76; Ref. Libn., Austin Pub. Lib., 1974–75. **Educ.:** Univ. of TX, Austin, 1969–73, BA (Eng.), 1974, MLS. **Orgs.:** SLA. Houston OLUG. **Activities:** 12; 17, 30, 49-Online srchs.; 60, 75, 91 **Addr.:** Research & Development Library, Badische Corporation, 602 Copper Rd., 605 Bldg., Freeport, TX 77541.

Tynan, Laurie F. (Jl. 14, 1951, North Tonawanda, NY) Asst. Dir., Meadville Pub. Lib., 1975–. **Educ.:** Bucknell Univ., 1969–73, AB (Eng.); Columbia Univ., 1973–75 MS (LS). **Orgs.:** PA LA: N.W. Chap. (Treas., 1976–78). ALA. Women's Srvs., Inc.: Treas. (1979–80). **Activities:** 9; 16, 39; 80, 91 **Addr.:** Meadville Public Library, 848 N. Main St., Meadville, PA 16335.

Tynes, Mary Savan Wilby (Ag. 19, 1944, Laurel, MS) Dir., Educ., MS ETV, 1981–; Dist. Media Dir., Biloxi Pub. Schs., 1977–80; Lib. Supvsr., Clarksdale Pub. Schs., 1970–77; Head Libn., Batesville Pub. Lib., 1966–69. **Educ.:** Univ. of South. MS, 1964–66, BS (Elem. Educ.); Univ. of MS, 1966–69, MLS. **Orgs.:** ALA. AECT. MS Assn. of Media Educs.: Pres.-Elect; Secy. MS LA: Sch. Sect. (Ch., 1975); Legis. Ch. (1977–78); Awds. Ch. (1976); LSCA Ch. (1976–77); Pres.-Elect (1980); Pres. (1981). **Activities:** 1, 9; 17, 31, 32 **Addr.:** P.O. Drawer 1101, Jackson, MS 39205.

U

Uebele, Dorothy Bonnifield (My. 5, 1930, Stockton, CA) Deputy Dir., Palos Verdes Lib. Dist., 1981–; Grad. Adv., Lectr., Grad. Sch. of Lib. and Info. Sci., Univ. of CA, Los Angeles, 1978–81; Catlgr., Ref. Libn., Palos Verdes Lib. Dist., 1974–78; Asst. Libn., Marymount Palos Verdes Coll., 1973–74. **Educ.:** Univ. of CA, Berkeley, 1948–52, BA (Soclgy.); Univ. of CA, Los Angeles, 1971–73, MLS. **Orgs.:** ALA. CA LA: Clearinghouse on Lib. Instr. (1977). Msc. LA. SLA. Leag. of Women Voters: Observer (1976–77). Peninsula Frnds. of the Lib. **Honors:** Univ. of CA, Los Angeles, Lib. Sch. Cand. for Women of the Year Awds., 1973; Beta Phi Mu. **Activities:** 9, 11; 25, 31, 46; 63 **Addr.:** 26767 Shadow Wood Dr., Rancho Palos Verdes, CA 90274.

Uibel, Barbara S. (Mr. 3, 1936, Salt Lake City, UT) Libn., Media Coord., Cheney HS, 1979–; Asst. Prof., Dept. of Educ., Libn., East. WA Univ., 1977–79; Lib. Media Spec., Univ. Mid. Sch., IN 1976–77; Lib. Media Spec., Windsor Sec. Sch., N. Vancouver, BC, 1970–72; AV Coord., East. WA Univ., 1968–69. **Educ.:** Brigham Young Univ., 1954–58, BS (Elem. Instr.), 1966–67, MLS. **Orgs.:** ALA. WA Lib. Media Assn.: Reg. Chap., Prog. Com. Natl. Educ. Assn. WA Educ. Assn. Cheney Educ. Assn. **Honors:** Beta Phi Mu, 1970. **Pubns.:** *Intercultural Bibliography* (1979). **Activities:** 10; 31, 32, 48; 63 **Addr.:** 448 Annie Pl., Cheney, WA 99004.

Ulm, Sandra W. (N. 5, 1942, Valdosta, GA) Admin., Sch. Lib. Media Srvs., FL Dept. of Educ., 1981–, Consult., 1974–81; Dept. Ch., Lib. Media Srvs., Edgewater HS, 1970–74, Asst. Libn., 1965–69; Asst. Libn., Leesburg HS, 1964–65. **Educ.:** FL State Univ., 1960–64, BS (Educ.), 1969–70, MS (LS). **Orgs.:** ALA: AASL, State Asm. (Del., 1973); Exec. Bd. (Rec. Secy., 1977–78), various coms. AECT: Div. of Educ. Media Mgt. (1975–81); Cncl. (Del., 1974), various confs., coms. FL Assn. of Sch. Libns.: Area Ch. (1971–72); Pres.-Elect (1972–73); various coms. SELA: Com. Relating to Stans. for Sch. Lib. Media Progs. (Ch., 1978); AASL Int. Frdm. Netwk. (SELA Rep., 1980–81); Nom. Com. (1981). Various other orgs. FL Assn. of Sch. Admins. FL Assn. of Supvsn. and Curric. Dev. FL Assn. for Media in Educ.: Pres. (1973–74); Exec. Bd., Past-Pres. (1974–75), Ex-Officio Mem. (1977–81); various coms. Natl. Assn. of State Educ. Media Profs.: Secy.-Treas. (1976); Pres.-Elect (1977); Pres. (1978); various coms. **Honors:** Beta Phi Mu; Phi Delta Kappa; Delta Kappa Gamma; Kappa Delta Pi. **Pubns.:** "School Library Media Pro-

Special Subjects/Services: 50. Adult educ.; 51. Advert./Mktg.; 52. Aerosp.; 53. Agric.; 54. Area std.; 55. Arts/Hum.; 56. Autom.; 57. Bibl./Prtg.; 58. Bio. sci.; 59. Bus./Fin.; 60. Chem.; 61. Copyrt.; 62. Documtn.; 63. Educ.; 64. Engin.; 65. Env.; 66. Eth. grps.; 67. Film; 68. Food/Nutr.; 69. Geneal.; 70. Geo.; 71. Geol.; 72. Handcpd.; 73. Hist.; 74. Int. frdm.; 75. Info. sci.; 76. Insr.; 77. Law; 78. Legis.; 79. Math./Comp. sci.; 80. Med.; 81. Metals; 82. Nat. resrcs.; 83. Newsp.; 84. Nuc. sci.; 85. Oral hist.; 86. Petr./Energy; 87. Pharm.; 88. Phys./Astr./Math.; 89. Readg.; 90. Relig.; 91. Sci./Tech.; 92. Soc. sci.; 93. Telecom.; 94. Transp.; 95. (other).

grams: Imperative for the 80's," *FL Libs.* (Mr.–Ap. 1980); "WHCLIS Impacts Florida Schools," *FL Media Qtly.* (Spr. 1980). **Activities:** 10, 14-State Educ. Agency; 17, 24, 32; 63, 78 **Addr.:** Florida Dept. of Education, School Library Media Services, 506 Knott Bldg., Tallahassee, FL 32301.

Ulrich, S. Jane (Je. 10, 1948, Beaumont, TX) Syst. Coord., TX Panhandle Lib. Syst., 1978–; Pub. Srvs. Libn., Deer Park Pub. Lib., 1975–77; Info. Spec., Southwest Info. Assoc., 1974–75. **Educ.:** Stephen F. Austin State Univ., 1966–71, BA, MA (Thea.); Univ. of TX, Austin, 1973–74, MLS. **Orgs.:** TX LA: JMRT (Ch. Elec., 1981–82; Secy.–Treas., 1979–80). ALA. **Honors:** Beta Phi Mu. **Pubns.:** Cmplr., *Austin Information–A Directory of Libraries and Information Centers* (1975); Ed., *Saddlebags* nsltr.; "Developing Skills in Planning Humanities–Based Library Programs," *SWLA Nsltr.* (O. 1975). Various articles. **Activities:** 3; 17, 24, 25 **Addr.:** P.O. Box 2171, Amarillo, TX 79189.

Underhill, Charles Sterling (My. 3, 1913, Buffalo, NY) Retired, 1976–; Assoc. Libn., Head, Per. Dept., SUNY Coll., Buffalo, 1969–74, Cat. Dept., 1965–69; Dir., Newark Pub. Lib., 1958–65; Dir., Corning Pub. Lib., 1955–58; various libn. positions, 1944–55. **Educ.:** Williams Coll., 1930–34, AB (Liberal Arts); Univ. of Buffalo, 1941–44, BLS. **Orgs.:** ALA. NY LA. **Pubns.:** Cmplr., *Handy Key to Your National Geographics* (1980); "Sketch for a Picture Collection," *Wilson Lib. Bltn.* (Mr. 1956). **Activities:** 1, 9; 17, 20, 39 **Addr.:** 7491 Center St., W. Falls, NY 14170.

Unruh, Elizabeth Lee (Ag. 28, 1943, Louisville, KY) Mktg. Rep., DIALOG Info. Srvs., Inc., 1980–; Mktg. Mgr., Online Srvs., Data Courier, Inc., 1978–80, Mktg. Rep., 1975–78. **Educ.:** Univ. of KY, 1962–65, BA (Fr.), 1967–70, MA (Eng.). **Orgs.:** ASIS. **Pubns.:** *User Education–The Channel for Communication* (1978); *Data Base User Aids and Materials–A Study* (1979); "Conference Papers Index," *Online* (Jl. 1978). **Activities:** 12; 26, 30; 51 **Addr.:** DIALOG Information Services, Inc., 3460 Hillview Ave., Palo Alto, CA 94304.

Unterburger, George William (Ap. 29, 1920, Dayton, OH) Chief, Tech. and Sci. Dept., Detroit Pub. Lib., 1980–, Chief, Gen. Info. Dept., 1975–80, Tech. Lit. Spec., 1961–75. **Educ.:** Otterbein Coll., 1937–41, AB (Liberal Arts); Univ. of MI 1947–48, ABLS. **Orgs.:** ALA. **Honors:** Detroit Pub. Lib., Staff Meml. and Flwshp. Awd., 1968. **Activities:** 9; 15, 17, 39; 91 **Addr.:** Detroit Public Library, 5201 Woodward Ave., Detroit, MI 48227.

Updegrove, Pat F. (D. 12, 1925, Jacksonville, FL) Lib. Coord., TX City Indp. Sch. Dist., 1967–; Tchr., Libn., TX City Jr. HS, 1951–67; Catlgr., Univ. of TX Lib., Austin, 1949–51; Libn., Armed Forces Staff Coll., 1945–49. **Educ.:** Coll. of William and Mary, 1936–40, BA (LS, Eng.); Univ. of Houston, 1953–55, MA (Educ.), 1970–72, Supvsr. Cert. (Elem., Sec. Educ.). **Orgs.:** TX Assn. of Sch. Libns.: Ch. (1976–77). TX LA: Nom. Com.; Constn. Com. ALA: AASL, Chrt. Affl. Asm. (TX Rep., 1977). Delta Kappa Gamma, Epsilon Tau: VP. (1976–80). **Honors:** TX Congs. of Parents and Tchrs., Hon. Life Mem., 1966. **Pubns.:** "TASL–Program, Issues, Problems," *TX Lib. Jnl.* (Win. 1977); Ed., *Media Matters* (1976–77). **Addr.:** TX City Indep. School Dist., 111 Seaside Ln., TX City, TX 77590.

Urbach, Peter F. (N. 13, 1935, London, Eng.) Pres., Pergamon Intl. Info. Corp., 1980–; Deputy Dir., Natl. Tech. Info. Srv., 1970–80; Dir., Prod. Plng., Leasco Info. Syst. Co., 1969–70; Assoc. Dir., Syst., Clearinghouse for Fed. Sci. and Tech. Info., 1965–69. **Educ.:** Carnegie Inst. of Tech., 1953–57, BS (Electrical Engin.); George Washington Univ., 1958–64, JD (Law), 1964–68, MEA (Engin. Admin.). **Orgs.:** ASIS. Natl. Micro. Assn.: Educ. Com. (Ch., 1976–79). Chemical Abs. Srv.: Adv. Bd. (1972–78). Engin. Indx.: Trustee (1977–80). **Pubns.:** "Access to Journal Article Copies Through NTIS," *IEEE Transactions on Professional Communication* (N. 1977); "Recent Developments in Government-owned Patent Licensing," *Licensing Executives Society LaNouvelles* (Je. 1973); "Agency Cooperation in Processing Technical Report Literature," *Jnl. of Chemical Documtn.* (1973); jt. auth., "An Experiment to Determine the Effectiveness of Various Announcement Media on CFSTI Sales," *Proc. of ASIS* (Fall 1968); jt. auth., "Experimentation, Modeling and Analysis to Establish a New Pricing Policy at the Clearinghouse for Federal Scientific and Technical Information," *Proc. of ASIS* (Fall 1968); various rpts., articles. **Activities:** 37; 56, 61 **Addr.:** Pergamon International Information Corp., 1340 Old Chain Bridge Rd., McLean, VA 22101.

Urban, Mary Jane (Jaine) (Ag. 12, 1944, Providence, RI) Asst. Dir., Info. Srvs., O'Melveny and Myers, 1979–; Mgr., Litigation Support Srvs., Un. Oil Co., CA, 1979–; Mgr., Litigation Support Srvs., O'Melveny and Myers, 1976–79. **Educ.:** Univ. of CA, Riverside, 1967, BA (Eng.), 1970, MA (Eng.); Univ. of South. CA, 1976, MS (LS). **Orgs.:** Assn. of Rec. Mgr. and Admin. Assoc. Info. Mgrs. AALL. ASIS. **Honors:** Beta Phi Mu. **Pubns.:** "Consumer-At-Law: Space Savers," *Los Angeles Lawyer* (Ja. 1980); "Enter The Information Manager: A Selected Bibliography of Journal Materials," *Private Law Library 1980's and Beyond* (1979). **Activities:** 12; 38, 39, 46; 56, 75, 77 **Addr.:** O'Melveny & Myers, 611 W. 6th St., Los Angeles, CA 90017.

U'Ren-Stubbings (Dr.), Hilda R. (Hayle, Cornwall, Untd. Kingdom) Bibl. Resrch., 1981–; Lib. Dir., St. John's Sch., 1976–81; Biblgphr., Intl. Schol. Bk. Srvs., 1974–75; Prof., Clackamas Cmnty. Coll., 1971–73; Prof., Willamette Univ., 1968–70; Prof., Warner Pac. Coll., 1967–68. **Educ.:** Stetson Univ., 1956–60, BA (Pol. Geog.), 1964–65, MA (Eng.) Vanderbilt Univ., 1965–68, PhD (Compar. Lit.); George Peabody Coll., 1976–77, MLS. **Orgs.:** ALA. **Honors:** Beta Phi Mu. **Pubns.:** *Renaissance Spain in Its Literary Relations with England and France: a Critical Bibliography* (1969); "The Celtic World," *An Baner Kernewek* (My. 1978). **Activities:** 10; 17, 41; 55, 57, 92 **Addr.:** 21443 S. Yeoman Rd., Beavercreek, OR 97004.

Urquidi, John de Belfort (Ja. 1, 1932, El Paso, TX) Lib. Consult., Asia Fndn., 1978–; Reg. Consult., Francophone Africa, IFLA, 1976–77, Liaison Ofcr. to UNESCO, 1977; various consult. assignments, The Asia Fndn., 1969–75; Head, Univ. of Alger Lib. Proj., The Ford Fndn., ALA, 1966–69; Gifts and Exch. Libn., Univ. of CA, Los Angeles, 1965–66; Asst. Ref. Libn., Univ. of CA, Riverside, 1963–65; Tchr., Los Angeles Sch. Dist., 1952–59. **Educ.:** Los Angeles State Univ., 1949–51, BA (Educ.); Univ. of South. CA, 1955–59, MSLS; Univ. of Paris, 1959–60 Dip. (Fr. Lit.); Inst. de Phonétique de Paris, 1960–62, Grad. cert. (Fr. phonetics). **Orgs.:** ALA. Pakistan LA. Afghanistan LA: Hon. Pres. (1973). Vietnam LA: Hue Univ. Chap. (Sponsor, 1972). Alpha Mu Gamma: Los Angeles City College Chap. (Secy., 1950). L'Amicale d'Ubu Roi: USC Secy. (1958). Anciens de la Cité Univ. de Paris: VP. (1968). **Honors:** Kabul Univ. Lib., Scroll of Apprec., 1974. **Pubns.:** "Afghanistan," *ALA Encyclopedia of Library and Information Services* (1980). **Activities:** 1, 3; 20, 26, 39; 54, 66, 75, 92 **Addr.:** 1820 S. Orange Ave., Monterey Park, CA 91754.

Urquiza, Rosina (N. 9, 1921, Matanzas, Cuba) Cat., Roux Lib., FL South. Coll., 1970–; Dir., Lib., Inst. del Vedado, Havana, Cuba, 1946–66, Libn., 1946–59; Ref., Cat., Sociedad Econ. de Amigos del Pais, Havana, Cuba, 1948–60; Prof., Ref., Cuban Bibl., Cuban Lib. Sch., 1950–53; Prof., Ref., Lib. Sch., Univ. of Havana, 1950. **Educ.:** Inst. de Matanzas, Cuba, 1935–39, Bachiller Letras y Ciencia; Univ. of Havana, Cuba, 1939–43, Dr (Phil., Letters), 1947–49, (Lib. Sci.). **Orgs.:** FL LA. Cuban LA: Chrt. Mem.; *Bltn.* Ed. (1949–52). Coll. Natl. de Bibtcr. Univ., Havana, Cuba. FL South. Coll. Women's Club. Lakeland Concert Assn. Coll. Natl. de Doctores en Ciencias y en Filosofía y Letras, Havana, Cuba. **Pubns.:** *Ensayo de una bibliografía para bibliotecas de centros secundarios* (1959); "Cuban Reference Sources," *Manual de fuentes de informacion* (1957); Editorials and some articles in the Bulletin of Cuban Library Association - 1949–52. **Activities:** 1, 9; 20, 39 **Addr.:** 213 W. Ariana St., Lakeland, FL 33803.

Uses, Anne Katherine (Ja. 14, 1922, Shenandoah, PA) Libn., Philadelphia HS for Girls, 1973–; Libn., John Bartram HS, 1954–73; Libn., Sayre Jr. HS, 1950–54; Libn., Holmes Jr. HS, 1946–50; Libn., Lewes Spec. Sch. Dist., 1944–46; Libn., John Bartram Evening Sch., 1966–70, Tchr., 1966–69. **Educ.:** Kutztown State Tchrs. Coll., 1939–43, BEd (LS Soc. Std.); Drexel Univ., 1943–44, BS (LS); Bucknell Univ., 1959–63, MA (Hist.); W. Chester State Coll., 1970–72, (Media). **Orgs.:** ALA. Cath. LA. PA Lrng. Resrcs. Assn. Assn. of Philadelphia Sch. Libns.: Com. for Constn. Rev. Various orgs. Pop. Culture Assn. Dickens Flwshp. Polish Amer. Hist. Assn. Kutztown Alum. Assn. Various orgs. **Pubns.:** Contrib., *Popular Culture Abs.* (1975). **Activities:** 10; 15, 17, 31; 63 **Addr.:** Philadelphia High School for Girls, Broad St. and Olney Ave., Philadelphia, PA 19141.

Usher, Elizabeth Reuter (Seward, NE) Chief Libn. Emeritus, Metro. Musm. of Art, 1980–, Chief Libn., Thomas J. Watson Lib., 1968–80, Chief, Art Ref. Lib., 1961–68, Asst. Libn., 1954–61, Asst. Libn., Actg. Libn., 1954–57, Head Catlgr., Head Ref. Libn., 1953–54, Cat., Ref. Libn., 1948–53; Libn., Cranbrook Acad. of Art, 1945–48; various libn. positions, 1943–45. **Educ.:** The Univ. of NE, 1941–42, BS Ed (Eng.); Univ. of IL, 1943–44, BS (LS); Concordia Tchrs. Coll., Dip. (Educ.); various crs. **Orgs.:** ARLIS/NA: Stan. Com. (1974–81); Pubshg. Awds. Com. (Ch., 1977). SLA: Pres. (1967–68); Bd. of Dir. (1960–63, 1966–69); NY Musm., Arts and Hum. Grp. (Ch., 1954–55); various coms., ofcs. Archons of Colophon: Conv. (1980–81). NY Lib. Club. Metro. Ref. and Resrch. Lib. Agency: Bd. of Trustees; Secy. (1971–77); VP. (1977–80). Heritage Village Country Club Women's Golf Assn.: Bd. of Dir. (1980–). Socty. of Archit. Hist.: NY Chap. **Honors:** SLA, Hall of Fame, 1980. **Pubns.:** "The Metropolitan Museum of Art Library," *Encyclopedia of Library and Information Science* (1976); "The Challenge for Library Schools An Employment View," *Spec. Libs.* (O., 1973); "Rare Books and the Art Museum Library," *Spec. Libs.* (Ja., 1961); "Continuing Bibliography for the Fine Arts in the United States," *Actes Colloques Internaux du Centre National de la Recherche Scientifique, Sciences Humaines* (1969). **Activities:** 8, 12; 15, 17, 24, 26, 35, 41; 55 **Addr.:** 557–A Heritage Village, Poverty Rd., Southbury, CT 06488.

Usher, Esther (O. 10, 1917, Lynn, MA) Retired, 1981–, Libn., Untd. Engin. and Constructors Inc., 1956–; Asst. Libn., Essex Inst., 1943–55, Catlgr., 1938–42; Asst. Ed., Essex Inst. Hist. Col., 1943–55. **Educ.:** Simmons Coll., 1934–38, BS (LS). **Orgs.:** SLA: Anl. Conf., Transp. and Tours (Ch., 1972). MA LA. ALA. Photographic Socty. of Amer. N. Shore Simmons Club: Treas. **Honors:** Simmons Coll., Alum. Srv. Awd., 1977. **Activities:** 12; 15, 17, 20; 64, 84, 91 **Addr.:** 22 Centre St., Danvers, MA 01923.

Utterback, Nancy (N. 15, 1947, Chicago, IL) Head, Pub. Srvs., Univ. of Louisville, 1977–; AHEC Libn., Univ. of ND, 1975–77; Dssm. Unit Spec., KY Dept. for Human Resrcs., 1974–75; ILL, Univ. of KY, 1971–74. **Educ.:** Univ. of IL, Chicago, 1966–70, BS (Pol. Sci.); Univ. of KY, 1971–74, MSLS; Med. LA, 1975–81, Cert. **Orgs.:** Med. LA: Midwest Reg. Grp., Bd. of Dir. (1979–81). KY LA. Amer. Bar Assn. **Activities:** 1, 12; 17, 22, 39; 80 **Addr.:** Kornhauser Health Sciences Library, University of Louisville, Louisville, KY 40292.

Uyehara, Harry Yoshimi (Ja. 6, 1934, Honolulu, HI) Asst. Prof., Univ. of HI, 1976–; Staff Spec. II, Sch. Lib. Srvs., Fed. Progs., HI State Dept. of Educ., 1975–76, Prog. Spec. I, Sch. Lib. Srvs., 1966–75; Sch. Libn., Wahiawa Intermediate Sch., 1962–66; Traveling Sch. Libn., Ctrl. Oahu Sch. Dist., 1961–62; Tchr.-Libn., Waiakea-Kai Elem. and Intermediate Sch., 1960–61. **Educ.:** Univ. of HI, 1954–58, BEd (Educ.); Univ. of MI, 1964–65, AMLS; 1957–58, Prof. Dip. (Educ.); Columbia Univ., 1969–70, MA (Instr. Media), 1971–78, EdD (Instr. Tech., Media). **Orgs.:** ALA: Mem. Com. (1974–77); Newbery-Caldecott Com. (1978–79); ALSC, Intl. Rel. Com. (1979–81); Newbery Com. (1981–82). HI LA: Treas., 1967–1969; Dir., 1975–1976; Pres. (1977–78); VP. (1976–77); various ofcs. AALS. Intl. Assn. of Sch. Libnshp; various orgs. **Honors:** Phi Delta Kappa; Kappa Delta Pi. **Pubns.:** "The Pohukaina School Library Media Center," *IL Libs.* (S. 1972); "Introducing HLA," *Pac. Assn. For Comm. and Tech. Jnl.* (Fall 1977); ed., *HI LA Jnl.* (1978); Ed., *The Golden Key: Jnl. of The HI Assn. of Sch. Libns.* (1980). **Addr.:** University of HI at Manoa, Graduate School of Library Studies, 2550 The Mall, Honolulu, HI 96822.

V

Vaden, William McGill (Ap. 30, 1921, Harriman, TN) Deputy Mgr., DOE Tech. Info. Ctr., 1963–; Chief, Pubshg. Branch, AEC Tech. Info. Ctr., 1962–63, Asst. Chief, Pubshg. Branch, 1955–62; Deputy Chief, Contract Grp., McGraw-Hill Bk. Co., Inc., 1953–55. **Educ.:** TN Tech., 1941–47, BS (Eng.). **Orgs.:** ASIS. IEA Coal Resrch. Tech. Info. Srv., London: US Tech. Rep. (1977–81). Intl. Nuc. Info. Syst.: US Std. Team. IAEA, Vienna. **Honors:** Dept. of Energy, Merit. Srv. Awd., 1979; Atomic Energy Comsn., Cert. of Apprec. for Spec. Srv., 1968; Atomic Energy Comsn., Superior Performance Awd., 1960. **Pubns.:** "USAEC Data Base Expansion to Include Non-nuclear Information," *Information Systems: Their Interconnection and Compatibility* (1975); *An Analysis of World-wide Contributions to Nuclear Science Abstracts, 1970* (1971); "Fossil Energy Information Resources in the US," *Lib. Sci.* (Je. 1977). **Activities:** 4; 17, 29, 30; 75, 84, 86 **Addr.:** 982 W. Outer Dr., Oak Ridge, TN 37830.

Vagt, J. Paul (N. 28, 1923, Jackson, MN) Dir., Lrng. Resrcs., Tarrant Cnty. Jr. Coll., 1967–; Dir., Libs., Midwestern Univ., 1964–67; Libn., Odessa Coll., 1961–64; Libn., Howard Cnty. Jr. Coll., 1953–61. **Educ.:** N. TX State Univ., 1947–49, BA (LS); Univ. of TX, Austin, 1951–53, MLS; TX Tech. Coll., 1960–61. **Orgs.:** TX LA: Conf. Lcl. Arrange. (Ch., 1978); Bylaws Com. (1977); VP. (1956); College Div. (Ch., 1961). ALA: Lib. Admin. Div., Bldgs. Com. (1977–78). TX Assn. of Educ. Tech. AECT. TX Lib. Systs. Act Adv. Bd. (Ch., 1980–81). Phi Delta Kappa: TX Christ. Univ. Chap. (Pres., 1970–71). Gideons, Intl. **Honors:** Phi Delta Kappa, Weldon Lucas Awd., 1974. **Activities:** 1; 17, 32 **Addr.:** 7329 Normandy Dr., Fort Worth, TX 76112.

Vaillancourt, Pauline M. (Fall River, MA) Assoc. Prof., Sch. of Lib. and Info. Sci., SUNY, Albany, 1970–; Consult., self-empl., 1968–70; Lib. Dir., Meml. Sloan-Kettering Cancer Ctr., 1960–68; Lib. Dir., Kings Park State Hosp., 1958–60; Libn., Sch. of Nursing Lib., Mary Immaculate Hosp., 1952–58. **Educ.:** St. John's Univ. Coll., Brooklyn, NY, BS (Bio.); Columbia Univ., MSLS; DLS, 1968. **Orgs.:** ALA: Ref. and Subscrpn. Bks. Review Com. (1980–); various coms. NY LA, 1958–61, Committee on Institutional Library Work, 1959–60. SLA: NY Chap., Ch. (1952–53), Nom. Com. (1953–54), various coms., ofcs.; Bio. Sci. Div., Nom. Com., (1952–53); various coms., ofcs. Med. LA: NY Reg. Grp. Mem. Com. (Ch., 1954–57), Hosplty. Com. (Ch., 1973–74); various coms., ofcs. AALS: Cont. Ed. Com. (Ch., 1977–78, 1978–79). Various orgs. AAAS. Amer. Chemical Socty.: Div. of Chemical Info. Natl. Comsn. on Libs. and Info. Sci. CLENE Proj.: Bd. of Dir., Nom. Com. (1975–76), Task Force on Implementation of the Recog. Syst. (1977–78). NY Acad. of Sci.: Sect. on Comp. and Info. Sci., Adv. Com. **Pubns.:** *International Directory of Acronyms in Library Information and Computer Science* (1980); jt. auth., "Library School Curricula," *Lib. Jnl.*, (My. 15, 1951); jt. auth., "A Faculty Writes a Minutes Manual," *Amer. Jnl. of Nursing* (Ag. 1955); "Periodical Checklist for Libraries in Catholic Schools of Nursing," *Cath. Lib. World* (F. 1956); "Hospital Nursing School Libraries," *Bltn. of the Med. LA* (Ap., 1956); various articles, bk. reviews. **Activities:** 11, 12; 17, 24, 37; 80, 91 **Addr.:** School of Library and Information Science, SUNY–Albany, Albany, NY 12222.

PROFESSIONAL ACTIVITIES: Institutions: 1. Acad. lib.; 2. Arch.; 3. Assn.; 4. Fed./Gvt. lib.; 5. Inst. lib.; 6. Mfr./Suppl.; 7. Milit. lib.; 8. Musm.; 9. Pub. lib.; 10. Sch. lib.; 11. Sch. of lib. sci.; 12. Spec. lib.; 13. State lib.; 14. (other). **Functions/Activities:** 15. Acq./Col. dev.; 16. Adult srvs.; 17. Admin.; 18. Apprais.; 19. Archit./Bldgs.; 20. Cat./Class.; 21. Chld. srvs.; 22. Circ.; 23. Cons./Pres.; 24. Consult.; 25. Cont. ed.; 26. Educ. lib. sci.; 27. Ext. srvs.; 28. Fund/Grants; 29. Gvt. pubs.; 30. Indx./Abs.; 31. Instr. lib. use; 32. Media srvs.; 33. Micro.; 34. Netwks./Coop.; 35. Persnl.; 36. PR; 37. Publshg.; 38. Recs. mgt.; 39. Ref. srvs.; 40. Repro.; 41. Resrch.; 42. Review.; 43. Secur.; 44. Serials; 45. Spec. col.; 46. Tech. srvs.; 47. Trustees/Bds.; 48. YA srvs.; 49. (other).

Vainstein, Rose (Ja. 7, 1920, Edmonton, AB) Margaret Mann Prof. of Lib. Sci. Sch. of Lib. Sci., Univ. of MI, 1974–, Prof., Sch. of Lib. Sci., 1968–74; Dir., Bloomfield Twp. Pub. Lib. (MI), 1964–68; Dir., Pub. Libs. Resrch. Std., Sch. of Libnshp., Univ. of BC, 1963–64, Assoc. Prof., Sch. of Libnshp., 1961–64; Pub. Lib. Spec., Lib. Srvs. Branch, US Ofc. of Educ., Dept. of HEW, 1957–61; Head, Ext. Dept. Gary Pub. and Lake Cnty. Lib., 1955–57; Pub. Lib. Consult., CA State Lib., 1953–55; various libn. positions, 1942–52. **Educ.:** Miami Univ., 1937–41, BA (Eng.); West. Rsv. Univ., 1941–42, BLS (Pub. Libnshp.); Univ. of IL, 1951–52, MS (Pub. Libnshp.). **Orgs.:** ALA: Cncl. (1956–60; 1974–78), Budget Asm. (1978–79); ASCLA, Nom. Com.; PLA, Actv. Com. (Ch., 1974–76), Stan. Com. (Ch., 1971–74), various coms., ofcs.; ASD; Lib. Admin. Div., various coms. AALS: various coms. Beta Phi Mu: Exec. Cncl. (1960–63); various com. CLENE: Inst. Rep. (1976–77). Various orgs. Univ. of MI Alum. Assn.: Alum. Athena Awd. Com. (1972–73). Woman's Resrch. Club, Univ. of MI: Treas. (1971–72); Loan Fund (Ch., 1975–79). LA of Eng. AAUP. **Honors:** Fulbright Awd., Eng., 1952–53; Cncl. on Lib. Resrcs., Fellow, 1974–75; Phi Beta Kappa, 1976; Women's Resrch. Club, 75th Anniv. Awd., 1978; other hons. **Pubns.:** "Public Libraries in British Columbia, A Survey with Recommendations," (1966); "State Standards for Public Libraries," *US Ofc. Educ. Bltn.* (1960); "The Trustee and Public Library Standards," *The Library Trustee, A Practical Guide* (1978); "Teaching the Elements of Community Analysis: Problems and Opportunities," *Lib. Trends* (Ja. 1976); "Aging in the Modern World," *OK Libn.* (O. 1960); various articles. **Activities:** 9, 11; 16, 17, 26; 50, 66, 89 **Addr.:** School of Library Science, University of Michigan, Ann Arbor, MI 48109.

Vaisey, G. Douglas (My. 22, 1946, Peterborough, ON) Head, Info. Srvs., St. Mary's Univ., 1973–; Ref. Libn., Dalhousie Univ., 1970–73. **Educ.:** Trent Univ., 1964–68, BA (Hist.); Dalhousie Univ., 1969–70, MLS. **Orgs.:** Atl. Provs. LA: Treas. (1974–76). NS LA. Can. Assn. Info. Sci. Marine Libns. Assn. NS On-Line Cnsrtm. Conv. (1980–). Atl. Provs. Bk. Review: Ed. Bd., (1980–). **Pubns.:** *The Labour Companion: A Bibliography of Canadian Labour History...1950–1975* (1980); *African Government Publications: A Selective Bibliography of Bibliographies* (1973); "Canadian Labour Bibliography," *Labour/Le Travailleur* (1981); "Canadian Labour Bibliography," *Com. on Can. Labour Hist. Bltn.* (1976–80). **Activities:** 1; 31, 39; 59, 75, 92 **Addr.:** Information Services, Patrick Power Library, St. Mary's University, Halifax, NS B3H 3C3 Canada.

Valint, Nancy Jean (Mr. 28, 1950, Trenton, MI) Libn., Foster Assoc., Inc., 1976–. **Educ.:** Wayne State Univ., 1971–74, BA (Hum.), 1974–75, MSLS; 1976, Cert. Med. Libn. **Orgs.:** SLA. **Honors:** Phi Beta Kappa, 1974. **Activities:** 4, 12; 15, 38, 39; 55, 82, 86 **Addr.:** Foster Associates, Inc., 1101 17th St. N.W., Washington, DC 20036.

Valk, Barbara G. (Mr. 27, 1945, San Francisco, CA) Coord., Bibl. Pubns. and Srvs., Univ. of CA, Los Angeles, Latin Amer. Ctr., 1981–, Ed., *Hisp. Amer. Per. Indx.*, 1976–81; Ref. Spec., Latin Amer. Std., Rom. Lang., AZ State Univ., 1973–76. **Educ.:** Smith Coll., 1963–68, AB (Latin Amer. Std.); Rosary Coll., 1972–73, MALS. **Orgs.:** SALALM: Pres. (1981–82); VP., Pres.-Elect (1980–81); Conf. Plng. Com. (Ch., 1979); Exec. Bd. (1979–82). ALA: RASD/Hist. Sect., Com. on Indexing and Abs. (1979–81). ASIS. Latin Amer. Std. Assn. **Honors:** Phi Beta Kappa, 1967; Beta Phi Mu, 1973; Natl. Endow. for the Hum., Resrch. tools grants, 1976, 1978, 1981. **Pubns.:** Ed., *Hispanic American Periodicals Index* (1975–); Cmplr., *HAPI Thesaurus and Name Authority, 1975–1977* (1980); "Cooperation in the Publication of Basic Bibliographic Works," *Latin Amer. Resrch. Review* (Fall 1977). **Activities:** 12; 17, 30, 37; 54, 56, 57 **Addr.:** Latin American Center, University of CA, 405 Hilgard, Los Angeles, CA 90024.

Valvoda, Mary Alice (O. 3, 1937, Detroit, MI) Corporate Info. Resrcs. Mgt. Consult., Stan. Oil Co., 1980–; Adjunct Prof., Case West. Rsv. Univ., 1979–81; Mgr., Resrch., Info. Srvs., McKinsey and Co. Inc., 1977–80; Dir. Inst. Resrch., Info. Srvs., Lakeland Cmnty. Coll., 1972–77; various resrch. positions, Grt. Cleveland Growth Bd., 1966–69; Resrch. Assoc., Supvsr., West. Rsv. Univ. Ctr. for Documtn. and Comm. Resrch., 1960–62; various tech. positions, TRW, Inc., Gen. Electric Co. Glass Tech. Lab.; various tchg. positions. **Educ.:** John Carroll Univ. 1955–72, BA (Eng.); Case West. Rsv. Univ., 1973–76, MSLS (Info. Sci.); Natl. Grad. Univ., Cert. of Completion (Grant, Contract Negtn. and Admin.). **Orgs.:** ASIS: Northeast OH Chap. Ch. (1980–81); Prog. Ch. (1979–80). SLA. AECT. Amer. Rec. Mgt. Assn. Amer. Mgt. Assn. Comp. Retrieval Srvs.: Spec. Interest Grp. Lake Cnty. Mental Hlth. Com. (Ch., 1973). Various orgs. **Honors:** Lakeland Cmnty. Coll., Bd. Recog. for dev. of inst. resrch. srvs. ofc., 1977. **Pubns.:** *Theory and Practical Application of Information Research Services at Lakeland Community College* (1975); *Development of a Communications Media Technology Program* (1974); *Comparison of Manual and Machine Literature Searching Techniques for Technical and Metallurgical Literature* (1963); *Mini-Guide Series of brief information profiles to orient new consultants and researchers* (1979); "Communication–A Point of View" TV prod. (1976). **Activities:** 11, 12; 17, 26, 38; 56, 59, 75 **Addr.:** The Standard Oil Co., Midland Bldg., Cleveland, OH 44115.

Vambery, Joseph Thomas (Je. 9, 1908, Sarajevo, Bosnia, Yugoslavia) Retired, 1980–, Head Law Libn., Pace Univ. Sch. of Law, 1978–80; Intl. Law Libn., Columbia Univ. Law Lib., 1967–76, Law Catlgr., 1960–67, Catlgr., 1960–62; Chief Attorney of Electrotrust, Budapest Hungary, 1950–56, Prac. Attorney at Law, 1935–49; Asst. Attorney, Hoffher, Schrantz, Clayton, Shuttleworth, Limited, 1931–35. **Educ.:** Pazmany Univ. of Sci., 1926–30 JD (Law), 1930–31, Doc Juris; Cncl. of Unfd. Judge and Lawyer Examinations, 1935, Judge and Lawyer Dip.; The Cath. Univ. of Amer., 1958–60, MS (LS). **Orgs.:** AALL. **Honors:** Beta Phi Mu, 1960. **Pubns.:** Jt. auth., *Cumulative List and Index of Treaties and International Agreements 1969–1974* (1977); *Annual Review of United Nations Affairs, 1975* (1976); *Annual Review of United Nations Affairs, 1974* (1976); "Documents and Publications of International Governmental Organizations," *Law Lib. Jnl.* (1971); "New Scope and Content of Cooperative Cataloging," *Law Lib. Jnl.* (1967). **Addr.:** 167 Chestnut St., Demarest, NJ 07627.

Van Allen, Neil Kennedy (Jl. 17, 1925, Little Falls, NY) Staff Libn., Gen. Motors Resrch. Labs., 1966–; Tech. Libn., Gen. Electric Co., 1964–66; Sci. Ed., Libn., Wyman-Gordon Co., 1960–64; Ofc. Mgr., R & H Mach., Inc., 1958–60; Advert. Mgr., Botwinik Bros. of MA, Inc., 1953–55. **Educ.:** Un. Coll., 1943, 1946–49, BA (Lit.); Cornell Univ., 1949–50, MA (Amer. Lit.); Simmons Coll., 1960–64, MS (LS). **Orgs.:** SLA: Metals. Div. Ch.-Elect (1977–78), Ch. (1978–79); Transp. Div. Secy.–Treas. (1972–73), Ch.-Elect (1973–74), Ch., (1974–75, 1975–77); Bylaws Com. **Pubns.:** Jt. Auth., *NHTSA/SASI Cooperative Thesaurus of Highway and Motor Vehicle Safety Literature Terms* (1973); *Air Cushion Restraint Systems: A Bibliography* (1975). **Activities:** 12; 17, 30, 39; 81, 94 **Addr.:** System on Automotive Safety Information–REB 225, General Motors Research Laboratories, General Motors Technical Center, Warren, MI 48090.

Van Benthuysen, Robert F. (Mr. 11, 1924, New York City, NY) Lib. Dir., Monmouth Coll., 1957–; Libn., Pascack Valley Reg. HS, 1956–57; Libn. II, Newark Pub. Lib., 1952–56; YA Libn., NY Pub. Lib., 1951–52. **Educ.:** Seton Hall Univ., 1946–50, BS (Eng.); Drexel Univ., 1950–51, MSLS. **Orgs.:** ALA. NJ LA: Coll. and Univ. Sect. (Pres., 1967–68); Ref. Sect. (Pres., 1964–65) Hist. and Bibl. Sect. (Pres., 1972–73). NJ Hist. Socty. **Honors:** Amer. Assn. for State and Lcl. Hist., Awd. of Merit, 1976; NJ Hist. Comsn., 1979. **Pubns.:** *Monmouth County, 1776–1973, A Bibliography of Published Works* (1975); various bk. reviews, *Choice, The American Reference Book Annual;* various abs., *American History and Life.* **Activities:** 1; 17, 45, 47; 57, 70 **Addr.:** Guggenheim Memorial Library, Monmouth College, W. Long Branch, NJ 07764.

Van Brunt, Virginia (F. 1, 1940, Cleveland, OH) Dir., Info Quest, Capital Syst. Grp. Inc., 1978–; Instr., Univ. of CO, 1975–78; Libn., Tech., Natl. Radio Astronomy Observatory, 1970–75; Libn., Univ. of CO, 1968–69. **Educ.:** Univ. of FL, 1958–62, BA (Eng.); Univ. of Denver, 1967–69, MA (Libnshp.). **Orgs.:** SLA: Phys. Astronomy Math. Div. (Ch., 1975–76), *Bltn.* Ed. (1973–74), Ch.-Elect (1974–75); CO Chap. (Treas., 1976–78); VA Chap. (*Bltn.* Co-Ed., 1973–74). VA LA. ASIS. COLA. **Pubns.:** Asst. Ed., Indxr., *Galactic and Extragalactic Radio Astronomy* (1974); Contrib., *PAM Nsltr., Columbine, CO Libs.* **Activities:** 12; 17, 34, 39; 59, 75, 88 **Addr.:** Capital Systems Group Inc., 11301 Rockville Pike, Kensington, MD 20795.

Van Buskirk, Elisabeth Lynne (O. 30, 1945, Philadelphia, PA) Assoc. Dir. of Resrch., NJ Educ. Assn., 1972–; Serials Ref. Libn., NJ State Lib., 1968–72. **Educ.:** Trenton State Coll., 1963–67, BA (Eng. Educ.); Drexel Univ., 1967–68, MLS; Trenton State Coll., 1970–75, MEd (Eng. Educ.). **Orgs.:** SLA: Princeton-Trenton Chap. (Treas., 1981–83; Dir., 1978–79, 1979–80). NJ State Plng. Grp. for Dev. of Libs. ALA. Natl. Cncl. of Tchrs. of Eng. Natl. Educ. Assn. Phi Delta Kappa: Resrch. Com. (1979–80); Prog. Com. (1980–81). **Pubns.:** *New Jersey School Law Decisions* anl. (1972–). **Activities:** 12; 30, 39, 41; 59, 63, 77 **Addr.:** NJ Education Association, 180 W. State St., Trenton, NJ 08608.

Van Camp, Ann J. (D. 3, 1931, Indianapolis, IN) Libn., Srch. Anal., IN Univ. Sch. of Med. Lib., 1977–, Assoc. Libn., Srch. Anal., 1974–77, Srch. Anal., 1972–74, Asst. Ref. Libn., 1967–72; Resrch. Chem., H.I. Thompson Fiber Glass Co. 1964; Staff Asst., Tech., Sandia Corp., 1961–64; Assoc. Phys. Chem., Eli Lilly and Co., 1954–61. **Educ.:** Hanover Coll., 1954, BA (Chem.); IN Univ., 1967, MLS. **Orgs.:** Med. LA: Nom. Com. (Ch., 1974). ASIS. Bibl. Retrieval Srvs.: User Bd. Tech. Subcom., Actg. Secy. (1976), Ch. (1977–). Cncl. of the Midwest Reg. Med. Lib. and Coop. Info. Srvs: ILL Com., (1970). Various orgs. Biomed. Comm. Netwk.: Bd. of Dir., (1975–77); Clearinghouse on Online Equip. (Dir., 1977–). **Honors:** Beta Phi Mu, 1967; 1st Anl. BIOSIS Srch. Tournament, 1st Place Prize, 2nd Place Prize, 1979. **Pubns.:** Jt. auth., "The Indiana Biomedical Information Program," *Bltn. of the Med. LA* (Ja. 1970); "TWX Network Plus MEDLINE – Rapid Transmission to Remote Physicians," *Lib. Netwk./MEDLARS Tech. Bltn.* (S. 1972); jt. auth., "Experience with MEDLINE and Author Searching," *Lib. Netwk./MEDLARS Tech. Bltn.* (My. 1973); jt. auth., "BIOSIS Previews and MEDLARS–A Biomedical Team. I. Complementary Use of the MEDLARS and BIOSIS Previews Databases in Biomedical Libraries," *Online* (Ja. 1977); jt. auth., "BIOSIS Previews and MEDLARS–A Biomedical Team. II. MEDLARS and BIOSIS Previews – What's in Them and How They're Indexed," *Online* (Ja. 1977); various articles. **Activities:** 1; 49-Online Srch.; 80 **Addr.:** Medical Science, 122, 1100 W. Michigan St., Indianapolis, IN 46223.

Van Camp, Beverley G. (Ja. 6, 1947, Rochester, NY) Dir., S. TX Lib. Syst., 1976–; Grants Admin., TX State Lib., 1974–76; Prints and Recs. Supvsr., Austin Pub. Lib., 1971–74. **Educ.:** Baylor Univ., 1964–68, BA (Drama); Univ. of TX, 1970–71, MLS (Info. Sci.). **Orgs.:** ALA: PLA/Pub. Lib. Syst. Sect., Secy. (1978–79); LAMA/PR Sect. PR for Libs. Com. (1978–80); ASCLA: Mem. Promo. Com. (1977); Legis. Com. (1979–80). SW LA. TX LA: various coms. Spindizzy Pubns. Com.: Bd. of Dir. **Addr.:** 6402 Weber Rd. #D–6, Corpus Christi, TX 78413.

Vance, Julia Marechal (Jl. 7, 1947, Manila, Philippine Islands) Dir., VCT Info. Assocs., 1981–; Dir., Lib. Srvs., Atlanta Newsp., 1979–80; Head Libn., The Dallas Morning News, 1978–79; Head Libn., The Houston Post, 1974–77; Head, Un. List of Serials Proj., Stanford Univ., 1972–74. **Educ.:** Univ. of Houston, 1966–69, BA (Hist.); Emory Univ., 1971–72, MLN (LS); various crs. **Orgs.:** SLA: Newsp. Div. (Ch., 1981); Lib. Mgt. Div. (Secy., 1981–83); Nom. Com.; various coms., ofcs. ASIS: Pubns. Com. (1979–83); SIG/IGP (Ch., 1980–82); Lcl. Arrange. Mid-Yr. Mtg. (Ch., 1978). ALA. Natl. Micro. Assn. **Honors:** Beta Phi Mu, 1972; Phi Kappa Phi, 1969; Mortar Bd., 1968. **Pubns.:** Ed., *Stanford Libraries Union List of Serials* (1977); ed., *Texas Chapter SLA Bltn.* (1977–78); jt. auth., "The Office of the Future Comes to Texas," *TX Chap. SLA Bltn.* (Fall 1978); "Supreme Court Ruling Threatens Confidential Business Files," *ASIS Bltn.* (O. 1978); "Introduction to Newspaper Libraries" slide/tape presentation (1978). **Addr.:** VCT Information Associates, 2665 Meadow Ct., Chamblee, GA 30341.

Vance, Kenneth E. (My. 20, 1917, Pewamo, MI) Asst. Prof. of LS, Prof. of Educ., The Univ. of MI, 1965–, Sch. Lib. Consult., 1950–65, Ext. Libn., 1950–60; Tchr., Clinton C.M. Schs., 1935–42. **Educ.:** Ctrl. MI Univ., 1943, BS (Eng.); The Univ. of MI, 1948, AM (Eng.), 1950, AMLS, 1962, EdD; Elem., Sec. Tchg. Cert. **Orgs.:** ALA: Com. on Accred. (1968–73); Cncl. (1968–71). AALS: Pres. (1975). MI LA. MI Assn. for Media in Educ.: Exec. Secy. (1954–65). **Pubns.:** "Certification and Library Education Media," *Spectrum* (1979); "Future of Library Education: 1975 Delphi Study," *Jnl. of Educ. for Libnshp.* (Sum. 1977). **Activities:** 10; 24, 25, 26; 63 **Addr.:** 415 Manor Dr., Ann Arbor, MI 48105.

Vance, Mary-Louise (Hinton) (Je. 29, 1909, Lumberton, MS) Retired, 1974–; Acq. Libn., Univ. of Houston, 1952–74; Asst. Libn., Med. Lib., Spec. Srvs., Valley Forge Army Hosp., 1950–51; Biblgphr., Acq. Dept., Univ. IL Lib., 1947–49; Asst. Ref. Libn., Univ. of AL, 1946–47; Ref. Asst., Econ. Div., NY Pub. Lib., 1943–46; Pvt. Tutor, New York, 1935–42; Tchr., Lumberton HS, 1931–35. **Educ.:** MS State Coll. for Women, 1931, BA, Voice Dip.; LA State Univ., 1943, BS (LS); various crs. **Orgs.:** TX LA: Conv. Treas.; Acq. RT, Co-fndr., 1st Ch. ALA. MS LA. MS Socty. of Archvsts. AAUW. Amer. Assn. of Retired Persons. Frnds. of Libs. Univ. of Houston Women's 20 Yr. Club. Various other orgs. **Honors:** Beta Phi Mu, 1949; Univ. of Houston, Assoc. Prof. Emerita, 1974. **Activities:** 1, 9; 15, 44, 45 **Addr.:** Edgewater Garden Apts. 2B, 109 W. Beach Blvd., Biloxi, MS 39531.

Van De Carr, Janet L. (O. 10, 1953, Chicago, IL) Head, Chld. Srvs., Park Ridge Pub. Lib., 1980–; Asst. Chld. Libn. Cols. Coord., Indian Trails Pub. Lib. Dist., 1977–80; Chld. Libn., Skokie Pub. Lib., 1977. **Educ.:** Univ. of Northeast. IL, 1971–74, BA (Eng. Lit.); Rosary Coll., 1976–77, MALS. **Orgs.:** Lib. Graph. Assn.: Secy. (1979–80); Pres. (1980–81). Reg. Lib. Adv. Cncl.: Chld. Libns. Unit (1977–81). ALA. **Activities:** 9; 15, 21, 40 **Addr.:** Park Ridge Public Library, 20 S. Prospect, Park Ridge, IL 60068.

Vandegrift, Barbara P. (N. 22, 1941, Philadelphia, PA) Archvst., Natl. Press Club, 1980–; Consult., Arch. and Lib. Srvs.; Lib. Dir., George C. Marshall Resrch. Lib., 1975–79; Ref., Pub. Srvs. Libn., Washington and Lee Univ., 1974–75; Film Libn., DC Pub. Lib., 1966–68. **Educ.:** Dickinson Coll., 1959–63, BA (Eng. Lit.); Cath. Univ., 1965–67, MSLS; NARS, 1978, Cert. (Arch.); GA Dept. of Arch. 1979, Cert. (Arch. Admin.). **Orgs.:** SAA: Copyrt. Task Frc. (1980–); Bus. Arch. Grp. (1980–). Oral Hist. Assn.: Com. on Legal Agmnt. (1979–80). Oral Hist. of Mid-Atl. Reg.: OHMAR Nom. Com. (1980–). Mid-Atl. Reg. Arch. Conf.: MARAC - DC Plng. Com. (1980–81). Vict. Socty. Columbia Hist. Socty.: Col. Dev. Com. (1980–). White Hse. Hist. Assn. **Honors:** Beta Phi Mu. **Activities:** 2, 3; 15, 17, 23; 55, 83, 86 **Addr.:** National Press Club Archives, National Press Bldg.–13th Floor, Washington, DC 20045.

Vandegrift, John Raymond (Ap. 27, 1928, Wilmington, DE) Libn., Dominican Coll. Lib., 1970–; Instr., Theo., Albertus Magnus Coll., 1968–70; Instr., Phil., St. Catharine Coll., 1965–68; Instr., Theo., Aquinas Coll., 1963–70, 1962–65. **Educ.:**

Special Subjects/Services: 50. Adult educ.; 51. Advert./Mktg.; 52. Aerosp.; 53. Agric.; 54. Area std.; 55. Arts/Hum.; 56. Autom.; 57. Bibl./Prtg.; 58. Bio. sci.; 59. Bus./Fin.; 60. Chem.; 61. Copyrt.; 62. Documtn.; 63. Educ.; 64. Engin.; 65. Env.; 66. Eth. grps.; 67. Film; 68. Food/Nutr.; 69. Geneal.; 70. Geo.; 71. Geol.; 72. Handcpd.; 73. Hist.; 74. Int. frdm.; 75. Info. sci.; 76. Insr.; 77. Law; 78. Legis.; 79. Math./Comp. sci.; 80. Med.; 81. Metals; 82. Nat. resrcs.; 83. Newsp.; 84. Nuc. sci.; 85. Oral hist.; 86. Petr./Energy; 87. Pharm.; 88. Phys./Astr./Math.; 89. Readg.; 90. Relig.; 91. Sci./Tech.; 92. Soc. sci.; 93. Telecom.; 94. Transp.; 95. (other).

Princeton Univ., 1945–49, AB (Chem.); Pontifical Fac. of the Immaculate Conception, DC, 1957–62, STB, STL, STLr, (Theo.); Columbia Univ., 1974–75, MS (Lib. Srv.). **Orgs.:** ALA: ACRL; RTSD. ATLA. DC LA. WA Theo. Cnsrtm.: Com. of Libns. Cluster of Indp. Theo. Schs. in the WA Metro. Area: Com. of Libns. Alpine of Club of Can. **Pubns.:** Proj. asst., *Union List of Periodicals of the Members of the Washington Theological Consortium and Contributing Institutions* (1979). **Activities:** 1, 12; 15, 17, 44; 55, 90 **Addr.:** Dominican College Library, 487 Michigan Ave., NE, Washington, DC 20017.

VandenBerge, Peter Nicholas (D. 16, 1915, Kalamazoo, MI) Dir., Lib. Srvs., Colgate Rochester, Bexley Hall/Crozer Theo. Semy., 1971–, Assoc. Libn., 1967–71; Libn., New Brunswick Theo. Semy., 1957–67, Secy. of Fac., 1960–67; various pastorial positions, 1943–56. **Educ.:** Hope Coll., 1933–37, AB (Hist.); Univ. of NE, 1937–38, MA (Hist.); NB Theo. Semy., 1940–43, BD (Theo.); Rutgers Univ., 1957–59, MLS; various crs. **Orgs.:** NY LA. ATLA: Exec. Com., (1962–67, 1971–74); Treas. (1964–67); Index Bd. (1979–); Com. on Fncl. Assistance from Fndns. (Ch., 1965–68); Com. on Apprais., (Ch., 1968–70); Pres., (1972–73). Reformed Church in Amer.: Com. on Hist. and Resrch. (Ch., 1957–67); Classis of Rochester, VP (1973); Pres. (1974). **Pubns.:** *Historical Directory of the Reformed Church in America, 1628–1978* (1978); "Reflections on the Naming of Churches," *Reformed Review* (Spr. 1979); "After One Year – An Appraisal of the New English Bible," *Reformed Review* (My. 1962); "Protestant Symbols – A Survey with Bibliography," *Encounter* (Win. 1965); "A Survey of Books of the Ten Commandments," *Earnest Worker* (Jl.–S. 1966); various articles, edshp. **Activities:** 10; 15, 17, 35; 90, 92 **Addr.:** Colgate Rochester Divinity School, 1100 S. Goodman St., Rochester, NY 14620.

Vanderbeck, Sr. Maria, O. P. (Je. 2, 1908, Green Bay, WI) Libn., Queen of the Holy Rosary Coll., 1973–; Libn., Marycrest HS, 1969–73, Tchr., 1966–68; Tchr., St. Michael's HS, 1961–65. **Educ.:** Queen of the Rosary Coll., Univ. of Portland, 1928–40, BA (Eng.); 1936–67, Tchg. Cred. (Educ.); Cath. Univ. of Amer., 1948–49, MA (Eng.); Univ. of Portland, 1969–71, MA (LS). **Orgs.:** Cath. LA. ALA. CA LA. **Activities:** 10; 20, 22, 39 **Addr.:** P.O. Box 3508, Mission San Jose, CA 94538.

Van Der Bellen, Liana (O. 20, 1925, Tartu, Estonia) Chief, Rare Bk., Div., Natl. Lib. of Can., 1973–; Assoc. Prof., Univ. de Montreal, Lib. Sch., 1961–73; Catlgr., McGill Univ., 1953–61. **Educ.:** McGill Univ., 1949–52, BA (Mod. Lang.), 1952–53, BLS, 1967, MLS; Columbia Univ., 1970–71 (LS). **Orgs.:** Bibl. Socty. of Can.: 1st VP (1980–81). ALA: ACRL/Rare Bks. and Mss. Sect. Can. LA: Amer. Prtg. Hist. Socty. Socty. for the Bibl. of Nat. Hist., London. Can. Hist. Assn. **Pubns.:** Chap. in "Bibliographie, Bibliography, Bibliologie: Quelques Remarques Sur La Terminologie," *Livre, Bibliothèque et Culture Québecoise. Mélanges Offerts à Edmond Desrochers* (1977). **Activities:** 4; 45; 54, 55, 57 **Addr.:** National Library of Canada – Rare Book Division, Ottawa, ON K1A 0N4 Canada.

Vandergrift, Kay E. (S. 20, 1940, Mechanicsburg, PA) Asst. Prof., Columbia Univ. Sch. of Lib. Srv., 1975–; Prin., Agnes Russell Sch., Tchrs. Coll., 1970–74, Co-Admin., Instr., PreSrv. Tchr. Educ., 1970–74, Libn., Dir., Media Ctr., Agnes Russell Sch., 1969–70, 1964–67, Classrm. Tchr., 1967–69, Lang., Lit. Consult., 1967–68, Asst. Libn., Chld. Bk. Rm., AV Dept., 1963–64; Libn., Snyder Jr. HS; various positions as instr., consult., 1966–75. **Educ.:** Millersville State Coll., 1962, BS (Lib. Educ.); Columbia Univ., 1965, MA (Educ.), 1973, EdD (Elem. Educ.). **Orgs.:** ALA: AASL, Lib. Educ. (Ch., 1978–80), Assoc. Orgs. for Profs. in Educ., Rep., Adv. Cncl. (1978–80), Stdg. Com. on Lib. Educ. Asm. (Rep., 1978–80); AASL/ALSC Ad Hoc Plng. Com. for the NY Conf. for Weston Woods Studios Prog. (1980); ALSC/YASD Jt. Com. on Sel. Aids for Bibls. Rev. (ALSC Ch., 1976–78); ALSC, Tchrs. of Chld. Lit. Grp. AALS. Assn. for Supvsn. and Curric. Dev. Chld. Lit. Assn. Assn. for Childhood Educ. Intl./Chld. Bk. Cncl. Jt. Com. Natl. Cncl. of Tchrs. of Eng.: Asm. on Chld. Lit.; Adlsnt. Lit. Asm. Intl. Readg. Assn.: Chld. Lit. Spec. Interest Grp.; Lib. Resrcs. and Readg. Improvement Com. (1978–80). various orgs. **Pubns.:** *Child and Story: The Literary Connection* (1980); *The Teaching Role of the School Media Specialist* (1979); "Field Work—Concern and Celebration," *Excellence in School Media Programs* (1980); Consult. Ed., *Sch. Media Qtly.* (1979–82); Ed. Bd., *Phaedrus;* various bk. chaps., articles. **Activities:** 11; 21, 32; 55, 63 **Addr.:** 353 Riverside Dr., Apt. 2B, New York, NY 10025.

Vanderhoff, Barbara Ann (F. 14, 1942, Boulder, CO) Head, Serial Recs., AZ State Univ., 1974–, Asst. Head, Cat. Srv., 1970–74, Cat. Libn., 1968–70; Cat. Libn., Univ. of NE, 1965–68. **Educ.:** Fort Hays State Univ., 1960–64, BA (Hist.); Univ. of Denver, 1964–65, MA (Libnshp.). **Orgs.:** AZ State LA. **Activities:** 1; 20, 44, 46 **Addr.:** Serial Records, Arizona State University, Tempe, AZ 85281.

Vandermolen, John F. (Ja. 2, 1929, Fond du Lac, WI) Head, Sci., Tech. Dept., Auburn Univ. Libs., 1979–; Head, Seaver Sci. Lib., Univ. of South. CA, 1967–79; Sci., Engin. Libn., WI State Univ., 1963–67; Asst. Libn., Acq. Dept., South. IL Univ., 1961–63; Cat. Libn., Main Lib., Gen. Electric Co., 1959–61; Asst. Cat. Libn., Purdue Univ., 1957–59; Libn. I, Cat. Dept., Free Lib. of Philadelphia, 1955–57. **Educ.:** LA State Univ., 1949–52, BA (Span.); Univ. of WI, 1954–55, MLS (Libnshp.); Univ. of IL, 1964–69, CAS (Lib.). **Orgs.:** ASIS. SE LA. SLA: South. CA Chap., Pubns. Dir., Treas. **Activities:** 1, 12; 15, 17, 20; 64, 87, 91 **Addr.:** P.O. Box 581, Auburn, AL 36830.

Vander Velde, John Jacob (Ag. 12, 1936, Emporia, KS) Spec. Proj. Libn., Ed. Consult., KS State Univ. Lib., 1977–, Acq. Libn., 1969–77, Catlgr., Biblgphr., 1968–69; Catlgr., William Allen White Meml. Lib., Emporia State Univ., 1966–68; Ling., Admin. Spec., U.S. Air Frc. Secur. Srv., 1960–65. **Educ.:** Emporia State Univ., 1954–58, 1965–67, BA (Msc.); Yale Univ., 1959–60, Cert. (Mandarin Chinese); Emporia State Univ., 1967–68, ML (Libnshp.); various crs. **Orgs.:** KS LA: Int. Frdm. Com. (Ch., 1969–70); Non-Print Media Task Frc. (1975); Coll. and Univ. Libs. Sect. (Secy.-Treas., 1974–76). Beta Phi Mu: Beta Epsilon (Secy., 1974–76). Frnds. of the Emporia Pub. Lib. Various other orgs. KS State Univ. Fac. Sen.: Constn. Rev. Com. (1974–75); Com. on Prsrvn. and Restoration of Campus Furnishings (1979–). KS Musm. Assn. Riley Cnty. Hist. Socty. KS State Univ. Hist. Socty. **Pubns.:** Ed., *Cavalry Journal/Armor Cumulative Indices, 1888–1968* (1974); indxr., *Military Affairs* (1970–); indxr., *Journal of the West* (1979–); ed., *Kansas State University Library Bibliography Series* (1971–); ed., *Farrell Footnotes* (1969–70). **Activities:** 1, 2; 23, 30, 36; 55 **Addr.:** 1916 Anderson Ave., Manhattan, KS 66502.

Van Der Voorn, Cornelius (Neal) P. (My. 24, 1944, Haarlem, the Netherlands) Inst. Lib. Srvs. Branch Libn., East. State Hosp./Lakeland Vlg./Interlake Sch./Pine Lodge Correct. Ctr., Geiger Fld. Correct. Ctr., 1980–; Branch Libn., Logan Correct. Ctr., 1978–80; Catlgr., Leavenworth Cnty., Leavenworth Pub. Lib., 1977–78; Indxr., May Massee Col. WAW Lib., Emporia State Univ., 1976–77; Tchr., Andale HS, 1969–76; Tchr., Caney Valley HS, 1967–69; Tchr., Burlingame Jr. HS, 1966–67. **Educ.:** Wichita State Univ., 1961–66, BA (Hist.); Emporia State Univ., 1976–77, MLS; various crs. **Orgs.:** ALA: ASCLA/Lib. Srv. to Prisoners Sect., Access and Censorship Problems in Insts. (1979–80); PLA. Common Cause. Amer. Cvl. Liberties Un. **Honors:** Natl. Educ. Socty., KS, Nom., Best Young Tchr. Awd., Sedgwick Cnty., KS, 1971. **Activities:** 5, 9; 15, 16, 39; 74, 92 **Addr.:** Library, Eastern State Hospital, Medical Lake, WA 99022.

Van De Voorde, Philip E. (Mr. 11, 1936, Moline, IL) Head, Gvt. Pubns. Dept., IA State Univ. Lib., 1969–, Serials Libn., 1966–69; Asst. Libn., Bethel Coll., 1965–66. **Educ.:** Bethel Coll., 1956–58, BA (Soclgy.); Univ. of MN, 1963–66, MA (LS); Ctrl. Bapt. Theo. Semy., Kansas City, KS, 1958–61, BD (Relig. Educ.). **Orgs.:** ALA: GODORT (Secy., 1978–80); Fed. Docum. Task Frc. (Coord., 1973–75). IA LA: Gvt. Docum. Sect. Ch., (1976–77); Secy., (1979–80). **Pubns.:** "Official Use Trend in the Monthly Catalog of United States Government Publications," *Lib. Resrcs. & Tech. Srvs.* (Sum. 1970); various reviews, *Gvt. Pubns. Review.* **Activities:** 1; 17, 29 **Addr.:** 1122 Scott, Ames, IA 50010.

Van Dusen-Jain, Rhe B. (Mr. 13, 1944, New York, NY) Libn., Naramore Bain Brady and Johanson, 1979–; Med. Libn., Schick's Shadel Hosp., 1977–79; Couns., Planned Parenthood, 1970–77. **Educ.:** Oberlin Coll., 1962–66, BA (Soclgy.); Univ. of WA, 1976–78, MLS (Libnshp.). **Orgs.:** SLA: Pubcty., PR (1981). Seattle Area Hosp. Lib. Cnsrtm.: VP (1981). Assn. of Archit. Libns. **Honors:** Beta Phi Mu, 1979. **Activities:** 12; 15, 20, 41; 64, 80, 91 **Addr.:** 7611 S.E. 22, Mercer Island, WA 98040.

VanGieson, Marilyn J. (Mr. 3, 1936, Madison, WI) Reg. Libn., Pearl City Reg. Lib., 1979–; Head Libn., Aiea Cmnty. Lib., 1976–79; YA Coord., HI State Lib., 1971–76; YA Libn., Kalihi Palama Cmnty. Lib., 1970–71. **Educ.:** Univ. of WI, Milwaukee, 1954–59, BS (Geo.); Univ. of WI, Madison, 1965–66, LS. **Orgs.:** HI LA: Mem. Ch. Harris Untd. Meth. Church: Admin. Bd. (Ch., 1981). Variety Club Sch. PTA: Secy. (1980–81). **Pubns.:** Producer, "Old Aiea Town" videotape (1978). **Activities:** 9, 13; 16, 17, 39 **Addr.:** 2333 Kapiolani Blvd. #3216, Honolulu, HI 96826.

van Grunsven, W. J. (Ja. 24, 1947, Forest Grove, OR) Dir., Lrng. Resrc. Ctr., State Cmnty. Coll., 1973–; Dir., Intl. Mktg., Natl. Educ. TV Films, 1968–72; Asst. Ed., Pubns., Assn. for Intl. Dev., 1964–67. **Educ.:** Coll. of the Maryknoll, 1963–67, BA, MA (Phil., Ancient Near E. Texts); IN Univ., 1968–72, EdD (Inst. Systs. Tech.); various crs. **Orgs.:** ALA: Black Caucus-Policy and Bylaws Com. (1975–81); Kaskaskia Lib. Syst.: Bd. of Dirs., Affl. Bd. E. St. Louis Pub. Lib.: Bd. of Trustees; Treas. (1981). South. IL Lrng. Resrc. Ctr., Inc.: Treas. (1979–80). Socty. for Intl. Dev.: Africa Del. (1974); Amsterdam Del. (1976). IL Ofc. of Educ.: Sch. Approval Eval. Team Del. Educ. Eval. Team: Various del. positions (1974–81). **Pubns.:** *The Opinion Leader and the Adoption of Innovations in Dynamic and Traditional Societies* (1970); *A Proposal: A Media Center to Coordinate the Centro de Recursos para la Ensenañza, Cali, Colombia* (1971); "The Use of the LRC by Black Students," *IL Libs.* (Ja. 1979); "Library Service: A Right or a Privilege?" multi-media (1978); "Siberian and Mongolian Education" multi-media (1979); various mono. **Activities:** 1; 17, 41, 47; 54, 90, 93 **Addr.:** 5328 State, East Saint Louis, IL 62203.

Van Haaften, Julia (N. 3, 1946, Lancaster, PA) Dir., Photograph Cols. Documtn. Proj., The NY Pub. Lib., 1979–, Libn. I, II, 1968–79. **Educ.:** Barnard Coll., 1964–68, BA (Art Hist.); Columbia Univ., 1969–70, MLS (Lib. Srv.). **Pubns.:** Jt. auth., *Francis Frith* (1980); "Photography," *Guide to Art Reference Books* (1980); "'Original Sun Pictures': A Checklist of The New York Public Library's Holdings of Early Works Illustrated with Photographs, 1844–1900," *Bltn. of The NY Pub. Lib.* (Spr. 1977); "Francis Frith and Negretti and Zambra," *Hist. of Photography* (Ja. 1980); "Francis Frith: The Grand Tour," *Portfolio* (Ap.–My. 1980); various bk. reviews, *Lib. Jnl.* **Activities:** 9, 12; 23, 41, 45; 55, 62 **Addr.:** Photograph Collections Documentation Project, The New York Public Library, 5th Ave. at 42nd St., New York, NY 10018.

Van Handel, Ralph A. (Ja. 17, 1919, Appleton, WI) Dir., Wells Meml. Pub. Lib., 1974–; Dir., Gary Pub. Lib., 1954–74; Dir., Hibbing Pub. Lib., 1951–54; Dir., Lawrence Pub. Lib., 1947–51. **Educ.:** Univ. of WI, 1946, BA (Econ.); Univ. of MI, 1947, ABLS (Lib.). **Orgs.:** ALA: Cncl. IN LA: Pres. (1964–65). Rotary Intl.: Bd. Knights of Columbus. **Honors:** IN Lib. Trustees Assn., Libn. of the Yr., 1974. **Addr.:** 3624 Winter St., Lafayette, IN 47905.

Van Horn, Martha P. (D. 22, 1915, Farmington, MO) Supvsr., Tech. Srvs., Kern Cnty. Lib. Syst., 1962–, Head, Cat. Dept., 1952–62, Catlgr., Juvenile Lit., 1947–51; Catlgr., Univ. of MO, 1940–47. **Educ.:** Univ. of MO, 1934–39, AB (Fr., Italian), 1939–40 (Fr.); Univ. of South. CA, 1956–58, MSLS. **Orgs.:** ALA: SORT (Secy. Treas., 1969–73); Mem.-at-Lg. (1974–76); Mem. Com. (CA Reg. Ch., 1975–76); South. CA Tech. Prcs. Grp., Nom. Com. (1965); Prog. Com. (1980–). CA LA: Cnclr.-at-Lg. (1969–71, 1978–80). Amer. Socty. for Pub. Admin. Kern Cnty. Mgt. Cncl. Zonta Intl. of Bakersfield: Treas. (1968–70); Pres. (1972–73). Bus. and Prof. Women's Clubs: E. Bakersfield Club: (Pres., 1978–79); Ctrl. Dist. (Nsltr. Ed., 1980–81). **Honors:** Beta Phi Mu. **Activities:** 9; 17, 20, 46; 50, 56, 75 **Addr.:** Kern County Library System, 1315 Truxtun Ave., Bakersfield, CA 93301.

Van House, Nancy A. (Ag. 3, 1950, Ogden, UT) Sr. Resrch. Assoc., King Research, Inc., 1979–; Actg. Instr., Sch. of LS, Univ. of CA (Berkeley), 1977–79); Coord., E. Bay Info. Srvs., 1976–77; Libn., San Mateo Cnty. Lib., 1973–76. **Educ.:** Univ. of CA (Berkeley), 1970–71, AB (Eng.), 1971–72, MLS, 1974–79, PhD (LS). **Orgs.:** ALA: RASD/MARS Com. on Costs and Finance (1978–79); PLA Com. on Educ. for Pub. Libn. 1979–). CA LA: Ad Hoc Com. on Fees (1977, Ch. 1978); Cncl. (1979); Dir., CA Socty. of Libns. (1979). DC LA: Legis. Day Com. (1979–80). ASIS. Amer. Econ. Assn. **Pubns.:** Jt. auth., *A Planning Process for Public Libraries* (1980); Jt. auth., "Effect of User Fees on the Cost of On-Line Searching in Libraries," *Jnl. of Lib. Auto.* (D. 1977); Jt. auth., "The Costs of On-Line Bibliographic Searching," *Jnl. of Lib. Auto.* (S. 1976); "On Line Searching in the Public Library," *ASIS Proceedings* (1976); other tech. reports. **Activities:** 9, 14-Consulting firm; 24, 41; 56, 75, 95-Economics of Information. **Addr.:** King Research, Inc., 6000 Executive Blvd., Rockville, MD 20852.

Van Hoven, William D. (N. 1, 1932, Montreal, PQ) Head Libn., NC Sch. of the Arts, 1965–; Head, Adult Srvs., Greensboro Pub. Lib., 1960–65; Tchr., Pearl River Schs., 1959–60. **Educ.:** Cornell Univ., 1950–53; Houghton Coll., 1953–55, BA (Eng.); Vanderbilt Univ., George Peabody Coll., 1955–56, MAT (Eng.); Univ. of NC, 1961–66, MSLS. **Orgs.:** ALA. SE LA. NC LA: Arch. Com. (1978–). **Pubns.:** "Accent on Tapes and Recordings," *NC Libs.* (Sum. 1967). **Activities:** 1; 15, 17, 39; 55 **Addr.:** Semans Library, North Carolina School of the Arts, P.O. Box 12189, Winston-Salem, NC 27107.

Van Jackson, Wallace M. (My. 6, 1900, Richmond, VA) Retired, 1970–; Asst. to Libn., Hampton Inst., 1969–70; Libn., Mary Holmes Coll., 1968–69; Lib. Dir., VA State Univ., 1954–68; Lib. Dir., TX South. Univ., 1949–54; Libn., Atlanta Univ., 1941–48; Prof., Atlanta Univ. Sch. of Lib. Srv., 1940–41; Libn., VA Un. Univ., 1927–39; Ed., *Richmond, VA, Voice,* 1925–27; Prin., Scottsville Grade Sch., 1926–27; various lib. positions in Liberia, Nigeria, Swaziland, Botswana, Lesotho. **Educ.:** VA Un. Univ., 1934, AB (Soclgy.); Hampton Inst., 1934, BLS; Univ. of MI, 1935, AMLS; Univ. of Chicago, 1939–41 (LS). **Orgs.:** ALA: Cncl. (1956–60); Com. on Int. Frdm. (1952–54); Cmnty. Econ. Oppt. Progs. (1965–67). TX LA: Dist. 5 Coll. Div. (Ch., 1952–53). Libns. Club of Atlanta: Pres. (1941–43). VA LA. Nigerian LA. VA Tchrs. Assn. **Honors:** ALA, Cent. Cit., 1976; Gvt. of Liberia, Star of Africa, 1949. **Pubns.:** "Role of the College Library: The Academic Core," *VA Libn.* (Sum. 1967); "The Importance of the Library in the Black Community," *Jnl. of African-Amer. Std.* (1972); "The Importance of Preserving Our Heritage," *Swaziland Tchrs. Jnl.* (N. 1975); "Library Development in Swaziland," *Intl. Lib. Review* (Ag. 1976); jt. cmplr., *Botswana, Lesotho and Swaziland. A Select Bibliography* (1977); various articles, reviews. **Activities:** 1; 15, 17 **Addr.:** 20400 Loyal Ave., Ettrick, VA 23803.

Van Laar, Myrtle June (S. 26, 1925, Leota, MN) Chld. Age-Level Spec., Prince George's Cnty. Meml. Lib. Syst., 1968–; Head, Curric. Ctr., Calvin Coll., 1965–68; Lib. Assoc., Chld. Dept., Montgomery Cnty. Lib. Syst., 1963–64; Tchr., WA Christ.

PROFESSIONAL ACTIVITIES: Institutions: 1. Acad. lib.; 2. Arch.; 3. Assn.; 4. Fed./Gvt. lib.; 5. Inst. lib.; 6. Mfr./Suppl.; 7. Milit. lib.; 8. Musm.; 9. Pub. lib.; 10. Sch. lib.; 11. Sch. of lib. sci.; 12. Spec. lib.; 13. State lib.; 14. (other). **Functions/Activities:** 15. Acq./Col. dev.; 16. Adult srvs.; 17. Admin.; 18. Apprais.; 19. Archit./Bldgs.; 20. Cat./Class.; 21. Chld. srvs.; 22. Circ.; 23. Cons./Pres.; 24. Consult.; 25. Cont. ed.; 26. Educ. lib. sci.; 27. Ext. srvs.; 28. Fund/Grants; 29. Gvt. pubs.; 30. Indx./Abs.; 31. Instr. lib. use; 32. Media srvs.; 33. Micro.; 34. Netwks./Coop.; 35. Persnl.; 36. PR; 37. Publshg.; 38. Recs. mgt.; 39. Ref. srvs.; 40. Repro.; 41. Resrch.; 42. Review.; 43. Secur.; 44. Serials; 45. Spec. col.; 46. Tech. srvs.; 47. Trustees/Bds.; 48. YA srvs.; 49. (other).

Sch., 1960–63. **Educ.:** Calvin Coll., 1945–49, AB (Eng. Educ.); Univ. of MI, 1957–58, AM (Art Educ.), 1964–65, MALS. **Orgs.:** MD LA. ALA: ALSC, Natl. Parks (1979–81). WA Christ. Sch. Bd.: Educ. Com. (1976–78); Bd. (Secy., 1978–79). **Pubns.:** "The Picture File," *Christ. Home and Sch. Mag.* (O. 1967). **Activities:** 9, 10; 17, 21, 32; 55, 63, 75 **Addr.:** #1006 6700 Belcrest Rd., Hyattsville, MD 20782.

Vann, J. Daniel, III (Je. 14, 1935, Raleigh, NC) Prof., Exec. Dir. Libs. and Lrng. Resrcs., Univ. of WI, Oshkosh, 1981–; Libn., Univ. Libs., SUNY, Buffalo, 1979–81, Asst. Dir. Plng., 1980–81, Head, Lockwood Meml. Lib., 1979–80; Prof., Lib., Coll. of Staten Island, CUNY, 1976–79; Chief Libn., Prof. of Lib., Ch., Lib. Dept., Staten Island Cmnty. Coll., CUNY, 1971–76; Libn., Keuka Coll., 1969–71; Dir., Lib., Prof. of Hist., Bapt. Coll., Charleston, 1966–69; Prof., Hist., CA Bapt. Coll., 1965–66; Biblgphr., European Hist. and Lit., Asst. Ref. Libn., Newberry Lib., 1963–65; Assoc. Prof., Hist., Campbell Coll., 1961–63. **Educ.:** Univ. of NC, 1953–57, BA (Hist.); Yale Univ., 1957–59, MA (Hist.), 1957–65, PhD (Hist.); Emory Univ., 1969–71, M Libnshp.; Tchrs. Coll., Columbia Univ., 1962–63, (Higher Educ. Admin.); Stanford Univ., Univ. Libs., 1977–78, Postdoct. Schol. **Orgs.:** ALA: Mem. Promo. Task Frc. (1978–80); ACRL, Acad./Resrch. Libn. of the Yr. Awd. Com. (1978), Bd. of Dirs. (1976–78), *Choice* Ed. Bd. (1978–80), Cmnty. and Jr. Coll. Libs. Sect. (Ch., 1977–78), various coms.; LAMA/Bldg. and Equip. Sect., Equip. Com. (1976–80). Assn. of Coop. Lib. Orgs. Com. LACUNY: Various coms. NY Metro. Ref. and Resrch. Lib. Agency: Various coms. Amer. Hist. Assn. Bibl. Socty. of Amer. Medvl. Acad. of Amer. Rotary Intl. **Honors:** Cncl. on Lib. Resrcs., Acad. Lib. Mgt. Internship, 1977–78; Beta Phi Mu; Phi Alpha Theta. **Pubns.:** *A Study of the Seigneurial Transactions and Possessions of the Temple in France (1120–1307)* (1965). **Activities:** 1; 15, 17, 19 **Addr.:** Forrest R. Polk Library, University of Wisconsin, Oshkosh, WI 54901.

Vann, Sarah Katherine (My. 15, 1916, Macon, GA) Prof., Univ. of HI, 1969–; Prof., SUNY, Buffalo, 1966–69; Resrch. Dir., Southeast. PA Prcs. Ctr. Feasibility Std., 1964–65; Dir., Fld. Srvy. of Dewey Decimal Class. Use Abroad, 1964–65; Assoc. Prof., Univ. of TX, 1962–64; Visit. Assoc. Prof., Columbia Univ., 1960–61; Assoc. Prof., Carnegie Lib. Sch., Carnegie Inst. of Tech., 1945–60; Catlgr., Ed., H.W. Wilson Co., 1946–48; various cat. positions, 1940–45; various tchg. positions at various univs., 1945–69. **Educ.:** Womans Coll. of GA, 1933–36, AB (Eng., Fr.); Univ. of NC, 1937–39, ABLS; Univ. of MI, 1940–44, AMLS; Univ. of Chicago, 1949–58, PhD (LS). **Orgs.:** ALA: Div. of Cat. and Class, Exec. Bd. (1952–56); RTSD/Cat. and Class Sect. (Ch., 1960–61), Exec. Bd. (1959–62), Margaret Mann Awd. (1963–64); Lib. Educ. Div./Tchrs. Sect., Exec. Bd. (1960–62, 1963–66), Pres. (1964–65); ACRL/Rare Bks. Sect.; various coms., RT's, chs. AALS: Exec. Bd. (1952–54); various coms., ofcs. SLA: Publshg. Div., Prog. Com. (Co-Ch., 1978–79). Frnds. of the Lib., HI. Various other orgs. AAUP. AAUW. Delta Kappa Gamma: Theta Chap. (Secy., 1980–). Beta Phi Mu: XI Chap. (HI Fac. Liaison, 1975–). **Honors:** Scarecrow Press, Scarecrow Press Awd. for Lib. Lit., 1962; GA Coll., Disting. Alum. Awd., 1966; U.S. Gvt., Hayes-Fulbright Awd., 1972. **Pubns.:** Ed., *Implications of White House Conference on Library and Information Services for Library Education* (forthcoming); auth., ed., *Melvil Dewey: His Enduring Presence in Librarianship* (1978); *The Williamson Reports: A Study* (1972); *Southeastern Pennsylvania Processing Center Feasibility Study* rpt. (1967); dir., ed., *Field Survey of Dewey Decimal Classification (DDC) Use Abroad* (1965); various articles, chaps., essays, reviews in *Amer. Ref. Bks. Anl., Lib. Qtly.* **Activities:** 11; 26, 30, 37; 57, 61, 74 **Addr.:** 1022 Prospect St., Apt. 1108, Honolulu, HI 96822.

Vannorsdall, Mildred M. (My. 10, 1918, Madison Cnty., OH) Libn., Prof. Lib., Chicago Pub. Lib., 1976–, Ref. Libn., Educ. Dept., 1972–75; Asst. Prof., LS, Grad. Sch. of LS, Rosary Coll., 1970–72; Lectr., Pre-Doct. Instr., Dept. of LS, Univ. of MI, 1964–67; Ref. Libn., Adult Srvs. Supvsr., Lane Pub. Lib., 1957–63; Subj. Spec. Exch. Libn., Tottenham Pub. Libs., London, Eng., 1956–57; various asst. libn. positions, Pub. Lib. of Cincinnati and Hamilton Cnty., 1953–56; Head, Ref. Dept., Cuyahoga Cnty. Pub. Lib., 1947–53; various catlgr. positions, 1940–47. **Educ.:** Miami Univ., Oxford, OH, 1936–39, AB (Eng.); Univ. of WI, 1939–40, BLS; Univ. of MI, 1963–64, AMLS (Advnc.), 1974, PhD (LS). **Orgs.:** ALA: Ref. and Subscrpn. Bks. Review Com. (1957–63, 1974–78), Guest Reviewer (1978–79); Ref. Sect. Srvy. Com. (Ch., 1953–54). IL LA. OH LA: Secy.-Treas. (1961–63). **Activities:** 9, 13; 15, 16, 39; 50, 75 **Addr.:** Professional Library, Chicago Public Library, 425 N. Michigan Ave., Rm. 1321, Chicago, IL 60611.

Van Nortwick, Barbara L. (Ja. 3, 1940, Johnson City, NY) Lib. Dir., NY State Nurses Assn., 1979–; Head Libn., Columbia HS, 1978–79; Head Libn., Westfield HS, 1976–78; AV Libn., S. Colonie HS, 1974–76. **Educ.:** SUNY, Binghamton, 1957–61, BA (Hum., Hist.); SUNY, Albany, 1974–76, MLS. **Orgs.:** ALA: Hlth. Care (1980–); Plng. Com. Multitype Libs. (1979–). Med. LA: Con. Hlth. Info. Strg. Com. (1981–82). NY/NJ Reg., Legis. Com. (1979–80); Upstate NY/ON Reg. Grp. NY LA: Con. Hlth. Info. (1980–81). SLA. Interagency Cncl. on Lib. Resrcs. for Nursing: New Eng. Reg. Grp. N. Atl. Hlth. Sci. LA. Mid. Atl. Reg. Arch. Assn. **Honors:** U.S. Dept. of Educ., Flwshp., 1981. **Activities:** 10, 12; 17, 32, 45; 80 **Addr.:** NY State Nurses Association, 2113 Western Ave., Guilderland, NY 12084.

Van Oosbree, Charlyne N. (Ja. 19, 1930, Alta, IA) Head, Branch Lib., Mid–Continent Pub., 1976–; Head, Sch. Lib., Trng. Sch. for Boys, MO, 1973–76; Hosp. Libn., Fort Leonard Wood Army Hosp., 1970–72. **Educ.:** IA State Univ., 1968–70, BS (Eng.); Univ. of MO, Columbia, 1972–73, MA (LS). **Orgs.:** MO LA: Outrch. RT. ALA. Park Hill Schs. Adv. Cncl. **Honors:** Beta Phi Mu, 1973. **Pubns.:** Contrib., *Show - Me* (1977–78). **Activities:** 9, 11; 17, 36, 37; 50, 72, 85 **Addr.:** Mid-Continent Public Library, Platte Woods Branch, 6500 Tower Dr., Kansas City, MO 64151.

Van Orden, Phyllis J. (Jl. 7, 1932, Adrian, MI) Prof., Sch. of LS, FL State Univ., 1977–; Assoc. Prof., Grad. Sch. of Lib. Srv., Rutgers Univ., 1970–76; Instr., Dept. of LS, Wayne State Univ., 1966–70; Head, Instr. Mtrls. Ctr., Oakland Univ., 1964–66; Instr. Mtrls. Consult., Royal Oak Pub. Schs., 1960–64; Chld. Libn., San Diego Pub. Lib., 1958–60; Sch. Libn., E. Detroit Pub. Schs., 1954–57. **Educ.:** East. MI Univ., 1950–54, BS (Elem. Educ.); Univ. of MI, 1957–58, AMLS; Wayne State Univ., 1966–70, EdD (Elem. Curric. Dev.). **Orgs.:** ALA: Com. on Accred. (1978–82); Cncl. (1972–73); ALSC, Newbery-Caldecott Com. (1976–77), Notable Chld. Bk. Com. (Ch., 1978–79); AASL, *Sch. Media Qtly.* Ed. Bd.; various ofcs. FL Assn. for Media in Educ.: Mem. Com. (Ch., 1978–79). NJ Sch. Media Assn.: Various coms. **Honors:** Pi Lambda Theta, 1968. **Pubns.:** Jt. ed., *Background Readings in Building Library Collections* (1979); ed., *Elementary School Library Collection* (1977); "Promotion, Review and Examination of Materials," *Sch. Media Qtly.* (Win. 1978); "Librarians and Publishers: an Idea Exchange Through Library Promotion," *Sch. Lib. Jnl.* (D. 1977); "Humanities: Resources for Teaching," *Sch. Libs.* (Win. 1972). **Activities:** 10, 11; 21, 26, 32; 63 **Addr.:** School of Library Science, Florida State University, Tallahassee, FL 32306.

Van Pulis, Noelle (D. 2, 1945, Freeport, NY) Info. Spec., OH State Univ. Libs., 1973–, Catlgr., 1970–73; Serials Libn., Fine Arts Lib., Univ. of Pittsburgh, 1969–70. **Educ.:** Allegheny Coll., 1963–67, BA (Eng.); McGill Univ., 1967–69, MLS. **Orgs.:** ALA. ASIS: Ctrl. OH Chap. (Secy., 1977). Acad. LA of OH. **Pubns.:** "User Education for an Online Catalog: A Workshop Approach," *RQ* (forthcoming); "Library Instruction at a University-based Information Center: The Informative Interview," *RQ* (Spr. 1976); jt. auth., "Periodical Usage in an Education-Psychology Library," *Coll. & Resrch. Libs.* (Jl. 1977); jt. auth., "The Online Library: Problems and Prospects for User Education," *New Horizons for Acad. Libs.* (1979). **Activities:** 1; 30, 31, 39; 75 **Addr.:** Mechanized Information Center, Ohio State University Libraries, 1858 Neil Ave. Mall, Columbus, OH 43210.

Van Slyke, Dorothy G. (F. 8, 1928, Perth, ON) Chief Libn., Niagara Falls Pub. Lib., 1972–, Dept. Head, Cat. and Ref., 1951–72. **Educ.:** McMaster Univ., 1946–49, BA; Univ. of Toronto, 1949–51, BLS, 1966–71, MLS. **Orgs.:** ON LA. Can. LA. **Pubns.:** Contrib., *Niagara Falls, Canada* (1967); weekly newsp. clmn. *Niagara Falls Review* (1977–). **Activities:** 9; 17 **Addr.:** Niagara Falls Public Library, 4848 Victoria Ave., Niagara Falls, ON L2E 4C5, Canada.

Van Staaveren, Elizabeth (Kelly) (N. 13, 1923, Adel, GA) Chief Biblgphr., U.S. Dept. of Labor Lib., 1975–, Biblgphr., 1972–75, Ref. Libn., 1970–72, Catlgr., 1967–70, Catlgr., 1958–61; Labor Econ., U.S. Dept. of Labor, 1949–53; Econ. Ed., Women's Bur., 1945–48; Econ., U.S. Dept. of Labor, Bur. of Labor Stats., 1948–49. **Educ.:** George Washington Univ., 1940–44, AB in Ed (Eng.); Univ. of CA, Berkeley, 1953–54, BLS (Libnshp.); Amer. Univ., 1945–47, (Labor Econ., Stats.); George Washington Univ. 1947, (Econ.). **Orgs.:** SLA. DC LA. WA Indus. Rel. Libns. Marlan Forest Citizens Assn.: Secy. (1978–79). Natl. Trust for Hist. Prsrvn. Sierra Club. Alexandria Assn. Virginians for Dulles. **Pubns.:** *Occupational Safety and Health; A Bibliography* (1978); *The Role of Labor Unions in the United States* bibl. (1978); "Flexible Working Hours," (1976); "Cost-Benefit Analysis of Manpower Programs," (1975); "Pensions and Pension Plans, 1971–1974," (1974); various rpts. **Activities:** 4; 20; 95-Labor, Indus. Rel. **Addr.:** 7115 Burtonwood Dr., Alexandria, VA 22307.

Van Velzer, Verna Jean (Ja. 22, 1929, State College, PA) Mgr., Resrch. Lib., ESL Inc., Subsidiary of TRW, 1966–; Mgr., Intelligence Lib., GTE Sylvania, West. Div., 1965–66; Head Libn., Tech. Lib., Fairchild Resrch. and Dev. Lab., 1964–65; Head Libn., Tech. Lib., G.E. Microwave Lab., 1958–64. **Educ.:** Univ. of IL, 1946–50, BS (LS); Syracuse Univ., 1954–57, MLS. **Orgs.:** SLA: 1974 Wkshp., Speaker on Acq. Assn. for Comp. Mach. Inst. of Electrical and Electronics Engin. Amer. Inst. of Aeronautics and Astronautics. **Honors:** Beta Phi Mu, 1956. **Activities:** 12; 15, 17, 41; 56, 88, 93 **Addr.:** 4048 Laguna Way, Palo Alto, CA 94306.

Van Vliet, Virginia (S. 20, 1949, Montreal, PQ) Chld. Libn., Etobicoke Pub. Lib., 1976–; Chld. Libn., Ottawa Pub. Lib., 1974–76. **Educ.:** Bishop's Univ., 1967–71, BA (Eng.); McGill Univ., 1972–74, MLS. **Orgs.:** Can. LA: Can. Assn. of Chld. Libns.: Com. on Srv. to the Handcpd. (1980–82); Bk. Awds. Review Com. (1979–80). ON LA: Subcom. on Can. Publshg. for Chld. (1978–80). Intl. Bd. on Bks. for Young People. Etobicoke Chld. Thea.: Bd. of Dirs. (1979–). **Pubns.:** "The Fault Lies Not in Our Stars: The Children's Librarian as Manager," *Can. Lib. Jnl.* (O. 1980); ed. adv. bd., *Emergency Libn.* (1980–); "Serving Deaf Children in the Library," *In Review* (Spr. 1978); "Pitfalls in Picture-Book Production," *Can. Chld. Lit.* (1976). **Activities:** 9; 21; 67, 72 **Addr.:** Etobicoke Public Library, Box 501, Etobicoke, ON M9C 5G1, Canada.

van Weringh, Janet (My. 10, 1948, Leeuwarden, Friesland, Netherlands) Info. Retrieval Libn., Clarkson Coll. of Tech., 1978–; Resrch. Assoc., Lib. Resrch. Ctr., Univ. of IL, 1976–78. **Educ.:** Univ. of IL, 1969–72, BS (Home Econ.), 1974–75, MS (LS); various crs. **Orgs.:** ASIS. ACRL: East. Chap. N. Country Ref. and Resrch. Resrcs. Cncl.: Prog. Com. (1979–). **Honors:** Beta Phi Mu. **Pubns.:** Jt. auth., *Modification and Extension of the Environmental Technical System for the Air Force* (1979); jt. auth., *Computer-Aided Environmental Legislative Data System User Manual* (1978). **Activities:** 1, 12; 30, 31, 39; 56, 64, 75 **Addr.:** Library, ERC, Clarkson College of Techology, Potsdam, NY 13676.

VanWiemokly, Jane G. (My. 11, 1951, Morristown, NJ) Sr. Libn., Morris Cnty. Free Lib., 1977–. **Educ.:** Douglass Coll., Rutgers Univ., 1971–73, BA (Art Hist.); Univ. of MD, 1973–74, MLS (Lib., Info. Sci.). **Orgs.:** ALA. NJ LA. ARLIS/NA. Coll. Art Assn. of Amer. **Pubns.:** Contrib., *Knowledge and Its Organization* (1976); "New Perspectives on Adolescence," *Voice of Youth Advocates* (Ag. 1980); various bk. reviews, *Voice of Youth Advocates* (1978–). **Activities:** 9; 15, 16, 48; 55 **Addr.:** 195 Madison Ave., Apt. 110, Convent Station, NJ 07961.

Van Wyk, Jan E. (S. 23, 1952, Dayton, OH) Libn., Lit. Dept., Seattle Pub. Lib., 1979–; King Cnty. Info. and Lib. Srv. Area: Prog. Coord. Vid. and Adult Prog. Srvs. Libn., Media Dept., Seattle Pub. Lib., 1977–79. **Educ.:** Fairhaven Coll., West. WA State Univ., 1970–74, BA (Creat. Comm.); Univ. of Chicago, 1974–76, AM (Grad. Lib. Sch.). **Orgs.:** ASIS. SIG/FIS, PNW Ch.; SIG/AH. WA LA: Cont. Educ. Com.; Ref. Interest Grp. **Pubns.:** "Model For Continuing Education," *Spec. Libs.* (Mr. 1976). **Activities:** 9; 26, 31, 39; 55, 75 **Addr.:** Literature Dept., Seattle Public Library, Seattle, WA 98104.

Van Zant, Nancy Patton (D. 9, 1947, Kingsport, TN) Dir. of Corporate and Fndn. Resrcs. Dev., Nat. Jewish Hosp./Natl. Asthma Ctr., 1981–; Ref. Libn., Dev. Assoc., Dev. Ofc., Earlham Coll., 1978–81; Adult Srvs. Consult., Rock Cnty. Lib. Syst., 1977–78; Visit. Libn., Georgian (USSR) Acad. of Sci. Lib., Tbilisi, 1976–77; Head, Reader Srvs., Cornell Coll., 1972–76. **Educ.:** Earlham Coll., 1966–70, BA (Psy.); Univ. of IL, 1970–71, MS (LS). **Orgs.:** ALA: GODORT, Fed. Docum. Task Frc. (Secy., 1979–80); ACRL, Cont. Educ. Com., Cat. in Pubn. Adv. Com. Cncl. for Advnc. and Support of Educ. **Pubns.:** Ed., *Personnel Policies in Libraries* (1980); *Selected U.S. Government Series* (1978); "Structuring Facilities and Services for Library Instruction," *Lib. Trends* (Sum. 1980); "An American in Georgia," *Wilson Lib. Bltn.* (Je. 1978); contrib., "Periodicals for College Libraries" clmn. *Choice;* various articles (1976–79). **Activities:** 1; 17, 31, 39; 92 **Addr.:** 401 Humboldt St., Denver, CO 80218.

Van Zanten, Frank (Veldhuyzen) (O. 21, 1932, Heemstede, The Netherlands) Dir., Mid-Hudson Lib. Syst., 1978–; Assoc. Dir., Lib. Dev., IL State Lib., 1976–78, Consult., Lib. Dev., 1973–76; Dir., Tucson Pub. Lib., 1968–73; Dir., St. Clair Cnty. Lib., 1965–68; Dir., Dickinson Cnty. Lib., 1962–65; Dir., Mid-Peninsula Lib. Fed., 1963–65; Prcs. Libn., MI State Lib., 1961–62. **Educ.:** Horticult. Sch., The Netherlands, 1950–52, Dip. (Horticulture); Calvin Coll., 1955–59, AB (Hist., Eng.); Univ. of MI, 1960–61, MA (LS). **Orgs.:** Chld. Bk. Review Srv. ALA. NY LA. **Activities:** 9; 17, 24, 34; 56, 74, 78 **Addr.:** Mid-Hudson Library System, 103 Market St., Poughkeepsie, NY 12601.

Van Zwalenburg, Joyce (Ap. 4, 1928, Jackson, CA) Maui Lib. Dist. Admin., State of HI, Dept. of Educ., Ofc. of Lib. Srvs., 1974–; Head, Circ., Univ. of HI, Hamilton Lib., 1969–74, Catlgr., 1968–69. **Educ.:** Mills Coll., 1946–50, BA (Hist.); Univ. of HI, 1967–68, MLS (Lib. Std.). **Orgs.:** ALA. HI LA: Dir. (1975–77). Maui Hui Malama (Alternative Educ.): Bd. of Dirs. (1976–). Maui Adult Educ. Adv. Com. Educ. Oppt. Ctr.: Adv. Com. (1977–79); Cmnty. Resrc. Com. (1979–). J. Walter Cameron Ctr.: PR Com. (1979–); Media Ctr. Com. (1978–). **Honors:** Beta Phi Mu, 1968. **Activities:** 4, 9; 17, 34; 50 **Addr.:** Maui Public Library, P. O. Box B, Wailuku, HI 96793.

Varieur, Normand L. (Mr. 15, 1927, Pawtucket, RI) Chief, Sci. and Tech. Info. Div., U.S. Army Armament Resrch. and Dev. Cmnd., 1974–; Chief, Col. Dev. and Tech. Srvs. Div., U.S. Milit. Acad., W. Point, 1972–74; Chief, Tech. Srvs. Branch, U.S. Army Picatinny Arsenal, 1968–72; Chief, Cat. Dept., Engin. Soctys. Lib., 1966–68; Chief, Info. and Pub. Cat. Dept., Queens Boro. Pub. Lib., 1964–66; Libn., St. Joseph's Coll., 1959–64. **Educ.:** Ottawa Univ., 1945–50, BA, BPh, STL (Phil., Theo.); Cath. Univ. of Amer., 1957–59, MLS; CUNY, 1973–75, Cert. (Info., LS); Amer. Univ., 1958–59 (Arch. Sci.); Indus. Coll. of the

Special Subjects/Services: 50. Adult educ.; 51. Advert./Mktg.; 52. Aerosp.; 53. Agric.; 54. Area std.; 55. Arts/Hum.; 56. Autom.; 57. Bibl./Prtg.; 58. Bio. sci.; 59. Bus./Fin.; 60. Chem.; 61. Copyrt.; 62. Documtn.; 63. Educ.; 64. Engin.; 65. Env.; 66. Eth. grps.; 67. Film; 68. Food/Nutr.; 69. Geneal.; 70. Geo.; 71. Geol.; 72. Handcpd.; 73. Hist.; 74. Int. frdm.; 75. Info. sci.; 76. Insr.; 77. Law; 78. Legis.; 79. Math./Comp. sci.; 80. Med.; 81. Metals; 82. Nat. resrcs.; 83. Newsp.; 84. Nuc. sci.; 85. Oral hist.; 86. Petr./Energy; 87. Pharm.; 88. Phys./Astr./Math.; 89. Readg.; 90. Relig.; 91. Sci./Tech.; 92. Soc. sci.; 93. Telecom.; 94. Transp.; 95. (other).

Armed Frcs., 1972–74, Cert. (Natl. Secur. Mgt.); FL Inst. of Tech., 1980–, MSc. **Orgs.:** ALA. SLA. SAA. Shared Bibl. Input Exper.: Chrt. Mem. (1977–). Dignity: Reg. II (Dir., 1978–79). Fed. Empl. Women: Rec. Secy. (1978–81). Resrc. Sharing Adv. Grp.: Ch. (1980–82). **Honors:** Fed. Exec. Bd. of North. NJ, Supervisory Awd., 1980; U.S. Army Armament Resrch. Dev. Cmnd., Sustained Superior Performance, 1979. **Pubns.:** *Charles Maurice Braibant: Dix ans au chantier ... du Temple* (1959); "Special, Small, or Church Archives," *Amer. Archvst.* (1959). **Activities:** 2, 4; 17, 20, 34; 64, 74, 91 **Addr.:** 87 Fox Hill Rd. POB-H, Denville, NJ 07834.

Varino, Mary (Pat) Gulley (Ja. 20, 1940, Farmerville, LA) Libn., St. Thomas More Sch., 1975–; Libn., Westdale Elem. Sch., 1968–69; Tchr., Istrouma Jr. HS, 1962–67. **Educ.:** N.E. LA State Coll., 1958–61, BA (Elem. Educ.); LA State Univ., 1963–67, MEd (Elem. Educ., LS). **Orgs.:** Cath. LA. LA LA. Baton Rouge Cath. LA: Instr. TV Reviewing Com. (1978–79); Libns. Wkshp. Com. (1979–80). Sherwood Forest Elem. Sch. Parent-Tchr. Org.: Parlmt. (1976–77); Corres. Secy. (1977–78); Pres. (1978–79). Episcopal Church Women: Treas. (1966–67). **Honors:** Phi Kappa Phi, 1967. **Pubns.:** Various bk. reviews, *Sch. Lib. Jnl.* (1978–79); various media reviews, *Previews* (1978–79). **Activities:** 10; 20, 21, 22 **Addr.:** 11530 Parkwood Dr., Baton Rouge, LA 70815.

Varlejs, Jana (Jl. 3, 1938, Riga, Latvia) Dir., Prof. Dev. Std., Rutgers Grad. Sch. of Lib. and Info. Std., 1979–; Consult., MA Bd. of Lib. Comsn., 1976–79; Head, AV, Arts, YA Srvs., Montclair Pub. Lib., 1968–75. **Educ.:** Bryn Mawr Coll., 1956–60, AB (Eng.); Rutgers Univ., 1967–68, MLS. **Orgs.:** ALA: Stans. Com. (1977–79); H.W. Wilson Lib. Per. Awd. Jury (Ch., 1978–79); YA Srvs. Div., Exec. Bd. (1976–79), various coms., ofcs.; PLA, Stans. Com. YA Srvs. Task Frc. (1972–73). NJ LA: Educ. Com. (Ch., 1971–73, 1979–81); Lib. Dev. Com. (1979–). ASIS. EF LA. Various other orgs. Litcy. Voluns. of NJ: Bd. of Dirs. (1979–). Assn. for Adult Educ. of NJ. NJ Libns. for Soc. Resp.: Cofndr. (1969). **Pubns.:** *The New Jersey Plan for Continuing Education in Library/Educational Media/Information Science* (1981); *Young Adult Literature in the Seventies: A Selection of Readings* (1978); jt. auth., *Akers Simple Library Cataloging* (1977); jt. auth., "From Within: Planning for Continuing Education," *The Sourdough* (Jl.–Ag. 1980); "Inside Our Schools: Rutgers GSLIS," *Wilson Lib. Bltn.* (Mr. 1980); various articles. **Activities:** 11; 17, 25, 26; 63 **Addr.:** Rutgers Graduate School of Library and Information Studies, Professional Development Studies, 4 Huntington St., New Brunswick, NJ 08903.

Varma, Divakara K. (Ag. 5, 1933, Trivandrum, Kerala, India) Admin. Std. Libn., York Univ., 1971–; Libn., Shriram Ctr. for Indus. Rel., New Delhi, India, 1964–71; Asst. Resrch. Libn., UNESCO Resrch. Ctr., Delhi, India, 1963–64; Adult Srvs. Libn., Brooklyn Pub. Lib., 1961–62. **Educ.:** Loyola Coll., Madras Univ., India, 1949–54, BA (Econ.); West. Rsv. Univ., 1960–61, MS (LS); Madras Univ., 1957–58, Dip. (Libnshp.). **Orgs.:** SLA: Toronto Chap. (Dir., 1976–77). Can. Assn. Info. Sci.: Toronto Chap., Coord. Bd. (1978–80). **Pubns.:** "Index of Periodical Articles on Industrial Relations in India," *Indian Jnl. of Indus. Rel.* (1966–); various bibls. **Activities:** 1; 15, 31, 39; 51, 59, 92 **Addr.:** York University, 113 Administrative Studies Bldg., 4700 Keele St., Downsview, ON M3J 2R6, Canada.

Varnet, Harvey (D. 2, 1946, Acushnet, MA) Asst. Dir., Lrng. Resrcs. Ctr., Bristol Cmnty. Coll., 1980–; Fulbright Prof., Univ. of Calabar, Nigeria, 1979–80; Asst. Dir., Lrng. Resrcs. Ctr., Bristol Cmnty. Coll., 1971–79; Head Libn., Resrch. and Dev. Dept., Norton Co., 1969–71; Supvsr., New Bedford Branch Lib., Southeast. MA Univ., 1967–69. **Educ.:** Southeast. MA Univ., 1965–69, BA (Eng.); Simmons Coll., 1969–71, MS (LS); Bridgewater State Coll., 1974–77, MEd (Instr. Media); Simmons Coll., 1977–79, DA (Lib. Admin.). **Orgs.:** ALA: ACRL/Cmnty. and Jr. Coll. Libs. Sect. (Secy., 1980–81), ACRL Natl. Conf. (AV Coord., N. 1978). ASIS. NLA. Southeast. MA Univ. Alum. Assn.: Gifts and Grants Com. (1980–); Bd. of Dirs. (1978–79). MA Walk-In ILL Com. (1976–79). Bristol Cmnty. Coll.: Athl. Adv. Bd. (Ch., 1972–74); Coll. Hon. Com. (Ch., 1976–77); Five-Yr. Plan Task Frc. (1980–); Student/Fac. Bd. (1974–76). MA Conf. of Chief Libns. of Pub. Higher Educ. Inst. **Pubns.:** "An Analysis of the Effectiveness and Cost Benefits of the Checkpoint Mark II Book Detection System Installed in the Library Section of Bristol Community College's Learning Resources Center," *Quantitative Measurement and Dynamic Library Service* (1978); "A Survey of Attitudes Toward Collection Development in College Libraries," *Collection Development in Libraries: A Treatise* (1980); *An Analysis of the Learning Resources Programs Provided by the Fifteen Colleges of the Massachusetts Community College System* (1979). **Activities:** 1; 15, 32, 39 **Addr.:** Bristol Community College, Learning Resources Center, 777 Elsbree St., Fall River, MA 02720.

Varoutsos, Mary Ann (Je. 6, 1947, Lynn, MA) Ref. Libn., U.S. Nvl. War Coll., 1975–; Libn., Essex Agr. and Tech. Inst., 1971–75; Asst. Libn., NY State Dept. of Law, 1969–71. **Educ.:** Univ. of MA, 1964–68, BA (Eng.); SUNY, Albany, 1968–69, MLS. **Orgs.:** ALA: JMRT, RI Chap. VP (1981–); Secy. (1979–80). RI LA. SLA. Daughters of Penelope: Ofcr. (1979–81). **Activities:** 4, 7; 20, 39; 77, 82 **Addr.:** 118 Ruggles Ave., Newport, RI 02840.

Vasilakis, Mary (Pittsburgh, PA) Mgr., Info. Resrcs., Westinghse. Electric Corp., 1979–; Visit. Instr., Sch. of LS, Univ. of Pittsburgh, 1976; Mgr., Lib., Info. Srvs., Westinghse. Electric Corp., 1967–78; Tech. Libn., Westinghse. Bettis Atomic Power Lab., 1956–67; Resrch. Assoc., Carnegie Mellon Inst., 1950–56. **Educ.:** Univ. of Pittsburgh, 1944–47, BS (Bio., Chem.); Duquesne Univ., 1960–63, MS (LS Educ.). **Orgs.:** SLA: Bd. of Dirs. (1979–82); various ofcs. ASIS: Various ofcs. **Honors:** Westinghse. Electric Corp., Ord. of Merit, 1977. **Pubns.:** Various pubns. **Activities:** 12; 17, 33; 64, 84, 91 **Addr.:** Westinghouse Electric Corp., P.O. Box 355, Pittsburgh, PA 15230.

Vaslef, Irene (Mr. 23, 1934, Budapest, Hungary) Libn., Dumbarton Oaks Resrch. Lib., Trustees for Harvard Univ., 1972–; Head Cat. Libn., CO Coll., 1968–72; Libn., CO Spr. Sch. Syst., 1964–67; Libn., Cambridge, MA Sch. Syst., 1962–64. **Educ.:** San José State Univ., 1960, BA (Fr.); Simmons Coll., 1963, MS (LS); Cath. Univ. of Amer., 1974–, PhD Cand. (Hist.); various postgrad. crs. **Orgs.:** SLA. ARLIS/NA. **Honors:** Pi Gamma Mu, 1979. **Pubns.:** "Byzantium: A Bibliographic Repertory of American and Canadian Publications," *Byzantine Std./Etudes Byzantines* (1980). **Activities:** 1; 15, 17 **Addr.:** 1703 32nd St., N.W., Washington, DC 20007.

Vassallo, Paul (Ag. 3, 1937, Marsa, Malta) Dean, Lib. Srvs., Univ. of NM, 1974–; Dir., Natl. Serials Data Prog., Lib. of Congs., 1972–74, Chief, Congsnl. Ref. Div., 1968–72; Asst. to Dean, Sch. of Lib. and Info. Srvs., Univ. of MD, 1967–68. **Educ.:** Wayne State Univ., 1954–59, BA (Pol. Sci.); Univ. of MI, 1961–62, MALS. **Orgs.:** Amigos Bibl. Cncl., Inc.: Bd. of Trustees (Ch., 1981–). Cncl. of Acad. Resrch. Libs. in Amigos: Ch. (1981). ALA:ACRL :Legis. Com. WHCOLIS: NM Del., Ch. Albuquerque Cham. of Cmrce.: Cult. Com. (1978–). **Honors:** Lib. of Congs., Merit. Srv. Awd., 1966. **Activities:** 1, 4; 17, 39, 44; 56, 78, 92 **Addr.:** General Library, University of New Mexico, Albuquerque, NM 87131.

Vasta, Bruno M. (Ap. 1, 1933, Washington, DC) Dir., Chem. Info. Div., Env. Protection Agency, 1978–; Chief, Bibl. Srvs. Div., Natl. Lib. of Med., 1976–78, Chief, Toxicology Info. Srvs., 1973–76, Chief, Tech. Files Implementation Branch, 1970–73. **Educ.:** Georgetown Univ., 1950–54, BS (Chem.); George Washington Univ., 1955–57, MS (Biochem.); Dept. of Agr., 1960, USDA Mgt. Cert. **Orgs.:** Med. LA. SLA. ASIS: SIG-Bio. Chem. (Ch.-Elect, 1979–80). Amer. Chem. Socty.: Chem. Info. Div. (Ch., 1975–76); Div. of Comps. in Chem., Prog. Ch., *Jnl. of Chem. Info. and Comp. Sci.* Ed. Bd., Adv. Bd. (1971–). Chem. Notation Assn. Chem. Socty. of WA. Drug Info. Assn. Various other orgs. **Honors:** Melpar, Inc., Outstan. Sr. Sci. Awd., 1963; FDA Awd., 1970; Amer. Chemical Socty., Outstan. Achvmt. Awd., 1976. **Pubns.:** *Drug Interactions–Annotated Bibliography* (1973–74); "CHEMLINE," *Natl. Lib. of Med. Medlars Tech. Bltn.* (F. 1975); "Searching Capabilities in CHEMLINE," *Natl. Lib. Med. TOXLINE Tech. Bltn.* (N. 1975); "CANCERLINE–A New NLM/NCI Data Base," *Jnl. Chem. Info. and Comp. Sci.* (My. 1976); jt. auth., "TOXLINE Inverted File Analysis," *Jnl. Chem. Info. and Comp. Sci.* (1976); various articles, presentations, patents. **Activities:** 4, 12; 17, 26, 34; 58, 75, 91 **Addr.:** 9111 Westerholme Way, Vienna, VA 22180.

Vastine, James P. (Ag. 20, 1941, Covington, KY) Asst. Head, Ref., Univ. of S. FL, 1977–, Circ., Rsv., ILL Libn., 1974–77, Asst. Ref. Libn., 1971–74, Asst. Cat. Libn., 1970–71. **Educ.:** Univ. of S. FL, 1960–64, BA (Hist.); FL State Univ., 1964–65, MS (LS). **Orgs.:** FL LA: ILL Caucus (Ch., 1975–76); Lib. Orien. and Bibl. Instr. Caucus Ch., (1979–80), Vice-Ch. (1978–79); Pubns. Com. (1979–81); Mem. Com. (1973–74). SE LA. **Activities:** 1; 31, 34, 39 **Addr.:** 11334 N. Rome Ave., Tampa, FL 33612.

Vaughn, (Mrs.) Florence E. (Fowler) (O. 30, 1907, Greenville, TX) Pub. Lib. Bd. Mem., Tyler Pub. Lib., 1972–; Cat. Libn., TX Coll., 1971–; HS Libn., Tyler Pub. Schs., 1956–71; Multi-Sch. Libn., Jr. HS Supvsr., Smith Cnty. Rural Schs., 1950–56; Assoc. State Supvsr., Sch. Libs., TX Dept. of Educ., 1947–50; Sch. Libn., Grades 1–12, Booker T. Washington Sch., 1946–47; various tchr., sch. libn. positions, 1927–46. **Educ.:** TX Coll., 1925–27, 1933–35, BA (Eng.); Prairie View Coll., 1940–43, MS (Eng., Educ., Admin.); Univ. of Denver, 1945–47, BS (LS); Univ. of WI, 1950–52, 1954, MS (LS). **Orgs.:** ALA: Mag. Com. (1954–56). TX LA: ALA Mem. Com. (1967–69); Trustee RT (Secy.-Treas., 1977–78). SW LA. Natl. Educ. Assn. TX State Tchrs. Assn. Lcl. Parent-Tchr. Assn. Natl. Cncl. of Negro Women. Various other orgs. **Honors:** Lcl. Parent-Tchr. Assn., Life Mem. and Trophy, 1968; Alpha Kappa Alpha. **Pubns.:** "The Instructional Materials Center Serving a System of Schools," *TX Lib. Jnl.* (Mr. 1955). **Activities:** 1, 11; 15, 20, 24 **Addr.:** 1620 N. Moore Ave., Tyler, TX 75702.

Vaughn, Kathryn Blair (Mr. 2, 1948, Ann Arbor, MI) Chief Libn., Montreal Gen. Hosp., 1981–; Docmlst., Univ. de Montréal, 1978–81; Libn., Intl. Planned Parenthood Fed., 1975–76. **Educ.:** Univ. of MI, 1966–70, BA (Anthro.); Columbia Univ., 1974–75, MS (Lib. Srv.); Med. LA, 1975, Cert. (Med. Libnshp.). **Orgs.:** SLA: Sect. de l'Est du Can., PR/Pubcty., (Ch., 1980–81). Corp. des Bibtcr. Prof. du PQ. **Activities:** 1, 12; 17, 39; 62, 80, 92 **Addr.:** 4858 Côte des Neiges #907, Montréal, PQ H3V 1G8, Canada.

Vaughn, Robert V. (N. 21, 1924, Carey, OH) Head Libn., The Ward M. Canaday Lib., The Good Hope Sch., 1970–; Libn., St. Dunstan's Episcopal Sch., 1966–70; Instr., Coll. of VI, 1966–67; Sr. Statistician, Anal., Gen. Motors Corp., 1962–66; Asst. to VP Mktg., Fenestra, Inc., 1955–62; various sales positions, 1951–54. **Educ.:** OH State Univ., 1947–50, BA, BS (Geo., Bus. Admin.); Univ. of MI, 1954–55, (LS); Univ. of WI, 1970, Cert. (Drug Educ.); Univ. of Denver, 1972, Cert. (Arch. Admin.); Goddard Coll., 1974–76, MALS; Univ. of Sarasota, 1976–79, EdD (Educ.); Natl. Afflt. for Litcy., 1981, Cert. (Advnc. Tutor). **Orgs.:** St. Croix LA: Fndr.; Past Pres.; Bd. ALA: AASL; ACRL. Intl. Assn. of Sch. Libns. SALALM. Various other orgs. Assn. of Caribbean Univ., Resrch., and Inst. Libs. Caribbean Std. Assn. Socty. for Caribbean Ling. St. Croix Cham. of Cmrce.: Lib. Com., Ch.; Bd. (1979–81). Various other orgs. **Honors:** St. Croix LA, Fndr., Past Pres. Awd., 1974. **Pubns.:** *West Indian Library and Archival Personnel* (1972); *The Virgin Islands . . . In . . . Periodical Literature* (1974); *To St Lucia with Love* bibl. (1980); *The Air Transport Industry Serving the Virgin Islands and the West Indies* (1975); *An Almanac for St. Thomas Airport Planners* (1974); various mono., articles. **Activities:** 1, 10; 17, 24, 41; 56, 83, 89 **Addr.:** P.O. Box 2513, Frederiksted, St. Croix, VI 00840.

Vaughn, Susan J. (Je. 13, 1941, Detroit, MI) Deputy Assoc. Libn., Ref. Srvs., Brooklyn Coll., 1971–; Ref. Libn., Grad. Sch. of Bus., Univ. of MI, 1968–71; Ref. Libn., Detroit Pub. Lib., 1964–68. **Educ.:** Marygrove Coll., 1959–63, BA (Hist.); Univ. of MI, 1963–64, AMLS; John Jay Coll. of Criminal Justice, 1973–75, MA (Criminal Justice). **Orgs.:** ALA: Lcl. Arrange. Com. (1980); Biblther. Com. (1974–75). NLA. NY LA: Legis. Com. (1979–); Inst. Libs. Com. (Ch., 1980). LA CUNY: Pres. (1978–79). **Honors:** Kappa Gamma Pi, 1963. **Pubns.:** *Private Reinvestment, Gentrification, and Displacement: Selected References* (1980); contrib., *Serials for Libraries* (1979); "Feminist Publishing: An Exploration," *Lib. Jnl.* (Je. 1, 1976); "Women: A Recommended List of Print and Non Print Materials," *Media Ctr.* (My. 1975). **Activities:** 1; 15, 17, 39; 59, 77, 92 **Addr.:** Brooklyn College Library, Brooklyn, NY 11210.

Veach, Lynn H. (O. 2, 1947, New Orleans, LA) Head, Bio. Lib., Oak Ridge Natl. Lab., 1971–. **Educ.:** LA State Univ., 1966–70, BS (Bio.); Univ. of KY, 1970–71, MSLS (Spec. Med. Libnshp.); Med. LA, 1971–, Cert. **Orgs.:** SLA: Lcl. Chap., Secy.; Lcl. Chap. Bltn. Ed. (1973). Med. LA. **Honors:** Beta Phi Mu, 1971. **Pubns.:** "Newscript," *Chem. and Engin. News* (1979). **Activities:** 4, 12; 15, 34, 39; 58, 80 **Addr.:** Biology Library, Bldg. 9207, POBY, Oak Ridge, TN 37830.

Veaner, Allen Barnet (Mr. 17, 1929, Harrisburg, PA) Univ. Libn., Univ. of CA, Santa Barbara, 1977–; Asst. Dir., Libs., Stanford Univ., 1967–77, Head, Acq. Dept., 1964–67; Spec., Docum. Reprodct., Harvard Univ., 1959–64; Catlgr., Harvard Coll. Lib., 1957–59; Chaplain, U.S. Army, 1954–56; various consult. positions. **Educ.:** Gettysburg Coll., 1946–49, BA (Phys.); Hebrew Un. Coll., 1949–54, BHL, MA (Rabbinics); Simmons Coll., 1958–60, MLS; Hebrew Un. Coll., 1969, MA. **Orgs.:** Natl. Micro. Assn.: Com. on Newsp. Stans.; Ed. Com. (1972–73); various coms. ALA: Cncl.; RTSD/Acq. Sect., Ch., Subcom. on Micropubshg., Ch., Com. on Accred. (1970–75); various coms. ASIS: Micro. Tutorials. Intl. Acad. at Santa Barbara: VP. Japan Socty. Amer. Natl. Stans. Inst.: Com. on The Romanization of Hebrew; Com. on the Romanization of Yiddish; Com. on Advert. Stans. for Micro. Collaborative Lib. Syst. Dev. Grp. Various other orgs. **Honors:** Phi Beta Kappa, 1949; Cncl. on Lib. Resrcs., Flwshp., 1972; Simmons Coll., 1981 Alum. Achvmt. Awd., 1981. **Pubns.:** *Studies in Micropublishing 1853–1976* (1976); *Evaluation of Micropublications* (1971); "Spires/Ballots Report" motion pic. (1969); ed.-in-chief, *Micro. Review* (1971–); chap. reviewer, *Anl. Review of Info. Sci. and Tech.* (1970–77); various articles, edshps. **Activities:** 1; 17, 33, 34; 55, 56, 75 **Addr.:** Office of the University Librarian, University of California, Santa Barbara, CA 93106.

Veatch, Julian Lamar, Jr., (Ap. 9, 1949, Atlanta, GA) Dir., High Plains Reg. Lib. Syst., 1979–; Libn., U.S. Geol. Srvy., Tallahassee, FL, 1977–79; Dir., Ohoopee Reg. Lib., 1973–76; Actg. Dir., Jefferson Cnty. Lib., 1971–72. **Educ.:** Young Harris Coll., Univ. of GA, 1967–71, AA, BA (Hist.); Emory Univ., 1972–73, MLn (Libnshp.); FL State Univ., 1976–79, AMD, PhD (LS). **Orgs.:** ALA: PLA, Goals, Guidelines and Stans. Com. (1979–81); Lib. Admin. Div./Bldg. and Equip. Sect., Exec. Com. (1980–82), Archit. for Pub. Libs. Com. (1976–81); Adv. Com. for Resrch. on Pub. Lib. Plng. (1979–81). CO LA: Constn. and Bylaws Com. (Ch., 1980–82). **Honors:** Beta Phi Mu, 1978. **Pubns.:** Ed., *Junior Members Roundtable: Affiliates Development Guidelines* (1976); "Reference Service in a Small Public Library," *PLA Nsltr.* (Sum. 1976). **Activities:** 9; 17, 19, 24 **Addr.:** High Plains Regional Library System, 2227 23rd Ave., Greeley, CO 80631.

Veblen, Marthanna E. (Seattle, WA) Docum. Libn., King Cnty. Lib. Syst., 1969–, Stockpile Libn., Coord. of Bkmobile.

PROFESSIONAL ACTIVITIES: Institutions: 1. Acad. lib.; 2. Arch.; 3. Assn.; 4. Fed./Gvt. lib.; 5. Inst. lib.; 6. Mfr./Suppl.; 7. Milit. lib.; 8. Musm.; 9. Pub. lib.; 10. Sch. lib.; 11. Sch. of lib. sci.; 12. Spec. lib.; 13. State lib.; 14. (other). **Functions/Activities:** 15. Acq./Col. dev.; 16. Adult srvs.; 17. Admin.; 18. Apprais.; 19. Archit./Bldgs.; 20. Cat./Class.; 21. Chld. srvs.; 22. Circ.; 23. Cons./Pres.; 24. Consult.; 25. Cont. ed.; 26. Educ. lib. sci.; 27. Ext. srvs.; 28. Fund/Grants; 29. Gvt. pubs.; 30. Indx./Abs.; 31. Instr. lib. use; 32. Media srvs.; 33. Micro.; 34. Netwks./Coop.; 35. Persnl.; 36. PR; 37. Publshg.; 38. Recs. mgt.; 39. Ref. srvs.; 40. Repro.; 41. Resrch.; 42. Review.; 43. Secur.; 44. Serials; 45. Spec. col.; 46. Tech. srvs.; 47. Trustees/Bds.; 48. YA srvs.; 49. (other).

Srvs., Reg. Supvsr., King Cnty. Lib. Syst., 1969–; Asst. Libn., Head Libn., Seattle Pac. Univ., 1960–66. **Educ.:** Univ. of WA, BA (Soclgy.), 1960, MLibr (Libnshp.). **Orgs.:** WA LA: WHCOLIS (Official Observer, 1979); Fed. Rel. Coord. (1974–79). WA State Adv. Com. on Depos. Stans. Pac, NW LA. Various other orgs. Seattle/King Cnty. Plng. Cncl. on Aging: 1st Ch. (1973–79). Episcopal Dio. of Olympia: Bd. of Trustees (1978–). Creat. Retirement Couns. Inc.: Pres. (1979–). Retirement Homes of West. WA Inc.: Comsn. on Aging (Ch., 1973–79). Various other orgs. **Pubns.:** *Aging Where to Turn in Washington State* (1976); *Giant Strides Since Andrew Carnegie: Creative Architecture in the King County Library System* (1974). **Addr.:** 4545 Sand Point Way N.E., Seattle, WA 98105.

Veit, Fritz (S. 17, 1907, Emmendingen, Baden, Germany) Dir., Libs. Chicago State Univ., 1949–73; Kennedy-King Coll., 1949–72; Supvsr., John Marshall Law Sch. Lib., 1949–57; Law Libn., U.S. Railroad Retirement Bd., 1943–49; Libn., Chicago City Jr. Coll., 1941–48; various libn. positions, Univ. of Chicago, 1937–43; Prof., Rosary Coll., Grad. Sch. of LS, 1950–77; various visit. prof. positions, 1959–78. **Educ.:** Univ. of Freiburg, Univ. of Berlin, Univ. of Heidelberg, 1926–32, DrJur (Frbg.); George Peabody Coll., 1935–36, BS (LS); Univ. of Chicago, 1936–41, PhD. **Orgs.:** ALA: Elec. Com. (Ch., 1959); ACRL/Tchr. Educ. Libs. Sect., (Secy., Ch., 1959–61); Assoc. Ed., *ACRL Mono.* (1952–60); 1963 Conf. (Lcl. ACRL Ch., 1963). IL LA. Chicago Lib. Club: Pres. (1964–65). AALS. Frdm. to Read Fndn. Chicago City Coll.: Lib. Tech. Prog., Adv. Com. (Ch., 1968–74). Univ. of IL Grad. Sch. of LS: Adv. Cncl. on Libns. (1971–74). **Honors:** Pi Gamma Mu, 1936. **Pubns.:** *The Community College Library* (1975); "Library Service to College Students," *Lib. Trends* (Jl. 1976); "Microforms, Microform Equipment and Microform Use in the Educational Environment," *Lib. Trends* (Ap. 1971); "Library Technical Assistant: Some General Observations," *IL Libs.* (S. 1970); "Training the Junior College Librarian," *Jnl. of Educ. for Libnshp.* (Fall 1968); various reviews, articles. **Activities:** 1, 4; 17, 24, 26; 54, 92 **Addr.:** 1716 E. 55th St., Chicago, IL 60615.

Veitch, Carol J. (O. 27, 1942, Irwin, PA) Asst. Prof., E. Carolina Univ., 1978–; Asst. Prof., Murray State Univ., 1976–78; Sch. Libn., Norwin Sch. Dist., 1964–76; Sch. of Nursing Libn., Jameson Hosp., PA, 1966. **Educ.:** Clarion State Coll., 1960–64, BSEd (LS, Soc. Std.); Univ. of Pittsburgh, 1965–66, MLS, 1975–78, PhD. **Orgs.:** ALA. NC LA. Chld. Lit. Assn. Natl. Cncl. Tchrs. Eng.: Asm. on Lit. for Adlsnt. Pitt Greenville Media Socty. **Honors:** Beta Phi Mu. **Activities:** 10, 11; 21, 48; 55, 63, 89 **Addr.:** Dept. of Library Science, East Carolina University, Greenville, NC 27834.

Velde, John Ernest, Jr. (Je. 15, 1917, Pekin, IL) **Educ.:** Univ. of IL, 1934–38, AB (Phil.). **Orgs.:** Natl. Cncl. on Libs. and Info. Sci. (1970–79). IL Valley Lib. Syst.: Pres. (1965–69). WHCOLIS: Adv. Bd. (1976–80). ALA: Endow. Trustee (1976–); ALTA, Fndn. Ch. (1976), Jury on Cits. (Ch., 1979–), Intl. Rel. Com. (Ch., 1973–76), Reg. VP (1970). Various other orgs. Univ. of CA, Los Angeles, Grad. Sch. of Lib. and Info. Sci.: Adv. Cncl. (1981–). Ctr. for Ulcer Resrch. and Educ.: Ch. (1977–). Jt. Cncl. on Econ. Educ.: Trustee (1977–). Univ. of CA, Los Angeles, Brain Resrch. Inst.: Bd. of Cnclrs. (1977–). Various other orgs. **Honors:** Natl. Lib. Week in IL, Hon. Ch., 1973. **Addr.:** 2003 La Brea Terr., Hollywood, CA 90046.

Vella, Sandra Agnes (Ap. 14, 1945, San Francisco, CA) Prin. Catlgr., Univ. of CA, Davis, 1981–, Catlgr., Assoc. Libn., 1980–81; Head, Copy Prcs. Unit, Catlgr., Stanford Univ., Green Lib., 1968–77. **Educ.:** San Francisco State Univ., 1963–67, BA (Hist.); Univ. of CA, Berkeley, 1967–68, MLS; 1976, CA Coll. Libn. Cred.; CA Cmnty. Coll., 1978, Instr. Cred. **Orgs.:** CA LA: Lib. Srv. to the Deaf and Hearing Impaired Chap. (Secy.-Treas., 1981); Tech. Srvs. Chap. CA Socty. of Libns. North. CA Tech. Prcs. Grp. ALA: RTSD; LITA; ACRL; ASCLA. **Activities:** 1; 17, 20; 72, 92 **Addr.:** 5000 Olive Oak Way, Carmichael, CA 95608.

Velleman, Ruth A. (Ap. 12, 1921, New York, NY) Lib. Dir., Human Resrcs. Sch., 1963–. **Educ.:** Smith Coll., 1938–42, BA (Hist.); C.W. Post, 1961–65, MS (LS). **Orgs.:** ALA: Stans. Com. for Libs. for the Blind and Phys. Handcpd.; ASCLA, Vocational Educ. for Handcpd.; Vocational Rehab. Com. (1980–81). Nassau LA: Bd. Long Island Lib. Resrcs. Cncl. Pres. Com. on Empl. of the Handcpd.: Lib. Com. **Pubns.:** "Rehabilitation Information: A Bibliography of Journals and Newsletters," *The Serials Libn.* (Win. 1981); "Library Service to Disabled People: A State of the Art Report for the 1970's," *The Bowker Annual of Library and Book Trade Information* (1980); "Special Education and Rehabilitation Librarianship," *Encyc. of Lib. and Info. Sci.* (1980); *Serving Physically Disabled People: An Information Handbook for All Libraries* (1979); "The Psychology of the Disabled," *Library Services to the Adult Handicapped* (1978); various articles, sps., rpts. **Activities:** 1, 10; 15, 21, 26; 72 **Addr.:** 15 Cliffway, Port Washington, NY 11050.

Vellucci, Matthew J. (D. 19, 1935, White Plains, NY) Pres., Spec. Info. Srvs., Inc., 1975–; Sr. Anal., Mgr., Lib. Srvs., Herner and Co., 1970–74; Resrch. Assoc., Spec. Asst. to Dean, Coll. of Lib. and Info. Srvs., Univ. of MD, 1968–70; Libn., Exxon Co., 1964–68; Libn., Queens Coll., 1963–64; Asst. to Tech. Srvs. Head, Westchester Lib. Syst., 1960–63. **Educ.:** St. Pius X Semy., 1953–58, BA (Phil.); Columbia Univ., 1960–62, MLS. **Orgs.:** SLA: Various NY, DC ofcs. ALA. **Pubns.:** Jt. ed., *Selected Federal Computer-Based Information Systems* (1972); jt. ed., *The National Directory of State Agencies* (1974); "New Information for the Congress: The Congressional Sourcebook," *GAO Review* (Fall 1976); various client srvy., plng. rpts. **Activities:** 12; 24; 62, 75 **Addr.:** 7212 13th Ave., Takoma Park, MD 20912.

Veltema, John H. (Je. 14, 1928, Hudsonville, MI) Dir., Media Srvs., Jenison Pub. Schs., 1970–, HS Libn., 1968–70; HS Libn., Grand Rapids Christ. HS, 1964–68. **Educ.:** Calvin Coll., 1946–50, AB (Eng.); Drake Univ., 1955–62, MA (Eng.); 1968, Lib. Cert. **Orgs.:** MI Assn. for Media In Educ.: Parlmt. (1974–80). Georgetown Pub. Lib. Bd.: Ch. Lakeland Lib. Fed.: Past Pres. (1974). Lakeland Lib. Coop.: Adv. Cncl. (Ch., 1980–81). Various other orgs. Amer. Assn. of Curric. Dirs. AECT. **Pubns.:** "The Media Specialist in the State of Michigan" cassette (1979). **Activities:** 10; 32 **Addr.:** Media Services, Jenison Public Schools, 2140 Bauer Rd., Jenison, MI 49428.

Veneziano, Velma D. (Jl. 10, 1921, Buffalo, WY) Lib. Systs. Anal., Northwest. Univ. Lib., 1967–; Systs. Anal., Chicago Pub. Sch., 1959–67; Systs. Anal., Sci. Resrch. Assoc., 1958–59. **Educ.:** Univ. of WY, 1939–43, BA (Hist.). **Orgs.:** ALA: Representation in Machine Readable Form of Bibl. Info. (1973–77). ASIS. **Pubns.:** "Library Automation," *Annual Review of Information Science and Technology* (1980); "Cost Advantages of Total System Devlopment," *Proceedings of the 1976 Clinic On Library Applications of Data Processing: The Economics of Library Automation* (1977); "An Interactive Computer-Based Circulation System for Northwestern University: The Library Puts It To Work," *Jnl. of Lib. Autom.* (Je. 1972). **Activities:** 1; 38, 46; 56, 62, 75 **Addr.:** Northwestern University Library, Evanston, IL 60201.

Verich, Thomas M. (Jl. 25, 1944, Superior, WI) Head, Dept. of Arch. and Spec. Cols., Univ. Archvst., John Davis Williams Lib., Univ. of MS, 1977–; Instr., Asst. Prof. of Hist., Clemson Univ., 1970–75. **Educ.:** Lawrence Univ., 1965, AB (Hist.); Duke Univ., 1973, PhD (Hist.); Univ. di Firenze, 1966, Dip. (Hist.); The Univ. of Chicago, 1977, AM (Libnshp.). **Orgs.:** SAA. Socty. of MS Archvsts. ALA. **Honors:** Lumber Arch. Proj., Natl. Hist. Pubns. and Recs. Comsn., Proj. Dir., 1979. **Pubns.:** *William Faulkner's Gifts of Friendship: Presentation and Inscribed Copies From the Collection of Louis Daniel Brodsky* (1980); *The European Powers and the Italo-Ethiopian War, 1935–1936: A Diplomatic Study* (1980); ed., *A Retrospective View of the University of Mississippi 1848–1906* (1979). **Activities:** 1, 2; 15, 17, 28 **Addr.:** Dept. of Archives and Special Collections, John Davis Williams Library, University of Mississippi University, MS 38677.

Vernon, Arrolyn H. (Ag. 10, 1927, Concord, NH) Libn., Beaver Country Day Sch., 1977–; Asst. Libn., Brimmer and May Sch., 1969–75. **Educ.:** Bates Coll., 1945–49, BA (Eng.); Penn State, 1949–51, MA (Eng.); Simmons Coll., 1970–74, MLS. **Orgs.:** ALA. New Eng. LA. Coop. LA. **Pubns.:** Various reviews, YA review clmn., *Sch. Lib. Jnl.* (1978–); adv. com., *Junior High School Library Catalog* (1980). **Activities:** 10; 21, 42, 48 **Addr.:** 189 Pond St., Westwood, MA 02090.

Veryha, Wasyl (Ja. 3, 1922, Kolodribka, Galicia, Ukraine) Libn. III, Head, Slavic Cat. Unit, Univ. of Toronto Lib., Bibl. Prcs. Dept., 1977–, Slavic Cat. Spec., Cat. Dept., 1976–77, West. European Lang. Catlgr., 1967–76, Slavic Catlgr., 1964–66, Ord. Dept. Libn., Ord. Dept., 1961–64. **Educ.:** Univ. of Toronto, 1955–59, BA (Hist.), 1960–61, BLS; Univ. of Ottawa, 1963–68, MA (Hist.). **Orgs.:** ALA: ACRL/Slavic and E. European Sect. (Ch., 1975–76). Can. LA. Libn. Assn. of the Univ. of Toronto. Ukrainian LA. Various other orgs. Shevchenko Sci. Socty. of Can.: Natl. Exec.; Conf. Org. (1976–). Ukrainian Natl. Fed. of Can.: Natl. Exec.; 2nd VP (1978–). Ukrainian Vets. Assn. of the 1st Div. UNA of Can.: Pres.; Natl. Exec. (1976–80). **Pubns.:** *Along the Roads of World War II* (in Ukrainian with English summary) (1980, 2nd ed. 1981); *Teachers' College in Zalishchyky; a Case Study of Education in Galicia* (in Ukranian) (1974); *Communication Media and Soviet Nationality Policy* (1972); "A Proposal for the Revision of the L.C. Classification Schedules in History for Eastern Europe," *Lib. Resrcs. & Tech. Srvs.* (Ap. 1977); "Library of Congress Classification and Subject Headings Relating to Slavic and Eastern Europe," *LRTS* (1972); various articles in Ukranian and English, edshps. **Activities:** 1; 20; 66, 75, 92 **Addr.:** 215 Grenadier Rd., Toronto, ON M6R 1R9 Canada.

Vesely, Marilyn L. (S. 19, 1932, Milwaukee, WI) Pub. Info. Ofcr., OK Dept. of Libs., 1977–, State Law Libn., 1974–77, 1970–71; Ref. Libn., OK City Pub. Lib., 1973–74; Sch. Libn., Prince George's Cnty., MD, 1966–70. **Educ.:** Univ. of WI, 1950–54, BA (Eng.); Univ. of MD, 1965–66, MLS. **Orgs.:** ALA. SW LA. OK LA: Bd. of Dirs. (1979). Southwest. Assn. of Law Libns. Frnds. of Libs. in OK: Bd. of Dirs. (1979–). **Honors:** John Cotton Dana Lib. Pubns. Awd., 1981; ALA Preconf. for Lib. Nsltr. Eds., Best Over-all Nsltr., 1979. **Pubns.:** "Project Worth" videotape (1980). **Activities:** 13; 16, 24, 36 **Addr.:** Oklahoma Dept. of Libraries, 200 N.E. 18th St., Oklahoma City, OK 73105.

Vestal, Alice M. (Ap. 5, 1945, Buffalo, NY) Head, Spec. Cols. Dept., Univ. of Cincinnati Libs., 1977–, Asst. Head, Spec. Cols. Dept., 1975–77; Cur., Nippert Col., Cincinnati Hist. Socty., 1971–75; Mss. Prcs., George Arents Resrch. Lib., Syracuse Univ., 1969–71. **Educ.:** Miami Univ., 1963–67, BA (Hist.); Univ. of NC, 1967–68 (Hist.); Syracuse Univ., 1969–70, MA (Educ.); various crs. **Orgs.:** SAA: Com. on Reg. Arch. Actv. (Ch., 1976–78); 1980 Lcl. Arrange. Com. (Ch., 1980). Socty. of OH Archvsts.: Cncl. (1973–75, 1978–80); VP (1975–77); *The SOA Nsltr.* Managing Ed. (1977–79). The Ms. Socty. Amer. Assn. for State and Lcl. Hist. **Pubns.:** "The American Etiquette Book; or How to Make Guests Feel at Home When They Wish They Were," *The Cincinnati Hist. Socty. Bltn.* (Win. 1976); "Arrangement and Description Problems Challenge Large and Small Repositories," *The OH Archvst.* (Spr. 1974); "Standardized Finding Aids and Volunteers Expedite Processing Demands," *The OH Archvst.* (Spr. 1974); "'Will You Come and Take an Indian Dinner...' An Invitation from Thomas Jefferson," *The Cincinnati Hist. Socty. Bltn.* (Fall–Win. 1972); "'I Am Satisfied With What I Have Done': Collis P. Huntington, 19th Century Entrepreneur," *The Courier* (Jl. 1971). **Activities:** 1, 2; 17, 38, 45 **Addr.:** Special Collections Department, Rm. 600–Blegen Library, University of Cincinnati, Cincinnati, OH 45221.

Veth, Terry R. (F. 11, 1947, Minneapolis, MN) Head, Acq. Dept., Minneapolis Pub. Lib., 1980–, Ref. Libn., 1978–80, Autom. Cat. Proj. Catlgr., 1977–78, Catlgr., 1974–77. **Educ.:** Univ. of MN, 1966–70, BA (Classics), 1972–74, MALS. **Orgs.:** ALA. MN LA. **Pubns.:** Jt. auth., *Detroit Public Library Cataloging Practices Study* (1980); jt. auth., *MPLIC/SPPL/MELSA Automated Cataloging Project Systems Design* (1978); "Searching for Foundation Grants," *MACAE Qtly.* (Spr. 1980). **Activities:** 9; 15, 24, 46 **Addr.:** 11810–36th Ave. N., Plymouth, MN 55441.

Viacava, Lillian D. (Brooklyn, NY) Assoc. Libn., Ryan Lib., Iona Coll., 1954–. **Educ.:** Coll. of New Rochelle, 1947–51, BA (Hist.); Columbia Univ., 1953–54, MS (Lib. Srv.). **Orgs.:** ALA. SLA. Metro. Cath. Coll. Libns. Unit: Secy.-Treas. (1955–58, 1975–77). Westchester LA: Coll. Libs. Sect. Vice-Ch. (1977–78), (1978–79). AAUP. Natl. Conf. of Christs. and Jews: Adult Bk. Com. (1959–76). **Activities:** 1; 31, 39, 49-Online srch.; 55, 59, 75 **Addr.:** Ryan Library, Iona College, New Rochelle, NY 10801.

Vick, Nancy Harper (Ja. 10, 1935, Edgecombe Cnty., NC) Dir., Reg. AV Srvs., Longwood Coll., 1972–; Media Coord., Charlotte Cnty. Schs., 1970–72; Media Coord., Norfolk City Schs., 1965–70; Tchr., Chesapeake Pub. Schs., 1959–65, 1952–56. **Educ.:** E. Carolina Univ., 1957, BS; Coll. of William and Mary, 1967, MED; IN Univ., 1977, EdD. **Orgs.:** AECT: Accred. Com.; Awds. Com.; Reg. Coord. Natl. Assn. of Reg. Media Ctrs.: Bd. (1979–80). VA Educ. Media Assn.: James Reg. Bd. (1979–81). Assn. of VA TV Reps. in Higher Educ.: Secy. (1978–79); Pres. (1979–80). Phi Delta Kappa: Piedmont VA Chap. (Secy., 1978–80). VA Educ. Assn.: Del. (1980). Natl. Educ. Assn. Longwood Educ. Assn.: Pres. (1981–82). **Pubns.:** "How State Laws Affect Regional Media Services," *AV Instr.* (D. 1978). **Activities:** 5; 32; 63, 67, 74 **Addr.:** Regional AVS, Longwood College, Farmville, VA 23901.

Vidor, Ann Bonner (Ag. 16, 1950, Montreal, PQ) Head, Serials Cat. Dept., GA Inst. of Tech., 1979–; Head, Serials Unit, Cat. Dept., Atlanta Pub. Lib., 1977–79; Head, Mono. Unit, Cat. Dept., GA State Univ., 1976–77; Rom. Lang. Catlgr., Univ. of AZ, 1973–76. **Educ.:** Colby Coll., 1968–72, BA (Fr.); Emory Univ., 1972–73, MLn (LS); Univ. de Caen, Caen, France, 1970–71, Dip. d'etudes supérieures. **Orgs.:** ALA: JMRT, Olofson Awd. Com. (Ch., 1978–79), Mid-Win. Actv. Com. (1979–80). Metro. Atlanta LA. **Honors:** ALA, JMRT, Olofson Awd., 1978. **Activities:** 1, 9; 20, 44; 55 **Addr.:** Price Gilbert Memorial Library, Georgia Institute of Technology, Atlanta, GA 30332.

Vidor, David L. (Mr. 25, 1949, Boston, MA) Ref. Libn., Woodruff Lib., Emory Univ., 1981–; Cat. Libn., Resrch. Lib., Fed. Rsv. Bank of Atlanta, 1978–81; Asst. Libn., Div. of Libnshp. Lib., Emory Univ., 1976–78; Cat. Libn., Univ. of AZ Lib., 1975–76. **Educ.:** Gettysburg Coll., 1966–70, BA (Bus. Admin.); Emory Univ., 1972–73, MLn (LS). **Orgs.:** ALA: JMRT, Students to ALA Com. (1979–80), Mem. Mtg. Com. (1978–79). Metro-Atlanta LA: VP (1976–77). GA LA. Amer. Inst. of Bankers. **Honors:** ALA, JMRT, Shirley Olofson Awd., 1978. **Pubns.:** Cat. consult., "Card catalog cinco I" educ. kit (1977). **Activities:** 4, 12; 20, 39; 59 **Addr.:** Reference Dept., Woodruff Library, Emory University, Atlanta, GA 30322.

Viele, George Brookins (Ap. 20, 1932, Flint, MI) Lib. Dir., Greensboro Pub. Lib., 1971–; Visit. Instr., Univ. of NC, Greensboro, 1977–79; Asst. Dir., Wake Cnty. Pub. Libs., 1968–71. **Educ.:** Ctrl. MI Univ., 1960, BS (Eng.), 1965, MA; Univ. of NC, 1969, MSLS. **Orgs.:** NC State Lib.: State Aid Formula Com. (1977–78); Multi-type Lib. Coop. Com. (1978–). NC LA: Pub. Lib. Sect., Stats. Com. (Ch., 1977–79); Bd. of Dirs. (1973–75). Torch Club, Intl.: VP (1972–73); Greensboro Chap. (Pres., 1973–74). **Honors:** Phi Delta Kappa. **Pubns.:** "Problems, Strategies, and Collective Bargaining in Public Libraries," *Strategies for Library Administration: Concepts and Approaches* (1981); jt. ed., *Greensboro Public Library: A Study of the Library*

Special Subjects/Services: 50. Adult educ.; 51. Advert./Mktg.; 52. Aerosp.; 53. Agric.; 54. Area std.; 55. Arts/Hum.; 56. Autom.; 57. Bibl./Prtg.; 58. Bio. sci.; 59. Bus./Fin.; 60. Chem.; 61. Copyrt.; 62. Documtn.; 63. Educ.; 64. Engin.; 65. Env.; 66. Eth. grps.; 67. Film; 68. Food/Nutr.; 69. Geneal.; 70. Geo.; 71. Geol.; 72. Handcpd.; 73. Hist.; 74. Int. frdm.; 75. Info. sci.; 76. Insr.; 77. Law; 78. Legis.; 79. Math./Comp. sci.; 80. Med.; 81. Metals; 82. Nat. resrcs.; 83. Newsp.; 84. Nuc. sci.; 85. Oral hist.; 86. Petr./Energy; 87. Pharm.; 88. Phys./Astr./Math.; 89. Readg.; 90. Relig.; 91. Sci./Tech.; 92. Soc. sci.; 93. Telecom.; 94. Transp.; 95. (other).

and Its Community, or, the Apex of Library Service (1977); "Tobacco Played Hefty Role in Century of Development," *The Greensboro Rec.* (Jl. 19, 1977). **Activities:** 9, 11; 17, 34 **Addr.:** 3409 Regents Park Ln., Greensboro, NC 27405.

Vierich, Richard Wallace (S. 28, 1926, Hollywood, CA) Head Libn., Phys. Scis. Lib., Univ. of CA, Riverside, 1970–, Chief Biblgphr., Phys. Scis.; Chief, Tech. Srvs. Div., CA State Polytech. Univ., 1966–69; Admin. Asst. Libn., Pomona Pub. Lib., 1960–66. **Educ.:** Univ. of Redlands, 1949–52, BA (Hum., Msc. Art); Univ. of South. CA, 1959–64, MS (LS); various crs. **Orgs.:** SLA: S. CA Chap., Sci.-Tech. Adv. Bd. (1979–80); Educ. Com. (Ch., 1980–). Inland Empire Acad. Libs. Coop.: Ch. (1975–). Jurupa Mts. Cult. Ctr., Riverside: VP; Bd. of Dirs. (1972–78); Adv. Bd. (1978–); Map Socty. of CA: Chrt. Mem. (1978–). **Honors:** Jurupa Mts. Cult. Socty., Apprec. of Merit, 1978; Beta Phi Mu, 1964; Phi Kappa Phi, 1964. **Pubns.:** "Maps at UCR," *Books at UCR* (1979). **Activities:** 1, 10; 15, 17, 39; 65, 70, 91 **Addr.:** Physical Sciences Library, University of California, Riverside, Riverside, CA 92521.

Viets, Lola M. (N. 19, 1927, Clyde, KS) Libn., Winfield HS, 1954–; Tchr.-Libn., Hanover HS, 1949–54. **Educ.:** Emporia State Univ., 1945–49, BS (Soc. Sci.), 1950–56, MS (LS). **Orgs.:** KS Assn. of Sch. Libns.: Dist. Dir. Coord. (1979–81). ALA: AASL. Natl. Educ. Assn. KS Natl. Educ. Assn. **Honors:** Winfield Jaycees, Outstan. Young Educ., 1959; Winfield Tchrs. Assn., Mstr. Tchr. Awd., 1974. **Activities:** 10; 31, 32, 48; 63 **Addr.:** 1615 Ames, Apt. 1, Winfield, KS 67156.

Vigeant, Robert J. (Ap. 26, 1928, Worcester, MA) Head Libn., Saint Joseph's Coll., IN, 1975–; Head, Tech. Srvs., WA and Lee Univ., 1971–75; Head Libn., Haverhill Pub. Lib., 1966–70; Tech. Srvs. Libn., Finger Lakes Lib. Syst., 1962–66; Consult., MI State Lib., 1961–62; Head Libn., Carnegie Pub. Lib., 1959–61; YA Libn., Detroit Pub. Lib., 1957–59; Ref. Libn., Worcester Free Pub. Lib., 1956. **Educ.:** Assumption Coll., Worcester, MA, 1946–50, AB (Phil.); Simmons Coll., 1955–57, MS (LS). **Orgs.:** ALA. IN LA: Coll. and Univ. Div., Vice-Ch. (1977–78), Ch. (1978–79). NW IN Area Lib. Srvs. Athrty.: VP (1978); Pres. (1978–79). Cath. LA. MA Bd. of Lib. Comsn. Adv. Com. on Statewide Lib. Srvs. (1969). **Honors:** Jaycees, Ithaca, NY, "Jaycee of the Month," Outstan. Srv., 1963; City Plng. Comsn., Sault Ste. Marie, MI, Cert. of Recog., 1961. **Addr.:** Library, Saint Joseph's College, Rensselaer, IN 47978.

Vigle, John Barry (S. 11, 1925, Chattanooga, TN) Dir., Lib. Srvs., Eckerd Coll., 1978–; Dir., Univ. Lib., Xavier Univ., 1972–78; Asst. Dir., Libs., Univ. of Dayton, 1959–72; Asst. Branch Libn., Brooklyn Pub. Lib., 1956–59. **Educ.:** Univ. of KY, 1946–49, AB (Psy.), 1949–50, Grad. Std. (Phil.), 1955–56, MSLS. **Orgs.:** ALA: ACRL. FL LA. Grt. Cincinnati Lib. Cnsrtm.: Pres. (1974). Tampa Bay Lib. Cnsrtm.: Pres. (1979–80). AAUP. **Pubns.:** *An Environment for Learning* (1970); assoc. ed., *Union List of Serials in the Libraries of the Miami Valley* (1968–69); "Catholic Library Association; the Golden Anniversary," *Amer. Libs.* (Je. 1974). **Activities:** 1, 9; 15, 17, 44 **Addr.:** Eckerd College Library, St. Petersburg, FL 33733.

Vincent, Donald Edward Perry (D. 26, 1922, Martins Ferry, OH) Dir., Libs., Univ. of NH, 1962–; Dir., Lib. Srvs., Univ. of MI, Dearborn, 1959–62; Biblgphr., Wayne State Univ., 1958–59, Catlgr., 1952–58, LS Lectr., 1957–59. **Educ.:** Univ. of Buffalo, 1940–49 (Math.); Univ. of MI, 1952, AMLS, 1957, AM (Pol. Sci.), 1974, PhD (LS). **Orgs.:** New Eng. LA: VP. (1975–76); Pres. (1976–77). NH LA: VP (1963–65). New Eng. Lib. Info. Netwk.: Bd. Dirs. (1981–); Exec. Com. (Co-Ch., Ch., 1967–72). ALA: ACRL, Com. on Grants (1968–70), Com. on Lib. Srvys. (1970–72). Various other orgs. U.S. Reg. I Arch. Adv. Cncl. Frdm. to Read Fndn. Durham Hist. Socty. **Honors:** Phi Kappa Phi; Phi Beta Mu. **Activities:** 1; 17, 24 **Addr.:** University of New Hampshire Library, Durham, NH 03824.

Vincent-Daviss, Diana (Ja. 13, 1943, Birmingham, Eng.) Assoc. Law Libn., NY Univ. Sch. of Law, 1981–, Pub. Srvs. Libn., 1978–81, Spec. Cols. Libn., 1976–78, Ref. Libn., 1973–76; Libn., VT Gvr.'s Comsn. on the Admin. of Justice, 1973. **Educ.:** Girton Coll., 1962–65, BA (Law), 1969, MA (Law); Columbia Univ., 1971–72, MLS. **Orgs.:** AALL: Pubns. Com. (1980–81); Stans. Com. (1980–81). **Pubns.:** Various abs., regular clmn., *Corp. Law Review* (Volume 1, 2); various abs., regular clmn., *Secur. Regulation Law Review*. **Activities:** 1; 15, 17, 23; 77 **Addr.:** New York University School of Law, Rm. 108, 40 Washington Sq. S., New York, NY 10012.

Vint, Patricia A. (Detroit, MI) Dir., Hlth. Instr. Ctr., Madonna Coll., 1977–; Media Consult., Media Inc., 1974–77; Ch., Media K–12, Woodhaven Sch. Dist., 1972–74; Coord., Instr. Mtrls., Crestwood Sch. Dist., 1967–72. **Educ.:** Univ. of Detroit, 1955, AB (Hist.); Univ. of MI, 1961, Mstrs. (LS); Wayne State Univ., 1969, Permanent Tchg. Cert. (LS); East. MI Univ., 1974, Mstrs. Educ. Leadership; Univ. of Sarasota, 1980, EdD (Admin.). **Orgs.:** ALA. MI Assn. For Media In Educ.: Chrt. Mem. AECT. Girl Scouts of Amer.: Merit Awd. (1960). **Pubns.:** *The Effect of Leadership Styles of Nursing Faculty in a Baccalaureate Program On Their Selection of Instructional Aids* (1979); *Training of Media Paraprofessionals* (1974); *Library Orientation for Nursing Students; Effective Use of Audio and Video Cassettes In Presenting Lecture Material* (1979). **Activities:** 1, 10; 17, 24, 32; 63, 75, 91 **Addr.:** 461 Robindale Ave., Dearborn, MI 48128.

Viola, Herman J. (F. 24, 1938, Chicago, IL) Dir., Natl. Anthro. Arch., Smithsonian Inst., 1972–; Ed., *Prologue*, Natl. Arch., 1968–72, Archvst., 1967–68. **Educ.:** Marquette Univ., 1956–60, BA (Hist.), 1962–64, MA (Hist.); IN Univ., 1964–70, PhD (Hist.). **Honors:** SAA, Waldo Gifford Leland Awd., 1972. **Pubns.:** *Diplomats in Buckskins: A History of Indian Delegations in Washington City* (1981); *Indian Legacy of Charles Bird King* (1976); *Thomas L. McKenney: Architect of America's Early Indian Policy* (1974); various articles, bk. reviews. **Activities:** 2; 17, 26, 45; 66 **Addr.:** National Anthropological Archives, Smithsonian Institution, Washington, DC 20560.

Virgo, Julie A. Carroll (Je. 14, 1944, Adelaide, S. Australia) Exec. Dir., ACRL, 1977–; Dir. of Educ., Med. LA, 1972–77; Lectr., Univ. of Chicago, 1968–; Libn., Repatriation Dept., 1961–66; Libn., State Lib. of S. Australia, 1960–61. **Educ.:** LA of Australia, 1960–64, Regis. Cert. (Libnshp.); Univ. of Chicago, 1966–68, MA (Libnshp.), 1968–74, PhD (Libnshp.). **Orgs.:** ALA: LED Com. on Lib./Media Tech. Assts. (1973–75), Com. on Lib. Support Staffs (1975–77). ASIS: Com. on Inter-Socty. Coop. (1973–79); Com. on Educ. (Ch., 1976–77); various ofcs. CLENE: Adv. Bd., Cont. Lib. Educ. Proj. (1973–74); Bd. of Dirs. (1975–77). SLA. Various other orgs. Amer. Mgt. Assns. Amer. Socty. for Assn. Exec. AAAS: Sect. T, Nom. Com. (1978–81). **Honors:** Beta Phi Mu, 1968. **Pubns.:** "The Review Article–Its Characteristics and Problems," *Lib. Qtly.* (O. 1971); "An Evaluation of Index Medicus and MEDLARS in the Field of Ophthalmology," *Jnl. of the Amer. Socty. for Info. Sci.* (Jl.–Ag. 1970); "Education for Medical Librarians," *Encyc. of Lib. and Info. Sci.* (1976); "Computer-Assisted Instruction and the Health Sciences Library," *Jnl. of Med. Educ.* (Ag. 1976); "Degree or License," *Wilson Lib. Bltn.* (D. 1976); various articles, rpts. **Activities:** 1, 3; 17, 24, 26; 75, 93 **Addr.:** Association of College and Research Libraries, 50 E. Huron St., Chicago, IL 60611.

Virta, Alan (Mr. 14, 1951, Arlington, VA) Sr. Catlgr., Natl. Un. Cat. of Ms. Cols., Lib. of Congs., 1979–, Catlgr., 1974–79. **Educ.:** Univ. of MD, 1969–73, BA (Hist.), 1973–74, MLS; Arch. Inst., 1977, Cert. **Orgs.:** SAA. ACRL: Mss. Com. (1975–77). Mid-Atl. Reg. Arch. Conf. Prince George's Cnty. Hist. and Cult. Trust: Trustee (1978–). Prince George's Cnty. Hist. Socty.: Ed. (1974–). Republican Natl. Conv., 1976: Del. from MD. Republican Ctrl. Com. for Prince George's Cnty.: Parlmt. (1975–77). **Honors:** Phi Beta Kappa, 1972; Phi Alpha Theta, 1972; Beta Phi Mu, 1974. **Activities:** 2, 4; 20, 30, 45; 55 **Addr.:** 8244 Canning Terr., Greenbelt, MD 20770.

Viskochil, Larry A. (Jl. 3, 1939, Traverse City, MI) Cur., Graph. Col., Chicago Hist. Socty., 1977–, Head, Ref. and Reader Srvs., Lib., 1967–77; Tchr., Highland Park HS, 1965–66; Tchr., Ubly HS, 1963–65. **Educ.:** Ctrl. MI Univ., 1961, BA (Soc. Sci.), 1963, MA (Hist.); Univ. of MI, 1967, MA (LS); Columbia Coll., 1976, BA (Photography). **Orgs.:** ALA: RASD/Hist. Sect., Nom. Com. (1971), Conf. Prog. Com. (1972), Exec. Com. (1977–80), Lcl. Hist. Com. (1980); various coms. SLA: Pic. Div. (Ch., 1981–82). SAA: Aural and Graph. Recs. Afnty. Grp., Strg. Com. (1979). **Pubns.:** "Arthur Siegel: A Life in Photography, 1913–1978," *Chicago Hist.* (1981); "Chicago's Bicentennial Photographer: C.D. Mosher," *Chicago Hist.* (1976); "Chicago and Lewis Hine," *Chicago Hist.* (1977–78). **Activities:** 2, 5; 15, 23, 45; 55, 67 **Addr.:** Graphics Collection, Chicago Historical Society, Clark St. at North Ave., Chicago, IL 60614.

Vita, Susan H. (Ag. 10, 1942, Pasadena, CA) Chief, Cat. Pubn. Div., Lib. of Congs., 1976–; Chief, Serials Sect., Interior Dept. Lib., 1971–76, Ref. Libn., 1970–71, Catlgr., 1969–70. **Educ.:** Holy Names Coll., 1960–64, AB (Eng.); Univ. of South. CA, 1968–69, MLS. **Orgs.:** ALA: Rep. to Amer. Natl. Stans. Inst., Stans. Com. on Lib. Work, Documtn. and Rel. Prac. (1977–81); FLRT (Secy., 1977–78); RTSD, Plng. Com. (Ch., 1979–80)/ Serials Sect., Policy and Resrch. Com. (Ch., 1975–77), Exec. Com. (1975–77)/ Resrcs. Sect., Bkdlr. Lib. Rel. Com. (1975–77), Exec. Com. (Rep.-at-Lg., 1978–81). **Pubns.:** *Pipeline Construction in Cold Regions: A Bibliography Excluding the Russian Literature* (1971); *Books on Conservation and Ecology for Youth Libraries* (1971). **Activities:** 1, 4; 17, 37, 46; 55, 75 **Addr.:** Library of Congress, Cataloging in Publication Division, Washington, DC 20540.

Vitek, Clement Gerard (Mr. 6, 1920, Baltimore, MD) Chief Libn., *The Baltimore Suny*, A. S. Abell, Co., Inc., 1953–, Actg. Libn., 1950–53, Asst. Libn. 1946–50, Chief Libn., 1946. **Educ.:** Loyola Coll., 1967–68. **Orgs.:** Hist. of MD Hist. Socty.: Musm. and Lib. MD LA. SLA: Schol. Com. (Ch., 1970–72); Pic. Div., Fndn. Mem.; Baltmore Chap., PR Com. (Ch., 1962–64), *Bltn.* Ed. (1962–64), Pres.-Elect (1964–65), Pres. (1965–66), Dir. (1966–67); Newsp. Div., various coms., ofcs. Natl. Microfilm Assn.: Stans. Com. for Newsp. **Honors:** Assn. Newsp. Div., Natl. Microfilm Assn., Cert. of Apprec. Stans. Com., Newsp. Microfilming, 1974. **Activities:** 12; 17, 30, 39; 83 **Addr.:** *Baltimore Sun*, 501 N. Calvert St., Baltimore, MD 21202.

Vivian, Zanier Downs Lane (Mr. 20, 1930, Thomaston, GA) Asst. Prof., Ref. Libn., Univ. of NM Gen. Lib., 1973–; Ref. Libn., Lawrence Lab., 1958–62; Ref. Libn., GA Inst. of Tech. Lib., 1955–56. **Educ.:** Univ. of AZ, 1950–52, BA (Span.); Univ. of GA, 1947–49; Univ. of IL, 1954–55, MSLS. **Orgs.:** SLA: Rio Grande Chap. (Pres., 1975–76). NM LA: VP, Prog. Ch. (1978–79); Anl. Conf. Exhibts (Ch., 1980–81). NM State Lib.: Adv. Cncl. (1975–76). NM Opera Gld., Inc.: Bd. of Dirs. (1970–72). Albuquerque Opera Gld.: Bd. of Dirs., Pres. (1970). Albuquerque Symph. Orch.: Bd. of Dirs. (1971–73). Amer. Socty. for Engin. Educ.: Engin. Libs. Div. (Ch.-Elect, 1980–82). **Honors:** Phi Kappa Phi, 1951; Beta Phi Mu, 1955. **Activities:** 1; 15, 31, 39; 64, 91 **Addr.:** P.O. Box 267, Tijeras, NM 87059.

Vlasic, Ivan (N. 23, 1933, Zagreb, Croatia, Yugoslavia) Head, Tech. Srvs., SUNY, Cortland, 1981–; Asst. Univ. Libn., Tech. Opers., Tulane Univ. Libs., 1978–81; Head, Tech. Srvs., North. IL Univ., Libs., 1975–78; Head, Div. of Prcs., Ball State Univ. Libs., 1971–75; Slavic, Gen. Catlgr., OH State Univ., 1968–71. **Educ.:** West. Rsv. Univ., 1960–66, BA (Slavic Lang.), 1966–67, MA (Slavic Lang.), 1967–68, MLS. **Orgs.:** ALA: ACRL. **Activities:** 1, 5; 20, 34, 46; 54, 56, 75 **Addr.:** State University College at Cortland Library, Cortland, NY 13045.

Vodra, Carol Jean (Ag. 1, 1941, Cincinnati, OH) Law Libn., Burns, Doane, Swecker and Mathis, 1981–; Law Libn., Wheatley and Wollesen, 1979–81; Law Libn., Thomas R. Ewald, Esquire, 1976–79; Pub. Srv. Libn., Univ. of Cincinnati, 1968–70; Ref. Libn., T.J. Watson Lib. of Bus. and Econ., Columbia Univ., 1965–68. **Educ.:** Coll. of Wooster, 1959–63, BA (Econ.); Univ. of MI, 1964–65, AMLS. **Orgs.:** AALL. Law Libns. Socty. of DC. Assn. of Legal Admins.: Cap. Chap. (Secy., 1979–81). **Activities:** 12; 17, 24, 39; 77 **Addr.:** Burns, Doane, Swecker and Mathis, 699 Prince St., Alexandria, VA 22314.

Voge, Susan A. (O. 15, 1948, New York City, NY) Med. Libn., Equitable Life Assurance Socty., 1979–; Asst. Libn., St. Luke's Hosp. Ctr., 1975–78. **Educ.:** Brooklyn Coll., 1971–74, BA (Soclgy.); Columbia Univ., 1974–75, MSLS; various crs. **Orgs.:** Med. LA: NY Reg. Grp., Legis. Com. (1979–81). NY LA: Inst. Libs. (1981–83). SLA: NY Chap., Insr. Grp. (1980–). Metro. Ref. and Resrch. Libs.: Legis. Com. (1980). **Activities:** 12; 15, 39, 41; 58, 80 **Addr.:** Medical and Health Information Center, Equitable Life Assurance Society, 1285 Ave. of the Americas, New York, NY 10019.

Vogel, Dorothy H. (My. 14, 1935, Elmira, NY) Supvsg. Libn., Asst. Bus. Libn., Bus. Lib., Brooklyn Pub. Lib., 1966–, Sr. Libn., 1962–65, Asst. Div. Chief, Sr. Libn., Sci. and Indus. Div., 1961–62, Libn., 1958–61. **Educ.:** Univ. of Buffalo, 1953–55; Syracuse Univ., 1955–57, BA (Eng. Lit., LS); Univ. of Denver, 1957–58, MALS. **Orgs.:** SLA. NY Lib. Club. **Activities:** 9, 12; 15, 17, 39; 59 **Addr.:** 280 Cadman Plz. W., Brooklyn, NY 11201.

Vogel, Marion L. (F. 8, 1921, Jersey City, NJ) Dean, Lrng. Resrcs., Trident Tech. Coll., 1973–; Dir., Lib. Srvs., Palmer Coll., 1969–73; Libn., Indus. Rel. Dept., Ebasco Srvs., Inc., 1946–48; Resrch., Ref. Libn., Amer. Geo. Socty., 1943–46. **Educ.:** Douglass Coll., Rutgers Univ., 1938–42, BA (LS); Columbia Univ., 1943–46, MA (Amer. Hist.). **Orgs.:** ALA. SE LA. SC LA. SC Tech. Educ. Libns.: Bd. (1976–77). Rutgers Univ. Grad. Sch. Libns. Assoc. Columbia Univ. Grad. Assn. Synagogue Emanu-El: VP (1966–70). Nat. Cncl. of Jewish Women: Past Pres. (1968–70). Mental Hlth. Assn.: VP (1973–75). Charleston Higher Educ. Cnsrtm.: Lib. Com. (Ch., 1979–80). Various other orgs. **Honors:** Emanu-El Synagogue, Citizenship Awd., 1961; Women in Cmnty. Srv., Srv. Awd., 1968. **Activities:** 1, 12; 17, 32, 46; 61, 63 **Addr.:** ILR/N Trident Technical College, P.O. Box 10367, Charleston, SC 29411.

Vogt, Howard Sheppard (O. 10, 1924, Orange, NJ) Lib. Dir., Bloomfield Pub. Lib., 1968–, Asst. Dir., 1964–68, Supvsg. Libn., 1962–64; Asst. Prof., Msc. Libn., North. IL Univ., 1956–61. **Educ.:** Univ. of Rochester, 1947–51, BMus (Voice), 1951–52, MMus (Msc. Lit.), 1952, Performer's Cert. (Voice); Rutgers Univ., 1957–59, MLS (Lib. Srv.). **Orgs.:** ALA. NJ LA: Pres. (1975–76); VP (1974–75); Spr. Conf. Com. (Ch., 1973–74); Fed. Rel. Com. (Ch., 1969–71). Msc. LA. Assn. for Rec. Snd. Cols. **Honors:** NJ State Cncl. on the Arts, Cert. of Merit, 1970; Bd. of Trustees, Bloomfield Pub. Lib., Bloomfield, NJ, Lib. Thea. named "Howard S. Vogt Thea. for the Performing Arts," 1972. **Pubns.:** *Flagstad: Her Life and Her Art* (forthcoming); "Opera at the Newark Public Library," *Lib. Jnl.* (S. 15, 1955); "Invitation to Listening," *IL Libs.* (F. 1958). **Activities:** 1, 9; 17, 24, 34; 50, 55, 74 **Addr.:** Bloomfield Public Library, 90 Broad St., Bloomfield, NJ 07003.

Voigt, Kathleen Jane (My. 30, 1933, Toledo, OH) Head Ref. Libn., Univ. of Toledo, 1969–; Ref. Libn., Assoc. Prof., Lib. Admin., Carlson Lib. Ref., 1976–, Ref. Libn., Asst. Prof., 1974–76, Asst. Ref. Libn., Asst. Prof., 1973–74, Asst. Prof., LS, 1972–73, Instr., LS, 1971–72, Actg. Head, Dept. of LS, Instr. in LS, 1969–71. **Educ.:** Univ. of Toledo, 1951–54, BA (Eng. Lit., Hist.); Univ. of MI, 1954–55, MA (LS). **Orgs.:** ALA. Acad. LA of OH. North. OH Tech. Srvs. Libns. AAUP. Ord. of the Rainbow for Girls: Mother Adv. Ord. of East. Stars. Delta Kappa Gamma: Pres. Zonta Club of Toledo II. **Honors:** Zeta Tau Alpha.

PROFESSIONAL ACTIVITIES: Institutions: 1. Acad. lib.; 2. Arch.; 3. Assn.; 4. Fed./Gvt. lib.; 5. Inst. lib.; 6. Mfr./Suppl.; 7. Milit. lib.; 8. Musm.; 9. Pub. lib.; 10. Sch. lib.; 11. Sch. of lib. sci.; 12. Spec. lib.; 13. State lib.; 14. (other). **Functions/Activities:** 15. Acq./Col. dev.; 16. Adult srvs.; 17. Admin.; 18. Apprais.; 19. Archit./Bldgs.; 20. Cat./Class.; 21. Chld. srvs.; 22. Circ.; 23. Cons./Pres.; 24. Consult.; 25. Cont. ed.; 26. Educ. lib. sci.; 27. Ext. srvs.; 28. Fund/Grants; 29. Gvt. pubs.; 30. Indx./Abs.; 31. Instr. lib. use; 32. Media srvs.; 33. Micro.; 34. Netwks./Coop.; 35. Persnl.; 36. PR; 37. Publshg.; 38. Recs. mgt.; 39. Ref. srvs.; 40. Repro.; 41. Resrch.; 42. Review.; 43. Secur.; 44. Serials; 45. Spec. col.; 46. Tech. srvs.; 47. Trustees/Bds.; 48. YA srvs.; 49. (other).

Pubns.: Various bk. reviews, *Amer. Ref. Bks. Anl., Lib. Jnl.* **Activities:** 1; 15, 17, 39; 55, 56, 75 **Addr.:** 3844 Brockton Dr., Toledo, OH 43623.

Voigt, Melvin J. (Mr. 12, 1911, Upland, CA) Univ. Libn. Emeritus, Univ. of CA, San Diego, 1976–, Univ. Libn., 1960–76; Dir., KS State Univ., 1959–60; Asst. Univ. Libn., Univ. of CA, Berkeley, 1952–59; Dir., Carnegie Inst. of Tech., 1946–52; Head, Lib. Pubns., Resrch. Dept., Gen. Mills Inc., 1942–46; Asst. Clasfr., Univ. of MI, 1938–42, Head, Phys. Lib., 1935–38; Libn., Bluffton HS, Pub. Lib., 1933–35; various positions in consult. **Educ.:** Bluffton Coll., 1931–33, AB (Math.); Univ. of MI, 1933–38, ABLS, AMLS. **Orgs.:** ALA: RTSD, Pres.; Lib. Educ. Div., Pres.; Cncl. SLA: VP, Bd. of Dirs. CA LA. Cncl. PA LA: Pres. Various other orgs. AAUP. AAAS: Cncl. Amer. Chem. Socty. Tuberculosis and Respiratory Disease Assn. of San Diego and Imperial Cntys.: Pres. **Honors:** Univ. of Copenhagen, Fulbright Resrch. Schol., 1958–59; Inst. für Documtn., Frankfurt, Fulbright Resrch. Schol., 1974–75; Phi Kappa Phi. **Pubns.:** Ed., *Progress in Communication Sciences* (volume 1, 1979; volume 2, 1980); ed., *Advances in Librarianship* (1970–77); ed., *Books for College Libraries* (1967); *Scientists' Approaches to Information* (1961); *Subject Headings in Physics* (1944); various articles, edshps. **Activities:** 1; 17, 26, 41; 62, 75, 93 **Addr.:** 624 Central University Library, University of California, San Diego C–075, La Jolla, CA 92093.

Voit, Irene E. (Ap. 18, 1945, Brooklyn, NY) Asst. Dir., OR State Univ., 1977–81, Spec. Asst. to Dir., Libs., 1974–77, Libn., 1970–74; Instr., Univ. of OR, 1971; Ref. Libn., Univ. of PA, 1968–69. **Educ.:** Brooklyn Coll., 1962–66, BA (Soclgy., Anthro.); Drexel Univ., 1966–68, MS (LS); OR State Univ., 1976–78, MA (Bus.). Ofc. Persnl. Assn.: Schol. Com. (1980–81). State Mgt. Assn. **Pubns.:** *Newspapers in the University of Pennsylvania Libraries, Temple University and the Free Library of Philadelphia: A Union List* (1970); jt. auth., "Library Group Practice," *Coll. & Resrch. Libs.* (Ja. 1973); jt. auth., "Library Orientation Videotape," ERIC (1973). **Activities:** 1; 17, 28, 35; 59 **Addr.:** R.R. 1, Box 32D, Arcadia, OK 73007.

Volkersz, Evert (O. 18, 1936, Amsterdam, Netherlands) Head, Dept. of Spec. Cols., SUNY, Stony Brook, Lib., 1969–; Asst. Spec. Cols. Libn., Univ. of CA, Los Angeles Lib., 1964–69, Bibl. Srch., 1963–64. **Educ.:** Univ. of WA, 1954–58, BA (Hist.), 1962–63, MLS (Libnshp.). **Orgs.:** ALA: IFRT, Prog. Com. (1974–76); Cncl. Ad Hoc Com. to Std. Intl. Rel. Resp. (1973–74); ACRL, Cont. Educ. Com. (1978–80), Com. on Constn. and Bylaws (Ch., 1974–76), Plng. Com. (1972–73, 1977–78)/Rare Bks. and Mss. Sect., various coms. SAA: SAA-ALA Jt. Com. on Lib.-Arch. Relshps. (Ch., 1978–80); various coms., ofcs. Mid-Atl. Reg. Arch. Conf.: Various coms. CA LA. Various other orgs. Long Island Arch. Conf.: Pres. (1974–80). Univ. of CA, Los Angeles Lib. Staff Assn.: VP, Pres. (1964–66). Long Island Std. Cncl.: Co-fndr., Secy. (1978–). Long Island Bk. Collectors. Various other orgs. **Honors:** SUNY, Chancellor's Awd. for Excel. in Libnshp., 1978. **Pubns.:** "Toward a New York Academic Library Community," *Bookmark* (Ja.–F. 1972); "Library Organization in Academia: Changes from Hierarchical to Collegial Relationships," *New Dimensions for Academic Library Service* (1975); "A Guide to Arranging and Handling Printed Ephemera," *Mid-Atl. Archvst.* (Jl. 1975); "Library Notes from the Netherlands," *Leads* (Je. 1977); "The Care and Feeding of Special Collections," *AB Bookman's Wkly.* (Je. 18, 1979); various articles, reviews. **Activities:** 1, 2; 15, 17, 45; 55, 57, 85 **Addr.:** Dept. of Special Collections, SUNY Library, Stony Brook, NY 11794.

Vollmar, William J. (O. 1, 1943, Milwaukee, WI) Recs. Admin., Archvst., Anheuser-Busch Co., Inc. 1978–; Archvst., Recs. Admin., OH State Univ., 1969–78; Fld. Rep., Asst. Cur., Milwaukee Cnty. Hist. Socty., 1966–68. **Educ.:** Marquette Univ., 1961–65, AB (Hist.), 1965–68, MA (Hist.); OH State Univ., 1968–70, PhD (Hist.). **Orgs.:** SAA: Coll. and Univ. Com. (1970–78). Assn. of Recs. Mgrs. and Admins. Socty. of OH Archvsts.: Cncl. (1975–78). **Pubns.:** "Breweriana," *Price Guide to Antiques* (Spr. 1980). **Activities:** 2, 12; 17, 38; 59, 73, 74 **Addr.:** Corporate Archives, Anheuser-Busch Co. Inc., 721 Pestolozzi St., St. Louis, MO 63118.

Volpe, Joan Semb (Ag. 1, 1931, Madison, WI) Biomed. Indxr., Cncl. for Tobacco Resrch.–U.S.A., Inc., 1981–; Indxr., *Readrs. Guide to Per. Lit.*, H. W. Wilson Co., 1978–81; Recs. Admin., Concast, Inc., 1977–78; Asst. Dir., WA Twp. Pub. Lib., 1976. **Educ.:** Purdue Univ., 1949–54, BS (Chem.); Pratt Inst., 1975–76, MLS. **Orgs.:** ALA. NY Lib. Club. Adirondack Mt. Club, Inc. **Honors:** Beta Phi Mu; Alpha Chi Omega. **Activities:** 14; 30, 37; 91 **Addr.:** 231 Knickerbocker Ave., Hillsdale, NJ 07642.

Volz, Arlene Ruth (Barron) (F. 12, 1949, Minneapolis, MN) Asst. Prof., Med. Lib. Ref., Univ. Miami, 1981–; Sci., Tech. Div. Head, Louisville Free Pub. Lib., 1978–80; Hlth. Sci. Lib. Mgr., St. Mary's Hosp., 1974–78; Pharm. Libn., Asst. Sci. Ref. Libn., Univ. of GA, 1972–74; Lib. Asst. II, Chem. Info. Srvs., Univ. of Pittsburgh, 1970–72. **Educ.:** Univ. of Pittsburgh, 1967–71, BA (Math., Eng. Lit.), 1971–72, MLS (Info. Sci.); Med. LA, 1973–88 Cert. Med. Libn.; Cmwlth. of KY, Cert. Libn. **Orgs.:** SLA: VA Chap. (Secy., 1976–78); KY Chap. (PR Ch., 1979–80); Sci. and Tech. Div., Natl. Ch., Mem. Ch. (1979–80). West End Jayceettes, Richmond, VA: Dir. (1977–78). Buechel-Fern Creek Jayceettes, Louisville, KY: Dir. (1978–79); 2nd VP (1979–80). Louisville Free Pub. Lib. Staff Assn.: Fund Raising Ch. (1979). **Honors:** Beta Phi Mu, 1972. **Pubns.:** "Implementing S.D.I.," *Hosp. Libs.* (Jl. 1977); *Locating a Journal Article Using Chemical Abstracts* (1973); *Iowa Drug Information Service (IDIS): Its Use for Rapid Retrieval of Clinical Information* (1973). **Activities:** 1, 12; 15, 17, 39; 56, 80, 91 **Addr.:** 11262 NW 14th Ct., Pembroke Pines, FL 33026.

von Brockdorff, Eric (Mr. 15, 1932, Königsberg, Germany) Dir., Libs., Hartwick Coll., 1967–; Ref. Libn., Colgate Univ., 1960–67; Credit Anal., Marine Midland Trust Co. of NY, 1955–59. **Educ.:** Hamilton Coll., 1951–55, BA (Hist.); Columbia Univ., 1959–60, MSLS (Lib. Srv.). **Orgs.:** ALA: ACRL. **Pubns.:** Transl., *Artistry of the Mentally Ill* (Hans Prinzhorn) (1972). **Activities:** 1; 15, 17, 39 **Addr.:** Hartwick College Library, Oneonta, NY 13820.

von Brockdorff, Hans (O. 3, 1938, Hamburg, W. Germany) Dir., Instr. Resrcs., SUNY, Canton, 1977–80; Libn., Colby-Sawyer Coll., 1974–77; Libn., Belknap Coll., 1969–74; Ref. Libn., Elmira Coll., 1968–69. **Educ.:** Hobart Coll., 1958–62, BA (Grmn., Fr., Soclgy.); Syracuse Univ., 1965–66, MSLS; various crs. **Orgs.:** SUNY LA: Head Libns. Exec. Bd. (1979–80); Agr. and Tech. Libns. (Conv., 1979–80). NH Lib. Cncl. Acad. Libns. of NH: Pres. (1972–73); VP (1971–72). ALA: ACRL, Natl. Legis. Netwk. **Activities:** 1; 17, 39; 92 **Addr.:** 16 Spears St., Canton, NY 13617.

Von der Porten, Amy Marguerite (O. 1, 1923, Kingston, Jamaica, B.W.I.) Libn., Rutgers Prep. Sch., 1968–; Supvsr., Coord., Elem. Sch. Libs., Madison Twp., Old Bridge, 1962–63; Botanist, Actg. Cur., Sci. Lib., Sci. Musm., Inst. of Jamaica, B.W.I., 1943–52, Asst. Libn., Chld. Div., 1942–43. **Educ.:** Cambridge Univ., Eng., 1942 (Bot., Eng.); Royal Schs. of Msc., London, Eng., Cert.; Royal Drawing Socty., Eng., Cert. **Orgs.:** ALA: AASL; ALTA. Educ. Media Assn.: Exec. Bd. (1973–75); NJ in the Classrm. Com. (1975). Old Bridge Pub. Lib.: Bd. of Trustees (Pres., 1973–81). Lib. of S. Middlesex: Pres. (1981–). Various other orgs. **Honors:** NJ Congs. of Parents and Tchrs., Life Mem. Awd., 1962; Matley Nat. Hist. Competition, Nat. Hist. Awd., 1939, 1940. **Pubns.:** Contrib., *Marine Algae of Jamaica* (1961–63); jt. ed., *Natural History Notes* (1949); contrib., *Glimpses of Jamaica Natural History* (1946, 1949); "Plants in Flower and Fruit in April in the Cockpit Country," *Nat. Hist. Notes* (My. 1949); "A True Fish Story; Old African Monarch," *Nat. Hist. Notes* (Ag. 1945); various articles. **Addr.:** Rutgers Preparatory School, 1345 Easton Ave., Somerset, NJ 08873.

von Lang, Frederick William (Scranton, PA) Lib. Dir., Geneal., Hibbing Pub. Lib., 1980–; Lib. Dir., St. Joseph Pub. Lib., 1977–79; Lib. Dir., Auburn Pub. Lib., 1973–77; Lib. Dir., Lehigh Cnty. Cmnty. Coll., 1966–73. **Educ.:** Kutztown State Coll., 1947–51, BS (Soc. Std., LS); Syracuse Univ., 1952–55, MSLS. **Orgs.:** ALA: Cncl (ME LA Del., 1974–77); ALA/ME LA Fed. Coord. (1974–77). ME LA: Exec. Bd. (1973–77); Legis. Com. (Ch., 1975–76). MO LA: Gvr.'s Conf. WHCOLIS (Del., 1977–78). PA LA: Cmnty. and Jr. Coll. Div. (Ch., 1970–71); various ofcs. Various other orgs. Bethlehem, PA Jr. Cham. of Cmrce: Pubns. Ch., Ed. (1964–68). Northampton Cnty. (PA) Assn. for the Blind: Exec. Bd. (1970–72). St. Joseph, MO Mental Hlth. Socty.: Exec. Bd. (1977–78). Kiwanis: Lewiston-Auburn Chap., Bd. of Dirs. (1976–77). Various other orgs. **Honors:** Beta Phi Mu, 1955. **Pubns.:** *Legislative Handbook of the Maine Library Association* (1976). **Activities:** 1, 9; 17, 34, 41; 69, 92, 95-Frnds. of the lib. grps. **Addr.:** Hibbing Public Library, 2020 E. 5th Ave., Hibbing, MN 55746.

Von Mechow, Sallie F. (Mr. 15, 1925, New York, NY) Head Catlgr., The Smithtown Lib., 1975–, Head, Acq., 1978–79, Catlgr., 1961–74; Army Libn., Army Lib. Srv., 1950–52; Resrch. Libn., Armstrong Cork Co., 1945–48. **Educ.:** Barnard Coll., 1941–45, BA (Chem.); Columbia Univ., 1948–50, MS (Lib. Srv.). **Orgs.:** SLA: Long Island Chap., Secy. (1980–81), Exec. Bd. (1977–80). Suffolk Cnty. LA: Tech. Srvs. Div. (Ch., 1981–82). **Activities:** 9, 12; 15, 20, 46; 60, 91 **Addr.:** 47 Arlington Ave., St. James, NY 11780.

von Nussbaumer, Aliyah W. M. (My. 11, 1925, Berlin, Germany) Resrch. Libn., Dresser Indus., Inc., 1967–; Serial and Exch. Libn., Centenary Coll., 1963–65; Base Libn., U.S. Armed Frcs. Base, Sidi Slimane, Morocco, 1959–62; Chief of Protocol, King Faisal II, Iraq, 1949–58. **Educ.:** Goethe Lyceum, Germany, 1943, BA; Sorbonne, 1945–47, BSLS, 1949, MS. **Orgs.:** SLA. ALA. TX LA. South. Meth. Univ. Sci. and Info. Ctr.: Adv Cncl. Grmn.-Amer. Club: VP (1971–73); Pres. (1974–75). Amer. Petr. Inst. Socty. of Petr. Engins. Weimaraner Club of Germany. **Honors:** Ed. Adv. Bd., Hist. Prsrvns. of Amer., Hon. Mem. Outstan. Women of Houston, 1976. **Activities:** 12; 20, 22, 24; 60, 62, 64 **Addr.:** Magcobar Research Library, Dresser Industries, Inc., 10201 Westheimer, Bldg. 1-A, Houston, TX 77042.

von Pfeil, Helena P. (Windhoek, Namibia) Sr. Acq. Libn., U.S. Dept. of State, 1980–; Libn., Cat. Coord., Worldwide Libs., U.S.I.C.A., 1979–; Law Libn., Lib. Admin., Corp. Couns., DC Gvt., 1977–79; Asst. Law Libn., Univ. of Puget Snd. Law Lib., 1975–77; Asst. Law Libn., Instr., Univ. of OR Law Lib., 1972–75. **Educ.:** Univ. of OR, 1968–70, BA, BS, Assoc. (Pol. Sci., Soclgy., Pub. Affairs), 1970–72, MSLS; various crs. **Orgs.:** AALL: *Law Lib. Jnl.* (1975–76); Pubns. Com. (Ch., 1978). IFLA: Official Del. (1979); Stdg. Com. on Intl. Admin. Libs. (1979–). SLA. ASIS. Various other orgs. AAUP. Amer. Socty. of Intl. Law. Intl. Law LA. Socty. of Abstctrs. and Indxrs. **Honors:** AALL, Joseph L. Andrews Awd. for Excel. in Legal Bibl., 1975. **Pubns.:** *Oceans, Coasts and Law: Bibliography and Union List of Books, Papers, Foreign and U.S. Articles Categorized by Topic* (1976); *Juvenile Rights since 1967: An Annotated, Indexed Bibliography* (1974); "Legislative History Research: Questions and Answers," *Fundamentals of Legal Research* (1977). **Activities:** 1, 4; 17, 30, 39; 54, 56, 77 **Addr.:** 333 2nd St., N.E. # 206, Washington, DC 20002.

von Wahlde, Barbara A. (O. 6, 1937, Pasadena, CA) Assoc. Dir., Tech. Srvs., Univ. of MI, Univ. Lib., 1980–; Staff Dev. Coord., Yale Univ. Libs., 1976–80; Assoc. Dir., Tech. Srv., Univ. of W. FL, 1972–76; Head, Cat. Dept., Univ. of South. MS, 1970–72, Catlgr., Actg. Head, Cat. Dept., 1969–70; Bibl. Cntrl. Consult., Manpower Resrcs. Resrch. Proj., Univ. of ME, 1969, Instr., Lib. Sch., 1969–71, Catlgr., Fogler Lib., 1966–69; Asst. Docum. Libn., IN Univ. Lib., 1965–66; Ref. Libn., Monroe Cnty. Pub. Lib., 1965. **Educ.:** IN Univ., 1955–61, BS (Educ.), 1964–66, MA (LS). **Orgs.:** ALA: Lib. Admin. Div./Persnl. Admin. Sect., Econ. Status, Welfare and Fringe Benefits Com. (1978–81); ACRL, Cont. Educ. Com. (1980–82), Staff Dev. Ofcrs. in Lg. Acad. Libs. Discuss. Grp. (Ch., 1980); LAMA/Persnl. Admin. Sect., Nom. Com. (1979–80, 1980–81). CT Gvrs. Conf. on Lib. and Info. Srvs. (1978). W. FL LA: VP (1973–74); Pres.-Elect (1974–75). CLENE. Various other orgs. Frnds. of Gulf Breeze Pub. Lib.: Dir. (1973–76). Yale Univ.: Lib. Assoc. (1976); Yale Bibliophiles (1976). **Honors:** Cncl. on Lib. Resrcs., Acad. Lib. Mgt. Intern, 1974–75; Delta Kappa Gamma, 1971. **Pubns.:** "CLR Academic Library Management Internship: A Symposium," *Jnl. of Acad. Libnshp.* (Jl. 1980); various articles. **Activities:** 1; 17, 35, 46 **Addr.:** University of Michigan Library, Ann Arbor, MI 48109.

Voorhees, Edward H. (O. 23, 1918, Winona, MN) Libn., Staff Dev. and Trng., Dallas Pub. Lib., 1979–, Branch Zone Mgr., 1976–79, Branch Mgr., 1971–76, Sci., Indus. Div. Head, 1969–71. **Educ.:** Univ. of MI, Univ. of MN, 1936–40, (Educ.); Univ. of MD, 1952–53, BA (Milit. Sci.); Univ. of MI, 1968–69, AMLS. **Orgs.:** ALA. SW LA. TX LA. Amer. Socty. for Trng. and Dev. **Activities:** 9; 17, 26; 91 **Addr.:** 3316 Northaven Rd., Dallas, TX 75229.

Voos, Henry (Ag. 10, 1928, Hamburg, Germany) Prof., Rutgers Univ., 1968–; Head, Tech. Srvs., U.S. Army Picatinny Arsenal, 1956–68; Libn., Intl. Ladies' Garment Workers Un., 1953–56; 1st Asst., Bk. Sect., NY Pub. Lib., 1948–53. **Educ.:** NY Univ., 1946–48, BA (Grmn.); NY Univ., 1948–53, MA (Grmn.); Columbia Univ., 1951–53, MLS; Rutgers Univ., 1958–65, PhD (Lib. Srv.). **Orgs.:** ASIS. SLA. Amer. Socty. of Indxrs. Natl. Micro. Assn. AAAS. ASLIB. **Pubns.:** "Implications of Holography for Information Systems," *JASIS* (N. 1980); "Telecommunications and Facsimile," *Spec. Libs.* (Ap. 1981); *Organizational Communication: A Bibliography* (1967); *Information Needs in Urban Areas* (1969); "Design of a Management Instrument for Technical Library Information Services," *Contemporary Problems in Technical Library and Information Center Management* (1974); "Inventory," *Essays for Ralph Shaw* (1975); various articles; papers. **Activities:** 11; 26 **Addr.:** Rutgers University Graduate School of Library and Information Studies, 4 Huntington St., New Brunswick, NJ 08903.

Vorwald, Doris Lauretta (Jl. 25, 1929, New York City, NY) Head, Educ. Lib., Queens Coll., CUNY, 1955–; Serials Libn., Hofstra Univ., 1953–55. **Educ.:** Queens Coll., CUNY, 1947–51, BA (Anthro., Soclgy.), Columbia Univ., 1951–53, MSLS. **Orgs.:** ALA. LA CUNY. AAUP. **Activities:** 1, 10; 15, 31, 39; 63, 92 **Addr.:** Paul Klapper Library, Education Library, Queens College, CUNY, Flushing, NY 11367.

Vosper, Robert Gordon (Je. 21, 1913, Portland, OR) Dir., W.A. Clark Meml. Lib., Univ. of CA, Los Angeles, 1966–81, Prof., Grad. Sch. of Lib. and Info. Sci., 1961–, Univ. Libn., 1961–73; Dir., Libs., Univ. of KS, 1952–61; Assoc. Univ. Libn., Univ. of CA, Los Angeles, 1949–52, Asst. Univ. Libn., 1948–49, Head., Acq. Dept., 1944–48; Asst. Ref. Libn., Stanford Univ., 1942–44; Jr. Libn., Univ. of CA, Berkeley, 1940–42. **Educ.:** Univ. of OR, 1933–37, BA (Classics), 1937–39, MA (Classics); Univ. of CA, Berkeley, 1939–40, Cert. (Libnshp.). **Orgs.:** ALA: Pres. (1965–66); Cncl. (1960–72); ACRL, Pres. (1955–56). ARL: Dir. (1962–64, 1969–72), Ch. (1963), Farmington Plan Com. (Ch., 1961–63). IFLA: VP (1971–77). AAUP. Natl. Sci. Fndn.: Sci. Info. Cncl. Chem. Abs. Adv. Bd. MA Inst. of Tech.: Visit. Com. for Libs. Various other orgs. **Honors:** Guggenheim Fndn., Fellow, 1959–60; Fulbright Prog., Lectr., 1959; Gvt. of Belgium, Ofcr. in the Ord. of the Crown, 1977; Phi Beta Kappa; other hons. **Pubns.:** Ed., *National and International Library Planning* (1976); ed., *European University Libraries* (1964); ed., *Acquisition of Latin American Library Materials* (1958); ed., *Acquisitions Trends in American Libraries* (1955); "Books for Libraries: Institutional Book Collecting," *Building Book Collections: Two Variations on*

Special Subjects/Services: 50. Adult educ.; 51. Advert./Mktg.; 52. Aerosp.; 53. Agric.; 54. Area std.; 55. Arts/Hum.; 56. Autom.; 57. Bibl./Prtg.; 58. Bio. sci.; 59. Bus./Fin.; 60. Chem.; 61. Copyrt.; 62. Documtn.; 63. Educ.; 64. Engin.; 65. Env.; 66. Eth. grps.; 67. Film; 68. Food/Nutr.; 69. Geneal.; 70. Geo.; 71. Geol.; 72. Handcpd.; 73. Hist.; 74. Int. frdm.; 75. Info. sci.; 76. Insr.; 77. Law; 78. Legis.; 79. Math./Comp. sci.; 80. Med.; 81. Metals; 82. Nat. resrcs.; 83. Newsp.; 84. Nuc. sci.; 85. Oral hist.; 86. Petr./Energy; 87. Pharm.; 88. Phys./Astr./Math.; 89. Readg.; 90. Relig.; 91. Sci./Tech.; 92. Soc. sci.; 93. Telecom.; 94. Transp.; 95. (other).

a Theme (1977); various chaps., articles. **Activities:** 1, 11; 15, 26, 45 **Addr.:** 10447 Wilkins Ave., Los Angeles, CA 90024.

Voss, Anne Elizabeth (D. 2, 1915, E. Stroudsburg, PA) Coord., Sch. and Coll. Media Srvs., NJ State Dept. of Educ., Div. of State Lib., Lib. Dev. Bur., 1957–; Ch., Undergrad. LS, NJ State Coll. at Trenton, 1954–57, Acq. Coll. Lib., 1945–54; Jr. High Libn., Summit, NJ, 1939–41; HS Libn., E. Rutherford, NJ, 1937–39. **Educ.:** Trenton State Coll., 1933–37, BSc (Hist., Eng.); Columbia Univ., 1939–44, MA (Eng.), 1950–54, MLS. **Orgs.:** ALA: AASL, Bd. (1965–69); LAMA/ Bldg. and Equip. Sect. (Secy., 1971–73); Chld. Srvs. Div., Sel. of Frgn. Chld. Bks. (1974–75). Educ. Media Assn., NJ: Bd. (Ex-officio Consult., 1957–). NJ Cncl. on Lib. Educ.: Secy. (1976–). NJ Hist. Socty. Educ. Com. **Pubns.:** Illustrator, *Animals of New Jersey* (1964); *Shrubs and Vines of New Jersey* (1965). **Activities:** 10, 13; 24, 25, 26; 63 **Addr.:** New Jersey State Library, 185 W. State St., CN 520, Trenton, NJ 08625.

Votaw, Floyd M. (F. 7, 1947, Fort Benjamin Harrison, IN) Head, Tech. Srvs., Grace Coll. and Semy., 1976–; Catlgr., Philadelphia Coll. of Bible, 1972–75. **Educ.:** CA State Univ., Fullerton, 1967–70, BA (Hist.); Univ. of South. CA, 1971–72, MLS; Grace Theo. Semy., 1976–80 Cert. (Biblical Std.). **Orgs.:** Christ. Libns. Flwshp. ATLA. Area Lib. Srvs. Assn.: ILL and Ref. Com. (1978–80). **Pubns.:** Cmplr., *Index to Monographs, Theses and Dissertations at Grace Theological Seminary, 1937–1979* (1980). **Activities:** 10; 20, 34, 46; 57, 90, 92 **Addr.:** 109 15th St., Winona Lake, IN 46590.

Voth, Sally J. (F. 3, 1940, Kansas City, KS) Assoc. Dean for Tech. Srvs., IN Univ., 1981–; Actg. Dean of Libs., KS State Univ., 1981, Assoc. Dir., Tech. Srvs., Budget and Autom., Univ. Lib., 1979–, Asst. Dir., 1977–79, Serials Libn., 1974–77; Catlgr., N.E. MO State Univ. Lib., 1970–74. **Educ.:** KS State Univ., 1958–62, BA (Soclgy.); Emporia State Univ., 1969–73, MS (LS). **Orgs.:** ALA: ACRL; RTSD; LITA; Lib. Admin. Div. KS LA: Coll. and Univ. Libs. Sect. Mt. Plains LA. Beta Phi Mu: Beta Epsilon Chap. (Pres., 1978). **Pubns.:** "Weeding of a Library Reserve Book Section–A Description of the Kansas State University System Using Floppy Diskettes," *Col. Mgt.* (1976–77); "Formatting the COM Catalog" cassette (1979). **Activities:** 1; 17, 46; 56 **Addr.:** 3462 John Hinkle Pl., Bloomington, IN 47401.

Vrooman, George H. (O. 27, 1935, New York City, NY) Assoc. Libn., Col. Dev., Yale Univ. Lib., 1974–, Hum. Biblgphr., 1966–74; Bibl. Asst., Univ. of IL Lib., 1964–66. **Educ.:** Univ. of IL, 1947–49, AB (Phil.), 1949–51, MA (Phil.), 1964–66, MA (LS). **Orgs.:** ALA: ACRL/West. European Spec. Sect., Nom. Com. (1979–80). Resrch. Libs. Grp.: Col. Dev. Ofcrs.-at-Lg., Chief. **Activities:** 1; 15, 17; 55, 57 **Addr.:** Yale University Library, New Haven, CT 06520.

Vyas, Shanker H. (O. 5, 1935, Gujarat, India) Dir., Libs., Assoc. Prof., Philadelphia Coll. of Osteopathic Med. 1972–; *Cit. Ed.*, Bio-Sci. Info. Srvs., 1970–71; Acq. Libn., Bowie State Coll., 1969–70; Dir., Prof. N.B. Divetia Grad. Lib., 1962–69; Prof., Elphinstone Coll., Univ. of Bombay, India, 1962–69; HS Tchr., India, 1954–62. **Educ.:** State of Bombay, India, 1956, STC (Educ.); State of Maharashtra, India, 1958, Kovid (Lang., Hindi), 1959, SR HSS (Educ.); Bombay Univ., India, 1958, BA, hons. (Lang., Psy.), 1960, MA (Classical Lit.), 1962, BEd (Educ.), 1966, PhD (Info. Sci., Medvl. Lit.); Drexel Univ., 1970–71, MS (Lib., Info. Sci.). **Orgs.:** Med. LA. Osteopathic Lib. Accred. Com. Osteopathic Libns. Grp.: Pres.-Elect (1980). Coll. of Physicians of Philadelphia: Reg. Med. Lib., Sub-Reg. Com., Resrc. Sharing Com. (1977–79), Pers. Com. (1978–79). ALA. Various other orgs. Prof. N. B. Divetia Lit. Assn., Bombay, India: VP (1962–69). Grp. of Poets in Gujarati Lit., Bombay, India. Boy Scouts of India: Hon. Scout Mstr. Adult Educ. Prog., State of Maharashtra, India: Appointed Ofcr. Various other orgs. **Pubns.:** *Union List of Osteopathic Literature* (1980); various articles, short stories, poems, reviews in Hindi pubns. **Activities:** 1, 2; 15, 17, 24; 63, 80 **Addr.:** 21 Mac Arthur Blvd., Somers Point, NJ 08244.

W

Wack, Helen M. (N. 27, 1927, Atchison, KS) Libn., Prof. Lib., CO State Hosp., 1972–; Syst. Libn., AR Valley Lib. Syst., 1971–72; Head Libn., St. Benedict's Coll., Atchison, KS, 1967–71, Ref. Libn., 1966–67, Cat. Libn., 1964–66. **Educ.:** Mt. St. Scholastica Coll., Atchison, KS, 1945–63, BA, cum laude (Eng.); Rutgers Univ., 1963–64, MLS (Lib. Srv.). **Orgs.:** Med. LA: Mental Hlth. Libns. Grp.; Midcontl. Chap. CO Cncl. of Med. Libns. Pueblo Med. Libns. **Activities:** 5; 15, 17, 39; 80 **Addr.:** Professional Library, Colorado State Hospital, 1600 W. 24th St., Pueblo, CO 81003.

Waddington, Susan R. (My. 23, 1934, Baltimore, MD) Head, Art and Msc. Dept., Providence Pub. Lib., 1966–, Ref. Asst., 1965–66; Head, Circ. Dept., Dartmouth Coll. Lib., 1962–65; Asst., Docum. Dept., IN Univ. Libs., 1960–62, Resrch. Assoc., 1960, Instr., LS, 1959–60. **Educ.:** Oberlin Coll., 1952–56, BA (Hist.); Rutgers Univ., 1967–58, MLS. **Orgs.:** RI LA: Persnl. Com. (1978–). ARLIS/NA. **Activities:** 1, 9; 15, 32, 41; 55 **Addr.:** Art & Music Department, Providence Public Library, 150 Empire St., Providence, RI 02903.

Wade, Betty Jane (Ja. 13, 1922, Morgantown, WV) Libn., Lincoln HS, 1978–; Libn., Shinnston HS, 1943–78; various visit. instr. positions, 1956–70; Dir., WV Univ. Sch. Lib. Assts. Wkshp., 1966–67; Dir., WV Sch. Lib. Dev. Proj., 1961–63. **Educ.:** Salem Coll., 1939–41; WV Univ., 1941–43, AB (Eng.); Univ. of IL, 1950–53, MSLS. **Orgs.:** WV LA: Pres. (1969). ALA: AASL, Del. Asm. (WV Rep., 1960–68). WV Educ. Assn. Natl. Educ. Assn. Delta Kappa Gamma: Kappa Chap. (Pres., 1974–1976). WV Fed. of Women's Clubs: N. Ctrl. Dist. Jr. Ch. (1952–54), Pres. (1970–72); Educ. Dept. (Ch., 1972–74); Lib. Div. (Ch., 1958–60, 1962–64); Motion Pic. Ch. (1960–62); Jr. Dept. (Rec. Secy., 1956–58). **Honors:** WV LA, Srv. Awd., 1980; Outstan. Sec. Educ. of Amer., 1973. **Activities:** 10; 17, 32; 63, 75 **Addr.:** 61 W. High St., Salem, WV 26426.

Wade, Gordon S. (D. 13, 1936, Minneapolis, MN) Lib. Dir., Carroll Pub. Lib., 1963–; Docum. Libn., Hennepin Cnty. Lib., 1962–63; Bkmobile. Libn., Hennepin Cnty. Lib., 1961–62. **Educ.:** Univ. of MN, 1954–58, BA (Soclgy.), 1961–63, MA (LS). **Orgs.:** NLA. IA LA. Films for IA Lib. Media Srvs.: Treas. (1973–75). Carroll Arts Cncl.: Dir. (1978). **Pubns.:** "Does Charging Fines Really Pay?" *Wilson Lib. Bltn.* (O. 1975); "Art Print Bin," *UNABASHED Libn.* (1977); various bk. reviews, *Lib. Jnl.* (1973–79). **Activities:** 9; 17 **Addr.:** 118 E. 5th St., Carroll, IA 51401.

Wadsworth, Carol Eckberg (D. 28, 1927, Rochester, NY) Supvsg. Libn., Branch Libn., Brooklyn Pub. Lib., 1965–; Adult Srvs. Libn., Branch Head, Farmingdale Pub. Lib., 1963–65; Asst. Dir., Actg. Dir., Mid-York Lib. Syst., 1961–63; Libn., Supvsg. Libn., Queens Boro. Pub. Lib., 1952–60; Bkmobile. Libn., Berkshire Athen., 1950–52. **Educ.:** Wellesley Coll., 1945–49, BA (Pol. Sci.); Geneseo Tchrs. Coll., 1949–50, BS (LS); Columbia Univ., 1955–57, MS (LS). **Orgs.:** NY LA: Outrch. Com. (1974–80). ALA: SRRT (1975–). NY Lib. Club. W. Park Presby. Church. **Pubns.:** Reviews. **Activities:** 9; 16, 17, 24; 50, 66, 74 **Addr.:** 102 W. 85 St., 8A, New York, NY 10024.

Wadsworth, Robert W(oodman) (My. 3, 1913, Chicago, IL) Retired, 1978–, Lectr., Grad. Lib. Sch., Univ. of Chicago, 1956–, Biblgphr. for Eng., Libnshp., Gen. Hum., 1973–78, Biblgphr. for Spec. Projs., 1967–73, Head Acq. Libn., 1952–66, Asst. Head, Acq. Dept., 1948–51, Head, Serials Dept., 1946–47, Chief Searcher Ord. Dept., 1945–46, various libn. positions, 1943–45. **Educ.:** Univ. of Chicago, 1930–34, PhB (Eng.); Columbia Univ., 1934–35, AM (Eng.); Univ. of Chicago, 1939–1943, AM (Libnshp.); various crs. **Orgs.:** ALA: Cnclr.-at-Lg. (1957–59); Bd. on Acq. of Lib. Mtrls. (1954–56); RTSD, Exec. Bd. (1957–59), Tech. Srvs. Coord. Routines Srvy. Com. (1963–66); Div. of Cat. and Class., Reg. Grp. of Catlgrs. and Clasfrs. (Pres., 1948–49). **Honors:** Phi Beta Kappa, 1934; Beta Phi Mu, 1954. **Pubns.:** "Some Lacunae in Foreign Bibliography," *International Aspects of Librarianship* (1954); "The Library Selector," *Coll. & Resrch. Libs. News* (O. 1979). **Activities:** 1, 11; 15, 26, 39; 57 **Addr.:** 5451 Woodlawn Ave., Chicago, IL 60615.

Wagar, Elsa I.W. Anderson (O. 1, 1915, Arlington, MA) Retired, 1976–; Libn., Bellevue Sr. HS, 1963–76; Head, Cat. Dept., Birchard Pub. Lib., 1952–56; Dir., Bellevue Pub. Lib., 1946–49; Libn., Bellevue HS, 1942–46; Head, Youth Dept., Parlin Lib., 1941–42; Chld. Libn., NY Pub. Lib., 1937–41. **Educ.:** Simmons Coll., 1933–37, BS (LS); Columbia Univ., 1940; Heidelberg Coll., 1963–64; OH Univ., 1965. **Orgs.:** ALA. OH LA: Dist. Ch. (1946). OH Assn. Sch. Libns. Natl. Lib. Wk.: Cmnty. Com., Ch. Bellevue Pub. Lib.: Bd. of Trustees (1964–72); Pres. (1966–68). Frnds. of the Bellevue Pub. Lib.: Treas. (1975–77). Tourist Club of Bellevue, OH: Pres.; Secy.; Constn. Rev. Com. (1979). Natl. Educ. Assn. Delta Kappa Gamma: Secy.; Treas. Various other orgs. **Activities:** 9, 10; 15, 17, 20 **Addr.:** 140 Huffman St., Bellevue, OH 44811.

Wagenknecht, Robert E. (D. 8, 1935, Seattle, WA) Dir., City Lib., Springfield, MA, 1978–; Dir., Lincoln Lib., Springfield, IL, 1967–78; Head Libn., Winchester (MA) Pub. Lib., 1963–67; Head Libn., Stoneham (MA) Pub. Lib., 1961–63; Ref. Asst., Detroit Pub. Lib., 1959–61. **Educ.:** Harvard Coll., 1954–58, AB (Eng.); Simmons Coll., 1958–59, MS (LS); Sangamon State Univ., 1974–75, MA (Lit.); Miami Univ., 1976, Exec. Dev. Prog. for Lib. Admins. **Orgs.:** Msc. LA: Dallas Sum. Conf. (Prog. Ch., 1971). IL LA: Pub. Lib. Sect. (Ch., 1971–72); Legis. Lib. Dev. Com. (1976–77). ALA: RASD, Nom. Com. (1976–77)/Hist. Sect. (Ch., 1978–79); Lib. Admin. Div./PR Sect., Bylaws Com. (1977–78). IL State Lib. Adv. Com. Various other orgs. Springfield, IL Symph. Orch.: Bd. of Dirs. (1969–78). Springfield (IL) Area Cncl. for Pub. Broadcasting. Cracker Barrel: Pres. (1976). Sangamon Cnty. (IL) Hist. Socty.: Pres. (1978). Springfield (MA) Adult Educ. Cncl.: Bd. of Dirs. (1979–). **Pubns.:** Ed., *The Bay State Libn.* (O. 1964–O. 1966); "Index to Orchestral Excerpts for Trombone," *Intl. Trombone Assn. Jnl.* (Ja. 1978); "The Reader's 'Thank You,'" *IL Hist.* (N. 1977); "Genealogy Reconsidered," *IL Libs.* (Je. 1976); "Toward a Policy Regarding Genealogy in the Public Library," *UNABASHED Libn.* (1976); various bk. reviews, *Lib. Jnl.* (1962–70). **Activities:** 9; 17 **Addr.:** Springfield City Library, 220 State St., Springfield, MA 01103.

Wagers, R. E. (N. 20, 1942, Lodi, CA) Assoc. Prof., San Jose State Univ., 1976–; Libn., Douglas Cnty. Lib., 1974–76. **Educ.:** San Jose State Univ., 1961–64, AB (Phil.), 1964–65, Cred. (Sec. Educ.); Univ. of OR, 1967–74, MA (Phil.), PhD (Hist.), MLS. **Orgs.:** ALA: RASD. ASIS. **Pubns.:** "American Reference Theory and the Information Dogma," *Jnl. of Lib. Hist.* (Sum. 1978); "ABI/INFORM and Management Contents on Dialog," *Database* (Mr. 1980); "Popular Culture Theories and Fiction Collections in Public Libraries," *Jnl. of Lib. Hist.* (Spr. 1981); jt. auth., "Online Bibliographic Search Strategy Development," *ONLINE* (Ja. 1982). **Activities:** 11; 26; 56, 59 **Addr.:** Division of Library Science, San Jose State University, San Jose, CA 95192.

Wages, Orland (Jack) (Ag. 2, 1915, Canton, TX) Dir., Lib., Bridgewater Coll., 1963–; Instr., LS, E. TX State Univ., 1959–63; Libn., Jacksonville Coll., 1951–59. **Educ.:** Stephen F. Austin State Coll., 1950–51, BS (LS); E. TX State Coll., 1957–58, MS (LS). **Orgs.:** ALA. TX LA: Dist. VI, Ch. VA LA: *The VA Libn.* Ed. (1965–70). SE LA. Various other orgs. Amer. Educ. Resrch. Assn. Christ. Libns. Flwshp.: Pres. Shenandoah Valley Folk Lore Socty. Rockingham Hist. Socty. Various other orgs. **Honors:** Phi Delta Kappa. **Pubns.:** *The Church Librarian's Handbook* (1961). **Activities:** 1, 2; 15, 17, 31; 86 **Addr.:** 210 W. Bank St., Bridgewater, VA 22812.

Wagman, Frederick H. (O. 12, 1912, Springfield, MA) Dir. Emeritus, Univ. Lib., Univ. of MI, 1978–, Prof., LS, 1953–, Dir., Univ. Lib., 1953–78, Dir., Admin., Deputy Chief Asst. Libn., Dir. Prcs. Dept., Asst. Dir., Ref. Dept., Actg. Dir., Persnl. and Admin. Srvs., Lib. of Congs., 1945–53; various positions as consult. **Educ.:** Amherst Coll., 1933, AB (Eng., Grmn. Lit.); Columbia Univ., 1934, MA (Grmn. Lit.), 1942, PhD (Grmn. Lit.); Amherst Coll., 1958, LHD; Alderson-Broaddus Coll., 1967, LLD; Luther Coll., 1969, LittD. **Orgs.:** Cncl. on Lib. Resrcs.: Bd. of Dirs. (1958); various coms. ARL: Exec. Bd. Task Frc. on ARL Mem. (Ch., 1976–78); various coms., ofcs. ALA: Pres. (1963–64); Exec. Bd. (1962–65); Cncl. (1957–61, 1964–72); various coms., ofcs.; RTSD, various ofcs., coms. Various other orgs. Univ. of MI: Clements Lib. Com. of Mgt. (Vice-Ch., 1953–78); MI Hist. Col. Exec. Com. (1953–78); Med. Campus Lib., Plng. Com.; various coms., ofcs. **Honors:** Phi Kappa Phi; Phi Beta Kappa. **Pubns.:** *Magic and Natural Science in German Baroque Literature* (1942); "The General Research Library and the Area Studies Programs," *Lib. Qtly.* (O. 1965); "The New Member and ALA," *ALA Bltn.* (D. 1965); "John Cronin and the Library of Congress Catalog Card Service," *Lib. Resrcs. & Tech. Srvs.* (Fall 1968); "Research Librarianship in a Transitional Phase," *Lib. Sch. Review* (O. 1968); various articles, reviews. **Activities:** 1, 4; 15, 17, 19; 54, 55, 74 **Addr.:** L116 Winchell, University of Michigan, Ann Arbor, MI 48109.

Wagner, Charlotte A. (D. 4, 1930, New York, NY) Asst. Libn., Gulf Refining and Mktg., 1975–. **Educ.:** Principia Coll., 1948–52, BA (Eng.); NY Univ., 1958–68, PhD (Eng.); Long Island Univ., 1973–74, MLS. **Pubns.:** "Of Roots and Trees...," *TX Spec. Libs. Bltn.* (Fall 1979); "...And Buildings", *TX Spec. Libs.* (Fall 1979). **Activities:** 12; 20, 29, 49-Comp. srchs. ILL; 59, 71, 86 **Addr.:** Gulf Refining and Marketing Company, Library & Information Center, P.O. Box 2100, Houston, TX 77001.

Wagner, Ernest C. (Crockett, TX) Coll. Libn., Coll. of the VI, 1963–; Coll. Libn., Dillard Univ., 1952–62; Acq. Libn., TX South. Univ., 1950–51; Coll. Libn., Shaw Univ., 1949–50. **Educ.:** Morehse. Coll., 1948, BA (Hist.); Atlanta Univ., 1949, BS (LS); Univ. of TX Grad. Lib. Sch., 1954; Univ. of IL, 1955–56, MS (LS). **Orgs.:** ALA. Assn. of Caribbean Univ. and Resrch. Libs.: Bd. of Dirs. (1975). **Honors:** ALA, Travel Grant, 1958. **Activities:** 1; 15, 17, 31; 66, 70, 89 **Addr.:** P.O. Box 2463, Charlotte Amalie, VI 00801.

Wagner, Frank Stevens (Ag. 26, 1925, Temple, TX) Info. Spec., Celanese Chem. Co., Tech. Ctr., 1965–, Tech. Libn., 1954–65, Chem., 1950–54; Prof., Chem., Schreiner Inst., 1948–50. **Educ.:** SW TX State Univ., 1941–46, BS (Chem.), 1946–47, MA (Chem.). **Orgs.:** SLA: TX Chap. (Pres., 1963–64). Amer. Chem. Socty.: S. TX Chap., Pres. (1965–66), Cnclr. (1970–78). **Pubns.:** *Dictionary of Documentation Terms* (1959); *Union List of Scientific Serials in Coastal Bend of Texas* (1962); various articles, *Kirk-Othmers Encyclopedia of Chemical Technology*. **Activities:** 12; 41; 56, 60, 75 **Addr.:** Celanese Chemical Co., Technical Center, P.O. Box 9077, Corpus Christi, TX 78408.

Wagner, Lloyd Felix (Je. 29, 1918, Dubuque, IA) Dir. of Lib., Hood Coll., 1978–; Dir. of Libs., Cath. Univ. of Amer., 1967–77; Chief, Lib. Srvs. Div., Fed. Aviation Agency, 1965–67; Head, Whippany Lib., Bell Telephone Labs., 1958–65; Head, Spec. Lib., Ctrl. Intelligence Agency, 1953–58. **Educ.:** Lafayette Coll., 1945–49, AB (Pol. Sci.); Cath. Univ. of Amer., 1949–51, MSLS. **Orgs.:** ALA. **Activities:** 1, 4; 17 **Addr.:** 9220 Manchester Rd., Silver Spring, MD 20901.

Wagner, Mary M. (F. 4, 1946, Minneapolis, MN) Ch., Dept. of LS, Coll. of St. Catherine, 1975–; Libn. I, St. Paul Pub. Lib., 1974–75; Ref. Lib., Guthrie Thea., 1969–74. **Educ.:** Coll. of

PROFESSIONAL ACTIVITIES: Institutions: 1. Acad. lib.; 2. Arch.; 3. Assn.; 4. Fed./Gvt. lib.; 5. Inst. lib.; 6. Mfr./Suppl.; 7. Milit. lib.; 8. Musm.; 9. Pub. lib.; 10. Sch. lib.; 11. Sch. of lib. sci.; 12. Spec. lib.; 13. State lib.; 14. (other). **Functions/Activities:** 15. Acq./Col. dev.; 16. Adult srvs.; 17. Admin.; 18. Apprais.; 19. Archit./Bldgs.; 20. Cat./Class.; 21. Chld. srvs.; 22. Circ.; 23. Cons./Pres.; 24. Consult.; 25. Cont. ed.; 26. Educ. lib. sci.; 27. Ext. srvs.; 28. Fund/Grants; 29. Gvt. pubs.; 30. Indx./Abs.; 31. Instr. lib. use; 32. Media srvs.; 33. Micro.; 34. Netwks./Coop.; 35. Persnl.; 36. PR; 37. Publshg.; 38. Recs. mgt.; 39. Ref. srvs.; 40. Repro.; 41. Resrch.; 42. Review.; 43. Secur.; 44. Serials; 45. Spec. col.; 46. Tech. srvs.; 47. Trustees/Bds.; 48. YA srvs.; 49. (other).

St. Catherine, 1964–69, BA (LS, Eng., Theo.); Univ. of WA, 1972–73, MLS. **Orgs.:** MN LA: Pres. (1982). ALA. CLENE. Perry Jones Adv. Bd. Coop. Fund Dr. **Pubns.:** "Continuing Education Needs of Minnesota Library/Information/Media Center Personnel," *MN Libs.* (Win. 1980); "Collection Development" 6 videotapes and manual (1980). **Activities:** 11; 24, 25, 26; 50, 63 **Addr.:** Dept. of Library Science, College of St. Catherine, 2004 Randolph, St. Paul, MN 55105.

Wagner, Rod G. (S. 14, 1948, Oakland, NE) Deputy Dir., NE Lib. Comsn. 1974–, Admin. Asst., 1973–74, Plng. Eval., Resrch. Coord., 1972–73. **Educ.:** Wayne State Coll., 1966–70, BA (Educ.); Univ. of NE, 1970–71, MA (Pol. Sci.); Univ. of MO, 1976–77 (LS); various crs. **Orgs.:** ALA: ASCLA/State Lib. Agency Sect., Plng. Com. (1978–80), Com. on the Std. of the Admin. Prcs. in State Lib. Agencies (1976–80); Budget & Fiscal Mgt. Discuss. Grp. (Ch., 1976–81); Assn. of State Lib. Agencies, Plng. Com. (1974), Cncl. (1980–). Mt. Plains LA: Exec. Bd. (1978–79); State Lib. Sect. (Ch. 1978–79); various coms. NE LA: Exec. Bd. (1980–); various coms., ofcs. **Pubns.:** *Networking for Library Legislation* (1974). **Activities:** 13; 17, 28, 34 **Addr.:** 3205 W. Pershing Rd., Lincoln, NE 68502.

Wagner, Rosalie Shreve (Je. 5, 1942, Traverse City, MI) Media Spec., Ludwigsburg Amer. Mid. Sch., Ludwigsburg, Germany, 1981–; Coord., Educ. Resrc. Ctr., Consult., Nuernberg Amer. HS, Germany, 1975–81; Libn., Head, Wagner Mid. Sch., Philippines, 1972–74; Libn., Molesworth Jr. HS, Eng., 1969–72; Head Libn., Interlochen Arts Acad., 1967–69. **Educ.:** Ctrl. MI Univ., 1962–64, BA (Hist.); West. MI Univ., 1965–68, MLS. Univ. of MD, 1968–79, MA (Educ.). **Orgs.:** ALA: AASL. Nuernberg-Erlangen Educ. Assn. S.E. Asia Educ. Assn. **Activities:** 10; 15, 20, 39; 66, 82 **Addr.:** Ludwigsburg Middle School, APO, NY 09154.

Wagner, Samuel Albin Mar (F. 23, 1942, Brighton, CO) Arch. Recs. Mgt. Anal., WY State Arch., 1979–; Instr., Los Angeles Cmnty. Coll. Overseas Prog.; Instr., Chapman Coll., Warren Air Frc. Base; City Archvst., Providence, RI, 1978–80; Cnty. Histn., Adams Cnty., CO, 1977–78; Sr. Asst. Archvst., Cornell Univ., 1971–73; Asst. Archvst., Univ. of CO, 1968–70; various archvst. positions, Harvard Univ., 1966–68. **Educ.:** Univ. of CO, 1961–64, BA (Hist.), 1964–65, MA (Hist.); Harvard Univ., 1965–68, (Hist. of World Relig.); Inst. for Advnc. Arch. Std., Univ. of Denver, 1978, Cert.; CA Tchg. Cert. for Cmnty. Coll. (Hist. and Ofc. Sci.). **Orgs.:** SAA. Assn. of Recs. Mgrs. and Admins. Data Prcs. Mgrs. Assn. Amer. Assn. for State and Lcl. Hist. Org. of Amer. Histns. West. Hist. Assn. WY Hist. Socty. **Honors:** Adams Cnty., CO, Hist. Prsrvn. Awd., 1978. **Pubns.:** *Crossroads of the West: Adams County, Colorado* (1977); *Brighton Reflections, 1776–1976* (1976); ed., *The Fort Lupton Story* (1976); various articles, TV progs., radio progs., films, slide shows, multi-media presentations. **Activities:** 2; 15, 26, 38; 66, 75, 95-Pub. recs. **Addr.:** 822 W. Pershing Blvd., Cheyenne, WY 82001.

Wahl, Kathryn Jane (Je. 27, 1925, Portland, OR) Assoc. Prof./Ref. and Circ. Libn., Univ. of Portland, 1972–, Ref. and Circ. Libn., 1968–, Circ. Libn., 1966–68, Circ. and Ref. Libn., 1964–65, Spec. Srvs. Libn., 1963–64. **Educ.:** Univ. of Portland, 1960–62, BA (Liberal Arts); 1962–63, MLS, 1964–66, MA (Hist.). **Orgs.:** Cath. LA. ALA. Pac. NW LA. Portland Area Spec. Libns.: Ch. (1971–72); Secy. (1969–70). Univ. of Portland REVIEW: Circ. Ed. (1969–). AAUP. AAUW. **Pubns.:** "Raiders of Sullivans Gulch," *Pac. Histn.* (V. 15 #2); ed., "Destination Toutle River," *Pac. Histn.* (18 #2). **Activities:** 1; 22, 31, 39 **Addr.:** 4810 N.W. Harney, Vancouver, WA 98663.

Wai, Lily C. (S. 29, 1939, Li-sui, Chekiang, China) Asst. Soc. Sci. Libn., Univ. of ID Lib., 1970–; Asst. Libn., Univ. of CA, Los Angeles, 1965–68. **Educ.:** Tunghai Univ., 1957–60, BA (Hist.); Univ. of KS, 1961–63, (Hist.); Univ. of IL, 1963–64, MLS; Univ. of ID, 1974–79, MA (Hist.). **Orgs.:** ID LA. West. Assn. Map Libs. ALA. **Pubns.:** *Formosan Resolution: Its Origin and Repeal* (1979); "Statistical Information", *Bookmark* (D. 1973); "How to Find U.S. Government Documents," *Bookmark* (Jl. 1973); "Map Collection," *Bookmark* (1974); *Pacific Northwest Reading List* (1971). **Activities:** 1, 5; 29, 31, 39; 59, 70, 92 **Addr.:** 716 East E, Moscow, ID 83843.

Wainwright, Alexander D. (Je. 26, 1917, Ventnor, NJ) Asst. Univ. Libn., Col. Dev., Princeton Univ. Lib., 1962–, Cur., Morris L. Parrish Col. of Vict. Novelists, 1948–, Cur., Rare Bks., Asst. Chief, Dept. of Rare Bks. and Spec. Cols., 1948–62, Asst., Prep. Dept., 1946–48; AUS, Ordnance Dept., 1942–46; Asst. Libn., Cooper Un., 1941–42. **Educ.:** Princeton Univ., 1935–39, AB (Eng.); Columbia Univ., 1940–41, BS (LS). **Orgs.:** Assn. Intl. de Bibl. ALA. Bibl. Socty. of Amer. Ms. Socty. Lib. Co. of Philadelphia. Various other orgs. Hist. Socty. of PA. NJ Hist. Socty. Grolier Club. Philobiblon Club. Various other orgs. **Pubns.:** *Robert Louis Stevenson: A Catalogue of Collections in the Princeton University Library* (1971); ed., *The Princeton Univ. Lib. Chronicle;* various articles (1949–62). **Activities:** 1; 15, 17, 45; 57 **Addr.:** 89 Hartley Ave., Princeton, NJ 08540.

Wait, Carol D. (Jl. 28, 1934, Seattle, WA) Serials Libn., Cap. Dist. Lib. Cncl., 1973–; Engin. Aide, Knolls Atomic Power Lab., 1955–57. **Educ.:** Coll. of William and Mary, 1951–55, BS (Phys.); SUNY, Albany, 1970–72, MLS. Phi Beta Kappa: Upper Hudson Assn., Exec. Com. (1977–), Pres. (1980–81). **Honors:** Beta Phi Mu, 1972. **Pubns.:** Ed., "Capital District Library Council," *Union List of Serials* (1980). **Activities:** 3; 34, 44, 49-Un. Listing of Serials; 84, 88, 91 **Addr.:** Capital District Library Council, 91 Fiddlers Ln., Latham, NY 12110.

Waity, Gloria A. (F. 27, 1933, Wausau, WI) Freelnc. Libn., 1979–; Instr., Univ. of WI, 1979–80, 1970–77; Lib. Career Spec., WI Dept. of Pub. Instr., Div. for Lib. Srvs., 1969–71. **Educ.:** Univ. of WI, Madison, 1951–55, BS Ed (Recreational Leadership), 1956–59, MLS (Libnshp.), 1967–70, Spec. Cert. **Orgs.:** ALA: Cncl.; YASD, Bd. (1965–69); ALSC, Presch. Srvs. and Parent Educ. Com. (1974–76). WI LA: Lib. Educ. Com. (Dir., 1978–80); Com. on Lib. Careers (Ch., 1970–71); various other coms. Hist. Madison, Inc.: Bd. of Dirs. (1978–81). Alliance for the Mentally Ill of Dane Cnty. (WI): Bd. of Dirs. (1979–). Natl. Alliance for the Mentally Ill. **Honors:** Pi Lambda Theta; Mortar Bd. **Pubns.:** Jt. auth., "Make a Thing not Made Before! Creative Utilization of Library Media Centers in Madison (WI)," *WI Lib. Bltn.* (Mr.–Ap. 1977). **Activities:** 9, 10; 21, 42, 48; 63 **Addr.:** 901 Crestview Dr., Madison, WI 53716.

Wakefield, Anne Kaye (Mrs. C.M. Belabi) (N. 13, 1947, Jamestown, VA) Libn., Admin. U.S. Army Libs., Fort Amador and Fort Clayton, Panama CZ, 1981–; Readers Srvs. Libn., Chattahoochee Valley Reg. Lib., 1978–80; Chief Admin. Libn., U.S. Army Lib., Wildflecken, Germany, 1977–78; Chief Libn., Atlanta Meml. Arts Ctr., 1969–76. **Educ.:** Univ. of Mex., 1962, Cert. (Span.); Emory Univ., 1962–67, BA (Art), 1967–68, MLS (Libnshp.). **Orgs.:** ARLIS/NA: GA Chap. (Fndn. Ch., 1974). The Un. of Indp. Colls. of Art: Chief Libns. Com. (1973–76). Univ. Ctr., GA: Lib. Adv. Com. (1970–76). *Contemporary Art Southeast:* Jnl. Co-fndr.; Bd. of Dirs. (1977). **Honors:** U.S. Army, Wildflecken Trng. Ctr., Germany, Merit. Srv. Awd. in Lib. Prog., 1978. **Pubns.:** Ed., *A Bookman's Guide to Valuable Books* 1976; "Atlanta International Film Festival" videotape (1974). **Activities:** 1, 12; 15, 16, 17; 50, 55, 74 **Addr.:** P. O. Box 354, Atlanta, GA 30301–0354.

Wakefield, Jacqueline M. (Je. 10, 1929, Pasadena, CA) Coord., Branch Srvs., Ventura Cnty. Lib. Srvs. Agency, 1980–, Coord., Chld. Srvs., 1969–81; Chld. Libn., Los Angeles Pub. Lib., 1968–69. **Educ.:** Pasadena City Coll., 1946, AA (Archit.); Univ. of South. CA, 1947–48 (Archit.); CA State Univ., Los Angeles, 1964–67, BA (Amer. Std.); Immaculate Heart Coll., 1967–68, MALS. **Orgs.:** CA LA: Couns.-at-lg. (1972–73, 1978–80); CA State Chld. Chap. (Ch., 1972); Cncl. Forum Coord. Com. (1978, 1980); Cncl. Com. on Org. (Ch., 1979). ALA: Newbery/Caldecott Com. (1976). South. CA Cncl. on Lit. for Chld. and Young People: Bd. (1974–78). **Pubns.:** "Combining Your Adult and Juvenile Collections: Certifiable Lunacy or Common Sense?" *Wilson Lib. Bltn.* (F. 1972); "Puppetry: An Alternate Expression," *CA Libn.* (Jl. 1975). **Activities:** 9; 17, 21, 27 **Addr.:** Ventura County Library Services Agency, P. O. Box 771, Ventura, CA 93001.

Walch, David B. (My. 19, 1936, La Grande, OR) Dir., Univ. Lib., CA Polytech. State Univ., 1981–; Dean, Acad. Srvs., State Univ. Coll., Buffalo, 1974–; Asst. Prof., Instr. Systs., Univ. of UT, 1971–74, Lrng. Resrcs., Asst. Prof., LS, 1967–71; Dir., Lib., Church Coll. of HI, 1965–67. **Educ.:** East. OR Coll., 1955–59 (Soc. Sci., Hum.); Univ. of IL, 1960–61, (Acad. Libnshp.), 1967–68, Cert. of Advnc. Std. in LS (Educ. for Libnshp.); Univ. of UT, 1970–73, PhD (Educ. Admin., Educ. Media, Instr. Systs.). **Orgs.:** ALA: ACRL, AV Com. (Ch., 1977). NY LA: Coll. and Univ. Lib. Sect., 2nd VP, Pres. (1976–79). AECT: Postsec. Stans. Com. (1979); Info. Systs. (Dir., 1974). West. NY Lib. Resrcs. Cncl.: Bd. of Trustees (Pres., 1977–). **Honors:** Phi Kappa Phi, 1973. **Pubns.:** "Budgeting for Non-Print Media in Academic Libraries," *New Horizons for Academic Libraries* (1979); "Slide Duplication and the New Copyright Law," *AV Instr.* (1979); "Film Transmission and the Law: A Survey of Film Producers," *AV Instr.* (1979); various papers. **Activities:** 1; 17 **Addr.:** California Polytechnic State University, R.E. Kennedy Library, San Luis Obispo, CA 93407.

Walch, Timothy (D. 6, 1947, Detroit, MI) Prog. Anal., Natl. Hist. Pubns. and Recs. Comsn., 1979–; Dir., Spec. Prog., SAA, 1975–79; Resrch. Assoc., Univ. Arch., Northwest. Univ., 1974–75. **Educ.:** Univ. of Notre Dame, 1966–70, BA (Hist.); Northwest. Univ., 1970–75, PhD (Hist.). **Orgs.:** SAA. Org. of Amer. Histns. **Honors:** Tchrs. Coll., Columbia Univ., Prize in Educ., 1969. **Pubns.:** *American Educational History: Guide to Information Sources* (1980); *Archives and Manuscripts: Security* (1977); spec. issue ed., *The Amer. Archvst.* (Jl. 1977); various articles. **Activities:** 2, 4; 28, 43 **Addr.:** 6308 King Louis Dr., Alexandria, VA 22312.

Walch, Victoria Irons (Ag. 26, 1950, Green Bay, WI) Archs. Spec., Machine-Readable Archs. Div., Natl. Archs. and Recs. Srv., 1979–; Asst. Cur. of Mss. (Actg.), Chicago Hist. Socty., 1978–79; Head, Pubns./Finding Aids Unit, IL State Archs., 1974–78, Archvst. I, 1973–74. **Educ.:** Mills Coll., 1968–72, BA (Art Hist.); Northwest. Univ., 1972–73, MA (Art Hist.). **Orgs.:** SAA: State and Lcl. Recs. Com. (1974–79); Descr. Prof. Afnty. Grp. (Ch., 1981–); Strg. Com. (1979–); Task Frc. on Autom. Recs. and Techqs. (1980–). Midwest Archs. Conf.: Nsltr. Co–ed. (1977–78). Natl. Arch. Asm. Exec. Bd. (1981–). Socty. of Archit. Histns. **Honors:** SAA, Waldo G. Leland Cert. of Cmdn., 1979. **Pubns.:** Jt. auth., *Descriptive Inventory of the Archives of the State of Illinois* (1978). **Activities:** 2, 4; 18, 20, 30; 55, 57, 91 **Addr.:** 9927 Capperton Dr., Oakton, VA 22124.

Walcott, Rosalind (Je. 29, 1946, Sydney, N.S.W., Australia) Earth and Space Scis. Libn., SUNY, Stony Brook, 1974–; Grad. Asst., Student Admin., Canberra Coll. of Adv. Educ., 1972; Geologist, Class 1, Bur. of Mineral Resrcs., 1968–71. **Educ.:** Univ. of New Eng. (Australia), 1964–67, BSc, hons. (Geol.); Australian Natl. Univ., 1968–70, BA (Psy.); Long Island Univ., 1973–74, MSLS. **Orgs.:** SLA: Long Island Chap. (Dir., 1978–80). LA of Australia. Geosci. Info. Socty.: Pres. (1979–80); Pres.–Elect (1978–79). **Honors:** Beta Phi Mu. **Pubns.:** "The Geoscience Librarian's View of the Publishing Process," *GIS Procs.* (1979); "Information Transfer to the Geoscientist Through the International Union of Geological Sciences," *Geosci. Info.* (1979); "A Survey of the Holdings of a Sample of IUGS Publications in Selected U.S. Geological Libraries," *GIS Procs.* (1978). **Activities:** 1, 12; 15, 17, 39; 70, 88, 91 **Addr.:** Earth and Space Sciences Library, SUNY at Stony Brook, Stony Brook, NY 11794.

Wald, Ingeborg (Ap. 24, 1933, Oberrissdorf, Germany) Asst. Libn., Fiske Icelandic Col., Cornell Univ. Libs., 1979–, Asst. Archvst., Dept. of Mss. and Univ. Archs., 1976–79; Acq. Dept., Lane Med. Lib., Stanford Univ., 1972–75; Libn., Goethe–Inst. (Boston), 1968–71. **Educ.:** Freie Univ. (Berlin), 1953–57; Boston Univ., 1967–68, MA; State Univ. of CA, 1974–75, MLS; Various crs. 1977, 1978. **Orgs.:** SAA: Prsrvn. Com. ALA: RTSD. Gld. of Bk. Workers. **Pubns.:** *A Guide to the Papers of Dorothy Whitney Straight Elmhirst; Combined Index to the Papers of Willard D. Straight and Dorothy Whitney Straight Rlmhirst;* jt. auth., *Ithaca Books and Book Arts* (1979); *Ex Libris Dorothy and Willard Straight. Bltn. No. 12.* Cornell Univ. Libs. (1979). **Activities:** 1, 2; 20, 23, 46; 55, 62 **Addr.:** 114 Cascadilla Park, Ithaca, NY 14850.

Walden, Bette Kent (My. 4, 1946, Bloomington, IN) Dir. of Lib. and Media Srvs., IN State Univ., Evansville, 1976–; Asst. Libn., Princeton (IN) Pub. Lib., 1974–76; Ref. Libn., IN State Univ., 1971–76; Eng./Span. Tchr., Edgewood HS (Ellettsville, IN), 1968–70. **Educ.:** IN Univ., 1964–68, AB (Eng.), 1970–71, MLS. **Orgs.:** IN LA: Exec. Bd., Ref. Div. (1979–). Four Rivers Area Lib. Srvs. Athrty.: Pres. (1980–). ALA. AAUW. Tri–State Epilepsy Assn. **Honors:** Phi Beta Kappa; Beta Phi Mu; IN State Univ., Evansville, Merit Recog., 1979. **Activities:** 1, 2; 17, 32, 35; 50, 61, 86 **Addr.:** Library Services, Indiana State University Evansville, 8600 University Blvd., Evansville, IN 47712.

Waldhart, Thomas James (Jl. 14, 1940, Spencer, WI) Assoc. Prof., Coll. of LS, Univ. of KY, 1970–; Asst. Engin. Libn., Engin. Lib., Univ. of WI, 1962–67. **Educ.:** Univ. of WI, 1958–62, BS (Zlgy.), 1962–64, MS (LS); IN Univ., 1967–73, PhD (LS). **Orgs.:** KY LA. AALS. ALA. ASIS: Educ. Com. (1979–81). **Honors:** Beta Phi Mu. **Pubns.:** *Communication Research in Library and Information Science* (1975); jt. auth., "User Fees in Publicly Funded Libraries," *Adv. in Libnshp.* (1979); "Implementation of Results-Oriented Management...," *Jnl. Acad. Libs.* (S. 1978); jt. auth., "Marketing Products and Services...," *LIBRI* (Fall 1977); jt. auth., "Productivity Measurement in Academic Libraries," *Adv. in Libnshp.* (1976); Various articles. **Activities:** 1, 12; 17, 26, 30; 56, 58, 75 **Addr.:** 425 Patterson Office Tower, College of Library Science, University of Kentucky, Lexington, KY 40506.

Waldhorn, Katharine Wohl (O. 13, 1923, Tampa, FL) Lib. Dir., Ypsilanti Area Pub. Lib., 1964–; Dir. of Pubns. and Pubcty., Dearborn Pub. Lib., 1957–64, Branch Libn., 1950–57; Med. Libn., City of Chicago, Tuberculosis Sanitorium, 1949–50; Bibl. Resrch., Univ. of WI Lib., Madison, 1948–50. **Educ.:** Univ. of Tampa, 1940–44, BS (Educ.); Univ. of WI, Madison, 1947–49, BS (LS); Univ. of MI, Ann Arbor, 1961–63, Advnc. MA (LS). **Orgs.:** ALA. MI LA. **Activities:** 1, 9; 15, 17, 36; 50, 57, 75 **Addr.:** Ypsilanti Area Public Library, 229 W. Michigan, Ypsilanti, MI 48197.

Waldrop, Ruth W. (Mr. 30, 1911, May, TX) Exec. Secy., AL LA, 1978–; Assoc. Prof. Grad. Sch. of Lib. Srv., Univ. of AL, 1969–78; State Sch. Lib. Consult., State Dept. of Educ. (AL), 1968–69. **Educ.:** Livingston Univ., BS (Educ.); Univ. of AL, Mstrs. (Educ.), 1970, EdS. **Orgs.:** ALA: Cncl.; Stans. Com. (1979–81); AALS, Dist. Dir.; Legis. Com. AL LA: Exec. Secy.; Pres.; various coms. SELA: Conv. Handbk. Com. (1978–80). Intl. Assn. of Sch. Libns.: Nom. Com. (1978). AL Inst. Media Assn.: Various coms. AL Educ. Assn.: Various coms. **Honors:** Mortar Bd., Hon. Mem.; Livingston Univ., Golden Key Awd., 1970. **Pubns.:** *Alabama Authors, Books in Print* (1980); *Simple Steps to Successful Legislation* (1976); *Santa Claus, A Brief Biography* (1981); *Bibliography of Southeastern Regional Literature for Elementary, Jr. High and Senior High School Students;* jt. auth., "Supervision of Instructional Media Services, Part 1 & 2," *Drexel Lib. Qtly.* (1977–78). **Activities:** 10, 11; 26, 31, 32; 63, 78 **Addr.:** P.O. BY, University, AL 35486.

Special Subjects/Services: 50. Adult educ.; 51. Advert./Mktg.; 52. Aerosp.; 53. Agric.; 54. Area std.; 55. Arts/Hum.; 56. Autom.; 57. Bibl./Prtg.; 58. Bio. sci.; 59. Bus./Fin.; 60. Chem.; 61. Copyrt.; 62. Documtn.; 63. Educ.; 64. Engin.; 65. Env.; 66. Eth. grps.; 67. Film; 68. Food/Nutr.; 69. Geneal.; 70. Geo.; 71. Geol.; 72. Handcpd.; 73. Hist.; 74. Int. frdm.; 75. Info. sci.; 76. Insr.; 77. Law; 78. Legis.; 79. Math./Comp. sci.; 80. Med.; 81. Metals; 82. Nat. resrcs.; 83. Newsp.; 84. Nuc. sci.; 85. Oral hist.; 86. Petr./Energy; 87. Pharm.; 88. Phys./Astr./Math.; 89. Readg.; 90. Relig.; 91. Sci./Tech.; 92. Soc. sci.; 93. Telecom.; 94. Transp.; 95. (other).

Walensky, Lucile R. (Sioux City, IA) Admin./Consult., SW IA Reg. Lib. Syst., 1973–; Dir., Yankton Carnegie Lib. and Yankton Cmnty. Lib., 1967–73; Adult Srvs. Libn., Marshalltown Pub. Lib., 1966–67; Reader's Adv., Sioux City Pub. Lib., 1964–66. **Educ.:** Grinnell Coll., 1940–42; Morningside Coll., 1943, BA (Eng., Soc. Scis.); TX Woman's Univ., 1963–65, MLS; Lifetime Tchg. Cert. (IA). **Orgs.:** SD LA: Pub. Lib. Sect. (Ch., 1968–70); Natl. Lib. Week Ch. (1970, 1977). ALA. IA LA. Jr. Leag., Sioux City. Sioux City PTA Cncl. **Activities:** 9; 16, 17, 24; 50, 89, 92 **Addr.:** P.O. Box 327, Missouri Valley, IA 51555.

Walford, Bess P. (Mr. 14, 1918, Richmond, VA) Indp. Consult., 1981–; Lit. Anal., Philip Morris U.S.A. Resrch. Ctr., 1979–80, Resrch. Libn., 1959–78; Libn., Fed. Rsv. Bank, 1949–59; Libn., Vets. Admin. Med. and Tech. Lib., 1947–49; Libn., Fort George G. Meade Post Lib. 3, 1945–46; Supvsr. of Libs., VA Dept. of Mental Hygiene and Hosps., 1941–45; Libn., Mathews Cnty. HS, 1940–41. **Educ.:** Univ. of Richmond, 1936–39, BA (Hist.); Drexel Univ., 1939–40, BS (LS). **Orgs.:** SLA: Div. Liaison Ofcr. (1970–72); Gvtl. Rels. Com. (Ch., 1968–70); Bus. and Fin. Div. (Co-Ch., 1958–59); Fin. Div. (Vice-Ch., 1957–58); VA Chap. (Pres., 1969–70). Lib. Adv. Com. of VA State Cncl. of Higher Educ.: Spec. Libs. Rep., (1972–78). VA LA: Pres. (1961–62). VA Lib. Inst.: First Ch. (1965). **Pubns.:** "The Evaluation of Special Librarians," *Spec. Libs.* (D. 1974); "Pros of Establishing a Library School in Virginia," *VA Libn.* (Win. 1969); "Special Library Resources in Virginia," *VA Libn.* (Win. 1965); "Planning the New Library: Philip Morris Research Center Library," *Spec. Libs.* (Ap. 1960). **Activities:** 12; 17, 24; 91 **Addr.:** 5014 Sulky Dr. 204, Richmond, VA 23228.

Walia, Rajinder S. (S. 1, 1930, Phillaur, Panjab, India) Law Libn. and Prof. of Law, Northeast. Univ. Law Sch., 1970–; Law Libn. and Assoc. Prof. of Law, Univ. of SK, 1968–70; Biblgphr., Harvard Law Sch., 1966–68; Lectr., Asst. Prof. of Law, Delhi Univ. (India), 1955–65. **Educ.:** Panjab Univ. (India), 1947–51, BSc (Phys., Chem.); Delhi Univ., 1951–55, LLB 7 LLM; Harvard Univ., 1961–63, LLM, Simmons Coll., 1968, MS (LS). **Orgs.:** AALL: Com. on Index to Legal Pers. (1975–). Law Libns. of New Eng.: Pres. (1972–74). Intl. Assn. of Law Libs. Amer. Socty. of Intl. Law. Amer. Assn. of Law Schs. **Activities:** 1, 12; 15, 17, 39; 54, 77, 78 **Addr.:** Northeastern University Law School, Boston, MA 02115.

Walker, Barbara Ann (D. 28, 1950, Detroit, MI) Farmington Branch Head, Coord. of YA Srvs., Farmington Cmnty. Lib., 1979–, Coord. of YA Srvs., 1977–79, YA Libn., 1975–77. **Educ.:** East. MI Univ., 1969–73, BA (Educ.); Wayne State Univ., 1974–76, MS (LS). **Orgs.:** ALA: YASD, Lib. Srvs. to YA's in Insts. Com. (1978–81). MI LA: YA Caucus (Ch., 1979–80). Wayne Oakland Lib. Fed.: YA Srvs. Com. (Ch., 1979–). **Honors:** MI LA YA Caucus, Frances H. Pletz Awd., 1978. **Pubns.:** Bk. reviews, *Voice of Youth Advocates* (1979–). **Activities:** 9; 16, 36, 48 **Addr.:** Farmington Branch Library, 23500 Liberty St., Farmington, MI 48024.

Walker, Catherine M. (My. 24, 1954, Monroe, LA) Asst. Catlgr., Nashotah Hse. Lib., 1980–; Circ. Libn., Ouachita Par. Pub. Lib. Syst., 1979–80, Ref. Libn., 1977–79, Chld. Libn., 1973–77. **Educ.:** NE LA Univ., 1972–75, BA (Eng., LS), 1975–78, MA (Eng.). **Orgs.:** ALA. WI LA. LA LA: JMRT Sect. (Secy., 1979–80). Mod. Lang. Assn. **Honors:** Phi Kappa Phi; LA LA–JMRT Srv. Awd., 1979; **Pubns.:** "How to Write For the *LLA Bulletin,*" *LA LA Bltn.* (Fall 1979); ed., *LA LA JMRT Nsltr.* (1977–79); ed., *LA LA Bltn.* (1979–); publshr., syst. staff nsltr. **Activities:** 9; 22, 39, 42; 55 **Addr.:** Nashotah House, Nashotah, WI 53058.

Walker, Celine F. (St. Lucia, W. Indies) Chief, Sci. Cols., Stanford Univ., 1978–; Instr., Univ. of CA, Berkeley, Sch. of Lib. and Info. Std., 1982; Chief, Sci. Libs., Stanford Univ., 1976–78; Lib. Mgr., R&D Assocs., 1971–76; Ref. Libn., Rand Corp., 1968–71; Catlgr., Aerosp. Corp., 1966–68. **Educ.:** Univ. of IL, 1959–62, BA (Liberal Arts and Sci.); Univ. of South. CA, 1972, MLS; Brit. LA, 1957, First Exam. **Orgs.:** SLA: San Andreas Chap. (Pres., 1980–81). ASIS. **Honors:** Untd. Nations, Human Rights Awd., 1964. **Activities:** 1, 12; 17, 24, 34; 64, 88, 91 **Addr.:** Library, Terman Engineering Center, Stanford University, Stanford, CA 94305.

Walker, Donald E. (N. 22, 1928, Green Bay, WI) Sr. Resrch. Ling., SRI Intl., 1971–; Head, Lang. and Text Prcs., MITRE Corp., 1961–71; Asst. Prof. of Psy., Rice Univ., 1953–61; Resrch. Psychologist, Houston Vets. Admin. Hosp., 1957–61. **Educ.:** Deep Springs Coll., 1945–47; Univ. of Chicago, 1947–52, PhD (Psy.); Yale Univ., 1952–53, (Ling.). **Orgs.:** Intl. Fed. for Documtn.: Com. on Ling. in Documtn. (Ch., 1972–80). Natl. Acad. of Scis.: U.S. Natl. Com. for FID (Ch., 1980–). ASIS: SIG Autom. Lang. Prcs. (Ch., 1970–72). Amer. Fed. of Info. Prcs. Soctys.: Bd. of Dirs. (1967–71, 1979–); Secy. (1971–72). Assn. for Computational Ling.: Pres. (1968); Secy./Treas. (1976–). Assn. for Comp. Mach. Ling. Socty. of Amer. **Honors:** Phi Beta Kappa; Sigma Xi; Soc. Sci. Resrch. Cncl., Fellow, 1952–53. **Pubns.:** Jt. ed., *Natural Language in Information Science: Perspectives and Directions ...* (1977); ed., *Understanding Spoken Language* (1978); ed., *Interactive Bibliographic Search: The User/Computer Interface* (1971); "Automated Language Processing," *Anl. Review of Info. Sci. and Tech.* (1973); "SRI Research on Speech Understanding," *Trends in Speech Recognition* (1979); various articles. **Activities:** 14-Nonprofit resrch. inst.; 17, 41; 56, 95-Ling. **Addr.:** Artificial Intelligence Center, SRI International, Menlo Park, CA 94025.

Walker, Elinor (Mr. 16, 1911, Enderlin, ND) Retired, 1976–; Bk. Reviewer, *Booklist,* ALA, 1971–76; Coord., Work with Young People, Carnegie Lib. of Pittsburgh, 1948–70; Instr., Adlsnt. Lit., Carnegie Inst. of Tech., 1948–60; Bk. Reviewer, *Booklist,* ALA, 1946–48; YA Libn., St. Paul Pub. Lib., 1943–46. **Educ.:** Macalester Coll., 1929–33, AB (Latin, Eng.); Univ. of MN, 1936–44, BS (LS). **Orgs.:** ALA: YASD (Pres., 1949–50); PLA (Pres., 1959–60). Pittsburgh Lib. Club. **Honors:** Macalester Coll., Disting. Citizen Cit., 1978. **Pubns.:** *Book Bait* (1957, 1969, 1979); *Doors to More Mature Reading* (1964, 1981). **Activities:** 9; 42, 48 **Addr.:** 5635 Minnetonka Blvd., Minneapolis, MN 55416.

Walker, Elizabeth (O. 29, 1948, Somerset, PA) Head Libn., Curtis Inst. of Msc., 1980–, Asst. Libn., 1977–80; Libn., Carnegie Lib. of Pittsburgh, 1974–76. **Educ.:** Hood Coll., 1966–70, BA (Msc.); PA State Univ., 1970–72, MFA (Voice); Univ. of Pittsburgh, 1973–74, MLS. **Orgs.:** Msc. LA: PA Chap., Vice-Ch./Ch.-Elect (1981), Nom. Com. (1978); Pubns. Com. (1980–). Hood Coll. Alum. Club of Philadelphia. Philadelphia Singers. **Honors:** Beta Phi Mu. **Pubns.:** Ed., *Notations* (1980–). **Activities:** 14-Cnsvty. of msc.; 15, 17, 45; 55 **Addr.:** The Curtis Institute of Music Library, 1726 Locust St., Philadelphia, PA 19103.

Walker, Estellene Paxton (S. 13, 1911, Washington Cnty., VA) Consult. to SC State Lib., 1979–, Libn., 1969–79; Dir., SC State Lib. Bd., 1946–69; Mtrls.–Supply Libn., Army Spec. Srvs. (ETO), 1945–46. **Educ.:** Univ. of TN, 1930–33, BA (Eng.); Emory Univ., 1934–35, BS (LS). **Orgs.:** ALA: Cncl. (1952–56). Amer. Assn. of State Libs.: Pres. (1968). SELA: Adv. Com. on Southeast. Coop. Lib. Srvy., Ch. SC LA: Pres. (1974–76). SC Com. for the Hum. S. Caroliniana Socty. **Honors:** Presby. Coll. (Clinton), Hon. DLitt, 1975; Lander Coll., Hon. DHum, 1979. **Pubns.:** *So Good and Necessary a Work: The Public Library in South Carolina, 1698–1980* (1981). **Activities:** 13; 17, 19, 24; 51, 75, 78 **Addr.:** 3208 Amherst Ave., Columbia, SC 29205.

Walker, Luise E(lisabeth) (N. 14, 1927, Ferndale, MI) Head Sci. Libn., Univ. of OR, 1967–; Readers' Srvs. Head, SUNY Coll. of Forestry, 1961–67; Head Math. Libn., Syracuse Univ., 1958–60; Head Bio. Libn., Univ. of Notre Dame, 1955–58. **Educ.:** Univ. of Washington, 1949–51, AB (Soclgy.); Univ. of MI, 1953–55, AMLS; SUNY Coll. of Forestry, 1958–61, MS (Bot.), PhD Cand. **Orgs.:** SLA: Archvst., Upstate NY Chap. (1964–67). Amer. Chem. Socty.: Div. of Chem. Lit., Mem. Recruiter, NW Reg. (1970). AAAS. Socty. of the Sigma Xi: Univ. of OR Chap. (Secy./Treas., 1976–79). AAUP: Univ. of OR Chap. (Treas., 1971–72). Amer. Rifle Assn. U.S. Nvl. Rsv. Various other orgs. **Pubns.:** Biblgphr., *Textbook of Dendrology* (1968); clmn., *Jnl. of Forestry* (1965–67). **Activities:** 1; 17, 39, 41; 58, 82, 91 **Addr.:** Science Library, University of Oregon, Eugene, OR 97403.

Walker, Lynn W. (Ag. 30, 1928, Okeechobee, FL) Dir. of Libs., Univ. of Ctrl. FL, 1966–; Libn., Engin. and Phys. Lib., Univ. of FL, 1954–66, Sci. Catlgr., Sci. Libn., 1952–54; Catlgr., Univ. of TN, 1950–52. **Educ.:** Univ. of FL, 1946–49, BA (Hist.); FL State Univ., 1949–50, MA (LS). **Orgs.:** ALA: Mem. Com.; Cnclr. SELA: Interstate Coop. Com.; Nom. Com. FL LA: Treas.; VP; Pres.; various coms. Natl. Micro. Assn. Nvl. Rsv. Assn. **Honors:** Beta Phi Mu. **Pubns.:** "Technical Processes in Small College Libraries," *Jnl. of Cat. and Class.* (Je. 1953); "Technical Processes in Small College Libraries," *Southeast. Libn.* (Sum. 1953); "Library Service for Florida Engineers," *FL Engin. Socty. Jnl.* (Ap. 1958); "Professionalism and the Library Profession," *Rub-Off* (Mr. 1969). **Activities:** 1; 17, 20; 64, 88, 91 **Addr.:** University of Central Florida, P.O. Box 25000, Orlando, FL 32816.

Walker, Mary Edith (Ja. 27, 1943, Nashville, TN) Sr. Libn., St. Jude Chld. Resrch. Hosp., 1980–; Mgr., Info. Retrieval Srvs., Memphis State Univ., 1978–80, Sr. Ref. Libn., 1975–78; Ref. Libn., GA State Univ., 1969–75. **Educ.:** Inst. for Amer. Univs. (France), 1963–64, Cert. in European Std.; Millsaps Coll., 1964–65, BA (Relig.); Emory Univ., 1968–69, MLS. **Orgs.:** SLA: Lcl. Pubcty. Ch. (1979–80). SELA. TN LA. Med. LA. Memphis Heritage. **Pubns.:** Ed., *The Atlanta Constitution: A Georgia Index* (1971–75); "From Migraines to Maddox: The Making of the *Atlanta Constitution* Index," *RQ* (Mr. 1975); various sps. **Activities:** 1, 12; 30, 31, 39; 56, 59, 80 **Addr.:** 4182 Chickasaw Rd., Memphis, TN 38117.

Walker, Mary Josephine (Duck) (Je. 22, 1932, Dallas, TX) Spec. Cols. Libn., East. NM Univ., 1969–; Libn., Ranger Jr. Coll., 1955–57. **Educ.:** George Peabody Coll. for Tchrs., 1951–52, BA (Eng.); Univ. of TX, Austin, 1959, MLS. **Orgs.:** NM LA: Lcl. Hist. and Archs. RT (Ch., 1978–79). SWLA: Nom. Com. (1979–80); Bk. Awds. Com. (1976). SAA: Lib.–Archs. Rels. (1978–79); Coll. and Univ. Com. (1980). Roosevelt Cnty. (NM) Hist. Socty. **Honors:** Delta Kappa Gamma; Hist. Socty., Contrib. to Cnty. Hist. Awd., 1978. **Pubns.:** "New Mexico Library Association," *Encyc. of Lib. and Info. Sci.* (1977); "A Memory Bank for Roosevelt County," *Grt. llano Estacado SW Heritage* (Spr. 1974); "Fantastic Tale: Science Fiction at Eastern New Mexico University," *Extrapolation* (My. 1973); various reviews, *Amer. Ref. Bks. Anl.* (1972–). **Activities:** 1; 45 **Addr.:** Golden Library, Eastern New Mexico University, Portales, NM 88130.

Walker, Patricia A. (Je. 12, 1946, Cameron, MO) HS Libn., Richmond R-XVI (MO), 1969–; Eng. Tchr., E. Buchanan Schs., 1968–69. **Educ.:** NW MO State Univ., 1964–68, BS (Sec. Educ.); Ctrl. MO State Univ., 1970–73, MSE (LS). **Orgs.:** MO Assn. of Sch. Libns.: Exec. Com. (1974, 1979); Nom. Com. (1981). NW Libns. Assn.: Pres. (1974). Richmond Tchrs. Assn. MO State Tchrs. Assn.: Legis. Com. (1981). **Honors:** Delta Kappa Gamma. **Activities:** 10; 20, 28, 41; 63, 77 **Addr.:** 108 S. College, Richmond, MO 64085.

Walker, Richard Dean (Ap. 17, 1930, Hammond, IN) Prof., Lib. Sch., Univ. of WI, 1964–; Asst. Prof., Instr. Mtrls. Dept., South. IL Univ., 1963–64; Dir. and Resrch. Assoc., Lib. Resrch. Ctr., Grad. Sch. of LS, Univ. of IL, 1961–63; Phys. Libn., Univ. of IL, 1958–61; Geol. Libn., IN Univ., 1955–58. **Educ.:** IN Univ., 1948–55, AB (Chem.), 1955–57, AM (LS); Univ. of IL, 1958–63, PhD (LS). **Orgs.:** ALA: ACRL. ASIS: Chap. Rep. (1975–78); WI Chap. (Pres., 1976–77). SLA: Career Guid. Com. (1976–78). Geosci. Info. Socty.: Pres. (1978); Exec. Bd. (1977–79); various coms. Various other orgs. Amer. Geol. Inst. Governing Bd. AAAS. Brit. LA. Univ. of WI: various coms. **Honors:** Beta Phi Mu. **Pubns.:** Cmplr., *Directory of Geoscience Libraries, U.S. and Canada* 2nd ed. (1974); *Independent Learning Materials in Library Science Instruction* (1968); *The Availability of Library Science and Academic Achievement* (1963); "Geo Ref (Plus Other Geoscience Data Bases)," *Online* (Ap. 1977); jt. auth., "Water Resources Abstracts Database," *Database* (Je. 1980); various other articles. **Activities:** 11; 26, 39, 41; 62, 75, 91 **Addr.:** Library School, University of Wisconsin, Madison, 600 N. Park, Madison, WI 53706.

Walker, Robin Gay (F. 26, 1948, Portland, OR) Head, Prsrvn. and Preps. Dept., 1972–, Cur., Arts of the Bk. Col., 1979–. **Educ.:** Reed Coll., 1965–69, BA (Eng. Lit.); Simmons Coll., 1971–72, MSLS; Wesleyan Univ., 1976–79, MA (Fine Arts, Eng.); Oxford Univ., Exeter Coll. 1977. **Orgs.:** Resrch. Libs. Grp.: Prsrvn. Com. (1975–). ALA: RTSD/Prsrvn. of Lib. Mtrls. Sect. (Ch., 1977–80), Nom. Com. (1980), Exec. Com., Past Ch. (1980), Vice-Ch./Ch.-Elect (1982–83); Reprodct. of Lib. Mtrls. Sect., various coms. Amer. Inst. for Cons. ARL/Ofc. of Mgt. Stds.: Ad Hoc Adv. Com.–Prsrvn. (1980–81). Cncl. on Lib. Resrcs.: Com. on the Prod. of Guidelines for the Longevity of Paper (1979–); ANSC 239 Subcom. S Paper for Lib. Bks. (Ch., 1981–). Amer. Prtg. Hist. Assn. Yale Bibliophiles: Ch. (1975–76, 1977–78, 1979–80). **Honors:** Beta Phi Mu. **Pubns.:** "Preservation Efforts in Larger U.S. Academic Libraries," *Coll. & Resrch. Libs.* (Ja. 1975); "The Quiet Disaster: People and Pests," *Procs. of a Disaster Conf., Stanford Univ.* (Ja. 1981); assoc. ed., *CAN Nsltr.* (1979–). **Activities:** 1; 23, 45; 55, 57 **Addr.:** Preservation & Preparations Dept. & Arts of the Book Collection, Yale University Library, P.O. Box 1603A Yale Station, New Haven, CT 06520.

Walker, Rubye M. (Columbus, GA) Supvsr. of Lib. Media Ctrs., Duval Cnty. Sch. Bd., Jacksonville, FL, 1976–, Sch. Lib. Media Spec., 1961–76. **Educ.:** Albany State Coll., 1956–59, BA (Soclgy., LS); Atlanta Univ., 1969–71, MSLS; FL State Univ., 1974–76, PhD (Prog. Dev. Supvsn. Media). **Orgs.:** ALA. FL LA. FL Assn. for Media in Educ. Assn. for Supvsn. and Curric. Dev. Various other orgs. AAUW: Comms. Com. Mayor's Adv. Cncl. Com. on the Status of Empl. for Women. **Honors:** Phi Delta Kappa; B'NAI B'RITH A.B. WeilLodge 800, Tchr. Student Hum. Awd., 1973; Alpha Kappa Alpha. **Pubns.:** *The Media Supervisor's Responsibility for Staff Development in Improving the Instructional Program* (1976). **Activities:** 10; 17, 32, 46; 50, 63, 66 **Addr.:** Educational Media Center, 31 Warren St., Jacksonville, FL 32206.

Walker, Sue A. (My. 1, 1943, Bloomsburg, PA) Prog. Spec. for Lib. Media Srvs., Sch. Dist. of Lancaster, 1975–; Libn., McCaskey HS, 1973–75; Media Coord., Fairfax Cnty. Schs., 1972–73; Libn., Glasgow Intermediate Sch. (VA), 1970–73. **Educ.:** Millersville State Coll., 1961–64, BS (Lib. Educ.); Syracuse Univ., 1964–67, MSLS. **Orgs.:** PA Sch. Libns. Assn.: Pres. (1980–82). PA Citizens for Better Libs.: Bd. of Dirs. (1979–1981). ALA: AASL, Afflt. Asm. Del. WHCOLIS: Del. (1979). **Honors:** PA Sch. Libns. Assn., Outstan. Prog., 1978. **Activities:** 10; 49-K-12 Supvsr. **Addr.:** 6065 Parkridge Dr., E. Petersburg, PA 17520.

Walker, William Bond (Ap. 15, 1930, Brownsville, TN) Chief Libn., Thomas J. Watson Lib., Metro. Musm. of Art, 1980–; Chief Libn., Lib. of the Natl. Col. of Fine Arts and the Natl. Portrait Gallery, Smithsonian Inst., 1964–80; Chief Libn., Art Ref. Lib., Brooklyn Musm., 1959–64; Catlgr./Ref. Libn., Metro. Musm. of Art, 1957–59. **Educ.:** Bisttram Sch. of Fine Arts, 1948–49; State Univ. of IA, 1949–53, AB (Fine Arts); Rutgers Univ., 1955–58, MSLS. **Orgs.:** ARLIS/NA: Ch. (1975); Chrt. Mem. (1972). ALA: ACRL/Art Sect. (Ch., 1971–72). SLA: Musm. Div. (Ch., 1961–62). Coll. Art Assn. of Amer. **Honors:** Phi Beta Kappa. **Pubns.:** Cmplr., "Sculpture" (annotated bibl.,

PROFESSIONAL ACTIVITIES: Institutions: 1. Acad. lib.; 2. Arch.; 3. Assn.; 4. Fed./Gvt. lib.; 5. Inst. lib.; 6. Mfr./Suppl.; 7. Milit. lib.; 8. Musm.; 9. Pub. lib.; 10. Sch. lib.; 11. Sch. of lib. sci.; 12. Spec. lib.; 13. State lib.; 14. (other). **Functions/Activities:** 15. Acq./Col. dev.; 16. Adult srvs.; 17. Admin.; 18. Apprais.; 19. Archit./Bldgs.; 20. Cat./Class.; 21. Chld. srvs.; 22. Circ.; 23. Cons./Pres.; 24. Consult.; 25. Cont. ed.; 26. Educ. lib. sci.; 27. Ext. srvs.; 28. Fund/Grants; 29. Gvt. pubs.; 30. Indx./Abs.; 31. Instr. lib. use; 32. Media srvs.; 33. Micro.; 34. Netwks./Coop.; 35. Persnl.; 36. PR; 37. Publshg.; 38. Recs. mgt.; 39. Ref. srvs.; 40. Repro.; 41. Resrch.; 42. Review.; 43. Secur.; 44. Serials; 45. Spec. col.; 46. Tech. srvs.; 47. Trustees/Bds.; 48. YA srvs.; 49. (other).

Sect. F) *Arts in America: A Bibliography* (1980); "Art Libraries: International and Interdisciplinary," *Spec. Libs.* (D. 1978); contrib., *Classification, Class N: Fine Arts* (1970). **Activities:** 8; 15, 17; 55 **Addr.:** 2166 Broadway, Apt. 7D, New York, NY 10024.

Wall, Carol (Jl. 5, 1941, New York, NY) Libn./Pub. Srvs., Youngstown State Univ., 1976–; Undergrad. and Circ. Libn., Kent State Univ., 1971–76; Head Ref. Dept., Shippensburg State Coll., 1966–71. **Educ.:** E. Stroudsburg State Coll., 1959–63, BS (Educ.); SUNY, Oneonta, 1964–65, MEd; SUNY, Albany, 1963–68, MLS. **Orgs.:** ALA. Acad. LA of OH. **Pubns.:** *Bibliography of Pennsylvania History: A Supplement* (1976); "Foreign Press in U.S. Libraries," *Lib. Jnl.* (F. 1, 1966); "Foreign Press and Academic Libraries," *Coll. & Resrch. Libs.* (My. 1968); "Updating Pennsylvania History," *PA LA Bltn.* (Ja. 1975). **Activities:** 1; 17, 22, 39 **Addr.:** William F. Maag Library, Youngstown State University, Youngstown, OH 44555.

Wall, Eugene (N. 25, 1922, Leeton, MO) VP and Sr. Sci., Aspen Systs. Corp., 1974–; Sr. Consult., Disclosure, Inc., 1972–74; Pres., Lex-Inc., 1966–72; Sr. Consult., Info. Dynamics Corp., 1965–66. **Educ.:** Univ. of MO, 1940–44, BS (Chem. Engin.). **Orgs.:** ASIS. Amer. Inst. of Chem. Engins. **Honors:** Tau Beta Pi. **Pubns.:** Various articles. **Activities:** 14-Corp.; 17, 30; 75, 91 **Addr.:** Aspen Systems Corporation, 1600 Research Blvd., Rockville, MD 20850.

Wall, Richard L. (Jl. 3, 1943, Sykesville, PA) Libn., Ref. Div., Queens Coll., CUNY, 1975–. **Educ.:** Fairleigh Dickinson Univ., 1962–66, BA (Eng.); Brandeis Univ., 1966–70, MA (Eng.); Simmons Coll., 1974–75, MS (LS). **Orgs.:** LA CUNY: Exec. Cncl. (1977–78, 1979–80); Secy. (1978–79); Inst. Com. (1979–80). Thea. LA. Amer. Socty. for Thea. Resrch. **Pubns.:** "Libraries and Librarians in the 80's," *1980 LA CUNY Institute Bibliography* ERIC; review ed., *Comps. and the Hum.* (1979–). **Activities:** 1; 39, 45; 55 **Addr.:** 301 W. 45th St., Apt. 15K, New York, NY 10036.

Wallace, Burma Morgan (My. 13, 19–, Eva, AL) Dir., Lrng. Resrcs., Jefferson State Jr. Coll., 1965–; Libn., Jefferson Cnty. Bd. of Educ., 1959–65; Libn., Birmingham Bd. of Educ., 1954–57; Libn., Misses Howard's Sch. for Girls, 1953–54. **Educ.:** Univ. of AL, 1965, BS, MA (LS), 1975, PhD (Admin. of Higher Educ.). AL Educ. Assn. **Activities:** 1; 25 **Addr.:** Jefferson State Junior College, Allen Library, 2601 Carson Rd., Birmingham, AL 35215.

Wallace, Harriet Evelyn (D. 10, 1914, New York, NY) Geol. Libn. and Prof. Emerita of Lib. Admin., Univ. of IL, 1979–, Geol. Libn., 1962–79; Geologist, Carl A. Bays and Assoc., 1955–58; Tech. Asst., IL State Nat. Hist. Srvy., 1953–54; Geologist, Corps of Engins., 1948–52; Instr., Geol., Univ. of TN, 1947–48; Asst. Geologist, Allied Chem. Corp., 1941–46; various other positions. **Educ.:** Northwest. Univ., 1936, BS (Geol.); Univ. of CA, Berkeley, 1936–37, (Geol.); Columbia Univ., 1939, MA (Tchg. Nat. Sci.); Univ. of IL, 1962, MS (LS). **Orgs.:** ALA. Geosci. Info. Socty: Secy. (1966); Pres. (1967). AAUW. IL State Geneal. Socty. Natl. Socty. of Daughters of Amer. Revolution. **Honors:** Beta Phi Mu. **Pubns.:** *Union List of Geologic Field Trip Guide Books of North America* (1978); "Basic Geology Collection for a Latin American University Library...," *Revista Géofisica* (Ja. 1976); "Geological Reference Publications," *Jnl. of Geol. Educ.* (1975); "Geological Field Trip Guidebooks, Bibliographic Problems," *Spec. Libs.* (1978); various papers. **Activities:** 1; 17, 26; 71 **Addr.:** 1312 S. Race St., Urbana, IL 61801.

Wallace, Marie G. (Ja. 21, 1929, CA) Law Libn., Kindel and Anderson, 1971–; Acq. Libn., Los Angeles Cnty. Law Lib., 1957–58; Acq. Libn., Univ. of CA, Los Angeles, 1956–57; Acq. Libn., Gen. Lib., Univ. of CA, Berkeley, 1951–56. **Educ.:** Univ. of CA, Berkeley, 1946–50, BS (Anthro.), 1950–51, MLS; AALL, 1976, Cert. **Orgs.:** South. CA Assn. of Law Libs.: Pres. (1973–74). AALL: Pvt. Law Libs. SIS (Ch., 1979–). CA LA. Univ. of W. Los Angeles Law Sch. Adv. Bd. (1979–). Practising Law Inst.: Progs. on Pvt. Law Libs. (Ch., 1977, 1979). Anl. Inst. on CA Law: Ch. (1973). **Pubns.:** Ed., *The Private Law Firm Library PLI Course Handbook* (1977); ed., *The Private Law Library - 1980's and Beyond PLI Handbook* (1979); "Manual Legal Memoranda System," *Legal Econ.* (Ja./F. 1980); "Your Library is Only as Good as Your Librarian," *Manual for Managing a Law office* (1977); wkshp. ch. **Activities:** 1, 12; 15, 24, 25; 75, 77, 78 **Addr.:** Kindel & Anderson Library, 555 S. Flower St., Los Angeles, CA 90071.

Wallace, Mary Gjermo (N. 7, 1948, Madison, WI) Libn., Cambridge Cmnty. Lib., 1979–; Cmnty. Info. Spec., Lexington Pub. Lib., 1978–79; Prog. and Resrch. Asst., Ofc. for Experiential Educ., Univ. of KY, 1975–78; AV and Ref. Libn., N. Ctrl. Coll., 1975. **Educ.:** Mundelein Coll., 1969–71, BA (Psy.); Rosary Coll., 1971–75, MALS; Univ. of KY, 1975–, MSHE (Fam. Std.). **Orgs.:** ALA. WI LA. Natl. Cncl. on Fam. Rel. WI Cncl. on Fam. Rel. Folk Coll. Assn. of Amer. AAUW. **Pubns.:** Contrib., *Family Economic Issues and Public Policy* (1979). **Activities:** 1, 9; 15, 17, 39; 50, 63, 92 **Addr.:** Box 586, Hwy. 12 and 18, Cambridge, WI 53523.

Wallace, Richard Edmund (F. 9, 1941, Schenectady, NY) Mgr., Info. Srvs., Archer Daniels Midland Co., 1971–; Ref. Libn., Case West. Rsv. Univ., 1970–71; Asst. Supvsr., Tech. Srvs., Deere and Co., 1968–70, Engin. Resrch. Libn., 1965–66. **Educ.:** MI State Univ., 1961–63, BS (Math.); Case West. Rsv. Univ., 1963–65, MSLS; IL State Univ., 1975–78, MBA. **Orgs.:** ALA: Oberly Awds. Com. (1977–79). ASIS. SLA: Food and Nutr. Div. (Ch., 1975–76); Publshr. Rels. Com. (1976–). **Honors:** Beta Phi Mu. **Pubns.:** Ed., *Food Science and Technology; A Bibliography of Recommended Materials* (1978); "Personnel Evaluation Bibliography," *Procs.: Personnel Performance Evaluation Institute* (1978). **Activities:** 12; 17, 39, 46; 59, 60, 68 **Addr.:** Research Library, Archer Daniels Midland Co., P.O. Box 1470, Decatur, IL 62525.

Wallach, John S. (Ja. 6, 1939, Steubenville, OH) Dir., Dayton and Montgomery Cnty. Pub. Lib., 1979–; Dir., Greene Cnty. Pub. Lib., 1970–78; Dir., Mercer Cnty. Pub. Lib., 1968–70. **Educ.:** Kent State Univ., 1957–63, BS (Educ.); Univ. of RI, 1966–68, MLS; Univ. of Dayton, 1975–77, MPA. **Orgs.:** ALA: Cnclr. (1976–80). OH LA: Pres. (1980–81). OHIONET: Dir. (1980–82). OHIONET OCLC Users Cncl.: Del. (1980–82). Dayton Musm. of Nat. Hist.: Bd. of Dirs. (1979–). Fam. Srv. Assn. Untd. Way Hlth. Div.: Bd. of Dirs. (1979–). **Activities:** 9; 17, 22, 24; 56, 78 **Addr.:** Dayton and Montgomery County Public Library, 215 E. Third St., Dayton, OH 45402.

Wallbridge, Allan Edward (Jl. 3, 1931, Pembroke, ON) Instr., Tech. Inst., Libn., SK Tech. Inst., 1976–; HQ Libn., Yellow Knife (NT) Lib. Srvs., 1975–76; Branch Libn., Windsor Pub. Lib., 1967–74; Catlgr., Edmonton Pub. Lib., 1965–66; Libn., Mines Branch Lib. (Ottawa), 1957–64. **Educ.:** Univ. of Toronto, 1950–53, BA (Eng.); Univ. of Ottawa, 1957, BLS; Univ. of MI, 1968–71, AMLS; Univ. of Windsor, 1972–76, MA (Eng. Lit.). **Orgs.:** Assn. of SK Gvt. Libs.: Secy. (1979–80). Assn. of Tech.-–Vocational Educs. of SK: PR–Info. (1977–79). Can. LA. SK Tech. Staff Club: Exec. Mem. (1980–81). Moose Jaw Lions Club. SK Writers Gld. Univ. of Toronto Alum. Assn. Univ. of MI Alum. Assn. **Pubns.:** "Three Poems Based on Themes from *Under the Volcano*," *North. Anthology* (Sum. 1975); ed. bd., *Jnl. of Assn. of Can. Cmnty. Colls.* (Spr.–Sum. 1978); **Activities:** 9, 13; 17, 20, 39; 59, 91, 95-Indus. arts. **Addr.:** Saskatchewan Technical Institute, P.O. Box 1420, Sask. St. & 6th Ave. N.W., Moose Jaw, SK S6H 4R4 Canada.

Walle, Dennis Francis (Ja. 10, 1938, Chicago, IL) Archvst. and Mss. Cur., Univ. of AK, 1979–; State Archvst. and Dir. of Archs. Resrc. Ctr., State of SD, 1977–79; Libn. and Mss. Cur., IL Hist. Srvy., Lib., Univ. of IL, 1972–77. **Educ.:** DePaul Univ., 1955–60, BA (Pol. Sci.), 1962–68, MA (Hist.); Univ. of IL, 1969–77, (Hist.); Amer. Univ./USNARS, 1976, Cert. (Arch. Admin.). **Orgs.:** SAA. Midwest Archs. Conf. AK LA. Natl. Rifle Assn. **Pubns.:** Jt. auth., *Guide to the Heinrich A. Rattermann Collection of German-American Manuscripts* (1979); *Guide to South Dakota Archives Resource Center* (1979); "Genealogical Research Materials in the Illinois Historical Survey Library," *IL State Geneal. Socty. Qtly.* (1977); "Institutional Spotlight: The Illinois Historical Survey Library," *Nsltr. of the Midwest Archs. Conf.* (Ap. 1975); "William Dudley," *Dictionary of Canadian Biography* (1974); various articles. **Activities:** 1, 2; 15, 17, 37; 62, 92 **Addr.:** Archives and Manuscripts Department, Library University of Alaska, Anchorage, 3211 Providence Dr., Anchorage, AK 99504.

Waller, Elaine Louise (Ag. 29, 1918, New Cristobal, Colon, CZ) Msc. Mtrls. Libn., Msc. Mtrls. Ctr., Msc. Dept., Andrews Univ., 1974–, Msc. Catlgr., James White Lib., 1970–74, Srch./Catlgr., 1960–70. **Educ.:** Pac. Un. Coll., 1937–42, BA (Eng.); Univ. of IL, 1965–70, MSLS. **Orgs.:** Msc. LA. Midwest Arch. Conf. Msc. (OH Coll. Lib. Ctr. Users Grp.) Intl. Assn. of Msc. Libs.: U.S. Branch (1979–). **Honors:** Beta Phi Mu, 1971. **Activities:** 45; 55 **Addr.:** Music Materials Center, Music Department, Andrews University, University Station, Berrien Springs, MI 49104.

Waller, Salvador B. (S. 14, 1930, Salisbury, MD) Dir., Parklawn Hlth. Lib., U.S. Pub. Hlth. Srv., 1981–; Deputy Chief, U.S. Natl. Insts. of Hlth. Lib., 1979–81; Deputy Chief, Parklawn Hlth. Lib., 1970–79; Chief Libn., Med. Lib., Dept. of Army, 1966–70; Chief Libn., Moran Lib., DC Gen. Hosp., 1965–66; Catlgr., Lib., Smithsonian Inst., 1962–64; Ref. Libn., Ofc. of Tech. Srvs., Dept. of Cmrce., 1961–62; Catlgr., Natl. Lib. of Med., 1958–61. **Educ.:** Howard Univ., 1949–53, BA (Fr.); Cath. Univ., 1957–58, MSLS; various crs., wkshps. **Orgs.:** Med. LA: Bylaws Com. (Ch., 1973–74); Mid Atl. Reg. Grp., Bylaws Com. (Ch., 1975–76, 1977–78). Reg. Med. Lib. Prog.: Secy.; Exec. Bd. U.S. Ofc. of Persnl. Mgt.: Com. for Dev. of Performance Stans. for Fed. Libs. (1980–81). NAACP. **Pubns.:** *MLA CE Syllabus - 33: Literature of Health Care Administration* (1978); "Thoughts on Cataloging and Classification in a Small Medical Library," *Med. LA Bltn.* (Ja. 1970); "Thoughts on Libraries, Managers and People," *Spec. Libs.* (S. 1975). **Activities:** 4, 12; 17, 20, 39; 58, 80, 92 **Addr.:** 9475 Maera Ct., Columbia, MD 21045.

Waller, Theodore (Ap. 25, 1916, Oakland, CA) Exec. Dir., Dem. Senatorial Campaign Com., 1981–; Exec. VP, Grolier, Inc., 1977–81; VP, Franklin Watts, 1954–; Ed. VP, New Amer. Lib. World Lit., 1953–54; Asst. to Pres., Managing Dir., Amer. Bk. Publshrs. Cncl., 1950–53; Various positions in gvt. srv., 1938–49. **Educ.:** Univ. of Chicago, 1933–37. **Orgs.:** Natl. Adv. Com. on Libs.: Mem. (1966–). ALA: Intl. Rel. Com. (1956–62, 1976–). Univ. of Pittsburgh Grad. Sch. of Lib. and Info. Sci.: Bd. of Visitors. Natl. Bk. Wk.: Exec. Com. Amer. Bk. Publshrs. Cncl.: Dir. UNESCO: Intl. Bk. Com. (Ch.). Hampshire Coll.: Natl. Adv. Com. (Ch.). Intl. Bk. Yr.: US Co-Ch. **Activities:** 6; 37 **Addr.:** Democratic Senatorial Campaign Committee 400 North Capitol Street NW Washington DC 20001.

Wallis, Carlton Lamar Sr. (O. 15, 1915, Blue Springs, MS) Lib. Consult., 1980–; Dir. of Libs., Memphis/Shelby Cnty. Pub. Lib. and Info. Ctr., 1958–80; City Libn., Richmond Pub. Lib., 1955–58; Head Libn., Rosenberg Lib., 1947–55. **Educ.:** MS Coll., 1932–36, BA (Eng.); Tulane Univ., 1945–46, MA (Eng.); Univ. of Chicago, 1946–47, BLS; Southwest. at Memphis, 1980, LHD. **Orgs.:** ALA: LAMA/Lib. Org. and Mgt. Sect. (Ch., 1971–72); PLA, Bd. of Dirs. (1973–76). TN LA: Pres. (1969–70). SELA: Pub. Lib. Sect. (Ch., 1960–62). Belhaven Coll.: Trustee (1978–). Egyptians (Lit. Club). Grt. Bks. Fndn.: Bd. of Dirs. (1960–68). **Honors:** TN LA, Disting. Srv. Awd., 1979; Memphis Rotary Club, Vocational Srv. Awd., 1980. **Pubns.:** *Libraries in the Golden Triangle* (1966); "Memphis and Shelby County Public Library and Info Center," *Encyc. of Lib. and Info. Sci.* (197–); "Confrontation in Memphis," *Lib. Jnl.* (N. 15, 1969); "Tennessee Reference Centers," *Southeast. Libn.* (Win. 1966); various articles, *The Egyptian Yrbk.* (1961–80). **Activities:** 9; 17, 19, 24; 50, 74, 85 **Addr.:** 365 Kenilworth, Memphis, TN 38112.

Walls, Edwina (Ja. 7, 1941, Little Rock, AR) Hist. of Med. Libn./Archvst., Univ. of AR for Med. Scis., 1978–, Chief, Tech. Srvs. Dept., 1974–78, 1970–72, Asst. Ref. Libn., 1972–74, 1966–69; Lib. Asst., Serials Dept., LA State Univ. Lib., 1963–65. **Educ.:** Ouachita Bapt. Coll., 1959–62, BSE, magna cum laude (Educ.); Case West. Rsv. Univ. Archs. Wkshp., 1979. **Orgs.:** Med. LA: Oral Hist. Com. (1979–81); S. Ctrl. Reg. Grp., Bylaws Com. (Ch., 1978–80). AR LA: Treas. (1973–74); Spec. Libs. Div. (Ch., 1976). AR Archvsts. and Recs. Mgrs.: Pres. (1979–80). Pulaski Cnty. Hist. Socty. Ozark Socty. **Pubns.:** "University of Arkansas for Medical Sciences Library, 1879-1979," *AR Libs.* (Mr. 1979); "Founders of the Arkansas Industrial University, Medical Department," *Pulaski Cnty. Hist. Review* (Fall 1979). **Activities:** 2, 12; 45; 80 **Addr.:** 910 N. Martin, Little Rock, AR 72205.

Walls, Esther Jean (My. 1, 1926, Mason City, IA) Assoc. Dir. of Libs., SUNY, Stony Brook, 1974–; Educ. Libn., Tchrs. Ctrl. Lab., Hunter Coll., 1973–74; Dir., U.S. Secretariat–Intl. Bk. Yr. 1972, Natl. Bk. Com., 1971–73; Prog. Ofcr./Asst. Dir. for Africa, Franklin Bk. Progs., 1965–71; various positions, NY Pub. Lib., 1956–65. **Educ.:** State Univ. of IA, 1946–48, BA (Rom. Langs.); Columbia Univ., 1949–50, MLS. **Orgs.:** ALA: Intl. Rel. Com., Past Ch.; IRRT. SUNY LA. Ctr. for the Bk., Lib. of Congs.: Natl. Adv. Bd. UNESCO: Comsn. for ALA (1973–79). UNICEF, U.S. Com.: VP, Bd. (1970–80). **Honors:** Phi Beta Kappa; Phi Sigma Iota. **Pubns.:** *International Book Year 1972: A Handbook for U.S. Participation* (1971); *African Encounter* (1963); *Some Observations on Nigerian Libraries* (1964); "International Book Year in the U.S.A.," *UNESCO Bltn. for Libs.* (My.–Je. 1972); "Children's Books and Reading in Developing Countries," *Top of the News* (Ja. 1973). **Activities:** 1; 17, 35, 36; 54, 66, 89 **Addr.:** 6 Dogwood Dr. - Box 443, Stony Brook, NY 11790.

Walsdorf, John J. (Je. 19, 1941, Sheboygan, WI) Sr. Libs. Srv. Adv., B.H. Blackwell, Ltd., 1967–; Sr. Lending Libn., Oxford City Lib., Eng., 1966–67; Gvt. Docum. and Ref. Libn., Milwaukee Pub. Lib., 1964–66. **Educ.:** WI State Univ., Oshkosh, 1959–63, BS (LS, Eng.); Univ. of WI, Madison, 1963–64, MLS. **Orgs.:** ALA. William Morris Socty. Bk. Club of CA. Pvt. LA. **Honors:** Natl. Lib. Week Essay Competition, UK, Sec. Prize, 1967. **Pubns.:** Ed., *Printers on Morris* (1981); *A Collector's Choice: William Morris in Private Press and Limited Editions* (1980); ed., *Men of Printing: Anglo-American Profiles* (1976); "The Antiquarian Book Trade in Great Britain," *AB Bookman's Yrbk.* (1969). **Activities:** 1, 12; 15, 45; 57, 95-Pvt. Press Prtg. **Addr.:** 18820 N.W. Astoria Dr., Portland, OR 97229.

Walsh, Bertrand M. (Mr. 21, 1915, Montreal, PQ) Libn., Jackson Lab. Lib., E.I. DuPont de Nemours and Co., 1951–; Ref. Asst., Sci.–Tech. Div., NY Pub. Lib., 1947–50; Jr. Chem., Can. Copper Refiners, Ltd., 1938–42. **Educ.:** McGill Univ., 1933–37, BA (Gen.); Sir George Williams Univ., 1938–42, B Sc (Gen. Sci.); McGill Univ., 1946–47, BLS; Columbia Univ., 1947–51, MS (LS). **Orgs.:** SLA. Amer. Chem. Socty. Du Pont Country Club. **Activities:** 12; 15, 20, 39; 60, 64, 91 **Addr.:** R.D. 1, Chadds Ford, PA 19317.

Walsh, Sr. M. Naomi (D. 2, 1909, Lackawanna, NY) Libn., Greensburg Ctrl. Cath. HS, 1971–; Supvsr. of Libs. for Srs. of Charity in Dio. of Greensburg–Baltimore, 1970–71; Asst. Libn., Seton Hill Coll., 1968–70; Libn., Sacred Heart HS (Pittsburgh), 1960–68. **Educ.:** Seton Hill Coll., 1928–32, BA (Hist.); Carnegie–Tech, 1935–36, BLS. **Orgs.:** PA Sch. LA. Westmoreland Assn. of Sch. Libns. Cath. LA: Exec. Bd. (1962–69); HS Sect., Secy.–Treas. (1955–63), Secy. (1963–65); West. PA Unit, HS Sect. (Ch., 1955–57); Cath. Bk. Week (Ch., 1955–56); Rep. in

Special Subjects/Services: 50. Adult educ.; 51. Advert./Mktg.; 52. Aerosp.; 53. Agric.; 54. Area std.; 55. Arts/Hum.; 56. Autom.; 57. Bibl./Prtg.; 58. Bio. sci.; 59. Bus./Fin.; 60. Chem.; 61. Copyrt.; 62. Documtn.; 63. Educ.; 64. Engin.; 65. Env.; 66. Eth. grps.; 67. Film; 68. Food/Nutr.; 69. Geneal.; 70. Geo.; 71. Geol.; 72. Handcpd.; 73. Hist.; 74. Int. frdm.; 75. Info. sci.; 76. Insr.; 77. Law; 78. Legis.; 79. Math./Comp. sci.; 80. Med.; 81. Metals; 82. Nat. resrcs.; 83. Newsp.; 84. Nuc. sci.; 85. Oral hist.; 86. Petr./Energy; 87. Pharm.; 88. Phys./Astr./Math.; 89. Readg.; 90. Relig.; 91. Sci./Tech.; 92. Soc. sci.; 93. Telecom.; 94. Transp.; 95. (other).

Dio. of Greensburg (1971–). **Honors:** Cath. LA, Silver Cup for Srv., 1969. **Pubns.:** Cmplr., *Basic Reference Books For High School Libraries* (1959, 1963); ed., *Cath. LA, HS Sect. Nsltr.* (1955–57). **Activities:** 1, 10; 15, 20, 32; 75, 89, 95-Trng. lib. aides. **Addr.:** Greensburg Central Catholic High School, 901 Armory Dr., Greensburg, PA 15601.

Walsh, Patricia Margaret (Je. 5, 1947, New York, NY) Managing Ed., *Visual Resrcs.*, 1980–; Managing Ed., *Micro. Review, Inc.*, 1978–80; Serials/Ref. Libn., Manhattan Coll., 1972–78; Serials/Ref. Libn., St. John's Univ., 1970–72. **Educ.:** NY Univ., 1965–69, BA (Classical Std.); Rutgers Univ., 1969–70, MLS; New Sch. for Soc. Resrch., 1971–74, MA, hons. (Phil., Arts). **Orgs.:** ALA. SLA. ARLIS/NA. Socty. of Archit. Histns. Metro. Musm. of Art. Amer. Assn. of Musms. Archlg. Assn. of Amer. Natl. Trust for Hist. Prsrvn. Various other orgs. **Pubns.:** *Serials Management and Microforms: A Reader* (1979); *Microforms and the Visual Arts* (1979); ed., *Micro. Equip. Review* (1978–79); ed., *Lib. Comp. Equip. Review* (1979); ed., *Micropublshrs.' Trade List Anl.* (1979). **Activities:** 1, 14-Publshg.; 33, 37, 44; 55, 57, 62 **Addr.:** P.O. Box 327, Redding Ridge, CT 06876.

Walsh, Robert Raymond (Ag. 14, 1943, Chicago, IL) Asst. to the Chief Libn., Paul Klapper Lib., Queens Coll., CUNY, 1981–; Lib. Plng. Consult., 1970–; Asst. Univ. Libn. for Bldg. Plng., Harvard Univ. Lib., 1971–76; Asst. VP, New Eng. Deposit Lib., 1972–76; Admin. Asst., Harvard Univ. Lib., 1967–71. **Educ.:** Harvard Univ., 1961–65, BA (Archit. Sci.); Univ. of Chicago, 1965–67 (LS). **Orgs.:** ALA: Lib. Admin. Div., Coll. and Univ. Lib. Bldgs. Com.; ACRL. **Pubns.:** "The New England Deposit Library," *Encyc. of Lib. and Info. Scis.* (1976); "Branch Library Planning in Universities," *Lib. Trends* (O. 1969); ed., *Harvard Libn., HUL Notes* (1971–74). **Activities:** 1; 17, 19, 24; 55 **Addr.:** 35-06 88th St., Suite 4D, Jackson Heights, NY 11372.

Walshak, Lynn Grice (Mr. 11, 1931, Taft, TX) Gvt. Docum. Libn., GA South. Coll., 1976–, Cat. Libn., 1971–76. **Educ.:** Southwest TX State Coll., 1966–68, BS (Hist., Bio.); N. TX State Univ., 1968–70, MLS (Lib. Srv., Bio.); Med. LA, 1977, Cert. **Orgs.:** GA LA: Pubcty. Com. (1980–81). SE LA. ALA. GA Chap. ACRL. AAUP. Archibald Bulloch Hist. Socty. **Honors:** Kappa Delta Phi, 1968; Alpha Chi, 1968. **Activities:** 1; 20, 29, 39 **Addr.:** 114 Wilton Dr., Statesboro, GA 30458.

Walsh-Brown, Jane S. (Ja. 18, 1947, Stamford, CT) Asst. Dir., Westchester Pub. Lib., 1975–; Asst. Prof., Lib. Dept., Baruch Coll., CUNY, 1974–75; Ed. Libn., Amer. Cncl. of Voluntary Agencies for Frgn. Srv., 1972–74. **Educ.:** Wells Coll., 1965–69, BA (Eng. Lit.); Northwest. Univ., 1969–70, MA (Eng. Lit.); Columbia Univ., 1972–73, MSLS (Lib. Srv.); State of IN, 1977, Cert. (Hold Libn. II). **Orgs.:** ALA. IN LA: Cmnty. Srvs. Div. (Vice-Ch., 1980). Coord. Com. for IN Folklore Adult Lrng. Ctr.: Bd. (1980). Hist. Prsrvn. of Porter Cnty.: Bd. (1980). Women's Netwk. of Northwest IN. Duneland Cncl. for Youth: Bd. (1980). **Honors:** IN LA, IN Lib. Trustee Assn., Libn. of the Yr., 1979. **Pubns.:** *Directory of Volunteer Opportunities in Porter County* (1978); *Directory of Medical Programs Abroad* (1973). **Activities:** 9; 16, 17, 36; 50, 66, 67 **Addr.:** Westchester Public Library, 200 W. Indiana Ave., Chesterton, IN 46304.

Walter, Gary Dean (N. 1, 1939, Fergus Falls, MN) Dir., Lrng. Resrcs. Ctr., Defense Lang. Inst., Presidio of Monterey (CA), 1976–; Dir., Tunghai Univ. Lib. (Taichung, Taiwan), 1972–75; Asst. Staff Libn., Eighth U.S. Army (Korea), 1968–72; Lectr., Dept. of LS, Yonsei Univ. (Korea), 1967–68. **Educ.:** Univ. of WA, 1962–64, BA (Chin.), 1964–67, MLS, MA (Korean). **Orgs.:** ALA. Korean LA. LA of China (Taiwan). **Honors:** LA of China (Taiwan), Outstan. Srv., 1974. **Pubns.:** "The Korean Mission to the US, 1883," *Jnl. of Korean Std.* (1968). **Activities:** 1; 17; 54, 74 **Addr.:** 2859 Ransford Ave., Pacific Grove, CA 93950.

Walter, Georgia Ann (My. 30, 1924, Des Moines, IA) Dir., Lib., Kirksville Coll. of Osteopathic Med., 1969–; Tchr., Kirksville Pub. Schs., 1963–69; Trainer, Camp Dir., Becky Thatcher Girl Scout Cncl., 1958–67. **Educ.:** NE MO State Univ., 1942–48, BSEd (Home Econ.), 1968–69, Cert. (LS); Med. LA, 1969–80 (Med. Libnshp.). **Orgs.:** Med. LA. Midcont. Reg. Med. Lib. Grp. MO LA: Lib. Dev. Com. NE MO Lib. Netwk.: Bd. of Dirs. Amer. Osteopathic Assn.: Com. on Colls. Accred. Team. Delta Zeta: Alum. Grp., Past Pres. MO WHCOLIS: Plng. Com. (Del., 1979). **Honors:** Med. LA, Murray Gottlieb Prize, 1979. **Pubns.:** *Osteopathic Medicine: Past and Present* (1981); "Osteopathic Roots in Kirksville," *Kirksville Daily Express* (Je. 4, 1980). **Activities:** 1, 12; 15, 17, 20; 80 **Addr.:** Still Memorial Library, Kirksville College of Osteopathic Medicine, Kirksville, MO 63501.

Walter, Kenneth G. (Mr. 14, 1932, Emory Univ., GA) Dir. of Libs., GA South. Coll., 1975–; Asst. Dir. of Libs. for Tech. Srvs., Univ. of SC, 1968–75; Head Cat. Libn., OH Univ., 1965–68, Asst. Cat. Libn., 1963–65. **Educ.:** Emory Univ., Univ. of GA, 1950–54, AB (Geol.), 1954–55, MS (Geol.); Univ. of NC, 1958–61, 1962–63, MSLS; Univ. Wien (Austria), 1961–62. **Orgs.:** ALA: Econ. Status, Welfare and Fringe Benefits Com. (1980–); Cncl. of Reg. Grps. (1972–76). SELA: Southeast. Reg. Grp. of Tech. Srvs. Libns., Ch. (1974–76), Vice Ch. (1972–74); South. Bk. Awds. Com. (1976–78). GA LA: Autom. Com. (Ch., 1977); Lib. Dev. Com. (1980–). Ctrl. GA Assoc. Libs. Cnsrtm.: Pres. (1980–). GA Acad. of Sci. Delta Tau Delta Fraternity: Chap. Adv. GA South. Coll. E. GA Lib. Triangle Cnsrtm.: Pres. (1977–). Univ. Syst. of GA Regents' Acad. Com. on Libs.: Various coms. **Honors:** Phi Delta Kappa; Beta Phi Mu; Fulbright to Universität Wien, 1961–62; Sigma Gamma Epsilon. **Pubns.:** *Cataloging Procedures for the University of South Carolina Libraries: A New Formulation* (1969); ed., *Library Guide of Ohio University* (1964); "Library Development for Areal Studies: Cameroons," *Nlstr. of the South. Assn. of Africanists* (My. 1973); "A Comparison of Stream Sediments from a Metamorphic Area with Those from an Igneous Source," *Bltn. of the GA Acad. of Sci.* (Ja. 1956); Various sps. **Activities:** 1; 17, 31, 46; 56 **Addr.:** Georgia Southern College Library, Landrum Box 8074, Statesboro, GA 30460.

Walter, Otto Wallace (Ja. 29, 1922, Norman, OK) Supvsr. of Lib. Srvs., MO Div. of Corrections Libs., 1970–; Asst. Libn., Circ., West. WY Cmnty. Coll., 1969–70; Libn., Riverton Sr. HS, 1968–69; Roving Libn. and Pers. Libn., OK Cnty. Libs., 1966–67; Asst. Libn., Del City Pub. Lib., 1964–66; Docums. Libn., OK State Lib., 1960–63; Branch Libn., Rider Coll., 1959–60; Rsv. Bk. Libn., Drew Univ., 1958–59; various other positions. **Educ.:** Washington Univ., 1948–50, AB (Soclgy., Anthro.); Iliff Sch. of Theo., 1950–51; George Peabody Coll. for Tchrs., 1953–54, MALS; 1970–79, various cert. from insts. or sems. on corrections progs. **Orgs.:** MO LA. MO State Tchrs. Assn. Correct. Tchrs. Assn.: Secy. (1979–80). MO Correct. Assn. **Honors:** Sigma Phi Epsilon, Jefftown Jaycees (MO State Penitentiary), Pres. Awd. of Hon., 1976. **Pubns.:** "A New Base for Corrections," *Jnl. of Inst. Educ. Assn.* (Ja. 1976); "The Library, a Catalytic Force for Change in Corrections," *Jnl. of IEA* (My. 1979); "Function of Criminal Justice," *Jnl. of IEA* (My. 1979); *The State of the Art of Correctional Librarianship Within the State of Missouri* (1978); *Basic Paralegal Program for the Law Research Center at the Missouri State Penitentiary* (1980); various mono. on MO libs. **Activities:** 5, 12; 16, 17, 20; 63, 77, 89 **Addr.:** Missouri Division of Corrections Libraries, 911 Missouri Blvd., Jefferson City, MO 65101.

Walters, Clarence R. (Je. 11, 1932, Detroit, MI) State Libn., CT State Lib., 1980–; Cnty. Libn., Contra Costa Cnty., CA, 1972–80; Asst. Cnty. Libn., Wayne Cnty. Fed. Library Syst., 1967–72; Lib. Bldg. Consult., MI State Lib., 1964–67; Libn., Detroit Pub. Lib., 1960–64. **Educ.:** Wayne Univ., 1950–54, BA (Hist.); Univ. of MI, 1957–60, MA (LS); Wayne State Univ., 1970, Cert. (Sem. in Pub. Admin.); CA State Coll., Hayward, 1977, Pub. Admin. Cert. **Orgs.:** ALA: Interlib. Coop. Com. (1975–76); Pub. Lib. Div. (Ch., 1969). CA LA: Cncl. (1976); Legis. Com. (Ch. 1973, 1977–78). MI LA: VP (1970); Legis. Com. (1969–72). CA Lib. Athrty. for Systs. and Srvs.: Adv. Cncl. (1976–78); Congs. of Mems. (VP, 1979). Various other orgs. Rotary. Concord Century Club. Contra Costa Cnty. Citizen Task Frc. on Cvl. Srv. Reform (1979). MI Socty. of Plng. Officials. **Pubns.:** Jt. auth., *A Logical Plan for Library Cooperation in Franklin County, Ohio* (1968). **Addr.:** Connecticut State Library, 231 Capitol Ave., Hartford, CT 06115.

Walters, Edward M. (Mr. 22, 1944, Rome, GA) Dir. of Libs., E. TN State Univ., 1977–; Univ. Archvst. and Head, Spec. Cols., Univ. of MS, 1975–77; Asst. Prof. of Hist., OK State Univ., 1972–75; Asst. Prof. of Hist., AL State Univ., 1970–72. **Educ.:** Baylor Univ., 1964–66, BA (Hist.); Univ. of GA, 1967–68, MA (Hist.), 1969–70, PhD (Hist.); Univ. of Chicago, 1974–75, MA (LS). **Orgs.:** ALA: Bhvl. Scis. Sect. (1979–); Bibl. Instr. Sect. (1979–). **Honors:** Cncl. on Lib. Resrcs., Post-Doct. Fellow, 1974. **Activities:** 1, 2; 15, 17, 45; 57, 91 **Addr.:** East Tennessee State University, P.O. Box 24331, Johnson City, TN 37601.

Walters, Gwen E. (N. 13, 1932, OH) Lib. Mgr., Univ. Cmnty. Hosp., 1974–; Lib. Trainee, Tampa Vets. Admin. Hosp., 1974; Asst. Libn., Arapahoe Reg. Lib., 1971. **Educ.:** Heidelberg Coll., 1951–55, BA (Fr.); Univ. of S. FL, 1972–74, MLS. **Orgs.:** Med. LA. SLA. FL Med. Libns. Assn.: Pres. (1980–81); VP (1979). Tampa Bay Med. Lib. Netwk.: Secy. (1975–77); Ch. (1978–79). **Honors:** Phi Kappa Phi; Beta Phi Mu. **Activities:** 12; 15, 17, 39; 80 **Addr.:** 310 Blount Rd., Lutz, FL 33549.

Walters, Mary Dawson (O. 6, 1923, Mitchell Cnty., GA) Col. Dev. Ofcr., CA State Univ., 1974–; Head, Acq. Dept. and Assoc. Prof. of Lib. Admin., OH State Univ., 1971–74, Head, Prcs. Div. and Asst. Prof., 1961–71; Dir. of Lib., Albany State Coll. (GA), 1957–61; Visit. Prof., Sch. of LS, Atlanta Univ., Sum. 1964. **Educ.:** Savannah State Coll., 1949, BSHE; Atlanta Univ., 1957, MSLS; OH State Hist. Socty., 1963, Cert. (Oral Hist.); Miami Univ. (OH), 1973, Cert. (Lib. Exec. Dev.). **Orgs.:** ALA: ACRL, Mem. Com. (1974–). CA LA: State Univ. and Colls. Chap. (Secy./Treas., 1974–75). **Honors:** OH State Univ. Libs., Dir's. Cit. of Merit, 1963. **Pubns.:** Ed., *Professional Development and Continuing Education in Librarianship* (1978); *Afro Americana, a Bibliography* (1969); *A Catalog of the Exhibition of Selected Private Presses in the U.S.* (1965). **Activities:** 1; 15, 17, 46; 57, 66, 85 **Addr.:** 1659 W. 81st St., Los Angeles, CA 90047.

Walton, Clyde C. (Mr. 8, 1925, Chicago, IL) Dir. of Libs., Univ. of CO, 1977–; Dir. of Libs., North. IL Univ., 1967–77; Exec. Dir. and IL State Histn., IL State Hist. Socty. and Lib., 1956–67; Head, Ref. Dept., Univ. of IA, 1955–56, Cur. of Rare Bks. and Head, Spec. Cols., 1952–55. **Educ.:** Cornell Coll., 1946–48, BA (Eng.); Univ. of Chicago, 1949–50, MA (LS). **Orgs.:** ALA/SAA Jt. Com. (1974–76, 1979–). ALA: ACRL, Mss. Com. (Ch., 1971–76). Abraham Lincoln Assn.: Secy. (1963–67); Dir. (1967–). **Honors:** IL Assn. of Coll. and Resrch. Libs., Cert. of Apprec., 1977; IL LA, Libn. of Yr., 1969. **Pubns.:** *An Illinois Reader* (1970); ed., *Private Smith's Journal* (1963); fndr., ed., *Cvl. War Hist.* (1955); ed., *Jnl. of the IL State Hist. Socty.* (1957–67); various articles, reviews. **Activities:** 1, 12; 15, 18, 45; 55, 57, 78 **Addr.:** Norlin Library, N210C, University of Colorado, Campus Box 184, Boulder, CO 80309.

Walton, Laurence R. (Mr. 27, 1939, Coffeyville, KS) Mgr., Corporate Info. Ctr., Pet Incorporated, 1973–, Tech. Libn., Pet Incorporated Resrch. and Dev. Ctr., 1965–73. **Educ.:** OK State Univ., 1957–65, BA (Chem.); WA Univ., St. Louis, 1968–72, BS (LS). **Orgs.:** SLA: Conf. Prog. Com. (Ch., 1980); Food Libn. Div. (Ch., 1975). ASIS. Inst. of Food Technologists. Amer. Assn. of Cereal Chems. Amer. Socty. for Microbiologists. **Pubns.:** Ed., *Food Publication Roundup, a Bibliographic Guide* (1976–). **Activities:** 12; 17, 39, 46; 51, 59, 68 **Addr.:** Corporate Information Center, P.O. Box 392, St. Louis, MO 63166.

Walton, Robert A. (My. 20, 1953, Houston, TX) Autom. Consult., Lib. Dev. Div., TX State Lib. Arch. Comsn., 1981–, Systs. Anal., Sr., 1979–81, Dir., TX State Pubns. Clearhse., 1977–79, Assoc. Dir., 1976–77; Assoc. Dir., TX Prog. of Educ. Resrcs. on Asia, Univ. of TX, Austin, 1974–76. **Educ.:** Univ. of TX Austin, 1971–75, BS (Educ.), 1977–80, MLIS. **Orgs.:** ASIS: Bd.; TX Chap., *Nsltr.* Ed. (1979–). ALA: State and Local Docums. *Documents to the People* Assoc. Ed.; GODORT (1979–80). TX LA. Assn. for Systs. Mgt. Data Prcs. Mgt. Assn.: TX Chap. Assn. for Comp. Mach. **Pubns.:** *Computer Network Security* (1980); jt. auth., *Texas State Documents Depository Survey: Findings and Results, 1978* (1978); *Texas State Documents: Development of a Program* (1977); *Guide to Texas Documents Reference* (1978); ed., *Pub. Docums. Highlights for TX* (1978–80); reviews. **Activities:** 13, 14-DP consult. firm; 29, 49-Lib. autom.; 56, 62, 93 **Addr.:** Library Development Division, Texas State Library & Archives Commission, P. O. Box 12927, Capitol Station, Austin, TX 78711.

Walton, Terence Michael (My. 28, 1938, Norwalk, CT) Assoc. Dean for Tech. Srvs. and Autom., Old Dominion Univ. Lib., 1978–; Adj. Instr. LS, Cath. Univ. of Amer., 1980–; Head of Acq., Univ. of Petr. and Minerals (Dhahran, Saudi Arabia), 1975–77; Head of Acq., Hunter College/CUNY, 1972–75, Soc. Work Libn., 1970–72, Sr. Ref. Libn., Lib. of Performing Arts, NY Pub. Lib., 1969–70; Adult Lib. Srvs. Coord., Phoenix Coll., 1968–69; Asst. Dir., Adult Educ. Div., AZ Dept. of Pub. Instr., 1964–67. **Educ.:** AZ State Univ., 1967, BA (Eng.); Univ. of HI, 1967–68, MLS; Coll. of Libnshp. (Wales), 1977, Cert. (LS); various grad. crs. **Orgs.:** ALA: LITA; RTSD; ACRL. VA LA: Lib. Dev. Com. (1978–). VA State Cncl. of Higher Educ.: VULS Task Frc. (1978–80). Tidewater Lib. Cnsrtm. State of VA (MASD): Autom. Lib. Systs. Eval. Com. (Co-Ch., 1980–). **Pubns.:** *Survey of Adult Basic Education Programs in Arizona, 1965-1967* (1967); "The Function of the Library in a School of Social Work," *Jnl. of Educ. for Soc. Work* (Win. 1974); "Automated Acquisitions," *LA CUNY Jnl.* (Spr. 1975); "Retrospective Conversion Project at Old Dominion University," *Jnl. of Lib. Autom.* (S. 1979). **Activities:** 1, 11; 17, 34, 46; 56, 75, 93 **Addr.:** 680 Masefield Cir., Virginia Beach, VA 23452.

Wampler, Dorris M. (S. 13, 1927, Eden, NC) Media Spec., John W. Wayland Intermediate Sch., 1966–; Instr., Bridgewater Coll., 1970–; Lectr., James Madison Coll., 1973–74; Libn., Dayton-Mt. Clinton Elem. Sch., 1965–66; Libn., Buffalo Gap HS, 1962–65; Tchr., Linville-Edom Elem., 1961–62. **Educ.:** Bridgewater Coll., 1944–47, BA (Chem., Bus. Educ.); James Madison Coll., 1958–60, Lib. Cert.; George Peabody Coll. for Tchrs., 1968–70, MLS; Univ. of Copenhagen, 1974. **Orgs.:** Rockingham Cnty. Sch. Libns.: Pres. (1966); Handbk. Com. (Ch., 1974). VA Educ. Assn.: Dist. 5 Libns.: Pres. (1973–75); Pres.-Elect (1981–); Reg. Spr. Conf. Plng. Com. (1979, 1981). ALA: AASL. Natl. Educ. Assn. VA Educ. Assn. Rockingham Cnty. Educ. Assn. **Honors:** Beta Phi Mu; Delta Kappa Gamma. **Activities:** 10; 15, 32, 48 **Addr.:** Box 25, Bridgewater College, Bridgewater, VA 22812.

Wamsley, Gail Noreen (O. 22, 1948, Windsor, ON) AV Srvs. Coord., Georgian Bay Reg. Lib. Syst., 1976–; Secy./Resrch. Asst., Info., Media and Lib. Planners, 1975–76; Branch Supvsr., Walkerton Branch Lib., 1971–74. **Educ.:** Univ. of Guelph, 1967–70, BA (Eng.); Univ. of Toronto, 1974–76, MLS. **Orgs.:** ON LA: Gvt. Pubns. Com. (Ch., 1977–79). Can. LA: Gvt. Pubns. Com. (Conv., 1978–80). ACCESS, Can. Com. for the Right to Pub. Info. **Pubns.:** Various articles, *Unravel* (N. 1976–); "Unravel II," *ON Lib. Review* (Je. 1977–); various articles, *Antenna*; "Anatomy of a Library Campaign," *Quill and Quire* (My. 1979). **Activities:** 9; 30 **Addr.:** Georgian Bay Regional Library System, 30 Morrow Rd., Barrie, ON L4N 3V8 Canada.

PROFESSIONAL ACTIVITIES: Institutions: 1. Acad. lib.; 2. Arch.; 3. Assn.; 4. Fed./Gvt. lib.; 5. Inst. lib.; 6. Mfr./Suppl.; 7. Milit. lib.; 8. Musm.; 9. Pub. lib.; 10. Sch. lib.; 11. Sch. of lib. sci.; 12. Spec. lib.; 13. State lib.; 14. (other). **Functions/Activities:** 15. Acq./Col. dev.; 16. Adult srvs.; 17. Admin.; 18. Apprais.; 19. Archit./Bldgs.; 20. Cat./Class.; 21. Chld. srvs.; 22. Circ.; 23. Cons./Pres.; 24. Consult.; 25. Cont. ed.; 26. Educ. lib. sci.; 27. Ext. srvs.; 28. Fund/Grants; 29. Gvt. pubs.; 30. Indx./Abs.; 31. Instr. lib. use; 32. Media srvs.; 33. Micro.; 34. Netwks./Coop.; 35. Persnl.; 36. PR; 37. Publshg.; 38. Recs. mgt.; 39. Ref. srvs.; 40. Repro.; 41. Resrch.; 42. Review.; 43. Secur.; 44. Serials; 45. Spec. col.; 46. Tech. srvs.; 47. Trustees/Bds.; 48. YA srvs.; 49. (other).

Wan, William W. (S. 4, 1936, Canton, China) Coord. for Acq., TX Woman's Univ. Lib., 1980–, Coord. for Pub. Srvs., 1977–80, Circ./ILL Libn., 1975–77; Libn., Amer. Christ. Coll., 1971–75. **Educ.:** Univ. of Hong Kong, 1957–60, BA (Econ., Bus.); Univ. of HI, 1963–66, MS (Econ.); Univ. of OK, 1969–70, MLS. **Orgs.:** Interuniv. Cncl. Circ. Subcom.: Ch. (1979–80). Chin. Amer. LA: Bd. of Dirs. (1979–82); SW Chap. (Pres., 1980–82). ALA. Beta Phi Mu: Beta Lambda Chap. (Treas., 1980–81). **Pubns.:** *Twentieth Century Chinese Works on Southeast Asia: A Bibliography* (1968). **Activities:** 1; 17, 22, 39; 59, 92 **Addr.:** 2520 Yellowstone, Denton, TX 76201.

Wang, Amy C. (Ag. 20, 1943, Chunking, Szechwan, China) Libn., John Hancock Mutual Life Insr. Co., 1971–, Asst. Libn., 1968–71; Asst. Libn., New Eng. Mutual Life Insr. Co., 1967–68; Asst. Ref. Libn., Boston Coll., Bapst Lib., 1966–67. **Educ.:** Baylor Univ., 1962–65, BA (Eng.); Atlanta Univ., 1965–66, MSLS; various cont. educ. crs. **Orgs.:** SLA: Insr. Div., Ch.–Elect (1979–80), Ch. (1980–81); Boston Chap., Dir. (1979–81), Treas. (1973–74), Nom. Com. (Ch., 1976–77), Fin. Com. (1977–78). Untd. Way of MA Bay. **Pubns.:** Managing ed., *Insr. Lit.* (1978); ed., *Insr. Lit.* (1978–79). **Activities:** 12; 17, 41; 59, 76 **Addr.:** John Hancock Mutual Life Insurance Co. Library, P.O. Box 111, Boston, MA 02117.

Wang, Ann C. (Mr. 23, 1923, Chia-hsin, Che-kiang, China) Sr. Catlgr. and Ed., Lib. of Congs., 1966–; Catlgr., West. MI Univ. Lib., 1964–66; Libn., Philippine Chin. Pub. Lib., 1955–63; Assoc. Ed. and Feature Writer, *Fookien Times* (Manila), 1953–54; Transl.–Ed., Radio Free Asia, Asia Fndn., 1953; Tchr., Chiang Kai-shek HS (Manila), 1953–58; Correspondent in Manila, *Sin Win Tien Ti* (wkly. news mag.), 1950–51. **Educ.:** Natl. SW Assoc. Univ. (China), 1940–42; Univ. of Manila, 1959–62, BA, magna cum laude (Hist.); George Peabody Coll. for Tchrs., 1963–64, MA (LS); West. MI Univ., 1965–66 (Hist.). **Orgs.:** ALA: ACRL, *Choice: Bks. for Coll. Libs.* Consult. (1965–74). Lib. of Congs. Prof. Assn. **Honors:** Beta Phi Mu. **Pubns.:** Various reviews, *Choice* (1965–74); various wkly. articles, *Saturday Mag., Fookien Times* (1953–54); various news features, *Sin Wen Tien Ti* (1950–51). **Activities:** 1, 4; 20, 41, 46; 54, 57, 83 **Addr.:** 4621 Seminary Rd., 202, Alexandria, VA 22304.

Wang, Chin Ling (My. 18, 1915, Peking, China) Assoc. Prof., Asst. to Dir. of Libs., Acq. Libn., St. John's Univ., New York, 1966–, Asst. Prof., LS, 1958–68, Asst. Libn., 1953–58; Cat. Libn., St. Ignatius Hse. of Std., Manhasset, NY, 1952–53; Lectr. in Eng., Natl. Peking Univ., Peking, China, 1946–48; Ed., Ta-Hua Daily Newsp., China, 1946–48; Lectr. in Eng., Natl. Yunnan Univ., Kunming, China, 1938–45; Instr. in Fr., Coll. Français-Chinois, Kunming, China, 1943–45. **Educ.:** Natl. Peking Univ., Peking, China, 1935–38, BA (Eng.); MI State Univ., 1948–50, MA (Eng.); Columbia Univ., 1951–52, MSLB (LS). AAUP: St. John's Univ. Chap. **Honors:** The China Acad., Huakang, Taiwan, China, Flwshp., 1972. **Pubns.:** *Comparative Study of the Nature Concept in Tao Yuan Ming and William Wordsworth* (1952); various articles and short stories in Chinese, published in Chinese pers. **Activities:** 1; 15 **Addr.:** 86–79 Palo Alto St., Jamaica, NY 11423.

Wang, Frances D. (Jl. 3, 1918, Soochow, Kiangsu, China) Cur., Asian Std. Col., Honnold Lib., Claremont Colls., 1969–; Asst. Libn., Far East. Lib., Univ. of WA, 1956–69, Resrch. Assoc., Far East. and Russ. Inst., 1955–56, Resrch. Asst., Dept. of Soclgy., 1953–55; Libn., Chin. Air Frc. Ofc. (DC), 1947–48; Head, Lib. PR, USIS HQ (Shanghai), 1945–46; Head, Distribution Dept., USOWI Chengtu Branch (China), 1943–45. **Educ.:** Ginling Coll. (China), 1938–41, BA (Soclgy.); Univ. of Chicago, 1948–50, Cert. (Soc. work); Univ. of WA, 1950–52, MA (Soclgy.), 1956–58, MA (LS). **Orgs.:** ALA. Assn. for Asian Std. Inc. Com. on E. Asian Libs.: Subcom. on Tech. Prcs. (1973–77); Exec. Grp. (1977–80); Std. Grp. on Access (1979–). South. CA Asian Libs. Grp.: Ch. (1971–73). Chin. Sr. Citizens Assn. (Los Angeles). Pomona Valley Chin. Club. Intl. Congs. of Human Scis. in Asia and N. Africa. **Honors:** Beta Phi Mu; Pacificulture-Asia Musm. (Pasadena), Hon. Adv., 1974–. **Pubns.:** "Trends of American Libraries," *Bltn. of LA of China* (D. 1969); "Social Value and Patterns of Living," *A General Handbook of China* (1956); "Social Value and Patterns of Living," *A Regional Handbook on Northwest China* (1956); "Social Value and Patterns of Living," *A Regional Handbook on Northeast China* (1956); jt. auth., "Attitudes and Reactions of the People," *A General Handbook of China* (1956). **Activities:** 1, 12; 15, 17, 23; 54, 55, 92 **Addr.:** 1662 Denver Ave., Claremont, CA 91711.

Wang, John Kuo-Chang (F. 17, 1936, Shantung, China) Asst. Prof., Lib. and Info. Sci., Univ. of West. ON, 1979–; Asst. Prof., Coord., Lib. Srvs., Niagara Cnty. Cmnty. Coll., 1978; Libn. II, SK Legis. Lib., 1973–74; Univ. Libn., Soochow Univ., Taipei, 1971–73. **Educ.:** Natl. Chengchi Univ., Taiwan, 1956–60, LLB (Intl. Law, Diplomacy); Northwest. Univ., 1968–69, MA (Pol. Sci.); Univ. of MI, 1969–70, MLS; Univ. of OK, 1974–77, PhD (Pol. Sci.). **Orgs.:** ALA. Can. LA. Chinese LA. Amer. Pol. Sci. Assn. Can. Pol. Sci. Assn. **Honors:** Pi Sigma Alpha, 1974. **Pubns.:** *UN Voting on Chinese Representation: An Analysis* (1980); *Introduction to the Study of Administrative Organization and Methods* (1966); "Political Behavior Analysis: Status and Problems," *Soochow Jnl. of Lit. and Soc. Std.* (S. 1972); "A Guide to Reference Materials in the Study of American Legislative Behavior," *Procs. of the 1st Natl. Conf. of Lib. Mgt. and Srvs.* (Jl. 1972); "Almond-Verba's Five Nation Study Data: A Behavioral Analysis," *Soochow Jnl. of Lit. and Soc. Std.* (S. 1973); various reviews, articles, chaps. in Chinese and Amer. pubns. **Activities:** 1, 11; 15, 17, 26; 54, 77, 92 **Addr.:** 1868 Main St. W. #704, Hamilton, ON L8S 1J1, Canada.

Wangsgard, Lynnda M. (Mr. 17, 1948, Ogden, UT) Asst. Dir., Weber Cnty. Lib., 1979–, Fine Arts Libn., 1973–79, Asst. Dept. Libn., 1970–73. **Educ.:** Weber State Coll., 1966–70, BS (Eng., Educ.); Brigham Young Univ., 1973–75, MLS; State of UT, 1966–, Tchg. Cert. **Orgs.:** UT LA: Pub. Lib. Sect., Pres. (1981–82), Secy. (1978–79); Int. Frdm. Com. (1977). Mt. Plains LA: Nom. Com. (1977). Ballet W. (Ogden Ballet Gld.). **Honors:** Mt. Plains LA, Beginning Prof. Awd., 1979; Phi Kappa Phi; Beta Phi Mu. **Pubns.:** *Hassle-Free Local Production* (1973); *Weber County Employee Handbook* (1980); "Employee Orientation: Weber County Library," *UT Jnl. of Arts Letters and Scis.* (Spr. 1977); "Material Selection of Minority Groups," *UT Libs.* (Fall 1977). **Activities:** 9, 11; 17, 26, 35; 55, 56, 66 **Addr.:** Weber County Library, 2464 Jefferson Ave., Ogden, UT 84401.

Wannarka, Marjorie B. (Fairmont, MN) Dir., Hlth. Scis. Lib., Creighton Univ., 1952–. **Educ.:** Coll. of St. Catherine, 1952, BS (LS); Univ. of MN, 1961–67, MA (LS); various crs. **Orgs.:** Assn. of Acad. Hlth. Scis. Lib. Dirs. Med. LA: Various coms., ofcs. Cath. LA. NE LA. Various other orgs. Amer. Assn. of Colls. of Pharm. Amer. Assn. for Hist. of Med. NY Acad. of Scis. NE Acad. of Scis. Various other orgs. **Honors:** Med. LA, Murray Gottlieb Essay Awd., 1967; Creighton Univ., Disting. Srv. Awd., 1978. **Pubns.:** "New Library Buildings: Creighton University Bio-Information Center," *Bltn. of the Med. LA* (Ap. 1980); "Forging CHEXS," *Biomed. Comms.* (S. 1979); "History of a Medical Collection Housed in the Omaha Public Library, 1906–1914," *NE State Med. Jnl.* (Je. 1968); "Dr. George Milbry Gould: Ophthalmologist...," *Bltn. of the Hist. of Med.* (My.–Je. 1968); "Medical Collections in Public Libraries of the United States: A Brief Historical Study," *Bltn. of the Med. LA* (Ja. 1968); various articles. **Activities:** 1, 12; 17, 19, 39; 58, 80, 87 **Addr.:** 3000 Farnam St. #2G, Twin Towers, Omaha, NE 68131.

Waranius, Frances B. (Mr. 29, 1931, Chicago, IL) Lib./Info. Ctr. Mgr., Lunar and Planetary Inst., 1971–; Documtn. Spec., ITT/Fed. Electric Corp., 1965–71; Libn., Meissner Engins., 1955–59. **Educ.:** Coll. of St. Francis, 1949–53, BS (Bio.). **Orgs.:** SLA: Phys.–Astro.–Math Div. (Bltn. Ed., 1976–78). Geosci. Info. Socty. **Honors:** Kappa Gamma Pi. **Pubns.:** "World Data Center Role in Lunar and Planetary Information Distribution," *NATO/AGARD Tech. Info. Panel Procs.* (1980); jt. auth., "Lunar Data Information Center," *Spec. Libs.* (1975); jt. auth., "Lunar Data and Where It's At," *Geosci. Info. Socty. Procs.* (1974); ed., *Lunar and Planetary Info. Bltn.* (1974–); assoc. ed., *The Moon And The Planets.* **Activities:** 12; 17, 36, 39; 88, 91 **Addr.:** Library/Information Center, Lunar & Planetary Institute, 3303 NASA Rd. One, Houston, TX 77058.

Ward, Dederick C. (Je. 22, 1934, Baltimore, MD) Head, Sci. Libs., Univ. of CO, 1966–, Earth Sci. Libn., 1961–. **Educ.:** WA Univ., Lee Univ., 1952–56, BA (Geol.); Univ. of CO, 1956–58, MA (Geol.); Univ. of Denver, 1960–61, MA (Libnshp.). **Orgs.:** Geosci. Info. Socty.: Secty. (1967); Pres. (1968); Tech. Prog. Com. (1967); Thesis Bibl. Com. (1967–74); Constn. Com. (1974–75); 1st Intl. Conf. on Geol. Info. (Co-ch., 1978). Amer. Geol. Inst.: GEOREF Adv. Com. (1978–80). **Pubns.:** *Geologic Reference Sources* (1972); *Bibliography of Theses in Geology 1967–1970* (1973); "State of the Art in Geoscience Information," *Proc. Ist International Conference on Geoscience Information* (1979). **Activities:** 1; 17, 31, 39; 70, 91 **Addr.:** Science Library, Univ. of CO Libraries, Boulder, CO 80309.

Ward, Edith (Jl. 17, 1928, New York, NY) Transnatl. Corps. Affairs Ofcr., Untd. Nations Ctr. on Transnatl. Corps., 1977–; Consult., 1972–77; Lib. Mgr., McKinsey and Co., 1969–72; Catlgr., Proj. URBANDOC, 1967–69. **Educ.:** Hunter Coll., 1944–48, BA (Eng. Lit.); Columbia Univ., 1966–67, MS (LS). **Orgs.:** ALA. Amer. Socty. of Indxrs.: Bd. of Dirs. (1979–). SLA: Data Base Users Grp., Fndr.; Plng. Com. (1979–). ASIS. **Pubns.:** *Bibliography on Transnational Corporations* (1979); *List of Company Directories and Summary of Their Contents* (1978); *Urban Affairs Subject Headings* (1975); *Thesaurus of Small Arms Terminology* (1972); *China Information Library - Index Design and Vocabulary Control* (1975); various manuals. **Activities:** 12; 15, 17, 39; 59 **Addr.:** Centre on Transnational Corporations, United Nations - BR 1075, New York, NY 10017.

Ward, Frank J. (Mr. 29, 1930, Blackburn, Eng.) Asst. Dir., Pub. Srvs., Univ. of Toledo Libs., 1979–, Lib. Mgt. Srvs., 1969–79; YA and Branch Libn., Toledo Pub. Lib., 1957–65; Bkmobile. Libn., Sarnia (ON) Pub. Lib., 1956–57; Deputy Boro. Libn., Accrington Pub. Lib., 1955–56; Head Catlgr., Blackburn Pub. Lib., 1951–55; Unit Libn., West. Cmnd. Signals Regiment, 1949–50. **Educ.:** Univ. of Toledo, 1965–68, BA (Pol. Sci.); Univ. of MI, 1968–69, AMLS; LA, (Eng.), 1951, Assoc. **Orgs.:** ALA. LA (Eng.). Acad. LA of OH. OH Lib. Fndn.: Bd. (1971–). AAUP. **Activities:** 1; 17, 22 **Addr.:** 1903 Evansdale, Toledo, OH 43607.

Ward, James E. (Ap. 10, 1934, Dardanelle, AR) Dir. of Lib., David Lipscomb Coll., 1966–, Assoc. Prof., Hlth. and Phys. Educ., 1963–66; Ch., Dept. of Hlth. and Phys. Educ. and Dir. of Athls., Ctrl. Meth. Coll., 1961–63; Tchr., Rogers HS, 1959–60; Tchr., Carlisle HS, 1955–57. **Educ.:** Hendrix Coll., 1951–54, BA (Hlth., PE, Eng.); Univ. of AR, 1954–55, MEd (Hlth., PE), 1959–61, EdD (Hlth., PE); George Peabody Coll., 1966–68, MLS. **Orgs.:** ALA: Cncl. (1978–80); ACRL, various coms.; Reg. VI Mem. Com. (Ch., 1974–78). SELA: Ref. and Adult Srvs. Sect. (Ch., 1974–76); Mem. Com. (Ch., 1978–80); Lib. Orien. and Bibl. Instr. Com. (Ch., 1976–78). TN LA: Pres. (1973–74); various ofcs., coms. Mid-State LA: Exec. Cncl. (Ch., 1971–72). Nashville Lib. Club: Pres. (1972–73). TN Coll. Phys. Educ. Assn. Amer. Alliance for Hlth., Phys. Educ., Recreation and Dance. TN Assn. for Hlth., Phys. Educ. and Recreation. **Honors:** Phi Delta Kappa; Kappa Delta Pi; Beta Phi Mu. **Pubns.:** *Education and Manpower in Tennessee Libraries* (1971); *Southeastern Bibliographic Instruction Directory: Academic Libraries* (1978); "Library Orientation and Bibliographic Instruction in Southeastern Academic Libraries," *Southeast. Libn.* (Fall 1976). **Activities:** 1; 17, 31, 35; 63 **Addr.:** Box 4146, David Lipscomb College, Nashville, TN 37203.

Ward, John Owen (S. 20, 1919, London, Eng.) Freelnc. consult., 1980–; Dir. of Serious Msc., Boosey and Hawkes Inc., 1972–80; Mgr., Msc. Dept., Oxford Univ. Press, 1957–72. **Educ.:** Oxford Univ., 1949–54, MA (Italian, Grmn.). **Orgs.:** Msc. LA. Intl. Msc. LA. Msc. Publshrs. Assn.: Pres. (1974–76). Royal Musical Assn. Amer. Musicological Assn. Socty. for Italian Std. **Pubns.:** *Careers in Music* (1968); ed., *Oxford Companion to Music* (1970); ed., *Concise Oxford Dictionary of Music* (1964); "P.A. Scholes," *Grove's Dictionary of Music* (1981); contrib. to various jnls. **Activities:** 14-Msc. publshr.; 20, 37, 41; 55, 57, 61 **Addr.:** 325 W. 76 St., New York, NY 10023.

Ward, Lynn Harmon (Mr. 26, 1952, Detroit, MI) Chlds. Libn., Woodrow Wilson Pub. lib. (Falls Church, VA.) 1980–; Asst. to the Dir., OIF, ALA, 1978–80; Sch. Libn., Dr. Jones Elem. Sch. (Racine, WI), 1977–78. **Educ.:** Univ. of WI, Parkside, 1970–73, BA (Eng.); Univ. of MO, 1975–76, MA (LS). **Orgs.:** ALA: IFRT. Frdm. to Read Fndn. **Activities:** 6; 25, 41, 49-Prog. Dev.; 74 **Addr.:** Woodrow Wilson Public Library, 6101 Knollwood Dr., Falls Church, VA 22041.

Ward, Robert Carl (My. 6, 1947, Louisville, KY) Admin., Ctrl. IA Reg. Lib. Syst., 1981–, Asst. Admin., 1980–81; Libn., U.S. Dept. of Justice, 1979; Gordon Ave. Branch Coord., Jefferson-Madison Reg. Lib., 1977–79; VP/Proj. Coord., Info. Consult. Srvs., 1975–77; Ref. Libn., Louisville Free Pub. Lib., 1972–75; Printer's Apprentice, Fawcett-Haynes Pubns., 1971; Asst. Dir., CONTACT, 1970–71. **Educ.:** Bellarmine Coll., 1965–70, BA (Hist., Pol. Sci.); Univ. of KY, 1975–76, MSLS; Drake Univ., 1980– (Pub. Admin.). **Orgs.:** IA LA: Legis. Com. (Ch., 1982); Guidelines Com. (1981–). ALA: LAMA Lib. Org. and Mgt. Sect., Prog. Com. (1981–); PLA. Dem. Party. Amer. Art Therapy Assn.: Legis. Resrch. Com. Amer. Socty. for Pub. Admin. **Honors:** Beta Phi Mu. **Pubns.:** Ed., reg. nsltr. **Activities:** 9; 17, 24 **Addr.:** 618-45th St., Des Moines, IA 50312.

Ward, Sandra N. (Jl. 10, 1943, Salem, MA) Assoc. Libn., J. Henry Meyer Meml. Lib., Stanford Univ., 1977–; Resrch. Asst., Ctr. for Occupational and Env. Safety and Hlth., SRI, 1976–77; Geosci. Libn., Lamont-Doherty Geol. Observatory, Columbia Univ., 1967–69, Phys. Libn., 1966–67. **Educ.:** Mt. Holyoke Coll., 1961–65, AB (Zlgy.); Columbia Univ., 1965–66, MLS. **Orgs.:** ALA: ACRL. SLA. CA ARL. Leag. of Women Voters: S. San Mateo Cnty. Chap., Educ. Com. (1974–76, 1978–80). **Pubns.:** "Columbia Libraries and the Upper Mantle," *Columbia Lib. Clmns.* (My. 1968). **Activities:** 1; 15, 31, 39; 58, 65, 91 **Addr.:** J. Henry Meyer Memorial Library, Stanford University, Stanford, CA 94305.

Ward, Victoria M. (F. 1, 1940, Philadelphia, PA) Lib. Dir., Morgan, Lewis and Bockius (DC), 1973–; Libn., U.S. Third Circuit Ct. of Appeals, 1972; Libn., Morgan, Lewis and Bockius (Philadelphia), 1963–71. **Educ.:** Ursinus Coll., 1959–61, BA (Pol. Sci.); Drexel Univ., 1961–62, MLS. **Orgs.:** AALL: Law and Legis. Com. (1977–78); Stans. Com. (1970–72); Educ. Com. (1975–76); Nom. Com. (1981–82); Pvt. Law Libns./Spec. Interest Sect. (Ch., 1981–1982). Law Libns. Socty. of DC: Lcl. Arrange. (Co–Ch., 1975–77); Bd. (1977–80). **Activities:** 12; 17; 77 **Addr.:** Morgan, Lewis & Bockius, 1800 M St., N.W., Washington, DC 20036.

Ward, William Dale (Jl. 1, 1940, Saskatoon, SK) Coord., Documtn. Srvs., Inst. for Intl. Dev. and Coop., Univ. of Ottawa, 1979–; Resrc. Ctr. Head, St. Lawrence Campus, Champlain Coll., 1976–79; Head, Derived Cat., Univ. Laval, 1974–76, Asst. Head of Cat., 1973–74, Cat. Verifier, 1969–1972. **Educ.:** Univ. of SK, 1959–63, 1965, AMus (Piano); BEd, BA, hons. (Fr., Msc.); Univ. D'Aix-Marseille, 1963–64, Univ. of Toronto, 1968–69, BLS. **Orgs.:** CAML: Pres. (1973–74, 1975–76); Cnclr. (1971–72); VP (1972–73); Past-Pres. (1974–75, 1976–78). **Activities:** 1; 17, 20, 39; 55 **Addr.:** 1045, Falaise Rd., Ottawa, ON K2C 0M6 Canada.

Warden, Carolyn L. (D. 1, 1945, Takoma Park, MD) Libn., Online Srvs., Gen. Electric Co. Corp. Resrch. and Dev.,

Special Subjects/Services: 50. Adult educ.; 51. Advert./Mktg.; 52. Aerosp.; 53. Agric.; 54. Area std.; 55. Arts/Hum.; 56. Autom.; 57. Bibl./Prtg.; 58. Bio. sci.; 59. Bus./Fin.; 60. Chem.; 61. Copyrt.; 62. Documtn.; 63. Educ.; 64. Engin.; 65. Env.; 66. Eth. grps.; 67. Film; 68. Food/Nutr.; 69. Geneal.; 70. Geo.; 71. Geol.; 72. Handcpd.; 73. Hist.; 74. Int. frdm.; 75. Info. sci.; 76. Insr.; 77. Law; 78. Legis.; 79. Math./Comp. sci.; 80. Med.; 81. Metals; 82. Nat. resrcs.; 83. Newsp.; 84. Nuc. sci.; 85. Oral hist.; 86. Petr./Energy; 87. Pharm.; 88. Phys./Astr./Math.; 89. Readg.; 90. Relig.; 91. Sci./Tech.; 92. Soc. sci.; 93. Telecom.; 94. Transp.; 95. (other).

1977–, Libn., Current Awareness, 1976–77; Asst. Libn., NY State Med. Lib., 1975–76; Comp. Lit. Srch. Asst., Univ. of CA, Berkeley, 1974; Lectr., Univ. of West. ON Sch. of LS, 1971–72. **Educ.:** Furman Univ., 1963–67, BS (Chem.); Emory Univ., 1967–68, MAT (Sci. Educ.); Univ. of West. ON, 1970–71, MLS; 1976, Cert. of Med. Libnshp. **Orgs.:** ALA: ACRL. ASIS. SLA. Cap. Dist. Lib. Cncl.: Comp.-Based Ref. Srvs. Com., Ch. (1978–79), Secy. (1977–78). BRS, Inc.: User Adv. Bd. Tech. Subcom. (1977–80). U.S. Dept. of Energy RECON Syst.: RECON User Grp. (1978–81). Amer. Chem. Socty.: Div. of Chem. Info. **Honors:** *Online Review,* Data Courier, 2d Prize, Srch. Corner Contest, 1979. **Pubns.:** "An Industrial Current Awareness Service: A User Evaluation Study," *Spec. Libs.* (D. 1978); "Database Usage," *Online* (Jl. 1978); "Update on Conference Call Searching," *Online* (Jl. 1979); "User Evaluation of a Corporate Library Online Search Service," *Spec. Libs.* (Ap. 1981); "Comparing the Bibliographic Utilities for Special Libraries," *Spec. Libs.* (D. 1980). **Activities:** 12; 39; 60, 80, 91 **Addr.:** 6 Film Ave., Troy, NY 12180.

Warden, Margaret S. (Mrs. R. D.) (Jl. 18, 1917, Glasgow, MT) Legis., Pub. Awareness Ch., NCLIS, 1980–84; Trustee, MT State Lib. Comsn., 1958–; Adv. Com., WHCOLIS, 1975–80; Sen., MT State Legis., 1975–79; Ch., MT State Lib. Comsn., 1973–75; Bd. Ch., Grt. Falls Pub. Lib. Bd., 1963–77; Civilian Ed., *NavAer Pubns. Index,* Bur. of Aeronautics, Dept. of Navy, 1942–44; Newsp. Histn. and Libn., Grt. Falls *Tribune,* 1935–42; various other cncls. and comsns., 1967–. **Orgs.:** ALA. Pac. NW LA: Legis. Ch. (1964). MT LA: Lay Pres. (1973–74); Legis. Com. (Ch., 1961–74); Lib. Dev. Com. (1959–76). ALTA: Secy. (1975–76); Speakers Bur. (1980–); various coms. Various other orgs. MT Com. for Hum. MT Multicult. Hist. Proj. Pres. Cncl., Coll. of Grt. Falls. Lewis and Clark Trail Comsn. (MT). Various other orgs. **Honors:** Grt. Falls Bus. Prof. Women, Woman of Yr., 1955; MT Env. Hlth. Assn., Disting. Srv. Awd., 1978; MT LA, First Trustee Awd., 1965; Delta Kappa Gamma. **Pubns.:** "MT LA History," *Encyc. of Lib. and Info. Sci.* (1976); "Great Falls, Heart of Golden Triangle," *MT Mag.* (S.–O. 1978); various articles, *MT Libs.* **Activities:** 3; 47, 49-Gvt. **Addr.:** 208 Third Ave. N., Great Falls, MT 59401.

Ware, Lucinda Frances (Je. 25, 1945, Niles, MI) Pub. Srv. Support Supvsr., Baltimore Cnty. Pub. Lib., 1977–; Supvsr., Chlds. Srvs., Cary Lib., 1975–77; Chlds. Spec. II, Baltimore Cnty. Pub. Lib., 1973–75; Chlds. Libn., Kanawha Cnty. Pub. Lib., 1972–73. **Educ.:** WV State Coll., 1966–70, BA (Hist.); Atlanta Univ., 1971–72, MS (LS). **Orgs.:** ALA: Newberry Com. (1980–81); Reeval. of Notable Bks. Com. (1971–75); Ad Hoc Com. for Storytel. (1976–77). MD LA: Chlds. Srvs. Programming Com.; Instr. for Chlds. Lit. (1973–75, 1977–). MD Lib. Reg. Plng. Comsn.: Howard Cnty. Rep. (1979–). New Eng. RT of Chlds. Libns. **Honors:** MD State Lib., Instr., 1974, 1975; WV State Lib., WV Pub. Lib. Grant, 1971, 1972. **Activities:** 9, 12; 16, 17, 21; 75 **Addr.:** 7158 Peace Chimes Ct., Columbia, MD 21045.

Ware, Malcolm Stewart (F. 20, 1933, Verona, MS) Sr. Libn., Gulf Coast Resrch. Lab., 1964–; Branch Libn., Univ. of South. MS, Biloxi Resident Ctr., 1962–64; Tchr.-Libn., Gulf Coast Milit. Acad., 1961–62. **Educ.:** Univ. of South. MS, 1959–61, BS (LS). **Orgs.:** SLA: AL Chap. Gulf Coast Biomed. Lib. Consortia: Ch. (Ja–Je. 1978). Intl. Assn. of Marine Sci. Libs. and Info. Ctrs. State Empls. Assn. of MS. Long Beach Air Marine Rescue Unit. **Activities:** 5, 13; 15, 20, 46; 58, 91 **Addr.:** The Gunter Library, Gulf Coast Research Lab., East Beach, Ocean Springs, MS 39564.

Warkentin, Katherine (S. 9, 1941, Birk, Translyvania, Rumania) Docum. Libn., Shippensburg State Coll., 1974–; Ref. Libn., Wilson Coll., 1969–74. **Educ.:** Univ. of Waterloo, ON, 1964–68, BA (Grmn. Lit.); Univ. of Toronto, 1968–69, BLS. **Orgs.:** PA LA: GODORT (Ch., 1978–79). ALA: GODORT, Constn. Com. (1981–). **Activities:** 1; 29, 31, 39; 57, 70 **Addr.:** Shippensburg State College, Ezra Lehman Memorial Library, Shippensburg, PA 17257.

Warne, Keith Warnell (N. 3, 1919, Hetland, SD) Ref. Libn., North. State Coll., 1963–; Docums. Libn., ND State Univ., 1958–63; Ref. Libn., Rochester (MN) Pub. Lib., 1957–58; Docums.–Ref. Libn., Univ. of NE Lib., 1955–57. **Educ.:** Yankton Coll., 1939–43, BA (Eng.); Univ. of SD, 1949 (Eng.); Univ. of MN, 1954 (LS). **Orgs.:** ALA. SD LA: Pres. (1972). **Activities:** 1; 15, 29; 57, 73 **Addr.:** Northern State College Library, Aberdeen, SD 57401.

Warner, Alice Sizer (D. 8, 1929, New Haven, CT) Owner/Consult., Info. Gld., 1980–; Pres., Warner-Eddison Assocs., Inc., 1973–80; Sch. Lib. Volun., Boston Pub. Schs., 1967–74; Ed. Consult., Harvard Univ., 1964–68. **Educ.:** Radcliffe Coll., 1946–50, AB (Rom. Langs.); Simmons Coll., 1971–72, MS (LS). **Orgs.:** ALA. ASIS. SLA. Info. Indus. Assn. 1980 White Hse. Conf. on Small Bus.: MA Del. Harvard Univ. Admis. Com. Smaller Bus. Assn. of New Eng. Phi Beta Kappa: Iota Chap. (Pres., 1971–74). **Honors:** Beta Phi Mu; **Pubns.:** Jt. auth., *Volunteers in Libraries* (1977); "Minicomputers in Libraries: State of the Art," *Law Lib. Jnl.* (Spr. 1981); "Noninstitutional Librarianship," *What Else You Can Do With a Library Degree* (1980); "Industry Trends: The Information Industry," *Minute-Man Pubns.* (Mr. 1980); "Bridging the Information Flow: A View from the Private Sector," *Lib. Jnl.* (S. 15, 1979); various articles. **Activities:** 14-Consult.; 24, 25, 49-Fncl. srvs.; 59, 95-Mgt. of info. procs. **Addr.:** The Information Guild, 546 Concord Ave., Lexington, MA 02173.

Warner, Beth Forrest (Mr. 20, 1954, Mechanicsburg, OH) Libn., Water Resrcs. Ctr., Univ. of WI, 1977–; Info. Spec., US Env. Protection Agency, 1977. **Educ.:** Coll. of Wooster, 1972–76, BA (Chem.); Univ. of Denver, 1976–77, MLS. **Orgs.:** SLA. ASIS. Madison Area Lib. Cncl.: Career Dev. Com. (Ch., 1979–80). Spec. Campus Libs. Grp.: Strg. Com. (1979–80). **Honors:** Phi Beta Mu, 1977. **Pubns.:** Jt. auth., "Using SDI's to Get Primary Journals–A New Online Way," *Online* (1978). **Activities:** 1, 4; 15, 17, 39; 65, 82 **Addr.:** Water Resources Reference Services, University of Wisconsin, Madison, WI 53706.

Warner, Edward S. (F. 29, 1936, Toledo, OH) Dir. of Libs., Univ. of ND, 1973–; Visit. Assoc. Prof., Univ. of IA, 1980–; Lib. Planner, Baltimore Reg. Plng. Cncl., 1971–73; Asst. Prof., Univ. of MD, 1968–71; Instr., Dept. of Libnshp., West. MI Univ., 1964–67; Asst. Ref. Libn., Miami Univ. (OH), 1963–64; Appts. as Ref. Libn., univ. or pub. libs., 1966–68; Adj. or Guest Lectr., Schs. of LS, 1979, 1971–73. **Educ.:** Miami Univ. (OH), 1954–58, BS (Bus.); Univ. of Toledo, 1961–62, MA (Pol. Sci.); Univ. of MI, 1963–64, AMLS; Amer. Univ., 1967–70, (Pol. Sci.). **Orgs.:** ALA. ND LA. **Pubns.:** Jt. auth., *Information Needs of Urban Residents* (1973); "Impact of Interlibrary Access to Periodicals on Subscription Continuation/Cancellation Decision-Making," *Jnl. of ASIS* (Mr. 1981); "Constituency Needs as Determinants of Library Collection and Service Configurations," *Drexel Lib. Qtly.* (Jl. 1977); jt. auth., "Utilizing Library Constituents' Perceived Needs in Allocating Journal Costs," *Jnl. of ASIS* (N. 1979); jt. auth., "Faculty Perceived Needs for Serials Titles: Measurement for Purposes of Collection Development and Management," *Serials Libn.* (Spr. 1980); various articles. **Activities:** 1, 11; 17, 41, 44 **Addr.:** 3007 E. Elmwood Dr., Grand Forks, ND 58201.

Warner, F. Eleanor (S. 6, 1921, Belfast, ME) Head Libn., New Eng. Coll. of Optometry, 1972–; Libn., Amer. Sci. and Engin., 1967–72. **Educ.:** Tufts Univ., 1940–44, AB (Eng.); Simmons Coll., 1963–67, MSLS. **Orgs.:** Assn. of Visual Sci. Libns.: Ch.-Elect (1978–80); Ch. (1980–82). SLA: Regis. Com., 1972 Anl. Mtg. Med. LA. ALA: ACRL. Gld. of Bk. Workers. Amer. Acad. of Optometry: Fellow. Socty. of Mayflower Descendants. Islesboro Hist. Socty. **Honors:** Class of 1977, New Eng. Coll. of Optometry, Outstan. Srv. in Educ., 1977. **Pubns.:** *Ancestry of Samuel, Freda, and John Warner* (1981); jt. auth., *Astronomical Charts, Catalogues, and Ephemerides* (1972). **Activities:** 1; 12; 17, 20, 39; 80, 91 **Addr.:** Library, The New England College of Optometry, 420 Beacon St., Boston, MA 02115.

Warner, Marnie M. (Ap. 15, 1950, Danbury, CT) Law Lib. Coord., Ofc. of the Chief Admin. Justice, 1980–; Consult. for the Disadv., MA Bd. of Lib. Comsns., 1979–80, Inst. Lib. Spec., 1975–79; Law Libn., Goodwin, Procter and Hoar, 1973–75. **Educ.:** Beloit Coll., 1968–72, BA (Hist.); Simmons Coll., 1972–73, MLS. **Orgs.:** ALA: ASCLA, Mem. Com. (1980–82), Plng., Org. and Bylaws Com. (1981–82), Lib. Srv. to Prisoners Com. AALL: Vice-Ch. (1977–78). Law Libns. of New Eng. New Eng. LA: Inst. Sect. (Secy., 1976–78). MA LA. **Pubns.:** Jt. auth., "Jail Library Game," *Workshops for Jail Library Service* (1981); "Statewide Library Card Study Committee Final Report," *Interface* (Spr./Sum. 1979); "Through the Legal Maze" slide/tapes (1977). **Activities:** 4, 13; 17, 24, 49-Plng.; 77, 89, 95-Institutionalized people. **Addr.:** 28 Eastman St., Dorchester, MA 02125.

Warner, Robert M. (Je. 28, 1927, Montrose, CO) Archvst. of The U.S. 1981–; Prof. of LS, Univ. of MI, 1974–81, Prof. of Hist., 1971–81, Dir., MI Hist. Cols., 1966–81, Asst. Dir., 1961–66, Asst. Cur., 1957–61. **Educ.:** Muskingum Coll., 1946–49, BA (Hist.); Univ. of MI, 1952–58, MA, PhD (Hist.). **Orgs.:** SAA. MI Arch. Assn. Midwest Arch. Assn. Org. of Amer. Histns. Hist. Socty. of MI: VP (1972–73); Pres. (1973–74). **Honors:** SAA, Fellow, 1967. **Pubns.:** Jt. auth., *Sources for the Study of Migration and Ethnicity* (1979); *The Anatomy of a Speech: Lyndon B. Johnson's Great Society Address* (1978); "The Prologue is Past," *Amer. Archvst.* (Ja. 1978); jt. auth., "Documenting the Great Migrations and a Century of Ethnicity in America," *Amer. Archvst.* (Jl. 1976); "Sources for Michigan Library History," *MI Libn.* (Fall 1976). **Activities:** 2; 17, 24, 45 **Addr.:** United States National Archives & Records Service, Pennsylvania Ave. at 8th St. NW, Washington, DC 20408.

Warren, Charles David (Je. 12, 1944, Martin, TN) Dir., Richland Cnty. Pub. Lib., 1979–; Dir., Cumberland Cnty. Pub. Lib., 1973–79; Dir., Shiloh Reg. Lib. Syst., 1969–72. **Educ.:** Univ. of TN, 1962–67, BS (Eng.); Univ. of IL, 1967–69, MS (LS). **Orgs.:** ALA: Pres.'s Prog. Plng. Com. (1981–82); Awds. Com. (1981–82); PLA, Plng. Com. (1980–82); LAMA; JMRT, Exec. Bd. (1973–79); ALTA; various other coms. SELA: Pub. Lib. Sect. (Ch., 1978–80). SC LA: Fed. Rels. Coord. (1980–84). **Honors:** Beta Phi Mu. **Activities:** 9; 17, 36 **Addr.:** Richland County Public Library, 1400 Sumter St., Columbia, SC 29201.

Warren, G. Garry (Ap. 22, 1948, Martin, TN) Dir. of Lrng. Resrcs., Henderson State Univ., 1978–; Dir. of Lib., Bainbridge Jr. Coll., 1973–76; Head of Docums. Dept., Memphis Pub. Lib. and Info. Ctr., 1970–72. **Educ.:** Murray State Univ., 1966–70, BS (LS); FL State Univ., 1972–73, MS (LS), 1976–77, Advnc. Mstrs. (LS), 1977–78, PhD (LS). **Orgs.:** ALA: RASD, Stans. Com. AR LA: Pubns. Com. Area Hlth. Educ. Ctr. **Pubns.:** *The Handicapped Librarian: A Study in Barriers* (1979). **Activities:** 1, 4; 15, 17, 29; 56, 72, 93 **Addr.:** Rte. 1, Box 791, Arkadelphia, AR 71923.

Warren, Hugh Parker (D. 3, 1922, Huron, SD) Persnl. Srvs. Admin., South Bend Pub. Lib., 1979–, Admin. Asst., 1963–78; Supvsr. of Ext. Work, Grace A. Dow Meml. Lib., 1957–63; Adult Libn., Depos. Dept., Chicago Pub. Lib., 1952–57. **Educ.:** SD State Coll., 1940–42 (Gen. Sci.); Univ. of SD, 1946–48, AB (Hist., Soclgy., Gvt.); Univ. of CA Berkeley, 1950–52, BLS. **Orgs.:** IN LA: Lib. Autom. and Tech. Div., Exec. Com. (1979–); Lib. Autom. RT (Ch., 1973–); Lib. Plng. Com. (1968–70); Dist. I (Ch., 1967–). ALA: LITA; LAMA. Amer. Socty. of Persnl. Admins. Leag. of Women Voters. South Bend Lions Club. Untd. Nations Assn./U.S.A. **Activities:** 9; 17, 27, 46; 56, 66 **Addr.:** South Bend Public Library, 122 W. Wayne St., South Bend, IN 46601.

Warren, Lois M. (Ap. 26, 1935, New York, NY) Pres., L. M. Warren Inc., 1979–; Mgr., West. Can. INFOMART, 1978–79; Cmnty. Consult., Lib. and AV Dept., Douglas Coll., 1975–78; Instr., Lib. Tech. Prog., Vancouver Cmnty. Coll., 1973–78; Lib. Consult., Dist. Sales Mgr., Info. Dynamics Corp., 1972–74; Libn., Vancouver Tech. Station, Fisheries Resrch. Bd. of Can., 1959–62. **Educ.:** Univ. of WA, Univ. of BC, 1953–57, BA (Psy., Eng.); Simmons Coll., 1971–72, MSc (LS). **Orgs.:** Can. Assn. Info. Sci. ASIS. SLA. Assoc. Info. Mgrs. **Honors:** Beta Phi Mu. **Pubns.:** *Fraser River Piledriving Company History 1911–1976* (1976). **Activities:** 12; 24, 30, 38; 56, 59, 91 **Addr.:** L. M. Warren Inc., 2000 W. 12th Ave., Vancouver, BC V6J 2G2, Canada.

Wartluft, David J(onathan) (S. 22, 1938, Stouchsburg, PA) Dir. of Lib., Luth. Theo. Semy. at Philadelphia, 1977–, Asst. Libn., 1969–77, Ref. and Cat. Libn., 1966–69; Pastor, Jerusalem Luth. Church (Allentown, PA), 1964–66. **Educ.:** Muhlenberg Coll., 1956–60, AB (Eng., Amer. Lit.); Luth. Theo. Semy. at Philadelphia, 1960–64, MDiv (Theo.); Univ. of PA, 1962–64, AM (Eng., Amer. Lit.); Drexel Univ., 1966–68, MS (LS); various crs., 1965–70, 1979–. **Orgs.:** ATLA: Exec. Secy. (1971–). CNLIA: Cnclr. (1978–). Cncl. on the Std. of Relig.: Cnclr. (1973–80); Liason Com. (1975–76, 1980–81); Nom. Com. (1978–79). Mid-Atl. Reg. Archs. Conf. Various other orgs. Luth. Church in Amer., Northeast. PA Synod: Archvst. (1979–). Luth. Hist. Socty. of East. PA: *The Per.* Ed. (1977–). Luth. Archs. Ctr. at Philadelphia: VP (1979–). N. Mt. Airy Neighbors Civic Assn. **Honors:** Assn. of Theo. Schs. in the U.S. and Can., Dev. Grant, 1976; Beta Phi Mu; Eta Sigma Phi; Phi Sigma Tau. **Pubns.:** "The Pastor as Historian," *Concordia Hist. Inst. Qtly.* (Sum. 1978); "Cooperative Ventures in Theological Libraries," *Drexel Lib. Qtly.* (Ja. 1970); "That the Church May Remember" slide/tape (1980); ed., *Summary of Procs., ATLA* (1971–); indxr. for five mono. **Activities:** 1, 2; 17, 24, 34; 55, 57, 90 **Addr.:** Lutheran Theological Seminary at Philadelphia, 7301 Germantown Ave., Philadelphia, PA 19119.

Wartman, William B., III (N. 27, 1951, Richmond, VA) Dir., Lib.–Media Srvs., Alderson–Broaddus Coll., 1980–; Head of Tech. Srvs., Glenville State Coll., 1976–80; Pub. Srvs. Libn., Kenyon Coll., 1975–76. **Educ.:** Univ. of VA, 1970–74, BA (Anthro.); Univ. of KY, 1974–75, MS (LS); Miami (OH) Univ., Exec. Dev. Prog. for Lib. Admins., 1979, 1981, Cert. **Orgs.:** ALA. WV LA: Coll. and Univ. Sect. (Secy., 1977–78). Pittsburgh Reg. Lib. Ctr.: Trustee (1980–). Tri-State ACRL. Mid-Atl. Reg. Archs. Conf. **Activities:** 1; 17, 31; 86, 89 **Addr.:** Box 34 Alderson-Broaddus College, Philippi, WV 26416.

Waserman, Barbara Anderson (Ja. 17, 1925, Evanston, IL) Reg. Mgr., Fairfax Cnty. Pub. Lib., 1977–; Asst. Reg. Libn., 1975–77, Branch Libn., 1969–75, Chld. Libn., 1963–69. **Educ.:** Northwest. Univ., 1942–48, BS (Educ.); Cath. Univ. of Amer., 1962–63, MS (LS). **Orgs.:** ALA: Prog. Com.; SO RT (1981–82); Strg. Com. (1984). VA LA: Mem. Com. (1981). Fairfax Cnty. Pub. Lib. Empls. Assn.: Pres. (1980). **Pubns.:** "The History of Medicine - A Bookshelf for the Public Library," *Lib. Jnl.* (Ja. 1972). **Activities:** 9; 16, 17, 35; 56, 63 **Addr.:** George Mason Regional Library, 7001 Little River Turnpike, Annandale, VA 22003.

Waserman, Manfred (Mr. 21, 1933, Free City of Danzig) Cur., Mod. Mss., Natl. Lib. of Med., 1965–; Libn., Yale Univ. Lib., 1963–65. **Educ.:** Univ. of MD, 1955–59, BA (Hist.), 1959–61, MA (Hist.); Cath. Univ. of Amer., 1962–63, MS (LS). **Orgs.:** Oral Hist. Assn. Amer. Hist. Assn. Amer. Assn. for the Hist. of Med. **Honors:** Natl. Lib. of Med., Bd. of Regents Awd., 1972. **Pubns.:** *A Bibliography on Oral History* (1975); "Manuscripts and Oral History," *Bltn. of Med. LA* (Ap. 1970); "Historical Chronology and Selected Bibliography Relating to the National Library of Medicine," *Bltn. of Med. LA* (O. 1972); "Fred L. Soper: Ambassador of Good Health," *Amer.'s* (O. 1975); "An Overview of Child Health Care in America," *Chld. Today* (My./Je. 1976). **Activities:** 4; 45; 80, 86, 92 **Addr.:** History of Medicine Division, National Library of Medicine, Bethesda, MD 20209.

PROFESSIONAL ACTIVITIES: Institutions: 1. Acad. lib.; 2. Arch.; 3. Assn.; 4. Fed./Gvt. lib.; 5. Inst. lib.; 6. Mfr./Suppl.; 7. Milit. lib.; 8. Musm.; 9. Pub. lib.; 10. Sch. lib.; 11. Sch. of lib. sci.; 12. Spec. lib.; 13. State lib.; 14. (other). **Functions/Activities:** 15. Acq./Col. dev.; 16. Adult srvs.; 17. Admin.; 18. Apprais.; 19. Archit./Bldgs.; 20. Cat./Class.; 21. Chld. srvs.; 22. Circ.; 23. Cons./Pres.; 24. Consult.; 25. Cont. ed.; 26. Educ. lib. sci.; 27. Ext. srvs.; 28. Fund/Grants; 29. Gvt. pubs.; 30. Indx./Abs.; 31. Instr. lib. use; 32. Media srvs.; 33. Micro.; 34. Netwks./Coop.; 35. Persnl.; 36. PR; 37. Publshg.; 38. Recs. mgt.; 39. Ref. srvs.; 40. Repro.; 41. Resrch.; 42. Review.; 43. Secur.; 44. Serials; 45. Spec. col.; 46. Tech. srvs.; 47. Trustees/Bds.; 48. YA srvs.; 49. (other).

Wash, Melba Eurydice Wilson (Ag. 6, 1918, Benton, TN) Dir., Reelfoot Reg. Lib., 1950–; Reg. Libn., W. TN Reg. Lib., 1948–50; Spec. Srvs. Libn., U.S. Army (Germany), 1946–48; Libn., McDonogh Sch., 1942–46; Libn., Oneida HS, 1941–42; Tchr., Old Fort Elem. Sch., 1939–41. **Educ.:** Berea Coll., 1935–39, AB (Eng.); George Peabody Coll., 1940–42, BS (LS). **Orgs.:** ALA: Cncl. (1951–54); Mem. Com. (1973–76); PLA, Pubns. Com. (1967–70). SELA: Lib. Dev. Com. (1979–81). TN LA: Treas. (1954–55); Pub. Lib. Sect. (Ch., 1966). W. TN LA: VP (1973); Pres. (1974). AAUW. TN Adv. Cncl. on Libs.: Secy. (1976–79). **Activities:** 9, 10; 17, 27, 47 **Addr.:** 126 Fonville Ave., Box 351, Martin, TN 38237.

Washburn, Keith E. (Ap. 3, 1944, Salem, OR) Dir., Pub. Srvs., Hamilton Coll., 1978–, Asst. Ref. Libn., 1973–78. **Educ.:** Bucknell Univ., 1962–64, 1969–71, AB (Eng.); SUNY, Albany, 1972–73, MLS; Bucknell Univ., 1972–78, MA (Eng.). **Orgs.:** ALA: ACRL; RASD. Ctrl. NY Lib. Resrcs. Cncl.: Prof. Dev. Com. (1980–81). **Pubns.:** Various bk. reviews, *Lib. Jnl.* **Activities:** 1; 17, 22, 39; 55, 74, 90 **Addr.:** Hamilton College Library, Clinton, NY 13323.

Wasick, Mary Ann (Jl. 19, 1946, Milwaukee, WI) Libn. I, W. Allis Pub. Lib., 1972–; Tchr.-Libn., Milwaukee Pub. Sch. Syst., 1969–71. **Educ.:** Univ. of WI, Milwaukee, 1964–69, BS Ed (Educ., Latin, LS); Univ. of WI, Oshkosh, 1971–72, MA (LS); Milwaukee Area Tech. Coll., 1970–81; Univ. of WI, Ext., 1976–79. **Orgs.:** ALA. WI LA. Amer. Classical Leag. W. Allis Art Alliance. Univ. of WI: Milwaukee Alum. Assn.; Oshkosh Alum. Assn. **Pubns.:** Various bk. reviews, *Lib. Jnl.* (1979–), *Kliatt YA Paperback Bk. Guide* (1980–), *Milwaukee Area Tech. Coll.* (1970–). **Activities:** 9; 32, 36, 39; 67 **Addr.:** 1310 S. 98 St., W. Allis, WI 53214.

Wasserman, Paul (Ja. 8, 1924, Newark, NJ) Prof., Coll. of Lib. and Info. Srvs., Univ. of MD, 1965–, Dean, 1965–70; Libn., Asst. Prof., Prof., Grad. Sch. of Bus. and Pub. Admin., Cornell Univ., 1953–65; Asst., Bus. Libn., Chief, Sci. and Indus. Div., Brooklyn Pub. Lib., 1949–53; Visit. Prof. or Lectr., 1960–64; sem. leader, UNESCO consult. **Educ.:** Coll. of City of NY, 1948, BBA; Columbia Univ., 1949, MS (LS), 1950, MS (Econ.); Univ. of MI, 1960, PhD (Lib. Admin., Pub. Admin.); West. Rsv. Univ., 1963–64, Post Doct. Schol. **Orgs.:** MD LA. ALA: RASD; Lib. Educ. Div.; Lib. Admin. Div.; Info. Sci. and Autom. Div; various coms. and ofcs. in each. SLA: Bus. Div. (Ch., 1952–53); various other coms. ASIS. Various other orgs. Intl. Fed. for Documtn. AAUP. **Pubns.:** Managing ed., various bks.; various articles, ed. bds. **Activities:** 11; 24, 26; 63, 75 **Addr.:** College of Library and Information Services, University of Maryland, Undergraduate Library Bldg., College Park, MD 20742.

Wassom, Earl Eugene (S. 20, 1923, Blackwell, OK) Dir. of Lib. Srvs., West. KY Univ., 1971–; Asst. Dean of Acad. Srvs., 1969–, Actg. Head, LS and Assoc. Dir. of Lib. Srvs., 1967–69; Docums., Soc. Std. Libn., OK State Univ., 1963–67; Media Libn., Montgomery Cnty., 1962–63; various positions as tchr., 1950–62. **Educ.:** Bethany Nazarene Coll., 1947–50, BA (Hist., Phil.); E. TN State Univ., 1960–62, MA (LS); OK State Univ., 1964–67, EdD (Higher Educ., Admin.). **Orgs.:** KY State Adv. Cncl. on Libs. (1981–). KY LA. SELA. WHCOLIS: Del. State Assisted Acad. Lib. Cncl. of KY. **Honors:** West. KY Univ., Disting. Srv. to the Univ. Excel. Awd., 1979. **Pubns.:** *Organization of the Libraries, University of the Andes, Merida, Venezuela* (1976); *Organizacion de los Bibliotecas, Universidad de los Andes, Merida, Venezuela* (1976); *On-Line Cataloging and Circulation at Western Kentucky University* (1973); "Bibliographic Access to Full Descriptive Cataloging with COM," *Jnl. of Lib. Autom.* (1978); "Some Perspectives Gleaned from Library Consulting Experiences in Latin America," *Educ.* (1977). **Activities:** 1, 2; 17, 32, 34; 56, 63, 75 **Addr.:** 548 Brentmoor Dr., Bowling Green, KY 42101.

Wasson, Betty (Jl. 29, 1921, Newport, AR) Coll. Libn., WA Coll., 1976–; Libn., West. Coll. of Miami Univ., 1974–76, Coll. Libn., 1966–74; Head, Readers' Srv., Mt. Holyoke Coll., 1960–66, Admin. Asst., 1958–60; Asst. Libn., Cleburne–Independence Reg. Lib., 1951–55; Lib. Asst., Sch. of Fine Arts, WA Univ., 1948–49; various other positions. **Educ.:** AR Coll., 1938–42, AB (Hist.); WA Univ., 1943–44, MA (Hist.); Carnegie Inst. of Tech., 1957–58, MLA. **Orgs.:** ALA. MD LA. **Honors:** Beta Phi Mu. **Activities:** 1; 15, 17, 39; 55, 92 **Addr.:** 115 Elm St., Chestertown, MD 21620.

Watanabe, Ruth T. (My. 12, 1916, Los Angeles, CA) Libn., Sibley Msc. Lib., and Prof. of Msc. Bibl., Eastman Sch. of Msc., Univ. of Rochester, 1947–. **Educ.:** Univ. of South. CA, 1932–37, BMus (Msc.), 1937–39, AB (Eng.), 1939–41, MA (Eng.), 1941–42, MMus (Msc.); Univ. of Rochester, 1952, PhD (Msclgy.); Columbia Univ., 1947 (LS). **Orgs.:** Msc. LA: Pres. (1979–81). Intl. Assn. of Msc. Libs. Amer. Musicological Socty. Intl. Musicological Socty. AAUW: Rochester Branch Pres. (1967–69). **Honors:** Mu Phi Epsilon; Rochester Assn. for the Untd. Nations, Outstan. Woman, 1976; Rochester Alum. Chap., Mu Phi Epsilon, Musician of the Yr., 1977; Phi Beta Kappa. **Pubns.:** *Introduction to Musical Research* (1967); *Antonio Il Verso: Madrigali a Cinque Voci, 1590* (1978); *Treasury of Four-Hand Piano Music* (1979); "Music Received," sect. *Notes* (1969–); various articles, reviews. **Activities:** 1; 17, 26; 55, 95-Msc. resrch. **Addr.:** Sibley Music Library, Eastman School of Music, University of Rochester, Rochester, NY 14604.

Watanabe, Stella K. (O. 15, 1930, Kahului, HI) Chief Libn., Hickam Air Force Base, Honolulu, 1965–; Air Force Libn., Japan, 1963–65; Army Libn., Okinawa, 1961–63; Branch Libn., Lib. of HI, Honolulu, 1957–61, Chld. Libn., 1955–57; Chld. Libn., Cuyahoga Cnty. Lib., 1954–55. **Educ.:** Univ. of HI, 1948–52, BA (Psy.); West. Rsv. Univ., 1953–54, MS (LS). **Orgs.:** HI LA: VP, Pres. Elect (1981). ALA: PLA; FLRT. Honolulu Zonta Club. **Activities:** 4; 20, 39 **Addr.:** 45 - 570 Awanene Pl., Kaneohe, HI 96744.*

Waters, Betsy M. (F. 4, 1931, Parkersburg, WV) Supvsr., Resrch. Lib., Moore Bus. Forms, Inc., 1976–; Elem. Libn., Starpoint Ctrl. Sch., 1970–75; Sub. Libn., Wilson Ctrl. Schs., 1970. **Educ.:** WV Univ., 1948–52, BS (Chem.); Niagara Univ., 1969–70, MS (Educ.); SUNY, Buffalo, 1970–73, MLS; NY State Lib. Media Spec., 1971; NY State Pub. Lib. 1975, Cert. **Orgs.:** SLA. Natl. Micro. Assn.: Exec. Bd., West. NY (1980). ASIS. West. NY Lib. Resrcs. Cncl. Data Base Networking Com. (1979–). Amer. Recs. Mgrs. Assn.: Buffalo Chap. (Secy., 1981–82). AAUW: Niagara Area Branch, various ofcs. (1974–). **Pubns.:** Various bk. reviews, *Previews* (1970–75). **Activities:** 10, 12; 17, 33, 41; 51, 56, 91 **Addr.:** Moore Research Center Library, Moore Business Forms, Inc., 300 Lang Blvd., Grand Island, NY 14072.

Waters, Edward N. (Jl. 23, 1906, Leavenworth, KS) Retired, 1976–, Chief, Msc. Div., Lib. of Congs., 1972–76, Asst. Chief, Msc. Div., 1937–72, Head, Ref. Sect., 1934–37. **Educ.:** Univ. of Rochester, 1923–27, BMus (Piano), 1927–28 (Msclgy.). **Orgs.:** Msc. LA: Pres. (1941–46). Amer. Musicological Socty.: Secy. (1947–48). U.S. Bk. Exch.: Bd. Ch. (1958–62). **Pubns.:** *Victor Herbert* (1955); *Frederic Chopin by Franz Liszt* (1963); various articles. **Activities:** 4; 17, 39; 55 **Addr.:** Apt 7-H Bldg. B, 3900 Watson Pl., N.W., Washington, DC 20016.

Waters, Marie Bell (Ag. 1, 1936, Long Beach, CA) Head, Col. Dev., Ref. Dept., Univ. of CA, Los Angeles, Univ. Resrch. Lib., 1980–, Adj. Lectr., Grad. Sch. Lib. Info. Sci., 1980–; Lectr. in Eng., Cuttington Coll., Monrovia, Liberia, 1970–71; Assoc. Libn., Ref. Dept., Univ. of CA, Los Angeles, Univ. Resrch. Lib., 1961–79. **Educ.:** Univ. of CA, Los Angeles, 1958, BA (Eng.), 1961, MS (Lib. Srv.). **Orgs.:** ALA: ACRL; RASD. CA ARL. Univ. of CA, Los Angeles, Grad. Sch. Lib. Info. Sci. Alum. Assn. **Pubns.:** *Worldwide Directory of Computer Companies, 1973–1974.* **Activities:** 1; 31, 39; 55, 67, 92 **Addr.:** 615 24th Pl., Hermosa Beach, CA 90254.

Waters, Richard L. (O. 7, 1937, Gloden City, MO) Assoc. Dir., Pub. Srvs., Dallas Pub. Lib., 1974–, Chief of Ctrl. Resrch. Lib., 1971–74, Chief of Branch Srvs., 1967–71, Head, Sci. and Indus. Dept., 1966–67; Prof. Asst., Seattle Pub. Lib., 1964–66; Admin. Asst., Wichita Pub. Lib., 1962–63; Head, Bus. and Tech. Dept., Pub. Libs. of Springfield and Greene Cnty., 1960–62. **Educ.:** SW MO State Coll., 1957–60, BS (Bus. Admin.); Univ. of WA, 1964–66, MLibr. **Orgs.:** ALA: Cnclr. (1973–77); Lib. Admin. Div. (Pres., 1977–78). TX LA: Exec. Bd. (1970–73). VNA, Inc. Bd. of Dirs. (1980–83). Musm. of African-Amer. Life and Culture Bd. of Trustees (1981–83). Bd. of Admin. Mgt. Socty.: Dir. (1976–80). HBW Assocs. Lib. Consults.: Partner (1979–). **Honors:** Dallas Cham. of Cmrce., Leadership Dallas, 1979; Beta Phi Mu. **Pubns.:** "Telefacsimile: An Effective Document Transfer Tool?" *Serials Libn.* (Win. 1979); "Tilting at the Windmill," *Lib. Jnl.* (Je. 1978); chap. contrib., *Reader in Public Librarianship* (1980); chap. contrib., *Libraries and the Political Process* (1980). **Activities:** 9; 17, 19, 24; 51, 59, 78 **Addr.:** Dallas Public Library, 1515 Young St., Dallas, TX 75201.

Waters, Samuel Theodore (Jl. 29, 1925, Boston, MA) Assoc. Dir., Natl. Agr. Lib., 1975–; Deputy Dir. for Resrc. Dev., 1970–75; Deputy Assoc. Dir., Lib. Oper., Natl. Lib. of Med., 1968–70, Chief, Ref. Srv., 1966–68; Asst. Libn., Georgetown Univ. Lib., 1960–1966. **Educ.:** Univ. of Rochester, Univ. of CO, 1947–50, BA summa cum laude; Cath. Univ., 1959, MS (LS). **Orgs.:** ALA: Stans. Com. (Ch., 19—); FLRT (Pres., 19—). SLA. ASIS. **Honors:** Phi Beta Kappa; Beta Phi Mu. **Pubns.:** "Creation and Use of Citation Data Bases," *Jnl. of ASIS* (Mr./Ap. 1975); "The Regional Medical Library and the Hospital Library", *Bltn. of Med. LA* (Ap. 1971); "The Proof of the Pudding: Using Library of Congress Proof Slips", *Coll. and Resrch. Libs.* (28:2); "Your Own Hands: Using Word Processors to Access and Interface Computer Systems," *Agr. Libs. Info. Notes* (My. 1980); "Federal Librarians Round Table," *The ALA Yrbk.* (1979); various articles. **Activities:** 1, 4; 17, 34; 56, 58 **Addr.:** National Agricultural Library, Rm. 100, Beltsville, MD 20705.

Watkins, Barbara Heather (S. 30, 1938, Horsley, Surrey, Eng.) Prog. Coord., Cariboo Coll., 1981–; Co-owner, Mgr., Spes Bona Bk. Srvs.; Partner, Watkins and Heather, Couns. and Consults., 1979–; Area Libn., Cariboo-Thompson Nicola Lib. Syst., Williams Lake Lib., 1978–81; Libn., Instr., N. Island Coll., 1976–78; Adult Srvs. Libn., Yakima Valley Reg. Lib., 1973–75; Libn., Radbrook Coll., 1966–68. **Educ.:** N.W. Polytech. Lib. Sch., 1959–60, ALA; Univ. of Keele, 1963–73, BA (Politics, Soclgy.); Univ. of WA, 1974, Cert. (Prof. Libn.). **Orgs.:** Can. LA. BC LA. **Pubns.:** Ed., publshr., *Cricket on the Hearth* (1975–78). **Activities:** 5, 9; 16, 17, 26; 50, 72, 92 **Addr.:** RR # 1, Box 38, Kinglet Rd., Williams Lake, BC V2G 2P1 Canada.

Watkins, Carolyn Kirkham (Ag. 14, 1940, Wichita Falls, TX) Head Libn., Walker Meml. Lib., 1980–; Libn., Casco Bay Coll., 1979; Ctrl. Lib. Srvs. Supvsr., Austin (TX) Pub. Lib., 1970–78; Branch Libn., Boston Pub. Lib., 1966–69. **Educ.:** TX Christ. Univ., 1958–62, BA (Relig.); Simmons Coll., 1964–66, MLS. **Orgs.:** ALA: YASD, Nom. Com. (1971). **Activities:** 9; 17, 25, 35; 66 **Addr.:** 32 Fellows St., Portland, ME 04103.

Watkins, Dorothy (Ag. 15, 1940, New York City, NY) VP, Fncl. Data Securs. Data Co., 1981–; Info. Mgr., Morgan Stanley and Co., 1972–80. **Educ.:** Brooklyn Coll., 1958–62, BA (Math.); Queens Coll., CUNY, 1970–72, MIS (Info. Sci.); CUNY Grad. Ctr., 1973–74, Cert. (Data Analysis). **Orgs.:** ASIS: NY Prog. Ch. SLA: Bus. and Fin. Com., NY Ch. Assn. for Info. Mgrs. **Activities:** 12; 17, 24, 38; 56, 59 **Addr.:** 147–18 27 Ave., Whitestone, NY 11354.

Watkins, Thomas T. (S. 21, 1918, Hazleton, PA) Libn., Msc. Lib., Columbia Univ., 1951–, Lectr., Grad. Msc. Dept., 1965–, Ref. Asst., Msc. Lib., 1950–51; Organist/Choir Dir., Meth. Church (Nesquehoning, PA), 1946–49; Instrumental Msc. Dir., E. Mauch Chunk Pub. Sch. Dist., 1941–43. **Educ.:** New Eng. Cnsvty. of Msc., 1936–38 (Msc.); State Tchrs. Coll. (W. Chester, PA), 1938–41, BS (Msc. Educ.); Columbia Univ., 1949–51, MS (LS), 1959–62, Cert. in Advnc. Libnshp. **Orgs.:** Msc. LA: Exec. Com. (1954–56). Grt. NY Msc. LA. NY Lib. Club. **Pubns.:** Various bk. and phonorec. reviews. **Activities:** 1; 15, 17, 31; 55, 57 **Addr.:** 61 Jane St. Apt. 17K, New York, NY 10014.

Watson, Elbert L. (My. 10, 1930, Birmingham, AL) Exec. Dir., IN Lib. and Trustee Assns., 1978–; Dir., Huntsville-Madison Cnty. Pub. Lib., 1969–78; Dir., Anniston-Calhoun Cnty. Pub. Lib., 1966–69; Sr. Archvst., TN State Lib. and Arch., 1962–66. **Educ.:** Bethany Coll., 1948–52, BA (Hist.); Univ. of OK, 1952–54, MA (Hist.); George Peabody Coll., 1965–66, MLS. **Orgs.:** AL LA: Pres. (1973–74); ALA Cnclr. (1974–75). ALA. IN State Cham. of Cmrce. Carmel-Clay Hist. Socty. IN Hist. Socty. Indianapolis Cvl. War RT. **Pubns.:** *A History of Etowah County, Alabama* (1968); *Tennessee at the Battle of New Orleans* (1965); *United States Senators from Alabama* (1981); "Constantine B. Sanders: The Sleeping Preacher of North Alabama," *The Huntsville Hist. Review* (Ap. 1971); "John Bell Hood's Tennessee Campaign in 1864," *The Huntsville Hist. Review* (O. 1972); various articles. **Activities:** 2, 9; 28, 36, 47; 69, 78, 92 **Addr.:** Indiana Library and Trustee Associations, 1100 W. 42nd St., Indianapolis, IN 46208.

Watson, Elizabeth S. (S. 27, 1940, Burlington, VT) Coord. of Chld. and Ext. Srvs., Fitchburg Pub. Lib., 1971–; Chld. Libn., Bacon Meml. Lib., 1969–70; Home Economist, NY State Ext. Srv., 1963–65. **Educ.:** Univ. of VT, 1958–62, BS (Home Econ.), 1963, Tchg. Cert. Univ. of MI, 1967–68, MALS. **Orgs.:** ALA: ALSC/U.S. Natl. Park Srv. Jt. Com. (Ch., 1980–81). New Eng. LA: RT of Chld. Libns. (Ch., 1979–80); New Eng. Outrch. Netwk. (Ch., 1972). MA LA. Women's Natl. Bk. Assn. Bus. and Prof. Women. Red Cross. Boston Globe/Horn Bk. Awds.: Judge (1981). **Pubns.:** "A/V Licensing Brings Kids and Media Together," *Previews* (D. 1975). **Activities:** 9; 21, 27, 32; 72 **Addr.:** 20 Round Rd., Lunenburg, MA 01462.

Watson, Jerry J. (S. 19, 1939, Pampa, TX) Asst. Prof., Chld. Lit., Univ. of IA, 1977–; Asst. Prof., Univ. of DE, 1974–77. **Educ.:** W. TX State Univ., 1958–62, BS (Educ.); MI State Univ., 1970–74, MA, PhD (Educ.). **Orgs.:** ALA: ALSC, Int. Frdm. Com. (1977–79), Caldecott Com. (1980). Natl. Cncl. of Tchrs. of Eng.: Various coms. **Honors:** MI State Univ., Excel.-in-Tchg. Awd., 1974. **Pubns.:** Contrib. reviewer, *Adventuring with Books* (1977); contrib. reviewer, *Picture Books for Children* (1973); "Selection Pressure on Teachers and Librarians," *Sch. Media Qtly.* (Win. 1981); "A Positive Image of the Elderly in Children's Books," *Readg. Tchr.* (Mr. 1981); consult., "Rudyard Kipling: Just So Stories," *Instr. Media* (1975); various other articles. **Activities:** 14-Univ. coll. of educ.; 21; 74, 89 **Addr.:** N248 Lindquist Center, University of Iowa, Iowa City, IA 52242.

Watson, Paula D. (Mr. 6, 1945, New York, NY) Asst. Dir., Gen. Srvs. for Ctrl. Ref. Srvs., Univ. of IL Lib., 1981–, Head, Docums. Lib., 1979–81, City Plng. and Landscape Archit. Libn., 1977–79, Asst. Ref. Libn., 1972–77. **Educ.:** Barnard Coll., 1961–65, AB (Eng.); Columbia Univ., 1965–66, MA (Eng.); Syracuse Univ., 1971–72, MSLS. **Orgs.:** ALA. **Pubns.:** "Publication Activity Among Academic Librarians," *Coll. & Resrch. Libs.* (S. 1977); jt. auth., *Report on Reference Services in Large Academic Libraries* ERIC (1978). **Activities:** 1; 17, 29, 39; 78, 92 **Addr.:** 305 Library, University of Illinois Library, 1408 W. Gregory Dr., Urbana, IL 61801.

Watson, Peter G. (My. 31, 1943, Oldham, Eng.) Ref. Libn./Data Srvs. Coord., CA State Univ., Chico, 1976–; Ref. Libn./Data Srvs. Coord., Univ. of CA, Los Angeles Resrch. Lib., 1974–76, Res. Libn., 1969–74; Sci. Asst., Brit. Lib.–Lending Div., 1967–68. **Educ.:** Univ. of Manchester (Eng.), 1961–65, BA (Eng., Phil.); Univ. of CA, Santa Barbara, 1965–67, MA (Eng.); Univ.

Special Subjects/Services: 50. Adult educ.; 51. Advert./Mktg.; 52. Aerosp.; 53. Agric.; 54. Area std.; 55. Arts/Hum.; 56. Autom.; 57. Bibl./Prtg.; 58. Bio. sci.; 59. Bus./Fin.; 60. Chem.; 61. Copyrt.; 62. Documtn.; 63. Educ.; 64. Engin.; 65. Env.; 66. Eth. grps.; 67. Film; 68. Food/Nutr.; 69. Geneal.; 70. Geo.; 71. Geol.; 72. Handcpd.; 73. Hist.; 74. Int. frdm.; 75. Info. sci.; 76. Insr.; 77. Law; 78. Legis.; 79. Math./Comp. sci.; 80. Med.; 81. Metals; 82. Nat. resrcs.; 83. Newsp.; 84. Nuc. sci.; 85. Oral hist.; 86. Petr./Energy; 87. Pharm.; 88. Phys./Astr./Math.; 89. Readg.; 90. Relig.; 91. Sci./Tech.; 92. Soc. sci.; 93. Telecom.; 94. Transp.; 95. (other).

of CA, Los Angeles, 1968–69, MLS. **Orgs.:** ALA: RASD, Info. Retrieval Com. (Ch., 1973–76), Goals and Objectives Com. (1979–), RASD/Machine—Assisted Ref. Sect., Discuss. Grp. (Ch., 1976–77); LAMA, Stats. for Non-Print Media Com. (1979–). ASIS: Los Angeles Chap. (Treas., 1975–76). **Pubns.:** Ed., *Charging for Computer Based Reference Services* (1978); ed., *On-Line Bibliographic Services–Where We Are, Where We're Going* (1977); jt. auth., *Computer Based Reference Service* (1973); *Great Britain's National Lending Library* (1970); "Dilemma of Fees for Service: Issues and Action for Librarians," *ALA Yrbk.* (1978). **Activities:** 1; 15, 17, 39; 56, 93 **Addr.:** Reference Department, Meriam Library, California State University, Chico, CA 95929.

Watson, Silvia D. (O. 15, 1947, Philadelphia, PA) Staff Dev./Affirmative Action Ofcr., Univ. of WI Libs., Madison, 1976–. **Educ.:** Temple Univ., 1966–70, BS (Soc. Admin.); Drexel Univ., 1974–76, MLS. **Orgs.:** ALA: Ofc. for Lib. Persnl. Resrcs./Equal Empl. Oppt. Subcom. (1976–); H.W. Wilson Staff Dev. Awds. Com. (1979–); Black Caucus (1976–); ACRL, Staff Dev. Ofcrs. of Lg. Acad. Libs. Discuss. Grp. **Pubns.:** "How to Develop An Affirmative Action Program," *Affirmative Action in Libraries* (1980). **Activities:** 1; 17, 25, 35; 63, 66 **Addr.:** Memorial Library, 728 State St., Madison, WI 53706.

Watson, Tom G. (Ap. 10, 1938, Ardmore, OK) Asst. to the Vice–Chancellor and Provost, Univ. of the S., 1981–; Univ. Libn., 1976–81; Dir. of Lib. and Media Srvs., Newberry Coll. (SC), 1973–76; Asst. Dir. of Lib., Bridgewater State Coll., 1970–73, Asst. Prof. of Eng., 1968–70; Eng. Master, Tabor Acad. (Marion, MA), 1967–68; Asst. Prof. of Eng., Univ. of South. MS, 1962–67. **Educ.:** OK Bapt. Univ., 1956–60, AB; Univ. of AR, 1962, MA (Eng.); Simmons Coll., 1971, MSLS. **Orgs.:** ALA: Com. on Accred.; Frdm. to Read Fndn. (Bd. of Trustees); ACRL, Com. on Stans. and Accred., Cont. Ed. Com., TN Chap. (Vice–Ch., Ch.–elect). SELA: Lib. Orien. and Bibl. Instr. Com. TN LA: Int. Frdm. Com. (Ch.). South. Coll. and Univ. Un.: Lib. Dirs. Grp. (Ch.). Eng.–Speaking Un., Hudson Stuck Chap. **Honors:** Phi Beta Kappa, 1961. **Pubns.:** "Accreditation: A Review of Issues," *ALA Yrbk.* (1981); "Johnson and Hazlitt on the Imagination in Milton," *South. Qtly.* (II); "Defoe's Attitude Toward Marriage and the Position of Women as Revealed in *Moll Flanders*," *South. Qtly.* (III). **Activities:** 1; 17, 26, 28; 55, 74 **Addr.:** Jessie Ball duPont Library, The University of the South, Sewanee, TN 37375.

Watson, Warren E. (Ap. 5, 1925, Quincy, MA) Dir., Libs., Thomas Crane Pub. Lib., 1968–; Dir., Libs., Framingham Pub. Lib., 1964–68, Asst. Dir., Libs., 1961–64; coverage of Sum. White Hse., WJAR-TV, Providence, RI, 1958; Spec. Frgn. Correspondent, Oper. Deep Freeze I, Antarctic, 1955–56; Tech. Writer, MA Inst. of Tech., Lincoln Lab., 1957–58; News Ed., WJAR-TV, 1952–55. **Educ.:** Boston Coll., 1945–48, AB (Hist., Gvt.), 1948, MA (Pol. Sci.); Simmons Coll., 1960–61, MS (LS). **Orgs.:** ALA: Subscrpn. Bks. Com. (1965–); Mem. Com. MA LA: Pres. (1971–72); VP (1970–71); Natl. Lib. Week (1964–65). Quincy Hist. Socty. US Power Squadrons. **Pubns.:** "Library Standards and Proposition 2 1/2," *Bay State Libn.* (Spr. 1981). **Activities:** 9; 17, 19, 34 **Addr.:** Thomas Crane Public Library, 40 Washington St., P.O. Box 379, Quincy, MA 02269.

Watson, William John (Ap. 12, 1928, Walkerville, ON) Asst. Libn., Phys. Plng. and Dev., Univ. of BC, 1973–; Univ. Libn., Univ. of Waterloo, 1969–72; Asst. Libn., Tech. Srvs., Univ. of BC, 1965–69; Islamic Std. Libn., McGill Univ., 1955–65. **Educ.:** Carleton Coll., 1947–50, BJ (Jnlsm.); McGill Univ., 1952–55, MA (Islamics), BLS. **Orgs.:** Can. LA. BC LA. **Activities:** 1; 17, 19, 43 **Addr.:** University of British Columbia Library, 2075 Wesbrook Mall, Vancouver, BC V6T 1W5 Canada.

Watt, Ronald G. (Ja. 2, 1939, Spring Canyon, UT) Mgr., Tech. Srvs., Hist. Dept., LDS Church, 1977–; Supvsr., Arch. Srch. Room, 1974–77, Sr. Catlgr., 1972–74; Instr., Hist., South. UT State Coll., 1966–68; Tchr., Carbon HS, Price, UT, 1964–65. **Educ.:** Coll. of East. UT, 1957–59, AS (Hist.); UT State Univ., 1961–63, BA (Hist.), 1965–66, MA (Hist.); Univ. of MN, 1966–72, PhD (Hist.). **Orgs.:** Conf. of Intermt. Archvsts.: Nom. Com. (1974–76); Nsltr. Ed. (1976–80); Cncl. Mem. (1980–). SAA. SPINDEX Users' Network: Ch., Interim exec. Com. (1978–79); Pubns. Com. (1979–). UT LA. UT State Hist. Socty. Mormon Hist. Assn. **Pubns.:** "LDS Church Records on Immigration," *Genealogical Jnl.* (1977); "Calligraphy in Brigham Young's Office," *UT State Hist. Qtly.* (1977); Jt. Auth., "Sources for Western History at the Church of Jesus Christ of Latter-day Saints," *West. Hist. Qtly.* (1977); "Sailing the Old Ship Zion: The Life of George D. Watt," *BYU Std.* (Aut. 1977); "Dry Goods and Groceries in Early Utah: An Account Book View of James Campbell Livingston," *UT Hist. Qtly.* (Fall 1978); other articles. **Activities:** 2, 12; 17, 18, 46 **Addr.:** Historical Department, LDS Church Office Building, 50 E. North Temple, Salt Lake City, UT 84150.

Watts, Shirley Marie (Ag. 1, 1935, Mooresville, NC) Msc. Libn., Vanderbilt Univ. Lib., 1957–. **Educ.:** George Peabody Coll., 1953–57, BM (Msc. Theory), 1957–61, MA (Msc. Educ.), 1963–67, MLS. **Orgs.:** Msc. Lib. Assn.: SE Chap., Exec. Bd. (1979–). TN LA. Msc. Educ. Natl. Conf. TN Msc. Educ. Assn. Sigma Alpha Iota. **Honors:** Beta Phi Mu, 1967. **Activities:** 1; 15, 17, 20, 22, 39; 55 **Addr.:** 913 Van Leer Dr., Nashville, TN 37220.

Waugh, Lucky Netuschil (S. 15, 1922, Yuma, CO) Dir., Head Libn., Norfolk Pub. Lib., 1973–81; Dir., Lewis and Clark Reg. Lib., 1973–81; Dir., Madison Cnty. Bkmobile., 1973–81; Admin. Asst., Norfolk Pub. Lib., 1969–73, Clerical and Ref. Asst., 1962–69. **Educ.:** Univ. of CO, Univ. of North. CO, 1940–43; Univ. of UT (LS). **Orgs.:** ALA. NE LA: Cits. Com., Ch.; Pub. Lib. Sect., Past Pres. North. Lib. Netwk. Cncl.: Past Pres. State Adv. Cncl. on Libs. Daughters of Amer. Revolution: Vice-regent. Bus. and Prof. Women: Woman of Achvmt. Awd., Ch. Cmnty. Concern, Inc.: Pres. Cham. of Cmrce. Women. various other orgs. **Honors:** Beta Sigma Phi, Woman of the Yr., 1977; Bus. and Prof. Women, Woman of Achvmt., 1979. **Activities:** 9; 17, 34, 35; 50, 69, 93†

Waugh, Richard P. (Ag. 5, 1932, Columbia City, IN) Head, Ref. Dept., Albany Pub. Lib., 1972–. **Educ.:** Purdue Univ., 1950–54, BS (Metals Engin.); Carnegie Inst. of Tech., 1957–59, MS (Indus. Admin.); Syracuse Univ., 1971–72, MS (LS). **Orgs.:** NY LA. ALA. Amer. Socty. for Metals. **Honors:** Tau Beta Pi, 1953. **Activities:** 9; 15, 16, 39; 59, 91 **Addr.:** Albany Public Library, 161 Washington Ave., Albany, NY 12210.

Waverchak, Gail A. (O. 3, 1952, Cleveland, OH) Med. Libn., St. Joseph's Hosp., Atlanta, GA, 1978–; Resrc. Libn., Outrch. Libn., Loretto Geriatric Ctr., Syracuse, NY, 1975–77. **Educ.:** State Univ. Coll., Fredonia, NY, 1970–74, BA (Liberal Arts, Eng.); Syracuse Univ., 1975–77, MLS. **Orgs.:** Atlanta Hlth. Sci. Libs. Cnsrtm.: Secy. (1979); Ch. (1981). GA Hlth. Sci. Libs. Assn. Med. LA: South. Reg. Grp., Legis. Com. (1981–). **Activities:** 5, 12; 15, 17; 72, 80 **Addr.:** 4109 W. Johnson Cir., Chamblee, GA 30341.

Waxman, Joanne (Ap. 16, 1934, Portland, ME) Libn., Slide Cur., Portland Sch. of Art, 1976–; Asst. Libn., Westbrook HS, 1974–76. **Educ.:** Simmons Coll., 1952–54; Univ. of South. ME, 1966–71, BA (Eng.); Univ. of ME, 1971–74, MLS; Grantsmanship Trng. Prog., 1977. **Orgs.:** ARLIS/NA. Art Libs. Socty./New Eng. South. ME Lib. Dist.: Exec. Bd. (1978–). ME LA. Coll. Art Assn. **Honors:** Phi Kappa Phi, 1975. **Activities:** 1, 12; 15, 17, 20; 55 **Addr.:** Portland School of Art Library, 97 Spring St., Portland, ME 04101.

Way, Harold E. (O. 21, 1942, Cresbard, SD) Tech. Srvs., Ref. Libn., NY State Sch. of Indus. and Labor Rel., Cornell Univ., 1976–; Asst. Head, Ref., West. MI Univ., 1973–76, Gen. Ref. Libn., 1971–73. **Educ.:** SD State Univ., 1961–65, BS (Soclgy.), 1974–76, MA (Urban Geo.); West. MI Univ., 1969–70, MLS. **Orgs.:** SLA. West. MI Univ. Lib. Sch. Alum. Assn.: Pres. (1971–73). Men's Garden Club of Cortland Cnty. **Honors** Beta Phi Mu, 1971. **Pubns.:** "Management Techniques," *RQ* (1972); Reviews. **Activities:** 1, 12; 15, 39, 49-Comp. Bibl. Srchg.; 59, 92 **Addr.:** Martin P. Catherwood Library, NYSSILR–Cornell University, P.O. Box 1000, Ithaca, NY 14853.

Way, Olivia Richman (Ja. 17, 1914, Lenola, NJ) Retired, 1976–; Elem. Sch. Media Spec., Ridgewood Pub. Schs., 1952–76; Chld. Libn., Girard Coll., Philadelphia, 1948–52; HS Libn., Manhasset (NY) Pub. Schs., 1947–48; Secy., Libn., Monmouth Cnty. Lib. Comsn., 1941–46; Libn., Neptune Twp. HS, Ocean Grove, NJ, 1936–41. **Educ.:** Trenton State Coll., 1932–36, BS (Educ.); Columbia Univ., 1942–47, MA (Educ.); Univ. of MI, 1952–56, MA (LS). **Orgs.:** ALA: Ref. and Subscrpn. Books Review Com. (1957–59); AASL, Exec. Bd., Reg. 2, (1962–64); Sch. Lib. Plng. Com. (1958–64); Stan. Implementation Com. (1958–64); ALSC, Newbery-Caldecott Awds. Com. (1966–67). Assn. of LS Alum., Univ. of MI. Natl. Educ. Assn. Pi Lambda Theta. **Honors:** Ridgewood Pub. Schs., Lloyd W. Ashby Awd., 1971; Beta Phi Mu. **Pubns.:** Jt. Auth., *British Children's Authors: Interviews at Home* (1976); "How Elementary School Teachers and Librarians Work Together," *Readg. Tchr.* (D., 1963); reprinted in *Educ. Digest* (Mr., 1964); and in *Readings on Reading Instruction* (1972). **Activities:** 10, 11; 26, 32, 42 **Addr.:** P.O. Box 117, Tenants Harbor, ME 04860.

Wayman, Sarah G. (O. 23, 1950, Pittsburgh, PA) Sr. Asst. Ref. Libn., PA State Univ., 1978–; Asst. Libn., Pub. Srvs., Lynchburg Coll., 1973–78. **Educ.:** PA State Univ., 1968–71, BA (Liberal Arts); Univ. of Pittsburgh, 1972, MLS (Ref., LS). **Orgs.:** SLA: Ctrl. PA Chap., Pres.–Elect. ALA: RASD, Bus. Ref. Srvs. Com. **Honors** Phi Beta Kappa, 1972; Beta Phi Mu, 1972. **Activities:** 1; 31, 39, 49-Data Base Srch.; 59, 92 **Addr.:** C/O E108 Pattee Library, Pennsylvania State University, University Park, PA 16802.

Weatherhead, Barbara A. B. (Jl. 7, 1929, Toronto, ON) Dir., Lib. Srvs., ON Mnstry. of Treasury & Econ., 1973–; Head Libn., ON Dept. of Mncpl. Affairs, 1963–72; Head Libn., Cmnty. Plng. Branch, ON Dept. of Plng. & Dev., 1953–62. **Educ.:** Univ. of Toronto, 1948–52, Honours BA (Geo.), 1968–69, BLS with Honours. **Orgs.:** SLA: Ch., Anl. Intl. Conf. (1974). Cncl. of Plng. Libns.: Conv., Prog. Com., Intl. Mtg. (1971). ON Gvt. Libns. Cncl.: Ch. (1978–79); Secy. (1970–72). **Honors:** Gvt. of Can., Centennial Medal, 1967. **Activities:** 12, 13; 17, 39; 59 **Addr.:** Library Services Branch, Ontario Ministry of Treasury & Economics, Queens Park, Toronto, ON M7A 1Y8 Canada.

Weaver, Barbara F. (Ag. 29, 1927, Boston, MA) Asst. Comsnr. of Educ./State Libn., NJ State Lib., 1978–; Reg. Admin., Ctrl. MA Reg. Lib. Syst., 1972–78; Dir., Lib. Srv. Ctr., CT State Lib., 1969–72; Head Libn., Thompson (CT) Pub. Lib., 1961–69. **Educ.:** Radcliffe Coll., 1945–49, BA (Math.); Univ. of RI, 1964–68, MLS; Boston Univ., 1974–78, EdM (Adult Educ.). **Orgs.:** ALA: ASCLA, Ch., Legis. Com. (1980–82); Exec. Bd. (1980–82). NJ LA. MA LA: VP (1977–78). CT LA: Exec. Bd.; Ch., Var. Coms. Amer. Socty. for Trng. Dev. Amer. Socty. for Pub. Admin. **Honors** Beta Phi Mu. **Activities:** 9, 13; 17, 24, 25; 50 **Addr.:** New Jersey State Library, 185 W. State St. (CN 520), Trenton, NJ 08625.

Weaver, Carolyn G. (F. 2, 1943, Joplin, MO) Assoc. Dir., Pub. Srv., Univ. of NE Med. Ctr. Lib., Omaha, 1981–; Head, Ref. Dept., 1977–81; Online Srvs. Libn., 1971–77; MEDLARS Anal./Reg. Ref. Libn., John Crerar Lib., 1968–71; Asst. Libn., Ref. Dept., Chicago Pub. Lib., 1965–68. **Educ.:** Pasadena Coll., 1961–65, AB (Eng.); Univ. of Chicago, 1965–67, AM (LS). **Orgs.:** Med. LA: Ad Hoc Com. to Dev. a Statement of Goals (1979–). ALA. NE LA. **Pubns.:** Cmplr., *Health Services Administration Collection Bibl.* (1977); *Excerpta Medica Intl. Congress Series Finding List* (1980); "Locating the Excerpta Medica Intl. Congress Series by Number," *Bltn. Med. Lib. Assn.* (Ap. 1980); "Medline," Slide-Tape (1977). **Activities:** 1, 12; 39; 80 **Addr.:** Leon S. McGoogan Library of Medicine, University of Nebraska Medical Center, 42nd & Dewey Ave., Omaha, NE 68164.

Weaver, John M. (My. 20, 1922, Kansas City, MO) Chief, Resrcs. Dev. Branch, Lib., US Dept. of Housing & Urban Dev., 1968–; Lib. Dir., NASA Goddard Space Flight Ctr., 1960–68; Asst. Libn., Army, Ofc. Chief of Engin., 1959–60; Head, Circ. Sect., Natl. Lib. of Med., 1956–59; Ref. Libn., Cncl. on Frgn. Rel., 1950–54. **Educ.:** Bucknell Univ., 1939–43, BA (Hist.); Univ. of AZ, 1946–47, MA (Hist.); Columbia Univ., 1949–54, MSLS. **Orgs.:** DC LA: Treas. (1964–65). SLA: Washington Chap., Bd. of Dir. (1971–72). ASIS. FLC: Tape Util. Com. (1968–). Silver Spring (MD) Lib. Adv. Com. **Honors** US Dept. of Housing & Urban Dev., Cert. of Spec. Achvmt., 1978. **Pubns.:** "Bibliographic control of HUD Comprehensive Planning Reports," *IL Libs.* (Ap. 1974); "Portrait of A Space Age Library," *DC Libs.* (Spr. 1962). **Activities:** 4; 17; 56, 92 **Addr.:** Library, Rm. 8141, U.S. Department of Housing & Urban Development, Washington, DC 20410.

Weaver, Virginia H. (Mr. 28, 1921, Anniston, AL) Libn. Coord. for Resrch. and Trng., Atlanta Pub. Lib., 1978–; Ctrl. Libn., 1976–78, Branch Supvsr., 1974–76, Head of Cat. Dept., 1970–74, Asst. Head of Ext. Srvs., 1965–70; Asst. to Libn., Agnes Scott Coll., 1944–46. **Educ.:** Jacksonville (AL) State Univ., 1939–41; Birmingham South. Coll., 1941–43, AB (Eng.); Emory Univ., 1943–44, AB (LS). **Orgs.:** ALA. SELA. GA LA: Ch., Pub. Lib. Div. (1979–81); various coms. (1975–80). Amer. Socty. for Trng. and Dev. Delta Zeta Fraternity. **Activities:** 9; 17, 25, 41 **Addr.:** Atlanta Public Library, 1 Margaret Mitchell Square N.W., Atlanta, GA 30303.

Weaver-Meyers, Patricia L. (D. 23, 1952, Wichita, KS) Gvt. Docum. Libn., Lamar Univ., 1979–; Media Libn., Coll. Hlth. Sci., 1977–79; Ref. Libn., Hlth. Sci. Ctn., Univ. of OK, 1975–77. **Educ.:** Univ. of OK, 1969–74, BS (Zlgy.), 1974–75, MLS; Med. LA Cert., 1975–82. **Orgs.:** Med. LA. Hlth. Sci. Comm. Assn. TX LA. Hlth. Educ. Resrc. Org.: Strg. Com. (1978); Prog. Com. (1978–79). **Pubns.:** Jt. Auth., "Health Information Sources and Services for the Small Public Library," *OK Libn.* (1978). **Activities:** 1, 12; 29, 32, 39; 58, 80 **Addr.:** Lamar University Library, P.O. Box 10021, Beaumont, TX 77710.

Webb, Barbara (S. 7, 1946, St. Louis, MO) Assoc. Dir. of Lib. Oper., Fairfax Cnty. Pub. Lib., 1981–; Head, Comm., Baltimore Cnty. Pub. Lib., 1980–81; Head, Prog. Srvs., 1976–80, Inst. Srvs. Libn., 1975–77, Chld. Spec., 1973–75; Young Peoples Libn., Elmhurst (IL) Pub. Lib., 1972–73. **Educ.:** Elmhurst Coll., 1964–68, BA (Eng.); Rosary Coll., 1970–71, MA (LS); Johns Hopkins Univ., 1976–81, MAS (Admin.). **Orgs.:** ALA: ASCLA Ch.-Elect, Lib. Srvs. to Impaired (1980–81); PLA, *Pub. Libs.* Elderly Sect. Ed. Com. (1981–82). MD LA. MD State Dept. of Educ., Div. of Lib. Srvs. & Dev.–LSCA Adv. Com. (1978–81). Natl. Assn. of Lcl. Cable Progmrs. **Honors:** Beta Phi Mu, 1971. **Pubns.:** Jt. Auth., *Gray and Growing* (1978); "Today's Libraries Work to Bring Elderly In," *Perspective on Aging* (Jl./Ag. 1979); "Gray & Growing: Programming with Older Adults," *Drexel Lib. Qtly.* (Ap., 1979). **Activities:** 9; 25, 32, 36 **Addr.:** Fairfax County Public Library, 5502 Port Royal Rd., Springfield, VA 22151.

Webb, David Aiken (Je. 3, 1917, Greenwood, SC) Retired, 1980–; Dir. of Libs., N. TX State Univ., 1953–78, Prof. of LS, 1953–80, Actg. Dean, Sch. of Lib. and Info. Sci., 1971–72. **Educ.:** Univ. of SC, 1935–39, AB (Eng.); Emory Univ., 1939–40, ABLA (LS); Univ. of MI, 1946–47, AMLS; Univ. of Chicago, 1963, PhD (LS). **Orgs.:** ALA. SWLA: Ch., Coll. & Univ. (1965–66, 1966–67). TX LA: Ch., Coll. Div. (1949–50). TX Assn. of Coll.

PROFESSIONAL ACTIVITIES: Institutions: 1. Acad. lib.; 2. Arch.; 3. Assn.; 4. Fed./Gvt. lib.; 5. Inst. lib.; 6. Mfr./Suppl.; 7. Milit. lib.; 8. Musm.; 9. Pub. lib.; 10. Sch. lib.; 11. Sch. of lib. sci.; 12. Spec. lib.; 13. State lib.; 14. (other). **Functions/Activities:** 15. Acq./Col. dev.; 16. Adult srvs.; 17. Admin.; 18. Apprais.; 19. Archit./Bldgs.; 20. Cat./Class.; 21. Chld. srvs.; 22. Circ.; 23. Cons./Pres.; 24. Consult.; 25. Cont. ed.; 26. Educ. lib. sci.; 27. Ext. srvs.; 28. Fund/Grants; 29. Gvt. pubs.; 30. Indx./Abs.; 31. Instr. lib. use; 32. Media srvs.; 33. Micro.; 34. Netwks./Coop.; 35. Persnl.; 36. PR; 37. Publshg.; 38. Recs. mgt.; 39. Ref. srvs.; 40. Repro.; 41. Resrch.; 42. Review.; 43. Secur.; 44. Serials; 45. Spec. col.; 46. Tech. srvs.; 47. Trustees/Bds.; 48. YA srvs.; 49. (other).

Tchrs. **Activities:** 1; 17, 19, 46 **Addr.:** 1214 Clover Le., Denton, TX 76201.

Webb, Dorothy M. (Je. 3, 1941, Montreal, PQ) Resrch. Supvsr., Can. Natl. Railways, 1967–; Libn., Can. Natl. Telecom. Lib., 1965–67; Libn., Can. Natl. Railways HQ Lib., 1963–65. **Educ.:** McGill Univ., 1957–61, BA (Hist.), 1962–63, BLS. **Orgs.:** SLA: Newsp. Div., Montreal Conf. (Lcl. Rep., 1967). **Activities:** 12; 17, 30, 41 **Addr.:** 3542 Garneys St., St. Laurent, PQ H4K 2M2 Canada.

Webb, Margaret L. (Je. 14, 19–, Philadelphia, PA) Libn., NJ Dept. Transp., 1967–; Asst. Lending Srvs. Libn., NJ State Lib., 1964–67, Ref. Libn., Lending, 1963–64; Tchr., Wildwood HS, 1957–58. **Educ.:** Chestnut Hill Coll., 1953–57, AB (Hist.); St. John's Univ., New York, NY, 1958–60, MA (Hist.); Rutgers Univ., 1961–63, MLS; various crs. **Orgs.:** SLA: Princeton-Trenton Chap. (Empl. Ch., 1973). Gvt. Docum. Assn. of NJ. **Activities:** 13; 15, 17, 29; 91, 92, 94 **Addr.:** 130 W. Farrel Ave. A4, Trenton, NJ 08618.

Webb, Mary Elizabeth (Roberts) (N. 16, —, Porter, OK) Media Coord., McLain HS, Tulsa Pub. Sch. Syst., 1970–; Head Libn., Ponca City (OK) HS, 1966–70; Head Libn., W. Jr. HS, Ponca City Pub. Sch. Syst., 1960–66; Info. and ILL Libn., Head of Circ. Dept., Univ. of OK Lib., 1951–60. **Educ.:** Northeast. OK State Univ., 1947, BS (Elem.); Univ. of OK, 1948–52, AB (LS), 1953–68, MLS; OK State Univ., 1966–80, (LS). **Orgs.:** ALA: Mem. Ch., State of OK (1976–80). SWLA. OK LA: Mem. Com. (1976–80); Sequoyah Chld. Book Awd. Com. (1973–76). OK AECT. OK Educ. Assn. Natl. Educ. Assn. Tulsa Classroom Tchrs. Assn. AAUW. **Activities:** 10; 32, 42, 48; 67, 89, 95-Graphics. **Addr.:** 7398 E. 24th St., Tulsa, OK 74129.

Webb, Thelma Elizabeth (Mr. 24, 1914, Bethlehem, PA) Lib. Media Supvsr., Sch. Dist. 89, IL, 1975–; Tchr.-Libn., Jane Addams Sch., 1963–74; Tchr., Lincoln Sch., 1961–63; Secy., Irving Sch., 1960–61; Fin. Ofcr., Mgr., Mid-Amer. Chap., Amer. Red Cross, 1942–43; Tchr., Wellington HS, 1936–40. **Educ.:** Baldwin-Wallace Coll., 1932–36, BA, cum laude (Span., Eng.); Rosary Coll., 1969, MALS; various crs. **Orgs.:** IL LA. ALA: AASL. Assn. of Supvsrs. and Curric. Dirs. AECT. Phi Delta Kappa: Secy. (1979–80). Alpha Phi Gamma: VP (1939–40). Gamma Sigma: Treas. (1938–40). Mensa. **Honors:** Pi Gamma Mu. **Activities:** 10; 17, 28, 31; 63, 67 **Addr.:** 913 N. 9th Ave., Maywood, IL 60153.

Webb, Ty (Carol T.) (Ag. 17, 1945, Knoxville, TN) Info. Broker, Info Webb, 1978–; Supvsr., Lib. Srvs., Mobay Chem. Corp., 1970–78. **Educ.:** Mt. Un. Coll., 1964–67, BA (Eng. Lit.); Univ. of MO, 1968, (Lib. and Info. Sci.); various sems. **Orgs.:** Kansas City Lib. Netwk., Inc.: Bd. of Dirs. (1976–78); various coms. Kansas City Metro. Lib. Netwk.: Adv. Cncl. (1978–81); various coms. ofcs. Kansas City OLUG: Bd. of Dirs. (1978–81); Lockheed Update Rep. (1978–). SLA: Welcoming Com.; Film Com.; Heart of Amer. Chap. (Pres., 1975); various ofcs. various orgs. Kansas City Ski Club: Pubcty. Com. (1977). Mobay Kansas City Credit Un.: Bd. of Dirs. (1978–81). **Pubns.:** Various articles, *Show-Me Libs.* **Activities:** 12; 39; 75, 91 **Addr.:** InfoWebb, 43 E. 106 Terr., Kansas City, MO 64114.

Webb, Tyrone T. (S. 17, 1950, Selma, AL) Lib. Media Spec., West End HS, 1980–; Lib. Media Spec., Whatley Elem. Sch., 1975–80; Libn., Vincent HS, 1975; Libn., E. Three Notch Elem. Sch., 1973–75; Libn., George W. Long HS, 1971–72. **Educ.:** AL State Univ., 1967–71, BS (Hist., Eng., LS), 1972–73, MEd (Sec. Educ.); Univ. of AL, 1974–77, MLS; Univ. of AL, Birmingham, 1980–. **Orgs.:** AL Instr. Media Assn.: Ch., Pubcty. Com. (1977–79); Ch., Nom. Com. (1980); Bd. of Dir. (1978–81); VP-Pres. Elect (1981–82). AL LA: Nom. Com. (1979); Sch. & Chld. Div., Secy. (1977). SELA. ALA. Other orgs. Birmingham Chap., ASU Alum. Assn. Inner City Jaycees. AL Educ. Assn. Other orgs. **Honors:** Birmingham News, Favorite Tchr. Nominee, 1978; Inner City Jaycees, Outstan. Young Educ., 1980. **Activities:** 9, 10; 17, 21, 24; 63, 74, 78 **Addr.:** 322 Stoneridge Rd., Birmingham, AL 35209.

Webber, John P. (Mr. 26, 1917, Newton, MA) Chief, Info. Resrcs. Dev. Branch, Lib. and Info. Srvs. Div., Env. Sci. Info. Ctr., Natl. Oceanic and Atmospheric Admin., 1977–, Spec. Asst. to Dir., 1975–77, Chief, Libs. Div., 1967–75. **Educ.:** Amherst Coll., 1935–39, BA; MA Inst. of Tech., 1939–41, MS (Meteorology); Cath. Univ. of Amer., 1957–61 (LS). **Orgs.:** SLA. ASIS. Amer. Meteorological Socty. **Activities:** 4, 12; 23, 33, 46; 52, 65, 82 **Addr.:** 2621 Sigmona St., Falls Church, VA 22046.

Webb-Ozmun, Mary Beth (Ja. 29, 1938, Tulsa, OK) Lib. and Musm. Dir., Bacone Coll., 1977–; Assoc. Dir., East. OK Dist. Lib., 1971–77; Media Consult., OK City Pub. Sch. Syst., 1970–71, Elem. Media Spec., 1968–70. **Educ.:** Univ. of OK, 1954–59, BS (Vocational Home Econ.), 1967–68, MLS, Univ. of OK, OK State Univ., 1971–79, postgrad. work; other courses, workshops, internship. **Orgs.:** SWLA: Mem. Ch. for all states, (1978–80). ALA: Mem. Ch., SW Reg. (1978–80). OK LA: Secy. (1972–73); Ch., Mem. Com. (1972–76). Ch., Pubcty. Com. (1972–73); Ch., Sequoyah Chld. Book Awd. (1971–72). OK AECT. other orgs. Muskogee Coal. for Equal Rights Amendment. AAUW. OK Educ. Assn. Natl. Educ. Assn. other orgs. **Pubns.:** "Library Service for Green Country," *OK Libn.* (Ap. 1972); "School Librarians Achieve Departmental Status in O.E.A.," *OK Libn.* (Jl. 1971). **Activities:** 1, 9; 17, 31, 45; 55, 66, 78 **Addr.:** 2503 Margaret Lynn Le., Muskogee, OK 74401.

Webby, Ernest J. Jr. (Je. 8, 1939, Brockton, MA) Lib. Dir., Brockton Pub. Lib. Syst., 1974–; Ch., Dept. of Instr. Resrcs., Brockton HS, 1969–74; Ref. Libn., Bay Shore (NY) Sr. HS, 1966–69; Tchr., Centereach (NY) Jr. HS, 1964–65. **Educ.:** Fairfield Univ., 1959–62, BSS (Hist.); Simmons Coll., 1965–66, MSLS; Boston State Coll., 1963–66, MEd (Hist.). **Orgs.:** MA LA. New Eng. LA. ALA. Rotary Club of Brockton. **Pubns.:** "Continuing Education in Many Directions," *Bay State Libn.* (Win. 1979). **Activities:** 9; 17, 50, 66 **Addr.:** Brockton Public Library System, 304 Main St., Brockton, MA 02401.

Weber, Benita M. (Ap. 5, 1947, Pittsburgh, PA) Head, Serials Dept., Univ. of NM, 1976–; Serials Libn., Montgomery Cnty. Cmnty. Coll., 1973–76. **Educ.:** Temple Univ., 1964–68, BA (Span.); Drexel Univ., 1972–74, MS (LS). **Orgs.:** ALA: Cnclr. (1980–84); RTSD/Serials Sect., Medium-Sized Resrch. Libs. Discuss. Grp. (Ch., 1977–78); Com. to Study Serials Recs. (1977–81, Ch., 1978–79). NM LA: Treas. (1978–79). **Honors:** Beta Phi Mu, 1974. **Pubns.:** "Education for Serials Librarians: A Survey," *Drexel Lib. Qtly.* (Jl. 1975); Jt. Ed., "Current Issues in Serials Librarianship," *Drexel Lib. Qtly.* (Jl. 1975). **Activities:** 1; 15, 26, 44; 50, 61 **Addr.:** Serials Department, General Library, University of New Mexico, Albuquerque, NM 87131.

Weber, David C. (Jl. 25, 1924, Waterville, ME) Dir. of Libs., Stanford Univ., 1969–; Assoc. Dir. of Libs., 1965–69, Asst. Dir. of Libs., 1961–65; Asst. Dir. of Libs., Harvard Univ., 1957–61, Asst., 1948–57. **Educ.:** Colby Coll., 1942–47, AB (Hist.); Columbia Univ., 1947–48, BS (LS); Harvard Univ., 1953, MA (Hist.); Rutgers Univ., Advnc. Sem. in Lib. Admin., 1956. **Orgs.:** ALA: ACRL, Pres. (1981–82); Com. on Future ALA Structure (1976–78); RTSD, Pres. (1967–68). Resrch. Libs. Grp.: Bd. of Gvrs. (1978–). CA Lib. Athrty. for Syst. and Srvs.: Bd. of Dir. (1978–80). NCLIS: Natl. Per. Syst. Adv. Com. (1978–80). **Honors:** Cncl. on Lib. Resrcs., Flwshp., 1970. **Pubns.:** Jt. Auth., *University Library Administration* (1971); Ed., *Studies in Library Administrative Problems* (1960); "The Next Fifty Years in Academic Libraries," *OK Libn.* (F. 1980); "A Century of Cooperative Programs Among Academic Libraries," Coll. & Resrch. Libs. (My. 1976). **Activities:** 1; 17, 34, 35; 56 **Addr.:** Stanford University Libraries, Green Library/Directors' Office, Stanford, CA 94305.

Weber, Donald John (Ag. 30, 1943, New York, NY) Dir., FL Reg. Lib. for the Blind and Phys. Handcpd., 1975–; Head, Netwk. Srvs., Natl. Lib. Srv. for the Blind and Phys. Handcpd., Lib. of Congs., 1974–75, Asst. Head, Natl. Col., 1970–75; Admin. Libn., Air Force Lib., Izmir, Turkey, 1968–70; Proj. Libn., Middle East Tech. Univ., Ankara, Turkey, Peace Corps, 1967–68; Head Libn., Patchogue-Medford (NY) Sch. Syst., 1965–67. **Educ.:** SUNY, Geneseo, 1960–64, BS (Educ.), 1964–65, MLS. **Orgs.:** ALA: ASCLA/Lib. Srv. to Blind and Phys. Handcpd. Sect., (Ch., 1978–79; Vice-ch. 1977–78); Ch., Campbell Awds. Com. (1977–78); Bd. of Dir. (1978–79); Ch., Prog. Plng. (1977–78). NLA. FL LA. Middle East Libns. Assn. Visual Aid Volun. of FL: Bd. of Dir. (1976–77; 1979–); Pres. (1977–79). Amer. Assn. of Workers for the Blind. Sunshine State Assn. of Workers for the Blind. Natl. Braille Assn. other orgs. **Pubns.:** "METU's Library: The First Decade," *UNESCO Bltn. for Libs.* (Mr.–Ap. 1970); "Library Services for the Blind & Physically Handicapped," *FL Libs.* (Mr.–Ap. 1976); Jt. Auth., "Volunteer Recognition: Report of the Ad Hoc Recognition Committee of the Sunshine State Association for the Blind," *Dikta* (Fall 1978); Jt. Auth., "Subject Bibliographies: A Modest Proposal," *Dikta* (Spr. 1979); "Volunteers: Telephone Pioneer Contributions to Library Service to the Blind and Physically Handicapped," *Keystone* (Je. 1979); other articles, reviews. **Activities:** 13; 17, 24, 34; 72, 95-Rehab. **Addr.:** 2231 Oriole Le., South Daytona, FL 32019.

Weber, E. Sue (Ag. 24, 1936, Detroit, MI) Asst. Dir. for Tech. Srvs., Univ. of TX Hlth. Sci. Ctr. Lib., 1977–; Asst. Head of Cat., SUNY at Stony Brook, 1974–77; Asst. Head of Cat., Columbia Univ., 1966–69. **Educ.:** MI State Univ., 1954–57, BA (Eng.); Purdue Univ., 1958–65, MA (Eng.); Columbia Univ., 1965–66, MS (LS). **Orgs.:** SLA: Ch., Lcl. Plng. Grp. (1980–). Med. LA: Ed. Com., *MLA News* (1979–); Ch., Policy Manual, Sub-Com.; S. Ctrl. Reg. Grp. Hlth. Sci. OCLC User's Grp.: Cont. Educ. Com. **Honors:** Beta Phi Mu. **Pubns.:** *Serials Workbook; a Problem-solving Manual for OCLC Serials Catalogers* (1977); "The art of helping," *Info. Reports and Bibl.* (1978). **Activities:** 1, 12; 15, 17, 46; 56, 72, 80 **Addr.:** 3121 Eanes Cir., Austin, TX 78746.

Weber, Milada (Mr. 2, 1911, Brno, Moravia, Czechoslovakia) Head, Cat., Class. Dept., Northwest. Univ., Sch. of Law, 1968–; Cat. Libn., Hofstra Univ., 1965–68; Catlgr., Elmont Meml. Lib., 1963–65. **Educ.:** Konsularakademie, Wienna, Austria, 1931–33, Dip.; Masaryk Univ., Brno, Czechoslovakia, 1934–39, JUDr (Law); Univ. of Parana, Curitiba, Brazil, 1950, Tchrs. Cert. (Eng., Fr.); Long Island Univ., 1962–63, MS (LS). **Orgs.:** AALL. **Activities:** 1; 20; 77 **Addr.:** Northwestern University School of Law Library, 357 E. Chicago Ave., Chicago, IL 60611.

Weber, Paul Michael (Jl. 27, 1947, Canton, OH) Dir., Greenville Pub. Lib., 1981–; Unit Head, Adams-Brown Bkmobile, State Lib. of OH, 1978–81; Head, Madge Youtz Branch, Stark Cnty. Dist. Lib., 1970–78. **Educ.:** St. Joseph's Coll., Rensselaer, IN, 1965–70, BS (Msc.); Kent State Univ., 1975–77, MLS. **Orgs.:** ALA. OH LA. **Honors:** ALA, JMRT, Shirley Olafson Awd., 1979. **Activities:** 9, 13; 27, 42; 55, 90 **Addr.:** Greenville Public Library, 520 Sycamore St., Greenville, OH 45331.

Weber, Pauline G. (Ap. 19, 1939, Kitchener, ON) Asst. Coord., Instr. Media, Halton Bd. of Educ., 1978–; Prin., Mnstry. of Educ., Evening Lib. Crs., ON Mnstry. of Educ., 1978–80; Lib. Consult., Wellington Bd. of Educ., 1976–77; Tchr.–Libn., Bennetto Sch., 1970–77. **Educ.:** McMaster Univ., 1969, BA (Msc., Psy.); ON Mnstry. of Educ., 1965–72, Lib. Spec. Cert. (Sch. Libs.). **Orgs.:** ON Educ. Comms. Athty. Reg. Adv. Cncl.: Cncl., Past Ch. ON Film Assn.: Bd. (1979–80). **Pubns.:** *Evaluation: The Key to Accountability and Excellence in Your School Libraries* (1979); educ. consult., "Hailey's Gift" 16mm film (1978); film scripts, "Flight of the Monarch," "Northern Spring" (1979); film std. guide, "Flight of the Monarch"; various film std. guides. **Activities:** 10, 12; 17, 26, 32 **Addr.:** Halton Board of Education, 2050 Guelph Line, Burlington, ON L7R 3Z2 Canada.

Webster, Alma A. (Ap. 13, 1920, SK) Lrng. Resrcs. Supvsr., Edmonton Pub. Sch. Bd., 1964–; Asst. Lib. Spec., 1962–64; Chief Libn., Port Arthur Pub. Lib., 1956–62; Asst. Chief Libn., Moose Jaw Pub. Lib., 1954–56; Sch. Libn., Edmonton Pub. Sch. Bd., 1949–54. **Educ.:** Univ. of SK, 1937–40, BA (Math), 1940–41 (Educ.); Univ. of Toronto, 1947–48, BLS, 1969, MLS; Univ. of AB, BEd. Delta Kappa Gamma Socty. Intl. **Activities:** 9, 10; 15, 32, 48; 63, 89, 92 **Addr.:** 10242-120 St., #2B, Edmonton, AB T5K 2A3 Canada.

Webster, Duane E. (Ag. 28, 1941, Rochester, NY) Dir., Ofc. of Mgt. Std., ARL, 1970–; Mgr., Lib. Systs., Srv. Tech. Corp., 1968–70; Tech. Info. Spec., Gen. Dynamics, 1967–68; Sr. Libn., Bus. Div., Rochester Pub. Lib., 1965–67; Lib. Schol., Bus. Admin. Lib., Univ. of MI, 1963–64. **Educ.:** Heidelberg Coll., 1959–63, BA (Hist.); Univ. of MI, 1963–64, MALS. **Orgs.:** ALA: ACRL. **Pubns.:** *Planning Program for Small Academic Libraries* (1980); *Preservation Planning Program* (1980); "Preparing Librarians as Consultants," *Jnl. of Acad. Libs.* (Spr. 1982); "Planning Program for Small Academic Libraries," *Jnl. of Lib. Admin.* (Win. 1982); *Collection Analysis Project: An Assisted Self Study Manual* (1980); various mono., articles. **Addr.:** Office of Management Studies, 1527 New Hampshire Ave. N.W., Washington, DC 20036.

Webster, James K. (My. 13, 1933, Buffalo, NY) Dir., Sci. & Engin. Lib., SUNY, Buffalo, 1976–; Head Libn., Calspan Corp., 1970–76, Asst. Libn., 1956–70. **Educ.:** Univ. of Buffalo, 1952–56, BA (Math.); State Univ., Coll. at Geneseo, 1963–66, MLS. **Orgs.:** SLA: Networking Com. (1979–82; Ch., 1979–82); Upstate NY Chap. (Pres. 1979–80); Transp. Div. (Ch., 1977–78); Lib. Mgt. Div., Nom. Com. (1978–80). NY LA: Acad. and Spec. Libs. Sect. (Pres. 1980–81). ALA: ACRL. West. NY Lib. Resrcs. Cncl.: Bd. of Trustees (1970–84). Other orgs. Amer. Socty. for Engin. Educ.: Engin. Libs. Div. **Pubns.:** Ed., "The Bibliographic Utilities: A Guide For The Special Librarian," *Spec. Libs. Assn.* (1980); Jt. Auth., "The Literature of Hazardous Wastes: Another Growing Problem," *Vance Bibliographies* (1980); Jt. Auth., "Love Canal, A Bibliography," *Vance Bibliographies* (1980); "Networking Notes," *Spec. Libs.* (1979–80); Jt. Auth., "The Impact of Modern Technology on a Technical Library," ASIS *Proc.* (1975); Articles, Reviews. **Activities:** 1; 17; 64, 91 **Addr.:** Science & Engineering Library, Capen Hall, State University of New York at Buffalo, Buffalo, NY 14260.

Wecker, Charlene Dudovitz (D. 19, 1945, St. Paul, MN) Head, Serials Cat. Sect., Wayne State Univ., 1979–; Catlgr., Univ. of CO, 1968–79; Ref. Libn., Univ. of MN, 1967–68. **Educ.:** Univ. of MN, 1963–66, BA (Italian), 1966–69, MA (LS). **Orgs.:** ALA. **Pubns.:** Jt. auth., *Doctoral Research in Educational Media, 1969–1972* ERIC (1975). **Activities:** 1; 20, 44, 46 **Addr.:** Serials Cataloging Section, Purdy Library, Wayne State University, Detroit, MI 48202.

Wecker, Steven (Ag. 3, 1948, Brooklyn, NY) Mgr. of Lib. Srvs., Natl. Bank of Detroit, 1979–; Bus. Libn., Univ. of CO, 1977–79; Ref. Libn., Lehman Coll., CUNY, 1971–76; Ref. Libn., SUNY Coll. at Oswego, 1970–71; **Educ.:** Brooklyn Coll., 1965–69, BA (Econ.); Columbia Univ., 1969–70, MS (LS); New Sch. for Soc. Resrch., 1972–75, MA (Econ.). **Orgs.:** SLA. Assoc. Info. Mgrs. **Honors:** Beta Phi Mu. **Activities:** 1, 12; 17, 38; 59, 75 **Addr.:** National Bank of Detroit, Library, P.O. Box 116, Detroit, MI 48232.

Wedgewood, Mary Elizabeth (Ap. 27, 1945, Grand Rapids, MN) Fine and Performing Arts Ref. Libn., Saskatoon Pub. Lib., 1979–; Msc. Libn., Otto Harrassowitz Exportbuchhandlung, W. Germany, 1977–78; Sessional Lect., Univ. of SK, 1969–74. **Educ.:** MacMurray Coll., 1963–64; Univ. of AR, 1964–67, BMus. (Msc.); Univ. of Chicago, 1974–75, MA (LS);

Special Subjects/Services: 50. Adult educ.; 51. Advert./Mktg.; 52. Aerosp.; 53. Agric.; 54. Area std.; 55. Arts/Hum.; 56. Autom.; 57. Bibl./Prtg.; 58. Bio. sci.; 59. Bus./Fin.; 60. Chem.; 61. Copyrt.; 62. Documtn.; 63. Educ.; 64. Engin.; 65. Env.; 66. Eth. grps.; 67. Film; 68. Food/Nutr.; 69. Geneal.; 70. Geo.; 71. Geol.; 72. Handcpd.; 73. Hist.; 74. Int. frdm.; 75. Info. sci.; 76. Insr.; 77. Law; 78. Legis.; 79. Math./Comp. sci.; 80. Med.; 81. Metals; 82. Nat. resrcs.; 83. Newsp.; 84. Nuc. sci.; 85. Oral hist.; 86. Petr./Energy; 87. Pharm.; 88. Phys./Astr./Math.; 89. Readg.; 90. Relig.; 91. Sci./Tech.; 92. Soc. sci.; 93. Telecom.; 94. Transp.; 95. (other).

Univ. of WI, 1971–72, (Musclgy.). **Orgs.:** Mus. LA. Amer. Musicological Socty. **Honors:** Beta Phi Mu, 1976; Phi Beta Kappa, 1967. **Pubns.:** "Avant-Garde Music: Some Publication Problems," *Lib. Qtly.* (Ap. 1976). **Activities:** 1, 9; 15, 37, 41; 55, 57 **Addr.:** 129 Dalhousie Crescent, Saskatoon, SK S7H 3R4 Canada.

Wedgeworth, Robert (Jl. 31, 1937, Ennis, TX) Exec. Dir., ALA, 1972–; Asst. Prof., Lib. Srv., Rutgers Univ., 1971–72; Asst. Chief Order Libn., Brown Univ., 1966–69; Head Libn., Meramec Cmnty. Coll., 1964–65; Actg. Head Libn., Park Coll., Parkville, MO, 1963–64; Asst. Head Libn., 1962–63; Catlgr., Kansas City Pub. Lib., 1961–62. **Educ.:** Wabash Coll., 1959, AB (Eng., Span.); Univ. of IL, 1961, MS (LS); Washington Univ., 1965, (Span.); Rutgers Univ., 1969–72, (LS). **Orgs.:** Natl. Lib. of Med.: Biomed. Lib. Review Com. (1975–79, Ch., 1978–79). Lib. of Congs.: Network Adv. Com. (1977–); Ctr. for the Bk. (Exec. Com.). ASIS. Univ. of Pittsburgh Grad. Sch. of Lib. and Info. Sci.: Bd. of Visitors (1977–). Other orgs. Amer. Assn. for Advnc. of Hum.: Bd. of Dir. Natl. Comsn. on New Tech. Uses of Copyrighted Works: Mem. (1975–78). Pub. Srv. Satellite Cnsrtm.: Bd. of Dirs. NAACP. Other orgs. **Honors:** Cncl. on Lib. Resrcs., Fellow, 1969; Park Coll., DLitt, 1973. **Pubns.:** Ed. in Chief, *ALA Yearbook* (1976–); Ed. in Chief, *ALA World Encyclopedia of Library and Information Services* (1980); "Organizing Librarians: Three Options for ALA," *Lib. Jnl.* (Ja. 1, 1976); "Libraries," *Dictionary of American History* (1976); "Global Library Diplomacy," *Amer. Libs.* (Ja. 1978); other articles. **Activities:** 3; 17 **Addr.:** American Library Association, 50 E. Huron St., Chicago, IL 60611.*

Weech, Terry L. (Jl. 8, 1937, Galesburg, IL) Assoc. Prof., Grad. Sch. of LS, Univ. of IL, 1980–; Asst. Prof., Sch. of LS, Univ. of IA, 1976–80; Head, LS Dept., MS Univ. for Women, 1973–76; Visit. Lect., Grad. Sch. of LS, Univ. of IL, 1972–73, Resrch. Assoc., Lib. Resrch. Ctr., 1967–68; Docum. Libn., IL State Lib., 1965–67, Libn. I, 1964–64. **Educ.:** Knox Coll., 1955–59, AB (Phil.); Univ. of IL, 1963–64, MS (LS), 1968–72, PhD (LS). **Orgs.:** ALA: LRRT Resrch. Awd. Com. (Ch., 1979–80). AALS: Resrch. Int. Grp. (Conv., 1976–77). IL LA. IA LA: Int. Frdm. Com. (Ch., 1979–80). **Pubns.:** "Public Library Standards and Rural Library Service," *Lib. Trends* (Spr. 1980); "Attitudes of School and Public Librarians towards Combined Facilities," *Pub. Lib. Qtly.* (Spr. 1979); "The Use of Government Publications ...," *Gvt. Pubns. Review* (N. 2, 1978); "Evaluation of Adult Reference Service," *Lib. Trends* (Ja. 1974); "Characteristics of State Government Publications, 1910–1969," *Gvt. Pubns. Review* (Fall 1973). **Activities:** 9, 11; 26, 29, 39; 55, 74, 75 **Addr.:** University of Illinois, Graduate School of Library and Information Science, 410 David Kinley Hall, 1407 W. Gregory Dr., Urbana, IL 61801.

Weekley, Shirley Ann (Shadyside, OH) Libn., Admin. Asst., Acad. of Vocal Arts, 1977–; Libn., Marlboro Msc. Sch. and Fest., 1962–; Asst. Libn., Curtis Inst. of Msc., 1973–77; Admin. Asst., Marlboro Sch. of Msc., 1971–73; Horn Player, Dallas Symph. Orch., 1962–71. **Educ.:** OH State Univ., 1954–57, B Music, (Horn) B Sci (Msc. Educ.); OH State, 1958–59 (grad. std. in Msc. Hist.); Drexel Univ., 1977–79, MLS. **Orgs.:** PA Msc. LA: Secy.-Treas. (1978–79). Msc. LA. **Pubns.:** Ed., cmplr., *Marlboro Music: 1951–1975* (1976); ed., cmplr., *Marlboro Music: 1976–1982* (forthcoming). **Activities:** 1, 14-Msc. Fest.; 15, 41; 55 **Addr.:** 1829 Spruce St., Philadelphia, PA 19103.

Weeks, Gerald Michael (My. 8, 1935, Vancouver, BC) Ref. Libn., Forestry and Prcs. Techs., 1981–; Ref. Coord., BC Inst. of Tech., 1979–81, Bus. Ref. Libn., 1975–79, Asst. Libn. 1968–75; Catlgr., Univ. of Toronto, 1963–68. **Educ.:** Univ. of BC, 1953–57, BA (Math., Eng.), 1957–58 (Tchr. Trng.), 1962–63, BLS; 1973–74, MLS. **Orgs.:** BC LA: Lib.-Bk. Trade Com. (Ch., 1977–78). Can. LA. Pac. NW LA. ALA. **Activities:** 1; 20, 31, 39; 51, 59, 77 **Addr.:** BCIT Library, 3700 Willingdon Ave., Burnaby, BC V5G 3H2, Canada.

Weeks, James Powell (Je. 24, 1950, Scranton, PA) Cat. Libn., IN Univ. of PA, 1978–; Libn./Archvst., Case West. Resrv. Univ., 1975–77. **Educ.:** PA State Univ., 1968–72, BA (Hist.), 1972–74, MA (Jrnlsm.); Univ. of Pittsburgh, 1974–75, MLS. **Orgs.:** ALA. PA LA. Pittsburgh Reg. Lib. Ctr.: OCLC Peer Cncl. (1979–). Tri-State Assn. of Coll. & Resrch. Libs. **Honors:** Beta Phi Mu, 1976. **Pubns.:** "The Bohn Housing & Planning Library of Case Western Reserve U.," *CPL Nsltr.* (Spr. 1976); "Baptism By Fire: Scranton Area Troops Had Bloody First Day of Battle," *Scrantonian* (S.29, O.6, O.13, 1979). **Activities:** 1, 2; 20, 32, 46; 92 **Addr.:** 672 Rustic Lodge Rd. A-22, Indiana, PA 15701.

Weeks, Kenneth R. (Ja. 15, 1941, San Francisco, CA) Asst. to the Univ. Libn., Univ. of CA, San Francisco, 1974–; Jr. Spec., Inst. of Lib. Resrch., Univ. of CA, Berkeley, 1973–74; Ref. & Docum. Libn., CT Coll., 1970–72. **Educ.:** Univ. of San Francisco, 1959–62, BS (Eng.); Marquette Univ., 1962–66, MA (Theo.); Univ. of CA, Berkeley, 1969–70, MLS. **Orgs.:** Med. LA: Intl. Coop. Com. (1981–). North. CA Med. Lib. Grp. N. Atl. Hlth. Sci. Libs. **Honors:** Cncl. on Lib. Resrcs./Natl. Lib. of Med., Hlth. Sci. Lib. Mgt. Intern, 1980. **Pubns.:** Jt. Auth., "The Duplication of Monograph Holdings in the University of California Library System," *Lib. Qtly.* (Jl. 1975). **Activities:** 1; 17, 35; 80 **Addr.:** The Library, University of California, San Francisco, CA 94143.

Weeks, Patsy Ann Landry (Mr. 3, 1930, Luling, TX) Libn., Bangs Indp. Sch. Dist., 1973–; Remedial Readg. Tchr., Anson Indp. Sch. Dist., 1971–73; Remedial Readg. Tchr., Taylor Cnty. Schs., 1965–66; Art, Coll. Algebra Tchr., Cisco Jr. Coll., 1957–58; Phys. Educ. Tchr., Beaumont Indp. Sch. Dist., 1953; Art, Readg., Math. Tchr., Grandview Indp. Sch. Dist., 1950–52. **Educ.:** SW TX State Univ., 1949–51, BS (Educ., Art, Math.); TX Scottish Rite Hosp. for Crippled Chld., 1967–69, Remedial Lang. Cert.; TX Woman's Univ., 1975–79, MLS. **Orgs.:** TX LA: Int. Frdm. and Prof. Resp. (1979–81). TX Assn. of Sch. Libns.: Reg. XV Wkshp. (Ch., 1976–77). ALA: AASL. Anson Pub. Lib.: Lib. Bd. (1972). Teenage LA: Dist. Sponsor (1978–79, 1979–80). Readg. is Fundamental, Inc.: Bangs Readg. Is Fundamental Proj. (Coord., 1978–79, 1979–80). **Honors:** Beta Phi Mu, 1980; Alpha Chi, 1951; Kappa Pi, 1950. **Activities:** 10; 15, 22, 32; 74, 89, 93 **Addr.:** P.O. Box 969, Bangs, TX 76823.

Weese, Dwain W. (S. 26, 1935, Cook Cnty., IL) Instr. Dev. Coord., Sch. Dist. No. 38, 1976–; Visit. Lectr., Univ. of BC, 1975–76; Educ. Libn., Univ. of AB, 1971–75; Ref. Libn., ON Inst. for Std. in Educ., 1970–71; Asst. Educ. Libn., Queen's Univ., 1966–69. **Educ.:** Bradley Univ., 1955–59, BSc (Cmrce.); Chicago State Univ., 1962–65, MEd (Sch. Lib.); Univ. of West. ON, 1969–70, MLS (Libnshp.). **Orgs.:** AECT. Assn. of Media and Tech. in Educ. in Can. BC Sch. LA. Can. Sch. LA. BC Tchrs. Fed. Can. Fndn. for Econ. Educ. Can. Socty. for the Std. of Higher Educ. Pac. Instr. Media Assn. **Honors:** Phi Delta Kappa. **Pubns.:** Com. mem., *Sources and Resources: A Handbook for Teacher-Librarians in BC* (1979); *Manual of Production Activities: How To Make Your Own Teaching Materials* (1978); contrib., *Selected Bibliography of Educational Administration: A Canadian Orientation* (1974); contrib., *Canadian Education and The Future; A Select Annotated Bibliography* (1972). **Activities:** 14-Sch. Dist. Media Ctr.; 15, 24, 32; 63, 67 **Addr.:** School District No. 38 (Richmond), 1891 Wellinton Crescent, Richmond, BC V7B 1G6 Canada.

Wegener, Judith Ellyn (N. 20, 1944, Chicago, IL) Exec. Dir., Ctrl. IN Area Lib. Srvs. Athrty., 1977–; Ref. Libn., Monroe Cnty. Pub. Lib., 1972–77. **Educ.:** IN Univ., 1967–70, AB (Fine Arts), 1971–74, MLS. **Orgs.:** IN LA: Div. on Women in IN Libs. (1978–); Legis. Com. (1979–); Conf. Plng. Team (1979). ALA. Adult Educ. Info. Ctr.: Adv. Bd. (1979–) in Vocational Tech. Coll.: Adv. Bd., Lib. Technicians Prog. (1979–). Bloomington Arts and Crafts Fest. **Pubns.:** Ed., *Free and Inexpensive Film Sources* (1979); "Developing a Computerized Organization File," *Lib. Jnl.* (1977); Ed., *Library Publicity* (1979); Reviews. **Activities:** 9, 14-Network-multi-type; 17, 24, 25; 50 **Addr.:** 7440 Lampkins Ridge, Bloomington, IN 47401.

Wehlacz, Joseph Theodore (My. 29, 1946, Chicago, IL) Info. Sci., Toxicology, Eli Lilly and Co., 1979–. Sr. Libn., Lib. Agr. Srv., 1974–79; Engin. Libn., Memphis State Univ., 1973–74; Sci. Catlgr., IN Univ. Libs. 1971–73. **Educ.:** Memphis State Univ., 1964–68, BSc (Chem.); IN Univ., 1968–72, MS, MLS (Organic Chem., Info. Sci.). **Orgs.:** SLA. Amer. Chem. Socty. **Activities:** 12; 38, 39, 49-Info. Retrieval; 60, 75, 91 **Addr.:** Toxicology Division, Greenfield Research Labs., P.O. Box 708, Eli Lilly & Co., Greenfield, IN 46140.

Wehmann, Howard Herman (My. 17, 1938, Jersey City, NJ) Archvst., Milit. Arch. Div., Natl. Arch. and Recs. Srv., 1967–. **Educ.:** Univ. of MD, 1956–62, BA (Hist.); Columbia Univ., 1965–68, MA (Hist.); Natl. Arch., Admin. of Mod. Arch., 1967–68, cert. **Orgs.:** SAA. Natl. Arch. Asm.: Descrpn., Prsrvn., Apprais., and Tech. Coms. Yale Lib. Assoc. Mt. Olivet Untd. Meth. Church. Papers of Gen. Friedrich von Steuben: Ed. Bd. (1976–). Co. of Milit. Histns. **Pubns.:** *Pre-Federal and Related Records in the National Archives* (1982); "Noise, Novelties, and Nullifiers," *SC Hist. Mag.* (Ja. 1975); "To Major Gibbs With Much Esteem," *Prologue: Jnl. of the Natl. Arch.* (Win. 1972); "Pennsylvania German Fraktur," *Prologue* (Fall 1970); Reviews. **Activities:** 2; 17, 18, 39; 73 **Addr.:** 955 N. Madison St., Arlington, VA 22205.

Wehmeyer, Lillian Biermann (O. 29, 1933, Milwaukee, WI) Asst. Supt. for Instr., San Mateo City Sch. Dist., 1979–; Lect., Univ. of CA, Berkeley, 1977–80; Asst. Supt. Instr., Lafayette Sch. Dist., 1973–79; Dist. Libn., 1969–73, Sch. Libn., 1965–69. **Educ.:** Univ. of CA, Berkeley, 1964–65, BA (Msc.), 1965–69, MLS, 1973–78, PhD (Educ.), 1969–73, Admin. cred. **Orgs.:** ALA: AASL. CA Media & Lib. Educ. Assn. Waukesha Cnty. (WI) LA: Secy. and Pres. (1960–62). CA Assn. of Tchrs. of Eng. **Honors:** Phi Beta Kappa, 1965; Beta Phi Mu, 1969; Phi Delta Kappa, 1977. **Pubns.:** *Images in a Crystal Ball: World Futures in Novels for Young People* (1981); *School Librarian as Educator* (1976); *School Library Volunteer* (1975); "Program Evaluation for Policy Setting," *Educ. Eval. & Policy Analysis* (S.-O. 1979); "Futuristic Children's Novels as a Mode of Communication," *Resrch. in the Tchg. of Eng.* (My. 1979); "Leaping from the Curriculum in a Single Bound," *CMLEA Jnl.* (Fall 1978); other books, articles, reviews. **Activities:** 10, 11; 17, 26, 41; 55, 63 **Addr.:** 1333 - 37th Ave., San Francisco, CA 94122.

Wehrung, Janet Lee Johnston (S. 7, 1947, Passaic, NJ) Dir., Three Rivers Pub. Lib., 1979–; Acq. Libn., East Brunswick Pub. Lib., 1976–78, Libn., Ref., Cat., Adult, 1971–75; Ref.

Libn., Park Coll. Lib., 1970–71. **Educ.:** Park Coll., 1965–69, BA (Lit.); Univ. of MI, 1969–70, AMLS (Gen.). **Orgs.:** ALA. MI LA. **Activities:** 9; 16, 17, 39; 69 **Addr.:** Three Rivers Public Library, 920 W. Michigan Ave., Three Rivers, MI 49093.

Weibel, Kathleen (F. 28, 1945, New York, NY) Freelance Consult., 1981–; Cont. Educ. Consult., NY State Lib., 1978–81; Proj. Dir., COLEPAC, Univ. of WI, 1976–77; Adult Spec., Chicago Pub. Lib., Ext., 1970–74. **Educ.:** Chestnut Hill Coll., 1963–67, BA (Eng.); Columbia Univ., 1967–69, MLS. **Orgs.:** ALA: Publshg. Com. (1978–). CLENE: Adv. Com. (1978–, Ch. 1980–). AALS: Cont. Educ. Com. (1980–). NY LA: Ref. and Adult Srvc. Sect., Bd. of Dir. (1979–). **Pubns.:** Jt. ed., *The Role of Women in Librarianship 1876–1976* (1978). **Activities:** 9, 13; 16, 25, 27; 50, 92 **Addr.:** 334 Manning Blvd., Albany, NY 12206.

Weick, Robert John (Jl. 15, 1925, Fort Wayne, IN) Media Ctr. Dir., Wayne HS, 1971–; Libn., S. Side HS, 1968–71; Asst. Consult., Sch. Lib., Fort Wayne Cmnty. Schs., 1965–68; Sum. Libn., IN Inst. of Tech., 1963–66. **Educ.:** Manchester Coll., 1950, BA (Hist.); West. MI Univ., 1958, MA (Libnshp.). **Orgs.:** ALA: AASL. Fort Wayne LA. AIME. Fort Wayne Educ. Assn. **Honors:** Phi Delta Kappa. **Activities:** 1, 10; 31, 32, 48; 55, 63, 95-Pers. **Addr.:** 6611 Winchester Rd., Fort Wayne, IN 46819.

Weidenaar, Evelyn J. (O. 9, 1929, Worthington, MN) Curric. Ctr. Dir., Calvin Coll., 1973–, Head, Ref., 1969–72, Head, Circ., 1967–69; various tchg. positions, 1951–65. **Educ.:** Calvin Coll., 1947–51, AB (Eng., Educ.); Univ. of MI, 1954–58, AM (Educ.), 1967, MALS. **Orgs.:** ALA: ACRL. **Pubns.:** Reviews **Activities:** 1, 10; 15, 17, 32; 63 **Addr.:** Curriculum Center, Calvin College, Instructional Resources Center, Grand Rapids, MI 49506.

Weidner, Ruth Irwin (My. 20, 1934, Philadelphia, PA) Msc. Libn., W. Chester State Coll., 1967–; Med. Resrch. Biblgphr., Med. Documtn. Srv., Lib. of the Coll. of Physicians of Philadelphia, 1966–67. **Educ.:** Hood Coll., 1952–56, BA (Hist. of Art); Drexel Univ., 1966–67, MSLS; Univ. of DE, 1971–79, MA (Hist. of Art). **Orgs.:** Msc. LA: PA Chap., VP/Pres. Elect (1979); Ch., Mem. Com. (1978, 1979); Ch., Nom. Com. (1977); Const. Com. (1975); Chap. Archvst. Msc. OCLC Users Grp. Sonneck Socty. Coll. Art Assn. Victorian Socty. in America. Amer. Assn. for State and Lcl. Hist. **Honors:** Beta Phi Mu. **Pubns.:** Jt. ed., *Essays on Mannerism in Art and Music; Papers Read at the West Chester State College Symposium on Interdisciplinary Studies* (1980); "The Majolica Wares of Griffen, Smith & Company," *Spinning Wheel* (Ja.-Fe. 1980, Mr. 1980). **Activities:** 1, 12; 15, 17, 39; 55, 57 **Addr.:** Music Library, Swope Hall, West Chester State College, West Chester, PA 19380.

Weigel, James S. (Jl. 2, 1951, Putnam, CT) Libn., Killingly Jr. HS, 1974–. **Educ.:** Univ. of Notre Dame, 1969–73, AB (Eng.); Univ. of RI, 1973–74, MLS. **Orgs.:** ALA. New Eng. Educ. Media Assn.: Finance Ch. (1979–). CT Educ. Media Assn.: Legis. Ch. (1978–). **Pubns.:** "School Media Programs and CLSU'S: Uneasy Truce or Grand Alliance?" *CEMA Bltn.* (N. 1979). **Activities:** 9, 10; 17, 32, 48; 63, 78, 89 **Addr.:** Killingly Junior High School, 52 Broad St., Danielson, CT 06239.

Weigel, John W. II (My. 15, 1934, Bellefonte, PA) Physical Sci. Physical Sci. Libn., Univ. of MI, 1964–80, 1982–; Libn., Univ. of MI, 1964–80, 1982–; Asst. for Persnl. & Staff Dev., 1980–82; Phys. Libn., Columbia Univ., 1962–64, Math. Libn., 1962; Assoc. Engin., Westinghouse Electric Corp., 1960–61. **Educ.:** Dickinson Coll., 1952–56, BA (Math.); Princeton Univ., 1956–57, (Phys.); Johns Hopkins Univ., 1957–60, MA (Phys.); Columbia Univ., 1961–62, MS (LS). **Orgs.:** SLA: Ch., Phys.-Astr.-Math. Div. (1972–73); Pres., MI Chap. (1975–76); VP, Astronomical Lib. Subsect. IFLA. **Honors:** Phi Beta Kappa, 1956. **Pubns.:** Reviews. **Activities:** 1, 12; 17, 39, 44; 76, 84, 88 **Addr.:** Physics-Astronomy Library, 290 Dennison Bldg., University of Michigan, Ann Arbor, MI 48109.

Weihs, Barbara Jean (N. 12, 1930, Ottawa, ON) Course Dir., Seneca Coll. of Applied Arts & Tech., 1969–; Head, Tech. Srvs., E. York Bd. of Educ., 1967–69; Catlgr., ON Inst. for Std. in Educ., 1966; Sch. Libn., Scarborough Bd. of Educ., 1965–66; Gen. Libn., N. York Pub. Lib., 1961–64; Biblgphr., Univ. of Toronto Lib., 1953–59. **Educ.:** Queen's Univ., 1948–51, BA (Pol., Econ.); Univ. of Toronto, 1952–53, BLS, Spec. Cert. in Sch. Libnshp., 1964–65. **Orgs.:** Can. LA: Com. on Lib. Tech. Role & Education (1979–); Can. Com. on Cat. (Ch.); Can. rep. to Jt. Strg. Com. ON LA. **Honors:** Gvr.-Gen. of Canada, Queen's Jubilee Medal, 1977; Can. Gvt., Can. Cncl. Grant, 1969; Can. LA, Ruby E. Wallace Travelling Flwshp., 1968. **Pubns.:** *Nonbook Cataloguing: The Organization of Integrated Collections* (1979); "Survey of Library Technician Programs in Canada," *Can. Lib. Jnl.* (D. 1979); "Nonbook Cataloguing: Problems and Prospects," *Hennepin Cnty. Lib. Cat. Bltn.* (Jl./Ag. 1977); "The Library Technician," *Canadian Libraries in their Changing Environment* (1977); "Problems of Subject Analysis for Audio/visual Materials in Canadian Libraries," *Can. Lib. Jnl.* (O. 1976); other books, articles, reviews. **Activities:** 11; 17, 25, 26 **Addr.:** Seneca College of Applied Arts & Technology, 1750 Finch Ave. E., Willowdale, ON M2J 2X5 Canada.

Weil, Lewis (S. 19, 1945, Pittsburgh, PA) Media Spec., Jackson Meml. HS, 1979–; Media Spec., Spotswood HS, 1977–79; Media Spec., Waldwick HS, 1976–77; Media Spec., Freehold HS, 1973–76. **Educ.:** Univ. of MO, 1963–67, BS (Educ.), 1967–68, MEd (Educ.); Univ. of Pittsburgh, 1973–74, MLS. **Orgs.:** ALA. NJ LA: New Mem. Sect. (Pres., 1979–80). **Activities:** 10; 31, 32, 48; 63, 75 **Addr.:** 1 Hazelwood Ct., Howell, NJ 07731.

Weilbrenner, Bernard (N. 3, 1929, Verdun, PQ) Asst. Dominion Archvst., Pub. Arch. of Can., 1971–; Dir., Hist. Branch, 1967–71; Dir., PQ Prov. Arch., 1963–67; Archvst., Hist. Branch, Pub. Arch. of Can., 1952–63. **Educ.:** Coll. De St.-Laurent, 1945–49, BA; Univ. De Montreal, 1949–51, MA (Hist.); Amer. Univ., Arch. Inst., 1958, Cert.; Pub. Srv. Comsn., 1957–58, Pub. Admin. Cert. **Orgs.:** Assn. des Archvsts. du PQ: Pres (1981–82). Assn. of Can. Archvsts. SAA. Intl. Cncl. on Arch.: Corresp. Mem., ARCHIVUM; Asst. Secy., Com. on Arch. Dev., (1976–); Ed., *CAD Info.*, (1978–). Can. Hist. Assn.: Cncl. (1961–62). Société Hist. De PQ: VP (1966–67). Fed. des Sociétés Hist. du PQ: VP (1966–67). **Honors:** Queen's Jubilee, Queen Elizabeth II Medal, 1977. **Pubns.:** Ed., *Guide des sources d'archives sur le Canada francais au Canada* (1975); Ed., *Etat Général des archives Du Québec* (1968); "L'homme politique et ses archives," *Arch.* (PQ) (D. 1978); "Les archives sur la scène internationale," *Arch.* (S. 1977); "Archives-Canada," *International Encyclopedia of Higher Education* (1977). **Activities:** 2; 17 **Addr.:** Public Archives of Canada, 395 Wellington St., Ottawa, ON K1A 0N3 Canada.

Weill, David P. (Mr. 23, 1941, Suffern, NY) Dir., E. Brunswick (NJ) Pub. Lib., 1979–; Assoc. Exec. Dir., New Eng. Lib. Bd., 1976–79; Exec. Dir., Southwest. CT Lib. Syst., 1972–75; Dir., Merrick (NY) Pub. Lib., 1968–72, Adult Srvs. Libn., 1966–68; Jr. Libn., Brooklyn Pub. Lib., 1965–66. **Educ.:** Colgate Univ., 1959–63, BA (Eng.); Columbia Univ., 1964–66, MLS. **Orgs.:** ALA: Com. on Org. (1972–73, 78–79); SRRT Action Cncl. (1970–71); ASCLA Plng., Org. & Bylaws, (1979–80). CT LA: Legis. Com. (1972–75); Dev. Com. (1977–78) White House Conf. Plng. Com. (1978). NJ LA. New Eng. LA. Other orgs. **Pubns.:** "Invisible Chains," *Lib. Jnl.* (S. 15, 1966). **Activities:** 9; 14-multi-type library coop.; 17, 24, 34; 56 **Addr.:** 9 Branchville Rd., Ridgefield, CT 06877.

Weimer, Jane Elliott (D. 27, –, Frankfort, KY) Head, Acq. Dept., Heterick Meml. Lib., OH North. Univ., 1974–; Circ./Ref. Libn., Arapahoe Cnty. (CO) Lib., 1973–74; Chld. Libn., Hardin Cnty. (OH) Reg. Lib., 1972–73; Head, Circ. Dept., OH North. Univ., 1969–72. **Educ.:** Transylvania Coll., AB (Eng.); Union Theo. Semy., New York, MA (Christ. Educ.); Columbia Univ., 1966, MA (Early Chld. Educ.); Univ. of Denver, 1969, MAL (Libnshp.). **Orgs.:** Acad. Libns. of OH. OH LA. West. OH Reg. Lib. Dev. Srv.: Secy. (1980). United Way Bd., Ada, OH. Untd. Meth. Women. **Honors:** Beta Phi Mu. **Pubns.:** Contrib., *Pop. Cult. Abs.* **Activities:** 1, 9; 15, 21, 22; 63, 90, 95-Chld. Lit. **Addr.:** Heterick Memorial Library, Ohio Northern University, Ada, OH 45810.

Weimer, Sally Willson (Je. 12, 1949, Santa Monica, CA) Ref. Libn., Univ. of CA, Santa Barbara, 1976–; Libn., Navy Env. Support Ofc. Lib., Port Hueneme, CA, 1974–76; Curric. Libn., Univ. of CA, Santa Barbara, 1974; Tchr., Santa Paula (CA) Sch. Dist., 1972–73. **Educ.:** Univ. of CA, Santa Barbara, 1967–71, BA (Soclgy.); San Jose State Univ., 1971–74, MLS; CA Cmnty. Coll. Libn. Cred.; CA State Univ., Northridge, 1977–, MA (Pub. Admin.) in progress. **Orgs.:** CA LA: CA Socty. of Libns., Com. on Prof. Stan. (Ch., 1976–77). CA Clearinghouse on Lib. Instr.: S. Stng. Com., Secy. (1978). ALA: RASD; ACRL. SLA: Soc. Sci. Div., S. CA Div. Pi Lambda Theta. **Honors:** Beta Phi Mu. **Pubns.:** Jt. auth., "An examination of search strategy and an on-line bibliographic system," *Spec. Lib.* (Mr., 1979); "CA Library Association Statement of Professional Responsibility for Librarians," *CA Libn.* (Ja. 1978). **Activities:** 1; 15, 31, 39; 63, 92 **Addr.:** 10264 Jamestown St., Ventura, CA 93004.

Weinberg, Bella Hass (Ag. 14, 1949, New York, NY) Assoc. Libn., YIVO Inst. for Jewish Resrch., 1971–; Visit. Instr., Hebrew Univ. of Jerusalem, 1980–81; Sr. Libn., Jewish Natl. and Univ. Lib., 1979–80; Lectr., Judaica Libnshp., Jewish Theo. Semy., NY, 1975; Instr., YIVO Inst. for Jewish Resrch., 1974–78. **Educ.:** City Coll., New York, 1967–70, BA magna cum laude (Langs.); Columbia Univ., 1970–71, MS (Lib. Srv.), 1973–81, DLS (Lib. Srv.); various crs. **Orgs.:** ALA. ASIS. AJL. Cncl. on Arch. and Resrch. Libs. in Jewish Std. **Honors:** Phi Beta Kappa, 1970. **Pubns.:** *Implications of Changes in LC Cataloging Policy for Judaica/Hebraica Librarians* (1978); "Hebraica cataloging and classification," *Cataloging and Class of Non-Western Material* (1980); "Transliteration in documentation," *Jnl. of Documtn.* (1974); "Bibliographic coupling: a review," *Info. Storage and Retrieval* (1974); Indxr., *History of the Yiddish Language* (1980); various articles, ed. works, reviews. **Activities:** 11, 12; 20, 26, 41; 55, 66, 75 **Addr.:** 2840 Shady Ave., Pittsburgh, PA 15217.

Weinbrecht, Ruby York (Mr. 19, 1927, Spartanburg, SC) Head Libn., Mary Washington Coll., 1972–; Chief, Tech. Info. Div., US Equal Empl. Oppt. Comsn., 1967–72; Ed., *Marketing Information Guide,* US Dept. of Cmrc., 1965–67, Supvsy. Libn., Mktg. Div., 1963–65; Ed., Sr. Decimal Clasfr., Lib. of Congs., 1959–63; Chief, Reader Srvs. Libn., Asst. Prof. of LS, IN State Univ., 1956–58; Ref. Srvs. Libn., Asst. Prof. of LS, Ball State Univ., 1955–56; Reg. Post Libn., US Army Lib. Srv., 1952–54; other prof. positions. **Educ.:** Mary Washington Coll., 1944–48, BA (Hist.); George Peabody Coll., 1949–50, MA (LS); Univ. of Chicago, 1954–55, (LS). **Orgs.:** ALA: Lib. Sch. Accred. Site Visit Mem. (1979–); ACRL, VA Chap. (Ch., 1977, 1978). VA LA: Secy. (1977); Ch., Coll. & Univ. Sect. (1978). SE LA: Dev. Com. (1978–80). DC LA: Ed. *DC Libs.* (1963–65). Frnds. of the Corcoran Art Gallery. VA Musm. Mary Washington Coll. Alum. Assn.: Pres. (1970–71). **Honors:** Mary Washington Coll., Disting. Alum., 1976. **Pubns.:** *History of the Equal Employment Opportunity Commission, 1965-1970* (1970); "Junior Librarian," *Jnl. of Educ. for Libnshp.* (Win. 1963); "What the Young Librarian Thinks of His Professional Association," *Lib. Jnl.* (Ap. 1, 1963). **Activities:** 1; 17 **Addr.:** Mary Washington College Library, Fredericksburg, VA 22401.

Weine, Mae (F. 17, 1912, New York, NY) Libn., Cong. Beth Abraham Hillel Moses, 1973–; Libn., Beth Israel Synagogue, 1953–72; Staff, Rutgers Coll. of S. Jersey, 1958–68. **Educ.:** Wayne State Univ./Columbia Univ., 1928–30, 1930–32, BLit (Jnlsm.); Wayne State Univ., 1932–34; Drexel Univ., 1954–57, MSLS. **Orgs.:** Jewish LA of Grt. Philadelphia: Pres. (1962–64). AJL: Pres. (1968). Jewish LA of Metro. Detroit: Pres. (1974–78). Natl. Women's Leag. **Honors:** Jewish LA of Grt. Philadelphia, Cit. of Hon., 1967. **Pubns.:** *Weine Classification Scheme for Judaica Libraries* (1975); "Libraries for the Jewish Layman," *Jewish Book Annual* (1966–67); "The Association of Jewish Libraries," *Church & Synagogue Libs.* (1980). **Addr.:** 13761 Sherwood, Oak Park, MI 48237.

Weiner, Anthony M. (Ja. 18, 1947, New York, NY) Tech. Info. Spec., Marathon Intl. Oil Co., 1977–; Asst. Sci. Libn., Miami (OH) Univ., 1974–77; Asst. Univ. Libn., Univ. of S. FL, 1972–74. **Educ.:** Univ. of MA, 1966–71, BS (Geol.); FL State Univ., 1971–72, MS (LS); Univ. of S. FL, 1972–74, (Comp. Sci.). **Orgs.:** Geosci. Info. Socty. SLA. Amer. Petroleum Inst.: Bus. Info. Task Force (1977–). AAAS. Amer. Geophys. Un. L-5 Socty. **Pubns.:** Jt. auth., "U.S.F. Library Lectures Revisited," *RQ* (Win. 1973); Jt. auth., "P/E News," *DATABASE* (Je. 1981); **Activities:** 1, 12; 17, 30, 39; 56, 86, 91 **Addr.:** Marathon International Oil Company, Technical Information Center, 539 S. Main St., Findlay, OH 45840.

Weiner, Betty Admin. Asst., Sci. Div., BIOSIS, 1980–; Lib. Consult., 1978–; Admin. Asst., Ed. Dept., BIOSIS, 1978–80, Head Libn., 1970–80; Asst. Libn., East. PA Psychiatric Inst., 1965–70. **Educ.:** PA State Univ., 1940–44, BS (Psy.); Drexel Univ., 1962–65, MLS, 1981– (Info. Syst.); PA State Univ., 1976–78, cert. (Mgt. Trng.). **Orgs.:** SLA. ASIS. Natl. Fed. of Abs. & Indx. Srvs.: Assoc. Ed., Nsltr. (1972–). **Honors:** Beta Phi Mu. **Pubns.:** "How to Organize A Small Library," *ERIC* (1972); Contrib., *Alternate Careers for Librarians* (1980). **Activities:** 6; 17, 24, 30 **Addr.:** 536 Atterbury Rd., Villanova, PA 19085.

Weingand, Darlene E. (Ag. 13, 1937, Oak Park, IL) Asst. Prof., Lib. Sci., Univ. of WI, Ext. and Madison, 1981–; IPCD/Lib. Coord., Cen. MI Univ., 1980–81; Comnty. Libn., Minneapolis Pub. Lib., 1973–80; Comnty. Fac., Met. State Univ., 1975–80. **Educ.:** Elmhurst Coll., 1970–72, BA (Hist.); Rosary Coll., 1972–73, MALS; Univ. of MN, 1975–80, PhD (Adlt. Educ.); Mankato State Univ., 1976–77 (Bus. Admin.). **Orgs.:** ALA: Lib. Admin. and Mgt. Assn.; Educ. for Pub. Libns. Com.; Alternative Educ. Prog. Sect. WI LA. MN LA: Secy. (1976–78); Ch., Media Roundtable (1973–76); Cont. Lib. Educ. Ntwk. and Exch. ASIS. Adult Educ. Assn.; Natl. Assn. of Pub. Cont. Adult Educ.; MN Assn. for Cont. Adult Educ.: VP, Lib. Sect. (1979–80); Board (1978–80). **Honors:** Pi Gamma Mu, 1973. **Pubns.:** *Reflections of Tomorrow: Lifelong Learning and the Public Library,* 1980; "Adult Education Pathfinder & Bibliography," *ERIC* (1979); "Learning Unlimited," *MACAE Qtly.* (1979). **Activities:** 1, 9; 16, 25, 27; 50, 59, 93 **Addr.:** University of Wisconsin-Extension Communication Programs and Madison Library School, Madison, WI 53706.

Weinreich, Gerane S. (Ap. 17, 1930, West Salem, WI) Freelnc. Info. Spec., The Answer Box, Ann Arbor, MI, 1981–; Libn., Ed., Urology, Dept. of Surgery, Univ. of MI, 1976–80, Coord., Media Lib. Srvs., Dept. Postgrad. Med., 1974–76; Ed. Resrch., Transl., Time-Life Intl., 1952–56. **Educ.:** MacMurray Coll., Univ. of WI, 1948–51, (Fr.); Univ. of MI, 1968–70, BA (Hist.), 1970–71, MALS. **Orgs.:** Med. LA: AV Grp. (Secy., 1978–79). SLA. MI Hlth. Sci. LA. S. Ctrl. MI Hlth. Sci. LA: *SCMHSLA News* Ed. Angell Sch. Parent Tchrs. Org.: Treas. (1964–65). Episcopal Church Women: St. Barnabas Pres. (1962–63). **Pubns.:** "Penile Prostheses," *The Principles of Ostomy Care: A Reference for Enterostomal Therapy Practice* (1980); "Media Library, A New Form of Continuing Medical Education," *For Your Info.* (1976); "Media Library Services," *The Bltn., MI Acad. of Fam. Physicians* (Je. 1976); "Behind the Scenes at Media Library," *The Bltn., MI Acad. of Fam. Physicians* (Ja. 1976); jt. auth., "Media Library Independent Study Centers," *The Bltn., MI Acad. of Fam. Physicians* (N. 1975); various confs., presentations. **Activities:** 12; 24, 39, 41; 58, 75, 80 **Addr.:** 2110 Tuomy Rd., Ann Arbor, MI 48104.

Weinrich, Gloria (D. 25, 1927, Bronx, NY) Sr. Libn., NY State Dept. of Labor Resrch. Lib., 1956–. **Educ.:** Hunter Coll., 1944–48, BA (Soclgy.); Columbia Univ., 1949–50, 1955–56, MS (LS). **Orgs.:** SLA: Mem. Ch., Soc. Sci. Div. (1980–81); NY Chapt., Rcrt. Ch. (1975–76); Dir. (1976–78); Awds. Com. Ch. (1977–78); Ch., Salary Survey (1978–79); Soc. Sci. Grp. Ch. (1972–73, 1980–81). Com. of Indus. Rel. Libns. Med. LA: NY Reg. Grp. New York Lib. Club. Other orgs. **Pubns.:** "SLA: New York Chapter. Salary survey, 1979," *ERIC report* (1981). **Activities:** 12, 13; 15, 17, 24; 66, 92 **Addr.:** New York State Dept. of Labor Research Library, Two World Trade Ctr., Rm. 6826, New York, NY 10047.

Weinstein, Ellen B. (N. 18, 1946, Brooklyn, NY) Head, Grad. Lib. Sch. Lib., Long Island Univ., 1979–; Acq. Libn., 1969–79. **Educ.:** Hofstra Univ., 1965–68, BA (Hist.); Long Island Univ., 1968–69, MS (LS), 1970–78, MA (Hist.). **Orgs.:** ALA. Nassau Cnty. LA: Coll. & Univ. Lib. Srvs. Div., Pres. (1982). Palmer Grad. LS Alum. Assn. Amer. Civil Liberties Un. Amer. Jewish Congs. **Activities:** 1, 11; 15, 26, 39 **Addr.:** C.W. Post College Library, Graduate Library School Library, Greenvale, NY 11548.

Weinstein, Lois (Ap. 20, 1943, Brooklyn, NY) Supvsr., Info. Resrcs., Gen. Foods Corp., 1977–; Info. Spec., Lederle Labs., 1970–77; Resrch. Asst., Amer. Musm. Nat. Hist., 1967–69. **Educ.:** SUNY, Binghamton, 1960–65, BA (Bio.); SUNY, Albany, 1969–70, MLS. **Orgs.:** SLA: Hudson Valley Chap., Pres. (1979–80); Pres. elect (1978–79); Food and Nutrition Div., Ch. Nom. Com. (1980–81). Assoc. Info. Mgrs. Hlth. and Indus. Libs. of Westchester. Inquire Users Grp.: NE Reg. (Ch. 1980–81). **Pubns.:** *Teratology and Congenital Malformations: A Comprehensive Guide to the Literature* (1976); Jt. auth., "Effects of Fluorine Following Short Term Inhalation," *Amer. Indus. Hygiene Assn. Jnl.* (Ja.-F. 1968). **Activities:** 12; 33, 38; 56, 68, 87, 91 **Addr.:** General Foods Technical Center, 250 North St., White Plains, NY 10625.

Weintraub, D. Kathryn (Jl. 29, 1932, Cincinnati, OH) Cat. Dept., Univ. of CA, Irvine, 1981–; Assoc. Prof., Grad. Lib. Sch., Univ. of Chicago, 1976–81; Assoc. Prof., Grad. Lib. Sch., IN Univ., 1972–75; Asst. Prof., Sch. of Lib. & Info. Sci., Univ. of WI, Milwaukee, 1970–72; Subj. Anal., Univ. of Chicago, 1969–70, Instr., 1961–64, Resrch. Asst., 1960–61. **Educ.:** Univ. of Chicago, 1951, AB, 1960, AM (LS), 1970, PhD (LS). **Orgs.:** ALA: ACRL; LITA; RTSD. ASIS. SLA. **Honors:** Beta Phi Mu. **Pubns.:** "Anglo-American cataloguing rules," *Lib. Qtly.* (O. 1979); "The Essentials or Desiderata of the Bibliographic Record as Discovered by Research," *Lib. Resrcs. and Tech. Srvs.* (Fall 1979); "An extended Review of PRECIS," *Lib. Resrcs. and Tech. Srvs.* (Sp. 1979); "The Use of Statistical Publications," *Gvt. Pubns. Review* (Fall 1974); Jt. ed., *North American Library Education Directory & Statistics* (1972); other articles, reviews. **Activities:** 1, 11; 15, 20, 30, 39, 46 **Addr.:** 183 Pergola, Irvine, CA 92715.

Weir, Katherine M. (Mr. 15, 1948, Waverly, NY) Archit. Env. Design Libn., Geo. Subj. Libn., SUNY, Buffalo, 1975–; Geo. Sub. Libn., 1973–75, Ref. Libn., 1972–73; Ref. & ILL Libn., Hofstra Univ., 1971–72. **Educ.:** SUNY, Coll. at Geneseo, 1966–70, BA magna cum laude (Hist.), 1970–71, MLS; Univ. of Würzburg, W. Germany, 1969–70, (Hist.); Univ. of MO, Kansas City, 1977, (Slide curatorship). **Orgs.:** Assn. of Archit. Libns. SLA: Secy., Upstate NY Chap. (1975–77). SUNY Libns. Assn. Assn. of Archit. Sch. Libns.: By-laws Com. (1979). Phi Alpha Theta. **Pubns.:** Contrib., *Articles on Twentieth Century Literature: An Annotated Bibliography* (1973); various conf. papers. **Activities:** 1; 15, 17, 39; 55, 70 **Addr.:** Architecture and Environmental Design Library, Hayes Hall, State University of New York at Buffalo, Buffalo, NY 14214.

Weir, Mary Jean (Ja. 15, 1921, Washington, DC) Asst. Prof., Sr. Asst. Libn., San Diego State Univ., 1970–; Sch. Libn., Spring Valley Jr. HS, CA, 1961–70; Cat. Libn., San Diego State Coll., 1960–61; Asst. Libn., Catlgr., Millikin Univ., 1959–60; Readers' Srvs. Libn., Colby Coll., 1958–59. **Educ.:** Bethany Coll., 1938–42, AB (Psy.); Drexel Univ., 1957–58, MS (LS); Univ. of IL, 1968–69, CAS (Libnshp.); Univ. of CO, 1971–, PhD in progress (Educ.). **Orgs.:** ALA: AASL, Com. on Eval. of Sch. Media Prog. (1975–78). CA Media & Lib. Educ. Assn.: Treas., South. Sect. (1970–72). Intl. Assn. of Sch. Libnshp.: Reporter (1976). AECT. CA Tchrs. Assn. Natl. Educ. Assn. Phi Delta Kappa. **Honors:** Beta Phi Mu. **Pubns.:** "Sources for Shaping the Bicentennial," *Wilson Lib. Bltn.* (Mr. 1975); Reviews. **Activities:** 1, 11; 20, 26, 39; 63 **Addr.:** 7374 Princeton Ave., La Mesa, CA 92041.

Weis, Ina J. (Mr. 12, 1921, Toledo, OH) Asst. to the Dir. for Spec. Proj., Prof. of Lib. Admin., Univ. of Toledo Libs., 1979–; Admin. of Lib. Info. Srvs., Prof. of Lib. Admin., 1971–79, Chief Circ. Libn., Asst. Prof., 1962–71, Chief Circ. Libn., Instr., 1951–62. **Educ.:** Univ. of Toledo, 1939–43, BA (Hist.); West. Resrv. Univ., 1946–49, BS (LS); 1961, MS (LS). **Orgs.:** Acad. LA of OH. ALA. North. OH Tech. Srvs. Libns. P.E.O. Chapter I. AAUP. Case West. Alum. Assn. Univ. of Toledo Alum. Assn. **Pubns.:** *Computerized Information Systems in Public Administration: a bibliography* (1979); *Women in Politics: a bibliography* (1979); *Libraries–Services to the Aged: a bibliography* (1978);

Special Subjects/Services: 50. Adult educ.; 51. Advert./Mktg.; 52. Aerosp.; 53. Agric.; 54. Area std.; 55. Arts/Hum.; 56. Autom.; 57. Bibl./Prtg.; 58. Bio. sci.; 59. Bus./Fin.; 60. Chem.; 61. Copyrt.; 62. Documtn.; 63. Educ.; 64. Engin.; 65. Env.; 66. Eth. grps.; 67. Film; 68. Food/Nutr.; 69. Geneal.; 70. Geo.; 71. Geol.; 72. Handcpd.; 73. Hist.; 74. Int. frdm.; 75. Info. sci.; 76. Insr.; 77. Law; 78. Legis.; 79. Math./Comp. sci.; 80. Med.; 81. Metals; 82. Nat. resrcs.; 83. Newsp.; 84. Nuc. sci.; 85. Oral hist.; 86. Petr./Energy; 87. Pharm.; 88. Phys./Astr./Math.; 89. Readg.; 90. Relig.; 91. Sci./Tech.; 92. Soc. sci.; 93. Telecom.; 94. Transp.; 95. (other).

Libraries–Services to the Disadvantaged: a bibliography (1978); *The Design of Library Areas and Buildings* (1981); Reviews. **Activities:** 1, 2; 25, 42, 45; 50, 57, 85 **Addr.:** 20600 N. River Rd., Elmore, OH 43416.

Weisbaum, Earl (My. 18, 1930, Chicago, IL) Frgn. Law Libn., Los Angeles Cnty. Law Lib., 1966–. **Educ.:** Los Angeles State Coll., 1948–52, BA (Eng.); Univ. of South. CA, 1960–61, MSLS; Loyola (Los Angeles) Law Sch., 1966–70, JD (Law). **Orgs.:** AALL. Intl. Assn. of Law Libs. State Bar of CA. Amer. Bar Assn. Los Angeles Cnty. Bar Assn.: Intl. Law Sect., Exec. Com. (1977–). **Honors:** Los Angeles Cnty. Bar Assn., Intl. Law Sect., Outstan. Srv., 1977. **Pubns.:** "Mexican Law for Norteamericanos," *Law Lib. Jnl.* (1975); "Hague Service Convention and C.C.P. 413.10," *Los Angeles Bar Bltn.* (1972); "Panama Canal Treaties," *Los Angeles Daily Jnl.* (D. 2, 1977). **Activities:** 12; 30, 39, 40; 77, 78 **Addr.:** Foreign Law Librarian, Los Angeles County Law Library, 301 W. First St., Los Angeles, CA 90012.

Weisberg, Ruth Dysken (Ap. 21, 1911, Dayton, OH) Libn., WQED TV and FM, Pub. TV, Pub. Radio, 1970–; Gift and Exch. Libn., Univ. of Pittsburgh Libs., 1965–69, Consult. to Univ. Libn., 1960–65. **Educ.:** Antioch Coll., 1930–36, BA (Lit.); Columbia Univ., 1937–38, BS (Adult Educ.). **Orgs.:** SLA. PA LA. **Pubns.:** "Television Station Libraries," *Encyc. of Lib. and Info. Sci.* (1980–81). **Activities:** 12; 39, 41; 55, 83, 93 **Addr.:** 6448 Nicholson St., Pittsburgh, PA 15217.

Weisbrod, David L. (N. 28, 1937, New York, NY) Head, Syst. Ofc., Yale Univ. Lib., 1964–; Sr. Progmr.-Anal., Syst. Dev. Corp., 1959–64. **Educ.:** Harvard Coll., 1955-59, AB (Phys.); Rutgers Univ., 1960–66, MS (Syst. Anal.). **Orgs.:** ALA: Rep., Amer. Natl. Stan. Inst. Comp. X3, Comp. and Info. Prcs. (1968–73); Subcom. on Character Sets, Interdiv. Com. on the Repr. in Machine-Readable Form of Bibl. Info. (1974–); Ch., Nom. Com., Info. Sci. and Autom. Div. (1974). ASIS: Ch., Spec. Int. Grp. on Lib. Autom. and Networks (1971–73). Assn. for Comp. Mach.: Com. on Chap. (1970–72); Ch., New Haven Area Chap. (1969–71). **Pubns.:** *New Technology for Libraries* (1979); "NUC Reporting and MARC Redistribution," *Jnl. of Lib. Autom.* (S. 1977); "Frederick G. Kilgour," *Lib. Resrcs. and Tech. Srvs.* (Fall 1974); "Acquisitions Systems: 1973 Application Status," *Proc.* of ALA Inst. Library Automation (1973); "An Integrated, Computerized, Bibliographic System for Libraries," *Drexel Lib. Qtly.* (Jl. 1968); Bk. Review Ed., *Jnl. of Lib. Autom./Info. Tech. and Libs.* (1981–). **Activities:** 1; 56 **Addr.:** Box 1603A Yale Sta., New Haven, CT 06520.

Weisel, Juanita L. (S. 26, 1931, Cleveland, OH) Dir., Lrng. Resrc. Ctr., Ursuline Coll., 1979–; Asst. Dir., Shaker Heights Pub. Lib., 1978–79; Lib. Dir., Taipei Amer. Sch., 1976–77; Catlgr./Serials Libn., John Carroll Univ., 1968–75. **Educ.:** Notre Dame Coll., 1949–53, AB (Hist., Eng.); Case West. Resrv. Univ., 1966–68, MSLS; State of OH Tchg. Cert., 1953–. **Orgs.:** ALA. Acad. Libs. of OH. OH LA. Med. LA. Other orgs. **Honors** Beta Phi Mu. **Activities:** 1; 15, 17, 19; 54, 63 **Addr.:** Ursuline College Library, Pepper Pike, OH 44124.

Weiser, Douglas E. (N. 1, 1925, Iron Mountain, MI) Asst. Dir., Wayne Oakland Lib. Fed., 1968–; Dir., Admin. Srvs., State Lib., MI, 1966–68, Asst. State Libn., 1964–66. **Educ.:** MI State Univ., 1946–49, BA (Bus., Pub. Srv.); Wayne State Univ., 1968–70, MLS. **Orgs.:** ALA: ASCLA. MI LA: PR Coms. (1958–). **Honors:** H.W. Wilson Co., Best pubcty. prog. by a State Lib., 1962; PR Cncl., ALA, Best lib. nsltr., 1967. **Activities:** 9, 13; 17, 32, 36, 37; 51, 67, 72 **Addr.:** 11749 Priscilla Le., Plymouth, MI 48170.

Weiss, Dianne (O. 22, 1951, New York, NY) Med. Libn., St. Clare's Hosp. and Hlth. Ctr., 1976–; Tchr., J.H.S. 211, Brooklyn, 1974–75. **Educ.:** Brooklyn Coll., 1968–72, BA (Eng.); Queens Coll., 1973–74, MLS. **Orgs.:** Med. LA: NY Reg. Grp., Small Hlth. Sci. Libs. Com. (Ch., 1979–80). Manhattan/Bronx Hlth. Sci. Libs. Grp.: Fndn. Mem.; Un. List Netwk. Mgr. **Activities:** 5, 12; 34, 41; 63, 80, 89 **Addr.:** 1465 Andrews Ln., East Meadow, NY 11554.

Weiss, Egon A. (Je. 7, 1919, Vienna, Austria) Lib. Dir., US Milit. Acad., 1963–; Asst. Libn., Actg. Libn., 1958–63; Branch Dir., Brookline (MA) Pub. Lib., 1951–58, Prof. Asst., 1949–51. **Educ.:** Berea College 1938–40; Harvard Coll., 1946–47, AB (Econ.); Boston Univ., 1948–49, MA (Germanic Lang.); Simmons Coll., 1949–51, MLS; Persnl. Mgt. for Exec., Sem. for Adv. Mgrs., 1966–79. **Orgs.:** ALA: Pres., Armed Forces Sect. (1966); John Cotton Dana Com. (1975–79). SLA: Ch., Milit. Libns. Div. (1970–71). Southeast. NY Lib. Resrcs. Cncl.: Trustee, VP (1969–). Musm. of the Hudson Highlands. Harvard-Radcliffe Club of the Hudson Valley. **Pubns.:** *Subject Catalog of the Military Art and Science Collection in the Library of the United State Military Academy* (1969); "Military Education," *Funk and Wagnall's New Encyclopedia* (1970–); "The New Library," in SLA *Milit. Lib. Bltn.* (F. 1966). **Activities:** 1, 4; 17, 24, 45; 54, 74, 85 **Addr.:** US Military Academy Library, West Point, NY 10996.

Weiss, Henry Allen (My. 16, 1947, New York, NY) City Libn., City of Palm Springs, CA, 1977–; Lib. Dir., City of Casa Grande, AZ, 1975–77; Interim Dir., Instr. Resrcs. Ctr., AZ State Univ., 1973. **Educ.:** SUNY, Stony Brook, 1965–69, BA (Econ.); SUNY, Buffalo, 1972–73, MLS; AZ State Univ., 1973–75 (Educ. Tech.). **Orgs.:** ALA. CA LA. Film Cncl. Circuit Comsn.: Pres. Inland Lib. Syst.: Exec. Com. **Honors:** Beta Phi Mu, 1973. **Pubns.:** Contrib., *The Administrative Aspects of Education for Librarianship* (1975); "How to Get What You Don't Pay For," *AZ Roadrunner* (Fall 1976). **Addr.:** Palm Springs Public Library, 300 S. Sunrise Way, Palm Springs, CA 92262.

Weiss, Irvin Joseph (My. 16, 1931, Pottsville, PA) Tech. Info. Expert, Env. Protection Agency, 1978–; Tech. Info. Spec., Consumer Product Safety Comsn., 1977–78, Prog. Mgr., 1977, Branch Chief, 1973–77; Comp. Syst. Anal., Natl. Agri. Lib., 1970–73; Sect. Mgr., Comp. Sci. Corp., 1969–70; Sr. Syst. Anal., Lib. of Congs., 1967–69; Actg. Chief, Ofc. of Educ., 1966–67; other positions in comp. sci. **Educ.:** Temple Univ., 1948–52, BS (Bus. Admin.), 1956–59, MBA (Persnl. Mgt.); Univ. of MD, 1972–76, MLS. **Orgs.:** SLA. **Honors:** Dept. of Cmrc., Sci. & Tech. Fellow, 1976; Phi Kappa Phi, 1976; Beta Phi Mu, 1976. **Pubns.:** Jt. auth., "Data Base Development," *Jnl. of Chem Info. & Comp. Sci.* (1977); "Evaluation of ORBIT & DIALOG," *Spec. Libs.* (1976); "Computer Aided Centralized Cataloging at the N.L.M.," *Lib. Resrch. & Tech. Srvs.* (Ja. 1967); "A new reference approach to chemicals found in consumer products," *N.T.I.S.* (1974). **Activities:** 4, 12; 17, 49-Online srchg.; 56, 75, 91 **Addr.:** 11408 Georgetowne Dr., Potomac, MD 20854.

Weiss, Judith M. (F. 19, 1954, Rockville Center, NY) Law Libn., Bd. of Gvrs. of the Fed. Resrv. Syst., 1981–; Legis. Libn., 1978–81; Team Leader, Informatics, Inc., 1977–78. **Educ.:** Univ. of CO, 1972–76, BA (Pol. Sci.); SUNY, Albany, 1976–77, MLS. **Orgs.:** AALL. SLA. **Activities:** 4; 17, 29, 39; 77, 78 **Addr.:** Law Library, Board of Governors of the Federal Reserve System, Washington, DC 20551.

Weiss, Sandra Leslie (F. 2, 1950, Irvington, NJ) Admin. Supvsr., Digital Equip. Corp., 1981–; Acq. Libn., Natl. Bur. of Stans., 1978–80; Libn., Phys. Sci. and Engin., Nvl. Resrch. Lab., DC, 1975–78. **Educ.:** Long Island Univ., 1967–71, BA (Soclgy.); S. CT State Coll., 1971–74, MSLS. **Orgs.:** ALA. ASIS. **Activities:** 4; 15, 36, 38; 60, 64, 88 **Addr.:** 4921 Seminary Rd. #422, Alexandria, VA 22311.

Weiss, Stephen Craig (Ag. 6, 1946, Minneapolis, MN) Docum. and Maps Libn., UT State Univ. Lib., 1973–. **Educ.:** UT State Univ., 1966–68, BA (Eng., Hist.), 1972–78, MEd IMLS. **Orgs.:** UT State Univ. Instr. Media Assn.: Pres. (1972–73). UT LA: GODORT, Coord. (1979–80, 1980–81), Pubns. Liaison (1981–82). Mt. Plains LA. ALA: GODORT, Nom. Com. (1980–81). **Activities:** 1; 29, 39, 44; 56, 65, 78 **Addr.:** Merrill Library UMC 30, Utah State University, Logan, UT 84322.

Weissman, Aaron (Mr. 6, 1922, New York, NY) Asst. Libn., Bowdoin Coll. Lib., 1967–. **Educ.:** City Coll. of New York, 1938–42, BA (Art); Columbia Univ., 1966–67, MLS. **Orgs.:** ALA. AAUP. **Honors:** Phi Beta Kappa, 1942; Beta Phi Mu, 1967. **Activities:** 1; 17, 22, 39 **Addr.:** Bowdoin College Library, Brunswick, ME 04011.

Weissmann, Steven L. (Jl. 26, 1947, New York, NY) Asst. Chief Libn., Port Athrty. of NY-NJ, 1976–; Legis. Ref. Libn., Mncpl. Ref. Lib., 1971–76. **Educ.:** Queens Coll., 1965–69, BA (Amer. Hist.), 1969–71, MLS; John Jay Coll., 1973–77, MPA (Gvt.). **Orgs.:** SLA: Secy., Soc. Sci. Grp. (1978–79). **Activities:** 4, 12; 17; 59, 94 **Addr.:** 144-20 68th Ave., Flushing, NY 11367.

Weiss-Moore, Carole (Ag. 15, 1944, Berkeley, CA) Actg. Head, Bibl. Prcs. Dept., Univ. of Toronto Lib., 1980–; Head, Ref. Dept., 1974–, Ref. Libn., 1968–74; Ref. Libn., Columbia Univ., 1967–68. **Educ.:** Stanford Univ., 1962–66, AB (Span.); Columbia Univ., 1966–67, MS (Lib. Srv.). **Orgs.:** ALA. Can. LA: Ethics Com. (1975). Univ. of Toronto Fac. Assn. Univ. of Toronto Libns. Assn. **Honors:** Soc. Sci. and Hum. Resrch. Cncl. of Can., Resrch. Grant, 1980. **Pubns.:** "Library Administration," *Canadian Libraries in Their Changing Environment* (1977); "Closing the Catalog: Impact on Reference Services," *Closing the Catalog* (1980); "Card Catalogue to Online Catalogue—the Transitional Process," *Alternative Cat. Nsltr.* (1979). **Activities:** 1; 17, 39, 46; 56 **Addr.:** University of Toronto Library, 130 St. George St., Toronto, ON M4K 1H6 Canada.

Weitkemper, Larry D. (Mr. 4, 1952, Mexico, MO) Chief, Lib. Srv., Vets. Med. Ctr., 1978–; Outreach Spec., Daniel Boone Reg. Lib., 1976–78. **Educ.:** Univ. of MO, 1970–75, BA cum laude (Hist.), 1975–76, MLS. **Orgs.:** ALA: ASCLA, Intl. Year of Disabled Persons Com. (1980–81); Lib. Srv. to the Impaired Elderly Sect. Mem.-At-Large (1980–81); Clearing House of Info. Com. (Ch., 1980–81); Hlth. Care Libs. Sect., Mem. Promo. Com. (Ch., 1980–81). Lib. Outreach Coop.: Ch. (1978–81). Cntrl. IN Hlth. Sci. Cnsrtm.: Ch. (1980–81). Other orgs. and coms. Univ. of MO Sch. of Lib. and Info. Sci. Alum. Assn.: Secy. (1979–81). **Honors:** ALA, JMRT/3M Co. Prof. Dev. Grant, 1978. **Pubns.:** Contrib., *The Librarian and the Patient* (1977); "Library Cooperates with a Triple A Information and Referral Program," *Show-Me Libs.* (My. 1978); "Service Program Planning, Record Keeping, and Evaluation," *Show-Me Libs.* (Jl. 1976); "Outreach Services, Daniel Boone Regional Library," *Show-Me Libs.* (F. 1975); "Improved Bookmobile Service to Rural Patrons," *Show-Me Libs.* (Ja. 1975). **Activities:** 4, 12; 17; 80 **Addr.:** 1 Polk Ave., East Northport, NY 11731.

Weitzel, Jacqueline N. (O. 16, 1927, Philadelphia, PA) Sr. Bus. Resrch. Anal., P.Q. Corp., 1971–; Info. Spec., E.I. duPont de Nemours Co., 1966–71; Engin. Libn., Widener Univ., 1964–66. **Educ.:** Univ. of PA, 1945–49, BS (Chem., Microbio.); Drexel Univ., 1963–68, MS (Info. Sci.). **Orgs.:** SLA. **Addr.:** P.Q. Corp., Box 840, Valley Forge, PA 19482.

Welch, Carolyn J. (O. 28, 1924, Indianapolis, IN) Med. Libn., Knoll Pharm. Co., 1976–. **Educ.:** DePauw Univ., 1942–46, AB (Psy.); Rutgers Univ., 1975–76 (Readrs. Srv. Ref.); 1977, Med. Libn. Cert. **Orgs.:** Med. LA. Amer. Socty. of Info. Specs. SLA. AAUW: Secy. (1966–68). Kappa Kappa Gamma, Lackawanna Alum. Chap.: Pubcty. (1979–80). **Honors:** Alpha Lambda Delta, 1943; Phi Beta Kappa, 1946. **Pubns.:** Contrib., *Courier News* (1964–). **Activities:** 12; 17, 39, 44; 80, 87, 93 **Addr.:** P.O. Box 314, Basking Ridge, NJ 07920.

Welch, Edgar Donnelly (D. 25, 1919, Rock Island, IL) Docum. Resrch., Natl. Med. Adv. Srv., 1978–; Asst. Law Libn., Howard Univ., 1974–78; Asst. Law Libn., Univ. of Baltimore, 1972–74; Law Libn., DE Law Sch., 1970–72. **Educ.:** South. Meth. Univ., 1934, JD (Law); State of OK, 1944, Life Tchg. Cert.; State of NM, 1950, Pub. Libn. Licn.; OK City Univ., 1952, BA (Hist., Pol. Sci.); Emporia State Univ., 1962, MSLS; U.S. Natl. Arch., Regis. Resrch., U.S. Natl. Lib. of Med., Regis. Resrch. **Orgs.:** DC LA. AALL. ALA. State Bar of TX. Bar of Supreme Ct. of U.S. Amer. Bar Assn. various fed. ct. bars. **Pubns.:** "Coordinate Indexing," *West. Bus. Review;* "Your Technical Library," *Jnl. of CO Socty. of Engins.* **Activities:** 1, 14-Corp. Lib.; 29, 30, 33; 62, 77, 87 **Addr.:** P.O. Box 10101, Glendale, CA 91209.

Welch, Edwin (Je. 18, 1927, Leicester, Grt. Britain) Consult., 1978–; City Archvst., City of Ottawa, ON, 1975–78; Assoc. Prof., Lib. Sch., Ottawa Univ., 1971–75; Coll. Archvst., Churchill Coll. Arch., Cambridge Univ., 1967–71. **Educ.:** Liverpool Univ., 1953, MA (Hist.); Southampton Univ., 1968, PhD (Hist.); Dipl. in Arch. Admin., Liverpool, 1949; Cert. Recs. Mgr., 1976. **Orgs.:** Socty. of Archivsts.: Treas. (1954–71). SAA: Educ. Com. Assn. of Can. Archvsts.: Educ. Com. Assn. of Recs. Mgrs. & Admin.: Chap. Pres. **Honors:** Fellow, Socty. of Antiquaries of London, 1970. **Pubns.:** "Security in an English Archive," *Archivaria* (1976); "Ignorance, Madam, Pure Ignorance," *Arch. Bltn.* (1976); "The London Society for the Extension of University Teaching 1875-1902," *Guildhall Studies in London History* (1977); "Archival Education," *Archivaria* (1977); "Oxford and University Extension," *Std. in Adult Educ.* (1978); other articles. **Activities:** 2; 23, 24, 38; 50, 55, 63 **Addr.:** 678 Morin St., Ottawa, ON K1K 3G9 Canada.

Welch, Eric Christian (Je. 3, 1947, New Haven, CT) Asst. Prof. and Ref. Libn., Univ. of IL, Rockford, 1978–; Instr., Circ./Serials Libn., 1975–78. **Educ.:** Univ. of PA, 1965–69, BA (Grm.); Univ. of WI, Madison, 1974–75, MALS; Med. LA Cert., 1976–. **Orgs.:** Med. LA. Midwest HSLN: Ch., Stats. Plng. Com. (1976–). Hlth. Sci. Libns. of IL. Rockford Amateur Radio Assn. Natl. Intercollegiate Soccer Ofcs. Assn. **Honors:** Beta Phi Mu, 1976. **Activities:** 1; 17, 24, 39; 56, 80, 93 **Addr.:** Library of the Health Sciences, Rockford School of Medicine, 1601 Parkview Ave., Rockford, IL 61101.

Welch, Janet M. (Ja. 12, 1945, Chicago, IL) Exec. Dir., Rochester Reg. Lib. Cncl., 1977–; Asst. Prof., N. Country Cmnty. Coll., 1976–77; Ed. Consult., Pahlavi Natl. Lib. Consults., 1975–76; Resrch. Assoc., Tucson Pub. Lib. Survey, 1973–74; Dir., Resrc. Ctr., Fort Ann (NY) Ctrl. Sch., 1971–72; Sr. Sci. Biblgphrs., SUNY, Albany, 1969–71. **Educ.:** Bucknell Univ., 1963–67, BA magna cum laude (Earth Sci.); Rutgers Univ., 1967–68, MLS; NY State Cert., Lib. Media Spec., other courses. **Orgs.:** NY LA: Legis. Com. (1980). ALA. NY NJ Reg. Med. Lib.: Reg. Plan Com. (1979–80). NY State Educ. Dept.: Comsn. Com. on Statewide Lib. Dev. (1980–82). **Honors:** Phi Beta Kappa, 1966. **Pubns.:** "An Evaluation of the Ghana Collection in the Rutgers University Library," *Readings in Building Library Collections* (1970); "Reference and Research Library Resources Systems in New York State," *Bookmark* (Spr. 1980). **Activities:** 14-Lib. Syst.; 17, 25, 34; 78 76. **Addr.:** Rochester Regional Research Library Council, 339 East Ave., Rochester, NY 14604.

Welch, Theodore F. (O. 10, 1933, Los Angeles, CA) Asst. Univ. Libn. for Dev., Northwestern Univ., 1975–; Chief, Info. Syst., UN Ctr. for Reg. Dev., Nagoya, Japan, 1973–75; Asst. Univ. Libn. for Pub. Srvs., Northwestern Univ., 1969–75; Reg. Libn., US Info. Srv., Tokyo, Japan, 1967–69; Catlgr., Lib. of Congs., 1965–67. **Educ.:** Univ. of South. CA, 1951–63, BA (Msc.); Univ. of CA, Berkeley, 1963–65, MSLS; Univ. of Tokyo, 1973–76, PhD (LS); Univ. of MD, Lib. Admin. Dev. Prog., 1970, cert. **Orgs.:** ALA: ACRL/Asian African Sect., Nom. Com. (Ch., 1980–81); Ref. Srvs. Div., Stans. Com. (1971–73); Adv. Com. on Liason with Japanese Libs. (1970–76); ACRL/Asia-N. Africa Sect. (Ch., 1970–72); Intl. Rel. Com. (1976–79). Midwest Acad. Libns. Conf.: Strg. Com. (Ch., 1971–73). Assn. for Asian Std.: Dev. Com. (1980–). Kobe Coll. Corp.: Bd. of Dir. (1979–). Japanese Amer. Srv. Com.: Bd. of Dir. (1980–). Japan-Amer. Socty.

PROFESSIONAL ACTIVITIES: Institutions: 1. Acad. lib.; 2. Arch.; 3. Assn.; 4. Fed./Gvt. lib.; 5. Inst. lib.; 6. Mfr./Suppl.; 7. Milit. lib.; 8. Musm.; 9. Pub. lib.; 10. Sch. lib.; 11. Sch. of lib. sci.; 12. Spec. lib.; 13. State lib.; 14. (other). **Functions/Activities:** 15. Acq./Col. dev.; 16. Adult srvs.; 17. Admin.; 18. Apprais.; 19. Archit./Bldgs.; 20. Cat./Class.; 21. Chld. srvs.; 22. Circ.; 23. Cons./Pres.; 24. Consult.; 25. Cont. ed.; 26. Educ. lib. sci.; 27. Ext. srvs.; 28. Fund/Grants; 29. Gvt. pubs.; 30. Indx./Abs.; 31. Instr. lib. use; 32. Media srvs.; 33. Micro.; 34. Netwks./Coop.; 35. Persnl.; 36. PR; 37. Publshg.; 38. Recs. mgt.; 39. Ref. srvs.; 40. Repro.; 41. Resrch.; 42. Review.; 43. Secur.; 44. Serials; 45. Spec. col.; 46. Tech. srvs.; 47. Trustees/Bds.; 48. YA srvs.; 49. (other).

of Chicago. **Honors:** Cncl. on Lib. Resrcs., Flwshp., 1970. **Pubns.:** *Toshokan; Libraries in Japanese Society* (1976); Jt. ed., *Japanese and U.S. Libraries at the Turning Point* (1977); "Metropolitan Central: the new super power; a bold thrust against tradition in Tokyo," *Wilson Lib. Bltn.* (Je. 1974); "Japanese Libraries," *ALA World Encyclopedia of Library and Information Services* (1980); "Meeting microforms halfway: Microtext library series book program," *Microform Review* (Jl. 1972); other books, articles. **Activities:** 1, 4; 17, 28; 54, 62 **Addr.:** 8612 Monticello Ave., Skokie, IL 60076.

Welch, Thomas L. (Je. 26, 1942, Merced, CA) Dir. of Libs., Org. of Amer. States, 1980–; Assoc. Dir. of Libs., CA State Polytech. Univ., Pomona, 1972–79; Asst. Libn., Ctr. for Cmnty. Change, 1970–71; Pub. Srvs. Libn., CA State Univ., Fresno, 1966–69; Pub. Srvs. Libn., Univ. of NM, 1964–66. **Educ.:** CA State Univ., Sacramento, 1958–62, BA (Soc. Sci.); Univ. of IL, 1962–63, MS (LS); Cath. Univ., 1970–72, MA (Hist.). **Orgs.:** ALA. DCLA. SALALM. Amer. Assn. of Tchrs. of Span. and Portuguese. **Honors:** Beta Phi Mu. **Activities:** 1, 12; 15, 17, 20; 54 **Addr.:** 1812 Calvert St., NW #B, Washington, DC 20009.

Welden, Stephanie H. (My. 25, 1932, Bronxville, NY) State Law Libn., NY State Lib., 1979–; Sr. Libn., 1977–79, Asst. Libn., 1966–77. **Educ.:** Columbia Univ., 1952–65, BS (Art Hist.); Univ. of KY, 1965–66, MSLS; Univ. of NC, 1970 (Legal Bibl.). **Orgs.:** AALL: Place. Com. (1977–79). Assn. of Law Libs. of Upstate NY: Place. Ofcr. (1977–79); Nom. Com. (1979). Law LA of Grt. NY. **Activities:** 13; 17, 39; 77, 78, 92 **Addr.:** Law/Social Sciences, New York State Library, Cultural Education Center, Albany, NY 12230.

Weldon, Edward L. (S. 12, 1936, Miami, FL) Deputy Archvst. of U.S., Natl. Arch. and Recs. Srv., 1980–; State Archvst., NY State Arch., 1975–80; Apprais. Archvst., Ed. and Chief, Ed. Branch, Natl. Arch. and Recs. Srv., 1971–74, Chief, Reg. Arch. Branch, Atlanta, 1969–71. **Educ.:** Oberlin Coll., 1954–58, AB (Econ.); Emory Univ., 1961–62, MA (Hist.), 1965–70, PhD (Hist.); GA Arch., 1968, Cert.; Amer. Univ., Natl. Arch., 1971, Cert.; Natl. Hist. Pubns. Recs. Com. 1974, Cert. **Orgs.:** SAA: Cncl.; VP; Pres. (1981–82). WHCOLIS: Del. (1979). Mid-Atl. Reg. Arch. Conf. Natl. Assn. of State Arch. and Recs. Admins.: Dir. (1978–81). Various other orgs. Albany Inst. of Hist. and Art. Boy Scouts of Amer. Untd. Meth. Church. Amer. Hist. Assn. **Honors:** SAA, Fellow, 1974. **Pubns.:** Jt. ed., *Access to the Papers of Recent Public Figures: The New Harmony Conference* (1977); "Lest We Forget: Setting Priorities for the Preservation & Use of Historical Records," *Amer. Archvst.* (Jl. 1977); "Copyrights in the Records of the U.S. District and Circuit Courts," *Prologue: The Jnl. of the Natl. Arch.* (Spr. 1970); ed., *Amer. Archvst.* (1971–75). **Activities:** 2, 4; 17, 38, 41; 69, 92 **Addr.:** National Archives and Records Service, GSA, Washington, DC 20408.

Weldon, Eunice Ward (Ap. 1, 1916, Cooleemee, NC) Media Libn., Asbury Coll., 1977–, Asst. Prof., Eng., 1968–77; Co-Coord., Elem. Lib. Srvs., L'Anse Cruise Pub. Schs., 1966–67; Asst. Prof., Eng., Macomb Cnty. Cmnty. Coll., 1965–66. **Educ.:** Asbury Coll., 1947–48, AB, cum laude (Eng.); George Peabody Coll., 1948–49, MA (Eng.); Univ. of MI, 1966–68, AM (LS); Univ. of KY, 1977–79, (Sch. Media Cert. Prog.). **Orgs.:** ALA. KY Sch. LA. KY Sch. Media LA. **Honors:** Kappa Delta Pi, 1949; Pi Gamma Mu, 1949. **Pubns.:** Contrib., *National Anthology of Poetry* (1953–55). **Activities:** 1; 32, 39; 56, 67 **Addr.:** 414 Akers Dr., Wilmore, KY 40390.

Welker, Kathy J. (Mr. 2, 1947, VanWert, OH) Asst. Dir., Law Lib., IN Univ. Sch. of Law, 1977–; Readers Srvs. Libn., 1976; Libn., Huntington Coll., 1976, Asst. Libn., 1972–76. **Educ.:** Huntington Coll., 1965–69, BA (Hist.); IN Univ., 1971–72, MLS; IN Univ. Sch. of Law, 1981–. **Orgs.:** OH Reg. Assn. of Law Libs.: Pres. (1979–80); Treas. (1978–79); Lcl. Arrang. Ch. (1978). AALL: Educ. Com. (1980–81); Copyrt. Com. (1979–80), AV Com. (1977–79). **Honors:** Beta Phi Mu, 1972. **Pubns.:** Jt. auth., *Model Bibliography of Indiana Legal Materials* (1978); Jt. auth., "The Library Game," *Amer. Libs.* (Ap. 1977). **Activities:** 1, 12; 17, 35, 39; 77, 78, 92 **Addr.:** Law Library-Indiana University, 735 W. New York St., Indianapolis, IN 46202.

Welles, Gordon S. (F. 18, 1950, Indianapolis, IN) Lcl. Hist. Libn., Oak Lawn Pub. Lib., 1978–; Sr. Libn., Port Jefferson Free Lib., 1974–78. **Educ.:** Wabash Coll., 1968–72, BA (Hist.); Syracuse Univ., 1973–74, MSLS. **Orgs.:** IL Reg. Lib. Cncl.: Ch., Lcl. Hist. & Geneal. Int. Grp. ALA. IL LA. **Pubns.:** *Port Jefferson: Story of a Village* (1978). **Activities:** 9; 16, 41, 45; 73, 85 **Addr.:** 9986 S. 84th Terrace #201, Palos Hills, IL 60465.

Wellington, Carol Strong (Ja. 30, 1948, Altadena, CA) Law Libn., Hill & Barlow, 1973–; Resrch. Mgr., State St. Bank & Trust Co., 1969–72. **Educ.:** Lake Forest Coll., 1965–69, AB (Art Hist.); Simmons Coll., 1972–73, MLS. **Orgs.:** AALL. SLA. Assn. of Boston Law Libns.: Pres. (1980–81); VP-Pres. Elect (1979–80); Nsltr. Com. (1979–). **Activities:** 12; 17, 39; 77 **Addr.:** Hill & Barlow, 225 Franklin St., Boston, MA 02110.

Wellington, Flora H. (Ap. 13, 1920, St. Louis, MO) Assoc. Libn. and Head, Tech. Srvs., Univ. of Miami Sch. of Med. Lib., 1972–; Assoc. Libn., Head Catlgr., 1963–72, Actg. Libn., 1961–63, Per. Libn., 1956–61; Libn., FL State Bd. of Hlth., 1954–55; Catlgr., Univ. of TN Coll. of Med., 1951–53; Intern, Tulane Univ. Sch. of Med., 1950–51; Tchr., 1941–42. **Educ.:** Coll. of William and Mary, 1937–41, BS (Math.); Univ. of NC, 1949–50, BS (LS); Med. LA Cert. Grade II, 1952–82. **Orgs.:** Med. LA: Ch., Subcom. on Internship (1956–57); South. Reg. Grp. (Secy.-Treas., 1964–65). Dade Cnty. LA: Pres. (1961–62). FL Med. Libns.: Pres. (1977–78). SLA: FL Chap., Secy.-Treas. (1964–65). Daughters of the Amer. Revolution. **Pubns.:** "The Public Health Library," *Bltn. Med. Libr. Assn.* (Ap. 1955). **Activities:** 1; 46; 80 **Addr.:** 3120 S.W. 27th St., Miami, FL 33133.

Wellisch, Hans H. (Ap. 25, 1920, Vienna, Austria) Prof., Coll. of Lib. & Info. Srvs., Univ. of MD, 1969–; Dir., Info. Ctr. & Lib., Tahal Consulting Engin., Tel Aviv, Israel, 1956–69; Libn., Signal Corps, Israel Defence Forces, 1953–56. **Educ.:** Univ. of MD, 1975, PhD (LS). **Orgs.:** Intl. Fed. of Documtn.: Ctrl. Class. Com. (1969–). Amer. Socty. of Indxrs.: Amer. Natl. Stans. Inst. Rep. (1978–). Assn. for the Bibl. of Hist.: Cncl. (1979–). Israel Socty. of Spec. Libs. and Info. Ctrs. **Honors** H.W. Wilson Co., Excel. in Indexing, 1979. **Pubns.:** *Conrad Gessner: a biobibliography* (1981); *Indexing and abstracting: an international bibliography* (1980); *The conversion of scripts: its nature, history and utilization* (1978); "Bibliographic access to multilingual collections," *Lib. Trends* (1980); "Ebla: the world's oldest library," *Jnl. of Lib. Hist.* (1981); other articles, reviews. **Activities:** 11; 30, 31, 41; 62, 75, 91 **Addr.:** College of Library and Information Services, University of Maryland, College Park, MD 20742.

Wellner, Cathryn J. (S. 5, 1946, Los Angeles, CA) Longridge Elem. Sch., Rochester, NY, 1981–; Lib. Media Spec., Greece Athena HS, Rochester, NY, 1978–80; Lib. Media Spec., Greece Olympia HS, 1976–78; AV Catlgr., Rochester Pub. Lib., 1975–76; Lib. Media Spec., Canyon Park Jr. HS, Bothell, WA, 1973–75. **Educ.:** Graceland Coll., 1964–66, AA (Fr.); Univ. of ID, 1966–68, BA (Fr., Eng.); Univ. of WA, 1972–73, MLS; Univ. de Clermont-Ferrand, France, 1968–69. **Orgs.:** Grt. Rochester Area Sch. Media Spec.: VP (1979–); Prog. Com. Co-Ch. (1979–80). Freedom to Read Fndn. NY LA: Sch. Lib. Media Sect., Awds. Com. (1977–79); Afflt. Asm. (1979–); John T. Short Awd./Sch. Lib. Media Day Com. (1979–). ALA: AASL; YASD. Natl. Educ. Assn. Greece Tchrs. Assn. **Honors** Phi Beta Kappa; Sch. of Libnshp., Univ. of WA, Byron Awd. for acad. perf., 1973; Beta Phi Mu, 1973; Sch. Lib. Media Sect., NY LA, John T. Short Awd. for pubcty., 1979. **Activities:** 10; 31, 36, 48; 63, 74, 89 **Addr.:** 158 Terrace Park, Rochester, NY 14619.

Wellner, Henry James (Ja. 31, 1936, Millville, WI) Coord., Instr. Media, Kenosha Unified Schs., 1963–; Visit. Lect., LS, Univ. of WI, Milwaukee, 1970–78; Tchr., Libn., Racine Unified Schs., 1958–63; Tchg. Prin., Racine Cnty. Sch., 1956–58. **Educ.:** Univ. of WI, Whitewater, 1959–62, BEd (Educ.); Univ. of WI, Madison, 1963–65; MSLS; other courses. **Orgs.:** WI LA: Secy., Exec. Bd. (1972–74); Com. on Org. (1969–71, 1981–82); Chld. & Young People's Srvs. Sect. (Ch. 1968–69). Kenosha Area LA: Pres. (1964–65). SE WI Reg. Lib. Conf.: Pres. (1972–73). SE WI Telecomm. Adv. Cncl.: Ch. (1974–75). Tri-Cnty. Lib. Cncl.: Pres. (1976–77). Other orgs., coms. **Pubns.:** "From order slips to shelves," *WI Lib. Bltn.* (Ja. 1968); "Dewey can be fun," *WI Lib. Bltn.* (Mr./Ap. 1979). **Activities:** 10, 11; 17, 26, 32 **Addr.:** 4919 S. Lakeshore Dr., Racine, WI 53403.

Wells, Anne S. (Mr. 25, 1952, Jackson, MS) Mss. Libn., MS State Univ., 1975–; Resrch. Asst., Douglas MacArthur Biograph-ical Proj., 1974–75. **Educ.:** Belhaven Coll., 1970–72; MS State Univ., 1972–74, BA (Hist.), 1974–75, MA (Hist.); Emory Univ./GA Arch., Archival Inst., 1976–76, Cert; Univ. of AL, 1980–81, MLS. **Orgs.:** Socty. of MS Archvsts.: VP (1981–); Treas. (1978–). SAA. Socty. of GA Archvsts. MS LA: JMRT. MS Hist. Socty. Phi Alpha Theta. AAUW. Other orgs. **Pubns.:** "Turner Catledge," *Mississippi Authors* (1979). **Addr.:** P.O. Box 4756, Mississippi State, MS 39762.

Wells, Donna L. (Ja. 19, 1951, Tisdale, SK) Asst. Head of Chld. Dept., STET Pub. Lib., 1979–; Chld. Libn., J.S. Wood Lib., 1977–79; Gen. Libn., Wheatland Reg. Lib., 1975–77. **Educ.:** Univ. of SK, 1970–73, BA (Hist., Fr.); Univ. of BC, 1973–75, MLS. **Orgs.:** SK LA: Secy. (1980/81). Can. LA. **Activities:** 9; 21, 31 **Addr.:** #2-625 6th Ave. N., Saskatoon, SK S7K 2S7 Canada.

Wells, Dorothy V. (F. 6, 1916, Boulder, CO) Asst. Dept. Head, Lcl. Docum. Libn., Univ. of CA, Los Angeles, 1942–; Actg. Head, Lib. Loan Dept., Univ. of WY, 1942; Asst. Libn., Docum., Fort Hays KS State Coll., 1939–42. **Educ.:** Univ. of WY, 1934–38, BA (Hist.); Univ. of IL, 1938–39 BS (LS). **Orgs.:** SLA: VP, South. CA Chap. (1948–49). Coll. of Plng. Libns. Intl. City Mgt. Assn. **Activities:** 1; 15, 29, 39; 65, 78, 92 **Addr.:** Public Affairs Service/Local, University Research Library, University of California, Los Angeles, CA 90024.

Wells, Ellen B. (Jl. 23, 1934, Berlin, Germany) Chief, Spec. Col., Smithsonian Institution Libs., 1979–; Assoc. Libn., Hist. of Sci. Col., Cornell Univ. Libs., 1972–78; Actg. Osler Libn., McGill Univ., 1968–72; Catlgr., print cur., Hist. of Med. Div., Natl. Lib. of Med., 1964–68. **Educ.:** OK State Univ., 1956–57, AB (Art Hist.); Cornell Univ., 1952–56; Univ. of CA, Berkeley, 1961–63, MLS; McGill Univ., 1971–73, MA (Hist.). **Orgs.:** Univ. of CA Lib. Schs. Alum. Assn. Socty. for the Bibl. of Nat. Hist. Hist. of Sci. Socty. **Pubns.:** *Horsemanship: A Guide to Information Sources* (1979); "Graphic Techniques of Medical Illustration in the 18th century," *Jnl. of Biocomm.* (Ag. 1976); "Dubois de Chemant's Lettre à M. Andouillé: A Translation, with Introduction, Notes and a Bibliography," *Bltn. Hist. Dentistry* (O. 1976); "The Horse in Science and Medicine: A Historical Review," *Animal Health* (S.-O. 1977); "Boncompagni Archive at Cornell University," *Hist. Math.* (N. 1978); other articles. **Activities:** 1, 4; 24, 45; 57, 73 **Addr.:** Dibner Room, MAH 5016, Smithsonian Institution, Washington, DC 20560.

Wells, Frances Dehnert (Ja. 1, 1926, Lewistown, MT) Coord. of Lib. Srvs., Billings Pub. Schs., 1970–; Libn., Billings West HS, 1961–70; Libn., Helena HS, 1956–61; Libn. Eng., Belgrade (MT) HS, 1954–56; Libn., Cheyenne HS, 1951–52; Libn., Albuquerque HS, 1949–51; Libn. Eng., Colstrip (MT) HS, 1947–48. **Educ.:** Univ. of MT, 1944–46; Rocky Mt. Coll., BA, 1946–47; MT State Univ., 1960, 1967, 1968; Univ. of MT, 1959, 1970, 1974; East. MT Coll., MS, 1961, 1963. **Orgs.:** ALA: Cnclr.-at-Large (1976–80); Plng. and Budget Asm. (1978–79); Dir. Reg. VII (1969–71); Pres. Awd. Selection Com. (1978–79). MT LA: Pres. (1972–73). MT Assn. of Sch. Libns.: Ch. (1960–61). Intl. Assn. of Sch. Libns. Other orgs., coms. Delta Kappa Gamma. Daughters of the Amer. Revolution. MT Dept. of Pub. Inst.: Sch. Lib./Media com. (1959–68). **Pubns.:** Guest ed., *MT Lib. Qtly.* (1961). **Activities:** 10, 11; 17, 24, 26; 50, 63, 89 **Addr.:** 2112 Fairview Pl., Billings, MT 59102.

Wells, Garron F. (D. 31, 1950, Toronto, ON) Mgr., Arch., Bank of NS, 1980–; Archvst., Hudson's Bay Co. Arch., Prov. Arch. of MB, 1975–80. **Educ.:** York Univ., 1969–73, BA (Hist.); Univ. of Toronto, 1973–75, MLS; Univ. of MB, 1976–, MA (Hist.) in progress. **Orgs.:** Assn. of Can. Archvsts.: Bus. Arch. Com. Toronto Area Archvsts. Grp. **Activities:** 2; 15, 17, 23; 59, 85 **Addr.:** Bank of Nova Scotia Archives, 44 King St. W., Toronto, ON M5H 1H1 Canada.

Wells, Gladys Ann (Jl. 31, 1948, Johannesburg, S. Africa) Spec. Asst. to the State Libn., NY State Lib., 1980–; Sen. Libn., NY State Sen., Resrch. Srv., 1975–80; Asst. Libn., Legis. Ref., NY State Lib., 1972–75; Libn., Empire State Coll., SUNY, 1971–72. **Educ.:** Greensboro Coll., 1966–70, BA (Eng.); SUNY, Albany, 1970–71, MLS. **Orgs.:** NY LA. SLA: Gvtl. Rel. Com. (Ch.); Gvtl. Affairs Ch., Upstate Chap.; Ch., Olympic Lib. Sierra Club. Porsche Club of Amer. **Pubns.:** Ed., *The Northeast: Managing a Way Out, Proceedings of a Symposium on Legislative Actions for Survival in the Credit Market* (1977); Upstate NY SLA *Nsltr.* (S.-D. 1979, Ja.-Mr. 1980, Mr.-My. 1980). **Activities:** 4, 12; 15, 29, 39; 50, 75, 78 **Addr.:** Office of the State Librarian, Rm. 10D36, Cultural Education Center, Empire State Plaza, Albany, NY 12230.

Wells, H. Lea (F. 4, 1946, Clover, SC) Persnl. Libn., Instr., Univ. of TN, Knoxville, 1978–1981. **Educ.:** Univ. of NC, Charlotte, 1965–73, BA (Eng.); Univ. of NC, Chapel Hill, 1976–77, MSLS. **Orgs.:** ALA: ACRL/LAMA/Persnl. Admin. Sect., Staff Dev. Com. (1979–81). SELA. TN LA: Staff Dev. Com. (1979–81). E. TN LA. **Honors:** Beta Phi Mu, 1978. **Pubns.:** "The Academic Library Development Program," *Coll. and Resrch. Libs.* (Ja. 1977). **Activities:** 1; 17, 25, 35; 50 **Addr.:** 5515 Country Dr. #45, Nashville, TN 37211.

Wells, Merle William (D. 1, 1918, Lethbridge, AB) State Archvst., ID State Arch., 1952–; Assoc. Prof. of Hist., Alliance Coll., 1950–56. **Educ.:** Boise Jr. Coll., 1937–39, AA; Coll. of ID, 1939–41, AB (Hist.); Univ. of CA, 1946–50, PhD (Hist.). **Orgs.:** SAA: State Recs. Com. Pac. NW LA: Mss. Com. (1962). ID LA. Cncl. on Pac. NW Reg. Resrch.: Pres. (1969–70). Other orgs. Amer. Assn. for State and Lcl. Hist.: Cncl. (1973–77). West. Hist. Assn.: Cncl. (1973–76). Natl. Conf. of State Hist. Prsrvn. Ofcrs.: Bd. of Dir. (1976–80). Amer. Hist. Assn. Other orgs. **Honors** SAA, Fellow, 1971. **Pubns.:** *Anti-Mormonism in Idaho, 1872-1892* (1978); *Gold Camps and Silver Cities* (1964); "Idaho Anti-Mormon Test Oath," *Pac. Hist. Review* (Ag. 1955); "Creation of the territory of Idaho," *Pac. NW Qtly.* (Ap. 1949). **Activities:** 2, 13; 29, 38, 41; 55, 75, 83 **Addr.:** 1325 Longmont, Boise, ID 83706.

Wells, Phyllis L. (O. 14, 1929, Riverhead, NY) Sr. Asst. Libn., Catlgr., SUNY, Plattsburgh, 1957–; Bkmobile. Libn., Clinton-Essex-Franklin Lib., 1955–57; Sch. Libn., Berlin Ctrl. Sch., 1953–55; Sch. Libn., Schoharie Ctrl. Sch., 1952–53. **Educ.:** State Tchrs. Coll., Geneseo, NY, 1948–52, BS (Educ., LS), 1955–58, MS (Educ.); various crs. **Orgs.:** ALA. NY State LA. SUNY LA. **Pubns.:** "Job Exchange, Anyone?" *SUNY LA Nsltr.* (Spr. 1979); various articles on hist. **Activities:** 1; 15, 20, 39; 55, 73, 90 **Addr.:** 13 Addoms St., Plattsburgh, NY 12901.

Welsch, Erwin Kurt (Ap. 17, 1935, Philadelphia, PA) Biblgphr., Univ. of WI, Madison, 1967–; Hist. Libn., IN Univ., 1962–65, Cat. Libn., 1959–62. **Educ.:** Univ. of PA, 1953–57, BA (Msc., Hist.); IN Univ., 1960, MA (LS), 1958–70, MA,PhD (Hist.). **Orgs.:** Assn. for the Bibl. of Hist.: Prog. Com. (1978–). Cncl. for European Std.: Publns. Com. (1970–75). **Honors:** George C. Marshall Meml. Fund in Denmark, Flwshp., 1980–81.

Special Subjects/Services: 50. Adult educ.; 51. Advert./Mktg.; 52. Aerosp.; 53. Agric.; 54. Area std.; 55. Arts/Hum.; 56. Autom.; 57. Bibl./Prtg.; 58. Bio. sci.; 59. Bus./Fin.; 60. Chem.; 61. Copyrt.; 62. Documtn.; 63. Educ.; 64. Engin.; 65. Env.; 66. Eth. grps.; 67. Film; 68. Food/Nutr.; 69. Geneal.; 70. Geo.; 71. Geol.; 72. Handcpd.; 73. Hist.; 74. Int. frdm.; 75. Info. sci.; 76. Insr.; 77. Law; 78. Legis.; 79. Math./Comp. sci.; 80. Med.; 81. Metals; 82. Nat. resrcs.; 83. Newsp.; 84. Nuc. sci.; 85. Oral hist.; 86. Petr./Energy; 87. Pharm.; 88. Phys./Astr./Math.; 89. Readg.; 90. Relig.; 91. Sci./Tech.; 92. Soc. sci.; 93. Telecom.; 94. Transp.; 95. (other).

Pubns.: *Libraries and Archives in France,* (1979); *Libraries and Archives in Germany* (1975); *The Negro in the United States; A Research Guide* (1965); "The University of Wisconsin Library Collection on East Germany," *East Central and Southeast Europe. A Handbook of Library and Archival Resources* (1976); "Historical Literature," *Encyclopedia of Library and Information Sciences* (1973); other articles. **Activities:** 1; 15, 29, 4S; 54, 73, 92 **Addr.:** 278 G Memorial Library, 728 State St., Madison, WI 53706.

Welsh, Eric L. (Ap. 17, 1952, Paterson, NJ) Ref. Libn., Dade Cnty. Law Lib., 1976–. **Educ.:** Westminster Coll., 1970–74, BA (Eng.); Drexel Univ., 1974–76, MS (LS). **Orgs.:** AALL. SE Assn. of Law Libns. S. FL Assn. Law Libns.: Pres. (1979–80). **Pubns.:** "WESTLAW: A Database Review and Searching Primer," *Online* (Jl. 1980); "Cases on Point Available By Computer," *FL Bar Jnl.* (N. 1978). **Activities:** 12; 29, 33, 39; 56, 77 **Addr.:** Dade County Law Library, 321A County Courthouse, 73 W. Flagler St., Miami, FL 33130.

Welsh, Harry E. (S. 19, 1940, Westernport, MD) Lib. Dir., SD Sch. of Mines & Tech., 1979–; Head, Gvt. Docum. Ctr., Univ. of WA, 1974–79; Asst. Inst., IN Univ., 1973–74; Asst. Libn., Wayne State Univ., 1970–73. **Educ.:** WV Univ., 1958–62, BA (Pol. Sci.); Drexel Univ., 1967–68, MS (LS); Wayne State Univ., 1971–73, MPA. **Orgs.:** ALA. SLA. Amer. Socty. for Pub. Admin. **Pubns.:** "What's New in Documents," *Gvt. Pubns. Review* (Volumes 1-5); "Some Questions and Answers About Environmental Impact Statements," *PNLA Qtly.* (Fall 1975); "U.S. Government Publications, Table of Catalogs, Checklists, Guides, Indexes, and Union List," *Reader's Advisory Service Topical Booklists* (1975); "An Acquisitions Up-Date for Government Publications," *Micro. Review* (S. 1977); "National Policy and Access to Federal Information," *Gvt. Pubns. Review* (Spr. 1979); Reviews. **Activities:** 15, 29; 91 **Addr.:** 320 Denver St., #103, Rapid City, SD 57701.

Welsh, Sue C. (Mr. 5, 1943, Denver, CO) Asst. Circuit Libn., U.S. Ct. of Appeals, 9th Circuit, 1981–; Info. Spec., Fed. Judicial Ctr., 1972–81; Asst. Libn., US Ct. of Custs. and Patents, 1968–72. **Educ.:** CO State Univ., 1961–65, BA (Pol. Sci.); Cath. Univ. of Amer., 1973–78, MS (LS). **Orgs.:** AALL: Mem. Com. (1975–77); Un. List of Legal Pers. (1977); Place. Com. (1981–82). Law Libns. Socty. of DC: Nom. Com. (1975); Mem. Ch. (1975–77). SLA. North. CA Assn. of Law Libs. CO State Univ. Alum. Assn. of DC: VP (1976–77); Secy.-Treas. (1977–78). **Honors:** Kappa Delta. **Activities:** 4; 17, 30; 77 **Addr.:** U.S. Court of Appeals Library, P.O. Box 5731, San Francisco, CA 94101.

Welsh, William J(oseph) (N. 15, 1919, Weatherly, PA) Deputy Libn. of Congs., Lib. of Congs., 1976–; Dir., Prcs. Dept., 1968–76, Assoc. Dir., Prcs. Dept., 1964–68, Assoc. Dir., Admin. Dept., 1960–64, Exec. Ofcr., Prcs. Dept., 1958–60, Head, East European Accessions Index Proj., 1952–58, Head, Order Unit, Prcs. Dept., 1949–52. **Educ.:** Univ. of Notre Dame, 1936–40, AB (Phil.), 1940–41, (Law). **Orgs.:** ALA: Cncl. (1978–). Cncl. on Lib. Resrcs.: Prog. Mgt. Com. (1979–). ARL: Lib. of Congs. Rep. IFLA: Prof. Bd. (1978–79); Ch., Unvsl. Bibl. Cntrl. Strg. Com. (1978–79); Secy., Sect. on Natl. Libs. (1978–79). Other orgs. **Honors:** ALA, Melvil Dewey Awd., 1971. **Pubns.:** "IFLA's Future – The View from the Library of Congress," *IFLA's First Fifty Years* (1977); "Libraries and the New Technology: Toward a National Bibliographic Data Base," *Academic Libraries in the Year 2000* (1977); "The Governance of Library Networks: Alternatives for the Future – Response," *The Structure and Governance of Library Networks* (1979); "Pamela Wood Darling," *Lib. Resrcs. & Tech. Srvs.* (Fall, 1979); "Progress in the United States Toward a National Periodicals System," *IFLA Jnl.* (1979); other articles, speeches. **Activities:** 4; 14; 17 **Addr.:** The Library of Congress, Washington, DC 20540.

Welwood, Ronald J. (F. 14, 1940, Penticton, BC) Lib. Dir., David Thompson Univ. Ctr., 1969–; Actg. Head, Newsp. Sect., Natl. Lib. of Can., 1968–69, Libn., 1967–68. **Educ.:** Univ. of BC, 1962–66, BA (Geo., Soclgy.), 1966–67, BLS; Cert. in Microrecording Tech., 1968. **Orgs.:** BC LA. Can. LA. Can. Assn. of Coll. & Univ. Libs.: Dir. (1971–73). Intl. Gyro. **Pubns.:** Ed., *Union list of Canadian newspapers held by Canadian libraries* (1968–69); "Book Budget Allocations: an objective formula for the small academic library," *Can. Lib. Jnl.* (Je. 1977); "Flexible Working Hours: guidelines for a small academic library," *Can. Lib. Jnl.* (Ag. 1976); "Kootenay Institute, Library System: a proposal," *BCLA Reporter* (Mr. 1974); other books. **Activities:** 1, 2; 17, 39; 55, 73 **Addr.:** David Thompson University Centre, Library, 820-10th St., Nelson, BC V1L 3C7 Canada.

Wember, Bertha Claire (Mr. 6, 1922, New York City, NY) Lib. Media Spec., Oak Park Schs., 1968–; Libn., Temple Israel, 1961–; Catlgr., Head of Frgn. Lang. Div., Film Ref., Detroit Pub. Lib., 1959–60, 1951–58; Chld. Libn., Lit. and Frgn. Lang. Ref., DC Pub. Lib., 1948–51, 1944–46; Circ. Dept. Asst., Brooklyn Coll., 1947–48. **Educ.:** Brooklyn Coll., 1939–43, BA (Eng., Educ.), 1943–44, (Eng. Lit.); Pratt Inst., 1946–47, BLS. **Orgs.:** AJL: Rec. Secy. (1966); Detroit Chap. (Treas., 1979–80). **Activities:** 5, 10; 20, 21, 39; 55, 66, 90 **Addr.:** Temple Israel Library, 5725 Walnut Lake Rd., West Bloomfield, MI 48033.

Wember, Lawrence (My. 1, 1921, West New York, NJ) Dir., Oak Park (MI) Pub. Lib., 1968–; Head, Detroit Mncpl. Ref. Lib., 1956–68; Branch Libn., Detroit Pub. Lib., 1955–56, Asst. Chief Tech. Dept., 1951–55; Libn. II, DC Pub. Lib., 1948–51. **Educ.:** Brooklyn Coll., 1938–42, BA (Eng.); Columbia Univ., 1947–48, MLS. **Orgs.:** ALA. MI LA. **Activities:** 9; 16, 17 **Addr.:** Oak Park Public Library, 14200 Oak Park Blvd., Oak Park, MI 48237.

Wemett, Lisa C. (D. 18, 1950, Rochester, NY) YA, AV Srvs. Libn., Fairport Pub. Lib., 1978–; YA Libn., Osterhout Free Lib., 1975–78. **Educ.:** Eckerd Coll., 1969–73, BA (Lit.); Univ. of NC, 1974–75, MS (LS). **Orgs.:** NY LA. ALA. Girl Scouts of USA: Fairport Div. (Ch. 1981–82). **Activities:** 9; 32, 48 **Addr.:** Fairport Public Library, 1 Village Landing, Fairport, NY 14450.

Wender, Ruth W. (My. 27, 1919, Laurel, MS) Assoc. Dir., Univ. of OK Hlth. Sci. Ctr., 1981–; Asst. Lib. Dir., 1972–81; Coord., Lib. Srvs. & Info. Proj., OK Reg. Med. Prog., 1970–72, ILL Libn., 1968–70, Assoc. Prof., Med. Lib. Sci., 1975–80, Prof. Med. Lib. Sci., 1980–, Asst. Prof., Instr., 1968–75. **Educ.:** Rice Inst., 1935–39, BA with distinction; Univ. of OK, 1966–68, MLS; TX Tchg. Cert.; Med. LA Cert. **Orgs.:** Beta Phi Mu: Secy.-Treas., OK Chap. (1971–72). Med. LA: Bd. of Dirs. (1981–84); S. Ctrl. Reg. Grp. (Ch., 1974–75); Cont. Educ. (Ch. 1977–78); ByLaws Ch. (1977–78); Ad hoc com. on MLA Grp. Structure Implementation (1978–). OK Hlth. Sci. LA. OK LA: Coll. and Univ. Div. (Ch., 1974–75). Other orgs., coms. Univ. Womens Assn. Hadassah. Sisterhood, Congregation Emanuel, Oklahoma City. **Honors:** Phi Beta Kappa, 1939; LRRT Resrch. Awd., 1976. **Pubns.:** Ed., *Organizing and Administering the Small Hospital Library* (1979); "Counting Journal Title Usage in the Health Sciences," *Spec. Libs.* (1979); "Management by objectives in Baptist Medical Center Library," *Hosp. Libs.* (Jl. 1978); "The Procedure Manual," *Spec. Libs.* (N. 1977); "Hospital Journal Usage," *Bltn. Med. LA* (Ap. 1978); other articles. **Addr.:** 2614 Meadow Brook, Norman, OK 73069.

Wenderoth, Christine (O. 12, 1949, Passaic, NJ) Reader Srvs. Libn., Columbia Theo. Semy., 1980–; Slide Cur., Emory Univ. Art Hist. Dept., 1977–80, Judaica Biblgphr., Woodruff & Pitts Libs., 1977–79; Libn., Fr.G.B.S.Hale HS, Raleigh, NC, 1974–75; Asst. Libn., Univ. of NC Plng. Dept., 1973–74. **Educ.:** Oberlin Coll., 1967–71, BA (Relig.); Univ. of NC, 1971–73, MSLS; Emory Univ., 1976–78, MA (Theo.), 1978, PhD cand. "Otto's Views on Language," *Perspectives in Religious Stud.* (Spr. 1982); Various **Orgs.:** ALA. ATLA. Amer. Acad. of Relig. **Pubns.:** Various speeches. **Activities:** 1, 12; 31, 39, 44; 55, 74, 90 **Addr.:** John Bulow Campbell Library, Columbia Theological Seminary, 701 Columbia Dr., Decatur, GA 30031.

Wenger, Charles B. (D. 7, 1940, Grand Junction, CO) Chief Libn., Natl. Ctr. for Atmospheric Resrch., 1979–; Syst. Libn., 1978–79; Recs. Mgr. and Sci. Libn., Johns-Manville Corp., 1977; Info. Spec., Biomed. Lib., Univ. of CA, Los Angeles, Cat., Acq., Natl. Oceanic & Atmospheric Admin., Boulder, 1975–76. **Educ.:** Univ. of Denver, 1958–63, BA (Chem.); Univ. of Miami, 1965–67, (Molecular Bio.); Univ. of Denver, 1973–74, MA (Libnshp.); Univ. of CO, 1977–79 (Bus.). **Orgs.:** SLA. ASIS. MLA. **Honors:** Phi Beta Kappa, 1963; Resrch. Socty. of Amer., Elected Mem. 1970. **Pubns.:** "Monograph Evaluation for Acquisition in a Large Research Library," *JASIS* (Mr. 1979); "Journal Evaluation in a Large Research Library," *Jul. of ASIS* (1977); **Activities:** 12; 15, 17, 36, 41; 56, 60, 88 **Addr.:** P.O. Box 3364, Boulder, CO 80307.

Wenger, Milton B. (S. 8, 1918, Brooklyn, NY) Info. Spec., Chem Systs. Inc., 1973–; Mgr., Info. Ctr., Halcon Intl. Inc., 1960–72; Tech. Ed., Libn., Vitro Engin. Co., 1956–60. **Educ.:** Miami Univ., 1939–41, BS (Chem., Bio.); George Peabody Coll., 1941–44, MSLS, 1942–44, MS (Chem. Bio.). **Orgs.:** SLA: Bio. Sect. (Ch., 1948); various coms. ASIS. Amer. Chem. Socty. The Chems. Club. **Activities:** 12; 30, 39, 41; 60, 64, 86 **Addr.:** 1411 E. 34th St., Brooklyn, NY 11210.

Wenglin, Barbara Nedell (Ap. 6, 1944, New York City, NY) Ref. Libn., White Plains Pub. Lib., 1979–, Chld. Libn., 1977–79; Sch. Libn., Hallen Ctr., 1976–77; Ref. Libn., Rochester (MN) Pub. Lib., 1966–67; Asst. to Libn., Fr. Inst., 1965–66. **Educ.:** Skidmore Coll., 1960–64, BA (Fr.); Sorbonne, 1964–65, Dip. de Lit. contemporaine (Contemporary Fr. Lit.) Univ. of AZ, 1973–75, MLS. **Orgs.:** ALA. Frdm. to Read Fndn. Westchester LA. **Honors:** Beta Phi Mu. **Pubns.:** "Library Life Unchanged by '73 Supreme Court," *Amer. Libs.* (Ap. 1975); "Zelda's Montgomery," *AL Sunday Mag.* (Ap. 29, 1973); "Effects on the Public Library of the 1973 Supreme Court Obscenity Ruling," ERIC (S. 1975). **Activities:** 9, 10; 16, 21, 39; 55, 85, 92 **Addr.:** White Plains Public Library, 100 Martine Ave., White Plains, NY 10601.

Wenman, Joan Mary (D. 2, 1947, Victoria, BC) Systs., Circ., ILL Libn., Douglass Cmnty. Coll., 1981–; Cmnty. Libn., Britannia Cmnty. Srvs. Ctr., 1977–81; Libn., Castlegar Pub. Lib., 1975–77. **Educ.:** Univ. of Victoria, 1969–73, BA (Hist., Art Hist., Eng.); Univ. of Toronto, 1973–75, MLS. **Orgs.:** BC LA. Can. LA. R.E.A.C.H. Med./Dental Clinic: Pres. (1978–80). **Activities:** 9, 10; 16; 31, 39; 50, 66, 77 **Addr.:** P.O. Box 2503, New Westminster, BC V3L 5B2 Canada.

Wente, LaVere Joyce (D. 7, 1931, Newington, CT) Dir., Coral Springs Branch, Broward Cnty. Lib., 1979–; Asst. Dir., Ft. Lauderdale Branch, 1978–79, Libn. for the Blind and Phys. Handcpd., 1977–78; Pub. Admin. Libn., Nova Univ., 1976–77. **Educ.:** Oakland Cmnty. Coll., 1967–69, AA (Educ.); Wayne State Univ., 1970–71, BS (Educ.); FL State Univ., 1975–76, MS (LS). **Orgs.:** ALA: ASCLA, Lib. Srv. Blind and Phys. Handcpd., Exec. Bd. (1978–79). FL LA: Awds. Com. (1976–77), Mem. Com. (1977–78), Online Searchers Caucus Secy. (1978–79), Pres. (1980–81). FL WHCOLIS: Wkshp. Leader (1978). Browncard Cnty LA. Wayne State Univ. Alum. Assn. FL State Univ. Alum. Assn. **Honors:** Beta Phi Mu. **Pubns.:** "Broward County Reader/Discussion Groups," *DIKTA* (Win. 1977–78); "What are 'Adult Services?'" *RQ* (Spr. 1979). **Activities:** 1, 9; 16, 17, 35; 50, 56, 72 **Addr.:** Broward County Library, P.O. Box 5463, Fort Lauderdale, FL 33310.

Wente, Sr. M. Therese (Jl. 11, 1935, Indianapolis, IN) Dir., Marian Coll. Lib., 1976–, Asst. Libn., 1970–76; Prin., Holy Trinity Elem. Sch., 1967–70; Elem. Sch. Tchr., 1955–67. **Educ.:** Marian Coll., 1961, BS (Educ.); Rosary Coll., 1965–70, MALS; Ball State Univ., Sum. 1971. **Orgs.:** ALA. IN Coop. Lib. Srvs. Athrty.: Bd. of Dirs. Ctrl. IN Lib. Srvs. Athrty.: Bd. of Dirs.; Exec. Com.; Cont. Educ. Com. Cath. LA. Various other orgs., ofcs. **Honors** Marian Coll. Alum. Assn., Leadership and Loyalty Awd., 1977; Ctrl. IN Lib. Srvs. Athrty., Outstan. Srv. Awd., 1979. **Activities:** 1, 10; 15, 17, 24; 50, 63, 93 **Addr.:** Marian College Library, 3200 Cold Spring Rd., Indianapolis, IN 46222.

Wente, Norman G. (Ja. 24, 1931, Waterloo, IA) Chief Libn., Luther-Northwest. Theo. Semy., 1968–; Bookstacks Libn., Univ. of IL, Urbana, 1966–68. **Educ.:** Wartburg Coll., 1949–53, BA (Liberal Arts); Wartburg Semy., 1953–57, M.Div. (Theo.); Univ. of IL, 1965–67, MS (LS); Univ. of MN, 1978–81, Spec. Cert. (LS). **Orgs.:** ATLA: Various coms. MN Theo. LA: Various ofcs. MN LA. MN Cnsrtm. of Theo. Schs.: Various ofcs. Luth. Hist. Conf. **Pubns.:** "A Librarian's Response," *Luth. Hist. Conf. Essays & Rpts.* (1974); "Footloose in Europe," *One Mag.* (1953). **Activities:** 1; 15, 17, 45 **Addr.:** Luther-Northwestern Seminary, 2375 Como Ave., St. Paul, MN 55108.

Wentz, Charlotte Marie (Jl. 25, 1920, Dayton, OH) Libn., Dir., Lrng. Resrcs., Southwest. MI Coll., 1967–; HS Libn., Trotwood Madison HS, 1956–67; Tchr., Garfield Sch., 1952–55; Tchr., Trotwood Madison Elem. Sch., 1950–52. **Educ.:** Univ. of Dayton, 1938–42, BS (Elem. Educ.); West. Rsv. Univ., 1955–56, MS (LS); various crs. **Orgs.:** NLA. ALA. Dowagiac Ladies LA. Christ. Women's Flwshp. Lib. Bd. of Dowagiac Pub. Lib.: Ch. (1975–76). **Activities:** 1, 10; 17, 32, 33 **Addr.:** 606 Fairlawn Dr., Dowagiac, MI 49047.

Werd, Margaret Paulsel (Jl. 3, 1938, Laredo, TX) Cust. Srv. Rep., *NY Times* Info. Srv., 1979–; Exec. VP, Ed., Campus and Cmnty. Pubns., 1977–79; Tchr., Pittsburgh Pub. Schs., 1973–76; Real Estate Sales Person, State of PA, 1974–76; Lib. Coord., Fairfield Jr. High, 1970–71. **Educ.:** Mary Baldwin Coll., 1956–60, BA (Eng.); Univ. of AL, 1971–73, MA (Educ., Eng.). **Orgs.:** OLUG: Reg. Conf. (Vendor Demonstrator, 1980). AALL. ASIS. **Pubns.:** Various trng. mtrls., booklets, guides, resrcs. for *NY Times* info. srvs. databases (1979–81). **Activities:** 10; 50, 63, 75 **Addr.:** New York Times Information Services, Inc., Suite 600, 134 S. La Salle, Chicago, IL 60603.

Werking, Richard H. (S. 29, 1943, Charleston, SC) Col. Dev. Libn., Trinity Univ., 1981–; Actg. Dir. of Libs., Univ. of MS, 1980–81; Asst. Dir., Ref. and Col. Dev., 1979–80, Head, Ref. Dept., 1977–79; Ref. Libn., Lawrence Univ., 1975–77. **Educ.:** Univ. of Evansville, 1961–66, BA (Hist.); Univ. of WI, 1966–67, MA (Hist.), 1969–73, PhD (Hist.); Univ. of Chicago, 1974–75, MA (LS). **Orgs.:** ALA: ACRL, Cont. Educ. Com. (Ch., 1977–79)/Bibl. Instr. Sect., Cont. Educ. Com. (1979–82); RTSD. Org. of Amer. Histns. Socty. for Histns. of Amer. Frgn. Rel. **Pubns.:** *The Master Architects: Building the U.S. Foreign Service, 1890-1913* (1977); "Bureaucrats, Businessmen, and Foreign Trade: The Origins of the U.S. Chamber of Commerce," *Bus. Hist. Rev.* (Aut., 1978); "Evaluating Bibliographic Education," *Lib. Trends* (Sum. 1980); "Using *Choice* As A Mechanism For Allocating Book Funds In An Academic Library," *Coll. & Resrch. Libs.* (Mr. 1981); various other articles in hist., LS. **Activities:** 1; 15, 17, 39; 54, 57, 92 **Addr.:** Trinity University Library, San Antonio, TX 78205.

Werling, Anita Laura (N. 26, 1946, Evansville, IN) Mgr., Cols. Dev., Univ. Micro. Intl., 1978–, Mgr., Ed., Photo., Bibl. Srvs., 1975–78, Supvsr., Bks. and Cols., 1972–74; Asst. Ref. Libn., Fairleigh Dickinson Univ., 1971–72. **Educ.:** IN Univ., 1964–68, BA (Eng.), 1970–71, MLS. **Orgs.:** ALA: RTSD/Reprodct. of Lib. Mtrls. Sect., Stans. Com. (1980–81); Bkdlr. Lib. Rel. Com. (1979–80). Natl. Micro. Assn. **Honors** Beta Phi Mu. **Activities:** 1, 14-Publshg.; 33, 37, 39; 57, 75 **Addr.:** University Microfilms International, 300 N. Zeeb Rd., Ann Arbor, MI 48106.

Werner, Gloria (D. 12, 1940, Seattle, WA) Biomed. Libn., Assoc. Univ. Libn., Dir., Pac. SW Reg. Med. Lib. Srv., Univ. of CA, Los Angeles, 1979–, Adj. Lectr. (LS), 1977–, Assoc. Biomed. Libn., Pub. Srvs., 1977–78, Asst. Biomed. Libn., Pub. Srvs.,

PROFESSIONAL ACTIVITIES: Institutions: 1. Acad. lib.; 2. Arch.; 3. Assn.; 4. Fed./Gvt. lib.; 5. Inst. lib.; 6. Mfr./Suppl.; 7. Milit. lib.; 8. Musm.; 9. Pub. lib.; 10. Sch. lib.; 11. Sch. of lib. sci.; 12. Spec. lib.; 13. State lib.; 14. (other). **Functions/Activities:** 15. Acq./Col. dev.; 16. Adult srvs.; 17. Admin.; 18. Apprais.; 19. Archit./Bldgs.; 20. Cat./Class.; 21. Chld. srvs.; 22. Circ.; 23. Cons./Pres.; 24. Consult.; 25. Cont. ed.; 26. Educ. lib. sci.; 27. Ext. srvs.; 28. Fund/Grants; 29. Gvt. pubs.; 30. Indx./Abs.; 31. Instr. lib. use; 32. Media srvs.; 33. Micro.; 34. Netwks./Coop.; 35. Persnl.; 36. PR; 37. Publshg.; 38. Recs. mgt.; 39. Ref. srvs.; 40. Repro.; 41. Resrch.; 42. Review.; 43. Secur.; 44. Serials; 45. Spec. col.; 46. Tech. srvs.; 47. Trustees/Bds.; 48. YA srvs.; 49. (other).

1972–77, Head, Ref. and Pub. Srvs., 1966–72, Asst. Head, Pub. Srvs., 1964–66, Ref. Libn., 1963–64. **Educ.:** Oberlin Coll., 1958–61, BA (Fr.); Univ. of WA, 1961–62, ML; Med. LA, 1962–63, Cert. **Orgs.:** Med. LA: *Bltn.* Ed. (1979–), Assoc. Ed. (1974–79); Pubn. Panel (1976–78); Nom. Com. (1973–76); various ofcs. Assn. for Acad. Hlth. Sci. Lib. Dirs.: Bd. of Dirs. (1981–), Nom. Com. (1979). Med. Lib. Grp. of South CA and AZ: Constn. Com. (Ch., 1971–72). Assn. for the Dev. of Comp.-based Instr. Systs. Med. Lib. Schol. Fndn.: Bd. of Dirs. (1979–). **Pubns.:** "Use of Online Bibliographical Retrieval Services in Health Sciences Libraries," *Bltn. Med. LA* (Ja. 1979). **Activities:** 1; 17, 26, 34; 58, 80 **Addr.:** University of California, Los Angeles, Biomedical Library, Center for the Health Sciences, Los Angeles, CA 90024.

Werner, O. James (Ja. 14, 1924, St. Louis, MO) Libn., San Diego Cnty. Law Lib., 1972–; Asst. Prof., Law Libn., Univ. of OK, 1971–72; Instr., Asst. Law Libn., Univ. of TX, 1969–71; Trust Ofcr., Seattle First Natl. Bank, 1956–68. **Educ.:** Univ. of Chicago, 1946–48, PhB (Liberal Arts), 1948–52, Cert. Adv. Std. (Phil.), 1953–56, JD; Univ. of WA, 1968–69, MLaw Libn. **Orgs.:** AALL: State, Ct. Cnty. Law Libs Sect. (Pres., 1981–82); Spec. Com. on Exch. of Persnl. (Ch., 1977–81). South. CA Assn. of Law Libs.: Pres. (1979–80). ALA. Intl. Assn. of Law Libs. (1975–). Various other orgs. San Diego Hist. Socty. **Honors:** Phi Beta Mu. **Pubns.:** *Manual for Prison Law Libraries* (1976); "Law Libraries for Correctional Facilities," *Lib. Trends* (Sum. 1977); "Present Legal Status and Conditions of Prison Law Libraries," *Law Lib. Jnl.* (1973); "Law Library Services to Prisoners," *Law Lib. Jnl.* (1970). **Activities:** 9, 12; 15, 17, 35; 77, 78 **Addr.:** San Diego County Law Library, 1105 Front St., San Diego, CA 92101.

Wernstedt, Irene J. (O. 18, 1924, Portland, OR) Head, Serial Rec., Acq., PA State Univ., 1981–, Head, Serial Rec., 1976–81, Serials Data Libn., 1973–76, Home Econ. Libn., 1965–66. **Educ.:** Univ. of OR, 1942–46, BA (Fr.); Univ. of CA, Los Angeles, 1946–48, MA (Grmn.); McGill Univ., 1945 (Fr.). **Orgs.:** ALA: RTSD, LITA. PA LA. PA Un. List of Serials Adv. Com. (1979–). Pittsburgh Reg. Lib. Ctr.: Ad Hoc Com. on the Un. List of Serials (1975–). **Pubns.:** "Planning for the Automation of Serials Check-in," *Technicalities* (My. 1981); "Two Thousand Claims Later," *Serials Libn.* (Spr. 1980); "The Effectiveness of Serials Claiming," *Lib. Resrcs. & Tech. Srvs.* (forthcoming). **Activities:** 1; 15, 38, 44; 54, 56, 83 **Addr.:** Pattee Library, Pennsylvania State University, University Park, PA 16802.

Wert, Alice L. (Mr. 29, 1922, Monroe, MI) Coord., Tech. Srvs., Vigo Cnty. Pub. Lib., 1972–, Ref. Libn., 1972–74; Lib. Supvsr., Vigo Cnty. Sch. Corp., 1966–72. **Educ.:** East. MI Univ., 1939–43, BS (Elem. Educ.); Univ. of MI, 1948–49, MALS. **Orgs.:** ALA. IN Sch. Libns. Assn.: Pres. (1970–71). IN LA: Gvr.'s Conf. on Libs. Com. (Ch., 1978). WHCOLIS: Alternate (1979). Various other orgs. **Pubns.:** "In Orbit," *Focus on IN Libs.* (Sum. 1973); "Indiana Governor's Conference on Libraries and Information Services - A Wrap-up," *Lib. Occurrent* (N. 1978). **Activities:** 9; 17, 46 **Addr.:** Vigo County Public Library, One Library Sq., Terre Haute, IN 47807.

Wert, Lucille Mathena (My. 24, 1919, Sioux City, IA) Asst. Dir., Phys. Sci. and Engin. Libs., Univ. of IL, 1981–, Prof. (LS), Chem. Libn., 1977–, Assoc. Prof. (LS), 1975–77, Dir., Lib. Resrch. Ctr., 1971–75, Resrch. Assoc. Prof., 1974–75, Resrch. Asst. Prof., 1969–74; Math-Phys. Libn., Univ. of Chicago, 1948–50; Math-Phys. Libn., Univ. of IA, 1946–48. **Educ.:** Morningside Coll., 1938–42, AB (Chem., Math); Simmons Coll., 1944–45, BS (LS); Univ. of IL, 1961–63, MS (LS), 1963–69 PhD (LS). **Orgs.:** ASIS: Spec. Interest Grp. on Educ. for Info. Sci., Doct. Forum. Com., Ch. AALS: Dir. at Lg. (1974–77); Bylaws Com. (1976–78), *Jnl. of Educ. for Libnshp.* Ed. (1976–80). ALA: ACRL/Col. Libs. Sect., Nom. Com. (1979–80), Plng. Com. (1972–74); LAMA; Lib. Educ. Div.; LRRT. SLA. Amer. Chem. Socty. Amer. Socty. for Engin. Educ.: Engin. Libs. Div., Accred. Com. **Honors:** Beta Phi Mu. **Pubns.:** "The Kinds of Books Requested by Books-by-Mail Patrons," *Books-by-Mail Service, A Conference Report* (1974); "Introduction to Online Searching of Bibliographic Databases," *Jnl. of Educ. Modules for Mtrls. Sci. and Engin.* (Sum. 1979); "Adequacy of School Library Reference Collections," *RQ* (Sum. 1974); "Illinois School Library Media Survey," *IL Libs.* (S. 1972); various other articles, talks, reviews. **Activities:** 1, 12; 17, 39, 41; 60, 75, 81 **Addr.:** Chemistry Library, 257 Noyes Laboratory, University of Illinois, Urbana, IL 61801.

Wertheimer, Leonard (Ag. 7, 1914, Berlin, Germany) Retired, 1979–; Langs. Coord., Metro. Toronto Lib. Bd., 1973–79, Head, Langs. Ctr., 1968–73; Head, Langs. and Lit. Ctr., Toronto Pub. Lib., 1963–68. **Educ.:** Univ. of Capetown, 1949, Cert. (LS); Univ. of S. Africa, 1950–54, BA; S. African LA, 1950–54, Dip. (LS). **Orgs.:** ASTED. ON Goethe Socty. **Pubns.:** *Books in Other Languages* (1979); "Serving Children in Multilingual Communities," *Can. Lib. Jnl.* (F.–Ap. 1979); "Quebec is Not Asleep; Impressions of a Quick Library Junket," *Bltn. PQ LA* (Jl.–S. 1977); "Multiculturalism: A Librarian's Perspective," *Multiculturalism* (1978); various other articles, presentations. **Activities:** 9; 15, 16, 36; 66 **Addr.:** 27 Maclean Ave, Toronto, ON M4E 2Z8, Canada.

Wertheimer, Marilyn L. (D. 1, 1928, Pueblo, CO) Ref. Libn., Pol. Sci. Biblgphr., Univ. of CO, 1968–; Sci. Serials Catlgr., Univ. of CA, San Diego, 1968. **Educ.:** Stanford Univ., 1946–50, BA (Russ.); Columbia Univ., 1950–53, MA (Law and Gvt.); Univ. of CA, Los Angeles, 1966–67, MLS; Columbia Univ. 1950–53, Cert. (Russ. Std.). **Orgs.:** ALA. CO LA. **Pubns.:** Jt. auth., *History of Psychology: A Guide to Information Sources* (1979). **Activities:** 1; 15, 31, 39; 54, 57, 92 **Addr.:** University Libraries, Campus Box 184, University of Colorado, Boulder, CO 80309.

Wesley, Eunice Carolyn (Jl. 25, 1947, Port Perry, ON) Instr., Cont. Ed., Sch. Libnshp., Fac. of Educ., Univ. of Toronto, 1979–, Primary/Jr. Coord., 1979, 1981; Libn., Northlea Elem. Sch., 1974–; Libn., St. Clair Jr. HS, 1970–74. **Educ.:** York Univ., 1964–67, BA (Hist.); Univ. of Toronto, 1969–70, BEd (Sch. Libnshp., Hist.), 1970–72; Spec. Cert. (Sch. Libnshp.). **Orgs.:** E. York Sch. Libns. Assn.: Pres. (1975–76); AV Conv. (1972–75). ON Sch. LA: Reviewer, *The Reviewing Libn.* Can. Sch. LA: Reviewer, *Can. Mtrls.* Intl. Assn. of Sch. Libns.: Can. Rpt., *Nsltr.* **Activities:** 1, 10; 21, 48; 63 **Addr.:** 48 Hood Crescent, Scarborough, ON M1W 3C1 Canada.

Wesley, Phillip (Je. 3, 1930, Los Angeles, CA) Dean, CA State Univ., Dominguez Hills, 1969–; Chief, Tech. Srvs., CA State Univ., Northridge, 1967–69, Head Cat. Libn., 1966–67; Acq., Ref., Head Cat. Libn., Los Angeles Cnty. Law Lib., 1960–66. **Educ.:** Glendale Coll., 1950, AA; Univ. of CA, Los Angeles, 1956, BA (Msc.); Univ. of South. CA, 1959, MS (LS). **Orgs.:** South. CA Assn. Law Libs.: Pres. (1964–65). SLA: South. CA Chap. (Treas., 1969–70). South. CA Tech. Prcs. Grp.: Pres. (1972–74). ALA. Various other orgs. Town Hall, Los Angeles. **Pubns.:** "Classification - the Choices," *Law Lib. Jnl.* (Ag. 1968); "Dignity and the S.P.C.A.," *CA Libn.* (Ja. 1972). **Activities:** 1; 15, 17, 22; 93 **Addr.:** California State University, Dominguez Hills, 1000 E. Victoria St., Carson, CA 90747.

Wessel, Carl John (O. 5, 1911, Pittsburgh, PA) Consult., 1979–; VP, Chief Sci., Tracor Jitco, Inc., 1966–79; Sci. Info. Coord., Food and Drug Admin., 1965–66; Dir., Prev. of Deterioration Ctr., Natl. Acad. of Sci. - Natl. Resrch. Ctr., 1946–65. **Educ.:** Canisius Coll., 1930–34, BS (PreMed.); Univ. of Detroit, 1936–38, MS (Chem.); Cath. Univ., 1938–41, PhD (Biochem.). **Orgs.:** ASIS. Natl. Fed. Sci. Abs. and Indx. Srvs.: Secy. (1963–65). Amer. Chem. Socty. AAAS. Amer. Inst. Chems. Biodeterioration Socty. Various other orgs. **Pubns.:** "Deterioration of Library Materials," *Encyc. of Lib. and Info. Sci.* (1971); "Environmental Factors Affecting the Performance of Library Materials," *Deterioration and Preservation of Library Materials* (1970); "Sources of Information for the Environmental Sciences," *Env. Qtly.* (S. and D. 1967); "New Directions in Materials Testing - Resistance to Deterioration," *Mtrls. in Dsgn. Engin.* (Je. 1961); various other articles, rpts., presentations. **Activities:** 6; 17, 23, 24; 58, 60, 65 **Addr.:** 5014 Park Pl., Bethesda, MD 20816.

Wessells, Helen E. (Mrs. Herman S. Hettinger) (Je. 3, 1903, Morristown, NJ) Retired 1978–; Dir., Bks.–Across–the–Sea, Eng.–Speaking Un., 1970–78; Lib. Consult., various state and fed. gvt. fndns., 1957–78; Ed., *Lib. Jnl.*, 1951–57; Chief, Lib. Branch, USIS, Dept. of State, 1949–50; USIS Dir. and Cult. Ofcr., U.S. Frgn. Srv. (Australia), 1943–47; Dir., Victory Bk. Campaign, 1942–43; Branch Libn., NY Pub. Lib., 1926–42. **Educ.:** NY Pub. Lib., Lib. Sch., 1925–26. **Orgs.:** ALA: Cncl. (1957–61); IRRT (Ch., 1949–50); Lib. Admin. Div./PR Sect., Ch.; various coms. SLA: Publshg. Div., Ch. CNLIA: Com. for Visit. Frgn. Libns. NY Lib. Club: Pres. (1952–54). Women's Natl. Bk. Assn. DC LA: Pres. (1950–52). **Pubns.:** Various articles; "The Public Library for Life Long Learning" pamphlet; "The Public Library: A tool for Modern Living," ALA Small Libs. Prog. #1. **Activities:** 9, 12; 24, 36, 37; 54, 89 **Addr.:** 433 W. 21st St., New York, NY 10011.

West, Carol C. (My. 23, 1944, Philadelphia, PA) Dir., Law Lib., MS Coll., 1975–; Legis. Ref. Libn., MS Legis., 1970–75; Cat. Libn., Law Lib., Univ. of MS, 1967–70; Pub. Srvs. Libn., Law Lib., Univ. of VA, 1966–67. **Educ.:** MS Univ. for Women, 1964–66, BA (LS); Univ. of MS, 1967–70, JD. **Orgs.:** Cnsrtm. for Lib. Autom. in MS: Pres. (1978). AALL: Exec. Bd. (1979–1981). MS LA: Ad Hoc Com. on Copyrt. (Ch., 1980). Southeast. Assn. of Law Libs.: Schol. Com. (Ch., 1979–80). Amer. Bar Assn. MS State Bar Assn. MS Assn. of Women Lawyers. **Activities:** 1, 12; 17; 77 **Addr.:** Law Library, Mississippi College School of Law, 151 E. Griffith St., Jackson, MS 39201.

West, Carolynn E. Bett (D. 12, 1943, Toronto, ON) Thesaural Proj. Dir., ON Educ. Resrch. Info. Syst., 1978–; Instr. (LS), Univ. of Regina, 1977; Head, AV, St. Catherines Pub. Lib., 1977–78, Libn.; SaskMedia Corp. Libn., 1976; Ed., *Can. Educ. Index,* 1973–76. **Educ.:** Univ. of Toronto, 1966, BA (Eng.), 1967, MA (Eng.), 1973, MS (LS). **Orgs.:** Can. LA. Can. Assn. Info. Sci. Can. Class. Resrch. Grp. SLA. Various other orgs. Bruce Trail Club. Westwood Sailing Club. Toronto Tai Chi Assn. **Pubns.:** "The Subject Access Project: A Comparison with PRECIS," *Indxr.* (Ap. 1979); "Project to Automate the Canadian Education Index," *Open Conf. on Info. Sci. in Can.* (1975); jt. auth., "Inside Information," *Educ. Can.* (Spr. 1975); "The Canadian Education Index," *Can. Socty. for the Std. of Educ. News* (F. 1975); various reviews. **Activities:** 13; 30, 34, 37; 56, 57, 63 **Addr.:** *ONTERIS* Mowat Block R2443, Queen's Park, Toronto, ON Canada.

West, Carrie Lynne (N. 10, 1935, Athens, AL) Asst. Dir. Libs., Pub. Srvs., Marquette Univ., 1969–79, Asst. to the Lib. Dir., 1966–69; Head Libn., Lambuth Coll., 1965; Asst. Acq. Libn., Jt. Univ. Libs., 1962–65. **Educ.:** TX Christ. Univ., 1952–54; Univ. of NE, 1954–56, BS (Intl. Affairs, Sp.); Columbia Univ., 1960–62, MS (LS); Univ. of WI, Milwaukee, 1979–80 (LS). **Orgs.:** ALA. SLA. WI LA. Metro. Milwaukee Lib. Cncl. **Honors:** Phi Beta Kappa. **Pubns.:** "New Space: Marquette University Library Addition," *WI Lib. Bltn.* (My.–Je., 1973); "Does Security Help?" *WI Lib. Bltn.* (Ja.–F., 1976). **Activities:** 1, 9; 15, 17, 22; 54, 91, 92 **Addr.:** 773 N. Prospect Ave., Milwaukee, WI 53202.

West, Harvey Gordon (Je. 11, 1945, Philadelphia, PA) Staff Asst. to Chief, Ord. Div., Lib. of Congs., 1978–, Head, Fiscal Cntrl. Sect., 1978, Head, Name Athty. Coop., 1977, Catlgr., Descr. Cat. Div., 1973–78. **Educ.:** Trinity Univ., 1970–72, BA (Politics, Econ.); Univ. of TX, Austin, 1972–73, MLS. **Orgs.:** SLA: Geog. and Map Div. **Activities:** 4; 15, 17, 20; 56, 70, 91 **Addr.:** 9965 Wood Wren Ct., Fairfax, VA 22032.

West, Linda G. (My. 30, 1941, Grand Rapids, MI) Cat. Libn., Cornell Univ. Libs., 1976–, Head, Soc. Sci. Cat. Team, 1973–76; Catlgr. Ithaca Coll. Lib., 1971–73; Cat. Ed., Univ. of MI Lib., 1970–71; Acq. Libn., MI State Lib., 1968–70. **Educ.:** Univ. of MI, 1958–62, BA (Soclgy.), 1965–68, AMLS. **Orgs.:** ALA: RTSD. **Activities:** 1, 9; 17, 20, 46; 92 **Addr.:** 110 Olin Library, Ithaca, NY 14853.

West, Lynda Glidewell (D. 5, 1946, Oklahoma City, OK) Libn., Christ the King Sch., 1981–; Media Coord., Heritage Hall Sch., 1975–81; Tchr., Adult Educ. Ext., OK Univ., 1974–75; Eng. Tchr., Zama, Japan, 1970–71. **Educ.:** Ctrl. State Univ., 1966–72, BS (Soc. Sci.), 1973–77, MED (Instr. Media); OK Real Estate License, 1979–81. **Orgs.:** ALA. OK LA: PR Com. (1978); Mem. Com. (1979); Natl. Lib. Wk. (Ch., 1977); Sequoyah Bk. Award Com (1981–). Libns. of OK Private Schs: Prog. Com. (1976–81). OK Bd. of Realtors. Omnipeople: Bibliomania Com. (1979–81). **Activities:** 10; 21, 32, 48; 63 **Addr.:** 2719 Tottingham, Oklahoma City, OK 73120.

West, Marian S. (F. 10, 1926, Grosse Pointe, MI) Lib. Media Spec., Plymouth Salem HS, 1973–; Lib. Media Spec., N. Farmington HS, 1972–73. **Educ.:** Univ. of MI, 1944–48, BA (Fr.), 1972, MALS; E. MI Univ., 1979– (Curric. and Instr.). **Orgs.:** ALA: AASL. MI Assn. for Media in Educ. MI LA. Various coms., ofcs. MI Educ. Assn. Natl. Educ. Assn. AAUW. **Honors:** Alpha Xi Delta; Beta Phi Mu. **Pubns.:** "If This is Tuesday, We Must Be on Service III," *Media Spectrum* (Spr. 1978); "Timely Tips," *Media Spectrum* (Sum. 1976); "Romanesque and Gothic Architecture in Detroit," AV Kit (1979). **Activities:** 10, 12; 15, 17, 24 **Addr.:** Plymouth Salem High School Library, 46181 Joy Rd., Canton, MI 48187.

West, Martha W. (Ap. 28, 1931, Greenville, SC) Info. Resrcs. Mgt. Consult., 1981–; Consult., Database Srvs., 1980–81; VP, Admin., Info. Access Corp., 1978–80; Assoc. Prof. (LS), San Jose State Univ., 1969–78; Sr. Systs. Anal., Info. Gen. Corp., 1967–69; Dir., Info. Srvs. EDEX Corp., 1965–66; Consult., 1964–65; Head, Info. Sect., Syntex Inst. for Molec. Bio., 1961–64; various prof. positions, 1954–61. **Educ.:** Dunbarton Coll. 1951, BA (Eng., Chem.); Univ. of SC, 1951–53, MA (Eng.); Emory Univ., 1953–54, MA (LS); Univ. of CA, Berkeley, 1966–67 (LS); Pepperdine Univ., 1980–81, MBA. **Orgs.:** ALA: Stans. Com. (1979–80); LITA/Info. Sci. and Autom. Sect., Autom. Indus.–Lib. Rel. Com. (1979–80); RTSD, Tech. Srvs. Costs Com. (1974–78). ASIS: Conf. Com. (Co-Ch., 1976). CA LA: Cncl. (1971–74); Treas. (1974–78). SLA: Conf. Com. (Treas., 1971). Various other ofcs. **Pubns.:** "Job Satisfaction, Productivity, and the Knowledge Worker," *The Info. Cmnty.: An Alliance for Progress; Procs. of the 44th ASIS Anl. Mtg.* (1981); Ed., *Access Information; An Online User's Guide to IAC Databases* (1979); jt. auth., "The Energy Validation Management System: Research and Prototype Implementation," *N. Amer. Networking; Procs. of the 8th ASIS Mid-Yr. Mtg.* (1979); jt. auth., "Basis for Resource Allocation," *Lib. Trends* (Ap. 1975); various other articles, rpts. **Activities:** 6; 17, 24; 56, 57, 75 **Addr.:** 717 Webster St., Palo Alto, CA 94301.

West, Mary Ellen Cox (My. 20, 1949, Phoenixville, PA) Actg. Head Libn., OH Hist. Socty., 1979–, Asst. Libn., Pub. Srvs., 1978–79, Asst. Libn., 1977–78, OH Docum. Libn., 1976–77; Libn., Tribhuvan Univ., Nepal, 1975, Ref. Libn., OH State Univ., 1975. **Educ.:** Miami Univ., 1967–69; OH State Univ., 1969–71, BA (Geo.); Kent State Univ., 1973–74, MLS; OH State Univ., 1976–, (Bus.); Franklin Univ., 1979, Cert. (Mgt.); Natl. Arch., 1979, Cert. (Geneal.). **Orgs.:** Acad. LA of OH. OH Geneal. Socty. **Honors:** Beta Phi Mu. **Pubns.:** "Henry S. Stebbins, 1835–1898," *Mapline* (S. 1978). **Activities:** 1, 2; 17, 39, 45; 55, 69, 70 **Addr.:** Ohio Historical Society, I-71 & 17th Ave., Columbus, OH 43211.

West, Sharon M. (Je. 4, 1947, Pueblo, CO) Head, Cat. Dept., Univ. of AK, 1975–, Bio-Med. Libn., 1973–75; Assoc. Ref.

Special Subjects/Services: 50. Adult educ.; 51. Advert./Mktg.; 52. Aerosp.; 53. Agric.; 54. Area std.; 55. Arts/Hum.; 56. Autom.; 57. Bibl./Prtg.; 58. Bio. sci.; 59. Bus./Fin.; 60. Chem.; 61. Copyrt.; 62. Documtn.; 63. Educ.; 64. Engin.; 65. Env.; 66. Eth. grps.; 67. Film; 68. Food/Nutr.; 69. Geneal.; 70. Geo.; 71. Geol.; 72. Handcpd.; 73. Hist.; 74. Int. frdm.; 75. Info. sci.; 76. Insr.; 77. Law; 78. Legis.; 79. Math./Comp. sci.; 80. Med.; 81. Metals; 82. Nat. resrcs.; 83. Newsp.; 84. Nuc. sci.; 85. Oral hist.; 86. Petr./Energy; 87. Pharm.; 88. Phys./Astr./Math.; 89. Readg.; 90. Relig.; 91. Sci./Tech.; 92. Soc. sci.; 93. Telecom.; 94. Transp.; 95. (other).

Libn., TX Tech. Univ., 1970–73. **Educ.:** Univ. of South. CO, 1965–69, BA (Langs.); Univ. of Denver, 1969–70, MA (LS). **Orgs.:** AK LA: Exec. Bd. (1974–75, 1979–82); Pres. (1980–81). Pac. NW LA: Exec. Bd. (1977–79), Acad. Div. (1977–79). ALA. **Pubns.:** "Washington Library Network: Better Service for Alaskans," *Sourdough* (D. 1979); "Washington Library Network: Implications for the University of Alaska," *Sourdough* (Ja. 1978); "A Statewide Plan for Continuing Education in Alaska," *Training the Trainers to Train for Interlibrary Cooperation and Networking* (1975); "People Change Places," *TX Lib. Jnl.* (Mr. 1974). **Activities:** 1; 20, 34, 44; 56 **Addr.:** Library, University of Alaska, Fairbanks, AK 99701.

West, Wilfred Laverne (My. 21, 1938) Tech. Srvs. Chief, Jefferson Cnty. Pub. Lib. 1973–; Pres., Prairie Hills (IA) Lib. Syst., 1972–73; Actg. Asst. Dir., IA State Traveling Lib., 1969–70; Admin., Prairie Hills Lib. Syst., 1966–72. **Educ.:** Carthage Coll., 1964, BA (Bus. Admin.); Univ. of Denver, 1965, MA (LS). **Orgs.:** ALA: Anl. Conf. Lcl. Arrange. Com. (1982). CO LA: Future Sites Com. (1979–80). CO State Lib.: LSCA Readg. Team, Networking Projs. (1980). ASIS: 1981 Mid-Yr. Strg. Com. (1979–). CO State Dept. Hws.: Passenger Rail Srv. Subcom. (1980–). CO Hist. Thea. Assn.: Pres. (1979–). Various other orgs. **Honors:** Mt. Plains LA, Srv. Awd., 1979. **Pubns.:** Various rpts., radio progs. **Activities:** 9, 10; 17, 28, 34; 74, 75, 93 **Addr.:** Jefferson County Public Library, 10200 W. 20th Ave., Lakewood, CO 80401.

Westbrook, Jack Hall (Ag. 19, 1924, Troy, NY) Mgr., Mtrls. Info. Srvs., CR and D, Gen. Electric Co., 1974–, Mgr., EMPIS, Engin. Consult., 1971–74, Metallurgist, CR and D, 1949–71. **Educ.:** RPI, 1941–47, BS, MS (Metallic Engin.); MA Inst. of Tech., 1947–49, ScD (Metallurgy); State of NY Prof. Engin. Licn. **Orgs.:** ASIS. CODATA: Adv. Panel on Data for Indus. Needs, Ch. Fed. of Mtrls. Soctys.: Mtrls. Info. Com., Ch. Natl. Acad. of Sci.: Mtrls. Adv. Bd., Subcom. on Inorganic Nonmetallics (1959–63); Adv. Com. on Chromium Cons. (1975–77). AAAS: Fellow (1976). Amer. Socty. for Metals: Ch. (1958–59); East. NY Chap., Transactions Com. (Ch., 1964–65); Mtrls. Sci. Cncl. (1970–72); various other coms. Electrochem. Socty.: Mohawk-Hudson Chap. (Ch., 1963–66); Electrothermics and Metallurgy Div. (Ch., 1961–63); various coms. **Honors:** Amer. Socty. for Metals, Jeffries Lectr., 1979; Amer. Socty. for Metals, Campbell Meml. Lectr., 1976, Natl. Acad. of Sci., Travelling Flwshp., US-USSR Sci. Exch., 1971; Lead Dev. Assn., Jt. Recipient, Hofmann Prize, 1971; AIME, Jt. Recipient, New Eng. Reg. Conf. Awd., 1963; other hons. **Pubns.:** Ed., "Non-ferrous Metals Section," *Mechanical Engineer's Handbook* (1958); ed., *Mechanical Properties of Intermetallic Compounds* (1960); ed., *Intermetallic Compounds* (1967); jt. ed., *The Science of Hardness Testing and its Research Applications* (1974); ed., *Grain Boundaries in Engineering Materials* (1975); various other pubns., U.S., Fr., Italian patents, ed. bds. **Activities:** 12; 24, 39, 46; 64, 81, 91 **Addr.:** Materials Information Services, General Electric Co., FNB/120 Erie Blvd., Schenectady, NY 12305.

Westbrook, Patricia Clarke (N. 28, 1926, New Haven, CT) Libn., Meriden-Wallingford Hosp., 1978–, Asst. Libn., 1976–78; Acq., Prcs. Libn., S. Windsor Pub. Lib., 1970–72, Ref. Libn., 1969–70. **Educ.:** Pembroke Coll., Brown Univ., 1944–48, BA (Eng. Lit.); South. CT State Coll., 1974–76, MLS. **Orgs.:** Med. LA. Hosp. LA. New Eng. LA. **Honors:** Phi Beta Kappa, 1948. **Activities:** 5; 15, 17, 20; 50, 80 **Addr.:** Meriden-Wallingford Hospital, 181 Cook Ave., Meriden, CT 06450.

Westby, Barbara Marietta (Ag. 20, 1919, Luverne, MN) Retired, 1981–; Chief, Cat. Mgt. Div., Lib. of Congs., 1970–81, Asst., Chief, Descr. Cat., 1969–70, Fld. Dir., Oslo Ofc., 1966–69; Coord. of Cat., Detroit Pub. Lib., 1963–66, Chief, 1956–63, Asst. Chief, 1955–56, Supvsr., Ref. Srv. Cat., 1953–54; Various prof. positions, 1945–53. **Educ.:** Augustana Coll., 1937–41, BA (Eng.); Univ. Denver, 1944–45, BS (LS). **Orgs.:** ALA: RTSD, (Pres., 1971–72), Descr. Cat. Com. (Ch., (1966–67); Nom. Com. (1957–58)/Cat. and Class. Sect., Exec. Com. (1958–61). Amer. Scandinavian Fndn. **Pubns.:** Ed., *Sears List of Subject Headings* (9th ed., 1965, 10th ed., 1972, 11th ed., 1977, 12th ed., 1982). **Activities:** 4 **Addr.:** 7700 Westfield Dr., Bethesda, MD 20817.

Wester-House, Mary (O. 16, 1954, Waterloo, IA) Libn., TN Dept. of Pub. Hlth., 1977–. **Educ.:** Morningside Coll., 1972–75, BA (LS, Fr.); George Peabody Coll., 1976–77, MLS; Med. LA, 1977–82, Cert. **Orgs.:** Med. LA. TN Hlth. Sci. Libns. Assn.: Spr. Wkshp. (Instr., 1980). Mid-TN Hlth. Sci. Libns.: Pres. (1979–80). **Activities:** 12, 13; 17, 39, 46; 80 **Addr.:** Tennessee Dept. of Public Health, Library, TDPH State Office Bldg., Ben Allen Rd., Nashville, TN 37216.

Westerman, Melvin Elliott (S. 2, 1939, Tarentum, PA) Bus. Libn., PA State Univ., 1969–; Libn. I, Bus., Sci., and Indus. Dept., Free Lib. of Philadelphia, 1967–69. **Educ.:** PA State Univ., 1957–66, BA (Sci.); Drexel Univ., 1966–69, MS (LS); PA State Univ., 1979– (Pub. Admin.). **Orgs.:** SLA: Com. on Guidelines for Bus. Libs. (1972–73); Lcl. Arrange. Com. (1973); Ctrl. PA Chap. (Ch., 1979–80). Full Gospel Businessmen's Flwshp. Intl. Alliance Christ. Sch.: Bd. of Dirs. **Pubns.:** "Libraries for the Business Community in Peru," *Spec. Libs.* (Ag. 1974). **Activities:** 1; 39; 59 **Addr.:** Pattee Library, The Pennsylvania State University, University Park, PA 16802.

Westermann, Mary L. (Mr. 11, 1953, Bronx, NY) Dir., John N. Shell Lib., Nassau Acad. of Med., 1977–; Consult. Med. Libn., Nassau-Suffolk Hlth. Systs. Agency, 1976–77. **Educ.:** Long Island Univ., 1971–75, BS (Bio.), 1975–76, MLS. **Orgs.:** Med. LA. SLA: Long Island Chap. (Secy., 1977–). ALA. Med. and Sci. Libs. of Long Island: Pres. (1980–81). Various other orgs., ofcs. Natl. Bio. Hon. Socty. **Activities:** 12; 17, 24, 34; 58, 80 **Addr.:** Shell Library, Nassau Academy of Medicine, Garden City, NY 11530.

Westfall, Gloria Dunn (S. 1, 1925, Fort Wayne, IN) Frgn. Docum. Libn., IN Univ. Libs., 1970–. **Educ.:** Mt. Holyoke Coll., 1943–47, BA (European Hist.); Univ. de Paris, 1948–49, Cert. (Fr.); Northwest. Univ., 1949–50, MA (Fr.); IN Univ., 1969–70, MLS. **Orgs.:** ALA: Intl. Docum. Task Frc. (Coord., 1977–78); GODORT (1975–). IN Univ. Libns. Assn.: Prog. Ch. (1976–77). Leag. of Women Voters. **Pubns.:** *French Official Publications* (1980); "British Statistical Information," *Gvt. Pubns. Review* (1976); "Nigerian Women: A Bibliographical Essay," *Africana Jnl.* (1974); frgn. docum. acq. clmn., *Gvt. Pubns. Review* (1977–). **Activities:** 1; 15, 29, 31; 54, 57, 92 **Addr.:** Indiana University Libraries, Bloomington, IN 47405.

Westhuis, Judith Anne Loveys (D. 1, 1941, Ithaca, NY) Law Libn., Catlgr., Albany Law Sch., 1974–; Pers. Libn., Schenectady Cnty. Cmnty. Coll., 1974–75; Lib. Dir., Canajoharie (NY) Pub. Lib., 1968, 1966–67; Catlgr., Grand Haven (MI) Pub. Schs., 1964–65; Ref. Libn., Rutherford (NJ) Pub. Lib., 1965–66. **Educ.:** Hope Coll., 1959–63, BA (Eng.) West. MI Univ., 1963–65, MA (LS). **Orgs.:** AALL: Cat. and Class. Com. (1976–78). Assn. of Law Libs. of Upstate NY. Hudson Mohawk LA. **Pubns.:** *Cataloging Manual for Nonbook Materials in Learning Centers and School Libraries* (1966–67). **Activities:** 1, 12; 20, 46; 77 **Addr.:** Albany Law School Library, 80 New Scotland Ave., Albany, NY 12208.

Westmoreland, N. Jean (Ag. 6, 1917, Wichita, KS) Libn., Media Spec., Rutledge Bus. Coll., 1978–; Libn., Instr., Media Spec., South. MO State Univ., 1965–77; Libn., Springfield-Greene Cnty Lib., 1962–65. **Educ.:** South. MO State Univ., 1935–62, BS (Elem. Educ.); Univ. of IL, 1963–64, MLS; Univ. of MO, 1975 (Media Spec.). **Orgs.:** MO LA. Springfield LA: Various ofcs. **Activities:** 10; 15, 17, 36; 59 **Addr.:** 1926 S. Delaware, Springfield, MO 65804.

Weston, Franklin Atwater (O. 25, 1934, Bangor, ME) Reg. Law Libn., West. Ctr. on Law and Poverty, 1978–; Law Lib. Consult., 1974–77; Circ. Libn., Los Angeles City Coll., 1975; Law Libn., Latham and Watkins, 1972–74; Law and Tax Libn., Exxon Corp., 1970–71; Corp. Libn., Ronson Corp., 1967–70; Libn., Simpson Thacher and Bartlett, 1964–66; various prof. positions, 1962–64. **Educ.:** Univ. of ME, 1953–57, BA (Phil.), 1957–58, Cert. (Educ.); Columbia Univ., 1959–62, MLS. **Orgs.:** AALL. SLA. South. CA Assn. of Law Libs.: VP (1973–74). ASIS. Eng. speaking Un. Unitarian Church of Studio City. **Pubns.:** Various articles. **Activities:** 4; 17, 39, 49-Tech. assistance; 66, 77, 78 **Addr.:** Western Center on Law and Poverty, Inc., 3535 W. 6th St., Los Angeles, CA 90020.

Weston, Janice Colmer (Ja. 3, 1944, Philadelphia, PA) Supervisory Libn., US Army Ordnance Ctr. and Sch., 1972–; Libn., Aberdeen Proving Ground Tech. Lib., 1971–72; Libn., US Army Gen. Equip. Test Actv., 1970–71; Branch Libn., Chesterfield Cnty. Lib., 1970; Ref. Libn., John Tyler Cmnty. Coll., 1969–70. **Educ.:** Univ. of MI, 1962–66, BA (Hist.); Wayne State Univ., 1967–69, MSLS; State of VA, 1969, Prof. Licn. **Orgs.:** SLA. TRADOC Lib. and Info. Netwk. Natl. Org. for Women. US Army Ordnance Ctr. and Sch.: Fed. Women's Com. (1977–). **Honors:** US Army Ordnance Ctr. and Sch., Outstan. Performance Awd., 1980–81; Aberdeen Proving Ground, MD, Dept. of the Army, Cert. of Achvmt., 1977. **Activities:** 1, 4; 15, 17, 39; 59, 63, 74 **Addr.:** ATTN.: Library, Bldg. 3071, US Army Ordnance Center & School, Aberdeen Proving Ground, MD 21005.

Westover, Keith R. (Ap. 14, 1945, Afton, WY) Head, Acq., WA State Univ. Lib., 1976–; Asst. Acq. Libn., IN Univ. Lib., 1970–76. **Educ.:** Brigham Young Univ., 1969, BA (Russ.), 1970, MLS; IN Univ., 1975, MA (Uralic Std.). **Orgs.:** ALA. Pac. NW LA. WA LA. Suomen Kirjastoseura. Various other orgs. **Honors:** Beta Phi Mu. **Pubns.:** *The Library in Finland* (1975). **Activities:** 1; 15, 44, 46; 54, 56 **Addr.:** Box 2585 College Station, Pullman, WA 99163.

Wetherbee, Louella Vine (Je. 20, 1946, LaSalle Cnty., TX) Assoc. Dir. of Libs., Fenwick Lib., George Mason Univ., 1980–; Dir. Mem. Srvs. Dept., Amigos Bibl. Cncl., 1977–80; Latin Amer. Proj. Coord., Univ. of TX, Austin, 1976–77; Exec. Secy., SALALM, 1977; Bibl. Cntrl. Libn., Univ. of TX, Austin, 1974–76; Serials Catlgr., 1972–74, Mono. Catlgr., 1970–72; Ref. Libn., Warren (MI) Pub. Lib., 1970. **Educ.:** Univ. of TX, 1964–67, BA (Portuguese), 1968–69, MLS. **Orgs.:** ALA: Intl. Rel. Com. (1979). ASIS. SWLA. SALALM. **Pubns.:** Guest ed., "Networking: North America," *Bltn. ASIS* (Je. 1979). **Activities:** 14-Netwk.; 20, 34, 46; 54 **Addr.:** Fenwick Library, George Mason University, 4400 University Dr., Fairfax, VA 22030.

Wetherby, Ivor Lois (My. 22, 1924, Louisville, KY) Med. Ref. Libn., Miami-Dade Cmnty. Coll., 1978–; Head Libn., Sebring (FL) Pub Lib., 1978; Catlgr., 1976–78. Serials Libn., Palm Beach Jr. Coll., 1965–76. **Educ.:** KY Wesleyan Coll., 1940–43, AB (Eng.); FL State Univ., 1964–65, MS (LS); various crs. **Orgs.:** SLA. FL LA. SELA. **Activities:** 1, 12; 31, 39, 44; 52, 63, 80 **Addr.:** Miami-Dade Community College, Medical Center Campus Library, 950 N.W. 20th St., Miami, FL 33127.

Wethey, Constance Chandler (Jl. 25, 1951, Quincy, MA) Med. Libn., Piedmont Hosp., 1979–; Libn., Palmer Davis Lib., MA Gen. Hosp., 1974–79. **Educ.:** Westfield State Coll., 1969–73, BA (Hist.); Univ. of RI, 1973–74, MLS; Natl. Lib. of Med., 1979 (Initial On-Line Trng.). **Orgs.:** New Eng. Cncl. on Lib. Resrcs. for Nurses: Ch. (1978); Adv. Cncl. (1979). Med. LA. ALA. **Activities:** 5, 12; 17, 39; 80 **Addr.:** Sauls Memorial Library, Piedmont Hospital, 1968 Peachtree Rd. N.W., Atlanta, GA 30309.

Wetmore, Rosamond Bayne (N. 1, 1914, Middlesboro, KY) Prof., LS, Ball State Univ., 1968–80; Asst., Cat., 1946–68. **Educ.:** Lincoln Meml. Univ., 1932–34; Earlham Coll., 1934–36, BA (Eng.); Columbia Univ., 1940, BLS; Ball State Univ., 1957 MA (Hist.). **Orgs.:** ALA. AALS. IN LA: Tech. Srvs. RT (Ch., 1974). OH Valley Tech. Srvs. Libns. AAUW. Assn. of IN Media Educs. **Pubns.:** *A Guide to the Organization of Library Materials* 5th rev. ed. (1976). **Activities:** 11; 15, 20, 29 **Addr.:** 1601 Riverside, Muncie, IN 47303.

Whalen, Catherine M. (Ag. 28, 1952, Canton, NY) Asst. Libn., SUNY, Agr. and Tech. Coll., Canton, 1978–; Libn., Carthage Free Lib., 1975–77. **Educ.:** Siena Coll., 1970–74, BA (Eng.); SUNY, Albany, 1974–75, MLS. **Orgs.:** NY LA. Canton Free Lib.: Trustee; Treas. (1979–). **Activities:** 1, 9; 20, 44, 47; 50, 78 **Addr.:** 42 Court St., Canton, NY 13617.

Whalen, George F. (N. 13, 1930, St. Stephen, NB) Educ. Ofcr., Libn., ON Mnstry. of Educ., 1967–; Tchr.-Libn., Sir James Dunn Collegiate, 1958–67; Tchr., Simonds Reg. HS, 1952–58. **Educ.:** Univ. of NB, 1947–51, BA; Univ. of West. ON, 1969–70, MLS. **Orgs.:** ON LA. Can. LA. **Pubns.:** Jt. auth., *Organizing the School Library* (1980). **Activities:** 4, 10; 21, 26, 39; 63 **Addr.:** Library, Ontario Ministry of Education, 7th Floor, 199 Larch St., Sudbury, ON P3E 5P9 Canada.

Whalen, James M. (Jl. 3, 1939, Sussex, NB) Archvst., Pub. Arch. of Can., 1968–. **Educ.:** Univ. of NB, 1966, BA (Hist.), 1968, MA (Hist.). **Orgs.:** Assn. Can. Archvsts. E. ON Archvsts. Assn. Can. Hist. Assn. **Pubns.:** "Almost as Bad as Ireland": Saint John, 1847," *Archivaria* (Sum. 1980); "Social Welfare in New Brunswick, 1784-1900," *Acadiensis* (Fall 1972); "The Nineteenth-Century Almshouse in Saint John County," *Hist. Sociale/Soc. Hist.* (Ap., 1971); various bibls. for *Dictionary of Can. Biog.* (1976). **Activities:** 2, 4; 15, 20, 24; 55, 75, 92 **Addr.:** 796 Fielding Dr., Ottawa, ON K1V 7G2, Canada.

Whalen, Lucille (Jl. 26, 1925, Los Angeles, CA) Prof., LS, SUNY-Albany, 1979–; Assoc. Dean, LS, 1971–79; Dean, LS, Immaculate Heart Coll., 1958–70, Ref. Libn., 1954–58; HS Libn., Conaty Mem. HS, Los Angeles, 1950–52. **Educ.:** Immaculate Heart Coll., 1943–49, BA (Eng.); Cath. Univ., 1953–54, MSLS; Columbia Univ., 1961–64, DLS. **Orgs.:** ALA: ASCLA, Resrch. Com. (1979–); Com. on Accred. (Ch., 1976–78). SLA: Soc. Sci. Div./Soc. and Hum. Srvs. Sect. (1980–); Resrch. Com. (Ch., 1976–80). AALS: Bd. of Dirs. (1978). ASIS: Conv. Plng. Com. (1966–67). Various other orgs., ofcs. Amer. Cvl. Liberties Un. Amer. Assn. for State and Lcl. Hist. Amnesty Intl. **Pubns.:** Jt. ed., *Library Service for the Adult Handicapped* (1978); "Role of the Assistant Dean in Library Schools," *Jnl. of Educ. for Libnshp.* (Sum. 1979); "Archival Education in NY State," *Bookmark* (Win. 1981); "Special Librarians in Human Services Fields," *Spec. Libnshp.: A New Reader* (1980). **Activities:** 11; 16, 25, 26; 50, 72 **Addr.:** School of Library & Information Science, SUNY, Albany, NY 12222.

Whalen-Levitt, Peggy (D. 1, 1946, Brooklyn, NY) Corres. Ed., *Chld. Lit. Assn. Qtly.*, 1976–; Bd. Mem., Puppet Resrcs., Inc. 1978–79; Sum. Fac., Univ. of PA, 1978, 1977; Libn., Info. Ctr. on Chld. Cultures, 1977–78; Coord., Ctr. for Resrch. in Lit. Com., 1975–77; Head, Chld. Dept., New Haven Pub. Lib., 1969–73. **Educ.:** Univ. of NC, Greensboro, 1964–68, BA (Eng.); Univ. of NC, Chapel Hill, 1968–69, MS (LS); Univ. of PA, 1973–75, MA (Com.), 1975–, ABD (Chld. Lit.). **Orgs.:** ALA. Chld. Lit. Asm. Chld. Lit. Assn. Intl. Resrch. Socty. for Chld. Lit. Mod. Lang. Assn. Natl. Cncl. of Tchrs. of Eng. Rosenbach Fndn. **Honors:** Phi Beta Kappa. **Pubns.:** "Jackie Torrence: 'I See Stories More Real'," *The New Era* (My.–Je. 1981); "Making Picture Books Real: Reflections on a Child's-Eye View," *Chld. Lit. Assn. Qtly.* (Win. 1982); "Picture Play," *Wilson Lib. Bltn.* (S. 1980); "Literature and Child Readers," *Chld. Lit. Assn. Qtly.* (Win. 1980); various other articles. **Activities:** 9, 12; 21, 26, 41; 55 **Addr.:** 611 N. Mendenhall St., Greensboro, NC 27401.

PROFESSIONAL ACTIVITIES: Institutions: 1. Acad. lib.; 2. Arch.; 3. Assn.; 4. Fed./Gvt. lib.; 5. Inst. lib.; 6. Mfr./Suppl.; 7. Milit. lib.; 8. Musm.; 9. Pub. lib.; 10. Sch. lib.; 11. Sch. of lib. sci.; 12. Spec. lib.; 13. State lib.; 14. (other). **Functions/Activities:** 15. Acq./Col. dev.; 16. Adult srvs.; 17. Admin.; 18. Apprais.; 19. Archit./Bldgs.; 20. Cat./Class.; 21. Chld. srvs.; 22. Circ.; 23. Cons./Pres.; 24. Consult.; 25. Cont. ed.; 26. Educ. lib. sci.; 27. Ext. srvs.; 28. Fund/Grants; 29. Gvt. pubs.; 30. Indx./Abs.; 31. Instr. lib. use; 32. Media srvs.; 33. Micro.; 34. Netwks./Coop.; 35. Persnl.; 36. PR; 37. Publshg.; 38. Recs. mgt.; 39. Ref. srvs.; 40. Repro.; 41. Resrch.; 42. Review.; 43. Secur.; 44. Serials; 45. Spec. col.; 46. Tech. srvs.; 47. Trustees/Bds.; 48. YA srvs.; 49. (other).

Whaley, Janie B. (S. 20, 1950, Lafayette, IN) Media Spec., Northaven Elem. Sch., 1981–; Assoc. Fac., IN Univ., SE Campus, 1980; Media Spec., Parkview Middle Sch., 1979–81; Media Spec., Crestview Jr. HS, 1976–79; Media Spec., Northside Jr. HS, 1973–76; Assoc. Fac., IN Univ., Purdue Univ., Ft. Wayne, 1978. **Educ.:** IN Univ., 1968–72, AB (Span., Eng.), 1972–73, MLS. **Orgs.:** IN AECT: Secy. (1977–78). IN Sch. Libns. Assn.: Corres. Secy. (1976–77). ALA: AASL, Eval. of Sch. Media Progs. Com. (1975–79). Assn. for IN Media Educs.: Mem. VP (1978–80). Various other orgs., ofcs. AAUW. First Presby. Church. Alpha Phi. Tri Kappa. **Honors:** Beta Phi Mu. **Activities:** 10; 31, 32, 48; 93 **Addr.:** 1731 DePauw Ave., New Albany, IN 47150.

Whaley, Roger E. (My. 23, 1940, Watertown, SD) Dir., Media Srvs., New Albany-Floyd Cnty. Schs., 1972–; Dir., Instr. Mtrls. Ctr., Floyd Ctrl. HS, 1967–72; Assoc. Fac., IN Univ., SE, 1968–; Tchr., Clinton Prairie HS, 1962–68. **Educ.:** Purdue Univ., 1958–62, BS (Hist.), 1962–68, MA (Hist., Media); Purdue Univ. and IN Univ., 1974, Supvsr. Cert. (Media). **Orgs.:** Assn. for IN Media Educs.: Pres. (1979–80); Consolidation Com. (1977–78); Mtrls. Ctr. Std. Com. (Ch., 1974–76). Heritage Hills Area Lib. Srvs.: Pres. (1977). ALA: AASL. AECT. **Honors:** Phi Delta Kappa. **Pubns.:** "Right Foot; Left Foot," *IN Media Jnl.* (Fall 1979); "AIME According to Pogo," *IN Media Jnl.* (Win. 1979). **Activities:** 10; 17, 32; 67 **Addr.:** Media Services, 802 E. Market St., New Albany, IN 47150.

Whaley, Sara Stauffer (Ap. 11, 1932, Chicago, IL) Pres., Publshr., Rush Publshg. Co., Inc., 1975–; Adj. Instr., Asst. Prof., SUNY Geneseo, 1973–78; Sub. Tchr., Rochester (NY) Schs., 1961–70; U.S. Frgn. Srv. Ofcr., 1958–61; Tchr. (Fr.), Frnds. Sch. (Wilmington, DE), 1955–57. **Educ.:** Univ. of RI, 1950–54, BA (Educ., Fr.); Middlebury Coll., 1954–55, MA (Fr.); Univ. of RI, 1957–61, MA (Pol. Sci.); Syracuse Univ., 1962–64, ABD (Pol. Sci.); SUNY, Geneseo, 1970–71, MLS. **Orgs.:** ALA. Natl. Women Std. Assn. **Honors:** Fulbright Schol., 1954, 1955. **Pubns.:** Ed., publshr., *Women Std. Abs.* (1971–). **Activities:** 14-Publshg.; 30, 37, 44; 54, 92 **Addr.:** 142 Farmcrest Dr., Rush, NY 14543.

Whalon, Marion K. (My. 24, 1913, Barnegat, NJ) Hum. and Fine Arts Col. Dev. Libn., Univ. of CA, Davis, 1969–, Ref. Libn., 1966–69; Hum. Div. Libn., ID State Univ., 1965–66; Libn., Msc. Rm. Head, Multnomah Cnty. (OR) Pub. Lib., 1963–65, Art Asst. Libn., 1962–63; Asst. Hum. Libn., Sacramento State Coll., 1959–62. **Educ.:** NJ Coll. for Women, 1930–34, BA (Grmn.); Sprachinstitut (Berlin), 1932 Cert. (Sp.). Univ. of CA, Berkeley, 1956–58, MA (Eng.), 1958–59, MLS. **Orgs.:** CA LA. Thea. LA. **Honors:** Phi Beta Kappa, 1934. **Pubns.:** *Performing Arts Research; A Guide to Information Sources* (1976); "Avant-Garde and Radical Theatre Holdings," *Broadside* (Win. 1976); reviews. **Activities:** 1; 15 **Addr.:** 708 E. 10th St., Davis, CA 95616.

Wharton, Betty Ann (Je. 26, 1911, Pasadena, CA) Resrch. Libn., NY Pub. Lib., 1962–; Volun. Libn., Dalton Sch., 1955–60; Asst. Casting Dir., Hal Prince (NY), 1951–55; Featured Actress, Thea., (NY), 1934–49; Featured Actress, Motion Pic., RKO, 20th Century Fox, 1931–34. **Educ.:** Pasadena Playhse. Coll. of Thea. Arts, 1929–31, Dip. (Drama); Columbia Univ., 1962–63 (LS). **Orgs.:** Thea. LA: Exec. Bd. (1976–). Amer. Socty. for Thea. Resrch. Edwin Booth-Walter Hampden Lib. and Col.: Bd. of Dirs. (1977–). Thea. Dev. Fund: Bd. of Dirs. (1979–). New Dramatists: Bd. of Dirs. (1978–). Plays for Living: Bd. of Dirs. (1976–). NY Univ.: Adv. Cncl., Sch. of the Arts (1978–). **Pubns.:** Pic. ed., *Life Among the Playwrights* (1974); various articles, *Performing Arts Resources* volume 1 (1974), *Grolier Encyc. Ency. Intl.* (1968). **Activities:** 1, 9; 20, 41, 45; 55, 67, 85 **Addr.:** Performing Arts Research Center, 111 Amsterdam Ave., New York, NY 10023.

Wharton, Martha E. (N. 23, 1923, McKenzie, TN) Ref., Pers. Libn., Wofford Coll., 1966–; Head, Adult Srvs. Dept., Spartanburg Cnty. Lib., 1960–66; Head Circ., Law Lib., Univ. of VA, 1955–59; Ref. Libn., Kanawha Cnty. Pub. Lib., 1945–51. **Educ.:** Bethel Coll., 1941–44, BA (Eng., Soc. Sci.); George Peabody Coll., 1944–45, MLS. **Orgs.:** SELA. SC LA. **Activities:** 1; 15, 33, 39 **Addr.:** 101 Old Salem Rd., Rte. 2, Moore, SC 29369.

Wheelbarger, Johnny J. (F. 15, 1937, Dayton, VA) Dir., Lrng. Resrcs., Trevecca Nazarene Coll., 1972–, Pres., SE Educ. Zone Fed. Credit Un., 1979–; Pastor, Santa Fe Circuit, Churches of the Nazarene, 1973–; Assoc. Prof. (Educ.), 1971–75; Asst. Prof. (Educ.), Media Dir., East. Nazarene Coll., 1971; Asst. Prof., Instr., Univ. of VA Ext. Div., 1969–71. **Educ.:** Bethany Nazarene Coll., 1963, AB (Relig.); Univ. of VA, 1967, MEd (Elem. Educ.), 1971 EdD (Curr., Instr.); George Peabody Coll., 1975, MLS, 1977, PhD (Educ. Admin.). **Orgs.:** ALA. TN LA. AECT. Natl. Educ. Assn. **Honors:** Phi Delta Kappa; Kappa Delta Pi; Beta Phi Mu. **Pubns.:** "Legal Ramifications of Computerized Library Networks and Their Implications for the Library Director," *SE Libn.* (Fall 1979); "Network Effectiveness Information for Tennessee Libraries," *TN Libn.* (Spr. 1978); "The Learning Resource Center at the Four-Year College Level," *AV Instr.* (Mr. 1973). **Activities:** 1; 17 **Addr.:** Learning Resources Center, Trevecca Nazarene College, Nashville, TN 37206.

Wheeler, Helen Rippier Sch. of Lib. & Info. Std., Univ. of CA, Berkeley, 1978–; Consult., 1973–; Assoc. Prof., LS, LA State Univ., 1971–73; Assoc. Prof., St. John's Univ., 1968–71. **Educ.:** Barnard Coll., 1947–50, BA (Latin Amer. Area Std.); Columbia Univ., 1950–51, MS (LS); Univ. of Chicago, 1953–55, MA (Soc. Sci.); Columbia Univ., 1956–64, EdD. (Curric. Tchg.: Instr. Support) **Orgs.:** ALA: ACRL; Intl. Rel. Com. (1974–75); Cncl. (1973–77); Status of Women Com. (1975–77); SRRT, Action Cncl. (Secy., Treas.). CA LA. CA Socty. of Libns.: Nom. Com. (1980). SLA: LA State Bd. (1974–75). Natl. Women Std. Assn. Intl. Hse. Assn. **Honors:** Pi Lambda Theta. Merritt Humanitarian Fund Awd. **Pubns.:** *Womanhood Media; Current Resources About Women* (1972, 1975); *A Basic Book Collection for the Community College* (1968); "The Community College Library; A Plan For Action;" various reviews, AV kits, articles. **Activities:** 1, 11; 17, 24, 26; 63, 92 **Addr.:** 2701 Durant Ave., #14, Berkeley, CA 94704.

Wheeler, James M. (N. 19, 1932, Jamestown, NY) Dir., Volusia Cnty. Pub. Lib. Syst., 1981–; Coord., of Lib. Srvs., Daytona Beach, 1979–81; Asst. Dir., NW (FL) Reg. Lib. Syst., 1977–79; Dir., Patterson Lib., 1969–77; Engin. Libn., Univ. of NB, 1967–69. **Educ.:** Univ. of Miami, 1951–55, BBA; Univ. of Pittsburgh, 1966–67, MLS. **Orgs.:** FL LA. **Honors:** ALA, Hammond Awd., 1972; NY LA, Moshier Awd., 1975. **Activities:** 9; 17, 29, 47 **Addr.:** Volusia County Public Library, City Island, Daytona Beach, FL 32014.

Wheeler, Margaret Alice (F. 11, 1925, Sackville, NB) Serials, Gvt. Docum. Libn., Mt. Allison Univ., 1970–; Chief Libn., Pictou-Antigonish Reg. Lib., 1960–70, 1951–52; Chld. Libn., Enoch Pratt Free Lib., 1949–50; Cnty. Libn., Knox Cnty. (OH), 1948–49. **Educ.:** Acadia Univ., 1943–47, BA (Eng., Math.); McGill Univ., 1947–48, BLS; Mt. Allison Cmrcl. Coll., 1941–42. **Orgs.:** Atl. Provs. LA. Can. LA. Sackville Pub. Lib. Bd. **Activities:** 1, 9; 29, 33, 44 **Addr.:** P.O. Box 1442, Sackville, NB E0A 3C0, Canada.

Whelan, John Francis (Jl. 4, 1929, Saint Paul, MN) Libn., Williams and Connolly, 1975–; Lib. Consult., 1968–; Lectr., DC Bar, 1977–; Deputy Dir., Law Libn., Dept. of Hlth., Educ., and Welfare Lib., 1975; Libn., Arnold and Porter, 1968–75; Chief, Fed. Aviation Agency Law Lib., 1964–68; Assoc. Libn., Illustrations, Natl. Geo. Socty. Lib., 1962–64; Chief, Fed. Aviation Admin. Law Lib., 1961–62; Chief, Army Lib., Law Branch, Pentagon, Ref. Libn., various fed. libs., 1955–60. **Educ.:** Coll. of St. Thomas, 1947–51, BA (Eng.); Univ. of MN, 1953–54 (Law); Cath. Univ., 1955–56 (LS). **Orgs.:** AALL: Fed. Actv. Com. (1961–62); Stats. Com. (1967–69). Law Libns. Socty. of DC: Treas. (1965–66). **Pubns.:** Jt. auth., *The Military Law Dictionary* (1960); cmplr., *Bibliography on the Philosophical and Historical Developments of the Regulatory Agencies* (1962); jt. auth., "The Basics of Building a Law Library," *Dist. Lawyer* (Mr.–Ap. 1980); jt. auth., "Building a Trial Library," *Trial* (Mr. 1981). **Activities:** 4, 12; 15, 17, 24; 56, 77 **Addr.:** Williams & Connolly, 839 17th St., N.W., Washington, DC 20006.

Whicker, Gene A. (N. 1, 1926, Harlan Cnty., KY) Gvt. Docum. Libn., W. KY Univ., 1975–; Head Libn., Marshfield Pub. Lib., 1969–74; Docum. Libn., E. KY Univ., 1964–69; Msc. Libn., Oberlin Coll., 1960–64. **Educ.:** Univ. of KY, 1943–47, AB (Msc.); Columbia Tchrs. Coll., 1947–50, MS (Msc.); Univ. of KY, 1958–60, MSLS. **Orgs.:** KY LA: GODORT (Ch., 1977–78). ALA. **Activities:** 1, 9; 17, 29, 39 **Addr.:** 1118 Nahm Dr., Bowling Green, KY 42101.

Whiffin, Jean Iris (N. 15, 1928, London, Eng.) Head, Serials, Univ. of Victoria Lib., 1966–, Spec. Acq. Libn., 1965–66; Head, Serials, Acq., Univ. of Toronto Lib., 1962–65. **Educ.:** Univ. of London, 1946–50 (Fr.); Univ. of Toronto, 1958–61, BA (Eng., Fr.), 1961–63, BLS, hons. **Orgs.:** BC LA: Dir. (1967–68). Assn. BC Libns.: Secy. (1969–70). ALA. IFLA: Consult. to UNESCO/IFLA (1979–81); Stdg. Com. on Serial Pubns. (1981–). Various other orgs., ofcs. **Honors:** Beta Phi Mu. **Pubns.:** *Guidelines for Union catalogues of Serials* (1981); "MARC II Serials at the University of Victoria Library," *Autom. in Libs.* (1971); "Serials Dynamics," *Serials Libn.* (Spr. 1979); ed. bd., *Serials Libn.* (1978–). **Activities:** 1; 15, 17, 44; 56, 57, 83 **Addr.:** Windfall Light, Rural Rte. 2, Sooke, BC V0S 1N0, Canada.

Whipkey, Harry E. (S. 23, 1933, Somerset, PA) State Arch., PA Hist. and Musm. Comsn., 1971–; Dir., Bur. of Arch. and Hist., 1975–, Chief, Div. of Arch. and Mss., 1971–75, Assoc. Archvst., 1968–71; Assoc. Prof., Hist., OH Univ., 1965–68; Asst. Prof., Hist., W. Liberty State Coll., 1964–65; Asst. Prof., Hist., Coll. of Emporia, 1962–64. **Educ.:** Juniata Coll., 1956–60, BA (Hist., Eng.); OH Univ., 1960–62, MA (Hist.); Natl. Arch. and Amer. Univ., 1968, Cert. (Recs. Mgt.), 1969, Cert. (Arch. Admin.); Pub. Srv. Inst. of PA, 1969, Cert. (Legal Resrch.). **Orgs.:** Natl. Assn. of State Arch. and Recs. Admins.: VP (1981–); Bd. of Dirs. (1980–); Policy Dev. Com. (1978–); various other coms. Natl. Micro. Assn.: Various coms. Mid-Atl. Reg. Arch. Conf. SAA: Com. on Micro. Stans. (1972–); Prog. Com. (1973). PA Hist. Assn. **Honors:** Phi Alpha Theta. **Pubns.:** *After Agnes: A Report on Flood Recovery Assistance* (1973); various reviews, articles in hist. pubns. **Activities:** 2; 17, 18, 23; 62, 75, 86 **Addr.:** Bureau of Archives and History, P.O. Box 1026, Harrisburg, PA 17120.

Whipple, Caroline Becker (Mr. 24, 1932, Pratt, KS) Dir. of Lib., Sch. of Theo. at Claremont, 1980–; Cat. Libn., Juniata Coll., 1974–80; Asst. Prof., Phil., Relig., OH North. Univ., 1967–73; Assoc. Prof., Relig., Wesley Coll., 1964–66; Tchr., Hist., The Gill Sch., 1963–64; Instr., Relig., TN Wesleyan Coll., 1961–62. **Educ.:** Southwest. Coll. (KS), 1951–54, AB (Soc. Sci.); Garrett Theo. Semy., 1954–58, BD (Relig.); Northwest. Univ., 1956–57, MA (Relig.); Drew Univ., 1958–67, PhD (New Testament); Kent State Univ., 1973–74, MLS. **Orgs.:** ALA: ACRL; LITA; RTSD. ATLA. Amer. Acad. of Relig. Socty. of Biblical Lit. **Honors:** Beta Phi Mu. **Pubns.:** Jt. auth., *The Jerusalem Conference as Seen by Twentieth Century Scholarship* (1973). **Activities:** 1; 20, 39, 46; 55, 56, 90 **Addr.:** 929 E. Foothill Blvd. No. 71, Upland, CA 91786.

Whisenton, Andre Carl (F. 4, 1944, Durham, NC) Lib. Dir., U.S. Dept. of Labor, 1976–; Lib. Dir., Nvl. Sea Syst. Cmnd., 1973–76; Chief, Ref. Srvs., Defense Intelligence Agency, 1971–73, Chief, Cat. Unit, 1968–71, Catlgr., 1966–68. **Educ.:** Morehse. Coll. 1961–65, BA (Pol. Sci.); Atlanta Univ., 1965–66, MSLS. **Orgs.:** SLA: DC Chap., various ofcs. **Activities:** 4, 12; 15, 22, 39; 95-Labor/Indus. Rel. **Addr.:** 1204 Canyon Rd., Silver Spring, MD 20904.

Whisler, John A. (Ja. 4, 1951, Beaverton, MI) Fine Arts Libn., Asst. Prof., East. IL Univ., 1981–; Libn. I, Memphis Pub. Lib., 1977–81. **Educ.:** Manchester Coll., 1969–73, BS (Msc.); Memphis State Univ., 1973–75, MM (Msc.); Univ. of IA, 1976–77, MA (LS). **Orgs.:** Msc. LA. Viola da Gamba Socty. of Amer.: Exec. Secy. (1979–). **Pubns.:** *Elvis Presley: Reference Guide and Discography* (1981); "Turner Clark Gallery at Memphis Public", *Southeast. Libn.* (Win. 1979); reviews. **Activities:** 9; 39; 55 **Addr.:** 1536 Third St., Apt. 6, Charleston, IL 61920.

Whistance-Smith, Ronald (D. 4, 1935, York Twp., ON) Map Cur., Univ. of AB, 1973–. **Educ.:** Waterloo Luth. Univ., 1967–70, BA, hons. (Geo.); Univ. of AB, 1970–73, MSc. (Geo.). **Orgs.:** Assn. of Can. Map Libns.: Cons. Com. (1975–); Ed. (1977–78); Conf. Ch. (1980). West. Assn. of Map Libs.: Pubns. Com. (1978–); Nom. Com. (1978). Can. Assn. of Geo. Amer. Assn. of Geo. Amer. Geo. Assn. AB Geo. Socty.: Dir. (1972–74); Pres. (1975–76). Various other orgs. and ofcs. **Activities:** 1; 15, 17, 20; 69, 70, 71 **Addr.:** University Map Collection, University of Alberta, Edmonton, AB T6G 2H4, Canada.

Whistler, Nancy N. (Ag. 25, 1939, Santa Rita, NM) Oral Hist. Consult., 1980–; Dir., Oral Histn., CO Ctr. for Oral Hist., Denver Pub. Lib., 1976–81; Proj. Dir., Amer. Issues Forum Grant Proj., 1975–76. **Educ.:** Univ. of CO, 1957–76, BA (Oral Hist.). **Orgs.:** ALA: Frnds. of Libs. Com. (1970–74). CO LA: Frnds. of Libs. RT. Frnds. of Denver Pub. Lib.: Pres. (1972–74); Bd. (1964–75). Oral Hist. Assn.: Nom. Com. (1978–81); Liaison Com. (1978–81); Wingspread Conf. (1979); Natl. Wkshp. (Ch., 1980). **Activities:** 2, 9; 24, 28, 34; 85 **Addr.:** 4990 S. Clinton, Englewood, CO 80111.

Whitaker, Susanne K. (S. 10, 1947, Clinton, MA) Vetny. Med. Libn., Cornell Univ., 1978–, Asst. Libn. 1977–78; Med. Libn., Hartford Hosp., 1972–77; Reg. Ref. Libn., Yale Med. Lib., 1970–72. **Educ.:** Clark Univ., 1969, BA (Bio.); Case West. Rsv. Univ., 1970, MS (LS); Med. LA, 1972 (Cert.). **Orgs.:** Med. LA. CT Assn. of Hlth. Sci. Libs.: Pres. (1975); Nsltr. Ed. (1973–75). **Honors:** Beta Phi Mu. **Activities:** 1; 15, 17, 39; 80 **Addr.:** Flower Veterinary Library, Cornell University, Ithaca, NY 14853.

Whitbeck, George W. (Lewiston, ME) Assoc. Dean, LS, IN Univ., 1975–; Ch., LS, Univ. of South. MS, 1973–75; Asst. Prof., LS, Univ. of MI, 1970–73; Assoc. Libn., Reader Srvs., SUNY, New Paltz, 1963–67; Ref. Libn., Levittown Pub. Lib., 1962–63; Cat. Libn., 1959–61. **Educ.:** Bates Coll., Columbia Coll., 1955–57, BA (Hist.); Columbia Univ., 1958–59, MS (LS); Columbia Univ., 1961–62, MA (Hist.). **Orgs.:** ALA: PLA, Resrch. Com. (1977–); ACRL. ASIS. AALS. IN LA: Exec. Bd. (1979–). AAUP. **Pubns.:** *The Influence of Librarians in Liberal Arts Colleges in Selected Decision Making Areas* (1972); "The Education of Archivists: Needs as Perceived By A Sampling of the Profession in the South," *South. Qtly.* (Ja. 1975); jt. auth., "Support for Research in Librarianship," *Advncs. in Libnshp.* (1979); jt. auth., "The Federal Depository Library System," *Gvt. Pubns. Review* (1978). **Activities:** 11; 25, 26; 50, 63, 92 **Addr.:** School of Library and Information Science, Indiana University, Bloomington, IN 47405.

Whitby, Thomas J. (Ja. 12, 1919, Chicago, IL) Assoc. Prof., LS, 1968–; Chief Libn., Martin-Marietta Corp., 1963–68; Info. Sci., Olin Mathieson Chem. Corp., 1961–63; Slavic Sci. Acq. Spec., Lib. of Congs., 1952–61. **Educ.:** Univ. of Chicago, 1938–47, PhB (Liberal Arts), 1947–52, MA (LS); Univ. de Montréal, 1947, (Cert.). **Orgs.:** SLA. CO LA. Cousteau Socty. AAAS. **Pubns.:** *Introduction to Soviet National Bibliography* (1979); "Classification and Definition in Serials Work," *Cath. Lib. World* (My.–Je. 1976); "Libraries and Bibliographical Projects in the Communist Bloc," *Lib. Qtly.* (1959). **Activities:** 20, 30, 44; 57, 88, 91 **Addr.:** Graduate School of Librarianship & Information Management, University of Denver, Denver, CO 80208.

Special Subjects/Services: 50. Adult educ.; 51. Advert./Mktg.; 52. Aerosp.; 53. Agric.; 54. Area std.; 55. Arts/Hum.; 56. Autom.; 57. Bibl./Prtg.; 58. Bio. sci.; 59. Bus./Fin.; 60. Chem.; 61. Copyrt.; 62. Documtn.; 63. Educ.; 64. Engin.; 65. Env.; 66. Eth. grps.; 67. Film; 68. Food/Nutr.; 69. Geneal.; 70. Geo.; 71. Geol.; 72. Handcpd.; 73. Hist.; 74. Int. frdm.; 75. Info. sci.; 76. Insr.; 77. Law; 78. Legis.; 79. Math./Comp. sci.; 80. Med.; 81. Metals; 82. Nat. resrcs.; 83. Newsp.; 84. Nuc. sci.; 85. Oral hist.; 86. Petr./Energy; 87. Pharm.; 88. Phys./Astr./Math.; 89. Readg.; 90. Relig.; 91. Sci./Tech.; 92. Soc. sci.; 93. Telecom.; 94. Transp.; 95. (other).

Whitcomb, Laurie A. (Jl. 3, 1951, Chicago, IL) Asst. Tech. Srvs. Libn., Roosevelt Univ. Lib., 1979–; Ref. Libn., Ryerson Lib., Art Inst. of Chicago, 1978–79; Libn. I, Chicago Pub. Lib., 1977–78. **Educ.:** Univ. of Rochester, 1969–73, BA (Art Hist., Eng.); Univ. of MI, 1976–77, MLS; Univ. of Chicago, 1974–76, MA (Art Hist.). **Orgs.:** ARLIS/NA ALA. **Honors:** Beta Phi Mu. **Pubns.:** Reviews. **Activities:** 1, 12; 20, 39, 44; 55 **Addr.:** 1369 E. Hyde Park Blvd., Apt #406, Chicago, IL 60615.

White, Beverly J. (Mr. 3, 1944, Fulton, MO) Supvsr., Lib. Srvs., Shawnee Missn. Pub. Schs., 1977–; Libn., Brookwood Sch., 1974–77; Libn., NW HS, 1970–74; Resrch. Asst., Mid-Continent Reg. Educ. Lab., 1969–70; Libn., Baptiste Jr. HS, 1967–69. **Educ.:** Univ. of MO, 1962–66, BS (Eng., LS), 1966–67, MEd. **Orgs.:** KS Assn. of Sch. Libns.: Elem. and Sec. Projs. (1979–81). Sch. Media Dirs. of KS: Pres. (1981). ALA. Un. Sch. Admins. Natl. Educ. Assn. **Activities:** 10; 17, 24, 35 **Addr.:** Mohawk Instructional Center, 6649 Lamar, Shawnee Mission, KS 66202.

White, Brenda H. (My. 17, 1940, Latrobe, PA) Lib. Media Consult., CT State Dept. of Educ., 1981–; Lib. Media Spec., Penn Hills Sch. Dist., 1979–81; Tchg. Fellow, Univ. of Pittsburgh, 1978–79; Lib. Media Spec., Penn Hills Sch. Dist., 1966–77, Tchr., 1961–65. **Educ.:** Thiel Coll., 1958–61, BA (Eng.); Univ. of Pittsburgh, 1964–66, MLS, 1977–80, PhD. **Orgs.:** ALA: AASL, Pubns. Adv. (1980–); Gen. Conf. (1981–). CT LA. CT Educ. Media Assn.: Int. Frdm. Ch. (1981–). **Honors:** Beta Phi Mu, 1966; AECT, Conv. Intern, 1978. **Pubns.:** *A Study of the Impact of ESEA Title II Funds on the Public School Library Media Centers of Pennsylvania* (1980); jt. ed., *Excellence in School Media Programs* (1980); "Cooperatives and Network: A Preliminary Survey and Suggested Sources of Information," *Networks for Networkers* (1980); "Spontaneous Interaction in Library Media Center Programming," *AR Libs.* (S. 1980). **Addr.:** Connecticut State Dept. of Education, Box 2219, Rm. 364, Hartford, CT 06115.

White, Cecil R. (O. 15, 1937, Hammond, IN) Libn., Golden Gate Bapt. Theo. Semy., 1980–; Asst. Libn., Pub. Srvs., SW Bapt. Theo. Semy., 1970–80, Actg. Ref. Libn., 1968–70; HS Libn., Herrin (IL) HS, 1964–66. **Educ.:** South. IL Univ., 1955–59, BS (Hist. Educ.); Syracuse Univ., 1960–61, Cert. (Czech.); SW Bapt. Theo. Semy., 1966–69, MDiv (Theo.); N. TX State Univ., 1969–70, MLS, 1977– (LS). **Orgs.:** ALA. ATLA: Consult. Srv. (Co-Coord., 1974–78). S. Bapt. Conv. Hist. (Comsn.: Bapt. Info. Retrieval Adv. Com. (1973–). CA LA. **Honors:** Beta Phi Mu. **Pubns.:** Jt. auth., "Special Concerns: Face the Issues," *Media* (O.–D. 1971, Ja.–Mr. 1972). **Activities:** 1, 12; 17, 34, 39; 55, 90, 92 **Addr.:** Golden Gate Baptist Theological Seminary, Strawberry Point, Mill Valley, CA 94941.

White, Charles Richard (Mr. 13, 1947, Greenwich, CT) Consult., Vocational Tech. Div., CT Dept. of Educ., 1981–; Dir., TV, AV, Ridgefield HS, 1978–81; Media Spec., Greenwich HS, 1972–78; Media Spec., Fitch Sr. HS, 1970–72. **Educ.:** Boston Coll., 1965–69, BA (Econ., Soclgy.); Pratt Inst. 1969–70, MLS; Univ. of CT, 1971–74, 6th. Yr. (Educ., AV). **Orgs.:** CT Educ. Media Assn.: VP (1975–77); Stans. Com. (1972–75). ALA: AASL/Admin. Div., Bldg. Equip. Subcom. (1972–74). New Eng. Educ. Media Assn.: Student Involvement Com. (1971–76); Schol. Com. (1975–79); Nom. Com. (Ch., 1980–81). AECT. Natl. Educ. Assn. **Honors:** ALA, Scribner Awd., 1971; Ridgefield Jaycee's, Tchr. of the Yr., 1980; U.S. State Dept., Sch.-to-Sch. Exch. Prog., 1980. **Pubns.:** Layout ed., *CT Educ. Media Assn. Bltn.* (1978–79). **Activities:** 4, 10; 24, 32; 63, 93 **Addr.:** Division of Vocational Technical Schools, State Office Bldg., P.O. Box 2219, Hartford, CT 06115.

White, Ernest Miller (My. 8, 1917, Robinson, IL) Libn., Prof., Louisville Presby. Theo. Semy., 1945–; Asst. Libn., Un. Theo. Semy. (Richmond, VA), 1941–44; Libn., Dalton HS, 1940–41. **Educ.:** Vanderbilt Univ., 1939, BA (Eng.); George Peabody Coll., 1941, BS (LS), 1959, MA. **Orgs.:** ATLA. SELA. KY LA: Various ofcs. **Activities:** 12; 90 **Addr.:** Louisville Presbyterian Theological Seminary, 1044 Alta Vista Rd., Louisville, KY 40205.

White, Herbert S. (S. 5, 1927, Vienna, Austria) Dean, Sch. of Lib. and Info. Sci., IN Univ., 1980–, Prof., LS, Dir., Resrch. Ctr. for Lib. and Info. Sci., 1975–80; Pres., Stechert Macmillan, Inc., 1974–75; Sr. VP, Inst. for Sci. Info., 1970–73; VP, Documtn., Inc., 1964–70; Exec. Dir., NASA Sci. and Tech. Info. Facility, 1964–68; Prog. Mgr., IBM Tech. Info. Ctr., 1959–64; Mgr., Engin. Lib., Chance Vought Aircraft, Inc., 1954–59; Libn., U.S. Atomic Energy Comsn. and Lib. of Congs., 1950–54. **Educ.:** Coll. of the City of NY, 1944–46, 1947–49, BS (Chem.); Syracuse Univ., 1949–50, MS (LS). **Orgs.:** FID: Exec. Com. (Treas., 1979–82); U.S. Del. to Cncl. (1977–80); Plng. Com. (1978, 1980). U.S. Natl. Acad. of Sci.: Com. for Intl. Info. Progs. (1976–). ASIS: Pres. (1973–74); various ofcs. SLA: Pres. (1968–69); various ofcs. Various other orgs., ofcs. Amer. Chem. Socty. **Honors:** Beta Phi Mu. **Pubns.:** *Copyright Dilemma* (1978); Jt. auth., *Publishers and Libraries* (1976); jt. auth., "Funding Support for Research in Librarianship," *Advncs. in Libnshp.* volume 9 (1979); "Critical Mass for Library Education," *Amer. Libs.* (S. 1979); various other articles, rpts. **Activities:** 11, 12; 17, 26, 41; 63, 75, 91 **Addr.:** School of Library and Information Science, Indiana University, Bloomington, IN 47405.

White, Howard S. (Hinsdale, IL) Ed., *Lib. Tech. Rpts.*, ALA, 1969–; Dept. Libn., Univ. of Chicago, 1964–69. **Educ.:** State Univ. of IA, BA; Univ. of Chicago, MA. **Orgs.:** Amer. Natl. Stans. Com. for Lib. Equip. and Supplies, Z85: Secy. (1978–). Amer. Natl. Stans. Com. for AV Systs., PH7: 1971–. **Activities:** 3; 37, 41 **Addr.:** American Library Association, 50 E. Huron St., Chicago, IL 60611.

White, J. Marshall (Je. 18, 1947, St. Joseph, MO) Archvst., Recs. Coord., Admin. Ofc. of the Cts., 1976–; State Recs. Archvst., KY Div. of Arch. and Recs., 1975–76. **Educ.:** W. GA Coll., 1973–75, BA (Hist.); various insts. and wkshps. **Orgs.:** SAA: Finding Aids Com. (1975–), State and Lcl. Recs. Com. (1976–), Minute Rev. Com. (1976–). KY Cncl. on Arch. Socty. GA Archvsts.: Wkshp. Plng. Com. (1975). Assn. of Recs. Mgrs. Various other orgs. KY Micro. Assn. Amer. Philatelic Assn. **Activities:** 2; 17, 24, 38; 77, 78 **Addr.:** Administrative Office of the Courts, Bush Bldg., 403 Wapping St., Frankfort, KY 40601.

White, James William (My. 5, 1935, Cedar Rapids, IA) Lib. Dir., LaCrosse Pub. Lib., 1976–; Lib. Dir., Muscatine Pub. Lib., 1968–76. **Educ.:** Univ. of IA, 1960–63, BA (Hist.), 1967–68, MLS. **Orgs.:** ALA: PLA. WI LA. **Pubns.:** "OCLC Helps a System," *WI Lib. Bltn.* (N.-D. 1978); "Wisconsin at the White House," *WI Lib. Bltn.* (Ja.-F. 1980). **Activities:** 9; 17, 19, 24; 50, 55, 63 **Addr.:** 800 Main St., La Crosse, WI 54601.

White, Janette Hunter (Ag. 6, 1921, Toronto, ON) Prof., LS, Asst. to Dean, Univ. of West. ON, 1967–; Head, Ref. and Circ., Educ. Ctr. Lib., Toronto Bd. of Educ., 1961–67; Genl. Libn. Meteorological Srvs. of Can. Lib., 1959–61; Ref. Libn., Toronto Pub. Lib., Gen. Ref. Div., 1957–59. **Educ.:** Univ. of Toronto, 1938–42, BA (Langs.); Columbia Univ., 1956–57, MS (LS); ON Coll. of Educ., 1942–43, Cert. (HS Educ.). **Orgs.:** SLA: Toronto Chap. (Pres., 1966–67). Can. Assn. of Lib. Schs.: Pres. (1971–73). ON LA: Cncl. (1971–73, 1977–78) Secy. (1978–79). **Pubns.:** Jt. auth., *A Select Bibliography of Education in the Commonwealth Caribbean, 1940–75* (1976). **Activities:** 11; 26 **Addr.:** School of Library and Information Science, University of Western Ontario, London, ON N6A 5B9 Canada.

White, Joyce L. (Je. 7, 1927, Philadelphia, PA) Libn., Archvst., Episcopal Dio. of West. KS, 1980–; Asst. Dir., Arch. Proj., Leadership Conf. Women Relig., 1979–81, Resrch. Asst., Hist. Socty. of Episcopal Church, 1976–78; Libn., Educ. Lib., Univ. of PA, 1957–76. **Educ.:** Univ. of PA, Drexel Univ., 1945–49, BA (LS); Drexel Univ., 1957–60, MSLS. **Orgs.:** CS LA: Exec. Secy. (1970–72), Pres. (1969–70), Conf. Ch. (1981). KS LA. SAA. TX LA. **Pubns.:** "Demography of Church Libraries in the U.S.," *Church and Synagogue Libs.* (1980); "Yarnall Library of Theology," *Lib. Chronicle* (Sum. 1979); "Affiliation of Seven Swedish Luthern Churches with the Episcopal Church," *Hist. Mag. of the Episcopal Church* (Je. 1977); "Church Libraries - Unrecognized Resources," *Amer. Libs.* (Ap. 1971). **Activities:** 2, 12; 24, 26, 41; 57, 90 **Addr.:** Episcopal Diocese of Western Kansas, Salina, KS 67401.

White, Lelia Cayne (F. 22, 1921, Berkeley, CA) Dir., Lib. Srvs., Oakland Pub. Lib., 1976–, Supvsg. Libn., 1973–76; Ref. Libn., Berkeley-Oakland Srv. Syst., 1970–73; Biblgphr., Adj. Lectr., LS, Univ. of CA, Berkeley, 1969–72. **Educ.:** Univ. of CA, Berkeley, 1943, BA, 1969, MLS. **Orgs.:** ALA: Instr. on the Use of Libs. Com. (1981); PLA. CA LA: CA Inst. of Libs. (Pres., 1982). Pub. Lib. Execs. of Ctrl. CA: Pres. (1979). Leag. of Women Voters. **Pubns.:** Contrib., *Public Library User Education* (1981). **Activities:** 9; 17, 28, 31; 66 **Addr.:** Oakland Public Library, 125 14th St., Oakland, CA 94612.

White, Lois A. (Ag. 9, 1921, Lake Benton, MN) Head, Ref. Srvs., IN Univ. N.W., 1980–; Cnsrtm. Coord., Libn., IN Univ. Med. Sch., 1979–80; Chem. Libn., Univ. of Chicago, 1971–79, Educ. Ref. Libn., 1969–71. **Educ.:** Moorhead State Univ., 1939–43, BS (Bio.); IN Univ., 1969–70, MLS; Univ. of IL, 1978, Cert. (Med. Libnshp.). **Orgs.:** SLA. Med. LA. Indian State LA. **Honors:** Beta Phi Mu. **Activities:** 1; 31, 39; 56 **Addr.:** Indiana University Northwest, 3500 Broadway, Gary, IN 46408.

White, Marilyn Domas (Ag. 16, 1940, Franklin, LA) Asst. Prof., LS, Univ. of MD, 1976–; Asst. Prof., SUNY, Buffalo, 1974–76. **Educ.:** Our Lady of the Lake Coll., 1958–62, BA (Hist.); Univ. of WI, 1962–63, MS (LS); Univ. of IL, 1968–71, PhD. **Orgs.:** ALA: RASD, various coms. ASIS. AALS. **Activities:** 11; 25, 26, 27; 57, 63, 76 **Addr.:** College of Library and Information Services, University of Maryland, College Park, MD 20742.

White, Mary Lou (My. 30, 1933, Akron, OH) Assoc. Prof. (Educ.), Wright State Univ., 1972–; Asst. Prof. (Educ.), Univ. of ME, 1968–71; Tchr., Curric. Asst., Shaker Heights City Schs., 1955–63. **Educ.:** Univ. of Akron, 1951–55, BS (Educ.); Univ. of WI, 1963–65, MS (Educ.); OH State Univ., 1965–72, PhD (Educ.). **Orgs.:** SW OH YA Mtrls. Rev. Grp. (1979–). OH Educ. Lib. Media Assn.: Pub. Com. (1978–80). ALA: ALSC, Intl. Rel. Com. (1980–81); AASL, Minorities in Chld. Lit. Com. (1975–76). OH LA: Higher Educ. Com. (1979–80), Higher Educ. Com. (Ch., 1978–79). Natl. Cncl. of Tchrs. of Eng.: Elem. Booklist Com. (Ch., 1977–81). OH Cncl. of Tchrs. of Eng.: Treas. (1980). West. OH Cncl. of Tchrs. of Eng.: Constn. Com. (1977); Liaison to Natl. Cncl. (1980). Intl. Reading Assn. other orgs. **Honors:** Miami Univ., Silver Gerlie Awd., 1978; Wright State Univ. Alum. Assn., Tchg. Excel. Awd., 1981. **Pubns.:** Ed., *Adventuring with Books* (1981); *Children's Literature* (1976); jt. auth., *Personalized Supervision* (1966); "Ethnic Literature for Children," *Cath. Lib. World* (Mr. 1980); ed., "Non Print Media," clmn. *Lang. Arts* (S. 1975, F. 1976, Ap. 1976); various other articles. **Activities:** 14-Coll. of educ.; 21, 48; 54, 63 **Addr.:** Wright State University, W495 Millett, Dayton, OH 45435.

White, R. Diane (Ag. 20, 1943, Cape Girardeau, MO) Lib. COord., Salem Cmnty. Coll., 1979–; Ref. Biblgphr., Univ. of Santa Clara, 1970–72; Eng. Lit. Catlgr., South. IL Univ. 1969–70; Latin-Amer. Lit. Catlgr., Stanford Univ., 1967–69. **Educ.:** S.E. MO State Univ., 1960–64, BS (Eng.); George Peabody Coll., 1966–67, MLS; San Francisco State Univ., 1972–74, MA (Eng.). **Orgs.:** Cumberland Cnty. Lib. Area Wide Coord. Cncl.: VP (1980). **Activities:** 1; 17, 20, 39 **Addr.:** Salem Community College Library, Penns Grove, NJ 08069.

White, R. Stephen S. (F. 19, 1948, Sackville, NB) ILL Libn., Ottawa Pub. Lib., 1980–, Ref. Libn., 1979–, Bus. and Tech. Libn., 1977–79, Boys and Girls Libn., 1975–77; Pers. Ref. Libn., Montreal Pub. Lib., 1973–75. **Educ.:** OH State Univ., 1965–70, BA (Fr.); Mt. Allison Univ., 1970–71, BEd; Univ. of West. ON, 1972–, MLS. **Orgs.:** Can. LA: Mem. Rcrt. Com. (1978–); Lcl. Arrange. Com. (1978–79). ON LA. Intl. Bd. of Bks. for Youth. **Pubns.:** Reviews. **Activities:** 9; 21, 29, 39; 51, 59, 91 **Addr.:** Ottawa Public Library, 120 Metcalfe St., Ottawa, ON K1P 5M2 Canada.

White, Ruth M. (S. 7, 1914, Ludlow, KY) Retired, 1981–; Volun. Libn., Natl. Park Srv., 1981–; Asst. Libn., Coord., Tech. Srvs., Pasadena (CA) Pub. Lib., 1971–75; Exec. Secy., Adult Srvs. Div. and Ref. Srvs. Div., various other positions, ALA, 1958–70; YA Libn., Detroit Pub. Lib., 1955–58. **Educ.:** OH State Univ., 1932–35, BS (Educ.); West. Rsv. Univ., 1937–38, BS (LS); Univ. of Chicago, 1958–63, AM (LS). **Orgs.:** ALA. Natl. Org. for Women. Common Cause. Sierra Club. The Nature Conservancy. **Activities:** 9; 16, 17, 20 **Addr.:** 311 Biltmore Garden Apts., Asheville, NC 28803.

White, Suellen Sebald (F. 4, 1949, Indianapolis, IN) Resrch. Info. Sci., Denver Resrch. Inst., 1981–; Info. Consult., Food and Agr. Org., Untd. Nations, 1980; Info. Spec., Denver Resrch. Inst., 1976–80. **Educ.:** Purdue Univ., 1967–71, BA (Hum.); Univ. of Denver, 1975–76, MA (LS). **Orgs.:** ASIS. AAAS. **Honors:** Beta Phi Mu. **Pubns.:** "Techniques and Tools for Scientific and Technical Information Service in Developing Countries," (forthcoming); jt. auth., "Information Types (Its) in International Development," *What Else You Can Do With a Library Degree* (1980); "Training in the Use of Scientific and Technical Information for Third World Countries," *Communicating Information, Proceedings ASIS-80* (1980). **Activities:** 12; 24, 28, 41; 75, 91 **Addr.:** 2441 S. Josephine St., Denver, CO 80210.

White, Tera Bailey (Mr. 4, 1920, Brantley, AL) Mgr., Corporate Info. Srvs., Blue Cross and Blue Shield, NC, 1977–, Mgr., Info. Ctr., 1975–77, Corporate Libn., 1972–75; Head, Adult Srvs., Pub. Lib. of Charlotte and Mecklenburg Cnty., 1948–51, Head, Ref., 1946–48, Ref. Libn., 1944–46; Ref. Libn., Washington Cnty. (MD) Free Lib., 1943–44. **Educ.:** Queens Coll., NC, 1937–41, AB (Eng.); Univ. of NC, 1942–43, BSLS. **Orgs.:** SLA: NC Chap. (Pres. 1979–80); Insr. Div., Dir. (1978–79), Secy. (1976–77). **Honors:** Beta Phi Mu. **Pubns.:** "Charlotte Experiments with Audio Charging," *Lib. Jnl.* (1950). **Activities:** 9, 12; 17, 39; 59, 76 **Addr.:** 109 Chase Ave., Chapel Hill, NC 27514.

Whitehead, James Madison (Jl. 16, 1929, Mobile, AL) Asst. Prof., LS, Atlanta Univ., 1980–; Asst. Prof., LS, SUNY, Geneseo, 1978–80; Assoc. Prof., Head Law Libn., Coll. of William and Mary, 1971–76; Admin. Asst., Head of Circ. and Dir. of Stacks, VA Polytech. Inst. and State Univ., 1967–71; Asst. Prof., Head Sci. Libn., Univ. of CO, 1965–67; various other prof. positions, 1963–65. **Educ.:** Univ. of Chicago, 1948–52, BA (Math); Tulane Univ., 1956–59, JD (Law); LA State Univ., 1962–63, MS (LS); Univ. of Pittsburgh, 1976–81, PhD (LS). **Orgs.:** ALA. NY LA. ASIS. AALS. LA Bar Assn. Amer. Bar Assn. Amer. Judicature Socty. **Honors:** Beta Phi Mu. **Pubns.:** Reviews. **Activities:** 1; 17, 22, 26; 56, 75, 77 **Addr.:** 30 F Cotswold Vlg., 1075 N. Hairston Rd., Stone Mountain, GA 30083.

Whitehead, Olive F. (N. 18, 1916, Washington, CT) Retired, 1981–; Mgr., Lib. Resrcs., RCA Gvt. Comms. Systs., 1978–, Libn., 1969–78; Asst. Libn., RCA Defense Electronic Prods., 1958–69; Libn., Amer. Sugar Refining Co., 1947–58; Asst. Libn., Hercules Powder Co., 1941–47. **Educ.:** Westminster Coll., 1934–39, BS (Math); Drexel Univ., 1940–41, BS (LS). **Orgs.:** SLA: Philadelphia Chap., Dir. Com. (1957–70); Treas. (1955–57); VP (1973–74); Pres. (1974–75); Dir. (1976–79). ASIS. ALA. **Honors:** SLA: Philadelphia Chap., Achvmt. Awd., 1970. **Pubns.:** "Groups - To Be or Not To Be," *Bltn. of Spec. Libs. Cncl. of Philadelphia* (F. 1968); jt. auth., "Technical Information:

PROFESSIONAL ACTIVITIES: Institutions: 1. Acad. lib.; 2. Arch.; 3. Assn.; 4. Fed./Gvt. lib.; 5. Inst. lib.; 6. Mfr./Suppl.; 7. Milit. lib.; 8. Musm.; 9. Pub. lib.; 10. Sch. lib.; 11. Sch. of lib. sci.; 12. Spec. lib.; 13. State lib.; 14. (other). **Functions/Activities:** 15. Acq./Col. dev.; 16. Adult srvs.; 17. Admin.; 18. Apprais.; 19. Archit./Bldgs.; 20. Cat./Class.; 21. Chld. srvs.; 22. Circ.; 23. Cons./Pres.; 24. Consult.; 25. Cont. ed.; 26. Educ. lib. sci.; 27. Ext. srvs.; 28. Fund/Grants; 29. Gvt. pubs.; 30. Indx./Abs.; 31. Instr. lib. use; 32. Media srvs.; 33. Micro.; 34. Netwks./Coop.; 35. Persnl.; 36. PR; 37. Publshg.; 38. Recs. mgt.; 39. Ref. srvs.; 40. Repro.; 41. Resrch.; 42. Review.; 43. Secur.; 44. Serials; 45. Spec. col.; 46. Tech. srvs.; 47. Trustees/Bds.; 48. YA srvs.; 49. (other).

Where to Get It," *RCA Engin.* (D. 1976–Ja. 1977). **Activities:** 12; 15, 17, 30; 64, 88, 93 **Addr.:** Library, Bldg. 10-6-5, RCA Government Communications Systems, Camden, NJ 08102.

Whitehead, Willard James (O. 30, 1934, Canton, IL) Dir., Bloomington Pub. Lib., 1977–; Asst. Dir., West. IL Lib. Syst., 1972–77; Lib. Systs. Anal., Circ. Libn., West. IL Univ., 1965–72; Gift and Exch. Libn., GA Inst. of Tech., 1964–65. **Educ.:** West. IL Univ., 1959–62, BA (Eng.); Univ. of IL, 1963–64, MLS; Univ. of IL, 1970–71, Cert. Adv. Std. (LS). **Orgs.:** ALA. IL LA. Mental Hlth Assn. of McLean Cnty. Macomb Lodge. **Activities:** 9; 17 **Addr.:** Bloomington Public Library, 205 E. Olive St., Bloomington, IL 61701.

Whitehill, Margaret E. (F. 3, 1935, Lander, WY) Base Libn., U.S. Air Frc., Zweibrucken Air Base, Germany, 1979–; Base Libn., Langley Air Frc. Base, VA, 1971–79; Base Libn., Udorn Air Frc. Base, Thailand, 1969–71; Libn., U.S. Marine Corps, Okinawa, 1966–68; Pub. Srvs. Libn., Juniata Coll., 1965–66; YA Libn., Tuscon Pub. Lib., 1963–64; Ref. Libn, Univ. of Pittsburgh, 1962–63; various positions as libn., 1958–62. **Educ.:** Univ. of MN, 1953–57, BA (Hist.); 1957–58, MS (LS); Univ. of MN, 1958–59, BS (Educ.). **Orgs.:** ALA. Amer. Forestry Assn. **Activities:** 7 **Addr.:** P.O. Box 1846, APO New York, NY 09860.

Whiteley, Sandra M. (My. 24, 1943, Ridley Park, PA) Prog. Ofcr., ACRL, 1981–, Asst. Ed., *Who's Who in Library and Info. Sci.*, ALA, 1980–81; Head, Ref. Dept., Northwest. Univ. Lib., 1975–80; Ref. Libn., Yale Univ. Lib., 1970–74. **Educ.:** PA State Univ., 1960–63, BA (Soclgy.); Columbia Univ., 1969–70, MS (LS); Univ. of PA, 1974–75, AM (Soclgy.). **Orgs.:** ALA: Elec. Com. (1980); Ref. Srvs. in Lg. Resrch. Libs. Discuss. Grp. (Ch., 1978); Alternate to the Card Cat. in Resrch. Libs. Discuss. Grp. (Ch., 1979); ACRL/Univ. Libs. Sect., Nom. Com. (1979); RASD, Cat. Use Com. (1979–81); RASD Rep. to RTSD Com. on Cat.: Descr. and Access (1979–81). AAUP: Northwest. Univ. Chap. (Secy.-Treas.) (1977–79). **Honors:** Beta Phi Mu, 1970. **Pubns.:** "Reference Services," *ALA Yrbk.* (1980); ed., "Newspapers in Review," *Serials Review* (1978–); reviews. **Activities:** 1; 17, 39, 42; 55, 83, 92 **Addr.:** 2124-A Maple Ave., Evanston, IL 60201.

Whitelock, Margaret M. (S. 19, 1935, Covington, TN) Catlgr., Princeton Theo. Semy., 1967–. **Educ.:** Maryville Coll., 1953–57, BA (Fr.); Cath. Univ., 1966–67, MS (LS). **Orgs.:** ATLA: Rec. Secy. (1975–78); Cat. and Class. Com. (Ch., 1971–74). **Activities:** 1; 20; 90 **Addr.:** Speer Library, Princeton Theological Seminary, Princeton, NJ 08540.

Whiteman, Merlin P. (S. 4, 1951, Columbus, IN) Readers' Srvs. Libn., IN Univ. Sch. of Law Lib., 1979–; Adult Srvs. Libn., Wyandotte (MI) Pub. Lib., 1974–79. **Educ.:** Hope Coll., 1969–73, BA (Pol. Sci); IN Univ., 1973–74, MLS. **Orgs.:** AALL. OH Reg. Assn. of Law Libs. **Activities:** 39; 77 **Addr.:** 5043 Wildflower Ct., Apt. A, Indianapolis, IN 46254.

Whitenack, Carolyn I. (Ap. 20, 1916, Mercer Cnty., KY) Retired, 1979–; Ch., Media Sci., and Prof., Dept. of Educ., Purdue Univ., 1967–79, Assoc. Prof., 1960–67, Asst. Prof., 1956–60; Dir., Div. of Sch. Libs. and Tchr. Mtrls., IN Dept. of Pub. Instr., 1953–56; Head, Cat. Dept., Louisville Pub. Schs., 1950–53; Instr., Libn., Dept. of LS, Univ. of KY, 1947–50. **Educ.:** Georgetown Coll., 1932–34, (Eng.); Univ. of KY, 1948, BA (Hist.); Univ. of IL, 1956, MS (LS). **Orgs.:** ALA: 2nd VP (1960–61); Cncl. (1955–60); AASL (Pres., 1968, Bd. of Dirs., 1955–60). KY Sch. LA: Pres. IN Sch. LA: Pres. AECT. Other orgs. Natl. Educ. Assn. Assn. for Supvsn. and Curric. Dev. Natl. Cncl. of Tchrs. of Eng. AAUP. **Honors:** Beta Phi Mu; Beta Phi Mu Awd. for Good Tchg., 1976. **Activities:** 10, 11; 32 **Addr.:** RD #3, Harrodsburg, KY 40330.*

Whitesides, William L. (Jl. 12, 1931, Gastonia, NC) Consult., 1981–; Dir., Fairfax Cnty. Pub. Lib., 1970–81, Asst. Dir. 1968–69, Asst. to Dir., 1966–67; Dir., Roanoke City Lib., 1961–65; Dir., Cobb Cnty. Pub. Libs., 1958–61; Branch Libn., Atlanta Pub. Lib., 1957–58; various prof. lib. positions, 1954–57. **Educ.:** Appalachian State Univ., 1949–53, BS; FL State Univ., 1953–54, MALS. **Orgs.:** SELA: Lib. Dev. Com. (1974–75); Interstate Coop. Com. (Ch., 1979–80); Pub. Lib. Sect. (Ch., 1981–82). ALA: Com. on Org. (1972–73); Cncl. (1976–79). VA LA: Treas. (1965–66); Fed. State Coord. (1975). DC LA: Pres. (1976). Various other orgs. WHCOLIS: VA Gvr's. Conf. (Del., 1979). North. VA Litey. Cncl.: Bd. (1981). North. VA Lib. Networking Com.: Ch. (1979). Kiwanis Intl.: Pres. (1969). **Honors:** Beta Phi Mu. **Pubns.:** Various articles and reviews, *ALA Yrbk.* **Activities:** 9; 17; 74, 78 **Addr.:** 12111 Wayland St., Oakton, VA 22124.

Whitlatch, Jo Bell (Je. 21, 1943, Hibbing, MN) Access Coord., San Jose State Univ., 1979–, Circ. Libn., 1974–79, Catlgr., 1973–74; Biblgphr., Stanislaus State Coll., 1970–72, Acq. Libn., 1968–69; Acq. Libn., Coll. of St. Thomas, 1965–67. **Educ.:** Univ. of MN, 1961–64, BA (Hist.), 1964–66, MA (LS); Univ. of CA, Berkeley, 1970–73, MA (Asian Std.). **Orgs.:** CA LA: State Univ. and Colls. Chap. (Pres., 1974); Acad. and Resrch. Libns. (Ch., 1981). ALA: LAMA/Prsnl. Admin. Sect., Staff Dev. Com. (1980–83). Assn. of Asian Std. **Honors:** Beta Phi Mu. **Pubns.:** Jt. auth., "Experiences with Faculty Status in Academic Libraries," *CA Libn.* (Ja. 1976); "Service at San Jose State University," *Jnl. of Acad. Libnshp.* (S. 1978); ed., gvt. docum. clmn., *RQ* (1976–79). **Activities:** 1; 15, 22, 49-Staff dev.; 54, 92 **Addr.:** 1801 Edgewood Ln., Menlo Park, CA 94025.

Whitlow, Cherrill Meyer (Ag. 1, 1936, Sheridan, WY) Libn., Rio Grande HS, Albuquerque, 1972–; Instr., LS, Univ. of NM, 1973–79; Tchr., San Manuel HS (AZ), 1971–72; Libn., Mayfield HS, 1969–71; Libn., Rawlins HS, 1968–69; Libn., Tchr., St. Joseph's Acad. (Tucson, AZ), 1963–64. **Educ.:** Univ. of NM, 1956–60, BS (Educ.); Univ. of AZ, 1963–68, MEd (LS); TX Woman's Univ., 1969–75, MLS. **Orgs.:** NM LA: Sch. Libs., Chld. and YA Div. (Ch., 1977–78); Mem. Ch. (1978–79). NM Media Assn.: Nsltr. Ed. (1977–80). SWLA: NM Mem. Com. (1979–). Grt. Albuquerque LA: Secy. (1973–74). **Honors:** Pi Lambda Theta; Beta Phi Mu. **Activities:** 10, 11; 15, 31, 32; 57, 75 **Addr.:** 2702 Morrow Rd. N.E., Albuquerque, NM 87106.

Whitlow, Hubert H., Jr. (F. 16, 1930, Atlanta, GA) Libn., Floyd Jr. Coll., 1970–; Asst. Univ. Libn., Circ., Emory Univ. Lib., 1968–70, Docum. Libn., 1967–68, Chief Circ. Libn., 1964–67, Chief, Serials and Binding Dept., 1960–64, Rsv. Libn., 1961–62; Head, Soc. Sci. Div., Univ. of GA Libs., 1958–60, Asst. Hum. Cat. Libn., 1956–58. **Educ.:** Emory Univ., 1947–51, BA (Hist.), 1955–56, MLn; Univ. of FL, 1960–61, MA (Pol. Sci.). **Orgs.:** ALA. SELA: Constn. and Bylaws Com. (Ch., 1976–80). GA LA: Lib. Dev. Com. (1977–79); Second VP (1975–77); Constn. and Bylaws Com. (Ch., 1973–75). AAUP. **Pubns.:** "SELA As Hypothesis...," *The Southeast. Libn.* (Sum. 1978); "The Present As Prologue?" *The GA Libn.* (N. 1976). **Activities:** 1; 15, 17, 35 **Addr.:** Library, Floyd Junior College, P.O. Box 1864, Rome, GA 30161.

Whitmore, Marilyn P. Univ. Archvst., Univ. of Pittsburgh, 1976–, Sp. and Thea. Biblgphr., 1974–78, Head, Gift and Exch., 1969–75, Head, Cat. Dept., 1966–69, Catlgr., 1961–66; Catlgr., PA State Univ., 1956–60. **Educ.:** Jamestown Coll., 1950–51; Univ. of ND, 1951–54, BA (Bus.); Rutgers Univ., 1959–64, MLS; Univ. of Pittsburgh, 1975–80, PhD (LS). **Orgs.:** ALA: Intl. Rel. Com. (1964–); RTSD, Subj. Anal. Com., Subcom. on Subj. Headings on Gay Liberation (1971–72)/Reprodct. of Lib. Mtrls. Sect., Discuss. Grp. SAA: Arch.-Libs. Relshps. Com. (1977–78). Mid-Atl. Arch. Conf.: Lcl. Arrange. Com. (1980–81); Prog. Com. (1980–81). SALALM: Mem. Com. (Ch., 1980–81). Thea. Lib. Assn. Various other orgs., ofcs. Church of the Ascension. Schenly Farms Civic Assn. Pittsburgh Civic Garden Ctr. Carnegie Inst. **Honors:** Beta Phi Mu; Univ. of Pittsburgh, Lancour Awd. in Intl. Libnshp., 1976. **Pubns.:** "The Library Scene in Chile and Public Library Development," ERIC (1981); "The Setting for Latin American Librarianship," ERIC (1981); "The Role of Education and National Development in Latin American Librarianship," *Intl. Lib. Review* (Ap., 1978); reviews. **Activities:** 1; 17, 31, 45; 54 **Addr.:** 348 Hillman, University of Pittsburgh, Pittsburgh, PA 15260.

Whitney, Janet Terry (O. 11, 1947, Burbank, CA) Supvsg. Libn., CA Attorney Gen.'s Lib., 1978–, Libn., 1970–78; YA Libn., Los Angeles Pub. Lib., 1969–70. **Educ.:** Univ. of CA, Los Angeles, 1964–68, BA (Art Hist.), 1968–69, MLS; AALL, 1976, Cert. **Orgs.:** AALL. South CA Assn. Law Libs. Los Angeles Jr. Cham. of Cmrce.: Mgt. and Leadership Com. (Vice-Ch., 1979–80). Women in Mgt. **Activities:** 4; 17, 39, 41; 65, 77, 78 **Addr.:** California Attorney General's Library, 3580 Wilshire Blvd., Rm. 701, Los Angeles, CA 90010.

Whitney, Karen A. (My. 20, 1941, Okemah, OK) Libn., Agua Fria Un. HS, 1979–; Dept. Ch., N. HS, 1978–79; Libn., Alhambra HS, 1974–78; Libn., Adobe Mt. Juvenile Correct. Inst., 1972–74. **Educ.:** Univ. of OK, 1959–63, BS (Lang. Arts), 1969–72, MLS. **Orgs.:** ALA: AASL/ESEA Title IV State Adv. Cncl. (Ch.-Elect, 1979–). AZ State LA: Sch. Lib. Div. (Pres.-Elect, 1979–80), Stans. Com. (Ch., 1977–79). Channeled AZ Info. Netwk. Adv. Cncl. **Activities:** 10; 15, 31, 48; 55, 91, 92 **Addr.:** 8247 W. Vale Dr., Phoenix, AZ 85033.

Whitney, Stephen Louis (Jl. 18, 1943, Chicago, IL) City Libn., San Bernardino Pub. Lib., 1977–; Cnty. Libn., Broward Cnty. Lib., 1974–77; Admin. Asst. to Dir., St. Louis Cnty. Lib., 1970–74; Coord., Mncpl. Lib. Coop. of St. Louis Cnty., 1967–70; Adult Srvs. Libn., St. Louis Pub. Lib., 1966–67. **Educ.:** Rockhurst Coll., 1961–65, AB (Eng.); Case-West. Rsv., 1965–66, MSLS. **Orgs.:** ALA: Constn. and Bylaws Com. (1972–74). Rotary. San Bernardino Symph. Lung Assn. of San Bernardino. **Pubns.:** "Library System Trustees," *Lib. Jnl.* (F. 15, 1970); "Model for a Statewide Public Relations Network," *WY Lib. Roundup* (Je. 1973); "Library Needs Assessment of the Spanish Speaking," *Lib. Jnl.* (Ap. 1, 1980). **Activities:** 9; 17, 36, 47; 51, 66, 67 **Addr.:** San Bernardino Public Library, 401 N. Arrowhead Ave., San Bernardino, CA 92401.

Whitney, Virginia P. (D. 1, 1914, Medford, MA) Retired, 1977; Actg. Dir., Dartmouth Coll., 1978–79; Univ. Libn., Dir., Rutgers Univ. Libs., 1971–77, Assoc. Libn., 1969–71, Douglass Coll. Libn., 1967–69, Urban Std. Ctr. Libn., 1962–67, Lectr., Grad. Sch. of Lib. Srvs., 1965–70. **Educ.:** Middlebury Coll., 1932–36, BS (Pol. Sci.); Rutgers Univ., 1961–62, MLS. **Orgs.:** ARL: Pres. (1975–76); Bd. (1973–77). ALA: Cncl. (1974–78). NJ LA: Exec. Com. (1971–73). Ctr. for Resrch. Libs.: Bd. (1973–76). Princeton Univ. Lib. Adv. Cncl. MA Inst. of Tech. Visit. Com. **Activities:** 1, 9; 17, 19, 22; 56 **Addr.:** P.O. Box 435, Blue Hill, ME 04614.

Whitson, Helene (O. 24, 1941, San Francisco, CA) Spec. Col. Libn., Archvst., San Francisco State Univ. Lib., 1981–, Gvt. Pubns. Dept. Head, 1976–81, Educ., Psy., ILL Libn., 1968–75, Asst. Libn., various depts., 1966–67. **Educ.:** City Coll. of San Francisco, 1960–62, AA (Eng.); Univ. of CA, Berkeley, 1962–64, BA (Eng.), 1964–65, MLS. **Orgs.:** CA LA: Lcl. Arrange. Com. (Ch., 1981); State Univ. and Coll. Libns. Chap. (Ch., 1979); Gvt. Pubns. Chap. Socty. CA Archvsts. SAA. Bay Area Educ. Libns. **Pubns.:** Ed., *CA State Univ. and Coll. Libns. Chap. Nsltr.* (N. 1978–); ed., *Socty. of CA Archvsts. Nsltr.* (1980–); *Strike!* (1977); *California State University and Colleges Board of Trustees Almanac* (1981); **Activities:** 1; 29 **Addr.:** J. Paul Leonard Library, San Francisco State University, 1630 Holloway Ave., San Francisco, CA 94132.

Whittaker, Edward L. (S. 3, 1937, Highland Park, MI) Lib. Dir., Genesee Dist. Lib., 1979–; Dir., E. Brunswick Pub. Lib, 1978–79; Dir., Corpus Christi Pub. Lib., 1975–78; Asst. Dir., Sioux City Pub. Lib., 1971–75; Dir. of Libs., Hope Coll., 1968–71; Head Libn., Whitworth, Coll., 1968–69; Ref. Libn., Pac. Luth. Univ., 1966–69; Libn., various prof. positions, 1960–66. **Educ.:** Murray State Univ., 1958–59, BS (Eng., Sp.); Univ. of MI, 1960–63, MALS; various wkshps. **Orgs.:** MI LA: Int. Frdm. Com. (Ch., 1981–82). ALA: PLA; Conf. Prog. Com. (Ch., 1978, 1980); ASCLA, Plng., Org., Bylaws Com. (1976–78); Int. Frdm. RT (Secy., 1974–76); LAMA/Persnl. Admin. Sect., Econ. Status Com., Pensions Subcom., Ch., various coms.; JMRT, Afflt. Com. (1973–74). **Pubns.:** *General Library Instruction* (1968); "Survey of Governmental Pension Plans Affecting Public Librarians," *LAMA Nsltr.* (Fall 1976). **Activities:** 9; 17, 36 **Addr.:** Genesee District Library, G-4195 W. Pasadena Ave., Flint, MI 48504.

Whitten, Benjamin Goodman, Jr. (O. 29, 1942, Whittier, CA) First Secy. (Lib. Rel.), U.S. Intl. Comm. Agency, Paris, 1980–, Reg. Lib. Consult., Tunis, 1978–80, Reg. Lib. Consult., Nairobi, 1975–78; Asst. Prof., LS, Univ. of South. CA, 1974–75; Lectr., Lit., LS, Hacettepe Univ., Ankara, 1973–75. **Educ.:** Whittier Coll., 1960–64, AB (Eng.); Univ. of CA, Los Angeles, 1964–65, MLS; Univ. of CA, Davis, 1967–71, PhD (Eng.). **Orgs.:** Prtg. Hist. Socty. Amer. Prtg. Hist. Assn. Assn. des Bibl. et Documentalistes Fr. Amer. Lib., Paris: Bd. of Trustees. **Pubns.:** *Jane Austen's Comedy of Feeling* (1974); "Education for Librarianship in Developing Nations," *Jnl. of Educ. for Libnshp.* (Spr. 1974); "Basic Undergraduate Education for Librarianship and Information Science," *Jnl. of Educ. for Libnshp.* (Spr. 1975); "The Social Sciences Bibliography Course," *Jnl. of Educ. for Libnshp.* (Sum. 1975). **Activities:** 1, 4; 17, 24; 54, 62, 92 **Addr.:** American Embassy/USICA Paris, APO New York, NY 09777.

Whitten, Joseph Nathaniel (N. 30, 1917, Jackson, MS) Prof., LS, Long Island Univ., 1970–; Libn., Prof., SUNY Maritime Coll., 1960–70; Libn., Prof., Cooper Un., 1953–60; Instr., LS, Univ. of KY, 1950–53; Libn., Asst. Prof., Lycoming Coll., 1947–49; Asst. Libn., Instr., Bethany Coll., 1945–46. **Educ.:** MS Coll., 1935–39, BA (Hist.); George Peabody Coll., 1941–46, BSLS; Columbia Univ., 1946–49, MS (LS); NY Univ., 1949–58, EdD. **Orgs.:** ALA: Tour Com. (Ch., 1974); various coms. (1950s). SLA: Long Island Chap. (Pres., 1975–76). NY LA: Coll. and Univ. Libs. Sect. (Pres., 1966–67); VP (1972–73). NY Lib. Club: Pres. (1968–69). Nassau Cnty. LA: Bd. (1975–76, 1981); Coll. and Univ. Libs. Div. (Pres., 1975). **Honors:** Beta Phi Mu; Phi Delta Kappa; Kappa Delta Pi. **Pubns.:** *The Melvil Dui Chowder and Marching Association* (1974); "Lycoming College Library: Audio-Visual Services," *Coll. & Resrch. Libs.* (1948); "Hard Cover Reprint Publishing," *Lib. Trends* (Jl. 1958); "The New York Library Club," *Encyc. of Lib. and Info. Sci.* (1981–). **Activities:** 1, 12; 20, 26, 46; 91 **Addr.:** Apt. 7-L, 8 Barstow Rd., Great Neck, NY 11021.

Whittington, Erma Elizabeth Paden (F. 14, 1917, Lawrence Cnty., PA) Hubbell Ctr. for Amer. Lit. Historiography, Duke Univ. Lib., 1976–, Head, Subj. Cat. Dept., 1962–76, First Asst., Subj. Cat. Dept., 1949–62; Tchr., Sharpsville HS, 1947–48; Tchr., New Castle, PA, 1941–47. **Educ.:** Westminster Coll., 1935–39, AB (Fr.); Slippery Rock State Univ., 1940–41, Cert. (Elem. Educ.); Duke Univ., 1945–51, MA (Amer. Lit.); Univ. of NC, 1948–49, BS (LS). **Orgs.:** ALA: ACRL. SELA. NC LA: Resrcs. and Tech. Srvs. Sect. (Secy.-Treas., 1960–61). Durham Cnty. LA. AAUP. AAUW. Disabled Amer. Vets. Auxiliary: NC Treas. (1952–1954). **Honors:** Kappa Delta Pi. **Pubns.:** Ed., *Duke Univ. Lib. Nsltr.;* "A Letter from John Bennett to Jay B. Hubbell," *SC Review* (1980); "The History of the Study and Teaching of American Literature," *Amer. Lit.* (N. 1981); "Wheelockiana in the Jay B. Hubbell Center," *Paumanok Rising* (1981); various articles (1977–79). **Activities:** 1; 20, 45; 63 **Addr.:** Perkins Library, Duke University, Durham, NC 27706.

Whittle, Susan Sellers (Ap. 11, 1948, Brooksville, FL) Pub. Lib. Consult., State Lib. of FL, 1978–; Libn., Ed. Asst., Tall Timbers Resrch. Station, 1974–78; Dir., Quincy Lib., 1974–77; Tchr., Eng., Hernando HS, 1971–73. **Educ.:** Univ. of FL, 1966–71, BA (Eng.); FL State Univ., 1972–73, MLS. **Orgs.:**

Special Subjects/Services: 50. Adult educ.; 51. Advert./Mktg.; 52. Aerosp.; 53. Agric.; 54. Area std.; 55. Arts/Hum.; 56. Autom.; 57. Bibl./Prtg.; 58. Bio. sci.; 59. Bus./Fin.; 60. Chem.; 61. Copyrt.; 62. Documtn.; 63. Educ.; 64. Engin.; 65. Env.; 66. Eth. grps.; 67. Film; 68. Food/Nutr.; 69. Geneal.; 70. Geo.; 71. Geol.; 72. Handcpd.; 73. Hist.; 74. Int. frdm.; 75. Info. sci.; 76. Insr.; 77. Law; 78. Legis.; 79. Math./Comp. sci.; 80. Med.; 81. Metals; 82. Nat. resrcs.; 83. Newsp.; 84. Nuc. sci.; 85. Oral hist.; 86. Petr./Energy; 87. Pharm.; 88. Phys./Astr./Math.; 89. Readg.; 90. Relig.; 91. Sci./Tech.; 92. Soc. sci.; 93. Telecom.; 94. Transp.; 95. (other).

Who's Who in Library and Information Services

CLENE: Bd. (1979–82). ALA: LAMA, various coms.; PLA, various coms. FL LA: PR Com. (1978–79); Stans. Com., Governance Subcom. (1981–82). **Pubns.:** "Friends of the Library and the Coordinating Role of the State Library of Florida," *FL Libs.* (N.–D. 1979); "Legal Basis of Library and Library Board in Florida Law," *FL Libs.* (Mr.–Ap., 1981); ed., contrib., "FL Library Trustee Education Program" audio cassette (1980). **Activities:** 4 **Addr.:** State Library of Florida, R. A. Gray Bldg., Tallahassee FL 32304.

Whitton, Donald Cleland (F. 14, 1940, San Francisco, CA) Head, Bayshore Lib., Daly City Pub. Lib., 1978–; Ref. Libn., San Mateo Pub. Lib., 1977–78; Libn., Kentfield Sch. Dist., 1973–75; Libn., San Mateo HS Dist., 1972–73. **Educ.:** Univ. of CA, Berkeley, 1958–62, BA (Grmn.); San Francisco State Univ., 1962–65, Cert. (Eng.); Univ. of San Francisco, 1970–71, Cert. (LS); Univ. of Denver, 1975–76, MA (LS). **Orgs.:** ARLIS/NA: N. CA Chap. (Ch., 1979–80). CA LA. ALA. **Pubns.:** *Percy Gray, 1869–1952* (1970); *The Grays of Salisbury: An Artist Family of Nineteenth Century England* (1976). **Activities:** 9, 10; 17, 21, 39; 55, 57, 89 **Addr.:** P.O. Box 562, Corte Madera, CA 94925.

Wiant, Sarah Kirsten (N. 20, 1946, Waverly, IA) Law Libn., Asst. Prof., Washington and Lee Univ., 1978–, Asst. Law Libn., 1972–77; Asst. Law Libn., TX Tech. Univ., 1970–72. **Educ.:** West. State Coll., 1964–68, BA (Soc. Std.); N. TX State Univ., 1968–70, MLS; Washington and Lee Univ., 1972–78, JD. **Orgs.:** AALL: Exec. Bd. (1981–82); Educ. Com. (Ch., 1977–80). ALA. SLA: VA Chap. (Pres., 1980–81). IALL. Various other orgs. Southeast. Admiralty Law Inst. VA State Bar Comp.-Assisted Legal Resrch. Com. U.S. Trademark Assn. U.S. Nvl. Inst. **Pubns.:** "Toward More Effective Continuing Education of Law Librarians," *Law Lib. Jnl.* (1979); "Government Documents Round Table, Legal Reference," *Southeast. Libn.* (O. 1975). **Addr.:** Law Library, Washington and Lee University, Lexington, VA 24450.

Wible, Joseph G. (F. 19, 1953, Washington, DC) Ref. Libn., Beverly Hills Pub. Lib., 1980–; Libn., Catalina Marine Sci. Ctr., 1977–79; Catlgr., GA Inst. of Tech., 1974–75. **Educ.:** GA State Univ., 1971–74, BS (Bio.); Emory Univ., 1974–75, MLn, (Med. Libnshp.); Univ. of South. CA, 1975– (Bio.). **Orgs.:** Med. LA. West. Socty. of Naturalists. **Honors:** Sigma Xi; Beta Phi Mu. **Pubns.:** Various presentations in bio. **Activities:** 1, 12; 39; 56, 58, 80 **Addr.:** Dept. of Biological Sciences, University of Southern California, Los Angeles, CA 90007.

Wichers, Jean Elaine (My. 24, 1925, Clay Center, KS) Assoc. Prof., LS, San Jose State Univ., 1965–; HS Libn., Monterey, 1963–65; Sch. Dist. Libn., San Jose, 1960–63. **Educ.:** KS State Univ., 1943–46, BS (Jnlsm.); San Jose State Univ., 1961–63, MA (LS). **Orgs.:** CA Assn. Sch. Libns.: Pres (1972–73); various other ofcs. ALA: AASL. AALS. Various other orgs. **Honors:** Tiger Awd., 1975. **Pubns.:** "Heart of the Humanities Program," *Wilson Lib. Bltn.* (1976); "Implementing the Multimedia Concept," *AV Instr.* (Ap. 1968); "Seaside High School Library," *CA Libn.* (v. 26, no. 1); lib. adv. com., *World Book* (1973–81); various other articles. **Activities:** 11; 63 **Addr.:** San Jose State University, San Jose, CA 95192.

Wick, Donald E. (F. 15, 1928, Enfield, Middlesex, Eng.) Actg. Univ. Libn., Univ. of Lethbridge, 1979–, Curric. Lab. Libn., 1975–79, Chief Libn., 1967–74; Libn., Selkirk Coll., 1965–67. **Educ.:** Cambridge Univ., 1949–52, MA (Hist.); Loushboro. Coll., 1952–53 (LS); LA UK, 1955–57, Assoc., 1957–, Fellow. **Orgs.:** Can. LA. Can. Assn. of Coll. and Univ. Libs. Bibl. Socty. of Can. **Activities:** 1, 2; 15, 17, 39; 55, 63, 92 **Addr.:** 1117 18th St. S., Lethbridge, AB T1K 2A4 Canada.

Wick, Hilda M. (My. 3, 1923, River Rouge, MI) Head, Ref. and Docum., OH Wesleyan Univ. Lib., 1962–, Assoc. Prof., 1968–, Asst. Prof., 1962–68; Bkmobile. Libn., DE Cnty. Dist. Lib., 1960–62; Instr., Eng., Drury Coll., 1958–60; Branch Libn., Chicago Pub. Lib., 1954; Head, Circ., Cedar Rapids Pub. Lib., 1950. **Educ.:** Univ. of MI, 1940–43, AB (Eng.), 1943–44, ABLS, 1945–47, AMLS. **Orgs.:** ALA: GODORT, Com. on the Constn. (1980–81). OH LA: Coll. and Univ. RT, Std. Com. on Fac. Status (Secy., 1969). Midwest Acad. Libns. Conf. Acad. Libns. Assn. of OH. AAUP. Natl. Org. for Women. Various OH Wesleyan Univ. coms. **Activities:** 1; 29, 31, 39; 55, 57, 61 **Addr.:** Beeghly Library, Ohio Wesleyan University, Delaware, OH 43015.

Wicker, William Walter (S. 11, 1930, Canaan, MS) Dir. of Libs., Univ. of Houston, Clear Lake City, 1973–; Assoc. Dir., Memphis State Univ., 1966–73; Head, Circ., MS State Univ., 1965–66; Libn., Fr .erick Coll., 1962–65; Serials Libn., Memphis State Univ., 1961–62; Head Libn., Sch. of the Ozarks, 1957–61; Dir. of Libs., Cap. Area Reg. Lib., MS, 1955–57. **Educ.:** Univ. of MS, 1947–51, BA (Eng.); LA State Univ., 1954–55, MS (LS); FL State Univ., 1970–77, AM (LS), PhD (LS). **Orgs.:** ALA. SWLA. TX LA: Exec. Bd. (1975–76). TX Cncl. of State Univ. Libns.: Exec. Bd. (1975–76). Various other orgs., ofcs. Rotary Club. Frnds. of Freeman Lib. **Pubns.:** "Planning a Library: The University of Houston at Clear Lake," *Lib. Scene* (Je. 1976); various other papers. **Activities:** 1; 17, 35 **Addr.:** University of Houston at Clear Lake City, 2700 Bay Area Blvd., Houston, TX 77058.

Wickliffe, Warren B. (Ag. 12, 1913, Louisville, KY) Ref. Libn. II, Burlingame Pub. Lib., 1955–; Acq. Libn., Univ. of OK Lib., 1953–55, Lower Div. Libn., 1951–53; Ref. Libn., Chicago Pub. Lib., 1950–51. **Educ.:** Olivet Coll., 1937–41, AB (Eng.); Univ. of Chicago, 1946–46, MA (Eng.), 1949–50, Cert. (LS). **Orgs.:** ALA. CA LA. Amer. Cvl. Liberties Un. **Activities:** 9; 15, 16, 39; 50, 55, 89 **Addr.:** 808 Edgehill Dr., Burlingame, CA 94010.

Wickman, Alma M. (N. 3, 1907, Bloomington, IL) Retired 1973–; Consult., NE Lib. Comsn., 1962–70; Head, Lewis and Clark Reg. Lib., 1968–73; Head Libn., Norfolk Pub. Lib., 1946–73; Asst. Libn., Grand Island Pub. Lib., 1945–46; Head Libn., Scottsbluff Pub. Lib., 1939–45; Libn., Morrill Pub. Lib., 1933–39. **Educ.:** NE Wesleyan Univ., 1927–32, BS (Bus. Admin); Univ. of Denver, 1939–41, BS (LS). **Orgs.:** ALA. Mt. Plains LA: Pubcty. Com. (1955). NE LA: Pres. (1959–60), Parlmt. (1962–63), Cit. Com. (1963–66), various ofcs. Wesleyan Srv. Gld. Bus. and Prof. Women's Club. Ord. of the East. Star. **Honors:** Norfolk Chamber of Cmrce., "Oscar," 1971–72; Delta Kappa Gamma; Norfolk Parent Tchr. Assn., NE Hon. Life Mem., 1973. **Activities:** 9; 17, 20, 24 **Addr.:** 1204 Norfolk Ave., Apt. 904, Norfolk, NE 68701.

Wickman, John E. (My. 24, 1929, Villa Park, IL) Dir., Dwight D. Eisenhower Lib., 1966–; Asst. Prof., Hist., Purdue Univ., 1965–66; Personal Asst. to Gvr., KS, 1964–65; Asst. Prof., Hist., NW MO State, 1962–64. **Educ.:** Elmhurst Coll., 1949–53, AB (Hist.); IN Univ., 1955–59, PhD (Hist.). **Orgs.:** SAA: Com. on Mss. (Ch., 1970–72); Ethics Com. (1977–79). Oral Hist. Assn.: Pres. (1972–73). West. Hist. Assn.: Cncl. (1972–75). KS State Hist. Socty: Pres. (1976–77). Various other orgs. **Honors:** Amer. Pol. Sci. Assn., Congsnl. Fellow, 1975; Elmhurst Coll., Disting. Alum., 1969; Natl. Ctr. for Educ. in Pol., Fac. Fellow, 1964. **Pubns.:** Ed., *D-Day: The Normandy Invasion in Retrospect* (1971); "Looking Forward: A Society at the Crossroads," *KS Hist.* (Spr. 1978); "The State of the Art: An Overview of Oral History," *Resrch. Qtly.* (Spr. 1973); jt. auth., "Gubernatorial Transitian in a One Party Setting," *Pub. Admin. Review* (Ja.–F. 1970); various other articles. **Activities:** 4; 17, 24, 41; 55, 86 **Addr.:** Dwight D. Eisenhower Library, Abilene, KS 67410.

Widener, Sarah A. (Je. 3, 1934, Wharton, TX) Lrng. Resrc. Spec., Westlake HS, 1969–; Libn., Eanes Elem. Sch., 1965–69. **Educ.:** Univ. of TX, 1953–56, BA (Eng.), 1964–65, Cert. (Sch. Lib.), 1974–76, MSLS. **Orgs.:** ALA: AASL. TX LA: Dist. 3 (Ch., 1979–80); Cncl. (1979–). TX Assn. Sch. Libns.: Resols. Com. (Ch., 1977–78). TX Assn. Educ. Tech.: Governing Bd. (1978–79). TX State Tchrs. Assn. Eanes Educ. Assn. **Honors:** Delta Kappa Gamma. **Pubns.:** Reviews. **Activities:** 10; 17, 32, 48; 63 **Addr.:** 203 Westbrook Dr., Austin, TX 78746.

Widenmann, Elizabeth A. (S. 6, 1935, Orange, NJ) African Biblgphr., Catlgr., Columbia Univ. Libs., 1972–, Catlgr., 1970–72; Ed., The Rockefeller Fndn., 1959–68. **Educ.:** Radcliffe Coll., 1953–57, AB (Pol. Sci.); London Sch. of Econ., 1957–58 (Pol. Sci.); Columbia Univ., 1968–69, MS (LS), 1969–70, Cert. (African Std.). **Orgs.:** ALA: ACRL/Asian and African Sect. Exec. Com. (Secy. 1973–76); IR RT, Plng. Com. (1980); RTSD/Cat. and Class. Sect., Com. on Cat., Asian and African Mtrls. (1979–), Com. on Cat., Descr. and Access. (IRRT Rep., 1980–); Subj. Anal. Com., Subcom. on Subj. Cat. of African and Asian Mtrls. (1976–78). African Std. Assn: Arch.-Libs. Com., Exec. Bd. (Ch., 1979–80), Subcom. on Cat. and Class. (Ch., 1975–78). Coop. Africana Micro. Proj.: Exec. Com. (1974–78, 1979–80). **Honors:** Beta Phi Mu. **Pubns.:** Reviews. **Activities:** 1; 15, 20, 39; 54, 92 **Addr.:** 159 W. 53rd St., New York, NY 10019.

Wiedenhoefer, Joyce C. (Jl. 28, 1944, Hancock, MI) Branch Libn., Cleveland Pub. Lib., 1978–, Asst. Head, Gen. Ref., 1974–78, Actg. Head, 1976–77, Ref. Libn., 1969–73. **Educ.:** Albion Coll., 1962–66, AB (Eng., Fr.); Univ. of MI, 1968–69, AMLS. **Orgs.:** OH LA. Cleveland Pub. Lib. Staff Assn. **Honors:** Phi Beta Kappa; Beta Phi Mu. **Activities:** 9; 17 **Addr.:** 3286 E. Scarborough, Cleveland Heights, OH 44118.

Wiegand, Wayne A. (Ap. 15, 1946, WI) Asst. Prof., LS, Univ. of KY, 1976–; Coll. Libn., Urbana Coll., 1974–76; Instr., Northwest. Acad. (Lake Geneva, WI), 1968–70. **Educ.:** Univ. of WI, Oshkosh, 1964–68, BA (Hist.); Univ. of WI, Milwaukee, 1968–70, MA (Hist.); West. MI Univ., 1973–74, MLS; South. IL Univ., 1970–74, PhD (Hist.). **Orgs.:** ALA: YASD, various coms.; LHRT; LRRT. Pop. Culture Assn. Beta Phi Mu: Chapbook Series, Ed. **Honors:** ALA, Herbert Putnam Awd., 1975, ALA, LRRT, Paper Prize, 1978; Phi Alpha Theta, Paper Prize, 1973. **Pubns.:** *History of A Hoax* (1979); "The Wayward Bookman," *Amer. Libs.* (Mr., Ap., 1977); Herbert Putnam's Appointment as Librarian of Congress," *Lib. Qtly.* (Jl., 1979); "Popular Culture: A New Frontier in Academic Libraries," *Jnl. of Acad. Libnshp.* (S. 1979); various other articles. **Activities:** 11; 95-Pop. culture. **Addr.:** College of Library Science, University of Kentucky, Lexington, KY 40506.

Wiener, Theodore (S. 28, 1918, Stettin, Prussia Germany) Judaica Catlgr., Subj. Cat. Div., Lib. of Congs., 1964–; Head Catlgr., Hebrew Un. Coll. Lib., 1963–64; Hebraica Libn., Cincinnati, OH 1959–63, Hebrew Catlgr., 1950–59; Rabbi, 1943–48. **Educ.:** Univ. of Cincinnati, 1936–40, BA (Hist.); Hebrew Un. Coll., 1936–43, Rabbi (Judaica). **Orgs.:** AJL: Resrch. and Spec. Libs. Div., various ofcs. (1966–). Cncl. of Natl. Lib. and Info. Assns.: Bd. (Ch., 1978–79). Untd. Jewish Appeal: Gvt. Div. (Bd., 1966–). Jewish Cmnty. Cncl., Washington. Ctrl. Conf. of Amer. Rabbis. **Pubns.:** "The writings of Leo Baeck," *Std. in Bibl. and Booklore* (1954); "The Writings of Samuel S. Cohon," *Std. in Bibl. and Booklore* (1956); various articles in *Universal Jewish Encyclopedia* (1943) and *Encyclopedia Judaica* (1971). **Activities:** 1, 4; 20, 39; 66, 90, 95-Judaica. **Addr.:** 1701 N. Kent St., Arlington, VA 22209.

Wiens, Allan L. (Jl. 30, 1929, Morse, SK) Dir., Lib. and Lrng. Resrcs., Olivet Nazarene Coll., 1970–, Asst. Dir. and Ref. Libn., 1968–70, Ref. Libn. 1967–68; Libn., Borgess Hosp., 1966–67. **Educ.:** Can. Nazarene Coll., 1950–54, ThB; Nazarene Theo. Semy., 1956–59, BD, Seattle Pac. Coll., 1963–65, BA (Hist.), West. MI Univ., 1965–66, MSL; Univ. of IL, 1979–80, crs. for Cert. of Advnc. Std. **Orgs.:** ALA. AECT. **Pubns.:** Bk. review ed., *Christ. Libn.* (1976–77); reviews. **Activities:** 1, 2; 17, 19, 32 **Addr.:** Library, Olivet Nazarene College, Kankakee, IL 60901.

Wigg, Ristiina M. (N. 16, 1946, Cheboygan, MI) Chld. Srvs. Consult., Mid-Hudson Lib. Syst., 1971–. **Educ.:** Oakland Univ., 1964–68, BA (Eng.); Univ. of MI, 1970–71, AMLS. **Orgs.:** NY LA: Chld. and YA Sect. Pres. (1981), VP (1980), Secy. (1977–78). Dutchess Cnty. LA: Pres. (1980), VP (1979–80). Natl. Org. for Women: Mid–Hudson Chap. (VP, 1978–80). **Pubns.:** "Spreading the News About Library Service," *The Bookmark* (Fall 1980); *We Want Sunshine in Our Houses* (1973); "Library Service to Children: What Makes it Effective," *The Bookmark* (Sum. 1978). **Activities:** 9; 21, 48 **Addr.:** Mid-Hudson Library System, 103 Market St., Poughkeepsie, NY 12601.

Wiggins, Beacher James Earl (My. 2, 1948, Warren Cnty., NC) Sect. Head, Descr. Cat. Spec., Lib. of Congs., 1972–. **Educ.:** Howard Univ., 1966–70, BA (Eng.); Univ. of WI, 1970–72, MA (LS). **Orgs.:** ALA: RTSD. **Activities:** 4; 20 **Addr.:** Descriptive Cataloging Division, Library of Congress, Washington, DC 20540.

Wiggins, Gary Dorman (S. 15, 1943, Ft. Knox, KY) Head, Chem. Lib., Dir., Chem. Info. Ctr., IN Univ., 1976–; Slavic Acq. Libn., Univ. of IL, 1972–76; Sci. Catlgr., IN Univ., 1970–71. **Educ.:** IN Univ., 1962–66, BA (Chem., Russ.), 1966–68, MA (Slavic), 1969–71, MLS, 1976–80 (LS). **Orgs.:** ALA: Slavic Sect. (1973). SLA: Chem. Div. (Secy., 1979–81). Amer. Chem. Socty. AAUP. Jaycees. **Pubns.:** *English-Language Sources for Reference Questions Related to Soviet Science* (1972); transl., "A Man" by Vladimir Mayakovsky, *Russ. Lit. Triqtly.* (Spr. 1975). **Activities:** 1, 12; 15, 26, 44; 60, 75, 91 **Addr.:** Chemistry Library, Indiana University, Bloomington, IN 47405.

Wiggins, Minnie Marguerite (Ap. 6, 1925, Mountolive, NC) Assoc. Prof., NC Libn., E. Carolina Univ., 1968–, Instr., 1964–68; Undergrad. Libn., Univ. of SC, 1964. **Educ.:** E. Carolina Univ., 1944–47, BA (Hist., Sci.); Univ. of NC, 1962–64, MSLS. **Orgs.:** NC LA. ALA: ACRL. NC Lit. and Hist. Assn. Assn. of Histns. of E. NC. NC Pres. Socty. Pitte Cnty. Hist. Socty. **Activities:** 1; 45; 69, 73 **Addr.:** 1108 E. 10th, Apt. 2C, Greenville, NC 27834.

Wiggins, Theresa Soulé (O. 28, 1950, Fresno, CA) Assoc. Libn., Med. Coll. of PA/East. PA Psyt. Inst., 1981–; Psy. Libn., Princeton Univ., 1973–80. **Educ.:** Univ. of South. CA, 1968–72, BA (Psy.), Univ. of IL, 1972–73, MSLS. **Orgs.:** ALA. Philadelphia Area Ref. Libns. Info. Exch. Med. LA. **Honors:** Beta Phi Mu. **Pubns.:** *Guide to Reference Books in Psychology* ED 183 171; "Guide to Reference Books in Psychology," *JSAS Cat. of Selected Docums. in Psy.* (1980). **Activities:** 1; 15, 17, 39; 92 **Addr.:** 9233 Wissinoming St., Philadelphia, PA 19114.

Wikander, Ethel Marie (F. 20, 1917, Washington, DC) Asst. Libn., Clark Art Inst. Lib., 1971–, Catlgr., 1968–71; Head, Circ., Smith Coll. Lib., 1964–68, Asst. Head, Cat. Dept., 1963–64, Catlgr., 1953–63; Head, Msc. Div., DC Pub. Lib., Asst. and Supvsr., various positions, 1937–45. **Educ.:** Amer. Univ., 1933–37, BA (Pol. Sci.); Columbia Univ., 1938–39, BS (LS). **Orgs.:** Msc. LA: Various coms. New Eng. LA. MA LA: Plng. Com. (1965–66). ARLIS/NA. Hampshire Choral Socty. Leag. of Women Voters. Northampton (MA) Sch. Bldg. Com. **Activities:** 5, 12; 20, 35, 39; 55 **Addr.:** Clark Art Institute Library, P.O. Box 8, Williamstown, MA 01267.

Wikander, Lawrence Einar (D. 16, 1915, Pittsburgh, PA) Coll. Libn., Williams Coll.; Libn., Forbes Lib. (Northampton, MA), 1950–68; Asst. Libn., Temple Univ., 1946–50. **Educ.:** Williams Coll., 1933–37, BA (Pol. Sci.); Columbia Univ., 1938–39, BS (LS); Univ. of PA, 1946–49, MA (Hist.). **Orgs.:** ALA: Cncl. (1962–68). New Eng. LA: Pres. (1967–68), Treas. (1963–65). MA LA: Pres. (1960–61). W. MA Lib. Club: Pres. (1953–55). Calvin Coolidge Meml. Fndn: Dir. (1969–). AAUP: Chap. Pres. (1974–76). S. Mt. Concert Assn.: Dir. (1975–). Com. for a New Eng. Bibl.: Bibl. **Pubns.:** *Disposed to Learn* (1972); *Calvin Coolidge: A Chronological Summary* (1957); "Symposium on Title IIA," *Jnl. of Acad. Libnshp.* (S. 1979); "Inside the New

PROFESSIONAL ACTIVITIES: Institutions: 1. Acad. lib.; 2. Arch.; 3. Assn.; 4. Fed./Gvt. lib.; 5. Inst. lib.; 6. Mfr./Suppl.; 7. Milit. lib.; 8. Musm.; 9. Pub. lib.; 10. Sch. lib.; 11. Sch. of lib. sci.; 12. Spec. lib.; 13. State lib.; 14. (other). **Functions/Activities:** 15. Acq./Col. dev.; 16. Adult srvs.; 17. Admin.; 18. Apprais.; 19. Archit./Bldgs.; 20. Cat./Class.; 21. Chld. srvs.; 22. Circ.; 23. Cons./Pres.; 24. Consult.; 25. Cont. ed.; 26. Educ. lib. sci.; 27. Ext. srvs.; 28. Fund/Grants; 29. Gvt. pubs.; 30. Indx./Abs.; 31. Instr. lib. use; 32. Media srvs.; 33. Micro.; 34. Netwks./Coop.; 35. Persnl.; 36. PR; 37. Publshg.; 38. Recs. mgt.; 39. Ref. srvs.; 40. Repro.; 41. Resrch.; 42. Review.; 43. Secur.; 44. Serials; 45. Spec. col.; 46. Tech. srvs.; 47. Trustees/Bds.; 48. YA srvs.; 49. (other).

Sawyer Library," *Williams Alum. Rev.* (Fall 1975); various bks. **Activities:** 1, 9; 17, 20, 45; 73, 92 **Addr.:** Williams College Library, Williamstown, MA 01267.

Wilbanks, Mary Elizabeth (Ap. 15, 1920, Eastaboga, AL) Hum. Libn., Auburn Univ. Lib., 1976–, Spec. Coll. Libn., 1963–76; Gift Exch. Libn., 1959–63. **Educ.:** Montevallo Univ., 1938–42, AB (Hist.); Emory Univ., 1946–48, MA (Eng.); Univ. of NC, 1951–56 (Eng.), 1957–59, MSLS. **Orgs.:** AL LA: Bibl. Com. (1966–71, 1972–78); Lit. Awds. Com. (1979–81); Legis. Com. (1981). SELA. ALA. AAUW. **Honors:** Beta Phi Mu. **Pubns.:** Various articles in *Auburn Lib. Topics.* **Activities:** 1; 39; 55 **Addr.:** 46 Woodland Terr., Auburn, AL 36830.

Wilbert, Shirley S. (Detroit, MI) Assoc. Dean, Univ. of WI, Oshkosh, 1980–, Asst. Prof., LS, 1977–; Instr., Wayne State Univ., 1976–77; Trng. Concepts, Prog. Dev. Anal., Chrysler Lrng., Inc., 1976; Media Spec., Detroit Pub. Schs., 1957–76. **Educ.:** Wayne State Univ., 1952–57, BS (LS), 1972–74, MSLS, 1974–76, PhD (Instr. Tech.). **Orgs.:** AALS. Univ. Club. Oshkosh Symph. Assn. Fac. Dames. **Honors:** Alpha Kappa Alpha. **Pubns.:** "Library Pathfinders Come Alive," *Jnl. of Educ. for Libnshp.* (Spr. 1982); *Learning in Today's Library/Media Center* (1981); *A Media Collection for the Disadvantaged and Handicapped* (1979). **Activities:** 10, 11 **Addr.:** College of Letters & Science, University of Wisconsin-Oshkosh 800 Algoma Blvd., Oshkosh, WI 54901.

Wilbur, Sharon Faye (My. 16, 1941, Fort Worth, TX) Cat. Libn., White Sands Missile Range Post Lib., 1980–; Cat. Libn., U.S. Milit. Acad. Lib., 1969–80; Supervisory Libn., Ft. Sill Post Lib. 1968–69, Ref. Libn., 1966–68. **Educ.:** Univ. of TX, Arlington, 1959–61; TX Woman's Univ., 1961–63, BA (LS), 1965–66, MLS. **Orgs.:** ALA. SLA. NM LA. AAUW. Sci. Fiction Resrch. Assn. **Activities:** 1, 9; 20, 39, 46; 56 **Addr.:** Post Library, Bldg. 464, White Sands Missile Range, NM 88002.

Wilcox, Alice Erlander (Jl. 2, 1925, Poy Sippi, WI) Dir., MINITEX, 1969–; Circ. Lib., Univ. of MN, 1964–68; Libn., Corp. of Trinity Church, New York, 1960–63; Mgr., Cross Current Bk. Store, 1957–59; Partner, Leslie Larson Lighting Dsgn., 1953–56; Deputy Zone Dir., Luth. World Fed., Srv. to Refugees, Germany, 1948–51. **Educ.:** St. Olaf Coll., 1943–47, BA (Hist., Soclgy.); Columbia Univ., 1962–64, MS (LS). **Orgs.:** MN LA: Acad. and Resrch. Div. (Secy., 1972–74), Bd. (1975–79). ALA: RASD, ILL Com. (Ch., 1975–76); Coll. and Resrch. Sect., various coms.; Cncl. (MN Rep., 1975–79); Legis. Com., Ad Hoc Copyrt. Subcom. (1978–). Assn. of Coop. Lib. Orgs.: Exec. Com. (Ch., 1977). MIDLNET: Exec. Com. (1975–76, 1980–). Perry Jones Fndn. Natl. Comsn. on New Tech. Uses of Copyrighted Works: Comsn. (1975–78). Pre-White Hse. Conf. on Netwks.: Adv. Com. (1978–). Lib. of Congs.: Adv. Com. on MARC-Newspapers. **Honors:** MN LA, MN Libn. of the Year, 1974; St. Olaf Coll., Doctor of Letters, honoris causa, 1978. **Pubns.:** *Minnesota Union List of Serials* (1974, 1977, 1979, 1980); "Networks: Description of Operational Systems—MINITEX," *Networks and the University Library, Proceedings of an Institute* (1973); "Minnesota Annual Review," *ALA Yearbk.* (1976, 1977, Jt. Auth., 1978, 1979); "Copyright," *ALA Yearbk.* (1979); "Library Resource Sharing," *ALA Encyc.* (1979). **Activities:** 1, 14-Netwk.; 34, 44; 56, 61, 78 **Addr.:** MINITEX, 30 Wilson Library, 309 19th Ave. S., University of Minnesota, Minneapolis, MN 55455.

Wilcox, June (Jl. 4, 1925, Los Angeles, CA) Head, Prep. Dept., Huntington Lib., 1974–, Assoc. Prep. Libn., 1967–74, Catlgr., 1958–67; Post Libn. U.S. Army Spec. Srvs. (Verdun, France) 1957–58; Fld. Libn. U.S. Army (Germany), 1956–57; Catlgr., Huntington Lib., 1950–55. **Educ.:** Occidental Coll., 1947, AB (Eng.); Univ. of MI, 1950, MALS. **Orgs.:** South. CA Tech. Prcs. Grp. **Activities:** 1; 15, 17, 46; 55 **Addr.:** Huntington Library, 1151 Oxford Rd., San Marino, CA 91108.

Wilde, Daniel U. (D. 27, 1937, Wilmington, OH) Dir., New Eng. Resrch. Application Ctr., Univ. of CT, 1972–, Prof., Info. Admin., 1974–, Assoc. Dir., NERAC, 1966–71, Assoc. Prof., 1972–74. **Educ.:** Univ. of IL, 1957–61, BS (Electrical Engin.); MA Inst. of Tech., 1962–66, MS, PhD (Comp. Sci.). **Orgs.:** Assn. of Sci. and Info. Ctrs.: Pres. (1979–), Secy.-Treas. (1976–79). Engin. Index: Trustee (1977–). **Honors:** NASA, Pub. Srv. Awd., 1975. **Pubns.:** *Introduction to Computing* (1972); "Using a Small Low-cost Computer in an Information Center," *Cost Reduction for Special Libraries and Information Centers* (1973); "Computerized Chemical Information Retrieval Techniques," *Jnl. Chem. Info. and Comp. Sci.* (1975); jt. auth., "Reduction of Data Generation Costs," *Jnl. ASIS* (1975); various other articles, reviews. **Activities:** 14-Tech. transfer ctr.; 17, 24, 46; 52, 59, 75 **Addr.:** New England Research Application Center Mansfield Professional Park, Storrs, CT 06268.

Wildemuth, Barbara Marie (Je. 13, 1950, Kewanee, IL) Assoc. Dir., ERIC/TM, Educ. Testing Srv., 1979–, Head, Test Col., 1978–79, ERIC User Srvs. Coord., 1976–78, ERIC Indxr/Abstctr., 1976. **Educ.:** N. Ctrl. Coll., 1968–71, BME (Msc. Educ.); Univ. of IL, 1975–76, MLS. **Orgs.:** ASIS: Info. Srvs. to Educ. Grp. Alternate Cabinet Rep. (1978–80), Ch.-Elect. (1980–81). SLA. Natl. Cncl. on Measur. in Educ.: *Measurement News* Ed. (1979–81). **Pubns.:** "Procedures for Identifying and Selecting a Minimum Competency Test," *Educ. Libs.* (Fall 1979). **Activities:** 4, 6; 17, 30, 36; 63 **Addr.:** ERIC Clearinghouse on Tests, Measurement, and Evaluation, Educational Testing Service, Princeton, NJ 08541.

Wilder, David T. (N. 26, 1917, Rochester, NY) Dir., Long Island Lib. Resrcs. Cncl., 1971–; Dir. of Libs., Univ. of MB, 1966–71; Prog. Spec., Univ. Libs., Mid. E. Reg., Ford Fndn., 1964–66; Univ. Libn., Oakland Univ., 1960–64; Asst. Dir. of Libs., Pub. Srvs., OH State Univ., 1954–60; Univ. Libn., Amer. Univ. of Beirut, 1951–54; Coll. Libn., Hamilton Coll., 1946–51; Fellow, Intl. Lib. Rel., ALA, 1946. **Educ.:** Un. Coll., 1936–40, AB (Soc. Std.); Univ. of Rochester, 1940–41, MA (Hist.); Columbia Univ., 1941–42, BS (LS). **Orgs.:** ALA: Cncl. (1948–51); Panel on UNESCO (1959–62); IR RT (Ch., 1966–67). NY LA: Cncl. (1948–51); Com. for Gvr.'s Conf. (1975–77). AAUP. **Pubns.:** *The Acquisition and Control of Publications from the Near and Middle East* (1959); "Regions' Colleges Should Cooperate," *Lib. Jnl.* (1949); "A Look at the Library of the Future," *Can. Lib. Jnl.* (1969); "Management Attitudes: Team Relationships," *Lib. Jnl.* (1969). **Activities:** 1, 14-Multi-type systs.; 17, 30, 34; 54, 74, 75 **Addr.:** 6 Broadview Ave., Bellport, NY 11713.

Wilder, Ulah (F. 18, 1916, Augusta, IN) Prof. Emeritus, Oakland City Coll., 1981–, Head Libn., Assoc. Prof., 1962–81, Asst. Libn., 1956–62. **Educ.:** Oakland City Coll., 1953–56, BA (Soc. Std.), IN State Univ., 1956–59, MA (LS). **Orgs.:** ALA. IN LA: Dist. V (Vice Ch., 1968), Dist. VII (Ch., 1975). Four Rivers Area Lib. Srv. Athrty. **Honors:** Sigma Kappa Sigma. **Activities:** 1, 12; 17, 20, 34; 63, 90, 92 **Addr.:** 218 N. Clay St., Oakland City, IN 47660.

Wildman, S. Kay (My. 6, 1942, Manhattan, KS) Msc. Libn., Marshall Univ., 1974–; Msc. Consult., KS City (KS) Pub. Schs., 1970–73; Elem. Msc. Tchr., Shawnee Missn., 1969–70; Elem. Msc. Tchr., Clay Ctr., 1965–68. **Educ.:** Emporia State Univ., 1960–65, BME (Organ), 1968–69, MM (Organ); George Peabody Coll., 1973–74, MLS. **Orgs.:** Msc. LA. WV LA. Amer. Gld. of Organists. Huntington Cham. Orch. AAUW. **Activities:** 1; 17, 20, 39; 55 **Addr.:** 1002 1/2 13th St., Huntington, WV 25701.

Wile, Raymond R. (Ja. 29, 1923, New York, NY) Coord., Bk. Sel., Queens Coll. (NY), Lib., 1978–, Biblgphr. for Hist., Ref. Libn., 1975–, Supvsr., Evening Srvs., 1967–75; HS Libn., Great Neck (NY), 1956–67. **Educ.:** Queens Coll., 1941–46, BA (Hist., Educ.); Columbia Univ., 1946–48, MA (Hist), 1948, 1954–55, MS (LS). **Orgs.:** ALA: ACRL. NY LA: Coll. Lib. Sect.; Resrcs. and Tech. Srv. Sect. LA City Univ. Assn. for Rec. Snd. Cols. **Pubns.:** *Edison Disc Recordings* (1978); "The Wonder of the Age" *Phonographs and Gramophones* (1977); various articles on the hist. of sound recs. **Activities:** 1; 15, 39; 55, 57, 92 **Addr.:** 195-28 37th Ave., Flushing, NY 11358.

Wiler, Linda Lou (Jl. 31, 1940, Chicago, IL) Head, Ref. Dept., FL Atl. Univ. Lib., 1972–; Libn. I, II, III, Chicago Pub. Lib., 1966–72; Catlgr., Univ. of Chicago, 1965–66; Sci. Libn., John Crerar Lib., 1963–65. **Educ.:** Univ. of CA, Los Angeles, 1961–62, BA (Hist.), 1962–63, MLS. **Orgs.:** ALA. FL LA. Palm Beach Cnty. LA: Pres. (1980–81). Org. Amer. Histns. Acad. of Pol. Sci. **Pubns.:** Cmplr., FL sect., *Municipal Government Reference Sources* (1978); contrib., *History and Historians Workbook* (1961). **Activities:** 1, 9; 36, 39, 47; 70, 77, 92 **Addr.:** Florida Atlantic University Library, Boca Raton, FL 33431.

Wiley, David Sherman (N. 9, 1935, Eldorado, IL) Dir., African Std. Ctr., African Media Ctr., Asst. Prof., Dept. of Soclgy., MI State Univ., 1977–; Assoc. Dir., African Std. Ctr., 1977; Ch., African Std. Prog., (Lang. and Area Std. Prog.), Univ. of WI, Madison, 1972–76, Asst. Prof., Dept. of Soclgy., 1970–76, Instr., 1968–70; Resrch. Afflt., Inst. for Soc. Resrch., Univ. of Zambia, 1966–67; Race Rel. Fld. Worker, Salisbury, Rhodesia, 1961–63. **Educ.:** Wabash Coll., 1953–57, BA (Zlgy., Chem.); Yale Univ., 1957–61, BD (Relig., Higher Educ.); Univ. Coll. of Rhodesia and Nyasaland, 1961–63 (Soc. Anthro. of Change, Law, Ethnography); Princeton Theo. Semy. and Univ., 1963–67, 1967–71, PhD (Soclgy., Soclgy. of Relig.). **Orgs.:** Assn. of African Std. Progs.: Exec. Com. (1978). Natl. Cncl. on Frgn. Langs. and Intl. Std.: Task Frc. on Elem., Sec., and Undergrad. Educ. (1980–82). Amer. Soclgy. Assn.: Com. on World Soclgy. (Ch., 1977–82), African Liaison Subcom. (Ch., 1978–82). **Honors:** Dept. of State, U.S. White Hse. Ofc. of Sci. and Tech. Policy, Africanist Adv. for Acad. Team, Del. to Nigeria, Zimbabwe, Kenya, and Senegal, 1980. **Pubns.:** *Africa in Film and Videotape: Reviews of Instructional Audiovisuals in the USA* (forthcoming); *Africa in Audiovisual Materials: Maps, Transparencies, Filmstrips, Slides, and Tapes in Critical Review* (1982); various soclgy. pubns., African std. **Activities:** 12; 25, 27, 32; 54, 67, 70 **Addr.:** African Studies Center, Michigan State University, 100 Center for International Programs, E. Lansing, MI 48824.

Wilford, Valerie Jane (D. 6, 19–, Indianapolis, IN) Asst. Prof., LS, IL State Univ., 1969–, HS Media Spec., Burbank, 1962–69; HS Libn., Moline, 1961–62. **Educ.:** IL State Univ., 1958–62, BS (Educ., Thea.); Univ. of IL, 1968, MS (LS); Univ. of MN, 1974 (LS). **Orgs.:** ALA: AASL, Jt. Com. with Amer. Sch., Couns. Assn. (Ch., 1973–77). IL LA: AACR2 Statewide Trng. Prog. (Proj. Dir., 1980–81); Cont. Educ. Com.; Exec. Bd. (1975–81). IL Assn. Sch. Libns.: Pres (1975–76). IL Assn. Media in Educ.: Stans. Com. (Ch., 1978–80). Various other orgs. and ofcs. **Honors:** IL Assn. for Media in Educ., Hon. Awd., 1980. **Pubns.:** "Questing for Competencies," *IL Libs.* (S. 1978); "Special Report on the IL WHCOLIS," *Illinois Public* (Win. 1978); *Illinois Public School Library/Media Centers: A Descriptive Report.* **Activities:** 10, 11; 20, 25, 32; 50, 63 **Addr.:** 1110 E. Jefferson, Bloomington, IL 61701.

Wilhelm, Mary Lou (S. 27, 1937, Custer, SD) Dir., Lib. Srvs., Cuesta Coll., 1976–; Head Libn., Orange Coast Coll., 1969–76, Pub. Srvs. Libn., 1966–69; Cat./Ref. Libn., San Marino Pub. Lib., 1964–66. **Educ.:** Concordia Tchrs. Coll., 1960, BS (Elem. Educ.); Univ. of South. CA, 1966, MS (LS). **Orgs.:** CA LA. Natl. Libns. Assn. Tri-Cnty. Film Coop.: Bd. (1976–). Lib. and Media People of San Luis Obispo Cnty.: Exec. Bd. (1977–). Various other orgs. and ofcs. AAUW. Natl. Org. of Women. **Activities:** 1; 17 **Addr.:** Cuesta College Library, P.O. Box J, San Luis Obispo, CA 93406.

Wilkas, Lenore Rae (Jl. 11, 1948, Geneva, IL) South. Sales Rep., Scholarly Bk. Ctr., Inc., 1981–; Head, Ord. Dept., Univ. of SC Lib., 1978–81; Asst. Serials Libn., Univ. of TX, 1976–78; Asst. Serials Catlgr., Northwest. Univ., 1973–76; Adult Srvs. Libn., Chicago Pub. Lib., 1973; Head, Serials Dept., Drake Univ. Lib., 1971–73. **Educ.:** Case West. Rsv. Univ., 1966–68; Univ. of WI, 1968–70, BA (Hist.); 1970–71, MALS. **Orgs.:** ALA. SC LA. SELA. **Honors:** Beta Phi Mu. **Activities:** 1; 15, 44, 46 **Addr.:** 400 Serpentine Rd., Irmo, SC 29063.

Wilken, Madeleine J. (S. 25, 1947, Alexandria, VA) Asst. Libn., Tech. Srvs., Univ. of TX Sch. of Law, 1981–; Assoc. Libn., West. New Eng. Coll. Sch. of Law, 1978–81; Asst. Libn., O'-Melveny and Myers, 1976–77. **Educ.:** Boston Univ., 1965–67; Amer. Univ., 1967–72, BA (Hist.); Boston Univ., 1973–76, JD; Cath. Univ., 1976–77, MLS. **Orgs.:** AALL: Autom. and Sci. Dev. Sect. (1980–); Rels. with Publshrs. and Dlrs. Com. (1980–), Rcrt. Com. (1981). Law Libns. of New Eng.: Actg. VP (1980–). Amer. Bar Assn. MA Bar. U.S. Dist. Court (MA) Bar. **Pubns.:** Ed., *Law Libs. of New Eng. Nsltr.* (1980–). **Activities:** 1, 12; 17, 35, 39; 56, 77, 78 **Addr.:** Tarlton Law Library, University of Texas at Austin School of Law, 727 E. 26th St., Austin, TX 78705.

Wilkens, Lea-Ruth C. (Jl. 19, 1934, Hamburg, Germany) Assoc. Prof., Univ. of Houston, Clear Lake City, 1974–; Asst. Prof., Univ. of IL, 1973–74; Asst. Prof., Univ. of Miami (FL), 1969–73. **Educ.:** Univ. of WI, Milwaukee, 1957–64, BS (Educ.); Univ. of IL, 1965–66, MS (LS); Univ. of Pittsburgh, 1969–73, PhD (LS). **Orgs.:** ALA. TX LA. Intl. Resrch. Socty. of Chld. Lit. **Honors:** Bay Area (TX) Litcy. Awd., 1980. **Pubns.:** *Why Your Child Can Read* (1980); "Love Gifts to Texas Children through Storytelling," *TX Lib. Jnl.* (Fall 1980); "The School Library-The Alpha and Omega of Your Elementary School Reading Program," *Readg. Horizons* (Fall 1979); reviews. **Activities:** 11; 63 **Addr.:** University of Houston at Clear Lake City, 2700 Bay Area Blvd., Houston, TX 77058.

Wilkerson, Mary I. (Ja. 24, 1921, West Helena, AR) Retired, 1981–; Lib. Consult., Jefferson Cnty. (KY) Pub. Schs., 1972–; Sch. Libn., Louisville, KY, 1965–72. **Educ.:** Univ. of Ctrl. AR, 1938–42, BSE (Eng.); Spalding Coll., 1964–67, MSLS; Univ. of Louisville, 1973–74, Spec. (Educ.). **Orgs.:** ALA. AECT: Prog. Plng. Com. (1977); Affirmative Action Com. (1978). KY Sch. Media Assn: Schol. Com. (Ch., 1979). KY LA: Lcl. Arrange. Com. (1975). Various other orgs., ofcs. **Honors:** Delta Kappa Gamma. Phi Kappa Phi. (KY Assn. for Comms. and Tech., Edgar Dale Awd., 1976. **Activities:** 10; 17, 24, 32; 85 **Addr.:** 209 Bellemeade Rd., Louisville, KY 40222.

Wilkes, Adeline W. (N. 5, 1926, Dalton, GA) Libn., LS Lib., FL State Univ., 1969–. **Educ.:** Wesleyan Coll., 1943–47, AB (Eng.); FL State Univ., 1966–68, MS (LS); 1977, AMD (LS). **Orgs.:** AALS: Teller's Com. (1981–82). FL LA: PR Com. (1979–81), Teller's Com. (Ch., 1980). ALA: ACRL. SELA. Various other orgs., ofcs. **Honors:** Beta Phi Mu. **Activities:** 1, 11; 15, 17, 20; 75 **Addr.:** Library Science Library, Florida State University, Tallahassee, FL 32306.

Wilkie, Everett C. (Je. 27, 1947, Kinston, NC) Biblgphr., J.C. Brown Lib., Brown Univ., 1981–; Ref. Libn., Lilly Lib., IN Univ., 1980–81; Resrch. Assoc., Brown Univ. 1978–80. **Educ.:** Campbell Coll., Wake Forest Univ., 1965–69, BA (Eng.); Wake Forest Univ., 1969–70, MA (Eng.); Univ. of SC, 1973–77, PhD (Comp. Lit.), Univ. of SC, 1977–78, ML. **Orgs.:** ALA. Medieval Acad. of Amer. Natl. Trust for Hist. Prsrvn. Southeast. Medvl. Assn. Amer. Lit. Transl. Assn. **Pubns.:** "'Marc-Antoine Eidous' Translation of Daniel Defoe's *A History of Discoveries and Improvements,*" *Papers of the Bibl. Socty. of Amer.* (1980); "Our Lady's Tumbler," *Allegorica* (Spr., 1979); "The Anglo-Norman Resurrection (C Text)," *Allegorica* (Win. 1978); various biog. articles; presentations. **Activities:** 1; 39, 45; 57 **Addr.:** John Carter Brown Library, Brown University, Providence, RI 02912.

Wilkins, Barratt (N. 6, 1943, Atlanta, GA) State Libn., State Lib. of FL, 1977–, Asst. State Libn., 1973–77; Inst. Libn., MO State Lib., 1971–73; Ref. Libn., SC State Lib., 1969–71. **Educ.:** Emory Univ., 1961–65, BA (Hist.); GA State Univ.,

Special Subjects/Services: 50. Adult educ.; 51. Advert./Mktg.; 52. Aerosp.; 53. Agric.; 54. Area std.; 55. Arts/Hum.; 56. Autom.; 57. Bibl./Prtg.; 58. Bio. sci.; 59. Bus./Fin.; 60. Chem.; 61. Copyrt.; 62. Documtn.; 63. Educ.; 64. Engin.; 65. Env.; 66. Eth. grps.; 67. Film; 68. Food/Nutr.; 69. Geneal.; 70. Geo.; 71. Geol.; 72. Handcpd.; 73. Hist.; 74. Int. frdm.; 75. Info. sci.; 76. Insr.; 77. Law; 78. Legis.; 79. Math./Comp. sci.; 80. Med.; 81. Metals; 82. Nat. resrcs.; 83. Newsp.; 84. Nuc. sci.; 85. Oral hist.; 86. Petr./Energy; 87. Pharm.; 88. Phys./Astr./Math.; 89. Readg.; 90. Relig.; 91. Sci./Tech.; 92. Soc. sci.; 93. Telecom.; 94. Transp.; 95. (other).

1965–68, MA (Hist.); Univ. of WI, 1968–69, MA (LS). **Orgs.:** Assn. of State Lib. Agencies: Pres. (1976–77). SELA: VP, Pres.-Elect (1980–82). Assn. of Hosp. and Inst. Libs.: Bd. of Dirs. (1973–74). ALA: Cncl. (1981–85); ASCLA, Com. on Stans. for Lib. Functions at the State Level (1979–81), various coms. Southeast. Lib. Netwk.: Bd. of Dirs. (1979–82); Treas. (1980–81); Vice-Ch. (1981–82). Amer. Correct. Assn.: Com. on Inst. Libs. (Ch., 1975–78). COSLA: Bd. of Dirs. (1980–82). **Honors:** Amer. Correct. Assn., Cert. of Apprec., 1978; Beta Phi Mu; Phi Alpha Theta. **Pubns.:** *Jails Need Libraries, Too!* (1974); "State Library Agencies," *Bowker Anl.* (1979); "Library Services for the Blind, Handicapped and Institutionalized," *Lib. Trends* (Fall 1978); "Correctional Facility Library; History and Standards," *Lib. Trends* (Sum. 1977); various other articles. **Activities:** 13; 34, 39, 49-Inst. lib. srvs.; 72 **Addr.:** State Library of Florida, R.A. Gray Bldg., Tallahassee, FL 32301.

Wilkins, Mary Ann V.C. (Ag. 19, 1945, Piqua, OH) Math Phys. Libn., Duke Univ., 1976–; Pub. Srvs. Libn., Cabot Sci. Lib., Harvard Univ., 1973–76; Asst. Libn., Phys. Sci. Lib., Cornell Univ., 1969–73. **Educ.:** Northwest. Univ., 1963–67, BA (Comp. Lit.); Univ. of MI, 1967–68, MSLS. **Orgs.:** SLA. NC OLUG. **Pubns.:** "Computerized Bibliographic Searching in the Duke Libraries," *Duke Univ. Lib. Nsltr.* (1979). **Activities:** 1, 12; 15, 17, 22; 84, 88, 91 **Addr.:** 233 Physics Bldg., Duke University, Durham, NC 27706.

Wilkins, Walter R. (D. 25, 1942, Chicago, IL) Hlth. Sci. Libn., Bradley Univ., 1977–, Resrcs. Libn., 1975–77; AV Libn., Coll. of Wooster, 1971–75; Soc. Sci. Libn., IL Wesleyan Univ., 1968–71, Pers. Libn., 1965–68. **Educ.:** IL Wesleyan Univ., 1960–64, BA (Hist.); Univ. of IL, 1964–65, MS (LS); IL State Univ., 1970–73, MS (Soclgy.); Med. LA, 1978, Cert. **Orgs.:** Med. LA. ALA. IL LA. **Honors:** Beta Phi Mu. **Activities:** 1; 29, 39, 46; 64, 80, 91 **Addr.:** Bradley University Library, Peoria, IL 61625.

Wilkinson, Ann M. (Mr. 8, 1940, Pottsville, PA) Sr. Staff Spec., Amer. Hosp. Assn. Lib., 1977–79; LS Libn., Columbia Univ., 1975–77, Catlgr., 1970–75, Libn., Coll. and Buregess-Carpenter Libs., 1968–69. **Educ.:** Wilson Coll., 1958–62, AB (Econ.); West. Rsv., Univ., 1962–63, MS (LS). **Orgs.:** ALA. Med. LA. **Activities:** 1, 12; 17, 46 **Addr.:** 222 W. Madison St., Baltimore, MD 21201.

Wilkinson, Billy R. (S. 8, 1933, Newton, NC) Dir., Univ. Lib., Univ. of MD, Baltimore Cnty., 1980–; Assoc. Univ. Libn., Univ. of IL, Chicago, 1977–79; Staff Rel. Ofcr., NY Pub. Lib., 1971–77, Prog. Ofcr., 1970–71; Chief Libn., Uris Undergrad. Lib., Cornell Univ., 1962–67, Goldwin Smith Libn., 1961–62, Asst. Ref. Libn., 1960–61, Actg. Goldwin Smith Libn., 1959–60. **Educ.:** Univ. of NC, 1951–55, AB (Eng.), 1955–56, 1958–60, MSLS; Columbia Univ., 1967–71, PhD (LS). **Orgs.:** ALA: ACRL, Acad. Status Com. (1973–77), Bd. of Dirs. (1973–81). AAUP. **Honors:** Phi Beta Kappa, 1954; Beta Phi Mu. **Pubns.:** *Reader in Undergraduate Libraries* (1978); *Reference Services for Undergraduate Students: Four Case Studies* (1972); "The Plethora of Personnel Systems in Academic Libraries," *New Horizons for Acad. Libs.* (1979); "Staff for Metropolitan Library Service," *Lib. Trends* (O. 1974); various other articles. **Activities:** 1; 17, 35, 39 **Addr.:** Library, University of Maryland Baltimore County, 5401 Wilkens Blvd., Catonsville, MD 21228.

Wilkinson, John P. (S. 12, 1927, Exeter, Eng.) Dir., Ctr. for Resrch. in Libnshp., Univ. of Toronto, 1976–81, Prof., 1965–; Dir. of Libs., Dalhousie Univ., 1960–65; Asst. Dir., Soc. Sci., Univ. of NE, 1957–60. **Educ.:** Univ. of Toronto, 1949, BA (Hist.), 1950, BLS, 1954, MLS; Univ. of Chicago, 1966, PhD (LS). **Orgs.:** Can. LA: Resrch. and Dev. Com. AALS. Inst. of Prof. Libns. of ON. Univ. of Toronto Fac. Assn. **Honors:** Beta Phi Mu. **Pubns.:** *Juvenile Fiction and the Canadian Library Market* (1976); "Trends in Library Education - Canada," *Advncs. in Libnshp.* (1978); "The Scope of Canadian Librarianship in the 1970s," *The Intl. Handbk. of Contemporary Dev. in Libnshp.* (forthcoming). **Activities:** 1; 17, 41; 92 **Addr.:** Faculty of Library Science, University of Toronto, 140 St. George St., Toronto, ON M5S 1A1 Canada.

Wilkinson, William A. (D. 16, 1926, Petrolia, ON) Mgr., Info. Ctr., Monsanto Co., 1964–; Lectr., LS, Washington Univ., 1971–; Tech. Libn., 1961–64, Resrch. Libn., 1956–61; Asst. Tech. Libn., Imperial Oil Ltd., 1953–56. **Educ.:** Univ. of West. ON, 1948–52, BA (Chem.); Carnegie Inst. of Tech., 1952–53, MLS. **Orgs.:** SLA: St. Louis Chap., various ofcs. ASIS. **Pubns.:** Jt. auth., "Machine-Assisted Serials Control," *Spec. Libs.* (D. 1971); "The Impact of Automation on the Special Library," *HI Lib. Jnl.* (Je. 1967); "A System for Machine-Assisted Serials Control," *Spec. Libs.* (Mr. 1967); "A Decentralized National Chemical Information System," *Amer. Docum.* (Ja. 1967); various other articles, reviews. **Activities:** 12; 17; 56, 60 **Addr.:** Information Center, Monsanto Co., P.O. Box 7090, St. Louis, MO 63177.

Willar, Arline (Jl. 23, 1932, Worcester, MA) Asst. Libn., Pub. Srv., Northeast. Univ., 1968–; Libn., Garland Jr. Coll., 1961–68; Actg. Libn., Pierce Coll. (Greece), 1965; Asst. Libn., Educ. Sch., Harvard Univ., 1960–61; Ref. Libn., Brown Univ., 1956–59; Readers Adv., Northwest. Univ., 1955–56. **Educ.:** Univ. of Chicago, 1948–51, PhB (Liberal Arts); Simmons Coll., 1954–55; various crs. in bus. and langs. **Orgs.:** ALA: ACRL, New Eng. Chap., Bibl. Instr. Com. (Ch., 1976–79). MA LA. New Eng. LA. New Eng. Tech. Srvs. Libns.: Various coms. Cambridge Civic Assn. **Activities:** 1; 17, 31; 50, 57 **Addr.:** 9 Commonwealth Rd., Watertown, MA 02172.

Willard, Barbara Bullock (N. 13, 1938, Glasco, KS) KS Rm. Libn., Hays Pub. Lib., 1978–; Pol. Sci., Hist. Libn., Kent State Univ., 1970–72; Tech. Srvs. Libn., Law Lib., Univ. of IL, 1968–70, Ref. Libn., 1963–68. **Educ.:** Univ. of KS, 1956–61, BA (Hist.); Univ. of IL, 1961–63, MS (LS), 1964–69, MA (Pol. Sci.). **Orgs.:** KS LA. Oral Hist. Assn. Assn. for State and Lcl. Hist. **Activities:** 1, 9; 15, 39, 45; 69, 73, 86 **Addr.:** Hays Public Library, 1205 Main St., Hays, KS 67601.

Willard, D. Dean (N. 22, 1930, Marble Hill, MO) Dir., Forsyth Lib., Fort Hays State Univ., 1977–; Prof., LS, IN Univ., South Bend, 1972–76; Asst. Law Libn., Univ. of IL, 1960–71. **Educ.:** Univ. of MO, 1945–53, AB (Pol. Sci.), 1957–59, BS (Educ.); Univ. of IL, 1959–60, MSLS, 1966–73, PhD (LS). **Orgs.:** ALA. KS LA. **Pubns.:** "Seven Realities of Library Administration," *Lib. Jnl.* (Ja. 15, 1976); "Marketing a College Education in a Buyer's Market," *Improving Instr.* (Ja. 1979). **Activities:** 1; 17 **Addr.:** 1711 Haney Dr., Hays, KS 67601.

Willett, Charles (Ja. 12, 1932, New York, NY) Ch., Acq. Dept., Univ. of FL Libs., 1978–; Head, Acq. Dept., SUNY Buffalo Libs., 1974–78; Admin. Asst. Ord. Libn., Harvard Coll. Lib., 1968–74; Frgn. Srv. Ofcr., various posts, U.S. Dept. of State, 1957–68. **Educ.:** Harvard Coll., 1950–55, AB (Hist.); Univ. of Munich (Germany), 1955–56, (Hist.); Frgn. Srv. Inst., 1959–60, Cert. (Czech); Simmons Coll., 1969–70, MS (LS). **Orgs.:** ALA: RTSD/Resrcs. Sect., Policy and Resrch. Com. (1976–78), Acq. of Lib. Mtrls. Discuss. Grp. (Ch., 1980–81), Nom. Com. (1981–82). Un. Fac. of FL. Amer. Cvl. Liberties Un. **Activities:** 1; 15, 17 **Addr.:** University of Florida Libraries, Gainesville, FL 32611.

Williams, Albert Louis (Jl. 13, 1937, Redfield, NY) Assoc. Cur., Pac. Biblgphr., Micronesian Area Resrch. Ctr., 1972–; Ref. Libn., Asst. Prof., Univ. of GU Lib., 1967–72; Lib. Consult., U.S. Dept. of Educ. (GU), 1965–67; Libn., Pulaski (NY) Acad. and Ctrl. Sch., 1962–65. **Educ.:** SUNY, Geneseo, 1957–61, BS (Educ.); Univ. of NY, 1961–62, MS (Educ. Media); various crs. **Orgs.:** ALA: Cncl. (1967). SLA. GU LA. GU Lib. Adv. Bd. Various other orgs. Amer. Philatelic Socty. **Pubns.:** Ed. com., *Governors Pre-White House Conference on Libraries and Information Services Proceedings* GU (1979); ed. staff, *GU Recorder* (1972–); *Pac. Asian Std. Assn. Jnl.* (1975–). **Activities:** 1, 12; 15, 20, 39; 54, 66, 92 **Addr.:** Micronesian Area Research Center, University of Guam, P. O. Box EK, Agana, GU 96910.

Williams, Alexander (Je. 6, 1922, Boston, MA) Ref. Libn., NASA Goddard Space Flight Ctr., 1968–; Ref. Libn., South. IL Univ., Edwardsville, 1965–68; Supvsr., Tech. Info. Ctr., Chrysler Corp. Space Div., 1962–65; Info. Retrieval Spec., Reactor Cat. Concept Proj., Argonne Natl. Lab., 1961–62; Bus. Libn., Northwest. Univ., 1958–61. **Educ.:** Harvard Coll., 1939–43, BA (Phys.); Syracuse Univ., 1949–50, MS (LS); OH State Univ., 1952–55, MA (Econ.); various crs., insts. **Orgs.:** SLA. **Activities:** 4, 12; 15, 20, 39; 52, 56, 91 **Addr.:** 6505 Blue Wing Dr., Alexandria, VA 22307.

Williams, Barbara J. (Je. 5, 1927, Alphoretta, KY) State Libn., KY Dept. of Lib. and Arch., 1977–, Asst. State Libn., 1976–77; Libn., KY Prog. Dev. Ofc., 1968–75; Libn., KY Dept. of Libs., 1965–68. **Educ.:** Centre Coll., 1945–49, AB (Span.); Columbia Univ., 1957; Univ. of KY, 1958–63, MS (LS). **Orgs.:** KY LA: Secy. (1973)/Spec. Lib. Sect. (Ch., 1976). COSLA: Liaison to Ofc. of Educ. (1979–80). Assn. of State Lib. Agencies: Index of State Lib. Actv. Com. (1979–80). ALA. Various other orgs. J. B. Speed Musm. KY Hist. Socty. Filson Club. **Activities:** 13 **Addr.:** Department of Library & Archives, Frankfort, KY 40602.

Williams, David Rees (Ja. 14, 1939, West Hartlepool, Cnty. Durham, Eng.) VP, Student Srvs., Kwantlen Coll., 1981–; Dir. of Libs., Douglas Coll., 1970–81; Supvsr. of Branches, Fraser Valley Reg. Lib., 1965–70; Libn., Manchester Pub. Lib., 1957–61. **Educ.:** Univ. of OK, BLS, MLS. **Orgs.:** Can. LA: Can. Assn. Coll. and Univ. Libs. BC LA. LA UK. BC Un. Cat.: Mgt. Com. (Ch., 1977–). **Activities:** 1; 17, 24, 49-Data prcs.; 50, 55, 56 **Addr.:** Kwantlen College, P.O. Box 9030, Surrey, BC V3T 5H8 Canada.

Williams, Dianne McAfee (D. 30, 1944, Houston, TX) Dir., Bur. of Instr. Media Prog., WI Dept. of Pub. Instr., 1977–; Sch. Lib. Media Consult., Univ. of MI, 1974–77; Media Spec., West Bloomfield HS, 1973–74; Sch. Lib. Spec., MI Dept. of Educ., 1972–73. **Educ.:** Fisk Univ., 1962–66, BA (Elem. Educ.); Atlanta Univ., 1966–67, MSLS; 1971–73, Eds (Libnshp.); 1981, PhD (Educ. Media and Tech.). **Orgs.:** AECT: Conf. Plng. Com. (Ch., 1981). ALA: AASL (Secy., 1976–77); IR RT, Exec. Com., Imroth Meml. Awd. (Ch., 1979–81). **Honors:** Phi Delta Kappa; MI Assn. for Media in Educ., Leadership Dev. Awd., 1977, Bd. of Dirs. Awd., 1977. **Pubns.:** "Instructional Media Programs: Status in Wisconsin 1978," *WI Lib. Bltn.* (Mr.–Ap. 1979); "Instructional Media Programs: Striving for Excellence" slide/tape (1979); "The Status of Instructional Media Programs in Wisconsin" audiotape (1979). **Activities:** 10, 13; 21, 24, 48; 63, 74, 89 **Addr.:** Wisconsin Dept. of Public Instruction, 125 S. Webster St., P.O. Box 7841, Madison, WI 53707.

Williams, Dorothy Payne (N. 24, 1938, Tallahassee, FL) Asst. Dir. of Libs., Assoc. Prof., Univ. of N. FL, 1971–; Head Libn., Raines HS, 1968–71; Head Libn., Johnson Jr. HS, 1962–68; Libn., Lincoln Meml. HS, 1960–61. **Educ.:** Florida A & M Univ., 1956–60, BS (LS), Syracuse Univ., 1964–67, MSLS; various crs. **Orgs.:** Duval Cnty. LA. FL LA. ALA: Black Caucus. Natl. Cncl. of Negro Women. Alpha Kappa Alpha Sorority. Links, Inc. **Honors:** James Weldon Johnson Jr. HS, Tchr. of the Yr., 1966; Gamma Rho Omega, Outstan. Srv. to Cmnty., 1981. **Activities:** 1; 17, 26, 39 **Addr.:** University of North Florida Library, P.O. Box 17605, Jacksonville, FL 32216.

Williams, Edwin Everitt (Jl. 13, 1913, Los Angeles, CA) Consult., Harvard Univ. Lib., 1980–, Assoc. Univ. Libn., Prof., Ed., *Harvard Lib. Bltn.,* Harvard Univ., 1966–80, Asst. Univ. Libn., 1964–66, Couns. to Dir. on the Cols., Harvard Univ. Lib., 1959–64, Asst. Libn. for Bk. Sel., Harvard Coll. Lib., 1956–59. **Educ.:** Stanford Univ., 1928–32, AB (Letters); Univ. of CA, Berkeley, 1934–36, AM (LS). **Orgs.:** ALA: Bd. of Acq. of Lib. Mtrls. (1953–56); Com. on Publshg. (1959–61); Cncl. (1948–52). **Pubns.:** *Tragedy of Destiny* (1940); *Racine depuis 1885: Bibliographie Raisonnée* (1940); *A Serviceable Reservoir* (1959); *Resources of Canadian University Libraries for Research in the Humanities and Social Sciences* (1962); various articles. **Activities:** 1; 17, 23, 37; 75 **Addr.:** Widener Library 183, Harvard University, Cambridge, MA 02138.

Williams, Evan W. (Je. 10, 1930, St. Louis, MO) Spec. Cols. Libn., Univ. Archvst., KS State Univ., 1968–, Catlgr., 1967–68, Asst. Soc. Sci. Libn., 1966–67, Asst. Ref. Libn., 1964–66. **Educ.:** Washington Univ., 1949–55, AB, (Soclgy.); Univ. of IL, 1955–56, MSLS. **Orgs.:** SAA. Oral Hist. Assn. KS LA. KS Corral of the Westerners. KS State Univ. Hist. Socty. **Pubns.:** *KSU Thesis Index, First Supplement, 1969–1973* (1975); jt. auth., *KSU Thesis Index, 1886–1968* (1969). **Activities:** 1, 2; 30, 33; 85 **Addr.:** 709 Dondee, Apt. 8, Manhattan, KS 66502.

Williams, Fred E. (Mr. 22, 1927, Jamieson, FL) Prof., Lib. and Educ. Media, Bowling Green State Univ., 1959–; Lectr., IN Univ., 1957–59; Film Libn., Ball State Univ., 1952–54. **Educ.:** FL State Univ., 1947–49, BS (Zlgy.), 1951–52, MA (LS); IN Univ., 1956–61, EdD (AV). **Orgs.:** OH Educ. Lib. Media Assn.: Bylaws and Policy (1978–81). AECT. ALA. **Honors:** AECT, Edgar Dale, 1979. **Activities:** 11; 26, 27, 32; 63 **Addr.:** 212 Williams St., Bowling Green, OH 43402.

Williams, Gayle Ann (Jl. 29, 1954, Hobart, OK) Assoc. Libn., Cat., Coll. of the VI, 1979–; Latin Amer. Mono. Catlgr., Univ. of TX, 1978–79. **Educ.:** OK State Univ., 1972–75, BA (Hum.); Univ. of TX, Austin, 1976–77, MLS. **Orgs.:** SALALM: Com. on Bibl. (1980–), Subcom. on Nonprint Media (1980–). St. Thomas LA. **Activities:** 1; 20, 30, 39; 54, 67 **Addr.:** Ralph M. Paiewonsky Library, College of the Virgin Islands, St. Thomas, VI 00801.

Williams, Gordon R. (Jl. 26, 1914, Ontario, OR) Dir. Emeritus, Ctr. for Resrch. Libs., 1980–, Dir., 1959–80; Asst. Univ. Libn., Univ. of CA, Los Angeles, 1952–59; Exec. Asst. to Dir., John Crerar Lib., 1950–52. **Educ.:** Stanford Univ., 1932–36, AB (Psy.); Univ. of Chicago, 1949–50, MA (LS). **Orgs.:** *Bio. Abs.:* Bd. of Trustees (1976–81). Mss. Socty.: Bd. of Dirs. (1958–63). SAA: Paper Resrch. Com. (Ch., 1970–75). ALA: Natl. Un. Cat. Com. (Ch., 1960–80). Caxton Club. Rounce and Coffin Club. **Pubns.:** *Ravens and Crows* (1966); *Bewick to Dovaston, Letters 1824–1828* (1968); *Cost of Owning vs. Borrowing Serials* (1969); "The Function and Methods of Libraries in the Diffusion of Knowledge," *Lib. Qtly.* (Jl. 1980); various other articles, reviews. **Activities:** 1, 14-Resrch. lib.; 15, 17, 23; 57 **Addr.:** 1662 Paulson Way, Napa, CA 94558.

Williams, Helen Elizabeth (D. 13, 1933, Timmonsville, SC) Lectr., Coord. of Undergrad. Educ. Media Prog., Univ. of MD, 1981–; Mgr., Prof. Publshg., Staff Libn., Brodart, Inc. 1976–81; Libn., White Plains City Schs., 1966–73; Libn., Dorchester Pub. Schs., 1964–66; Libn., Mt. Vernon Pub. Lib., 1963–64; Libn., Brooklyn Pub. Lib., 1960–62. **Educ.:** Morris Coll., 1954, BA (Eng.); Atlanta Univ., 1960, MS (LS); Univ. of IL, 1969, CAS (LS); various crs. **Orgs.:** ALA: AASL, Ad Hoc Elem. Sch. Mtrls. Sel. Com. (Ch., 1981–83), Prof. Dev. Com. (1977–79); YASD; Black Caucus, ALA Rel. Com. (1980–). PA Sch. Libns. Assn.: Exec. Com. (1980–81); Media Rev. and Sel. (1978–). Lycoming Cnty. Libns. Assn.: Prog. Com. (1979). AAUW. NAACP. Leag. of Women Voters. Women's Natl. Bk. Assn. **Honors:** Beta Phi Mu. **Pubns.:** *The High/Low Consensus* (1980); *Independent Reading, K–3* (1980). **Activities:** 14-Cmrcl. firm; 17, 24, 37; 51 **Addr.:** 9883 Good Luck Rd., Lanham, MD 20801.

Williams, J. Linda (Je. 30, 1945, Bethesda, MD) Lib. Media Spec., White Marsh Sch., 1981–; Lib. Media Spec., Choptico HS, 1977–81, Actg. Dir., Instr. Dsgn. and Support Ctr., Univ. of MD, 1977; Tchr., 1966–76. **Educ.:** Radford Coll.,

PROFESSIONAL ACTIVITIES: Institutions: 1. Acad. lib.; 2. Arch.; 3. Assn.; 4. Fed./Gvt. lib.; 5. Inst. lib.; 6. Mfr./Suppl.; 7. Milit. lib.; 8. Musm.; 9. Pub. lib.; 10. Sch. lib.; 11. Sch. of lib. sci.; 12. Spec. lib.; 13. State lib.; 14. (other). **Functions/Activities:** 15. Acq./Col. dev.; 16. Adult srvs.; 17. Admin.; 18. Apprais.; 19. Archit./Bldgs.; 20. Cat./Class.; 21. Chld. srvs.; 22. Circ.; 23. Cons./Pres.; 24. Consult.; 25. Cont. ed.; 26. Educ. lib. sci.; 27. Ext. srvs.; 28. Fund/Grants; 29. Gvt. pubs.; 30. Indx./Abs.; 31. Instr. lib. use; 32. Media srvs.; 33. Micro.; 34. Netwks./Coop.; 35. Persnl.; 36. PR; 37. Publshg.; 38. Recs. mgt.; 39. Ref. srvs.; 40. Repro.; 41. Resrch.; 42. Review.; 43. Secur.; 44. Serials; 45. Spec. col.; 46. Tech. srvs.; 47. Trustees/Bds.; 48. YA srvs.; 49. (other).

Who's Who in Library and Information Services

1963–66, BS (Eng., Hist.); Univ. of MD, 1976–77, MS (LS). **Orgs.:** ALA: JMRT, *Cognotes* Asst. Ed. (1978–79), Ed. (1979–80), Com. on Governance (Ch., 1980–82), Prof. Dev. Grant Sel. Com. (1981–82), Midwin. Actv. Com. (1980–81), Orien. Com. (1981). AASL, Student Involvement in the Media Ctr. (1979–81). Natl. LA MD LA. MD Educ. Media Org. Natl. Educ. Assn. MD State Tchrs. Assn. **Honors:** Beta Phi Mu; 3M/JMRT, Prof. Dev. Grant, 1981. **Activities:** 10; 17, 31, 32; 63 **Addr.:** Rte. 4, Box 4146, La Plata, MD 20646.

Williams, James F., II (Ja. 22, 1944, Montgomery AL) Med. Libn., Wayne State Univ., 1972–; Dir., KY-OH-MI Reg. Med. Lib. Netwk., 1973–. **Educ.:** Morehse. Coll., 1962–66, BA (Soclgy., Psy.); Atlanta Univ., 1966–67, MS (LS), U.S. Pub. Hlth. Srv. Flwshp., 1967–68 (Med. Libnshp.). **Orgs.:** Med. LA: Com. on Structure (Ch., 1975–78), Assoc. Acad. Hlth. Sci. Lib. Dirs: Com. on Tech. (Ch., 1979–). MI Hlth. Sci. LA. **Pubns.:** "Medical Libraries," *ALA Yrbk.* (1981); "A MEDLARS Perspective," *The Special Library Role in Networks* (1980); "A Medical Librarian's Perspective," *Patient/Health Education - The Librarian's Role* (1979); jt. auth., "A Study of Access to the Scholarly Record from a Hospital Health Science Core Collection," *Bltn. Med. LA* (O. 1973). **Activities:** 1, 12; 17, 34; 80 **Addr.:** Shiffman Medical Library, Wayne State University, 4325 Brush St., Detroit, MI 48201.

Williams, James G. (Ap. 18, 1939, Johnstown, PA) Prof., Info. Sci., Univ. of Pittsburgh, 1974–; Asst. Prof., Univ. of SC, 1972–74; Instr., Univ. of Pittsburgh, 1969–72; Asst. Prof., Lorain Cnty. Cmnty. Coll., 1966–68. **Educ.:** Clarion State Coll., 1957–61, BS (Sci.); Univ. of Pittsburgh, 1963–72, MS, PhD (Info. Sci.). **Orgs.:** ASIS: Prof. Dev. Com. (1979–81). **Pubns.:** *Introduction to Computers and Programming* (1980); "WEBNET - A Demonstration of a Full Service Library Network," *Lib. Jnl.* (1979); "Information Science Education," *Procs. of ASIS Conf.* (1979). **Activities:** 1, 9; 24, 34, 46; 56, 75, 93 **Addr.:** P.O. Box 271, Murrysville, PA 15668.

Williams, James W. (Je. 8, 1945, LaPorte, IN) Instr., Hist. Dept., U.S. Nvl. Acad., 1981–; Consult., J. W. Williams and Assocs., 1980–; Hist. Ed., IN State Comsn. on Pub. Recs., 1977–79; Contract Coord., Hist. Prsrvn. IN Univ., 1976–77; Assoc. Instr., U.S. Hist., 1973–75. **Educ.:** Wabash Coll., Univ. of Edinburgh, 1964–68, AB (Hist.); Amer. Univ., 1976 (Arch. Admin.); IN Univ., 1972–81, MA, PhD (Hist.). **Orgs.:** SAA. Assn. of Recs. Mgrs. and Admins. Midwest Arch. Conf. Socty. IN Archvsts. Socty. for Values in Higher Educ. U.S. Nvl. Rsv. **Honors:** Danforth Fndn., Flwshp., 1968; Woodrow Wilson Fndn., Grad. Flwshp., 1968. **Pubns.:** "Storage, Space and Equipment," *A Manual of Archival Techniques* (1981). **Activities:** 2; 24, 38, 41; 62, 74, 92 **Addr.:** I-1 Perry Cir., Annapolis, MD 21402.

Williams, Janet L. (Ag. 6, 1949, Noblesville, IN) Libn., Educ. Testing Srv., 1977–, Assoc. Libn., 1976–77; Asst. Libn., CA Fed. Savings and Loan, 1973–75; Staff Writer, *Los Angeles Herald Examiner,* 1971–73. **Educ.:** Purdue Univ., 1967–71, BS (Food Sci.); Univ. of South. CA, 1972–74, MLS; Rutgers Univ., 1980– (LS). **Orgs.:** SLA: Princeton–Trenton Chap., Pres. (1981–82), Secy. (1978–79). **Honors:** Beta Phi Mu, 1974. **Pubns.:** "Best of Both Worlds: Librarian/Working Mother," *Amer. Libs.* (S. 1978); "Computer Searching and ILL: Where's the Connection" ERIC (1978). **Activities:** 12; 17; 63, 92 **Addr.:** Educational Testing Service, Rosedale Rd., Princeton, NJ 08541.

Williams, Joan Frye (Jl. 11, 1952, San Francisco, CA) CLSA Prog. Coord., CA State Lib., 1980–, Lib. Syst. Spec., 1978–80, CA Docum. Libn., 1975–78. **Educ.:** Univ. of CA, Santa Barbara, 1970–73, BA (Eng.); Univ. of CA, Berkeley, 1974–75, MLS. **Orgs.:** ALA. CA LA. SLA: Sierra Nevada Chap., Dir., Pubcty. & Pubns. (1978/79); Dir., Prog. (1979/80). **Honors:** Phi Beta Kappa, 1973. **Pubns.:** Ed., *SLA Gold & Silver Gazette* (1978/79). **Activities:** 13; 24, 34; 56 **Addr.:** 2930 Bendmill Way, Sacramento, CA 95833.

Williams, John A. (F. 1, 1919, Hartford, CT) Head Libn., Williston-Northampton Sch., 1981–; Head of Libs., Cranbrook Schs., 1977–81; Libn., OR Episcopal Sch., 1975–76; Libn., Pomfret Sch., 1968–75. **Educ.:** Hobart Coll., 1946–49, BA (Hist.); Trinity Coll., 1956, MA (Hist.); Univ. of RI, 1968, MLA (LS). **Orgs.:** ALA: AASL/Non-pub. Sch. Sect. MI LA. **Pubns.:** Jt. ed., *Books for Secondary School Libraries* (1976). **Activities:** 10; 17, 20, 31; 92 **Addr.:** Library, Williston-Northampton School, Easthampton, MA 01027.

Williams, John E. (Mr. 9, 1948, Rogers, TX) Supvsr., Tech. Srvs., Mesquite Pub. Lib., 1979–; Tchr., Mesquite HS, 1974–79; Supvsr., Pub. Srvs., Mesquite Pub. Lib., 1973–74, Adult Ref. Libn., 1971–73. **Educ.:** Univ. of TX, Arlington, 1968–70, BS (Bio.); N. TX State Univ., 1971–73, MLS; E. TX State Univ., 1975–77, MS (Bio.). **Orgs.:** TX LA. Dallas Cnty. LA. Frnds. of the Mesquite Pub. Lib. **Activities:** 9; 15, 17, 20; 58, 60, 65 **Addr.:** Mesquite Public Library, 300 Grubb St., Mesquite, TX 75149.

Williams, John Troy (Mr. 11, 1924, Oak Park, IL) Visit. Schol., Univ. of MI, 1980–82; Asst. Dean, Asst. Univ. Libn., Wright State Univ., 1975–80; Head, Readers Srvs., North. IL Univ., 1972–75; Head, Ref. Srvs., Purdue Univ., 1965–72. **Educ.:** Ctrl. MI Univ., 1946–49, AB (Soc. Sci.); Univ. of MI, 1949–51, MA (LS), MA (Hist.); MI State Univ., 1959–62, PhD (Soc. Sci.); 1966–79, Insts. on Bibl., Autom., Gvt. Docum., Stats. **Orgs.:** ALA: Ref. and Subscrpn. Bks. Review Com. (1980–); RASD, Pubns. Com. (1974–78), Stans. Com. (1979–); ACRL, Constn. Com. (1978). SLA: Consult. Srvs. Com. (1976–77). ASIS: Proprietary Use/Rights Com. (1975–76). Intl. Assn. for Soc. Sci. Info.: Srv. and Tech.: Mem. Com. Amer. Soclgy. Assn. AAUP. **Pubns.:** "Who Runs ALA?" *Focus On IN Libs.* (Je. 1969); "Census Tapes," *IN SLANT* (O. 1972); "Conflict Theory," *Soc. Sci.* (Spr. 1976); abstctr., *Hist. Abs., Amer.* **Activities:** 1; 17, 29, 39; 56, 66, 92 **Addr.:** 1453 Marlborough St., Ann Arbor, MI 48104.

Williams, Judith L. (S. 3, 1948, Jacksonville, FL) Asst. Dir., of Libs., Jacksonville Pub. Lib., 1979–, Admin. Asst., 1976–78, Branch Libn., 1972–76, Gen. Srvs. Libn., 1971–72. **Educ.:** FL State Univ., 1966–70, BA (Hist., LS), 1970–71, MLS. **Orgs.:** ALA. FL LA: Secy. (1981–82). Duval Cnty. LA. **Activities:** 9; 17, 35, 36; 56, 74, 89 **Addr.:** Jacksonville Public Library, 122 N. Ocean St., Jacksonville, FL 32202.

Williams, Lauren Sapp (Ag. 22, 1945, Smithfield, NC) Asst. Dept. Head., Lib., FL State Univ., 1981–, Assoc. Univ. Libn., Asst. Dept. Head, 1977–81, Assoc. Univ. Libn., Ref., 1976–77, Asst. Univ. Libn., Ref., 1974–76; Instr., Libn., Voorhees Coll., 1971–74. **Educ.:** NC Ctrl. Univ., 1963–67, BA (Eng.); Univ. of MI, 1970–71, AMLS; FL State Univ., 1978–79, Advnc. Mstr.'s (LS). **Orgs.:** ALA. SELA. FL LA. **Honors:** Beta Phi Mu. **Activities:** 1; 29, 39; 63 **Addr.:** 950 Richardson Rd., Tallahassee, FL 32301.

Williams, Lee H., Jr. (Mr. 18, 1921, Madison Cnty., GA) Cur., Latin Amer. Col., Yale Univ. Lib., 1967–; Dir., Tech. Srvs., SUNY, Stony Brook, 1964–67; Dir., Tech. Srvs., Univ. of PR, 1960–64; Head, Cat. Dept., Wesleyan Univ., 1955–60; Catlgr., Columbia Univ., 1954–55. **Educ.:** Univ. of WA, 1941–46, BA (Span.); Columbia Univ., 1953–54, MS (LS). **Orgs.:** SALALM: Exec. Bd. (1978–); various coms. Latin Amer. Microfilm Proj.: Exec. Bd. (1978–). Latin Amer. Std. Assn. **Pubns.:** *The Allende Years...* (1977); "Problems of Acquisition of Cuban Library Materials by United States University Research Libraries," *Intl. Conf. Cuban Acq. and Bibl., Lib. of Congs.* (1970). **Activities:** 1; 15; 54 **Addr.:** Yale University Library, New Haven, CT 06520.

Williams, Mabel (My. 31, 1887, Newton Center, MA) Retired, 1952–; Head, YA Srvs., New York Pub. Lib., 1919–52, Supvsr., Work with Schs., 1916–19; Libn., Somerville HS, 1915–16; Ref. Libn., Somerville Pub. Lib., 1912–15; Staff, Radcliffe Coll. Lib., 1911–12; Asst., Simmons Coll. Lib., 1909–11. **Educ.:** Simmons Coll., 1909, BS (LS). **Orgs.:** ALA: Young People's Readg. RT (Fndr.); PLA; YASD. NY LA. **Honors:** ALA, Grolier Fndn. Awd., 1980. **Pubns.:** Ed., *Books for the Teen Age* (1930–). **Activities:** 9; 21, 48 **Addr.:** 63 Lakeside Trail, c/o Waller, Kinnelon, NJ07405.*

Williams, Margaret T. (D. 11, 1931, St. John's, NF) Univ. Libn., Meml. Univ. of NF, 1953–, Assoc. Libn., 1975–80, Assoc. Libn., Tech. Srvs., 1974–75, 1971–72, Actg. Univ. Libn., 1972–74, 1967–68, Asst. Libn., Tech. Srvs., 1968–71, Asst. Libn., 1961–67. **Educ.:** Meml. Univ., NF, 1949–53, BA (Classics); Univ. of Toronto, 1960–61, BLS. **Orgs.:** Can. LA: Can. Assn. of Coll. and Univ. Libs., Pres. (1973–74), Secy. (1967–68). NF LA: Pres. (1969–71). Atl. Prov. LA: VP (1969–70). Natl. Lib. Bd.: Com. on Bibl. Srvcs. (Ch., 1975–78). **Activities:** 1; 17; 75 **Addr.:** Library, Memorial University of Newfoundland St. John's, NF A1B 3Y1 Canada.

Williams, Marilyn Simpson (F. 14, 1928, Nashville, TN) Chief, Ref., Air Univ. Lib., 1972–, Bibl., Air Cmnd. and Staff Coll., 1962–72, Bibl., Com. and Electronics Div., 1960–62, Bibl., Chaplain's Writer's Bd. and Squadron Ofcrs. Sch., 1958–60. **Educ.:** Mary Baldwin Coll., 1946–50, BA (Sp. and Drama), George Peabody Coll., 1950–51, MA (LS). **Orgs.:** SLA: AL Chap. (Histn., 1972–73). AL LA. Rsv. Ofcrs. Assn. Ladies: State Pres. (1971–72). Air Frc. Assn. **Addr.:** 3813 Marie Cook Dr., Montgomery, AL 36119.

Williams, Martha E. (Chicago, IL) Prof., Info. Sci., Univ. of IL, 1972–. **Educ.:** Barat Coll, 1955, AB (Chem.); Loyola Univ., 1957, MA (Phil.). **Orgs.:** ASIS: *Anl. Review of Info. Sci. and Tech* Ed. (1975); Cnclr. (1971–72); Pub. Com. (1971–72, 1975–79), Com. on Intersocty. Coop. (Ch., 1972–73); various other coms. Engin. Index: Pres. (1980–81, 1981–82); VP (1978–79); Trustee (1974–83); Bd. of Dirs. (1976–). AAAS: Comps, Info., and Comm. Sect. Amer. Chem. Socty. Assn. for Sci. Info. Dssm. Ctrs.: Various coms., ofcs. Natl. Lib. of Med.: Bd. of Regents (Ch., 1981–82). **Honors:** H. W. Wilson Co., Best Paper of the Yr., 1975. **Pubns.:** Ed.-in-Chief, *Computer-Readable Databases–A Directory and Data Sourcebook;* ed., *Online Review* (1977–); "Databases and Online Statistics for 1979," *Bltn. ASIS* (D. 1980); "Chance vs. Stability in Data Bases," *Bltn. ASIS* (Je. 1979); various articles, presentations. **Activities:** 14-Coll. of engin.; 41 **Addr.:** Coordinated Science Laboratory, College of Engineering, University of Illinois, Urbana, IL 61801.

Williams, Maudine B. (Ag. 23, 1929, Yosemite, KY) Head Libn., Herron Sch. of Art, IN Univ., 1970–. **Educ.:** Berea Coll., 1948–52, BA (Educ.); Butler Univ., 1968–70, MA (LS); IN Univ. Sch. of Lib. & Info. Sci., Spec. Degree, 1982. **Orgs.:** ARLIS/NA. IN LA: SLA: IN Chap., Past Pres. **Activities:** 1; 17, 39; 55 **Addr.:** Herron School of Art Library, 1701 N. Pennsylvania St., Indianapolis, IN 46202.

Williams, Mitsuko (S. 20, 1943, Mie Prefechire, Japan) Asst. Bio. Libn., Asst. Prof., LS, Univ. of IL, 1974–. **Educ.:** Hokusei Coll., 1962–66, BA (Eng.); Westmar Coll., 1966–68, BA (Eng.); Univ. of IL, 1971–74. **Orgs.:** Japan LA. SLA. Med. LA: Intl. Ed. (1980–); Resrch. Libs. Grp. (Ch., 1980–81); Intl. Coops. Com. (1979–80); Midwest Reg. Grp., Exec. Com. (1980–82), Prog. Com. (1976–77). **Pubns.:** "The Impact of the Recent Development at the University of Illinois Library," *Daigaku Toshokan Kenkyu* (1979); "Evaluation of PLATO Library Instruction Program," *Jnl. of Acad. Libnshp.* (1979); "Library Instruction Activities in American University Libraries," *Gendai no Toshokan* (1978); "Wanted: Middle-aged Women Librarians," *Toshokan Zasshi* (1978); various other articles. **Activities:** 1; 31, 39; 58, 80 **Addr.:** University of Illinois at Urbana-Champaign, 407 S. Goodwin Ave., Urbana, IL 61801.

Williams, Nancy Lynne (D. 11, 1946, Flint, MI) Ch., Cat. Dept., Univ. of FL Libs., 1980–, Asst. Ch., Cat. Dept., 1975–79, Serials Catlgr., 1971–75. **Educ.:** Univ. of MI, 1965–69, AB (Hist.); FL State Univ., 1970–71, MS (LS). **Orgs.:** ALA. SELA. FL LA: Tech. Srvs. Caucus (Ch., 1975–76); Per./Serials Caucus (Ch., 1979–80). **Honors:** Beta Phi Mu, 1972; Phi Kappa Phi, 1969. **Activities:** 1; 17, 20, 44; 56 **Addr.:** 1309 N.W. 39th Dr., Gainesville, FL 32605.

Williams, Nyal Zeno (D. 20, 1930, Spindale, NC) Prof., LS, Msc. Libn., Ball State Univ., 1971–; Asst. Msc. Libn., Univ. of NC, 1959–68. **Educ.:** Gardner-Webb Coll., 1947–49, AA (Msc.); Baylor Univ., 1950–53, BM (Piano), 1955–57, MM (Msc.); Univ. of NC, 1958–71, PhD (Msclgy.); Ball State Univ., 1973–75, MLS. **Orgs.:** Msc. LA: Exhibits Dir. (1972–75). IN LA. OH Valley Grp. of Tech. Srv. Libns. Midwest Acad. Libns. Conf. Amer. Msclgy. Socty. **Pubns.:** Jt. ed., *Library Instruction and Faculty Development* (1980); "Periodicals and Yearbooks," *A Basic Music Library* (1978); "Music Reference Materials: An Examination of the Reviews," *Ref. Qtly.* (Fall 1977); reviews. **Activities:** 1; 15, 17, 20; 55 **Addr.:** 4516 N. Tillotson Ave., Muncie, IN 47304.

Williams, Patricia Frances (Ap. 26, 1931, Clinton, TN) HS Lib. Media Spec., Toney, AL, 1969–; Elem. Tchr., Ft. Payne, AL, 1968–69; Libn., NE (AL) State Jr. Coll., 1966–68. **Educ.:** Univ. of N. AL, 1951–52, 1956–59, BA (Hist., Fr.); Univ. of NC, 1959–61, (LS); Univ. of N. AL, 1968–70, (Educ.). **Orgs.:** ALA: AASL; YASD; LIRT. AL LA: AIMA, Dist. 2. Natl. Cncl. Tchrs. of Eng. Adlsnt. Lit. Assn. Natl. Educ. Assn. AL Educ. Assn. **Activities:** 10; 31, 32, 48; 55, 89, 92 **Addr.:** 2811-H Academy Dr., N.W., Huntsville, AL 35811.

Williams, Pauline C. (O. 31, 1942, Northport, AL) Pers. Ref. Libn., Univ. of Montevallo, 1973–; Patients' Libn., Ctrl. State Hosp. Lib., Norman, OK, 1972–73; Tchr., Math., Roosevelt Jr. HS, 1968–72; Asst. Catlgr., Univ. of South. MS, 1967–68. **Educ.:** Univ. of AL, 1961–65, BS (LS); Univ. of OK, 1972–73, MS (Libnshp.); various certs. **Orgs.:** ALA. AL LA: Coll. Univ. Spec. Libs. Div., Secy. (1975–76), Vice-Ch. (1981–82), Ch. (1982–83), Newsp. Indexing Com. (Ch., 1975–77), Roll of Hon. Com. (Ch., 1981–82), Nom. Com. (Ch., 1979–80); GODORT (Secy., 1981–82). AAUW. Church of Jesus Christ of LDS. **Pubns.:** Index, *Shelby Cnty. Rpt.* (1975–). **Activities:** 1; 31, 39, 44; 59, 63, 83 **Addr.:** Rte. 2, Box 145, Montevallo, AL 35115.

Williams, Richmond Dean (D. 10, 1925, Reading, MA) Dir., Eleutherian Mills Hist. Lib., 1962–; Interim Dir., Reg. Econ. Hist. Resrch. Ctr., Eleutherian Mills-Hagley Fndn., 1975–76; Assoc. Dir., Eleutherian Mills Hist. Lib., 1961–62; Asst. Dir., Amer. Assn. for State and Lcl. Hist., 1960–61; Dir., WY Hist. and Geol. Socty., Wilkes-Barre, PA, 1956–60; Asst. Dean, Instr., Williams Coll., 1954–56. **Educ.:** Williams Coll., 1950, BA (Amer. Hist., Lit.); Univ. of PA, 1952, MA, 1959, PhD (European Hist.). **Orgs.:** Amer. Micro. Acad. Assn. of Recs. Mgrs. and Admins. Natl. Hist. Pubns. and Recs. Comsn.: Comsn. (1977–78). SAA. Econ. Hist. Assn.: Secy-Treas. (1975–). Amer. Assn. State and Lcl. Hist.: Pres. (1974–76); Cnclr. (1964–80). Amer. Cncl. of Learned Soctys.: Conf. of Secys. (Secy., 1979–81). **Honors:** Phi Beta Kappa, 1949. **Pubns.:** *They Also Served* (1966); jt. auth., *A Look at Ourselves* (1962); various articles, reviews in prof. jnls. **Activities:** 12; 15, 17, 24; 55, 59, 91 **Addr.:** Eleutherian Mills Historical Library, P.O. Box 3630, Wilmington, DE 19807.

Williams, Robert V. (O. 10, 1938, Brooksville, FL) Asst. Prof., LS, Univ. of SC, 1978–; Mgr., Recs. Srvs., Ford Fndn., 1969–74; Archvst., GA Dept. of Arch. and Hist., 1965–69. **Educ.:** Harding Coll., 1959–61, BA (Soc. Sci.); FL State Univ., 1963–64, MS (LS); NY Univ., 1970–74, MA (Hist.); Univ. of WI, 1974–78, PhD (LS). **Orgs.:** SLA: Resrch. Com. (1970–74). SALALM: Oral Hist. Com. (1974–78). SAA: Intl. Rel. Com. (1970–74). ALA. Various other orgs. Assn. for the Bibl. of Hist. **Honors:** GA State Univ., John Hancock Prize, 1968. **Pubns.:** "Latin American Library Development," *A Search for New Insights....* (1975); "Of Historical Value?" *Jnl. of Lib. Hist.* (1968); "George Whitefield's

Special Subjects/Services: 50. Adult educ.; 51. Advert./Mktg.; 52. Aerosp.; 53. Agric.; 54. Area std.; 55. Arts/Hum.; 56. Autom.; 57. Bibl./Prtg.; 58. Bio. sci.; 59. Bus./Fin.; 60. Chem.; 61. Copyrt.; 62. Documtn.; 63. Educ.; 64. Engin.; 65. Env.; 66. Eth. grps.; 67. Film; 68. Food/Nutr.; 69. Geneal.; 70. Geo.; 71. Geol.; 72. Handcpd.; 73. Hist.; 74. Int. frdm.; 75. Info. sci.; 76. Insr.; 77. Law; 78. Legis.; 79. Math./Comp. sci.; 80. Med.; 81. Metals; 82. Nat. resrcs.; 83. Newsp.; 84. Nuc. sci.; 85. Oral hist.; 86. Petr./Energy; 87. Pharm.; 88. Phys./Astr./Math.; 89. Readg.; 90. Relig.; 91. Sci./Tech.; 92. Soc. sci.; 93. Telecom.; 94. Transp.; 95. (other).

Bethesda..," *Jnl. of Lib. Hist.* (1967); clmn. ed., *Jnl of Lib. Hist.* (1969–74). **Activities:** 2, 12; 26, 30, 41; 56, 57, 92 **Addr.:** College of Librarianship, University of South Carolina, Columbia, SC 29208.

Williams, Roberta S. (S. 24, 1936, Burlington, NC) Dir., Duplin Cnty. Lib., 1980–; Asst. Serials Libn., Univ. of NC, Greensboro, 1969–80; Libn., Advnc. Tchrs. Coll., Kano, Nigeria, 1965–68; Ref. Libn., Kern Cnty. Free Lib., 1964–65. **Educ.:** Longwood Coll., 1954–57, BA (Eng.); Univ. of NC, 1957–59, MA (Eng.); Univ. of Denver, 1962–63, MA (LS). Pilot Club of Greensboro: Pres. (1977–78). **Activities:** 1, 9; 15, 44, 46; 54, 92 **Addr.:** Duplin County Library, P.O. Box 718, Kenansville, NC 28349.

Williams, Roger M. (Ja. 24, 1928, Chicago, IL) Libn., Archvst., Nazarene Bible Coll., 1974–; Ref., Circ. Libn., Point Loma Coll., 1971–74; Pastor, various states, 1951–71. **Educ.:** East. Nazarene Coll., 1945–49, BA (Phil.); Nazarene Theo. Semy., 1949–52, MDiv (Bible Lit.); Univ. of OK, 1968–71, MLS. **Orgs.:** ATLA: Lib. Mtrls. Exch. Com. Assn. of Christ. Libns. CS LA: Sites Com., Ch. CO LA. **Pubns.:** *The Sunday School Superintendent and the Church Library* (1975); "Inspirational Articles," *Herald of Holiness;* "Devotions," *Come Ye Apart;* reviews. **Addr.:** Nazarene Bible College, Box 15749, Colorado Springs, CO 80935.

Williams, Ronald David (Mr. 5, 1947, Selma, AL) Asst. Prof., Media Srvs., Emory Univ., 1974–; Media Spec., Fairbanks N. Star Boro. Lib., 1971–72; Telecom. Consult., AK Educ. Broadcasting Comsn., 1972. **Educ.:** Auburn Univ., 1965–69, BA (Eng.); Univ. of AK, 1970–72, MFA; Emory Univ., 1973–74, MLn; Rutgers Univ. 1976–, PhD Cand. (LS). **Orgs.:** AALS. SELA. GA LA: Pubcty. Com. (Ch., 1975–77). ALA: Cncl., Com. on Org. (1973–75); PLA/Alternative Educ. Prog. Sect., Bylaws Com. (Ch., 1975–79), Visual Lit. and AV Comm. Task Frc. (1976–79), Com. (1979–). **Honors:** Beta Phi Mu, 1974; Sigma Tau Delta, 1968; Gamma Beta Phi, 1969; Phi Mu Alpha, 1967. **Pubns.:** Cmplr., *Film Production Workbook* (1971); jt. auth., *ARC Training Program* (1972); jt. auth., *ARC–Alaska Resources Challenge: An Attack on Poverty Through Knowledge* (1972). **Activities:** 11; 24, 26, 32; 67, 75, 93 **Addr.:** Division of Librarianship, Emory University, Atlanta, GA 30322.

Williams, Sally F. (F. 6, 1944, Norwood, MA) Budget and Plng. Ofcr., Harvard Coll. Lib., 1980–, Head, Serial Recs., Asst. for Plng., Cat. Dept., 1975–79; Head, Ref. Dept., Drexel Univ., 1974–75; Head, Acq. and Serials, 1973–74; Head, Serials, 1970–73, Bus. Ref. Libn., 1969–70; Asst. Libn., AVCO Everett Resrch. Lab. Lib., 1967–69. **Educ.:** Marietta Coll., 1962–66, BA (Bio., Phil.); Simmons Coll., 1966–67, MS (LS); Drexel Univ., 1974, MBA (Fin., Mgt.). **Orgs.:** ALA: RTSD/Resrcs. Sect., Exec. Com. (Secy., 1981–83), Lib. Mtrls. Price Index Com. (Ch., 1979–81)/Serials Sect., Ad Hoc Com. on Dynamic Care Lists of Serials (Ch., 1979–81), Com. to Review ANSC Stan. Z39. 20-1974 (1980–); ACRL. **Pubns.:** "Construction and Application of a Periodical Price Index," *Col. Mgt.* (Win. 1978); "Prices of U.S. and Foreign Published Materials," *Bowker Anl. of Lib. and Bk. Trade Info.* (1980–81). **Activities:** 1; 15, 17, 46; 59 **Addr.:** Harvard College Library, Cambridge, MA 02138.

Williams, Shelagh C. (O. 21, 1939, Aklavik, NT) Head Libn., Rideau HS Lib., Ottawa, 1968–; Catlgr., Natl. Sci. Lib., 1967–68; HS Tchr., Kingston, ON, 1963–64. **Educ.:** Queen's Univ., ON, 1957–61, BSc, hons. (Chem.), 1961–66, MSc (Chem.); Univ. of London, 1966–67, Postgrad. Dip. (Libnshp.); Univ. of W. ON, 1977–80, MLS. **Orgs.:** Can. LA. LA (UK). ON LA. LA of Ottawa–Hull: Couns. (1973–75). ON Sec. Sch. Tchrs. Fed: Ottawa Lib. Subj. Cncl., Secy. (1974–75), Pres. (1975–76). Chem. Socty., (UK). **Pubns.:** Two articles in *Can. Jnl. of Chem.* **Activities:** 10; 31, 48; 60, 63 **Addr.:** 180 Patricia Ave., Ottawa, ON K1Y 0C4 Canada.

Williams, Thomas L. (F. 1, 1944, Schenectady, NY) Med Libns., Vets. Admin. Med. Ctr., New York, 1981–; Adjunct Asst. Cur., NY Univ. Sch. of Med., 1981–; Med. Libn., Vets. Admin. Med. Ctr., Lyons, NJ, 1980–81; Head, Circ. Dept., Westchester Med. Ctr. Lib., NY Med. Coll., 1977–80; Cat., Ref. Libn., NY Med. Coll., Flower and Fifth Ave. Hosp., 1976–77. **Educ.:** Columbia Univ., 1974, BA (Eng. Lit.), 1976, MS (LS). **Orgs.:** Med. LA: NY Reg. Grp., Legis. Com. (1976–77), Prog. Com. (1979–80), Exec. Com. (1980–82). **Addr.:** VA Medical Center, 408 1st Ave., New York, NY 10010.

Williams, Virginia F. (Ap. 24, 1927, Cleveland, OH) Media Spec., Cleveland Pub. Schs., 1966–, Elem. Tchr., 1955–66. **Educ.:** Philander Smith Coll., 1946–49, AB, cum laude (Eng.); Case West. Rsv., 1954–55, MA (Educ.); Kent State Univ., 1978–79, MLS; various insts. **Orgs.:** OH LA. ALA: AASL. **Honors:** Alpha Kappa Mu, 1948; Alpha Kappa Alpha. **Activities:** 10; 21, 22, 32; 63 **Addr.:** Cleveland Public Schools, 1380 E. 6th St., Cleveland, OH 44114.

Williams, Wallace D. (O. 23, 1946, Campbellsville, KY) Head Libn., Florence Williams Pub. Lib., Coord. Pub. Libs., St. Croix, 1977–; Branch Libn., Chicago Pub. Lib., 1974–77, Lrng. Skills Instr., Univ. of NH, 1975; Jet Aircraft Mechanic, U.S. Air Frc., 1966–70. **Educ.:** Northeast. IL Univ., 1970–73, BA (Pol. Sci.); Rosary Coll., 1973–75, MALS; various lib. insts. **Orgs.:** St Croix LA: Insts. Com., Ch. ALA: Black Caucus. Gvr.'s Conf. on Lib. and Info. Srvs.: Pub. Com. (Ch., 1979); Del. Various other orgs. St. Croix Arts Cncl. Emancipation a Sec. Look. Frnds. of the F. Williams Pub. Lib. Amer. Running and Fitness Assn. Various other orgs. **Honors:** Spec. Olympics Prog., Cert. of Apprec., 1980. **Pubns.:** Various articles, slide-tape presentations. **Activities:** 9, 13; 17, 27; 50, 66, 72 **Addr.:** Box 2720, Christiansted, St. Croix, VI 00820.

Williams, Wiley J. (Mr. 3, 1924, Headland, AL) Prof., LS, Kent State Univ., 1979–; Asst. Prof. to Prof., Peabody Lib. Sch., 1965–79, Asst. Prof., LS, Univ. of WA, 1965; Visit. Instr., Univ. of NC, 1963; Instr., Libn., Bowling Green State Univ., 1961–64; Ref. Libn., Bus. Lib., Univ. of AL, 1952–59. **Educ.:** Univ. of NC, 1945–49, BS (Mktg.); Peabody Coll., 1951–52, MALS; Univ. of MI, 1959–60, MPA (Pub. Admin.); Univ. of MI, 1957–64, PhD (LS). **Orgs.:** ALA: RASD, Outstand. Ref. Srvs. Com. (1978–80); Ref. and Subscrpn. Bks. Review Com. (1968–74, 1981–). AALS. SLA. **Honors:** Alpha Kappa Psi. **Pubns.:** Jt. auth., *Fundamental Reference Sources* (1980); "The Years of a Popularly Elected Public Printer in Michigan, 1850–1851," *Jnl. of Lib. Hist.* (Jl. 1970); "Memo Writing–A Classroom Experiment," *Jnl. of Educ. for Libnshp.* (Spr. 1977); "Economics and Business Administration," annotated bibl. *Sources of Information in the Social Sciences* (1973). **Activities:** 11; 15, 29, 39; 59, 91, 92 **Addr.:** School of Library Science, Kent State University, Kent, OH 44242.

Williamson, Harriet L. (Mr. 30, 1941, Crawfordsville, IN) Lib. Dir., Mercy Hosp., 1976–. **Educ.:** Hunter Coll., 1959–61; Cornell Univ., 1961–62; Boston Univ., 1963–65, BA (Art Hist.); Univ. of IL, 1971–72, MA (Educ.), 1975–76, MS (LS); Med. LA 1976, Cert. **Orgs.:** Med. LA: Midwest Chap., Educ. Com. (Ch., 1981–83); Hosp. Lib. Sect. (Secy., 1981–82). Hlth. Sci. Libns. of IL: Pres. (1981–82). Champaign-Urbana Cnsrtm.: Coord. (1979–81). **Pubns.:** Ref. chap., *Basic Library Management for Health Science Librarians* (1981). **Activities:** 5; 15, 17, 39; 80 **Addr.:** Mercy Hospital Library, 1400 W. Park, Urbana, IL 61810.

Williamson, Jane (Ja. 13, 1950, Gaylord, MN) Dir., Info. Srvs., Women's Action Alliance, 1977–; Freelnc. Libn.; Clearinghse. Coord., Managing Ed., Clearinghse. on Women's Std., The Feminist Press, 1974–76. **Educ.:** Antioch Coll., 1968–73, BA (Hist.); Columbia Univ., 1973–74, MLS. **Orgs.:** ALA. SLA. NY LA: RT on Women's Concerns, Strg. Com. Women's Info. Srvs. Netwk. Various other orgs. Amer. Prtg. Hist. Assn. Feminist Writers Gld. Women's Natl. Bk. Assn. Amer. Socty. of Indxrs. **Pubns.:** Jt. auth., *Women's Action Almanac* (1979); *New Feminist Scholarship: A Guide to Bibliographies* (1979); jt. auth., *Feminist Resources: A Guide to Curricular Materials* (1977); jt. auth., *Women's Work and Women's Studies: An Annotated Bibliography* (1975); jt. auth., *Who's Who and Where in Women's Studies* (1974). **Activities:** 12; 15, 17, 39; 95-Women's issues. **Addr.:** 615 W. 113 St., New York, NY 10025.

Williamson, John G. (Ja. 29, 1933, Winthrop, MN) Dir., St. Mary's Coll. of MD Lib., 1978–; Hum. Biblgphr., Yale Univ. Lib., 1972–78, Assoc. Acq. Libn., Univ. of DE Lib., 1971–72; Asst. Prof., European Hist., Swarthmore Coll., 1966–70. **Educ.:** Cornell Univ., 1950–54, AB (Hist.); Johns Hopkins Univ., 1958–63, PhD (Hist.); Drexel Univ., 1970–71, MS (LS). **Orgs.:** ALA. **Honors:** Phi Beta Kappa, 1964; Beta Phi Mu, 1971. **Pubns.:** *Karl Helfferich, 1872–1924: Economist, Financier, Politician* (1971); transl., Rudolf von Albertini, *European Colonial Rule* (forthcoming); "The 'Mussolini Collection'," *Yale Univ. Lib. Gazette* (Jl. 1978); "Swarthmore College's Teaching Library Proposals," *Drexel Lib. Qtly.* (Sum.–Fall 1971). **Activities:** 1; 15, 17, 34 **Addr.:** St. Mary's College of Maryland Library, St. Mary's City, MD 20686.

Williamson, Linda Eileen (Ag. 5, 1947, San Diego, CA) Gvt. Docum. Libn., Vanderbilt Univ. Lib., 1975–, Visit. Instr., Dept. of LS, 1980; Ref. Libn., Jt. Univ. Libs., 1973–75; Gvt. Docum. Libn., Univ. of CA, San Diego, 1972–73; Visit. Lectr., LS, George Peabody Coll., 1978; Indexing Consult., Natl. Indexing Ctr. for Educ. Media, 1971–72. **Educ.:** PA State Univ., 1965–68, BS (Fam. Std.); Univ. of South. CA, 1971–72, MS (LS). **Orgs.:** Gvt. Docum. Org. of TN: Prog. Dir. (1976–77); Nsltr. Ed. (1977–78); Vice–Ch., Prog. Dir. (1978–79); Ch. (1979–80). TN State Data Ctr. Adv. Cncl.: Ch. (1981–82). SELA. ALA: GODORT; IRRT. Various other orgs. Jt. Univ. Libs. Lib. Fac. Cncl: Vice–Ch. (1977–78); Ch. (1978–79). Nashville Univ. Women's Cncl. **Pubns.:** Various articles, reviews. **Activities:** 1; 29, 39, 46; 62, 78 **Addr.:** Documents Unit, Central Library, Vanderbilt University Library, Nashville, TN 37203.

Williamson, Marilyn L. (Ja. 27, 1943, Pontiac, IL) Bk. Acq. Libn., GA Inst. of Tech., 1981–, Asst. Acq. Libn., Serials, 1971–80. **Educ.:** Agnes Scott Coll., 1963–65, BA (Eng.); Emory Univ., 1970–71, MLn; GA State Univ., 1975, MA (Eng.). **Orgs.:** ALA: ACRL. **Pubns.:** "Serials Evaluation at the Georgia Institute of Technology Library," *Serials Libn.* (Win. 1977). **Activities:** 1; 15, 44, 46 **Addr.:** Price Gilbert Memorial Library, Georgia Institute of Technology Atlanta, GA 30332.

Williamson, Mary F. (Je. 14, 1933, Toronto, ON) Fine Arts Libn., York Univ., 1970–; Assoc. Instr., Fac. of LS, Univ. of Toronto, 1978–; Ref. Libn., Educ. Ctr., Toronto Bd. of Educ., 1965–69; Libn., Fine Art Sect., Toronto Pub. Lib., 1960–65. **Educ.:** Univ. of Toronto, 1951–55, BA (Fine Art), 1959–60, BLS, 1962–64, MA (Fine Art), 1969–70, MLS. **Orgs.:** Can. LA: Can. Art Libs. *Nsltr.* Ed. (1979–81). ARLIS/NA: Can. Rep. to Exec. Bd. (1976–78); Pubns. Com. (Ch., 1981–). ARLIS/UK. Bibl. Socty. of Can. Univs. Art Assn. of Can. Assn. of Can. Thea. Hist. **Honors:** Beta Phi Mu, 1960. **Pubns.:** Jt. ed., *The Art and Pictorial Press in Canada; Two Centuries of Art Periodicals* (1979); ed. adv. bd., *Art Libs. Jnl.* (1981–). various short articles. **Activities:** 1, 11; 15, 24, 26; 55, 57 **Addr.:** Scott Library, York University, Downsview, ON M3J 2R2 Canada.

Williamson, William Landram (Ag. 13, 1920, Lexington, KY) Prof., LS, Univ. of WI, 1966–; Lib. Consult., USAID–Indonesia Higher Educ., 1970; Head Libn., Montclair State Coll., 1964–66; Nicholas Murray Butler Libn., Columbia Univ., 1954–64; Lib. Consult., Ford Indonesia Tchr. Trng. Proj., SUNY, 1960–62; Assoc. and Actg. Libn., Baylor Univ., 1949–51, Asst. Libn., 1947–48; various tchg. and consult. positions, 1964–70. **Educ.:** Univ. of WI, 1938–41, BA, hons. (Amer. Hist.); Emory Univ., 1941–42, BA (LS); Columbia Univ., 1948–49, MS (LS); Univ. of Chicago, 1951–59, PhD (LS). **Orgs.:** ALA: LLib. Admin. Div./Circ. Srvs. Sect. (Ch., 1968–69). WI LA. Archons of Colophon. AAUP. **Pubns.:** *William Frederick Poole and the Modern Library Movement* (1963); "A Quest for Copies of the Articles," *Bk. Collector* (Spr. 1978); ed., *A Search for New Insights in Librarianship; Proceedings...* (1976); "William Frederick Poole," *Encyc. of Lib. and Info. Sci.* (v. 23); "William Frederick Poole," *Dictionary of American Library Biography* (1978); "Thomas Bennet and the Origins of Analytical Bibliography," *Jnl. of Lib. Hist.* (Win. 1981); various articles, eds. (1970–71). **Activities:** 1, 11; 15, 26, 41; 54, 57, 73 **Addr.:** Library School, University of Wisconsin, Helen C. White Hall, 600 N. Park St., Madison, WI 53706.

Willis, Paul A. (O. 1, 1941, Edwardsville, IN) Dir. of Libs., Univ. of KY, 1974–, Actg. Dean, Coll. of LS, 1975–76, Law Libn., Coll. of Law, 1969–74, Circ. Libn., 1966–69; Catlgr., NASA Sci. and Info. Facility, 1963–66; Catlgr., Copyrt. Ofc., Lib. of Congs., 1963. **Educ.:** Univ. of KY, 1960–63, AB (Arts, Law); Univ. of MD, 1965–66, MLS; Univ. of KY, 1966–69, JD. **Orgs.:** AALL: Place. Com. (Ch., 1971–73). ALA. KY LA. KY Judicial Retirement and Removal Comsn.: Exec. Secy. (1977–). **Honors:** Omicron Delta Kappa. **Pubns.:** *Jnl. of Legal Educ. Cumulative Index, 1948–1970* (1971); "Call on the U.K. Law Library," *KY Bar Jnl.* (1972); "Law Libraries and the Depository Program," *Law Lib. Jnl.* (1972); "A Brief Survey of the Kentucky Court of Appeals Legal Opinions Published 1968–1971," *KY Law Jnl.* (1973); chap., *Fundamentals of Legal Research* probs. booklet (1973); various articles, reviews in LS and law (1969–71). **Activities:** 1; 17 **Addr.:** 2055 Bridgeport Dr., Lexington, KY 40502.

Willis, Stephen Charles (D. 17, 1946, Collingwood, ON) Head, Mss. Col., Msc. Div., Natl. Lib. of Can., 1975–; Prof., CEGEP Vanier, 1975; Catlgr., Radio–Can., 1974–75. **Educ.:** Univ. of West. ON., 1965–69, BA, hons. (Msc.); Columbia Univ., 1969–71, MA (Msclgy.), 1971–75, PhD (Msclgy.); Pub. Arch. of Can., 1975, Dip. (Arch.). **Orgs.:** CAML: Mem. Secy. (1975–80); Pubns. Com. (1978–). Assn. des Archvsts. du PQ. Mss. Socty. **Honors:** Woodrow Wilson Fellow, 1969; Can. Cncl., Flwshp., 1972–74. **Activities:** 2, 4; 15, 39, 45; 55 **Addr.:** Manuscript Collection, Music Division, National Library of Canada, 395 Wellington St., Ottawa, ON K1A ON4 Canada.

Willmering, William Joseph (Ja. 7, 1944, St. Louis, MO) Head, Serial Recs. Sect., Natl. Lib. of Med., 1980–; Head, Serials Dept., Northwest. Univ. Lib., 1973–80; Serials Libn., Univ. of MT, 1971–73, Asst. Serials Libn., 1970–71, Asst. Ref. Libn., 1967–70. **Educ.:** Marian Coll., 1962–66, BA; Univ. of IL, 1966–67, MLS. **Orgs.:** ALA: RTSD/Serials Sect., Policy and Resrch. Com. (1980–82). **Pubns.:** "Serial Control with Northwestern University Library's NOTIS 3 System," *ASIS Procs.* (1977); "On-line Centralized Serial Control," *Serials Libn.* (Spr. 1977). **Activities:** 1; 15, 44, 46 **Addr.:** National Library of Medicine, 8600 Rockville Pike, Bethesda, MD 20209.

Willmert, J. Allen (Ja. 25, 1926, Lakeville, IN) Libn. of the Coll., Funderburg Lib., Manchester Coll., 1969–, Cat. Libn., 1966–69; Libn., Montague Pub. Schs., 1957–66; Tchr./Libn., Bourbon Pub. Schs., 1954–57. **Educ.:** Miami Univ., OH, Manchester Coll., 1944–48, AB (Eng.); Untd. Theo. Semy., 1948–51, MDiv (New Testament); Univ. of MI, 1961–63, AMLS. **Orgs.:** ALA: ACRL. IN LA: Coll. and Univ. Div. Untd. Meth. Church: N. IN Conf. **Honors:** Beta Phi Mu, 1963. **Activities:** 1; 17, 40, 44; 61, 90 **Addr.:** Funderburg Library, Manchester College, North Manchester, IN 46962.

Willocks, Robert Max (O. 10, 1924, Maryville, TN) Assoc. Dir. of Libs., Univ. of FL, 1976–; Asst. Dir. of Libs., Syracuse Univ., 1970–76; Dir. of Lib., Columbia Coll., 1967–70; Assoc. Dir., Heidelberg Coll., 1965–67; Bapt. Missn. to Korea, Frgn. Missn. Bd., South. Bapt. Conv., 1956–65. **Educ.:** Maryville Coll., 1942–49, BA (Phil.); Golden Gate Bapt. Theo. Semy. 1949–52, BD; George Peabody Coll., 1961–62, MALS; Golden Gate Bapt.

PROFESSIONAL ACTIVITIES: Institutions: 1. Acad. lib.; 2. Arch.; 3. Assn.; 4. Fed./Gvt. lib.; 5. Inst. lib.; 6. Mfr./Suppl.; 7. Milit. lib.; 8. Musm.; 9. Pub. lib.; 10. Sch. lib.; 11. Sch. of lib. sci.; 12. Spec. lib.; 13. State lib.; 14. (other). **Functions/Activities:** 15. Acq./Col. dev.; 16. Adult srvs.; 17. Admin.; 18. Apprais.; 19. Archit./Bldgs.; 20. Cat./Class.; 21. Chld. srvs.; 22. Circ.; 23. Cons./Pres.; 24. Consult.; 25. Cont. ed.; 26. Educ. lib. sci.; 27. Ext. srvs.; 28. Fund/Grants; 29. Gvt. pubs.; 30. Indx./Abs.; 31. Instr. lib. use; 32. Media srvs.; 33. Micro.; 34. Netwks./Coop.; 35. Persnl.; 36. PR; 37. Publshg.; 38. Recs. mgt.; 39. Ref. srvs.; 40. Repro.; 41. Resrch.; 42. Review.; 43. Secur.; 44. Serials; 45. Spec. col.; 46. Tech. srvs.; 47. Trustees/Bds.; 48. YA srvs.; 49. (other).

Theo. Semy., 1962, ThM. **Orgs.:** ALA: RTSD/Reprodct. of Lib. Mtrls. Sect., Tech. Com. (Ch., 1980–82), Telefac. Com. (Ch., 1976–1978), Consult., Resrch. and Policy Com. (1978–80); LAMA, Circ. Systs.' Eval. Com. (1980–). FL LA. SELA. **Pubns.:** "4 Million Catalog Cards on Seven Little Platters; Library Spinoffs from Videodisc Technology," *Amer. Libs.* (D. 1975); ed. bd., *Videodisc/Teletext Jnl.* **Activities:** 1; 17, 22, 24; 56, 93 **Addr.:** Libraries, 210 Library W., University of Florida, Gainesville, FL 32611.

Willoughby, Nona C. (Je. 3, 1923, Racine, WI) Hlth. Scis. Libn., Dept. Head, North. Westchester Hosp. Ctr., 1979–; Ref. Libn., Gen., Bus. and Indus., Atlanta Pub. Lib., 1954–55. **Educ.:** Univ. of CA, Berkeley, 1945–48, BA (Anthro.), 1948–50, MA (Anthro.); FL State Univ., 1953–55, MALS. **Orgs.:** Med. LA. Hlth. Info. Libs. of Westchester. ALA. NY LA. Various other orgs. **Honors:** Phi Beta Kappa, 1948; Beta Phi Mu, 1955. **Pubns.:** "Division of Labor Among the Indians of California," *Indians of California* (1974). **Activities:** 5, 9; 15, 17, 49-On-Line srch.; 56, 58, 80 **Addr.:** 14 Garey Dr., Chappaqua, NY 10514.

Wills, Floreid (S. 15, 1909, Tyler, TX) Libn., Gambrell St. Bapt. Church, 1976–; Cat. Libn., Fleming Lib., Southwest. Bapt. Theo. Semy., 1954–75; Head Catlgr., Baylor Univ., 1945–54; Tchr.-Libn., Un. Grove Pub. Schs., 1944–45; Libn., Sequin HS, 1941–44. **Educ.:** TX Woman's Univ., 1939–40, BA (Eng., LS), 1944–48, BS (LS); Baylor Univ., 1952–56, MA (LS, Eng.). **Orgs.:** ATLA. TX LA. AAUW. Semy. Woman's Club. **Honors:** Phi Theta Kappa, 1938. **Activities:** 12; 15, 17, 20; 89, 90 **Addr.:** 1313 W. Boyce, Fort Worth, TX 76115.

Wills, Keith Cameron (Ag. 11, 1917, McCleary, WA) Dir. of Libs., Southwest. Bapt. Semy., 1966–; Lib. Dir., Midwest. Bapt. Semy., 1958–66; Ref. Libn., Southwest. Bapt. Semy., 1957–58, Circ. Libn., 1953–57. **Educ.:** Univ. of WA, 1936–41, AB (Gvt. Srv.); Southwest. Bapt. Semy., 1947–50, MDiv (Theo.), 1951–58, ThD (Christ. Ethics); Univ. of Denver, 1965–66, MA (LS). **Orgs.:** ATLA: Mem. Com., Ch.; Exec. Bd. TX LA. Civitan. South. Bapt. Hist. Socty.: Exec. Bd. TX Bapt. Hist. Socty.: Secy.–Treas. Various other orgs. **Pubns.:** "L. R. Elliott, Librarian of Vision," *Southwest. Jnl. of Theo.* (Fall 1969); "L. R. Elliott and Southern Baptist History," *Bapt. Hist. and Heritage* (Jl. 1971). **Activities:** 1; 15, 17, 35; 85, 90, 92 **Addr.:** 6133 Wrigley Way, Fort Worth, TX 76133.

Willson, Elizabeth Mgr., Data Conversion, Chicago Pub. Lib., 1981–, Asst. to Dir., Cult. Ctr., 1979–81; Spec. Cols. Libn., Galesburg Pub. Lib., 1973–79. **Educ.:** Knox Coll., 1968–71, BA (Msc.); Univ. of IL, 1972–73, MLS. **Orgs.:** ALA. IL LA. **Activities:** 9; 17, 49-Lib. autom. **Addr.:** Data Processing Dept., Chicago Public Library, 425 N. Michigan Ave., Chicago, IL 60611.

Willson, Richard Eugene (Ja. 1, 1933, Kenton, OH) Exec. Dir., Starved Rock Lib. Syst., 1977–; Instr., LS, Lorain Cnty. Cmnty. Coll., 1970–77; Dir., Lorain Pub. Lib., 1967–77; Head Libn., Amos Meml. Lib., 1963–67; Head Libn., Hum. Div., Kent State Univ., 1958–63; Art and Msc. Libn., S. Euclid Reg. Branch, Cuyahoga Cnty. Pub. Lib., 1957–58. **Educ.:** Bowling Green State Univ., 1951–54, BA (Hist.); Case West. Rsv. Univ., 1955–57, MSLS; Miami Univ. 1968, Lib. Exec. Dev. Prog. **Orgs.:** IL LA: Spec. Lib. Srvs. Sect. (VP and Pres.–Elect, 1979–81). IL Valley Cmnty. Coll.: Adv. Com. for Lib. Tech. Assts. (1977–). ALA: LAMA, Com. on Stats. for Lib. Persnl. Resrcs. (1979–81); Natl. Lib. Week. Com. (1971–73); PLA, Actv. Com. (1971–74). Various other orgs. Sons of the Amer. Revolution: Natl. Socty. Lib. Com. (1978–); IL Socty. Constructive Citizenship Com.: Ch. (1980–). Amer. Coll. of Genealogists: Secy. (1979–). Socty. of Colonial Wars. Hereditary Ord. of Descendants of Colonial Gvrs. Various other orgs. **Honors:** Sons of the Amer. Revolution, OH Socty., Silver Good Citizenship Medal, 1975; Sons of the Amer. Revolution, Natl. Mem. Awds., 1976, 1977. **Pubns.:** *The Willson Family Supplement 1959–1979* (1979); *The Willson Family 1672–1959* (1959); *English Benedictine Monastic Libraries During the Middle Ages* (1957). **Activities:** 9, 13; 17, 24, 34; 66, 69 **Addr.:** Starved Rock Library System, 900 Hitt St., Ottawa, IL 61350.

Wilmeth, Don B. (D. 15, 1939, Houston, TX) Prof. and Ch., Dept. of Thea. Arts, Brown Univ., 1967–; Asst. Prof. and Ch., Dept. of Drama, East. NM Univ., 1964–67. **Educ.:** Abilene Christ. Univ., 1957–61, BA (Thea.); Univ. of AR, 1961–62, MA (Thea.); Univ. of IL, 1962–64, PhD (Thea.). **Orgs.:** Thea. LA: VP; George Freedley–Thea. LA Bk. Awd. Com. (Ch., 1974–). Amer. Socty. for Thea. Resrch: Exec. Bd. (1976–79). Amer. Thea. Assn.: Pubns. Com. (Ch., 1976–78); *Theatre Jnl.* Bk. Review Ed. (1977–80). Core Col. for Coll. Libs.: Consult. (1970–). Socty. for Thea. Resrch., Eng. Socty. for the Advnc. of Educ.: Bd. of Trustees (1977–). Int. Fed. for Thea. Resrch. **Honors:** Barnard Hewitt Thea. Hist. Awd.; Phi Beta Kappa, 1977; Phi Kappa Phi, 1964. **Pubns.:** *George Frederick Cooke* (1980); *American and British Popular Entertainment: An Information Guide* (1980); *The American Stage to World War I: An Information Guide* (1978); "American Popular Entertainment: Historical Perspective," *Amer. Pop. Entertainment* (1979); "Stage Entertainments," *A Handbook of American Popular Culture* (1978). **Activities:** 1, 2; 17, 24, 41; 55, 57 **Addr.:** Dept. of Theatre Arts, Box 1897, Brown University, Providence, RI 02912.

Wilner, Isabel (F. 17, 1920, Shanghai, China) Libn., Lida Lee Tall Lib., Towson State Univ., 1949–; Instr. in Storytel., Towson State Coll., 1972–76; Storytel. Spec., Ctrl. Atl. Reg. Educ. Lab., 1967–68, Consult. in Chld. Lit., 1967; Exch. Chld. Libn., Merton and Morden Pub. Lib., Surrey, Eng., 1956–57; Chld. Libn., NY Pub. Lib., 1948–49; Libn., Army Lib. Srv., 1946–48; Chld. Libn., Carnegie Lib. of Pittsburgh, 1945–46. **Educ.:** William Smith Coll., 1938–42, BA (Eng.); Carnegie Inst. of Tech., 1944–45, BS (LS). **Orgs.:** ALA: ALSC, Booklist Subcom. of Jaycees Good Readg. Com. (1966–72), Newbery–Caldecott Awds. Com. (1968–69), Intl. Rel. Com. Booklist Subcom. (1969–71), Laura Ingalls Wilder Awd. Com. (1973–75); *Top of the News* Assoc. Ed. (1967–69). Assn. for Childhood Educ. Intl.: Com. to Rev. "Children's Books for $1.50 and Less" (Ch., 1967–69); Lit. Com. for "Told Under the City Umbrella" (1969–72). Frnds. of the Intl. Bd. of Bks. for Young People. Natl. Assn. for the Prsrvn. and Perpet. of Storytel. **Pubns.:** "Making Poetry Happen: the Birth of a Poetry Troupe," *Chld. Lit. in Educ.* (Sum. 1979); *The Poetry Troupe, an Anthology of Poems to Read Aloud* (1977); "Poetry Troupe: Answers to Questions," *Sch. Media Qtly.* (Win. 1979); "Grandmothers in Residence," *Sch. Media Qtly.* (N. 1975); "A Beginner's Card Catalog," *Sch. Media Qtly.* (Sum. 1974); various articles (1966–72). **Activities:** 10, 12; 21 **Addr.:** 316 Garden Rd., Towson, MD 21204.

Wilroy, Jo Ann (D. 7, 1935, Guntown, MS) Asst. Dir., 1st Reg. Lib., 1979–, Reg. Ref. Libn., 1967–79; HS Libn., Whitehaven HS, 1961–63; Readers Adv., Memphis–Shelby Cnty. Pub. Lib., 1958–61; HS Libn., Haines City HS, 1957–58. **Educ.:** Univ. of MS, 1955–57, BAE (Eng.), 1977, MLS; George Peabody Coll., 1978, MLS. **Orgs.:** ALA. MS LA: *Ms Libs.* Pub. Libs. Rpt. (1981–); Rcrt. Com. (1980–); Awds. Com. (Ch., 1980); Gvr.'s Conf. (Grp. Leader, 1979); Conv. Com. (1977); Pub. Lib. Sect. (Secy., 1973), MS Per. Index Com. (1976–77); Legis. Com. (1978). DeSoto Cnty. Hist. Socty.: Bd. of Dirs. (1977–). Reg. II Mental Hlth. Ctr.: Bd. of Dirs. (1977–); Secy. (1980–). Hernando Woman's Club. **Honors:** Beta Phi Mu, 1979. **Activities:** 9; 16, 24, 39; 69, 78, 86 **Addr.:** 59 Commerce St., Hernando, MS 38632.

Wilson, Amy Seetoo (Ag. 24, 1946, Taipei, Taiwan, Repub. of China) Asst. Ref. Libn., Univ. of IL, 1974–. **Educ.:** Natl. Chengchi Univ., 1964–68, BA (West. Lang. and Lit.); Univ. of IL, 1968–70, MA (Eng. as a Sec. Lang.); North. IL Univ., 1971–73, MA (LS). **Orgs.:** ALA: ACRL; RASD/Machine–Assisted Ref. Sect., Eval. Com.; GODORT, Educ. Task Frc. Chin. Amer. LA: Bd. **Pubns.:** "China Viewed Through Stories for American Children," *Jnl. of Lib. and Info. Sci.* (O. 1978); "Instructional and Promotional Activities for Government Documents in Illinois Libraries," *IL Libs.* (forthcoming). **Activities:** 1; 39 **Addr.:** 2007 S. Crescent Dr., Champaign, IL 61820.

Wilson, Barbara J. (Jl. 9, 1948, Mansfield, OH) Adj. Lectr., Sch. of LS, Univ. of MI, 1979–; Mgr., Sales Admin., Univ. Microfilms Intl., 1971–, Supvsr., 1977–78, Publshr. Rep., 1973–76, Prog. Admin., 1971–73. **Educ.:** Univ. of MI, 1966–70, BA (Psy.), 1971–74, MA (Educ.), 1974–, PhD Cand. **Orgs.:** ALA. Natl. Micro. Assn. Assn. of Info. Mgrs. SLA. **Activities:** 12; 17, 26, 33; 63, 75, 95-Micro. **Addr.:** University Microfilms International, 300 N. Zeeb Rd., Ann Arbor, MI 48106.

Wilson, Barbara L. (N. 12, 1927, Hartford, CT) Chief, Div. of Spec. Lib. Srvs., RI Dept. of State Lib. Srvs., 1973–; Head Libn., RI Reg. Lib. for the Blind and Phys. Handcpd., 1969–73; Interim Dir., RI Lib. Film Coop., 1975. **Educ.:** RI Sch. of Dsgn., 1945–49, BFA (Textile Dsgn.); Univ. of RI, 1967–69, MLS; various crs. (1973–77). **Orgs.:** New Eng. LA: Inst. Lib. Sect. RI LA: Corres. Secy. (1971–72); Nom. Com. (1978). WHCOLIS: Alternate Del. (1979). ALA: ASCLA, Com. to Assess Needs for Vocational Info. by Handcpd. (Ch., 1974–), RT for the Blind (Exhibits Ch., 1973) State Lib. Agency Sect.; Lib. Admin. Div./Bldg. Equip. Sect., Com. on Archit. Barriers (1972–74). RI Gvr.'s Conf. on Libs.: Conf. Coord. (1979). Gvr.'s Com. on Empl. of the Handcpd.: PR Com. (Head, 1978–79). Univ. of RI, Grad. Lib. Sch.: Adv. Bd. (1978–). Amer. Assn. of Workers for the Blind: NE Chap., Prog. Com. (1971–72), Secy. (1971), Nom. Com. (1972–73). RI Adult Educ. Assn.: Nom. Com. (1976–77). Various other orgs., ofcs. **Honors:** Untd. Cerebral Palsy, RI Chap., Outstan. Srv. Awd., 1977; Jamestown Rotary Club, Srv. Awd., 1976; Natl. Fed. of the Blind, RI Chap., Achvmt. Awd., 1979. **Pubns.:** "Assessment Needs: Materials," *HRLSD Jnl.* (Fall 1976). **Activities:** 13; 17, 27, 36; 55, 72, 95-Labor rel. **Addr.:** Rhode Island Dept. of State Library Services, 95 Davis St., Providence, RI 02908.

Wilson, Bernard E. (Je. 26, 1915, Detroit, MI) Catlgr. of Spec. Mtrls., Newberry Lib., 1959–; Msc. Catlgr., Univ. of MI, 1954–59; Ed., Intelligence, US Air Frc., Austria, 1948–52; Place. Ofcr., US Cvl. Srv., Austria, 1945–47. **Educ.:** Univ. of Toledo, 1932–37, BS (Chem.); Univ. of MI, 1937–38, MS (Math.), 1953–54, AMLS. **Orgs.:** Msc. LA. **Pubns.:** "An Unpublished Letter of Stendhal," *Newberry Lib. Bltn.* (D. 1965); various reviews of msc. and bks. about msc., *Msc. LA Notes* (1956–80). **Activities:** 12, 20, 41, 45; 55 **Addr.:** Newberry Library, 60 W. Walton St., Chicago, IL 60610.

Wilson, C. Daniel, Jr. (N. 8, 1941, Middletown, CT) Assoc. Dir., Birmingham Pub. Lib., 1979–; Dir., Wilton Pub. Lib., 1976–79; Asst. Dir., Perrot Meml. Lib., 1970–76; Biblgphr., Univ. of IL, 1968–70. **Educ.:** Univ. of the S., Elmhurst Coll., 1967, BA (Hist.); Rosary Coll., 1968, MLS. **Orgs.:** AL LA. SELA. ALA. **Honors:** Pi Gamma Mu, 1966. **Activities:** 9; 17 **Addr.:** 2020 Park Pl., Birmingham, AL 35203.

Wilson, Connie M. (Ja. 26, 1950, Merced, CA) Libn., Assoc. Prof., Area Hlth. Educ. Ctr., Univ. of AR for Med. Scis., Area Hlth. Educ. Ctr., 1977–; Libn., Ext. Div., Univ. of OK Hlth. Scis., 1973–76. **Educ.:** Univ. of OK, 1968–72, BA (Eng. Lit.), 1972–73, MLS; 1975, Cert. (Med. Libn. I). **Orgs.:** OK Hlth. Sci. Libns. Assn.: Pres. (1975–76). AR LA. Med. LA: S. Ctl. Reg. Grp., Nom. Com. (1976, 1979), Cont. Ed. Com. (1978). **Honors:** Phi Beta Kappa, 1972; ALA, LRRT Resrch. Awd., 1976. **Pubns.:** "Determination of Continuing Medical Education Needs of Clinicians from a Literature Search Study, Parts I and II," *Bltn. of the Med. LA* (Jl. 1977). **Activities:** 12; 27, 39; 80 **Addr.:** Area Health Education Center, Northwest Library, Washington Regional Medical Center, 1125 N. College, Fayetteville, AR 72701.

Wilson, DeEtta Catherine (N. 23, 1931, Harrisonburg, LA) Head Libn., Windward Cmnty. Coll., 1972–; Prog. Spec., Sch. Libs. and Instr. Mtrls. Branch, Ofc. of Lib. Srvs., State of HI, 1971–72; Libn., Waianae HS, 1966–71; Elem. Tchr., 1957–66. **Educ.:** LA State Univ., 1952, BA (Span.); Univ. of TX, Austin, 1969, MLS; Univ. of HI, 1978, MEd (Educ. Comm., Tech.). **Orgs.:** HI LA: Spr. Conf. Prog. Plng. (Co–Ch., 1970). ALA. ASIS. Delta Kappa Gamma Socty. Intl.: Chap. Pres. (1970–72); State Prog. Ch. (1973–75); Pioneer Women Ch. (1975–). **Pubns.:** "On the Way to Intershelving: Elements In the Decision," *HI Lib. Jnl.* (1976); various slide/tape progs. (1974–78). **Activities:** 1; 17, 31; 56, 75 **Addr.:** Windward Community College Library, 45–720 Keaahala Rd., Kaneohe, HI 96744.

Wilson, Eugene Holt (My. 13, 1909, Harrison, AR) Consult., 1979–; Exec. Dir., CO Comsn. on Higher Educ., 1976–77; Ch., Cent. Comsn., Univ. of CO, 1973–77, Pres., Emeritus, 1972–, Secy., Bd. of Regents, 1970–72, Pres., 1969, VP for Bus. Affairs, 1964–71, Prof. of Educ., 1960–72; various prof. positions, 1930–59. **Educ.:** Univ. of Ctrl. AR, 1930, BA; Univ. of IL, 1932, BS, 1933, MA, 1937, PhD; Yale Univ., 1940–41, Post–doct. fellow. **Orgs.:** ALA: Exec. Bd.; Cncl.; various coms.; ACRL, various ofcs., coms. ARL: Vice–Ch. CO LA: Pres. Various other orgs. AAUP: Natl. Cncl.; Com. on Org. and Policy; Univ. of CO Chap., Pres. Rocky Mt. Asm. on Natl. Goals: Dir. Wingspread Asm. on Natl. Goals. Beta Phi Mu: Pres. (1958–59). Various other orgs. **Honors:** US Air Frc. ROTC, Outstan. Srv. Medal, 1964; Univ. of CO, Assoc. Alum., Robert L. Stearns Awd., 1965; Univ. of CO, Recog. Medal, 1973. **Pubns.:** Jt. auth., *A Survey of the Library of MT State University* (1951); various articles, sps. **Activities:** 1, 14-Univ. admin.; 17, 20; 63 **Addr.:** 4295 Caddo Pkwy., Boulder, CO 80303.

Wilson, Evie YA Srvs. Spec., Tampa-Hillsborough Cnty. Pub. Lib. Syst., 1977–; YA Libn., Finkelstein Meml. Lib., Spring Valley, NY, 1974–77, Chld., Adult Ref., 1970–74; Media Spec., George W. Carver HS, Newport News, VA, 1968–69. **Educ.:** MS State Coll. for Women, 1965, BS; George Peabody Coll., 1968, MLS. **Orgs.:** ALA: YASD, Pres. (1981–82); VP, Pres. Elect (1980–81); Legis. Com. (Ch., 1981); Prog. and Budget Dev. (Ch., 1981); Bd. of Dir. FL LA: YA Srvs. Caucus. FL Netwk. of Youth and Fam. Srvs. Hills Cnty. (FL) Chld. Study Comsn. **Pubns.:** "The YA Advisory Board," *Voice of Youth Advocates* (Ap. 1979); "Cooperative Grantsmanship," *Top of the News* (Win. 1979); Reviews. **Activities:** 9; 48 **Addr.:** 8602 Champlain Ct., Apt. 85, Tampa, FL 33614.*

Wilson, Florabelle (Ja. 12, 19–, Indianapolis, IN) Libn., IN Ctrl. Univ., 1971–, Asst. Libn., 1957–71; Elem. Tchr., Indianapolis Pub. Schs., 1949–57. **Educ.:** IN Ctrl. Univ., 1946–49, BS (Educ.); IN Univ., 1961, MA (LS). **Orgs.:** ALA. IN LA: Coll. and Univ. Div. (Secy.–Treas., 1980). Ctrl. IN Area Lib. Srvs. Athrty.: Bd. of Dirs. (1979–). IN Coop. Lib. Srvs. Athrty. **Honors:** Beta Phi Mu. **Addr.:** Krannert Memorial Library, Indiana Central University, 1400 E. Hanna Ave., Indianapolis, IN 46227.

Wilson, Florence J. (D. 16, 1946, Las Vegas, NM) Coord. of Lib. Autom., George Mason Univ., 1981–, Circ. Libn., 1977–80, Ref. Libn., 1974–77. **Educ.:** Northwest. Univ., 1964–68, BA (Econ.); Emporia State Univ., 1972–73, ML (LS). **Orgs.:** ALA: LAMA/Stats. Sect., Exec. Com. (1980–82), Coord. Com. (1979–82), Stats. for Ref. Srvs. Com. (Ch., 1977–81, 1979–81), Stats. for Coll. and Univ. Libs. (Ch., 1981–82, 1981–83); GODORT, Lcl. Docums. Task Frc., Coord. (1977–78), Secy. (1976–77). Natl. Ctr. for Educ. Stats.: Feasibility Std. of Pub. Lib. User Srvy. **Activities:** 1; 22, 39; 56, 92 **Addr.:** 7805 McLean St., Manassas, VA 22111.

Wilson, Ian E. (Ap. 2, 1943, Montreal, PQ) Prov. Archvst., SK Arch. Bd., 1976–; Univ. Archvst., Queen's Univ., 1970–76, Asst. Archvst., 1967–70. **Educ.:** Queen's Univ., 1964–67, BA (Hist.), 1967–74, MA (Hist.). **Orgs.:** Soc. Scis. and Hum. Resrch. Cncl. of Can.: Consult. Grp. on Arch. (Ch., 1978–80). SK Heritage Adv. Bd.: Ch. (1977–). Can. Hist. Assn.: Arch. Sect., Exec. Mem. (1970–75), Ch. (1971–72). Natl. Arch. Apprais. Bd.: Prai-

Special Subjects/Services: 50. Adult educ.; 51. Advert./Mktg.; 52. Aerosp.; 53. Agric.; 54. Area std.; 55. Arts/Hum.; 56. Autom.; 57. Bibl./Prtg.; 58. Bio. sci.; 59. Bus./Fin.; 60. Chem.; 61. Copyrt.; 62. Documtn.; 63. Educ.; 64. Engin.; 65. Env.; 66. Eth. grps.; 67. Film; 68. Food/Nutr.; 69. Geneal.; 70. Geo.; 71. Geol.; 72. Handcpd.; 73. Hist.; 74. Int. frdm.; 75. Info. sci.; 76. Insr.; 77. Law; 78. Legis.; 79. Math./Comp. sci.; 80. Med.; 81. Metals; 82. Nat. resrcs.; 83. Newsp.; 84. Nuc. sci.; 85. Oral hist.; 86. Petr./Energy; 87. Pharm.; 88. Phys./Astr./Math.; 89. Readg.; 90. Relig.; 91. Sci./Tech.; 92. Soc. sci.; 93. Telecom.; 94. Transp.; 95. (other).

rie Reg. Ch. (1976–). SAA. Various other orgs. ON Hist. Socty.: Exec. Mem. (1970–76); Pres. (1975–76). Can. Cncl. Explorations Prog.: ON Sel. Com. (Ch., 1975–76). **Honors:** Woodrow Wilson Fndn., Flwshp. (hon.), 1967; Gvt. of Can., Queen Elizabeth II Silver Jubilee Medal, 1977. **Pubns.:** Jt. auth., *Heritage Kingston* (1973); ed., *Kingston City Hall* (1975); jt. auth., *Regina Before Yesterday* (1978); ch. and prin. auth., *Canadian Archives* (1980); "Opening Remarks," "Conclusion," *Report: Saskatchewan Heritage Conference* (1978); various articles, ed. coms., and videos. (1966–75). **Activities:** 2; 17; 55, 92 **Addr.:** Saskatchewan Archives Board, C/o University of Regina, Regina, SK S4S 0A2 Canada.

Wilson, Jane (S. 1, 1925, Chicago, IL) Intl. Rel. Ofcr., ALA, 1976–81; Chief Acq. Libn., Roosevelt Univ., 1971–74; Asst. to Dir./Persnl. Libn., Univ. of IL, Chicago, Med. Ctr., 1969–71; Actg. Head, Dept. of Spec. Cols., Univ. of CA, Davis, 1967–68; Libn., Asia Fndn., 1954–67, Asst. Libn., 1951–54; Air Frc. Libn., European Cmnd., U.S. Air Frc., 1948–51; Libn., CA Hist. Socty., 1947–48. **Educ.:** Knox Coll., Univ. of IL, 1942–46, BA (Hist.); Univ. of CA, Berkeley, 1946–47, BLS. **Orgs.:** ALA: Intl. Rel. Com. (1974–76); ACRL/Law and Pol. Sci. Subsect. (Ch., 1966–67); IRRT (Ch., 1958–59); various coms., ch.; ALA IRC Panel on UNESCO (1958–64). Frdm. to Read Fndn.: Dir. (1973–75). IL LA: Int. Frdm. Com. (Ch., 1971–73). CA LA: Various coms., ofcs. (1960–69). SLA: Various coms., ofcs. (1956–73). Chicago Map Socty. AAUP. **Pubns.:** "The Christmas Printer, or, The Printing Career of James D. Hart; with Checklist," *Bk. Club of CA Qtly. Nsltr.* (Win. 1963); "Adrian Wilson: The Book Designer in Tuscany Alley," *Bk. Club of CA Qtly. Nsltr.* (Spr.–Sum. 1968); "It's Still Christmas; or, a Continuation of the Printing Career of James D. Hart. Checklist," *Bk. Club of CA Qtly. Nsltr.* (Win. 1975–76); "Adrian Wilson, The Book Designer in Tuscany Alley: A Continued Checklist," *Bk. Club of CA Qtly. Nsltr.* (Spr. 1979); jt. auth., "Library and Archives Development Program: Organization of American States," *Encyc. of Lib. and Info. Sci.* (1977). **Activities:** 1, 12; 15, 39, 45; 54, 57 **Addr.:** c/o E.B. Stofft, 2315 W. Cherry, Park Ridge, IL 60068.

Wilson, Jane Bliss (F. 24, 1914, Durham, NC) Retired, 1976–; Chld. Consult., NC Dept. of Cult. Resrcs., 1968–75; Dir. of Sch. Libs., Durham City Schs., 1945–68; HS Libn., R. J. Reynolds HS, 1943–45; Chld. Libn., Wake Cnty. Pub. Lib., 1941–43; YA Libn., Durham Cnty. Pub. Lib., 1940–41; Chld. Libn., Detroit Pub. Lib., 1937–40; Visit. Lectr., various univs., 1938–78. **Educ.:** Duke Univ., 1931–34, AB (Amer. Lit.); Univ. of NC, 1936–37, BSLS; Duke Univ., 1945–47, MA (Amer. Lit.). **Orgs.:** ALA: Resrch. Com. (1972–73); Cncl. (1950–53). SELA: Adv. Com. to Exec. Bd. (1965). NC LA: Pres. (1950–53). Delta Kappa Gamma: Various coms. (1967–). **Honors:** ALA, Grolier Awd., 1975; NC LA, Life Mem., 1979. **Pubns.:** *The Story Experience* (1979); jt. ed., *North Carolina Authors* (1951); jt. producer, *Reading is the Family* film (1973); various articles (1945–75). **Activities:** 10, 13; 17, 21, 24; 55, 67, 89 **Addr.:** Rte. 6, Box 133, Farrington Rd., Chapel Hill, NC 27514.

Wilson, Joan W. (O. 15, 1944, Atlanta, GA) Head of Lib. Srvs., Fred Hutchinson Cancer Resrch. Ctr., 1977–; Head of Pub. Srvs., Univ. of VA Hlth. Scis. Lib., 1975–76; Ref. Coord., Univ. of WA Hlth. Scis. Lib., 1972–75, Ref. Libn., 1971–75; Bk. Ord. Libn., 1969–70. **Educ.:** Emory Univ., 1962–66, BA (Educ.), 1968–69, MLS; Med. LA, 1969, Cert. (Grade 1). **Orgs.:** Med. LA: Mem. Com. (1979–82); Cancer Libns. Grp. (Ch., 1979–80). Seattle Area Hosp. Lib. Cnsrtm. **Pubns.:** "Evaluation of a Clinical Medical Librarianship Program at a University Health Sciences Library," *Bltn. of Med. LA* (1976); "Continuing Education in Cancer for the Community Physician: Design and Evaluation of a Regional Table of Contents Service," *Bltn. of Med. LA* (1981). **Activities:** 1, 14-Resrch. ctr.; 15, 17, 39; 80 **Addr.:** 2304 N. 57th St., Seattle, WA 98103.

Wilson, Lesley Pauline (Je. 3, 1951, Sheboygan, WI) Head, Autom. Cat., Univ. of WA, 1981–, Proj. Mgr., HEA Title II-C, Forest Resrcs. Proj., 1980–81, Sci. Catlgr., Orig. Cat. Div., 1979–80; Head, Cat. Dept., IN Univ., Purdue Univ., 1978–79; Catlgr., N.E. MO State Univ., 1975–78. **Educ.:** Univ. of WI, Milwaukee, 1969–73, BA (Fr.), 1974–75, MA (LS). **Orgs.:** ALA. Pac. NW LA. **Activities:** 1; 17, 20, 46; 56, 58 **Addr.:** University of Washington Libraries, Suzzallo Library, Seattle, WA 98195.

Wilson, Lucy (D. 27, 1938, Cincinnati, OH) Coll. Libn., Dir. of Lib. Instr. Media Tech. Prog., Raymond Walters Coll., Univ. of Cincinnati, 1979, Adj. Asst. Prof. of Lib. Tech., 1979–, Adj. Instr. of Lib. Tech., 1977–79, Pub. Srvs. Libn., 1974–79; Sch. Libn., Coll. Prep. Sch., Cincinnati, OH, 1969–74; Tech. Libn., Chanute Air Frc. Base, 1963–65. **Educ.:** Middlebury Coll., 1956–60, BA (Fr.); Univ. of IL, 1962–63, MS (LS). **Orgs.:** ASIS: South. OH Chap., Prog. Com. (Secy., 1980–81). Grt. Cincinnati Lib. Cnsrtm.: Fin. and Grant Com. (1979–80); Treas. (1980–81). Participating Lib. Adv. Com. of the KY, OH, MI Reg. Med. Lib. Netwk. AAUP. **Pubns.:** "Teaching Online Retrieval in a Library Technology Program," *Natl. Online Mtg. Procs.* (Mr. 1981). **Activities:** 1; 17, 26; 75 **Addr.:** Raymond Walters College, 9555 Plainfield Rd., Cincinnati, OH 45236.

Wilson, Marion C. (Conroy) (Ja. 28, 1916, Edmonton, AB) Exec. Secy., Natl. Lib. of Can., 1979–, Asst. Dir., Pub. Srvs. Branch, 1973–79, Chief, Lib. Documtn. Ctr., 1970–73; Exec. Secy., Can. LA, 1967–70; Assoc. Ed., *Can. Per. Index*, 1962–67. **Educ.:** Univ. of AB, 1933–36, BA (Eng.); Univ. of WA, 1941–42, BA (Libnshp.). **Orgs.:** Can. LA. Bibl. Socty. of Can. Indexing and Abs. Socty. of Can. Notre Dame de Grace Cmnty. Cncl., Montreal. Bd. of Mgt. NDG Lib. for Boys and Girls: Ch. (1953–59). **Honors:** NDG Kinsmen's Club, Citizen of the Yr., 1959. **Pubns.:** Ed., *Women in Federal Politics, a Bio-bibliography* (1975); *Survey of Library Technician Training Programs in Western Canada and Ontario* (1968); ed., *Feliciter* (1968–70). **Activities:** 4; 17, 36, 39; 57, 92 **Addr.:** R.R. 2, Merrickville, ON K0G 1N0 Canada.

Wilson, Mary Love (Jl. 29, 1927, Charlotte, NC) Dir., Lrng. Ctr., Charlotte Country Day Sch., 1970–; Ref. Libn., Charlotte Pub. Lib., 1969–70; Classrm. Tchr., Eastover Sch., 1965–68. **Educ.:** Queens Coll., 1960–63, BA (Educ.); Appalachian State Univ., 1970–73, MA (LS), 1981, EdS. **Orgs.:** NC LA: Prog. Non-Pub. Schs. (1979–80). SELA. ALA: AASL/Non-Pub. Schs. Sect. (1979–80). NC Assn. of Educs. NC Parents-Tchrs. Assn. Congs. **Activities:** 1, 10; 15, 17, 31, 36; 63 **Addr.:** 5138 Dunes Ct.–Carmel S., Charlotte, NC 28211.

Wilson, Michael Edward (D. 31, 1949, Long Beach, CA) Asst. Archvst., Rosenberg Lib., 1977–; Resrch. Consult., AIA Resrch. Corp., 1975–76. **Educ.:** Univ. of Denver, 1972–74, BA (Hist.), 1974–75, MA (LS), 1974, Cert. (Arch. Std.). **Orgs.:** SAA: Com. on Aural and Graph. Recs. (1978–); Bus. Arch. Afnty. Grp. (1979–); Prsrvn. Methods Afnty. Grp. (1979–). Socty. of SW Archvsts. Various other orgs. Vict. Socty. in Amer.: TX Chap., Bd. (1977–), Pres. (1979–). Thea. Hist. Socty. of Amer.: Com. on Arch. and Resrch. (1979–). Socty. of Archit. Histns. **Pubns.:** Ed., *Guide to Manuscripts in The Rosenberg Library* (1980); "Managing Architectural Records," *Prsrvn. News* (Mr. 1977). **Activities:** 2, 12; 19, 20, 45; 69 **Addr.:** Rosenberg Library, 2310 Sealy Ave., Galveston, TX 77550.

Wilson, Mildred Ford (N. 5, 1927, High Point, NC) Sch. Libn., McGavock HS, Metro. Nashville Pub. Schs., 1978, Sch. Libn., Rose Park Jr. HS, Donelson HS, 1969–78; Eng. Tchr., Roanoke Rapids HS, 1952–56; Soc. Std. Tchr., Halifax Cnty. Schs., 1951–52. **Educ.:** Univ. of NC, Greensboro, 1945–49, BA (Eng. Lit.); George Peabody Coll., 1976–77, MLS; various lib. crs. **Orgs.:** ALA. TN LA. Nashville LA. Untd. Tchg. Prof. **Honors:** Alpha Delta Kappa; Beta Phi Mu. **Activities:** 10; 31, 39, 48 **Addr.:** 2740 Windemere Dr., Nashville, TN 37214.

Wilson, Patrick (D. 29, 1927, Santa Cruz, CA) Prof., Sch. of Lib. and Info. Std., Univ. of CA, Berkeley, 1965–, Dean, 1970–75. **Educ.:** Univ. of CA, Berkeley, 1945–49, AB (Phil.), 1952–53, BLS, 1957–60, PhD (Phil.). **Orgs.:** ASIS. AALS. **Pubns.:** *Public Knowledge, Private Ignorance* (1977); *Two Kinds of Power* (1968). **Activities:** 11; 27, 42 **Addr.:** School of Library & Information Studies, University of California, Berkeley, CA 94720.

Wilson, Pauline C. (Cleveland, OH) Assoc. Prof., Grad. Sch. of Lib. and Info. Sci., Univ. of TN, 1972–; Soc. Scis. Libn., IL State Univ., 1967–69; Head, YA Dept., Lakewood Pub. Lib., 1961–67. **Educ.:** Baldwin Wallace Coll., 1959–60, BA (Hist.); Case West. Rsv. Univ., 1960–61, MS (LS); Univ. of IL, 1968–70, MA (Interdisciplinary Soc. Sci.); Univ. of MI, 1969–72, PhD (LS). **Orgs.:** AALS: Resrch. Com. (Ch., 1979–80). ALA: YASD/*Top of the News* Ed. (1965–66), Consult. Ed. (1967), Pubns. Com. (1968–69). TN LA: Pub. Lib. Stans. Com. (1973–77). E. TN LA: Mary U. Rothrock Lect. (1972). **Honors:** ALA, LRRT, Resrch. Competition Awd., 1979; *Amer. Libs.*–ALA Goals Awd., Article Competition, 1977. **Pubns.:** *A Community Elite and the Public Library: The Uses of Information in Leadership* (1977); "Librarians as Teachers: The Study of an Organization Fiction," *Lib. Qtly.* (Ap. 1979); "Factors Effecting Research Productivity," *Jnl. of Educ. for Libnshp.* (Sum. 1979); "Children's Services in a Time of Change," *Sch. Lib. Jnl.* (F. 1979); "Librarianship and ALA in the Post-Industrial Society," *Amer. Libs.* (Mr. 1978); various articles (1976–81). **Activities:** 11; 27, 34, 47; 74, 78, 92 **Addr.:** Graduate School of Library & Information Science, University of Tennessee, 804 Volunteer Blvd., Knoxville, TN 37916.

Wilson, Phillis M. (N. 26, 1943, Chicago, IL) Dir., Rochester MN Pub. Lib., 1970–; Chld. Libn., Enoch Pratt Free Lib., 1967–69. **Educ.:** Fontbonne Coll., 1961–65, BA (Eng.); Rosary Coll., 1965–66, MALS. **Orgs.:** MN LA: State Conf. Lcl. Arrange. (Ch., 1970); Nom. Com. (1971); Pubcty. and PR Com. (1972); Lib. Mgt. RT (1976–81). ALA: Stans. Com. (1980–82); ALSC, Bd. of Dirs. (1975–79), various ofcs., coms. (1969–); PLA, various coms. (1972–75). Inst. on Consult. Skills for State Lib. Consults.: Mgr. (1979). U.S. Frnds of IBBY. AAUW: Bd. of Dirs. (1973–74, 1975–76). Mayo Clinic Hist. of Med. Socty. Rochester Cham. of Cmrce.: Bd. of Dirs. Rochester Exempt Empls. Assn.: Exec. Bd. Various other orgs. **Honors:** Delta Kappa Gamma, Recog. in Admin., 1972. **Pubns.:** "Planning for Children," *Amer. Libs.* (Ja. 1975). **Activities:** 9; 17, 21, 47 **Addr.:** Rochester Public Library, Broadway at 1st St. S.E., Rochester, MN 55901.

Wilson, Richard Arave (N. 14, 1951, Seattle, WA) Spec. Progs. Consult., ID State Lib., 1976–; Dir., Sandpoint–E. Bonner Cnty. Lib. Dist., 1975–76. **Educ.:** Graceland Coll., 1969–73, BA (Soc. Std.); Univ. of IA, 1973–74, MA (LS). **Orgs.:** ID LA: PR Com. (1975); Cont. Ed. Com. (Ch., 1976–). Pac. NW LA: Lib. Educ. Div. (Ch., 1977–79); Lcl. Arranges. Com. (Ch., 1979); Ref. Div. (1976–). ALA: ASCLA, various coms. CLENE. Various other orgs. Benevolent and Protective Ord. of Elks: Secy. (1975–76). Natl. Assn. of Realtors. ID Assn. of Realtors. Boise Bd. of Realtors. Various other orgs. **Pubns.:** "Can We Survive?" *ID Libn.* (Ja. 1979); "IL Profile," *ID Libn.* (O. 1978); "Librarians Want to Do Well What They Do," *ID Libn.* (Ja. 1977). **Activities:** 13; 17, 24, 26; 50 **Addr.:** 2902 Grover, Boise, ID 83705.

Wilson, Robert E. (F. 13, 1951, Pittsburgh, PA) Coll. Archvst., Carlow Coll., 1981–; Fld. Proj. Dir., Univ. of Pittsburgh, 1978–80; Archvst., Proj. Dir., Old Economy Musm., 1977–78; Proj. Dir., Archvst., Pittsburgh Cncl. on Higher Educ., 1975–77. **Educ.:** Marquette Univ., 1970–73, BA (Pol. Sci.); Univ. of Pittsburgh, 1973–74, MLS, 1976 (Eth. Stds., Hist.). **Orgs.:** SAA: Eth. Arch. Com. (1976–); Prof. Afnty. Grp. on Theme Cols. Mid-Atl. Reg. Arch. Conf.: Lcl. Arranges. and Prog. Com. (1977–81). Immigration Hist. Socty. Pittsburgh Reg. Lib. Ctr.: Eth. Cols. Com. Marquette Alum. Assn. Pittsburgh Cncl. on Higher Educ.: Eth. Std. Plng. Com. (Secy., 1976–78). **Pubns.:** *Resources on the Ethnic and the Immigrant in the Pittsburgh Area* (1976, 1979); various articles, *PA Eth. Heritage Std. Nsltr.*, lcl newsps. (1976). **Activities:** 2; 17, 23, 24; 55, 66, 86 **Addr.:** 310 Dolores Cir., RD#4, Mars, PA 16046.

Wilson, Sally M. (D. 17, 1925, Providence, RI) Asst. Libn., Spec. Cols., Adams Lib., RI Coll., 1977–, Asst. Dir., 1971–77, Head, Tech. Srvs., 1966–71, Catlgr., 1965–66; Catlgr., Emerson Coll., 1963–65; Asst. Ref. Libn., NS Reg. Libs., 1952–54. **Educ.:** Hood Coll., 1944–48, BA (Hist.); Simmons Coll., 1951–52, MS (LS); Univ. of RI, 1978 (Mgt. of Arch.) **Orgs.:** New Eng. Archvsts.: Actg. Secy. (1978–79). ALA: ACRL; RTSD; LHRT. New Eng. LA: Exec. Bd. (1977–78). New Eng. Tech. Srvs. Libns.: Rec. Secy. (1973–75); VP (1976–77); Pres. (1977–78); Nom. Com. (Ch. 1979–80). Various other orgs., ofcs. AAUP: RI Coll. Chap. Amer. Fed. of Tchrs. **Pubns.:** Jt. auth., "Unionization at RIC and the Librarians," *RI LA Bltn.* (F. 1976); "Robinson Hall Reaches Hundredth Anniversary," *PPS News* (Mr. 1978). **Activities:** 1, 2; 23, 45; 63, 66 **Addr.:** Special Collections, James P. Adams Library, Rhode Island College, Providence, RI 02908.

Wilson, Thomas C. (Ag. 3, 1930, Detroit, MI) Assoc. Prof., Dept. of Lib., Media and Info. Std., Univ. of S. FL, 1968–; Tchr., TV Tchr., Admin., Detroit Pub. Schs., 1954–68. **Educ.:** Wayne State Univ., 1952–54, BS (Educ.), 1967–70, EdD (Instr. Tech.); various LS crs., 1976–78. **Orgs.:** AALS. FL Assn. for Media in Educ.: Dir. (1978–81). AECT: Reg. Coord. (1972–77). **Pubns.:** Jt. auth., *The Matrix System: A Practical Basis for Stimulus Selection* (1978); "A Model for The Systematic Integration of Instructionel Materials into Individualized Learning Systems," *AV Instr.* (My. 1974). **Activities:** 11, 14-Dir., open univ.; 26; 63, 93 **Addr.:** Open University, University of S. Florida, SVC 116, Tampa, FL 33620.

Wilson, William G. (O. 3, 1936, Shreveport, LA) Libn., Lectr., Coll. of Lib. and Info. Srvs., Univ. of MD, 1972–; Libn., Catawba Coll., 1967–70; Ref. Libn., Enoch Pratt Free Lib., 1964–67; Cat., Ref. Libn., Beloit Coll., 1960–64. **Educ.:** LA State Univ., 1955–58, BA (Econ.); Univ. of MI, 1958–60, AMLS; Emory Univ., 1967, Cert. (Lib. Mgt.); Claremont Grad. Sch., 1970–71, MA (Educ.). **Orgs.:** ALA. MD LA: Acad. and Resrch. Libs. Div., Vice Ch. (1977–78), Ch. (1978–79). MD Cons. Cncl.: Treas. (1975–78); 1st VP (1979–80); Pres. (1980–). **Honors:** Beta Phi Mu, 1960; Univ. of MI, Margaret Mann Awd., 1960; Phi Kappa Phi, 1960. **Pubns.:** "Library USA, 1965," *LA LA Bltn.* (Win. 1965); "Continuing Library Education Network and Exchange (CLENE)," *CRAB* (D. 1974); various reviews, "General Reference Sources," videotape, print std. package (1977). **Activities:** 1, 11; 17, 26, 39; 65, 72 **Addr.:** College of Library and Information Services, University of Maryland, College Park, MD 20742.

Wilsted, Thomas Peter (Ap. 16, 1943, Detroit, MI) Archvst., Dir., Salvation Army Arch. and Resrch. Ctr., 1978–; Mss. Libn., Alexander Turnbull Lib., 1973–78; Fld. Archvst., IL State Hist. Lib., 1968–73. **Educ.:** Kalamazoo Coll., 1962–66, BA (Hist.); Univ. of WI, 1966–68, MA (Hist.). **Orgs.:** SAA: Relig. Arch. Com. (1978–); Col. Personal Papers and Mss. (1971–73). Arch. and Recs. Assn. of NZ: Pres. (1976–78). Midwest Arch. Conf.: Prog. Com. (1973). NY Arch. RT: Strg. Com. (1979–). Various other orgs. **Honors:** Archs. and Recs. Assn. of NZ, Hon. Life Mem., 1978. **Pubns.:** "Underneath the Archives," *NZ Listener* (1977); "Starting an Archives or Manuscripts Collection: Some Basic Procedures," *A NZ Sem., Procs. of an Arch. Sem. Held in Wellington, 21–26 S., 1975* (1978); "Scoring Archival Goals," *Arch. Conf. Procs. 1977, Conf. of the Australian Socty. of Archvsts.* (1978); "Preserving Army History," *War Cry* (1979); "Kiwis, Kangaroos and Bald Eagles, Archival Development in Three Countries," *Midwest. Archvst.* (1979); various articles, (1975–77). **Addr.:** Salvation Army Archives & Research Center, 145 W. 15th St., New York, NY 10011.

Wilt, Lawrence J. M. (Je. 2, 1948, Buffalo, NY) Col. Mgt. Libn., Univ. of MD, Baltimore Cnty., 1981–; Head of Ref., Dickinson Coll., 1979–81. Ref. Libn., 1977–79. **Educ.:** SUNY, Bing-

PROFESSIONAL ACTIVITIES: Institutions: 1. Acad. lib.; 2. Arch.; 3. Assn.; 4. Fed./Gvt. lib.; 5. Inst. lib.; 6. Mfr./Suppl.; 7. Milit. lib.; 8. Musm.; 9. Pub. lib.; 10. Sch. lib.; 11. Sch. of lib. sci.; 12. Spec. lib.; 13. State lib.; 14. (other). **Functions/Activities:** 15. Acq./Col. dev.; 16. Adult srvs.; 17. Admin.; 18. Apprais.; 19. Archit./Bldgs.; 20. Cat./Class.; 21. Chld. srvs.; 22. Circ.; 23. Cons./Pres.; 24. Consult.; 25. Cont. ed.; 26. Educ. lib. sci.; 27. Ext. srvs.; 28. Fund/Grants; 29. Gvt. pubs.; 30. Indx./Abs.; 31. Instr. lib. use; 32. Media srvs.; 33. Micro.; 34. Netwks./Coops.; 35. Persnl.; 36. PR; 37. Publshg.; 38. Recs. mgt.; 39. Ref. srvs.; 40. Repro.; 41. Resrch.; 42. Review.; 43. Secur.; 44. Serials; 45. Spec. col.; 46. Tech. srvs.; 47. Trustees/Bds.; 48. YA srvs.; 49. (other).

hamton, 1966–70, BA (Hum.); IN Univ., 1975–77, MLS (Info. Sci.), 1970–80, PhD (Phil.). **Orgs.:** ALA: ACRL, Pubns. Com. (Ch., 1980–82)/Bibl. Instr. Sect., Policy and Plng. Com. (1979–). **Honors:** Beta Phi Mu, 1977. **Pubns.:** "Symbol Signs for Libraries," *Sign Systems for Libraries: Solving the Wayfinding Problem* (1979). **Activities:** 1; 31, 39, 49-Lib. autom.; 55, 56, 74 **Addr.:** University Library, University of Maryland, Baltimore County, Catonsville, MD 21228.

Wilt, Matthew Richard (Ap. 14, 1924, Hollidaysburg, PA) Exec. Dir., Cath. LA, 1960–; Acq. Libn., Georgetown Univ., 1957–60; Frgn. Bk. Buyer, Sidney Kramer Bks., 1956–57; Acq. Libn., Dept. of Defense, 1955–56. **Educ.:** San Luis Rey Coll., 1942–46, BA (Phil.); Cath. Univ., 1948–49, MA (Hist.); Columbia Univ., 1954–55, MSLS. **Orgs.:** PA LA: Conf. Plng. (1965); Exec. Com. (1968); Treas. (1968); Exec. Bd. (1968–69); Natl. Lib. Week (1969). Cncl. of Natl. Lib. and Info. Assn.: Pres. (1965–67). Booksellers Assn. of Philadelphia. **Honors:** PA LA, Awd. of Merit, 1975. **Pubns.:** Jt. ed., *Catholic Subject Headings* (1981); ed., *Cath. Lib. World* (1962–63); contrib., *ALA Yrbk.* (1975–). **Activities:** 1, 10; 15, 17, 25; 50, 90 **Addr.:** Catholic Library Association, 461 W. Lancaster Ave., Haverford, PA 19041.

Winckler, Paul Albert (My. 17, 1926, Brooklyn, NY) Prof., LS, Palmer Grad. Lib. Sch., Long Island Univ., C.W. Post Ctr., 1968–, Assoc. Prof., LS, 1962–68; Libn., Asst. Prof., Suffolk Cnty. Cmnty. Coll., 1960–62; Lib. Dir., Bryant Lib., 1956–60; Libn., Asst. Prof., St. John's Univ., 1951–56; Libn., Grade 2, Brooklyn Pub. Lib., 1950–51. **Educ.:** St. John's Univ., 1944–48, BA (Eng. Lit.); Pratt Inst., 1949–50, MLS, NY Univ., 1948–53, MA (Eng. Lit.), 1962–68, PhD (Higher Educ.). **Orgs.:** AALS. ALA: Lib. Educ. Div., Spec. Com. on Illustrated Mtrls. for Hist. of Bks. and Libs. (1966–67). NY LA: Lib. Educs. Sect., Bd. of Dirs. (1971–74). Various other orgs. Melvil Dui Chowder and Marching Assn. Amer. Prtg. Hist. Assn.: Conf. Plng. Com., Fall 1976 Inst. on "Typographic America"; Educ. Com. (1974–); Ad Hoc Com. to Std. Tchg. Methods and Mtrls. in the Hist. of Bks. and Prtg. (Ch., 1976–79); NY Chap. Ctr. for Bk. Arts: *Bk. Arts* Mag. Adv. Com. Prtg. Hist. Socty., Eng. **Honors:** NY Univ., Fndrs. Day Awd., 1969. **Pubns.:** *History of Books and Printing: A Guide to Information Sources* (1979); *Reader in the History of Books and Printing* (1978); "Materials and Sources for Teaching the History of Books and Printing," *Jnl. of Educ. for Libnshp.* (Sum.–Fall 1972) "Charles C. Williamson," *Dictionary of American Library Biography* (1978); "Marcus Musurus," *Encyc. of Lib. and Info. Sci.* (1976); various articles, reviews (1956–). **Activities:** 11; 26, 37, 41; 55, 57, 73 **Addr.:** Palmer Graduate Library School, Long Island University, C.W. Post Center, Greenvale, NY 11548.

Windham, Eula H. (F. 3, 1919, Tifton, GA) Libn., Mid. GA Coll., 1961–; Asst. Libn., Hardin Simmons Univ., 1957–61. **Educ.:** GA Coll., 1936–40, AB (Hist.); South. Bapt. Theo. Semy., 1948–50, MRE (Relig. Educ.); Emory Univ., 1956–57, MLS. **Orgs.:** ALA: ACRL/Cmnty. and Jr. Coll. Sect. (GA Ch., 1968–72). SELA. GA LA: Tech. Srv. Div. (Ch., 1968). Ctrl. GA Assoc. Libs.: Secy. (1976–77). Hlth. Sci. Libs. of Ctrl. GA: Constn. Com. (Ch., 1978–80). Various other orgs. Cochran Pilot Club. Cochran Woman's Club. GA Assn. of Jr. Colls.: Ch. **Pubns.:** "Title IIA–A Bargain at the Price, a Symposium," *Jnl. of Acad. Libnshp.* (S. 1979). **Activities:** 1; 15, 17, 34 **Addr.:** C2, 1003 8th St., Cochran, GA 31014.

Windheuser, Christine S. (Je. 4, 1952, Orange, NJ) Cartograph. Libn., World Bank, 1978–; Map Libn., Metro. DC Cncl. of Gvts., 1975–78. **Educ.:** Univ. of WI, 1970–74, BA (Anthro., Grmn.), 1974–75, MLS. **Orgs.:** SLA: Geo. and Map Div., DC Chap. Pres. (1979–80), VP (1978–79), Secy.–Treas. (1977–78). **Activities:** 12; 45; 70 **Addr.:** World Bank, Cartographic Information System, 1818 H St. N.W., Washington, DC 20433.

Windsor, Donald Arthur (Mr. 22, 1934, Chicago, IL) Leader, Lib. and Srch. Grp., Norwich–Eaton Pharm., 1966–. **Educ.:** Univ. of IL, 1956–59, BS (Zlgy.), 1959–66, MS (Zlgy.). **Orgs.:** ASIS. Inst. of Info. Scis. Socty. for Gen. Systs. Resrch. Assn. for Comp. Mach. NY Acad. of Scis. AAAS. **Pubns.:** *The Literature on the Freshwater Leeches of North America* (1972); "Using Bibliometric Analyses of Patent Literature for Predicting the Clinical Fates of Developing Drugs," *Jnl. of Chem. Info. and Comp. Sci.* (1979); "Adverse–Reactions Literature: a Bibliometric Analysis," *Methods of Info. in Med.* (1977). **Addr.:** Library, Norwich–Eaton Pharmaceuticals, P.O. Box 191, Norwich, NY 13815.

Winearls, D. Joan (N. 4, 1937, Toronto, ON) Map Libn., Univ. of Toronto Lib., 1964–; Ref. Libn., Catlgr., India Ofc. Lib., UK, 1962–64; Libn., Bibl. Ctr., Toronto Pub. Lib., 1960–62. **Educ.:** Univ. of Toronto, 1955–59, BA (Hist.), 1959–60, BLS, 1974, MLS. **Orgs.:** Assn. Can. Map Libns.: Pres. (1972–73); various coms. (1967–). SLA. Bibl. Socty. of Can. Can. Cartograph. Assn.: Hist. of Cartography Interest Grp. (1976–). Socty. for the Hist. of Discoveries. **Pubns.:** "Reference Work in a Current Map Collection," *Assn. Can. Map Libns. Procs. of the 8th Conf., 1974* (1975); introductory essay, *County Maps: Land Ownership Maps of Canada in the 19th Century...* (1976); "Cartobibliography and Map Cataloguing in Canada," *AB Bookman's Yrbk. 1976 Pt. 1* (1977); "A Comprehensive Bibliography of Manuscript and Printed Maps of Upper Canada from Circa 1774 to 1867," *Assn. Can. Map Libns. Procs. of 10th Anl. Conf.* (1976); "Map Collections and Map Librarianship in Canada: Review and Prospects," *The Map Librarian in the Modern World: Essays in Honour of Walter W. Ristow* (1979); various articles, reviews (1967–). **Activities:** 1, 12; 26, 39, 41; 57, 70 **Addr.:** University of Toronto Library, 130 St. George St., Toronto, ON M5S 1A5 Canada.

Winfree, Waverly Keith (Jl. 15, 1933, Chesterfield Cnty., VA) Cur. of Mss., VA Hist. Socty., 1975–, Asst. Cur. of Mss., 1961–75; Archvst., VA State Lib., 1959–61. **Educ.:** Univ. of Richmond, 1953–57, BA (Hist.); Coll. of William and Mary, 1958–59, MA (Hist.). **Orgs.:** SAA. Mid–Atl. Reg. Arch. Conf. **Pubns.:** Cmplr., *The Laws of Virginia: Supplement to Hening's Statutes, 1700–1750* (1971). **Activities:** 2, 3; 18, 20, 39; 69, 78, 73 **Addr.:** 6105 Hokie Ct., Richmond, VA 23234.

Winfrey, Dorman H. (S. 4, 1924, Henderson, TX) Dir., Libn., TX State Lib., 1962–; Archvst., Univ. of TX, 1960–61; State Archvst., TX State Lib., 1958–60; Soc. Sci. Resrch. Assoc., TX State Hist. Assn., Univ. of TX, 1946–58. **Educ.:** Univ. of TX, 1950, BA (Hist., Gvt.), 1951, MA (Hist., Gvt.), 1962, PhD (Hist., Gvt.). **Orgs.:** Amer. Assn. for State and Lcl. Hist.: Cncl. ALA. SWLA. SAA: Fellow; Cncl. Various other orgs. TX Inst. of Letters. Phil. Socty. of TX. Austin Com. on Frgn. Rel. TX State Hist. Assn.: Pres.; Fellow; Exec. Cncl. **Honors:** Phi Alpha Theta; Pi Sigma Alpha. **Pubns.:** *Julien Sidney Devereux and his Monte Verdi Plantation* (1964); *Arturo Toscanini in Texas: The 1950 NBC Symphony Orchestra Tour* 1967; ed., *Procs. of the Phil. Socty. of TX* (1976–); *Seventy-five Years of Texas History* (1975); ed., *Presidents and Governors of Texas Series* (1969–); various articles in arch., hist., LS jnls. **Activities:** 2, 13; 34, 38, 39; 57, 69, 72 **Addr.:** 6503 Willamette Dr., Austin, TX 78723.

Winger, Anna K. (O. 13, 1930, Waynesboro, PA) Libn., Defense Logistics Srvs. Ctr., 1966–; Libn., Franklin Cnty. Lib., 1963–66; Catlgr., Univ. of DE, 1961–63; Asst. Libn., Juniata Coll., 1956–61; Libn., James Buchanan Jr.–Sr. HS, 1954–56. **Educ.:** Juniata Coll., 1949–53, AB (Eng.); Drexel Inst. of Tech., 1953–54, MS (LS). **Orgs.:** SLA. Altrusa Intl., Inc.: Dist. 5 (Gvr., 1980–82). Amer. Bus. Women's Assn. **Honors:** Amer. Bus. Women's Assn., Battle Creek Chap., Woman of the Yr., 1969. **Activities:** 4, 12; 15, 17, 20; 56, 59, 81 **Addr.:** 34 Everett Ave., Battle Creek, MI 49017.

Winger, Howard W. (O. 29, 1914, Marion, IN) Prof. Emeritus, Univ. of Chicago, 1981–, Prof., 1953–81; Asst. Prof., Univ. of WI, 1950–53. **Educ.:** Manchester Coll., 1932–36, AB (Hist.); George Peabody Coll., 1941–45, BS (LS); Univ. of IL, 1945–48, MS (LS), 1948–53, PhD (LS). **Orgs.:** AALS: Secy.–Treas. (1954–57). ALA. Beta Phi Mu: Pres. (1976–77). **Pubns.:** Ed., *American Library History, 1876–1976* (1976); *Printers' Marks and Devices* (1976); "Scholarly Use of Renaissance Printed Books," *Lib. Trends* (Ap. 1977); "Leon Carnovsky," *Lib. Qtly.* (Ap. 1976); ed., *Lib. Qtly.* (1961–72; 1980–). **Activities:** 11; 37, 49-Tchg.; 73 **Addr.:** 121 Walnut St., Park Forest, IL 60466.

Winkel, Lois H. (Ag. 5, 1939, New York, NY) Ed., *Elementary School Library Collection*, 1979–; Adj. Fac., Univ. of NC, Chapel Hill, 1978–79; Adj. Fac., Univ. of NC, Greensboro, 1975–; Adj. Fac., Grad. Sch. of Lib. and Info. Sci., Rutgers Univ., 1973–75; Adj. Fac., Sch. of LS, Columbia Univ., 1972–75; Lib. Media Spec., Darien, CT, 1969–72; Tchr., Lib. Media Spec., P.S. 144, 1962–65. **Educ.:** Hunter Coll., 1957–61, BA (Presoc. Work); Pratt Inst., 1967–69, MLS (Sch. Media Ctrs.); Columbia Univ., 1972–75, Advnc. Cert. (LS). **Orgs.:** ALA: AASL, Educ. (1980–82), Networking (1975–80), Lib. Mtrls. for Minority Grps. (1970–74), Self-Std. (1970–74); ALSC, Cont. Ed. (1980–82), Resrch. and Dev. (1974–76), Batchelder Awd. Com. (1972–74). **Pubns.:** Jt. auth., "The Children's Media Date Bank," *Top of the News* (Win. 1980); jt. auth., "Microcomputer-Aided Production of Indexes," *Indxr.* (Fall 1979); jt. auth., "Microcomputers and the Serials Librarian," *Serials Libn.* (Sum. 1980); jt. auth., "A Simple Way to Reduce Keyboarding Effort," *Microcomp.*; various articles. **Activities:** 11, 6–Mtr./Suppl.; 24, 26, 37; 56, 75, 95-Chld.'s mtrls. **Addr.:** 1113 Hill St., Greensboro, NC 27408.

Winkels, Mary (Ag. 4, 1923, Winona, MN) Mgr., Tech. Info. Div., Brookhaven Natl. Lab., 1979–; Dir., Hlth. Scis. Lib., SUNY, Stony Brook, 1973–79, Assoc. Dir., 1970–73, Ref. Libn., 1969–70. **Educ.:** Coll. of St. Teresa, 1953, BA; Univ. of MI, 1968, AMLS. **Orgs.:** Med. LA: Mem. Com. (1972–75); NY Reg. Grp. Audit. (1977–79). SLA: Consult. Ofcr. (1976–79); Long Island Chap. (Pres., 1974–75). Long Island Lib. Resrcs. Cncl.: Bd. of Trustees (1977–). **Activities:** 1, 12; 17, 39, 46; 65, 80, 84 **Addr.:** 9 Linda Ln., Setauket, NY 11733.

Winkler, Paul W(alter) (Jl. 15, 1912, Buda, IL) Sr. Descr. Cat. Spec., Lib. of Congs., 1979–; Ed., *Anglo–Amer. Cat. Rules* 1975–78, Prin. Descr. Catlgr., Descr. Cat. Div., 1968–74, Asst. Chief, Shared Cat. Div., 1966–68, Head, Eng. Lang. Sect., Descr. Cat. Div., 1964–66; Dir., Cat. Dept., Prof. Lib. Srvs., 1962–64; Assoc. Prof., Sch. of LS, Univ. of South. CA, 1959–62; Asst. and Assoc. Prof., Sch. of Libnshp., Univ. of Denver, 1954–59; various prof. positions, 1936–. **Educ.:** IL State Univ., 1931–39, BEd (Soc. Sci.); Univ. of IL, 1940–41, BS (LS), 1943–49, MS (LS). **Orgs.:** ALA. **Honors:** ALA, Margaret Mann Cit., 1979. **Activities:** 1, 11; 20, 29; 57, 92 **Addr.:** 955 S. Columbus St., Apt. 515, Arlington, VA 22204.

Winn, Carolyn P. (Je. 5, 1927, Detroit, MI) Resrch. Libn., Woods Hole Oceanograph. Inst., 1975–; Sci. Ref. Libn., Univ. of RI, 1968–75, Resrch. Asst., 1965–67; Catlgr. of Fishes, Univ. of MI, 1950–54. **Educ.:** Univ. of MI, 1945–49, BS (Zlgy.), 1949–50, AM (Zlgy.); Univ. of RI, 1967–70, MLS. **Orgs.:** Intl. Assn. of Marine Sci. Libs. and Info. Ctrs.: Org. and Pres. (1975–77); Exec. Bd. (1978–79). Natl. Micro. Assn. ALA: ACRL/Bibl. Instr. Sect., Policy and Plng. Com. (1977–79), Cont. Ed. Com. (1980); LAMA/Bldgs. and Equip. Sect. (1979–), Women Admins. Discuss. Grp.; LITA/Vid. and Cable Sect. (1980–). RI LA. AAAS. **Pubns.:** Ed., cmplr., *Directory of Marine Science Libraries* (1976); "Goals and Timetable for Implementation of Library Instruction Program," *Handbook of Bibliographic Instruction* (forthcoming); *Library Resources for Nursing Students* slide/tape (1974–75). **Activities:** 1, 12; 17, 31, 39; 58, 91 **Addr.:** Woods Hole Oceanographic Institution, Woods Hole, MA 02543.

Winn, J. Karyl Mss. Libn., Univ. of WA Lib., 1970–, Catlgr., 1967–70; Libn., Milwaukee Pub. Lib., 1965–67. **Educ.:** Univ. of MI, 1960–64, BA (Eng.), 1964–65, MLS; Univ. of WA, 1973–77, MA (Hist.). **Orgs.:** SAA: Ref./Access (Ch., 1979–81); Replevin (1978–79); Copyrt. Task Frc. (1980–); Prog. Com. (1981). NW Archvsts. Oral Hist. Assn. **Pubns.:** "Common Law Copyright and The Archivist," *Amer. Archvst.* (37:3); *North Cascades Archival Resources in Washington State* (1974). **Activities:** 1, 2; 45; 61, 66 **Addr.:** University of Washington Library FM–25, Seattle, WA 98195.

Winner, Marian C. (Je. 29, 1929, Toledo, OH) Head Sci. and Math. Libn., Miami Univ., 1978–, Asst. Sci. Libn., 1977–78. **Educ.:** Otterbein Coll., 1947–51, BA, cum laude (Comp. Sci.), BS (Bot.); Univ. of KY, 1976–77, MSLS. **Orgs.:** ALA: ACRL. Acad. LA of OH. SLA. AAUP. **Honors:** Beta Phi Mu. **Pubns.:** *The Marketing of Computer-Based Bibliographic Search Services by the Library: A Study of the Marketing of Miami University* ERIC. **Addr.:** Science Library, Miami University, Oxford, OH 45056.

Winowich, Nicholas (O. 6, 1922, Pittsburgh, PA) Lib. Dir., Kanawha Cnty. Pub. Lib., 1956–; Lib. Dir., McKeesport Pub. Lib., 1952–56; Branch Libn., Carnegie Lib., Pittsburgh, PA, 1950–52. **Educ.:** Bethany Coll., 1946–49, BA (Hist., Pol. Sci.); Carnegie Inst. of Tech., 1949–50, MLS (Pub. Lib.). **Orgs.:** WV LA: Pres. (1959–60); various coms., assignments. Mid. Atl. Reg. Lib. Fed.: Pres. (1975–77). ALA: Chap. Cnclr. (1970–74); PLA, Legis. Com. (1980–). Charleston Job Corps Ctr.: Pres. (1979–). Chld.'s Musm. and Planetarium. Camp Galahad. Hum. Fndn. of WV. **Honors:** Natl. Secys. Assn., Charleston Chap., Boss of the Yr., 1961; WV LA, Outstan. Libn., 1970; Charleston Oppts. Indus. Ctr., Cert. of Apprec., 1971; Bethany Coll., Alum. Awd. for Cmnty. Srv., 1976. **Pubns.:** "Bringing Public Library Service to the Hospital," *Auxiliary Leader: Jnl. of Hosp. Auxiliaries* (Je. 1963). **Activities:** 9, 12; 17, 19, 47 **Addr.:** Kanawha County Public Library, 123 Capitol St., Charleston, WV 25301.

Winslow, Carol M. (N. 18, 1933, Rochester, MN) Trustee, Evansville Pub. Lib., 1971–; Sch. Media Spec., Ctrl. HS, Evansville, IN, 1966–; Ref. Libn., Univ. of Evansville, 1979, Instr., 1974, Bkmobile. Libn., E. Fairbanks Pub. Lib. 1955–57. **Educ.:** IN State Tchrs. Coll., 1951–55, BS (Home Econ.); IN State Univ., 1972, MLS. **Orgs.:** IN Lib. Trustees Assn.: Pres. (1979); VP (1978). Four Rivers Area Lib. Srv. Athrty.: Pres. (1978–79); VP (1978). Assn. for IN Media Educs. ALTA: State Orgs. Com. Various other orgs. **Pubns.:** Various reviews. **Activities:** 9, 10; 26, 47, 48; 55, 63 **Addr.:** Central High School Media Center, 5400 1st Ave., Evansville, IN 47710.

Winter, Bernadette G. (My. 20, 1925, Belleville, IL) Coord. of Lib. Srvs., Rockford Pub. Schs., 1975–; Elem. Media Spec., Whitehead Sch., 1966–75; Elem. Tchr., Addison Pub. Schs., 1960–66. **Educ.:** Univ. of IL, 1942–45, BS (Acct.); North. IL Univ., 1966–69, MA (LS). **Orgs.:** IL LA: Awds. Com. (1979). IL Assn. for Media in Educ.: Treas. (1976–77); Conf. Regis. Com. (1975); Nom. Com. (Ch., 1979–80). **Honors:** IL State Bd. of Educ., Those Who Excel, 1978. **Activities:** 10; 20, 32, 35; 63, 66, 89 **Addr.:** 2308 Silverthorn Dr., Rockford, IL 61107.

Winter, Eugenia Bull (Ag. 6, 1945, Highland Park, IL) Acq./Biblgphr., CA State Coll., 1981–; Coord. of Adult Srvs., Stockton–San Joaquin Cnty., 1976–81; Ref. Spec., Suffolk Coop. Lib. Syst., 1974–75; Head, Ref. Dept., Omaha Pub. Lib., 1970–74; Ref. Libn., Yale Univ. Lib., 1968–70. **Educ.:** Sweet Briar Coll., 1963–67, BA (Eng.); George Peabody Coll., 1967–68, MLS; Jagiellonian Univ. of Krakow, 1974, Cert. (Polish); Oxford Univ., 1978, Cert. (Eng.). **Orgs.:** ALA. CA LA: Int. Frdm. Com. (1978–81). Lib. Admins. Assn. of North. CA NE LA: Conf. Exhibits Grp. (Ch., 1971). Kosciuszko Fndn.: Assoc. Amer. Philatelic Socty. **Honors:** Beta Phi Mu, 1968. **Activities:** 1, 9; 15, 16, 17; 55, 67, 74 **Addr.:** California State College, Bakersfield, 9001 Stockdale Hwy., Bakersfield, CA 93309.

Winter, Frank H. (Ag.–, 1948, Vancouver, BC) Lib. Persnl. Ofcr., Univ. of SK Lib., 1980–; Head, Reader Srvs. Dept., Paul Martin Law Lib., Univ. of Windsor, 1975–, Head, Gvt. Docums. Sect., Leddy Lib., 1973–75, Ref. Libn., 1970–73. **Educ.:** Univ. of BC, 1967–69, BA (Eng.), 1969–70, BLS; Univ. of Windsor, 1972–77, B. Comm.; Univ. of Toronto, 1977–78, MBA. **Pubns.:** "Timeliness of Canadian Law Reporting," *C.A.L.L. Nsltr.* (1978); *An Introduction to Computerized Legal Research* videotape (1979); "Using the QL System" videotape (1979); "Legalese, Bafflegab, and 'Plain Language' Laws," *Can. Cmnty. Law Jnl.* (1980); "A Proposal for an Automated Ontario Statute Citator," *C.A.L.L. Nsltr.* (1980). **Activities:** 1; 17, 29, 39 **Addr.:** University of Saskatchewan Library, Saskatoon, SK S7N 0W0, Canada.

Winters, Wilma E. (Mr. 27, 1918, Woonsocket, RI) Libn., Harvard Ctr. for Popltn. Std., 1965–; Libn., Dept. Clinical Eye Resrch., Retina Fndn., 1962–65; Asst. Libn., Boston Med. Lib., 1958–62; Med. Libn., VA Hosp. (Brockton, MA), 1954–58; Asst. Libn., Boston Univ. Sch. of Med., 1943–54. **Educ.:** Larson Jr. Coll., 1936–38, AA (LS); Boston Univ., 1940–43, BS (Educ.); 1945–50, MA (Hist.); Simmons Coll., 1958–60, MS (LS); Med. LA, Cert. **Orgs.:** Med. LA. N. Atl. Hlth. Sci. Lib. Grp. Assn. for Popltn./Fam. Plng. Libs. and Info. Ctrs.–Intl.: Pres. (1973–74); Bd. of Dirs. (1969–71; 1977–80); Nom. Com. (1974–75); Cont. Educ. Com. (1979–). AAAS. Popltn. Assn. of Amer. **Pubns.:** Ed., *APLIC-International Directory of On-Site Orientation to Population/Family Planning Resources* (1975). **Activities:** 1; 15, 17, 39; 95-Popltn. and fam. plng. **Addr.:** Harvard Center for Population Studies Library, 665 Huntington Ave., Boston, MA 02115.

Wiren, Harold N. (Ja. 31, 1924, Teaneck, NJ) Engin. Libn., Univ. of WA, 1969–; Head, Engin. Libs., OH State Univ., 1965–69; Asst. Dir. of Libs. for Sci. and Tech., Univ. of NE; 1962–65; Asst. Libn., Sci. and Tech., Rochester Pub. Lib., 1957–62. **Educ.:** Univ. of IL, 1947–51, BS (Mktg. Mgt.), 1954–56, MS (LS); Univ. of Stockholm, Amer. Coll., 1948–49, Cert. **Orgs.:** ALA. Amer. Socty. for Engin. Educ.: Engin. Libs. Div., Ed. (1968–69), Prog. Ch. (1969, 1978). SLA. ASIS: SIG Lib. Autom. Prog. Com. (1968). **Pubns.:** *Guide to Literature on Nuclear Engineering* (1972); "Applied Science and Technology Index," *MO LA Bltn.* (Je. 1969). **Activities:** 1, 9; 15, 17, 39; 64, 81, 91 **Addr.:** Engineering Library, FH-15, University of Washington, Seattle, WA 98195.

Wirt, Michael James (My. 21, 1947, Sault Ste. Marie, MI) Dir., Spokane Cnty. Lib., 1979–, Asst. Dir., 1976–79, Inst. Srvs. Libn., 1972–76; Actg. Libn., Ctr. for Resrch. on Econ. Dev., Univ. of MI, 1971–72. **Educ.:** MI State Univ., 1965–69, BA (Psy.); Univ. of MI, 1971, AMLS. **Orgs.:** ALA. Pac. NW LA. WA State Adv. Cncl. on Libs. **Honors:** Beta Phi Mu, 1971. **Pubns.:** "Library Services in Washington State Mental Hospitals–Eastern State Hospital," *IL Libs.* (Spr. 1975). **Activities:** 9; 17, 35; 56 **Addr.:** Spokane County Library, N2901 Argonne Rd., Spokane, WA 99206.

Wirtanen, Lyle E. (N. 28, 1942, Duluth, MN) Lib. Spec., Grants Mgr., OR Dept. of Educ., 1970–; Libn., Edmonds Sch. Dist., 1969–70; Libn., Fed. Way Sch. Dist., 1967–69; Libn., St. Helens Sch. Dist., 1965–67. **Educ.:** East. WA Univ., 1960–65, BA (Hist.); Univ. of WA, 1967–70, MLS (Libnshp.). **Orgs.:** ALA: AASL. OR Educ. Media Assn. OR LA. **Pubns.:** "Federal Funding—Block Grants," *Interchange* (Fall 1981); "Questions Related to Media Standards," *Interchange* (Win. 1981). **Activities:** 13; 24, 28, 32; 63, 74 **Addr.:** Oregon Dept. of Education, 700 Pringle Pkwy. S.E., Salem, OR 97310.

Wirth, Mary K. (S. 4, 1942, St. Louis, MO) Dir. of Danforth Lib., New England Coll., 1976–, Ref. Libn. and Head of Reader Srvs., 1972–76; Asst. Libn., Circ., Colby Jr. Coll., 1971–72; Med. Abstctr.-Indxr., Chas. Pfizer Co. Lib., 1964–66. **Educ.:** Washington Univ., 1959–63, AB (Zlgy.), 1963–64, Grad Work (Grmn.); Univ. of MD, 1970–71, MLS. **Orgs.:** NH LA: Exec. Bd. (1978–80). Acad. Libns. of NH: VP (1978–79); Pres. (1979–80). NH Adv. Cncl. on Libs. New Eng. Assn. of Schs. and Colls.: Eval. for Peer Accred. (1981–). NH Coll. and Univ. Cncl.: Lib. Policy Com. (Ch., 1980–82). **Activities:** 1; 17, 30, 39; 58, 80 **Addr.:** H. Raymond Danforth Library, New England College, Henniker, NH 03242.

Wisdom, Donald Farrell (Ag. 24, 1928, St. Louis, MO) Chief, Serial Div., Lib. of Congs., 1976–, Asst. Chief, Serial Div., 1971–76, Asst. Dir., Hisp. Fndn., 1966–70, Head, Ref. Sect., Serial Div., 1963–66, Asst. Head, Gvt. Pubns. Sect., Serial Div., 1958–63. **Educ.:** Georgetown Univ., Sch. of Frgn. Srv., 1948–52, BS (Frgn. Srv.). **Orgs.:** SALALM: Exec. Bd. (1968–71); VP (1971–72); Pres., (1972–73); Ed. Bd. (Ch., 1973–75); Budget and Fin. (Ch., 1978–). ALA. Amer. Natl. Stans. Inst. Z39/SC 44. *Index to Current Urban Documents:* Ed. Bd. (1972–). **Pubns.:** Jt. cmplr., *Popular Names of U.S. Government Reports: A Catalog* (1966); *Foreign Government Publications in American Research Libraries: A Survey* (1961); "American Librarians and the UNESCO Library Programme, 1946–66," *UNESCO Bltn. for Libs.* (O. 1966); jt. auth., "Bibliography and General Works," *Handbook of Latin American Studies* (1967, 1968, 1969, 1970); "The Spanish Newspaper Acquisition Project," *Nsltr. of the Socty. for Span. and Portuguese Hist. Std.* (F. 1975). **Activities:** 1, 4; 15, 29, 39; 57, 83, 95-Prsrvn. **Addr.:** 5812 Massachusetts Ave., Bethesda, MD 20086.

Wise, Donald A. (Ja. 25, 1930, Mercedes, TX) Head, Acq. Unit, Lib. of Congs., 1970–; Geographer, Dept. of State, 1963–70; Instr., St. Louis Univ., 1960–63; Cartographer, Dept. of the Air Frc., 1956–60. **Educ.:** OK State Univ., 1951–53, BA (Geo.); St. Louis Univ., 1957–60, MA (Geo.). **Orgs.:** West. Assn. Map Libns. SLA: Geo. and Maps Div., DC Chap., Nom. Com. (Ch., 1974). Assn. of Amer. Geographers: Mid. Atl. Div., Bylaws Com. (1975); Treas. (1971–74); Fin. Com. (1975–77); various ofcs., coms. VA Hist. Fed.: Dir. (1970–72); Pres. (1973–75). Arlington Hist. Socty.: Pres. (1969–70); Hist. Resrch. Com. (Ch., 1976–). Arlington Cnty. Hist. Comsn. Various other orgs. **Honors:** Ramon Magsaysay Awd. Fndn. Lib., Consult., 1978. **Pubns.:** "Cartographic Sources and Acquisition Techniques," *West. Assn. Map Libns. Info. Bltn.* (Mr. 1979); "Cartographic Acquisitions at the Library of Congress," *Spec. Libs.* (D. 1978); "Cartographic Sources and Procurement Problems: Appendixes F-K," *SLA Geo. and Map Div. Bltn.* (Mr. 1979); "Young Washington as a Surveyor," *North. VA Heritage* (O. 1979); "Bazil Hall of Hall's Hill," *Arlington Hist. Mag.* (O. 1979); various articles (1956–78). **Activities:** 4; 15, 18, 24; 70 **Addr.:** 5920 4th Rd., N., Arlington, VA 22203.

Wise, Jo Goodwin (Jl. 15, 1936, Stuttgart, AR) Supvsr. of Media Srvs., N. Little Rock Sch. Dist., 1975–, Media Spec., Indian Hills Elem., 1971–75, Fourth Grade Tchr., Belwood Elem., 1969–71; Fourth Grade Team Leader, Douglas MacArthur Elem., Indianapolis, 1968–69, Fourth Gr. Tchr., 1966–68. **Educ.:** Ball State Univ., 1966, BS; IN Univ., 1974, MS (Instr. Systs. Tech.). **Orgs.:** ALA: AASL, Vid. Comm. Com. (1976–78). AR LA: VP/Pres.-Elect. AECT. AR AV Assn.: Bd. of Dirs. (1980–). Delta Kappa Gamma Socty.: Beta Phi Chap. (Treas., 1978–80). **Pubns.:** "Program for Effective Teaching (PET) Implemented in North Little Rock Schools," *AAVA News and Views* (Ap. 1980); "NLR Media Services Uses New Mini-Computer," *AAVA News and Views* (D. 1980). **Activities:** 10; 24, 32, 36; 63, 67 **Addr.:** North Little Rock School District, P.O. Box 687, North Little Rock, AR 72115.

Wise, Kenda Carolyn (Jl. 19, 1929, Warren, AR) Biblgrphr., Air Univ. Lib., 1975–, Ref. Libn., 1969–75; Ref. Libn., Bus. Lib., Univ. of AL, 1959–69, Asst. Ref. Libn., 1951–59. **Educ.:** Univ. of AL, 1947–51, BS (Educ, LS); FL State Univ., 1954–55, MS (LS). **Orgs.:** AL LA: Coll., Univ. and Spec. Div. Secy–Treas. (1961–62); Schol. Com. (1967–79); Roll of Hon. Com. (1979–80). SLA: AL Chap., Secy.–Treas. (1962–63); VP (1966–67); Pres. (1967–68), Adv. Cncl. (1967–68). SELA. Altrusa. **Activities:** 1, 4; 30, 39, 41; 54, 63, 74 **Addr.:** 602 A Lynwood Dr., Montgomery, AL 36111.

Wise, Mintron Suzanne (O. 19, 1946, Florence, SC) Ref. Libn., Appalachian State Univ., 1979–; Educ. Ref. Libn., WA State Univ., 1976–79; Asst. Ref. Libn., Univ. of GA, 1971–76; Asst. Ref. Libn., West Hartford Pub. Lib., 1969–71. **Educ.:** Univ. of SC, 1964–68, BA (Educ.); Univ. of KY, 1968–69, MSLS; Appalachian State Univ., 1979–81, MA (Hist.). **Orgs.:** SLA: H.W. Wilson Awd. Com. (1981–83); Educ. Div. *Bltn.* Ed.; Educ. Div. Nom. Com. (1981). SELA. NC LA. NC OLUG. ERIC Vocabulary Review Grp. **Activities:** 1; 31, 36, 39; 63, 67, 92 **Addr.:** Reference Department, Belk Library, Appalachian State University, Boone, NC 28608.

Wise, Olga B. (Ja. 14, 1941, St. Louis, MO) Ref. Libn., TX Woman's Univ. Lib., 1981–; Resrch. Assoc. in Info. Sci., N. TX State Univ., 1979–81; Libn., Washington Univ., 1979; Engin. Docums. Libn., Univ. of IL, 1978, Pubns. Coord., 1975–77. **Educ.:** Washington Univ., 1958–62, BA (Grmn.), 1962–64, MA (Grmn.); Univ. of IL, 1971–72, MSLS; N. TX State Univ., CAS Cand. **Orgs.:** SLA. ASIS. TX LA. SWLA. **Honors:** Univ. of IL, Grad. Sch. of LS, Anna Boyd Awd., 1972; Beta Phi Mu. **Pubns.:** *Planning a Legal Library for a Correctional Institution* (1976); various reviews, *Lib. Jnl.* (1974–77). **Activities:** 1, 12; 15, 20, 30; 55, 64, 91 **Addr.:** 3406 Valley View Dr., Dento, TX 76201.

Wise, Virginia J. (N. 8, 1950, Midland, MI) Asst. Libn. for Pub. Srvs., Harvard Law Lib., 1979–; Head, Ref. Dept., Tarlton Law Lib., Univ. of TX, 1978–79; Asst. Libn., Miller, Canfield, Paddock and Stone, 1975–77. **Educ.:** Univ. of MI, 1970–73, BGS (Hist.), 1973–75, AMLS; Wayne State Univ., 1974–77, JD. **Orgs.:** AALL: AV Com. (1978–79); *Law Lib. Jnl.* Com. (1980–81). TX State Bar Assn. CA State Bar Assn. Amer. Bar Assn. **Pubns.:** "Law Librarianship," *Special Librarianship: A Reader* (1980); jt. ed., *Fundamentals of Legal Research* assignment bk. (1980). **Activities:** 1; 17, 33, 39; 77 **Addr.:** Harvard Law Library, Langdell Hall, Cambridge, MA 02138.

Wiseman, John Austin (My. 13, 1931, Liverpool, Lancashire, Eng.) Actg. Univ. Libn., 1981–82; Assoc. Libn., Trent Univ., 1967–; Coll. Libn., Flintshire Coll. of Tech., Wales, 1965–67; Head, Circ., Univ. of VT, 1964–65. **Educ.:** Loughboro. Univ., M Phil (LS); Fellow of the LA (UK). **Orgs.:** LA (UK) Bibl. Socty. of Can. Resrch. Socty. for Vict. Pers. Can. Resrch. Socty. for Chld. Lit. **Pubns.:** "Historical Bibliography: Its Role in Canadian Descriptive Bibliography," *Bibl. Socty. of Can. Papers* (1980); jt. auth., "Library Service to Parttime Students," *Can. Lib. Jnl.* (F. 1977); "Library Service to Parttime Students at Trent University; A Study" (1976); "Community Use of University Libraries," *Can. Lib. Jnl.* (O. 1975); "Library Networks: Pandora' Box or Aladdin's Cave?" *Can. Lib. Jnl.* (D. 1974). **Activities:** 1, 5; 17, 35, 41; 50, 57, 89 **Addr.:** Thomas J. Bata Library, Trent University, Peterborough, ON K9J 7B8, Canada.

Wiseman, Teko (Ja. 1, 1928, Piave, MS) Info., Mobile Pub. Lib., 1975–; Sunday Columnist, Mobile Press Regis., 1973–74; Span. Tchr., St. Luke's Episcopal Sch., 1970–73; Dir. of Voluns., Mobile Gen. Hosp., 1964–66; Resrch. Assoc. in Teratology, Cincinnati Gen. Hosp., 1952–54; Med. Ed., Boston Chld. Hosp., 1950–52. **Educ.:** Univ. of AL, 1946–49, BA (Jnslm., Creat. Wrtg.); Pub. Mgt. Inst., 1979, Cert. (PR). **Orgs.:** AL LA: Natl. Lib. Week (Ch., 1979–80); Conv. Ch. (1980–81). ALA. SELA. Mobile Press Club: Exec. Bd. (1979–81). PR Cncl. of AL. **Honors:** ALA, John Cotton Dana Awds., 1978, 1979, 1980). **Activities:** 9; 16, 21, 36 **Addr.:** Mobile Public Library, 701 Government St., Mobile, AL 36602.

Wishart, H. Lynn (D. 29, 1948, New Eagle, PA) Asst. Law Libn., Resrch. Srvs., Georgetown Univ., Law Ctr., 1981–; Assoc. Law Libn., Washington and Lee Univ. Law Sch., 1978–81; Info. Srvs. Libn., Washington Univ., 1977–78, Interlib. Rel. Coord., 1975–77, ILL Libn., 1973–75, Ref. Libn., 1971–73. **Educ.:** WV Univ., 1966–69, AB (Pol. Sci.); Univ. of MI, 1970–71, AMLS; Washington Univ., 1972–77, JD. **Orgs.:** ALA: RASD, Nom. Com. (Ch., 1979–80), Outstan. Ref. Bks. Com. (Ch., 1976–78). AALL: Micro. and AV Spec. Interest Sect. (Ch., 1980–81); AV Com. (1979–80). **Pubns.:** Ed., "Reference Books of 1977," *Lib. Jnl.* (Ap. 15, 1978); ed., "Reference Books of 1976," *LJ* (Ap. 15, 1977). **Activities:** 1; 17, 34, 39; 61, 77, 92 **Addr.:** Georgetown University Law Center Library, Washington, DC 20001.

Wishingrad, Vivian D. (Ap. 28, 1953, Queens, NY) Dir. of Resrch., Canny Bowen Inc., 1981–; Resrch. Assoc., Handy Assocs., 1979–81; Asst. Dept. Head for Mgt. Anal., Queensboro. Pub. Lib., 1979; Head, Ref. Dept., Framingham Pub. Lib., 1975–78. **Educ.:** SUNY, Buffalo, 1970–73, BA, summa cum laude (Psy.); Simmons Coll., 1973–74, MLS. **Orgs.:** NY Metro. Ref. and Resrch. Lib. Agency: Admin. Com. (1979–80). ALA: LAMA/Circ. Srvs. Sect., Circ. Systs. Eval. Com. (1979). NY LA. Lib. PR Cncl. Various other orgs. **Honors:** Phi Beta Kappa, 1973. **Pubns.:** "Reference and Information Services Performance Standards at the Framingham Public Library," *UNABASHED Libn.* (N. 1979); "Framingham Registers with the Natl. Criminal Justice Reference Service," *UNABASHED Libn.* (N. 1977); contrib. series on LSCA, *Bay State Libn.* (D. 1976–77). **Activities:** 9, 14-Consult.; 17, 39, 41; 59, 91, 93 **Addr.:** 97 Rolling Wood Dr., Stamford, CT 06905.

Wismer, Donald R. (D. 27, 1946, Chicago, IL) Coord. of Autom. Data Srvs., ME State Lib., 1981–; Coord. of Circ./State Agencies Libn., 1977–81; Libn., Bigelow Lab. for Ocean Scis., 1977. **Educ.:** IN Univ., 1966–68, BA (Soclgy.), 1970–73, MA (Comp. Rel.); South. CT State Coll., 1976, MS (LS). **Orgs.:** NLA. ME LA: Exec. Bd. (1980–); Spec. Lib. Grp. (ME Pres., 1980–81). SLA. **Pubns.:** *The Islamic Jesus: An Annotated Bibliography of Sources in English and French* (1977); ed., *Downeast Libs.* (1981–); ed., *SLG News* (Spr. 1981); "Energy Information," *Downeast Libs.* (F. 1981); "AIM for Maine?" *Downeast Libs.* (S. 1980); various other articles (1976–79). **Activities:** 12, 13; 22, 36, 49-Online srch.; 56, 61, 93 **Addr.:** Maine State Library, State House Station 64, Augusta, ME 04333.

Witczak, Matthew W. (Je. 19, 1911, Chicago, IL) Pres., Bd. of Dirs., Cicero Pub. Lib., 1954–. **Educ.:** YMCA Coll., 1932–36 (Bus. Admin.). **Orgs.:** ALTA. IL LA: Exec. Bd. (1972–75); Legis. Com. (1972–75). IL Lib. Trustee Assn.: Exec. Bd. (1968–69); Secy. (1970–71); Pres. (1972–75). **Honors:** IL Trustee Assn., Disting. Srv. Awd. for Trustee, 1970; Hawthorne Bus. Men's Assn., Trustee of the Yr. for Lib. Work and Lib. Legis., 1971; Town of Cicero Town Bd., Outstan. Contrib. to Lib., 1972. **Activities:** 9; 47; 78 **Addr.:** 3143 S. 52nd Ct., Cicero, IL 60650.

Witherell, Julian Wood (Ag. 29, 1935, Washington, DC) Chief, African and Mid. East. Div., Lib. of Congs., 1978–, Head, African Sect., 1966–78, Ref. Libn., African Sect., 1963–66, Ref. Libn., Serial Div., 1962–63. **Educ.:** Bowdoin Coll., 1952–56, BA (Hist.); Univ. of WI, 1956–62, MA, PhD (African Std.). **Orgs.:** ALA: ACRL/Asian and African Sect. African Stds. Assn.: Arch.-–Libs. Com. (1964–). Mid. E. LA. South. Assn. of Africanists. Amer. Oriental Socty. Assn. of African Std. Progs. Mid. E. Std. Assn. **Honors:** U.S. Gvt., William Jump Awd., 1968; African Std. Assn., Conover–Porter Awd. for Bibl. Achvmt., 1980. **Pubns.:** *The United States and Africa* (1978); *Africana in Great Britain and the Netherlands: Report of a Publication Survey Trip, March-April 1977* (1977); "Africana in the Library of Congress," *Qtly. Jnl. of the Lib. of Congs.* (1970); *French-Speaking Central Africa: A Guide to Official Publications in American Libraries* (1973); *Africana Acquisitions: Report of a Publication Survey Trip to Nigeria, Southern Africa, and Europe, 1972* (1973); various mono. (1965–69). **Activities:** 4; 15, 29, 39; 54 **Addr.:** African & Middle Eastern Division, Library of Congress, Washington, DC 20540.

PROFESSIONAL ACTIVITIES: Institutions: 1. Acad. lib.; 2. Arch.; 3. Assn.; 4. Fed./Gvt. lib.; 5. Inst. lib.; 6. Mfr./Suppl.; 7. Milit. lib.; 8. Musm.; 9. Pub. lib.; 10. Sch. lib.; 11. Sch. of lib. sci.; 12. Spec. lib.; 13. State lib.; 14. (other). **Functions/Activities:** 15. Acq./Col. dev.; 16. Adult srvs.; 17. Admin.; 18. Apprais.; 19. Archit./Bldgs.; 20. Cat./Class.; 21. Chld. srvs.; 22. Circ.; 23. Cons./Pres.; 24. Consult.; 25. Cont. ed.; 26. Educ. lib. sci.; 27. Ext. srvs.; 28. Fund/Grants; 29. Gvt. pubs.; 30. Indx./Abs.; 31. Instr. lib. use; 32. Media srvs.; 33. Micro.; 34. Netwks./Coop.; 35. Persnl.; 36. PR; 37. Publshg.; 38. Recs. mgt.; 39. Ref. srvs.; 40. Repro.; 41. Resrch.; 42. Review.; 43. Secur.; 44. Serials; 45. Spec. col.; 46. Tech. srvs.; 47. Trustees/Bds.; 48. YA srvs.; 49. (other).

Witiak, Joanne L. (O. 6, 1949, Ft. Dodge, IA) Info. Sci., Rohm and Haas Co., 1976–, Resrch. Chem., 1973–76. **Educ.:** IA State Univ., 1967–71, BS (Chem.), 1971–72, MS (Org. Chem.); Drexel Univ., 1976–79, MLS. **Orgs.:** ASIS: SIG/BC, Secy; Amer. Chem. Socty. **Pubns.:** "Online Database Searching via Telephone Conferencing," *Online* (Ap. 1979). **Activities:** 12; 31, 39; 58, 60, 91 **Addr.:** Information Services, Rohm and Haas Co., 727 Norristown Rd., Spring House, PA 19477.

Witmer, John A. (N. 29, 1920, Lancaster, PA) Dir., Mosher Lib., Dallas Theo. Semy., 1977–, Libn., 1964–77; Actg. Libn., 1963–64. **Educ.:** Wheaton Coll., 1938–42, AB (Eng. Lit.), 1942–46, MA (Theo.); Dallas Theo. Semy., 1944–46, ThM (Sys. Theo.); 1946–53, ThD (Sys. Theo.); E. TX State Univ., 1964–69, MSLS. **Orgs.:** Dallas Cnty. LA: Pres. (1969–70). Christ. Libns. Flwshp.: Pres. (1970–71). TX LA: Pubns. Com. (1979–81). SWLA. Various other orgs. Evang. Theo. Socty. Evang. Phil. Socty. **Honors:** Kappa Delta Pi. Phi Delta Kappa. **Pubns.:** "What Think Ye of Christ?" *Jerusalem and Athens* (1971); "Biblical Authority in Contemporary Theology," *Truth for Today* (1963); "He Fought at Stalingrad," *These Live On* (1945). **Activities:** 1; 17, 30, 42; 57, 61, 90 **Addr.:** Mosher Library, Dallas Theological Seminary, Dallas, TX 75204.

Wittkopf, Barbara Jean (Jl. 28, 1943, Yonkers, NY) Assoc. Libn., Univ. of FL, 1975–, Asst. Libn., 1970–75; Jr. Libn., Syracuse Pub. Lib., 1968–70; Tchr., Grade 2, Nassau Luth. Sch., 1965–67. **Educ.:** Valparaiso Univ., 1961–65, BS (Educ.); Syracuse Univ., 1967–68, MLS. **Orgs.:** ALA: ACRL/Bibl. Instr. Sect., Coop. Com. (1980–82). SELA: Law and Pol. Sci. Sect., Nom. Com. (Ch., 1981–82). FL LA: Ref., Acad. and Spec. Online, ILL, LOBI Caucuses. Alachua Cnty. Lib. Leag.: Pres. (1978–80); VP (1977–78). Various other orgs. UN/USA. Assn. of Women Fac. Untd. Fac. of FL. Various other orgs. **Honors:** Beta Phi Mu, 1968. **Pubns.:** Jt. auth., *Guide to Academic Libraries* (1981); jt. auth., "Computerized Census Data: Meeting Demands in an Academic Library," *RQ* (Spr. 1980); "Card Catalog: A Users Approach" slide/tape (1979). **Activities:** 1; 31, 39, 49-Online srch.; 63, 92 **Addr.:** University of Florida Libraries, 114 Library W., Gainesville, FL 32605.

Wittman, Sr. Patricia (F. 19, 1928, Portland, OR) Lib. Dir., Holy Fam. Coll., 1976–; Rel. Educ. Tchr. and Supvsr., Srs. of the Holy Fam., 1953–76; Ref. Staff, Cath. Info. Bur. and Lending Lib. of the Cath. Truth Socty., 1951–53. **Educ.:** Holy Fam. Coll., 1968, BA (Theo.); Univ. of HI, 1975–76, MLS. **Orgs.:** ALA: ACRL. CA LA. CA Acad. and Resrch. Libns. Various other orgs. Washington Twp. Hist. Socty.: Cur. (1977–). Lib. Adv. Com. (Fremont, CA). **Activities:** 1; 15, 20, 39; 63, 90, 92 **Addr.:** Holy Family College Library, 159 Washington Blvd., Mission San Jose, Fremont, CA 94539.

Wittorf, Robert H. (S. 27, 1938, New York City, NY) Sr. Lib. Systs. Anal., OCLC, Inc., 1977–; Asst. Prof., Lib. and Comm. Sci., Wright State Univ., 1972–77; Head, Lib. Autom. and Syst. Dept., Brigham Young Univ. Lib., 1965–70. **Educ.:** Brigham Young Univ., 1955–59, BA (Hist.); Pratt Inst., 1959–60, MLS. **Orgs.:** ALA: RTSD, Bk. Cats. Com. (1976–). **Pubns.:** *Index to L.D.S. Church Periodicals, 1966–1970* (1967–71). **Activities:** 11, 6; 26, 38, 49-Lib. autom.; 56 **Addr.:** P.O. Box 02164, Clintonville Station, Columbus, OH 43202.

Witucke, A. Virginia (My. 7, 1937, Oak Park, IL) Assoc. Prof., Univ. of AZ, 1978–; Assoc. Prof., Pratt Inst., 1976–78; Asst. Prof., Univ. of IA, 1973–76; Asst. Prof., Purdue Univ., 1966–70. **Educ.:** IL State Univ., 1953–57, BS (Educ.); West. MI Univ., 1960–61, MA (LA); Columbia Univ., 1974, DLS. **Orgs.:** ALA: Ref. and Subscrpn. Bks. Review Com. (1978–82); AASL, Netwk. Resrch. (1976–80); ALSC, Newbery–Caldecott Awd. Com. (1980) Amer. Cvl. Liberties Un. Natl. Cncl. of Tchrs. of Eng. **Pubns.:** *Poetry in the Elementary School* (1970); "A Comparative Analysis of Juvenile Book Review Media," *Sch. Media Qtly.* (Spr. 1980); "Library School Policies Toward Preprofessional Work Experience," *Jnl. of Educ. for Libnshp.* (Win. 1976); various reviews. **Activities:** 10; 21, 26 **Addr.:** Graduate Library School, University of Arizona, Tucson, AZ 85719.

Woeckel, Allan J. (O. 3, 1944, LaSalle, IL) Dir., Reddick Lib., 1971–; Instr., Hum. Dept., IL Valley Cmnty. Coll., 1971–72; Ref. Libn., Coll. of DuPage, 1970–72; Asst. Dir., Helen M. Plum Meml. Lib., 1969–71. **Educ.:** North. IL Univ., 1964–66, BA (Hist.), 1966–67, Cert. (Educ.), 1967–69, MA (LS). **Orgs.:** ALA. DuPage Cnty. Libns. Assn.: VP, Pres.-Elect (1970–71). IL LA: PR Com. (Ch., 1974–75); Natl. Lib. Wk. Com. (1973–74); Conf. Arrange. Com. (1972–73, 1969–70); Conf. Exhibits Com. (1971–72); Audit Com. (1970–71). Lib. Admins. Conf. of North. IL. Ottawa Area Cham. of Cmrce. Ottawa Lions Club.: Various ofcs. Parents Without Partners, Inc.: Various ofcs. Loyal Ord. of Moose. **Honors:** Ottawa Lions Club, Disting. Srv. Awd., 1976. **Activities:** 9; 17, 36, 39 **Addr.:** 420 Park Ave., Ottawa, IL 61350.

Woerner, W. Robert (Ja. 29, 1941, Louisville, KY) Lib. Dir., Ithaca Coll., 1980–; Dir. of Lib. Srvs. (Interim), Greensboro Coll., 1980; Dir. of Libs., Salem Coll., 1973–79; Head Libn., Behrend Coll., PA State, 1969–73; Soc. Scis. Libn., Rutgers Univ., 1967–68; Head, Readg. Rm. and Chief Ref. Libn., NY Hist. Socty., 1966–67. **Educ.:** Univ. of Louisville, 1959–63, BA (Hist.), 1963–68, MA (Hist.); Columbia Univ., 1965–66, MS (LS). **Orgs.:** ALA. SELA. Bibl. Socty. of Amer. Filson Club. Eng.–Speaking Un.: Bd. of Dirs. (1977–80). **Activities:** 1; 15, 17, 36; 55, 57, 89 **Addr.:** Ithaca College Library, Ithaca, NY 14850.

Wojan, Phyllis Hoecker (My. 4, 1924, New York, NY) Asst. Libn., Hotchkiss Sch., 1972–; Resrch. Biblgrphr., Downstate Med. Ctr., 1971; Dir. of Sales Presentations, RKO–Gen. Teleradio, Inc., 1955–57; Exec. Staff Writer, Columbia Broadcasting Syst., Inc., 1946–55. **Educ.:** Barnard Coll., 1942–46, AB (Eng.); Pratt Inst., 1969–1971, MLS. **Orgs.:** ASIS. ALA. New Eng. LA. Beta Phi Mu: Theta Chap., Bd. of Dirs. (1972–74). Intl. Radio and TV Socty.: Hosplty. Com. (1954–55). AAAS. Willoughby Settlement Hse.: Bd. of Gvrs. (1967–72). Housetonic Valley Assn.: Pubcty. Ch. (1972–73). Various other orgs. ofcs. **Honors:** Natl. Inst. of Hlth. Conf. on the Hist. of the Inbred Mouse, "In recognition of a dedicated amateur in the field of inbred mice," 1978; Pratt Inst. Grad. Sch. of Lib. and Info. Sci. Student Assn., Fndrs. Awd. for Leadership and Srv., 1971. **Pubns.:** Ed., *The Friendly Gourmet* (1966); "A First Report on Bright Woods Breeders: Research and Stocks," *Mouse Nsltr.* (Jl. 1980); "Man Builds, Man Destroys–It Can Be Done" film (1971). **Activities:** 1, 10; 20, 24, 41; 58, 75, 91 **Addr.:** Bright Woods, Rte. 45, Cornwall Bridge, CT 06754.

Wolcott, Merlin Dewey (O. 22, 1920, Sandusky, OH) Emeritus Dir., Stark Cnty. Dist. Lib., 1980–, Dir., 1962–80; Dir., Elyria Pub. Lib., 1957–62; Dir., Avon Lake Pub. Lib., 1955–56; Asst. Sci. and Tech. Div., Cleveland Pub. Lib., 1952–53. **Educ.:** Bowling Green State Univ., 1946–50, BS (Educ.); Kent State Univ., 1952–53, MLS. **Orgs.:** ALA: Bylaws Com. OH LA: Legis. Com. Mayflower Socty. Grt. Canton Econ. Cncl. Natl. Assn. of Accts. Sons of the Amer. Revolution: VP. Various other orgs. **Pubns.:** "Alexander Clemons' Bible Record," *Amer. Genealogist* (51:4); "Marblehead Limestone for the Soo Lock," *Inland Seas* (Sum. 1976); "Duvelle Cemetery, Ottawa County, Ohio," *Rpt.: The OH Genealogical Socty.* (Fall 1978); "Family History of Harriet (Hill) Johnson," *Amer. Genealogist* (Ja. 1979); "Southard Family Cemetery, Bellmore, Long Island," *NY Genealogical and Biographical Rec.* (O. 1979); various articles on hist., geneal. (1954–72). **Activities:** 9; 17, 35; 69 **Addr.:** 327 Shelby St., Sandusky, OH 44870.

Wold, Shelley Thurman (Ja. 27, 1935, Edgerton, WI) Gvt. Docums. Libn., Univ. of AR (Little Rock), 1980–; Serials and Gifts Libn., 1977–79, Ref. Libn., 1976–77, Instr., LS, 1970–76; Asst. Circ. Libn., IN Univ., 1964–67; Lectr., LS, Univ. of the Punjab, 1959–62; Gifts Libn., Univ. of WI, 1957. **Educ.:** Univ. of WI, 1952–56, BA (Hisp. Std.), 1956–57, MA (LS). **Orgs.:** ALA. AR LA: Arkansiana Awd. Com. (1979); Educ. Com. (Ch., 1974–75); Constn. Com. (Ch., 1980–81). WI Lib. Sch. Alum. Assn.: Nom. Com. (1972). AAUW: Charlie May Simon Chld. Bk. Awd. Com. (1974–). Amer. Recorder Socty. **Honors:** Phi Beta Kappa, 1956. **Activities:** 1; 15, 29, 44 **Addr.:** 38 Pine Manor Dr., Little Rock, AR 72207.

Wolf, Carolyn E. (Jl. 15, 1941, New York, NY) Ref. Libn., Hartwick Coll., 1969–; Asst. Libn., NY State Lib., 1967–69; Tchr., Bethlehem Ctrl. Sch., 1965–67; Tchr., Broadalbin Ctrl. Sch., 1963–67. **Educ.:** SUNY, Albany, 1959–63, BS (Bio.), 1964–68, MLS. **Orgs.:** ALA: ACRL, East. NY Chap. Hartwick Coll. Women's Club. Oneonta Cmnty. Art Ctr. Oneonta Country Club: Women's Golf Assn. AAUP. **Pubns.:** *Basic Library Skills: A Short Course* (1981); "Library Services to the Visually Handicapped in the South Central Research Library Council," *Info. Rpts. and Bibls.* (1978); "Hartwick Serves Blind," *Amer. Libs.* (D. 1971); "Field Report: When Pupils Grow Crystals," *Prof. Growth for Tchrs., Sci., Jr. HS Ed.* (3rd quarter 1966–67); "Independent Studies with Light," *Prof. Growth for Tchrs., Sci., Jr. HS Ed.* (F. 1966); various other articles. **Activities:** 1; 22, 39, 44; 63, 72, 91 **Addr.:** Hartwick College Library, Oneonta, NY 13820.

Wolf, Coralie Ann (Ja. 16, 1941, New York, NY) Wilmot Lib. Branch Mgr., Tucson Pub. Lib., 1979–, Valencia Branch Mgr., 1969–79; Medford Jr. HS Lib., Medford Pub. Schs., 1965–68; HS Tchr., Sunnyside Pub. Schs., 1963–65. **Educ.:** Hope Coll., 1958–62, AB (Latin, Grk., Math.); Simmons Coll., 1965–68, MS (LS). **Orgs.:** SWLA: Nom. Com. (1978–80). AZ LA: Conf. (Ch., 1981); Awds. Com. (Ch., 1978–79); Pres. (1976–77); Lib. Dev./Legis. Com. (1974–77); various other coms., ofcs. ALA: State Mem. Ch. (1975–76); various coms., ofcs. La Reforma. Various other orgs. Fam. Violence Coal. Educ. Com. Una Noche Plateada: Assoc.; Pres. (1977–78). IMAGE de Tucson. Various other orgs., ofcs. **Honors:** Victim–Witness Spec. Merit Awd., 1979–80; Pima Cmnty. Coll., Cert. of Recog. (1977, 1978); Sunnyside Optimist Club, Cert. of Apprec., 1978; Una Noche Plateada, Spec. Recog. Awd., 1976; other hons. **Activities:** 9; 17; 66 **Addr.:** 2601 S. Enchanted Hills Dr., Tucson, AZ 85713.

Wolf, Edward G. (Je. 6, 1930, Greensburg, PA) Coord., Media Resrcs., IN Univ. of PA, 1962–; Sch. Tchr./Libn., Abington Twp. Schs., 1958–62; Tchr., Soc. Stds., Shaler Twp. Schs., 1953–58. **Educ.:** Duquesne Univ., 1949–53, BEd (Hist.); Univ. of Pittsburgh, 1954–58, ML (Hist.); Drexel Inst. of Tech., 1959–62, MLS; Univ. of Pittsburgh, 1966–72, PhD (LS). **Orgs.:** ALA: LRTS; ACRL. **Pubns.:** "Local History in American Libraries," *Ency. of Lib. and Info. Sci.* **Activities:** 1; 15, 20, 32; 57, 67, 92 **Addr.:** Media Resources, University Library, Indiana University of Pennsylvania, Indiana, PA 15705.

Wolf, Edwin (D. 6, 1911, Philadelphia, PA) Libn., Lib. Co. of Philadelphia, 1955–, Cur., 1953–55; Catlgr., Biblgphr., Mgr., Rosenbach Co. Rare Bks. and Mss., 1930–52. **Orgs.:** Bibl. Socty. of Amer.: Past Pres. Grolier Club. Frnds. of Univ. of PA Lib.: Past Pres. Grt. Philadelphia Cult. Alliance: Pres. (1977–78). Jewish Publshg. Socty. of Amer.: Past Pres. Amer. Phil. Socty. Amer. Antiq. Socty. Other orgs. **Honors:** Coll. of Jewish Std., DHL, 1965; Univ. of PA, Rosenbach Fellow, 1964; Guggenheim Fellow, 1961; Athen. Lit. Awd., 1961; Penn Awd., 1979; other hons. **Pubns.:** *At the Instance of Benjamin Franklin* (1976); *Philadelphia: a Portrait of an American City* (1975); *The Library of James Logan* (1974); Jt. auth., *Rosenbach: a Biography* (1960); Jt. auth., *William Blake's Illuminated Books* (1953); Other bks., articles. **Activities:** 14-Resrch. Lib.; 45 **Addr.:** 1314 Locust St., Philadelphia, PA 19107.*

Wolf, Marta S. (Mr. 25, 1946, Newark, NJ) Asst. Dir., Col. Devel., Div. for Blind and Phys. Handcpd., TX State Lib., 1980–, Resrch. Libn., Netwk. Dev., 1980; Dir., Tech. Info. Srvs., Ctr. for Soc. Work Resrch., Univ. of TX, 1975–79, Branch Libn., Gen. Libs., 1972–75; Asst. Libn., Hosp. Admin. Lib., Univ. of MI, 1970–72; Sch. Libn., Brooks Jr. Sec. Sch., 1969–70. **Educ.:** Bowling Green Univ., 1964–68, BS (Eng., Sp., LS); Univ. of TX, 1975–77, MLS. **Orgs.:** SLA: Prog. Plng. Com. (1977–). Alliance of Info. and Ref. Srvs.: Stans. and Accred. Com. (1978–); Lib. Com. (1976–); Jnl. Ed. Bd. (1978–). TX Alliance of Info. and Ref. Srvs: Exec. Com.; Stans. Com., Ch.; Conf. Ch. (1979). ALA. State Agency Libs. of TX: Pres. (1981–82). Various other orgs. **Pubns.:** "Cooperation Between Libraries and Other Agencies in Information and Referral," *Pub. Libs.* (Sum. 1981); "Concept of Information Services–Old and New," *Contact* (1976). **Activities:** 12, 13; 15, 17; 72, 92 **Addr.:** Texas State Library–DBPH, 1201 Brazos, Austin, TX 78711.

Wolfe, Carl F. (O. 2, 1951, Harlingen, TX) Resrch. Libn., Dow Chem., TX Div., 1976–. **Educ.:** Univ. of AK, 1970–74, BA (Eng.); N. TX State Univ., 1975, MLS. **Orgs.:** SLA: TX Chap. Networking Com. (Ch., 1979–80), Empl. Com. (Ch., 1980–81). ALA. TX LA. ASIS. **Honors:** Beta Phi Mu. **Activities:** 12; 20, 39, 46; 60, 64, 91 **Addr.:** Library B-1210, Dow Chemical USA, Texas Div., Freeport, TX 77541.

Wolfe, Charles B. (D. 1, 1945, Milwaukee, WI) State Law Libn., MI State Lib., 1978–, Asst. State Law Libn., 1973–78. **Educ.:** Univ. of WI, Milwaukee, 1963–68, BS (Soclgy.); Univ. of WI, 1968–72, JD, 1972–73, MS (LS). **Orgs.:** AALL: *Law Lib. Jnl.* Asst. Ed. (1978–). MI Assn. of Law Libs.: Pres. (1977–78). OH Reg. Assn. of Law Libs. State Bar of WI. **Pubns.:** "Current Problems Facing State Law Libraries," *Law Lib. Jnl.* (F. 1978). **Activities:** 13; 17; 77 **Addr.:** State Law Library, P.O. Box 30012, Lansing, MI 48909.

Wolfe, Gary D. (Mr. 19, 1941, Altoona, PA) Dist. Ctr. Admin., Ctr. Cnty. Lib., 1975–; Asst. Prof. of Libnshp., St. Francis Coll., 1970–74, Circ. and Pers. Libn., 1963–69; Actg. Chld. Libn., Coyle Free Lib., 1961–62. **Educ.:** St. Francis Coll., 1966–70, BS (Educ., Lib. Cert.); Univ. of Pittsburgh, 1970–72, MLS. **Orgs.:** Cambria Cnty. LA: Pres. (1974–75). Cath. LA: Various coms. Cresson Pub. Lib.: Various ofcs. PA LA: Juniata–Conemaugh Chap. Ch. (1974–75); Ch.-Elect. (1973–74); Natl. Lib. Week State Com. (1974); Cnty./Pub. Div., Nom. Com. (Ch., 1979); Bd. of Dirs. (1974–75); Conf. Eval. Com. (1979–80); various other coms., ofcs. Various other orgs., ofcs. Untd. Mnstry. of Penn State: Bd. of Dirs. (1980–). **Pubns.:** *Training Manual for Consultant Librarians* (1977); "Homework Hotline," *Lrng. and Media* (Win. 1979). **Activities:** 1, 9; 17, 26, 34; 50, 63, 67 **Addr.:** Centre County Library, 203 N. Allegheny St., Bellefonte, PA 16823.

Wolfe, Judith A. (Jl. 27, 1935, Chicago, IL) Coord. of Lib. Resrcs., MO State Lib., 1978–, Gvt. Srvs. Libn., 1975–78, Ref. Libn., 1974–75; Tchr., Rockbridge Elem. Sch., 1968–73. **Educ.:** East. IL Univ., 1967, BS (Educ.); Univ. of MO, 1974, MA (LS), 1978, MA (Pub. Admin.). **Orgs.:** SLA: Chap. Pres. (1975); Legis. Ref. Sect. (Ch., 1979); Soc. Sci. Div. (Ch. Elect, 1980). MO LA: Awds. Com. (Ch., 1977–78). ALA. Amer. Socty. for Pub. Admin. **Honors:** Beta Phi Mu, 1974. **Pubns.:** Various articles, *Show Me Libs.* (1974–); reviews, *Amer. Ref. Bk. Anl.* (1978–). **Activities:** 13; 17, 24, 39; 56, 78, 92 **Addr.:** Missouri State Library, P.O. Box 387, 308 E. High St., Jefferson City, MO 65102.

Wolfe, Marice M. (Ag. 3, 1935, Warren, OH) Head, Spec. Cols., Vanderbilt Univ. Lib., 1973–. **Educ.:** Clarke Coll., 1952–56, BA (Eng.); Marquette Univ., 1956–58, MA (Eng.); George Peabody Coll., 1975–77, MLS. **Orgs.:** SAA. TN Archvsts.: Pres. (1979–81); VP (1977–79). TN LA. **Activities:** 1, 2; 17, 39, 45; 55 **Addr.:** Special Collections, Vanderbilt University Library, Nashville, TN 37203.

Wolfe, Peggy Richter (Je. 17, 1930, Chicago, IL) Libn., Urban Transp. Col., Univ. of MN, 1969–; Libn., Pillsbury Co., 1960–67. **Educ.:** Coll. of St. Catherine, 1948–52, BA (Eng.); Univ. of MN, 1962–66, MA (LS). **Orgs.:** SLA: MN Chap. VP (1973–74); Pres., (1974–75); Dir. (1975–76). **Pubns.:** "A Look at Advertising and Marketing Libraries," *Spec. Libs.* (S. 1969). **Ac-**

Special Subjects/Services: 50. Adult educ.; 51. Advert./Mktg.; 52. Aerosp.; 53. Agric.; 54. Area std.; 55. Arts/Hum.; 56. Autom.; 57. Bibl./Prtg.; 58. Bio. sci.; 59. Bus./Fin.; 60. Chem.; 61. Copyrt.; 62. Documtn.; 63. Educ.; 64. Engin.; 65. Env.; 66. Eth. grps.; 67. Film; 68. Food/Nutr.; 69. Geneal.; 70. Geo.; 71. Geol.; 72. Handcpd.; 73. Hist.; 74. Int. frdm.; 75. Info. sci.; 76. Insr.; 77. Law; 78. Legis.; 79. Math./Comp. sci.; 80. Med.; 81. Metals; 82. Nat. resrcs.; 83. Newsp.; 84. Nuc. sci.; 85. Oral hist.; 86. Petr./Energy; 87. Pharm.; 88. Phys./Astr./Math.; 89. Readg.; 90. Relig.; 91. Sci./Tech.; 92. Soc. sci.; 93. Telecom.; 94. Transp.; 95. (other).

tivities: 1; 15, 17, 39; 94 **Addr.:** Urban Transportation Collection, 150 Experimental Engineering, 208 Union St., University of Minnesota, Minneapolis, MN 55455.

Wolfermann, Nancy B. (Ag. 26, 1947, New York, NY) Tech. Srvs. Libn., Mt. Sinai Med. Ctr., 1980–, Head, Cat. Dept., 1972–79, Asst. Catlgr., 1970–72. **Educ.:** Queens Coll., CUNY, 1965–69, BA (Fr.); SUNY, Albany, 1969–70, MLS. **Orgs.:** Med. LA: NY Reg. Grp., Cont. Educ. Com. (1972–73), Exec. Bd. (1973–75). **Pubns.:** "Integrating the Records of Two Separately Owned Library Collections," *Spec. Libs.* (1975). **Activities:** 1, 12; 17, 20, 31; 80 **Addr.:** 3240 Henry Hudson Pkwy., Bronx, NY 10463.

Wolfgram, Patricia B. (Ag. 13, 1942, Wilmington, DE) Dir. of Libs., Saginaw Osteopathic Hosp., 1975–; Consult. Libn., Hills and Dales Gen. Hosp., 1977–; Clare Osteopathic Hosp.; Traverse City Osteopathic Hosp. **Educ.:** Ctrl. MI Univ., 1974, BS (Educ., LS); West. MI Univ., 1981 (MLS). **Orgs.:** Valley Reg. Hlth. Sci. Libns.: VP (1977–79); Pres. (1979–80). MI State Univ. Participating Lib. Adv. Com.: Ch. (1977–79). Med. LA: Midwest Reg. Grp. and Hosp. Lib. Sect. KY–OH–MI Reg. Med Lib. Exec. Com.: Basic Unit Rep. for MI (1978–80). CETA Adv. Cncl. for Saginaw Cnty. Dept. of Manpower. Leag. of Women Voters of Saginaw Cnty.: Bd. YWCA Bd. Jr. Leag. of Saginaw: Bd. Various other orgs. **Activities:** 12; 20, 39, 41; 80, 95-Osteopathic lit. **Addr.:** Saginaw Osteopathic Hospital Library, 515 N. Michigan Ave., Saginaw, MI 48602.

Wolfinger, Audrey Jane (Je. 21, 1933, Mt. Penn Reading, PA) Libn., Neshaminy Sch. Dist., 1955–; Resrch. Libn., Balke Resrch. Assocs., 1970–79. **Educ.:** Kutztown State Coll., 1951–55, BS in ED (LS, Eng.); Temple Univ. 1958, Cert. (Tchg.); FL State Univ., 1970, MLS. **Orgs.:** ALA. PA LA PA Sch. Libns. Assn. AECT. Amer. Fed. of Tchrs. Neshaminy Fed. of Tchrs.: Lcl. 1417. Assn. for Supvsn. and Curric. Dev. **Activities:** 10; 15, 31, 48; 63 **Addr.:** Neshaminy–Langhorne Sr. High School, Langhorne, PA 19047.

Wolford, Betty J. (D. 27, 1932, Bourbon Cnty., KY) Media Dir., Princeton Jr. HS, 1964–; Libn., Cleveland Pub. Lib., 1957–58; Asst. Libn., Shaker Hts. HS Lib., 1953–57. **Educ.:** Univ. of KY, 1949–53, BA (Educ.); Case-West. Rsv. Univ., 1954–60, MS (LS). **Orgs.:** OH Educ. Lib./Media Assn.: 1st VP, Pres.–Elect (1979–80). AECT. ALA: AASL. **Honors:** Phi Delta Kappa. **Pubns.:** "Getting the Itch for ITV," *OH Media Spectrum* (Win. 1979). **Addr.:** Princeton Junior High School, 11157 Chester Rd., Cincinnati, OH 45246.

Wolford, Janet (Jl. 19, 1939, McKinney, TX) Tech. Libn., Mobil Resrch. and Dev. Corp. Fld. Resrch. Lab., 1966–; Asst. Catlgr., N. TX State Univ., 1965–66; Tchr., Weatherford Pub. Schs., 1963–64; Tchr., Amarillo Pub. Schs., 1962–63; Tchr., Weatherford Pub. Schs., 1960–62. **Educ.:** TX Christ. Univ., 1956–60, BMscEd (Msc.); N. TX State Univ., 1964–65, MLS. **Orgs.:** SLA: Mem. Ch. (1968–70); Consult Com. (1970–72); Nom. Com., (Ch., 1969). **Activities:** 12; 15, 22, 46; 86 **Addr.:** 222 S. Alexander Ave., Duncanville, TX 75116.

Wolfson, Catherine Lincoln (F. 25, 1946, Louisville, KY) Acq. Libn., Hlth. Scis. Ctr. Lib., Univ. of AZ, 1975–, Asst. Cat. Libn., 1974–75; Head Cat. Libn., Med. Lib., Univ. of NM, 1973–74. **Educ.:** Univ. of AZ, 1965–68, BA (Fr.); Univ. of MO, 1972–73, MA (LS). **Orgs.:** Med. LA: South. CA and AZ Grp. AZ LA: Spec. Libs. Div. (Prog. Ch., 1978–79). Beta Phi Mu: Beta Pi Chap. (Pres., 1980–81). AZ Hlth. Sci. Ctr. Lib. Fac. Asm.: Secy. (1977–78). **Honors:** Phi Beta Kappa, 1968. **Activities:** 5, 12; 15, 17, 44; 58, 80, 91 **Addr.:** 1821 E. 9th St., Tucson, AZ 85719.

Wolk, Robert S. (Ag. 5, 1947, Brooklyn, NY) Libn., Cur., Joseph Conrad Lib., Seamen's Church Inst. of NY, 1976–. **Educ.:** Brooklyn Coll., 1966–70, BA (Hist.), 1970–75, MA (Hist.); Pratt Inst., 1972–74, MLS. **Orgs.:** SLA. NY State Hist. Assn. Amer. Assn. for State and Lcl. Hist. **Honors:** Beta Phi Mu, 1974. **Pubns.:** Series ed., *Seafaring Men: Their Ships and Their Times* (1979). **Activities:** 8, 12; 17, 28; 73, 94 **Addr.:** Joseph Conrad Library, Seamen's Church Institute of New York, 15 State St., New York, NY 10004.

Woll, Christina Glass (D. 14, 1934, Madison, WI) Consult., Lib. Media Srvs., El Paso Pub. Schs., 1965–, Comms. Spec., 1964–65, Jnslm. Tchr., 1959–64. **Educ.:** NM State Univ., 1953–59, BS (Educ.); AZ State Univ., 1962–63, MA (Curric., LS). **Orgs.:** TX Assn. of Sch. Libns.: Pres. (1970); Exec. Bd. (1969–71). TX LA: Cncl. (1969–74). Border Reg. LA: Pres. (1967). TX Lib. Systs. Act Adv. Bd. TX ESEA IVB-C Adv. Cncl.: Ch. (1979–). *Elem. Sch. Lib. Col.:* Adv. Bd. (1971–74). El Paso Cncl. on the Arts and Hum. El Paso Day Care Ctr. Various other orgs. **Honors:** Border Reg. LA, Libn. of the Yr., 1969. **Pubns.:** Ed., *Bilingual/Bicultural Materials; A Listing for Library Learning Resource Centers* (1974, 1975). **Activities:** 10; 17, 24 **Addr.:** P.O. Box 20100, El Paso, TX 79998.

Wolohan, Juliet Francis (N. 7, 1905, Albany, NY) Retired, 1970–; Assoc. Libn., Mss. and Hist., NY State Lib., 1966–70, Sr. Libn., 1961–65, Actg. Head, 1956–61. **Educ.:** Siena Coll., 1941–45, BA (Soclgy.); SUNY, Albany, 1949–50, MS (LS); Arch. Inst., Amer. Univ., 1958, Cert. (Arch.). **Orgs.:** ALA: RASD/Hist. Sect., Exec. Com. (1970–71). NY LA. Cath. LA: Albany Chap., Past Treas. SAA. NY State Hist. Assn. Arch. Assocs. Rensselaer City Hist. Socty. Natl. Trust for Hist. Prsrvn. Various other orgs. **Activities:** 2; 15, 38, 45; 70, 92 **Addr.:** 210 Lindbergh Ave., Rensselaer, NY 12144.

Wolter, John Amadeus (Jl. 25, 1925, St. Paul, MN) Chief, Geo. and Map Div., Lib. of Congs., 1978–, Asst. Chief, 1968–78; Asst. Prof., Univ. of WI, River Falls, 1966–68; Asst. to Dir. of Libs., Univ. of MN, 1965–66. **Educ.:** Univ. of MN, 1952–56, BA (Geo.), 1963–65, MA (LS), 1968–75, PhD (Geo.). **Orgs.:** SLA: Geo. and Map. Div. (Secy.–Treas., 1965–66). ALA: Org. Com. on Stans. for Map Micro. (Ch., 1974–75). IFLA: Geo. and Map Libs. Sect., Com. on Educ. for Map. Libnshp. (1976–78), World Dir. of Map Colls. Com. (Ch., 1979–). Univ. of MN Lib. Staff Assn: VP and Exec. Com. (1962–64). U.S. Bd. on Geographic Names: Ch. (1980–); Frgn. Names Com. (Ch., 1978–80). U.S. Natl. Com. for the Intl. Geographical Un. (1972–80.) Amer. Congs. on Surveying and Mapping: Pubns. Com. Ch. (1977–78); ed. bds., *The Amer. Cartographer Surveying and Mapping; Imag Mundi* and *Cartographica 1972–80* Cartography Div. Dir. (1973–75). Socty. for the Hist. of Discoveries: Various ofcs. Various other orgs., ofcs. **Pubns.:** "The Heights of Mountains and the Lengths of Rivers," *Surveying and Mapping* (1972); "Geographical Libraries and Map Collections," *Encyc. of Lib. and Info. Sci.* (1973); "Cartography–An Emerging Discipline," *Can. Cartographer* (1975); "Research Tools and the Literature of Cartography," *AB Bookman Yrbk. Part I* (1976); "Source Materials for the History of American Cartography," *Amer. Std. Topics and Sources* (1976). **Activities:** 4; 17, 41; 70 **Addr.:** Chief, Geography and Map Division, Library of Congress, Washington, DC 20540.

Woltz, Lillian Martha (Ag. 17, 1940, Okeman, OK) Asst. Libn., Pub. Srvs., Nash Lib., Univ. of Sci. and Arts of OK, 1976–; Spec. Instr., Dept. of Eng., Univ. of OK, 1968–74. **Educ.:** OK City Univ., 1958–61, BA (Eng.); Univ. of OK, 1975–76, MLS. **Orgs.:** SWLA. OK LA: Mem./Rcrt. Com. (1980–81); Un. List of Serials Com. (Ch., 1979–80); Rcrt. Com. (1977–80); Ref. RT Sect. (1981–82). Higher Educ. Alum. Cncl. of OK. **Activities:** 1; 31, 39, 44; 55 **Addr.:** Nash Library, University of Science & Arts of Oklahoma, Chickasha, OK 73018.

Womack, (Sharon) Kay (Jl. 23, 1943, Hominy, OK) Assoc. Prof., Soc. Sci. Div., Univ. of NE-Lincoln Lib., (1973–; Ref. Libn., IN Univ., Kokoma, 1971–73; Asst. Circ. Libn., Univ. of WA, 1970–71, Ref. Libn., 1967–70. **Educ.:** Univ. of OK, 1962–66, BA (French), 1966–67, MLS, Univ. of NE, 1975–79, MS (Human Dev.). **Orgs.:** ALA: ACRL/EBSS, Ad Hoc Psy./Psyt. Com., (1979–81). NE OLUG. **Honors:** Omicron Nu, 1978. **Pubns.:** Jt. auth., *Death, Dying and Grief; a Bibliography* (1978). **Activities:** 1; 31, 39, 49-Comp. srchg.; 63, 92 **Addr.:** 3742 L, Lincoln, NE 68510.

Womack, Sharon G. (Je. 13, 1940, Flora, IL) Dir., AZ State Dept. of Lib., Arch. and Pub. Recs., 1979–, Deputy Dir., 1977–79; Dir., Maricopa Cnty. Lib., 1976–77; Dir., Miami Meml. Gila Cnty. Lib., 1972–76. **Educ.:** Univ. of AZ, 1967–72, BS (Bus. Admin.), 1976, MLS. **Orgs.:** AZ LA: Pres. (1977–78). SWLA: Exec. Bd. (1977–78). ALA: Adv. Com., for Lib. Outrch. Srvs. (1976–). AZ State Adv. Cncl. on Lib.: Ex–Officio Mem. (1979–80). AZ Hist. Recs. Adv. Bd.: State Coord. (1979–80). AZ Hist. Adv. Comsn.: Secy. (1979–80). Amer. Bus. Women's Assn. **Activities:** 9, 13; 17, 25, 38; 50, 59, 78 **Addr.:** Arizona State Department of Library, Archives & Public Records, Third Floor, State Capitol, 1700 W. Washington, Phoenix, AZ 85007.

Womeldorf, Ann Clark (Ag. 8, 1945, Portsmouth, VA) Asst. Libn., U.S. Sen. Lib., 1975–; Catlgr., Georgetown Univ. Lib., 1973–75, Asst. Head, Acq. Dept., 1971–73, Ref. Libn., 1968–70. **Educ.:** Coll. of William and Mary, 1963–67, BA (Eng.); Univ. of NC, 1967–68, MSLS. **Orgs.:** ALA. SLA. DC LA. **Activities:** 4, 12; 17, 29, 39; 56, 62, 78 **Addr.:** U.S. Senate Library, S–332, The Capitol, Washington, DC 20510.

Wong, Anita Y. (Ap. 26, 1942, Hong Kong). Dir., Hlth. Sci. Lib., St. Michael's Hosp., 1972–; Libn. II, Sci. and Med. Dept., Univ. of Toronto Lib., 1970–72, Libn. II, Circ. Dept., Hum. and Soc. Scis., 1968–70, Libn. I, 1966–67. **Educ.:** St. Dunstan's Univ., 1962–65, BSc (Bio.); Univ. of Toronto, 1965–66, BLS. **Orgs.:** CH LA. Med. LA. Toronto Med. Libs. Grp. **Activities:** 12; 15, 35, 39; 80 **Addr.:** Health Science Library, St. Michael's Hospital, 30 Bond St., Toronto, ON M5B 1W8, Canada.

Wong, Clark Chiu-Yuen (O. 9, 1937, Canton, Kwong Tung, China) Asst. Dir., Admin. Srvs., Univ. Libs., CA State Univ., Northridge, 1980–; Dir. of Lrng. Mtrls. Ctr., Cmnty. Coll. of Denver, N. Campus, 1973–80; Asst. Dir., 1969–73, Instr., Lib. Tech. Prog., 1969–71; Libn., Reno HS, 1965–69; Eng. Tchr., Oriental Coll., Hong Kong, 1960–61; Eng. Tchr., Hong Kong Buddhist Elem. Sch., 1960. **Educ.:** Natl. Chengchi Univ., 1956–60, BA (Eng. Lit.); Univ. of NV, 1962–64, MA (Couns., Psy.); Univ. of MI, 1964–65, AMLS; Univ. of CO, 1973–75, PhD (Lib. Media Admin.). **Orgs.:** ALA. AECT. CA LA. Natl. Educ. Assn. **Activities:** 1, 10; 17, 24, 32; 63 **Addr.:** California State University, Northridge, Oviatt Library, 18111 Nordhoff St., Northridge, CA 91330.

Wong, William Sheh (China) Asst. Dir. of Tech. Srvs., Dept. for Asian Lib. Univ. of IL 1981–, Prof. of Lib. Admin., 1978–; Head, E. Asian Lib., Univ. of MN, 1971–78; Chief Biblgrphr., Loyola Univ., Chicago, 1970–71; Cur., E. Asian Col., Northwest. Univ., 1967–70; Asst. E. Asian Libn., Univ. of KS, 1964–67. **Educ.:** Taiwan Normal Univ., 1950–54, BA (Chin.); Meiji Univ., 1958–60, MA (Pol. Sci.); George Peabody Coll., 1962–63, MA (LS); Northwest. Univ., 1968–71, PhD (Soc. Sci.). **Orgs.:** ALA. Assn. for Asian Std.: Com. on E. Asian Libs., Exec. Com. (1979–82). **Honors:** Cncl. on Lib. Resrcs., Fellow, 1977–78. **Pubns.:** "Alfred Kaiming Chiu and Chinese American Librarianship," *Coll. & Resrch. Libs.* (1978); "Chinese Literature and Bibliography," *Encyc. of Lib. and Info. Sci.* (1977); "The Development of Archives and Libraries in China," *Libri* (1976); "Opening Up the People's Republic: Library Cooperation With China," *Wilson Lib. Bltn.* (1981). **Activities:** 1; 45; 54, 92 **Addr.:** Asian Library, 329 Library, University of Illinois, Urbana, IL 61801.

Wong-Cross, Philip W. (Je. 8, 1942, Saco, ME) Asst. Head, Ref. Sect. and Consult. to Netwk. Libs. of the Midlands Conf., Natl. Lib. Srvs. for the Blind and Phys. Handcpd., Lib. of Congs., 1980–; Chief, Telephone Ref. Srv., DC Pub. Lib., 1978–80; Ref. Libn., 1975–78, Coord., Lorton Proj., 1973–75; Gen. Ref. Libn., Sam Houston State Univ., 1972–73; Spec. Educ. Classrm. Tchr., Elem., OK City Pub. Schs., 1969–70; Classrm. Tchr., 5th-Grade, TX State Sch. for the Blind, 1968–69. **Educ.:** Barrington Coll., 1961–66, BA (Hist., Lit., Relig.); Univ. of TX, 1970–72, MLS. **Orgs.:** ALA: LAMA; ASCLA; PLA; RASD. ASIS. SLA: Soc. Sci. Sect. DC LA: Ref. Interest Grp. Amer. Correct. Assn.: Com. on Inst. Libs. (1975). **Activities:** 4, 9; 17, 39; 63, 74, 75 **Addr.:** 1616 18th St., N.W., Apt. 511, Washington, DC 20009.

Wonsmos, Dorothy Arlene (O. 7, 1925, Thornton, IA) ILL Libn., Gen. Lib., Univ. of NM, 1978–, Actg. Head, Spec. Cols. Dept., 1976–77, Asst. Spec. Cols. Libn., 1974–76, Ref., ILL, Bibl., Acq. Depts., 1961–74, Acq. and Ref. Depts., 1957–59. **Educ.:** Waldorf Coll., 1943–45, AA (Gen.); St. Olaf Coll., 1945–47, BA (Eng.); George Peabody Coll., 1955–56, MA (LS). **Orgs.:** NM LA. Grt. Albuquerque LA. St. Paul Luth. Church Sr. Choir. St. Paul Luth. Church Women. **Activities:** 1; 22, 34, 49-ILL; 61 **Addr.:** General Library, University of New Mexico, Albuquerque, NM 87131.

Wood, Alberta Gjertine Auringer (F. 19, 1942, Detroit, MI) Head, Info. Srvs. Div., Meml. Univ. of NF, 1980–, Info. Srvs. Libn., 1979–80; Sci. Coll. Libn., 1978–79; Cartograph. Libn., World Bank, 1976–77; Map Catlgr., Univ. of WI, 1975–76; Map Spec., Detroit Pub. Lib., 1974–75, Ref. Libn., 1974; Actg. Map Ref. Libn., Univ. of MI, 1973, Asst. Map Ref. Libn., 1968–73; Ref. Libn., Geo. and Maps, Lib. of Congs., 1965–68. **Educ.:** Univ. of MI, 1960–64, BA (Geo.), 1964–65, AMLS, 1970–73, MA (Geo.). **Orgs.:** SLA: Geo. and Map. Div., Ch. (1974–75), Ch. Elect and Prog. Ch. (1973–74), Bltn. Assoc. Ed. (1970–76), Stans. Com. (1972–73; 1975–76), Hons. Com. (1975–77); Jt. Cabinets Std. Com. on Lcl. and Subj. Oriented Grps. (1975). West. Assn. Map Libs. Assn. of Can. Map Libs. NF LA: Lib. Week Com. (1978). Intl. Socty. for the Hist. of Cartography. Assn. of Amer. Geographers. Can. Cartograph. Assn. Amer. Congs. on Surveying and Mapping: Dir. (1979–84); Cartography Div. Ch. (1979–80); Vice–Ch. (1978–79), Dir., (1976–78), Cartograph. Info. Srv. Com. (1974–78), Hons. Com. (1976–78). Various other orgs. **Pubns.:** "Joseph Gaspard Chaussegros de Léry: Cartographer of Early Detroit" *Detroit in Perspective; A Jnl. of Reg. Hist.* (Fall 1978); Library Map Collection," *Bltn., Geo. and Map Div., SLA* (Je. 1976); jt. auth., "Maps and Map Collections," *Nonprint Media in Academic Libraries* (1975); "Acquisition Philosophy and Cataloging Priorities for University Map Libraries," *Spec. Libs.* (N. 1972); "The New Map Room of the University of Michigan Library," *Bltn. Geo. and Map Div., SLA* (S. 1971); various articles, reviews, lists (1970–76). **Activities:** 1, 9; 15, 31, 39; 70 **Addr.:** University Library, Memorial University of Newfoundland, St. John's NF A1B 3Y1, Canada.

Wood, Ann L. (Je. 5, 1939, Cambridge, MA) Soc. Sci./ICPSR Biblgrphr., SUNY, Albany, 1979–; S. Asian Biblgrphr., Columbia Univ., 1968–79. **Educ.:** Beloit Coll., 1958–62, BA (Anthro.); Univ. of WI, 1962–67, MA (Anthro.), MA (S. Asian Std.); Columbia Univ., 1970–72, MS (LS). **Orgs.:** ALA: ACRL/Asian and African Sect., Nom. Com. (1975–76, 1980–81). S. Asia Micro. Proj.: Exec. Com. (Ch., 1978). Amer. Anthro. Assn. Assn. for Asian Std. **Honors:** Beta Phi Mu. **Activities:** 1; 15; 54, 92 **Addr.:** University Library, State University of New York, 1400 Washington Ave., Albany, NY 12222.

Wood, Beulah C. (Mr. 7, 1918, Fincastle, VA) Assoc. Libn., Un. Carbide Corp., 1969–, Libn., Tech. Srv. Lab., 1958–68, Supvsr., Mktg. Info. Ctr., 1955–57, various other positions, 1942–54. **Educ.:** Roanoke Coll., 1936–40, BS (Chem.); Columbia Univ., 1964, MS (LS). **Orgs.:** SLA: Chem. Div. (Ch., 1969–70); NY Chap., Tech. Scis. Grp. (Ch., 1971–72). ASIS. Amer. Chem. Socty.: Div. of Chem. Info. **Activities:** 12; 33, 44; 60, 61, 91

PROFESSIONAL ACTIVITIES: Institutions: 1. Acad. lib.; 2. Arch.; 3. Assn.; 4. Fed./Gvt. lib.; 5. Inst. lib.; 6. Mfr./Suppl.; 7. Milit. lib.; 8. Musm.; 9. Pub. lib.; 10. Sch. lib.; 11. Sch. of lib. sci.; 12. Spec. lib.; 13. State lib.; 14. (other). **Functions/Activities:** 15. Acq./Col. dev.; 16. Adult srvs.; 17. Admin.; 18. Apprais.; 19. Archit./Bldgs.; 20. Cat./Class.; 21. Chld. srvs.; 22. Circ.; 23. Cons./Pres.; 24. Consult.; 25. Cont. ed.; 26. Educ. lib. sci.; 27. Ext. srvs.; 28. Fund/Grants; 29. Gvt. pubs.; 30. Indx./Abs.; 31. Instr. lib. use; 32. Media srvs.; 33. Micro.; 34. Netwks./Coop.; 35. Persnl.; 36. PR; 37. Publshg.; 38. Recs. mgt.; 39. Ref. srvs.; 40. Repro.; 41. Resrch.; 42. Review.; 43. Secur.; 44. Serials; 45. Spec. col.; 46. Tech. srvs.; 47. Trustees/Bds.; 48. YA srvs.; 49. (other).

Addr.: Union Carbide Corporation, Tarrytown Technical Center, Tarrytown, NY 10591.

Wood, David A. (Ap. 24, 1935, Concord, NH) Head, Hum. and Soc. Sci. Dept., Head, Msc. Lib., 1981–; Univ. of WA, 1967–81; Biblgrphr., Msc. Lib., Harvard Univ., 1964–67, Circ. Head, Msc. Lib., 1960–64. **Educ.:** Univ. of NH, 1953–57, BA (Msc.); Harvard Univ., 1957–59, MA (Msc.); Simmons Coll., 1961–64, MS (LS). **Orgs.:** Msc. LA: Mem. Com. (1968–70); Fndn. Ch., Pac. NW Chap. (1969–71); Lcl. Arrange. Ch., Natl. Conv. (1976). Intl. Assn. of Msc. Libs **Honors:** Woodrow Wilson Flwshp., 1957; Phi Beta Kappa. **Pubns.:** *Music in Harvard Libraries, a Catalogue...* (1980). **Activities:** 1; 15, 17, 39; 55 **Addr.:** Music Library DN-10, University of Washington, Seattle, WA 98195.

Wood, Don E. (Mr. 9, 1942, Mt. Vernon, IL) Serials Libn., South. IL Univ., 1970–; Head, Serials Div., OH State Univ., 1968–70, Math. Libn., 1966–68, Intern, 1965–66. **Educ.:** Univ. of IL, 1960–64, BS (Math.), 1964–65, MS (LS). **Orgs.:** ALA. IL LA. **Honors:** Beta Phi Mu, 1966. **Pubns.:** Jt. auth., "The Human Element," *Amer. Libs.* (Mr. 1970). **Activities:** 1; 17, 20, 44; 56 **Addr.:** P.O. Box 378, De Soto, IL 62924.

Wood, Ellen D. (Je. 5, 1951, Evansville, IN) Libn., *Contra Costa Times,* 1978–; Asst. Libn., *Oakland Tribune,* 1977; Asst. Libn., *AZ Daily Star,* 1973–76. **Educ.:** Univ. of AZ, 1969–74, BA (Jnlsm.); 1974–76, MLS. **Orgs.:** SLA: Newsp. Div., Bltn. Com. (Ch., 1978–80), Ad Hoc Salary Srvy. Com. (1979–80), PR and Prof. Dev. Com. (1977–79), Cont. Educ. Com. (Ch., 1981–82); Mgt. Div., Bltn. Co-ed. (1977–78); Bay Reg., Hosplty. Com. (1978–79), Secy. (1980–82). ASIS. Royal Scottish Country Dance Socty. **Honors:** Beta Phi Mu, 1976. **Pubns.:** "Librarians May Feel Impact of Libel Decision," *Ed. and Publshr.* (Jl. 21, 1979); "New Copyright Act Changes Rights/Protection for Photos," *Ed. and Publshr.* (Jl. 15, 1978). **Activities:** 12; 15, 17, 39; 83 **Addr.:** Contra Costa Times Library, P.O. Box 5088, Walnut Creek, CA 94596.

Wood, Irene (D. 6, 1943, Berkeley, CA) Ed., Nonprint Reviews, *Booklist,* ALA, 1973–, Reviewer, Nonprint Reviews, 1970–73; Asst. Film Libn., NY Pub. Lib., 1969, Adult Srvs. Libn., 1967–69. **Educ.:** C.W. Post Coll., 1961–65, BA (Eng.); Univ. of WA, 1966–67, MLS. **Orgs.:** ALA: LITA; YASD. **Honors:** Flaherty Film Sem., Lib. Flwshp., 1979–; Amer. Film Fest., Jury Ch., 1972–80; Chicago Intl. Film Fest., Jury Ch., 1976. **Pubns.:** "Filmstrips, Films," *ALA Yrbk.* (1976–80); "Audiovisual Services," *ALA World Encyc.* (1980). **Activities:** 17, 26, 32; 67 **Addr.:** American Library Association, 50 E. Huron, Chicago, IL 60611.

Wood, John Brent (D. 21, 1931, Montgomery Cnty., TX) Head, Continuations Sect. and Continuations Biblgrphr., CA State Univ., Los Angeles, 1971–, Head, Pers. Acq. Sect., 1968–71, Prin. Pers. Libn., 1964–68, Supvsg. Per. Libn., 1962–64; Head, Circ. Dept., San Diego State Univ., 1959–62, Ref. and Pers. Libn., 1956–59. **Educ.:** Univ. of TX, 1950–55, BA (Liberal Arts); Univ. of Denver, 1955–56, MA (LS). **Orgs.:** CA LA. ALA. South. CA Tech. Prcs. Grp. Untd. Profs. of CA. **Pubns.:** Contrib., *Magazines for Libraries* (1972; 1978); jt. auth., "Periodicals Deacquisitions in Academic Libraries: Proceedings of a Seminar," *Serials Libn.* (Spr. 1979); various per. reviews, *Lib. Jnl.* **Activities:** 1; 15, 44, 46; 66, 74 **Addr.:** 297 S. Madison Ave. #5, Pasadena, CA 91101.

Wood, Karen G. (O. 3, 1947, Pasadena, CA) Dir., Law Lib., Glendale Univ. Coll. of Law, 1980–; Pvt. Lib. Consult. for Law and Bus. Libs., 1976–81; Firm Law Libn., Frandzel and Share, 1979–80; Firm Law Libn., Foonberg and Frandzel, 1978–79; Ref. Libn., Whittier Coll. Sch. of Law, 1977–78; Head, Resrch. Lib., CBS TV City, 1976–79; Libn., U.S. Army Libs., Germany, 1974–76; Tech. Srvs. Libn., City of Scottsdale, AZ, 1969–70; Bkmobile. Libn., City of Tempe, AZ, 1969. **Educ.:** AZ State Univ., 1966–69, BA (Anthro., LS); Univ. of South. CA, 1976–77, MSLS; Whittier Coll., 1977–80, JD; 1980, admitted to prac. of law in CA and fed. cts. **Orgs.:** AALL. South. CA Assn. of Law Libs. **Activities:** 1, 12; 15, 17, 20; 61, 63, 77 **Addr.:** 825 1/2 N. Edinburgh Ave., Los Angeles, CA 90046.

Wood, Linda K. (O. 27, 1945, Kenton, OH) Head, Gen. Ref. Div., Pub. Lib. of Columbus and Franklin Cnty., 1979–, Asst. Head, 1977–79, Libn. I, 1969–76. **Educ.:** OH State Univ., 1963–67, BA (Hist.); Univ. of Pittsburgh, 1967–68, MLS. **Orgs.:** ALA. OH LA. **Honors:** Beta Phi Mu. **Activities:** 9; 17, 29, 39 **Addr.:** 485 Chase Rd., Columbus, OH 43214.

Wood, Linda May (N. 6, 1942, Fort Dodge, IA) Lib. Dir., Riverside City and Cnty. Pub. Lib., 1980–; Asst. City Libn., Los Angeles Pub. Lib., 1977–80; Asst. Libn., Multnomah Cnty. Lib., 1973–77, Admin. Asst. to the Libn., 1972–73, Branch Libn., Gregory Hts. Branch, 1969–72, Branch Libn., Albina Branch Lib., 1967–68, Ref. Libn., Lit. and Hist. Dept., 1965–67. **Educ.:** Portland State Univ., 1960–64, BA (Eng.); Univ. of WA, 1964–65, MLibn. **Orgs.:** CA LA: Gvt. Rel. Com. (Ch., 1981). CA Lib. Athrty. for Systs. and Srvs.: Bd. of Dirs. (1978–80). ALA: LAMA/LOMA Circ. Srvs. Sect. Ch. (1977–78); Vice Ch. (1976–77), Bd. of Dirs. (1976–78); PLA, Metro. Area Lib. Srv. Com. (1975–77). Various other orgs. Inland Area Urban Leag. Leag. of Women Voters. **Pubns.:** "Defending Right to Read in Oregon," *Nsltr. on Int. Frdm.* (Mr. 1975). **Activities:** 9; 17, 27, 47; 78 **Addr.:** Riverside City & County Public Library, P.O. Box 468, Riverside, CA 92502.

Wood, M. Sandra (Ap. 29, 1947, Mechanicsburg, PA) Head, Ref., George T. Harrell Lib., Milton S. Hershey Med. Ctr., PA State Univ., 1972–, Ref. Libn., 1970–72. **Educ.:** Univ. of Pittsburgh, 1965–69, BA (Anthro.); IN Univ., 1969–70, MLS. **Orgs.:** Med. LA. Ctrl. PA Hlth. Scis. LA: Ch. (1974–76). SLA: Ctrl. PA Chap. Vice–Pres./Pres.–Elect. (1979–80), Pres. (1980–81). **Honors:** Beta Phi Mu. **Pubns.:** Jt. auth., "Development of SDI Services from a Manual Current Awareness Service to SDILINE," *Bltn. Med. LA* (O. 1974); ed., *Union List of Serials in Central Pennsylvania Hospital Libraries* (D. 1976); jt. auth., "Departmental Libraries - Why do They Exist?" *Bltn. Med. LA* (O. 1977); jt. auth., "Effect of Fees on an Information Service for Physicians," *Bltn. Med. LA* (Ja. 1978). **Activities:** 1, 12; 39; 80 **Addr.:** George T. Harrell Library, Milton S. Hershey Medical Center, Pennsylvania State University, Hershey, PA 17033.

Wood, Marjorie J. (N. 20, 1948, Spokane, WA) Media Spec. (Lib.), Pine Hill Mid. Sch., 1978–; Libn., St. Paul's Sch., 1978; Ref. and Chld. Libn., Yakima Valley Reg. Lib., 1977–78; Ref. Libn., King Cnty. Lib., 1976. **Educ.:** Univ. of Puget Snd., 1967–70, BA (Educ.); Univ. of WA, 1975–76, MLS. **Orgs.:** Sch. LA of West. NY: Secy. (1979–80). ALA: AASL. Prime Time Sch. TV. **Activities:** 9, 10; 21, 32, 39; 50, 63 **Addr.:** Pine Hill Middle School, Cheektowaga, NY 14215.

Wood, Sr. Mary John (Mr. 5, 1924, Appleton, WI) Head Libn., Silver Lake Coll., 1974–; Libn., Xavier HS, 1970–74; Prin. and Sch. Libn., St. Mary's, Algoma, WI, 1964–70; Elem. Sch. Tchr., WI Schs., 1944–64. **Educ.:** Holy Fam. Coll., 1942–58, BA (Educ.); Cath. Univ. of Amer., 1962–70, MSLS. **Orgs.:** ALA. Cath. LA. WI LA. WI Cath. LA: Treas. (1977–). **Activities:** 1; 15, 17, 24, 34; 55, 63, 90 **Addr.:** 2406 S. Alverno Rd., Silver Lake College Library, Manitowoc, WI 54220.

Wood, Norma W(ode) (My. 26, 1927, Borger, TX) Head, Tech. Srvs., E. Chicago Pub. Lib., 1969–; Head, Tech. Prcs., MS Lib. Comsn., 1955–57; Base Libn., Vance Air Frc. Base, 1953–54; Catlgr., LA of Portland, OR, 1952–53, Branch Libn., Lents Branch, 1951–52; Night Supvsr., Loan Desk, Univ. of OK Lib., 1950–51; Asst. Libn., Doane Coll., 1948–50; Visit. Tchr., Catlgr., various univs., 1968–. **Educ.:** Univ. of OK, 1944–48, BA (LS), 1950–51, BA (Grmn.). **Orgs.:** ALA. IN LA. Chicago Lib. Club. **Addr.:** 5504 Wegg Ave., East Chicago, IN 46312.

Wood, Patricia A. (My. 22, 1948, Ann Arbor, MI) Libn., Evans, Kitchel and Jenckes, P.C., 1979–; Head, Ref. Dept., Morrisson–Reeves Lib., 1975–79; Asst. Libn., Circ. Dept., 1972–75; Asst. Libn., Biog., Hist., Travel Div., Columbus Pub. Lib., 1971–72. **Educ.:** Univ. of MI, 1966–69, BA (Eng.), 1970–71, MA (LS). **Orgs.:** ALA. IN LA: Ref. Div., Exec. Com. (1977–78). AALL. **Activities:** 9, 12; 16, 29, 39; 59, 77 **Addr.:** Evans, Kitchel & Jenckes, P.C., 363 N. 1st Ave., Phoenix, AZ 85003.

Wood, R(ulon) Kent (Je. 15, 1934, Cedar City, UT) Prof. and Dir., Viddisc Innovation Projs., UT State Univ., 1981–, Asst. Dept. Head, 1970–77; Resrch. Asst. to the Dir., West. MI Univ., 1968–69; Dir. of Acads., UT State Univ., 1966–67, Dir., Div. of LS, 1963–65. **Educ.:** Univ. of UT, 1954–57, BS (Pol. Sci.); Univ. of Denver, 1959–61, MA (LS); West. MI Univ., 1967–69, EdS (LS); Brigham Young Univ., 1972–77, EdD (Higher Educ. Admin.). **Orgs.:** UT LA: PR Ch. and Lib. Week (1962–65). MT Plains LA: Schol. Com. (Ch., 1963–66). AECT: Definitions Com. (Ch., 1978–81). AALS. Various other orgs. Natl. Cnsrtm. of Univs. for Instr. Dev.: Inst. Dir. (1971–76). UT Congs. of Parents and Tchrs.: State Dir. (1966–67). UT Educ. Media Assn. UT Acad. of Scis., Arts and Letters. Various other orgs. **Honors:** Beta Phi Mu, 1968. **Pubns.:** *Community Resources* (1981); chap., *Learning Via Telecommunications* (1978); chap., *Educational Technology: A Glossary of Terms* (1979); "The Utah State University Videodisc Innovations Project," *Amer. Libs.* (Ap. 1981); "So You Want to Buy A Computer," *Instr.* (Mr. 1980); various articles, vids. **Activities:** 1, 10; 17, 26; 93 **Addr.:** Department of Instructional Technology, Videodisc Innovation Projects, UMC #30, Logan, UT 84322.

Wood, Raymund F. (N. 9, 1911, London, Eng.) Retired, 19–; Assoc. Dean and Prof. of LS, Grad. Sch. of Lib. and Info. Sci., Univ. of CA, Los Angeles, 1966–67; Ref. Libn., Fresno State Coll., 1950–66. **Educ.:** St. Mary's Univ., 1927–31, AB (Classics); Gonzaga Univ., 1936–39, MA (Phil.); Univ. of CA, Los Angeles, 1946–49, PhD (Hist.); Univ. of South. CA, 1949–50, MS (LS). **Orgs.:** ALA: *Ref. and Subscrpn. Bks. Rev.* Com. (1969–). CA LA: Various coms. Oral Hist. Assn. The Westerners, Los Angeles Corral. Hist. Socty. of South. CA. Fresno Cnty. Hist. Socty. San Fernando Valley Hist. Socty. Various other orgs. **Honors:** Alliance Française de Fresno, Awd. of Merit, 1966; Westerners Intl., "Best Hist. Wrtg.," 1978, 1979. **Pubns.:** *Ina Coolbrith: Librarian and Laureate* (1973); *California's Agua Fria: Early History of Mariposa County* (1954); *Life and Death of Peter Lebec* (1954); ed., *History of Mission San Jose, 1797–1835* (1958); *Mariana la Loca, Prophetess of the Cantua* (1970); various articles in LS and hist., various reviews (1951–). **Activities:** 1, 11; 26, 31, 39; 57, 85, 92 **Addr.:** 18052 Rosita St., Encino, CA 91316.

Wood, Robert D(illon) (My. 29, 1919, Chicago, IL) Dir., E. Chicago Pub. Lib., 1969–, Asst. Dir. and Branch Libn., 1957–69; Fld. Rep., MS Lib. Comsn., 1955–57; City Libn., Enid, Pub. Lib., 1953–55; Request Asst., Branches Dept., LA of Portland, OR, 1952–53, Bkmobile. Libn., 1951–52. **Educ.:** Doane Coll., 1946–50, BA (Psy.); Univ. of OK, 1950–51, BA (LS). **Orgs.:** IN LA: Int. Frdm. Com. (1969–71), Audit. Com. (1974–75); Legis. Com. (1980–81). ALA: Elecs. Com.; IFRT, Nom. Com. (1976–77). Untd. Church of Christ NW Assn. IN-KY Conf.: Church and Mnstry. Com. (1977–). First Congregational Untd. Church of Christ. Rotarian, East Chicago. East Chicago Salvation Army Adv. Bd. Various other orgs. **Pubns.:** "The Truth Shall Make You Free–or Will It?" *Focus on IN Libs.* (Spr. 1972); "Idea Is a Four–Letter Word," *Focus on IN Libs.* (Je. 1968). **Activities:** 9; 16, 17 **Addr.:** 5504 Wegg Ave., East Chicago, IN 46312.

Wood, Thor E. (N. 3, 1932, Washington, DC) Chief, Performing Arts Resrch. Ctr., NY Pub. Lib., 1965–; Msc. Libn., Univ. of IL, 1960–65; Sum. Sub., Msc. Div., NY Pub. Lib., 1958–60. **Educ.:** Pomona Coll., 1950–54, BA (Msc.); Univ. of CA, Berkeley, 1956–57, MLS; Princeton Univ., 1957–60, MFA (Msclgy.). **Orgs.:** Intl. Assn. of Msc. Libs.: Pres. (1972–73); U.S. Branch (Ch., 1968–75); Pub. Libs. Com. (VP, 1968–81). Msc. LA: Bd. of Dirs. (1962–64); Place. Secy. (1960–67). Amer. Msc. Ctr.: Bd. of Dirs. (1968–79); Lib. Com. Thea. LA. Various other orgs. Amer. Frnds. of the Aldeburgh Fest.: Bd. of Dirs. (1973–); Treas. (1977–). Princeton Univ., Adv. Couns. Dept. of Msc. (1980–). Harvard Univ.: Visit. Com., Dept. of Msc. (1974–80). Amer. Musicological Socty. Amer. Soc. for Thea. Resrch. Assoc. for Rec. Snd. Col. **Pubns.:** "History of the Public Libraries Commission," *Fontes artis musicae* (1980); "Performing Arts Resources–Lincoln Center–New York–USA," *Arts Information in Australia Seminar* (1979); "American Music Libraries," "Music Librarianship in U.S.," "The International Association of Music Libraries," *Encyc. of Lib. and Info. Sci.;* ed., two issues, *Fontes artis musicae* (1969, 1971). **Activities:** 1, 9; 15, 17, 28; 55 **Addr.:** Performing Arts Research Center, 111 Amsterdam Ave., New York, NY 10023.

Wood, Vivian F. (Ja. 28, 1945, Plainfield, NJ) Ref. Libn.–Asst. Prof., Livingston Coll., Rutgers Univ., 1974–; Reader's Adv. Libn., Oxon Hill Pub. Lib., 1971–73; Elem. Sch. Tchr., DC, 1969–71. **Educ.:** Howard Univ., 1963–67, BA (Soclgy.); Cath. Univ. of Amer., 1967–69, MA (Educ.); Rutgers Univ., 1973–74, MLS. **Orgs.:** ALA: Black Caucus; ACRL. NJ Women Lib. Workers: Ofcr. (1976–78). NJ LA: Coll. and Univ. Sect. (VP, 1979–80), User Educ. Com. (Ch., 1979–80). Livingston Coll., Rutgers Univ. Black Fac. and Staff Assn. AAUP Oper. PUSH: New Brunswick Chap. **Pubns.:** "The Image Problem of Librarians," *Women Lib. Workers* (D. 1977); "Library Workers Demand Rights," *New Directions for Women* (Win. 1977–78). **Activities:** 1; 15, 31, 39; 63, 66, 92 **Addr.:** 43 Manor Crescent Ave., New Brunswick, NJ 08901.

Wood, William Bliss (Mr. 19, 1914, Arlington, MA) Retired and Asst. Prof. Emeritus, San Jose State Univ., 1978–; Asst. Prof., Div. of LS, San Jose State Univ., 1967–78; Asst. Prof., Sch. of Libnshp., Univ. of BC, 1964–67; Head Libn., LA of Portland, OR, Multnomah Cnty. Lib., 1961–64; Asst. Chief Libn., St. Louis Pub. Lib., 1950–60; Cnty. Libn., Van Buren Cnty., 1949–50; Libn., Gordon Coll. and Dvnty. Sch., 1945–49; Tech. Adv., Power Tube Lib., Raytheon Mfr. Co., 1944–45; Asst., Ref. Dept., NY Pub. Lib., 1942–44; Asst. Cat. Dept., Harvard Coll. Lib., 1941–42. **Educ.:** Brown Univ., 1933–41, AB (Eng.); Columbia Univ., 1942–43, BS (LS); Univ. of Denver, 1960–64, MA (LS). **Orgs.:** ALA: LAMA/Lib. Org. and Mgt. Sect., Insr. for Libs. Com. (Ch., 1954–56); Lib. Educ. Div./Tchrs.'s Sect. Secy.–Treas. (1959–60); Reg. I, Mem. Com. (Ch., 1962–64); Subscrpn. Bks. Com. (1962–64). SLA. Bibl. Socty. of Amer. CA LA. City Club of Portland. Cmwlth. Club of CA. OR Hist. Socty. CA Hist. Socty. **Pubns.:** "Some Thoughts on Trustee Responsibilities," *PNLA Qtly.* (Jl. 1963); "Libraries in a Neighboring State, Oregon," *ID Libn.* (Jl. 1963). **Activities:** 9, 11; 17, 26, 39; 55, 57, 75 **Addr.:** P.O. Box 985, Morro Bay, CA 93442.

Woodall, Nancy C. (D. 9, 1934, Englewood, NJ) Coord., Adult Mtrls. Sel., Fairfax Cnty. Pub. Lib., 1971–; Branch Coord., Anne Arundel Cnty. Pub. Lib., 1968–71; Dir., Irvington-on-Hudson Pub. Lib., 1966–68; Dir., Prince William Cnty. Pub. Lib., 1965–66. **Educ.:** Middlebury Coll., 1952–54 (Eng.); Univ. of MD, 1954–56, AB (Eng.); Cath. Univ. of Amer., 1959–60, MSLS. **Orgs.:** VA LA: Int. Frdm. Com. (Ch., 1972–73). ALA: LAMA/PR Sect. Secy. (1974–76); PR Srvs. to Libs. Com. (1979–83). Pi Beta Phi Sorority. AAUW. **Honors:** Beta Phi Mu, 1960. **Activities:** 9; 15, 36, 39; 74, 75, 93 **Addr.:** 4103 S. 32nd. Rd., Arlington, VA 22206.

Woodard, Paul Esty (O. 24, 1921, Chico, CA) Chief Med. Libn., New Eng. Bapt. Hosp., 1970–, Dir., Insrv. Educ., 1963–69; Nursing Srv. Dept., MA Gen. Hosp., 1955–62; Dir., Student Hlth. Dept., Frnds. Univ., 1950–52. **Educ.:** Frnds. Univ., 1947–52, BA (Educ.); Wichita-St. Joseph Hosp. Sch. of Nursing, 1948–50, RN (Hlth. Care); West. Univ., 1952–55, PhD (Educ.);

MA State Coll., 1972–73, Cert. (LS). **Orgs.:** Med. LA. Boston Biomed. Lib. Cnsrtm. Men Libns. Club. Royal Numismatic Socty. (London): Fellow. Medvl. Acad. of Amer. **Honors:** Amer. Red Cross, Awd. of Recog., 1955, 1963; Amer. Frnds. Srv. Com., Awd. of Recog., 1946. **Pubns.:** "Eliminate the Unfit," *The Psyt. Aid* (D. 1946); "The College Health Program," *The KS Nurse* (Ap. 1952). **Activities:** 12; 15, 17, 39; 58, 80 **Addr.:** New England Baptist Hospital, Medical Staff Library, 91 Parker Hill Ave., Boston, MA 02120.

Woodburn, David M. (Ag. 3, 1946, Bloomington, IN) Dir., MS Lib. Comsn., 1980–, Asst. Dir. for Admin., 1979–80; Dir., Washington Cnty. Lib. Syst., 1977–79; Dir., Yazoo–Sharkey–Issaquena Lib. Syst., 1972–77. **Educ.:** CO State Univ., 1964–68, BA (Hist.); Univ. of Denver, 1970–72, ML (LS); various crs., 1972–80. **Orgs.:** ASCLA: LSCA Coord. Grp. (1980–). MS LA: ILL Code (1980–81); Secy. (1979). MS Natl. Lib. Wk.: Exec. Dir. (1979). MS Pub. LA: Spec. Com. on Pub. Lib. Salary (1977–79). Various orgs., coms. Greenville Symph. St. James Episcopal Church. **Pubns.:** *Personnel Incentive Grants Program Handbook* (1979); "Director's Page," *MS Libs.* (ea. qtly. issue). **Activities:** 9, 13; 17, 24, 34; 72, 78 **Addr.:** P.O. Box 3260, Jackson, MS 39207.

Woodburn, Judy I. (O. 18, 1943, Raleigh, NC) Col. Libn., Duke Univ. Med. Ctr. Lib., 1971–, Serials Libn., 1968–70; Serials Libn., Guilford Coll. Lib., 1965–67. **Educ.:** Duke Univ., 1961–64, BA (Hist.); Univ. of NC, 1964–65, MS (LS). **Orgs.:** NC LA: *NC Libs.* Ed. Bd. (1977–79). SLA: NC Chap., Rcrt. Com. (Ch., 1975), Mem. Com. (1977). Med. LA: *Vital Notes* Ed. Com. (1973–); Mid-Atl. Reg. (Secy., 1978–79); Pubn. Com., 1980 Natl. Mtg. **Pubns.:** *North Carolina Union List of Biomedical Serials* (1969; 1970; 1973; 1978); "The Nation's Attic," *MLA News* (N.–D. 1979). **Activities:** 1, 12; 15, 44, 46; 80, 91 **Addr.:** Medical Center Library, Duke University, Durham, NC 27710.

Woodbury, Ella M. (Ja. 25, 1934, Marianna, FL) Head, Ref. Sect., State Lib. of FL, 1978–, Pub. Lib. Consult., 1976–78, Asst. ILL Libn., 1972–76; Tchr. and Sch. Libn., Pinellas Cnty. Bd. of Pub. Instr., 1956–72. **Educ.:** FL Agr. and Mech. Univ., 1951–56, BS (Elem. Educ.); Univ. of Denver, 1969–72, MA (LS); various cont. educ. crs. **Orgs.:** FL LA: PR Caucus Ch. (1977–78). ALA: Lib. Admin. Div. WHCOLIS, PR Task Frc. (1977–79). **Activities:** 9, 13; 28, 39, 41; 63, 69, 75 **Addr.:** 1410 California St., Tallahassee, FL 32304.

Woodford, Susan E. (Jl. 3, 1941, Muskegon, MI) Fac. Mem., Cont. Educ. Inst., Simmons Grad. Sch. of Lib. and Info. Sci., 1978–79; Info. Spec., MA Inst. of Tech., 1975–, Asst. Sci. Libn., 1973–75; MEDLARS Srch. Spec., Countway Lib. of Med., Harvard Univ., 1969–72; Catlgr., Lib. of Hlth. Scis., Univ. of IL, 1966–69. **Educ.:** Hood Coll., 1959–64, AB (Chem.); West. MI Univ., 1965–66, MSL. **Orgs.:** ASIS. Med. LA. New Eng. OLUG: Treas. (1978–80). **Pubns.:** Jt. auth., "Planning and Implementation Guidelines for an Academic Online Search Service," *Sci. and Tech. Libs.* (Fall 1980); jt. auth., "Patterns of Growth in a University's Fee-for-service Online Search Center," *Information Management in the 1980's: Proceedings of the 40th ASIS Annual Meeting* (1977); jt. auth., "Continuing User Education to Promote the Effective Use of an Established Online Search Service in a University Community," *Information Management in the 1980's* (1977). **Activities:** 1; 39, 49-Online bibl. srch.; 60, 80, 91 **Addr.:** Computerized Literature Search Service, M.I.T. Libraries, Rm. 14SM–48, Cambridge, MA 02139.

Woodruff, Brenda Ann (Jl. 10, 1945, Palestine, TX) Toledo Law Assn., 1981–; Law Libn., Wood Cnty. Law Lib., 1977–81; Catlgr., Cambridge Univ. Lib., 1974–76; Catlgr., Austin Pub. Lib., 1971–74; Clinical Lab. Tech., U.S.D.A., Poisonous Plant Lab., 1967–71. **Educ.:** E. TX State Univ., 1963–66, BS (Bio.), 1966–67, MS (LS). **Orgs.:** OH Reg. Assn. of Law Libs.: Mem. Com. (Ch., 1980). AALL. **Pubns.:** Jt. indxr., *Biology and Genetics of Drosophila* (1977–). **Addr.:** Toledo Law Association, Lucas County Courthouse, Toledo, OH 43624.

Woodrum, Frances L. (N. 3, 1934, Springfield, IL) Head Libn., Jacksonville Pub. Lib., 1970–; Head, Circ. Srvs., Lincoln Lib., 1968–70, Asst. Ref. Libn., 1958–68, Circ. Asst., 1957–58. **Educ.:** Univ. of IL, 1952–56, BA (Eng.), 1956–57, MS (LS). **Orgs.:** ALA. IL LA. Jacksonville Bus. and Prof. Woman's Club. Altrusa Club of Jacksonville. **Activities:** 9; 16, 17 **Addr.:** Jacksonville Public Library, Jacksonville, IL 62650.

Woodrum, Patricia Ann (O. 11, 1941, Hutchinson, KS) Dir., Tulsa City Cnty. Lib. Syst., 1976–, Asst. Dir., 1973–76, Chief of Pub. Srv., 1970–73, Chief of Ext., 1967–70. **Educ.:** KS State Coll., 1963, BA (Lit.); Univ. of OK, 1966, MLS. **Orgs.:** ALA: Com. on Org.; Cncl.; PLA, Bd. of Dirs.; various other coms. OK LA: Stans. Com., Ch.; other past coms., ofcs. SWLA: Past coms. Lib. Srv. and Construct. Act Adv. Cncl. Various other orgs. Tulsa Area Cncl. on Aging. Arts and Hum. Cncl. Metro. Tulsa Cham. of Cmrce. Cmnty. Srv. Cncl. Adv. Cncl. Various other orgs. **Pubns.:** "Motivating Employees," *Jnl. of Educ. Media Sci.* (Win. 1980); "Farming in Tulsa," *Lib. Jnl. Spec. Rpt. #9* (1977); "Regional Centers - Sharing Service," *Lib. Jnl.* (Ja. 15 1977). **Activities:** 9; 17 **Addr.:** 400 Civic Center, Tulsa, OK 74103.

Woods, Frances Babcock (N. 20, 1926, Hartford, CT) Head, Cat. Dept., Yale Law Lib., 1965–, Rev., 1959–64, Sr. Catlgr., 1953–59; Catlgr., Brooklyn Pub. Lib., 1948–53. **Educ.:** Smith Coll., 1944–48, BA (Hist.); Columbia Univ., 1949–51, MS (LS). **Orgs.:** ALA. AALL. NY Tech. Srvs. Libns. Law Libns. of New Eng.: Pres. (1964–65). South. New Eng. Law LA: VP (1980–81). **Activities:** 1; 20, 44; 77 **Addr.:** 572 Whitney Ave., New Haven, CT 06511.

Woods, Janice Thumm (Ag. 28, 1924, Malden, WV) Branch Libn., Half Hollow Hills Cmnty. Lib., 1980–, Interim Dir., 1978–80, Branch Libn., 1973–78, Ref. Asst., 1966–73; Ref. Asst., Huntington Pub. Lib., 1961–72; Ref. Asst., Levittown Pub. Lib., 1959–60; Supvsr., AV Cat. Rev., Montgomery Cnty. Bd. of Educ. Lib., AV Educ., 1959; Asst. in Hum. Div., Univ. of NE Lib., 1948–49; Ref. Libn., Baldwin–Wallace Coll. Lib., 1947–48. **Educ.:** Morris Harvey Coll., 1941–45, AB (Eng.); Univ. of IL, 1946–47, BS (LS). **Orgs.:** ALA. NY LA. Suffolk Cnty. LA. Huntington Hist. Socty. Suffolk Cnty. Archlg. Assn. Walt Whitman Birthplace Assn. NY Pub. Lib. Frnds. Various other orgs. **Activities:** 9; 17, 39 **Addr.:** Half Hollow Hills Community Library, 510 Sweet Hollow Rd., Melville, NY 11747.

Woods, Joyce C. (D. 18, 1939, St. Johns, MI) Dir., Saline Area Pub. Lib., 1978–; Dir., Tecumseh Pub. Lib., 1968–73; Circ., Ann Arbor Pub. Lib., 1966–68. **Educ.:** West. MI Univ., 1958–61, BA (Soc. Work); Univ. of MI, 1966–68, MLSA (LS). **Orgs.:** ALA. MI LA. AAUW: Play Readg. Exper. Aircraft: Prog. Ch. **Activities:** 9; 17 **Addr.:** Saline Area Public Library, 201 S. Ann Arbor, Saline, MI 48176.

Woods, L. B. (S. 23, 1938, Gilmer, TX) Ed., Current Std. in Libnshp., 1977–; Assoc. Prof., Univ. of RI, 1976–; Dir., Tyler Pub. Lib., 1970–74; Libn., Los Angeles City Schs., 1969–70; Sci. Tchr., Los Angeles, Marshall, TX, New London, TX, 1960–68. **Educ.:** Henderson State Tchrs. Coll., 1955–60, BSE (Chem., Bio.); Univ. of TX, 1968–69, MLS, 1975–77, PhD (Curric., Instr.). **Orgs.:** Frdm. to Read Fndn.: Bd. of Trustees (1980–82); Exec. Com. (1980–81). ALA: IFRT (Dir., 1980–82). RI LA: Com. on Governance (1977–78); Int. Frdm. Com. (1978–). New Eng. LA. Various other orgs. Sch. of Educ., Univ. of TX: Com. for Self–eval., Dept. of Curric. and Instr. Grad. Prog. (1976). **Honors:** *Bay State Libn.*, First Prize, Article Wrtg. Competition, 1979. **Pubns.:** "The Sixteen Most Censored Books in the U.S.," *Directory of Learning Resources for Reading* (1979); *A Decade of Censorship in America; The Threat to Classrooms and Libraries, 1966–1975* (1979); "Is Academic Freedom Dead in Public Schools?" *Education 80/81* (1980); "Intellectual Freedom; Guiding Principle of Democracy," *KY Libs.* (Win. 1981); "Censorship in Kansas: Thinking About the Problem," *Lib. Sch. Review* (1980); various articles, edshps., AV (1973–). **Activities:** 9, 11; 17, 37, 41; 74 **Addr.:** Graduate Library School, University of Rhode Island, Rodman Hall, Kingston, RI 02881.

Woods, Lawrence A. (Mr. 27, 1939, Springfield, VT) Head, Resrch. and Dev., Purdue Univ. Libs., 1977–; Chief, Lib. Autom., Dartmouth Coll., 1975–77; Asst. Chief, Lib. Autom., 1972–75. **Educ.:** Valley Forge Christ. Coll., 1956–59, Dip.; Dartmouth Coll., 1964–67; East. Nazarene Coll., 1967–68, BA (Hist.); Simmons Coll., 1970–72, MLS. **Orgs.:** IN LA: Lib. Autom. and Tech. Div., Ch. ALA: LITA/Info. Sci. and Autom. Sect., Tech. Stans. for Lib. Autom. Com. (1979–81). ASIS: SIG Cabinet Rep. (1979–81); Mem. Com. (1980–82); IN Chap. (Ch., 1980–81). **Honors:** Beta Phi Mu, 1972. **Pubns.:** Jt. auth., "An Information System for Practicing Veterinarians," *Med. LA Bltn.* (O. 1978). **Activities:** 1; 17, 41, 46; 56, 75 **Addr.:** Head, Research & Development, Purdue University Libraries, West Lafayette, IN 47907.

Woods, Lawrence J. (D. 6, 1944, Baltimore, MD) Ed., Pub. Affairs Info. Srv., Inc., 1981–; Mktg./Prod. Mgr., *CHOICE Mag.*, 1979–81, Soc. Sci. Ed., 1973–79; Ed. Staff, Soc. Sci. and Hum. Index, 1967–73. **Educ.:** Brown Univ., 1962–67, BA (Econ., Pol. Sci.); Pratt Inst., 1968–71, MLS; Univ. of CT, 1976–79, MBA. **Orgs.:** ALA: ACRL; RASD. SLA. ASIS. **Honors:** Beta Phi Mu, 1971. **Pubns.:** Jt. ed., *Opening Day Collection* (1974). **Activities:** 1, 12; 30, 37, 39; 59, 62, 92 **Addr.:** Public Affairs Information Service, Inc., 11 W. 40th St., New York, NY 10018.

Woods, Linda A. (Ap. 24, 1943, Reading, PA) Ref. Libn., Kutztown State Coll., 1968–; Elem. Sch. Libn., Tyson-Schoener Elem. Sch., 1966–68; Elem. Schs. Libn., Pottsgrove Sch. Dist., 1964–66. **Educ.:** Kutztown State Coll., 1961–64, BS (LS, Educ.); Drexel Univ., 1965–67, MSLS, 1978–79, Cert. of Advnc. Std. (Ref., ILL). **Orgs.:** ALA. PA LA. St. Paul's Evang. Luth. Church: Evangelism Com. (1979–). **Pubns.:** "An Introduction to ERIC: Why, What, and How," vid. cassette (1978); "An Introduction to ERIC: What and How," vid. cassette (1978). **Activities:** 1; 31, 34, 39 **Addr.:** 237 E. Main St., Fleetwood, PA 19522.

Woods, Mary S. (Ag. 9, 1940, Willmar, MN) Mgr., Lib. Srvs., Untd. Srvs. Auto. Assn., 1977–; Part-time Consult., TX State Lib., 1975; Libn., Comal Indp. Sch. Dist., 1971–72. **Educ.:** Univ. of ND, 1958–62, BS, magna cum laude (Eng.); Univ. of TX, 1970–71, MLS, 1972–77, PhD (Instr. Media). **Orgs.:** SLA: TX Chap. (Pres., 1979–80), San Antonio Cont. Educ. Subcom. (Ch., 1978–79). ASIS: TX Chap., Awds. Com. (1979–80). Cncl. of Resrch. and Acad. Libs.: VP (1979–80); Secy. (1978–79). San Antonio OLUG: Pres. (1979–80). **Pubns.:** Jt. auth., *Planning Audiovisual Services in Public Libraries* (1975); "Sex Discrimination: The Question of Valid Grounds," *Protean: Admin., Systs., Mgt. in Lib.* (1971); "Bexar County Jail Library" slide/tape (1974). **Activities:** 12; 17, 39; 56, 59, 76 **Addr.:** USAA Library, USAA Bldg., San Antonio, TX 78288.

Woods, Sr. Regina Clare (S. 7, 1912, Woodside, NY) Coord., Med. Libs., Cath. Med. Ctr. of Brooklyn and Queens, 1969–; Assoc. Prof., LS, St. John's Univ. Grad. Sch.; Med. Libn., Mary Immaculate Hosp., 1966–69; Nursing Libn., Schs. of Nursing, 1962–66; Libn., Sec. Sch., Dio. of Brooklyn, 1950–61. **Educ.:** St. John's Univ., 1949, BA (Eng.), 1954, MLS; Univ. of IL, 1967 (Med. Ref.). **Orgs.:** ALA. Med. LA: NY Reg. Grp., Exec. Com. (1978–). Untd. Hosp. Fund: Adv. Mem. (1975–77). **Honors:** St. John's Univ., Alum. Assn., 4th Anl. Awd., Lib. and Info. Sci., 1980. **Pubns.:** Jt. auth., "Three Pronged Approach for Centralized Services," *Spec. Libs.* (N. 1972). **Activities:** 5, 11; 17, 24, 32; 63, 75, 80 **Addr.:** Catholic Medical Center, Central Medical Library, 88-25 153 St., Jamaica, NY 11432.

Woods, Richard (N. 8, 1948, Burlington, IA) Lib. Systs. Coord., Univ. of Houston Libs., 1979–; Lib. Srvs. Coord., WA Lib. Netwk., 1977–79; Systs. Libn., WA State Lib., 1975–77. **Educ.:** West. WA Univ., 1972–74, BA (LS); Univ. of WA, 1974–75, MLibn. **Orgs.:** ALA: RTSD/Cat. and Class. Sect., Nom. Com. (1979–80). **Pubns.:** Jt. auth., *Library Resource Sharing II, A Comparison of Ballots, UCLC, and WLN* (1979); "Washington Library Network Computer System," *Online Review* (S. 1979); "The Reality and The Dream for WLN Reference Librarians," *Ref. Qtly.* (Fall 1979). **Activities:** 1, 14-Netwk.; 17, 34; 56 **Addr.:** University of Houston Libraries, Houston, TX 77004.

Woods, William E. (Ja. 21, 1928, Chicago, IL) Coord., Lib. Tech. Prog., Richard J. Daley Coll., 1968–; Admin. Libn., Kennedy–King Coll., 1967–68; Libn. of the Mtrl. Ctr., Chicago State Univ., 1965–67, Head, Circ. Dept., 1960–65; Tchr.–Libn., Chicago Pub. Schs., 1951–60. **Educ.:** Chicago Tchrs. Coll., 1947–51, BEd (Math.), 1954–58, MEd (LS); Univ. of Chicago, 1962–65, MA (LS). **Orgs.:** ALA. IL LA. Chicago Lib. Club. CLENE. Cncl. on Lib./Media Tech.: Ctrl. Reg. (Ch., 1969–73). **Pubns.:** *Manual and List of Subject Headings Used on the Woods Cross Reference Cards* (1978); "Barebones Acquisitions," *UNABASHED Libn.* (Fall 1978); "On the Other Hand," *Sch. Lib. Jnl.* (N. 1976); "Card Catalog Companions" slides and casettes (forthcoming); *Woods Cross Reference Card System* (1978); various articles (1951–). **Activities:** 1, 11; 25, 31, 46 **Addr.:** Woods Library Publishing Company, 9159 Clifton Park, Evergreen Park, IL 60642.

Woodson, Nancy J. (Jl. 12, 1944, Selma, AL) Ref. Libn., Div. of Pub. Lib. Srvs., GA Dept. of Educ., 1979–; Branch Libn., Atlanta Pub. Lib., 1975–78, Chld. Libn., various branches, 1972–75. **Educ.:** Tuskegee Inst., 1962–67, BS (Soc. Std., Educ.); Atlanta Univ., 1971–72, MLS (Lib. Srv.); Univ. of GA, Ctr. for Cont. Ed., City of Atlanta Trng. Ctr., 1975, Cert. (Supervisory Dev.). **Orgs.:** ALA. SE LA. Metro Atlanta LA: Treas. (1978–79). GA LA. Amer. Bus. Women's Assn.: Tara Chap., Boss Night (Ch., 1980); Correspondent Secy. (1980–81). Atlanta Lawn Tennis Assn. Coretta Scott King Bk. Awd. Com. (1976–78). **Activities:** 9, 13; 16, 39 **Addr.:** 4415 Kimball Rd., S.W., Atlanta, GA 30331.

Woods–Robinson, Ruby O. (My. 13, 1939, Mt. Clemens, MI) Resrch., Natl. Comsn. on Libs. and Info. Sci., 1981–; Reg. Consult. to W. Africa, U.S. Info. Agency, 1974–76; Chief Libn., Martin Luther King Meml. Lib., DC Pub. Lib., 1973–74; Lib. Consult., CA State Lib., 1971–73; Dir. of Libs., Sacramento City Untd. Schs., 1969–71; Coord., Lib. Srvs., Overseas Dependent Schs., Dept. of Defenses, 1966–67; Sch. and Pub. Srvs. Libn., Detroit Pub. Schs., 1962–66. **Educ.:** Wayne State Univ., 1958–62, BS (Educ.), 1963–66; CA State Univ., Sacramento, 1966–71. **Orgs.:** ALA. Alliance for Info. and Ref. Srvs. DC LA. Urban Leag. NAACP. **Honors:** Alpha Kappa Alpha. **Activities:** 4, 9; 24, 39, 41; 63 **Addr.:** National Commission on Libraries and Information Science, 1717 K St. N.W., Suite 601, Washington, DC 20036.

Woodsworth, Anne (F. 10, 1941, Frederica, Denmark) Dir., York Univ. Libs., 1978–; Persnl. Libn., Toronto Pub. Lib., 1975–78; Resrch. Proj. Ofcr., ON Educ. Comm. Athrty., 1974–75; Head, Ref. Dept., Univ. of Toronto Lib., 1971–74, Admin. Asst. to Chief Libn., 1970–71; Med. Libn., Toronto West. Hosp., 1969–70; Ref. Libn., Univ. of Toronto Lib., 1967–68; various other prof. positions, 1964–67. **Educ.:** Univ. of MB, 1958–62, BFA; Univ. of Toronto, 1963–64, BLS, 1968–69, MLS. **Orgs.:** Can. LA: Cnclr. (1977–80). CARL: Secy. (1979–80). Can. Assn. of Spec. Libs. and Info. Srvs.: Treas. (1974–76); Ch. (1976–77). ALA. Various other orgs. Popltn. Resrch. Fndn. (Toronto): Bd. of Dirs. **Pubns.:** Jt. auth., "Survey of Physician Self-Education Patterns in Toronto. Part 1: Use of Libraries," *Can. Lib. Jnl.* (Ja.–F. 1972); jt. auth., "Survey of Physician Self-Education Patterns in Toronto. Part 2: Use of Journals and Filing Systems," *Can. Lib. Jnl.* (Mr.–Ap. 1972); "One Vacancy: Thirty-two Applicants," *IPLO Qtly.* (Jl. 1971); "The Underground Press in Canada...," *Lib. Jnl.* (Mr. 1, 1971); ed., *MB LA Bltn.* (1967).

PROFESSIONAL ACTIVITIES: Institutions: 1. Acad. lib.; 2. Arch.; 3. Assn.; 4. Fed./Gvt. lib.; 5. Inst. lib.; 6. Mfr./Suppl.; 7. Milit. lib.; 8. Musm.; 9. Pub. lib.; 10. Sch. lib.; 11. Sch. of lib. sci.; 12. Spec. lib.; 13. State lib.; 14. (other). **Functions/Activities:** 15. Acq./Col. dev.; 16. Adult srvs.; 17. Admin.; 18. Apprais.; 19. Archit./Bldgs.; 20. Cat./Class.; 21. Chld. srvs.; 22. Circ.; 23. Cons./Pres.; 24. Consult.; 25. Cont. ed.; 26. Educ. lib. sci.; 27. Ext. srvs.; 28. Fund/Grants; 29. Gvt. pubs.; 30. Indx./Abs.; 31. Instr. lib. use; 32. Media srvs.; 33. Micro.; 34. Netwks./Coop.; 35. Persnl.; 36. PR; 37. Publshg.; 38. Recs. mgt.; 39. Ref. srvs.; 40. Repro.; 41. Resrch.; 42. Review.; 43. Secur.; 44. Serials; 45. Spec. col.; 46. Tech. srvs.; 47. Trustees/Bds.; 48. YA srvs.; 49. (other).

Activities: 1, 14-Consult.; 17, 24 **Addr.:** 310 Scott Library, York University, 4700 Keele St., Downsview, ON M3J 2R2 Canada.

Woodward, Daniel H. (O. 17, 1931, Ft. Worth, TX) Libn., Huntington Lib., 1972–; Libn., Mary Washington Coll., Univ. of VA, 1969–72, Asst. Prof., Assoc. Prof., Prof., Eng., 1957–72. **Educ.:** Univ. of CO, 1948–51, BA (Phil.), 1954–55, MA (Eng.); Yale Univ., 1955–58, PhD (Eng.); Cath. Univ. of Amer., 1968–69, MS (LS). **Orgs.:** Grolier Club. Zamorano Club: Secy. (1977–). Bibl. Socty. of Amer. Renaissance Socty. **Honors:** Phi Beta Kappa; Beta Phi Mu. **Pubns.:** Ed., *Poems and Translations of Robert Fletcher* (1970); various reviews. **Activities:** 1, 12; 15, 17, 45; 55, 57, 91 **Addr.:** Huntington Library, 1151 Oxford Rd., San Marino, CA 91108.

Woodward, Edith S. (Je. 4, 1917, Kiowa, KS) Lib. Admin., OH Legis. Srv. Comsn., 1969–; Head, Docums. Div., State Lib. of OH, 1957–69; Head, Linden Branch, Lib. of Columbus and Franklin Cnty., 1955–57, Asst. Libn., 1947–55. **Educ.:** George Washington Univ., 1942–46, BA (Span–Amer. Lit.); Univ. of MI, 1958, MALS. **Orgs.:** SLA: Ctrl. OH Chap. (Pres., 1973–74); Soc. Welfare Sect. (Ch., 1974–75). Franklin Cnty. LA. **Honors:** Beta Phi Mu, 1969. **Activities:** 4, 12; 17, 39, 41; 77, 78, 92 **Addr.:** 4160 Lyon Dr., Columbus, OH 43220.

Woodward, Frances M. (D. 13, 1938, Golden, BC) Ref. Libn., Spec. Cols., Univ. of BC Lib., 1966–; Archvst., Prov. Arch. of BC, 1961–66. **Educ.:** Univ. of BC, 1960, BA (Eng.); McGill Univ., 1960–61, BLS; Univ. of WA, 1962 (Arch. Mgt.). **Orgs.:** Assn. Can. Map Libns.: Secy. (1969–70); VP/Ed. (1973–74); Pres. (1974–75); Past Pres. (1975/76); Conf. Com. (1969–70, 1972–73, 1977–78). BC LA. Assn. of BC Archvsts. West. Assn. Map Libs.: VP (1977–78); various ofcs., coms (1975–). Various other orgs. Vancouver Hist. Socty. Can. Cartograph. Assn. Intl. Socty. for the Hist. of Cartography. Archlg. Socty. of BC. **Pubns.:** *Theses on British Columbia History and Related Subjects (and supplements)* (1971); "Fire Insurance Plans and British Columbia Urban History," *BC Std.* (Sum. 1979); "The Influence of the Royal Engineers on the Development of British Columbia," *BC Std.* (Win. 1974–75); "Bibliography of British Columbia," *BC Std.* (1968–69–); various bibls. and indxs. in various jnls. **Activities:** 1, 2; 30, 39, 45; 69, 70, 73 **Addr.:** Library, Special Collections, 1956 Main Mall, University of British Columbia, Vancouver, BC V6T 1Y3, Canada.

Woodward, Mary Hardin Morris (Mr. 18, 1925, Louisville, KY) Head Libn., KY Country Day Sch., 1975–, Upper Sch. Libn., 1972–75; Sch. Libn., KY Home Sch. for Girls, 1969–72. **Educ.:** Univ. of Louisville, 1943–67, BA (Eng.); Spalding Coll., 1969–72, MALS. **Orgs.:** ALA: AASL. KY LA. KY Sch. Media Assn. Jefferson Cnty. Sch. Media Assn.: Prog. Ch. (1980–81); Secy. (1981–82). various other orgs. Woman's Club of Louisville. Daughters of the Amer. Revolution: John Marshall Chap. (Chaplain, 1979–81). KY Hist. Socty. Hist. Homes Fndn. various other orgs. **Activities:** 10; 15, 39, 48; 69 **Addr.:** 4415 Signal Hill Rd., Louisville, KY 40207.

Woodward, Mary Margaret (N. 29, 1922, Westernport, MD) Asst. Head/Pub. Srvs., Assoc. Prof., Davis and Elkins Coll. Lib., 1962–; Libn., Tygart Valley HS, 1955–62. **Educ.:** Davis and Elkins Coll., 1940–44, BA (Bus.); WV Univ., 1956–62, MA (LS). **Orgs.:** ALA. SELA. WV LA. AAUW. AAUP. Elkins Randolph Cnty. Pub. Lib.: Trustee (1978–). Ord. of the East. Star: Randolph Chap. #74. Various other orgs. **Activities:** 1; 34, 36, 39; 57, 61, 63 **Addr.:** 167 Guy St., Elkins, WV 26241.

Woodward, Robert C. (My. 26, 1924, Lancaster, NH) Dir., Bangor Pub. Lib., 1962–; Dir., Dedham Pub. Lib., 1956–62; Ref. Libn., Hist. Dept., Boston Pub. Lib., 1953–56; Asst., Ref. Dept., 1951–53. **Educ.:** Bates Coll., 1942–48, AB (Hist.); Boston Univ., 1948–49, AM (Hist.). **Orgs.:** ME Lib. Comsn.: Ch. (1973–81). New Eng. LA: Pres. (1964–65); Reg. Plng. Com. (1956–62); Bibl. Com. (1968–71). OCLC–NELINET: ILL Com. (1980–). ME LA: Treas. (1963–65). Various other orgs., ofcs. ME Cncl. on Hum. and Pub. Policy: Vice-Ch. (1974–75). **Pubns.:** Various reviews, *Lib. Jnl.* (1959–69). **Activities:** 9, 13; 15, 17, 24; 55, 75, 78 **Addr.:** Bangor Public Library, 145 Harlow St., Bangor, ME 04401.

Woodward, Wayne W. (My. 4, 1930, Greensburg, IN) Dir. of Lib. Srv., Wesley Biblical Semy., 1978–; Ref. Libn., Asbury Coll., 1977–78, Head Libn., 1967–77; Admin. Asst. to Libn., Asbury Theo. Semy., 1965–67; Untd. Meth. Mnstr., NC, 1955–63. **Educ.:** Coll. of the Sequoias, 1948–50, AA; Taylor Univ., IN, 1950–52, AB (Rel.); Asbury Theo. Semy., 1952–55, BD; Appalachian State Tchrs. Coll., 1957–60, MA (Educ.); Univ. of KY, 1965–67, MS (LS). **Orgs.:** ATLA. MS LA. Christ. Libns. Flwshp.: Pres. (1973–74). SELA. Various other orgs. **Activities:** 1; 90 **Addr.:** Wesley Biblical Seminary, P.O. Box 9938, Jackson, MS 39206.

Woodworth, Bonnie-Jean (Mr. 30, 1941, Oswego, NY) Corporate Libn., Hartford Insr. Grp., 1968–; Libn., Diebold Grp., 1967–68; Asst. Libn., Gen. Motors, 1965–67; Libn., Bechtel Corp., 1963–65. **Educ.:** SUNY, Geneseo, 1959–63, BS (LS). **Orgs.:** Cap. Reg. Lib. Cncl.: Pres. SLA: CT Valley Chap., Pres. **Activities:** 12; 15, 17, 39; 59, 76 **Addr.:** Hartford Insurance Group, Hartford Plz., Hartford, CT 06115.

Woodworth, Mary L. (Richland Ctr., WI) Prof., Lib. Sch., Univ. of WI, Madison 1976–, Instr., Asst. Prof., Assoc. Prof., 1964–76; Libn., WI HS, 1958–64; Libn., W. HS (Green Bay), 1956–58. **Educ.:** Univ. of WI, 1946–48, BS (Educ.), 1955–56, MS (LS), 1964–68, PhD (LS, Educ.). **Orgs.:** AALS. ALA: AASL, Exec. Bd. (1962–64); YASD (Pres., 1968), Exec Bd. (1964–65; 1967–69), Int. Frdm. Com. (1977–79); Cncl. (1962–65, 1967–68). WI Int. Frdm. Coal. **Pubns.:** Ed., *Young Adult and Intellectual Freedom* (1977); *Intellectual Freedom, the Young Adult and Schools; A Wisconsin Study* (1976); "Intellectual Freedom and The Young Adult," *Libraries and Young Adults* (1979); various other articles. **Activities:** 10; 26, 32, 48; 74, 95-YA Lit. **Addr.:** Library School, University of Wisconsin–Madison, 600 N. Park St., Madison, WI 53706.

Wooldridge, Connie Nordhielm (Je. 16, 1950, Asheville, NC) Freelnc. Ed. Work, Scott, Foresman and Co., 1979–; Libn., Sieden Prairie Elem. Sch., 1977–78; Tchr., Seoul Frgn. Sch., 1973–75. **Educ.:** Mt. Holyoke Coll., 1968–72, BA (Latin); Univ. of Chicago, 1975–77, MA (LS), 1975–77, MS (Tchg.). **Orgs.:** ALA: ALSC, Newbery–Caldecott Com. (1978); Notable Bks. Com. (1980–82). **Pubns.:** "Masquerading as Realism - Child Abuse in Juvenile Novels," *Sch. Lib. Jnl.* (Mr. 1978); various reviews, *Sch. Lib. Jnl., Serials Review, Lib. Qtly.* (1977–). **Activities:** 10; 37, 42; 89, 95-Chld.'s and YA lit. **Addr.:** 921 Argyle Ave., Pontiac, MI 48053.

Woollet, Bonnie L. (D. 14, 1946, Buchanan, MI) Head Media Ctr. Libn., Univ. of AZ Lib., 1979–; Dir., Lrng. Resrcs., John Wesley Coll., 1974–78; Libn., Grt. Lakes Bible Coll., 1969–74. **Educ.:** Andrews Univ., 1967–69, BA (Eng.); Univ. of MI, 1970–73, MALS. **Orgs.:** ALA. MI Lib. Cnsrtm.: Libn. Trustee (1976–78). AZ State LA. Assn. Christ. Libns.: Bk. Review Ed. (1976–81). **Activities:** 1, 12; 17, 32, 39; 63, 92 **Addr.:** 3647 E. 2nd St., Apt. H, Tucson, AZ 85716.

Woolley, Robert D. (D. 11, 1945, Portland, OR) Asst. Prof., Instr., Tech. Dept., Syst. Anal., Curric. Libn., Merrill Lib., UT State Univ.; various consult. positions, 1980–. **Educ.:** UT State Univ., 1970, MEd (Instr. Media, LS), BS (Hist., Bus. Admin.). **Orgs.:** ALA. AECT. Assn. for Comp. Mach. Natl. Assn. of Lrng. Lab. Dirs. **Pubns.:** Jt. auth., *Videodisc Technology: Applications to Library, Information and Instructional Sciences* ERIC (1981); jt. auth., *Coloney Intelligent Learning System* (1981); jt. auth., "So You Want to Buy a Computer?" *Instr.* (Mr. 1980); jt. auth., "Microcomputers and Videodisc: New Dimensions for Computer Based Education," *Interface Age* (D. 1979); jt. producer, "Videodisc in Education" videotape (1980); various articles, videodiscs, mono. **Addr.:** 921 E. 320 N., Logan, UT 84321.

Woolls, Esther Blanche (Mr. 30, 1935, Louisville, KY) Prof., Univ. of Pittsburgh, 1973–; Coord., Sch. Libs., Roswell Indp. Schs., 1967–70; Coord., Sch. Libs., Hammond Pub. Schs., 1965–67; Elem. Libn., Edison Sch. (Hammond), 1958–65. **Educ.:** IN Univ., 1958, AB (Fine Arts), 1962, MA (LS), 1973, PhD (LS). **Orgs.:** ALA. Beta Phi Mu: Pres. (1978–79). AECT: Info. Systs. Div. (Pres., 1978–79). CLENE: Secy. (1978). Various other orgs. Woman's Natl. Bk. Assn. Delta Kappa Gamma. **Pubns.:** Jt. ed., *Critical Issues In Cooperative Library Network Development* (1980); jt. auth., *Multi-Media Indexes, Tools and Review Sources: A Bibliographic Guide* (1975); "District-Level Program Evaluation," *Drexel Lib. Qtly.* (Jl. 1978). **Activities:** 10, 11; 17, 26, 32; 55, 67 **Addr.:** 270 Tennyson Ave., Pittsburgh, PA 15213.

Wooster, Harold (Ja. 3, 1919, Hartford, CT) Spec. Asst. for Prog. Dev., Lister Hill Natl. Ctr. for Biomed. Comm., Natl. Lib. of Med., 1974–; Chief, Resrch. and Dev. Branch, 1970–74; Adj. Instr., Grad. Sch. of LS, Drexel Inst. of Tech., 1967; Exec. Secy. of COSATI Panel on Info. Scis. Tech., 1965–66; Dir., Info Scis., Directorate of Info. Scis., Air Frc. Ofc. of Sci. Resrch., 1962–70, Proj. Sci., 1959–62, Dir., Resrch. Info., 1956–59; Sr. Fellow, Mellon Inst., 1947–56. **Educ.:** Syracuse Univ., 1935–39, AB, magna cum laude (Chem.); Univ. of WI, 1939–41, MS (Chem.), 1941–43, PhD (Chem.). **Orgs.:** ASIS. AAAS: Sect. T, Nom. Com., Ch. **Honors:** Phi Beta Kappa; Sigma Xi. **Pubns.:** "Bibliotaphic Libraries of the Year 2000," *Lib. Resrcs. & Tech. Srvs.* (Ja.–Mr. 1981); "The Users Last," *Bltn. of ASIS* (Ag., 1979); "Information for Poison Centers," *Vetny. and Human Toxicology* (1979); "The LHNCBC Experimental CAI Network, 1971–75," *Info. Tech. in Hlth. Sci. Educ.* (1978); "Confessions of a CAI Ignoramus," *Computers and Communication* (1977); various articles and bks. in LS, info sci., chem. (1949–77). **Activities:** 4; 17, 24, 34; 75, 93 **Addr.:** Lister Hill National Center for Biomedical Communication, National Library of Medicine, 8600 Rockville, Bethesda, MD 20209.

Wootton, Norris (D. 25, 1947, Kingsport, TN) Dir., Chesterfield Cnty. Lib., 1976–; Adult Srvs. Libn., Lake Lanier/Piedmont Reg. Libs., 1975–76. **Educ.:** Univ. of AZ, 1969–72, BA (Drama); George Peabody Coll., 1974–75, MLS. **Orgs.:** SC LA: Pub. Lib. Sect. (Ch., 1979). SELA. ALA. SC Gvr.'s Conf.: Pub. Libs. Plng. Com. (1979). ERA SC. Palmetto Alliance. **Activities:** 9; 17, 36, 39; 55, 59 **Addr.:** Chesterfield County Library, 130 Main St., Chesterfield, SC 29709.

Worden, Diane D. (N. 23, 1937, Milwaukee, WI) Info. Spec. II, The Upjohn Co., 1981–; Libn., Kalamazoo Nature Ctr., 1971–81; Tchr., Delton–Kellogg Schs., 1968–69; Tchr., Arrowhead Jr. HS, 1960–61. **Educ.:** Kalamazoo Coll., 1955–59, BA (Bio.); Univ. of KS, 1959–60, Cert. (Sec. Tchg.); West. MI Univ., 1970–71, MSL. **Orgs.:** SLA: Nat. Resrcs. Div., Exec. Com. (1975–77). Grt. Lakes Env. Info. Sharing: Treas. (1976–81). Frnds. of Charles A. Ransom Pub. Lib.: Exec. Com. (1978–81). Cncl. of Plng. Libns. Leag. of Women Voters. MI Musms. Assn.: Secy. (1973–74); Dir. (1971–73, 1976–78); Prof. Stans. Com. (1974). Plainwell Cmnty. Schs.: Citizens Adv. Com. for Educ. Assess. (1977–78). **Honors:** Beta Phi Mu, 1971; Unitarian Universalist Cncl. of MI, Outstan. Srv., 1968. **Pubns.:** Cmplr., *Role of Earthworms* bibl. (1981); ed., *Special Delivery: A Collection of Papers 1974–1977* (1978); ed., *Curriculum Resources for Environmental Progress* (1975); *Potpourri: A Medley of Recipes...* (1969); "EnviroAlert," *Nature Ctr. News* (D. 1973–); "A Beginning Glossary of Ecology" 110 frames (1973); various reviews, articles. **Activities:** 5, 12; 15, 17, 30; 65, 82 **Addr.:** 235 West E. Ave., Kalamazoo, MI 49007.

Worley, Joan H. (Houston, TX) Ref. Libn., Univ. of TN, 1975–; Sales Rep., Encyc. Britannica, 1970–75. **Educ.:** TX Tech. Univ., BA (Hist.); Univ. of TN, 1974–75, MLS. **Orgs.:** TN LA: *TN Libn.* Ed. (1980–). ALA: ACRL/Educ. and Bhvl. Scis. Sect., Bibl. Instr. for Educs. Com. (Ch., 1979–81)/Bibl. Instr. Sect., Educ. for Bibl. Instr. Com. (1979–81). Leag. of Women Voters. **Pubns.:** Ed., "Local Color: A Conversation With Wilma Dykeman and Richard Marius," *TN Libn.* (Win. 1979); ed., "Perspectives on Reference Service: A Visit With Miss Eleanor Goehring," *TN Libn.* (Win. 1978); various reviews, *Amer. Ref. Bks. Anl.* (1977–78). **Activities:** 1; 15, 31, 39 **Addr.:** Library, University of Tennessee, Knoxville, TN 37916.

Worley, Merry Penelope (F. 26, 1949, Vicksburg, MS) Lib. Srvs. Coord., Exxon Prod. Resrch. Co., 1981–; Head of Info. Srvs., TX Med. Ctr. Lib., 1980–81; Coord. for Ref. Srvs., 1979–80, Asst. Head of Info. Srvs., 1978–80, Coord. for Autom. Info. Srvs., 1976–78; MCRMLP Medline/Ref. Coord., Midcontl. Reg. Med. Lib. Prog., 1975–76; Outrch. Libn., Unger Meml. Lib., 1975; Coord. of Comp. Info. Srvs., TX Med. Ctr. Lib., 1973–74, Chief Medlars Anal., 1972–73, Medlars Anal., 1971. **Educ.:** Univ. of AL, 1967–70, BS (Math.); Univ. of MO, 1974–75, MA (LS). **Orgs.:** Natl. Lib. of Med.: Stdg. Com. for Online Retrieval Educ. (1976–79). SLA: TX Chap., Nom. Com. (1980–81), Mem. Com. (Ch., 1978–79). Houston OLUG: Various ofcs. ASIS: Constn. and Bylaws Com. (1980–81); TX Chap., Asm. Rep. Alternate (1979–81); Mem. Com. (Ch., 1979–81); Midyr. Mtg. Conf. Com., Prog. Coord. Subcom. (1978). Various other orgs. **Honors:** Beta Phi Mu. **Activities:** 1, 12; 39; 80 **Addr.:** Exxon Production Research Co., P.O. Box 2189, Houston, TX 77001.

Worley, Parker (F. 25, 1920, Muskogee, OK) Libn., Rutgers Camden Lib., 1961–; Readers Adv., Trenton State Coll., 1958–61; Libn., Thiel Coll., 1952–57; Asst. Libn., Ursinus Coll., 1949–52; Intern, Lib. of Congs., 1948–49. **Educ.:** Univ. of OK, 1939–47, BA (Letters), 1947–48, BA (LS); Rutgers Univ., 1957–58, MLS, 1958–61, MA (Hist.). **Orgs.:** ALA. NJ LA. Amer. Prtg. Hist. Assn.: Exec. Bd. **Activities:** 1; 15, 17; 57 **Addr.:** 310 Jess Ave., Haddonfield, NJ 08033.

Worthen, Dennis Brent (Je. 3, 1943, Wilmington, DE) Chief, Info. Srvs. Sect., Norwich-Eaton Pharm., 1976–; Instr., LS and Coord., Clinical Drug Info. Prog., Case West. Rsv. Univ., 1974–76; Med. Sales Rep., E. R. Squibb and Sons, 1966–72. **Educ.:** Univ. of MI, 1964, BA (Eng.); Case West. Rsv. Univ., 1973, MS (LS), 1974, MS (Hlth. Sci. Educ.), 1976, PhD (Info. Sci.). **Orgs.:** Drug Info. Assn.: Mem. Com.; PR Com. ASIS. Assoc. Info. Mgrs. Sch. of LS, Case West. Rsv. Univ.: Visit. Com. of the Bd. of Overseers. **Honors:** Beta Phi Mu. **Pubns.:** Jt. auth., *Enteral Hyperalimentation With Chemically Defined Elemental Diets: A Source Book* (1978, 1979); "Characteristics of the Enteral Hyperalimentation Literature," *J Pen* (N.–D. 1979); "Ideal Qualifications for Professional Personnel in the Technical Information Center," *Innovative Management of the Technical Information Functions; Proceedings of the Engineering Foundation Conference* (1979); jt. auth., "The Drug Information Communication Network - An Overview," *Drug Info. Jnl.* (1979); "Short Lived Technical Literature: A Bibliometric Analysis," *Methods of Info. in Med.* (1978); various articles in LS and med. (1973–77). **Activities:** 12; 17, 41; 58, 80, 87 **Addr.:** Norwich-Eaton Pharmaceuticals, P.O. Box 191, Norwich, NY 13815.

Worthington, Anne Perry (Ja. 1, 1930, London, Eng.) Med. Ref. Libn./MEDLINE Anal., Thompson Med. Lib., NRMC, 1978–; Temporary Ref. Libn., San Diego Cmnty. Coll., 1975–77. **Educ.:** Univ. of CA, San Diego, 1967–69, BA (Lit.); San Diego State Univ., 1970–71, MA (Eng.); CA State Univ., Fullerton, 1973–74, MS (LS); Univ. of CA, Los Angeles, 1978, Cert. (Med. Libnshp.). **Orgs.:** Med. LA. Med. Lib. Grp. of South. CA and AZ: Mem. Com. (1978–79); Un. List Com. (1980–81). SLA: San Diego Chap. Pres. (1980–81); Pres. Elect (1979–80); Bltn. Ed. (1977–78). Phi Kappa Phi. Univ. of CA, San Diego Alum.

Special Subjects/Services: 50. Adult educ.; 51. Advert./Mktg.; 52. Aerosp.; 53. Agric.; 54. Area std.; 55. Arts/Hum.; 56. Autom.; 57. Bibl./Prtg.; 58. Bio. sci.; 59. Bus./Fin.; 60. Chem.; 61. Copyrt.; 62. Documtn.; 63. Educ.; 64. Engin.; 65. Env.; 66. Eth. grps.; 67. Film; 68. Food/Nutr.; 69. Geneal.; 70. Geo.; 71. Geol.; 72. Handcpd.; 73. Hist.; 74. Int. frdm.; 75. Info. sci.; 76. Insr.; 77. Law; 78. Legis.; 79. Math./Comp. sci.; 80. Med.; 81. Metals; 82. Nat. resrcs.; 83. Newsp.; 84. Nuc. sci.; 85. Oral hist.; 86. Petr./Energy; 87. Pharm.; 88. Phys./Astr./Math.; 89. Readg.; 90. Relig.; 91. Sci./Tech.; 92. Soc. sci.; 93. Telecom.; 94. Transp.; 95. (other).

Who's Who in Library and Information Services

Activities: 4, 5; 15, 20, 39; 56, 80, 74 **Addr.:** Thompson Medical Library, Naval Regional Medical Center, San Diego, CA 92134.

Wortzel, Murray N. (Jl. 1, 1923, Brooklyn, NY) Pers. Libn., Herbert H. Lehman Coll., CUNY, 1979–; Ref. Libn., 1966–79, Soc. Sci. Libn., 1964–66; Asst. to Soc. Sci. Libn., Hunter Coll., 1963–64. **Educ.:** Stanford Univ., 1945–46, AB (Far East Std.); Columbia Univ., 1960–62, MS (LS), 1970–77 (LS). **Orgs.:** ALA: ACRL/Bibl. Instr. Sect., Cont. Educ. Com. (1977–78); LRRT; RASD. AAUP: Various lcl. ofcs. Cncl. on Soc. Work Educ. Natl. Conf. on Soc. Welfare. **Pubns.:** Contrib., *Magazines For Libraries* (1972). **Addr.:** Herbert H. Lehman College, Periodicals Division, Bedford Park Blvd. W., Bronx, NY 10468.

Woy, James B. (My. 19, 1927, Moorefield, WV) Head, Mercantile Lib., Free Lib. of Philadelphia, 1964–; various positions, 1953–64; Head, Circ. Dept., Univ. of DE Lib., 1952–53; various positions, Brooklyn Pub. Lib., 1950–52. **Educ.:** WV Univ., 1945–49, AB (Soclgy.); Univ. of IL, 1949–50, MSLS. **Orgs.:** ALA: RASD (Sec. VP, 1971–72); Bsns. Ref. Srv. Com. (Ch., 1968–72). **Pubns.:** Jt. ed., *Encyclopedia of Business Information Sources* 5th ed. (forthcoming); *Commodity Futures Trading Methods, a Bibliographic Guide* (1976); *Investment Methods, a Bibliographic Guide* (1973); *Investment Information, a Guide to Information Sources* (1970); *Business Trends and Forecasting Information Sources* (1965). **Activities:** 9, 12; 30, 39, 42; 59 **Addr.:** Mercantile Library, Free Library of Philadelphia, 1021 Chestnut St., Philadelphia, PA 19107.

Wozniak, Grace I. (D. 28, 19–, New York, NY) Prof. Col. Libn., State Lib. of PA, 1967–; Ref. Libn., Reading Pub. Lib., 1963–65. **Educ.:** Wilkes Coll., 1957–60, BA (Fine Art); Drexel Univ., 1964–66, MSLS. **Orgs.:** PA LA. Appalachian Trail Conf. Keystone Trails Assn. **Activities:** 13; 15, 39, 42; 95-LS Lit. **Addr.:** State Library of Pennsylvania, Harrisburg, PA 17101.

Wozny, John J. (Ja. 1, 1947, Detroit, MI) Dir., Pettigrew Reg. Lib., 1978–; Ext. Libn., Wake Cnty. Pub. Libs., 1974–78; Asst. Dir., Fontana Reg. Lib., 1973–74. **Educ.:** Wayne State Univ., 1964–68, BA (Eng.); Univ. of MI, 1972–73, MA (LS); NC State Univ., 1976–80 (Pub. Affairs). **Orgs.:** NC LA: Dir., Exec. Bd.; JMRT. NC Pub. Lib. Dirs. Assn.: Secy. ALA. SELA. Plymouth Lions Club. **Honors:** Beta Phi Mu, 1973. **Pubns.:** *Pettigrew Regional Library Community Analysis* (1979). **Activities:** 9; 17; 92, 95-Pub. admin. **Addr.:** 127 Anne St., Plymouth, NC 27962.

Wray, Martha Catherine (S. 4, 1939, Bedford, IN) Dir., Media Srvs., Olympia Cmnty. Schs., 1976–, HS Libn., 1970–76; Asst. Dir., Bedford Pub. Lib., 1966–70; Asst. to Libn., Vincennes Univ., 1965–66; Asst. Libn., Bedford Pub. Lib., 1957–65. **Educ.:** IN Univ., 1966–68, BS (Sch. Lib. and AV Srvs.), 1968–72, MS (Sec. Educ., LS), 1979–81, SpLS (Lib. and Info. Sci.). **Orgs.:** IL Assn. of Media in Educ.: Reg. V (Dir., 1979–). McLean Cnty. Media Spec. Assn.: Plng. Com. (1979–). Olympia Dist. Sch. and Pub. Libn. Assn.: Org., Ch. (1978–). Natl. Educ. Assn. IL Educ. Assn. **Activities:** 10, 11; 21, 32, 48; 63 **Addr.:** 1811 Widermere Dr., Normal, IL 61761.

Wray, Wendell L. (Ja. 30, 1926, Pittsburgh, PA) Chief, Schomburg Ctr. for Resrch. in Black Culture, NY Pub. Lib., 1981–; Prof., Sch. of Lib. and Info. Sci., Univ. of Pittsburgh, 1973–81; Dir. of N. Manhattan Proj., NY Pub. Lib., 1966–73, Actg. Dir., Schomburg Ctr., 1964–65, Adult Grp. Spec., 1959–63; Pub. Affairs Div., Carnegie Lib. of Pittsburgh, 1952–59. **Educ.:** Bates Coll., 1946–50, AB (Psy.); Carnegie Lib. Sch., 1951–52, MS (LS). **Orgs.:** ALA: Notable Bks. Cncl. (1978–81). PA LA: Adult Srvs. Div. EFLA. Assn. for the Std. of Afro-Amer. Life and Hist. Oral Hist. Assn. **Honors:** Univ. of Pittsburgh, Sch. of Lib. and Info. Sci., Disting. Alum. Awd., 1973; Beta Phi Mu, 1973; Phi Beta Kappa, 1950; Phi Sigma Iota, 1948. **Pubns.:** "Library Services for Black Americans," *Handbook on Black Librarians* (1977); "Why We Need Black Librarians," *Opportunities for Minorities in Librarianship* (1977); *Pictorial Report of the North Manhattan Project* (1972); "Library Services for the Poor: Implications for Library Education," *Cath. Lib. Jnl.* (Mr. 1976). **Activities:** 9, 11; 16, 17, 39; 50, 66, 86 **Addr.:** 2186 Fifth Ave., NY, NY 10037.

Wright, Aileen H. (N. 18, 1935, Edmonton, AB) Dept. Libn., AB Solicitor Gen., 1977–; Asst. Prof., Admin. Prof. Ofcr., Fac. of LS, Univ. of AB, 1975–77; Asst. Libn., Douglas Coll., 1973–74; Instr., Boise State Coll., 1970–; Assoc. in Admis. and Place., Sch. of Libnshp., Univ. of WA, 1968–72; Fld. Consult., ID State Lib., 1967–68; Libn., First Untd. Presby. Church, Coeur d'Alene, 1962–66; Asst. Branch Libn., Multnomah Cnty. Lib., 1957–58. **Educ.:** Royal Cnsvty. of Toronto, 1953, ARCT (Piano); Univ. of AB, 1953, AMusA (Piano), 1956, BA (Msc.); Univ. of WA, 1957, MLibn. **Orgs.:** AB Lib. Trustee Assn.: Lib. Legis. Com. (Consult., 1975–76). Can. LA: Cncl. (1977–78). AB LA: Cnclr. (1975–76); First VP (1976–77); Com. on Lib. Legis. (Ch., 1976–78); Pres. (1977–78). Pac. NW LA: Various coms., ofcs. Various other orgs. **Pubns.:** "Public Relations...Why Bother?" *ID Libn.* (Ja. 1968). **Activities:** 4, 5; 15, 17, 26; 50, 90, 92 **Addr.:** 5820-114A St., Edmonton, AB T6H 3N1 Canada.

Wright, Charlotte (Je. 11, 1940, Brockport, NY) Lib. Media Spec., Ginther Elem. Sch., 1976–; Lib. Media Spec., Brockport Mid. Sch., 1974–76; Libn., Lakeshore Elem. Sch., 1962–66. **Educ.:** SUNY, Geneseo, 1958–62, BS (LS), 1965–69, Mstrs. (LS). **Orgs.:** NY LA. ALA. Grt. Rochester Area Sch. Media Specs. NY State Untd. Tchrs. **Activities:** 10; 21, 31, 32 **Addr.:** 433 Gallup Rd., Spencerport, NY 14559.

Wright, Dianne H. (My. 4, 1941, Clyattville, GA) ILL Libn./Asst. Prof., LS, Valdosta State Coll., 1981–, Serials Libn./Asst. Prof., LS, 1972–80, Asst. Ref. Libn., 1970–72; Tchr., Valdosta Jr. HS, 1967–68. **Educ.:** Valdosta State Coll., 1964–66, BS (Educ.); FL State Univ., 1969–70, MS (LS). **Orgs.:** ALA. SELA. GA LA: Resrch. and Tech. Srvs. Sect. Secy./Treas. (1973–75); Ch. (1975–77). **Honors:** Beta Phi Mu. **Pubns.:** Ed., *South Georgia-Central Georgia Union List of Serials* (1979); ed., *Collection Development Policy* (1980). **Addr.:** 103 Starmount Dr., Valdosta, GA 31601.

Wright, Donald Eugene (Jl. 25, 1930, Boulder, CO) Dir., Evanston Pub. Lib., 1967–; Assoc. State Libn., IL State Lib., 1965–67; Chief, Bur. of Lib. Srvs., CT Dept. of Educ., 1964–65; Exec. Secy., RASD, (ALA), ALTA, 1963–64; Dir., ALA Small Libs. Proj., 1961–63; Asst. Dir., Lincoln City Libs., 1960–61; Consult., NE Pub. Libs. Comsn., 1958–60; Libn., N. Platte Pub. Lib., 1956–58; Ref. Asst., Detroit Pub. Lib., 1953–56. **Educ.:** Univ. of CO, 1948–52, BA (Eng., Hist.); Denver Univ., 1952–53, MA (LS). **Orgs.:** ALA: Ed. Com. (Ch., 1969–72); Assn. of State Libs. (Bd. of Dirs., 1966–69); PLA, Bd. of Dirs. (1969–73); LAMA, Pres. (1977–78). IL LA: Lib. Dev. Com. (1966–72); Pres. (1972); various coms. WHCOLIS: Various IL ofcs. Caxton Club. Rotary Club of Evanston. **Addr.:** Evanston Public Library, 1703 Orrington Ave., Evanston, IL 60201.

Wright, F. Gwendolyn (O. 25, 1921, Sydney, NS) Hlth. Sci. Libn., Queen's Univ., 1982–, Chief Educ. Libn., 1966–81; Libn., McGill Univ., 1964–66; Libn., Legis. Lib., SK, 1957–64. **Educ.:** Univ. of SK, 1938–41, BA (Eng.); Univ. of Toronto, 1956–57, BLS. **Orgs.:** Can. LA. **Activities:** 1, 4; 17, 29, 39; 63 **Addr.:** Bracken Library, Botterell Hall, Queen's University, Kingston, ON K7L 3N6 Canada.

Wright, Gerry R. (Ag. 11, 1944, Lawton, OK) Biblgphr., Barker TX Hist. Ctr., Univ. of TX, Austin, 1981–, Head Libn., Serials Dept., 1980–81, Actg. Head Libn., 1979, Asst. Head Libn., 1979; Serials Cat. Libn., Univ. of OK, 1977–79, Asst. Acq. Libn., 1976–77; Actg. Acq. Libn., Univ. of WI, LaCrosse, 1974–76. **Educ.:** Univ. of OK, 1966–68, BA (Eng.); Univ. of TX, 1968–70, MA (Eng.), 1973–74, MLS. **Orgs.:** ALA. TX LA. **Pubns.:** "Thornton Wilder: A Bibliography of Secondary Sources, 1963–1978," *Bltn. of Bibl.* (O.–D. 1979). **Activities:** 1; 15, 44, 46; 55, 57 **Addr.:** Barker Texas History Center, The General Libraries, University of Texas Austin, TX 78712.

Wright, Gordon H. (Ag. 9, 1922, London, Eng.) Dir., Plng., Budgeting and Admin. Srvs., Univ. of Toronto Lib., 1975–; Dir., Coll. Biblctr., Toronto, 1969–75; Cnty. Tech. Libn., Hatfield Polytech. and Hertfordshire Cnty. Cncl., 1956–69; Peripatetic Libn., London Cnty. Cncl., 1946–56. **Educ.:** LA (UK), Assoc.; Inst. of Repro. Tech., Fellow. **Orgs.:** Can. LA: Com. on Lib. Netwk. (Ch., 1975–77); Bk. and Per. Dev. Cncl., Task Frc. on Distribution (1978–). Can. Assn. of Info. Scis.: Com. on Info. Policy. Natl. Lib. of Can.: Can. Marc Task Frc.; Subcom. for Serials (Ch., 1970–71). UK Secy. of States' Lib. Adv. Cncl.: Various working parties (1968–69). LA (UK): Various coms. ASLIB: Various coms., ofcs. Can. Micro. Socty.: Pres.; Dir.; Treas. (1971–75). Inst. of Reprograph. Tech.: Cncl. (1964–69); Educ. Com. (1963–69); Pubn. Com. (1965–69). Micro. Assn. of Grt. Brit.: Past Ch., Vice Ch. **Pubns.:** *The Library in Colleges of Commerce and Technology* (1966); *Microcopying Methods by the late H.R. Verry* (1967); "Fire! Anquish! Dumb Luck! or Contingency Planning," *Can. Lib. Jnl.* (O. 1979); "Canadian Mosaic - Planning or Shared Partnership in a National Network," *ASLIB Proc.* (F. 1978); "What Happened to the Technological Innovation in Libraries?" *Proceedings, 7th Anl. Can. Conf. on Info. Sci.* (1979); various articles, chaps., sps. (1955–). **Activities:** 1; 17, 33, 46; 56 **Addr.:** 226 Timberbank Blvd., Agincourt, ON M1W 2A3, Canada.

Wright, Helen K. (S. 23, 1927, Indianapolis, IN) Publshg. Ofcr. III, ALA, 1958–; Libn., Chicago Pub. Lib., 1957–58; Asst. Prof. of LS, Univ. of UT, 1954–57; Ref. and YA Libn., Brooklyn Pub. Lib., 1953–54. **Educ.:** Butler Univ., 1941–45, AB, magna cum laude (Latin, Span.), 1948–50, MS (Educ.); Columbia Univ., 1950–52, MS (LS). **Pubns.:** "Where to Go For Further Information," *Encyclopedia of Careers* (1979); "Reference and Subscription Books Review Committee," *Encyc. of Lib. and Info. Sci.* (1980), **Activities:** 37, 39; 89 **Addr.:** American Library Association, 50 E. Huron St., Chicago, IL 60611.

Wright, Helena E. (O. 30, 1946, Madison, WI) Libn., Merrimack Valley Textile Musm., 1976–, Keeper of Prints and Mss., 1968–76. **Educ.:** Bryn Mawr Coll., 1964–68, AB (Hist.); Simmons Coll., 1972–74, SM (LS). **Orgs.:** Amer. Prtg. Hist. Assn. Ephemera Socty. Amer. Socty. of Pic. Profs. New Eng. Archvsts. Socty. for the Hist. of Tech.: Exec. Com.; Tech. Musms. Spec. Interest Grp. (1980–). Women in Technological Hist.: Biblgphr. Socty. for Indus. Archlg.: South. New Eng. Chap. (Prog. Ch., 1981). **Honors:** Natl. Endow. for the Arts Flwshp. for Mus. Profs., 1973. **Pubns.:** Jt. auth., *Documents in American Industrial History—Vol. IV, 1860–1920* (forthcoming); "Sarah G. Bagley: A Biographical Note," *Labor Hist.* (Sum. 1979); "The Harcourt Bindery of Boston," *Gld. of Bk. Workers Jnl.* (1975–76); "Views of Lowell, 1825–1976" exhibit cat. (1976); "New City on the Merrimack: Prints of Lawrence (MA) 1845–1876" exhibit cat. (1974). **Activities:** 8; 15; 39, 45; 55, 92 **Addr.:** Merrimack Valley Textile Museum, 800 Massachusetts Ave., North Andover, MA 01845.

Wright, James R. (My. 12, 1941, Fayette, AL) Dir., Phillis Wheatley/Lib., Rochester Pub. Lib., 1969–; Asst. Libn., AL A&M Univ. Lib., 1968–69; Branch Libn., Gary Pub. Lib., 1966–67; Libn., St. Jude Educ. Inst., 1962–65. **Educ.:** AL State Univ., 1958–62, BS (Soc. Std.); SUNY, Geneseo, 1969–71, MLS; Un. Grad. Sch., Un. for Exper. Colls. and Univs., 1974–77, PhD (Mgt.). **Orgs.:** NY LA: Schol. and Cont. Educ. (Ch., 1972–76). Adult Educ. Assn. ALA: PLA, Actv. Com. (1973); Lib. Admin. Div., Arch. for Pub. Libs. Com.; Nom. Com. (1976–77); Black Caucus (Ch., 1973–74); Subcom. on Equal Empl. Oppt. (1974–76); various coms., ofcs. Rochester Urban Leag. Montgomery Neighborhood Ctr. Rochester Chap. Untd. Nations. Rochester Black Pol. Caucus. Various other orgs. **Honors:** Church of God in Christ, Disting. Srv., 1975–; Rochester Urban Leag. Outstan. Srv., 1976. **Pubns.:** "Bring Them Into the Main Stream," *Focus on IN Libs.* (Je. 1968); "Help Change the Pecking Order," *Lib. Jnl.* (Ja. 1969); "Fringe Benefits for Academic Library Personnel," *Coll. & Resrch Libs.* (Ja. 1970); "Staffing Inner-City Libraries," *Wilson Lib. Bltn.* (Je. 1971); chap., *What Black Librarians are Saying* (1972); various articles. **Activities:** 9, 12; 16, 32, 39; 50, 66, 86 **Addr.:** 52 Elmford Rd., Rochester, NY 14606.

Wright, Jean Acker (F. 24, 1928, Springfield, MO) Head, Serials Dept., Vanderbilt Univ. Lib., 1976–, Head, Reclass. Unit, 1972–76, Serials/Analytics Libn., 1962–72; Catlgr., TN State Lib., 1952–56; Admin. Asst., Nashville Pub. Lib., 1951–52. **Educ.:** Vanderbilt Univ., 1945–49, BA (Span.); George Peabody Coll. 1949–51, MA (LS). **Orgs.:** SOLINET Data Base Adv. Com. (1980–). TN LA: Various coms. Nashville Lib. Club. ALA: RTSD/Cat. and Class. Sect., Policy and Resrch. Com. (Ch., 1979), Nom. Com. (Ch., 1980–81); ACRL; LITA. Phi Beta Kappa: Chap. Mem. Com. (1980–). TN Hist. Socty. **Pubns.:** "Vanderbilt University Libraries Detail Retrospective Conversion Project," *SOLINEWS* (O.–N. 1979, Ja.–F. 1980). **Activities:** 1; 20, 44, 46 **Addr.:** 2709 Wortham Ave., Nashville, TN 37215.

Wright, John Garrick (O. 24, 1928, Star City, SK) Prof. Fac. of LS, Univ. of AB, 1968–; Supvsr., Sch. Libs., SK Dept. of Educ., 1963–68; Libn., Aden Bowman Collegiate, Saskatoon Bd. of Educ., 1958–63; Libn., Ctrl. Unit Lib., Wadena Sch. Unit, 1957–58. **Educ.:** Univ. of SK, 1949–52, BEd (Hist., Lit.); Columbia Univ., 1956–57, MS (LS). **Orgs.:** Can. LA: Cncl. (1968–71); Restructure Com. (1971); Schol. and Awds. Com. (Ch., 1978–80); Cont. Educ. Com. (1980–). Can. Sch. LA: Conf. Plng. and Arrange. (Ch., 1977–78); Constn. Com. (1968–69); various coms., ofcs. ALA: Various sects. Can. Assn. of Lib. Schs.: Various coms. Various other orgs., ofcs. Edmonton City Ctr. Church Corp. McDougall Untd. Church. **Honors:** Can. Sch. LA, Margaret C. Scott Merit Awd., 1976; Beta Phi Mu, 1958. **Pubns.:** "School Libraries in Canada," *Sch. Libs. in Can.* (Win. 1981); "Las Bibliotecas Escolares en Canada," *IX Conf. Anl. de la Assn. Intl. de Bibliofecarios Escolares* (1980); "Survey of Recipients of CLA Awards and Scholarships," *Can. Lib. Jnl.* (Je. 1980); "Information Materials for Canadian Children," *Elements* (O. 1979); "CSLA: A National Voice by Default or Design," *Emergency Libn.* (My. 1979); various articles (1967–78). **Activities:** 10, 11; 21, 32, 39; 55, 89 **Addr.:** Faculty of Library Science, University of Alberta, Edmonton, AB T6G 2J4, Canada.

Wright, Joyce C. (D. 17, 1951, Charleston, SC) Head, Mags./Newsp. Dept., Memphis/Shelby Cnty. Pub. Lib. and Info. Ctr., 1978–; Head, Outrch. Tech. Srvs., Hampton Pub. Lib., 1976–78; Ref. Docums. Libn., Trident Tech. Coll., 1974–76. **Educ.:** Voorhees Coll., 1969–73, BA (Soc. Std.); Univ. of MI, 1973–74, AMLS. **Orgs.:** SELA: Pub. Lib. Sect., Mem. Com. TN LA: Pub. Lib. Sect., Mem. Com. ALA: W. TN Chap.; JMRT; ASCLA. AAUW. Natl. Exec. Female Cncl. Univ. of MI Alum. Assn. **Activities:** 9; 16, 17, 31; 83 **Addr.:** Memphis/Shelby County Public Library and Information Center, 1850 Peabody Ave., Memphis, TN 38103.

Wright, Judith M. (Ag. 16, 1944, Jackson, TN) Lectr., Grad. Lib. Sch. and Law Sch., Univ. of Chicago, 1977–, Law Libn., Law Sch., 1980–, Ref. Libn., 1974–77, Docums. Libn., 1970–74. **Educ.:** Memphis State Univ., 1962–66, BS (Hist.); Univ. of Chicago, 1969–70, MA; DePaul Univ., 1975–80, JD. **Orgs.:** AALL. Chicago Assn. of Law Libs. **Activities:** 1, 12; 15, 17; 77 **Addr.:** University of Chicago Law Library, 1121 E. 60th St., Chicago, IL 60637.

Wright, Kathleen J. (Je. 25, 1942, Orange, CA) Libn., Nvl. Ocean Systs. Ctr., 1971–; Chem., Rocketdyne, 1965–70. **Educ.:** Univ. of South. CA, 1962–65, BS (Chem.); Univ. of CA, Los Angeles, 1970–71, MLS. **Orgs.:** SLA: San Diego Chap. Pres.

PROFESSIONAL ACTIVITIES: Institutions: 1. Acad. lib.; 2. Arch.; 3. Assn.; 4. Fed./Gvt. lib.; 5. Inst. lib.; 6. Mfr./Suppl.; 7. Milit. lib.; 8. Musm.; 9. Pub. lib.; 10. Sch. lib.; 11. Sch. of lib. sci.; 12. Spec. lib.; 13. State lib.; 14. (other). **Functions/Activities:** 15. Acq./Col. dev.; 16. Adult srvs.; 17. Admin.; 18. Apprais.; 19. Archit./Bldgs.; 20. Cat./Class.; 21. Chld. srvs.; 22. Circ.; 23. Cons./Pres.; 24. Consult.; 25. Cont. ed.; 26. Educ. lib. sci.; 27. Ext. srvs.; 28. Fund/Grants; 29. Gvt. pubs.; 30. Indx./Abs.; 31. Instr. lib. use; 32. Media srvs.; 33. Micro.; 34. Netwks./Coop.; 35. Persnl.; 36. PR; 37. Publshg.; 38. Recs. mgt.; 39. Ref. srvs.; 40. Repro.; 41. Resrch.; 42. Review.; 43. Secur.; 44. Serials; 45. Spec. col.; 46. Tech. srvs.; 47. Trustees/Bds.; 48. YA srvs.; 49. (other).

(1977–78), Bltn. Ed. (1975–76). Grossmont Coll., Lib. Tech. Prog.: Adv. Com. (1979–). **Honors:** Iota Sima Pi. **Pubns.:** *NUC-TP-499, Library Management and Retrieval System* (1976). **Activities:** 4, 12; 39, 49-Autom.; 60, 75, 91 **Addr.:** Naval Ocean Systems Center, Attn: Technical Library, Code 4473, San Diego, CA 92152.

Wright, Katie Harper (Mrs. Marvin Wright) (O. 5, 1923, Crawfordsville, AR) Adj. Asst. Prof., Educ., Harris/Stowe State Coll., 1980–; Asst. Supt. of Schs., E. St. Louis Pub. Schs., 1977–79, Dir. of Spec. Educ., 1971–77, Dir. of Instr. Media, 1966–71, Classrm. Tchr., 1944–66. **Educ.:** Univ. of IL, 1940–44, AB (Soc. Sci.), 1957–59, MEd (Spec. Ed.); St. Louis Univ., 1974–79, EdD (Spec. Ed.). **Orgs.:** ALA. ALTA: Secy. (1979–80); Reg. VP (1977–79); Int. Frdm.; Litcy. Com.; Mem. Task Frc. (Ch., 1976); Speakers Bur. Com.; various other coms. E. St. Louis Lib. Bd. St. Clair Cnty. Mental Hlth. Bd. IL Comsn. on Chld.: VP (1980–). St. Louis Urban Leag. Bd. St. Clair Cnty. Untd. Way Bd. Various other orgs., ofcs. **Honors:** IL Ofc. of Educ., Top Admin., 1975; St. Louis Globe, Dem. Woman of Achvmt. in Educ., 1974; St. Louis, Outstan. Working Woman, 1967; other hons. **Pubns.:** *The Improvement of Special Education* (1978); "The Challenge Instr. Media Program," *IL Libs.* (S. 1970); "Emphasis Needed on Dev. Handicapped Child's Voc. Skills," *Career Educ. Jnl.* (1979); "A Backward Look: Did We Help or Hurt?" *ICEC Jnl.* (1980); "Dressing for Special Teaching," *ICEC Jnl.* (1981). **Activities:** 14-State coll.; 47; 63, 83 **Addr.:** 733 N. 40th St., East St. Louis, IL 62205.

Wright, Marjorie P. (My. 15, 1923, Perry, FL) Sch. Media Spec., Ortona Sch., 1967–; Libn., Oakland Hts. Elem. Sch., 1961–64; Instr., OK State Univ. Lib., 1954–55; Tchr., Nagoya Amer. HS, Japan, 1950–51; Libn., Lib. Sch., FL State Univ., 1947–48; Libn., Port St. Joe HS, 1945–47. **Educ.:** FL State Coll., 1941–45, BS (Chem.); FL State Univ., 1946–49, MA (Lib.); various crs. **Orgs.:** ALA. FL LA: Sch. and Chld. Sect. (Ch., 1947–48). FL Assn. Media Educ.: Ethics Com. (1980). Volusia Assn. Media Educ.: Book-a-Roo Kit (1974–76); Position Paper (1977); Proj. Ch. (1978–80). Natl. Educ. Assn. FL Tchg. Prof. Volusia Educ. Assn. Ormond Beach Lib. Adv. Bd. **Honors** Alpha Delta Kappa; Phi Beta Mu; Delta Delta Delta. **Activities:** 10, 11; 21, 31, 32; 63, 89 **Addr.:** 128 Windward Ln., Ormond Beach, FL 32074.

Wright, Meredith S. (Ag. 15, 1920, Cleveland, OH) Mgr., Tech. Info. Srv., Un. Carbide Corp., Parma Tech. Ctr., 1945–; Petrographer, Repub. Steel Corp., 1942–45. **Educ.:** Barnard Coll., 1937–41, BA (Geo.); Case West. Rsv. Univ., 1944–45, BS (LS), 1952–54, MA (Eng.). **Orgs.:** SLA. ASIS. **Pubns.:** *Properties of Carbon and Graphite at High Temperatures* (1956); "Microfilming Laboratory Notebooks," *Spec. Libs.* (O. 1960). **Activities:** 12; 17, 30, 38; 75, 81, 91 **Addr.:** Technical Information Service, Union Carbide Corp., P.O. Box 6116, Cleveland, OH 44101.

Wright, Nan J. (Cleveland, OH) Supvsg. Libn., Trenton Free Pub. Lib., 1972–; Sr. Ref. Libn., Marin Cnty. Lib., 1969–71. **Educ.:** Univ. of KS, BA (Fine Arts); Univ. of CA, Berkeley, 1969, MLS. **Orgs.:** NJ LA. **Activities:** 9; 16, 39 **Addr.:** Reference Dept., Free Public Library, 120 Academy St., Trenton, NJ 08608.

Wright, Nancy Kirkpatrick (My. 8, 1926, Knoxville, TN) Pub. Srvs. Libn., Yavapai Coll., 1972–. **Educ.:** Univ. of MN, 1944–47, BA (Psy.); Univ. of AZ, 1971–72, MLS. **Orgs.:** ALA. AZ State LA. AZ Resrcs. Cnsrtm.: Pub. Srvs. Com., Ch. Frnds. of the Prescott Pub. Lib.: Secy. AZ Hist. Socty. **Honors:** AZ State LA, Rosenzweig Awd., 1967. **Activities:** 1; 31, 34, 39 **Addr.:** Yavapai College Library, 1100 E. Sheldon, Prescott, AZ 86301.

Wright, Patricia E. (My. 4, 1954, Carbondale, PA) Frgn. Docums. Libn., Univ. of CA, Los Angeles, 1979–; Soc. Sci./Bus. Ref. Libn., CA State Univ., Long Beach, 1978–79. **Educ.:** Muhlenberg Coll., 1972–76, BA (Soc. Sci.); Simmons Coll., 1976–77, MSLS. **Orgs.:** ALA: GODORT. CA LA: Gvt. Docum. Chap. **Pubns.:** "Federal Government Publications for Legal Research," *Forum* (Mr.–Ap. 1981); ed., for Africa and Europe, "Africa, Asia, Europe, and Latin America," *Gvt. Pubns. Review* (Spr. 1981); various reviews. **Activities:** 1, 4; 29, 39, 49-Online srch.; 54, 56, 92 **Addr.:** 1034 Las Lomas Ave., Pacific Palisades, CA 90272.

Wright, Pauline A. Williams (O. 14, 1931, Kilgore, TX) Libn., L.M. Goza Jr. HS, Arkadelphia Pub. Schs., 1967–; Libn., Alpine HS, 1965–67; HS Libn., Hale Ctr., 1964; Estab. Centralized Elem. Libs., Plainview Pub. Schs., 1963; Tchr., Jr. HS Eng., Carlsbad Pub. Schs., 1956–61; Tchr., Jr. HS Eng., Pecos Pub. Schs., 1953–56. **Educ.:** Ranger Jr. Coll., 1949–51, AA (Gen.); Hardin-Simmons Univ., 1951–53, BA (Eng., Sec. Educ.); TX Woman's Univ., 1955–59, MLS. **Orgs.:** ALA. AR LA. AR Assn. of Sch. Libns. Natl. Educ. Assn. AR Educ. Assn. **Pubns.:** *The Wright Book: Worthy Heritage, Enduring Challenge* (1974); *Clark County, Arkansas: A Genealogical Source Book* (1981). **Activities:** 10; 17, 32; 63, 69 **Addr.:** 722 S. 22nd, Arkadelphia, AR 71923.

Wright, Raymond Clifford (My. 4, 1917, Winnipeg, MB) Dir. of Libs., Univ. of Winnipeg, 1967–; Chief Libn., Untd. Coll., 1961–67; Asst. Libn., MB Ext. Lib., 1955–61; Docum. Libn., Legis. Lib., MB Gvt., 1947–55. **Educ.:** Univ. of MB, 1935–39, BA; McGill Univ., 1946–47, BLS. **Orgs.:** MB LA: Pres. (1966, 1967). Cncl. of West. Can. Univ. Libs.: Secy. (1972–). Cncl. of Prairie Univ. Libs.: Ch. (1981). **Activities:** 1, 9; 17, 27, 29; 55, 58, 88 **Addr.:** 488 Queenston St., Winnipeg, MB R3N 0X2, Canada.

Wright, Raymond Sanford III (S. 14, 1941, Ogden, UT) Mgr., Pub. Srvs. Sect., Lib. Srvs. Div., Geneal. Dept. Lib. Church of Jesus Christ of Latter-Day Saints, 1979–, Grp. Mgr., Europe-Africa-Mid. E. Fld. Opers., 1977–79, Supvsr., Recs. Spec. Dept., 1975–77, Resrch. Spec., East. Europe, 1972–75. **Educ.:** Univ. of UT, 1967, BA (Grmn., Hist.), 1973, MA (Hist.), 1977, PhD (Hist.). **Orgs.:** ALA. Amer. Hist. Assn. Univ. of UT Ctr. for Hist. Popltn. Std.: Adv. Com. 1980 World Conf. on Recs.: European Subcom., Ch. Medvl. Acad. of Amer. **Pubns.:** "The Individual and the Family in Historical Research: Sources," *Nsltr. of the Ctr. for Reformation Resrch.* (Je. 1975); "An International Center for the Study of the Family," *The Jnl. of Fam. Hist.* (Sum. 1977); "Tracing Family Origins in Europe," *Genealogy and Local History Reference Services. An ALA RASD History Preconference Syllabus.* **Activities:** 2, 12; 16, 39, 41; 55, 69, 92 **Addr.:** Public Services, Genealogical Dept. Library, Church of Jesus Christ of Latter-Day Saints, 2WW, 50 E. North Temple, Salt Lake City, UT 84150.

Wrigley, Elizabeth S. (O. 4, 1915, Pittsburgh, PA) Dir., Francis Bacon Lib., 1960–; Pres., Francis Bacon Fndn. Inc., 1954–; Dir., Resrch., 1954–60; Libn., Francis Bacon Lib., 1950–54, Cur., Rare Bks., 1945–50; Resrch. Asst., Francis Bacon Fndn., Inc., 1944–45. **Educ.:** Univ. of Pittsburgh, 1931–35, AB (Lit.); Carnegie Inst. of Tech., 1935–36, BS (LS); various crs. **Orgs.:** ALA. CA LA. SLA. SAA: Com. on Collecting Personal Papers and Mss. (1978–79). Mod. Hum. Resrch. Assn. Mod. Lang. Assn. Renaissance Socty. of Amer. Conf. on Brit. Std. **Honors:** Amer. Cryptogram Assn., Hon. VP, 1978; Alpha Delta Pi. **Pubns.:** Jt. ed., *A Concordance to The Essays of Francis Bacon* (1973); cmplr., *Lee-Bernard Collection in American Political Theory* (1972); "The Bacon Collection in the Francis Bacon Library," *Claremont Qtly.* (Win. 1962); "The Francis Bacon Library," *Lib. Jnl.* (D. 1, 1960). **Activities:** 2, 12; 17, 41, 45; 55, 57 **Addr.:** The Francis Bacon Library, 655 N. Dartmouth Ave., Claremont, CA 91711.

Wrisley, Lois E. (O. 25, 1929, Burlington, PA) Head Media Spec., Stranahan HS, 1961–, Media Spec., 1960–61; Media Spec., Annapolis Sr. HS, 1957–60; Media Spec., Athens HS, 1951–57. **Educ.:** Millersville State Tchrs. Coll., 1947–51, BS Ed (LS); Syracuse Univ., 1953–57, Mstrs. (LS); FL Atl. Univ., Cert.; Univ. of MD, 1955, Cert.; Johns Hopkins Univ., 1958, Cert. **Orgs.:** ALA. FL Assn. of Media in Educ. Broward Cnty. Assn. of Media Specs.: Pres. (1973–74). Natl. Educ. Assn. **Honors:** Winipeg, Can., Exch. Tchr., Fulbright Schol., 1954–55. **Pubns.:** "Student Staff Assistants," *Wilson Lib. Bltn.* (Ap. 1957). **Activities:** 10; 17, 24, 31 **Addr.:** 5261 S.W. 3rd St., Plantation, FL 33317.

Wszolek, Sr. Mary Maurita (Mr. 14, 1916, Gary, IN) Med. Libn., St. Anthony Med. Ctr., Crown Point, IN, 1978–; Libn., St. John Med. Ctr., Huron, SD, 1971–78; Prin., Blessed Sacrament Sch., Gary, IN, 1968–71; Libn., St. John Sch. of Nursing, Huron, SD, 1959–68. **Educ.:** De Paul Univ., 1943, BS in ED (Educ.); Rosary Coll., 1958, MSLS. **Orgs.:** Cath. LA. Med. LA. Natl. Assn. of Pastoral Musicians. **Activities:** 12; 22, 39, 46 **Addr.:** St. Anthony Medical Center, Main at Franciscan Rd., Crown Point, IN 46307.

Wu, Ai-Hwa (O. 18, 1939, Surabaja, Java, Indonesia) Cat. Libn., Subj. Spec., AZ State Univ. Lib., 1964–. **Educ.:** Natl. Taiwan Univ., 1958–62, BA (Frgn. Lang., Lit.); Univ. of WA, 1962–64, MLS (Libnshp.). **Orgs.:** Msc. LA. AZ State LA. AZ State Univ. Fac. Women Assn. **Activities:** 1; 15, 20, 45; 54 **Addr.:** Hayden Library, Arizona State University, Tempe, AZ 85287.

Wu, Daisy Te-Hsien (Ag. 15, 1930, Shanghai, Kiang-Su, China) Dir., Steenbock Life Scis. Lib., 1980–; Assoc. Dir., W. S. Middleton Hlth. Sci. Lib., 1959–80; Asst. Libn., Amer. Jnl. of Nursing Co. Lib., 1958–59; Catlgr., Univ. of IL Lib., 1957–58. **Educ.:** Coll. of St. Benedict, 1951–55, BA (Eng.); Cath. Univ. of Amer., 1955–57, MS (LS). **Orgs.:** ALA. Med. LA: Intl. Coop. Com. (1979–); Midwest Reg. Grp., Plng. Com. (1978). WI Hlth. Sci. LA. Midwest HSLN Cncl. Zonta Intl. of Exec. Women: WI Chap., Bd. of Dirs. (1978–). Org. of Chinese Amers.: WI Chap., VP (1978), Bd. of Dirs. (1979–). **Activities:** 1, 12; 17, 39, 46; 58, 75, 80 **Addr.:** Steenbock Life Sciences Library, University of Wisconsin, 550 Babcock Dr., Madison, WI 53706.

Wu, Dorothea Wan Lien (Jl. 19, 1927, Peking, China) Head, Art and Msc. Div., Queens Boro. Pub. Lib., 1968–, Asst. Head, Art and Msc. Div. Head, Pic. Div., 1960–68; Gen. Asst., Msc. Dept., Chicago Pub. Lib., 1958–60; Chinese Catlgr., Harvard–Yenching Lib., Harvard Univ., 1951–58. **Educ.:** Fu Jen Univ., 1944–46, (Eng. Lit.); Yenching Univ., 1946–48, BA (Eng. Lit.); Univ. of CA, Berkeley, 1949 (Fr.); Univ. of AL, 1949–50 (LS); Simmons Coll., 1950–51, MS (LS). **Orgs.:** ALA. Chin.-Amer. Libns. Assn. Intl. Assn. of Msc. Libs. Msc. LA. Various other orgs. Metro. Musm. of Art. Musm. of Mod. Art. **Activities:** 9; 15, 16, 17; 55, 67 **Addr.:** 110–45 71 Rd., Apt. 2B, Forest Hills, NY 11375.

Wu, Harry Pao-Tung (My. 1, 1932, Chinan, Shantung, China) Dir., Blue Water Lib. Fed., 1974–; Dir., St. Clair Cnty. Lib. Syst., 1968–; Pres., MI Lib. Film Circuit, 1977–79; Dir., Flesh Pub. Lib., 1966–68; Asst. Dir., Head, Adult Srvs., Massillon Pub. Lib., 1966, Actg. Asst. Dir., 1965; Ref. Libn., 1964–65. **Educ.:** Natl. Taiwan Univ., 1955–59, BA (Frgn. Langs., Lit.); Kent State Univ., 1960–66, MLS; various crs. **Orgs.:** ALA. AECT. Detroit Suburban Libns. RT. MI LA: Lib. Syst. RT (Ch., 1974). Amer. Mgt. Assn. Port Huron Intl. Club. Port Huron Rotary Club: Bd. of Dirs. (1972–74); Intl. Youth Com. (Ch., 1971–73); Intl. Srv. (Gen. Ch., 1973–74); World Srv. Com. (Ch., 1975–77, 1979–80); Cult. Com. (Ch., 1976–77, 1978–79). **Activities:** 9, 14-Reg. coop. lib. syst.; 17, 24, 36; 50, 72, 78 **Addr.:** 1518 Holland Ave., Port Huron, MI 48060.

Wu, Julia Li (Jl. 2, 1936, Nankin, China) Head Libn., Virgil Jr. HS, Los Angeles Unfd. Schs. Dist., 1969–; Asst. Inst. Libn., Los Angeles Cnty. Lib., 1962–69; Voice of Amer., USA, W. Coast Correspondent, 1962–68; Mnstry. of Educ., Asst. to Mnstr., Repub. of China, 1958–59. **Educ.:** Taiwan Natl. Normal Univ., 1954–58, BA (Eng.); Immaculate Heart Coll., Hollywood, CA, 1960–62, MA (LS); CA State Univ., 1975–76, MA (Educ. Admin.); Cmnty. Coll. Tchg. Cred., Stan. Sec. Tchg. Cred. **Orgs.:** ALA: AASL. CA Media and Lib. Educ. Assn. Chin. Libns. Assn. Los Angeles Sch. Libns. Assn. Com. to Conserve Chin. Culture: Bd. of Dirs. Chin.-Amer. Citizen Alliance. **Honors:** Appointed to Natl. Comsn. on Libs. and Info. Sci., 1973–78; SLA, CA Chap., Spec. Awd., 1977; Appointed to Asian-Amer. Educ. Comsn., Los Angeles City Schs., 1975. **Pubns.:** *Bibliography on Asian American Culture* (1975); *Dragon Boat Festival–A Bilingual Chinese Book* (1972); "What's Your Programs in Library Profession?" *Lib. Jnl.* (1974); "The Future Role of Chinese-American Librarians from the Viewpoint of a National Library Program Planner," *Jnl. of Lib. and Info. Sci.* (Ja. 1980). **Addr.:** 2383 W. Silverlake Dr., Los Angeles, CA 90039.

Wujcik, Dennis S. (Ag. 19, 1950, South Bend, IN) Msc. Catlgr., Memphis/Shelby Cnty. Pub. Lib. and Info. Ctr., 1978–; Msc. Catlgr., Miami Univ. 1975–78; Msc. Asst., Cleveland Inst. of Msc., 1974–75. **Educ.:** Hanover Coll., 1968–72, AB (Msc.); Case West. Rsv. Univ., 1972–73, MSLS. **Orgs.:** Msc. LA: Subcom. on Subj. Heading Access. Msc. OCLC Users Grp.: Ch. Nominee. Coll. Msc. Socty. JMRT: Memphis Chap. (Pres., 1980). Amer. Gld. of Organists. **Activities:** 9; 20; 55 **Addr.:** 45 N. Belvedere #101, Memphis, TN 38104.

Wulfekoetter, Gertrude (Mr. 3, 1895, Cincinnati, OH) Volun. Libn., Univ. Congregational Church, 1968–; Asst. Libn., Law Lib., Univ. of WA, 1953–62, Prof., Lib. Sch., 1945–48; Asst. Libn., Univ. of Cincinnati, 1925–44. **Educ.:** Univ. of Cincinnati, 1913–17, BA (Rom. Lang.); Univ. of IL, 1918–25, BLS (Libnshp.); Univ. of Cincinnati, 1935–38, MA (Eng.). **Orgs.:** ALA. CS LA. Zonta Intl.: Dist. Histn. **Pubns.:** *Acquisition Work; Processes Involved in Building Library Collections* (1962); various articles. **Activities:** 1, 12; 15, 17, 26 **Addr.:** 2451 Perkins Ln., W., Seattle, WA 98199.

Wulff, L. Yvonne (N. 23, 1940, Seattle, WA) Head, Alfred Taubman Med. Lib., Coord., Med. and Sci./Tech. Libs., Univ. of MI, 1978–; Coord., Lrng. Resrcs. Dev. Proj., Biomed. Lib., Univ. of MN, 1976–77, Asst. to Dir., 1975–76, Coord., Hlth. Sci. Libs., 1973–75; Staff Asst., Head, Srch. Unit, Info. Ctr. for Sp., Johns Hopkins Univ., 1971–72; MEDLARS Anal., Hlth. Sci. Lib., Univ. of WA, 1968–69; Prin. Inv., Terrestrial Hypoxia Proj., OH State Univ. Lib., 1966–67, Head, Docum. Div., 1964–66, Prof. Intern, 1963–64. **Educ.:** WA State Univ., 1958–62, BS (Psy.); Univ. of WA, 1962–63, MLS (Libnshp.). **Orgs.:** Med. LA: Anl. Mtg. Lcl. Arrange. Com. (Asst. Ch., 1976), Prog. and Conv. Com. (1977–80). ALA. ASIS: Mu Chap., Symp. Com. (Co-Ch., 1977–78). Assn. of Acad. Hlth. Sci. Lib. Dirs.: Prog. Com. (Ch., 1980); Adv. Com.; Anl. Stats. (1978–79). MN LA: Nsltr. Ed. (1976–77). Womens Conf. in the Visual Arts: Strg. Com. (1972). **Honors:** Syracuse Univ., Gaylord Doct. Flwshp., 1969. **Pubns.:** Jt. auth., *Physiology Factors Relating to Terrestrial Altitudes* (1968); contrib., *Basic Library Management for Health Science Libraries* (1975); jt. auth., "An Information Service Program for Rural Physician Associate Students," *MN Med.* (1976); "Book Availability in the University of Minnesota Bio-Medical Library," *Bltn. of the Med. LA* (1978). **Activities:** 1; 17; 80 **Addr.:** Alfred Taubman Medical Library, University of Michigan, 1135 E. Catherine, Ann Arbor, MI 48109.

Wurfel, Clifford Randall (Mr. 24, 1927, Oakland, CA) Head, Univ. of CA, Riverside, 1968–, Cat. Dept., 1957–68; Biomed. Lib., Univ. of CA, Los Angeles, 1954–57; Cat. Dept., Univ. of UT, 1952–54. **Educ.:** San Jose State Coll., 1947–50, AB (Fr.); Univ. of CA, Berkeley, 1951–52, BLS (Lib.). **Orgs.:** ALA. SAA. Socty. of CA Archvsts.: Pres. (1976–78). Bibl. Socty. (Grt. Brit.). Bibl. Socty. of Amer. **Activities:** 1; 23, 45; 55, 57 **Addr.:** 8272 Briarwood Dr., Riverside, CA 92504.

Wurzburger, Marilyn J. (My. 30, 1931, Kirkwood, IL) Head, Spec. Cols., AZ State Univ., 1973–, Rare Bks. Catlgr., 1971–73, Lit. Catlgr., 1970–71, Head, Lib. of Congs. Reclass. Proj., 1963–71. **Educ.:** MacMurray Coll., 1949–53, AB (Eng.); AZ State Univ., 1959–60 (LS). **Orgs.:** ALA: ACRL. AZ State LA. AZ State Univ. Lib. Assocs.: Bd. of Dirs. (1978–). **Activities:**

Special Subjects/Services: 50. Adult educ.; 51. Advert./Mktg.; 52. Aerosp.; 53. Agric.; 54. Area std.; 55. Arts/Hum.; 56. Autom.; 57. Bibl./Prtg.; 58. Bio. sci.; 59. Bus./Fin.; 60. Chem.; 61. Copyrt.; 62. Documtn.; 63. Educ.; 64. Engin.; 65. Env.; 66. Eth. grps.; 67. Film; 68. Food/Nutr.; 69. Geneal.; 70. Geo.; 71. Geol.; 72. Handcpd.; 73. Hist.; 74. Int. frdm.; 75. Info. sci.; 76. Insr.; 77. Law; 78. Legis.; 79. Math./Comp. sci.; 80. Med.; 81. Metals; 82. Nat. resrcs.; 83. Newsp.; 84. Nuc. sci.; 85. Oral hist.; 86. Petr./Energy; 87. Pharm.; 88. Phys./Astr./Math.; 89. Readg.; 90. Relig.; 91. Sci./Tech.; 92. Soc. sci.; 93. Telecom.; 94. Transp.; 95. (other).

Who's Who in Library and Information Services

1; 15, 23, 45 **Addr.:** Special Collections, Arizona State University Library, Tempe, AZ 85287.

Wyatt, James F. (Jl. 4, 1934, Mullins, WV) Dir. of Libs., Univ. of Rochester, 1980–; Dean of Libs., Univ. of AL, 1973–80; Dir. of Lib., Mars Hill Coll., 1966–73. **Educ.:** Univ. of Richmond, 1953–56, BA (Eng.); Colgate Rochester Dvnty. Sch., 1956–57, 1963–65; Univ. of NC, 1965–66, MS (LS); FL State Univ., 1970–73, PhD (LS). **Orgs.:** ALA: Acad. Status Com. (1974–76). ARL: Bd. of Dirs. (1978–81); Mem. Com. (1979–80). NY LA. **Activities:** 1; 17, 26, 34; 56 **Addr.:** Rush Rhees Library, The University of Rochester, Rochester, NY 14627.

Wygant, Alice Chambers (Je. 26, 1948, Clinton, LA) Asst. Libn., Pub. Srvs., TX A and M Univ. at Galveston, Lib., 1977–; Libn., O'Connell HS, 1974–76; Bibliother., Ctrl. LA State Hosp., 1972–74. **Educ.:** LA Coll., 1966–70, BA (Fr., Hist.); LA State Univ., 1970–72, MS (LS). **Orgs.:** TX LA. ALA. SLA. SW LA. AAUP. World Future Socty. **Activities:** 1; 17, 31, 39; 91, 94 **Addr.:** Texas A&M at Galveston, Library, P.O. Box 1675, Galveston, TX 77553.

Wygant, Larry James (Je. 25, 1945, Dallas, TX) Assoc. Dir., Hist. of Med. and Arch., Univ. of TX Med. Branch, Moody Med. Lib., 1977–, Archvst., 1977; Cur., Spec. Cols., Rosenberg Lib., 1975–76, Archvst., 1973–74. **Educ.:** Univ. of TX, Arlington, 1963–67, BA (Hist.); LA State Univ., 1971–72, MS (LS); Univ. of Denver, 1974, Cert. (Arch. Admin.); Univ. of Houston, 1974–78, MA (Hist.). **Orgs.:** SAA. Socty. of SW Archvsts.: Prog. Com. (1973–75); Site Sel. Com. (Ch., 1975–78); Exec. Bd. (1976); Prof. Dev. Com. (Ch., 1978–80). Assn. of Libns. in the Hist. of the Hlth. Sci. Houston Area Resrch. Lib. Cnsrtm.: Spec. Cols. Com. (1979–80). Various other orgs. Galveston Hist. Fndn., Inc.: Exec. Com. (1974–79); Bd. of Dirs. (1978–80); Resrch. Com. (Ch., 1974–78). Galveston Cnty. Hist. Musm.: Bd. of Trustees (Pres., 1977–78). Frnds. of the Rosenberg Lib. **Pubns.:** "The John Sealy Hospital: A Study of Late Nineteenth Century Hospital Design," *TX Archit.* (S. 1980); "P.S. Thanks for 'Smell' Reference," *The Bookman* (N. 1978). **Activities:** 1, 2; 17, 45; 55, 80, 85 **Addr.:** History of Medicine and Archives Dept., Moody Medical Library, University of Texas Medical Branch, Galveston, TX 77550.

Wygnanski, Jadwiga (My. 18, 1923, Warsaw, Poland) Head, Engin. Lib., McGill Univ., 1973–, Head, Bot.-Genetics Lib., 1971–73, Head, Serials Dept., McLennon, 1968–71, Head, Fac. of Dentistry, 1965–68. **Educ.:** Univ. de Montreal, 1965, BA, BLS, 1967 MA, MLS. **Orgs.:** SLA. **Activities:** 1; 17, 46; 64, 91 **Addr.:** Engineering Library, McGill University, 817 Sherbrooke St. W., Montreal, PQ H3A 2K6 Canada.

Wylie, Margaret M. (My. 25, 1916, Sault Ste Marie, MI) Retired, 1981–; Libn., MacDonald Mid. Sch., 1967–81; Libn. Asst., MI State Lib., 1965–67; Cat. and Sch. Dept. Ref. Libn. Asst., Lansing Pub. Lib., 1949–53; Dir., Kent Cnty. Lib., 1942–46; Chld. Libn., W. Side Lib., 1941–42. **Educ.:** Coll. of St. Catherine, 1934–38, BA (Hist.), 1938–39, BS (LS); MI State Univ., 1946–48, MA (Soclgy.); Univ. of MI, 1968–69 (LS). **Orgs.:** MI LA: State Lib. Sch. Lib. Com., Rep.; Cnty. Lib. Div. MI Assn. for Media in Educ. ALA. MI Educ. Assn.: Reg. 8, Retirement Concerns Ch. AAUW: Various coms. **Honors:** AAUW, Flwshp., 1979. **Pubns.:** *Characteristics of Rural Library Users in Twenty-three County Libraries* (1948). **Activities:** 9, 10; 17, 20, 21; 50, 89 **Addr.:** 321 Clarendon Rd., East Lansing, MI 48823.

Wyllie, Stanley Clarke, Jr. (N. 19, 1935, Clearwater, FL) Libn. II, Soc. Sci. Ref. and Geneal., Dayton and Montgomery Cnty. Pub. Lib., 1973–, Libn., Dayton Col., Soc. Sci., 1967–73, Ref. Libn., Indus. and Sci. Div., 1964–66; Dir., Chestatee Reg. Lib. and Hall Cnty. Pub. Lib., 1963–64; Libn. I, Tampa Pub. Lib., 1962; Tchr., Lakeland Jr. HS, 1960–61; Spec. Libn., Park Trammell Pub. Lib., 1958–60. **Educ.:** FL South. Coll., 1954–58, BS (Soc. Sci.); FL State Univ., 1961–63, MS (LS). **Orgs.:** OH LA: Dupls. Exch. (Ch., 1978); JMRT, Mem. Com. (Ch., 1967). Tau Kappa Epsilon: Dayton Alum. Treas. (1968). Dayton Philatehic Socty.: Pres. (1967). Dayton and Montgomery Cnty. Pub. Lib. Staff Assn.: Pres. (1966). Montgomery Cnty. Young Republicans: 1st VP (1966). Various other orgs. **Honors:** Jr. Cham. of Cmrce., Gainesville, GA, Pres. Awd., 1964. **Pubns.:** *Education in Americanism* (1954); "Presidential Oaths," *Miscellanea* (1978); "What is This? A Pot of Manna!" *Royal Arch Mason* (Spr. 1970); "Who Comes Here?" *OH Lodge of Resrch. Nsltr.* (D. 1974); "There Can Be No Doubt as to His Death," *Philalethes Mag.* (1980); various articles, reviews, coll. and HS poetry anthologies. **Activities:** 2, 9; 16, 39, 42; 69, 74, 92 **Addr.:** P.O. Box 1452, Dayton, OH 45401.

Wyllys, Ronald Eugene (My. 14, 1930, Phoenix, AZ) Assoc. Prof., Grad. Sch. of LS & Info., Univ. of TX, Austin, 1972–; Lectr., Comp. Sci. Dept., Univ. of WI, 1966–72, Chief Systs. Anal., Univ. Libs., 1966–69; Comp. Systs. Spec., Syst. Dev. Corp., 1961–66; Assoc., Info. Retrieval, Plng. Resrch. Corp., 1959–61; Mathematician, Dept. of Defense, DC, 1954–59; Assoc., Math., George Washington Univ., 1954–59. **Educ.:** AZ State Univ., 1945–50, BA (Math.); Univ. of WI, 1969–74, PhD (Info. Sci.). **Orgs.:** ASIS: Educ. Com. (1977–79). AALS. Assn. for Comp. Mach.: Madison (WI) Area Chap. Ch. (1969–70) ALA: Com. on Tech. Stans. for Lib. Autom. (1974–78). Amer. Stats. Assn. AAAS. Assn. for Comp. Ling. **Pubns.:** Jt. auth., *National Document-Handling Systems for Science and Technology* (1967); "System Design–Principles and Techniques," *Annual Review of Information Science and Technology* (1979); "Teaching Descriptive and Inferential Statistics in Library Schools," *Jnl. of Educ. for Libnshp.* (Sum. 1978); "On the Analysis of Growth Rates of Library Collections and Expenditures," *Col. Mgt.* (Sum. 1978); "What's Sleek, Contemporary, and Up To Data?" *Alcalde: The Univ. of TX at Austin Alum. Mag.* (Ja.–F. 1979); various articles, chaps., papers. **Activities:** 1, 10; 24, 26, 41; 56, 75, 95-Stats. **Addr.:** Graduate School of Library and Information Science, University of Texas at Austin, Austin, TX 78712.

Wyly, Mary Porter (Je. 11, 1940, Sheridan, WY) Deputy Dir., Lib. Srvs., Newberry Lib., 1976–; Assoc. Libn., Grinnell Coll., 1968–76; Ref. Libn., Elmhurst Coll., 1967–68. **Educ.:** Grinnell Coll., 1958–62, BA (Msc.); Univ. of Chicago, 1962–64, MA (Msc.), 1966–68, MA (LS). **Orgs.:** ALA. Chicago Lib. Club. C. G. Jung Ctr., Chicago: Lib. Com. Lakeview Mental Hlth. Ctr.: Adv. Bd. **Activities:** 1, 12; 17, 35; 55 **Addr.:** Newberry Library, 60 W. Walton, Chicago, IL 60610.

Wynar, Bohdan S. (S. 7, 1926, Lviv, Ukraine) Pres., Libs. Unlimited, 1969–; Dean, Sch. of LS, SUNY, Geneseo, 1966–69; Assoc. Prof., Grad. Sch. of Libnshp., Univ. of Denver, 1963–66; Head, Tech. Srvs., Univ. of Denver Libs., 1958–62; Resrch., E. European Prog., Ford Fndn. Grants, 1954–57; Methods Anal., Tremco Corp., 1951–53. **Educ.:** Univ. of Munich, 1949, Dip. (Econ.), 1950, PhD (Econ.); Univ. of Denver, 1958, MA (LS). **Orgs.:** ALA: Slavic and E. European Sect., Ch.; ACRL (1966–67). CO LA: Exec. Bd. (1963–64). NY LA. Amer. Assn. for the Advnc. of Slavic Std. Ukrainian Acad. of Arts and Sci.: Exec. Bd. (1974–79). Shevchenko Sci. Socty.: Exec. Bd. (1964–66). Ukrainian Resrch. Fndn.: Pres. (1974–). **Honors:** ALA, Isadora Mudge Cit., 1977. **Pubns.:** *Introduction to Cataloging and Classification* (1980); ed., *Colorado Bibliography* (1980); ed., *Best Reference Books* (1980); ed., *Recommended Reference Books for Small and Medium-sized Libraries and Media Centers* (1981); ed., *American Reference Books Annual* (1969–); various bks. **Activities:** 1, 14-Publshg.; 15, 17, 26; 50, 57, 92 **Addr.:** Libraries Unlimited, Inc., PO Box 263, Littleton, CO 80160.

Wynar, Christine Lorraine (Gehrt) (Mr. 14, 1933, Rockford, IL) Pres., Corona Press, Inc., 1981–; Managing Ed., Libs. Unlimited, Inc., 1965–; Dist. Libn., Alamitos Sch. Dist., 1963–65. **Educ.:** Quincy Coll., 1951–55, BA (Hist.); Univ. of Denver, 1961–63, MS (LS). **Orgs.:** ALA: AASL. **Pubns.:** *Guide to Reference Books for School Media Centers* (1973); *Supplement 1974–75* (1976); *Index to American Reference Books Annual 1975–1979* (1979); "Ukrainian Children's Literature in North America," *Phaedrus: An Intl. Jnl. of Chld. Lit. Resrch.* (Spr. 1979); contrib. ed., gvt. pubns. clmn. *Sch. Media Qtly.* (1973–78). **Activities:** 10; 15, 37, 39 **Addr.:** 7788 S. Ogden Way, Littleton, CO 80122.

Wyngaard, Susan E. (O. 16, 1947, Madison, WI) Head, Fine Arts Lib., OH State Univ., 1981–; Dir., Arch., Intl. Musm. of Photography, George Eastman Hse., 1979–81; Assoc. Art Libn., Univ. of CA, Santa Barbara, 1973–78. **Educ.:** Univ. of WI, 1965–69, BA (Art Hist., Italian), 1972–73, MLS; Univ. di Lingua e Cultura, Siena, Italy, 1968; Univ. of NM, 1978–, MA (Art Hist.). **Orgs.:** ARLIS/NA: Vice-Ch., Ch.-Elect (1977). **Pubns.:** Past ed., *Catalog of the Art Exhibition Catalog Collection at the University of California–Santa Barbara* bi-anl. pubn. (1977–); various bk. reviews, *Nsltr. ARLIS/NA* (1975–). **Activities:** 2, 8; 15, 17, 39; 55, 67 **Addr.:** Fine Arts Library, Ohio State University, 166 Sullivant Hall, 1813 N. High St., Columbus, OH 43210.

Wynne, Allen Dean (D. 25, 1935, Great Falls, MT) Instr., Head of Math., Phys. Lib., Univ. of CO, 1967–; Sci. Acq. Libn., CO State Univ., 1965–67. **Educ.:** Univ. of NE, 1953–58, BS (Geo.); Univ. of Denver, 1964–65, MA (Libnshp.). **Orgs.:** SLA: Phys.-Astronomy-Math. Div., Ch. (1973–74), Rcrt. Ch. (1974–75), Conf. Prog. (Ch., 1974, 1976), Nom. Com. (1977); CO Chap., Nom. Com. (1968, 1970, 1972), various other coms. CO LA: Schol. Com. (1967–69); contrib. ed., *CO Libs.* clmn. (1974–78). Univ. of CO Fac. Cncl.: Lib. Rep. (1978–81). **Pubns.:** Ed., phys. sect., *Magazines for Libraries* (1982); *Specialized Library Resources of Colorado* 2nd ed., consult. ed., 3rd ed., 4th ed. (1970, 1975, 1979); "A Computer-based Index to Book Reviews in the Physics Literature," *Spec. Libs.* (Mr. 1979); various eds. *CO Libs.* (D. 1975–Je. 1978); "Introduction to the CUBoulder Math-Physics Library" slide/snd. tape (1977). **Activities:** 1; 15, 39; 88 **Addr.:** 2750 Heidelberg Dr., Boulder, CO 80303.

Wynne, Marjorie Gray (Mr. 7, 1917, Petersburg, VA) Resrch. Libn., Beinecke Rare Bk. and Ms. Lib., Yale Univ., 1963–, Libn., Rare Bk. Rm., 1947–63, Asst., Rare Bk. Rm., 1943–47, Serial Catlgr., 1942–43. **Educ.:** Duke Univ., 1934–38, BA (Eng.), Sch. of Libnshp., Univ. of CA, Berkeley, 1940–41, Cert.; Yale Univ., 1944–48, MA (Eng.). **Orgs.:** ALA: ACRL/Rare Bks. and Mss. Sect. (Ch., 1958, 1978). Assn. Intl. de Bibliophilie. Bibl. Socty. of Amer. The Grolier Club. **Honors:** Phi Beta Kappa, 1973. **Pubns.:** Various articles, bk. reviews. **Activities:** 1; 45 **Addr.:** 309 St. Ronan St., New Haven, CT 06511.

Wypyski, Eugene M. (Je. 20, 1926, New York, NY) Law Libn., Prof. of Law, Hofstra Univ., 1968–; Libn., Asst. Prof., Fordham Univ. Law Sch., 1957–62; Libn., Law Dept., City of NY, 1955–57; Asst. to Libn., NY Cnty. Lawyers Assn., 1950–55. **Educ.:** St. John's Univ., 1950, LLB (Law); Admitted to Prac. in NY, 1950; Pratt Inst., 1955, MLS. **Orgs.:** AALL: Treas. (1970–76). Law LA of Grt. NY: Pres. (1957). NY Cnty. Lawyers Assn. Nassau Cnty. Bar Assn. **Honors:** Hofstra Univ. Sch. of Law, Disting. Fac. Srv. Awd., 1980. **Pubns.:** *Legal Periodicals in English* (1975–81); jt. auth., *Bankruptcy Reform Act of 1978. A Legislative History* (1979); *Law of Inheritance* (1976). **Activities:** 1, 12; 17; 77 **Addr.:** Hofstra University School of Law Library, Hempstead, NY 11550.

X

X, Laura (St. Louis, MO) Pres., Women's Hist. Resrch. Ctr., Dir., Women's Hist. Lib., 1968–. **Educ.:** Univ. of CA, Berkeley, BA (Soc. Sci.); Vassar Coll., 1958–61; Bank St. Coll. of Educ., 1961–62. **Orgs.:** ALA: ACRL. CA LA. Mod. Lang. Assn. of Amer. Natl. Women's Std. Assn. **Honors:** *Mademoiselle*, Women of Achvmt., Ja., 1974; Soroptimists, Honorariums, 1974; Miss Hall's Sch., Pittsfield, MA, Honorarium, 1974; Northwest. Univ., Honorarium, 1975; other hons. **Pubns.:** *Herstory* micro. (1975); *Women and Health/Mental Health* micro. (1975); *Women and Law* micro. (1975); *Female Artists, Past and Present* (1974); "Grow Your Own...Women's History Research Center," *Sch. Lib. Jnl.* (Ja. 1973); various articles. **Activities:** 2; 15, 24, 33; 77, 80, 92 **Addr.:** National Clearinghouse on Marital Rape and Women's History Research Center, 2325 Oak St., Berkeley, CA 94708.

Xerxes, Edward Irabert (D. 14, 1936, Syracuse, NY) Msc. Libn. to Pres., Lyndonville State Coll., 1980–; Msc./Choral Spec., Syracuse Ctrl. Univ., 1971–80; Head, Spec. Cat., Ctrl. FL Msc. Inst., 1965–70; Mnstr., Choir Dir., Elmwood Presby. Church, 1961–65. **Educ.:** Univ. Coll., Davidson, 1954–58, BS (Relig.); Denver Ext. Univ., 1960–61, MS (LS); 1979, Comm. Networking Cert. **Orgs.:** NLA. PA LA: Tech. Srvs. RT. NY LA: Msc. Div. (Ch., 1973–74). **Pubns.:** *Japanese Music Materials, a Bibliography* (1974); "Music on a Soroban??" *Msc. in Higher Educ. in PA Libs.* (1979). **Activities:** 1; 20, 31, 39; 56, 84, 90 **Addr.:** c/o Hildman, 112 Carlton Rd., Syracuse, NY 13212.

Y

Yaffe, Phyllis N. (My. 1, 1949, Winnipeg, MB) Dir., The Chld. Bk. Ctr., 1977–; Ref. Libn., Seneca Coll., 1973–77; Branch Libn., Winnipeg Pub. Lib., 1971–73. **Educ.:** Univ. of MB, 1966–69, BA (Eng.); Univ. of AB, 1971–72, BLS (Lib.); Univ. of Toronto, 1974–76, MLS (Lib.). **Orgs.:** Can. LA. **Pubns.:** Jt. ed., *Emergency Libn.* (1973–79). **Activities:** 12; 17, 21, 48; 89, 92 **Addr.:** The Children's Book Centre, 229 College St., 5th Floor, Toronto, ON M5T 1R4 Canada.

Yagello, Virginia E. (S. 10, 1919, Cleveland, OH) Head, Chem. and Phys. Libs., Prof. of Lib. Admin., OH State Univ., 1966–, Head, Chem. Lib., 1963–66, Asst. to Head, Dept. Libs., 1961–63; Cmnd. Libn., HQ, U.S. Army Spec. Srvs., 1959–61. **Educ.:** Case West. Rsv. Univ., 1937–44, BA (Hist.); Carnegie Tech, Univ. of Pittsburgh, 1949–50, MLS. **Orgs.:** SLA: Div. Cabinet, Ch.-Elect (1977–78), Ch. (1978–79); Chem. Div., Ch.-Elect (1973–74), Ch. (1974–75); Dayton Chap., Pres.-Elect (1970–71); Pres. (1971–72). ASIS. Franklin Cnty LA. Assn. for Women in Sci.: Ctrl. OH Chap., Nom. Com., Pubns. Com. (1977–79); Amer. Chem. Socty.: Columbus (OH) Chap., Patterson-Crane Awd. Com. (1977–81). **Pubns.:** "Division Cabinet Report," *Spec. Libs.* (S. 1979); "Chemistry Library Linked to Laboratory," *OH State Univ. Frnds. Line* (D. 1977); jt. auth., "The Effect of Reduced Loan Periods on High Use Items," *Coll. & Resrch. Libs.* (S. 1975); "The Model Library Program of Project Intrex," *Amer. Jnl. of Pharm. Educ.* (D. 1972); "Increasing User Participation in *Chemical Titles* Search Program," *Quantitative Methods in Librarianship* (1972). **Activities:** 1; 15, 17, 39; 60, 64, 88 **Addr.:** Chemistry Library, 310 McPherson Chemical Laboratory, 140 W. 18th Ave., Ohio State University, Columbus, OH 43210.

Yager, Ellen K. Libn., NY Pub. Lib., 1981–, Libn., 1978–80, Libn., 1977–78; Resrch. Assoc. to Auth. John Davis, for *The Guggenheims*, 1976–77; HS Libn., St. Stephens HS, Brooklyn, NY, 1974–75. **Educ.:** Univ. of MN, BA (Hist.), BS (Educ.), MA (Hist.); St. John's Univ., 1972–74, MLS; Grad. Ctr., CUNY, 1979, Cert. (Bk. Ed.). **Orgs.:** NY Lib. Club. NY LA. SLA. Law Libns. Assn. of Grt. NY. Amer. Hist. Assn. **Activities:** 9; 15, 17, 39; 59, 77 **Addr.:** 201 E. 21 St., New York, NY 10010.

Yamasaki, Lorraine H. (N. 30, 1954, Tokyo, Japan) Libn., Leag. of CA Cities, 1977–. **Educ.:** Sacramento City Coll., 1971–74, AA (Bus. Admin.); CA State Univ., Sacramento, 1974–76, BS (Bus. Admin.); San Jose State Univ., 1976–77, MLS. **Orgs.:** SLA: Sierra NV Chap., Hosp. Com. (1977–78); Secy./Treas. (1978–79); Prog. Com. (1977–78). CA LA: Edna Yelland

PROFESSIONAL ACTIVITIES: Institutions: 1. Acad. lib.; 2. Arch.; 3. Assn.; 4. Fed./Gvt. lib.; 5. Inst. lib.; 6. Mfr./Suppl.; 7. Milit. lib.; 8. Musm.; 9. Pub. lib.; 10. Sch. lib.; 11. Sch. of lib. sci.; 12. Spec. lib.; 13. State lib.; 14. (other). **Functions/Activities:** 15. Acq./Col. dev.; 16. Adult srvs.; 17. Admin.; 18. Apprais.; 19. Archit./Bldgs.; 20. Cat./Class.; 21. Chld. srvs.; 22. Circ.; 23. Cons./Pres.; 24. Consult.; 25. Cont. ed.; 26. Educ. lib. sci.; 27. Ext. srvs.; 28. Fund/Grants; 29. Gvt. pubs.; 30. Indx./Abs.; 31. Instr. lib. use; 32. Media srvs.; 33. Micro.; 34. Netwks./Coop.; 35. Persnl.; 36. PR; 37. Publshg.; 38. Recs. mgt.; 39. Ref. srvs.; 40. Repro.; 41. Resrch.; 42. Review.; 43. Secur.; 44. Serials; 45. Spec. col.; 46. Tech. srvs.; 47. Trustees/Bds.; 48. YA srvs.; 49. (other).

Sch. Com. (1978–81). **Addr.:** 3323 Monterey Ave., Davis, CA 95616.

Yamashita, Kenneth Akira (S. 11, 1945, Topaz, UT) Rep., C L Systs., Inc., Newtonville, MA, 1978–79; Asst. to the Comsn., Chicago Pub. Lib., 1975–78; Supvsr. of Ext. Srvs., Decatur Pub. Lib., 1973–75; Ref./Info. Srvs. Libn., Montclair Pub. Lib., 1970–73. **Educ.:** Rutgers Univ., State Univ. of NJ, 1963–67, BA (Eng. Lit.); IN Univ., 1967–70, MA Cand. (Fine Arts); Rutgers Univ., State Univ. of NJ, 1971–72, MLS; Simmons Coll., 1979–81, DA in progress (Lib. Admin.). **Orgs.:** ALA: Ref. and Subscrpn. Bks. Review Com. MA LA. Frdm. to Read Fndn. Miklós Rózsa Socty. Elmer Bernstein's Filmsc. Col. The Amer. Film Inst. Metro. Opera Gld. **Honors:** Beta Phi Mu, 1972. **Pubns.:** Contrib., "Asian American Public Librarians," *Opportunities for Minorities in Librarianship* (1977); "Rutgers Report," *NJ Libs.* (D. 1971); "Montclair Public Library's Summer Outreach Program–1972," *NJ Libs. for Soc. Resp. Nsltr.* (N. 1972). **Activities:** 9, 13; 17, 35, 36; 55, 66, 67 **Addr.:** 280 Commonwealth Ave., G-5, Boston, MA 02116.

Yanarella, Marie Thérèse (N. 28, 1918, Yonkers, NY) Prof., LS, Northwest. CT Cmnty. Coll., 1969–; Lectr., NY Univ. Sch. of Cont. Educ., 1967–69; Branch Admin., Yonkers Pub. Lib., 1964–69, Fine Arts Libn., 1962–64; Cat. Libn., Gen. Foods Tech. Ctr., Tarrytown, NY, 1960–62; Asst. Libn., Natl. Indus. Conf. Bd., 1959–60. **Educ.:** Coll. of New Rochelle, 1935–39, BA (Eng. Lit.); Columbia Univ., 1939–40, MA (Lit.), MSLS. **Orgs.:** CT LA: Pres. (1974–75). SLA. Cncl. on Lib. Tech. **Activities:** 9, 11; 17, 20, 26; 55 **Addr.:** Box 559, Canaan, CT 06018.

Yanez, Elva Kocalis (S. 4, 1953, Los Angeles, CA) Info. Mgr., State of HI, Ofc. of the Gvr., Ofc. of Chld. and Youth, 1979–; Lib. Consult., Univ. of CA, Berkeley, 1978–79; Resrch. Asst., Univ. of South. CA, 1977–78. **Educ.:** Univ. of CA, Berkeley, Mills Coll., 1974–76, BA (Span. Lit.); Univ. of South. CA, 1976–79, MS (LS); various crs. **Orgs.:** ASIS. HI LA. Beta Phi Mu: Beta Chap. Univ. of South. CA Alum. Assn. Mills Coll. Alum. Assn. **Honors:** SLA, Positive Action for Minority Grps. Stipend, 1978. **Pubns.:** "The Spanish Speaking Mental Health Research Center Bibliographic Data Base," *Ref. Qtly.* (Spr. 1980). **Activities:** 12; 24, 37, 41; 56, 66, 95-Data Bases. **Addr.:** 223-A Namilimili St., Honolulu, HI 96813.

Yang, Basil Pei-nai (Ag. 11, 1934, Hsüchou, Kiangsu, China) Afflt. Libn., Brigham Young Univ., 1981–; Sr. Catlgr., Geneal. Socty. of UT Lib., 1974–81; Tchr. of Eng., Taipei Chienkuo Sr. HS, 1967–72; Tchr. of Eng., Pan-ch'iao Sr. HS, 1960–67. **Educ.:** Natl. Normal Univ., Taipei, Taiwan, 1944–48, BEd (Educ.); Brigham Young Univ., 1972–74, MLS. 1975, Accredited Genealogist, (China, Hong Kong, and Taiwan Resrch.). **Orgs.:** ALA. UT LA. Chinese-Amer. Libns. Assn. UT-Asian Libns. Assn. Assn. for Asian Std.: Com. on E. Asian Libs. (1980–81). **Honors:** Natl. Endow. for Hum., Resrch. Grant, 1978. **Pubns.:** Jt. auth., *Annotated Bibliography of Chinese Clan Genealogies at the Genealogical Society of Utah Library* (published in Taipei 1981); *Experimental English Grammar for High School Students* (published in Taipei 1966–68); *English Review for High School Students* (1966–67). **Activities:** 2, 12; 20, 39, 46; 57, 66, 69 **Addr.:** 411 E. Springhill Cir., North Salt Lake, UT 84054.

Yankee, Paula M. (Ag. 2, 1951, Ashland, WI) Recs. and Info. Mgr., Natl. Broadcasting Co., Inc., 1980–, Admin., Recs. Admin., 1978–80; Legal Recs. Spec., Pac. Lighting Corp., 1978; Assessor's Libn., LA Cnty. Assessor, 1977. **Educ.:** Univ. of WI, Oshkosh, 1969–73, BA (LS, Fr.); Univ. of South. CA, 1975–78, MLS; Assn. of Recs. Mgrs. and Admins., Natl. Micro. Assn., 1979, Recs. Mgt. Cert. **Orgs.:** ASIS: Mktg. Com. (1982); Los Angeles Chap. (Ch., 1980–81); Natl. Asm. Rep., Ch.-Elect, Prog. Dir. (1980); Hosplty. Ch. (1979). CA LA: State Cnclr. (1981–83). ALA. SAA. Frdm. to Read Fndn. Assn. of Recs. Mgrs. and Admins.: Grt. Los Angeles Chap. (Legis. Ch., 1979–81). Athl. Assn. **Honors:** Beta Phi Mu, 1979; Chap. Mem. of the Yr., 1981. **Pubns.:** Various articles, *OASIS* (ASIS Nsltr. (1979–81); *ARMA Nsltr.; News and Views* (1980–81); various poems, ... *a different drummer, Poetry* (1977). **Activities:** 12; 17, 38, 49-Systs. analysis; 59, 78, 93 **Addr.:** 3000 W. Alameda Ave., Burbank, CA 91523.

Yaple, Henry M. (My. 30, 1940, Vicksburg, MI) Acq. Libn., Univ. of WY Libs., 1978–; Hum. Biblgphr., MI State Univ. Libs., 1974–78, Ord. Libn., 1973–74. **Educ.:** Kalamazoo Coll., 1963, BA (Eng.); Univ. of ID, 1966, MA (Eng.); West. MI Univ., 1972, MSL. **Orgs.:** ALA. Mt. Plains LA. WY LA: Acad. Sect. (Pres., 1980–81); Exec. Bd. (1980–81). Natl. Ski Ptl. Syst., Inc.: Med. Bow Ptl. **Honors:** Rotary Fndn. Flwshp. (to Univ. d'Aix-Marseille), 1965–66; Beta Phi Mu, 1972. **Pubns.:** *Programmed Instruction in Librarianship: A Classified Bibliography* (1976); *Spartan Poets: A Preliminary Checklist 1855-1978* (1978); "Gold in the Snowy Range!" *Pop. Culture Assn. Nsltr.* (Jl. 1979); ed., *Title Varies* (D. 1973–75). **Activities:** 1; 15, 18 **Addr.:** University of Wyoming Libraries, Laramie, WY 82071.

Yaple, Marilyn V. (F. 26, 1932, Wilmington, OH) Dir., Bellaire City Lib., City of Bellaire, TX, 1979–, Asst. Dir., 1977–79; Branch Libn., W. Univ. Branch Lib., Harris Cnty., TX, 1972–77; Chldrn's. Libn., Price Hill Branch Pub. Lib. of Cincinnati and Hamilton Cnty. (OH), 1955–61. **Educ.:** Wilmington Coll., 1950–54, BA (Eng., Hist.); Univ. of IL, 1954–55, MSLS. **Orgs.:** ALA. TX LA. SW LA. Lib. Dirs. Assn. of TX Mun. Leag. **Activities:** 9; 15, 17 **Addr.:** Bellaire City Library, 5111 Jessamine, Bellaire, TX 77401.

Yarmal, Ann (Ja. 1, 1933, New York, NY) Chld. Libn., Ferguson Lib., Stamford, CT, 1980–; Libn. and AV Coord., The Brearley Sch., NY, 1979–80; Head of Chld. Srvs., The Howard Whittemore Meml. Naugatuck, CT, 1970–79; Head Libn., The Oakville Pub. Lib., 1969–70, Asst. to Head Libn., 1964–69. **Educ.:** South. CT State Coll., 1971–76, BA (Eng.); Columbia Univ., 1977–79, MSLS; Northwest. CT Cmnty. Coll., 1969–71, LTA. **Orgs.:** CT LA.: Chld. Sect. (Vice-Ch., 1978–79); Spec. Child Com. 1977–79. ALA. Hudson Valley LA. Coop. Libs. in Ctrl. CT: of Chld. RT (Co-Ch., 1977–79). CT Poetry Socty.: Hartford Chap. (Pres., 1978–79). Yale Bibliophiles: New Haven Chap. (VP, 1977–78). **Pubns.:** "CETA, HRD, LTA–Mutually Beneficial?" *CT Libs.* (Sum. 1978); jt. auth., "Libraries and P.L. 94-142; Awareness Planning Makes a Difference," *Top of the News* (Fall 1978); "An Educational Role," *Lib. Lookout Sunday Republican Mag.* (Feb. 1974). **Activities:** 11; 15, 21, 36; 67, 72, 89 **Addr.:** 29 Tremont St., Hartford, CT 06105.

Yates, Dudley V. (O. 31, 1932, Henleyfield, MS) Dir. of Lib. Srvs., TN Tech. Univ., 1974–; Dir. of Lib., Stetson Univ., 1968–74; Asst. Dir., Univ. of Southwest. LA, 1964–68; Pub. Srvs. Libn., Parsons Coll., 1963–64. **Educ.:** N.E. LA Univ., 1957–61, BA (Eng.); LA State Univ., 1961–63, MSLS. **Orgs.:** TN LA: Coll. and Univ. Sect. Vice-Ch. (1977–78); Ch. (1978–79). SE LA: Jnl. Advert. Ed. (1976–78). ALA. Mid-State LA: Adv. Bd. **Activities:** 1; 26 **Addr.:** P.O. Box 5066, Tennessee Tech University, Cookeville, TN 38501.

Yates, Marguerite W. (O. 12, 1906, Niagara Falls, NY) Lib. Trustee. **Educ.:** SUNY, Buffalo, 1924–27 (Educ.); Univ. of Buffalo, 1927–29, BE (Educ.). **Orgs.:** ALA: ALTA, Task Frc. on Litcy. (1975–); Prog. Plng. Com. (1972–77). Pubcty. Com. (1978–80). NY State Assn. Lib. Bds.: Pres. (1977–78). Nioga Lib. Syst.: Bd. (1965–79); Pres. (1969–72). NY Gvr.'s Conf. Adv. Bd. (1977–78). Litcy. Voluns.: NY State Bd. (Dir., 1979). Zonta Club of Lockport: Secy. (1975–76); Nsltr. Ed. (1978–). **Honors:** ALTA, Awd. for Litcy., 1980; Lib. Trustees Fndn. of NY State, Velma K. Moore Awd., 1976; Amer. Heritage Resrch. Assn., Human Resrc. Awd., 1975. **Pubns.:** *America's Millions Who Can't Read* (1980); various articles, *Litcy.* (1975–80), *PLA* (1975–80), state lib. pubns. (1973–80). **Activities:** 49-Educ. of lib. trustees; 95-Litcy. **Addr.:** 190 Windemere Rd., Carlisle Gardens, Lockport, NY 14094.

Yates-Edwards, Ella Gaines (Je. 14, 1927, Atlanta, GA) Pres., Yates-Edwards Lib. Consults., 1981–; Lectr., Univ. of WA, 1982; Lib. Dir., Atlanta Pub. Lib., 1976–81, Asst. Dir., 1972–76; Asst. Dir., Montclair Pub. Lib., 1970–72; Branch Libn., East Orange Pub. Lib., 1960–70; Med. Libn., Orange Mem. Hosp., 1963–66; Head Chld. Dept., Orange Pub. Lib., 1956–60; Asst. Branch Libn., Brooklyn Pub. Lib., 1951–55. **Educ.:** Spelman Coll., 1945–49, AB (Eng.); Atlanta Univ., 1950–51, MSLS; Atlanta Law Sch., 1976–79, JD; Intl. City Mgt. Assn., 1972, Cert. for Prof. Mgt. Trng.; 1974, HUD Cert. for Black Admins. in Mncpl. Admin.; 1975, Cert. for Adv. Prof. Mgt. Trng. **Orgs.:** WA LA: Int. Frdm. Com. (1981–); Frdm. to Read Fndn. Bd. (1982–84). ALA: Exec. Bd. (1978–83); Cncl. (1976–79); Legis. Com. (1978–81). Int. Frdm. Com. (1974–78). SE LA. GA LA: Strg. Com. on Pre-White Hse. Conf. on Libs. (1977–79); various other coms. Metro-Atlanta LA. Pub. Broadcasting Assn. of Grt. Atlanta: Bd. of Dirs. (1980–81). YMCA of Grt. Atlanta: Bd. of Dirs. (1980–81). Cham. of Cmrce., Atlanta. Atlanta Women's Cham. of Cmrce. Frnds. of the Fulton Cnty. Jail: Ch. (1974–81). **Honors:** City of Atlanta, Phoenix Awd., 1980; Umoja Fest., Outstan. Citizens Awd., 1978. **Pubns.:** Jt. ed., *The Role of the Humanities in the Public Library* (1979); ed., *What Black Librarians Are Saying* (1972); "Sexism in the Library Profession," *Lib. Jnl.* (D. 1979). **Activities:** 5, 9; 16, 17, 19; 74, 78, 93 **Addr.:** Yates-Edwards Library Consultants, P.O. Box 18188, Seattle, WA 98118.

Yauer, Loretta Orndorff (O. 8, 1949, Baltimore, MD) Law Libn., Gordon, Feinblatt, Rothman, Hoffberger and Hollander, 1975–; YA Libn., Enoch Pratt Gordon, Free Lib., 1975–76. **Educ.:** Univ. of MD, 1967–71, BA (Russ.), 1974–75, MLS (Info. Sci.); Univ. of Baltimore, 1976–80, JD (Law). **Orgs.:** AALL. Washington, DC Socty. of Law Libns. **Activities:** 14-Pvt. Law Firm; 15, 17, 39; 77 **Addr.:** Gordon, Feinblatt, Rothman, Hoffberger & Hollander, 233 E. Redwood St., Baltimore, MD 21215.

Yazgoor, Donald (Je. 29, 1936, New Haven, CT) Lib. Dir., Norwalk Pub. Lib., 1966–. **Educ.:** Univ. of CT, 1954–58, BA (Hist.); South. CT State Coll., 1959–60, MLS. **Orgs.:** ALA. CT LA. **Activities:** 9; 17 **Addr.:** Norwalk Public Library, 1 Belden Ave., Norwalk, CT 06850.

Yeamans, George Thomas (N. 7, 1929, Richmond, VA) Prof. of LS, Ball State Univ., 1972–, Assoc. Prof. of LS, 1966–72, Asst. Prof., 1961–66, Film Libn., 1961–69, Asst. Film Libn., 1958–61; Admin. Asst., AV Ctr., IN State Univ., 1957–58. **Educ.:** Univ. of Richmond, 1947–48; Univ. of VA, 1948–50, AB (Econ.); Univ. of KY, 1953–55, MSLS; IN Univ., 1955–57, EDD. **Orgs.:** AECT. ALA. AALS. Assn. of IN Media Educs.: Audit Com. Ch. **Honors:** Phi Delta Kappa. **Pubns.:** *Tape Recording Made Easy* (1978); *Linear Programming Workbook* (1977); *Mounting and Preserving Pictorial Materials* (1976); *Principles of Photography-Developing and Printing* (1981); *Principles of Photography-Taking Pictures* (1980). **Activities:** 11; 25, 26, 32; 63, 67, 93 **Addr.:** 4507 W. Burton Dr., Muncie, IN 47304.

Yeandle, Laetitia (Jl. 11, 1930, Hong Kong) Cur. of Mss., Folger Shakespeare Lib., 1957–; Asst. archvst., Shropshire Record Off., Eng., 1955–57; Asst., Vestry House Mus., Eng., 1953–54. **Educ.:** Trinity Coll., Dublin, 1949–53, BA (Mod. Hist.); Univ. Coll., London, 1954–55, Dipl. Arch. Admin. **Orgs.:** SAA. Br. Record Assn. The Conference on British Stds. The Renaissance Soc. of Amer. **Honors:** American Council of Learned Societies, "Grant-in-aid" 1975; Folger-British Acad., Flwshp., 1975. **Pubns.:** "The Evolution of Handwriting in the English-speaking Colonies of America," *Amer. Archvst.* (Sum. 1980); jt. auth., "Three Manuscript Sermon Fragments by Richard Hooker," *Mss.* (1977); "Theatrical Holdings of the Folger Shakespeare Library," *Performing Arts Resrcs.* (1974); "An Autograph Manuscript by Richard Hooker," *Mss.* (1974); jt. auth., *Elizabethan Handwriting, 1500–1650, Manual* (1966). **Activities:** 1, 12; 20, 39, 45; 55 **Addr.:** Folger Shakespeare Library, 201 E. Capitol St., Washington, DC 20003.

Yeargain, Eloisa Gomez (D. 12, 1946, Manila, Philippines) Actg. Unit Head, Univ. of CA, Los Angeles Grad. Sch. of Mgt. Lib., 1975–; Eth. Bk. Coord., Eth. Bk. Proj., Los Angeles Pub. Lib., 1975; Subj. Spec., Bus. and Econ., South. CA Answering Netwk., 1973–75; Ref. Libn., West Valley Reg. Branch, Los Angeles Pub. Lib., 1970–73. **Educ.:** St. Paul Coll., Manila, 1963–67, BS (Bus. Admin.); Univ. of CA, Los Angeles, 1969–70, MLS. Philippine Coll. of Cmrce., 1968, Cert. (Jnlsm.). **Orgs.:** SLA. Bus. Libns. Grp., Los Angeles. ALA: ACRL. Assn. for Asian Std.: Philippine Std. Grp. Econ. Hist. Assn. **Honors** Los Angeles Pub. Lib., Empl. Cmdn., 1972. **Pubns.:** Ed., *ETHNO-BIBLIO* (1972); ed., *GSM Library Guides* (1975–); reviews. **Activities:** 1, 12; 17, 39, 42; 51, 59 **Addr.:** UCLA Graduate School of Management Library, University of California, Los Angeles, 405 Hilgard Ave., Los Angeles, CA 90024.

Yeatman, Ted P. (O. 16, 1951, Nashville, TN) Asst. Libn., Current River Reg. Lib, 1977–; Per. Asst., Jt. Univ. Educ. Lib., TN, 1977. **Educ.:** George Peabody Coll., 1970–76, BA (Hist.), 1976–77, MLS. **Orgs.:** ALA: JMRT, Afflt. Cncl. (1978); MO Alternate Del. MO LA: Area Rep.; Exec. Bd., Outrch. RT (1978–81). Carter Cnty. (MO) Arts Socty.: Bd. of Advs. (1978–79). **Pubns.:** Ed., *The Big Springs Lib. Netwks. Dir. of Soc. Srvs.* (1978); "Unserved Area Gains New Libraries," *Show-Me Libs* (Je. 1979); various radio series. **Activities:** 9; 16, 27, 34; 67, 72, 92 **Addr.:** Box 481, Van Buren, MO 63965.

Yeatts, Wendell A., Jr. (O. 15, 1936, Richmond, VA) Head, Serials Conversion Proj., Cat. Dept., Purdue Univ. Libs., 1979–; Asst. Media Coord., Instr. Media Srv., Univ. of South. CA, 1976–78; Netwk. Cat. Spec., IN Coop. Lib. Srvs. Athrty., 1975–76; Catlgr. and Ref. Libn., Beverly Hills Pub. Lib., 1973–74; Head, Tech. Lib., Info. Corp., 1970–73; Head, Tech. Srvs. Dept., Biomed. Lib., Univ. of CA, 1967–70; Head, Data Prcs. Dept., Univ. of MO Lib., Columbia, 1965–67; Serials Libn., Baker Lib., Harvard Univ. Grad. Sch. of Bus., 1962–65. **Educ.:** Harvard Coll., 1954–58, BA (Eng., Psy.); U.S. Army Lang. Sch., Presidio of Monterey, CA, 1959–60, Cert. (Russ.); Simmons Coll., 1962–64, MSLS; **Orgs.:** SLA. **Pubns.:** Contrib., *The MARC Pilot Project: Final Report* (1968); *Experience with Library of Congress MARC Tapes, Los Angeles* (1969); "A Bucket of Information Science," *Lib. Jnl.* (Ja. 1966). **Activities:** 1, 9; 20, 44, 46; 52, 75, 80 **Addr.:** Purdue University Libraries and Audio-Visual Center, West Lafayette, IN 47907.

Yedlin, Deborah K. (Fe. 23, 1949, Pontiac, MI) Head of Tech. Srvs., WA Univ. Med. Sch. Lib., 1981–, Asst. Libn. for Tech. Srvs., 1975–81; Acq. Libn., 1973–75; Head Libn., Hazelwood Jr. HS, 1972–73. **Educ.:** Univ. of MI, 1967–71, BA (Eng., Jnlsm.); Wayne State Univ., 1971–72, MSLS. **Orgs.:** Med. LA. Hlth. Sci. OCLC Users Grp.: Vice Ch./Ch. (1980); Ch. (1981). St. Louis Med. Libns. Midcontl. Reg. Med. Lib. Grp. **Pubns.:** "Closing the Card Catalog," *Alternative Cat. Nsltr.* (D. 1979); "Information Needs of Health Science Librarians Using OCLC: A Survey," *Bltn. of the Med. LA* (Ja. 1979). **Activities:** 12; 17, 20, 46; 80, 91 **Addr.:** Washington University School of Medicine Library, 4580 Scott, St. Louis, MO 63110.

Yeh, Thomas Yen-Ran (S. 27, 1936, Nanking, China) Assoc. Prof. and Head, Cat. Dept., Ctrl. WA Univ. Lib., 1965. **Educ.:** Soochow Univ., 1954–58, BA (Pol. Sci.); Univ. of MN, 1960–62, MA (Intl. Rel.), 1963–65, MALS. **Orgs.:** ALA. Pac. NW LA. AAUP. **Pubns.:** "The Treatment of the American Indian in the Library of Congress E-F Schedule," *Lib. Resrcs. & Tech. Srvs.* (Spr. 1971); "Library Peer Evaluation for Promotion and Merit Increase: How It Works," *Coll. & Resrch. Libs.* (Jl. 1973). **Activities:** 1; 20; 54, 56, 92 **Addr.:** 2019 Mt. Daniels Dr., Ellensburg, WA 98926.

Special Subjects/Services: 50. Adult educ.; 51. Advert./Mktg.; 52. Aerosp.; 53. Agric.; 54. Area std.; 55. Arts/Hum.; 56. Autom.; 57. Bibl./Prtg.; 58. Bio. sci.; 59. Bus./Fin.; 60. Chem.; 61. Copyrt.; 62. Documtn.; 63. Educ.; 64. Engin.; 65. Env.; 66. Eth. grps.; 67. Film; 68. Food/Nutr.; 69. Geneal.; 70. Geo.; 71. Geol.; 72. Handcpd.; 73. Hist.; 74. Int. frdm.; 75. Info. sci.; 76. Insr.; 77. Law; 78. Legis.; 79. Math./Comp. sci.; 80. Med.; 81. Metals; 82. Nat. resrcs.; 83. Newsp.; 84. Nuc. sci.; 85. Oral hist.; 86. Petr./Energy; 87. Pharm.; 88. Phys./Astr./Math.; 89. Readg.; 90. Relig.; 91. Sci./Tech.; 92. Soc. sci.; 93. Telecom.; 94. Transp.; 95. (other).

Yeh, Yi Y. (Ja. 24, 1939, Kweiyang, Kweichow, China) Sch. Lib. Media Spec., Binghamton W. Jr. HS, 1978–; Sub. Sch. Libn., Binghamton and Vestal Sch., 1975–78; Asst. Libn., Univ. of New Haven, 1963–66; Asst. Libn., Princeton Univ., 1963; Asst. Biblgphr., Natl. Ctrl. Lib., 1960. **Educ.:** Natl. Taiwan Univ., 1956–60, BA; Columbia Univ., 1960–63, MSLS; SUNY, Binghamton, 1975–77 (Educ.); State Univ. Coll., Geneseo, 1978, (LS); NY State Pub. Libns. Prof. Cert.; NY State Sch. Media Spec. Cert. **Orgs.:** NY LA. ALA. **Pubns.:** "Meet John Newbery" slide (1977), "Tangrams" videotape (1977). **Activities:** 10; 15, 32, 46 **Addr.:** 4844 Country Club Rd., Binghamton, NY 13903.

Yellis, Jo L. (O. 8, 1943, Harrisburg, PA) Legis. Libn., Edison Electric Inst., 1979–; Libn., Amer. Pub. Power Assn., 1975–79; Head, Soc. Sci. Lib., Cath. Univ., 1973–75; Ref. Libn., Boston Univ., 1969–73. **Educ.:** Antioch Coll., 1961–66, BA (Hist.); Univ. of MI, 1968–69, AMLS. **Orgs.:** SLA. Law Libns. Socty. of DC. **Activities:** 12; 29, 39, 41; 78, 84, 86 **Addr.:** Edison Electric Institute, Legislative Library - 9th Floor, 1111 19th St. N.W., Washington, DC 20036.

Yen, Charles Chih-Hung (Ap. 20, 1937, Peijing, China) Chief Ref. Libn./Prof., Seton Hall Univ. Lib., 1967–; Catlgr., Univ. of New Orleans, 1964–67. **Educ.:** Tunghai Univ., Taiwan, 1956–60, BA (Eng. Lit.); Vanderbuilt Univ., 1962–64, MALS; Seton Hall Univ., 1968–70, MA (Asian Std.); Univ. of Chicago, 1969, Cert. (Chin. Libnshp.); NY Univ., 1970–, PhD in progress (Hist.). **Orgs.:** NJ Coll. Lib. Stans. Subcom. Chin.-Amer. LA. Seton Hall Univ. Lib. Fac. Caucus. **Honors:** Univ. of Chicago, Flwshp., 1969. **Pubns.:** "A Short History of the Seton Hall Asian Department," *Chin. Std. in the U.S.* (D. 1976); reviews. **Activities:** 1; 54, 92 **Addr.:** Reference Dept., McLaughlin Library, Seton Hall University, South Orange, NJ 07079.

Yen, David S. (S. 28, 1936) Dir., Law Lib., Prof. of Law, Southwest. Univ., 1973–; Asst. Prof., West. WA State Univ., 1972–73; Biblgphr.-Libn., CA State Univ., Los Angeles, 1969–72. **Educ.:** Baylor Univ., 1956–60, BA (Hist., Econ.); Amer. Bapt. Semy. of the W., 1960–64, MDiv (Biblical Theo.); Claremont Coll., 1968–76, PhD (Gvt.); Univ. of South. CA, 1969–70, MSLS; Claremont Coll., 1968–69, MA (Asian Std., Comp. Gvt.). **Orgs.:** AALL: SIS on Contemporary Soc. Problems (Ch., 1980). Intl. Assn. of Law Libs. South. CA Assn. of Law Libs. The Amer. Acad. of Pol. and Soc. Sci. The Acad. of Pol. Sci. **Honors:** Delta Theta Phi, 1977; Baylor Univ., O.S. Boggess Schol. Awd., 1959; Univ. of Cambridge (Eng.), LLB, hons., 1981. **Pubns.:** *Computer Law Bibliography* (1979); "Computer Related Evidence Law," *Comp. Law Jnl.* (Spr. 1979). **Activities:** 1; 17, 28, 36; 77 **Addr.:** Southwestern University School of Law Library, 675 S. Westmoreland Ave., Los Angeles, CA 90005.

Yeo, Ronald Frederick (N. 13, 1923, Woodstock, ON) Chief Libn., Regina Pub. Lib., 1972–; Pub. Srvs. Coord., North York Pub. Lib., 1968–71; Mgr., Trade Div., Collier-Macmillan Can. Ltd., 1963–65; Sales Mgr./Dir., Brit. Bk. Srvs., 1953–63. **Educ.:** Univ. of Toronto, 1946–48, BA, 1966–67, BLS. **Orgs.:** Can. LA: Pres. (1978–79). Can. Assn. of Pub. Libs.: Ch. (1975–76). Admin. of Lg. Pub. Libs.: Ch. (1973–74). SK LA. Regina Kiwanis Club. **Honors:** Can. Gvt., Silver Jubilee Medal, 1977. **Activities:** 9; 17 **Addr.:** Regina Public Library, 2311 - 12th Ave., Regina, SK S4P 0N3 Canada.

Yeoh, Josephine W. (Jl. 22, 1938, Moscow, U.S.S.R.) Dir., Med. Lib., Riverside Hosp., 1973–; Info. Sci., Dept. Head, Johns Hopkins Med. Inst., 1972–73. **Educ.:** Cornell Univ., 1956–60, BSc (Psy., Soclgy.); Case West. Rsv. Univ., 1971–72, MLS. **Orgs.:** Med. LA. Mid-OH Hlth. Sci. LA: Secy. (1976). Ctrl. OH Hosp. Lib. Cnsrtm.: Coord. (1977–). OH Hlth. Info. Org.: Treas. (1979–). Parent-Tchr. Assn.: Lcl. Bd. Del. (1976–77), Lcl. VP (1977–78), Lcl. Secy. (1978–79), Lcl. Treas. (1979–80). Natl. Org. of Women. **Honors:** Beta Phi Mu, 1972. **Pubns.:** "Use of the OCLC System in a Hospital Library," *Bltn. Med. LA* (Ja. 1976); "Where Is the Medical Librarian?" *Jnl. Amer. Med. Assn.* (Ja. 1976); "Clinical Medical Librarians," (Ag. 1976). "Planning a New or Remodelled Hospital Library," *Hosp. Topics* **Activities:** 12, 14-Hosp.; 15, 17, 39; 58, 80, 87 **Addr.:** Medical Library, Riverside Hospital, 3535 Olentangy River Rd., Columbus, OH 43214.

Yerkey, A. Neil (F. 4, 1938, Akron, OH) Asst. Prof., Sch. of Info. and Lib. Std., SUNY, Buffalo 1977–; Visit. Asst. Prof., Kent State Univ., 1976–77, Resrch. Libn., Univ. of Akron, 1972–73; Libn., Goodyr. Aerosp. Corp., 1966–72; Asst. Coord. for Grp. Srvs., Akron Pub. Lib., 1961–66. **Educ.:** Univ. of Akron, 1955–59, BA (Sp.); West. Rsv. Univ., 1961–62, MSLS; Kent State Univ., 1973–76, PhD (Comm.). **Orgs.:** SLA: Cleveland Chap. (Treas., 1972–73). ASIS. AALS. **Pubns.:** Jt. auth., *Cogent Communication; Overcoming Reading Overload* (1980); "Values of Library School Student, Faculty, and Librarians," *Jnl. of Educ. for Libnshp.* (Fall 1981); "Adoptability Criteria for Information Systems," *Jnl. of Lib. Autom.* (Je 1979). **Activities:** 11; 24, 26, 41; 56, 75, 93 **Addr.:** School of Information and Library Studies, Bell Hall 217, State University of New York at Buffalo, Buffalo, NY 14260.

Yim, Sr. Mary Ancilla, OSF (F. 17, 1927, Honolulu, HI) Assoc. Prof. and Dir. of Lib.-Media Ctr., Maria Regina Coll., 1975–; Asst. Prin., Oswego Cath. HS (NY), 1971–75; Prin., St. Joseph HS, Hilo, HI 1965–71, Tchr.-Libn., 1952–65. **Educ.:** Univ. of Dayton, 1957, BS (Educ.); Univ. of HI, 1961–69; Cath. Univ. of Amer., 1962, MSLS; SUNY, Oswego, 1971–75, CAS; **Orgs.:** ALA. NY LA. Cath. LA: Syracuse Chap., Pres. (1979–81); VP (1977–79). Libs. Unltd. Fac. Org.: Pres. (1979–80). **Activities:** 1; 17, 26; 63, 75, 76 **Addr.:** Maria Regina College Library, 1024 Court St., Syracuse, NY 13208.

Yirka, Carl A. (F. 28, 1952, Cleveland, OH) Head, Acq. Dept., Northwest. Univ. Law Sch. Lib., 1978–; Ref. Libn./Asst. Prof., LS, Chase Law Sch., North. KY Univ., 1976–78; Circ. Libn., Cincinnati Law LA, 1975–76. **Educ.:** Columbia Univ., 1970–74, AB (Eng.); Case West. Rsv. Univ., 1974–75, MSLS. **Orgs.:** AALL: Com. on Rel. with Publshrs. and Dlrs. *Pubns. Clearinghse. Bltn.* Ed. (1979–81), (Ch., 1981–82), Chicago Assn. of Law Libns. **Activities:** 1; 15, 29, 44; 77 **Addr.:** Northwestern University, Law School Library, 357 E. Chicago Ave., Chicago, IL 60611.

Yirka, Manja (Ja. 18, 1951, Cleveland, OH) Ref. Libn., Dana Med. Lib., Univ. of VT, 1977–, Cat. Libn., 1973–77. **Educ.:** Case West. Rsv. Univ., 1968–72, BA (Russ.), 1972–73, MSLS (Hlth. Sci. Libnshp.). **Orgs.:** Med. LA. N. Atl. Hlth. Sci. Libs. **Activities:** 1, 12; 39, 58, 80 **Addr.:** Dana Medical Library, Given Bldg., University of Vermont, Burlington, VT 05405.

Yliniemi, Hazel A. (Ja. 30, 1941, Rural Becker Cnty., MN) Dir., Instr. Resrcs., Fargo Pub. Sch., 1980–; Libn./AV Dir., S. HS, 1973–80; Eng. Tchr., Indp. Sch., Carlton, MN, 1969–71; Eng. Tchr., Hibbing, MN, 1967–69. **Educ.:** Moorhead State Univ., 1964–67, BS (Eng.); Mankato State Univ., 1972–73, MS (Media Educ.). **Orgs.:** ALA: AASL. AECT. YA Srvs. Div. ND LA: Sch. Sect. (Ch., 1979). MN Educ. Media Org. ND Assn. of Tchr. Educ. Valley Readg. Assn. **Honors:** Delta Kappa Gamma. **Activities:** 10; 17, 32, 35; 63, 89, 93 **Addr.:** 341 Prairiewood Cir. #103, Fargo, ND 58103.

Yngve, Victor H. (Jl. 5, 1920, Niagara Falls, NY) Prof. of Info. Sci., Univ. of Chicago, 1965–; Asst Prof., MA Inst. of Tech., 1953–65. **Educ.:** Antioch Coll., 1938–43, BS (Phys.); Univ. of Chicago, 1946–53, PhD (Phys.). **Pubns.:** *Computer Programming with COMIT II* (1972); "Stoic Influences in Librarianship: A Critique," *Jnl. Lib. Hist.* (1981); "A Model and an Hypothesis for Language Structure," *Procs. Amer. Phil. Socty.* (1960). **Activities:** 11; 41; 63, 75 **Addr.:** University of Chicago, 1100 E. 57th St., Chicago, IL 60637.

Yochim, Charmaine Stander (S. 29, 1940, Saginaw, MI) Coord. of Tech. Srvs., Prince George's Cmnty. Coll., 1967–; Ref. Libn., Arlington Cnty. Pub. Libs., 1966–67. **Educ.:** Univ. of MI, 1960–62, BA (Hist.), 1966, MA (LS). **Orgs.:** MD LA: Pres. (1978–79); Acad. and Resrch. Libs. Div. (Ch., 1976); Fed. Rel. Com. (Ch., 1972–74); PR Com. (Ch., 1975–76). DC LA. Legis. Day Com. (Ch., 1976); Legis. Com. (Ch., 1979–81). ALA. **Honors:** Beta Phi Mu; MD LA, Awd., 1981. **Activities:** 1; 15, 19, 20; 67 **Addr.:** Learning Resources Center, Prince George's Community College, Largo, MD 20772.

Yoder, Myra Suzanne (Je. 6, 1949, Gainesville, FL) Ref. Libn., Assoc. Univ. Libn., Univ. of FL (Gainesville), 1982–; Assoc. Univ. Libn., State Univ. Syst. of FL, Ext. Lib., 1979–81; Asst. Libn., Coll. of Dsgn., Arch. and Art, Univ. of Cincinnati, 1975–77; Libn., Pub. Lib. of Cincinnati and Hamilton Cnty., 1973–74; Asst. Libn., Robert Manning Strozier Lib., FL State Univ., 1973. **Educ.:** Univ. of MD, 1967–69; Univ. of S. FL, 1969–71, BA (Art Hist.); FL State Univ., 1972, MSLS; Univ. of Cincinnati, 1974 (Art Hist.). **Orgs.:** SLA: FL Chap. Advert. Mgr. (1979–81), Secy. (1980–81), Pres.-Elect (1981–). FL LA. ARLIS/SE. SELA. **Activities:** 1, 12; 17, 39, 46; 50, 55, 63 **Addr.:** University of Florida, Extension Library, 1500 Norman Hall, Gainesville, FL 32611.

Yoho, Betty E. (N. 6, 1921, Warren, OH) Libn., Lombardy Sch., 1957–; Libn., Oak Grove Sch., 1951–57; Tchr., Drew Sch. for Girls, 1948–51. **Educ.:** OH Wesleyan Univ., 1945, BA (Span.); Katharine Gibbs Sch., NY, 1949; Drexel Univ., 1965, MSLS; Univ. of WI, 1966; NDEA Inst. (Lib. Non-Print Media). **Orgs.:** ALA. DE Sch. LA: Pres. DE LA: Treas.; Pres. Natl. Educ. Assn. DE State Educ. Assn. New Castle Cnty. Ed. Assn. **Honors:** Phi Beta Kappa, 1943. **Activities:** 10 **Addr.:** 2300 Riddle Ave., Wilmington, DE 19806.

Yontz, Bob, Jr. (Ap. 14, 1939, Aurora, IL) Head, Serials, Murray State Univ., 1979–; Lib. Dir., Westmar Coll., 1977–79; Acq. Libn., Furman Univ., 1976–77; AV Srvs. Libn., Newberry Coll., 1974–76. **Educ.:** East. IL Univ., 1963–66, BEd (Hist.), 1967, MEd (Hist.); Univ. of IL, 1973–74, MLS. **Orgs.:** SELA. KY LA. **Activities:** 1; 15, 29, 44; 90, 95-Sports. **Addr.:** Serials Dept., University Library, Murray State University, Murray, KY 42071.

York, Grace Ann (Ja. 4, 1946, Detroit, MI) Docum. Ref. Libn., Univ. of MI, 1975–, Asst. Docum. Ref. Libn., 1970–75, Serials Catlgr., 1969–70. **Educ.:** Wayne State Univ., 1963–68, BA (Hist.); Univ. of MI, 1968–69, AMLS. **Orgs.:** ALA. GODORT of MI: VP (1978–79). Gamma Delta: Natl. Secy. (1966–67). Common Cause: Dist. Mem. Rcrt. Ch. (1975). **Honors:** Phi Beta Kappa, 1967; Phi Kappa Phi, 1970; Beta Phi Mu, 1969; Sigma Kappa. **Pubns.:** Jt. auth., *Documents Handbook* (1973); *The American Revolution, 1763-1783: Selected Reference Works* (1976); "Michigan Legislative Histories" pamphlet (1979). **Activities:** 1; 29, 39; 78, 92 **Addr.:** 405 Nob Hill Pl., Apt. 6, Ann Arbor, MI 48103.

York, Michael C. (Ja. 2, 1947, Newton, MA) Dir., Merrimack Valley Coll. Lib., 1981–; Asst. Dir., Castleton State Coll. Lib., VT, 1977–81; Ref. Libn., Ithaca Coll., 1973–77. **Educ.:** Univ. of NH, 1968–71, BA (Hist.); LA State Univ., 1971–72, MSLS. **Orgs.:** VT LA: Ch., Bylaws Com. (1980–81). **Addr.:** Merrimack Valley College, Manchester, NH 03102.

Yost, Charles E., S.C.J. (My. 4, 1932, Pittsburgh, PA) Dir. of Fund Raising Ofc., 1981–; Head Libn., Sacred Heart Sch. of Theo., 1963–; Prof. of Pastoral Std., Libn., St. John Coll., Indonesia, 1962–63. **Educ.:** Sacred Heart Monastery, 1951–55, (Hum.), 1955–59, STB (Theo.); Cath. Univ., 1959–60, STL (Theo.), 1960–61, MSLS. **Orgs.:** Cath. Hist. Assn. Cath. LA. ALA. Amer. Phil. Socty. **Pubns.:** *Preaching to the Sick* (1975); *Notes for Advent Homilies* (1972); "Problem Areas in Religious Living," *Homiletic and Pastoral Review* (F. 1973); "The Major Seminary Library," *Cath. Educ. Review* (O. 1961). **Activities:** 1, 2; 15, 20, 41; 50, 90 **Addr.:** Sacred Heart Monastery, 7335 S. Lovers Ln. Rd., Hales Corners, WI 53130.

Young, Alda Helena (Ag. 7, 1921, Weymouth, MA) Supvsr. of Lib./Media Srvs., Wheaton Pub. Sch., 1977–, Dir. of Lib. Srvs., 1969–77, Lib. Consult., 1964–68. **Educ.:** North. Bapt. Semy., 1948, BRE; North. IL Univ., 1959, MS (Educ.), 1968, MA (LS). **Orgs.:** ALA. IL LA: Bd. of Dirs. IL Assn. for Media in Educ.: Pres. (1977–78). Stepping Stone Day Care Ctr.: Bd. of Dirs. **Honors:** Delta Kappa Gamma. **Pubns.:** "Cooperation: Try It, You'll Like It," *IL Libs.* (My. 1972); "Literary Gems for Children," *Christ. Bookseller* (S. 1978). **Activities:** 10; 17, 32, 46; 63, 89 **Addr.:** 1490 Briar Cove, Wheaton, IL 60187.

Young, Amy Y. (Je. 20, 1948, Canton, China) Sr. Libn./Catlgr., Queens Boro. Pub. Lib., 1973–; Gen. Ref. Asst., Sci. and Tech. Div., 1972–73; Libn., Chem Systs., Inc., 1971–72; Asst. Sci.-Eng. Lib., Univ. of NM, 1970–71. **Educ.:** OK Bapt. Univ., 1965–69, BSc (Bio.); Univ. of CA, Berkeley, 1969–70, MLS. **Orgs.:** ALA. AAUP. **Activities:** 9; 20; 58, 60, 88 **Addr.:** 33 Hitching Post Ln., Glen Cove, NY 11542.

Young, Arthur Price (Jl. 29, 1940, Boston, MA) Dean, Univ. Lib., Univ. of RI, 1981–; Asst. Dean for Pub. Srvs., Univ. of AL, 1976–81; Head of Reader Srvs. and Soc. Sci. Bibl., SUNY, Cortland, 1969–72. **Educ.:** Tufts Univ., 1958–62, BA (Pol. sci.); Univ. of MA, 1962–64, MAT (Hist. and Educ.); Syracuse Univ., 1968–69, MSLS; Univ. of IL, 1972–76, PhD (Lib. Sci.). **Orgs.:** ALA: Bibl. Instr. Sect., Com. on Educ. for Bibl. Instr. (1977–80). AL LA. NY LA. RI LA. *Jnl. of Lib. Hist.*: Adv. Ed. Bd. (1979–). **Honors:** Phi Kappa Phi, 1974; Beta Phi Mu, 1969. **Pubns.:** *Books for Sammies: The American Library Association and World War I* (1981); "And Gladly Teach: Bibliographic Instruction and the Library," *Advncs. in Libnshp.* (1980); "Aftermath of a Crusade," *Lib. Qtly.* (Ap. 1980); "Bibliographic Instruction," *Progress in Educating the Library User* (1978); "Scholarly Book Reviewing in America," *LIBRI* (S. 1975). **Activities:** 1; 15, 17, 39; 57, 74, 92 **Addr.:** 12 Grey Birch Ct., Peace Dale, RI 02879.

Young, Bernadette C. (S. 7, 1909, Chicago, IL) Libn., St Daniel Church Lib., Clarkston, MI, 1969–; Tchr., Detroit Bd. of Educ., 1929–73; Libn., St Lucian Lib., 1957–63. **Educ.:** Marygrove Coll., 1927; Detroit Tchrs. Coll., 1927–29, Cert. (Educ.); Wayne State Univ., 1929–44. **Orgs.:** Cath. LA: MI Chap., Par. Sect. (Ch., 1959–63); Par. and Cmnty. Lib. Sect., Ch., (1963–64). Vice-Ch. (1972–74). Luth. Church LA. CS LA. **Honors:** Cath. LA, Aggiornamento Awd., 1981. **Pubns.:** Contrib., "Catholic Library Association Parish and Community Libraries Section," *Church and Synagogue Libs.* (1980); jt. auth., *Guide for the Organization and Operation of Religious Resource Centers* (1977); *Check It!* (1961–64); "Needs Assessment," *Cath. Lib. World.* (S. 1976). **Activities:** 12; 16, 21, 32; 90 **Addr.:** 3990 Sashabaw Rd., Clarkston, MI 48016.

Young, Betty I. (Mr. 23, 1928, Elk Falls, KS) Head of Circ. Dept., Actg. Head of E. Campus Lib., Duke Univ., 1978–, Head of Circ. Dept., 1970–78. **Educ.:** Univ. of NC, Chapel Hill, 1964–68, AB (Hist.), 1968–70, MSLS. **Orgs.:** ALA: Prog. Com. of Lib. Hist. RT (1977–78). SE LA. NC LA: Ad Hoc Com. for Reorg. (1974–75). Univ. of NC Sch. of LS Alum. Assn.: Pres. (1977–78). Carolinas Symp. on Brit. Std.: Bibl. Com. (1976–); Exec. Bd. (1979–82). **Honors:** Phi Beta Kappa, 1968; Beta Phi Mu, 1970. **Pubns.:** *The Library of the Woman's College, Duke University, 1930-1972* (1978); "Circulation Service. Is It Meeting the User's Needs," *Jnl. of Acad. Libnshp.* (Jl. 1976); "Josephus Larned and the Public Library Movement," *Jnl. of Lib. Hist.* (O. 1975); jt. auth., *A Methodist Guide to London and the Southeast* (1980); "Lillian Baker Griggs," *Dictionary of American Library Biography* (1978). **Activities:** 1; 17, 22; 55, 57 **Addr.:** 2929 Welcome Drive, Durham, NC 27705.

Young, Cecil T. (O. 27, 1903, Maynard, IA) Bd., Frnds. of Minneapolis Pub. Lib., 1974–; Bd., Frnds. of Libs., U.S.A., 1979–;

PROFESSIONAL ACTIVITIES: Institutions: 1. Acad. lib.; 2. Arch.; 3. Assn.; 4. Fed./Gvt. lib.; 5. Inst. lib.; 6. Mfr./Suppl.; 7. Milit. lib.; 8. Musm.; 9. Pub. lib.; 10. Sch. lib.; 11. Sch. of lib. sci.; 12. Spec. lib.; 13. State lib.; 14. (other). **Functions/Activities:** 15. Acq./Col. dev.; 16. Adult srvs.; 17. Admin.; 18. Apprais.; 19. Archit./Bldgs.; 20. Cat./Class.; 21. Chld. srvs.; 22. Circ.; 23. Cons./Pres.; 24. Consult.; 25. Cont. ed.; 26. Educ. lib. sci.; 27. Ext. srvs.; 28. Fund/Grants; 29. Gvt. pubs.; 30. Indx./Abs.; 31. Instr. lib. use; 32. Media srvs.; 33. Micro.; 34. Netwks./Coop.; 35. Persnl.; 36. PR; 37. Publshg.; 38. Recs. mgt.; 39. Ref. srvs.; 40. Repro.; 41. Resrch.; 42. Review.; 43. Secur.; 44. Serials; 45. Spec. col.; 46. Tech. srvs.; 47. Trustees/Bds.; 48. YA srvs.; 49. (other).

Pres., Frnds. of Minneapolis Pub. Lib., 1975–79. **Educ.:** Univ. of IA, 1922–25, BA (Econ.). **Orgs.:** ALA: PR (1978). **Honors:** Phi Beta Kappa, 1925; Ord. of Artus, 1924. **Activities:** 9 **Addr.:** 1770 Bryant Ave. S., Minneapolis, MN 55403.

Young, Charles F. J. (Ja. 1, 1936, Nassau Cnty., NY) Head, Ctrl. Lib., Queens Boro. Pub. Lib., 1978–; Head, Soc. Sci. Div., 1976–78, Admin. Asst. to Dir., 1967–76, Head, various divs., 1963–67. **Educ.:** City Coll., NY, 1953–57, BA (Soc. Sci.); Columbia Univ., 1958–60, MSLS. **Orgs.:** ALA. NY LA. Linnaean Socty. of NY. Royal Socty. for the Protection of Birds. **Activities:** 2, 9; 16, 17, 39; 59, 82, 92 **Addr.:** 11 Millford Dr., Lattingtown, Locust Valley, NY 11560.

Young, Christina Carr (D. 20, 1928, Baltimore, MD) Consult., Natl. Comsn. on Lib., Info. Sci., 1977–; Lectr., George Washington Univ., 1977–; Instr., Cath. Univ., 1974–76; Educ. Spec., Pub. Sch. of DC, 1972–74. **Educ.:** Boston Univ., 1945–49, AB (Bio.); Cath. Univ., 1965–68, MSLS. **Orgs.:** ALA: AASL; Task Frc. I (1970–73). DC Assn. of Sch. Libns.: Pres. (1969–71). DC LA: Chld. and YA Discuss. Grp. (Ch., 1973). Chld. Bk. Gld. of DC: Prog. Ch. (1979). Alum. Assn. of LS of the Cath. Univ.: Pres. (1979–80). Delta Kappa Gamma: Resrch. Com. (Ch., 1979–80). Assn. for Childhood Educ. Intl.: "Books for Children" Com. (Ch., 1976–78). **Honors:** DC Assn. of Sch. Libns., Merit. Srvs., 1971. **Activities:** 21, 24, 34 **Addr.:** 1253 Girard St. N.E., Washington, DC 20017.

Young, Diana Dent (Je. 28, 1944, Chicago, IL) Pub. Lib. Consult. for Chld. Srvs., NC State Lib., 1975–; Chld. Libn., Dallas Pub. Lib., 1970–75, YA Libn., 1969–70; Head, Ref. and Adult Srvs., Lubbock City-Cnty. Libs., 1966–67. **Educ.:** Henderson Cnty. Jr. Coll., 1962–64, AA (Math); N. TX State Univ., 1965–66, BS (LS), 1968, MLS. **Orgs.:** ALA: Cncl. (1978–81); ALSC, Bd. (1978–80); PLA: Ed. Bd.; Srv. to Chld. (1976–82); AASL, Afflt. Cncl. (1981–83). SE LA: Sch. and Chld. Sect. (Ch., 1981–83). **Pubns.:** *Small Public Libraries Series #6, Serving Children in Small Public Libraries* (1981); "Literacy, Libraries and the Whole Child in North Carolina," *Cath. Lib. World* (S. 1980); "I Know a Book," *NC Libs.* (Spr. 1978); "We Can Grow," *Sch. Lib. Jnl.* (My. 1977); "People Puppets and You," *Top of the News* (Ja. 1975); ed., "Service to Children," clmn. *Pub. Libs.* (1976–). **Activities:** 9, 13; 21, 24, 42; 57, 61, 89 **Addr.:** North Carolina State Library, 109 E. Jones, Raleigh, NC 27611.

Young, Frances Elizabeth (Je. 5, 1954, Point Pleasant, NJ) Ref. Libn., The Frick Art Ref. Lib., 1981–; Sr. Art Libn., Newark Pub. Lib., 1978–81; Asst. Art Libn., Rutgers Univ. Art Lib., 1976–78. **Educ.:** Douglass Coll., 1974–76, BA (Art Hist.); Rutgers Univ., 1976–78, MLS. **Orgs.:** ARLIS/NA: NJ Chap. (Treas., 1980–81). **Honors:** Beta Phi Mu. **Pubns.:** Reviews. **Activities:** 9; 15, 30, 39; 55 **Addr.:** 1256 Waverly Pl. Apt. B-1, Elizabeth, NJ 07208.

Young, Harold Chester (O. 26, 1932, Cambridge, MA) Dir., Wilson Lib., Univ. of MN, 1977; Prof., 1975–77; Dir., Lrng. Resrcs. Ctr., Washtenaw Cmnty. Coll., 1966–69; Ref. Libn., Actg. Dir., Univ. of MI, Dearborn, Lib., 1962–66; Consult., Gale. Resrch. Co., 1961–75. **Educ.:** Boston Univ., 1954–58, BA (Hist.); Univ. of MI, 1960, AMLS, 1966, MBA, 1974, PhD. **Orgs.:** ALA. SLA. ASIS. MN LA: Legis. Com. Walker Art. Ctr. Frnds. of Minneapolis Pub. Lib. **Pubns.:** *Planning, Programming and Budgeting Systems in University Libraries* (1976); *Subject Dir. of Spec. Libs.* (1975); *Dir. of Spec. Libs. and Info. Ctrs.* (1974). **Activities:** 1, 12; 17, 24, 37; 56, 57, 74 **Addr.:** 313 Farmdale Rd., Hopkins, MN 55343.

Young, James Bradford (N. 3, 1951, Princeton, NJ) Asst. Prof., Asst. Msc. Cat. Libn., Univ. of IL, 1979–; Msc. Cat. Libn., South. IL Univ., 1976–78. **Educ.:** McGill Univ., 1970–74, BA (Msc.); Emory Univ., 1975–76, MLS. **Orgs.:** Msc. LA: Midwest Chap. Msc. OCLC Users' Grp. Amer. Musicological Socty. **Activities:** 1; 20; 55 **Addr.:** Music Cataloguing Dept., 2150 Music Bldg., University of Illinois, Urbana, IL 61801.

Young, Jerry F. (S. 3, 1937, Springfield, MO) Dir., Anoka Cnty. Lib., 1969–; Pub. Lib. Consult., WI Dept. of Pub. Instr., Dir. for Lib. Srvs., 1966–69; Dir., Rolling Hills Reg. Lib., 1961–66. **Educ.:** SW MO State Univ., 1955–60, AB (Eng.); Univ. of Denver, 1960–61, MALS. **Orgs.:** ALA. MN LA: Pres. (1979–80); VP (1978–79). MN Lib. Film Cir.: Pres. (1975–76). MN LA: Pub. Lib. Div. (Pres., 1974). Blaine Area Cham. of Cmrce.: VP (1978–79), Bd. of Dirs. (1978–82). Cir. Pines-Lexington Lions Club: Pres. (1979–80); VP (1977–79); Bd. of Dirs. (1975–77). Blaine Chrt. Comsn. (1976–80). **Activities:** 9; 17, 19, 24 **Addr.:** 4673 104th Ave. N.E., Circle Pines, MN 55014.

Young, K. Penny (Jl. 27, 1947, Cincinnati, OH) Asst. Dir. for Supportive Srvs., Med. Ctr. Libs., Univ. of Cincinnati, 1976–; Actg. Dir., 1980, Coord. for Info. Srvs., 1974–76, Libn., Coll. of Med., 1972–74. **Educ.:** Coll. of Wooster, 1965–69, BA (Bio., Relig.); Univ. of IL, 1969–70, MS (Biomed. Info. Sci.). **Orgs.:** SLA: Cincinnati Chap. (Pres., 1978–79). ASIS: South. OH Chap. Med. LA. **Honors:** Coll. of Wooster, 1966; Beta Phi Mu, 1970. **Pubns.:** Jt. auth., "New Information Transfer Therapies," *Lib. Trends* (1974). **Activities:** 1, 12; 17, 31, 34; 80 **Addr.:** Medical Center Libraries, 231 Bethesda Ave., Cincinnati, OH 45267.

Young, Margaret Labash (Ag. 17, 1926, Bridgeport, CT) Libn., Salzburg Sem. in Amer. Std., Salzburg, Austria, 1981–83; Ed., Gale Resrch. Co., 1972–81; Indxr., Ford Motor Co., 1964–72; Ref., Cir. Libn., Univ. of MI, Dearborn, 1959–62. **Educ.:** Cornell Univ., 1944–48, BA (Gvt.); Univ. of MI, Ann Arbor, 1958–59, AMLS; Harvard Univ., 1959–64, (Adult Educ.). **Orgs.:** SLA: MI Chap., Bltn. Ed. (1967–68). Amer. Fld. Srv. Sel.: Coord. Walker Art Ctr. Guthrie Thea. Cncl. for Basic Educ. **Pubns.:** *Dir. of Spec. Libs. and Info. Ctrs.* (1981). *Subj. Dir. Spec. Libs.* (1977). **Activities:** 12; 30, 34, 37; 59, 92 **Addr.:** Gale Research Company, 8800 Highway 7, Suite 300, Minneapolis, MN 55426.

Young, Marna Jo (N. 21, 1948, Neosho, MO) Admin. Srvs. Libn., Wichita State Univ., 1977–; Head, Sci. and Tech. Libs., Univ. of KS, 1971–77, Asst. Sci. Libn., 1970–71. **Educ.:** Univ. of MO, Columbia, 1966–68, BA (Zlgy.), 1969–70, MALS; Wichita State Univ., 1978–, MBA. **Orgs.:** Med. LA: Pharm. Grp. (Ch., 1972–73). ALA. KS LA: Coll. and Univ. Lib. Sect. (1977–80). Amer. Assn. of Colls. of Pharm.: Del. (1975–77). **Honors:** Beta Phi Mu, 1971. **Pubns.:** "Literature of Pharmacognosy and Medicinal Chemistry," *Amer. Jnl. of Pharm. Educ.* (1972). **Activities:** 1, 12; 22; 56, 91 **Addr.:** Wichita State University Library, Box 68, Wichita State University, Wichita, KS 67208.

Young, Sr. Mary Bernita (O. 29, 1905, Ennismore, ON) Archvst., Srs. of St. Joseph of Toronto Arch., 1974–; Supvsr. of Schs., 1965–74; Vice-Prin., Danis Morris HS, 1962–65; Prin., Srs. of St. Joseph's HS, Islington, 1957–62, Libn., 1950–57; Tchr., St. Michael's Coll., Univ. of Toronto, 1931–49. **Educ.:** Univ. of Toronto, 1922–27, BA (Eng., Fr.), 1939, MA (Eng. Lang., Lit.); various crs. **Orgs.:** Assn. Can. Archvsts. Toronto Area Archvst. Grp. Can. Cath. Hist. Assn. ON Hist. Socty. Can. Coll. of Tchrs. Superannuated Tchrs. of ON. Eng. Cath. Tchrs. of ON. **Pubns.:** Various articles, transls. from Fr. **Activities:** 2; 39; 90 **Addr.:** 3377 Bayview Ave., Willowdale, Toronto, ON M2M 3S4 Canada.

Young, Micki Jo (N. 16, 1939, Kansas City, KS) Lib. Systs. Anal., Cap Gemini, Inc, 1980–; Pres./Owner, Resrcs. on Request Ltd., 1976–; Lib. Consult., Informatics Inc, 1975–76; Coord., Media Prcs. Srvs., North. VA Cmnty. Coll., 1970–75. **Educ.:** TX Christ. Univ., 1957–61, BS (Elem. Educ.); Cath. Univ., 1968–75, MSLS, PhD (Educ. Tech.). **Orgs.:** ALA: LITA, Tech. Stans. Com. (1978–80). Assoc. Info. Mgrs. Natl. Assn. of Women Bus. Owners. **Honors:** Beta Phi Mu. **Pubns.:** *Introduction to Minicomputers in Federal Libraries* (1978); *A Program for Quality in Continuing Education for Information, Library, and Media Personnel; Final Report* (1980); "The Library and the Computer Center," *Jnl. of Lib. Autom.* (D. 1979). **Activities:** 24, 25, 46; 50, 56, 62 **Addr.:** Resources on Request Ltd., P.O. Box 2249, Reston, VA 22090.

Young, Olivia K. (S. 3, 1922, Benton, AR) Dir., Lib. Dev. and Ext. Srvs., TN State Lib. and Arch., 1972–; Consult., Pub. Libs. Sect., 1970–72; Dir., Watauga Reg. Lib. Syst., 1963–70; Chief Libn., U.S. Army, Ft. Stewart, 1958–63. **Educ.:** TN Tech. Inst., 1938–42, BS (Fr.); George Peabody Coll. for Tchrs., 1945–46, BSLS. **Orgs.:** ALA. SELA. TN LA. **Activities:** 13; 17, 24, 27 **Addr.:** 511 Capitol Towers, Nashville, TN 37219.

Young, Peter R. (Ag. 13, 1944, Washington, DC) Cust. Srvs. Ofcr., Cat. Distribution Srv., Lib. of Congs., 1980–; Lib. Systs. Anal., C L Systs., Inc, 1976–80; Asst. Dir., Grand Rapids Pub. Lib., 1978; Asst. Libn. for Pub. Srvs., Rice Univ. Libs., 1975–76; Ref. Libn., Head Catlgr., Franklin and Marshall Coll. Lib., 1971–75. **Educ.:** Coll. of Wooster, OH, 1961–66, AB (Phil.); Columbia Univ., 1967–68, MSLS; George Washington Univ., 1966–67 (Phil.). **Orgs.:** ALA: LAMA/Stats. Sect., Circ. Stats. Com. (1978–). MI WHCLIS: Strg. Com. (1979). Fed. Docum. Wkshp., Reg. Six, Prog. Plng. Com. (1976). **Pubns.:** Various sps. **Activities:** 1, 9; 17, 23, 31; 56, 75 **Addr.:** 338 Gambrills Rd., Gambrills, MD 21054.

Young, Rosemary M. (D. 13, 1923, Independence, MO) Coord. of Chld. and YA Srvs., Denver Pub. Lib., 1970–, Libn. III, Head of YA Lib., 1968–70, Libn. II, Chld. Lib., 1967–68; Asst. to Dir., Bibl. Ctr. for Resrch., Rocky Mt. Reg., 1951–54; Libn. I, Child. Libn., Denver Pub. Lib, 1950; Sr. Asst. to Chld. Libn., West Branch of KS City Pub. Lib., 1945–49. **Educ.:** Kansas City Tchrs. Coll., 1940–44, BS (Educ.); Univ. of Denver, 1946–50, MLS. **Orgs.:** ALA: Conf. Simplification Com. (1979–); YASD, Pres. (1977–78), Coms. Media Sel. and Usages, Re-eval. of Goals and Objectives. CO LA. CO Educ. Media Assn. Mt. Plains LA. **Honors:** DCIRA, Grt. Increase Cncl. Mem., 1980. **Pubns.:** *Pres.'s Nsltr., CO LA* (1973); "The Young Adult Librarian as an Administrator," *Drexel Lib. Qlty.* (Ja. 1978). **Activities:** 9; 21, 36, 48; 93 **Addr.:** Denver Public Library – Library Administrative Center, 3840 York St., Bldg. 2, Unit I, Denver, CO 80205.

Young, Stephen R. (My. 31, 1943, Cleveland, OH) Head, Rare Bk. Cat. Div., Yale Univ. Lib., 1979–, Cat. Libn., 1975–79, Ref. Libn., 1973–75; Tech. Asst., Columbia Univ. Msc. Lib., 1970–73. **Educ.:** Amherst Coll., 1961–65, BA (Msc); Columbia Univ., 1966–69, MA, 1971–73, MSLS. **Orgs.:** ALA: ACRL Rare Bks. and Mss. Div., Lcl. Arrange. for Conf. (Co.-Ch., 1978). NY Tech. Srvs. Libns.: Cit. Com., Ch. (1977–78), Secy. (1979–80). Yale Bibliophiles: Secy., (1975–76); Pres., (1976–77, 1979–82), Co-Pres. (1977–78). **Activities:** 1; 20, 45 **Addr.:** Rare Book Cataloguing Division - SML, Yale University Library, New Haven, CT 06520.

Young, Tommie Morton (Ap. 20, 19–, Nashville, TN) Dir., Instr. Srvs., NC A & T State Univ., 1975–; Asst. Prof., Prog. Dir., NC Ctrl. Univ, Durham, 1969–74; Assoc. Prof., Univ. of AR, Pine Bluff, 1966–69; Asst. Prof., LS, Atlanta Univ., 1964–66; Asst. Prof., Dir. of Lib. Educ., South. Univ., 1961–64; Instr., Coord. LS, Prairie View Coll., 1959–61; Chief Libn., Wilberforce Univ., 1961; Head Ref., Serial Docum., TN State Univ., 1956–59. **Educ.:** TN State Univ., 1948–51, BA (Eng.); Peabody Coll., 1954–55, MALS; Duke Univ., 1972–77, PhD (Educ.); Univ. of OK. **Orgs.:** ALA: Persnl. Com., (1964); Chld. Srv. Com. (1973–75); ACRL. Guilford Cnty. Lib. Club: Pres. AAUW. Zeta Phi Beta: Reg. Ch., Pol. Action. **Honors:** NAACP, Cert. Apprec., 1972; Zeta Phi Beta Woman of the Yr. Awd., 1976; Beta Phi Mu. **Pubns.:** *Multicultural Academic Library Service...* (1976); *See How They Learn* (1973); "Your Child and Reading," *LA Educ. Assn.* (1961); "Parent Programs," *Start Early for Early Start* (1975); "Afro-American Genealogy," "Sexism and Human Rights," *Proj. Afro-Amer. Geneal.* (1979). **Activities:** 1, 2; 26, 28, 41; 66, 69, 85 **Addr.:** P. O. Box B-20, North Carolina A & T State University, Greensboro, NC 27411.

Young, Virginia G. (Ja. 16, 1919, Mountain View, MO) Ch., Bd., Coord. Bd. for Higher Educ., MO State Lib., 1974–80; Ch., Bd., Columbia Pub. Lib., 1951–65; Guest Lectr., Columbia Univ., Univ. NC, LA State Univ., Univ. of MO, Univ. of CO, Case West. Rsv., Sch. of Lib. Srv., Visit. Com., 1968–74. **Educ.:** SW MO State Univ., Univ. of MO, 1936–39, AB (Eng.); Univ. of OK, 1939–40, MLS; Tariko Coll., 1979, Doctor Humane Letters. **Orgs.:** WHCOLIS: Adv. Com. BALA: ALTA, Pres. (1959–61); Educ. Com. (1979–80); White Hse. Conf. Com. (1977–80); Legis. (1960–69); Com. on Org. (1962–); Intl. Rel. (1970–74); Awds. (1968–72). IFLA: Del. (1965–80). Amer. Lib. in Paris: Trustee (1968–73). MO LA: Pres. (1967–68). Carnegie Fndn. for Advnc. of Tchg. Com. on Governance and Higher Educ. Assn. of Governing Bd.: Mentor (1977–). MO Press-Bar Comsn.: Secy. (1974–). Leag. of Women Voters of MO: Bd. (1943, 1974). Columbia Leag. of Women Voters: Pres. (1943–45). **Honors:** Univ. of OK, Outstan. Srv. to Libnshp., 1979; ALA, Trustee Cit. of Merit, 1962; MO LA Achvmt. Awd., 1956. **Pubns.:** *Trustee of a Small Public Library* (1962); *The Library Trustee* (1964); various articles in natl., intl. and state jnls. **Activities:** 9, 13; 24, 26, 47; 63, 78, 89 **Addr.:** 10 E. Parkway Dr., Columbia, MO 65201.

Younger, Jennifer A. (N. 3, 1947, Milwaukee, WI) Prin. Catlgr., Univ. of WI, Madison, 1977–; Cat. Ed., Northwest. Univ., 1974–77; Catlgr., U.S. Dept. of State, 1971–73. **Educ.:** Univ. of WI, Madison, 1965–69, BA (Hist.), 1969–71, MALS. **Orgs.:** ALA: RTSD; Subj. Anal. Com. (1977–79, 1979–81)/Cat. and Class. Sect. WI LA: Pres.-Elec. and VP; Tech. Srvs. Sect. (Ch., 1980–81). **Activities:** 1; 20, 46; 56 **Addr.:** Memorial Library, 728 State St., Madison, WI 53706.

Younger, Mildred L. (Jl. 7, 1924, Long Branch, NJ) Educ. Media Spec., Freehold Reg. HS Dist., 1958–; Chld. Libn., Monmouth Cnty. Lib., 1948–58; Asst. Libn., Mt. Hermon Sch., 1947–48. **Educ.:** Monmouth Coll., 1941–45, AA; Simmons Coll., 1945–47, BSLS; Columbia Univ., 1950–53, MSLS; Rutgers Univ.; Kean Coll.; Monmouth Coll.; Georgian Ct. Coll.; 1964–81. **Orgs.:** NJ LA: Secy. (1953–54). NJ Sch. Media Assn.: Pres. (1972–73). ALA: AASL, Reg. 2 Dir., 1977–80). Freehold Reg. HS Dist. Tchr. Assn.: Bldg. Rep. (1979–81); Prof. Rel. Com. (Ch., 1979–81). **Activities:** 10 **Addr.:** 85 Laurel Dr., Fair Haven, NJ 07701.

Younger, William Carl (N. 5, 1919, Sulligent, AL) State Law Libn. and Dir., AL Supreme Ct. and State Law Lib., 1965–; Asst. Attorney Gen., State of AL, 1964–65, 1957–59; Lawyer, Montgomery, AL, 1962–64; Dir., Dept. of Cons., State of AL, 1959–63; Law Clerk, AL Supreme Ct., 1957. **Educ.:** Univ. of AL, 1951–54, BS (Bus. Admin.), 1953–56, JD (Law), 1971–73, MLS; AALL, 1969, Cert. Law Libn. **Orgs.:** AALL: Southeast. Chap., Secy.-Treas. (1970–72), VP (1972–74), Pres. (1974–76); Cert. Bd. (Ch., 1975–76); Schol. Com. (1970–71); Mem. Com., Vice-Ch. (1973–74), Co-Ch. (1970–71). AL LA. Montgomery Cnty. LA. E. Montgomery Exch. Club: Pres. (1967). Exch. Club of Metro. Montgomery: Bd. of Dirs. (1968). **Honors:** Univ. of AL., Sesquicent. Hon. Prof. LS, 1981. **Pubns.:** Ed. bd., *AL Law Review* (1954–56). **Addr.:** Alabama Supreme Court and State Law Library, Judicial Bldg. - 445 Dexter Ave., Montgomery, AL 36130.

Youngholm, Philip (N. 5, 1948, Quincy, MA) Msc. Libn., CT Coll., 1977–; Tech. Srvs. Libn., Wellesley Free Lib., 1976–77, Head Catlgr., 1974–76. **Educ.:** Dartmouth Coll., 1965–69, AB (Msc.); Univ. of MI, 1973–74, AMLS. **Orgs.:** Msc. LA: AV Com. (Ch., 1981–); New Eng. Chap. (Secy./Treas., 1977–78), Vice-Ch. (1978–79); Ch. (1979–80). Msc. OCLC Users Grp. Phi Beta Kappa: CT Coll. Chap. (Secy./Treas., 1979–); New Eng. Dist., (Secy./Treas., 1979–). **Activities:** 1; 15, 16, 20; 55 **Addr.:** Greer Music Library, Box 1534, Connecticut College, New London, CT 06320.

Special Subjects/Services: 50. Adult educ.; 51. Advert./Mktg.; 52. Aerosp.; 53. Agric.; 54. Area std.; 55. Arts/Hum.; 56. Autom.; 57. Bibl./Prtg.; 58. Bio. sci.; 59. Bus./Fin.; 60. Chem.; 61. Copyrt.; 62. Documtn.; 63. Educ.; 64. Engin.; 65. Env.; 66. Eth. grps.; 67. Film; 68. Food/Nutr.; 69. Geneal.; 70. Geo.; 71. Geol.; 72. Handcpd.; 73. Hist.; 74. Int. frdm.; 75. Info. sci.; 76. Insr.; 77. Law; 78. Legis.; 79. Math./Comp. sci.; 80. Med.; 81. Metals; 82. Nat. resrcs.; 83. Newsp.; 84. Nuc. sci.; 85. Oral hist.; 86. Petr./Energy; 87. Pharm.; 88. Phys./Astr./Math.; 89. Readg.; 90. Relig.; 91. Sci./Tech.; 92. Soc. sci.; 93. Telecom.; 94. Transp.; 95. (other).

Youngs, Willard Oliver (D. 23, 1910, Berkeley, CA) Libn. Emeritus, Seattle Pub. Lib., 1975–, City Libn., 1957–74, Asst. Libn. and Coord. of Ref. Srvs., 1950–57, Head Ref. Dept., 1948–50; Supvsg. Libn., Bus. and Tech. Dept., San Diego Pub. Lib., 1946–48; Exec. Assoc., Stanford Univ. Libs., 1939–40, Ref. Libn., 1941–46; Libn., Jr. Grade, Univ. of CA Lib., 1939–40. **Educ.:** Univ. of CA, Berkeley, 1928–32, BS, 1932–35, (Econ.), 1935–36, LS Cert.; Univ. of MD, 1967 (Lib. Admin.). **Orgs.:** ALA: Cncl. (1964–71); Exec. Bd. (1967–71); PLA VP (1967–68); Pres. (1968–69). WA LA. Pac. NW LA. Kiwanis Club of Seattle: Pres. (1968). KCTS-TV Pub. TV: Adv. Bd. (1957–81). **Honors:** Fed. Repub. of Germany, Guest Prog., 1963. **Activities:** 1, 9; 16, 19, 39 **Addr.:** 8230 43rd Ave., N.E., Seattle, WA 98115.

Yu, Clement T. (Ag. 3, 1948, Hong Kong) Assoc. Prof., Univ. of IL, Chicago, 1978–; Assoc. Prof., Univ. of AB, 1977, Asst. Prof., 1973–77. **Educ.:** Columbia Univ., 1967–70, BS (Appld. Math.); Cornell Univ., 1970–73, PhD (Comp. Sci.). **Orgs.:** ASIS. Assn. for Comp. Mach. **Honors:** Can. Natl. Resrch. Cncl., Resrch. Grants, 1974–80; Natl. Sci. Fndn., Resrch. Grants, 1979–83. **Pubns.:** "A Clustering Algorithm Based on Use Queries," *Jnl. of the Amer. Assn. for Info. Sci.* (1974); "A Methodology for the Construction of Term Classes," *Info. Storage and Retrieval* (1974); "A Formal Construction of Term Classes," *Jnl. of the Assn. for Comp. Mach.* (1975); jt. auth., "A Theory of Term Importance in Automatic Text Analysis," *JASIS* (1975); "Precision Weighting–An Affective Automatic Indexing Method," *Jnl. of the Assn. for Comp. Mach.* (1976); various articles, papers. **Activities:** 1, 30, 31, 41 **Addr.:** Dept. of Information Engineering, Univ. of Illinois at Chicago Circle, Chicago, IL 60680.

Yu, Nancy S. (Nanking, China) Catlgr., Lib. of Congs., 1980–; Catlgr., Jersey City State Coll., Lib., 1972–79; Head Libn., RCA Srv. Co., 1971–72; Asst. Libn., Pennie, Edmonds Law, 1970–71. **Educ.:** Chung-Hsing Univ., Taipei, Taiwan, China, 1956–60, LLB (Law); Queens Coll., 1968–70, MLS. **Orgs.:** Chin. LA. NJ LA. **Activities:** 1, 4; 20 **Addr.:** Library of Congress, Washington, DC 20540.

Yucht, Donald J. (D. 30, 1939, Brooklyn, NY) Head, Instr. Media Ctr., NY Univ., 1977–; Asst. Univ. Libn. for Readers' Srvs., 1972–77, Lib. Coord., 1969–72, Circ. Libn., 1965–69; Libn., Brooklyn Pub. Lib., 1962–65. **Educ.:** Brooklyn Coll., 1957–61, AB; Pratt Inst., 1961–65, MLS; NY Univ., 1971–75, AM (Educ. Admin.). **Orgs.:** ALA: ACRL. NY Tech. Srvs. Libn. **Honors:** Beta Phi Mu; Phi Beta Kappa; Epsilon Pi Tau. **Pubns.:** "A Tab Card Circulation System," *UNABASHED Libn.* (1978); "Towards Some Standards for the Library Card Catalog Tray," *Lib. Resrcs. & Tech. Srvs.* (1972). **Activities:** 1; 32 **Addr.:** 11 Honeysuckle Ln., Matawan, NJ 07747.

Yueh, Norma N. (Ja. 21, 1928, Peking, China) Dir. of Lib. Srvs., Ramapo Coll. of NJ, 1974–; Assoc. Libn., William Paterson Coll. of NJ, 1970–74, Acq. Libn., 1964–70; Libn., Yonkers Pub. Sch. Syst., 1960–63; Asst. Branch and Adult Srvs. Libn., NY Pub. Lib., 1958–60; Admin. Asst. to Univ. Libn., Univ. of South. CA, 1955–57. **Educ.:** St. Joseph Coll., 1950, BS (Eng.); Stanford Univ., 1951, (English); Univ. of South. CA, 1955, MSLS; Columbia Univ., 1974, DLS. **Orgs.:** ALA. NJ LA: Inst. Com.; Admin. Sect. Prog. Com.; Persnl. Admin. Com.; Educ. for Libnshp. Com. (1974–). Coord. Cncl. of Ridgewood Area Libs.: Steering Com. (1974–). Natl. Micro. Assn.: Metro. NY Chap. Beta Phi Mu: (Nu Chap. Pres., 1979–). Org. of Chinese Amer.: NJ Chap., (Founding Bd. Mem., 1978–). **Pubns.:** "Alan Swallow, Publisher, 1915–1966," *Lib. Qtly.* (Jl., 1969). **Activities:** 1; 17, 25, 26; 63, 72, 75 **Addr.:** Ramapo College of New Jersey, Ramapo Valley Rd., Mahwah, NJ 07430.

Yukawa, Masako (My. 5, 1931, Odawara City, Kanagawa Prefecture, Japan) Libn., Head of the Gvt. Docum. Dept., Schwartz Mem. Lib., 1971–; Assoc. Prof., Long Island Univ. C.W. Post Ctr., 1971–, Libn., Asst. Head, Ref. Dept., 1967–71; Libn. and Ofcr., Women's Prog., Yokohama Amer. Cult. Ctr., 1965–67; Libn., Palmer Grad. Lib. Sch., Long Island Univ., C.W. Post Ctr., 1963–65. **Educ.:** Tsuda Coll., Tokyo, Japan, 1950–54, BA (Eng.); Long Island Univ., 1961–63, MSLS, 1973, (Pub. Admin.); Columbia Univ.; Mnstry. of Educ., Japan. **Orgs.:** ALA. NY LA. Nassau Cnty LA. Long Island Resrcs. Cncl.: Com. on Gvt. Info. (1974–). AAUP. **Honors:** Fulbright, 1961; Phi Be Mu, 1978. **Pubns.:** *The Congressional Subcommittee Index* (1980, 1981); jt. auth., "Using Government Documents to Obtain Information on National Parks, Monuments and Forests," *Jnl. of Geol. Educ.* (My. 1980); *List of Subject Headings for the Library Science Vertical File* (1965); *Resources in Politics of Environmental Control in U.S. Government Documents . . .* (1973); *Playing with Documents* (1974). **Activities:** 1; 29, 39 **Addr.:** B. Davis Schwartz Memorial Library, C. W. Post Center, Greenvale, NY 11548.

Yun, James M. (S. 28, 1938, Kyungpuk, Korea) Dir., Sci. Comms., Exec. Dir., Resrch. and Dev., Purdue Frederick Co., 1977–; Dir., Tech. Info., Hoechst Roussel, 1974–76; Mgr., Tech. Documtn., Schering Corp., 1967–74; Asst. Dir., Pharmgy., USV Pharms., 1965–67. **Educ.:** SUNY, New Paltz, 1961–63, BA (Bio.); Cornell Univ., 1963–64 (Physio.); Fairleigh Dickinson, 1970–73, MBA (Intl. Bus.). **Orgs.:** ASIS. Drug Info. Assn. Amer. Chem. Socty. Proj. Mgt. Inst. Pharm. Mfrs. Assn. **Pubns.:** "Use of a Project Management System on New Drug Development," *Drug Info. Jnl.* (O.–D. 1976). **Activities:** 5; 17, 41, 46; 60, 87, 91 **Addr.:** Research & Development, The Purdue Frederick Co., 50 Washington St., Norwalk, CT 06856.

Yungmeyer, Elinor (Chicago, IL) Accred. Ofcr., ALA, 1975–; Coord., Instr. Media, Oak Park Elem. Sch., 1960–75; Sch. Lib. Consult., MI State Lib., 1954–60; Sch. Libn., Phoenix Elem. Sch., 1951–54; Sch. Libn., Battle Creek Pub. Sch., 1946–51. **Educ.:** Univ. of Chicago, 1941–45, BA (Hist.), 1945–46, BLS (Libnshp.), 1954, AMLS, 1969–70, CAS (LS). **Orgs.:** ALA. **Pubns.:** Various educ. and lib. articles. **Activities:** 10, 11; 17, 21, 24; 63 **Addr.:** American Library Association, 50 E. Huron St., Chicago, IL 60611.

Yunker, J. Olivia (S. 19, 1929, Hudson, NY) Supvsr., Lib. Srvs., Knolls Atomic Power Lab., 1978–; Spec., Cat., Gen. Electric Co., Lib., 1965–78. **Educ.:** NY State Coll. for Tchrs., 1945–49, BA (Sp., Eng.); SUNY, 1949–50, MA (Eng.), 1966, MLS. **Orgs.:** SLA: Bltn. Co-Ed (1966–68). Hudson Mohawk LA: Pres. (1978–80). Cap. Dist. Lib. Cncl. SUNY Alum. Assn. **Activities:** 12; 17, 20, 39; 75, 84, 91 **Addr.:** 1319 Trinity Ave., Schenectady, NY 12306.

Z

Zabel, Jean Marie (Mr. 14, 1950, Milwaukee, WI) Libn. II, Legis. Ref. Bur., 1981–, Libn. I, 1980–81, Lib. Asst., 1973–80. **Educ.:** Univ. of WI, 1968–72, BFA (Thea. Arts), 1974–76, MALS. **Orgs.:** SLA. Milwaukee Cnty. Zoological Socty.: Zoo Pride, Bd. of Dirs., Lib. Com. (1981), Libn. (1979). **Pubns.:** "Prison Libraries," *Spec. Libs.* (Ja. 1976). **Activities:** 4; 20, 39, 41; 78, 83 **Addr.:** Legislative Reference Bureau, City Hall, Rm. 404, 200 E. Wells St., Milwaukee, WI 53202.

Zack, Daniel G. (O. 1, 1943, Waukegan, IL) Dir., Burlington Pub. Lib., 1978–; Asst. Dir., Charles White Pub. Lib., 1976–78; Ed., Memorex Corp., 1970–73; Writer, Anal., IBM Corp., 1968–70. **Educ.:** West. IL Univ., 1963–67, BA (Psy.); Univ. of IL, 1974–75, MS (LS). **Orgs.:** ALA: Pub. Lib. Div. (1979–). IA LA: Min. Guidelines (Ch., 1978). **Pubns.:** Jt. auth., *Evaluation of the Illinois Interlibrary Loan Network* (1977). **Activities:** 9; 17 **Addr.:** Burlington Public Library, 501 N. 4th St., Burlington, IA 52601.

Zaehringer, David John (Ag. 11, 1931, Clinton, IA) Bus. Biblgphr., Univ. of NC at Charlotte, 1980–; Libn., Inst. of Indus. Rel., Univ. of CA, Berkeley, 1977–80; Head, Tech. Srvs., Bus. Biblgphr., Univ. of San Diego, 1973–77; Head, Reader Srvs., Ref., Jackson Lib., Bus. Sch., Stanford Univ., 1967–73; Bus. Libn., Univ. of IA, 1962–67 **Educ.:** Loras Coll., 1949–53, BA (Eng.); Columbia Univ., 1956–59, MS (Libnshp. Ref.). **Orgs.:** SLA: Bus. and Fin. Div. (Treas., 1965–66); San Francisco Bay Area Chap. Com. of Indus. Rel. Libns. **Honors:** Beta Gamma Sigma; Delta Epsilon Sigma. **Activities:** 1; 15, 39, 46; 59 **Addr.:** 6328 Countryside Dr. #15, Charlotte, NC 28213.

Zafran, Enid L. (Ap. 15, 1949, Malden, MA) Mgr., Indexing Dept., Banks-Baldwin Law Publshg. Co., 1979–; Self-empl. as Indxr., Abstctr., 1978–79; Indxr., Banks-Baldwin Law Publshg. Co., 1975–78; ILL Libn., Univ. of Louisville, 1973–75. **Educ.:** Mt. Holyoke Coll., 1966–70, BA (Latin); Univ. of KY, 1972–74, MSLS; various crs. **Orgs.:** Amer. Socty. of Indxrs. ASIS. **Pubns.:** *Ohio Bank Manual* (1979); indxr., *Ohio Administrative Code* (1978); *Abstracts: Research in Education* ERIC (1979). **Activities:** 14-Publshg. Co.; 30, 37; 63, 77, 78 **Addr.:** Banks-Baldwin Law Publishing Co., P.O. Box 1974, Cleveland, OH 44106.

Zafren, Herbert C. (Ag. 25, 1925, Baltimore, MD) Prof., Jewish Bibl. 1968–; Co-Dir., Hebrew Un. Coll.-Jewish Inst. of Relig., 1980–, Dir., Libs., 1966–; Exec. Dir., Amer. Jewish Per. Ctr., 1958–; Libn., Hebrew Un. Coll.-Jewish Inst. of Relig., 1950–; Bibl. Srch., Univ. of MI Law Lib., 1949–50. **Educ.:** Johns Hopkins Univ., 1941–44, AB (Latin); Baltimore Hebrew Coll., 1941–44, Dip. (Jewish Std.); Univ. of MI, 1949–50, AMLS. **Orgs.:** AJL: Natl. Pres. (1965–66). Cncl. of Arch. and Resrch. Libs. in Jewish Std.: Natl. Pres. (1975–78). World Cncl. of Jewish Arch.: Intl. VP (1977–81). ALA: Ref. and Subscrpn. Bks. Com. (1973–74). Various other orgs. AAUP: Chap. Pres. (1964–68). Amer. Hist. Assn. Amer. Jewish Hist. Socty. Amer. Acad. of Jewish Resrch. Various other orgs. **Honors:** Amer. Phil. Socty., Resrch. Grant, 1974; Beta Phi Mu, 1972; Phi Beta Kappa, 1944. **Pubns.:** Jt. cmplr., *The Writings of Jacob Rader Marcus: A Bibliographic Record* (1978); *A Gathering of Broadsides* (1967); "The Freeze, AACR2 and GCLC," *Update: GCLC* (Jl.–Ag. 1978); ed., *Std. of Bibl. and Booklore* (1953–); "Among Recent Acquisitions," *Std. in Bibl. and Booklore* (1979); various reviews, edshps., mono. **Activities:** 1; 17, 41, 45; 57, 66 **Addr.:** Hebrew Union College-Jewish Institute of Religion, 3101 Clifton Ave., Cincinnati, OH 45220.

Zalewski, Wojciech (Mr. 20, 1937, Gdynia, Poland) Cur., Russ. and E. European Cols., Stanford Univ. Libs., 1971–. **Educ.:** Cath. Univ., Lublin, Poland, 1960–65, Mstr. (Theo.); Pontifical Biblical Inst., Rome, Italy, 1965–67, Licenc (Bible); Gregorianum Univ., Rome, Italy, 1967–68, Doctor of Theo.; San Jose State Univ., 1970–71, MA (Libnshp.). **Orgs.:** ALA: ACRL, Ch. (1980–81)/Slavic and E. European Sect. Amer. Assn. for the Advnc. of Slavic Std. **Pubns.:** *Guide to Selected Reference Materials, Russia and East Europe* (1973); *Russian-English Dictionaries with Aids for Translators, A Selected Bibliography* (1981); "Reference Materials in Russian-Soviet Area Studies," *Russ. Review* (anl Ap. issue, 1975–); "The Impact of Microforms on the Future of Slavic Collections in America," *Micro. Review* (My.–Je. 1978); "Polish Libraries Outside Poland," *Migrant Echo* (Ja.–Ap. 1980). **Activities:** 1; 15, 31; 54, 57 **Addr.:** 162 Highland Ave., San Carlos, CA 94070.

Zalin, Fern Renee (Je. 5, 1950, OH) Dir., Prof. Lib., Philadelphia Psyt. Ctr., 1978–; Ref. Libn., Van Pelt Lib., Univ. of PA, 1980–; Supvsr., Srch. Srvs., Inst. for Sci. Info., 1978; Libn., Santa Barbara Pub. Lib., 1974–77. **Educ.:** Univ. of CA, 1969–72, BA (Eng.), 1972–74, MLIS. **Orgs.:** Med. LA. **Pubns.:** "Homebaked Bread–Bibliographic Essay," *Booklegger Mag.* (F. 1972). **Activities:** 12; 15, 17, 20; 80 **Addr.:** Professional Library, Philadelphia Psychiatric Center, Ford Rd. and Monument Ave., Philadelphia, PA 19131.

Zambusi, William Joseph (Je. 11, 1941, Matachewan, ON) Asst. Dir., Head, Prcs. Srvs. Ctr., and Srvs., Midwest. Reg. Lib. Syst., 1974–; Branch Libn., Hamilton Pub. Lib., 1968–74; Tchr., Libn., Mater Amabilis Sec. Sch., Nigeria, 1965–67. **Educ.:** Univ. of Ottawa, 1961–65, BA (Hist., Fr.); Univ. of Toronto, 1967–68, BLS, 1971–73, MLS. **Orgs.:** Can. LA. Can. Assn. of Pub. Libs.: Reg. Lib. Div. (Ch., 1979–80). Inst. of Prof. Libns. of ON: Bd. of Dirs. (1973–74). ON LA: Reg. and Pub. Lib. Div. (Reg. Rep. 1971–72). **Activities:** 4, 9; 17, 24, 36; 51 **Addr.:** Midwestern Regional Library System, 637 Victoria St. N., Kitchener, ON N2H 5G4, Canada.

Zamora, Antonio (D. 6, 1942, Nuevo Laredo, Mex. Sr. Info. Sci., Chem. Abs. Srv., 1965–. **Educ.:** Univ. of TX, 1958–62, BS (Chem.); OH State Univ., 1966–69, MS (Info. Sci.). **Orgs.:** Assn. for Comp. Mach. ASIS: Exec. Com. (1979–80). Amer. Chem. Socty.: Chem. Info. Plng. (1980). **Honors:** ASIS, Best Paper of the Yr., 1971. **Pubns.:** "Automatic Detection and Correction of Spelling Errors in Large Data Bases," *JASIS* (Ja. 1980); jt. auth., "Automatic Abstracting and Indexing," *JASIS* (Jl. 1971); jt. auth., "Automatic Abstracting Research at Chemical Abstracts Service," *Jnl. Chem. Info. Comp. Sci.* (Ap. 1975). **Activities:** 12; 41; 60, 62 **Addr.:** Chemical Abstracts Service, Dept. 23, P.O. Box 3012, Columbus, OH 43210.

Zaporozhetz, Laurene Elizabeth (N. 25, 1950, Detroit, MI) Asst. Prof., Univ. of OR, 1979–; Actg. Ref. Dept. Head, Educ. Spec., Univ. of NE (Omaha), 1977–78, Soc. Sci. Libn., 1976–77; Educ. Spec., MA Dept. of Educ., Bur. of Lib. Ext., 1974–75. **Educ.:** MI State Univ., 1968–72, BA (Educ.); West. MI Univ., 1972–74, MSL (Libnshp.). **Orgs.:** ALA. MA Sch. LA: Treas. (1974–75). New Eng. Educ. Media Assn.: Exec. Bd. (1974–75). NE LA: Coll., and Univ. Sect. (Ch., 1976–77, 1977–78). **Honors:** State of NE, Named Admiral in the Grt. Navy of the State of NE, 1978. **Activities:** 1, 10; 17, 39, 41; 63, 74, 92 **Addr.:** 3970 Hayden Bridge Rd., Springfield, OR 97477.

Zarechnak, Galina V. (S. 27, 1916, Novocherkassk, Russia) Pubn. Prog. Admin., Natl. Lib. of Med., 1972–, Libn., 1952–72. **Educ.:** Komensky (Slovak) Univ., Bratislava, Czechoslovia, 1936–41, PhD (Slavic Lang., Lit.); Cath. Univ. of Amer., 1954–58, MS (LS). **Orgs.:** Med. LA. SLA. Socty. of Fed. Lings. Amer. Assn. for the Advnc. of Slavic Std. **Pubns.:** *Academy of Medical Sciences of the USSR* pub. hlth. mono. no. 63 (1960); "Russian Medicine from Russian Language Sources," *Guide to Russian Medical Literature* (1958); various bk. reviews. **Activities:** 4; 15, 17, 37; 57, 80 **Addr.:** 1308 Farragut St. N.W., Washington, DC 20011.

Zarins, Paul (N. 30, 1947, Nuremberg, Germany) Coord., Comp. Assisted Ref. Srv., Intl. Docum. Libn., Univ. of CA, San Diego, 1978–, Ref. Libn., Biblgphr., 1971–78. **Educ.:** Univ. of WA, 1965–69, BA (Hist.); Stanford Univ., 1969–70, MA (Hist.); Univ. of OR, 1970–71, MLS. **Orgs.:** ALA. Intl. Assn. for Soc. Sci. Info. Srv. and Tech. Univ. of CA Data Srvs. Coords. Grp.: Ch. (1979–80). **Honors:** Phi Beta Kappa, 1969. **Activities:** 1; 29, 39; 54, 56, 92 **Addr.:** Central University Library, C-075, University of California, San Diego, La Jolla, CA 92093.

Zaslavsky, Gerald L. (Je. 5, 1943, Philadelphia, PA) Broadcast Dir., Temtron Electronics, 1980–; Lib. Media Spec., Baldwin HS, 1977–79; Dir., Head, Instr. Mtrls./Media Ctr., NY Univ., Bobst Lib., 1973–77; Lib. Media Spec., Port Washington Schs., Schreiber HS, 1971–73; Fndr., Owner, Zaslavsky and Assocs., 1969–; Educ. Curric. Media Spec., Title III, Evanston Twp. HS, 1968–70; Tchr., Sch. Dist. of Philadelphia, 1966–68. **Educ.:** Temple Univ., 1961–65, BS (Soc. Std., Hist.); Northeast. IL State Univ., 1969–70, (Comm., Radio, TV); Long Island Univ., 1972–75, MS (LS); various crs., tchg., libn. cert. **Orgs.:** ALA: AASL Facilities (1976–79), Vid. (1976–78, 1980–82); LITA Vid. and Cable Comms. Sect., Vid. Distribution and Exch. (1980–82). NY LA. AECT. Long Island Sch. Media Assn. Palmer Grad. Lib. Sch. Alum.: Pres. (1978–80); VP (1977–78); Treas. (1980–82). Beta Pi Mu: Beta Mu Chap., Pres. (1980–81), VP (1979–80). Amer. Film Inst. Long Island Educ. Sales Assn. Various other orgs. **Honors:** Kappa Delta Pi. **Pubns.:** "Passover" slide tape

PROFESSIONAL ACTIVITIES: Institutions: 1. Acad. lib.; 2. Arch.; 3. Assn.; 4. Fed./Gvt. lib.; 5. Inst. lib.; 6. Mfr./Suppl.; 7. Milit. lib.; 8. Musm.; 9. Pub. lib.; 10. Sch. lib.; 11. Sch. of lib. sci.; 12. Spec. lib.; 13. State lib.; 14. (other). **Functions/Activities:** 15. Acq./Col. dev.; 16. Adult srvs.; 17. Admin.; 18. Apprais.; 19. Archit./Bldgs.; 20. Cat./Class.; 21. Chld. srvs.; 22. Circ.; 23. Cons./Pres.; 24. Consult.; 25. Cont. ed.; 26. Educ. lib. sci.; 27. Ext. srvs.; 28. Fund/Grants; 29. Gvt. pubs.; 30. Indx./Abs.; 31. Instr. lib. use; 32. Media srvs.; 33. Micro.; 34. Netwks./Coop.; 35. Persnl.; 36. PR; 37. Publshg.; 38. Recs. mgt.; 39. Ref. srvs.; 40. Repro.; 41. Resrch.; 42. Review.; 43. Secur.; 44. Serials; 45. Spec. col.; 46. Tech. srvs.; 47. Trustees/Bds.; 48. YA srvs.; 49. (other).

prog. (1977); "Sabbath: Religious Traditions and Rituals" slide tape presentation (1976); "Until the Computer Arrives: Using Edge Notched Cards to Catalog Nonprint Materials," *AV Instr.* (N. 1977); "Library Media Services in An Academic Library" ERIC (D. 1975); "Lights Camera Action: A Mediography on Filmmaking" ERIC (Spr. 1974); various mono., articles, papers, sps. **Activities:** 1, 10; 15, 17, 24; 63, 93 **Addr.:** 34 3rd Ave., Port Washington, NY 11050.

Zaslavsky, Judith Marcus (Mrs.) (Ja. 14, 1920, Philadelphia, PA) Supvsr., Sch. Lib. Media Ctrs., Dist. 6 and 8, Philadelphia Pub. Schs., 1981–; Libn., Pepper Mid. Sch., 1977–80; Supvsr., Sch. Lib. Media Ctrs. Dist. 6, Philadelphia Pub. Schs., 1966–77; Demonstration Libn., Masterman Lab. and Demonstration Sch., 1960–66; Libn., Rowland and Wayne Elem. Schs., 1959–60; Libn., William Penn HS for Girls, 1952–57; Libn., John Bartram HS, 1944–49; Libn., Stoddart Jr. HS, 1942–44. **Educ.:** Temple Univ., 1937–41, BS (Educ.); Drexel Univ., 1941–42, BS (LS); Columbia Univ., 1945–51, MS (Lib. Srv.); various crs. **Orgs.:** ALA: AASL, Intl. Rel. Com. (1954–55); ALSC. Sch. Libns. of Philadelphia and Vicinity Assn.: Pres. (1956–58); Com. to Plan Lib. Mtg. for Univ. of PA Schoolmen's Week (Ch., 1954–63). Assn. of Philadelphia Sch. Libns.: Exec. Bd. (1979–). Frnds. of Philadelphia Sch. Libs.: VP (1979–). Various other orgs. Intl. Readg. Assn. DE Valley Readg. Assn. Amer. Indian Hist. Assn. Frnds. of the Free Lib. of Philadelphia. Various other orgs. **Honors:** Women in Educ., Cert. for 25 Yrs. of Srv. to Educ., 1975; Chapel of the Four Chaplains, Cert., Hon. Dedicated Srv. to Cmnty., 1956. **Pubns.:** Various articles, *Book of Knowledge* (1953); ed., *Drexel Lib. Sch. Alum. Assn. Nsltr.* (1953–62). **Activities:** 10; 17, 19, 24; 63, 89 **Addr.:** 23 Rolling Rd., Carroll Park, PA 19151.

Zavitz, (Mary) Jane Vandervort (My. 19, 1930, Columbus, OH) Libn., Pickering Coll., 1976–; Cur., Frnds. Discipline Col., Quakers, 1979–; Tchr., Olney Frnds. Sch., 1955–75; Ofc. (sbtcl. Leave), Quaker Untd. Nations, Frnds. World Com. (short term sbtcl.) 1973; Tchr. (sbtcl. leave), Norwich Dist. HS, 1962–63. **Educ.:** Earlham Coll., 1948–52, AB (Hist., Eng.); ON, 1963, Certs. (Sec. Tchg., Libns. Spec.); Univ. of West. ON, 1975–76, MLS; Univ. of MD, 1979 (Arch., Cons., Prsrvn.). **Orgs.:** Can. LA. Can. Assn. of Spec. Libs. for Info. Sci.: Toronto Branch, Ex-Treas. ALA: ACRL/Rare Bks. and Mss. ON LA. Can. Frnds. Hist. Assn.: Exec.; Nsltr. Ed.; Resrch. Com. ON Geneal. Socty. Socty. of Frnds.: Can. **Pubns.:** "An Afternoon in Appreciation of Arthur G. Dorland," *Can. Frnds. Hist. Assn. Nsltr.* (N. 1979); "History of Pickering College," *Can. Frnds. Hist. Assn. Nsltr.* (Je. 1977); "History of Sparta Friends Meeting," *Can. Frnds. Hist. Assn. Nsltr.* (Je. 1976); "How to Use Quaker Records for Genealogical Search," *Fams.* (Ja. 1980); various sps. **Activities:** 2, 10; 15, 17, 23; 57, 69, 74 **Addr.:** Pickering College Library, Pickering College, Newmarket, ON L3Y 4X2 Canada.

Zealy, Yolande M. (Jl. 22, 1948, Washington, DC) Tech. Info. Spec., Xerox Corp., 1977–. **Educ.:** Univ. of Rochester, 1972–75, BS (Eng.); SUNY, Geneseo, 1975–76, MLS. **Orgs.:** SLA. Assoc. Info. Mgrs. ALA: Black Caucus. Metro. Women's Netwk. Rochester Reg. Resrch. Lib. Cncl. **Activities:** 12; 30, 41; 59, 66, 91 **Addr.:** Xerox Corp., 800 Phillips Rd. Bldg. 105B, Webster, NY 14580.

Zeidlik, Hannah M. (Jl. 26, 1922, Middle River, MN) Supervisory Archvst., U.S. Army Ctr. of Milit. Hist., 1978–, Supervisory Histn., Ref., 1977–78, Archvst., Ref., 1970–77, Histn., Ref., 1967–70, Archvst., 1950–67. **Educ.:** Amer. Univ., 1956–70, BA (Hist.). **Orgs.:** SAA. Intl. Cncl. of Archvsts. U.S. Comsn. of Milit. Histns. Milit. Histns. and Collectors. **Honors:** Various hons. **Pubns.:** *Guide to Historical Manuscripts Collection* (1979). **Activities:** 2, 4 **Addr.:** U.S. U.S. Army Center of Military History, Washington, DC 22314.

Zeugner, Lorenzo A., Jr. (D. 29, 1942, Reading, PA) Head, Acq. Dept., Univ. of Notre Dame, 1978–; Chief Acq. Libn., PA State Univ., 1977–78, Acq. Libn. for Campuses, 1974–77, Head, York Campus Lib., 1969–74. **Educ.:** Fairfield Univ., 1961–65, AB (Hist.), 1965–66, MA Ed (Educ.); Univ. of Pittsburgh, 1967–69, MLS. **Orgs.:** ALA. PA LA: Bd. of Dirs. (1977–78); Nom. Com. (Ch., 1973); S. Ctrl. Chap. (Mem. Coord., 1971). **Honors:** Beta Phi Mu, 1969. **Activities:** 1; 15, 17, 46 **Addr.:** 51800 E. Gatehouse Dr., South Bend, IN 46637.

Zeydel, Jeanne R. (Jl. 13, 1925, Montclair, NJ) Agency Libn., US Info. Agency, 1975–, Chief, Ref. Branch, 1962–74. **Educ.:** George Washington Univ., 1945–49, AB (Eng. Lit.); Columbia Univ., 1949–51, MS (LS). **Orgs.:** Fed. Lib. Com. **Honors:** US Intl. Comm. Agency, Merit. Hon., 1967. **Pubns.:** *US Constitution Used as a Model* (1962); ed., *USIA; A Bibliography* (1976). **Activities:** 4; 17, 39, 41; 54 **Addr.:** U.S. Information Agency, The Agency Library, 1750 Pennsylvania Ave., N.W., Washington, DC 20547.

Ziaian, Mahmonir (Mr., 1939, Tehran, Iran) Libn., Univ. of South CA, 1979–; Libn., Natl. Cncl. of Alcl., 1976–79; Med. Libn., St. Joseph Med. Ctr., 1973–76. **Educ.:** Univ. of CA, Los Angeles, 1967–70, BS (Ling.), 1970–72, MLS. **Orgs.:** Med. LA. SLA. ARLIS/NA. **Activities:** 1, 5; 15, 17, 27 **Addr.:** Safety & Systems Management Library, Institute of Safety & Systems Mgt., University Southern California, University Park, Los Angeles, CA 90007.

Zibilich, Bernice G. (Ag. 26, 19–, San Antonio, TX) Chld. Libn., New Orleans Pub. Lib., 1961–, Ref. Libn., 1947–61. **Educ.:** Our Lady of the Lake Coll., 1937–41, BA (Eng.); Our Lady of the Lake Univ., 1946–47, MS (LS). **Orgs.:** Cath. LA: Chld. Srvs. Div., Bd. SW LA: Jt. Mtg. with SE LA, Pubcty. Ch. LA LA: PR Com., Pubcty. Ch.; Mem. Com. New Orleans Lib. Club: Secy. (1961–62); Pres. (1975–76). Puppet Playhse. Thea.: Bd. of Dirs. Open Door Proj. of U.S. State Dept.: Coord. Boy Scouts of Amer.: Bd. **Honors:** Assn. for Chld. Educ. Intl., Awd. of the Yr.; Our Lady of the Lake Univ., Alum. of the Yr. **Pubns.:** "Selected Books for Preschool Children," *Day Care in Louisiana* (1974). **Activities:** 9; 21 **Addr.:** New Orleans Public Library, 219 Loyola Ave., New Orleans, LA 70140.

Zibrat, Jan (Ag. 15, 1951, Akron, OH) Med. Libn., Swedish Covenant Hosp., 1978–; Asst. Libn., Chld. Meml. Hosp., 1977–78; Libn., Villa Maria Coll., 1975–76; Admin. Libn., Erie Vets. Admin. Hosp., 1974–75. **Educ.:** Kent State Univ., 1969–72, BA (European Hist.); Case West. Rsv. Univ., 1973–74, MSLS; 1975, Cert. Medline Anal.; Med. LA, 1975, Cert. Med. Libn. **Orgs.:** Chicago OLUG. Med. LA: Hosp. Libs. Sect.; Midwest Chap. Hlth. Sci. Libns. of IL: Prog. Ch. (Spr. 1980). Metro. Cnsrtm., Chicago: Deputy Coord. (1980–81); Coord. (1981–82). **Activities:** 12; 15, 17, 39; 80 **Addr.:** Stromberg Library, Swedish Covenant Hospital, 5145 N. California, Chicago, IL 60625.

Zich, Robert (Ja. 18, 1939, Omaha, NE) Planner, Lib. of Congs., 1977–, Asst. Head, Pub. Ref. Sect., 1972–76, Ref. Libn., 1964–72, Spec. Rcrt., 1963–64. **Educ.:** Univ. of Omaha, 1956–60, BA (Eng. Lit., Hist.); Univ. of MN, 1960–63, MA (LS). **Orgs.:** DC LA: Ref. RT (Ch., 1972–75). Lib. of Congs. Prof. Assn.: Pres. (1970). Amer. Phil. Assn. **Pubns.:** Various articles, *Lib. of Congs. Info. Bltn.* **Activities:** 1, 4; 15, 17, 39; 55, 75 **Addr.:** Planning Office, Library of Congress, Washington, DC 20540.

Zick, Kenneth A. (S. 3, 1949, Mt. Pleasant, MI) Dir., Assoc. Prof. of Law, Wake Forest Univ. Law Lib., 1978–, Ref. Libn. Asst. Prof. of Law, 1975–78. **Educ.:** Albion Coll., 1967–71, AB (Pol. Sci.); Wayne State Univ., 1971–74, JD (Law); Univ. of MI, 1974–75, MLS. **Orgs.:** AALL: *Law Lib. Jnl.* Com. (1979–81); Southeast. Chap., Nom. Com. (1980). Scribes, Amer. Socty. of Writers on Legal Subjs.: Admin. NC State Bar. Amer. Bar Assn. **Pubns.:** "A Westlaw Primer on Computer-Assisted Legal Research," *Law Lib. Jnl.* (1979); "Developing and Implementing a Law School Westlaw Orientation Program," *Law Lib. Jnl.* (1979). **Activities:** 1; 15, 17, 31; 77 **Addr.:** P.O. Box 7206, Reynolda Station, Winston-Salem, NC 27109.

Ziegler, Janet M. (My. 10, 1940, Rhinelander, WI) Ref. ILL Libn., Univ. of CA, Los Angeles, 1969–, Cat. Libn., 1964–69. **Educ.:** Univ. of CA, Los Angeles, 1961–63, BA, 1964, MLS, 1974, MA (Hist.). Amer. Com. on the Hist. of The Sec. World War: Biblgphr. (1973–); Dir. (1976–). Hist. Abs. Bibl. Srvs. User Bd. **Pubns.:** *World War II: Books in English, 1945–65* (1971); "Repertoire international des bibliographies publiees de 1945 a 1965 sur la seconde guerre mondiale," *Revue d'histoire de la deuxieme querre mondiale* (1966); "Bibliographies dur la seconde guerre mondiale," *Revue d'histoire de la deuxieme querre mondiale* (1971). **Activities:** 1; 34, 39; 54, 92 **Addr.:** Reference Dept., University Research Library, University of California, Los Angeles, CA 90024.

Ziegler, Ronald M. (Ag. 10, 1935, Cuyahoga Falls, OH) Ref. Libn., WA State Univ., 1970–; Ref. Libn., FL Atl. Univ., 1968–70. **Educ.:** Univ. of Miami, 1960–66, AB (Lit.); FL State Univ., 1967–68, MS (LS). **Orgs.:** NLA. West. European Lang. Specs. **Honors:** Beta Phi Mu. **Pubns.:** *Wilderness Waterways: A Guide to Information Sources* (1979); *Ski Northwest & Canada West: A New Descriptive Guide to Over 90 Ski Areas in Alberta, British Columbia, Idaho, Oregon and Washington,* (1981); "Canoe, Kayak and Raft Periodicals for Libraries," *The Serials Libn.* (Fall 1980); series ed., *Sports, Games and Pastimes Series* (1980). **Activities:** 1; 19, 28, 39; 55 **Addr.:** Washington State University, Holland Library, Pullman, WA 99164.

Zieleniewski, Janet Louise (Ag. 31, 1942, Cincinnati, OH) Lib. Supvsr., PEDCO Grp. Cos., 1974–; Libn., Lockland HS, 1969–73; Libn., Deer Park HS, 1967–68. **Educ.:** OH Univ., 1960–63 (Eng.); Univ. of Cincinnati, 1968–69, BSEd (Eng.), 1971–73, MEd (Educ.). **Orgs.:** SLA: Cincinnati Chap., Hosplty. Com. (1978–79), Secy. (1979–80), Audit. (1980–81). OH Sch. Libns. Assn. PEDCO Grp. Empls. Credit Un.: Bd. of Dirs.; Secy. (1979–81); VP (1981). Sigma Kappa Sorority: Cincinnati Alum. Chap., various ofcs. **Activities:** 6, 12; 15, 17, 20; 64, 65, 91 **Addr.:** PEDCO Group Companies, 11499 Chester Rd., Cincinnati, OH 45246.

Zielinska, (Mrs.) Marie F. (Je. 26, 1927, Cracow, Poland) Chief, Multilingual Bibliosrv., Natl. Lib. of Can., 1973–; Chief, Serials, Dir. des bib., Univ. de Montreal, 1970–73, Bib. de bio., 1964–70, Catlgr., 1963–64, Libn., Loans, Ref., Bib. ctrl., 1962–63, Chief Libn., Inst. de med. exper., 1962, Resrch. Tech., McGill Univ., Allan Meml. Inst., 1957–61; Libn., Mfr. "Siew," Cracow, 1953–56; Head, Documtn. Ctr., 1951–53. **Educ.:** Jagiellonian Univ., Cracow, Poland, 1943–47, BSc, MSc (Agr. Sci.); Univ. de Montreal, 1961–62, BBibl (Libnshp.); McGill Univ., 1967–69, MLS; various crs. in jnlsm. **Orgs.:** Can. LA: Cncl. Adv. Grp. (1967–73); Intl. Rel. Com. (Ch., 1973–75); Can. Comsn. for UNESCO (Del., 1973–79); various coms. Polish-Can. Libns. Assn.: Pres. (1978–79). ALA. Intl. Assn. of Sch. Libs. Various other orgs. Assn. of Polish Engins. Ladies Auxiliary: Pres. (1974–76, 1978–). Polish Sch. Cncl.: Sch. Bd. Ch. (1964–68). Com. for Can.-Polish Univ. and Sci. Coop.: Secy.–Treas. (1970–). Ctrl. and E. European Std. Assn. of Can. Various other orgs. **Pubns.:** "The Botanical Library at the University of Montreal" *Agova* (Jl. 1970); "A New Concept in Library Service," *Perspectives: A Polish Amer. Educ. and Cult. Qtly.* (O.–D. 1974); "Multiculturalism: The Idea Behind the Policy," *Can. Lib. Jnl.* (Je. 1976); "Libraries in the Canadian Ethnic Mosaic: the Multilingual Biblioservice," *Can. Lib. Jnl.* (O. 1976); "Multiculturalism and Library Services to Ethnic Communities," *Unesco Bltn. for Libs.* (Volume 32, no 1); various articles. **Activities:** 4, 9; 15, 17, 22; 55, 58, 66 **Addr.:** 330 Driveway, Apt. 601, Ottawa ON K1S 3M9 Canada

Zilonis, Mary Frances (S. 17, 1947, Boston, MA) Ch., Media Dept., Randolph Pub. Schs., (1981–; Visit. Lectr., Boston Coll., Spr. 1981; Consult. for fourth ed., *Junior High School Library Catalog,* H.W. Wilson Co., 1979–; Asst. Prof., Bridgewater State Coll., 1977; Libn., Media Spec., Randolph Pub. Schs., 1969–. **Educ.:** Bridgewater State Coll., 1965–69, BS (Educ.), 1970–73, MEd (Sch. Libnshp.); Boston Univ., 1973–79, EdD (Educ. Media, Tech.). **Orgs.:** ALA: AASL. AECT. Natl. Educ. Assn. MA Tchrs. Assn. Norfolk Cnty. Tchrs. Assn. Randolph Tchrs. Assn. **Honors:** Pi Lambda Theta. **Pubns.:** *Characteristics of School Librarians and Audiovisual Media Specialists Affecting Acceptance of Unified Media* (1979). **Activities:** 10, 11; 26, 32, 48; 63, 67, 89 **Addr.:** Gerrish Rd., Rochester, MA 02770.

Zimmer, Gail Enid (Jl. 10, 1942, Jersey City, NJ) Prin. Libn., Ref., Maurice M. Pine Free Pub. Lib., 1976–, Sr. Libn., Ref., 1967–76; Libn., NY Pub. Lib., 1964–66. **Educ.:** Trenton State Coll., 1959–63, BA (Sci., Eng.); Rutgers Univ., 1963–64, MLS. **Orgs.:** Bergen-Passaic LA. Fair Lawn Lib. Empl. Grp. Untd. Fed. of Doll Clubs. Natl. Inst. of Amer. Doll Artists. Intl. Doll Makers Assn. **Pubns.:** Various articles about doll collecting. **Activities:** 9; 16, 31, 39; 55, 67 **Addr.:** Maurice M. Pine Free Public Library, 10–01 Fair Lawn Ave., Fair Lawn, NJ 07410.

Zimmer, Naomi Marie (S. 29, 1937, Gallupville, NY) Gen. Srvs. Consult., Adult Spec., Mohawk Valley LA, 1977–, ILL, Ref. Libn., 1965–77; Chld. Libn., Schenectady Cnty. Pub. Lib., 1961–65; Chld. Libn., Burnt Hills Sch. Syst., 1960–61. **Educ.:** SUNY, Oneonta, 1955–59, BS (Educ.); SUNY, Albany, 1959–60, MS (LS). **Orgs.:** ALA. NY LA. Cap. Dist. Lib. Cncl. **Activities:** 9; 15, 16, 24 **Addr.:** Gallupville, NY 12073.

Zimmerman, Barbara T. (My. 22, 1942, Trenton, NJ) Libn., Memphis Correct. Ctr., 1976–; Soc. Worker, Memphis Mental Hlth. Inst., 1975–76; Libn., Memphis Hebrew Acad., 1973–75; Lib. Asst., Memphis Pub. Lib. Info. Ctr., 1969–70; Libn., Shelby City Schs., 1966–67; Asst. Libn., Brooks Art Gallery, 1964–65. **Educ.:** Memphis State Univ., 1960–65, BS (Soclgy., LS, Grmn.); 1979, Cert. Prog. in Correct. Inst. Title IIB–HEA; various crs. **Orgs.:** ALA: Biblther. Discuss. Grp. (1976); Lib. Srvs. to Prisons Lcl. Srv. to Jail Resol. (1979–81); Nom. Com. (1979); Secy. (1978–79); ASCLA, Amer. Correct. Assn. Jt. Comsn. on Inst. Libs. (1977–78), ALA Anl. Conv., Prog. Com. "Playing the Jail Game" (1978–79). TN Adv. Cncl. on Libs.: Correct. Libs. (Rep., 1979–81, 1981–84). Amer. Correct. Assn.: ACA/ALA Jt. Comsn. on Inst. Libs. (1976–78). **Honors:** Memphis Correct. Ctr. Lib., Arts in Prison Prog., Grant Proposal Accepted, Awd., 1980. **Pubns.:** Various projs. on improving correct. libs. **Activities:** 5, 9; 15, 16, 22; 50, 77, 89 **Addr.:** 4099 Sequoia Rd., Memphis, TN 38117.

Zimmerman, H. Neil (Jl. 18, 1945, New York City, NY) Libn., Popltn. Cncl., 1974–; Libn., SLA, 1973–74; Asst. Libn., Cncl. on Frgn. Rel., 1969–73; Supvsr., Untd. Nation Col., NY Univ., 1967–69. **Educ.:** PA State Univ., 1963–67, BA (Pol. Sci.); Long Island Univ., 1967–69, MLS. **Orgs.:** Assn. for Popltn./Fam. Plng. Libs. and Info. Ctrs.: Bd. (1975–77); Treas. (1979–). Cnsrtm. of Fndn. Libs.: Pres. (1978). SLA. **Activities:** 12; 15, 20, 39; 54, 68, 92 **Addr.:** Population Council Library, 1 Dag Hammarskjold Plz., New York, NY 10017.

Zimmerman, John Jacob (N. 4, 1918, Westmoreland County, PA) Lib. Dir., Frostburg State Coll., 1957–; Acq. Libn., Univ. of GA, 1950–57; Instr., Admiral Farragur Acad., 1945–48; Tchr., Apollo HS, 1943–45. **Educ.:** Muhlenberg Coll., 1937–41, PhB (Eng.); Univ. of FL, 1948, MA (Eng.); Emory Univ., 1949–50, MA (Libnshp.); various crs. **Orgs.:** MD LA: Pres. (1966–67); various coms. MD Congs. of Acad. Lib. Dirs.: Exec. Dir. (1979–81). SE LA: Various coms. MD State Lib. Resrc. Ctr. Adv. Com.: Ch. (1980–). Various other orgs. AAUP. MD State Coll. Com. to Review Prof. Status of Libns.: Bd. of Trustees (Ch., 1972). MD Cncl. on Higher Educ.: Lib. Std. Comsn. (1964). **Honors:** MD LA, Awd., 1979; Tau Kappa Epsilon; Alpha Psi Omega. **Pubns.:** *In The Poet's Hand* (1965); "So Catalogers Are Scarce," *Coll. & Resrch. Libs.* (Ja. 1963); "A School Librarian's

Special Subjects/Services: 50. Adult educ.; 51. Advert./Mktg.; 52. Aerosp.; 53. Agric.; 54. Area std.; 55. Arts/Hum.; 56. Autom.; 57. Bibl./Prtg.; 58. Bio. sci.; 59. Bus./Fin.; 60. Chem.; 61. Copyrt.; 62. Documtn.; 63. Educ.; 64. Engin.; 65. Env.; 66. Eth. grps.; 67. Film; 68. Food/Nutr.; 69. Geneal.; 70. Geo.; 71. Geol.; 72. Handcpd.; 73. Hist.; 74. Int. frdm.; 75. Info. sci.; 76. Insr.; 77. Law; 78. Legis.; 79. Math./Comp. sci.; 80. Med.; 81. Metals; 82. Nat. resrcs.; 83. Newsp.; 84. Nuc. sci.; 85. Oral hist.; 86. Petr./Energy; 87. Pharm.; 88. Phys./Astr./Math.; 89. Readg.; 90. Relig.; 91. Sci./Tech.; 92. Soc. sci.; 93. Telecom.; 94. Transp.; 95. (other).

Who's Who in Library and Information Services

Summer," *MD Libs.* (Fall 1963); "Libraries in Maryland Post Secondary Education Institutions" rpt. (1977); ed. bd., *MD Libs.* (1963–65). **Activities:** 1, 12; 17, 34; 69, 93 **Addr.:** 169 Ormand St., Frostburg, MD 21532.

Zimmerman, Walter Evan (Jl. 29, 1947, Brookline, MA) Can. Consult., Bibl. Retrieval Srvs., Inc., 1979–; Visit. Lectr., SLIS, Univ. of West. ON, 1981–, Online Srvs. Libn., Univ. of West. ON, 1977–, Ref. Libn., The D.B. Weldon Lib., 1974–77, Admin. Asst. to Chief Libn., 1971–74. **Educ.:** Brandeis Univ., 1965–69, BA (Econ.); Univ. of West. ON, 1970–71, MLS. **Orgs.:** ON LA. Can. Assn. Info. Sci. London ON Spec. Libns. Univ. of West. ON Alum. Cncl. **Pubns.:** "Psychological Abstracts Database," *Residents Guide to Psychiatric Education* (1978); jt. auth., "A Canadian Online BRS Consortium: First Impressions," *Procs. of the 7th Anl. Can. Conf. on Info. Sci.* (1979). **Activities:** 1; 24, 39, 49-Info. retrieval; 75, 92 **Addr.:** The D. B. Weldon Library, The University of Western Ontario, London, ON N6A 3K7, Canada.

Zimon, Kathy E. (F. 20, 1941, Szeged, Hungary) Fine Arts Libn., Univ. of Calgary Lib., 1969–. **Educ.:** Univ. of BC, 1961–66, BA (Art Hist.), 1968–69, BLS, 1967–70, MA (Art Hist.). **Orgs.:** Can. LA. Can. Assn. of Spec. Libs. and Info. Srvs./Can. Art Libs. Sect. (Ch., 1979–80). ARLIS/NA. Calgary Reg. Arts Fndn.: Bd. (1977–). **Pubns.:** Ed., *Can. Art Libs. Nsltr.* (1975–78). **Activities:** 1; 15, 39; 55 **Addr.:** Library, Fine Arts Division, University of Calgary, 2500 University Dr. N.W., Calgary, AB T2N 1N4, Canada.

Zimpfer, William Edward (Je. 3, 1926, Columbus, OH) Dir. of Lib., Asst. and Prof. of Resrch. Methods, Boston Univ. Sch. of Theo., 1964–; Co-Pastor, Zion Luth. Church, Brentwood, PA, 1960–62; Pastor, St. John Luth. Church, Pittsburgh, PA, 1950–60. **Educ.:** Cap. Univ., 1943–46, AB (Hist., Classics); Univ. of MI, 1946–48, MA (Hist., Classics); Evang. Luth. Semy., Columbus, OH, 1946–50, BD (Theo.); Columbia Univ., 1962–64, MSLS (Theo.). **Orgs.:** ATLA: Readers Srv. Com. (1978–81); Col. Dev. Com. (1978–80). Gen. Theo. Lib., Boston: Bd. of Dirs.; Bk. Sel. Com. **Activities:** 1, 2; 15, 17, 31; 50, 90, 92 **Addr.:** 745 Commonwealth Ave., Boston, MA 02215.

Zink, Esther (Ja. 18, 1941, Clearwater, FL) Head Libn., Trinity Bible Inst., 1975–; Ref. Libn., FL Jr. Coll., 1974–75; Head Libn., Sch. of Pharm., Univ. of MS, 1968–74. **Educ.:** FL South. Coll., 1962–65, BS (Elem. Educ., Relig.); Univ. of MS, 1969–71, MLS; State of FL, Tchr.-Libn. Cert. **Orgs.:** ALA. ATLA. ND LA. Christ. Libns. Flwshp. Various other orgs. Natl. Hon. Socty. Parents-Tchr.-Student Assn. **Honors:** Tchr.-Student Hum. Awd., 1974; Jacksonville Investor's Assn., Cert. of Bravery Awd., 1968; Cert. of Merit for Leadership, 1959; Dean's Staff Cert. of Awd., 1959. **Activities:** 1, 5; 20, 22, 39; 80, 90 **Addr.:** Box 420, Trinity Bible Institute, Ellendale, ND 58436.

Zink, James K. (F. 9, 1933, Seminole, OK) Dir., Lib., SE MO State Univ., 1979–; Dvnty. Libn., Jt. Univ. Libs., 1978; Dir., Univ. Libs., Univ. of OK, 1973–77, Assoc. Dir., Pub. Srvs., 1971–73. **Educ.:** Harding Univ., 1951–54, BA (Relig.); Univ. of Chicago, 1968–69, MA; Duke Univ., 1958–60, PhD (Relig.). **Orgs.:** ALA. OK LA: *OK Libn.* Ed. (1972–76). Socty. of Biblical Lit. **Activities:** 1; 17; 57, 90 **Addr.:** 1578 Parksite Dr., Cape Girardeau, MO 63701.

Zink, Steven D. (Ag. 30, 1954, Salem, IN) Head of Dept., Gvt. Pubns. Libn., Univ. of NV, 1980–; Docum. Libn., Coll. of Wooster, 1979–80. **Educ.:** IN State Univ., 1972–74, BS (Hist.); Univ. of WI, 1974–75, MA (Hist.); LA State Univ., 1978–79, MLS; various crs. **Orgs.:** Assn. for the Bibl. of Hist.: Cncl. (1980–82). ALA: RASD/Hist. Sect., Bibl. and Indxs. Com. (1980–82); GODORT, Col. Dev. and Review Docum. Task Frcs. SLA. Coll. and Resrch. Libs. Org. of Amer. Histns. **Honors:** WI Mag. of Hist., William Hesseltine Awd., 1980; Hist. New Orleans Col., Gen. L. Kemper Williams Prize, 1977; Beta Phi Mu, 1979; Phi Alpha Theta, 1974. **Pubns.:** *U.S. Government Publications Catalogs* (1981); "Putting Reference in the *Publications Reference File*," *RQ* (Jl. 1980); "Journal Publishing in the Field of U.S. History," *Schol. Publshg.* (Ag. 1980); ed., "Government Publications," clmn. *Ref. Srvs. Review* (1981–). **Activities:** 1; 29, 33; 57, 78, 92 **Addr.:** Government Publications Dept., University of Nevada Library, Reno, NV 89557.

Zinn, Nancy Whitten (Je. 28, 1935, Oak Park, IL) Head, Spec. Cols., Univ. of CA, San Francisco, 1966–; Head, Circ., Ref., Coll. of Physicians, 1963–65. **Educ.:** Univ. of DE, 1953–57, BA (Hist.); Bryn Mawr Coll., 1957–59, MA (Hist.); Drexel Univ., 1961–62, MSLS; Emory Univ., 1962–63, Med. Lib. Internship; various crs. **Orgs.:** North. CA Med. Lib. Grp. Socty. of CA Archvsts.: Cncl. (1979–81). Med. LA: Mem. Com. (Ch., 1966–69); Internship Com. (Ch., 1971–72); Ad Hoc Com. to Review the Goals and Stans. of Med. LA (1970–71); Hist. Med. Grp. (Ch., 1970–72); Murray Gottlieb Prize Subcom. (Ch., 1978–79); Nom. Com. (1973–74); various coms. Various other orgs. Bk. Club of CA. Amer. Assn. Hist. of Med. Hand Bookbinders of CA: Pres. (1977–79). Assn. Libns. Hist. Hlth. Sci.: Pres. (1977–79). **Honors:** Beta Phi Mu; Phi Kappa Phi; Cncl. of Lib. Resrcs., Fellow, 1976–77. **Pubns.:** *Handbook of Medical Library Practice;* volume 3, chap. 11, *Rare Books and Special Collections* (forthcoming); "Philadelphia's Medical Libraries," *Bltn. Med. LA* (Ap. 1965); "The Rosencrantz Collection of Osleriana, San Francisco," *Osler Lib. Nsltr.* (Je. 1971); *Materials for the History of the Health Sciences* (1974); various bk. reviews. **Activities:** 1, 2; 23, 31, 45; 57, 80, 86 **Addr.:** 1410–21st Ave., San Francisco, CA 94122.

Zins, Martha Lee (D. 14, 1945, Mankato, MN) Sch. Libn., Hopkins W. Jr. HS, 1967–; Tchr., Worthington HS, 1966–67. **Educ.:** Coll. of St. Catherine, St. Paul, MN, 1963–64; Mankato State Univ., 1964–67, BS (Soc. Std., Eng., LS), 1966–67, BA (Hist., Eng.); West. MI Univ., 1967–71, MLS (LS, Media); various crs. **Orgs.:** MN Assn. of Sch. Libns.: Treas. (1975–76). MN Educ. Media Org.: Merge Com. (1976); Co-treas. (1976–78); Bylaws Com. (Ch., 1976–78). ALA: AASL; YASD. MN Gvr.'s Pre-WHCOLIS: Del. (1979). Various other orgs. Hopkins Educ. Assn.: Pres. (1974–75); Negotiator (1977–). MN Educ. Assn.: VP (1977–). Natl. Educ. Assn.: Various task frcs.; Dir. (1976). Delta Kappa Gammi (Phi): Legis. Ch. (1978–80). **Honors:** MN Educ. Assn., Human Rights Awd., 1978; MN Educ. Media Org., Cotreas. Awd., 1979; Natl. Educ. Assn., 1 of 5 Outstan. Women in Educ. in MN, 1977. **Activities:** 10; 21, 31, 48 **Addr.:** 155 Gleason Lake Rd. #411, Wayzata, MN 55391.

Ziolko, Joseph F. (Jl. 7, 1949, Buffalo, NY) Dir., Libs., MS Cnty. and MS Cnty. Comm. Coll. Lib. Syst., 1977–; Libn., Buffalo and Erie Cnty. Pub. Lib., 1971–77. **Educ.:** St. Bonaventure Univ., 1967–71, BA (Jnlsm.); SUNY, Buffalo, 1967–73, Mstrs. of LS. **Orgs.:** AR LA: VP–Pres–Elect (1981–); PR Com. (1978–); Nom. Com. (1979). SW LA: Coll. Lib. Div. (Secy., 1979). ALA. N.E. AR Hosp. Lib. Cnsrtm.: Secy. (1980). Various other orgs. Rotary Intl.: *Bltn.* Ed. (1979). MS Cnty. Cmnty. Coll. Booster Club: Prog. Ed. (1978–); PR Dir. (1978). Knights of Columbus: Advocate (1978). **Honors:** March of Dimes, Cmnty. Leadership Awd., 1980. **Pubns.:** "Multitype Library Networking: Is It an Answer to Current Fiscal Problems?" cassette (1978). **Activities:** 1, 9; 17, 36, 39; 51, 59 **Addr.:** Mississippi County Library System, 200 N. 5th, Blytheville, AR 72315.

Zionkowski, Walter John (My. 31, 1939, Nanticoke, PA) Asst. Dir., Pub. Srvs., Savitz Lib., Glassboro State Coll., 1974–80, Soc. Sci. Libn., 1971–74; Asst. Archvst., Paley Lib., Temple Univ., 1970–71. **Educ.:** Wilkes Coll., 1957–61, AB (Hist.); Univ. of VA, 1961–64, AM (Frgn. Affairs); Univ. of Pittsburgh, 1969–70, MLS: Polish Natl. Lib., (Socialist Libs.,) 1977, Cert.; Oxford Univ. Brit. Libs., 1978, Cert. (Admin. of Libs.); various crs. **Orgs.:** ALA: Anthro. Com. (1971–73); ACRL, DE Valley Chap., Exec. Bd. (Dir.-at-Lg., 1977–). SLA. Amer. Pol. Sci. Assn. Amer. Hist. Assn. **Honors:** Polish Natl. Lib., Warsaw, Invitation to Std. Socialist Libs., 1977; Phi Delta Gamma. **Activities:** 1; 15, 17, 35; 54, 92†

Zipin, Amnon (Ap. 10, 1946, Haifa, Israel) Jewish Std. Biblgphr., OH State Univ., 1977–; Near E. Libn., Univ. of WA, 1976–77; Lang., Subj. Spec., Yale Univ., 1973–76. **Educ.:** Hebrew Univ., Jerusalem, 1968–70, BA (Arabic); Yale Univ., 1970–72, MA; South. CT State Coll., 1973–75, MLS. **Orgs.:** Mid. E. Libn. Assn.: Com. on Machine Readable Arabic Data (1977–); Pubn. Com. (1980–). AJL: Task Frc. on Un. List of Serials, Ch. Assn. for Jewish Std. **Pubns.:** *Fihrest Al-Adab Al-Ibri Al-Hadith Al-Mutarjam Ila Al-Arabiyah* (1980); jt. auth., *Bibliography of Modern Hebrew Literature in Translation* (1979); "Kitlug Ha-Ivrit Be-Idan Ha-Mehashev," *Yad La-Kore* (S. 1978); "Serials Cost Efficiency: A Model and Case Study," *AJL Bltn.* (Win. 1979). **Activities:** 1, 2; 15, 20, 39; 54, 90 **Addr.:** Ohio State University Library, 1858 Neil Ave., Columbus, OH 43210.

Zipkowitz, Fay (N. 11, 1938, New York City, NY) Dir., RI Dept. of State Lib. Srvs., 1981–; Coord., Lib. Systs., Worcester Area Coop. Libs., 1977–80; Docum. Ref. Libn., Univ. of MA, 1975–77, Lib. Systs. Anal., 1973–75, Head, Info. Prcs. 1970–73, Sr. Catlgr., 1968–70, Asst. to Dir., 1966–68, Archvst., Abba Hillel Silver Meml. Arch. and Lib., The Temple, Cleveland, OH, 1964–66; Asst., Pop. Lib., Cleveland Pub. Lib., 1959–63. **Educ.:** Long Island Univ., 1955–58, BA (Eng.); Case West. Rsv. Univ., 1958–59, MSLS (LS); Univ. of MA, 1967–70, MA (Eng.); Simmons Coll., 1973–77, DA (Acad. Lib. Admin.). **Orgs.:** ALA: ACRL; ASCLA, Prog. Com. (1979–80); LAMA, Women Admin. Discuss. Grp., Strg. Com. New Eng. Chap. ACRL: Nom. Com. (Ch., 1977–78); Pres. (1980–81); Conf. Prog. (Ch., 1979–80). MA Bd. of Lib. Comsns.: Serials Adv. Com. (Co-ch., 1978–79). New Eng. Lib. Info. Netwk., Inc.: Bd. of Dirs. Worcester Cnsrtm. for Higher Educ. Media Comm. Com. Univ. of MA Med. Sch. Subcom. on the Lib. Com. for Worcester Online Srch. Srv. Univ. of MA: Fac. Sen. (1971–74); Univ. of MA Press, Subcom. on Ed. Policy (1974–77); Campus Phys. Plng. Com. (Ch., 1976–77); Jt. Com. on Lit. (1974–77); Various other coms. Oper. Friendship. Various confs. **Honors:** Cncl. on Lib. Resrcs., Flwshp., 1973. **Pubns.:** Various pubn. reviews, *Coll. & Resrch. Libs.;* "Catalogs and Catalogers: Revolution through Evolution," *Jnl. of Acad. Libnshp.* (S. 1976); indxr., *Index to Jewish Periodicals* (1964–66); various sps. **Activities:** 1, 3; 17, 20, 34; 56, 75 **Addr.:** 95 Davis St., Providence, RI 02908.

Ziplans, Emilija E. (Je. 17, 1917, Aduliena, Vidzeme, Latvia) Head, Multiple Copies and Undergrad. Sect., Bk. Sel. Dept., Univ. of Toronto Lib., 1967–, Head Libn., New Coll., 1964–67, Libn., Circ. Dept., 1961–64. **Educ.:** Univ. of Latvia, 1941–44, (Philology); Univ. of Toronto, 1956–60, BA (Psy.), 1960–61, BLS. **Orgs.:** Can. LA. ALA: Mem. Com. (ON Rep., 1968–70). Libns. Assn., Univ. of Toronto. Assn. for Advnc. of Baltic Std.: Baltic Resrcs. Netwk. Coord. Com.; Can. Com. Latvian-Can. Cult. Ctr.: Latvian Resrc. Ctr. Com. (Ch., 1980–). Ctrl. and E. European Std. Assn. of Can. **Pubns.:** Cmplr., *Baltic Material in the University of Toronto Library* (1972, 1978); "Bibliographical Implications in the Baltic Studies Area," *Jnl. of Baltic Std.* (Sum. 1976). **Activities:** 1, 12; 15, 17, 28; 55, 57, 66 **Addr.:** The Summerhill, Apt. 1106, 7 Jackes Ave., Toronto, ON M4T 1E3 Canada.

Zirbes, Sr. Colette Mary (N. 11, 1924, Milwaukee, WI) Libn., Dir., Cardinal Stritch Coll., 1976–, Asst. Prof., Chld. and Advnc. Lit., 1972–, Asst. Libn., 1970–76; Asst. Libn., Univ. of WI, 1968–70. **Educ.:** Cardinal Stritch Coll., 1943–50, BA (Eng., Educ.); San Francisco Coll. for Women, 1952–56, MA (Eng. Lit.); Univ. of WI, 1967–69, MA (LS). **Orgs.:** ALA. Cath. LA. WI Cath. LA: Exec. Bd. (1975–). Intl. Readg. Assn.: SIGNAL Sect., Exec. Bd. (1975–81); Secy. (1978–80). Various other orgs. Lib. Cncl. of Metro. Milwaukee: Exec. Bd. (1972–75). WI ILL Srvs.: Adv. Bd. (1975–77). **Honors:** Cath. LA Schol. Awd., 1980; Childcraft Schol. Awd., 1977, 1980; Assoc. Prof., 1979. **Pubns.:** Consult., reader ed., *Harper-Row Reading Series* (1977); asst. ed., *Pilot Series in Youth Ministry* (1975); "Reading: An Open Door to Personal Insights," *MARC* (F. 1977); various bk. reviews., *SIGNAL* (1974–); ed., *ALA Biblther. Nsltr.* (Win. 1980). **Activities:** 1; 15, 17, 41; 50, 63, 75 **Addr.:** 7979 N. Port Washington Rd., Milwaukee, WI 53217.

Zlatich, Marko (Jl. 4, 1932, Chicago, IL) Chief, Documtn. Systs. Sect., Recs. Mgt. Div., World Bank, 1976–, Chief, Resrch. Files and Lib. Srvs. Sect., 1962–76; Ed., World List of Future Intl. Mtgs., Gen. Ref. and Bibl. Div., Lib. of Congs., 1960–62. **Educ.:** Univ. of Chicago, 1948–52, BA; Georgetown Univ., 1952–53, BS (Intl. Std.), 1954–57, MS (Intl. Std.). **Orgs.:** Assn. of Intl. Libs.: Treas. (1974–81). SLA. Assn. of Recs. Mgrs. and Admins. **Activities:** 12; 54, 62 **Addr.:** World Bank, 1818 H St. N.W., Washington, DC 20433.

Zobrist, Benedict K. (Ag. 21, 1921, Moline, IL) Dir., Harry S. Truman Lib., 1969–; Prof., Hist., Dept. Ch., Augustana Coll., 1960–69; Cmnd. Histn., US Army Ordnance Weapons Cmnd., 1954–60. **Educ.:** Augustana Coll., 1946, AB (Hist.); Northwest. Univ., 1947–53, MA, PhD (Hist.); Fed. Exec. Inst., 1974. **Orgs.:** SAA. ALA: ACRL. SLA. Amer. Hist. Assn. Org. of Amer. Histns. Jackson Cnty. MO Hist. Socty.: VP. (1972–). Davenport IA Pub. Musm.: Bd. of Dirs. (1969). **Honors:** Tunghai Univ., Taiwan, Fullbright Fellow, 1962; E. Asian Inst., Columbia Univ., Tchg. Fellow in Orien. Std., 1962–63; Harry S. Truman Resrch. Inst., Hebrew Univ. of Jerusalem, Martin Fellow, 1978; Augustana Coll., Oustan. Alum. Achvmt. Awd., 1975. **Pubns.:** "Resources of Presidential Libraries for the History of the Second World War," *Milit. Affairs* (Ap. 1975); "Resources of Presidential Libraries for the History of Post World War II American Military Government in Germany and Japan," *Milit. Affairs* (F. 1978); various articles, reviews. **Activities:** 2, 4; 17; 73, 92 **Addr.:** Harry S. Truman Library, Independence, MO 64050.

Zoccola, Donna Marie (Jl. 28, 1949, Princeton, NJ) Med. Libn., Frnds. Hosp., 1976–; Asst. Libn., Princeton Univ., Geol. Lib., 1971–74. **Educ.:** Georgian Ct. Coll., 1967–71, AB (Eng. Lit.); Univ. Italiana per Stranieri, Perugia, Italy, 1973, Cert. (Italian, Hist., Lang., Art); Drexel Univ., 1975–76, MS (Lib., Info. Sci.). **Orgs.:** SLA: Philadelphia Chap., Treas.; various other chaps. Med. LA. Geosci. Info. Socty. Socty. of Vertebrate Paleon. **Activities:** 12; 15, 17, 46; 80 **Addr.:** Friends Hospital, Weiner Professional Library, Roosevelt Blvd. at Adams Ave., Philadelphia, PA 19124.

Zolton, Ronald G. (Jl. 30, 1937, Marquette, MI) Dir., Media Srvs., Reg. Educ. Media Ctr.-9, Saginaw Intermediate Sch. Dist., 1973–, Asst. Dir., 1971–73, Media Consult., 1969–71; Tchr., Saginaw Pub. Schs., 1959–68. **Educ.:** Ctrl. MI Univ., 1957–60, BS (Cmrce., Soc. Std.), 1961–65, MS (Admin., AV, LS); West. MI Univ., MI State Univ., 1975–79 (LS).**Orgs.:** Mid-MI Socty. for Instr. Tech. MI Assn. for Sch. Libns.: Legis. Ch. (1972–73). MI Intermediate Media Assn.: Pres. (1972–73); Legis. Ch. (1977–79). Amer. Assn. of Sch. Admins. Kiwanis Club: Bd.; Youth Com.; Pres.-Elect (1980–81). Untd. Way: Saginaw Cnty. (Educ. Coord., 1973–75). MI Assn. for Media in Educ.: Reg. 9 (Pres., 1975–76). MI Assn. of Intermediate Sch. Admins.: Com. on Media (1975–80). various other orgs. **Pubns.:** "Storage Ideas," *Mod. Media Tchr.* (1973); "REMC's and the Concept of Levels," *MI Libns.* (1973); "REMC's Communication Network," *Media Spectrum* (1979); "Media in the Curriculum–Especially Film," *Focus* (Mr. 1979); "We Also Book Skeletons," *Media Spectrum* (1978); various articles in *Reg. 9* nsltr. (1973–79). **Activities:** 10, 12; 17, 22, 32 **Addr.:** Regional Educational Media Center–9, Saginaw Intermediate School District, 6235 Gratiot Rd., Saginaw, MI 48603.

Zorach, Margaret B. (Ja. 26, 1917, E. Orange, NJ) Chief Libn., Art Ref. Lib., Brooklyn Musm., 1964–, Catlgr., 1961–64. **Educ.:** Radcliffe Coll., 1934–38, BA (Pol. Theory); Pratt Inst., 1961–64, MLS. **Orgs.:** ARLIS/NA: Nom. Com. (1980). SLA:

PROFESSIONAL ACTIVITIES: Institutions: 1. Acad. lib.; 2. Arch.; 3. Assn.; 4. Fed./Gvt. lib.; 5. Inst. lib.; 6. Mfr./Suppl.; 7. Milit. lib.; 8. Musm.; 9. Pub. lib.; 10. Sch. lib.; 11. Sch. of lib. sci.; 12. Spec. lib.; 13. State lib.; 14. (other). **Functions/Activities:** 15. Acq./Col. dev.; 16. Adult srvs.; 17. Admin.; 18. Apprais.; 19. Archit./Bldgs.; 20. Cat./Class.; 21. Chld. srvs.; 22. Circ.; 23. Cons./Pres.; 24. Consult.; 25. Cont. ed.; 26. Educ. lib. sci.; 27. Ext. srvs.; 28. Fund/Grants; 29. Gvt. pubs.; 30. Indx./Abs.; 31. Instr. lib. use; 32. Media srvs.; 33. Micro.; 34. Netwks./Coop.; 35. Persnl.; 36. PR; 37. Publshg.; 38. Recs. mgt.; 39. Ref. srvs.; 40. Repro.; 41. Resrch.; 42. Review.; 43. Secur.; 44. Serials; 45. Spec. col.; 46. Tech. srvs.; 47. Trustees/Bds.; 48. YA srvs.; 49. (other).

Musm. Div. (Ch., 1968). Asia Socty. Arch. of Amer. Art. Metro. Musm. of Art. **Honors:** Beta Phi Mu, 1964. **Activities:** 5; 15, 17, 38; 54, 55 **Addr.:** 276 Hicks St., Brooklyn, NY 11201.

Zubatsky, David Samuel (S. 17, 1939, Milwaukee, WI) Asst. Dir., Tech. and Autom. Srvs., WA Univ., St. Louis, MO 1975–78, Chief, Acq. Dept., 1970–75, Biblgphr., Latin Amer. and Iberian Peninsula, 1967–69. **Educ.:** Univ. of WI, 1957–62, BA (Span.), 1962–66, MA (Hist.); Univ. of IL, 1966–67, MSLS. **Orgs.:** ALA: RTSD/Resrcs. Sect., Col. Dev. Com. (Ch., 1973–78), Col. Dev. Ofcrs. for Medium-Size Resrch. Libs. Discuss. Grp. (Ch., 1975–76), Tech. Srvs. Admins. for Medium-Size Resrch. Libs. Discuss. Grp. (Ch., 1973–74). Untd. States Bk. Exch.: Bd. of Dirs. (1972–74). SALALM: Exec. Bd. (1971–74); *SALALM Nsltr.* Ed. (1972–75). **Pubns.:** *A Bibliographical Essay on the History of American Colleges and Their Libraries in the 17th and 18th Centuries* (1979); jt. auth., *Recommended Procedures for the Internal Financial Auditing of University Libraries* (1977); "An Annotated Bibliography of 20th Century Catalan and Spanish Author Bibliographies," *Hispania* (O. 1978). **Activities:** 1; 15, 17, 46; 54, 57 **Addr.:** 2404 Southwood, Champaign, IL 61820.

Zubkoff, Helene (Ja. 12, 1930, Buffalo, NY) Ref., Info. Srvs. Spec., Amer. Coll. of Nursing Home Admins., 1976–; Libn., AV, George Washington Univ. Med. Lib., 1969–75; Libn., Resrch. Assn., DC, 1968–69. **Educ.:** NY State Coll. for Tchrs., 1948–52, BS (Educ.); Univ. of MD, 1966–68, MLS. **Orgs.:** SLA: Hlth. Sci. Comm. Assn.: Biomed. Libs. Sect. (Ch., 1974–75). **Honors:** Beta Phi Mu, 1968. **Pubns.:** *Bibliography of Audiotapes and Tape-Slide Programs Applicable to Undergraduate Medical Education* (1972); "Long Term Care Administration Bookshelf," *Jnl. of Long-Term Care Admin.* (Mr. 1981); "Library Services in Nursing Homes," *Procs.: Sec. N. Amer. Symp. on Long-Term Care Admin.* (1977). **Activities:** 12; 17, 39; 80 **Addr.:** 3204 Woodbine St., Chevy Chase, MD 20815.

Zubrow, Marcia Lee Singal (Jl. 19, 1945, Boston, MA) Head Ref. Libn., Charles B. Sears Law Lib., SUNY, Buffalo, 1979–, Serials Catlgr., 1977–79; Catlgr., Heafey Law Lib., Univ. of Santa Clara, 1973–77. **Educ.:** Boston Univ., 1963–67, BA (Amer. Hist., Cvlztn.); CA State Univ., San Jose, 1972–73, MLS (Libnshp.). **Orgs.:** AALL. Assn. of Law Libns. of Upper NY. SUNY LA. **Pubns.:** Ed., *Checklist of Basic American Legal Publications* (1979–). **Activities:** 1; 31, 39; 77 **Addr.:** Charles B. Sears Law Library, John Lord O'Brian Hall, State University of NY/ Buffalo, Amherst Campus, Buffalo, NY 14260.

Zuckerman, Arline (Je. 11, 1940, New York City, NY) Libn., Head, Athty. Sect., Univ. of CA, Los Angeles, 1962–. **Educ.:** Long Beach State Coll., 1958–61, AB (Eng.); Univ. of CA,

Los Angeles, 1961–62, MLS. **Orgs.:** ALA: Subj. Analysis Com. (Ch., 1979–80); Ad Hoc Subcom. on Subj. Analysis of African and Asian Mtrls. (Ch., 1976–78), Cat. Maintenance Discuss. Grp. (Ch., 1980–81). CA LA. South. CA Tech. Prcs. Grp. **Activities:** 1; 20; 54, 77 **Addr.:** 11315 Victoria Ave., Los Angeles, CA 90066.

Zuest, Patricia A. (N. 10, 1944, Vancouver, BC) Head, Plng., Metro. Toronto Lib. Bd., 1977–; Plng., Dev. Libn., Toronto Pub. Lib., 1976–77; Info. Systs. Consult., Digital Methods Ltd., 1972–76; Head, Tech. Srvs., Food and Drug Directorate Lib., Dept. of Natl. Hlth. and Welfare, 1969–72. **Educ.:** Univ. of BC, 1962–66, BSc (Zlgy.); Univ. of WA, 1968–69, MLS. **Orgs.:** Can. Assn. Info. Sci. ASIS. Can. LA: Com. on Pubns. (1978–79). ON LA. **Activities:** 9; 17, 34, 49-Plng.; 56, 95-Plng. **Addr.:** Metropolitan Toronto Library, 789 Yonge St., Toronto, ON M4W 2G8 Canada.

Zuga, Connie (D. 19, 1945, Holmesville, OH) DIALOG Cust. Srvs., DIALOG Info. Srvs., 1979–; Libn., Bur. of Soc. Sci. Resrch., 1978–79; Demog., US Bur. of the Census, 1977; Libn., Popltn. Ref. Bur., 1975–77. **Educ.:** OH State Univ., 1963–67, BA, BS (Educ.); San Jose State Univ., 1973–74, MA (Libnshp.); Georgetown Univ., 1976–78, MA (Demog.). **Orgs.:** ASIS. SLA. Assn. for Popltn./Fam. Plng. Libs. and Info. Ctrs.: Treas. (1977–79); Washington/Baltimore Chap. (Ch., 1978–79). Popltn. Assn. of Amer. **Pubns.:** Ed., *Sourcebook on Population 1970–1976* (1976). **Activities:** 12; 17, 36; 59 **Addr.:** DIALOG Customer Services, DIALOG Information Services, 3460 Hillview Ave., Palo Alto, CA 94304.

Zula, Floyd Michael (My. 23, 1945, Shawnee, OK) Acq. Libn., Christopher Newport Coll., 1978–; Head Acq. Libn., AR State Univ., 1976–78; Head Libn., Thomas More Coll., 1975–76; Coord., Lib. Srvs., Muskegon Cmnty. Coll., 1968–73. **Educ.:** Northwest. Univ., 1963–67, BA (Hist.); Univ. of MI, 1967–68, AMLS. **Orgs.:** ALA: ACRL, Nom. Com. (1980). ARLIS/NA. Intl. Ctr. of Medvl. Art. **Pubns.:** two bk. review annotations, *Lib. Jnl.* (1976); "The New Copyright Bill" radio talk, KASU, State Univ., AR (D. 1, 1976). **Activities:** 1; 15, 46; 55 **Addr.:** 554 Logan Pl., Apt. #13, Newport News, VA 23601.

Zumwalt, Orlow 'R.' (Je. 1, 1928, Kansas City, MO) AV Media Spec., Rockville HS, 1976–; Film Libn., Montgomery Cnty. Pub. Schs., 1970–76; Drafting Instr., Rockville HS, 1969–70; Ofcr. in Charge, Trng. Aids Lib., Marine Corps. Dev. and Educ. Cmnd., 1966–69. **Educ.:** Univ. of MO, 1947–51, BS (Educ., Soc. Std.), 1953–54, M (Indus. Educ.); Univ. of MD, 1967–77, Media Spec. Cert. (Educ. Tech.). **Orgs.:** AECT. MD LA: WA Film Cncl. Montgomery Cnty. Educ. Media Specs. Assn. Natl. Educ. Assn. MD State Tchrs. Assn. Rsv. Ofcrs. Assn.

Honors: Phi Delta Kappa, 1973. **Activities:** 10; 12; 22, 32, 46; 63, 67, 74 **Addr.:** Rockville High School, 2100 Baltimore Rd., Rockville, MD 20851.

Zussy, Nancy L. (Mr. 4, 1947, Tampa, FL) Deputy State Libn., WA State Lib., 1981–; Dir., Libs., Clearwater Pub. Lib., 1978–81, Admin. Asst., Ref. Prof., 1972–78; Media Spec., DeKalb Cnty., GA, 1970–71. **Educ.:** St. Petersburg Jr. Coll., 1965–67, AA; Univ. of FL, 1967–69, BAE (LS); Univ. of S. FL, 1974–77, MA (LS), 1978–80, MS (Mgt.); State of WA, 1981, Prof. Libn. Cert. **Orgs.:** ALA. FL LA: Legis. and Plng. Com. (1979–81). Tampa Bay Lib. Cnsrtm. Pinellas Cnty. LA: Countywide Lib. Syst. Com. (1979–80). **Honors:** Phi Kappa Phi, 1965–80. **Activities:** 9, 13; 17, 25, 35; 59, 74, 78 **Addr.:** Washington State Library, AJ-11, Olympia, WA 98504.

Zvigaitis, Sr. Marie de Brebeuf, I.H.M. (S. 21, 1915, Philadelphia, PA) Asst. Libn., Catlgr., OCLC Terminal Oper., Immaculata Coll., 1969–; Libn., Lancaster Cath. HS, Lancaster, PA, 1965–69; Tchr.-Libn., Archbishop Prendergast HS, Drexel Hill, PA, 1959–65; Tchr.-Libn., Immaculate Conception HS, Jim Thorpe, PA, 1948–49; Tchr.-Libn., Immaculate Heart HS, Fountain Springs, PA, 1944–46; Tchr., Archdio. of Philadelphia, 1939–44. **Educ.:** Immaculata Coll., Immaculata, PA, 1934–38, AB (Eng., Soc. Std.); Temple Univ., 1946 (LS); Villanova Univ., 1951–53, Tchr. Cert.; Marywood Coll., 1959–65, MSLS (Libnshp.); 1967, State Cert. (LS); various std. tours. **Orgs.:** Cath. LA: Bk. Fair Com. (Ch., 1969–71). Tri-state Coll. Lib. Coop. (PA, NJ, DE): Tech. Prcs. Com., Ch. PA LA: Natl. Lib. Week Com. (1968). Mid. Atl. States Assn.: Eval. Com. of Sec. Sch. Libs. (1966–69). **Honors:** Chapel of the Four Chaplains, Nom. to Legion of Hon., 1980. **Pubns.:** *A Bibliography of the Works By and About the Sisters, Servants of the Immaculate Heart of Mary, 1845–1962* microfilm (1970). **Activities:** 1, 10; 17, 20, 34; 55, 63, 90 **Addr.:** Immaculata College, Immaculata, PA 10901.

Zweizig, Douglas Lough (Ap. 3, 1938, York, PA) Asst. Prof., Sch. of Libnshp., Univ. of WA, 1975–; Asst. Prof., Dept. of Lib. and Info. Srvs., Univ. of Toledo, 1972–75; Asst. Prof., Asst. to Dean, Sch. of LS, Syracuse Univ., 1968–69, Lectr., 1967–68; Instr., Lib. Admin., Head, Eng. and Sp., Grad. Lib., OH State Univ., 1965–67; Instr., Dept. of Eng., Univ. of NH, 1961–64. **Educ.:** Lafayette Coll., 1956–60, BA (Eng.); Harvard Univ., 1960–61, MA (Eng.); Rutgers Univ., 1964–65, MLS (Lib. Srv.); Syracuse Univ., 1967–73, PhD (Info. Transfer). **Orgs.:** ALA: Com. on Resrch. (1979–81); PLA, Resrch. Com. (Ch., 1974–78). AALS: Resrch. Com. (1979–80). Alliance of Info. and Ref. Srvs. **Honors:** Beta Phi Mu, 1965. **Addr.:** School of Librarianship, FM-30, University of Washington, Seattle, WA 98195.

Special Subjects/Services: 50. Adult educ.; 51. Advert./Mktg.; 52. Aerosp.; 53. Agric.; 54. Area std.; 55. Arts/Hum.; 56. Autom.; 57. Bibl./Prtg.; 58. Bio. sci.; 59. Bus./Fin.; 60. Chem.; 61. Copyrt.; 62. Documtn.; 63. Educ.; 64. Engin.; 65. Env.; 66. Eth. grps.; 67. Film; 68. Food/Nutr.; 69. Geneal.; 70. Geo.; 71. Geol.; 72. Handcpd.; 73. Hist.; 74. Int. frdm.; 75. Info. sci.; 76. Insr.; 77. Law; 78. Legis.; 79. Math./Comp. sci.; 80. Med.; 81. Metals; 82. Nat. resrces.; 83. Newsp.; 84. Nuc. sci.; 85. Oral hist.; 86. Petr./Energy; 87. Pharm.; 88. Phys./Astr./Math.; 89. Readg.; 90. Relig.; 91. Sci./Tech.; 92. Soc. sci.; 93. Telecom.; 94. Transp.; 95. (other).